D1221246

ANALYTICAL HEBREW AND CHALDEE

LEXICON

COMPANION TEXTS FOR
OLD TESTAMENT STUDIES

A Concordance of the Septuagint (Morrish)

Hebrew-English Lexicon (Osborn)

The Analytical Hebrew-Chaldee Lexicon (Davidson)

The Englishman's Hebrew and Chaldee Concordance of the Old Testament (Wigram)

The Englishman's Hebrew-English Old Testament (Magil)

The Hebrew-English Old Testament (Lee)

The Hebrew Old Testament Slidaverb Conjugation Chart (Peterson and Barker)

The Interlineary Hebrew-English Psalter

The Septuagint: Greek and English

The Septuagint with Apocrypha: Greek and English (Brenton)

THE ANALYTICAL HEBREW AND CHALDEE LEXICON

BENJAMIN DAVIDSON

EVERY WORD AND INFLECTION OF
THE HEBREW OLD TESTAMENT
ARRANGED ALPHABETICALLY AND
WITH GRAMMATICAL ANALYSES

A Complete Series of Hebrew and Chaldee Paradigms,
With Grammatical Remarks and Explanations

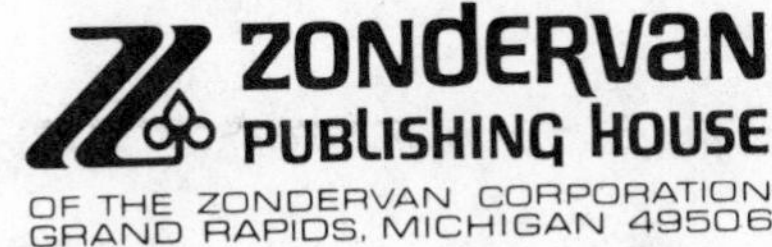

The Analytical Hebrew and Chaldee Lexicon

Originally published by Samuel Bagster & Sons, Ltd., London, 1848; second edition, 1850.

Library of Congress Catalog Card Number 76-106439
ISBN 0-310-20290-6

First Zondervan printing January 1970
Eleventh printing 1978

Printed in the United States of America

PREFACE

Of the several languages which constitute the group commonly designated the Shemitic Family, as those spoken by the descendants of Shem, two have always held the foremost place of interest and importance, namely, the Hebrew and the Chaldee. This distinction is owing to the fact of their being the channel through which the Divine Revelation was imparted directly to the chosen people of Israel, to show them the way of salvation and prepare them for the coming of that Just One to whom the Law of Moses, the Prophets, and the Psalms, successively bore their continuous witness as the Saviour of mankind.

The study of the " Oracles of God " in their original form never relaxed among the favoured people to whom they had been committed, but continued to be jealously treasured when, on their rejection of the Gospel, it was preached to the Gentiles, and the Scriptures transferred to European language. Few, however, among the doctors of the early Christian Church, were learned in the Hebrew tongue; through the mediæval ages the Old Testament of their Bible was the Septuagint Greek Version in the East, and the Latin Vulgate in the West of Europe, until, on the Revival of Learning in the fifteenth century, this among other branches of knowledge began to be increased, Christian Hebraists to flourish, Grammars and Lexicons to be issued in abundance. Eminent among lexicographers were Pagninus, the Buxtorfs, Simonis, and others, who retained the Etymological arrangement of words in vogue among the Jews, according to derivation from their verbal roots.

After them the renowned Gesenius adopted the Alphabetical arrangement of Nouns and Particles, by which a great facility was afforded to students, who often experienced a difficulty in tracing their Radical derivation. Other famous Hebraists, as Lee and Fürst, followed the Alphabetical example set by Gesenius, and the result has been that in modern times the knowledge of Hebrew has greatly advanced, both in Universities and Collegiate Schools, and also among those who, without the advantage of professorial instruction, study for themselves.

A still further step, however, remained to be taken for the benefit of these. Not only the derivation of Nouns, but the inflections of Verbs also, and the combination of Particles, are often difficult to a beginner, and to such as for want of leisure cannot acquire or afterwards retain for themselves the mastery of all the Hebrew forms as they could wish. Accordingly, the ANALYTICAL HEBREW AND CHALDEE LEXICON has been compiled, in which every separate word of the Old Testament original, in every variety of conformation, is exhibited in its Alphabetical place, accompanied with a full grammatical Analysis of its composition, the indication of its root, and its English meaning after the best authorities. The utility of such a work is obvious, and can hardly be overrated. To augment its value, a complete Series of Paradigms, both of Nouns and Verbs, with explanatory remarks, is prefixed.

Although the primary design of this Lexicon has been to supply the learner with the utmost possible assistance, it is no less serviceable for permanent use by those who have attained a scholarly proficiency in the study of the Hebrew and Chaldee Scriptures.

THE CONTENTS

			PAGE
OBJECT AND PLAN			vii
LIST OF ABBREVIATIONS			x

GRAMMATICAL OBSERVATIONS, WITH TABLES OF PARADIGMS OF THE HEBREW LANGUAGE.

SECTION I.	The Personal Pronoun	(TABLE A)	9
	The Separate Pronoun		10
II.	The Verbal Suffix		10
III.	Suffixes to the Noun in the Singular		12
IV.	Suffixes to the Noun in the Plural		12
V.	Suffixes attached to the Prefix Prepositions לְ and בְּ, the Conjunction כְּ, אֵת (Sign of the Accusative) and the Prepositions מִן and עִם		13
VI.	Unusual Conjugations		15
VII.	Quadriliterals		17
VIII.	Regular Verb—KAL	(TABLE B, p. 15)	17
IX.	Niphal		20
X.	Piel and Pual		21
XI.	Hiphil and Hophal		22
XII.	Hithpael		24
XIII.	Verb Pe Guttural	(TABLE C, p. 25)	26
XIV.	Ayin Guttural	(TABLE D, p. 25)	28
XV.	Lamed Guttural	(TABLE E, p. 26)	29
XVI.	Regular Verb with Suffixes	(TABLE F, p. 29)	30
XVII.	Irregular Verbs—Pe Nun	(TABLE G, p. 32)	33
XVIII.	Ayin doubled	(TABLE H)	34
XIX.	Pe Aleph	(TABLE I)	39
XX.	Pe Yod	(TABLE K)	41
XXI.	Ayin Vav	(TABLE L, p. 44)	45
XXII.	Ayin Yod	(Ditto)	47
XXIII.	Lamed Aleph	(TABLE M)	48
XXIV.	Lamed He	(TABLE N, p. 50)	51
XXV.	Verbs doubly Anomalous		54
XXVI.	Nouns derived from the Regular Verb		55
XXVII.	Irregular Verbs		56
XXVIII.	The Vowel-changes of Nouns		57
XXIX.	On the Declension of the Masculine Nouns in General	(TABLE O, pp. 59, 60)	58

THE CONTENTS.

			PAGE
SECTION XXX.	First Declension of the Masculines		61
XXXI.	Second Declension of the Masculines		62
XXXII.	Third Declension of the Masculines		63
XXXIII.	Fourth Declension of the Masculines		64
XXXIV.	Fifth Declension of the Masculines		64
XXXV.	Sixth Declension of the Masculines		65
XXXVI.	Seventh Declension of the Masculines		68
XXXVII.	Eighth Declension of the Masculines		69
XXXVIII.	Ninth Declension of the Masculines		70
XXXIX.	Vowel-changes in the Formation of Feminine Nouns		71
XL.	On the Declension of the Feminine Nouns in General	(TABLE O, p. 60)	73
XLI.	Tenth Declension, or the *First* of the Feminines		73
XLII.	Eleventh Declension, or the *Second* of the Feminines		73
XLIII.	Twelfth Declension, or the *Third* of the Feminines		74
XLIV.	Thirteenth Declension, or the *Fourth* of the Feminines		75
XLV.	Irregular Nouns		76

OF THE CHALDEE LANGUAGE.

	The Personal Pronoun	(TABLE P)	78
XLVI.	On the Suffixes to Nouns Singular and Plural		78
XLVII.	On the Regular Verb	(TABLE Q, p. 79)	80
XLVIII.	Unfrequent Conjugations		80
XLIX.	Verbs with Gutturals		81
L.	On the Regular Verb with Suffixes	(TABLE R, p. 81)	82
	TABLE T. Verbs Ayin doubled		82
LI.	On Verbs Pe Nun	(TABLE S, p. 82)	83
LII.	On Verbs Pe Yod (and Pe Vav)	(TABLE U)	83
LIII.	Verbs Pe Aleph		83
LIV.	On Verbs Ayin Vav (and Ayin Yod)	(TABLE V)	84
LV.	On Verbs Lamed Aleph (and Lamed He)	(TABLE W, p. 85)	86
LVI.	Verbs doubly Anomalous		86
	TABLE X. Declension of Masculine and Feminine Nouns		87
LVII.	First Declension of Masculines		88
LVIII.	Second Declension of Masculines		88
LIX.	Third Declension of Masculines		88
LX.	Fourth Declension of Masculines		89
LXI.	Fifth Declension of Masculines		89
LXII.	Sixth Declension of Masculines		89
LXIII.	Seventh Declension of Masculines		89
LXIV.	Eighth Declension, or the *First* of Feminines		89
LXV.	Ninth Declension, or the *Second* of Feminines		89
LXVI.	Tenth Declension, or the *Third* of Feminines		89
LXVII.	Eleventh Declension, or the *Fourth* of Feminines		89
LXVIII.	Irregular Nouns		90

THE ANALYTICAL HEBREW AND CHALDEE LEXICON, Containing the Alphabetical Arrangement of the Words of the Entire Hebrew Scriptures, with parsing Analysis and Lexicography . . . 1 to 784

THE OBJECT AND PLAN

OF THE

ANALYTICAL HEBREW AND CHALDEE

LEXICON

FROM what has been briefly stated in the Preface, it will sufficiently appear that this Work is intended, not so much to teach the first principles of Hebrew Grammar, as to provide the Student who has already begun to read a little (ever so little) with the means of making *speedy and sure after progress.* Its object is to assist him in his practice of the Sacred Text, by enabling him to apply the Rules he has learned, and may be learning; and, by supplying him with the Analysis of every single word in the entire language, under every form it can assume, it promises him exemption from the tedium and disappointment of uncertainty in his investigations.

Experience has shown that multitudes of Hebrew students, after having overcome the first difficulties under the instruction of a living Teacher, abandon further study for lack of a Guide through the yet untrodden intricacies of the Language. Our aim has been to provide a permanent Instructor, to succeed the living Teacher in his function of solving the difficulties of the inquiring Student; and we have endeavoured neither to mislead by imperfect information, nor to disappoint by suppressing the explanation of apparently trifling matters.

As an ANALYTICAL LEXICON, this work embraces especially the ETYMOLOGY and SIGNIFICATION of WORDS.

The following summary will exhibit the mode of treatment adopted:—

THE ETYMOLOGY OF WORDS.

I. The entire body of Words, contained in the Hebrew Scriptures, exactly as they are found in the Text, have been thrown into Alphabetical order; so that each, accompanied by its prefixes, suffixes, and under every modification of form, may be immediately found by an alphabetical reference.

II. Each word thus arranged is concisely and fully *parsed*, its composition is explained, and its simple form and root given.

III. Whenever the form of the word analysed agrees with the Tables of Paradigms, a plain but full statement of the nature of the word has been considered sufficient; but where any peculiar difficulty or irregularity exists, reference has also been made to the section of the Grammatical Introduction in which the deviation is explained.

IV. To provide standards of inflexion and comparison, a complete series of PARADIGMS of the Verbs, Pronouns, and Nouns, of both the Hebrew and Chaldee languages, has been prepared.

V. These Tables are accompanied with Explanations and Remarks, which account for every deviation from the Tables, and comprise a COLLECTION OF EVERY SINGLE EXCEPTIONAL CASE. In the body of the work, these *Explanations* are indicated by reference to their number.

VI. Every form that happens to occur but once in the Bible has its reference to the passage given at the foot of the page. To this we have attended in the minutest difference of the forms, in order to increase the references, so valuable to the beginner who has no Concordance. When, however, the form is especially peculiar, more than one reference is given.

*** It is an interesting and important fact, that this collection of citations constitutes a Concordance of more than three-fourths of the forms of the Language.

VII. The place of the Accent is throughout indicated by a perpendicular line (ˌ) under the tone-syllable, except when the form is affected by a pausal accent, where (֭) is used to indicate the tone-syllable; while the absence of pausal accent and influence are marked with (ˏ).

VIII. Kamets Hhattuph (ŏ) is distinguished from the long Kamets (ā) by this sign (ָ). But this is used only in the forms analysed, in the leading forms of the derivatives under their respective roots, and in those forms where its use requires particular notice.

THE SIGNIFICATION OR LEXICOGRAPHY OF WORDS.

IX. A full explanation of the various meanings of the words will be found under their respective Roots, in their alphabetical place.

X. In preparing the Lexicography, Gesenius has been chiefly relied on for definitions; but the works of Dr. Lee, Winer, Biesenthal, Fürst, and others, have been compared throughout.

XI. In addition to the various significations of each root, a Synoptical List of all the words derived from each is given, to aid the student in remembering the connection between the root and its derivatives.

BENJAMIN DAVIDSON.

LIST OF ABBREVIATIONS

IN THE WORK.

abs. st.	absolute state
acc.	accent, accusative
a. & act.	active
adj.	adjective
adv.	adverb
anom.	anomaly & anomalous
ap. & apoc.	apocopated
Aph.	Aphel
aphær.	aphæresis
Arab.	Arabic
art.	article
bef.	before
c. & com.	common
causat.	causative
Ch. & Chald.	Chaldee
coll.	collated
collect.	collectively
comp.	compare
compd.	compounded
compos.	composition
concr.	concrete
conj.	conjunction & conjunctive
const.	construed
constr.	construct
contr.	contracted
conv.	conversive
cop.	copulative
d. & dec.	declension
Dag.	Dagesh
def. & defect.	defective
demon.	demonstrative
denom.	denominative
deriv.	derivative
dist.	distinctive
du.	dual [tically.
emph.	emphatic & empha-
Eng. vers.	English version
epenth.	epenthetic
Ethiop.	Ethiopic
euph.	euphony
f. & fem.	feminine
f.	for
foll.	following
fr.	from
fut.	future
gen.	gender
genit.	genitive
gent.	gentile & gentilic
gutt.	guttural
Hiph.	Hiphil
Hithpa.	Hithpael
Hithpal.	Hithpalel
Hithpol.	Hithpolel
Hoph.	Hophal
Hothp.	Hothpael
i. q.	id quod
id.	idem
imp.	imperative
impl.	implied
inf. & infin.	infinitive
interrog.	interrogative
intrans.	intransitive
irr. & irreg.	irregular
Ithpe.	Ithpeel
Ishtaph.	Ishtaphal
K.	Keri
Kh. & Kheth.	Khethiv
l. c.	loco citato
lab.	labial
lett.	letter
loc.	local
m. & masc.	masculine
Mak.	Makkeph
metaph.	metaphorically
meton.	metonymy & metonymically
monos.	monosyllable & monosyllabic
n. f. s.	noun, feminine, singular
n. m. s.	noun, masculine, singular
n. m. p.	noun, masculine, plural
Niph.	Niphal
Nith.	Nithpael
numb. card.	cardinal number
obsol.	obsolete
p. & pass.	passive
Pa.	Pael
Pal.	Palel
parad.	paradigm
parag.	paragogic
part.	participle
patronym.	patronymi
perh.	perhaps
pers.	person
Pi.	Piël
Pil.	Pilel
pl.	plural
Pol.	Polal & Polel
Polp	Polpal
preced.	preceding
pref.	prefix
prep.	preposition
pret.	preterite
prim.	primary
pr. n. m	proper name, masculine
prob.	probably
pron. demon.	demonstrative pronoun
pron. relat.	relative pronoun
prop.	properly
prosth.	prosthetic
Pu.	Pual
Pul.	Pulal
q. v.	quod vide
R.	Root
Seg. n.	Segolate noun
Shaph.	Shaphel
sc.	scilicet
Sept.	Septuagint
suff.	suffix
s. & sing.	singular
Talm.	Talmud
term.	termination
Tiph.	Tiphal
trop.	tropically
ult.	ultimate
Vulg.	Vulgate
§ & rem.	refers to the Paradigms and remarks at the commencement of the work
1 p., 2 p.,	1 pers. & 2 pers., &c., 1st or 2nd person
3 p. s. m.	3rd person singular masculine, &c.

[a], [b], or [c], &c. after any word, refers to the passage at the foot of the page.

וּ, וַ, וָ, or וְ, placed before any word indicates that such word occurs only with this conjunction.

׳וּ, ׳וַ, ׳וָ, or ׳וְ, placed before any word indicates that such word occurs with and without this conjunction.

)(This sign divides the explanation of the word's prefix from the analysis of the word itself.

[ ] inclose forms which do not actually occur in the Scriptures.

TABLES OF PARADIGMS

OF

THE HEBREW LANGUAGE

WITH

REMARKS AND OCCASIONAL EXPLANATIONS

SECTION I.—THE PERSONAL PRONOUN

TABLE A. THE PERSONAL PRONOUN.

SEPARATE PRONOUN.		VERBAL SUFFIX. A. SIMPLE FORM.		VERBAL SUFFIX. B. WITH נ EPENTHETIC.	NOMINAL SUFFIX. A. SUFF. TO NOUNS SINGULAR.		NOMINAL SUFFIX. B. TO NOUNS PLURAL AND DUAL.	
Singular.								
1. *com.* אָנֹכִי, in pause אָנֹכִי; אֲנִי, in pause אָנִי	*I.*	־ַנִי; ־ֵנִי; נִי	*me.*	־ֶנִּי, ־ֶנִּי	־ִי	*my.*	־ַי	*my.*
2. *m.* אַתָּה (אַתְּ), in pause אָתָּה	*thou.*	ךָ, in pause ־ֶךָּ	*thee.*	־ֶךָּ	ךָ, in pause ־ֶךָ	*thy.*	־ֶיךָ	*thy.*
f. אַתְּ (אַתִּי, prop. אַתִּי) in p. אָתְּ		־ֶךְ; ־ֵךְ; ־ָךְ; ךְ		not found.	־ֵךְ, ךְ		־ַיִךְ	
3. *m.* הוּא	*he.*	־ֵהוּ, ־ָהוּ; וֹ, הוּ; (־ָמוֹ); וֹ, הֹ	*him.*	־ֶנּוּ, (נּוֹ)	הוּ, וֹ; ־ֵהוּ, וֹ, הֹ	*his.*	־ֵיהוּ, ־ָו, ־ָיו	*his.*
f. הִיא	*she.*	־ֶהָ; ־ָהּ; הָ	*her.*	־ֶנָּה	־ֶהָ; ־ָהּ; הָ	*her.*	־ֶיהָ	*her.*
Plural.								
1. *com.* אֲנַחְנוּ (נַחְנוּ), (אָנוּ)	*we.*	־ֵנוּ (*nos*); ־ָנוּ; נוּ	*us.*	־ֶנּוּ	־ֵנוּ; נוּ	*our.*	־ֵינוּ	*our.*
2. *m.* אַתֶּם	*ye.*	כֶם	*you.*	not found.	כֶם	*your.*	־ֵיכֶם	*your.*
f. אַתֵּנָה, אַתֶּן		כֶן			כֶן		־ֵיכֶן	
3. *m.* הֵמָּה, הֵם	*they.*	־ֵם, ־ָם; ם, הֶם; ־ֵמוֹ, ־ָמוֹ (*eos*)	*them.*	not found.	־ָמוֹ, ־ָם; הֶם	*their.*	־ֵימוֹ, ־ֵיהֶם	*their.*
f. הֵנָּה, הֵן		־ֵן, ־ָן; ן, הֶן; ־ֵן (*eas*)			־ָן, הֶן, הֵן		־ֵיהֶן	

SECTION I.—THE SEPARATE PRONOUN. (Table A).

REMARKS.

1. *First Person Singular.*

אָנֹכִי is the ancient and full form, of which אֲנִי is an abbreviation, and from the latter are formed the suffixes attached to nouns, verbs, &c.

2. *Second Person Singular.*

Instead of Dagesh forte in אַתְּ, אַתָּה (pl. אַתֶּם), the kindred dialects have נ before ת (Chald. & Arab. אַנְתְּ), which, however, is not the original form, but ת alone is the characteristic consonant.*

אַתְּ without ה occurs only in 1 Sa. 24. 19; Ps. 6. 4; Job 1. 10; Ec. 7. 22; Ne. 9. 6; it is, however, in each place corrected in the Keri. The *feminine* form אַתִּי in Ju. 17. 2; 1 Ki. 14. 2; 2 Ki. 4. 16, 23; 8. 1; Je. 4. 30; Eze. 36. 13, was originally pronounced אַתִּי (with the feminine designation ִי, probably from הִיא *she*, properly *thou she*, comp. תִּקְטְלִי) as in the Syriac and the vulgar Arabic. The pointing with Sheva is agreeably to the Keri אַתְּ, because the Jewish critics, as it appears, did not recognise the form אַתִּי. The same final י appears likewise in the unfrequent form of the suffix ֵכִי, ֵיכִי.

3. *Third Person Singular.*

The masculine הוא is of common gender in the Pentateuch, and signifies also *she* (which is expressed by הִיא only eleven times, viz., Ge. 14. 2; 20. 5; 38. 25; Le. 2. 15; 11. 39; 13. 10, 21; 16. 31; 21. 9; Nu. 5. 13). The punctuators, however, either from want of appreciating such an idiom, or for the sake of distinction, whenever הוא stands in the text for הִיא, give it the appropriate pointing of this form, (הִוא), and require it to be read הִיא. It is, however, to be sounded rather according to the old form הוא. Besides the Pentateuch, הִיא occurs also in 1 Ki. 17. 15; Job 31. 11; Is. 30. 33.

4. *First Person Plural.*

אֲנַחְנוּ is manifestly the plural of אָנֹכִי, with the exchange of כ for ח, as אֲנוּ is of אֲנִי. The form אֲנוּ, from which the suffixes (ֵנוּ, ָנוּ, נוּ) are derived, is found only in Je. 42. 6, Khethib. The Masorites, however, did not recognize so unusual a form, and instead of it put אֲנַחְנוּ, which, indeed, some MSS. and editions have even as the reading of the text itself. Nevertheless, אֲנוּ appears also in the Rabbinical. The abbreviated form נַחְנוּ is found only six times, viz., Ge. 42. 11; Ex. 16. 7, 8; Nu. 32. 32; 2 Sa. 17. 12; La. 3. 42.

5. *Second Person Plural.*

אַתֶּם & אַתֶּן are blunted forms of אַתּוּם (Arab. *antum*, Chald. אַתּוּן, a form which lies at the foundation of some verbal inflexions, comp. the preterite with suffix), and אַתִּין, the full final vowel giving place to the obtuse sound of *e*, somewhat in the manner of the third person (הֵם). אַתֵּן is found only once, Eze. 34. 31 (where another reading is אַתֶּן); and אַתֵּנָה (for which some MSS. have also אַתֶּנָה) occurs only in Ge. 31. 6; Eze. 13. 11, 20; 34. 17.

6. *Third Person Plural.*

הֵם & הֵן are got from הוא and הִיא in the same manner as אַתֶּם from אַתָּה. The ָה in both forms (ה *paragogic*) has a *demonstrative* force.

SECTION II.—THE VERBAL SUFFIX.† (Table A).

REMARKS.

1. *First Person Singular*

Has this peculiarity, that the union vowel of the form ַנִי is invariably *Pattah*, though in an open syllable we expect *Kamets*, as in ָנוּ, ָהוּ; but this Kamets is found only in pause, e. g. Ex. 5. 22. For ֵנִי, the full form ֵינִי is found with the *fut.* in 1 Ki. 2. 24, Kheth. For ִנִי see Ps. 118. 18; Ge. 30. 6; with the *fut.* Job 7. 14; 9. 34; ֶנִּי Je. 50. 44.

* Comp. Sansc. *toa*; Egypt. *entok*, fem. *ento*; ancient and modern Pers. *tu*; Greek τυ (συ); Germ. *tu*, *du* [Engl. *thou*], see Gesenius's Heb. Gram. § 33, note.

† Just as the separate suffixes stand for the nominative, so the inseparable, when appended to verbs, stand for the accusative, and but rarely for the dative, as with intransitive verbs. Particles having the force of a verb, or where the substantive verb must be supplied, take the verbal suffixes. As, הִנְנִי *behold me!* but on the contrary אֵינֶנּוּ *he* (is) *not*, עוֹדֶנּוּ *he* (is) *yet*, where the nominative is designated by the same suffix. The suffixes are but seldom employed with prepositions. Comp. § 3, note.

2. *Second Person Singular.*

The pausal form for the masculine, ־ֶךָּ, commonly found with the verbs ל״ה & ל״א (Is. 30. 19; Je. 23. 37; Eze. 28. 15), is seldom attached to other verbs (Is. 55. 5; De. 28. 24, 45), but ־ְךָ is the more usual form (Is. 43. 5; 44. 2; Ps. 30. 13); the reverse, however, obtains when appended to the particles.

Unfrequent forms are, כָּה 1 Ki. 18. 44, and ־ֶכָּה Pr. 2. 11. אֶמְאָסְאךָ Ho. 4. 6 is probably pointed incorrectly for אֶמְאָסְאךְ, a Syriac form of the suffix, which occurs a few times in the Codex Sam. (Ge. 22. 26.)

The form ־ֶךְ for the *feminine* is unusual with the verb (Is. 54. 6), as is also ־ִךְ when appended to the *preterite*, and ־ֵךְ, the tone being thrown back (Is. 47. 10, comp. Is. 60. 7). כִי, ־ָכִי (as in the Syriac) are frequently found in the later Psalms, comp. Ps. 137. 6.

3. *Third Person Singular.*

The forms ־ֶנּוּ, ־ֶנָּה occur frequently, and are most common in pause, comp. Ps. 65. 10; Job 5. 27; 41. 2. The two forms (viz., with and without epenth. נ) are found in immediate succession in Is. 26. 5, יַשְׁפִּילֶנָּה יַשְׁפִּילָהּ עַד אֶרֶץ *he casts her down, casts her down to the earth.* The first word ought, doubtless, to conclude the first hemistich, though the accents decide differently.

־ָהּ is frequently written without Mappik, comp. וַתַּחְמְרָה Ex. 2. 3; הִוָּסְדָה Ex. 9. 18; שְׁמָרָה Amos 1. 11 (the best mode of explaining the latter passage).

־ֶנָּה is of common occurrence.

4. *First Person Plural.*

In Is. 85. 7, several MSS. and editions have ־ֵינוּ instead of ־ֵנוּ.

For this suffix the Chaldee uses the form נָא. Some discover such a Chaldaism in תִּקְרֶאנָה Ex. 1. 10, for תִּקְרָאנוּ (*she befalls us*). But נָה here may be regarded as the afformative of the fut. 3 pers. pl. fem. agreeing with מִלְחָמָה, which follows it, in a collective sense (*wars*).* The Samaritan text indeed has such a Chaldaism in De. 32. 3, where לאלהינה stands for לאלהינו, and in Nu. 16. 13.

5. *Third Person Plural.*

That the forms of מוֹ belong exclusively to the poetical style, may be seen from the examples in Noldius, Concordd. Particul. ed. Tympe, pp. 438, 498, 563, 564. But comp. § 5. No. 2, note. In Ex. 15. 5, occurs יְכַסְיֻמוּ with י which is found nowhere else. This is, however, the common form in the Ethiopic.

For the suffix ן (fem.), ם is frequently substituted (prob. to prevent its being mistaken for the paragogic Nun), so that the distinction between masc. and fem. entirely ceases: e. g. וַיְגָרְשׁוּם *and they drove them* (the daughters) *away*, Ex. 2. 17; וַיַּאַסְרוּם *and they tied them* (the kine), 1 Sa. 6. 10. Comp. Ge. 26. 15; Nu. 17. 3, 4; Jos. 4. 8; Ho. 2. 14; Pr. 6. 21. Just the reverse is found in the word יְדַעְתִּין Is. 48. 7, where ן stands for ם.

6. The tone invariably rests on the union vowel, or, in the absence of this, on the last syllable of the word. כֶם, כֶן and הֶם, הֶן are excepted, and are therefore called *grave*, the others *light* suffixes.

7. The participles and infinitives may take either the verbal, or nominal suffixes. The participle is but slightly affected by their difference, as עֹשֵׂנִי *he who created me*, Job 32. 22, and עֹשִׂי *my creator;* רֹאֵנִי Is. 47. 10, comp. Is. 28. 4. With the infinitive, however, they effect a change in the signification. E. g. קָרְאִי *my calling*, Ps. 141. 1, פָּקְדִי *my visiting*, Je. 32. 5; but לְהָרְגֵנִי *to slay me*, Ex. 2. 14, לְעָזְרֵנִי *to help me*, 1 Ch. 12. 17. In the first examples, the suffix denotes the genitive, in the latter the accusative. A single exception is found in Eze. 47. 7, בְּשׁוּבֵנִי *in my returning*, for בְּשׁוּבִי.

* In the same manner may be explained in Job 17. 16, תֵּרַדְנָה, as agreeing with תִּקְוָתִי (collect. *expectations*) of the preceding verse; in Is. 28. 3, תֵּרָמַסְנָה, instead of agreeing with the subject עֲטֶרֶת, agrees with the instrumental רַגְלַיִם; and so in Ju. 5. 26, תִּשְׁלַחְנָה, agrees with the accusative יָדָהּ (collect. *her hands*), comp. Ge. 27. 39; 31. 8; Is. 18. 5, where the verb, instead of agreeing with the subject, agrees with the predicate. Moreover, תִּשְׁלַחְנָה Ob. 13, may refer to the people addressed there, in the feminine. Hence several grammarians and commentators have been induced to observe, that the plural form of the future, תִּקְטֹלְנָה, frequently stands for the singular תִּקְטֹל, which, indeed, suits well the several passages.

SECTION III.—SUFFIXES TO THE NOUN IN THE SINGULAR.* (TABLE A).

REMARKS.

1. When the *First Person* ִי is to be appended to a noun terminating in ִי, one Yod is dropped, as גּוֹיִ my people, Zep. 2. 9, for גּוֹיִי.

ִי has the tone, which it loses when the word following is either monosyllabic, or dissyllabic, having the tone on the first syllable (Milêl); e. g. אֲחֹתִי אָתְּ (thou art my sister) Ge. 12. 13; כְּכֹחִי עָתָּה Jos. 14. 11, comp. Ge. 20. 2, 5; 26. 7, 9; 49. 3; Je. 2. 27; 31. 9; 2 Sa. 23. 17; Job 19. 25; 20. 2; Ps. 140. 7.

2. *Second Person Singular.*

Unfrequent forms: masc. כַּפֶּכָה (thy hand) Ps. 139. 5, חֵלְכָה (thy host) Ps. 10. 14, but see the analysis of this form in the alphabetical order. Fem. ֵיךְ Eze. 5. 12; ָךְ (like the suffix of the verb) for ֵךְ, Eze. 23. 28; ֵכִי Je. 11. 15; Ps. 103. 3.

3. *Third Person Singular.*

The form ה for ו seems to belong to an older orthography. It is generally corrected in the Keri, as in Ge. 49. 11 (twice); Ex. 22. 26; Le. 23. 13; 2 Ki. 19. 23; 20. 13; but is not corrected in Je. 2. 21; Eze. 20. 40.

ָה is also found without Mappik, as in Nu. 15. 28 (Job 31. 22): so that even ָא is substituted for it in Eze. 36. 5, אֱדוֹם כֻּלָּא (Edom, the whole of her) for כֻּלָּה.

The forms ֵהוּ and ֶהָ are usually attached to nouns ending in ֶה, e. g. מַרְאֶה (sight)—מַרְאֵהוּ, מַרְאֶהָ; שָׂדֶה (field)—שָׂדֵהוּ; עָלֶה (leaf)—עָלֵהוּ; and so with מֵרֵעַ, רֵעַ for מֵרֵעֶה, רֵעֶה (friend). With other words they are seldom used, as לְמִינֵהוּ Ge. 1. 12, comp. Ju. 19. 24; Na. 1. 13; Job 25. 3.

4. *First Person Plural.*

The form ָנוּ (like the suff. of the verb) instead of ֵנוּ, must be regarded as an exception, as Job 22. 20; Ru. 3. 2, comp. No. 2.

5. *Second and Third Person Plural.*

Anomalous and unfrequent forms are: 2 pers. כֶנָה Eze. 23. 48 (comp. Eze. 13. 20); 3 pers. masc ָהֵם 2 Sa. 23. 6, for ָהֶם (whence contr. ָם); fem. ָהֶנָה 1 Ki. 7. 37; ֶנָה e. g. כֻּלָּנָה Ge. 42. 36; Pr. 31. 29; בֹּאֲנָה Ru. 1. 19; Je. 8. 7; לְדָתָּנָה Job 39. 2; לְבַדְּנָה Ge. 21. 29; ֶנָה Ge. 41. 21; הֶן and הֵן e. g. מַלְכָּהֶן Eze. 13. 17, פָּתְהֵן Is. 3. 1

SECTION IV.—SUFFIXES TO THE NOUN IN THE PLURAL. (TABLE A).

REMARKS.

1. The י which distinguishes these suffixes, is occasionally omitted in most of the persons; e. g. דְּרָכֶךָ (similar to the pausal form of the singular) for דְּרָכֶיךָ *thy ways*, Ex. 33. 13; Ps. 119. 37; Jos. 1. 8; רֵעֵהוּ for רֵעֵיהוּ *his friends*, Job 42. 10; 1 Sa. 30. 26; אַשְׁרֵהוּ for אַשְׁרֵיהוּ *his felicities*, Pr. 29. 18; חֶלְבְהֶן *their fat*, Ge. 4. 4; גּוֹיֵהֶם *their nations*, Ge. 10. 5; לְמִינֵהֶם *after their kinds*, Ge. 1. 21; לִבְּהֶן *their hearts*, Na. 2. 8. This is most frequent in suffixes of the 3 pers. sing. masc., ָיו, which is very often, and in all the copies alike, written ָו, but the Keri almost always substitutes the common form ָיו. The word יַחְדָּו (*together*, properly *his unions*) is alone excepted, in which the Keri has made no change, probably because ָו was not regarded as a suffix. יַחְדָּיו occurs only in Je. 46. 12, 21; 49. 3.

2. Although ֵי, or the י prefixed to these suffixes, is, doubtless, originally the plural termination of the masculine, they are yet regularly attached to the feminine plural וֹת also; as קוֹלוֹתַי *my voices*, קוֹלוֹתֶיךָ *thy voices.* It is hence to be regarded as an exception, when these suffixes are occasionally found appended to וֹת without this י. As, עֵדֹתַי *my testimonies*, Ps. 132. 12; מַכֹּתְךָ *thy strokes*, De. 28. 59; אֲחוֹתֵךְ *thy sisters*, Ex. 16. 52; אֲבוֹתָם *their fathers*, Ex. 4. 5; אוֹתֹתָם *their signs*, Ps. 74. 4; עַצְּבוֹתָם *their pains*, Ps. 16. 4; צָרוֹתָם *their distresses*, Ps. 34. 18.

3. These suffixes with י are found, on the other hand, also with forms of the *singular;* as, תְּהִלָּתֶיךָ *thy praise*, Ps. 9. 15; שִׂנְאָתֶיךָ *thy hatred*, Eze. 35. 11; בְּנוֹתַיִךְ *thy building*, Eze. 16. 31; הַזְּנוּתֵיכֶם *your dis-*

* The suffixes appended to the noun properly stand for the genitive, as סוּסִי *the horse of me*, i. e. my horse. The prepositions, being originally substantives, take likewise these suffixes with a few exceptions (as בַּעֲדֵנִי, תַּחְתֵּנִי) comp. § 2, note.

person, Eze. 6. 8. To these may be added חֲמִישִׁתָיו Le. 5. 24, as it has, at least, the signification of the singular, *his fifth part.*

4. *Second Person Singular.*

Yod in ־ַ֫יִךְ is furtive (like that in בַּיִת for בַּ֫יְתְ), and the original form ־ַיְךְ is found in the Syriac and Chaldee. The feminine in these dialects is ـܶܟܝ, ־ָ֫יְכִי, and so it is likewise in the Hebrew, by a Syriacism, as in Ps. 103. 3, 4, 5; 116. 7, and in Kheth. 2 Ki. 4. 3, 7. ־ֵיךְ Ec. 10. 17, is formed in imitation of the singular ־ֵךְ. The suffix in מַלְאָכֵכֵה (*her messengers*) Nah. 2. 14, can hardly be accounted for; other codices read ־ֵכֶה and ־ֶכָה.

5. *Third Person Singular.*

The poetic ־ָיְהוּ is formed in imitation of the singular ־ֵהוּ, e. g. Job 24. 23; Na. 2. 4.—וֹהִי in תַּגְמוּלוֹהִי Ps. 116. 12, is strictly a Chaldee form. For ־ֶיהָ is found ־ֶהָא in Eze. 41. 15, comp. Chald. ־ַהָא *her*. Here we meet, finally, with an epenthetic נ, viz. in מָעֻזְנֶיהָ Is. 23. 11, for מָעֻזֶּיהָ *her fortresses.*

6. For the poetic form ־ֵימוֹ, comp. De. 32. 37; Job 20. 23; 22. 2; 27. 23; Ps. 11. 7. Some of the older grammarians* observe, that this form stands occasionally also for the singular. Kimchi (incorrectly) assigns as a reason, that this form exhibits both characteristics of the plural and of the singular. But though it cannot be denied that in the passages cited above (De. 32. 37 excepted) this suffix has reference to nouns singular, nevertheless, those nouns being collectives, do not lose their plural signification. Another instance is in Ps. 11. 7, where פָּנֵימוֹ as referring to יְהוָה may be regarded as a *Pluralis majestatis.* But were this form even to be admitted as strictly a singular, e. g. in Ps. 11. 7, we should then have to suppose it a misuse arising from its frequent occurrence in connection with collective nouns. The passages (Lu. 2. 4; Jo. 19. 27; Ac. 1. 20, from the Ethiopic version) cited by Lud. de Dieu (Crit. Sacra, p. 226, on Is. 53. 6), seem at all events to prove, that the suffix ሙ, answering to the Hebrew ־ֵימוֹ, does in the Ethiopic stand for the singular.†

Other unfrequent forms are, ־ֵיהֵמָה Eze. 40. 16, ־ֵיהֶנָה Eze. 1. 11; ־ֵיכֶמָה Eze. 13. 20.

SECTION V.

Suffixes attached to the Prefix Prepositions לְ and בְּ, the Conjunction כְּ, אֵת (Sign of the Accusative) and the Prepositions מִן and עִם.‡

(*a*) לְ *to*, sign of the dative. | (*b*) בְּ *in*.

		Sing.		*Plur.*		*Sing.*		*Plur*	
1.	c.	לִי . .	*to me.*	לָנוּ . .	*to us.*	בִּי . .	*in me.*	בָּנוּ	*in us.*
2.	m.	לְךָ, in pause לָךְ	*to thee.*	לָכֶם	*to you.*	בְּךָ, in p. בָּךְ	*in thee.*	בָּכֶם	*in you.*
	f.	לָךְ . .		לָכֶן		בָּךְ .		——	
3.	m.	לוֹ, (לָמוֹ comp. r. 2)	*to him.*	לָהֶם, poet. לָמוֹ	*to them.*	בּוֹ . .	*in him.*	בָּם	*in them.*
	f.	לָהּ . .	*to her.*	לָהֶן . .		בָּהּ .	*in her.*	בָּהֵן, בָּהֶן	

(*c*) כְּ *as* (for which also כְּמוֹ, כָּמוֹ). | (*d*) אֵת (sign of the accusative).

		Sing.		*Plur.*		*Sing.*		*Plur.*	
1.	c.	כָּמוֹנִי . .	*as I.*	כָּמוֹנוּ . .	*as we.*	אֹתִי, אוֹתִי .	*me.*	אֹתָנוּ	*us.*
2.	m.	כָּמוֹךָ . .	*as thou.*	כָּכֶם seldom כְּמוֹכֶם	*as ye.*	אֹתְךָ, in p. אֹתָךְ	*thee.*	אֶתְכֶם	*you.*
	f.	——		—— — —		אֹתָךְ .		——	
3.	m.	כָּמוֹהוּ . .	*as he.*	כָּהֶם, כָּהֵם, כְּמוֹהֶם	*as they.*	אֹתוֹ . .	*him.*	אֹתָם	*them.*
	f.	כָּמוֹהָ . .	*as she.*	—— — —		אֹתָהּ .	*her.*	אֹתָן	

* Kimchii Michlol, fol. 266, comp. l' Empereur on M. Kimchii, *ὁδοιπορια*, p. 243; Noldii Concordd. Partic. pp. 904, 916.

† We have given this remark of Gesenius in full, chiefly on account of his admission with regard to the use of this suffix in the Ethiopic, which is important, and may assist in the explanation of the form לָמוֹ in the following §, rem. 2.

‡ We exhibit these in particular, because of some peculiar forms they take when connected with the suffixes.

(*e*) מִן *from* (for which also מִמֶּן, properly, *a part*).

		Sing.		Plur.	
1.	c.	מִמֶּנִּי, poet. מִנִּי, מֶנִּי	*from me.*	מִמֶּנּוּ . .	*from us.*
2.	m.	מִמְּךָ, in pause מִמֶּךָּ	*from thee.*	מִכֶּם	*from you.*
	f.	מִמֵּךְ . .		מִכֶּן . .	
3.	m.	מִמֶּנּוּ, poet. מֶנְהוּ, מִנֵּהוּ	*from him.*	מֵהֶם, poet. מִנְהֶם	*from them.*
	f.	מִמֶּנָּה . .	*from her.*	מֵהֶן . .	

(*f*) עִם *with.*

		Sing.		Plur.	
1.	c.	עִמִּי . .	*with me.*	עִמָּנוּ	*with us.*
2.	m.	עִמְּךָ, in p. עִמָּךְ	*with thee.*	עִמָּכֶם	*with you.*
	f.	עִמָּךְ .		——	
3.	m.	עִמּוֹ .	*with him.*	עִמָּם, עִמָּהֶם	*with them.*
	f.	עִמָּהּ . .	*with her.*	——	

REMARKS.

I. On the Suffixes with לְ.

1. Instead of לוֹ the form לֹא is found several times (according to the Masora on Nu. chap. 11, 21 times) in Kheth., e. g. Ex. 21. 8; Le. 11. 21; 1 Sa. 2. 3, &c.

2. As regards the form לָמוֹ, grammarians maintain that it is also a singular, i. q. לוֹ, because it often agrees with nouns singular. Those singulars, however, are all collectives, and can therefore not serve as a proof. The examples are, Ge. 9. 26 (where it refers to שֵׁם, i. e. the descendants of Shem); Ps. 28. 8 (where it refers to the people of ver. 9, and hence some copies read לְעַמּוֹ); Ps. 73. 10 (also in reference to עַם); Is. 44. 15 (in reference to אֵל and פֶּסֶל, which may likewise be taken in a collective sense); and finally Is. 53. 8. Though the subject of this last chapter is throughout given in the singular, yet the change to the plural form in ver. 8 is fully accounted for, when the *servant of God* (chap. 51. 13, like 42. 1, and 49. 3, 6) is considered to stand collectively for *the prophets*, which to me seems quite evident. Some copies have in Is. 44. 15 and 53. 8, לוֹ, which is an exegetical gloss. (Gesenius.)*

3. Unfrequent forms are :—2 pers. masc. לְכָה Ge. 27. 37; 2 pers. pl. fem. לָכֶנָה Eze. 13. 18 (לָכֶן does not occur at all). לָהֵן Ru. 1. 13, is different from לָהֶן, and signifies *therefore*, as in the Chaldee.

II. On the Suffixes with אֵת.

4. The forms in the paradigm are the usual ones; unfrequent forms are:—2 pers. masc. אוֹתָכָה (in pause) Ex. 29. 35, אוֹתְכֶם Jos. 23. 15, אֶתְהֶם Ge. 32. 1, אוֹתְהֶם Eze. 23. 45; fem. אוֹתְהֶן Eze. 23. 47, אוֹתָנָה Ex. 35. 26.

III. On the Suffixes with מִן.

5. מִנִּי (*from me*) must not be confounded with מִנִּי where י is paragogic.

6. מִמֶּנּוּ *from him* (for מִמֶּנְהוּ), and מִמֶּנּוּ *from us* (for מִמֶּנְנוּ) can only be distinguished by the context.

7. The pronouns הֵמָּה and הֵנָּה often retain their full form after the prepositions, as, בָּהֵמָּה Ex. 36. 1; Hab. 1. 16; כָּהֵמָּה Je. 36. 32; לָהֵמָּה Je. 14. 16; מֵהֵמָּה Ec. 12. 12; Je. 10. 2; fem. בָּהֵנָּה Le. 5. 22; Nu. 13. 19; כָּהֵנָּה Ge. 41. 19; לָהֵנָּה Eze. 1. 5, 23; 42. 9; מֵהֵנָּה Le. 4. 2.

* But if there were even no other passage to establish the use of לָמוֹ in the singular, the passages Is. 53. 8, and 44. 15 alone might have been sufficient for this purpose: the former, where throughout the chapter only the singular appears; and the latter, where the plural does not at all suit the sense, and the writer himself explains it in the same connection by לוֹ in ver. 17. Comp. Hengstenberg's "Christology of the Old Testament," p. 523 of Prof. Keith's translation. In confirmation of this we may add the facts, that some copies do really read לוֹ instead of לָמוֹ in both passages, and that the form ומו in the Ethiopic, answering to the Hebrew ־ֵימוֹ, is used in that version for the singular, as Gesenius himself admits (comp. § 5. rem. 6). When we, moreover, consider that this poetic syllable, which never receives the tone as a suffix, almost everywhere occurs in pause, or, which amounts to the same thing, stands with a word preceding the pause (comp. De. 32. 27; Ps. 11. 7; Job 20. 23; and Lehrgeb. § 52, 4 anm. 1 in reference to Jos. 3. 9; De. 32. 37, comp. Is. 21. 14; Ps. 4. 3, comp. also below, § 24. rem. 5), its specific use, in the poetical books, appears to be, that it takes the place of other forms, which must necessarily have the tone upon the ultimate, to suit the pause, the tendency of which is to throw the tone back upon the penultimate. Thus לָמוֹ which occurs 55 times, is everywhere in pause, except three times (Ps. 66. 7; 119. 165; Job 24. 17) before the word in pause, most probably for לָהֶם or לוֹ, which, the former with grave suffix and the latter as a monosyllable, never can change the tone. Nor is it improbable that the מ of לָמוֹ in the singular is merely epenthetic, as in כָּמוֹנִי, comp. the poetical forms לְמוֹ, כְּמוֹ, בְּמוֹ, as independent words formed from the prefixes בְּ, כְּ, לְ, and the syllable מוֹ.

TABLE B. REGULAR VERB.

	KAL.		NIPHAL.	PIEL.	PUAL.	HIPHIL.	HOPHAL.	HITHPAEL.
PRET. 3. *m.*	קָטַל	כָּבֵד	נִקְטַל	קִטֵּל	קֻטַּל	הִקְטִיל	הָקְטַל	הִתְקַטֵּל
3. *f.*	קָֽטְלָה	כָּֽבְדָה	נִקְטְלָה	קִטְּלָה	קֻטְּלָה	הִקְטִילָה	הָקְטְלָה	הִתְקַטְּלָה
2. *m.*	קָטַלְתָּ	כָּבַדְתָּ	נִקְטַלְתָּ	קִטַּלְתָּ	קֻטַּלְתָּ	הִקְטַלְתָּ	הָקְטַלְתָּ	הִתְקַטַּלְתָּ
2. *f.*	קָטַלְתְּ	כָּבַדְתְּ	נִקְטַלְתְּ	קִטַּלְתְּ	קֻטַּלְתְּ	הִקְטַלְתְּ	הָקְטַלְתְּ	הִתְקַטַּלְתְּ
1. *c.*	קָטַלְתִּי	כָּבַדְתִּי	נִקְטַלְתִּי	קִטַּלְתִּי	קֻטַּלְתִּי	הִקְטַלְתִּי	הָקְטַלְתִּי	הִתְקַטַּלְתִּי
Plur. 3. *c.*	קָֽטְלוּ	כָּֽבְדוּ	נִקְטְלוּ	קִטְּלוּ	קֻטְּלוּ	הִקְטִילוּ	הָקְטְלוּ	הִתְקַטְּלוּ
2. *m.*	קְטַלְתֶּם	כְּבַדְתֶּם	נִקְטַלְתֶּם	קִטַּלְתֶּם	קֻטַּלְתֶּם	הִקְטַלְתֶּם	הָקְטַלְתֶּם	הִתְקַטַּלְתֶּם
2. *f.*	קְטַלְתֶּן	כְּבַדְתֶּן	נִקְטַלְתֶּן	קִטַּלְתֶּן	קֻטַּלְתֶּן	הִקְטַלְתֶּן	הָקְטַלְתֶּן	הִתְקַטַּלְתֶּן
1. *c.*	קָטַלְנוּ	כָּבַדְנוּ	נִקְטַלְנוּ	קִטַּלְנוּ	קֻטַּלְנוּ	הִקְטַלְנוּ	הָקְטַלְנוּ	הִתְקַטַּלְנוּ
INF. *absol.*	קָטוֹל		הִקָּטֹל, נִקְטֹל	קַטֹּל	קֻטֹּל	הַקְטֵיל		
constr.	קְטֹל		הִקָּטֵל	קַטֵּל	קֻטַּל	הַקְטִיל	הָקְטַל	הִתְקַטֵּל
IMP. *m.*	קְטֹל	כְּבַד	הִקָּטֵל	קַטֵּל	wanting	הַקְטֵל	wanting	הִתְקַטֵּל
f.	קִטְלִי	כִּבְדִי	הִקָּטְלִי	קַטְּלִי		הַקְטִילִי		הִתְקַטְּלִי
Plur. m.	קִטְלוּ	כִּבְדוּ	הִקָּטְלוּ	קַטְּלוּ		הַקְטִילוּ		הִתְקַטְּלוּ
f.	קְטֹלְנָה	כְּבַדְנָה	הִקָּטֵלְנָה	קַטֵּלְנָה		הַקְטֵלְנָה		הִתְקַטֵּלְנָה
FUT. 3. *m.*	יִקְטֹל	יִכְבַּד	יִקָּטֵל	יְקַטֵּל	יְקֻטַּל	יַקְטִיל	יָקְטַל	יִתְקַטֵּל
3. *f.*	תִּקְטֹל	תִּכְבַּד	תִּקָּטֵל	תְּקַטֵּל	תְּקֻטַּל	תַּקְטִיל	תָּקְטַל	תִּתְקַטֵּל
2. *m.*	תִּקְטֹל	תִּכְבַּד	תִּקָּטֵל	תְּקַטֵּל	תְּקֻטַּל	תַּקְטִיל	תָּקְטַל	תִּתְקַטֵּל
2. *f.*	תִּקְטְלִי	תִּכְבְּדִי	תִּקָּטְלִי	תְּקַטְּלִי	תְּקֻטְּלִי	תַּקְטִילִי	תָּקְטְלִי	תִּתְקַטְּלִי
1. *c.*	אֶקְטֹל	אֶכְבַּד	אֶקָּטֵל	אֲקַטֵּל	אֲקֻטַּל	אַקְטִיל	אָקְטַל	אֶתְקַטֵּל
Plur. 3. *m.*	יִקְטְלוּ	יִכְבְּדוּ	יִקָּטְלוּ	יְקַטְּלוּ	יְקֻטְּלוּ	יַקְטִילוּ	יָקְטְלוּ	יִתְקַטְּלוּ
3. *f.*	תִּקְטֹלְנָה	תִּכְבַּדְנָה	תִּקָּטֵלְנָה	תְּקַטֵּלְנָה	תְּקֻטַּלְנָה	תַּקְטֵלְנָה	תָּקְטַלְנָה	תִּתְקַטֵּלְנָה
2. *m.*	תִּקְטְלוּ	תִּכְבְּדוּ	תִּקָּטְלוּ	תְּקַטְּלוּ	תְּקֻטְּלוּ	תַּקְטִילוּ	תָּקְטְלוּ	תִּתְקַטְּלוּ
2. *f.*	תִּקְטֹלְנָה	תִּכְבַּדְנָה	תִּקָּטֵלְנָה	תְּקַטֵּלְנָה	תְּקֻטַּלְנָה	תַּקְטֵלְנָה	תָּקְטַלְנָה	תִּתְקַטֵּלְנָה
1. *c.*	נִקְטֹל	נִכְבַּד	נִקָּטֵל	נְקַטֵּל	נְקֻטַּל	נַקְטִיל	נָקְטַל	נִתְקַטֵּל
FUT. *apoc.*						יַקְטֵל		
PART. *act.*	קֹטֵל		נִקְטָל	מְקַטֵּל	מְקֻטָּל	מַקְטִיל	מָקְטָל	מִתְקַטֵּל
pass.	קָטוּל							

SECTION VI.—UNUSUAL CONJUGATIONS.

Besides the five usual forms of conjugation exhibited in the preceding paradigm (viz. Kal, Niphal, Piel and Pual, Hiphil and Hophal, Hithpael), there are other unusual forms, which, although they occur but seldom in the regular verb, are, nevertheless, *usual* in certain classes of the irregular verb. Of the latter conjugations some are connected in form with Piel, and are made by the doubling or repetition of one or more radical letters, or by the insertion of a long vowel, i. e. by changes within the root itself;

others are analogous to Hiphil, and are formed by the addition of prefix letters or syllables. To the former class, besides a Passive distinguished by the more obscure vowels in the final syllable, belongs also a reflective form with the prefix הִתְ after the analogy of Hithpael.

Those which are analogous to Piel, and which follow it in their inflexion are :—

1. *Poel ;* as קוֹטֵל, reflexive הִתְקוֹטֵל, fut. יְקוֹטֵל, part. מְקוֹטֵל, fut. pass. יְקוֹטַל. In the regular verb it occurs very seldom. Examples are :—מְשֹׁפְטִי *my judge,* Job 9. 15 ; יוֹדַעְתִּי *I have appointed,* 1 Sa. 21. 3 ; שֹׁרֵשׁ *to take root,* Is. 40. 24, denom. from שֹׁרֶשׁ *root.* In verbs ע״ע it is far more frequent; e. g. הוֹלֵל, סוֹבֵב, חוֹנֵן. Its signification is mostly analogous to Piel.

2. *Pilel, Pulal, Hithpalel ;* as קִטְלֵל and קֻטְלַל, pass. קֻטְלַל, reflexive הִתְקַטְלֵל (the last radical letter being repeated). In the regular verb, the following are the only examples :—נִפְלַל Eze. 28. 23, i. q. נָפַל *to fall ;* צִמְּתַתְנִי *it has consumed me,* Ps. 119. 139, צִמְּתֻתוּנִי Ps. 88. 17, which probably is to be read צִמְּתְתוּנִי* (from צָמַת) *they consume me* (Dagesh in both instances is euphonic) ; with guttural שַׁאֲנַן *to be at rest,* רַעֲנַן *to be green ;* pass. אֻמְלַל *to be withered.* It is more frequent in verbs ע״ו, where it takes the place of Piel and Hithpael.

3. *Pealal,* as קְטַלְטַל (the two last letters being repeated) used especially of slight motions repeated in quick succession ; e. g. סְחַרְחַר *to go about with quick motion,* hence of the heart, *to beat quick, to palpitate,* Ps. 38. 11, from סָחַר *to go about ;* pass. (Poalal) חֳמַרְמַר *to ferment with violence, to make a rumbling sound,* La. 1. 20.

4. *Pilpel,* formed from a *biliteral root* by doubling both radical letters, as סָבַב, סִבְסֵב ; כּוּל, כִּלְכֵּל. This also is used of motion rapidly repeated, e. g. צִפְצֵף *to chirp,* צִלְצֵל *to tinkle,* גַּרְגַּר *to gargle,* עִפְעֵף *to flutter* (from עוּף *to fly*) ; reflex. הִתְגַּלְגַּל *to roll oneself down.*

With Hiph. are connected :—

5. *Tiphel,* as תִּקְטֵל, with ת prefixed ; e. g. תִּרְגֵּל *to teach one to walk, to lead,* denom. from רֶגֶל *a foot ;* תַּחֲרָה, fut. יְתַחֲרֶה *to emulate,* Je. 12. 5 ; 22. 15 (from חָרָה *to be ardent, eager*).

6. *Shaphel,* as שַׁקְטֵל frequent in the Syriac ; e. g. שַׁלְהֵב *to burn,* from להב. In the Hebrew it is found only in the noun שַׁלְהֶבֶת *flame.*

Forms of which single examples occur :—

7. קַטְלַט, pass. קְטַלַט ; as מְחֻסְפָּס *scaled off, having the form of scales,* Ex. 16. 14, from חָשַׂף=חָסַף *to peel, to scale.*

8. קַטְקַל, as זַרְזִיף Ps. 72. 6, *a violent rain,* from זָרַף.

9. קְטַקְטַל (the two first letters repeated) a passive, only יָפְיָפִיתָ *thou art fair,* Ps. 45. 3, from יָפָה.

10. נִתְקַטֵּל (frequent in the Rabbinic) a form compounded of Niph. and Hiph., found in the examples נִוַּסְּרוּ for נִתְוַסְּרוּ *they permit themselves to be admonished,* Eze. 23. 48 ; נִכַּפֵּר De. 21. 8 ; נִשְׁתָּוָה Pr. 27. 15.†

11. קְטוֹטֵל, in חֲצוֹצֵר *to blow the trumpet,* from חָצַר. The participle מחצצרים occurs 1 Ch. 15. 24 ; 2 Ch. 5. 13 ; 7. 6 ; 13. 14 ; 29. 28 in Kheth., and is doubtless to be read מַחֲצֹצְרִים ; but the Keri invariably rejects one צ, pointing it either as Hiph. or Piel, מַחְצְרִים or מְחַצְּרִים.

* The supposition that תְּתוּ stands for תְּתוּ may be founded upon the principle, that the feeble subordinate sound of *vocal Sheva* often conforms to the following proper vowel of the syllable, e. g. סְדֹם, LXX Σοδόμ, Sodom ; שְׁלֹמֹה Σολομών, Solomon (Lehrg. § 14. Gram. § 10. 2).

† The form נִגֹּאֲלוּ La. 4. 14, is supposed to be likewise a compound, viz. of Niph. and Pual (נִגְאֲלוּ and גֹּאֲלוּ), in which form Gesenius discovers a passive of Niphal. Passives of Hithpael are : הָתְפָּקְדוּ for הִתְפַּקְדוּ, Nu. 1. 47 ; 2. 33 ; הֻטַּמָּא for הִתְטַמָּא, De. 24. 4 ; הֻכַּבֵּס Le. 13. 55, 56 ; הֻדַּשְּׁן Is. 34. 6. Lehrg. § 71. 4.

SECTION VII.—QUADRILITERALS.

The few verbs of this kind are formed after the analogy of Piel. The following are all the examples which occur:—

Pret. פַּרְשֵׁז *he spread out*, Job 26. 9 (with Pattahh under the first syllable, as in the Chaldee).

Fut. יְכַרְסְמֶנָּה *he will devour it*, Ps. 80. 14.

Pass. רֻטֲפַשׁ *to become green*, Job 33. 25.

Part. מְכֻרְבָּל *girded*, 1 Ch. 15. 27.

SECTION VIII.—REGULAR VERB. (TABLE B.)

REMARKS.

I. ON THE PRETERITE OF KAL.

1. The verbs of *middle O* (as קָטֹן)* retain this Hholem in the 2nd and 1st persons, as יָכֹלְתִּי *I am able*, Ge. 30. 8; Ju. 8. 3; Ps. 40. 13; יָגֹרְתִּי, יָגֹרְתָּ *thou wast, I was, afraid*, De. 28. 60; 9. 19; קָטֹנְתִּי *I am small*, Ge. 32. 11; יָקֹשְׁתִּי *I lay snares*, Je. 50. 24. This and the usual form (*middle A*) are found together in Ge. 43. 14, כַּאֲשֶׁר שָׁכֹלְתִּי שָׁכָלְתִּי *as I am bereaved, I am bereaved*. In those cases, however, where (according to rem. 7) the tone is shifted to the ultimate, viz. in the 2nd pers. pl., before suffixes, and Vav conversive of the preterite, Hholem is shortened to Kamets Hhatuph; as וְיָכָלְתָּ *and thou shalt be able*, Ex. 18. 23, יְכָלְתִּיו Ps. 13. 5.

The verbs *middle E* generally lose the sound (..) in their inflexion, e. g. חָפֵץ, חָפַצְתָּ (like קָטַל, קָטַלְתָּ), and this original vowel appears again only:—

(*a*) in the 3 pers. sing. and pl. standing in pause, as גָּבֵרוּ *they are strong*, 2 Sa. 1. 23; דָּבֵקָה *she cleaves*, Job 29. 10; דָּבֵקוּ Job 41. 15. Several verbs, properly *middle E*, have *Pattahh* in the 3 pers. when not in pause, and the E sound appears again only *in pause;* e. g. דָּבַק, גָּבַר, comp. שָׁכֵן Ex. 40. 35; Jos. 22. 19, *in pause* שָׁכֵן De. 33. 12, 20; Ju. 5. 17 (comp. in Piel גִּדַּל, in pause גִּדֵּל).†

(*b*) In forms with the tone on the ultimate, in which case (..) is shortened into (.:) or (.), as, שְׁאֶלְתֶּם *ye have asked*, 1 Sa. 12. 13; 25. 5; וִירִשְׁתָּם *and thou shalt succeed them in possession*, De. 19. 1; וִירִשְׁתָּהּ De. 30. 5; יְלִדְתִּיךָ *I have begotten thee*, Ps. 2. 7; שְׁאִלְתִּיו 1 Sa. 1. 20, שְׁאִלְתִּיהוּ Ju. 13. 6, comp. Je. 2. 27; 15. 10; Nu. 11. 12; Jos. 1. 15.‡

2. In some instances the 3 pers. has (..) in the second syllable, although not in pause; as, שָׁפֵט *he judged*, 1 Sa. 7. 17, גָּזֵל *he robbed*, Eze. 18. 12,§ שָׁגֵג *he erred*, Le. 5. 18.

3. *Third Person Feminine.* ־ַת, the usual form in the Syriac and Arabic, is some times used also in the Hebrew; as, אָזְלַת De. 32. 36. Another Aramaic termination is ־ָא in Eze. 31. 5.

An example with *euphonic Dagesh*, in pause, is נָשַׁתָּה (for נָשְׁתָה) *she dries up*, Is. 41. 17.

4. *Third Person Plural.* The form וּא (with parag. א), usual in the Arabic, is found in the Hebrew; as הָלְכוּא Jos. 10. 24.

It is but seldom that parag. ן is appended to the preterite; as, יָדְעוּן De. 8. 3, 16. Examples with *euphonic Dagesh*, in pause, are:—חָדֵלּוּ Ju. 5. 7; 1 Sa. 2. 5 (where, however, MSS. vary); נָתַנּוּ Eze. 27. 19.

5. *Second Person Singular.* Besides the common form תָּ for the masculine, the full form תָּה also occurs; e. g. בָּגַדְתָּה Mal. 2. 14, זָקַנְתָּה Jos. 13. 1.

2 pers. fem. As was observed above (§ 1. rem. 2), that besides the pronoun אַתְּ, there occurs another form אַתִּי in Kheth., so it should be remembered in this afformative derived from it, there occurs, besides תְּ, also the form תִּי in Kheth., e. g. הָלַכְתִּי Je. 31. 21,

* The common form of the 3 pers. pret. has, in the final syllable of the ground-form, either *A* (*Pattahh*), *E* (*Tseri pure*), or *O* (*Hholem pure*),—as מָלַךְ *to reign*, חָמֵץ *to be sour*, יָכֹל *to be able*,—which are found likewise in the irregular verb, e. g. מֵת (for מָוֵת) *to die*, אוֹר (for אָוֹר) *to be light, bright*. For the sake of brevity, these are called, after the example of the Arabic grammarians, verbs *middle A*, *middle E*, and *middle O*. The two latter are usual in *intransitive* verbs, e. g. זָקֵן *to be old*, קָטֹן *to be small* (Lehrg. § 66. 3).

† It is better, however, to view these as two different forms of the same verb, comp. the Lexicon.

‡ This shortening, however, into (.:) & (.) may properly be from *Pattahh*, occasioned by the removal of the tone to the next following syllable, comp. יֶדְכֶם for יַדְכֶם, מַדּוּ for מַדּוּ from מַד, comp. especially § 11. rem. 1; so that there is no need to suppose here a ground-form *middle E*, as שָׁאֵל, יָרֵשׁ, יָלֵד.

§ Nevertheless, Zakeph-katon may in this instance have the force of a pausal accent.

comp. Eze. 16. 13, which is to be read הָלַכְתִּי. In such instances the Keri has the note יָתִיר י׳ (abundat י), and in thus rejecting י the vowel points are suited accordingly.

6. *Second Person Plural Feminine.* Instead of תֶּן, the form תֶּנָה is used in Am. 4. 3, corresponding to a similar form of the pronoun, § 1. rem. 5.

7. In combination with the afformatives תָּ, תִּי, נוּ the tone is on the penultima, and the word is said to be *Milêl* (above), but with the other afformatives the tone is on the ultimate, and the word is said to be *Milra* (below). The tone, however, is shifted, (*a*) by *conversive Vav* of the preterite from the penultima to the ultimate (comp. § 18. rem. 1), e. g. וּפָקַדְתָּ *and thou shalt visit*, Job 5. 24, וּפָקַדְתִּי Ex. 32. 34, except in pause, comp. however, De. 8. 6; (*b*) by the suffixes, comp. the table of the verb with suffixes; (*c*) by the *pause* in several of the persons from the ultimate to the penultima, where the original vowel, if it has fallen away, is likewise restored, as קָטָלְתָּ; מָלֵאוּ, קָטָלוּ, קָטָלָה, &c.; the tone, however, remains fixed with the grave afformatives, as קְטַלְתֶּם.

II. On the Infinitive of Kal.

8. There is but one form for the *inf. abs.* which is קָטוֹל (with Hholem impure). The Hholem is found written either *in full*, or *defectively* (קָטֹל); the former, however, is the original.

9. For the *inf. constr.* the usual form is קְטֹל (with Hholem pure), besides which there is also an unusual form קְטַל, as שְׁכַב *to lie down*, Ge. 34. 7; 2 Ki. 14. 22; שְׁפַל *to be humbled*, Pr. 16. 19; Ec. 12. 4. That they are strictly *Segolate* forms is seen from their inflexion (שָׁכְבִי, קָטְלִי), which perfectly agrees with the declension of the *Segolates* (קֶטֶל, קֹטֶל or קְטֹל; קַטֵל or קֹטֶל) comp. § 35. rem. 10.

10. The various infinitive forms, which occur as *verbal nouns*, will be enumerated farther on (§ 26). Here belong only such as are really construed as infinitives. They are :—

(*a*) קִטְלָה, קָטְלָה and קְטָלָה, as feminine forms from קְטֹל, קְטַל; e. g. לְגָבְהָה *to be lifted up*, Zep. 3. 11; לְטָמְאָה *to become unclean*, Le. 15. 32; לְחֶמְלָה *to have compassion*, Eze. 16. 5; לְמָשְׁחָה *to anoint*, Ex. 29. 29; לְרָחְצָה *to wash*, Ex. 30. 18; לְקָרְבָה *to draw near*, Ex. 36. 2; לְקָרַאת, instead of which by *Syriasm*, לִקְרָאת *to meet* (i. e. *against*). Moreover, יִרְאָה *to fear*, De. 4. 10, and שִׂנְאָה *to hate*, De. 1. 27, occur construed as infinitives, but are besides, more usually *verbal* nouns. Forms like אַשְׁמָה, חֶזְקָה, are produced by the effect of the gutturals.

(*b*) With a preformative מ, as in the Syriac and Chaldee, as מִגְרַשׁ *to drive*, Eze. 36. 5; מִקְרָא *to convoke*, Nu. 10. 2; so likewise in some verbs of פ״נ, as מַשָּׂא for מִנְשָׂא *to carry*, Nu. 4. 24; מַסַּע *to remove*, De. 10. 11.*

(*c*) Other examples are יֵשַׁע Hab. 3. 13, אֲפֻדָּה Ex. 28. 8, which may, however, be regarded as *verbal nouns*.*

(*d*) דְּרִיוֹשׁ Ezr. 10. 16, for דְּרֹשׁ is quite anomalous. (Gesenius, in his Thesaurus, is inclined to regard it as an *inf. Piel*, for דָּרוֹשׁ, comp. דַּלְיוֹ Pr. 26. 7, for דַּלּוּ.)

III. On the Imperative of Kal.

11. The verbs which have *A* in the second syllable of the future retain the same also in the imperative; as שְׁכַב *lie down*, 2 Sa. 13. 5; Eze. 4. 4; לְבַשׁ *put on*, 1 Ki. 22. 30; שְׁלַם *be peaceable*, Job 22. 20.

With parag. ה ָ the form קְטֹל becomes קָטְלָה, the form קְטַל becomes קִטְלָה; as, שָׁמְרָה *watch over* (from שְׁמֹר) Ps. 25. 20, זָכְרָה *remember* (from זְכֹר) 2 Ch. 6. 42; שִׁכְבָה *lie down*, Ge. 39. 12, מִכְרָה *sell*, Ge. 25. 31, נִצְּרָה (with euphonic Dagesh) from נְצֹר for נְצֹר *keep*, Ps. 141. 3.†

12. The form קִטְלִי, קִטְלוּ is more directly derived from קְטַל than קְטֹל, and is chiefly found with imperatives of the first form, e. g. שִׁכְבִי, לִבְשִׁי, though also with those of the latter form. The form קָטְלִי, however, is comparatively unfrequent; as, מָלְכִי *reign*, Ju. 9. 10, 12; עָלְזִי *rejoice*, Zep. 3. 14; קָרְחִי *make bald*, Mi. 1. 16; מָשְׁכוּ *draw*, Eze. 32. 20 (but also מִשְׁכוּ Ex. 12. 21); with composite Sheva, קָסֳמִי *use enchantment*, 1 Sa. 28. 8, Keri. Segol is found only with gutturals (§ 13. rem. 3).

In pause the long *O* or *A* returns again; as, שְׁפֹטוּ *judge ye*, Zec. 7. 9. Such forms, however, are found also without pause, as Da. 9. 19, with which the following may be classed: רְגָזָה—פְּשֹׁטָה וְעֹרָה *tremble—strip thyself and make thee bare*, Is. 32. 11, and according to some, also חֲגוֹרָה (*gird thyself*) which immediately follows in this passage.

* The infinitives of *b* and *c*, on account of their small number, must, in the Lexicon, be sought for among the nouns.

† The *lengthened imperative* or *imp. parag.* is, as may be seen from a comparison of the references given above, expressive of *wish* and *entreaty*; and is often *emphatic*, as קוּם *stand up*, קוּמָה *up!* (comp. rem. 13, and § 11. rem. 5).

In some instances Hholem has been retained in the inflexion according to Keth.; as צרופה *try*, Ps. 26. 2, מלוכה *reign*, Ju. 9. 8, קסומי *use enchantment*, 1 Sa. 28. 8, where the Keri has invariably cancelled ו.

IV. On the Future of Kal.

13. The Hholem in the second syllable of the future is almost exclusively confined to the *transitive verbs* (middle *A*); while the verbs middle *E* and *O* (קָטֵל, קָטֹל) have regularly Pattahh in the future; e. g. גָּדַל, fut. יִגְדַּל *to be great*, כָּבֵד, fut. יִכְבַּד *to be honoured;* קָטֹן, fut. יִקְטַן *to be small*, שָׁכֹל, fut. יִשְׁכַּל *to be childless.* In several verbs, however, this difference of form exists only in the future, so that the future *O* stands for the transitive, and the future *A* for the intransitive signification; as קָצַר *to cut off, to reap* (Le. 25. 5; De. 24. 19, &c.), future *A*, *to be cut*, i. e. *to be short* (Ju. 10. 16; 16. 16); חָרַשׁ, future *O*, *to cut, to plough*, future *A*, *to be dumb*, (properly, *to be blunted*); חָלַשׁ, future *O*, *to subdue*, Ex. 17. 13, future *A*, *to be subdued*, Job 14. 10; קָרַם *to overlay, cover*, fut. *A* intrans. ver. 8. In a few instances the difference in the signification is of another character; e. g. יִגְזֹר *he shall cut (eat)*, Is. 9. 19, יִגְזַר trop. *he shall decide*, Job 22. 28; חָבַשׁ fut. *O*, *to saddle*, fut. *A* and *O*, *to bind up*, Job 5. 18; Eze. 34. 16; עָרַב fut. *O*, *to be surety for*, עָרֵב fut. *A*, *to be sweet.*

Very frequently both occur without any difference of signification; as יִשְׁבֹּת (Le. 26. 35) and יִשְׁבַּת (ver. 34) *he shall rest;* טָרַף, future *O* (Ps. 7. 3; Ho. 5. 14), and future *A* (Ge. 49. 27), *to tear;* נָדַר fut. *O* (Nu. 6. 21; De. 12. 17, &c.), and fut. *A* (Ge. 28. 20, &c.), *to vow;* נָשַׁךְ fut. *O*, Ec. 10. 11, and fut. *A*, Pr. 23. 22, *to bite;* בָּגַד fut. *O*, Mal. 2. 15, fut. *A*, ver. 10, *to be treacherous.*

With parag. ה, the form אֶקְטֹל becomes אֶקְטְלָה. This (so called) *lengthened future* (comp. note to rem. 11) is usually attached to the 1 pers. sing. and pl., and is found in all classes of the regular and irregular verbs, except in the *passives*, and has the tone, wherever it is taken, by the afformatives וּ and ִי, and hence affects in precisely the same manner the final vowel of the ground-form, e. g. Kal אֶשְׁמְרָה, Piel נְנַתְּקָה Ps. 2. 3; but Hiph. אַזְכִּירָה.*

It is, however, sometimes found attached to other persons, as the second and third, comp. Is. 5. 19; Eze. 23. 20; Ps. 20. 4. The form ֶה is also sometimes found instead of ָה, as אֶקְרָאֶה 1 Sa. 28. 15, יְדַשְּׁנֶה Ps. 20. 4.

14. In the forms in which, according to the paradigm, Hholem is dropped, something of the O sound seems to have been expressed in the time when the Hebrew was a living language. Thus the vowel of the last syllable is constantly retained in the Arabic, and is lost only in the vulgar dialect. Traces of this are observable, (*a*) in the old *matres lectionis*, which the Keri has cancelled:—ואשקולה *and I weighed*, Ezr. 8. 25, אשקוטה *I will rest*, Is. 18. 4, יכשולו *they stumble*, Pr. 4. 16; (*b*) where the vowel remains and is pointed ֻ, being considered shorter than וֹ; as יִשְׁפּוּטוּ *they shall judge*, Ex. 18. 26, תַּעֲבוּרִי *thou shalt pass on*, Ru. 2 8, תִּשְׁמוּרֵם *thou shalt observe them*, Pr. 14. 3; (*c*) in (ֳ) which the punctuators have occasionally substituted for simple Sheva, e. g. וָאֶשְׁקֳלָה and אֶשְׁקֳטָה in the Keri of the passages quoted above, comp. Ezr. 8. 26; Je. 32. 9; אֶשְּׁקָה *I might kiss*, 1 Ki. 19. 20, אֶסֳּרֵם Ho. 10. 10; comp. Is. 27. 3; 62. 2; Eze. 35. 6.

15. The vowel of the last syllable is regularly restored again *in pause*, with which it receives the tone. *Pattahh* is then lengthened into Kamets, e. g. תִּקְטֹלִי, יִלְכֹּדוּ, תִּלְבָּשִׁי.

16. For the 3 pers. pl. fem. תִּקְטֹלְנָה, the form יִקְטֹלְנָה is substituted, in three instances, to distinguish it from the 2 pers., viz. יַעֲמֹדְנָה *they shall arise*, Da. 8. 22, comp. Ge. 30. 38; 1 Sa. 6. 12. The parag. ה in נָה, both for the masc. and fem. is often dropped, so that only ן remain; e. g. תִּגַּשְׁןָ Ge. 33. 6.

A single anomaly is וַתִּגְבְּהֶינָה, Eze. 16. 50, for תִּגְבַּהְנָה (comp. Verb *Ain gutt.*) where ֶי is inserted after the manner of verbs ע״ו and ע״ע.

17. To the forms ending in וּ or ִי a parag. ן is often appended, most frequently at the end of a period, where the vowel of the second syllable is restored, though this vowel does not (as in No. 15) receive the tone; e. g. יִרְגָּזוּן Ex. 15. 14, תִּשְׁמָעוּן De. 1. 17, comp. Ps. 104. 9, 22, 28, 29; Joel 3. 1; Ex. 9. 29. For instances of this *without pause* comp. Ru. 2. 8, 9; Ps. 4. 3; but the vowel is then more frequently not restored, comp. Hab. 3. 7; Ps. 104. 28, 29; De. 8. 20; Ex. 4. 9.

V. On the Infinitive, Imperfect, and Future of Kal.

18. Hholem of the *inf. constr.* and *fut.*, being a

* The *future parag.* expresses excitement (in the sing., *of oneself*, in the pl., *of one another*), determination, wish, entreaty, &c., e. g. אָגִילָה וְאֶשְׂמְחָה *let me be glad and rejoice!* Ps. 31. 8; נֵלְכָה *let us go!* Ge. 22. 5 (comp. § 11. rem. 6).

pure vowel, is in most instances written without ו. The full form occurs most frequently in pause or in the later books, comp. תִּקְצוֹר Le. 25. 5, לִבְלוֹם Ps. 32. 9, תִּבְגּוֹד Is. 48. 8, אֶסְגּוֹד Is. 44. 19.

Before Makkeph, Hholem is changed into Kamets-hhatuph, as:—לִשְׁאָל־לוֹ 2 Sa. 8. 10; Ps. 78. 18, דְּרָשׁ־נָא Je. 21. 2, תִּגְבָּל־בָּהּ Zec. 9. 2. Where ו stands in the text, it is cancelled in the Keri, so that it remains only in the Kheth.; e.g. לגאול־לו Ru. 4. 6 Kh. (Keri לִגְאָל־לוֹ), כתוב־לך Eze. 24. 2 Kh. (Keri כְּתָב־לְךָ), אכתוב־לו Ho. 8. 12 Kh. (Keri אֶכְתָּב־לוֹ).

VI. On the Participle of Kal.

19. קוֹטֵל is the regular participle of the verbs middle *A*, like קָטַל. The Hholem is *impure*, and ought, therefore, to be written *fully;* it is, however, more frequently written *defectively*, not only before an accession at the end, but even in the ground form, קֹטֵל.

Like the noun, it often has parag. י appended to the construct state; as שֹׁכְנִי סְנֶה *the inhabitant of the thorn-bush*, De. 33. 16, הַהֹפְכִי הַצּוּר *who changes the rock*, Ps. 114. 8, יֹשְׁבִי בַּשָּׁמָיִם *who dwells in heaven*, Ps. 123. 1, אֹסְרִי לַגֶּפֶן *who binds to the vine*, Ge. 49. 11, עֹזְבִי הַצֹּאן Zec. 11. 17.

In its inflexion it differs in nothing from the noun (comp. dec. 7), and by the same analogy is formed the feminine; only that it must be noticed, that the feminine form קֹטֶלֶת (with gutt. שֹׁמַעַת) is here more frequent than קֹטְלָה.

When the tone is thrown back on account of a word, with the tone on the *penultima*, following it, Segol is substituted in the final syllable, as in Is. 41. 7, הוֹלֶם פָּעַם *who smites the anvil.*

An unfrequent form is תּוֹמִיךְ *upholding*, Ps. 16. 5, for תּוֹמֵךְ; הִנְנִי יוֹסִף *behold I am adding*, Is. 29. 14; 38. 5.*

20. The participles of the verbs middle *E* and *O* do not differ in form from the preterite; as מָלֵא *he is full*, and *full;* יָשֵׁן *he slept*, and *sleeping;* יָגֹר *he was afraid*, and *fearing*. Where these forms do not occur as participles, they are at least *verbal adjectives* †

SECTION IX.—NIPHAL.

REMARKS.

1. *Preterite.* There is no positive proof for the existence of preterites like נִקְטֹל, נִקְטֵל, corresponding to קָטֹל, קָטֵל of the Kal (comp. § 8. rem. 1, note), in addition to the form נִקְטַל; for נַחְתּוֹם Est. 8. 8, נַעְתּוֹר 1 Ch. 5. 20, נַהֲפוֹךְ Est. 9. 1, usually regarded as such preterites, are properly *infinitives abs.*

With regard to the tone and its changes, the remarks already made upon Kal (§ 8. rem. 7) are also applicable to Niphal.

2. The first *inf. abs.* (נִקְטֹל), connects itself, in form, with the preterite, to which it bears the same relation as קָטוֹל to קָטַל, and is the only infinitive of this kind. Examples are—נִלְחֹם *warring*, Ju. 11. 25, נִכְסֹף *longing*, Ge. 31. 30, נִשְׁאֹל *asking for oneself*, 1 Sa. 20. 6, נִשְׁלֹחַ *sending*, Est. 3. 13. Examples for the second form are—הִנָּתֹן Je. 32. 4, הֵאָכֹל Le. 7. 18, once אִדָּרֹשׁ *being inquired of*, Eze. 14. 3, which is quite an Arabic form. The construct form is but seldom used instead of the absolute, e. g. הִשָּׁמֵד De. 4. 26. In Ps. 68. 3, כְּהִנְדֹּף עָשָׁן תִּנְדֹּף *as smoke is driven away thou drivest* (them) *away*, the form הִנְדֹּף, as the construct of הִנָּדֵף, is chosen instead of הִנָּדֵף, probably for its agreement of sound with the following תִּנְדֹּף.

3. The *infinitive*, *imperative*, or *future*, in those persons which have no afformatives, when immediately followed by a word of one syllable, have the tone commonly drawn back to the penultima, and the final syllable having lost the tone receives Segol instead of Tseri; as יִלָּכֶד בָּהּ Ec. 7. 26, יִכָּשֶׁל בָּהּ Eze. 33. 12, תִּכָּתֶב זֹאת Ps. 102. 19, וַיֵּעָתֶר לוֹ Ge. 25. 21; 2 Ch. 33. 13, יֵאָמֶן נָא 1 Ki. 8. 26, יֵאָמֶר לוֹ Is. 4. 3, יֵחָלֶק אוֹר Job 38. 24; so in the *inf.* לְהִסָּתֶר שָׁם Job 34. 22; in the *imp.* הִלָּחֶם בּוֹ Ju. 9. 38. In some words, however, this form with the retracted tone has become the usual one; e. g. הִשָּׁמֶר Ex. 23. 21, and with *conversive Vav*, וַיִּלָּחֶם Nu. 21. 23; Jos. 24. 9; Ju. 9. 39; 1 Sa. 14. 47; וַיִּנָּגֶף 1 Sa. 4. 2, 10; 2 Sa. 2. 17; 2 Ki. 14. 12.

4. In a similar case, Pattahh is sometimes, though but seldom, put for Tseri, as תֵּעָזַב אֶרֶץ Job 18. 4; it is, however, more frequently found with distinctive

* This form is, however, not universally acknowledged as a participle. Thus is תּוֹמִיךְ regarded as fut. of Hiph. *thou makest wide, glorious,* from יָמַךְ, Arab. *amplus fuit* (Schult., instit. ad fundam. 1 Hebr. p. 298). יוֹסִף is likewise taken as Hiph. with אֲשֶׁר supplied, and rendered, *I am he who shall add.*

† This is indeed true in principle; we find it, however, more convenient to class even the participle cited here, among the adjectives, where they will be found in the Lexicon.

accents, e. g. וַיִּגָּמַל *he was weaned*, Ge. 21. 8; וַיִּנָּפַשׁ *he was refreshed*, Ex. 31. 17; יֵאָמַר *it is said*, Ge. 10. 9; Nu. 21. 14; וַיֵּאָמַר Jos. 2. 9, וַיֵּאָנַשׁ *he became sick*, 2 Sa. 12. 15. In the 2 and 3 pers. pl. the form with Pattahh is more common than that with Tseri, not only in pause (as תִּשָּׁגַלְנָה Zec. 14. 2, תֵּרָמַסְנָה Is. 28. 3), and with gutturals or ר (as תִּזָּכַרְנָה Is. 65. 17, תִּפָּתַחְנָה Is. 35. 5), but even in the absence of either of these, e. g. תֵּאָכַלְנָה Je. 24. 2.

5. The fut. 1 pers. sing. has frequently also Hhirek under the preformative, as אִשָּׁבַע *I swear*, Ge. 21. 24, אִדָּרֵשׁ Eze. 14. 3, comp. Ge. 19. 20; 1 Sa. 20. 29; 27. 1; Job 1. 15, 16, 17; Is. 1. 24, &c.

6. When the prepositions בְּ, כְּ, לְ, are to be prefixed to the infinitive the ה is frequently contracted, but not so frequently as in the Hiphil; e. g. בִּכָּשְׁלוֹ for בְּהִכָּשְׁלוֹ Pr. 24. 17. This contraction, however, is more usually with verbs of *first guttural*, as בֵּעָטֵף for בְּהֵעָטֵף La. 2. 11, comp. Eze. 26. 15; Is. 1. 12, &c.

SECTION X.—PIEL AND PUAL.

REMARKS.

I. ON PIEL.

1. The *pret.* of Piel has frequently (ַ) in the final syllable instead of (ֵ); e. g. אִבַּד 2 Ki. 21. 3; La. 2. 9; especially before a Makkeph and in the *middle of a period*, whereas in the end of a period (ֵ) is preferred, e. g. לִמַּד־דַּעַת *he teaches wisdom*, Ec. 12. 9, וּמִלַּט־הוּא אֶת־הָעִיר *he delivered the city*, Ec. 9. 15, comp. Eze. 33. 5, וְהוּא נִזְהַר נַפְשׁוֹ מִלֵּט *he who is warned saves his life*. See גִּדֵּל Is. 49. 21, and גִּדַּל Jos. 4. 14; Est. 3. 1.

A few verbs, of which the following are all the examples, have (ֶ) in the final syllable—וְכִבֶּס *and he shall wash*, Le. 13. 6, 34; 14. 8, 9, &c. (comp. כִּבֵּס Ge. 49. 11; 2 Sa. 19. 25); וְכִפֶּר *and he shall atone*, Le. 4. 20, 26, 31, &c.; דִּבֶּר *he spoke*, frequently דִּבֵּר at the end of a period.

A single instance of (ַ) in the first syllable in the manner of Aramaic and Arabic, is found in Ge. 41. 51, נַשַּׁנִי אֱלֹהִים וגו׳ *God makes me forget*, which is occasioned by a play upon the name מְנַשֶּׁה.

2. *Infinitive.* The distinguishing form of the inf. abs. is יַסֹּר Ps. 118. 18, קַנֹּא 1 Ki. 19. 10, רַפֹּא Ex. 21. 19; and in the same relation is נִאֵץ 2 Sa. 12. 14.

The latter form, which resembles the 3 pers. pret., is found also in Le. 14. 43 as an inf. constr. אַחַר חִלֵּץ *after drawing out*. Here, it is true, אֲשֶׁר or כִּי may be supplied, and אַחַר taken as a conjunctive, *after one has drawn out;* see, however, the remarks on Hiph. § 11. rem. 4.

Somewhat more frequent are here the forms with the feminine termination—זַמְּרָה *to sing*, Ps. 147. 1; יַסְּרָה *to chasten*, Le. 26. 18; צַדֶּקְתֵּךְ *thy justifying* (comp. § 8. rem. 10) Eze. 16. 52.

3. An *imperative* with Pattahh in the final syllable is פַּלַּג Ps. 55. 10.

4. The *inf. imp.* and *fut.*, when followed by a Makkeph, or a word which has the tone on the penultima, take generally (ֶ) in the final syllable, e, g. דַּבֶּר־עֹשֶׁק Is. 59. 13; Je. 9. 4; קַדֶּשׁ־לִי Ex. 13. 2; יְבַקֶּשׁ־לוֹ Is. 40. 20; and so, moreover, with *Vav conversive*, e. g. וַתְּגָרֶשׁ Jos. 24. 12.

Instead of תְּקַטֵּלְנָה the form also with Pattahh in the second syllable is found, as תְּרַטַּשְׁנָה, Is. 13. 18.

The following are examples with parag. ן—יְהַלֵּכוּן Ps. 104. 10, יְיַחֵלוּן Is. 51. 5, comp. Kal § 8. rem. 17.

II. ON PUAL.

5. The less frequent form of Pual, with Kametshhatuph instead of Kibbuts, is found in the following examples—מְאָדָּם *dyed red*, Na. 2. 4; יְחָבְרְךָ *he is joined to thee*, Ps. 94. 20 (beside יְחֻבַּר Ec. 9. 4); כָּרַּת *he is cut off*, Eze. 16. 4; and in the regular syllables of some irregular verbs, as שָׁדְּדָה *she is desolate*, Na. 3. 7 (usually שֻׁדַּד, שֻׁדְּדָה); כָּלּוּ *they are at an end*, Ps. 72. 20, כָּסּוּ *they are covered*, Ps. 80. 11; Pr. 24. 31.

It is merely an orthographical variation when Shurek takes the place of Kibbuts, as יוּלַּד, in pause יוּלָּד Ju. 13. 8; 18. 29; Job 5. 7 (which may also be taken for Hophal, comp. הוּלֶּדֶת Eze. 16. 4); זוּנָּה *fornication is committed*, Eze. 16. 34; מְאוּזָּל *spun*, Eze. 27. 19; הוּלָּלוּ *they were praised*, Ps. 78. 63, comp. also Ec. 9. 12.

6. The participle of Pual occurs sometimes without the prefix מְ; it is then distinguished, like the part. of Niph., by the Kamets only in the last syllable; as לֻקָּח for מְלֻקָּח *taken away*, 2 Ki. 2. 10; הַהֻלָּלָה* *the praised*, Eze. 26. 17; לֹא נֻחָמָה *not comforted*, Is. 54. 11; לֹא רֻחָמָה *not pitied*, Ho. 1. 6, 8; יוּקָשִׁים or יוּקָּשִׁים *ensnared*, Ec. 9. 12; מֹרָט for מְמֹרָט Eze. 21. 15, 16.

* This and the two next following examples are to be taken rather as preterites, in consequence of their having the tone retracted to the penultima by the pause accent, which is hardly to be met with in participles and adjectives.

III. In General.

7. In those forms of Piel and Pual, which have Sheva under the radical letter, the characteristic Dagesh is often dropped; e. g. שִׁלְחָה for שִׁלְּחָה *she stretched out*, Eze. 17. 7, שִׁלְחוּ Ps. 74. 7; תְּבֻקְשִׁי *thou shalt be sought*, Eze. 26. 21; though in most instances it is inserted.

The absence of this Dagesh is sometimes intimated (*a*) by the lengthening of the preceding vowel, e. g. יְחָלְקֵם for יְחַלְּקֵם 1 Ch. 23. 6; (*b*) by a Hhatuph under the letter which was to have had the Dagesh, e. g. לֻקֳחָה for לֻקְּחָה Ge. 2. 23, comp. Ju. 16. 16.

SECTION XI.—HIPHIL AND HOPHAL.

REMARKS.

I. On Hiphil.

1. The characteristic ִי impure of the final syllable is only retained in the 3 *pers. preterite* of Hiph. (in the participle also, but with some exceptions) so as not to have another form with Tseri. In the imp. inf. and fut. there exists also a form with Tseri in the final syllable, which however differs from the other in signification, as the following remarks will show.

Forms in the *preterite* deviating from the paradigm are, (*a*) with (ֶ) under ה, e. g. הֶכְלַמְנוּ *we are ashamed*, 1 Sa. 25. 7, which is still more usual in verbs ל״ה, e. g. הֶפְדָּה, הֶגְלָה, הֶלְאָה; (*b*) with א, as in the Aramaic; אֶגְאַלְתִּי *I have polluted*, Is. 63. 3; (*c*) with (ִ) in the 2 and 3 pers., however only with suffix, as הִשְׁאִלְתִּיהוּ 1 Sa. 1. 28.

2. The *inf. absol.* has generally Tseri with or without Yod; as הַשְׁכֵּם *to rise up early*, Je. 7. 13, and הַשְׁכֵּים Je. 44. 4, &c.; הַשְׁמֵד *destroying*, Is. 14. 23, and הַשְׁמֵיד Am. 9. 8; הַשְׁלֵךְ *casting*, Je. 22. 19; הַקְטֵיר *burning incense*, 1 Ki. 9. 25; הַעֲמֵיד Ne. 7. 3: הַעֲנֵיק De. 15. 14, &c.

A form with א, by Chaldaism, is אַשְׁכֵּים Je. 25. 3. As such may be taken אַבְרֵךְ Ge. 41. 42, viz. as an *inf. abs.* for the *imperative*, *bow the knee*, if regarded according to Hebrew etymology.

When followed by Makkeph the inf. takes Segol, as הַכֶּר־פָּנִים Pr. 24. 23; 28. 21.

Unfrequent exceptions are, when the form with *Tseri* occurs for the *inf. constr.*, as הַנְחֵל De. 32. 8, comp. ch. 26. 12; Da. 11. 35, and the form with ִי for the *inf. abs.* Jos. 7. 7.

3. When the prepositions בְּ, כְּ, לְ are prefixed to the inf. constr. generally no contraction takes place, and the form remains לְהַקְטִיל, בְּהַקְטִיל, &c., differing in this respect from the future, where יַקְטִיל stands for יְהַקְטִיל. There are, however, some few exceptions; e. g. לַשְׁמִיד *to destroy*, Is. 23. 11; לַשְׁבִּית *to put an end to*, Am. 8. 4; לַלְבֵּן *to make white*, Da. 11. 35; לַנְפִּל Nu. 5. 22; לַאֲדִיב *to cause to languish*, 1 Sa. 2. 33; לַעְשֵׂר, בַּעְשֵׂר *to pay tithes*, Ne. 10. 39; De. 26. 12, comp. Ex. 13. 21; Ps. 78. 17, and in Keth., as לעזיר 2 Sa. 18. 3, for which the Keri has לַעְזוֹר; לַגִּיד 2 Ki. 9. 15.

4. *Infinitives* not differing in form from the *preterite*, are more frequent here than in Piel (§ 10. rem. 2); e. g. עַד הִשְׁאִיר 2 Ki. 3. 25; לְמַעַן הִרְגִּיעַ וְהִרְגִּיז Je. 50. 34; גָּנֹן יְהוָה—גָּנוֹן וְהִצִּיל פָּסֹחַ וְהִמְלִיט Is. 31. 5. These examples may yet be doubted, as they can be regarded as real preterites, and the prepositions before them as mere conjunctions (for עַד אֲשֶׁר, לְמַעַן אֲשֶׁר); there are, however, others which must be recognised as infinitives, e. g. הִשְׁמִידְךָ De. 7. 24; moreover אַחֲרֵי הִקְצוֹת אֶת־הַבַּיִת *after the scraping of the house*, Le. 14. 43 (where the ending וֹת of the verb ל״ה decides for the inf.)

5. In the *imp.* the leading form (הַקְטִיל) does not occur at all;* instead of it are employed the shortened and lengthened forms, הַקְטֵל and הַקְטִילָה (§ 8. rem. 13); e. g. הַשְׁמֵן *make fat*, Is. 6. 10; הַקְשֵׁב *attend*, Job 33. 31; הַקְשִׁיבָה Ps. 5. 3; 17. 1; הַצְלַח *prosper*, 1 Ki. 22. 12, 15, and הַצְלִיחָה Ps. 118. 25 (nowhere הַצְלִיחַ); הַבֵּט *look*, Job 35. 5, and הַבִּיטָה La. 1. 11; הַגֵּד *tell*, 1 Sa. 25. 11; הַבְדֵּל *separate*, Is. 56. 3; הַקְשִׁיבָה *hearken*.

Before Makkeph (..) is changed into (ֶ), as הַסְכֶּן־נָא Job 22. 21; הַבֶּט־נָא Ge. 15. 5.

6. In the future, the more usual form is that with Tseri for the *shortened future*, and has in general the

* This remains, however, the ground-form whenever the suffixes are added, as הַשְׁמִיעֵנִי Ps. 143. 8, and is analogous to the forms with the afformatives having a union vowel, as הַקְטִילִי, הַקְטִילוּ.

signification of the subjunctive, similar to the lengthened future (§ 8. rem. 13), with some modification occasioned by the difference of person. It is found—

(*a*) In the expression of command and wish; e. g. יַכְרֵת *may be cut off*, Ps. 12. 4; 109. 15 (comp. יַכְרִית *he shall cut off*, De. 12. 29; 19. 1; 1 Ki. 14. 14); יוֹסֵף *may he add, may he increase*, Ge. 30. 24; Le. 5. 16, 24; 27. 31; Nu. 5. 7; 22. 19; De. 1. 11 (comp. יוֹסִיף Jos. 23. 13; 2 Sa. 14. 10); תּוֹצֵא *let her bring forth* (comp. תּוֹצִיא Is. 61. 11; Hag. 1. 11); יַפְקֵד *let him appoint*, Ge. 41. 34; Est. 2. 3 (יַפְקִיד Is. 10. 28); יַשֵּׂג *let him overtake*, Ps. 7. 6; תַּאֲכֵל Eze. 3. 3; תּוֹחֵל 1 Sa. 10. 8, &c.

(*b*) More usually in the expression of prohibition with אַל; e. g. אַל תַּסְתֵּר *hide not*, Ps. 27. 9; 69. 18; 102. 3; 119. 19 (comp. תַּסְתִּיר Ps. 13. 2; 44. 25); אַל תַּשְׁחֵת *destroy not*, De. 9. 26; Ps. 57. 1, &c.; אַל תַּסְגֵּר *shut not up*, Ob. 14; תַּצֵּל *deliver not*, Ps. 119. 43 (comp. 1 Sa. 30. 8); אַל תַּפֵּל *let not fail*, Est. 6. 10 (comp. Pr. 1. 14); אַל תַּבֵּט *look not*, 1 Sa. 16. 7; אַל יַאֲמֵן *let him not trust*, Job 15. 31; אַל יוֹתֵר *let him not leave*, Ex. 16. 19; see also Pr. 30. 10; Ob. 12.

(*c*) Less frequently with a וְ preceding it, expressive of the conjunction *that, in order that*, as in Ju. 14. 15, *entice thy husband* וְיַגֶּד־לָנוּ *that he declare to us*, and so Job 11. 6; 12. 7; Je. 42. 3; וְיַצֵּל *that he deliver*, 1 Sa. 7. 3.

(*d*) With a negation, e. g. לֹא־תֹסֵף *she shall not continue*, Ge. 4. 12, comp. Job 40. 32 (27); לֹא אֹסֵף De. 18. 16; Ho. 9. 15; אַל תּוֹתֵר *thou shalt not have the pre-eminence*, Ge. 49. 4; see also Is. 13. 20.

(*e*) After *conversive Vav;* the first person, however, is excepted, which generally retains the form with ִי; e. g. וָאַשְׁמִיד *and I destroyed*, Am. 2. 9; וָאַשְׁלִיךְ *and I cast*, Zec. 11. 13; וָאַגִּיד *and I told*, Is. 48. 5; וָאַמְלִיךְ *and I made king*, 1 Sa. 12. 1; וָאַסְתִּיר *and I hid*, Eze. 39. 23, 24. It is likewise so pointed when י is omitted in the text—וָאַעְשִׁר *and I enriched*, Zec. 11. 5; וָאַחְבִּא *and I hid*, 1 Ki. 18. 13; וָאַצִּל *and I delivered*, Jos. 24. 10; Ju. 6. 9; 1 Sa. 10. 18.

Exceptions where יַקְטֵל is used for the plain *future* (or *present*), are only found with the poets, e. g. יַשְׁלֵךְ *he casts*, Job 15. 33; 27. 22; יַמְטֵר *he causes to rain*, Job 20. 23; Ps. 11. 6; see also Job 18. 9; 34. 29; 37. 4; 40. 9, 19; Ps. 25. 9; 2 Sa. 22. 14; 1 Sa. 2. 10; Mi. 3. 4. Also with somewhat later authors, e. g. יַדְבֵּק *he shall make to cleave*, De. 28. 21; יוֹלֵךְ *he shall lead*, De. 28. 36; אָז יַקְהֵל *then he assembled*, 1 Ki. 8. 1, for which 2 Ch. 5. 2 אָז יַקְהִיל (doubtless to be read יַקְהִיל); וְאַחְזֵק *and I shall lay hold*, Is. 42. 6.

7. Before Makkeph this Tseri of the shortened future becomes Segol; e. g. וַיַּחֲזֶק־בּוֹ *and he laid hold upon him*, Ju. 19. 4; וַיַּגֶּשׁ־לוֹ *and he drew near to him*, Ge. 27. 25; וַנַּגֶּד־לוֹ *and we told him*, Ge. 43. 7. In pause it occurs with Pattahh—וַיַּגַּשׁ Ju. 6. 19. In the plural Tseri is sometimes entirely dropped, as is the case with the *e* of the final syllable in the Aramaic—וַיַּדְרִכוּ for וַיַּדְרִיכוּ *and they bent* (the bow), Je. 9. 2; וַיַּדְבְּקוּ *and they pursued*, 1 Sa. 14. 22; 31. 2.

8. In the participle the form with (..) seldom occurs in the singular, see however מַסְתֵּר for מַסְתִּיר *hiding*, Is. 53. 3, and in the fem. מַזְכֶּרֶת Nu. 5. 15, מַגֶּדֶת Est. 2. 20. Hence are the plurals מַחְלְמִים *dreaming*, Je. 29. 8, מַעְזְרִים *helping*, 2 Ch. 28. 23, מַהְלְכִים *leading* (*leaders*), Zec. 3. 7, comp. the Chaldee מַהְלְכִין Da. 3. 25; 4. 34.

9. The tone in Hiph. differs from that of the rest of the conjugations, inasmuch as it does not rest upon the afformatives וּ and ִי in the pret., imp. and fut. In the pret. however, they receive the tone by *conversive Vav;* וְהִבְדִּילָה *and she shall divide*, Ex. 26. 33, but is retained in וְהִגִּידָה *and she told*, 2 Sa. 17. 17.

II. ON HOPHAL.

10. Besides the form with Kamets-Hhatuph given in the paradigm, there is another with Kibbuts equally frequent, and often in one and the same verb, e. g. הֻשְׁלַךְ *he is cast*, Da. 8. 11, הֻשְׁלַכְתָּ Is. 14. 19, הָשְׁלַכְתִּי Ps. 22. 11, fut. יֻשְׁלַךְ Is. 34. 3, Eze. 16. 5, part. מֻשְׁלָךְ 2 Sa. 20. 21; הֻשְׁכַּב *to be laid*, Eze. 32. 32, imp. הָשְׁכְּבָה ver. 19; הָפְקַד *to be appointed*, Je. 6. 6, part. מָפְקָדִים 2 Ch. 34. 10; תָּקְטַר *to be burned*, Le. 6. 15, part. מֻקְטָר Mal. 1. 11.

11. The *inf. abs.* is distinguished by (..) in the final syllable, e. g. הָחְתֵּל *to be swaddled*, Eze. 16. 4; הֻגֵּד Jos. 9. 24. Of the *inf. constr.* as given in the paradigm, there happens to occur no example in the regular verb.

12. Of the *participle* there occurs, in Eze. 46. 22, the uncontracted form מְהֻקְצָעוֹת for מֻקְצָעוֹת. This form occurs likewise in the fut. of the verbs פ״ו, as יְהוֹדֶה for יוֹדֶה (comp. § 20. rem. 10).

SECTION XII.—HITHPAEL.

REMARKS.

1. The *preterite*, as in Piel, has frequently also *Pattahh* in the final syllable, e. g. הִתְחַזַּק *to show oneself courageous*, 2 Ch. 13. 7; 15. 8. This vowel occurs also in the future and imperative, as יִתְחַכַּם *he thinks himself wise*, Ec. 7. 16; הִתְעַנַּג *delight thyself*, Ps. 37. 4; הִתְקַדַּשׁ *sanctify thyself*, Jos. 3. 5, comp. 1 Ki. 20. 22. In pause these forms take Kamets, as pret. הִתְאַזָּר *he girded himself*, Ps. 93. 1; fut. יִתְאַבָּל *he mourns*, Eze. 7. 12, 27, יִתְאַדָּם *it sparkles*, Pr. 23. 31.

2. The *preterite* with conversive Vav has sometimes *Hhirek* instead of *Pattahh* in the penultima which has lost the tone, as וְהִתְגַּדִּלְתִּי וְהִתְקַדִּשְׁתִּי *I will show myself great and holy*, Eze. 38. 23; וְהִתְקַדִּשְׁתֶּם *and ye shall show yourself holy*, Le. 11. 44; 20. 7, comp. in Kal the form יְלִדְתִּיךָ (§ 8. rem. 1 b).

3. The Syriac form with אֶת occurs in 2 Ch. 20. 35, אֶתְחַבַּר for הִתְחַבַּר *he joined himself*.

Note. The ת of the syllable הִתְ suffers the following changes:—(*a*) when the first radical of the verb is a sibilant (ס, צ, שׁ) it changes place with ת, as הִשְׁתַּמֵּר for הִתְשַׁמֵּר, הִסְתַּבֵּל for הִתְסַבֵּל; צ causes, moreover, a change of ת into the more nearly related ט, as הִצְטַדֵּק for הִצְתַּדֵּק; (*b*) before ד, ז, ט & ת it is assimilated, e. g. הִדַּבֵּר from דָּבַר, הִזַּכּוּ from זָכָה Is. 1. 16, הִטַּהֵר, הִתַּמֵּם; sometimes also before נ & כ, as הִנַּבֵּא, elsewhere הִתְנַבֵּא; הִכּוֹנֵן for הִתְכּוֹנֵן.

4. Forms followed by Makkeph are:—הִתְהַלֶּךְ־נֹחַ *Noah walked*, Ge. 6. 9; יִתְעַלֶּם־שָׁלֶג *the snow hides itself*, Job 6. 16; with parag. ן, יִתְהַלָּכוּן *they walk*, Ps. 12. 9 (comp. Kal fut. § 8. rem. 17); with parag. ה, אֶתְהַלְּכָה *I will walk*, Ps. 119. 45 (comp. Kal § 8. rem. 13).

5. In forms, in which the middle radical has Sheva, so that Dagesh may be dropped (§ 10. rem. 7), this latter is sometimes compensated by lengthening (ַ) into (ָ), as הִתְפָּקְדוּ for הִתְפַּקְּדוּ, Ju. 20. 15, and from habit of the punctuator, also in the sing. יִתְפָּקֵד (for יִתְפַּקֵּד) Ju. 21. 9.*

* Some have adopted here another conjugation הִתְקָאֵטֵל.

TABLES OF THE VERBS WITH GUTTURALS.

TABLE C. VERB PE GUTTURAL.

	KAL.		NIPHAL.	HIPHIL.	HOPHAL.
PRET. 3. m.	עָמַד		נֶעֱמַד	הֶעֱמִיד	הָעֳמַד
3. f.	עָמְדָה		נֶעֶמְדָה	הֶעֱמִידָה	הָעָמְדָה
2. m.	עָמַדְתָּ		נֶעֱמַדְתָּ	הֶעֱמַדְתָּ	הָעֳמַדְתָּ
2. f.	עָמַדְתְּ		נֶעֱמַדְתְּ	הֶעֱמַדְתְּ	הָעֳמַדְתְּ
1. c.	עָמַדְתִּי		נֶעֱמַדְתִּי	הֶעֱמַדְתִּי	הָעֳמַדְתִּי
Plur. 3. c.	עָמְדוּ		נֶעֶמְדוּ	הֶעֱמִידוּ	הָעָמְדוּ
2. m.	עֲמַדְתֶּם		נֶעֱמַדְתֶּם	הֶעֱמַדְתֶּם	הָעֳמַדְתֶּם
2. f.	עֲמַדְתֶּן		נֶעֱמַדְתֶּן	הֶעֱמַדְתֶּן	הָעֳמַדְתֶּן
1. c.	עָמַדְנוּ		נֶעֱמַדְנוּ	הֶעֱמַדְנוּ	הָעֳמַדְנוּ
INF. absol.	עָמוֹד		נַעֲמוֹד	הַעֲמֵד	
constr.	עֲמֹד		הֵעָמֵד	הַעֲמִיד	הָעֳמַד
IMP. m.	עֲמֹד	חֲזַק	הֵעָמֵד	הַעֲמֵד	wanting
f.	עִמְדִי	חִזְקִי	הֵעָמְדִי	הַעֲמִידִי	
Plur. m.	עִמְדוּ	חִזְקוּ	הֵעָמְדוּ	הַעֲמִידוּ	
f.	עֲמֹדְנָה	חֲזַקְנָה	הֵעָמַדְנָה	הַעֲמֵדְנָה	
FUT. 3. m.	יַעֲמֹד	יֶחֱזַק	יֵעָמֵד	יַעֲמִיד	יָעֳמַד
3. f.	תַּעֲמֹד	תֶּחֱזַק	תֵּעָמֵד	תַּעֲמִיד	תָּעֳמַד
2. m.	תַּעֲמֹד	תֶּחֱזַק	תֵּעָמֵד	תַּעֲמִיד	תָּעֳמַד
2. f.	תַּעַמְדִי	תֶּחֶזְקִי	תֵּעָמְדִי	תַּעֲמִידִי	תָּעָמְדִי
1. c.	אֶעֱמֹד	אֶחֱזַק	אֵעָמֵד	אַעֲמִיד	אָעֳמַד
Plur. 3. m.	יַעַמְדוּ	יֶחֶזְקוּ	יֵעָמְדוּ	יַעֲמִידוּ	יָעָמְדוּ
3. f.	תַּעֲמֹדְנָה	תֶּחֱזַקְנָה	תֵּעָמַדְנָה	תַּעֲמֵדְנָה	תָּעֳמַדְנָה
2. m.	תַּעַמְדוּ	תֶּחֶזְקוּ	תֵּעָמְדוּ	תַּעֲמִידוּ	תָּעָמְדוּ
2. f.	תַּעֲמֹדְנָה	תֶּחֱזַקְנָה	תֵּעָמַדְנָה	תַּעֲמֵדְנָה	תָּעֳמַדְנָה
1. c.	נַעֲמֹד	נֶחֱזַק	נֵעָמֵד	נַעֲמִיד	נָעֳמַד
FUT. apoc.				יַעֲמֵד	
PART. act.	עֹמֵד		נֶעֱמָד	מַעֲמִיד	מָעֳמָד
pass.	עָמוּד				

TABLE D. VERB AYIN GUTTURAL.

	KAL.	NIPHAL.	PIEL.	PUAL.	HITHPAEL.
PRET. 3. m.	שָׁחַט	נִשְׁחַט	בֵּרַךְ	בֹּרַךְ	הִתְבָּרֵךְ
3. f.	שָׁחֲטָה	נִשְׁחֲטָה	בֵּרְכָה	בֹּרְכָה	הִתְבָּרְכָה
2. m.	שָׁחַטְתָּ	נִשְׁחַטְתָּ	בֵּרַכְתָּ	בֹּרַכְתָּ	הִתְבָּרַכְתָּ
2. f.	שָׁחַטְתְּ	נִשְׁחַטְתְּ	בֵּרַכְתְּ	בֹּרַכְתְּ	הִתְבָּרַכְתְּ
1. c.	שָׁחַטְתִּי	נִשְׁחַטְתִּי	בֵּרַכְתִּי	בֹּרַכְתִּי	הִתְבָּרַכְתִּי
Plur. 3. c.	שָׁחֲטוּ	נִשְׁחֲטוּ	בֵּרְכוּ	בֹּרְכוּ	הִתְבָּרְכוּ
2. m.	שְׁחַטְתֶּם	נִשְׁחַטְתֶּם	בֵּרַכְתֶּם	בֹּרַכְתֶּם	הִתְבָּרַכְתֶּם
2. f.	שְׁחַטְתֶּן	נִשְׁחַטְתֶּן	בֵּרַכְתֶּן	בֹּרַכְתֶּן	הִתְבָּרַכְתֶּן
1. c.	שָׁחַטְנוּ	נִשְׁחַטְנוּ	בֵּרַכְנוּ	בֹּרַכְנוּ	הִתְבָּרַכְנוּ
INF. absol.	שָׁחוֹט	נִשְׁחוֹט	בָּרוֹךְ		
constr.	שְׁחֹט	הִשָּׁחֵט	בָּרֵךְ	בֹּרַךְ	הִתְבָּרֵךְ
IMP. m.	שְׁחַט	הִשָּׁחֵט	בָּרֵךְ	wanting.	הִתְבָּרֵךְ
f.	שַׁחֲטִי	הִשָּׁחֲטִי	בָּרְכִי		הִתְבָּרְכִי
Plur. m.	שַׁחֲטוּ	הִשָּׁחֲטוּ	בָּרְכוּ		הִתְבָּרְכוּ
f.	שְׁחַטְנָה	הִשָּׁחַטְנָה	בָּרַכְנָה		הִתְבָּרַכְנָה
FUT. 3. m.	יִשְׁחַט	יִשָּׁחֵט	יְבָרֵךְ	יְבֹרַךְ	יִתְבָּרֵךְ
3. f.	תִּשְׁחַט	תִּשָּׁחֵט	תְּבָרֵךְ	תְּבֹרַךְ	תִּתְבָּרֵךְ
2. m.	תִּשְׁחַט	תִּשָּׁחֵט	תְּבָרֵךְ	תְּבֹרַךְ	תִּתְבָּרֵךְ
2. f.	תִּשְׁחֲטִי	תִּשָּׁחֲטִי	תְּבָרְכִי	תְּבֹרְכִי	תִּתְבָּרְכִי
1. c.	אֶשְׁחַט	אֶשָּׁחֵט	אֲבָרֵךְ	אֲבֹרַךְ	אֶתְבָּרֵךְ
Plur. 3. m.	יִשְׁחֲטוּ	יִשָּׁחֲטוּ	יְבָרְכוּ	יְבֹרְכוּ	יִתְבָּרְכוּ
3. f.	תִּשְׁחַטְנָה	תִּשָּׁחַטְנָה	תְּבָרַכְנָה	תְּבֹרַכְנָה	תִּתְבָּרַכְנָה
2. m.	תִּשְׁחֲטוּ	תִּשָּׁחֲטוּ	תְּבָרְכוּ	תְּבֹרְכוּ	תִּתְבָּרְכוּ
2. f.	תִּשְׁחַטְנָה	תִּשָּׁחַטְנָה	תְּבָרַכְנָה	תְּבֹרַכְנָה	תִּתְבָּרַכְנָה
1. c.	נִשְׁחַט	נִשָּׁחֵט	נְבָרֵךְ	נְבֹרַךְ	נִתְבָּרֵךְ
PART. act.	שֹׁחֵט	נִשְׁחָט	מְבָרֵךְ	מְבֹרָךְ	מִתְבָּרֵךְ
pass.	שָׁחוּט				

TABLE E. VERB LAMEDH GUTTURAL.

	KAL.	NIPHAL.	PIEL.	PUAL.	HIPHIL.	HOPHAL.	HITHPAEL.
PRET. 3. *m.*	שָׁלַח	נִשְׁלַח	שִׁלַּח	שֻׁלַּח	הִשְׁלִיחַ	הָשְׁלַח	הִשְׁתַּלַּח
3. *f.*	שָֽׁלְחָה	נִשְׁלְחָה	שִׁלְּחָה	שֻׁלְּחָה	הִשְׁלִיחָה	הָשְׁלְחָה	הִשְׁתַּלְּחָה
2. *m.*	שָׁלַחְתָּ	נִשְׁלַחְתָּ	שִׁלַּחְתָּ	שֻׁלַּחְתָּ	הִשְׁלַחְתָּ	הָשְׁלַחְתָּ	הִשְׁתַּלַּחְתָּ
2. *f.*	שָׁלַחַתְּ	נִשְׁלַחַתְּ	שִׁלַּחַתְּ	שֻׁלַּחַתְּ	הִשְׁלַחַתְּ	הָשְׁלַחַתְּ	הִשְׁתַּלַּחַתְּ
1. *c.*	שָׁלַחְתִּי	נִשְׁלַחְתִּי	שִׁלַּחְתִּי	שֻׁלַּחְתִּי	הִשְׁלַחְתִּי	הָשְׁלַחְתִּי	הִשְׁתַּלַּחְתִּי
Plur. 3. *c.*	שָֽׁלְחוּ	נִשְׁלְחוּ	שִׁלְּחוּ	שֻׁלְּחוּ	הִשְׁלִיחוּ	הָשְׁלְחוּ	הִשְׁתַּלְּחוּ
2. *m.*	שְׁלַחְתֶּם	נִשְׁלַחְתֶּם	שִׁלַּחְתֶּם	שֻׁלַּחְתֶּם	הִשְׁלַחְתֶּם	הָשְׁלַחְתֶּם	הִשְׁתַּלַּחְתֶּם
2. *f.*	שְׁלַחְתֶּן	נִשְׁלַחְתֶּן	שִׁלַּחְתֶּן	שֻׁלַּחְתֶּן	הִשְׁלַחְתֶּן	הָשְׁלַחְתֶּן	הִשְׁתַּלַּחְתֶּן
1. *c.*	שָׁלַחְנוּ	נִשְׁלַחְנוּ	שִׁלַּחְנוּ	שֻׁלַּחְנוּ	הִשְׁלַחְנוּ	הָשְׁלַחְנוּ	הִשְׁתַּלַּחְנוּ
INF. *absol.*	שָׁלוֹחַ	נִשְׁלֹחַ	שַׁלֵּחַ		הַשְׁלֵחַ		
constr.	שְׁלֹחַ	הִשָּׁלַח	שַׁלַּח	שֻׁלַּח	הַשְׁלִיחַ	הָשְׁלַח	הִשְׁתַּלַּח
IMP. *m.*	שְׁלַח	הִשָּׁלַח	שַׁלַּח		הַשְׁלַח		הִשְׁתַּלַּח
f.	שִׁלְחִי	הִשָּֽׁלְחִי	שַׁלְּחִי	wanting	הַשְׁלִיחִי	wanting	הִשְׁתַּלְּחִי
Plur. *m.*	שִׁלְחוּ	הִשָּֽׁלְחוּ	שַׁלְּחוּ		הַשְׁלִיחוּ		הִשְׁתַּלְּחוּ
f.	שְׁלַחְנָה	הִשָּׁלַחְנָה	שַׁלַּחְנָה		הַשְׁלַחְנָה		הִשְׁתַּלַּחְנָה
FUT. 3. *m.*	יִשְׁלַח	יִשָּׁלַח	יְשַׁלַּח	יְשֻׁלַּח	יַשְׁלִיחַ	יָשְׁלַח	יִשְׁתַּלַּח
3. *f.*	תִּשְׁלַח	תִּשָּׁלַח	תְּשַׁלַּח	תְּשֻׁלַּח	תַּשְׁלִיחַ	תָּשְׁלַח	תִּשְׁתַּלַּח
2. *m.*	תִּשְׁלַח	תִּשָּׁלַח	תְּשַׁלַּח	תְּשֻׁלַּח	תַּשְׁלִיחַ	תָּשְׁלַח	תִּשְׁתַּלַּח
2. *f.*	תִּשְׁלְחִי	תִּשָּֽׁלְחִי	תְּשַׁלְּחִי	תְּשֻׁלְּחִי	תַּשְׁלִיחִי	תָּשְׁלְחִי	תִּשְׁתַּלְּחִי
1. *c.*	אֶשְׁלַח	אֶשָּׁלַח	אֲשַׁלַּח	אֲשֻׁלַּח	אַשְׁלִיחַ	אָשְׁלַח	אֶשְׁתַּלַּח
Plur. 3. *m.*	יִשְׁלְחוּ	יִשָּֽׁלְחוּ	יְשַׁלְּחוּ	יְשֻׁלְּחוּ	יַשְׁלִיחוּ	יָשְׁלְחוּ	יִשְׁתַּלְּחוּ
3. *f.*	תִּשְׁלַחְנָה	תִּשָּׁלַחְנָה	תְּשַׁלַּחְנָה	תְּשֻׁלַּחְנָה	תַּשְׁלַחְנָה	תָּשְׁלַחְנָה	תִּשְׁתַּלַּחְנָה
2. *m.*	תִּשְׁלְחוּ	תִּשָּֽׁלְחוּ	תְּשַׁלְּחוּ	תְּשֻׁלְּחוּ	תַּשְׁלִיחוּ	תָּשְׁלְחוּ	תִּשְׁתַּלְּחוּ
2. *f.*	תִּשְׁלַחְנָה	תִּשָּׁלַחְנָה	תְּשַׁלַּחְנָה	תְּשֻׁלַּחְנָה	תַּשְׁלַחְנָה	תָּשְׁלַחְנָה	תִּשְׁתַּלַּחְנָה
1. *c.*	נִשְׁלַח	נִשָּׁלַח	נְשַׁלַּח	נְשֻׁלַּח	נַשְׁלִיחַ	נָשְׁלַח	נִשְׁתַּלַּח
FUT. *apoc.*					יַשְׁלַח		
PART. *act.*	שֹׁלֵחַ	נִשְׁלָח	מְשַׁכֵּחַ	מְשֻׁלָּח	מַשְׁלִיחַ	מָשְׁלָח	מִשְׁתַּלֵּחַ
pass.	שָׁלוּחַ						

SECTION XIII.—VERB PE GUTTURAL. (TABLE C.)

REMARKS.

I. ON KAL.

1. In the *preterite* no other deviation exists except הֱיִיתֶם (with Hhateph-Segol) *ye are*, Job 6. 21, and the same word with simple Sheva וִהְיִיתֶם Ge. 3. 5 (comp. rem. 13).

2. In the verbs פ״א the *inf. constr.* takes (ֱ) under the first letter, as אֱכֹל especially with the prefixes, בֶּאֱחֹז ,לֶאֱחֹז *to seize*, בֶּאֱסֹף ,לֶאֱסֹף *to collect*, Is. 17. 5; 2 Ki. 5. 7; לֶאֱכֹל Ge. 24. 33, and בַּאֲכֹל* Nu. 26. 10. With simple Sheva לֶאְסֹר (for לֶאֱסֹר) *to bind*, Ps. 105. 22. With the feminine termination:—אַשְׁמָה *to become guilty*, Le. 5. 26, אַהֲבָה *to love*, De. 10. 12; 11. 22; חֶזְקָה, whence בְּחֶזְקָתוֹ *when he gained strength*, 2 Ch. 12. 1; 26. 16.

3. *Imperative.* In the verbs פ״א the first letter takes (ֱ), as אֱזֹר *gird on*, Job 38. 3, אֱחֹז *lay hold*, Ex. 4. 4, אֱסֹף *collect*, Nu. 21. 16; אֱהַב *love*, Ho. 3. 1. The rest of the persons have generally the regular form, only in a few instances Segol is retained, e. g. אֶסְפָה, *collect*, Nu. 11. 16, עֶרְכָה *order*, Job 33. 5, חֶשְׂפִּי *make bare*, Is. 47. 2, which more especially happens when the second radical is likewise a guttural, אֶהֱבוּ Ps. 31. 24, אֶחֱזוּ Ca. 2. 15, אֶחֱזִי Ru. 3. 15.

4. The form of the *future* exhibited in the paradigm is that of the verbs *fut. O*, as יַחֲלֹם *to dream*, יַעֲבֹד *to serve*, יַעֲבֹר *to pass over*, יַעֲרֹךְ *to set in order*. The verbs *fut. A* take Segol under the preformatives, as יֶאֱבַל *to mourn*, יֶחֱזַק *to be strong*, יֶחֱרַד *to tremble*, יֶעֱרַב *to be sweet*. Less frequently do verbs *fut. O* occur with Segol, as יֶאֱסֹף *to collect*, יֶחֱשֹׂף *to make bare*, and once in pause יֶחְדָּל Job 10. 20 (elsewhere יֶחְדַּל). Both futures, like יַעֲמֹד & יֶחֱזַק, are found in one and the same verb (with or without a difference of signification), as in חָבַשׁ *to bind*, חָלַשׁ *to be weak*, חָרַשׁ *to cut*, חָפֵץ *to delight in*, עָרַב (§ 8. rem. 18). Moreover, יַהֲלֹךְ *to go*, תְּהַלֵּךְ (*grassari*) for תֶּהֱלַךְ (comp. rem. 12) Ex. 9. 23; Ps. 73. 9.

Examples with afformatives are:—יַהֲרֹג, יַהַרְגוּ, אַהַרְגֶנָּה (*to kill*), יַהֲפֹךְ, יַהַפְכוּ (*to turn*); יֶחֱזַק, יֶחֶזְקוּ; יֶחֱרַד, יֶחֶרְדוּ (*to tremble*).

5. Other verbs have very constantly simple Sheva under the guttural; but in the same relation as mentioned above. This is most frequently the case with ח, as יַחְגֹּר (for יַחֲגֹר) *to gird on*, יַחְמֹל *to pity*, יַחְשֹׁב *to think;* יֶחְדַּל *to cease*, יֶחְכַּם *to be wise*. The persons with afformatives remain quite regular, as יַחְגְּרוּ, יַחְדְּלוּ. Less frequently are both forms found in the same verb, e. g. יֶאֱהַב Pr. 3. 12, and יֶאֱהַב Pr. 15. 9, 12, and especially when the leading form has composite Sheva; but with the afformatives and suffixes, simple Sheva is introduced, as יַחֲבשׁ, but יַחְבְּשׁוּ 1 Ki. 13. 13, יַחְבְּשֵׁנוּ Ho. 6. 1; יַחֲבֹל De. 24. 6, pl. יַחְבֹּלוּ Job 24. 3; יַחֲלֹק, pl. יַחְלְקוּ Jos. 14. 5; so also יַעֲזֹר, pl. יַעְזְרוּ; יַעֲבֹר, but אֶעְבְּרָה, נַעְבְּרָה.

6. Since the punctuation (ַ ֲ), (ַ) is considered shorter than (ֶ ֱ), (ֶ), the former is sometimes used where the form is augmented by afformatives, suffixes, &c., while the leading form has the latter punctuation. E. g. יֶאֱסֹף (*to collect*), but יַאַסְפִי, תַּאַסְפִּי, and so with suffix; יֶאְסֹר (*to bind*), with suff. יַאַסְרֵהוּ, יַאַסְרוּהוּ &c.; יֶחְסַר (*to want*), pl. יַחְסְרוּ Ps. 34. 11; Eze. 4. 17. According to the same principle we find יַחְפְּרוּ (*to blush*), Ps. 35. 4, 26, in pause יֶחְפָּרוּ Ps. 34. 6; Job 6. 20; יַחְפְּצוּ, in pause יֶחְפָּצוּ (comp. rem. on Niph. and Hiph.).

II. On Niphal.

7. *Preterite.* Besides the form exhibited in the paradigm there is another with simple Sheva, as נֶאְשַׁם (*to be guilty*), נֶהְדַּר (*to be glorified*). The shorter (ַ ֲ) is introduced only with the augmentation at the end of the participle, as נֶעְלָם *hid*, Ec. 12. 14, but on the contrary, נַעֲלָמָה Na. 3. 11, and נַעֲלָמִים Ps. 26. 4; so נֶחֱרָבוֹת *waste*, Eze. 30. 7; a single exception is נַעֲרָץ *terrible*, Ps. 89. 8. A few infinitives absol. formed according to the preterite (§ 9. rem. 1) have likewise this *a*, as נַהֲפוֹךְ.†

8. The *future* is once written *fully* תֵּיעָשֶׂה for תֵּעָשֶׂה Ex. 35. 31. In a few instances Segol is found instead of Tseri, e. g. בֶּהָרֵג (for בְּהֵהָרֵג) Eze: 26. 15, and so likewise in a few earlier editions in Eze. 43. 18; Job 19. 7.

III. On Hiphil and Hophal.

9. The forms with (ֱ ֶ) in the preterite, and (ַ ֲ) in the infinitive, imperative and future, as exhibited in the paradigm, are as regular here as in the non-guttural verb the forms with (ִ) and (ַ) to which they correspond; only that here occurs also the form with simple Sheva, as הֶחְסִיר, fut. יַחְסִיר *shall cause to want;* מַחְפִּיר *causing shame*.

10. In the *preterite*, the punctuation is remarkably

* Pattahh is found here (as the shorter form, comp. rem. 6) because the tone is forcibly thrown forward, בַּאֲכֹל הָאֵשׁ. For the same reason they wrote אֲמַרְתֶּם not אֱמַרְתֶּם.

† There are, however, preterites as well as participles (in the leading form) of verbs ל״ה and ל״א which have this (ַ ֲ ַ ֲ), as נַעֲוֵיתִי Ps. 38. 7; Is. 21. 3; נַעֲלָה Nu. 9. 21; 10. 11; נַעֲנֶה Is. 53. 7; נַעֲנֵיתִי Ps. 119. 107; נַעֲשָׂה Le. 7. 9; נַעֲשׂוּ Le. 18. 30, but also נֶעֶשְׂתָה Nu. 15. 24; נַחְבֵּאתָ Ge. 31. 27; נַחְבֵּתֶם Jos. 2. 16.

affected by the *conversive Vav*, since the tone connected with it changes (ֱ : ֲ) into the shorter (ַ : ֲ). E. g. הֶחֱרַמְתִּי *I have devoted*, 1 Sa. 15. 20; וְהַחֲרַמְתִּי *and I shall devote*, Nu. 21. 2; Mi. 4. 13; וְהַחֲרַמְתָּה 1 Sa. 15. 18, וְהַחֲרַמְתֶּם 1 Sa. 15. 3; הֶעֱמַדְתָּ *thou hast appointed*, Ne. 6. 7; Ps. 31. 9; וְהַעֲמַדְתָּ *and thou shalt appoint*, Nu. 3. 6; 8. 13; 27. 19; Eze. 29. 7; הֶעֱבַרְתִּי *I caused to pass*, Zec. 3. 4; וְהַעֲבַרְתִּי *and I shall cause to pass*, Je. 15. 14; וְהַעֲבַרְתָּ Ex. 13. 12; Le. 25. 9; Nu. 27. 7; Eze. 5. 1; הֶאֱכַלְתִּי Ex. 16. 32; וְהַאֲכַלְתִּי Is. 49. 26; הֶאֱבַדְתִּי & וְהַאֲבַדְתִּי &c. The like change is effected by the *conversive Vav* even in the 3rd person, comp. הֶאֱזִין *he hearkened*, De. 1. 45, and וְהַאֲזִין *and he shall hearken*, Ps. 77. 2.*

11. Of *Hophal* only a few instances occur with simple and composite Sheva under the guttural, as הָהְפַּךְ, fut. יָחֳרַם, part. מָעֳמָד.

12. In the *part. of Hiph.* (ֱ : ֲ) is sometimes changed into (ַ : ֲ), and in Hoph. (ָ : ֳ) into (ָ : ֳ), prolonging the short vowel which was sustained by Metheg, e. g. הֶעֱבַרְתָּ (elsewhere הֶעֱבַרְתָּ) Jos. 7. 7; הֶעֱלָה Hab. 1. 15 (elsewhere הֶעֱלָה); הֹעֲלָה Na. 2. 8, and that often, for הֹעֲלָה. Comp. in Kal תְּהֲלֵךְ for תֵּהָלֵךְ (§ 13. rem. 4), Ex. 9. 23; Ps. 73. 9; but—Note, on the contrary, (ֱ : ֲ) is put for (ַ : ֲ) in אֶחֱרוּ (Piel for אִחֲרוּ) Ju. 5. 28; יֶחֱמוּ Ge. 30. 39; יֶחֱמַתְנִי Ps. 51. 73.

IV. In General.

13. A few verbs ל״ה with Pe guttural differ from the above inasmuch as their ה & ח are not at all treated as gutturals, viz. הָיָה *to be* (except the pret., see rem. 1), fut. יִהְיֶה, with prepositions לִהְיוֹת, Niph. נִהְיָה; so also חָיָה *to live*, pret. וִחְיִיתֶם Eze. 37. 5, 6, inf. לִחְיוֹת, imp. with copulative Vav וִחְיוּ, fut. יִחְיֶה. Only in a few examples the guttural character is retained (viz. when the guttural begins the word), as הֱיוֹת, הֱיֵה Eze. 21. 15. The same analogy is observed in the apocopated future יִחַד, וַיִּחַן (otherwise יֶחֱנֶה) & וַיִּחַר.

14. The letter ר as first radical comes within this anomaly only in the *inf.* and *fut. of Niph.*, e. g. יֵרָאֶה *he is seen*. The unusual form with Pattahh under the preformative is found only in the apocopated fut. וַיֵּרָא, and in Hiph. וְהַרְאֵתִי Na. 3. 5, with conversive Vav, otherwise הֶרְאָה & הֶרְאָה.

SECTION XIV.—VERB AYIN GUTTURAL. (Table D.)

REMARKS IN GENERAL.

1. In *Piel*, *Pual* and *Hithpael*, Dagesh forte of the middle radical letter is lost, but in the greater number of examples, particularly before ה, ח & ע, the preceding vowel remains short, and the guttural has *Dagesh forte implicitum*, or Dagesh forte implied, e. g. Piel נִהַג *to lead*, נִחַם *to comfort*, בִּעֵר *to destroy*, inf. צַחֵק *to mock*, fut. יְטַהֵר *to cleanse*, part. מְטַהֵר; Pual רֻחַץ *to be washed*; Hithpa. הִטַּהֲרוּ. Before א the vowel is commonly prolonged (but comp. נִאֵץ, יְנַאֵץ, Pu. רֻאּוּ Job 33. 21), and always before ר.

2. In *Pi.* and *Hiph.* the tone is sometimes drawn back to the penultima, and Tseri of the final syllable is shortened to Segol, viz.:—

(*a*) When a monosyllabic word, or one with the tone on the penultima follows, e. g. לְשָׁרֶת שָׁם *to minister there*, De. 17. 12 (otherwise לְשָׁרֵת); לְצַחֶק בִּי, בָּנוּ *to mock me* or *us*, Ge. 39. 14, 17; כִּחֶשׁ בִּי, בָּהּ *he denies him, her*, Job 8. 18; Le. 5. 22, comp. כִּחֵשׁ Le. 5. 21, יְכַחֶשׁ בָּהּ Ho. 9. 2, but וַתְּכַחֵשׁ Ge. 18. 15; יְחָרֶף צָר *shall the adversary reproach*, Ps. 74. 10, but וַיְחָרֵף 2 Sa. 21. 21.

(*b*) After conversive Vav, as וַיְבָרֶךְ אוֹתָם *and he blessed them*, Ge. 1. 22, 28; 2. 3; 5. 2 (without a tone syllable following it); וַיְגָרֶשׁ *and he drove away*, Ex. 10. 11; De. 33. 27, &c.; וַיְשָׁרֶת אֹתוֹ *and he scared him*, Ge. 39. 4; וַתִּתְפָּעֶם רוּחוֹ *and his spirit was troubled*, Da. 2. 1. The (ֵ) is, however, retained in both these cases, especially in the latter, e. g. וַיְמָאֵן *and he refused*, Ge. 48. 19; Nu. 20. 21, וַיְמַהֵר *and he made haste*, Ge. 18. 6, 7.

3. In the *Hithpa.*, when the second radical takes Kamets on account of the pause, the preceding syllable takes (ֶ) instead of (ַ) or (ָ). E. g. הִטֶּהָרוּ *cleanse yourselves*, Nu. 8. 7; הִנֶּחָמְתִּי Eze. 5. 13.

* As an exception of this rule must be regarded הַחִיתֶם (for הֶחֱיִתֶם) Ju. 8. 19.

REMARKS.

1. In the *inf.* and *fut. of Niphal*, and in the *pret.*, *inf.* and *fut. of Piel*, the form with (ַ) is employed at the beginning and in the middle of a period (with conjunctive accent), that with (ֵ) and furtive Pattahh is used at the end of a period (with distinctive accent). E. g. Niph. הִכָּנַע 2 Ch. 33. 23, but on the contrary לְהִבָּקֵעַ Eze. 30. 16; fut. יִגָּרַע Nu. 27. 4; 36. 4; comp. יִגָּרֵעַ chap. 36. 3; יִזָּרַע Na. 1. 14, but יִזָּרֵעַ Le. 11. 37; De. 21. 4. Piel pret. פִּתַּח Job 30. 11, and פִּתֵּחַ chap. 12. 18; גִּדַּע 2 Ch. 34. 7, and גִּדֵּעַ ver. 4; inf. בַּלַּע Hab. 1. 13; Nu. 4. 20, comp. בַּלֵּעַ La. 2. 8; שַׁלַּח Ex. 5. 2; 7. 14, and שַׁלֵּחַ chap. 7. 27; 9. 2; fut. יְבַקַּע Hab. 3. 9; Ps. 78. 15; Ge. 22. 3, comp. יְבַקֵּעַ Eze. 13. 11; 2 Ki. 8. 12; יְגַלַּח & יְגַלֵּחַ Le. 14. 9; אֲבַלַּע 2 Sa. 20. 20, comp. אֲבַלֵּעַ Is. 19. 3.

2. The *participle of Niphal* must be supposed to admit of another form like נִשְׁלֵחַ, which loses (ֵ) before an accession at the end (comp. dec. 7); hence נִדָּחוּ 2 Sa. 14. 13, נִדַּחֲכֶם Ne. 1. 9 (comp. § 23. rem. 6).

REGULAR VERB WITH SUFFIXES.

TABLE F. REGULAR VERB WITH SUFFIXES.

SUFFIXES *for*	1 *Sing.*	2 *Sing. m.*	2 *Sing. f.*	3 *Sing. m.*	3 *Sing. f.*	1 *Plur.*	2 *Plur. m.*	2 *Plur. f.*	3 *Plur. m.*	3 *Plur. f.*
PRET. *Kal.* 3. *m.*	קְטָלַנִי	קְטָלְךָ	קְטָלֵךְ	קְטָלָהוּ קְטָלוֹ	קְטָלָהּ	קְטָלָנוּ	קְטַלְכֶם	קְטַלְכֶן	קְטָלָם	קְטָלָן
3. *f.*	קְטָלַתְנִי	קְטָלַתְךָ	קְטָלָתֶךְ	קְטָלַתְהוּ קְטָלַתּוּ	קְטָלַתָּה	קְטָלַתְנוּ	קְטָלַתְכֶם	קְטָלַתְכֶן	קְטָלָתַם	קְטָלָתַן
2. *m.*	קְטַלְתַּנִי קְטַלְתָּנִי	—	—	קְטַלְתָּהוּ קְטַלְתּוֹ	קְטַלְתָּהּ	קְטַלְתָּנוּ	—	—	קְטַלְתָּם	קְטַלְתָּן
2. *f.*	קְטַלְתִּינִי	—	—	קְטַלְתִּיהוּ קְטַלְתִּיו	קְטַלְתִּיהָ	קְטַלְתִּינוּ	—	—	קְטַלְתִּים	קְטַלְתִּין
1. *c.*	—	קְטַלְתִּיךָ	קְטַלְתִּיךְ	קְטַלְתִּיו	קְטַלְתִּיהָ	—	קְטַלְתִּיכֶם	קְטַלְתִּיכֶן	קְטַלְתִּים	קְטַלְתִּין
Plur. 3. *c.*	קְטָלוּנִי	קְטָלוּךָ	קְטָלוּךְ	קְטָלוּהוּ	קְטָלוּהָ	קְטָלוּנוּ	קְטָלוּכֶם	קְטָלוּכֶן	קְטָלוּם	קְטָלוּן
2. *m.*	קְטַלְתּוּנִי	—	—	קְטַלְתּוּהוּ	קְטַלְתּוּהָ	קְטַלְתּוּנוּ	—	—	קְטַלְתּוּם	קְטַלְתּוּן
1. *c.*	—	קְטַלְנוּךָ	קְטַלְנוּךְ	קְטַלְנוּהוּ	קְטַלְנוּהָ	—	קְטַלְנוּכֶם	קְטַלְנוּכֶן	קְטַלְנוּם	קְטַלְנוּן
INF. *Kal.*	קָטְלִי קָטְלֵנִי	קָטְלְךָ קְטָלְךָ	קָטְלֵךְ	קָטְלוֹ	קָטְלָהּ	קָטְלֵנוּ	קָטְלְכֶם קְטָלְכֶם	קָטְלְכֶן	קָטְלָם	קָטְלָן
IMP. *Kal.*	קָטְלֵנִי	—	—	קָטְלֵהוּ	קָטְלֶהָ קָטְלָהּ	קָטְלֵנוּ	—	—	קָטְלֵם	—
FUT. *Kal.* 3. *m.*	יִקְטְלֵנִי	יִקְטָלְךָ	יִקְטְלֵךְ	יִקְטְלֵהוּ	יִקְטְלֶהָ יִקְטְלָהּ	יִקְטְלֵנוּ	יִקְטָלְכֶם	יִקְטָלְכֶן	יִקְטְלֵם	יִקְטְלֵן
3. *m.* *with Nun epenthet.*	יִקְטְלֶנִּי	יִקְטְלֶךָּ	—	יִקְטְלֶנּוּ	יִקְטְלֶנָּה	יִקְטְלֶנּוּ	—	—	—	—
Plur. 3. *m.*	יִקְטְלוּנִי	יִקְטְלוּךָ	יִקְטְלוּךְ	יִקְטְלוּהוּ	יִקְטְלוּהָ	יִקְטְלוּנוּ	יִקְטְלוּכֶם	יִקְטְלוּכֶן	יִקְטְלוּם	יִקְטְלוּן
PRET. *Piël.*	קִטְּלַנִי	קִטֶּלְךָ	קִטְּלֵךְ	קִטְּלוֹ	קִטְּלָהּ	קִטְּלָנוּ	קִטֶּלְכֶם	קִטֶּלְכֶן	קִטְּלָם	קִטְּלָן

SECTION XVI.—REGULAR VERB WITH SUFFIXES. (TABLE F.)

REMARKS.

I. ON THE PRETERITE OF KAL.

1. *Third Person Masculine.* In the verbs *middle E* (§ 8. rem. 1) this characteristic vowel remains also before the suffix, as אֲהֵבְךָ De. 7. 13; 15. 16; 23. 6, from אָהֵב; לְבֵשָׁם Le. 16. 4; שְׂנֵאָהּ De. 24. 3.

2. *Third Person Feminine.* The form קָטְלַת designating the *fem.* has a twofold peculiarity—(*a*) it takes the suffixes which form a syllable by themselves (נִי, ךָ, הוּ, הָ, נוּ, כֶם, כֶן) without a union-vowel, though itself ends with a consonant; (*b*) with the rest of the suffixes it indeed takes the union-vowel, but the tone is drawn back to the penultima, so that they appear in the shortened form ַ־ךָ, ַ־ם, ַ־ן. E. g. אֲהֵבָתֶךְ *she loves thee*, Ru. 4. 15; שׁוֹבְבָתֶךְ *it has perverted thee*, Is. 47. 10; שְׂרָפָתַם *she burns them*, Is. 47. 14; אֲכָלָתַם *it consumes them*, Ho. 2. 14; גְּנָבָתַם *she had stolen them*, Ge. 31. 32; נְצָרָתַם *it observes them*, Ps. 119. 129; מְצָאָתַם *it befell them*, Ex. 18. 8; but on the contrary עֲנָקָתְמוֹ Ps. 73. 6.

3. In the suffix of the third person a kind of contraction takes place, which may be compared with the form ֶ־נּוּ for ֶ־נְהוּ, viz. ַ־תְהוּ contr. ַ־תּוּ, and ַ־תָּה contracted from ַ־תְהָ. In the masculine both occur, the contracted and uncontracted form, as גְּמָלַתְהוּ *she shows him*, Pr. 31. 12; גְּמָלַתּוּ *she weaned him*, 1 Sa. 1. 24; סְמָכָתְהוּ Is. 59. 16, comp. Ge. 37. 20; 1 Sa. 18. 28, and גְּנָבַתּוּ Job 21. 18, comp. Ru. 4. 15. With the suffix of the feminine only the contracted form exists, אֲחָזַתָּה Je. 49. 24; Is. 34. 17.

For ַ־תְנִי, ַ־תְנוּ, ַ־תְךָ the pause exhibits ָ־תְנִי &c., e. g. אֲכָלָתְנִי Ps. 69. 10; מְצָאָתְנוּ Nu. 20. 14; יְלָדַתְךָ Ca. 8. 5 (where חִבְּלַתְךָ in the first member of the sentence is so pointed for the sake of consonance).

4. The *Second Person Masculine* assumes in all cases the form קְטַלְתָּ, wherefore the suffix has no union-vowel, except with the suffix of the 1 and 2 pers. sing. masc., where sometimes קְטַלְתִּ appears as the ground-form, and so to it is attached the suffix (ַ־נִי, ֹו) by its union-vowel. Hence חֲקַרְתַּנִי *thou searchest me*, Ps. 139. 1; חֲזַקְתַּנִי *thou hast overcome me*, Je. 20. 7 (elsewhere, however, עֲזַבְתָּנִי Ps. 22. 2); אֲסַפְתּוֹ *thou gatherest him*, 2 Ki. 5, 6, comp. Nu. 23. 27; Ps. 89. 44; Hab. 1. 12 (elsewhere also כִּפַּרְתָּהוּ Eze. 43. 20).

5. *Second Person Feminine.* All the forms exhibited in the paradigm assume the ground-form קְטַלְתִּי, so that the suffix has no union-vowel. ִ־י is often written defectively, as יְלִדְתִּנִי *thou hast borne me*, Je. 15. 10; comp. Ca. 4. 9; 1 Sa. 19. 17. The form קְטַלְתְּ, however, occurs also with suffixes which have the union-vowel, as יְלִדְתָּנוּ *thou hast brought us forth*, Je. 2. 27; Jos. 2. 17; Ca. 5. 9 (for (ִ) in the final syllable comp. § 8. rem. 1 b).

6. All the *persons of the plural* follow one rule, as all the verbal forms end here alike in ּו, and the suffixes have therefore no union-vowel. These are frequently written *defectively*, as דְּרַשְׁנֻהוּ 1 Ch. 13. 3, which, of course, is immaterial.

II. ON THE INFINITIVE OF KAL.

7. The shortened form קְטֹל is found most frequently before the suffixes כֶם & כֶן, אֲכָלְכֶם *your eating*, Ge. 3. 5, אֲמָרְכֶם *your saying*, Mal. 1. 7; somewhat less frequent are forms like עָבְרְכֶם De. 27. 4; קְצָרְכֶם Le. 23. 22. The same inconstancy is found before the suff. ךָ, e. g. עָבְרְךָ *thy passing over*, De. 29. 11; שָׁמְעֲךָ *thy hearing*, 2 Ki. 22. 19; but also עֲמָדְךָ Ob. 11; אֲכָלְךָ Ge. 2. 17. There is also a form קְצָרְךָ Le. 23. 22, which agrees with קְצָרְכֶם in the same verse.

8. When the middle letter is a guttural it takes (ֳ) instead of simple Sheva, e. g. בָּחֳרִי *my choosing*, Eze. 20. 5; אָהֳבָם *their loving*, Ho. 9. 10; and in the 2 pers., Kamets-Hhatuph, as מָאָסְכֶם Is. 30. 12, and so also (with ר) קָרָבְכֶם De. 20. 2.

9. An anomalous form, otherwise found with guttural (comp. § 13. rem. 12) is מֹצַאֲכֶם for מָצְאֲכֶם Ge. 32. 20. In the same way some explain the form בּוֹשַׁסְכֶם for בָּשְׁסְכֶם Am. 5. 11; this, however, may be regarded as a form of Poel (§ 6. No. 1).

10. The inf. קְטֹל assumes with suffix the form קִטְל (comp. § 35. rem. 10), also קָטְל, with כֶם only the form קְטָל is used. As פִּתְחִי *my opening*, Eze. 37. 13; בִּקְעָם *their cleaving*, Am. 1. 13; לְשִׂטְנוֹ *to hinder him*, Zec. 3. 1; רַקְעֲךָ *thy stamping*, Eze. 25. 6; לַחֲנַנְכֶם *to be gracious to you*, Is. 30. 18. With the middle guttural לְפַעֲמוֹ *to drive him on*, Ju. 13. 25.

III. On the Imperative of Kal.

11. Examples are—זָכְרֵנִי *remember me*, Je. 15. 15; רָדְפֵהוּ *pursue him*, Ps. 34. 15; כָּתְבֵם *write them*, Pr. 3. 3; נִצְּרֶהָ (with euphonic Dagesh) *preserve them*, Pr. 4. 13, or (in the other form of the suffix) like כָּתְבָהּ Is. 30. 8.

When a guttural happens to be in the final syllable, the vowel of the final syllable is retained and lengthened to Kamets, as שְׁמָעֵנִי *hear me*, Ge. 23. 11; שְׁמָעֶנָּה *hear it*, Job 5. 27; אֱהָבֶהָ *love her*, Pr. 4. 6. *Plur.* שְׁמָעוּנִי *hear me*, Ge. 23. 8; שְׁאָלוּנִי *ask me*, Is. 45. 11.

IV. On the Future of Kal.

12. The verbs future *A* (§ 8. rem. 13), to which belong all those with 2nd and 3rd radical guttural, retain this A-sound in the sing. and pl., and besides, lengthen Pattahh to Kamets; e. g. יַלְבִּשֵׁנִי *he will clothe me*, Job 29. 14; יִלְבָּשֵׁם Ex. 29. 30, comp. Ca. 5. 3; יִשְׁכָּבֶנָּה De. 28. 30; יִשְׁמָעֵנִי Ex. 6. 12; יֶאֱהָבֵנִי Ge. 29. 32, comp. also Job 22. 27; Je. 42. 5. *Plur.* יְגָאֲלוּהוּ *they pollute him*, Job 3. 5; יִבְעָלוּךְ Is. 62. 5; יִמְצָאֻהוּ Job 20. 8, &c. An example, where this is not the case, is וָאֶנְעָלֵךְ *and I shod thee*, Eze. 16. 10.

A few examples are already given above (§ 8. rem. 14) in which there are some traces left of the O-sound, either by (ֳ) or ו, in the final syllable before suffix.

13. Besides the union-vowel, there is another mode of connecting the suffix with the verbal form, by means of an inserted נ or the syllable ֶנ, ֵנ, ָנ, commonly called epenthetic Nun. It is found only with the future before the suffix of the singular, and usually in pause. E. g. יְכַבְּדָנְנִי *he will honour me*, Ps. 50. 23; אֶתְּקֶנְךָּ *I will pluck thee*, Je. 22. 24; יַעַבְרֶנְהוּ *he passes over it*, Je. 5. 22; יְבָרֲכֶנְהוּ *he will bless him*, Ps. 72. 15, comp. De. 32. 10; Ex. 15. 2. This נ is for the most part assimilated to the suffix, and hence the separate form of the suffixes with epenthetic Nun in the paradigm.

14. By a Syriacism, the suffixes are sometimes attached, without a union-vowel, to the form יִקְטְלוּן with the paragogic Nun. E. g. יִקְרָאֻנְנִי *they shall call me*, Pr. 1. 28; יִמְצָאוּנְנִי ibid.; יְשַׁבְּחוּנְךָ *they shall praise thee*, Ps. 63. 4; יְשָׁרְתוּנֶךָ *they shall serve thee*, Is. 60. 7, 10; יַעַבְרֶנְהוּ *it shall pass it*, Je. 5. 22; יִלְכְּדוּנוֹ *they shall take him*, Pr. 5. 22; יִמְצָאוּנְהָ *they shall find her*, Je. 2. 24. With a union-vowel occurs יְדַכְּאוּנַנִי *they crush me*, Job 19. 2, for which Athias's bible reads יְדַכְּאוּנְנִי more consistently with analogy.

V. On Piel and Hiphil with Suffix.

15. Examples of Piel are—*Pret.* קִבֶּצְךָ *he gathers thee*, De. 30. 3; בֵּרַכְךָ *he blesses thee*, De. 2. 7. *Inf.* רַחֶמְכֶם *your pitying*, Is. 30. 18; פָּרִשְׂכֶם *your spreading out*, Is. 1. 15; שַׁחֶתְכֶם *your destroying*, Eze. 5. 16. *Fut.* יְקַבֶּצְךָ *he will gather thee*, De. 30. 4; אֲחַלֶּלְךָ *I will pollute thee*, Eze. 28. 16; אֹסִפְךָ *I will gather thee*, 2 Ki. 22. 20; אֲאַמִּצְכֶם *I will strengthen you*, Job 16. 5. *Part.* מְקַדִּשְׁכֶם *who sanctifies you*, Ex. 31. 13.

The same is observed in Poel, e. g. אֲרוֹמִמְךָ *I will extol thee*, Is. 25. 1.

In a few instances Tseri has been retained, even before ךָ, as אֲשַׁלֵּחֲךָ *I will send thee*, Ge. 31. 27; מְשַׁלֵּחֲךָ Je. 28. 16; תְּכַבֵּדְךָ *she will honour thee*, Pr. 4. 8.

16. The only example, in which the form of Tseri is assumed in Hiph. before suffix (by a Syriacism) is יַעְשִׁרֶנּוּ for יַעְשְׁרֶנּוּ *he will enrich him*, 1 Sa. 17. 25.*

* Here, however, must be added וַיַּגֵּדְךָ for וַיַּגִּידְךָ De. 32. 7; יֹשִׁעֲכֶם for יֹשִׁיעֲכֶם Is. 35. 4.

TABLE G. VERB PE NUN (פ״ן).

	KAL.	NIPHAL.	HIPHIL.	HOPHAL.
PRET. 3. *m.*	נָגַשׁ	נִגַּשׁ	הִגִּישׁ	הֻגַּשׁ
3. *f.*		נִגְּשָׁה	הִגִּישָׁה	הֻגְּשָׁה
2. *m.*		נִגַּשְׁתָּ	הִגַּשְׁתָּ	הֻגַּשְׁתָּ
2. *f.*		נִגַּשְׁתְּ	הִגַּשְׁתְּ	הֻגַּשְׁתְּ
1. *c.*	regular	נִגַּשְׁתִּי	הִגַּשְׁתִּי	הֻגַּשְׁתִּי
Plur. 3. *c.*		נִגְּשׁוּ	הִגִּישׁוּ	הֻגְּשׁוּ
2. *m.*		נִגַּשְׁתֶּם	הִגַּשְׁתֶּם	הֻגַּשְׁתֶּם
2. *f.*		נִגַּשְׁתֶּן	הִגַּשְׁתֶּן	הֻגַּשְׁתֶּן
1. *c.*		נִגַּשְׁנוּ	הִגַּשְׁנוּ	הֻגַּשְׁנוּ
INF. *absol.*	נָגוֹשׁ	הִנָּגֵשׁ	הַגֵּישׁ	הֻגַּשׁ
constr.	גֶּשֶׁת	הִנָּגֵשׁ	הַגִּישׁ	
IMP. *m.*	גַּשׁ	הִנָּגֵשׁ	הַגֵּשׁ	
f.	גְּשִׁי	הִנָּגְשִׁי	הַגִּישִׁי	wanting
Plur. m.	גְּשׁוּ	הִנָּגְשׁוּ	הַגִּישׁוּ	
f.	גַּשְׁנָה	הִנָּגַשְׁנָה	הַגֵּשְׁנָה	
FUT. 3. *m.*	יִגַּשׁ	יִנָּגֵשׁ	יַגִּישׁ	יֻגַּשׁ
3. *f.*	תִּגַּשׁ		תַּגִּישׁ	תֻּגַּשׁ
2. *m.*	תִּגַּשׁ		תַּגִּישׁ	תֻּגַּשׁ
2. *f.*	תִּגְּשִׁי		תַּגִּישִׁי	תֻּגְּשִׁי
1. *c.*	אֶגַּשׁ	regular	אַגִּישׁ	אֻגַּשׁ
Plur. 3. *m.*	יִגְּשׁוּ		יַגִּישׁוּ	יֻגְּשׁוּ
3. *f.*	תִּגַּשְׁנָה		תַּגֵּשְׁנָה	תֻּגַּשְׁנָה
2. *m.*	תִּגְּשׁוּ		תַּגִּישׁוּ	תֻּגְּשׁוּ
2. *f.*	תִּגַּשְׁנָה		תַּגֵּשְׁנָה	תֻּגַּשְׁנָה
1. *c.*	נִגַּשׁ		נַגִּישׁ	נֻגַּשׁ
FUT. *apoc.*			יַגֵּשׁ	
PART. *act.*	נֹגֵשׁ	נִגָּשׁ	מַגִּישׁ	מֻגָּשׁ
pass.	נָגוּשׁ			

SECTION XVII.—VERBS פ״ן.

REMARKS.

I. ON KAL.

1. *Inf. constr.* In some instances both the full, regular, and the defective forms are found in one and the same verb, in others the irregular only are in use. E. g. נָגַע *to touch*, Ge. 20. 6, with suff. נָגְעוֹ Le. 15. 23, but also גַּעַת 2 Sa. 14. 10; נָטַע *to plant*, Is. 51. 16; Je. 1. 10, but also טַעַת Ec. 3. 2; נְתֹן Ge. 38. 9; Nu. 20. 21, along with תֵּת for תֶּנֶת. Examples without the defective forms are—נְצֹר *to preserve*, Pr. 2. 8, נְבֹל *to fade*, Is. 34. 4; נְקֹם *to avenge*, Eze. 24. 8; 25. 12. An example of the inf. with suff. is גִּשְׁתּוֹ Ge. 33. 3.

2. In the *imp.* the defective form has *Pattahh* as well as Tseri and Hholem, comp. גַּשׁ 2 Sa. 1. 15; גְּשִׁי Ge. 19. 9; גֹּשִׁי Ru. 2. 14; גֹּשׁוּ Jos. 3. 9; 1 Sa. 14. 38. Other examples are—שַׁל *put off*, Ex. 3. 5; תֵּן *give*, Ge. 14. 21.

These forms frequently take parag. ה, and then the vowel is lost; e. g. תְּנָה *give;* גְּשָׁה *draw near*, &c. (comp. § 8. rem. 11).

Examples of the full regular form are—נְטֹשׁ *leave*, Pr. 17. 14; נִדְרוּ *vow ye*, Ps. 76. 12; נִטְעוּ *plant ye*, 2 Ki. 19. 29.

3. *Future.* Examples of the full regular form occur even in verbs not Ayin-guttural,* but invariably only when the contracted form is likewise found in use; as תִּנְגְּשׂוּ Is. 58. 3, and יִגֹּשׂ De. 15. 2 (*to oppress*); תִּנְדֹּף Ps. 68. 3, and יִדֹּף Ps. 1. 4 (*to drive*); יִנְטוֹר Je. 3. 5, and יִטּוֹר Ps. 103. 9 (*to preserve*); יִנְצֹר Ps. 78. 7; 140. 2; 61. 8, and יִצֹּר (*to preserve*); יִנְקֹב Job 40. 24, and יִקֹּב Le. 24. 11 (*to bore through*).

The vowel *Pattahh* in the final syllable is found only in a few other verbs besides נָגַשׁ of the paradigm; e. g. יִשַּׁל De. 28. 40, יִשַּׁק Ge. 41. 40; the *future O*, however, occurs most frequently. Future *E* occurs only in the verb נָתַן.

II. ON NIPHAL.

4. Since Piel has sometimes also Pattahh in the second syllable (§ 10. rem. 1), it follows that the pret. of Niph. and Piel are occasionally similar in form, and can only be distinguished by the context. E. g. נִחַת (*to descend*), Niph. in Ps. 38. 3, and Piel in Ps. 18. 35; 65. 11; נִקַּם (*to be avenged*) Niph. in 1 Sa. 14. 24, and Piel in 2 Ki. 9. 7; Je. 51. 36; and so נִשָּׂא (*to be borne*) comp. Ex. 25. 28, and 1 Ki. 9. 11. With regard to נִגַּשׂ Is. 3. 5, it is doubtful whether it is Piel or Niph., since the construction admits of either.

5. The only example of an *inf. absol.* is נִגּוֹף Ju. 20. 39.

III. ON HIPHIL AND HOPHAL.

6. In a very few instances only is נ retained in Hiphil, as לְהַנְתִּיךְ *to pour out*, Eze. 22. 20; לַנְפִּל *to cause to fall*, Nu. 5. 22; with gutturals, as וַיַּנְעִלוּם *and they shod them*, 2 Ch. 28. 15, הִנְחַלְתִּי *I have given for an inheritance*, Je. 3. 18.

7. In Hophal, the form with *Kibbuts* is general, and the only exception is הָנְתְּקוּ *they were drawn away*, Ju. 20. 31.

IV. IN GENERAL.

8. The anomalies of the verbs פ״ן are also in part exhibited in the verb לָקַח, in which ל is treated like the *Nun* of these verbs. Hence *imp.* קַח (seldom לְקַח, as Ex. 29. 1), קְחוּ, קְחִי, קְחָה (seldom לִקְחִי, as 1 Ki. 17. 11); *fut.* יִקַּח; *inf. abs.* לָקוֹחַ, *constr.* קַחַת (once קְחַת 2 Ki. 12. 9), with *suff.* קַחְתִּי; *Hoph. fut.* יֻקַּח; but *Niph.* always like נִלְקַח.

Some of the old grammarians (as Buxtorf Thes. Gramm. p. 154) derive נִתָּעוּ *they are broken out*, (spoken of the teeth), Job 4. 10, from לָתַע, and combine it with מַלְתָּעוֹת. The Nun, however, in this word is perfectly certain, so that נָתַע is the same as נָתַץ, and the verb with Lamed is to be rejected.

9. The verb נָתַן (*to give*) has this peculiarity, that the final Nun is likewise assimilated, at least so in the *pret.* and *inf.* of *Kal.* Hence נָתַתָּ, נָתַתִּי, נְתַתֶּם; *inf.* תֵּת for תֶּנֶת, with *suff.* תִּתִּי, &c. תַּתָּה 2 Sa. 22. 44, is by aphæresis for נָתַתָּה of the parallel passage, Ps. 18. 44.

* Most of the verbs Ayin-guttural are perfectly regular, as יִנְאַץ; יִנְחַל.

TABLE H. VERB AYIN DOUBLED (ע״ע). § 66.

		KAL.		NIPHAL.	HIPHIL.	HOPHAL.	POEL.	POAL.
Pret.	3. *m.*	סַב		נָסַב	הֵסֵב	הוּסַב	סוֹבֵב	סוֹבַב
	3. *f.*	סַבָּה		נָסַבָּה	הֵסֵבָּה	הוּסַבָּה	סוֹבְבָה	סוֹבְבָה
	2. *m.*	סַבּוֹתָ		נְסַבּוֹתָ	הֲסִבּוֹתָ	הוּסַבּוֹתָ	סוֹבַבְתָּ	סוֹבַבְתָּ
	2. *f.*	סַבּוֹת		נְסַבּוֹת	הֲסִבּוֹת	הוּסַבּוֹת	סוֹבַבְתְּ	סוֹבַבְתְּ
	1. *c.*	סַבּוֹתִי		נְסַבּוֹתִי	הֲסִבּוֹתִי	הוּסַבּוֹתִי	סוֹבַבְתִּי	סוֹבַבְתִּי
Plur.	3. *c.*	סַבּוּ		נָסַבּוּ	הֵסֵבּוּ	הוּסַבּוּ	סוֹבְבוּ	סוֹבְבוּ
	2. *m.*	סַבּוֹתֶם		נְסַבּוֹתֶם	הֲסִבּוֹתֶם	הוּסַבּוֹתֶם	סוֹבַבְתֶּם	סוֹבַבְתֶּם
	2. *f.*	סַבּוֹתֶן		נְסַבּוֹתֶן	הֲסִבּוֹתֶן	הוּסַבּוֹתֶן	סוֹבַבְתֶּן	סוֹבַבְתֶּן
	1. *c.*	סַבּוֹנוּ		נְסַבּוֹנוּ	הֲסִבּוֹנוּ	הוּסַבּוֹנוּ	סוֹבַבְנוּ	סוֹבַבְנוּ
Inf.	*absol.*	סָבוֹב		הִסּוֹב	הָסֵב	הוּסַב	סוֹבֵב	סוֹבַב
	constr.	סֹב		הִסַּב	הָסֵב			
Imp.	*m.*	סֹב		הִסַּב	הָסֵב	wanting	סוֹבֵב	wanting
	f.	סֹבִּי		הִסַּבִּי	הָסֵבִּי		סוֹבְבִי	
	Plur. m.	סֹבּוּ		הִסַּבּוּ	הָסֵבּוּ		סוֹבְבוּ	
	f.	סֻבֶּינָה		הִסַּבֶּינָה	הֲסִבֶּינָה		סוֹבֵבְנָה	
Fut.	3. *m.*	יָסֹב	יִסֹּב	יִסַּב	יָסֵב (יֵסֵב)	יוּסַב (יֻסַּב)	יְסוֹבֵב	יְסוֹבַב
	3. *f.*	תָּסֹב	תִּסֹּב	תִּסַּב	תָּסֵב	תּוּסַב	תְּסוֹבֵב	תְּסוֹבַב
	2. *m.*	תָּסֹב	תִּסֹּב	תִּסַּב	תָּסֵב	תּוּסַב	תְּסוֹבֵב	תְּסוֹבַב
	2. *f.*	תָּסֹבִּי	תִּסְּבִי	תִּסַּבִּי	תָּסֵבִּי	תּוּסַבִּי	תְּסוֹבְבִי	תְּסוֹבְבִי
	1. *c.*	אָסֹב	אֶסֹּב	אֶסַּב	אָסֵב	אוּסַב	אֲסוֹבֵב	אֲסוֹבַב
Plur.	3. *m.*	יָסֹבּוּ	יִסְּבוּ	יִסַּבּוּ	יָסֵבּוּ	יוּסַבּוּ	יְסוֹבְבוּ	יְסוֹבְבוּ
	3. *f.*	תְּסֻבֶּינָה	תִּסֹּבְנָה	תִּסַּבֶּינָה	תְּסִבֶּינָה	תּוּסַבֶּינָה	תְּסוֹבֵבְנָה	תְּסוֹבַבְנָה
	2. *m.*	תָּסֹבּוּ	תִּסְּבוּ	תִּסַּבּוּ	תָּסֵבּוּ	תּוּסַבּוּ	תְּסוֹבְבוּ	תְּסוֹבְבוּ
	2. *f.*	תְּסֻבֶּינָה	תִּסֹּבְנָה	תִּסַּבֶּינָה	תְּסִבֶּינָה	תּוּסַבֶּינָה	תְּסוֹבֵבְנָה	תְּסוֹבַבְנָה
	1. *c.*	נָסֹב	נִסֹּב	נִסַּב	נָסֵב	נוּסַב	נְסוֹבֵב	נְסוֹבַב
Fut. *with Vav conv.*		וַיָּסָב			וַיָּסֶב			
Part.	*act.*	סוֹבֵב		נָסָב	מֵסֵב	מוּסָב	מְסוֹבֵב	מְסוֹבָב
	pass.	סָבוּב						

SECTION XVIII.—VERBS ע״ע.

REMARKS.

I. On Kal.

1. In the pret. there occur a few examples of *middle O* (according to יָכֹל, § 8. rem. 1), as רֹמּוּ *they are lifted up*, Job 24. 24 (for רָמְמוּ); רֹבּוּ *they shoot arrows*, Ge. 49. 23 (for רָבְבוּ), by which form it is distinguished from רַבּוּ *they are many*.

Examples, in which the geminate letter is a guttural, are—וְאָרוֹתִי *and I curse*, Mal. 2. 2; שַׁחוֹתִי *I was bowed down*, Ps. 35. 14; צַחוּ *they are bright*, La. 4. 7 (the two last with dag. forte implied, comp. § 14. rem. 1).

When conversive Vav is prefixed to the preterite, the tone is shifted from the penultima to the ultimate (comp. § 8. rem. 7); e. g. וְקַלּוּ *and they shall be quick*, Hab. 1. 8; וְרַבָּה *and she will be great*, Is. 6. 12. The tone is, however, also found upon the ultimate without any apparent cause; as רַבּוּ Ps. 3. 2; קַלּוּ Je. 4. 13; זַכּוּ Job 15. 15; דַּלּוּ Is. 38. 14; שַׁתּוּ Ps. 73. 9; רַכּוּ Ps. 55. 22; שַׁחוּ Hab. 3. 6, and in the *first person*, דַּלּוֹתִי Ps. 116. 6; חַמּוֹתִי Is. 44. 16; שַׁנּוֹתִי De. 32. 41.

2. *Hholem* of the *inf.*, *imp.* and *fut.* (סֹב, יָסֹב, answering to קְטֹל, יִקְטֹל from which they originated), being a pure vowel, is written *defectively*. There are, however, some few exceptions, especially in the later orthography; e. g. inf. לָבוֹז *to plunder*, Est. 3. 13; 8. 11; imp. גּוֹל Ps. 37. 5 (comp. גֹּל Ps. 22. 9), דּוֹם *be silent, stand still*, Jos. 10. 12; Ps. 37. 7; דּוֹמִּי Ps. 62. 6; צוֹר *bind together*, Is. 8. 16; קוֹשׁוּ *gather*, Zep. 2. 1; fut. יָעוֹז *he becomes powerful*, Da. 11. 12; יָגוֹדּוּ *they gather themselves together*, Ps. 94. 21; וַיָּבוֹל *and he gave fodder*, Ju. 19. 21 Khethib, (Keri וַיָּבָל).

3. The common form of the *inf.*, סֹב, is shortened before Makkeph into סָב־, e. g. רָן *to shout*, Job 38. 7; with suff. like בְּחֻקּוֹ *when he established*, Pr. 8. 27.

Other verbs have the form סַב (according to שְׁכַב), e. g. שַׁךְ *to bow down*, Je. 5. 26; לָרַד *to lay to the ground*, Is. 45. 1; with suff. בְּשַׁגָּם *because they have erred*, Ge. 6. 3; לְבָרָם *to select them*, Ec. 3. 18; הִלּוֹ (from הַל) *his shining*, Job 29. 3.

A form with the fem. designation (comp. § 8. rem. 10) is רֹעָה *to break* (from רָעַע) Is. 24. 19, used as an inf. absol. Here belong doubtless also the forms שַׁמּוֹת *to lay waste*, Eze. 36. 3; חַנּוֹת *to be gracious*, Ps. 77. 10; חַלּוֹתִי *my being wounded*, Ps. 77. 11; זַמּוֹתִי *my thinking*, Ps. 17. 3; all of which, according to their occurrence, must be taken as infinitives of the verbs שָׁמַם, חָנַן, חָלַל, זָמַם, and can only be regarded as original plurals, after the form שַׁךְ, fem. שַׁכָּה.

4. Besides the form סֹב of the *imp.*, there is another with *Pattahh*, גַּל *roll*, Ps. 119. 22; with parag. ה, as אָרָה (for אֹרָה) *curse*, Nu. 22. 6.*

Before suffixes the tone is shifted to the afformative, and the vowel before dagesh is shortened from Hholem to Kamets-hhatuph; e. g. סָלּוּהָ *cast her up*, Je. 50. 26; but sometimes also without suffix, e. g. גָּזִּי *shear*, Je. 7. 29; רָנִּי *shout*, Zec. 2. 14; רָנּוּ Is. 44. 23; Je. 31. 7; חָגִּי *keep a festival*, Na. 2. 1.

Before parag. ה the tone remains, hence עוּזָּה *be strong*, Ps. 68. 29. קָבְנוֹ *curse him*, Nu. 23. 13, has epenthetic Nun before the suffixes.

5. When the *future* receives conversive Vav, the tone is drawn back to the penultima, and Hholem is changed into Kamets-hhatuph, וַיָּגָז *and he shaved*, Job 1. 20, וַיָּסָב *and he compassed*, Ju. 11. 18, וַיָּהָם *and he troubled*, Ex. 14. 24; but in pause וַיָּהֹם 2 Sa. 22. 15 Keri. (The form here is precisely the same as in the verbs ע"ו).

The same change of Hholem takes place, when the tone is shifted to the afformatives at the addition of suffixes, e. g. יְחָנֵּנוּ *may he be gracious unto us*, Ps. 67. 2; 123. 2; תְּחָגֻּהוּ *ye shall solemnize it*, Ex. 12. 14; יְשָׁדֵּם *he shall destroy them*, Pr. 11. 3 Keri; or Kibbuts is chosen instead, e. g. יְמֻשֵּׁנִי Ge. 27. 12; יְחֻנֶּנּוּ, יְחֻנֶּךָּ *he will be gracious to thee, him*, Nu. 6. 25; Is. 27. 11.

In יְחֻנְךָ *he will be gracious unto thee*, there is a transposition of the vowels, for יְחָנְךָ.

6. The *future A* (comp. § 8. rem. 13) of these verbs, which are often mistaken for an anomalous form of Niph., has Tseri under the preformative. The examples which occur of these are—יֵמַר *it is bitter*, Is. 24. 9 (from מָרַר); וָאֵקַל *and I am despised*, Ge. 16. 5; תֵּקַל ver. 4; יֵקַלּוּ from קָלַל; יֵחַם *it is hot*, De. 19. 6; Eze. 24. 11; יֵחַמּוּ Ho. 7. 7 (from חָמַם), along with יָחֹם Is. 44. 16; אֵיתָם *I am blameless*, Ps. 19. 14 (along with יִתּוֹם of a different signification) with Yod as a *mater lectionis*, which, however, is omitted in several MSS.

As a *future A*, with Kamets under the preformative, may be regarded יָחַד *it is sharpened*, Pr. 27. 17 (יַחַד in the second member is to be taken as a Chaldaizing fut. of Hiph. for יָחֵד comp. rem. 14).

* This view is grounded upon the supposition that the Kamets under א of the form אָרָה in the last verse is lengthened from Pattahh. The form קָבָה־לִּי, however, which is found in the same chapter, ver. 17, being an analogous form (from קָבַב), proves this vowel to be Kamets-hhatuph, shortened from Hholem on account of the loss of the accent before Makkeph. It is also to be observed that the form קָבָה has unnecessarily been derived by some from נָקַב, for נְקָבָה=נִקְבָה.

II. On Niphal.

7. Besides the usual form with Pattahh in the second syllable, as exhibited in the paradigm, there are two others to be met with throughout the whole of this conjugation, with Tseri and Hholem (like קָטַל, קָטֵל, קָטֹל).

Examples with Tseri:—

Pret. נָקַל *it is a light thing,* 2 Ki. 20. 10; Is. 49. 6 (along with נָקַל 2 Ki. 3. 18). נָמֵס *it faints,* Ps. 22. 15; נָסֵבָּה *she is turned,* Eze. 26. 2.

Inf. הִמֵּס *to melt,* Ps. 68. 3, הֵחֵל *to be polluted,* Eze. 20. 9, 14; with suff. הֵחַלּוֹ Le. 21. 15.

Fut. תֵּחֵל *she is polluted,* Le. 21. 9, which, however, may also be taken as a fut. of Hiph., *she begins.*

Part. נָמֵס *dissolved, refuse,* 1 Sa. 15. 9.

Examples with Hholem:—

Pret. נָגֹלּוּ *they are rolled together,* Is. 34. 4, נָגוֹזּוּ *they are cut off,* Na. 1. 12; נָבֹזּוּ *they are spoiled,* Am. 3. 11; נָרוֹץ *he is broken,* Eze. 29. 7; נָקֹטּוּ *they loathe themselves,* Eze. 6. 9.

Inf. abs. twice in Is. 24. 3, הִבּוֹק תִּבּוֹק הָאָרֶץ וְהִבּוֹז תִּבּוֹז *the land shall be emptied and spoiled.*

Imp. הֵרֹמּוּ *rise up,* Nu. 17. 10.

Fut. תֵּרוֹץ *thou art broken,* Eze. 29. 7; תִּדֹּמִּי *thou shalt be cut off,* Je. 48. 2 (along with יִדַּמּוּ 1 Sa. 2. 9); יֵרֹמּוּ *they are raised up,* Eze. 10. 17.

Note. Since the fut. of Kal may likewise have dag. forte in the first radical (according to the analogy of the Chaldee, see rem. 14), and since the last syllable may in both conjugations have either the vowel A or E, it follows that in some forms it may become doubtful as to whether they are to be taken as Kal or Niphal. Thus, for instance, יִתֹּם has been taken as the fut. of Niphal; but this and its plural יִתְּמוּ differ in signification from יִתַּמּוּ, which latter is undoubtedly Niphal, so that the former must be taken as Kal.

8. In the preterite and participle there occurs, besides the usual form with Kamets under the preformative, another with Hhirek and Tseri, especially when the first radical happens to be a guttural, as נִחַל *he was profaned* (from חָלַל); נִחַן *he is pitied* (from חָנַן). These forms may be explained in a twofold manner; either that the usual form of Niphal, נִקְטַל, is here at the foundation, so that נִחַל stands for נִחְלַל, like נָסַב, for נִסְבַב, or they are Chaldaizing forms referred to below (rem. 14). The latter seems the most suitable explanation, (*a*) because that Chaldaizing formation is found in all the conjugations besides Niphal, and were probably not wanting in this; (*b*) because the doubling of the last radical before the afformatives is omitted in these as well as in the Chaldaizing forms referred to below.

9. The future 1 pers. אִכַּף *I bow down,* Mi. 6. 6, stands for אֶכַּף comp. § 9. rem. 5.

III. Hiphil.

10. Instead of Tseri, in the final syllable of Hiphil, the vowel Pattahh is frequently found throughout the whole of this conjugation, not only when one radical happens to be a guttural, as in הֵמַר *he has embittered,* Job 27. 2; הֵרַךְ *he has intimidated,* Job 23. 16; inf. הָבַר *to cleanse,* Je. 4. 11, and in pause, as הֵתַז *he cuts off,* Is. 18. 5,† but even in the absence of these accidents, as pret. הֵדַק *he stamped small,* 2 Ki. 23. 15; הֵקַל *he made light,* Is. 8. 23; הֵמַסּוּ *they intimidated,* De. 1. 28, הֵסַבּוּ 1 Sa. 5. 10; הֵשַׁמּוּ Je. 10. 25; 2 Sa. 20. 18; inf. הָדַק *to beat in pieces,* 2 Ch. 34. 7; part. מֵצַל *shading,* Eze. 31. 3.

11. In the *future* the accent is drawn back to the penultima, on account of which Tseri is shortened to Segol, (*a*) after conversive Vav, as וַיָּגֶל *and he rolled down,* Ge. 29. 10; וַיָּסֶךְ *and he covered,* Job 38. 8; (*b*) before a monosyllabic word, as יָסֶךְ לְךָ Ps. 91. 4.

With gutturals Pattahh is used instead of Segol, as יָצַר-לוֹ *he straitens him,* 1 Ki. 8. 37; אַל תָּצַר De. 2. 9.

An example with suffix is יְסִבֵּנִי Eze. 47. 2.

IV. In General.

12. The verbs ע"ע are closely related to the verbs ע"ו, as appears from the similarity in their conjugations, which are parallel throughout. In form the verb ע"ע is generally shorter than the other (comp. יָקוּם and יָסֹב, הֵקִים and הֵסֵב). In some cases they have precisely the same form, as in the fut. convers. of Kal and Hiphil, in Hophal, &c. On account of this relation they have sometimes borrowed forms from each other. Thus, for instance,

(*a*) Kal inf., לָבוּר for לָבֹר *to search out,* Ec. 9. 1. With suffix בְּחוּקוֹ for בְּחֻקּוֹ Pr. 8. 29. Fut. יָרוּן *he shouts* for יָרֹן Pr. 29. 6; יָרוּץ *he breaks,* for יָרֹץ Is. 42. 4.

(*b*) Hiph. inf. הֲתִימְךָ* for הֲתִמְּךָ *thy ceasing,* Is. 33. 1.

† This last only assumes the form as if from תָּזַז, but is to be derived from תִּיז q. v.

* The forms, however, as הֲתִימְךָ, אֲדִיקֵם, יְחִיתַן find their analogy in nouns in which, instead of sharpening the syllable

Fut. אֲדִיקֵם* for אֲדִקֵּם *I beat them small*, 2 Sa. 22. 43; יַשִּׁים Je. 49. 20, and נַשִּׁים Nu. 21. 30, *he, she shall lay waste* (for which comp. rem. 14), from שָׁמַם; וַתָּרִץ* *and she broke*, Ju. 9. 53; יְחִיתַן *he terrifies them*, for יְחִתַּן*, Hab. 2. 17. This is frequently the case in the Chald. e. g. אָעִילוּ Aph. of עלל Ca. 2. 5. Targ.

13. Besides the contracted defective forms hitherto treated upon, there are also found, especially in certain conjugations and tenses, others which are quite regular, as:—

Kal pret. דָּלְלוּ *they languish*, Is. 19. 6, also דַּלּוּ Job 28. 4; גָּלְלוּ *they roll*, Ge. 29. 3, 8, but גַּלּוֹתִי Jos. 5. 9; זָמַמְתִּי *I devise*, Zec. 8. 14, 15, and זַמּוֹתִי Ps. 17. 3. Thus it is with בָּזַז *to plunder*, מָדַד *to measure*, שָׁדַד *to spoil*, שָׁלַל *to rob*, &c.

Inf. סְבֹב Nu. 21. 4, and סֹב De. 2. 3, so גְּזֹז, שְׁדֹד; with suff. חֲנַנְכֶם *your pitying*, Is. 30. 18.

Imp. חָנְנֵנִי (like קָטְלֵנִי) *have mercy upon me*, Ps. 9. 14, elsewhere חָנֵּנִי Ps. 4. 2; 6. 3; שָׁדְדוּ *spoil ye*, Je. 49. 28, for שֹׁדּוּ.

Fut. יֶחֱנַן *he will have mercy*, Am. 5. 15. With suff. יְשָׁדְדֵם *he shall spoil them*, Je. 5. 6, but also יְשָׁדֵּם Pr. 11. 3.

Hiph. pret. הִרְנִין, fut. יַרְנִין (*to shout*) is nowhere found written defectively; וְהַחְתַּתִּי *and I break*, Je. 49. 37 (but also הַחִתּוֹתָ *thou hast broken*, Is. 9. 3). Inf. הַשְׁמֵם *laying waste*, Mi. 6. 13. Part. מַשְׁמִים *astonished*, Eze. 3. 15.

V. CHALDAISMS.

14. In a great number of these verbs the vowel of the preformative in Kal, Niphal, Hiphil, and Hophal is a short instead of a long vowel, and Dag. forte is inserted in the next (first radical) letter. This formation is general in the Chaldee, as Peal fut. יִדּוֹק for for יָדֹק (from דְּקַק); Aph. pret. אַדֵּק for אָדֵק, Heb. הֵדֵק, fut. יַדֵּק for יָדֵק. That this Dagesh in the first radical is a compensation for the one omitted in the second radical, is evident from the forms with afformatives in which the Dagesh is wanting in the second radical, as יִדְקוּ, אַדְקוּ, יַדְקוּ.

Examples in the Hebrew are:—

Kal fut. יִסֹּב and יָסֹב (from סָבַב); יִדֹּם, pl. יִדְּמוּ (from דָּמַם); יִשֹּׁם *shall be established*, 1 Ki. 9. 8, but pl. יִשְּׁמוּ Ps. 40. 16; so יִקֹּד, pl. יִקְּדוּ (*to bow down*) from קָדַד. Examples of *fut. A* are—יִתַּמּוּ Ps. 102. 28; יִמַּלּוּ Job 24. 24; Ps. 37. 2; with Kibbuts in the final syllable, תִּתֻּם Eze. 24. 11 (comp. the forms with ֻ in the regular verb, § 8. rem. 14).

Niph. pret. נִחַל *he is polluted*, Eze. 25. 3; נִחַר *he is burned*, Ps. 69. 4; 102. 4 (but also נָחַר Je. 6. 29), pl. נִחֲרוּ Ca. 1. 6; נִחַת *he is broken, terrified*, Mal. 2. 5; נֵחַנְתְּ *thou art to be pitied*, Je. 22. 23. Part. נֵאָרִים *cursed*, Mal. 3. 9; נֵחָמִים *inflamed*, Is. 57. 5 (without Dagesh as in יִתַּמּוּ above).

Hiph. fut. וַיַּסֵּב Ex. 13. 18; תַּתֵּם Job. 22. 3; יַחֵל Nu. 30. 3; and אַחֵל *shall be profaned* (with Dag. forte impl. in ח) to distinguish it from יָחֵל, אָחֵל *to begin*; pl. וַיַּכְּתוּ *and they destroyed*, De. 1. 44, with suff. וַיַּכְּתוּם Nu. 14. 45; וַיַּסִּבּוּ† Ju. 18. 23; 1 Sa. 5. 8.§

Hophal יֻכַּת Is. 24. 12, with Shurek יוּסַּב Is. 28. 27; יוּשַּׁד Ho. 10. 14; תּוּשַּׁד Is. 33. 1; הָשַּׁם Le. 26. 34 (Dagesh is here incorrectly omitted in several copies); pl. הֻמַּכּוּ† Job 4. 20; Je. 46. 5.

15. We have seen from the preceding examples, that in the future of the Chaldee form the Dagesh of the third radical, together with the preceding vowel, is omitted before afformatives. Of the same omission in the Hebrew form there are unquestionable examples:—

Kal fut. נָבְלָה Ge. 11. 7, *let us confound*, for נָבֹלָּה (from בָּלַל, with parag. ה); יָזְמוּ Ge. 11. 6, *they will devise*, for יָזֹמּוּ (from זָמַם).

Niph. pret. נָסְבָה for נָסַבָּה *she turned round*, Eze. 41. 7; וְנָבְקָה for נָבַקָּה *and she shall be made empty*, Is. 19. 3; fut. נִדְּמָה for נִדַּמָּה (1 pers. pl. with parag. ה) Je. 8. 14, *let us perish*. This last, however, is best taken as Kal fut. (see No. 14), *and let us be quiet*.‡

by Dagesh forte in the final consonant, the vowel is prolonged by the insertion of a vowel letter, as מוֹרִיגִים 1 Ch. 21. 23, for מוֹרִגִּים 2 Sa. 24. 22, פִּילֶגֶשׁ and פִּלֶגֶשׁ, קִימוֹשׁ and קִמּוֹשׁ, &c.—וַתָּרִץ may be thus pointed only to distinguish it from וַתָּרֶץ Hiph. of רוּץ.

† The forms marked with † are the only examples in which the geminates have retained Dagesh in the lengthened form.

§ Here may also be added as examples for pret. and inf. of Hiph. הַחִלּוֹתָ *thou hast begun*, De. 3. 24; 2. 31; הַחִתּוֹתָ *thou hast broken*, Is. 9. 3; inf. הַחִלָּם *their beginning*, Ge. 11. 6, in which Pattahh under the preformative seems to indicate a Dag. forte implicit.

‡ In the examples given above both the Dagesh and the preceding vowel are omitted. In other examples the vowel is retained, and even prolonged by the pause, as יֻחָקוּ for יֻחַקּוּ Job 19. 23; יִדָּמוּ 1 Sa. 2. 9, for יִדַּמּוּ; חָיָה *she lives*, Ex. 1. 16,

16. In the Chaldee, both the epenthetic וֹ and ־ֵי in those forms in which the Hebrew has them, and the Dagesh in the last radical, are omitted. The like formation is also found in the Hebrew, by way of exception, especially in those forms which have likewise the Chaldaism of No. 14. E. g.

Kal pret. תַּמְנוּ *we are consumed*, Ps. 64. 7, for תַּמּוֹנוּ; fut. תִּצַּלְנָה *they tingle*, Je. 19. 3; תִּמַּקְנָה *they consume away*, Zec. 14. 12. The two last, however, may be Niphal.

Niph. pret. נִחַלְתְּ (Dag. forte impl.) *thou art polluted*, Eze. 22. 16; נֶחֱנְתְּ *thou art to be pitied*, Je. 22. 23.

Instead of the epenthetic וֹ there is (ְ) put in נְשַׁדֻּנוּ Mi. 2. 4, for נְשַׁדּוֹנוּ *we are destroyed*.

17. In the Aramaic, the verbs ע״ע borrow several forms from the verbs ע״א. An example of this kind in the Hebrew is שֹׁאֲסַיִךְ (as it ought to be pointed) *those that spoil thee*, Je. 30. 16, in Khethib for שֹׁסַיִךְ.

Note. Other examples referred to in the Lehrgebäude (§ 103, 17) and by other grammarians are—

Niph. fut. יִמָּאֵס *it melts*, for יִמַּס, Job 7. 5; pl. יִמָּאֲסוּ, Ps. 58. 8.

Hiph. fut. תַּכְאִיבוּ 2 Ki. 3. 19, *ye shall mar*, for תַּכְבִּיבוּ from כבב Syr. and Arab. *to injure*; part. מַמְאִיר for מַמְרִיר *causing pain*, Eze. 28. 24, fem. מַמְאֶרֶת Le. 13. 51, 52. A similar example is the noun צֶאֱלִים Job 40. 21, for צֶלָלִים *shades, shady trees*.

But this is unnecessary, since all these forms may be derived immediately from roots ע״א, as כָּאַב, מָאַס, צָאַל, מָאַר, as kindred roots of כָּבַב, מָסַס, &c.

18. In the Piel, Pual, and Hithpael these verbs are without any contraction. There is, however, one form which seems to be inflected like the Chaldee, Ithpeel or Ittaphal, viz. תִּתָּבָר 2 Sa. 22. 27, *thou showest thyself pure*, for תִּתְבָּרָר of the parallel passage in Ps. 18. 27. In the Chaldee, the Ithpeel (passive of Kal) would be אִתְבַּר, fut. יִתְבַּר, Ittaphal (passive of Hiphil) אִתַּבַּר, precisely like the above form.* This shorter form seems to be chosen for the sake of harmony with the immediately preceding תִּתַּמָּם Ps. 18. 26. A more difficult form is תִּתַּפָּל ver. 27, which, according to the context, must necessarily be derived from פָּתַל. This difficulty can only be solved by supposing that תִּתְתַּפַּל (contr. תִּתַּפָּל) is a transposition for תִּתְפַּתַּל.

for חַיָּה. Some of the like forms, however, occur without being in pause, as הֶעֱזָה for הֵעֵזָּה Pr. 7. 13; נֵחָמִים Is. 57. 5, for נִחַמִּים; comp. also תְּרַנֵּנָּה Ps. 71. 23, for תְּרַנֵּנָה (to avoid the concurrence of four Nuns), and תֵּעָגֵנָה Ru. 1. 13, for תֵּעָגֵנָּה.

* i. e. only as regards the preformatives תִּתְ; but as regards the second syllable, תִּתָּבַר must then be supposed to stand for תִּתַּבַּר, comp. הִתְפָּקֵד for הִתְפַּקֵּד § 12. rem. 5.

TABLE I. VERB PE ALEPH (פ״א).

		KAL.	NIPHAL.	HIPHIL.	HOPHAL.
PRET.	3. *m.*	אָכַל	נֶאֱכַל	הֶאֱכִיל	הָאֳכַל
	3. *f.*	Like the Verb *Pe guttural*, in Paradigm C.			
	2. *m.*				
	2. *f.*				
	1. *c.*				
Plur.	3. *c.*				
	2. *m.*				
	2. *f.*				
	1. *c.*				
INF.	*absol.*	אָכוֹל	הֵאָכֹל		
	constr.	אֱכֹל	הֵאָכֵל	הַאֲכִיל	הָאֳכַל
IMP.	*m.*	אֱכֹל	הֵאָכֵל	הַאֲכֵל	
	f.	אִכְלִי	ETC.	ETC.	wanting.
Plur.	*m.*	אִכְלוּ			
	f.	אֱכֹלְנָה			
FUT.	3. *m.*	יֹאכֵל	יֵאָכֵל	יַאֲכִיל	יָאֳכַל
	3. *f.*	תֹּאכֵל			
	2. *m.*	תֹּאכֵל			
	2. *f.*	תֹּאכְלִי	ETC.	ETC.	ETC.
	1. *c.*	אֹכֵל			
Plur.	3. *m.*	יֹאכְלוּ			
	3. *f.*	תֹּאכֵלְנָה			
	2. *m.*	תֹּאכְלוּ			
	2. *f.*	תֹּאכֵלְנָה			
	1. *c.*	נֹאכֵל			
FUT. *with Vav conv.*		וַיֹּאכַל,	וַיֹּאמֶר		
PART.	*act.*	אֹכֵל	נֶאֱכָל	מַאֲכִיל	מָאֳכָל
	pass.	אָכוּל			

SECTION XIX.—VERBS פ״א. (TABLE I.)

REMARKS.

I. ON FUT. OF KAL.

1. The relation between *Tseri* and *Pattahh* in the final syllable is the same here as in the Piel pret. of the regular verb (§ 10. rem. 1), and in several forms of the verb with gutturals (§ 15. rem. 1). That with Tseri seems, however, to be the original

and here the peculiar form. Examples are—יֹאבַד Job 3. 3, and יֹאבֵד Job 20. 7; תֹּאבַד De. 22. 3, comp. תֹּאבֵד Job 8. 13; Ps. 1. 6; תֹּאכַל Ge. 2. 16, comp. תֹּאכֵל ver. 17, and so constantly יֹאמַר and יֹאמֵר. The form with Tseri appears also in the plural, where this vowel is again introduced on account of the *pause;* e. g. יֹאכֵלוּ De. 18. 1, 8, comp. וְאֹכְלָה *that I may eat*, Ge. 27. 4.

2. With *conversive Vav*, the tone is drawn back to the penultima, e. g. וַיֹּאכַל *and he ate*, Ge. 25. 34; 31. 15; וַיֹּאמֶר *and he spoke* (where Tseri of the final syllable is shortened to Segol). But the tone is retained,

(*a*) Where the word stands at the end of a period, hence with a distinctive accent; e. g. וַיֹּאכַל Ge. 27. 25, וַיֹּאמַר Ge. 14. 19; Ex. 2. 14.

(*b*) In the first person; e. g. וָאֹמַר Ge. 20. 13; 24. 39; וָאֹכַל Ge. 27. 33. This is precisely the case with the verbs ע״ו in the first person.

The tone may, moreover, be drawn back on account of a monosyllabic word following it; e. g. יֹאבַד יוֹם Job 3. 3.

3. Examples, in which א becomes quiescent in *Tseri*, are—תֵּאתֶה *she shall come*, Mi. 4. 8; אֵהַב *I will love*, Pr. 8. 17 (along with אֹהַב, Mal. 1. 2); וַיֵּתֵא *and he came*, De. 33. 21 (for יֶאֱתֶה from אָתָה); תֵּזְלִי for תֵּאזְלִי (from אָזַל) *she goes away*.* In וַיַּאת *and he came*, Is. 41. 25, the א is indeed quiescent after *Pattahh*, but it is only so on account of being apocopated for יֶאֱתֶה, and properly stands for וַיֵּאת, and the vowel already in the syllable is retained.

4. Both forms (viz. the one in which א is quiescent, and the other in which it is moveable) are found also in one and the same verb; as וְתֹאחֵז *and it takes hold*, De. 32. 41, also תֶּאֱחֹז; אֹסְפָה Mi. 4. 6; וַיֹּסֶף 2 Sa. 6. 1; תֹּסֵף Ps. 104. 29, but also יֶאֱסֹף; אֵהַב and אֹהַב (comp. rem. 3), also יֶאֱהַב. An example with a full Hholem is הַאוֹכַל (*do I eat?*) Ps. 50. 13; several MSS., however, have it without ו.

5. א which is regularly omitted in the first pers. fut., is also omitted in the following instances, יֹמְרוּךָ for יֹאמְרוּךָ Ps. 139. 20; תֹּמְרוּ 2 Sa. 19. 14; וַתֹּפֵהוּ *and she baked it*, 1 Sa. 28. 24; תֹּבֵא for תֹּאבֶה *she is willing*, Pr. 1. 10.

II. ON THE INF. AND IMP. OF KAL.

6. In the *inf.* א is quiescent only in the frequent form לֵאמֹר for לֶאֱמֹר, but is otherwise moveable, as בֶּאֱמֹר De. 4. 10; כֶּאֱמֹר Jos. 6. 8. In the imp. the Aramaic punctuation is often introduced, as אֱפוּ for אֶפוּ Ex. 16. 23; אֱתָיוּ for אֵתָיוּ Is. 21. 12; 56. 9, 13

III. ON THE PRET. OF NIPHAL.

7. The only example is נֹאחֲזוּ *he has taken possession of*, Jos. 22. 9, along with the part. נֶאֱחָז *held*, Ge. 22. 13.

IV. ON HIPHIL AND HOPHAL.

8. In the *inf.*, *imp.*, and *fut.* of *Hiphil*, א is sometimes quiescent after *Hholem*, *Tseri*, and *Kamets*, and then it is altogether omitted.

Inf. הָכִיל for הַאֲכִיל *to eat*, Eze. 21. 33.

Imp. הָתָיוּ for הַאֲתָיוּ *bring* (from אָתָה), Is. 21. 14; Je. 12. 9.

Fut. (*a*) with Hholem, as אוֹכִיל *I feed*, Ho. 11. 4; אֹצְרָה for אוֹצִירָה (comp. § 11. rem. 7) = אַאֲצִירָה *I make treasures*, Ne. 13. 13; אֹבִידָה *I will destroy*, Je. 46. 8; אֹסִפְךָ 1 Sa. 15. 6; וַיֹּחֶר 2 Sa. 20. 5. In the Chald. and Syr. this is the usual form, e. g. אוֹכֵל; so in the Hebrew ו is likewise sometimes substituted for א.

(*b*) With Kamets, as וַיָּאצֶל *he separated*, Nu. 11. 25; אָזִין for אַאֲזִין *I hearken*, Job 32. 11; וַיָּרֶב for וַיַּאֲרֶב *and he set an ambush*, 1 Sa. 15. 5.

Part. מֵזִין for מַאֲזִין *hearkening*, Pr. 17. 4.

9. In Hophal יוּכְלוּ Eze. 42. 5, stands for יֻאכְלוּ *they are cut off*, i. e. become shorter. In the Chaldee of Daniel—as the Targums have no Hophal—there occurs a Hophal in the form הוּבַד Da. 7. 11.

V. ON PIEL.

10. There are a few anomalous forms in Piel in which א is not quiescent, but entirely dropped with its preceding Sheva, so that the preformative takes its place in the punctuation: viz. וַתְּזְרֵנִי *and thou girdest me*, 2 Sa. 22. 40, for וַתְּאַזְּרֵנִי in the parallel passage, Ps. 18. 40; וָאַבֶּדְךָ for וָאֲאַבֶּדְךָ *and I destroy thee*, Eze. 28. 16; מַלְּפֵנוּ for מְאַלְּפֵנוּ *our teacher*, Job 35. 11; יַהֵל for יְאַהֵל *shall pitch his tent*, Is. 13. 20.

* The Tseri, however, in these forms is not the original vowel of the preformative, but is introduced in consequence of a contraction from the form in which א is moveable, so תֵּאתֶה for תֶּאֱתֶה, comp. לֵאמֹר for לֶאֱמֹר, לֵאלֹהִים for לֶאֱלֹהִים.

TABLE K. VERB PE YOD פ״י (orig. פ״ו).							Properly Pe Yod (פ״י).	
		KAL.		NIPHAL.	HIPHIL.	HOPHAL.	KAL.	HIPHIL.
Pret. 3. *m.*		יָשַׁב		נוֹשַׁב	הוֹשִׁיב	הוּשַׁב	יָטַב	הֵיטִיב
3. *f.*				נֽוֹשְׁבָה	הוֹשִׁיבָה	הֽוּשְׁבָה		הֵיטִיבָה
2. *m.*				נוֹשַׁבְתָּ	הוֹשַׁבְתָּ	הוּשַׁבְתָּ		הֵיטַבְתָּ
2. *f.*				נוֹשַׁבְתְּ	הוֹשַׁבְתְּ	הוּשַׁבְתְּ		הֵיטַבְתְּ
1. *c.*		regular		נוֹשַׁבְתִּי	הוֹשַׁבְתִּי	הוּשַׁבְתִּי	regular	הֵיטַבְתִּי
Plur. 3. *c.*				נוֹשְׁבוּ	הוֹשִׁיבוּ	הֽוּשְׁבוּ		הֵיטִיבוּ
2. *m.*				נֽוֹשַׁבְתֶּם	הֽוֹשַׁבְתֶּם	הֽוּשַׁבְתֶּם		הֱיטַבְתֶּם
2. *f.*				נֽוֹשַׁבְתֶּן	הֽוֹשַׁבְתֶּן	הֽוּשַׁבְתֶּן		הֱיטַבְתֶּן
1. *c.*				נוֹשַׁבְנוּ	הוֹשַׁבְנוּ	הוּשַׁבְנוּ		הֵיטַבְנוּ
Inf. *absol.*		יָשׁוֹב			הוֹשֵׁב, הוֹשִׁיב		יָטוֹב	הֵיטֵב
constr.		שֶׁבֶת	יְסֹד,	הִוָּשֵׁב	הוֹשִׁיב	הוּשַׁב	יְטֹב	הֵיטִיב
Imp. *m.*		שֵׁב	יְרַשׁ	הִוָּשֵׁב	הוֹשֵׁב		יְטַב	הֵיטֵב
f.		שְׁבִי	יְרְשִׁי	הִוָּשְׁבִי	הוֹשִׁיבִי	wanting	יִטְבִי	הֵיטִיבִי
Plur. m.		שְׁבוּ	יִרְשׁוּ	הִוָּשְׁבוּ	הוֹשִׁיבוּ		יִטְבוּ	הֵיטִיבוּ
f.		שֵׁבְנָה	יְרַשְׁנָה	הִוָּשֵׁבְנָה	הוֹשֵׁבְנָה		יְטַבְנָה	הֵיטֵבְנָה
Fut. 3. *m.*		יֵשֵׁב	יִירַשׁ	יִוָּשֵׁב	יוֹשִׁיב	יוּשַׁב	יִיטַב	יֵיטִיב
3. *f.*		תֵּשֵׁב	תִּירַשׁ	תִּוָּשֵׁב	תּוֹשִׁיב	תּוּשַׁב	תִּיטַב	תֵּיטִיב
2. *m.*		תֵּשֵׁב	תִּירַשׁ	תִּוָּשֵׁב	תּוֹשִׁיב	תּוּשַׁב	תִּיטַב	תֵּיטִיב
2. *f.*		תֵּשְׁבִי	תִּירְשִׁי	תִּוָּשְׁבִי	תּוֹשִׁיבִי	תּֽוּשְׁבִי	תִּיטְבִי	תֵּיטִיבִי
1. *c.*		אֵשֵׁב	אִירַשׁ	אִוָּשֵׁב	אוֹשִׁיב	אוּשַׁב	אִיטַב	אֵיטִיב
Plur. 3. *m.*		יֵשְׁבוּ	יִירְשׁוּ	יִוָּשְׁבוּ	יוֹשִׁיבוּ	יֽוּשְׁבוּ	יִיטְבוּ	יֵיטִיבוּ
3. *f.*		תֵּשַׁבְנָה	תִּירַשְׁנָה	תִּוָּשַׁבְנָה	תּוֹשֵׁבְנָה	תּוּשַׁבְנָה	תִּיטַבְנָה	תֵּיטֵבְנָה
2. *m.*		תֵּשְׁבוּ	תִּירְשׁוּ	תִּוָּשְׁבוּ	תּוֹשִׁיבוּ	תּֽוּשְׁבוּ	תִּיטְבוּ	תֵּיטִיבוּ
2. *f.*		תֵּשַׁבְנָה	תִּירַשְׁנָה	תִּוָּשַׁבְנָה	תּוֹשֵׁבְנָה	תּוּשַׁבְנָה	תִּיטַבְנָה	תֵּיטֵבְנָה
1. *c.*		נֵשֵׁב	נִירַשׁ	נִוָּשֵׁב	נוֹשִׁיב	נוּשַׁב	נִיטַב	נֵיטִיב
Fut. *apoc.*					יוֹשֵׁב			יֵיטֵב
Fut. *with Vav conv.*		וַיֵּשֶׁב			וַיּוֹשֶׁב		וַיִּיטַב, וַיִּיקַץ	
Part. *act.*		יֹשֵׁב		נוֹשָׁב	מוֹשִׁיב	מוּשָׁב	יֹטֵב	מֵיטִיב
pass.		יָשׁוּב					יָטוּב	

SECTION XX.—VERBS פ״י. (Table K.)

EXPLANATORY.

1. The Hebrew verbs פ״י are divided into three principal classes the distinction of which is not manifest in the ground-form, but in the inflexion and derivation. By far the greater number are :—

(*a*) Verbs originally פ״ו, which in the Arabic are written with ו in the ground-form, e. g. יָלַד, Arab. ولد, יָרַד, Arab. ورد. In the Hebrew, the radical Vav appears only in the conjugations Niphal, Hiphil, and Hophal, but so that in the pret. and part. of Niphal it becomes quiescent in Hholem, and in the Hophal in Shurek, as נוֹשַׁב for נִוְשַׁב, הוֹשִׁיב for הִוְשִׁיב, הוּשַׁב for הֻוְשַׁב. In the inf., imp. and future of Niphal, the Vav remains a consonant, and the inflexion is regular, as הִוָּשֵׁב, יִוָּשֵׁב; and so likewise in the Hithpael of some verbs, הִתְוַדָּה, הִתְוַכַּח, הִתְוַדַּע, from יָדָה, יָכַח, יָדַע.

(*b*) Verbs originally פ״י, which are the same in the Arabic. In the Hiphil the original Yod is retained quiescent in Tseri, as הֵימִין, הֵינִיק, הֵילִיל, הֵיטִיב, and is but seldom moveable, e. g. מַיְמִינִים *who use the right hand*, 1 Ch. 12. 2; יַיְשִׁירוּ *they are upright*, Pr. 4. 25; comp. הַיְשַׁר Ps. 5. 9, Keri.

(*c*) A few verbs, the Yod of which is assimilated like נ in verbs פ״ן, e. g. יָצַע Hiph. הִצִּיעַ.

REMARKS.

On the first class or verbs originally פ״ו.

I. KAL.

1. In the *fut. imp.* and *inf. constr.* of Kal there is a twofold form. About half the number of these verbs have the *fut. E.* Hence fut. יֵיְשֵׁב, contracted יֵישֵׁב, but written, without exception, *defectively* יֵשֵׁב; imp שֵׁב (by *aphæresis*) for יְשֵׁב; inf. שֶׁבֶת for יְשֶׁבֶת (with the fem. termination ־ֶת, to distinguish it from the imp. The other half have *fut. A*, and retain Yod quiescent in Hhirek, as יִירַשׁ, imp. יְרַשׁ, inf. יְסֹד *to lay the foundation*, Is. 51. 16; יְבֹשׁ *to be dry*, Is. 27. 11. To the first mode of inflexion belong, for instance, יָלַד *to bear;* הָלַךְ *to go;* יָצָא *to go out;* יָרַד *to go down;* יָשַׁב *to sit.*

Those of the latter class take *Pattahh* instead of *Tseri* in the final syllable when it has guttural or ר; e. g. יֵדַע, imp. דַּע, inf. דַּעַת (from יָדַע *to know*); הַב, pl. הָבוּ *give* (from יָהַב); יֵקַר Ps. 72. 14 (from יָקַר *to be precious*); יֵקַד, however, in Is. 10. 16, is an instance with Pattahh where the syllable does not contain a guttural.

2. In some verbs the full forms occur along with the defective, as יִיקַד De. 32. 22, and יֵקַד Is. 10. 16 (from יָקַד *to burn*); יִיקַר 1 Sa. 18. 30, and יֵקַר Ps. 72. 14 (from יָקַר *to be precious*); imp. רֵשׁ 1 Ki. 21. 15, רַשׁ De. 2. 24, 31, but also יְרַשׁ, in pause with ה parag. יְרָשָׁה De. 33. 23; צַק 2 Ki. 4. 41, and יְצֹק Eze. 24. 3 (from יָצַק *to pour out*); יְרַד Ju. 5. 13, and frequently רֵד (from יָרַד *to go down*).

A full form with Tseri is exhibited in יֵיקַר Ps. 72. 14, and אֵילְכָה *I will go*, Mi. 1. 8.

The form יִירַשׁ is frequently written *defectively*, but this is not an essential difference; e. g. וַיִּרָא 1 Sa. 18. 12; יִרְאוּ (with Metheg) 2 Ki. 17. 28; יִבַשׁ Job 8. 12, pl. יִבָשׁוּ Job 12. 15.

3. The *inf.* of Kal, without the radical Yod, has very seldom the masculine form like דַּע *to know*, Job 32. 6, 10, or the feminine termination ־ָה, like לְדָה *to bear*, 2 Ki. 19. 3; רְדָה *to go down*, Ge. 46. 3. With suffix the form שֶׁבֶת is used, as שִׁבְתִּי, רִדְתִּי (from רֶדֶת). With guttural the latter takes the form ־ַ־ַת instead of ־ֶ־ֶת; e. g. דַּעַת. Examples for the full form of the infinitive with the feminine termination are, יְבֹשֶׁת *to become dry*, Ge. 8. 7; יְכֹלֶת *to be able*, Nu. 14. 16 (comp. § 8. rem. 1). With prepositions are, לִיסוֹד *to lay the foundation*, Is. 51. 16; לְרֹא *to fear*, for לִירֹא 1 Sa. 18. 29.

The defective *imperative* has frequently parag. ה, as רְדָה *go down*, Ge. 45. 9; לְכָה *go;* instead of which also לָךְ Nu. 23. 13; Ju. 19. 13; once דְּעָה Pr. 24. 14, for דְּעָה, comp. § 8. rem. 11.

4. The *future* יֵשֵׁב has, in some cases, the accent drawn back to the penultima, when the final syllable takes *Segol* instead of *Tseri.*

(*a*) *Before monosyllabic words*, or immediately preceding another tone-syllable, e. g. אֵלֶךְ־לִי *let me go*, Ca. 4. 6; יֵשֶׁב־בָּהּ *he dwells therein*, Job 22. 8; תֵּרֶד אֵשׁ *fire descends*, 2 Ki. 1. 10, 12.

(*b*) *After conversive Vav*, as וַיֵּשֶׁב, וַיֵּרֶד, וַיֵּלֶךְ. The tone, however, is in this case retained (1) in the first person, as וָאֵשֵׁב, וָאֵרֵד, וָאֵלֵךְ, and (2) in pause, as וַיֵּשֵׁב.

Pattahh instead of *Tseri* is found in this defective form, as noticed above (rem. 1), only by concurrence with a guttural, and besides also in pause; e. g. וַיֵּלַךְ *and he disappears*, Job 27. 21; וַיֵּלַךְ *and he went*, Ge. 24. 61; 25. 34; Nu. 12. 9, &c.

II. NIPHAL.

5. In the *pret.* and *part.* there are a few examples where ו is quiescent in Shurek, as נוּגֵי Zep. 3. 18, and נוּגוֹת *mourning*, La. 1. 4; נוּלְּדוּ (with euphonic Dagesh) *they were born*, 1 Ch. 3. 5; 20. 8.

6. In two instances moveable י occurs instead of moveable ו, and that in verbs which are undoubtedly פ״ו, viz. יִיָּרֶה *he shall be shot through*, Ex. 19. 13, and וַיִּיָּחֶל *and he waited*, Ge. 8. 12 (pret. נוֹחַל, Hiph. הוֹחִיל).

7. The fut. 1 pers. takes here invariably *Hhirek* under the preformative, as אִוָּלֵד (not אֶוָּלֵד) Job. 3. 3, comp. Pr. 30. 9; Eze. 20. 5; 2 Sa. 22. 4; Ps. 18. 4; 119. 117; Je. 17. 4; 1 Ki. 19. 10.

III. Piel.

8. The only deviation to be met with in Piel is, that in a few examples the radical Yod is dropped after the preformative, and the latter adopts its punctuation, as is the case in verbs פ״א (§ 19. rem. 10): as וַיַּבְּשֵׁהוּ for וַיְיַבְּשֵׁהוּ *and he dries it up*, Na. 1. 14; וַיַּדּוּ for וַיְיַדּוּ *and they threw*, La. 3. 5, 3; וַיַּגֶּה *and he afflicted*, La. 3. 33; וַיַּשְּׁרֵם 2 Ch. 32. 30, Khethib for וַיְיַשְּׁרֵם.

IV. Hiphil and Hophal.

9. The apocopated form of the future, יוֹשֵׁב, has the tone drawn back to the penultima, and the final syllable takes Segol (comp. rem. 4)—

(*a*) *Before another tone-syllable*, as יוֹסֶף לֶקַח *he shall add knowledge*, Pr. 1. 5.

(*b*) *After conversive Vav*, as וַיּוֹלֶךְ *and he led*, Ex. 14. 21; וַיּוֹלֶד *and he begat*, Ge. 5. 3; 4. 6; but not in the first person, as וָאוֹלֵךְ Le. 26. 13. The toneless helping Segol is omitted, and even Sheva put instead, in אַל־תּוֹסְףְּ *add not*, Pr. 30. 6, for תּוֹסֶף (comp. the nominal form קֹשְׁטְ for קֹשֶׁט).

10. Almost peculiar to these verbs is the uncontracted form of the Hiph. fut. in which ה is retained: as, יְהוֹשִׁיעַ *he will save*, 1 Sa. 17. 47; Ps. 116. 6; יְהוֹדֶה *he shall praise*, Ne. 11. 17; אֲהוֹדֶנּוּ *I shall praise him*, Ps. 28. 7 (comp. § 11. rem. 12).

11. Vav may also be omitted, as וַיֹּלֶךְ 2 Ki. 6. 19; 25. 20.

12. In Hophal הוּדַע appears in Le. 4. 23 for הוֹדַע.

V. Hithpael.

13. The only deviating form in Hithp. is תֵּתַצַּב Ex. 2. 4, for תִּתְיַצֵּב *and she placed herself*. The omission of the radical Yod here is analagous to the cases in Piel (rem. 8), and the omission of the first radical א in the Chaldee; e. g. אִתְמַר for אִתְאֲמַר.

On the second class or verbs properly פ״י.

14. The number of the verbs really belonging to this class is very limited. They are properly only the verbs יָטַב, יָלַל, יָנַק, יָצַר. Along with these some single forms occur of real פ״ו, and *vice versâ;* viz. הַיְצֵא *bring forth*, Ge. 8. 17, Keri, for Khethib הוֹצֵא (which is the common form); אַיְסִירֵם *I will chastise them*, Ho. 7. 12 (along with Niph. נוֹסַר and the noun מוּסָר); הֵילִיכִי *bring*, Ex. 2. 9 (elsewhere always הוֹלִיךְ); הוֹשַׁר Ps. 5. 9 Khethib, but יַיְשִׁירוּ Pr. 4. 25; and תֵּיטְבִי Na. 3. 8, for תֵּיטְבִי.

15. Some forms of the *Hiphil* are sometimes written *defectively;* e. g. הֵטִיב, הֵמִין for הֵיטִיב, הֵימִין. There is an uncontracted form also of this class in Is. 52. 5, where יְהֵילִילוּ stands for יְיֵלִילוּ *they howl* (comp. rem. 10).

A few forms of Hiph. fut. have occasioned much difficulty to grammarians, viz. יֵיטִב for יֵיטִיב Job 24. 21; יְיֵלִיל Is. 15. 2; 16. 7; יְיֵלִילוּ Ho. 7. 14; אֲיֵלִיל Je. 48. 31, and constantly so in this verb (excepting אֵילִילָה Mi. 1. 8), to which another example of Kal fut. is added, viz. יְיֵדַע *he knows*, for יֵדַע Ps. 138. 6. The oldest grammarians regard י as changed from the characteristic ה, so that יְיֵלִיל stands for יְהֵלִיל. This seems of all others the best explanation, only that it does not suit יְיֵדַע, which cannot be Hiphil.

On the third class, or verbs פ״י, *whose Yod is assimilated.*

16. Yod in these verbs does not remain quiescent, but is assimilated like נ in the verbs פ״ן. Some verbs belong exclusively to this class; e. g. יָצַע, Hiph. הִצִּיעַ, Hoph. fut. יֻצַּע, derivative מַצָּע; יָצַת, Hiph. הִצִּית. Others have two forms; one in which Yod is assimilated, and another in which it is quiescent; e. g. יָצַק, fut. יִצֹּק *he shall pour*, Le. 14. 26, and וַיִּיצֹק 1 Ki. 22. 35, Hoph. part. מֻצָּק Job 11. 15; יָצַר fut. יִצְּרֵהוּ *he fashions it*, Is. 44. 12; אֶצָּרְךָ Je. 1. 5 Keri, but also וַיִּיצֶר.

The same assimilation takes place in some Chaldee verbs, e. g. יְכֵל, fut. יִכֻּל; יְדַע, fut. יִדַּע; but so that Dagesh is again resolved in Nun, as יִנְדַּע for יִדַּע.

17. The *future O* of the verbs פ״י is only to be met with in this class, as יִצֹּק, יִצֹּר, יִסֹּר.

	TABLE L. VERB AYIN VAV (ע״ו).						AYIN YOD (ע״י).		
	KAL.	NIPHAL.	HIPHIL.	HOPHAL.	PILEL.	PULAL.	KAL.		NIPHAL.
Pret. 3. *m.*	קָם	נָקוֹם *	הֵקִים	הוּקַם	קוֹמֵם	קוֹמַם	בָּן	בִּין	נָבוֹן
3. *f.*	קָמָה	נָקוֹמָה	הֵקִימָה	הוּקְמָה	קוֹמְמָה	קוֹמְמָה	בָּנָה	בִּינָה	נָבוֹנָה
2. *m.*	קַמְתָּ	נְקוּמוֹתָ	הֲקִימוֹתָ	הוּקַמְתָּ	קוֹמַמְתָּ	קוֹמַמְתָּ	בַּנְתָּ	בִּינוֹתָ	נְבוּנוֹתָ
2. *f.*	קַמְתְּ	נְקוּמוֹת	הֲקִימוֹת	הוּקַמְתְּ	קוֹמַמְתְּ	קוֹמַמְתְּ	בַּנְתְּ	בִּינוֹת	נְבוּנוֹת
1. *c.*	קַמְתִּי	נְקוּמוֹתִי	הֲקִימוֹתִי	הוּקַמְתִּי	קוֹמַמְתִּי	קוֹמַמְתִּי	בַּנְתִּי	בִּינוֹתִי	נְבוּנוֹתִי
Plur. 3. *c.*	קָמוּ	נָקוֹמוּ	הֵקִימוּ	הוּקְמוּ	קוֹמְמוּ	קוֹמְמוּ	בָּנוּ	בִּינוּ	נָבוֹנוּ
2. *m.*	קַמְתֶּם	נְקוּמוֹתֶם	הֲקִימוֹתֶם	הוּקַמְתֶּם	קוֹמַמְתֶּם	קוֹמַמְתֶּם	בַּנְתֶּם	בִּינוֹתֶם	נְבוּנוֹתֶם
2. *f.*	קַמְתֶּן	נְקוּמוֹתֶן	הֲקִימוֹתֶן	הוּקַמְתֶּן	קוֹמַמְתֶּן	קוֹמַמְתֶּן	בַּנְתֶּן	בִּינוֹתֶן	נְבוּנוֹתֶן
1. *c.*	קַמְנוּ	נְקוּמוֹנוּ	הֲקִימוֹנוּ	הוּקַמְנוּ	קוֹמַמְנוּ	קוֹמַמְנוּ	בַּנּוּ	בִּינוֹנוּ	נְבוּנוֹנוּ
Inf. *absol.*	קוֹם	הִקּוֹם	הָקֵם, הָקִים					בֹּן	הִבּוֹן
constr.	קוּם	הִקּוֹם	הָקִים	הוּקַם	קוֹמֵם	קוֹמַם		בִּין	הִבּוֹן
Imp. *m.*	קוּם	הִקּוֹם	הָקֵם		קוֹמֵם			בִּין	הִבּוֹן
f.	קוּמִי	הִקּוֹמִי	הָקִימִי	wanting	קוֹמְמִי	wanting		בִּינִי	as הִקּוֹם
Plur. m.	קוּמוּ	הִקּוֹמוּ	הָקִימוּ		קוֹמְמוּ			בִּינוּ	
f.	קֹמְנָה	הִקֹּמְנָה	הָקֵמְנָה		קוֹמֵמְנָה			—	
Fut. 3. *m.*	יָקוּם	יִקּוֹם	יָקִים	יוּקַם	יְקוֹמֵם	יְקוֹמַם		יָבִין	יִבּוֹן
3. *f.*	תָּקוּם	תִּקּוֹם	תָּקִים	תּוּקַם	תְּקוֹמֵם	תְּקוֹמַם		תָּבִין	as יִקּוֹם
2. *m.*	תָּקוּם	תִּקּוֹם	תָּקִים	תּוּקַם	תְּקוֹמֵם	תְּקוֹמַם		תָּבִין	
2. *f.*	תָּקוּמִי	תִּקּוֹמִי	תָּקִימִי	תּוּקְמִי	תְּקוֹמְמִי	תְּקוֹמְמִי		תָּבִינִי	
1. *c.*	אָקוּם	אֶקּוֹם	אָקִים	אוּקַם	אֲקוֹמֵם	אֲקוֹמַם		אָבִין	
Plur. 3. *m.*	יָקוּמוּ	יִקּוֹמוּ	יָקִימוּ	יוּקְמוּ	יְקוֹמְמוּ	יְקוֹמְמוּ		יָבִינוּ	
3. *f.*	תְּקוּמֶינָה	תִּקֹּמְנָה	תָּקֵמְנָה	תּוּקַמְנָה	תְּקוֹמֵמְנָה	תְּקוֹמַמְנָה		תְּבִינֶינָה	
2. *m.*	תָּקוּמוּ	תִּקּוֹמוּ	תָּקִימוּ	תּוּקְמוּ	תְּקוֹמְמוּ	תְּקוֹמְמוּ		תָּבִינוּ	
2. *f.*	תְּקוּמֶינָה	תִּקֹּמְנָה	תָּקֵמְנָה	תּוּקַמְנָה	תְּקוֹמֵמְנָה	תְּקוֹמַמְנָה		תְּבִינֶינָה	
1. *c.*	נָקוּם	נִקּוֹם	נָקִים	נוּקַם	נְקוֹמֵם	נְקוֹמַם		נָבִין	
Fut. *apoc.*	יָקֹם		יָקֵם					יָבֵן	
Fut. *with* ו *conv.*	וַיָּקֹם, וַיָּקָם		וַיָּקֶם					וַיָּבֶן	
Part. *act.*	קָם	נָקוֹם	מֵקִים	מוּקָם	מְקוֹמֵם	מְקוֹמָם		בָּן	נָבוֹן
pass.	קוּם							בּוּן	

* The few instances of *Piel* and *Hithp.* from ע״ו are הִצְטַיֵּד, חִיֵּב, קִיֵּם, עִוֵּד.

SECTION XXI.—VERBS ע"ו. (TABLE L.)

REMARKS.

I. Pret. and Part. of Kal.

1. We class these two forms together, on account of their similarity in these verbs. The form of the paradigm, in which the pret. is *middle A* (קָוַם, contr. קָם), is very seldom written *in full*. Examples, however, are—קָאם *he arises*, Ho. 10. 14; part. שָׁאטִים *despising*, Eze. 28. 24, 26; fem. שָׁאטוֹת Eze. 16. 57; and in the adjective, as לָאט *secretly*, Ju. 4. 21; רָאשׁ *poor*, Pr. 10. 4; 13. 23. Here must be referred the form כָּאֲרִי Ps. 22. 17, which, according to the present punctuation, seems to stand for כָּאֲרִים, or, with a slight change of the vowels, for כָּאֲרִי, in both cases from כּוּר. Two codices read כארו, in the preterite, for כָּרוּ.*

2. In the intransitive verbs *middle E* and *O*, which in the regular verb have likewise the pret. and part. alike (§ 8. rem. 20), the latter are formed like מֵת (for מֵית from מָוֵת), אוֹר (from אָוֹר). Examples are:—

Pret. מֵתָה *she died*, Ex. 7. 21; מֵתוּ Ex. 4. 19, 2 pers. מַתָּה Eze. 28. 8; פִּשְׁתֶּם Mal. 3. 20, from פּוּשׁ, 3 pers. pret. פָּשׁ; בּוֹשׁ, 2 and 1 pers. בֹּשְׁתָּ, בֹּשְׁנוּ *thou art, we are, ashamed;* אוֹר, pl. אוֹרוּ *they are enlightened*, 1 Sa. 14. 29; טֹבוּ *they are good*, Nu. 24. 5; זֹרוּ *they are estranged*, Ps. 58. 4 (also זֹרוּ), *they are pressed out*, Is. 1. 6. בּאוּ Je. 27. 18 is the only example in this verb, elsewhere always בָּאוּ.

Part. עֵר *waking*, Ca. 5. 2; לָנִים *lodging*, Ne. 13. 21; and written *in full* גֵּירִים *stranger*, 2 Ch. 2. 16. With *O*, קוֹמִים *arising*, 2 Ki. 16. 7 (also קָמִים); בּוֹשִׁים *being ashamed*, Eze. 32. 30.

The part. fem. קָמָה is distinguished from the pret. 3 pers. fem. קָמָה by the tone.

II. Inf., Imp. and Fut. of Kal.

3. In some verbs the ו of the *inf., constr., imp.* and *fut.* is always quiescent in Hholem, as אוֹר *to be light*, בּוֹא *to come*, בּוֹשׁ *to be ashamed;* in all the rest it is quiescent in Shurek only, like קוּם. Both forms are found also in one and the same verb, as דּוּשׁ *to thresh*, imp. דּוֹשִׁי Mi. 4. 13; inf. מוֹט *to totter*, Ps. 46.3, fut. יָמוּט. חוּס *to spare*, has a double fut. יָחוּס and יָחוֹס; the latter, however, seems everywhere to be the apocopated future (but written *in full* contrary to rule). Those, however, with וּ have regularly וֹ in the inf. abs., and apocopated fut. and imp.

4. Examples of the *inf. abs.* are—גּוֹר יָגוּר *dwelling he shall dwell*, Is. 54. 15; מוֹת תְּמוּתוּן *dying ye shall die*, Ge. 3. 4; קוֹם יָקוּמוּ *arising they shall arise*, Je. 44. 29; נוֹחַ Est. 9. 16, &c. Here belongs likewise the adv. עוֹד properly *repeating*.

5. There are also some examples of the *imp.* with Kibbuts, as מֻת *die*, De. 32. 50; קֻם לְךָ *get thee up*, Jos. 7. 10; שֻׁב *return*, Ex. 4. 19; רֻץ *run*, 2 Ki. 4. 26. This form is certainly to be regarded as an apocopated imperative, and not as accidently written *defectively*, since Kibbuts is found also in the future besides the form with defective Hholem (comp. rem. 7).

Lengthened imperatives are קוּמָה, שׁוּבָה (comp. § 8. rem. 11).

6. In one verb alone the preformatives of the future have Tseri, viz. יֵבוֹשׁ (for יָבוֹשׁ), strictly after the form יִקְטֹל.

7. The *apocopated future* is יָקֹם, very seldom יָקֻם, or in full יָקוֹם; e. g. תָּמֹת *may she die*, Nu. 23. 10; Ju. 16. 30; יָשֹׁב *let him return*, Ju. 7. 3; יָרֹם *let him be exalted*, 2 Sa. 22. 47; אַל יָשֹׁב *let him not return*, Ps. 74. 21; וְיָמֹת *that he may die*, 1 Ki. 21. 10. Examples of the full orthography (יָקוֹם) are very frequent in the verb חוּס, besides which there are also single instances found in other verbs, as וַיָּצוֹם *and he fasted*, 1 Ki. 21. 27; וַתָּמוֹג *and she melted away*, Am. 9. 5; moreover a few times in Khethib, where, in the Keri, Vav is cancelled, as וַתָּלוֹשׁ *and she kneaded*, 2 Sa. 13. 8; וַיָּשׁוֹב *and he returned*, Eze. 18. 28. In both these last instances we are doubtless to sound it וֹ and not וּ.

8. When the tone of the *apocopated future* is drawn back to the penultima, Hholem is shortened to Kamets-hhatuph, יָקָם. This takes place—

(*a*) *Before monosyllabic words*, as יָקָם לְךָ Job 22. 28; frequently with Makkeph (which otherwise is not usual in the like combination); e. g. יָשָׁב־נָא 2 Sa. 19. 38; Da. 9. 16; תָּשָׁב־נָא 1 Ki. 17. 21.

* This is likewise the reading of the Masora on Nu. 24. 9; comp. Prof. Lee's Heb. Lex. under כּוּר.

(*b*) After *conversive Vav*, as וַיָּקָם, וַיָּמָת. In pause, however, the tone remains on the ultimate, as וַיָּקֹם, וַיָּמֹת, comp. Ge. 11. 28, 32, with ch. 5. 5, 8. The *first person* of the *future* forms another exception, which generally retains the full form after *conversive Vav* (§ 11. rem. 6); e. g. וָאָקוּם 2 Ch. 6. 10; Ne. 2. 12; 4. 8; Da. 8. 27.

9. When the first or last letter of the monosyllabic root is a guttural or ר, the *apocopated future with conversive Vav* may take *Pattahh* in the final syllable; e. g. וַיָּסַר *and he turned aside*, Ru. 4. 1; וַיָּזַר *and he wringed out*, Ju. 6. 38; וַיָּנַח *and he rested*, Ex. 10. 14; וַיָּעַף *and he became weary*, Ju. 4. 21.

10. For the *fut.* 2 and 3 *pers. pl.*, the form given in the paradigm (תְּקוּמֶינָה) is the usual one; e. g. תְּשׁוּבֶינָה Eze. 16. 55, comp. Is. 54. 10; 60. 8; Zec. 1. 17; 13. 7; there occurs, however, also a form like תָּשֹׁבְןָ besides תְּשׁוּבֶינָה in Eze. 16. 55, and תָּבֹאנָה Est. 4. 4; 1 Sa. 10. 17 in Keri.

III. NIPHAL.

11. In the *preterite* occurs the form נֵעוֹר for נָעוֹר (according to נִקְטַל) Zec. 2. 17, which corresponds to the Kal fut. יֵבוֹשׁ (comp. rem. 6). This, however, may be compared with the form נִמּוֹל and referred to the Chaldee or Rabbinic punctuation of *rem.* 24.

12. The וֹ is sometimes retained in those forms in which, according to the paradigm, it is to be changed to וּ on account of the accession at the end. Thus נְפֹצוֹתֶם (for נְפוּצוֹתֶם) *ye are dispersed*, Eze. 11. 17; 20. 41; נְקֹטֹתֶם Eze. 20. 43. The וּ is, on the other hand, inserted contrary to the paradigm in the inf. כְּהִדּוּשׁ Is. 25. 10, and part. נְבֻכִים Ex. 14. 3 (comp. § 32. rem. 5).

IV. HIPHIL.

13. *Preterite.* Besides the forms with epenthetic וֹ, there are others without it, after the form הֲקַמֹתָ (הִקְטַלְתָּ); e. g. הֲנַפְתָּ *thou liftest up*, Ex. 20. 25, besides הֲנִיפוֹתִי Job 31. 21; הֵבֵאתִי (according to הִמְצֵאתִי) Ge. 27. 12, besides הֲבִאוֹתִי Eze. 38. 16 (comp. Je. 25. 13); הֵטַלְתִּי *I cast*, Je. 16. 13. The וֹ is especially omitted in verbs ל״ת and ל״ן before the afformatives with ת and נ, as הֵמַתָּה, הֵמַתִּי, pl. הֵמַתֶּם, with suff. הֲמִתִּיהָ Ho. 2. 5; הֵכַנּוּ *we prepare*, 2 Ch. 29. 19, besides הֲכִינוֹנוּ 1 Ch. 29. 16.

There is, on the other hand, epenthetic ־ֵי instead of וֹ in the fut. תְּהִימֶנָּה for תְּהִימֶינָה Mi. 2. 12.* (The change of תְּהִי״ from תָּהֶ is occasioned by the shifting of the tone, comp. the pret. הֲקִימוֹתָ, הֲקִימוֹתִי, but imp. הֲקִמְנָה).

14. Less important deviations from the paradigm are:—

(*a*) Forms like הֲרֵמֹת (for הֲרִימוֹת) Nu. 31. 28, especially before suffix הֲקִמֹתוֹ 2 Ki. 9. 2 (comp. 1 Ki. 8. 34; Ex. 19. 23; Ca. 3. 4 Keri); and written *fully* הֲשִׁיבוֹתָם 2 Ch. 6. 25. (*b*) With *Segol* instead of *Pattahh* under the preformatives, as הֱטִיבוֹתָ 1 Ki. 8. 18; הֱבִישׁוֹתָ Ps. 44. 8; הֱקִיצוֹתִי Ps. 139. 18; comp. also rem. 24.

15. Of the *inf.* there once occurs a Chaldee form with the fem. termination, viz. הֲנָפָה (with impure Kamets) for הָנִיף Is. 30. 28 (comp. הֲזָדָה Da. 5. 20), from נוּף.

16. In the *imp.* the shortened and lengthened form הָקֵם, הָקִימָה have wholly supplanted the regular form הָקִים.†

17. The *apocopated future* has the form יָקֵם. Examples are, וְיָרֵם *that he take up*, Nu. 17. 2; יָסֵר *let him take away*, Job 9. 34; וְיָסֵר *that he may remove*, Ex. 10. 17; Nu. 21. 7. As the poetic future and present, יָעֵר Da. 11. 25; יָפֵץ Job 38. 24; יָרֵם 1 Sa. 2. 10.

18. When the tone is drawn back, the final syllable takes *Segol* instead of *Tseri*, as (after a negation) אַל־תָּשֶׁב *turn not away*, 1 Ki. 2. 20, or after *conversive Vav*, וַיָּרֶם, וַיָּנֶף &c. The 1 pers., however, forms an exception here as in Kal (rem. 8), as וָאָשִׁיב Ne. 2. 20; 6. 4; וָאָעִיד vers. 13, 15, besides וָאָעֵד Je. 32. 10; וָאָקִים Am. 2. 11.

19. When one of the letters is a guttural or ר the final syllable takes *Pattahh*, as in Kal (rem. 9), and the context must decide between Kal and Hiphil, as וַיָּסַר *and he removed*, Ge. 8. 13; וַיָּנַח *and he gave rest*, Jos. 21. 42.

V. PILEL, PULAL AND HITHPALEL.

20. In the *Hithpal* the final syllable has some-

* The form ־ֶנָּה for ־ֶינָה is found also in תְּמוּתֶנָּה Zec. 13. 19, תְּפוּצֶנָה Zec. 1. 17, but not in all MSS. and editions (comp. § 24. rem. 6).

† This, however, remains the ground-form whenever the suffixes are added, as הֲקִימוֹ Je. 23. 20; 30. 24; comp. § 11. rem. 5.

times also *Pattahh*, as in the Hithpa. of the regular verb (§ 12. rem. 1), and hence Kamets in pause, as pret. הִתְבּוֹנָן Is. 1. 3; מִתְקוֹמָמָה Job 20. 27; imp. הִתְרוֹעָעִי Ps. 60. 10; fut. תִּתְמוֹגָג Ps. 107. 26, comp. Ps. 119. 158; 139. 21; 58. 8.

21. The form וַיְכוּנֶנּוּ *he has prepared us*, Job 31. 15, stands for וַיְכוֹנְנֵנוּ (from יְכוֹנֵן) the first Nun being compensated for by Dagesh, and וֹ having lost the tone is shortened to וּ (comp. Niph. נָקוֹם, 2 pers. נְקוּמוֹת). The omission of Dagesh in the נ of the suffix seems to be designed for avoiding the concurrence of too many Nuns.

VI. In General.

22. On account of the intimate relation between verbs ע״ו and ע״ע (see above § 18. rem. 12), some of the former class borrow forms from the latter, as Kal pret. בַּז *he despised* for בָּז (from בּוּז), Zec. 4. 10; מַח *he besmeared*, for מָח, Is. 44. 18.

23. The verbs whose middle radical is a moveable Vav are, in respect to this letter, quite regular. They are, however, comparatively few. E. g. חָוַר, fut. יֶחְוַר *to be white;* גָּוַע, fut. יִגְוַע *to die;* רָוַח, fut. יִרְוַח *to be wide*, Pu. מְרֻוָּח; צָוַח, fut. יִצְוַח *to cry;* עָוַל, Pi. עִוֵּל *to act perversely;* עָוַר, Pi. עִוֵּר *to blind;* and several others which are also ל״ה, as כָּוָה, חָוָה, הָוָה, קָוָה, לָוָה &c.

24. The verbs ע״ו have also this in common with the verbs ע״ע (§ 18. rem. 14) that some forms take Dagesh forte in the first radical letter like the verbs פ״ן, and the preformative takes a short vowel instead of the long, which is more usual in the Chaldee and Rabbinic; e. g. יַלִּינוּ, מַלִּינִים Ex. 16. 7, 8; Nu. 14. 27 (from לוּן *to murmur*); יַלִּיזוּ *they depart* (from לוּז); הַסִּית, יַסִּית, מַסִּית, along with הֵסִית, יָסִית (*to stimulate*); Niph. נִמּוֹל *he was circumcised*, Ge. 17. 26, 27; 34. 22 (from מוּל); with gutt. נֵעוֹר Zec. 2. 17 (comp. rem. 11). In the same way may be explained הַעִירוֹתִי Is. 41. 25; הַעֲדֹתִי Je. 11. 7 (with Dagesh forte implicit) for הַעֲדֹתִי. Here belong, moreover, some forms of verbs *Pe guttural* with *Dagesh forte implicit*, as Kal fut. וַתָּחַשׁ for וַתָּחַשׁ *and she hastened* (from חוּשׁ) Job 31. 5; וַיַּעַט, וַתַּעַט 1 Sa. 15. 19, and 14. 32 Keri, from עוּט or עִיט *to rush upon.*

SECTION XXII.—ON THE VERBS ע״י. (Table L.)

REMARKS.

1. In the *preterite* some verbs have both the forms exhibited in the paradigm, as בִּינוֹתִי Da. 9. 2; בַּנְתָּה Ps. 139. 2; רִיבוֹתָ *thou contendest*, Job 33. 13; רַבְתָּה La. 3. 58; דִּיגוּם *they fish them*, Je. 16. 16. The participle exhibits here also two forms, as בָּן *middle A*, and לֵנִים *middle E*, Ne. 13. 21 (comp. § 21. rem. 2).

2. Examples of the *inf. abs.* are—רֹב *striving*, Ju. 11. 25; Job 40. 2; שׂוֹת *putting*, Is. 22. 7; also רִיב Je. 50. 34.

3. Examples of the *apocopated fut.* are—(*a*) יָרֵב *let him plead*, 1 Sa. 24. 16; יָשֵׂם *may he give*, 1 Sa. 2. 20; יָגֵל *may he rejoice*, Ps. 13. 6; אַל יָרֵב Ho. 4. 4. (*b*) וְיָבֵן *that he may observe*, Je. 9. 11; Ho. 14. 10. (*c*) As a positive future of poesy, as יָשֵׂם *he shall put*, Job 33. 11; 24. 25; Ps. 107. 33 (comp. § 11. rem. 6). With the retracted tone the final syllable takes Segol (*a*) before *a monosyllabic word*, as יָרֶב לוֹ Ju. 6. 31, 32; (*b*) after אַל, as אַל תָּלֶן 2 Sa. 17. 16; (*c*) with *conversive Vav*, as וַיָּשֶׂם, וַיָּבֶן.

Pattahh occurs instead of *Tseri* (*a*) on account of a *guttural*, as יָרַח *he may smell*, 1 Sa. 26. 19; (*b*) in *pause*, as אַל־תָּלַן Ju. 19. 20; תָּלַן Job 17. 2.

II. Niphal.

4. נָזִיד *pottage* (properly *sodden*), Ge. 25. 29, from זִיד, is the only example in which Yod is retained in Niphal. (There is at least no trace of a root זִיד=נָזַד).

III. Hiphil.

5. The *fut.* of Hiph. can be distinguished from the fut. of Kal by the signification only; e. g. יָבִין *he understands;* Hiph. תְּבִינֵם *he gives them understanding*, Job 32. 8.

TABLE M. VERB LAMED ALEPH (ל״א).

	KAL.	NIPHAL.	PIEL.	PUAL.	HIPHIL.	HOPHAL.	HITHPAEL.
Pret. 3. *m.*	מָצָא	נִמְצָא	מִצֵּא	מֻצָּא	הִמְצִיא	הֻמְצָא	הִתְמַצֵּא
3. *f.*	מָצְאָה	נִמְצְאָה	מִצְּאָה	מֻצְּאָה	הִמְצִיאָה	הֻמְצְאָה	הִתְמַצְּאָה
2. *m.*	מָצָאתָ	נִמְצֵאתָ	מִצֵּאתָ	מֻצֵּאתָ	הִמְצֵאתָ	הֻמְצֵאתָ	הִתְמַצֵּאתָ
2. *f.*	מָצָאת	נִמְצֵאת	מִצֵּאת	מֻצֵּאת	הִמְצֵאת	הֻמְצֵאת	הִתְמַצֵּאת
1. *c.*	מָצָאתִי	נִמְצֵאתִי	מִצֵּאתִי	מֻצֵּאתִי	הִמְצֵאתִי	הֻמְצֵאתִי	הִתְמַצֵּאתִי
Plur. 3. *c.*	מָצְאוּ	נִמְצְאוּ	מִצְּאוּ	מֻצְּאוּ	הִמְצִיאוּ	הֻמְצְאוּ	הִתְמַצְּאוּ
2. *m.*	מְצָאתֶם	נִמְצֵאתֶם	מִצֵּאתֶם	מֻצֵּאתֶם	הִמְצֵאתֶם	הֻמְצֵאתֶם	הִתְמַצֵּאתֶם
2. *f.*	מְצָאתֶן	נִמְצֵאתֶן	מִצֵּאתֶן	מֻצֵּאתֶן	הִמְצֵאתֶן	הֻמְצֵאתֶן	הִתְמַצֵּאתֶן
1. *c.*	מָצָאנוּ	נִמְצֵאנוּ	מִצֵּאנוּ	מֻצֵּאנוּ	הִמְצֵאנוּ	הֻמְצֵאנוּ	הִתְמַצֵּאנוּ
Inf. *absol.*	מָצוֹא	נִמְצֹא	מַצֵּא		הַמְצֵא		
constr.	מְצֹא	הִמָּצֵא	מַצֵּא	מֻצָּא	הַמְצִיא	הֻמְצָא	הִתְמַצֵּא
Imp. *m.*	מְצָא	הִמָּצֵא	מַצֵּא	wanting	הַמְצֵא	wanting	הִתְמַצֵּא
f.	מִצְאִי	הִמָּצְאִי	מַצְּאִי		הַמְצִיאִי		הִתְמַצְּאִי
Plur. m.	מִצְאוּ	הִמָּצְאוּ	מַצְּאוּ		הַמְצִיאוּ		הִתְמַצְּאוּ
f.	מְצֶאנָה	הִמָּצֶאנָה	מַצֶּאנָה		הַמְצֶאנָה		הִתְמַצֶּאנָה
Fut. 3. *m.*	יִמְצָא	יִמָּצֵא	יְמַצֵּא	יְמֻצָּא	יַמְצִיא	יֻמְצָא	יִתְמַצֵּא
3. *f.*	תִּמְצָא	תִּמָּצֵא	תְּמַצֵּא	תְּמֻצָּא	תַּמְצִיא	תֻּמְצָא	תִּתְמַצֵּא
2. *m.*	תִּמְצָא	תִּמָּצֵא	תְּמַצֵּא	תְּמֻצָּא	תַּמְצִיא	תֻּמְצָא	תִּתְמַצֵּא
2. *f.*	תִּמְצְאִי	תִּמָּצְאִי	תְּמַצְּאִי	תְּמֻצְּאִי	תַּמְצִיאִי	תֻּמְצְאִי	תִּתְמַצְּאִי
1. *c.*	אֶמְצָא	אֶמָּצֵא	אֲמַצֵּא	אֲמֻצָּא	אַמְצִיא	אֻמְצָא	אֶתְמַצֵּא
Plur. 3. *m.*	יִמְצְאוּ	יִמָּצְאוּ	יְמַצְּאוּ	יְמֻצְּאוּ	יַמְצִיאוּ	יֻמְצְאוּ	יִתְמַצְּאוּ
3. *f.*	תִּמְצֶאנָה	תִּמָּצֶאנָה	תְּמַצֶּאנָה	תְּמֻצֶּאנָה	תַּמְצֶאנָה	תֻּמְצֶאנָה	תִּתְמַצֶּאנָה
2. *m.*	תִּמְצְאוּ	תִּמָּצְאוּ	תְּמַצְּאוּ	תְּמֻצְּאוּ	תַּמְצִיאוּ	תֻּמְצְאוּ	תִּתְמַצְּאוּ
2. *f.*	תִּמְצֶאנָה	תִּמָּצֶאנָה	תְּמַצֶּאנָה	תְּמֻצֶּאנָה	תַּמְצֶאנָה	תֻּמְצֶאנָה	תִּתְמַצֶּאנָה
1. *c.*	נִמְצָא	נִמָּצֵא	נְמַצֵּא	נְמֻצָּא	נַמְצִיא	נֻמְצָא	נִתְמַצֵּא
Fut. *apoc.* (*Jussive*)					יַמְצֵא		
Part. *act.*	מֹצֵא	נִמְצָא	מְמַצֵּא	מְמֻצָּא	מַמְצִיא	מֻמְצָא	מִתְמַצֵּא
pass.	מָצוּא						

SECTION XXIII.—ON THE VERBS ל״א. (Table M.)

REMARKS.

I. Kal.

1. The verbs *middle E*, like יָרֵא, retain *Tseri* throughout the rest of the persons, as יָרֵאתָ *thou didst fear;* מָלֵאתִי *I have filled.* The 3 pers. fem. assumes sometimes the Aramaic form, as קָרָאת Is. 7. 14; and so in Niph. נִפְלָאת Ps. 118. 23; in Hoph. הֻבָאת Ge.

33. 11. There are also examples where א is omitted, מָצָתִי Nu. 11. 11; יָצָתִי Job 1. 21; מָלֵתִי Job 32. 18.

2. Forms of the *infinitive* deviating from the paradigm are—(*a*) like יִרְאָה, חֲטָאָה, טָמְאָה, also לִקְרָאת* by Syriacism for לִקְרַאת (constr. of קִרְאָה); (*b*) מְלֹאת for מְלֹאת (after יְכֹלֶת) Le. 12. 4; קְרֹאת *to call*, Ju. 8. 1; שְׂנֹאת *to hate*, Pr. 8. 13; (*c*) מַשְּׂאוֹת *to carry*, Eze. 17. 9, for מַשְּׂאֵת.

א is omitted in חֲטוֹ Ge. 20. 6.

3. In the *imperative* there is an anomalous form, יְרָאוּ *fear ye*, Ps. 34. 10 (comp. נִרְפְּאוּ Niph. Eze. 47. 8), where א is passed over in the pronunciation. The punctuators have given to this word the character of ל״ה probably to distinguish it from יִרְאוּ *they shall see.*

A striking anomaly is presented in צְאֶינָה וּרְאֶינָה *go out and see*, Ca. 3. 11, where the first word stands for צֶאנָה, comp. the fut. תְּשֶׂאינָה Eze. 23. 49. The epenthetic ◌ֶי is as anomalous here as it is in the regular verb § 8. rem. 16, only that here it is chosen for the sake of consonance with רְאֶינָה.

4. The *part. fem.* is commonly, by contraction, מֹצֵאת, seldom with the Syriac punctuation מֹצֶאֶת for מֹצֵאת, Ca. 8. 10; 1 Ki. 10. 22; and defective יוֹצֵת De. 28. 57.

In the *masculine* a Syriac punctuation is introduced in חֹטְאִים for חֹטְאִים *sinners*, 1 Sa. 14. 33; בֹּדָאם for בֹּדְאָם Ne. 6. 8.

II. Niphal.

5. In a few instances א is omitted, as נִטְמֵתֶם *ye are polluted*, Le. 11. 43; נַחְבֵּתֶם *ye have hid yourself*, Jos. 2. 16. In the 3 pers. fem. the same kind of contraction is found as in Kal (rem. 1), as נִפְלָאת Ps. 118. 23; נִפְלֵאת† De. 30. 11; נִטְמָאת Nu. 5. 20; Eze. 23. 30.

6. In the *participle* there are traces of a form like נִמְצָא, viz. in the plurals נִמְצְאִים Est. 1. 5; 4. 16; נִטְמְאִים Eze. 20. 30; נֶחְבְּאִים Jos. 10. 17 (comp. § 15. rem. 2, and dec. 7).

III. Hiphil.

7. Anomalous forms are הֶחֱטִי 2 Ki. 13. 6; inf. הַחֲטִי Je. 32. 35, for הֶחֱטִיא, הַחֲטִיא.

IV. In General.

8. In addition to the anomalous forms exhibited above there are others, the irregularity of which consists in assuming forms of verbs ל״ה. The ל״א and ל״ה of the Hebrew form but one class in the Aramaic. The Syriac has א only, and the Chaldee has א and ה promiscuously forming but one class. In the Hebrew this is either peculiar to certain verbs, and the two exist as distinct verbs ל״א and ל״ה, and as such occupy separate places in the Lexicon, e. g. קָרָא and קָרָה *to meet*, פָּלָא and פָּלָה *to be distinguished*, &c., or in the real ל״א there occur some isolated forms which borrow either the punctuation only or the inflexion altogether from ל״ה; comp. the following remarks.

9. Examples of such verbs, where א is retained, and only the punctuation of ל״ה is adopted, are—כָּלָאתִי *I have refrained*, Ps. 119. 101; part. מֹצָא, חֹטָא Ec. 7. 26; 8. 12; Piel מִלָּא *he accomplished*, Je. 51. 34; דִּכָּא Ps. 143. 3; רִפֵּאתִי *I heal*, 2 Ki. 2. 21; fut. יְגַמֶּא *he swallows*, Job 39. 24; inf. מַלֹּאות 2 Ch. 36. 21; מַלֹּאת Ex. 31. 5; Hithp. הַמִּתְנַבְּאוֹת Eze. 13. 17; Hiph. הִפְלָא Is. 28. 29; De. 28. 59; הֶחְבְּאָתָה *she concealed* (with ה parag.), Jos. 6. 17.

10. In the following examples there is, on the contrary, the punctuation of ל״א retained, and ה only is adopted. Kal imp. רְפָה for רְפָא *heal*, Ps. 60. 4; נְסָה for נְשָׂא, נְסָא Ps. 4. 7. Niph. inf. abs. נֶחְבָּה Je. 49. 10, constr. הֵחָבֵה *to hide oneself*, 1 Ki. 22. 25; הֵרָפֵה Je. 19. 11. Piel יְמַלֶּה *he shall fill*, Job 8. 21.

11. Finally, forms which are entirely inflected after ל״ה—צָמִת *thou art thirsty*, Ru. 2. 9; מָלוּ for מָלְאוּ *they are full*, Eze. 28. 16; כָּלוּ for כָּלְאוּ 1 Sa. 6. 10; נָשׂוּא Ps. 139. 20 (with parag. א § 8. rem. 4), for נָשׂוּ, נָשְׂאוּ; fut. תִּרְפֶּינָה Job 5. 18; part. fem. יֹצָא for יֹצְאָה, יֹצָה Ec. 10. 5; pass. נְשׂוּי Ps. 32. 1. Niph. נִבֵּיתָ *thou hast prophesied*, Je. 26. 9; נִטְמִינוּ *we are polluted*, Job 18. 3; נִרְפְּתָה Je. 51. 9; fut. (perhaps) יִמָּצוּ *they are found*, Ps. 73. 10; יִנָּשׂוּא Je. 10. 5 (with parag. א). Piel יְרַפּוּ, Je. 8. 11. Hithp. הִתְנַבֵּיתָ 1 Sa. 10. 6; הִתְנַבּוֹת 1 Sa. 10. 6. Hiph. הִמְצִיתִךָ 2 Sa. 3. 8; part. מַקְנֶה for מַקְנִיא Eze. 8. 3.

* Comp. חֹטְאִים for חֹטְאִים rem. 4.

† This, however, must be taken as a participle, comp. rem. 4.

TABLE N. VERB LAMED HE (ל״ה).

	KAL.	NIPHAL.	PIEL.	PUAL.	HIPHIL.	HOPHAL.	HITHPAEL.
PRET. 3. *m.*	גָּלָה	נִגְלָה	גִּלָּה	גֻּלָּה	הִגְלָה	הָגְלָה	הִתְגַּלָּה
3. *f.*	גָּלְתָה	נִגְלְתָה	גִּלְּתָה	גֻּלְּתָה	הִגְלְתָה	הָגְלְתָה	הִתְגַּלְּתָה
2. *m.*	גָּלִיתָ	נִגְלֵיתָ	גִּלִּיתָ	גֻּלֵּיתָ	הִגְלֵיתָ	הָגְלֵיתָ	הִתְגַּלֵּיתָ
2. *f.*	גָּלִית	נִגְלֵית	גִּלִּית	גֻּלֵּית	הִגְלֵית	הָגְלֵית	הִתְגַּלֵּית
1. *c.*	גָּלִיתִי	נִגְלֵיתִי	גִּלִּיתִי	גֻּלֵּיתִי	הִגְלֵיתִי	הָגְלֵיתִי	הִתְגַּלֵּיתִי
Plur. 3. *c.*	גָּלוּ	נִגְלוּ	גִּלּוּ	גֻּלּוּ	הִגְלוּ	הָגְלוּ	הִתְגַּלּוּ
2. *m.*	גְּלִיתֶם	נִגְלֵיתֶם	גִּלִּיתֶם	גֻּלֵּיתֶם	הִגְלֵיתֶם	הָגְלֵיתֶם	הִתְגַּלֵּיתֶם
2. *f.*	גְּלִיתֶן	נִגְלֵיתֶן	גִּלִּיתֶן	גֻּלֵּיתֶן	הִגְלֵיתֶן	הָגְלֵיתֶן	הִתְגַּלֵּיתֶן
1. *c.*	גָּלִינוּ	נִגְלֵינוּ	גִּלִּינוּ	גֻּלֵּינוּ	הִגְלֵינוּ	הָגְלֵינוּ	הִתְגַּלֵּינוּ
INF. *absol.*	גָּלֹה	נִגְלֹה	גַּלֹּה	גֻּלֹּה	הַגְלֵה	הָגְלֵה	הִתְגַּלֹּה
constr.	גְּלוֹת	הִגָּלוֹת	גַּלּוֹת	גֻּלּוֹת	הַגְלוֹת	הָגְלוֹת	הִתְגַּלּוֹת
IMP. *m.*	גְּלֵה	הִגָּלֵה	גַּלֵּה	wanting	הַגְלֵה	wanting	הִתְגַּלֵּה
f.	גְּלִי	הִגָּלִי	גַּלִּי		הַגְלִי		הִתְגַּלִּי
Plur. m.	גְּלוּ	הִגָּלוּ	גַּלּוּ		הַגְלוּ		הִתְגַּלּוּ
f.	גְּלֶינָה	הִגָּלֶינָה	גַּלֶּינָה		הַגְלֶינָה		הִתְגַּלֶּינָה
FUT. 3. *m.*	יִגְלֶה	יִגָּלֶה	יְגַלֶּה	יְגֻלֶּה	יַגְלֶה	יָגְלֶה	יִתְגַּלֶּה
3. *f.*	תִּגְלֶה	תִּגָּלֶה	תְּגַלֶּה	תְּגֻלֶּה	תַּגְלֶה	תָּגְלֶה	תִּתְגַּלֶּה
2. *m.*	תִּגְלֶה	תִּגָּלֶה	תְּגַלֶּה	תְּגֻלֶּה	תַּגְלֶה	תָּגְלֶה	תִּתְגַּלֶּה
2. *f.*	תִּגְלִי	תִּגָּלִי	תְּגַלִּי	תְּגֻלִּי	תַּגְלִי	תָּגְלִי	תִּתְגַּלִּי
1. *c.*	אֶגְלֶה	אֶגָּלֶה	אֲגַלֶּה	אֲגֻלֶּה	אַגְלֶה	אָגְלֶה	אֶתְגַּלֶּה
Plur. 3. *m.*	יִגְלוּ	יִגָּלוּ	יְגַלּוּ	יְגֻלּוּ	יַגְלוּ	יָגְלוּ	יִתְגַּלּוּ
3. *f.*	תִּגְלֶינָה	תִּגָּלֶינָה	תְּגַלֶּינָה	תְּגֻלֶּינָה	תַּגְלֶינָה	תָּגְלֶינָה	תִּתְגַּלֶּינָה
2. *m.*	תִּגְלוּ	תִּגָּלוּ	תְּגַלּוּ	תְּגֻלּוּ	תַּגְלוּ	תָּגְלוּ	תִּתְגַּלּוּ
2. *f.*	תִּגְלֶינָה	תִּגָּלֶינָה	תְּגַלֶּינָה	תְּגֻלֶּינָה	תַּגְלֶינָה	תָּגְלֶינָה	תִּתְגַּלֶּינָה
1. *c.*	נִגְלֶה	נִגָּלֶה	נְגַלֶּה	נְגֻלֶּה	נַגְלֶה	נָגְלֶה	נִתְגַּלֶּה
FUT. *apoc.*	יִגֶל	יִגָּל	יְגַל		יֶגֶל		יִתְגַּל
PART. *act.*	גֹּלֶה	נִגְלֶה	מְגַלֶּה	מְגֻלֶּה	מַגְלֶה	מָגְלֶה	מִתְגַּלֶּה
pass.	גָּלוּי						

SECTION XXIV.—VERBS ל״ה. (TABLE N.)

REMARKS.

I. KAL.

1. Instead of the *pret.* 3 fem. גָּֽלְתָה, there occurs an Aramaic form like גָּלַת properly for גָּלְיַת,* after the form קָטְלַת, comp. § 8. rem. 3, and § 23. rem. 1, hence גָּלַת, נִגְלָאת); e. g. עָשָׂת *she brings forth*, Le. 25. 21. The like inflexion is found in Hiphil and Hophal (see rem. 14).

2. The *inf. abs.* assumes also the form גָּלוֹ, which probably stands for גָּלוֹ (galov) with the radical ו (properly from the root גָּלוֹ*), and hence is derived the form גְּלוֹת for גְּלוֹת constr. st. E. g. רָאוֹ *seeing*, Ge. 26. 28; בָּכוֹ *weeping*, Is. 30. 19. As the *inf. constr.* occurs also, though seldom, a form like קְנֹה *to buy*, Pr. 16. 16; עֲשֹׂה Ge. 50. 20; רְאוֹ Ge. 48. 11; and, on the other hand, as the *inf. abs.* the form שָׁתוֹת Is. 22. 13; רָאוֹת Is. 42. 20 Keri. Another *inf. constr.* is רַאֲוָה *to see*, Eze. 28. 17 (like אַהֲבָה, comp. § 8. rem. 10, and § 13. rem 2).

3. The *apocope* of the *future* occasions the following changes:—

(*a*) The first radical letter most commonly receives the auxiliary vowel *Segol*, or, when the middle radical is a guttural, *Pattahh*, e.g. יֶגֶל for יִגְל; וַיִּשַׁע *and he looked* (from שָׁעָה), וַיִּמַח *and he destroyed* (from מָחָה).

(*b*) The *Hhirek* of the preformative is also sometimes lengthened into *Tseri* (because it is brought into an open syllable); the two forms, however, are commonly found in one and the same verb, as וַיִּפֶן *and he turned himself*, Ex. 2. 12; but in the 1 & 2 pers. וָאֵפֶן De. 9. 15; וַנֵּפֶן De. 2. 1; תֵּפֶן De. 9. 27; יֶרֶב and וַיֵּרֶב *he was multiplied*, but also וַתֵּרֶב; the latter form occurs in תֵּתַע, וַתֵּתַע Ge. 21. 14; Pr. 7. 25 (from תָּעָה); וַתֵּכַהּ Job 17. 7 (from כָּהָה); וַתֵּלַהּ Ge. 47. 13 (from לָהָה).

(*c*) In both these cases Segol is sometimes omitted, especially when the middle letter is an aspirate, as וַיִּשְׁבְּ *and he took captive*, Nu. 21. 1; וַיִּפְתְּ *and he persuaded*, Job 31. 27; וַיֵּבְךְּ, וַתֵּבְךְּ *and he, she wept*; וְיֵרְדְּ Nu. 24. 19; אַל יֵשְׁטְ Pr. 7. 25 (comp. § 11. r. 6). The verb רָאָה has the two forms, יֵרֶא, תֵּרֶא, וַתֵּרֶא, and with conv. Vav also וַיַּרְא (the latter with Pattahh on account of ר).

(*d*) Examples of verbs which are *Pe guttural* as well as *Lamed He*: וַיַּעַן, וַיַּעַשׂ, and in pause אֶחַז *I see* (from חָזָה), Job 23. 9; וַיָּחַל *and he was sick*, 2 Ki. 1. 2 (from חָלָה). Sometimes, however, the punctuation of the first syllable is not affected by the guttural, as וַיִּחַר *and it was kindled* (from חָרָה), וַיִּחַן *and he encamped*, וַיִּחַד *and he rejoiced*.

(*e*) The verbs הָיָה *to be*, and חָיָה *to live*, which would properly have in the fut. apoc. יִהְי, יִחְי, change these forms into יְהִי and יְחִי (like the derivative פְּרִי for פֶּרְי § 27. V). Another example is תֶּשִׁי. De. 32. 18 (in pause for תְּשִׁי, comp. § 35. r. 14), if directly derived from שָׁיָה. A perfectly Syriac form is יְהוּא Ec. 11. 3, for יִהְיֶה, ap. יְהוּ (from הָוָה *to be*).

4. In the *part. act.* the *fem.* frequently assumes the form of גּוֹלִיָּה, evidently from a masc. גּוֹלִי for גּוֹלִיי* (after the form תּוֹמִיךְ, see § 8. r. 19). E. g. פּוֹרִיָּה *fruitful*, Ps. 128. 3; בּוֹכִיָּה *weeping*, La. 1. 16; צוֹפִיָּה *watching*, Pr. 31. 27; הוֹמִיָּה *making a noise*, Pr. 7. 11; pl. אוֹתִיּוֹת *coming, future things*, Is. 41. 23. (This is not to be confounded with the form גּוֹלִיָּה of rem. 5.)

The *part. pass.* is sometimes without י, as עָשׂוּ for עָשׂוּי (properly for עָשׂוּו, with moveable Vav*) *made*, Job 41. 25; צָפוּ for צָפוּו Job 15. 22; hence the pl. fem. נְטוּוֹת Is. 3. 16; עֲשׂוּוֹת 1 Sa. 25. 18, in the Khethib; in the Keri, however, it is נְטוּיוֹת, עֲשׂוּיוֹת; the form גָּלוֹ, as it appears, was not recognised by the Masorites.

5. The original י* is sometimes retained and usually preceded by (ָ) before the afformatives beginning with a vowel, especially where, for any reason, emphasis rests upon the word, as *in pause*, or *before pause*, and *before Nun parag.* of the future. Pret. חָסָיוּ בוֹ *they take refuge in him*, De. 32. 37; before pause, חָסָיָה Ps. 57. 2; נָטָיוּ Ps. 73. 2; imp. אִם־תִּבְעָיוּן בְּעָיוּ שֻׁבוּ אֵתָיוּ Is. 21. 12; Fut. יִשְׁלָיוּ Job 12. 6; יִרְבָּיֻן

* The verbs ל״ה, like those of פ״י, properly embrace two different classes of the irregular verbs, viz. ל״י and ל״ו, which in Arabic are perfectly distinguished from each other, being actually written with י and ו. But in Hebrew the original י and ו have passed over into a feeble ה, in all those forms which end with the third radical, and which hence appear as verbs ל״ה, as גָּלָה for גָּלַי, שָׁלָה for שָׁלַו (Ges. Gram. § 74).

De. 8. 13; יִרְוְיֻן Ps. 36. 9; in pause, יִשְׁתָּיֻן Ps. 78. 44, יֶחֱסָיֻן Ps. 36. 8; comp. Is. 26. 11; 41. 5; Job 3. 25, with ה parag. אֶהֱמָיָה *I mourn*, Ps. 77. 4. Part. עֹטְיָה *covered*, Ca. 1. 7.

6. A variation from the form תִּגְלֶינָה is תִּרְאֶנָּה Mi. 7. 10, תַּעֲנֶנָּה Ju. 5. 29, the termination of which must not be confounded with the suffix of the same form. Comp. § 21. rem. 13.

7. The ־ִי, ־ֵי of the second syllable is but seldom written *defectively*, e. g. הָיִתָ for הָיִיתָ 2 Sa. 15. 33; בָּנִתִי 1 Ki. 8. 44; תַּעֲשֶׂנָּה Job 5. 12.

II. Niphal.

8. In the *pret.* occurs also the form נִגְלִינוּ (instead of נִגְלֵינוּ) 1 Sa. 14. 8; נִקִּית Ge. 24. 8. In pause is נִטָּיוּ Nu. 24. 6, comp. rem. 5.

9. An anomalous form of the *inf. abs.* is נִגְלוֹת 2 Sa. 6. 20; כְּהִגָּלוֹת נִגְלוֹת אַחַד הָרֵקִים lit. *as uncovering uncovers himself one of the vain fellows;* where the second inf. is to be regarded as pleonastic, and this form is probably chosen to agree in sound with the termination of the preceding הִגָּלוֹת, comp. also rem. 2.

Another inf. abs., with the termination ־ָה (which occurs also in Hiph.), is נֶחְבָּה *to hide oneself*, Je. 49. 10, instead of נֶחְבֹּה.

10. The *apocope* of the *future* occasions here no further changes, e. g. וָאֶפָּת *and I was persuaded*, Je. 20. 7; וַיִּקָּר *and he met*, Nu. 23. 16. There is, however, יִמַּח Ps. 109. 13; וַיִּמַּח Ge. 7. 23, for יִמָּח (from מָחָה).

III. Piel.

11. In the *pret.* the second syllable has *Hhirek* in the greater number of examples, as דִּמִּיתִי, קִוִּיתִי, which is therefore adopted in the paradigm.

12. The *fut. apoc.* loses the Dagesh forte of the second radical, e. g. וַיְצַו *and he commanded; יְקַו let him look for*, Job 3. 9. Hithp. וַיִּתְגַּל *and he uncovered himself*, Ge. 9. 21. In but few instances the vowel is lengthened, as וַיְתָו, *and he made marks*, 1 Sa. 21. 14; יִתְאָו *he desires*, Ps. 45. 12.

The *apocope* occurs also in the *imp.* of Piel and Hithp., as הַס for הַסֵּה *be silent*, Am. 6. 10; הִתְחַל *feign thyself sick*, 2 Sa. 13. 5; with ר as the second radical הִתְגָּר (for הִתְגָּרֵה = ׳גַּרֶּה) De. 2. 24.

13. Examples where the original י has been retained (comp. rem. 5): imp. דַּלְיוּ* prop. *draw off*, i. e. *take away*, Pr. 26. 7. Fut. תְּדַמְּיוּנִי Is. 40. 25; יְכַסְיֻמוּ *they cover them*, Ex. 15. 5; אֲרַיָּוֶךְ by transp. for אֲרַוֶּיךְ *I will water thee*, Is. 16. 9.

IV. Hiphil.

14. In the *pret.* the forms הִגְלִיתָ and הִגְלֵיתָ are about equally common; before suffixes the latter is used as being somewhat shorter than the other.

For the 3 pers. fem. there occurs also the Aramaic form of ־ָת (as in Kal), e. g. הִרְצָת, Le. 26. 34; הֶלְאָת Eze. 24. 12. Hoph. הָגְלָת Je. 13. 19.

15. The Tseri of the *inf. abs.* is the regular vowel (as הַגְלֵה), to this corresponds the inf. abs. of Hoph., as הָפְדֵּה Le. 19. 20 (comp. rem. 20).

The verb רָבָה *to be much* or *many*, has three forms of the infinitive, viz. הַרְבֵּה *much* (used adverbially), הַרְבָּה used when the inf. is pleonastic, and הַרְבּוֹת the inf. constr.

16. The *fut. apoc.* either remains a monosyllabic like יַרְדְּ *that he may have dominion over*, Is. 41. 2; יַפְתְּ *may he enlarge*, Ge. 9. 27, or it takes the helping vowel as in יֶגֶל for which, however, is invariably substituted the form יָגֶל (comp. § 35. No. 1), as וַיֶּגֶל 2 Ki. 18. 11; יֶפֶר *he makes fruitful*, Ps. 105. 24. Examples with gutturals: וַיַּתַע *he made to err*, 2 Ch. 33. 9; אַל תֵּמַח Ne. 13. 14; when the first radical is a guttural, like וַיַּעַל, יַעַל Eze. 14. 7; Nu. 23. 2. The latter forms can be distinguished from the *fut. Kal* only by the context.

17. The *imp. apoc.* has invariably the auxiliary vowel, hence הֶרֶב *increase*, for הַרְבֵּ; הֶרֶף *let alone*, for הַרְפֵּה ,הַרְף De. 9. 14; הַעַל for הַעֲלֵה, Ex. 33. 12.

18. In the Aramaic the *preterite* (as in all conjugations) terminates in ־ִי, the *fut.* in ־ֵי. The form with ־ִי is found also in the Hebrew with the pret. and future. Pret. הֶחֱלִי for הֶחֱלָה *he made sick*,

* This seems the only way of accounting for this form, if derived from דָּלָה. Prof. Lee, who takes it as the *pret. of* Kal, does not sufficiently account for the form; for we should then expect דָּלְיוּ. Gesenius has finally declared himself in favour of the Rabbinic opinion, that דַּלְיוּ stands for דַּלּוּ, comp. his Man. and Thes. under דָּלַל.

Is. 53. 10; pl. הֶמְסִיו *they caused to faint*, Jos. 14. 8 (which is quite Aramaic, comp. רְמִיו Da. 3. 21; הַיְתִיו Da. 5. 3). Fut. וַתִּזְנִי Je. 3. 6; תֶּמְחִי Je. 18. 23, for תִּמְחֶה (masc.).

V. ARAMAISMS.

19. In the same manner as the verbs ל״א have occasionally some forms inflected after the analogy of ל״ה (§ 23. rem. 8—11), so it happens, *vice versâ*, that the latter borrow forms from the former, though not so frequently, according to the following division:—

(*a*) The ה is retained and the punctuation alone of ל״א is adopted, e. g. Kal fut. אֶשְׁעָה *I will have respect to*, for אֶשְׁעֶה, Ps. 119. 117; תִּכְלָה for תִּכְלֶה 1 Ki. 17. 14, comp. Da. 10. 14. Niph. part. יוֹם נַחְלָה, for נַחְלֶה *a grievous day*, Is. 17. 11,* and defective אָתָנוּ *we come*, Je. 3. 22.

(*b*) The א is adopted and the punctuation of ל״ה is retained, e. g. Kal pret. רָצָאתִי *I delight*, Eze. 43. 27; fut. יִשְׁנֶא *it is changed*, La. 4. 1; וַיֶּחֱלֶא *he became sick*, 2 Ch. 16. 12; inf. נְשֹׁא for נְשֹׁה, *to forget*, Je. 23. 39. Piel שִׁנָּא 2 Ki. 25. 29. Pual יְשֻׁנֶּא Ec. 8. 1. Comp. also וַיֹּרְאוּ הַמּוֹרְאִים *and the archers shot*, 2 Sa. 11. 24.

(*c*) The consonant and the vowels of ל״א are adopted, as תְּלָאוּם *they hanged them*, 2 Sa. 21. 12; יַפְרִיא for יַפְרֶה *he is fruitful*, Ho. 13. 15. (But here we may suppose roots תָּלָא and פָּרָא i. q. תָּלָה and פָּרָה, comp. Gesenius' Manuale.)

20. In the Aramaic, where the verbs ל״א and ל״ה flow into one another, both classes terminate, in the fut. and part. of all the conjugations, in the Syriac in ־ֵא, in the Chald. in ־ֵי. As intimations of this mode of formation we are to regard those forms of the inf., imp. and fut. in ־ֵה, less frequently ־ֵא and ־ֵי, which are found in Hebrew also. Inf. הֱיֵה Eze. 21. 15. Imp. הֱוֵא *be thou*, Job 37. 6. Fut. תִּהְיֵה Je. 17. 17; תֹּבֵא for תֹּאבֶה *thou wilt*, Pr. 1. 10; וַיֵּתֵא for וַיֶּאֱתֶה *he came*, De. 33. 21. Piel inf. עַנֵּה Ex. 22. 22; imp. כַּלֵּה 1 Sa. 3. 12; 2 Ch. 24. 10; חַכֵּי Ho. 6. 9; fut. תְּגַלֵּה Le. 18. 7. Hiph. (comp. rem. 15). Hoph. הָפְדֵּה Le. 19. 20.

VI. FORMS WITH SUFFIXES.

21. The annexing of the suffixes to the verbs ל״ה occasions various changes, viz.:—

(*a*) In all the forms which end in ה, the ה is dropped with the preceding vowel. E. g. עָנָנִי *he answered me*, Ps. 118. 5; צִוְּךָ *he has commanded thee*, De. 6. 17;† קָנֶךָ *he has bought thee*, De. 32. 6; fut. יַעַנְךָ Ps. 20. 2. Piel אֲכַלְּךָ for אֲכַלֶּךָ *I consume thee*, Ex. 33. 3 (comp. Chald. מַנִּי for מַנִּי Ezr. 7. 25). Hiph. הֶעֶלְךָ Ne. 9. 18; seldom fut. like יַחְתְּךָ *he shall take thee away*, Ps. 52. 7.

(*b*) Very seldom does ־ֵי take the place of ־ָה, ־ֶה, as חַיֵּיהוּ *revive it*, Hab. 3. 2; יְחַיֵּנוּ Ho. 6. 2; הַכֵּינִי *smite me*, 1 Ki. 20. 35; אַפְאֵיהֶם (Hiph. fut. from פָּאָה) De. 32. 26, perhaps also נוֹטֵיהֶם Is. 42. 5, in reference to Jehovah, which may be regarded as a plural.

(*c*) The *pret.* 3 pers. sing. fem. takes invariably the form גָּלַת. E. g. עָשָׂתְנִי Job 33. 4; רָאָתְךָ Job 42. 5; כִּסָּתְנִי Ps. 44. 16; כִּלַּתּוּ for כִּלָּתְהוּ Zec. 5. 4; צִוָּתָה Ru. 3. 6; הֶעֱלָתַם Jos. 2. 6.

VII. PILEL (comp. § 6. No. 2).

22. This conjugation with its reflexion occurs in three verbs ל״ה, where the third radical, which the conjugation requires to be doubled, appears under the form וה, as

נָאָה (*to be comely*) in Kal not used, Pil. נַאֲוָה, contracted נָאוָה, pl. נָאווּ Ca. 1. 5; 2. 14. Deriv. adj. נָאוֶה.

טָחָה, in Kal not used, Pil. part. מְטַחֲוֵי קֶשֶׁת *archers*, Ge. 21. 16.

שָׁחָה *to bow down* (usual in Kal and Hiph.), Pil. שַׁחֲוָה, hence Hithpal. הִשְׁתַּחֲוָה (comp. § 9 & 12. rem. 3), fut. יִשְׁתַּחֲוֶה, apoc. יִשְׁתַּחוּ for יִשְׁתַּחֲו (analogous with יְהִי for יִהְיֶ). Inf. Chald. הִשְׁתַּחֲוָיָה 2 Ki. 5. 18.

* Unless we prefer to take נַחְלָה (with Gesenius, comp. his Manuale) as a substantive, and render *day of possession*, i. e. day of harvest.

† The form ־ָךְ for the masc. *thy*, which is seldom found with other verbs (§ 2. rem. 2), is here somewhat more usual, e. g. עָנָךְ Is. 30. 19; Je. 23. 37.

SECTION XXV.—VERBS DOUBLY ANOMALOUS.

1. Such is the designation of verbs which have two radical letters affected by the anomalies which are exhibited in the paradigms of irregular verbs. These verbs exhibit no new changes; and even in cases where two anomalies might occur, usage must teach whether the verb is actually subject to both or but one of them, or, as it sometimes happens, to neither.

Thus from נָדַד (*to flee*) are formed יִדֹּד Na. 3. 7; יִדַּד Ge. 31. 40 (after the analogy of verb פ״ן); Hiph. הֵנֵד (after ע״ע); Hoph. הֻנַּד, but fut. יֻדַּד (after פ״ן).

Thus the verbs פ״ן and ע״ו, as נוּעַ, נוּד, are irregular only in respect to the middle radical letter, not in respect to the Nun.

2. The following are examples of doubly anomalous verbs, and of difficult forms derived from them:—

(*a*) Verbs פ״ן and ל״א, as

נָשָׂא (*to bear, carry*) Kal imp. שָׂא; inf. constr. שְׂאֵת (for שֶׂאֶת), also שְׂאֵת, with suff. שְׂאֵתִי; fut. יִשָּׂא, תִּשֶּׂנָה (for תִּשֶּׂאנָה) Ru. 1. 14.

נָשָׁא (*to deceive*) Hiph. fut. יַשִּׁי (for יַשִּׁיא) Ps. 55. 16 Keri.

(*b*) Verbs פ״ן and ל״ה:

נָטָה (*to bow, incline*) Kal fut. יִטֶּה, apoc. יֵט Zep. 2. 12; fem. תֵּט Ps. 4. 5, 27; Hiph. imp. הַטֵּה, apoc. הַט Ps. 17. 6; fut. יַטֶּה, apoc. וַיַּט 2 Sa. 19. 15; 1 pers. אַט Job 23. 11; וָאַט Je. 15. 6; 2 pers. אַל תַּט Ps. 27. 9; with suff. יַטְּךָ.

נָכָה (*to smite*) Hiph. הִכָּה; inf. הַכּוֹת; imp. הַכֵּה, apoc. הַךְ Ex. 8. 12; fut. יַכֶּה, apoc. יַךְ Ho. 14. 6; 1 pers. וָאַךְ Ex. 9. 15, with suff. יַכּוּ 2 Sa. 14. 6; יַכֶּכָּה Ps. 121. 6.

נָזָה (*to sprinkle*) Kal fut. apoc. יֵז Is. 63. 3; וַיֵּז 2 Ki. 9. 33. Hiph. fut. apoc. וַיַּז Le. 8. 11, 30.

(*c*) Verbs פ״א and ל״ה, as

אָתָה (*to come*) Kal pret. אָתָנוּ Je. 3. 22; imp. אֵתָיו (for אֱתָיו ,אֱתוּ, § 19. rem. 6, & § 24. rem. 5) Is. 21. 12; 56. 9; fut. וַיֵּתֵא (for וַיֶּאֱתֶה, § 19. rem. 3) De. 33. 21; apoc. וַיֵּאת (for וַיֶּאֱתֶה ,וַיֵּאַת, § 19. rem. 3). Hiph. imp. הֵתָיוּ (for הַאֲתָיוּ, § 19. rem. 8) Is. 21. 14.

אָלָה (*to swear*) Hiph. fut. ap. וַיֹּאֶל (from יֹאלֶה, § 24. rem. 3) 1 Sa. 14. 24.

אָפָה (*to bake*) Kal imp. אֵפוּ (for אֱפוּ § 19. rem. 6) Ex. 16. 23; וַתֹּפֵהוּ (for וַתֹּאפֵהוּ § 19. r. 5) 1 Sa. 28. 24.

(*d*) Verbs פ״י and ל״א, as

יָצָא (*to go out*) Kal inf. צֵאת (for צֶאֶת, comp. § 23. rem. 4); imp. צֵא, Hiph. הוֹצִיא.

(*e*) Verbs פ״י and ל״ה:

יָדָה (*to throw*, Hiph. *to confess*) Piel fut. וַיַּדּוּ (for וַיְיַדּוּ § 20. rem. 8) La. 3. 53. Hiph. fut. יוֹדֶה, with suff. אוֹדְךָ Ps. 35. 18; אוֹדֶךָּ Ps. 30. 13, and ה retained יְהוֹדוּךָ (§ 20. rem. 10).

יָנָה (*to oppress*) Kal fut. with suff. נִינָם Ps. 74. 8. Hiph. הוֹנָה fut. with suff. תּוֹנֶנּוּ De. 23. 17; part. מוֹנַיִךְ Is. 49. 26.

יָפָה (*to be fair*) Kal fut. apoc. וַיִּיף (fr. וַיִּיפֶה) Eze. 31. 7. Unusual conj. Pu. יָפְיָפִיתָ Ps. 45. 3, see § 6. No. 9.

יָרָה (*to throw*, Hiph. *to show, instruct*) Kal imp. יְרוּ; inf. יָרֹה, יְרוֹת; fut. with suff. נִירָם Nu. 21. 30. Hiph. הוֹרָה; inf. הוֹרוֹת; fut. יוֹרֶה, apoc. וַיּוֹר 2 Ki. 13. 17, with suff. תּוֹרְךָ Ps. 45. 5; Job 12. 7, 8; יוֹרֶנּוּ Ps. 25. 12.

(*f*) Verbs ע״ו and ל״א, as

בּוֹא (*to come*) Kal pret. בָּא, pl. בָּאנוּ 1 Sa. 25. 8; inf. בּוֹא; fut. יָבוֹא, once וַיָּבוֹ 1 Ki. 12. 12 Kheth. Hiph. הֵבִיא, 2 pers. הֵבֵאתָ; fut. יָבִיא, 1 pers. אָבִי for אָבִיא 1 Ki. 21. 29; Mi. 1. 15; imp. הָבִיא once הָבִי Ru. 3. 15.

נוּא Hiph. הֵנִיא (*to withhold, refuse*) fut. יָנִי for יָנִיא Ps. 141. 5.

(*g*) One verb ע״ע and ע״י is

חָיָה=חָיַי (*to live*) only in the pret. חַי, in such connection where it cannot be the adj. חַי (*living*), e. g. Ge. 5. 5; 11. 12, 14; 25. 7.

REM. A few other anomalies must be mentioned here, which are occasioned by the verbs ל״ן and ל״ת, of which ן and ת are assimilated with the afformatives. Such are: לַנּוּ Ju. 19. 13, for לַנְנוּ (from לוּן); from מוּת (*to die*) מַתָּה, מַתִּי *thou diest, I die*, Eze. 28. 8, for מַתְתָּה, מַתְתִּי Ge. 19. 19. Pil. מוֹתַתִּי *I put to death*, 2 Sa. 1. 16. Hiph. הֵמַתָּה, הֵמַתִּי *thou puttest, he put, to death*, with suff. הֲמִיתִיו 1 Sa. 17. 35, with the *mater lexionis* in Kheth., for הֲמִתִּיו Keri.

Finally, the anomaly of the verb ל״ד, viz. יָלַד, inf. לֶדֶת, contracted לַת 1 Sa. 4. 19.

SECTION XXVI.—NOUNS DERIVED FROM THE REGULAR VERB.

We distinguish here—

I. *Forms originally Participles, and Participial Nouns, from Kal.*

1. קָטָל, *fem.* קְטָלָה the most simple participial form of verbs *middle A* (comp. § 8. r. 1); in use as a participle only in verbs ע״ו (e. g. קָם for קָוֵם). It is most frequently employed as an adjective expressing *quality*, as חָכָם *wise*, חָדָשׁ *new*, יָקָר *precious*, יָשָׁר *straight*, נָבָל *foolish*. It occurs, however, also as an infinitive form (No. 12).

2. קָטֵל, *fem.* קְטֵלָה, seldom קְטֶלֶת. Part. of verbs *middle E* (§ 8. r. 1), is likewise the form of adjectives of quality, e. g. זָקֵן *old*, *old man*, יָבֵשׁ *dry*. The Tseri is sometimes *immutable*, and the form is then related to No. 5, e. g. אָבֵל *mourning* (in other dialects אביל), *fem.* גְּזֵלָה *that which is plundered.*

3. קָטֹל and קָטוֹל (with Hholem *immutable*), *fem.* קְטֹלָה, Part. of verbs *middle O;* e. g. יָגֹר *fearing*, יָקֹשׁ *fowler;* then frequently as an adjective, even when no preterite with Hholem is found, as גָּדוֹל *great*, רָחוֹק *far*, עָשֹׁק=עָשׁוֹק *oppressor* (comp. No. 21).

4. קוֹטֵל ,קֹטֵל, *fem.* קֹטְלָה ,קֹטֶלֶת, the usual participial form of transitive verbs; e. g. אֹיֵב *enemy*, יוֹנֵק *suckling*, hence of the instrument by which the action is performed, as חֹרֵשׁ *a cutting instrument, a tool.* A feminine with collective signification is אֹרְחָה *caravan.*

5. קָטוּל and קָטִיל passive participles of Kal, the latter (Chaldaizing) form employed rather as a substantive, like the Greek verbals in τός, e. g. אָסוּר *imprisoned*, מָשׁוּחַ *anointed*, אָסִיר *prisoner*, מָשִׁיחַ *one anointed.*

In intransitive verbs, also with an active signification, as צָעִיר *small*, עָצוּם *strong*. Some words of this form indicate the *time* of the action, as קָצִיר *time of harvest*, חָרִישׁ *time of ploughing*. The feminines and the plurals are apt to take the abstract signification, as יְשׁוּעָה *deliverance* (*the being delivered*), חֲנֻטִים *the act of embalming.*

6. קַטָּל (Arab. קַטָּאל) with Kamets *immutable* in the Arabic, the usual intensive form of the participle, hence in the Hebrew expresses what is habitual, e. g. נַגָּח *apt to butt*, חַטָּא *sinner* (different from חֹטֵא *sinning*), גַּנָּב *thief;* so of occupation, trades, e. g. טַבָּח *cook*, חָרָשׁ (for חַרָּשׁ) *smith*. Here, again, the feminine often takes the abstract signification, as חַטָּאת for חַטָּאַת) *sinfulness, sin.* Such intensive forms are also the three following.

7. קַטִּיל and קַטּוּל, of which forms are most adjectives in the Chaldee, צַדִּיק *righteous*, אַבִּיר *strong*, חַנּוּן *compassionate.* In Hebrew from intransitive verbs alone.

8. קַטּוֹל, as יִסּוֹר *censurer*, שִׁכּוֹר *one drunken*, גִּבּוֹר *strong one, hero;* rarely in a passive sense, יִלּוֹד *born*, אִיּוֹב proper name (*persecuted*).

9. קִטֵּל indicates very great intensity, often excessive, so as to become a fault and a defect; e. g. קֵרֵחַ, *bald-headed*, אִלֵּם *dumb*, עִוֵּר *blind*, פִּסֵּחַ *lame*, חֵרֵשׁ *deaf.* The abstract signification is found in the feminine, as עִוֶּרֶת *blindness.*

II. *Forms which were originally infinitives of Kal.**

10. קְטַל ,קְטֹל ,קְטֵל (with *mutable* vowels) the simplest forms of the infinitive, of which the first and last are employed in the verb (§ 8. rem. 9). They seldom occur as nominal forms, e. g. גְּבַר *man*, פְּאֵר *ornament*, צְחֹק *laughter*. Instead of these, the three following—

11. קֶטֶל ,קֵטֶל ,קֹטֶל, called Segolate forms, are the more frequent; e. g. מֶלֶךְ *king* (for מַלְךְ , מַלֶךְ), סֵפֶר (for סִפְר) *book*, קֹדֶשׁ (for קֹדְשׁ) *holiness*. These have the characteristic vowel in the first syllable, and the auxiliary vowel Segol in the second. When the second or third radical letter is a guttural, *Pattahh* is used instead of *Segol*, as זֶרַע *seed*, נֵצַח *eternity*, פֹּעַל *work*. Examples of feminines: מַלְכָּה *queen*, יִרְאָה *fear*, עֶזְרָה *help*, חָכְמָה *wisdom.*

In masculines as well as feminines the *abstract* is the prevailing signification, and is the original one even in cases where the *concrete* occurs; e. g. מֶלֶךְ and מַלְכָּה prop. *royalty;*† נַעַר *a youth* (prop. *the season of youth*, comp. in Eng. *youth* and *a youth*); בַּעַר *brutish* (prop. *brutishness*). For the abstract in such cases another form is employed, as מַלְכוּת *royalty*, נֹעַר *youth.*

* All these forms are found, *mutatis mutandis*, in the Arabic as infinitives, or the so called *nomina actionis.*

† As there is a tendency to employ abstract terms for names of offices, e. g. פֶּחָה *governor* (prop. *office of governor*, comp. the English *lordship*).

12. קָטָל, like No. 1, and קְטַל, *fem.* קְטָלָה, often from verbs *middle E*, with the abstract signification, e. g. רָעָב *hunger*, אָשָׁם *guilt*, along with the concretes of the form No. 2 (רָעֵב *hungry*, אָשֵׁם *guilty*), very frequent in the feminine, as צְדָקָה *righteousness*.

13. קָטָל (for קְטָאל), קְטֵל, (for קְטֵיל), קְטִיל, קְטוֹל, קְטוּל, with an *immutable* vowel between the second and third radical, as כְּתָב *book*, כְּאֵב *pain*, שְׁבִיל *way*, חֲלוֹם *dream*, זְבוּל *habitation;* sometimes also with prosthetic Aleph as אַכְזָב (prop. *deception*), *deceitful stream*, i. e. whose waters fail in the summer; אֶפְרֹחַ *brood*. The corresponding feminines will suggest themselves; but the forms קְטִילָה, קְטוּלָה coincide with the feminines of No. 5.

14. מִקְטָל, the Chaldee form of the infinitive, e. g. מִשְׁפָּט *judgment*. Related forms are מִזְמוֹר *song*, מַחְמָד *desire*, מַלְקוֹחַ *booty*, מַמְלָכָה *kingdom*, מַשְׂכֹּרֶת *wages*. This form indicates, not only the action itself, but also often the place of the action, as מִזְבֵּחַ *altar*, מִדְבָּר *a place of driving*, i. e. to which cattle are driven, whence *a desert*.

15. קִטְלוֹן, קִטְלָן, and other similar forms with the terminations וֹן & ָן, which are generally appended to the Segolates, as חֶשְׁבּוֹן *reckoning* (from חֵשֶׁב), קָרְבָּן *offering* (immediately from קֶרֶב); but there are also forms like זִכָּרוֹן *remembrance*.

16. With the feminine termination וּת appended to the Segolate form, e. g. רִפְאוּת *healing*. In the Syriac this is the usual termination of the infinitive. The ת is properly the sign of the feminine, and the masculine form would be רִפְאוּ (like עִבְרִי, עִבְרִית).

III. *Participles of the derived conjugations.*

17. From Niph. נִקְטָל, as נִפְלָאוֹת *wonders*.

18. 19. From *Piel* and *Hiph.*; e. g. מְזַמֶּרֶת *snuffers*, מַזְמֵרָה *pruning-knife*.

20. From *Poel*, as חוֹתָם, *signet-ring*, prop. *that which seals*.

21. From *Pil.* קְטֹל, *fem.* קְטָלָה; and 22. קְטַלָל for the most part adjectives of colour, as אָדֹם *fem.* אֲדֻמָּה *red*, רַעֲנָן *green*.

23. קְטַלְטַל, קְטַלְטֹל, adjectives with a *diminutive* signification, as אֲדַמְדָּם *reddish*, שְׁחַרְחֹר *blackish;* hence in a contemptuous sense (like *miser*, *misellus*), as אֲסַפְסֻף *collected rabble* (with the passive form, for אָסוּף).

IV. *Infinitives of the derived conjugations.*

24. From *Niph.*, as נַפְתּוּלִים *struggles*.

25. From *Piel*, like נַפֵּץ *dispersion*, more frequently in the fem., as בַּקָּשָׁה *request*, with Kamets *immutable*.

26. קִטּוּל, and 27. תַּקְטוּל, תַּקְטִיל, likewise infinitives of *Piel* (the latter very common in the Arabic); e. g. חִבּוּק *folding of the hands*, תַּגְמוּל *benefit*, תַּכְרִיךְ *mantle*.

28. From *Hiph.*, like אַזְכָּרָה *remembrance-offering*, הַשְׁמָעוּת *annunciation* (with Kamets *immutable*), an Aramaic infinitive.

29. From *Hithpa.* הִתְיַחֵשׂ *register*.

30. From *Poel*, like הוֹלֵלָה *folly*, and 31. like קִיטוֹר *smoke*, the latter form common in Arabic.

32. From *Pil.*, אֲפֻדָּה *a putting on*, and 33, נַאֲפוּף *adultery*.

34. פְּקַחְקוֹחַ *opening*, inf. of No. 23.

35. שַׁקְטֵל, e. g. שַׁלְהֶבֶת *flame* (comp. § 7. No. 6).

36. Quadriliterals, like סָלְעָם *locust*.

SECTION XXVII.—NOUNS DERIVED FROM THE IRREGULAR VERBS.

The formation of these is perfectly analagous to that of the regular verb, and whatever is differently modified is caused merely by the peculiar structure of these verbs. We shall therefore follow the preceding order, and exhibit such verbs and forms only in which the irregularity has been of some important influence.

I. From Verbs פ״ן.

Connected with the *infinitive* of *Kal*, 14. מַתָּן *gift*, מַגֵּפָה *overthrow;* of Hiph. 28. הַצָּלָה *deliverance*. The noun מַדָּע *knowledge* from יָדַע; comp. § 20. 16.

II. From Verbs ע״ע.

From the *part.* of *Kal*—1. תָּם *upright* (like קָטָל) more frequently with *Pattahh* (to indicate the sharpening of the syllable), דַּל *abject*, רַב *much*, fem. דַּלָּה, תַּמָּה. 2. מֵחַ *fat*. From the inf. 10. 11. בַּז *booty*, חֵן *favour*, חֹק *law*, fem. מִלָּה *word*, חֻקָּה *law*. 14. מָעֹז *fastness*, מֵסַב *that which surrounds anything*, fem.

מְגִלָּה *roll.* The form מֵסַב sometimes, by retraction of the tone, becomes a Segolate form, as מֶמֶר *bitterness,* מֹרֶךְ *timidity* (from רָכַךְ). 22. קְלֹקֵל *contemned,* עֲרוֹעֵר *naked* (a collateral form of Pilpel). 27. תְּהִלָּה *praise,* תְּפִלָּה *prayer,* with the Segolate form also תֶּמֶס *a melting away* (from מָסַס), תֹּרֶן *mast* (from רָנַן *to shout*). From the unfrequent conjugation Pilpel (§ 6. No. 4), גַּלְגַּל *wheel,* from גָּלַל *to roll.*

III. From Verbs פ״ו and פ״י.

The *participial* forms are regular. Forms originally *infinitives* are—10. דֵּעַ, fem. דֵּעָה, דַּעַת *knowledge,* עֵצָה *counsel.* 13. סוֹד for יְסוֹד *divan.* 14. מוֹרָא *fear,* מוֹקֵשׁ *snare,* מוֹלֶדֶת *birth,* מוּסָר *punishment;* and from a verb properly פ״י, מֵיטָב *the best.* 27. תּוֹשָׁב *inhabitant,* תּוֹלֶדֶת *generation,* תֵּימָן *the south.*

IV. From Verbs ע״ו and ע״י.

Participles: 1. זָר *foreign.* 2. גֵּר *stranger,* עֵדָה *a witness, testimony.* 3. טוֹב *good,* טוֹבָה *what is good.* *Infinitives:* 11. the different Segolate forms, as מָוֶת *death,* and בַּיִת *house,* קוֹל *voice,* רוּחַ *spirit,* and in the *fem.* בֹּשֶׁת, עַוְלָה. 14. מָנוֹחַ, *fem.* מְנוּחָה *rest,* מָקוֹם *place,* also מִשׁוֹט *oar* (from שׁוּט). 27. תְּבוּנָה *intelligence,* תְּעוּדָה *testimony,* תָּמִיד *continuance.* 28. הֲנָחָה *rest.*

Rem. A ו in one of these nouns is not sufficient warrant to limit its derivation to ע״ו, nor is י sufficient to limit it to ע״י, since each of these classes sometimes borrow forms from the other, e. g. תְּבוּנָה from בִּין.

V. From Verbs ל״ה.

Participles: 2. יָפֶה *fair,* קָשֶׁה *hard, fem.* יָפָה, קָשָׁה. Some lose ֶה, as תָּו *sign,* for תָּוֶה. 4. רֹאֶה *seer, fem.* עוֹלָה *burnt-offering.* 5. כָּסוּי *covering,* נָקִי *pure,* עָנִי *poor.* Originally *infinitives:* 11. the Segolates in different forms, not often with ה retained, as בֶּכֶה *a weeping,* רֵעֶה *friend,* חָזֶה, רֹאֶה *vision, revelation,* commonly without it, as רֵעַ (for רֵעֶה), or with the original י or ו, which then becomes quiescent in Hhirek (comp. on יְהִי § 24. rem. 3), e. g. פְּרִי *fruit,* חֳלִי *sickness,* בֹּהוּ *waste,* and in the masc. seldom *moveable,* as קֵצֶו *end,* but always in the fem. עֲנָוָה *humility,* לִוְיָה *garland.* 13. סְתָו *winter,* שְׁתִי fem. שְׁתִיָּה *a drinking,* fem. מְנָת (for מְנָאָת, מְנָאַת) *part,* חֲצוֹת *the midst,* שְׁבוּת *captivity.* 14. מִקְנֶה *possessions,* מַרְאֶה *appearance; fem.* מִצְוָה *command.* Apocopated form מַעַל for מַעֲלֶה. 15. קִנְיָן *wealth,* כִּלָּיוֹן *destruction.* 27. תַּבְנִית *structure,* תַּרְבּוּת *brood,* also perh. תֶּבֶן (for תִּבְנֶה) *straw.* 28. אֶשֶׁךְ *testicle,* for אַשְׁכֶּה from שָׁכָה.

VI. From Doubly Anomalous Verbs.

We exhibit only some cases of special difficulty:—

1. From פ״ן and ל״א, שֵׂת for שְׂאֵת, from נָשָׂא.
2. From פ״י and ל״ה, תּוֹרָה *precept, law,* מוֹפֵת *sign,* perh. from יָפָה; but see the analysis.
3. From ע״א and ל״ה, שֵׁת, Nu. 24. 17, from שָׁאָה for שְׁאֵת.
4. From ע״ו and ל״ה, אִי *island,* from אָוָה *to dwell,* for אֱוִי; אוֹת *sign,* for אֹוֶת from אָוָה; קָו *cord,* from קָוָה, תָּא *chamber,* for תָּו from תָּוָה *to dwell,* גּוֹי *people,* from גָּוָה.

The root is also often obscured by contraction of Nun, Daleth, He, e. g. גַּת *wine-press,* for גֶּנֶת, יֶגֶנֶת (from יָגַן); אַף *anger,* for אֶנֶף; אֵת *coulter,* for אֶדֶת; זִו for זִהְיו (from זָהָה) *brightness.*

SECTION XXVIII.—THE VOWEL-CHANGES OF NOUNS.*

1. The consideration of the *cases* of the noun does not belong to this part of Hebrew Grammar,† but to the syntax, because the cases do not at all affect the inflexion of the noun, as they are merely indicated by prepositions without any change of the *form* of the word itself. On the contrary, the connection of the noun with suffixes—with the feminine, dual and plural terminations—or with a noun following in the genitive, produces numerous changes in its form, and thus originates another species of declension. The theory of this peculiar, but important, system of inflexion can be displayed conspicuously only by a full exhibition of paradigms, inasmuch as the term declension is used in Hebrew Grammar, with a meaning differing considerably from that it bears in the Grammar of the Greek and Latin languages.‡

* The adjective entirely agrees in form with the substantive, so that in treating of the declension of nouns, adjectives are included.

† This work having especially the etymology of words alone for its object.

‡ In these latter, the term *declension* (*κλίσις*) properly denotes the variation of the ground-form by cases (*casus, πτώσεις*). We may, however, be permitted to retain the term *declension,* though it does not properly express the mode of inflexion of Hebrew nouns, just as the term *conjugation* is employed, though not in its ordinary sense (Gesen. Gram. 78. 2).

These vowel-changes are caused (*a*) by a noun following in the genitive; (*b*) by the suffixes; (*c*) by the dual and plural terminations; to which is added, again, the effect of a genitive following, or suffix.

2. The tone in all these cases is moved forward more or less, or even thrown upon the following word. We here distinguish three cases, viz.:—

(*a*) *When the tone is moved forward only one place.* This is the case when the appendage to the noun is either monosyllabic, or at least has the tone on the penultima, and likewise begins with a vowel. Such are (1) the terminations for the plural and dual (ִ־ים; ַ־יִם; וֹת); (2) the light suffixes for the singular nouns (ִ־י; ְ־ךָ; ֵ־ךְ; וֹ, ֵ־הוּ; ָ־הּ, ֶ־הָ; ֵ־נוּ; ָ־ם, ָ־מוֹ); (3) the light suffixes for the plural nouns (ַ־י; ֶ־יךָ, ַ־יִךְ; ָ־יו, ֵ־יהוּ, ֶ־יהָ; ֵ־ינוּ; ֵ־ימוֹ). In this case, generally, only one of two mutable vowels in the noun is dropped, e. g. from דָּבָר—דְּבָרִים, דְּבָרִי, דְּבָרַי; in a few forms the second only is dropped, e. g. אֹיֵב—אֹיְבִים, or the ground-form of the word, which, in the leading form, has undergone some change, appears again, as from מֶלֶךְ (for מַלְךְ)—מַלְכִּי.

(*b*) *When the tone is moved forward two places*, as in the plural *constr. st.*, and when the *grave* suffixes are appended to the plural (ֵ־יכֶם, ֵ־יהֶם ֵ־יכֶן, ֵ־יהֶן). In this case both vowels, if mutable, are dropped, as דִּבְרֵי הָעָם *words of the people*; דִּבְרֵיכֶם *your words*, דִּבְרֵיהֶם *their words*.

(*c*) When the suffix begins with a consonant without a union-vowel, and forms a syllable by itself, as the suffixes of the singular, as ךָ, כֶם, כֶן, הֶם, הֶן, הֵן (more commonly ָ־ם, ָ־ן). Of these the first is a light suffix, and regularly affects the tone in just the same manner, as ִ־י, וֹ, e. g. דְּבָרְךָ, דָּמְךָ, זְקֵנְךָ. The others are grave suffixes, and have more effect in shortening the vowels, as דִּבְרְכֶם, &c. A similar effect is seen in the *constr. st.* of the singular number, as דְּבַר אֱלֹהִים; חֲצַר הַבַּיִת (from חָצֵר).

The application of these three cases to the different forms of the masculine noun is exhibited in the nine paradigms of the *Masculines* given below, to which also the necessary explanations are subjoined. For the sake of brevity, we will use the terms *first*, *second*, *third*, &c. *declension*.

3. In the formation of the Feminine from the Masculine, by appending the termination ָ־ה, the same change of vowels is introduced as in No. 2 (*a*), since the tone is moved forward in the very same proportion as shown there. The vowel-change is somewhat different when the second feminine termination ֶ־ת is appended. Both will be shown in § 39.

SECTION XXIX.—ON THE DECLENSION OF THE MASCULINE NOUNS IN GENERAL.

1. The following paradigms exhibit—of each noun —the *absolute* and *construct state* in the sing., plur., and dual, and the singular and plural forms with *light* and *grave* suffixes. To render this subject easier, it should be noticed that:

(*a*) The shortening of the vowels is the same in the dual and the plural, except in the sixth declension, where the dual is more shortened than the plural, e. g. pl. מְלָכִים, but du. רַגְלַיִם.

(*b*) In the plural, *light suffixes* are, without exception, attached to the *absolute*, and *grave suffixes* to the *constr. state*, e. g. דְּבָרִים, דְּבָרַי; דִּבְרֵי, דִּבְרֵיכֶם.

2. According to the nine paradigms of the masculines alluded to, are also declined those feminine and common nouns which are without a distinctive feminine termination, e. g. אֶבֶן *stone*, חֶרֶב *sword;* except that in most cases they take in the plural the ending וֹת, which remains unchanged in the constr. st. and before suffixes.

3. The changes of the vowels generally affect the two last syllables, and in a very few instances only the third from the end is affected (comp. § 31. r. 3). Changes of consonants occur in the ninth declension alone.

TABLE O. DECLENSION OF MASCULINE NOUNS.

	I. a.	I. b.	II. a.	II. b.	III. a.	III. b.	III. c.	IV. a.	IV. b.	IV. c.	IV. d.	V. a.	V. b.	V. c.
Sing. *absol.*	סוּס (horse)	גִּבּוֹר (hero)	דָּם (blood)	עוֹלָם (eternity)	פָּקִיד (overseer)	מֵלִיץ (interpreter)	זִכָּרוֹן (remembrance)	דָּבָר (word)	לֵבָב (heart)	חָכָם (wise)	שֵׂעָר (hair)	זָקֵן (old)	כָּתֵף (shoulder)	חָצֵר (court)
constr.	סוּס	גִּבּוֹר	דַּם	עוֹלַם	פְּקִיד	מֵלִיץ	זִכְרוֹן	דְּבַר	לְבַב	חֲכַם	שְׂעַר	זְקַן	כֶּתֶף	חֲצַר
light suff.	סוּסִי	גִּבּוֹרִי	דָּמִי	עוֹלָמִי	פְּקִידִי	מְלִיצִי	זִכְרוֹנִי	דְּבָרִי	לְבָבִי	חֲכָמִי	שְׂעָרִי	זְקֵנִי		חֲצֵרִי
grave suff.	סוּסְכֶם	גִּבּוֹרְכֶם	דִּמְכֶם	עוֹלַמְכֶם	פְּקִידְכֶם	מְלִיצְכֶם	זִכְרוֹנְכֶם	דְּבַרְכֶם	לְבַבְכֶם	חֲכַמְכֶם	שְׂעַרְכֶם	זְקַנְכֶם		חֲצַרְכֶם
Plur. *absol.*	סוּסִים	גִּבּוֹרִים	דָּמִים	עוֹלָמִים	פְּקִידִים	מְלִיצִים	זִכְרוֹנִים	דְּבָרִים	לְבָבִים	חֲכָמִים	שְׂעָרִים	זְקֵנִים		חֲצֵרִים
constr.	סוּסֵי	גִּבּוֹרֵי	דְּמֵי	עוֹלְמֵי	פְּקִידֵי	מְלִיצֵי	זִכְרוֹנֵי	דִּבְרֵי	לִבְבֵי	חַכְמֵי	שַׂעֲרֵי	זִקְנֵי		חַצְרֵי
light suff.	סוּסַי	גִּבּוֹרַי	דָּמַי	עוֹלָמַי	פְּקִידַי	מְלִיצַי	זִכְרוֹנַי	דְּבָרַי	לְבָבַי	חֲכָמַי	שְׂעָרַי	זְקֵנַי		חֲצֵרַי
grave suff.	סוּסֵיכֶם	גִּבּוֹרֵיכֶם	דְּמֵיכֶם	עוֹלְמֵיכֶם	פְּקִידֵיכֶם	מְלִיצֵיכֶם	זִכְרוֹנֵיכֶם	דִּבְרֵיכֶם	לִבְבֵיכֶם	חַכְמֵיכֶם	שַׂעֲרֵיכֶם	זִקְנֵיכֶם		חַצְרֵיכֶם
Dual *absol.*	יוֹמַיִם (two days)	רִבּוֹתַיִם (two myriads)	יָדַיִם (hands)	מֶלְקָחַיִם (pair of tongs)	שְׁבֻעַיִם (two weeks)			כְּנָפַיִם (wings)		חֲלָצַיִם (hips)		יְרֵכַיִם (loins)		עֲקֵבַיִם (heels)
constr.			יְדֵי					כַּנְפֵי		חַלְצֵי				עִקְבֵי

VI.

	a.	a.	b.	c.	d.	e.	f.	g.	h.	i.	k.
Sing. *absol.*	מֶלֶךְ (king)	קֶבֶר (grave)	סֵפֶר (book)	קֹדֶשׁ (sanctuary)	נַעַר (a youth)	נֵצַח (perpetuity)	פֹּעַל (work)	מָוֶת (death)	זַיִת (olive)	פְּרִי (fruit)	חֳלִי (sickness)
constr.	מֶלֶךְ	קֶבֶר	סֵפֶר	קֹדֶשׁ	נַעַר	נֵצַח	פֹּעַל	מוֹת	זֵית	פְּרִי	חֳלִי
light suff.	מַלְכִּי	קִבְרִי	סִפְרִי	קָדְשִׁי	נַעֲרִי	נִצְחִי	פָּעֳלִי	מוֹתִי	זֵיתִי	פִּרְיִי	חָלְיִי
grave suff.	מַלְכְּכֶם	קִבְרְכֶם	סִפְרְכֶם	קָדְשְׁכֶם	נַעַרְכֶם	נִצְחֲכֶם	פָּעָלְכֶם	מוֹתְכֶם	זֵיתְכֶם	פֶּרְיְכֶם	חָלְיְכֶם
Plur. *absol.*	מְלָכִים	קְבָרִים	סְפָרִים	קֳדָשִׁים	נְעָרִים	נְצָחִים	פְּעָלִים	מוֹתִים	זֵיתִים	צְבָיִים (gazelles)	חֳלָיִים
constr.	מַלְכֵי	קִבְרֵי	סִפְרֵי	קָדְשֵׁי	נַעֲרֵי	נִצְחֵי	פָּעֳלֵי	מוֹתֵי	זֵיתֵי		חָלְיֵי
light suff.	מְלָכַי	קְבָרַי	סְפָרַי	קֳדָשַׁי	נְעָרַי	נְצָחַי	פְּעָלַי	מוֹתַי	זֵיתַי		חֳלָיַי
grave suff.	מַלְכֵיכֶם	קִבְרֵיכֶם	סִפְרֵיכֶם	קָדְשֵׁיכֶם	נַעֲרֵיכֶם	נִצְחֵיכֶם	פָּעֳלֵיכֶם	מוֹתֵיכֶם	זֵיתֵיכֶם		חָלְיֵיכֶם
Dual *absol.*	רַגְלַיִם (feet)	בִּרְכַּיִם (knees)		מָתְנַיִם (hips)	נַעֲלַיִם (shoes)		צָהֳרַיִם (noon)		עֵינַיִם (eyes)	לְחָיַיִם (cheeks)	
constr.	רַגְלֵי	בִּרְכֵּי		מָתְנֵי	נַעֲלֵי				עֵינֵי		

Declension of Masculine Nouns—*continued.*

	VII. a.	VII. b.	VII. c.	VIII. a.	VIII. b.	VIII. c.	VIII. d.	VIII. e.	VIII. f.	IX. a.	IX. b.
Sing. absol.	שֵׁם (name)	אֹיֵב (enemy)	מִזְבֵּחַ (altar)	יָם (sea)	אֵם (mother)	חֹק (statute)	רַב (much)	מַד (garments)	לֵוִי (Levite)	חֹזֶה (seer)	שָׂדֶה (field)
constr.	שֵׁם	אֹיֵב	מִזְבַּח	יָם	אֵם	חָק־	רַב	מַד		חֹזֵה	שְׂדֵה
light suff.	שְׁמִי	אֹיְבִי	מִזְבְּחִי	יַמִּי	אִמִּי	חֻקִּי	רַבִּי	מִדִּי		חֹזִי	שָׂדִי
grave suff.	שִׁמְכֶם	אֹיִבְכֶם	מִזְבַּחֲכֶם	יַמְּכֶם	אִמְּכֶם	חָקְכֶם	רַבְּכֶם	מִדְּכֶם		חֹזְכֶם	שָׂדְכֶם
Plur. absol.	שֵׁמוֹת	אֹיְבִים	מִזְבְּחוֹת	יַמִּים	אִמּוֹת	חֻקִּים	רַבִּים	מִדִּים	לְוִיִּם	חֹזִים	שָׂדִים
constr.	שְׁמוֹת	אֹיְבֵי	מִזְבְּחוֹת	יְמֵי	אִמּוֹת	חֻקֵּי	רַבֵּי	מִדֵּי		חֹזֵי	שְׂדֵי
light suff.	שְׁמוֹתַי	אֹיְבַי	מִזְבְּחוֹתַי	יָמַי	אִמּוֹתַי	חֻקַּי	רַבַּי	מִדַּי		חֹזַי	שָׂדַי
grave suff.	שְׁמוֹתֵיכֶם	אֹיְבֵיכֶם	מִזְבְּחוֹתֵיכֶם	יְמֵיכֶם	אִמּוֹתֵיכֶם	חֻקֵּיכֶם	רַבֵּיכֶם	מִדֵּיכֶם		חֹזֵיכֶם	שְׂדֵיכֶם
Dual absol.		מֹאזְנַיִם (balances)		כַּפַּיִם (hands)	שִׁנַּיִם (teeth)						
constr.		מֹאזְנֵי		כַּפֵּי	שִׁנֵּי						

DECLENSION OF FEMININE NOUNS.

	(I.) X.*	(II.) XI.* a.	XI.* b.	XI.* c.	(III.) XII.* a.	XII.* b.	XII.* b.	XII.* c.	XII.* d.	(IV.) XIII.* a.	XIII.* a.	XIII.* b.	XIII.* c.
Sing. absol.	בְּתוּלָה (virgin)	שָׁנָה (year)	שֵׁנָה (sleep)	צְדָקָה (righteousness)	מַלְכָּה (queen)	שִׂמְלָה (garment)	חֶרְפָּה (reproach)	חָרְבָּה (waste)	נַעֲרָה (maid)	מִסְגֶּרֶת (inclosure)	גְּבֶרֶת (mistress)	אֵשֶׁת (wife)	כְּתֹנֶת (coat)
constr.	בְּתוּלַת	שְׁנַת	שְׁנַת	צִדְקַת	מַלְכַּת	שִׂמְלַת	חֶרְפַּת	חָרְבַּת	נַעֲרַת	מִסְגֶּרֶת	גְּבֶרֶת	אֵשֶׁת	כְּתֹנֶת
light suff.	בְּתוּלָתִי	שְׁנָתִי	שְׁנָתִי	צִדְקָתִי	מַלְכָּתִי	שִׂמְלָתִי	חֶרְפָּתִי	חָרְבָּתִי	נַעֲרָתִי	מִסְגַּרְתִּי	גְּבִרְתִּי	אִשְׁתִּי	כְּתָנְתִּי
grave suff.	בְּתוּלַתְכֶם	שְׁנַתְכֶם	שְׁנַתְכֶם	צִדְקַתְכֶם	מַלְכַּתְכֶם	שִׂמְלַתְכֶם	חֶרְפַּתְכֶם	חָרְבַּתְכֶם	נַעֲרַתְכֶם	מִסְגַּרְתְּכֶם	גְּבִרְתֵּךְ	אִשְׁתְּךָ	כְּתָנְתְּךָ
Plur. absol.	בְּתוּלוֹת	שָׁנוֹת	שֵׁנוֹת	צְדָקוֹת	מְלָכוֹת	שְׂמָלוֹת	חֲרָפוֹת	חֲרָבוֹת	נְעָרוֹת	מִסְגְּרוֹת			כֻּתֳּנוֹת
constr.	בְּתוּלוֹת	שְׁנוֹת	שְׁנוֹת	צִדְקוֹת	מַלְכוֹת	שִׂמְלוֹת	חֶרְפוֹת	חָרְבוֹת	נַעֲרוֹת	מִסְגְּרוֹת			כָּתְנוֹת
light suff.	בְּתוּלוֹתַי	שְׁנוֹתַי	שְׁנוֹתַי	צִדְקוֹתַי	מַלְכוֹתַי	שִׂמְלוֹתַי	חֶרְפוֹתַי	חָרְבוֹתַי	נַעֲרוֹתַי	מִסְגְּרוֹתַי			
grave suff.	בְּתוּלוֹתֵיכֶם	שְׁנוֹתֵיכֶם	שְׁנוֹתֵיכֶם	צִדְקוֹתֵיכֶם	מַלְכוֹתֵיכֶם	שִׂמְלוֹתֵיכֶם	חֶרְפוֹתֵיכֶם	חָרְבוֹתֵיכֶם	נַעֲרוֹתֵיכֶם	מִסְגְּרוֹתֵיכֶם			
Dual absol.	אַמָּתַיִם (two cubits)	שְׂפָתַיִם (lips)	פֵּאָתַיִם (corners)		יַרְכָתַיִם (sides)	רִקְמָתַיִם (double embroidery)				עֲצַלְתַּיִם (slothfulness)		מְצִלְתַּיִם (cymbals)	נְחֻשְׁתַּיִם (double fetters)
constr.		שִׂפְתֵי	פַּאֲתֵי		יַרְכְּתֵי								

* See note to the heading of § 41.

SECTION XXX.—FIRST DECLENSION OF THE MASCULINES. (TABLE O.)

EXPLANATORY.

1. In this declension the noun itself undergoes no change of vowels before the suffixes, and stands, as an indeclinable, merely for comparison with the others. It is, however, important to know the various forms which are thus indeclinable.

2. To this paradigm belong all nouns whose vowels are immutable,* e. g. (according to the note given below, No. 1) עִיר *city,* קוֹל *voice,* לְבוּשׁ *garment,* זְרוֹעַ *arm;* (No. 2) קָם, part. of קוּם, *arising,* גָּר, part. of גּוּר, *stranger,* נֵר (for נֵיר) *lamp,* כְּתָב (כְּתָאב) *book;* (No. 3) גִּבּוֹר *hero,* צַדִּיק *righteous,* מַלְכוּת *kingdom,* אֶבְיוֹן *poor,* מַשְׁחִית *destruction;* (No. 4) פָּרָשׁ for פַּרָּשׁ *horseman.*

3. The vowels (ָ) and (ֵ) occasion here peculiar difficulty, as it often cannot be determined, at first sight, whether they are *pure* or *impure,* or whether a Dagesh is omitted in the form (comp. note No. 2). There is, however, no difficulty in forms like קָם, גֵּר, as soon as we are aware of their derivation from קוּם, גּוּר, from which it becomes evident that they stand for קָאם, גֵּיר (§ 21. rem. 1); in קָטָל, קְטָל, the general formation of nouns that (ָ) is *impure,* and therefore immutable (§ 25. No. 6); but with regard to forms like כְּאֵב *pain,* פָּרָשׁ *horseman,* it can be known only from the existing inflexions (as, constr. state כְּאֵבֵי, פָּרָשֵׁי) that they stand for כְּאֵיב, פָּרָשׁ, since there are also words of the like forms in which the vowels are *pure,* and therefore mutable.

4. Hence, of the classes of *verbal nouns* (of § 26), the following belong to this declension:

(*a*) Of the derivatives from the regular verb, the forms of No. 6. חַטָּא *sinner,* פֶּחָר (for פַּחָּר) *potter,* פָּרָשׁ (for פַּרְאשׁ) *horseman,* חַנּוּן *compassionate,* צַדִּיק *righteous;* 8. גִּבּוֹר *hero;* 13. כְּתָב *book,* כְּאֵב *pain* (though the forms קְטָל, קָטֹל, occur also with *pure* vowels, and are inflected according to dec. 6. § 35. rem. 10); 14. מִזְמוֹר *song,* מַלְבּוּשׁ *garment;* 15. שִׁלְטוֹן *government,* חֶסְרוֹן *want;* 16. גְּבֻלוֹת *border,* &c.; 19. מַשְׁחִית *destruction;* 26. חִבּוּק *a folding,* זֵרוּעַ (for זֵרּוּעַ *herbs;* 27. תַּלְמִיד, תַּגְמוּל.

(*b*) Of the derivatives from the irregular verbs (of § 27), II. 16. סֻכּוֹת *tabernacle;* 27. תַּעֲלוּל *action;* IV. 13. סוֹד, בּוּל; 14. מִישׁוֹר; 28. תִּירוֹשׁ; V. 1. קָם; 2. גֵּר; 3. 5. 8; VIII. 13. שְׁבוּת, שְׁבִית, מְנָת; 15. רַעְיוֹן; 16. גָּלוּת (note, with *Kamets impure*).

REMARKS.

1. That Kamets is *impure,* and therefore *immutable,* in the form קָטָל, is sufficiently evident from a comparison with the Arab. קָטָאל, and also from many examples where it remains unchanged in the declension, e. g. חַטָּאֵי Am. 9. 10, comp. אִכָּרֵיכֶם *their husbandmen,* Is. 61. 5. The punctuators, however, have sometimes from neglect shortened this Kamets. E. g. דַּיַּן אַלְמָנוֹת *judge of the widows,* Ps. 68. 6, חָרָשׁ *smith,* constr. state חָרַשׁ Ex. 28. 11; Is. 44. 12, 13, פָּרָשׁ, constr. state פָּרַשׁ Eze. 26. 10. Moreover, צַוָּאר (which even in the Hebrew is written *in full*), pl. constr. צַוְּארֵי. This plural, however, must doubtless be derived from a feminine צַוָּארֶת, with the pl. termination ־ִים (comp. שִׁבֹּלֶת, pl. שִׁבֳּלִים), according to the 4th declension of the feminines.

2. Of the form קָטוֹל there occurs also an example which changes *Hholem,* viz. צִפּוֹר (*a small bird, sparrow*), pl. צִפֳּרִים Le. 14. 4, 49; Ec. 9. 12; Is. 31. 5. Here, however, the plural appears to be derived from a sing. fem. צִפֹּרֶת, Hholem of which is *pure,* comp. קָטוֹר, fem. קְטֹרֶת with suff. קְטָרְתִּי (§ 39. No. 4 d), as in צַוָּאר, comp. rem. 1.

3. As regards the forms of No. 15 (of § 26), we might reasonably expect the Kamets to be *impure* in קָרְבָּן, שֻׁלְחָן, since in the Arabic they assume the form like קֻרְבָּאן. The punctuators, however, have seldom attended to it, and have usually shortened that Kamets. E. g. אָבְדָן, constr. אָבְדַן *destruction,* Est. 8. 6; שֻׁלְחַן Nu. 4. 7; קָרְבַּן

* Immutable vowels are: 1. Those in which their homogeneous vowel is quiescent, as ָא ; ֵי ; וֹ, וּ, e. g. רָאשׁ, הֵיכָל, פָּקִיד, קוֹל, זְבוּל. These are sometimes written *defectively,* which, however, is not an essential shortening.

2. Those which must originally have been written *in full,* but from which the vowel letter has been omitted; hence called *impure* (*vocalis impuræ*). E. g. רָשׁ for רָאשׁ, מָשַׁח for מָשִׁיחַ, קֹלוֹת for קוֹלוֹת, זְבֻל for זְבוּל. Whether a vowel is thus made *impure,* can be known only from etymology, flexion, and comparison of the kindred dialects. The cases are noticed in the grammars and lexicons.

3. A short vowel in a sharpened syllable followed by *Dagesh forte,* as גִּבּוֹר, גַּנָּב; also a short vowel in a compound syllable, when another such syllable immediately follows, e. g. מִדְבָּר, מִשְׁקָל, אֶבְיוֹן, מַלְכוּת.

4. Vowels after which a *Dagesh forte* has been omitted on account of a guttural. E. g. חָרָשׁ for חַרָּשׁ, אַחִים for אַחִּים, חֵרֵשׁ for חִרֵּשׁ.

Le. 2. 1; קָרְבְּנֵיהֶם Le. 7. 38 (but where several MSS. have קָרְבָּנֵיהֶם).

4. Among the indeclinables here, there are yet a few with וֹ in the final syllable, which they change to ֹ before suffixes and in the plural. E. g. מַחְסוֹר *want*, pl. מַחְסֹרֶיךָ Pr. 24. 34 (according to some copies); שְׁפוֹט, pl. שְׁפוֹטִים Eze. 23. 10; מַטְמוֹן, pl. מַטְמוֹנִים, but constr. מַטְמֻנֵי Is. 45. 3, comp. § 32. rem. 5.

5. Several forms which belong here will be noticed also among the exceptions of the following declension.

SECTION XXXI.—SECOND DECLENSION OF THE MASCULINES. (TABLE O.)

EXPLANATORY.

1. To this declension belong all nouns which have a *pure changeable Kamets* in their final syllable, and are either monosyllabic or have their preceding vowels immutable. E. g. יָד *hand*, הֵיכָל *palace*, מֵיכָל *little water*, אוֹצָר *treasure*, מוּסָר *chastisement*, מִשְׁמָר *custody*, &c., comp. § 26. Nos. 14, 20; § 27. III. 14, 27. Here belong also the plurals, נָשִׁים *women*, יָמִים *days*, the particle עָל *above*, constr. state עַל *upon*, pl. constr. עֲלֵי, with suff. עָלָיו, עֲלֵיכֶם.

2. The vowel-change consists simply in this, that

(*a*) In the *constr. state* and before the *grave suffixes* of the *singular* (ָ) is changed into (ַ);

(*b*) This (ָ) is altogether dropped in the *constr. state*, and before the *grave suffixes* in the plural.

3. There are nouns which resemble in form the above examples, but which have an *impure* Kamets in their final syllable, and therefore do not belong to this declension, comp. § 30. No. 4. Other exceptions are contained in the following remarks.

REMARKS.

1. Certain nouns of the form מַקְטָל have Kamets *impure* in their final syllable, especially derivatives from the irregular verbs. E. g. מַעֲבָדֵיהֶם *their works*, Job 34. 25; מַטָּעֵי כֶרֶם *plantings of a vineyard*, Mi. 1. 6; מוֹרָשֵׁי לְבָבִי *possessions of my heart*, Job 17. 11, comp. מוֹרָשֵׁיהֶם Ob. 17; מַתָּן אָדָם *gift of a man*, Pr. 18. 18. This is especially the case in the derivatives from verbs ל״א (where א seems to have some hold upon the vowel Kamets), as מִקְרָאֵי *assemblies*, Le. 23. 2, 4, 37; מוֹצָאֵי *goings out*, Ps. 65. 9; מוֹצָאֵיהֶם Nu. 33. 2, and so צֶאֱצָאֵי *shoots*, Is. 48. 19. Comp. Is. 61. 9; Job 21. 8.

Kamets is, moreover, immutable in תּוֹשָׁב *inhabitant*, whence תּוֹשָׁבֵי 1 Ki. 17. 1, to which there is a corresponding form in the Arabic תִּפְעָאל.

2. In the word יָם Kamets has been retained even before Makkeph, e. g. always יָם־הַמֶּלַח *salt-sea*; יָם כִּנֶּרֶת *sea Chinereth*, i. e. Genesareth; except in the combination יַם־סוּף *sea of reeds*. (Notwithstanding the constancy of this punctuation, no ground can be assigned for the difference.) There are, moreover, found in the constr. st. the forms אוּלָם *porch, portico*, Eze. 40. 7; פִּתְגָּם *word*, Est. 1. 20, without changing Kamets.

3. With the suffix כֶם, יָד becomes יֶדְכֶם (for יַדְכֶם,) Ge. 9. 2; דָּם becomes דִּמְכֶם Ge. 9. 5 (because the forms (ֶ ְ), and (ִ ְ) are shorter than (ַ ְ), comp. אֶכְלְךָ for אֲכָלְךָ, מִדּוֹ for מַדּוֹ). An instance of regular formation before כֶם, though terminating with א (comp. rem. 1), is מוֹרַאֲכֶם *fear of you*, Is. 8. 13.

The form like נֶחְבָּאִים, נִטְמָאִים is doubtless the plural of a Niph. part. with (ֵ) in the final syllable, from נֶחְבֵּא, נִטְמֵא comp. § 23. rem. 6.

4. For מִבְטָח with suff. מִבְטַחוֹ, pl. מִבְטַחִים see below § 37. rem. 7.

5. The few words with *Pattahh* in the ultimate, preceded by an immutable syllable (comp. § 30. No. 2, note), follow the analogy of this declension in their inflexion, as far as regards the suffixes and the plural. They are, אֶצְבַּע *finger*, with suff. אֶצְבָּעוֹ, pl. אֶצְבָּעוֹת; אַרְבַּע *four*, pl. אַרְבָּעִים *forty*; שַׁד dual שָׁדַיִם *breasts*; כּוֹבַע *helmet*, pl. כּוֹבָעִים. The latter noun is written with the tone on the ultimate, כּוֹבַע, in Eze. 27. 10; but כֹּובַע in 1 Sa. 17. 5; Is. 59. 17, according to which it is a Segolate form written, by way of exception, with a full Hholem. The first form, however, is favoured by the fact that וֹ is retained in the plural, which is inconsistent with the Segolate forms.

SECTION XXXII.—THIRD DECLENSION OF THE MASCULINES. (Table O.)

EXPLANATORY.

1. This declension embraces all nouns which have an *immutable vowel* in the final syllable, and *mutable Kamets* or *Tseri* in the penultima, as פָּקִיד, or some other syllables may precede, as כִּלָּיוֹן. Of the derivatives from the regular verb (§ 26) belong here those of No. 3. קָדוֹשׁ *holy,* גָּדוֹל *great;* No. 5. עָצוּם *mighty,* פָּקִיד *officer;* No. 15. רְעָבוֹן *famine,* עֵרָבוֹן (for עִרְבוֹן) *pledge,* זִכָּרוֹן *remembrance.* Of the derivatives from the irregular verbs (§ 27), from פ״א, as אֵזוֹר *girdle,* אֵמוּן *faithfulness;* from ע״ו No. 14. מָקוֹם *place;* No. 27. תָּמִיד *continuance;* moreover, the participles of Hiphil, as מֵקִים, מֵשִׁיב, מֵלִיץ. From ל״ה No. 15. הָמוֹן *multitude,* גִּלָּיוֹן *roll.* The primitives and denominatives follow the same analogy.

2. The vowel-change here consists in this, that Kamets (or Tseri) of the penultima is dropped in all the forms, except the absol. state of the singular. In the forms like זִכָּרוֹן, כִּלָּיוֹן, Dagesh of the middle radical is likewise dropped, and the first two syllables are combined into one, as זִכְרוֹן, כִּלְיוֹן. Another combination of the letters is effected in פִּרָזוֹן, with suff. פִּרְזוֹנוֹ, with guttural רְעָבוֹן, constr. רַעֲבוֹן (for רְעְבוֹן).

3. Here also are to be distinguished nouns which resemble the above forms, but which have *impure* Kamets, and as such do not belong here, as בָּרִיחַ (for בַּרִּיחַ) *fugitive,* עָרִיץ (for עַרִּיץ) *tyrant,* חָרוּץ (for חַרּוּץ) *diligent* (according to § 26. No. 7), and the derivatives of ל״ה of the form חָזוּת, גָּלוּת, the Kamets of which is likewise *impure.*

REMARKS.

1. Of the forms קָטוֹל, קָטוּל, קָטִיל (§ 26. Nos. 3 & 4) there are some few words in which Kamets is *impure.* E. g. שָׁלִישׁ *charioteer,* pl. שָׁלִישִׁים Ex. 14. 7, with suff. שָׁלִישׁוֹ, שָׁלִישָׁיו 2 Ki. 15. 25; Ex. 15. 4; שָׁבוּעַ *week,* pl. שָׁבֻעוֹת, שָׁבֻעִים Da. 9. 24, 25, with suff. שָׁבֻעֹתֵיכֶם Nu. 28. 26 (though also שְׁבֻעוֹת Je. 5. 24; Eze. 45. 21), and in the Gentilic nouns מָכִירִי, יָמִינִי Nu. 26. 12, 29; comp. 2 Sa. 20. 26, instead of which we would expect מְכִירִי, יְמִינִי.

2. With regard to some words with middle guttural, the punctuators seem to have disagreed among themselves, as to whether they belong to the form קָטִיל or קַטִּיל, i. e. whether Kamets is to be changed or not. Hence inconsistencies like the following: בָּרִיחִים *fugitives,* Is. 43. 14 (from בַּרִּיחַ); but, on the contrary, בְּרִיחֶיהָ Is. 15. 5; סָרִיס *eunuch,* constr. state סְרִיס Ge. 37. 36, pl. סָרִיסִים 2 Ki. 9. 32, constr. state סָרִיסֵי Est. 2. 21, and סְרִיסֵי Ge. 40. 7, with suff. סָרִיסָיו Ge. 40. 2; פָּרִיץ *violent,* constr. state פְּרִיץ Is. 35. 9, but pl. פָּרִיצִים Je. 7. 11; פָּרִיצֵי Da. 11. 14.

3. Some nouns of the form זִכָּרוֹן, when shortened, take Segol instead of Hhirek. Thus, חִזָּיוֹן *vision,* constr. state חֶזְיוֹן Job 33. 15, pl. חֶזְיֹנוֹת Job 4. 13; עִשָּׂרוֹן *tenth deal* (dry measure), pl. עֶשְׂרֹנִים Ex. 29. 40; Le. 14. 10. This is doubtless the effect of the first letter which is a guttural (§ 35. rem. 6), though עִצָּבוֹן has the constr. state עִצְּבוֹן, and חִשָּׁבוֹן the pl. חִשְּׁבוֹנוֹת.

4. In the forms like אֵבוּס, אֵזוֹר where, on account of א, Tseri stands, by Syriacism, for (ֱ) (comp. § 19. r. 6), it is retained also in the constr. state, because the same cause continues to exist here as in the abs. state, as אֵבוּס בְּעָלָיו Is. 1. 3; אֵטוּן מִצְרָיִם Pr. 7. 16; אֵפוֹד בַּד 1 Sa. 2. 18; but, in the plural, where the shorter (ֲ) is to be introduced, the Syriacism is no longer employed; hence אֲבוּסִים *cribs,* Job 39. 9; אֲסוּרִים *bands,* Ju. 15. 14; also אֱמוּנִים *faithful,* Ps. 31. 24.*

5. In several nouns of the form מָקוֹם, especially such as are derived from verbs ע״ו, וֹ is changed to וּ in the shortening. E. g. מָנוֹחַ *rest,* pl. מְנוּחִים; מָנוֹס *flight,* with suff. מְנוּסִי; מָעוֹן *habitation,* pl. מְעוּנִים; מָגוֹר *fear,* pl. מְגוּרִים; מָצוֹר, with suff. מְצוּרֵךְ, as there exists no ground-form with Kibbuts for any of these forms. This is moreover the case in the adj. מָתוֹק of which the pl. is מְתוּקִים (comp. § 39. No. 3. r. 1).

6. Among the derivatives from ע״ו there are a few of the form לָצוֹן (from לוּץ) in which Kamets is shortened, contrary to analogy (comp. § 30. Nos. 2 & 3), as זָדוֹן *arrogance,* constr. זְדוֹן Ob. 3, with suff. זְדוֹנְךָ 1 Sa. 17. 28; שָׂשׂוֹן *joy,* constr. שְׂשׂוֹן Ps. 51. 14, from זִיד or זוּד and שׂוּשׂ. The vowel-change here gives them the character of derivatives from (as it were) שָׂשָׂה, שָׂדָה.

7. In some few instances *Hholem* of the form קָטוֹל (§ 26. No. 3) is treated as a *pure* vowel, and is shortened to *Kamets-hhatuph,* as שְׁלָשׁ־אֵלֶּה *these three,* Ex. 21. 11; גְּדָל־ Ps. 145. 8; Na. 1. 3 Keri; טְהָר־ Job 17. 9; Pr. 22. 11 Keri. Still more striking is the kind of shortening in הֲמָנְכֶם Eze. 5. 7, for הֲמוֹנְכֶם *your noise.* Comp. also קִנְּמָן־ Ex. 30. 23, from קִנָּמוֹן *cinnamon.*

8. מָדוֹן *contention,* (from דִּין or דּוּן) has the pl. מִדְוָנִים with moveable Vav, comp. § 35. rem. 13.

* Comp. § 13. rem. 2, note; also rem. 7 and 9.

SECTION XXXIII.—FOURTH DECLENSION OF THE MASCULINES. (Table O.)

EXPLANATORY.

1. This declension embraces nouns of two syllables, either with *Kamets pure* in both, or *Tseri pure* in the first and Kamets in the second. Here belong only the derivatives from the regular verb (§ 26. Nos. 1 & 2), as זָהָב *gold*, זָנָב *tail*, שֵׁכָר *strong drink*, and with gutturals, אָשָׁם *guilt*, רָעָב *famine*, שָׂבָע *satiety*, שֵׂעָר *hair*, עֵנָב *cluster of grapes*.

2. The vowel-change in this declension consists in this, that

(*a*) Kamets or Tseri of the first syllable is always dropped, except in the ground-form;

(*b*) in the constr. st. sing., and before the suffix כֶם, (ָ) of the final syllable is changed to (ַ);

(*c*) in the plural, Kamets is altogether dropped in the constr. st. and before the *grave* suffixes, and the two Shevas, now coming to stand under the first two radicals (דְּבְ), are combined in one syllable by Hhirek, with a guttural by Pattahh, hence שַׂעֲרֵי ,חַכְמֵי ,דִּבְרֵי. E. g. עָפָר *dust*, pl. constr. עַפְרוֹת; עָנָו *afflicted*, pl. constr. עַנְוֵי, &c.

3. For some exceptions like חָרָשׁ *smith*, פָּרָשׁ *horseman*, see § 30. No. 4, also rem. 1.

REMARKS.

1. In the pl. constr. there is *Pattahh* found under the first radical, even where there is no guttural, e. g. כָּנָף *wing*, du. constr. כַּנְפֵי; זָנָב *tail*, pl. constr. זַנְבוֹת; צֵלָע *rib*, pl. constr. צַלְעוֹת. On the contrary, *Hhirek* is found also under guttural instead of *Pattahh*, as עִמְקֵי *deep*, Is. 33. 19, from עָמֹק; עִנְּבֵי *grapes*, De. 32. 32 (with euphonic Dagesh for עִנְבֵי); חִזְקֵי *strong*, Eze. 2. 4; 3. 7, from חָזָק.

2. This class of nouns derived from ל״א retain in the constr. st. the (ָ) in which א is quiescent, as צָבָא *host*, constr. צְבָא; צָמָא *thirst*, constr. צְמָא.

3. For a few nouns of this class (קָטָל and קֵטָל), the Segolate form is used in the constr. st. and before suffixes (comp. dec. 5). E. g. עָשָׁן *smoke*, constr. עֲשַׁן and עֶשֶׁן; עָנָף *branch*, with suff. עַנְפְּכֶם Eze. 36. 8; צֵלָע *rib*, constr. צֶלַע and צֶלַע (Milêl), with suff. צַלְעִי.

The case is reversed in חֶדֶר *chamber*, with suff. חֶדְרוֹ, but constr. חֲדַר (as if from חָדָר).

SECTION XXXIV.—FIFTH DECLENSION OF THE MASCULINES. (Table O.)

1. This declension embraces nouns of two syllables, which have *Tseri pure* in the final, and *Kamets* in the preceding syllable, hence chiefly derivations of the regular verb only of No. 2 (§ 26). The two forms exhibited in the paradigm differ only with respect to the first radical when a guttural.

2. This declension is very similar to the preceding, as regards the vowel-change, and is properly a mere variation of the same. In this the *Tseri* of the final syllable is treated like final *Kamets* in the foregoing, except that the form קְטֵל, which might be expected in the constr. st., occurs but very seldom (see, however, לְבֶן *white*, Ge. 49. 12; אֲבֶל *mourning*, Ps. 35. 14), and instead of it the forms like either that of זְקַן or כְּתֶף are used. According to the latter form are inflected, גָּדֵר, constr. גֶּדֶר *wall*; יָרֵךְ, constr. יֶרֶךְ *hip*; גָּזֵל, constr. גֶּזֶל *robbery, any thing taken by violence*; אָרֵךְ, constr. אֶרֶךְ *long*; to the first belong יָתֵד, constr. יְתַד *peg, pin*; קָצֵר, constr. קְצַר *short*, &c. Both forms appear in כָּבֵד *heavy*, constr. כְּבַד Ex. 4. 10, and כֶּבֶד Is. 1. 4; עָרֵל *uncircumcised*, constr. עֲרַל Ex. 6. 12, 30, and עֶרֶל Eze. 44. 9.

REMARKS.

1. The nouns of this form derived from ל״א retain *Tseri* in the constr. st., e g. מָלֵא ,מְלֵא; טָמֵא ,טְמֵא; יָרֵא ,יְרֵא (§ 33. rem. 2); this, however, is not confined to forms with א merely, comp. יָוֵן *mire*, constr. יְוֵן Ps. 69. 3; עָקֵב *heel*, constr. עֲקֵב Ge. 25. 26; יָפֵחַ *puffing out*, constr. יְפֵחַ Ps. 27. 12; finally, חָמֵשׁ *five*, constr. חֲמֵשׁ.

2. Some nouns retain *Tseri* in the pl. constr. st., e. g. יָשֵׁן *sleeping*, constr. יְשֵׁנֵי Da. 12. 2; אָבֵל *mourning*, אֲבֵלֵי Is. 61. 3; שָׂמֵחַ *joyful*, שְׂמֵחֵי Ps. 35. 26 (but also שִׂמְחֵי Is. 24. 7); שָׁכֵחַ *forgetful*, שְׁכֵחֵי Ps. 9. 18; חָפֵץ *delighting*, חֲפֵצֵי Ps. 40. 15; 70. 3.

3. אָבֵל *(grassy place)* remains entirely unchanged in the pr. names אָבֵל הַשִּׁטִּים Ju. 7. 22, אָבֵל מְחוֹלָה 11. 33, &c.; comp. also כָּתֵף פְּלִשְׁתִּים Is. 11. 14.

4. *Hhirek* under the first radical when a guttural, like עִקְּבֵי in paradigm *c*, is a mere exception; it occurs in Ca. 1. 8, and with euphonic Dagesh, עִקְּבֵי Ge. 49. 17; Ju. 5. 22; for the like Dagesh, comp. עַצְּבֵיכֶם Is. 58. 3, from עָצֵב. (This, however, may be derived from עֶצֶב in the sense of *labour*.)

SECTION XXXV.—SIXTH DECLENSION OF THE MASCULINES. (TABLE O.)

EXPLANATORY.

1. This declension embraces the large class of nouns denominated *Segolate forms,* i. e. those dissyllabic nouns which have the tone and characteristic vowels in the first, and an auxiliary Segol (with guttural Pattahh) in the second syllable. The characteristic vowel may be either A, E, or O; hence the following forms :—

(*a*) From the regular verb, like מֶלֶךְ for מַלְךְ, סֵפֶר, קֹדֶשׁ; (*b*) with gutturals, like נַעַר, נֵצַח, פֹּעַל; (*c*) from the verb ע״ו, like מָוֶת, חַיִל, or שׁוֹר for שׁוֶֹר (§ 27. IV); (*d*) from verbs ל״ה, like אֲרִי, לְחִי, חֳלִי (§ 27. V). They are closely related to the forms like שְׁבַב, שְׁכֶם, קְטֹל (§ 26. No. 10), which in the Aramaean occupy the place of the Hebrew Segolates.

2. The peculiarity in their inflexion is as follows :—

(*a*) In the constr. st. the form remains unchanged, with the exception of חֵיל מוֹת, in which ו and י become quiescent.

(*b*) Before the suffixes the original monosyllabic form is introduced, which they have in the Arabic (מַלְךְ, סִפְר or סֵפְר, קֹדְשׁ), hence מַלְכִּי, סִפְרִי, &c. This is likewise the case in the constr. st. of the plural and dual.

(*c*) The plural is not formed immediately from the Segolate form of the singular, but from the kindred form מְלַךְ, סְפַר, קְדַשׁ or קֳדַשׁ, which they have in the Aramaean, hence מְלָכִים, סְפָרִים, so that Pattahh, which in this case would stand in an open syllable, is changed into Kamets, like שַׁד dual שָׁדַיִם (§ 31. rem. 5).

REMARKS.

I. ON THE FORM מֶלֶךְ (& נַעַר).

1. In the form of two Segols, like מֶלֶךְ, the first *generally* stands for *Pattahh* (מַלֶךְ), and this again for the monosyllabic מַלְךְ. The latter form is the Arabic, which the Arabian usually pronounces *mĕlk*, and the vulgar even *mĕlek*. The Hebrew language exhibits this original form in the word גַּיְא *a valley*, and the proper name אַרְדְּ Ge. 46. 21; Nu. 26. 40. The Greek translators of the Old Testament have also sometimes expressed this form in the same way, e. g. קֶרֶן Aqu. & Symm. *καρν* Job 42. 14; חֶרֶשׂ *αρς* Is. 17. 9.

2. In a few words only the original *a*, as (ַ) & (ָ), appears already in the ground-form, viz., (*a*) in the nouns which have a guttural for their second radical, as נַעַל, נַעַר, בַּעַל; (*b*) in the derivatives from ע״ו, as מָוֶת, חַיִל; (*c*) in the contracted forms like אַף from אֶנֶף *wrath*, בַּת from בֶּנֶת; (*d*) in the word הָאָרֶץ, but only with the article (for הָאֶרֶץ); (*e*) in pause, as מָלֶךְ, כָּרֶם, and with paragogic ה, אַרְצָה *to the ground.*

3. There is, however, a considerable number of nouns of this form, in which, seemingly, the first Segol does not stand for Pattahh or Kamets, but for *Tseri*, as לֶדֶת for לֵדֶת, קֹטֶלֶת for קֹטֵלֶת. These, though similar to the preceding in the ground-form, are nevertheless inflected like the form סֵפֶר (to which they originally belong) with *Hhirek*, seldom *Segol*, in the first syllable. An example of this kind is presented in the paradigm קֶבֶר.

Nouns inflected in this manner with *Hhirek*, the ground-form being קֶטֶל not קָטֶל, are the following: בֶּגֶד *garment*, בֶּטֶן *belly*, בֶּרֶךְ *knee*, גֶּזַע *stem*, גֶּשֶׁם *rain*, גֶּרֶשׂ *something pounded*, דֶּגֶל *banner*, דֶּשֶׁן *fat*, זֶבַח *sacrifice*, טֶבַח *slaughter*, יֶתֶר *string*, כֶּלֶא *confinement*, לֶקַח *doctrine*, מֶתֶג *bridle*, נֶגַע *stroke*, נֶזֶם *ring*, נֶטַע *planting*, נֶשֶׁר *eagle*, נֶשֶׁף *twilight*, פֶּגֶר *carcase*, פֶּלֶךְ *district*, פֶּסֶל *image*, צֶדֶק *righteousness*, צֶמַח *sprout*, קֶרֶב *midst*, קֶשֶׁר *conspiracy*, רֶכֶב *chariot*, רֶסֶן *bridle*, רֶשֶׁף *flame*, שֶׁקֶר *falsehood*, שֶׁמֶשׁ *sun.* In others this characteristic of the word becomes apparent in its change to the feminine, e. g. גֶּבַע fem. גִּבְעָה *hill.* With Segol in the first syllable are inflected חֶלֶד *life-time*, נֶגֶב (with ה parag. נֶגְבָּה) *south*, נֶגֶד *before*, נֶכֶד *progeny.*

4. Sometimes both forms (like מַלְכִּי and בִּגְדִי) are found with one ground-form like קֶטֶל, e. g. יֶלֶד *child*, hence יַלְדֵי Is. 57. 4, and יִלְדֵי Ho. 1. 2 (fem. יַלְדָּה); חֶדֶר *chamber*, with suff. חֶדְרִי, but with ה parag. חַדְרָה, pl. constr. חַדְרֵי; הֶבֶל *vanity*, with suff. הֶבְלִי, but pl. constr. הַבְלֵי; חֶבֶל *band*, pl. חֲבָלִי, but with pref. בּ always בְּחַבְלֵי Is. 5. 18; Job 36. 8. So likewise in the change to the feminine, as כֶּבֶשׂ *lamb*, fem. כַּבְשָׂה and כִּבְשָׂה.

5. When the third radical is a guttural, the pointing is like that of זֶרַע *seed*, פֶּתַח *door*, סֶלַע *rock*, פֶּסַח *passover*, when the second is a guttural, like that of נַעַר (parad. d). The cases, however, are but rare where the punctuation is not affected by the guttural, e. g. לֶחֶם *bread*, רֶחֶם (but also רַחַם) *womb.* In the

word כִּנְעָנֶיהָ *her merchants*, Is. 23. 8, from כְּנַעַן, the Sheva coming, in the plural, to stand under נ is combined into one syllable with the Sheva under כְּ (for כְּנַעֲנֶיהָ). כְּנַעַן stands for כְּנַעֲנִי *Canaanite*, which latter is used for *a merchant* in general.

Nouns of the form נַעַר are often found with simple Sheva, in those combinations where the latter exhibits a composite Sheva, as יַעְרִי for יַעֲרִי from יַעַר *wood, forest* (comp. § 13. rem. 5).

II. On the form סֵפֶר (& נֵצַח).

6. The nouns of the form סֵפֶר (seldom in the monosyllabic form like חֵטְא, נֵרְדְּ) are all inflected according to the paradigm, e. g. סֵתֶר *covering*, שֵׁבֶט *rod*, נֵדֶר *vow;* those, however, with the first radical guttural, take nearly all of them *Segol* instead of *Hhirek* in the first syllable, as אֵבֶר *pinion*, with suff. אֶבְרוֹ, חֵלֶב *fat*, חֵלֶק *part*, חֵפֶץ *delight*, חֵרֶם *net*, עֵבֶר *country on the other side*, עֵגֶל *calf*, עֵדֶר *flock*, עֵזֶר *help*, עֵרֶךְ *valuation*. There are, however, some few with guttural which retain *Hhirek*, as חֵקֶר *searching*, עֵמֶק *valley*, pl. constr. חִקְרֵי, עִמְקֵי. The noun יֵשַׁע *salvation* has both forms, יִשְׁעֲךָ 2 Sa. 22. 36, and יֶשְׁעֲךָ Ps. 85. 8.

חֵטְא *sin*, has in the pl. constr. חֲטָאֵי 2 Ki. 10. 29; Am. 9. 10, with suff. חֲטָאֵיכֶם Is. 1. 18, where (ָ) is retained on account of א (comp. § 30. rem. 1).

7. Some few Segolates of the forms נֵצַח, זֶרַע, have their constr. state like זֶרַע Nu. 11. 7, as שֶׁבַע *seven*, and תֵּשַׁע *nine*, constr. שְׁבַע and תְּשַׁע, so likewise in the proper name יְשַׁעְיָהוּ (for יְשַׁע יָהוּ) *salvation of the Lord*. The same analogy follows חֶדֶר *chamber*, in the constr. state חֲדַר.

III. On the Form קֹדֶשׁ (& פֹּעַל).

8. The form קֹדֶשׁ takes sometimes *Kibbuts* in the inflexion before suffix, as סְבֹךְ *thicket*, סֻבְּכוֹ Is. 4. 7, גֹּדֶל *greatness*, גֻּדְלוֹ Ps. 150. 2 (also גָּדְלוֹ), קֹמֶץ *handful*, קֻמְצוֹ.

Those with the middle letter guttural like פֹּעַל take sometimes, though not often, simple Sheva under the guttural, as בָּאְשׁוֹ *his stink*, Joel ii. 20; רָחְבּוֹ *his breadth*, Ex. 25. 10. In some instances the vowels ֳ־ָ are put instead of ָ־ֳ, as פָּעֳלוֹ for פָּעֳלוֹ *his work*, Is. 1. 31; תָּאֳרוֹ *his visage*, Is. 52. 14, for תָּאֳרוֹ 1 Sa. 28. 14.

With the suffix ךָ the form becomes פָּעָלְךָ Is. 45. 9; Hab. 3. 2, אָהָלְךָ (*thy tent*), Ps. 61. 5, and even so without the influence of a guttural, as קָטָבְךָ Ho. 13. 14, from קֹטֶב *destruction;* the usual form, however, is like קָדְשְׁךָ, קָדְשְׁכֶם. (The same form is found under the infinitive, § 16. rem. 7—9.)

9. The plural with *Hhateph-Kamets* under the first letter is found (besides קֳדָשִׁים of the parad.) only in חֳדָשִׁים *months*, from חֹדֶשׁ, and אֳרָחוֹת *ways*, from אֹרַח, but everywhere else with simple Sheva (like in the plural of מֶלֶךְ, סֵפֶר); as בֹּקֶר, בְּקָרִים *mornings;* גֹּרֶן, גְּרָנוֹת *threshing-floors;* סְבֹךְ, סְבָכִים *thickets;* קֹמֶץ, קְמָצִים *handfuls;* שֹׁעַל, שְׁעָלִים *hollow hands;* כֹּפֶר, כְּפָרִים *cyprus flowers;* רֹמַח, רְמָחִים *spears;* רֹתֶם, רְתָמִים *genista;* פֹּעַל, פְּעָלִים *actions;* and so probably כְּמָרִים *idol-priests*, from an obsolete כֹּמֶר*.

Kamets-Hhatuph (instead of *Hhateph-Kamets*) under the first radical occurs in שָׁרָשִׁים (shŏrashim) and קָדָשִׁים (so usually with the article, but without it, קֳדָשִׁים, according to the paradigm).

The noun אֹהֶל (*tent*) has by Syriacism pl. אֹהָלִים for אֳהָלִים, whence אֹהָלָיו, אֹהָלֶיךָ for אֳהָלָיו, אֳהָלֶיךָ, but again, אָהֳלֵי, אָהֳלֵיכֶם; אֹרַח also makes אֹרְחֹתָיו, אֹרְחֹתָם.

בֹּהֶן *thumb*, has for its plural בְּהֹנוֹת, so that, instead of קֹטֶל, the parallel form קְטֹל is used.

IV. On the Forms קְטֹל, קְטֹל, קְטֶל.

10. The Chaldee has, instead of the forms מֶלֶךְ, סֵפֶר, the corresponding forms מְלֶךְ, מְלֵךְ, מְלֹךְ, with the vowel between the last two radicals. Examples of this kind are found also in the Hebrew, which agree with the Segolates in the inflexion: they are, however, of too rare occurrence for a paradigm and general rule to be given for them. They are:— דְּבַשׁ *honey*, with suff. דִּבְשִׁי; גְּבַר i. q. גֶּבֶר *man;* שְׁכֶם *shoulder*, in pause שֶׁכֶם Ps. 21. 13, with suff. שִׁכְמִי, with ה parag. שֶׁכְמָה (*to Shechem*) Ho. 6. 9; בְּאֵר *cistern*, pl. בְּאֵרוֹת, constr. בֶּאֱרוֹת; פְּאֵר *head-dress*, pl. פְּאֵרִים, constr. פַּאֲרֵי (also, on the contrary, פַּאֲרֵיכֶם Eze. 24. 23); הֲבֵל *vanity*, Eze. 1. 2; 12. 8; בְּאשׁ *ill-savour*, with suff. בָּאְשׁוֹ Joel 2. 20.

Here belong also the infinitives of Kal of the form קְטֹל, קְטֹל, for the inflexion of which see § 16. rem. 7—10.

For שְׂלָו *quails*, pl. שַׂלְוִים, see below, rem. 16.

V. On the Forms מָוֶת, זַיִת.

11. Of the form מָוֶת are the following nouns:— אָוֶן *adversity*, with suff. אוֹנִי, pl. אוֹנִים; תָּוֶךְ *midst*,

* Hence it is, that some have in the pl. constr. the form קִ..דְ..י instead of קָדְשֵׁי, viz. סְבֹךְ, pl. סְבָכִים, סִבְכֵי; שֶׁקֶת, pl. constr. שִׁקְתוֹת, so that there is no *necessity* to suppose other ground-forms, like סֶבֶךְ, שֶׁקֶת.

constr. תּוֹךְ, with suff. תּוֹכִי; and the monosyllabic שָׁוְא *nothingness*. The only instance without the contraction is עָוֶל, constr. עֲוֶל, with suff. עַוְלוֹ Eze. 18. 26; 33. 13. The plurals מוֹתִים, אוֹנִים (not מְוָתִים, אֲוָנִים, which one would naturally expect here; comp. מְלָכִים, סְפָרִים) are the only instances which occur of this form, which properly is a contraction of the shortened form אֲוָנִים, מָוְתִים (rem. 16).

12. Of the form זַיִת are, אַיִל *ram*, לַיִל *night*, צַיִד *hunting*. A few others have ־ִי instead of ־ַי before suffix, e.g. עַיִר *foal*, עִירֹה Ge. 49. 11; שַׁיִת *thorns*, שִׁיתוֹ Is. 10. 17; לַיִל *night*, pl. לֵילוֹת, but derivative לִילִית.

The plural is generally contracted, as in the paradigm. There are, however, some instances with *moveable Yod* in the plural, as חֲיָלִים *forces*, עֲיָנוֹת *fountains* (from עַיִן, but dual עֵינַיִם), עֲיָרִים *foals*. Here belongs also גַּיְא, pl. גֵּיָאוֹת Khethib (see under the irreg. nouns, § 45). Compare the following remark.

13. It has already been noticed, § 27. No. 11, of the verbs ע״ו, that nouns of the form קוֹל, קִיל may likewise be *originally* Segolate forms, for קָוֶל, קַיֶל. As such they are inflected, at least in the plural, like the Segolates, so that ו and י may again become moveable. E. g. שׁוֹר, pl. שְׁוָרִים *oxen;* חוֹחַ *thorn*, pl. חוֹחִים 2 Ch. 33. 11, and חֲוָחִים 1 Sa. 13. 6; דּוּד, pl. דְּוָדִים *pots;* שׁוּק, pl. שְׁוָקִים *streets*.

VI. ON THE FORMS חֳלִי, פְּרִי.

14. For the origin of this form see § 27. No. 11, of the verbs ל״ה. Nouns of this form may also be properly divided into three classes, likewise distinguished by the sounds *A*, *E*, and *O*, e. g. לְחִי, אֲרִי, חֳלִי, in pause אֲרִי, לֶחִי (חֵצִי), חֹלִי, with suff. לְחָיִי, אַרְיִי, חָלְיִי, in the plural and dual אֲרָיִים, לְחָיַיִם, חֳלָיִים. Those of the second class have almost always *Hhirek* before suffixes which begin with a vowel, and *Segol* before ךָ; e. g. פְּרִי, פִּרְיוֹ Le. 19. 23; Ps. 1. 3; פֶּרְיְךָ Ho. 14. 9; שְׁבִי *captivity*, שִׁבְיוֹ De. 21. 10; שֶׁבְיְךָ Ju. 5. 12; מְרִי *rebellion*, מִרְיָם Ne. 9. 17; מֶרְיְךָ De. 31. 27, and so כֶּלְיְךָ *thy vessel*, De. 23. 25; תֶּלְיְךָ *thy quiver*, Ge. 27. 3. Before the suffixes כֶם, כֶן, הֶם, הֶן, the ground-form usually remains unchanged, as פִּרְיָהֶם Am. 9. 14; פִּרְיָהֶן Je. 29. 28; שִׁבְיְכֶם Nu. 31. 19 (otherwise פִּרְיָם, פִּרְיָן, שִׁבְיָם), comp. however פֶּרְיְכֶם Eze. 36. 8.

Examples in which the first radical is a guttural: חֲלִי *necklace;* עֲדִי *ornament*, with suff. עֶדְיוֹ; עֱלִי *pestle;* with the middle guttural, לְחִי *jaw-bone*, with suff. לֶחְיוֹ Job 40. 26; לֶחְיָהּ La. 1. 2.

15. Examples of the plural, according to the paradigm: אֲרִי *lion*, pl. אֲרָיִים, אֲרָיוֹת; גְּדִי *kid*, pl. גְּדָיִים; צְבִי *gazelle*, pl. צְבָיִים 2 Sa. 2. 18; פְּתִי *simple*, pl. פְּתָיִים. On account, however, of the preceding characteristic Kamets, the third radical י is often changed into א. Hence חֲלִי, pl. חֲלָאִים *necklaces;* לְבִי, pl. לְבָאִים, לְבָאוֹת *lions, lionesses;* and צְבִי, פְּתִי take, besides the form *exhibited* in the paradigm, also that of צְבָאִים 1 Ch. 12. 8, and צְבָאוֹת Ca. 2. 7, פְּתָאִים Pr. 1. 4.*

The dual לְחָיַיִם, as given in the paradigm, corresponds to the form of the plural, though the greater shortening, as לְחַיַיִם, לְחָיַיִם, would have been expected here.

The interchange of י and א is doubtless the reason why Kamets remains immutable in גְּדָיֵי Ge. 27. 9, 16, and לְחָיֵי Is. 30. 28 (instead of גְּדָיֵי, לְחָיֵי) they resemble the form חֲטָאֵי (see rem. 6). For the form לְחָיֵיהֶם *your cheeks*, Ho. 11. 4, an abs. לְחָיִם must be supposed, like כְּלִי, כֵּלִים (see irreg. nouns, § 45).

VII. IN GENERAL.

16. Some few plurals of this class deviate from the general formation in this, that in the abs. state and before light suffixes the greater shortening is introduced, which otherwise is used only in the constr. state. Such are, עֶשְׂרִים *twenty* (not עֲשָׂרִים, from עֶשֶׂר *ten*); שִׁבְעִים *seventy* (from שֶׁבַע *seven*); תִּשְׁעִים *ninety* (from תֵּשַׁע *nine*); בָּטְנִים *pistacia-nuts* (comp. the Arab. בָּטְם); פִּילַגְשִׁים *concubines* (from פִּילֶגֶשׁ); שַׂלְוִים *quails* (from שְׂלָו, שְׂלָו); דָּלְיָו *his buckets*, Nu. 24. 7 (from דְּלִי, for דְּלָיָו); אַשְׁרֶיךָ, אַשְׁרָיו, אַשְׁרֵהוּ *thine, his happiness* (i. e. happiness to thee, him); עַל אָפְנָיו *at a suitable season*, Pr. 25. 11; שִׁקְמִים *sycamore trees*, הָבְנִים *ebony*. The singulars אֶשֶׁר, אֹפֶן, שֶׁקֶם †, הֹבֶן are merely supposed forms, and do not really occur.

17. In the pl. constr. a euphonic Dagesh is often inserted in the letter which has Sheva, e. g. (*a*) of the form מֶלֶךְ there is חַלְּקֵי for חֶלְקֵי; (*b*) of the form סֵפֶר there are עִשְּׂבוֹת, שִׁבֳּלֵי; (*c*) of the form קֹדֶשׁ,

* In a similar manner may be accounted for the plurals דּוּדָאִים *mandrakes*, לוּלָאוֹת *winding stairs*, viz. probably from lost singulars דּוּדַי, לוּלַי, with the Aramaean adjective termination ־ַי, hence דּוּדַי signifies properly *pertaining to love*, from דּוּד=דּוֹד *love*. The plural which was to have been דּוּדָיִים is become דּוּדָאִים, similar to the Chaldee קַדְמַי, emph. קַדְמָאָה.

† In the Mishna (tract. Kilaim. No. 8, ed. Surenh.) is found the sing. שקמה.

סִבְּלוֹ, also שְׁקָתוֹת in which Dagesh is omitted and compensated by composite Sheva under the following letter, comp. כִּנֹּרוֹת and כִּנֳּרוֹת, וַתְּאַלְּצֵהוּ and וַתְּאַלְצֵהוּ, עֲנָיִי for עֲנִיִּי; comp. also יִצְחַק, רָמְשׁ, אֲמָרוֹת, which forms are to be regarded as if they had euphonic Dagesh in *syllaba brevi* (Lehrg. § 15. 4, lit. *c*).

18. The paragogic ה effects no further change in the form of these words than that the auxiliary Segol becomes Sheva. Hence אֶרֶץ, אַרְצָה (rem. 2); קֶדֶם and קֵדְמָה, קֶדֶם. *towards the east;* אֹהֶל, אֹהֱלָה *into the tent;* גֹּרֶן, גָּרְנָה *to the threshing-floor*, Mi. 4. 2; מָוְתָה *death*, לַיְלָה *night*, from לַיִל, מָוֶת. שְׁכֶם becomes שְׁכְמָה (rem. 10).

SECTION XXXVI.—SEVENTH DECLENSION OF THE MASCULINES. (Table O.)

EXPLANATORY.

1. To this declension belong nouns which have Tseri *pure* in their final syllable, and are either monosyllabic or have their preceding vowels immutable. It accordingly embraces participles in Kal (§ 26. No. 4); those in Piel and Hithpael, and other words of a similar form, e. g. כֹּהֵן *priest*, עֹרֵב *raven* (also the Chaldee שָׂהֵד *witness*, Job 16. 19); to which must be added of the verbal nouns from the regular verb (§ 26) No. 9. קָטֵל; No. 14. the forms מַכְתֵּשׁ, מִסְפֵּד; No. 25. קָטֵל; and the primitives of the like forms, as כִּסֵּא *throne*, מַקֵּל *staff*, or pluriliterals, as צְפַרְדֵּעַ *frog*. Nouns derived from verbs פ״י, as מוֹעֵד *time;* and those from verbs ל״ה, as בֵּן *son*. The verbal nouns, however, of No. 19 do not belong to this declension, e. g. מַקְהֵל, pl. מַקְהֵלִים.

2. This declension is characterised by the following peculiarities:

(*a*) Most of the words of this class do not change at all in the constr. state of the singular, e. g. שֵׁם, אֹיֵב, in others Tseri is changed into Pattahh, e. g. מִזְבֵּחַ, מִזְבַּח.

(*b*) In all the forms, other than the ground-form of the singular, the vowel of the final syllable is entirely lost, except the monosyllabic words which retain Tseri in the plural abs. e. g. שֵׁמוֹת.

(*c*) In the singular, where two Shevas would occur together before the suffixes ךָ, כֶם, כֶן, they are combined into one syllable by Hhirek, e. g. אֹיִבְךָ, אֹיִבְכֶם.

For the numerous deviations see the remarks.

REMARKS.

1. The words in which (..) is changed to (-) are, besides the one given in the paradigm, מַעֲשֵׂר *tenth*, מִסְפֵּד *lamentation*, מַקֵּל *staff* (constr. מַקַּל Ge. 30. 37, and מַקַּל Je. 1. 11), and in participles of Kal and Piel of the verbs with guttural, e. g. שֹׁסַע Le. 11. 7, and without guttural in אֹבַד עֵצוֹת *of corrupt counsel*, De. 32. 28.

It is, moreover, to be observed, that some nouns of the form מִקְטֵל have for their constr. state מִקְטַל; e. g. מַפְתֵּחַ *key*, constr. מִפְתַּח; מַרְבֵּץ *place of lying down*, constr. מִרְבַּץ; מַשְׁבֵּר *matrix*, constr. מִשְׁבַּר; מַרְזֵחַ *cry*, constr. מִרְזַח; מַשְׁחֵת *destruction*, constr. מִשְׁחַת; מַשְׁעֵן *stay*, constr. מִשְׁעַן; this last, however, may be referred to the ground-form מִשְׁעָן which actually occurs.

2. Some monosyllabic words *retain Tseri* in the singular before the *light suffixes*, e. g. גֵּו *back*, גֵּוִי Is. 50. 6; גֵּוְךָ Is. 38. 17; עֵץ *wood*, עֵצִי, עֵצְךָ; דֵּעַ *knowledge*, דֵּעִי Job 33. 6, 10; רֵעַ *companion, friend*, also *thought*, רֵעִי Ps. 139. 2; רֵעֲךָ Le. 19. 18. Those monosyllabic words are, of course, excepted which from the nature of their derivation have Tseri *impure*, e. g. the participles of ע״ו, as מֵת *dead*, גֵּר *stranger*, אֵל *God* (from אול).

3. Before the suffixes ךָ, כֶם, כֶן some of these nouns take Segol, as מַקֶּלְכֶם *your staff*, Ex. 12. 11; יֶשְׁךָ *thou art* (as a particle belongs also to this declension); אֶשְׁכֶם *your fire*, Is. 50. 11 (with gutturals they take Pattahh, as אֹהַבְךָ 2 Ch. 20. 7; שֹׂנַאֲךָ Ex. 23. 5); on the contrary, however, with Sheva is כִּסְאֲךָ 2 Sa. 7. 16; Ps. 45. 7; 89. 5; 93. 2 (for כִּסְאֲךָ, comp. § 10. r. 7, not כִּסַּאֲךָ, from כִּסֵּא); others have immutable Tseri, as אַבְנֵטְךָ *thy girdle*, Is. 22. 21.

Changes of (..) into (..) occur only in the words בֵּן constr. בֶּן *son*, six times, the form שֶׁם־ from שֵׁם; עֵת *time*, constr. עֵת, but also עֶת־ Le. 15. 25; Hag. 1. 2.

4. In the *plural abs.* all the monosyllabic words retain Tseri, e. g. עֵץ *wood*, pl. abs. עֵצִים, constr. עֲצֵי; דֵּעַ *knowledge*, pl. דֵּעִים; du. רֵחַיִם *hand-mill*. There are, however, several plurisyllabic nouns which follow the same analogy, e. g. רִבֵּעִים, שִׁלֵּשִׁים *descendants of the third, fourth generation;* שׁוֹמֵמוֹת *desolations*, Da. 9. 26; and quadriliterals, עֲטַלֵּפִים *bats*, סַנְוֵרִים *blindness*, פַּרְדֵּסִים *parks*, אַבְנֵטִים *girdles*. רֵעַ *friend*, מֵעִים *intestines*, retain Tseri even before the *grave* suffixes; רֵעֵיכֶם Ps. 28. 3; מֵעֵיהֶם Eze. 7. 19 (but also מְעַי). These examples are better regarded as so many irregularities than *forma dagessanda*, according to which רֵעַ is to be supposed to stand for רֵעֶה, רֵעָה; מֵעִים for מְעַיִם.

5. The analogy of these nouns is followed also in several nouns which have *Pattahh* in the final syllable, and are derived from verbs ל״ה, or, at least, they assume a similar form, and are consequently of the same origin as the form שֵׁם, בֵּן. They are בַּר *son*, with suff. בְּרִי Pr. 31. 2 (from בְּרָא=בָּרָה); זַן, pl. זְנִים *kind;* מְתִים *men*, from a lost singular מַת, Ethiopic מת (with the sixth vowel) *man, husband.*

Here is to be noticed also other nouns with *Pattahh*, in which this vowel is substituted for *Tseri* on account of a guttural, e. g. הִכָּנַע (for הִכָּנֵעַ Niph. inf.), with suff. הִכָּנְעוֹ 2 Ch. 12. 12.

6. There are a few nouns ending with *Hholem pure*, in which this vowel is dropped like Tseri in this declension, as קָדְקֹד *crown of the head*, with suff. קָדְקְדוֹ; אֶשְׁכֹּל *cluster*, pl. אֶשְׁכְּלוֹת; צִפֹּר *bird*, pl. constr. צִפְּרֵי, though the two last may be derived from a fem. צִפֹּרֶת, אֶשְׁכֹּלֶת (according to § 30. rem. 2). In the same manner the punctuators have inflected the original plural בָּמוֹת *heights*, viz. בָּמֳתֵי, בָּמֳתִים (bamŏthim, bamŏthai).

7. תֵּבֵל is without vowel-change, prob. for תֵּיבֵל from יָבַל.

SECTION XXXVII.—EIGHTH DECLENSION OF THE MASCULINES. (TABLE O.)

EXPLANATORY.

1. This declension embraces nouns which double the final consonant whenever a sufformative is added at the end, e. g. יָם *sea*, pl. יַמִּים; אֵם *mother*, pl. אִמּוֹת. This reduplication lies doubtless already in the character of the ground-form יָם itself, only that, according to a rule of Hebrew orthography, no such reduplication is to be expressed at the end of the word.*

2. According to the original form with Dagesh, the forms mentioned above would have had short vowels (יַם, אִם, כֻּל), but having lost the sharpening, they are changed into long vowels, יָם, אֵם, כֹּל.† When the sharpening is now again introduced, by an accession at the end, the long vowel is again shortened, viz., *Kamets* into *Pattahh*, *Tseri* into *Hhirek*, *Hholem* (and *Shurek*) into *Kibbuts*. *Pattahh* is either retained or attenuated to *Hhirek*.

In the *constr. st.* of the singular, the vowel-change depends upon the general character of the form, e. g. עָם, constr. עַם (according to the second declension), but on the contrary אֵם, constr. אֵם (according to the seventh declension).

If the word is of more than one syllable, the penultimate vowel conforms to the principles which regulate the vowel-changes, as אוֹפָן pl. אוֹפַנִּים, גַּלְגַּל pl. גַּלְגַּלִּים, where the first syllable is immutable (according to the second declension), but on the other hand גָּמָל pl. גְּמַלִּים, constr. גְּמַלֵּי (according to the fourth declension).

3. This reduplication of the final radical is found, however, in nouns of the most heterogeneous forms; and whether or not a noun is to be inflected according to the scheme mentioned above, can seldom be known from the ground-form, though its etymology will generally decide. Etymology refers to this declension the following classes of nouns:—

(*a*) All the derivatives of the verbs ע״ע (§ 27. II), in which the geminate terminates the word,‡ e. g. יָתֹם רַב, No. 10. גַּן, חֵן, חֹק, No. 14. מֵסַב, מָעֹז, מָגֵן, and the primitives which follow the same analogy, יָם *sea*, אֵשׁ *fare*, גַּג *roof*.

(*b*) Many contracted forms in which נ is assimilated in the final letter. E. g. אַף (for אֱנַף, אַנְף) *wrath*, with suff. אַפִּי; בַּת (for בְּנַת) *daughter*, with suff. בִּתִּי; תֵּת (for תֵּנֶת) *to give*, תִּתִּי; אֱמֶת (for אֱמֶנֶת) *truth*, אֲמִתִּי; חֵךְ (Arab. חנך) *palate*, חִכִּי; עֵז (Arab. עזז) *goat*, pl. עִזִּים.

(*c*) Derivatives from the regular verb (§ 26) of the following forms: No. 1. עָצָב *idol*, pl. עֲצַבִּים, עֲצַבֵּי; קָטֹן *small*, fem. קְטַנָּה. No. 5. חָרוּל *nettle*, pl. חֲרֻלִּים; No. 6. שַׁבָּת *sabbath*, with suff. שַׁבַּתּוֹ. No. 10. זְמָן *time*, לְשַׁד *juice*, אֶשְׁנָב *window-lattice*, אַשְׁמַנִּים *darkness*. No. 14. מַחְשָׁךְ *darkness*, מַחְמָד *loveliness*, מִשְׂגָּב *height*, מִשְׁמָן *fatness*, מַשְׁבֵּת *destruction*, מַאֲמָץ *strength*, &c. No. 20. אוֹפָן *wheel*. No. 21. אָדֹם *red*, pl. אֲדֻמִּים; נָקֹד *spotted*, pl. נְקֻדִּים. No. 22. שַׁאֲנָן *quiet*, pl. שַׁאֲנַנִּים. No. 34. גַּבְנֹן, pl. גַּבְנֻנִּים *summits*. Finally, several quadriliterals, as עַקְרָב *scorpion*, pl. עַקְרַבִּים; חַרְטֹם *magician*, pl. חַרְטֻמִּים; גַּרְזֶן *axe*, with suff. גַּרְזִנִּי. Primitives of the forms mentioned are, גָּמָל *camel*, שָׁפָן *coney*, מוֹרַג *threshing instrument*, pl. מוֹרַגִּים.

4. Here also are to be noticed other derivatives from irregular verbs of the following forms: (*a*) like עָנִי *afflicted*, pl. עֲנִיִּים, for עָנִיי (after the form קָטִיל); (*b*) אִי *island*, pl. אִיִּים; עִי *heap*, pl. עִיִּים, for עֱוִי, אֱוִי (the geminate Yod properly stands for וי); קַו *cord*, with suff. קַוּם (from קוה, קוו, properly for קָוֻו). Finally, several patronymic and gentilic nouns terminating in ִ־י, as לֵוִי, pl. לְוִיִּם, כּוּשִׁי, pl. כּוּשִׁיִּים, (on the contrary יְהוּדִי has the pl. יְהוּדִים *Jews*).

* Comp. אַף *anger* for אַף, (aff) אֱנַף, וַיְצַו for וַיְצַוּ (y'tzavv) &c.

† Comp. בָּרֵךְ for בָּרֵךְ, בֵּרֵךְ for בֵּרֵךְ, בָּרֵךְ for בָּרֵךְ, יָגֵל for יָגֵל.

‡ In others, where the geminate stands in the middle, as מְגִלָּה, חַלּוֹן, the reduplication has already been effected on account of the terminations ָ־ה, וֹן.

REMARKS.

1. Some nouns of the form אֵם take *Pattahh* before the accession, as כֵּן *pedestal*, with suff. כַּנּוֹ (from כָּנַן); עֵת *time*, with suff. עִתִּי, but with ה parag. עַתָּה *at this time, now.*

2. The nouns of the form חֹק generally have *Makkeph* in the *constr. st.*, and thence *Kamets-hhatuph* for their vowel, e. g. כֹּל *all*, כָּל־; רֹב *multitude*, רָב־; עֹז *strength*, עָז.

Before the suffixes which begin with a vowel, *Kamets-hhatuph* occurs also, though but seldom, as עָזִּי Ex. 15. 2; Ps. 118. 14; but more frequently before the suffixes ךָ, כֶם, כֶן, as עָזְּךָ Ex. 15. 13; Ps. 21. 2 (also עֻזְּךָ Ps. 63. 3), where, however, *Kibbuts* is not unfrequent, e. g. כֻּלְּכֶם.

Instead of Kibbuts, *Shurek plene* is sometimes found, as עוּזֵּנוּ Ps. 81. 2, comp. § 10. rem. 5.

3. According to paradigm מַד (lett. e) are inflected, סַף *threshold*, pl. סִפִּים; פַּת *morsel*, pl. פִּתִּים; בַּז *spoil*, גַּלְגַּל *wheel*, מוֹרַג *threshing instrument*, חַת *fear*; מֵסַב *divan*, with suff. מְסִבּוֹ. מוֹרִיגִים 1 Ch. 21. 23, is written *in full* for מוֹרִגִּים from מוֹרַג.

Nouns having *Segol* in the final syllable follow the same analogy, בַּרְזֶל, בַּרְזִלּוֹ; גַּרְזֶן, גַּרְזְנּוֹ, &c. All others with *Pattahh* retain this vowel in the inflexion.

4. Some of the derivatives from ע״ע, with the preformative מ (from No. 14) do not shorten Kamets under מ, e. g. מָעֹז *fortress*, pl. מָעֻזִּים; מָסָךְ *covering*, constr. מָסַךְ; מָגֵן *shield*, with suff. מָגִנִּי, pl. מָגִנִּים.

5. Some few nouns are, in different passages, inflected either with or without Dagesh, which in some instances may be ascribed to a mere inconsistency of the punctuators. E. g. אֵת *ploughshare*, whence אִתּוֹ, אִתִּים 1 Sa. 13. 20, 21 (in several MSS. even איתו, איתים), but also אִתִּים Is. 2. 4; Joel 4. 10; מַעֲדַנִּים *dainties*, Je. 51. 34, and מַעֲדַנִּים Pr. 29. 17; Ge. 49. 20, comp. מַעֲדַנּוֹת Job 38. 31; נִכְבָּדִים *honourable*, Nu. 22. 15, with suff. נִכְבַּדֵּיהֶם Ps. 149. 8, but also נִכְבַּדֵּי Is. 23. 8, 9; Pr. 8. 24; נִכְבַּדֶּיהָ Na. 3. 10; כַּרְמֶל *fruitful field* (also pr. name), with suff. כַּרְמִלּוֹ 2 Ki. 19. 23, but gentile noun כַּרְמְלִי 1 Sa. 30. 5; 2 Sa. 23. 35. Especially fluctuating in the inflexion is ִי in the patronymic and gentilic nouns, as יְהוּדִי, pl. יְהוּדִים and יְהוּדִיִּים.

In some cases the signification is affected by this difference of inflexion, עֲרֻמִּים *naked* (from עָרוֹם), Job 22. 6, and עֲרוּמִים *wise*, Job 5. 12; so also the particle אֵת, whence אוֹתִי *me*, and אִתִּי *with me*.

6. The noun חַי *living, life*, from חָיַי is inflected in the same manner, e. g. pl. חַיִּים, fem. חַיָּה, with this difference, that it is contracted in the constr. state of the singular to חֵי. So also דַּי *sufficient*, constr. דֵּי, with suff. דַּיּוֹ דַּיִי.

7. When the geminate letter is a guttural or ר, the omission of the Dagesh is compensated by lengthening the preceding vowel. E. g. שַׂר *prince*, with suff. שָׂרוֹ (for שַׂרּוֹ), pl. שָׂרִים, but with grave suff. שָׂרֵכֶם. There are, however, a few exceptions as regards ר, e. g. שָׁרֵּךְ *thy navel*, Eze. 16. 4, from שֹׁר. Others have the so called *Dagesh forte implicit.*, e. g. לַח *fresh* pl. לַחִים (for לַחִּים); אָח *brother*, pl. אַחִים; מִבְטָח, with suff. מִבְטַחוֹ, pl. מִבְטַחִים.

SECTION XXXVIII.—NINTH DECLENSION OF THE MASCULINES. (Table O.)

EXPLANATORY.

1. This declension comprises derivatives from verbs ל״ה (§ 27. V) which terminate in ֶה, as No. 2. יָפֶה *beautiful;* No. 4. רֹאֶה *seer;* No. 11. קָצֶה *end;* רֵעֶה *friend;* No. 14. מַרְאֶה *appearance;* from Pilel נָאוֶה *comely* (§ 24. rem. 22); finally, the primitives analogous to the above, as שָׂדֶה *field.*

2. The first syllable is treated according to the nature of its form; ֶה, however, undergoes the following changes:—

(*a*) In the constr. state of the singular it becomes ֵה.

(*b*) Before any of the afformatives it is entirely dropped.

REMARKS.

1. The original termination ַי for which ֶה is substituted* is often restored, and affects the inflexion of the word. Thus, with suff. מְכַסֶּיךָ (sing. *thy covering*, which might also be expressed by מְכַסְּךָ),

* As יִגְלֶה prop. for יִגְלַי, מַרְאֶה for מַרְאַי, comp. שָׂדֶה, poet. שָׂדַי, Gesen. gram. § 42. 2; comp. also above, § 24. r. 4 & 5.

Is. 14. 11; מִקְנֶיךָ Is. 30. 23; מַרְאֶיךָ (almost universally, though erroneously, taken for the plural), Ca. 2. 14; מַרְאֵיהֶם, מַרְאָיו Da. 1. 15; Eze. 1. 5. In the plural מְמֻחָיִם from מְמֻחֶה for מְמֻחַי Pual part., Is. 25. 6 (Ges. Gram. § 90. 9).

2. To this declension is properly to be referred the plural שָׁמַיִם (from a singular שְׁמַי, comp. rem. 1), constr. שְׁמֵי, with suff. שָׁמֶיךָ. The form שָׁמַיִם is only an apparent dual, but is a plural in fact, on account of the final י, like גּוֹי which makes the plural גּוֹיִם (not גּוֹיִים), מַי pl. מַיִם, which latter has likewise the dual form, comp. Lehrg. p. 537.

3. In a few instances ֶה is retained even before a genitive, e. g. רֵעֶה הַמֶּלֶךְ *friend of the king*, 1 Ki. 4. 5; מִשְׁנֶה שִׁבָּרוֹן *double destruction*, Je. 17. 18.

SECTION XXXIX.—VOWEL-CHANGES IN THE FORMATION OF FEMININE NOUNS.

EXPLANATORY.

1. A substantive or adjective feminine is formed from its corresponding masculine, by appending either of the two terminations ָה and ֶת (with gutturals ַת). Where the one or the other termination is used, and how the masculine is thereby modified, especially with respect to the vowels, has already become evident from the examples given in § 26 and 27, being everywhere accompanied by the corresponding feminine forms; a closer consideration, however, of the general analogy of this formation is still necessary in this place.

2. The termination ָה is more general than ֶת (ַת), since, in most cases, the latter occurs only in connection with the other, and is commonly used for the *constr. state*, because ת with Pattahh or Segol affords a convenient transition to the following word. E. g. מַמְלָכָה and מַמְלֶכֶת *kingdom*, מִשְׁפָּחָה and מִשְׁפַּחַת *family*, אַשְׁמוּרָה and אַשְׁמֹרֶת *night-watch*, the latter invariably as the *constr. state*. With the participles, however, and certain infinitives, the termination ֶת is, on the contrary, more commonly in use, e. g. קֹטֶלֶת is more frequent than קֹטְלָה, לֶדֶת more frequent than לֵדָה. In like manner the feminine of nouns terminating in ִי is seldom ִיָּה, but frequently ִית (for ִיַּת). The latter termination, however, is very seldom appended to words which have a quiescent letter, especially ִי, וּ, in the final syllable, e. g. צַדִּיק, עָצוּם.

3. The termination ָה appended to a masculine noun affects the tone of the word, and consequently its vowel, in the same manner as the light suffixes beginning with a vowel (§ 28. No. 21). The following are examples of the formation of feminines in the several declensions:—

Decl.	Masc.		Fem.	
1.	סוּס	*horse*	fem. סוּסָה	*mare*
	תַּחְתּוֹן		תַּחְתּוֹנָה	*lower*
2.	מוֹצָא		מוֹצָאָה	*origin*
3.	גָּדוֹל		גְּדוֹלָה	*great*
	עָצוּם		עֲצוּמָה	*mighty*
	בָּרִיא		בְּרִיאָה	*fat*
	מֵקִים		מְקִימָה	*raising*
4.	נָקָם		נְקָמָה	*vengeance*
5.	זָקֵן	*old man*	זְקֵנָה	*old woman*
6.	מֶלֶךְ	*king*	מַלְכָּה	*queen*
	גֶּבַע		גִּבְעָה	*hill*
	אֵמֶר		אִמְרָה	*word*
	עֵגֶל	*vitulus*	עֶגְלָה	*vitula*
	אֹכֶל		אָכְלָה	*food*
	חֹזֶק		חָזְקָה	*strength*
	עָוֶל		עַוְלָה	*wrong*
	צַיִד	*hunting*	צֵידָה	*game, provison*
7.	אֹרֵחַ	*traveller*	אֹרְחָה	*caravan*
	מוֹקֵד		מוֹקְדָה	*burning*
	דֵּעַ		דֵּעָה	*knowledge*
8.	תָּם		תַּמָּה	*innocent*
	נֵץ		נִצָּה	*flower*
	כֵּן		כַּנָּה	*pedestal*
	חֹק		חֻקָּה	*law*
	בַּז		בִּזָּה	*spoil*
	גַּן		גַּנָּה	*garden*
	שַׂר	*prince*	שָׂרָה	*princess*
9.	יָפֶה		יָפָה	*fair*
	מַרְאֶה		מַרְאָה	*appearance.*

REMARKS.*

ON DECLENSION 3.

1. In some few words וֹ of the final syllable is changed in the feminine into וּ (comp. § 32. rem. 5). E. g. מָתוֹק *sweet*, fem. מְתוּקָה; מָלוֹן *lodging*, fem.

* The reader, when directed to the remarks of this section, should bear in mind that there are other remarks, besides these, after No. 4.

מְלוּנָה; מָנוֹחַ *rest*, fem. מְנוּחָה; מָנוֹס *flight*, fem. מְנוּסָה; מָצוֹר *fortress*, fem. מְצוּרָה.

2. An example of *Kamets pure* in the first syllable is בָּגוֹדָה Je. 3. 7, 10, comp. § 32. rem. 1.

On Declensions 4 & 5.

3. The forms קְטַל and קָטֵל have sometimes feminines which seem to be derived from *Segolate forms*, which, from their close relation, is quite natural. E. g. יָעֵל, fem. יַעֲלָה (not יְעֵלָה) *wild goat*, יָעֵן, fem. יַעֲנָה *ostrich*; יָרֵךְ, fem. יַרְכָה *thigh*;* שֵׂעָר, fem. שַׂעֲרָה *hair*.

On Declension 7.

4. *Tseri* of the final syllable is even more frequently retained here than in the accession of the suffixes (§ 36. rem. 4). As עֵץ *wood*, fem. עֵצָה (collect.); מִשְׁעֵן *stay*, fem. מַשְׁעֵנָה; especially so with the participles, as בֹּגֵדָה *treacherous*, Je. 3. 8, 11; יוֹלֵדָה *bearing*, Is. 21. 3; נֹטֵרָה *watching*, Ca. 1. 6; סֹרֵרָה *rebellious*, Ho. 4. 16; זוֹלֵלָה *despised*, La. 1. 11; אֹכֵלָה *eating*, Is. 30. 30 (but also אֹכְלָה De. 4. 24); בֹּעֵרָה *burning*, Is. 34. 9 (but בֹּעֲרָה ch. 30. 33); שֹׁמֵמָה *desolate*, Is. 54. 1; שֹׁקֵקָה *eager*, Ps. 107. 9; Piel מְשַׁכֵּלָה *miscarrying*, Ex. 23. 26; מְכַשֵּׁפָה *sorceress*, Ex. 22. 17; מְרַקֵּדָה *dancing*, Na. 3. 2; Hithp. מִתְנַכֵּרָה *feigning a stranger*, 1 Ki. 14. 5, 6.

4. The penultimate vowel is affected in the same manner (No. 3) when the feminine termination ־ֶת (־ַת) is employed, e. g. עֲטָרָה, עֲטֶרֶת *crown* (from masc. עֶטֶר); עָקָר *barren*, fem. עֲקֶרֶת; חָבֵר *companion*, fem. חֲבֶרֶת; but remains immutable in declensions 2 and 7, as חוֹתָם fem. חוֹתֶמֶת, קֹטֵל fem. קֹטֶלֶת. The final vowel is also affected in several ways, viz.:—

(*a*) *Kamets* and *Pattahh* are both changed to *Segol* (like מֶלֶךְ for מַלְךְ, מָלְךְ), e. g. מִשְׁעָן *staff*, fem. מִשְׁעֶנֶת.

(*b*) *Tseri* is retained in some words, in others it is changed to *Segol*, e. g. חָמֵשׁ *five*, fem. חֲמֵשֶׁת; גָּדֵר *wall* fem. גְּדֶרֶת; inf. לֵד *to bear*, fem. לֶדֶת.

(*c*) ־ַת, employed when a word ends with a guttural, changes the preceding *Kamets* or *Tseri* to *Pattahh*, as מוֹדָע fem. מוֹדַעַת *acquaintance*; דֵּעַ fem. דַּעַת *knowledge*; נַחַת *rest*, שַׁחַת (perhaps from masculines שַׁח, נַח).

(*d*) In the few examples which admit of this termination, though they have an *immutable* vowel (וּ, וֹ, ־ִי, ־ָא) in the final syllable (comp. No. 2), this vowel is exchanged for its corresponding mutable one, as אִישׁ, fem. אֵשֶׁת (for אִישֶׁת); שַׁלִּיט, fem. שַׁלֶּטֶת *imperious*, Eze. 16. 30; מַקְטִיל, fem. מַקְטֶלֶת (§ 11. rem. 8); גְּבִיר *master*, fem. גְּבֶרֶת (but also גְּבִירָה); בּוֹשׁ *shame*, fem. בֹּשֶׁת (with suff. בָּשְׁתִּי); שָׁלוֹשׁ, fem. שְׁלֹשֶׁת, נְחוּשָׁה and נְחֹשֶׁת *brass*; אַשְׁמוּרָה and אַשְׁמֹרֶת *night-watch* (from a masc. אַשְׁמוּר; in תְּשׂוּמֶת however, in Le. 5. 21, וּ has remained unchanged, and so in the pr. name תַּנְחוּמֶת 2 Ki. 25. 23; Je. 40. 8.

The like feminines most probably existed from צַוָּאר and צִפּוֹר, viz. צַוָּארֶת, צִפֹּרֶת, which accounts for the plurals צִפֳּרִים, צַוְּארֵי § 30. rem. 1 & 2. This gives rise to another three Segolate forms for the declension of the feminines, like מֶלֶךְ, סֵפֶר, קֹדֶשׁ, viz. קְטֶלֶת, אֵשֶׁת, בֹּשֶׁת.

When the word terminates in a quiescent vowel-letter, the *Segol*, as a toneless vowel, is entirely dropped, hence חַטָּאת *sin*, for חַטָּאֶת (from חַטָּא), עִבְרִית for עִבְרִיֶּת.

REMARKS.†

I. On the Termination ־ֶת.

1. This termination is not generally appended to masculine nouns of the eighth declension which have the final letter doubled, but where this does take place, the reduplication of the last radical is omitted. E. g. אֲדַמְדָּם *reddish*, pl. אֲדַמְדַּמִּים Le. 14. 37, but fem. אֲדַמְדֶּמֶת Le. 13. 19; קַשְׂקַשִּׂים *scales*, 1 Sa. 17. 5, but fem. sing. קַשְׂקֶשֶׂת, whence the plural קַשְׂקְשׂוֹת Eze. 29. 4. The same analogy exists in the feminines of the patronymics, gentilics, and ordinals terminating in ־ִי, which are inflected ־ִיָּה, and ־ִית by solving the reduplication. E. g. מוֹאֲבִיָּה Ru. 4. 5, and מוֹאֲבִית 2 Ch. 24. 26, *a Moabitish woman*; אֲרַמִּיָּה *Syrian woman* 1 Ch. 7. 14, and אֲרָמִית *in the Syrian language*, 2 Ki. 18. 26; שְׁלִישִׁיָּה Is. 15. 5, and שְׁלִישִׁית *third*; and in like manner the cardinal numerals חֲמִשָּׁה and חֲמֵשֶׁת *five*, שִׁשָּׁה and שֵׁשֶׁת *six*.‡

2. Where the Hebrew has the Segolate termination (ֶ ֶ) the Aramaean has usually (ְ ֵ), as מְלֵךְ, מֶלֶךְ. The like Syriacism is found here in the feminine termination, as שְׂאֵת for שֶׂאֶת *to bear*; מַשְׂאֵת for מַשְׂאֶת

* In this word, however, there appears to be a twofold derivation, viz. יְרֵכָה (with suff. יַרְכָתוֹ, du. יַרְכָתַיִם) from יָרֵךְ; and יַרְכָּה (whence du. יַרְכְּתֵי) from the Segolate form יֶרֶךְ, the constr. of יָרֵךְ.

† For other remarks in this section see above, after No. 3.

‡ This accounts for the plural termination ־ִיּוֹת used for the nouns of ־ִית as עִבְרִית pl. עִבְרִיּוֹת), namely, an original form of ־ִיָּה must likewise be supposed as the ground-form, comp. Ges. Lehrg. § 124. 3.

gift; מִצֵּאת for מְצֶאת *finding*, invariably, as it appears, when the last radical is א.

3. The reverse of the inflexion just mentioned is that of the Arabic, which has (ַ ְ) instead of (ֶ ֶ) as מַלְךְּ for מֶלֶךְ. A similar form in the Hebrew is יֹלַדְתְּ *bearing*, for יֹלֶדֶת Ge. 16. 11; Ju. 13. 5.

II. IN GENERAL.

4. The vowels are shortened in the same manner when the formative syllables ִי, וֹן, ָן, וּת are appended, as when the termination ָה is appended, which affords the explanation for the vowel-changes of § 26. Nos. 15, 16, &c.

5. Finally, it is to be observed that, since there are not masculines extant for every feminine, it is often doubtful to which class a certain feminine is to be referred. Thus, for instance, there is an entire want of masculine forms corresponding to the feminines of וּת; there can, however, be no doubt that they must have ended in וּ.

SECTION XL.—ON THE DECLENSION OF THE FEMININE NOUNS IN GENERAL.

The declension of these nouns is much more simple than that of the masculines, since the addition of the feminine termination has already occasioned a shortening of the vowels. In the plural no distinction is made between the *light* and *grave* suffixes, both being appended to the *constr. state*. The inflexion of the feminine nouns is best exhibited in four declensions (comp. the note to the following section).

SECTION XLI.—TENTH DECLENSION, OR THE *FIRST* OF THE FEMININES.* (TABLE O.)

EXPLANATORY.

1. This declension, like the first of the masculines, has no vowel-change, and is inserted merely for the sake of comparison.

2. After what has been said, it is hardly necessary to point out the nouns belonging to this declension, viz. the feminines terminating in ָה from the masc. dec. 3. גְּדוֹלָה, 7. קְטֻלָּה, 8. חֻקָּה, בִּצָּה, תַּמָּה.

SECTION XLII.—ELEVENTH DECLENSION, OR THE *SECOND* OF THE FEMININES. (TABLE O.)

EXPLANATORY.

1. To this declension belong those nouns which have a *pure Kamets* or *Tseri* before the feminine termination ָה. Such are the following derivatives from the regular verb (§ 26), the feminine forms of Nos. 1. as נְבָלָה *foolish*, חֲכָמָה *wise*; 2. לְבֵנָה *brick*; 4. תּוֹעֵבָה *abomination*; 12. נְקָמָה *vengeance*; 14. מַמְלָכָה *kingdom*, מַצֵּבָה *pillar*; 17. נִפְלָאָה *wonder*; also the following derivatives from the regular verbs (§ 27) are, e. g. from פ"ו, Nos. 10. עֵצָה *counsel*, חֵמָה *wrath*; 14. מוֹעֵצָה *counsel*; from ל"ה, Nos. 2. יָפָה *fair*; 11. כֵּרָה *pit*; 12. כָּלָה *destruction*; consequently the feminine forms from dec. 2, 4, 5, 9.

2. This inflexion is analogous to that of the second declension of the masculines, whether the vowel is *Kamets* or *Tseri*. When Sheva precedes the terminations ָָה, ֵָה, as in paradigm c, the two Shevas of the shortened form (צְדְקַת) are combined in one syllable, צִדְקַת.

3. The following are regular exceptions, in which (ָ) and (ֵ) are *immutable*, either as being *impure* vowels, or as standing in sharpened syllables with Dagesh, *syllaba dagessanda*:—

Of the derivatives from the regular verb (§ 26), the feminine forms of Nos. 6. יַבָּשָׁה *dry land*; 13. חֲשֵׁכָה (for חֲשֵׁיכָה) *darkness*, and several others; בַּקָּשָׁה *request*, נֶאָצָה *reproach*,† פָּרָשָׁה (for פַּרָשָׁה) *exposition*; 28. אַזְכָּרָה *memorial*; also from פ"ן, as הַצָּלָה *deliverance*, הַכָּרָה *a knowing*; and so all the

* Gesenius gives two separate tables: one for the masculines, consisting of nine declensions, and another for the feminines, consisting of four. For the sake of convenience, we have given both in one table, making together *thirteen* declensions; here, however, in the explanations, where they must necessarily be kept distinct, we have in this manner contrived to point out both orders.

† נֶאָצָה with *Dagesh forte implicit.* for נַאָצָה, *Pattahh* is changed to *Segol* before the *guttural* with *Kamets*, comp. אָח § 45, also § 37. rem. 7 and § 14. rem. 3.

feminines whose geminate letter is a guttural, on account of which it cannot be doubled, and are therefore preceded by (ָ) or (ֵ); e. g. (§ 27) Nos. 1. צָרָה *enemy* (from צַר), רָעָה *evil* (from רַע), בָּרָה *pure* (from בַּר); 2. גֵּרָה *rumination* (from גָּרַר); 14. מְאֵרָה *curse* (from אָרַר), מְגֵרָה *a saw* (from גָּרַר); so also derivatives from ע״ו and ע״י (whose Kamets and Tseri are invariably *impure*), as Nos. 1. זָרָה *strange*, בָּמָה *height*; 2. עֵדָה *witness*; and finally, derivatives from ל״א, No. 2. מְלֵאָה *full*, טְמֵאָה *unclean*.

REMARKS.

I. On the form with ָ-ה.

1. Forms of parad. c, when their first or second letter is a guttural, take in the shortened form either (ֲ) or (ֳ); e. g. חֲכָמָה *wise*, pl. c. חַכְמוֹת; עֲגָלָה *waggon*, with suff. עֶגְלָתוֹ; זְעָקָה *cry*, constr. זַעֲקַת.

2. In a small number of derivatives from ל״ה Kamets of the penultima is immutable, as תְּלָאָה *travail* (from לָאָה), תְּעָלָה *aqueduct* (from עָלָה), אָלָה *oath*, with suff. אָלָתִי, אָלָתוֹ Ge. 24. 41; De. 29. 11; מָנָה *portion*, whence מָנוֹתֶיהָ Est. 2. 9 (but sing. constr. מְנָת Je. 13. 25); הָרָה *pregnant*, whence הָרוֹתֶיהָ 2 Ki. 15. 16; הָרוֹתֵיהֶם 2 Ki. 8. 12 (but sing. constr. הֲרַת Je. 20. 17); יָפָה *fair*, with suff. יָפָתִי Ca. 2. 10, 13 (elsewhere constr. יְפַת, pl. יְפוֹת).

3. An irregularity similar to the preceding is found in the word קְעָרָה *dish*, of which the pl. constr. is קַעֲרוֹת, and yet with suff. קְעָרֹתָיו.

II. On the form with ֵ-ה.

4. By far the greater number of this class of nouns retain the Tseri in the inflexion, and but few occur with *mutable Tseri* besides those given in No. 1 of this section, viz., אֲשֵׁדָה *outpouring*, pl. constr. אַשְׁדוֹת; שְׁדֵמָה *field*, pl. constr. שַׁדְמוֹת; בְּהֵמָה *cattle*, constr. בֶּהֱמַת, pl. בַּהֲמוֹת; comp. also שְׁאֵלָה, with suff. שֶׁאֱלָתִי. With *immutable Tseri* are, אֲבֵדָה *something lost*, גְּזֵלָה *robbery*, אֲפֵלָה *darkness*, בְּרֵכָה *pool*, גְּנֵבָה *something stolen*, מְרֵרָה *gall*, שְׂרֵפָה *burning*, תְּאֵנָה *fig*; from (§ 26) No. 14. מַהְפֵּכָה *overthrow*, מַגֵּפָה *plague*, &c.

With some nouns both the contracted and uncontracted forms are found to consist together, as נְבֵלָה *dead body*, whence נִבְלָתִי, but constr. נִבְלַת, with suff. נִבְלָתוֹ Le. 5. 2; De. 21. 3; שְׁאֵלָה *request*, whence שְׁאֵלָתִי 1 Sa. 1. 27, and שֶׁאֱלָתִי Job 6. 8; גְּדֵרָה *wall*, pl. גְּדֵרוֹת 1 Sa. 24. 4, but pl. with suff. גְּדֵרוֹתָיו Ps. 89. 41.

III. In General.

5. Several nouns of both the foregoing forms take in the constr. st., and before suffixes, the secondary Segolate form ֶ-ֶת, ַ-ַת, a case similar to that of the masculines (§ 34. No. 2), as the following examples show:—

מַמְלָכָה *kingdom*,	constr.	מַמְלֶכֶת,	with suff.	מַמְלַכְתִּי
מִשְׁפָּחָה *family*	„	מִשְׁפַּחַת	„	מִשְׁפַּחְתִּי
מְלָאכָה *work*	„	מְלֶאכֶת	„	מְלַאכְתְּךָ
מֶרְכָּבָה *chariot*	„	מִרְכֶּבֶת	„	מֶרְכַּבְתּוֹ
מֶמְשָׁלָה *government*	„	מֶמְשֶׁלֶת	„	מֶמְשַׁלְתּוֹ
מִלְחָמָה *war*	„	. . . . .	„	מִלְחַמְתִּי
תִּפְאָרָה *ornament*	„	תִּפְאֶרֶת	„	תִּפְאַרְתּוֹ

Comp. also עֲטָרָה, constr. עֲטֶרֶת *crown*; דְּבֵלָה, constr. דְּבֶלֶת *a lump of figs*; נֶחֱרָצָה *determined*, constr. נֶחֱרֶצֶת; גְּבִירָה *mistress*, constr. גְּבֶרֶת; לֶהָבָה *flame*, constr. לַהֶבֶת; אַיָּלָה, constr. אַיֶּלֶת *hind*; בְּהֵמָה *cattle*, with suff. בְּהֶמְתְּךָ, בְּהֶמְתֵּנוּ, and of the numerals אַרְבָּעָה, constr. אַרְבַּעַת *four*, עֲשָׂרָה, constr. עֲשֶׂרֶת *ten*.

Several of these, e. g. תִּפְאֶרֶת, אַיֶּלֶת, occur also in the absolute state, which is sufficient warrant that the Segolate is a ground-form; the latter, however, is so frequently used as the construct in connection with the form ָ-ה, that constructs like תִּפְאֲרַת, אַיַּלַת do not occur any longer.

SECTION XLIII.—TWELFTH DECLENSION, OR THE *THIRD* OF THE FEMININES. (Table O.)

1. To this declension belong the feminines derived from the Segolate form of the regular verb (§ 26. No. 11), or of the irregular verbs, as long as this form is unaffected by the irregularity, e. g. from פ״י, as יַלְדָּה *maiden*, and ל״ה, as שַׁלְוָה *rest*, רַעְיָה *companion*; hence the feminines from the masculine forms of declension 6.

2. The inflexion is analogous to that of the masculines, and is especially distinguished by the peculiar formation of the plural, for which see explanation § 35. No. 2 c.

3. There are other nouns resembling this in form, but as they are not feminines derived from the Segolate forms, they do not belong to this declension, especially derivatives from ל״ה like מִצְוָה *commandment* (from צָוָה), מִרְמָה *deceit*, &c., which form their plural without any vowel-change מִצְוֹת, מִרְמוֹת.

REMARK.

There are a few words which deviate from the paradigm, in having their middle Vav *moveable* in the ground-form, but *quiescent* in the shortening; as עַוְלָה *wickedness*, with ה parag. עַלָתָה Job 5. 16, pl. עוֹלוֹת Ps. 58. 3; 64. 7; לִוְיָה *garland*, pl. לֹיוֹת 1 Ki. 7. 29, 30, 36.

SECTION XLIV.—THIRTEENTH DECLENSION, OR THE *FOURTH* OF THE FEMININES. (TABLE O.)

1. To this declension belong the feminines formed by the addition of the feminine termination ־ֶ־ֶת or ־ַ־ַת (§ 39. Nos. 2 & 3). They are properly Segolate forms, and as such correspond in the inflexion to the masculine Segolates.

2. Their inflexion is,

(*a*) In the singular, in every respect the same as that of the masculines. There is, therefore, no change of vowels in the constr. state, and before the suffixes *Segol* of the penultima is changed to *Pattahh* (and *Hhirek*), *Tseri* to *Hhirek*, *Hholem pure* to *Kamets-hhatuph*, like in מֶלֶךְ (קֶבֶר), סֵפֶר, קֹדֶשׁ.

(*b*) In the plural there exists this peculiarity, that the vowel preceding the final Segol (or Pattahh) is dropped even in the absolute state; the form ־ֹ־ֶת, however, either leaves some trace behind in the vowel (־ֳ), as שִׁבֹּלֶת, pl. שִׁבֳּלִים, as in the paradigm, or is entirely dropped, as גֻּלְגֹּלֶת, pl. גֻּלְגְּלוֹת.

These vowels are invariably *pure* and mutable, viz. (־ָ), (־ֵ), (—) *pure*. The entire rejection of these vowels in the inflexion will be easier understood, if it is borne in mind that the terminations (־ָ־ֶ), (־ֵ־ֶ), ־ֹ־ֶ, are also elsewhere interchanged with (־ְ־ָ), (־ְ־ֵ), ־ְ (comp. § 26. Nos. 10 & 11, & § 35. rem. 10). Here also may be adduced as an instance, מַשְׂאֵת for מַשְׂאֶת, pl. מַשְׂאוֹת.

REMARKS.

I. ON THE SING. WITH SUFFIX.

1. According to the paradigm, the form ending in ־ֶ־ֶת takes, before suffixes, in some words, Pattahh; in others, Hhirek. This, however, is not merely arbitrary, but depends upon the origin of the form. If the masculine from which it is derived terminates in (־ָ) or (־ַ), as is the case with most of them, the *Pattahh* appears in the inflexion of the feminine; but if the masculine terminates in (־ֵ) or ־ִי, the feminine takes *Hhirek* (comp. § 35. rem. 3). Thus the following are inflected :—

With *Pattahh*, e. g. מִשְׁמֶרֶת *custody* (from מִשְׁמָר), מִשְׁמַרְתִּי; דֶּלֶת *door* (from דַּל), comp. the examples given in § 42. rem. 5).

With *Hhirek*, all the infinitives of the verbs פ״י, e. g. שֶׁבֶת *to dwell* (masc. שֵׁב), with suff. שִׁבְתִּי; רֶדֶת *to descend* (masc. רֵד), רִדְתִּי; לֶדֶת *to bear*, לִדְתִּי; in the same manner גְּבֶרֶת *mistress* (masc. גְּבִיר), with suff. גְּבִרְתִּי; מֵינֶקֶת *nurse* (masc. מֵינִיק), מֵנִקְתּוֹ; זֶפֶת *pitch* (masc. Chald. זִפְתִּי ;(זְפָא ,זִף; אֲמֶנֶת contracted אֱמֶת *thrust* (masc. אָמֵן), with suff. אֲמִתּוֹ; בַּת contr. from בֶּנֶת *daughter* (masc. בֵּן), with suff. בִּתּוֹ for בִּנְתּוֹ.

There are, comparatively, but few examples in which the punctuation does not conform to the origin of the form. Such are, e. g. יוֹנֶקֶת *sprout* (masc. יוֹנֵק), יוֹנַקְתּוֹ, and so אִגֶּרֶת *letter*, אִוֶּלֶת *folly*, מַצֶּבֶת *pillar*, which have Pattahh, though (according to § 26. No. 9) we must suppose them derived from masc. אִגֵּר ,אֱוִל ,מַצֵּב (for which comp. מַצֵּבָה). There occurs, moreover, שִׁבְתִּי *my dwelling*. Ps. 23. 6, which elsewhere is שִׁבְתִּי, comp. Ps. 27. 4.

2. Of the form (־ֵ־ֶ) the shortening is constantly Hhirek, e. g. אֵשֶׁת, אִשְׁתִּי.

3. The forms ־ֵ־ֶת and ־ֶ־ֶת, which have commonly (־ַ) and (־ִ) in the shortening, occur also with *Segol*, but almost exclusively before the suffix, ךָ, e. g. אֶשְׁתְּךָ *thy wife*, Ps. 128. 3; otherwise, אִשְׁתִּי, אִשְׁתּוֹ; and even אֶשְׁתְּךָ Ge. 6. 18; Am. 7. 17; חֲבֶרֶת *companion*, חֲבֶרְתְּךָ Mal. 2. 14; בְּהֶמֶת, בְּהֶמְתְּךָ Le. 19. 19; 25. 7; but also בְּהֶמְתֵּנוּ Nu. 32. 26; Ne. 9. 37. So, finally, לֶכֶת *to go*, with all the suffixes, לֶכְתִּי, לֶכְתְּךָ ,לֶכְתּוֹ ,לֶכְתָּם.

4. The form ־ֹ־ֶת, besides its inflexion given in the paradigm, is in certain words also inflected with *Kibbuts*. Here, however, like in rem. 1, reference must be made to the origin of the form, viz. where the masculine has originally וֹ, the feminine takes *Kamets-hhatuph*; but *Kibbuts* when the masculine has וּ. E. g. בֹּשֶׁת *shame* (from בּוּשׁ), with suff. בָּשְׁתִּי; גֻּלְגֹּלֶת *skull* (as if from גֻּלְגֹּל, with suff. גֻּלְגָּלְתִּי; שְׁלֹשֶׁת *three* (from שָׁלוֹשׁ), with suff. שְׁלָשְׁתְּכֶם; but נְחֹשֶׁת

brass (masc. נְחוּשׁ, comp. the other form נְחוּשָׁה), with suff. נְחֻשְׁתִּי; and so מַשְׂכֹּרֶת *wages*, מַתְכֹּנֶת *measure*, מַחֲלֹקֶת *division*, may be derived from forms like מַשְׂכּוֹר. An exception is נְחֻשְׁתַּי La. 3. 7.

II. ON THE FORM OF THE PLURAL.

5. The characteristic of the inflexion of the plural, which is the rejection of the vowel preceding the final syllable, may be seen in numerous examples, as אִגֶּרֶת, pl. אִגְּרוֹת *letters;* יוֹנֶקֶת, pl. יוֹנְקוֹת *sprouts;* מַחֲלֹקֶת, pl. מַחְלְקוֹת *divisions;* גֻּלְגֹּלֶת, pl. גֻּלְגְּלוֹת *skulls;* and with (ְ:) צִפֳּרִים *birds* (from a fem. צִפֹּרֶת). Several nouns, however, of this class, borrow their plural from the coexisting fem. form ָה—, ֶה— (though this form does not actually occur), so that the vowel of the original masculine appears again in full. Such are:—כֹּתֶרֶת *chapiter* (from כּוֹתֶר), pl. כּוֹתָרוֹת; מַאֲכֶלֶת *knife* (as if from מַאֲכָל), pl. מַאֲכָלוֹת; תּוֹכַחַת *reproof*, pl. תּוֹכָחוֹת (as if from תּוֹכָחָה); טַבַּעַת *ring*, pl. טַבָּעוֹת (as if from טַבָּעָה); מִשְׁפַּחַת *family*, pl. מִשְׁפָּחוֹת; מִקְלַעַת, pl. מִקְלָעוֹת *carved work;* מֵינֶקֶת *nurse*, pl. מֵינִיקוֹת (as if from מֵינִיקָה); מַחֲרֶשֶׁת, pl. מַחֲרֵשׁוֹת *ploughshares*. A few, however, of the form ֶת— occur likewise with the pl. ָוֹת—, e. g. עַשְׁתֹּרֶת *Astarte*, pl. עַשְׁתָּרוֹת; בַּצֹּרֶת *draught*, pl. בַּצָּרוֹת. Thus the plurals אַרְמְנוֹת *palaces*, אַשְׁכְּלוֹת *clusters*, should probably be derived from singulars אַרְמֹנֶת, אַשְׁכֹּלֶת, though only the masculines אַרְמוֹן, אֶשְׁכּוֹל occur.

Here belongs, moreover, חַטָּאת *sin*, for חַטָּאֶת, pl. חַטָּאוֹת.

SECTION XLV.—IRREGULAR NOUNS.

There are several anomalous forms of inflexion chiefly occurring in single examples only, or, at the most, in very few. Most of these irregularities of inflexion consist in the derivation of the *constr. state*, or of the *plural*, not from the absolute state of the singular, but from another wholly different form.

These irregularities require the more attention, because, as in all languages, the words which they affect are those in most common use. And though most of these nouns are primitives, they nevertheless follow the analogy of verbal nouns without even their roots occurring as verbs. They follow here in alphabetical order:—

אָב, *father*, for אָבֶה; as if from אָבָה (like a derivative from a verb ל״ה § 27. V. No. 2); constr. state אֲבִי (like a Segolate form from ל״ה No. 11); with light suff. אָבִי, אָבִיךָ, אָבִיךְ, אָבִינוּ, with grave suff. אֲבִיכֶם, אֲבִיהֶם, (from אָב). Plur. אָבוֹת (with fem. termination).

The regular form of the constr. state, viz. אַב, occurs only in Ge. 17. 4, 5, in order to bring in the etymology of אַבְרָהָם, as in the like cases rare forms are often introduced. This form occurs also besides in several proper names, e. g. אַבְנֵר, אַבְשָׁלוֹם. The Chald. and Arab. form אֲבוּ is found, according to Khethib, in the proper name אֲבוּגַיִל 1 Sa. 25. 18.

אָח, *brother*, constr. אֲחִי with suff. אָחִיו, אָחִיךָ, אֲחִיכֶם, plur. constr. אֲחֵי, אֲחֵיכֶם. All these forms follow the analogy of verbs ל״ה, as if אָח stood for אָחֶה, from אָחָה, comp. the preceding אָב. But the plur. abs. is אַחִים with *Dag. forte implicit.* (comp. § 37. r. 7), as if from אָחַח; hence אַחַי, אַחֶיהָ אַחֶיךָ, &c. But אֶחָיו, אֶחָי for אַחָיו, אַחַי, where Segol takes the place of Pattahh before the guttural ח with Kamets (ָח), comp. הֶחָזוֹן for הַחָזוֹן, כֶּחָשׁ for כַּחָשׁ.

אֶחָד, *one* (for אַחָד, with *Dag. forte implicit.*, comp. the preceding אָח), constr. state אַחַד, fem. אַחַת for אַחֶדֶת, אַחַדְתְּ, in pause אֶחָת (for אַחַת comp. אֶחָיו above). In one instance, Eze. 33. 30, it takes the form חַד by aphaeresis. Pl. masc. אֲחָדִים as if from אָחָד or אַחַד.

אָחוֹת, *sister* (contr. for אֲחֹוֶת from a masculine for אָחוּ, comp. חֲצוֹת § 27. V. No. 13, & § 24. rem. 2). Plur. only with suff. אַחְיוֹתַי, אַחְיוֹתָיו (from a sing. אֲחִיָּה, fem. of אֲחִי), also אַחוֹתַיִךְ (as if from a sing. אָחָה fem. from אָח, אָחָה).

אַחֵר, *another*, fem. אַחֶרֶת (with *Dag. forte implicit.*); but plur. אֲחֵרִים, אֲחֵרוֹת, as if from a form אָחֵר (after dec. V).

אִישׁ *man*, a softened form from אֱנָשׁ; in the plural it has very seldom אִישִׁים, the usual form being אֲנָשִׁים (from אֱנָשׁ) constr. אַנְשֵׁי.* Comp. אִשָּׁה.

* This is true as far as the use of these forms is concerned; but it seems more natural to class together אִישִׁים with אִישׁ, אֲנָשִׁים with אֱנוֹשׁ; so that there remains the only one irregularity, that the plural of אֱנָשׁ is used for אֱנוֹשׁ. This is the order we have followed in this work, and have accordingly adopted two roots אנשׁ, and אישׁ, the latter being secondary, and softened from the former. Under אנשׁ we have put אִשָּׁה for אִנְשָׁה, plur. נָשִׁים. Under אישׁ we have put אֵשֶׁת for אִישֶׁת (§ 39. 4. d).

אָמָה maid-servant, plur. (with ה inserted) אַמָהוֹת, אֲמָהוֹת. Comp. in Chaldee אֲבָהָן fathers.

אִשָּׁה woman (for אִנְשָׁה fem. from אֱנָשׁ), plur. נָשִׁים by aphaeresis for אֲנָשִׁים. For אֵשֶׁת see the note under אִישׁ above.

בַּיִת house, constr. בֵּית, plur. בָּתִּים, with light suff. בָּתָּיו, but with grave suff. בָּתֵּיהֶם, בָּתֵּיכֶם (with Metheg). The root of this word is doubtful. It is usually derived from בּוּת, to pass the night, and the plur. בָּתִּים for בָּתְתִים from a sing. בֹּתֶת (after the form בֹּשֶׁת from בּוֹשׁ). Or בַּיִת is supposed to be a softened form from בֶּנֶת (like אִישׁ for אֱנָשׁ) derived from בָּנָה to build; plur. בָּתִּים (bottim) for בָּנְתִּים from another sing. בֹּנֶת. For this plural form comp. § 35. rem. 16.

בֵּן son (for בֶּנֶה from בָּנָה), constr. state בֶּן־, seldom בִּן, once בְּנִי, and finally בְּנוֹ. With suff. בְּנִי, בִּנְךָ; plur. בָּנִים (as if from בַּן, for בָּנֶה), constr. state בְּנֵי.

בַּת daughter (for בֶּנֶת, fem. from בֵּן), with suff. בִּתִּי (for בִּנְתִּי), plur. בָּנוֹת (from the sing. בָּנָה comp. בָּנִים sons, pl. of בֵּן), constr. state בְּנוֹת.

גַּי fully, גַּיְא valley. The Khethib גיאות, 2 Ki. 2. 16, ought, doubtless, to be pointed גְּיָאוֹת, which is the regular plural (§ 35. rem. 12); but it is often transposed גְּאָיוֹת.

חָם stepfather, with suff. חָמִיךְ, and חָמוֹת stepmother, comp. אָח brother, אָחוֹת sister.

יוֹם day, with suff. יוֹמִי, dual יוֹמַיִם. Plur. יָמִים by Chaldaism יָמִין (as if from יָם for יָמֶה) constr. יְמֵי and poet. יְמוֹת.

כְּלִי vessel, plur. כֵּלִים (as if from כֶּלֶה, כֵּל).

כְּנָת associate, prop. for כְּנָאת, כְּנָאֶת (§ 39. No. 4), plur. with suff. כְּנָוֹתָיו. As if from כְּנָוָה, comp. מְנָת.

מַיִם plur. water, constr. state מֵי, and also מֵימֵי, with suff. מֵימֵיכֶם. The last two are regular plural forms from מַיִם regarded as a singular, like בַּיִת.

מְנָת portion (from מָנָה), for מְנָאת, whence plur. מְנָאוֹת and מְנָיוֹת (both with (ָ) pure).

This inflexion is best accounted for in the following manner:—the form מְנָאת=מְנָת is derived from a masc. מְנָא, which stands for מְנָי (after the form כְּתָב § 26. No. 13). Hence מְנָאת for מְנָית, מְנָיֶת. Whence the plural, but not immediately from the form ָת, but from מְנָיָה, מְנָאָה, according to § 44. rem. 5, as the termination ֹת would lose the preceding long vowel.

עִיר city, plur. עֲיָרִים (according to § 35. rem. 12), only Ju. 10. 4, elsewhere עָרִים. This might indeed be taken as a contraction from עֲיָרִים; but better from עִיר=עָר, which still occurs in the proper names, e. g. עָר מוֹאָב.

עַם, with distinctive accent and with the article עָם, people, plur. עַמִּים, but also by Aramaism עֲמָמִים, עַמְמֵי (as if from a Segolate form עֶמֶם).

פֶּה mouth (prop. for פֶּאֶה, comp. שֶׂה), constr. state פִּי (for פְּאִי), with suff. פִּי (my mouth), פִּיו, פִּיךָ, &c. Plur. פִּים, also פִּיּוֹת. Fem. פִּיָה from פֶּה.

פֶּחָה governor, for פַּחָה (with Dag. forte implicit.), comp. אָחִיו under אָח), plur. פַּחוֹת, with suff. פַּחוֹתֶיהָ, but constr. state פַּחֲוֹת, like the Chald. פַּחֲוָתָא.

The sing. with suff. is פֶּחָם Ne. 5. 14, as if from פַּח.

ראשׁ head (for רְאָשׁ Segolate form), plur. רָאשִׁים (for רְאָשִׁים) once with suff. רָאשָׁיו.

שֶׂה sheep or goat, for שֶׂיֶה (like פֶּה), constr. state שֵׂה, with suff. שֵׂיוֹ and שֵׂיֵהוּ.

CHALDEE PARADIGMS.

Since the Biblical Chaldee occupies only a few chapters, viz. Ezr. 4. 8; 6. 18; 7. 12—26; Da. 2. 4—7. 21; Je. 10. 11, it needs hardly to be noticed, that but an exceedingly small number of examples can be found in the Bible itself applicable to the Chaldee paradigms. But it must be remarked, that were we, agreeably to the purpose of this work, to form paradigms for the Biblical portion alone, they would not only be incomplete, but they would likewise, in a measure, misrepresent its true Chaldee character, because this portion is so replete with Hebraisms. We give, accordingly, the paradigms as they are found in Winer's Chaldee Grammar; but confine our remarks to the occurrences of the Biblical portion.

TABLE P. THE PERSONAL PRONOUN.

	SEPARATE PRONOUN.		VERBAL SUFFIX.		NOMINAL SUFFIX. A. SUFFIXES TO NOUNS SINGULAR.		NOMINAL SUFFIX. B. SUFFIXES TO NOUNS PLURAL.	
Singular.								
1. *com.*	אֲנָא, אֲנָה	*I.*	ַ־נִי, נִי	*me.*	ִ־י	*my.*	ַ־י	*my.*
2. *com.*	אַתְּ, אַנְתְּ, אַנְתָּה	*thou.*	ָ־ךְ, ךְ	*thee.*	ָ־ךְ	*thy.*	ָ־ךְ, ָ־יךְ	*thy.*
2. *f.*			ֵ־ךְ, ַ־יִךְ, ִ־יךְ		ֵ־ךְ, (ִ־יךְ)		ַ־יִךְ, ַ־יְכִי	
3. *m.*	הוּא	*he.*	ֵ־הּ, ִ־יהּ (וֹהִי, הִי)	*him.*	ֵ־הּ	*his.*	וֹהִי, וֹי	*her.*
3. *f.*	הִיא	*she.*	ַ־הּ, הָא	*her.*	ַ־הּ (in Bibl. Ch. ָ־הּ)	*her.*	ָ־הָא, (ַ־יהּ Da. 7. 7, 19)	
Plural.								
1. *com.*	נַחְנָא, אֲנַחְנָא	*we.*	ָ־נָא; נָא	*us.*	ָ־נָא	*our.*	ָ־ינָא	*our.*
2. *m.*	אַתּוּן, אַנְתּוּן	*ye.*	כוֹן	*you.*	כוֹן, (כוֹם)	*your.*	ֵ־יכוֹן	*your.*
2. *f.*	אַתֵּין, אַנְתֵּין		כֵן		כֵן		ֵ־יכֵן	
3. *m.*	הִמּוֹ, הִמּוֹן, הִנּוּן, אִנּוּן	*they.*	ִ־נּוּן; נוּן	*them.*	הוֹן (הוֹם)	*their.*	ֵ־יהוֹן	*their.*
3. *f.*	הִנֵּין, אִנֵּין		ִ־נֵּן; נֵין		הֵין, הֵן		ֵ־יהֵן	

SECTION XLVI.*—ON THE SUFFIXES TO NOUNS SINGULAR AND PLURAL.

REMARKS.

I. On the Suffix to Nouns Singular.

1. Instead of ַ־הּ there is twice found ֵ־א in פִּשְׁרֵא *its interpretation*, Da. 4. 15; 5. 8 Kheth., but which is not recognised by the Masorites, who give ַ־הּ in the Keri.

Appended to the words אַב, אַח, which before suffix become אֲבוּ, &c., the suffixes of the 2nd and 3rd pers. sing. take the forms ךְ, הִי, הָא; which forms do not elsewhere occur (in the Bible) as nominal suffixes. E. g. אֲבוּךְ Da. 5. 11, 18; אֲבוּהִי Da. 5. 2.

2. The same forms are attached to prepositions

* We continue the sections from the Hebrew to the Chaldee, for the sake of convenience to the reader.

(especially such as are originally plural nouns) and to signs of cases, בְּ, לְ, יַת, &c.; as, יָתֵהּ, לִי, בִּי.

II. On the Suffix to Nouns Plural.

3. These suffixes are regularly appended, however, only to plurals masculine. Feminines frequently take the singular suff. ־ֵי, ־ֵהּ, &c. E. g. יַרְכָּתֵהּ *his sides;* Da. 2. 32; שֵׁגְלָתֵהּ, וּלְחֵנָתֵהּ *his wives and his concubines*, Da. 5. 2; כְּנָוָתְהוֹן *their companies*, מַחְלְקָתְהוֹן, פְּלֻגָּתְהוֹן Ezr. 4. 17; 6. 18.

4. The suffix ־ָיִךְ frequently appears abbreviated ־ָךְ; e. g. רַעְיוֹנָךְ Da. 5. 10, comp. Da. 2. 29.

5. Prepositions, which are originally plural nouns, take the suffixes of plur. nouns; e. g. קֳדָמַי, קֳדָמוֹהִי, עֲלֵיהוֹן, עֲלוֹהִי.

TABLE Q. REGULAR VERB.

		PEAL.	ITHPEAL.	PAEL.	ITHPAAL.	APHEL.	ITTAPHAL.
Pret.	3. *m.*	קְטַל	אִתְקְטֵל	קַטֵּל	אִתְקַטַּל	אַקְטֵל	אִתַּקְטַל
	3. *f.*	קִטְלַת	אִתְקְטְלַת	קַטְּלַת	אִתְקַטְּלַת	אַקְטְלַת	אִתַּקְטְלַת
	2. *m.*	קְטַלְתְּ	אִתְקְטֵלְתְּ	קַטֵּלְתָּא, קַטֵּלְתְּ	אִתְקַטַּלְתְּ	אַקְטֵלְתָּא, אַקְטֵלְתְּ	אִתַּקְטַלְתְּ
	2. *f.*	קְטַלְתְּ	אִתְקְטֵלְתְּ	קַטֵּלְתְּ	אִתְקַטַּלְתְּ	אַקְטֵלְתְּ	אִתַּקְטַלְתְּ
	1. *c.*	קִטְלֵת	אִתְקְטְלֵת	קַטְּלֵת	אִתְקַטְּלֵת	אַקְטְלֵת	אִתַּקְטְלֵת
Plur.	3. *m.*	קְטַלוּ	אִתְקְטִלוּ	קַטִּלוּ	אִתְקַטַּלוּ	אַקְטִלוּ	אִתַּקְטַלוּ
	3. *f.*	קְטַלָא	אִתְקְטַלָא	קַטִּלָא	אִתְקַטָּלָא	אַקְטִלָא	אִתַּקְטַלָא
	2. *m.*	קְטַלְתּוּן	אִתְקְטַלְתּוּן	קַטֵּלְתּוּן	אִתְקַטַּלְתּוּן	אַקְטֵלְתּוּן	אִתַּקְטַלְתּוּן
	2. *f.*	קְטַלְתֵּן	אִתְקְטַלְתֵּן	קַטֵּלְתֵּן	אִתְקַטַּלְתֵּן	אַקְטֵלְתֵּן	אִתַּקְטַלְתֵּן
	1. *c.*	קְטַלְנָא	אִתְקְטַלְנָא	קַטֵּלְנָא	אִתְקַטַּלְנָא	אַקְטֵלְנָא	אִתַּקְטַלְנָא
Inf		מִקְטַל	אִתְקְטָלָא	קַטָּלָא	אִתְקַטָּלָא	אַקְטָלָא	אִתַּקְטָלָא
Imp.	2. *m.*	קְטֻל	אִתְקְטֵל	קַטֵּל	אִתְקַטַּל	אַקְטֵל	אִתַּקְטַל
	2. *f.*	קְטֻלִי	אִתְקְטַלִי	קַטֵּלִי	אִתְקַטַּלִי	אַקְטֵלִי	אִתַּקְטַלִי
Plur.	2. *m.*	קְטֻלוּ	אִתְקְטַלוּ	קַטֵּלוּ	אִתְקַטַּלוּ	אַקְטֵלוּ	אִתַּקְטַלוּ
	2. *f.*	קְטֻלָנָא	אִתְקְטֵלָנָא	קַטֵּלָנָא	אִתְקַטַּלְנָא	אַקְטֵלָנָא	אִתַּקְטַלְנָא
Fut.	3. *m.*	יִקְטֻל	יִתְקְטֵל	יְקַטֵּל	יִתְקַטַּל	יַקְטֵל	יִתַּקְטַל
	3. *f.*	תִּקְטֻל	תִּתְקְטֵל	תְּקַטֵּל	תִּתְקַטַּל	תַּקְטֵל	תִּתַּקְטַל
	2. *m.*	תִּקְטֻל	תִּתְקְטֵל	תְּקַטֵּל	תִּתְקַטַּל	תַּקְטֵל	תִּתַּקְטַל
	2. *f.*	תִּקְטְלִין	תִּתְקַטְלִין	תְּקַטְּלִין	תִּתְקַטְּלִין	תַּקְטְלִין	תִּתַּקְטְלִין
	1. *c.*	אֶקְטֻל	אֶתְקְטֵל	אֲקַטֵּל	אֶתְקַטַּל	אַקְטֵל	אֶתַּקְטַל
Plur.	3. *m.*	יִקְטְלוּן	יִתְקַטְלוּן	יְקַטְּלוּן	יִתְקַטְּלוּן	יַקְטְלוּן	יִתַּקְטְלוּן
	3. *f.*	יִקְטְלָן	יִתְקַטְלָן	יְקַטְּלָן	יִתְקַטְּלָן	יַקְטְלָן	יִתַּקְטְלָן
	2. *m.*	תִּקְטְלוּן	תִּתְקַטְלוּן	תְּקַטְּלוּן	תִּתְקַטְּלוּן	תַּקְטְלוּן	תִּתַּקְטְלוּן
	2. *f.*	תִּקְטְלָן	תִּתְקַטְלָן	תְּקַטְּלָן	תִּתְקַטְּלָן	תַּקְטְלָן	תִּתַּקְטְלָן
	1. *c.*	נִקְטֻל	נִתְקְטֵל	נְקַטֵּל	נִתְקַטַּל	נַקְטֵל	נִתַּקְטַל
1. *Part.*	*m.*	קָטֵל	מִתְקְטֵל	מְקַטֵּל	מִתְקַטַּל	מַקְטֵל	מִתַּקְטַל
	f.	קָטְלָא	מִתְקַטְלָא	מְקַטְּלָא	מִתְקַטְּלָא	מַקְטְלָא	מִתַּקְטְלָא
2. *Part.*	*m.*	קְטִיל		מְקַטַּל		מַקְטַל	
	f.	קְטִילָא		מְקַטְּלָא		מַקְטְלָא	

SECTION XLVII.—ON THE REGULAR VERB. (TABLE Q.)

I. GENERAL REMARKS.

1. Forms with (..) often take (.) instead; e. g.

(*a*) *Part. act.* of *Peal*, נָחֵת Da. 4. 10, 20; יָכֵל Da. 3. 17; 4. 34.

(*b*) *Pret.* of *Ithpeel*, אִתְרְחִצוּ Da. 3. 28.

(*c*) *Pret.* of *Pael*, קַטֵּל Da. 3. 22, בָּרֵךְ Da. 2. 19.

(*d*) The *part. pass.* sometimes, though seldom, appears in a contracted form, like קְטֵל, as תְּקֵל Da. 7. 25.

2. *Preterite.* Instead of the afformative תְּ for the 2 pers. masc., sometimes appears תָּ, by a Hebraism, e. g. יְדַעְתָּ Da. 5. 22; רְשַׁמְתָּ Da. 6. 13, 14; Pael שַׁבַּחְתָּ Da. 5. 13; and even the full form חֲזַיְתָה Da. 2. 41.

3. *Future.* The 3 pers. pl. masc. takes sometimes the termination וּ instead of וּן, as יַחִיטוּ Ezr. 4. 12.

4. In those conjugations in which א is preformative, ה is generally used instead in the Biblical Chaldee. E. g. *Ithpeel*, הִתְרְחִצוּ Da. 3. 28, for אִתְרְחִצוּ (comp. No. 1); *Ithpael*, הִתְנַדַּבוּ Ezr. 7. 15; *Aphel*, הַכְרִזוּ Da. 5. 29; so in the fut. and part., even after the characteristic prefix, as יְהַשְׁפִּל Da. 7. 24; מְהַקְרְבִין Ezr. 6. 10. Comp. also note to Table T.

5. *Infinitive.* The Biblical Chaldee has everywhere ָ◌ָא instead of ָ◌ָה of the Targums, a termination of all infinitives excepting Peal. E. g. הוֹבָדָה Da. 2. 12 (Aph. of אֲבַד); קַטָּלָה ver. 14; בַּקָּרָה Ezr. 7. 14; הַשְׁכָּחָה Da. 6. 5. Once, however, occurs לְהַשְׁנָיָא Ezr. 6. 12.

II. ON THE SEVERAL CONJUGATIONS.

6. *Peal.* (*a*) Some verbs, especially such as are intransitive, take (..), (.), or even ִי as the characteristic vowel of the *preterite*; e. g. בְּאֵשׁ *to be evil*, טְאֵב *to be good*, יְתִב *to sit*, עֲשִׁית *to think*. These vowels remain in those persons, where (-) is usually retained; e. g. שְׁאֵלְנָא *we asked*, Ezr. 5. 9; סְלִקוּ *they went up*, Ezr. 4. 12. The 3 pers. sing. fem. also retains its vowel, as בְּטֵלַת *it ceased*, Ezr. 4. 24.

(*b*) The *future* has also in the final syllable (-) instead of (.), as תִּלְבַּשׁ *thou shalt be clothed*, Da. 5. 16.

7. *Ithpeel.* The preformative sometimes takes אֶת instead of אִת, Da. 7. 15. The final syllable takes (.) instead of (..), תִּשְׁתְּבִק Da. 2. 44, comp. No. 1.

8. *Pael.* As in Hebrew, Dagesh forte is sometimes omitted when the middle radical has Sheva, comp. § 10. rem. 7.

9. *Aphel.* Hiphil (and pass., Hoph.) sometimes takes the place of Aphel in the Biblical Chaldee; comp. No. 4.

10. *Ittaphal.* The place of this conjugation, which occurs very seldom anywhere, is supplied in the Biblical Chaldee, by Hophal. E. g. Ezr. 4. 15; Da. 4. 33; 7. 11. There occurs, however, one form of this conjugation, usually taken for *Ithpeel*, viz. יִתְּזִין Da. 4. 9, fut. of זוּן; but comp. § 54. rem. 3.

III. PERSONAL INFLEXION OF THE PARTICIPLE PEIL.

11. In the Biblical Chaldee a kind of *Preterite passive* tense is in use, formed by appending the afformatives of the Preterite to the participle Peil. It takes the place of Ithpeel.*

	3 *m.*	3 *f.*	2 *m.*	2 *f.*	1 *c.*
Sing.	קְטִיל	קְטִילַת	קְטִילְתְּ, תָּא	קְטִילְתְּ	קְטִילֵת
Plur.	קְטִילוּ	קְטִילָא	קְטִילְתּוּן	קְטִילְתֵּן	קְטִילְנָא

E. g. תְּקִילְתָּא Da. 5. 27, יְהִיבַת ver. 28; comp. ver. 30; 7. 4; 6. 11; יְהִיבוּ Ezr. 5. 14.

SECTION XLVIII.—UNFREQUENT CONJUGATIONS.

As in Hebrew, there are here certain unfrequent conjugations, some of which are confined to particular classes of irregular verbs.

(*a*) *Poel* and *Ithpoal*, especially in verbs ע״ע; the characteristics are the same as in the Hebrew. E. g. מְסוֹבְלִין Ezr. 6. 3.

(*b*) *Palel* and *Ithpalel* in verbs ע״ו; e. g. רוֹמֵם Da. 4. 34; הִתְרוֹמַם (for אִתְ׳) Da. 5. 23.

(*c*) *Shaphel* and *Ishtaphal*; e. g. שַׁכְלֵל Ezr. 4. 12; יִשְׁתַּכְלְלוּ Ezr. 4. 13; שֵׁיצִיא Ezr. 6. 15, is Shaphel from יְצָא.

(*d*) Altogether peculiar is the verb שֵׁיזִיב (שֵׁיזִיב) Da. 3. 28. Fut. יְשֵׁיזִב ver. 17. Inf. שֵׁיזָבוּת ibid. Part. מְשֵׁיזִב Da. 6. 28. Passive אִשְׁתֵּיזִיב in the Targum. Ge. 32. 30.

* In the Targums *both participles* are inflected by the addition of pronominal fragments, which forms there the present tense; as קָטֵלְנָא *I slay*, קְטִילְנָא *I am slain*.

SECTION XLIX.—VERBS WITH GUTTURALS.

1. The gutturals (א, ה, ח, ע, and in part ר) present the same peculiarities as in Hebrew. It will be sufficient, therefore, to give examples of the most important forms.

2. *Verbs Pe guttural.* *Peal* pret. עֲבַד f. עַבְדַת 1 c. עַבְדֵת; imp. עֲבַדִי, עֲבֵד; inf. מֶהֱדַר, מֶעְבַּד (comp. § 13. rem. 1, 2, 3, 4); fut. יֶעְרֹק, יַחֲזוֹר (§ 139. 4); participles עָבֵד, עֲבִיד. *Ithpeel* אִתְעֲבֵד, אִתְעֲבַד. *Pael* pret. עַבֵּד; fut. יְעַבַּד. *Ithpaal* אִתְעַבַּד. *Aphel* pret. אַעֲבֵד, אַחְסֵן, אַחְרִיב; fut. יַחֲלִיף, יַחְסֵן; part. מַחְלֵף.

3. *Verbs Ayin guttural.* *Peal* pret. בְּחַן; imp. בְּחַן; inf. מִבְחַן; fut. יִבְחַן; part. בָּחֵן, בְּחִין. *Ithpeel* אִתְבְּחַן, אִתְבְּחִין. *Pael* חָרֵשׁ. *Aphel* אַבְחַן.

4. *Verbs Lamed guttural.* *Peal* pret. שְׁכַח, שְׁכַחַת; imp. שְׁכַח, שְׁכַחִי; fut. יִשְׁכַּח, יִשְׁלַח; part. שָׁכַח, שְׁכִיחַ. *Ithpeel* אִשְׁתְּכַח, fem. אִשְׁתְּכַחַת. *Pael* pret. שַׁכַּח; fut. יְשַׁכַּח. Ithpaal אִשְׁתַּכַּח. Aphel אַשְׁכַּח, אַשְׁכִּיחַ, 1st pers. אַשְׁכַּחַת.

Rem. 1. *Verbs Lamed guttural* have the pret. 3 pers. sing. fem. sometimes terminating in (-ַ-) with the tone on the penultima, of which there is no example in the Bible (comp. Targ. אֲמַרַת Ge. 30. 16), though there are some without gutt., as אֲמֶרֶת Da. 5. 10; אִתְגְּזֶרֶת Da. 2. 45; הַדֶּקֶת Da. 2. 34, 45 (from דְּקַק).

2. Instead of שְׁמַעַת (1 pers. com.) Da. 5. 14, Buxtorf, and after him Dr. Fürst, in his Concordance, give the form שְׁמַעַת Da. 5. 16, but we cannot tell on what authority.

3. When the first radical takes a composite Sheva, verbs פ״א and פ״ה have (ֱ), as אֱמַרוּ Da. 2. 9; verbs פ״ח and פ״ע take generally (ֲ).

4. Forms like חֶחֱסִין Da. 7. 22, belong not to Aphel but to Hiphel, and are Hebraisms.

TABLE R. REGULAR VERB WITH SUFFIXES.

Suffixes *for*	1 *Sing.*	2 *Sing. m.*	2 *Sing. f.*	3 *Sing. m.*	3 *Sing. f.*	1 *Plur.*	2 *Plur. m.*	2 *Plur. f.*	3 *Plur. m.*	3 *Plur. f.*
Pret.										
Peal 3. *m.*	קַטְלַנִי	קַטְלָךְ	קַטְלֵךְ	קַטְלֵהּ	קַטְלָהּ	קַטְלָנָא	קְטַלְכוֹן	קְטַלְכֵן	קְטַלִנּוּן } קַטְלִנּוּן	קְטַלִנֵּן
3. *f.*	קְטַלְתַּנִי	קְטַלְתָּךְ	קְטַלְתֵּךְ	קְטַלְתֵּהּ	קְטַלְתָּהּ	קְטַלְתָּנָא	קְטַלַתְכוֹן	קְטַלַתְכֵן	קְטַלְתִּנּוּן	קְטַלְתִּנֵּן
2. *m.*	קְטַלְתַּנִי	—	—	קְטַלְתֵּהּ	קְטַלְתָּהּ	קְטַלְתָּנָא	—	—	קְטַלְתִּנּוּן	קְטַלְתִּנֵּן
2. *f.*	קְטַלְתִּינִי	—	—	קְטַלְתִּיהִי	קְטַלְתִּיהָא	קְטַלְתִּינָא	—	—	קְטַלְתִּינוּן	קְטַלְתִּינֵן
1. *c.*	—	קְטַלְתָּךְ	קְטַלְתֵּךְ	קְטַלְתֵּיהּ	קְטַלְתָּהּ	—	קְטַלְתְּכוֹן	קְטַלְתְּכֵן	קְטַלְתִּנּוּן	קְטַלְתִּנֵּן
Plur. 3. *c.*	קַטְלוּנִי	קַטְלוּךְ	קַטְלוּךְ	קַטְלוּהִי	קַטְלוּהָ	קַטְלוּנָא	קַטְלוּנְכוֹן	קַטְלוּנְכֵן	קַטְלוּנוּן	קַטְלוּנֵן
2. *m.*	קְטַלְתּוּנִי	—	—	קְטַלְתּוּנֵהּ	קְטַלְתּוּנָהּ	קְטַלְתּוּנָא	—	—	קְטַלְתּוּנוּן	קְטַלְתּוּנֵן
1. *c.*	—	קְטַלְנָךְ	קְטַלְנֵךְ	קְטַלְנָהִי	קְטַלְנָהָא	—	קְטַלְנָכוֹן	קְטַלְנָכֵן	קְטַלְנָנוּן	קְטַלְנָנֵן
Inf.										
Peal	מִקְטְלִי	מִקְטְלָךְ	מִקְטְלֵךְ	מִקְטְלֵהּ	מִקְטְלָהּ	מִקְטְלָנָא	מִקְטַלְכוֹן	מִקְטַלְכֵן	מִקְטַלְהוֹן	מִקְטַלְהֵין
Imp.										
Peal m.	קְטֻלְנִי	—	—	קְטֻלֵהּ	קְטֻלָהּ	קְטֻלְנָא	—	—	קְטֻלִנּוּן	קְטֻלִנֵּן
f.	קְטֻלִינִי	—	—	קְטֻלִיהִי	קְטֻלִיהָ	קְטֻלִינָא	—	—	קְטֻלִינוּן	קְטֻלִינֵן
Plur. m.	קְטֻלוּנִי	—	—	קְטֻלוּהִי	קְטֻלוּהָ	קְטֻלוּנָא	—	—	קְטֻלוּנוּן	קְטֻלוּנֵן
Fut.										
Peal 3. *m.*	יִקְטְלִנַּנִי	יִקְטְלִנָּךְ	יִקְטְלִנֵּךְ	יִקְטְלִנֵּהּ	יִקְטְלִנָּהּ	יִקְטְלָנָא	יִקְטְלִנְכוֹן	יִקְטְלִנְכֵן	יִקְטְלִנּוּן	יִקְטְלִנֵּן
Plur. 3. *m.*	יִקְטְלוּנַנִי	יִקְטְלוּנָּךְ	יִקְטְלוּנֵּךְ	יִקְטְלוּנֵּהּ	יִקְטְלוּנָּהּ	יִקְטְלוּנָא	יִקְטְלוּנְכוֹן	יִקְטְלוּנְכֵן	יִקְטְלוּנּוּן	יִקְטְלוּנֵּן

SECTION L.—ON THE REGULAR VERB WITH SUFFIXES.

REMARK.

An epenthetic נ is frequently inserted between the verb and the suffix. This occurs as the prevailing usage in the *fut.* and *imp.*, less frequently in the pret., and still less frequently in the inf. In the Biblical Chaldee examples are only found with the future. Once the union-vowel is (ֶ) instead of (ֵ), יְשְׁאֲלֶנְכוֹן Ezr. 7. 21.

TABLE S. VERBS פ״ן.

		PEAL.	APHEL.	ITTAPHAL.
PRET.	3. *m.*	נְפַק	אַפֵּק	אִתַּפַּק
	3. *f.*	נִפְקַת	אַפְּקַת	אִתַּפְּקַת
	2. *m.*	נְפַקְתָּ	אַפֵּקְתָּ	אִתַּפַּקְתָּ
	2. *f.*	נְפַקְתְּ	אַפֵּקְתְּ	אִתַּפַּקְתְּ
	1. *c.*	נִפְקֵת	אַפְּקֵת	אִתַּפְּקֵת
Plur.	3. *m.*	נְפַקוּ	אַפֵּקוּ	אִתַּפַּקוּ
	3. *f.*	נְפַקָא	אַפֵּקָא	אִתַּפַּקָא
	2. *m.*	נְפַקְתּוּן	אַפֵּקְתּוּן	אִתַּפַּקְתּוּן
	2. *f.*	נְפַקְתֵּן	אַפֵּקְתֵּן	אִתַּפַּקְתֵּן
	1. *c.*	נְפַקְנָא	אַפֵּקְנָא	אִתַּפַּקְנָא
INF.		מִפַּק	אַפָּקָא	אִתַּפָּקָא
IMP.	*m.*	פֻּק, פַּק	אַפֵּק	אִתַּפַּק
	f.	פֻּקִי	אַפִּקִי	אִתַּפַּקִי
Plur.	*m.*	פֻּקוּ, פַּקוּ	אַפִּקוּ	אִתַּפַּקוּ
	f.	פֻּקְנָא	אַפֵּקְנָא	אִתַּפַּקְנָא
FUT.	3. *m.*	יִפֻּק, יִפַּק	יַפֵּק	יִתַּפַּק
	3. *f.*	תִּפֻּק, תִּפַּק	תַּפֵּק	תִּתַּפַּק
	2. *m.*	תִּפֻּק, תִּפַּק	תַּפֵּק	תִּתַּפַּק
	2. *f.*	תִּפֻּקִין	תַּפְּקִין	תִּתַּפְּקִין
	1. *c.*	אֶפֻּק, אֶפַּק	אַפֵּק	אֶתַּפַּק
Plur.	3. *m.*	יִפְּקוּן	יַפְּקוּן	יִתַּפְּקוּן
	3. *f.*	יִפְּקָן	יַפְּקָן	יִתַּפְּקָן
	2. *m.*	תִּפְּקוּן	תַּפְּקוּן	תִּתַּפְּקוּן
	2. *f.*	תִּפְּקָן	תַּפְּקָן	תִּתַּפְּקָן
	1. *c.*	נִפֻּק, נִפַּק	נַפֵּק	נִתַּפַּק
1. *Part.*	*m.*	נָפֵק	מַפֵּק	מִתַּפַּק
	f.	נָפְקָא	מַפְּקָא	מִתַּפְּקָא
2. *Part.*	*m.*	נְפִיק	מַפַּק	
	f.	נְפִיקָא	מַפְּקָא	

TABLE T. VERBS ע״ע.*

		PEAL.	APHEL.	ITTAPHAL.
PRET.	3. *m.*	דַּק	אַדֵּק	אִתַּדַּק
	3. *f.*	דַּקַּת	אַדְּקַת	אִתַּדְּקַת
	2. *m.*	דַּקְתָּא, דַּקְתְּ	אַדֵּקְתְּ	אִתַּדַּקְתְּ
	2. *f.*	דַּקְתְּ	אַדֵּקְתְּ	אִתַּדַּקְתְּ
	1. *c.*	דַּקֵּת	אַדְּקֵת	אִתַּדְּקֵת
Plur.	3. *m.*	דַּקּוּ	אַדֵּקוּ	אִתַּדַּקוּ
	3. *f.*	דַּקָּא	אַדֵּקָא	אִתַּדַּקָא
	2. *m.*	דַּקְתּוּן	אַדֵּקְתּוּן	אִתַּדַּקְתּוּן
	2. *f.*	דַּקְתֵּן	אַדֵּקְתֵּן	אִתַּדַּקְתֵּן
	1. *c.*	דַּקְנָא	אַדֵּקְנָא	אִתַּדַּקְנָא
INF.		מִדַּק	אַדָּקָא	אִתַּדָּקָא
IMP.	2. *m.*	דֹּק	אַדֵּק	אִתַּדַּק
	2. *f.*	דֹּקִּי	אַדִּקִי	אִתַּדַּקִי
Plur.	2. *m.*	דֹּקּוּ	אַדִּקוּ	אִתַּדַּקוּ
	2. *f.*	דֹּקְנָא	אַדֵּקְנָא	אִתַּדַּקְנָא
FUT.	3. *m.*	יְדֹק	יַדֵּק	יִתַּדַּק
	3. *f.*	תְּדֹק	תַּדֵּק	תִּתַּדַּק
	2. *m.*	תְּדֹק	תַּדֵּק	תִּתַּדַּק
	2. *f.*	תִּדְּקִין	תַּדְּקִין	תִּתַּדְּקִין
	1. *c.*	אֱדֹק	אַדֵּק	אֶתַּדַּק
Plur.	3. *m.*	יִדְּקוּן	יַדְּקוּן	יִתַּדְּקוּן
	3. *f.*	יִדְּקָן	יַדְּקָן	יִתַּדְּקָן
	2. *m.*	תִּדְּקוּן	תַּדְּקוּן	תִּתַּדְּקוּן
	2. *f.*	תִּדְּקָן	תַּדְּקָן	תִּתַּדְּקָן
	1. *c.*	נְדֹק	נַדֵּק	נִתַּדַּק
1. *Part.*	*m.*	דָּקֵק	מַדֵּק	מִתַּדַּק
	f.	דָּקְקָא	מַדְּקָא	מִתַּדְּקָא
2. *Part.*	*m.*	דְּקִיק	מַדַּק	
	f.	דְּקִיקָא	מַדְּקָא	

* All that may be remarked here is, (*a*) that the *Dagesh forte* is sometimes resolved in נ, as הַנְעֵל Da. 2. 25; comp. Da. 4. 3 (for הַעֵּל, הַעֵל, comp. § 52. rem. 2); (*b*) that several Hebraisms occur, as Aph. הַדִּקוּ Da. 6. 25; הָעֵלְנִי Da. 2. 24; Hoph. הֻעַל, הֻעֲלוּ Da. 5. 13, 15 (comp. § 47. rem. 4 & 9).

SECTION LI.—ON VERBS PE NUN.

REMARKS.

1. Some verbs of this class are inflected regularly, e. g. תִּנְתֵּן Ezr. 7. 20; יִנְתֵּן Da. 2. 16; הַנְפֵּק Ezr. 5. 14. This is especially the case when the second radical is a guttural, of which, in the Bible, we have the only example in Hophal of נְחַת, viz. הָנְחַת Da. 5. 20. But this verb is defective throughout Aphel, as תַּחֵת Ezr. 6. 5; מְהַחֲתִין Ezr. 6. 1 (with *Dag. forte impl.* comp. § 14. rem. 1); but the imp. is אֲחֵת Ezr. 5. 15, for אַחֵת, probably to distinguish it from the 1st pers. fut.

2. In the Targums, the verb נְתַן takes (..) in the future as its characteristic vowel, e. g. אֶתֵּן Ex. 25. 16. Instead of this, the Biblical Chaldee exhibits the full form יִנְתְּנוּן, תִּנְתֵּן Ezr. 4. 13; 7. 20. Once (with Makkeph) יִנְתֶּן־ Da. 2. 16.

SECTION LII.—ON VERBS PE YOD (AND PE VAV).

TABLE U.		VERBS פ״ו.	VERBS פ״י.	
PAEL.	*Preter.* 3. *p.*	יְלַד, יִלְדַת	יְלִיד, יְלִידַת	יְטַב
	1. *p.*	יִלְדֵת etc.	יְלִידֵת etc.	
	Imper.	הַב	(תִּיב) תֵּב	
	Inf.	מֵילַד		
	Fut.	יֵילַד		יִיטַב
	Part.	יְלִיד, יָלֵד		
ITHPEEL.	*Pret.*	אִתְיְלֵד (אִתְיְלִיד), אִתְיְדַע		
PAEL.	*Pret.*	יַלֵּד		יַטֵּב
	Fut.	יְיַלֵּד		יְיַטֵּב
ITHPAAL.	*Pret.*	אִתְיַלַּד		
APHEL.	*Pret.*	אוֹלִיד		אֵיטִיב
	Fut.	יוֹלִיד		יֵיטִיב

REMARKS.

1. As in Hebrew there are three classes of verbs, viz., (1) verbs originally פ״ו; (2) verbs properly פ״י; and (3) those in which י is not treated as a quiescent, but is *assimilated* like the נ of verbs פ״ן.

2. For the inflexion of the first and second classes see parad.* They assimilate their first radical to the following letter in the *inf.* and *fut. Peal*, and in *Aphel;* so that they are in those forms entirely analogous to verbs פ״ן. Of this class all the occurring examples in the Biblical Chaldee are:—יְדַע *to know;* where, however, Dagesh is always resolved in נ as fut. תְּנְדַּע Da. 2. 30; 4. 22, 23, 29; אִנְדַּע Da. 2. 9, for תִּדַּע, אִדַּע (comp. note to Table T); יְכִל *to be able;* fut. יִכֻּל Da. 3. 29; תִּכּוּל Da. 5. 16, Keri; יְצַב Aph. inf. יַצָּבָא Da. 7. 19, formed after Hiphil with the termination א ָ.

SECTION LIII.—VERBS PE ALEPH.

1. A few verbs פ״א are treated not only as gutturals, but at the same time as quiescents, viz., אֲמַר, אֲכַל, אֲתָא, אֲבַד. The א of these verbs, in the fut. and inf. Peal, is quiescent in (..), e. g. יֵאכֻל, and sometimes even changed in י, as יֵיבַד, מֵימַר (in the Biblical Chaldee defective, comp. inf. מֵתֵא, מֵמַר (and מֵאמַר), from אֲתָא, אֲמַר). Throughout Aphel it becomes וֹ as הוֹבְדָה, תְּהוֹבֵד. An instance of Hophal is הוּבַד Da. 7. 11.

REM. 1. The form of the imp. אֱזֶל־ Ezr. 5. 15, stands with Makkeph, where it has lost the tone, for אֱזֶל, as Syriacism for אֲזֻל, comp. § 19. rem. 3 & 6.

2. For the verb אֲתָא see the doubly anomalous verbs, section 25.

* The ה of Aphel is frequently retained in the future, as תְּהוֹדְעַ Da. 2. 5, comp. § 53. No. 1.

TABLE V. VERBS ע״ו.

		PEAL.	ITHPEAL.	PAEL.	ITHPAAL.	APHEL.	ITTAPHAL.	POEL.	ITHPOAL.
PRET.	3. *m.*	קָם	אִתְּקָם	קַיֵּם	אִתְקַיַּם	אֲקִים	אִתָּקִים	קוֹמֵם	אִתְקוֹמַם
	3. *f.*	קָמַת	אִתְּקָמַת	קַיְּמַת	אִתְקַיְּמַת	אֲקִימַת, אֲקֵימַת·	אִתָּקִימַת	קוֹמְמַת	אִתְקוֹמְמַת
	2. *m.*	קָמְתָּ, קֳמְתְּ	אִתְּקָמְתָּ	קַיֵּמְתָּ	אִתְקַיֵּמְתָּ	אֲקִימְתָּ, אֲקֵימְתָּ	אִתָּקִימְתָּ	קוֹמֵמְתָּ	אִתְקוֹמַמְתָּ
	2. *f.*	קָמְתְּ	אִתְּקָמְתְּ	קַיֵּמְתְּ	אִתְקַיֵּמְתְּ	אֲקִימְתְּ	אִתָּקִימְתְּ	קוֹמַמְתְּ	אִתְקוֹמַמְתְּ
	1. *c.*	קָמֵת	אִתְּקָמֵת	קַיְּמֵת	אִתְקַיְּמֵת	אֲקִימֵת, אֲקֵימֵת	אִתָּקִימֵת	קוֹמְמֵת	אִתְקוֹמְמֵת
Plur.	3. *m.*	קָמוּ	אִתְּקָמוּ	קַיִּמוּ	אִתְקַיַּמוּ	אֲקִימוּ	אִתָּקִימוּ	קוֹמִמוּ	אִתְקוֹמַמוּ
	3. *f.*	קָמָא	אִתְּקָמָא	קַיִּמָא	אִתְקַיַּמָא	אֲקִימָא	אִתָּקִימָא	קוֹמִמָא	אִתְקוֹמַמָא
	2. *m.*	קָמְתּוּן, קַמְתּוּן	אִתְּקָמְתּוּן	קַיֵּמְתּוּן	אִתְקַיֵּמְתּוּן	אֲקֵמְתּוּן	אִתָּקִימְתּוּן	קוֹמַמְתּוּן	אִתְקוֹמַמְתּוּן
	2. *f.*	קָמְתֵּן, קַמְתֵּן	אִתְּקָמְתֵּן	קַיֵּמְתֵּן	אִתְקַיֵּמְתֵּן	אֲקֵמְתֵּן	אִתָּקִימְתֵּן	קוֹמַמְתֵּן	אִתְקוֹמַמְתֵּן
	1. *c.*	קָמְנָא, קַמְנָא	אִתְּקָמְנָא	קַיֵּמְנָא	אִתְקַיֵּמְנָא	אֲקֵמְנָא	אִתָּקִימְנָא	קוֹמַמְנָא	אִתְקוֹמַמְנָא
INF.		מְקָם (מְקוּם)	אִתְּקָמָא	קַיָּמָא	אִתְקַיָּמָא	אֲקָמָא	אִתָּקָמָא	קוֹמָמָא	אִתְקוֹמָמָא
IMP.	2. *m.*	קוּם	אִתְּקָם	קַיֵּם	אִתְקַיַּם	אֲקִים	אִתָּקִים	קוֹמֵם	אִתְקוֹמַם
	2. *f.*	קוּמִי	אִתְּקָמִי	קַיִּמִי	אִתְקַיַּמִי	אֲקִימִי	אִתָּקִימִי	קוֹמִמִי	אִתְקוֹמַמִי
Plur.	2. *m.*	קוּמוּ	אִתְּקָמוּ	קַיִּמוּ	אִתְקַיַּמוּ	אֲקִימוּ	אִתָּקִימוּ	קוֹמִמוּ	אִתְקוֹמַמוּ
	2. *f.*	קוּמְנָא	אִתְּקָמְנָא	קַיֵּמְנָא	אִתְקַיֵּמְנָא	אֲקֵמְנָא	אִתָּקִימְנָא	קוֹמֵמְנָא	אִתְקוֹמַמְנָא
FUT.	3. *m.*	יְקוּם	יִתְּקָם	יְקַיֵּם	יִתְקַיַּם	יְקִים	יִתָּקִים	יְקוֹמֵם	יִתְקוֹמַם
	3. *f.*	תְּקוּם	תִּתְּקָם	תְּקַיֵּם	תִּתְקַיַּם	תְּקִים	תִּתָּקִים	תְּקוֹמֵם	תִּתְקוֹמַם
	2. *m.*	תְּקוּם	תִּתְּקָם	תְּקַיֵּם	תִּתְקַיַּם	תְּקִים	תִּתָּקִים	תְּקוֹמֵם	תִּתְקוֹמַם
	2. *f.*	תְּקוּמִין	תִּתְּקָמִין	תְּקַיְּמִין	תִּתְקַיְּמִין	תְּקִימִין	תִּתָּקִימִין	תְּקוֹמְמִין	תִּתְקוֹמְמִין
	1. *c.*	אֲקוּם	אִתְּקָם	אֲקַיֵּם	אֶתְקַיַּם	אֲקִים	אֶתָּקִים	אֲקוֹמֵם	אֶתְקוֹמַם
Plur.	3. *m.*	יְקוּמוּן	יִתְּקָמוּן	יְקַיְּמוּן	יִתְקַיְּמוּן	יְקִימוּן	יִתָּקִימוּן	יְקוֹמְמוּן	יִתְקוֹמְמוּן
	3. *f.*	יְקוּמָן	יִתְּקָמָן	יְקַיְּמָן	יִתְקַיְּמָן	יְקִימָן	יִתָּקִימָן	יְקוֹמְמָן	יִתְקוֹמְמָן
	2. *m.*	תְּקוּמוּן	תִּתְּקָמוּן	תְּקַיְּמוּן	תִּתְקַיְּמוּן	תְּקִימוּן	תִּתָּקִימוּן	תְּקוֹמְמוּן	תִּתְקוֹמְמוּן
	2. *f.*	תְּקוּמָן	תִּתְּקָמָן	תְּקַיְּמָן	תִּתְקַיְּמָן	תְּקִימָן	תִּתָּקִימָן	תְּקוֹמְמָן	תִּתְקוֹמְמָן
	1. *c.*	נְקוּם	נִתְּקָם	נְקַיֵּם	נִתְקַיַּם	נְקִים	נִתָּקִים	נְקוֹמֵם	נִתְקוֹמַם
1. *Part.*	*m.*	קָאֵם, קָיֵם	מִתְּקָם	מְקַיֵּם	מִתְקַיַּם	מְקִים	מִתָּקִים	מְקוֹמֵם	מִתְקוֹמַם
	f.	קָיְמָא	מִתְּקָמָא	מְקַיְּמָא	מִתְקַיְּמָא	מְקִימָא	מִתָּקִימָא	מְקוֹמְמָא	מִתְקוֹמְמָא
2. *Part.*	*m.*	קִים		מְקַיַּם		מְקָם		מְקוֹמַם	
	f.	קִימָא		מְקַיְּמָא		מְקָמָא		מְקוֹמְמָא	

SECTION LIV.—ON VERBS AYIN VAV (AND AYIN YOD).

REMARKS.

1. Peal future. Instead of the form יְקוּם there also occurs the contracted form יְהָךְ Ezr. 5. 5; 6. 5, from הוּךְ.

2. The *second participle* (*Peil*) takes also, like the inf., the form קוּם, from which a new *pret. passive* is formed, thus שִׂימַת (3 p. f.) Da. 6. 18, comp. § 47. r. 11.

3. *Ithpeel.* Besides the form אִתְּקָם with (ְ) under the first radical, there are also instances in the Targums of the form אִתָּקִים, comp. Je. 33. 22; Ge. 38. 26, to which may also be reckoned יִתְּזִין Da. 4. 9; but comp. § 47. rem. 10.

4. *Aphel.* Instead of the characteristic ־ִי, some-

times ـֵי is used, as הֲקֵים Da. 3. 2, 3, 5, 7; 6. 2, comp. Da. 3. 18, and in the 1st pers. with (ְ) under the last radical, הֲקֵימֶת Da. 3. 14.

HEBRAISMS.

5. Hebraisms, besides the constant use of ה for א, are:—*Peal* pret. שָׂמְתְּ Da. 3. 10, for שָׂמְתְּ. *Aphel* pret. הֲקֵימְתָּ Da. 3. 18; fut. תָּסֵף Da. 2. 44; for תְּסִיף, יְחִיטוּ Ezr. 4. 12; part. מָרִים Da. 5. 19.

6. Examples of verbs inflected like ע״י are only רִם Da. 5. 20, which, however, may be the part. Peil pret., comp. No. 2, and § 47. rem. 11. Imp. שִׂימוּ Ezr. 4. 21; part. pass. שִׂים Da. 3. 29; 4. 3, &c.

TABLE W. VERB ל״א.

	PEAL.		ITHPAEL.	PAEL.	ITHPAAL.	APHEL.	ITTAPHAL.
PRET. 3. *m.*	גְּלָא	סְנִי (סְגִי)	אִתְגְּלִי (ـִי)	גַּלִּי	אִתְגַּלִּי (ـִי)	אַגְלִי (ـִי)	אִתַּגְלִי
3. *f.*	גְּלָת	סְנִיאַת, סְנִיַּת	אִתְגְּלִיַת (ـיאַת)	גַּלִּיַת, גַּלִּיאַת	אִתְגַּלִּיַת	אַגְלִיַת	אִתַּגְלִיַת (ـיאַת)
2. *m.*	גְּלֵיתָ, גְּלַיְתָּ	סְנִיתָ	אִתְגְּלֵיתָ	גַּלִּיתָ	אִתְגַּלִּית	אַגְלֵיתָ (ـִיתָ)	אִתַּגְלִית
2. *f.*	גְּלֵית, גְּלַיְתְּ	סְנִית, צְבִית	אִתְגְּלֵית	גַּלִּית	אִתְגַּלִּית	אַגְלֵת (ـִית)	אִתַּגְלִית
1. *c.*	גְּלֵיתִי, גְּלֵית	סְנִיתִי	אִתְגְּלֵיתִי	גַּלִּיתִי, גַּלֵּית	אִתְגַּלֵּיתִי	אַגְלֵיתִי	אִתַּגְלֵיתִי
Plur. 3. *m.*	גְּלוֹ	סְנִיאוּ, סְנִיו	אִתְגְּלִיו (ـִיאוּ)	גַּלִּיו, גַּלִּיאוּ	אִתְגַּלִּיו (ـִיאוּ)	אַגְלִיו (ـִיאוּ)	אִתַּגְלִיו
3. *f.*	גְּלָאָה	סְנִיאָה	אִתְגְּלִיָא	גַּלִּיָא	אִתְגַּלִּיאָה	אַגְלִיָא (ـִיאָה)	אִתַּגְלִיָא
2. *m.*	גְּלֵיתוּן	סְנִיתוּן	אִתְגְּלֵיתוּן	גַּלִּיתוּן, גַּלֵּיתוּן	אִתְגַּלִּיתוּן	אַגְלִיתוּן	אִתַּגְלִיתוּן
2. *f.*	גְּלֵיתֶן	סְנִיתֶן	אִתְגְּלֵיתֶן	גַּלִּיתֶן, גַּלֵּיתֶן	אִתְגַּלִּיתֶן	אַגְלִיתֶן	אִתַּגְלִיתֶן
1. *c.*	גְּלֵינָא	סְנֵינָא	אִתְגְּלֵינָא	גַּלִּינָא, גַּלֵּינָא	אִתְגַּלִּינָא	אַגְלִינָא	אִתַּגְלִינָא
INF.	מִגְלֵא (מִגְלְיָה, מִגְלָא		אִתְגְּלָאָה	גַּלָּאָה	אִתְגַּלָּאָה	אַגְלָיָה, אַגְלָאָה	אִתַּגְלָאָה
IMP. *m.*	גְּלִי, (גְּלָא) גְּלִי		אִתְגְּלֵא	גַּלִּי, גַּלַּי	אִתְגַּלֵּי	אַגְלִי (ـִי)	אִתַּגְלִי
f.	גְּלִי, גְּלָא		אִתְגְּלָא	גַּלָּא	אִתְגַּלָּא	אַגְלָא	אִתַּגְלָא
Plur. *m.*	גְּלוֹ		אִתְגְּלוֹ	גַּלּוֹ	אִתְגַּלּוֹ	אַגְלוֹ	אִתַּגְלוֹ
f.	גְּלֶן, גְּלָאנָה		אִתְגְּלָנָא	גַּלָּנָא	אִתְגַּלָּנָא	אַגְלִינָא	אִתַּגְלִינָא
FUT. 3. *m.*	יִגְלֵא (ـֵי)		יִתְגְּלֵי (ـֵא)	יְגַלֵּי (ـֵא)	יִתְגַּלֵּי (ـֵא)	יַגְלֵי (ـֵא)	יִתַּגְלֵא (ـֵי)
3. *f.*	תִּגְלֵא (ـֵי)		תִּתְגְּלֵי (ـֵא)	תְּגַלֵּי (ـֵא)	תִּתְגַּלֵּי (ـֵא)	תַּגְלֵי (ـֵא)	תִּתַּגְלֵא (ـֵי)
2. *m.*	תִּגְלֵא (ـֵי)		תִּתְגְּלֵי (ـֵא)	תְּגַלֵּי (ـֵא)	תִּתְגַּלֵּי (ـֵא)	תַּגְלֵי (ـֵא)	תִּתַּגְלֵא (ـֵי)
2. *f.*	תִּגְלַיִן		תִּתְגְּלַיִן	תְּגַלַּיִן	תִּתְגַּלַּיִן	תַּגְלַיִן	תִּתַּגְלַיִן
1. *c.*	אֶגְלֵא (ـֵי)		אֶתְגְּלֵי (ـֵא)	אֲגַלֵּי (ـֵא)	אֶתְגַּלֵּי (ـֵא)	אַגְלֵי (ـֵא)	אֶתַּגְלֵא (ـֵי)
Plur. 3. *m.*	יִגְלוֹן		יִתְגְּלוֹן	יְגַלּוֹן	יִתְגַּלּוֹן	יַגְלוֹן	יִתַּגְלוֹן
3. *f.*	יִגְלְיָן		יִתְגַּלְיָן	יְגַלְּיָן	יִתְגַּלְּיָן	יַגְלְיָן	יִתַּגְלְיָן
2. *m.*	תִּגְלוֹן		תִּתְגְּלוֹן	תְּגַלּוֹן	תִּתְגַּלּוֹן	תַּגְלוֹן	תִּתַּגְלוֹן
2. *f.*	תִּגְלְיָן		תִּתְגַּלְיָן	תְּגַלְּיָן	תִּתְגַּלְּיָן	תַּגְלְיָן	תִּתַּגְלְיָן
1. *c.*	נִגְלֵא (ـֵי)		נִתְגְּלֵי (ـֵא)	נְגַלֵּי (ـֵא)	נִתְגַּלֵּי (ـֵא)	נַגְלֵי (ـֵא)	נִתַּגְלֵא (ـֵי)
1. *Pt.* *m.*	גָּלֵא, גָּלֵי		מִתְגְּלֵי	מְגַלֵּי (ـֵא)	מִתְגַּלֵּי (ـֵא)	מַגְלֵי (ـֵא)	מִתַּגְלֵא
f.	גָּלְיָא		מִתְגַּלְיָא	מְגַלְּיָא	מִתְגַּלְּיָא	מַגְלְיָא	מִתַּגְלְיָא
2. *Pt.* *m.*	גְּלֵא, גְּלִי			מְגַלַּי		מַגְלַי	
f.	גְּלְיָא			מְגַלְּיָא		מַגְלְיָא	

SECTION LV.—ON VERBS LAMED ALEPH (AND LAMED HE*).

REMARKS.

1. Pret. The 3 pers. sing. fem. Peal appears sometimes in the full orthography, as מְלָאת Da. 2. 35. It takes, however, also (ַ) instead of (ָ), as הֲוָת Da. 2. 35; מְטָת Da. 4. 19. The 2 *pers. sing. masc.* is also written *fully*, terminating in תָה, as חֲזַיְתָה Da. 2. 41. Instead of ֵי in the 1 *pers. sing.* there is ִי in צְבִית Da. 7. 19. The 3 *pers. pl. masc.* sometimes follows the analogy of the other derived conjugations (Ithpe., Pa., &c.), as רְמִיו Da. 3. 21. An example with prosthetic א is אִשְׁתִּיו Da. 5. 3, 4.

2. *Future.* The 3 *pers. sing. masc.* terminates also in ֵי in יִתְקְרֵי Da. 5. 12. The 3 pers. pl. takes also the termination וֹן instead of וֹן, as יְהַעְדּוֹן Da. 7. 26.

3. The *infinitive* of *Peal* takes sometimes the termination ָא, in the Biblical Chaldee, as צְבָא Da. 7. 19; more usually ָה, as לְמִבְנְיָה Ezr. 5. 9; and in the other conjugations ָיָה, e. g. Da. 2. 10; 5. 2.

4. *Part. Peil.* In some instances the first radical takes composite Sheva, though a non-guttural, as קֱרִי Ezr. 4. 18, 23; גֱּלִי Da. 2. 30, and גֱּלִי ver. 19.

SECTION LVI.—VERBS DOUBLY ANOMALOUS (COMP. § 25).

1. פ״ן and ל״א:—נְשָׂא. Imp. שָׂא Ezr. 5. 15.

2. פ״א and ל״א:—אֲתָא, אֲזָא. *Peal inf.* מִתֵא Da. 3. 2; מֵזֵה Da. 3. 19, by syncope for מֶאֱתֵא, &c.; *Part. pass.* אֵזֵה Da. 3. 22; by Syriacism for אֱזֵה (comp. § 53. rem. 1). *Aphel*, pret. 3 pers. sing. masc. הַיְתִי Da. 5. 13; 3 pers. plur. הַיְתִיו Da. 5. 3; (comp. inf. הַיְתָיָה Da. 5. 2). Altogether peculiar are the anomalies of Hophal, 3 pers. fem. הֵיתָיִת Da. 6. 18; 3 pers. plur. masc. הֵיתָיוּ Da. 3. 13.

3. פ״י and ל״א. Only יְדָא, *Aph.* Part. מְהוֹדֵא Da. 2. 23, and מוֹדֵא 6. 11.

* In the Biblical Chaldee ה is promiscuously used instead of א, comp. § 46. rem. 4, & § 54. rem. 5.

TABLE X. DECLENSION OF MASCULINE NOUNS.

	I. a.	I. b.	II. a.	II. b.	III. a.	III. b.	III. c.	III. d.
Sing. absol.	טְוּר (mount)	אִילָן (tree)	עָלַם (eternity)	כָּהֵן (priest)	מֶלֶךְ (king)	זְמַן (time)	חֵלֶם (dream)	עַיִן (eye)
constr.	טְוּר	אִילַן	עָלַם	כָּהֵן	מְלֵךְ	זְמַן	חֵלֶם	עֵין
emphat.	טוּרָא	אִילָנָא	עָלְמָא	כָּהֲנָא	מַלְכָּא	זִמְנָא	חֶלְמָא	עֵינָא (עַיְנָא)
with suff.	טוּרֵהּ	אִילָנֵהּ	עָלְמֵהּ	כָּהֲנֵהּ	מַלְכֵּהּ	זִמְנֵהּ	חֶלְמֵהּ	עֵינֵהּ (עַיְנֵהּ)
	טוּרְכוֹן	אִילַנְכוֹן	עָלַמְכוֹן	כָּהֵנְכוֹן	מַלְכְּכוֹן	זִמְנְכוֹן	חֶלְמְכוֹן	עֵינְכוֹן
Plur. absol.	טוּרִין	אִילָנִין	עָלְמִין	כָּהֲנִין	מַלְכִין	זִמְנִין	חֶלְמִין	עַיְנִין
constr.	טוּרֵי	אִילָנֵי	עָלְמֵי	כָּהֲנֵי	מַלְכֵי	זִמְנֵי	חֶלְמֵי	עֵינֵי (עַיְנֵי)
emphat.	טוּרַיָּא	אִילָנַיָּא	עָלְמַיָּא	כָּהֲנַיָּא	מַלְכַיָּא	זִמְנַיָּא	חֶלְמַיָּא	עֵינַיָּא (עַיְנַיָּא)
with suff.	טוּרוֹהִי	אִילָנוֹהִי	עָלְמוֹהִי	כָּהֲנוֹהִי	מַלְכוֹהִי	זִמְנוֹהִי	חֶלְמוֹהִי	עֵינוֹהִי (עַיְנוֹהִי)
	טוּרֵיכוֹן	אִילָנֵיכוֹן	עָלְמֵיכוֹן	כָּהֲנֵיכוֹן	מַלְכֵיכוֹן	זִמְנֵיכוֹן	חֶלְמֵיכוֹן	עֵינֵיכוֹן (עַיְנֵיכוֹן)

	IV.	V. a.	V. b.	V. c.	VI. a.	VI. b.	VII.
Sing. absol.	מְתַקְטֵל (murderer)	גַּב (back)	עֵז (goat)	אֻם (people)	גָּלֵא revealer)	מְגַלֵּי	קַדְמַי (first)
constr.	מְתַקְטֵל	גַּב	עֵז	אֻם	גָּלֵא	מְגַלֵּי	קַדְמַי
emphat.	מְתַקְטְלָא	גַּבָּא	עִזָּא	אֻמָּא	גָּלְיָא	מְגַלְיָא	קַדְמָאָה
with suff.	מְתַקְטְלֵהּ	גַּבֵּהּ	עִזֵּהּ	אֻמֵּהּ	גָּלְיֵהּ	מְגַלְיֵהּ	קַדְמָאֵהּ
Plur. absol.	מְתַקְטְלִין	גַּבִּין	עִזִּין	אֻמִּין	גָּלַיִן	מְגַלַּיִן	קַדְמָאִין
constr.	מְתַקְטְלֵי	גַּבֵּי	עִזֵּי	אֻמֵּי	גָּלֵי	מְגַלֵּי	קַדְמָאֵי
emphat.	מְתַקְטְלַיָּא	גַּבַּיָּא	עִזַּיָּא	אֻמַּיָּא	גָּלַיָּא	מְגַלַּיָּא	קַדְמָאֵי
with suff.	מְתַקְטְלֵיכוֹן	גַּבֵּיכוֹן	עִזֵּיכוֹן	אֻמֵּיכוֹן	גָּלֵיכוֹן	מְגַלֵּיכוֹן	קַדְמָאֵיכוֹן

DECLENSION OF FEMININE NOUNS.

	(A) VIII.* a.	(A) VIII.* b.	(A) VIII.* c.	(B) IX.*	(C) X.*	(D) XI.*
Sing. absol.	מְדִינָא (province)	מַשְׁרֵי (army)	מַלְכוּ (kingdom)	אַרְמְלָא (widow)	גָּלְיָא (discoverer)	קַדְמָאָה (first)
constr.	מְדִינַת	מַשְׁרִית	מַלְכוּת	אַרְמְלַת	גָּלְיַת	קַדְמָאַת
emphat.	מְדִינְתָּא	מַשְׁרִיתָא	מַלְכוּתָא	אַרְמַלְתָּא	גָּלִיתָא	קַדְמִיתָא
with suff.	מְדִינְתֵּהּ	מַשְׁרִיתֵהּ	מַלְכוּתֵהּ	אַרְמַלְתֵּהּ	גָּלִיתֵהּ	קַדְמִיתֵהּ
	מְדִינַתְהוֹן	מַשְׁרִיתְהוֹן	מַלְכוּתְהוֹן	אַרְמַלַתְהוֹן		
Plur. absol.	מְדִינָן	מַשְׁרְיָן	מַלְכְוָן	אַרְמְלָן	גָּלְיָן	קַדְמָאָן
constr.	מְדִינָת	מַשְׁרְיָת	מַלְכְוָת	אַרְמְלָת	גָּלְיָת	קַדְמָאָת
emphat.	מְדִינָתָא	מַשְׁרְיָתָא	מַלְכְוָתָא	אַרְמְלָתָא	גָּלְיָתָא	קַדְמָיָתָא
with suff.	מְדִינָתְהוֹן	מַשְׁרְיָתְהוֹן	מַלְכְוָתְהוֹן	אַרְמְלָתְהוֹן	גָּלְיָתְהוֹן	קַדְמָיָתְהוֹן

SECTION LVII.—FIRST DECLENSION OF MASCULINES.

EXPLANATORY.

This declension includes all nouns, which have all their vowels immutable. It comprehends,

(*a*) Nouns which have ִי, ֵי, ו or וֹ before their final consonant, e. g. דִּין *judgment,* יוֹם *day,* אַתּוּן *furnace.*

(*b*) Those which have (ָ) in their final syllable; as טָב *good,* גַּנָּב *thief.* There are, however, a few of those which change (ָ) to (ַ), compare the following remark.

REMARK.

Nouns with (ָ) in the ultimate are chiefly of six classes:—

(1) Nouns derived from ע״ו, e. g. קָל, דָּר (Heb. דּוֹר, קוֹל);

(2) Nouns of the form שְׁלָם, כְּתָב (Heb. שָׁלוֹם);

(3) Nouns of the form קַטָּל (Arab. קַטָּאל, and also in the Heb. with (ָ) *impure*);

(4) Nouns like קְטָל (also in the Heb. with (ָ) *impure*).

(5) Nouns which have the formative ending ָן, e. g. קָרְבָּן (Arab. קרבאן).

(6) Nouns of the form קוֹטָל, e.g. אוֹצָר, עוֹבָד. They have a twofold inflexion :—

(*a*) The first three of these classes retain (ָ) in all the inflexions, and consequently belong regularly to Declension 1.

(*b*) Nouns of the fourth, fifth, and sixth classes sometimes take (ַ) instead of (ָ) in the constr. sing.; and before the suffixes, כוֹן and הוֹן. Elsewhere (ָ) is retained. The punctuation of these nouns is, however, variable; and as they present no other irregularity, they may better be regarded as exceptions from Declension 1, than as forming a separate declension.

SECTION LVIII.—SECOND DECLENSION OF MASCULINES.

EXPLANATORY

The second declension embraces nouns with final (ַ) or (ֵ), either monosyllabic, as שֵׁם, יַד, or having the preceding vowels immutable, as עָלַם, קְטַל, אֶדְרַע, מִסְפֵּד. These vowels are dropped before suffixes beginning with a vowel.

REM. 1. The forms like קַטְלִין for קָטְלִין, pl. of קָטֵל (part. act.), must be attributed to the variable vocalization of the Chaldee; as פַּרְסִין Da. 5. 25; חַשְׁחָן for חָשְׁחָן (plur. fem. of חָשַׁח) Ezr. 6. 9.

2. To this paradigm belongs also פַּרְזֶל, emph. st. פַּרְזְלָא

3. Before כוֹן and הוֹן, monosyllables, as in Hebrew, take (ַ), (ֶ), or (ִ); e. g. יֶדְכוֹן, דִּמְהוֹן.

SECTION LIX.—THIRD DECLENSION OF MASCULINES.

This declension embraces all nouns which correspond to the Segolate forms in the Hebrew. They may either be written with two vowels (the second of which is always considered an auxiliary vowel), as מֶלֶךְ, חֵלֶם (almost exclusively in the Biblical Chaldee), בַּיִת (קֹדֶשׁ; or with only *one* vowel between the last two consonants, as מְלַךְ, סְפַר. They are inflected, however, for the most part, as in Hebrew; except,

(*a*) In the plural absol. the forms מְלַךְ and סְפַר become, as they do in most other inflexions מַלְךְ and סִפְר.

(*b*) The form קֹדֶשׁ either follows the analogy of the Hebrew, as תָּקְפָּא Da. 2. 37, or takes (ֻ), as כֻּתְלַיָּא Ezr. 5. 8.

(*c*) In the form בַּיִת, the י often remains moveable in the inflexion, as עַיְנֵי Da. 7. 8; עַיְנֵי Da. 4. 31; בַּיְתָא Ezr. 5. 3; בַּיְתֵהּ Da. 5. 23.

(*d*) The forms מְלַךְ and סְפַר, in the course of inflexion, usually take (ַ), (ִ), or rarely (ֶ), under their first radical.

Nouns having gutturals for their first or second radical, naturally take (ַ), as טְעֵם, טַעֲמָא, עֲבֵד, עַבְדָּא.

SECTION LX.—FOURTH DECLENSION OF MASCULINES.

The fourth declension comprehends those nouns in which the vowel of the final syllable falls away in the course of inflexion, and the third consonant from the end receives then, (ִ) or (ַ). To this declension belong the participles of Ithpeel.

SECTION LXI.—FIFTH DECLENSION OF MASCULINES.

The fifth declension embraces those nouns which double the final consonant when they receive any accession. They are mostly monosyllables derived from verbs ע״ע. The long vowels (ֵ) and וֹ are changed in the course of inflexion into the corresponding short vowels. In some nouns (ַ) becomes (ִ), as גַּלְגַּל, גַּלְגִּלִּין Da. 7. 9.

Rem. כֹּל has in the emph. st. כֹּלָּא, &c. with the tone on the penultima (Da. 2. 40); but with suff. כָּלְּהוֹן Da. 2. 38; 7. 19.

SECTION LXII.—SIXTH DECLENSION OF MASCULINES.

The sixth declension includes nouns, participles, and infinitives, derived from verbs ל״א (ל״ה) and terminating in ־ָא (־ֵה), ־ֵי, ־ִי, ־ֵי, e. g. גְּלָא, גֵּלָא, מִתְגְּלֵי, מְגַלֵּי, בְּכִי. The general rule is, that י appears in the course of declension, as the third radical, displacing א in forms like גְּלָא. That י is joined to the suffix throughout the singular, and thus becomes moveable; in forms like רְבִי, בְּכִי a short vowel is pronounced under the first radical. The termination ־ַיִן of the plural absol. is sometimes contracted into ־ִן. In the constr. and emph. plur. no trace of the radical י remains.

SECTION LXIII.—SEVENTH DECLENSION OF MASCULINES.

Here belong nouns which terminate in the formative syllable ־ָי (־ָאי). They are mostly *gentilic* or *patronymic nouns*, or *ordinal numerals*. They all have this in common, (*a*) that in the course of inflexion their final י is changed into א, which is likewise *moveable*, and commences the following syllable. As a consequence, (ַ) is here changed into (ָ). (*b*) The plur. emph. terminates in ־ֵי, agreeing in form with the construct.

Exceptions from *b*: כַּשְׂדָּיֵא Da. 2. 5; תִּפְתָּיֵא Da. 3. 2, 3; יְהוּדָיֵא Da. 3. 8; Ezr. 4. 12, 23; 5. 1, 5.

SECTION LXIV.—EIGHTH DECLENSION OR *FIRST* OF FEMININES.

This declension includes all invariable feminines, i. e. all nouns with the feminine terminations, ־ָא, ־ָה, ־ִי, and וּ, the final syllable of which commences with only one consonant; as מְגִלָּא, גְּבוּרָא, עֵצָא, בָּמָא, מַרְבִּי, גְּזֵרָה, סְגִירוּ, טָבוּ.

SECTION LXV.—NINTH DECLENSION, OR THE *SECOND* OF FEMININES.

This declension embraces all those feminines the final syllable of which commences with two consonants, as שִׁפְּא *lip;* אִצְטְלִי *a robe;* זְכוּ *purity.*

(*a*) Nouns in ־ָא, to avoid, in the emph. and suff. states, two consonants with sheva under each in immediate succession, as שִׁפְתָא, אַרְמְלְתָא, &c., a short vowel must necessarily be supplied for the first of these. The supplied vowel is *Hhirek* or *Pattah* (the latter with gutturals); more rarely Segol; e. g. חֶמְתָא, חֲמָא, אַמְתָא, אֲמָא, שִׁפְתָא, שְׁפָא.

(*b*) The forms in ־ִי and וּ are regular in the singular (like Dec. VIII). In the plural, as becomes necessary, they also take a supplied vowel, *Hhirek* or *Pattahh.*

SECTION LXVI.—TENTH DECLENSION, OR THE *THIRD* OF FEMININES.

This declension includes all feminines in יָא (derived from ל״א) which have a consonant without a vowel immediately preceding this termination, as מִגְלְיָא, גָּלְיָא. In the sing. emph. and suff. states, this consonant takes the supplied vowel Hhirek (for the cause stated in the preceding section), so that י becomes quiescent in it.

SECTION LXVII.—ELEVENTH DECLENSION, OR THE *FOURTH* OF FEMININES.

Here belong feminines in ־ָאָה derived from masculines in ־ִי (Dec. VII). In the emphatic state and before suffixes, א is changed in *moveable* י, though ordinal numerals take also ־ִי or ־ֵי; e. g. רְבִיעֲתָא, קַדְמִיתָא (but רְבִיעָיְתָא Da. 7. 19). In the plural absol. and constr. the usual forms are קַדְמָאָן, קַדְמָאַת.

REM. When feminine nouns are formed from masculines by adding the terminations ־ָא, וּ or ־ִי, the changes in the ground-form are precisely the same as those which appear in the emph. state of masculines. E. g. עוֹלָם, עוּלְמָא; מְלַךְ, מַלְכָּא and מַלְכוּת; צְדִי, צַדְיָא.

SECTION LXVIII.—IRREGULAR NOUNS (COMP. § 45).

אַב *father*, with suff. אֲבִי, but also אֲבוּהִי, אֲבוּךְ (from אֲבוּ as if from R. אָבָה comp. Heb. אָב § 45. rem). Plur. with suff. אֲבָהָתִי, אֲבָהָתָךְ, אֲבָהָתַנָא from the abs. אֲבָהָן (as if from a sing. אֲבָהָא).

אָח *brother*, plur. with suff. אֶחָיךְ Ezr. 7. 18, by Hebraism (comp. אָח § 45), for אֲחִיךְ, from אֲחִי=אֲחוּ R. אחה.

אֱנָשׁ, אֱנַשׁ *man*, emph. state אֱנָשָׁא, אֲנָשָׁא, but also אֱנוֹשָׁא Khethib (as if from אֱנוֹשׁ). Plur. (by Hebraism) אֲנָשִׁים.

אֲרִי, אַרְיֵה *lion*, plur. emph. אַרְיָוָתָא, from the absolute אַרְיָוָן (as if from a sing. אַרְיוּ, comp. Dec. VIII).

בַּיִת *house*, emph. בַּיְתָא, בַּיְתָה, constr. בֵּית, with suff. בֵּיתִי and בַּיְתֵה (comp. Dec. III, c), but plur. with suff. בָּתֵּיכוֹן from בָּתִּין (comp. Heb. בַּיִת § 45).

נְבִיא *prophet*, emph. state נְבִיָּאה (for נְבִיאָה, נְבִיאָא). Plur. emph. נְבִיַּאיָּא with א in otio, for נְבִיַּיָּא (as if from an absolute נְבִיִּין).

עַם *people*, emph. state עַמָּא, but pl. emph. עַמְמַיָּא (comp. Heb. עַם § 45).

רֵאשׁ *head*, emph. state רֵאשָׁה, with suff. רֵאשֵׁהּ. Plur. רֵאשִׁין, but with suff. רָאשֵׁיהֶם (as if from רָאשׁ).

שְׁם *name*, but with suff. שְׁמֵהּ (from שֵׁם, comp. Dec. II). Plur. constr. שְׁמָהַת, with suff. שְׁמָהַתְהוֹם (as if from שְׁמָהָא).

THE ANALYTICAL
HEBREW AND CHALDEE
LEXICON

LEXICON

א

אֲאַזֶּרְךָ[a] Piel fut. 1 pers. s. [אֲאַזֵּר], suff. 2 s. m. (§ 16. r. 15) אזר

אֲאַלֶּפְךָ[b] וֲ Piel fut. 1 pers. sing. [אֲאַלֵּף], suff. 2 pers. sing. masc. (§ 16. rem. 15); וֲ before (־ׄ) . אלף

אֲאַמִין[c] Hiph. fut. 1 pers. sing. . . . . אמן

אֲאַמִּצְכֶם[d] Piel fut. 1 s. [אֲאַמֵּץ], suff. 2 pl. m. (§ 16. r. 15) אמץ

אֶאֱסֹף[e] Kal fut. 1 pers. sing. . . . . אסף

אָאֹר[f] Kal fut. 1 pers. sing. . . . . . ארר

אַאֲרִיךְ Hiph. fut. 1 pers. sing. . . . . . ארך

אָב 'וֲ masc. irreg. (§ 45).—I. *father*.—II. *forefather, ancestor*.—III. *author, inventor*.—IV. *father*, as an honorary appellation to priests and prophets in the character of teachers.—Hence, V. an *adviser*. Ge. 45. 8.

אַב Ch. masc. irreg. (§ 68), i. q. Heb. אָב *father*.

Proper names compounded with אֲבִי, אֲבוּ, אֱב, אַב:

אֲבוּגַיִל Khethib, 1 Sa. 25. 18, for the usual אֲבִיגַיִל q. v.

אֲבִי fem. mother of Hezekiah, also called אֲבִיָּה, compare 2 Ki. 18. 2 with 2 Ch. 29. 1.

אֲבִי־עַלְבוֹן (*father of strength*, i. e. *strong*, עלב collated with the Arab. *to be strong*) masc. one of David's heroes, called also אֲבִיאֵל, compare 2 Sa. 23. 31 with 1 Ch. 11. 32.

אֲבִיאֵל (*father of strength*, i.e. *strong*) masc.—I. grandfather of Saul, called also נֵר, compare 1 Sa. 9. 1 with 1 Ch. 9. 39.—II. one of David's heroes, compare the preceding.

אֲבִיאָסָף (*father of gathering*, i.e. *gatherer*) masc. a Korahite, called also אֶבְיָסָף, compare Ex. 6. 24 with 1 Ch. 6. 8.

אב

אֲבִיגַיִל (*father of exultation*, i. e. *exulting*, גִּיל i. q. גִּיל) fem.—I. wife of David; before of Nabal.—II. sister of David, called also אֲבִיגַל, compare 1 Ch. 2. 16 with 2 Sa. 17. 25.

אֲבִידָן (*father of the judge*, see דָּן) masc. chief of the tribe of Benjamin.

אֲבִידָע (*father of knowledge*, i. e. *knowing*, R. יָדַע) masc. a son of Midian.

אֲבִיָּהוּ, אֲבִיָּה (whose *father is the Lord*, see יָהּ) name of several persons, especially—I. of the second son of Samuel.—II. of a king of Judah, son of Rehoboam, called also אֲבִיָּם, compare 2 Ch. 13. 1 with 1 Ki. 14. 31.—III. of the wife of Hezron, 1 Ch. 2. 24.

אֲבִיהוּא (whose *father is He*, viz. God) masc. a son of Aaron.

אֲבִיהוּד (*father of glory*, הוּד i.q. הוֹד) m. 1 Ch. 8. 3.

אֲבִיהַיִל (perhaps for אֲבִיחַיִל) fem.—I. wife of Rehoboam.—II. wife of Abishur, 1 Ch. 2. 29.

אֲבִיחַיִל (*father of valour*, i. e. *valiant*) masc.—I. a Levite.—II. a Gadite.—III. father of Esther.

אֲבִיטוּב (*father of goodness*) masc. a Benjaminite, 1 Ch. 8. 11.

אֲבִיטַל (*father of dew*) fem. wife of David.

אֲבִימָאֵל (*father of fatness*, מאל Arab. *to be fat*) masc. a son of Joktan.

אֲבִימֶלֶךְ (*father of the king*) masc.—I. name of several Philistine kings.—II. son of Gideon.—III. 1 Ch. 18. 16, for אֲחִימֶלֶךְ 2 Sa. 8. 17.

אֲבִינָדָב (*noble father*, see נָדַב) masc. name of several men, especially—I. of a son of Jesse.—II. of a son of Saul.

---

[a] Is. 45. 5. [b] Job 33. 33. [c] Job 9. 16. [d] Job 16. 5. [e] Mi. 2. 12. [f] Ge. 12. 3.

אֲבִינֹעַם (*father of pleasantness*) m. father of Barak.

אֲבִינֵר (*father of light*) masc. Saul's commander-in-chief; elsewhere אַבְנֵר.

אֲבִיעֶזֶר (*father of help*) masc.—I. son of Gilead.—Patronymic אֲבִי הָעֶזְרִי. An abridged form is אִיעֶזֶר, Nu. 26. 30, and patronymic אִיעֶזְרִי.—II. one of David's heroes.

אֲבִירָם (*father of height*, רָם from רוּם) masc.—I. one of the conspirators against Moses, Nu. 16. 1.—II. son of Hiel restorer of Jericho, 1 Ki. 16. 34.

אֲבִישַׁג (*father of error*, R. שָׁגַג) fem. a concubine of David.

אֲבִישׁוּעַ (*father of prosperity*, R. יָשַׁע or שׁוּעַ) masc.—I. a Benjaminite, son of Bela.—II. a son of Phinehas, 1 Ch. 5. 30.

אֲבִישׁוּר (*father of song*, שׁוּר i. q. שִׁיר) a man of the posterity of Judah.

אֲבִישַׁי (*father of gift*, compare שַׁי) masc. a brother of Joab, also called אַבְשַׁי, 2 Sa. 10. 10; 1 Ch. 2. 16.

אֲבִישָׁלוֹם (*father of peace*) masc. father-in-law of Rehoboam, called also אַבְשָׁלוֹם, compare 1 Ki. 15. 2 with 2 Ch. 11. 20.

אֶבְיָתָר (*father of abundance*) masc. a son of Ahimelech the priest.

אַבְנֵר (*father of light*) masc. Saul's commander-in-chief, also called אֲבִינֵר q. v.

אַבְרָהָם (*father of a great multitude*, lit. *father great of* (i. e. as to) *multitude*, for אַב רַב הָם see הָם, R. הָמָה) masc. the Father and founder of the Hebrews, called אַבְרָם (*father of height*) before the covenant by circumcision, Ge. 17. 5.

אַבְשָׁלוֹם (*father of peace*) masc. third son of David, famous for his rebellion against his father.

[a] אֲבִי id. construct state . . . . . אב

וָאָבָא defect. for אָבִיא (q. v.) . . . . בוא

[rr] וָאָבֹא Kal fut. 1 pers. sing.; וָ for וַ conversive בוא

[b] אָבֹאָה id. with paragogic ה . . . . בוא

[c] וַאֲבִאֵם וָ defect. for אֲבִיאֵם (q. v.) . . . . בוא

אָבַב in the Heb. not used; Chald. Pa. אַבֵּב *to bear fruit.*

אֵב masc. dec. 8b, *greenness, verdure.* אִבֵּי הַנַּחַל *green herbs of the valley.* Ca. 6. 11.

אֵב Ch. *fruit*, with suff. אִנְבֵּהּ for אִבֵּהּ Dag. forte resolved in Nun, (compare § 52. rem. 2) Da. 4. 9.

אָבִיב masc. *green ears of corn.* חֹדֶשׁ הָאָבִיב *month of green ears*, viz. the month in which the earing of the barley took place, beginning with the new moon of April.

אֲבִגַיִל, אֲבִגַל } pr. name masc. defect. for אֲבִיגַיִל q. v. } אב

וַאֲבַגְתָא וָ pr. name of a Persian eunuch. Est. 1. 10.

אָבַד fut. יֹאבַד—I. *to stray, wander, be lost.*—II. *to perish*, const. with לְ and מִן of the person. Piel I. *to cause to stray, to disperse.*—II. *to cause to perish, to destroy.* Hiph. הֶאֱבִיד fut. once, אֹבִידָה (q. v.) causat. of Kal i. q. Piel.

אֲבַד Chald. *to perish.* Aph. *to destroy.* Hoph. *to be destroyed.*

אֹבֵד masc. *destruction, ruin.* Nu. 24. 20, 24.

אֲבֵדָה fem. dec. 10.—I. *something lost.*—II. i. q. אֲבַדּוֹן Pr. 27. 20. Khethib.

אֲבַדּוֹן masc.—I. *destruction.*—II. *place of destruction, abyss.*

אַבְדָן, אָבְדָן masc. *destruction, ruin.* Est. 8. 6; 9. 5.

אָבַד, וְאָבַד } Kal preter. 3 pers. sing. masc. (compare § 8. rem. 2) . . . } אבד

[d] אַבֵּד וְ Piel infin. construct used for the absolute אבד

אָבֹד Kal infin. absolute . . . . . אבד

[e] אֲבֹד id. infin. construct . . . . . אבד

[f] וְאִבַּד Piel pret. 3 pers. sing. masc. (§ 10. rem. 1) אבד

[g] אֹבַד construct of the following (§ 36. rem. 1) . אבד

אֹבֵד Kal part. act. sing. masc. dec. 7b. . . אבד

[h] אֹבֵד noun masc. sing. . . . . . אבד

אָבְדָה Kal preter. 3 pers. sing. fem. for אָבְדָה . אבד

[i] וַאֲבַדֹּה וָ Kh. אֲבַדָּה (q.v.), K. אֲבַדּוֹן (q.v.); וָ bef. (-:) אבד

אֲבֵדָה noun fem. sing. dec. 10. . . . אבד

וְאָבְדָה Kal preter. 3 pers. sing. fem. . . . אבד

[k] אָבְדוּ, וְאָבְדוּ } id. preter. 3 pers. pl. (§ 8. rem. 7) } אבד

[l] וַאֲבַדּוֹן וָ noun masc. sing.; וָ before (-:) . . אבד

[m] אֹבְדוֹת Kal part. act. fem., pl. of אֹבֶדֶת dec. 13a אבד

[n] וָאַבְדִּילָה וָ Hiph. fut. 1 pers. s. with parag. ה; וָ f. וַ conv. בדל

[o] וָאַבֶּדְךָ וָ contr. from [וָאֲאַבֶּדְךָ] Piel fut. 1 pers. sing. [וָאֲאַבֵּד] suff. 2 pers. sing. m.; וָ f. וַ conv. אבד

[p] אֲבָדְךָ Kal inf., suff. 2 pers. sing. m. (§ 16. rem. 7) אבד

[q] אֲבָדֶךָ id. id. in pause for [אֲבָדְךָ] . . . אבד

[r] אַבֶּדְכֶם id., suff. 2 pers. pl. masc. . . . אבד

[s] וָאַבְדִּל וָ for [וָאַבְדִּיל] Hiph. fut. 1 pers. s.; וָ f. וַ conv. בדל

[t] אָבְדָם Kal infin., suff. 3 pers. pl. masc. . . אבד

[u] אִבְּדָם Piel pret. 3 p. s. m. (אִבֵּד) suff. 3 pl. m. (§ 16. r. 15) אבד

[x] וְאָבְדָן וְ noun masc. sing. . . . . אבד

[y] אָבַדְנוּ, [z] אָבָדְנוּ } Kal preter. 1 pers. pl. (§ 8. rem. 7) } אבד

[a] Ge. 17. 5. [b] Ju. 15. 1. [c] Eze. 20. 28. [d] De. 12. 2. [e] De. 7. 20. [f] Je. 51. 55. [g] De. 32. 28. [h] Nu. 24. 20, 24. [i] Pr. 27. 20. [k] Je. 48. 36. [l] Pr. 15. 11. [m] Je. 50. 6. [n] Ezr. 8. 24. [o] Eze. 28. 16. [p] De. 28. 20. [q] De. 28. 22. [r] Jos. 23. 13. [rr] Ge. 24. 42. [s] Le. 20. 26. [t] Ob. 1. 12. [u] 2 Ki. 13. 7. [x] Est. 9. 5. [y] Nu. 17. 27. [z] Nu. 17. 27.

אֲבֶדֶת noun fem. sing., construct of אֲבֵדָה dec. 10 . אבד
אָבַדְתָּ[a] Kal preter. 2 pers. sing. masc. . . . אבד
אָבַדְתְּ[b] id. preter. 2 pers. sing. fem. . . . אבד
אִבַּדְתָּ[c] Piel preter. 2 pers. sing. masc. . . . אבד
אָבַדְתִּי[d] / אָבָדְתִּי } Kal preter. 1 pers. sing. (§ 8. rem. 7) . } אבד
אִבַּדְתִּי[e] Piel preter. 1 pers. sing. . . . אבד
אִבַּדְתִּי[f] וְ id.; acc. shifted to ult. by conv. וְ . . אבד
אֲבַדְתֶּם וַ Kal preter. 2 pers. pl. masc.; וַ for וְ conv. אבד
אִבַּדְתֶּם וְ Piel preter. 2 pers. pl. masc. . . . אבד

אָבָה fut. יֹאבֶה *to be willing, inclined, desirous.* Is followed by an infin. with or without pref. לְ.
אֵבֶה masc. *reed, bulrush,* אֳנִיּוֹת אֵבֶה *vessels of reed,* probably *the papyrus,* only Job 9. 26.
אָב masc. *desire,* Job 34. 36, according to the Targum.
אֲבוֹי *poverty, misery,* only Pr. 23. 29.
אֶבְיוֹן adj. dec. 1 b.—prop. *wishing, desiring,* hence —I. *poor, needy.*—II. *miserable, wretched.*
אֲבִיּוֹנָה fem. *desire,* only Ec. 12. 5.

אֵבֶה[g] noun masc. sing. . . . . אבה
אֶבָּהֵל[h] Niph. fut. 1 pers. sing. . . . . בהל
אֲבָהָתִי[i] Ch. n. m. pl., suff. 1 p. s. fr. [אַב] irr. (§ 68) אב
אֲבָהָתָךְ[k] Ch. id., suff. 2 pers. sing. masc. . . . אב
אֲבָהָתַנָא[l] Ch. id., suff. 1 pers. pl. . . . . אב
אָבוּ Kal pret. 3 pers. pl. . . . . אבה
אָבוֹא וָ׳, וְ׳ Kal fut. 1 pers. sing.; וָ for וַ conv. . בוא
אָבוּא[m] Kal pret. 3 pers. pl. for אָבוּ (§ 8. rem. 4) . אבה
אָבוֹאָה וְ Kal fut. 1 pers. sing. with paragogic ה . בוא
אֲבוֹנְיַל Kh. אֲבוּנִיַל, K. אֲבִינַיִל (q. v.) . . אב
אֲבוּהִי[n] Ch. n. m. s., suff. 3 p. s. m. fr. [אַב] irr. (§ 68) אב
אֲבוֹי noun masc. sing. (after the form קְטוֹל) . אבה
אֲבוּךְ Ch. n. m. s., suff. 2 p. s. m. from [אַב] irr. (§ 68) אב
אָבוּס[o] Kal part. pass. sing. masc. . . . אבס
אָבוּס[p] וְ Kal fut. 1 pers. sing. . . . . בוס
אֵבוּס noun masc. sing. dec. 3 b. . . . אבס
אֲבוּסִים Kal part. pass. masc., pl. of אָבוּס dec. 3 a. . אבס
אֲבוּסֶךָ[r] noun masc. sing., suff. 2 pers. sing. masc. for [׳סְךָ] from אֵבוּס dec. 3 b. . . אבס
אֲבוּסֶנּוּ[s] Kal fut. 1 pers. sing., suff. 3 pers. sing. masc. בוס
אֵבוֹשׁ Kal fut. 1 pers. sing. (§ 21. rem. 6) . . בוש
אֵבוֹשָׁה id. with paragogic ה . . . . בוש
אָבוֹת n. m. with pl. fem. term. from אָב irr. (§ 45) אב
אֲבוֹת וַ׳ id., construct state; וַ before (-:) . . אב
אֲבוֹתָי / אֲבוֹתַי[t] וַ׳ } id., suff. 1 pers. sing. ·וַ before (-:) . } אב

אֲבוֹתֵיהֶם[u] וַ׳ id., suff. 3 pers. pl. masc.; וַ id. . . אב
אֲבוֹתָיו id., suff. 3 pers. sing. masc. . . . אב
אֲבוֹתֶיךָ id., suff. 2 pers. sing. masc. . . . אב
אֲבוֹתֵיכֶם[pp] וַ׳ id., suff. 2 pers. pl. masc.; וַ before (-:) . אב
אֲבוֹתֵינוּ וַ׳ id., suff. 1 pers. pl.; וַ id. . . . אב
אֲבוֹתָם וַ׳ id., suff. 3 pers. pl. masc. (§ 4. rem. 2); וַ id. אב
אֶבְחָנְךָ[x] Kal fut. 1 pers. sing. [אֶבְחֹן], suff. 2 p. sing. m בחן
אֶבְחַר וָ׳ Kal fut. 1 pers. sing.; וָ for ·וַ conv. . בחר
אֶבְחֲרָה id. with paragogic ה . . . . בחר
אֶבְחָרֵהוּ id., suff. 3 pers. sing. masc. (§ 16. rem. 12) בחר

אָבַח Root not used, whence אִבְחָה fem. only Eze. 21. 20, אִבְחַת חָרֶב *threatening of the sword,* i. e. the threatening sword. Prof. Lee, *resting, remaining.*

אֶבְטָח / אֶבְטַח } Kal fut. 1 pers. sing. (§ 8. rem. 15) } בטח
אָבִי[y] n. m. s., suff. 1 pers. sing. from [אָב] dec. 2 a. אבה
אָבִי וְ׳ n. m. s., suff. 1 p. s. from אָב irr. (§ 45) אב
אָבִי Kh. for אָבִיא Hiph. fut. 1 pers. sing. (§ 25, 2 f.) בוא
אֲבִי[z] Ch. n. m. s., suff. 1 p. s. from [אַב] irr. (§ 68) אב
אֲבִי וַ׳ n. masc. sing., construct of אָב irr. (§ 45); also pr. name fem., and in compos. as, אֲבִי הָעֶזְרִי (see אֲבִיעֶזֶר), and אֲבִי עַלְבוֹן אב
אָבִיא וָ׳ Hiph. fut. 1 pers. sing.; וָ for ·וַ conv. . בוא
אָבִיאָה[a] וָ id. with paragogic ה (Kh. אָבִיאָה), Keri אָבִיא (q. v.) . . . . . בוא
אֲבִיאֲךָ[b] id., suff. 2 pers. sing. masc. . . . בוא
אֲבִיאֵל pr. name masc. . . . . . אב
אֲבִיאֵם[c] וַ׳ Hiph. fut. 1 s., suff. 3 p. pl. m.; וָ for ·וַ conv. בוא
אֲבִיאֶנָּה[d] id., suff. 3 pers. sing. fem. . . . בוא
אֲבִיאֶנּוּ id., suff. 3 pers. sing. masc. . . . בוא
אֲבִיאָסָף וַ pr. name masc.; וַ before (-:) . . אב
אָבִיב noun masc. sing. . . . . . אבב
אֲבִיגַיִל / אֲבִינָיִל } וַ׳ pr. name fem.; וַ before (-:) . . } אב
אֲבִיגַל id. by contraction . . . . . אב
אֹבִידָה[e] Hiph. fut. 1 pers. s. with paragogic ה (§ 19. r. 8) אבד
אֲבִידָן, וַאֲבִידָע pr. name masc. . . . . אב
אָבִיהָ[f] וְ׳ n. m. s., suff. 3 p. sing. f. from אָב irr. (§ 45) אב
אֲבִיָּה וַ׳ pr. name masc. or (1 Ch. 2. 24) fem. . אב
אָבִיהוּ n. m. s., suff. 3 p. sing. m. from אָב irr. (§ 45) אב
אֲבִיהוּ masc., וַאֲבִיהוּא & וַ׳ masc., וַאֲבִיהוּד masc., אֲבִיהַיִל fem., pr. names . . . אב
אֲבִיהֶם[g] וַ׳ noun masc. sing., suff. 3 pers. pl. masc. from אָב irreg. (§ 45); וַ before (-:) . אב
אֲבִיהֶן id., suff. 3 pers. pl. fem. . . . אב
אָבִיו וְ׳ id., suff. 3 pers. sing. masc. . . . אב

[a] Nu. 21. 29. [b] Eze. 26. 17. [c] Ps. 9. 6. [d] Es. 4. 16. [e] Je. 15. 7. [f] Eze. 6. 3. [g] Job 9. 26. [h] Job 23. 15. [i] Da. 2. 23. [k] Ezr. 4. 15. [l] Ezr. 5. 12. [m] Is. 28. 12. [n] Da. 5. 2. [o] Pr. 15. 17. [p] Is. 63. 6. [pp] Je. 44. 21. [q] 1 Ki. 5. 3. [r] Job 39. 9. [s] Is. 14. 25. [t] 2 Ch. 32. 13. [u] Je. 19. 4. [x] Ps. 81. 8. [y] Job 34. 36. [z] Da. 5. 13. [a] Jos. 24. 8. [b] Ca. 8. 2. [c] Zec. 10. 10. [d] Is. 46. 11. [e] Je. 46. 8. [f] Nu. 12. 14. [g] Ge. 42. 35.

אֶבְיוֹן וְ׳ adj. masc. sing. dec. 1b. . . . . אבה
אֶבְיוֹנֵי[a] וְ id. pl., construct state . . . . אבה
אֶבְיוֹנֶיהָ[b] id. pl., suff. 3 pers. sing. fem. . . . אבה
אֶבְיוֹנִים וְ׳ id. pl., absolute state . . . . אבה
אֲבִיחַיִל, אֲבִיהַיִל } pr. name masc., or (2 Ch. 11. 18) fem. . } אב
אַבִּיט[c] וְ׳ Hiph. fut. 1 pers. sing. . . . נבט
אַבִּיטָה וְ id. with paragogic ה . . . נבט
אֲבִיטוּב masc., אֲבִיטָל fem., pr. names . . . אב
אָבִיךָ[d] וְ n. m. s., suff. 2 p. s. m. from אָב irr. (§ 45) אב
אָבִיךְ id., suff. 2 pers. sing. fem. . . . אב
אֲבִיכֶם id., suff. 2 pers. pl. masc. . . . אב
אֲבִיכֶן וְ׳ id., suff. 2 pers. pl. fem.; וּ before (-:) אב
אֲבִיָּם pr. name masc., see אֲבִיָּהוּ . . . . אב
אֹבִים[e] Kal part. masc., pl. of [אֹבֶה] dec. 9a. . אבה
אֲבִימָאֵל, אֲבִימֶלֶךְ and וְ׳ pr. names masc. . . אב
אָבִין Kal fut. 1 pers. sing. . . . . . בין
אֲבִינָדָב וְ׳ pr. name masc.; וּ before (-:) . . אב
אָבִינָה[f] וְ׳, וָ׳, Kal fut. 1 p. s. with parag. ה; וָ for וַ conv. בין
אָבִינוּ n. m. s., suff. 1 pers. pl. from אָב irr. (§ 45) אב
אֶבְיֹנֵי[g] construct of the following . . . אבה
אֶבְיֹנִים adj. masc., pl. of אֶבְיוֹן dec. 1b. . . אבה
אֶבְיֹנְךָ[h] id. sing., suff. 2 pers. sing. masc. . . . אבה
אֲבִינֹעַם, אֲבִינֵר, אֶבְיָסָף (see אֲבִיאָסָף) pr. names masc. אב
אַבִּיעָה Hiph. fut. 1 pers. sing. with paragogic ה . נבע
אֲבִיעֶזֶר pr. name masc. . . . . . אב
אַבִּיר adj. masc. sing. dec. 1b. . . . . אבר
אֲבִיר noun masc. sing., constr. of [אָבִיר] dec. 3a. אבר
אַבִּירַי[i] adj. m. pl., suff. 1 pers. sing. from אַבִּיר dec. 1b. אבר
אַבִּירֵי id. pl., construct state . . . . אבר
אַבִּירָיו id. pl., suff. 3 pers. sing. masc. . . . אבר
אַבִּירֶיךָ[k] id. pl., suff. 2 pers. sing. masc. . . . אבר
אַבִּירִים id. pl., absolute state . . . . אבר
אֲבִירָם וְ׳ masc., אֲבִישַׁג & וַ׳ fem., אֲבִישׁוּעַ & וַ׳ masc., אֲבִישׁוּר & וַ׳ masc., אֲבִישַׁי & וַ׳ masc., אֲבִישָׁלוֹם masc., pr. names . . . אב
אָבִיתִי Kal pret. 1 pers. sing. . . . . אבה
אֲבִיתֶם id. pret. 2 pers. pl. masc. . . . . אבה
אֶבְיָתָר וְ׳ pr. name masc. . . . . . אב

אָבַךְ Hith. only Is. 9. 17, וַיִּתְאַבְּכוּ גֵּאוּת עָשָׁן *they shall roll* or *swell up* in the mounting up of smoke.

אֶבְכֶּה[l] וְ׳, וָ׳ Kal. fut. 1 pers. sing.; וָ for וַ conv. . בכה

אָבַל[m] וְ׳ fut. יֶאֱבַל *to mourn*; with עַל of the pers. mourned over. Hiph. *to cause to mourn*. Hithp. i. q. Kal.

אָבֵל adj. dec. 5c (§ 34, 2 & r. 2), *mourning*. אָבֵל מִצְרַיִם (*mourning of* Egypt) pr. name of a place near Jordan, Ge. 50. 11.

אֵבֶל m. dec. 6b. (§ 35. r. 6) *mourning*, *lamentation*.

אָבֵל Root not used. Arab. *to be moist*, sc. with the moisture of grass; hence Syr. יַבָל grass.

אָבֵל *grassy place, meadow*, 1 Sa. 6. 18, where the Sept. and Syr. express אֶבֶן, comp. *vv.* 14, 15. Hence the following pr. names.—I. אָבֵל בֵּית־מַעֲכָה Abel near Beth Maacha, a city in the north of Palestine, eastward of Jordan, not far from Antilibanus, in the tribe of Manasseh, called also אָבֵל־מַיִם, comp. 1 Ki. 15. 20 with 2 Ch. 16. 4, and perhaps simply אָבֵל 1 Sa. 6. 18, see above.—II. אָבֵל הַשִּׁטִּים (*Acacia-meadow*) a place in the land of Moab, Nu. 33. 49.—III. אָבֵל כְּרָמִים (*meadow of vineyards*) a village of the Ammonites on the other side of Jordan, Ju. 11. 33.—IV. אָבֵל מְחוֹלָה (*meadow of dancing*) a village in the land of Issachar, the birth-place of the prophet Elisha.

אוֹבִיל (*chief of the camels*, coll. with the Arab.) pr. name of an Ishmaelite who had the charge of David's camels, 1 Ch. 27. 30.

אֲבָל adv. . . . . בלה
אָבֵל adj. masc. sing. dec. 5c. (§ 34. 2, & rem. 2), also pr. name in composition as אָ׳ הַשִּׁטִּים, אָ׳ בֵּית מַעֲכָה, &c. . . . . . . אבל
אֵבֶל[n] וְ׳ noun masc. sing. dec. 6. (§ 35. rem. 6) . אבל
אָבֵלָה pr. name of a place (אָבֵל) with local ה . אבל
אָבְלָה Kal pret. 3 sing. fem. . . . . אבל
אָבְלוּ[o] וְ׳ id. pret. 3 pers. pl. . . . . אבל
אֲבֵלוֹת[p] adj. pl. fem. from אָבֵל masc. . . . אבל
אַבְלִיגָה וְ Hiph. fut. 1 sing. with paragogic ה . בלג
אֲבֵלִים adj. m., pl. of אָבֵל dec. 5c. (§ 34, 2 & r. 2) אבל
אֶבְלֵךְ[q] n. m. s., suff. 2 p. s. from אֵבֶל dec. 6. (§ 35. r. 6) אבל
אֶבְלָם[r] id., suff. 3 pers. pl. masc. . . . אבל
אֲבַלַּע, אֲבַלֵּעַ[s] } Piel fut. 1 pers. sing. (§ 15. rem. 1) } בלע

אֶבֶן com. (mostly fem.) with suff. אַבְנוֹ dec. 6a.—I. *a stone*, generally; אֶבֶן הַשָּׂדֶה *the common stone of the field*; אֶבֶן יָד *a stone which may be thrown with the hand*; אֶבֶן בָּרָד *hail-stones*; אַבְנֵי אֵשׁ *shining-stones*; לֵב הָאֶבֶן *obdurate heart*.—II. *precious stone, gem*, also fully, אֶבֶן יְקָרָה.—III. *rock*, Ge. 49. 24.—IV. *weight*; אֶבֶן וָאֶבֶן *divers*

[a] Is. 29. 19. [b] Ps. 132. 15 [c] Is. 63. 5. [d] 2 Sa. 17. 8. [e] Eze. 3. 7. [f] Job 23. 5. [g] Ex. 23. 11. [h] Ex. 23. 6. [i] La. 1. 15. [k] Je. 46. 15. [l] Is. 16. 9. [m] Am. 8. 8. [n] Mi. 1. 8. [o] Joel 1. 9. [p] La. 1. 4. [q] Is. 60. 20. [r] Je. 31. 13. [s] 2 Sa. 20. 20. [t] Is. 19. 3.

weights; אַבְנֵי כִיס *weights of* (i. e. carried in) *the bag.*—V. *plummet,* Is. 34. 11. אַבְנֵי תֹהוּ *stones of desolations;* i. e. minutely measured off for desolation.—VI. pr. names; *a.* אֶבֶן הָאֶזֶל (*stone of departure*), a stone not far from Jerusalem, 1 Sa. 20. 19. *b.* אֶבֶן הַזֹּחֶלֶת (*smooth stone,* coll. with Chald. and Arab.) a stone near Jerusalem, 1 Ki. 1. 9. *c.* אֶבֶן עֵזֶר (*stone of help*), a stone set up by Samuel.

אֶבֶן Chald. emph. אַבְנָא dec. 3 a—*a stone.*

אֲבָנָה 2 Ki. 5. 12. Kheth. in Keri אֲמָנָה q. v.

אֹבֶן masc. only in dual. אָבְנַיִם.—I. *potter's wheel,* Je. 18. 3.—II. Ex. 1. 16. where it is doubtful what it refers to; according to Kimchi, *the seat* or *stool* of a woman in labour.

אֶבֶן וְ׳ } noun com. (suff. אַבְנוֹ) dec. 6 a. Chald. 3 a; for וְ see letter ו. . . אבן
אָבֶן וָ׳,וְ׳ }

אַבְנָא וְ Chald. n. m. s. emph. of אֶבֶן dec. 3 a. (§ 59) אבן

אֲבָנָה Kh., אֲמָנָה K. (q. v.) . . . . אמן

אֶבְנֶה [a] וְ׳, וָ׳ Kal fut. 1 pers. sing.; וָ for ·וַ conv. . בנה

אִבָּנֶה [b] [c] וְ Niph. fut. 1 pers. sing. (§ 10. rem. 5) . בנה

אַבְנוֹ [d] noun com. sing., suff. 3 pers. sing. masc. from אֶבֶן dec. 6 a . . . . אבן

אַבְנֵט וְ׳ noun, masc. sing. dec. 1 b. (§ 36. No. 1) . בנט

אַבְנֵטְךָ [e] וְ id., suff. 2 pers. sing. masc. . . בנט

אַבְנֵטִים [f] id. pl., absolute state . . . . בנט

אַבְנֵי וְ׳ noun com. pl. construct from אֶבֶן dec. 6 a. אבן

אֲבָנֶיהָ id. pl., suff. 3 pers. sing. fem. . . אבן

אַבְנֵיהֶם [g] id. pl., suff. 3 pers. pl. masc. . . . אבן

אֲבָנָיו id. pl., suff. 3 pers. sing. masc. . . אבן

אֲבָנַיִךְ [h] [i] וְ׳,וַ id. pl., suff. 2 pers. sing. fem.; וַ before (-:) אבן

אֲבָנִים [k] וְ׳,וַ id. pl., absolute state; וַ id. . . אבן

אֶבְנֵךְ [l] Kal fut. 1 pers. sing. (אֶבְנֶה), suff., 2 pers. sing. fem. (§ 24. rem. 21) . . . בנה

אֶבְנֶנָּה [m] וְ id., suff. 3 pers. sing. fem. (§ 2. rem. 3) . בנה

אַבְנֵר וְ pr. name masc. . . . . . אב

[אָבַס] *to feed,* or *fatten* cattle.

אֵבוּס (by Syriasm for אֱבוּס) masc. pl. אֲבוּסִים, *a crib* or *stall* in which animals are fed.

מַאֲבוּס masc. dec. 1 b, *barn, granary,* Je. 50. 26.

אֶבְעֵא [n] Chald. Peal fut. 1 pers. sing. R. בְּעָא see בעה

אֲבַעְבֻּעֹת [o] n. f., pl. of [אֲבַעְבֻּעָה] from [בַּעְבּוּעַ] & א prosth. בוע

אֶבֶץ וְ for אֶבֶץ (perhaps *tin,* i. q. Chald. אַבְצָא) pr. n. of a city in the tribe of Issachar, Jos. 19. 20.

אִבְצָן (*labour,* i. q. Chald. אוּבְצָן) pr. n. of a judge of Israel, Ju. 12. 8, 10.

אָבָק [p] masc. dec. 4 c.—*fine dust,* different to עָפָר thick and heavy dust. Niph. denom. *to wrestle,* prop. *to dust each other* by wrestling, Ge. 32. 25, 26.

אֲבָקָה fem. only in the construct אַבְקַת (§ 42. rem. 1), *powder,* aromatic powder, Ca. 3. 6.

אֲבַק [q] id. construct state . . . . אבק

אֲבָקָם [r] id., suff. 3 pl. masc. . . . . . אבק

אֲבַקֵּר [s] Piel fut. 1 pers. sing. . . . . בקר

אֲבַקֵּשׁ [t] וְ׳,וָ Piel fut. 1 pers. sing.; וָ for ·וַ conv. . בקש

אֲבַקֶּשׁ־ [u] id. with Mak. (§ 10. rem. 4) . . . בקש

אֲבַקְשָׁה [x] וְ׳,וָ id. with parag. ה (§ 10. r. 7), וָ for ·וַ conv. בקש

אֲבַקְשֵׁהוּ [y] וָ id. with suff. 3 pers. sing. masc.; וָ id. . בקש

אֲבַקְשֶׁנּוּ [z] id., suff. 3 pers. sing. masc. . . בקש

אַבְקַת [a] noun fem. sing., constr. of [אֲבָקָה] dec. 11 c. (§ 42. rem. 1) . . . . . אבק

אָבַר Kal, not used, in the deriv. *to be strong.* Hiph. *to fly, soar,* Job 39. 26.

אָבִיר m. dec. 3 a—*the mighty one,* spoken of God.

אַבִּיר adj. dec. 1 b.—I. *strong, mighty, brave;* אַבִּירֵי לֵב *stout-hearted;* אַבִּירֵי בָשָׁן *strong ones* (i.e. bulls) *of Bashan.*—II. nobles, princes; אַבִּיר הָרֹעִים *chief of the shepherds.*

אֵבֶר masc. *wing-feather, pinion.*

אֶבְרָה fem. with suff. אֶבְרָתוֹ (no pl. absolute) id.

אֵבֶר noun masc. sing. . . . . . . אבר

אֶבְרָה [b] noun fem. sing. (no pl. absolute) . . אבר

אֶבְרֶה [c] וָ Kal fut. 1 pers. sing.; וָ for ·וַ conv. . ברה

אַבְרָהָם וְ׳ pr. name masc. . . . . . אב

אֶבְרוֹתֶיהָ [d] וְ n. f. pl., suff. 3 pers. s. f. from אֶבְרָה (q. v.) אבר

אֶבְרַח [e] Kal fut. 1 pers. sing. for [אֶבְרַח] . . ברח

אַבְרִיחֵהוּ [f] וָ Hiph. fut. 1 pers. sing. suff. 3 pers. sing. masc.; וָ for ·וַ conv. . . . . ברח

אֲבָרֵךְ [g] וְ׳,וָ Piel fut. 1 pers. sing.; וָ for ·וַ conv. . ברך

אַבְרֵךְ [h] noun masc. formed like אַבְנֵט; or a Syriasm for הַבְרֵךְ Hiph. inf. . . . . ברך

אֲבָרְכָה [i] וְ׳ Piel fut. 1 pers. s. with parag. ה; וַ bef. (-:) ברך

אֲבָרְכֵהוּ [k] } וָ id. with suff. 3 pers. sing. masc.; וָ for ·וַ conversive; וַ before (-:) . . ברך
אֲבָרְכֵהוּ [l] } וַ

אֲבָרֶכְךָ [m] [n] } וְ׳,וָ id., suff. 2 pers. sing. masc. (§ 16. rem. 15 & 13. § 2. rem. 3); וַ before (-:) ברך
אֲבָרֶכְךָ [o] } וְ׳,וַ

אֲבָרֶכְכָה [p] וְ׳ id. id. (§ 2. rem. 2); וַ id. . . ברך

אֲבָרְכֵם [q] [r] וְ׳,וַ id., suff. 3 pers. pl. masc.; וַ id. . . ברך

אַבְרָם וְ׳ pr. n. masc. see אַבְרָהָם . . . . אב

אֶבְרָתוֹ n. f. s., suff. 3 p. s. m. fr. אֶבְרָה (no pl. abs.) אבר

אֲבִשַׁי [s] defect for אֲבוּשַׁי (q. v.) . . . . בוש

[a] 1 Ch. 21. 22. [b] Ge. 16. 2. [c] Ge. 30. 3. [d] 2 Ki. 3. 25. [e] Is. 22. 21. [f] Ex. 28. 40. [g] Ne. 3. 35. [h] Is. 54. 11. [i] Eze. 26. 12. [k] 1 Ch. 22. 14. [l] Je. 31. 4. [m] Ne. 2. 5. [n] Da. 7. 16. [o] Ex. 9. 9, 10. [p] De. 28. 24. [q] Na. 1. 3. [r] Eze. 26. 10. [s] Eze. 34. 12. [t] Eze. 22. 30. [u] Ru. 3. 1. [x] Da. 8. 15. [y] Ps. 37. 36. [z] Pr. 23. 35. [a] Ca. 3. 6. [b] Job 39. 13. [c] 2 Sa. 13. 6, 10. [d] Ps. 68. 14. [e] Ps. 139. 7. [f] Ne. 13. 28. [g] Ge. 24. 48. [h] Ge. 41. 43. [i] Ps. 34. 2. [k] Ge. 27. 33. [l] Is. 51. 2. [m] Ps. 145. 2. [n] Ge. 26. 3. [o] Ge. 12. 2. [p] Ge. 27. 7. [q] Nu. 6. 27. [r] Ge. 48. 9. [s] De. 32. 11. [t] Je. 17. 18.

אַבְשַׁי — וְ׳ (see אֲבִישַׁי, אַבְשָׁלוֹם, וְ׳ אַבְשָׁלֹם) pr.n.m. — אב
אֲבַשְּׂרָה[a] — וָ Piel fut. 1 p.s. with parag. ה; וַ before (-:) for וְ — בשׂר
אָבֹת — for אָבוֹת noun masc. with pl. fem. term. from אָב irreg. (§ 45) — אב
אֲבֹתַי / אֲבֹתָי — id., suff. 1 pers. sing. — אב
אֲבֹתֵיהֶם[b] — וְ׳ id., suff. 3 pers. pl. masc.; וַ bef. (-:) — אב
אֲבֹתָיו — id., suff. 3 pers. sing. masc. — אב
אֲבֹתֶיךָ — וָ id., suff. 2 pers. sing. masc.; וַ before (-:) — אב
אֲבֹתֵיכֶם — וְ׳ id., suff. 2 pers. pl. masc.; וַ id. — אב
אֲבֹתֵינוּ — וְ׳ id., suff. 1 pers. pl.; וַ id. — אב
אֲבֹתָם — id., suff. 3 pers. pl. masc. (§ 4. rem. 2) — אב
אָגֵא — (*fugitive* coll. with the Arab.) pr. name masc. 2 Sam. 23. 11.
אֶגְאָל[c] — Kal fut. 1 pers. sing. for [אֶגְאַל] — גאל
אֶגְאָלֵם[d] — id., suff. 3 pers. pl. masc. (§ 16. rem. 12) — גאל
אֶגְאָלְתִּי[e] — in pause for [אֶגְאַלְתִּי] Chaldaism for [הִגְאַלְתִּי] Hiph. pret. 1 pers. sing. — גאל
אֲגַג / אָגָג — pr. name of Amalekitish kings. אגג Arab. *to burn.*
אֲגָגִי — gent. name of Haman.

אגד Heb. not used. Chald. *to bind together.*
אֲגֻדָּה fem. dec. 10.—I. *bands, knots,* Is. 58. 6.—II. *bundle, bunch,* Ex. 12. 22.—III. *band of men, troop,* 2 Sam. 2. 25.—IV. *vault* of heaven, Am. 9. 6.

אַגִּד[f] — וָ defect. for אַגִּיד (q. v.) — נגד
אֲגֻדּוֹת[g] — noun fem., pl. of אֲגֻדָּה dec. 10 — אגד
אַגְדִּיל[h] — Hiph. fut. 1 pers. sing. — גדל
אֶגְדַּל[i] — Kal fut. 1 pers. sing. — גדל
אֲגַדְּלָה[k] — וָ Piel fut. 1 pers. sing. with parag. ה; וַ bef. (-:) — גדל
אֲגַדְּלֶנּוּ[l] — וָ id., suff. 3 pers. sing. masc.; וַ id. — גדל
אֲגַדֵּעַ — Piel fut. 1 pers. s. for [אֲגַדַּע] (§ 15. rem. 1) — גדע
אֶגְדַּע[m] — וָ Kal fut. 1 pers. sing.; וָ for וַ· conversive — גדע
אֲגֻדַּת[n] — noun fem. sing., construct of אֲגֻדָּה dec. 10 — אגד
אֲגֻדָּתוֹ[o] — וָ id. with suff. 3 pers. sing. masc.; וַ before (-:) — אגד
אֱגוֹז — *a nut,* Cant. 6. 11. Arab. جوز, Syr. גּוֹזָא.
אֶגְוָע / אֶגְוַע[p] — וְ׳ Kal fut. 1 pers. sing. — גוע
אֶגֹּף[q] — Kal fut. 1 pers. sing. — נגף
אָגוּר[r] — Kal fut. 1 pers. sing. — גור
אָגוּר — pr. name masc. — אגר
אָגוּרָה[s] — Kal fut. 1 pers. sing. with parag. ה — גור
אַגִּיד — וְ׳ Hiph. fut. 1 pers. sing.; וָ for וַ· conv. — נגד
אַגִּידָה — וְ׳ id. with paragogic ה — נגד
אַגִּידֶנּוּ[t] — id. with suff. 3 pers. sing. masc. (§ 2. rem. 3) — נגד
אָגִילָה — Kal fut. 1 pers. sing. with parag. ה — גיל

אגל Heb. not used. Arab. *to flow together, be collected.*
אֵגֶל masc. only in pl. constr. אֶגְלֵי טָל *reservoirs,* or *drops of dew,* Job 38. 28.
אֶגְלַיִם (*two ponds*) pr. name of a village in the territory of Moab, Is. 15. 8.

אֲגַלֶּה — Piel fut. 1 pers. sing. — גלה
אֶגְלֶה[u] — Kal fut. 1 pers. sing. — גלה
אֶגְלֵי[x] — n. masc. pl. constr. fr. [אֵגֶל] dec. 6 (§ 35. r. 6) — אגל
אֶגְלַיִם — pr. name of a place — אגל

אגם Heb. not used. Arab. *to be hot, to be warm, stagnant,* of water; Chald. (אֲגַם) *to be pained, grieved.*
אֲגַם masc. with dist. acc. אֲגַם Is. 35. 7, pl. constr. אַגְמֵי dec. 6. (§ 35. rem. 10.), abs. אֲגַמִּים dec. 8b.—I. *pool, marsh.*—II. *marshy, reedy place,* Jer. 51. 32.
אָגֵם adj. dec. 5c. only pl. constr. אַגְמֵי, Is. 19. 10.
אַגְמוֹן masc.—I. *caldron,* Job 41. 13.—II. *reed, bulrush.*—III. *rope of rushes,* Is. 40. 25.

אֲגַם[y] — n. masc. sing. dec. 6. (§ 35. r. 10) but pl. אֲגַמִּים — אגם
אַגְמוֹן — וְ noun masc. sing. — אגם
אַגְמֵי — וְ׳[z] noun masc. pl. const. of אֲגַם (q.v.) — אגם
אַגְמֵי[a] — adj. masc. pl. construct from [אָגֵם] dec. 5c. — אגם
אַגְמֵיהֶם[b] — n. masc. pl., suff. 3 pers. pl. masc. fr. אֲגַם (q.v.) — אגם
אֲגַמִּים — וַ id. pl. absolute dec. 8a; וַ before (-:) — אגם
אַגְמֹן[c] — וְ׳[d] noun masc. sing. — אגם

אגן Root not used, whence אַגָּן masc. dec. 2b. *bason, bowl.*

אַגַּן[e] — noun masc. sing. construct of [אַגָּן] dec. 1b. (comp. § 30. Nos. 3. 4. & rem. 1) — אגן
אֶגֹּף[f] — וָ Kal fut. 1 sing. וָ for וַ· conversive — נגף
אֲגַפֶּיהָ[g] — n. m. pl., suff. 3 pers. s. fem. fr. [אֲגַף] dec. 8a. — גפף
אֲגַפָּיו — id., suff. 3 pers. sing. fem. — גפף
אֲגַפֶּיךָ — id., suff. 2 pers. sing. masc. — גפף

[אָגַר] *to gather, collect.*
אָגוּר (*collected*) pr. name of a wise man, the son of Jakeh, Prov. 30. 1.
אֲגוֹרָה f. only constr. אֲגוֹרַת, *a small coin,* 1 Sa. 2. 36.
אִגֶּרֶת fem. dec. 13a.—*letter, epistle, edict.*
אִגְּרָא fem. dec. 9.—*epistle.*

אֹגֵר[h] — Kal part. act. sing. masc. — אגר
אִגְּרָא[i] — Chald. noun fem. sing. dec. 9. — אגר
אָגְרָה[k] — Kal preter. 3 pers. sing. fem. — אגר
אִגְּרוֹת — noun fem., pl. of אִגֶּרֶת dec. 13a. — אגר
אֲגַרְטְלֵי[l] — noun masc. pl. construct from אֲגַרְטָל *bason, charger.* Its etymology is not defined.
אֶגְרַע[m] — וָ׳[n] Kal fut. 1 pers. sing.; וָ for וַ· conv. — גרע

[a] 2 Sa. 18. 19. [b] 1 Ch. 9. 19. [c] Ru. 4. 4. [d] Ho. 13. 14. [e] Is. 63. 3. [f] Je. 42. 21, etc. [g] Is. 58. 6. [h] Eze. 24. 9. [i] Ge. 41. 40. [k] Ge. 12. 2. [l] Ps. 69. 31. [m] Zec. 11. 10, 14. [n] Ex. 12. 22. [o] Am. 9. 6. [p] Job 10. 18. [q] Ps. 89. 4. [r] De. 32. 27. [s] Ps. 61. 5. [t] Job 31. 37. [u] Ru. 4. 4. [x] Job 38. 28. [y] Ps. 114. 8. [z] Is. 14. 23. [a] Is. 19. 10. [b] Ex. 7. 19. [c] Job 40. 26. [d] Job 41. 12. [e] Ca. 7. 3. [f] Jos. 24. 5. [g] Eze. 38. 6. [h] Pr. 10. 5. [i] Ezr. 4. 8. [k] Pr. 6. 8. [l] Ezr. 1. 9. [m] Eze. 5. 11. [n] Eze. 16. 27.

[a]אֲגָרֵשׁ [b]וְ׳ Piel fut. 1 pers. sing.; וָ id. . . . גרש
[c]אֲגָרְשֵׁם id., suff. 3 pers. pl. masc. . . . . גרש
[d]אֲגָרְשֶׁנּוּ [e]וְ׳ id., suff. 3 pers. sing. masc.; וָ before (‑:) גרש
[ee]אִגֶּרֶת וְ׳ noun fem. sing. dec. 13 a. . . . אגר
אִגַּרְתָּא Chald. noun fem. sing., emph. of אִגְּרָא dec. 9. אגר
[f]אִגְּרֹתֵיהֶם n. fem. pl., suff. 3 pers. pl. m. fr. אִגֶּרֶת dec. 13 a. אגר
[g]אֵד וְ noun masc. sing. dec. 1 a. . . . . אוד

אָדַב Kal not used, Hiph. *to languish, faint,* 1 Sa. 2. 33.
[h]אֶדְאָג Kal fut. 1 pers. sing. . . . . . דאג
אַדְבְּאֵל וְ (*miracle of God*, coll. with the Arab.; or *finger of God*, Chald. אַדְבְּעָא *finger*) pr. name of a son of Ishmael, Gen. 25. 13.
[i]אַדְבִּיק Hiph. fut. 1 pers. sing. . . . . דבק
אֲדַבֵּר / אֲדַבֶּר־ [k]וְ׳, וָ׳ Piel fut. 1 pers. sing. (§ 10. rem. 4); וֵ for וְ cop., וָ for ‑וַ conversive . } דבר
אֲדַבְּרָה / אֲדַבֵּרָה [l]וָ׳, וְ׳ id. with paragogic ה; וְ, וָ id. . } דבר

אָדַד Heb. not used, i. q. הדד Arab. *to befall* any one, as a misfortune.

אֲדַד pr. name of an Edomite, 1 Ki. 11. 17; called also הֲדַד ver. 14.

אִדּוֹ pr. name masc. Ez. 8. 17.

אַדָּן pr. n. masc. Ez. 2. 59; called אַדּוֹן, Neh. 7. 61.

אֲדַד pr. name masc. . . . . . אדד
[cc]אֶדַּדֶּה Hithp. fut. 1 pers. sing. contr. for [אֶתְדַּדֶּה] דדה
[ff]אֶדַּדֵּם id. with suff. 3 pers. masc. pl. . . . דדה
אִדּוֹ pr. name masc. . . . . . . אדד
אֱדוֹם וְ׳ pr. name of a man or nation; וֶ before (‑:) אדם
[m]אֱדוֹם וְ written *fully* for אָדֹם (q. v.) . . . אדם
אֲדוֹמִים gent. noun masc., pl. of אֲדוֹמִי from אֱדוֹם אדם
אָדוֹן noun masc. sing. dec. 3 a. . . . . דון
אַדּוֹן pr. name masc. . . . . . . אדד
אֲדוֹן noun masc. sing., construct of אָדוֹן dec. 3 a. דון
[n]אֲדוֹנָי id. pl. spoken only of God, elsewhere אֲדֹנָי (q. v.) דון
[o]אֲדוֹנֶיהָ id. pl. with suff. 3 pers. sing. fem. . . . דון
אֲדוֹנִיָּה pr. name masc. . . . . . דון
[p]אֲדוֹנֵיהֶם n. m. pl., suff. 3 pers. pl. m. fr. אָדוֹן dec. 3 a. דון
[q]אֲדוֹנִים id. pl. absolute state . . . . . דון
אֲדוֹרַיִם pr. name of a place . . . . אדר
[qq]אָדוֹשׁ Kal inf. absolute . . . . . אדש
אֲדוֹת defect. for אודות noun fem. pl. . . . אוד
[r]אֲדוֹתַי id. with suff. 1 pers. pl. . . . . אוד
[s]אֲדוֹתֶיךָ id. with suff. 2 pers. s. masc. . . . אוד
אַדִּיחֵם Hiph. fut. 1 pers. sing., suff. 3 pers. pl. masc. נדח
[t]אֱדַיִן וֶ׳ Chald. adv. *then, at that time;* בֵּאדַיִן id.; מִן אֱדַיִן *since that time.*

אַדִּיר adj. masc. sing. dec. 1 b. . . . . אדר
[u]אַדִּירוֹ id., suff. 3 pers. sing. masc. . . . אדר
[x]אַדִּירֵי וְ׳ id. pl., construct state . . . . אדר
[y]אַדִּירֵיהֶם וְ׳ id. pl., suff. 3 pers. pl. masc. . . . אדר
[z]אַדִּירָיו id. pl., suff. 3 pers. sing. masc. . . . אדר
[a]אַדִּירַיִךְ id. pl., suff. 2 pers. sing. masc. . . . אדר
אַדִּירִים / [hh]אַדִּירִם } id. pl., absolute state . . . } אדר
אֲדַלֶּג־ with Mak. for [אֲדַלֵּג] Piel. fut. 1 pers. sing. דלג
אֲדַלְיָא pr. n. of a son of Haman, Est. 9. 8. As a Pers. name Gesenius conjectures, *heart* or *eagle.*

[אָדַם] *to be red, ruddy.*—Pu. part. *made,* or *dyed red.*—Hiph. *to be red,* Is. 1. 18.—Hithp. *to be red, sparkling,* Prov. 23. 31.

אָדָם masc. (has no pl. number)—I. *a man,* human being irrespective of sex; more frequently collect. *men,* for which also is used בְּנֵי אָדָם *sons of man;* בֶּן אָדָם *son of man,* i. e. weak and mortal man; פֶּרֶא אָדָם *wild ass of a man,* i. e. a wild man, Ge. 16. 12; in the construct (without change of vowels) אָדָם בְּלִיַּעַל *a man of worthlessness,* Prov. 6. 12.—II. *a man,* not a woman, i. q. אִישׁ, Eccl. 7. 28.—III. pr. name—(*a.*) of the first man, 1 Ch. 1. 1.—(*b.*) of a city near Jordan.

אָדֹם, אָדוֹם adj. pl. אֲדֻמִּים dec. 8 c. (§ 37. Nos. 2 & 3) fem. אֲדֻמָּה *red, ruddy,* or *a reddish brown,* comp. § 26. No. 23.

אֱדֹם, אֱדוֹם pr. name.—I. of the elder son of Isaac, Ge. 25. 30, usually called עֵשָׂו.—II. *Edomite,* collect. *Edomites;* fully בְּנֵי אֱדֹם, בַּת אֱדֹם; also as the name of the country *Idumea.* Gent. n. אֲדֹמִי *Edomite,* fem. אֲדֹמִית *Edomitish woman,* pl. אֲדֹמִיּוֹת comp. § 39. No. 4. rem. 1, note.

אֹדֶם masc. *a ruby,* or *cornelian.* Sept. Vulg. *Sardius.*

אֲדַמְדָּם, fem. אֲדַמְדֶּמֶת, pl. אֲדַמְדַּמּוֹת (§ 39. No. 4. rem. 1), adj. *reddish,* comp. § 26. No. 23.

אֲדָמָה fem. dec. 11 c. (§ 42. rem. 1).—I. *ground, soil, land.*—II. *land, region, country.*—III. pr. name of a city in the tribe of Naphtali, Jos. 19. 36.

אַדְמָה pr. name of a city destroyed with Sodom and Gomorrah.

אֲדָמִי (*human*) pr. name of a city in the tribe of Naphtali, Jos. 19. 33.

אַדְמֹנִי, אַדְמוֹנִי adj. *red-haired.*

אַדְמָתָא pr. n. of a Persian nobleman, Est. 1. 14.

[a] Ju. 2. 3. [b] Ju. 6. 9. [c] Ho. 9. 15. [cc] Is. 38. 15. [d] Ex. 23. 29, 30. [e] Nu. 22. 6. [ee] Es. 9. 29. [ff] Ps. 42. 5. [f] Ne. 6. 17. [g] Ge. 2. 6. [h] Ps. 38. 19. [hh] Zec. 11. 2. [i] Eze. 3. 26. [k] Eze. 2. 1. [l] Da. 10. 16. [m] Ca. 5. 10. [n] Ju. 13. 18. [o] Ju. 19. 26. [p] Ps. 123. 2. [q] Mal. 1. 6. [qq] Is. 28. 28. [r] Jos. 14. 6. [s] Jos. 14. 6. [t] Ezr. 5. 5. [u] Je. 30. 21. [x] Ps. 16. 3. [y] Ne. 10. 30. [z] Na. 2. 6. [a] Na. 3. 18.

דָּם (for אָדָם) m. dec. 2 a.—I. *blood;* אָכַל עַל־הַדָּם *to eat* (flesh) *with the blood;* דָּם נָקִי *innocent blood;* but דַּם נָקִי *blood of the innocent.*—II. *blood-shed, blood-guiltiness;* אֵין לוֹ דָם *he is not guilty of blood;* in the plural, אִישׁ, עִיר דָּמִים *bloody man, city;* דָּמָיו בּוֹ *his blood is upon him,* is guilty of his own blood.—III. *blood of grapes, wine.*

אָדָם וְ׳ noun masc. sing., also pr. name . . אדם
אָדֹם adj. m. s., pl. אֲדֻמִּים dec. 8 c. (§ 37. Nos. 2 & 3) אדם
[a] אֶדֹּם וָ Kal fut. 1 pers. s. (§ 18. r. 14); וָ for וַ conv. דמם
אֱדֹם see עֹבֵד אֱדֹם . . . . . עבד
אֹדֶם noun masc. sing. . . . . . אדם
[b] אֲדַמְדָּם adj. masc. sing. (§ 39. 4. rem. 1) . . אדם
[c] אֲדַמְדָּמֶת in pause for אֲדַמְדֶּמֶת (q. v.) . . . אדם
[d] אֲדַמְדַּמֹּת pl. of the following . . . . . אדם
[e] אֲדַמְדֶּמֶת adj. fem. sing. from אֲדַמְדָּם m. (§ 39. 4. rem. 1) אדם
אֲדָמָה וְ׳ noun fem. sing. dec. 11 c. (§ 42. rem. 1), also pr. name; וַ before (־ֲ) . . . . אדם
אֲדַמֶּה Piel fut. 1 pers. sing. . . . . דמה
אַדָמָה וְ׳ pr. name of a place . . . . אדם
[bb] אֲדֻמָּה adj. fem. s. from אָדֹם m. (§ 39. No. 3. parad.) אדם
[f] אֶדַּמֶּה contr. for [אֶתְדַּמֶּה], Hithp. fut. 1 pers. sing. דמה
[g] אָדְמוּ Kal pret. 3 pers. pl. . . . . . אדם
אַדְמוֹנִי adj. masc. sing. . . . . . . אדם
[h] אֲדָמוֹת noun fem. pl. absolute from אֲדָמָה dec. 11 c. אדם
אֲדָמִי וַ pr. name of a place; וַ before (־ֲ) . . אדם
אֲדֹמִי gent. noun masc. from אֱדוֹם . . . אדם
אֲדֹמִיִּים id. pl. dec. 8. . . . . . . אדם
אֲדֻמִּים see מַעֲלֵה אֲדֻמִּים . . . . . עלה
אֲדֻמִּים adj. masc., pl. of אָדֹם dec. 8 c. (§ 37. Nos. 2 & 3) אדם
אֲדֹמִיֹּת gent. noun fem., pl. of אֲדֹמִית (§ 39. No. 4. rem. 1) from אֲדֹמִי masc. (q. v.) . . . אדם
[i] אַדְמֹנִי וְ adj. masc. sing. . . . . . . אדם
אַדְמַת n. f. s., constr. of אֲדָמָה dec. 11 c. (§ 42. r. 1) אדם
אַדְמָתָא pr. name masc. . . . . . . אדם
[k] אַדְמָתָהּ noun fem. sing., suff. 3 pers. sing. fem. from אֲדָמָה dec. 11 c. (§ 42. rem. 1) . . . אדם
אַדְמָתוֹ id., suff. 3 pers. sing. masc. . . . . אדם
אַדְמָתִי id., suff. 1 pers. sing. . . . . . . אדם
אַדְמָתְךָ, אַדְמָתֶךָ וְ׳ id., suff. 2 pers. sing. masc. . . . אדם
אַדְמַתְכֶם id., suff. 2 pers. pl. masc. . . . . אדם
אַדְמָתָם id., suff. 3 pers. pl. masc. . . . . אדם
[dd] אַדְמָתֵנוּ וְ׳ id., suff. 1 pers. pl. . . . . . אדם

[אֶדֶן] masc. in pause אָדֶן dec. 6 a.—I. *base of a column.*—II. trop. *foundation,* Job 38. 6.

אַדָּן pr. name masc. . . . . אדד
[l] אֲדֹנָו Kheth. for אֲדֹנָיו (q. v.) . . . . דון
אַדְנֵי noun masc. pl. constr. from [אֶדֶן] dec. 6 a. . אדן
אֲדֹנָי noun pl. *the Lord,* spoken of God, different from אֲדֹנַי pl. with suff. (q. v.) . . . דון
אדֹנָי וַ id. contracted for [וַאֲדֹנָי] . . . . דון
אֲדֹנַי noun m. pl., suff. 1 pers. s. from אָדוֹן dec. 3 a. דון
[m] אֲדֹנֵי וַ׳ id. pl. construct state; וַ bef. (־ֲ) . . דון
אֲדֹנִי, אדֹנִי וַ id. s., suff. 1 pers. s., with pref. for [וַאֲדֹנִי]; also pr. name in compos. as אֲדֹנִי־בֶזֶק &c. דון
אֲדָנֶיהָ n. m. pl., suff. 3 pers. s. fem. fr. [אֶדֶן] dec. 6 a. אדן
אֲדֹנֶיהָ n. m. pl., suff. 3 pers. s. f. from אָדוֹן dec. 3 a. דון
אֲדֹנִיָּה וְ׳ & אֲדֹנִיָּהוּ וַ׳ pr. names masc. . . . דון
אַדְנֵיהֶם וְ׳ n. m. pl., suff. 3 pers. pl. m. fr. [אֶדֶן] dec. 6 a. אדן
אֲדֹנֵיהֶם n. m. pl., suff. 3 pers. pl. m. fr. אָדוֹן dec. 3 a. דון
אֲדָנָיו וְ׳ noun masc. pl., suff. 3 pers. sing. masc. from [אֶדֶן] dec. 6 a.; וַ before (־ֲ) . . . . אדן
אֲדֹנָיו n. m. pl., suff. 3 pers. s. m. from אָדוֹן dec. 3 a. דון
אֲדֹנֶיךָ id., suff. 2 pers. sing. masc. . . . . דון
אֲדֹנַיִךְ id., suff. 2 pers. sing. fem. . . . . דון
אֲדֹנֵיכֶם id., suff. 2 pers. pl. masc. . . . . דון
אֲדָנִים noun masc., pl. of [אֶדֶן] dec. 6 a. . . . אדן
אֲדֹנִים noun masc., pl. of אָדוֹן dec. 3 a. . . . דון
אֲדֹנֵינוּ וְ׳ id. with suff. 1 pers. pl.; וַ before (־ֲ) . דון
אֲדֹנִיקָם, וַאֲדֹנִירָם pr. names masc. . . . . דון
[n] אֲדֹנֵנוּ n. m. s., suff. 1 pers. pl. from אָדוֹן dec. 3 a. דון
אֵדַע, וְ׳ אֵדָע Kal fut. 1 pers. sing.; וָ for וַ conv. . ידע
[o] אֵדַע וְ Kh. אֵדַע q. v., K. אֵדְעָה (q. v.) . . ידע
[p] אֵדְעָה, [q] וְ׳ וָ׳ אֵדָעָה Kal fut. 1 pers. sing. with paragogic ה; וָ for וַ conv. . . . . ידע
[r] אֵדָעֲךָ וְ, וָ׳ id. with suff. 2 p. s. m. (§ 16. r. 12); וָ id. ידע
[s] אֲדִקֵּם Hiph. fut. 1 pers. sing. [אָדֵק], suff. 3 pers. pl. masc. (§ 18. rem. 11) . . . דקק

אָדַר. Niph. *to become glorious,* Ex. 15. 6, 11.—Hiph. *to make honourable, glorious,* Is. 42. 21.

אֲדוֹרַיִם pr. name of a city of Judah, 2 Chr. 11. 9. Its etymology is uncertain. Gesenius, *two princes* or *two mounds;* others derive it from דּוּר, *two dwellings.*

אַדִּיר adj. m. dec. 1 b.—I. *great, mighty.*—II. *noble, excellent;* hence—III. *prince.*

אַדָּר pr. name of a Benjaminite, 1 Chr. 8. 3. see also חֲצַר אַדָּר

אֲדָר the twelfth month of the Hebrew year, beginning with the new moon of March, and ending with that of April. The etymology is uncertain. Chald. id. Ezr. 6. 15.

---

[a] Job 31. 34. [b] Le. 13. 42, 49. [bb] Nu. 19. 2. [c] Le. 13. 19. [d] Le. 14. 37. [dd] Ge. 47. 18, 19. [e] Le. 13. 24, 43. [f] Is. 14. 13. [ff] Ne. 13. 10. [g] La. 4. 7. [h] Ps. 49. 12. [i] 1 Sa. 17. 42. [k] Am. 5. 2. [l] Pr. 30. 10. [m] De. 10. 17. [n] 1 Sa. 16. 16. [o] Ru. 4. 4. [p] Ge. 18. 21. [q] Je. 11. 18. [r] Ex. 33. 13, 17. [s] 2 Sa. 22. 43.

אֶדֶר masc.—I. *cloak, mantle*, Mi. 2. 8.—II. *greatness, splendour*, Zec. 11. 13.

אַדֶּרֶת fem. with suff. אַדַּרְתּוֹ dec. 13a.—I. *cloak, mantle.*—II. *magnificence.*

אֲדַרְגָּזְרִין Chald. *chief judges*, Da. 3. 2, 3. From אֲדַר greatness, and גָּזְרִין part. of גְּזַר q. v.

אַדְרַמֶּלֶךְ (*splendour of the king*, contracted from אֶדֶר הַמֶּלֶךְ) pr. n.—I. of an idol, 2 Ki. 17. 31.—II. of a son of Sennacherib, 2 Ki. 19. 37.

אַדָּר pr. name masc. . . . . . אדר
אֲדָר name of a month . . . . אדר
אֶדֶר noun masc. sing. . . . . אדר
אֲדַרְגָּזְרַיָּא[a] Chald. n. masc. pl. emph. from [גָּזֵר״] dec. 2b. אדר
אַדָּרָה pr. name of a place [אַדָּר] with parag. ה . אדר
אֶדְרוֹשׁ[b] Kal fut. 1 pers. sing. (comp. § 8. rem. 18) דרשׁ
אַדְרַזְדָּא Chald. adv. *quickly, diligently*, Ezr. 7. 23. .
אִדְּרֵי Chald. n. m. pl. constr. from [אִדַּר] dec. 2a. נדר
אַדְרִיכֵם[c] Hiph. fut. 1 pers. sing., suff. 2 pers. pl. masc. דרך
אֶדְרְכֵם[d] וְ Kal fut. 1 pers. s. [אֶדְרֹךְ], suff. 3 pers. pl. m. דרך
אֲדַרְכֹּנִים[e] וַ *darics*, a Persian gold coin, see also דַּרְכְּמוֹנִים
אַדִּרָם[ee] for אַדִּירִים, adj. m., pl. of אַדִּיר dec. 1b. . אדר
אֲדֹרָם וַ׳ pr. name, see אֲדֹנִירָם . . . דון
אַדְרַמֶּלֶךְ וְ pr. name masc. . . . . אדר
אֶדְרֶעִי וְ׳ pr. name of a place for [אֶדְרְעִי] . דרע
אֶדְרֹשׁ Kal fut. 1 pers. sing. . . . . דרשׁ
אִדָּרֵשׁ Niph. fut. 1 pers. sing. (§ 10. rem. 5) . דרשׁ
אֶדְרְשָׁה[f] וְ Kal fut. 1 pers. s. (אֶדְרֹשׁ) with parag. ה . דרשׁ
אֶדְרְשֶׁנּוּ[g] id. with suff. 3 pers. sing. masc. (§ 2. rem. 3) דרשׁ
אַדֶּרֶת[h] / אַדֶּרֶת } noun fem. sing. dec. 13a. . . } אדר
אַדַּרְתּוֹ id., suff. 3 pers. sing. masc. . . . אדר
אַדַּרְתָּם[i] id., suff. 3 pers. pl. masc. . . . אדר

[אָדַשׁ] *to thresh*, once, Is. 28. 28.

אָהַב, אָהֵב fut. יֶאֱהַב, יֶאֱהַב, 1 pers. אֹהַב, אֱהַב—I. *to love*, with the acc., rarely with לְ and בְּ; part. אֹהֵב *friend.*—II. *to love* to do anything, followed by an infin. with לְ.—Niph. part. *lovely, amiable*, 2 Sa. 1. 23.—Pi. part. *a lover.*

אַהַב masc. only pl. אֲהָבִים.—I. *amours, loves*, Ho. 8. 9.—II. *loveliness*, Pr. 5. 19.

אֹהַב m. only pl. אֳהָבִים *amours, loves*, Pr. 7. 18.

אַהֲבָה fem.—I. infin. of the verb אָהַב e. g. לְאַהֲבָה אֶת־שֵׁם יְהוָֹה *to love the name of the Lord.*—II. subst. *love, beloved.*—III. adv. *delightfully*, Ca. 3. 10.

אֶאֱהָב[k] Kal fut. 1 p. s. in pause for [אֶאֱהַב] (§ 19. r. 3) אהב
אֱהַב־[l] id. imp. sing. masc. . . . . אהב
וָאֹהַב[m] וָ id. fut. 1 pers. sing.; וָ for וַ· conv. . אהב
וְאֹהֵב וְ׳ id. part. act. sing. masc. dec. 7b. . אהב
וְאַהֲבָה וְ׳[n] (prop. inf. § 8. rem. 10. & 13. rem. 2) noun fem. only in the sing. (§ 26. No. 11) . אהב
אֲהֵבָהּ Kal pret. 3 pers. sing. masc. (אָהֵב), suff. 3 pers. sing. fem. (§ 16. rem. 1) . . . אהב
אֱהָבֶהָ[o] id. imp. s. m. (אֱהַב), suff. 3 p. s. f. (§ 16. r. 11) אהב
וָאֹהֲבֵהוּ[p] וָ id. fut. 1 pers. sing. (אֹהַב), suff. 3 pers. sing. masc. (§ 16. rem. 12); וָ for וַ· . אהב
אָהֲבוּ id. pret. 3 pers. pl. . . . . אהב
אֲהֵבוֹ id. pret. 3 pers. s. m. (אָהֵב), suff. 3 pers. s. m. אהב
אֱהָבוּ[q] / וֶאֱהָבוּ[r] וְ׳[s] } id. imp. pl. masc. (§ 8. rem. 12) . } אהב
וְאֹהֲבוֹ[t] וְ id. part. act. s. m. (אֹהֵב) suff. 3 s. m. dec. 7b. אהב
אֲהֵבוּךָ id. pret. 3 p. pl. (s. אָהֵב), suff. 2 p. s. m. . אהב
אֲהֵבוּם[u] id. id., suff. 3 pers. pl. masc. . . אהב
וְאֹהֲבַי id. part. act. pl. m., suff. 1 pers. s. dec. 7b. . אהב
וְאֹהֲבֵי וְ׳ id. id. pl., construct state . . . אהב
וְאֹהֲבִי[x] id. id. sing., suff. 1 pers. sing. . . . אהב
וְאֹהֲבַיהָ[y] Kh. אֹהֲבֶיהָ q. v., K. אֹהֲבַי (q. v.) . אהב
וְאֹהֲבֶיהָ וְ׳[a] Kal part. act. pl. m., suff. 3 pers. s. f. dec. 7b. אהב
וְאֹהֲבָיו וְ׳[b] id., suff. 3 pers. sing. masc. . . אהב
וְאֹהֲבֶיךָ id., suff 2 pers. sing. masc. . . אהב
וְאֹהֲבַיִךְ[c] id., suff. 2 pers. sing. fem. for [־בַיִךְ] . אהב
אֲהָבִים noun masc., pl. of [אַהַב] dec. 6d. . אהב
וְאֹהֲבִים[d] Kal part. act. pl. masc., from אֹהֵב dec. 7b. . אהב
וַאֲהֵבְךָ וַ׳[e] id. preter. 3 pers. sing. masc. (אָהֵב), suff. 2 pers. sing. m. (§ 16. r. 1); וַ for וְ conv. אהב
וְאֹהַבְךָ[f] id. part. act. sing. masc. (אֹהֵב), suff. 2 pers. sing. masc., dec. 7b. (§ 36. rem. 3) . אהב
וָאֹהֲבֵם[g] וָ׳[h] id. fut. 1 pers. s. (אֹהַב), suff. 3 pers. pl. masc.; וָ for וַ conv. . . . אהב
וְאַהֲבַת וְ׳ n. fem. sing., construct of אַהֲבָה (q. v.) . אהב
אֲהֻבַת[i] Kal part. pass. sing. fem., construct of אֲהוּבָה dec. 10, from אָהוּב masc. . . אהב
וְאֹהֶבֶת[k] id. part. act. sing., fem. of אֹהֵב . . אהב
אָהַבְתָּ id. preter. 2 pers. sing. masc. . . אהב
וְאָהַבְתָּ וְ׳ id. id., acc. shifted by conv. וְ (§ 8. rem. 7) אהב
אָהַבְתְּ id. preter. 2 pers. sing. fem. . . אהב
אֲהֵבַתְהוּ[l] id. pret. 3 pers. s. f., suff. 3 p. s. m. (§ 16. r. 1) אָהֵב
אַהֲבָתִי n. f. s. with suff. 1 pers. s. from אַהֲבָה (q. v.) אהב
אָהַבְתִּי / אָהָבְתִּי } Kal preter. 1 pers. sing. (§ 8. rem. 7) } אהב
[m] אֹהַבְתִּי id. part. act. s. f. (אֹהֶבֶת) with parag. י, dec. 13a. אהב
[n] אֲהַבְתִּיךָ id. pret. 1 pers. sing., suff. 2 pers. sing. masc. אהב

[a] Da. 3. 2, 3. [b] Eze. 20. 40. [c] Is. 42. 16. [d] Is. 63. 3. [e] 1 Ch. 29. 7. [ee] Eze. 32. 18. [f] 1 Sa. 28. 7. [g] Ge. 9. 5. [h] Eze. 17. 8. [i] Zec. 11. 3. [k] Pr. 8. 17. [l] Ho. 3. 1. [m] Mal. 1. 2. [n] Pr. 15. 17. [o] Pr. 4. 6. [p] Ho. 11. 1. [q] Zec. 8. 19. [r] Ps. 31. 24. [s] Am. 5. 15. [t] Pr. 13. 24. [u] Je. 8. 2. [x] Is. 41. 8. [y] Pr. 8. 17. [a] Pr. 18. 21. [b] Ju. 5. 31. [c] Ps. 122. 6. [d] De. 13. 4. [e] De. 7. 13. [f] 2 Ch. 20. 7. [g] Ho. 14. 5. [h] Ps. 119. 167. [i] Ho. 3. 1. [k] Ge. 25. 28. [l] 1 Sa. 18. 28. [m] Ho. 10. 11. [n] Is. 43. 4.

אֲהַבְתִּיךְ Kal preter. 1 pers. sing., suff. 2 pers. sing. fem. אהב

אֲהֲבָתְךָ[a] n. f. s., suff. 2 pers. s. m. from אַהֲבָה (q. v.) אהב

אֲהֵבָתֶךְ[b] Kal pret. 3 p. s. f., suff. 2 p. s. f. (§ 16. r. 2) אָהֵב

אַהֲבָתָם n. f. s., suff. 3 pers. pl. m. from אַהֲבָה (q. v.) אהב

אֲהַבְתֶּם[c] [d]וְ׳ Kal preter. 2 pers. pl. masc.; וְ before (־ֲ) אהב

אֲהַבְתָּנוּ[e] id. preter. 2 pers. sing. masc., suff. 1 pers. pl. אהב

אֲהַבְתָּנִי[f] id. with suff. 1 pers. sing. . . . . אהב

אֶהְגֶּה Kal fut. 1 pers. sing. (§ 13. rem. 5) . הגה

אֹהַד וְ pr. name of a son of Simeon, Ge. 46. 10. The etymology is uncertain; coll. with the Samar. *portion*. According to Gesenius, *union*, אָהַד i. q. אָחַד.

אֵהוּד (by Syr. for אֲחוּד) pr. name of a judge in Israel.

אֲהָהּ interj. expressive of grief, *ah! alas!*

אַהֲוָא pr. name of a country and a river. Ezr. 8. 21, 31.

אָהוּב[g] וְ Kal part. p. sing. masc. . . . . אהב

אֲהוּבָה[h] id. fem. (§ 38. No. 3. dec. 3) dec. 10. . אהב

אֵהוּד וְ׳ pr. name masc. . . . . . אהד

אֲהוֹדֶנּוּ[i] Hiph. fut. 1 pers. sing., suff. 3 pers. sing. masc. (§ 20. rem. 10. § 25. No. 2e) . ידה

אֲהוֹדְעִנֵּהּ[k] Chald. Aph. fut. 1 pers. sing., suff. 3 pers. sing. masc. (§ 47. rem. 4, compare 53. 1) ידע

אֱהִי i. q. אַיֵּה *where!* Ho. 13. 10. Others take it as an interj. expressive of derision, *ha!*

אֱהִי וְ׳ apocopated for the following (§ 24. r. 3) היה

אֶהְיֶה וְ׳, וָ׳ Kal fut. 1 pers. sing.; וָ for וַ· conv. היה

אָהִימָה[l] וְ Hiph. fut. 1 pers. sing. with paragogic ה הום

אהל i. q. הָלַל, only Hiph. *to shine*, Job 25. 5. See also the following article.

אֹהֶל וְ׳ masc. dec. 6, with suff. אָהֳלִי, אָהָלְךָ (§ 35. r. 8), with ה paragogic אֹהֱלָה, pl. אֹהָלִים (rem. 9).—I. *tent, tabernacle, dwelling*.—II. pr. name of a son of Zerubbabel. 1 Ch. 3. 20.

אָהַל *to pitch a tent, to live in tents.* Piel id. Is. 13. 20.

אָהֳלָה (*her tent*, for אָהֳלָהּ, see § 3. rem. 3) an allegorical name given to Samaria by Ezekiel, 23. 4, sq.

אָהֳלִיאָב (*tent of* (his) *father*) pr. name of an artificer employed in the work of the tabernacle.

אָהֳלִיבָה (*my tent* (is) *in her*, בָה for בָּהּ, see § 3. rem. 3) an allegorical name given to Jerusalem by Ezekiel, 23. 4.

אָהֳלִיבָמָה (*tent of the high place*) pr. name of a wife of Esau. Ge. 36. 2, 14.

אָהֳלָה pr. name fem. . . . . . . אהל

אֹהֳלֹה noun masc. sing., suff. 3 pers. sing. masc. from אֹהֶל (§ 35. rem. 9) . . . . אהל

אָהֳלוֹ id., with suff. 3 pers. sing. masc. . . אהל

אֲהָלוֹת וַ noun pl. fem. see אֲהָלִים

אָהֳלֵי n. masc. pl., constr. from אֹהֶל (§ 35. rem. 9) אהל

אָהֳלִי id. sing., suff. 1 pers. sing. . . . . אהל

אֹהָלַי[m] id. pl., suff. 1 pers. sing. (note א) . . אהל

אָהֳלִיאָב וְ׳ m., וְ׳ אָהֳלִיבָה f., וְ׳ אָהֳלִיבָמָה f., pr. n. m. אהל

אָהֳלֵיהֶם [n]וְ׳ noun masc. pl., suff. 3 pers. pl. masc. from אֹהֶל (§ 35. rem. 9) . . . . אהל

אֹהָלֶיךָ[o] id. pl., suff. 2 pers. sing. masc. (note א) . אהל

אָהֳלֵיכֶם[p] id. pl., suff. 2 pers. pl. masc. . . . אהל

אֲהָלִים[q] masc. pl. and אֲהָלוֹת fem. pl. *lign-aloes*, or *aloes wood*, a perfumed wood.

אֹהָלִים וְ׳ noun masc., pl. of אֹהֶל, dec. 6. (note א, § 35. rem. 9) . . . . . אהל

אָהֳלֶךָ id. sing., suff. 2 pers. sing. masc. for [אָהָלְךָ] אהל

אֲהַלֵּךְ Piel fut. 1 pers. sing. . . . . . הלך

אָהֳלֵךְ[r] n. m. s., suff. 2 pers. s. f. from אֹהֶל (q. v.) אהל

אֶהֱלֹךְ Kal fut. 1 pers. sing. . . . . . הלך

אֲהַלֵּל Piel fut. 1 pers. sing. . . . . . הלל

אֲהַלְלָה [uu]וַ׳ id. with parag. ה; לְ for לֵ, (§ 10. rem. 7) הלל

אֲהַלְלֶךָּ id., suff. 2 pers. sing. masc. for [אֲהַלֶּלְךָ] (§ 2. rem. 3. and 16. rem. 15) . . הלל

אֲהַלְלֶנּוּ[yy] id. with suff. 3 pers. sing. masc. . . הלל

אֶהֱמֶה[s] וְ Kal fut. 1 pers. sing. . . . . המה

אֶהֱמָיָה[t] וְ id. (§ 24. rem. 5) . . . . . המה

אֶהְפֹּךְ[u] Kal fut. 1 pers. sing. (§ 13. rem. 5) . הפך

אֶהֱרֹג[x] Kal fut. 1 pers. sing. . . . . . הרג

אַהַרְגָה[y] וְ id. with paragogic ה (§ 13. rem. 4) . הרג

אֶהֶרְגֵהוּ וָ id., suff. 3 pers. s. m.; וָ for וַ· conv. הרג

אֶהֱרוֹג[z] *fully* for אֶהֱרֹג (q. v.) . . . . הרג

אֶהֱרוֹס[a] Kal fut. 1 pers. sing. . . . . . הרס

אַהֲרֹן וְ׳ pr. name of the brother of Moses, and the first high-priest.

אֶהֱרֹס Kal fut. 1 pers. sing. . . . . . הרס

אוֹ conj.—I. *or, either*; אוֹ—אוֹ *whether*—*or*.—II. *or else*.—III. *if, but if*; יָמִים אוֹ עָשׂוֹר *some days, if* it were *perhaps* ten, i. e. about ten days.

אוּאֵל וְ pr. name of a man. Ezr. 10. 34. Simonis, *strength of God*, for אוּל אֵל; Gesenius, perhaps *will of God*, for אַו אֵל see R. אָוָה.

אוב Root not used; whence, אוֹב masc. pl. אוֹבוֹת.—I. *leathern bottle*, Job 32. 19.—II. *a spirit of divina-*

---

2 Sa. 1. 26. Ru. 4. 15. Am. 4. 5. [d] De. 10. 19. [e] Mal. 1. 2. [f] Ju. 14. 16. [g] Ne. 13. 26. [h] De. 21. 15. [i] Ps. 28. 7. [k] Da. 5. 17. [l] Ps. 55. 3. [m] Je. 4. 20. [n] Ju. 6. 5. [o] Nu. 24. 5. [p] Jos. 22. 8. [q] Pr. 7. 17. [r] Is. 54. 2. [s] Ps. 55. 18. [t] Ps. 77. 4. [u] Zep. 3. 9. [uu] Ps. 145. 2. [x] Am. 9. 1. [y] Ge. 27. 41. [yy] Ps. 109. 30. [z] Am. 2. 3. [a] Mal. 1. 4.

tion, or *necromancy*.—III. *necromancer, one who calls up spirits to learn of them the future.*

אֹבֹת (*water skins*) pr. name of a station of the Israelites in the wilderness.

אוֹב noun masc. sing. dec. 1 a. . . . . אוב

אוֹבֵד Kal part. act. sing. masc. dec. 7 b. . . אבד

אוֹבִיל pr. name masc. . . . . . . אבל

[a] אוֹבִילֵם Hiph. fut. 1 pers. sing., suff. 3 pers. pl. masc. יבל

אוֹבִישׁ Hiph. fut. 1 pers. sing. . . . . יבש

[b] אוּבָל [for אוֹבַל] Hoph. fut. 1 pers. sing. . יבל

[c] אוּבַל n. masc. sing., construct of יָבָל dec. 2 b. . יבל

אוד Root not used; Arab.—I. *to bend, to turn, to surround.*—II. *to be strong.*

אֵד masc. dec. 1 a., *mist, vapour*, the exhalations arising from, and surrounding, the earth.

אוּד masc. dec. 1 a., *a wooden poker*, for turning or stirring the fire, Is. 7. 4; hence, *a fire-brand.*

אוֹדוֹת pl. fem. dec. 10, *causes*, (prop. *turnings*, compare סִבָּה ,גָּלָל, Eng. *circumstances*), עַל אוֹדוֹת *for the causes*, i. e. *on account of*; עַל אוֹדוֹתַי *on my account.*

אֵיד m. dec. 1 a., *straitness, calamity, destruction.*

מְאֹד masc. dec. 1 a.—I. *might, power, excess*; בִּמְאֹד מְאֹד *in excess of excess*, i. e. *very exceedingly*; עַד לִמְאֹד *even to excess*, עַד מְאֹד *till* (it amounted) *to excess, exceedingly.*—II. adv. *exceedingly*; מְאֹד מְאֹד *very exceedingly*; טוֹב מְאֹד *very good*; נִמְצָא מְאֹד *he is very present*; מַהֵר מְאֹד *go down quickly.*

[d] אוּד noun masc. sing. dec. 1 a. . . . . אוד

אוֹדֶה [e] וְ' Hiph. fut. 1 pers. sing. (§ 25. No. 2 e) ידה

אוֹדִיעַ Hiph. fut. 1 pers. sing. . . . . ידע

אוֹדִיעָה id. with paragogic ה . . . . ידע

אוֹדִיעֲךָ id., suff. 2 pers. sing. masc. . . . ידע

[bb] אוֹדִיעֵם id., suff. 3 pers. pl. masc. . . . ידע

אוֹדְךָ [f] וְ' } Hiph. fut. 1 pers. sing. (אוֹדֶה), suff. 2 p. } ידה
אוֹדֶךָּ [g] וְ' } sing. masc. (§ 25. No. 2 e. & § 2. r. 3) }

אוֹדֶנּוּ id., suff. 3 pers. sing. masc., (§ 2. rem. 3) . ידה

[h] אֵדְעָ וָ Kal fut. 1 pers. sing. (§ 20. rem. 7); וָ before gutt. for וַ· conversive . . . . ידע

[i] אוֹדֹת noun pl. fem. from the form [אוֹד] . . אוד

I. **אָוָה** Kal, not used. Arab. *to bend, inflect*, also *turn aside, take lodgings, dwell.* Pi. *to desire, to long for.* Hithp.—I. id.—II. *to take for a dwelling.*

אַו masc. *desire.* Pr. 31. 4. Khethib.

אַוָּה fem. dec. 10.—I. *desire, longing.*—II. *lust.*

אֱוִי (*desire*) pr. name of a king of Midian.

אִי masc. (for אֱוִי) pl. אִיִּים (§ 37. No. 4) *habitable earth* or *land, coast, sea-coast, island.* See also אִי R. אוה II.

מַאֲוַי masc. only, pl. מַאֲוַיִּים *desires.* Ps. 140. 9.

תַּאֲוָה fem. dec. 10.—I. *desire, appetite, lust.*—II. *object of desire, a delight.*

II. **אָוָה** Root not used. Arab. *to howl.*

אוֹי I. *wailing.*—II. interj. *wo! alas!* expressive of grief.—III. *ho!* expressive of threatening.

אוֹיָה id. *alas!* Ps. 120. 5.

אִי masc. (for אֱוִי)—I. *jackal*, only in the plural, אִיִּים—II. interj. *wo! alas!* אִי לוֹ *wo to him*, Ec. 4. 10.

אַיָּה fem.—I. the name of a bird of prey, Sept. and Vulg. *vulture*; *kite.*—II. pr. name of a man.

III. **אָוָה** Root not used; supposed to signify, *to mark, describe with a mark.*

אוֹת (for אֱוֹת) com. dec. 1 a., pl. אֹתוֹת—I. *mark, memorial, warning.*—II. *sign, portent, miracle.*

אָת Chald. masc. id.

[k] אִוָּה Piel preter. 3 pers. sing. masc. . . . אוה

[l] אוֹהֵב Kal part. act. sing. masc. dec. 7 b. . . אהב

אוּזַי pr. name of a man. Ne. 3. 25. אוּז Arab. *quick.*

אוּזָל pr. name masc. . . . . . . אזל

[m] אוֹחִוֹלָה (Kh. אוֹחוּלָה ?) K. אוֹחִילָה Hiph. fut, 1 pers. s. ה parag. in form from יָחַל, in sense fr. חול

אוֹחִיל Hiph. fut. 1 pers. sing. . . . . יחל

[n] אוֹחִילָה id., with paragogic ה . . . . יחל

אוֹי interj. . . . . אוה

אֱוִי pr. name masc. . . . . . . אוה

אוֹיֵב וְ' Kal part. act. sing. masc. dec. 7 b. . . איב

אוֹיְבַי [o] } id. pl., suff. 1 pers. sing. . . . } איב
אוֹיְבִי }

אוֹיְבֵי id. pl., construct state . . . . איב

[p] אוֹיְבִי id. sing., suff. 1 pers. sing. . . . איב

אוֹיְבֵיהֶם id. pl., suff. 3 pers. pl. masc. . . . איב

אוֹיְבָיו id. pl., suff. 3 pers. sing. masc. . . איב

אוֹיְבֶיךָ id. pl., suff. 2 pers. sing. masc. . . איב

[q] אוֹיְבֶיךָ id. id. (Kh. אוֹיְבֶיךָ; K. אוֹיִבְךָ (q. v.) . איב

אוֹיְבֵיכֶם id. pl., suff. 2 pers. pl. masc. . . . איב

[r] אוֹיְבִים id. pl., absolute state . . . . איב

אוֹיְבֵינוּ id. pl., suff. 1 pers. pl. . . . . איב

[s] אוֹיִבְךָ id. sing., suff. 2 pers. sing. masc. . . איב

[dd] אוֹיְבֵנוּ id., sing., suff. 1 pers. pl. . . . איב

אוֹיָה interj. . . . . אוה

אֱוִיל וֶ' noun masc. sing., dec. 1 a.; also pr. name in compos. אֱ' מְרֹדַךְ; וֶ before (ֱ) . . אול

---

[a] Je. 31. 9. [b] Job 10. 19. [bb] Je. 16. 21. [c] Da. 8. 2. [d] Zec. 3. 2. [dd] Ju. 16. 23, 24. [e] Ps. 138. 2. [f] Ps. 34. 4 [g] Ps. 118. 28. [h] Eze. 20. 5. [i] Ge. 21. 11. [k] Ps. 132. 13. [l] Pr. 27. 6. [m] Je. 4. 19. [n] Mi. 7. 7. [o] Ps. 102. 9. [p] 1 Ki. 21. 20. [q] Pr. 24. 17. [r] Ps. 127. 5. [s] Pr. 24. 17.

אֱוִילִים[a] וְ n. masc., pl. of אֱוִיל dec. 1 a.; וְ id. . אול

אִוִּתִיהָ[b] Piel preter. 1 pers. sing., suff. 3 pers. sing. fem. אוה

אִוִּתִךְ[c] id. with suff. 2 pers. sing. masc. for [תִיךְ] . אוה

אוֹכִיחַ[d] Hiph. fut. 1 pers. sing. . . . יכח

אוֹכִיחֲךָ[e] / אוֹכִיחֲךָ[f] } id., suff. 2 pers. sing. masc. . . יכח

אוֹכִיל[g] [for אַאֲכִיל] Hiph. fut. 1 pers. s. (§ 19. r. 8) אכל

אוֹכֵל Kal part. act. sing. masc. dec. 7 b. . . אכל

אוּכַל / אוּכָל } Hoph. fut. 1 pers. sing. . . יכל

אֹכְלָה Kal part. act. fem. for [אֹכְלָה] . . אכל

אֹכְלֶיהָ[h] id. pl. m., suff. 3 pers. s. f. from אוֹכֵל dec. 7 b. אכל

אִוָּלֵד[i] Niph. fut. 1 pers. sing. (§ 20. rem. 7); Milêl before monos. for [אִוָּלֵד] . . . ילד

אָוַל Root not used; i. q. יָאַל *to be foolish.*

אֱוִיל masc. dec. 1 a., *a fool*, by implication *an impious wicked person.*

אֱוִילִי adj. *foolish*, Zec. 11. 15.

אֱוִיל מְרֹדַךְ pr. name of a king of Babylon, successor of Nebuchadnezzar. See מְרֹדַךְ the name of a Babylonian idol; *the fool of Merodach*, perhaps so called by the Jews by way of opprobrium for, *the wise of Merodach.*

אִוֶּלֶת f. with suff. אִוַּלְתִּי dec. 13 a., *folly, impiety.*

אוּל & **אִיל** Root not used;—Arab.—I. *to be the first, chief.*—II. *to be strong.*

אוּל masc. dec. 1 a.—I. *prince, chief*, 2 Ki. 24. 15. Kh.—II. *body*, Ps. 73. 4.

אוּלַי pr. name of a river flowing by Susa in Persia, Da. 8. 2. See also analyt. order.

אוּלָם, אֻלָם, masc., pl. אֻלַמִּים.—I. *vestibule, porch.*—II. pr. name of a man. *Note.*—Some editions have also the form אֵלָם.

אַיִל masc. dec. 6 h.—I. *ram.*—II. a certain ornament over doors or windows.

אַיָּל com. *a stag, hart*, or *deer*, also fem. *hind.*

אַיָּלָה fem. dec. 11 a., *hind* or *female deer.*

אַיֶּלֶת fem. id. אַיֶּלֶת הַשַּׁחַר *hind of the morning*, in the heading of Ps. 22, to designate the subject of the Psalm.

אַיָּלוֹן (*belonging to deer, deer-field*), pr. name of a city in the tribe of Dan, and another in the tribe of Zebulun.

אֱיָל masc. *strength, force*, Ps. 88. 5.

אֱיָלוּת fem. id., Ps. 22. 20.

אַיִל masc. dec. 1 a.—I. *the mighty, noble.*—II. applied to strong trees, as *the oak, the pine*, or *terebinth*, &c.

אֵילִם pr. name of a station of the Israelites in the wilderness.

אֵילוֹן (*oak*).—I. pr. name of several men.—II. of a city in the tribe of Dan.

אֵילַת, אֵילוֹת pr. name of a sea-coast town in Idumea.

אֵילָם only pl. אֵילַמִּים, אֵלַמּוֹת *vestibules, porticos.*

אִילָן Chald. masc. dec. 1., *a tree.*

אֵל masc. dec. 1 a.—I. *strong, mighty man, hero.*—II. *power*, יֶשׁ לְאֵל יָדִי *it is in the power of my hand.*—III. *God, the Mighty One.*—IV. *a supposititious god, an idol.*

אֵלִיָּהוּ, אֵלִיָּה (*my God is the Lord*), pr. name of the celebrated prophet, *Elijah*, during the reign of Ahab, king of Israel, and likewise of two other but obscure persons.

לָאֵל (*to God*, sc. dedicated), pr. name masc. Nu. 3. 24.

אֵלָא (i. q. אֵלָה *terebinth*), pr. name masc. 1 Ki. 4. 18.

אֵלָה fem.—I. *terebinth.*—II. pr. name of one of the dukes of Idumea.—III. of a king of Israel, son of Baasha, and others.

אֵלוֹן masc. dec. 1 b.—I. *oak*, others, *terebinth.*—II. pr. name masc. Ge. 46. 14.

אוּלֵי[k] Kh. אוּלֵי, K. אֵילֵי noun masc. pl. construct from אוּל or אַיִל . . . . אול

אוּלַי pr. name of a river, for [אוּלָי] . . אול

אוּלַי (compounded of אוֹ=אוּ, and לִי i.q. לֹא compare לוּלֵי) adv.—I. *if not, unless.*—II. *perhaps, peradventure.*

אֱוִלִי[l] for [אֱוִילִי] adj. masc. sing. . . . אול

אוֹלִיד[m] Hiph. fut. 1 pers. sing. . . . ילד

אוֹלִיךְ Hiph. fut. 1 pers. sing. . . . ילד

אוֹלִיכָה[n] וְ id. with paragogic ה . . . ילד

אוֹלִיכֵם[o] id., suff. 3 pers. pl. masc. . . . ילד

אֱוִלִים def. for אֱוִילִים n. masc., pl. of אֱוִיל dec. 1 a. אול

אוֹלֵךְ וָ apoc. for אוֹלִיךְ (q. v.); וָ for וַ· conversive ילך

אוּלָם pr. name masc. . . . . אול

אוּלָם[p] n. m. s., suff. 3 pers. pl. m. from [אוּל] dec. 1 a. אול

אוּלָם וְ' noun masc. sing., pl. c. אֻלַמֵּי dec. 8 a. . אול

אוּלָם וְ' (compounded of אוֹ=אוּ, and לָם Arab. *not*) adv. prop. *whether not*, i. q. *but perhaps, but.*

אִוֶּלֶת וְ' n. fem. sing. dec. 13 a. (see the following) אול

---

[a] Pr. 1. 7. [b] Ps. 132. 14. [c] Is. 26. 9. [d] Job 13. 15. [e] Ps. 50. 21. [f] Ps. 50. 8. [g] Ho. 11. 4. [h] Ec. 5. 10. [i] Job 3. 2. [k] 2 Ki. 24. 15. [l] Zec. 11. 15. [m] Is. 66. 9. [n] 2 Ki. 6. 19. [o] Je. 31. 9. [p] Ps. 73. 4.

אִוַּלְתּוֹ n. f. s., suff. 3 pers. s. m. from אִוֶּלֶת dec. 13a. אול
אִוַּלְתִּי[a] id., suff. 1 pers. sing. . . . . אול
אוֹמָר ו׳ pr. name masc. . . . . אמר
אוֹמַר וָ Kal fut. 1 pers. sing.; וָ for וַ· conversive אמר
אוֹמֵר id. part. act. sing. masc. dec. 7b. . . אמר
אוֹמְרָה[b] id. fut. 1 pers. sing. with paragogic ה . אמר

אוּן, אוֹן אֵין Heb. not used, in the derivatives.—I. *to be nothing, to be light, easy.*—II. *to be strong.*

אָוֶן masc. dec. 6h.—I. *nothingness, falsehood, vanity.*—II. *idol, idols;* בֵּית אָוֶן *house of idols;* בִּקְעַת אָוֶן *valley of idols,* Am. 1. 5.—III. *wickedness, iniquity;* מְתֵי אָוֶן *wicked men;* פֹּעֲלֵי אָוֶן *workers of iniquity.*—IV. *adversity, calamity, sorrow.*

אוֹן masc. dec. 1a.—I. *power, strength, vigour,* רֵאשִׁית הָאוֹן *beginning of strength,* i. e. first-born. —II. *wealth, riches.*—III. pr. name masc. Nu. 16. 1. —IV. אוֹן & אֹן (sun), *Heliopolis,* an Egyptian city.

אוֹנוֹ (*strong,* for אוֹנוֹן) pr. name of a city in Benjamin.

אוֹנָם (id.) pr. name of a man.

אוֹנָן (id.) pr. name of a son of Judah.

אַיִן masc. dec. 6i., construct אֵין.—I. *nothingness,* Is. 40. 23.—II. as an adv. *not,* including the idea of the subst. verb *to be* (compare יֵשׁ); אֵין אִישׁ *there is no man,* אֵין פּוֹתֵר *there was none interpreting;* אָדָם אַיִן *there was no man,* לֶב־אַיִן *there is no heart;* אֵין לָבוֹא *it is not to enter,* i. e. none dare enter; אֵין עֲרוֹךְ *there is no comparing,* i. e. cannot be compared; אֵין דָּבָר מְאוּמָה *nothing;* אֵין כֹּל *nothing at all.*—III. If a personal pronoun is the subject of the proposition, the particle takes the verbal suffixes, אֵינֶנִּי *I am,* or *was not, shall not be,* אֵינְךָ, אֵינֶנּוּ, אֵינֶנָּה, &c.—IV. When followed by the dative, אֵין לִי *there is not to me,* i. e. *I have not,* אֵין לָהֶם *they have not.*—V. Combined with prepositions; בְּאֵין (*a*) *without,* (*b*) *before there was, were,* Pr. 8. 24; כְּאַיִן (*a*) *as nothing,* (*b*) *almost.* Ps. 73. 2; לְאֵין (*a*) *to him who has not,* (*b*) *that there should be no,* &c.; מֵאֵין (*a*) *so as not to be,* מֵאֵין יוֹשֵׁב *so that there shall be no inhabitants,* Is. 5. 9; Je. 34. 22. (*b*) *because there is not;* מֵאֵין מַיִם *for want of water,* Is. 50. 2.

אִין i. q. אֵין. 1 Sa. 21. 9.

תְּאֻנִים masc. pl., *vanity, falsehood,* Ez. 24. 12.

אָוֶן ו׳, וְ׳ n. m. s. dec. 6g; also pr. n.; וְ see lett. ו און
אוֹן[c] ו׳ noun masc. sing. dec. 1a; also pr n. m. . און

אוֹנוֹ ו׳ pr. name of a place . . . און
אוֹנוֹ[d] ו׳ n. m. s. from אוֹן, or אָוֶן, (q. v.) . . און
אוֹנִי noun masc. sing. from אוֹן, dec. 1a. . און
אֳנִיּוֹת[e] Kh. אוֹנִיוֹת, K. אֳנִיּוֹת, noun fem., pl. of אוֹנִיָּה (participial form like הוֹמִיָּה) or אֳנִיָּה . אנה
אוֹנִים noun masc., pl. of אוֹן dec. 1a. . . . און
אוֹנִים[f] noun masc., pl. of אָוֶן dec. 6g. . . און
אוֹנֵךְ[g] id. sing., suff. 2 pers. sing. fem. . . און
אוֹנָם[h] id. sing., suff. 3 pers. pl. masc. . . און
אוֹנָם[i] n. m. s., suff. 3 pers. pl. m. from אוֹן dec. 1a. און
אוֹנָם ו׳ pr. name masc. . . . . . און
אוֹנָן ו׳ pr. name masc. . . . . . און
אוֹסִיף Hiph. fut. 1 pers. sing. . . . . יסף
אוֹסֵף[k] ap. for the preceding . . . יסף
אִוָּסֵר[l] וָ Niph. fut. 1 pers. s. (§ 20. r. 7); וָ for וַ· conv. יסר
אִוָּעֵד Niph. fut. 1 pers. sing. (§ 20. rem. 7) . יעד
אוּפָז pr. name of a country rich in gold, the situation of which is not known.
אוֹפִיר pr. name of a region . . . . אפר
אוֹפִירָה id. with paragogic ה . . . . אפר
אוֹפַן[m] noun masc. sing.; pl. אוֹפַנִּים dec. 8.
אוֹפָן ו׳ (§ 37. No. 2) . . . . . אפן
אוֹפַנֵּי[n] id. pl., construct state . . . . אפן
אוֹפַנֵּיהֶם[o] id. pl., suff. 3 pers. pl. masc. . . אפן
אוֹפַנִּים[p] id. pl., absolute state . . . . אפן
אֹפִר defect. for אוֹפִיר (q. v.) . . . אפר

[אוּץ] I. *to be narrow.* Jos. 17. 15.—II. trans. *to press on, to urge.*—III. *to urge oneself, to hasten;* const. with מִן *to hasten away.* Je. 17. 16. Hiph. *to press on, urge,* const. with בְּ.

אֹצִא[q] וָ defect. for אוֹצִיא (q. v.) . . . יצא
אֲצַוֶּאָה[r] וָ Kh. אוֹצְאָה Hiph. fut. 1 pers. sing. R. יצא; K. אֲצַוֶּה (q. v.) . . . . צוה
אוֹצִיא וָ׳ Hiph. fut. 1 pers. sing.; וָ for וַ· conv. . יצא
אוֹצִיאָה id. with paragogic ה . . . . יצא
אוֹצִיאֵם[s] וָ id. with suff. 3 pers. pl. masc.; וָ for וַ· . יצא
אוֹצָר[t] noun masc. sing., dec. 2b. . . . אצר
אוֹצַר id. construct state . . . . אצר
אוֹצְרָה[u] וָ Hiph. fut. 1 pers. sing. with paragogic ה, for [אַאֲצִירָה] (§ 19. r. 8. & § 11. r. 7); וָ for וַ· אצר
אוֹצָרוֹ noun masc. sing., suff. 3 pers. sing. masc. from אוֹצָר dec. 2b. . . . . אצר
אוֹצָרוֹת[a] וָ id. pl., absolute state . . . אצר
אוֹצְרוֹת וְ׳ id. pl., construct state . . . אצר
אוֹצְרוֹתֶיךָ[y] id. pl., suff. 2 pers. sing. masc. . . אצר
אוֹצְרוֹתָם[z] id. pl., suff. 3 pers. pl. masc. . . אצר

---

[a] Ps. 38. 6. [b] Ps. 42. 10. [c] Ho. 12. 8. [d] Job 40. 16. [e] 2 Ch. 8. 18. [f] Pr. 11. 7;—& perhaps Ho. 9. 4. [g] Je. 4. 14. [h] Ps. 94. 23. [i] Ps. 105. 36. [k] Ho. 9. 15. [l] Je. 31. 18. [m] Na. 3. 2. [n] 1 Ki. 7. 30. [o] Eze. 10. 12. [p] Eze. 10. 9. [q] Eze. 28. 18. [r] Ezr. 8. 17. [s] Eze. 20. 10. [t] Pr. 21. 20. [u] Ne. 13. 13. [x] 2 Ch. 32. 27. [y] Je. 17. 3. [z] Is. 30. 6.

אֽוֹצָרֹת[a] noun m. with pl. f. term. from אוֹצָר dec. 2b. אצר

אֽוֹצְרֹתֶ֫יהָ[b] id. pl., suff. 3 pers. sing. fem. . . . אצר

אֽוֹצְרֹתֶ֫יךָ[c] וְ id. pl., suff. 2 pers. sing. masc. . . . אצר

אוֹקִיר[d] Hiph. fut. 1 pers. sing. . . . . יקר

אוֹר (§ 21. rem. 2) *to become light, to shine, to be enlightened,* and impers. *it is light.* Niph. *to become bright.* Part. *glorious.* Hiph.—I. *to give light, to enlighten, illuminate.* Meton. *to cheer, enliven,* const. with אֵל ,עַל ,בְּ ,לְ ,אֵת; הֵאִיר פָּנִים אֶל פּ׳ *to cause* one's face *to shine upon any one,* to be propitious to him.—II. *to kindle.*

אוֹר masc. dec. 1a—I. *light, lightning, luminary.* —II. Meton. *prosperity.*—III. *knowledge.*

אוּר m. dec. 1a—I. *fire.*—II. *light;* אוּר אֵשׁ *the light of fire;* הָאֻרִים וְהַתֻּמִּים *light,* i. e. *revelation and truth,* the Urim and Thummim worn by the high-priest.—III. pr. name masc. 1 Ch. 11. 35.—IV. pr. name of a city in Chaldea, fully אוּר כַּשְׂדִּים *Ur of the Chaldeans,* the native place of Abraham.

אוֹרָה fem. dec. 10.—I. *light,* Ps. 139. 12.—II. *prosperity,* Est. 8. 16.—III. *herbs.*

אוּרִי (*shining*) pr. name of several men.

אוּרִיאֵל (*light of God*) pr. n. of two different men.

אוּרִיָּה (*light of the Lord*) pr. name—I. of the husband of Bath-sheba, afterwards the wife of David. —II. of a priest in the time of Ahaz and Isaiah.

אוּרִיָּהוּ (id.) pr. name of a prophet, contemporary with Jeremiah. Je. 26. 20. sq.

יָאִיר (*he shall enlighten*) pr. name.—I. of a son of Manasseh, Nu. 32. 41.—II. of a judge of Israel, Ju. 10. 3.—Patronym. יָאִירִי, 2 Sa. 20. 26.—III. Est. 2. 5.

מָאוֹר masc. dec. 3a, pl. מְאֹרִים ,מְאוֹרוֹת.—I. *light, luminary,* the sun, the moon; מְנֹרַת הַמָּאוֹר *the candlestick* in the tabernacle.—II. *the candlestick.* Ex. 25. 6.

מְאוּרָה fem. only construct מְאוּרַת *a hole, viper's den,* Is. 11. 8.

אוֹר[e] וְ'[f], וְ'[g] Kal pret. 3 pers. sing. masc. (§ 21. rem. 2); וָ see lett. ו . . . . . אור

אוֹר וְ'[h], וְ' noun masc. sing. dec. 1a; וָ id. . אור

אֽוֹר noun masc. sing. dec. 1a; also pr. name . אור

אוֹרֵב וְ'[i] Kal part. act. sing. masc. dec. 7b. . ארב

אוֹרִדְךָ[k] וְ Hiph. fut. 1 pers. sing., suff. 2 pers. sing. m. ירד

אוֹרָה[l] noun fem. sing. . . . . . אור

אוֹרֶה Hiph. fut. 1 pers. sing. . . . . ירה

אוֹרֵהוּ[m] n. m. s. suff. 3 pers. s. masc. from אוֹר dec. 1a אור

אוֹרוֹ וְ'[n] id., suff. 3 pers. sing. masc. . . . אור

אֹ֫רוּ[o] Kal pret. 3 pers. pl. (§ 21. rem. 2) . אור

אוֹרוּ[p] *fully* for אֹרוּ Kal imp. pl. masc. . . . ארר

א֫וֹרִי[mm] Kal imp. sing. masc. (§ 21. rem. 2) . אור

אוֹרִי[q] noun m. s., suff. 1 pers. s. from אוֹר dec. 1a. אור

אוּרִי אוּרִיאֵל, וְ' pr. names masc. . . . אור

אוֹרִיד וְ Hiph. fut. 1 pers. sing. . . . ירד

אוֹרִידְךָ id., suff. 2 pers. sing. masc. . . . ירד

אוֹרִידֵם id., suff. 3 pers. pl. masc. . . . ירד

אוּרִיָּה אוּרִיָּהוּ, וְ' pr. names masc. . . . אור

אוֹרֶיךָ[r] וְ noun masc. pl., suff. 2 pers. sing. masc. from אוֹר dec. 1a. . . . אור

אוֹרִים[s] noun masc., pl. of אוֹר dec. 1a. . . אור

אוֹרִישׁ[t] Hiph. fut. 1 pers. sing. . . . ירש

אוֹרִישֵׁם[u] id., suff. 3 pers. pl. masc. . . . ירש

אוֹרְךָ, אוֹרֶ֫ךָ[x] } noun masc. sing., suff. 2 pers. sing. masc. from אוֹר dec. 1a. . . . } אור

אוֹרְךָ[y] וְ Hiph. fut. 1 pers. sing. (אוֹרֶה), suff. 2 pers. sing. masc. (§ 25. No. 2e. § 24. rem. 21) ירה

אוֹרֵךְ[z] noun masc. sing., suff. 2 pers. sing. fem. from אוֹר dec. 1a. . . . . . אור

אוֹרָם id., suff. 3 pers. pl. masc. . . . אור

אִוָּרֵשׁ[a] Niph. fut. 1 pers. sing. (§ 20. rem. 7) . ירש

אוֹרִשֶׁנּוּ[b] וְ Hiph. fut. 1 pers. sing., suff. 3 pers. sing. masc. (§ 2. rem. 3) . . . ירש

אוֹרֹת[c] noun pl. fem. from אוֹרָה or אוֹר . . אור

אוֹשִׁיבְךָ[d] Hiph. fut. 1 pers. sing., suff. 2 pers. s. masc. ישב

אוֹשִׁיעַ Hiph. fut. 1 pers. sing. . . . ישע

אוֹשִׁיעָה[e] וְ id., with paragogic ה; וָ for וַ . . ישע

אוֹשִׁיעֵךְ[f] id., suff. 2 pers. sing. fem. . . ישע

אוֹשִׁיעֵם[g] id., suff. 3 pers. pl. masc. . . ישע

אִוָּשֵׁעַ וְ'[h] Niph. fut. 1 pers. sing. (§ 20. rem. 7) for [אִוָּשֵׁעַ] (§ 15. rem. 1) . . . ישע

אִוָּשֵׁעָה[i] וְ id. with paragogic ה for [אִוָּשְׁעָה] . ישע

אֲוַשֵּׁר[k] Kh. אוֹשֵׁר, K. אֲיַשֵּׁר Hiph. or Piel fut. 1 p. s. ישר

אוּת or **אוֹת**. Niph. *to consent, to agree to* any one.

אַוַּת noun fem. sing., construct of [אַוָּה] dec. 10. אוה

אוֹת noun com. sing. dec. 1a. . . . אוה

אִוְּתָה Piel pret. 3 pers. sing. fem. . . . אוה

אוֹתָהּ וְ' as if [אוֹת] with suff. 3 pers. sing. fem., see אֵת sign of the accus. (§ 5. parad.) . את

אוֹתָם id., suff. 3 pers. pl. masc. . . . את

אוֹתָן[m] id., suff. 3 pers. pl. fem. . . . את

אוֹתוֹ id., suff. 3 pers. sing. masc. . . . את

אוֹתִי וְ' id., suff. 1 pers. sing. . . . את

[a] Je. 51. 13. [b] Je. 50. 37. [c] Je. 15. 13. [d] Is. 13. 12. [e] Ge. 44. 3. [f] 1 Sa. 29. 10. [g] Pr. 4. 18. [h] Is. 5. 30. [i] Ezr. 8. 31. [k] 1 Sa. 30. 15. [l] Est. 8. 16. [m] Job 25. 3. [n] Job 37. 3. [o] 1 Sa. 14. 29. [p] Ju. 5. 23. [q] Ps. 27. 1. [r] De. 33. 8. [s] Ps. 136. 7. [t] Ex. 34. 24. [u] Jos. 13. 6. [x] Ps. 43. 3. [y] Ps. 32. 8. [z] Is. 60. 1. [a] Pr. 30. 9. [b] Nu. 14. 12. [c] Is. 26. 19. [d] Ho. 12. 10. [e] Ju. 10. 12. [f] 2 Ki. 6. 27. [g] Ho. 1. 7. [h] Je. 17. 14. [i] Ps. 119. 117. [k] Is. 45. 2. [l] Eze. 23. 45. [m] Eze. 23. 47. [mm] Is. 60. 1.

אוֹתִיהָ[a] Piel pret. 1 pers. sing [אִוִּיתִי], suff. 3 p. s. f. . אוה

אוֹתִיר[b] Hiph. fut. 1 pers. sing. . . . . . יתר

אוֹתְךָ as if [אוֹת] with suff. 2 pers. sing. masc., see אֵת sign of the accus. (§ 5. parad.) . את

אוֹתָךְ id., suff. 2 pers. sing. fem., or אוֹתָךְ in pause 2 pers. sing. masc. . . . . . את

אוֹתְכֶם[c] id., suff. 2 pers. pl. masc. . . . . את

אוֹתָם ו׳ id., suff. 3 pers. pl. masc. . . . . . את

אוֹתָנָה[d] id., suff. 3 pers. pl. fem. (§ 5. rem. 4) . את

אוֹתָנוּ ו׳ id., suff. 1 pers. pl. . . . . . את

אוּתַר[e] וָ Niph. fut. 1 pers. s. (§ 20. r. 7); וָ for וַ conv. יתר

אוֹתֹת noun masc., pl. of אוֹת (q. v.) dec. 1 a. . אוה

אוֹתֹתָם[f] id., suff. 3 pers. pl. masc. (§ 4. rem. 2) אוה

אָז ו׳ adv. *then, at that time,* referring either to past or future time. מֵאָז & מִן־אָז prop. *from then,* hence—I. *from ancient times, from old.* —II. *from the time, since.*

אֱזַי adv. *then, at that time,* Ps. 124. 3, 4, 5.

אֲזָא, אֲזָה Chald. *to kindle.*

אָזֹב Root not used, whence

אֵזוֹב, אֵזֹב masc. *hyssop.*

אֶזְבָּי (perh. *dwarf*) pr. name, masc. 1 Ch. 11. 37.

אֶזְבַּח[g] Kal fut. 1 pers. sing. . . . . זבח

אֲזַבֵּחַ[h] Piel fut. 1 pers. sing. . . . . . זבח

אֶזְבְּחָה ו׳[i] id. with paragogic ה . . . . זבח

אֶזְבָּי pr. name masc. for אֶזְבַּי . . . . אזב

[אֲזַד] Chald. *to go away, depart,* only Da. 2. 5, 8, אַזְדָּא part. f. for אָזְדָה from אֲזַד masc. (§ 67 rem.)

אַזְדָּא Chald. see the preced. R.

אֵזֵה[k] Ch. Peal part. pass. s. m. (§ 56. No. 2. § 23. r. 8) אזא

אֵזוֹב ו׳[l] noun masc. sing. . . . . . אזב

אָזוּר[m] Kal part. pass. sing. masc. . . . . אזר

אֵזוֹר ו׳[n] noun masc. sing. . . . . . אזר

אֱזַי adv. . . . . אז

אָזִין[o] for [אַאֲזִין] Hiph. fut. 1 pers. sing. (§ 19. r. 8) אזן

אַזְכִּיר Hiph. fut. 1 pers. sing. . . . . זכר

אֶזְכִּיר[p] Kheth id., K. אֶזְכּוֹר Kal fut. 1 pers. sing. זכר

אַזְכִּירָה[q] Hiph. fut. 1 pers. sing. with parag. ה . זכר

אֶזְכֹּר, אֶזְכְּרִי־ ו׳, וָ[r] } Kal fut. 1 pers. sing. (§ 8. rem. 18); וָ for וַ conv. . . . . . } זכר

אֶזְכְּרָה id. with paragogic ה . . . . . זכר

אֶזְכָּרְךָ[s] id., suff. 2 pers. sing. masc. . . . . זכר

אֶזְכְּרֵכִי[t] id., suff. 2 pers. sing. fem. (§ 2. rem. 2) . זכר

אֶזְכְּרֶנּוּ[u] id., suff. 3 pers. sing. masc. . . . . זכר

אַזְכָּרָתָהּ[x] n. f. s., suff. 3 pers. s. f. from רָה׳ dec. 10. זכר

אָזַל[y] *to go away, to depart,* Pu. part. מְאוּזָּל for מְאֻזָּל *something spun,* Talm. אַזְלָאָה *weaver.*

אֲזַל Chald. id. *to go away, to depart.*

אֶזֶל *departure,* see אֶבֶן אֶזֶל

אוּזָל pr. name masc. Ge. 10. 27.

אֲזַל Chald. Peal pret. 3 pers. sing. masc. . אזל

אֱזֶל־[z] Chald. Peal imp. sing. masc. with Mak. for [אֱזַל by Syr. for אֲזַל] . . . . אזל

אֹזֵל[a] וְ Kal part. act. sing. masc. . . . . אזל

אֲזַלוּ[b] Chald. Peal 3 pers. pl. masc. . . . אזל

אָזְלוּ[c] Kal pret. 3 pers. pl. . . . . . אזל

אֲזַלְנָא[d] Chald. Peal preter. 1 pers. sing. . . אזל

אָזְלַת[e] Kal preter. 3 pers. fem. sing.; Milêl before monos. for [אָזְלָה=אָזְלַת § 8. rem. 3] . אזל

אֲזַמֵּר Piel fut. 1 pers. sing. . . . . . זמר

אֲזַמְּרָה ו׳[f], אֲזַמֵּרָה ב׳ } id. with paragogic ה; וָ before (-:) . זמר

אֲזַמֶּרְךָּ[g] ב׳[h], אֲזַמְּרֶךָּ[i] } id., suff. 2 pers. sing. masc. (§ 16. rem. 15, and § 2. rem. 3); וָ id. . } זמר

I. **אָזַן** Kal not used. Hiph. denom. of אֹזֶן, *to give ear, to listen, to attend,* const. with עַל ,עַד ,אֶל ,לְ.

II. **אָזַן** Kal not used. Pi. *to weigh,* trop. *to consider,* Ec. 12. 9.

אָזֵן masc. dec. 5 c, a kind of instrument or weapon, only De. 23. 14, Chald. אֲזַן *to be armed.*

אֹזֶן fem. dec. 6 c, *the ear,* בְּאָזְנֵי פ׳ *in the ears,* i. e. in the hearing *of any one.*

אָזְנִי (*hearing well*) pr. name masc. Nu. 26. 16.

אֲזַנְיָה (whom *the Lord hears*) pr. n. m. Ne. 10. 10.

אֻזֵּן שֶׁאֱרָה pr. name of a city built by Sherah, 1 Ch. 7. 24.

אַזְנוֹת־תָּבוֹר (*ears,* i. e. *summits of Tabor*) pr. name of a city, Jos. 19. 34.

יַאֲזַנְיָה (whom *the Lord hears*) pr. name of two different men.

יַאֲזַנְיָהוּ (id.) pr. name masc. 2 Ki. 25. 23, called יְזַנְיָה יְזַנְיָהוּ Je. 40. 8; 42. 1.

מֹאזְנַיִם dual (of מֹאזֶן dec. 7 b) *balances, a balance.*

מֹאזְנַיִן Chald. id. only emph. בְּמֹאזַנְיָא, Da. 5. 27.

אִזֵּן[k] וְ Piel pret. 3 pers. sing. masc. . . . אזן

אֹזֶן ו׳[l] noun fem. sing. dec. 6 c. . . . אזן

אֻזֵּן pr. name, see אֻזֵּן שֶׁאֱרָה . . . . אזן

אָזְנוֹ[m] Kh. אָזְנוֹ q. v., K. אָזְנִי (q. v.) . . . אזן

אָזְנוֹ n. fem. s., suff. 3 pers. s. m. from אֹזֶן dec. 6 c. אזן

אַזְנוֹת pr. name, see אַזְנוֹת תָּבוֹר . . . אזן

---

[a] Ps. 132. 14. [b] Eze. 39. 28. [c] Jo. 23. 15. [d] Eze. 34. 21. [e] 1 Ki. 19. 10, 14. [f] Ps. 74. 4. [g] Ps. 116. 17. [h] 2 Ch. 28. 23. [i] Ps. 27. 6. [k] Da. 3. 22. [l] Nu. 19. 6. [m] 2 Ki. 1. 8. [n] 2 Ki. 1. 8. [o] Job 32. 11. [p] Ps. 77. 12. [q] Ps. 45. 18. [r] Ex. 6. 5. [s] Je. 31. 34. [t] Ps. 42. 7. [u] Ps. 137. 6. [x] Le. 2. 2, 9. [y] 1 Sa. 9. 7. [z] Ezr. 5. 15. [a] Pr. 20. 14. [b] Ezr. 4. 23. [c] Job 14. 11. [d] Ezr. 5. 8. [e] De. 32. 36. [f] Ps. 57. 8. [g] Ps. 57. 10. [h] Ps. 108. 4. [i] Ps. 138. 1. [k] Ec. 12. 9. [l] Pr. 18. 15. [m] 1 Sa. 22. 17.

אָזְנַי[pp] | ⎫ noun fem. dual, suff. 1 pers. sing. from ⎫ אזן
אָזְנָי[a] ן׳ | ⎭ אֹזֶן dec. 6c. . . . . ⎭

אָזְנִי id. sing., suff. 1 pers. sing. . . . . אזן

אָזְנֵי ן id. dual, construct state . . . אזן

אֲזַנְיָה pr. name masc. . . . . . אזן

[b] אָזְנֵיהֶם [c] ן׳ noun fem. dual, suff. 3 pers. pl. masc. from אֹזֶן dec. 6c. . . . . . אזן

אָזְנָיו ן׳ id. dual, suff. 3 pers. sing. masc. . . אזן

אָזְנֶיךָ[qq] ן׳ id. dual, suff. 2 pers. sing. masc. . . אזן

אָזְנַיִךְ[d] ⎫
אָזְנַיִךְ[e] ן ⎭ id. dual, suff. 2 pers. sing. fem. . . אזן

אָזְנַיִם[f] ⎫
אָזְנָיִם ן׳ ⎭ id. dual, absolute state . . אזן

[g] אֲזֵנֶךָ for [אֲזֵנְךָ] noun masc. sing., suff. 2 pers. sing. masc. from [אָזֵן] dec. 5c. . . . אזן

אָזְנֶךָ defect. for אָזְנֶיךָ q. v., or in pause for the foll. אזן

אָזְנְךָ noun f. s., suff. 2 p. s. m. from אֹזֶן, dec. 6c. אזן

אָזְנֵךְ[h] id., suff. 2 pers. sing. fem. . . . . אזן

אָזְנְכֶם id., suff. 2 pers. pl. masc. . . . . אזן

אָזְנָם id., suff. 3 pers. pl. masc. . . . . אזן

[i] אֶזְעֹם Kal fut. 1 pers. sing. . . . . . זעם

אֶזְעַק ⎫ Kal fut. 1 pers. sing. (§ 8. rem. 15); ⎫
אֶזְעָק ן׳ ⎭ ן for ·ן conversive. . . . ⎭ זעק

[אָזַר] I. *to bind, gird about,* spoken of a girdle, a garment, and trop. of strength.—II. *to gird up,* spoken of the loins. Niph. *to be girded.* Pi. *to gird,* with a double acc. of the person, and of the girdle. Hithp. *to gird oneself.*

אֵזוֹר (Syriacism for אֲזוֹר) m.—I. *girdle, belt.*—II. *fetters.*

אֱזָר־ Kal imp. sing. masc. with Mak. for [אֱזֹר] (§ 8. rem. 18) . . . . . . אזר

אֲזָרֶה Piel fut. 1 pers. sing. for [אֲזָרֶּה] . . זרה

אָזְרוּ[k] Kal pret. 3 pers. pl. . . . . . אזר

[l] אֶזְרֵם ן Kal fut. 1 pers. sing. [אֶזְרֶה], suff. 3 pers. pl. masc. (§ 24. rem. 21); ן for ·ן conv. זרה

[m] אֶזְרְעָה Kal fut. 1 pers. sing. with paragogic ה . זרע

[n] אֶזְרֹעִי ן noun fem. sing., suff. 1 pers. s. from אֶזְרוֹעַ dec. 1b. . . . . זרע

[o] אֶזְרָעֵם ן Kal fut. 1 pers. sing. [אֶזְרַע], suff. 3 pers. pl. masc. (§ 16. rem. 12) . . . זרע

אָח [p] ן׳, [q] ן׳ masc. irreg. (§ 45).—I. *brother.*—II. *relative, kinsman.*—III. *countryman.*—IV. *friend.*—V. *fellow,* used both of persons and things; אִישׁ אֶל אָחִיו *one towards another.*

אַח Chald. *brother,* Ezr. 7. 18.

אַחְאָב (*brother of the father*) pr. name—I. of a king of Israel.—II. of a false prophet, Je. 29. 21, called אֶחָב *v.* 22.

אַחְבָּן (*brother of the wise* בָּן from בִּין) pr. name masc. 1 Ch. 2. 29.

אֲחוּמַי (*brother of water*) pr. name m. 1 Ch. 4. 2.

אֶחָי (*brother,* comp. אֵבִי) pr. name of a man.

אֲחִיאָם (*brother of the mother, uncle* אָם i. q. אֵם) pr. name of a man.

אֲחִיָּה (*friend of the Lord*) pr. name of several men, especially—I. of a priest in the time of Saul, 1 Sa. 14. 3, 18.—II. of a prophet in the time of Jeroboam, called also אֲחִיָּהוּ.

אֲחִיהוּד (*friend of the Jews,* for אֲחִי יְהוּד) pr. name masc. Nu. 34. 27.

אַחְיוֹ (*brotherly,* for אַחְיוֹן) pr. name of several men.

אֲחִיחֻד (*brother of union,* for אֲחִי יְחוּד) pr. name masc. 1 Ch. 8. 7.

אֲחִיטוּב (*brother of goodness*) pr. name of several men.

אֲחִילוּד (*brother of Lud*) pr. name of the father of Jehoshaphat.

אֲחִימוֹת (*father of death*) pr. name m. 1 Ch. 6. 10.

אֲחִימֶלֶךְ (*brother of the king*) pr. name—I. of a priest and friend of David put to death by Saul.—II. of a high-priest in the time of David.

אֲחִימָן (*the brother's likeness,* מָן root מוּן) pr. name—I. one of the Anakims.—II. 1 Ch. 9. 17.

אֲחִימַעַץ (*brother of anger*) pr. name masc.—I. 1 Sa. 14. 50.—II. son of Zadok the high-priest in the time of David.

אַחְיָן (*brotherly*) pr. name masc. 1 Ch. 7. 19.

אֲחִינָדָב (*noble* or *liberal brother*) pr. name masc. 1 Ki. 4. 14.

אֲחִינֹעַם (*brother of pleasantness*) pr. name fem. —I. of a wife of Saul, 1 Sa. 14. 50.—II. of a wife of David, comp. 1 Sa. 25. 43.

אֲחִיסָמָךְ (*brother of support*) pr. name of a man.

אֲחִיעֶזֶר (*brother of help*) pr. name—I. of a chief of the tribe of Dan.—II. of an ally of David, 1 Ch. 12. 3.

אֲחִיקָם (*the rising brother,* קָם part. of קוּם) pr. name of a man.

אֲחִירָם (*exalted brother* רָם part. of רוּם) pr. name masc. Nu. 26. 38. Patronym. אֲחִירָמִי ibid.

אֲחִירַע (*unfortunate brother,* i. e. *unfortunate*) pr. name of a chief of the tribe of Naphtali.

[a] 2 Ch. 7. 15. [b] Mi. 7. 16. [c] Zec. 7. 11. [d] Eze. 16. 12. [e] Eze. 23. 25. [f] Eze. 24. 26. [g] De. 23. 14. [h] Ps. 45. 11. [i] Nu. 23. 8. [k] 1 Sa. 2. 4. [l] Je. 15. 7. [m] Job 31. 8. [n] Job 31. 22. [o] Zec. 10. 9. [p] Pr. 17. 17. [pp] Ps. 92. 12. [q] Ec. 4. 8. [qq] Ps. 130. 2.

אֲחִישַׁחַר (*brother of the morning*) pr. name masc. 1 Ch. 7. 10.

אֲחִישָׁר (*brother of the singer*, שָׁר part. of שִׁיר) pr. name masc. 1 Ki. 4. 6.

אֲחִיתֹ֫פֶל (*brother of folly*) pr. name of a courtier of David and conspirator with Absalom.

אַחֲוָה fem. *brotherhood*, Zec. 11. 14.

אָחוֹת fem. irreg. (§ 45).—I. *sister*.—II. *relative, kinswoman*.—III. *countrywoman*, Nu. 25. 18.—IV. *an ally*.—V. *fellow*, of persons and things, אִשָּׁה אֶל אֲחוֹתָהּ *one to another*.

אָהּ[a] interj. expressive of grief, *ah! alas!*

אֹחַ m., only pl. אֹחִים, a kind of *howling animals*. Is. 13. 21.

אַח[b] apocopated for אֶחָד . . . . . אחד

אַחְאָב וְ' pr. name masc. . . . . . אח

אֵחָבֵא[c] וָ for [אֶחָבֵא] Niph. fut. 1 pers. sing.; וָ for וַ· conversive . . . . . חבא

אַחְבִּא[d] וָ for [אַחְבִּיא] Hiph. fut. 1 pers. sing.; וָ id. חבא

אַחְבִּירָה[e] Hiph. fut. 1 pers. sing. with paragogic ה חבר

אֶחְבֹּל[f] Kal fut. 1 pers. sing. . . . . . חבל

אַחְבָּן pr. name masc. . . . . . . אח

אֶחֱבֹשׁ[g] Kal fut. 1 pers. sing. (§ 13. rem. 4, 5) . חבש

אֶחְבְּשָׁה[h] id. with paragogic ה . . . . חבש

אֶחְבְּשֵׁךְ[i] וָ id., suff. 2 pers. sing. fem.; וָ for וַ· conv. חבש

אֶחָד וְ' irr. constr. אַחַד; אַחַת and in pause אֶחָת fem. (§ 45).—I. *one*.—II. *first*, only in the enumerating of time, where the cardinal stands for the ordinal, בְּאֶחָד לַחֹדֶשׁ *on the first* (day) *of the month*; שְׁנַת אַחַת *the first year*.—III. *some one, any one*; אַחַד הָעָם *one of the people*, אֶחָד מֵאֶחָיו *one of his brethren*, לֹא אֶחָד, אֵין אֶחָד *no one*. Hence—IV. as the indef. art., אַיִל אֶחָד *a ram*, נָבִיא אֶחָד *a prophet*, a certain prophet.—V. אֶחָד־אֶחָד *one-another*; אִישׁ אֶחָד אִישׁ אֶחָד לְמַטֶּה *one man from each tribe*.—V. כְּאֶחָד, כְּאַחַת *as one, together, at once*.—VI. fem. אַחַת, *one time, once*; (*a*) בְּאַחַת *at once*.—Pl. אֲחָדִים *the same*; (*b*) *joined into one*; (*c*) *a few*.

אִחֵד Hithpa. *to unite oneself*, Eze. 21. 21.

אֵהוּד (*union*) pr. name masc., called also אֲחִי, comp. 1 Ch. 8. 6, with Ge. 46. 21.

אַח (apocopated for אֶחָד) *one*. Eze. 18. 10.

חַד Eze. 33. 30, by Chaldaism for אֶחָד *one*.

חַד Ch. emph. חַדָא, חֲדָה.—I. *one*.—II. *first*.—III. חַד שִׁבְעָה עַל דִּי *seven times more*.—IV. כַּחֲדָה *at the same time, together*.

אַחַד[k] וְ' id. construct state . . . . . אחד

אֲחָדִים id. pl., absolute state . . . . . אחד

אֶחְדָּל Kal fut. 1 pers. sing. for [אֶחְדַּל] (§ 13. r. 5) חדל

אֶחְדָּלָה[l] וָ id. with paragogic ה (§ 13. rem. 5) . חדל

אָחוּ[m] *grass, reeds, bulrushes*, an Egyptian word.

אֲחַוֵּא[n] Ch. Pael fut. 1 pers. sing. . . . . חוא

אֵחוּד pr. name, masc. . . . . . . אחד

אָחוּדָה[o] Kal fut. 1 pers. sing. with paragogic ה . חוד

אֲחַוֶּה[p] Piel fut. 1 pers. sing. . . . . . חוה

אָחוּז[q] Kal part. p. sing. masc. dec. 3a. . . . אחז

אֲחוּזִים* id. pl. absolute state. *Eze. 41. 6, 6. . אחז

אָחוֹחַ וְ pr. name, masc.; וּ before (-:) . . . אחח

אַחֲוָיַת[r] וְ Chald. noun fem. sing., constr. of [אַחֲוָיָה] dec. 8a. . . . . חוה

אֲחַוְּךָ[s] וַ Piel fut. 1 pers. sing. [אֲחַוֶּה] suff. 2 pers. sing. masc. (§ 2. rem. 3); וָ for וַ· conv.

אֲחַוְּךָ[t] (as above) . . . . חוה

אֲחוּמַי pr. name masc. . . . . . . אח

אָחוּס Kal fut. 1 pers. sing. . . . . . חוס

אָחוֹר וְ' noun masc. sing. dec. 3a., used also as an adv. . . . . אחר

אָחוֹת n. fem. sing. contr. for [אֲחֶוֶת] irr. (§ 45) אח

אֲחוֹת וְ' id. construct state; וּ before (-:) . . אח

אֲחֹתָהּ id., suff. 3 pers. sing. fem. . . . . אח

אַחֲוָתִי[u] וְ noun fem. sing., suff. 1 pers. s. from [אַחֲוָה] dec. 10 (§ 43. rem. 3) . . . . . חוה

אַחוֹתַי[v] n. f. pl., suff. 1 pers. s.; Kh. אַחוֹתַי as if from a sing. [אָחָה], K. אַחְיוֹתַי as if from [אַחְיָה] see אָחוֹת irr. § 45 . . . . . . אח

אֲחוֹתִי id. sing., suff. 1 pers. sing. . . . . אח

אַחְיוֹתַיִךְ[w] וְ' id. pl., suff. 2 pers. sing. fem. as if from a sing. [אָחָה]; וּ before (-:) . . . . . אח

אֲחוֹתֵךְ[x] וְ' id. sing., suff. 2 pers. sing. fem.; וּ id. אח

אֲחֹתְךָ[a] id. sing., suff. 2 pers. sing. masc. . . . אח

אֲחוֹתָם id. sing., suff. 3 pers. pl. masc. . . . אח

אֲחֹתֵנוּ[b] id. sing., suff. 1 pers pl. . . . . . אח

אָחַז וְ' fut. יֹאחַז and יֶאֱחֹז.—I. *to seize*, construed with acc. and בְּ.—II. *to take, catch*, in hunting.—III. *to hold*, const. with בְּ; אֲחֻזֵי חֶרֶב *holding the sword*.—IV. *to join*.—V. *to shut up, close*. Ne. 7. 3.—VI. *to cover, overlay*. 1 Ki. 6. 10.—VII. *to draw out by lot*. Niph.—I. *to be caught*. Ec. 9. 12.—II. *to be held*. Ge. 22. 13.—III. *to take or have possession*. Pi. *to shut up*. Job 26. 9. Hoph. *to be joined, fastened*.

---

[a] Eze. 6. 11; & 21. 20. [b] Eze. 18. 10 [c] Ge. 3. 10. [d] 1 Ki. 18. 13. [e] Job 16. 4. [f] Job 34. 31. [g] Eze. 34. 16. [h] 2 Sa. 19. 27. [i] Eze. 16. 10. [k] Ge. 37. 9. [l] Job 16. 6. [m] Job 8. 11. [n] Da. 2. 24. [o] Ju. 14. 12. [p] Job 32, 10. 17. [q] Est. 1. 6. [r] Da. 5. 12. [s] Job 36. 2. [t] Job 15. 17. [u] Job 13. 17. [v] Jos. 2. 13. [w] Eze. 16. 51, 61. [y] Eze. 16. 55. [x] Eze. 16. 46, 46. [a] Le. 18. 9, 11. [b] Ge. 34. 31.

אָחָז (*possessor*) pr. name—I. of a king of Judah.—II. of another person, compare 1 Ch. 8. 35.

אֲחֻזָּה fem. dec. 10, *possession*.

אַחְזַי pr. name masc. Ne. 11. 13, called יַחְזֵרָה in 1 Ch. 9. 12.

אֲחַזְיָה, אֲחַזְיָהוּ (whom *the Lord holds*) pr. name —I. of a son of Ahab king of Israel.—II. of a son of Joram king of Judah.

אֲחֻזָּם (*their possession*) pr. name m. 1 Ch. 4. 6.

אֲחֻזַּת (*possession*) pr. name masc. Ge. 26. 26.

[a] אֶחַז Kal fut. 1 pers. sing. for [אֶחֱז] apoc. for אֶחֱזֶה, אֶחֱזֶה . . . . . חזה

אָחָז ו' pr. name masc. . . . . . אחז

[b] אֱחֹז Kal inf. construct . . . . . אחז

אֱחֹז ו id. imp. sing. masc.; וֶ before (־:) . . אחז

אָחֻז ו' [c] id. part. pass. sing. masc. dec. 3 a. . . אחז

[d] אֹחֵז id. part. act. sing. masc. . . . . אחז

[e] אֹחֵז וָ id. fut. 1 pers. sing.; וָ for ·וַ conv. . אחז

אָחֲזָה id. preter. 3 pers. sing. fem. . . . אחז

אֲחֻזָּה [f] ו' noun fem. sing. dec. 10; וַ before (־:) . אחז

אֶחֱזֶה [g] ו' Kal fut. 1 pers. sing.; וָ for ·וַ conv. חזה

[h] אֹחֲזָה [i] ו' Kal fut. 1 pers. sing. with parag. ה; וָ id. אחז

[k] אָחֲזוּ id. preter. 3 pers. pl. . . . . . אחז

[l] אֶחֱזוּ, [m] אֶחֱזוּ ו } id. imp. pl. masc. (§ 8. rem. 12); וֶ before (־:) . . . . } אחז

[n] אֲחָזוּנִי id. preter. 3 pers. pl., suff. 1 pers. sing. . אחז

אַחְזַי pr. name masc. . . . . . אחז

[o] אֲחֻזֵי Kal part. p. pl. construct from אָחוּז dec. 3 a; Milêl before penacute, (חֶרֶב) . . אחז

[p] אֶחֱזִי־ וֶ id. imp. sing. fem. (§ 13. rem. 3, & § 8. r. 12) אחז

אֲחַזְיָה ו', אֲחַזְיָהוּ ו', אֲחֻזָּם pr. names masc. . אחז

[q] אֲחָזַנִי Kal preter. 3 pers. sing. masc., suff. 1 pers. sing. אחז

[r] אַחֲזֵק וְ Hiph. fut. 1 pers. sing., ap. for [אַחֲזִיק] (§ 11. rem. 6) . . . . . חזק

אֲחַזֵּק Piel fut. 1 pers. sing. . . . . חזק

[s] אֲחַזְּקֶנּוּ id., suff. 3 pers. sing. masc. . . . חזק

אֲחֻזַּת וַ' noun fem. sing., construct of זָּה' dec. 10; וַ before (־:) . . . . . . אחז

אֲחֻזַּת וַ pr. name masc.; וַ id. . . . . אחז

[t] אֹחֶזֶת Kal part. act. s. fem., from אֹחֵז m. (§ 8. r. 19) אחז

אָחַזְתָּ Kal preter. 2 pers. sing. masc. . . . אחז

[u] אֲחָזַתְהָ id. preter. 3 pers. sing. f., suff. 3 pers. sing. f. אחז

אֲחֻזָּתוֹ noun fem. sing., suff. 3 pers. sing. masc. from אֲחֻזָּה dec. 10. . . . . . אחז

[x] אֲחַזְתִּיו Kal preter. 1 pers. sing., suff. 3 pers. sing. m. אחז

[y] אֲחֻזָּתְךָ וַ noun fem. sing., suff. 2 pers. sing. masc. from אֲחֻזָּה dec. 10; וַ before (־:) . . . אחז

אֲחֻזַּתְכֶם id., suff. 2 pers. pl. masc. . . . אחז

[a] אֲחָזָתַם Kal preter. 3 pers. sing. fem., suff. 3 pers. pl. masc. (§ 16. rem. 2) . . . אחז

אֲחֻזָּתָם וַ' noun fem. sing., suff. 3 pers. pl. masc. from אֲחֻזָּה dec. 10. . . . . . אחז

[b] אֲחָזַתְנִי Kal preter. 3 pers. sing. fem., suff. 1 pers. sing. אחז

אחח Root not used; Arab. *to be warm, hot.*

אָח masc. *fire-pot* or *pan*, for warming rooms. Jer. 36. 22, 23.

אֲחוֹחַ pr. name masc. 1 Ch. 8. 4, for which *v.* 7, אֲחִיָּה.—Patronym. אֲחֹחִי. 2 Sa. 23. 9, 28.

אֵחִי pr. name masc. Ge. 46. 21.

[c] אֶחֱטָא Kal fut. 1 pers. sing. . . . . . חטא

אֲחִטוּב defect. for אֲחִיטוּב (q. v.) . . . אח

[d] אֶחֱטָם־ for [אֶחְטֹם] Kal fut. 1 pers. sing. . . חטם

[e] אֲחַטֶּנָּה for [אֲחַטְּאֶנָּה] Piel fut. 1 pers. sing., suff. 3 pers. sing. fem. . . . . . חטא

אַחַי וְ' noun masc. pl., suff. 1 pers. sing. [for אַחַי], from אָח irr. (§ 45) . . . . אח

אֲחֵי id. pl., construct state . . . . אח

אָחִי id. sing., suff. 1 pers. sing. . . . . אח

אֲחִי [f] וַ' id. sing., construct state.; also pr. n. m. . אח

אָחִי in pause for אַחַי (§ 45) . . . . אח

אֲחִי pr. name masc. see אֲחוֹחַ . . . . אחח

אֲחִיאָם pr. name masc. . . . . . אח

[g] אֲחִידָן Chald. noun fem., pl. of [אֲחִידָא] dec. 8 a. . חוד

[h] אֲחַיֶּה [i] וַ' Piel fut. 1 pers. sing.; וַ for וְ . . חיה

אַחֶיהָ noun masc. pl., suff. 3 pers. sing. fem. [for אַחֶיהָ] from אָח irr. (§ 45) . . . אח

אֲחִיָּה וַ' pr. name masc.; וַ before (־:) . . אח

אָחִיהָ noun masc. sing., suff. 3 pers. sing. fem. from אָח irr. (§ 45) . . . . . . אח

אֶחְיֶה וְ' Kal fut. 1 pers. sing. . . . . חיה

אָחִיהוּ noun masc. sing., suff. 3 pers. sing. masc. from אָח irr. (§ 45) . . . . . . אח

אֲחִיָּהוּ וַ', אֲחִיהוּד pr. names masc. . . . אח

אֲחֵיהֶם וְ' noun masc. pl., suff. 3 pers. pl. masc. from אָח irr. (§ 45); וַ before (־:) . . . אח

אֲחִיהֶם id. sing., suff. 3 pers. pl. masc. . . . אח

אָחִיו וְ' id. sing., suff. 3 pers. sing. masc. . . אח

אֶחָיו וְ' id. pl., suff. 3 pers. s. m. [for אַחָיו § 45] אח

אַחְיוֹ וְ pr. name masc. . . . . . אח

[k] אַחְיוֹתֵךְ noun fem. pl., suff. 2 pers. sing. f. as if from [אֲחָיָה] see אָחוֹת irreg. (§ 45, for suff. see § 4. rem. 2) . . . . . . אח

אֲחִיטוּב, אֲחִיחֻד & וַ' pr. names masc. . . אח

---

[a] Job 23. 9. [b] 1 Ki. 6. 6. [c] 1 Ch. 24. 6. [d] 2 Ch. 25. 5. [e] Ju. 20. 6. [f] Eze. 44. 28. [g] Pr. 24. 32. [h] Ca. 7. 9. [i] 2 Sa. 4. 10. [k] Job 18. 20. [l] Ca. 2. 15. [m] Ne. 7. 3. [n] Is. 21. 3. [o] Ca. 3. 8. [p] Ru. 3. 15. [q] 2 Sa. 1. 9. [r] Is. 42. 6. [s] Is. 22. 21. [t] Ge. 25. 26. [u] Je. 49. 24. [x] Ca. 3. 4. [y] Ps. 2. 8. [a] Ps. 48. 7. [b] Ps. 119. 53. [c] Ps. 119. 11. [d] Is. 48. 9. [e] Ge. 31. 39. [f] Ge. 14. 13. [g] Da. 5. 12. [h] Je. 49. 11. [i] De. 32. 39. [k] Eze. 16. 52.

אַחֶיךָ וְ' noun masc. pl., suff. 2 pers. sing. masc. [for אַחֶיךָ] from אָח irreg. (§ 45) . . . אח

אָחִיךָ id. sing., suff. 2 pers. sing. masc. . . . אח

[a] אַחַיִךְ id. pl., suff. 2 pers. sing. fem. for [אַחַיִךְ § 45] אח

אָחִיךְ id. sing., suff. 2 pers. sing. fem. . . . אח

[b] אַחָיךְ Chald. noun masc. pl., suff. 2 pers. sing. masc. [from אַח § 68] . . . . . אח

אֲחֵיכֶם וְ' noun masc. pl., suff. 2 pers. pl. masc. from אָח irreg. (§ 45); וּ bef. (-:) . . . . אח

אֲחִיכֶם id. sing., suff. 2 pers. pl. masc. . . . אח

[c] אֹחִילָה def. for אוֹ', Hiph. fut. 1 pers. s. with parag. ה יחל

אֲחִילוּד pr. name masc. . . . . . . אח

[aa] אַחִים וְ' noun m. pl. for [אַחִים] from אָח irr. (§ 45) אח

[d] אֹחִים noun masc., pl. of [אֹחַ] dec. 1 a, see אָח interj.

אֲחִימוֹת, וַ' אֲחִימֶלֶךְ, & וַ' אֲחִימָן, & וְ' אֲחִימַעַץ and אֲחִינָדָב, אַחְיָן וְ' & אֲחִימַעַץ . . . אח

אֲחִינוּ noun masc. pl., suff. 1 pers. pl. [for אַחֵינוּ] from אָח irreg. (§ 45) . . . . אח

[e] אָחִינוּ וְ' id. sing., with suff. 1 pers. pl. . . . אח

אֲחִינֹעַם, אֲחִיסָמָךְ, אֲחִיעֶזֶר, אֲחִיקָם & וַ' אֲחִירַע pr. names masc. . . . . אח

[f] אָחִישָׁה Hiph. fut. 1 pers. sing. with paragogic ה . חוש

אֲחִישָׁחַר וַ' pr. name masc.; וַ before (-:) . . . אח

[g] אֲחִישֶׁנָּה Hiph. fut. 1 pers. sing. [אָחִישׁ], suff. 3 pers. sing. fem. (§ 2. rem. 3) . . . . חוש

אֲחִישָׁר וַ' pr. name. masc.; וַ before (-:) . . . אח

[h] אַחְיוֹתֵיהֶם וְ' noun fem. pl., suff. 3 pers. pl. masc. as if from [אַחְיָה] see אָחוֹת irreg. (§ 45) אח

[k] אַחְיֹתָיו id. with suff. 3 pers. sing. masc. . . . אח

[dd] אֲחִיתֹפֶל וַ' pr. name masc.; וַ before (-:) . . . אח

אֶחְכָּמָה for [אֶחְכְּמָה], Kal fut. 1 pers. s. with parag. ה חכם

[l] אָחֵל Hiph. fut. 1 pers. sing. . . . . חלל

[m] אֵחַל id.; Dag. impl. [for אֶחַל], Ch. form (§ 18. r. 14) חלל

[n] וָאֵחַל [for אֶחַל] Niph. fut. 1 pers. sing.; וָ before gutt. for וַ conv. . . . . . . חלל

אַחְלָב pr. name of a place . . . . . חלב

[o] אַחֲלַי, [p] אַחֲלֵי adv. expressive of wish, *O that!*

אַחְלַי for אַחְלַי pr. name masc. and fem.

[gg] וַאֲחַלֵּל וַ' Piel fut. 1 pers. sing.; וָ for וַ . . חלל

[r] וָאֲחַלֶּלְךָ וָ id., suff. 2 pers. sing. masc.; וָ for וַ conv. חלל

אַחְלָמָה וְ noun masc. sing. [אַחְלָם] with paragogic ה חלם

[s] וָאֲחַלְּצָה וָ Piel fut. 1 pers. sing. with parag. ה; וָ for וַ חלץ

[t] אֲחַלְּצֵהוּ id., suff. 3 pers. sing. masc. . . . חלץ

[u] אֲחַלֶּצְךָ, וָאֲחַלֶּצְךָ id., suff. 2 pers. sing. masc. (§ 2. rem. 3); וָ for וַ conv. . . . . חלץ

[z] אֲחַלֵּק, [a] אֲחַלֶּק־ Piel fut. 1 pers. sing. (§ 10. rem. 4) . חלק

אֲחַלְּקָה id. with paragogic ה . . . . חלק

[b] אֲחַלְּקֵם id., suff. 3 pers. pl. masc. . . . חלק

[c] וָאֶחְמְדֵם וָ Kal fut. 1 pers. sing. [אֶחְמֹד], suff. 3 pers. pl. masc. (§ 13. rem. 5), וָ for וַ conv. . חמד

אֶחְמוֹל Kal fut. 1 pers. sing. (§ 13. rem. 5); [d] אֶחְמֹל [e] וְ' וָ id. . . . . . חמל

[אַחְמְתָא] pr. name *Ecbatana*, the metropolis of Media, Ezr. 6. 2.

[f] אָחֹן Kal fut. 1 pers. sing. . . . . חנן

אַחַסְבַּי pr. name masc. . . . . . חסה

אֶחֱסֶה Kal fut. 1 pers. sing. . . . . חסה

[kk] אֶחְסָר for [אֶחְסַר] Kal fut. 1 pers. sing. (§ 13. rem. 5) חסר

[g] אֶחְפָּץ in pause for [אֶחְפַּץ], and אֶחְפֹּץ Kal fut. 1 pers. sing. (§ 13. rem. 4, 5) . חפץ

[h] וָאֶחְפֹּר וָ Kal fut. 1 pers. s. (§ 13. r. 5); וָ for וַ conv. חפר

אֲחַפֵּשׂ Piel fut. 1 pers. sing. . . . . חפש

[i] אֶחְקֹר Kal fut. 1 pers. sing. . . . . חקר

[k] אֶחְקְרֵהוּ id., suff. 3 pers. sing. masc. . . . חקר

[אָחַר] *to stay, tarry,* Ge. 32. 5. Pi.—I. *to retard, hinder.*—II. intrans. *to stay long, to linger,* constr. with עַל.

אַחֵר I. adj. irr. (§ 45) *another;* אֱלֹהִים אֲחֵרִים *other* i. e. strange *gods;* שָׁנָה אַחֶרֶת *next year.*—II. pr. name masc. 1 Ch. 7. 12.

אַחַר I. prep. *behind, after;* הָלַךְ אַחַר פּ' *to go after,* to follow any one; מֵאַחַר עָלוֹת *from behind,* i. e. from following *the ewes.*—II. of time, *after,* אַ' הַדְּבָרִים הָאֵלֶּה *after these things.*—III. adv. of time, *afterwards, then.*—IV. conj. *after that,* and fully אַחַר אֲשֶׁר id.—Pl., construct אַחֲרֵי, with suff. אַחֲרֵיכֶם, אַחֲרַי, &c.—I. *the hinder part,* 2 Sa. 2. 23. —II. prep. of place, *after, behind* any one.—III. of time, *after, after that;* אַחֲרֵי אֲשֶׁר *after that;* אַחֲרֵי כֵן, *afterwards.*—IV. מֵאַחֲרֵי *from after,* i. e. from going after, hence מֵאַחֲרֵי כֵן *afterwards;* אֶל אַחֲרֵי, עַל *after, behind.*

אַחַר Chald. id. only in the phrase אַחֲרֵי דְנָה *after this,* Da. 2. 29, 45, and with suff. 7. 24.

אָחוֹר masc. dec. 3 a.—I. *the hinder side, back part.* —II. *the west.*—III. adv. מֵאָחוֹר, לְאָחוֹר, בְּאָחוֹר *behind;* לְאָחוֹר *hereafter.*

אַחֲרוֹן adj.—I. *hinder;* hence, *western.*—II. *following, future,* pl. אַחֲרֹנִים *posterity.*—III. *last,* compare Is. 44. 6; fem. לָאַחֲרֹנָה, בָּאַחֲרֹנָה, אַחֲרֹנָה *last, the last.*

[a] Jos. 2. 18. [b] Ezr. 7. 18. [c] 2 Sa. 18. 14. [d] Is. 13. 21. [e] Ge. 44. 26. [f] Ps. 55. 9. [g] Is. 60. 22. [h] Job 1. 4. [i] 1 Ch. 2. 16. [k] Job 42. 11. [l] De. 2. 25; & Jos. 3. 7. [m] Eze. 39. 7. [n] Eze. 22. 26. [o] Ps. 119. 5. [p] 2 Ki. 5. 3. [r] Eze. 28. 16. [s] Ps. 7. 5. [t] Ps. 91. 15. [u] Ps. 50. 5. [x] Ps. 81. 8. [z] Ex. 15. 9. [a] Is. 53. 12. [aa] 1 Ch. 26. 9, 11. [b] Ge. 49. 7. [c] Jos. 7. 21. [d] Eze. 9. 10. [dd] Ec. 7. 23. [e] Eze. 36. 21. [f] Ex. 33. 19. [g] Job 13. 3. [gg] Is. 43. 28; Ps. 89. 35. [h] Je. 13. 7. [i] 1 Sa. 20. 12. [k] Job 29. 16. [kk] Ps. 23. 1.

אַחְרַח (*after the brother*, for אֲחִי־אָח) pr. name masc. 1 Ch. 8. 1.

אַחַרְחֵל (*behind the wall*) pr. name m. 1 Ch. 4. 8.

אָחֳרִי Chald. adj. fem. *another*.

אַחֲרִין Chald. adj. *last*, preceded by עַד, *at last*, Da. 4. 5. Kheth.

אַחֲרִית fem. dec. 1b.—I. *the last*, or *uttermost part*, Ps. 139. 9.—II. *the latter time*, אַחֲרִית הַיָּמִים *the latter days*, אַחֲרִית הַשָּׁנָה *the end of the year*.—III. *posterity*.

אַחֲרִית Chald. fem. i. q. Hebr. No. II.

אָחֳרָן Chald. masc. *another*.

אֲחֹרַנִּית adv. *backwards*.

אַחַר	ו׳ [for אַחַר] adv. and prep.	אחר
אַחֵר	pr. name masc.	אחר
אַחֵר	ו׳ adj. masc. sing. irr., pl. אֲחֵרִים (§ 45) .	אחר
[a]אִחַר	for [אִחַר] Piel pret. 3 pers. sing. masc.	אחר
[b]אֵחַר	ו׳ for [אֶאֱחַר] Kal fut. 1 pers. s. (§ 19. r. 3)	אחר
[c]אַחֲרִב [d]אַחֲרִב	ו׳ ו׳ } Hiph. fut. 1 pers. sing. (§ 13. rem. 9)	חרב
אַחֲרָו	ו׳ Kheth for K. אַחֲרָיו (q. v.) . . .	אחר
[e]אֵחֲרוּ	for [אִחֲרוּ] Piel pret. 3 pers. pl. (§ 13. r. 12)	אחר
אַחֲרוֹן	[f]ו׳ adj. masc. sing. dec. 1 b. . . .	אחר
אַחֲרוֹת	adj. fem., pl. of אַחֶרֶת, from אַחֵר masc. irr. (§ 45)	אחר
אַחְרַח	ו׳, אַחַרְחֵל pr. names masc. . . .	אחר
אַחֲרַי אַחֲרָי	prep., pl. with suff. 1 pers. sing. from [g]ו׳ אַחַר . . . . . }	אחר
אַחֲרֵי	ו׳ id. pl., construct state	אחר
[h]אֲחֹרָי	noun masc. pl., suff. 1 pers. sing. for [אֲחוֹרַי] from אָחוֹר dec. 3a	אחר
[i]אֲחֹרֵי	id. pl., construct state	אחר
אָחֳרִי	[k]ו׳ Chald. adj. f. s. by apocope for [אָחֳרִית]	אחר
אַחֲרִיב	Hiph. fut. 1 pers. sing.	חרב
אַחֲרֶיהָ	[l]ו׳ prep., pl. with suff. 3 pers. sing. fem. from אַחַר	אחר
אַחֲרֵיהֶם	ו׳ id., suff. 3 p. pl. masc.	אחר
אֲחֹרֵיהֶם	noun masc. pl., suff. 3 pers. pl. masc. from [אָחוֹר] dec. 3a	אחר
אַחֲרֵיהֶן	prep., pl. with suff. 3 pers. pl. fem. from אַחַר	אחר
[m]אַחֲרֵיהוֹן	Chald. id., suff. 3 pers. pl. masc. . .	אחר
אַחֲרָיו	ו׳ Heb. id., suff. 3 pers. sing. masc. . .	אחר
אַחֲרַיִךְ	[n]ו׳ id., suff. 2 pers. sing. fem. . . .	אחר
אַחֲרֶיךָ	ו׳ id., suff. 2 pers. sing. masc. . . .	אחר
אַחֲרֵיכֶם	id., suff. 2 pers. pl. masc.	אחר
אֲחֵרִים	adj. masc., pl. of אַחֵר irr. (§ 45) . .	אחר
[o]אֲחֵרִין	id. with Chald. term.	אחר
[p]אַחֲרוֹן	Chald., Keri אָ׳ adj. sing. masc. . . .	אחר
אַחֲרֵינוּ	prep., pl. with suff. 1 pers. pl. from אַחַר .	אחר
אַחֲרִישׁ	Hiph. fut. 1 pers. sing.	חרש
אַחֲרִית	[q]ו׳ noun fem. sing. dec. 1b . . .	אחר
אַחֲרִיתָהּ	וְ׳ id., suff. 3 pers. sing. fem. . . .	אחר
אַחֲרִיתוֹ	ו׳ id., suff. 3 pers. sing. masc. . . .	אחר
[r]אַחֲרִיתִי	id., suff. 1 pers. sing.	אחר
[s]אַחֲרִיתְךָ	וְ id., suff. 2 pers. sing. masc. . . .	אחר
[t]אַחֲרִיתֵךְ	וְ id., suff. 2 pers. sing. fem. . . .	אחר
[u]אַחֲרִיתְכֶן	וְ id., suff. 2 pers. pl. fem. . . .	אחר
[x]אַחֲרִיתָם	[y]ו׳ id., suff. 3 pers. pl. masc. . . .	אחר
[z]אַחֲרִיתָן	id., suff. 3 pers. pl. fem.	אחר
[a]אַחֲרִיתֵנוּ	id., suff. 1 pers. pl.	אחר
אָחֳרָן	ו׳ Chald. adj. masc. sing.	אחר
אַחֲרֹנִים	adj. masc., pl. of אַחֲרוֹן, dec. 1b . .	אחר
אֲחֹרַנִּית	adv., a fem. form from a masc. [אֲחֹרַנִּי] .	אחר
[b]אַחֲרִשׁ	for [אַחֲרִישׁ] Hiph. fut. 1 pers. sing. .	חרש
אַחֶרֶת	adj. fem. sing. from אַחֵר masc. (q. v.) .	אחר
[c]אַחְשְׁבָה	וָ Piel fut. 1 pers. sing. with parag. ה ; וָ for וְ	חשב
[אֲחַשְׁדַּרְפַּן]	only in the pl., *chief satraps*, officers of the Persian court, Chald. id.	
[d]אֲחַשְׁדַּרְפְּנֵי	id. pl., construct state.	
אֲחַשְׁדַּרְפְּנַיָּא	וַ׳ Chald. id. pl., emph. st.; וַ before (-:)	
אֶחֱשֶׁה	Kal fut. 1 pers. sing.	חשה
אֲחַשְׁוֵרוֹשׁ, אֲחַשְׁוֵרֹשׁ	pr. name of several kings of Persia and Media.	
[e]אֶחְשֹׂךְ	וָ Kal fut. 1 pers. s. (§ 13. r. 5); וָ for וְ conv.	חשך
[f]אֶחֱשָׂךְ־	id. with Mak. (§ 8. rem. 18) . . .	חשך
אֲחַשְׁרֹשׁ	Kh. for אֲחַשְׁוֵרוֹשׁ q. v.	
[אֲחַשְׁתָּרִי]	only with the art., pr. name m. of Persian origin.	
[אֲחַשְׁתְּרָן]	only in the pl. אֲ׳תְּרָנִים, *mules*, Est. 8. 10, 14, a word of Persian origin.	
אַחַת	ו׳ [for אַחְדְתְּ=אַחֶדֶת] card. num., fem. of אֶחָד (§ 45)	אחד
[g]אַחִת	Chald. Aph. imp. sing. masc. (§ 51. No. 1)	נחת
אֶחָת	[for אַחַת] in pause for אַחַת f. of אֶחָד (§ 45)	אחד
אֲחֹתָהּ	noun fem. sing. with suff. 3 pers. sing. fem. from אָחוֹת irr. (§ 45)	אח
[h]אֵחַתָּה	Kal fut. 1 pers. sing. [אֵחַת] § 18. rem. 6] with paragogic ה . . .	חתת
אֲחֹתוֹ	[i]וַ׳ noun fem. sing., suff. 3 pers. sing. masc. from אָחוֹת irr. (§ 45) וַ before (-:) .	אח
אֲחֹתִי	[k]וַ׳ id. with suff. 1 pers. sing.; וַ id. .	אח
[l]אֲחִתְּךָ	Hiph. fut. 1 pers. sing. [אָחֵת], suff. 2 pers. sing. masc. (§ 18. rem. 11) .	חתת
אֲחֹתָם	noun fem. sing., suff. 3 pers. pl. masc. from אָחוֹת irr. (§ 45)	אח

[a] Ge. 34. 19. [b] Ge. 32. 5. [c] 2 Ki. 19. 24. [d] Is. 37. 25. [e] Ju. 5. 28. [f] Job 19. 25. [g] Is. 43. 10. [h] Ex. 33. 23. [i] Ex. 26. 12. [k] Da. 7. 20. [l] 2 Ch. 11. 20. [m] Da. 7. 24. [n] Eze. 16. 34. [o] Job 31. 10. [p] Da. 4. 5. [q] Ec. 10. 13. [r] Nu. 23. 10. [s] Job 8. 7. [t] Eze. 23. 25. [u] Am. 4. 2. [x] De. 32. 20. [y] Am. 9. 1. [z] Is. 41. 22. [a] Je. 12. 4. [b] Je. 4. 19. [c] Ps. 73. 16. [d] Est. 3. 12. [e] Ge. 20. 6. [f] Job 7. 11. [g] Ezr. 5. 15. [h] Je. 17. 18. [i] 1 Ch. 7. 18. [k] Job 17. 14. [l] Je. 1. 17.

[a]אֶחְתֹּם וְ Kal fut. 1 p. s. (§ 13. r. 5); וְ for וַ· conv. חתם

אֲחֹתֵנוּ n. f. s., suff. 1 pers. pl. from אָחוֹת irr. (§ 45) אח

[b]אֶחְתֹּר וְ Kal fut. 1 pers. sing. (§ 13. rem. 5); וְ for וַ· conv. . . . . . חתר

[c]אֵט, [d]אֵט וְ, [e]וְ׳ } ap. for אַטֶּה (q. v.); וְ for וַ· conv. נטה

[f]אַט adv. . . . . אטט

[g]אָטָד masc.—I. *blackthorn;* rhamnus paliurus of Linn.—II. pr. name of a place beyond Jordan, Ge. 50. 10, 11.

[h]אֶטְבָּעָה Kal fut. 1 pers. sing. [אֶטְבַּע] with paragogic ה for [יִבְעָה] § 8. rem. 15] . . . טבע

אַטֶּה Hiph. fut. 1 pers. sing. (§ 25. 2 b) . . . נטה

[i]אֲטַהֵר Piel (dag. forte impl. § 14. r. 1) fut. 1 pers. s. טהר

[rr]אֶטְהַר וְ Kal fut. 1 pers. sing. for [יִהַר] § 8. rem. 15] טָהֵר

אֵטוּן masc. a kind of Egyptian *thread,* or *linen,* Prov. 7. 16. The word is probably of Egyptian origin.

[k]אֶטּוֹר Kal fut. 1 pers. sing. (§ 17. rem. 3) . . נטר

אָטַט Root not used; Arab. *to utter a gentle sound, to murmur.*

אִט masc. pl. אִטִּים dec. 8 e.—I. *necromancer,* only Is. 19. 3.—II. *gentleness, softness,* hence adv. *gently, slowly,* 1 Ki. 21. 27, and with pref. לְאַט, לְאַט; לְאִטִּי *at my ease, convenience.*

[l]אֲטִילְךָ for [לְךָ] Hiph. fut. 1 p. s., suff. 2 p. s. m. טול

[אָטַם] *to shut, to close,* Hiph. id. Ps. 58. 5.

אֹטֵם Kal part. act. sing. masc. . . . . אטם

[m]אֲטַמֵּא וְ Piel fut. 1 pers. sing.; וְ for וַ· conv. . טמא

אֲטֻמוֹת Kal part. p. fem., pl. of [אֲטוּמָה] dec. 10 . אטם

[n]אֲטֻמִים id. masc., pl. of [אָטוּם] dec. 3 a . . אטם

[o]אֶטְמְנֵהוּ וְ Kal fut. 1 pers. sing. [אֶטְמֹן], suff. 3 pers. sing. masc.; וְ for וַ· conv. . . . טמן

[p]אֲטַנְּפֵם Piel fut. 1 pers. sing., suff. 3 pers. pl. masc. טנף

[q]אֶטְעַם Kal fut. 1 pers. sing. . . . . טעם

[r]אַטִּף for [אַטִּיף] Hiph. fut. 1 pers. sing. . . נטף

[אָטַר] fut. תֶּאְטַר, *to shut, to close,* Ps. 69. 16.

אָטֵר (*lame?*) pr. name masc.

אִטֵּר adj. prop. *shut up, bound, impotent,* אִטֵּר יַד יְמִינוֹ *having his right hand bound,* i. e. being left-handed.

אֶטְרֹף Kal fut. 1 pers. sing. . . . . טרף

[אַי] construct אֵי (§ 37. rem. 6) adv. of interrog. *where?* with suff. אַיֶּכָּה *where art thou?* אַיּוֹ *where is he?* אַיָּם *where are they?* With adverbs and pronouns, אֵי זֶה מִזֶּה *which? what? where? whither? whence? from what?* אֵי לָזֹאת *on what account? wherefore?* Je. 5. 7.—With parag. ה, אַיֵּה *where?*

אֵיךְ (for the next אֵיכָה q. v.) *how?* Also as an exclamation of grief, *how!*

אֵיכָה (from אֵי, and כָה i. q. כֹּה *so*) *where? how?* As an exclamation of grief, *ah, how!*

אֵיכֹה *where?* 2 Ki. 6. 13, where Keri has אֵיכוֹ

כָּכָה *how?* compare אֵיכָכָה.

אַיִן adv. of interrog. (where?) only in the form מֵאַיִן *whence?*

אֵיפֹה *where? how?* comp. פֹּה.

אָן (contr. from אַיִן) *where?* מֵאָן *whence?* 2 Ki. 5. 25. in Kheth; עַד־אָן *until when? how long?* Job 8. 2. With parag. ה, אָנָה *whither? where?* עַד אָנָה *how long?* אָנָה וְאָנָה *hither and thither,* 1 Ki. 2. 36, 42.

[s]אִי וְ׳ noun masc. sing., pl. אִיִּים, dec. 8. (§ 37, No. 4. a); or interj. . . . . . . אוה

אִי i. q. אַיִן, אֵין *not,* Job 22. 30. Hence the name אִי־כָבוֹד (*inglorious,* others *where is the glory,* i. q. אֵי־כָבוֹד) 1 Sa. 4. 20, compare also אִיזֶבֶל.

[אָיַב] *to hate, to be an enemy,* Ex. 23. 22. Part. אוֹיֵב as a subst. dec. 7 b, *adversary, enemy.* Fem. אוֹיֶבֶת id.

אֵיבָה fem. dec. 10, *enmity.*

אִיּוֹב (*persecuted*) pr. name, *Job,* the patriarch.

אֹיֵב Kal part. act. sing. masc. dec. 7 b. . . . איב

[t]אֵיבָה [u]וְ׳ noun fem. sing. dec. 10. . . . . איב

אֹיְבוֹ Kal part. act. sing. masc., suff. 3 pers. sing. masc. from אֹיֵב dec. 7 b. . . . . איב

אֹיְבַי, אֹיְבַי וְ׳ } id. pl., suff. 1 pers. sing. . . . . איב

[x]אֹיְבֵי וְ׳ id. pl., construct state . . . . איב

אֹיְבִי id. sing., suff. 1 pers. sing. . . . . איב

אֹיְבֶיהָ id. pl., suff. 3 pers. sing. fem. . . . איב

אֹיְבֵיהֶם id. pl., suff. 3 pers. pl. masc. . . . איב

אֹיְבָיו וְ׳ id. pl., suff. 3 pers. sing. masc. . . . איב

אֹיְבֶיךָ id. pl., suff. 2 pers. sing. masc. . . . איב

[y]אֹיְבָיִךְ, [z]אֹיְבַיִךְ } id. pl., suff. 2 pers. sing. fem. . . . איב

אֹיְבְךָ id. pl., (Kh. אֹיְבֶיךָ), suff. 2 pers. sing. masc. K. אֹיִבְךָ (q. v.) . . . . . איב

---

[a] Je. 32. 10. [b] Eze. 8. 8. [c] Job 23. 11. [d] Ho. 11. 4. [e] Je. 15. 6. [f] 1 Ki. 21. 27. [g] Ps. 58. 10. [h] Ps. 69. 15. [i] Eze. 36. 25. [k] Je. 3. 12. [l] Eze. 32. 4. [m] Eze. 20. 26. [n] 1 Ki. 6. 4. [o] Je. 13. 5. [p] Ca. 5. 3. [q] 2 Sa. 3. 35. [r] Mi. 2. 11. [rr] Ps. 51. 9. [s] Ec. 4. 10. [t] Nu. 35. 22. [u] Ge. 3. 15. [x] Ps. 37. 20. [y] Mi. 4. 10. [z] La. 2. 16.

אֹיְבֵיכֶם	Kal part. act. pl. m., suff. 2 p. pl. m. fr. אוֹיֵב d. 7b.	איב
אֹיְבֵינוּ	ו֯' id. pl., suff. 1 pers. pl. . . .	איב
אֹיְבֶךָ[a]	id. s., suff. 2 p. s. m. in pause for אֹיִבְךָ (q.v.)	איב
אֹיְבֵךְ[b]	id. sing., suff. 2 pers. sing. fem. . .	איב
אֹיִבְךָ	id. sing., suff. 2 pers. sing. masc. . .	איב
אֹיְבֵנוּ[zz]	id. sing., suff. 1 pers. sing.	איב
אִיבַשׁ[c]	Kal fut. 1 pers. sing. for [יְבַשׁ'] (§ 8. rem. 15)	יבש
אֵיבַת	noun fem. sing. construct of 'בָה dec. 10.	איב
אָיַבְתִּי[d]	ו֯ Kal pret. 1 pers. sing.; acc. shifted by conv. ו֯ (§ 8. rem. 7) . . .	איב
אֹיַבְתִּי[e]	id. part. act. sing. fem. [אֹיֶבֶת] with paragogic י (§ 9. rem. 19) . . .	איב
אִיגָע[f]	Kal fut. 1 pers. sing. for [יְגַע'] (§ 8. rem. 15)	יגע
אֵיד	[g]ו֯' noun masc. sing. dec. 1a. . . .	אוד
אֵידוֹ	id., suff. 3 pers. sing. masc. . . .	אוד
אֵידִי	id., suff. 1 pers. sing.	אוד
אֵידֶךָ[h]	id., suff. 2 pers. sing. masc. for [אֵידְךָ] .	אוד
אֵידְכֶם[i]	ו֯ id., suff. 2 pers. pl. masc. . . .	אוד
אֵידָם	id., suff. 3 pers. pl. masc.	אוד
אַיָּה[k]	noun fem. sing.; also pr. name masc.	אוה
אַיֵּה	ו֯' interrog. adv. [אַי], with paragogic ה construct אֵי (q. v.)	אי
אַיּוֹ	ו֯' id., suff. 3 pers. sing. m. dec. 8d. (§ 37. r. 6)	אי
אַיּוֹ[l]	Kh. אַיּוֹ q. v., K. אַיֵּה (q. v.) . . .	אי
אִיּוֹב	ו֯' pr. name masc.	איב
אִיזֶבֶל / אִיזָבֶל	ו֯' } pr. n. f. (*non-inhabited*) comp. אִי & R. זָבַל) pr. n. f. the wife of Ahab king of Israel.	
אֲיַחֵל	Piel (dag. f. impl. § 14. r. 1) fut. 1 pers. s.	יחל
אֲיַחֲלָה[m]	ו֯ id. with paragogic ה ; ו֯ for ו֯ . .	יחל
אֵיטִיב[n]	Hiph. fut. 1 pers. sing. . . .	יטב
אֵיטִיבָה[o]	ו֯' id. with paragogic ה	יטב
אֵין	[p]ו֯' construct of the following	אוה
אִיִּים	[tt]ו֯' noun masc., pl. of אִי dec. 8. (§ 37. No. 4a)	אוה
אֵיךְ	ו֯' interrog. adv.	אי
אַיֶּכָּה[q]	interr. adv. [אַי], suff. 2 pers. sing. masc. dec. 8d. (§ 37. rem. 6) . . .	אי
אֵיכָה	interrog. adv.	אי
אֵיכֹה[r]	id. Kh. אֵיכָה, K. אֵיכוֹ . . .	אי
אֵיכָכָה	[s]ו֯' interrog. adv.	אי
אֱיָל[t]	noun masc. sing. dec. 1b. . . .	אול
אַיִל	ו֯', ו֯' noun masc. sing. dec. 6 h; ו֯ see lett. ו	אול
אֵיל	id., construct state	אול
אֱיָל[u]	noun masc. sing.	אול
אַיָּלָה[x]	noun fem. sing. (§ 42. rem. 5) . . .	אול
אֵילָו	ו֯' Kh. for [אֵילָיו § 4. rem. 1], noun masc. pl., suff. 3 pers. sing. m. from אַיִל dec. 6h.	אול
אַיָּלוֹן	ו֯' pr. name of a place	אול
אֵילוֹן	ו֯' pr. name of a man or place . .	אול
אַיָּלוֹת	noun fem., pl. of אַיָּלָה dec. 10. (§ 42. rem. 5)	אול
אֵילוֹת	pr. name of a place	אול
אֱיָלוּתִי[y]	noun fem. sing., suff. 1 pers. sing. from ['לוּת] dec. 1b.	אול
אֵילֵי[z]	[aa]ו֯' n. m. pl. constr. fr. אַיִל dec. 6 h., or [cc]אֵיל	אול
אֵילִיל[ee]	Hiph. fut. 1 pers. sing. (§ 20. rem. 15) .	ילל
אֵילִילָה[b]	ו֯ Hiph. fut. 1 pers. sing. with parag. ה .	ילל
אֵילִים	ו֯' noun masc., pl. of אַיִל dec. 6h. .	אול
אֵילְכָה[bb]	Kal fut. 1 pers. sing. with parag. ה . .	ילך
אֵילִם	pr. name of a place	אול
אֵלִם	ו֯' defect. for אֵילִים (q. v.) . . .	אול
אֵילִמָה	pr. name of a place (אֵילִם) with loc. ה .	אול
אֵילַמּוֹ[c]	ו֯ noun masc. pl., suff. 3 pers. sing. masc. from אֵילָם dec. 8a. for ['לַמָּיו § 4. rem. 1]	אול
אֵילֹן	pr. name masc. see אֵילוֹן . . .	אול
אִילָן[d]	Chald. noun masc. sing. dec. 1b. . .	אול
אִילָנָא	Chald. id., emph. st.	אול
אַיָּלֹנָה	pr. name of a place (אַיָּלוֹן) with loc. ה .	אול
אַיֶּלֶת	noun fem. sing. construct of אַיָּלָה; but as abs. Je. 14. 5 (§ 42. rem. 5) . .	אול
אֵילַת	pr. name of a place, see אֵילוֹת . .	אול

אים Root not used; Chald. Pa. *to terrify*.

אָיֹם adj. *terrible*, fem. אֲיֻמָּה

אֵים or אֵים masc. pl. אֵימִים.—I. *terror, dread.* —II. *idols*, Je. 50. 38.—III. pr. name of the original inhabitants of Moab.

אֵימָה fem. dec. 10, *terror, dread.*

אַיָּם	interrog. adv. [אַי], suff. 3 pers. pl. masc. dec. 8d. (§ 37. rem. 6) . . .	אי
אָיֹם[e]	adj. masc. sing.	אים
אֵימָה	noun fem. sing. dec. 10. . . .	אים
אֲיֻמָּה[f]	adj. fem. sing. from אָיֹם masc. (§ 39. No. 3)	אים
אֵימוֹת[g]	ו֯ noun fem., pl. of אֵימָה dec. 10. . .	אים
אֵימִנָה[h]	ו֯ Hiph. fut. 1 pers. sing. with paragogic ה	ימן
אֵימַת[i]	noun fem. sing., construct of אֵימָה dec. 10.	אים
אֵימָתָה[k]	id. with paragogic ה	אים
אֵימָתִי	id., suff. 1 pers. sing. . . .	אים
אֵימָתְךָ[l]	ו֯ id., suff. 2 pers. sing. masc. . .	אים
אֵימַתְכֶם[m]	id., suff. 2 pers. pl. masc. . . .	אים
אַיִן / אָיִן	ו֯' ו֯' } (prim. subst.) used as an adv.; for ו֯ see lett. ו	און
אִין[n]	ו֯ adv. i. q. אַיִן	און

[a] De. 28. 53. [b] Zep. 3. 15. [c] Ps. 102. 12. [d] Ex. 23. 22. [e] Mi. 7. 8, 10. [f] Job 9. 29. [g] Job 18. 12. [h] Pr. 27. 10. [i] Pr. 1. 27. [k] Job 28. 7. [l] Je. 37. 19. [m] Job 30. 26. [n] Ge. 32. 13. [o] Ge. 32. 10. [p] Est. 10. 1. [q] Ge. 3. 9. [r] 2 Ki. 6. 13. [s] Est. 8. 6. [t] Deu. 14. 5. [tt] Ps. 72. 10. [u] Ps. 88. 5. [x] Ge. 49. 21. [y] Ps. 22. 20. [z] Is. 60. 7. [zz] 2 Sa. 19. 10.

[a] Ge. 31. 38. [b] Mi. 1. 8. [bb] Mi. 1. 8. [c] Eze. 40. 21, 22, 24, 26, 29, 31, 33, 34, 36. [cc] Is. 61. 3. [d] Da. 4. 7. [e] Hab. 1. 7. [ee] Je. 48. 31. [f] Ca. 6. 4, 10. [g] Ps. 55. 5. [h] Ge. 13. 9. [i] Pr. 20. 2. [k] Ex. 15. 16. [l] Job 13. 21. [m] Jos. 2. 9. [n] 1 Sa. 21. 9.

אֵין וְ' adv., prop. construct of אַ֫יִן dec. 6h. . . און

אֵינֵימוֹ[a] וְ'[b] id. pl., suff. 3 pers. pl. masc. . . און

אֵינְךָ וְ' id. sing., suff. 2 pers. sing. masc. . און

אֵינֵךְ וְ id sing., suff. 2 pers. sing. fem. . . און

אֵינְכֶם id., suff. 2 pers. pl. masc. . . . און

אֵינָם וְ' id., suff. 3 pers. pl. masc. . . . און

אֵינֶנָּה id., (verbal) suff. 3 pers. sing. fem. . און

אֵינֶנּוּ וְ' id., (verbal) suff. 3 pers. s. m. or 1 pers. pl. און

אֵינֶנִּי וְ' id., (verbal) suff. 1 pers. sing. . . און

אִינָק[c] Kal fut. 1 pers. sing. for [אִינַק § 8. rem. 15] ינק

אַיְסִירֵם[d] Hiph. fut. 1 pers. sing., suff. 3 pers. pl. masc. (§ 20. rem. 14) . . . . יסר

אֲיַסֵּר[e] Piel fut. 1 pers. sing. . . . . יסר

אִיעֶזֶר contr. for אֲבִיעֶזֶר (q. v.) . . . אב

אִיעֲצָה[f] Kal fut. 1 pers. sing. with paragogic ה . יעץ

אִיעָצְךָ id., suff. 2 pers. sing. masc. (§ 16. rem. 12) יעץ

אִיעָצֵךְ[g] id., suff. 2 pers. sing. fem. . . . יעץ

אֵיפָה וְ'[ll] fem. dec. 10, *an Ephah*, a corn measure.

אֵיפֹה וְ' interrog. adv. . . . . . אי

אֵיפַת וְ' noun fem. sing., construct of אֵיפָה dec. 10. איף

אִיקָץ[h] וָ for [אִיקַץ] Kal fut. 1 pers. sing. (§ 8. rem. 15); וָ for וַ· conv. . . יקץ

אִירָא וָ' Kal fut. 1 pers. sing.; וָ id. . . ירא

אִירָאֶנּוּ[i] id., suff. 3 pers. sing. masc. (§ 2. rem. 3) ירא

אִירָשֶׁנָּה[k] Kal fut. 1 pers. sing., suff. 3 pers. sing. fem. (§ 2. rem. 3) . . . . ירש

אִישׁ[nn][l] וְ', וָ masc. dec. 1a.—I. *man*, Lat. *vir*, with reference to strength; hence as denoting sex, *a male*, of the human species or brutes.—II. *husband*.—III. *man*, as opposed to God, to animals, Lat. *homo*.—IV. used before other nouns to denote the qualities or qualifications of men; אִישׁ אֱמֶת *a faithful man*; אִישׁ אָוֶן *a wicked man*; אִישׁ תֹּאַר *a handsome man*; אִישׁ מִלְחָמָה *a warrior*.—V. *any one. any person*.—VI. *each, every one*; אִישׁ אִישׁ *every one*; אִישׁ וְאִישׁ *each and every one*. Plur. אִישִׁים only occurs three times, more frequently is אֲנָשִׁים, see אֱנוֹשׁ (comp. § 45.)

אִישׁ denom. Hithpal. הִתְאוֹשֵׁשׁ *to show oneself a man*, Is. 46. 8.

אִישׁ־בֹּשֶׁת (*man of shame*) pr. name of a son of Saul; also called אֶשְׁבַּעַל (*man of Baal*.)

אִישְׁהוֹד (*man of glory*) pr. name of a man, 1 Ch. 7. 18.

אִישׁוֹן masc. prop. dimin. *the little man*, the small image of a person as seen in the eye.—I. אִישׁוֹן בַּת עַיִן *the pupil of the eye*.—II. Metaph. *the middle*, followed by לַיְלָה, חֹשֶׁךְ *midnight, midst of darkness*.

אֵשֶׁת fem. dec. 13 b.—I. *woman*; *female* (of animals,) Ge. 7. 2.—II. *wife*; אֵשֶׁת אָב *father's wife*, a stepmother. It is used as the construct of אִשָּׁה q. v.

אֶשְׁתּוֹן (*womanish*) pr. name m. 1 Ch. 4. 11, 12.

אִישָׁהּ וְ' id. with suff. 3 pers. sing. fem. . . איש

אִישְׁהוֹד pr. name masc. . . . . איש

אִישׁוֹ[l] noun masc. sing., suff. 3 pers. sing. masc. from אִישׁ dec. 1a. (but see § 45) . איש

אִישַׁי וְ pr. name masc., see יִשַׁי . . . ישה

אִישִׁי noun masc. sing., suff. 1 pers. sing. from אִישׁ dec. 1a. (but see § 45) . . איש

אִישִׁים id. pl., absolute state . . . . איש

אִישֵׁךְ id. sing., suff. 2 pers. sing. fem. . . איש

אָאִישְׂמָה[m] וָ Kal fut. 1 pers. s. with parag. ה, Kh. אִישְׂמָה R. ישׂם, K. אָשִׂימָה R. שִׂים see . שום

אִישָׁן[n] } אִישַׁן[o] } Kal fut. 1 pers. sing. (§ 8. rem. 15) . ישן

אִישָׁנָה[p] וָ id. with parag. ה, for [וָאִישְׁנָה § 8. rem. 15]; וָ for וַ· conv. . . . ישן

אֲיַשֵּׁר Piel fut. 1 pers. sing. . . . . ישר

אִיתוֹהִי[q] Chald. the following with suff. 3 pers. s. m.

אִיתַי Chald. i. q. Heb. יֵשׁ *there is*; with the suff. of the pl. אִיתָךְ *thou art*; אִיתוֹהִי *he is*; אִיתָנָא *we are*; אִיתֵיכוֹן *ye are*. Hence the two following names.

אִיתַי pr. name of a man, 1 Ch. 11. 31, for which אִתַּי, 2 Sa. 23. 29.

אִיתִיאֵל (*there is a God*) pr. name of a man, Pr. 30. 1.

אִיתֵיכוֹן[r] Chald. adv. (אִיתַי) with suff. 2 pers. pl. m.

אֵיתָם[s] Kal fut. 1 pers. sing., for [אֵתַם, § 18. rem. 6] . . . . . תמם

אִיתָמָר וְ' pr. name masc. . . . . אוה

אֵיתָן וְ' adj. or subst. masc. sing. (no vowel change); also pr. name . . . . יתן

אִיתָנָא[t] Chald. adv. (אִיתַי) with suff. 1 pers. pl. .

אֵיתָנִים[u] וְ noun masc., pl. of אֵיתָן (no vowel change) יתן

אַךְ וְ' adv.—I. *only*; אַךְ הַפַּעַם *only this once*; אַךְ חֹשֶׁךְ *darkness only*; i. e. nothing but darkness.—II. *only, but*.—III. *only now, just now*.—IV. *surely, certainly*.

אַךְ[x] וָ' Hiph. fut. 1 pers. sing., ap. for אַכֶּה (§ 25. No. 2 b); וָ for וַ· conv. . נכה

אֲכַבֵּד Piel fut. 1 pers. sing. . . . . כבד

[a] Ps. 73. 5.
[b] Ps. 59. 14.
[c] Job 3. 11.
[d] Ho. 7. 12.
[e] 1 Ki. 12. 11, 14.
[f] Ps. 32. 8.
[g] 1 Ki. 1. 12
[h] Ge. 41. 21.
[i] Job 9. 35.
[k] Ge. 15. 8.
[l] 1 Ki. 20. 20.
[ll] Job 4. 7.
[m] Ju. 12. 3.
[n] Ps. 4. 9.
[nn] Est. 1. 8.
[o] Ps. 13. 4.
[p] Ps. 3. 6.
[q] Da. 2. 11.
[r] Da. 3. 14, 15.
[s] Ps. 19. 14.
[t] Da. 3. 18.
[u] Job 12. 19.
[x] Ex. 9. 15.

אֶכָּבֵד[a] [b]וְ׳ Niph. fut. 1 pers. sing. . . כבד

אֶכְבְּדָ[c] וְ id., (Kh. אֶכָּבֵד), K. אֶכְבְּדָה (q. v.) כבד

אֲכַבְּדָה[d] וָ Piel fut. 1 pers. sing. with parag. ה; וָ for וְ כבד

אֶכָּבְדָה / אֶכָּבְדָה[e] וְ } Niph. fut. 1 pers. sing. with parag. ה (§ 10. rem. 5). 2 Sa. 6. 22. . . } כבד

אֲכַבְּדֶהוּ[f] וָ Piel fut. 1 pers. sing., suff. 3 pers. sing. masc.; וָ for וְ . . . . . כבד

אֲכַבֶּדְךָ id., suff. 2 pers. sing. masc. . . . כבד

אַכַּד וְ pr. name of a city, Ge. 10. 10; supposed to signify *fortress*, אכד i. q. אָנַד, עָקַד *to bind, to strengthen*.

אַכֶּה [g]וְ״א וְ׳ Hiph. fut. 1 pers. sing. (§ 25. No. 2 b); וְ for ·וַ conv. . . . . . נכה

אַכֵּהוּ[h] וְ׳ id., suff. 3 pers. sing. masc. . . . נכה

אָכוֹל Kal inf. absolute . . . . אכל

אֱכוֹל[i] וְ׳ id. imp. sing. masc.; וֶ bef. (ֵ:) . . אכל

אָכוֹלְ[k] וְ Kh. אָכוֹל Kal inf. absolute, K. אָכְלוּ (q.v.) אכל

אֲכַזֵּב Piel fut. 1 pers. sing. . . . . כזב

אַכְזָב[l] adj. masc. sing. . . . . . כזב

אַכְזִיב וְ׳ pr. name of a place . . . . כזב

אַכְזִיבָה id. with loc. ה . . . . . כזב

אַכְזָר adj. masc. sing. . . . . . כזר

אַכְזָרִי id. with the adj. term. ־ִי . . . . כזר

אַכְזְרִיּוּת[n] noun fem. sing., formed from the preceding כזר

אֲכַחֵד[o] Piel (dag. f. impl. § 14. r. 1) fut. 1 pers. sing. כחד

אַכְחִד[p] וָ Hiph. fut. 1 pers. sing.; וָ for ·וַ conv. . כחד

אָכִין Hiph. fut. 1 pers. sing. . . . . כון

אָכִינָה[q] id. with paragogic ה . . . . כון

אַכִּיר Hiph. fut. 1 pers. sing. . . . . נכר

אַכִּירָה[r] וָ id. with parag. ה; וָ for ·וַ conv. . . נכר

אָכִישׁ pr. name of a king of the Philistines.

אַכֶּכָּה[s] Hiph. fut. 1 pers. sing. (אַכֶּה § 25. No. 2), suff. 2 pers. sing. masc. (§ 2. rem. 2) נכה

אָכַל (§ 19. rem. 1. and 2.)—I. *to eat, to eat up*, const. with acc., בְּ, לְ, מִן.—II. *to devour, to consume*, const. with בְּ.—III. *to enjoy*, const. with בְּ.—IV. יוֹכְלוּ אַתִּיקִים *the columns occupied*, Eze. 42. 5. Niph. *to be eaten*; also *to be fit for food*. Pi. *to consume*, Job 20. 26. Pu. *to be consumed*. Hiph. —I. *to give to eat, to feed*.—II. *to cause to consume*, Eze. 21. 33. Hoph. (§ 19. rem. 9.)

אֲכַל Ch. (§ 53.) id., comp. קְרַץ.

אֹכֶל masc. dec. 6c.—I. *an eating*, the act of eating.—II. *food*.

אָכְלָה fem. *food, meat*.

אֲכִילָה fem. id.

מַאֲכָל masc. dec. 2b, *food*; עֵץ מַאֲכָל *fruit-tree*; צֹאן מַאֲכָל *flock of* (i. e. slaughtered for) *food*.

מַאֲכֶלֶת fem. pl. מַאֲכָלוֹת (§ 44. rem. 5) *a knife*, both for eating and slaughtering.

מַאֲכֹלֶת fem. *food*, trop. for fire, Is. 9. 4, 18.

מַכֹּלֶת fem. *food*. מַאֲכֹלֶת 1 Ki. 5. 25.

אָכַל / אָכָל [t]וְ׳ / וְ } Kal pret. 3 pers. sing. masc. (§ 8. rem. 7) . . . . . } אכל

אֲכַל[u] וְ Piel fut. 1 pers. sing., ap. for אֲכַלֶּה; וָ for ·וַ conv. . . . . . . כלה

אָכֹל וְ׳ Kal inf. abs. . . . . . אכל

אֱכֹל / אֱכָל[v] } id. inf. constr. (§ 8. rem. 18) . . אכל

אֱכֹל / אֱכָל־ וְ / [x]וְ״ } id. imp. sing. masc. (§ 8. rem. 18); וֶ before (ֵ:) . . . . } אכל

אֹכַל / אֹכֵל [a]וְ׳, [b]וְ / [c]וְ, [d]וְ׳ } id. fut. 1 pers. sing. (§ 19. r. 1); וָ for ·וַ conv. . . } אכל

אֹכֵל [e]וְ׳ id. part. act. sing. masc. dec. 7b . . אכל

אֹכֶל noun masc. sing. dec. 6c. . . . אכל

אֻכָּל[f] Pual part. sing. masc. for [מְאֻכָּל § 10. r. 6] אכל

אֻכָל וְ pr. name masc. Prov. 30. 1.

אֶכְלָא[g] Kal fut. 1 pers. sing. . . . . כלא

אָכְלָה[h] [i]וְ׳ in pause for אָכְלָה q. v. (§ 8. rem. 7) אכל

אֲכָלָהּ[k] וַ Kal pret. 3 pers. sing. masc., suff. 3 pers. sing. fem.; וַ for וְ conv. . . . אכל

אֲכַלֶּה וְ׳ Piel fut. 1 pers. sing.; וַ for וְ . . כלה

אָכְלָה וְ׳ Kal pret. 3 pers. sing. fem. . . אכל

אָכְלָה[l] Chald. Peal part. act. sing. fem. from [אָכֵל] masc. . . . . אכל

אָכְלָה[m] Kal inf. const. (§ 8. rem. 10) . . . אכל

אִכְלָה[n] וְ id. imp. sing. masc. with paragogic ה (§ 8. rem. 11) . . . . . . אכל

אֹכְלָה id. part. act., fem. of אֹכֵל (§ 8. rem. 19) אכל

אֹכְלָה[o] / אֹכְלָה[r] [p]וְ׳, [q]וְ׳ / וְ } id. fut. 1 pers. sing. with parag. ה (§ 19. r. 1); וָ for ·וַ conv. } אכל

אֲכָלֻהוּ וַ id. pret. 3 pers. pl., suff. 3 pers. sing. masc.; וַ for וְ conv. . . . . אכל

אִכְלֻהוּ[s] id. imp. pl. masc., suff. 3 pers. sing. masc., [for אִכְלוּהוּ] . . . . . אכל

אֲכָלוֹ [t]וְ׳ id. pret. 3 pers. sing. masc., suff. 3 pers. sing. masc.; וַ for וְ conv. . . . אכל

אָכָלוּ[u] in pause for אָכְלוּ q. v. (§ 8. rem. 7) . אכל

אֲכַלוּ[x] [y]וְ׳ Ch. Peal pret. 3 pers. pl. masc.; וַ bef. (ֲ:) אכל

אָכְלוּ וְ׳ Kal pret. 3 pers. pl. masc. . . . אכל

---

[a] Le. 10. 3. [b] Is. 49. 5. [c] Hag. 1. 8. [d] Ps. 86. 12. [e] Ex. 14. 4, 17. [f] Ps. 91. 15. [g] Je. 40. 15. [h] Ne. 13. 25. [i] Is. 57. 17. [k] 1 Sa. 28. 22. [l] Is. 37. 30. [m] Je. 15. 18. [n] Pr. 27. 4. [o] Job 27. 11. [p] Zec. 11. 8. [q] 1 Ch. 22. 5. [r] Ne. 6. 12. [s] 2 Sa. 2. 22. [t] Ge. 27. 10. [u] Eze. 43. 8. [x] De. 12. 23. [y] Ge. 3. 11. [z] Am. 7. 12. [a] Job 31. 17. [b] Ge. 27. 33. [c] Is. 44. 19. [d] Ge. 3. 12, 13. [e] Ec. 4. 5. [f] Ex. 3. 2. [g] Ps. 40. 10. [h] Eze. 19. 14. [i] Ho. 11. 6. [k] De. 14. 21. [l] Da. 7. 7, 19. [m] 1 Sa. 1. 9. [n] Ge. 27. 19. [o] De. 12. 20. [p] Ge. 27. 25. [q] Eze. 3. 3. [r] Ge. 27. 4. [s] Ex. 16. 25. [t] 2 Sa. 9. 10. [u] Eze. 22. 25. [x] Da. 6. 25. [y] Da. 3. 8.

וְ' אֱכֹלוּ, [a]וֶ אֱכֹלוּ } id. imp. pl. masc. (§ 8. rem. 12) . אכל

אָכְלוֹ id. inf.; or noun masc. with suff. 3 pers. sing. masc. from אֹכֶל dec. 6c. . . . אכל

אֻכְּלוּ Pual pret. 3 pers. pl. masc. . . . אכל

[b]אִכְלוּהָ וְ Kal imp. pl. masc., suff. 3 pers. sing. fem. אכל

[c]אֲכָלוּם [d]וַ' id. pret. 3 pers. pl. with suff. 3 pers. pl. masc.; וַ for וְ conv. . . . . אכל

[e]אֱכֻלִי Chald. Peal imp. sing. fem. . . . אכל

[f]אֹכְלֵי וְ' Kal part. act. pl. constr. masc. from אֹכֵל dec. 7b . . . . . אכל

[g]אֹכְלָיו וְ' id. pl., suff. 3 pers. sing. masc. . . אכל

[h]אֹכְלַיִךְ id. pl., suff. 2 pers. sing. fem. . . . אכל

[i]אֹכְלִים וְ' id. pl., abs. st. . . . . אכל

[k]אֲכָלְךָ Kal inf. with suff. 2 pers. sing. masc. from אֱכֹל . . . . . אכל

[l]אֲכַלֶּךָ Piel fut. 1 pers. sing. (אֲכַלֶּה), suff. 2 pers. sing. masc. (§ 24. rem. 21a. & § 10. r. 7) כלה

[m]אָכְלֶךָ for לְּךָ', noun masc. sing., suff. 2 pers. sing. masc. from אֹכֶל dec. 6c . . . אכל

[n]אֲכַלְכֵּל Pilpel fut. 1 pers. sing. (§ 6. No. 4) . כול

[o]אֲכַלְכֵּלְם וָ id., suff. 3 pers. pl. masc.; וָ for וַ conv. כול

[p]אֲכָלְכֶם Kal inf., suff. 2 pers. pl. masc. (§ 16. r. 7) אכל

אָכְלָם noun masc. sing. with suff. 3 pers. pl. masc. from אֹכֶל dec. 6c. . . . . אכל

אֲכַלֵּם [q]וָ, [r]וָ' Piel fut. 1 pers. s. (אֲכַלֶּה), suff. 3 pers. pl. masc. (§ 24. r. 21a); וָ for וְ, וָ for וַ. כלה

אֹכְלֵם וָ', וְ' Kal fut. 1 pers. sing., suff. 3 pers. pl. masc.; וָ id. . . . . אכל

[s]אֲכַלְנֻהוּ וַ id. pret. 1 pers. pl., suff. 3 pers. sing. masc.; וַ for וְ . . . . אכל

[t]אֲכָלַנוּ id. pret. 3 pers. sing. masc., suff. (Kh. נוּ, K. נִי) 1 pers. pl. or sing. . . אכל

[y]אָכַלְנוּ id. pret. 1 pers. pl. . . . . אכל

[z]אֲכָלָנִי id. pret. 3 pers. sing. masc., suff. 1 pers. sing. אכל

[a]אָכַלְתָּ, [b]אָכָלְתָּ } id. pret. 2 pers. sing. masc. (§ 8. rem. 7) אכל

אָכַלְתָּ וְ id. id.; acc. shifted by conv. וְ (§ 8. r. 7) אכל

[c]אָכַלְתְּ וְ id. pret. 2 pers. sing. fem. . . . . אכל

[d]אֹכֶלֶת, אֹכֶלֶת } id. part. act. sing. fem. . . . . אכל

אֲכָלַתְהוּ, [e]אֲכָלַתְהוּ } id. pret. 3 pers. sing. fem. with suff. 3 pers. sing. masc. . . . . אכל

[f]אָכַלְתִּי id. pret. 2 pers. sing. fem. Kh. אָכַלְתְּ, K. תִּי' (§ 8. rem. 5) . . . . . אכל

אָכַלְתִּי, וְ' אָכַלְתִּי } id. pret. 1 pers. sing. (§ 8. rem. 7) . אכל

[g]אֲכָלַתְךָ id. pret. 3 pers. sing. f., suff. 2 pers. sing. m. אכל

אֲכָלְתֶם וָ id. id., suff. 3 pers. pl. masc.; וָ for וְ conv. אכל

אֲכַלְתֶּם וְ' id. pret. 2 pers. pl. masc.; וַ id. . אכל

[h]אֲכָלַתְנִי id. pret. 3 pers. sing. fem., suff. 1 pers. sing. [for לַתְנִי'] . . . . . . אכל

אָכֵן adv. . . . . כון

[i]אֲכַנֶּה Piel fut. 1 pers. sing. . . . . כנה

אַכֶּנּוּ Hiph. fut. 1 pers. sing. (אַכֶּה § 25, No. 2b), suff. 3 pers. sing. masc. . . . . נכה

[k]אַכְנִיעַ Hiph. fut. 1 pers. sing. . . . . כנע

[l]אֲכַנְּךָ Piel fut. 1 pers. sing. (אֲכַנֶּה), suff. 2 pers. sing. masc. (§ 24. rem. 21) . . . כנה

[m]אֲכַסֶּה [n]וָ' Piel fut. 1 pers. sing.; וָ for וַ conv. כסה

[o]אֲכַסֵּךְ וָ id., suff. 2 pers. sing. fem. (§ 24. rem. 21); וָ id. . . . . . כסה

[p]אֲכַסֶּנּוּ id., suff. 3 pers. sing. masc. . . . כסה

[q]אַכְעִיסֵם Hiph. fut. 1 pers. sing., suff. 3 pers. pl. masc. כעס

[r]אֶכְעָס Kal fut. 1 pers. sing. . . . . כעס

אָכַף *to bow down*, cogn. כָּפַף, hence *to compel*, Pr. 16. 26. אֶכֶף masc. i. q. כַּף *the palm of the hand*, only with suff. אַכְפִּי, Job 33. 7.

[s]אִכַּף Niph. fut. 1 pers. sing. . . . . כפף

[t]אַכְפִּי וְ' noun masc. sing. with suff. 1 pers. sing. from [אֶכֶף] dec. 6a. . . . אכף

[u]אֲכַפֵּר Piel fut. 1 pers. sing. . . . . כפר

אֲכַפְּרָה id. with paragogic ה . . . . כפר

אכר Root not used; Arab. *to dig*, whence אִכָּר masc. dec. 1b (§ 30. rem. 1) *ploughman, husbandman*.

[x]אֶכְּרֶהָ וָ Kal fut. 1 pers. s., suff. 3 pers. s. fem. with euph. dag. for [אֶכְרֶהָ]; וָ for וַ conv. . כרה

אֶכְרוֹת Kal fut. 1 pers. sing. . . . . כרת

[y]אֶכְרָת־ id.; Kh. רוֹת', K. רָת־' with Mak. (§ 8. r. 18) כרת

[z]אִכָּרֵיכֶם noun masc. pl., suff. 2 pers. pl. masc. from אִכָּר dec. 1b . . . . . אכר

אִכָּרִים id. pl., absolute state . . . . אכר

אַכְרִית [a]וָ' Hiph. fut. 1 pers. sing.; וָ for וַ conv. . כרת

[b]אֶכְרְעָה וָ Kal fut. 1 pers. sing. [אֶכְרַע] with parag. ה; וָ id. . . . . כרע

אֶכְרֹת וְ' Kal fut. 1 pers. sing. . . . . כרת

[a] Is. 55. 1. [b] Le. 10. 12. [c] Je. 50. 7. [d] Ob. 1. 18. [e] Da. 7. 5. [f] Da. 11. 26. [g] Le. 19. 8. [h] Je. 30. 16. [i] Am. 6. 4. [k] Ge. 2. 17. [l] Ex. 33. 3. [m] Le. 25. 37. [n] Ge. 50. 21. [o] 1 Ki. 18. 13. [p] Ge. 3. 5. [q] Ex. 32. 10. [r] 2 Sa. 22. 39. [s] Ho. 13. 8. [t] Je. 15. 16. [u] 1 Ki. 17. 12. [x] Je. 51. 34. [y] 2 Sa. 19. 43. [z] Ge. 31. 40. [a] Ge. 3. 11. [b] Pr. 23. 8. [c] Ru. 2. 14. [d] Is. 30. 27. [e] Eze. 15. 5. [f] Eze. 16. 13. [g] Eze. 28. 18. [h] Ps. 69. 10. [i] Job 32. 21, 22. [k] Ps. 81. 15. [l] Is. 45. 4. [m] Je. 46. 8. [n] Eze. 16. 8. [o] Eze. 16. 10. [p] Eze. 32. 7. [q] De. 32. 21. [r] Eze. 16. 42. [s] Mic. 6. 6. [t] Job 33. 7. [u] 2 Sa. 21. 3. [x] Ho. 3. 2. [y] Jos. 9. 7. [z] Is. 61. 5. [a] 1 Ch. 17. 8. [b] Ezr. 9. 5.

אַכְרִתָה[a] וְ Hiph. fut. 1 pers. sing. with parag. ה; וְ for וַ· conv. . . . . . כרת

אֶכְרְתָה[b] וְ Kal fut. 1 pers. sing. (אֶכְרֹת with parag. ה) כרת

אַכְשָׁף וְ׳ pr. name of a place . . . . . כשף

אֶכֹּת[c] וְ Kal fut. 1 pers. sing., for [אֶכְתֹּת § 18. rem. 14]; וְ for וַ· conv. . . . . כתת

אֶכְתֹּב[d] וְ׳, וָ׳[e] Kal fut. 1 pers. sing.; וָ id. . . . כתב

אֶכְתֳּבֶנָּה[f] id., suff. 3 pers. sing. fem. (§ 8. r. 14, & § 2. r. 3) כתב

אֶכְתֹּוב־[g] Kh. תּוֹב׳, K. תָּב־ Kal. fut. 1 pers. sing. (§ 8. rem. 18.) . . . . . כתב

אֵל (only 1 Ch. 20. 8. elsewhere הָאֵל) and אֵלֶּה pron. pl. com., *these*, used as the pl. of זֶה and זֹאת.—Chald. id.

אֵלִּין and אֵלֵּךְ Chald. id.

אֵל וְ׳ noun m. s. dec. 1 a., or def. of אֵיל[ll] (q.v.) אול

אַל וְ׳ adv. of negation . . . . . אלל

אֶל וְ׳ more frequently אֶל־, prop. constr. of אֵל (following the analogy of ל״ה, as if for אֵלֶה comp. § 27, V. § 36. rem. 2, 3, 4, hence) pl. constr. אֱלֵי, with suff. אֵלַי, אֵלֶיךָ, אֵלָיו, אֲלֵיהֶם, once אֵלֵהֶם, poet. אֵלֵימוֹ, prep. expressing, in general, motion or direction towards any thing, whether physically or intellectually, but also a state of rest attained to, equivalent to עַל.—I. *to*, sign of the dative case, like לְ.—II. *to, towards.*—III. *about, concerning.*—IV. *for, on account of.*—V. *in, into.*—VI. denoting rest, *at, on, near; among; through, by.*—VII. with other particles its force is sometimes entirely lost, אֶל־אַחֲרַי *behind me;* אֶל־מִחוּץ לְ *without;* אֶל־תַּחַת יָדִי *under my hand*, 1 Sa. 21. 5; אֶל־מִן *out of*, Job 5. 5.

אֵלָא pr. name masc. . . . . . . אול

אַלְבִּין[h] Hiph. fut. 1 pers. sing. . . . . לבן

אַלְבִּישׁ Hiph. fut. 1 pers. sing. . . . . לבש

אַלְבִּשֵׁךְ[i] וָ id., suff. 2 pers. sing. fem.; וָ for וַ· conv. לבש

אֶלְבָּשֶׁנָּה[k] Kal fut. 1 pers. sing. [אֶלְבַּשׁ], suff. 3 pers. sing. fem. (§ 16. rem. 12, & § 2. rem. 3) לבש

אֶלְגָּבִישׁ noun masc. sing. . . . . . גבש

אַלְגּוּמִּים[l] וְ׳[m] noun pl. masc., see אַלְמֻגִּים.

אֵלֵד[n] וָ׳[o] Kal fut. 1 pers. sing.; וָ for וַ· conv. . ילד

אֶלְדָּד, וְאֶלְדָּעָה pr. names masc. . . . . אלה

אָלַהּ Root not used; Arab. *to worship, to adore.*

אֱלוֹהַּ masc. dec. 1; sing. and pl. (אֱלֹהִים).—I. *God*, the true God, especially with the art. הָאֱלֹהִים.—II. applied *to false gods*, or *idols*.—III. applied to *angels*, Ps. 8. 6. אֱלֹהִים in the sense of the singular, spoken of God, is followed by the verb or adj. in the singular very rarely in the plural; comp. Ge. 20. 13; 1 Sa. 17. 26; 2 Sa. 7. 23.

אֱלָהּ Chald. masc. dec. 1 a, *God.*

I. אָלָה denom. of אֵל (R. אול) prop. *to invoke God.*—I. *to swear.*—II. *to curse*, Ju. 17. 2.—III. *to howl*, cogn. אלל, ילל. Hiph. *to cause to swear.*

אָלָה fem. dec. 10. with suff. אָלָתִי.—I. *oath*, especially a covenant made by an oath.—II. *imprecation, curse, cursing;* שְׁבֻעַת הָאָלָה *an oath of imprecation*, i. e. joined with cursing; הָיָה לְאָלָה *to be for a curse;* נָתַן לְאָלָה *to give over unto cursing;* לִשְׁאוֹל בְּאָלָה נַפְשׁוֹ *to wish a curse for his soul.*

תַּאֲלָה fem. dec. 10, *curse*, La. 3. 65.

אֵל (with tseri pure) and אֱלִי in composition with the following pr. names i. q. אֵל *God*, R. אול.

אֶלְדָּד (whom *God loves*, R. דוד) pr. name masc. Nu. 11. 26, 27.

אֶלְדָּעָה (whom *God calls*, דעא Arab. *to call*), pr. name masc. Ge. 25. 4.

אֶלְזָבָד (whom *God has given*) pr. name masc.

אֶלְחָנָן (whom *God favours*) pr. name of one of David's heroes.

אֱלִיאָב (*God* is his *father*) pr. name of several men, especially—I. of a chief of the tribe of Zebulun.—II. of a brother of David.

אֱלִיאֵל (*God* is his *strength*) pr. name of several men, especially—I. of a hero of David.—II. of a chief of the tribe of Manasseh.—III. of a chief of the tribe of Benjamin.

אֱלִיאָתָה (to whom *God comes*) pr. name masc. 1 Ch. 25. 4, called ver. 27 אֱלִיָּתָה (Simonis, *lamentation* from אלה).

אֱלִידָד (whom *God loves*, comp. אֶלְדָּד) pr. name of a chief of Benjamin, Nu. 34. 21.

אֶלְיָדָע (whom *God knows*) pr. name of several men, especially of a son of David, 2 Sa. 5. 16, for which בְּעֶלְיָדָע 1 Ch. 14. 7.

אֱלִיהוּ (*God* is *He*, i. e. the Lord) pr. name masc., see the following.

אֱלִיהוּא (id.) pr. name of several men, especially of one of Job's friends, written also אֱלִיהוּ.

אֶלְיַחְבָּא (*God will hide* (protect) him) pr. name of one of David's heroes, 2 Sa. 23. 32.

---

[a] 2 Sa. 7. 9. [b] Is. 55. 3. [c] De. 9. 21. [d] De. 10. 2. [e] Je. 32. 10. [f] Je. 31. 33. [g] Ho. 8. 12. [h] Ps. 51. 9. [i] Eze. 16. 10. [k] Ca. 5. 3. [l] 2 Ch. 9. 10 [ll] Eze. 40. 48. [m] 2 Ch. 2. 7. [n] Ge. 18. 13. [o] 1 Ki. 3. 17.

אֱלִיחֹרֶף (*God is his recompense* חרף Arab. *to recompense*) pr. name masc. 1 Ki. 4. 3.

אֱלִימֶלֶךְ (*God is his king*) pr. name of the father-in-law of Ruth.

אֶלְיָסָף (whom *God has added*) pr. name masc.—I. of a chief of the tribe of Gad.—II. Nu. 3. 24.

אֱלִיעֶזֶר (*God is his help*) pr. name of several men, especially—I. of a servant of Abraham.—II. of the second son of Moses.

אֱלִיעֵינַי (*God is mine eye*, i. e. directs me) pr. name masc. 1 Ch. 8. 20.

אֱלִיעָם (*God's people*) pr. name masc.—I. 2 Sa. 11. 3, for which עַמִּיאֵל 1 Ch. 3. 5.—II. 2 Sa. 23. 34.

אֱלִיפַז (*God is strength*, or *precious*, R. פזז) pr. name masc.—I. of a son of Esau.—II. of a friend of Job.

אֱלִיפָל (whom *God judges*, R. פלל) pr. name masc. 1 Ch. 11. 35.

אֱלִיפְלֵהוּ (*whom God distinguishes*) pr. name masc. 1 Ch. 15. 18, 21.

אֱלִיפֶלֶט, אֶלְפֶּלֶט (*God is his deliverance*) pr. name of various men.

אֱלִיצוּר (*God is his rock*) pr. name masc.

אֱלִיצָפָן, אֶלְצָפָן (whom *God protects*) pr. name masc.

אֱלִיקָא (*God's congregation*, comp. אֱלִיעָם, קָא for קְהָא Chald. *to congregate*) pr. name masc. 2 Sa. 23. 25.

אֶלְיָקִים (*God establishes* him) pr. name masc.—I. of a prefect of the palace under King Hezekiah.—II. of a king of Judah, afterwards changed to יְהוֹיָקִים.—III. Ne. 12. 41.

אֱלִישֶׁבַע (*God is her oath*) pr. name fem. Ex. 6. 23.

אֱלִישׁוּעַ (*God is his salvation*) pr. name of a son of David.

אֶלְיָשִׁיב (*God will restore*) pr. name of various men.

אֱלִישָׁמָע (whom *God hears*) pr. name masc.—I. of a son of David.—II. of a son of Ammihud, a chief of Ephraim.—III. of the grandfather of Ishmael who slew Gedaliah, comp. 2 Ki. 25. 25.—IV. of a priest in the time of Jehoshaphat, 2 Ch. 17. 8.—V. 1 Ch. 2. 41.

אֱלִישָׁע (*God is his salvation*, for אֵלִי יֶשַׁע) pr. name masc. prophet and successor of Elijah.

אֱלִישָׁפָט (whom *God judges*) pr. name masc. 2 Ch. 23. 1.

אֶלְנַעַם (*God is his delight*) pr. name masc. 1 Ch. 11. 46.

אֶלְנָתָן (whom *God has given*, i. e. given of God) pr. name masc.—I. of the grandfather of King Jehoiakim.—II. Ezr. 8. 16.

אֶלְעָד (apoc. for אֶלְעָדָה q. v.) pr. name masc. 1 Ch. 7. 21.

אֶלְעָדָה (whom *God adorns*) pr. name masc. 1 Ch. 7. 20.

אֶלְעוּזַי (*God my strength* or *praise*, for עֻזִּי R. עזז) pr. name masc. 1 Ch. 12. 5.

אֶלְעָזָר (whom *God helpeth*) pr. name of various men.

אֶלְעָלֵה, אֶלְעָלֵא (*God ascending*) pr. name of a town in the tribe of Reuben.

אֶלְעָשָׂה (*God has done it!*) pr. name of various men.

אֶלְפַּעַל (*God of recompense*, comp. פֹּעַל, פְּעֻלָּה) pr. name of a man.

אֶלְקָנָה (whom *God created*) pr. name of various men, especially—I. of a son of Korah.—II. of the father of Samuel.

אֶלְתּוֹלַד (*God of posterity*, see תּוֹלֵד R. ילד) pr. name of a city.

אֶלְתְּקֵא, אֶלְתְּקֵה (*God of worship*, תקא Arab. *to fear*) pr. name of a city in the tribe of Dan.

אֶלְתְּקֹן (*God is its establishment*) pr. name of a city in the tribe of Judah, Jos. 15. 59.

II. אָלָה Arab. *to be stout, fat*, cogn. אול.

אַלְיָה fem. the large *tail* of the eastern sheep.

אָלָה noun fem. sing. dec. 10. (§ 42. rem. 2) . אלה

אָלֹה[a] Kal infin. absolute . . . . . אלה

אֵלֶּה[b] Chald. Kh. אֵלֶּה, K. אֵל pron. demon. pl. . אל

אֵלָה[c] ׳וְ noun fem. sing.; also proper name masc. אול

אֱלָהּ Chald. noun masc. sing. dec. 1 a. . . אלה

אֵלֶּה ׳וְ pron. demon. pl. com. gen. . . . אל

אֱלוֹהַּ noun masc. sing. dec. 1 a. . . . . אלה

אֱלָהָא } Chald. n. m. s., emph. of אֱלָהּ dec. 1 a; } אלה
אֱלָהָא[d] ׳וְ } with pref. contr. [for וֶאֱלָהָא] . }

אֱלָהֵהּ Chald. id., suff. 3 pers. sing. masc. . . אלה

אֱלָהֲהוֹן[e] Chald. id., suff. 3 pers. pl. masc. . . אלה

אֱלָהֲהֹם Chald. id., suff. 3 pers. pl. masc., ם by Hebraism for ן . . . . . אלה

אֱלָהִי[f] Chald. id., suff. 1 pers. sing. . . . אלה

אֱלֹהָי in pause for אֱלֹהַי (q. v.) . . . אלה

[a] Ho. 4. 2. [b] Ezr. 5. 15. [c] Eze. 6. 13; Ho. 4. 13. [d] Ezr. 6. 12. [e] Da. 3. 28, 29. [f] Da. 6. 23.

אֱלֹהָי וֶ' id. contracted [for וֶאֱ'] . . . . אלה

אֱלֹהַי } noun m. pl., suff. 1 pers. s. from אֱלוֹהַּ
וֵ' אלֹהַי } dec. 1 a; with pref. contr. [for וֶאֱ'] . אלה

אֱלֹהֵי } id. pl., construct state; with pref. id. . אלה
וֵ' אלֹהֵי }

אֱלָהַיָּא[a] Chald. noun masc. pl. emph. from אֱלָהּ dec. 1 a. . . . . אלה

אֱלֹהֶיהָ noun masc. pl., suff. 3 pers. sing. fem. from אֱלוֹהַּ dec. 1 a. . . . . אלה

אֱלֹהֵיהֶם } id., suff. 3 pers. pl. masc.; with pref.
וֵ' אלֹהֵיהֶם[b] } contr. [for וֶאֱ'] . . . אלה

אֱלֹהֵיהֶן id., suff. 3 pers. pl. fem. . . . אלה

אֱלֹהָיו } id., suff. 3 pers. sing. masc.; with pref.
וֵ' אלֹהָיו[c] } con. [for וֶאֱ'] . . . אלה

אֱלֹהֶיךָ id., suff. 2 pers. sing. masc. . . . אלה

אֱלֹהָיִךְ } id., suff. 2 pers. sing. fem. . . . אלה
אֱלֹהַיִךְ }

וֵ' אלֹהָיִךְ id. id.; contracted [for וֶאֱ'] . . . אלה

אֱלֹהֶיךָ[d] id., suff., Kh. ־הָיִךְ q. v., K. ־הִים (q. v.) . אלה

אֱלֹהֵיכֶם id., suff. 2 pers. pl. masc. . . . אלה

אֱלֹהִים } id. pl., absolute state; with pref. contr.
וֵ' אלֹהִים } [for וֶאֱ'] . . . . אלה

אֱלֹהֵימוֹ[e] id., suff. 3 pers. pl. masc. . . . אלה

אֱלָהִין Chald. noun masc. pl. abs. from אֱלָהּ dec. 1 a. אלה

אֱלֹהֵינוּ } noun m. pl., suff. 1 pers. pl. from אֱלוֹהַּ
וֵ' אלֹהֵינוּ } dec. 1 a; with pref. contr. [for וֶאֱ'] אלה

אֱלָהָךְ Chald. noun masc. sing., suff. 2 pers. sing. masc. from אֱלָהּ dec. 1 a. . . . אלה

אֱלָהֲכוֹן[f] Chald. id., suff. 2 pers. pl. masc. . . אלה

אֱלָהֲכֹם[g] Chald. id., suff. 2 pers. pl. masc., ם by Hebraism for ן . . . . . אלה

אֲלֵהֶם[h] וַ' for אֲלֵי', prep. (אֶל), with pl. suff. 3 pers. pl. masc. . . . . . אל

אֲלֵהֶן[i] id., suff. 3 pers. pl. fem. . . . אל

אֱלָהַנָא[k] Chald. noun masc. sing., suff. 1 pers. pl. from אֱלָהּ dec. 1 a. . . . . אלה

אֲלוּ וַ Chald. i. q. אֲרוּ *see! behold!*

אִלּוּ וְ conj. (contr. from אִם־לוּ) *if, though.*

אֵלוֹ Kh., for K. אֵלָיו (q. v.) . . . . אל

אֵלָו[l] וְ' Kh. id.; noun masc. pl., suff. 3 pers. sing. masc. from אַיִל dec. 6 h. . . . אול

אֱלוֹהַּ[m] וֶ' noun masc. sing. dec. 1 a; וֶ before (ֱ) . אלה

אֱלוֹהַי[n] } id. pl. with suff. 1 pers. sing. . . . אלה
אֱלוֹהַי[o] }

אֱלוּל[p] וְ' Kh. אֱלוּל, K. אֱלִיל noun masc. sing. dec. 1 a; וֶ before (ֱ) . . . . . . אלל

אַלּוֹן[q] וְ' noun masc. sing. dec. 1 b; also pr. name masc. . . . . אלל

אֵלוֹן[cc] וְ' noun masc. sing. dec. 1 b; also pr. name m. אול

אַלּוֹנֵי noun masc. pl. construct from אַלּוֹן dec. 1 b. אלל

אֵלוֹנֵי[r] noun masc. pl. construct from אֵלוֹן dec. 1 b. אול

אַלּוֹנִים[s] noun masc. pl. absolute from אַלּוֹן dec. 1 b. אלל

אַלּוּף noun masc. sing. dec. 1 b. . . . אלף

אַלּוּפֵי id. pl., construct state . . . . אלף

אַלּוּפִי[t] id. sing., suff. 1 pers. sing. . . . אלף

אַלּוּפֵיהֶם[u] id. pl., suff. 3 pers. pl. masc. . . . אלף

אַלּוּפֵינוּ[ff] id. pl., suff. 1 pers. pl. . . . אלף

אָלוֹת[ii] n. f., pl. of אָלָה d. 10 (§ 42. r. 2), or Kal inf. con.[mm] אלה

אֶלְזָבָד pr. name masc. . . . . . אלה

אלח. Niph. *to be corrupt,* in a moral sense.

אֶלְחַם[x] Kal fut. 1 pers. sing. . . . . לחם

אֶלְחָנָן pr. name masc. . . . . . אלה

אֵלַי } prep. (אֶל) with pl. suff. 1 pers. sing. . אל
וְ' אֵלָי }

אֱלֵי id. pl., construct state . . . . אל

אֵלִי noun masc. sing., suff. 1 pers. sing from אֵל dec. 1 a. . . . . . . אול

אֱלִי[y] Kal imp. sing. fem. . . . . . אלה

אֻלַי[z] defect. for אוּלַי adv. . . . . . אול

אֱלִיאָב ,וְ' & אֱלִיאֵל ,וְ' & אֱלִיאָתָה ,אֱלִידָד ,אֱלִידָע & וְ' pr. names masc.; וֶ before (ֱ) . . אלה

אֵלֶיהָ prep. (אֶל) with pl. suff. 3 pers. sing. fem. . אל

אֵלִיָּה ,וְ' & אֵלִיָּהוּ ,וְ' pr. names masc. . . אול

אֱלִיהוּ ,וֶ' & אֱלִיהוּא ,וֶ' pr. names masc.; וֶ before (ֱ) אלה

אֶלְיְהוֹעֵינַי (*towards the Lord are mine eyes,* compare R. הוה יְהוָה) contr. אֶלְיוֹעֵינַי pr. name of various men.

אֲלֵיהֶם[a] וְ' prep. (אֶל) with pl. suff. 3 pers. pl. masc. אל

אֵילֵיהֶם[b] noun masc. pl., suff. 3 pers. pl. masc. from אַיִל dec. 1 a. . . . . . איל

אֵילֵיהֶמָּה[c] noun masc. pl., suff. 3 pers. pl. masc. from אַיִל dec. 6 h. (§ 4. rem. 6) . . איל

אֲלֵיהֶן prep. (אֶל) with pl. suff. 3 pers. pl. fem. . אל

אֵלָיו[d] וְ' id., suff. 3 pers. sing. masc. . . . אל

[a] Je. 10. 11. [b] Ju. 2. 3. [c] 2 Sa. 7. 23. [cc] Ho. 4. 13. [d] 1 Ki. 1. 47. [e] De. 32. 37. [f] Da. 2. 47. [ff] Ps. 144. 14. [g] Ezr. 7. 17, 18. [h] Le. 17. 8. [i] Ex. 1. 19. [ii] De. 29. 20. [k] Da. 3. 17. [l] Eze. 40. 29, 33. [m] Job 24. 12. [mm] Ho. 10. 4. [n] Ps. 143. 10. [o] Ps. 145. 1. [p] Je. 14. 14. [q] Is. 44. 14. [r] De. 11. 30. [s] Eze. 27. 6. [t] Ps. 55. 14. [u] Ge. 36. 19. [x] Ps. 141. 4. [y] Joel 1. 8. [z] Ge. 24. 39. [a] 2 Sa. 20. 3. [b] Eze. 31. 14. [c] Eze. 40. 16. [d] De. 24. 15.

אֶלְיוֹעֵינַי וְ' / אֶלְיוֹעֵנַי } pr. name masc., see אֶלְיְהוֹעֵינַי.

אֱלִיחֹרֶף, אֶלְיַחְבָּא pr. names masc. . . . אלה

אֵלֶיךָ וְ' prep. (אֶל) with pl. suff. 2 pers. sing. masc. אל

אֵלַיִךְ / אֵלָיִךְ[a] וְ' } id. with suff. 2 pers. sing. fem. . אל

אֲלֵיכֶם id., suff. 2 pers. pl. masc. . . . אל

אֱלִילֵי[b] וְ' n. masc. pl. construct from אֱלִיל dec. 1 a. אלל

אֱלִילִים / אֱלִלִים[c] } id. pl., absolute state . . אלל

אֵלִים noun masc., pl. of אַיִל or אֵיל dec. 6 h. or 1 a. אול

אֵלֵימוֹ[d] prep. (אֶל) with pl. suff. 3 pers. pl. masc. . אל

אֱלִימֶלֶךְ pr. name masc. . . . . אלה

אָלִין Kal fut. 1 pers. sing. R. לִין see . . לון

אִלֵּין Chald. pron. demon. pl. com. gen. . אל

אֵלֵינוּ prep. (אֶל) with pl. suff. 1 pers. pl. . . אל

אֱלִיסָף, אֱלִיעֶזֶר & וְ' אֱלִיעֵינַי, וְאֱלִיעָם, אֱלִיפָז &
וֶאֱלִיפְלֵהוּ, וֶאֱלִיפָלֶט, אֱלִיפָל, אֱלִיפָז &
אֱלִיקָא, אֱלִיצָפָן, אֱלִיצוּר, וְ' & אֱלִיפֶלֶט,
אֱלִישֶׁבַע, אֶלְיָקִים (fem.), pr. names masc. אלה

אֱלִישָׁה pr. name of a region . . . אלש

אֱלִישׁוּעַ, וְ' אֱלְיָשִׁיב, & וְ' אֱלִישָׁמָע, וְ' אֶלְיְשָׁמָע & וְ' אֱלִישָׁע &
אֱלִישָׁפָט pr. names masc. . . . אלה

אָלִית[e] Kal preter. 2 pers. sing. fem. . . . אלה

אֵלֵךְ[f] וְ' / אֵלֵךְ וְ' & וְ' } Kal fut. 1 pers. sing. (§ 20. rem. 4); וָ for וַ· conv. . } ילך

אֵלֵךְ id.; Milêl before monos. . . . . ילך

אִלֵּךְ Chald. pron. demon. pl. . . . . אל

אֲלַכֵּד[g] Kal fut. 1 pers. sing. . . . . לכד

אֵלְכָה[h] וְ' / אֵלְכָה וְ' } Kal fut. 1 pers. sing. with paragogic ה . ילך

אֲלֵכֶם def. [for אֲלֵי'כֶם] prep. (אֶל) with pl. suff. 2 pers. sing. masc. . . . . . אל

אָלַל Root not used, in the deriv.—I. *to be nothing.*—II. *to howl,* cogn. יָלַל.—III. *to be strong,* cogn. אוּל.

אַל prop. subst. *nothing,* Job 24. 25.—Adv.—I. abs. *nay! not so!* אַל בְּנֹתַי *nay,* or *not so, my daughters!*—II. conj. *that not;* especially before the future, to express prohibition and dehortation; אַל יֵצֵא אִישׁ *let no man go out;* אַל אֵבוֹשָׁה *let me not be ashamed;* but rarely like לֹא, as אַל יֶחֱרַשׁ *he will not be silent,* Ps. 50. 3. —III. once before a pret. interrogatively, 1 Sa. 27. 10.

אַל Chald. i. q. Heb. No. II.

אֵלָה fem. *terebinth,* others, *an oak,* Jos. 24. 26.

אֵלוֹן masc. dec. 1 b.—I. *an oak.*—II. pr. name masc., 1 Ch. 4. 37.

אֱלוּל masc.—I. i. q. אֱלִיל, *vanity,* Je. 14. 14. Kheth.—II. *Elul,* the sixth month of the Hebrew year, answering nearly to our September, Ne. 6. 15. Its etymology is uncertain.

אֱלִיל masc. dec. 1 a.—I. adj. *nought, vain,* hence, pl. *idols*—II. *vanity.*

אַלְלַי interj. expressive of grief, *wo! alas!*

אַלַּמֶּלֶךְ (*the king's oak* for אַל הַמֶּלֶךְ, comp. fem. אֵלָה) pr. name of a place in the tribe of Asher, Jos. 19. 26.

אֱלִילֵי def. for אֱלִיל noun masc. sing., dec. 1 a. . אלל

אַלְלַי interj. . . . . . . אלל

אָלַם Kal not used, in the deriv. *to bind.* Niph.—I. *to be dumb.*—II. *to be silent.* Pi. *to bind,* as sheaves, Ge. 37. 7.

אֵלֶם masc. *silence,* Ps. 58. 2; *is there indeed silence* (when) *ye ought to decree justice* (though contrary to the accents), Ps. 56. 1; correctly Gesenius, *the silent dove among strangers,* designating the subject of the Psalm.

אִלֵּם masc. dec. 7 b, adj. *dumb.*

אֲלֻמָּה fem. dec. 10. pl. ־ִים & ־וֹת, *a sheaf of corn*

אַלְמָן masc. adj. *forsaken, widowed,* Je. 51. 5.

אַלְמֹן masc. *widowhood,* Is. 47. 9.

אַלְמָנָה fem. dec. 11 b.—I. *a widow.*—II. *desolate places,* Is. 13. 22.

אַלְמָנוּת fem. dec. 3 a, *widowhood.*

אַלְמֹנִי *some one,* a certain one, always joined with פְּלֹנִי.

אֵלֶם noun masc. sing. . . . . . אלם

אִלֵּם adj. masc. sing. dec. 7 b. . . . אלם

אֵלָם[k] וְ' not in all copies, for אוּלָם (q. v.) . אול

אֵלָמָּיו[l] וְ' accord. to some copies אֵלָם for אוּלָם (q.v.) אול

אַלְמֻגִּים pl. *almug-trees,* a kind of precious wood, by some supposed to be the red *sandal-wood.* It is also found by transposition אַלְגּוּמִּים.

אֶלְמַד[m] Kal fut. 1 pers. sing. . . . . למד

---

[a] Is. 45. 14. [b] Is. 31. 7. [c] Le. 26. 1. [d] Ps. 2. 5. [e] Ju. 17. 2. [f] Job 19. 10. [g] 2 Sa. 12. 28. [h] Is. 38. 10. [i] Job 13. 4. [k] Eze. 40. 9. [l] Job 17. 10. [m] Ps. 119. 71.

Hiph. denom. from אֶלֶף, *to bring forth thousands.*

אַלּוּף adj. masc. dec. 1 b.—I. *tame, gentle,* Je. 11. 19.—II. *familiar, friend.*—III. *ox, bullock,* Ps. 144. 14.—IV. *head of a family* or *tribe.*

אֶלֶף masc. dec. 6 a. with suff. אַלְפִּי.—I. *thousand;* מֵאָה אֶלֶף *a hundred thousand;* אֶלֶף אֲלָפִים *a thousand thousands;* אַלְפֵי רְבָבָה *thousands of myriads.*—II. *family,* as a subdivision of a tribe.—III. pl. *oxen,* comp. אַלּוּף.—IV. pr. name of a city, Jos. 18. 28.

אֲלַף, אֶלֶף (by Hebraism, Da. 7. 10.) Chald. masc. dec. 3 a. *thousand.*

אֲלַף[z] Chald. noun masc. sing. dec. 3 a. . . אלף

אָלֶף ן' / אֶלֶף ן', ן' [a] } noun m. sing. dec. 6 a. (with suff. אַלְפִּי); ן see lett. ו . . } אלף

אַלְפָּא[b] Chald. noun m. sing., emph. of אֲלַף, dec. 3 a. אלף

אַלְפֵי noun masc., pl. constr. from אֶלֶף dec. 6 a. . אלף

אַלְפִּי[c] id. sing., suff. 1 pers. sing. . . . אלף

אַלּוּפֵי[d] noun masc. pl. constr. from אַלּוּף dec. 1 b. . אלף

אֲלָפֶיךָ noun masc. pl., suff. 2 pers. sing. masc. from אֶלֶף (q. v.) . . . . . אלף

אֲלָפִים [e] ן' id. pl. absolute state; ן before (-:) . אלף

אַלּוּפִים[f] noun masc., pl. of אַלּוּף dec. 1 b. . . אלף

אַלְפַּיִם / אַלְפָּיִם [g] ן' } noun masc., dual of אֶלֶף dec. 6 a. . אלף

אַלְפִים[h] Chald. by Hebraism for Keri ־פִין pl. of אֲלַף (q. v.) . . . . . אלף

אֶלְפֶּלֶט ן for ־פֶּלֶט (see אֱלִיפֶלֶט), אֶלְפַּעַל & pr. names masc. . . . . אלה

אָלַץ Pi. *to urge, press,* Ju. 16. 16.

אֶלְצָפָן ן' pr. name masc. see אֱלִיצָפָן . . אלה

אַלְקוּם Pr. 30. 31. מֶלֶךְ אַלְקוּם עִמּוֹ *a king against whom there is no rising up* (from אַל *not,* and קוּם). Most of the moderns, *a king with whom is the people,* i. e. surrounded by his people, (אַל the Arab. art. and קוּם Arab. *people*). Prof. Lee, *a king* (having) *provision with him* (coll. with the Arab. לקם).

אֶלָּקֵחַ[i] Niph. fut. 1 pers. sing. . . . . לקח

אֲלַקֳּטָה[k] [l] ן' Piel fut. 1 pers. sing. with parag. ה (§ 10. rem. 7); ן for ן . . . . לקט

אֶלְקָנָה ן' pr. name masc. . . . . אלה

אֶלְקֹשִׁי gent. noun Elkoshite, spoken of the prophet Nahum, from a place אֶלְקֹשׁ, Na. 1. 1.

אֲלַמְּדָה[a] Piel fut. 1 pers. sing. with parag. ה . . למד

אֶלְמְדָה[b] ן Kal fut. 1 pers. sing. (אֶלְמַד) with parag. ה למד

אֲלַמֶּדְכֶם[c] Piel fut. 1 pers. sing., suff. 2 pers. pl. masc. למד

אֲלַמְּדֵם[d] id., suff. 3 pers. pl. masc. . . . למד

אֵלַמָּו[e] ן noun masc. pl., suff. 3 pers. pl. masc. (§ 4. rem. 1) from [אֵילָם] dec. 8 a. . . . אול

אַלְמוֹדָד pr. name of a son of Joktan.

אֵלַמּוֹת[f] ן n. m. with pl. fem. term. from אֵילָם dec. 8 a. אול

אֻלַמֵּי[g] ן noun masc. pl. constr. from אוּלָם dec. 8 a. אול

אֲלֻמִּים[h] noun fem. with pl. masc. term. from אֲלֻמָּה dec. 10. . . . . . אלם

אִלְּמִים adj. masc., pl. of אִלֵּם dec. 7 b. . . . אלם

אַלַּמֶּלֶךְ ן pr. name of a place . . . . אלל

אַלְמָן[i] adj. masc. sing. . . . . . אלם

אַלְמֹן[k] ן noun masc. sing. . . . . אלם

אַלְמָנָה ן' noun fem. sing. dec. 11 a. . . . אלם

אַלְמָנוֹת [l] ן' id. pl., absolute state . . . אלם

אַלְמְנוּת[m] noun fem. sing., constr. of [־מָנוּת] dec. 3 c. אלם

אַלְמְנוּתָהּ[n] id., suff. 3 pers. sing. fem. . . . . אלם

אַלְמְנוֹתָו[o] noun fem. pl., suff. (K. ־תָיו, § 4. rem. 1) 3 pers. sing. masc. from ־מָנָה dec. 11 a. אלם

אַלְמְנוֹתֶיהָ[p] id., suff. 3 pers. sing. fem. . . . אלם

אַלְמְנוֹתָיו id., suff. 3 pers. sing. masc. . . . אלם

אַלְמְנוֹתֶיךָ[q] ן id., suff. 2 pers. sing. masc. . . אלם

אַלְמְנוּתַיִךְ[r] noun fem. pl., suff. 2 pers. sing. fem. from [־מָנוּת] dec. 3 a. . . . . . אלם

אַלְמֹנִי adj. masc. sing. . . . . אלם

אַלְמְנֹתָיו ן defect for אַלְמְנוֹתָיו (q. v.) אלם

אֲלֻמָּתִי[s] noun fem. sing., suff. 1 pers. sing. from [אֲלֻמָּה] dec. 10. . . . . . אלם

אֲלֻמֹּתָיו[t] id. pl., suff. 3 pers. sing. masc. אלם

אֲלֻמֹּתֵיכֶם[u] id. pl., suff. 2 pers. pl. masc. . . אלם

אִלֵּן[x] Chald. elsewhere אִלֵּין pron. demon. pl. com. אל

אֶלְנֹעַם for ־נַעַם & אֶלְנָתָן pr. names masc. . אלה

אֶלָּסָר pr. name of a city, Ge. 14. 1, 9.

אֶלְעַג[y] Kal fut. 1 pers. sing. . . . . לעג

אֶלְעָד ן, אֶלְעָדָה וְאֶלְעוּזַי, אֶלְעָזָר, אֶלְעָלֵא, אֶלְעָלֵה, אֶלְעָשָׂה pr. names masc. . . . אלה

[אָלַף] fut. תֶּאֱלַף (§ 13. rem. 5), *to learn,* only Pr. 22. 25. In the deriv. and prim. *to accustom oneself, to become familiar; to join together, to associate,* Pi. *to teach.*

[a] Ps. 51. 15. [b] Ps. 119. 73. [c] Ps. 34. 12. [d] Ps. 132. 12. [e] Eze. 40. 21. [f] Eze. 40. 30. [g] Eze. 41. 15. [h] Ge. 37. 7. [i] Je. 51. 5. [k] Is. 47. 9. [l] Je. 18. 21. [m] 2 Sa. 20. 3. [n] Ge. 38. 14, 19. [o] Je. 15. 8. [p] Eze. 22. 25. [q] Je. 49. 11. [r] Is. 54. 4. [s] Ge. 37. 7. [t] Ps. 126. 7. [u] Ge. 37. 7. [x] Da. 6. 7. [y] Pr. 1. 26. [z] Da. 5. 1. [a] Ezr. 2. 69. [b] Da. 5. 1. [c] Ju. 6. 15. [d] Zec. 12. 5, 6. [e] Ps. 8. 8. [f] Je. 13. 21. [g] Ex. 38. 29. [h] Da. 7. 10. [i] 2 Ki. 2. 9. [k] Ru. 2. 7. [l] Ru. 2. 2.

אֶ֫לֶשׁ Root not used, whence
אָלוּשׁ (according to the Talmud, *a crowd of people*) pr. name of a station in the wilderness, Nu. 33. 13.
אֱלִישָׁה pr. name of a region situated on the Mediterranean.

אֱלָתוֹ[a] noun fem. sing., suff. 3 pers. sing. masc. from אָלָה dec. 10. (§ 42. rem. 2) . . . אלה

אֶלְתּוֹלַד ן pr. name of a place . . . אלה

אֱלָתִי[b] noun fem. sing., suff. 1 pers. sing. from אָלָה dec. 10. (§ 42. rem. 2) . . . אלה

אֶלְתְּקֵא / **אֶלְתְּקֵה** ן' } pr. name of a place . . . אלה

אֶלְתְּקֹן ן pr. name of a place . . . אלה

אֵם fem. dec. 8b.—I. *mother.*—II. *grandmother.*—III. *mother-city* or *metropolis.*—IV. metaph. of a nation, also of the earth, Job 1. 21.—V. אֵם הַדֶּרֶךְ *mother* (i. e. head) *of the way*, i. e. a place whence two ways diverge.
אַמָּה fem. dec. 10.—I. *the fore-arm*, cubitus, prop. *the mother* of the arm; whence—II. *a cubit*, a measure; אַרְבַּע בָּאַמָּה *four by the cubit*, i. e. four cubits.—III. *mother-city*, or *metropolis*, 2 Sa. 8. 1.—IV. *basis* or *pedestal*, Is. 6. 4.—V. pr. name of a hill, 2 Sa. 2. 24.
אַמָּה Chald. fem. pl. אַמִּין, *a cubit.*

אִם ן' mostly אִם־.—I. conj. *if, supposing, that;* אִם—אִם *whether—or;* אִם in swearing is properly conditional, *if*, as in 1 Sa. 3. 17, *God do so to thee, and more so, if thou*, &c.; but the form of imprecation is elsewhere omitted, and it is conveniently rendered by a negation, *not*, and אִם לֹא by an affirmative.—II. *though, although.*—III. adv. *when*, referring either to time past or future; עַד אִם, עַד אֲשֶׁר אִם *till when, till that.*—IV. *surely, truly.*—V. interrog. i. q. הֲ *if? whether?* הֲ—אִם, אִם—אִם, *whether—or?* and without interrog. in an indirect inquiry.—VI. הַאִם i. q. הֲלֹא *is not?*—VII. אִם־לֹא *if not, unless*, compare also No. 1.

אֶמְאָס Kal fut. 1 pers. sing. . . . מאס

אֶמְאָסְאךָ[c] ן id., suff. 2 pers. sing. masc. (§ 2. rem. 2); ן for ·וַ conv. . . . מאס

אֲמַגֶּנְךָ[d] Piel fut. 1 pers. sing., suff. 2 pers. sing. masc. . . . מגן

אֲמַדֵּד Piel fut. 1 pers. sing. . . . מדד

אָמָה[e] [f] ן' fem. irr. (§ 45) *a maid-servant, handmaid;* בֶּן־אָמָה *servant.*

אַמָּה ן' noun fem. sing. dec. 10. . . . אם

אַמָּהּ ן' noun fem. sing., suff. 3 pers. sing. fem. from אֵם dec. 8b. . . . אם

אַמָּה[g] Chald. noun fem. sing., pl. emph. אַמַּיָּא . . . אמם

אַמְהוֹת[h] noun fem. pl., constr. of אֲמָהוֹת' from אָמָה, irr. (§ 45) . . . אמה

אַמְהֹתַי[i] ן id., suff. 1 pers. sing. . . . אמה

אַמְהֹתֶיהָ[k] ן id., suff. 3 pers. sing. fem. . . . אמה

אַמְהֹתֵיהֶם ן id., suff. 3 pers. pl. masc. . . . אמה

אַמְהֹתָיו[l] ן id., suff. 3 pers. sing. masc. . . . אמה

אַמְהֹתֵיכֶם[m] ן id., suff. 2 pers. pl. masc. . . . אמה

אִמּוֹ ן' noun fem. sing., suff. 3 pers. sing. masc. from אֵם dec. 8b. . . . אם

אֶמּוֹט Niph. fut. 1 pers. sing. . . . מוט

אָמוֹן[n] noun masc. sing., also pr. name . . . אמן

אֱמוּנָה [o]ן' noun fem. sing. dec. 10; ן before (:;) . . . אמן

אֱמוּנוֹת[p] pl. of the preceding . . . אמן

אֱמוּנֵי[q] Kal part. p. pl. masc. constr. from [אָמוּן] dec. 3a. . . . אמן

אֱמוּנִים id. pl. abs.; or noun masc., pl. of [אֵמוּן] dec. 3b. . . . אמן

אֱמוּנַת[r] noun fem. sing., constr. of נָה' dec. 10. . . . אמן

אֱמוּנָתוֹ[s] [t]ן' id., suff. 3 pers. sing. masc.; ן before (:;) . . . אמן

אֱמוּנָתִי[u] ן id., suff. 1 pers. sing.; ן id. . . . אמן

אֱמוּנָתְךָ / **אֱמוּנָתֶךָ** ן' } id., suff. 2 pers. sing. masc.; ן' before (:;) . . . אמן

אָמוֹץ pr. name masc. . . . אמץ

אָמוֹר Kal inf. abs. . . . אמר

אַמּוֹת [x]ן' noun fem., pl. of אַמָּה dec. 10. . . . אם

אָמוּת Kal fut. 1 pers. sing. . . . מות

אַמּוֹת[y] Kh. אַמּוֹת q. v., K. מֵאוֹת (q. v.) . . . מאה

אֲמוֹת[z] noun fem., pl. of אָמָה dec. 10. . . . אמם

אָמוּתָה[a] Kal fut. 1 pers. sing. with parag. ה . . . מות

אֶמְחֶה [b]ן' Kal fut. 1 pers. sing. . . . מחה

אֶמְחֶנּוּ[c] id., suff. 3 pers. sing. masc. . . . מחה

אֶמְחָצֵם[d] [e]ן' Kal fut. 1 pers. sing., suff. 3 pers. sing. masc. (§ 16. rem. 12); ן for ·וַ conv. . . . מחץ

אַמְטִיר Hiph. fut. 1 pers. sing. . . . מטר

אָמִי pr. name masc., see אָמוֹן . . . אמן

אִמִּי ן n. fem. sing., suff. 1 pers. sing. from אֵם dec. 8b. . . . אם

אִמַּיָּא Chald. noun fem. with pl. (emph.) masc. term. from אֻמָּה . . . אמם

אַמֶּיךָ[f] noun masc. pl. with suff. 2 pers. sing. masc. from [אַיִם or אַם] . . . אים

[a] Eze. 17. 16. [b] Eze. 17. 19. [c] Ho. 4. 6. [d] Ho. 11. 8. [e] Ex. 21. 32. [f] Le. 25. 44. [g] Da. 3. 29. [h] 2 Sa. 6. 20. [i] Job 19. 15. [k] Na. 2. 8. [l] Ge. 20. 17. [m] De. 12. 12. [n] Pr. 8. 30. [o] Ps. 119. 75, 138. [p] Pr. 28. 20. [q] 2 Sa. 20. 19. [r] Is. 33. 6. [s] Ps. 100. 5. [t] Ps. 98. 3. [u] Ps. 89. 25. [x] 2 Ch. 6. 13. [y] Eze. 42. 16. [z] Nu. 25. 15. [a] Ge. 46. 30. [b] De. 9. 14. [c] Ex. 32. 33. [d] Ps. 18. 39. [e] 2 Sa. 22. 39. [f] Ps. 88. 16.

אֲמִילֵם[a] Hiph. fut. 1 pers. sing. [אָמִיל], suff. 3 pers. pl. masc. . . . . מול

אֵמִים[b] noun masc. pl. abs. def. for אֵימִים (q. v.); also pr. name . . . . . . אים

אַמִּין Chald. noun fem., with pl. masc. term. from [אַמָּה] . . . . אם

אַמִּיץ ו׳ adj. masc. sing. . . . . . אמץ

אָמִיר[c] noun masc. sing. . . . . . אמר

אָמִיר[d] Hiph. fut. 1 pers. sing. . . . . . מור

אָמִישׁ[e] Hiph. fut. 1 pers. sing. . . . . . מוש

אָמִית[f] Hiph. fut. 1 pers. sing. . . . . . מות

אֲמִיתֶךָ, אֲמִיתְךָ[g] } id., suff. 2 pers. sing. masc. . . . מות

אֲמִיתֵךְ[h] id., suff. 2 pers. sing. fem. . . . . מות

אִמֶּךָ[i] ו׳, אִמְּךָ[k] ו׳ } noun fem. sing., suff. 2 pers. sing. masc. from אֵם dec. 8b. . . } אם

אִמֵּךְ[l] ו׳ id., suff. 2 pers. sing. fem. . . . . אם

אִמְּכֶם id., suff. 2 pers. pl. masc. . . . . אם

אִמְּכֶן id., suff. 2 pers. pl. fem. . . . . אם

[אָמַל] *to languish, to be sick*, Eze. 16. 30. Pul. (§ 6. No. 2) *to languish, to droop, to waste away*.

אֲמֵלָל adj. masc. *feeble*, only pl. אֲמֵלָלִים Ne. 3. 34.

אֻמְלָל adj. masc. *languishing, wasting*, Ps. 6. 3.

אֲמַלֵּא[m] ו׳ Piel fut. 1 pers. sing.; וָ for וְ . . מלא

אִמָּלְאָה[n] Niph. fut. 1 pers. sing. with paragogic ה (§ 9. rem. 5) . . . . . . מלא

וָאֲמַלְאֵהוּ[o] ו Piel fut. 1 pers. sing., suff. 3 pers. sing. masc. (§ 10. rem. 7); וָ for וְ . . . מלא

אֲמֻלָה[p] Kal part. p. sing. fem. from [אָמוּל] masc. . . אמל

אֶמְלוֹךְ[q] Kal fut. 1 pers. sing. . . . . . מלך

אֲמַלֵּט[r] ו׳ Piel fut. 1 pers. sing.; וָ for וְ . . מלט

אִמָּלֵט[t] Niph. fut. 1 pers. sing. (§ 9. rem. 5) . . מלט

אִמָּלְטָה[u] ו׳ id. with paragogic ה; וְ for וַ conversive מלט

אֲמַלֶּטְךָ[x] Piel fut. 1 pers. sing., suff. 2 pers. sing. masc. מלט

אַמְלִיךְ[y] ו Hiph. fut. 1 pers. sing.; וְ for וַ conversive מלך

אֶמְלֹךְ[z] Kal fut. 1 pers. sing. . . . . . מלך

אֻמְלַל, אֻמְלָל[a] ו׳ } Pulal preter. 3 pers. sing. masc.; adj. Ps. 6. 3, (§ 6. No. 2) . . . } אמל

אֻמְלְלָה, אֻמְלָלָה } id. preter. 3 pers. sing. fem. (§ 8. rem. 7) אמל

אֻמְלָלוּ, אֻמְלְלוּ[zz] } id. preter. 3 pers. pl. . . . . אמל

אָמַם Root not used, Arab. *to be related*, cogn. עָמַם.

אֻמָּה (*union?*) pr. name of a city in the tribe of Judah, Jos. 15. 26.

אֻם masc. dec. 8c. i. q. אֻמָּה, Ps. 117. 1.

אֻמָּה fem. dec. 10. *people, nation*.

אֻמָּה Chald. pl. emph. אֻמַּיָּא id.

אִמָּם[b] noun fem. sing., suff. 3 pers. pl. masc. from אֵם dec. 8b. . . . . . אם

[אָמַן] I. *to stay, to support*, La. 4. 5.—II. *to nurse, to bring up*; part. אֹמֵן, *nursing-father, foster-father*.—III. intrans. *to be firm, true, faithful*. Niph.—I. *to be borne*, Is. 60. 4.—II. *to be firm, established, sure*.—III. *to be true, faithful*. Hiph.—I. *to trust, confide, believe in, rely upon*, const. with בְּ, לְ.—II. for הֵימִין *to turn to the right*, Is. 30. 21.

אֲמַן Chald. Aph. *to confide in*; part. pass. *true, faithful*.

אָמוֹן masc.—I. Pr. 8. 30, *foster-child*. Prof. Lee, *constant, unwearying*. Others, *artificer*.—II. for הָמוֹן *multitude*, Je. 52. 15.—III. pr. name of various persons, especially of a king of Judah. Amon of Ne. 7. 59, is also called אָמִי Ezr. 2. 57.—IV. pr. name of an Egyptian idol, Je. 46. 25.

אֵמוּן masc. (by Syriasm for אֱמוּן), *faithfulness, truth*, De. 32. 20. Pl. אֱמוּנִים id. Ps. 31. 24.

אֱמוּנָה fem. dec. 10.—I. *steadiness*, Ex. 17. 12.—II. *truth*, Is. 33. 6.—III. *faithfulness*.

אֲמִינוֹן (*faithful*) pr. name i. q. אַמְנוֹן q. v.

אָמָּן masc. *artificer*, Ca. 7. 2.

אָמֵן masc.—I. *truth*, Is. 65. 16.—II. adv. *Amen, so be it*.

אֹמֶן masc. *truth, faithfulness*, Is. 25. 1.

אֲמָנָה fem.—I. *covenant*, Ne. 10. 1.—II. *fixed allowance*, Ne. 11. 23.—II. pr. name of a river and the region near Damascus.

אֹמְנָה fem. *a beam, lintel*, 2 Ki. 18. 16.

אָמְנָה fem.—I. *education, nursing*, Est. 2. 20.—II. adv. *truly, indeed*.

אַמְנוֹן (*faithful*) pr. name.—I. the eldest son of David, called אֲמִינוֹן 2 Sa. 13. 20.—II. 1 Ch. 4. 20.

אָמְנָם, אֻמְנָם adv. *verily, truly, indeed*, אָמְנָם כִּי *true that, it is true that*.

אֱמֶת fem. (for אֱמֶנֶת) with suff. אֲמִתּוֹ (§ 37, No. 3).—I. *firmness, stability*.—II. *faithfulness, fidelity*.—III. *truth*, as opposed to falsehood.

[a] Ps. 118. 10, 11, 12. [b] Job 20. 25. [c] Is. 17. 6. [d] Ho. 4. 7. [e] Job 23. 12. [f] De. 32. 39. [g] 1 Ki. 2. 8. [h] 1 Sa. 19. 17. [i] Pr. 23. 25. [k] Ge. 37. 10. [l] Eze. 16. 45. [m] Ex. 31. 3. [n] Eze. 26. 2. [o] Ps. 81. 11. [p] Eze. 16. 30. [q] Eze. 20. 33. [r] Job 29. 12. [s] Is. 46. 4. [t] 1 Sa. 27. 1. [u] Job 1. 15. [x] Je. 39. 18. [y] 1 Sa. 12. 1. [z] 1 Ki. 1. 5. [zz] Je. 14. 2. [a] Ho. 4. 3. [b] Ho. 2. 7.

אֲמִתַּי (*veracious*), pr. name of the father of the prophet Jonah.

הֵימָן (*faithful* for מְהֵימָן) pr. name of two different men.

מְהוּמָן (*faithful*), pr. name of a Persian eunuch, Est. 1. 10.

[a]אָמֵן noun masc. sing. . . . . . . אמן

אָמֵן ו׳ subst. and adv. . . . . . . אמן

אָמוֹן pr. name masc. . . . . . . אמן

[b]אֵמֻן defect. for [אֵמוּן] noun masc. sing. dec. 3 b. אמן

[c]אֹמֵן Kal part. act. sing. masc. dec. 7 b. . אמן

[d]אֹמֶן noun masc. sing. . . . . . . אמן

[e]אֲמָנָה ו׳, ו׳ noun fem. sing.; also pr. name, וּ before (-:) אמן

אֲמָנָה noun fem. sing. . . . . . אמן

אַמְנוֹן pr. name masc. . . . . . . אמן

[g]אֹמְנַיִךְ Kal part. act. pl. masc., suff. 2 pers. sing. fem. from אֹמֵן dec. 7 b. . . . . אמן

[h]אֱמֻנִים noun masc., pl. of אֵמֻן dec. 3 b. . . אמן

אָמְנָם, [i]אֻמְנָם } adv.; from אֹמֶן with the term. ־ָם . . אמן

אַמְנֹן pr. name masc. . . . . . . אמן

אֶמְנַע [k] ו׳, וָ Kal fut. 1 pers. sing.; וָ for ·וַ conv. מנע

[l]אֱמֻנָתוֹ noun fem. sing., suff. 3 pers. sing. masc. from אֱמוּנָה dec. 10. . . . . . אמן

[m]אֹמַנְתּוֹ Kal part. act. sing. fem., (אֹמֶנֶת׳) suff. 3 pers. sing. masc. dec. 13 a. (§ 8. rem. 19) . אמן

[n]אַמְסֶה Hiph. fut. 1 pers. sing. . . . . מסה

[o]אָמְעָד [for אֶעֱמֹד § 8. rem. 15], Kal fut. 1 pers. sing. . . . . מעד

[אָמֵץ] *to be strong, courageous.* Pi.—I. *to strengthen, make strong; to encourage.*—II. *to repair, restore.*—III. *to harden,* spoken of the heart. Hiph. *to strengthen, confirm.* Hithp. *to strengthen one-self, to take courage.*

אַמִּיץ adj. *strong, powerful.*

אָמוֹץ (*strong*) pr. name of the father of the prophet Isaiah.

אָמֹץ adj. masc., only pl. אֲמֻצִּים (§ 32. rem. 5), *active, fleet,* or *vigorous.*

אֹמֶץ masc. *strength,* Job 17. 9.

אַמְצָה fem. id. Zec. 12. 5.

אַמְצִי (*strong*) pr. name masc.

אֲמַצְיָה (whom *the Lord strengthens*) pr. name of several men, especially,—I. of a king of Judah, also called אֲמַצְיָהוּ.—II. of an idolatrous priest. Am. 7. 10, sq.

מַאֲמָץ masc. only pl. c. מַאֲמַצֵּי *powers, forces,* Job 36. 19.

[p]אַמֵּץ Piel imp. sing. masc. . . . . . אמץ

[q]אַמֵּץ ו׳ defect. for אַמֵּיץ (q. v.) . . . . אמץ

אֱמָץ, אֱמָץ } וֶ, וֶ Kal imp. sing. masc. (§ 8. rem. 11 & 12); וֶ before (-:) . . . } אמץ

[r]אַמֵּץ וְ Piel fut. 3 pers. sing. masc. . . . אמץ

[s]אֹמֶץ noun masc. sing. . . . . . . אמץ

אֶמְצָא ו׳, וָ Kal fut. 1 pers. sing.; וָ for ·וַ conv. מצא

[u]אֶמְצָאֵהוּ וְ id., suff. 3 pers. sing. masc. . . מצא

[x]אֶמְצָאֲךָ, [y]אֶמְצָאֵךְ } וָ id., suff. 2 pers. sing. masc.; וָ for ·וַ conv. מצא

[z]אַמְצָה noun fem. sing. . . . . . אמץ

[a]אַמְּצֵהוּ וְ Piel imp. s. m. (אַמֵּץ), suff. 3 pers. s. m. אמץ

[b]אַמְּצוּ [for אַמְּצוּ] Piel imp. pl. masc. . . . אמץ

אָמְצוּ Kal preter. 3 pers. pl. . . . . אמץ

אִמְצוּ וְ id. imp. pl. masc. . . . . . אמץ

אַמְצִי pr. name masc. . . . . . . אמץ

אֲמַצְיָה, אֲמַצְיָהוּ } וַ׳ pr. name masc.; וּ before (-:) . . אמץ

[c]אִמַּצְתִּיךָ Piel pret. 1 pers. sing., suff. 2 pers. sing. m. אמץ

[d]אֲמֻצִּים adj. masc., pl. of [אָמֹץ] dec. 8 c. (§ 37. No. 2) אמץ

[e]אִמַּצְתָּ, [f]אִמַּצְתָּה } Piel pret. 2 pers. sing. masc. (§ 8. rem. 5) אמץ

אָמַר fut. וַיֹּאמֶר, יֹאמַר, with conjunctive accent וַיֹּאמַר (§ 19. rem. 2 & 1.)—I. *to say, declare,* (different from דִּבֵּר *to speak*) mostly followed by the words spoken, constr. with לְ, אֶל before the person *to* or *of* whom any thing is said, and rarely with an acc. comp. Ge. 43. 27, De. 1. 39, Ps. 139. 20.—II. *to command.*—III. *to think,* either followed by בְּלֵב, לְלֵב or not. Niph.—I. *to be said,* constr. with לְ, אֶל; impers. *it is said,* on dit.—II. *to be called,* constr. with לְ. Hiph. *to cause to say, promise,* De. 26. 17, 18. Hithp. *to speak of oneself, to boast oneself,* Ps. 94. 4.

אֲמַר Chald. (§ 53. No. 1. & § 49. rem. 1.)—I. *to say.*—II. *to command.*

אָמִיר masc., English version, *bough, branch.* Others, *top, summit,* lit. something prominent, manifest; or simply from the idea of *height,* supposed to be contained in the root. Prof. Lee, the *pod* which contains the fruit of the palm tree.

אֹמֶר masc. dec. 6 b.—I. *word, discourse.*—II. *appointment, declaration,* Job 20. 29.

---

[a] Ca. 7. 2. [b] De. 32. 20. [c] Est. 2. 7. [d] Is. 25. 1. [e] Ne. 10. 1. [f] Ne. 11. 23. [g] Is. 49. 23. [h] Is. 26. 2. [i] Ge. 18. 13. [k] Eze. 31. 15. [l] 1 Sa. 26. 23. [m] 2 Sa. 4. 4. [n] Ps. 6. 7. [o] Ps. 26. 1. [p] Na. 2. 2. [q] 2 Sa. 15. 12. [r] De. 2. 30. [s] Job 17. 9. [t] Ne. 7. 5. [u] Job 23. 3. [x] Ca. 8. 1. [y] Pr. 7. 15. [z] Zec. 12. 5. [a] De. 3. 28. [b] Je. 35. 5. [c] Is. 41. 10. [d] Zec. 6. 3. [e] Ps. 80. 18. [f] Ps. 80. 16.

אַמְרָה & אִמְרָה fem. dec. 12b. *word, saying, discourse.*

אִמַּר Chald. only pl. אִמְּרִין *lambs.*

אִמֵּר (*loquacious*, others, *tall*, comp. אָמִיר) pr. name of two different men.

אֹמֶר m.—I. *word, saying, discourse.*—II. *thing, matter*, Job 22. 28.

אוֹמָר (*eloquent*, others, *tall*, comp. אָמִיר) pr. name of a man.

אֱמֹרִי gent. noun *Amorite*, collect. *Amorites*, a Canaanitish people. Simonis conjectures its signification to be *mountaineer*, comp. אָמִיר.

אִמְרִי (*eloquent*) pr. name of two different men.

אֲמַרְיָה, אֲמַרְיָהוּ (whom *the Lord promised*) pr. name of several men, especially of two high-priests.

מַאֲמָר masc. only constr. מַאֲמַר *edict, command.*

מֵאמַר Chald. masc. id.

אָמַר } Kal pret. 3 pers. sing. masc. (compare § 8. rem. 7) . . . . } אמר
אָמָר ו׳ }

אָמַר ו׳ Chald. Peal part. act. sing. masc. dec. 2a. (§ 49. No. 4) . . . . . אמר

אֲמַר ו׳ Ch. id. pret. 3 pers. sing. masc.; וַ before (-:) אמר

אמרו[a] Kh. אָמַר q. v., K. אָמְרוּ (q. v.) . . אמר

אָמֹר Kal inf. abs. . . . . . אמר

אֱמָר־[b] id. inf. constr., with Mak. for אֱמֹר (§ 8. r. 18) אמר

אֱמָר־ ו׳ id. imp. sing. masc. with Mak. for אֱמֹר (§ 8. rem. 13) וֶ before (:‥) . . אמר

אֱמַר } Chald. Peal imp. sing. masc. (§ 49. No. 2) אמר
אֱמַר[c] }

אֱמֹר Kal inf. constr. or imp. sing. masc. . . אמר

אִמֵּר ו׳ pr. name masc. . . . . אמר

אֹמַר [d]ו׳, וָ׳, Kal fut. 1 pers. sing. (§ 19. rem. 2 & 1); וָ for וַ· conv. . . . אמר

אֹמֵר [e]ו׳ id. part. act. sing. masc. dec. 7b. . אמר

אֹמֶר noun masc. sing. . . . . אמר

אָמְרָה ו׳ Kal pret. 3 pers. sing. fem. . . אמר

אֹמְרָה[f] ו, ו׳; id. fut. 1 pers. sing. with parag. ה; וָ for וַ· conv. . . . . . אמר

אֲמַרוּ[g] Chald. Peal pret. 3 pers. pl. masc. (§ 49. No. 2) אמר

אָמְרוּ ו׳ Kal pret. 3 pers. pl. . . . אמר

אֱמַרוּ[h] Chald. Peal imp. pl. masc. (§ 49. No. 2) . אמר

אִמְרוֹ[i] noun masc. sing., suff. 3 pers. sing. masc. from [אֵמֶר] dec. 6b. . . . אמר

אִמְרוּ ו׳ Kal imp. pl. masc. . . . אמר

אֲמָרוֹת[k] noun fem., pl. of [אִמְרָה] dec. 12b. . . אמר

אִמְרוֹת[l] id. pl., construct state . . . אמר

אֶמְרְטָה[m] וָ Kal fut. 1 pers. sing. with parag. ה; וָ for וַ· conversive . . . . . מרט

אֶמְרְטֵם[n] וָ id., suff. 3 pers. pl. masc.; וָ id. . מרט

אֲמָרַי } noun masc. pl., suff. 1 pers. sing. from [אֵמֶר] dec. 6b. . . . } אמר
אֲמָרָי }

אֱמֹרִי gent. noun masc. . . . . אמר

אִמְרֵי noun masc. pl. constr. from [אֵמֶר] dec. 6b. אמר

אִמְרִי pr. name masc. . . . . . אמר

אִמְרִי Kal imp. sing. fem. . . . . אמר

אָמְרִי Kal inf., suff. 1 pers. sing. . . . אמר

אֲמָרֶיהָ noun masc. pl., suff. 3 pers. sing. fem. from [אֵמֶר] dec. 6b. . . . . אמר

אֲמַרְיָה } ו׳ } pr. name masc.; וַ before (-:) . . אמר
אֲמַרְיָהוּ }

אֲמָרָיו noun masc. pl., suff. 3 pers. sing. masc. from [אֵמֶר] dec. 6b. . . . . מר

אִמְרֵיכֶם[o] id., suff. 2 pers. pl. masc. . . מר

אֲמָרִים id. pl., absolute state . . . מר

אֹמְרִים ו׳ Kal part. act. masc., pl. of אֹמֵר dec. 7b. . מר

אָמְרִין ו׳ Chald. Peal part. act. masc., pl. of אָמַר dec. 2a. (§ 49. No. 4) . . . מר

אִמְּרִין[p] ו׳ Chald. noun masc., pl. of [אִמַּר] dec. 2b. מר

אֲמָרְךָ[q] Kal inf., suff. 2 pers. sing. masc., (§ 16. r. 7) מר

אָמְרֵךְ id., suff. 2 pers. sing. fem. . . . מר

אֲמָרְכֶם[r] id., suff. 2 pers. pl. masc. comp. אֲמָרְךָ . מר

אֲמַרְנָא[s] Chald. Peal pret. 1 pers. pl. (§ 49. No. 2) מר

אָמַרְנוּ ו׳ Kal pret. 1 pers. pl. . . . מר

אַמְרָפֶל ו׳ pr. name of a king of Shinar in the time of Abraham, Ge. 14. 1, 9.

אֲמָרֵר[t] Piel fut. 1 pers. sing. [for אֲמַרֵּר] . . רר

אָמַרְתָּ } ו } Kal pret. 2 pers. sing. masc. (§ 8. r. 7) מר
אָמַרְתָּ }

אָמַרְתָּ ו׳ id. id.; acc. shifted by conv. וְ (§ 8. rem. 7) מר

אָמַרְתְּ ו׳ id. pret. 2 pers. sing. fem. . . . מר

אַמְרֵת[u] Chald. Peal pret. 1 pers. sing. (§ 49. No. 2) מר

אֲמֶרֶת[x] וַ Chald. id. pret. 3 pers. sing. fem. (§ 49. No. 2. and rem. 1); וַ before (-:) . מר

אִמְרַת noun fem. sing. constr. of [אִמְרָה] dec. 12b. מר

אֹמֶרֶת Kal part. act. sing. fem. (§ 8. rem. 19) . מר

אֹמְרֹת[y] id. id. pl. dec. 13a. . . . . מר

אֶמְרָתוֹ[z] noun fem. sing., suff. 3 pers. sing. masc. [from אֶמְרָה] . . . . . מר

אִמְרָתוֹ[a] noun fem. sing., suff. 3 pers. sing. masc. from [אִמְרָה] dec. 12b. . . . מר

אָמָרְתִּי[b] } Kal pret. 1 pers. sing. (§ 8. rem. 7) . מר
אָמַרְתִּי }

[a] 1 Sa. 13. 19. [b] Pr. 25. 7. [c] Da. 2. 4. [d] Eze. 13. 15. [e] Pr. 28. 24. [f] Ge. 46. 31. [g] Da. 4. 23. [h] Da. 2. 9. [i] Job 20. 29. [k] Ps. 12. 7. [l] Ps. 12. 7. [m] Ezr. 9. 3. [n] Ne. 13. 25. [o] Is. 41. 26. [p] Ezr. 6. 9. [q] Eze. 35. 10. [r] Je. 23. 38. [s] Ezr. 5. 4. [t] Is. 22. 4. [u] Da. 4. 5. [x] Da. 5. 10. [y] Je. 38. 22. [z] La. 2. 17. [a] Ps. 147. 15 [b] Ps. 40. 11.

אָמַרְתִּי וְ' Kal pret. 1 pers. s.; acc. shifted by conv. וְ (§ 8. rem. 7) . . . . . . אמר

אִמְרָתִי noun fem. sing., suff. 1 pers. sing. from [אִמְרָה] dec. 12b. . . . . . אמר

אִמְרָתֶךָ / אִמְרָתְךָ } id., suff. 2 pers. sing. masc. . . אמר

[a] אִמְרָתֵךְ id., suff. 2 pers. sing. fem. . . . אמר

אֲמַרְתֶּם וַ' Kal pret. 2 pers. pl. masc.; וַ for conv. וְ אמר

[b] אֶמֶשׁ / אֶמֶשׁ } prop. past night—I. adv. *last night, yesterday*.—II. *night, darkness*, Job 30. 3.

[c] אֲמֻשְׁךָ וַ Kal fut. 1 pers. sing. [אָמוּשׁ], suff. 2 pers. sing. masc.; וַ for וְ . . . מושׁ

[d] אֶמְשְׁכֵם Kal fut. 1 pers. sing., suff. 3 pers. pl. masc. משׁך

[e] אֶמְשֹׁל Kal fut. 1 pers. sing. . . . משׁל

[f] אָמֻת וְ for אָמוּת, Kal fut. 1 pers. sing. (compare § 28. rem. 7) . . . . . מות

[g] אַמַּת noun fem. sing., constr. of אַמָּה dec. 10. אם

אַמֹּת pl. of the preceding . . . . אם

אֱמֶת וֶ' noun fem. sing., contr. [for אֲמֶנֶת], with suff. אֲמִתּוֹ (§ 37. No. 3) . . . אמן

[h] אֲמָתָהּ noun fem. sing., suff. 3 pers. sing. fem. from אָמָה irr. (§ 45) . . . . אמה

אֲמָתוֹ וַ' id., suff. 3 pers. sing. masc.; וַ before (-:) אמה

[i] אֲמִתּוֹ וַ' noun fem. sing., suff. 3 pers. sing. masc. from אֱמֶת (q. v.); וַ id. . . . אמן

[k] אֵימָתוֹ וְ noun fem. sing., suff. 3 pers. sing. masc. from אֵימָה dec. 10. . . . אים

[l] אַמְתַּחַת noun fem. sing. dec. 13a. . . . מתח

[m] אַמְתְּחֹת id., pl. . . . . . . מתח

[n] אַמְתַּחְתּוֹ id. sing., suff. 3 pers. sing. masc. . . מתח

אַמְתְּחֹתֵיכֶם id. pl., suff. 2 pers. pl. masc. . . מתח

אַמְתְּחֹתֵינוּ id. pl., suff. 1 pers. pl. . . . מתח

[o] אֲמָתִי [p] וַ' noun fem. sing., suff. 1 pers. sing. from אָמָה irr. (§ 45) . . . . אמה

אֲמִתַּי pr. name masc. . . . . . אמן

אַמָּתַיִם וְ' noun fem., dual of אַמָּה dec. 10. . אם

[q] אִמֹּתֵינוּ n. fem. pl., suff. 1 pers. pl. from אֵם dec. 8b. אם

אֲמָתֶךָ וַ' / אֲמָתְךָ וַ' } noun fem. sing., suff. 2 pers. sing. masc. אָמָה irr. (§ 45); וַ bef. (-:) . } אמה

אֲמִתֶּךָ / [r] אֲמִתְּךָ וַ' } noun fem. sing., suff. 2 pers. sing. masc. from אֱמֶת (q. v.); וַ id. . . } אמן

אִמֹּתָם noun fem. pl., suff. 3 pers. pl. masc. from אֵם dec. 8b. . . . . אם

[s] אֶמְתָּנִי וְ Ch. adj. masc. sing. by apoc. [for אֶמְתָּנִית] מתן

[t] אֲמֹתְתֵהוּ וַ Pilel fut. 1 pers. sing., suff. 3 pers. sing. masc.; וַ for וְ. . . . . מות

אָן interrog. adv. . . . . . אי

אֹן pr. name for און . . . . . און

אָנָּא (*anna*, with double accent except Ps. 118. 25. before a penacute) interj. of entreaty, *I pray*, &c.; also written אָנָּה.

אֲנָא Ch. pers. pron. sing. com. *I*, also written אֲנָה

[u] אִנְבֵּהּ [x] וְ' Ch. [for אִבֵּהּ], n. m. s. with suff. 3 p. s. m. from אֵב dec. 5b. (comp. § 52. rem. 2) אבב

[y] אִנְדַּע וְ Chald. Peal fut. 1 pers. sing. [for אִדַּע] (§ 52. rem. 2) . . . . ידע

I. [אָנָה] *to sigh, to mourn.*

אֲנִיָּה fem. *mourning, sorrow.*

תַּאֲנִיָּה fem. id.

אֲנִיעָם (*mourning of the people*) pr. name masc. 1 Ch. 7. 19.

II. אָנָה Kal not used, Arab. *to meet; to be in good time.* Pi. *to cause to come*, or *happen*, Ex. 21. 13. Pu. *to befall* any one. Hithp. *to seek occasion* against any one, const. with לְ, 2 Ki. 5. 7.

אֳנִי masc. *ship*, collect. *ships, a fleet.*

אֳנִיָּה fem. dec. 10. *a ship.*

אוֹנִיָּה fem. id. 2 Ch. 8. 18. Kheth.

תַּאֲנָה fem. dec. 10. *sexual impulse*, Je. 2. 24.

תֹּאֲנָה fem. *occasion, cause*, Ju. 14. 4.

תַּאֲנַת שִׁלֹה (*approach to Shiloh*) pr. name of a place in Ephraim, Jos. 16. 6.

אָנָּה i. q. אָנָּא (q. v.) . . . . . אנא

אָנָה וְ', וָ', interrog. adv. (אָן) with parag. ה; וָ see lett. ו . . . . . . אי

אֲנָה וַ' Chald. for אֲנָא (q. v.) . . . אנא

אָנֶה adv. (אָן) with parag. ה . . . . אי

[z] אִנָּה Piel pret. 3 pers. sing. masc. . . . אנה

[a] אֶנְהָגְךָ Kal fut. 1 pers. sing. [אֶנְהַג], suff. 2 pers. sing. masc. (§ 16. rem. 12) . . נהג

אָנוּ וְ Kal pret. 3 pers. pl. . . . . אנה

אֹנוֹ noun masc. sing., suff. 3 pers. sing. masc. from און or אָוֶן dec. 1. or 6g. . . און

אֹנוֹ וְ pr. name of a place . . . . און

[b] אַנְוֵהוּ וְ Hiph. fut. 1 pers. sing., suff. 3 pers. sing. m. נוה

[c] אָנוּחַ Kal fut. 1 pers. sing. . . . נוח

אִנּוּן Chald. pron. pers. pl. masc. *they*, fem. אִנִּין

[d] אָנוּסָה Kal fut. 1 pers. sing. with parag. ה . . נוס

[e] אֲנוֹעֲךָ [Kh. אֲנִעֲ׳], [K. אֲנִי׳], Kal or Hiph. fut. 1 pers. sing., suff. 2 pers. sing. masc. . . נוע

אָנוּשׁ Kal part. pass. sing. masc. . . . אנשׁ

---

[a] Is. 29. 4, 4. [b] Ge. 31. 42. [c] Ge. 27. 21. [d] Ho. 11. 4. [e] Ju. 8. 23. [f] 2 Sa. 19. 38. [g] Je. 51. 13. [h] Ex. 2. 5. [i] Ps. 91. 4. [k] Job 9. 34. [l] Ge. 44. 2. [m] Ge. 44. 1. [n] Ge. 43. 12. [o] Ge. 30. 3. [p] Job 31. 13. [q] La. 5. 3. [r] Ps. 71. 22. [s] Da. 7. 7. [t] 2 Sa. 1. 10. [u] Da. 4. 11. [x] Da. 4. 9, 18. [y] Da. 2. 9. [z] Ex. 21. 13. [a] Ca. 8. 2. [b] Ex. 15. 2. [c] Hab. 3. 16. [d] Ex. 14. 25. [e] 2 Sa. 15. 20.

אֱנוֹשׁ noun masc. sing., pl. אֲנָשִׁים irr. (comp. אִישׁ § 45); also pr. name . . . . אנש

אֱנָשָׁא[a] Chald. Kh. אֱנוֹשָׁא as if from אֱנוֹשׁ, K. אֲנָשָׁא q. v. (§ 68) . . . . אנש

אָנוּשָׁה[b] וְ Kal fut. 1 pers. sing. with parag. ה; וָ for וַ conv. . . . . נוש

אֲנוּשָׁה Kal part. pass. sing. fem. from אָנוּשׁ masc. אנש

אָנַח. Niph. *to sigh*, const. with עַל, מִן.

אֲנָחָה fem. dec. 11 c. suff. אַנְחָתִי (§ 42. rem. 1) *sighing, sigh.*

אֲנָחָה[c] וַ noun fem. sing. dec. 11 c. (§ 42. rem. 1); וַ before (-:) . . . . אנח

אַנְחֵהוּ[d] וְ Hiph. fut. 1 pers. sing., suff. 3 pers. sing. m. נחה

אֶנָּחֵם Niph. fut. 1 pers. sing. . . . . נחם

אֲנַחֲמֵךְ[e] וַ′ Piel (§ 14. rem. 1) fut. 1 pers. sing., suff. 2 pers. sing. fem.; וַ for וְ . . . נחם

אֲנַחֶמְכֶם[g] id., suff. 2 pers. pl. masc. (§ 16. rem. 15) נחם

אֲנַחְנָא / אֲנַחְנָה[h] } Chald. pron. pers. 1 pers. com. *we.*

אַנְחֶנָּה[i] Hiph. fut. 1 pers. sing., suff. 3 pers. sing. fem. (§ 24. rem. 21) . . . . . נחה

אֲנַחְנוּ / אֲנַחְנוּ וַ′ } pers. pron. 1 pl. com. *we*, by aphæresis נַחְנוּ.

אֲנָחֲרַת וַ pr. name of a city belonging to the tribe of Issachar, Jos. 19. 19.

אַנְחָתָה[k] noun fem. sing. (אֲנָחָה) with paragogic ה dec. 11 c. (§ 42. rem. 1) . . . . אנח

אַנְחָתִי[l] וְ′ id., suff. 1 pers. sing. . . . . אנח

אַנְחֹתַי[m] id. pl., suff. 1 pers. sing. . . . . אנח

אֲנִי / אֲנִי וַ′ } pers. pron. 1 pers. sing. com. *I*, i. q. אָנֹכִי

אֳנִי[n] וָ′ (vo-ŏnee′), noun masc. sing.; וָ before (т:) for וְ . . . . אנה

אֲנִיָּה וַ noun fem. sing.; וַ before (-:) . . . אנה

אֳנִיָּה noun fem. sing. dec. 10. . . . . אנה

אֳנִיּוֹת[o] וָ′ (vo-ŏniy-′) id. pl.; וָ before (т:) for וְ . אנה

אִנְיָן[p] Chald. fem. of אִנּוּן (q. v.)

אֲנִיעָה[q] וְ Hiph. fut. 1 pers. sing. with paragogic ה . נוע

אֲנִיעָם וַ pr. name masc. . . . . . . אנה

אֳנִיֹּת[oo] noun fem., pl. of אֳנִיָּה dec. 10. . . . אנה

אֲנָךְ masc.—I. *lead.*—II. *plummet*, Am. 7. 7, 8.

אָנֹכִי וְ′ pers. pron. 1 pers. sing. com. *I*, whence the shorter form אֲנִי.

אָנַן. Hithpo. *to complain, murmur.*

[אָנַס] *to urge, compel*, only part. אֹנֵס, Est. 1. 8.

אֲנַס Chald. *to trouble*, only part. אָנֵס, Da. 4. 6.

אֲנַסֶּה Piel fut. 1 pers. sing. . . . . נסה

אֲנַסְּכָה[r] Piel fut. 1 pers. sing., suff. 2 pers. sing. masc. (§ 2. rem. 2) . . . . . נסה

אֲנַסֶּנּוּ[s] id., suff. 3 pers. sing. masc. . . . נסה

אֶנְעָלֵךְ[t] וָ Kal fut. 1 pers. sing., suff. 2 pers. sing. fem. (§ 16. rem. 12); וָ for וַ conv. . נעל

אִנָּעֵר[u] וְ Niph. fut. 1 pers. sing. (§ 9. rem. 5) . נער

[אָנַף] *to breathe through the nose, snort;* hence *to be angry*, construed with בְּ. Hithp. *to be* or *become angry.*

אֲנַף Chald. masc. dec. 3 a. *face*, comp. אַף.

אֲנָפָה fem. an unclean bird, according to Bochart, a species of *eagle.*

אַף (for אַנְף=אֱנֶף) masc. with suff. אַפִּי dec. 8 d. (§ 37. No. 3).—I. *nose.*—II. *anger*, בַּעַל אַף, אִישׁ אַף *an angry man.* Dual אַפַּיִם.—I. *the nostrils.*—II. meton. *face, countenance;* אַפַּיִם אַרְצָה *the face to the ground;* לְאַפֵּי *at the face of, before.*—III. *two persons*, מָנָה אַחַת אַפָּיִם *a portion of two persons*, i. e. a double portion.—IV. *anger;* אֶרֶךְ אַ′ *slow to anger*, קְצַר אַ′ *quick to anger, impatient.*

אַנְפּוֹהִי Chald. noun masc. pl., suff. 3 pers. sing. masc. from [אֲנַף] dec. 3 a. . . . . אנף

אָנַפְתָּ Kal pret. 2 pers. sing. masc. . . . אנף

אָנַפְתָּ וְ id.; acc. shifted by conv. וְ (§ 8. rem. 7) אנף

אִנָּצְלָה[x] Niph. fut. 1 p. sing. with parag. ה (§ 9. r. 5) נצל

אָנַק fut. יֶאֱנֹק *to groan.* Niph. *to moan, lament.*

אֲנָקָה fem. construct אֶנְקַת (§ 42. rem. 1).—I. *a groaning, lamentation.*—II. a kind of *lizard* Le. 11. 30.

אֲנָקָה[y] וַ noun fem. sing., dec. 11 c. construct אֶנְקַת (§ 42. rem. 1) . . . . . אנק

אֲנַקֶּךָּ Piel fut. 1 pers. sing., suff. 2 pers. sing. masc. (§ 24. rem. 21. & § 2. rem. 3) . נקה

אִנָּקְמָה וְ Niph. fut. 1 pers. sing. with paragogic ה (§ 9. rem. 5) . . . . . . נקם

אֶנְקַת noun fem. sing., constr. of אֲנָקָה dec. 11 c. (§ 42. rem. 1) . . . . . אנק

[אָנַשׁ] only in part. pass.—I. *incurable, mortal.*—II. *troublesome, grievous, sorrowful*, of pain, of a day; *malignant*, of the human heart.

[a] Da. 4. 13, 14. [b] Ps. 69. 21. [c] Is. 35. 10. [d] Is. 57. 18. [e] Is. 51. 19. [f] La. 2. 13. [g] Is. 66. 13. [h] Ezr. 4. 16. [i] Job 31. 18. [k] Is. 21. 2. [l] Ps. 38. 10. [m] La. 1. 22. [n] 1 Ki. 9. 26. [o] Is. 60. 9. [oo] Ge. 49. 13. [p] Da. 7. 17. [q] Job 16. 4. [r] Ec. 2. 1. [s] Ex. 16. 4. [t] Eze. 16. 10. [u] Ju. 16. 20. [x] Ps. 69. 15. [y] Mal. 2. 13.

אֱנוֹשׁ masc. (see אִישׁ § 45).—I. *man, mankind.* —II. *the common people.*—Pl. אֲנָשִׁים, construct אַנְשֵׁי, with suff. אֲנָשָׁי, *men,* commonly used for אִישִׁים the plural of אִישׁ.—III. pr. name masc. grandson of Adam.

אֱנָשׁ, אֱנָשׁ Chald. masc. irr. (§ 68) *man, mankind.*

אִשָּׁה f. irr. (§ 45) pl. נָשִׁים.—I. *woman, female;* —אִשָּׁה פִּלֶגֶשׁ *a concubine;* אִשָּׁה אַלְמָנָה *a widow.* II. *wife.*—III. *every one;* א׳—רְעוּת, א׳—אֲחוֹת *one-another.* Comp. also אֵשֶׁת under אִישׁ.

אֱנֹשׁ[zz] ן defect. for אֱנוֹשׁ (q. v.) . . . אנש

אֱנָשׁ[a] ן׳ן Chald. noun masc. sing. (§ 68); אֱנָשׁ[b] ן before (ּ:) . . . . אנש

אֲנָשָׁא, אֲנָשָׁא Chald. id., emph. state . . . אנש

אֶנָּשֵׂא[c] Niph. fut. 1 pers. sing. . . . . נשא

אֲנָשַׁי[d] noun masc. pl., suff. 1 pers. sing. [as if from אֱנָשׁ], see אֱנוֹשׁ (& אִישׁ § 45) . . אנש

אַנְשֵׁי ן׳ id. pl., construct state . . . אנש

אֲנָשֶׁיהָ[e] id. pl., suff. 3 pers. sing. fem. . . . אנש

אַנְשֵׁיהֶם ן id. with suff. 3 pers. pl. masc. . . אנש

אַנְשֵׁיהֶן[f] id. pl., suff. 3 pers. pl. fem. . . . אנש

אֲנָשָׁיו ן׳ id. pl., suff. 3 pers. sing. m.; ן before (-:) אנש

אֲנָשֶׁיךָ[g] ן׳ id. pl., suff. 2 pers. sing. masc.; ן id. אנש

אֲנָשִׁים ן׳ id. pl., absolute state, Chald. Da. 4. 14. אנש

אֲנָשֵׁינוּ[h] id. pl., suff. 1 pers. pl. . . . . אנש

אַנְתְּ[i] ן, אַנְתָּה ן׳ Kheth. אַנְתָּה Chald. pers. pron. 2 pers. s. masc. *thou.* For נ comp. § 1. r. 2.

אַנְתּוּן Chald. pl. of the preceding, *you, ye,* Da. 2. 8.

אַתָּה (for אַנְתָּה but compare § 1. rem. 2) *thou,* in pause אָתָּה.

אַתְּ *thou,* f., in Kh. אַתִּי, read אַתְּ (§ 1. r. 2)

אַתֶּם *you, ye,* fem. אַתֶּן, with parag. ה, אַתֵּנָה.

אֲנַתְּקֵהוּ[k] ן ן Piel fut. 1 p. s., suff. 3 p. s. fem.; ן for ן נתה

אֲנַתֵּק Piel fut. 1 pers. sing. . . . . נתק

אָסָא ן׳ pr. name masc. . . . . אסה

אֲסֹבְבָה * ן Pilel fut. 1 p. s. with parag. ה; ן bef. (-:) *Ps. 26. 6. סבב

אֶסְבֹּל[l] Kal fut. 1 pers. sing. . . . . סבל

אֶסְגּוֹד[m] Kal fut. 1 pers. sing. (§ 8. rem. 18) . סגד

אסה Root not used, coll. with the Arab. אזה *to be hurt, injured,* and trans. *to hurt, injure.*

אָסָא (*injurious*) pr. name.—I. of a king of Judah, son of Abijam, grandson of Rehoboam.— II. 1 Ch. 9. 16.

אָסוֹן masc. *hurt, injury, mischief.*

אֲסוֹבְבָה[bb] ן Pilel fut. 1 pers. sing. with paragogic ה; ן for ן . . . . . סבב

אָסוּךְ[n] noun masc. sing. . . . . סוך

אָסוֹן noun masc. sing. . . . . . אסה

אָסוֹר[o] Kal inf. absolute . . . . אסר

אָסוּר Kal fut. 1 pers. sing. . . . . סור

אָסוּר Kal part. p. sing. masc. dec. 3 a. . . אסר

אֲסוּרֵי[p] Kh. אֲסוּרֵי id. pl. constr., K. אֲסִירֵי (q. v.) אסר

אֲסוּרָיו[q] noun masc. pl., suff. 3 pers. sing. masc. from אֵסוּר dec. 3 b. . . . . . אסר

אֲסוּרִים id. pl. abs. (Ec. 7. 26); or pl. of אָסוּר (q. v.) אסר

אַסִּיךְ[r] Hiph. fut. 1 pers. sing. . . . נסך

אֹסִיף defect. for או׳, Hiph. fut. 1 pers. sing. . יסף

אֲסִיפֵם[s] Hiph. fut. 1 pers. sing., suff. 3 pers. pl. m. סוף

אָסִיר[t] ן׳ & [u] ן׳ Hiph. fut. 1 pers. s.; ן for ן conv. סור

אָסִיר noun masc. sing. dec. 3 a. . . . אסר

אַסִּיר ן׳ noun masc. sing.; also pr. name masc. . אסר

אָסִירָה ן Hiph. fut. 1 pers. sing. with paragogic ה סור

אֲסִירֵי noun masc. pl. construct from אָסִיר dec. 3 a. אסר

אֲסִירָיו id., suff. 3 pers. sing. masc. . . . אסר

אֲסִירַיִךְ[x] id., suff. 2 pers. sing. fem. . . . אסר

אֲסִירִים id. pl., absolute state . . . . אסר

אֲסֻכֵךְ[y] ן Kal fut. 1 pers. sing. [אָסוּךְ], suff. 2 pers. sing. fem.; ן for ן conv. . . . . סוך

אֲסַלְּדָה[z] ן Piel fut. 1 pers. sing. with paragogic ה; ן for ן . . . . סלד

אֶסְלוֹחַ־[a] אֶסְלָח ן׳ Kal fut. 1 pers. sing.; Kh. אֶסְלוֹחַ־ (§ 8. rem. 18) . . . . סלח

אָסָם masc. only in the pl. אֲסָמֶיךָ *thy storehouses,* Pr. 3. 10, compare De. 28. 8.

אַסְנָה (*thorn-bush,* compare סְנֶה) pr. name masc. Ezr. 2. 50.

אָסְנַפַּר pr. name of an Assyrian general, Ezr. 4. 10.

אָסְנַת pr. name of the wife of Joseph, daughter of the priest Potiphar. Coll. with the Egyptian by Gesenius it signifies, *belonging to Neith,* the Minerva of the Egyptians.

אֲסָעֲרֵם[b] ן Piel fut. 1 pers. sing., suff. 3 pers. pl. m., by Syriasm for אֲסַ׳ (compare § 19. rem. 6) סער

אָסַף ן׳—I. *to collect, to gather, to assemble,* const. with אֶל, עַל to designate the person or place to or in which.—II. *to take,* or, *receive to oneself.*—III. *to take in, to draw back,* as the hand.—IV. *to take away;* hence, *to destroy.*—V. *to gather in,* or *up,*

Da. 6. 8, 13. Da. 2. 10. Is. 33. 10. [d] 1 Sa. 23. 12. [e] Jos. 10. 2. [f] Eze. 16. 45. [g] 1 Sa. 28. 1. [h] Je. 44. 19. [i] Ezr. 7. 25. [k] Ju. 20. 6. [l] Is. 46. 4, 4. [m] Is. 44. 19. [n] 2 Ki. 4. 2. [o] Ju. 16. 11. [p] Ge. 39. 20. [q] Ju. 15. 14. [r] Ps. 16. 4. [s] Je. 8. 13. [t] Is. 10. 13. [u] Eze. 16. 50. [x] Zec. 9. 11. [y] Eze. 16. 9. [z] Job 6. 10. [zz] Je. 17. 9. [a] Je. 5. 7. [b] Zec. 7. 14. [bb] Ca. 3. 2.

as the rear does an army. Niph. pass. of Kal No. I. II. IV. constr. with עַל, לְ, אֶל. Pi.—I. i.q. Kal No. I. Is. 62. 9.—II. *to receive*, as a guest, Ju. 19. 15, 18.—III. i. q. Kal No. V.—Pu. *to be gathered.* Hithp. *to be gathered together*, Deut. 33. 5.

אָסָף (*collector*) pr. name of several men, especially of a Levite and chief singer of David.

אֹסֶף only in pl. אֲסֻפִּים (§ 37. No. 3c) *stores, storehouses.*

אֹסֶף masc. dec. 6c. *ingathering, harvest of fruits.*

אָסִיף masc. id. Ex. 23. 16; 34. 22.

אֲסֵפָה fem. *gathering, collection*, Is. 24. 22.

אֲסֻפָּה fem. *assembly, a council*, Ec. 12. 11.

אֲסַפְסֻף masc. *mixed multitude*, Nu. 11. 4.

אָסָף ו׳ pr. name masc. . . . . . אסף

[a]אָסֵף Hiph. fut. 1 pers. sing., ap. for אָסִיף . . סוף

אָסֹף Kal inf. abs. . . . . . . אסף

אֱסֹף id. imp. sing. masc. . . . . . אסף

אֹסֵף Hiph. fut. 1 pers. sing. ap. for אוֹסִיף . יסף

אֹסֶף noun masc. sing. . . . . . אסף

אֹסֵף defect for אוֹסִיף Hiph. fut. 1 pers. sing. . יסף

אֻסַּף ו Pual pret. 3 pers. sing. masc. . . . אסף

[b]אֶסְפְּדָה Kal fut. 1 pers. sing. with parag. ה . . ספד

[c]אֲסֵפָה noun fem. sing. . . . . . אסף

[d]אַסְפֶּה Hiph. fut. 1 pers. sing. . . . . ספה

[e]אֶסָּפֶה Niph. fut. 1 pers. sing. . . . . ספה

[f]אֶסְפָה־ Kal imp. sing. masc. with parag. ה (§ 13. r. 3) אסף

[g]אֹסְפָה id. fut. 1 pers. sing. [אֹסֵף] with parag. ה (§ 19. rem. 4) . . . . . . אסף

[h]אֹסִפָה ו Hiph. fut. 1 pers. sing. (אוֹסִיף) with parag. ה יסף

אָסְפוּ ו׳ Kal pret. 3 pers. plur. . . . . אסף

אִסְפוּ id. imp. pl. masc. . . . . . אסף

אֻסְּפוּ ו Pual pret. 3 pers. pl. . . . . אסף

[i]אֲסֻפּוֹת noun fem., pl. of [אֲסֻפָּה] dec. 10. . . אסף

[k]אֲסֻפֵי Kal part. p. pl. construct masc. fr. [אָסוּף] dec. 3a. . . . . . . אסף

[l]אִסְפִּי id. imp. sing. fem. . . . . . אסף

[m]אֹסִפְךָ־ id. fut. 1 pers. sing. [אֹסֵף] suff. 2 pers. sing. masc. (§ 19. rem. 4) . . . . אסף

[n]אֹסִפְךָ id. part. act. sing. masc. with suff. 2 pers. sing. masc. from אֹסֵף dec. 7b. . . אסף

[o]אֹסְפָם id. id. with suff. 3 pers. pl. masc. . . אסף

[p]אֲסַפֵּר [q]ו׳ Piel fut. 1 pers. sing.; וַ for וְ . . ספר

[r]אֲסַפְּרָה ו׳ / [s]אֲסַפֵּרָה ו׳ } id. with parag. ה ; וַ id. . . ספר

[t]אֶסְפְּרֵם Kal fut. 1 pers. sing., suff. 3 pers. pl. masc. ספר

אָסְפַּרְנָא Ch. adv. *diligently*, comp. Ez. 5. 8; 6. 8; 7. 17.

[u]אֲסַפְּרֶנָּה Piel fut. 1 pers. sing., suff. 3 pers. sing. fem. (§ 2. rem. 3) . . . . . ספר

[x]אָסַפְתָּ Kal pret. 2 pers. sing. masc. . . . אסף

אָסַפְתָּ ו׳ id.; acc. shifted by conv. ו (§ 8. rem. 7) אסף

אַסְפָּתָא pr. name of a son of Haman, Est. 9. 7.

[y]אָסַפְתָּה ו Kal pret. 2 pers. sing. masc. (§ 8. r. 5. & 7) אסף

אֲסַפְתּוֹ וַ id. with suff. 3 pers. sing. m.; וַ for וְ conv. אסף

[z]אָסַפְתִּי / אָסָפְתִּי } id. pret. 1 pers. sing. (§ 8. rem. 7) . אסף

אָסַפְתִּי ו׳ id.; acc. shifted by conv. ו (§ 8. rem. 7) אסף

[a]אֶסַּק Kal fut. 1 pers. sing. . . . . סק

[אָסַר] I. *to bind.*—II. *to put in bonds, to fetter*; part. אָסוּר *captive, prisoner.*—III. *to bind, tie, fasten to* any thing, const. with בְּ, לְ; whence, *to harness a* chariot, with acc.—IV. אָסַר אִסָּר עַל נַפְשׁוֹ *to bind an oath upon oneself*, i. e. bind oneself by an oath. Niph. *to be bound*, Ju. 16. 6, 13; *to be imprisoned.* Pu. *to be reduced to bondage.*

אָסִיר masc. dec. 3a, *captive, prisoner.*

אַסִּיר masc. I. id.—II. pr. name masc.

אֱסָר m. dec. 2b, *obligation*, or *vow of abstinence*.

אִסָּר masc. dec. 1a, id.

אֱסָר Chald. dec. 1a, *an interdict*, Da. 6. 8, 13. sq.

אֵסוּר masc. dec. 3b, *bond, fetter*; בֵּית הָאֵסוּר *prison.*

אֱסוּר Chald. masc. dec. 1a, id.

מָסֹרֶת (for מַאֲסֹרֶת) *bond, obligation*, Ez. 20. 37.

מוֹסֵר (for מַאְסֵר) masc. dec. 7b, pl. ־ים & ־וֹת *bands, bonds, fetters.*

מוֹסֵר De. 10. 6, and מֹסֵרָה Nu. 33. 30. (*bands*) pr. name of a station of the Israelites in the wilderness.

אַסִּר pr. name masc. for אַסִּיר . . . אסר

[b]אָסֹר Kal inf. abs. . . . . . . אסר

אֵסַר־חַדּוֹן / אֵסַר־חַדֹּן } pr. name of a king of Assyria, son of Sennacherib.

[c]אֱסָר Chald. noun masc. sing. dec. 1b. . . אסר

[d]אֱסַר Chald. id. construct state . . . אסר

[e]אֱסֹר Kal imp. sing. masc. . . . . אסר

אִסָּר noun masc. sing. dec. 2b. . . . אסר

[f]אֱסָרָא [g]ו׳ Chald. noun masc. sing., emph. of אֱסָר dec. 1b; וֶ before (־:) . . . . אסר

אָסְרָה [h]ו׳ Kal pret. 3 pers. sing. fem. . . אסר

[i]אָסֻרָה־ Kal fut. 1 pers. sing. with parag. ה for אָסוּרָה סור

[k]אֱסָרֶהָ וֶ noun masc. sing., suff. 3 pers. sing. fem. from [אֱסָר] dec. 1. (§ 30. No. 3) וֶ bef. (־:) אסר

[a] Zep. 1. 2, 3. [b] Mi. 1. 8. [c] Is. 24. 22. [d] De. 32. 23. [e] 1 Sa. 27. 1. [f] Nu. 11. 16. [g] Mi. 4. 6. [h] 2 Sa. 12. 8. [i] Ec. 12. 11. [k] Eze. 34. 29. [l] Je. 10. 17. [m] 1 Sa. 15. 6. [n] 2 Ki. 22. 20; & 2 Ch. 34. 28. [o] Ps. 39. 7. [p] Ps. 22. 18. [q] Ps. 118. 17. [r] Job 15. 17. [s] Ps. 66. 16. [t] Ps. 139. 18. [u] Ps. 145. 6. [x] Ps. 85. 4. [y] Ju. 18. 25. [z] Is. 10. 14. [a] Ps. 139. 8. [b] Ju. 15. 13. [c] Da. 6. 8; 13. 16. [d] Da. 6. 13. [e] 1 Ki. 18. 44. [f] Da. 6. 9, 14. [g] Da. 6. 10. [h] Nu. 30. 4. [i] Ex. 3. 3. [k] Nu. 30. 5.

Word	Analysis	Root
אֲסָרֶהָ[a]	וְ id. pl., suff. 3 pers. sing. fem. for אֱסָרֶיהָ	אסר
אִסְרוּ	Kal imp. pl. masc.	אסר
אֻסְּרוּ[b] אֻסָּרוּ[c]	Pual pret. 3 pers. pl. masc. (comp. § 8. rem. 7)	אסר
אֲסָרוּךָ[d]	וְ Kal pret. 3 pers. pl., suff. 2 pers. sing. masc.; וַ for וְ	אסר
אֲסֻרוֹת[e]	id. part. p. fem., pl. of [אֲסוּרָה] dec. 10.	אסר
אֹסְרִי[f]	id. part. act. sing. m. with parag. י (§ 8. r. 19)	אסר
אֱסָרֶיהָ[g]	וְ, noun masc. pl., suff. 3 pers. sing. fem. from אֱסָר dec. 1 a. (§ 30. No. 3) . . .	אסר
אֲסָרָם[h]	Kal pret. 3 pers. sing. masc., suff. 3 pers. pl. masc.	אסר
אֶסֳּרֵם[i]	וְ Kal fut. 1 pers. sing., suff. 3 pers. pl. masc. (§ 20. rem. 16. & § 8. rem. 14) .	יסר
אֲסַרְנֻהוּ[k]	וַ Kal pret. 1 pers. plur., suff. 3 pers. sing. masc.; וַ for וְ conv.	אסר
אֲסַרְתֶּם[l]	וַ id. pret. 2 pers. pl. masc.; וַ id. .	אסר
אַסְתִּיר	וְ, וְ[m] Hiph. fut. 1 pers. sing.; וְ for וַ conv. .	סתר
אַסְתִּירָה[n]	id. with parag. ה	סתר
אֶסָּתֵר	וְ, וְ[o] Niph. fut. 1 pers. sing. . . .	סתר
אֶסְתֵּר	וְ (*star*, Pers. sitareh) pr. name fem. foster-daughter of Mordecai, afterwards wife of Ahasuerus and queen of Persia.	
אָע[p]	וְ[q] Chald. masc. dec. 1. i. q. Heb. עֵץ *wood*.	
אָעָא[r]	Chald. id., emph. st.	
אֶעֱבֹד[s]	Kal fut. 1 pers. sing.	עבד
אֶעֱבְדָךְ[t]	id., suff. 2 pers. sing. masc. . . .	עבד
אֶעֱבוֹר[u]	Kh. Kal fut. 1 p. s. R. עבר; K. אֶעֱבוֹר (q.v.)	עבר
אֶעֱבוֹר	וְ, Kal fut. 1 pers. sing. (§ 8. rem. 18); וְ for וַ conv.	עבר
אַעֲבִיר	Hiph. fut. 1 pers. sing.	עבר
אֶעֱבֹר	וְ, Kal fut. 1 pers. sing.; וְ for וַ conv. .	עבר
אֶעְבְּרָה אֶעֱבֹרָה	וְ[x] וְ id. with parag. ה (§ 8. rem. 15); וְ id.	עבר
אָעֵד	וָ ap. for אָעִיד (q. v.)	עוד
אֶעְדֵּךְ[y]	וְ Kal fut. 1 pers. sing. [אֶעְדֶּה], suff. 2 pers. sing. fem. (§ 24. rem. 21); וְ for וַ conv.	עדה
אֲעוּדֵךְ[z]	Kh. אֲעוּ׳, K. אֲעִי׳, Kal or Hiph. fut. 1 pers. sing., suff. 2 pers. sing. fem. . . .	עוד
אָעוּפָה[a]	Kal fut. 1 pers. sing. with parag. ה .	עוף
אֶעֱזֹב[b]	Kal fut. 1 pers. sing.	עזב
אֶעֶזְבָה	וְ[c] id. with parag. ה	עזב
אֶעֶזְבֶךָּ אֶעֶזְבֶךָ[d]	id., suff. 2 pers. sing. masc. (§ 2. rem. 3)	עזב
אֶעֶזְבֵם[e]	id., suff. 3 pers. pl. masc.	עזב
אָעִיד[f]	וְ Hiph. fut. 1 pers. sing.; וְ for וַ conv.	עוד

Word	Analysis	Root
אָעִידָה	וְ, וְ[g] id. with paragogic ה; וְ id. . .	עוד
אֹעִיל[h]	Hiph. fut. 1 pers. sing. [for אוֹעִיל] . .	יעל
אָעִירָה	Hiph. fut. 1 pers. sing. with parag. ה .	עור
אַעַל	וְ Kal (De. 10. 3) or Hiph. (Nu. 23. 4) fut. 1 pers. sing. ap. for אֶעֱלֶה or אַעֲלֶה (§ 24. rem. 3 & 15); וְ for וַ conv. . .	עלה
אַעֲלֶה	וְ, Hiph. fut. 1 pers. sing.; וְ id. . .	עלה
אֶעֱלֶה	Kal fut. 1 pers. sing.	עלה
אֶעֱלוֹזָה[i]	*fully*, for אֶעֱלְזָה q. v. (§ 8. rem. 14) .	עלז
אֶעֱלֹז[k]	וְ Kal fut. 1 pers. s. (§ 13. r. 5); וְ for וַ conv.	עלז
אֶעֱלֹזָה	id. with parag. ה in pause [for אֶעֶלְזָה] .	עלז
אַעְלִים[l]	וְ[m] Hiph. fut. 1 pers. sing. (§ 13. rem. 9)	עלם
אַעַלְךָ[n]	Hiph. fut. 1 pers. sing. (אַעֲלֶה), suff. 2 pers. sing. masc. (§ 24. rem. 21) . . .	עלה
אֶעֶלְצָה[o]	וְ Kal fut. 1 pers. sing. with paragogic ה	עלץ
אֶעֱמֹד[p]	וְ, וְ Kal fut. 1 pers. sing.; וְ for וַ conv. .	עמד
אֶעֱמֹדָה[q]	id. with parag. ה in pause [for אֶעֶמְדָה] (§ 8. rem. 15)	עמד
אַעֲמִדֵם[r]	וְ the following with suff. 3 pers. pl. masc.	עמד
אַעֲמִיד	וְ Hiph. fut. 1 pers. sing.; וְ for וַ conv.	עמד
אַעֲמִידָה	וְ id. with parag. ה; וְ id. . . .	עמד
אָעַן	וְ Kal fut. 1 p. s., ap. for אֶעֱנֶה (§ 24. r. 3); וְ id.	ענה
אֶעֶנְדֶנּוּ[s]	Kal fut. 1 pers. sing., suff. 3 pers. sing. masc.	ענד
אֶעֱנֶה[t] אֶעֱנֶה	וְ Kal fut. 1 pers. sing.	ענה
אֵעָנֶה[u]	Niph. fut. 1 pers. sing.	ענה
אַעַנֶּה[x]	וְ with א quiescent [for וַאֲעַנֶּה] Piel fut. 1 p. s.	ענה
אֶעֱנֵהוּ[y]	וְ Kal fut. 1 pers. sing., suff. 3 pers. sing. masc.	ענה
אֲעַנֵּךְ[z]	Piel fut. 1 p. s., suff. 2 p. s. fem. (§ 24. r. 21)	ענה
אֶעֱנְךָ[a] אֶעֱנֶךָּ	וְ[b] Kal fut. 1 p. s. (אֶעֱנֶה), suff. 2 p. s. m. (§ 24. rem. 21. & § 2. rem. 3) .	ענה
אֶעֱנֵם[c]	וְ[d] id., suff. 3 pers. pl. masc. . . .	ענה
אֶעֱנֶנּוּ[e]	id., suff. 3 pers. sing. masc. (§ 2. rem. 3)	ענה
אֶעְצֹר[f]	Kal fut. 1 pers. sing. (§ 13. rem. 5) .	עצר
אֶעֶרְבֶנּוּ[g]	Kal fut. 1 pers. sing., suff. 3 pers. sing. masc.	ערב
אֶעֱרוֹץ[h]	Kal fut. 1 pers. sing. (§ 8. rem. 18) .	ערץ
אֶעֱרָךְ[i]	Kal fut. 1 pers. sing., (§ 8. rem. 18)	ערך
אֶעֶרְכָה[k]	וְ[l] id. with parag. ה	ערך
אַעַשׂ	וְ ap. for the following (§ 24. rem. 3) .	עשה
אֶעֱשֶׂה	וְ, וְ, Kal fut. 1 pers. sing.; וְ for וַ conv.	עשה
אֶעֶשְׂךָ[m]	וְ[n] id., suff. 2 pers. sing. masc. . .	עשה
אֶעֱשֶׂנָּה	id., suff. 3 pers. sing. fem. (§ 2. rem. 3) .	עשה
אַעְשִׁר[o]	וְ with quiescent א and def. [for וַאַעְשִׁיר] Hiph. fut. 1 pers. sing.	עשר
אֲעַשְּׁרֶנּוּ[p]	Piel fut. 1 pers. sing., suff. 3 pers. sing. masc.	עשר

[a] Nu. 30. 8. [b] Is. 22. 3. [c] Is. 22. 3. [d] Eze. 3. 25. [e] 2 Sa. 3. 34. [f] Ge. 49. 11. [g] Nu. 30. 6, 15. [h] Job 36. 13. [i] Ho. 10. 10. [k] Ju. 16. 5. [l] 1 Sa. 6. 7. [m] Eze. 39. 23, 24. [n] De. 32. 20. [o] Ps. 55. 13. [p] Ezr. 6. 4, 11. [q] Ezr. 5. 8. [r] Da. 5. 4, 23. [s] 2 Sa. 16. 19. [t] Ge. 29. 18. [u] Je. 2. 20. [x] Ju. 12. 3. [y] Eze. 16. 11. [z] La. 2. 13. [a] Ps. 55. 7. [b] 1 Ki. 6. 13. [c] Je. 9. 1. [d] Ge. 28. 15. [e] Is. 41. 17. [f] Ne. 13. 15. [g] Ne. 13. 21. [h] Job 35. 3. [i] Hab. 3. 18. [k] Je. 15. 17. [l] Is. 1. 15. [m] 1 Sa. 12. 3. [n] Ge. 46. 4. [o] Ps. 9. 3. [p] 2 Sa. 1. 10. [q] Hab. 2. 1. [r] Ne. 13. 11. [s] Job 31. 36. [t] Job 32. 17. [u] Job 19. 7. [x] 1 Ki. 11. 39. [y] Ps. 91. 15. [z] Na. 1. 12. [a] Ps. 81. 8. [b] Je. 33. 3. [c] Is. 41. 17. [d] Zec. 10. 6. [e] Job 9. 14, 32. [f] 2 Ch. 7. 13. [g] Ge. 43. 9. [h] Job 31. 34. [i] Ps. 5. 4. [k] Job 23. 4. [l] Ps. 50. 21. [m] Eze. 35. 6. [n] Ge. 12. 2. [o] Zec. 11. 5. [p] Ge. 28. 22.

[a] אַעְתִּיר Hiph. fut. 1 pers. sing. (§ 13. rem. 9) . עתר

אַף, וְ׳ אַף } noun masc. sing. dec. 8d. contr. [for אַנְף § 37. No. 3] . . . } אנף

וְ׳ אַף conj. *also, moreover, indeed, yea;* אַף כִּי (*a*) *how much more, how much less;* (*b*) *yea more, yea furthermore;* [הַ] אַף כִּי אָמַר *is it even so, that* (God) *has said?* Ge. 3. 1.

וְ אַף Chald. *also,* Da. 6. 23.

[b] אַפְאֵיהֶם Hiph. fut. 1 pers. sing. [אַפְאֶה], suff. 3 pers. pl. masc. (§ 24. rem. 21) . . . פאה

[c] אֲפָאֵר Piel fut. 1 pers. sing. . . . . פאר

[d] אֶפְגַּע Kal fut. 1 pers. sing. . . . . פגע

[e] אֶפְגְּשֵׁם Kal fut. 1 pers. sing., suff. 3 pers. pl. masc. פגשׁ

[אָפַד] *to gird on, put on,* const. with לְ of the person and בְּ of the thing.

אֵפֹד, אֵפוֹד masc.—I. *ephod,* especially that of the high-priest, a kind of short coat without sleeves girded on over all the garments.—II. perhaps *an idol* dressed in an ephod.—III. pr. name masc. Nu. 34. 23.

אֲפֻדָּה fem. dec. 10.—I. *a putting on* of the ephod.—II. *a vestment* in which idols were dressed, Is. 30. 22.

[f] אֵפֹד noun m. s., defect for אֵפוֹד; also pr. name אפד

[g] אֶפְדֶּה Kal fut. 1 pers. sing. . . . . פדה

אֶפְדֵּם id., suff. 3 pers. pl. masc. (§ 24. rem. 21) פדה

[h] אַפַּדְנוֹ noun masc. sing., suff. 3 pers. sing. masc. from [אַפֶּדֶן] dec. 6a. . . . . פדן

[i] וְאָפַדְתָּ Kal pret. 2 pers. sing. masc.; acc. shifted to ult. by conv. וְ (§ 8. rem. 7) . אפד

[k] אֲפֻדַּת noun fem. sing., constr. of [דָּה] dec. 10. אפד

אֲפֻדָּתוֹ id., suff. 3 pers. sing. masc. . . אפד

[l] אָפָה [m] וְ׳״ *to bake;* part. אֹפֶה dec. 9a. *baker.* Niph. *to be baked.*

מַאֲפֶה masc. *a baking, something baked,* Le. 2. 4.

תֻּפִינִים masc. pl. *bakings, baked pieces,* Le. 6. 14.

[n] אַפָּהּ noun masc. sing., suff. 3 pers. sing. fem. from אַף (q. v.) dec. 8d. . . . . אנף

[o] אֹפֶה Kal part. act. sing. masc. dec. 9a. . אפה

[p] אֹפֵהֶם id., suff. 3 pers. pl. masc. . . אפה

[q] וְאָפוּ id. pret. 3 pers. pl. . . . אפה

[r] וְ׳״ אַפּוֹ noun masc. sing., suff. 3 pers. sing. masc. from אַף (q. v.) dec. 8d. . . . אנף

[s] אֵפוּ Kal imp. pl. masc. by Syriacism [for אֱפוּ § 19. rem. 6]. . . . . אפה

אֵפוֹ, אֵפוֹא } adv. *now, then;* אַיֵּה אֵפוֹא *where now?* מָה, מִי אֵ׳ *who, what then?* לְכָה אֵ׳ *come on now!* אִם כֵּן אֵ׳ *if then it be so;* דְּעוּ אֵ׳ *know then!*

וְ׳ אֵפוֹד noun masc. sing. Ex. 28. 4. . . אפד

[t] אָפוּנָה Kal fut. 1 pers. sing. with parag. ה . פון

אֶפְחַד, [u] וְאֶפְחָד } Kal fut. 1 pers. sing. (§ 8. rem. 15) . פחד

וְ׳ אַפִּי noun masc. sing., suff. 1 pers. sing. from אַף (q. v.) dec. 8d. . . . . אנף

[x] אַפֶּיהָ id. du., suff. 3 pers. sing. fem. . . אנף

אַפָּיו id. du., suff. 3 pers. sing. masc. . . אנף

[y] אָפִיחַ Hiph. fut. 1 pers. sing. . . . פוח

אֲפִיחַ pr. name masc. 1 Sa. 9. 1. אפח perhaps i. q. פּוּחַ *to breathe.*

אַפֶּיךָ noun masc. pl., suff. 2 pers. sing. masc. from אַף (q. v.) dec. 8d. . . . . אנף

אַפִּיל Hiph. fut. 1 pers. sing. . . . נפל

[z] אֲפִילֹת adj. fem. pl., from [אָפִיל] masc. . אפל

[a] אַפַּיִם, אַפָּיִם } noun masc., du. of אַף (q. v.) dec. 8d; also pr. name masc. . . . } אנף

[b] אַפֵּינוּ id., suff. 1 pers. pl. . . . . אנף

[c] אָפִיץ [d] וָ׳ Hiph. fut. 1 pers. sing.; וָ for וַ conv. פוץ

[e] וָ׳ אֲפִיצֵם id., suff. 3 pers. pl. masc.; וָ for וַ . פוץ

אֲפִיק pr. name of a place, see אֲפֵק . . אפק

אֲפִיקֵי adj. and subst. m. pl. constr. from אָפִיק dec. 3a אפק

[f] אֲפִיקָיו id., (subst.) pl., suff. 3 pers. sing. masc. אפק

[g] אֲפִיקֶיךָ id. id., suff. 2 pers. sing. masc. . . אפק

[h] אֲפִיקִים id. id. pl., absolute state . . אפק

[i] אָפִיר Hiph. fut. 1 pers., as if from פּוּר, see פרר

[k] וְאָפִיתָ Kal pret. 2 pers. sing. masc.; acc. shifted to ult. by conv. וְ (§ 8. rem. 7) . . אפה

[l] אָפִיתִי id. pret. 1 pers. sing. . . . . אפה

אַפְּךָ, אַפֶּךָ } noun masc. sing., suff. 2 pers. sing. masc. from אַף (q. v.) dec. 8d. . . } אנף

אַפֵּךְ id., suff. 2 pers. sing. fem. . . . . אנף

אָפַל Root not used, Arab. *to set, go down,* as the sun.

אָפִיל adj., f. אֲפִילָה, *late,* as to growth, Ex. 9. 32.

אָפֵל adj. masc. *dark, obscure,* Am. 5. 20.

אֲפֵלָה fem. *darkness, thick darkness.*

אֹפֶל masc. *thick darkness;* trop. *misfortune.*

מַאֲפֵל masc. *darkness,* Jos. 24. 7.

מַאְפֵּלְיָה *great darkness,* comp. of the preceding and יָהּ, lit. *darkness of the Lord,* Je. 2. 31.

[m] וְאָפֵל adj. masc. sing. . . . . אפל

[n] וָ׳ אֶפְּלָה Kal fut. 1 p. s. (§ 17. r. 3); וָ for וַ conv. נפל

[a] Ex. 8. 5. [b] De. 32. 26. [c] Is. 60. 7. [d] Is. 47. 3. [e] Ho. 13. 8. [f] Ex. 28. 15. [g] Ex. 13. 15. [h] Da. 11. 45. [i] Ex. 29. 5. [k] Is. 30. 22. [l] Ge. 19. 3. [m] Is. 44. 15. [n] Ge. 24. 47. [o] Ge. 40. 17. [p] Ho. 7. 6. [q] Le. 26. 26. [r] Ezr. 8. 22. [s] Ex. 16. 23. [t] Ps. 88. 16. [u] Job 23. 15. [x] 2 Sa. 14. 4. [y] Eze. 21. 36. [z] Ex. 9. 32. [a] 1 Sa. 1. 5. [b] La. 4. 20. [c] Na. 1. 8. [d] Eze. 36. 19. [e] Je. 18. 17. [f] Is. 8. 7. [g] Eze. 35. 8. [h] Job 12. 21. [i] Ps. 89. 34. [k] Le. 24. 5. [l] Is. 44. 19. [m] Am. 5. 20. [n] 1 Ch. 21. 13.

אֹפֶל noun masc. sing. . . . . . אפל

[a] אֲפֵלָה וְ׳ noun fem. sing. dec. 10; וַ before (-:) . אפל

[b] אֶפְּלָה } Kal fut. 1 pers. sing. with parag. ה (§ 8. rem. 15); וָ for וַּ . . . } נפל
[c] וְ׳ אֶפְּלָה

[d] אֲפַלְּטָה וָ Piel fut. 1 p. s. [אֲפַלֵּט] with parag. ה; וָ for וַ פלט

[e] אֲפַלְּטֵהוּ וָ id., suff. 3 pers. sing. masc.; וַ id. . פלט

אֶפְלָל וְ׳ pr. name masc. . . . . . פלל

[f] אֲפֵלָתֶךָ וַ noun fem. sing., suff. 2 pers. sing. masc. from אֲפֵלָה dec. 10; וַ id. . . . אפל

אַפָּם noun masc. sing., suff. 3 pers. sing. masc. from אַף (q. v.) dec. 8d. . . . אנף

אָפַן Root not used, prob. cogn. with פָּנָה, *to turn, revolve.*

אוֹפָן & אֹפָן masc. dec. 8. pl. אוֹפַנִּים, *a wheel.*

אֹפֶן masc. *season*, comp. תְּקוּפָה; only אָפְנָיו (for אֳפָנָיו § 35. rem. 16) Pr. 25. 11.

אֵפֶן וָ ap. for אֶפְנֶה q. v. (§ 24. rem. 3); וָ for וַ conversive . . . . . . פנה

[g] אֹפֶן noun masc. sing. constr. dec. 8. (§ 37. No. 2) אפן

[h] אֶפְנֶה וְ Kal fut. 1 pers. sing. . . . . . פנה

[i] אָפְנָיו noun masc. pl., suff. 3 pers. sing. masc. from [אֹפֶן] dec. 6c. (§ 35. rem. 16) . . . אפן

אָפֵס *to cease, fail, have an end.*

אֶפֶס masc. dec. 6a.—I. *end, extremity.*—II. dual אַפְסַיִם *two extremities*, i. e. the *soles* or *ankles* of the feet, Eze. 47. 3.—III. adv. (*a*) *no more; none besides*, and so with paragogic Yod אַפְסִי; (*b*) *not, non;* בְּאֶפֶס *without;* (*c*) *nothing;* מֵאֶפֶס *of nothing;* בְּאֶפֶס *for nothing;* (*d*) *nothing but, only;* אֶפֶס כִּי prop. only that, *except, unless.*

אֶפֶס דַּמִּים pr. name of a town in the tribe of Judah, 1 Sa. 17. 1, for which פַּס דַּמִּים 1 Ch. 11. 13.

אֶפֶס } noun m. s., (pl. c. אַפְסֵי) dec. 6a. (also as an adv.), and pr. name in אֶפֶס דַּמִּים } אפס
וְ׳ אָפֶס

אַפְסִי וְ׳ noun masc. s. (אֶפֶס dec. 6a) with parag. י as an *adv.* . . . . . . אפס

אַפְסֵי id. pl., construct state . . . . אפס

[k] אָפְסָיִם id. dual, absolute state [for אַפְסַיִם] . . אפס

[l] אֶפְסֹל וָ Kal fut. 1 pers. sing.; וָ for וַ conv. פסל

אָפַע Root not used, prob. cogn. with פָּאָה, פָּעָה *to breathe;* whence—

אֶפַע masc. *breath, nothingness, vanity*, Is. 41. 24.

[m] אֶפְעֶה Kal fut. 1 pers. sing. . . . . פעה

אֶפְעֶה noun masc. sing. . . . . . . אפע

אֶפְעַל Kal fut. 1 pers. sing. . . . . . פעל

[אָפַף] *to surround, encompass.*

[n] אָפְפוּ Kal preter. 3 pers. pl. . . . . . אפף

אֲפָפוּנִי } id. with suff. 1 pers. sing. . . . אפף
[o] אֲפָפֻנִי

אָפַק Kal not used, coll. with the Arab. the ideas of *motion* and *force*, or *strength*, are ascribed to it. Hithp. prop. to put force upon oneself.—I. *to restrain oneself.*—II. *to constrain oneself* to act, 1 Sa. 13. 12.

אֲפֵק (*fortress*) pr. name.—I. of a town in the tribe of Asher, also called אֲפִיק comp. Jos. 19. 30 with Ju. 1. 31.—II. of a city in the tribe of Issachar.

אֲפֵקָה (*fortress*) pr. name of a town in the mountains of Judah, Jos. 15. 53.

אָפִיק masc. dec. 3a.—I. adj. *mighty, eminent*, Job 12. 21.—II. *the boss* of a shield, Job 41. 7.—III. *brook, torrent;* also applied to the bed of a brook or stream, *a channel;* hence,—IV. Metaph. *a tube*, spoken of the bones of the Behemoth.

אֲפֵק וְ׳ pr. name of a place . . . . . אפק

[p] אֶפְקֹד וָ׳ } Kal fut. 1 pers. sing. (§ 8. rem. 18); וָ for וַ conversive . . . } פקד
[q] אֶפְקָד־

אֲפֵקָה וְ׳ pr. name of a place; וַ before (-:) . . אפק

אֶפְקוֹד Kal fut. 1 pers. sing. (§ 8. rem. 18) . פקד

[r] אֶפְקַח Kal fut. 1 pers sing. . . . . . פקח

[s] אַפְקִיד Hiph. fut. 1 pers. sing. . . . . פקד

[t] אֲפִקִים וַ defect. for אֲפִיקִים (q. v.) . . . . אפק

אָפַר Root not used, Arab. *to be light, fleet.*

אֵפֶר masc.—I. *ashes.*—II. *anything worthless.*

אֲפֵר masc. a kind of *head-band, turban*, from אָפַר i. q. עָפַר *to cover.* According to others it is by transposition for פְּאֵר a *tiara, crown.*

אֶפְרַיִם (*double fruitfulness, double fruit*, with the signification of פָּרָה, comp. Ge. 41. 52; Ho. 13. 15.)—I. pr. name of the second son of Joseph. —II. of the tribe descended from him, afterwards the chief tribe of the kingdom of Israel.

אֶפְרָת, אֶפְרָתָה (*fertility*, comp. אֶפְרַיִם) pr. name.—I. of a city in the tribe of Judah, called also Bethlehem.—II. i. q. אֶפְרַיִם, Ps. 132. 6.—III. of the wife of Caleb.

---

[a] Ex. 10. 22. [b] 2 Sa. 24. 14. [c] 1 Ch. 21. 13. [d] Job 23. 7. [e] Ps. 91. 14. [f] Is. 58. 10. [g] Ex. 14. 25. [h] Ge. 24. 49. [i] Pr. 25. 11. [k] Eze. 47. 3. [l] De. 10. 3. [m] Is. 42. 14. [n] Ps. 40. 13. [o] 2 Sa. 22. 5. [p] Le. 18. 25. [q] Je. 9. 8. [r] Zec. 12. 4. [s] Ps. 31. 6. [t] Eze. 32. 6.

אֶפְרָתִי gent. noun.—I. an Ephrathite.—II. an Ephraimite, comp. אֶפְרָת No. II.

אוֹפִיר pr. name of a place celebrated for its gold.

אָפֵר[a] Hiph. fut. 1 pers. sing. . . . . פרר

אֵפֶר וְ' noun masc. sing.; for וָ see letter ו . אפר

אֶפְרוֹשׂ[b] Kal fut. 1 pers. sing. (§ 8. rem. 18) . פרשׂ

אֶפְרֹחָיו[c] וְ noun masc. pl., suff. 3 pers. sing. masc. (§ 4. rem. 1) from [אֶפְרֹחַ] dec. 1 b. . פרח

אֶפְרֹחֶיהָ[d] id. pl. with suff. 3 pers. sing. fem. . פרח

אֶפְרֹחִים[e] id. pl., absolute state . . . פרח

אַפִּרְיוֹן[f] noun masc. sing. . . . . פרה

אֶפְרַיִם וְ' / אֶפְרָיִם וְ' } pr. name of a man and a country . אפר

אֲפָרְסָיֵא Chald. pr. name of a people . . פרס

אֲפַרְסְכָיֵא Chald. pr. name of a people . . פרס

אֲפַרְסַתְכָיֵא וַ Chald. pr. name of a people; וַ before (-:) פרס

אֶפְרַע[g] Kal fut. 1 pers. sing. . . . פרע

אֶפְרֹשׂ[h] וְ'[i] Kal fut. 1 pers. sing.; וָ for וַ conv. . פרשׂ

אֶפְרְשָׂה[k] וָ id. with paragogic ה; וָ id. . . פרשׂ

אֶפְרָת / אֶפְרָתָה } pr. name of a place and a woman . אפר

אֶפְרָתִי gent. noun from the preceding . . אפר

אֶפְרָתִים id. pl. absolute . . . . אפר

אַפְשִׁיטֶנָּה[l] Hiph. fut. 1 pers. sing., suff. 3 pers. sing. f. פשט

אֶפְשְׁעָה[m] Kal fut. 1 pers. s. with parag. ה (§ 8 r. 14) פשע

אֶפֶּת[n] וָ Niph. fut. 1 pers. sing. ap. [for אֶפָּתֶה § 24. rem. 10]; וָ for וַ conv. . . פתה

אֶפְתַּח[o] / אֶפְתַּח וָ'[p] } Kal fut. 1 pers. sing. (§ 8. rem. 15); וָ for וַ conversive } פתח

אֲפַתֵּחַ[q] [for תַּח'] Piel fut. 1 pers sing. (§ 15. r. 1) פתח

אֶפְתְּחָה[r] Kal fut. 1 pers. sing. with paragogic ה . פתח

אַפְתֹּם וְ Chald. adv. *at last*, Ezr. 4. 13.

אֲפַתֶּנּוּ Piel fut. 1 pers. s., suff. 3 p. s. m. (§ 2. r. 3) פתה

אָץ וְ' Kal pret. 3 pers. sing. m.; or part. dec. 1 a. אוץ

אֵצֵא וָ'[s] Kal fut. 1 pers. sing.; וָ for וַ conv. . יצא

אֵצְאָה וָ'[t] & וָ'[u] id. with paragogic ה; וָ id. יצא

אֶצְבּוֹן וְ' pr. name.—I. Ge. 4. 16.—II. 1 Ch. 7. 7.

אֶצְבַּע noun fem. sing., comp. dec. 2 b. (§ 31. r. 5) צבע

אֶצְבָּעוֹ id., suff. 3 pers. sing. masc. . . צבע

אֶצְבָּעוֹת[x] id. pl., absolute state . . . . צבע

אֶצְבְּעוֹת[y] וְ id. pl., construct state . . . צבע

אֶצְבְּעוֹתַי[z] id. pl., suff. 1 pers. pl. . . . . צבע

אֶצְבְּעוֹתֵיכֶם[a] וְ id. pl., suff. 2 pers. pl. masc. . צבע

אֶצְבְּעָן[b] Chald. noun fem., pl. of אֶצְבַּע dec. 2 a. . צבע

אֶצְבְּעָת[c] וְ Chald. id. pl., construct state . . צבע

אֶצְבְּעֹת[d] וְ noun fem., pl. of אֶצְבַּע (q. v.) . . צבע

אֶצְבְּעָתָא[e] וְ Chald. noun f. pl. emph. of אֶצְבַּע dec. 2 a. צבע

אֶצְבְּעֹתַי[f] וְ noun f. pl., suff. 1 p. pl. from אֶצְבַּע (q. v.) צבע

אֶצְבְּעֹתָיו[g] וְ' id., suff. 3 pers. sing. masc. . . צבע

אֶצְבְּעֹתֶיךָ id., suff. 2 pers. sing. masc. . . . צבע

אַצְדִּיק Hiph. fut. 1 pers sing. . . . . צדק

אֶצְדָּק[h] / אֶצְדָּק[i] } Kal fut. 1 pers. sing. (§ 8. rem. 15) צדק

אֲצַו[k] וָ apoc. for the following . . . צוה

אֲצַוֶּה וָ Piel fut. 1 pers. sing.; וָ for וַ . . צוה

אֲצַוְּךָ[l] / אֲצַוֶּךָּ { id. with suff., in pause without נ epenth. & id. with suff. in pause with נ epenth., for: } צוה

אֲצַוְּךָ[m] id. with suff. 2 p. s. m. (§ 24. r. 21. & § 2. r. 2) צוה

אָצוּם[n] Kal fut. 1 pers. sing. . . . . צום

אֲצַוֶּנּוּ[o] וַ' Piel fut. 1 pers. sing. (אֲצַוֶּה), suff. 3 pers. sing. masc. (§ 24. r. 21. & § 2. r. 3); וַ for וָ צוה

אֶצָּוֹרְךָ[p] Kh. אֶצוֹרְךָ from צוּר; K. אֶצָּרְךָ Kal fut. 1 pers. sing., suff. 2 pers. s. m. (§ 20. r. 16) יצר

אַצִּיגָה[q] Hiph. fut. 1 p. s. with parag. ה (§ 20. r. 16) יצג

אַצִּיל[r] וָ'[s] Hiph. fut. 1 pers. sing.; וָ for וַ conv. . נצל

אַצִּילָה[t] noun fem. sing. dec. 10. . . . אצל

אַצִּילוֹת[u] pl. of the preceding . . . . אצל

אַצִּילֵי[x] noun masc. pl. constr. of [אַצִּיל] dec. 1 b. אצל

אֲצִילֵי[y] noun masc., pl. constr. of [אָצִיל] dec. 3 a. אצל

אַצִּילְךָ Hiph. fut. 1 pers. sing., suff. 2 pers. sing. masc. נצל

אָצִים[z] Kal part. act. masc., pl. of אָץ dec. 1 a. . אוץ

אַצִּיעָה[a] וְ Hiph. fut. 1 p. s. with parag. ה (§ 20. r. 16) יצע

אַצִּיתֶנָּה[b] Hiph. fut. 1 pers. sing., suff. 3 pers. sing. fem. צות

[אָצַל] I. *to hold back, withhold*, const. with מִן.—II. *to reserve*, const. with לְ. Niph. *to be contracted*, Eze. 42. 6.—Hiph. *to withhold*, const. with מִן, Nu. 11. 25.

אָצִיל masc. dec. 3 a. prop. adj. set aside, select; secluded.—I. *nobleman*, Ex. 24. 11.—II. *remote part*, Is. 41. 9.

אַצִּיל masc. dec. 1 b. pl. ־ִים and וֹת, *juncture, joint;* אַצִּילֵי יָדַיִם *the wrists*, which others take to be the *armpits*, taking יָד for the whole arm.

אָצֵל (*noble*, see אָצִיל) pr. name—I. of a man, in pause אָצַל.—II. of a town near Jerusalem, Zec. 14. 5.

אֵצֶל masc. dec. 6. (§ 35. rem. 6).—I. *the side*.—II. prep. *by, near*.

אֲצַלְיָהוּ (whom *the Lord has reserved*) pr. name masc. 2 Ch. 34. 8.

אָצֵל / אָצַל } pr. name of a man and of a place . אצל

[a] Ju. 2. 1. [b] Ho. 7. 12. [c] Job 39. 30. [d] Ps. 84. 4. [e] De. 22. 6. [f] Ca. 3. 9. [g] Eze. 24. 14. [h] Ex. 9. 29. [i] Eze. 16. 8. [k] Ezr. 9. 5. [l] Ho. 2. 5. [m] Is. 27. 4. [n] Je. 20. 7. [o] Job 31. 32. [p] Eze. 3. 2. [q] Is. 45. 1. [r] Ps. 78. 2. [s] Eze. 3. 23. [t] 2 Ch. 1. 10. [u] Nu. 2. 13. [x] Je. 52. 21. [y] 2 Sa. 21. 20. [z] Ps. 144. 1. [a] Is. 59. 3. [b] Da. 5. 5. [c] Da. 2. 42. [d] 2 Sa. 21. 20. [e] Da. 2. 41. [f] Ca. 5. 5. [g] 1 Ch. 20. 6. [h] Job 13. 18. [i] Job 9. 20. [k] De. 3. 18. [l] 1 Ki. 11. 38. [m] Je. 1. 7. [n] Est. 4. 16. [o] De. 31. 14. [p] Je. 1. 5. [q] Ge. 33. 15. [r] Zec. 11. 6. [s] 1 Sa. 10. 18. [t] Eze. 41. 8. [u] Je. 38. 12. [x] Eze. 13. 18. [y] Ex. 24. 11. [z] Ex. 5. 13. [a] Ps. 139. 8. [b] Is. 27. 4.

Form	Explanation	Root
אַצִּל	וְ defect for אַצִּיל (q. v.)	נצל
אֵצֶל	[a] וְ' (prim. a subst.) prep. dec. 6. (§ 35. rem. 6)	אצל
אֶצְלָהּ	id., suff. 3 pers. sing. fem.	אצל
אֶצְלֶה[b]	Kal fut. 1 pers. sing.	צלה
אֶצְלוֹ	prep., suff. 3 pers. sing. masc. from אֵצֶל (q. v.)	אצל
אֶצְלִי	id., suff. 1 pers. sing.	אצל
אֲצַלְיָהוּ	pr. name masc.	אצל
אֶצְלָם	prep., suff. 3 pers. pl. masc. from אֵצֶל (q. v.)	אצל
אָצַלְתָּ[c]	Kal pret. 2 pers. sing. masc. . . .	אצל
אָצַלְתִּי[d]	id. pret. 1 pers. sing.	אצל
אֲצַלְתִּי[e]	וְ id. id.; acc. shifted by conv. וְ (§ 8. rem. 7)	אצל
אֹצֶם	וְ' pr. name masc. 1 Ch. 2. 15, 25.	
אַצְמִיחַ	Hiph. fut. 1 pers. sing.	צמח
אַצְמִית[f]	Hiph. fut. 1 pers. sing.	צמת
אַצְמִיתֵם[g]	[h] וְ' id., suff. 3 pers. pl. masc. . . .	צמת
אֶצְעָדָה[i]	[k] וְ' noun fem. sing., pl. צְעָדוֹת . . .	צעד
אֶצְעַק[l]	Kal fut. 1 pers. sing.	צעק
אֶצְעָקָה[m]	וְ id. with parag. ה, in pause [for אֶצְעֲקָה § 8. r. 15]	צעק
אֲצַפֶּה[n]	וְ' Piel fut. 1 pers. sing.; וְ for וַ . .	צפה
אֲצַפְצֵף[o]	Pilpel (§ 6. No. 4) fut. 1 pers. sing. . .	צפף
אֶצֹּק[p] / אֶצָּק־[q]	Kal fut. 1 pers. sing. (§ 20. r. 16. § 8. r. 18)	יצק

[אָצַר] *to lay up, treasure up*, Niph. pass. Is. 23. 18. Hiph. *to appoint as treasurer*, Ne. 13. 13.

אוֹצָר masc. dec. 2 b. pl. אוֹצָרוֹת.—I. *store, treasure.*—II. *store-house, treasury.*

אֵצֶר (*treasure*) pr. name masc. Ge. 36. 21, 30.

Form	Explanation	Root
אֶצֹּר[r]	Kal fut. 1 pers. sing.	נצר
אֶצֳּרָה[s] / וְאֶצְּרָה[t]	id. with parag. ה (§ 8. rem. 15) . .	נצר
אָצְרוּ	Kal pret. 3 pers. pl.	אצר
אֹצָרוֹת	noun masc. with pl. (abs.) fem. term. from אוֹצָר dec. 2 b.	אצר
אֹצְרוֹת	וְ' id. pl., construct state . . .	אצר
אֶצָּרְךָ[u]	וְ Kal fut. 1 pers. sing. (אֶצֹּר), suff. 2 pers. sing. masc. (R. יצר § 20. r. 16) or .	נצר
אֶצְּרֶנָּה[x]	וְ id., suff. 3 pers. sing. fem. . . .	נצר
אֶצְּרֶנָּה[y]	id. id. (§ 8. rem. 14)	נצר
אֶצְרֹף[z]	וְ Kal fut. 1 pers. sing.	צרף
אֶצְרְפֶנּוּ[a]	וְ id., suff. 3 pers. sing. fem. . . .	צרף
אוֹצְרֹתֵיהֶם[b]	וְ noun masc. with pl. fem. term. and suff. 3 pers. pl. masc. from אוֹצָר dec. 2 b. .	אצר
אַצְתִּי[c]	Kal pret. 1 pers. sing.	אוץ
אֶקֹּב[d]	Kal fut. 1 pers. sing.	נקב
אֲקַבֵּץ	Piel fut. 1 pers. sing.	קבץ
אֶקְבֹּץ[e]	Kal fut. 1 pers. sing.	קבץ
אֲקַבְּצָה[f]	Piel fut. 1 p. s. with parag. ה [for אֲקַבְּצָה]	קבץ
אֶקְבְּצָה[g]	וְ', וָ, Kal fut. 1 s. with parag. ה; וְ for וַ conv.	קבץ
אֲקַבְּצֵךְ[h]	Piel fut. 1 pers. sing. id., suff. 2 pers. sing. fem.	קבץ
אֲקַבְּצֶךָּ[gg]	id., suff. 2 pers. sing. masc. (§ 2. rem. 2)	קבץ
אֲקַבְּצֵם	[i] וְ', [k] וָ, id., suff. 3 p. pl. m.; וַ for וְ, וָ for וַ conv.	קבץ
אֶקְבְּצֵם[l]	וָ Kal. fut. 1 p. s., suff. 3 p. pl. m.; וָ id. .	קבץ
אֶקָּבֵר[m]	Niph. fut. 1 pers. sing.	קבר
אֶקְבְּרָה	וְ Kal fut. 1 pers. sing. with parag. ה .	קבר
אֶקְבְּרֶהָ[n]	וָ id., suff. 3 pers. sing. fem.; וָ for וַ conv.	קבר
אֶקֹּד[o]	וָ Kal fut. 1 p. s. [for אֶקֹּד § 14. r. 18]; וָ id.	קדד
אֶקְדַּח[p]	noun masc. sing.	קדח
אַקְדִּר[q]	וָ Hiph. fut. 1 pers. sing.; וָ for וַ conv. .	קדר
אַקְדִּירֵם[r]	id., suff. 3 pers. pl. masc. . . .	קדר
אֲקַדֵּם[s]	Piel fut. 1 pers. sing.	קדם
אֲקַדֵּשׁ[t]	Piel fut. 1 pers. sing.	קדש
אֶקָּדֵשׁ[u]	Niph. fut. 1 pers. sing.	קדש
אַקּוֹ	וְ m. a sort of *wild goat* or *gazelle*, De. 14. 5.	
אֶקּוֹב[x]	וָ Kal fut. 1 pers. sing. (§ 17. rem. 3. & § 8. rem. 18); וָ for וַ conv. . . .	נקב
אֲקַוֶּה[y]	[z] וְ', [a] וָ, Piel fut. 1 p. s.; וַ for וְ, וָ for וַ conv.	קוה
אָקוּט[b]	Kal fut. 1 pers. sing.	קוט
אָקוּם	וָ' Kal fut. 1 pers. sing.; וָ for וַ conv. .	קום
אָקוּמָה	[c] וְ' id. with parag. ה	קום
אֲקוֹמֵם[d]	Pilel fut. 1 pers. sing.	קום
אֶקַּח / וָאֶקַּח	Kal fut. 1 pers. sing. (§ 8. rem. 15. & § 17. rem. 8); [e] וָ', וְ, וָ for וַ conv.	לקח
אֶקְחָה[f]	[g] וְ', [h] וָ', id. with parag. ה (for אֶקְּחָה comp. § 10. rem. 7); וָ id.	לקח
אֶקָּחֵהוּ[i]	וְ id., suff. 3 pers. sing. masc. (§ 16. rem. 12)	לקח
אֶקָּחֵךְ	id., suff. 2 pers. sing. masc. (§ 16. rem. 12)	לקח
אֶקָּחֵם[k]	וָ id., suff. 3 p. pl. m. (§ 16. r. 12); וָ for וַ conv.	לקח
אֶקְטֹף[l]	Kal fut. 1 pers. sing.	קטף
אָקִים	[m] וָ' Hiph. fut. 1 pers. sing.; וָ for וַ conv. .	קום
אֲקַיְּמָה[n]	וָ Piel fut. 1 pers. sing. with parag. ה [for אֲקַיְּמָה]; וָ id.	קום
אֲקִימֵהּ[o]	Chald. Aph. pret. 3 pers. s., suff. 3 pers. s. m.	קום
אָקִיץ[p]	Hiph. fut. 1 pers. sing.	קוץ
אֵקַל[q]	וָ Kal fut. 1 p. s. (§ 18. r. 6); וָ for וַ conv.	קלל
אֲקַלְלֵם[r]	וָ Piel fut. 1 p. s., suff. 3 p. pl. m. (§ 10. r. 7); וָ id.	קלל
אָקֻם	וָ Kal fut. 1 pers. sing. for אָקוּם (but comp. § 21. rem. 7); וָ id.	קום
אֶקְנֶה	וָ' Kal fut. 1 pers. sing.; וָ id. . .	קנה

[a] Pr. 7. 12. [b] Is. 44. 19. [c] Ge. 27. 36. [d] Ec. 2. 10. [e] Nu. 11. 17. [f] Ps. 101. 5, 8. [g] Ps. 18. 41. [gg] Is. 43. 5.
[h] 2 Sa. 22. 41. [i] Nu. 31. 50. [k] 2 Sa. 1. 10. [l] Job 19. 7. [m] Ps. 77. 2. [n] Mi. 7. 7. [o] Is. 38. 14.
[p] Is. 44. 3. [q] Is. 44. 3. [r] Ps. 119. 69. [s] Ps. 119. 145. [t] Ps. 119. 34, 115. [u] Is. 42. 6; 49. 8. [x] Ps. 119. 33.
[y] Is. 27. 3. [z] Is. 1. 25. [a] Ju. 7. 4. [b] Pr. 8. 21. [c] Je. 17. 16. [d] Nu. 23. 8. [e] Eze. 22. 20.
[f] Mi. 4. 6. [g] 2 Sa. 3. 21. [h] Is. 54. 7. [i] Zec. 10. 8. [k] Ne. 13. 11. [l] Ezr. 8. 15. [m] Ru. 1. 17.
[n] Ge. 48. 7. [o] Ge. 24. 48. [p] Is. 54. 12. [q] Eze. 31. 15. [r] Eze. 32. 8. [s] Mi. 6. 6. [t] Ex. 29. 44.
[u] Le. 10. 3. [x] Job 5. 3. [y] Job 17. 14. [z] Ps. 52. 11. [a] Ps. 69. 21. [b] Ps. 95. 10. [c] 2 Sa. 17. 1.
[d] Is. 44. 26. [e] Ho. 13. 11. [f] Is. 56. 12. [g] Ge. 18. 5. [h] Zec. 11. 13. [i] 2 Ki. 6. 13. [k] Jos. 7. 21.
[l] Eze. 17. 22. [m] Am. 2. 11. [n] Ps. 119. 106. [o] Da. 3. 1. [p] Pr. 23. 35. [q] Ge. 16. 5. [r] Ne. 13. 25.

[a] אַקְנִיאֵם Hiph. fut. 1 pers. sing., suff. 3 pers. pl. masc. קנא

[b] אָקִיץ וְ Kal fut. 1 pers. sing. for [אָקוּץ, but comp. § 21. rem. 7]; וָ for וְ· conv. . קוץ

[c] אֶקְצוֹף
[d] אֶקְצֹף } וְ' } Kal fut. 1 pers. sing. (§ 8. rem. 18) . קצף

אֶקְרָא וְ' Kal fut. 1 pers. sing.; וָ for וְ· conv. . קרא

[e] אֶקְרֵא Chald. Peal fut. 1 pers. sing. . . . קרא

[f] אֶקְרָאָה וְ' Kal fut. with parag. ה; וָ for וְ· conv. קרא

אֶקְרָאֲךָ id., suff. 2 pers. sing. masc. (§ 2. rem. 3) קרא

אֶקְרַב וָ Kal fut. 1 p. s. (§ 8. r. 13); וָ for וְ· conv. קָרַב

[g] אֲקָרְבֶנּוּ Piel fut. 1 p. s., suff. 3 p. s. m. (§ 2. r. 3.) קרב

[h] אִקָּרֵה Niph. fut. 1 pers. sing. (§ 10. rem. 5) . קרה

[i] אֶקְרָעֵ
[k] אֶקְרַע וְ' & [m] וְ'' וְ' } Kal fut. 1 pers. sing. (§ 8. rem. 15); וָ for וְ· conv. . } קרע

[n] אֶקְרָעֶנָּה id., suff. 3 pers. sing. f. (§ 10. r. 5. § 2. r. 3) קרע

[o] אַקְשֶׁה Hiph. fut. 1 pers. sing. . . . קשה

אֲרָא וָ pr. name masc.; וְ before (-:) . . ארה

[p] אֵרָא וָ ap. for אֶרְאֶה (q. v.) § 24. r. 10; וָ for וְ· conversive . . . . . . ראה

[q] אֵרֶא וָ & וְ' ap. for אֶרְאֶה (q.v.) § 24. r. 3c; וָ id. ראה

אֵרָאֶה [r] וְ' Niph. fut. 1 pers. sing. . . . ראה

[s] אֶרְאֶה Kh. אֶרְאֶה q. v., K. אֵרֶא (q. v.) . . ראה

אֶרְאֶה וְ' & וְ' Kal fut. 1 pers. sing.; וָ for וְ· conv. ראה

[t] אַרְאֵהוּ וְ Hiph. fut. 1 pers. sing., suff. 3 pers. sing. masc. (§ 24. rem. 21) . . . ראה

אַרְאֶךָ [u] וְ'' id., suff. 2 pers. sing. masc. . . ראה

[xc] אֶרְאֶךָ Kal fut. 1 pers. s., suff. 2 p. s. m. (§ 2. r. 3) ראה

[x] אֶרְאֵךְ וָ id., suff. 2 pers. s. f.; וָ for וְ· conv. . ראה

[y] אֲרִאֵל noun masc. sing. compound of אֲרִי & אֵל ארה

אַרְאֵלִי וְ pr. name masc. . . . . ארה

[z] אֶרְאֶלָּם noun masc. sing. [אֶרְאֵל], suff. 3 pers. pl. m. ארה

[a] אֶרְאֵם Kal fut. 1 p. s., suff. 3 p. pl. m. (§ 24. r. 21) ראה

אַרְאֶנּוּ Hiph. fut. 1 p. s., suff. 3 p. s. m. (§ 24. r. 21) ראה

אֶרְאֶנּוּ [b] וְ' Kal fut. 1 p. s., suff. 3 p. s. m. (§ 24. r. 21) ראה

[c] אָרַב וְ *to lie in wait* or *ambush*, const. with לְ, עַל, and acc.; part. אֹרֵב *a lier-in-wait*, collect. *liers-in-wait, an ambush.* Pi. i. q. Kal, const. with עַל; abs. Ju. 9. 25. Hiph. *to place an ambush*, 1 Sa. 15. 5.

אֲרָב (*ambush*) pr. name of a city in the mountains of Judah, Jos. 15. 52, gent. n. אַרְבִּי, 2 Sa. 23. 35.

אֶרֶב masc.—I. *a lying-in-wait*, Job 38. 40.—II. *a place of lying-in-wait, a lair* of wild beasts, Job 37. 8.

אֹרֶב masc. dec. 6c. *fraud, plot*, Je. 9. 7.

אֻרָּבָה fem. dec. 12c. id. only in pl. constr. אָרְבּוֹת, Is. 25. 11.

אֲרֻבָּה fem. dec. 10. a kind of *net-work* or *wicker-work*, to guard various apertures, and applied to—I. *a window*, Ec. 12. 3.—II. *a pigeon-house*, Is. 60. 8.—III. *a chimney*, Ho. 13. 3.—IV. Meton. of the visible heavens.

מַאֲרָב masc. dec. 2b.—I. *a place of ambush.*—II. *persons in an ambush*, 2 Ch. 13. 13.

אֲרָב pr. name of a place . . . . . ארב

אֶרֶב for [אֶרֶב] noun masc. sing. (§ 35. rem. 2) ארב

[d] אַרְבֶּה וְ Hiph. fut. 1 pers. sing., Kh. אֶרֶב ap. K. אַרְבֶּה; וָ for וְ· conv. . . . רבה

[e] אֱרֹב
[f] אֱרָב־ } וְ } Kal imp. sing. masc. (§ 8. rem. 18); וְ before (-:) . . . } ארב

אֹרֵב [g] וְ' id. part. act. sing. masc. dec. 7b. . ארב

אַרְבְּאֵל pr. name, see בֵּית אַרְבְּאֵל . . . בית

אַרְבֶּה noun masc. sing. . . . . רבה

אַרְבֶּה [h] וְ' Hiph. fut. 1 pers. sing. . . . רבה

[i] אַרְבֵּהוּ וְ id., suff. 3 pers. sing. masc. (§ 24. rem. 21) רבה

אָרְבוּ Kal preter. 3 pers. pl. . . . . ארב

[k] אָרְבּוֹ n. m. s., suff. 3 p. s. m. from אֹרֶב dec. 6c. ארב

[l] אָרְבּוֹת noun fem. pl. constr. from [אֻרָּבָה] dec. 12c. ארב

אֲרֻבּוֹת noun fem., pl. of אֲרֻבָּה dec. 10. . ארב

אֹרְבִים Kal part. act. masc., pl. of אֹרֵב dec. 7b. ארב

[m] אַרְבִּיצֵם Hiph. fut. 1 pers. sing., suff. 3 pers. pl. masc. רבץ

אַרְבַּע
אַרְבַּע } וְ' } num. card. fem. (§ 31. rem. 5) . רבע

אַרְבָּעָה וְ' id. masc., constr. אַרְבַּעַת (§ 42. rem. 5) . רבע

אַרְבְּעָה [n] וְ' Chald. num. card. masc. . . רבע

אַרְבָּעִים וְ' num. card. com., pl. of אַרְבַּע (§ 31. r. 3) רבע

[o] אַרְבַּעְתְּ Kh. בַּעַת' q. v., K. בַּע' (q. v.) . . רבע

אַרְבַּעַת וְ' num. card. m., constr. of אַרְבָּעָה (§ 42. r. 5) רבע

[p] אַרְבַּעְתָּיִם id., dual (of בַּעַת' comp. dec. 13a), for תַּיִם' רבע

[q] אַרְבַּעְתָּם id. sing., suff. 3 pers. sing. masc. . . רבע

אֲרֻבֹּת וְ defec. for אֲרֻבּוֹת q. v.; וַ before (-:) . ארב

[r] אָרַבְתִּי Kal pret. 1 pers. sing. [for אָרַבְתִּי § 8. r. 7] ארב

[s] אֲרֻבֹּתֵיהֶם n. f. pl., suff. 3 p. pl. m. from אֲרֻבָּה d. 10. ארב

[t] אֲרַבְתֶּם וְ Kal pret. 2 pers. pl. masc.; וְ for וַ . ארב

[אָרַג] I. *to plait* the hair, Ju. 16. 13.—II. *to weave*; אֹרֵג *weaving, a weaver.*

אֶרֶג masc. I. *texture, web*, Ju. 16. 14.—II. *weaver's shuttle*, Job 7. 6.

[u] אֶרֶג noun masc. sing. [for אֶרֶג § 35. r. 2] . ארג

אֹרֵג [x] וְ'' Kal. part. act. sing. masc. dec. 7b. . ארג

[a] De. 32. 21. [b] Le. 20. 23. [c] Is. 57. 16. [d] Is. 57. 17. [e] Da. 5. 17. [f] 1 Sa. 28. 15. [g] Job 31. 37. [h] Nu. 23. 15. [i] 1 Ki. 11. 13. [k] 1 Ki. 11. 11. [l] Ho. 13. 8. [m] 1 Ki. 14. 8. [n] 1 Ki. 11. 12. [o] Ex. 7. 3. [p] Ex. 6. 3. [q] Is. 41. 28. [r] Ps. 42. 3. [s] Jos. 7. 21. [t] Ps. 91. 16. [u] Ju. 4. 22. [x] Eze. 16. 6, 8. [y] 2 Sa. 23. 20. [z] Is. 33. 7. [a] Je. 18. 17. [b] Ge. 45. 28. [c] De. 19. 11. [d] Jos. 24. 3. [e] Ju. 9. 32. [f] Pr. 12. 6. [g] Ju. 20. 33. [h] Ge. 17. 2. [i] Is. 51. 2. [k] Je. 9. 7. [l] Is. 25. 11. [m] Eze. 34. 15. [n] Da. 7. 6. [o] Eze. 7. 2. [p] 2 Sa. 12. 6. [q] Da. 1. 17. [r] Job 31. 9. [s] Is. 60. 8. [t] Ju. 21. 20. [u] Job 7. 6. [x] Ex. 35. 35. [xc] 2 Ki. 3. 14.

אַרְגֹּב pr. name of a region . . . . רגב

אַרְגְּוָן *purple*, i.q. אַרְגָּמָן, only 2 Ch. 2. 6, and Chald. emph. אַרְגְּוָנָא Da. 5. 7, 16, 29.

אֹרְגוֹת[a] Kal part. act. pl. f. from אֹרֵג m. (§ 8. r. 19) ארג

אֶרְגָּז[b] Kal fut. 1 pers. sing. [for אֶרְגַּז § 8. rem. 15] רגז

אַרְגִּיז[c] Hiph. fut. 1 pers. sing. . . . . רגז

אֹרְגִים [d]וְ' Kal part. act. masc., pl. of אֹרֵג dec. 7 b. ארג

אַרְגִּיעַ[e] Hiph. fut. 1 pers. sing. . . . רגע

אַרְגִּיעָה id. with parag. ה . . . . . רגע

אַרְגָּמָן וְ' *purple, reddish purple*, both of the colour itself and clothes dyed with purple. The etymology is uncertain.

אָרַד Root not used, perhaps i. q. עָרַד *to flee*; in the Chald. אַרְדָּא *mushroom*. Whence—

אַרְדְּ (*mushroom?*) pr. name of a son or grandson of Benjamin, Ge. 46. 21; Nu. 26. 40. called אַדָּר 1 Ch. 8. 3. Gent. n. אַרְדִּי.

אֲרוֹד (*flight*, or perhaps i. q. עָרוֹד *wild ass*) pr. name masc. Nu. 26. 17. Gent. n. אֲרוֹדִי Ge. 46. 16.

אַרְדּוֹן (*fugitive*) pr. name masc. 1 Ch. 2. 18.

אֲרִידַי (*strong*, coll. with the Pers.) pr. name of a son of Haman, Est. 9. 9.

אֲרִידָתָא (id.) pr. name of a son of Haman, Est. 9. 8.

אֵרֵד וְ' Kal fut. 1 pers. sing.; וָ for וַ conv. . ירד

אֵרְדָה[f] id. with paragogic ה . . . . . ירד

אֶרְדּוֹף[g] Kal fut. 1 pers. sing. (§ 8. rem. 18) . רדף

אַרְדִּי pr. name masc. for אֲרִידַי . . . . ארד

אֶרְדֹּף Kal fut. 1 pers. sing. . . . . רדף

אֶרְדְּפָה[h] [i]וְ' id. with paragogic ה . . . . רדף

[אָרָה] I. *to pull*, or *pluck off*, Ps. 80. 13.—II. *to gather*, Ca. 5. 1.

אֲרָא (*lion*, comp. אֲרִי) pr. name masc. 1 Ch. 7. 38.

אֻרְוָה (for אֻרְוָה, fem. of אֻרְוֹ, pl. abs. אֻרְוֹת for אֻרָוֹת, constr. אֻרְוֹת comp. dec. 12 c) and אֻרְיָה, fem. *a stall, a stable.*

אָרוֹן com. dec. 3 a.—I. *ark, chest.*—II. *coffin*, Ge. 50. 26.

אֲרִי masc. dec. 6. pl. אֲרָיִים and אֲרָיוֹת, *lion.*

אַרְיֵה i. q. אֲרִי, with parag. ה *a lion.*

אַרְיֵה Chald. id. irr. comp. § 68.

אֲרִיאֵל masc. prop. *a lion of God*, hence—I. *a hero*, applied also to the altar of burnt-offering, Eze. 43. 15, 16. and Jerusalem, Is. 29. 1, 2.—II. pr. name masc. Ezr. 8. 16.

אֶרְאֵל contr. from the preceding, *a hero*, only with suff. אֶרְאֶלָּם, Is. 33. 7.

אַרְאֵלִי (*hero*) pr. name masc. Ge. 46. 16.

אַרְיוֹךְ (*lion-like*, the syllable אך being an adj. term. in the Pers., Gesenius) pr. name—I. a king of Ellasar, Ge. 14. 1, 9.—II. a Chaldean, Da. 2. 14.

אֲרִיסַי (*lion-like*, Pers. סא, סה *like*) pr. name of a son of Haman, Est. 9. 9.

אָרָה־ Kal imp. sing. masc., [אַר] with parag. ה [for אֹרָה § 18. rem. 4] . . . ארר

אֲרוּ וְ Chald. *lo, behold!* Da. 7. 2, 5, 6, 7, 13.

אֹרוּ[k] Kal pret. 3 pers. pl. (§ 21. rem. 2) . אור

אֹרוּ[l] Kal imp. pl. m. from [אֹר] sing., comp. אָרָה ארר

אַרְוַד וְ' pr. name of a place . . . . רוד

אַרְוָדִי וָ gent. noun from אַרְוַד . . . ארד

אָרוּהָ[m] וְ Kal pret. 3 pers. pl., suff. 3 pers. sing. fem. ארה

אֲרוּכָה noun fem. sing. dec. 10. . . . ארך

אָרוּם[n] Kal fut. 1 pers. sing. . . . . רום

אֲרֻמִּים וְ Kh., for אֲדֹמִים K., see אֱדוֹם . אדם

אֵרוֹמָם[o] [for אֶתְרוֹ'] Hithpal fut. 1 pers. s. (§ 21. r. 20) רום

אֲרוֹמְמֶךָּ[p] / אֲרוֹמְמֶךָ } Pilel fut. 1 pers. sing., suff. 2 pers. sing. masc. (§ 2. rem. 3) . . } רום

אֲרוֹן וְ' noun com., constr. of אָרוֹן dec. 3 a; וּ bef. (ֿ) ארה

אֲרַוְנָה pr. name masc. . . . . . ארן

אָרוּץ Kal fut. 1 p. s. (2 Sa. 22. 30, perh. R. רצץ) רוץ

אָרוּצָה[q] [r]וְ' id. with paragogic ה . . . רוץ

אֲרוּצֵם[s] Kh. אֲרוּצֵם Kal fut. with suff. R. רצץ (§ 18. r. 12) K. אֲרִיצֵם Hiph. fut. 1 p. s. with suff. 3 p. pl. m. רוץ

אָרוֹר[t] Kal inf. abs. . . . . . ארר

אָרוּר וְ' id. part. p. sing. masc. dec. 3 a. . ארר

אֲרוּרָה[u] id. id. fem. . . . . . ארר

אֲרוּרִים id. id. pl. masc. . . . . . ארר

אֻרְוֹת[x] וְ' noun fem., pl. of [אֻרְוָה] q. v. . . ארה

אֻרְוֹת[y] id. pl., construct state . . . . ארה

אָרוֹתִי[z] וְ' Kal pret. 1 pers. sing. [for אָרוֹתִי]; acc. shifted by conv. וְ (§ 8. rem. 7) . . ארר

אָרוֹתִיהָ[a] id., suff. 3 pers. sing. fem. . . . ארר

[אָרַז] *to be firm, fast*, only in part. pass. Eze. 27. 24.

אֶרֶז masc. dec. 6 a. (pl. c. אַרְזֵי) *cedar.*

אַרְזָה fem. *cedar wainscot*, Zep. 2. 14.

מֵרוֹז (built of *cedar* for מֵאֶרוֹז) pr. name of a town in Palestine, Ju. 5. 23.

אֶרֶז [a]וְ' / אָרֶז [b]וְ' } noun masc. sing., (pl. c. אַרְזֵי § 35. rem. 1, 2) dec. 6 a; for וָ see lett. ו } ארז

אַרְזָה[c] noun fem. sing. . . . . . ארז

אַרְזֵי noun masc. pl. constr. from אֶרֶז dec. 6 a. ארז

---

[a] 2 Ki. 23. 7. [b] Hab. 3. 16. [c] Is. 13. 13. [d] Is. 19. 9. [e] Is. 51. 4. [f] Ge. 18. 21. [g] Ps. 18. 38. [h] 2 Sa. 22. 38. [i] 2 Sa. 17. 1. [k] 1 Sa. 14. 29. [l] Ju. 5. 23. [m] Ps. 80. 13. [n] Ps. 46. 11, 11. [o] Is. 33. 10. [p] Ps. 118. 28. [q] 2 Sa. 18. 19. [r] 2 Ki. 4. 22. [s] Je. 50. 44. [t] Ju. 5. 23. [u] Ge. 3. 17. [x] 2 Ch. 32. 28. [y] 1 Ki. 5. 6. [z] Mal. 2. 2. [a] 1 Ki. 7. 11. [b] 1 Ki. 6. 18. [c] Zep. 2. 14.

אֲרָזָיו id. pl., suff. 3 pers. sing. masc. . . ארז

אֲרָזַיִךְ[a] id. pl., suff. 2 pers. sing. masc. . . ארז

אֲרָזִים [b]וְ' id. pl., absolute state; וֻ before (ְ:) . ארז

אֲרֻזִים[c] וְ Kal part. pass. pl. of [אָרוּז] dec. 3a; וֻ id. ארז

אָרַח[d] וְ *to go, to be on the way,* Job 34. 8; part. אֹרֵחַ *a way-farer, traveller.*

אָרַח (*wanderer*) pr. name masc.

אֹרַח com. dec. 6c. pl. אֳרָחוֹת constr. and with suff. אָרְחוֹת, by Syr. אָרְחֹתָם (§ 35. rem. 5 & 9).—I. *way, road, path.*—II. *manner, mode.*—III. poet. for אֹרֵחַ *traveller,* Job 31. 32.

אֹרַח Chald. id. dec. 3c. pl. אָרְחָן.

אֹרְחָה fem. dec. 10. *a company of travellers, a caravan.*

אֲרֻחָה fem. dec. 10.—I. *appointed portion.*—II. *portion, generally,* Pr. 15. 17.

אָרַח pr. name masc. . . . . . . ארח

אֹרַח וְ' noun com. sing. dec. 6. pl. אֳרָחוֹת, more under the Root . . . . . ארח

אֹרְחָה[e] noun fem. sing. dec. 10. . . . ארח

אָרְחוֹ[f] n. com. s., suff. 3 pers. s. m. from אֹרַח (q. v.) ארח

אֳרָחוֹת[u] id. pl., absolute state . . . . ארח

אֹרְחוֹת[g] noun fem., pl. of [אֹרְחָה] dec. 10. . ארח

אָרְחוֹת וְ'[h] noun com. pl. constr. from אֹרַח (q. v.) . ארח

אָרְחוֹתֶיךָ[i] id., suff. 2 pers. sing. masc. (א̇ § 35. r. 9) ארח

אָרְחֹתָם id., suff. 3 pers. pl. masc. (א̇ ibid.) . ארח

אָרְחִי id. sing., suff. 1 pers. sing. . . . ארח

אֹרְחִים[k] Kal part. act. masc., pl. of אֹרֵחַ' dec. 7b. ארח

אַרְחִיק Hiph. fut. 1 pers. sing. . . . . רחק

אָרְחֶךָ[l] [for אָרְחֲךָ'] noun com. sing., suff. 2 pers. sing. masc. from אֹרַח dec. 6c. (more under R.) ארח

אֲרַחֵם Piel fut. 1 pers. sing. (§ 14. rem. 1) . רחם

אֶרְחָמְךָ[m] Kal fut. 1 pers. s. [אֶרְחַם], suff. 2 pers. s. m. רחם

אֲרַחֲמֶנּוּ[n] Piel fut. 1 p. s., suff. 3 p. s. m. (§ 14. r. 1) רחם

אֶרְחַץ [o]וָ' Kal fut. 1 pers. sing.; וָ for וַ· conv. רחץ

אֶרְחָצֵךְ[p] וָ id., suff. 2 pers. sing. fem. (§ 16. r. 12); וָ id. רחץ

אֲרֻחַת noun fem. sing. constr. of [חָה'] dec. 10. . ארח

אֹרְחַת[oo] noun fem. sing., constr. of [חָה'] dec. 10. ארח

אָרְחָתְהּ[q] וְ Chald. noun com. pl. [אָרְחָן], suff. 3 pers. sing. masc., comp. Heb. אֹרַח . . ארח

אֲרֻחָתוֹ וֻ noun fem. sing., suff. 3 pers. sing. masc. from אֲרֻחָה dec. 10; וֻ before (ְ:) . . ארח

אָרְחֹתָיו[r] noun com., pl., suff. 3 pers. sing. masc. from אֹרַח q. v. (א̇ § 35. rem. 9) . . ארח

אָרְחֹתַי id., suff. 1 pers. sing. [for אָרְחוֹתַי] . . ארח

אָרְחֹתֵיהֶם[s] id., suff. 3 pers. pl. masc. . . . ארח

אָרְחֹתֶיךָ id., suff. 2 pers. sing. masc. (א̇ § 35. rem. 9) ארח

אָרְחָתָךְ[t] Chald. id. pl. with suff. 2 pers. s. m. dec. 3c. ארח

אֲרִי noun masc. sing. dec. 6i. (§ 35. rem. 14) . ארה

אֻרִי pr. name masc. for אוּרִי . . . . אור

אֲרִיאֵל noun masc. sing. compound of אֲרִי & אֵל . ארה

אָרִיב [u]וָ' Kal fut. 1 pers. sing.; וָ for וַ· conv. ריב

אָרִיבָה וָ id. with parag. ה; וָ id. . . . ריב

אָרִיד[x] Hiph. fut. 1 pers. sing. . . . . רוד

אֲרִידַי pr. name masc. . . . . . ארד

אֲרִידָתָא pr. name masc. . . . . . ארד

אֲרִיֵּה[y] Kh. אַרְיֵה q. v., K. אֲרִי (q. v.) . . ארה

אַרְיֵה וְ' n. m. s., from אֲרִי with parag. ה (§ 35. r. 14) ארה

אֲרַיֶּךָ[z] Piel fut. 1 pers. s. [אֲרַיֶּה] from pret. רִיָּה, like קִיֵּם from קוּם] with suff. 3 p. s. f., rad. ה changed to ו, comp. רַאֲוָה from רָאָה. Or it may stand by transp. for אֲרַוֶּךְ (§ 24. r. 13) רוה

אַרְיוֹךְ וְ' pr. name masc. . . . . ארה

אֲרָיוֹת n. masc. with pl. fem. term. from אֲרִי (q. v.) ארה

אֲרָיוֹת[a] noun fem., pl. of [אֲרָיָה] dec. 10. . ארה

אַרְיָוָתָא Chald. noun masc. with pl. fem. term., emph. st. from אַרְיֵה irr. (§ 68) . . ארה

אָרִיחַ Hiph. fut. 1 pers. sing. . . . רוח

אֲרִיךְ[b] Chald. Peal part. pass. sing. . . ארך

אֲרָיִים[c] noun masc., pl. of אֲרִי dec. 6i. . ארה

אָרִים Hiph. fut. 1 pers. sing. . . . רום

אֲרִיסַי pr. name masc. . . . . ארה

אֲרִיצֶנּוּ[d] Hiph. fut. 1 p. s. [אָרִיץ], suff. 3 p. s. m. (§ 2. r. 3) רוץ

אָרִיק Hiph. fut. 1 pers. sing. . . . רוק

אֲרִיקֵם[e] id., suff. 3 pers. pl. masc. . . . רוק

אָרִיתִי[f] Kal pret. 1 pers. sing. . . . ארה

[אָרַךְ] *to be* or *become long,* spoken of boughs (Eze. 31. 5), and of time; אָרְכוּ לוֹ שָׁם הַיָּמִים *he had been there a long time.* Hiph.—I. *to make long, to prolong,* הֶאֱרִיךְ יְמֵי פ' *to prolong one's life.*—II. *to defer,* הֶאֱרִיךְ אַפּוֹ *to defer one's anger, to be patient.*—III. intrans. *to be long,* 1 Ki. 8. 8; הֶאֱרִיכוּ יָמָיו *his days are long,* i. e. lives long.

אֲרַךְ Chald. only part. pass. *meet, fit,* Ezr. 4. 14.

אָרֵךְ masc. adj. only fem. אֲרֻכָּה (§ 39. No. 3. dec. 8. & § 26. III. No. 22) *long,* of space and time.

אֹרֶךְ masc.—I. *length,* Eze. 17. 3, אֶרֶךְ הָאֵבֶר *length of wing* for the concrete *long-winged.*—II. *slowness, tardiness,* אֶרֶךְ אַפַּיִם *slowness of anger,* i. e. *forbearance,* Je. 15. 15, elsewhere in this phrase and אֶרֶךְ רוּחַ (slowness of spirit) for the concrete *patient, long-suffering,* spoken of God or men.—

[a] Je. 22. 7. [b] Is. 9. 9. [c] Eze. 27. 24. [d] Job 34. 8. [e] Je. 40. 5. [f] Ps. 119. 9. [g] Is. 21. 13. [h] Pr. 2. 29. [i] Ps. 25. 4. [k] Je. 9. 1. [l] Ps. 44. 19. [u] Ju. 5. 6. [m] Ps. 18. 2. [n] Je. 31. 20. [o] Ps. 73. 13. [oo] Ge. 37. 25. [p] Eze. 16. 9. [q] Da. 4. 34. [r] Pr. 22. 25. [s] Pr. 2. 15. [t] Da. 5. 23. [u] Ne. 13. 25. [x] Ps. 55. 3. [y] La. 3. 10. [z] Is. 16. 9. [a] 2 Ch. 9. 25. [b] 1 Ki. 10. 20. [c] Ezr. 4. 14. [d] Je. 49. 19. [e] Ps. 18. 43. [f] Ca. 5. 1.

III. pr. name of a city of Babylonia, Ge. 10. 10. Gent. noun אַרְכִּי.

אֹרֶךְ masc. dec. 6c. *length*, of time and space; אֹרֶךְ אַפַּיִם *forbearance*, comp. אֶרֶךְ.

אַרְכָּא & אַרְכָה Chald. fem. *length, duration*, Da. 4. 24; 7. 12.

אֲרוּכָה, אֲרֻכָה fem. dec. 10. (prop. prolongation) *a repairing, restoring, healing*.

אַרְכְּוָי Chald. gent. noun from אֶרֶךְ q. v. pl. אַרְכְּוָיֵ Kheth. אַרְכְּוָאֵי K. (§ 63) Ezr. 4. 9.

אֶרֶךְ[rr] וְ' noun masc. sing.; also pr. name of a place . ארך
אֹרֶךְ וְ' noun masc. sing. dec. 6c. . . . ארך
אֶרְכַּב[a] וְ Kal fut. 1 pers. sing. . . . . רכב
אַרְכֻּבָתֵהּ[b] וְ Chald. noun fem. sing., suff. 3 pers. sing. masc. from [אַרְכֻּבָא] dec. 8a. . . רכב
אַרְכָּא[c] / אַרְכָה[d] וְ } Chald. noun fem. sing. . . . ארך
אֲרֻכָה defect. for אֲרוּכָה, noun fem. sing. dec. 10. ארך
אֲרֻכָּה adj. fem. sing. fr. [אָרֹךְ] masc. (§ 37. No. 3. & § 39. rem. 3. dec. 8) . . . . ארך
אָרְכָּהּ n. m. s., suff. 3 pers. s. f. from אֹרֶךְ dec. 6c. ארך
אָרְכוּ[e] Kal pret. 3 pers. pl. . . . . . ארך
אָרְכּוֹ וְ' n. m. s., suff. 3 pers. s. m. from אֹרֶךְ dec. 6c. ארך
אַרְכְּוָיֵ Chald. gent. noun pl. Kh. (more under R.) ארך
אַרְכִּיב[f] Hiph. fut. 1 pers. sing. . . . . רכב
אָרְכָּם[g] n. m. s., suff. 3 p. pl. m. from אֹרֶךְ dec. 6c. ארך
אֲרֻכַת[h] noun fem. sing., constr. of אֲרוּכָה dec. 10. ארך
אֲרֻכָתְךָ[i] וְ id., suff. 2 pers. sing. masc.; וְ before (-:) ארך

אָרַם Root not used, i. q. רוּם, רָאַם, רָמַם, &c. *to be high*, whence

אֲרוּמָה (*lofty*) pr. name of a city near Sichem, Ju. 9. 41, called רוּמָה 2 Ki. 23. 36.

אֲרָם, constr. אֲרַם (*high*) pr. name.—I. son of Kamuel and grandson of Nahor, Ge. 22. 21, but according to chap. 10. 22, he was a son of Shem.—II. 1 Ch. 7. 34.—III. *Aramea, Syria*, the whole region between Phenicia, the Taurus, Tigris and Palestine; the principal part is, אֲרַם דַּמֶּשֶׂק *Syria of Damascus*, the territory of and round Damascus; אֲרַם נַהֲרַיִם *Syria of the two rivers*, i. e. Mesopotamia, also called פַּדַּן אֲרָם *plain of Syria*, and שְׂדֵה אֲרָם *field of Syria*.

אֲרַמִּי gent. noun *Aramean, Syrian*, fem. אֲרַמִּיָּה; pl. אֲרַמִּים.

אֲרָמִית (formed of the preceding, see § 39. No. 4. rem. 1) adv. *in the language of Syria, in Syriac*.

אַרְמוֹן masc. pl. constr. אַרְמְנוֹת [as if from אַרְמֹנֶת § 44. rem. 5], *castle, palace*.

אַרְמֹנִי (*palastine*) pr. name of a son of Saul, 2 Sa. 21. 8.

אַרְמוֹן[k] וְ' noun masc. sing. (q. v.) . . . ארם
אֲרַמִּי gent. noun from אֲרָם . . . . ארם
אֲרַמִּים id. pl. absolute . . . . . ארם
אֲרָמִית adv. from the gentilic n. אֲרַמִּי (§ 39. No. 4. r. 1) ארם
אֲרֹמְמֶנְהוּ[l] וְ Pilel fut. 1 pers. sing. with epenth. נ (§ 16. r. 13) and suff. 3 pers. sing. masc.; וְ for וְ רום
אַרְמְנוֹת noun masc. with pl. fem. term. const. [as if from אַרְמֹנֶת § 44. r. 5] see אַרְמוֹן . ארם
אַרְמְנוֹתֶיהָ id. with suff. 3 pers. sing. fem. . . ארם
אַרְמְנוֹתַיִךְ[m] id., suff. 2 pers. sing. fem. for ־ַיִךְ . ארם
אַרְמֹנִי pr. name masc. . . . . . ארם
אַרְמְנֹתֶיהָ noun masc. with fem. term. and suff. 3 pers. sing. fem. from אַרְמֹן (q. v.) . . ארם
אַרְמְנֹתָיו[n] וְ id., suff. 3 pers. sing. masc. . . . ארם
אֶרְמְסֵם[o] וְ Kal fut. 1 pers. sing. [אֶרְמֹס], suff. 3 pers. pl. masc. . . . . . רמס

אָרַן Root not used, Arab. *to be active, nimble*.

אֹרֶן (*wild goat*, Syriac ארנא id.) pr. n. of a man.

אֹרֶן masc.—I. a kind of tree, supposed to be the *mountain ash*, Vulg. *pinus*, Is. 44. 14. Its connexion with the Root is uncertain.—II. pr. name masc. 1 Ch. 2. 25.

אַרְנָן (*nimble*) pr. name masc. 1 Ch. 3. 21.

אָרְנָן (id.) pr. name of a Jebusite, on the site of whose threshing-floor Solomon built the temple, 1 Ch. 21. 15; 2 Ch. 3. 1.

אֲרַוְנָה pr. name, stands for אָרְנָן in 2 Sa. 24. 20, sq. which is called in *v.* 16, אוֹרְנָה Kheth., in *v.* 18, אֲרַנְיָה Kheth.

אֹרֶן וְ pr. name masc.; וְ before (-:) . . ארן
אֲרוֹן noun masc. sing. constr. of אָרוֹן dec. 3a. ארה
אֹרֶן[p] וְ' noun masc. sing.; also pr. name . ארן
[אַרְנֶבֶת] f. *hare*; only with the art. Le. 11. 6; De. 14. 17.
אַרְנוֹן pr. name of a river . . . . רנן
אֲרַנְיָה pr. name masc., K. אֲרַוְנָה . . . ארן
אֲרַנֵּן[q] וְ' Piel fut. 1 pers. sing. . . . רנן
אָרְנָן pr. name masc. . . . . . ארן
אַרְנִן[r] [for אֲרַנִּין] Hiph. fut. 1 pers. sing. . . רנן
אַרְנֹן pr. name of a river, for אַרְנוֹן . . רנן
אָרְנָן וְ' pr. name masc. . . . . ארן

אֲרַע Chald. only in the emph. st. אַרְעָא (dec. 3a).—I.

---

[a] 2 Sa. 19. 27. [b] Da. 5. 6. [c] Da. 4. 24. [d] Da. 7. 12. [e] Ge. 26. 8. [f] Ho. 10. 11. [g] 2 Ch. 3. 11. [h] Je. 8. 22. [i] Is. 58. 8. [k] Je. 30. 18. [l] Ex. 15. 2. [m] Am. 3. 11. [n] Am. 6. 8. [o] Is. 63. 3. [p] Is. 44. 14. [q] Ps. 59. 17. [r] Job 29. 13. [rr] Pr. 15. 18.

the earth, i. q. Heb. אֶרֶץ.—II. adv. *low, inferior*, Da. 2. 39.

אַרְעִית Chald. fem. (prop. constr. of אַרְעִי, comp. dec. 8b) *the bottom*, Da. 6. 25.

אָרֵעַ Hiph. fut. 1 pers. sing. (§ 18. rem. 11) . רעע

[a]אַרְעָא Chald. Kh. אַרְעָא, K. אֲרַע adv. . ארע

[b]אַרְעָא ו׳ Chald. noun f. s. emph. of [אֲרַע] dec. 3a. ארע

[c]אֶרְעַב Kal fut. 1 pers. sing. . . . . רעב

[d]אֶרְעֶה ו׳ Kal fut. 1 pers. sing.; וָ for וַ conv. . רעה

[e]אֶרְעֶנָּה id., suff. 3 pers. sing. fem. (§ 24. rem. 21) רעה

[f]אֵרָפֵא וְ Niph. fut. 1 pers. sing. . . . רפא

[g]אֶרְפָּא ו׳ Kal fut. 1 pers. sing. . . . . רפא

[h]אֶרְפָּאֵהוּ וְ id., suff. 3 pers. sing. masc. . . . רפא

[i]אֶרְפָּאֵךְ id., suff. 2 pers. sing. fem. . . . רפא

אַרְפָּד ו׳ pr. name of a region . . . . רפד

אַרְפֶּהָ Hiph. fut. 1 p. s., suff. 3 p. s. f. (§ 24. r. 21) רפה

[k]אֶרְפָּה Kal fut. 1 pers. sing. (§ 23. rem. 10) . רפא

[l]אַרְפֶּךָּ Hiph. fut. 1 pers. sing. [אַרְפֶּה], suff. 2 pers. sing. masc. (§ 24. rem. 21) . . רפה

אַרְפַּכְשַׁד ו׳ pr. name of the third son of Shem.

[m]אַרְפֶּנּוּ Hiph. fut. 1 pers. sing. [אַרְפֶּה], suff. 3 pers. sing. masc. (§ 24. rem. 21, & § 2. rem. 3) רפה

אֶרֶץ fem. rarely masc. dec. 6a. with the art. הָאָרֶץ, with suff. אַרְצִי.—I. *the earth*, opp. to שָׁמַיִם.—II. *earth, land*, opposed to יָם.—III. *land, ground.*—IV. *land, country.* Pl. אֲרָצוֹת *lands, countries*, especially *Gentile countries*.

אַרְצָא pr. name of a man, 1 Ki. 16. 9.

אֶרֶץ ו׳ / אָרֶץ ו׳ } noun fem. sing. dec. 6a. (§ 35. rem. 2); for וָ see lett. ו . . } ארץ

[n]אָרִיץ Kal fut. 1 p. s. (perhaps from רצץ § 18. r. 12) רוץ

אַרְצָא pr. name masc. . . . . . ארץ

אַרְצָה / אָרְצָה } [o]ו׳ noun f. s. (אֶרֶץ), with parag. ה dec. 6a. ארץ

אַרְצָהּ id., suff. 3 pers. sing. fem. . . . . ארץ

[p]אָרֻצָה Kal fut. 1 pers. sing. with parag. ה for אָרוּצָה רוץ

[q]אֶרְצֶה ו׳ Kal fut. 1 pers. sing. . . . . רצה

אַרְצוֹ noun f. s., suff. 3 p. s. m. from אֶרֶץ dec. 6a. ארץ

אֲרָצוֹת id. pl. absolute state . . . . ארץ

אַרְצוֹת id. pl. constr. state . . . . ארץ

[r]אֵרָצֵחַ Niph. fut. 1 pers. sing. [for צַח § 15. rem. 1] רצח

אַרְצִי noun f. s., suff. 1 pers. s. from אֶרֶץ dec. 6a. ארץ

אַרְצְךָ / אַרְצֶךָ } id., suff. 2 pers. sing. masc. . . ארץ

[s]אַרְצֵךְ ו׳ id., suff. 2 pers. sing. fem. . . . ארץ

אַרְצְכֶם id., suff. 2 pers. pl. masc. . . . ארץ

אַרְצָם id., suff. 3 pers. pl. masc. . . . . ארץ

[t]אֶרְצֵם Kal fut. 1 pers. sing. (אֶרְצֶה), suff. 3 pers. pl. masc. (§ 24. rem. 21) . . . רצה

[u]אַרְצֵנוּ ו׳ noun f. s., suff. 1 p. pl. from אֶרֶץ dec. 6a. ארץ

אֲרַק Chald. only emph. st. אַרְקָא (dec. 3a) Je. 10. 11. *the earth.*

[x]אֶרְקָעֵם Kal fut. 1 pers. sing. [אֶרְקַע], suff. 3 pers. pl. masc. (§ 16. rem. 12) . . רקע

[אָרַר] *to curse, execrate.* Niph. *to be cursed*, Mal. 3. 9. Pi.—I. *to curse*, Ge. 5. 29.—II. *to bring on a curse*, Nu. 5. 18, 19. sq. Hoph. *to be cursed*, Nu. 22. 6.

מְאֵרָה fem. dec. 10. *curse, execration.*

[y]אֵרְרָהּ Piel pret. 1 pers. sing., suff. 3 pers. sing. fem. ארר

אֲרָרַט / אֲרָרָט } pr. name of a province in Armenia, upon whose mountains the ark of Noah rested.

[z]אֹרְרֵי Kal part. act. m., pl. c. from [אֹרֵר] dec. 7b. ארר

[a]אֹרְרֶיךָ ו׳ id. pl., suff. 2 pers. s. m. (ךָ anom. for ךָ) ארר

אָרַשׂ Pi. *to betroth*; the price paid for a wife is put with בְּ. Pu. *to be betrothed.*

אָרַשׁ Root not used, Arab. *to desire.*

אֲרֶשֶׁת fem. *desire, request*, Ps. 21. 3.

[c]אֵרַשׂ Piel pret. 3 pers. sing. masc. (§ 10. rem. 1) ארשׂ

אֹרָשָׂה Pual pret. 3 pers. sing. fem. [for אֹרְשָׂה.] ארשׂ

אַרְשִׁיעַ Kal fut. 1 pers. sing. [for אֶרְשַׁע § 8. rem. 15] רשע

[d]אֲרֶשֶׁת וַ noun fem. sing.; וַ before (ֲ) . . ארש

[e]אֵרַשְׂתִּי Piel pret. 1 pers. sing. . . . . ארשׂ

[f]אֵרַשְׂתִּיךְ וְ id., suff. 2 pers. sing. masc. . . ארשׂ

[g]אֹרֹת noun m., with pl. f. term. from אוֹר dec. 1a. אור

אַרְתַּחְשַׁשְׁתָּא / אַרְתַּחְשַׁשְׂתְּא / אַרְתַּחְשַׁסְתְּא ו׳ } Artaxerxes pr. name of several Persian kings.

אֵשׁ ו׳ וָ ו׳ com. dec. 8b.—I. *fire*; used of lightning, of the sun, and trop. of anger.—II. *shining brightness*, Na. 2. 4; אַבְנֵי אֵשׁ *stones of fire*, glittering gems, Ez. 28. 14, 16.

אֵשׁ Chald. emph. אֶשָּׁא, id. Da. 7. 11.

אֶשָּׁה f. *fire*, only in Kheth. אֶשָּׁתָם (מְ) Je. 6. 29.

אִשֶּׁה masc. dec. 9a. an offering made by fire.—I. *a burnt-offering.*—II. *incense-offering.*

אִשׁ i. q. יֵשׁ *there is, there are*, comp. Ch. אִית.

[h]אֶשָּׁא Chald. noun masc. sing. emph. of אֵשׁ dec. 5b. אשׁ

אֶשָּׂא ו׳, וָ, ו׳ Kal fut. 1 pers. sing.; וָ for וַ conv. נשׂא

---

[a] Da. 2. 39. [b] Ezr. 5. 11. [c] Ps. 50. 12. [d] Zec. 11. 7, 7. [e] Eze. 34. 16. [f] Je. 17. 14. [g] 2 Ch. 7. 14. [h] Is. 57. 18. [i] Je. 30. 17. [k] Je. 3. 22. [l] Jos. 1. 5. [m] Ca. 3. 4. [n] Ps. 18. 30. [o] Is. 8. 23. [p] 2 Sa. 18. 22. [q] Hag. 1. 8. [r] Pr. 22. 13. [s] Is. 62. 4. [t] Eze. 20. 40. [u] Ps. 85. 13. [x] 2 Sa. 22. 43. [y] Ge. 5. 29. [z] Job 3. 8. [a] Ge. 27. 29. [b] Nu. 24. 9. [c] De. 20. 7. [d] Ps. 21. 3. [e] 2 Sa. 3. 14. [f] Ho. 2. 21, 22. [g] 2 Ki. 4. 39. [h] Da. 7. 11.

[a]אֶשְׁאָב Kal fut. 1 pers. s. [for אֶשְׁאַב § 8. rem. 15] שאב

אַשְׁאִיר Hiph. fut. 1 pers. sing. . . . . שאר

[b]אֶשְׁאַל [c]ו׳, וָ Kal fut. 1 pers. sing.; וָ for וַ conv. . שאל

[d]אֶשְׁאֲלָה id. with paragogic ה . . . . שאל

[e]אֶשְׁאָלְךָ וְ id., suff. 2 pers. sing. m. (§ 16. rem. 12) שאל

[f]אֶשְׁאָלֵם וְ & [g]וָ id., suff. 3 pers. pl. masc. (§ 16. rem. 12); וָ for וַ . . . שאל

[h]אֶשָּׂאֶנּוּ [i]ו׳ Kal fut. 1 pers. sing., suff. 3 pers. sing. masc. (§ 2. rem. 3) . . . . נשא

[k]אֶשְׁאַף וְ Kal fut. 1 pers. sing. . . . . שאף

[l]אֶשְׁאֲפָה וָ id. with paragogic ה, [for אֶשְׁאָפָה' § 8. rem. 15]; וָ for וַ conv. . . . שאף

[m]אָשֵׁב וָ ap. for אָשִׁיב (q. v.) . . . . שוב

[n]אָשֵׁב וָ defect. for אָשׁוּב (q. v.) . . . שוב

אֵשֵׁב ו׳ & וָ׳ Kal fut. 1 pers. sing.; וָ for וַ conv. ישב

[o]אֵשְׁבָה וְ & [p]ו׳ id. with parag. ה (§ 8. rem. 15); } ישב
[q]אֵשְׁבָה וְ וָ id. . . . . }

[r]אֶשְׁבּוֹר Kal fut. 1 pers. sing. (§ 8. rem. 18) . שבר

[s]אַשְׂבִּיעַ Hiph. fut. 1 pers. sing. . . . . שבע

[t]אַשְׂבִּיעֵהוּ id., suff. 3 pers. sing. masc. . . . שבע

[u]אַשְׂבִּיעֶךָּ וְ Hiph. fut. 1 pers. sing. with suff. 2 p. s. m. שבע

[v]אַשְׂבִּעֶךָּ Hiph. fut. 1 pers. sing. with suff. 2 pers. sing. masc. (for ךָ' § 2. rem. 3) . . . שבע

[y]אַשְׁבִּיעֵם וָ Hiph. fut. 1 pers. sing., suff. 3 pers. pl. masc.; וָ for וַ conv. . . . . שבע

[z]אַשְׁבִּיר Hiph. fut. 1 pers. sing. . . . . שבר

[a]אַשְׁבִּיתָה Hiph. fut. 1 pers. sing. with paragogic ה . שבת

אַשְׁבֵּל ו׳ pr. name of a son of Benjamin. Patronym. אַשְׁבֵּלִי, Nu. 26. 38.

אֶשְׁבָּן וְ pr. name masc. Ge. 36. 26.

אַשְׁבֵּעַ pr. name. masc. . . . . . שבע

[b]אַשְׁבִּעַ וָ Hiph. fut. 1 pers. sing.; וָ for וַ conv. שבע

[c]אֶשְׁבַּע Kal fut. 1 pers. sing. . . . . שבע

אִשָּׁבֵעַ ו׳, וָ Niph. fut. 1 pers. sing.; וָ for וַ conv. } שבע
[d]אִשָּׁבֵעַ (§ 9. rem. 5. & § 15. rem. 1) . }

[e]אִשָּׁבְעָה Kal fut. 1 pers. sing. with paragogic ה שבע

אֶשְׁבַּעַל for בַּעַל' pr. name masc. see אִישׁ־בֹּשֶׁת . איש

[f]אֲשַׁבֵּר Piel fut. 1 pers. sing. . . . . שבר

אֶשְׁבֹּר ו׳ Kal fut. 1 pers. sing.; וָ for וַ conv. שבר

[g]אֲשַׁבְּרָה וָ Piel fut. 1 pers. sing. with parag. ה; וָ שבר

[h]אֲשַׁבְּרֵם וָ id., suff. 3 pers. pl. masc.; וָ id. שבר

[i]אֲשַׂגְּבֵהוּ Piel fut. 1 pers. sing., suff. 3 pers. sing. m. שגב

[k]אֶשְׁגֶּה וָ Kal fut. 1 pers. sing.; וָ for וַ conv. . שגה

אָשַׁד Root not used; Chald. and Syr. *to pour out*.
אֶשֶׁד *a pouring out*, Nu. 21. 15, אֶשֶׁד הַנְּחָלִים i. e. places where the torrents from the mountains are poured out or flow down into the valleys and plains below, q. d. *ravines*. (Gesenius.)

אֲשֵׁדָה fem. dec. 11 c. (§ 42. rem. 1. & 4) *a low place* or *ravine*, at the foot of a mountain, see the preceding.

אֶשֶׁד' וְ noun masc. sing. . . . . . אשד

אַשְׁדּוֹד pr. name of a place . . . . . שדד

אַשְׁדּוֹדָה id. with local ה . . . . . שדד

אַשְׁדֳּדִיּוֹת gent. noun pl. fem. from אַשְׁדּוֹד, Kh. דּוֹדִיּוֹת', Kr. דֳּדִיּוֹת' . . . . . שדד

אַשְׁדּוֹדִים id. pl. masc. . . . . . שדד

אַשְׁדּוֹדִית adv. from a gent. noun אַשְׁדּוֹד=אַשְׁדּוֹדִי' . שדד

[m]אַשְׁדּוֹת [n]וְ׳ noun fem. pl. constr. of אֲשֵׁדוֹת' from } אשד
אַשְׁדֹּת [דָה'] sing. dec. 11 c. (§ 42. No. 1) }

אָשָׁה Root not used; i. q. אָשַׁשׁ *to found*; Arab. *to heal*.
אָשְׁיָה fem. *foundation*, only pl. with suff. אָשְׁיוֹתֶיהָ, Je. 50. 15 Keri, but Kheth. אֲשׁוּיֹתֶיהָ from אֲשׁוּיָה.
יֹאשִׁיָּה (whom *the Lord heals*) pr. name masc. Zec. 6. 10.
יֹאשִׁיָּהוּ (id.) pr. name of a king of Judah.

אִשָּׁה ו׳ noun fem. sing. dec. 10. (compare § 45) . אנש

אֵשֶׁת constr. of the foll. . . . . . אש

אִשֶּׁה [o]ו׳ noun masc. sing. dec. 9 a. . . . אש

אִשּׁוֹ n. com. s., suff. 3 p. s. m. from אֵשׁ dec. 8 b. אש

אָשׁוֹב Kh. אָשׁוּב q. v., K. אָשִׁיב (q. v.) . . שוב

אָשׁוּב [p]ו׳ & וָ׳ Kal fut. 1 pers. sing.; וָ for וַ conv. שוב

אָשׁוּבָה ו׳ id. with paragogic ה . . . . שוב

[q]אַשְׁוֶה Hiph. fut. 1 pers. sing. . . . . שוה

[r]אֶשְׁוֶה וְ Kal fut. 1 pers. sing. . . . . שוה

[s]אֻשּׁוֹהִי וְ Chald. noun masc. pl., suff. 3 pers. sing. m. from אשׁ dec. 5 c. . . . . . אשש

אָשׂוּחַ Pilel fut. 1 pers. sing. for [חַ'ח] § 15. rem. 1] שיח

[t]אֲשׁוּיֹתֶיהָ Kh. אֲשׁוּיֹתֶ', K. אָשְׁיוֹתֶ', noun fem. with suff. [from אֲשׁוּיָה or אָשְׁיָה] . . . . אשה

[u]אָשׁוֹם Kal inf. absolute . . . . . אשם

אֲשַׁוֵּעַ } Piel fut. 1 pers. sing. (§ 15. rem. 1); } שוע
אֲשַׁוַּע [v]ו׳ } וְ for וַ . . . . }

[w]אֲשַׁוְּעָה וָ id. id. with parag. ה; וָ for וַ conv. . שוע

[x]אָשׁוּר Kal fut. 1 pers. sing. . . . . שור

אַשּׁוּר ו׳ pr. name of a man, people and country . אשר

אַשּׁוּרָה pr. name of a country (אַשּׁוּר) with loc. ה אשר

אַשּׁוּרִים gent. noun, pl. of אַשּׁוּרִי' . . . אשר

---

[a] Ge. 24. 19, 44. [b] Is. 7. 12. [c] Ge. 24. 47. [d] Ju. 8. 24. [e] Job 38. 3; 40. 7. [f] Is. 41. 28. [g] Ne. 1. 2. [h] Job 31. 36. [i] Je. 10. 19. [k] Is. 42. 14. [l] Ps. 119. 131. [ll] Ps. 119. 147. [m] Jos. 14. 7. [n] Zec. 6. 1. [o] 1 Sa. 27. 5. [p] Ezr. 9. 3. [q] Is. 49. 20. [r] Ho. 2. 20. [s] Ps. 132. 15. [t] Ps. 91. 16. [u] Ge. 24. 3. [v] Ps. 81. 17. [y] Ne. 5. 12. [z] Is. 66. 9. [a] De. 32. 26. [b] Je. 5. 7. [c] Pr. 30. 9. [d] Ge. 21. 24. [e] Ps. 17. 15. [f] Is. 45. 2. [g] Job 29. 17. [h] De. 9. 17. [i] Ps. 91. 14. [k] 1 Sa. 26. 21. [l] Nu. 21. 15. [m] Jos. 12. 3. [n] Jos. 13. 20. [o] Le. 22. 22. [p] Zec. 1. 3. [q] La. 2. 13. [r] Is. 40. 25. [s] Ezr. 6. 3. [t] Ps. 143. 5. [u] Je. 50. 15. [w] Eze. 25. 12. [y] La. 3. 8. [x] Ho. 13. 7.

אֲשׁוּרֶנּוּ [a] ו״ן Kal fut. 1 p.s. (אָשׁוּר), suff. 3 p.s.m.; וְ for וַ . שור

אֶשְׁחֶה [b] Hiph. fut. 1 pers. sing. . . . . שחה

אַשְׁחוּר pr. name masc. . . . . . שחר

אֶשְׁחָט [c] וָ Kal fut. 1 pers. sing.; וָ for ·וַ conv. . שחט

אַשְׁחִית Hiph. fut. 1 pers. sing. . . . . שחת

אַשְׁחִיתֵךְ [d] וָ id., suff. 2 pers. sing. fem.; וָ for ·וַ conv. שחת

אַשְׁחִיתֵם [e] id., suff. 3 pers. pl. masc. . . . שחת

אֶשְׂחָק [f] } Kal fut. 1 pers. sing. (§ 8. rem. 15) שחק
אֶשְׂחָק [g] }

אֶשְׂחָקֵם וְ Kal fut. 1 pers. sing. [אֶשְׁחַק], suff. 3 pers. pl. masc. (§ 16. rem. 12) . . שחק

אֲשַׁחֲרֶךָ Piel fut. 1 pers. sing., suff. 2 pers. sing. masc. (§ 14. rem. 1. & § 2. rem. 2) . . שחר

אֶשְׁטֹף [h] וָ Kal fut. 1 pers. sing.; וָ for ·וַ conv. . שטף

אַנְשֵׁי noun masc., pl. constr. from אִשָּׁה dec. 9a. אש

אֻשַּׁיָּא [i] [k]וְ Chald. n. m., pl. emph. from [אֻשׁ] dec. 5c. אש

אָשִׁיב [l]וָ & וְ׳ ו״ן Hiph. fut. 1 pers. s.; וָ for ·וַ conv. שוב

אָשִׁיבָה וְ & וְ׳ id. with paragogic ה; וָ id. . שוב

אֲשִׁיבְךָ [m] } id., suff. 2 pers. sing. masc. (§ 3. r. 2); } שוב
אֲשִׁיבְךָ [n] } [o]וְ וְ for וַ . . . . }

אֲשִׁיבֶנָּה [p] id., suff. 3 pers. sing. fem. (§ 2 rem. 3) . שוב

אֲשִׁיבֶנּוּ id., suff. 3 pers. sing. masc. . . . שוב

אַשִּׂיג [q] Hiph. fut. 1 pers. sing. . . . . נשג

אַשִּׂיגֵם [r] וְ id., suff. 3 pers. pl. masc. . . . נשג

אָשִׂיחַ [s] Kal fut. 1 pers. sing. . . . . . שיח

אָשִׂיחָה וְ׳ id. with paragogic ה . . . . שיח

אָשִׂים [t]וְ׳ & וָ׳ ו״ן Kal fut. 1 p. s.; וָ for ·וַ; R. שִׂים see שום

אֲשִׁימָא pr. name of an idol of the city of Hamath, 2 Ki. 17. 30.

אָשִׂימָה [uu] [u]וְ׳ & [x]וְ׳ ו״ן Kal fut. 1 pers. s. with parag. ה; וָ for ·וַ; R. שִׂים see . . . . שום

אֲשִׂימְךָ id., suff. 2 pers. sing. masc. . . . שום

אֲשִׂימֵךְ [y] id., suff. 2 pers. sing. fem. . . . שום

אֲשִׂימֵם [z] id., suff. 3 pers. pl. masc. . . . שום

אֲשִׂימֶנָּה [cc] id., suff. 3 pers. sing. fem. (§ 2 rem. 3) . שום

אֲשִׂימֶנּוּ id., suff. 3 pers. sing. masc. (id.) . . שום

אָשִׁיר [a] Kal fut. 1 pers. sing. . . . . . שיר

אָשִׁירָה id. with paragogic ה . . . . שיר

אֲשֵׁירָה [b] noun fem. sing. dec. 10. . . . אשר

אֲשֵׁירֵיהֶם וַ id. pl. with masc. term. and suff. 3 pers. pl. masc.; וַ before (-:) . . . אשר

אֲשֵׁירֶיךָ [ii] id., suff. 2 pers. sing. masc. . . . אשר

אָשִׂישׂ [c] Kal fut. 1 pers. sing. R. שׂישׂ see . . שוש

אֲשִׁישָׁה וַ noun fem. sing. dec. 10; וַ before (-:) אשש

אֲשִׁישֵׁי [d] id., with pl. masc. term., construct state . אשש

אָשִׁית Kal fut. 1 pers. sing. . . . . . שית

אֲשִׁיתֵהוּ [e] וְ id., suff. 3 pers. sing. masc.; וְ for וַ . שית

אֲשִׁיתֵךְ [f] id., suff. 2 pers. sing. masc. . . . שית

אֲשִׁיתֵךְ [g] id., suff. 2 pers. sing. fem. . . . שית

אֶשֶׁךְ [for אֶשֶׁךְ § 35. r. 2] m. *testicle*, Le. 21. 20.

אֶשְׁכָּב [h] Kal fut. 1 pers. sing. [for ׳כַּב § 8. rem. 16] שכב

אֶשְׁכָּבָה id. with paragogic ה . . . . . שכב

אֶשְׁכּוֹל pr. name of a place, see אֶשְׁכֹּל . . . שכל

אֶשְׁכּוֹל [i]ו״ן n.m., pl. אֶשְׁכְּלוֹת & ׳כָּלוֹת, אַשְׁ (§ 44. r. 5) שכל

אֶשְׁכּוֹן [k] ו״ן Kal fut. 1 pers. sing. (§ 8. rem. 18) . שכן

אֶשְׁכַּח Kal fut. 1 pers. sing. . . . . . שכח

אֶשְׁכָּחָה [m] id. with paragogic ה . . . . שכח

אֶשְׁכָּחֵךְ id., suff. 2 pers. sing. fem. (§ 16. rem. 12) . שכח

אַשְׂכִּילָה [n] Hiph. fut. 1 pers. sing. with. paragogic ה שׂכל

אַשְׂכִּילְךָ [o] id., suff. 2 pers. sing. masc. . . . שׂכל

אַשְׁכֵּים [p] by Chaldaism for הַשְׁכֵּים (q.v.) § 11. rem. 2. שכם

אַשְׁכִּיר [q] Hiph. fut. 1 pers. sing. . . . . שכר

אֶשְׁכַּל [r] Kal fut. 1 pers. sing. . . . . שכל

אֶשְׁכֹּל noun masc. sing., pl. אֶשְׁכְּלוֹת & ׳כֹּלֹת, אַשְׁ (§ 44. rem. 5); also pr. name masc. . שכל

אִשְׁכְּלְלוּ [s] Chald., Kh. אִשְׁכְּלִלוּ [for אִשְׁתַּכְלִלוּ] Ishtaph., K. שַׁכְלִלוּ Shaph., pret. 3 p. pl. m. (§ 48. 1) כלל

אַשְׁכְּלֹת [t] noun pl. fem., as if from אַשְׁכֹּלֶת (comp. dec. 13. § 44. rem. 5) see אֶשְׁכֹּל . . שכל

אַשְׁכְּלֹתֶיהָ [u] id. with suff. 3 pers. sing. fem. . . . שכל

אֶשְׁכֶּם [x] noun com. sing., suff. 2 pers. pl. masc. from אֵשׁ dec. 8b. (§ 36. rem. 3) . . אש

אֶשְׁכָּן [y] Kal fut. 1 pers. sing. for ׳כֹּן (§ 8. rem. 18) . שכן

אֲשַׁכְּנָה [z] וַ Piel fut. 1 pers. s. with parag. ה; וַ for וְ שכן

אֶשְׁכְּנָה [a] } וְ Kal fut. 1 pers. sing. with paragogic ה } שכן
אֶשְׁכֹּנָה [b] } (§ 8. rem. 15) . . . . }

אַשְׁכְּנַז וְ׳ pr. name of a son of Gomer, Ge. 10. 3, and a province called after him.

אֶשְׁכָּר [c] noun masc. sing. (no vowel change) . . שכר

אֶשְׁכָּרֵךְ [d] id., suff. 2 pers. sing. fem. . . . שכר

אֲשַׁכְּרֵם [e] וַ Piel fut. 1 p. s., suff. 3 p. pl. m.; וַ for וְ שכר

אֵשֶׁל [pp] masc. *the tamarisk*, a middle-sized prickly tree.

אֲשַׁלַּח [f]וְ׳ Piel fut. 1 pers. sing.; וַ for וְ . . שלח

אֶשְׁלַח [g] } Kal fut. 1 pers. sing. (§ 8. rem. } שלח
אֶשְׁלָח [h]וְ׳ & וָ׳ ו״ן } 15); וָ for ·וַ conv. . . }

אֲשַׁלֵּחַ [i] Piel fut. 1 pers. sing. [for ׳לַּח § 15. rem. 1] שלח

אֲשַׁלְּחֶהָ [k] וַ id., suff. 3 pers. sing. fem.; וַ for וְ . שלח

אֲשַׁלְּחָה וַ id. with paragogic ה; וַ id. . . . שלח

אֶשְׁלְחָה וְ & וָ׳ Kal fut. 1 p. s. with parag. ה; וָ for ·וַ conv. שלח

---

[a] Ho. 14. 9. [b] Ps. 6. 7. [c] Ge. 40. 11. [d] Je. 15. 6. [e] 2 Ch. 12. 7. [f] Pr. 1. 26. [g] Job 29. 24.
[h] Eze. 16. 9. [i] Ezr. 5. 16. [k] Ezr. 4. 12. [l] 1 Sa. 12. 3. [m] Job 40. 4. [n] Job 35. 4. [o] Je. 15. 19.
[p] Nu. 23. 20. [q] Ex. 15. 9. [r] Ps. 18. 38. [s] Ps. 119. 78. [t] Je. 40. 4. [u] Ge. 44. 21. [uu] De. 17. 14.
[x] Ezr. 8. 17. [y] Je. 6. 8. [z] 1 Ki. 5. 23. [a] Ps. 59. 17. [b] 2 Ki. 17. 16. [c] Is. 61. 10. [cc] Eze. 21. 32.
[d] Ho. 3. 1. [e] Is. 5. 6. [f] Je. 22. 6. [g] Je. 3. 19. [h] Job 7. 21. [i] Nu. 13. 23. [ii] Mic. 5. 13.
[k] Is. 57. 15. [l] Job 29. 25. [m] Job 9. 27. [n] Ps. 101. 2. [o] Ps. 32. 8. [p] Je. 25. 3. [pp] Ge. 21. 33.
[q] De. 32. 42. [r] Ge. 27. 45. [s] Ezr. 4. 12. [t] De. 32. 32. [u] Ge. 40. 10. [x] Is. 50. 11.
[y] Eze. 43. 7. [z] Je. 7. 3. [a] Ps. 55. 7. [b] Ps. 139. 9. [c] Ps. 72. 10. [d] Eze. 27. 15.
[e] Is. 63. 6. [f] Zec. 8. 10. [g] Is. 42. 19. [h] 2 Ki. 6. 13. [i] Ex. 5. 2. [k] Ju. 20. 6.

[a] אֲשַׁלְּחֵהוּ וְ Piel fut. 1 pers. s., suff. 3 p. s. m.; וָ id. שׁלח
[b] אֲשַׁלְּחֶךָּ [c] וְ', id., suff. 2 pers. sing. m. (§ 2. rem. 2); } שׁלח
אֲשַׁלֵּחֲךָ [d] וָ', וָ for וְ . . .
אֶשְׁלָחֲךָ וְ' Kal fut. 1 pers. sing. (אֶשְׁלַח), suff. 2 p. sing. masc. (§ 16. rem. 12) . . . שׁלח
[e] אֶשְׁלָחֵם וְ id., suff. 3 pers. pl. masc. שׁלח
[f] אֲשַׁלְּחֶנּוּ Piel fut. 1 pers. s., suff. 3 p. s. m. (§ 2. r. 3) שׁלח
אַשְׁלִיךְ [g] וְ' Hiph. fut. 1 pers. sing. . . . שׁלך
[h] אַשְׁלִיכָה וְ id. with paragogic ה; וָ for וַ conversive שׁלך
[i] אַשְׁלִךְ וְ id. defect. for אַשְׁלִיךְ q. v.; וָ id. . . שׁלך
[k] אַשְׁלִכֵהוּ וְ id., suff. 3 pers. sing. masc.; וָ id. . . שׁלך
[l] אַשְׁלִכֵם וְ id., suff. 3 pers. pl. masc.; וָ id. . . שׁלך
אֲשַׁלֵּם וְ' Piel. fut. 1 pers. sing. . . . שׁלם
[m] אֲשַׁלְּמָה } id. with paragogic ה; (comp. § 8. rem. } שׁלם
[n] אֲשַׁלְּמָה [o] וָ' 15); וָ for וְ . . . .

אָשַׁם, אָשֵׁם וְ—I. *to be* or *become guilty, to transgress,* with לְ of the person against whom, and בְּ, לְ, of the thing in which.—II. *to feel one's guilt.*—III. *to bear one's guilt, suffer punishment.*—IV. *to be laid waste,* i. q. שָׁמַם יָשַׁם, Eze. 6. 6. Niph. *to be destroyed,* Joel 1. 18. Hiph. *to bring the consequences of sin* upon any one, Ps. 5. 11.

אָשָׁם masc. dec. 4c.—I. *guilt.*—II. *damage.*—III. *a sacrifice for guilt, trespass-offering.*

אָשֵׁם adj. masc. dec. 5c. *guilty.*

אַשְׁמָה fem. dec. 12a.—I. prop. inf. (§ 8. rem. 10), לְאַשְׁמָה בָהּ *to trespass therein.*—II. *guilt, trespass.*—III. *trespass-offering,* Le. 5. 24.

אָשָׁם noun masc. sing. dec. 4c. . . . . אשם
אָשָׂם וְ defect. for אָשִׂים (q. v.) . . . שׂום
[p] אָשֹׁם Kal inf. absolute, compare אָשׁוֹם . . . אשם
[q] אָשֹׁם Kal fut. 1 p. s. from שׁמם (§ 18. r. 14), or נשׁם
[r] אִשָּׁם וְ n. com. s., suff. 3 pl. m. from אִשׁ dec. 8b. אשׁ
אַשְׂמְאִילָה וְ Hiph. fut. 1 pers. sing. with paragogic ה שׂמאל
[s] אָשְׁמָה וְ Kal pret. 3 pers. sing. fem. . . . אשם
[nn] אָשִׂמָה וְ defect. for אָשִׂימָה (q. v.) . . . שׂום
[u] אָשְׁמוּ וְ Kal pret. 3 p. pl. [for אָשְׁמוּ § 8. rem. 1] אשם
אַשְׁמָה noun fem. sing. dec. 12a. . . . . אשם
אֲשָׁמוֹ n. m. s., suff. 3 p. s. m. from אָשָׁם dec. 4c. אשם
[x] אֶשְׁמוֹר־ Kh. מוֹר׳, K. מָר־׳ Kal fut. 1 p. s. (§ 8. r. 18) שׁמר
[y] אַשְׁמוּרָה וְ noun fem. s., constr. אַשְׁמֹרֶת, pl אַשְׁמֻרֹת (§ 39. No. 4) . . . . שׁמר

[a] אַשְׁמוֹת noun fem., pl. abs. from אַשְׁמָה dec. 12a . אשם
[b] אַשְׁמוֹתַי וְ id. with suff. 1 pers. sing. . . . אשם
אֶשְׂמַח Kal fut. 1 pers. sing. . . . . שׂמח
[u] אֶשְׂמְחָה [c] וְ' id. with parag. ה . . . . שׂמח
אַשְׁמִיד [d] וָ' Hiph. fut. 1 pers. sing.; וָ for וַ conv. שׁמד
[e] אַשְׁמִידְךָ id., suff. 2 pers. sing. masc. . . . שׁמד
[f] אַשְׁמִידֵם וְ', וָ, id., suff. 3 pers. pl. m.; וָ for וַ conv. שׁמד
[g] אֲשֵׁמִים [h] וְ' adj. m., pl. of אָשֵׁם dec. 5c; וּ before (‑:) אשם
אַשְׁמִיעַ Hiph. fut. 1 pers. sing. . . . . שׁמע
[i] אַשְׁמִיעֲךָ [k] וְ' id., suff. 2 pers. sing. masc. . . שׁמע
[cc] אַשְׁמִיעֵם וְ id., suff. 3 pers. pl. masc. . . . שׁמע
[l] אֲשָׁמָם n. m. s., suff. 3 pers. pl. m. from אָשָׁם dec. 4c. אשם
[m] אַשִּׁמֵּם Hiph. fut. 1 p. s. [אַשֵּׁם], suff. 3 pers. pl. m. שׁמם
[n] אָשִׂמֵם וְ defect. for אָשִׂימֵם q. v.; וָ for וְ . . שׂום
אֶשְׁמַע [o] וָ' } Kal fut. 1 pers. sing. (§ 8. rem. 15); } שׁמע
אֶשְׁמָע וָ' } וָ for וַ conv. . . . . .
אֶשְׁמְעָה [p] וְ', [q] וָ' id. with parag. ה; וָ id. . . שׁמע
[r] אַשְׁמִעֵם וְ defect. for אַשְׁמִיעֵם (q. v.) . . שׁמע
אֶשְׁמֹר Kal fut. 1 pers. sing. . . . . שׁמר
[s] אֶשְׁמְרָה } id. with parag. ה (§ 8. rem. 15); } שׁמר
[t] אֶשְׁמְרָה וָ', וְ' } וָ for וַ conv. . . . .
אַשְׁמֻרוֹת noun fem., pl. of אַשְׁמוּרָה, sing. const. אַשְׁמֹרֶת (§ 39. No. 4) . . . שׁמר
[u] אֶשְׁמְרֶנָּה וְ Kal. future, 1 p. s. (אֶשְׁמֹר), suff. 3 p. s. f. שׁמר
[x] אָשַׁמְתָּ וְ Kal pret. 2 p. s. m. [for וְאָשַׁמְתָּ § 8. r. 7] אשם
[y] אָשַׁמְתְּ id. pret. 2 pers. sing. fem. . . . אשם
[z] אַשְׁמַת noun fem. sing., const. of מָה׳ dec. 12a. . אשם
[a] אַשְׁמָתוֹ id., suff. 3 pers. sing. masc. . . . אשם
[b] אַשְׁמָתָם id., suff. 3 pers. pl. masc. . . . אשם
[c] אַשְׁמָתֵנוּ [d] וְ' id., suff. 1 pers. pl. . . . . אשם
[e] אֶשְׂנָא Kal fut. 1 pers. sing. . . . . שׂנא
[f] אֶשְׁנַבִּי n. masc. sing., suff. 1 pers. sing. from אֶשְׁנָב׳ dec. 8a. (§ 37. No. 3) . . . שׁנב
[g] אֲשַׁנֶּה Piel fut. 1 pers. sing. . . . . שׁנה
אַשְׁנָה וְ (*fortified*) pr. name of two cities in the tribe of Judah, Jos. 15. 33, 43; from אשן Arab. *to be strong,* to which Root Pr. 20. 20, (Keri) is referred.
[h] אֶשְׁנֶה Kal fut. 1 pers. sing. . . . שׁנה
[i] אֶשְׁעָה וְ Kal fut. 1 pers. sing. [for עֶה׳ § 24. r. 18] שׁעה
[k] אֶשָּׁעֵן וְ Niph. fut. 1 pers. sing. . . . שׁען
אֶשְׁעָן וְ pr. name of a place . . . שׁען

אשף Root not used; Syr. *to use enchantment,* perhaps primarily *to cover.*

[a] Ps. 81. 13. [b] Ge. 32. 27. [c] Ge. 31. 27. [d] 1 Sa. 9. 26. [e] Jos. 18. 4. [f] Is. 10. 6. [g] Zec. 11. 13. [h] Ne. 13. 8. [i] De. 9. 21. [k] Ex. 32. 24. [l] De. 9. 17. [m] Jon. 2. 10. [n] Pr. 20. 22. [nn] 1 Sa. 28. 22. [o] Ps. 41. 11. [p] Le. 5. 19. [q] Is. 42. 14. [r] Is. 66. 24. [s] Ge. 13. 9. [t] Nu. 5. 6. [tt] Ps. 9. 3. [u] Le. 4. 13. [x] Ps. 89. 29. [y] Ps. 90. 4. [a] 2 Ch. 28. 10. [b] Ps. 69. 6. [c] Ps. 31. 8. [cc] Is. 48. 3. [d] Am. 2. 9. [e] Eze. 25. 7. [f] De. 9. 14. [g] Ge. 42. 21. [h] Ezr. 10. 19. [i] Je. 18. 2. [k] 1 Sa. 9. 27. [l] Nu. 18. 9. [m] Eze. 20. 26. [n] De. 1. 13. [o] Je. 8. 6. [p] Nu. 9. 8. [q] Da. 8. 13. [r] De. 4. 10. [s] Ps. 59. 10. [t] Ps. 119. 55. [u] Ps. 119. 34. [x] Pr. 30. 10. [y] Eze. 22. 4. [z] Ezr. 10. 10. [a] Le. 5. 24. [b] Ezr. 10. 19. [c] 2 Ch. 28. 13. [d] Ezr. 9. 6. [e] Ps. 139. 21. [f] Pr. 7. 6. [g] Ps. 89. 35. [h] 1 Sa. 26. 8. [i] Ps. 119. 117. [k] Ju. 16. 26.

אָשַׁף Chald. dec. 2b. (prop. participle), *an enchanter, magician.*

אַשָּׁף masc. id. pl. אַשָּׁפִים; Chald. Da. 2. 2.

אַשְׁפָּה fem. (no pl.) *a quiver,* בְּנֵי אַ׳ *sons of the quiver,* i. e. *arrows.*

אַשְׁפָּה noun fem. sing. dec. 10. . . . . שפה
אֶשְׁפּוֹט Kal fut. 1 pers. sing. (§ 8. rem. 18) . שפט
אֶשְׁפּוֹךְ Kal fut. 1 pers. sing. (§ 8. rem. 18) . שפך
אֶשְׁפֹּט Kal fut. 1 pers. sing. . . . . שפט
אִשָּׁפֵט[a] Niph. fut. 1 pers. sing. (א § 10. rem. 5) . שפט
אִשָּׁפְטָה[b] וְ id. with parag. ה . . . . . שפט
אֶשְׁפָּטְךָ[c] Kal fut. 1 pers. sing. (אֶשְׁפֹּט), suff. 2 pers. sing. masc. [for ׳פָּטְךָ] . . . שפט
אֶשְׁפְּטֵם[d] id., suff. 3 pers. pl. masc. . . . שפט
אָשְׁפַיָּא Chald. noun m. pl. emph. from [אָשַׁף] dec. 2b. אשף
אַשְׁפִּיל[e] Hiph. fut. 1 pers. sing. . . . . שפל
אָשְׁפִין Chald. noun m. pl. abs. from [אָשַׁף] dec. 2b. אשף
אֶשְׁפֹּךְ וָ׳ Kal fut. 1 pers. sing.; וָ for וַ conv. . שפך
אֶשְׁפְּכָה[f] וְ id. with parag. ה . . . . שפך
[אַשְׁפְּנַז] ׳ pr. name of one of the eunuchs of Nebuchadnezzar, Da. 1. 3.
אֶשְׁפָּר וְ noun masc. sing. . . . . שפר
אַשְׁפָּתוֹ noun f. s., suff. 3 p. s. m. from ׳פָּה dec. 10. שפה
אַשְׁפַּתּוֹת[g] noun pl. f., from a sing. אַשְׁפַּתָּה or אַשְׁפֹּת (comp. § 37. No. 3) . . . שפת
אֶשְׁקֹד[h] Kal fut. 1 pers. sing. . . . . שקד
אַשְׁקֶה[i] וָ׳[k] Hiph. fut. 1 pers. sing.; וָ for וַ conv. . שקה
אֶשְׁקָה־[l] Kal fut. 1 pers. sing. [אֶשַּׁק] with parag. ה (§ 8. rem. 14) . . . . נשק
אֶשְׁקוֹט[m] וְ׳[n] Kal fut. 1 pers. sing. (§ 8. rem. 18) . שקט
אֶשְׁקוֹטָה[o] id. with parag. ה, Kh. אֶשְׁקוֹטָה, K. אֶשְׁקֳטָה (§ 8. rem. 14) . . . . שקט
אֶשְׁקוֹל[p] Kal fut. 1 pers. sing. (§ 8. rem. 18) . שקל
אֶשְׁקוֹלָה[q] וְ id. with parag. ה Kh. אֶשְׁקוֹלָה, K. אֶשְׁקֳלָה (§ 8. rem. 14); וְ for וַ conv. . . שקל
אַשְׁקִיעַ[r] Hiph. fut. 1 pers sing . . . . שקע
אַשְׁקְךָ[s] Hiph. fut. 1 pers. sing. (אַשְׁקֶה), suff. 2 pers. sing. masc. (§ 24. rem. 21) . . שקה
אֶשָּׁקְךָ[t] Kal fut. 1 p. s. [אֶשַּׁק], suff. 2 p. s. m. (§ 16. r. 12) נשק
אֶשְׁקֹל[u] וָ Kal fut. 1 pers. sing.; וָ for וַ conv. . שקל
אֶשְׁקְלָה[x] וָ id. with parag. ה (§ 8. rem. 14); וָ id. שקל
אֶשְׁקֲלָה־[y] וָ id. id., [as if from אֶשְׁקָל] . . שקל
אַשְׁקְלוֹן וְ׳ pr. name of a place . . . . שקל
אַשְׁקֶנָּה[z] Hiph. fut. 1 pers. sing. (אַשְׁקֶה), suff. 3 pers. sing. fem. (§ 2. rem. 3, & § 24. rem. 21) שקה
אֲשַׁקֵּר[a] Piel fut. 1 pers. sing. . . . . שקר

אשר Root not used, probably i. q. אָסַר *to bind.*

אֲשַׂרְאֵל (whom *God has bound*) pr. name masc 1 Ch. 4. 16.

אַשְׂרִיאֵל (*vow of God*) pr. name masc. Patronym. אַשְׂרִיאֵלִי Nu. 26. 31.

[אָשַׁר] *to go straight on,* Pr. 9. 6. Pi.—I. *to guide, direct aright.*—II. *to pronounce happy, to call blessed.* Pu.—I. *to be guided,* Is. 9. 15.—II. *to be made or pronounced happy, blessed.*

אָשֵׁר (*happy, blessed*) pr. name—I. a son of Jacob, from whom came the tribe of *Asher*. Gent. n. אָשֵׁרִי Ju. 1. 32.—II. of a city near Sichem, Jos. 17. 7.

אֲשֵׁרָה, אֲשֵׁירָה, fem. dec. 10. pl. וֹת & ִים English version after the Sept. and Vulg. "*grove.*" Modern interpreters, *fortune, goddess of fortune,* put for the image of Astarte, and in the pl. *images.* Prof. Lee conjectures, *shrine, shrines.*

אֶשֶׁר masc. *happiness, blessedness;* only in pl. constr. in the character of an interj. אַשְׁרֵי הָאִישׁ *O the happiness of the man!* With suff. אַשְׁרֶיךָ *happy art thou!* אַשְׁרֵהוּ, אַשְׁרָיו, for אַשְׁרֶיךָ, &c. see § 35. rem. 16, for ֵהוּ, § 3. rem. 1, 5.

אֹשֶׁר masc. dec. 6c. *happiness,* Ge. 30. 13.

אֲשֻׁר or אַשּׁוּר fem. dec. 1 or 3a.—I. *step, going.*—II. *wood of the box-tree,* Eze. 27. 6.

אַשּׁוּר fem.—I. *step,* Job 31. 7.—II. pr. name *Assyria, the Assyrian empire.*

אַשּׁוּרִי pr. name of an Arabian tribe, Ge. 25. 3. called אֲשׁוּרִי 2 Sa. 2. 9.

אֲשַׂרְאֵלָה (*upright towards God*) pr. name masc. 1 Ch. 25. 2. written also יְשַׂרְאֵלָה *v.* 14.

אֻשַּׁרְנָא Chald. masc. *a wall,* Ezr. 5. 3.

תְּאַשּׁוּר masc. *the box-tree.*

אָשֵׁר וְ׳ pr. name of a man and a place . . אשר
אַשְּׁרוּ[b] וְ Piel imp. sing. masc. . . . אשר
אֲשֶׁר וְ׳—I. relat. pron. of both genders and numbers, *who, which;* often including the pers. pronoun, *he which, she which, what, that which;* וַאֲשֶׁר תָּאֹר *and he whom thou cursest,* אֲ׳ אָכְלוּ הַנְּעָרִים *that which the young men have eaten;* especially after prepositions, לַאֲשֶׁר *to him who, to them who,* אֶת־אֲשֶׁר *him who, that which,* מֵאֲשֶׁר *from or of that which;* when the prep. refers to place, לַאֲשֶׁר *whither,* בַּאֲשֶׁר *where,* see No. IV.—II.

[a] Eze. 20. 36. [b] 1 Sa. 12. 7. [c] Eze. 35. 11. [d] Eze. 7. 27. [e] Is. 13. 11. [f] Ps. 42. 5. [g] La. 4. 5. [h] Je. 31. 38. [i] Ge. 24. 14, 46. [k] Je. 25. 17. [l] 1 Ki. 19. 20. [m] Is. 62. 1. [n] Job 3. 13. [o] Is. 18. 4. [p] Est. 3. 9. [q] Ezr. 8. 25. [r] Eze. 32. 14. [s] Ca. 8. 1. [t] Ca. 8. 1. [u] Je. 32. 10. [x] Ezr. 8. 26. [y] Je. 32. 9. [z] Is. 27. 3. [a] Ps. 89. 34. [b] Pr. 23. 19.

note of the relative before adverbs and pronouns; אֲשֶׁר־שָׁם *where;* אֲשֶׁר מִשָּׁם *whence;* אֲשֶׁר הוּא חַי *which liveth;* אֲשֶׁר לוֹ *to whom;* אֲשֶׁר בּוֹ *in whom;* אֲשֶׁר לְשֹׁנוֹ *whose tongue;* אֲשֶׁר אֶת־עָפָר *which dust,* acc. אֲשֶׁר אֹתִי *me, whom;* אֲשֶׁר לְ׳ בְּחַרְתִּיךָ *thee whom I have chosen.*—III. circumscribing the genitive, שִׁיר הַשִּׁירִים אֲשֶׁר לִשְׁלֹמֹה *the song of songs of Solomon,* i. e. Solomon's Song of Songs.—IV. conj. (*a*) *that, to the end that;* (*b*) *because, because that;* (*c*) *if, that if;* (*d*) *when;* (*e*) of place, *where;* (*f*) with prefixes, בַּאֲשֶׁר *in that, because,* see also No. I.;—כַּאֲשֶׁר *according to, as; as if; because; when;*—מֵאֲשֶׁר *since,* see also No. I.

[a] אֵשֵׁר וָ Kh. אֲשֶׁר, K. וָאֵשֵׁב (q. v.) . . . ישב
אַשֻּׁר pr. name of a people, for אַשּׁוּר . . . אשר
אֲשַׂרְאֵל וָ pr. name masc.; וָ before (-:) . . . אשר
אֲשַׂרְאֵלָה וָ pr. name masc.; וָ id. . . . אשר
אֲשֵׁרָה noun fem. sing. dec. 10. . . . אשר
[b] אַשְׁרֵהוּ noun m. pl., suff. 3 pers. s. m. [from אֶשֶׁר dec. 6a. for אֲשָׁרֵיהוּ § 35. r. 16, & § 4. r. 1] אשר
[c] אַשְּׁרוּ Piel imp. pl. masc. . . . . . אשר
[d] אִשְׁרוּ וְ Kal imp. pl. masc. . . . . . אשר
[e] אִשְּׁרוּ וְ Piel pret. 3 pers. pl. . . . . אשר
[f] אִשְּׁרוּנִי id. pret. 3 pers. pl., suff. 1 pers. sing. . אשר
[g] אֲשֵׁרוֹת noun fem., pl. of רָה׳, dec. 10. . . . אשר
אַשְׁרֵי וְ׳ noun masc. pl. const. [from אֶשֶׁר dec. 6a. § 35. rem. 16] . . . . . אשר
אֲשֻׁרָי / [h] אֲשֻׁרִי } noun masc. pl., suff. 1 pers. sing. [from אֲשׁוּר׳ or אָשׁוּר dec. 1 or 3 a.] . } אשר
[i] אַשְׁרִי noun m. s., suff. 1 p. s. [from אַשּׁוּר dec. 1 b.] אשר
אַשְׂרִיאֵל וְ׳ pr. name masc. . . . . . אשר
[k] אֲשֵׁרֵיהֶם וְ׳ noun fem. with pl. masc. term. and suff. 3 pers. pl. masc. from אֲשֵׁרָה dec. 10. אשר
[l] אֲשֵׁרָיו id. with suff. 3 pers. pl. masc. . . . אשר
אַשְׁרָיו noun masc. pl., suff. 3 pers. sing. masc. [from אֶשֶׁר dec. 6a. for אֲשָׁרָיו § 35. rem. 16] . אשר
[m] אֲשֻׁרָיו noun m. pl. with suff. 3 pers. s. m. see אֲשֻׁרַי אשר
אַשְׁרֶיךָ noun masc. pl., suff. 2 pers. sing. masc. [from אֶשֶׁר dec. 6a. for אֲשָׁרֶיךָ § 35. rem. 16] אשר
[n] אַשְׁרַיִךְ id., suff. 2 pers. sing. fem. [for אֲשָׁרַיִךְ]; id. אשר
[o] אַשְׁרֵיכֶם id., suff. 3 pers. pl. masc. . . . . אשר
[p] אֲשֵׁרִים וְ׳ n. f. with pl. m. term. from אֲשֵׁרָה dec. 10. אשר
אַשּׁוּרִים pr. name of a people, pl. of אַשּׁוּרִי . . אשר
[r] אַשְׁרֵנוּ noun m. s., suff. 1 p. pl. from אַשּׁוּר dec. 1 b אשר
[s] אֲשֻׁרֵנוּ noun m. sing., suff. 1 pers. sing. (see אֲשֻׁרַי) אשר

[q] אֻשַּׁרְנָא וְ Chald. noun masc. sing. . . . . אשר
[t] אֶשְׂרֹף וָ Kal fut. 1 pers. sing.; וָ for וַ׳ conv. . שרף
[u] אֶשְׁרְקָה Kal fut. 1 pers. sing. with parag. ה׳ . . שרק

אשׁשׁ Root not used; Arab. *to found, make firm.*
אָשִׁישׁ masc. dec. 3 a. *foundation,* Is. 16. 7.
אֲשִׁישָׁה fem. dec. 10. pl. וֹת & ־ִים, *cake.*

[x] אֶשְׁתְּ וָ ap. for אֶשְׁתֶּה q. v. (§ 24. r. 3); וָ for וַ׳ conv. שתה
אֵשֶׁת וְ׳ noun fem. sing. abs. and const. dec. 13 b. (see אִשָּׁה § 45) . . . . איש
[y] אִשֹּׁת noun fem., pl. of אִשָּׁה dec. 10. (§ 45) . אנש
אֶשְׁתָּאוֹל / אֶשְׁתָּאֹל } וְ׳ pr. name of a place . . . שאל
[z] אֶשְׁתַּדּוּר וְ Chald. noun masc. sing. . . . שדר
אֶשְׁתֶּה וְ׳ Kal fut. 1 pers. sing. . . . . שתה
אִשְׁתּוֹ וְ׳ noun fem. sing., suff. 3 pers. sing. m. from אֵשֶׁת dec. 13 c. (see אִשָּׁה § 45) . . איש
[a] אֶשְׁתּוֹלְלוּ [for אֶתְשׁוֹלְלוּ by Syriacism for הִתְשׁ׳ § 12. rem. 3] Hithpo. pret. 3 pers. pl. . שלל
[b] אֶשְׁתּוֹמַם Chald. [for אֶתְשׁוֹמַם] Ithpo. pret. 3 pers. s. masc. (comp. § 21. rem. 20) . . שמם
[c] אֶשְׁתּוֹמֵם [d] וָ׳, וָ Hithpoel, fut. 1 p. s.; וָ for וַ׳ conv. שמם
אֶשְׁתּוֹן וְ׳ pr. name masc. . . . . . איש
[e] אֶשְׁתּוֹנָן [for אֶתְשׁוֹנָן] Hithpal. fut. 1 pers. sing. (comp. § 21. rem. 20) . . . שנן
אֶשְׁתַּחֲוֶה [f] וָ׳, [g] וְ׳ Hithpal. fut. 1 pers. s. [for אֶתְשַׁחֲוֶה § 24. r. 25, & § 6. No. 2]; וָ for וַ׳ conv. שחה
אִשְׁתִּי noun fem. sing., suff. 1 pers. sing. from אֵשֶׁת dec. 13 b. (see אִשָּׁה § 45) . . . איש
[h] אִשְׁתִּיו [i] וְ׳ Chald. Peal pret. 3 pers. pl. masc. with prosth. א [for שְׁתִיו § 55. rem. 1] . שתא
[k] אֶשְׁתְּךָ / אִשְׁתְּךָ / אִשְׁתְּךָ וְ׳ } noun fem. sing., suff. 2 pers. sing. masc. from אֵשֶׁת dec. 13 c. (§ 45, & 44. r. 3) } איש
[l] אֶשְׁתֳּלֶנּוּ Kal fut. 1 pers. sing. [אֶשְׁתֹּל], suff. 3 pers. sing. masc. (§ 8. rem. 14, & § 2. rem. 3) שתל
אֶשְׁתְּמֹה, וְ׳ אֶשְׁתְּמֹעַ, אֶשְׁתְּמוֹעַ, וְ pr. name of a place . . . . . שמע
[m] אֶשְׁתַּמֵּר וָ [for אֶתְשַׁמֵּר] Hith. fut. 1 pers. s.; וָ for וַ׳ שמר
[n] אֶשְׁתַּמְּרָה וָ id. with parag. ה . . . שמר
[o] אֲשִׁתֶנּוּ Kal fut. 1 pers. sing. (אָשִׁית), suff. 3 pers. sing. masc. (§ 2. rem. 3) R. שִׁית see שות
[p] אֶשְׁתַּנִּי Chald. [for אֶתְשַׁ׳] Ithpa. pret. 3 pers. sing. masc., K. נִּי׳; Kh. נּוֹ׳ or נּוֹ׳ 3 pers. pl. m. שנא
[q] אֶשְׁתַּעֲשָׁע / [r] וְ אֶשְׁתַּעֲשַׁע } [for אֶתְשַׁ׳] Hithpalp. fut. 1 pers. sing. (§ 6. No. 4) . . . } שעע

[a] Eze. 3. 15. [b] Pr. 29. 18. [c] Is. 1. 17. [d] Pr. 9. 6. [e] Mal. 3. 12. [f] Ge. 30. 13. [g] 2 Ch. 33. 3. [h] Ps. 17. 5. [i] Job 31. 7. [k] 1 Ki. 14. 15. [l] Ex. 34. 13. [m] Ps. 37. 31. [n] Ec. 10. 17. [o] Is. 32. 20. [p] Is. 27. 9. [r] Ps. 17. 11. [s] Ps. 44. 19. [q] Ezr. 5. 3. [t] De. 9. 21. [u] Zec. 10. 8. [x] Ge. 24. 46. [y] Eze. 23. 44. [z] Ezr. 4. 15, 19. [a] Ps. 76. 6. [b] Da. 4. 16. [c] Is. 63. 5. [d] Da. 8. 27. [e] Ps. 73. 21. [f] 1 Sa. 15. 25. [g] Ge. 24. 48. [h] Da. 5. 4. [i] Da. 5. 3. [k] Ps. 128. 3. [l] Eze. 17. 23. [m] Ps. 18. 24. [n] 2 Sa. 22. 24. [o] 1 Ki. 11. 34. [p] Da. 3. 19. [q] Ps. 119. 16. [r] Ps. 119. 47.

I. [אֵת] masc. with suff. אִתּוֹ, pl. אִתִּים & אֵתִּים (§ 37. rem. 5) *ploughshare.*

II. אֵת, אֶת־ sign of—I. the accusative.—II. the nominative with verbs passive and neuter; יִקָּרֵא אֶת־שִׁמְךָ *thy name shall be called,* יֻתַּן אֶת־הָאָרֶץ *let the land be given;* אַל יֵרַע אֶת־הַדָּבָר *let the thing not displease.* With suff. אֶתְכֶם, אוֹתִי, אֹתִי see § 5. For מֵאוֹתִי see the following.

III. אֵת, אֶת־ with suff. אִתְּךָ, אִתָּךְ, אִתִּי, אִתָּךְ fem. &c. prep.—I. *with, by, near.*—II. *with, in company with.*—III. *towards.*—IV. מֵאֵת prop. *from with,* i. e. *from,* מֵאִתִּי *from me,* מֵאִתְּךָ *from thee,* &c.; but also מֵאוֹתִי, מֵאוֹתְךָ.

אִתַּי (*near*) pr. name—I. 2 Sa. 15. 19; 18. 2.—II. 2 Sa. 23. 29, written also אִיתַי q. v.

אַתְּ ו׳ Kh., K. אַתָּה pron. pers. 2 pers. sing. masc. אנת

אַתְּ, אַתְּ ו׳ } id. 2 pers. sing. fem. . . . אנת

אָתָא[a] Kal pret. 3 pers. s. m. for אָתָה (§ 24. r. 18) אתה

אֲתָא[b] Chald. Peal pret. 3 pers. sing. masc. see אתה

אֶתְאַבְּלָה[c] וָ Hith. fut. 1 pers. s. with parag. ה; וָ for וַ conv. אבל

אֶתְאַפַּק[d], אֶתְאַפָּק[e] ו׳ } Hith. fut. 1 pers. sing. (§ 12. rem. 1); וָ for וַ conv. . . . . } אפק

אֶתְבּוֹנָן, אֶתְבּוֹנָן ו׳[f] } Hithpal. fut. 1 pers. sing. (§ 21. rem. 20); וָ for וַ conv. . . . } בין

אֶתְבַּעַל (*with Baal*) pr. name of a king of Sidon, 1 Ki. 16. 31.

אִתְגְּזֶרֶת[g] Chald. Ithpe. pret. 3 pers. s. fem. (§ 49. r. 1) גזר

אָתָה[h], אָתָא ו׳ (§ 24. rem. 18. & 20, & § 25. No. 2c) *to come,* const. with לְ, עַד of the pers. to whom; part. אוֹתִיּוֹת (§ 24. rem. 4) *things to come.*

אֲתָה Chald. (§ 55. rem. 1 note. & § 56. No. 2) *to come,* const. with עַל of the pers. Aph. *to cause to come, to bring.*

אִיתוֹן masc. *entrance,* Eze. 40. 15. Keri.

אַתָּה, אַתָּה ו׳ ו׳[k] } pers. pron. 3 pers. sing. masc.; for וָ see lett. ו . . . . } אנת

אֲתָה Ch. Peal pret. 3 pers. s. m. (§ 55. r. 1 note) אתה

אָתֵה[i] Chald. id. part. act. sing. masc. (id.) . אתה

אִתָּהּ prep. (אֵת) with suff. 3 pers. sing. fem. . . את

אֹתָהּ ו׳[m] prop. [אוֹת] sign of the accus. with suff. 3 pers. sing. fem. see אֵת (§ 5) . . את

אֶתְהַלֵּךְ Hith. fut. 1 pers. sing. . . . הלך

אֶתְהַלְּכָה[n] וָ id. with parag. ה . . . . הלך

אֶתְהֶם (אֵת), sign of the accus. with suff. 3 pers. pl. masc. (§ 5) . . . . את

אֶתְהֶן ו׳[o] id. with suff. 3 pers. pl. fem. . . את

אֲתוֹ[p] Ch. Peal pret. 3 p. pl. m. R. אתא see אתה

אִתּוֹ[q] noun m. s., suff. 3 p. s. m. from אֵת (q. v.) את

אֱתוֹ[r] וֶ Chald. id. imp. pl. masc.; וֶ before (:) ; R. אֲתָא see . . . . אתה

אִתּוֹ ו׳ prep. (אֵת) with suff. 3 pers. sing. masc. את

אֹתוֹ ו׳ prop. [אוֹת] sign of the accus. with suff. 3 pers. sing. masc. see אֵת (§ 5) . . את

אֶתְוַדֶּה[s] וָ Hith. fut. 1 p.s. (§ 20. No. 1); וָ for וַ conv. ידה

אֶתְוַדַּע[t] [for אֶתְיַדַּע] Hith. fut. 1 pers. sing. (§ 20. No. 1) ידע

אָתוֹהִי[u] Chald. noun masc. pl., suff. 3 pers. sing. masc. from [אָת] dec. 1 a. . . . . אוה

אַתּוּן[x] Chald. noun com. sing. dec. 1 a. [for אַתְנוּן] תנן

אַתּוּנָא[y] וְ Chald. id. emph. st. . . . . . תנן

אֲתֹנוֹת noun fem., pl. of אָתוֹן dec. 3 a. . . אתן

אַתּוּקֶיהָא[z] וְ Kh. אַתּוּ׳, K. אַתִּי׳, noun m. pl., suff. 3 pers. s. f. (§ 4. r. 5) [from אַתּוּק or אַתִּיק q. v.] אתק

אֶתּוֹשׁ Kal fut. 1 pers. sing. . . . . נתש

אֹתוֹת noun com., pl. of אוֹת dec. 1 a. . . אוה

אֹתוֹתָיו id., suff. 3 pers. sing. masc. . . . אוה

אוֹתֹתֵינוּ[a] id., suff. 1 pers. pl. . . . . אוה

אֶתְחַבַּר[b] for הִתְ׳ (§ 12. rem. 3) Hith. pret. 3 pers. sing. masc. (§ 12. rem. 1) . . . חבר

אֶתְחַנָּן[c] ו׳ Hith. fut. 1 pers. sing. [for יִתְ׳ § 12. r. 1] חנן

אֶתְחַנֶּן־[d] id. before Mak. [for תְחַנֵּן׳] . . חנן

אָתִּי in pause for the following . . }
אַתִּי ו׳ Kh. אַתִּי, K. אַתְּ pers. pron. 2 pers. sing. fem. (§ 1. rem. 2) . . . } אנת

אִתַּי pr. name masc. . . . . את

אִתִּי prep. (אֵת) with suff. 1 pers. sing. . . את

אֹתִי ו׳ prop. [אוֹת] sign of the accus. with suff. 1 pers. sing. see אֵת (§ 5) . . את

אָתַיָּא[e] Chald. noun m. pl. emph. from [אָת] dec. 1 a. אוה

אֵתָיוּ Kal imp. pl. masc.; [for אֱתָיוּ § 19. rem. 6, § 25. No. 2, & § 24. rem. 5] . . אתה

אֹתִיּוֹת[f] וָ Kal part. act. pl. fem., as if from a masc. [אֹתִין § 24. rem. 4, & § 39. No. 2] . אתה

אִתֵּיכֶם[g] noun m. pl., suff. 2 p. pl. m. from אֵת (q.v.) את

אָתִין[h] Chald. noun masc., pl. of [אָת] dec. 1 a. . אוה

אִתְיָעַטוּ[i] Chald. Ithpa. pret. 3 pers. pl. masc. . יעט

אֶתְיַצְּבָה[k] וְ Hith. fut. 1 pers. sing. . . . יצב

אַתִּיק[l] noun masc. sing. dec. 1 b. . . . אתק

אַתִּיקִים[m] id. pl., absolute state . . . . אתק

אִתָּךְ prep. (אֵת) with suff. 2 pers. sing. fem., or in pause for the following . . את

[a] Is. 21. 12. [b] Ezr. 5. 16. [c] Ne. 1. 4. [d] Is. 42. 14. [e] 1 Sa. 13. 12. [f] 1 Ki. 3. 21. [g] Da. 2. 45. [h] De. 33. 2. [i] Is. 21. 12. [k] 2 Ki. 9. 25. [l] Da. 7. 13. [m] Le. 10. 17. [n] Ps. 119. 45. [o] Le. 20. 14. [p] Ezr. 4. 12. [q] 1 Sa. 13. 20. [r] Da. 3. 26. [s] Da. 9. 4. [t] Nu. 12. 6. [u] Da. 3. 33. [x] Da. 3. 6, 11, 15, 17, 21, 23, 26. [y] Da. 3. 22. [z] Eze. 41. 15. [a] Ps. 74. 9. [b] 2 Ch. 20. 35. [c] De. 3. 23. [d] Job 19. 16. [e] Da. 3. 32. [f] Is. 44. 7. [g] Joel 4. 10. [h] Da. 6. 28. [i] Da. 6. 8. [k] Hab. 2. 1. [l] Eze. 42. 3, 3. [m] Eze. 42. 5.

אִתָּךְ prep. (אֵת) with suff. 2 pers. sing. masc. . את

אֹתָךְ[a] וְ׳ prop. [אוֹת] sign of the accus. (see אֵת § 5), suff. 2 pers. sing. fem., or in pause for ; את

אֹתָךְ, אֹתְכָה[b], אֹתָכָה[c] וְ׳ } id., suff. 2 pers. sing. masc. (§ 5. rem. 4) את

אֶתְכֶם וְ׳ id., suff. 2 pers. pl. masc. strictly from אֵת את

אִתְּכֶם וְ׳ prep. (אֵת) with suff. 2 pers. pl. masc. . את

אֶתְכְּרִיַּת[d] Chald. Ithpe. pret. 3 pers. sing. fem. . כרא

אַתֶּם וְ׳ pers. pron. 2 pers. pl. masc. see אַתָּה . אנת

אִתָּם prep. (אֵת) with suff. 3 pers. pl. masc. . את

אֹתָם וְ׳ prop. [אוֹת] sign of the accus. with suff. 3 pers. pl. masc. see אֵת (§ 5) . . את

אֶתְמוֹל, אֶתְמוֹלִי[e] וְ׳ } adv.; תְּמוֹל with prosth. א . . תמל

אֶתְמָךְ־[f] Kal fut. 1 p. s. before Mak. [for ׳מֹךְ § 8. r. 18) תמך

אֶתְמַלְּטָה[g] וָ Hithp. fut. 1 pers. sing.; וָ for וַ· conv. . מלט

אֶתְמַשֵּׁל[h] וָ Hithp. fut. 1 pers. sing.; וָ id. . . משל

אָתַן Root not used; Arab. *to step slowly.*
 אָתוֹן fem. dec. 3 a. *she-ass.*

אֵתָן[i] (prim. adj.) noun masc. sing. dec. 1. for אֵיתָן יתן

אַתֵּן[k] וְ׳ pers. pron. 2 pers. pl. fem. see אַתָּה . אנת

אֶתֵּן וְ׳, וָ׳, אֶתֶּן וְ׳[l], וָ׳[m] } Kal fut. 1 pers. sing. (§ 17. rem. 2 & 3); וָ for וַ· conv. . } נתן

אֹתָן[n] prop. [אוֹת] sign of the accus. with suff. 3 pers. sing. fem. see אֵת (§ 5) . . את

אַתֵּנָּה[o] וְ׳ for אַתֵּן q. v. (§ 1. rem. 5) . . אנת

אֶתְּנָה וָ, אֶתְּנָה וָ׳, וְ׳ } Kal fut. 1 p. s. with parag. ה (comp. § 8. r. 15, § 17. r. 3); וָ for וַ· conv. } נתן

אֶתְּנֶהָ[p] וָ id. with suff. 3 pers. sing. fem. . . נתן

אֶתְנָה[q] noun fem. sing., [תְּנָה] with prosth. א . תנה

אֹתָנָה[r] for אֹתָן q. v. (§ 5. rem. 4) . . את

אֶתְּנֵהוּ[s] וְ׳[t] Kal fut. 1 pers. sing., suff. 3 pers. s. m. נתן

אֶתְנַהֲלָה[u] Hithp. fut. 1 pers. sing. with paragogic ה (§ 14. rem. 1) . . . . נהל

אָתָנוּ[x] Kal pret. 1 pers. pl. R. אָתָא (§ 24. rem. 18) אתה

אֲתֹנוֹ noun fem. sing., suff. 3 pers. sing. masc. from אָתוֹן dec. 3 a. . . . . . אתן

אִתָּנוּ וְ׳ prep. (אֵת) with suff. 1 pers. pl. . את

אֹתָנוּ prop. [אוֹת], sign of the accus. with suff. 1 p. pl. see אֵת (§ 5) . . . . . את

אֲתֹנוֹת noun fem., pl. of אָתוֹן dec. 3 a. . . אתן

אֶתְנֶחָם[y] וָ Hithp. fut. 1 pers. sing. (§ 14. r. 1 & 3); וָ for וַ· conv. . . . . . נחם

אֶתְנִי pr. name masc. . . . . . תנה

אֲתֹנְךָ[z] noun masc. sing., suff. 2 pers. sing. masc. from אָתוֹן dec. 3 a. . . . . אתן

אֶתְּנֶךָּ וְ׳, וָ׳ Kal fut. 1 pers. sing., suff. 2 pers. sing. masc. (§ 17. rem. 3); וָ for וַ· conv. . נתן

אֶתְּנֵךְ[a] וְ׳[b], וָ׳[ff] id., suff. 2 pers. sing. fem.; וָ id. . נתן

אֶתְּנֵם וָ id., suff. 3 pers. pl. masc.; וָ id. . נתן

אֶתְנַן וְ׳ with dist. acc. for the foll.; also pr. name m. תנה

אֶתְנַן וְ׳[c] noun masc. sing. dec. 8 d. . . . תנה

אֶתְנַנָּהּ[d] וְ id., suff. 3 pers. sing. fem. . . תנה

אֶתְּנֶנָּה וְ׳[e] Kal fut. 1 p. s., suff. 3 p. s. f.; וָ for וַ· conv. נתן

אֶתְּנֶנּוּ[f] וְ׳[g] id., suff. 3 pers. sing. masc. . . נתן

אֶתְנַנֶּיהָ[h] noun masc. pl., suff. 3 pers. sing. fem. from אֶתְנַן dec. 8 d. . . . . . תנה

אֶתְנַפָּלִי[i] וָ Hithp. fut. 1 pers. sing.; וָ for וַ· conv. . נפל

אֲתֹנֹת וְ׳[k] noun f., pl. of אָתוֹן dec. 3 a; וָ before (־:) אתן

אֶתְעַבָּה[l] וָ [for אֶתְעֲבָה] Piel fut. 1 pers. sing. with paragogic ה (§ 14. rem. 1) וָ id. . תעב

אֶתְעֲקָרוּ[m] Chald. Ith. pret. 3 pers. pl., Kh. ׳קָרוּ masc. (by Hebraism), K. ׳קָרָה fem. . עקר

אֶתְפָּאָר[n] Hithp. fut. 1 pers. sing. [for ׳פָּאֵר § 12. r. 1] פאר

אֶתְפַּלָּל[o] in pause [for ׳פַּלֵּל § 12. rem. 1] . . } פלל

אֶתְפַּלֵּל וְ[p] & וָ׳ Hithp. fut. 1 p. s.; וָ for וַ· conv. }

אֶתְפַּלְלָה[q] וָ id. with paragogic ה; וָ id. . . פלל

אֶתְפֹּשׂ[r] וָ Kal fut. 1 pers. sing.; וָ id. . . תפש

אֶתֹּץ[s] Kal fut. 1 pers. sing. (§ 17. rem. 3) . . נתץ

אָתַק Root not used; whence perhaps אַתִּיק masc. dec. 1 b. an obscure term in architecture, Sept. *peristyle,* Vulg. *portico.* In Kheth. אַתּוּק, Eze. 41. 15.

אֶתְקוֹטָט[t] Hithpal. fut. 1 pers. s. [for ׳טֵט § 21. r. 20] קוט

אֶתְקוֹטְטָה[u] וָ id. with parag. ה [for ׳קוֹטְטָה]; וָ for וַ· conv. קוט

אֶתְּקֶנְךָּ[x] Kal fut. 1 pers. s. with epenth. נ (§ 16. r. 13) and suff. 2 pers. sing. masc. . . נתק

אֲתַר Chald. masc. dec. 3 a.—I. *place;* אֲתַר דִּי *in the place where.*—II. prep. בָּאתַר (for בַּאֲתַר) *after,* Da. 7. 6, 7, בַּתְרָךְ *after thee,* Da. 2. 39.
 אֲתָרִים (*places*) pr. name of a place in the south of Palestine, Nu. 21. 1.

אַתְרֵהּ Chald. id., suff. 3 pers. sing. masc. . . אתר

אַתַּרוּ[y] Chald. Aph. imp. pl. masc. . . . נתר

אֶתְרוֹעָע[z] Hithpal. fut. 1 pers. sing. [for ׳עֵע] . רוע

אֹתֹת[a] noun com. gen., pl. of אוֹת dec. 1 a. . אוה

אֹתֹתַי id., suff. 1 pers. sing. . . . . אוה

אֹתֹתָיו[b] id., suff. 3 pers. sing. masc. . . אוה

אֹתֹתָם[c] וְ id., suff. 3 pers. pl. masc. (§ 4. rem. 2) . אוה

---

[a] Ge. 12. 12. [b] Ex. 29. 35. [c] Nu. 22. 33. [d] Da. 7. 15. [e] Mi. 2. 8. [f] Is. 42. 1. [g] Job 19. 20. [h] Job 30. 19. [i] Job 33. 19. [k] Eze. 34. 31. [l] Je. 3. 19. [m] Jos. 24. 3. [n] Eze. 16. 54. [o] Eze. 13. 20. [p] 1 Ki. 14. 8. [q] Ho. 2. 14. [r] Ex. 35. 26. [s] Ps. 89. 28. [t] Eze. 31. 11. [u] Ge. 33. 14. [x] Je. 3. 22. [y] Ps. 119. 52. [z] Nu. 22. 30, 32. [a] Eze. 26. 21. [b] Eze. 5. 14. [c] Eze. 16. 34. [d] Is. 23. 18. [e] Ju. 15. 2. [f] Ju. 20. 28. [ff] Eze. 16. 27. [g] 2 Ch. 7. 20. [h] Mi. 1. 7. [i] De. 9. 18, 25. [k] Ge. 12. 16. [l] Ps. 119. 163. [m] Da. 7. 8. [n] Is. 49. 3. [o] Ps. 5. 3. [p] 1 Sa. 7. 5. [q] Da. 9. 4. [r] De. 9. 17. [s] Ju. 8. 9. [t] Ps. 139. 21. [u] Ps. 119. 158 [x] Je. 22. 24. [y] Da. 4. 11. [z] Ps. 108. 10. [a] Ne. 9. 10. [b] De. 11. 3. [c] Job 21. 29.

ב

בְּ everywhere with Sheva except in the following cases:—בִּ before a word beginning with Sheva, as בִּבְשַׂר for בְּבְשַׂר;—בַּ, בֶּ, בֳּ before the composites ֲ, ֱ, ֳ, as בַּעֲמַל, (and contr. בַּאדֹנָי for בַּאֲדֹנָי), בֶּאֱמֹר, (contr. בֵּאלֹהֵי for בֶּאֱלֹהֵי), בֳּחֳרִי;—בַּ, בֶּ, בָּ, when displacing the art. ה (q. v.), as בַּדָּם for בְּהַדָּם, בָּאָרֶץ for בְּהָאָרֶץ, בֶּחָלָל for בְּהֶחָלָל;—בָּ rarely before the tone-syllable, as בָּזֶה, בָּהֶם. For ב with suffixes see § 5.

Prep.—I. of place and time, *in, within, among*, and rarely after verbs of motion, *into*.—II. noting nearness, *at, near, by, on, before*, (in the presence of), and of motion, *to, unto, upon, against; for*, of price and exchange; *for, on account of, because of*.—III. noting accompaniment and instrument, *with, by, through*.—IV. after verbs often lost in the translation, as וַיִּגְעַר־בּוֹ *and he rebuked him*, Ge. 37. 10, comp. *v.* 11.—V. prefixed to the inf. of verbs, *in* or *when*.

בָּא וּ' Kal pret. 3 pers. sing. masc.; וּ before lab. — בוא
בָּא וָ' id. part. act. s. m. dec. 1 a; for וָ see lett. ו — בוא
בֹּא וָ' id. inf. abs. and const. (§ 21. No. 2); וָ id. — בוא
בֹּא[a] וּ' id. imp. sing. masc.; וּ before lab. — בוא
בַּאֲבֹד[b] וּ pref. בַּ before (ֲ)) (Kal inf. constr.; וּ id. — אבד
בָּאֲבַדּוֹן[c] pref. בָּ for בְּהָ, בְּהַ·) (noun masc. sing. — אבד
בְּאָבְדָם[d] וּ pref. בְּ) (Kal inf. with suff. 3 pers. pl. m.; וּ bef. (:) — אבד
בְּאָבְדַן[e] pref. id.) (noun m. s., constr. of [אָבְדָן] dec. 2 a. — אבד
בְּאִבּוֹ[f] pref. id.) (n. m. s., suff. 3 p. s. m. fr. [אֵב] dec. 8 b. — אבב
בַּאֲבוֹתֵיכֶם[g] pref. בַּ before (ֲ)) (noun m. with pl. f. term. and suff. 2 p. pl. m. from אָב irr. (§ 45) — אב
בְּאִבֵּי[h] pref. בְּ) (n. m. pl. constr. from [אֵב] dec. 8 b. — אבב
בַּאֲבִיגַיִל pref. בַּ before (ֲ)) (pr. name fem. — אב
בַּאֲבִימֶלֶךְ pref. id.) (pr. name masc. — אב
בַּאֲבִירָם pref. id.) (pr. name masc. — אב
בְּאָבֵל pref. בְּ) (pr. name of a place — אבל
בְּאָבֵלָה pref. id.) (id. with parag. ה id. — אבל
בָּאֶבֶן pref. } בָּ for בְּהָ, בְּהַ· } noun f. s. (suff. — אבן
בָּאֶבֶן[i] וּ' pref. } אַבְנוֹ) d. 6 a;
בְּאֶבֶן[k] וּ' pref. בְּ q. v. } וּ before labial }
בָּאַבְנֵט[l] pref. בָּ for בְּהָ, בְּהַ· } noun masc. sing. dec. — בנט
בְּאַבְנֵט[m] וּ pref. בְּ q. v. } 1 b; וּ before (:) }

בְּאַבְנֵי[n] pref. בְּ) (noun fem. with pl. masc. term., constr. st. from אֶבֶן dec. 6 a. — אבן
בָּאֲבָנִים וּ' pref. בָּ for בְּהָ, בְּהַ·) (id. pl. abs. st.; וּ bef. lab. — אבן
בְּאַבְרָם pref. בְּ) (pr. name masc., see אַבְרָהָם — אב
בְּאֶבְרָתוֹ[o] pref. id.) (noun fem. sing., suff. 3 pers. sing. masc. from אֶבְרָה (no pl. absolute) — אבר
בְּאַבְשָׁלוֹם pref. id.) (pr. name masc. — אב
בְּאֹבֹת pref. id.) (pr. name of a place — אוב
בַּאֲבֹתֶיךָ[p] pref. בַּ before (ֲ)) (noun masc. with pl. fem. term. and suff. 2 p. s. m. from אָב irr. (§ 45) — אב
וּבַאֲבֹתֵיכֶם[q] pref. id.) (id. pl., suff. 2 p. pl. m.; וּ bef. lab. — אב
בָּאַגָּנֹת[r] pref. בָּ for בְּהָ, בְּהַ·) (noun masc. with pl. fem. term. from אַגָּן dec. 1. (§ 30. rem. 1) — אגן
בְּאֶגְרוֹף[s] pref. בְּ) (noun masc. sing. — גרף
בָּאִגְּרוֹת[t] pref. בָּ for בְּהָ, בְּהַ·) (n. f., pl. of אִגֶּרֶת dec. 13 a. — אגר
בְּאֶגְרֹף[u] pref. בְּ) (noun masc. sing. — גרף
בֶּאֱדוֹם וּ' pref. בֶּ) (pr. name of a people and country — אדם
בֵּאדַיִן Chald. pref. בֵּ, contr. for בֶּאֱדַיִן, adv. — אדין
בְּאַדִּיר[x] pref. בְּ) (adj. masc. sing. dec. 1 b. — אדר
בָּאָדָם[y] וּ' pref. בָּ from בְּהָ, בְּהַ· } n. m. s.; also (Jos. — אדם
בְּאָדָם[z] וּ' pref. בְּ q. v. } 3. 16) pr. name of a place; וּ before labial }
בֶּאֱדֹם pref. בֶּ before (ֱ)) (pr. name of a people — אדם
בַּאֲדָמָה pref. בַּ bef. (ֲ)) (n. f. s. dec. 11 c. (§ 42. r. 1) — אדם
בַּאדֹנָי pref. בַּ, contr. for בַּאֲדֹנָי) (noun masc. pl. the name of God, different from נִי', pl. suff. — דון
בַּאדֹנִי pref. בַּ id.) (noun masc. sing., suff. 1 pers. sing. for אָדוֹן dec. 3 a. — דון
בְּאֶדְרָע[a] Chald. pref. בְּ) (noun com. sing. — דרע
בְּאֶדְרֶעִי וּ' pref. id.) (pr. n. of a place [for אֶדְרֶעִי]; וּ bef. (:) — דרע
בְּאַדַּרְתּוֹ[b] pref. id.) (noun fem. sing., suff. 3 pers. sing. masc. from אַדֶּרֶת dec. 13 a. — אדר
בָּאֹה[c] וּ'[d] Kh. בָּאָה q. v., K. בָּא (q. v.) — בוא
בָּאָה Kal part. act. s. fem. dec. 10, from בָּא masc. — בוא
בָּאָה וּ' id. pret. 3 pers. sing. fem.; וּ for וְ conv. — בוא
בֹּאָה[e] וָ'[f] id. imp. sing. masc. with parag. ה (§ 25. No. 2); for וָ see lett. ו — בוא
בָּאַהֲבָה[g] pref. בָּ for בְּהָ, בְּהַ·) (noun fem. s. (no pl.) — אהב
בָּאֳהָבִים[h] pref. בָּ before (ֳ) for בְּ) (noun masc., pl. [of אֹהַב dec. 6. § 35. rem. 9] — אהב
בְּאַהֲבַת pref. בְּ) (noun f. s. constr. of אַהֲבָה (no pl.) — אהב
בְּאַהֲבָתָהּ[i] pref. id.) (id., suff. 3 pers. sing. fem. — אהב
בְּאַהֲבָתוֹ pref. id.) (id., suff. 3 pers. sing. masc. — אהב

[a] Est. 5. 14. [b] Pr. 11. 10. [c] Ps. 88. 12. [d] Pr. 28. 28. [e] Est. 8. 6. [f] Job 8. 12. [g] Je. 11. 7. [h] Ca. 6. 11. [i] 1 Sa. 17. 50. [k] Da. 11. 38. [l] Le. 8. 7. [m] Le. 16. 4. [n] Jos. 10. 11. [o] Ps. 91. 4. [p] De. 10. 15. [q] 1 Sa. 12. 15. [r] Ex. 24. 6. [s] Is. 58. 4. [t] 2 Ch. 30. 6. [u] Ex. 21. 18. [x] Is. 10. 34. [y] Je. 32. 20. [z] Pr. 28. 2. [a] Ezr. 4. 23. [b] 1 Ki. 19. 13. [c] Je. 15. 9. [d] Je. 43. 11. [e] 1 Ki. 13. 7. [f] 1 Sa. 20. 21. [g] Ca. 8. 7. [h] Pr. 7. 18. [i] Pr. 5. 19.

בָּאֹהֶל pref. בָּ for בְּהָ, בְּהַ· } noun m. sing. dec. 6. (§ 35.r.9) וּ before lab. אהל
בְּאֹהֶל ['a] וּ pref. בְּ q. v. אהל
בְּאָהֳלוֹ pref. בְּ (id., suff. 3 pers. sing. masc. . אהל
בְּאָהֳלֵי pref. id. (id. pl., construct state . . אהל
בְּאָהֳלֵיהֶם pref. id. (id. pl., suff. 3 pers. pl. masc. אהל
בְּאֹהָלֶיךָ pref. id. (id. pl., suff. 2 p. s. m. (אֹ § 35. r. 9) אהל
בְּאָהֳלֵיכֶם[b] pref. id. (id. pl., suff. 2 pers. pl. masc. אהל
בָּאֳהָלִים pref. בָּ before (ְָ) for בְּ (id. pl., abs. st. אהל
בְּאָהָלְךָ / בְּאָהָלֶךָ[c] } pref. בְּ (id. sing., suff. 2 pers. sing. masc. אהל
בְּאַהֲרֹן וּ pref. id. (pr. name masc.; וּ before (ְ) . אהר
בָּאוּ ['d] וּ ,'וְ, Kal pret. 3 p. pl.; וּ for וְ, וָ see lett. וְ בוא
בֹּאוֹ id. inf. (בּוֹא) suff. 3 pers. sing. masc. dec. 1a. (§ 25. No. 2) . . . . . בוא
בֹּאוּ 'וּ, 'וָ, id. imp. (or pret. Je. 27. 18. § 21. r. 2) pl. masc.; וּ for וְ, וָ see lett. וָ . בוא
בָּאוֹב pref. בָּ for בְּהָ, בְּהַ· (noun m. s. dec. 1a. אוב
בָּאוּלָם[e] pref. id. (noun m. s., pl. c. אֵלַמֵּי, dec. 8a. אול
בְּאִוַּלְתּוֹ pref. בְּ (noun fem. sing., suff. 3 pers. sing. masc. from אִוֶּלֶת dec. 13a. . . אָוַל
בְּאוֹנוֹ[f] וּ pref. id. (noun masc. sing., suff. 3 pers. sing. masc. from אוֹן dec. 1a; וּ before (ְ) און
בָּאוֹפַנִּים[g] pref. בָּ for בְּהָ, בְּהַ· (noun masc., pl. of אוֹפַן dec. 8d. (§ 37. rem. 2 & 3) . . אפן
בְּאוֹצָרוֹת[h] pref. בְּ (noun masc. with pl. fem. term., abs. st. from אוֹצָר dec. 2b. . . אצר
בְּאוֹצְרוֹת 'וּ pref. id. (id. const. st.; וּ before (ְ) . אצר
בְּאוֹצְרוֹתֶיךָ[k] pref. id. (id., suff. 2 pers. sing. masc. אצר
בְּאוֹצְרוֹתַיִךְ[l] וּ pref. id. (id., suff. 2 pers. s. f.; וּ bef. (ְ) אצר
בְּאוֹצְרֹתֵי pref. id. (id., suff. 1 pers. pl. [for 'תֵי] אצר
בְּאוֹצְרֹתָיו pref. id. (id., suff. 3 pers. sing. masc. . אצר
בָּאוֹר[m] pref. בָּ for בְּהָ, בְּהַ· (noun m. s. dec. 1a. אור
בָּאוּר[n] pref. id. (noun masc. sing. dec. 1a. . אור
בְּאוֹר pref. בְּ (noun masc. sing. dec. 1a. . אור
בְּאוּר[o] pref. id. (n. m. s. dec. 1a; also pr. n. of a place אור
בָּאוּרִים[p] pref. בָּ for בְּהָ, בְּהַ· (id. pl., abs. st. . אור
בְּאוֹרֶךָ[q] pref. בְּ (n. m. s., suff. 2 p. s. m. fr. אוֹר dec. 1a. אור
וּבְאוּשְׁתָּא[r] וּ Ch. adj. fem. s., emph. of [בְּאוּשָׁא dec. 8a. fr. בְּאוּשׁ masc. § 67. rem.]; וּ bef. labial באש
בָּאוֹת ['s] וּ Kal part. act. fem., pl. of בָּאָה dec. 10, from בָּא masc.; וּ id. . . . בוא
בְּאַוַּת[t] pref. בְּ (n. f. s., constr. of [אַוָּה] dec. 10. אוה
בְּאַוָּתִי[u] pref. id. (id., suff. 1 pers. sing. . . אוה
בָּאֵזוֹב[v] וּ pref. בָּ for בְּהָ, בְּהַ· } noun masc. sing. . אזב
בְּאֵזוֹב[w] pref. בְּ q. v. אזב

בְּאָזְנוֹ[z] pref. בְּ (n. f. s., suff. 3 p. s. m. fr. אֹזֶן dec. 6c. אזן
בְּאָזְנַי / בְּאָזְנָי } pref. id. (id. du. suff. 1 pers. sing. . אזן
בְּאָזְנֵי 'וּ pref. id. (id. du., constr. st.; וּ before (ְ) אזן
בְּאָזְנֵיהֶם pref. id. (id. du., suff. 3 pers. pl. masc. . אזן
בְּאָזְנָיו ['zz] וּ pref. id. (id. du., suff. 3 p. s. m.; וּ bef. (ְ) אזן
בְּאָזְנַיִךְ[a] pref. id. (id. du., suff. 2 pers. sing. fem. אזן
בְּאָזְנֶיךָ 'וּ pref. id. (id. du., suff. 2 p. s. m.; וּ bef. (ְ) אזן
בְּאָזְנֵיכֶם pref. id. (id. du., suff. 2 pers. pl. masc. אזן
בְּאָזְנֵינוּ pref. id. (id. du., suff. 1 pers. pl. . . אזן
בָּאֲזִקִּים[b] pref. בָּ, contr. from 'בְּהָאֲ, 'בָּאֲ (noun masc. pl. of [אָזֵק] dec. 8b. . . זקק
בְּאֶזְרוֹעַ[c] וּ pref. בְּ (noun com. s. dec. 1b; וּ bef. (ְ) זרע
בָּאֶזְרָח[d] pref. בָּ for בְּהָ, בְּהַ· (n. m. s. dec. 2b. . זרח
בְּאֶזְרַח[e] וּ pref. בְּ (id., construct state; וּ bef. (ְ) זרח
בְּאַחַד[f] Kh. בְּאֶחָד q. v., K. בְּאַחַת (q. v.) . . אחד
בְּאַחַד pref. בְּ (constr. of the following . אחד
בְּאֶחָד ['g] וּ pref. id. (num. card. masc. irr. (§ 45) אחד
בָּאָחוּ[h] pref. בָּ, for בְּהָ, בְּהַ· (noun fem. sing. . אחו
בְּאָחוֹר[i] pref. בְּ (noun masc. sing. dec. 3a. . אחר
בֶּאֱחֹז[k] pref. בָּ bef. (ֱ) (Kal inf. constr. . . אחז
בַּאֲחֻזָּתוֹ pref. בַּ before (ֲ) (noun fem. sing., suff. 3 pers. sing. masc. from אֲחֻזָּה dec. 10. אחז
בַּאֲחֻזָּתָם[l] pref. id. (id., suff. 3 pers. pl. masc. . אחז
בְּאָחִיהוּ[m] pref. בְּ (noun masc. sing., suff. 3 pers. sing. masc. from אָח irr. (§ 45) . . אח
בְּאָחִיו ['n] וּ pref. id. (id., suff. 3 p. s. m.; וּ bef. (ְ) אח
בְּאֶחָיו pref. id. (id. pl., suff. 3 pers. sing. masc., (as if from אַח R. אחח see § 45) . אח
בְּאָחִיךָ pref. id. (id. sing., suff. 2 pers. sing. masc. אח
בַּאֲחֵיכֶם[o] וּ pref. בַּ before (ֲ) (id. pl., suff. 2 pers. pl. masc. comp. בְּאֶחָיו; וּ before labial . אח
בְּאַחְמְתָא pref. בְּ (pr. name of a place, see אַחְמְתָא
בָּאַחֲרוֹנָה[p] pref. בָּ for בְּהָ, בְּהַ· (adj. f. s. fr. אַחֲרוֹן masc. אחר
בְּאַחֲרֵי[q] pref. בְּ (n. m. pl. constr. from אַחַר (q. v.) אחר
בְּאַחֲרִית ['r] וּ pref. id. (noun fem. s. dec. 1b; וּ bef. (ְ) אחר
בְּאַחֲרִיתָהּ[s] pref. id. (id., suff. 3 pers. sing. fem. . אחר
בְּאַחֲרִיתוֹ[t] וּ pref. id. (id., suff. 3 pers. s. m.; וּ bef. (ְ) אחר
בְּאַחֲרִיתֶךָ pref. id. (id., suff. 2 p. s. m. [for אַחֲרִיתְךָ] אחר
בָּאַחֲרֹנָה defect. for בָּאַחֲרוֹנָה (q. v.) . . אחר
בְּאַחַת ['u] וּ pref. בְּ (num. card., [for אַחֶדֶת], fem. of אֶחָד irr. (§ 45); וּ before (ְ) . . אחד
בְּאֶחָת[x] pref. id. (id. in pause (comp. אֶחָיו under אָח § 45) . . . . אחד
בַּאֲחֹתָהּ[y] pref. בַּ bef. (ֲ) (noun fem. sing., suff. 3 pers. sing. fem. from אָחוֹת irr. (§ 45) . . אח

[a] Ge. 31. 33, 33. [b] De 1. 27. [c] Ps. 61. 5. [d] Ec. 8. 10. [e] 1 Ki. 7. 19. [f] Ho. 12. 4. [g] Eze. 1. 20, 21. [h] Ps. 33. 7. [i] 2 Ki. 14. 14. [k] Eze. 28. 4. [l] Je. 48. 7. [m] Job 33. 28. [n] Eze. 5. 2. [o] Is. 50. 11. [p] 1 Sa. 28. 6. [q] Ps. 36. 10. [r] Ezr. 4. 12. [s] Eze. 41. 6. [t] Je. 2. 24. [u] Ho. 10. 10. [v] Le. 14. 52. [w] Ps. 51. 9. [z] De. 15. 17. [zz] Is. 6. 10. [a] Is. 49. 20. [b] Je. 40. 1. [c] Je. 32. 21. [d] Le. 17. 15 [e] Ex. 12. 19 [f] Ca. 4. 9. [g] Ezr. 7. 9. [h] Ge. 41. 2, 18. [i] Pr. 29. 11. [k] Ps. 56. 1. [l] 1 Ch. 9. 2. [m] Job 41. 9. [n] Ex. 32. 29. [o] Le. 25. 46. [p] 2 Sa. 2. 26. [q] 2 Sa. 2. 23. [r] Da. 8. 23. [s] Pr. 25. 8. [t] Je. 17. 11. [u] Je. 10. 8. [x] Pr. 28. 18. [y] Ge. 30. 1.

בָּאֵי Kal part. act. pl. constr. from בָּא dec. 1 a. בוא

בֹּאִי id. inf. (בּוֹא), suff. 1 p. s. dec. 1 a. (§ 25. No. 2)

בֹּאִי ו׳ id. imp. sing. fem.; וּ bef. labial . בוא

בְּאֵיבָה[a] pref. בְּ)(noun fem. sing. dec. 10. . איב

בְּאֹיְבַי[b] וּ pref. id.)(the foll. with suff. 1 p. s.; וּ bef. (:) איב

בְּאֹיְבֵי pref. id.)(Kal part. act. pl. constr. masc. from אוֹיֵב dec. 7 b. . . . איב

בְּאֵידְכֶם[c] pref. id.)(n. m. s., suff. 2 p. pl. m. fr. אֵיד d. 1 a. אוד

בָּאֶיהָ[d] Kal part. act. pl. m., suff. 3 p. s. f. fr. בָּא dec. 1 a. בוא

בְּאִיּוֹב pref. בְּ)(pr. name masc. . . . איב

בְּאֵין pref. id)(constr. of the following: Is. 24. 15.

בָּאִיִּים pref. בָּ, for בְּהַ·, בְּהָ)(noun masc., pl. of אִי dec. 8. (§ 37. No. 4) . . . אוה

בָּאַיִל[e] pref. id.)(noun m. s. dec. 6 h. (§ 35. r. 12) אול

בְּאֵיל pref. בְּ)(id., construct state . . אול

בְּאֵילוֹן pref. id.)(pr. name of a place . . אול

בְּאַיָּלוֹת pref. id.)(n. f., pl. of אַיָּלָה or אַיֶּלֶת (§ 42. r. 5) אול

בְּאֵילִים[f] pref. id.)(noun masc., pl. of אַיִל dec. 6 h. אול

בְּאֵילִם ו pref. id.)(pr. name of a place; וּ bef. lab. אול

בָּאִים ו׳ Kal part. act. m., pl. of בָּא dec. 1 a; וּ id. בוא

בָּאֵימָה[g] pref. בָּ)(noun fem. sing. dec. 10. . אים

בָּאֵימִים[h] ו pref. בָּ for בְּהָ, בְּהַ·)(noun masc. pl. of [אֵים, or אַיִם]; וּ bef. lab. . . . אים

בְּאַיִן[i] ו׳ pref. בְּ)(adv., prop. noun masc. sing., constr. of אַיִן dec. 6 h; וּ id. . . און

בָּאִישׁ pref. בָּ, f. בְּהָ, בְּהַ· } noun masc. s. dec. 1. } איש
בְּאִישׁ pref. בְּ q. v. } (comp. § 45) }

בְּאִישָׁהּ[k] pref. id.)(id., suff. 3 pers. sing. fem. . איש

בְּאִישׁוֹן[l] Kh. בְּאִישׁוֹן see the following, K. בֶּאֱשׁוּן, pref. בְּ)(noun masc. sing. R. אשן

בְּאִישׁוֹן[m] pref. בְּ)(noun masc. sing. . . . איש

בְּאֵיתָן[n] pref. id.)(noun m. sing. (no vowel change) יתן

בָּאֶךָ[o] וְ Kh. וּבְאֶךָ (q. v.?), K. יְבִאֲךָ, defect. for יְבִיאֲךָ (q. v.) . . . . . בוא

בֹּאֶךָ ו׳ } Kal inf. (בּוֹא), suff. 2 pers. sing. masc. } בוא
בֹּאֶךָ[p] } dec. 1 a. (§ 25. No. 2); וּ bef. lab. }

בֹּאֲכָה id. for בֹּאֲךָ (§ 3. rem. 2) . . . בוא

בֶּאֱכֹל[q] pref. בֶּ bef. (-:))(Kal inf. constr. . אכל

בָּאֹכֵל[r] pref. בָּ for בְּהַ·, בְּהָ)(Kal part. act. s. m. d. 7 b. אכל

בְּאֹכֶל[s] pref. בְּ)(noun masc. sing. dec. 6 c. . אכל

בְּאֹכְלֵי pref. id.)(Kal part. act. pl. constr. masc. from אֹכֵל dec. 7 b. . . אכל

בַּאֲכָלְכֶם[t] pref. בַּ bef. (-:))(Kal inf., suff. 2 pers. pl. m. אכל

בְּאָכְלָם pref. בְּ)(id., suff. 3 pers. pl. masc. . אכל

בְּאָכְלֵנוּ[u] pref. id.)(id., suff. 1 pers. pl. . אכל

בֹּאֲכֶם Kal inf. (בּוֹא), suff. 2 pers. pl. masc. dec. 1 a. (§ 25. No. 2) . . . . . בוא

בְּאֵל[x] pref. בְּ)(noun masc. sing. dec. 1 a. . אול

בָּאֵלָה[y] pref. בָּ, for בְּהַ·, בְּהָ)(noun fem. sing. . אול

בָּאֵלֶּה pref. id. bef. tone-syl. s. ב)(pron. demon. pl. com. אל

בְּאָלָה pref. בְּ)(noun fem. sing. dec. 10. (§ 42. r. 2) אלה

בְּאֵלֶּה[z] ו׳ pref. id.)(pron. demon. pl. com.; וּ bef. (:) אל

בֵּאלָהֵהּ[a] Chald. pref. בֵּ contr. [for בְּאֶ׳])(noun masc. sing., suff. 3 pers. sing. masc. אֱלָהּ dec. 1 a. אלה

בֵּאלֹהַי[b] ו׳ pref. id.)(noun masc. pl., suff. 1 pers. sing. from אֱלוֹהַּ dec. 1; וּ bef. lab. . אלה

בֵּאלֹהֵי[c] ו׳ pref. id.)(id., construct state; וּ id. . אלה

בֵּאלֹהֶיהָ[d] pref. id.)(id., suff. 3 pers. sing. fem. . אלה

בֵּאלֹהֵיהֶם[e] ו pref. id.)(id., suff. 3 pers. pl. m.; וּ bef. lab. אלה

בֵּאלֹהָיו[f] ו׳ pref. id.)(id., suff. 3 pers. s. m.; וּ id. אלה

בֵּאלֹהֶיךָ[g] pref. id.)(id., suff. 2 pers. sing. masc. . אלה

בֵּאלֹהֵיכֶם[h] pref. id.)(id., suff. 2 pers. pl. masc. . אלה

בָּאֱלֹהִים pref. בָּ for בְּהַ·, בְּהָ } id. pl., absolute st. אלה
בֵּאלֹהִים pref. בֵּ, [for בְּאֶ׳] }

בֵּאלֹהֵינוּ pref. id.)(id., suff. 1 pers. pl. . . אלה

בְּאַלּוּף[i] pref. בְּ)(noun masc. sing. dec. 1 a. . אלף

בְּאָלוּשׁ pref. id.)(pr. name of a place. . . אלש

בָּאֱלִילִים[k] pref. בָּ for בְּהַ·, בְּהָ)(n. m., pl. of אֱלִיל d. 1 a. אלל

בָּאֵלִים[l] }
בָּאֵלִם[m] } pref. id.)(noun masc., pl. of אֵל dec. 1 a. אול

בָּאֻלָּם[n] ו pref. בָּ)(n. m. s. for אוּלָם q. v.; וּ bef. (:) אול

בְּאַלְמְנוֹתָיו[o] pref. id.)(noun fem. pl., suff. 3 pers. sing. masc. from אַלְמָנָה dec. 11 a. . . אלם

בְּאַלֹּנֵי pref. id.)(n. m. pl. constr. from אֵלוֹן dec. 1 b. אול

בְּאֶלֶף pref. id.)(noun m. s., (suff. אַלְפִּי) dec. 6 a. אלף

בַּאֲלָפָיו pref. בַּ before (-:))(id. pl., suff. 3 pers. sing. masc., K. פָּיו׳ (§ 4. rem. 1) . . אלף

בְּאַלְפֵי pref. בְּ)(id. pl., construct state . . אלף

בְּאָלָתוֹ[p] ו pref. id.)(n. f. s., suff. 3 p. s. m.; וּ bef. (:). אלה

בֹּאָם Kal inf. (בּוֹא) suff. 3 p. pl. m. d. 1 a. (§ 25. No. 2) בוא

בָּאַמָּה pref. בָּ for בְּהַ·, בְּהָ)(noun fem. sing. dec. 10. אם

בְּאִמָּהּ[q] pref. בְּ)(n. f. s., suff. 3 p. s. f. fr. אֵם d. 8 b. אם

בֶּאֱמוּנָה pref. בֶּ bef. (∵))(noun fem. sing. dec. 10. אמן

בֶּאֱמוּנָתוֹ pref. id.)(id., suff. 3 pers. sing. masc. . אמן

בֶּאֱמוּנָתִי[r] pref. id.)(id., suff. 1 pers. sing. . אמן

בֶּאֱמוּנָתֶךָ[s] pref. id.)(id., suff. 2 pers. s. m. [for נָתְךָ] אמן

בֶּאֱמוּנָתָם pref. id.)(id., suff. 3 pers. pl. masc. אמן

בָּאַמּוֹת[t] pref. בָּ for בְּהַ·, בְּהָ)(n. f., pl. of אַמָּה d. 10. אם

בְּאִמְּכֶם[u] pref. בְּ)(n. f. s., suff. 2 p. pl. m. fr. אֵם d. 8 b. אם

[a] Nu. 35. 21. [b] Ps. 54. 9. [c] Pr. 1. 26. [d] Pr. 2. 19. [e] Da. 8. 7. [f] Eze. 40. 38. [g] Ezr. 3. 3. [h] Je. 50. 38. [i] Pr. 26. 20. [k] Nu. 5. 27. [l] Pr. 20. 20. [m] Pr. 7. 9. [n] Ge. 49. 24. [o] Ex. 13. 11. [p] 1 Ki. 2. 13. [q] Nu. 26. 10. [r] Mal. 3. 11. [s] La. 1. 11. [t] Nu. 15. 19. [u] Ex. 16. 3. [x] Ex. 6. 3. [y] 2 Sa. 18. 9, 10. [z] Nu. 26. 64. [a] Da. 6. 24. [b] Ps. 18. 30. [c] Is. 48. 1. [d] Ho. 14. 1. [e] Nu. 33. 4. [f] Is. 8. 21. [g] Ho. 12. 7. [h] Jos. 24. 27. [i] Mi. 7. 5. [k] Ps. 97. 7. [l] Is. 57. 5. [m] Ex. 15. 11. [n] Eze. 40. 39. [o] Is. 13. 22. [p] De. 29. 11. [q] Mi. 7. 6. [r] Ps. 89. 34. [s] Ps. 89. 50. [t] Eze. 43. 13. [u] Ho. 2. 4.

Word	Analysis	Root
בֶּאֱמֻנָה	defect. for בֶּאֱמוּנָה (q. v.)	אמן
[a] בֶּאֱמֻנָה	pref. בְּ (noun fem. sing.	אמן
[b] בֶּאֱמֻנָתְךָ	pref. בְּ bef. (ֱ) (noun fem. sing., suff. 2 pers. sing. masc. from אֱמוּנָה dec. 10.	אמן
[c] בְּאַמְּצוֹ	pref. בְּ (Piel inf. (אַמֵּץ), suff. 3 p. s. m. d. 7 b.	אמץ
בַּאֲמַצְיָהוּ	pref. בַּ bef. (ֲ) (pr. name masc.	אמץ
בֶּאֱמֹר	pref. בְּ bef. (ֱ) (Kal inf. constr.	אמר
בְּאִמְרֵי	pref. בְּ (n. m. pl. constr. fr. [אֵמֶר] dec. 6 b.	אמר
בְּאָמְרִי	[d] וּ pref. id. (Kal inf., suff. 1 p. s.; וּ bef. (:)	אמר
[e] בְּאִמְרֵיכֶם	וּ pref. id. (noun masc. pl., suff. 2 pers. pl. masc. from [אֵמֶר] dec. 6 b; וּ id.	אמר
[f] בְּאֹמְרִים	pref. id. (Kal part. act. m., pl. of אֹמֵר d. 7 b.	אמר
בֶּאֱמָרְכֶם	pref. בְּ bef. (ֱ) (id. inf., suff. 2 pers. pl. m.	אמר
בְּאָמְרָם	pref. בְּ (id. id., suff. 3 pers. pl. masc.	אמר
[g] בְּאִמְרָתֶךָ	pref. id. (noun fem. sing., suff. 2 pers. sing. masc. from [אִמְרָה] dec. 12 b. [for רָתְךָ]	אמר
[h] בְּאַמַּת	pref. id. (noun f. s., constr. of אַמָּה dec. 10.	אם
בֶּאֱמֶת	[i] וּ pref. בְּ before (ֱ) (noun fem. sing. (suff. אֲמִתּוֹ) dec. 6 b. [for אֱמֶנֶת]; וּ bef. lab.	אמן
[k] בְּאַמְתַּחַת	pref. בְּ (noun f. s. dec. 13 a. (§ 44. No. 1)	מתח
[l] בְּאַמְתַּחְתִּי	pref. id. (id., suff. 1 pers. sing.	מתח
[m] בְּאַמְתְּחֹתֵיכֶם	pref. id. (id., suff. 2 pers. pl. masc.	מתח
[n] בְּאַמְתְּחֹתֵינוּ	pref. id. (id., suff. 1 pers. pl.	מתח
בַּאֲמִתְּךָ / [o] בַּאֲמִתֶּךָ	pref. בַּ before (ֲ) (noun fem. sing., suff. 2 p. s. m. from אֱמֶת (q. v.) dec. 8 b.	אמן
[p] בֹּאָנָה	Kal inf. (בּוֹא), suff. 3 p. pl. fem. (§ 4. r. 5) d. 1 a.	בוא
בָּאנוּ	[q] וּ id. pret. 1 pers. pl. (§ 25. 2); וּ bef. lab.	בוא
[r] בֹּאֵנוּ	id. inf. (בּוֹא), suff. 1 pers. pl. dec. 1 a.	בוא
בֶּאֱנוֹשׁ	pref. בְּ bef. (ֱ) (n. m. s. (comp. אִישׁ § 45)	אנש
[s] בַּאֲנָחָה	pref. בְּ for בְּהַ, בְּהָ (n. f. s. d. 11 c. (§ 42. r. 1)	אנח
בְּאַנְחָתִי	pref. בְּ (id. with suff. 1 pers. sing.	אנח
[t] בָּאֳנִי	pref. בָּ before (ֳ) (noun masc. sing.	אנה
[u] בְּאוֹנִי	pref. בְּ (n. m. s., suff. 1 p. s. from אוֹן dec. 1 a.	און
[x] בָּאֳנִיָּה	pref. בְּ for בְּהַ, בְּהָ (noun fem. sing. dec. 10.	אנה
בָּאֳנִיּוֹת	[y] וּ pref. בָּ before (ֳ) (id. pl.; וּ bef. lab.	אנה
[z] בֶּאֱנֹק	pref. בְּ bef. (ֱ) (Kal inf. constr.	אנק
בְּאַנְשֵׁי	[a] וּ pref. בְּ (constr. of the foll.; וּ bef. (:)	אנש
בָּאֲנָשִׁים / [b] בַּאֲנָשִׁים	pref. בְּ for בְּהַ, בְּהָ (/ pref. בַּ before (ֲ) (} n. m. pl., as if from [אֱנָשׁ] d. 6, see אֱנוֹשׁ	אנש
[c] בֶּאֱסוּר	וּ Ch. pref. בְּ bef. (ֱ) (n. m. s. d. 1 a; וּ bef. lab.	אסר
[d] בַּאֲסָמֶיךָ	pref. בַּ bef. (ֲ) (noun masc. pl., suff. 2 pers. sing. masc. [from אָסָם]	אסם
[e] בְּאַסְפֵּי	pref. id. (noun masc. pl. constr. [from אָסֹף dec. 8 c. § 37. No. 3.]	אסף
בְּאָסְפְּךָ	pref. בְּ (Kal inf., suff. 2 pers. sing. masc.	אסף
[f] בְּאָסְפְּכֶם	pref. id. (id., suff. 2 pers. pl. masc.	אסף
[g] בְּאָסְרָם	pref. id. (Kal inf., suff. 3 pers. pl. masc.	אסר
[h] בָּאַף / [i] בְּאַף	pref. בְּהַ, בְּהָ=בָּ / pref. בְּ q. v. } noun masc. sing. dec. 8 d. for [אַנְף]; וּ bef. (:)	אנף
בְּאַפּוֹ	pref. id. (id., suff. 3 pers. sing. masc.	אנף
בְּאַפִּי	pref. id. (id., suff. 1 pers. sing.	אנף
בְּאַפָּיו	pref. id. (id. du., suff. 3 pers. sing. masc.	אנף
[i] בְּאַפַּיִם	pref. id. (id. du., absolute state	אנף
[k] בָּאֲפִיקִים	pref. בְּ for בְּהַ, בְּהָ (n. m., pl. of [אָפִיק] d. 3 a.	אפק
בְּאַפְּךָ / בְּאַפֶּךָ	pref. בְּ (noun masc. sing., suff. 2 pers. sing. masc. from אַף dec. 8 d.	אנף
[l] בְּאַפְּכֶם	וּ pref. id. (id., suff. 2 p. pl. m.; וּ bef. (:)	אנף
[m] בָּאֹפֶל	pref. בְּ for בְּהַ, בְּהָ (noun masc. sing.	אפל
בַּאֲפֵלָה	pref. id. (noun fem. sing. dec. 10. (§ 42. r. 4)	אפל
[n] בַּאֲפֵלוֹת	pref. בַּ before (ֲ) (id. pl.	אפל
[o] בְּאַפָּם	pref. בְּ (noun masc. sing., with suff. 3 pers. pl. masc. from אַף dec. 8 d.	אנף
בְּאֶפֶס	וּ pref. id. (noun masc. sing., as an *adv.* also pr. name masc. אֶפֶס דַּמִּים; וּ bef. labial	אפס
בַּאֲפֵק	pref. בַּ before (ֲ) (pr. name of a place	אפק
[p] בָּאֵפֶר	pref. בְּ for בְּהַ, בְּהָ (noun masc. sing.	אפר
בְּאֵפֶר	pref. id. (noun masc. sing.	אפר
בְּאֶפְרַיִם	וּ pref. בְּ (pr. name of a tribe; וּ before (:)	אפר
בְּאֶפְרָתָה	pref. id. (pr. name of a place	אפר
בְּאֶצְבַּע	pref. בְּ (noun fem. sing. dec. 2 b. (§ 31. r. 5)	צבע
בְּאֶצְבָּעוֹ	pref. id. (id., suff. 3 pers. sing. masc.	צבע
בְּאֶצְבָּעֲךָ	pref. id. (id., suff. 2 pers. sing. m., [for בָּעֲךָ]	צבע
[q] בְּאֶצְבְּעֹתָיו	pref. id. (id. pl., suff. 3 pers. sing. masc.	צבע
בְּאֹצְרוֹת	[r] וּ pref. id. (noun masc. with pl. fem. term., constr. state from אוֹצָר dec. 2 b; וּ before (:)	אצר
[s] בְּאֹצְרֹתָי	pref. id. (id., suff. 1 pers. sing [for תַי]	אצר
[t] בְּאֹצְרֹתֶיהָ	pref. id. (id., suff. 3 pers. sing. fem.	אצר

בָּאַר Kal not used; Pi.—I. *to engrave*, as upon a tablet, Hab. 2. 2.—II. *to expound, explain.*

בְּאֵר fem. with suff. בְּאֵרְךָ, pl. בְּאֵרוֹת, constr. בְּאֵרוֹת (§ 35. rem. 10).—I. *a well, cistern.*—II. *pit.*—III. pr. name of a station of the Israelites in the desert, probably the same which is called בְּאֵר אֵלִים (*well of heroes*) in Is. 15. 8.—IV. a place in Judah, Ju. 9. 21.

בְּאֵר לַחַי רֹאִי pr. name of the well where the angel appeared to Hagar. The etymology according to Ge. 16. 14 is, "*well of life of vision,*" i. e. life retained notwithstanding the vision of God. רֹאִי in pause for רְאִי=רֹאִי (comp. § 35. rem. 14) probably to avoid the concurrence of this accent with that of the preceding לַחַי.

[a] Est. 2. 20. [b] Ps. 143. 1. [c] Pr. 8. 28. [d] Eze. 33. 14. [e] Job 32. 14.
[f] Ps. 122. 1. [g] Ps. 119. 133, 148. [h] De. 3. 11. [i] Jos. 24. 14. [k] Ge. 44. 12.
[l] Ge. 42. 28. [m] Ge. 43. 23. [n] Ge. 43. 18, 22. [o] Ps. 54. 7. [p] Je. 8. 7.
[q] 2 Sa. 17. 12. [r] Ex. 10. 26. [s] Ps. 31. 11. [t] 1 Ki. 9. 27. [u] De. 26. 14.
[x] Jon. 1. 5. [y] Da. 11. 40. [z] Eze. 26. 15. [a] 2 Sa. 2. 31. [b] 1 Sa. 17. 12.
[c] Da. 4. 12, 20. [d] De. 28. 8. [e] Ne. 12. 25. [f] Le. 23. 39. [g] Ho. 10. 10.
[h] La. 3. 43; Is. 14. 6. [i] Da. 11. 20. [k] Eze. 34. 13. [l] Am. 4. 10.
[m] Ps. 91. 6. [n] Is. 59. 9. [o] Ge. 49. 6. [p] 1 Ki. 20. 38.
[q] Pr. 6. 13. [r] 2 Ki. 16. 8. [s] 2 Ki. 20. 15. [t] Je. 49. 4.

בְּאֵר שֶׁבַע (*well of oath*) pr. name of a city in the tribe of Judah, afterwards of Simeon.

בְּאֵרָא (*well*) pr. name masc. 1 Ch. 7. 37.

בְּאֵרָה (id.) pr. name masc. 1 Ch. 5. 6.

בְּאֵרוֹת (*wells*) pr. name of a city in the tribe of Benjamin. Gent. noun בְּאֵרֹתִי and contr. בֵּרֹתִי.

בְּאֵרוֹת בְּנֵי יַעֲקָן (*wells of the sons of Jaakan*) pr. name of a station of the Israelites in the desert. De. 10. 6, called בְּנֵי יַעֲקָן in Nu. 33. 31.

בְּאֵרִי (*belonging to a well*) pr. name.—I. the father of Hosea, Ho. 1. 1.—II. father-in-law of Esau, Ge. 26. 34.

בֹּאר masc. pl. בֹּארוֹת i. q. בּוֹר *a cistern.*

בּוֹר (for בְּאֹר=בֹּאר) masc. dec. 1a. pl. בֹּרוֹת.—I. *pit.*—II. *cistern.*—III. *dungeon* or *prison*; בֵּית הַבּוֹר *prison-house.*—IV. *grave, sepulchre.*

בּוֹר הַסִּרָה (*cistern of departure*) pr. name of a place, 2 Sa. 3. 26.

בַּיִר i. q. בְּאֵר *a cistern*, Je. 6. 7, Keri.

בֵּרִי (for בְּאֵרִי q. v.) pr. name masc. 1 Ch. 7. 36.

בֵּרוֹתָה, בֵּרוֹתַי (*my well*) pr. name of a city between Damascus and Hamath, Eze. 47. 16; 2 Sa. 8. 8.

בָּאֵר[a] [b]ו׳ Piel inf.; וּ before labial . . . באר

בֵּאֵר[c] id. pret. 3 pers. sing. masc. . . . באר

בְּאֵר [d]ו׳ noun fem. sing. (§ 35. r. 10); וּ before labial באר

בְּאֵרָא וּ pr. name masc.; וּ before (:) . . . באר

בָּאֲרָבֶּה[e] pref. בָּ, for בְּהָ, בְּהַ· (noun masc. sing. . . רבה

בָּאֲרֻבּוֹת[f] pref. id. (noun fem., pl. of אֲרֻבָּה dec. 10; also pr. name of a place . . . ארב

בְּאָרְבָּם[g] pref. בְּ (noun masc. sing. suff. 3 pers. pl. masc. from [אֹרֶב] dec. 6c. . . ארב

בְּאַרְבַּע ו׳ pref. id. (num. card. f. (§ 30. r. 5); וּ before (:) רבע

בְּאַרְבָּעָה [h]ו׳ pref. id. (id. m. constr. בַּעַת׳ (§ 42. r. 5); וּ id. רבע

בְּאַרְבָּעִים pref. id. (id. pl. com. (§ 30. rem. 5) . רבע

בְּאַרְבַּעַת[i] pref. id. (id. s. m., constr. of אַרְבָּעָה (§ 42. r. 5) רבע

בָּאַרְגָּוָן[k] וּ pref. id. (n. m. s.; וּ before labial, see R. ארג׳

בָּאַרְגָּז[l] pref. בָּ (for בְּהָ, בְּהַ·; noun masc. sing. רגז

בְּאַרְגָּמָן[m] ו׳ pref. id. (noun masc. sing.; וּ id. . ארג׳

בְּאֵרָה pr. name masc. . . . . . באר

בְּאֵרָה pr. name of a place (בְּאֵר) with local ה . באר

בָּארוּמָה pref. בָּ [for בְּאַ׳] (pr. name of a place . ארם

בָּאָרוֹן pref. id. (noun masc. sing. dec. 3a. . ארה

בַּאֲרוֹן[n] pref. בַּ before (-:) (id., construct state . ארה

בְּאֵרוֹת ו׳ pr. name of a place . . . באר

בֹּארוֹת[o] noun m. with pl. fem. term. from בֹּאר, dec. 1a. באר

בָּאֶרֶז[p] / בָּאָרֶז[q] } pref. בָּ for בְּהָ, בְּהַ· (noun masc. sing., pl. c. אַרְזֵי dec. 6a. (§ 35. rem. 2) } ארז

בַּאֲרָזֶיךָ[r] pref. בַּ before (-:) (id. pl. with suff. 2 p. s. m. ארז

בָּאֲרָזִים pref. בָּ for בְּהָ, בְּהַ· (id. pl., absolute state ארז

בְּאֹרַח pref. בְּ (noun com. sing. dec. 6c. . . ארח

בְּאֹרְחֹתָיו pref. id. (id. pl., suff. 3 p. s. m. (אֹ § 35. r. 9) ארח

בְּאֵרִי pr. name masc. . . . . באר

בָּאֵרִים[s] pref. בָּ for בְּהָ, בְּהַ· (n. m., pl. of אוּר dec. 1a. אור

בְּאֹרֶךְ pref. id. (noun masc. sing. dec. 6c. . . ארך

בְּאֵרְךָ[t] pref. בְּ (noun masc. sing., suff. 2 pers. sing. masc. from בְּאֵר dec. 1 & 6. (§ 35. rem. 10) באר

בְּאֹרֶךְ pref. id. (noun masc. sing. dec. 6c. . ארך

בַּאֲרָם pref. בַּ before (-:) (pr. name of a people and region . . . . . ארם

בַּאֲרַם pref. id. (pr. name of a region . . ארם

בְּאַרְמוֹן[u] pref. id. (noun masc. sing. (§ 37. rem. 6) ארם

בְּאַרְמְנוֹתֶיהָ[x] pref. id. (id. pl., suff. 3 pers. sing. fem. as if from [אַרְמֶנֶת § 44. rem. 5] . . ארם

בְּאַרְמְנוֹתֵיהֶם[y] pref. id. (id. pl., suff. 3 pers. pl. masc. ארם

בְּאַרְמְנוֹתָיִךְ[z] pref. id. (id. pl., suff. 2 pers. sing. masc. ארם

בְּאַרְמְנוֹתֵינוּ pref. id. (id. pl., suff. 1 pers. pl. . ארם

בְּאַרְנוֹן pref. id. (pr. name of a region . . רנן

בְּאַרְעָא [a]ו׳ Chald. pref. id. (noun fem. sing., emph. of [אֲרַע] dec. 3a; וּ before lab. . ארע

בָּאָרֶץ ו׳ pref. בָּ for בְּהָ, בְּהַ· / בְּאֶרֶץ ו׳ pref. בְּ q. v. } noun fem. sing., (suff. אַרְצִי) dec. 6a; וּ id. } ארץ

בְּאַרְצוֹ pref. id. (id., suff. 3 pers. sing. masc. . ארץ

בָּאֲרָצוֹת pref. בָּ for בְּהָ, בְּהַ· / בַּאֲרָצוֹת pref. בַּ before (-:) } id. pl., absolute state ארץ

בְּאַרְצוֹת[b] pref. בְּ (id. pl., construct state . . ארץ

בְּאַרְצִי pref. id. (id. sing., suff. 1 pers. sing. . ארץ

בְּאַרְצֶךָ / בְּאַרְצְךָ } pref. id. (id. sing., suff. 2 pers. sing. masc. ארץ

בְּאַרְצֵךְ[c] pref. id. (id. sing., suff. 2 pers. sing. fem. ארץ

בְּאַרְצְכֶם [d]ו׳ pref. id. (id. s., suff. 2 p. pl. m.; וּ before (:) ארץ

בְּאַרְצָם pref. id. (id. sing., suff. 3 pers. pl. masc. ארץ

בְּאַרְצֵנוּ pref. id. (id. sing., suff. 1 pers. pl. . ארץ

בְּאַרְצֹת[e] pref. id. (id. pl., construct state . . ארץ

בְּאַרְצֹתָם pref. id. (id. pl., suff. 3 pers. pl. masc. . ארץ

בְּאֵרֹת[f] noun fem., pl. constr. from בְּאֵר, dec. 1a. . באר

בֶּאֱרֹת[g] id. pl. constr., dec. 6. (§ 35. rem. 10) . באר

בָּאַשׁ[h] וּ *to stink.* Niph. metaph. *to become odious* to any one, const. with בְּ, אֵת of pers. Hiph.—I. *to cause to stink*, Ec. 10. 1.—II. metaph. *to make loathsome, odious*, const. with בְּ.—III. intrans. *to stink*: metaph. *to be odious*, 1 Sa. 27. 12.—IV. *to act*

---

[a] De. 27. 8. [b] Hab. 2. 2. [c] De. 1. 5. [d] Pr. 23. 27. [e] Ex. 10. 12. [f] Ec. 12. 3. [g] Ho. 7. 6. [h] Est. 9. 18. [i] Eze. 46. 22. [k] 2 Ch. 2. 6. [l] 1 Sa. 6. 8. [m] 2 Ch. 2. 13. [n] 1 Sa. 6. 19. [o] Je. 2. 13. [p] Je. 22. 14, 15. [q] 1 Ki. 7. 3, 7. [r] Zec. 11. 1. [s] Is. 24. 14. [t] Pr. 5. 15. [u] 2 Ki. 15. 25. [x] Ps. 48. 4. [y] Am. 3. 10. [z] Ps. 122. 7. [a] Da. 6. 28. [b] Ps. 116. 9. [c] Is. 60. 18. [d] Le. 22. 24. [e] Le. 26. 36, 39. [f] Ge. 26. 18. [g] Ge. 14. 10. [h] Ex. 7. 18.

badly, wickedly, Pr. 13. 5. Hithp. *to make oneself odious*, const. with עִם, 1 Ch. 19. 6.

בְּאֵשׁ Chald. *to be evil*, only Da. 6. 15, const. with עַל, *to be displeased at.*

בְּאֹשׁ masc. with suff. בָּאְשׁוֹ (§ 35. r. 10) *stench.*

בְּאֻשִׁים masc. pl. *bad, unripe* or *sour grapes*, Is. 5. 2, 4.

בְּאִישׁ Chald. masc. adj. (§ 67. rem.) *bad, wicked*, Ezr. 4. 12.

בָּאְשָׁה fem. *a bad plant, weed*, Job 31. 40.

בָּאֵשׁ [a] ו׳ pref. בָּ for בְּהָ·, בְּהַ } n. com. sing. dec. 8b; וּ before lab. — אשׁ
בְּאֵשׁ [b] ו׳ pref. בְּ
בְּאַשְׁדּוֹד ו׳ pref. id.) pr. name of a place; וּ id. — שׁדד
בָּאֲשֵׁדוֹת [c] וּ pref. בָּ for בְּהַ·, בְּהָ) n. fem., pl. of אֲשֵׁדָה dec. 11c. (§ 42. rem. 4); וּ id. — אשׁד
בְּאִשָּׁה [d] ו׳ noun fem. s. dec. 10. (comp. § 45); וּ id. — אנשׁ
בָּאְשָׁה [e] noun fem. sing. — באשׁ
בָּאְשׁוֹ [f] noun masc. sing., suff. 3 pers. sing. masc. from בְּאֹשׁ dec. 6. (§ 35. rem. 10) — באשׁ
בְּאַשּׁוּר ו׳ pref. בְּ) pr. name of a country; וּ before (:) — אשׁר
בְּאֻשִׁים [g] noun masc. pl. — באשׁ
בָּאֲשִׁישׁוֹת [h] pref. בָּ for בְּהַ·, בְּהָ) n. f., pl. of אֲשִׁישָׁה dec. 10. — אשׁשׁ
בְּאֶשְׁכּוֹל [i] pref. id.) noun masc. sing., pl. אֶשְׁכֹּלוֹת (§ 36. rem. 6. & § 44. rem. 5) — שׁכל
בָּאְשָׁם [k] n. m. s., suff. 3 pl. m. from בְּאֹשׁ dec. 6. (§ 35. r. 10) — באשׁ
בְּאַשְׁמָה [l] pref. בְּ) noun fem. sing. dec. 12a. — אשׁם
בַּאֲשָׁמָיו [m] pref. בַּ before (-:)) noun masc. pl., suff. 3 pers. sing. masc. from אָשָׁם dec. 4c. — אשׁם
בָּאַשְׁמַנִּים [n] pref. בָּ for בְּהָ·, בְּהַ) n. m., pl. of [אַשְׁמָן] dec. 8a. — שׁמן
בְּאַשְׁמֻרוֹת [o] pref. בְּ) noun fem., pl. of אַשְׁמוּרָה dec. 10. — שׁמר
בְּאַשְׁמֹרֶת pref. id.) id. s., constr. st. (§ 39. No. 3. rem. 4) — שׁמר
בְּאַשְׁמַת [p] pref. id.) n. f. s., constr. of אַשְׁמָה dec. 12a. — אשׁם
בְּאַשְׁמָתֵינוּ [q] pref. id.) id. suff. 1 pers. pl. (for ׳ see § 4. r. 3) — אשׁם
בְּאַשְׁמָתָם [r] pref. id.) id., suff. 3 pers. pl. masc. — אשׁם
וּבְאַשְׁמָתֵנוּ [s] וּ pref. id.) id., suff. 1 pers. pl.; וּ before (:) — אשׁם
בְּאַשְׁפָּתוֹ [t] pref. id.) noun fem. sing., suff. 3 pers. sing. masc. from אַשְׁפָּה (no vowel change) — אשׁף
בַּאֲשֶׁר ו׳ pref. בַּ before (-:)) pron. relat. and conj. — אשׁר
בְּאָשֵׁר ו׳ pref. בְּ) pr. name of a tribe; וּ before (:) — אשׁר
בַּאֲשֻׁרוֹ [u] pref. בַּ before (-:)) noun masc. sing., suff. 3 pers. sing. masc. from [אָשׁוּר] dec. 3a. — אשׁר
בְּאָשְׁרִי [x] pref. בְּ) n. m. s., suff. 1 p. s. from [אֹשֶׁר] dec. 6c. — אשׁר
בְּאֵשֶׁת וּ pref. id.) noun f. s. dec. 13c; וּ before (:) — אישׁ
בְּאִשְׁתּוֹ [z] ו׳ pref. id.) id., suff. 3 pers. sing. m.; וּ id. — אישׁ
בְּאֶשְׁתְּמֹעַ pref. id.) pr. name of a place — שׁמע
בָּאתָ ו׳ Kal pret. 2 p. s. m. (§ 25. No. 2. f.); וּ bef. lab. — בוא

בָּאת ו׳ / בָּאתְ [a] וּ } Kal pret. 2 pers. sing. fem.; וּ id. — בוא
בָּאתָה [b] id. pret. 2 pers. s. m. for בָּאתָ (§ 8. rem. 5) — בוא
בְּאֹתוֹת [c] [d] ו׳ pref. בְּ) noun com., pl. of אוֹת dec. 1a. [for אֹתוֹת]; וּ before lab. — אוה
בָּאתִי ו׳ Kal pret. 1 pers. sing. (§ 29. rem. 2); וּ id. — בוא
בָּאתֶם ו׳ id. pret. 2 pers. pl. masc.; וּ id. — בוא
בְּאֵתָם pref. בְּ) pr. name of a place — יתם
בָּאַתְנוּ [e] Kal pret. 3 pers. sing. fem., suff. 1 pers. pl. — בוא
בְּאַתְרַ [f] Chald. pref. בְּ [contr. בְּאַתַר]) noun m. s. — אתר
בְּאֹתֹת defect. for בְּאֹתוֹת (q. v.) — אוה
בְּבֹא ו׳ pref. בְּ) Kal inf. constr. (§ 21. r. 2); וּ bef. (:) — בוא
בַּבָּאָה [g] pref. בַּ for בְּהַ) noun fem. sing. — בוא
בְּבֹאָה [h] pref. בְּ) Kal inf. (בּוֹא) with parag. ה (§ 21. r. 2) — בוא
בְּבֹאָהּ וּ pref. id.) id. with suff. 3 p. s. f.; וּ bef. (:) — בוא
בְּבֹאוֹ ו׳ pref. id.) id. with suff. 3 pers. s. m.; וּ id. — בוא
בְּבֹאִי pref. id.) id., suff. 1 pers. sing. — בוא
בְּבֹאֲךָ [i] / בְּבֹאֲךָ [k] } pref. id.) id., suff. 2 pers. sing. masc. — בוא
בְּבֹאֲכֶם pref. id.) id., suff. 2 pers. pl. masc. — בוא
בְּבֹאָם pref. id.) id., suff. 3 pers. pl. masc. — בוא
בְּבֹאָן [l] pref. id.) id., suff. 3 pers. pl. fem. — בוא
בִּבְאֵר ו׳ pref. בְּ bef. (:)) pr. n. in compos. בְּאֵר שֶׁבַע — באר
בְּבָבֶל pref. בְּ) pr. name of a city and country — בלל
בְּבָבַת [m] pref. id.) noun f. s., constr. of [בָּבָה] d. 10. — בוב
בַּבָּגֶד [n] pref. בַּ for בְּהַ) in pause as if from [בֶּגֶד] § 25. rem. 2.] } — בגד
בְּבֶגֶד pref. id. / בְּבֶגֶד [o] pref בְּ } noun masc. sing. (with suff. בִּגְדִי) dec. 6a. } — בגד
בְּבִגְדוֹ pref. id.) id., Ge. 39. 12 (inf. Ex. 21. 8) suff. 3 p. s. m. — בגד
בִּבְגָדָו [p] pref. id.) id. pl. suff. 3 p. pl. m. K. יו׳ (§ 4. r. 1) — בגד
בְּבִגְדֵי [q] pref. id.) id. pl., constr. st. — בגד
בְּבִגְדֵיהֶם [r] pref. id.) id. pl., suff. 3 pers. pl. masc. — בגד
בִּבְגָדָיו [s] pref. id.) id. pl., suff. 3 pers. sing. masc. — בגד
בַּבְּגָדִים [t] pref. בַּ for בְּהַ) id. pl., absolute state — בגד
בְּבַד [u] pref. בְּ) noun masc. sing. dec. 8d. — בדד
בִּבְהִילוּ [v] Chald. pref. בְּ before (:)) noun fem. sing. — בהל
בַּבֶּהָלָה [y] pref. בַּ for בְּהַ) n. f. s. dec. 10. (§ 42. No. 3) — בהל
בַּבְּהֵמָה ו׳ pref. id. / בִּבְהֵמָה *ו׳ pref. בְּ bef. (:) }) noun f. s. dec. 11 (§ 42. r. 5); וּ bef. lab. *Ezr. 1. 4 } — בהם
בְּבַהֲמוֹת [z] pref. בְּ) id. pl., constr. st. (comp. § 42. r. 1) — בהם
בְּבֶהֱמַת [a] pref. id.) id. sing., constr. state (comp. id.) — בהם
וּבִבְהֶמְתְּךָ [b] וּ pref. בְּ bef. (:)) id. sing., suff. 2 pers. sing. masc. [from בְּהֶמֶת dec. 13. see § 44. r. 3] — בהם
וּבִבְהֶמְתֵּנוּ [c] וּ pref. id.) id. sing., suff. 1 pers. pl. see the preceding; וּ bef. labial — בהם

[a] 2 Sa. 23. 7. [b] Zep. 1. 18. [c] Jos. 12. 8. [d] Ho. 12. 13. [e] Job 31. 40. [f] Joel 2. 20. [g] Is. 5. 2, 4. [h] Ca. 2. 5. [i] Is. 65. 8. [k] Is. 34. 3 [l] Ezr. 9. 7. [m] Ps. 68. 22. [n] Is. 59. 10. [o] Ps. 63. 7. [p] Am. 8. 14. [q] Ezr. 9. 15. [r] 2 Ch. 24. 18. [s] Ezr. 9. 13. [t] Is. 49. 2. [u] Job 23. 11. [x] Ge. 30. 13. [y] Ge. 2. 24. [z] Ge. 26. 11. [a] 2 Sa. 14. 3.
[b] 2 Sa. 3. 7. [c] Je. 32. 21. [d] De. 26. 8. [e] Ps. 44. 18. [f] Da. 7. 6, 7. [g] Eze. 8. 5. [h] 1 Ki. 14. 12. [i] 2 Sa. 3. 13. [k] De. 28. 6, 19. [l] Ge. 30. 38. [m] Zec. 2. 12. [n] 1 Sa. 19. 13. [o] Le. 13. 47, 47. [p] 2 Sa. 1. 11. [q] Eze. 27. 20. [r] Eze. 44. 19. [s] 2 Ki. 2. 12. [t] 1 Ki. 1. 1. [u] Ex. 30. 34. [v] Ezr. 4. 23. [y] Ps. 78. 33. [z] Mi. 5. 7. [a] Nu. 3. 41. [b] De. 7. 14. [c] Ne. 9. 37.

Word	Analysis	Root
בַּבַּהֶרֶת[a]	pref. בַּ for בְּהַ)(noun fem. sing., pl. בֶּהָרוֹת (§ 42. No. 3, & § 44. rem. 5)	בהר
בְּבוֹא	ו׳ pref. בְּ)(Kal inf. constr. dec. 1. (§ 21. rem. 2); וּ bef. (:)	בוא
בְּבוֹאוֹ	pref. id.)(id., suff. 3 pers. sing. masc.	בוא
בְּבוֹאָם	pref. id.)(id., suff. 3 pers. pl. masc.	בוא
בְּבוֹאָן[b]	pref. id.)(id., suff. 3 pers. pl. fem.	בוא
בַּבּוּץ[c]	וּ pref. בַּ for בְּהַ)(noun m. s.; וּ bef. labial	בוץ
בַּבּוֹר	[d]ו׳ pref. id. } noun masc. sing. dec. 1, for בְּאֵר q.v.; but Job 9.30, see R.	ברר
בְּבוֹר[e]	pref. בְּ q.v. } (id.)	ברר
בַּבִּזָּה	וּ pref. בַּ f. בְּהַ } noun sing. fem.)(וּ id.	בזז
בְּבִזָּה[f]	וּ pref. בְּ q. v. } (id.)	בזז
בְּבֶזֶק / בְּבָזֶק	pref. id.)(pr. name of a place (§ 35. r. 2)	בזק
בְּבַחֻרִים	pref. id.)(pr. name of a place	בחר
בְּבִטְחָה[g]	וּ pref. id.)(noun sing. fem.; וּ bef. (:)	בטח
בַּבֶּטֶן	pref. בַּ for בְּהַ } noun fem. sing. (suff. בִּטְנִי) dec. 6a.	בטן
בְּבֶטֶן	pref. בְּ q. v. } (id.)	בטן
בְּבִטְנָהּ	pref. id.)(id., suff. 3 pers. sing. fem.	בטן
בְּבִטְנוֹ	pref. id.)(id., suff. 3 pers. sing. masc.	בטן
בְּבִטְנֶךָ[h]	pref. id.)(id., suff. 2 pers. sing. masc. [for ־ךָ]	בטן
בְּבִטְנֵךְ[i]	pref. id.)(id., suff. 2 pers. sing. fem.	בטן
בֵּבָי	[for בֵּבַי] pr. name masc. etymon not known.	
בְּבֵין[k]	pref. בְּ)(prep., prop. constr. of [בַּיִן] d. 6h.	בין
בַּבִּינָה[l]	pref. בַּ for בְּהַ)(noun fem. sing. dec. 10.	בין
בְּבִירְתָא[m]	Ch. pref. בְּ)(n. f. s., emph. of [בִּירָא] d.8a.	ביר
בַּבַּיִת / בַּבָּיִת	pref. בַּ f. בְּהַ } noun masc. sing. irr. (§ 45)	בית
בְּבַיִת	pref. בְּ q. v. } (id.)	בית
בְּבֵית	ו׳ pref. id.)(id. constr. st. Heb. & Ch. (§ 68), also pr. n. in compos. בְּבֵית־אֵל, &c.; וּ bef. (:)	בית
בְּבֵית	Kh. בְּבֵית, K. בֵּית (q. v.)	בית
בְּבֵיתָהּ[n]	pref. בְּ)(noun masc. sing., suff. 3 pers. sing. fem., from בַּיִת irr. (§ 45)	בית
בְּבֵיתוֹ	[o]ו׳ pref. id.)(id., suff. 3 pers. s. m.; וּ bef. (:)	בית
בְּבֵיתִי	[p]ו׳ pref. id.)(id., suff. 1 pers. sing. Heb. and Chald. (§ 68); וּ id.	בית
בְּבֵיתֶךָ / בְּבֵיתָךְ	pref. id.)(id., suff. 2 pers. sing. masc.	בית
בְּבִכּוּרֵיהֶם[q]	pref. בְּ bef. (:))(noun masc. pl., suff. 3 pers. pl. masc. from בִּכּוּר dec. 1a.	בכר
בַּבֶּכִי	pref. בַּ for בְּהַ } noun masc. sing. dec. 6i. (§ 35.r.14); וּ bef. lab.	בכה
בְּבֶכִי	[r]ו׳ pref. בְּ bef. (:) } (id.)	בכה
בִּבְכֹר[s]	pref. id.)(noun masc. sing. dec. 1a.	בכר
בִּבְכֹרוֹ[t]	pref. id.)(id., suff. 3 pers. sing. masc.	בכר
בָּבֶל	ו׳ pr. name of a city and province; וּ bef. lab.	בלל
בָּבֶלָה	id. with parag. ה	בלל
בְּבִלְהָה	וּ pref. בְּ)(pr. name fem.; וּ bef. (:)	בלה
בִּבְלִי	pref. בְּ bef. (:))((prop. subst.) adv.	בלה
בַּבְלָיֵא	Chald. pr. name of a people, pl. emph. [from בַּבְלָי § 63]	בלל
בְּבַלַּע[u]	pref. בְּ)(Piel inf. constr.	בלע
בַּבָּמָה	pref. בַּ for בְּהַ)(noun fem. sing. dec. 10.	בום
בַּבָּמוֹת	pref. id.)(id. pl.	בום
בְּבָמוֹתָם[x]	pref. בְּ)(id. pl., suff. 3 pers. pl. m. (§ 4. r. 2)	בום
בְּבֵן[ff]	pref. id.)(noun m. s. constr. of בֵּן irr. (§ 45)	בנה
בִּבְנָהּ[y]	וּ pref. בְּ bef. (:))(id., suff. 3 p.s.f.; וּ bef. lab.	בנה
בִּבְנוֹ[z]	pref. id.)(id., suff. 3 pers. sing. masc.	בנה
בִּבְנוֹת[a]	וּ pref. id.)(Kal inf. constr.; וּ bef. lab.	בנה
בִּבְנוֹת	pref. id.)(noun fem. pl., constr. of בָּנוֹת see בַּת irr. (§ 45)	בנה
בִּבְנוֹתֶיהָ	וּ pref. id.)(id., suff. 3 pers. s. f.; וּ bef. lab.	בנה
בִּבְנוֹתַיִךְ[b]	pref. id.)(Kal inf. (בְּנוֹת), suff. 2 p.s.f. for ־ֵךְ	בנה
בִּבְנוֹתְכֶם[c]	pref. id.)(id., suff. 2 pers. pl. masc.	בנה
בִּבְנוֹתֵנוּ[d]	וּ pref. id.)(noun fem. pl. (בָּנוֹת), suff. 1 pers. pl. see בַּת irr. (§ 45); וּ bef. labial	בנה
בִּבְנֵי	ו׳ pref. id.)(n. m. pl., constr. of בָּנִים, see בֵּן irr. (§45); also pr. n. in compos. בִּבְנֵי יַעֲקָן; וּ id.	בנה
בְּבָנֶיהָ[e]	וּ pref. בְּ)(id. pl., suff. 3 pers. s. f.; וּ id.	בנה
בְּבָנָיו[f]	pref. id.)(id., pl. suff. 3 pers. sing. masc.	בנה
בְּבָנֶיךָ[g]	[h]ו׳ pref. id.)(id. pl., suff. 2 p. s. m.; וּ bef. (:)	בנה
בַּבָּנִים	pref. בַּ for בְּהַ)(id. pl., absolute state	בנה
בְּבִנְיָמִן	ו׳ pref. בְּ)(pr. name of a tribe, see בִּנְיָמִין	בנה
בְּבָנֵינוּ[i]	pref. בְּ)(noun masc. pl. (בָּנִים), suff. 1 pers. pl., see בֵּן irr. (§ 45)	בנה
בִּבְנֹתֶיהָ[k]	וּ pref. בְּ bef. (:))(noun fem. pl. (בָּנוֹת), suff. 3 pers. sing. fem. see בַּת irr (§ 45)	בנה
בִּבְנֹתְכֶם[l]	pref. id.)(Kal inf. (בְּנוֹת), suff. 2 pers. pl. m.	בנה
בַּבַּעַל / בַּבָּעַל	pref. בַּ for בְּהַ)(n. m. s. dec. 6d, also pr. name in compos. as בְּבַעַל הָמוֹן, &c.	בעל
בִּבְעָלָיו[m]	pref. בְּ bef. (:))(id. pl., suff. 3 pers. s. m.	בעל
בַּבֹּץ[n]	pref. בַּ for בְּהַ)(noun masc. sing.	בצץ
בְּבֶצַע[o]	pref. בְּ)(n. m. s., (suff. בִּצְעוֹ) d.6a (§ 35.r.5)	בצע
בְּבָצְרָה	pref. id.)(pr. name of a place	בצר
בַּבִּקְעָה	pref. בַּ for בְּהַ)(noun fem. sing. dec. 12b.	בקע
בְּבִקְעַת	pref. בְּ)(id., construct state	בקע
בַּבָּקָר	[p]ו׳ pref. בַּ for בְּהַ)(n. m. s. d. 4a; וּ bef. lab.	בקר
בַּבֹּקֶר	ו׳ pref. id.)(n. m. s. d. 6c. (§ 35. r. 9); וּ id.	בקר
בַּבְּקָרִים[ll]	pref. id.)(noun masc., pl. of בָּקָר dec. 4a.	בקר
בִּבְקָרְךָ[q]	pref. בְּ bef. (:))(id. sing., suff. 2 pers. s. m.	בקר
בִּבְקָרָם[r]	וּ pref. id.)(id., suff. 3 pers. pl. m.; וּ bef. lab.	בקר
בִּבְקָרֵנוּ[s]	וּ pref. id.)(id., suff. 1 pers. pl.; וּ id.	בקר

[a] Le. 13. 25, 26. [b] Eze. 42. 12. [c] 2 Ch. 2. 13. [d] Je. 38. 6. [e] Ps. 88. 7. [f] Da. 11. 33. [g] Is. 30. 15. [h] Pr. 22. 18. [i] Ge. 25. 23. [k] Is. 44. 4. [l] Job 39. 17. [m] Ezr. 6. 2. [n] Pr. 7. 11. [o] 2 Ch. 7. 11. [p] Is. 3. 7. [q] Ps. 136. 10. [r] Joel 2. 12. [s] De. 15. 19. [t] Jos. 6. 26. [u] Hab. 1. 13. [x] Ps. 78. 58. [y] De. 28. 56. [z] Ex. 32. 29. [a] Eze. 17. 17. [b] Eze. 16. 31. [c] Jos. 22. 16. [d] Ex. 10. 9. [e] De. 28. 57. [f] 1 Sa. 16. 1. [ff] Pr. 17. 2. [g] Ex. 13. 13. [h] 2 Ch. 21. 14. [i] Ex. 10. 9. [k] Ne. 11. 28. [ll] Am. 6. 12. [l] Jos. 22. 19. [m] Ex. 21. 29. [n] Je. 38. 22. [o] Is. 33. 15. [p] 1 Ch. 12. 40. [q] De. 15. 19. [r] Ho. 5. 6. [s] Ex. 10. 9.

Word	Analysis	Root
בְּבַקָּשָׁתִי [a]	pref. בְּ)(n. f. s., suff. 1 p. s. from בַּקָּשָׁה d. 10.	בקש
בַּבָּר [b]	pref. בַּ for בְּהַ)(noun masc. sing. [for בַּר]	ברר
בְּבֹר [c]	pref. בְּ)(noun masc. sing. dec. 1 a.	ברר
בַּבָּרָד [d]	[e] ׳ו pref. בַּ for בְּהַ)(noun m. s.; וּ bef. lab.	ברד
וּבַבֹּרוֹת [f]	׳ו pref. id.)(noun masc. with pl. fem. term. from בּוֹר dec. 1; ׳ו id.	באר
בִּבְרוּתִי [g]	pref. בְּ)(noun f. s., suff. 1 pers. sing. d. 1 b.	ברה
בַּבַּרְזֶל * ׳ו בְּבַרְזֶל [h] ׳ו	pref. בַּ f. בְּהַ pref. בְּ } noun masc. sing.; וּ before labial, *2 Ch. 2. 6	ברזל
בִּבְרֹחַ [k]	pref. בִּ bef. (:))(Kal inf. constr.	ברח
בְּבָרְחוֹ	pref. בְּ)(id., suff. 3 pers. sing. masc.	ברח
בְּבָרְחִי [l]	pref. id.)(id., suff. 1 pers. sing.	ברח
בְּבָרְחֲךָ [m]	pref. id.)(id., suff. 2 pers. sing. masc.	ברח
בַּבְּרִית בִּבְרִית	pref. בַּ for בְּהַ pref. בִּ bef. (:) } noun fem. sing. dec. 1 a.	ברה
בִּבְרִיתוֹ [n]	pref. id.)(id., suff. 3 pers. sing. masc.	ברה
בִּבְרִיתִי [o]	pref. id.)(id., suff. 1 pers. sing.	ברה
בִּבְרִיתֶךָ [p]	pref. id.)(id., suff. 2 pers. s. m. [for בְּרִיתְךָ]	ברה
בִּבְרָכָה [q]	pref. id.)(noun fem. sing. dec. 11 c.	ברך
בְּבָרְכוֹ [r]	pref. בְּ)(Piel inf. (בָּרֵךְ), suff. 3 pers. sing. masc. [for בָּרְכוֹ dec. 7 b.]	ברך
בְּבִרְכַּת [s]	pref. id.)(n. f. s., constr. of בְּרָכָה dec. 11 c.	ברך
בַּבְּשָׂמִים [t]	pref. בַּ for בְּהַ)(noun m., pl. of בֶּשֶׂם dec. 6.	בשם
בַּבָּשָׁן ׳ו	׳ו pref. id.)(pr. name of a region; וּ bef. lab.	בשן
בַּבָּשָׂר	pref. id.)(noun masc. sing. dec. 4 c.	בשׂר
בִּבְשַׂר [u]	pref. בִּ bef. (:))(id., construct state	בשׂר
בִּבְשָׂרָהּ	pref. id.)(id., suff. 3 pers. sing. fem.	בשׂר
בִּבְשָׂרִי [x]	[y] ׳ו pref. id.)(id., suff. 1 pers. sing.; וּ bef. lab.	בשׂר
בִּבְשַׂרְכֶם	pref. id.)(id., suff. 2 pers. pl. masc.	בשׂר
בִּבְשָׂרָם [z]	׳ו pref. id.)(id., suff. 3 pers. pl. m.; וּ bef. lab.	בשׂר
בְּבֹשֶׁת	[a] ׳ו pref. בְּ)(noun fem. sing. dec. 13 c. (§ 39. No. 4. d.); וּ id.	בוש
בְּבָשְׁתֵּנוּ [b]	pref. id.)(id., suff. 1 pers. pl.	בוש
בְּבַת	pref. id.)(noun fem. sing. irr. (§ 43)	בנה
בְּבִתָּהּ [c]	׳ו pref. id.)(id., suff. 3 pers. sing. fem. comp. dec. 8 e; וּ bef. (:)	בנה
בִּבְתוּאֵל	׳ו pref. בִּ bef. (:))(pr. name of a place, see בְּתוּאֵל; וּ id.	
בִּבְתוּלֶיהָ [d]	pref. בִּ bef. (:))(noun masc. pl., suff. 3 pers. sing. fem. [from בְּתוּל dec. 1 a.]	בתל
בְּבָתֵּי	[e] ׳ו pref. בְּ)(noun masc. pl., constr. of בָּתִּים, see בַּיִת irr. (§ 45); וּ bef. (:)	בית
בְּבָתֵּיהֶם [f]	׳ו pref. id.)(id. pl., suff. 3 pers. pl. masc.	בית
בְּבָתֵּיךְ [g]	׳ו pref. id.)(id. pl., suff. 2 p. pl. m.; וּ bef. (:)	בית
בְּבָתֵּיכֶם	pref. id.)(id. pl., suff. 2 pers. pl. masc.	בית
בַּבָּתִּים	pref. בַּ for בְּהַ)(id. pl., absolute state	בית
בְּבִתְּכֶם [h]	pref. בְּ)(noun fem. sing., suff. 2 pers. pl. masc. from בַּת irr. (§ 45)	בנה
[בַּג]	*food*, only Eze. 25. 7. Kheth. (K. בַּז) found besides in the compound פַּתְבַּג q. v.	
בְּגַאֲוָה	pref. id.)(noun fem. sing. (no vowel change)	גאה
בִּגְאוֹן	pref. בִּ bef. (:))(n. m. s., constr. of גָּאוֹן d. 3 a.	גאה
בִּגְאוֹנָם [i]	pref. id.)(id., suff. 3 pers. pl. masc.	גאה
בְּגַאֲוַת [k]	pref. בְּ)(noun fem. sing., constr. of גַּאֲוָה (no vowel change)	גאה
בְּגֵאוּת	pref. id.)(noun fem. sing.	גאה
וּבְגַאֲוָתוֹ [l]	[m] ׳ו pref. id.)(noun fem. sing., suff. 3 pers. sing. masc. from גַּאֲוָה (q. v.); וּ bef. (:)	גאה
בְּגֹב	pref. id.)(pr. name of a place	גוב
בְּגַבָּהּ [n]	pref. id.)(noun masc. sing. dec. 6 c. (§ 35. r. 5)	גבה
בְּגַבָּהוּ	pref. id.)(id., suff. 3 pers. sing. masc.	גבה
בְּגַבֵּהֶם [o]	pref. id.)(id., suff. 3 pers. pl. masc.	גבה
בִּגְבוּל	pref. בִּ bef. (:))(noun masc. sing. dec. 1 a.	גבל
בִּגְבוּלַיִךְ [p]	pref. id.)(id. pl., suff. 2 pers. s. m. [for לַיִךְ]	גבל
בִּגְבוּלָם [q]	pref. id.)(id. sing., suff. 3 pers. pl. masc.	גבל
בִּגְבוּלֵנוּ [r]	pref. id.)(id. sing., suff. 1 pers. pl.	גבל
בְּגִבּוֹר [s]	pref. בְּ)(noun masc. sing. dec. 1 b.	גבר
בִּגְבוּרָה	pref. בִּ bef. (:))(noun fem. sing. dec. 10.	גבר
בִּגְבוּרוֹת [t]	pref. id.)(id. pl.	גבר
בַּגִּבֹּרִים	pref. בַּ for בְּהַ)(noun m., pl. of גִּבּוֹר dec. 1 b.	גבר
בִּגְבוּרַת [u]	pref. בִּ bef. (:))(noun fem. sing., constr. of גְּבוּרָה dec. 10.	גבר
בִּגְבוּרֹת [x]	pref. id.)(id. pl.	גבר
בִּגְבוּרָתוֹ	pref. id.)(id. sing., suff. 3 pers. sing. masc.	גבר
בִּגְבוּרֹתָיו [y]	pref. id.)(id. pl., suff. 3 pers. sing. masc.	גבר
וּבִגְבוּרָתְךָ [z]	׳ו pref. id.)(id. s., suff. 2 p. s. m.; וּ bef. lab.	גבר
בִּגְבוּרָתָם [a]	pref. id.)(id. sing., suff. 3 pers. pl. masc.	גבר
בַּגַּבַּחַת [b]	pref. בַּ for בְּהַ)(noun fem. sing. dec. 13 a.	גבח
בְּגַבַּחְתּוֹ	pref. בְּ)(id., suff. 3 pers. sing. masc.	גבח
בִּגְבֻלוֹ	pref. בִּ bef. (:))(noun masc. sing., suff. 3 pers. sing. masc. from גְּבוּל dec. 1 a.	גבל
בִּגְבֻלֵךְ [c]	pref. id.)(id., suff. 2 p. s. m. [for גְּבוּלְךָ=גְּבֻלְךָ]	גבל
בִּגְבֻלֹת [d]	pref. id.)(noun fem., pl. of [גְּבוּלָה] dec. 10.	גבל
בְּגֶבַע	pref. בְּ)(pr. name of a place	גבע
בַּגִּבְעָה	pref. בַּ for בְּהַ)(pr. name of a place	גבע
בְּגִבְעוֹן	׳ו pref. בְּ)(pr. name of a place; וּ bef. (:)	גבע
בְּגִבְעַת	pref. בְּ)(n. f. s., constr. of גִּבְעָה dec. 12 b, also pr. name בְּגִבְעַת בִּנְיָמִין	גבע
בִּגְבָרוֹת [e]	pref. בִּ bef. (:))(n. fem., pl. of גְּבוּרָה d. 10.	גבר
בִּגְבַרְתּוֹ [f]	pref. id.)(id. sing., suff. 3 pers. sing. masc.	גבר
בְּגִבְּתוֹן	pref. בְּ)(pr. name of a place	גבב

[a] Est. 7. 3. [b] Job 39. 4. [c] Job 22. 30. [d] Ps. 78. 47. [e] Hag. 2. 17. [f] 1 Sa. 13. 6.
[g] Ps. 69. 22. [h] Pr. 27. 17. [i] Jos. 22. 8. [k] 1 Sa. 23. 6. [l] 1 Ki. 2. 7. [m] Ge. 35. 1.
[n] Ps. 78. 37. [o] Is. 56. 4, 6. [p] Ps. 44. 18. [q] Ps. 109. 17. [r] Ge. 28. 6. [s] Pr. 11. 11.
[t] Est. 2. 12. [u] Le. 15. 7. [x] Ps. 38. 4, 8. [y] Job 19. 20. [z] Le. 21. 5. [a] Ezr. 9. 7.
[b] Je. 3. 25. [c] De. 28. 56. [d] Le. 21. 13. [e] Is. 42. 22. [f] De. 19. 1. [g] Ex. 8. 17.
[h] Ge. 34. 8. [i] Ps. 59. 13. [k] Ps. 10. 2. [l] Ps. 46. 4. [m] De. 33. 26. [n] 2 Ch. 32. 26.
[o] Eze. 31. 14. [p] Is. 60. 18. [q] 1 Ch. 6. 39. [r] Mi. 5. 5. [s] Je. 46. 12. [t] Ps. 20. 7.
[u] Ps. 147. 10. [x] Ps. 90. 10. [y] Ps. 150. 2. [z] Ps. 54. 3. [a] Eze. 32. 29.
[b] Le. 13. 42. [c] Ex. 10. 4. [d] Nu. 32. 33. [e] Ps. 71. 16. [f] Ju. 5. 31.

[בָּגַד] *to act covertly, to deal falsely, treacherously*, const. absol. also with מִן, oftener with בְּ; part. בּוֹגֵד *treacherous person.*

בָּגוֹד adj. only fem. בָּגוֹדָה (Kamets impure, § 39. No. 3. rem. 2) *treacherous*, Je. 3. 7, 10.

בֶּגֶד masc. with suff. בִּגְדִי dec. 6a. (but in pause בָּגֶד § 35. rem. 2 & 4)—I. *a covering, wrapper.*—II. *cloak, garment.*—III. *faithlessness, treachery*, Je. 12. 1.—IV. *rapine, violence*, Is. 24. 16.

בֹּגְדוֹת fem. pl. *treachery*, Zeph. 3. 4.

בְּגָד[a] Kh. בְּגָד (pref. בְּ) n. m.; K. בָּא גָד (q. v.) — בוא, גדד

בָּגֶד in pause, as if from [בֶּגֶד § 35. r. 2] and וּ בֶגֶד n. m. s. (suff. בִּגְדִי) dec. 6a; וּ bef. lab. — בגד

בֹּגֵד[b] Kal part. act. sing. masc. dec. 7b. — בגד

בָּגְדָה id. pret. 3 pers. sing. fem. — בגד

בֹּגֵדָה[c] id. part. act. s. f. fr. בֹּגֵד m. (§ 39. No. 3. r. 4) — בגד

בָּגְדוּ, בָּגָדוּ id. pret. 3 pers. pl. (§ 8. rem. 7) — בגד

בִּגְדוֹ n. m. s., suff. 3 pers. s. m. from בֶּגֶד dec. 6a. — בגד

בַּגְּדוּד[d] pref. בַּ for בְּהַ) noun masc. sing. dec. 1a. — גדד

בַּגָּדֹל[e] pref. id.) adj. masc. sing. dec. 3a. — גדל

בֹּגְדוֹת[f] noun fem. pl. — בגד

בִּגְדִי n. m. pl., suff. 1 p. s. from בֶּגֶד d. 6. (§ 35. r. 3) — בגד

וּ בִגְדֵי id. pl., construct state; וּ bef. lab. — בגד

בִּגְדִי[g] id. sing., suff. 1 pers. sing. — בגד

בִּגְדִי[h] pref. בְּ bef. (:)) noun masc. sing. dec. 6i. — גדה

בֹּגְדֵי Kal part act. pl. constr. m. from בֹּגֵד d. 7b. — בגד

בְּגָדֶיהָ noun m. pl., suff. 3 pers. s. f. from בֶּגֶד d. 6a. — בגד

בִּגְדֵיהֶם id. pl., suff. 3 pers. pl. masc. — בגד

וּ בְגָדָיו id. pl., suff. 3 pers. sing. masc.; וּ bef. (:) — בגד

בְּגָדַיִךְ[i], בְּגָדָיִךְ[k] id. pl., suff. 2 pers. sing. fem. — בגד

וּ בְגָדֶיךָ[l] id. pl., suff. 2 pers. sing. masc.; וּ bef. lab. — בגד

וּ בִגְדֵיכֶם[m] id. pl., suff. 2 pers. pl. masc.; וּ id. — בגד

וּ בְגָדִים id. pl., absolute state; וּ id. — בגד

בֹּגְדִים Kal part. act. masc., pl. of בֹּגֵד dec. 7b. — בגד

בְּגָדֵינוּ[n] n. m. pl., suff. 1 pers. pl. from בֶּגֶד dec. 6a. — בגד

בִּגְדֹל[o] pref. בְּ bef. (:)) n. m. s., constr. of גָּדוֹל d. 3a. — גדל

וּ בְגֹדֶל pref. בְּ) noun masc. sing. dec. 6c; וּ bef. (:) — גדל

בְּגָדְלוֹ[p] pref. id.) id., suff. 3 pers. sing. masc. — גדל

בִּגְדֹלוֹת[q] pref. בְּ bef. (:)) adj. fem., pl. of גְּדוֹלָה dec. 10, from גָּדוֹל masc. — גדל

בְּגָדְלֶךָ pref. בְּ) n. m. s., suff. 2 p. s. m. fr. גֹּדֶל d. 6c. — גדל

בַּגְּדֵרוֹת pref. בַּ for בְּהַ) noun fem., pl. of גְּדֵרָה dec. 11c. (§ 42. rem. 4) — גדר

בָּגַדְתָּה[r] Kal pret. 2 pers. sing. masc. (§ 8. rem. 5) — בגד

בָּגַדְתִּי[s] id. pret. 1 pers. sing. [for בָּגַדְתִּי § 8. r. 7] — בגד

בִּגְדֹתָיִךְ[t] noun masc. with pl. fem. term. and suff. 2 pers. sing. masc. from בֶּגֶד dec. 6a. — בגד

בְּגַדְתֶּם Kal pret. 2 pers. pl. masc. — בגד

בְּגוֹ[u], בְּגוֹא[u] Ch. pref. בְּ) noun masc. sing., constr. of גַּו irr. (§ 68) *Da. 7. 15. — גוה

בְּגוֹב pr. name of a place — גוב

בָּגוֹד Kal inf. abs. — בגד

בָּגוֹדָה[x] adj. fem. s. [from בָּגוֹד m. § 39. No. 3. r. 2] — בגד

בְּגַוַּהּ[y], בְּגַוַּהּ[z] Ch. pref. בְּ) noun masc. sing., suff. 3 pers. sing. fem. from גַּו irr. (§ 68) — גוה

בְּגַוֵּהּ[a] Ch. pref. id.) id., suff. 3 pers. sing. masc. — גוה

בְּגֵוָה[b] Chald. pref. id.) noun fem. sing. — גאה

בִּגְוַי, בִּגְוָי pr. name masc. etymon doubtful.

בְּגוֹי pref. בְּ) noun masc. sing. dec. 1a. — גוה

בְּגוֹיֵהֶם pref. id.) id. pl., suff. 3 p. pl. m. (§ 4. r. 1) — גוה

וּ בַגּוֹיִם pref. בַּ f. בְּהַ; בְּגוֹיִם[c] pref. בְּ q. v. — id. pl., absolute state — גוה

בִּגְוִיַּת[d] pref. בְּ bef. (:)) n. f. s., constr. of גְּוִיָּה d. 10. — גוה

בִּגְוִיֹּתָם[e] pref. id.) id., suff. 3 pers. pl. masc. — גוה

וּ בַגּוֹלָה[f] pref. בַּ for בְּהַ) noun fem. sing.; וּ bef. lab. — גלה

בִּגְוֹעַ[g] pref. בְּ bef. (:)) Kal inf. constr. — גוע

בְּגוּר־ pref. בְּ) pr. name in compos. בְּגוּר־בַּעַל — גור

בַּגּוֹרָל pref. בַּ f. בְּהַ; בְּגוֹרָל pref. בְּ q. v. — noun masc. sing. dec. 2b. — גרל

בְּגוֹרַל[h] pref. id.) id., construct state — גרל

בְּגוֹרָלוֹת[i] pref. id.) id. pl., absolute state — גרל

בְּגוֹרָלֶךָ[k] pref. id.) id. s., suff. 2 p. s. m. [for רָלְךָ] — גרל

בַּגִּזָּה[l] pref. בַּ for בְּהַ) noun fem. sing. dec. 10. — גזז

בִּגְזֹז[m] pref. בְּ bef. (:)) Kal inf. constr. — גזז

בְּגָזִית[n] pref. בְּ) noun fem. sing. — גזה

וּ בְגָזֶל[o] pref. id.) noun masc. sing. — גזל

בְּגֶזֶר, בְּגָזֶר pref. id.) pr. name of a place (§ 35. r. 2) — גזר

בִּגְזֵרַת[q] pref. בְּ bef. (:)) n. f. s., constr. of גְּזֵרָה d. 10. — גזר

בְּגִיחוֹן pref. בְּ) pr. name of a stream — גיח

בַּגַּיְ[r] pref. בַּ for בְּהַ) noun com. sing. irr. (§ 45) — גיא

וּ בְגֵי pref. בְּ) id., constr. st. (§ 37. r. 6); וּ bef. (:) — גיא

בַּגַּיְא[s], בַּגַּיְא pref. בַּ for בְּהַ) noun com. sing. irr. (§ 45) — גיא

בְּגֵיא pref. בְּ) id., construct state (§ 37. rem. 6) — גיא

בְּגִיד[w] pref. id.) noun masc. sing. dec. 1a. — גיד

בְּגִיחוֹ[x] pref. id.) Kal inf., suff. 3 pers. sing. masc. — גיח

בַּגֹּיִים[y] Kheth., but Keri בַּגּוֹיִם (q. v.) — גוה

[a] Ge. 30. 11. [b] Pr. 22. 12. [c] Ja. 3. 8. [d] Job 29. 25. [e] Ge. 44. 12. [f] Zep. 3. 4. [g] Ezr. 9. 3, 5. [h] Ju. 15. 1. [i] Eze. 23. 26. [k] Eze. 16. 39. [l] Is. 63. 2. [m] Le. 10. 6. [n] Ne. 4. 17. [o] Ex. 15. 16. [p] Eze. 31. 7. [q] Ps. 131. 1. [r] Mal. 2. 14. [s] Ps. 73. 15. [t] Ps. 45. 9. [u] Da. 3. 25; 4. 7. [x] Je. 3. 7, 10. [y] Ezr. 4. 15. [z] Ezr. 6. 2. [a] Ezr. 5. 7. [b] Da. 4. 34. [c] De. 15. 6. [d] Ju. 14. 8. [e] Na. 3. 8. [f] Je. 48. 11. [g] Nu. 20. 3. [h] Jos. 14. 2. [i] 1 Ch. 24. 5. [k] Ju. 1. 3. [l] Ju. 6. 39. [m] 1 Sa. 25. 2. [n] La. 3. 9. [o] Le. 5. 21. [p] Ps. 62. 11. [q] Da. 4. 14. [r] De. 34. 6. [s] Jos. 19. 27. [t] De. 3. 29. [w] Ge. 32. 33. [x] Job 38. 8. [y] Ps. 79. 10.

בַּגִּלְבֹּעַ	pref. בַּ for בְּהַ)(pr. name of a place .	גלל
[a] בַּגַּלְגַּל	pref. id.)(noun m. s. dec. 8 d. (§ 37. No. 2)	גלל
בַּגִּלְגָּל	pref. id.)(pr. name of a place . .	גלל
[b] בְּגִלּוּלֵי	וּ pref. בְּ)(noun masc. pl. constr. from [גִּלּוּל] d. 1 b; וּ bef. (:)	גלל
בְּגִלּוּלֵיהֶם	וּ/ pref. id.)(id. pl., suff. 3 pers. pl. masc.; וּ id.	גלל
[c] בְּגִלּוּלָיו	pref. id.)(id. pl., suff. 3 pers. sing. masc.	גלל
[d] בְּגִלּוּלַיִךְ	וּ pref. id.)(id. pl., suff. 2 p. s. f.; וּ bef. (:)	גלל
בְּגִלּוּלֵיכֶם	וּ pref. id.)(id. pl., suff. 2 pers. pl. m.; וּ id.	גלל
[f] בִּגְלוֹמֵי	pref. בְּ bef. (:))(n.m.pl.constr.fr.[גְּלוֹם] d.1a.	גלם
[g] בַּגְּלוֹתוֹ	pref. בַּ, contr. for בְּהַגְלוֹתוֹ, Hiph. inf., suff. 3 pers. sing. masc. (§ 11. rem. 3) .	גלה
[h] בְּגַלְּחוֹ	וּ pref. בְּ)(Piel inf. [גַּלַּח], suff. 3 pers. sing. masc.; וּ before (:)	גלח
בַּגָּלִיל	pref. בַּ for בְּהַ)(pr. name of a region .	גלל
בִּגְלַל	i/ וּ pref. בְּ bef. (:))(prep.; prop. noun masc. constr. of גָּלָל dec. 4 c; וּ id. . .	גלל
[k] בְּגִלְלֵי	pref. בְּ)(n.m.pl.constr.fr.[גֵּלֶל] d.6. (§ 35.r.3.)	גלל
[l] בִּגְלָלְךָ	pref. בְּ bef. (:))(noun masc. sing., suff. 2 pers. sing. masc. from גָּלָל dec. 4 a. . .	גלל
[m] בִּגְלָלֵךְ	pref. id.)(id., suff. 2 pers. sing. fem.	גלל
בִּגְלַלְכֶם	pref. id.)(id., suff. 2 pers. pl. masc. .	גלל
בַּגִּלְעָד / בְּגִלְעָד	pref. בַּ f. בְּהַ / pref. בְּ q. v. } pr. name of a region, see גִּלְעָד	
[n] בַּגְּמַלִּים	o/ וּ pref. בַּ for בְּהַ)(noun masc., pl. of גָּמָל dec. 8 a. (§ 37. rem. 2) . . .	גמל
[p] בַּגָּן / בְּגָן	pref. id. / pref. בְּ } noun com. sing. dec. 8 d. .	גנן
[q] בַּגְּנָבִים	pref. id.)(noun m. s. dec. 1 b. (§ 30. No. 3)	גנב
[r] בִּגְנֵבָתוֹ	pref. בְּ bef. (:))(noun fem. sing., suff. 3 pers. sing. masc. from גְּנֵבָה dec. 10. . .	גנב
[s] בַּגַּנּוֹת	pref. בַּ for בְּהַ)(noun f., pl. of גַּנָּה dec. 10.	גנן
[t] בְּגִנְזֵי	וּ pref. בְּ)(noun masc. pl. constr. from [גֶּנֶז] dec. 6 b; וּ bef. (:)	גנז
בַּגַּנִּים	pref. בַּ for בְּהַ)(n. com., pl. of גַּן dec. 8 d.	גנן
[u] בְּגֹעַל	pref. בְּ)(noun masc. sing. . . .	געל
[v] בְּגַעֲרַת	pref. בְּ)(n.f.s., constr. of גְּעָרָה d.11 c. (§ 42.r.1)	גער
[w] בְּגַעֲרָתִי	pref. id.)(id., suff. 1 pers. sing. . .	גער
[x] בְּגַפּוֹ	pref. id.)(noun masc. sing., suff. 3 pers. sing. masc. from [גַּף] dec. 8 d. . . .	גפף
[a] בַּגֶּפֶן	b/ וּ pref. בַּ for בְּהַ)(noun com. sing., (suff. גַּפְנִי) dec. 6 a; וּ bef. labial . .	גפן
[c] בַּגְּפָנִים	pref. id.)(id. pl., absolute state .	גפן
[d] בַּגֵּר	e/ וּ pref. id.)(noun m. s. dec. 1 a; וּ bef. lab.	גור
[f] בְּגָרָב	וּ pref. id.)(noun masc. sing.; וּ id. .	גרב
[g] בְּגָרוֹן	pref. בְּ)(noun masc. sing. dec. 3 a. . .	גרה
בִּגְרוֹנָם	pref. בְּ bef. (:))(id., suff. 3 pers. pl. masc.	גרה
[h] בְּגֵרוּת	pref. בְּ)(noun fem. sing. . . .	גור
[i] בַּגַּרְזֶן	pref. בַּ for בְּהַ)(noun masc. sing. . .	גרז
[k] בְּגֹרָלִי	pref. בְּ)(n. m. s., suff. 1 p. s. fr. גּוֹרָל d. 2 b.	גרל
[l] בַּגֹּרֶן / בְּגֹרֶן	pref. בַּ f. בְּהַ / pref. בְּ q. v. } noun fem. sing. dec. 6 c. .	גרן
בִּגְרָר	pref. בְּ bef. (:))(pr. name of a place .	גרר
בִּגְשׁוּר	pref. id.)(pr. name of a place, see גְּשׁוּר	
[m] בְּגֶשְׁמְהוֹן	Ch. pref. בְּ)(noun masc. sing., suff. 3 pers. pl. masc. [from גֶּשֶׁם dec. 3. § 59] .	גשם
[n] בְּגֶשֶׁת	pref. id.)(Kal inf. constr. dec. 13 a. .	נגש
בְּגִשְׁתָּם	pref. id.)(id., suff. 3 pers. pl. masc. .	נגש
[o] בַּגַּת / [p] בְּגַת	pref. בַּ f. בְּהַ / pref. בְּ q. v. } noun fem. sing. dec. 6 e. .	גת
בִּגְתָא	pr. name of a eunuch of Ahasuerus, Est. 1. 10.	
בִּגְתָן / בִּגְתָנָא	} pr. name of a eunuch of Ahasuerus, Est. 2. 21; 6. 2.	
בַּד / בָּד	} noun masc. sing. dec. 8 d. . .	בדד
בָּדָא [q]	*to devise, feign.*	
[r] בִּדְאָגָה	וּ/ וּ pref. בְּ bef. (:))(noun fem. s.; וּ bef. lab.	דאג
בַּדְּבִיר	pref. בַּ for בְּהַ)(noun masc. sing. . .	דבר
בְּדָבָר	וּ/ וּ pref. id.)(noun m. s. dec. 4 a; וּ bef. lab.	דבר
בַּדֶּבֶר [s] / בַּדָּבֶר	t/ וּ / u/ וּ } pref. בַּ for בְּהַ)(noun masc. sing. dec. 6 a. (§ 35. r. 2); וּ bef. lab.	דבר
בְּדָבָר	pref. בְּ)(noun masc. sing. dec. 4 a. .	דבר
בְּדַבֵּר	w/ וּ pref. id.)(Piel inf. constr. d. 7 b; וּ bef. (:)	דבר
בְּדֶבֶר	pref. id.)(noun masc. sing. dec. 6 a. . .	דבר
בִּדְבַר	y/ וּ pref. בְּ bef. (:))(noun masc. sing., constr. of דָּבָר dec. 4 a; וּ bef. lab. . .	דבר
בְּדַבְּרוֹ	z/ וּ pref. בְּ)(Piel inf. (דַּבֵּר), suff. 3 pers. sing. masc. dec. 7 b; וּ id. . .	דבר
בִּדְבָרוֹ	pref. בְּ bef. (:))(noun masc. sing., suff. 3 pers. sing. masc. from דָּבָר dec. 4 a. .	דבר
[a] בְּדַבְּרִי	b/ וּ pref. בְּ)(Piel inf. (דַּבֵּר), suff. 1 pers. sing. dec. 7 b; וּ bef. (:) . . .	דבר
בְּדִבְרֵי	pref. id.)(n. m. pl. constr. from דָּבָר d. 4 a.	דבר
[c] בִּדְבָרַי	pref. בְּ bef. (:))(id. pl., suff. 1 pers. sing.	דבר
[d] בִּדְבָרֶיהָ	pref. id.)(id. pl., suff. 3 pers. sing. fem.	דבר
בִּדְבָרָיו	pref. id.)(id. pl., suff. 3 pers. sing. masc. .	דבר
[e] בִּדְבָרֶיךָ	pref. id.)(id. pl., suff. 2 pers. sing. masc.	דבר
[f] בִּדְבָרֶיךָ	וּ pref. id.)(id. id. (Kh. בִּדְבָרֶיךָ, K. בִּדְבָרְךָ), sing. with suff. 2 pers. sing. masc.	דבר

[a] Ps. 77. 19. [b] Eze. 20. 7. [c] 2 Ki. 21. 11. [d] Eze. 22. 4. [e] Eze. 20. 39. [f] Eze. 27. 24.
[g] Je. 27. 20. [h] 2 Sa. 14. 26. [i] De. 18. 12. [k] Eze. 4. 12. [l] Ge. 30. 27. [m] Ge. 12. 13.
[n] Ex. 9. 3. [o] 1 Ch. 12. 40. [p] Ge. 3. 8, 10. [q] Je. 48. 27. [r] Ex. 22. 2. [s] Is. 65. 3.
[t] Eze. 27. 24. [u] Eze. 16. 5. [v] 2 Sa. 22. 16. [w] Is. 50. 2. [x] Ex. 21. 3, 4. [a] Je. 8. 13.
[b] Ge. 40. 10. [c] Hab. 3. 17. [d] Ex. 12. 19. [e] Le. 17. 15. [f] De. 28. 27. [g] Is. 58. 1.
[h] Je. 41. 17. [i] De. 19. 5. [k] Ju. 1. 3. [l] Ju. 6. 37. [m] Da. 3. 27. [n] Nu. 8. 19.
[o] Ju. 6. 11. [p] Is. 63. 2. [q] 1 Ki. 12. 33. [r] Eze. 12. 19. [s] Ex. 9. 15. [t] Je. 21. 9.
[u] Je. 14. 12. [w] Is. 32. 7. [y] 2 Ch. 8. 13. [z] 2 Ki. 1. 16. [a] Ex. 19. 9.
[b] Eze. 3. 27. [c] Eze. 3. 4. [d] Ju. 16. 16. [e] Da. 10. 12. [f] 1 Ki. 18. 36.

בְּדִבְרֵיכֶם[a] pref. בְּ)(id. pl., suff. 2 pers. pl. masc. . דבר

בַּדְּבָרִים pref. בַּ for בְּהַ } id. pl., absolute state . דבר
בִּדְבָרִים pref. בִּ bef. (:) }

בְּדַבֶּרְךָ[b] pref. בְּ)(Kal inf., suff. 2 p. s. m. [for רְךָ] דבר

בִּדְבָרֶךָ[c] pref. בִּ bef. (:))(noun m. sing., suff. 2 pers. sing. masc. [for בִּדְבָרְךָ] from דָּבָר dec. 4a. דבר

בְּדַבֶּרְכֶם[d] pref. בְּ)(Piel inf. (דַּבֵּר), suff. 2 pers. pl. masc. dec. 7b. (§ 36. rem. 3) . דבר

בְּדִבְרָם pref. id.)(id., suff. 3 pers. pl. masc. . דבר

בִּדְבַשׁ[e] pref. בִּ bef. (:))([for בִּדְבַשׁ] noun m. sing. dec. 6. (§ 35. rem. 10) . דבש

בְּדַבָּשֶׁת pref. בְּ)(pr. name of a place, for דַּבֶּשֶׁת דבש

בִּדְגַת[f] pref. בִּ bef. (:))(n. f. s., constr. of דָּגָה d. 11a. דגה

[בָּדַד] I. *to be separate, solitary,* only part. בּוֹדֵד *solitary.*—II. in the deriv. *to devise, feign,* comp. בָּדָא, בָּטָא, see בַּד below.

בָּדָד masc. prop. *separation,* only as an adv. לְבָדָד and בָּדָד *solitary, alone.*

בְּדַד (*separation*) pr. name masc. Ge. 36. 35.

בַּד masc. dec. 8d.—I. *a part.*—II. pl. בַּדִּים *parts of a body, members, limbs.*—III. *branches.*—IV. *staves, poles;* metaph. *princes,* Ho. 11. 6.—V. בַּד, *fine linen,* pl. *linen garments.*—VI. pl. *lies,* comp. בָּדָד No. II.—VII. לְבַד *separately, alone;* לְבַדִּי, לְבַדְּךָ, לְבַדּוֹ, &c. *I, thou, he alone;* לְבַד מִן and מִלְּבַד *besides;* לְבַד עַל, Eze. 1. 6, and מִלְּבַד אֲשֶׁר, Nu. 6. 21. *besides that which.*

בָּדָד adv. . . . . בדד

בְּדַד pr. name masc. . . . . . בדד

בַּדּוּד[g] pref. בַּ for בְּהַ)(noun masc. sing. pl. דּוּדִים & דְּוָדִים (§ 35. rem. 13) . . . דוד

בְּדָוִד pref. בְּ)(pr. name masc. . . . דוד

בְּדוּדָאֵי[h] pref. id.)(n. m. pl. constr. [from דּוּדַי § 35. r. 15] דוד

בַּדּוּדִים[ll] pref. בַּ for בְּהַ)(noun m., pl. of דּוּד d. 1a. דוד

בִּדְוָדִים[i] ו pref. id.)(id. pl. abs. (§ 35. r. 13); ו bef. labial דוד

בְּדָוִיד pref. בְּ)(pr. name masc. . . . דוד

בַּדּוֹר[k] pref. בַּ f. בְּהַ } noun masc. sing. dec. 1a. דור
בְּדוֹר pref. בְּ q.v. }

בַּדֵּי noun masc. pl. constr. from בַּד dec. 8d. בדד

בְּדֵי pref. בְּ)(prep., prop. subst. masc. constr. of דַּי dec. 8d. (§ 37. rem. 6) . . די

בְּדִיבֹן ו׳ pref. id.)(pr. name of a place . . דוב

בַּדֶּיהָ[l] noun m. pl., suff. 3 pers. s. f. from בַּד d. 8d. בדד

בֵּדְיָה (perh. for בְּאֵד יָהּ *in the strength of the Lord,* comp. R. אוד) pr. name m. Ezr. 10. 35.

בַּדָּיו noun m. pl., suff. 3 pers. s. m. from בַּד d. 8d. בדד

בַּדְּיוֹ[m] pref. בַּ for בְּהַ)(noun masc. sing. . דיה

בַּדֶּיךָ[n] noun m. pl., suff. 2 pers. s. m. from בַּד d. 8d. בדד

בְּדִיל[o] ו״ noun masc. sing. dec. 1a; ו before (:) . בדל

בְּדִילָיִךְ* id. pl., suff. 2 pers. s. f. [for לַיִךְ], *Is. 1. 25. בדל

בַּדִּים noun masc., pl. of בַּד dec. 8d. . . בדד

בְּדִינָה pref. בְּ)(pr. name fem. . . . דין

בְּדִישׁוֹ[q] pref. id.)(Kal inf. [דִּישׁ], suff. 3 pers. sing. masc. dec. 1a. . . . . . דיש

בָּדַל Niph. I. *to be separated,* with מִן from, *to be chose[n] out,* with לְ *to* any thing.—II. *to depart,* with מִן of the place and אֶל of the person. Hiph. I. *[to] separate, to make a division,* const. with בֵּין.—I[I.] *to distinguish,* const. with בֵּין—לְ, בֵּין—לְבֵין, בֵּין—וּבֵין, —III. *to separate, select,* with מִן, מֵעַל, לְ.

בָּדָל masc. d. 4a, *part, portion,* only, Am. 3. 12.

בְּדִיל masc. dec. 1a, *tin.*

מִבְדָּלָה fem. *separation, separate place,* Jos. 16. [9.]

בְּדֹלַח masc. Eng. vers., after most of the an[-]cient interpreters, *bdellium,* a transparent gum [of] the Arab., and so the Rabbies and Bochart, *pearl.*

בְּדַל[r] noun masc. sing., constr. of [בָּדָל] dec. 4a. . בדל

בַּדַּלֶּקֶת[s] ו pref. בַּ for בְּהַ)(noun f. s.; ו before lab. דלק

בַּדֶּלֶת[t] ו״ pref. בַּ for בְּהַ)(noun fem. sing. see דֶּלֶת. דלה

בְּדַלְתּוֹ[x] pref. בְּ)(id., suff. 3 pers. sing. masc. . דלה

בְּדַלְתוֹת[y] pref. id.)(id. pl., constr. of דְּלָתוֹת (§ 44. rem. 5), ת treated as if radical . . דלה

בִּדְלָתַיִם[z] pref. בִּ bef. (:))(n. f., du. of [דְּלָה] d. 11a. דלה

בַּדָּם pref. בַּ f. בְּהַ } noun m. s. d. 2b.)(ו bef. (:) דם
בְּדָם[a] ו״ pref. בְּ }

בְּדַם[b] ו״ pref. id.)(id., constr. state; ו id. . דם

בִּדְמוּת[c] pref. בִּ bef. (:))(noun fem. sing. dec. 1a. דמה

בִּדְמוּתוֹ[d] pref. id.)(id., suff. 3 pers. sing. masc. . דמה

בְּדָמִי[e] pref. בְּ)(noun masc. sing., suff. 1 pers. sing. from דָּם dec. 2a. . . . . דם

בִּדְמֵי pref. בִּ before (:))(id. pl., constr. state . דם

בִּדְמִי[f] pref. id.)(noun masc. sing. . . . דמה

בְּדָמַיִךְ[g] } pref. בְּ)(noun masc. pl., suff. 2 pers. sing. fem. from דָּם dec. 2b . } דם
בְּדָמָיִךְ[h] }

בַּדָּמִים[i] pref. בַּ for בְּהַ } id. pl., absolute state . דם
בְּדָמִים pref. בְּ q.v. }

בְּדָמֵךְ pref. id.)(id. s., suff. 2 pers. sing. fem. . דם

בִּדְמֶךָ[k] pref. id.)(noun masc. sing., suff. 2 pers. sing. masc. [from דֳּם] . . . . דמה

בְּדִמְעָה[l] pref. id.)(noun fem. sing. dec. 12b. . דמע

[a] Mal. 2. 17. [b] Ps. 51. 6. [c] Ps. 119. 42. [d] De. 5. 25.
[e] Ex. 16. 31. [f] Ge. 1. 26, 28. [g] 1 Sa. 2. 14. [h] Ge. 30. 16.
[i] 2 Ch. 35. 13. [k] Ge. 7. 1. [l] Eze. 19. 14. [m] Je. 36. 18.
[n] Job 11. 3. [o] Eze. 27. 12. [p] Eze. 22. 18, 20. [q] De. 25. 4.
[r] Am. 3. 12. [s] De. 28. 22. [t] 2 Ki. 6. 32. [u] De. 15. 17.
[x] 2 Ki. 12. 10. [y] Ju. 16. 3. [z] Job 38. 8. [a] Eze. 38. 22.
[b] Ge. 49. 11. [c] Ge. 5. 1. [d] Ge. 5. 3. [e] Ps. 30. 10.
[f] Is. 38. 10. [g] Eze. 16. 6. [h] Eze. 16. 6. [i] Ps. 106. 38.
[k] Eze. 19. 10. [ll] Ps. 126. 5. [ll] 2 Ki. 10. 7.

בַּדְּמָעוֹת pref. בַּ f. בְּהַ } id. pl., absolute state . דמע
בִּדְמָעוֹת pref. בְּ bef. (:) } id. pl., absolute state . דמע
בְּדִמְעָתִי pref. בְּ)(id. sing., suff. 1 pers. sing. . דמע
בַּדַּמֶּשֶׂק } pref. id.)(pr. name of a place . דמשק
בְּדַמֶּשֶׂק } pref. id.)(pr. name of a place . דמשק
וּבְדַמֶּשֶׂק וּ pref. בְּ bef. (:))(noun m. s.; וּ bef. lab. דמשק
בְּדָן pref. בְּ)(proper name of a place . דין
בְּדָן (for בֶּן־דָּן *Danite*, comp. בִּדְקַר) proper name, masc.—I. 1 Sa. 12. 11.—II. 1 Ch. 7. 17.
בְּדָנִיֵּאל pref. בְּ)(pr. name masc. . . . דין
[e] בְּדַעַת } pref. id.)(noun fem. sing. dec. 13a. (§ 44. No. 1); וּ before (:) . ידע
[f] וּבְדַעַת ו׳ } pref. id.)(noun fem. sing. dec. 13a. (§ 44. No. 1); וּ before (:) . ידע
בְּדַעְתּוֹ pref. id.)(id., suff. 3 pers. sing. masc. . ידע
בְּדָפְקָה pref. id.)(pr. name of a place . . דפק

[בָּדַק] Arab. *to tear, rend,* in Heb. only as denom. of בֶּדֶק *to repair a breach,* 2 Ch. 34. 10.

בֶּדֶק masc. dec. 6 a, with suff. בִּדְקֵךְ *a breach, rupture,* in a building.

[g] בָּדֶק in pause; Seg. n. as if from [בַּדְק] } בדק
בֶּדֶק noun m. sing. dec. 6a. (see the following) } בדק
[h] בִּדְקֵךְ id., suff. 2 pers. sing. fem. . . . בדק
בִּדְקַר (for בֶּן־דֶּקֶר *son of stabbing,* i. e. *stabber,* comp. בִּלְדַּד) pr. name masc., 2 Ki. 9. 25.

[בְּדַר] Chald. Pa. *to scatter,* Da. 4. 11.

בְּדֹר[i] pref. בְּ)(noun masc. sing. for דּוֹר . דור
[k] וּבַדַּרוּ וּ Ch. Pael pret. 3 pers. pl. m.; וּ bef. labial בדר
[l] בַּדָּרוֹם pref. בַּ for בְּהַ)(noun masc. sing. [for דָּרוֹם] דרר
בַּדֶּרֶךְ pref. בַּ f. בְּהַ } noun com. sing., (suff. דַּרְכִּי) dec. 6a; וּ before labial. דרך
[m] בַּדָּרֶךְ ו׳ pref. id. } noun com. sing., (suff. דַּרְכִּי) dec. 6a; וּ before labial. דרך
[n] בְּדָרֶךְ ו׳ pref. בְּ q.v. } noun com. sing., (suff. דַּרְכִּי) dec. 6a; וּ before labial. דרך
בְּדֶרֶךְ ו׳ pref. id. } noun com. sing., (suff. דַּרְכִּי) dec. 6a; וּ before labial. דרך
[o] בְּדַרְכּוֹ וּ pref. id.)(id. s. with suff. 3 pers. s. m.; וּ id. דרך
[p] בִּדְרָכָו pref. בְּ bef. (:))(id. pl., suff. 3 pers. sing. masc. (for ־כָיו § 4. rem. 1) . דרך
בְּדַרְכֵי [q] ו׳ pref. בְּ)(id. pl., constr. state; וּ bef. (:) דרך
בִּדְרָכַי pref. בְּ before (:))(id. pl., suff. 1 pers. sing. דרך
בְּדַרְכֵיהֶם pref. בְּ)(id. pl., suff. 3 pers. pl. masc. . דרך
בְּדַרְכֵיהֶן pref. id.)(id. pl., suff. 3 pers. pl. fem. . דרך
בִּדְרָכָיו pref. בְּ bef. (:))(id. pl., suff. 3 pers. sing. m. דרך
בִּדְרָכֶיךָ pref. id.)(id. pl., suff. 2 pers. sing. masc. דרך
בְּדַרְכְּךָ pref. בְּ)(id. sing., suff. 2 pers. sing. masc. דרך
בִּדְרָכֶךָ pref. בְּ before (:))(id. pl., suff. 2 pers. sing. masc. for דְּרָכֶיךָ (§ 4. rem. 1) . דרך
בְּדַרְכְּכֶם pref. בְּ)(id. sing., suff. 3 pers. pl. masc. . דרך

בְּדַרְמֶשֶׂק pref. id.)(pr. name of a place . . דמשק
[r] בְּדֹרֹתָיו pref. id.)(noun m. with pl. fem. term. and suff. 3 pers. sing. masc. from דּוֹר dec. 1 a. דור
[s] בַּדֶּשֶׁן pref. בַּ for בְּהַ)(n. m. s., (pl. c. דִּשְׁנֵי) d. 6a. דשן
בְּדָת Ch. pref. בְּ)(noun fem. s. (constr.) d. 1 b. דת
[t] בְּדָת Chald. pref. id.)(id. construct state . . דת
[a] בְּדִתְאָא Ch. pref. id.)(n.m.s., emph. of [דִּתְא] d. 3 b. דתא
[b] בְּדִתְאָה Chald. pref. id.)(id. by Hebraism . דתא
[c] בְּדָתִי pref. id.)(n. f. s. dec. 1 a. (but constr. דַּת) דת
בְּדֹתָן pref. id.)(pr. name of a place, see דֹּתָן
בָּהּ ו׳ pref. prep. בְּ with suff. 3 pers. s. fem. (§ 5) ב
בֵּהּ Chald. id. with suff. 3 pers. sing. masc. . ב
[d] בֹּהּ Kh. בָּהּ q. v., K. בּוֹ q. v. . . . ב
[e] בְּהֵאָבְקוֹ pref. בְּ)(Niph. inf. [הֵאָבֵק], suff. 3 p. s. m. d. 7 b. אבק
[f] בְּהַאֲרִיךְ [g] ו׳ pref. id.)(Hiph. inf. constr.; וּ before (:) ארך
בַּהֲבִיאִי pref. בַּ before (-:))(Hiph. inf. (הָבִיא), suff. 1 pers. sing., dec. 3a. . . בוא
[h] בַּהֲבִיאֲכֶם pref. id.)(id., suff. 2 pers. pl. masc. . בוא
[i] בְּהַבִּיטִי pref. בְּ)(Hiph. inf., suff. 1 p. sing., dec. 1 b. נבט
[k] בַּהֶבֶל pref. בַּ for בְּהַ)(n. m. s. dec. 6a. (§ 35. r. 4) הבל
בְּהַבְלֵי pref. בְּ)(id. pl., construct state . . הבל
בְּהַבְלֵיהֶם pref. id.)(id. pl., suff. 3 pers. pl. masc. הבל
[l] בְּהִבָּנֹתוֹ pref. id.)(Niph. inf., suff. 3 p. s. m., dec. 1 b. בנה
[m] בְּהִבָּרְאָם pref. id.)(Niph. inf. [הִבָּרֵא], suff. 3 pers. pl. masc., dec. 7 b. . . . . ברא
[n] בַּהֲגִיגִי pref. בַּ bef. (-:))(noun masc. sing., suff. 1 p. sing. from [הָגִיג] dec. 3 a. . . הגג
[o] וּבְהַגִּיעַ וּ pref. בְּ)(Hiph. inf. constr. dec. 1 b; וּ bef. (:) נגע
[p] בְּהַגְלוֹת pref. id.)(Hiph. inf. construct dec. 1 a. . גלה
[q] בְּהִגָּלוֹת pref. id.)(Niph. inf. construct גלה
[r] בְּהַגְלוֹתִי pref. id.)(Hiph. inf., suff. 1 pers. s. dec. 1 b. גלה
בַּהֲדַדְעֶזֶר pref. בַּ before (-:))(pr. name masc. הדד
[s] בַּהֲדֹף pref. id.)(Kal inf. construct . . הדף
[t] בַּהֲדַר pref. בֶּ for בְּהַ, בְּהֶ)(noun m. sing. dec. 4 c. הדר
[u] בַּהֲדָרִי pref. בַּ before (-:))(id., suff. 1 pers. sing. . הדר
[x] בְּהַדְרֵי pref. בְּ)(id. pl., construct state . הדר
[y] בַּהַדֶּרֶךְ pref. הַ art. & בְּ)(n. com. s., (suff. דַּרְכִּי) dec. 6a. דרך
בַּהֲדַדְעֶזֶר pref. בַּ bef. (-:))(pr. name m., see הֲדַדְעֶזֶר הדד
בְּהַדְרַת pref. בְּ)(noun fem. sing. constr. [of הֲדָרָה dec. 11 c, § 42. rem. 1] . . . הדר

בָּהָה Root not used; Arab. בהו *to be void.* Hence—

[z] בֹּהוּ ו׳ (for בֹּהוּ) masc. *emptiness.*

[a] וּבְהוֹדֹת וּ pref. בְּ)(Hiph. inf. constr. (§ 25. No. 2); וּ before (:) . . . . ידה
[b] בְּהִוָּלֵד pref. id.)(Niph. inf. constr., bef. monos. for הִוָּלֵד ילד

La. 2. 11. Ps. 80. 6. Ps. 6. 7. Am. 3. 12. Pr. 13. 16. Job 34. 35.
[g] 2 Ki. 12. 6. [h] Eze. 27. 9, 27. [i] Ps. 90. 1. [k] Da. 4. 11. [l] Ec. 11. 3. [m] Je. 6. 25.
[n] 1 Sa. 15. 18. [o] Eze. 46. 8. [p] 1 Sa. 8. 3. [q] 2 Ch. 21. 12. [r] Eze. 16. 47. [s] Ho. 10. 13.
[t] Ps. 119. 37. [u] Eze. 36. 17. [x] Ge. 6. 9. [y] Is. 55. 2. [z] Ezr. 7. 14.
[a] Da. 4. 12. [b] Da. 4. 20. [c] Est. 1. 19. [d] Je. 17. 24. [e] Ge. 32. 26.
[f] Nu. 9. 22. [g] Nu. 9. 19. [h] Eze. 44. 7. [i] Ps. 119. 6. [k] Ec. 6. 4.
[l] 1 Ki. 6. 7, 7. [m] Ge. 2. 4. [n] Ps. 39. 4. [o] Est. 2. 12, 15. [p] 1 Ch. 5. 41.
[q] Eze. 21. 29. [r] Eze. 39. 28. [s] De. 9. 4. [t] Ps. 29. 4. [u] Eze. 16. 14.
[x] Ps. 110. 3. [y] Ne. 9. 19. [z] Is. 34. 11. [a] Ezr. 3. 11. [b] Ge. 21. 5.

בְּהוֹלְלִים[a] pref. בְּ for בְּהַ ✕ Kal part. act. masc., pl. of [הוֹלֵל] dec. 7 b. . . . . . הלל

בְּהוֹן Chald. pref. prep. בְּ with suff. 3 p. pl. masc. ב

בְּהִוָּסְדָם[b] pref. בְּ ✕ Niph. inf. [הִוָּסֵד], suff. 3 p. s. m., dec. 7 b. יסד

בְּהוֹצִיאוֹ pref. id. ✕ Hiph. inf., suff. 3 p. s. m., dec. 1 b. יצא

בְּהוֹצִיאִי pref. id. ✕ id., suff. 1 pers. sing. . . יצא

בְּהוֹצִיאֲךָ pref. id. ✕ id., suff. 2 pers. sing. masc. . יצא

וּבְהוֹצִיאָם[c] ו pref. id. ✕ id., suff. 3 pers. pl. m.; ו bef. (:) יצא

בְּהוֹרִדִי[d] pref. id. ✕ Hiph. inf. (הוֹרִיד), suff. 1 p. s., dec. 1 b. ירד

בְּהוֹשֻׁעַ pref. id. ✕ pr. name masc. . . . . ישע

וּבְהַוַּת[e] ו pref. id. ✕ noun fem. sing., constr. of [הַוָּה] dec. 10; ו before (:) . . . . הוה

בְּהַוָּתוֹ[f] pref. id. ✕ id., suff. 3 pers. sing. masc. . הוה

בְּהִזָּרוֹתֵיכֶם[g] pref. id. ✕ Niph. inf. [הִזָּרוֹת], suff. 2 pers. pl. masc., dec. 1 b. contrary to rule, for הִזָּרוֹתְכֶם; comp. בִּבְנוֹתַיִךְ, Eze. 16. 31. זרה

בְּהֵחָבֵא[h] pref. id. ✕ Niph. inf. construct . . . הבא

בְּהֵחָפְזָם[i] pref. id. ✕ Kh. בְּהֵחָפְזָם, Niph. inf. [הֵחָפֵז] dec. 7 b], K. בְּחָפְזָם Kal inf., suff. 3 p. pl. m. חפז

בַּהַט masc. a species of *marble*, only Est. 1. 6.

בִּהְיוֹת pref. בְּ bef. (:) ✕ Kal inf. constr. (הֱיוֹת § 13. rem. 13, comp. rem. 1 and 2) . . . היה

בִּהְיוֹתוֹ pref. id. ✕ id., suff. 3 pers. sing. masc. . היה

בִּהְיוֹתֵךְ[k] pref. id. ✕ id., suff. 2 pers. sing. fem. . היה

בִּהְיוֹתְכֶם pref. id. ✕ id., suff. 2 pers. pl. masc. . היה

בִּהְיוֹתָם pref. id. ✕ id., suff. 3 pers. pl. masc. . היה

בִּהְיוֹתֵנוּ[l] pref. id. ✕ id., suff. 1 pers. pl. . . היה

בְּהֵיטִיבוֹ[m] pref. בְּ ✕ Hiph. inf., suff. 3 pers. sing. masc. יטב

בַּהֵיכָל pref. בַּ for בְּהַ ✕ noun masc. sing., dec. 2 b. היכל

בְּהֵיכַל pref. בְּ ✕ id.; construct state . . . היכל

בְּהֵיכְלָא[n] Chald. pref. id. ✕ n. m., emph. of [הֵיכַל] dec. 2 a. היכל

וּבְהֵיכָלוֹ[o] ו'' pref. id. ✕ noun masc. sing., suff. 3 pers. sing. masc. from הֵיכָל dec. 2 b; ו bef. (:) היכל

בְּהֵיכְלֵי pref. id. ✕ id. pl., construct state . . היכל

בְּהֵיכְלִי[p] Chald. pref. id. ✕ noun masc. sing., suff. 1 p. sing. from הֵיכַל dec. 2 a. . . . היכל

בָּהִיר[q] adj. masc. sing. . . . . . . בהר

בִּהְיֹת[r] pref. בְּ before (:) ✕ Kal inf. constr. dec. 1 a, comp. בִּהְיוֹת . . . . . . היה

בִּהְיֹתוֹ pref. id. ✕ id., suff. 3 pers. sing. masc. . היה

בְּהִכָּבְדִי[s] pref. בְּ ✕ Niph. inf. [הִכָּבֵד], suff. 1 p. s., dec. 7 b. כבד

בְּהַכּוֹתִי[t] pref. id. ✕ Hiph. inf., suff. 1 pers. s., dec. 1 b, (§ 25. No. 2) . . . . . . נכה

בְּהֵכִין[u] pref. בְּ with the relat. art. for בְּהַ (comp. 2 Ch. 29. 36); Hiph. pret. 3 pers. sing. m. כון

בַּהֲכִינוֹ[w] pref. בְּ before (-:) ✕ Hiph. inf. (הָכִין), suff. 3 pers. sing. masc., dec. 3 a. . . כון

בְּהַכְלִים[y] pref. בְּ ✕ Hiph. inf. construct . . כלם

וּבְהִכָּנְעוֹ[z] ו pref. id. ✕ Niph. inf. (הִכָּנַע § 36. rem. 5) suff. 3 pers. sing. masc.; ו before (:) . כנע

בְּהַכְרִית[a] } pref. id. ✕ Hiph. inf. construct dec. 1 b. . כרת
בְּהַכְרִת[b] }

בְּהִכָּרֵת[c] pref. id. ✕ Niph. inf. construct . . כרת

וּבְהִכָּשְׁלָם[d] ו pref. id. ✕ Niph. inf. [הִכָּשֵׁל], suff. 3 pers. pl. masc., dec. 7 b; ו before (:) . . כשל

בְּהַכֹּתִי[e] pref. id. ✕ Hiph. inf., suff. 1 pers. s. (§ 25. No. 2) נכה

בָּהַל. Niph.—I. *to be agitated, terrified, amazed.*—II. *to hasten*, with לְ *after* Pr. 28. 22.—III. *to be ruined.* Pi.—I. *to terrify, confound.*—II. *to cause to hurry, hasten*, const. acc., בְּ, עַל.—Pu. part. *hurried, hastened.* Hiph. i. q. Piel.

בְּהַל Chald. Ithpe. inf. *haste.* Pa. *to terrify, alarm.*

בֶּהָלָה fem., pl. בֶּהָלוֹת *fear, terror.*

בְּהִילוּ Chald. fem. *haste*, Ezr. 4. 23.

בֶּהָלָה[f] noun f. s. dec. 10. (§ 42. No. 3 comp. note) בהל

בְּהִלּוֹ[g] pref. בְּ ✕ Kal inf. [הַל § 18. rem. 3], suff. 3 p. sing. masc. dec. 8 e. . . . . הלל

וּבֶהָלוֹת[h] ו n. f. pl. abs. from בֶּהָלָה (q. v.); ו bef. lab. בהל

בְּהִלָּחֲמוֹ[i] pref. בְּ ✕ Niph. inf. [הִלָּחֵם], suff. 3 pers. sing. masc., dec. 7 b. . . . . . לחם

בַּהֲלִיכוֹתָם[k] pref. בַּ bef. (-:) ✕ Kh. כּוֹתָם' noun f. pl., K. כָתָם' sing. with suff. from הֲלִיכָה dec. 10. הלך

וּבְהַלֵּל[l] ו'' pref. בְּ ✕ Piel inf. constr.; ו before (:) הלל

בָּהַם Root not used; Arab. *to be dumb.*

בְּהֵמָה fem. constr. בֶּהֱמַת, pl. בְּהֵמוֹת, constr. בַּהֲמוֹת (comp. § 42. rem. 4) sing. with suff. בְּהֶמְתּוֹ (as if from בְּהֶמֶת § 42. rem. 5).—I. *cattle.*—II. *wild beast.* By the plural, in Job 40. 15 some stupendous quadruped is understood, according to some the *hippopotamus*, others, the *elephant.*

וּבָהֶם[m] ו'' pref. prep. בְּ with suff. 3 p. pl. m. (§ 5); ו id. ב

בָּהֶם pref. בְּ ✕ pr. name of a region . . המה

בָּהֵמָּה pref. בְּ q. v. ✕ pron. pers. 3 pl. masc. with paragogic ה (§ 5. rem. 7) . . . הם

וּבְהֵמָה ו'' n. f. s. dec. 11. (§ 42. r. 4 & 5); ו bef. (:) בהם

בְּהִמּוֹל[n] pref. בְּ ✕ Niph. inf. construct, dec. 1 b. . מול

בַּהֲמוֹן[o] pref. בְּ before (-:) ✕ construct of the following המה

בֶּהָמוֹן[p] pref. בְּ for בְּהַ · בְּהָ ✕ noun masc. s. dec. 3 a. המה

בַּהֲמוֹת construct of the following . . . בהם

[a] Ps. 73. 3. [b] Ps. 31. 14. [c] 2 Ch. 34. 14. [d] Eze. 31. 16. [e] Pr. 11. 6. [f] Ps. 52. 9. [g] Eze. 6. 8. [h] Da. 10. 7. [i] 2 Ki. 7. 15. [k] Eze. 16. 22. [l] 1 Sa. 25. 15. [m] Ex. 30. 7. [n] Ezr. 5. 15. [o] Ps. 29. 9. [p] Da. 4. 1. [q] Job 37. 21. [r] Ex. 19. 16. [s] Ex. 14. 18. [t] Eze. 32. 15. [u] 2 Ch. 1. 4. [w] Pr. 8. 27. [y] Pr. 25. 8. [z] 2 Ch. 12. 12. [a] 1 Ki. 18. 4. [b] 1 Sa. 20. 15. [c] Ps. 37. 34. [d] Da. 11. 34. [e] Ex. 12. 13. [f] Le. 26. 16. [g] Job 29. 3. [h] Je. 15. 8. [i] 2 Ki. 8. 29. [k] Na. 2. 6. [l] 2 Ch. 5. 13. [m] Mal. 2. 17. [n] Ge. 37. 22. [o] Je. 51. 42. [p] Ec. 5. 9.

בְּהֵעָצֵר pref. id.)(Niph. inf. construct . . עצר
בְּהַפִּילְכֶם[l] וּ Hiph. inf., suff. 2 p. pl. m. d. 1b; וּ bef. (:) נפל
בַּהֲפִיצִי[g] pref. בַּ bef. (-:))(Hiph. inf. [הָפִיץ], suff. 1 p. s. d. 3a. פוץ
בַּהֲפֹךְ[h] pref. id.)(Kal inf. construct . . הפך
בְּהַפְרִידוֹ[i] pref. בְּ)(Hiph. inf., suff. 3 p. s. m. dec. 1b. פרד
בְּהַצּוֹתוֹ[k] pref. id.)(Hiph. inf., suff. 3 p. s. m. dec. 1b. נצה
בְּהַצֹּתָם[l] pref. id.)(id., suff. 3 p. pl. m. (§ 25. No. 2) נצה

בָּהַק Root not used; Arab. *to be white, shining.* Hence—
בֹּהַק masc. only Le. 13. 39, a kind of harmless *leprosy*, consisting of dull whitish spots.

בְּהִקָּבֵץ[m] וּ[n] pref. בְּ)(Niph. inf. construct; וּ bef. (:) קבץ
בְּהִקָּדְשִׁי pref. id.)(Niph. inf. [הִקָּדֵשׁ], suff. 1 p. s. d. 7b. קדש
בְּהַקְהִיל[o] וּ pref. id.)(Hiph. inf. constr.; וּ before (:) קהל
בְּהִקָּהֵל[p] pref. id.)(Niph. inf. construct . . קהל
בְּהָקִיץ[q] pref. id.)(Hiph. inf. construct . . קוץ
בְּהַקְצִיף[r] pref. id.)(Hiph. inf. construct . . קצף
בְּהַקְרִבָם[s] pref. id.)(Hiph. inf. (הַקְרִיב) suff. 3 p. pl. m. d. 1b. קרב
בְּהַקְרִיבְכֶם pref. id.)(id., suff. 3 pers. pl. masc. . קרב
בְּהַקְרִיבָם[t] pref. id.)(id., suff. 3 pers. pl. masc. . . קרב
בְּהַקְשֹׁתָהּ[u] pref. id.)(Hiph. inf., suff. 3 p. s. f. dec. 1b. קשה

בָּהַר Root not used; Arab. *to shine.*
בַּהֶרֶת fem., pl. בֶּהָרוֹת (§ 42. No. 3 note, and § 44. rem. 5) *a shining, whitish scurf,* sinking in the skin and having white hair.
בָּהִיר masc. adj. *bright, shining,* Job 37. 21.

בָּהָר וּ[v] pref. בַּ f. בְּהַ· ,בָּהָ ,בַּה } noun m. s. dec. 8. (§ 37. rem. 7); וּ before (:) . הרר
בְּהָר וּ[v] pref. בְּ q. v. }
בְּהֹר pref. id.)(pr. name of a mountain . הרר
בְּהֵרָאוֹתוֹ[x] pref. id.)(Niph. inf., suff. 3 p. s. m. dec. 1b. ראה
בְּהַרְאֹתוֹ[y] pref. id.)(Hiph. inf., suff. 3 p. s. m. dec. 1b. ראה
בַּהֲרֹג pref. בַּ before (-:))(Kal inf. construct . הרג
בֵּהָרֵג[z] pref. בְּ [for בְּהֵהָרֵג ,בְּהֵהָרֵג], Niph. inf. constr. (§ 13. rem. 8) . . . . הרג
בַּהֲרוּגִים[a] pref. בַּ before (-:))(Kal part. pass. masc., pl. of [הָרוּג] dec. 3a. . . . . הרג
בְּהַרְרֵי[b] וּ[v] pref. בְּ)(noun masc. pl. constr. [for הַרְרֵי] from הַר dec. 8. (§ 37. rem. 7); וּ bef. (:) הרר
בַּהֲרִיחוֹ[c] pref. בַּ bef. (-:))(Hiph. inf. [הָרִיחַ], suff. 3 pers. sing. masc. dec. 3a. . . רוח
בֶּהָרִים pref. בֶּ for בְּהָ ,בְּהַ·)(noun m. [for הַרִים], pl. of הַר dec. 8. (§ 37. rem. 7) . הרר
בַּהֲרִימְכֶם[d] pref. בַּ before (-:))(Hiph. inf. (הָרִים), suff. 2 pers. pl. masc. dec. 3a. . . רום
בַּהֲרִיעַ[e] pref. בַּ)(Hiph. inf. constr. . . רוע

בְּהֵמוֹת n.f.pl.abs.from בְּהֵמָה dec. 11c. (§ 42. r. 4 & 5) בהם
בְּהָמִיר[a] pref. בְּ)(Hiph. inf. construct . . . מור
בְּהִמֹּלוֹ[b] pref. id.)(Niph. inf., suff. 3 p. s. m. dec. 1b. מול
בְּהִמָּצְאוֹ pref. id.)(Niph. inf. (הִמָּצֵא), suff. 3 pers. sing. masc. dec. 7b. . . . . מצא
וּבְהַמְרוֹתָם[c] pref. id.)(Hiph. inf., suff. 3 p. pl. m.; וּ bef. (:) מרה
בֶּהֱמַת n.f.s., constr. of בְּהֵמָה dec. 11c. (§ 42. r. 4 & 5) בהם
בְּהֵמֹת[e] id. pl., absolute state . . . בהם
בְּהֶמְתָּהּ וּ[f] id. sing., suff. 3 p. s. f. [from בֶּהֱמַת]; וּ bef. (:) בהם
בְּהֶמְתּוֹ id. sing., suff. 3 pers. sing. masc. . . בהם
בְּהֶמְתְּךָ
בְּהֶמְתֶּךָ וּ[g] } id. sing., suff. 2 pers. sing. m.; וּ bef. (:) בהם
בְּהֶמְתְּכֶם וּ[i] id. sing., suff. 2 pers. pl. masc.; וּ id. . בהם
בְּהֶמְתָּם וּ[k] id. sing., suff. 3 pers. pl. masc.; וּ id. . בהם
בְּהֶמְתֵּנוּ וּ[m] id. sing., suff. 1 pers. pl.; וּ id. . . בהם

בָּהַן Root not used; Arab. *to shut up.*
בֹּהֶן masc., pl. בְּהֹנוֹת (as if from בֹּהוֹן § 35. rem. 9).—I. *the thumb.*—II. *the great toe.*
בֹּהַן (*thumb*) pr. name of a son of Reuben; whence אֶבֶן־בֹּהַן, the name of a place in Judah, Jos. 15. 6; 18. 17.

בָּהֵן pref. בָּ, see lett. ב)(pron. pers. pl., fem. of הֵם הם
בָּהֶן pref. prep. בְּ with suff. 3 pers. sing. fem. (§ 5) ב
בֹּהַן pr. name of a place . . . . בהן
בֹּהֶן noun fem. sing., pl. בְּהֹנוֹת (§ 35. rem. 9) . בהן
בְּהִנָּבְאוֹ[n] pref. בְּ)(Niph. inf. (הִנָּבֵא), suff. 3 p. s. m., d. 7b. נבא
בְּהִנָּבְאֹתוֹ[o] pref. id.)(id. [from הִנָּבְאוֹת § 23. rem. 9) נבא
בְּהִנָּגֵף[p] pref. id.)(Niph. inf. construct . . נגף
בָּהֵנָּה pref. בָּ, see lett. ב)(pron. pers. pl. fem. with parag. ה, from הֵם masc. . . . . הם
בְּהֹנוֹת[q] noun fem., pl. of בֹּהֶן (§ 35. rem. 9) . בהן
בְּהַנְחִל[r] pref. בְּ)(Hiph. inf. constr. for הַנְחִיל (§ 11. r. 2) נחל
בְּהָנִיחִי[s] pref. id.)(Hiph. inf. construct dec. 3a. . נוח
בְּהִנָּשֵׂא[t] וּ pref. id.)(Niph. inf. constr. d. 7b; וּ bef. (:) נשא
בְּהִנָּשְׂאָם[u] וּ pref. id.)(id., suff. 3 pers. pl. masc.; וּ id. נשא
בְּהַעֲבִיר pref. id.)(Hiph. inf. construct dec. 1b. . עבר
בְּהַעֲוֺתוֹ[x] pref. id.)(Hiph. inf., suff. 3 p. s. m. dec. 1b. עוה
בְּהַעֲטִיף[y] וּ pref. id.)(Hiph. inf. construct; וּ before (:) עטף
בְּהַעֲלוֹת pref. id.)(Hiph inf. construct dec. 1b. . עלה
בְּהֵעָלוֹת[z] וּ[a] pref. id.)(Niph. inf. constr. d. 1b; וּ bef. (:) עלה
בְּהַעֲלוֹתִי[b] וּ pref. id.)(foll. with suff. 1 pers. sing.; וּ id. עלה
בְּהַעֲלֹת[c] וּ pref. id.)(Hiph. inf. constr. dec. 1b; וּ id. עלה
בְּהֵעָלֹתוֹ[d] וּ pref. id.)(Niph. inf. with suff. 3 pers. sing. masc. dec. 1b; וּ id. . . . . עלה
בְּהַעֲלֹתְךָ[e] pref. id.)(Hiph. inf., suff. 2 p. s. m. dec. 1b. עלה

[a] Ps. 46. 3. [b] Ge. 17. 24, 25. [c] Is. 55. 6. [d] Job 17. 2. [e] De. 32. 24. [f] Jos. 8. 2. [g] Ex. 20. 10. [h] Le. 26. 22. [i] 2 Ki. 3. 17. [k] Ps. 107. 38. [l] Nu. 32. 26. [m] Ne. 10. 37. [n] Zec. 13. 3. [o] Zec. 13. 4. [p] 1 Ki. 8. 33. [q] Ju. 1. 6, 7. [r] De. 32. 8. [s] De. 25. 19. [t] Eze. 1. 19. [u] Eze. 1. 21. [x] 2 Sa. 7. 14. [y] Ge. 30. 42. [z] Jer. 37. 11. [a] Ex. 40. 36. [b] Eze. 37. 13. [c] Ex. 30. 8. [d] Nu. 9. 22. [e] Nu. 8. 2. [f] Eze. 45. 1. [g] Eze. 12. 15. [h] Ge. 19. 29. [i] De. 32. 8. [k] Ps. 60. 2. [l] Nu. 26. 9. [m] Ps. 102. 23. [n] Est. 2. 8, 19. [o] Nu. 10. 7. [p] Nu. 17. 7. [q] Ps. 17. 15. [r] Zec. 8. 14. [s] Nu. 3. 4. [t] Nu. 26. 61. [u] Ge. 35. 17. [v] Mal. 3. 2. [y] Est. 1. 4. [z] Eze. 26. 15. [a] Eze. 37. 9. [b] Eze. 34. 14. [c] Ju. 16. 9. [d] Nu. 18. 30, 32. [e] 2 Ch. 13. 15.

בְּהַרְרֵי pref. בְּ)(n. m. pl. constr. from [הָרָר] d. 4c. הרר

בְּהַרְרָם[a] pref. id.)(id., suff. 3 pers. pl. masc. . . הרר

בַּהֶרֶת noun fem. sing. see the following . . בהר

בֶּהָרֹת[b] id. pl. absolute (§ 42. No. 3. & § 44. rem. 5) בהר

בְּהַשְׁבִּיעַ[c] pref. בְּ)(Hiph. inf. construct . . . שׁבע

בַּהֹשֶׂדֶה[d] Kh. בְּהַשָּׂדֶה preff. הַ & בְּ, K. contr. בַּשָּׂדֶה, q.v. שׂדה

בְּהַשְׂכִּיל[e] pref. בְּ)(Hiph. inf. absolute as subst. . שׂכל

בְּהַשְׂכִּיל[f] וּ pref. id.)(id. inf. constr.; וּ before labial שׂכל

בְּהָשַּׁמָּה[g] pref. בְּ)(בְּהָשַּׁמָּה (comp. יָחְנְךָ for יְחָנְךָ)
Hoph. inf. construct (§ 18. rem. 14) . שׁמם

בְּהַשָּׁמַיִם[h] preff. הַ art. & בְּ)(n. m. pl. [of שָׁמַי § 38. r. 2) שׁמה

בְּהִשָּׁמַע[i] pref. בְּ)(Niph. inf. construct . . . שׁמע

בְּהִשָּׁעֶנְךָ[k] וּ[l] pref. id.)(Niph. inf. (הִשָּׁעֵן), suff. 2 pers.
sing. masc., dec. 7b; וּ before (:) . שׁען

בְּהִשָּׁעֲנָם[m] וּ pref. id.)(id., suff. 3 pers. pl. masc.; וּ id. שׁען

בְּהִשָּׁפְטוֹ[n] pref. id.)(Niph. inf. constr. dec. 7b. . שׁפט

בְּהִשָּׁפְטוֹ pref. id.)(id., suff. 3 pers. sing. masc. . שׁפט

בְּהַשְׁקֵט[o]
בְּהַשְׁקֵט[p] } pref. id.)(Hiph. inf. constr. (§ 11. r. 2) שׁקט

בְּהִשְׁתַּחֲוָיָתִי[q] pref. id.)(a Čhald. form of Hithpal. inf.
[הִשְׁתַּחֲוָיָה § 47. r. 5] and suff. 1 p. s. שׁחה

בְּהִשְׁתַּפֵּךְ[r] pref. id.)(Hithpa. inf. constr. [for הִתְשַׁפֵּךְ] שׁפך

בְּהִתְאַסֵּף[s] pref. id.)(Hithpa. inf. constr. . . אסף

בְּהִתְבְּהָלָה וּ[t] Ch. pref. id.)(Ithpe. inf. (§ 47. rem. 5) בהל

בְּהִתְגַּלּוֹת[u] pref. id.)(Hithpa. inf. constr. . . גלה

בְּהִתְהַלֶּכְךָ[x] pref. id.)(Hithpa. inf. (הִתְהַלֵּךְ), suff. 2 pers.
sing. masc. dec. 7b. (§ 16. r. 15. & § 36. r. 3) הלך

בְּהִתְוַדַּע[y] pref. id.)(Hithpa. inf. constr. (§ 20. rem. 1) ידע

בְּהִתְחַבֶּרְךָ[z] pref. id.)(Hithpa. inf. [הִתְחַבֵּר], suff. 2 pers.
sing. masc. d. 7b. (§ 16. r. 15. & § 36. r. 3) חבר

בְּהִתְחַנְנוֹ[a] pref. id.)(Hithpa. inf. [הִתְחַנֵּן], suff. 3 pers.
sing. masc. dec. 7b. (§ 10. rem. 7) . חנן

בְּהִתְיַחֵשׂ[b] pref. id.)(Hithpa. inf. constr. d. 7b. (§ 14. r. 1) יחשׂ

בְּהִתְנַדֵּב[c] pref. id.)(Hithpa. inf. constr. dec. 7b. . נדב

בְּהִתְנַשֵּׂא[d] pref. id.)(Hithpa. inf. constr. . . נשׂא

בְּהִתְעַטֵּף pref. id.)(Hithpa. inf. constr. dec. 7b. . עטף

בְּהִתְעַטְּפָם[e] pref. id.)(id., suff. 3 pers. pl. masc. . עטף

בְּהִתְפַּלְלוֹ[f] pref. id.)(Hithpa. inf. (הִתְפַּלֵּל), suff. 3 pers.
sing. masc. dec. 7b. (§ 10. rem. 7) . . פלל

בוֹ וּ' pref. prep. בְּ with suff. 3 pers. s. m. (§ 5) ב

בּוֹא fut. יָבוֹא (§ 21. r. 2, 3. & § 25. No. 2 f).—I. *to enter, come* or *go in*, const. with בְּ, אֶל, לְ, also acc.; בָּא הַשֶּׁמֶשׁ *the sun went down*; צֵאת וָבוֹא *to go out and come in*, i. e. to manage one's affairs, with לִפְנֵי הָעָם *to go before, lead on a people*; בּוֹא בְּ *to have intercourse with*, Jo. 23. 7, 12; בּוֹא בְמִשְׁפָּט עִם *to enter into judgment with*, i. e. to arraign; בּוֹא בִבְרִית *to enter into a covenant*, i. e. to engage in it; בּוֹא בְדָמִים *to enter into blood-shed*, i. e. commit it; בּוֹא בַיָּמִים *to advance in years*; בּוֹא אֶל, עַל אִשָּׁה *to have connection with a woman*.—II. *to come*, const. with אֶל, עַל, עַד of pers. or place, *unto*, with בְּ *with* any thing.—III. rarely i. q. הָלַךְ *to go*. Hiph. I.—*to cause to come in, to lead, bring in*.—II. *to cause to come, to lead, bring*. Hoph. pass. of Hiph.

בִּאָה fem. *entrance*, Eze. 8. 5.

מָבוֹא masc. dec. 3 a.—I. *an entering*, Eze. 26. 10.—II. *entrance*, place of entering; מְבוֹא הַשֶּׁמֶשׁ *place of sunset, the west*.

מוּבָא masc. (no vowel change) *entrance*, only Eze. 43. 11, and Keri 2 Sam. 3. 25.

תְּבוּאָה fem. dec. 10.—I. *a coming in, being stored up*, Ps. 107. 37.—II. *income, profit*.—III. *produce, fruit*; trop. *result*, Prov. 18. 20.

בּוֹא Kal inf. or imp. sing. masc. (§ 21. rem. 2) . בוא

בוֹא[g] וָ id. inf. dec. 1a; for וָ see lett. ו . . בוא

בּוֹאוֹ[h] id. id., suff. 3 pers. sing. masc. . . בוא

בּוֹאִי[i] id. id., suff. 1 pers. sing. . . . בוא

בוֹאִי[k] וּ[l] id. imp. sing. fem.; וּ bef. labial . . בוא

בוֹאֲךָ וּ[m]
בוֹאֶךָ וּ[n] } id. inf., suff. 2 pers. s. m. d. 1a; וּ id. בוא

בּוֹאָנָה[oo] id. inf., suff. 3 pers. pl. fem. (§ 3. rem. 5) . בוא

בּוּב *to be hollow*, whence the forms נָבוּב, נְבוּב are supposed to be Niph., but see נָבַב.

בָּבָה fem. only in the constr. בָּבַת (Kamets impure, comp. § 30. No. 2) Zech. 2. 12, *apple of the eye, pupil*. Talm. בִּיב *hollow place*, Arab. בָּאב *gate*.

בּוֹגֵד וּ[o] Kal part. act. s. m. dec. 7b; וּ bef. labial בגד

בּוֹגְדִים וּ' id. pl., absolute state; וְ id. . . בגד

בּוֹרְאָם[p] Kal part. act. sing. masc., suff. 3 pers. pl.
masc. [for בּוֹרְאָם § 23. rem. 4] . . ברא

בּוֹדֵד Kal part. act. sing. masc. . . . בדד

[בּוּז] *to despise, contemn*.

בּוּז masc.—I. *contempt*.—II. pr. name of the second son of Nahor, Ge. 22. 21, and of a people in Arabia Deserta, Je. 25. 23. Gent. noun בּוּזִי Job 32. 2.—III. pr. name masc. 1 Ch. 5. 14.

בּוּזָה fem. *object of contempt*, Ne. 3. 36.

[a] Ge. 14. 6. [b] Le. 13. 38, 39. [c] 1 Sa. 14. 27. [d] 2 Ki. 7. 12. [e] Job 34. 35. [f] Pr. 21. 11. [g] Le. 26. 43. [h] Ps. 36. 6. [i] Est. 2. 8. [k] 2 Ch. 16. 7. [l] 2 Ch. 16. 8. [m] Eze. 29. 7. [n] 2 Ch. 22. 8. [o] Is. 30. 15. [oo] Ruth 1. 19. [p] Job 37. 17. [q] 2 Ki. 5. 18. [r] La. 2. 12. [s] De. 33. 5. [t] Da. 6. 20. [u] Pr. 18. 2. [x] Pr. 6. 22. [y] Ge. 45. 1. [z] 2 Ch. 20. 37. [a] Ge. 42. 21. [b] 1 Ch. 5. 7 [c] Ju. 5. 2. [d] Pr. 30. 32. [e] La. 2. 12. [f] Job 42. 10. [g] 2 Ch. 18. 29. [h] Mal. 3. 2. [i] 1 Sa. 10. 8. [k] 2 Sa. 13. 11. [l] Ca. 4. 16. [m] Is. 37. 28. [n] Ps. 121. 8. [o] Is. 33. 1. [p] Ne. 6. 8.

בּוּזִי pr. name of the father of the prophet Ezekiel, Eze. 1. 3.

בּוֹז[a] Kal inf. abs. . . . . . בוז

בּוּז[b] ו׳ & ו׳ְ noun masc. sing. also pr. name; וּ bef. labial, for וְ see lett. ו . . . . . בוז

בּוֹזֶה Kal part. act. sing. masc. dec. 9a. . . . בזה

בּוּזָה[c] noun fem. sing. . . . . . בוז

בּוֹזֵהוּ[d] Kal part. act. s. m. (בּוֹזֶה), suff. 3p. s. m. d. 9a. בזה

בּוֹזֵי[e] id. pl., constr. state . . . . . בזה

בּוּזִי pr. name masc. . . . . . . בוז

בּוֹזִים[f] וּ pl. of בּוֹזֶה q. v. וּ before labial . . . בזה

בְּוֹזָנַי pr. name, see שְׁתַר בּוֹזְנַי . . . . שתר

בּוֹטֶה[g] Kal part. act. sing. masc. . . . . בטה

בּוֹטֵחַ ו׳ Kal part. act. sing. masc. dec. 7b; וּ bef. lab. בטח

בַּוַּי pr. name masc. Ne. 11. 18.

בּוּךְ. Niph. part. *perplexed, confused.*

מְבוּכָה fem. dec. 10. *perplexity, confusion.*

בּוֹכֶה[h] וּ Kal part. act. sing. masc. dec. 9a. . . בכה

בֹּוכִיָּה[i] id. fem. (§ 24. rem. 4) . . . . בכה

בּוֹכִים id. pl. absolute masc. . . . . . בכה

בּוּל[k] noun masc. sing. . . . . . . יבל

בּוֹלֵס[l] וּ Kal part. act. sing. masc.; וּ bef. labial . בלס

בּוֹלְקָהּ[m] וּ Kal part. act. sing. masc. [בּוֹלֵק], suff. 3 pers. sing. fem. dec. 7b; וּ id. . . . בלק

בּוּם Root not used; probably *to be high*, Syr. בִּים *a raised place, a pulpit.*

בָּמָה f. dec. 10. (pl. c. בָּמוֹתֵי Kh. with double plural, בָּמֳתֵי K. see § 36. r. 6).—I. *high place, hill, hillock,* usually *dedicated to religious worship,* whether true or false; בָּתֵּי הַבָּמוֹת *houses* or *temples* erected upon *high places;* כֹּהֲנֵי הַבָּמוֹת *idolatrous priests.* Metaph. spoken of *the waves* of the sea, Job 9. 8; of *the clouds,* Is. 14. 14.—II. *height, strong place.*

בָּמוֹת (*heights*) and בָּמוֹת בַּעַל (*heights of Baal*) pr. name of a town in Moab on the river Arnon.

בּוּנָה וּ (*discretion*) fr. בּוּן i. q. (בִּין) pr. n. m. 1 Ch. 2. 25.

בּוֹנֶה Kal part. act. sing. masc. dec. 9a. . . בנה

בּוֹנֵה[n] id., constr. state . . . . . בנה

בּוּנִּי pr. name masc., see בָּנִי . . . . בנה

בּוֹנָיו[o] Kal part. act. pl., suff. 3 p. s. m. fr. בּוֹנֶה d. 9a. בנה

בּוֹנִים[p] ו׳ id. pl., absolute state . . . . בנה

[בּוּס] *to trample upon, tread under foot.* Pil. *to tread down,* (profane). Hoph. part. *trodden under foot,* Is. 14. 19. Hithpal. part. id. Eze. 16. 6, 22.

בֻּסַּי (*trampler*) pr. name of a man.

יְבוּס (*place trodden down*) the ancient name of Jerusalem. Gent. n. יְבוּסִי.

מְבוּסָה fem. *a treading down.*

תְּבוּסָה fem. dec. 10a. *a treading down, destruction,* 2 Ch. 22. 7.

בּוֹסִים[q] Kal part. act. pl. masc. (§ 21. rem. 2) . בוס

בּוֹסְסוּ[r] Pilel pret. 3 pers. pl. . . . . בוס

בּוּעַ Root not used; Chald. *to boil, to swell up.*

אֲבַעְבֻּעֹת fem. *blains, pustules,* Ex. 9. 9, 10.

בּוּץ Root not used; Arab. *to be white, shining.*

בּוּץ masc. *fine linen, byssus.*

בֵּיצָה (Chald. בֵּיעָה & בֵּיצָה) fem. dec. 10. only pl. בֵּצִים *eggs.*

בֵּצַי (*white*) pr. name of a man.

בּוּץ ו׳ noun masc. sing.; וּ before labial . . בוץ

בּוֹצֵעַ Kal part. act. sing. masc. . . . . בצע

בּוֹצֵץ pr. name of a rock . . . . . בצץ

בּוּק Root not used; i. q. בָּקַק *to empty.*

בּוּקָה fem. *emptiness, devastation,* Na. 2. 11.

מְבוּקָה fem. *emptiness,* Na. 2. 11.

בּוּקָה[s] noun fem. sing. . . . . . בוק

בּוֹקֵעַ Kal part. act. sing. masc. . . . . בקע

בּוֹקֵק Kal part. act. sing. masc. dec. 7b. . . . בקק

בּוֹקֵר[t] noun masc. sing. . . . . . בקר

[בּוּר] cogn. בָּרַר *to examine, prove,* Eccl. 9. 1.

בּוֹר[u] Kh. בּוֹר q. v., K. בַּיִר noun masc. sing. . באר

בּוֹר[x] ו׳ וּ noun masc. sing. dec. 1a. . . . באר

בּוֹרֵא ו׳ Kal part. act. s. m. dec. 7b; וּ bef. labial ברא

בּוֹרְאֶיךָ[y] id. pl., suff. 2 pers. sing. masc. . . ברא

בּוֹרוֹ[z] noun m. s., suff. 3 pers. s. m. fr. בּוֹר d. 1a. באר

בּוֹשׁ (§ 21. r. 2, 3, 6)—I. *to be ashamed,* const. with מִן.—II. *to be disappointed, to be confused, perplexed.* Pil. *to delay.* Hiph. *to make ashamed, cause shame, disgrace.* Hithpal. *to be ashamed.*

בּוּשָׁה fem. *shame, ignominy.*

בָּשְׁנָה fem. *shame,* Hos. 10. 6.

בֹּשֶׁת fem. dec. 13c. (§ 39. No. 4d).—I. *shame, confusion.*—II. *ignominy.*—III. *an idol.*

מְבוּשׁ m. d. 3a., only in pl. *secret parts,* De. 25. 11.

---

[a] Ca. 8. 7. [b] Job 31. 34. [c] Ne. 3. 36. [d] Pr. 14. 2. [e] Mal. 1. 6. [f] 2 Ch. 36. 16. [g] Pr. 12. 18. [h] 2 Sa. 15. 30. [i] La. 1. 16. [k] Job 40. 20. [l] Am. 7. 14. [m] Is. 24. 1. [n] Ps. 147. 2. [o] Ps. 127. 1. [p] Ne. 4. 12. [q] Zec. 10. 5. [r] Is. 63. 18. [s] Na. 2. 11. [t] Am. 7. 14. [u] Je. 6. 7. [x] Le. 11. 36. [y] Ec. 12. 1. [z] Is. 36. 16.

בֹּושׁ Kal inf., or pret. 3 pers. s. m. (§ 21. r. 2) בוש
בֹּושָׁה[a] ו׳ id. pret. 3 pers. sing. fem.; וּ bef. labial בוש
בּוּשָׁה noun fem. sing. . . . . . בוש
בֹּשׁוּ Kal imp. pl. m., or pret. 3 pers. pl. (§ 21. r. 2) בוש
בֹּושִׁי id. imp. sing. fem. . . . . . בוש
בֹּושִׁים[b] id. part. act. sing. masc. (§ 21. rem. 2) . בוש
בּוֹשַׁסְכֶם[c] Poel inf. [בּוֹשֵׁס § 6. No. 1], suff. 2 p. pl. m. [for בּוֹשֶׁסְכֶם or בּוֹשֶׁסְכֶם comp. § 16. r. 15] בשס

[בּוּת] Ch. *to pass the night*, Da. 6. 19. Hence commonly derived בַּיִת *a house*, q. v.

בָּז Kal part. act. sing. masc. . . . . בוז
בָּז[d] Kal pret. 3 p. s. m. (as if fr. בזז § 21. r. 22) בוז
בַּז noun masc. sing. dec. 8e. . . . . בזז

[בָּזָא] i. q. בָּזַז *to spoil*, Is. 18. 2, 7. Others, i. q. בָּזַע *to cleave, divide*.

בָּזְאוּ[e] Kal pret. 3 pers. pl. . . . . בזא
בָּזֹאת[f] ו׳ pref. בָּ for בְּ } pron. demon. fem. s., see זה
בְּזֹאת pref. בְּ q. v.
בִּזְבֻלֻן / בִּזְבוּלוּן } pref. בְּ bef. (:))(pr. n. of a tribe; וּ bef. lab. זבל
בַּזֶּבַח[g] pref. בַּ for בְּהַ } noun masc. sing., (suff. זִבְחִי) dec. 6a. (§ 35. rem. 5) } זבח
בְּזֶבַח[h] pref. בְּ q. v.
בְּזָבְחוֹ[i] pref. id.)(Kal inf., suff. 3 pers. sing. masc. זבח
בְּזִבְחִי[k] pref. id.)(noun masc. sing., suff. 1 pers. sing. from זֶבַח dec. 6a. (§ 35. rem. 5) . זבח
בְּזִבְחֵינוּ[l] וּ pref. בְּ bef. (:))(id. pl., suff. 1 pers. pl.; וּ before labial . . . . . זבח
בְּזָדוֹן pref. בְּ)(noun masc. sing. d. 3a. (§ 32. r. 6) זוד

בָּזָה ו׳״ *to despise, contemn*, const. with acc., לְ, עַל. Niph. part. *despised*. Hiph. *to render contemptible*, Est. 1. 17.

בָּזֶה adj. masc. dec. 3a, *despised*, Is. 49. 7.

בִּזָּיוֹן masc. *contempt*, Est. 1. 18.

בִּזְיוֹתְיָה (*contempt of the Lord*) pr. name of a town in Judah, Jos. 15. 28.

נִמְבְזָה *contemptible*, 1 Sa. 15. 9, Niph. part. denom. of a subst. מְבְזָה.

בָּזֶה[m] ו׳״ pref. בָּ, see ב } pron. demon. sing. masc.; וּ bef. labial } זה
בַּזֶּה[n] pref. בַּ for בְּהַ
בִּזָּה noun masc. sing. . . . . . . בזז
בִּזָּהּ[p] noun m. s., suff. 3 pers. sing. f. fr. בַּז d. 8e. בזז
בַּזָּהָב ו׳ pref. בַּ f. בְּהַ } n. m. s. d. 4a; וּ bef. labial זהב
בְּזָהָב[q] ו׳ pref. בְּ q. v.

בָּזוּ[r] Kal pret. 3 pers. sing. masc. . . . בוז
בֹּזוּ[s] Kal imp. pl. masc. . . . . . בוז
בְּזוֹבוֹ[t] pref. בְּ)(n. m. s., suff. 3 p. s. m. fr. זוֹב d. 1a. זוב
בָּזוּז[u] Kal part. pass. sing. masc. . . . בזז
בָּזוּי Kal part. pass. sing. masc. dec. 3a. . בזה
בְּזוּי[w] וּ id., constr. state; וּ bef. lab. . . בזה
בְּזוּיָה[y] id., fem. of בָּזוּי . . . . . בזה
בַּזּוֹנָה[z] pref. בַּ for בְּהַ)(Kal part. pass. sing. fem. dec. 10. [from זוֹנֶה masc.] . . זנה
בַּזּוֹנוּ[a] Kal pret. 1 pers. pl. . . . . בוז

בָּזַז וּ[b] (§ 18. rem. 13) *to take as a prey, to spoil, plunder*. Niph. *to be spoiled*. Pu. id. Jer. 50. 37.

בַּז masc. dec. 8e. *prey, spoil, booty*; הָיָה לָבַז *to become a prey*; נָתַן לָבַז *to give as a prey, to be spoiled*.

בִּזָּה fem. *prey, booty*.

בִּזְתָא (*prey for* בִּזְתָא) pr. name of a eunuch of Ahasuerus, Est. 1. 10.

בָּזְזוּ[c] / בָּזָזוּ[d] / ו׳ בָּזֲזוּ } Kal pret. 3 pers. pl. (§ 18. r. 13. & § 8. r. 7) בָּזְזוּ anom. for בָּזְזוּ; וּ bef. lab. } בזז
בֻּזָּזוּ[e] וּ Pual pret. 3 p. pl. [for בֻּזְזוּ comp. § 8. r. 7) בזז
בְּזָזוּם[f] וּ Kal pret. 3 p. pl., suff. 3 p. pl. m.; וּ bef. lab. בזז
בֹּזְזֵיהֶם[g] id. part. act. masc., pl. of [בֹּזֵז] dec. 7 b. . בזז
בֹּזְזַיִךְ[h] id. pl., suff. 2 pers. sing. fem. . . . בזז
בֹּזְזִים[i] id. pl., absolute state . . . . בזז
בָּזַזְנוּ[k] Kal pret. 1 pers. pl. . . . . . בזז
בֹּזַי[l] וּ Kal part. act. pl. masc., suff. 1 pers. pl. fr. בּוֹזֶה dec. 9a; וּ id. . . . . בזה
בִּזָּיוֹן[m] noun masc. sing. . . . . . בזה
בִּזְיוֹתְיָה וּ pr. name of a place . . . . בזה
בָּזִינוּ[n] Kal pret. 1 pers. sing. . . . . בזה
בְּזִיקוֹת[o] וּ pref. בְּ)(noun pl. fem. for זִקּוֹת (comp. § 18. r. 12 note) from a sing. [זֵק for זֵנֶק] זנק
בָּזִית Kal pret. 2 pers. sing. fem. . . . בזה
בָּזִיתָ[p] id. pret. 2 pers. sing. masc. . . . בזה
בְּזָכְרֵנוּ[q] pref. בְּ)(Kal inf., suff. 1 pers. pl. . . זכר
בְּזֹלְלֵי[r] pref. id.)(Kal part. pl. constr. m. from זֹלֵל d. 7b. זלל
בְּזִמָּה pref. id.)(noun. fem. sing. dec. 10. . זמם
בִּזְמַנֵּיהֶם[s] pref. בְּ bef. (:))(noun masc. pl., suff. 3 pers. pl. masc. from זְמָן dec. 8a. . . זמן
בִּזְמִרוֹת[t] pref. id.)(n. m. with pl. f. term. from זָמִיר d. 1a. זמר
בִּזְנָבוֹ[u] pref. id.)(n. m. s., suff. 3 p. s. m. from זָנָב d. 4a. זנב
בִּזְנוּנֶיהָ[w] pref. id.)(n. m. pl., suff. 3 p. s. f. [from זְנוּן d. 1a.] זנה
בִּזְנוּתַיִךְ[y] pref. id.)(n. f. pl., suff. 2 p. s. f. from זְנוּת d. 1a. זנה

a Is. 24. 23. b Eze. 32. 30. c Am. 5. 11. d Zec. 4. 10. e Is. 18. 2, 7. f 2 Ch. 19. 2. g 1 Sa. 16. 3, 5. h 1 Sa. 3. 14. i 2 Sa. 15. 12. k 1 Sa. 2. 29. l Jos. 22. 27. m Eze. 17. 18. n Est. 2. 13. o 1 Sa. 21. 11. p Eze. 29. 19. q Da. 11. 38. r Pr. 1. 7. s Na. 2. 10. t Le. 15. 3. u Is. 42. 22. w Ps. 22. 6. y Ec. 9. 16. z Joel 4. 3. a De. 3. 7. b Eze. 29. 19. c Nu. 31. 9. d Nu. 31. 53. e Je. 50. 37. f Je. 20. 5. g Eze. 39. 10. h Je. 30. 16. i 2 Ch. 20. 25. k De. 2. 35. l 1 Sa. 2. 30. m Est. 1. 18. n Mal. 1. 6. o Is. 50. 11. p 2 Sa. 12. 9. q Ps. 137. 1. r Pr. 23. 20. s Est. 9. 31. t Ps. 95. 2. u Ex. 4. 4. w Na. 3. 4. y Je. 3. 2.

בִּזְנוּתֵךְ[a] pref. id.)(Kal inf. [זְנוּת] suff. 2 pers. s. f. זנה
בִּזְנוּתָם[b] pref. id.)(n. f. s., suff. 3 p. pl. m. from זְנוּת d. 1 a. זנה
בְּזַעַם pref. בְּ)(noun masc. sing. dec. 6 d. . זעם
בְּזַעַף pref. id.)(noun masc. sing. dec. 6 d. . . זעף
בְּזַעְפּוֹ וּ Kal inf., suff. 3 p. s. m. (§ 16. r. 10); וּ bef. (:) זעף
בְּזַעֲקֵךְ[d] pref. id.)(Kal inf., suff. 2 p. s. f. (§ 16. r. 10) זעק
בְּזֵעַת[e] pref. id.)(n. f. s., construct of [זֵעָה] dec. 10. יזע
בַּזֶּפֶת[f] וּ pref. בַּ for בְּהַ)(for זֶפֶת, n. f. s.; וּ bef. lab. זוף

בָּזָק Root not used; Syr. and Chald. *to scatter*.
בָּזָק masc. *lightning*, Eze. I. 14.
בֶּזֶק (*lightning*) pr. name of a Canaanitish city.

בֶּזֶק pr. name, see אֲדֹנִי בֶזֶק . . . דון
בַּזִּקִּים pref. בַּ f. בְּהַ } noun masc. pl. [of זִק dec. 8 b.] זקק
בְּזִקִּים[g] pref. בְּ q. v. }
בַּזָּקֵן[h] pref. בַּ for בְּהַ)(adj. masc. sing. dec. 5 a. . זקן
בְּזָקָן pref. בְּ)(noun com. sing. dec. 4 a. זקן
בִּזְקַן[k] pref. בְּ before (:))(id. construct state . זקן
בִּזְקָנוֹ[l] pref. id.)(id., suff. 3 pers. sing. masc. . זקן
בִּזְקֵנֵינוּ[m] וּ adj. pl. masc., suff. 1 pers. pl. from זָקֵן dec. 5 a; וּ before labial . . . זקן

[בָּזַר] *to scatter, disperse*, Da. II. 24. Pi. id. Ps. 68. 31.

בִּזַּר[n] Piel pret. 3 pers. sing. masc. . . . . בזר
בְּזָרָה[o] pref. בְּ)(Kal part. s. f. dec. 10. from זָר masc. זור
בִּזְרוֹעַ ׳וּ pref. בְּ bef. (:))(n. com. s. d. 1 a; וּ bef. lab. זרע
בִּזְרוֹעִי[p] וּ pref. id.)(id., suff. 1 pers. sing.; וּ id. . זרע
בְּזָרִים[q] pref. בְּ)(Kal part. act. m. pl. of זָר dec. 1 a. זור
בִּזְרַע[r] pref. בְּ bef. (:))(n. m. s., constr. of זֶרַע (§ 35. r. 7) זרע
בִּזְרֹעַ[s] וּ defect. for בִּזְרוֹעַ q. v. . . . . זרע
בְּזַרְעוֹ pref. בְּ)(noun masc. sing., suff. 3 pers. sing. masc. from זֶרַע dec. 6 a. (§ 35. rem. 7) . זרע
בִּזְרֹעוֹ[t] pref. בְּ bef. (:))(noun com. sing., suff. 3 pers. sing. masc. from זְרוֹעַ dec. 1 a. . . זרע
בְּזַרְעֲךָ[u] ׳וּ } pref. בְּ)(noun masc. sing., suff. 2 pers.
בְּזַרְעֶךָ[x] וּ } sing. masc. from זֶרַע dec. 6 a; וּ bef. lab. זרע
בִּזְרֹעֲךָ וּ pref. בְּ bef. (:))(noun com. sing., suff. 2 p. sing. masc. from זְרוֹעַ dec. 1 a; וּ id. . זרע
בְּזַרְעָם[y] pref. בְּ)(noun masc. sing., suff. 3 pers. pl. masc. from זֶרַע dec. 6 a. (§ 35. rem. 7) זרע
בַּזֶּרֶת[z] pref. בַּ for בְּהַ)(noun fem. sing. . . זרה
בִּזְתָא pr. name masc. . . . . . בזז
בִּזִּיתַנִי[a] Kal pret. 2 pers. s. m. (בָּזִיתָ), suff. 1 p. s. בזה
בְּחָבוֹר וּ pr. name of a river; וּ before (:) . . חבר
בְּחֻבִּי[b] pref. בְּ)(n. m. s., suff. 1 p. s. [from חֹב dec. 8 c.] חבב

בַּחֶבֶל pref. בַּ f. בְּהַ } noun m. sing. dec. 6 a. (§ 35. חבל
בְּחֶבֶל[c] ׳וּ pref. בְּ q. v. } rem. 4); וּ before lab. .
בְּחַבְלֵי[d] ׳וּ pref. id.)(id. pl., construct state; וּ id. חבל
בַּחֲבָלֶיהָ[e] pref. בַּ bef. (-:))(noun masc. pl., suff. 3 pers. sing. fem. from חֶבֶל dec. 6. (§ 35. rem. 6) חבל
בַּחֲבָלִים pref. id.)(n. m. pl. of חֶבֶל dec. 6. (§ 35. r. 4) חבל
בְּחֶבְרוֹן pref. בְּ)(pr. name of a place . . . חבר
בַּחֲבֵרָיִךְ[f] pref. בַּ for בְּהַ)(noun masc. pl., suff. 2 p. sing. fem. from חָבֵר dec. 6 a. . . חבר
בַּחֹבֶרֶת[g] pref. בַּ for בְּהַ)(noun fem. sing. for [חֹבֶרֶת] חבר
בַּחֲבֻרָתוֹ[h] וּ pref. בַּ bef. (-:))(noun fem. sing. with suff. 3 p. s. m. from [חֲבֻרָה] dec. 10; וּ bef. lab. חבר
בֶּחָג pref. בֶּ for בְּהָ, בְּהַ)(noun masc. sing. dec. 8 a. חגג
בְּחַג ׳וּ pref. בְּ)(id. construct state; וּ before (:) חגג
בְּחַגְוֵי pref. id.)(noun masc. pl. constr. [of חֲגָוִים] חגה
בַּחַגִּים[k] ׳וּ pref. בַּ for בְּהַ)(noun masc., pl. of חַג dec. 8 a; וּ before labial . . . חגג
בְּחַגֶּךָ[l] pref. בְּ)(id. sing., suff. 2 p. s. m. [for חַגְּךָ] חגג
בַּחֲגֹרָתוֹ[m] pref. בַּ bef. (-:))(n. f. s., const. of חֲגֹרָה d. 10. חגר
בַּחֶדְוָה[n] Chald. noun fem. sing. . . . . חדה
בַּחֲדַר[o] ׳וּ pref. בַּ bef. (-:))(constr. of the foll. (§ 33. r. 3) חדר
בַּחֶדֶר[p] pref. בַּ for בְּהַ }
בֶּחָדֶר[q] pref. בֶּ f. בְּהַ, בְּהָ, בֶּ & } noun masc. s. dec. 6. (§ 35. rem. 4) . חדר
בְּחֶדֶר }
בְּחֵדֶר } pref. בְּ q. v. & ה
בְּחַדְרֵי[r] ׳וּ pref. id.)(id. pl., const. state; וּ bef. (:) חדר
בַּחֲדָרֶיךָ[s] pref. בַּ bef. (-:))(id. pl., suff. 2 pers. sing. m. חדר
בַּחֹדֶשׁ ׳וּ pref. בַּ f. בְּהַ } noun masc. sing. dec. 6 c. חדש
בְּחֹדֶשׁ pref. בְּ q. v. }
בְּחָדְשָׁהּ[t] pref. id.)(id., suff. 3 pers. sing. fem. . חדש
בְּחָדְשׁוֹ pref. id.)(id., suff. 3 pers. sing. masc. . חדש
בֶּחֳדָשִׁים וּ pref. בֶּ for בְּהָ, בְּהַ)(id. pl., abs. st.; וּ bef. lab. חדש
בְּחוֹחַ[u] וּ pref. ב)(n. m. sing. d. 1 a. & 6; וּ bef. lab. חוח
בַּחֲוָחִים[x] ׳וּ } pref. בַּ for בְּהַ)(id. pl. absolute (§ 35. חוח
בַּחוֹחִים[y] } rem. 13); וּ id. . . .
בַּחוֹל[z] pref. id.)(noun masc. sing. . . . הול
בַּחוֹמָה[a] ׳וּ pref. id. } noun f. s. dec. 10; וּ bef. lab. חמה
בְּחוֹמָה[b] pref. בְּ }
בְּחוֹמַת[c] ׳וּ pref. id.)(id., construct state; וּ id. . חמה
בְּחוֹמֹת[d] pref. id.)(id. pl. . . . . . חמה
בְּחוֹמֹתַי[e] וּ pref. id.)(id. pl., suff. 1 pers. sing.; וּ id. חמה
בָּחוֹן[f] adj. masc. sing. . . . . . בחן
בְּחוֹף[g] וּ pref. בְּ)(noun masc. s. (for חֹף); וּ bef. (:) חפף
בַּחוּץ pref. בַּ for בְּהַ)(noun masc. sing. dec. 1 a. . חוץ
בַּחוּצוֹת pref. id. } id. pl. with fem. term.; וּ bef. (:) חוץ
בְּחוּצוֹת[h] ׳וּ pref. בְּ }

[a] Eze. 23. 30. [b] Eze. 43. 7. [c] 2 Ch. 26. 19. [d] Is. 57. 13. [e] Ge. 3. 19. [f] Ex. 2. 3. [g] Ps. 149. 8. [h] Is. 3. 5. [i] Le. 13. 29. [k] 2 Sa. 20. 9. [l] 1 Sa. 17. 34. [m] Ex. 10. 9. [n] Ps. 68. 31. [o] Pr. 5. 20. [p] Je. 27. 5. [q] De. 32. 16. [r] Da. 2. 43. [s] De. 5. 15. [t] De. 4. 37. [u] Is. 40. 11. [x] Ge. 28. 14. [y] De. 10. 15. [z] Is. 40. 12. [a] 2 Sa. 12. 10. [b] Job 31. 33. [c] Ps. 78. 55. [d] Pr. 5. 22. [e] Is. 26. 17. [f] Is. 47. 12. [g] Ex. 26. 4, 10. [h] Is. 53. 5. [i] Eze. 45. 17. [k] Eze. 46. 11. [l] De. 16. 14. [m] 1 Ki. 2. 5. [n] Ezr. 6. 16. [o] Ex. 7. 28. [p] Ju. 16. 9. [q] Ju. 16. 12. [r] Ec. 10. 20. [s] Is. 26. 20. [t] Je. 2. 24. [u] Job 40. 26. [x] 1 Sa. 13. 6. [y] 2 Ch. 33. 11. [z] Ex. 2. 12. [a] Jos. 2. 15. [b] Is. 30. 13. [h] Je. 7. 17. [i] Job 40. 25. [c] 2 Ch. 27. 3. [d] Ne. 2. 13. [e] Is. 56. 5. [f] Je. 6. 27. [g] De. 1. 7.

בְּחוּצוֹתֶיהָ pref. id.)(id. pl., suff. 3 pers. sing. fem. . חוץ
בְּחוּצוֹתֵינוּ[a] pref. id.)(id. pl., suff. 1 pers. pl. . . חוץ
בְּחוּצֹת[b] pref. id.)(id. pl., defect. for חוּצוֹת . חוץ
בְּחוּצֹתֶיו pref. id.)(id. pl., suff. 3 pers. s. m. Is. 15. 3. חוץ
בְּחוּקוֹ[c] pref. id.)(Kal inf., suff. 3 pers. sing. masc., for חֻקּוֹ (§ 18. rem. 12) . . . . חקק
בְּחֻקֵּי[d] pref. id.)(noun masc. pl. constr. (for חֻקֵּי § 37. rem. 2) from חֹק dec. 8 c. . . חקק
בָּחוֹר* וּ Kal inf. absolute; וּ before lab. *Is. 7. 15, 16. בחר
בָּחוּר וּ' id. part. pass. sing. masc. dec. 3 a; וּ id. . בחר
בָּחוּר n. m. s. [for בַּחוּר], pl. בַּחוּרִים (dag. for impl.) בחר
בְּחוּרוֹתֶיךָ[aa] noun f. pl. (בְּחוּרוֹת), suff. 2 p. s. m. dec. 10. בחר
בַּחוּרַי[e] / בַּחוּרַי } noun masc. pl., suff. 1 pers. sing. from בָּחוּר (q. v.); וּ before lab. . . } בחר
בַּחוּרֵי[f] וּ' id. pl., construct state; וּ id. . . בחר
בְּחוּרֵי Kal part. pass. pl. constr. m. from בָּחוּר d. 3 a. בחר
בַּחוּרֶיהָ n. m. pl., suff. 3 p. s. f. from בָּחוּר [for בַּחוּר] בחר
בַּחוּרֵיהֶם id. pl., suff. 3 pers. pl. masc. . . בחר
בַּחוּרָיו[g] וּ' id. pl., suff. 3 pers. sing. masc.; וּ bef. lab. בחר
בַּחוּרֵיכֶם id. pl., suff. 2 pers. pl. masc. . . בחר
בַּחוּרִים[h] וּ' id. pl., abs. state, also pr. name; וּ bef. lab. בחר
בַּחוֹרִים[i] pref. בַּ for בְּהַ)(n. m., pl. of [חוֹר] dec. 1 a. חור
בְּחֶזְוָא[k] Chald. pref. בְּ)(n. m. s., emph. of [חֱזוּ] dec. 3 c. חזא
בְּחֶזְוֵי Chald. pref. id.)(id. pl. construct state . חזא
בְּחֶזְוִי[l] Chald. pref. id.)(id. sing., suff. 1 pers. sing. חזא
בַּחֲזוֹן[m] pref. בַּ bef. (-:))(construct of the following: חזה
בֶּחָזוֹן / בְּחָזוֹן[n] pref. בֶּ f. בְּהָ, בֶּהָ / pref. בְּ q.v. & ה } noun masc. sing. dec. 3 a. חזה
בַּחֲזוֹת[o] pref. בַּ before (-:))(Kal inf. construct . חזה
בַּחֲזוֹת[p] וּ pref. id.)(noun masc. sing. construct [of חָזוֹת] dec. 3 a; וּ before lab. . . חזה
בְּחָזָק[q] pref. בְּ)(adj. m. s. dec. 4 c. (§ 33. rem. 1) חזק
בְּחֹזֶק pref. id.)(noun masc. sing. dec. 6 c. . חזק
בְּחָזְקָה[r] וּ' pref. id.)(noun fem. sing.; וּ before (:) חזק
בְּחָזְקֵנוּ[s] pref. id.)(n. m. s., suff. 1 p. pl. from חֹזֶק d. 6 c. חזק
בְּחֶזְקַת[t] pref. id.)(noun fem. sing., constr. of חֶזְקָה (no vowel change) . . . חזק
בַּחַחִים[u] pref. בַּ for בְּהַ)(noun masc., pl. of חָח § 37. rem. 7. (as if from a Root ע"ע) see . חוח
בְּחֵטְא[x] וּ pref. בְּ)(n. m. s. d. 6. (§ 35. r. 6); וּ bef. (:) חטא
בְּחֶטְאָהּ[y] pref. id.)(id., suff. 3 pers. s. f. (for ה without Mak. § 3. rem. 3) . . . . חטא
בְּחֶטְאוֹ pref. id.)(id., suff. 3 pers. sing. masc. . חטא
בְּחַטֹּאות[z] וּ' pref. id.)(n. f. pl. [for חַטָּאוֹת comp. § 23. No. 4] construct of חַטָּאוֹת, from חַטָּאת (§ 39. No. 4 d. & 44. rem. 5) . חטא

בְּחַטֹּאותֶיךָ[a] pref. id.)(id. pl., suff. 2 pers. sing. masc. חטא
בְּחַטֹּאתֵינוּ[b] pref. id.)(id. pl., suff. 1 pers. pl. . חטא
בַּחֲטָאִים[c] pref. בַּ for בְּהַ)(n. m., pl. of [חֲטָא] d. 1 b. חטא
בַּחֲטָאֵינוּ[d] pref. בַּ bef. (-:))(noun masc. pl., suff. 1 pers. pl. from חֵטְא dec. 6. (§ 35. rem. 6) . חטא
בְּחַטָּאת[e] pref. בְּ)(noun f. s. (§ 39. No. 4 d. & 44. r. 5) חטא
בְּחַטֹּאת[f] pref. id.)(id. pl. construct state [for חַטָּאוֹת comp. § 23. rem. 4] . . . חטא
בְּחַטָּאתוֹ[g] וּ' pref. id.)(id. sing., suff. 3 p. s. m.; וּ bef. (:) חטא
בְּחַטֹּאתָו[h] וּ pref. id.)(id. pl., with suff. (Kh. בְּחַטֹּאתָיו), K. בְּחַטָּאתוֹ (q. v.); וּ id. . . . חטא
בְּחַטֹּאתַיִךְ[i] pref. id.)(id. pl., suff. 2 pers. sing. fem. חטא
בְּחַטֹּאתָם pref. id.)(id. pl., suff. 3 pers. pl. masc. . חטא
בְּחִטֵּי[k] pref. id.)(noun masc. with pl. fem. term., construct state from חִטָּה . . חטה
בְּחֵי[l] pref. id.)(adj. m. s. constr. of חַי d. 8 d. (§ 37. r. 6) חיי
בְּחִידוֹת / בְּחִידֹת[m] } pref. id.)(noun fem., pl. of חִידָה dec. 10. חוד
בַּחַיָּה[n] וּ pref. בַּ for בְּהַ)(n. f. s. dec. 10; וּ bef. lab. חיי
בְּחַיָּו[o] Kh., for K. בְּחַיָּיו (q. v. & § 4. rem. 1) . חיי
בְּחַיַּי / בְּחַיָּי[p] } pref. בְּ)(noun masc. pl., suff. 1 pers. sing. from חַי dec. 8 d. (§ 37. rem. 6) } חיי
בְּחַיֶּיהָ[q] pref. id.)(id. pl., suff. 3 pers. sing. fem. . חיי
בְּחַיֵּיהֶם pref. id.)(id. pl., suff. 3 pers. pl. masc. . חיי
בְּחַיָּיו pref. id.)(id. pl., suff. 3 pers. sing. masc. . חיי
בְּחַיֶּיךָ[r] pref. id.)(id. pl., suff. 2 pers. sing. masc. . חיי
בַּחַיִּים pref. בַּ for בְּהַ)(id. pl., absolute state . חיי
בְּחַיִּין pref. id.)(id. pl., absolute state, Chald. form חיי
בְּחַיִּין[s] Chald. pref. בְּ)(adj. m., pl. of חַי dec. 5 a. . חיי
בְּחַיִל[u] / בְּחָיִל } pref. id.)(noun masc. sing. dec. 6 h. (§ 35. rem. 12), Chald. dec. 3 d. . . } חול
בְּחֵיל pref. id.)(id., construct st. Chald. Da. 4. 32. חול
בְּחֵילַהּ[x] Chald. pref. id.)(id., suff. 3 pers. sing. fem. חול
בְּחִילָה[y] pref. id.)(noun fem. sing. . . . חול
בְּחֵילוֹ[z] pref. id.)(noun masc. sing., suff. 3 pers. sing. masc. from חַיִל dec. 6 h. (§ 35. rem. 12) חול
בְּחֵילְךָ[a] / בְּחֵילֶךָ[b] } pref. id.)(id., suff. 2 pers. sing. masc. חול
בְּחֵילֵךְ pref. id.)(id., suff. 2 pers. sing. fem. . חול
בְּחִינָיו[c] Kh. בְּחִינָיו, K. בַּחוּנָיו, noun masc. pl. with suff. from [בַּחוּן or בַּחִין] . . בחן
בַּחִיצוֹן[d] וּ pref. בַּ for בְּהַ)(adj. masc. sing.; וּ bef. lab. חוץ
בְּחֵיק[e] / בַּחֵיק[f] pref. id. / pref. בַּ } noun masc. sing. dec. 1 a. . חוק
בְּחֵיקָהּ pref. id.)(id., suff. 3 pers. sing. fem. . חוק

[a] Ps. 144. 13. [b] 2 Sa. 1. 20. [c] Pr. 8. 29. [d] Eze. 20. 18. [e] La. 1. 15. [f] Ps. 78. 31. [g] Is. 31. 8. [h] Is. 40. 30. [i] Is. 42. 22. [k] Da. 2. 19. [l] Da. 7. 2. [m] 2 Ch. 32. 32. [n] Ps. 89. 20. [o] Eze. 21. 34. [p] 2 Ch. 9. 29. [q] Is. 40. 10. [r] Eze. 34. 4. [s] Am. 6. 13. [t] Is. 8. 11. [u] Eze. 19. 4, 9. [x] Ps. 51. 7. [y] Nu. 15. 28. [z] Mi. 1. 5. [a] Is. 43. 24. [b] Ne. 9. 37. [c] Pr. 23. 16. [d] Da. 9. 16. [e] Je. 17. 3. [f] 2 Ki. 24. 3. [g] Eze. 3. 20. [h] 1 Ki. 16. 26. [i] Eze. 16. 52. [k] Eze. 27. 17. [l] Da. 12. 7. [m] Nu. 12. 8. [n] Ge. 7. 21. [o] 2 Sa. 18. 18. [p] Ge. 27. 46. [q] Le. 18. 18. [r] De. 28. 66. [s] Job 24. 22. [t] Da. 7. 12. [u] Da. 3. 4. [x] Da. 3. 20. [y] Job 6. 10. [z] Ob. 1. 13. [a] Eze. 28. 5. [aa] Ec. 11. 9. [b] Ps. 59. 12. [c] Is. 23. 13. [d] Eze. 41. 17. [e] Pr. 16. 33. [f] Ec. 7. 9.

Word	Analysis	Root
בְּחֵיקוֹ וּ׳	pref. id.)(id., suff. 3 pers. sing. masc.	חוק
בְּחֵיקִי	pref. id.)(id., suff. 1 pers. sing. . . .	חוק
בְּחֵיקֶךָ	pref. id.)(id., suff. 2 pers. s. m. [for חֵיקְךָ]	חוק
[a] בְּחִיר	adj. masc. sing., constr. of [בָּחִיר] dec. 3a. .	בחר
[b] בְּחִירוֹ	id., suff. 3 pers. sing. masc. . .	בחר
[c] בְּחִירָי / [d] בְּחִירַי	} id. pl., suff. 1 pers. sing. . . .	בחר
בְּחִירִי	id. sing., suff. 1 pers. sing. . . .	בחר
בְּחִירָיו	id. pl., suff. 3 pers. sing. masc. . .	בחר
[e] בְּחִירֶיךָ	id. pl., suff. 2 pers. sing. masc. .	בחר
[f] בְּחַיַּת	pref. בְּ)(noun fem. s., constr. of חַיָּה d. 10.	חיה
בְּחִכָּה	pref. id.)(noun fem. sing. . . .	חנך
[g] בְּחִכִּי	pref. id.)(n. m. s., suff. 1 p. s. fr. חֵךְ d. 8b.	חנך
בַּחָכְמָה / בְּחָכְמָה	pref. בַּ for בְּהַ / pref. בְּ q. v. & ה } n. f. s. (no vowel change); Chald. (Da. 2. 30) d. 8a.	חכם
[h] בְּחָכְמָתָהּ	pref. id.)(id., suff. 3 pers. sing. fem. .	חכם
בְּחָכְמָתוֹ	pref. id.)(id., suff. 3 pers. sing. masc. .	חכם
[i] בְּחָכְמָתִי	וּ pref. id.)(id., suff. 1 pers. sing.; וּ bef. (:)	חכם
[k] בְּחָכְמָתְךָ	pref. id.)(id., suff. 2 pers. sing. masc. .	חכם

[בָּחַל] I. as in Syr. *to loathe*, with בְּ, Zec. 11. 8.—II. as in Arab. *to be greedy*, only Pu. part. *greedily gotten*, Prov. 20. 21. Kheth.

Word	Analysis	Root
[l] בַּחֵל / [m] בְּחֵל	pref. בַּ f. בְּהַ / pref. בְּ q. v. } noun masc. sing. dec. 1a. .	חול
בַּחֲלֵב	pref. בַּ bef. (-:))(n. m. s., constr. of [חָלָב] d. 5c.	חלב
[n] בֶּחָלָב	pref. בֶּ for בְּהֶ, בְּהַ)(noun masc. sing. dec. 4c.	חלב
[o] בְּחֶלְבּוֹ	pref. בְּ)(noun masc. sing., suff. 3 pers. sing. masc. from חֵלֶב dec. 6. (§ 35. rem. 6) .	חלב
[p] בְּחֶלְבֵי	pref. id.)(id. pl., construct state . .	חלב
[q] בָּחֲלָה	Kal pret. 3 pers. sing. fem. . . .	בחל
בַּחֲלוֹם	pref. בַּ bef. (-:))(noun masc. sing. dec. 1a.	חלם
בַּחֲלוֹמִי	pref. id.)(id., suff. 1 pers. sing. Ge. 40. 9, 16.	חלם
[r] בַּחֲלוֹמֹתָם	pref. id.)(id. pl., suff. 3 pers. pl. masc.	חלם
בַּחַלּוֹן / [s] בְּחַלּוֹן	pref. בַּ f. בְּהַ / pref. בְּ q. v. } noun com. sing. dec. 1a. .	חלל
[t] בְּחַלּוֹנֵינוּ	pref. id.)(id. pl., suff. 1 pers. pl. . .	חלל
[u] בַּחֲלוֹתָם	pref. בַּ bef. (-:))(Kal inf., suff. 3 p. pl. m. d. 1b.	חלה
בַּחֲלַח	pref. id.)(pr. name of a province .	חלח
בְּחָלְיוֹ	pref. בְּ)(n. m. s., suff. 3 p. s. m. fr. חֳלִי d. 6k.	חלה
[x] בָּחֳלָיִים	pref. בָּ bef. (т:))(id. pl. absolute state .	חלה
[y] בֶּחָלִיל	pref. בֶּ for בְּהֶ, בְּהַ)(noun masc. sing. dec. 3a.	חלל
[z] בַּחֲלַל	pref. בַּ bef. (-:))(constr. of the following .	חלל
בֶּחָלָל	pref. בֶּ for בְּהֶ, בְּהַ)(adj. masc. sing. dec. 4c.	חלל
[a] בְּחַלְּלוֹ	וּ pref. בְּ)(Piel inf. (חַלֵּל), suff. 3 pers. sing. masc. dec. 7b; וּ bef. (:) . .	חלל
[b] בַּחֲלִלִים	pref. בַּ bef. (-:))(noun m., pl. of חָלִיל d. 3a.	חלל
בַּחֲלֹם	pref. id.)(noun masc. sing. dec. 1a. .	חלם
בַּחֲלֹמוֹת	pref. id.)(id. pl. with fem. term. .	חלם
[c] בַּחֲלֹמִי	pref. id.)(id. sing., suff. 1 pers. sing. .	חלם
[d] בַּחַלָּמִישׁ	pref. בַּ for בְּהַ)(noun masc. sing. dec. 3c.	חלם
בְּחֵלֶק	pref. בְּ)(noun masc. sing. dec. 6b. (§ 35. r. 6.)	חלק
[e] בַּחֶלְקָה	pref. בַּ for בְּהַ)(noun fem. sing. dec. 12b.	חלק
[f] בַּחֲלָקוֹת	pref. בַּ bef. (-:))(id. pl. absolute state .	חלק
[g] בַּחֲלֻקּוֹת	pref. id.)(noun fem., pl. of [חֲלֻקָּה] dec. 10.	חלק
[h] בְּחַלְקֵי	pref. בְּ)(noun masc. pl. constr. from חֵלֶק with dag. euph. (§ 35. rem. 17) .	חלק
[i] בַּחֲלַקְלַקּוֹת	pref. בַּ bef. (-:))(n. pl. fem. [from חֲלַקְלַק]	חלק
[k] בְּחַלְּקָם	pref. בְּ)(Piel inf. [חַלֵּק], suff. 3 p. pl. m. d. 7b.	חלק
בְּחֶלְקַת	pref. id.)(noun f. s., constr. of חֶלְקָה d. 12b.	חלק
[l] בַּחֲלֹתוֹ	pref. בַּ bef. (-:))(Kal inf., suff. 3 p. s. m. d. 1a.	חלה
בְּחֹם	pref. בְּ)(noun masc. sing. . . .	חמם
[m] בְּחֵמָא	by Chaldaism for בְּחֵמָה (q. v.) . .	יחם
[n] בַּחֲמֻדוֹת	וּ pref. בַּ bef. (-:))(noun fem. pl.; וּ bef. lab.	חמד
בְּחֵמָה	וּ׳ pref. בְּ)(noun fem. sing. dec. 11b; וּ id.	יחם
[o] בְּחֵמָה	pref. id.)(noun s. fem. by syncope for חֶמְאָה	חמא
[p] בְּחֻמּוֹ	pref. id.)(Kal inf. (חֹם), suff. 3 p. s. m. d. 8c.	חמם
[q] בַּחֲמוּדוֹ	pref. בַּ bef. (-:))(Kal part. pass. [חָמוּד], suff. 3 pers. sing. masc. dec 3a. .	חמד
[r] בַּחֲמוֹרִים	pref. id.)(noun masc., pl. of חֲמוֹר dec. 1a.	חמר
[s] בְּחוֹמֹתַיִךְ	pref. בְּ)(n. m. pl., suff. 2 p. s. m. fr. חוֹמָה d. 10.	חמה
[t] בַּחֲמִישִׁי	pref. בַּ for בְּהַ)(num. ord. sing. masc.	חמש
[u] בְּחֶמְלַת	pref. בְּ)(noun fem. sing., constr. of חֶמְלָה	חמל
[x] בְּחֶמְלָתוֹ	וּ pref. id.)(id., suff. 3 pers. s. m.; וּ bef. (:)	חמל
[y] בְּחֻמָּם	pref. id.)(Kal inf. (חֹם), suff. 3 pers. pl. m. d. 8c.	חמם
[z] בֶּחָמֵץ	pref. בַּ for בְּהַ)(noun masc. sing. .	חמץ
[a] בַּחֲמוֹר	וּ pref. בַּ bef. (-:))(n. m. s. d. 1a; וּ bef. lab.	חמר
בַּחֹמֶר*	pref. בַּ for בְּהַ)(noun masc. sing. *Ex. 2. 3.	חמר
בַּחֹמֶר* / [b] בְּחֹמֶר	pref. id. / pref. בְּ })(noun masc. sing. *Na. 3. 14.	חמר
[c] בַּחֲמֹרִים	וּ׳ pref. בַּ bef. (-:))(noun masc., pl. of חֲמוֹר dec. 1a; וּ bef. lab. . . .	חמר
[d] בַּחֲמֵשׁ	pref. id.)(num. card. sing. fem. constr. of חָמֵשׁ (§ 34. rem. 1)	חמש
בַּחֲמִשָּׁה	וּ׳ pref. id.)(id. masc., constr. חֲמֵשֶׁת .	חמש
[e] בַּחֲמִישִׁי	pref. בַּ for בְּהַ)(num. ord. m. s. from חָמֵשׁ	חמש
בַּחֲמִשִּׁים	pref. בַּ bef. (-:))(num. card. com., pl. of חָמֵשׁ	חמש
בַּחֲמָת	pref. id.)(pr. name of a place . .	חמה

a 2 Sa. 21. 6. b Ps. 106. 23. c Is. 65. 22. d Is. 65. 9. e Ps. 106. 5. f Ho. 4. 3. g Job 33. 2. h 2 Sa. 20. 22. i Is. 10. 13. k Eze. 28. 4. l 2 Sa. 20. 15. m 1 Ki. 21. 23. n Ca. 5. 12. o Job 15. 27. p 2 Ch. 29. 35. q Zec. 11. 8. r Je. 23. 27. s Pr. 7. 6. t Je. 9. 20. u Ps. 35. 13. x 2 Ch. 21. 15. y Is. 30. 29. z Nu. 19. 16. a 1 Ch. 5. 1. b 1 Ki. 1. 40. c Ge. 41. 17, 22. d Job 28. 9. e 2 Ki. 9. 26, 26. f Ps. 73. 18. g Da. 11. 32. h Is. 57. 6. i Da. 11. 21, 34. k Is. 9. 2. l Is. 38. 9. m Da. 11. 44. n Da. 11. 38. o Job 29. 6. p Job 6. 17. q Job 20. 20. r 1 Ch. 12. 40. s Eze. 26. 9. t Zec. 7. 5. u Ge. 19. 16. x Is. 63. 9. y Je. 51. 39. z Ru. 2. 14. a De. 22. 10. b Ex. 1. 14. c Ge. 47. 17. d Eze. 45. 2. e Eze. 20. 1.

בַּחֲמַת pref. id.)(n. f. s., constr. of חֵמָה dec. 11b. — יחם

בַּחֲמָתָהּ[a] pref. id.)(noun fem. sing., suff. 3 pers. sing. fem. from [חֲמוֹת] dec. 3a. — חם

בַּחֲמָתוֹ[b] [c] ו׳ pref. id.)(noun fem. sing., suff. 3 pers. sing. masc. from חֵמָה dec. 11b; וּ bef. lab. — יחם

בַּחֲמָתִי ו׳ pref. id.)(id., suff. 1 pers. sing.; וּ id. — יחם

בַּחֲמָתְךָ[d] ו׳ pref. id.)(id., suff. 2 pers. sing. masc.; וּ id. — יחם

[בָּחַן] *to try, prove, test.* Niph. *to be tried.* Pu. id. Eze. 21. 18, but see בֹּחַן.

בַּחַן masc. *watch-tower,* Is. 32. 14.

בֹּחַן masc. *proof, trial,* Is. 28. 16, to which some refer also Eze. 21. 18, see the verb.

בָּחוֹן masc. adj. *trier, assayer* of metals, Je. 6. 27.

בַּחוּן· (after the form קָטוּל) *a watch-tower,* Is. 23. 13 Keri, בַּחִין Kheth.

בֹּחַן[e] וָ noun masc. sing.; for וָ see lett. ו — בחן

בֹּחַן noun masc. sing. — בחן

בֹּחֵן ו׳ Kal part. act. sing. masc.; וּ bef. labial — בחן

בָּחֲנוּ[f] id. pret. 3 pers. pl. — בחן

בְּחָנוּנִי[g] id. id., suff. 1 pers. sing. — בחן

בְּחָנוּנִי[h] וּ id. imp. [בְּחַן], pl. masc., suff. 1 pers. sing. (§ 16. rem. 11); וּ bef. lab. — בחן

בַּחֲנִית ו׳ pref. בַּ bef. (-:))(n. fem. sing. d. 1a; וּ id. — חנה

בַּחֲנִיתוֹ pref. id.)(id., suff. 3 pers. sing. masc. — חנה

בַּחֲנֻכַּת[i] וּ pref. id.)(noun fem. sing., constr. of חֲנֻכָּה dec. 10; וּ bef. lab. — חנך

בַּחֲנָמַל[k] pref. בַּ for בְּהַ)(noun masc. sing. — חנמל

בְּחָנַנִי[l] Kal pret. 3 pers. sing. masc., suff. 1 pers. sing. — בחן

בְּחָנֵנִי id. imp. s. m., [בְּחַן], suff. 1 p. s. (§ 16. r. 11) — בחן

בְּחַנְפֵי[m] pref. בְּ)(noun m. pl. constr. from חָנֵף d. 5c. — חנף

בָּחַנְתָּ[n] Kal pret. 2 pers. sing. masc. — בחן

בָחַנְתָּ וּ id. id.; acc. shifted by וּ (bef. lab. for וְ) conv. (§ 8. rem. 7) — בחן

בַּחֲנֹת[o] וּ pref. בַּ bef. (-:))(Kal inf. constr.; וּ bef. lab. — חנה

בְּחַנְתִּים וּ Kal pret. 1 pers. s., suff. 3 pers. pl. m.; וּ id. — בחן

בְּחַנְתָּנוּ[p] id. pret. 2 pers. sing. masc., suff. 1 pers. pl. — בחן

בַּחֶסֶד pref. בַּ for בְּהַ } noun m. sing., (suff. חַסְדִּי) dec. 6a; וּ bef. (:) — חסד
בְחֶסֶד ו׳ pref. בְּ q. v. }

בְּחַסְדְּךָ / בְחַסְדְּךָ } [q] ו׳ pref. id.)(id., suff. 2 pers. s. m.; וּ id. — חסד

בַּחֲסַף[r] Chald. pref. בַּ bef. (-:))(noun m. s. dec. 3a. — חסף

בַּחֲסַר[s] pref. id.)(adj. masc. sing. constr. of חָסֵר d. 5c. — חסר

בְּחֹסֶר[t] pref. בְּ)(noun masc. sing. — חסר

בְחֹסֶר[u] [x] ו׳ pref. id.)(noun masc. sing.; וּ bef. (:) — חסר

בְּחָפְזָהּ[y] pref. id.)(Kal inf., suff. 3 pers. sing. fem. — חפז

בְּחִפָּזוֹן pref. id.)(noun masc. sing. — חפז

בְּחָפְזִי pref. id.)(Kal inf., suff. 1 pers. sing. — חפז

בְּחָפְנָיו[z] pref. id.)(n. m. du., suff. 3 p. s. m. fr. [חֹפֶן] d. 6c. — חפן

בְּחֶפֶץ[a] pref. id.)(noun masc. sing. dec. 6b. (§ 35. r. 6) — חפץ

בְּחָצוֹר pref. id.)(pr. name of a place — חצר

בַּחֻצוֹת וּ noun masc. with pl. fem. term. def. for חוצות from חוץ dec. 1a; וּ bef. (:) — חוץ

בַּחֲצִי pref. בַּ bef. (-:) } noun masc. sing. dec. 6i. — חצה
בַּחֲצִי pref. בַּ for בְּהַ } (§ 35. rem. 14)

בְּחִצִּים [b] ו׳ pref. id. } noun masc., pl. of חֵץ dec. 8b; — חצץ
בַּחִצִּים[c] וּ pref. בְּ } וּ bef. lab.

בְּחֹצֶן[d] pref. id.)(noun masc. sing. dec. 6c. — חצן

בֶּחָצָץ[e] pref. בֶּ for בְּהַ, בְּהָ)(noun masc. sing. dec. 4c. — חצץ

בְּחַצְצוֹן / בְּחַצְצֹן } pref. בְּ)(pr. name of a place, see חַצְצוֹן תָּמָר — חצץ

בַּחֲצֹצְרוֹת / בַּחֲצֹצְרֹת } ו׳ pref. בַּ bef. (-:))(n. f., pl. of חֲצֹצְרָה d. 10. — חצר

בַּחֲצַר pref. בַּ bef. (-:))(constr. of the following; also pr. name in compos. as בַּחֲצַר סוּסִים — חצר

בֶּחָצֵר pref. בֶּ for בְּהַ, בְּהָ)(noun com. sing. dec. 5c. — חצר

בַּחֲצֵרוֹ[f] pref. בַּ bef. (-:))(id., suff. 3 pers. sing. masc. — חצר

בַּחֲצֵרוֹת pref. id.)(id., pl. abs. st. and pr. name of a place — חצר

בְּחַצְרוֹת [g] ו׳ pref. בְּ)(id. pl., constr. st. fem. term. — חצר

בְּחַצְרֵי[h] pref. id.)(id. pl. constr. masc. term. — חצר

בְּחַצְרֵיהֶם pref. id.)(id., pl., suff. 3 pers. pl. masc. — חצר

בַּחֲצֵרֶיךָ[i] pref. בַּ bef. (-:))(id. pl., suff. 2 pers. sing. masc. — חצר

בַּחֲצֵרִים[k] pref. id.)(id. pl. masc., as a pr. name of a place — חצר

בְּחַצְרֹתֵיהֶם[l] וּ pref. בְּ)(id. pl. fem., suff. 3 pers. pl. m. — חצר

בַּחֵק[m] pref. בַּ for בְּהַ)(noun m. sing. for חֵיק d. 1a. — חוק

בְּחֻקּוֹ[n] pref. בְּ)(noun masc. sing. dec. 8c. — חקק

בְּחֻקּוֹת pref. id.)(noun fem., pl. of חֻקָּה dec. 10. — חקק

בְּחֻקּוֹתַי pref. id.)(id. with suff. 1 pers. sing. — חקק

בְּחֵקִי[o] pref. id.)(n. m. s., suff. 1 pers. s. fr. חֵיק d. 1a. — חוק

בְּחֻקַּי pref. id.,)(n. m. pl., suff. 1 p. s. fr. חֹק d. 6c. — חקק

בְּחֻקָּיו[p] pref. id.)(id., suff. 3 pers. sing. masc. — חקק

בְּחֻקֶּיךָ pref. id.)(id., suff. 2 pers. sing. masc. — חקק

בְּחֵקֶר[q] וּ pref. id.)(noun masc. sing. d. 6b; וּ bef. (:) — חקר

בְּחֻקֹּת[r] pref. id.)(noun fem., pl. of חֻקָּה dec. 10. — חקק

בְּחֻקֹּתַי[s] ו׳ pref. id.)(id., suff. 1 pers. sing.; וּ bef. (:) — חקק

בְּחֻקֹּתֵיהֶם[t] וּ pref. id.)(id., suff. 3 pers. pl. masc.; וּ id. — חקק

בְּחֻקֹּתָיו[u] וּ pref. id.)(id., suff. 3 pers. sing. masc.; וּ id. — חקק

בְּחֻקֹּתֶיךָ[w] pref. id.)(id., suff. 2 pers. sing. masc. — חקק

בָּחַר ו׳ I. *to prove, examine* (so in the Syr.) Job 34. 3; Is. 48. 10; and 2 Ch. 34. 6. Kheth.—II. *to choose, elect, select,* const. with acc., בְּ, לְ, once עַל, with

[a] Mi. 7. 6. [b] Est. 7. 7. [c] De. 29. 22. [d] Ps. 6. 2. [e] Is. 32. 14. [f] Mal. 3. 15. [g] Ps. 95. 9. [h] Mal. 3. 10. [i] Ne. 12. 27. [k] Ps. 78. 47. [l] Job 23. 10. [m] Ps. 35. 16. [n] Ps. 17. 3. [o] Nu. 1. 51. [p] Ps. 66. 10. [q] Ps. 143. 12. [r] Da. 2. 41, 43. [s] Pr. 10. 21. [t] Job 30. 3. [u] De. 28. 57. [x] De. 28. 48. [y] 2 Sa. 4. 4. [z] Pr. 30. 4. [a] Pr. 31. 13. [b] 1 Ch. 12. 2. [c] Eze. 39. 9. [d] Is. 49. 22. [e] La. 3. 16. [f] 2 Sa. 17. 18. [g] Ne. 8. 16. [h] Ne. 13. 7. [i] Ps. 84. 11. [k] De. 2. 23. [l] Ne. 8. 16. [m] Pr. 21. 14. [n] Pr. 8. 27. [o] Job 19. 27. [p] 1 Ki. 8. 61. [q] Job 38. 16. [r] Le. 20. 23. [s] Je. 44. 10. [t] Le. 18. 3. [u] Je. 44. 23. [w] Ps. 119. 16.

מִן *to be better than.* Niph. part. *chosen, choice, excellent,* with לְ *by*; with מִן *more.*

בָּחוּר (for בָּחוּר) masc., pl. בַּחוּרִים (dag. forte implied), *a youth,* prop. *choice* for vigour and activity.

בַּחֻרִים (*place of youths*) pr. name of a town in the tribe of Judah, Gent. n. בַּחֲרוּמִי, 1 Ch. 11. 33. and transp. בַּרְחֻמִי, 2 Sa. 23. 31.

בְּחֻרִים masc. pl. (prop. from a sing. בְּחוּר § 26. No. 13) *youth, youthful age,* see the prec. Nu. 11. 28.

בְּחֻרוֹת fem. pl. id. Ec. 11. 9; 12. 1.

בָּחִיר masc. dec. 3 a, *chosen, elect.*

יִבְחָר (whom *He chooses*) pr. name of a son of David.

מִבְחָר masc. dec. 2 b.—I. *choice, best.*—II. pr. name masc. 1 Ch. 11. 38.

מִבְחוֹר masc. id. 2 Ki. 3. 19; 19. 23.

בָּחַר [a] Kal pret. 3 pers. sing. m. for בָּחַר (§ 8. r. 7) בחר

בָּחֹר [b] וּ id. inf. absolute; וּ bef. labial . בחר

בְּחַר id. imp. sing. masc. . . . . בחר

בְּחַרְבֹתֵיהֶם Kh. בְּחַרְבֹתֵיהֶם q. v.; K. בְּחַר בָּתֵּיהֶם, pref. בְּ) noun fem. pl., suff. 3 pers. pl. masc. from חֶרֶב dec. 6 a. . . . . . חרב

בְּחֹר pref. בְּ) pr. n. in compos., see חֹר הַגִּד׳ under R. גדד

בֹּחֵר [d] Kal part. act. sing. masc. . . . בחר

בַּחֶרֶב [e] וּ׳ pref. בַּ f. בְּהַ } noun fem. s. (suff. חַרְבִּי) dec. 6 a; וּ bef. (:) חרב
בֶּחָרֶב pref. בֶּ f. בְּהֶ, בְּהַ
בְּחֶרֶב [f] וּ׳ pref. בְּ q. v. & ה

בְּחֹרֵב וּ׳ pref. id.) pr. name of a place; וּ bef. (:) . חרב

בֶּחָרְבָה pref בֶּ for בְּהֶ, bef. חָ for בְּהַ) noun f. s. חרב

בְּחַרְבּוֹ [f] [g] וּ׳ pref. בְּ) noun fem. sing., suff. 3 pers. sing. masc. from חֶרֶב dec. 6 a. . . . חרב

בְּחַרְבֹנַי [h] pref. id.) noun masc. pl. c. [from חֲרָבוֹן d. 3 c. § 32. No. 2]; Milêl before monos. . חרב

בֶּחֳרָבוֹת [i] pref. בַּ for בְּהַ) n. f. pl. abs. fr. חֶרֶב d. 6 a. חרב

בָּחֳרָבוֹת pref. בָּ bef. (:‏)) n. f. pl. abs. fr. חָרְבָּה d. 12 c. חרב

בְּחַרְבוֹת [k] pref. בְּ) noun fem. pl., constr. of חֲרָבוֹת from חֶרֶב dec. 6 a. . . . . חרב

בֶּחֳרָבוֹת [l] pref. בֶּ for בְּהֶ, בְּהַ) noun fem. pl. abs. from חָרְבָּה dec. 12 c. . . . . . חרב

בְּחַרְבוֹתָיו [m] וּ pref. בְּ) noun fem. pl., suff. 3 pers. sing. masc. from חֶרֶב dec. 6 a. . . . . חרב

בְּחַרְבוֹתָם pref. id.) id. pl., suff. 3 pers. pl. masc. . חרב

בְּחַרְבִּי [n] pref. id.) id. sing., suff. 1 pers. sing. . . חרב

בְּחַרְבְּךָ pref. id.) id. sing., suff. 2 pers. sing. masc. חרב

בְּחַרְבָּם [o] pref. id.) id. sing. 3 pers. pl. masc. . . חרב

בַּחֲרָדָה pref. בַּ bef. (-:)) pr. name of a place . חרד

בָּחֲרוּ
בָּחֲרוּ [p] [q] וּ׳ } Kal pret. 3 pers. pl. (§ 8. r. 7); וּ bef. lab בחר

בַּחֲרוּ id. imp. pl. masc. . . . בחר

בַּחֲרוּזִים [r] pref. בַּ bef. (-:)) noun masc. pl. [of חָרוּז] חרז

בַּחֲרוֹן [s] pref. id.) noun m. s., constr. of חָרוֹן d. 3 a. חרה

בַּחֲרוֹנוֹ [t] וּ pref. id.) id., suff. 3 pers. s. m.; וּ bef. lab. חרה

בֶּחָרוּץ [u] pref. בֶּ for בְּהֶ, bef. חָ for בְּהַ) n. m. s. d. 3 a. חרץ

בַּחֲרוֹת [x] pref. בַּ, bef. (-:)) Kal inf. constr. . חרה

בְּחוּרוֹתֶיךָ [y] noun f. pl. [בְּחֻרוֹת], suff. 2 pers. sing. m. בחר

בְּחַרְחֻר [z] וּ pref. בְּ) noun masc. sing.; וּ bef. (:) חרר

בַּחֶרֶט [a] pref. בַּ for בְּהַ } noun masc. sing. . חרט
בְּחֶרֶט [b] pref. בְּ q. v.

בַּחַרְטֻמִּים [c] pref. בַּ for בְּהַ) noun masc. pl. [of חַרְטֹם dec. 8 c. § 37. No. 4] . . . . חרט

בָּחֳרִי pref. בָּ bef. (:‏)) noun masc. sing. . חרה

בָּחֳרִי [d] Kal inf., suff. 1 pers. sing. (§ 16. rem. 8) בחר

בַּחוּרֶיהָ [e] noun masc. pl., suff. 3 pers. sing. fem. (dag. forte impl. in ח) from בָּחוּר [for בַּחּוּר] בחר

בַּחוּרֵיהֶם [f] וּ id. with suff. 3 pers. pl. masc.) וּ bef. lab. בחר

בְּחוֹרֵיהֶן [g] pref. בְּ) n. m. pl., suff. 3 p. pl. f. fr. חוֹר d. 1 a. חור

בַּחֻרִים pr. name of a place . . . . בחר

בַּחֻרִים [h] וּ defect. for בַּחוּרִים (q.v.) . . . בחר

בַּחֲרִיצֵי [i] וּ pref. בַּ bef. (-:)) noun masc. pl. const. fr. [חָרִיץ] dec. 3 a; וּ bef. labial . . חרץ

בֶּחָרִישׁ [u] pref. בֶּ for בְּהֶ, bef. חָ for בְּהַ) n. m. s. d. 3 a. חרש

בַּחֵרֶם pref. בַּ for בְּהַ) noun m. s. d. 6 (§ 35. r. 6) חרם

בְּחָרְמָה וּ׳ pref. בְּ) pr. name of a place . חרם

בְּחֶרְמוֹ [k] pref. id.) id., suff. 3 pers. sing. masc. . חרם

בְּחֶרְמִי [l] pref. id.) id., suff. 1 pers. sing. . . חרם

בְּחָרָן pref. id.) pr. name of a place . חרר

בֶּחָרֶם [m] וּ pref. בֶּ for בְּהֶ, bef. חָ for בְּהַ) noun m. sing., for חֵרֶם׳ dec. 6 a. (§ 35. r. 1); וּ bef. labial חרם

בַּחֹרֶף [n] וּ pref. בַּ for בְּהַ) noun m. s. dec. 6 c; וּ id. חרף

בְּחֶרְפָּה [o] וּ׳ pref. בְּ) noun fem. sing. dec. 12 b; וּ id. חרף

בְּחָרְפָם [p] pref. id.) Piel inf., חָרֵף suff. 3 pers. pl. m. חרף

בַּחֲרֻצוֹת [q] pref. בַּ bef. (-:)) adj. pl. fem. from חָרוּץ m. חרץ

בַּחֲרִצֵי [r] וּ defect. for בַּחֲרִיצֵי (q.v.) . . . חרץ

בַּחֹרֶשָׁה [s] pref. בַּ for בְּהַ) noun masc. sing. (חֹרֶשׁ) with parag. ה dec. 6 c. (§ 35. rem. 18) . חרש

בֶּחֳרָשִׁים [t] וּ pref. בֶּ for בְּהֶ, bef. חָ for בְּהַ) id. pl. abs.; וּ bef. labial . . . . . חרש

בַּחֲרֹשֶׁת וּ pref. בַּ bef. (-:)) noun fem. sing., also pr. name, see חֲ׳ הַגּוֹיִם . . . חרש

בָּחַרְתָּ
בָּחָרְתָּ } Kal pret. 2 pers. sing. masc. (§ 8. rem. 7) בחר

---

[a] Ps. 78. 67. [b] 1 Sa. 2. 28. [c] 2 Ch. 34. 6. [d] 1 Sa. 20. 30. [e] De. 28. 22. [f] Is. 27. 1. [g] Is. 66. 16. [h] Ps. 32. 4. [i] 1 Ki. 18. 28. [k] Eze. 32. 12. [l] Eze. 33. 27. [m] Eze. 26. 9. [n] Ge. 48. 22. [o] Ps. 44. 4. [p] Is. 66. 3. [q] Is. 56. 4. [r] Ca. 1. 10. [s] Na. 1. 6. [t] Ps. 2. 5. [u] Is. 28. 27. [x] Ps. 124. 3. [y] Ec. 12. 1. [z] De. 28. 22. [a] Ex. 32. 4. [b] Is. 8. 1. [c] Ex. 9. 11. [d] Eze. 20. 5. [e] Je. 51. 3. [f] 2 Ki. 8. 12. [g] Zec. 14. 12. [h] Je. 31. 13. [i] 1 Ch. 20. 3. [k] Hab. 1. 15. [l] Eze. 32. 3. [u] Ex. 34. 21. [m] De. 28. 27. [n] Zec. 14. 8. [o] Ne. 1. 3. [p] 2 Sa. 23. 9. [q] Am. 1. 3. [r] 2 Sa. 12. 31. [s] 1 Sa. 23. 15, 18. [t] 2 Ch. 27. 4.

בְּחַרְתָּ[a] וּ id. id. acc. shifted by וּ (bef. labial for וְ) conv. (§ 8. r. 7) . . . . בחר

בְּחַרְתִּי / בָּחַרְתִּי } [b] וּ id. pret. 1 pers. sing.; וּ bef. labial . בחר

בְּחַרְתִּיךָ[c] id. id., suff. 2 pers. sing. masc. . . . בחר

בְּחַרְתֶּם id. pret. 2 pers. pl. masc. . . . . בחר

בְּחֵשֶׁב pref. בְּ)(noun masc. sing. . . . חשב

בְּחֶשְׁבּוֹן pref. id.)(pr. name of a place . . . חבש

בַּחֲשׁוֹכָא[d] Chald. pref. בַּ bef. (-:))(noun masc. sing., emph. of [חֲשׁוֹךְ] dec. 1 a. . . . חשך

בַּחֹשֶׁךְ[e] וּ pref. בַּ for בְּהַ)(n. m. s. d. 6 c; וּ bef. lab. חשך

בַּחֲשֵׁכָה[f] pref. בַּ bef. (-:))(noun fem. sing. dec. 10. . חשך

בְּחַשְׁמֹנָה pref. בְּ)(pr. name of a place . . . חשם

בְּחֹשֶׁן[g] pref. id.)(noun masc. sing. . . . . חשן

בְּחִתִּיתָם[h] pref id.)(n. f. s., suff. 3 p. pl. m. from חִתִּית d. 1 b. חתת

בְּחֹתָמוֹ[i] pref. id.)(noun masc. sing., suff. 3 pers. sing. masc. from חוֹתָם (no vowel change) . חתם

בָּטָא. Pi. *to utter*, or *talk rashly*, or *unadvisedly*, comp. בָּטָה.

מִבְטָא masc. *rash utterance*, Nu. 30. 7, 9.

בַּטַּבָּעֹת pref. בַּ for בְּהַ)(pl. abs. from the following: טבע

בְּטַבַּעַת pref. בְּ)(noun fem. sing. (§ 4. rem. 5) . טבע

בְּטַבְּעֹת[k] pref. id.)(id. pl., construct state . . טבע

בָּטָה i. q. בָּטָא, only part. בֹּטֶה *an idle talker*, Pr. 12. 18.

בַּטָּהוֹר[l] pref. בַּ for בְּהַ)(adj. m. s. d. 3 a (§ 32. r. 7) טהר

בְּטָהֳרָתוֹ[m] pref. בְּ)(n. f. s., suff. 3 p. s. m. from טָהֳרָה (no pl.) טהר

בַּטּוֹב pref. בַּ for בְּהַ } adj. and subst. masc. sing. dec. 1 a. } טוב

בְּטוֹב pref. בְּ q. v.

בְּטוּב[n] וּ pref. id.)(noun m. s. dec. 1 a; וּ before (:) טוב

בַּטּוֹבָה[o] pref. בַּ for בְּהַ)(noun fem. sing. dec. 10. . טוב

בְּטוּבְךָ[p] [q] וּ pref. בְּ)(noun masc. sing., suff. 2 pers. sing. masc. from טוּב dec. 1 a; וּ before (:) טוב

בְּטוֹבַת[r] pref. id.)(noun f. s., constr. of טוֹבָה dec. 10. טוב

בְּטוֹבָתְךָ[s] pref. id.)(id., suff. 2 pers. sing. masc. . טוב

בָּטוֹחַ[t] Kal inf. absolute . . . . . בטח

בָּטוּחַ[u] id. part. pass. sing. masc. . . . . בטח

בָּטַח prop. *to cling to*, comp. Hiph., hence—I. *to rely upon, trust, confide in*, const. with בְּ, אֶל, עַל.—II. abs. *to be confident, secure*, in a good and bad sense. Hiph.—I. *to cause to cling to* or *hang upon*, Ps. 22. 10.—II. *to cause to trust, confide*, with אֶל, עַל.

בֶּטַח masc.—I. *trust, confidence, security*; לָבֶטַח and בֶּטַח *confidently, securely, safely*.—II. pr. name of a city in Syria, 2 Sa. 8. 8, for which טִבְחַת 1 Ch. 18. 8.

בִּטְחָה fem. *confidence*, Is. 30. 15.

בִּטָּחוֹן masc. *confidence, hope*.

בַּטֻּחוֹת fem. pl. *security, tranquillity*, Job 12. 6.

אֲבַטִּיחַ masc. *melon*, by transp. from טבח Arab *to cook, ripen*, Nu. 11. 5.

מִבְטָח masc. with suff. מִבְטַחִי dec. 2 b, but als מִבְטְחִי (§ 37. rem. 7) *trust, confidence, security* meton. *object of confidence*.

בָּטָח Kal preter. 3 pers. sing. masc. for בָּטַח (comp. § 8. rem. 1 and 7) . . בטח

בָּטֻחַ[x] defect. for בָּטוּחַ (q. v.) . . . . בטח

בֶּטַח[y] וָ noun masc. sing.; for וָ see letter ו . בטח

בְּטַח[z] וּ Kal imp. sing. masc.; וּ before labial . בטח

בֹּטֵחַ וּ id. part. act. sing. masc. dec. 7 b; וּ id. . בטח

בָּטָחָה[a] id. pret. 3 pers. sing. f. [for בָּטְחָה § 8. r. 7] בטח

בָּטְחוּ id. preter. 3 pers. pl. . . . . בטח

בִּטְחוּ[b] וּ id. imp. pl. masc.; וּ before labial . בטח

בִּטָּחוֹן[c] noun masc. sing. . . . . . בטח

בַּטֻּחוֹת pref. בַּ for בְּהַ)(noun fem. pl. [of טוּחָה] טוח

בַּטֻּחוֹת[d] וּ noun fem. pl. [of בַּטֻּחָה]; וּ before labial בטח

בַּטֻּחוֹת[mm] Kal part. act. f., pl. of בֹּטְחָה d. 10. from בֹּטֵחַ m. בטח

בַּטָּחִים[e] וּ pref. בַּ for בְּהַ)(Kal part. act. masc., pl. of [טָח] dec. 1 a; וּ before labial . טוח

בֹּטְחִים Kal part. act. masc., pl. of [בֹּטֵחַ] dec. 7 b. . בטח

בִּטְחֵךְ[f] Kal inf. [בְּטֹחַ], suff. 2 p. s. m. (§ 16. r. 10) בטח

בָּטָחְנוּ id. pret. 1 pers. pl. [for בָּטַחְנוּ § 8. rem. 7] בטח

בָּטָחְתָּ / בָּטַחְתָּ } id. pret. 2 pers. sing. masc. (§ 8 rem. 7) בטח

בָּטַחְתָּ[g] וּ id. id.; acc. shifted by וּ (before labial for וְ) conversive (§ 8. rem. 7) . . . בטח

בָּטָחְתִּי / בָּטַחְתִּי } id. pret. 1 pers. sing. (§ 8. rem. 7) . בטח

בַּטִּיט pref. בַּ for בְּהַ } noun masc. sing. . . טוא

בְּטִיט[h] pref. בְּ q. v.

בְּטִירֹתָם[i] וּ pref. בְּ)(noun fem. pl., suff. 3 pers. pl. masc. from [טִירָה] dec. 10; וּ before (:) טור

בָּטֵל *to cease, rest from*, Ec. 12. 3.

בְּטֵל Chald. (§ 47. rem. 6) id. Ezr. 4. 24. Pa *to cause to cease, to hinder*.

בִּטְלַל[k] וּ Chald. pref. בְּ)(noun m. s.; וּ before labial טלל

בָּטְלָא[l] Chald. Peal part. act. fem. [of בְּטֵל m.] בטל

בַּטְּלָאִים pref. בַּ for בְּהַ)(pr. name of a place, see טְלִי טלה

בָּטְלוּ[m] וּ Kal pret. 3 pers. pl.; וּ before labial . בטל

---

a De. 30. 19. b 2 Ch. 7. 12. c Is. 41. 8, 9. d Da. 2. 22. e Ec. 6. 4, 4. f Ps. 82. 5. g Ex. 28. 29. h Eze. 32. 30. i 1 Ki. 21. 8. k Ex. 25. 15. l Le. 15. 8. m Le. 14. 32. n De. 28. 47. o Job 21. 25. p Ne. 9. 25. q Ne. 9. 35. r Ps. 106. 5. s Ps. 68. 11. t Is. 59. 4. u Is. 26. 3. x Ps. 112. 7. y Is. 32. 17. z Ps. 37. 5. a Zep. 3. 2. b Ps. 4. 6. c Ec. 9. 4. d Job 12. 6. e Eze. 13. 15. f Je. 48. 7. g Job 11. 18. h Zec. 10. 5. i Ge. 25. 16. k Da. 4. 12, 20. l Ezr. 4. 24. m Ec. 12. 3. mm Job 38. 36.

בְּטַלוּ[a] [b]ו׳ Chald. Pael pret. 3 p.pl.m. (§ 47.r.1); וּ id. בטל

בְּטִלַת[c] Chald. Peal pret. 3 pers. sing. f. Ezr. 4. 24. בטל

בְּטָמֵא[d] pref. בְּ)(adj. m. sing. dec. 5a. (§ 34. rem. 1) טמא

בְּטַמַּאֲכֶם[e] pref. id.)(Piel inf. (טַמֵּא), suff. 2 pers. pl. masc. dec. 7b. (§ 36. rem. 3) . . טמא

בְּטֻמְאָם[f] pref. id.)(id., suff. 3 pers. pl. masc. . טמא

בְּטֻמְאַת pref. id.)(noun f. s., constr. of טֻמְאָה d. 10. טמא

בְּטֻמְאָתֵךְ[g] pref. id.)(id., suff. 2 pers. sing. masc. טמא

בְּטֻמְאֹתָם pref. id.)(id., suff. 3 pers. pl. masc. . טמא

בַּטָּמוּן[h] pref. בַּ for בְּהַ)(Kal part. pass. sing. masc. טמן

בֶּטֶן [i]ו׳, feminine, dec. 6a. (with suff. בִּטְנִי).—I. *belly*.—II. *womb*; פְּרִי בֶטֶן *fruit of the womb*, i. e. offspring; בַּר בִּטְנִי *mine own son*; בְּנֵי בִטְנִי *mine own children*.—III. *the inmost part*, spoken of the heart, the mind, also of שְׁאוֹל.—IV. *a protuberance* in a column, 1 Ki. 7. 20.—V. pr. name of a town in Asher, Jos. 19. 25.

בֹּטֶן masc. only pl. בָּטְנִים (§ 35. rem. 16) *pistachio nuts*, Ge. 43. 11.

בְּטֹנִים (*pistachio nuts*) pr. name of a town in Gad, Jos. 13. 26.

בָּטֶן for בֶּטֶן Seg. n. as if from [בָּטְן § 35. r. 2] בטן

בַּטֶּנֶא[k] pref. בַּ for בְּהַ)(n. m. s. (suff. טַנְאֲךָ) d. 6a. טנא

בִּטְנָהּ noun f. s., suff. 3 pers. s. f. from בֶּטֶן d. 6a. בטן

בִּטְנוֹ id., suff. 3 pers. sing. masc. . . . בטן

בִּטְנִי [l]ו׳ id., suff. 1 pers. sing.; וּ bef. labial . בטן

בְּטֹנִים וּ pr. name of a place; וּ id. . . . בטן

בָּטְנִים[m] noun masc. pl. [of בֹּטֶן § 35. r. 16] . בטן

בִּטְנְךָ noun fem., suff. 2 pers. s. m. fr. בֶּטֶן d. 6a. בטן

בִּטְנֵךְ id., suff. 2 pers. sing. fem. . . . בטן

בִּטְנָם [n]ו׳ id., suff. 3 pers. pl. masc.; וּ bef. labial בטן

בִּטְנֵנוּ[o] id., suff. 1 pers. pl. . . . . . בטן

בִּטְעֵם[p] Chald. pref. בְּ bef. (:))(noun m. s. d. 3a. טעם

בַּטָּף[ll] pref. בַּ for בְּהַ)(noun m. s. for טַף d. 8d. טפף

בְּטֶרוֹם[q] Kh. בטרום pref. בְּ)(adv., K. בְּטֶרֶם (q.v.) טרם

בְּטֶרֶם ו׳ pref. בְּ)(adv.; וּ bef. (:) . . . . טרם

בִּי particle of entreaty; always with אֲדֹנִי ,אֲדֹנָי *I pray my Lord*. It is supposed to be contr. from בְּעִי *entreaty*. R. בָּעָה.

בִּי pref. prep. בְּ with suff. 1 pers. sing. (§ 5) ב

בַּיְאוֹר / בַּיְאֹר } pref. בַּ for בְּהַ)(noun masc. sing. d. 1a. יאר

בַּיְאֹרִים[r] pref. id.)(id. pl. absolute . . . יאר

בְּיֵבֶל ו׳ pref. id.)(noun m. s. d. 7b; וּ bef. lab. יבל

בְּיַבֵּשׁ pref בְּ)(pr. name of a place יבש

בִּיבֹשׁ[s] pref. בְּ [for בִּיבֹשׁ ,בִּיְ]; Kal inf. constr. יבש

בַּיַּבָּשָׁה pref. בַּ for בְּהַ)(noun fem. sing. . יבש

בְּיָבֵשָׁה pref. בְּ)(pr. name of a place, ה parag. . יבש

בַּיַּבֶּשֶׁת[u] pref. בַּ for בְּהַ)(noun f. s. for יַבָּשֶׁת׳ . יבש

בְּיָגוֹן pref. בְּ)(noun masc. sing. dec. 3a. . . יגה

בְּיָד ו׳ pref. id.)(noun com. s. d. 2a; וּ bef. (:) יד

בְּיַד ו׳ pref. id.)(id., constr. st. (Ch. d. 2a); וּ id. יד

בְּיָדָהּ pref. id.)(id., suff. 3 pers. sing. fem. . יד

בִּידַהּ Chald. pref. בְּ [for בִּידַהּ ,בִּיְ]; noun fem. sing., suff. 3 pers. sing. fem. from יַד d. 2a. יד

בִּידְהֹם[x] Chald. pref. בְּ)(id., suff. 3 pers. pl. masc. יד

בְּיָדוֹ ו׳ pref. בְּ)(noun com. sing., suff. 3 pers. sing. masc. from יָד dec. 2a; וּ bef. (:) . יד

בְּיָדִי pref. id.)(id., suff. 1 pers. sing. . . יד

בִּידֵי pref. בְּ [for בִּידֵי ,בִּיְ])(id. du., constr. st. יד

בְּיָדֶיהָ pref. בְּ)(id. du., suff. 3 pers. sing. fem. . יד

בִּידֵיהֶם pref. בְּ [f. בִּידֵי ,בִּיְ])(id. du., suff. 3 p. pl. m. יד

בִּידֵיהֶן[y] pref. id.)(id. du., suff. 3 pers. pl. fem. . יד

בְּיָדָיו[z] [a]ו׳ pref. בְּ)(id. du., suff. 3 pers. s. m.; וּ bef. (:) יד

בְּיָדֶיךָ[b] pref. id.)(id. du., suff. 2 masc. (Kh. בְּיָדֶיךָ), K. בְּיָדְךָ q.v. . . . . . . יד

בִּידֵיכֶם[c] וּ pref. בְּ [for בִּידֵי ,בִּיְ])(id. du. with suff. 2 pers. pl. masc.; וּ bef. labial . . יד

בְּיָדַיִם[d] pref. בְּ)(id. du., absolute state . . יד

בִּידַיִן[e] Chald. pref. בְּ [for בִּידַ׳ ,בִּיְ]; noun fem., du. of יַד dec. 2a. . . . . . יד

בְּיָדְךָ / בְּיָדֶךָ ו׳ } pref. בְּ)(noun com. sing., suff. 2 pers. sing. masc. from יָד dec. 2a; וּ bef. (:) יד

בְּיָדֵךְ pref. id.)(id., suff. 2 pers. sing. fem. . יד

בִּידָךְ Chald. pref. בְּ [for בִּידָךְ ,בִּיְ]; noun fem. sing., suff. 2 pers. sing. m. from יַד d. 2a. יד

בְּיֶדְכֶם pref. בְּ)(noun com. sing., suff. 2 pers. pl. masc. from יָד dec. 2a. (§ 31. rem. 2) יד

בְּיֶדְכֶן[f] pref. id.)(id., suff. 2 pers. pl. fem. . יד

בְּיָדָם pref. id.)(id., suff. 3 pers. pl. masc. יד

בְּיָדֵנוּ pref. id.)(id., suff. 1 pers. pl. . . יד

בְּיָהּ pref. id.)(abbrev. from יְהוָֹה (q.v.) . הוה

בִּיהוּד pref. בִּ, for [בִּיהוּד]; pr. name of a country ידה

בִּיהוּדָה ו׳ pref. id.)(pr. name of a tribe and country ידה

בַּיהוָֹה ו׳ pref. בַּ)(the most sacred name of God, יהוה, with the vowels of אֲדֹנָי (בַּ)אֲדֹנָי contr. בַּאדֹנָי הוה

בִּיהוּדִי pref. בִּ, [for בִּיהוּדִי])(gent. n. m. fr. יְהוּדָה ידה

בַּיְּהוּדִיִּים pref. בַּ for בְּהַ)(id. pl., Kh. ׳דִים, K. ׳דִיִּים ידה

בִּיהוֹנָתָן pref. בִּ, [for בִּיהוֹ׳])(pr. name masc. . הוה

בִּיהוֹסֵף pref. id.; pr. name masc. . . . יסף

בִּיהוֹשֻׁעַ pref. id.)(pr. name masc. . . . הוה

בְּיַהְצָה pref. בְּ)(pr. name of a place . . יהץ

בְּיוֹאָב pref. id.)(pr. name masc. . . . הוה

[a] Ezr. 5. 5. [b] Ezr. 4. 23. [c] Ezr. 4. 24. [d] De. 26. 14. [e] Le. 18. 28. [f] Le. 15. 31. [g] Eze. 24. 13. [h] Job 40. 13. [i] Pr. 13. 25. [k] De. 26. 2. [l] Ps. 31. 10. [ll] Nu. 31. 17. [m] Ge. 43. 11. [n] Job 15. 35. [o] Ps. 44. 26. [p] Da. 5. 2. [q] Ru. 3. 14. [r] Na. 3. 8. [s] Le. 25. 31. [t] Is. 27. 11. [u] Ex. 4. 9. [x] Ezr. 5. 8. [y] Eze. 23. 37, 45. [z] Ex. 17. 12. [a] 2 Ch. 6. 4. [b] Jos. 10. 8. [c] Je. 44. 25. [d] Pr. 30. 28. [e] Da. 2. 34, 35. [f] Eze. 13. 21.

בַּיּוֹם ו׳ pref. בְּ for בְּהַ } n. com. s. irr. (§ 45); וּ bef. (:) — יום
בְּיוֹם ו׳ pref. בְּ q. v. }
בְּיוֹמָא[a] Chald. pref. id. ⟩ id., emph. st. — יום
בְּיוֹמוֹ pref. id. ⟩ id., suff. 3 pers. sing. masc. — יום
בְּיוֹמֵי[b] וּ Ch. pref. id. ⟩ id. pl., constr. st.; וּ bef. (:) — יום
בְּיוֹמֵיהוֹן[c] וּ Ch. pref. id. ⟩ id. pl., suff. 3 p. pl. m.; וּ id. — יום
בְּיוֹמָם[d] pref. id. ⟩ id. sing., suff. 3 pers. pl. masc. — יום
בְּיָוֵן[e] pref. בְּ [for בְּיְ׳, בְּיָוֵן]; noun masc. sing., constr. of יָוֵן dec. 5a. (§ 34. rem. 1) — יון
בִּיהוֹנָתָן pref. בְּ ⟩ pr. name masc., see יְהוֹנָתָן — הוה
בְּיוֹשְׁבֵי[f] ו׳ pref. id. ⟩ Kal part. act. pl. constr. masc. from יוֹשֵׁב dec. 7b; וּ bef. (:) — ישב
בַּיֶּזַע[g] pref. בְּ for בְּהַ ⟩ noun masc. sing. for [יֶזַע] — יזע
בְּיִזְרְעֶאל pref. בְּ ⟩ pr. name of a place — זרע
בְּיָטְבָתָה pref. id. ⟩ pr. name of a place — יטב
בַּיָּוֵן[h] } בְּ for בְּהַ } noun m. s. dec. 6h; וּ bef. lab. — יון
בַּיָּוֵן ו׳ }
בְּיָוֵן[k] pref. בְּ q. v.
בְּיָוֵן[l] ו׳ m׳ pref. id. ⟩ id. construct state; וּ id. — יון
בַּיֶּלֶד[n] pref. בְּ for בְּהַ ⟩ n. m. s. (pl. c. יַלְדֵי) d. 6a. — ילד
בְּיַלְדוּתֶךָ[o] pref. בְּ ⟩ n. f. s., suff. 2 p. s. m. fr. יַלְדוּת d. 1b. — ילד
בְּיַלְדֵי[p] וּ pref. id. ⟩ noun masc. pl. constr. from יֶלֶד dec. 6a; וּ bef. (:) — ילד
בְּיִלְדֵי[q] defect. for בְּיִלְדֵי (q. v.) — ילד
בְּיַלֶּדְכֶן[r] pref. בְּ ⟩ Piel inf. [יַלֵּד], suff. 2 pers. pl. masc. dec. 7b. (§ 16. rem. 15) — ילד
בִּילִידֵי[s] pref. בְּ [for בְּיְ׳, בְּיְלִי׳]; noun masc. pl. constr. from [יָלִיד] dec. 3a. — ילד
בַּיַּלְקוּט[t] וּ pref. בְּ for בְּהַ ⟩ noun masc. s.; וּ bef. lab. — לקט
בַּיָּם pref. בְּ for בְּהַ ⟩ noun masc. sing. dec. 8a. — ים
בְּיַם pref. בְּ ⟩ id., construct state — ים
בְּיָמַי } pref. id. ⟩ n. com. pl., suff. 1 p. s. [as if from יָם] see יוֹם (§ 45) } — יום
בִּימֵי[u] וּ }
בִּימֵי ו׳ pref. בְּ [for בְּיְ׳, בְּיְמֵי] ⟩ id. pl., constr. st. — יום
בִּימֵיהֶם[x] pref. id. ⟩ id. pl., suff. 3 pers. pl. masc. — יום
בְּיָמָיו pref. בְּ ⟩ id. pl., suff. 3 pers. sing. masc. — יום
בְּיָמֶיךָ[y] pref. id. ⟩ id. pl., suff. 2 pers. sing. masc. — יום
בִּימֵיכֶם[z] ו׳ pref. בְּ [for בְּיְ׳, בְּיְמֵי] ⟩ id. pl., suff. 2 p. pl. m. — יום
בַּיָּמִים[a] ו׳ pref. בְּ f. בְּהַ } id. pl., absolute state — יום
בְּיָמִים[b] [c] ו׳ pref. בְּ q. v. }
בַּיַּמִּים pref. בְּ for בְּהַ ⟩ noun masc., pl. of יָם dec. 8a. — ים
בְּיָמִין[d] Kh. בְּיָמִין, K. מִיָּמִין (pref. בְּ or מִ) n. m. s. d. 3a. — ימן
בִּימִין[e] pref. בְּ [for בְּיְ׳, בְּיְמִין] ⟩ id., construct state — ימן
בִּימִינָהּ[f] pref. id. ⟩ id., suff. 3 pers. sing. fem. — ימן
בִּימִינוֹ pref. id. ⟩ id., suff. 3 pers. sing. masc. — ימן
בִּימִינִי[g] pref. id. ⟩ id., suff. 1 pers. sing. — ימן

בִּימִינֶךָ[h] } pref. id. ⟩ id., suff. 2 pers. sing. masc. — ימן
בִּימִינְךָ[i] }

בִּין, בּוּן I. *to distinguish, discern.*—II. *to mark, attend.*—III. *to understand, know*; const. with עַל, לְ, בְּ, אֶל.—IV. abs. *to have understanding, be intelligent, wise.* Niph. i. q. Kal No. IV.; part. נָבוֹן *intelligent, discreet, knowing,* Pil. *to make to discern, to instruct,* De. 32. 10. Hiph. I. *to cause to understand, to explain, to teach.*—II. i. q. Kal No. I. II. III. const. with אֶל, בְּ; part. מֵבִין *intelligent, wise.* Hithpal. I. *to mark, attend to;* const. with אֶל, בְּ, עַל, עַד.—II. *to understand,* Job 26. 14.—III. *to be wise,* Ps. 119. 100.

בַּיִן dec. 6h.—I. *interval, midst,* אִישׁ הַבֵּנַיִם *a middle man, umpire,* 1 Sa. 17. 4.—II. prep. *between, betwixt;* and *within,* of space and time. בֵּין—לְ, בֵּין—לְבֵין, בֵּין—וּבֵין *between—and,* sometimes also *whither—or;* אֶל־בֵּין and אֶל־בֵּינוֹת *between, among,* with motion implied; בְּבֵין *as among,* Is. 44. 4; עַל־בֵּין *from between, out of;* מִבֵּין and מִבֵּינוֹת לְ *among,* with motion implied.

בֵּין Chald. *between,* Da. 7. 5, 8.

בִּינָה fem. dec. 10, *understanding, intelligence, discernment, prudence.*

בִּינָה Chald. id. Da. 2. 21.

יָבִין (*whom He knows*) pr. name—I. of two Canaanitish kings.—II. Ju. 4. 2; Ps. 83. 10.

מְבוֹנִים masc. pl. *wisdom,* for concr. *wise teachers,* 2 Ch. 25. 3 Kheth.; Keri מְבִינִים.

תָּבוֹן masc. d. 3a, *understanding, prudence,* Ho. 13. 2.

תְּבוּנָה fem. dec. 10. id.; also *intelligent words,* or *speeches,* Job 32. 11.

תּוֹבֻנָה id. Job 26. 12. Kheth.

בֵּין ו׳ prep.; prop. constr. of [בַּיִן] dec. 6h. — בין
בִּין[k] ו׳ Kal inf. abs. or imp. s. m. & pret. Da. 10. 1; וּ bef. lab. — בין
בִּינָה[l] id. imp. sing. masc. with parag. ה — בין
בִּינָה ו׳ noun masc. sing. dec. 10; וּ bef. lab. — בין
בֵּינוֹ[m] ו׳ n׳ prep. בֵּין [prop. from בַּיִן dec. 6h] with pl. suff. 3 pers. sing. masc. (§ 4. rem. 1) — בין
בֵּינוֹ id. sing., suff. 3 pers. sing. masc. — בין
בִּינוּ Kal imp. pl. masc. — בין
בֵּינוֹת[o] prep.; pl. fem. of בֵּין, constr. of [בַּיִן] d. 6h. — בין
בִּינוֹת[p] noun fem., pl. of בִּינָה dec. 10. — בין
בֵּינוֹתֵינוּ prep. בֵּין [prop. from בַּיִן dec. 6h] with pl. fem., suff. 1 pers. pl. — בין

---

[a] Da. 6. 11. [b] Da. 5. 11. [c] Da. 2. 44. [d] Ne. 9. 19. [e] Ps. 69. 3. [f] 2 Ch. 20. 23. [g] Eze. 44. 18. [h] Est. 1. 10. [i] De. 14. 26. [k] Pr. 9. 5. [l] Eze. 27. 18. [m] Da. 1. 8. [n] Ge. 42. 22. [o] Ec. 11. 9. [p] Is. 2. 6. [q] 2 Sa. 21. 18. [r] Ex. 1. 16. [s] 2 Sa. 21. 16. [t] 1 Sa. 17. 40. [u] Ps. 116. 2. [x] Ps. 44. 2. [y] 1 Ki. 11. 12. [z] Je. 16. 9. [a] Ju. 18. 1. [b] Eze. 38. 17. [c] Da. 11. 20. [d] 2 Ki. 12. 10. [e] Is. 41. 10. [f] Pr. 3. 16. [g] Is. 44. 20. [h] Ps. 17. 7. [i] Ps. 16. 11. [k] Pr. 23. 1. [l] Ps. 5. 2. [m] Jos. 8. 11. [n] Jos. 3. 4. [o] Eze. 10. 2, 7. [p] Is. 27. 11.

בֵּינִי id. sing. suff. 1 pers. sing. . . . בין

בֵּינֵיהוֹן[a] Chald. id. pl. masc., suff. 3 pers. pl. Kh. הוֹן׳ masc., K. הֵן fem. . . . בין

בֵּינֵיהֶם [b] וּ׳ id. pl. masc., suff. 3 pers. pl. m.; וּ bef. lab. בין

בֵּינֶיךָ וּ id. pl. masc., suff. 2 pers. sing. masc.; וּ id. בין

בֵּינֵיכֶם[dd] וּ׳ id pl. masc., suff. 2 pers. pl. masc.; וּ id. בין

בֵּינֵינוּ id. pl. masc., suff. 1 pers. pl. . . . בין

בֵּינֵךְ[c] וּ id. sing., suff. 2 pers. sing. fem.; וּ bef. lab. בין

בֵּינְךָ וּ / בֵּינֶךָ[hh] וּ׳ } id. sing., suff. 2 pers. sing. m.; וּ bef. lab. בין

בֵּינֵכֶם[d] defect. for בֵּינֵיכֶם (q. v.) . . . בין

בִּינַת[e] [f] וּ׳ noun f. s., constr. of בִּינָה d. 10; וּ bef. lab. בין

בִּינֹתִי[g] Kal pret. 1 pers. sing. . . . בין

בֵּינֹתֵינוּ[h] prep. בֵּין [prop. from בַּיִן dec. 6h] with pl. fem. term. suff. 1 pers. pl. . . . בין

בִּינָתְךָ[mm] noun f. sing., suff. 2 pers. s. m. fr. בִּינָה d. 10. בין

בִּינַתְכֶם וּ id., suff. 2 pers. pl. masc.; וּ bef. lab. . בין

בֵּינֹתָם prep. בֵּין [prop. בַּיִן dec. 6h] with pl. fem. term. suff. 3 pers. pl. masc. (§ 4. rem. 2) בין

בְּיָסְדוֹ[qq] pref. בְּ)(Kal inf., suff. 3 pers. sing. masc יסד

בְּיָסְדִי[uu] pref. id.)(id., suff. 1 pers. sing. . יסד

בַּיְּעוֹרִים[k] pref. בַּ for בְּהַ)(Kh. יְעוֹרִים׳, noun masc., pl. [of יָעוֹר]; K. יְעָרִים, pl. of יַעַר dec. 6a. . יער

בְּיַעְזֵיר pref. בְּ)(pr. name of a place . . עזר

בְּיַעַן וּ׳ pref. id.)(prop. subst. used as a conj. . ענה

בִּיעָף[m] pref. בְּ [for בְּיְ׳, בִּיְעָף]; noun masc. sing. יעף

בְּיַעֲקֹב pref. בְּ)(pr. name masc. . . . עקב

בַּיַּעַר / בַּיָּעַר } pref. בַּ for בְּהַ; בְּיַעַר[n] pref. בְּ q. v. } noun masc. sing. dec. 6d. יער

בְּיַעְרָהּ[o] pref. id.)(id., suff. 3 pers. s. fem. (§ 35. r. 5) יער

בְּיַעֲרַת[p] pref. id.)(noun fem. sing., constr. of [יַעֲרָה] comp. § 35. rem. 5] . . . יער

בְּיָפְיוֹ pref. בְּ)(n. m. s., suff. 3 p. s. m. fr. [יְפִי] d. 6k. יפה

בְּיָפְיֵךְ[q] pref. id.)(id., suff. 2 pers. sing. m. [for יָפְיְךָ] יפה

בְּיָפְיֵךְ[r] pref. id.)(id., suff. 2 pers. sing. fem. . יפה

בְּיִצְחָק pref. id.)(pr. name masc. . . . צחק

בֵּיצֵי noun fem. with pl. masc. term., constr. st., from [בֵּיצָה] dec. 10. . . . בוץ

בֵּיצֶיהָ[t] id. pl., suff. 3 pers. sing. fem. . . בוץ

בֵּיצִים id. pl., absolute state . . . בוץ

בְּיָצְקָתוֹ[u] pref. בְּ, [for בְּיְ׳, בִּיְצְ׳]; noun fem. sing., suff. 3 pers. sing. masc. from [יְצֻקָה] dec. 10. יצק

בְּיֶקֶב[aa] pref. בְּ)(noun masc. sing. (pl. c. יִקְבֵי) d. 6a. יקב

בַּיְקָבִים[x] pref. בַּ for בְּהַ)(id. pl. absolute state . יקב

בִּיקַבְצְאֵל וּ pref. בְּ [for יְקַבְ׳]; pr. name of a place; וּ bef. lab. . . . קבץ

בִּיקָר[y] pref. בְּ [for בְּיְ׳, בִּיְקָר])(noun m. s. d. 1a. יקר

בִּיקָרוֹ pref. id.)(id. with suff. 3 pers. sing. masc. יקר

בִּיקְּרוֹתֶיךָ[z] pref. id., contr. for בִּיְקִרוֹתֶיךָ)(adj. pl. fem. (constr. יְקָרוֹת dag. euph.), suff. 2 pers. sing. fem. from יְקָרָה dec. 11c. from יָקָר m. יקר

בְּיִרְאָה[a] pref. בְּ)(noun fem. sing. (no pl.) . ירא

בְּיִרְאַת [b] וּ׳ pref. id.)(id., construct state; וּ bef. (:) ירא

בְּיִרְאָתְךָ[c] pref. id.)(id., suff. 2 pers. s. m., for יִרְאָתְךָ׳ ירא

בַּיַּרְדֵּן pref. בַּ for בְּהַ)(pr. name of a river . ירד

בִּירָה׳ fem. I. *castle, palace.*—II. *the temple*, 1 Ch. 29. 1. 19.
בִּירָא Chald. dec. 8a. id. Ezr. 6. 2.
בִּירָנִית fem. only pl. בִּירָנִיּוֹת (§ 39. No. 4. r. 1, note) *palaces.*

בִּירוּשָׁלַם וּ׳ / בִּירוּשָׁלָם וּ׳ / בִּירוּשָׁלַיִם וּ׳ / בִּירוּשָׁלָיִם } pref. בְּ)(pr. name of a place; וּ bef. lab. ירה

בְּיֶרַח pref. בְּ)(noun masc sing., dec. 6a. (pl. con. יַרְחֵי § 35. rem. 5) . . . ירח

בִּירְחוֹ / בִּירִיחוֹ } pref. בְּ [for בְּיְ׳]; pr. name of a place רוח

בַּיְרִיעָה pref. בַּ for בְּהַ)(noun fem. sing. dec. 10. . ירע

בִּירִיעֹת[d] pref. בְּ [for בְּיְ׳, בִּיְרִ׳])(id. pl. . . ירע

בְּיַרְכְּתֵי pref. בְּ)(noun fem. du. constr. [fr. יַרְכָּתַיִם from יֶרֶךְ=יַרְכָּה § 39. No. 3. rem. 3] . ירך

בְּיַרְכָתַיִם pref. בַּ for בְּהַ)(n. f., du. of [יְרֵכָה] d. 11c. ירך

בְּיַרְכָתָם[e] K. בְּיַרְכָתַיִם id.; Kh. כָתָם׳ sing. with suff. 3 pers. pl. masc. . . . . ירך

בְּיַרְמוּת וּ pref. בְּ)(pr. name of a place; וּ bef. (:) . ירם

בְּיִרְמְיָהוּ pref. בְּ)(noun masc. sing. . . . רמה

בִּירָנִיּוֹת noun fem. pl. [of בִּירָנִית § 39, No. 4. rem. 1] ביר

בַּיֵּרָקוֹן וּ pref. בַּ for בְּהַ)(noun m. sing.; וּ bef. lab. ירק

בִּירַקְרַק[f] pref. בְּ [for בְּיְ׳, בִּירַקְ׳]; noun masc. sing. ירק

בְּיֹשֵׁב[g] pref. בְּ)(Kal part. act. sing. masc. dec. 7b. ישב

בְּיֹשְׁבֵי וּ pref. id.)(id. pl., construct state; וּ bef. (:) ישב

בִּישׁוּעָה[h] pref. בְּ [for בְּיְ׳ בִּישׁ׳])(noun fem. sing. d. 10. ישע

בִּישׁוּעָתוֹ pref. id.)(id., suff. 3 pers. sing. masc. . ישע

בִּישׁוּעָתִי[i] pref. id.)(id., suff. 1 pers. sing. . . ישע

בִּישׁוּעָתֶךָ / בִּישׁוּעָתְךָ[k] וּ } pref. id.)(id., suff. 2 pers. sing. masc.; וּ before labial . . } ישע

בִּישִׁימוֹן pref. id.)(noun masc. sing. . . . ישם

בִּישִׁישִׁים[l] pref. id.)(noun m., pl. of יָשִׁישׁ dec. 3a. ישש

בְּיֶשַׁע pref. בְּ)(n. m. s., d. 6a. (suff. יִשְׁעִי § 35. r. 5) ישע

בְּיֹשֶׁר וּ׳ pref. id.)(noun m. sing. dec. 6c; וּ bef. lab. ישר

בְּיִשְׂרָאֵל וּ׳ pref. id.)(pr. name of a people; וּ id. . שׂהר

בְּיָשְׁרוֹ[m] pref. id.)(n. m. s., suff. 3 p. s. m. fr. יֹשֶׁר d. 6c. ישר

[a] Da. 7. 8. [b] Eze. 43. 8. [c] Ru. 1. 17. [d] Is. 59. 2. [dd] Jos. 3. 4. [e] Pr. 30. 2. [f] Is. 29. 14. [g] Da. 9. 2. [h] Jos. 22. 34. [hh] Ge. 3. 15. [i] De. 4. 6. [k] Eze. 34. 25. [l] Eze. 36. 3. [m] Da. 9. 21. [mm] Pr. 3. 5. [n] 2 Sa. 18. 6. [o] Je. 21. 14. [p] 1 Sa. 14. 27. [q] Eze. 28. 17. [qq] Ezr. 3. 12. [r] Eze. 16. 14, 15. [s] Is. 59. 5. [t] Job 39. 14. [u] 1 Ki. 7. 24. [uu] Job 38. 4. [x] Is. 16. 10. [y] Ps. 49. 13, 21. [z] Ps. 45. 10. [a] Ps. 2. 11. [aa] Ju. 7. 25. [b] Pr. 16. 6. [c] Ps. 5. 8. [d] Ex. 26. 12. [e] Eze. 46. 19. [f] Ps. 68. 14. [g] Ge. 34. 30. [h] Ps. 149. 4. [i] Ps. 91. 16. [k] Ps. 21. 2. [l] Job 12. 12. [m] Pr. 14. 2.

בִּישֻׁרוּן[a] pref. בְּ, [for 'בְּיְ, 'בְּיִשְׁ]; noun masc. sing. ישר

בִּישְׁרַת[b] וּ pref. בְּ X noun fem. sing. constr. [of יְשֻׁרָה or יְשָׁרָה]; וּ bef. (:) . . . . ישר

בְּיִשָּׂשכָר וּ' pref. בְּ X pr. name of a tribe; וּ id. . שכר

בַּיִת, וּ' בָּיִת } masc. irr. (§ 45).—I. *house, dwelling*; בֶּן־בַּיִת, יְלִיד בַּיִת, *home-born slave*; בֵּית הָעוֹלָם *long home*, i. e. the grave; בָּתֵּי חֹמֶר *houses of clay*, of the human bodies; בֵּ' הַנָּשִׁים *harem*; בֵּ' עַכָּבִישׁ *spider's web*.—II. *tent, tabernacle*.—III. *temple*, of God or idols.—IV. *palace*.—V. *place, space, a receptacle* in general; בָּתֵּי נֶפֶשׁ *perfume boxes*; בָּתִּים לַבַּדִּים *places, receptacles for the bars*.—VI. *the inside, within* (opposed to חוּץ without, out of doors); בַּיְתָה, מִבַּיִת, מִבַּיְתָה *within*; בַּיִת לְ, מִבַּיִת לְ, מִבֵּית לְ, לְמִבֵּית לְ *within*.—VII. *household, family*; בֵּית אָב *father's house, family tribe*.—VIII. put before pr. names of towns.—בֵּית אָוֶן (*house of vanity, idols*) in the tribe of Benjamin.—בֵּית אֵל (*house of God*) between Jerusalem and Sichem (formerly לוּז Ge. 28. 19); Gent. n. בֵּית הָאֱלִי.—בֵּית הָאֵצֶל (*house of firmness*, אצל Arab. *to take root*) Mi. 1. 11.—בֵּית אַרְבֵּאל (*house of God's ambush*, for אֱרֶב אֵל) in Galilee, Ho. 10. 14.—בֵּית בַּעַל מְעוֹן, בֵּית מְעוֹן and בַּעַל מְעוֹן (*house of habitation*) in the tribe of Reuben.—בֵּית בִּרְאִי (*house of Biri, or my making*) in the tribe of Simeon, 1 Ch. 4. 31.—בֵּית בָּרָה (for בֵּית עֲבָרָה *house of passage*) a place near Jordan, Ju. 7. 24.—בֵּית גָּדֵר (*house of wall*) in the tribe of Judah, 1 Ch. 2. 51.—בֵּית גִּלְגָּל Ne. 12. 29, i. q. גִּלְגָּל q. v. R. גָּלַל.—בֵּית גָּמוּל (*house of the weaned child or camel*, see גָּמָל) in the land of Moab, Je. 48. 23.—בֵּית דִּבְלָתַיִם see דִּבְלָתַיִם.—בֵּית דָּגוֹן (*temple of Dagon*, see R. דגה), (*a*) in the tribe of Judah, Jos. 15. 41; (*b*) in the tribe of Asher, Jos. 19. 27.—בֵּית הָרָם (*house of the height*, R. הרם) in the tribe of Gad, Jos. 13. 27, called בֵּית הָרָן Nu. 32. 36.—בֵּית חָגְלָה (*partridge-house*; see חָגְלָה) in the tribe of Benjamin. בֵּית חָנָן (*house of Hanan or grace*) in the tribe of Judah or Dan, 1 Ki. 4. 9.—בֵּית חוֹרוֹן (*house of cavern*, R. חור) two towns in the tribe of Ephraim.—בֵּית הַיְשִׁימוֹת (*house desolations*, R. ישם) in the tribe of Reuben near the Dead Sea.—בֵּית כַּר (*house of pasture*, R. כָּרַר) in the tribe of Judah, 1 Sa. 7. 11.—בֵּית הַכֶּרֶם (*house of the vineyard*) in the tribe of Judah.—בֵּית לְבָאוֹת (*house of lionesses*) in the tribe of Simeon, Jos. 19. 6.—בֵּית לֶחֶם (*house of bread*) (*a*) in the tribe of Judah, Gent. n. בֵּית הַלַּחְמִי; (*b*) in the tribe of Zebulun, Jos. 19. 15.—בֵּית מְעוֹן see בֵּ' בַּעַל.—בֵּית מַעֲכָה (*house of Maachah*, R. מָעַךְ) on the foot of Hermon, 2 Sa. 20. 14.—בֵּית הַמֶּרְחָק (*house of remoteness*, R. רָחַק) place near the brook of Kedron, 2 Sa. 15. 17.—בֵּית הַמַּרְכָּבוֹת (*house of chariots*, R. רָכַב) in the tribe of Simeon.—בֵּית נִמְרָה (*house of pure water*, R. נמר), also נִמְרָה, in the tribe of Gad; hence Is. 15. 6, מֵי נִמְרִים *limpid waters* for the waters of Nimrah.—בֵּית עֶדֶן (*house of pleasantness*) a town near Damascus, Am. 1. 5.—בֵּית עַזְמָוֶת, and עַזְמָוֶת a village in Judah or Benjamin, see עזז.—בֵּית הָעֵמֶק (*house of the valley*) a place in the tribe of Asher, Jos. 19. 27.—בֵּית עֲנוֹת (*house of answer*, R. עָנָה) in Judah, Jos. 15. 59.—בֵּית עֲנָת (id.) in Naphtali.—בֵּית עֵקֶד הָרֹעִים (*house of the shepherds' union*) a place near Samaria, 2 Ki. 10. 12, and without הָרֹעִים ver. 14.—בֵּית הָעֲרָבָה (*house of the desert*) on the confines of Judah and Benjamin, also without בֵּית.—בֵּית פֶּלֶט (*house of escape*) in the tribe of Judah, Jos. 15. 27.—בֵּית פְּעוֹר, (*temple of Peor*, see פְּעֹר) in the tribe of Judah.—בֵּית פַּצֵּץ (*house of dispersion*) in the tribe of Issachar, Jos. 19. 21.—בֵּית צוּר (*house of the rock*) in the mountains of Judah.—בֵּית רְחֹב (*house of streets*) a city in Syria, see אֲרָם.—בֵּית שְׁאָן (*house of quiet*) contr. בֵּית שָׁן, שַׁן in the tribe of Manasseh.—בֵּית הַשִּׁטָּה (*acacia-house*, see שִׁטָּה) a place near Jordan, Ju. 7. 22.—בֵּית שֶׁמֶשׁ (*house of the sun*) (*a*) a Levitical city in the tribe of Judah. Gent. n. בֵּית הַשִּׁמְשִׁי; (*b*) a city in Naphtali; (*c*) in Issachar, Jos. 19. 22; (*d*) in Egypt, i. e. Heliopolis, i. q. אֹן Je. 43. 13.—בֵּית תַּפּוּחַ (*house of apples*) a place in Judah, Jos. 15. 53.

בַּיִת Chald. irr. (§ 68) *house, palace, temple*.

בִּיתָן masc. dec. 2 b, *a great house, palace*.

בֵּית וּ' Heb. and Chald. noun masc., constr. of בַּיִת (§ 45); וּ bef. labial . . . בית

בַּיְתָא Chald. id. emph. state . . . בית

בְּיַתֵד[c] pref. בְּ for בַּ X noun com. sing. dec. 5a. . יתד

בַּיְתָה וְ', בַּיְתָה[d] } noun masc. sing. with parag. ה from בַּיִת irr. (§ 45); for וְ see lett. ו . } בית

[a] De. 33. 5. [b] 1 Ki. 3. 6. [c] Ju. 16. 14. [d] Ps. 68. 7.

בַּיְתָה [a] [b] ו' Chald. noun masc. sing. (for בַּיְתָא), emph. of בַּיִת irr. (§ 68); ו bef. labial . . בית
בַּיְתֵהּ ו' Chald. id., suff. 3 pers. sing. masc.; ו id. בית
בֵּיתָהּ ו' noun masc. sing., suff. 3 pers. sing. fem. from בַּיִת irr. (§ 45) . . בית
בַּיְתָה id., constr. state with paragogic ה . בית
בֵּיתוֹ ו' id., suff. 3 pers. sing. masc.; ו bef. labial בית
בֵּיתִי ו' id., suff. 1 pers. sing.; ו id. בית
בֵּיתְךָ ו' / בֵּיתֶךָ ו' } id., suff. 2 pers. sing. masc.; ו id. . בית
בֵּיתֵךְ [c] [d] ו' id., suff. 2 pers. sing. fem.; ו id. . בית
בֵּיתְכֶם [e] ו id., suff. 2 pers. pl. masc.; ו id. . בית
בֵּיתָם id., suff. 3 pers. pl. masc. . בית
בִּיתַן [f] noun masc., constr. of [בִּיתָן] dec. 2b. . בית
בְּיַתִּר pref. בְּ)(pr. name of a place יתר
בְּיֶתֶר [g] [h] ו' pref. id.)(noun masc. sing., (suff. יִתְרוֹ) dec. 6a; ו bef. (:) . יתר
בָּךְ pref. prep. בְּ with suff. 2 pers. sing. fem. (§ 5) ב
בְּךָ [i] ו' / בָּךְ ו' } id., with suff. 2 pers. sing. masc. (§ 5); ו bef. (:), for ךָ see ךְ . ב

בָּכָא Root not used; i. q. בָּכָה *to weep.*

בָּכָא masc. dec. 4a.—I. *a weeping*, only as a pr. name עֵמֶק הַבָּכָא (*valley of weeping*), a valley in Palestine, Ps. 84. 7.—II. the name of a *shrub* distilling a white sort of acrid gum.

בְּכָאִים [k] noun masc., pl. of בָּכָא' dec. 4a. . בכא
בַּכָּבֵד [l] pref. בַּ for הַבְּ)(noun masc. sing. dec. 5a. כבד
בִּכְבֹדִי [m] pref. בְּ bef. (:))(noun masc. sing., suff. 1 pers. sing. from כָּבוֹד dec. 3a . . כבד
בִּכְבֶדֶת [n] pref. id.)(noun fem. sing. . כבד
בְּכָבוֹד pref. בְּ)(noun masc. sing. dec. 3a. . כבד
בִּכְבוֹדוֹ pref. בְּ bef. (:))(id., suff. 3 pers. sing. masc. כבד
וּבִכְבוֹדָם [o] ו pref. id.)(id., suff. 3 pers. pl. m.; ו bef. lab. כבד
בְּכַבּוֹתְךָ [rr] pref. בְּ)(Piel inf., suff. 2 pers. s. m., dec. 1b. כבה
בַּכֶּבֶל [p] pref. בַּ for הַבְּ)(noun masc. sing. dec. 6a. כבל
בְּכַבְלֵי [q] pref. בְּ)(id. pl., constr. st. כבל
בַּכְּבָרָה [r] pref. בַּ for הַבְּ)(noun fem. sing. . כבר
בַּכְּבָשִׂים [s] pref. id.)(noun masc., pl. of כֶּבֶשׂ dec. 6a. כבשׂ
בַּכַּד [t] pref. id.)(noun com. sing. dec. 8d. . כדד

בָּכָה I. *to weep.*—II. *to mourn, lament*; const. with acc., לְ, אֶל, עַל. Pi. *to mourn, deplore*, const. acc., עַל.

בֶּכֶה masc. *a weeping*, Ezr. 10. 1.

בְּכִי masc. dec. 6i.—I. *a weeping, lamentation.*—II. *a dropping* or *trickling* of water, Job 28. 11.

בֹּכִים (*weepers*) pr. name of a place near Gilgal, Ju. 2. 1, 5.

בָּכוּת fem. *a weeping, mourning*, Ge. 35. 8.

בְּכִית fem. dec. 1a, id. Ge. 50. 4.

בָּכֹה ו Kal inf. abs.; ו bef. lab. . בכה
בְּכָה [u] ו' pref. prep. בְּ with suff. 2 p. s. m. (§ 5); ו id. ב
בֶּכֶה [x] noun masc. sing. . בכה
בְּכֹה pref. בְּ)(adv. Je. 41. 6. . כה
בֹּכֶה ו' Kal part. act. sing. masc. dec. 9a; ו bef. lab. בכה
בְּכֹהֲנֵי [y] pref. בְּ)(n. m. pl. constr. from כֹּהֵן dec. 7b. כהן
בְּכֹהֲנָיו [z] pref. id.)(id. pl., suff. 3 pers. sing. masc. כהן
בַּכֹּהֲנִים [a] ו' pref. בַּ for הַבְּ)(id. pl., abs. st.; ו bef. lab. כהן
בָּכוֹ [b] ו' Kal inf. abs. (§ 24. rem. 2); ו id. . בכה
בָּכוּ [c] ו' id. pret. 3 pers. pl.; ו id. . בכה
בְּכוּ [d] [e] ו' id. imp. pl. masc.; ו id. . בכה
בְּכוֹבָעִים [f] pref. בְּ)(noun masc., pl. of כּוֹבַע dec. 2. (§ 31. rem. 5) . כבע
בַּכּוֹכָבִים [g] pref. בַּ for הַבְּ)(n. m., pl. of כּוֹכָב dec. 2b. כבב
בְּכוֹר noun masc. sing. dec. 1. . בכר
בְּכוֹר pref. בְּ)(pr. name in compos. כּוֹר עָשָׁן . כור
בְּכוּר [h] pref. id.)(noun masc. sing. . כור
בְּכוּרָה [i] noun fem. sing. . בכר
בְּכוֹרוֹ n. m. s., suff. 3 pers. s. m. from בְּכוֹר dec. 1a. בכר
בְּכוֹרֵי id. pl., constr. state . בכר
בְּכוֹרִי id. sing., suff. 1 pers. sing. . בכר
בִּכּוּרֵי [k] ו' noun masc. pl. const. from [בִּכּוּר] dec. 1b; ו bef. lab. . בכר
בִּכּוּרֶיךָ [l] id. pl., suff. 2 pers. sing. masc. . בכר
בִּכּוּרִים id. pl., absolute state . בכר
בְּכוֹרַת pr. name masc. . בכר
בְּכוּשׁ pref. בְּ)(pr. name of a country . כושׁ
בַּכּוֹשָׁרוֹת [m] pref. בַּ for הַבְּ)(noun fem. pl. [of כּוֹשָׁרָה] כשׁר
בְּכוּת [n] noun fem. sing. . בכה
בְּכַזֶּבְכֶם [o] pref. בְּ)(Piel inf. [כַּזֵּב], suff. 2 p. pl. m. d. 7b. כזב
בִּכְזִיב pref. בְּ bef. (:))(pr. name of a place כזב
בַּכֹּחַ pref. בַּ f. הַבְּ / בְּכֹחַ pref. בְּ q. v. } noun masc. sing. dec. 1a. . כחח
בְּכֹחוֹ pref. id.)(id., suff. 3 pers. sing. masc. . כחח
בְּכֹחִי [p] pref. id.)(id., suff. 1 pers. sing. . כחח
בְּכֹחֲךָ pref. id.)(id., suff. 2 pers. sing. masc. כחח
בְּכַחַשׁ [q] pref. id.)(noun masc. sing. dec. 6d. כחשׁ
וּבְכַחֲשֵׁיהֶם [r] ו pref. id.)(id. pl., suff. 3 p. pl. m.; ו bef. (:) כחשׁ
בֶּכִי / בֶּכִי [s] ו' } noun m. s. dec. 6i (§ 35. rem. 14); ו id. בכה
בַּכִּידוֹן [t] pref. בַּ for הַבְּ / וּבְכִידוֹן [u] ו pref. בְּ q. v. } noun masc. sing.; ו id. . כיד
בַּכִּיּוֹר [x] pref. בַּ for הַבְּ)(noun masc. sing. dec. 1b. כור

[a] Ezr. 6. 15. [b] Ezr. 5. 12. [c] Jos. 2. 19. [d] 2 Ki. 8. 1. [e] Nu. 18. 31. [f] Est. 1. 15. [g] Jos. 23. 12. [h] De. 28. 54. [i] Nu. 21. 7. [k] 2 Sa. 5. 23. [l] Eze. 21. 26. [m] Ex. 29. 43. [n] Ex. 14. 25. [o] Is. 61. 6. [p] Ps. 105. 18. [q] Ps. 149. 8. [r] Am. 9. 9. [s] Nu. 15. 11. [t] 1 Ki. 17. 12. [u] Ex. 7. 29. [x] Ezr. 10. 1. [y] 1 Sa. 22. 17. [z] Ps. 99. 6. [a] Ezr. 8. 15. [b] Je. 50. 4. [c] Eze. 27. 31. [d] Je. 22. 10. [e] Joel 1. 5. [f] Je. 46. 4. [g] Is. 47. 13. [h] Is. 48. 10. [i] Mi. 7. 1. [k] Ne. 10. 36. [l] Le. 2. 14. [m] Ps. 68. 7. [n] Ge. 35. 8. [o] Eze. 13. 19. [p] Je. 27. 5. [q] Ho. 12. 1. [r] Ho. 7. 3. [s] Est. 4. 3. [t] Jos. 8. 18, 18, 26. [u] 1 Sa. 17. 45. [x] 1 Sa. 2. 14. [rr] Eze. 32. 7.

בְּכְיִי [a] noun m. s., suff. 1 pers. s. from בְּכִי dec. 6 i. בכה
בֹּכִים Kal part. act. m., pl. of בֹּכֶה d. 9 a. (also) pr. n. בכה
בְּכֶינָה [b] id. imp. pl. fem. . . . . בכה
בָּכִינוּ [c] id. pret. 1 pers. pl. . . . . בכה
בַּכִּיֹּס [d] pref. בַּ for בְּהַ)(Kh. כִּיס׳ q. v., K. כּוֹס׳ (q. v.) כוס
בְּכִיס [e] וּ pref. בְּ)(noun m. sing. dec. 1 a; וּ bef. (:) כוס
בְּכִיסְךָ [f] pref. id.)(id., suff. 2 pers. sing. masc. . כוס
בַּכִּישׁוֹר [g] pref. בַּ for בְּהַ)(noun masc. sing. . . כשר
בְּכִיתוֹ [h] n. fem. s., suff. 3 p. s. m. from [בְּכִית] dec. 1 a. בכה
בָּכִיתִי [i] Kal pret. 1 pers. sing. . . . בכה
בְּכִיתֶם [k] id. pret. 2 pers. pl. masc. . . . בכה
בְּכִכַּר pref. בְּ)(noun m. s., constr. of כִּכָּר dec. 2 b. כרר
בְּכִכְּרַיִם [l] pref. id.)(id. dual, in the constr. for כִּכָּרִים כרר
בַּכֹּל pref. בַּ for בְּהַ
בְּכֹל וּ, בְּכָל־ וּ } pref. בְּ q. v. } noun masc. sing. dec. 8 c; וּ bef. (:) . כלל
בְּכָלֵב pref. id.)(pr. name in compos. כָּלֵב אֶפְ׳ . כלב
בְּכָלְהוֹן [m] Chald. pref. id.)(noun masc. sing., suff. 3 pers. pl. masc. (§ 61. rem.) . . כלל
בִּכְלוֹת [n] pref. בְּ bef. (:))(Kal inf. constr. . . כלה
בְּכַלּוֹתִי [o] pref. בְּ)(Piel inf., suff. 1 pers. sing. dec. 1 b. כלה
בְּכַלֹּתְךָ [p] pref. id.)(id., suff. 2 pers. sing. masc. . כלה
בְּכֶלַח [q] pref. id.)(noun masc. sing. . . . כלח
בַּכֶּלִי [r], בַּכֶּלִי [s] } pref. בַּ for בְּהַ)(noun masc. sing. irr. (§ 45. & § 35. rem. 14) . . } כלה
בִּכְלֵי וּ pref. בְּ bef. (:))(id. pl., constr. st.; וּ bef. lab. כלה
בִּכְלִי [t] וּ pref. id.)(id. sing., absolute state; וּ id. כלה
בִּכְלֵיהֶם [u] pref. id.)(id. pl., suff. 3 pers. pl. masc. . כלה
בְּכֵלָיו [v] וּ pref. בְּ)(id. pl., suff. 3 p. s. m.; וּ bef. (:) כלה
בִּכְלֵיכֶם pref. בְּ bef. (:))(id. pl., suff. 2 pers. pl. m. כלה
בַּכֵּלִים [y] pref. בַּ for בְּהַ)(id. pl., absolute state . כלה
בִּכְלוּלֹתָי [z] pref. בְּ)(n. f. pl., suff. 1 p. s. fr. [כְּלוּלָה] d. 12 b. כלה
בְּכֻלָּם [a] pref. id.)(n. m. s., suff. 3 p. pl. m. fr. כֹּל (q. v.) כלל
בַּכְּלִמָּה [b] pref. בַּ for בְּהַ)(noun fem. sing. dec. 10. . כלם
בָּכֶם pref. prep. בְּ with suff. 2 pers. pl. m. (§ 5) ב
בְּכֵן וּ pref. בְּ)(adv.; וּ bef. (:) . . כון
בַּכִּנּוֹר pref. בַּ f. בְּהַ
בְּכִנּוֹר [c] וּ pref. בְּ q. v. } noun masc. sing. d. 1 b; וּ id. כנר
בַּכְּנַעֲנִי pref. בַּ for בְּהַ)(gent. n. fr. כְּנַעַן . . כנע
בִּכְנַף pref. בְּ bef. (:))(n. f. s., constr. of כָּנָף d. 4 a. כנף
בִּכְנָפוֹ [d] pref. id.)(id., suff. 3 pers. sing. masc. . כנף
בְּכַנְפוֹת [e] pref. בְּ)(id. pl., constr. state (§ 33. rem. 1) כנף
בִּכְנָפֶיהָ pref. בְּ bef. (:))(id. du., suff. 3 pers. sing. f. כנף
בְּכַנְפֵיהֶם pref. בְּ)(id. du., suff. 3 pers. pl. m. (§ 33. r. 1) כנף

בִּכְנָפָיו [f] pref. בְּ bef. (:))(id. du., suff. 3 pers. s. m. כנף
בִּכְנָפֶיךָ [g] pref. id.)(id. du., suff. 2 pers. sing. masc. כנף
בִּכְנָפֶיךָ [h] pref. id.)(id. du., suff. 2 pers. sing. masc. כנף
בְּכִנֹּרוֹת וּ pref. בְּ)(noun masc. with pl. fem. term. from כִּנּוֹר dec. 1 b; וּ before (:) . . כנר
בַּכֵּסֶה [i] pref. בַּ for בְּהַ)(noun masc. s. [for כֶּסֶא] כסא
בִּכְסִילִים pref. id.)(noun masc., pl. of כְּסִיל dec. 1 a. כסל
בְּכִסְלֵו* pref. בְּ)(name of a month, see כִּסְלֵו *Zec. 7. 1.
בְּכִסְלֶךָ [k] pref. id.)(noun masc. sing., suff. 2 pers. sing. masc. from כֶּסֶל dec. 6 a. . . כסל
בַּכֶּסֶף, בַּכֶּסֶף וּ } pref. בַּ f. בְּהַ } noun masc. sing., dec. 6 a. (§ 35. rem. 2); וּ bef. lab. } כסף
בְּכֶסֶף [l], בְּכֶסֶף [m] וּ } pref. בְּ q. v.
בְּכַסְפָּא [n] Chald. pref. id.)(noun masc. sing., emph. of כְּסַף dec. 3 a. . . . כסף
בְּכָסִפְיָא pref. id.)(pr. name of a place . . כסף
בְּכַעַס [o] pref. id.)(noun masc. sing. dec. 6 d. . כעס
בְּכַעְסוֹ [p] pref. id.)(id., suff. 3 pers. sing. masc. . כעס
בַּכַּף [q], בַּכַּף [r] } pref. בַּ f. בְּהַ } noun fem. sing. dec. 8 d. . כפף
בְּכַף pref. בְּ q.v.
בְּכַפּוֹ pref. id.)(id., suff. 3 pers. sing. masc. . כפף
בְּכַפַּי, בְּכַפַּי [t] וּ } pref. id.)(id. du., suff. 1 p. s.; וּ bef. (:) כפף
בְּכַפִּי pref. id.)(id. sing., suff. 1 pers. sing. . כפף
בְּכַפֵּיהֶם pref. id.)(id. du., suff. 3 pers. pl. masc. כפף
בַּכֵּפִים [u] וּ pref. בַּ for בְּהַ)(n. m. pl. [of כֵּף]; וּ bef. lab. כף
בַּכַּפְךָ [v] Kh. בְּכַפְּךָ q. v., K. בְּכַף (q. v.) . כפף
בְּכַפְּךָ [y] pref. בְּ)(n. f. s., suff. 2 p. s. m. fr. כַּף d. 8 d. כפף
בְּכֶפֶל [z] pref. id.)(noun masc. s. (du. כִּפְלַיִם) d. 6 a. כפל
בְּכָפָן [a] וּ pref. id.)(noun masc. sing.; וּ bef. (:) . כפן
בַּכֹּפֶר [b] pref. בַּ for בְּהַ)(noun masc. sing. dec. 6 c. כפר
בְּכַפְּרִי [c] pref. בְּ)(Piel inf. (כַּפֵּר), suff. 1 pers. s. d. 7 b. כפר
בַּכְּפָרִים [d] [e] וּ pref. בַּ for בְּהַ)(n. m., pl. of [כָּפָר] d. 4 a. כפר
בִּכְפִירִים [f] pref. id.)(noun masc., pl. of כְּפִיר dec. 1 a. כפר
בְּכַפֶּרְךָ [g] pref. בְּ)(Piel inf. (כַּפֵּר), suff. 2 pers. sing. masc. dec. 7 b. (§ 16. rem. 15) . כפר
בְּכַפְתֹּרֶיהָ [h] pref. id.)(noun masc. pl., suff. 3 pers. sing. fem. from כַּפְתֹּר dec. 1 b. כפתר

בָּכַר Kal not used; Arab. *to be early*. Pi.—I. *to bear early fruit*, Eze. 47. 12.—II. *to constitute* (one) *first-born*, De. 21. 16.

בֵּכֶר masc. dec. 6 b, *a young camel*, Is. 60. 6.

---

[a] Ps. 6. 9. [b] 2 Sa. 1. 24. [c] Ps. 137. 1. [d] Pr. 23. 31. [e] Mi. 6. 11. [f] De. 25. 13. [g] Pr. 31. 19. [h] Ge. 50. 4. [i] Job 30. 25. [k] Nu. 11. 18. [l] 1 Ki. 16. 24. [m] Da. 2. 38. [n] Pr. 5. 11. [o] Eze. 5. 13. [p] Eze. 43. 23. [q] Job 5. 26. [r] 1 Sa. 21. 6. [s] 1 Ki. 17. 10. [t] 1 Ki. 19. 21. [u] Jos. 7. 11. [v] Nu. 4. 16. [y] 1 Ch. 23. 5. [z] La. 3. 13. [a] Ec. 11. 8. [b] Is. 45. 16. [c] Ge. 31. 27. [d] Hag. 2. 12. [e] Job 38. 13. [f] Le. 1. 17. [g] Je. 2. 34. [h] Eze. 5. 3. [i] Ps. 81. 4. [k] Pr. 3. 26. [l] Is. 48. 10. [m] Da. 11. 38. [n] Ezr. 7. 17. [o] Ps. 31. 10. [p] 1 Ki. 15. 30. [q] Eze. 21. 16. [r] Eze. 21. 29. [s] 1 Ch. 12. 17 [t] Job 31. 7. [u] Je. 4. 29. [v] Eze. 29. 7. [y] Eze. 6. 11. [z] Job 41. 5. [a] Job 30. 3. [b] Ge. 6. 14. [c] Eze. 16. 63. [d] Ca. 7. 12. [e] 1 Ch. 27. 25. [f] Ne. 6. 2. [g] Ex. 29. 36. [h] Zep. 2. 14.

בֶּכֶר (*young camel*) pr. name.—I. of a son of Ephraim, Nu. 26. 35. Gent. n. בַּכְרִי ibid.—II. of a son of Benjamin, Ge. 46. 21.

בִּכְרָה fem. *a young she-camel*, Je. 2. 23.

בִּכְרִי (*juvenile*) pr. name masc. 2 Sa. 20. 1.

בִּכּוּר masc. dec. 1 b. *first-fruit*, in the sing. only Is. 28. 4; יוֹם הַבִּכּוּרִים *the feast of the first-fruits, Pentecost*.

בִּכּוּרָה, בִּכּוּרָה (Je. 24. 2) f. *the early fig*, Ho. 9. 10; Mi. 7. 1.

בְּכוֹר masc. dec. 1 a.—*the first-born, firstling*, both of man and beast; בְּכוֹרֵי דַלִּים *the first-born of the poor*, i.e. *the poorest*; בְּכוֹר מָוֶת *mortal disease*.

בְּכֹרָה, בְּכוֹרָה fem. dec. 10.—I. *first-born, firstling* both of man and beast.—II. *earlier birth, primogeniture*; מִשְׁפַּט הַבְּכֹרָה *birth-right*.

בְּכוֹרַת (*primogeniture*) pr. name m. 1 Sa. 9. 1.

בְּכִיר masc. adj., only fem. *first-born daughter*.

בֹּכְרוּ (for בֹּכֶר הוּא *he is the first-born*) pr. n. m.

בָּכֶר in pause for בֶּכֶר (q.v.) . . . בכר

[a]בְּכַר pref. בְּ)(noun masc. sing. d. 8. (§ 37. r. 7) כרר

בֶּכֶר וָ׳ pr. name masc.; for וָ see lett. ו . בכר

בְּכֹר noun masc. sing. dec. 1 a. for בְּכוֹר . . בכר

[b]בְּכֹרָה noun fem. sing. dec. 10. for בְּכוֹרָה . בכר

[c]בִּכְרָה noun fem. sing. . . . . . בכר

בְּכֹרוֹ noun m. s., suff. 3 pers. s. m. fr. בְּכוֹר d. 1 a. בכר

בֹּכְרוּ proper name masc. . . . . בכר

[d]בִּכּוּרוֹת noun fem., pl. of בִּכּוּרָה dec. 10. . . בכר

בְּכֹרִי noun m. s., suff. 1 pers. sing. fr. בְּכוֹר d. 1 a. בכר

[e]בִּכְרֵי noun masc. pl. constr. from [בֶּכֶר] dec. 6 b. בכר

בִּכְרִי pr. name of a man.

[f]בְּכָרִים pref. בְּ)(n. m. pl. [f. כָּרִים] fr. כַּר d. 8. (§ 37. r. 7) כרר

בְּכֹרְךָ, [g]בְּכֹרֶךָ } n. m. s., suff. 2 pers. s. m. fr. בְּכוֹר d. 1 a. בכר

בְּכַרְכְּמִישׁ, בְּכַרְכְּמִשׁ } pref. בְּ)(pr. name of a place . . כרך

[h]בַּכִּרְכָּרוֹת וּ pref. בַּ for בְּהַ)(noun f. pl.; וּ bef. labial כרר

[i]בְּכָרֶם, בְּכֶרֶם וּ׳ } pref. בְּ)(n. m. s. d. 6 a. (see the foll.); וּ bef. (:) כרם

[k]בְּכַרְמֵי pref. id.)(id. pl., constr. state . . כרם

[l]בַּכַּרְמִיל וּ pref. בַּ f. בְּהַ)(n. m. s.; וּ bef. lab. see כַּרְמִיל

[m]בִּכְרָמִים וּ׳[n] pref. id.)(noun masc., pl. of כֶּרֶם, (suff. כַּרְמִי) dec. 6 a; וּ id. . . . . כרם

[o]בַּכַּרְמֶל pref. id. / בְּכַרְמֶל וּ׳ pref. בְּ } noun masc. sing. dec. 8 b. (§ 37. rem. 5) also pr. name; וּ id. } כרם

[p]בְּכֶרֶת־ pref. בְּ bef. (:))(Kal inf. constr. with Mak. for כְּרֹת (§ 8. rem. 18) . . . כרת

בְּכֹרֹת וּ adj. fem., pl. of בְּכוֹרָה dec. 10; וּ bef. (:) בכר

בְּכֹרָתוֹ noun f. s., suff. 3 pers. s. m. fr. בְּכוֹרָה d. 10. בכר

[q]בְּכֹרָתִי id. id, suff. 1 pers. sing. . . . בכר

[r]בְּכָרְתִי pref. בְּ)(Kal inf., suff. 1 pers. sing. . כרת

[s]בְּכֹרָתְךָ noun f. s., suff. 2 pers. s. m. fr. בְּכוֹרָה d. 10. בכר

בַּכְּשָׂבִים pref. בַּ f. בְּהַ)(noun m., pl. of כֶּשֶׂב d. 6 a. כשב

[t]בְּכַשִּׁילִ pref. בְּ)(noun masc. sing. . . . . כשל

[u]בִּכָּשְׁלוֹ וּ pref. בְּ [for בְּהִכָּשְׁלוֹ § 10. r. 6]; Niph. inf. [הִכָּשֵׁל], 3 pers. s. m. d. 7 b; וּ bef. lab. כשל

[x]בִּכְשָׁפֶיהָ pref. בְּ bef. (:))(noun masc. pl., suff. 3 pers. sing. fem. from [כֶּשֶׁף] dec. 6. . כשף

[y]בְּכִשְׁרוֹן וּ pref. בְּ)(noun masc. s.; וּ bef. lab. . כשר

[z]בִּכְתָב וּ׳ pref. בְּ bef. (:))(noun m. s. d. 1 a; וּ id. כתב

[a]בְּכָתְבוֹ pref. בְּ)(Kal inf., suff. 3 pers. sing. masc. כתב

[b]בַּכְּתֻבִים pref. בַּ for בְּהַ)(id. pt. p. m., pl. of כָּתוּב d. 3 a. כתב

[c]בָּכְתָה וּ Kal pret. 3 pers. sing. fem.; וּ bef. labial בכה

[d]בִּכְתוֹב pref. בְּ bef. (:))(Kal inf. constr. . . כתב

[e]בְּכֻתְלַיָּא Chald. pref. בְּ)(noun masc. pl. emph. [from כְּתַל § 59 b] . . . . כתל

בְּכֶתֶם pref. id.)(noun masc. sing. . . . כתם

[f]בְּכֻתֳּנֹתָם pref. בְּ)(noun fem. pl., suff. 3 pers. pl. masc. [from כְּתֹנֶת dec. 13 c. § 44. No. 2] כתן

בַּכָּתֵף pref. בַּ for בְּהַ / [g]בְּכָתֵף וּ׳[h] pref. בְּ q.v. } noun f. s. dec. 5 b; וּ bef. (:) כתף

[i]בִּכְתֵפָם pref. בְּ bef. (:))(id., suff. 3 pers. pl. masc. כתף

[k]בְּכֶתֶר pref. בְּ)(noun masc. sing. . . . כתר

בַּל Chald. masc. *the heart*, Da. 6. 15.

בַּל וּ׳ adv.; וּ before labial . . . . בלה

בֵּל proper name of an idol . . . בעל

בְּלֹא pref. בְּ)(adv. . . . . . לא

בַּלְאֲדָן pr. name masc. . . . . בעל

[l]בַּלָּאט pref. בַּ for בְּהַ)(prop. Kal part., with the pref. as an adv. . . . . לוט

בִּלְאֻמִּים pref. id.)(noun masc., pl. of לְאֹם dec. 8 c. . לאם

בְּלֵב, בְּלֶב־ וּ׳ } pref. בְּ)(n. masc. sing. dec. 8 b. (comp. § 36. rem. 3); וּ bef. (:) } לבב

בִּלְבָב וּ׳ pref. id.)(noun masc. sing. dec. 4 b; וּ id. לבב

[m]בִּלְבַב pref. בְּ bef. (:))(id., construct state . לבב

בִּלְבָבָהּ pref. id.)(id., suff. 3 pers. sing. fem. . לבב

בִּלְבָבוֹ וּ׳[n] pref. id.)(id., suff. 3 p. s. m.; וּ bef. lab. לבב

בִּלְבָבִי pref. id.)(id., suff. 1 pers. sing. . . לבב

בִּלְבָבְךָ, בִּלְבָבֶךָ וּ׳[o] } pref. id.)(id., suff. 2 p. s. m.; וּ bef. lab. לבב

בִּלְבָבֵךְ pref. id.)(id., suff. 2 pers. sing. fem. . לבב

בִּלְבַבְכֶם pref. id.)(id., suff. 2 pers. pl. masc. . לבב

[a] Ge. 31. 34. [b] Ge. 25. 32. [c] Je. 2. 23. [d] Ne. 10. 37. [e] Is. 60. 6. [f] Eze. 27. 21. [g] Ge. 27. 32. [h] Is. 66. 20. [i] Is. 1. 8. [k] Ca. 1. 14. [l] 2 Ch. 2. 13. [m] Ju. 21. 20. [n] Is. 16. 10. [o] Is. 32. 16. [p] 1 Sa. 22. 8. [q] Ge. 27. 36. [r] 1 Sa. 24. 12. [s] Ge. 25. 31. [t] Ps. 74. 6. [u] Pr. 24. 17. [x] Na. 3. 4. [y] Ec. 2. 21. [z] Eze. 13. 9. [a] Je. 45. 1. [b] Nu. 11. 26. [c] De. 21. 13. [d] Ps. 87. 6. [e] Ezr. 5. 8. [f] Le. 10. 5. [g] Is. 11. 14. [h] Eze. 34. 21. [i] 1 Ch. 15. 15. [k] Est. 1. 11. [l] Ju. 4. 21. [m] Jon. 2. 4. [n] Da. 8. 25. [o] De. 30. 14.

בִּלְבָבָם pref. id.)(id., suff. 3 pers. pl. masc. . לבב

בִּלְבָהּ pref. בְּ)(noun masc. sing., suff. 3 pers. sing. fem. from לֵב dec. 8b. . . . לבב

בִּלְבּוֹ pref. id.)(id., suff. 3 pers. sing. masc. . לבב

[a] בִּלְבוֹנָה pref. בְּ bef. (:))(noun fem. sing. dec. 10. . לבן

בִּלְבוּשׁ pref. id.)(noun masc. sing. dec. 1a. . לבש

[b] בִּלְבוּשׁוֹ pref. id.)(id., suff. 3 pers. sing. masc. . לבש

[c] בִּלְבּוֹתָם pref. בְּ)(noun fem., pl. of [לִבָּה] dec. 10. לבב

בִּלְבִּי pref. id.)(noun masc. sing., suff. 1 pers. sing. from לֵב dec. 8b, Chald. dec. 5b. . . לבב

[d] בִּלְבֶּךָ pref. id.)(id., suff. 2 pers. sing. m., for לִבְּךָ לבב

[e] בִּלְבֵּךְ pref. id.)(id., suff. 2 pers. sing. fem. . לבב

בִּלְבָּם pref. id.)(id., suff. 3 pers. pl. masc. . לבב

בִּלְבָן pref. id.)(pr. name masc. . . . . לבן

בִּלְבְנָה pref. id.)(pr. name of a place . . לבן

[f] וּבַלְּבָנוֹן pref. בַּ for בְּהַ)(pr. n. of a region; וּ bef. lab. לבן

[ll] וּבִלְבֵנִים pref. בְּ bef. (:))(n. fem. with pl. m. term. from לְבֵנָה d. 11c. (§ 42. r. 4); וּ bef. lab. לבן

בִּלְבֻשֵׁיהֶם pref. id.)(noun masc. pl., suff. 3 pers. pl. masc. from לְבוּשׁ dec. 1a. . . לבש

[g] בְּלַבַּת pref. בְּ)(noun fem. sing., constr. of [לַבָּה] contr. for [לְהָבָה] . . . . להב

בָּלַג Kal not used; Arab. *to open; to shine;* hence Hiph.—I. *to open,* or *cause to break out, upon,* with עַל, Am. 5. 9.—II. *to make cheerful, to enliven,* with פָּנִים *the face,* also without it, *to be cheerful, glad.*

בִּלְגָּה (*joy*) pr. name masc. Ne. 12. 5, 18, written בִּלְגַּי chap. 10. 9.

מַבְלִיגִית fem. *exhilaration, cheerfulness,* Je. 8. 18.

בִּלְגָּה pr. name masc. . . . . . . בלג

בִּלְגַּי pr. name masc. . . . . . בלג

וּבִלְדַּד (for בֶּן־לְדַד *son of strife,* לדד Arab. *to strive,* see בִּלְשָׁן) pr. n. of a friend of Job; וּ bef. lab.

בְּלֶדֶת pref. בְּ)(Kal inf. constr. dec. 13b. . . ילד

בְּלִדְתָּהּ pref. id.)(id., suff. 3 pers. sing. fem. . ילד

בָּלַהּ Pi. *to harass, trouble,* Ezr. 4. 4. Keri.

בַּלָּהָה fem. dec. 11a.—I. *terror.*—II. *calamity.*

בִּלְהָה (*feebleness*) pr. name—I. of a hand-maid of Rachel.—II. of a place in the tribe of Simeon, 1 Ch. 4. 29, comp. בַּעֲלָה.

בִּלְהָן (*feeble*) pr. name masc.—I. Ge. 36. 27.—II. 1 Ch. 7. 10.

[בָּלָה] I. *to grow old.*—II. *to waste away.* Pi. *to caus[e] to waste away, to consume.*

בְּלָא Pa. *to destroy,* Da. 7. 25.

בָּלֶה masc. dec. 9, adj., fem. בָּלָה; *old, worn out*

בָּלָה pr. name of a place, Jos. 19. 3, for בִּלְהָה q. v.

בְּלוֹ Chald. masc. *custom, tax.*

בְּלוֹי masc. only pl. com. בְּלוֹיֵ & בְּלוֹאֵי (lik[e] פְּתָאִים for פְּתָיִים) *old clothes, rags.*

בַּל adv.—I. *not.*—II. *nothing.*

בְּלִי masc.—I. *consumption, destruction,* Is. 38. 17 —II. *want,* only adverbially, *not; without;* בִּבְלִי לִבְלִי *without;* מִבְּלִי *because not;* lit. *from wan[t] of;* עַד בְּלִי *as long as,* lit. *until the wanting of.* עַל בְּלִי *because not,* Ge. 31. 20.

בְּלִימָה (compounded of בְּלִי & מָה *not any thing*) *nothing,* Job 26. 7.

בְּלִיַּעַל (compounded of בְּלִי *without,* and יַעַל *use*).—I. *worthlessness.*—II. *wickedness,* אִישׁ בְּ׳ *a wicked man;* also ellipt. without אִישׁ.—III. *injury, destruction.*

בִּלְעֲדֵי (compounded of בַּל *not,* and עֲדֵי *to,* R. עָדָה), also בִּלְעֲדֵי, with suff. בִּלְעָדַי, בִּלְעָדֶיךָ.—I. *not,* or *nothing to, as far as regards,* Ge. 14. 24; 41. 16.—II. *besides, without.*

בֵּלֶת, with suff. בִּלְתְּךָ, בִּלְתִּי only Ho. 13. 4, & 1 Sa. 2. 2, elsewhere בִּלְתִּי with parag. Yod.—I. adv. *not,* 1 Sa. 20. 26.—II. *without, besides.*—III. conj. *besides that; except that, unless;* בִּלְתִּי אִם *unless it be that;* לְבִלְתִּי chiefly as the negation before an inf. (בִּלְתִּי אֱכֹל for לְבִלְתִּי אֲכֹל) *not to, so that not;* מִבִּלְתִּי *because not;* עַד בִּלְתִּי *until not; so long as.*

אֲבָל adv.—I. *nay indeed, nay rather.*—II. *truly, certainly.*—III. *but, yet, nevertheless.*

תַּבְלִית fem. dec. 1b, *destruction,* Is. 10. 25.

וּבָלָה pr. name of a place, contr. for בִּלְהָה; וּ bef. lab. בלה

[h] בִּלָּה Piel pret. 3 pers. sing. masc. . . . בלה

[i] בְּלַהַב pref. בְּ)(noun masc. sing. dec. 6d. . להב

[k] וּבְלֶהָבָה pref. id.)(n. fem. sing. dec. 11a; וּ bef. (:) להב

[l] בְּלַהֲבֵי pref. id.)(n. m. pl. constr. from לַהַב dec. 6d. להב

[m] בַּלָּהָה noun fem. sing. dec. 11a. . . . בלה

בִּלְהָה pr. name fem. . . . . . בלה

בַּלָּהוֹת noun fem. pl., of בַּלָּהָה dec. 11a. . . בלה

[n] בַּלְהוֹת id. pl., construct state . . . בלה

[o] בְּלַהֲטֵיהֶם pref. בְּ)(noun masc. pl. with suff. for לָטֵיהֶם (comp. Ex. 7. 22). R. לוּט, or from לָהַט . להט

---

[a] Is. 43. 23. [b] Is. 63. 1. [c] Ps. 125. 4. [d] Pr. 2. 10. [e] Is. 47. 10. [f] La. 4. 14. [g] Ex. 3. 2. [h] La. 3. 4. [i] Ju. 13. 20. [k] Da. 11. 33. [l] Is. 66. 15. [ll] Ex. 1. 14. [m] Is. 17. 14. [n] Job 24. 17. [o] Ex. 7. 11.

בְּלָהָן pr. name masc. . . . . . בלה

בָּלוּ Kal pret. 3 pers. pl. . . . . בלה

בְּלוֹ Chald. noun masc. sing. . . . . בלה

בְּלוֹ pref. בְּ)(pr.n. in compos. לוֹ דְבָר, see לֹא דְבָר

[a] בְּלוֹא וּ׳ pref. בְּ)(adv. more frequently לֹא; וּ bef. (:) לא

[b] בְּלוֹאֵי for בְּלוֹיֵ, בְּלוֹיֵ like פְּתָאִים for פְּתָיִים (§ 35. r. 15) בלה

בְּלוּז pref. בְּ)(pr. name of a place . . . לוז

בְּלוּט pref. id.)(pr. name masc. . . . לוט

[c] בְּלוֹיֵ וּ׳ noun masc. pl. constr. [for בְּלוֹיֵי from בְּלוֹי comp. § 3. rem. 1]; וּ bef. (:) . בלה

בַּלְוִיִּם pref. בַּ for בְּהַ)(patronym., pl. of לֵוִי dec. 8f. לוה

בָּלוּל Kal part. pass. sing. masc. . . . בלל

בְּלוּלָה id. fem. dec. 10. . . . . בלל

[d] בְּלוּלִים וּ pref. בְּ)(noun m., pl. of [לוּל]; וּ bef. (:) לול

בְּלוּלֹת Kal part. pass. fem., pl. of בְּלוּלָה dec. 10. from בָּלוּל masc. . . . בלל

[e] בָּלוֹת adj. fem., pl. of בָּלָה, fr. [בָּלֶה] masc. . בלה

[f] בִּלְחוּמוֹ pref. בְּ bef. (:))(noun masc. sing., suff. 3 pers. sing. masc. from [לְחוּם] . לחם

בַּלְּחִי pref. בַּ for בְּהַ)(pr. name of a place, for לְחִי (§ 35. rem. 14) . . . לחה

[zz] בִּלְחִי pref. בְּ bef. (:))(noun masc. sing. dec. 6 i. (§ 35. rem. 14. & 15) . . . לחה

בִּלְחָיֶיךָ pref. id.)(id. du. (לְחָיַיִם) with suff. 2 p. s. m. לחה

[g] בַּלֶּחֶם [h] וּ׳ } pref. בַּ for בְּהַ } noun com. sing. dec. 6a; וּ bef. lab. } לחם
בַּלָּחֶם
[i] בְּלֶחֶם pref. בְּ q. v.

בְּלַחְמוֹ pref. id.)(id., suff. 3 pers. sing. masc. . לחם

[k] בְּלַחְמִי pref. id.)(id., suff. 1 pers. sing. . . לחם

[l] בְּלַחְמֶךָ pref. id.)(id., suff. 2 pers. s. m. from לַחְמְךָ לחם

[m] בַּלַּחַץ pref. בַּ f. בְּהַ } noun masc. sing. dec. 6d. . לחץ
בְּלַחַץ pref. בְּ q. v. }

בַּלָּט pref. בַּ for בְּהַ)(prop. Kal part., with the pref. as an adv. . . . . לוט

בְּלָטֵיהֶם pref. בְּ)(id. as a subst. pl., suff. 3 pers. pl. m. לוט

בֵּלְטְשַׁאצַּר } pr. name given to Daniel at the court of Nebuchadnezzar.
בֵּלְטְשַׁאצַּר }

[n] בְּלִי Kh. בְּלִי q. v., K. בַּל q. v. . . . בלה

בְּלִי noun masc. sing. (Is. 38. 17), otherwise adv. בלה

בַּלֵּיל pref. בַּ for בְּהַ)(Kh. לַיִל noun masc. sing. dec. 6h, K. בַּלַּיְלָה (q.v.) . . . ליל

[o] בְּלֵיל pref. בְּ)(id., constr. state . . . ליל

[p] בְּלִיל noun masc. sing. dec. 1a. . . . בלל

[q] בַּלַּיְלָה וּ׳ } pref. בַּ f. בְּהַ } noun m. s. (לַיִל d. 6h) with parag. ה; וּ bef. lab. } ליל
בַּלַּיְלָה וּ׳
בְּלַיְלָה pref. בְּ q. v.

בְּלִילוֹ noun m. s., suff. 3 pers. s. m. fr. בְּלִיל d. 1a. בלל

בַּלֵּילוֹת pref. בַּ for בְּהַ)(noun masc. with pl. fem. term. from לַיִל dec. 6h. . . . ליל

[r] בְּלֵילְיָא Chald. pref. בְּ)(noun m. s. emph., [fr. לֵילֵי] ליל

[s] בָּלִים adj. masc., pl. of [בָּלֶה] dec. 9b. . . בלה

[t] בְּלִימָה compound of בְּלִי & מָה see . . בלה

בְּלִיַּעַל } noun m. s., compound of בְּלִי & יַעַל see בלה
בְּלִיַּעַל וּ׳ }

בְּלֶכֶת וּ׳ pref. בְּ)(Kal inf. constr. dec. 13. (§ 44. rem. 3); וּ bef. (:) . . . . ילך

בְּלֶכְתּוֹ pref. id.)(id., suff. 3 pers. sing. masc. . ילך

בְּלֶכְתְּךָ וּ׳ pref. id.)(id., suff. 2 pers. s. m.; וּ bef. (:) ילך

[u] בְּלֶכְתָּם וּ׳ pref. id.)(id., suff. 3 pers. pl. masc.; וּ id. ילך

[bb] בְּלֶכְתָּן pref. id.)(id., suff. 3 pers. pl. fem. . . ילך

[x] בָּלַל I. *to suffuse*, Ps. 92. 3.—II. *to mingle, mix, confound.*—III. *to give fodder*, Ju. 19. 21, denom. of בְּלִיל. Hithpo. *to mix oneself, to be mixed*, Ho. 7. 8.

בָּבֶל (for בַּלְבֵּל *confusion*) *Babylon;* also used for the kingdom of Babylon, *Babylonia.*

בַּבְלִי Chald. only pl. emph. בַּבְלָיֵא *Babylonians*, Ezr. 4. 9.

בְּלִיל masc. dec. 1a, *mixed provender, fodder.*

תֶּבֶל masc. *mixture* or *confusion* of species by bestiality, or of relation by incest.

תְּבַלֻּל masc. some *disorder* or *blemish* in the eye, Le. 21. 20.

[y] בַּלֻּלָאֹת pref. בַּ for בְּהַ)(noun pl. fem. defect. [for לוּלָאוֹת fr. לוּלִי comp. § 35. r. 15, note] לול

[בָּלַם] *to bind, to bridle*, Ps. 32. 9.

[z] בְּלָמְדִי pref. בְּ)(Kal inf., suff. 1 pers. sing. . . למד

[a] בְּלִמֻּדָי pref. id.)(adj. masc. pl., suff. 1 pers. sing. fr. לִמּוּד dec. 1b. . . . . למד

[בָּלַס] *to pluck* or *gather figs*, Am. 7. 14.

[b] בָּלַע I. *to swallow.*—II. *to consume, to destroy.* Niph. *to be swallowed up, lost.* Pi. i. q. Kal. Pu. *to be destroyed, to perish.* Hithpa. id.

בֶּלַע m. d. 6a. (§ 35. r. 5) with suff. בַּלְעִי—I. *a thing swallowed*, Je. 51. 44.—II. *destruction*, Ps. 52. 6.—

[a] Is. 55. 1. [b] Je. 38. 12. [c] Je. 38. 11, 11. [d] 1 Ki. 6. 8. [e] Jos. 9. 5. [f] Job 20. 23. [g] Ge. 47. 19. [h] Le. 8. 32. [i] Ne. 5. 15. [k] Pr. 9. 5. [l] Ju. 13. 16. [m] Job 36. 15. [n] Ho. 9. 16. [o] Is. 15. 1, 1. [p] Is. 30. 24. [q] Is. 28. 19. [r] Da. 5. 30. [s] Jos. 9. 4. [t] Job 26. 7. [u] 2 Ch. 24. 25. [x] Ge. 11. 9. [y] Ex. 26. 11. [z] Ps. 119. 7. [zz] Ju. 15. 16, 16. [a] Is. 8. 16. [b] Job 20. 15. [bb] Eze. 1. 9, 12, 17.

III. pr. name (*a*) of a city near the Dead sea. Gent. n. בַּלְעִי; (*b*) of a man.

בִּלְעָם (for בְּלַע עָם *wasting of the people*) pr. name.—I. of the prophet Balaam.—II. of a city in Manasseh, called also יִבְלְעָם (for יְבַלַּע עָם)

בֶּלַע[a] [for בֶּלַע] noun m. s., (suff. בִּלְעוֹ) dec. 6a. בלע

בַּלַּע[b] Piel imp. sing. masc. . . . . בלע

בֶּלַע ו׳ pr. name of a man and city . בלע

בָּלַע[c] ו׳ id. pret. 3 pers. sing. masc.; ו bef. labial בלע

בְּלַעֲגֵי[d] pref. בְּ) adj. pl. const. masc. fr. [לָעֵג] d. 5. לעג

בִּלְעָדַי / בִּלְעָדֵי[e] } the following with suff. 1 pers. sing. . בלה

בִּלְעֲדֵי[f] adv., in form pl. constr., compound of בַּל & עַד see . . . . בלה

בִּלְעָדֶיךָ ו id. with suff. 2 pers. sing. m.; ו bef. lab. בלה

בָּלְעָה[h] ו Kal pret. 3 pers. sing. fem.; ו bef. lab. בלע

בִּלְעוֹ[i] noun masc. sing., suff. 3 pers. sing. masc. fr. [בֶּלַע] dec. 6a. (§ 35. rem. 5) . בלע

בִּלְּעוּ[k] Piel pret. 3 p. pl. [for בִּלְּעוּ comp. § 8. r. 7] בלע

בְּלָעוּנוּ[l] Kal pret. 3 pers. pl., suff. 1 pers. pl. בלע

בִּלְעִי[m] id. inf. [בְּלֹעַ], suff. 1 pers. sing. (§ 16. r. 10) בלע

בְּלֹעֶךָ[n] pref. בְּ) noun masc. sing., suff. 2 pers. sing. m. [for לֹעֲךָ fr. לֹעַ] . . . לוע

בִּלְעָם ו׳ pr. name masc.; ו bef. lab. . . בלע

בְּלָעָנוֹ[o] Kal pret. 3 pers. sing. masc., suff., Kh. ־ָנוֹ, 1 pers. pl., K. ־ַנִי 1 pers. sing. . . בלע

בִּלַּעֲנוּ[p] Piel pret. 1 p. pl. [for בִּלַּעְנוּ comp. § 8. r. 7] בלע

בִּלַּעֲנוּהוּ id., suff. 3 pers. sing. masc. . . בלע

בַּלַּפִּדִים / בַּלַּפִּידִים } pref. בַּ for בְּהַ) noun masc., pl. of לַפִּיד dec. 1b. . . . . . . } לפד

[בָּלַק] *to empty out, make waste*, Is. 24. 1. Pu. *to be made waste*, Na. 2. 11. Hence

בָּלָק ו׳ (*empty*) pr. name of a king of Moab in the time of Moses . . . . בלק

בֵּלְשַׁאצַּר pr. name of the last of the Chaldean kings, written בֵּלְאשַׁצַּר in Da. 7. 1.

בַּלָּשׁוֹן[t] pref. בַּ for בְּהַ / בְּלָשׁוֹן[u] ו pref. בְּ q. v. } noun com. s. d. 3a; ו bef. (:) לשן

בִּלְשׁוֹן[x] pref. בְּ bef. (:)) id., constr. state . לשן

בִּלְשׁוֹנוֹ pref. id.) id., suff., 3 pers. sing. masc. . לשן

בִּלְשׁוֹנִי pref. id.) id., suff. 1 pers. sing. . . לשן

בִּלְשׁוֹנָם[y] ו pref. id.) id., suff. 3 p. pl. m.; ו bef. lab. לשן

בַּלְּשָׁכֹת[z] pref. בַּ for בְּהַ) noun fem. pl. abs. from לִשְׁכָּה dec. 12b. . . . . לשך

בְּלִשְׁכַּת pref. בְּ) id. sing., constr. state . . לשך

בְּלִשְׁכֹת[a] pref. id.) id. pl., constr. state . . לשך

בִּלְשָׁן (for בֶּן־לָשׁוֹן *son of tongue*, i. e. *eloquent*, comp. בְּמֹהַל) pr. name of a man.

בָּלְתָה Kal pret. 3 pers. sing. fem. . . בלה

בַּלֹּתִי[b] Kal pret. 1 pers. sing. . . . בלל

בְּלֹתִי[c] Kal inf. [בְּלוֹת], suff. 1 pers. sing. . בלה

בִּלְתִּי adv. and prep., [בֶּלֶת with parag. י] . בלה

בִּלְתִּי[d] prep. [בֶּלֶת] with suff. 1 pers. sing. . בלה

בִּלְתֶּךָ[e] id., suff. 2 pers. sing. masc., [for בִּלְתְּךָ] . בלה

בָּם[f] ו׳ pref. prep. בְּ with suff. 3 pers. pl. m. (§ 5); ו bef. lab. . . . ב

בִּמְאֹד pref. בְּ bef. (:)) adv. . . . . אוד

בְּמֵאָה pref. בְּ) noun fem. sing. dec. 11b. . מאה

בְּמֹאזְנֵי pref. id.) n. m. du. constr. fr. [מֹאזֶן] d. 7b. אזן

בְּמֹאזַנְיָא[g] Chald. pref. id.) id. du., emph. state . אזן

בְּמֹאזְנַיִם / בְּמֹאזְנָיִם } pref. id.) id. du., abs. state . . אזן

בְּמַאֲרַב[h] pref. id.) n. m. s., constr. of [מַאֲרָב] d. 2b. ארב

בַּמְּאֵרָה[i] pref. בַּ for בְּהַ) noun f. s. dec. 10. (§ 42. r. 3) ארר

בְּמָבוֹא pref. id.) noun masc. sing. dec. 3a. . בוא

בְּמִבְחַר[k] pref. בְּ) n. m. s., constr. of [מִבְחָר] d. 2b. בחר

בְּמִבְטַחַיִךְ[l] pref. id.) noun masc. pl., suff. 2 pers. sing. masc. fr. [מִבְטָח] dec. 2b. (§ 37. rem. 7) בטח

בְּמֵבִין[m] pref. id.) Hiph. part. sing. masc. . בין

בְּמִבְצָרֶיהָ[n] pref. id.) noun masc. pl., suff. 3 pers. sing. fem. fr. מִבְצָר dec. 2b. . . . בצר

בְּמִבְצָרִים[o] pref. id.) id. pl., abs. state . . בצר

בִּמְבַקְשֵׁי[p] pref. בְּ bef. (:)) Piel part. pl. constr. masc. dec. 7b. (comp. § 10. rem. 7) . בקש

בִּמְבֻשָׁיו[q] pref. id.) noun masc. pl., suff. 3 pers. sing. masc. from [מָבוּשׁ] dec. 3a. . . בוש

בְּמִגְדּוֹל pref. בְּ) pr. name of a place . . גדל

בַּמִּגְדָּלוֹת[r] ו pref. בַּ for בְּהַ) noun masc. with pl. fem. term. from מִגְדָּל dec. 2b.; ו bef. lab. גדל

בְּמִגְדְּלוֹתַיִךְ[s] pref. בְּ) id. pl., suff. 2 pers. sing. fem. גדל

בַּמִּגְדָּנוֹת[t] ו pref. בַּ for בְּהַ) noun fem. pl.; ו bef. lab. מגד

בְּמָגוֹג pref. בְּ) pr. name of a region . . גוג

בַּמְּגוּרָה[u] pref. בַּ for בְּהַ) noun fem. sing. dec. 10. . גור

בִּמְגוּרָיו[x] pref. בְּ bef. (:)) noun masc. pl., suff. 3 pers. sing. masc. from [מָגוּר] dec. 3a. . גור

בִּמְגוּרָם[y] pref. id.) id. pl., suff. 3 pers. pl. masc. גור

[a] Ps. 52. 6. [b] Ps. 55. 10. [c] Is. 25. 7. [d] Is. 28. 11. [e] Ge. 14. 24. [f] Job 34. 32. [g] Ge. 41. 44. [h] Nu. 16. 30. [i] Je. 51. 44. [k] Is. 3. 12. [l] Ps. 124. 3. [m] Job 7. 19. [n] Pr. 23. 2. [o] Je. 51. 34. [p] La. 2. 16. [q] Ps. 35. 25. [r] Ju. 7. 20. [s] Ju. 15. 5. [t] Je. 18. 18. [u] Is. 28. 11. [x] Pr. 21. 6. [y] Ps. 78. 36. [z] 1 Ch. 9. 33. [a] Eze. 44. 19. [b] Ps. 92. 11. [c] Ge. 18. 12. [d] Ho. 13. 4. [e] 1 Sa. 2. 2. [f] Eze. 33. 10. [g] Da. 5. 27. [h] Ps. 10. 8. [i] Mal. 3. 9. [k] Ge. 23. 6. [l] Je. 2. 37. [m] Pr. 17. 10. [n] Is. 34. 13. [o] Nu. 13. 19. [p] Est. 9. 2. [q] De. 25. 11. [r] 1 Ch. 27. 25. [s] Eze. 27. 11. [t] Ezr. 1. 6. [u] Hag. 2. 19. [x] Job 18. 19. [y] Ps. 55. 16.

בְּמַגְזְרוֹת[a]	וּ pref. בְּ)(noun fem. pl. constr. from [מַגְזֵרָה] dec. 11 b; וּ bef. (:)	גזר
בַּמְּגִלָּה[b]	pref. בַּ for בְּהַ)(noun fem. sing. dec. 10.	גלל
בִּמְגִלַּת[c]	pref. בְּ bef. (:))(id., construct state	גלל
בַּמַּגֵּפָה	pref. בַּ f. בְּהַ } noun fem. sing. dec. 10.	נגף
בְּמַגֵּפָה[d]	pref. בְּ q. v. }	
בַּמְּגֵרָה	pref. בַּ for בְּהַ)(n. fem. s. dec. 10. (§ 42. r. 3)	גרר
וּבַמְּגֵרוֹת[e]	וּ pref. id.)(id. pl.; וּ bef. lab.	גרר
בְּמִגְרוֹן	pref. בְּ)(pr. name of a place	מגר
בַּמִּדְבָּר	וּ׳ pref. בַּ for בְּהַ)(noun m. s. dec. 2 b; וּ id.	דבר
בְּמִדְבַּר	pref. בְּ)(id., construct state	דבר
בַּמִּדָּה	pref. בַּ f. בְּהַ } noun fem. sing. dec. 10.	מדד
בְּמִדָּה[mm]	pref. בְּ q. v. }	
בְּמָדַי	pref. id.)(pr. name of a region, see מָדַי	
בְּמַדִּין	pref. id.)(pr. name of a region R. דִּין see	דון
בַּמְּדִינָה	pref. בַּ for בְּהַ)(n. fem. s. dec. 10. R. דִּין see	דון
בַּמְּדִינוֹת[f]	pref. בַּ for בְּהַ } id. pl.	דון
בִּמְדִינוֹת[g]	pref. בְּ bef. (:) }	
בִּמְדִינַת[h]	Ch. pref. id.)(n. f. s., constr. of [מְדִינָא] d. 8 a.	דון
בַּמַּדְכֵהָ[i]	pref. בַּ for בְּהַ)(noun fem. sing.	דוך
בְּמַדָּעֲךָ[k]	pref. בְּ)(n. m. s., suff. 2 pers. s. m. from מַדָּע	ידע
בְּמִדְרַשׁ[l]	pref. id.)(n. m. s., constr. of [מִדְרָשׁ] dec. 2 b.	דרשׁ
בָּמָה	noun fem. sing. dec. 10. (pl. c. בָּמֳתֵי)	בום
בַּמָּה	וּ׳[m'] pref. בַּ for בְּהַ)(pron. interrog. in pause (2 Ki. 22. 21; 2 Ch. 18. 20), and bef. the gutt. ה & א	מה
בַּמֶּה	pref. id. } pron. interrog. bef. non-gutt., and	מה
בַּמָּה[n]	pref. בְּ } once (2 Ch. 7. 21) bef. ע	
בִּמְהָל	וּ (for בֶּן־מְהָל circumcised, מהל i. q. מול comp. בַּעֲלִים) pr. name masc. 1 Ch. 7. 33.	
בְּמַהֲמֹרוֹת[o]	pref. id.)(noun fem. pl.	המר
בְּמַהֵר[p]	pref. id.)(noun masc. sing.	מהר
בִּמְהֵרָה[q]	pref. בְּ bef. (:))(noun fem. sing.	מהר
בְּמוֹ	pref. בְּ with the parag. syllable, מוֹ q. v.	
בְּמוֹאָב	וּ׳ pref. בְּ)(pr. name of a people and country, see מוֹאָב; וּ bef. (:)	
בַּמּוֹט[r]	pref. בַּ for בְּהַ)(noun masc. sing. dec. 1 a.	מוט
בְּמוֹט[s]	וּ׳[t'] pref. בְּ)(Kal inf. constr.; וּ bef. (:)	מוט
בַּמּוּסָר[u]	pref. בַּ for בְּהַ)(noun masc. sing. dec. 2 b.	יסר
בְּמוֹעֲדוֹ	pref. בְּ)(n. m. s., suff. 3 p. s. m. fr. מוֹעֵד d. 7 b.	יעד
בְּמוֹעֲדֶיהָ[x]	pref. id.)(id. pl., suff. 3 pers. sing. fem.	יעד
בְּמוֹעֲדָיו[y]	pref. id.)(noun masc. pl., suff. 3 pers. sing. masc. from [מוֹעָד] dec. 2 b.	יעד
וּבְמוֹעֲדֵיכֶם[z]	וּ׳[a'] pref. id.)(noun masc. pl., suff. 2 pers. pl. masc. from מוֹעֵד dec. 7 b; וּ bef. lab.	יעד
בַּמּוֹעֲדִים[b]	וּ׳ pref. בַּ for בְּהַ)(id. pl., abs. state; וּ id.	יעד
בְּמוֹעֲדָם[c]	pref. בְּ)(id. sing., suff. 3 pers. pl. masc.	יעד
בְּמוֹעֲצוֹתֵיהֶם[d]	pref. id.)(noun fem. pl., suff. 3 pers. pl. masc. from [מוֹעֵצָה] dec. 11 b.	יעץ
וּבְמוֹפְתִים	וּ pref. id.)(noun masc., pl. of מוֹפֵת dec. 7 b; וּ bef. (:)	יפת
בְּמוּצָק[e]	pref. id.)(noun masc. sing. for מוּצָק׳	צוק
בְּמוֹקְשִׁים[f]	pref. id.)(noun masc., pl. of מוֹקֵשׁ dec. 7 b.	יקשׁ
וּבְמוֹרָא[rr]	וּ pref. id.)(noun masc. sing. dec. 1 b. (§ 31. rem. 1 & 3); וּ bef. lab.	ירא
וּבְמוֹרָאִים[g]	וּ pref. id.)(id. pl., absolute state; וּ id.	ירא
בַּמּוֹרָד[h]	pref. בַּ f. בְּהַ } noun masc. sing. dec. 2 b.	ירד
בְּמוֹרָד[i]	pref. בְּ q. v. }	
בְּמוֹרַד	pref. id.)(id. construct state	ירד
וּבְמוֹשַׁב	וּ pref. id.)(noun masc. sing., constr. of מוֹשָׁב dec. 2 b; וּ bef. (:)	ישׁב
בְּמוֹשְׁבֹתָם[k]	pref. id.)(id. pl., suff. 3 pers. pl. masc.	ישׁב
בַּמָּוֶת	pref. בַּ for בְּהַ)(noun masc. sing. dec. 6 g.	מות
בָּמוֹת	וּ׳ n. f., pl. of בָּמָה d. 10, also pr. name; וּ bef. lab.	בום
בְּמוֹת	וּ׳[l'] pref. בְּ)(n. m. s., constr. of מָוֶת dec. 6 g; וּ id.	מות
בְּמוֹתוֹ	pref. id.)(id., suff. 3 pers. sing. masc.	מות
בָּמוֹתַי	noun fem. pl. suff. 1 pers. s. from בָּמָה dec. 10.	בום
בָּמוֹתֵי	id. constr. st., Kh. בָּמוֹתֵי, K. בָּמֳתֵי, (§ 36. r. 6)	בום
בְּמוֹתִי[m]	pref. בְּ)(n. m. s., suff. 1 p. s. fr. מָוֶת dec. 6 g.	מות
בָּמוֹתָיו[n]	n. fem. pl., suff. 3 p. s. m. from בָּמָה dec. 10.	בום
בָּמוֹתֶיךָ[o]	id. pl., suff. 2 pers. sing. masc.	בום
בָּמוֹתֵיכֶם[yy]	id. pl., suff. 2 pers. pl. masc.	בום
בָּמוֹתֵימוֹ[p]	id. pl., suff. 3 pers. pl. masc.	בום
בָּמוֹתָם	id. pl., suff. 3 pers. pl. masc. (§ 4. rem. 2)	בום
וּבְמוֹתָם[q]	וּ׳ pref. בְּ)(noun masc. sing., suff. 3 pers. pl. masc. from מָוֶת dec. 6 g; וּ bef. (:)	מות
בַּמִּזְבֵּחַ	pref. בַּ for בְּהַ)(noun masc. sing. dec. 7 c.	זבח
בִּמְזִמּוֹת[r]	pref. בְּ bef. (:))(n. fem., pl. of מְזִמָּה dec. 10.	זמם
בַּמְּזַמֵּרוֹת[s]	pref. בַּ for בְּהַ)(n. fem., pl. [מְזַמֵּרָה] dec. 11 b.	זמר
וּבַמִּזְרֶה[t]	וּ pref. id. } noun masc. sing.; וּ bef. lab.	זרה
בַּמִּזְרֶה[u]	pref. בְּ }	
בְּמִזְרְקֵי[x]	pref. id.)(n. m. pl. constr. fr. מִזְרָק dec. 2 b.	זרק
בַּמַּחְבֶּרֶת / בַּמַּחְבָּרֶת	pref. בַּ for בְּהַ)(noun fem. sing. dec. 13 a.	חבר
וּבַמְּחוּגָה[y]	וּ pref. id.)(noun fem. sing.; וּ bef. lab.	חוג
בְּמָחוֹל	pref. בְּ)(noun masc. sing. dec. 3 a.	חול
בִּמְחוֹל[z]	pref. בְּ bef. (:))(id., construct state	חול
בַּמַּחֲזֶה[a]	pref. בַּ for בְּהַ)(noun masc. sing. dec. 9 a.	חזה
בִּמְחִיר	pref. בְּ bef. (:))(noun masc. sing. dec. 1 a.	מחר
בִּמְחִירֵיהֶם[b]	pref. id.)(id. pl., suff. 3 pers. pl. masc.	מחר
בְּמַחֲלֵה[c]	pref. בְּ)(n. m. s. constr. of [מַחֲלֶה] dec. 9 a.	חלה
וּבִמְחֹלוֹת[d]	וּ pref. בְּ bef. (:))(noun fem., pl. of [מְחֹלָה] dec. 10; וּ bef. lab.	חלל

[a] 2 Sa. 12. 31. [b] Je. 36. 6. [c] Ps. 40. 8. [d] Eze. 24. 16. [e] 1 Ch. 20. 3. [f] La. 1. 1. [g] Est. 9. 16. [h] Da. 3. 1, 30. [i] Nu. 11. 8. [k] Ec. 10. 20. [l] 2 Ch. 13. 22. [m] 2 Sa. 21. 3. [n] Ec. 3. 22. [o] Ps. 140. 11. [p] 1 Sa. 18. 25. [q] Ec. 4. 12. [r] Nu. 13. 23. [s] Ps. 38. 17. [t] Ps. 46. 3. [u] Pr. 4. 13. [x] Eze. 36. 38. [y] Is. 14. 31. [z] Nu. 29. 39. [a] Nu. 10. 10. [b] Eze. 46. 9, 11. [c] Le. 23. 4. [d] Ps. 81. 13. [e] Job 37. 10. [f] Job 40. 24. [g] De. 4. 34. [h] Jos. 7. 5. [i] Mi. 1. 4. [k] Nu. 31. 10. [l] Est. 2. 7. [m] 1 Ki. 13. 31. [mm] Job 28. 25. [n] 2 Ch. 32. 12. [o] 2 Sa. 1. 19, 25. [p] De. 33. 29. [q] 2 Sa. 1. 23. [r] Ps. 10. 2. [rr] Je. 32. 21. [s] Is. 18. 5. [t] Is. 30. 24. [u] Je. 15. 7. [x] Am. 6. 6. [y] Is. 44. 13. [yy] Eze. 6. 3. [z] Je. 31. 4. [a] Ge. 15. 1. [b] Ps. 44. 13. [c] 2 Ch. 21. 15. [d] Is. 2. 19.

בַּמְּחֹלוֹת pref. בַּ for בְּהַ } noun fem., pl. of [מְחֹלָה] dec. 10; וּ bef. lab. — חול
וּבִמְחֹלוֹת[a] pref. בְּ bef. (:)

בַּמַּחֲלָיִים[b] pref. בְּ)(noun masc., pl. of [מַחֲלִי] dec. 1b. — חלה

בְּמַחְלְקוֹת[c] pref. id.)(noun fem., pl. of מַחֲלֹקֶת dec. 13c. — חלק

בְּמַחְלְקוֹתֵיהֶם[d] pref. id.)(id. pl., suff. 3 pers. pl. masc. — חלק

בְּמַחְלְקוֹתֵיכֶם[e] pref. id.)(id. pl., suff. 2 pers. pl. masc. — חלק

בְּמַחְלְקוֹתָם[f] pref. id.)(id. pl., suff. 3 pers. pl. m. (§ 4. r. 2) — חלק

בְּמַחְלְקָתְהוֹן[g] Chald. pref. id.)(noun fem. pl., suff. 3 pers. pl. masc. from [מַחְלְקָא] dec. 9a. — חלק

וּבִמְחֹלֹת[h] pref. בְּ bef. (:))(n. fem., pl. of [מְחֹלָה] d. 10. — חול

בְּמֵחַן[i] Chald. pref. בְּ)(Peal inf. (dag. forte impl. in ח) — חנן

בַּמַּחֲנֶה pref. בַּ for בְּהַ)(noun com. sing. dec. 9a. — חנה

בְּמַחֲנֵה pref. בְּ)(id., construct state — חנה

בַּמַּחֲנוֹת[k] pref. בַּ for בְּהַ)(id. pl. fem. — חנה

בְּמַחֲנַיִם pref. בְּ)(pr. name of a place — חנה

בִּמְחֹקְקִי[l] pref. בְּ bef. (:))(Poel part. sing. m. dec. 7b. — חקק

בַּמַּחְשָׁךְ[m] pref. בְּ)(noun masc. sing. dec. 8a. — חשך

בְּמַחֲשַׁכִּים pref. id.)(id. pl. absolute — חשך

בַּמַּחְתֶּרֶת pref. בַּ for בְּהַ)(noun fem. sing. — חתר

בְּמַטְאֲטֵא[n] pref. בְּ)(noun masc. sing. — טוא

בַּמַּטֶּה pref. בַּ for בְּהַ)(noun masc. sing. dec. 9a. — נטה

בַּמִּטָּה[ff] pref. id.)(noun fem. sing. dec. 10. — נטה

בְּמַטֵּהוּ pref. בְּ)(n. m. s., suff. 3 p. s. m. fr. מַטֶּה dec. 9a. — נטה

בַּמֹּטוֹת[o] pref. בַּ for בְּהַ)(n. fem., pl. of מוֹטָה dec. 10. — מוט

בְּמַטָּיו[p] pref. בְּ)(n. m. pl., suff. 3 p. s. m. fr. מַטֶּה dec. 9a. — נטה

בְּמַטֶּךָ[q] pref. id.)(id. s., suff. 2 pers. s. m. [for מַטְּךָ] — נטה

בְּמֵו[r] Kh. בְּמוֹ q. v., K. בְּמֵי q. v.

בְּמֵי pref. בְּ)(noun masc. pl., constr. of מַיִם, [sing. מַי § 38. rem. 2. & § 45] — מי

בַּמִּי pref. id.)(pron. interrog. — מי

בְּמוֹ[s] Kh. בְּמֵי q. v., K. בְּמוֹ q. v.

בְּמֵיטַב[t] pref. בְּ)(n. m. s., constr. of [מֵיטָב] dec. 2b. — יטב

בַּמַּיִם וּ pref. בַּ f. בְּהַ } n. m., pl. [of מַי § 38. r. 2. § 45]; וּ bef. lab. — מי
בַּמָּיִם וּ
בְּמַיִם וּ pref. בְּ q. v.

בַּמִּישׁוֹר וּ pref. בַּ f. בְּהַ } noun m. sing.; וּ bef. lab. — ישר
בְּמִישׁוֹר וּ pref. בְּ q. v.
בַּמִּישֹׁר[v] pref. בַּ for בְּהַ

בְּמֵישָׁרִים pref. בְּ)(noun masc. pl., also as an adv. — ישר

בְּמֵיתָרֶיךָ pref. id.)(noun masc. pl., suff. 2 pers. sing. masc. from [מֵיתָר] dec. 2b. — יתר

בְּמַכְאוֹב pref. id.)(noun masc. sing. dec. 1b. — כאב

בַּמִּכְוָה[b] pref. בַּ for בְּהַ)(noun fem. sing. dec. 10. — כוה

בִּמְכוֹנָה[c] pref. id.)(noun fem. sing. dec. 10. — כון

בִּמְכוֹנֵי[d] pref. בְּ bef. (:))(n. m. pl. constr. fr. מָכוֹן d. 3a. — כון

בְּמַכְלֻלִים[e] pref. בְּ)(noun masc. pl. [of מַכְלוּל] — כלל

בְּמִכְמַנֵּי[f] pref. id.)(n. m. pl. constr. from [מִכְמָן] d. 8a. — כמן

בְּמִכְמָרָיו[g] pref. id.)(noun masc. pl., suff. 3 pers. sing. masc. from [מִכְמֹר] dec. 1b. — כמר

בְּמִכְמַרְתּוֹ[h] pref. id.)(noun fem. sing., suff. 3 pers. sing. masc. from מִכְמֶרֶת dec. 13a. — כמר

בְּמִכְמָשׂ pref. id.)(pr. name of a place, see מִכְמָס — כמס

וּבִמְכֹנָה pref. בְּ bef. (:))(pr. name of a place; וּ bef. (:) — כון

בְּמִכְסֵה[u] pref. בְּ)(n. m. s., constr. of מִכְסֶה dec. 9a. — כסה

בְּמִכְסַת[i] pref. id.)(noun fem. sing., constr. [of מִכְסָה], from מֶכֶס masc. — כסס

בַּמַּכְפֵּלָה pref. בַּ for בְּהַ)(pr. name of a region — כפל

בִּמְכַשְּׁפִים[tt] pref. id.)(Piel part. m., pl. of מְכַשֵּׁף dec. 7b. — כשף

בְּמִכְתָּב pref. בְּ)(noun masc. sing. dec. 2b. — כתב

וּבְמִכְתַּב[k] pref. id.)(id., construct state; וּ bef. lab. — כתב

בַּמַּכְתֵּשׁ[l] pref. בַּ for בְּהַ)(noun masc. sing. — כתש

בִּמְכִתָּתוֹ[m] pref. בְּ bef. (:))(noun fem. sing., suff. 3 pers. sing. masc. from [מְכִתָּה] dec. 10. — כתת

בִּמְלֹאות[n] pref. id.)(Kal inf. constr. [for מְלֹאת=מְלֹאות= מְלֹאת § 23. rem. 2. 4. & 9] — מלא

בַּמְּלָאכָה pref. בַּ for בְּהַ)(n. fem. s. see under the R. — לאך

בְּמַלְאֲכוּת[o] pref. בְּ)(n. f. s., constr. of [מַלְאָכוּת] d. 3a. — לאך

בְּמַלְאָכַי[p] pref. id.)(n. m. pl. constr. from מַלְאָךְ dec. 2b. — לאך

וּבְמַלְאָכָיו[q] pref. id.)(id., suff. 3 pers. s. m.; וּ bef. lab. — לאך

בַּמְּלֶאכֶת[r] pref. בַּ for בְּהַ } noun fem. sing., constr. of מְלָאכָה (§ 42. rem. 5) — לאך
בִּמְלֶאכֶת pref. בְּ bef. (:)

בִּמְלַאכְתּוֹ pref. id.)(id., suff. 3 pers. sing. masc. — לאך

וּבִמְלֹאת[s] pref. id.)(Kal inf. constr. (see בִּמְלֹאות); וּ bef. lab. — מלא

בְּמִלֻּאֹתָם[t] pref. בְּ)(noun fem. pl., suff. 3 pers. pl. masc. from [מִלּוּאָה] dec. 10. — מלא

בַּמַּלְבֵּן[u] pref. בַּ for בְּהַ)(noun masc. sing. — לבן

וּבְמֹלָדָה pref. בְּ)(pr. name of a place; וּ bef. (:) — ילד

וּבְמִלּוֹאת[x] pref. בְּ bef. (:))(Kal inf. constr., see בִּמְלֹאות; וּ bef. lab. — מלא

בְּמִלּוּאֹתָם[y] pref. בְּ)(n. fem. pl., suff. fr. [מִלּוּאָה] dec. 10. — מלא

בַּמָּלוֹן pref. בַּ for בְּהַ)(noun masc. sing. dec. 3a — לון

בַּמֶּלַח[z] pref. id.)(n. masc. sing. (segolate § 35. r. 5) — מלח

בַּמִּלְחָמָה pref. id. } noun fem. sing. dec. 11a. (comp. § 42. rem. 5); וּ bef. (:) — לחם
וּבְמִלְחָמָה[a] pref. בְּ

וּבְמִלְחֲמוֹת[b] pref. id.)(id. pl., construct state; וּ id. — לחם

בַּמֶּלֶט[c] pref. בַּ for בְּהַ)(noun masc. sing. — מלט

בְּמִלִּים pref. בְּ } noun fem. with pl. masc. term. from מִלָּה dec. 10. — מלל
בְּמִלִּין pref. id.

[a] Ju. 11. 34. [b] 2 Ch. 24. 25. [c] 2 Ch. 31. 15. [d] 2 Ch. 31. 17. [e] 2 Ch. 35. 4. [f] 2 Ch. 8. 14. [g] Ezr. 6. 18. [h] Ex. 15. 20. [i] Da. 4. 24. [k] Zec. 14. 15. [l] Nu. 21. 18. [m] Is. 29. 15. [n] Is. 14. 23. [o] 1 Ch. 15. 15. [p] Hab. 3. 14. [q] Ex. 8. 1. [r] Job 9. 30. [s] Is. 25. 10. [t] Ge. 47. 6, 11. [u] 2 Ch. 26. 10. [x] Mal. 2. 6. [y] Jos. 20. 8. [z] Ps. 21. 13. [a] Job 33. 19. [b] Le. 13. 25. [c] 1 Ki. 7. 32. [d] Is. 18. 4. [e] Eze. 27. 24. [f] Da. 11. 43. [ff] Sa. 19. 13. [g] Ps. 141. 10. [h] Hab. 1. 15. [i] Ex. 12. 4. [k] 2 Ch. 35. 4. [l] Pr. 27. 22. [u] Nu. 4. 8, 11, 12. [m] Is. 30. 14. [n] Job 20. 22. [o] Hag. 1. 13. [p] 2 Ch. 36. 16. [q] Job 4. 18. [tt] Mal. 3. 3. [r] 2 Ch. 13. 10. [s] Le. 12. 6. [t] Ex. 39. 13. [u] Je. 43. 9. [u] 2 Sa. 12. 31. Je. 43. 9. [x] Est. 1. 5. [y] Ex. 28. 20. [z] Le. 2. 13. [a] Da. 11. 20. [b] Is. 30. 32. [c] Je. 43. 9.

[a]בִּמְלִיצֵי pref. בְּ bef. (:))(Hiph. part. pl. constr. masc. from מֵלִיץ dec. 3b. . . . . . לוץ

בַּמֶּלֶךְ pref. בַּ for בְּהַ } noun masc. sing. dec. 6a. מלך
בְּמֶלֶךְ pref. בְּ q. v. }

[b]בְּמֹלְךְ Kh. בְּמָלְכוֹ, K. מִמְּלֹךְ; pref. בְּ or מִ)(Kal inf. constr. מלך

[c]בַּמַּלְכָּה pref. בַּ for בְּהַ)(noun fem. sing. dec. 12a. מלך

[d]בְּמַלְכּוֹ pref. בְּ)(noun masc. sing., suff. 3 pers. sing. masc. fr. מֶלֶךְ dec. 6a. . . . מלך

בְּמָלְכוֹ pref. id.)(Kal inf., suff. 3 pers. sing. masc. מלך

בַּמַּלְכוּת pref. בַּ f. בְּהַ } n. f. s. d. 1b. Ch. constr. of מַלְכוּ dec. 8c; וּ bef. (:) מלך
וּבְמַלְכוּת ו׳ pref. בְּ q. v. }

בְּמַלְכוּתָא Ch. pref. id.)(n. f. s., emph. of מַלְכוּ d. 8c. מלך

בְּמַלְכוּתוֹ pref. id.)(noun fem. sing., suff. 3 pers. sing. masc. fr. מַלְכוּת dec. 1b. . . . מלך

[e]בְּמַלְכוּתִי Chald. pref. id.)(noun fem. sing., suff. 1 pers. sing. fr. מַלְכוּ dec. 8c. . . . מלך

[f]וּבְמַלְכוּתִי pref. id.)(noun fem. sing., suff. 1 pers. sing. fr. מַלְכוּת dec. 1b.; וּ bef. (:) . מלך

[g]בְּמַלְכוּתָךְ Chald. pref. id.)(noun fem. sing., suff. 2 pers. sing. masc. fr. מַלְכוּ dec. 8c. . . מלך

[h]בְּמַלְכוּתָם pref. id.)(noun fem. sing., suff. 3 pers. pl. masc. fr. מַלְכוּת dec. 1b. . . מלך

בַּמְּלָכִים pref. בַּ for בְּהַ)(noun m., pl. of מֶלֶךְ dec. 6a. מלך

[i]וּבְמַלְכֵי pref. בְּ)(id. pl., constr. st.; וּ bef. (:) מלך

בְּמַלְכְּכֶם pref. id.)(id. sing., suff. 3 pers. pl. masc. מלך

[k]בַּמַּלְכֵּן pref. בַּ for בְּהַ)(Kh. perh. מַלְכֵּן (i. q. מַלְכָּם the name of an idol, and meton. for the temple); K. מַלְבֵּן, noun masc. sing. . לבן

[l]בְּמַלְמַד pref. בְּ)(n. m. s., constr. of [מַלְמָד] d. 2b. למד

[m]בְּמֶלְקָחַיִם pref. id.)(noun masc., du. of [מֶלְקָח] d. 2b. לקח

[n]בַּמַּמְלָכָה pref. בַּ f. בְּהַ } noun fem. sing. (§ 42. rem. 5) מלך
[o]בְּמַמְלָכָה pref. בְּ q. v. }

[p]וּבַמְנָאֲפִים pref. בַּ for בְּהַ)(Piel part. masc., pl. of מְנָאֵף dec. 7b; וּ bef. labial . נאף

[q]וּבִמְנוּחֹת pref. בְּ bef. (:))(noun fem., pl. of מְנוּחָה dec. 10; וּ id. . . . . . נוח

[r]וּבִמְנוּסָה pref. id.)(noun fem. sing. dec. 10; וּ id. . נוס

[s]בַּמִּנְחָה pref. בַּ f. בְּהַ } noun f. s. d. 12b; וּ bef. (:) מנח
[t,ll]וּבְמִנְחָה ו׳ pref. בְּ q. v. }

[u]וּבְמִנְחַת pref. id.)(id., constr. state; וּ id. . מנח

[x]וּבְמִנְחָתִי pref. id.)(id., suff. 1 pers. sing.; וּ id. . מנח

[y]בְּמִנִּים pref. id.)(noun m., pl. of [מֵן] dec. 8b. . מנן

בִּמְנַשֶּׁה pref. בְּ bef. (:))(pr. name of a tribe . נשה

[z]בְּמַנְעַמֵּיהֶם pref. בְּ)(noun masc. pl., suff. 3 pers. pl. masc. fr. [מַנְעָם] dec. 8a. . . נעם

[a]וּבִמְנַעַנְעִים pref. בְּ bef. (:))(noun m. pl. [for מְנַעַנְעִים fr. נֵעַ, מְנַעֲנַע § 36. r. 5]; וּ bef. labial . נוע

וּבַמְּנֹרָה pref. בַּ for בְּהַ)(noun fem. s. dec. 10; וּ id. נור

[b]בִּמְסִבּוֹ pref. בְּ bef. (:))(noun masc. sing., suff. 3 p. s. m. fr. מֵסַב d. 8e. (§ 37. No. 2, & r. 3) סבב

בַּמַּסָּה pref. בַּ f. בְּהַ } pr. name of a place; וּ bef. (:) נסה
וּבְמַסָּה ו׳ pref. בְּ q. v. }

[c]בְּמִסְכֵּנֻת pref. id.)(noun fem. sing. . . . . סכן

בַּמְּסִלָּה pref. בַּ בְּהַ } noun fem. sing. dec. 10. . סלל
[d]בִּמְסִלָּה pref. בְּ bf. (:) }

[e]בַּמְסִלּוֹת pref. בַּ for בְּהַ)(id. pl. . . . . סלל

[f]בִּמְסִלּוֹתָם pref. בְּ bef. (:))(id. pl., suff. 3 pers. pl. m. סלל

בִּמְסִלַּת pref. id.)(id. sing., constr. state . . סלל

[g]בִּמְסִלָּתוֹ pref. id.)(id. sing., suff. 3 pers. sing. masc. סלל

[h]בְּמַסְמְרוֹת pref. בְּ)(noun masc. with pl. fem. term. fr. [מַסְמֵר] dec. 7b. . . . . . סמר

[i]בְּמַסְמְרִים pref. id.)(id. with pl. masc. term. . סמר

[k]וּבְמִסְפֵּד pref. id.)(noun masc. sing. dec. 7c. (§ 36. rem. 1); וּ bef. (:) . . . ספד

[l,ll]וּבְמִסְפָּר ו׳ pref. id.)(noun masc. sing. dec. 2b; וּ id. ספר

וּבְמִסְפַּר ו׳ pref. id.)(id., constr. state . . ספר

בְּמִסְפָּרָם pref. id.)(id., suff. 3 pers. pl. masc. . ספר

בְּמֹסֵרוֹת pref. id.)(pr. name of a place, see מוֹסֵר אסר

[m]וּבְמֹסָרָם pref. id.)(noun masc. sing., suff. 3 pers. pl. masc. fr. [מֹסָר]; וּ bef. (:) . . יסר

[n]בְּמָסֹרֶת pref. id.)(noun fem. sing. [for מַאֲסֹרֶת]. אסר

[o]בְּמַסֹּת pref. id.)(noun fem., pl. of מַסָּה dec 10. נסה

בַּמִּסְתָּר pref. בַּ for בְּהַ)(noun masc. sing. dec. 2b. סתר

בַּמִּסְתָּרִים pref. id. } id. pl., absolute state . . סתר
בְּמִסְתָּרִים pref. בְּ }

[p]בְּמַעֲבֵה pref. id.)(n. m. s., constr. of [מַעֲבֶה] d. 9b. עבה

[q]בַּמַּעְגָּל pref. בַּ for בְּהַ)(noun masc. sing. dec. 2b. עגל

[r]בְּמַעְגְּלוֹתֶיךָ pref. בְּ)(noun fem. pl., suff. 2 pers. sing. masc. fr. מַעְגָּלָה dec. 11a. . . . עגל

[s]וּבְמַעְגְּלוֹתָם pref. id.)(id. pl., suff. 3 pers. pl. masc. . עגל

בְּמַעְגְּלֵי pref. id.)(n. m. pl. constr. fr. מַעְגָּל d. 2b. עגל

[t]בְּמַעְגְּלֹתָם pref. id.)(noun fem. pl., suff. 3 pers. pl. masc. fr. מַעְגָּלָה dec. 11a. . . עגל

[u]בְּמֹעֵד pref. id.)(noun masc. sing. dec. 7b. . יעד

[ll]בְּמֹעֲדוֹ pref. id.)(id., suff. 3 pers. sing. masc. יעד

[x]בְּמֹעֲדֵיכֶם pref. id.)(id. pl., suff. 2 pers. pl. masc. . יעד

[y]בַּמַּעְדֵּר pref. בַּ for בְּהַ)(noun masc. sing. . . עדר

בְּמָעֻזּוֹ pref. בְּ)(noun masc. s. (suff. מָעֻזּוֹ) dec. 8c. עזז

בְּמָעוֹן pref. id.)(pr. name of a place . . עון

[z]בִּמְעוֹן pref. בְּ bef. (:))(noun masc. sing., constr. of מָעוֹן dec. 3a. . . . . . עון

---

a 2 Ch. 32. 31.
b 2 Ki. 23. 33.
c Est. 1. 15.
d Is. 8. 21.
e Ezr. 7. 13.
f 1 Ch. 17. 14.
g Da. 5. 11.
h Ne. 9. 35.
i 1 Sa. 14. 47.
k 2 Sa. 12. 31.
l Ju. 3. 31.
ll Nu. 9. 3, 7, 13.
m Is. 6. 6.
n Am. 9. 8.
o Is. 19. 2.
p Mal. 3. 5.
q Is. 32. 18.
r Is. 52. 12.
s Ge. 32. 21.
t 1 Sa. 3. 14.
u Ezr. 9. 5.
x 1 Sa. 2. 29.
y Ps. 150. 4.
z Ps. 141. 4.
a 2 Sa. 6. 5.
b Ca. 1. 12.
c De. 8. 9.
d 1 Sa. 6. 12.
e Ju. 20. 31, 45.
f Is. 59. 7.
g Joel 2. 8.
h Je. 10. 4.
i Is. 41. 7.
k Joel 2. 12.
l 1 Ch. 9. 28.
m Job 33. 16.
n Eze. 20. 37.
o De. 4. 34.
p 1 Ki. 7. 46.
q 1 Sa. 26. 5, 7.
r Ps. 17. 5.
s Pr. 2. 15.
t Is. 59. 8.
u De. 31. 10.
x Nu. 15. 3.
y Is. 7. 25.
z Ps. 68. 6.

[a] בַּמְּעוֹנוֹת	pref. בַּ for בְּהַ)(noun f., pl. מְעוֹנָה dec. 10.	עון
[b] בִּמְעוֹנֹתֶיהָ	וּ pref. בְּ bef. (:))(id. pl., suff. 3 pers. sing. fem.; וּ bef. labial	עון
[c] בִּמְעוֹנֹתֵינוּ	pref. id.)(id. pl., suff. 1 pers. pl. .	עון
[d] בְּמָעֻזִּי	pref. בְּ)(noun masc. sing., suff. 1 pers. sing. fr. מָעֹז dec. 8c. (§ 37. rem. 4) . .	עזז
[e] בִּמְעַט [f] בִּמְעַט־	} pref. בְּ bef. (:))(noun masc. sing. d. 8d.	מעט
[g] בְּמֵעַי	pref. בְּ)(noun masc. pl., suff. 1 pers. sing. fr. [מֵעַ] dec. 7a. (§ 36. rem. 4) . .	מע
[h] בִּמְעֵי	pref. בְּ bef. (:))(id. pl., constr. state .	מע
בְּמֵעָיו	pref. בְּ)(id. pl., suff. 3 pers. sing. masc.	מע
[i] בְּמֵעַיִךְ	pref. id.)(id. pl., suff. 2 pers. sing. fem. .	מע
[k] בִּמְעִיל	pref. בְּ bef. (:))(noun masc. sing. dec. 1a.	מעל
[l] בַּמַּעַל [m] בְּמַעַל	pref. בְּהַ f. בַּ pref. בְּ q. v. } noun masc. sing. dec. 6d. .	מעל
[n] בְּמַעַל	pref. id.)(noun masc. sing. . .	עלה
[o] בַּמַּעֲלֶה	pref. בַּ for בְּהַ)(noun masc. sing. dec. 9a.	עלה
בְּמַעֲלֵה	pref. בְּ)(id., constr. state . . .	עלה
בְּמַעֲלוֹ	pref. id.)(n. m. s. or inf., suff. 3 s. m. fr. מַעַל d. 6d.	מעל
בַּמַּעֲלוֹת בְּמַעֲלוֹת	[p] וּ/ pref. בַּ f. בְּהַ [q] וּ/ pref. בְּ q. v. } noun fem., pl. of מַעֲלָה dec. 10; וּ bef. (:) .	עלה
[r] בְּמַעַלְלֵיהֶם	pref. id.)(noun masc. pl., suff. 3 pers. pl. masc. [for מַעַלְלֵי] from מַעֲלָל dec. 2b. .	עלל
[s] בְּמַעֲלָלָיו	pref. id.)(id. pl., suff. 3 pers. sing. masc.	עלל
בְּמַעֲלָם	pref. id.)(n. m. s. or inf., suff. 3 pl. m. fr. מַעַל d. 6d.	מעל
[t] בְּמַעֲלֹת	pref. id.)(noun fem., pl. of מַעֲלָה dec. 10.	עלה
[u] בְּמַעֲלֹתָו	pref. id.)(id. pl., 3 pers. sing. masc. (K. תָיו § 4. rem. 1)	עלה
בְּמַעֲמַקֵּי	pref. id.)(n. m. pl. constr. from [מַעֲמָק] d. 8a.	עמק
[x] בְּמַעֲנֵה	pref. id.)(n. m. s., constr. of מַעֲנֶה dec. 9b.	ענה
[y] בַּמַּעֲצָד	pref. בַּ for בְּהַ)(noun masc. sing.	עצד
בְּמֹעֵצוֹת	pref. בְּ)(noun m., pl. of [מוֹעֵצָה] dec. 11b.	יעץ
[z] בְּמֹעֲצוֹתָם	pref. id.)(id. pl., suff. 3 pers. pl. masc. .	יעץ
[a] בְּמַעֲרָבֵךְ	pref. id.)(noun masc. sing., suff. 2 pers. sing. fem. from [מַעֲרָב] dec. 2b. . . .	ערב
בַּמְּעָרָה	pref. בַּ for בְּהַ)(noun fem. sing. dec. 10. .	עור
[b] בַּמְּעָרוֹת [d] בִּמְעָרוֹת	[c] וּ/ pref. id. pref. בְּ bef. (:) } id. pl.	עור
בַּמַּעֲרָכָה	pref. בַּ for בְּהַ)(noun fem. sing. dec. 11a.	ערך
[e] בְּמַעֲרָצָה	pref. בְּ)(noun fem. sing. . . .	ערץ
[f] בִּמְעָרַת	pref. בְּ bef. (:))(n. f. s., constr. of מְעָרָה d. 10.	עור
בְּמַעֲשֵׂה	pref. בְּ)(n. m. s., constr. of מַעֲשֶׂה dec. 9a.	עשה
בְּמַעֲשֵׂי	pref. id.)(id. pl., construct state .	עשה
בְּמַעֲשֵׂיהֶם	pref. id.)(id. pl., suff. 3 pers. pl. masc. .	עשה

בְּמַעֲשָׂיו	pref. id.)(id. pl., suff. 3 pers. sing. masc. .	עשה
[g] בְּמַעֲשַׂיִךְ	pref. id.)(id. pl., suff. 2 pers. sing. fem.	עשה
[h] בְּמַעֲשֵׂינוּ	pref. id.)(id. pl., suff. 1 pers. pl. .	עשה
[i] בְּמַפְגִּיעַ	pref. id.)(Hiph. part. sing. masc. . .	פגע
[k] בְּמַפַּלְתָּם	pref. id.)(noun fem. sing., suff. 3 pers. pl. masc. from מַפֶּלֶת dec. 13a. . .	נפל
בְּמִפְקַד	pref. id.)(n. m. s., constr. of [מִפְקָד] d. 2b.	פקד
[l] בַּמֹּפְתִים	וּ pref. בַּ for בְּהַ)(noun masc., pl. of מוֹפֵת dec. 7b; וּ bef. lab. . . .	יפת
[m] בְּמֹצַאֲכֶם	pref. בְּ)(Kal inf., suff. 2 pers. pl. masc. [for מֹצַאֲכֶם=מֹצְאֲכֶם § 16. rem. 9] .	מצא
[n] בַּמָּצֹד	pref. בַּ for בְּהַ)(noun masc. sing. dec. 1a.	צוד
[o] בַּמְּצֹדָה	pref. id.)(noun fem. sing. dec. 10. .	צוד
בַּמְּצֹדוֹת	pref. id.)(noun masc. with pl. fem. term. from מָצוֹד dec. 1a. . . .	צוד
[p] בַּמְּצוֹדוֹת	pref. id.)(noun fem., pl. of [מְצוֹדָה] dec. 10.	צוד
[q] בִּמְצֹדוֹת	pref. בְּ bef. (:))(n. masc., pl. of מָצוֹד dec. 1a.	צוד
בַּמְּצוּדָה	pref. בַּ for בְּהַ)(noun fem. sing. dec. 10. .	צוד
[r] בִּמְצוּדָה	pref. בְּ bef. (:))(noun fem. sing. dec. 10.	צוד
[s] בִּמְצוּדָתִי	pref. id.)(n. f. s., suff. 1 p. s. fr. [מְצוּדָה] d. 10.	צוד
[t] בַּמִּצְוָה	וּ pref. בַּ for בְּהַ)(n. fem. s. dec. 10; וּ bef. lab.	צוה
[u] בִּמְצוּלָה	pref. בְּ bef. (:))(noun fem. sing. dec. 10. .	צול
[x] בִּמְצוּלוֹת	pref. id.)(id. pl.	צול
בִּמְצוּלֹת	pref. id.)(noun fem., pl. of [מְצוּלָה] dec. 10.	צול
בְּמָצוֹק	וּ pref. בְּ)(noun masc. sing.; וּ bef. (:) .	צוק
בַּמָּצוֹר בְּמָצוֹר	pref. בַּ f. בְּהַ pref. בְּ q. v. } n. m. s. dec. 3a. (§ 32. rem. 5)	צור
[y] בַּמַּצּוֹת	וּ pref. בַּ for בְּהַ)(n. f., pl. of מַצָּה d. 10; וּ bef. lab.	מצץ
בְּמִצְוַת	pref. בְּ)(n. fem. s., constr. of מִצְוָה dec. 10.	צוה
[z] בְּמִצְוֹתָיו	[a] וּ/ pref. id.)(id. pl., suff. 3 p. s. m.; וּ bef. (:)	צוה
[b] בְּמִצְוֹתֶיךָ	pref. id.)(id. pl., suff. 2 pers. sing. masc.	צוה
בְּמִצְחוֹ	pref. id.)(n. m. s., suff. 3 p. s. m. fr. מֵצַח d. 6e.	מצח
[c] בַּמְּצֻלָה	pref. בַּ for בְּהַ)(n. fem. s. (for מְצוּלָה) d. 10.	צול
[d] בִּמְצֻלוֹת	pref. בְּ bef. (:))(noun fem., pl. מְצוּלָה dec. 10.	צול
[e] בְּמַצְלִיחַ	pref. בְּ)(Hiph. part. sing. masc. . .	צלח
בַּמְצִלְתַּיִם בִּמְצִלְתַּיִם בִּמְצִלְתָּיִם	pref. בַּ for בְּהַ וּ pref. בְּ bef. (:) וּ/ pref. id. } n. fem., du. of [מְצֶלֶת] d. 13c. (comp. § 39. No. 4. rem. 1); וּ bef. lab.	צלל
[f] בְּמִצְנֶפֶת	וּ pref. בְּ)(noun fem. sing.; וּ id. .	צנף
[g] בְּמִצְעָדָיו	pref. id.)(noun masc. pl., suff. 3 pers. sing. masc. from [מִצְעָד] dec. 2b. . .	צעד
[h] בְּמִצְעַר	pref. id.)(n. m. s., constr. of מִצְעָר dec. 2b.	צער
בַּמִּצְפָּה	pref. בַּ for בְּהַ)(pr. name of a place .	צפה
[i] בְּמֻצַקְתּוֹ	pref. בְּ)(noun fem. sing., suff. 3 pers. sing. masc. from [מֻצֶקֶת] dec. 13a. .	יצק

[a] Job 38. 40. [b] Job 37. 8. [c] Je. 21. 13. [d] Is. 27. 5. [e] 1 Sa. 14. 6. [f] Da. 11. 23. [g] Ruth 1. 11.
[h] Jon. 2. 1. [i] Nu. 5. 22. [k] 1 Ch. 15. 27. [l] Ezr. 9. 2. [m] Jos. 22. 22. [n] Ne. 8. 6.
[o] Ne. 12. 37. [p] Eze. 40. 49. [q] Eze. 40. 22. [r] Ps. 106. 29. [s] Pr. 20. 11. [t] Ex. 20. 26.
[u] Eze. 40. 6. [x] Pr. 15. 23. [y] Je. 10. 3. [z] Mi. 6. 16. [a] Eze. 27. 19. [b] 1 Sa. 13. 6.
[c] Eze. 33. 27. [d] Is. 2. 19. [e] Is. 10. 33. [f] Ge. 50. 13. [g] Je. 48. 7. [h] Ezr. 9. 13.
[i] Job 36. 32. [k] Pr. 29. 16. [l] De. 26. 8. [m] Ge. 32. 20. [n] 1 Ch. 11. 7. [o] 2 Sa. 5. 9.
[p] Eze. 19. 9. [q] 1 Sa. 24. 1. [r] Ec. 9. 12. [s] Eze. 12. 13. [t] 2 Ch. 31. 21. [u] Ps. 107. 24.
[x] Mic. 7. 19. [y] Ju. 6. 21. [z] Ps. 112. 1. [a] 2 Ch. 17. 4. [b] Ps. 119. 47, 66. [c] Zec. 1. 8.
[d] Ps. 88. 7. [e] Ps. 37. 7. [f] Le. 16. 4. [g] Da. 11. 43. [h] 2 Ch. 24. 24. [i] 2 Ch. 4. 3.

בְּמִצְרַיִם	pref. בְּ)(pr. name of a country . .	מצר
וּבְמִצְרָיִם	וּ' id.	
בַּמַּקָּבוֹת[a]	וּ pref. בַּ f. בְּהַ } noun fem., pl. of [מַקָּבָה];	נקב
בְּמַקָּבוֹת[b]	וּ pref. בְּ q. v. } וּ bef. lab. . .	
בְּמַקֵּדָה	pref. id.)(pr. name of a place . .	נקד
בְּמִקְדַּשׁ	pref. id.)(n. m. s., constr. of מִקְדָּשׁ dec. 2 b.	קדש
בְּמִקְדָּשׁוֹ[c]	pref. id.)(id., suff. 3 pers. sing. masc. .	קדש
בְּמִקְדָּשִׁי[d]	pref. id.)(id., suff. 1 pers. sing. .	קדש
בְּמַקְהֵלוֹת[e]	pref. id.)(noun pl. fem. and masc. [from	קהל
בְּמַקְהֵלִים[f]	מַקְהֵל § 36. No. 1] . . .	
בְּמַקְהֵלֹת	pref. id.)(pr. name of a place	קהל
בַּמָּקוֹם[g]	וּ' pref. בַּ f. בְּהַ } noun com. sing. dec. 3 a;	קום
בְּמָקוֹם	pref. בְּ q. v. } וּ bef. lab. .	
בִּמְקוֹם	וּ' pref. בְּ bef. (:))(id. constr. state; וּ id. .	קום
בִּמְקוֹמוֹ	pref. id.)(id., suff. 3 pers. sing. masc. .	קום
בִּמְקוֹמֵנוּ[h]	pref. id.)(id., suff. 1 pers. pl. . .	קום
בַּמַּקֵּל[i]	pref. בַּ for בְּהַ)(n. m. s. dec. 7 b. (§ 36. r. 1)	מקל
וּבְמַקֵּל[k]	וּ pref. בְּ)(id., constr. st.; וּ bef. (:) .	מקל
בַּמַּקְלוֹת	pref. בַּ for בְּהַ)(id. pl. [for מַקְּלוֹת comp. § 10. rem. 7]	מקל
בְּמַקְלִי[l]	pref. בְּ)(id. sing., suff. 1 p. s. [for מַקְּלִי comp. id.]	מקל
בְּמָקֹם[m]	pref. id.)(noun com. sing. for מָקוֹם dec. 3 a.	קום
בִּמְקֹמוֹ[n]	pref. בְּ bef. (:))(id., suff. 3 pers. sing. masc.	קום
בַּמִּקְנֶה[o]	pref. בַּ f. בְּהַ } noun m. s. dec. 9 a; וּ bef. (:)	קנה
וּבְמִקְנֶה[p]	וּ pref. בְּ	
וּבְמִקְנֵה[q]	וּ pref. id.)(id., constr. st.; וּ id. .	קנה
בְּמִקְנֵיכֶם[r]	pref. id.)(id. pl., suff. 2 pers. pl. masc. .	קנה
בְּמִקְנְךָ[s]	pref. id.)(sing., suff. 2 pers. sing. masc.	קנה
בְּמָקֵץ	pref. id.)(pr. name of a place .	קצץ
בְּמִקְצֹעַ[t]	pref. id.)(noun masc. sing. dec. 1 b. .	קצע
בַּמִּקְצֹעוֹת[u]	pref. בַּ for בְּהַ)(n. fem., pl. of [מִקְצֹעָה] d. 10.	קצע
בַּמִּקְרָא[x]	pref. id.)(noun m. sing. dec. 1 b. (§ 31. r. 1)	קרא
בְּמִקְשָׁה[y]	pref. בְּ)(noun fem. sing., [for מִקְשָׁאָה]	קשא
בְּמַר	pref. id.)(noun masc. sing. dec. 8. (§ 37. r. 7)	מרר
וּבְמוֹרָא[z]	וּ pref. id.)(n. m. s. d. 1 b. (§ 31. r. 1. & 2); וּ bef. (:)	ירא
בַּמַּרְאָה	pref. בַּ for בְּהַ)(noun fem. sing. dec. 10. .	ראה
בַּמַּרְאֶה	pref. id.)(noun masc. sing. dec. 9 a. .	ראה
בְּמַרְאוֹת	pref. בְּ)(noun fem., pl. of מַרְאָה dec. 10. .	ראה
וּבְמַרְאֵי[a]	וּ pref. id.)(Kh. מַרְאֵי', K. מַרְאֵה' n. m. pl. or sing. constr. from מַרְאֶה dec. 9 a. .	ראה
בְּמַרְאֹת[b]	pref. id.)(noun fem., pl. of מַרְאָה' dec. 10.	ראה
וּבְמַרְבִּית[c]	וּ pref. id.)(noun fem. s. dec. 1 b; וּ bef. (:)	רבה
בְּמַרְגֵּמָה[d]	pref. id.)(noun fem. sing. . .	רגם
בְּמֶרֶד[e]	pref. id.)(noun masc. sing. . .	מרד
בְּמֹרְדֵי[f]	pref. id.)(Kal part. pl. constr. masc. from [מוֹרֵד] dec. 7 b. . . .	מרד

בְּמָרְדְּכַי	pref. id.)(pr. name masc., see מָרְדְּכַי	
בְּמָרָה	pref. id.)(pr. name of a fountain . .	מרר
בַּמָּרוֹם	pref. בַּ for בְּהַ)(noun masc. sing. dec. 3 a.	רום
בִּמְרוֹם[g]	pref. בְּ bef. (:))(id., construct state .	רום
בִּמְרוֹמָיו[h]	pref. id.)(id. pl., suff. 3 pers. sing. masc.	רום
בַּמְּרוֹמִים	pref. בַּ for בְּהַ)(id. pl., absolute state .	רום
בִּמְרוֹרִים[i]	pref. id.)(noun masc., pl. of [מָרוֹר] dec. 3 a.	מרר
בַּמֶּרְחָב	pref. id.)(noun masc. sing. dec. 2 b.	רחב
וּבְמֶרְחַקִּים[k]	וּ pref. id.)(n. m., pl. of מֶרְחָק d. 8 a; וּ bef. lab.	רחק
בְּמַרְחֶשֶׁת[l]	pref. id.)(noun fem. sing. . . .	רחש
בִּמְרִיבַת[m]	pref. בְּ bef. (:))(n. f. s., constr. of מְרִיבָה d. 10.	ריב
בְּמִרְיָם[n]	pref. בְּ)(n. m. s., suff. 3 p. pl. m. fr. מְרִי d. 6 i.	מרה
וּבִמְרִירוּת[o]	וּ pref. בְּ bef. (:))(noun fem. sing.; וּ bef. lab.	מרר
בַּמֶּרְכָּבָה[p]	וּ' pref. בַּ for בְּהַ)(n. fem. s. (§ 42. r. 5); וּ id.	רכב
בְּמִרְכֶּבֶת[q]	pref. בְּ)(id. construct state . . .	רכב
בְּמֶרְכַּבְתּוֹ[r]	pref. id.)(id., suff. 3 pers. sing. masc. .	רכב
בְּמַרְכֻּלְתֵּךְ[s]	pref. id.)(noun fem. sing., suff. 2 pers. sing. fem. from [מַרְכֹּלֶת] dec. 13 c. . .	רכל
בְּמִרְמָה[t]	וּ' pref. id.)(n. fem. sing. dec. 10; וּ bef. lab.	רמה
בְּמִרְעֶה[u]	pref. id.)(noun masc. sing. dec. 9 b. .	רעה
בַּמְּרֵעִים	pref. בַּ for בְּהַ)(Hiph. part. masc., pl. of מֵרַע [for מֵרֵעַ] dec. 3 b. . .	רעע
בִּמְרֻצוֹתָם[x]	pref. בְּ bef. (:))(Kh. מְרוּצוֹתָם', K. מְרֻצָתָם', pl. or sing. with suff. 3 pers. pl. m. from [מְרוּצָה]	רוץ
בַּמַּרְצֵעַ[y]	pref. בַּ for בְּהַ)(noun masc. sing. .	רצע
בְּמִרְקַחַת[z]	pref. בְּ)(noun fem. sing. . . .	רקח
בַּמַּשָּׂא[a]	pref. בַּ f. בְּהַ } noun m. s. d. 1 a. (§ 31. r. 1)	נשא
בְּמַשָּׂא	pref. בְּ q. v.	
בְּמַשָּׁאוֹן[b]	pref. id.)(noun masc. sing.	נשא
וּבְמִשְׁאֲרוֹתֶיךָ[c]	וּ pref. id.)(noun fem. pl., suff. 2 pers. s. m. fr. [מִשְׁאֶרֶת] d. 13 a; וּ bef. (:)	שאר
בְּמַשְׁבֵּר[d]	pref. id.)(noun masc. sing., constr. of מַשְׁבֵּר (§. 36. rem. 1)	שבר
בְּמוֹשְׁבֹתָם[e]	pref. id.)(noun masc. pl., suff. 3 pers. pl. masc. fr. מוֹשָׁב dec. 2 b. . . .	ישב
בְּמֹשֶׁה	וּ' pref. id.)(pr. name masc.; וּ bef. (:)	משה
בִּמְשׁוֹךְ	pref. בְּ bef. (:))(Kal inf. constr. . .	משך
בַּמְּשׂוּרָה[f]	וּ pref. בַּ f. בְּהַ } noun fem. sing.; וּ bef. lab.	שור
בִּמְשׂוּרָה[g]	pref. בְּ bef. (:)	
בִּמְשִׁיחַ	pref. id.)(noun m. s., constr. of מָשִׁיחַ d. 3 a.	משח
בִּמְשִׁיחָי	pref. id.)(id. pl., suff. 1 pers. sing. for מְשִׁיחַי'	משח
בְּמֹשֵׁךְ[h]	pref. בְּ)(Kal part. act. sing. masc. dec. 7 b.	משך
בִּמְשֹׁךְ	pref. בְּ bef. (:))(id. inf. constr.	משך
בַּמִּשְׁכָּב[i]	pref. בַּ for בְּהַ)(noun masc. sing. dec. 2 b.	שכב
בְּמִשְׁכָּבָהּ[k]	pref. בְּ)(id., suff. 3 pers. sing. fem.	שכב
בְּמִשְׁכָּבוֹ	pref. id.)(id., suff. 3 pers. sing. masc.	שכב

a Is. 44.12. b Je. 10.4. c Ps. 96.6. d Eze. 44.7, 8, 11. e Ps. 68.27. f Ps. 26.12. g Hag 2.9. h Ge. 29.26. i Nu. 22.27. k Eze. 39.9. l Ge. 32.11. m Ex. 29.31. n 1 Ch. 16.27. o Ge. 13.2. p Jos. 22.8. q Ge. 47.17. r Ge. 47.16. s Ex. 9.3. t Eze. 46.21. u Is. 44.13. x Ne. 8.8. y Is. 1.8. z De. 26.8. a Ec. 11.9. b Ex. 38.8. c Le. 25.37. d Pr. 26.8. e Jos. 22.22. f Job 24.13. g Je. 31.12. h Job 25.2. i La. 3.15. k Zec. 10.9. l Le. 7.9. m Nu. 27.14. n Ne. 9.17. o Eze. 21.11. p Zec. 6.2, 3, 3. q Ge. 41.43. r 1 Sa. 8.11. s Eze. 27.24. t Ho. 12.1. u Eze. 34.14. x Jer. 8.6. y Ex. 21.6. z 2 Ch. 16.14. a 1 Ch. 15.22. b Pr. 26.26. c Ex. 7.28. d Ho. 13.13. e Ex. 10.23. f Le. 19.35. g Eze. 4.11, 16. h Am. 9.13. i 2 Ch. 16.14. k Le. 15.21.

בְּמָשְׁכוֹ[a] pref. בְּ)(Kal inf., suff. 3 pers. sing. masc. משך
בְּמַשְׂכִּיּוֹת[b] pref. id.)(n. f., pl. of מַשְׂכִּית (§ 39. No. 4. r. 1) שׂכה
וּבְמִשְׁכָּן[c] pref. id.)(noun masc. sing. d. 2b; וּ bef. (:) שׁכן
וּבְמִשְׁכְּנוֹת[d] id. pl. fem., constr. state; וּ id. . . שׁכן
בְּמַשְׂכִּתוֹ[e] pref. id.)(noun fem. sing., suff. 3 pers. sing. masc. fr. מַשְׂכִּית dec. 1b. . . . שׂכה
בְּמָשָׁל[f] pref. id.)(noun masc. sing. dec. 4a. . משל
וּבִמְשֹׁל[g] pref. בְּ bef. (:))(Kal inf. constr. וּ bef. lab. משל
וּבְמִשְׁמַנֵּי[h] pref. בְּ)(noun masc. pl. constr. fr. [מִשְׁמָן] dec. 8a; וּ id. . . . . . שמן
בְּמִשְׁמַנֵּיהֶם[i] pref. id.)(id., suff. 3 pers. pl. masc. . שמן
בְּמִשְׁמַנָּיו[k] pref. id.)(id., suff. 3 pers. sing. masc. . שמן
בַּמִּשְׁמָר pref. בַּ f. בְּהַ } noun masc. sing. dec. 2b. . שמר
בְּמִשְׁמָר[l] pref. בְּ q. v. } noun masc. sing. dec. 2b. . שמר
בְּמִשְׁמַר pref. id.)(id., constr. state . . שמר
בְּמִשְׁמָרוֹ[m] pref. id.)(id., suff. 3 pers. sing. masc. . שמר
בְּמִשְׁמְרוֹתֵיהֶם[n], בְּמִשְׁמְרוֹתָם[o] pref. id.)(noun f. pl., suff. 3 pers. pl. m. fr. מִשְׁמֶרֶת d. 13a. (§ 4. r. 2) שמר
וּבְמִשְׁמָרָיו[p] pref. בְּ)(noun masc. pl., suff. 3 pers. sing. masc. fr. מִשְׁמָר dec. 2b; וּ bef. (:) . שמר
בְּמִשְׁמֶרֶת[q] pref. id.)(noun fem. sing. dec. 13a, pl. מִשְׁמָרוֹת (§ 44. rem. 5) . . . שמר
בְּמִשְׁמַרְתָּם[r] pref. id.)(id. pl., suff. 3 p. pl. m. (§ 4. r. 2) שמר
בַּמִּשְׁנֶה pref. בַּ for בְּהַ)(noun masc. sing. dec. 9a. שנה
בְּמִשְׁעוֹל[s] pref. בְּ)(noun masc. sing. . . . שעל
בְּמִשְׁעֲנֹתָם[t] pref. id.)(noun fem. pl., suff. 3 pers. pl. m. fr. מִשְׁעֶנֶת dec. 13a. . . . שען
בְּמִשְׁפְּחוֹתֵיהֶם[u], בְּמִשְׁפְּחוֹתָם[x] pref. id.)(noun fem. pl., suff. 3 pers. pl. masc. fr. מִשְׁפַּחַת, constr. of מִשְׁפָּחָה' (§ 42. r. 5. & § 4. r. 2) שפח
וּבְמִשְׁפַּחְתּוֹ[y] pref. id.)(id. s., suff. 3 p. s. m.; וּ bef. (:) שפח
בַּמִּשְׁפָּט pref. בַּ for בְּהַ } noun masc. sing. dec. 2b; וּ bef. (:) . . שפט
וּבְמִשְׁפָּט[z] 'וּ pref. בְּ q. v. } noun masc. sing. dec. 2b; וּ bef. (:) . . שפט
בְּמִשְׁפַּט[a] pref. id.)(id., constr. state . . שפט
וּבְמִשְׁפָּטַי 'וּ pref. id.)(id. pl., suff. 1 pers. s.; וּ bef. (:) שפט
וּבְמִשְׁפְּטֵיהֶם[b] 'וּ[c] pref. id.)(id. pl., suff. 3 p. pl. m.; וּ id. שפט
וּבְמִשְׁפָּטֶיךָ[d] pref. id.)(id. pl., suff. 2 pers. s. m.; וּ id. שפט
בְּמִשְׁקוֹל[e] pref. id.)(noun masc. sing. . . שקל
בַּמִּשְׁקָל pref. בַּ f. בְּהַ } noun masc. sing. dec. 2b. שקל
בְּמִשְׁקָל pref. בְּ q. v. } noun masc. sing. dec. 2b. שקל
בְּמִשְׁקַל[f] pref. id.)(id., constr. state . . שקל
בְּמִשְׁקָלוֹ[g] pref. id.)(id., suff. 3 pers. sing. masc. . שקל
וּבְמִשְׂרְפוֹת[h] pref. id.)(noun f. pl. constr. fr. [מִשְׂרָפָה] dec. 11a; וּ bef. (:) . . . . שרף
בְּמִשְׁתֵּה pref. id.)(noun masc. sing., constr. of מִשְׁתֶּה dec. 9a. . . . . שתה

בַּמֵּת[i] pref. בַּ for בְּהַ } Kal part. sing. masc. d. 1a. מות
בְּמֵת[k] pref. בְּ q. v. } Kal part. sing. masc. d. 1a. מות
בְּמֶתֶג[l] pref. id.)(n. m. s., (suff. מִתְגִּי) d. 6a. . מתג
בְּמוֹתוֹ pref. id.)(noun masc. sing., suff. 3 pers. s. m. fr. מָוֶת dec. 6g. . . . מות
בָּמוֹתַי[m] noun fem. pl., suff. 1 pers. s. fr. בָּמָה d. 10. בום
בָּמֳתֵי id. pl. constr. [fr. בָּמֳתִים § 4. r. 2. & § 36. r. 6] בום
בִּמְתֵי pref. בְּ bef. (:))(noun masc. pl. constr. [fr. מַת § 36. r. 5] . . . . מתה
בָּמוֹתָיו noun f. pl., suff. 3 pers. s. m. fr. בָּמָה d. 10. בום
בְּמֹתָיו[n] pref. בְּ)(noun masc. pl., suff. 3 pers. sing. masc. fr. מָוֶת dec. 6g. . . . מות
בָּמוֹתֶיךָ[o] noun f. pl., suff. 2 pers. s. m. fr. בָּמָה d. 10. בום
בָּמוֹתֵיכֶם[p] id. pl., suff. 2 pers. pl. masc. . . . בום
בַּמֵּתִים[q] pref. בַּ for בְּהַ)(Kal part. m., pl. of מֵת d. 1a. מות
בְּמַתְכֻּנְתָּהּ[r] pref. בְּ)(noun fem. sing., suff. 3 pers. sing. fem. fr. מַתְכֹּנֶת dec. 13c. . . . תכן
וּבְמַתְכֻּנְתּוֹ[s] pref. id.)(id., suff. 3 p. s. m.; וּ bef. (:) . תכן
בְּמוֹתָם pref. id.)(noun masc. sing., suff. 3 pers. pl. masc. fr. מָוֶת dec. 6g. . . . מות
בְּמַתְּנוֹתֵיכֶם[t] pref. id.)(noun fem. pl., suff. 2 pers. pl. masc. fr. מַתָּנָה dec. 11a. . . . נתן
בְּמַתְּנוֹתָם[u] pref. id.)(id. pl., suff. 2 p. pl. m. (§ 4. r. 2) נתן
בְּמָתְנֵיהֶם pref. id.)(noun masc., du., suff. 3 pers. pl. masc. fr. [מֹתֶן] dec. 6c. . . . מתן
בְּמָתְנָיו pref. id.)(id. du., suff. 3 pers. sing. masc. מתן
בְּמָתְנֵינוּ pref. id.)(id. du., suff. 1 pers. pl. . . מתן
בְּמִתְקָה pref. id.)(pr. name of a place . . מתק
בְּמַתַּת[aa] pref. id.)(noun fem. sing., [for מַתֶּנֶת] . נתן
בֵּן[x] Kh. בֵּן q. v., K. בַּת (q. v.) . . . בנה
בֵּן 'וּ n. m. s. irr. (§ 45), also pr. n. m.; וּ bef. lab. בנה
בֶּן 'וּ id., constr. state (§ 36. r. 3), also pr. name in compos. as בֶּן־אוֹנִי, &c. . . . בנה
בֶּן 'וּ[y] id. constr. state; וּ id. . . . בנה
בְּנֹא pref. בְּ)(pr. n. of a place, see נֹא
בְּנֹאדֶךָ[z] pref. id.)(n. m. s., suff. 2 p. s. m. fr. נֹאד d. 1a. נאד
בִּנְאוֹת[a] pref. בְּ bef. (:))(noun fem. pl. constr. fr. [נָאָה] dec. 11a. . . . . נאה
בְּנֶאֱמְנֵי[b] pref. בְּ)(Niph. part. pl. constr. [for נֶאֶמְנֵי] fr. נֶאֱמָן dec. 2b. . . . . אמן
בְּנֹב pref. id.)(pr. name of a place . . נבה
וּבִנְבִאֵי[c] וּ defect. for 'בִּנְבִיאֵי' q. v. . . . נבא
בִּנְבוּאַת[d] Ch. pref. בְּ bef. (:))(noun fem. sing., constr. of נְבוּאָה dec. 8a. . . . . נבא
וּבְנָבִיא[e] וּ pref. בְּ)(noun m. s. dec. 3a; וּ bef. lab. נבא
וּבִנְבִיאֵי[f] וּ pref. בְּ bef. (:))(id. pl. constr. state . נבא

[a] Ps. 10. 9.
[b] Pr. 25. 11.
[c] 2 Sa. 7. 6.
[d] Is. 32. 18.
[e] Pr. 18. 11.
[f] Ps. 78. 2.
[g] Pr. 29. 2.
[h] Da. 11. 24.
[i] Ps. 78. 31.
[k] Is. 10. 16.
[l] Ge. 40. 4.
[m] Ne. 7. 3.
[n] 2 Ch. 31. 17.
[o] 2 Ch. 31. 16.
[p] Ne. 13. 14.
[q] Nu. 4. 27.
[r] Nu. 8. 26.
[s] Nu. 22. 24.
[t] Nu. 21. 18.
[u] 1 Ch. 6. 45.
[x] 1 Ch. 4. 38.
[y] Le. 20. 5.
[z] Ho. 2. 21.
[a] Nu. 27. 21.
[b] Eze. 23. 24.
[c] Eze. 7. 27.
[d] Ne. 9. 29.
[e] Eze. 4. 10.
[f] 1 Ch. 28. 15.
[g] Ge. 43. 21.
[h] Je. 34. 5.
[i] Nu. 19. 18.
[k] Nu. 19. 11, 13, 16.
[l] Ps. 32. 9.
[m] 2 Sa. 22. 34.
[n] Is. 53. 9.
[o] Je. 17. 3.
[p] Le. 26. 30.
[q] Ps. 88. 6.
[r] Ex. 30. 37.
[s] Ex. 30. 32.
[t] Eze. 20. 39.
[u] Eze. 20. 26.
[x] 2 Ch. 11. 18.
[y] Jon. 4. 10.
[z] Ps. 56. 9.
[a] Ps. 23. 2.
[aa] Pr. 25. 14.
[b] Ps. 101. 6.
[c] Je. 23. 14.
[d] Ezr. 6. 14.
[e] Ho. 12. 14, 14.
[f] Je. 23. 13.

בִּנְבִיאָ֑י [a] וּ pref. id.)(id. pl., suff. 1 pers. sing. . נבא

בִּנְבִיאָיו pref. id.)(id. pl., suff. 3 pers. sing. masc. נבא

בַּנְּבִיאִים, בַּנְּבִאִם [b] } pref. בַּ for בְּהַ)(id. pl., absolute state נבא

בְּנֵבֶל, בְּנֶ֫בֶל [c] } pref. בְּ)(noun masc. sing, pl. constr. נִבְלֵי, dec. 6b. & a. . . . נבל

בִּנְבָלִים וּ pref. בְּ bef. (:))(id. pl., abs. st.; וּ id. . נבל

בְּנִבְלַת pref. בְּ)(noun fem. sing., constr. of נְבֵלָה dec. 11. (§ 42. rem. 4) . . . נבל

בְּנִבְלָתָהּ [d] pref. id.)(id., suff. 3 pers. sing. fem. . נבל

בְּנִבְלָתָם [e] וּ pref. id.)(id., suff. 3 pers. pl. masc. . נבל

בַּנֶּגֶב וּ pref. בַּ f. בְּהַ } noun masc. sing. dec. 6. (§ 35. rem. 3) . נגב
בְּנֶגֶב [f] pref. בְּ q. v.

בַּנֶּגְבָּה [g] pref. בַּ for בְּהַ)(id. with parag. ה . . נגב

בְּנַגְהָא [h] Ch. pref. בְּ)(noun masc. sing., emph. of נְגַהּ dec. 3e. . . . . . נגה

בִּנְגִינוֹת pref. בְּ bef. (:))(n. f., pl. of [נְגִינָה] d. 10. נגן

בִּנְגִינוֹתָי [i] pref. id.)(id. pl., suff. 1 pers. sing. for ־תַי נגן

בִּנְגִינֹת defect. for נְגִינוֹת (q. v.) . . . נגן

בַּנֶּגַע [k] pref. בַּ f. בְּהַ } noun masc. sing. (d. 6a. pl. constr. נִגְעֵי § 35. r. 5) נגע
בְּנֶגַע [l] pref. בְּ q. v.

בְּנָגְעוֹ [m] pref. id.)(Kal inf., suff. 3 pers. sing. masc. נגע

בְּנִגְעֵי [n] וּ pref. id.)(constr. of the following . . נגע

בִּנְגָעִים [o] וּ pref. בְּ bef. (:))(noun masc., pl. of נֶגַע dec. 6a. (§ 35. rem. 5); וּ bef. labial . נגע

בְּנָגְפּוֹ [p] pref. בְּ)(Kal inf., suff. 3 pers. sing. masc. . נגף

בְּנֹגְשֵׂיהֶם [q] pref. id.)(Kal part. act. pl. masc., suff. 3 pers. pl. masc. fr. נֹגֵשׂ dec. 7b. . . . נגש

בִּנְדָבָה pref. בְּ bef. (:))(noun fem. sing. dec. 11c. נדב

בִּנְדִיבִים pref. id.)(noun masc., pl. of נָדִיב dec. 3a. נדב

בְּנִדַּת pref. בְּ)(noun fem. sing. dec. 10. . נדד

בְּנִדָּתָהּ [r] pref. id.)(id., suff. 3 pers. sing. fem. . נדד

בָּנָה וּ I. *to build, to construct*, as a house, temple, &c. The materials of which something is built is mostly put in the acc. but rarely with בְּ; the place where, with בְּ, עַל.—II. *to repair, restore.*—III. metaph. *to establish, prosper*; בָּנָה בַּיִת לְ *to build a house to* or *for* any one, to give him posterity, or increase his family. Niph.—I. pass. of Kal Nos. I. & II.—II. *to be built up*, i. e. obtain children, spoken of a woman, Ge. 16. 2.

בְּנָא, בְּנָה Chald. *to build.* Ithpe. *to be built.*

בֵּן masc. irr. (§ 45).—I. *a son; also used for child;* בֵּן זָכָר *male-child.*—II. *foster-son;* hence applied to *pupils.*—III. *descendant*, as *a grandson*, &c. בְּנֵי בָנִים *grandsons;* בְּנֵי יִשְׂרָאֵל Israelites; בְּנֵי עַמּוֹן *Ammonites;* applied to the inhabitants of a country בְּנֵי צִיּוֹן *inhabitants of Zion.*—IV. metaph. בֶּן־מָוֶת *son of death*, i. e. one worthy of or destined for death; בִּן־הַכּוֹת *worthy of stripes;* בֶּן־חַיִל *son of strength*, i. e. warrior; בֶּן־בְּלִיַּעַל *son of wickedness*, i. e. a wicked man; בֶּן־עַוְלָה *son of perverseness*, i. e. a perverse man; בֶּן־עָנִי *son of affliction*, i. e. afflicted.—V. with a genit. of time, בֶּן־שָׁנָה *son of a year*, i. e. a year old; בֶּן־שְׁמוֹנִים שָׁנָה *eighty years old;* בִּן־לַיְלָה *a night old.*—VI. *the young of brutes;* בֶּן־אֲתֹנוֹ *son of the ass*, i. e. foal; בֶּן־יוֹנָה *young dove;* applied to plants, בֵּן־פֹּרָת *a twig of a fruitfull tree.*—VII. pr. name masc. 1 Ch. 15. 18.

בֵּן Chald. masc. dec. 2b, *son.*

בֶּן־אוֹנִי (*son of my sorrow*) pr. name given to Benjamin by his mother, Ge. 35. 18.

בֶּן־הֲדַד (*son of Hadad*, an Assyrian idol) pr. name of the kings of Damascus.

בֶּן־חַיִל (*son of strength*) pr. name of a man, 2 Ch. 17. 7.

בֶּן־חָנָן (*son of the gracious*) pr. name of a man, 1 Ch. 4. 20.

בִּן־יָמִין (*son of* my *right hand*) pr. name masc. of two different persons.

בִּנּוּי (*building*) pr. name masc. of several persons.

בְּנֵי־בְרַק (*sons of Berak*, i. e. of lightning) pr. name of a town in the tribe of Dan, Jos. 19. 45.

בְּנֵי יַעֲקָן pr. name of a place, see בְּאֵרוֹת בְּ׳ יְ׳.

בָּנִי (*built up*) pr. name masc. of several persons.

בֻּנִּי (*built up*) pr. name of two different men.

בְּנָיָה (whom *the Lord built up*) pr. name masc. of several persons.

בְּנָיָהוּ (id.) pr. name masc. of several persons.

בִּנְיָה fem. *a building*, Eze. 41. 13.

בִּנְיָמִן, בִּנְיָמִין (*son of* my *right hand*) pr. name of Benjamin the youngest son of Jacob, and the tribe descended from him. Gent. n. בֶּן־יְמִינִי, אִישׁ יְמִינִי, בֶּן־הַיְמִינִי, and ellipt. יְמִינִי *Benjaminite.*

בִּנְיָן masc. *a building.* In Chald. id. only emph. בִּנְיָנָא Ezr. 5. 4.

בְּנִינוּ (*our son*, from Seg. בְּנִי) pr. name masc. Ne. 10. 14.

בַּת fem. irr. (§ 45).—I. *daughter.*—II. *foster-daughter.*—III. *a female descendant;* בְּנוֹת יִשְׂרָאֵל *the daughters of Israel*, i. e. Hebrew women; בְּנוֹת הַפְּלִשְׁתִּים *Philistine women;* and applied to the inhabitants of a place, בְּנוֹת צִיּוֹן *the daughters,*

[a] 1 Ch. 16. 22. [b] 1 Sa. 19. 24. [c] Ps. 33. 2. [d] Le. 11. 39. [e] Le. 11. 24, 27, 36. [f] Ju. 1. 16. [g] Jos. 15. 21. [h] Da. 6. 20. [i] Hab. 3. 19. [k] Le. 13. 3. [l] De. 24. 8. [m] Le. 15. 23. [n] 2 Sa. 7. 14. [o] Ps. 89. 33. [p] Ex. 12. 27. [q] Is. 14. 2. [r] Le. 15. 19, 20, 33.

female inhabitants, of Zion; in the sing. collect. for בַּת־צִיּוֹן *daughter of Zion* for the inhabitants in general, so בַּת־צֹר *Tyrians;* בַּת־עַמִּי *my country people.*—IV. with the genit. of time, בַּת־תִּשְׁעִים שָׁנָה *a woman ninety years old.*—V. metaph. בַּת־עַיִן *daughter of the eye,* i. e. *the pupil;* בְּנוֹת הַשִּׁיר *daughters of song,* i. e. songstresses; applied to the produce of animals, trees, and places; בַּת הַיַּעֲנָה *the female ostrich;* pl. בָּנוֹת *branches,* Gen. 49. 22; by *daughters,* when spoken of a city, are understood the *small towns* and *villages* dependent upon it.

בַּת־רַבִּים (*daughter of many*) pr. name of a gate in Heshbon, Ca. 7. 5.

בַּת־שֶׁבַע (*daughter of oath*) pr. name of the wife of Uriah, afterwards of David, mother of Solomon.

בִּתְיָה (*daughter,* i. e. worshipper *of the Lord*) pr. name fem. 1 Ch. 4. 18.

יַבְנֶה (which *He causes to be built*) pr. name of a town of the Philistines.

יַבְנְאֵל (which *God causes to be built*) pr. name of a town—I. in the tribe of Judah, Jos. 15. 11.—II. in Naphtali, Jos. 19. 33.

יִבְנְיָה (whom *the Lord will build up*) pr. name masc. 1 Ch. 9. 8.

יִבְנִיָּה (id.) pr. name masc. 1 Ch. 9. 8.

מִבְנֶה masc. dec. 9, *a building,* Eze. 40. 2.

מְבֻנַּי (*built up*) pr. name of a warrior of David, 2 Sa. 23. 27, elsewhere סִבְּכַי q. v.

תִּבְנִי (for תִּבְנִיָּה *building of the Lord*) pr. name masc. 1 Ki. 16. 21, 22.

תַּבְנִית fem. dec. 1 b.—I. *model.*—II. *form, resemblance.*—III. *building.*

בָּנֹה[a] Kal inf. abs. . . . . . . בנה

בְּנָהּ pref. בְּ) n. m. s., suff. 3 p. s. f. fr. בֵּן irr. (§ 45) בנה

בְּנֵה[b] Chald. Peal part. pass. sing. masc. . בנה

בְּנֵה Kal imp. sing. masc. . . . . בנה

בֹּנֶה id. part. act. sing. masc. dec. 9 a. . . בנה

בְּנָהִי[c] Chald. Peal pret. 3 p. s. m., suff. 3 p. s. m. בנה

בַּנָּהָר[d] pref. בַּ for בְּהַ) noun masc. sing. dec. 4 a. . נהר

בִּנְהַר pref. בְּ bef. (:)) id., construct state . נהר

וּבַנְּהָרוֹת pref. בַּ for בְּהַ) id. pl. f., abs. st.; וּ bef. lab. נהר

בִּנְהָרִים[e] pref. id.) id. pl. masc., absolute state . נהר

בְּנַהֲרֹתֶיךָ[f] pref. בְּ) id. pl. fem., suff. 2 pers. sing. masc. נהר

בָּנוֹ[g] וּ' Kh. for בָּנָיו (q. v. § 4. rem. 1) . בנה

בָּנוּ וּ' Kal pret. 3 pers. pl.; וּ bef. lab. . . בנה

בָּנוּ[h] Kal pret. 1 pers. pl. for בָּאנוּ (§ 25. No. 2. f.) בוא

בָּנוּ pref. prep. בְּ with suff. 1 pers. pl. (§ 5) . ב

בְּנוֹ Kh. בְּנוֹ q. v., K. בְּנִי (q. v.) . . בנה

בְּנוֹ וּ' noun m. s., suff. 3 p. s. m. or (Nu. 24. 3, 15) with ו parag. from בֵּן irr. (§ 45); וּ bef. (:) בנה

בְּנוֹ[k] וּ Chald. Peal pret. 3 pers. pl. masc.; וּ id. בנה

בְּנוּ וּ' Kal imp. pl. masc.; וּ id. . . . בנה

בְּנָוֶה pref. בְּ) noun masc. sing. dec. 9 b. . נוה

בִּנְוֵה pref. בְּ bef. (:)) id., construct state . נוה

בָּנוּהוּ[l] Kal pret. 3 pers. pl., suff. 3 pers. sing. masc. בנה

בְּנוֹהִי וּ Chald. n. m. pl., suff. 3 p. s. m. fr. בֵּן d. 2 b. בנה

בְּנוּי[m] Kal part. pass. sing. masc. dec. 3 a. . בנה

בִּנּוּי וּ' pr. name masc.; וּ bef. lab. . . . בנה

בְּנוּיִם[n] Kal part. pass. [for בְּנוּיִים comp. § 3. rem. 1] from בְּנוּי dec. 3 a. . . . . . בנה

בְּנָוֹית pref. בְּ) Kh. נָוֹית, K. נָיוֹת' pr. name of a place נוה

בְּנוּסָם pref. id.) Kal inf. (נוּס), suff. 3 p. pl. m. d. 1 a. נוס

בָּנוֹת וּ' noun fem. pl. [as if from בָּנָה dec. 11 a] see בַּת irr. (§ 45); וּ bef. lab. . בנה

בְּנוֹת וּ' id., construct state; or Kal inf. constr.; וּ id. בנה

בְּנוֹתַי[o] וּ' id., suff. 1 pers. sing.; וּ id. . . בנה

בְּנוֹתֶיהָ וּ' id., suff. 3 pers. sing. fem.; וּ id. . . בנה

בְּנוֹתֵיהֶם וּ' id., suff. 3 pers. pl. masc.; וּ id. . . בנה

בְּנוֹתָיו וּ id., suff. 3 pers. sing. masc.; וּ id. . . בנה

בְּנוֹתַיִךְ[p] וּ', בְּנוֹתַיִךְ וּ' } id., suff. 2 pers. sing. fem.; וּ bef. lab. בנה

בְּנוֹתֶיךָ[q] וּ' id., suff. 2 pers. sing. masc.; וּ id. . בנה

בְּנוֹתֵיכֶם[r] וּ' id., suff. 2 pers. pl. masc.; וּ id. . בנה

בְּנוֹתֵינוּ[t] וּ' id., suff. 1 pers. pl.; וּ id. . . בנה

בַּנּוֹתָר[u] pref. בַּ for בְּהַ) Niph. part. sing. masc. . יתר

בְּנֵזֶק[x] pref. בְּ) noun masc. sing. . . . נזק

בְּנֻחֹה[y] וּ pref. id.) Kal inf. (נוּחַ'), suff. 3 pers. sing. masc.; וּ bef. lab. . . . נוח

בַּנַּחַל, בַּנָּחַל } pref. בַּ f. בְּהַ; בְּנַחַל pref. בְּ q. v. } noun masc. sing. dec. 6 d. נחל

בַּנַּחֲלָה pref. בַּ f. בְּהַ; בְּנַחֲלָה[z] pref. בְּ q. v. } noun fem. sing. 12 d. . נחל

בְּנַחֲלֵי[a] pref. id.) constr. of the following: . נחל

בַּנְּחָלִים[b] וּ' pref. בַּ for בְּהַ) noun masc., pl. of נַחַל dec. 6 d; וּ bef. lab. . . . . נחל

בְּנַחֲלַת pref. בְּ) n. fem. s., constr. of נַחֲלָה dec. 12 d. נחל

בְּנַחֲלָתוֹ[c] וּ' pref. id.) id., suff. 3 pers. s. m.; וּ bef. lab. נחל

בְּנַחֲלָתֶךָ[d], בְּנַחֲלָתְךָ[e] } pref. id.) id., suff. 2 pers. sing. masc. . נחל

בְּנַחֲלַתְכֶם[f] pref. id.) id., suff. 2 pers. pl. masc. . נחל

בְּנַחֲלָתָם pref. id.) id. sing., suff. 3 pers. pl. masc. . נחל

[a] 1 Ki. 8. 13. [b] Ezr. 5. 11. [c] Ezr. 5. 11. [d] Ps. 66. 6. [e] Hab. 3. 8. [f] Eze. 32. 2. [g] Da. 11. 10. [h] 1 Sa. 25. 8. [i] 1 Ch. 22. 7. [k] Ezr. 6. 14. [l] Ne. 3. 13. [m] Ca. 4. 4. [n] Ne. 7. 4. [o] Is. 43. 6. [p] Eze. 16. 48. [q] Ge. 31. 31. [r] Eze. 24. 21. [s] Ps. 144. 12. [t] 2 Ch. 29. 9. [u] 2 Ki. 4. 7. [x] Est. 7. 4. [y] Nu. 10. 36. [z] Je. 12. 14. [a] Is. 7. 19. [b] Le. 11. 9, 10. [c] Ps. 78. 62. [d] Ps. 79. 1. [e] De. 19. 14. [f] Nu. 18. 26.

בְּנַחֲמֵךְ[a] pref. בְּ)(Piel inf. (נַחֵם § 14. rem. 1), suff. 2 pers. sing. masc. dec. 7b . . נחם

בַּנְּחֹשֶׁת ׳ו pref. בַּ for בְּהַ } noun fem. sing. dec. 13c;
בִּנְחֹשֶׁת[b] ו pref. בְּ bef. (:) } ו bef. lab. . } נחש

בַּנְּחֻשְׁתַּיִם pref. בַּ for בְּהַ)(id. dual, abs. st. (comp. § 35. r. 8) נחש

בְּנַחַת[c] pref. בְּ)(noun fem. sing. . . . נוח

בָּנַט Root not used; probably *to bind*, comp. Pers. *bando*, Germ. and Eng. *band*.
אַבְנֵט masc. dec. 1b, *a girdle* worn by the priests.

בִּנְטֹתִי[d] ׳ו pref. בְּ bef. (:))(Kal inf. constr., suff. 1 pers. sing. dec. 1a . . . . . נטה

בָּנַי
בָּנָי ׳ו[e] } noun m. pl. (בָּנִים), suff. 1 pers. sing. irr. of בֵּן (§ 45); ו bef. lab. . } בנה

בָּנִי ׳ו pr. name masc.; ו id. . . . בנה

בְּנֵי[f] Kh. בְּנִי q. v., K. בֵּן (q. v.) . . בנה

בְּנֵי ׳ו n. m. pl., constr. of בָּנִים irr. of בֵּן (§ 45); also pr. name in compos. as בְּנֵי־בְרַק &c. בנה

בְּנִי[g] ׳ו id. sing. construct state (Ge. 49. 11), or with suff. 1 pers. sing.; ו bef. lab. . בנה

בֹּנֵי[h] ׳ו[i] Kal part. pl. constr. m. fr. בֹּנֶה d. 9a; ו id. בנה

בֻּנִּי pr. name masc. . . . . . . בנה

בָּנֶיהָ ו[k] noun masc. pl. (בָּנִים), suff. 3 pers. sing. fem. irr. of בֵּן (§ 45); ו bef. lab. . בנה

בְּנָיָה ׳ו pr. name masc.; ו id. . . . בנה

בְּנָיָהוּ ׳ו pr. name masc.; ו id. . . . בנה

בְּנֵיהוֹן[l] Ch. n. m. pl., suff. 3 pers. pl. m. from בֵּן d. 2b בנה

בְּנֵיהֶם ׳ו id. pl., suff. 3 pers. pl. masc.; ו bef. (:) . בנה

בִּנְוֵהֶם[m] pref. בְּ)(noun masc. sing., suff. 3 pers. pl. masc. [from נֵי for נְהִי] . . . נהה

בְּנֵיהֶן[n] ׳ו[o] noun masc. pl. (בָּנִים), suff. 3 pers. pl. fem. irr. of בֵּן (§ 45); ו bef. lab. . בנה

בָּנָיו ׳ו id. pl., suff. 3 pers. sing. masc.; ו id. . בנה

בָּנַיִךְ
בָּנָיִךְ } id., suff. 2 pers. sing. fem. . . בנה

בָּנֶיךָ ׳ו id., suff. 2 pers. sing. masc.; ו bef. lab. . בנה

בֹּנַיִךְ[p] Kal part. act. pl. masc., suff. 2 pers. sing. fem. from בֹּנֶה dec. 9a . . . בנה

בָּנַיִכִי[q] noun masc. pl. (בָּנִים), suff. 2 pers. sing. fem. Kh. בָּנַיְכִי (§ 4. r. 4) K. בָּנַיִךְ, see בֵּן (§ 45) בנה

בְּנֵיכֶם ׳ו id. pl., suff. 2 pers. pl. masc.; ו bef. lab. בנה

בָּנִים ׳ו id. pl. absolute state; ו id. . . בנה

בִּנְיָמִין
בִּנְיָמִן } ׳ו pr. name masc.; ו id. . . בנה

בָּנַיִן[r] ׳ו Chald. Peal part. act. masc., pl. of [בָּנֵא] dec. 6a; ו id. see . . . . בנה

בִּנְיָן[s] noun masc. sing. . . . . . בנה

בִּנְיָנָא[t] Chald. id., emph. state dec. 1a . . בנה

בָּנֵינוּ ׳ו[u] noun masc. pl. (בָּנִים), suff. 1 pers. pl., irr. of בֵּן (§ 45); ו bef. lab. . . בנה

בָּנִינוּ[x] ו Kal pret. 1 pers. pl.; ו id. . . בנה

בִּנֵינוּ[y] defect. for בֵּינֵינוּ (q. v.) . . . בין

בְּנִינוּ pr. name masc. . . . . . בנה

בְּנִינְוֵה pref. בְּ)(pr. name of a place, see נִינְוֵה.

בָּנִיתָ[z] ׳ו Kal pret. 2 pers. sing. masc.; ו bef. lab. בנה

בָּנִיתָ[a] id. pret., Kh. בָּנִיתָ 2 p. s. m., K. בָּנִיתִי 1 p. s. בנה

בָּנִית[b] id. pret. 2 pers. sing. fem. . . . בנה

בְּנַיְתַהּ[c] Chald. Peal pret. 1 p. s., suff. 3 p. s. fem., see בנה

בָּנִיתִי ׳ו Kal pret. 1 pers. sing.; ו bef. lab. . בנה

בְּנִיתִיהָ[d] ו id. id., suff. 3 pers. sing. fem.; ו id. . בנה

בְּנִיתִים[qq] ו id. id., suff. 3 pers. pl. masc.; ו id. . בנה

בְּנִיתֶם id. pret. 2 pers. pl. masc. . . . בנה

בְּנֶךָ in pause for בִּנְךָ (q. v.) . . . . בנה

בְּנֵךְ ׳ו[e] noun masc. sing., suff. 2 pers. sing. fem. from בֵּן irr. (§ 45); ו bef. lab. . . בנה

בִּנְךָ ׳ו id., suff. 2 pers. sing. masc.; ו id. . . בנה

בַּנִּכְבָּד[f] pref. בַּ for בְּהַ)(Niph. part. sing. masc. dec. 2 & 8 (§ 37. rem. 5) . . . כבד

בְּנִכְלֵיהֶם[g] pref. בְּ)(n. m. pl., suff. 3 p. pl. m. fr. [נֵכֶל] d. 6b נכל

בִּנְכָסִים[h] pref. בְּ bef. (:))(noun m., pl. of [נֶכֶס] dec. 6a נכס

בְּנֵנוּ[i] noun m. s., suff. 1 pers. pl. from בֵּן irr. (§ 45) בנה

בְּנַס Chald. *to be angry*, Da. 2. 12.

בַּנְּסָכִים[k] ו pref. בַּ for בְּהַ)(noun masc., pl. of נֶסֶךְ dec. 6b; ו bef. lab. . . . . . נסך

בִּנְסֹעַ ׳ו[l] ו pref. בְּ bef. (:))(Kal inf. constr.; ו id. נסע

בִּנְסֹעָם pref. בְּ)(id., suff. 3 pers. pl. masc. . . נסע

בִּנְעָא
בִּנְעָה } pr. name of a man, 1 Ch. 8. 37; 9. 43.

בִּנְעוּרֶיהָ[m] pref. בְּ bef. (:))(noun masc. pl., suff. 3 pers. sing. fem. from [נְעוּר] dec. 1a . . נער

בִּנְעוּרֵיהֶם[n] pref. id.)(id., suff. 3 pers. pl. masc. נער

בִּנְעוּרֵיהֶן[o] pref. id.)(id., suff. 3 pers. pl. fem. . נער

בִּנְעוּרָיו[p] pref. id.)(id., suff. 3 pers. sing. masc. נער

בַּנְּעִימִים pref. בַּ for בְּהַ)(adj. m., pl. of נָעִים dec. 3a נעם

בְּנַעֲלוֹ[q] ו pref. בְּ)(noun masc. sing., suff. 3 pers. sing. masc. from נַעַל dec. 6d; ו bef. lab. נעל

בַּנְּעָלִים pref. בַּ for בְּהַ)(id. pl., absolute state . נעל

בְּנֹעַם[r] pref. בְּ)(noun masc. sing. . . . נעם

בַּנַּעַר[s] pref. בַּ for בְּהַ)(noun masc. sing. dec. 6d נער

בַּנַּעַר[t] pref. id.)(noun masc. sing. . . . נער

בְּנַעֲרוֹת[u] pref. בְּ)(noun f. pl. constr. fr. נַעֲרָה d. 12d נער

---

a Eze. 16. 54. b Jos. 22. 8. c Ec. 9. 17. d Ex. 7. 5. e 1 Sa. 12. 2. f 2 Ki. 23. 10. g Ge. 49. 11. h 1 Ki. 5. 32. i 1 Ki. 5. 32. k Eze. 16. 45. l Da. 6. 25. m Eze. 27. 32. n Eze. 23. 37. o Eze. 16. 45. p Eze. 27. 4. q 2 Ki. 4. 7. r Ezr. 5. 11. s Eze. 42. 5. t Ezr. 5. 4. u 2 Ch. 29. 9. x Ne. 2. 18, 20. y Jos. 22. 25, 27. z De. 6. 10. a 1 Ki. 8. 48. b Eze. 16. 25. c Da. 4. 27. d Am. 9. 11. e 1 Ki. 3. 22. f Is. 3. 5. g Nu. 25. 18. h Jos. 22. 8. i De. 21. 20. k 2 Ch. 29. 35. l Nu. 1. 51. m Eze. 23. 8. n Ps. 144. 12. o Eze. 23. 3. p La. 3. 27. q 1 Ki. 2. 5. qq Je. 24. 6. r Ps. 27. 4. s 2 Sa. 18. 12. t Job 36. 14. u Ru. 2. 23.

Word	Analysis	Root
בִּנְעָרֵי [a]	pref. בְּ)(noun m. pl. constr. fr. נַעַר d. 6d.	נער
בִּנְעָרֶיהָ [b]	pref. בְּ bef. (:))(noun masc. pl., suff. 3 pers. sing. fem. fr. [נְעוּר] dec. 1a.	נער
וּבַנְּעָרִים [c]	pref. בַּ for בְּהַ)(noun masc., pl. of נַעַר dec. 6d; וּ bef. labial	נער
בִּנְעָרֵינוּ [d]	pref. בְּ bef. (:))(id. pl., suff. 1 pers. pl.	נער
וּבְנֹף	pref. בְּ)(pr. n. of a place, see מֹף; וּ bef. (:)	
וּבְנָפוֹת [e]	pref. id.)(noun f., pl. of [נָפָה] d. 10; וּ id.	נוף
בְּנֶפֶךְ [f]	pref. id.)(noun masc. sing.	נפך
בִּנְפֹל	pref. בְּ bef. (:))(Kal inf. constr.	נפל
וּבְנִפְלָאוֹת [g]	pref. בְּ)(Niph. part. pl. abs. fr. [נִפְלָאָה] dec. 11a, fr. נִפְלָא masc.	פלא
בְּנִפְלְאוֹתֶיךָ [h]	pref. id.)(id. pl., suff. 2 pers. sing. masc.	פלא
בְּנִפְלְאֹתָיו [i]	pref. id.)(id. pl., suff. 3 pers. sing. masc.	פלא
בַּנֹּפְלִים	pref. בַּ for בְּהַ)(Kal part. act. masc., pl. of נֹפֵל dec. 7b.	נפל
בַּנֶּפֶשׁ	pref. id. } noun com. sing., (suff. נַפְשִׁי) dec. 6a; וּ bef. (:)	נפש
וּבְנֶפֶשׁ [k]	pref. בְּ } noun com. sing., (suff. נַפְשִׁי) dec. 6a; וּ bef. (:)	נפש
וּבְנַפְשׁוֹ	pref. id.)(id., suff. 3 pers. sing. m.; וּ id.	נפש
בְּנַפְשׁוֹ [l]	pref. id.)(id., suff., Kh. נַפְשׁוֹ 3 pers. sing. masc. K. נַפְשִׁי 1 pers. sing.	נפש
בְּנַפְשׁוֹתֵיכֶם	pref. id.)(id. pl., suff. 2 pers. pl. masc.	נפש
בְּנַפְשׁוֹתָם	pref. id.)(id. pl., suff. 3 pers. pl. m. (§ 4. r. 2)	נפש
וּבְנַפְשִׁי [m]	pref. id.)(id. s., suff. 1 pers. s.; וּ bef. (:)	נפש
בְּנַפְשֵׁךְ [n]	pref. id.)(id. sing., suff. 2 pers. sing. fem.	נפש
בְּנַפְשָׁם [o]	pref. id.)(id. sing., suff. 3 pers. pl. masc.	נפש
בְּנַפְשֵׁנוּ [p]	pref. id.)(id. sing., suff. 1 pers. pl.	נפש
בְּנַפְשֹׁתָם [q]	pref. id.)(id. pl., suff. 3 pers. pl. m. (§ 4. r. 2)	נפש
בְּנָפַת [r]	pref. id.)(noun f. s., constr. of [נָפָה] d. 10.	נוף
וּבְנַפְתָּלִי	pref. id.)(pr. name of a tribe	פתל
וּבַנְּצוּרִים [s]	pref. בַּ for בְּהַ)(Kal part. p. masc., pl. of נָצוּר dec. 3a; וּ bef. lab.	נצר
בְּנֹצָתָהּ [t]	pref. בְּ)(noun fem. sing., suff. 3 pers. sing. fem. fr. [נוֹצָה] dec. 10.	יצא
בְּנָקְבוֹ [u]	pref. id.)(Kal inf., suff. 3 pers. sing. masc.	נקב
בַּנֹּקְדִים [x]	pref. בַּ for בְּהַ)(noun m., pl. of נֹקֵד d. 7b.	נקד
בִּנְקוֹר [y]	pref. בְּ bef. (:))(Kal inf. constr.	נקר
בִּנְקִיק [z]	pref. id.)(noun masc. sing. dec. 1a.	נקק
בְּנִקָּיוֹן	pref. בְּ)(noun masc. sing. dec. 3c.	נקה
וּבְנִקְיֹן [a]	pref. id.)(id., constr. state; וּ bef. labial	נקה
וּבִנְקִיקֵי [b]	pref. בְּ bef. (:))(noun masc. pl. constr. fr. נָקִיק dec. 1a; וּ id.	נקק
בִּנְקֹם [c]	pref. id.)(Kal inf. constr.	נקם
בִּנְקָמָה [d]	pref. id.)(noun fem. sing. dec. 11c.	נקם
בְּנִקְרוֹת [e]	pref. בְּ)(noun fem., pl. of [נְקָרָה] dec. 11c.	נקר
בְּנִקְרַת [f]	pref. id.)(id. sing., constr. state	נקר
בַּנֵּרוֹת [g]	pref. בַּ for בְּהַ)(noun masc. with pl. f. term. fr. נֵר dec. 1a.	נור
בְּנַשְּׂאִי [h]	pref. בְּ)(Kal inf., suff. 1 pers. sing.	נשא
וּבַנִּשְׁבָּעִים [i]	pref. בַּ f. בְּהַ)(Niph. part. pl. m.; וּ bef. lab.	שבע
וּבְנָשֶׁיךָ [k]	pref. בְּ)(the following with suff. 2 pers. sing. masc.; וּ bef. labial	אנש
בַּנָּשִׁים	pref. בַּ for בְּהַ)(noun fem. with pl. masc. term. see אִשָּׁה in (§ 45)	אנש
בַּנֶּשֶׁךְ [l]	pref. id. } noun masc. sing. (§ 35. rem. 2)	נשך
בְּנֶשֶׁךְ	pref. בְּ } noun masc. sing. (§ 35. rem. 2)	נשך
בַּנֶּשֶׁךְ	pref. id. } noun masc. sing. (§ 35. rem. 2)	נשך
בַּנֶּשֶׁף	pref. בַּ f. בְּהַ } noun masc. sing., (suff. נִשְׁפּוֹ) dec. 6a.	נשף
בְּנֶשֶׁף [m]	pref. בְּ q. v. } noun masc. sing., (suff. נִשְׁפּוֹ) dec. 6a.	נשף
בַּנֶּשֶׁק [n]	pref. בַּ f. בְּהַ } noun masc. sing.	נשק
בְּנֶשֶׁק [o]	pref. בְּ q. v. } noun masc. sing.	נשק
בָּנְתָה	Kal pret. 3 pers. sing. fem.	בנה
בַּנְתָּה [p]	Kal pret. 2 pers. sing. masc. (§ 8. rem. 5)	בין
בָּנִתָה [q]	Kal pret. 2 pers. sing. masc. (§ 8. rem. 5)	בנה
בְּנֹתַי	noun fem. pl. (בָּנוֹת), suff. 1 pers. sing. irr. of בַּת (§ 45)	בנה
בִּנְתִיב [r]	pref. בְּ bef. (:))(noun masc. sing., constr. of נָתִיב dec. 3a.	נתב
בִּנְתִיבוֹת [s]	pref. id.)(noun fem., pl. of נְתִיבָה dec. 10.	נתב
בִּנְתִיבֹתֶיהָ [t]	pref. id.)(id. pl., suff. 3 pers. sing. fem.	נתב
בִּנְתִיבֹתָיו [u]	pref. id.)(id. pl., suff. 3 pers. sing. masc.	נתב
וּבְנֹתֶיהָ	noun fem. pl. (בָּנוֹת), suff. 3 pers. sing. fem., irr. of בַּת (§ 45); וּ bef. (:)	בנה
וּבְנֹתֵיהֶם	id. pl., suff. 3 pers. pl. masc.	בנה
וּבְנֹתָיו	id. pl., suff. 3 pers. sing. masc.	בנה
וּבְנֹתַיִךְ	id. pl., suff. 2 pers. sing. fem.	בנה
וּבְנֹתֶיךָ	id. pl., suff. 2 pers. sing. masc.	בנה
וּבְנֹתֵיכֶם	id. pl., suff. 2 pers. pl. masc.	בנה
וּבְנֹתֵינוּ	id. pl., suff. 1 pers. pl.	בנה
בְּנֹתָם [x]	id. pl., suff. 3 pers. pl. masc. (§ 4. rem. 2)	בנה
בַּנֶּתֶר [y]	pref. בַּ for בְּהַ)(noun masc. sing.	נתר
בְּסַאסְּאָה [z]	pref. בְּ)(noun fem. sing.	סאה
בְּסֹבְאֵי [a]	pref. id.)(Kal part. act. pl. constr. masc. from סֹבֵא dec. 7b.	סבא
וּבִסְבִיבֵי	pref. בְּ bef. (:))(noun masc. pl. constr. from סָבִיב dec. 3a; וּ bef. labial	סבב
בַּסְּבַךְ [b]	pref. בַּ for בְּהַ)(noun masc. sing.	סבך
בִּסְבָךְ־ [c]	pref. בְּ bef. (:))(n. m. s. with mak. [for סְבַךְ]	סבך
בְּסִבְכֵי [d]	pref. בְּ)(noun masc. pl. constr. [for סִבְכֵי without metheg fr. סְבָךְ dec. 6b; or perhaps from סְבַךְ § 35. rem. 10]	סבך
בַּסֵּבֶל [e]	pref. בַּ for בְּהַ)(noun masc. sing.	סבל

[a] 1 Ki. 20. 14. [b] Nu. 30. 4, 17. [c] Job 1. 16. [d] Ex. 10. 9. [e] Jos. 11. 2. [f] Eze. 27. 16. [g] Ps. 131. 1. [h] Ps. 119. 27. [i] Ps. 78. 32. [k] 1 Ch. 28. 9. [l] 2 Sa. 18. 13. [m] 1 Sa. 2. 35. [n] Est. 4. 13. [o] Ps. 106. 15. [p] La. 5. 9. [q] Nu. 17. 3. [r] Is. 30. 28. [s] Is. 65. 4. [t] Le. 1. 16. [u] Le. 24. 16. [x] Am. 1. 1. [y] 1 Sa. 11. 2. [z] Je. 13. 4. [a] Ge. 20. 5. [b] Is. 7. 19. [c] Eze. 25. 12. [d] Eze. 25. 15. [e] Is. 2. 21. [f] Ex. 33. 22. [g] Zep. 1. 12. [h] Ps. 28. 2. [i] Mal. 3. 5. [k] 2 Ch. 21. 14. [l] Eze. 18. 8, 13. [m] Pr. 7. 9. [n] Eze. 39. 10. [o] Eze. 39. 9. [p] Ps. 139. 2. [q] 1 Ki. 9. 3. [r] Ps. 119. 35. [s] Is. 42. 16. [t] Pr. 7. 25. [u] Job 24. 13. [x] Ge. 34. 21. [y] Je. 2. 22. [z] Is. 27. 8. [a] Pr. 23. 20. [b] Ge. 22. 13. [c] Ps. 74. 5. [d] Is. 9. 17. [e] Ne. 4. 11.

בְּסִבְלֹתָם pref. בְּ)(noun fem. pl., suff. 3 pers. pl. masc. [§ 4. rem. 2; from סִבְלָה or סְבָלָה] . סבל
בַּסַּד pref. בַּ for בְּהַ)(noun masc. sing. . סדד
בְּסֹדָם[a] pref. בְּ)(noun masc. sing., suff. 3 pers. pl. masc. from סוֹד dec. 1a. . . . יסד
בִּסְדֹם pref. בְּ bef. (:))(pr. name of a place . סדם
בַּסּוּגַר[b] pref. בַּ for בְּהַ)(noun masc. sing. . . סגר
בְּסוֹד pref. בְּ)(noun masc. sing. d. 1a. [for יְסוֹד] יסד
בְּסוֹדִי[c] pref. id.)(id., suff. 1 pers. sing. . . יסד
בְּסוֹדְיָה pr. name masc. . . . . . יסד
בְּסוּס[d] pref. id.)(noun masc. sing. dec. 1a. . סוס
בְּסוּסָו[e] pref. id.)(id. pl., suff. 3 p. s. m. (§ 4. r. 1) סוס
וּבַסּוּסִים pref. בַּ f. בְּהַ / בְּסוּסִים pref. בְּ q. v. } id. pl., absolute state; וּ bef. labial סוס
בַּסּוּף[g] pref. בַּ for בְּהַ)(noun masc. sing. . . סוף
בְּסוֹף[h] pref. בְּ)(noun masc. sing. dec. 1a. . סוף
בְּסוּפָה pref. id.)(noun fem. sing. dec. 10. . סוף
בֵּסַי / בֵּסָי } pr. name masc. . . . . . בוס
וּבְסוּפָתְךָ וּ pref. בְּ)(noun fem., suff. 2 pers. sing. masc. fr. סוּפָה dec. 10; וּ bef. labial . סוף
בַּסִּיר pref. בַּ for בְּהַ)(noun com. sing. dec. 1a. סיר
בַּסִּירוֹת pref. id. / בְּסִירוֹת pref. בְּ } id. pl. fem. . . . . סיר
בַּסִּירִים pref. בַּ for בְּהַ)(id. pl. masc. . . . סיר
בַּסָּךְ[n] pref. id.)(noun masc. sing. . . . סכך
בַּסֻּכָּה[o] pref. id. / בְּסֻכָּה[p] pref. בְּ } noun fem. sing. dec. 10. . . סכך
בְּסֻכֹּה pref. id.)(noun masc. sing., suff. 3 pers. sing. masc. (§ 3. rem. 3) fr. [סֹךְ] dec. 8c. סכך
בַּסֻּכּוֹת pref. בַּ for בְּהַ)(noun f., pl. of סֻכָּה d. 10. סכך
בְּסִכְלוּת pref. בְּ)(noun fem. sing. . . . . סכל
בַּסֻּכֹּת pref. בַּ for בְּהַ)(noun f., pl. of סֻכָּה dec. 10. סכך
בְּסֻכֹּת pref. בְּ)(pr. name of a place . . סכך
בַּסַּל[r] / וּבַסַּל[s] pref. בַּ f. בְּהַ וּ / בְּסַל[u] pref. בְּ q. v. } noun masc. sing. dec. 8d; וּ bef. lab. סלל
וּבְסַלְכָה וּ pref. id.)(pr. name of a place; וּ id. . סלך
בַּסֶּלַע pref. בַּ f. בְּהַ / בְּסֶלַע[x] pref. בְּ q. v. } noun masc. s., (suff. סַלְעִי) dec. 6a. (§ 35. rem. 5) . סלע
וּבַסְּלָעִים וּ pref. בַּ for בְּהַ)(id. pl., abs. st.; וּ bef. lab. סלע
בְּסֹמְכֵי pref. בְּ)(Kal part. act. pl. constr. masc. from סֹמֵךְ dec. 7b. . . . . סמך
בַּסַּנְוֵרִים pref. בַּ for בְּהַ)(noun masc., pl. of [סַנְוֵר] סנור
בְּסַנְסִנָּיו pref. בְּ)(noun masc. pl., suff. 3 pers. sing. masc. from [סַנְסִן] dec. 8c. . . סנן

בֹּסְסוּ Pilel pret. 3 pers. pl. Je. 12. 10. . . בוס
בִּסְעִיף[b] pref. בְּ bef. (:))(noun masc. sing. dec. 1a. סעף
וּבִסְעִפֵּי[c] וּ pref. id.)(id. pl., constr. st.; וּ bef. labial סעף
בִּסְעִפֶיהָ[d] pref. id.)(id. pl., suff. 3 pers. sing. masc. . סעף
בִּסְעַפֹּתָיו[e] pref. id.)(noun fem. pl., suff. 3 pers. sing. masc. from [סְעַפָּה] dec. 10. . . סעף
בְּסַעַר[f] pref. בְּ)(noun masc. sing. dec. 6d. . סער
בַּסְּעָרָה[g] pref. בַּ for בְּהַ)(noun fem. sing. . . סער
בִּסְעָרָה[h] pref. id.)(noun fem. sing. dec. 11c. (§ 42. r. 1) סער
בְּסַעֲרוֹת[i] pref. בְּ)(id. pl., construct state . סער
בְּסַעֲרֶךָ[k] pref. id.)(noun masc. sing., suff. 2 pers. sing. masc. [for סַעַרְךָ], from סַעַר dec. 6d. סער
בַּסַּף[l] / בַּסָּף pref. בַּ f. בְּהַ / בְּסַף[m] pref. בְּ q. v. } noun masc. sing. dec. 8e. . ספף
בַּסִּפִּים[n] pref. בַּ for בְּהַ)(id. pl., absolute state . ספף
בַּסַּפִּירִים[o] pref. id.)(noun masc., pl. of סַפִּיר dec. 1b. ספר
בְּסֵפֶל[p] pref. בְּ)(noun masc. sing. . . . ספל
בַּסֵּפֶר pref. בַּ for בְּהַ / בְּסֵפֶר pref. בְּ q. v. } noun masc. sing. dec. 6b. . ספר
בִּסְפַר[q] Chald. pref. בְּ bef. (:))(noun m. s. dec. 3b. ספר
בִּסְפָרַד pref. id.)(pr. name of a region . ספרד
בַּסְּפָרִים pref. בַּ for בְּהַ)(n. m., pl. of סֵפֶר dec. 6b. ספר
בְּסִפְרָתֶךָ[r] pref. בְּ)(n. f. s., suff. 2 p. s. m. [for ־רָתְךָ fr. סִפְרָה] ספר

בָּסַר

Root not used; Arab. *to do any thing too soon;* also *to look sour.*

בֹּסֶר m. d. 6b, coll. *unripe, sour grapes,* Job 15.33. Also

וּבֹסֶר וּ[s] noun masc. i. q. בֶּסֶר; וּ bef. lab. . בסר
בְּסַרְבָּלֵיהוֹן[t] Chald. pref. בְּ)(noun masc. pl., suff. 3 pers. pl. masc. from [סַרְבָּל] dec. 1a. . סרבל
בִּסְרוֹ[u] n. m. s., suff. 3 p. s. m. from [בֶּסֶר] dec. 6b. בסר
בְּסִרְיֹנוֹ[x] pref. בְּ)(noun masc. sing., suff. 3 pers. sing. masc. from [סִרְיוֹן] dec. 1b. see . שׁרה
וּבְסָתֻם[y] וּ pref. id.)(Kal part. pass. sing. masc. for סָתוּם dec. 3a; וּ bef. (:) . . סתם
בַּסָּתֶר pref. בַּ for בְּהַ)(seg. n. in pause [as if from סֵתֶר=סָתֶר § 35. rem. 2] see the following: סתר
בַּסֵּתֶר pref. id. / בְּסֵתֶר pref. בְּ } noun masc. sing. dec. 6b. . . סתר
בָּעֵא[z] Chald. Peal part. act. sing. masc. dec. 6a. בעא
וּבְעָא[a] [b] וּ Chald. Peal pret. 3 pers. s. m.; וּ bef. (:) בעא
בְּעָב[c] pref. בְּ)(noun masc. sing., constr. of עָב, as if from עָבָה, see עָב R. . . . עוב
בַּעֲבֹדָה pref. בַּ for בְּהַ)(noun fem. sing. dec. 10. עבד

Ge. 49. 6. / Eze. 19. 9. / Je. 23. 22. / Eze. 26. 7. / 2 Ki. 5. 9. / Ho. 1. 7.
[g] Ex. 2. 3. [h] 2 Ch. 20. 16. [i] Ps. 83. 16. [k] 2 Ch. 35. 13. [l] Am. 4. 2. [m] Ho. 2. 8.
[n] Ps. 42. 5. [o] Job 38. 40. [p] Ps. 31. 21. [q] Ec. 2. 3. [r] Ex. 29. 3, 32. [s] Ju. 6. 19.
[t] Ge. 40. 17. [u] Le. 8. 31. [x] Ju. 20.47; 21.1[illegible]. [y] 1 Sa. 13. 6. [z] Ps. 54. 6. [a] Ca. 7. 9.
[b] Ju. 15. 8. [c] Is. 2. 21. [d] Is. 17. 6. [e] Eze. 31. 6. [f] Am. 1. 14.
[g] 2 Ki. 2. 1. [h] 2 Ki. 2. 11. [i] Zec. 9. 14. [k] Ps. 83. 16. [l] Ex. 12. 22.
[m] 1 Ki. 14. 17. [n] 1 Ch. 9. 22. [o] Is. 54. 11. [p] Ju. 5. 25. [q] Ezr. 4. 15.
[r] Ps. 56. 9. [s] Is. 18. 5. [t] Da. 3. 21. [u] Job 15. 33. [x] Je. 51. 3.
[y] Ps. 51. 8. [z] Da. 6. 14. [a] Da. 2. 49. [b] Da. 2. 16. [c] Ex. 19. 9.

[ע]בְּעַבְדּוֹ pref. בְּ)(n. m. s., suff. 3 p. s. m. fr. עֶבֶד d. 6a. עבד

בְּעַבְדִּי[a] pref. id.)(id., suff. 1 pers. sing. . . עבד

בַּעֲבָדָיו pref. בַּ bef. (-:))(id. pl., suff. 3 pers. sing. m. עבד

בַּעֲבָדֶיךָ וּ pref. id.)(id. pl., suff. 2 p. s. m.; וּ bef. lab. עבד

בְּעַבְדֶּךָ, בְּעַבְדְּךָ } pref. בְּ)(id. sing., suff. 2 pers. sing. masc. עבד

בַּעֲבֹדַת pref. בַּ bef. (-:))(n.f.s., constr. of עֲבוֹדָה d. 10. עבד

בַּעֲבֹדָתָם pref. id.)(id., suff. 3 pers. pl. masc. . עבד

בְּעַבְדֻתֵנוּ[d] וּ pref. בְּ)(n.f.s., suff. 1 p.s.fr. [עַבְדוּת] d. 10. עבד

בַּעֲבוּר וּ pref. בַּ bef. (-:))(prep. and conj.; וּ bef. lab. עבר

בַּעֲבוּרָהּ[e] pref. id.)(id., suff. 3 pers. sing. fem. . עבר

בַּעֲבוּרִי[f] pref. id.)(id., suff. 1 pers. sing. . . עבר

בַּעֲבוּרֶךָ[g] pref. id.)(id., suff. 2 pers. s. m. [for בַּעֲבוּרְךָ] עבר

בַּעֲבוּרֵךְ[h] pref. id.)(id., suff. 2 pers. sing. fem. . עבר

בַּעֲבוּרָם pref. id.)(id., suff. 3 pers. pl. masc. . עבר

בַּעֲבֹטוֹ[i] pref. id.)(n.m.s., suff. 3 p. s. m. fr. עֲבוֹט d. 1 a. עבט

בַּעֲבִי pref. id.)(noun masc. sing. . . עבה

בְּעָבָיו[k] pref. בְּ)(the following with suff. 3 pers. s. m. עוב

בֶּעָבִים pref. בֶּ f. בְּהַ, בְּהָ; בְּעָבִים[l] pref. בְּ q. v. } noun m., pl. of עָב d. 1 a. עוב

בַּעֲבַר Chald. pref. בַּ bef. (-:))(noun masc. sing. . עבר

בַּעֲבֹר[m] pref. id.)(Kal inf. constr. . . . עבר

בַּעֲבֻר[n] defect. for בַּעֲבוּר (q. v.) . . . עבר

בְּעֵבֶר pref. בְּ)(noun masc. sing. dec. 6. (§ 35. r. 6) עבר

בְּעֵבֶר[o] Kh. בְּעֵבֶר q. v., K. מֵעֵבֶר (q. v.) . עבר

בְּעֶבְרָה pref. בְּ)(noun fem. sing. dec. 12 b. . עבר

בְּעָבְרוֹ pref. id.)(Kal inf., suff. 3 pers. sing. masc. עבר

בְּעַבְרוֹת pref. id.)(n. fem. pl., constr. from עֲבָרָה d. 12 a. עבר

בְּעַבְרוֹת pref. id.)(Kh. constr. of עֲבָרָה' q. v., K. בְּעַרְבוֹת (q. v.)

בְּעֶבְרֵי pref. id.)(n. m. pl. constr. fr. עֵבֶר d. 6. (§ 35. r. 6) עבר

בְּעָבְרְךָ pref. id.)(Kal inf., suff. 2 pers. s. m. for עָבְרְךָ' עבר

בְּעָבְרְכֶם pref. id.)(id., suff. 2 pers. pl. masc. . עבר

בְּעַבְרֹנָה pref. id.)(pr. name of a place . . עבר

בְּעֶבְרַת pref. id.)(n. fem. s., constr. of עֶבְרָה d. 12 b. עבר

בְּעֶבְרָתוֹ pref. id.)(id., suff. 3 pers. sing. masc. . עבר

בְּעֶבְרָתִי pref. id.)(id., suff. 1 pers. sing. . . עבר

בְּעֶבְרָתֶךָ pref. id.)(id., suff. 2 pers. sing. m. [for עֶבְרָתְךָ'] עבר

בַּעֲבֹתוֹ pref. בַּ for בְּהָ)(noun com. with pl. fem. term. from עֲבֹת dec. 1 a. . . . . עבת

בַּעֲבֹתִי pref. id.)(id. pl. masc. . . . עבת

בָּעֲגָלָה pref. בָּ f. בְּהַ, בְּהָ; בַּעֲגָלָה pref. בַּ before (-:) } noun fem. sing. dec. 11 c. (§ 42. rem. 1) . עגל

בַּעֲגָלוֹת pref. id.)(id. pl., absolute state . . עגל

בְּעֶגְלֵי pref. בְּ)(noun masc. pl. constr. from עֵגֶל dec. 6. (§ 35. rem. 6) . . . עגל

בַּעֲגָלִים[d] pref. בַּ bef. (-:))(id. pl. absolute state . גל

בְּעֶגְלָתִי[e] pref. בְּ)(n. f. s., suff. 1 p. s. from עֶגְלָה d. 12 b. גל

בַּעַד Root not used; Arab. *to be distant.* Hence

בַּעַד וּ, [and בְּעַד'] dec. 6 d. (§ 35. rem. 10) prep.—I. *after, behind, about;* מִבַּעַד לְ *behind.*—II. *abou[t] round about,* and especially after the verbs o[f] *shutting up,* &c.—III. *for, in behalf of.*

בְּעֹד[f] pref. בְּ)(prop. inf., used as an adv. . . וד

בַּעֲדָהּ prep. [בַּעַד dec. 6 d] with suff. 3 pers. s. fem. עד

בָּעֵדָה[g] pref. בָּ for בְּהָ, בְּהַ)(n. fem. s. dec. 11 b. עד

בַּעֲדוֹ prep. [בַּעַד] with suff. 3 pers. sing. masc. עד

בְּעֵדְוֹתָיו[h] וּ pref. בְּ)(noun fem. pl., suff. 3 pers. s. m. from עֵדוּת (comp. Ch. dec. 8 c); וּ bef. (:) וד

בְּעֵדְוֹתֶיךָ[i] וּ pref. id.)(id., suff. 2 pers. sing. m.; וּ id. וד

בַּעֲדִי[k] pref. בַּ bef. (-:))(noun masc. sing., (suff. עֶדְיוֹ) dec. 6 i. (§ 35. rem. 14) . . . דה

בַּעֲדִי prep. [בַּעַד dec. 6 d] with suff. 1 pers. sing. עד

בַּעֲדֵינוּ[l] id. pl., suff. 1 pers. pl. . . . . עד

בַּעֲדֵךְ[m] id. sing., suff. 2 pers. sing. fem. . . עד

בַּעַדְךָ[n], בַּעֲדֶךָ } id. sing., suff. 2 pers. sing. masc. . עד

בַּעַדְכֶם id. sing., suff. 2 pers. pl. masc. . . עד

בַּעֲדָם id. sing., suff. 3 pers. pl. masc. . . עד

בְּעֵדֶן pref. בְּ)(pr. name of a place . . דן

בְּעִדָּנָא[o] Chald. pref. id.)(n. m. s., emph. of עִדָּן dec. 1 b. דן

בַּעֲדֵנוּ prep. [בַּעַד dec. 6 d] with suff. 1 pers. pl. . עד

בַּעֲדֵנִי[p] id. with suff. 1 pers. sing. . . . עד

בָּעֹדֵף[q] pref. בָּ for בְּהָ, בְּהַ)(Kal part. s. m. d. 7 b. דף

בְּעֵדֶר[r] pref. id.)(noun masc. sing. dec. 6. (§ 35. r. 6) דר

בְּעֶדְרוֹ[s] pref. בְּ)(id., suff. 3 pers. sing. masc. . דר

בְּעֶדְרֵי[t] pref. id.)(id. pl., construct state . . דר

בַּעֲדַת pref. בַּ bef. (-:))(n. f. s., constr. of עֵדָה dec. 11 b. יד

בְּעֵדֹתֶיךָ[u] pref. בְּ)(n. f. pl., suff. 2 p. s. m. fr. עֵדָה d. 10. יד

בַּעֲדָתָם[x] pref. בַּ bef. (-:))(noun fem. sing., suff. 3 pers. sing. fem. from עֵדָה dec. 11 b. . . וד

בָּעָה I. *to make to swell, boil up,* Is. 64. 1.—II. *to see[k] ask, request.* Niph. I. *to swell out,* Is. 30. 13.—II. *to be sought out,* Obad. 6.

בְּעָא Chald.—I. *to seek, search after,* const. wi[th] acc.—II. *to ask, request,* with מִן קֳדָם, מִן. P[a.] *to search after,* with לְ.

בָּעוּ fem. dec. 8 c. *petition,* Da. 6. 8, 14.

בְּעִי masc. *prayer,* Job 30. 24; comp. בִּי'.

בָּעֵה[y] Chald. Peal part. act. s. m. [for בָּעֵא § 62] d. 6 a. עה

[a] Nu. 12. 8. [b] 1 Ch. 24. 3. [c] Ezr. 9. 8. [d] Ezr. 9. 9. [e] Ge. 12. 16. [f] 1 Sa. 23. 10. [g] Ge. 3. 17. [h] Ge. 12. 13. [i] De. 24. 12. [k] Job 26. 8. [l] Ps. 147. 8. [m] Ex. 33. 22. [n] Ge. 27. 10, 31. [o] Jos. 24. 15. [p] Is. 14. 6. [q] Ps. 7. 7. [r] 2 Sa. 15. 28. [s] De. 27. 3. [t] La. 2. 2. [u] Ho. 13. 11. [x] Ps. 90. 9. [y] Ho. 11. 4. [z] 1 Sa. 6. 7, 10. [a] 1 Ch. 13. 7. [b] Ge. 46. 5. [c] Ps. 68. 31. [d] Mi. 6. 6. [e] Ju. 14. 18. [f] Je. 15. 9. [g] Ex. 34. 31. [h] Je. 44. 23. [i] Ps. 119. 31. [k] Eze. 16. 7. [l] Am. 9. 10. [m] 2 Ki. 4. 4. [n] Is. 26. 20. [o] Da. 3. 5, 15. [p] Ps. 139. 11. [q] Ex. 26. 13. [r] Je. 31. 24. [s] Mal. 1. 14. [t] Mi. 5. 7. [u] Ps. 119. 46. [x] Ps. 106. 18. [y] Da. 6. 12.

בְּעוּתֵי [g] noun fem. pl. constr. from [בְּעוּת] dec. 1b. בעת
בְּעוּתֶיךָ [h] id. pl., suff. 2 pers. sing. masc. . . בעת
בְּעֹז [i] pref. בְּ) noun masc. sing. dec. 8c. . . עזז
בֹּעַז [ו״] (*alacrity*) pr. name—I. of the husband of Ruth.—II. of a pillar in Solomon's temple.
בְּעַזָּא pref. בְּ) pr. name masc. . . . עזז
בְּעִזְבוֹנַיִךְ [k] pref. id.) noun masc. pl., suff. 2 pers. sing. fem. from עִזָּבוֹן dec. 3c. . . עזב
בְּעִזְבוֹנַיִךְ [l]
בְּעָזְבְכֶם [m] pref. בְּ bef. (-:)) Kal inf., suff. 2 p. pl. m. עזב
בְּעָזְבָם [n] pref. בְּ) id., suff. 3 pers. pl. masc. . עזב
בְּעַזָּה pref. id.) pr. name of a place . . עזז
בְּעֻזָּה pref. id.) pr. name masc. . . . עזז
בְּעֻזּוֹ [o] pref. id.) noun masc. sing., suff. 3 pers. sing. masc. fr. עֹז dec. 8c. . . עזז
בַּעֲזוֹז [p] pref. בַּ bef. (-:)) Kal inf. constr. . עזז
בְּעִזִּים [q ו״] pref. בָּ for בְּהַ־, בָּהָ) noun fem., pl. of עֵז dec. 8b; וּ bef. labial . . . עזז
בְּעֻזְּךָ pref. בְּ) noun m. s., with suff. 2 p. s. masc. from עֹז dec. 8c. (§ 37. rem. 2) עזז
בְּעֻזֶּךָ [r]
בְּעָזְקַת [s] וּ Ch. pref. id.) noun fem. sing., constr. of עִזְקָא dec. 8a; וּ bef. (:) . . . עזק
בְּעִזְקְתֵהּ [t] Ch. pref. id.) id., suff. 3 pers. sing. masc. עזק
בַּעֲזֹר [u] pref. בַּ bef. (-:)) Kal inf. constr. . . עזר
בְּעֶזְרוֹ [x] pref. בְּ) noun masc. sing., suff. 1 pers. sing. from עֵזֶר dec. 6. (§ 35. rem. 6) . עזר
בְּעֶזְרִי [y] pref. id.) id., suff. 1 pers. sing. . . עזר
בְּעֹזְרָי [z] pref. id.) Kal part. act. pl., suff. 1 pers. sing. from עֹזֵר dec. 7b. . . . עזר
בְּעֶזְרֶךָ pref. id.) noun sing. masc., suff. 2 pers. sing. masc. [for עֶזְרְךָ] from עֵזֶר (§ 3. r. 6) עזר
בְּעֶזְרָתִי [a] pref. id.) noun fem. sing., suff. 1 pers. sing. from עֶזְרָה (no pl. absolute) . עזר
בְּעֶזְרָתֵךְ [b] pref. id.) id., suff. 2 pers. sing. fem. . עזר

בָּעַט

I. *to kick, kick up,* Deu. 32. 15.—II. *to kick, spurn at,* with בְּ 1 Sa. 2. 29.

בְּעֵט pref. בְּ) noun masc. sing. . . . עוט
בַּעֲטֹף [c] pref. בַּ bef. (-:)) Kal inf. constr. . . עטף
בְּעָטֵף [d] pref. בְּ, [for בְּהֵעָטֵף], Niph. inf. constr. (§ 10. rem. 6) . . . . עטף
בָּעֲטָרָה [e] pref. בָּ for בְּהַ־, בָּהָ) noun fem. sing., constr. עֲטֶרֶת (§ 42. rem. 5) . . . . עטר
בְּעַי pref. id.) pr. name of a place . . עוה
בְּעִי [f] n. m. s. R. בעה, or pref. בְּ, עִי n. m. s. R. עוה
בְּעַיוּ [g] Kal imp. pl. masc. (§ 24. rem. 5) . . בעה
בְּעִיֵּי pref. בְּ) n. m. pl. constr. pr. n., עִיֵּי הָעֲבָרִים עוה

בְּעוֹ [a] וּ Chald. id. pret. 3 p. pl. m. R. בְּעָא; וּ bef. (:) בעה
בָּעוּ [b] Chald. noun fem. sing. dec. 8c. . . בעה
בְּעוֹד [c ו״] pref. בְּ) adv. dec. 1a; וּ bef. (:) . . עוד
בְּעוֹדָהּ [d] pref. id.) id., suff. 3 pers. sing. fem. . עוד
בְּעוֹדִי pref. id.) id., suff. 1 pers. sing. . . עוד
בְּעוֹדֶנּוּ [e] pref. id.) id., (verbal) suff. 3 p.s.m. (§ 2. note) עוד
בְּעוֹדֶנִּי [f] pref. id.) id., (verbal) suff. 1 p. s. (§ 2. note) עוד
בְּעָוֺן [g] pref. בְּ) noun masc. sing. dec. 3a. . . עוה
בָּעֹז [h] pref. בָּ f. בְּהַ, בָּהָ) noun m. s., for עֹז dec. 8c. עזז
בְּעֹז [i] pref. בְּ q. v.
בְּעָוֶל [k] pref. id.) noun masc. sing. (§ 35. rem. 11) עול
בְּעֹלִי [l] pref. id.) noun masc. sing. for עֹל dec. 8c. עלל
בְּעַוְלָה pref. id.) noun fem. sing. . . . עול
בְּעוֹלָה pref. id.) noun fem., contr. for עַוְלָה R. עול (Is. 61. 8); or for עֹלָה (q. v.) . . עלה
בְּעוּלָה Kal part. p. sing. fem. dec. 10, from [בָּעוּל] m. בעל
בְּעַוְלוֹ [m n ו״] pref. בְּ) noun m. sing., suff. 3 pers. sing. masc. from עָוֶל (§ 35. rem. 11); וּ bef. lab. עול
בְּעוֹלוֹת pref. id.) noun fem., pl. of עוֹלָה dec. 10. . עלה
בְּעַוְלָתָה [o] pref. id.) n. fem. sing. (עַוְלָה) with parag. ה עול
בַּעֲוֺן pref. בַּ bef. (-:)) constr. for the following: עוה
בֶּעָוֺן [p] pref. בֶּ for בְּהֶ, בָּהֶ) noun masc. sing. dec. 3a. עוה
בַּעֲוֺנָהּ [q] pref. בַּ bef. (-:)) id., suff. 3 pers. sing. fem. עוה
בַּעֲוֺנוֹ pref. id.) id., suff. 3 pers. sing. masc. . עוה
בַּעֲוֺנוֹת [r ו״] pref. id.) id. pl. fem. term.; וּ bef. lab. עוה
בַּעֲוֺנִי [u] pref. id.) id. sing., suff. 1 pers. sing. . עוה
בְּעוֹנִי [s] Kh. בְּעוֹנִי (pref. בְּ), in pause for עֲנִי R. ענה; K. בְּעֵינִי, עַיִן with suff. 1 pers. sing. עין
בַּעֲוֺנֶךָ [y] pref. בַּ bef. (-:)) noun masc. sing., suff. 2 pers. sing. masc. from עָוֺן dec. 3a. עוה
בַּעֲוֺנָם pref. id.) id., suff. 3 pers. pl. masc. . עוה
בַּעֲוֺנֹתַיִךְ [z] pref. id.) id. pl. fem., suff. 2 pers. sing. m. עוה
בַּעֲוֺנֹתֵינוּ [zz] וּ pref. id.) id. pl., suff. 1 pers. pl.; וּ id. עוה
בַּעֲוֺנֹתֵיכֶם pref. id.) id. pl., suff. 2 pers. pl. masc. עוה
בָּעוֹף [a ו״] pref. בָּ f. בְּהַ־, בָּהָ) noun masc. sing.; וּ bef. (:) . . עוף
בְּעוֹף וּ pref. בְּ q. v.
בְּעוֹפְפִי [b] pref. id.) Pilel inf. [עוֹפֵף], suff. 1 pers. sing. dec. 7b. . . . . עוף
בָּעוֹר pref. בָּ f. בְּהַ־, בָּהָ) noun masc. sing. dec. 1a. עור
בְּעוֹר pref. בְּ q. v.
בְּעוֹר pr. name masc. . . . . בער
בְּעִוָּרוֹן [c] pref. בְּ for בְּהַ) noun masc. sing. . . עור
בְּעִוָּרוֹן [d] וּ pref. בְּ q. v.
בְּעוֹרִי [e] pref. id.) noun masc. sing. dec. 1a. . עור
בְּעוּתֵהּ [f] Ch. noun fem. sing., suff. 3 pers. sing. masc. from בָּעוּ dec. 8c. . . . בעה

[a] Da. 2. 13. [b] Da. 6. 8. [c] Is. 7. 8. [d] Is. 28. 4. [e] Ge. 25. 6. [f] De. 31. 27. [g] Ps. 51. 7. [h] Pr. 24. 5. [i] Pr. 31. 17. [k] Eze. 28. 18. [l] De. 21. 3. [m] Eze. 18. 26. [n] Eze. 33. 13. [o] Ps. 125. 3. [p] Is. 59. 3. [q] Je. 51. 6. [r] Le. 26. 39. [s] Da. 9. 16. [u] Ps. 31. 11. [x] 2 Sa. 16. 12. [y] Ho. 14. 2. [z] Is. 43. 24. [zz] Ezr. 9. 7. [a] Le. 20. 25. [b] Eze. 32. 10. [c] Zec. 12. 4. [d] De. 28. 28. [e] Job 19. 20. [f] Da. 6. 14. [g] Job 6. 4. [h] Ps. 88. 17. [i] Mi. 5. 3. [k] Eze. 27. 16. [l] Eze. 27. 19. [m] 1 Ki. 18. 18. [n] 2 Ch. 28. 6. [o] Ps. 78. 26. [p] Pr. 8. 28. [q] Le. 22. 19. [r] Ps. 21. 14. [s] Da. 6. 18. [t] Da. 6. 18. [u] 1 Ch. 15. 26. [x] Ps. 146. 5. [y] Ex. 18. 4. [z] Ps. 118. 7. [a] Ps. 35. 2. [b] Na. 3. 9. [c] Ps. 61. 3. [d] La. 2. 11. [e] Ca. 3. 11. [f] Job 30. 24. [g] Is. 21. 12.

בְּעֵילָם pref. בְּ X pr. name of a province, see עֵילָם

בְּעָיִם[a] for בְּעַיִּם, pref. בְּ bef. (ֲ) X n. m. s. constr. — עים

בְּעַיִן[b] Ch. Peal part. act. m., pl. R. בְּעָא see בְּעָא, d. 6a. — בעה

בָּעַיִן[c] pref. בָּ, f. בְּהַ·, בְּהָ } noun com. sing. dec. 6 h., also p. n.; וּ bef. lab. — עין
בְּעַיִן וּ pref. בְּ q. v.

בְּעֵין pref. id. X id., constr. state, also pr. name in compos. as עֵין דּאר &c. — עין

בְּעֵינָא[d] Ch. Peal pret. 1 pers. pl. R. בְּעָא see — בעה

בְּעֵינוֹ Kh. for בְּעֵינָיו Keri (q. v. § 4. rem. 1) — עין

בְּעֵינוֹ[e] pref. בְּ X noun com. sing., suff. 3 pers. sing. masc. from עַיִן dec. 6h. — עין

בְּעֵינַי
בְּעֵינַי } pref. id. X id., du., suff. 1 pers. sing. — עין

בְּעֵינֵי וּ pref. id. X id. du., constr. state; וּ bef. lab. — עין

בְּעֵינֶיהָ[f] pref. id. X id. du., suff. 3 pers. sing. fem. — עין

בְּעֵינֵיהֶם pref. id. X id. du., suff. 3 pers. pl. masc. — עין

בְּעֵינֵיהֶן[g] pref. id. X id. du., suff. 3 pers. pl. fem. — עין

בְּעֵינָיו pref. id. X id. du., suff. 3 pers. sing. masc. — עין

בְּעֵינַיִךְ[h]
בְּעֵינַיִךְ[i] } pref. id. X id. du., suff. 2 pers. sing. fem. — עין

בְּעֵינֶיךָ pref. id. X id. du., suff. 2 pers. sing. masc. — עין

בְּעֵינֵיכֶם pref. id. X id. du., suff. 2 pers. pl. masc. — עין

בָּעֵינַיִם pref. בָּ for בְּהָ·, בְּהַ· X id. du. abs. st. pr. n. — עין

בְּעֵינֵינוּ pref. בְּ X id. du., suff. 1 pers. pl. — עין

בְּעֵינֶךָ[k] defect. for בְּעֵינֶיךָ (q. v.) — עין

בָּעִיר[l] for בְּהָעִיר pref. בְּ X n. m. with the art. R. עיר q.v.; or, better (הָעִיר) Hiph. inf. constr. — עור

בָּעִיר pref. בָּ f. בְּהַ·, בְּהָ } noun fem. sing. irr. (§ 45) — עור
בְּעִיר pref. בְּ q. v.

בְּעִיר[m] pref. id. X noun masc. sing. — עיר

בְּעִירֹה[n] noun masc. sing., suff. 3 pers. sing. masc. from [בְּעִיר] dec. 1a. — בער

בְּעִירוֹ[o] וּ pref. בְּ X noun fem. sing., suff. 3 pers. sing. masc. from עִיר irr. (§ 45); וּ bef. (:) — עור

בְּעִירִי[p] pref. id. X id., suff. 1 pers. sing. — עור

בְּעִירְכֶם[q] noun masc. sing., suff. 2 pers. pl. masc. from [בְּעִיר] dec. 1a. — בער

בְּעִירָם[r] וּ id., suff. 3 pers. pl. masc.; וּ bef. (:) — בער

בְּעֵירֹם[s] וּ pref. בְּ X noun masc. sing. dec. 8c; וּ id. — ערם

בְּעִירֵנוּ[t] וּ noun masc. sing., suff. 1 pers. pl. from [בְּעִיר] dec. 1a; וּ id. — בער

בְּעֹכְרַי[u] pref. בְּ X Kal part. act. pl., suff. 1 pers. sing. from עֹכֵר dec. 7b. — עכר

בָּעַל[x] וּ I. *to have dominion, be lord over, possess* any thing.—II. *to become a husband* of any one, *to marry a wife*; part. pl. בֹּעֲלַיִךְ *thy* (sc. God's) *husband*; pass. fem. בְּעוּלָה and בְּעֻלַת בַּעַל *one married*.—III. *to disdain, despise*, const. with בְּ. Niph. *to be married.*

בַּעַל masc. dec. 6 d.—I. *lord, possessor, owner*, and sometimes pl. majest. בְּעָלִים *lord*, &c.—II. *husband*.—III. from the idea of *possessor* various phrases are formed, as בַּעֲלֵי שְׁכֶם *inhabitants of Shechem, Shechemites;* בַּעַל הַקְּרָנַיִם *having two horns;* בַּעַל כְּנָפַיִם *winged;* בַּעַל הַחֲלֹמוֹת *the dreamer;* בַּעַל בְּרִית *confederate;* בַּעַל דְּבָרִים *one having a law-suit*.—IV. הַבַּעַל pr. name *Baal*, the tutelary god of the Phenicians; in pl. *images of Baal*. He was worshipped also under the following names, as בַּעַל בְּרִית *lord of covenant;* בַּעַל זְבוּב *fly-god, fly-destroyer;* בַּעַל פְּעוֹר see פְּעוֹר.—V. pr. name of a town on the borders of Simeon, 1 Ch. 4. 33, probably the same as בַּעֲלַת בְּאֵר Jos. 19. 8.—VI. compounded in the names of towns: בַּעַל גָּד (*Baal of fortune*) a town at the foot of Hermon, Jos. 11. 17.—בַּעַל הָמוֹן (*place of multitude*) at the foot of Lebanon, Cant. 8. 11.—בַּעַל חָצוֹר (*having a village*) a town in the tribe of Benjamin, 2 Sa. 13. 23.—בַּעַל חֶרְמוֹן near mount Hermon.—בַּעַל מְעוֹן (*place of dwelling*) in the tribe of Reuben, see בֵּית מ׳.—בַּעַל פְּרָצִים (*place of defeats*) where David routed the Philistines, comp. 2 Sa. 5. 20.—בַּעַל צְפוֹן (*place of Typhon*, a divinity) a town in Egypt near the Red sea.—בַּעַל שָׁלִשָׁה place in the district of Shalishah, 2 Ki. 4. 42, comp. 1 Sa. 9. 4.—בַּעַל תָּמָר (*place of palms*) not far from Gibeah, Ju. 20. 33.—VII. בַּעַל pr. name masc. of two different persons.—בַּעַל חָנָן (*lord of grace*) pr. name (*a*) of a king of Edom; (*b*) 1 Ch. 27. 28.

בְּעֵל Ch. masc. *lord*, Ez. 4. 8, 9, 17, see טְעֵם.

בַּעֲלָה fem.—I. *a mistress*, comp. בַּעֲלַת אוֹב; בַּעֲלַת כְּשָׁפִים *a sorceress*.—II. pr. name (*a*) of a city in the north of Judah, called also קִרְיַת בַּעַל & קִ׳ יְעָרִים; (*b*) another in the south of Judah, Jos. 15. 29, perhaps the same as בִּלְהָה, בָּלָה.

בְּעָלוֹת pr. name of a city in the tribe of Judah, Jos. 15. 24.

בַּעֲלָת pr. name of a city in the tribe of Dan. For בַּעֲלַת בְּאֵר see בַּעַל No. VI.

בְּעֶלְיָדָע (whom *the Lord knows*) pr. name of a son of David, 1 Ch. 14. 7, called אֶלְיָדָע 2 Sa. 5. 16.

[a] Is. 11. 15. [b] Da. 6. 5. [c] 1 Sa. 29. 1. [d] Da. 2. 23. [e] Le. 21. 20. [f] Ge. 16. 4, 5. [g] Est. 1. 17. [h] Ge. 16. 6. [i] 1 Sa. 1. 23. [k] De. 15. 18. [l] Ps. 73. 20. [m] Ho. 11. 9. [n] Ex. 22. 4. [o] 1 Sa. 28. 3. [p] 2 Sa. 19. 38. [q] Ge. 45. 17. [r] Nu. 20. 11. [s] De. 28. 48. [t] Nu. 20. 4. [u] Ju. 11. 35. [x] Mal. 2. 11.

בַּעַלְיָה (whose *lord is the Lord*) pr. name masc. 1 Ch. 12. 5.

בֵּל (contr. from בְּעֵל i. q. בַּעַל) pr. name of the god of the Babylonians.

בַּלְאֲדָן (whose *lord is Baal*) pr. name of a king of Babylon, father of Merodach-Baladan, 2 Ki. 20. 12.

בַּעַל / וּ בָּעַל } n. m. s. d. 6d, also pr. n. of an idol, and in compos, as בַּעַל בְּרִית &c. . } בעל

[a] בְּעֵל Ch, noun masc. sing. . . . . בעל

[b] בְּעֹל pref. בְּ)(noun masc. sing. dec. 8c. . . עלל

בַּעֲלָה pr. name of a place . . . . בעל

בַּעְלָהּ noun masc. sing., suff. 3 pers. sing. fem. dec. 6d. [for בַּעֲלָהּ § 35. rem. 5] . . בעל

[c] וּ בְעָלָהּ Kal pret. 3 pers. sing. masc., suff. 3 pers. sing. fem.; וּ bef. labial . . . בעל

[d] בְּעָלוּ id. pret. 3 pers. pl. . . . . . בעל

[e] בְּעָלוּנוּ id. id., suff. 1 pers. pl. . . . . בעל

בַּעֲלוֹת pref. בַּ bef. (-:))(Kal inf. constr. . . עלה

[f] בַּעֲלוֹת Kh. i. q. prec.; K. כַּעֲלוֹת (q. v.) . . עלה

וּ בְעָלוֹת pr. name of a place; וּ bef. (:) . . בעל

[g] בְּעֹלוֹת pref. בְּ)(noun fem., pl. of עֹלָה dec. 10. . עלה

בַּעֲלוֹתָהּ pref. בַּ bef. (-:))(Kal inf., suff. 3 pers. sing. fem. dec. 1a. . . . . . . עלה

בַּעֲלוֹתוֹ pref. id.)(id., suff. 3 pers. sing. masc. . עלה

בְּעֹלֹתֵינוּ pref. בְּ)(noun fem. pl., suff. 1 pers. pl. from עֹלָה dec. 10. . . . . . עלה

בַּעֲלוֹתָם pref. בַּ bef. (-:))(Kal inf., suff. 3 p. pl. m. d. 1a. עלה

בַּעֲלָטָה pref. בָּ for בְּהַ·, בְּהָ)(noun fem. sing. . עלט

[l] וּ בַעֲלֵי n. m. pl. constr. fr. בַּעַל d. 6d; וּ bef. lab. בעל

[m] בַּעְלִי id. sing. with suff. 1 pers. sing. . . בעל

[n] בָּעֳלִי pref. בַּ for בְּהַ)(noun masc. sing. . . עלה

וּ בְעֶלְיָדָע pr. name masc.; וּ bef. (:) . . . בעל

וּ בְעַלְיָה pr. name masc.; וּ id. . . . . בעל

בְּעָלֶיהָ noun m. pl., suff. 3 p. s. f. fr. בַּעַל dec. 6d. בעל

בַּעְלֵיהֶן id., suff. 3 pers. pl. fem. . . . . בעל

בְּעָלָיו id., suff. 3 pers. sing. masc. . . . בעל

[p] בְּעֶלְיוֹן pref. בְּ)(adj. masc. sing. dec. 1b. . . עלה

[q] בֹּעֲלַיִךְ Kal part. act. pl, suff. 2 p. s. f. fr. [בֹּעֵל] dec. 7b בעל

[r] בַּעֲלִיל pref. בַּ bef. (-:))(noun masc. sing. . עלל

וּ בַעֲלִילוֹתֶיךָ pref. id.)(noun fem. pl., suff. 2 pers. sing. masc. from עֲלִילָה dec. 10; וּ bef. labial עלל

וּ בַעֲלִילוֹתָם pref. id.)(id., suff. 3 pers. pl. masc.; וּ id. עלל

בַּעֲלִיס [for בֶּן־עֲלִיס *son of exultation*, R. עלס comp. בַּעְנָא] pr. name of a king of the Ammonites, Je. 40. 14.

[ii] בַּעֲלִית pref. id.)(n. f. sing., constr. of עֲלִיָּה d. 10. עלה

[u] בְּעִלִּיתֵהּ Ch. pref. בְּ)(noun fem. sing., suff. 3 pers. sing. masc. from [עִלִּי] dec. 8c. . . עלה

[x] בַּעֲלִיָּתוֹ pref. בַּ bef. (-:))(noun fem. sing., suff. 3 pers. sing. masc. from עֲלִיָּה dec. 10. . עלה

[y] בְּעַלְמָה pref. בְּ)(noun fem. sing. dec. 12a. . . עלם

בְּעַלְמֹן pref. id.)(pr. name of a place, עַלְמֹן דִּבְלָתַיִם, with parag. ה Nu. 33. 46. . . עלם

[z] בַּעֲלֹץ pref. בַּ bef. (-:))(Kal inf. constr. . . עלץ

וּ בַעֲלַת pr. name of a place; וּ bef. labial . . בעל

בַּעֲלַת noun fem. sing., constr. of [בַּעֲלָה], also pr. name in compos. בַּעֲלַת בְּאֵר . בעל

בְּעֻלַת Kal part. p. fem., constr. of בְּעוּלָה, [from בָּעוּל masc.] . . . . בעל

בַּעֲלָתָה pr. name of a place (בַּעֲלָת with loc. ה . בעל

[a] וּ בְעַלְתָּהּ Kal pret. 2 pers. sing. masc., suff. 3 pers. sing. fem.; וּ bef. labial . . . בעל

[b] בַּעֲלֹתוֹ pref. בַּ bef. (-:))(Kal inf. (עֲלוֹת), suff. 3 pers. sing. masc. dec. 1a. . . . עלה

בָּעַלְתִּי Kal pret. 1 pers. sing. . . . . בעל

[c] בַּעֲלֹתִי pref. בַּ bef. (-:))(Kal inf., suff. 1 p. s. d. 1a. עלה

[d] בַּעֲלֹתְךָ pref. id.)(id., suff. 2 pers. sing. masc. . עלה

בָּעָם / [e] וּ בְעַם } pref. בָּ f. בְּהַ·, בְּהָ | pref. בְּ q. v. } noun com. s. d. 8, pl. irr. (§ 45); וּ bef. (:) } עמם

[f] וּ בְעַמֻּד defect. for עַמּוּד (q. v.) . . עמד

[g] בְּעָמְדוֹ pref. בְּ)(Kal inf., suff. 3 pers. sing. masc. עמד

[h] וּ בְעָמְדָם pref. id.)(id., suff. 3 p. pl. m.; וּ bef. (:) עמד

בְּעַמּוֹ pref. id.)(noun com. sing., suff. 3 pers. sing. masc. from עַם or עָם dec. 8. (§ 45) עמם

וּ בְעַמּוּד pref. id.)(noun m. s. dec. 1b; וּ bef. lab. עמד

[i] בְּעַמֵּי pref. id.)(noun com. pl. constr. from עַם or עָם dec. 8. (§ 45) . . . . עמם

בְּעַמִּי pref. id.)(id. sing., suff. 1 pers. sing. . עמם

בְּעַמָּיו pref. id.)(id. pl., suff. 3 pers. sing. masc. עמם

בְּעַמֶּיךָ pref. id.)(id. pl., suff. 2 pers. sing. masc. עמם

בָּעַמִּים pref. בָּ f. בְּהַ·, בְּהָ)(id. pl. abs. . . עמם

[k] בְּעָמִיר pref. בְּ)(noun masc. sing. . . עמר

בַּעֲמִיתוֹ pref. בַּ bef. (-:))(noun fem. sing., suff. 3 pers. sing. masc. from [עָמִית] dec. 3a. עמה

וּ בְעַמְּךָ / [l] וּ בְעַ֫מְּךָ } pref. בְּ)(noun com. s., suff. 2 pers. sing. masc. from עַם or עָם dec. 8. (§ 45) } עמם

בַּעֲמַל pref. בַּ bef. (-:))(constr. for the following עמל

[m] [n] וּ בֶעָמָל pref. בֶּ for בְּהַ·, בְּהֶ)(noun masc. sing. dec. 4c; וּ bef. labial . . . עמל

בַּעֲמָלוֹ pref. בַּ bef. (-:))(id., suff. 3 pers. sing. masc. עמל

[o] וּ בַעֲמָלְךָ pref. id.)(id., suff. 2 p. s. m.; וּ bef. lab. עמל

Ezr. 4. 8, 9, 17. Je. 27. 8, 11, 12. De. 24. 1. 1 Ch. 4. 22. Is. 26. 13.
[f] Jos. 4. 18; 6. 15. [g] 1 Sa. 15. 22. [h] 1 Sa. 2. 19. [i] Ju. 11. 13. [ii] Ju. 3. 20.
[k] Jos. 22. 27. [l] 2 Sa. 1. 6. [m] Ho. 2. 18. [n] Pr. 27. 22.
[o] Est. 1. 17. [p] Ps. 73. 11. [q] Is. 54. 5. [r] Ps. 12. 7.
[s] Ps. 77. 13. [t] Eze. 36. 17. [u] Da. 6. 11. [x] 2 Ki. 1. 2.
[y] Pr. 30. 19. [z] Pr. 28. 12. [a] De. 21. 13. [b] 1 Sa. 15. 2.
[c] De. 9. 9. [d] Ex. 34. 24. [e] Eze. 17. 9. [f] Nu. 14. 14.
[g] Ge. 41. 46. [h] Eze. 1. 21. [i] Ezr. 9. 2, 14. [k] Zec. 12. 6.
[l] Ex. 22. 27. [m] Ps. 107. 12. [n] Ec. 2. 11. [o] Ec. 9. 9.

בַּעֲמָלָם [a] pref. id.)(id., suff. 3 pers. pl. masc. . עמל
בַּעֲמָלֵק pref. id.)(pr. name of a people . . עמלק
בַּעֲמָמֶיךָ [b] pref. id.)(noun com. pl., suff. 2 pers. sing. masc. irr. of עַם (§ 45) . . עמם
בָּעֵמֶק [c] וּ׳ pref. בָּ f. בְּהָ, בְּהַ· } noun masc. sing. dec. 6b; וּ bef. lab. } עמק
בְּעֵמֶק pref. בְּ q. v. }
בְּעִמְקֵי [d] pref. id.)(id. pl., construct state . . עמק
בָּעֲמָקִים [e] pref. בָּ f. בְּהָ, בְּהַ· } id. pl., absolute state . עמק
בַּעֲמָקִים [f] pref. בַּ before (ֲ) }
בָּעֹמֶר [g] pref. בָּ for בְּהָ, בְּהַ·)(noun masc. sing. dec. 6c. עמר
בָּעֳמָרִים [h] pref. id.)(id. pl. absolute state . עמר
בְּעֹן וּ pr. name see בֵּית בַּעַל מְעוֹן under . בית
בַּעֲנָא } [for בֶּן־עֲנָא son of affliction R. ענה, see
בַּעֲנָה } בִּשְׁלָם] pr. name m. of several persons.
בָּעֳנִי [i] pref. בָּ bef. (ֳ))(n. m. s. (constr. st.) d. 6k. ענה
בְּעָנְיוֹ [k] pref. בְּ)(id., suff. 3 pers. sing. masc. . ענה
בְּעָנְיִי pref. id.)(id., suff. 1 pers. sing. . . ענה
בְּעִנְיַן [l] pref. id.)(noun m. s., constr. of עִנְיָן dec. 2b. ענה
בֶּעָנָן [m] וּ׳ pref. בֶּ for בְּהָ, בְּהַ)(n. m. s. d. 4c; וּ bef. lab. ענן
בְּעַנְנִי [n] pref. בְּ)(Piel inf. [עַנֵּן], suff. 1 pers. sing. dec. 7b. [for עַנְּנִי comp. § 10. rem. 7] . ענן
בְּעַנְפּוֹהִי [qq] וּ Ch. pr. בְּ)(n. m. pl., suff. 3 m. s. [fr. עֲנַף] d. 3a. ענף
בָּעֲנָקִים pref. בָּ for בְּהָ, בְּהַ·)(pr. name of a people, pl. of עֲנָק . . . . . ענק
בַּעֲנֹשׁ־ [o] pref. בַּ bef. (ֲ))(Kal inf. c., for עֲנֹשׁ (§ 8. r. 18) ענש
בַּעֲנָתוֹת }
בַּעֲנָתֹת } pref. id.)(pr. name of a place . . ענה
בָּעֹפֶל pref. בָּ for בְּהָ, בְּהַ·)(pr. name of a place עפל
בַּעְפָלִים [p] [q] וּ׳ K. בַּטְּחֹרִים; pref. בַּ, n. m. pl. R. טָחַר; Kh. בָּעֳפָלִים, pref. בָּ, pl. of עֹפֶל dec. 6c. . עפל
בְּעַפְעַפֵּי [r] pref. בְּ)(n. m. du. constr. fr. [עַפְעַף] dec. 8d. עוף
בְּעַפְעַפֶּיהָ [s] pref. id.)(id., suff. 3 pers. sing. fem. . עוף
בֶּעָפָר [t] וּ׳ pref. בֶּ for בְּהָ, בְּהַ)(noun m. s. dec. 4c. עפר
בְּעָפְרָה pref. בְּ)(pr. name of a place . . . עפר
בְּעֶפְרוֹן pref. id.)(pr. name masc. . . . עפר
בְּעָפְרַת pref. id.)(pr. name of a place, constr. of עָפְרָה עפר
בָּעֵץ pref. בָּ f. בְּהָ, בְּהַ· } noun masc. sing. dec. 7a. } עצה
בְּעֵץ [u] [x] וּ׳ pref. בְּ q. v. } (§ 36. rem. 2) }
בְּעֶצֶב [y] pref. id.)(noun masc. sing., dec. 6a. . עצב
בְּעֹצֶב [z] pref. id.)(noun masc. sing. dec. 6c. . עצב
בְּעִצָּבוֹן [a] pref. id.)(noun masc. sing. dec. 3c. . . עצב
בְּעַצְּבַת [b] וּ pref. id.)(noun fem. sing. constr., [as if from עַצְּבָה] see עַצֶּבֶת; וּ bef. lab. . עצב
בְּעֵצָה pref. id.)(noun fem. sing. dec. 11b. . יעץ
בְּעֵצוֹ [c] pref. id.)(noun masc. sing., suff. 3 pers. sing. masc. from עֵץ dec. 7a. (§ 36. rem. 2) . עצה

בַּעֲצוּמָיו [d] pref. בַּ bef. (ֲ))(noun masc. pl. (עֲצוּמִים), suff. 3 pers. sing. masc. . . . ם
בַּעֲצֵי [e] וּ׳ pref. בַּ bef. (ֲ))(noun masc. pl. constr. from עֵץ dec. 7a. (§ 36. rem. 2); וּ bef. lab. ה
בְּעֶצְיוֹן pref. בְּ)(pr. name in compos. עֶצְיוֹן גֶּבֶר . ה
בָּעֵצִים וּ pref. בָּ f. בְּהָ, בְּהַ· } noun masc. pl. abs. fr. } ה
בְּעֵצִים [e] pref. בְּ q. v. } עֵץ dec. 7a; וּ bef. lab. }
בְּעֶצְיֹן pr. name defect. for עֶצְיוֹן (q. v.) . ה
בַּעֲצַלְתַּיִם [f] pref. בַּ bef. (ֲ))(n. fem., dual of [עַצֶלֶת] d. 13a. ל
בָּעֶצֶם [g] pref. בָּ for בְּהָ } n. f. s., (suff. עַצְמִי) dec. 6a, } ם
בְּעֶצֶם pref. בְּ q. v. } also pr. n. of a place; וּ bef. (ְ) }
בְּעֹצֶם [h] pref. id.)(noun masc. sing. dec. 6c. . ם
בַּעֲצָמוֹת [i] וּ pref. בַּ bef. (ֲ))(noun fem. pl. abs. from עֶצֶם dec. 6a. (comp. the following) . ם
בְּעַצְמוֹת [k] pref. id.)(id. pl., construct state . ם
בְּעַצְמוֹתַי [l] pref. id.)(id. pl., suff. 1 pers. sing. . ם
בְּעַצְמוֹתָיו pref. id.)(id. pl., suff. 3 pers. sing. masc. . ם
בַּעֲצָמַי pref. בַּ bef. (ֲ))(id. pl. m., suff. 1 pers. sing. ם
בְּעָצְמַת [m] pref. בְּ)(n. fem. s. constr. [of עָצְמָה; no pl.] ם
בְּעַצְמֹתַי [n] } pref. בְּ)(noun fem. pl., suff. 1 pers. sing. } ם
בְּעַצְמֹתָי [o] } from עֶצֶם dec. 6a. . . . }
בְּעַצְּרֹתֵיכֶם [p] pref. id.)(n. f. pl., suff. 2 pers. pl. masc. from עֲצָרָה dec. 11c. (§ 42. rem. 1) ר
בַּעֲצַת pref. בַּ bef. (ֲ))(n. f. s., constr. of עֵצָה d. 11b.
בַּעֲצָתְךָ [q] pref. id.)(id., suff. 2 pers. sing. masc. .
בַּעֲצָתָם pref. id.)(id., suff. 3 pers. pl. masc. . .
בַּעֲקֵב [r] pref. id.)(constr. of the following (§ 34. r. 1) ב
בְּעָקֵב [s] pref. בְּ)(noun masc. sing. dec. 5. (§ 35. r. 4) ב
בְּעָקְבָהּ [t] pref. id.)(noun sing. fem. . . . ב
בְּעִקְבֵי [u] pref. id.)(n. m. pl. constr. fr. עָקֵב d. 5. (§ 35. r. 4) ב
בַּעֲקְרַבִּים pref. בָּ for בְּהָ, בְּהַ·)(n. m., pl. of עַקְרָב d. 8a. רב

בָּעַר I. to consume, burn up with fire; metaph. of ang[er], const. mostly with בְּ.—II. intrans. to burn.—[...] denom. of בְּעִיר, to be brutish, part. בֹּעֲרִים bru[tish] men. Niph. to become brutish. Pi.—I. to f[eed] upon, to consume, as a field, vineyard, with בְּ[...] II. to consume with fire; to kindle, to set on f[ire] with בְּ.—III. to remove, to destroy, with מִן, [אַח]ֲרֵי [...] Pu. to be kindled, to burn. Hiph.—I. to feed upon[...] II. to consume with fire; to kindle, to set on f[ire] with בְּ.—III. to remove, destroy.

בַּעַר masc. stupid, brutish.

בַּעֲרָא (stupid) pr. name fem. 1 Ch. 8. 8.

בְּעֵרָה fem. a burning, Ex. 22. 5.

בְּעוֹר (torch) pr. name—I. of the father of Bala[am] —II. of the father of Bela king of the Edomite[s]

---

[a] Ec. 4. 9.
[b] Ju. 5. 14.
[c] Jos. 13. 27.
[d] Pr. 9. 18.
[e] Je. 49. 4.
[f] 1 Ch. 27. 29.
[g] Ex. 16. 18.
[h] Ruth 2. 7.
[i] 1 Sa. 1. 11.
[k] Job 36. 15.
[l] Ec. 5. 13.
[m] De. 1. 33.
[n] Ge. 9. 14.
[o] Pr. 21. 11.
[p] 1 Sa. 5. 6, 12.
[q] De. 28. 27.
[r] Job 3. 9.
[s] Pr. 6. 25.
[t] Job 14. 8.
[u] Eze. 15. 6.
[x] Le. 14. 52.
[y] Ge. 3. 16.
[z] 1 Ch. 4. 9.
[a] Ge. 3. 17.
[b] Pr. 15. 13.
[c] Ho. 4. 12.
[d] Ps. 10. 10.
[e] Zec. 12. 6.
[f] Ec. 10. 18.
[g] Nu. 19. 18.
[h] Job 30. 21.
[i] Job 10. 11.
[k] 2 Ki. 13. 21.
[l] Ps. 42. 11.
[m] Is. 47. 9.
[n] Je. 20. 9.
[o] La. 1. 13.
[p] Am. 3. 21.
[q] Ps. 73. 24.
[qq] Da. 4. 9, 10.
[r] Ge. 25. 26.
[s] Job 18. 9.
[t] 2 Ki. 10. 1[...]
[u] Ca. 1. 8.

בְּעִיר masc. dec. 1b.—I. *beasts, cattle*, generally, collect.—II. *beasts* of burden.

תַּבְעֵרָה (*burning*) pr. name of a place in the desert.

[a]בְּעַר, [b]וָ׳ בְעַר } noun masc. sing.; וָ see וּ — בער

בָּעֵר Piel inf. constr. — בער

בְּעָר pref. בְּ)(pr. name of a place — עור

בְּעֹר pr. name masc. for בְּעוֹר — בער

בִּעֵר וּ׳ Pi. (dag. forte impl. § 14. r. 1) pret. 3 p. s. m. — בער

בֹּעֵר Kal part. act. sing. dec. 7b. — בער

בַּעְרָא pr. name fem. — בער

בָּעֲרָב, בַּעֲרָב } pref. בַּ bef. (-:))(pr. name of a country — ערב

בָּעֲרָב in pause for בַּעֲרָב (q. v.) — ערב

[c]בָּעֶרֶב pref. בָּ for בְּהַ, בְּהָ)(noun masc. sing. — ערב

בָּעֶרֶב וּ׳ pref. id.)(noun masc. sing., (du. עַרְבַּיִם) dec. 6a; וּ bef. lab. — ערב

[d]בְּעֶרֶב pref. בְּ)(noun masc. sing. — ערב

[e]בְּעֶרֶב pref. id.)(noun m. sing. (du. עַרְבַּיִם) dec. 6a. — ערב

בָּעֲרָבָה וּ׳ pref. בָּ for בְּהַ, בְּהָ)(noun fem. sing. dec. 11c. (§ 42, rem. 1); וּ bef. lab. — ערב

בָּעֲרָבוֹת pref. id.)(id. pl., absolute state — ערב

בְּעַרְבוֹת pref. בְּ)(id. pl., construct state — ערב

בָּעַרְבִים pref. בָּ for בְּהַ, בְּהָ)(gent. noun masc., pl. of עַרְבִי, from עֲרָב — ערב

בָּעֹרְבִים pref. בָּ for בְּהַ)(Kal part. act. m., pl. of עֹרֵב d. 7b. — ערב

בְּעַרְבֹת pref. בְּ)(noun fem. pl. constr. from עֲרָבָה dec. 11c. (§ 42. rem. 1) — ערב

בָּעֲרָה וּ׳ Kal pret. 3 pers. sing. fem.; וּ bef. lab. — בער

[h]בֹּעֵרָה, בֹּעֲרָה } id. part. act., sing. fem. from בֹּעֵר masc. (§ 39. No. 3. rem. 4) — בער

בָּעֲרוּ וּ׳ id. pret. 3 pers. pl.; וּ bef. lab. — בער

[k]בִּעֲרוּ וּ Piel (dag. forte impl. § 14. r. 1) pret. 3 p. pl.; וּ id. — בער

[l]בְּעוֹרוֹ pref. בְּ)(n. m. s., suff. 3 p. s. m. fr. עוֹר d. 1a. — עור

בַּעֲרוֹעֵר pref. בַּ bef. (-:))(pr. name of a place — ערר

בַּעֲרֹעֵר וּ pref. בְּ)(pr. n. of a place, see עֲרוֹעֵר; וּ bef. (:) — ערר

[m]בַּעֲרִיץ pref. בַּ bef. (-:))(noun masc. sing. — ערץ

[n]בֹּעֲרוֹת Kal part. act. fem., pl. of בֹּעֵרָה or בֹּעֶרֶת [from בֹּעֵר masc.] — בער

בְּעָרֵי וּ׳ pref. בְּ)(noun fem. pl. constr. of עָרִים irr. of עִיר (§ 45); וּ bef. (:) — עור

[o]בְּעָרֶיהָ pref. id.)(id. pl., suff. 3 pers. sing. fem. — עור

בְּעָרֵיהֶם pref. id.)(id. pl., suff. 3 pers. pl. masc. — עור

בְּעָרָיו וּ׳ pref. id.)(id. pl., suff. 3 p. s. m.; וּ bef. (:) — עור

בְּעָרֵיכֶם pref. id.)(id. pl., suff. 2 pers. pl. masc. — עור

בֶּעָרִים pref. בֶּ for בְּהַ, בְּהָ)(id. pl., absolute state — עור

בֹּעֲרִים Kal part. act. masc., pl. of בֹּעֵר dec. 7b. — בער

[q]בְּעָרֵינוּ pref. בְּ)(noun fem. pl. (עָרִים), suff. 1 pers. pl., irr. of עִיר (§ 45) — עור

[r]בַּעֲרִיפֶיהָ pref. בַּ bef. (-:))(noun masc. pl., suff. 3 pers. sing. fem. from [עָרִיף] dec. 1a. — ערף

[s]בְּעֶרְכְּךָ, בְּעֶרְכְּךָ } pref. בְּ)(noun masc. sing., suff. 2 pers. sing. m. from עֵרֶךְ dec. 6. (§ 35. r. 6) — ערך

[t]בְּעָרְלָה pref. id.)(noun fem. sing. dec. 12c. — ערל

בְּעָרְמָה pref. id.)(noun fem. sing. — ערם

[u]בְּעָרְמָם pref. id.)(n. m. s., suff. 3 p. pl. m. fr. [עֹרֶם] d. 6c. — ערם

בַּעֲרֹעֵר defect for עֲרוֹעֵר (q. v.) — ערר

[x]בְּעָרֶף pref. בְּ)(noun masc. sing. dec. 6c. — ערף

[y]בְּעָרְפִּי pref. id.)(id., suff. 1 pers. sing. — ערף

[z]בָּעֲרָפֶל pref. בָּ f. בְּהַ, בְּהָ }
[a]בַּעֲרָפֶל pref. בַּ bef. (-:) } noun masc. sing. — ערף

[b]בִּעַרְתָּ Piel (dag. forte impl. § 14. r. 1) pret. 2 p. s. m. — בער

בִעַרְתָּ וּ׳ id. id.; acc. shifted by conv. וּ (bef. lab.) — בער

[c]בֹּעֶרֶת Kal part. act. sing. fem. dec. 13, from בֹּעֵר m. — בער

[d]בִּעַרְתִּי וּ׳ Piel (dag. forte impl. § 14. r. 1) pret. 1 pers. s. — בער

בִעַרְתִּי וּ id. id.; acc. shifted by conv. וּ (bef. lab.) — בער

[e]בִּעַרְתִּיהָ id. id. with suff. 3 pers. sing. fem. — בער

בִּעַרְתֶּם id. pret. 2 pers. pl. masc. — בער

בַּעְשָׁא pr. name of a king of Israel.

[f]בַּעֲשַׂב Chald. pref. בַּ bef. (-:))(noun m. s. dec. 3b. — עשב

[g]בְּעֵשֶׂב וּ pref. בְּ)(n. m. s. d. 6. (§ 35. r. 6); וּ bef. lab. — עשב

[h]בֶּעָשׂוֹר וּ׳ pref. בֶּ for בְּהַ, בְּהָ)(noun masc. sing. — עשר

[i]בַּעֲשׂוֹת pref. בַּ bef. (-:))(Kal inf. constr. dec. 1a. — עשה

בַּעֲשׂוֹתִי pref. id.)(id., suff. 1 pers. sing. — עשה

[k]בַּעֲשׂוֹתְךָ pref. id.)(id., suff. 2 pers. sing. masc. — עשה

[l]בַּעֲשׂוֹתֵךְ pref. id.)(id., suff. 2 pers. sing. fem. — עשה

בְּעֹשֵׂי pref. בְּ)(Kal part. pl. constr. m. fr. עֹשֶׂה d. 9a. — עשה

בַּעֲשֵׂיָה (perhaps for מַעֲשֵׂיָה *work of the Lord*) pr. name masc. 1 Ch. 6. 25.

[m]בְּעֹשָׂיו pref. id.)(Kal part. pl. masc., suff. 3 pers. sing. masc. from עֹשֶׂה dec. 9a. — עשה

[n]בָּעֲשִׂירִי pref. בָּ for בְּהַ, בְּהָ)(adj. ord. sing. masc. — עשר

בֶּעָשָׁן pref. בֶּ f. בְּהַ, בְּהָ }
[o]בְּעָשָׁן pref. בְּ q. v. } noun masc. sing. dec. 4c. — עשן

[p]בָּעֹשֶׁק pref. בָּ f. בְּהַ }
בְּעֹשֶׁק pref. בְּ q. v. } noun masc. sing. — עשק

[q]וּבְעֹשְׁקֵי וּ pref. id.)(Kal part. act. pl. constr. masc. from עֹשֵׁק dec. 7b. — עשק

[r]בַּעְשֵׂר [for בְּהַעְשֵׂר] pref. בְּ; Hiph. inf. constr. (§ 11. rem. 3. & § 13. rem. 9. also 1, 2) — עשר

[s]בָּעֶשֶׂר pref. בָּ for בְּהַ, בְּהָ)(noun masc. sing. — עשר

בְּעָשְׂרוֹ pref. בְּ)(n. m. s., suff. 3 p. s. m. fr. עֹשֶׁר d. 6c. — עשר

בָּעֲשִׂרִי defect. for בָּעֲשִׂירִי (q. v.) — עשר

---

[a] Pr. 12. 1. [b] Ps. 49. 11. [c] Le. 13. 49, 51, 53, 57. [d] Le. 13. 48. [e] Pr. 7. 9. [f] Ps. 68. 5. [g] Pr. 22. 26. [h] Is. 30. 33. [i] Is. 1. 31. [k] Eze. 39. 9, 9. [l] Le. 13. 18, 24. [m] Job 30. 6. [n] Eze. 1. 13. [o] 2 Ki. 17. 24. [p] Je. 31. 23. [q] Ezr. 10. 14. [r] Is. 5. 30. [s] Le. 27. 27, 27. [t] Je. 9. 24. [u] Job 5. 13. [x] Ge. 49. 8. [y] Job 16. 12. [z] 1 Ki. 8. 12. [a] 2 Ch. 6. 1. [b] 2 Ch. 19. 3. [c] Je. 20. 9. [d] De. 26. 13, 14. [e] Eze. 21. 4. [f] Da. 4. 12. [g] Ex. 10. 15. [h] Nu. 29. 7. [i] Eze. 23. 21. [k] Is. 64. 2. [l] Eze. 16. 30. [m] Ps. 149. 2. [n] Ge. 8. 5. [o] Ps. 102. 4. [p] Eze. 22. 7, 12. [q] Mal. 3. 5. [r] Ne. 10. 39. [s] Ex. 12. 3.

בְּעֶשְׂרִים pref. בְּ) num. card. com. gen., pl. of עֶשְׂרָה see עָשָׂר . . . . . עשר

בַּעֲשֹׂתָהּ[a] pref. בַּ bef. (-:)) Kal inf. (עֲשׂוֹת) suff. 3 pers. sing. fem. dec. 1a. . . . . . עשה

בַּעֲשֹׂתוֹ pref. id.) id., suff. 3 pers. sing. masc. . עשה

בְּעַשְׁתֵּי pref. בְּ) n. m. pl. constr. from עֶשֶׁת dec. 6a. עשת

בְּעֶשְׁתְּרָה (for בֵּית עֶשְׁתְּרָה *temple of Astarte*) pr. name of a Levitical city in Manasseh, Jos. 21. 27. called עַשְׁתָּרוֹת 1 Ch. 6. 56.

בְּעַשְׁתָּרוֹת, בְּעַשְׁתֹּרֶת } pref. בְּ) pr. name of a place, see עַשְׁתֹּרֶת

בְּעַשְׁתְּרֹת pref. id.) pr. name in compos. עַשְׁתְּרֹת קַרְנַיִם see עַשְׁתֹּרֶת.

בָּעַת. Niph. *to be terrified*, const. with מִפְּנֵי. Pi.—I. *to terrify, alarm.*—II. *to come upon suddenly*, 1 Sa. 16. 14.

בְּעָתָה fem. *terror.*

בִּעוּתִים masc. pl. (of בִּעוּת dec. 1b) *terrors.*

בָּעֵת ו׳ pref. בָּ f. בְּהַ·, בְּהָ) noun com. sing. dec. 8b; ו bef. (:) . עדה

בְּעֵת ו׳ pref. בְּ (q. v.) } (as above) עדה

בְּעָתָה noun fem. sing. . . . . . . בעת

בְּעִתָּהּ[b] pref. בְּ) noun com. sing., suff. 3 pers. sing. fem. from עֵת dec. 8b. . . . . עדה

בִּעֲתֻהוּ[c] Piel (dag. forte impl. § 14. rem. 1) pret. 3 pers. pl., suff. 3 pers. sing. masc. [for בִּעֲתוּהוּ] בעת

בְּעִתּוֹ pref. בְּ) noun com. sing., suff. 3 pers. sing. masc. from עֵת dec. 8b. . . . . עדה

בָּעִתִּים[d] ו׳ pref. בָּ f. בְּהַ·, בְּהָ) id. pl., absolute state; ו bef. lab. עדה

בְּעִתִּים[e] pref. בְּ q. v. } (as above) עדה

בַּעֲתָךְ pref. בַּ bef. (-:)) pr. name of a place עתך

בְּעִתָּם pref. בְּ) id. sing., suff. 3 pers. sing. masc. עדה

בִּעֲתַתּוּ[f] ו Piel pret. 3 pers. sing. fem. [בִּעֲתָה § 14. rem. 1], suff. 3 pers. s. m. [for בִּעֲתַתְהוּ] בעת

בִּעֲתַתְנִי[g] id., suff. 1 pers. sing. [for בִּעֲתַתְנִי] . בעת

בִּפְאַת[h] pref. בִּ bef. (:)) noun fem. sing., constr. of פֵּאָה dec. 11b. . . . פאה

בְּפִגְעוֹ[i] pref. בְּ) Kal inf. (פְּגֹעַ), suff. 3 pers. sing. masc. (§ 16. rem. 10) . . . פגע

בְּפִגְרֵי[k] ו׳׳ pref. id.) noun masc. pl. constr. from פֶּגֶר dec. 6a; ו bef. (:) . . . פגר

בְּפַדַּן pref. id.) pr. name in compos. פַּדַּן אֲרָם פדן

בְּפֹה[m] pref. id.) noun masc. sing. [for פֵּאָה § 45] פאה

בַּפּוּךְ pref. בַּ for בְּהַ) noun masc. sing. פוך

בְּפוּנֹן pref. בְּ) pr. name of a place . פון

בַּפָּז[n] pref. בַּ for בְּהַ) noun masc. sing. פזז

בְּפַח pref. id.) for פַּח, n. m. s., pl. פַּחִים (§ 37. r. 7) פחח

בְּפַחַד[o] pref. בְּ) noun masc. sing. dec. 6d. . פחד

בְּפַחֲזוּתָם[p] ו pref. id.) noun fem. sing., suff. 3 pers. pl. masc. from [פַּחֲזוּת] dec. 1; ו bef. lab. . פחז

בַּפֶּחָם[q] pref. בַּ for בְּהַ) noun masc. sing. . פחם

בְּפִי[r] ו׳ pref. בְּ) n. m. s. constr., or with suff. 1 p. s. [for פִּאִי] from פֶּה irr. (§ 45); ו bef. (:) פאה

בְּפִידִי pref. id.) noun masc. sing. dec. 1a. . פיד

בְּפִידוֹ pref. id.) id., suff. 3 pers. sing. masc. . פיד

בְּפִיהָ pref. id.) noun masc. sing., suff. 3 pers. sing. fem. from פֶּה irr. (§ 45) . . . פאה

בְּפִיהוּ pref. id.) id., suff. 3 pers. sing. masc. . פאה

בְּפִיהֶם pref. id.) id., suff. 3 pers. pl. masc. . פאה

בְּפִיו pref. id.) id., suff. 3 pers. sing. masc. . פאה

בְּפִיךָ pref. id.) id., suff. 2 pers. sing. masc. . פאה

בְּפִיךְ[s] pref. id.) id., suff. 2 pers. sing. fem. . פאה

בְּפִיכֶם pref. id.) id., suff. 2 pers. pl. masc. . פאה

בְּפִילַגְשׁוֹ[x] pref. id.) noun fem. sing., suff. 3 pers. sing. masc. from פִּילֶגֶשׁ dec. 6a. (§ 35. rem. 16) פלגש

בְּפִילַגְשִׁי[y] pref. id.) id., suff. 1 pers. sing. . . פלגש

בְּפִימוֹ[z] pref. id.) noun masc. sing., suff. 3 pers. pl. from פֶּה irr. (§ 45) . . . פאה

בִּפְלַגּוֹת pref. בִּ bef. (:)) n. fem., pl. of [פְּלַגָּה] d. 10. פלג

בִּפְלֻגָּתְהוֹן[a] Chald. pref. id.) noun fem. pl., suff. 3 pers. pl. masc. from [פְּלֻגָּה] dec. 8a. . פלג

בַּפֶּלֶךְ[b] pref. בַּ for בְּהַ) n. m. s., [suff. פִּלְכוֹ] d. 6a. פלך

בִּפְלִלִים[c] pref. בִּ bef. (:)) n. m., pl. of [פָּלִיל] d. 3a. פלל

בַּפֶּלֶס[d] pref. בַּ for בְּהַ) noun masc. sing. . פלס

בַּפְּלִשְׁתִּים ו׳ pref. id.) gent. noun masc., pl. of פְּלִשְׁתִּי from פְּלֶשֶׁת . . . . פלש

בְּפֻם[e] Chald. pref. בְּ) noun masc. sing. dec. 3c. . פום

בְּפֻמַּהּ[f] Chald. pref. id.) id., suff. 3 pers. sing. fem. פום

בִּפְנוֹתָם[g] pref. בִּ bef. (:)) Kal inf. (פְּנוֹת), suff. 3 pers. pl. masc. dec. 1a. . . . . פנה

בְּפָנַי[h] pref. בְּ) noun masc. pl., suff. 1 pers. sing. from [פָּנֶה] dec. 9b. . . . . פנה

בִּפְנֵי pref. בִּ bef. (:)) id. pl., constr. state . פנה

בְּפָנֶיהָ[k] pref. בְּ) id. pl., suff. 3 pers. sing. fem. . פנה

בִּפְנֵיהֶם pref. בִּ bef. (:)) id. pl., suff. 3 pers. pl. m. פנה

בְּפָנָיו pref. בְּ) id. pl., suff. 3 pers. sing. masc. . פנה

בְּפָנֶיךָ pref. id.) id. pl., suff. 2 pers. sing. masc. פנה

בִּפְנֵיכֶם pref. בִּ bef. (:)) id. pl., suff. 2 pers. pl. m. פנה

בְּפָנִים[l] pref. בְּ) id. pl., absolute state . פנה

בַּפְּנִימִי[m] pref. בַּ for בְּהַ) adj. masc. sing. dec. 1a. פנם

בְּפַס דַּמִּים pref. id.) pr. n. of a place, see אֶפֶס דַּמִּים

בִּפְסִילֵיהֶם[n] ו pref. בִּ bef. (:)) noun masc. pl., suff. 3 pers. pl. masc. from [פָּסִיל] dec. 3a. פסל

בַּפָּסֶל[o] pref. בַּ for בְּהַ) for פֶּסֶל noun masc. sing. פסל

---

[a] Le. 4. 27. [b] Is. 60. 22. [c] Job 18. 11. [d] Da. 11. 6. [e] Ne. 13. 31. [f] 1 Sa. 16. 14. [g] Is. 21. 4. [h] Am. 3. 12. [i] Nu. 35. 19, 21. [k] Is. 66. 24. [l] Eze. 43. 7. [m] Pr. 11. 9. [n] La. 4. 2. [o] Ge. 31. 53. [p] Je. 23. 32. [q] Is. 44. 12. [r] Pr. 11. 11.

[s] Job 31. 29. [t] Job 30. 24. [u] Eze. 16. 56. [x] Ju. 19. 25, 29. [y] Ju. 20. 6. [z] Ps. 58. 7. [a] Ezr. 6. 18. [b] 2 Sa. 3. 29. [c] Ex. 21. 22. [d] Is. 40. 12. [e] Da. 4. 28. [f] Da. 7. 5. [g] Eze. 29. 16. [h] Job 16. 8. [i] Eze. 42. 12. [k] Nu. 12. 14. [l] De. 5. 4. [m] Eze. 41. 17. [n] Ps. 78. 58. [o] Is. 42. 17.

בִּפְסִלֵיהֶם[a] defect. for בִּפְסִילֵיהֶם (q. v.) . . . פסל
בְּפֹעַל[b] pref. בְּ) noun masc. sing. dec. 6f. . . פעל
בְּפָעָלְךָ[c] pref. id.) id., suff. 2 pers. s. m., for פָּעָלְךָ פעל
בְּפָעֳלָם[d] pref. id.) id., suff. 3 pers. pl. masc. . פעל
בַּפַּעַם pref. בַּ for בְּהַ } noun fem. sing. dec. 6 d. פעם
בְּפַעַם } pref. בְּ q. v.
בַּפָּעַם
בִּפְקֹד[e] pref. בְּ bef. (:)) Kal inf. constr. . . פקד
בְּפִקָּדוֹן[f] pref. בְּ) noun masc. sing. . . . פקד
בְּפִקֻּדֶיךָ[g] } pref. בְּ) noun masc. pl., suff. 2 pers. sing. masc. [פִּקּוּד] dec. 1 b. . פקד
בְּפִקּוּדֶיךָ[h]
בַּפָּרִ[i] pref. בַּ for בְּהַ } noun masc. sing. pl. פָּרִים (§ 37. rem. 7) . פרר
בְּפַר pref. בְּ q. v.
וּבַפְּרָדִים pref. בַּ for בְּהַ) noun masc., pl. of פֶּרֶד (suff. פִּרְדּוֹ) dec. 6 a; וּ bef. labial . פרד
בַּפָּרוּר pref. id.) noun masc. sing. . . . פרר
בַּפַּרְוָרִים[k] pref. id.) noun m., pl. of פַּרְוָר, see פַּרְבָּר
וּבַפְּרִזִּי pref. id.) pr. n. of a people; וּ bef. labial פרז
בִּפְרֹחַ[l] pref. בְּ bef. (:)) Kal inf. constr. . . פרח
וּבִפְרִי pref. id.) noun masc. s. d. 6i; וּ bef. lab. פרה
בְּפִרְיוֹ[m] pref. בְּ) id., suff. 3 pers. sing. masc. . פרה
בַּפָּרִים[n] pref. id.) noun m., pl. of פַּר (§ 37. r. 7) פרר
בְּפָרֶךְ[o] וּ } pref. בְּ) noun masc. sing. (§ 35. r. 2) פרך
בְּפָרֶךְ[p]
בְּפַרְסוֹת[q] pref. id.) noun fem., pl. of פַּרְסָה dec. 12 a. פרס
בִּפְרֹעַ[r] pref. בְּ bef. (:)) Kal inf. constr. . . פרע
בְּפַרְעֹה pref. בְּ) pr. name masc., see פַּרְעֹה
בְּפִרְעָתוֹן pref. id.) pr. name of a place . . פרע
בַּפֶּרֶץ pref. בַּ for בְּהַ) noun masc. sing. (pl. with suff. פִּרְצֵיהֶם) dec. 6 a. . . . פרץ
בַּפְּרָצוֹת[s] pref. id.) id. pl., absolute state . פרץ
בְּפָרֵשׂ[t] pref. בְּ) Piel inf. constr. . . . פרש
וּבְפָרָשָׁיו pref. id.) noun masc. pl., suff. 3 pers. sing. m. fr. פָּרָשׁ dec. 1 b. (§ 30. r. 1); וּ bef. (:) פרש
וּבַפָּרָשִׁים[u] pref. id.) id. pl., absolute state; וּ id. . פרש
וּבְפָרֶשְׂכֶם[x] pref. id.) Piel inf. (פָּרֵשׂ), suff. 2 pers. pl. masc. dec. 7 b; וּ id. . . . פרשׂ
בִּפְרָת pref. בְּ bef. (:)) pr. name of a river . פרת
בַּפּשׁ[y] pref. בַּ for בְּהַ) noun masc. sing. . . פוש
בְּפֶשַׁע[z] } pref. בְּ) noun masc. sing., d. 6 a. (suff. פִּשְׁעִי dec. 6 a. § 35. rem. 5) . פשע
בַּפֶּשַׁע
וּבְפִשְׁעֵיכֶם[a] pref. id.) id. pl., suff. 2 p. pl. m.; וּ bef. (:) פשע
בְּפִשְׁתֵּי[b] pref. id.) constr. of the following . פשת
בַּפִּשְׁתִּים[c] pref. בַּ for בְּהַ) noun fem. with pl. masc. term. fr. פִּשְׁתָּה dec. 10. . . . פשת
בַּפְּתָאִים[d] pref. id.) n. m., pl. of פֶּתִי d. 6i. (§ 35. r. 15) פתה

בְּפִתְאֹם[e] pref. בְּ) adv. for פִּתְעֹם . . פתע
בְּפַתְבַּג[f] pref. id.) n. m. s., constr. of [פַּתְבָּג] d. 2 b. פתבג
וּבְפִתּוֹתֵי[g] pref. בְּ bef. (:)) noun masc. pl. constr. fr. [פְּתוֹת] dec. 1 a; וּ bef. labial . פתת
בַּפֶּתַח[h] } pref. בַּ f. בְּהַ } noun masc. sing., d. 6 a. (suff. פִּתְחוֹ § 35. r. 5) פתח
בְּפֶתַח[i]
בְּפֶתַח pref. בְּ q. v.
וּבְפִתְחֵי[k] וּ pref. id.) id. pl., constr. state; וּ bef. (:) פתח
בְּפִתְחִי[m] pref. id.) Kal inf. [פְּתֹחַ], suff. 1 pers. sing. (§ 35. rem. 5) . . . . פתח
בִּפְתָחֶיהָ[n] pref. בְּ bef. (:)) noun masc. pl., suff. 3 pers. sing. fem. (see בְּפֶתַח) . . . פתח
בִּפְתִיל pref. id.) n. m. s., constr. of פָּתִיל d. 3 a. פתל
בְּפֶתַע pref. בְּ) prop. masc. n., used as an *adv.* פתע
בְּפַתְרוֹס pref. id.) pr. name of a region, see פַּתְרוֹס
בַּצֹּאן וּ pref. בַּ f. בְּהַ } noun masc. sing. dec. 1 a. צאן
בְּצֹאן pref. בְּ q. v.
בְּצֹאנְךָ[o] } pref. id.) id., suff. 2 pers. sing. masc.; וּ bef. labial . . . . צאן
וּבְצֹאנְךָ[p]
בְּצֹאנָם[q] pref. id.) id., suff. 3 pers. pl. masc. . צאן
בְּצֹאנֵנוּ[r] pref. id.) id., suff. 1 pers. pl. . . צאן
בְּצֵאת pref. id.) Kal inf. constr. [for צֵאת § 25. No. 2, comp. § 23. rem. 2 & 4] . . יצא
וּבְצֵאתוֹ pref. id.) id., suff. 3 pers. s. m.; וּ bef. (:) יצא
בְּצֹאתָיו[s] noun fem. pl., suff. 3 pers. sing. masc., for [בְּצוֹתָיו] from בִּצָּה dec. 10. . . בצץ
בְּצֵאתִי pref. בְּ) Kal inf. with suff. 1 p. s. comp. בְּצֵאת יצא
בְּצֵאתְךָ } pref. id.) id., suff. 2 pers. sing. masc. יצא
בְּצֵאתְךָ
בְּצֵאתְכֶם[t] pref. id.) id., suff. 2 pers. pl. masc. . יצא
וּבְצֵאתָם pref. id.) id., suff. 3 p. pl. m.; וּ bef. lab. יצא
בַּצָּבָא pref. בַּ for בְּהַ) n. m. s. d. 4 a. (§ 34. r. 2) צבא
בִּצְבָאוֹת pref. בְּ bef. (:)) noun masc. with pl. fem. term. from צְבִי dec. 6i. (§ 35. rem. 15) צבה
בְּצִבְאוֹתֵינוּ } pref. בְּ) n. m., with pl. fem. term. & suff. 1 pers. pl. from צָבָא dec. 4 a. צבא
בְּצִבְאֹתֵינוּ[u]
וּבַצַּבִּים[x] pref. בַּ for בְּהַ) noun masc., pl. of צָב dec. 8 a; וּ bef. labial . . צבב
בְּצַד pref. בְּ) noun masc. sing. dec. 8 e. . צדד
בְּצִדָּהּ[y] pref. id.) id., suff. 3 pers. sing. fem. . צדד
בִּצְדִיָּה[z] pref. בְּ bef. (:)) noun fem. sing. . צדה
בְּצִדֵּיכֶם pref. בְּ) noun masc. pl., suff. 2 pers. pl. masc. from צַד dec. 8 e. . . . צדד
בַּצֶּדֶק[a] pref. בַּ f. בְּהַ } noun masc. sing., suff. צִדְקִי dec. 6 a. . . צדק
בְּצֶדֶק pref. בְּ q. v.
בְּצִדְקָה[b] Chald. pref. id.) noun fem. sing. . צדק

[a] Je. 8. 19. [b] Ps. 9. 17. [c] Ps. 92. 5. [d] Job 24. 5. [e] Ex. 30. 12, 12. [f] Le. 5. 21. [g] Ps. 119. 78. [h] Ps. 119. 15. [i] Eze. 43. 22. [k] 2 Ki. 23. 11. [l] Ps. 92. 8. [m] Ca. 8. 11. [n] 1 Sa. 1. 24. [o] Eze. 34. 4. [p] Le. 25. 53. [q] Eze. 26. 11. [r] Ju. 5. 2. [s] Eze. 13. 5. [t] Ps. 68. 15. [u] Joel 2. 4. [x] Is. 1. 15. [y] Job 35. 15. [z] Da. 8. 12. [a] Is. 50. 1. [b] Jos. 2. 6. [c] Le. 13. 52. [d] Pr. 7. 7. [e] 2 Ch. 29. 36. [f] Da. 1. 8. [g] Eze. 13. 19. [h] 2 Ki. 4. 15. [i] 1 Ki. 14. 6. [k] Pr. 1. 21. [l] Eze. 33. 30. [m] Eze. 37. 13. [n] Mi. 5. 5. [o] Ge. 31. 41. [p] De. 15. 19. [q] Ho. 5. 6. [r] Ex. 10. 9. [s] Eze. 47. 11. [t] De. 23. 5, etc. [u] Ps. 108. 12. [x] Is. 66. 20. [y] Ge. 6. 16. [z] Nu. 35. 20. [a] Pr. 25. 5. [b] Da. 4. 24.

בִּצְדָקָה וּ' pref. בְּ bef. (:))(n. f. s. d. 11c; וּ bef. lab. — צדק

בְּצִדְקוֹ[a] pref. בְּ)(noun masc. sing., suff. 3 pers. sing. masc. from צֶדֶק dec. 6a. — צדק

בְּצִדְקָתוֹ pref. id.)(noun fem. sing., suff. 3 pers. sing. masc. from צְדָקָה dec. 11c. — צדק

בְּצִדְקָתִי pref. id.)(id., suff. 1 pers. sing. — צדק

בְּצִדְקָתְךָ, בְּצִדְקָתְךָ[b] וּ' pref. id.)(id., suff. 2 pers. sing. masc.; וּ bef. labial — צדק

בְּצַדֶּקְתֵּךְ[c] pref. id.)(Piel inf. [צַדֶּקֶת § 10. r. 2], suff. 2 pers. sing. fem. dec. 13b. — צדק

בְּצִדְקָתָם[d] pref. id.)(noun fem. sing., suff. 3 pers. pl. masc. from צְדָקָה dec. 11c. — צדק

בִּצָּה[e] וּ'[f] noun fem. sing. dec. 10; וּ bef. labial — בצץ

בַּצָּהֳרַיִם, בַּצָּהֳרָיִם pref. בַּ for בְּהַ)(noun fem., du. of צֹהַר dec. 6f. (§ 35. rem. 9. & 16) — צהר

בְּצַוָּאר pref. בְּ)(n. m. s. d. 2b. (comp. § 30. r. 1) — צור

בְּצַוָּארוֹ[g] pref. id.)(id., suff. 3 pers. sing. masc. — צור

בְּצַוְּארֵי[h] pref. id.)(id. pl., constr. state — צור

בַּצּוֹם pref. בַּ for בְּהַ; בְּצוֹם וּ'[i] pref. בְּ q. v. } noun masc. sing. dec. 1; וּ bef. (:) — צום

בְּצֹעַר pref. id.)(pr. name of a place — צער

בְּצוֹק[k] וּ pref. id.)(noun masc. sing.; וּ bef. (:) — צוק

בַּצּוּר pref. בַּ for בְּהַ; בְּצוּר וּ'[l] pref. בְּ q. v. } noun masc. s. d. 1a; וּ id. — צור

בְּצוּרָה Kal part. pass. s. f. d. 10, [from בָּצוּר m.] — בצר

בַּצּוּרוֹת[m] pref. בַּ for בְּהַ)(noun masc. with pl. fem. term. from צוּר dec. 1a. — צור

בְּצוּרוֹת[n], בְּצוּרֹת[o] וּ' Kal part. pass. fem., pl. of בְּצוּרָה d. 10 [from בָּצוּר masc.]; וּ bef. (:) — בצר

בְּצַוֹּת[p] pref. בְּ)(Kal inf. const. dec. 1b. — צוה

בְּצַוֹּתוֹ[q] pref. id.)(id., suff. 3 pers. sing. masc. — צוה

בַּצַּחְיֳיִם[r] pref. בַּ for בְּהַ)(adj. masc. Kh. צְחִיִים, K. צְחִים [pl. of צְחִיחִי] — צחח

בְּצַחְצָחוֹת[s] pref. בְּ)(noun fem. pl. [of צַחְצָחָה] — צחח

בֵּצַי for בֵּצָי pr. name masc. — בוץ

בַּצִּיָּה[t] pref. בַּ for בְּהַ)(noun fem. sing. dec. 10. — ציה

בְּצִיּוֹן pref. בְּ)(noun masc. sing. — ציה

בְּצִיּוֹן pref. id.)(pr. name of a place — ציה

בַּצִּיּוֹת[u] pref. בַּ for בְּהַ)(noun fem., pl. of צִיָּה d. 10. — ציה

בְּצִיִּים[x] pref. id.)(noun m., pl. of צִי (comp. § 3. r. 1) — ציה

בְּצִיצִת[y] pref. בְּ)(noun fem. sing. — צוץ

בָּצִיר וּ'[z] noun masc. sing. dec. 3a; וּ bef. lab. — בצר

בְּצִירֵךְ[a] id. with suff. 2 pers. sing. fem. — בצר

בָּצַל Root not used; Arab. *to strip, peel.*

בָּצָל masc. only pl. בְּצָלִים *onions* Nu. 11. 5.

בַּצְלוּת (*nakedness*) pr. name masc. Ezr. 2. 52, called בַּצְלִית Ne. 7. 54.

בַּצֵּל[b] pref. בַּ for בְּהַ; בְּצֵל וּ' pref. בְּ q. v. } noun masc. sing. dec. 8b; וּ bef. (:) — צלל

בְּצַלְאֵל וּ' pref. id.)(pr. name masc. — צלל

בְּצִלָּהּ[c] pref. id.)(n.m.s., suff. 3 p. s. fem. fr. צֵל d. 8b. — צלל

בְּצִלּוֹ[d] וּ' pref. id.)(id., suff. 3 pers. sing. masc. — צלל

בַּצְלוּת pr. name masc. — בצל

בַּצַּלַּחַת pref. בַּ for בְּהַ)(noun fem. sing. — צלח

בַּצֵּלָחוֹת[e] וּ pref. id.)(n. fem. pl. [of צְלָחָה]; וּ bef. lab. — צלח

בְּצִלִּי[f] pref. בְּ)(n. m. s., suff. 1 p. s. from צֵל d. 8b. — צלל

בַּצְלִית pr. name masc., see בַּצְלוּת — בצל

בְּצֶלֶם pref. בְּ)(noun m. s. dec. 6a. (see the foll.) — צלם

בְּצַלְמוֹ pref. id.)(id., suff. 3 pers. sing. masc. — צלם

בְּצַלְמוֹן pref. id.)(pr. name of a mountain — צלם

בְּצַלְמָוֶת[g] pref. id.)(n. f. s., compound of צֵל and מָוֶת — צלל

בְּצַלְמֹנָה pref. id.)(pr. name of a place — צלם

בְּצַלְמֵנוּ[h] pref. id.)(n. m. s., suff. 1 p. pl. fr. צֶלֶם d. 6a. — צלם

בְּצֶלַע[i] pref. id.)(n. fem. s., constr. of צֵלָע dec. 4c. (§ 33. No. 2. r. 3); also pr. name of a place — צלע

בְּצַלְעוֹת[k] pref. id.)(id. pl., construct state — צלע

בְּצַלְעִי[l] וּ pref. id.)(noun m. sing., suff. 1 pers. sing. from צֶלַע dec. 6a. (§ 35. rem. 5); וּ bef. (:) — צלע

בְּצֶלְצַח pref. id.)(pr. name of a place — צלל

בְּצִלְצַל[m] וּ pref. id.)(noun m. s. [for צִלְצַל, constr. of צְלָצַל] for צֵל comp. d. 4, & 12c; וּ bef. (:) — צלל

בְּצִלְצְלֵי[n] pref. id.)(id. pl., constr. st.; (for צל comp. § 36. r. 5) — צלל

בְּצֶלְצְלִים[o] וּ pref. id.)(id. pl., absolute state; וּ bef. (:) — צלל

בַּצָּמָא pref. בַּ for בְּהַ; בְּצָמָא וּ pref. בְּ q. v. } noun m. sing. dec. 4a; וּ id. — צמא

בַּצֶּמֶר[p] pref. בַּ for בְּהַ)(n. m. s. (suff. צַמְרִי) d. 6a. — צמר

בְּצִנָּה[q] pref. בְּ)(noun fem. sing. dec. 10. — צנן

בַּצִּנּוֹר[r] pref. בַּ for בְּהַ)(noun masc. sing. dec. 1b. — צנר

בְּצִנּוֹת[s] pref. בְּ)(noun fem., pl. of צִנָּה dec. 10. — צנן

בָּצַע I. *to break,* or *cut off, to break in pieces.* In Joel 2. 8, perhaps intrans., or the word *course* is to be implied.—II. *to spoil, plunder;* hence *to acquire unjust gain.* Pi.—I. *to cut off,* (as the weaver his web from the loom Is. 38. 12).—II. *to defraud,* Eze. 22. 12.—III. *to finish, complete.* Hence

בֶּצַע, בָּצַע } m. d. 6a. (with suff. בִּצְעוֹ § 35. r. 5. & 3. 2). —I. *plunder, unjust gain.*—II. *gain, profit* in general — בצע

[a] Ec. 7. 15. [b] Ps. 89. 17. [c] Eze. 16. 52. [d] Eze. 14. 14, 20. [e] Job 8. 11. [f] Job 40. 21. [g] Job 41. 14. [h] Ju. 8. 21, 26. [i] Joel 2. 12. [k] Da. 9. 25. [l] Job 22. 24. [m] Job 28. 10. [n] Eze. 36. 35. [o] Ne. 9. 25. [p] 2 Sa. 18. 5. [q] Eze. 10. 6. [r] Ne. 4. 7. [s] Is. 58. 11. [t] Ps. 78. 17. [u] Ps. 105. 41. [x] Eze. 30. 9. [y] Eze. 8. 3. [z] Le. 26. 5. [a] Je. 48. 32. [b] Jon. 4. 5.

[c] Is. 34. 15. [d] Eze. 31. 6. [e] 2 Ch. 35. 13. [f] Ju. 9. 15. [g] Ps. 44. 20. [h] Ge. 1. 26. [i] 2 Sa. 16. 13. [k] 1 Ki. 6. 15, 15, 16. [l] Ps. 35. 15. [m] Job 40. 31. [n] Ps. 150. 5. [o] 2 Sa. 6. 5. [p] Le. 13. 52. [q] 1 Ch. 12. 34. [r] 2 Sa. 5. 8. [s] Am. 4. 2.

[a]בְּצֹעַ Kal inf. constr. . . . . . בצע

[b]בִּצַּע Piel pret. 3 pers. sing. masc. . . . בצע

בֹּצֵעַ [c]וְ Kal part. act. sing. masc.; וּ bef. lab. . בצע

בְּצַעֲדְךָ pref. בְּ)(Kal inf. [צְעֹד], suff. 2 pers. sing. masc. (§ 16. rem. 10) . . . . צעד

[d]בִּצְעוֹ n.m.s., suff. 3 p.s.m.fr. בֶּצַע d. 6a. (§ 35. r. 5) בצע

[e]בַּצָּעִיף pref. בַּ for בְּהַ)(noun masc. sing. dec. 3a. . צעף

[f]בִּצְעִירוֹ וּ pref. בְּ bef. (:))(adj. masc. sing., suff. 3 pers. sing. masc. from צָעִיר dec. 3a; וּ bef. lab. צער

[g]בִּצְעֲךָ noun masc. sing., suff. 2 pers. sing. masc. [for בִּצְעֲךָ] from בֶּצַע dec. 6a. (§ 35. rem. 5) . בצע

בִּצְעֵךְ id., suff. 2 pers. sing. fem. . . . בצע

בִּצְעָם id., suff. 3 pers. pl. masc. . . . בצע

[h]בַּצְּעֵם וּ Kal imp. sing. masc. [בְּצַע], suff. 3 pers. pl. masc. [for בַּצְּעֵם] § 16. rem. 11; וּ bef. lab. בצע

בְּצֹעַן pref. בְּ)(pr. name of a place . צען

בְּצַעֲנַנִּים Kh. / בְּצַעֲנַנִּים K. } pref. id.)(pr. name of a place . צען

[i]בַּצָּפוֹן pref. בַּ for בְּהַ)(noun masc. sing. dec. 3a. צפן

[k]בַּצַּפַּחַת pref. id.)(noun fem. sing. צַפַּחַת . צפח

[l]בְּצִפִּיָּתֵנוּ pref. בְּ)(n.fem.s., suff. 1 p.pl.fr. [צִפִּיָּה] d. 10. צפה

[m]בְּצִפֹּר וּ pref. id.)(noun com. sing. (pl. צִפֳּרִים § 30. rem. 1); וּ before labial . . צפר

[n]בַּצְפַרְדְּעִים pref. בַּ for בְּהַ)(n.com., pl. of צְפַרְדֵּעַ d. 7b. צפרדע

[o]בְּצִפָּרְןָ pref. בְּ)(noun masc. sing. dec. 6c. . צפר

בָּצַץ Root not used; Arab. *to flow slowly, trickle.*

בֹּץ masc. *mire, mud,* Jer. 38. 22.

בִּצָּה fem. *a marsh, fen;* pl. with suff. בִּצֹּאתָיו for בִּצּוֹתָיו.

בּוֹצֵץ (*shining,* בצץ Arab. *to shine* comp. בּוּץ) pr. name of a rock near Gibeah, 1 Sa. 14. 4.

[בָּצַק] *to swell,* spoken of the feet.

בָּצֵק masc. dec. 5a, *dough.*

בָּצְקַת (*elevation*) pr. name of a city in the tribe of Judah.

בָּצֵק noun masc. sing. dec. 5a. . . . בצק

[p]בָּצֵקָה Kal pret. 3 p. s. fem. [for בָּצְקָה § 8. r. 1. & 7] בצק

[q]בָּצֵקוּ id. pret. 3 pers. pl. [for בָּצְקוּ see prec.] . בצק

[r]בְּצֵקוֹ n. m. s., suff. 3 pers. s. m. from בָּצֵק dec. 5a. בצק

בְּצִקְלַג וּ pref. בְּ)(pr. name of a place; וּ bef. (:) צקלג

[s]בְּצִקְלֹנוֹ pref. id.)(noun masc. sing., suff. 3 pers. sing. masc. from [צִקָּלוֹן] dec. 1b. . . צקל

[t]בְּצֶקֶת pref. id.)(Kal inf. constr. . . יצק

בָּצְקַת וּ pr. name of a place; וּ bef. lab. . בצק

[בָּצַר] I. *to cut off.*—II. *to prune the vine.*—III. *to gather the vintage;* part. בֹּצֵר *a vintager,* metaph. of a destructive enemy.—IV. part. pass. בָּצוּר *inaccessible, fortified, strong,* access to it being *cut off;* metaph. *incomprehensible,* Je. 33. 3. Niph. *to be cut off, restrained,* with מִן. Pi. *to make inaccessible, to fortify.*

בָּצִיר masc. dec. 3a.—I. *vintage.*—II. adj. *fortified* (comp. R. No. IV.) Zec. 11. 2. Keri.

בְּצַר masc. *gold,* Job 36. 19.

בֶּצֶר masc. dec. 6, in pause בָּצֶר.—I. *gold.*—II. pr. name of a city in the tribe of Reuben.—III. pr. name masc. 1 Ch. 7. 37.

בָּצְרָה fem.—I. *fold for cattle,* Mic. 2. 12.—II. pr. name of the capital of Edom.

בִּצָּרוֹן masc. *fortress, strong-hold,* Zec. 9. 12.

בַּצֹּרֶת fem. pl. בַּצָּרוֹת (§ 44. rem. 5) *withholding of rain, drought.*

מִבְצָר masc. dec. 2b. pl. ־ִים & ־וֹת.—I. *fortification;* עִיר מִבְצָר *a fortified city.*—II. pr. name of a prince of the Edomites, Ge. 36. 42.

[u]בַּצָּר / בַּצָּר } pref. בַּ for בְּהַ)(noun masc. sing. pl. צָרִים (§ 37. rem. 7) . . . צרר

[x]בֶּצֶר noun masc. sing. for [בֶּצֶר] dec. 6a. . . בצר

[y]בְּצָר noun masc. sing. [for בֶּצֶר] . . . בצר

[z]בְּצָר pref. בְּ)(noun m. sing., pl. צָרִים (§ 37. r. 7) צרר

בֶּצֶר pr. name of a man and a place . בצר

[a]בָּצְרָה perhaps noun fem. sing., (after the form קָלְסָה, בַּקָּשָׁה) . . . בצר

בַּצָּרָה pref. בַּ for בְּהַ / [b]בְּצָרָה [c]וְ pref. בְּ q. v. } n.fem.s.d.10. [for צָרָה fr. צַר m. § 37. r. 7; וּ bef. (:) צרר

בָּצְרָה noun fem. sing. (Mic. 2. 12); also pr. name בצר

בִּצְרוֹר pref. בְּ bef. (:))(noun masc. sing. dec. 1a. צרר

בְּצָרוֹת pref. בְּ)(noun fem., pl. of צָרָה dec. 10. . צרר

בְּצֻרוֹת וְ Kal part. pass. fem., pl. of בְּצוּרָה dec. 10. [from בָּצוּר masc.] . . . בצר

[d]בַּצְּרִחִים וּ pref. בַּ for בְּהַ)(noun masc., pl. of [צְרִיחַ] dec. 3a; וּ bef. lab. . . . צרח

[e]בְּצָרָיו pref. בְּ)(noun masc. pl., suff. 3 pers. sing. masc. from צַר (§ 37. rem. 7) . צרר

[f]בְּצָרֶיךָ n. m. pl., suff. 2 p. s. m. from [בֶּצֶר] dec. 6. בצר

בֹּצְרִים Kal part. act. m., pl. of [בֹּצֵר] dec. 7b. . בצר

[g]בַּצֹּרֶת noun fem. sing., (comp. בַּצָּרָה) . . בצר

[h]בַּצֹּרֶת וְ defect. for בַּצּוֹרוֹת (q. v.) . . בצר

[i]בַּצָּרָתָה pref. בַּ for בְּהַ)(n.f.s. (צָרָה q.v.) with ה parag. צרר

בַּקְבֻּק pr. name masc. . . . . בקק

[k]בִּקְבוּרָה pref. בְּ bef. (:))(noun fem. sing. dec. 10. . קבר

a Eze. 22. 27. b La. 2. 17. c Ps. 10. 3. d Is. 57. 17. e Ge. 38. 14. f Jos. 6. 26. g Je. 22. 17. h Am. 9. 1. i Ec. 11. 3. k 1 Ki. 17. 12. l La. 4. 17. m Le. 14. 52. n Ex. 7. 27. o Je. 17. 1. p De. 8. 4. q Ne. 9. 21. r Ex. 12. 34. s 2 Ki. 4. 42. t Job 38. 38. u Ps. 4. 2. x Job 22. 24. y Job 36. 19. z Job 7. 11. a Ps. 10. 1. b Ps. 91. 15. c Ne. 9. 37. d 1 Sa. 13. 6. e Ps. 112. 8. f Job 22. 25. g Je. 17. 8. h De. 3. 5; 9. 1. i Ps. 120. 1. k Is. 14. 20.

Word	Analysis	Root
בְּקַבְּצִי[a]	pref. בְּ)(Piel inf. (קַבֵּץ), suff. 1 p. s. d. 7 b.	קבץ
בַּקְבֻּק[b]	[c] וּ' noun masc. sing.)(וּ bef. lab. . .	בקק
בַּקְבֻּקְיָה	וּ pr. name masc.; וּ id. . . .	בקק
בַּקְבַּקַּר	וּ pr. name masc.; וּ id. . . .	בקק
בַּקָּבֶר[d], בַּקֶּבֶר	pref. בַּ f. בְּהַ } noun masc. sing. dec. 6 a. (§ 35. rem. 2; but with suff. קִבְרוֹ) .	קבר
בְּקָבֶר[e], בְּקֶבֶר	pref. בְּ q.v. } noun masc. sing. dec. 6 a. (§ 35. rem. 2; but with suff. קִבְרוֹ) .	קבר
בְּקִבְרוֹ[f]	pref. id.)(id., suff. 3 pers. sing. masc. .	קבר
בְּקִבְרוֹת	[g] וּ' pref. id.)(id. pl. constr. fem. . .	קבר
בְּקִבְרִי[h]	pref. id.)(id. sing., suff. 1 pers. sing. .	קבר
בַּקְּבָרִים[i]	pref. בַּ for בְּהַ)(id. pl., absolute state .	קבר
בְּקִבְרֹת	וּ pref. בְּ)(pr. name in compos. קִבְרֹת הַתַּאֲוָה	קבר
בִּקְבֻרָתוֹ	pref. בְּ bef. (:))(noun fem. sing., suff. 3 pers. sing. m. from קְבוּרָה dec. 10. . .	קבר
בְּקִבְרֹתָיו[k]	pref. בְּ)(noun masc. with pl. fem. term. and suff. 3 pers. sing. masc. from קֶבֶר dec. 6 a.	קבר
בִּקְבֻרָתָם[l]	pref. בְּ bef. (:))(noun f. sing., suff. 3 pers. pl. masc. from קְבוּרָה dec. 10. . .	קבר
בַּקַּדַּחַת[m]	וּ pref. בַּ for בְּהַ)(noun fem. sing.; וּ bef. lab.	קדח
בִּקְדוֹשׁ	pref. בְּ bef. (:))(adj. m. s., constr. of קָדוֹשׁ d. 3 a.	קדשׁ
בַּקֹּדֶשׁ	pref. בַּ for בְּהַ } noun masc. sing. dec. 6 c. .	קדשׁ
בְּקֹדֶשׁ	pref. בְּ q. v. } noun masc. sing. dec. 6 c. .	קדשׁ
בְּקָדֵשׁ	pref. id.)(pr. name of a place, also in compos. קָדֵשׁ בַּרְנֵעַ	קדשׁ
בְּקָדְשׁוֹ	pref. id.)(noun masc. sing, suff. 3 pers. sing. masc. from קֹדֶשׁ dec. 6 c. . . .	קדשׁ
בִּקְדֹשָׁו[n]	pref. בְּ bef. (:))(adj. pl. masc., suff. 3 pers. sing. masc. (§ 4. rem. 1) from קָדוֹשׁ dec. 3 a.	קדשׁ
בְּקָדְשִׁי[o]	pref. בְּ)(n. m. s., suff. 1 p. s. fr. קֹדֶשׁ d. 6 c.	קדשׁ
בַּקְּדֵשִׁים[p]	pref. בַּ for בְּהַ)(n. masc. pl. of קָדֵשׁ dec. 5 a.	קדשׁ
בַּקֳּדָשִׁים[q]	pref. id.)(noun masc., pl. of קֹדֶשׁ dec. 6 c. .	קדשׁ
בַּקָּהָל	pref. id. } noun m. sing. dec. 4 a; וּ bef. lab.	קהל
בְּקָהָל	[r] וּ' pref. בְּ } noun m. sing. dec. 4 a; וּ bef. lab.	קהל
בִּקְהַל	[s] וּ' pref. בְּ bef. (:))(id., constr. st.; וּ id.	קהל
בִּקְהָלָם[t]	pref. id.)(id., suff. 3 pers. pl. masc. . .	קהל
בִּקְהֵלָתָה	pref. id.)(pr. name of a place . .	קהל
בַּקָּו[u]	pref. בַּ for בְּהַ)(n. m. s. d. 8 a. (§ 37. No. 4)	קוה
בְּקוֹל	וּ' pref. בְּ)(noun m. sing. dec. 1 a; וּ bef. (:)	קול
בְּקוֹלָהּ	pref. id.)(id., suff. 3 pers. sing. fem. .	קול
בְּקוֹלוֹ	[x] וּ' pref. id.)(id., suff. 3 pers. s. m.; וּ bef. (:)	קול
בְּקוֹלִי	[y] וּ' pref. id.)(id., suff. 1 pers. sing.; וּ id.	קול
בְּקוֹלֵךְ[z]	pref. id.)(id., suff. 2 pers. sing. fem. .	קול
בְּקוֹלֶךָ	pref. id.)(id., suff. 2 pers. sing. m. for קוֹלְךָ	קול
בְּקוֹלָם	pref. id.)(id., suff. 3 pers. pl. masc. .	קול
בְּקוֹלֵנוּ[a]	pref. id.)(id., suff. 1 pers. pl. . . .	קול
בְּקוּם	[b] וּ' pref. id.)(Kal inf. constr.; וּ bef. lab.	קום
בְּקוֹמָה[c]	pref. id.)(noun fem. sing. dec. 10. .	קום
בְּקוּמָהּ[d]	וּ pref. id.)(Kal inf., suff. 3 p. f. s. d. 1 a; וּ bef. lab.	קום
בְּקוּמוֹ[e]	pref. id.)(id., suff. 3 pers. sing. masc. .	קום
בְּקוּמֶךָ	וּ pref. id.)(id., suff. 2 pers. sing. masc. [for קוּמְךָ]; וּ bef. (:)	קום
בְּקוֹמָתָם[f]	pref. id.)(noun fem. sing., suff. 3 pers. pl. masc. from קוֹמָה dec. 10. . . .	קום
בַּקּוֹצֵר[g]	pref. בַּ for בְּהַ)(Kal part. act. s. m. d. 7 b.	קצר
בְּקַחְתּוֹ	pref. בְּ)(Kal inf. (קַחַת § 17. rem. 8), suff. 3 pers. sing. masc. dec. 13 a. (§ 44. No. 1)	לקח
בְּקַחְתֵּךְ[h]	pref. id.)(id., suff. 2 pers. sing. fem. .	לקח
בַּקָּטֹן[i]	וּ pref. בַּ for בְּהַ)(adj. m. s., d. 3 a; וּ bef. lab.	קטן
בֻּקִּי	וּ' pr. name masc.	בקק
בְּקִיאוֹ	pref. בְּ)(noun masc. sing., suff. 3 pers. sing. masc. from קִיא dec. 1 a.	קוא
בֻּקִּיָּהוּ	pr. name masc.	בקק
בְּקִיטוֹר[k]	pref. בְּ)(noun masc. sing.	קטר
בְּקִינוֹתֵיהֶם[l]	pref. id.)(noun fem. pl., suff. 3 pers. pl. masc. from קִינָה dec. 10. . . .	קון
בְּקִיעֵי[m]	noun masc. pl. constr. of [בְּקִיעַ] dec. 1 a.	בקע
בַּקַּיִץ	pref. בַּ for בְּהַ)(noun masc. sing. 6 h. .	קוץ
בַּקִּיר	וּ' pref. id. } noun masc. sing. dec. 1 a; וּ bef. labial . .	קיר
בְּקִיר	pref. בְּ q.v. } noun masc. sing. dec. 1 a; וּ bef. labial . .	קיר
בְּקִירוֹת[n], בְּקִירֹת[o]	pref. id.)(id. pl. fem. . . .	קיר
בְּקָל[p]	Ch. pref. id.)(noun masc. sing. . .	קול
בְּקֹלָהּ[q]	pref. id.)(noun masc. sing., suff. 3 pers. sing. fem. from קוֹל dec. 1 a. . .	קול
בְּקֹלוֹ	[r] וּ' pref. id.)(id., suff. 3 p. s. m.; וּ bef. lab.	קול
בְּקָלוֹן[s]	pref. id.)(noun masc. sing. dec. 3 a. . .	קלה
בַּקַּלַּחַת[t]	pref. בַּ for בְּהַ)(noun fem. sing. . .	קלח
בְּקֹלִי	pref. בְּ)(n. m. s., suff. 1 p. s. fr. קוֹל d. 1 a.	קול
בְּקֹלֶךָ[u]	pref. id.)(id., suff. 2 pers. s. m., for קוֹלְךָ	קול
בְּקֹלְכֶם	pref. id.)(id., suff. 2 pers. pl. masc. .	קול
בְּקַלְלוֹ[x]	pref. id.)(Piel inf. (קַלֵּל § 10. rem. 7), suff. 3 pers. sing. masc. dec. 7 b. . .	קלל
בְּקֹלֵנוּ[y]	pref. id.)(noun masc. sing., suff. 1 pers. pl. from קוֹל dec. 1 a.	קול
בַּקֶּלַע[z]	pref. בַּ for בְּהַ)(n. m. s., (suff. קַלְעוֹ) d. 6 a.	קלע
בַּקָּמָה[a]	pref. id.)(noun fem. sing. dec. 10. .	קום
בְּקָמוֹן	pref. בְּ)(pr. name of a place . .	קום
בְּקֻמָהּ[b]	וּ defect. for בְּקוּמָהּ (q. v.) . . .	קום
בְּקָמוֹת[c]	pref. בְּ)(noun fem., pl. of קָמָה dec. 10.	קום

[a] Eze. 28. 25. [b] Je. 19. 1. [c] 1 Ki. 14. 3. [d] Nu. 19. 18. [e] Nu. 19. 16. [f] 1 Ki. 13. 30. [g] De. 9. 22. [h] Ge. 50. 5. [i] Is. 65. 4. [k] 2 Ch. 16. 14. [l] Ge. 47. 30. [m] De. 28. 22. [n] Job 15. 15. [o] Ps. 89. 36. [p] Job 36. 14. [q] Le. 22. 4. [r] Eze. 17. 17. [s] Eze. 23. 24. [t] Ge. 49. 6. [u] Is. 34. 17. [x] Jos. 24. 24. [y] Je. 3. 13. [z] 1 Sa. 25. 35. [a] 2 Sa. 12. 18. [b] Pr. 28. 12. [c] Eze. 31. 10. [d] Ge. 19. 33. [e] Is. 2. 19, 21. [f] Eze. 31. 14. [g] Am. 9. 13. [h] Eze. 16. 61. [i] Ge. 44. 12. [k] Ps. 119. 83. [l] 2 Ch. 35. 25. [m] Is. 22. 9. [n] 1 Ki. 6. 6. [o] Le. 14. 37, 39. [p] Da. 6. 21. [q] Ge. 21. 12. [r] De. 13. 5. [s] Ho. 4. 7. [t] 1 Sa. 2. 14. [u] Da. 9. 11. [x] 2 Sa. 16. 7. [y] De. 21. 20. [z] 1 Sa. 17. 50. [a] De. 16. 9. [b] Ge. 19. 35. [c] Ju. 15. 5.

בְּקָמֵיהֶם[a] pref. בְּ) Kal part. pl. masc., suff. 3 pers. pl. masc. from קָם dec. 1 a. . . קום

בַּקָּמִים[b] pref. בַּ for בְּהַ) id. pl., absolute state . קום

בְּקָמְצוֹ[c] pref. בְּ) noun masc. sing., suff. 3 pers. sing. masc. fr. [קֹמֶץ] dec. 6 c. (§ 35. r. 8) קמץ

בְּקָמַת[d] pref. id.) noun f. s. constr. of קָמָה d. 10. קום

בְּקַנְאוֹ[e] pref. id.) Piel inf. [קַנֵּא], suff. 3 pers. sing. masc. dec. 7 b. (comp. § 10. rem. 7) . קנא

בְּקַנְאתוֹ[f] pref. id.) id. [קַנֹּאת § 23. r. 2 & 9], suff. 3 p. s. m. קנא

בְקִנְאָתִי[g] ו' pref. id.) noun sing. fem., suff. 1 pers. sing. fr. קִנְאָה dec. 12 b; ו before (:) . קנא

בַּקָּנֶה pref. בַּ f. בְּהַ } noun masc. sing. dec. 9 b. קנה

בְּקָנֶה pref. בְּ q. v. }

בִּקְנֵה pref. בְּ bef. (:)) id. constr. state . . קנה

בִּקְסָם־[h] pref. id.) Kal inf. constr., with Mak. [for קְסֹם § 8. rem. 18] . . . . קסם

בָּקַע[i] I. *to cleave, divide;* const. with בְּ *to break through.* —II. *to break* or *lay open*, as a fortified city; hence *to break open* or *hatch eggs*, Is. 34. 15.—III. *to rip open* a woman with child, Am. 1. 13. Niph.—I. *to be cleft, to divide itself.*—II. *to be opened, laid open; to be hatched*, comp. Kal No. II. Pi.—I. i. q. Kal Nos. I. II. III.—II. *to rend, tear in pieces*, as wild beasts. Pu. pass. of Pi.—Hiph. I. i. q. Kal No. II.—II. with אֶל *to break through to* any one, 2 Ki. 3. 26. Hoph. pass. of Hiph. No. I. Je. 39. 2. Hithp. *to be cleft, rent.*

בֶּקַע masc. *half a shekel.*

בִּקְעָה f. dec. 12 b, *a valley;* also used for a *low plain.*

בִּקְעָא Ch. fem. dec. 8 a, id. Da. 3. 1.

בְּקִיעַ masc. dec. 1, *fissure, cleft.*

בֶּקַע noun masc. sing. . . . . . בקע

בִּקַּע Piel pret. 3 pers. s. m. [for בִּקַּע § 15. r. 1] בקע

בֹּקֵעַ[k] ו Kal part. act. sing. masc.; ו bef. lab. . בקע

בִּקְעָה[l] noun fem. sing. dec. 12 b. . . . בקע

בִּקְּעוּ[m] Piel pret. 3 p. pl. [for בִּקְעוּ comp. § 8. r. 7] בקע

בָּקְעָה[n] ו Kal pret. 3 pers. sing. fem.; ו bef. lab. בקע

בְּקָעֵהוּ[o] ו id. imp. sing. masc. [בְּקַע], suff. 3 pers. sing. masc. (§ 16. rem. 11) ו id. . בקע

בְּקָעוֹת noun fem. pl. absolute from בִּקְעָה dec. 12 b. בקע

בִּקְעִילָה pref. בְּ bef. (:)) pr. n. of a place, see קְעִילָה

בְּקִעִים[p] noun masc., pl. of [בְּקִיעַ] dec. 1 a. . . בקע

בְּקָעָם[q] Kal inf. [בְּקַע], suff. 3 p. pl. m. (§ 16. r. 10) בקע

בָּקַעְתָּ id. pret. 2 pers. sing. masc. . . בקע

בָקַעְתָּ[r] ו id. id.; ac. shifted by conv. ו, bef. lab. for וְ (§ 8. r. 7) בקע

בְּקָעֹת[cc] ו noun fem., pl. abs. of בִּקְעָה dec. 12 b; ו id. בקע

בִּקְעַת noun fem. sing., constr. of בִּקְעָה dec. 12 b. בקע

בִקַּעְתִּי[s] ו Piel pret. 1 pers. sing.; acc. shifted to ult. by conv. ו, bef. labial for וְ (§ 8. rem. 7) בקע

בִקְצֵה[t] ו' pref. בְּ bef. (:)) noun masc. sing., constr. of קָצֶה dec. 9 b; ו bef. lab. . . . קצה

בְּקָצֵהוּ[u] pref. בְּ) id., suff. 3 pers. sing. masc. . קצה

בַקָּצִיר[x] ו' pref. בַּ for בְּהַ) noun masc. sing. dec. 3 a; ו bef. labial . . . . קצר

בִּקְצִירִי[y] pref. בְּ bef. (:)) id., suff. 1 pers. sing. . קצר

בְקֶצֶף ו pref. בְּ) noun masc. sing. dec. 6 a (see the following); ו bef. (:) . . . קצף

בְּקִצְפִּי[z] pref. id.) id., suff. 1 pers. sing. . . . קצף

בְּקֶצְפְּךָ[a] pref. id.) id., suff. 2 p. s. m. (§ 35. r. 3 & 4) קצף

בְּקֻצְרְךָ[b] pref. id.) Kal inf., suff. 2 pers. sing. masc. [for קָצְרְךָ § 16. rem. 7, comp. § 35. rem. 8] קצר

בְקֻצְרְכֶם ו pref. id.) id., suff. 2 p. pl. m.; ו bef. lab. קצר

בָּקַק I. *to empty, make empty*, as a land of its inhabitants, *to depopulate;* of counsel, *to empty, pour out*, deprive one of it.—II. *to pour itself out*, of a tree, גֶּפֶן בּוֹקֵק *spreading* or *luxuriant vine*, Ho. 10. 1. Niph. pass. of Kal No. 1. Po. i. q. Kal *to make empty*, Je. 51. 2.

בַּקְבֻּק masc. I. *a bottle.*—II. pr. name of a man, Ezr. 2. 51; Neh. 7. 53.

בַּקְבֻּקְיָה (*profusion of the Lord*) pr. name of a man.

בַּקְבַּקַּר (for בַּקְבַּק הַר *profusion of the mountain*) pr. name masc. 1 Ch. 9. 15.

בֻּקִּי (for בֻּקִּיָּהוּ q. v.) pr. name of two different men.

בֻּקִּיָּהוּ (*profusion of the Lord*) pr. name of a man, 1 Ch. 25. 4, 13.

יַבֹּק (*effusion*) pr. name of a stream flowing into the Jordan.

בְּקָקוּם[c] Kal pret. 3 pers. pl., suff. 3 pers. pl. masc. בקק

בֹּקְקִים[d] id. part. act. masc., pl. of בּוֹקֵק dec. 7 b. . בקק

בָּקַר Kal not used; in the deriv. *to plough; to break forth* (as light); *to search.* Pi.—I. *to search, look after.*—II. *to consider, observe.*—III. *to take care of*, const. with acc. לְ, בֵּין—לְ, בְּ.

בַּקַּר Ch. Pa. *to search, examine.* Ithpe. pass. Ezr. 5. 17.

בָּקָר com. dec. 4 a, coll. *oxen*, without distinction of sex; חֶמְאַת בָּ׳ *milk of kine;* בָּ׳ עָלוֹת *milch cows;* בֶּן־בָּקָר *a calf;* עֵגֶל בֶּן־בָּ׳ id.; rarely pl. בְּקָרִים *oxen.*

---

[a] Ex. 32. 25. [b] Ps. 92. 12. [c] Le. 6. 8. [cc] De. 11. 11. [d] De. 23. 26. [e] Nu. 25. 11. [f] 2 Sa. 21. 2. [g] Eze. 38. 19. [h] Eze. 21. 34. [i] Ps. 78. 13. [k] Ps. 141. 7. [l] Ge. 11. 2. [m] Is. 59. 5. [n] Is. 34. 15. [o] Ex. 14. 16. [p] Am. 6. 11. [q] Am. 1. 13. [r] Eze. 29. 7. [s] Eze. 13. 13. [t] Ps. 19. 5. [u] Ex. 19. 12. [x] Ex. 34. 21. [y] Job 29. 19 [z] Is. 60. 10. [a] Ps. 38. 2. [b] Le 23. 22. [c] Na. 2. 3. [d] Na. 2. 3.

בּוֹקֵר masc. *herdsman*, Am. 7. 14.

בֹּקֶר masc. pl. בְּקָרִים (§ 35. rem. 9)—I. *the dawn, morning* (prop. *day-break*); לַבֹּקֶר, בַּבֹּקֶר *in the morning;* לַבְּקָרִים, בַּבֹּקֶר בַּבֹּקֶר *every morning.*—II. *the morrow,* adv. *to-morrow;* לַבֹּקֶר *early soon,* Ps. 49. 15.

בַּקָּרָה fem. dec. 10. (§ 42. No. 3) *a looking after, caring,* Eze. 34. 12.

בִּקֹּרֶת fem. *chastisement,* Lev. 19. 20, from the idea of *searching, visiting,* comp. פְּקֻדָּה, פָּקַד.

בָּקָר וּ׳ noun com. sing. dec. 4 a; וּ bef. labial . בקר
[a]בְּקַר id. constr. state . . . . . בקר
בָּקָר [b]ו׳, [c]וָ׳ noun m. s. d. 6c. § 35. r. 9; וּ bef. lab. בקר
[d]בִּקְרֹא pref. בְּ bef. (:))(Kal inf. constr. . . קרא
בְּקָרְאִי pref. בְּ)(id. inf. with suff. 1 pers. sing. קרא
[e]בְּקֹרְאֵי pref. id.)(id. part. act. pl. constr. masc. fr. קֹרֵא dec. 7 b. . . . . . קרא
[f]בַּקֶּרֶב pref. בַּ for בְּהַ)(noun masc. sing. dec. 1 a. קרב
בְּקֶרֶב [g]ו׳ pref. בְּ)(n. m. s., (suff. קִרְבִּי) d. 6 a; וּ bef. (:) קרב
[h]בִּקְרֹב, [i]בִּקְרָב־ pref. בְּ bef. (:))(Kal inf. constr. (§ 8. r. 18) קרב
בְּקִרְבָּהּ pref. בְּ)(n. m. s., suff. 3 p. s. f. fr. קֶרֶב d. 6 a. קרב
בְּקִרְבּוֹ ו׳ pref. id.)(id., suff. 3 pers. s. m.; וּ bef. (:) קרב
בְּקִרְבִּי pref. id.)(id., suff. 1 pers. sing. . . קרב
[k]בִּקְרֹבַי pref. בְּ bef. (:))(adj. masc. pl., suff. 1 pers. sing. from קָרוֹב dec. 3 a. . . . . קרב
בְּקִרְבְּךָ, בְּקִרְבֶּךָ pref. בְּ)(noun masc. sing., suff. 2 pers. sing. masc. from קֶרֶב dec. 6 a. . קרב
בְּקִרְבֵּךְ pref. id.)(id., suff. 2 pers. sing. fem. . קרב
בְּקִרְבְּכֶם pref. id.)(id., suff. 2 pers. pl. masc. קרב
בְּקִרְבָּם [l]ו׳ pref. id.)(id., suff. 3 p. pl. m.; וּ bef. (:) קרב
בְּקִרְבֵּנוּ pref. id.)(id., suff. 1 pers. pl. . . קרב
[m]בְּקָרְבָתָם [n]ו׳ pref. id.)(Kal inf., [קָרְבָה] § 8. rem. 10] suff. 3 pers. pl. m.; וּ bef. lab. . . קרב
[o]בְּקַרְדֻּמּוֹת וּ pref. id.)(noun masc. with pl. fem. term. from [קַרְדֹּם] dec. 8 c; וּ id. . . . קרדם
[p]בַּקָּרָה pref. בַּ for בְּהַ)(noun fem. sing. d. 10. [for קָרָה § 37. rem. 7] from קַר masc. . . קרר
[q]בְּקָרוֹב pref. בְּ)(prop. adj. with the pref. as an *adv.* קרב
[r]בַּקָּרַחַת pref. בַּ for בְּהַ)(n. f. s. d. 13 a (§ 44. No. 1) קרח
[s]בְּקָרַחְתּוֹ pref. בְּ)(id., suff. 3 pers. sing. masc. . קרח
בַּקַּרוּ וּ Ch. Pael pret. 3 pers. pl. masc.; וּ bef. lab. בקר
בְּקֶרִי pref. בְּ)(n. m. s. [for קְרִי § 35. r. 14] . קרה
[t]בְּקִרְיָה Ch. pref. id.)(noun fem. sing. dec. 8 a. . קרה
[u]בְּקָרִים noun com., pl. of בָּקָר dec. 4 a. . . בקר
[x]בְּקָרֵינוּ id. pl., suff. 1 pers. pl. . . . . בקר

בְּקִרְיַת pref. בְּ)(noun fem. sing., constr. of קִרְיָה d. 10, also pr. n. in compos., as קִרְיַת אַרְבַּע &c. קרה
[y]בְּקָרְךָ, בְּקָרֶךָ [z]ו׳, ו׳ pref. בְּ)(noun com. sing., suff. 2 pers. sing. masc. fr. בָּקָר d. 4 a; וּ bef. (:) בקר
בְּקַרְכֶם [a]ו׳ pref. id.)(id., suff. 2 pers. pl. masc.; וּ id. בקר
בְּקָרָם ו׳ pref. id.)(id., suff. 3 p. pl. m.; וּ id. . בקר
בְּקֶרֶן pref. id.)(noun fem. sing., (suff. קַרְנִי) d. 6 a. קרן
[b]בְּקַרְנָא Ch. pref. id.)(id., emph. state dec. 3 a. . קרן
בְּקַרְנוֹת pref. id.)(id. pl., constr. of קְרָנוֹת . . קרן
[c]בְּקַרְנַיָּא Ch. pref. id.)(id. du., emph. state dec. 3 a. קרן
[d]בְּקַרְנָיו pref. id.)(id. du., suff. 3 pers. sing. masc. קרן
[e]בְּקַרְנֵיכֶם וּ pref. id.)(id. du., suff. 2 p. pl. m.; וּ bef. (:) קרן
בַּקְּרָסִים pref. בַּ for בְּהַ)(noun masc. pl. (constr. קַרְסֵי) from קֶרֶס dec. 6 a. . . קרס
[f]בְּקָרְעִי וּ pref. בְּ)(Kal inf., suff. 1 pers. s.; וּ bef. (:) קרע
בְּקַרְקַע pref. id.)(noun masc. sing. . . . קרקע
בַּקַּרְקֹר pref. בַּ for בְּהַ)(pr. name of a place . קור
[g]בִּקֹּרֶת noun fem. sing. . . . . . בקר
[h]בִּקַּרְתִּים וּ Piel pret. 1 p. s., suff. 3 p. pl. m.; וּ bef. lab. בקר

בִּקֵּשׁ [i]ו׳ Pi. I. *to seek,* with acc., *to seek after,* with לְ; בִּקֵּשׁ אֶת־יְהוָֹה *to seek the Lord,* to apply to him by acts of worship, or to apply for an oracle; בִּקֵּשׁ נֶפֶשׁ פּ׳ *to seek the life of* any, i. e. to endeavour to kill him; בִּקֵּשׁ רָעַת פּ׳ *to seek one's hurt.*—II. *to require, demand,* with acc.; מִיַּד, מִן *of, at the hand of* any one.—III. *to ask, request,* with acc. of the thing and מִן of pers.; with עַל *to supplicate for.* Pu. *to be sought.*

בַּקָּשָׁה fem. d. 10. (§ 42. No. 3) *request, petition.*

בַּקֵּשׁ [k]ו׳ Piel imp. sing. m., inf. Ec. 7. 25; וּ bef. lab. בקש
[u]בִּקֶּשׁ־ id. pret. 3 pers. masc. for בִּקֵּשׁ . . בקש
בִּקְשָׁה id. pret. 3 pers. sing. fem. (§ 10. rem. 7) בקש
בִּקְשֻׁהוּ id. pret. 3 p. pl. (בִּקְשׁוּ), suff. 3 p. s. m. (§ 10. r. 7) בקש
בַּקְּשׁוּ [l]ו׳ id. imp. pl. masc.; וּ bef. lab. . . בקש
בִּקְשׁוּ ו׳ id. pret. 3 pers. pl. (§ 10. rem. 7); וּ id. בקש
[m]בַּקְּשׁוּנִי id. imp. pl. masc., suff. 1 pers. sing. . בקש
[n]בִּקְשֻׁנִי id. pret. 3 p. pl. (בִּקְשׁוּ § 10. r. 7), suff. 1 p. s. בקש
[o]בְּקַשְׂקְשֹׂתֶיךָ pref. בְּ)(noun fem. pl., suff. 2 pers. sing. m. from קַשְׂקֶשֶׂת d. 13 a. (§ 39. No. 4. r. 1) קשה
[p]בַּקֹּשְׁרִים pref. בַּ for בְּהַ)(Kal part. act. masc., pl. of [קֹשֵׁר] dec. 7 b. . . . . קשר
בַּקֶּשֶׁת, בַּקָּשֶׁת [q]ו׳ pref. id.; בְּקֶשֶׁת pref. בְּ — n. com. s., with suff. קַשְׁתִּי, pl. קְשָׁתוֹת, constr. קַשְׁתוֹת, ת treated as if radical, comp. dec. 6 a. . . קוש

[a] Nu. 7. 88. [b] Ex. 16. 7. [c] Ps. 55. 18. [d] Je. 36. 13. [e] Ps. 99. 6. [f] 2 Sa. 17. 11. [g] Pr. 14. 33. [h] Ps. 27. 2. [i] 2 Sa. 15. 5. [k] Le. 10. 3. [l] Ps. 62. 5. [m] Le. 16. 1. [n] Ex. 40. 32. [o] Je. 46. 22. [p] Job 24. 7. [q] Eze. 11. 3. [r] Le. 13. 42. [s] Le. 13. 43, 55. [t] Ezr. 4. 10. [u] Pr. 14. 6. [x] 2 Ch. 4. 3. [x] Ne. 10. 37. [y] Ex. 20. 24. [z] Je. 5. 17.

[a] Ex. 10. 24. [b] Da. 7. 8. [c] Da. 7. 8. [d] Ge. 22. 13. [e] Eze. 34. 21. [f] Ezr. 9. 5. [g] Le. 19. 20. [h] Eze. 34. 11. [i] 1 Sa. 20. 16. [k] Ecc. 7. 25. [l] Je. 5. 1. [m] Is. 45. 19. [n] Is. 65. 1. [o] Eze. 29. 4. 4. [p] 2 Sa. 15. 31. [q] Is. 7. 24.

בַּקָּשָׁתוֹ [a] ו׳ noun fem. sing., suff. 3 pers. sing. masc. from [בַּקָּשָׁה] dec. 10. (§ 42. No. 3) — בקשׁ

בַּקָּשָׁתִי [b] [c] ו׳ id., suff. 1 pers. sing.; וּ bef. lab. — בקשׁ

בִּקַּשְׁתִּי Piel pret. 1 pers. sing. — בקשׁ

בְּקַשְׁתִּי [d] [e] ו׳ pref. בְּ) noun com. sing., suff. 1 pers. sing. (see בְּקֶשֶׁת); וּ bef. (:) — קושׁ

בִּקַּשְׁתִּיה Pie pret. 1 pers. sing., suff. 3 pers. sing. masc. — בקשׁ

בִּקַּשְׁתִּיו id. id., suff. 3 pers. sing. masc. — בקשׁ

בַּקָּשָׁתֵךְ noun fem. sing., suff. 2 pers. sing. fem. from [בַּקָּשָׁה] dec. 10. (§ 42. No. 3) — בקשׁ

בְּקַשְׁתֶּךָ [h] } pref. בְּ) noun com. sing., suff. 2 pers.
בְּקַשְׁתְּךָ [i] ו } sing. masc. (see בְּקֶשֶׁת); וּ bef. lab. — קושׁ

בִּקַּשְׁתֶּם [k] ו׳ Piel pret. 2 pers. pl. masc.; וּ id. — בקשׁ

בִּקְשָׁתַם [l] ו id. pret. 3 pers. sing. fem. suff. 3 pers. pl. masc. (§ 10. rem. 7. & 16. rem. 2); וּ id. — בקשׁ

בַּקֹּתִי [u] ו Kal pret. 1 pers. sing.; וּ id. — בקק

בָּר }
בַּר } noun masc. sing.; adj. Pr. 14. 4. — ברר

בַּר noun masc. sing., dec. 2a. (§ 36. rem. 5) — ברא

בַּר ו adj. masc. sing. (pl. constr. בָּרֵי § 37. rem. 7); וּ before labial — ברר

בֹּר [n] noun masc. sing. dec. 1a. (for בְּאֹר, בּוֹר) — באר

בָּרָא [o] ו׳ *to create, form, make.* Niph.—I. *to be created.*—II. *to be born.* Pi.—I. *to cut, cut down.*—II. *to form, fashion.* Hiph. *to feed, fatten.*

בַּר masc. with suff. בְּרִי (§ 36. rem. 5) *a son.*

בַּר Chald. masc. dec. 2a.—I. *son.*—II. *grandson,* Ezr. 5. 1.

בָּרִיא masc. dec. 3a. adj. fem. בְּרִיאָה dec. 10.—*fat, fattened.*

בְּרִיאָה fem. *a new, wonderful thing,* Nu. 16. 30.

בְּרָאיָה (whom *the Lord created*) pr. name masc. 1 Ch. 8. 21.

בָּרָא Chald. noun masc. sing. [for בַּרָא] emph. of [בַּר] (comp. § 37. r. 7) — ברר

בָּרֵא [p] Piel imp. sing. masc. — ברא

בָּרֵא [q] ו id. inf. abs.; וּ bef. lab. — ברא

בְּרֹא [r] Kal inf. constr. — ברא

בְּרָא [s] id. imp. sing. masc. — ברא

בֹּרֵא [t] ו id. part. act. sing. masc. dec. 7b; וּ bef. lab. — ברא

בְּרֹאדַךְ pr. name see מְרֹאדַךְ

בָּרֹאֶה [u] pref. בָּ for בְּהָ, בְּהַ·) Kal part. act. s. m. d. 9a. — ראה

בְּרָאָהּ Kal pret. 3 pers. sing. m., suff. 3 pers. sing. fem. — ברא

בְּרִאָה [pp] adj. fem. for בְּרִיאָה, from בָּרִיא masc. — ברא

בִּרְאוֹת [x] ו׳ pref. בְּ bef. (:)) Kal inf. const. d. 1a; וּ bef. lab. — ראה

בִּרְאוֹתָם pref. id.) id., suff. 3 pers. pl. masc. — ראה

בְּרָאִי pr. name see בֵּית בִּרְאִי under — בית

בְּרָאיָה ו pr. name masc.; וּ bef. (:) — ברא

בְּרִאִים [z] adj. masc., pl. of בָּרִיא dec. 3a. — ברא

בֹּרַאֲךָ [a] Kal part. act. sing., suff. 2 pers. sing. masc. from בֹּרֵא dec. 7b. (§ 36. rem. 3) — ברא

בְּרָאָם [b] id. pret. 3 pers. sing. masc., suff. 3 pers. pl. m. — ברא

בְּרָאָנוּ [c] id. id. suff. 1 pers. pl. — ברא

בָּרֹאשׁ pref. בָּ f. בְּהָ, בְּהַ· } noun masc. sing. irr.
בְּרֹאשׁ ו׳ pref. בְּ q. v. } (§ 45); וּ bef. (:) — ראשׁ

בְּרֹאשָׁהּ [d] pref. id.) id., suff. 3 pers. sing. fem. — ראשׁ

בְּרֵאשַׁהּ [e] Chald. pref. id.) noun masc. s., suff. 3 pers. sing. masc. from רֵאשׁ dec. 1. — ראשׁ

בְּרָאשֵׁיהֹם [f] Ch. pref. id.) id., suff. 3 pers. pl. m. (§ 68) — ראשׁ

בְּרֹאשׁוֹ pref. id.) noun masc. sing., suff. 3 pers. sing. masc. from רֹאשׁ irr. (§ 45) — ראשׁ

בָּרִאשׁוֹן pref. בָּ for בְּהָ, בְּהַ·) adj. masc. sing. dec. 1b. — ראשׁ

בָּרִאשׁוֹנָה pref. id.) id. fem. dec. 10. — ראשׁ

בְּרָאשֵׁי ו׳ pref. בְּ) noun masc. pl. constr. from רֹאשׁ irr. (§ 45); וּ bef. (:) — ראשׁ

בְּרָאשֵׁיהֶם pref. id.) id. pl., suff. 3 pers. pl. masc. — ראשׁ

בְּרָאשֵׁיכֶם [g] pref. id.) id. pl., suff. 2 pers. pl. masc. — ראשׁ

בְּרָאשֵׁינוּ [h] pref. id.) id. pl., suff. 1 pers. pl. — ראשׁ

בְּרֵאשִׁית pref. id.) noun fem. sing. dec. 1b. — ראשׁ

בְּרֵאשִׁיתָהּ [i] pref. id.) id., suff. 3 pers. sing. fem. — ראשׁ

בְּרֹאשְׁךָ pref. id.) noun masc. sing., suff. 2 pers. sing. masc. from רֹאשׁ irr. (§ 45) — ראשׁ

בְּרֹאשֵׁךְ [k] pref. id.) id., suff. 2 pers. sing. fem. — ראשׁ

בְּרֹאשְׁכֶם [l] pref. id.) id., suff. 2 pers. pl. masc. — ראשׁ

בְּרֹאשָׁם pref. id.) id., suff. 3 pers. pl. masc. — ראשׁ

בָּרִאשֹׁן [m] pref. בָּ for בְּהָ, בְּהַ·) adj. m. sing. dec. 1b. — ראשׁ

בָּרִאשֹׁנָה pref. id.) id. fem. dec. 10. — ראשׁ

בְּרֹאשֵׁנוּ pref. בְּ) noun masc. sing., suff. 1 pers. pl. from רֹאשׁ irr. (§ 45) — ראשׁ

בָּרִאשֹׁנִים [n] pref. בָּ for בְּהָ, בְּהַ·) adj. m., pl. of רִאשׁוֹן d. 1b. — ראשׁ

בָּרָאתָ [o] Kal pret. 2 pers. sing. masc. — ברא

בֵּרֵאתָ [p] ו Piel pret. 2 pers. sing. masc.; acc. shifted by conv. וּ, bef. lab. for וְ (§ 8. rem. 7) — ברא

בֵּרֵאתוֹ [q] ו id. with suff. 3 pers. sing. masc.; וּ bef. lab. — ברא

בִּרְאֹתוֹ pref. בְּ bef. (:)) Kal inf. (רְאוֹת) with suff. 3 pers. sing. masc. dec. 1a. — ראה

בָּרָאתִי Kal pret. 1 pers. sing. — ברא

בִּרְאֹתִי [r] pref. בְּ bef. (:)) Kal inf. (רְאוֹת), suff. 1 p. s. — ראה

בְּרָאתִיו Kal pret. 1 pers. sing., suff. 3 pers. sing. masc. — ברא

בְּרָאתָם [s] id. pret. 2 pers. sing. masc., suff. 3 pers. pl. m. — ברא

בִּרְאֹתָם pref. בְּ bef. (:)) Kal inf. (רְאוֹת), suff. 3 pers. pl. masc. dec. 1a. — ראה

בְּרַב [t] pref. בְּ) adj. masc. sing. dec. 8d. — רבב

---

[a] Ezr. 7. 6. [b] Est. 5. 8. [c] Est. 5. 7. [d] Ps. 44. 7. [e] Ge. 48. 22
[f] Ca. 5. 6. [g] Ca. 3. 1, 2. [h] Jos. 24. 12. [i] 2 Ki. 6. 22. [k] Eze. 34. 4.
[l] Ho. 2. 9. [m] Je. 19. 7. [n] Ex. 21. 33. [o] Is. 4. 5. [p] Eze. 21. 24, 24.
[q] Eze. 23. 47. [r] Ge. 5. 1. [s] Ps. 51. 12. [t] Am. 4. 13. [u] Is. 28. 7.
[x] 2 Ch. 12. 7. [y] 1 Sa. 17. 24. [z] 1 Ki. 5. 3. [a] Is. 43. 1. [b] Ge. 5. 2.
[c] Mal. 2. 10. [d] Est. 2. 17. [e] Da. 7. 20. [f] Ezr. 5. 10. [g] De. 1. 13.
[h] 1 Ch. 12. 19. [i] Ho. 9. 10. [k] Eze. 16. 12. [l] Joel 4. 4, 7. [u] Je. 19. 7.
[m] Ex. 12. 18. [n] 2 Sa. 21. 9. [o] Ps. 89. 48. [p] Jos. 17. 15. [pp] Hab. 1. 16.
[q] Jos. 17. 18. [r] Da. 8. 2, 15. [s] Ps. 89. 13. [t] 1 Sa. 14. 6.

בְּרֹב / בְּרָב־ ו׳ pref. בְּ)(noun masc. sing. dec. 8c. (§ 37. rem. 2); וּ bef. (:) . — רבב
בְּרִבְבוֹת[a] pref. id.)(n. fem. pl. constr. from רְבָבָה d. 11c. — רבב
בְּרִבְבֹתָו / בְּרִבְבֹתָיו[b] pref. id.)(id. pl., suff. 3 pers. sing. masc. (§ 4. rem. 1) . . . — רבב
בְּרַבָּה pref. id.)(pr. name of a place . . — רבב
בִּרְבוֹת pref. בְּ bef. (:))(Kal inf. constr. . . — רבה
בִּרְבִיבִים[c] pref. id.)(noun masc. pl. . . . — רבב
בָּרַבִּים pref. בָּ f. בְּהָ / בְּרַבִּים[d] pref. בְּ q. v. } adj. masc., pl. of רַב dec. 8d. — רבב
בָּרְבִיעִי[ff] pref. בָּ for בְּהַ·, בְּהָ)(adj. ord. masc. . — רבע
בְּרִבְלָה pref. בְּ)(pr. name of a place . . — רבל
בְּרִבְלָתָה pref. id.)(id. with parag. ה . . . — רבל
בְּרִבָם[e] pref. בְּ)(noun masc., pl. of רִיב dec. 1a. — ריב
בִּרְבִעִית[f] pref. בְּ bef. (:))(adj. ord., fem. of רְבִיעִי — רבע
בְּרֻבְּרִים[g] וּ noun masc. pl.; וּ before labial . . — ברר
בְּרַבַּת pref. בְּ)(pr. name of a place, constr. of רַבָּה — רבב
בְּרֹגֶז pref. id.)(noun masc. sing. dec. 6c. . . — רגז
בִּרְגַז[h] Chald. pref. בְּ bef. (:))(noun masc. sing. — רגז
בְּרָגְזָה[i] pref. בְּ)(noun fem. sing. . . . — רגז
בְּרֶגֶל / בְּרָגֶל[k] } pref. id.)(n. fem. sing. dec. 6a. (§ 35. r. 2) — רגל
בְּרַגְלָו pref. id.)(id. du., suff. 3 p. s. m. (§ 4. r. 2) — רגל
בְּרַגְלוֹ[m] pref. id.)(id. sing., suff. 3 pers. sing. masc. — רגל
בְּרַגְלַי / בְּרַגְלָי[n] } pref. id.)(id. dual, suff. 1 pers. sing. . — רגל
בְּרַגְלֵי[o] pref. id.)(id. du., construct state . — רגל
בְּרַגְלֵיהּ[p] Chald. pref. id.)(id. du., suff. 3 pers. sing. fem. (§ 46. parad.) . . . . . — רגל
בְּרַגְלֵיהֶם[q] ו׳ pref. id.)(id. du., suff. 3 p. pl. m.; וּ bef. (:) — רגל
בְּרַגְלָיו pref. id.)(id. du., suff. 3 pers. sing. masc. . — רגל
בְּרַגְלֶיךָ pref. id.)(id. du., suff. 2 pers. sing. masc. — רגל
בְּרַגְלֵיכֶם pref. id.)(id. du., suff. 2 pers. pl. masc. — רגל
בְּרַגְלַיִם pref. id.)(id. du., absolute state . . — רגל
בְּרַגְלְךָ pref. id.)(id. sing., suff. 2 pers. sing. masc. — רגל
בְּרֶגַע[r] ו׳ pref. id.)(noun masc. sing. dec. 6. (§ 35. rem. 5); וּ bef. (:) . . . . — רגע
בְּרֶגֶשׁ[s] pref. id.)(noun m. s. [for רֶגֶשׁ § 35. rem. 2] — רגש

בָּרַד[u] וּ *to hail*, Is. 32. 19.

בָּרֹד masc. adj. only pl. בְּרֻדִּים (§ 8. No. 9) *spotted*. Also the two following—

בָּרָד ו׳ masc. *hail*; אַבְנֵי בָרָד *hail-stones*, i. q. *hail* — ברד
בֶּרֶד / בָּרֶד ו׳ } (*hail*) pr. name—I. of a place in the desert of Shur.—II. of a man, 1 Ch. 7. 20. — ברד

בְּרֻדִּים[x] ו׳[y] adj. masc., pl. of [בָּרֹד] dec. 8c. (§ 37. No. 3); וּ bef. (:) . . . . — רד
בְּרֹדְפַי[z] pref. בְּ)(Kal part. act. pl. masc., suff. 1 pers. sing. from רֹדֵף dec. 7b. . . . — רף
בְּרָדְפָם[a] pref. id.)(id. inf., suff. 3 pers. pl. masc. . — רף
בְּרֶדֶת ו׳[b] pref. id.)(Kal inf. constr. d. 13b. (§ 44. r. 1) — ד
בְּרִדְתּוֹ[c] pref. id.)(id., suff. 3 pers. sing. masc. . — ד
בְּרִדְתִּי[d] pref. id.)(id., suff. 1 pers. sing. . . — ד

בָּרָה[e] prop. *to cut*, i. q. Pi. of בָּרָא; hence—I. *to eat*.—II. *to choose, select*, 1 Sa. 17. 8. Pi. *to eat*, La. 4. 10, but see בָּרוּת. Hiph. *to give to eat*.

בָּרוּת fem. (after the form אָחוֹת) *food*, La. 4. 10, but see Pi. above.

בָּרוּת fem. dec. 1b. id. Ps. 69. 22.

בָּרִי only fem. בְּרִיָה—I. adj. *fat*, Eze. 34. 20.—II. subs. *food*.

בְּרִית fem. dec. 1a.—I. *agreement, league, covenant* (from the idea of cutting, comp. כָּרַת, see also בַּעַל Nos. III., IV.—II. *sign of the covenant*, i. e. circumcision; מַלְאַךְ הַבְּרִית *the angel of the covenant*, the Messiah, comp. Jud. 2. 1; Ro. 15. 8.

בָּרָה adj. fem. sing. for [בָּרָה § 37. rem. 7] from בַּר m. (also pr. name in compos. see בַּיִת) — רר
בְּרֵהּ[f] Ch. noun m. s., suff. 3 p. s. m. from בַּר d. 2b. — רא
בָּרְהָטִים pref. בָּ for בְּהַ·, בְּהָ)(n. m., pl. of [רַהַט] d. 6d. — הט
בְּרוּ Kal imp. pl. masc. . . . . — רה
בֹּרוֹ[g] noun m. s., suff. 3 pers. s. m. from בּוֹר d. 1a. — אר
בָּרוֹחַ[h] Kal inf. absolute . . . . — רח
בָּרוּחַ pref. בָּ for בְּהָ / בְּרוּחַ ו׳ pref. בְּ q. v. } n. com. s. dec. 1a; וּ bef. (:) — וח
בְּרוּחוֹ pref. id.)(id., suff. 3 pers. sing. masc. . — וח
בְּרוּחִי[i] pref. id.)(id., suff. 1 pers. sing. . . — וח
בְּרוּחֲךָ pref. id.)(id., suff. 2 pers. sing. masc. . — וח
בְּרוּחֲכֶם[k] pref. id.)(id., suff. 2 pers. pl. masc. . — וח
בָּרוֹךְ[l] Kal inf. abs. or [for בָּרֵךְ] Piel inf. abs. (§ 10. r. 2) — רך
בָּרוּךְ ו׳ id. part. pass. sing. masc. dec. 3a; also pr. name masc.; וּ bef. lab. . . . — רך
בְּרוּךְ id., construct state . . . — רך
בְּרוּכָה[m] ו׳[n] id. fem.; וּ bef. (:) . . . — רך
בְּרוּכֵי[o] id. pl. const. masc. dec. 3a. . . — רך
בְּרוּכִים[p] id. pl., absolute state . . . . — רך
בְּרוֹמִים[q] noun masc. pl. [of בְּרוֹם] . . — רם
בְּרוּמָם[r] וּ pref. בְּ)(Kal inf. [רוּם § 21. rem. 3], suff. 3 pers. pl. masc. . . . — ום
בְּרוֹק[s] Kal imp. sing. masc. . . . — רק

---

a Mi. 6. 7. b 1 Sa. 18. 7. c Ps. 65. 11. d Ps. 55. 19. e Job 31. 13. f Nu. 15. 4. g 1 Ki. 5. 3. h Da. 3. 13. i Eze. 12. 18. k De. 19. 21. l Pr. 6. 13. m 2 Sa. 15. 18. n Nu. 20. 19. o 1 Sa. 25. 27. p Da. 7. 7, 19. q Is. 3. 16. r Is. 54. 7. s Job 21. 13. t Ps. 55. 15. u Is. 32. 19. x Zec. 6. 3. y Ge. 31. 10, 12. z Ps. 119. 84. a De. 11. 4. b Nu. 11. 9. c Ex. 34. 29. d Ps. 30. 10. e 2 Sa. 12. 17. f Da. 5. 22. ff Eze. 1. 1. g 2 Ki. 18. 31. h Job 27. 22. i Zec. 4. 6. k Mal. 2. 15, 16. l Jos. 24. 10. m Ruth 3. 10. n 1 Sa. 25. 33. o Is. 65. 23. p Ps. 115. 15. q Eze. 27. 24. r Eze. 10. 17. s Ps. 144. 6.

בָּרוּר Kal part. pass. sing. masc. dec. 3a. . ברר
[a] בְּרוּרָה id. fem. dec. 10. . . . . . ברר
[b] בְּרוּרִים id. pl. masc., dec. 3a. . . . ברר
[aa] בְּרוֹשׁ noun masc. sing. dec. 1a. . . . ברשׁ
בְּרוֹשָׁיו id. pl., suff. 3 pers. sing. masc. . . ברשׁ
בְּרוֹשִׁים id. pl., absolute state . . . ברשׁ
בְּרוֹת noun m. with pl. fem. term. from בּוֹר dec. 1a. באר
בֵּרוֹתָה pr. name of a place . . . . . באר
[c] בָּרוֹתִי וּ Kal pret. 1 pers. sing. [for בַּרּוֹתִי]; וּ bef. lab. ברר
בְּרוֹתִים n.m., pl. of [בְּרוֹת] i.q. בְּרוֹשׁ *cypress*, Cant. 1. 17.
בִּרְזָוִת Kh. בִּרְזוֹת, K. בִּרְזַיִת pr. name fem. 1 Ch. 7. 31. בְּרַז Chald. *to pierce.*

בַּרְזֶל וּ' masc.—I. *iron*; metaph. of a thing *hard, inflexible.*—II. *instrument of iron.*

בַּרְזִלַּי | וּ' בַּרְזִלָּי } (*of iron, austere*) pr. name—I. of an intimate friend of David.—II. Ezr. 2. 61. } ברזל

בָּרַח I. *to pass* or *shoot along*, as a bar Ex. 36. 33.—II. *to flee* constr. with אֶל, לְ of the place *whither*, מִפְּנֵי, מֵאֵת, מִן *from* whom, אַחֲרֵי *after* whom one flees; בְּרַח לְךָ *flee, get away*, Hiph.—I. i. q. Kal No. 1.—II. *to cause to flee, put to flight.*

בָּרִחַ, בָּרֵחַ masc. dec. 1b, (for בַּרִּיחַ)—I. *fleeing, fugitive.*—II. pr. name masc. 1 Ch. 3. 22.

בְּרִיחַ masc. dec. 1a.—I. *bar, cross-bar.*—II. *bar, bolt.*—III. *fugitive*, Is. 15. 5.

מִבְרָח masc. dec. 2b, *fugitives*, Eze. 17. 21.

בָּרִחַ adj. masc. sing. dec. 1b. [for בַּרִּיחַ] . ברח
בְּרַח Kal imp. sing. masc. . . . . . ברח
בֹּרֵחַ id. part. act. sing. masc. . . . . ברח
[d] בָּרְחֹב pref. בְּ for הַבְּ | בִּרְחֹב pref. בְּ q. v. } noun masc. sing. dec. 6f. רחב
בִּרְחֹב pref. בְּ bef. (:)) (noun fem. sing. dec. 1a. . רחב
[f] בִּרְחָבָה pref. בְּ for בְּהַ·, בְּהָ) (adj. fem. s. from רָחָב m. רחב
[g] וּ' בָּרְחֹבוֹת pref. id. | בִּרְחֹבוֹת pref. בְּ bef. (:) } noun fem., pl. of רְחוֹב dec. 1a; וּ bef. lab. } רחב
וּ' בִּרְחֹבֹתֶיהָ pref. id.) (id. pl., suff. 3 pers. s. fem.; וּ id. רחב
בִּרְחֹבֹתֵינוּ pref. id.) (id. pl., suff. 1 pers. pl. . . רחב
[h] בָּרְחוּ | [i] בָּרָחוּ } Kal pret. 3 pers. pl. (§ 8. rem. 7) . ברח
[k] בִּרְחוּ id. imp. pl. masc. . . . . . ברח
בָּרְחוֹב pref. בְּ f. בְּהַ·, בְּהָ | וּ' בִּרְחוֹב pref. בְּ bef. (:) } noun fem. sing. dec. 1a; וּ bef. lab. } רחב
בִּרְחוֹבוֹתֶיהָ pref. id.) (id. pl., suff. 3 pers. sing. fem. רחב
[m] בְּרָחוֹק pref. בְּ) ((prop. adj.) noun m. sing. dec. 3a. רחק

[o] בְּרִחֶיהָ n. m. pl., suff. 3 p. s. fem. from בְּרִיחַ d. 1a. ברח
[p] בָּרֵחַיִם pref. בְּ for בְּהַ·, בְּהָ) (noun masc. dual, see רח
בְּרָחֵל pref. בְּ) (pr. name fem. . . . . רחל
[q] בְּרָחֶם pref. בְּ for בְּהַ·, בְּהָ) (n. m. s. (suff. רַחְמָה), d. 6a. רחם
[r] בְּרַחֲמֶיךָ וּ' pref. בְּ) (the following with suff. 2 p. s. m. רחם
[s] בְּרַחֲמִים וּ' pref. id.) (noun fem. pl. [for רְחָמִים § 35. rem. 16, from רַחַם]; וּ bef. (:) . רחם
[u] בִּרְחֹץ pref. בְּ bef. (:)) (Kal inf. constr. . . רחץ
[x] בָּרַחַת pref. בְּ for בְּהַ·, בְּהָ) (noun fem. sing. . רוח
בֹּרַחַת Kal part. act. fem. of בֹּרֵחַ (§ 8. rem. 19) ברח
[y] בְּרִי noun masc. sing., either from R. ברה, or pref. בְּ & רִי (for רְוִי) R. . . רוה
[z] בְּרִי n. m. s., suff. 1 pers. s. from בַּר (§ 36. r. 5) ברא
בֵּרִי וּ pr. name masc.; וּ before labial . באר
[a] בְּרִיא [b] וּ' adj. masc. sing. dec. 3a; וּ id. . . ברא
[c] בְּרִיאָה noun fem. sing. . . . . . ברא
[d] בְּרִיאוֹת adj. fem., pl. of בְּרִיאָה' d. 10, from בָּרִיא m. ברא
[e] בְּרִיאֵי וּ id. m. pl. constr. from בָּרִיא d. 3a; וּ bef. (:) ברא
[f] בְּרִיאֹת וּ defect. for בְּרִיאוֹת q. v.; וּ id. . . ברא
[g] בָּרִיב pref. בְּ) (noun masc. sing. dec. 1a. . ריב
בְּרִיבוֹ pref. id.) (id., suff. 3 pers. sing. masc. ריב
[h] בְּרִיָּה adj. fem. sing. from [בָּרִי] masc. . . ברה
בָּרִיחַ וּ pr. name masc.; וּ before labial . ברח
בְּרִיחַ pref. בְּ) (noun masc. sing. dec. 1a. רוח
בְּרִיחַ וּ' noun masc. sing. dec. 1a; וּ before (:) . ברח
[i] בְּרִיחֶהָ id. pl., suff. 3 pers. sing. fem. for בְּרִיחֶיהָ (according to some copies) . ברח
בְּרִיחָו id. pl., suff. 3 pers. s. m. for בְּרִיחָיו (§ 4. r. 2) ברח
בְּרִיחֵי וּ' id. pl., construct state; וּ before (:) . ברח
בְּרִיחֶיהָ id. pl., suff. 3 pers. sing. fem. . . ברח
[k] בְּרִיחָיו וּ' id. pl., suff. 3 pers. sing. masc.; וּ bef. (:) ברח
[l] בְּרִיחַיִךְ id. pl., suff. 2 pers. sing. fem. [for יִךְ'] ברח
[m] בָּרִיחִים noun masc. pl. [of בָּרִיחַ for בַּרִּיחַ] dec. 1b. ברח
[n] וּ בְּרִיחִים | בְּרִיחִם } noun masc., pl. of בְּרִיחַ dec. 1a; וּ bef. (:) ברח
[o] בְּרִיךְ Chald. Peal part. pass. sing. masc. . ברך
בְּרִיעָה וּ' pr. name—I. of a son of Ephraim 1 Ch. 7. 31, in which passage the signification is defined to be, *in calamity*, (רִיעָה from רוּעַ). —II. masc. Ge. 46. 17.—III. 1 Ch. 8. 13. —IV. 1 Ch. 23. 10.—Patronym. from No. II בְּרִיעִי Nu. 26. 44.
[p] בְּרִיר pref. בְּ) (noun masc. sing. dec. 1a. . רור
[q] בֹּרִית noun fem. sing. . . . . . ברר
בְּרִית וּ' noun fem. sing. dec. 1a; וּ bef. (:) . ברה
בְּרִיתוֹ וּ' id., suff. 3 pers. sing. masc.; וּ id. . ברה
בְּרִיתִי וּ' id., suff. 1 pers. sing.; וּ id. . ברה

[a] Zep. 3. 9. [b] 1 Ch. 7. 40. [c] Eze. 20. 38. [d] Eze. 48. 15. [e] Ju. 19. 17. [f] Ps. 119. 45. [g] Ca. 3. 2. [h] Is. 22. 3. [i] Job 9. 25. [k] Is. 48. 20. [l] Ne. 8. 16, 16 [m] Je. 5. 1. [n] Ps. 10. 1. [o] Jon. 2. 7. [p] Nu. 11. 8. [q] Job 31. 15. [r] Ne. 9. 19. [s] Ne. 9. 31. [t] Zec. 1. 16. [u] Job 29. 6. [x] Is. 30. 24. [y] Job 37. 11. [z] Pr. 31. 2. [a] Ju. 3. 17. [aa] Is. 37. 24. [b] Ps. 73. 4. [c] Nu. 16. 30. [d] Ge. 41. 5, 18. [e] Da. 1. 15. [f] Ge. 41. 2. [g] Pr. 18. 6. [h] Eze. 34. 20. [i] Is. 15. 5. [k] Ex. 40. 18. [l] Na. 3. 13. [m] Is. 43. 14. [n] 2 Ch. 14. 6. [o] Da. 3. 28. [p] Job 6. 6. [q] Je. 2. 22. [r] Ps. 25. 14.

בְּרִיתֵךְ[a] id., suff. 2 pers. sing. fem. . . . ברה

בְּרִיתְךָ / וּבְרִיתְךָ[b] } id., suff. 2 pers. sing. masc.; וּ bef. (:) ברה

בְּרִיתְכֶם[c] id., suff. 2 pers. pl. masc. . . . ברה

[בָּרַךְ] I. *to bend the knee, to kneel.*—II. *to worship, to bless,* בָּרוּךְ יְהוָה *blessed be the Lord.* Niph. *to be blessed.* Pi.—I. *to praise, adore, bless* God, const. with acc., לְ.—II. *to bless, to pronounce a blessing* upon any one, of men towards men.—III. meton. by a euphemism, *to curse* God, comp. Job 1. 5, 11. —IV. *to salute, greet.* Pu. pass. of Pi. Nos. I. II. Hiph. *to make to kneel* Ge. 24. 11; perhaps *to bend the knee* 41. 43. Hithp. *to be blessed,* with בְּ *in* or *through* whom; reflex. De. 29. 18.

בְּרַךְ Chald.—I. *to kneel.*—II. *to bless.* Pa. *to bless, praise.*

בֶּרֶךְ fem. dec. 6a, (du. בִּרְכַּיִם) *knee.*

בְּרַךְ Chald. dec. 3b, id. Da. 6. 11.

בְּרָכָה once בְּרָכָה fem. dec. 11c.—I. *a blessing,* either an ascription of praise to God, or *blessing* received of God.—II. *gift, present.*—III. *peace.*— IV. pr. name, (*a*) of a valley 2 Ch. 20. 26; (*b*) masc. 1 Ch. 12. 3.

בְּרֵכָה fem. dec. 10, *a pool of water.*

בָּרוּךְ (*blessed*) pr. name of the companion of Jeremiah and various other men.

בָּרַכְאֵל (whom *God has blessed*) pr. name masc. Job 32. 2, 6. Other MSS. read בַּרַכְאֵל.

בֶּרֶכְיָה (whom *the Lord has blessed,* for יְבָרֶכְיָה) pr. name masc.—I. of a son of Zerubabel, 1 Ch. 3. 20.—II. ib. 9. 16.—III. Ne. 3. 4, 30.

בֶּרֶכְיָהוּ (id.) pr. name masc.—I. of the father of the prophet Zechariah, Zec. 1. 7, but בֶּרֶכְיָה ver. 1. —II. 1 Ch. 6. 24.—III. 2 Ch. 28. 12.

יְבֶרֶכְיָהוּ (*the Lord blesses* him!) pr. name m. Is. 8. 2.

בָּרֵךְ[d] Chald. Peal part. act. sing. masc. . . . ברך

בָּרֵךְ Piel inf. or imp. sing. masc. . . . ברך

בָּרֵךְ 'וּ id. imp. sing. masc.; וּ before labial . ברך

בָּרֵךְ[e] Ch. Pael pret. 3 pers. sing. masc. (§ 47. r. 1) ברך

בֵּרֵךְ 'וּ / בֵּרֵךְ[f] 'וּ[g] } Piel pret. 3 pers. sing. masc. (§ 10. rem. 1); וּ before labial . . } ברך

בֶּרֶךְ[h] noun fem. sing. (du. בִּרְכַּיִם) dec. 6a. . ברך

בָּרַכְאֵל pr. name masc. . . . . . ברך

בְּרֶכֶב 'וּ[i] pref. בְּ f. בְּהָ / בְּרֶכֶב 'וּ[k] pref. בְּ q. v. } noun masc. sing., (suff. רִכְבִּי) d. 6a; וּ bef. (:) } רכב

בִּרְכֹב[l] K. בְּרֹב q.v.; Kh. בִּרְכֹב pref. בְּ, Kal inf. constr. רכב

בְּרִכְבּוֹ 'וּ[m] pref. בְּ (noun masc. sing., suff. 3 pers. sing. masc. from רֶכֶב dec. 6a; וּ bef. (:) רכב

בְּרִכְבֵי[n] pref. id. (id. pl., constr. state . . רכב

בְּרָכָה 'וּ[o] noun fem. sing. dec. 11c, also pr. name masc.; וּ before labial . . . . ברך

בָּרְכוּ 'וּ[q] / בָּרְכוּ[p] 'וּ[nn] } Piel imp. pl. masc.; וּ id. . . ברך

בֵּרְכוֹ / בֵּרְכוֹ[r] } id. pret. 3 pers. sing. masc. (בֵּרֵךְ), suff. 3 pers. sing. masc. . . . } ברך

בֵּרְכוּ[s] 'וּ[t] id. pret. 3 pers. pl.; וּ bef. labial . ברך

בִּרְכָּיו[u] noun fem. du., suff. 3 pers. sing. masc. (§ 4. rem. 2) fr. בֶּרֶךְ dec. 6a. . . . . ברך

בִּרְכוֹהִי[w] Ch. id. du., suff. 3 pers. sing. masc. . . ברך

בֵּרְכוּנִי[y] Piel pret. 3 pers. pl., suff. 1 pers. sing. . ברך

בִּרְכוּשׁ[z] pref. בְּ for בְּהָ / בִּרְכוּשׁ[a] 'וּ pref. בְּ bef. (:) } noun masc. sing. dec. 1a. רכש

בְּרָכוֹת noun fem. pl. abs. fr. בְּרָכָה dec. 11c. . ברך

בְּרֵכוֹת noun fem., pl. of בְּרֵכָה dec. 10. . . ברך

בִּרְכוֹת[b] noun fem. pl. constr. fr. בְּרָכָה dec. 11c. . ברך

בִּרְכוֹתֵיכֶם[c] id. pl., suff. 2 pers. pl. masc. . . ברך

בָּרְכִי Piel imp. sing. fem. . . . . . ברך

בִּרְכַּי noun fem. du., suff. 1 pers. s. fr. בֶּרֶךְ d. 6a. ברך

בִּרְכֵּי[d] id. du., constr. state . . . . . ברך

בֶּרֶכְיָה וּ pr. name masc.; וּ bef. labial . . ברך

בִּרְכֶּיהָ noun f. du., suff. 3 pers. s. f. fr. בֶּרֶךְ d. 6a. ברך

בֶּרֶכְיָהוּ pr. name masc. . . . . . ברך

בִּרְכֵיהֶם[e] noun f. pl., suff. 3 pers. pl. m. fr. בֶּרֶךְ d. 6a. ברך

בִּרְכָּיו id. du., suff. 3 pers. sing. masc. . . ברך

בְּרֻכִים Kal part. pass. m., pl. of בָּרוּךְ dec. 3a. . ברך

בִּרְכַּיִם / בִּרְכַּיִם 'וּ } noun fem., du. of בֶּרֶךְ dec. 6a; וּ before labial . . . . } ברך

בֵּרַכְךָ[f] וּ / בֵּרַכְךָ 'וּ } Piel pret. 3 pers. sing. m. (בֵּרֵךְ), suff. 2 pers. sing. m. (§ 2. r. 2); וּ bef. lab. } ברך

בְּרָכָל pref. בְּ (pr. name of a place . . . רכל

בִּרְכֻלָּתְךָ[g] pref. בְּ bef. (:) (noun fem. sing., suff. 2 pers. sing. masc. fr. [רְכֻלָּה] dec. 10. . . רכל

בֵּרַכְנוּ[h] Piel pret. 1 pers. sing. . . . . ברך

בֵּרַכְנוּכֶם[i] id. id., suff. 2 pers. pl. masc. . . ברך

בָּרְכֵנִי[k] id. imp. sing. masc. (בָּרֵךְ), suff. 1 pers. sing. ברך

בֵּרְכָנִי[l] id. pret. 3 pers. s. m. (בֵּרֵךְ), suff. 1 pers. s. ברך

בִּרְכֻשׁ[m] defect. for בִּרְכוּשׁ (q. v.) . . . . רכש

בָּרְכֵת[n] Ch. Pael pret. 1 pers. sing. . . . ברך

בֵּרַכְתָּ Piel pret. 2 pers. sing. masc. . . . ברך

בֵּרַכְתָּ[o] וּ id. acc. shifted by conv. וּ, bef. lab. for וְ; (§ 8. rem. 7) . . . . . ברך

[a] Zec. 9. 11. [b] De. 33. 9. [c] Is. 28. 18. [d] Da. 6. 11. [e] Da. 2. 19. [f] Ps. 10. 3. [g] Nu. 23. 20. [h] Is. 45. 23. [i] Is. 66. 20. [ii] Is. 28. 18. [k] Eze. 26. 7. [l] 2 Ki. 19. 23. [m] 2 Ki. 5. 9. [n] Ca. 1. 9. [nn] Ps. 134. 2. [o] Pr. 11. 26. [p] Ju. 5. 9. [q] 2 Sa. 21. 3. [r] 1 Ch. 26. 5. [s] 2 Ch. 20. 26. [t] Job 1. 5. [u] 1 Ki. 18. 42. [w] Da. 6. 11. [y] Job 31. 20. [z] Ezr. 1. 6. [a] Da. 11. 28. [b] Ps. 21. 4. [c] Mal. 2. 2. [d] Ge. 50. 23. [e] Ju. 7. 6. [f] De. 24. 13. [g] Eze. 28. 5. [h] Ps. 129. 8. [i] Ps. 118. 26. [k] Ge. 27. 34, 38. [l] Jos. 17. 14. [m] Ge. 15. 14. [n] Da. 4. 31. [o] De. 8. 10.

בְּרֶכֶת noun fem. sing., constr. of בְּרֵכָה dec. 10. — ברך
בִּרְכַּת noun fem. sing., constr. of בְּרָכָה dec. 11c. — ברך
בִּרְכֹת id. pl., constr. state . . . . — ברך
[a]בֵּרַכְתִּי Piel pret. 1 pers. sing. . . . — ברך
[b]בֵּרַכְתִּי וּ id. acc. shifted by conv. וְ, bef. lab., (§ 8. r. 7) — ברך
בִּרְכָתִי [c]וּ noun fem. sing., suff. 1 pers. sing. from בְּרָכָה dec. 11c; וּ bef. lab. . . — ברך
[d]בֵּרַכְתִּיהָ וּ Piel pret. 1 pers. s., suff. 3 pers. s. f.; וּ id. — ברך
בֵּרַכְתִּיךָ וּ id., suff. 2 pers. sing. masc.; וּ id. . — ברך
בִּרְכָתֶךָ noun f. s., suff. 2 pers. s. m. fr. בְּרָכָה d. 11c. — ברך
[e]בֵּרַכְתֶּם וּ Piel pret. 2 pers. pl. masc.; וּ bef. lab. . — ברך
[f]בֵּרַכְתָּנִי id. pret. 2 pers. sing. masc., suff. 1 pers. s. — ברך

בָּרַם Root not used; Arab. *to twist threads together*.
בְּרֹמִים masc. pl. *cloth interwoven with various colours*, Eze. 27. 24.

בְּרַם Ch. adv. *but, yet, nevertheless.*
בָּרָמָה pref. בָּ for בְּהָ, בְּהַ·)(pr. name of a place — רום
בָּרָמוֹת pref. בְּ)(pr. name of a place . . — רום
[g]בְּרֹמַח וּ pref. בְּ)(noun masc. sing. dec. 6c; (§ 35. rem. 5) וּ bef. lab. . . . . — רמח
[h]בָּרְמָחִים [i]וּ pref. בָּ for בְּהָ, בְּהַ·)(id. pl., abs. state (§ 35. rem. 9); וּ id. . . . — רמח
בְּרִמֹּן pref. בְּ)(pr. name רִמּוֹן פֶּרֶץ . . . — רמם
[k]בְּרָן־ pref. בְּ)(Kal inf. constr., with mak. [for רֹן § 18. rem. 3] . . . . — רנן
בְּרִנָּה pref. id.)(noun fem. sing. dec. 10. . . — רנן
[l]בִּרְנָנָה pref. בִּ bef. (:))(noun fem. sing. dec. 11c. — רנן
בַּרְנֵעַ pr. name, see קָדֵשׁ בַּרְנֵעַ under — קדש
בְּרִסָּה pref. בְּ)(pr. name of a place . . — רסס
בָּרָע pref. בָּ f. בְּהַ·, בְּהָ (for רַע) adj. & subst. m. dec. 8. (§ 37. rem. 7)
בְּרָע pref. בְּ q. v. — רעע
בֶּרַע (*gift*; coll. Arab.) pr. name of a king of Sodom, Ge. 14. 2.
[m]בְּרֵעַ pref. בְּ)(noun masc. sing. dec. 1. (§ 36. r. 4) — רעה
[n]בְּרֹעַ pref. id.)(noun masc. sing. . . . — רעע
בָּרָעָב [i]וּ pref. בָּ f. בְּהַ·, בְּהָ noun masc. sing. dec. 4a; וּ bef. labial
בְּרָעָב pref. בְּ q. v. — רעב
[o]בִּרְעָדָה pref. בִּ bef. (:))(noun fem. sing. . . — רעד
בָּרָעָה pref. בָּ f. בְּהַ·, בְּהָ noun fem. sing. dec. 10. [for רָעָה fr. רַע m.
בְּרָעָה pref. בְּ q. v. — רעע
בְּרִעָה וּ defect. for בְּרִיעָה q. v.
[p]בְּרֵעֹה pref. בְּ)(noun masc. sing., suff. 3 pers. sing. masc. fr. רֵעַ dec. 1a. . . — רוע
בְּרֵעֵהוּ pref. id.)(noun masc. sing., suff. 3 pers. sing. masc. fr. רֵעַ dec. 1. (§ 36. rem. 4) . — רעה

[q]בָּרָעוֹת pref. בָּ)(noun fem., pl. of רָעָה dec. 10, fr. רַע masc. (§ 37. rem. 7) . . . — רעע
[r]בְּרָעוֹתֵיהֶם pref. id.)(id. pl., suff. 3 pers. pl. masc. . — רעע
בְּרַעְיוֹן וּ pref. id.)(noun masc. sing.; וּ bef. (:) — רעה
בְּרֵעֲךָ pref. id.)(noun masc. sing., suff. 2 pers.
[t]בְּרֵעֶךָ sing. masc. fr. רֵעַ dec. 1. (§ 36. rem. 4) — רעה
[u]בְּרַעַם pref. id.)(noun masc. sing. dec. 6d. . — רעם
[x]בָּרַעַשׁ pref. בָּ f. בְּהַ· בְּהָ noun masc. sing. dec. 6d; וּ bef. (:) .
בְּרַעַשׁ [y]וּ pref. בְּ q. v. — רעש
בְּרָעָתוֹ pref. id.)(noun fem. sing., suff. 1 pers. sing. fr. רָעָה dec. 10, fr. רַע masc. (§ 37. r. 7) — רעע
[z]בִּרְעֹתוֹ pref. בִּ bef. (:))(Kal inf., suff. 3 p. s. m. d. 1a. — רעה
[a]בְּרָעָתִי pref. בְּ)(noun fem. sing., suff. 1 pers. sing. fr. רָעָה dec. 10, fr. רַע masc. (§ 37. r. 7) — רעע
[b]בְּרָעָתֶךָ pref. id.)(id., suff. 2 pers. s. m. for רָעָתְךָ — רעע
[c]בְּרָעָתֵךְ [d]וּ pref. id.)(id., suff. 2 pers. s. f.; וּ bef. (:) — רעע
[e]בְּרָעָתָם [f]וּ pref. id.)(id., suff. 3 pers. pl. m.; וּ id. — רעע
[g]בָּרְפָאִים pref. בָּ for בְּהָ, בְּהַ·)(Kal part. act. masc., pl. of רֹפֵא dec. 7b. . . . . — רפא
בִּרְפִידִים / בִּרְפִידִם pref. בִּ bef. (:))(pr. name of a place . — רפד
[h]בָּרְפָתִים pref. בָּ for בְּהָ, בְּהַ·)(n. m., pl. of [רֶפֶת] d. 6. — רפת
[i]בִּרְצוֹן pref. בִּ bef. (:))(noun masc. sing., constr. of רָצוֹן dec. 3a. . . . . — רצה
[k]בִּרְצוֹנוֹ pref. id.)(id., suff. 3 pers. sing. masc. . — רצה
[l]בִּרְצוֹנִי וּ pref. id.)(id., suff. 1 pers. sing.; וּ bef. lab. — רצה
בִּרְצוֹנְךָ [m]וּ pref. id.)(id., suff. 2 pers. sing. m.; וּ id. — רצה
[n]בִּרְצוֹת pref. id.)(Kal inf. constr. dec. 1a. . . — רצה
[o]בִּרְצוֹתִי pref. id.)(id., suff. 1 pers. sing. . . — רצה
בְּרֶצַח pref. בְּ)(noun masc. sing. . . . — רצח
[p]בִּרְצֵי pref. id.)(n. m. pl. constr. fr. [רַץ] dec. 8d. — רצץ
[q]בִּרְצֹנָם וּ pref. בִּ bef. (:))(noun masc. sing., suff. 3 pers. pl. masc. fr. רָצוֹן dec. 3c.; וּ bef. lab. — רצה
[u]בִּרְצֹתוֹ pref. id.)(Kal inf. (רְצוֹת), suff. 3 p. s. m. d. 1. — רצה

בָּרַק *to lighten, send forth lightning*, Ps. 144. 6.

בָּרָק masc. dec. 4a.—I. *lightning*.—II. *glitter of a sword*, Job 20. 25.—III. pr. name of an Israelitish captain who with Deborah defeated the Canaanites, Jud. 4. 6, &c.

בָּרְקַת, בָּרֶקֶת fem., a species of *gem*, supposed to be the *emerald.*

בַּרְקָן masc. only pl. בַּרְקָנִים *threshing wagons*, or *sledges* furnished underneath with pointed stones (prob. *fire-stones*) which were drawn over the grain. Symm. τρίβολοι *briers*.

---

[a] Ge. 17. 20. [b] Ge. 17. 16. [c] Is. 44. 3. [d] Ge. 17. 16. [e] Ex. 12. 32. [f] Ge. 32. 27. [g] Eze. 39. 9. [h] Ne. 4. 15. [i] 1 Ki. 18. 28. [k] Job 38. 7. [l] Ps. 100. 2. [m] Mi. 7. 5. [n] Ec. 7. 3. [o] Ps. 2. 11. [p] Ex. 32. 17. [q] Ps. 88. 4. [r] Ps. 141. 5. [s] Ec. 2. 22. [t] Pr. 24. 28. [tt] Job 34. 9. [u] Is. 29. 6. [x] 1 Ki. 19. 11. [y] Is. 29. 6. [z] Ge. 36. 24.
[a] Nu. 11. 15. [b] 2 Sa. 16. 8. [c] Is. 47. 10. [d] Je. 3. 2. [e] Ho. 7. 3. [f] Ps. 94. 23. [g] 2 Ch. 16. 12. [h] Hab. 3. 17. [i] Ps. 106. 4. [k] Ps. 30. 6. [l] Is. 60. 10. [m] Ps. 89. 18. [n] Pr. 16. 7. [o] 1 Ch. 29. 3. [p] Ps. 68. 31. [q] Ge. 49. 6.

בָּרָק [a] ו' noun masc. sing. dec. 4a, also pr. name masc.; ו bef. (:) . . . . . ברק

בְּרַק [b] ו' id., constr. st.; (also pr. name see בֵּן R. (בְּנֵה); ו id. . . . . . ברק

בַּרְקוֹס pr. n. m. Ezr. 2. 53; Ne. 7. 55; etym. uncertain.

בְּרָקָיו [c] noun m. pl., suff. 3 p. s. m. fr. בָּרָק d. 4a. ברק

בְּרָקִים ו' id. pl., absolute state; ו bef. (:) . . ברק

בִּרְקִיעַ pref. בְּ bef. (:))(noun masc. sing., constr. of רָקִיעַ dec. 3a. . . . . . רקע

בְּרִקְמָה [d] pref. בְּ)(noun fem. sing. dec. 12b. . . רקם

בָּרֶקֶת [e] ו noun fem. sing.; ו bef. lab. . . . ברק

בָּרֶקֶת ו noun fem. sing.; ו id. . . . . . ברק

בְּרַקָּתוֹ [f] pref. בְּ)(noun fem. sing., suff. 3 pers. sing. masc. from רַקָּה dec. 10. . . . . רקק

בָּרַר I. *to separate*, with מִן Eze. 20. 38; hence, *to select, choose out.*—II. *to purge, purify;* only part. בָּרוּר *pure, chaste.*—III. *to examine, prove.* Niph. *to purify oneself;* part. נָבָר *pure*, morally. Pi. *to purify*, Da. 11. 35. Hiph.—I. *to cleanse, clear*, as corn.—II. *to polish, furbish* a sword. Hithpa. *to be purified*, Da. 12. 10; *to show oneself pure*, morally.

בַּר masc. בָּרָה fem. (§ 37. r. 7) adj.—I. *chosen, beloved*, Ca. 6. 9.—II. *pure, clear;* also *pure* in a moral sense.—III. *empty*, Pr. 14. 4.

בַּר, בָּר masc.—I. *corn, grain*, purified from the chaff; also of growing corn, Ps. 65. 14.—II. *open fields, country*, Job 39. 4.

בַּר Ch. masc. emph. בָּרָא (for בַּרָּא § 37. r. 7) *open fields, country.*

בֹּר masc. d. 1a.—I. *cleanness, purity.*—II. *soap.*

בֹּרִית fem. *soap*, Je. 2. 22; Mal. 3. 2.

בַּרְבֻּרִים masc. pl. 1 Ki. 5. 3, Vulg. *birds, fowls;* Kimchi, *capons;* Gesenius *geese*, from their whiteness; Prof. Lee, *choice beasts.*

בְּרֻרוֹת [g] Kal part. pass. f., pl. of בְּרוּרָה d. 10, fr. בָּרוּר m. ברר

בָּרַשׁ Root not used; signification uncertain.

בְּרוֹשׁ masc. dec. 1, *fir-tree.* Gesenius, Lee, *cypress.*—II. any thing made of that wood, as *a lance*, Nah. 2. 4; *musical instrument*, 2 Sa. 6. 5.

בְּרֹשָׁיו [h] noun m. pl., suff. 3 p. s. m. fr. בְּרוֹשׁ d. 1a. ברש

בְּרָשִׁים [i] pref. בְּ)(Kal part. act. m., pl. of רָשׁ d. 1a. רוש

בְּרֶשַׁע pref. id.)(n. m. s. d. 6a. (suff. רִשְׁעוֹ; § 35. r. 5) רשע

בִּרְשַׁע (for בֶּן־רֶשַׁע *son of wickedness*, comp. בִּשְׁלָם) pr. name of a king of Gomorrah, Ge. 14. 2.

בְּרִשְׁעוֹ [k] pref. בְּ)(id., suff. 3 pers. sing. masc. fr. רֶשַׁע dec. 6a. (§ 35. rem. 5) . . רשע

בָּרְשָׁעִים [l] pref. בָּ for בְּהַ·, בְּהָ)(adj. m., pl. of רָשָׁע d. 4a. רשע

בְּרִשְׁעַת [m] ו' pref. בְּ)(noun fem. s., constr. of רִשְׁעָה (no pl.); ו bef. (:) . . . רשע

בְּרִשְׁעָתוֹ [o] ו pref. id.)(id. suff. 3 pers. s. masc.; ו id. רשע

בְּרֶשֶׁת pref. id.)(noun fem. sing. dec. 13a. . . ירש

בְּרִשְׁתּוֹ [p] pref. id.)(id., suff. 3 pers. sing. masc. . ירש

בְּרַתִּיקוֹת [q] pref. id.)(n. f. pl. Kh. רַתִּיקוֹת, K. רַתּוּקוֹת רתק

בֹּרֹת [r] ו n. m. with pl. f. term. fr. בּוֹר d. 1; ו bef. lab. באר

בְּרִתְמָה pref. בְּ)(pr. name of a place . . . רתם

בֹּשׁ [s] ו' Kal pret. 3 p. s. m. (§ 21. r. 2); ו bef. lab. בוש

בְּשַׁאֲנָתִי [t] pref. בְּ)(noun fem. sing., suff. 1 pers. sing. from שַׁאֲנָה dec. 11c. (§ 42. rem. 1) . שאג

בִּשְׁאוֹל pref. בְּ bef. (:))(noun masc. sing. . . שאל

בְּשָׁאוֹן [u] pref. בְּ)(noun masc. sing. dec. 3a. . שאה

בִּשְׁאָט pref. בְּ bef. (:))(noun masc. sing. . . שאט

בְּשֶׁאֱלָתִי [w] pref. id.)(noun fem. sing., suff. 1 pers. sing. from שְׁאֵלָה dec. 10 & 11, (§ 42. rem. 4) שאל

בִּשְׁאָר [y] pref. id.)(noun masc. sing. . . . שאר

בִּשְׁאָר [z] Ch. pref. id.)(n. m. s., constr. of שְׁאָר d. 1a. שאר

בַּשְׂאֵת [a] pref. בַּ for בְּהַ)(noun f. s. (§ 39. No. 4. r. 2) נשא

בִּשְׂאֵת [b] ו' pref. בְּ bef. (:))(Kal inf. constr. (§ 25. No. 2. § 39. No. 4. rem. 2) dec. 1a; ו bef. lab. נשא

בְּשׁוּבוֹ [c] pref. בְּ)(Kal inf. (שׁוּב), suff. 3 p. s. m. d. 1a. שוב

בִּשְׁבוּעָה [d] ו pref. בְּ bef. (:))(noun f. s. d. 10; ו bef. lab. שבע

בַּשָּׁבֶט pref. בַּ for בְּהַ)(Seg. n. in pause as if for [שֶׁבֶט=שָׁבֶט § 35. r. 2], but see the foll. . שבט

בְּשֵׁבֶט pref. id. } noun com. sing. dec. 6b; ו bef. lab. . . . } שבט
בְּשֵׁבֶט [e] ו' pref. בְּ }

בְּשִׁבְטֵי pref. id.)(id. pl., constr. state . . שבט

בְּשִׁבְטָיו [f] pref. בְּ bef. (:))(id. pl., suff. 3 pers. s. m. שבט

בְּשִׁבְטֶךָ [g] pref. בְּ)(id. s., suff. 2 pers. s. m. for שִׁבְטְךָ שבט

בַּשֶּׁבִי } pref. בַּ for בְּהַ } n. m. s. d. 6i. (§ 35. r. 14) שבה
בַּשֶּׁבִי }
בַּשְּׁבִי [h] } pref. בְּ bef. (:) }

בַּשִּׁבְיָה pref. בַּ for בְּהַ)(noun fem. sing. . . שבה

בַּשְּׁבִיעִי ו' pref. id.)(adj. ordin. m.; ו bef. lab. שבע

בִּשְׁבִית [k] pref. id.)(noun fem. sing. dec. 1a. . שבה

בְּשִׁבֳּלִים [l] pref. id.)(noun fem. with pl. masc. term. from שִׁבֹּלֶת (§ 44. rem. 2) . . שבל

בְּשֶׁבַע [m] ו' pref. בְּ)(num. card. fem. (constr. שְׁבַע § 35. rem. 7); ו bef. (:) . . . שבע

בְּשִׁבְעָה [n] ו' pref. id.)(id. fem., constr. שִׁבְעַת; ו id. שבע

בְּשִׁבְעָה pref. בְּ bef. (:))(noun fem. sing., constr. of שְׁבוּעָה dec. 10. . . . . שבע

[a] Job 20. 25. [b] Na. 3. 3. [c] Ps. 97. 4. [d] Eze. 27. 7. [e] Eze. 28. 13. [f] Ju. 4. 21, 22. [g] Ne. 5. 18. [h] 2 Ki. 19. 23. [i] Pr. 22. 7. [k] Eze. 31. 11. [l] Pr. 24. 19. [m] De. 9. 5. [n] De. 9. 4. [o] Pr. 11. 5. [p] Ps. 10. 9. [q] 1 Ki. 6. 21. [r] De. 6. 11. [s] Je. 48. 13. [t] Ps. 32. 3. [u] Am. 2. 2. [w] Est. 7. 3. [y] Est. 9. 12. [z] Ezr. 7. 18. [a] Le. 13. 10. [b] Ex. 27. 7. [c] 2 Sa. 8. 13. [d] Ne. 10. 30. [e] Ps. 78. 67. [f] Ps. 105. 37. [g] Mic. 7. 14. [h] Da. 11. 33. [i] Zec. 7. 5. [k] Nu. 21. 29. [l] Ruth 2. 2. [m] Ge. 41. 34, 47. [n] Job 5. 19. [o] De. 28. 7, 25.

בְּשִׁבְעִים[a] pref. בְּ)(num. card. com. pl. of שֶׁבַע (§ 35. r. 16) שבע

בַּשְּׁבִעִת[b] ו'' [c] pref. בַּ for בְּהַ)(adj. ordin., fem. of שְׁבִיעִי; וּ bef. lab. . . . . . שבע

בִּשְׁבֻעַת[d] pref. בְּ bef. (:))(n. f. s., constr. of שְׁבוּעָה d. 10. שבע

בִּשְׁבֻעֹתֵיכֶם[zz] pref. בְּ)(noun masc. pl. fem., suff. 2 pers. pl. masc. from שָׁבוּעַ (§ 32. rem. 1) . שבע

בַּשֶּׁבֶר[f] pref. בַּ for בְּהַ }
בְּשֶׁבֶר[g] pref. בְּ q. v. } noun masc. sing. (suff. שִׁבְרִי) dec. 6a. . שבר

בְּשִׁבְרוֹן[h] pref. id.)(n. m. s., constr. of שִׁבָּרוֹן dec. 3c. שבר

בְּשִׁבְרִי pref. id.)(Kal inf. [שְׁבֹר], suff. 1 pers. sing. 16. rem. 10) . . . . שבר

בַּשַּׁבָּת pref. בַּ for בְּהַ)(noun com. sing. dec. 8a, (but pl. שַׁבָּתוֹת constr. שַׁבְּתוֹת) . שבת

בַּשָּׁבֶת[i] pref. id.)(in pause seg. as if for שַׁבָּת=שָׁבֶת (§ 32. rem. 2) but see the following: . ישב

בְּשֶׁבֶת[k] pref. id. }
בְּשֶׁבֶת pref. בְּ } Kal inf. and subst. fem. (suff. שִׁבְתִּי) dec. 13a. . ישב

בְּשַׁבַּתּוֹ pref. id.)(n. com. s., suff. 3 p. s. m. (see בַּשַּׁבָּת) שבת

בְּשִׁבְתּוֹ[l] pref. id.)(Kal inf. (שֶׁבֶת), suff. 3 pers. sing. masc. dec. 13a. . . . . . ישב

בַּשַּׁבָּתוֹת[m] ו'' pref. בַּ for בְּהַ)(noun com. pl. abs. (see בַּשַּׁבָּת); וּ bef. lab. . . . שבת

בְּשִׁבְתִּי[o] pref. בְּ)(Kal inf. (שֶׁבֶת), suff. 1 p. s. d. 13a. ישב

בְּשִׁבְתְּךָ pref. id.)(id., suff. 2 pers. sing. masc. . ישב

בְּשִׁבְתְּכֶם[p] pref. id.)(id., suff. 2 pers. pl. masc. . ישב

בְּשִׁבְתָּם[q] pref. id.)(id., suff. 3 pers. pl. masc. . . ישב

בְּשִׁבְתֵּנוּ[r] pref. id.)(id., suff. 1 pers. pl. . . ישב

בְּשַׁבְּתֹתֵיכֶם[s] pref. id.)(noun com. pl., suff. 2 pers. pl. masc. (see בַּשַּׁבָּת) . . . . שבת

בִּשְׁגָגָה pref. בְּ bef. (:))(noun fem. sing. dec. 11c. שגג

בְּשָׂגִיב וּ pref. id.)(pr. name m., Kh. שָׂגִיב, K. שָׂגוּב שגב

בְּשַׁגָּם[t] preff. בְּ and שַׁ with גַּם adv.; or, Kal inf. [שַׁג § 18. rem. 3] with suff. 3 pers. pl. masc. שגג

בַּשִּׁגָּעוֹן[u] pref. בַּ f. בְּהַ }
בְּשִׁגָּעוֹן pref. בְּ q. v. } noun masc. sing. . . . שגע

בַּשָּׂדֶה[x] ו'' pref. בַּ f. בְּהַ }
בְּשָׂדֶה pref. בְּ q. v. } noun masc. sing. dec. 9b; וּ before labial . שדה

בִּשְׂדֵה pref. בְּ bef. (:))(id., construct state . שדה

בִּשְׂדֵי[y] ו'' pref. id.)(id. pl., constr. st.; וּ bef. lab. שדה

בְּשָׂדְךָ[z] }
בְּשָׂדְךָ[a] } pref. בְּ)(id. sing., suff. 2 pers. sing. masc. שדה

בְּשַׁדְמוֹת[ee] pref. id.)(noun fem. pl. constr. from שְׁדֵמָה dec. 11. (§ 42. rem. 4) . . . שדם

בַּשִּׁדָּפוֹן ו'' [c] pref. בַּ for בְּהַ)(noun masc. sing. . שדף

בִּשְׂדֹתָם[d] pref. בְּ bef. (:))(noun masc. pl., suff. 3 pers. pl. masc. from שָׂדֶה dec. 9a. . . שדה

בְּשֶׂה pref. בְּ)(noun com. sing. irr (§ 45) . שיה

בְּשֹׁהַם[e] pref. id.)(noun masc. sing. . . . שהם

בַּשָּׁו[kk] pref. בַּ for בְּהַ)(noun masc. sing., K. שָׁוְא שוא

בָּשׁוּ וְ', ו'' Kal pret. 3 pers. pl. (§ 21. rem. 2); וּ bef. lab., for וְ see lett. ו . בוש

בְּשׂוֹא[f] pref. בְּ)(Kal inf. constr. for נְשֹׂא (§ 17. r. 1) נשא

בְּשׁוֹאָה[g] pref. id.)(noun fem. sing. dec. 10. . שאה

בְּשׁוּב ו'' pref. id.)(Kal inf. constr.; וּ bef. (:) . שוב

בְּשׁוֹבְבִי[h] pref. id.)(Pilel inf. (שׁוֹבֵב), suff. 1 p. s. d. 7b. שבב

בְּשׁוּבָה[i] pref. id.)(noun fem. sing. . . . שוב

בְּשׁוּבוֹ[k] pref. id.)(Kal inf. (שׁוּב), suff. 3 pers. s. m. שוב

בְּשׁוּבִי pref. id.)(id., suff. 1 pers. sing. . . שוב

בְּשׁוּבְכֶם[l] pref. id.)(id., suff. 2 pers. pl. masc. . שוב

בְּשׁוּבֵנִי[m] pref. id.)(id., suff. 1 pers. sing. . . שוב

בְּשָׁוֵה pref. id.)(pr. name in compos. שָׁוֵה קִרְיָתַיִם שוה

בְּשׁוֹט[n] pref. id.)(noun masc. sing. dec. 1a. . שוט

בַּשּׁוֹטִים pref. בַּ for בְּהַ)(id. pl. abs. . . . שוט

בְּשׁוּלֶיהָ[o] pref. בְּ)(n. m. pl., suff. s. fem. fr. [שׁוּל] d. 1. שול

בַּשּׁוּלַמִּית pref. בַּ for בְּהַ)(gent. noun fem. . . שלם

בְּשׂוּם[p] pref. בְּ)(Kal inf. constr. dec. 1a. . שום

בְּשׂוּמוֹ pref. id.)(id., suff. 3 pers. sing. masc. . שום

בְּשׂוּמִי pref. id.)(id., suff. 1 pers. sing. . . שום

בְּשׁוּנֵם pref. id.)(pr. name of a place . . שאן

וּבְשַׁוְּעוֹ[q] וּ pref. id.)(Piel inf. [שַׁוַּע], suff. 3 pers. sing. masc. dec. 7b; וּ bef. (:) . . . שוע

בְּשַׁוְּעִי pref. id.)(id. with suff. 1 pers. sing. . שוע

בַּשּׁוֹפָר pref. בַּ f. בְּהַ }
בְּשׁוֹפָר[r] pref. בְּ q. v. } noun masc. sing. dec. 2b. שפר

בַּשּׁוֹפָרוֹת ו'' pref. בַּ f. בְּהַ }
בְּשׁוֹפָרוֹת[s] וּ pref. בְּ q. v. } id. pl., abs. state; וּ bef. (:) שפר

בַּשּׁוּק pref. בַּ for בְּהַ)(noun masc. sing. (pl. שְׁוָקִים § 35. rem. 13) . . . . שוק

בְּשׁוֹקֵי[t] pref. בְּ)(n. fem. pl. constr. from שׁוֹק d. 1a. שוק

בַּשְּׁוָקִים[u] pref. בַּ for בְּהַ)(noun masc., pl. of שׁוּק (§ 35. rem. 13) . . . . שוק

בְּשׁוֹר[x] pref. בְּ)(noun masc. sing. dec. 1a. (pl. שְׁוָרִים § 35. rem. 13) . . . . . שור

בְּשֹׂרָה[y] noun fem. sing. . . . . בשר

בְּשׁוּרֵי[z] pref. בְּ)(noun masc. pl., suff. 1 pers. pl. from [שׁוּר] dec. 1a. . . . . שור

בְּשׁוּרִי[a] pref. id.)(Kal inf. [שׁוּר], suff. 1 pers. sing. שור

בְּשׁוֹרְרָי[b] pref. id.)(Kal part. act. pl., suff. 1 pers. sing. from [שׁוֹרֵר] dec. 7b. . . . שרר

בְּשׁוּשַׁן }
ו'' בְּשׁוּשַׁן } pref. id.)(pr. name of a place; וּ bef. (:) שוש

בַּשֹּׁשַׁנִּים pref. בַּ for בְּהַ)(noun m., pl. of שׁוֹשָׁן d. 8a. שוש

[a] De. 10. 22. [b] 1 Ki. 18. 44. [c] Ex. 21. 2. [d] Nu. 5. 21. [e] Nu. 26. 28. [f] Ge. 47. 14. [g] La. 4. 10. [h] Eze. 21. 11. [i] 2 Sa. 23. 7. [k] 2 Sa. 23. 8. [l] Pr. 31. 23. [m] Eze. 46. 3. [n] Eze. 45. 17. [o] 2 Sa. 15. 8. [p] Le. 26. 35. [q] Eze. 39. 26. [r] Ex. 16. 3. [s] Le. 26. 35. [t] Ge. 6. 3. [u] Zec. 12. 4. [x] Ge. 39. 5. [y] Pr. 23. 10. [z] De. 24. 19. [zz] Nu. 28. 26. [a] De. 11. 15. [b] 2 Ki. 23. 4. [c] De. 28. 22. [d] Ne. 11. 25. [e] Job 28. 16. [ee] 2 Ki. 23. 4. [f] Ps. 89. 10. [g] Ps. 35. 8. [h] Eze. 39. 27. [i] Is. 30. 15. [k] Eze. 18. 23. [kk] Job 15. 31. [l] 2 Ch. 30. 9. [m] Eze. 47. 7. [n] Job 5. 21. [o] La. 1. 9. [p] Job 37. 15. [q] Ps. 22. 25. [r] Is. 27. 13. [s] 2 Ch. 15. 14. [t] Ps. 147. 10. [u] Ca. 3. 2. [x] De. 22. 10. [y] 2 Sa. 18. 25, 27. [z] Ps. 92. 12. [a] Ho. 9. 12. [b] Ps. 59. 11.

בַּשַּׁחַר[a] pref. בַּ for בְּהַ } noun masc. sing. . . שחר
בְּשַׁחַר pref. בְּ q. v. }
בִּשְׂחוֹק[b] pref. בִּ bef. (:))(Kal inf. constr. . . שחק
בְּשַׁחוּתוֹ[c] pref. id.)(noun fem. sing., suff. 3 pers. sing. masc. from [שְׁחוּת] dec. 1a. . . שחה
וּבְשַׁחֲטָם[d] וּ pref. בְּ)(Kal inf. [שְׁחֹט], suff. 3 pers. pl. m. (§ 16. r. 10, comp. § 35. r. 10. & d. 6d. שחט
בַּשְּׁחִין[e] pref. בַּ for בְּהַ } noun masc. sing. . שחן
בִּשְׁחִין pref. בִּ bef. (:) }
בִּשְׁחִיתוֹתָם[f] pref. id.)(noun fem. pl., suff. 3 pers. pl. masc. from [שְׁחִית] dec. 1a. . . שחה
בַּשַּׁחֶפֶת[g] pref. בַּ for בְּהַ)(noun fem. sing. . . שחף
בַּשַּׁחַק pref. id.)(noun masc. sing. dec. 6d. . . שחק
בִּשְׂחֹק[h] pref. בִּ bef. (:))(noun masc. sing. . שחק
בַּשְּׁחָקִים pref. בַּ for בְּהַ)(n. m., pl. of שַׁחַק dec. 6d. שחק
בַּשַּׁחַר[i] pref. id.)(noun masc. sing. dec. 6d. . שחר
בַּשָּׁחַת[k] pref. id. }
בַּשַּׁחַת[l] pref. id. } noun fem. sing. dec. 13a. . שוח
בְּשַׁחַת pref. בְּ }
בְּשַׁחֵת[m] pref. id.)(Piel inf. constr. (§ 14. rem. 1) . שחת
בְּשַׁחְתָּם[n] pref. id.)(n. fem. sing., suff. 3 pers. pl. m. [for שַׁחַתָּם comp. § 35. r. 5] from שַׁחַת d. 13a. שוח
בַּשִּׁטִּים pref. בַּ for בְּהַ)(pr. name of a place . שטה
בַּשֶּׁטֶף[o] pref. id. } noun masc. sing.; וּ bef. (:) . שטף
וּבְשֶׁטֶף[p] וּ pref. בְּ }
בְּשֵׂיבָה pref. id.)(noun fem. sing. dec. 10. . שיב
בְּשִׁבְתּוֹ[q] pref. id.)(noun fem. sing., suff. 3 pers. sing. masc. from שִׁיבָה dec. 10. . . . ישב
בַּשִּׂיד[r] pref. בַּ for בְּהַ)(noun masc. sing. . שיד
וּבְשִׁיחוֹר וּ pref. בְּ)(pr. name of a river; וּ bef. (:) . שחר
בְּשִׂיחִי pref. id.)(noun masc. sing., suff. 1 pers. sing. from שִׂיחַ dec. 1a. . . . שיח
בְּשִׁילֹה }
בְּשִׁילוֹ } pref. id.)(pr. name of a place . . שלה
בַּשִּׁיר pref. בַּ for בְּהַ } noun m. s. d. 1a; וּ bef. (:) שיר
בְּשִׁיר[s] וּ/ pref. בְּ q. v. }
וּבְשִׁירִים[t] וּ pref. id.)(id. pl., absolute state; וּ id. שיר
בְּשִׁכְבָהּ[u] pref. id.)(Kal inf. (שְׁכַב), suff. 3 pers. sing. fem. (§ 16. rem. 10) . . . שכב
בְּשָׁכְבוֹ[x] pref. id.)(id. (שְׁכֹב), suff. 3 pers. sing. masc. שכב
בְּשָׁכְבְּךָ[y] וּ/ pref. id.)(id. id., suff. 2 p. s. m.; וּ bef. (:) שכב
בְּשֶׁכְּבָר[z] preff. בְּ & שֶׁ (q. v.))(adv. . . . כבר
בַּשֵּׂכוּ pref. בַּ for בְּהַ)(pr. name of a place . שכה
בְשֻׂכּוֹת[a] pref. בְּ)(noun fem., pl. of [שֻׂכָּה] dec. 10. שכך
בְּשֵׂכֶל[b] pref. id.)(noun m. sing., (suff. שִׂכְלוֹ) dec. 6a. שכל
בִּשְׁכֶם pref. בִּ bef. (:))(pr. name of a place . שכם

בְּשָׁכְנוֹ[c] pref. id.)(Kal inf. constr. . . . שכן
בַּשֵּׁכָר[d] וּ/ pref. בַּ for בְּהַ)(n. m. sing.; וּ bef. lab. שכר
בִּשְׂכָרוֹ[e] pref. בִּ bef. (:))(n. m. s., suff. שָׂכָר dec. 4a. שכר

בָּשַׁל[f] I. *to boil* intrans. Eze. 24. 5.—*to ripen, become ripe,* Joel 4. 13. Pi. *to boil, cook, seethe.* Pu. pass. of Pi.—Hiph. *to ripen,* bring to maturity, Ge. 40. 10.

בָּשֵׁל adj., fem. בְּשֵׁלָה *boiled, sodden,* Ex. 12. 9; Nu. 6. 19.

מְבַשְּׁלוֹת fem. pl. (of מְבַשֶּׁלֶת dec. 13) *boilers,* Eze. 46. 23.

בָּשֵׁל[g] וּ adj. masc. sing.; וּ bef. lab. . . . בשל
בַּשֵּׁל[h] וּ Piel imp. sing. masc.; וּ id. . . בשל
בְּשֶׁלִּי[i] pref. בְּ)(particle made up of the preff. שׁ & ל see שׁ
בְּשֵׁלָה[k] adj. fem. sing. from בָּשֵׁל masc. . . בשל
בְּשִׁלֹה pref. בְּ)(pr. name of a place, see שִׁילֹה . שלה
בֻּשָּׁלָה[l] Pual pret. 3 p. s. fem. [for בֻּשְּׁלָה comp. § 8. r. 7] בשל
בָּשְׁלוּ[m] Kal pret. 3 pers. pl. . . . . בשל
בַּשְּׁלוּ[n] Piel imp. pl. masc; p. בַּשֵּׁלוּ Ex. 16. 23. . בשל
בְּשִׁלוֹ pref. בְּ)(pr. name of a place, see שִׁילֹה שלה
בִּשְּׁלוּ וּ/ Piel pret. 3 pers. pl.; וּ bef. lab. . בשל
בְּשַׁלְוָה[o] וּ/[p] pref. בְּ)(n. fem. sing. (no pl. abs.); וּ id. שלה
בְּשַׁלְוִי[q] pref. בְּ)(noun masc. sing., suff. 1 pers. sing. from [שֶׁלֶו] dec. 6a. . . . . שלה
בַּשָּׁלוֹם pref. בַּ for בְּהַ } (prim. adj.) noun masc. s. dec. 3a; וּ before (:) } שלם
בְּשָׁלוֹם וּ/[r] pref. בְּ q. v. }
בַּשִּׁלּוּם[s] pref. בַּ for בְּהַ)(noun masc. sing. dec. 1b. שלם
בִּשְׁלוֹמָהּ[t] pref. בִּ bef. (:))(noun masc. sing., suff. 3 pers. sing. fem. from שָׁלוֹם dec. 3a. . . שלם
בִּשְׁלוֹשָׁה pref. id.)(num. card. masc. (constr. שְׁלֹשֶׁת) from שָׁלֹשׁ fem. . . . . שלש
בְּשַׁלְוֹתַיִךְ[u] pref. בְּ)(noun fem. pl., suff. 2 pers. sing. fem. from שַׁלְוָה (no pl. abs.) . . . שלה
בַּשָּׁלַח[x] pref. בַּ for בְּהַ)(n. m. s. for שֶׁלַח as if from שְׁלַח (§ 35. rem. 2) but with suff. שִׁלְחוֹ שלח
בְּשַׁלַּח[y] pref. בְּ)(Piel inf. constr. . . . שלח
בְּשֶׁלַח[z] pref. id.)(n. m. s. (suff. שִׁלְחוֹ § 35. r. 5) d. 6a. שלח
בִּשְׁלֹחַ וּ/[a] pref. בִּ bef. (:))(Kal inf. constr.; וּ bef. lab. שלח
בְּשַׁלְּחָהּ[b] pref. בְּ)(Piel inf. [שַׁלַּח] suff. 3 pers. sing. fem. dec. 7b. (§ 36. rem. 5) . . שלח
בְּשַׁלְּחוֹ[c] pref. id.)(id. with suff. 3 pers. sing. masc. שלח
בְּשַׁלְּחִי[d] pref. id.)(id., suff. 1 pers. sing. . . שלח
בְּשָׁלְחִי[e] pref. id.)(Kal inf., suff. 1 pers. sing. . שלח

---

[a] Is. 33. 15. [b] Ju. 16. 27. [c] Pr. 28. 10. [d] Eze. 23. 39. [e] Le. 13. 20. [f] La. 4. 20. [g] De. 28. 22. [h] Pr. 14. 13. [i] Ho. 10. 15. [k] Job 33. 28. [l] Job 9. 31. [m] Ge. 19. 29. [n] Eze. 19. 4, 8. [o] Da. 9. 26. [p] Na. 1. 8. [q] 2 Sa. 19. 33. [r] De. 27. 2, 4. [s] Ps. 69. 31. [t] 1 Ch. 13. 8. [u] Ge. 19. 33, 35. [x] Ruth 3. 4. [y] Pr. 6. 22. [z] Ec. 2. 16. [a] Job 40. 31. [b] 1 Ch. 26. 14. [c] Ge. 35. 22. [d] Is. 28. 7. [e] Ex. 22. 14. [f] Joel 4. 13. [g] Ex. 12. 9. [h] 2 Ki. 4. 38. [i] Ec. 8. 17. [k] Nu. 6. 19. [l] Le. 6. 21. [m] Eze. 24. 5. [n] Le. 8. 31. [o] Da. 11. 21, 24. [p] Da. 8. 25. [q] Ps. 30. 7. [r] Is. 55. 12. [s] Mi. 7. 3. [t] Je. 29. 7. [u] Je. 22. 21. [x] Job 33. 18. [y] Ex. 13. 17. [z] Job 36. 12. [a] De. 9. 23. [b] Is. 27. 8. [c] Eze. 31. 5. [d] Eze. 5. 16. [e] Nu. 32. 8.

[a] בְּשַׁלֵּחֲךָ pref. בְּ)(Piel inf. with suff. 2 pers. sing. m. [strictly from the form שַׁלַּח instead of שַׁלֵּחַ, comp. § 16. rem. 15] . שלח

[b] בַּשַּׁלִי pref. בַּ for בְּהַ)(n. m. s. [for שַׁלְיָ § 35. r. 14] שלה

[c] בְּשֶׁלִּי pref. בְּ)(particle שֶׁל (from the preff. שֶׁ & לְ) with suff. 1 pers. sing. . . . ש

[d] וּבְשִׁלְיָתָהּ וּ pref. id.)(noun fem. sing. with suff. 3 pers. sing. fem. [from שִׁלְיָה]; וּ bef. (:) . שלה

[e] בַּשְּׁלִישִׁי pref. בַּ for בְּהַ)(adj. ordin. masc. . שלש

[f] בַּשְּׁלִישִׁת pref. id.)(id. fem. defect. for שִׁית . שלש

[g] בְּשַׁלֶּכֶת pref. בְּ)(noun fem. sing. . . . שלך

[h] בַּשָּׁלָל pref. בַּ for בְּהַ)(noun masc. sing. dec. 4a. שלל

בְּשָׁלֵם pref. בְּ)(pr. name of a place . . . שלם

[i] בְּשָׁלֹם defect. for בְּשָׁלוֹם (q. v.) . . . שלם

[k] בִּשְּׁלָם Piel pret. 3 p. s. m. [בִּשֵּׁל], suff. 3 p. pl. m. בשל

בִּשְׁלָם (for בֶּן־שְׁלָם *son of peace*, comp. בִּדְקַר) pr. name masc. Ezr. 4. 7.

[l] בַּשַּׂלְמָה pref. בַּ for בְּהַ } noun fem. sing. dec. 12a. שלם
[m] בְּשַׂלְמָה pref. בְּ q. v.

בִּשְׁלֹמֹה pref. בִּ bef. (:))(pr. name masc. . . שלם

[n] וּבִשְׁלָמוֹת וּ pref. בִּ bef. (:))(n. f., pl. of שַׂלְמָה d. 12a . שלם

[o] בְּשֶׁלְּמִי pref. בְּ)(compound of שֶׁל (see בְּשֶׁל) & מִי pron. interrog. . . . . ש

[p] בִּשְׁלָמָיו pref. בִּ bef. (:))(adj. masc. pl., suff. 3 pers. sing. masc. from שָׁלוֹם dec. 3a. . . שלם

[q] וּבִשְׁלָמֵינוּ וּ pref. בִּ bef. (:))(noun masc. pl., suff. 1 pers. pl. from שֶׁלֶם dec. 6a; וּ bef. lab. . שלם

[r] בְּשַׂלְמָתוֹ pref. בְּ)(noun fem. sing., suff. 3 pers. sing. masc. from שַׂלְמָה dec. 12a. . . שלם

[s] בַּשָּׁלִשׁ pref. בַּ for בְּהַ)(noun masc. sing. defect. for שָׁלִישׁ dec. 1b. (§ 32. rem. 1) . . שלש

[t] בְּשָׁלֹשׁ pref. בְּ)(num. card. sing. fem. . . שלש

[u] וּבִשְׁלֹשׁ וּ' pref. בִּ bef. (:))(id. constr. st.; וּ bef. lab. שלש

[aa] בַּשְּׁלֹשָׁה pref. בַּ for בְּהַ } id. fem. (constr. שְׁלֹשֶׁת) שלש
בִּשְׁלֹשָׁה pref. בִּ bef. (:)

[x] וּבִשְׁלִשִׁים וּ pref. בְּ)(noun masc., pl. of שָׁלִישׁ dec. 1b. (§ 32. rem. 1); וּ bef. (:) . . . שלש

[y] בַּשְּׁלִשִׁים pref. בַּ for בְּהַ)(adj. ordin. m., pl. of שְׁלִישִׁי שלש

בִּשְׁלֹשִׁים pref. id. } num. card. com., pl. of שָׁלֹשׁ שלש
בִּשְׁלֹשִׁים pref. בִּ bef. (:)

[z] וּבִשְׁלֹשֶׁת וּ pref. id.)(id. sing. masc., constr. of שְׁלֹשָׁה (§ 42. rem. 5); וּ bef. lab. . . . שלש

וּבִשַּׁלְתָּ וּ Piel pret. 2 pers. sing. masc.; acc. shifted by conv. וּ, bef. lab. for וְ (§ 8. rem. 7) בשל

בָּשָׂם Root not used; Chald. and Syr. *to be sweet, pleasant, fragrant.*

בָּשָׂם masc. dec. 4a, *the balsam-tree,* Ca. 5. 1.

בֹּשֶׂם & בֶּשֶׂם masc. pl. בְּשָׂמִים.—I. *scent, odour of perfume.*—II. *perfumes themselves.*—III. *balsam tree,* Ca. 5. 13; 6. 2.

בָּשְׂמַת (*fragrant*) pr. name.—I. of a wife of Esau.—II. of a daughter of Solomon, 1 Ki. 4. 15.

יִבְשָׂם (*pleasant*) pr. name masc. 1 Ch. 7. 2.

מִבְשָׂם (*fragrance*) pr. name masc.—I. Ge. 25. 13.—II. 1 Ch. 4. 25.

[a] בֹּשֶׂם noun masc. sing. dec. 6. . . . בשם

וּבְשֵׁם וּ' pref. בְּ)(noun masc. s. d. 7a; וּ bef. (:) שם

[b] בְּשֻׁם Ch. pref. id.)(noun masc. sing. irr. (§ 68) שם

בֶּשֶׂם noun masc. sing. . . . . . בשם

[c] בִּשְׂמֹאולָהּ pref. בִּ bef. (:))(noun masc. sing., suff. 3 pers. sing. fem. from שְׂמֹאול dec. 1a. . שמאל

בִּשְׂמֹאלוֹ pref. id.)(id., suff. 3 pers. sing. masc. שמאל

וּבִשְׁמוֹ וּ' pref. id.)(noun masc. sing., suff. 3 pers. sing. masc. from שֵׁם dec. 7a; וּ bef. lab. . שם

[d] בִּשְׁמוֹנָה [e] וּ' pref. id.)(num. card. fem.; וּ id. . שמן

[f] בִּשְׁמוֹנִים pref. id.)(id. pl. com. gen. (comp. dec. 9) שמן

[g] בַּשְּׁמוּעָה pref. בַּ for בְּהַ)(noun fem. sing. dec. 10. . שמע

[h] בִּשְׁמוֹר pref. בִּ bef. (:))(Kal inf. constr. (§ 8. r. 18) שמר

בִּשְׁמוֹת pref. בִּ)(n. m. with pl. f. term., abs. fr. שֵׁם d. 7a. שם

[ee] בִּשְׁמוֹתָם pref. בִּ bef. (:) id. with suff. 3 pers. pl. masc. שם

בְּשִׂמְחָה pref. בְּ)(noun fem. sing. dec. 12b. . שמח

בְּשִׂמְחַת pref. id.)(id., constr. state . . . שמח

[i] בִּשְׂמָחוֹת pref. בִּ bef. (:))(id. pl., absolute state . שמח

[k] וּבְשִׂמְחָתוֹ וּ pref. בְּ)(id. s., suff. 3 p. s. m.; וּ bef. (:) שמח

[l] בְּשִׂמְחַתְכֶם pref. id.)(id. sing., suff. 2 pers. pl. masc. שמח

[m] בְּשָׂמִי noun m. s., suff. 1 pers. s. fr. [בָּשָׂם] d. 4a. בשם

[n] בִּשְׁמֵי pref. בִּ bef. (:))(noun masc., pl., constr. of שָׁמַיִם [fr. sing. שְׁמַי comp. § 38. rem. 2] שמה

[o] וּבִשְׁמִי וּ' pref. id.)(noun masc. sing. with suff. 1 pers. sing. fr. שֵׁם dec. 7a; וּ bef. lab. . שם

[p] בִּשְׁמַיָּא Ch. pref. id.)(noun masc. pl., emph. of שְׁמַיִן, comp. בִּשְׁמֵי . . . שמה

[q] בְּשָׂמָיו noun m. pl., suff. 3 pers. s. m. fr. בֶּשֶׂם d. 6. בשם

[r] בַּשְּׂמִיכָה pref. בַּ for בְּהַ)(noun fem. sing. see סמך

בַּשָּׁמַיִם } pref. id.)(noun m. pl. [of שָׁמַי comp. § 38. rem. 1] . . } שמה
בַּשָּׁמָיִם

וּבְשָׂמִים וּ' noun masc., pl. of בֶּשֶׂם dec. 6a; וּ bef. (:) בשם

בְּשָׁמִיר pref. בְּ)(pr. name of a place . . . שמר

וּבְשִׁמְךָ וּ pref. id. } noun m. s., suff. 2 p. s. m. fr. שֵׁם d. 7a; וּ bef. (:) } שם
בִּשְׁמֶךָ pref. בִּ bef. (:)

[a] De. 15. 18. [b] 2 Sa. 3. 27. [c] Jon. 1. 12. [d] De. 28. 59. [e] Eze. 31. 1. [f] 1 Sa. 3. 8. [g] Is. 6. 13. [h] Jos. 7. 21. [i] 1 Ki. 2. 5, 6. [k] 1 Ki. 19. 21. [l] 1 Ki. 11. 30. [m] 1 Ki. 11. 29. [n] Jos. 22. 8. [o] Jon. 1. 7. [p] Ps. 55. 21. [q] Jos. 22. 27. [r] De. 24. 13. [s] Is. 40. 12. [t] Is. 16. 14. [u] Ju. 7. 8. [x] 1 Sa. 18. 6. [y] Eze. 42. 3. [z] Job 32. 3. [a] Ex. 30. 23. [aa] 2 Sa. 23. 18. [b] Ezr. 5. 1. [c] Pr. 3. 16. [d] 2 Ch. 35. 19. [e] 2 Ch. 34. 3. [ee] Ps. 49. 12. [f] 1 Ki. 6. 1. [g] Je. 51. 46. [h] 2 Sa. 11. 16. [i] Ps. 45. 16. [k] Pr. 14. 10. [l] Is. 66. 5. [m] Ca. 5. 1. [n] Ps. 68. 34. [o] Ps. 89. 25. [p] Da. 6. 28. [q] Ca. 4. 16. [r] Ju. 4. 18.

בְּשִׁמְכָה [a] pref. בְּ)(id. id. for שִׁמְךָ (comp. § 3. r. 2) — שם

בַּשִּׂמְלָה pref. בַּ for בְּהַ)(noun fem. sing. dec. 12 b. — שמל

בְּשִׂמְלֹתָם [b] pref. בְּ)(id. pl., suff. 3 pers. pl. masc. — שמל

בִּשְׁמָם [c] pref. בְּ bef. (:))(noun masc. sing., suff. 3 pers. pl. masc. from שֵׁם dec. 7 a. — שם

בְּשִׁמָּמוֹן [d] e/ וּ pref. בְּ)(noun masc. sing.; וּ bef. (:) — שמם

בַּשֶּׁמֶן, בַּשָּׁמֶן } pref. בַּ f. בְּהַ; בְּשֶׁמֶן pref. בְּ q. v. } noun masc. sing., dec. 6 a. (with suff. שַׁמְנִי § 35. rem. 2) — שמן

בִּשְׁמֹנָה [f] pref. בְּ bef. (:))(masc. of the foll., (constr. שְׁמֹנַת) — שמן

בִּשְׁמֹנֶה וּ/ pref. id.)(num. card. fem.; וּ bef. labial — שמן

בִּשְׁמֹנִים [g] pref. id.)(id. pl. com. gen. — שמן

בִּשְׁמֹעַ [h] pref. id.)(Kal inf. construct — שמע

בְּשָׁמְעוֹ pref. בְּ)(id., suff. 3 pers. sing. masc. — שמע

בְּשָׁמְעוֹ [i] pref. id.)(id., suff. 3 p. s. m., K. כְּשָׁמְעוֹ (q.v.) — שמע

בְּשָׁמְעֲךָ [k] pref. id.)(id., suff. 2 p. s. m., K. כְּשָׁמְעֲךָ (q.v.) — שמע

בְּשָׁמְעֲךָ pref. id.)(id., suff. 2 pers. sing. masc. — שמע

בְּשָׁמְעֲכֶם [l] pref. id.)(id., suff. 2 pers. pl. masc. — שמע

בְּשָׁמְעָם [m] pref. id.)(id., suff. 3 pers. pl. masc. — שמע

בְּשֹׁמְרוֹן pref. id.)(pr. name of a place — שמר

בְּשָׁמְרָיִן Chald. pref. id.)(pr. name of a place — שמר

בְּשָׁמְרָם [n] pref. id.)(Kal inf., suff. 3 pers. pl. masc. — שמר

בַּשֶּׁמֶשׁ [o] pref. בַּ f. בְּהַ)(n. com. s. (suff. שִׁמְשֵׁךְ) dec. 6 a. — שמש

בָּשְׂמַת וּ/ pr. name, fem.; וּ before labial — בשם

בְּשֵׁמוֹת [p] q/ וּ pref. בְּ)(noun m. pl. abs. from שֵׁם d. 7 a. id. — שם

בִּשְׁמֹתָם pref. בְּ before (:))(id., suff 3 pers. pl. masc. — שם

בָּשָׁן (*light sandy soil*, coll. with the Arab. Gesen.) pr. name of a region beyond Jordan, between Hermon and the brook of Jabbok. נִבְשָׁן (*soft soil*) pr. name of a place in the desert, Jos. 15. 62.

בְּשֵׁן [r] pref. בְּ)(noun com. sing. dec. 8 b. — שנן

בְּשִׂנְאָה pref. id.)(noun fem. sing. (no pl.) — שנא

בְּשֹׂנְאַי [s] pref. id.)(Kal part. act. pl., suff. 1 p. s. fr. שֹׂנֵא d. 7 b. — שנא

בְּשֹׂנְאֵיהֶם pref. id.)(id. pl., suff. 3 pers. pl. masc. — שנא

בְּשִׂנְאַת [t] pref. id.)(n. f. s., constr. of שִׂנְאָה (no pl.) — שנא

בַּשָּׁנָה וּ/ pref. בַּ f. בְּהַ; בְּשָׁנָה pref. בְּ q. v. } noun fem. sing. dec. 11 a; וּ before labial — שנה

בָּשְׁנָה [u] noun fem. sing. — בוש

בָּשְׁנוּ Kal pret. 1 pers. sing. (§ 21. rem. 2) — בוש

בְּשַׁנּוֹתוֹ [v] pref. בְּ)(Piel inf., suff. 3 pers. sing. masc. — שנה

בַּשֵּׁנִי [w] pref. בַּ for בְּהַ)(adj. ord. masc. from שְׁנַיִם — שנה

בְּשִׁנָּי [x] pret. בְּ)(n. com. du., suff. 1 p. s. fr. שֵׁן dec. 8 b. — שנן

בִּשְׁנֵי a/ וּ pref. בְּ before (:))(num. card. masc., constr. of שְׁנַיִם; וּ before labial — שנה

בִּשְׁנֵי [b] וּ pref. id.)(n. m. s., constr. of שָׁנִי d. 3 a; וּ id. — שנה

בְּשִׁנֵּיהֶם [c] pref. בְּ)(n. com. du., suff. 3 p. pl. m. fr. שֵׁן d. 8 b. — שנן

בְּשִׁנָּיו [d] pref. id.)(id. du., suff. 3 pers. sing. masc. — שנן

בַּשָּׁנִים pref. בַּ for בְּהַ)(noun fem. with pl. fem. term. from שָׁנָה dec. 11 a. — שנה

בַּשְּׁנַיִם [e] pref. בַּ for בְּהַ; בִּשְׁנַיִם [f], בִּשְׁנָיִם [g] pref. בְּ bef. (:) } num. card. du. masc. — שנה

בִּשְׁנַיִם h/ וּ pref. id.)(id., construct state only before עָשָׂר; וּ before labial — שנה

בִּשְׁנַת וּ/ pref. id.)(n. f. s., constr. of שָׁנָה d. 11 a; וּ id. — שנה

בִּשְׁנַת Ch. pref. id.)(n. f. s., constr. of שְׁנָה dec. 8 a. — שנה

בַּשָּׁנָת [i] Kh. בִּשְׁנַת q. v., K. בַּשָּׁנָה (q. v.) — שנה

בָּשַׁס. Po. *to trample upon*, with עַל, Amos 5. 11.

בְּשֵׂעִיר וּ/ pref. בְּ)(pr. name of a region; וּ bef. (:) — שער

בְּשַׁעַלְבִים וּ pref. id.)(pr. name of a place; וּ id. — שעל

בְּשָׁעֳלוֹ [k] pref. id.)(n. m. s., suff. 3 p. s. m. fr. [שֹׁעַל] d. 6 f. — שעל

בְּשָׁעֳלֵי [l] pref. id.)(n. m. pl. constr. from [שֹׁעַל] dec. 6 d. — שעל

בִּשְׂעִפִּים [m] pref. בְּ before (:))(noun masc., pl. of [שְׂעִף] dec. 8 b. (§ 37. No. 3), see — סעף

בַּשַּׁעַר, בַּשָּׁעַר } pref. בַּ for בְּהַ; בְּשַׁעַר pref. בְּ q. v. } noun com sing. masc. dec. 6 d. — שער

בִּשְׁעָרָה [n] o/ וּ pref. בְּ bef. (:))(noun fem. s.; וּ bef. lab. — שער

בְּשַׁעֲרֵי pref. בְּ)(n. com. pl. constr. from שַׁעַר dec. 6 d. — שער

בִּשְׁעָרֶיהָ [p] pref. בְּ bef. (:))(id. pl., suff. 3 pers. sing. fem. — שער

בִּשְׁעָרַיִךְ pref. id.)(id. pl., suff. 2 pers. sing. fem. — שער

בִּשְׁעָרֶיךָ q/ וּ pref. id.)(id. pl., suff. 2 p. s. m.; וּ bef. lab. — שער

בְּשַׁעֲרֵיכֶם pref. בְּ)(id. pl., suff. 2 pers. pl. masc. — שער

בַּשְּׁעָרִים pref. בַּ for בְּהַ)(id. pl., absolute state — שער

בְּשַׁעֲרַיִם וּ pref. בְּ)(id. du. pr. name of a place; וּ bef. (:) — שער

בְּשָׂפָה [r] pref. id.)(noun fem. sing. dec. 11 a. — שפה

בְּשִׁפְחָתֵךְ [s] pref. id.)(noun fem. sing., suff. 2 pers. sing. masc. (for שִׁפְחָתְךָ) from שִׁפְחָה dec. 12 b. — שפח

בִּשְׁפָטִים [t] u/ וּ pref. בְּ before (:))(noun masc., pl. of [שֶׁפֶט] dec. 6; וּ before labial — שפט

בְּשָׁפְטֵךְ [w] pref. בְּ)(Kal inf., suff. 2 p. s. m. [for שָׁפְטְךָ] — שפט

בִּשְׁפֹּךְ [y] pref. בְּ before (:))(Kal inf. construct — שפך

בְּשָׁפְכֵךְ [z] pref. בְּ)(id. suff. 2 pers. sing. masc. — שפך

בַּשָּׁפֵל [a] pref. בַּ for בְּהַ)(noun masc. sing. dec. 6 b. — שפל

בִּשְׁפַל [b] pref. בְּ bef. (:))(adj. m. s., constr. of שָׁפָל d. 4 a. — שפל

בַּשְּׁפֵלָה [c] וּ pref. בַּ for בְּהַ)(noun fem. sing.; וּ bef. lab. — שפל

בַּשְּׁפֵלָה וּ/ pref. id.)(noun fem. sing. dec. 10; וּ id. — שפל

בְּשִׁפְלוּת [d] וּ pref. בְּ)(noun fem. sing.; וּ id. — שפל

בְּשִׁפְמוֹת pref. id.)(pr. name of a place — שפם

---

[a] Je. 29. 25. [b] Ex. 12. 34. [c] Ho. 2. 19. [d] Eze. 12. 19. [e] Eze. 4. 16. [f] Je. 41. 15.
[g] 2 Ki. 6. 25. [h] Ex. 16. 8. [i] 1 Sa. 11. 6. [k] 2 Sa. 5. 24. [l] Jos. 6. 5. [m] 2 Ch. 20. 29.
[n] Ps. 19. 12. [o] Is. 38. 8. [p] Nu. 32. 38. [q] Nu. 4. 32. [r] De. 19. 21. [s] Ps. 118. 7.
[t] De. 1. 27. [u] Ho. 10. 6. [x] Ps. 34. 1. [y] 2 Ch. 3. 2. [z] Job 13. 14. [a] Job 42. 7.
[b] Le. 14. 52. [c] Mi. 3. 5. [d] Job 16. 9. [e] 1 Ch. 11. 21. [f] Nu. 13. 23. [g] Ju. 15. 13.
[h] Est. 9. 1. [i] Je. 28. 1. [k] Is. 40. 12. [l] Eze. 13. 19. [m] Job 4. 13.
[n] Job 9. 17. [o] Na. 1. 3. [p] Je. 17. 27. [q] De. 6. 9; 11. 20. [r] Ps. 22. 8.
[s] 2 Ki. 4. 16. [t] Ex. 7. 4. [u] Ex. 6. 6. [x] Ps. 51. 6. [y] Eze. 17. 17.
[z] Eze. 9. 8. [a] Ec. 10. 6. [b] Ec. 12. 4. [c] Is. 32. 19. [d] Ec. 10. 18.

בְּשֶׁפֶק[a] pref. בְּ)(noun m. s. [for שֶׁפֶק § 35. rem. 2] שפק
בַּשֹּׁפָר[b] pref. בַּ for בְּהַ)(noun masc. sing. dec. 2b. שפר
בִּשְׁפַרְפָּרָא[c] Ch. pref. בְּ bef. (:))(n. m. s. emph. [of שְׁפַרְפַּר] שפר
בִּשְׂפַת pref. id.)(n. f. s., constr. of שָׂפָה dec. 11 a. שפה
בִּשְׂפָתָו[d] pref. id.)(id. du., suff. 3 pers. sing. masc., K. ־ָתִיו (§ 4. rem. 1) . . . שפה
בְּשִׂפְתוֹתֵיהֶם[e] pref. בְּ)(id. pl., suff. 3 pers. pl. masc. . שפה
בְּשִׂפְתוֹתֶיךָ[f] pref. id.)(id. pl., suff. 2 pers. sing. masc. שפה
בְּשִׂפְתֵי[g] pref. id.)(id. du., construct state . שפה
בִּשְׂפָתַי[h] pref. בְּ before (:))(id. du., suff. 1 pers. sing. שפה
בִּשְׂפָתָיו ו״[i] pref. id.)(id. du., suff. 3 p. s. m.; וּ bef. lab. שפה
בִּשְׂפָתֶיךָ pref. id.)(id. du., suff. 2 pers. sing. masc. . שפה
בִּשְׂפָתַיִם[k] pref. id.)(id. du., absolute state . . שפה
בְּשֶׁצֶף[l] pref. בְּ)(noun masc. sing. . . . שצף
בַּשָּׂק pref. בַּ for בְּהַ)(for שַׂק noun m. s. dec. 8 d. שקק
בְּשַׂקּוֹ[m] pref. בְּ)(id., suff. 3 pers. sing. masc. . שקק
בְּשִׁקּוּצֵיהֶם וּ pref. id.)(noun masc. pl., suff. 3 pers. pl. masc. from שִׁקּוּץ dec. 2b; וּ before (:) . שקץ
בַּשַּׂקִּים pref. בַּ f. בְּהַ } noun m., pl. of שַׂק dec. 6d; } שקק
בְּשַׂקִּים[n] וּ pref. בְּ q.v. } וּ id. . . . } שקק
בְּשֶׁקֶל pref. id.)(noun m. s. (pl. c. שִׁקְלֵי), dec. 6 a. שקל
בַּשָּׁקֶר pref. בַּ for בְּהַ)(noun masc. sing. for שֶׁקֶר as if from שָׁקַר (§ 35. rem. 2) but see the foll. שקר
בַּשֶּׁקֶר ו״[o] pref. id. } noun masc. sing. dec. 6 a. (see the foll.); וּ before labial } שקר
בְּשֶׁקֶר pref. בְּ } שקר
בְּשִׁקְרֵיהֶם[p] pref. id.)(id. pl. suff. 3 pers. pl. masc. . שקר
בְּשִׁקֲתוֹת[q] pref. id.)(noun fem., pl. of [שֶׁקֶת]; (but comp. § 35. rem. 9, note) . . שקה

בִּשֵּׂר. Pi.—I. *to announce, declare.*—II. *to bring, tell good tidings.*—Hithp. *to receive good tidings,* 2 Sa. 18. 31.

בְּשׂוֹר (*cool, cold,* coll. with the Arab. Gesenius) pr. name of a torrent near Gaza, 1 Sa. 30. 9, 10, 21.

בְּשֹׂרָה, בְּשׂוֹרָה fem.—I. *good tidings, news.*—II. *reward for good tidings,* 2 Sa. 4. 10.

בָּשָׂר ו״ masc. dec. 4 a.—I. *flesh.*—II. *body.*—III. כָּל־בָּשָׂר *all flesh,* i. e. all creatures or animate beings.—IV. *near relation, consanguinity.*—V. *the secret parts* (viri).

בְּשַׂר Chald. m. dec. 3 b, i.q. Heb. בָּשָׂר Nos. I, III.

בְּשַׂר ו״ n. m. s., constr. of בָּשָׂר dec. 4 a; וּ bef. (:) בשר
בְּשַׂר[r] Chald. noun masc. sing. dec. 3 b. . . בשר
בִּשֵּׂר[s] Piel pret. 3 pers. sing. masc. (§ 10. rem. 1) בשר
בִּשְׂרָא Chald. noun masc. s., emph. of בְּשַׂר dec. 3 b. בשר
בַּשֶּׂרֶד[t] pref. בַּ for בְּהַ)(noun masc. sing. . שרד

בְּשָׂרָהּ[u] noun m. s., suff. 3 pers. s. f. from בָּשָׂר dec. 4 a. בשר
בְּשֹׂרָה noun fem. sing. . . . . . בשר
בַּשְּׂרוּ Piel imp. pl. masc. . . . . בשר
בְּשָׂרוֹ ו״[x] noun masc. sing., suff. 3 pers. sing. masc. from בָּשָׂר dec. 4 a; וּ before (:) . . בשר
בַּשָּׁרוֹן pref. בַּ for בְּהַ)(pr. name of a region . ישר
בְּשָׁרוֹתֶיהָ[y] pref. בְּ)(noun fem. pl., suff. 3 pers. sing. fem. from [שָׁרָה] dec. 10. . . שור
בְּשָׂרִי ו n. m. s., suff. 1 p. s. from בָּשָׂר dec. 4 a; וּ bef. (:) בשר
בַּשְּׂרִידִים[z] וּ pref. בַּ for בְּהַ)(noun masc., pl. of שָׂרִיד dec. 3 a; וּ before labial . . שרד
בְּשָׁרִים[a] pref. id.)(noun masc., pl. of שִׁיר dec. 1 a. . שיר
בְּשָׂרִים[b] noun masc., pl. of בָּשָׂר dec. 4 a. . . בשר
בְּשָׂרִים[c] pref. בְּ)(noun masc. pl. of שַׂר (§ 37. r. 7) שרר
בְּשָׁרִים[d] וּ pref. id.)(noun masc., pl. of שִׁיר dec. 1 a. שיר
בִּשְׁרִירוּת pref. בְּ before (:))(noun fem. sing. . שרר
בְּשָׁרִירֵי[e] pref. id.)(adj. m. pl. constr. from [שָׁרִיר] d. 3 a. שרר
בְּשָׂרְךָ[f] } noun masc. sing., suff. 2 pers. sing. masc. } בשר
בְּשָׂרֶךָ ו״ } from בָּשָׂר dec. 4 a; וּ before (:) . } בשר
בְּשַׂרְכֶם[g] ו״[h] id., suff. 2 pers. pl. masc.; וּ id. . בשר
בְּשָׂרָם ו״[i] id., suff. 3 pers. pl. masc.; וּ id. . בשר
בְּשָׂרֵנוּ id., suff. 1 pers. pl. . . . . בשר
בַּשֶּׁרֶץ[k] pref. בַּ for בְּהַ)(noun masc. sing. . שרץ
בִּשְׁרִרוּת defect. for בִּשְׁרִירוּת (q. v.) . . שרר
בַּשַּׁרְשְׁרוֹת[l] pref. בַּ for בְּהַ)(n. f., pl. of [שַׁרְשְׁרָה] dec. 10. שרר
בִּשַּׂרְתָּ[m] וּ Piel pret. 2 pers. sing. masc.; acc. shifted by conv. וּ, before labial for וְ (§ 8. rem. 7) בשר
בִּשַּׂרְתִּי[n] id. pret. 1 pers. sing. . . . בשר
בְּשָׁרְתָם[o] pref. בְּ)(Piel inf. (שָׁרֵת), suff. 3 p. pl. m. d. 7 b. שרת
בַּשֵּׁשׁ[p] וּ pref. בַּ for בְּהַ)(noun masc. s.; וּ bef. lab. שש
בְּשֵׁשׁ pref. בְּ)(num. card. fem. . . . שש
בּשֵׁשׁ Pilel pret. 3 pers. sing. masc. . . בוש
בְּשֻׁשָׁן pref. בְּ)(noun m. s. dec. 3 a. (§ 32. rem. 6) שוש
בַּשִּׁשִּׁי pref. בַּ for בְּהַ)(adj. ordin. masc. from שֵׁשׁ שש
בְּשִׁשִּׁים[q] וּ pref. בְּ)(num. card. com., pl. of שֵׁשׁ שש
בַּשָּׁשַׁר pref. בַּ for בְּהַ)(noun masc. sing. [for שָׁשֵׁר ששר
בֹּשֶׁת ו״[r] n. f. s. dec. 13 c. (§ 39. No. 4); וּ bef. lab. בוש
בֹּשְׁתְּ[s] ו״ Kal pret. 2 p. s. f. (§ 21. r. 2); for וְ see lett. ו בוש
בָּשְׁתִּי[t] וּ noun f. s., suff. 1 pers. s. from בֹּשֶׁת (q. v.) בוש
בַּשְּׁתִי pref. בַּ for בְּהַ } noun masc. sing. . . שתה
בִּשְׁתִי[u] pref. בְּ bef. (:) } שתה
בִּשְׁתֵּי ו״[y] construct of בִּשְׁתַּיִם (q. v.) . . שנה
בֹּשְׁתִּי Kal pret. 1 pers. sing. (§ 21. rem. 2) . בוש
בִּשְׁתַּיִם ו״ pref. בְּ before (:))(num. card., constr. שְׁתֵּי, fem. of שְׁנַיִם; וּ before labial שנה
בִּשְׁתֵּים[x] ו״[a] pref. id.)(id., constr. state, only bef. עֶשְׂרֵה שנה

[a] Job 36. 18. [b] 2 Sa. 20. 22. [c] Da. 6. 20. [d] Pr. 26. 24. [e] Ps. 59. 8. [f] Ps. 45. 3.
[g] Pr. 10. 13. [h] Ps. 119. 13. [i] Is. 29. 13. [k] Le. 5. 4. [l] Is. 54. 8. [m] Ge. 42. 35.
[n] Ne. 9. 1. [o] Is. 28. 15. [p] Je. 23. 32. [q] Ge. 30. 38. [r] Da. 7. 5.
[s] Je. 20. 15. [t] Is. 44. 15. [u] Nu. 19. 5. [x] Le. 17. 16. [y] Je. 5. 10.
[z] Joel 3. 5. [a] Pr. 25. 20. [b] Pr. 14. 30. [c] Pr. 19. 10. [d] Ge. 31. 27.
[e] Job 40. 16. [f] Ec. 5. 5. [g] Ju. 8. 7. [h] Ju. 9. 2. [i] Nu. 18. 18.
[k] Le. 11. 29. [l] 2 Ch. 3. 16. [m] 2 Sa. 18. 20. [n] Ps. 40. 10. [o] Eze. 44. 17.
[p] Eze. 16. 10. [q] 2 Ch. 12. 3. [r] Ps. 44. 16. [s] Je. 2. 36. [t] Eze. 16. 63.
[u] Ps. 69. 20. [x] Le. 13. 48. [y] Ju. 16. 3. [z] Eze. 43. 16. [a] 2 Ch. 34. 3.

בָּשְׁתְּכֶם[a] noun fem. sing., suff. 2 pers. pl. masc. from בֹּשֶׁת dec. 13c. (§ 39. No. 4) . . . בוש

בָּשְׁתָּם id. with suff. 3 pers. pl. masc. . . בוש

בָּת[b] וּ Chald. Peal pret. 3 pers. s. m.; וּ bef. lab. בות

בַּת וּ noun fem. sing. irr., pl. בָּנוֹת (§ 45); also pr. name in compos. as בַּת־רַבִּים, &c. . בנה

בַּת[c] וּ' noun masc. sing. dec. 8d. . . בתת

בַּתְּאֵנָה[d] pref. בַּ for בְּהַ } noun fem. sing. dec. 10. . תאן
בִּתְאֵנָה[e] pref. בְּ bef. (:) }

בַּתֵּבָה[f] pref. בַּ for בְּהַ)(noun fem. sing. dec. 10. תבה

בַּתְּבוּאֹת[g] pref. id.)(noun fem., pl. of תְּבוּאָה dec. 10. בוא

בִּתְבוּאַת[h] וּ pref. בְּ bef. (:))(id. sing., constr. st.; וּ bef. lab. בוא

בִּתְבוּנָה וּ' pref. id.)(noun fem. sing. dec. 10; וּ id. בין

בִּתְבוּנוֹת[i] וּ pref. id.)(id. pl.; וּ id. . . בין

בִּתְבוּנָם[k] pref. id.)(n. m. s., suff. 3 p. pl. m. fr. [תָּבוֹן] d. 3a. בין

בִּתְבוּנָתוֹ וּ pref. id.)(noun fem. sing., suff. 3 pers. sing. masc. from תְּבוּנָה dec. 10; וּ before lab. בין

בִּתְבוּנָתְךָ[l] וּ pref. id.)(id., suff. 2 pers. sing. masc.; וּ id. בין

בְּתֵבֵל[m] pref. בְּ)(noun fem. sing. . . . יבל

בְּתַבְנִית[n] pref. id.)(noun fem. sing. dec. 1b. . בנה

בְּתַבְנִיתָם[o] pref. id.)(id., suff. 3 pers. pl. masc. . בנה

בְּתַבְעֵרָה וּ pref. id.)(pr. name of a place; וּ before (:) בער

בְּתֶבֶץ pref. id.)(pr. name of a place, see תֵּבֵץ.

בִּתְדִירָא[p] Ch. pref. בְּ bef. (:))(properly noun fem. s., with the pref. as an adv. . . . דור

בָּתָּה[q] noun fem. sing., as if fr. בּוֹת or בָּתָה see בתת

בִּתָּהּ[r] וּ' noun fem. sing., suff. 3 pers. sing. fem. from בַּת irr. (§ 45); וּ bef. lab. . בנה

בַּתֹּהוּ pref. בַּ for בְּהַ } noun masc. sing.; וּ bef. (:) תהה
בְּתֹהוּ[s] וּ' pref. בְּ q. v. }

בִּתְהִלָּה[t] pref. בְּ bef. (:))(noun fem. sing. dec. 10. הלל

בִּתְהִלָּתֶךָ pref. id.)(id., suff. 2 p. s. m. (for תְּהִלָּתְךָ) הלל

בַּתְּהֹמוֹת pref. בַּ for בְּהַ)(noun com. with pl. fem. term. from תְּהוֹם dec. 1a. . . הום

בְּתַהְפֻּכוֹת[u] pref. בְּ)(noun fem., pl. of [תַּהְפֻּכָה] d. 10. הפך

בִּתּוֹ וּ' noun fem. sing. with suff. 3 pers. sing. masc. from בַּת irr. (§ 45); וּ bef. lab. בנה

בְּתוּאֵל (for בְּתוּל אֵל *set apart of God,* comp. בָּתַל) pr. name.—I. of the father of Laban.—II. of a place in the tribe of Simeon, 1 Ch. 4. 30, called בְּתוּל Jos. 19. 4.

בְּתוֹדָה pref. בְּ)(noun fem. sing. dec. 10. ידה

בְּתוֹדוֹת[x] וּ' pref. בְּ)(id. pl.; וּ bef. (:) . . ידה

בַּתָּוֶךְ pref. בַּ for בְּהַ)(noun masc. sing. dec. 6g. תוך

בְּתוֹךְ וּ' pref. בְּ)(id. const. state; וּ bef. (:) . תוך

בְּתוֹכָהּ pref. בְּ)(id., suff. 3 pers. sing. fem. . תוך

בְּתוֹכֹה[y] pref. id.)(id., suff. 3 pers. sing. masc. . תוך

בְּתוֹכְהֶנָה[z] pref. id.)(id., suff. 3 pers. pl. f. (§ 3. r. 5) תוך

בְּתוֹכוֹ pref. id.)(id., suff. 3 pers. sing. masc. . תוך

בְּתוֹכָחוֹת[a] pref. id.)(n. f., pl. abs. fr. תּוֹכַחַת (§ 44. r. 5) יכח

בְּתוֹכְחוֹת[b] pref. id.)(id. pl., constr. state . יכח

בְּתוֹכַחְתּוֹ[c] pref. id.)(id. sing., suff. 3 pers. sing. masc. (prop. fr. תּוֹכַחַת dec. 13a) . יכח

בְּתוֹכִי[d] pref. id.)(noun masc. sing., suff. 1 pers. sing. from תָּוֶךְ dec. 6g. . . תוך

בְּתוֹכֵךְ } pref. id.)(id., suff. 2 pers. sing. fem. (§ 3. rem. 2) . . . } תוך
בְּתוֹכֵכִי }

בְּתוֹכְכֶם[e] } pref. id.)(id. with suff. 2 pers. pl. masc. תוך
בְּתוֹכְכֶם }

בְּתוֹכָם[f] וּ' pref. id.)(id., suff. 3 p. pl. m.; וּ bef. (:) תוך

בְּתוֹכֵנוּ pref. בְּ)(id. with suff. 1 pers. pl. . תוך

בְּתוּל וּ contr. for בְּתוּאֵל q. v.

בְּתוֹלָד וּ pref. בְּ)(pr. name of a place; וּ bef. (:) ילד

בְּתוּלָה וּ' noun fem. sing. dec. 10; וּ bef. (:) . בתל

בְּתוּלוֹת pl. of the prec. . . . . בתל

בְּתוּלַי[g] noun m. pl., suff. 1 pers. s. fr. [בְּתוּל] d. 1a. בתל

בְּתוּלֵי[h] id. pl., constr. state . . . בתל

בְּתוּלֶיהָ[i] id. pl., suff. 3 pers. sing. fem. . בתל

בְּתוּלֵיהֶן[k] id. pl., suff. 3 pers. pl. fem. . . בתל

בְּתוּלִים id. pl., absolute state . . בתל

בְּתוֹלַעַת[l] [m]וּ' pref. בְּ)(noun fem. s. d. 13a; וּ bef. (:) תלע

בְּתוּלַת noun fem. sing., constr. of בְּתוּלָה dec. 10. בתל

בְּתוּלֹת id. pl. of the prec. . . . . בתל

בְּתוּלֹתַי id. pl., suff. 1 pers. sing. . . בתל

בְּתוּלֹתֶיהָ[n] id., suff. 3 pers. sing. fem. . . בתל

בְּתוּלֹתָיו[o] וּ' id., suff. 3 pers. sing. masc.; וּ bef. (:) . בתל

בַּתֹּם[p] pref. בַּ for בְּהַ)(for תֹּם, noun m. s. d. 8c. תמם

בְּתוֹעֲבוֹתָם[q] pref. בְּ)(noun fem. pl., suff. 3 pers. pl. masc. (§ 4. rem. 2) fr. תּוֹעֵבָה dec. 11b. תעב

בְּתוֹעֵבֹת[r] pref. id.)(id. pl., absolute state . תעב

בְּתוֹעֲבֹתֵיהֶם[s] pref. id.)(id. pl., suff. 3 pers. pl. masc. תעב

בַּתּוֹרָה[t] וּ' pref. בַּ for בְּהַ)(n. f. s. d. 10; וּ bef. lab. ירה

בַּתֹּרִים[u] pref. id.)(noun masc., pl. of תּוֹר dec. 1a. תור

בְּתוֹרַת pref. בְּ)(noun f. s. constr. of תּוֹרָה d. 10. ירה

בְּתוֹרָתוֹ[x] וּ' pref. בְּ)(id., suff. 3 pers. s. m.; וּ bef. (:) ירה

בְּתוֹרָתִי pref. בְּ)(id., suff. 1 pers. sing. . . ירה

בְּתוֹרֹתָיו[y] pref. id.)(id. pl., suff. 3 pers. sing. masc. . ירה

בְּתַזְנוּתַיִךְ[z] } pref. בְּ)(noun fem. pl., suff. 2 pers. sing. fem. from [תַּזְנוּת] dec. 1b. . } זנה
בְּתַזְנוּתָיִךְ[a] }

בְּתַזְנוּתָם[b] pref. id.)(id. sing., suff. 3 pers. pl. masc. זנה

[a] Is. 61. 7. [b] Da. 6. 19. [c] Eze. 45. 10. [d] Je. 8. 13. [e] Ho. 9. 10. [f] Ge. 8. 1. [g] Ge. 47. 24. [h] Pr. 15. 6. [i] Ps. 78. 72. [k] Ho. 13. 2. [l] Eze. 28. 4. [m] Pr. 8. 31. [n] Ps. 106. 20. [o] Ex. 25. 40. [p] Da. 6. 17, 19. [q] Is. 5. 6. [r] Le. 18. 17. [s] De. 32. 10. [t] Ps. 100. 4. [u] Pr. 2. 14. [x] Ne. 12. 27. [y] Eze. 48. 15, 21. [z] Eze. 16. 53. [a] Ps. 39. 12. [b] Eze. 25. 17. [c] Pr. 3. 11. [d] Ps. 143. 4. [e] Eze. 6. 7. [f] Nu. 16. 3. [g] Ju. 11. 37. [h] De. 22. 15, 17. [i] Eze. 23. 8, ect. [k] Eze. 23. 3. [l] Ex. 35. 35. [m] Ex. 38. 23. [n] La. 1. 4. [o] Ps. 78. 63. [p] Pr. 10. 9. [q] Eze. 43. 8. [r] De. 32. 16. [s] Ezr. 9. 11. [t] 2 Ch. 31. 21. [u] Ca. 1. 10. [x] Is. 42. 24. [y] Da. 9. 10. [z] Eze. 16. 33. [a] Eze. 16. 34, 36. [b] Eze. 23. 17.

בְּתוּלִים masc. pl. (of בְּתוּל) dec. 1a.—I. *virginity.*—II. *tokens of virginity,* De. 22. 14, 15, &c.

בִּתְלַאשָּׂר pref. בְּ bef. (:)) pr. n. of a region, see תְּלַאשָּׂר

בְּתוּלֹת [r] noun fem., pl. of בְּתוּלָה dec. 10. . בתל

בְּתֶלֶם [s] pref. בְּ) noun m. sing. (pl. c. תַּלְמֵי) dec. 6a. תלם

בִּתְלַשָּׂר pr. name of a place; see תְּלַאשָּׂר

בְּתֻלֹת [t] noun fem., pl. of בְּתוּלָה dec. 10. . בתל

בְּתָם־ pref. בְּ) bef. Mak. for תֹּם noun m. s. d. 8c. תמם

בַּתִּמָּהוֹן [u] pref. בַּ for בְּהַ) noun masc. sing. dec. 3c. תמה

בְּתִמְהוֹן [x] וּ' pref. בְּ) id. construct state; וּ bef. (:) . תמה

בְּתֻמּוֹ [y] pref. בְּ) noun masc. sing., suff. 3 pers. sing. masc. from תֹּם dec. 8c. . תמם

בְּתֻמִּי pref. id.) id. with suff. 1 pers. sing. . תמם

בְּתָמִים [z] וּ' pref. בְּ) adj. m. sing. dec. 3a; וּ bef. (:) תמם

בְּתִמְנַת pref. id.) pr. name in compos. תִּמְנַת חֶרֶס &c. מנה

בְּתִמְנָתָה pref. id.) pr. name. of a place, (תִּמְנַת) with paragogic ה . מנה

בְּתָמָר [a] pref. בְּ) noun masc. sing. dec. 4a. . תמר

בְּתַמְרוּקֵי [b] וּ pref. id.) noun masc. pl. constr. from תַּמְרוּק dec. 1b; וּ bef. (:) . מרק

בְּתֻמָּתוֹ [c] pref. id.) noun fem. sing., suff. 3 pers. sing. masc. from תֻּמָּה dec. 10. . תמם

בְּתֻמָּתֶךָ [d] pref. id.) id., suff. 2 pers. s. m. [for תֻּמָּתְךָ] תמם

בִּתֵּנוּ [e] n. fem. s., suff. 1 pers. pl. from בַּת, irr. (§ 45) בנה

בִּתְנוּמוֹת [f] pref. בְּ bef. (:)) n. fem., pl. of תְּנוּמָה d. 10. נום

בַּתַּנּוּר [g] pref. בַּ f. בְּהַ } noun masc. sing. dec. 1b. . תנר

בְּתַנּוּר [h] pref. בְּ q. v. }

בְּתַנּוּרֶיךָ [i] וּ pref. בְּ) id. pl., suff. 2 p. s. m.; וּ bef. (:) תנר

בִּתְעוֹת pref. בְּ bef. (:)) Kal inf. constr. . . תעה

בַּתְּעָלָה [k] pref. בַּ for בְּהַ) noun fem. sing. dec. 10. . עלה

בְּתַעֲלוּלֵיהֶם [l] pref. בְּ) noun masc. pl., suff. 3 pers. pl. masc. from [תַּעֲלוּל] dec. 1b. . עלל

בִּתְעָלַת pref. בְּ bef. (:)) noun fem. sing., constr. of תְּעָלָה dec. 10. . . . עלה

בַּתַּעֲנוּגִים [m] pref. בַּ for בְּהַ) noun m., pl. of תַּעֲנוּג d. 1b. ענג

בְּתַעְנָךְ pref. בְּ) pr. name of a place, see תַּעְנָךְ

בְּתַעַר pref. בְּ) n. m. s. comp. dec. 6d [for תַּעְרָה] ערה

בְּתַעְרָהּ [n] pref. בְּ) id. suff. 3 pers. sing. masc. [for תַּעְרָהּ comp. § 35. rem. 5] . . ערה

בְּתֹף pref. id.) noun masc. sing. dec. 8c. . תפף

בַּתַּפּוּחִים [o] pref. בַּ for בְּהַ) noun m., pl. of תַּפּוּחַ d. 1b. נפח

בְּתֻפִּים וּ' pref. בְּ) n. m., pl. of תֹּף d. 8c; וּ bef. (:) תפף

בַּתְּפִלָּה [p] pref. בַּ for בְּהַ) noun fem. sing. dec. 10. . פלל

בִּתְפִלַּת [q] pref. בְּ bef. (:)) id., construct state פלל

בְּתָפְשָׂם [r] pref. בְּ) Kal inf., suff. 3 pers. pl. masc. . תפש

בְּתֹפֶת וּ' pref. id.) pr. name of a place; וּ bef. (:) תוף

בְּתַחְבּוּלֹתָיו [a] וּ pref. בְּ) noun fem. pl., suff. 3 pers. pl. m. (§ 4. r. 2) from [תַּחְבֻּלָה] dec. 10. חבל

בְּתַחְבֻּלוֹת [b c] וּ' pref. id.) id. pl., absolute st.; וּ bef. (:) חבל

בְּתַחֲלֻאִים [d] pref. בְּ) noun m., pl. of [תַּחֲלוּא] d. 1b. חלא

בַּתְּחִלָּה pref. בַּ for בְּהַ) noun fem. sing. dec. 10. חלל

בִּתְחִלַּת pref. בְּ bef. (:)) id., constr. state . . חלל

בְּתַחֲנוּנִים [e] וּ pref. בְּ) noun masc., pl. of [תַּחֲנוּן] dec. 1b; וּ bef. (:) . . חנן

בִּתְחַפְנְחֵס · וּ pref. בְּ bef. (:) } pr. name of a place, see תַּחְפַּנְחֵס .

בְּתַחְפַּנְחֵס וּ' pref. בְּ q. v. }

בְּתַחַת pref. id.) pr. name of a place, for תַּחַת . תוח

בְּתַחְתִּיּוֹת pref. id.) pl. of the following . . תוח

בְּתַחְתִּית [f] pref. id.) adj. fem. sing. from [תַּחְתִּי] m. תוח

בָּתֵּי וּ' noun masc. pl., constr. of בָּתִּים irr. of בַּיִת (§ 45); וּ before labial . . בית

בִּתִּי noun f. s., suff. 1 pers. s. fr. בַּת irr. (§45) בנה

בִּתְיָה pr. name fem. . . . . . בנה

בָּתֵּיהֶם וּ' noun masc. pl. (בָּתִּים), suff. 3 pers. pl. masc. irr. of בַּיִת (§ 45); וּ bef. labial . בית

בָּתֵּיהֶן [g] וּ id., suff. 3 pers. pl. fem.; וּ id. . . בית

בָּתָּיו [h] id., suff. 3 pers. sing. masc. . . בית

בָּתַּיִךְ [i] id., suff. 2 pers. sing. fem. . . . בית

בָּתֶּיךָ [k] id., suff. 2 pers. sing. masc. . . בית

בָּתֵּיכוֹן [l] וּ' Ch. id., suff. 2 pers. pl. masc.; וּ bef. lab. בית

בָּתֵּיכֶם וּ' Heb. id., suff. 2 pers. pl. masc.; וּ id. . בית

בָּתִּים וּ' id. pl., absolute state; וּ id. . . בית

בַּתִּים noun masc., pl. of בַּת dec. 8d. . . בתת

בָּתֵּימוֹ [m] noun masc. pl. (בָּתִּים), suff. 3 pers. pl. masc. from בַּיִת, irr. (§ 45) . . בית

בְּתֵימָן pref. בְּ) pr. name of a region . . ימן

בַּתִּין [n] Chald. noun masc., pl. of בַּת dec. 5a. . בתת

בָּתֵּינוּ [o] וּ' noun masc. pl. (בָּתִּים), suff. 1 pers. pl. from בַּיִת irr. (§ 45); וּ before labial . בות

בִּתֵּךְ וּ' } noun fem. sing., suff. 2 pers. sing. masc. from בַּת, irr. (§ 45); וּ bef. lab. } בנה

בִּתֶּךָ }

בְּתֹכְחוֹת [p] וּ pref. בְּ) noun fem. pl., constr. of תּוֹכָחוֹת from תּוֹכַחַת (§ 44. rem. 5); וּ id. . יכח

בְּתוֹכְכֶם pref. id.) noun masc. sing., suff. 2 pers. pl. masc. from תָּוֶךְ dec. 6g. . . תוך

בַּתִּכְלֶת pref. בַּ for בְּהַ) noun fem. sing. . . תכל

בְּתוֹכָם [q] pref. בְּ) noun masc. sing., suff. 3 pers. pl. masc. from תָּוֶךְ dec. 6g. . . תוך

בָּתַל Root not used; Arab. *to separate.*

בְּתוּלָה fem. dec. 10.—I. *a virgin.*—II. applied to cities and countries, comp. בַּת.

---

[a] Job 37. 12. [b] Pr. 24. 6. [c] Pr. 20. 18. [d] 2 Ch. 21. 19. [e] Je. 31. 9. [f] Ex. 19. 17. [g] Eze. 23. 47. [h] 1 Ch. 28. 11. [i] Eze. 16. 41. [k] Ex. 10. 6. [l] Da. 2. 5. [m] Ps. 49. 12. [n] Ezr. 7. 22, 22. [o] Ne. 5. 3. [p] Eze. 5. 15. [q] Job 2. 1. [r] Zec. 9. 17. [s] Job 39. 10. [t] La. 5. 11. [u] Zec. 12. 4. [x] De. 28. 28. [y] Pr. 28. 6. [z] Ju. 9. 16, 19. [a] Ca. 7. 9. [b] Est. 2. 12. [c] Job 2. 3. [d] Job 2. 9. [e] Ge. 34. 17. [f] Job 33. 15. [g] Le. 7. 9. [h] Le. 26. 26. [i] Ex. 7. 28. [k] 1 Ki. 18. 38. [l] Is. 66. 4. [m] Ca. 7. 7. [n] 2 Sa. 20. 8. [o] Ca. 2. 5. [p] Da. 9. 21. [q] Ps. 80. 5. [r] Eze. 29. 7.

בִּתֵּק. Pi. *to cut, pierce,* only in the following form—

בִּתְּקוּךְ[a] ו Piel pret. 3 p. pl., suff. 2 p. s. fem.; ו bef. lab. בתק

בְּתְקוֹמְמֶיךָ[b] ו pref. בְּ bef. (:))(noun masc. pl., suff. 2 pers. s. m. from [תְּקוֹמֵם] d. 7b; ו bef. lab. קום

בַּתָּקוֹעַ[c] pref. בַּ for בְּהַ)(noun masc. sing. . . תקע

בִתְקוֹעַ ו pref. בְּ bef. (:))(pr. n. of a place; ו bef. lab. תקע

בְּתֵקַע[d] pref. בְּ)(noun masc. sing. . . . . תקע

בְּתֹקְעֵי־[e] pref. id.)(Kal part. act. m. pl. c. fr. תֹּקֵעַ d. 7b. תקע

בְּתֹקֶף[f] pref. id.)(noun masc. sing. dec. 6c. . תקף

בִּתְקָף[g] Chald. pref. בְּ bef. (:))(noun masc. sing., a better reading is בִּתְקַף . . . . תקף

[בָּתַר] *to cut in pieces, to divide,* Ge. 15. 10. Pi. id. ibid.

בֶּתֶר m. dec. 6a. (suff. בִּתְרוֹ, but in pause בֶּתֶר § 35. r. 2).—I. *piece, part.*—II. *separation,* Ca. 2. 17.

בִּתְרוֹן (*section*) pr. name of a place on the Jordan, 2 Sa. 2. 29.

בָּתָר[h] Kal pret. 3 pers. s. m. [for בָּתַר § 8. rem. 7] בתר

בָּתֶר[i] noun masc. sing. for [בֶּתֶר § 35. rem. 2] dec. 6a, but with suff. בִּתְרוֹ; also pr. name בתר

בְּתַרְבִּית[k] ו Kh. preff. בְּ & ו bef. lab.; K. וְתַרְבִּית n. f. s. רבה

בִּתְרוֹ[l] noun masc. sing., suff. 3 pers. sing. masc. from [בֶּתֶר] dec. 6a. . . . . בתר

בִּתְרוּמַת[m] pref. בְּ bef. (:))(n. f., constr. of תְּרוּמָה d. 10. רום

בִּתְרוּעָה[n] ו pref. id.)(noun fem. sing. d. 10; ו bef. lab. רוע

בְּתֹרֹתֶךָ[o] ו pref. בְּ)(Kh. תֹּרוֹתֶךָ, K. תּוֹרָתְךָ, n. fem. pl. or s., suff. 2 p. s. m. from תּוֹרָה d. 10; ו id. ירה

בְּתָרַח pref. id.)(pr. name of a place, for תֶּרַח . תרח

בִּתְרֵי[p] noun masc. pl. constr. from [בֶּתֶר] dec. 6a. בתר

בְּתָרָיו[q] id. pl., suff. 3 pers. sing. masc. . . בתר

בְּתַרָךְ[r] ו Ch. [for בְּאַתְרָךְ] pref. בְּ; n. m. s., suff. 2 pers. s. m. from אֲתַר dec. 3a; ו bef. lab. אתר

בְּתַרְמָה[s] pref. בְּ)(noun fem. sing. . . . רמה

בַּתַּרְמִית[t] pref. בַּ for בְּהַ)(noun fem. sing. dec. 1b. רמה

בִּתְרַע[u] Chald. pref. בְּ bef. (:))(noun masc. sing. תרע

בַּתְּרָפִים[x] pref. בַּ for בְּהַ)(noun masc. pl. . . תרף

בְּתִרְצָה pref. בְּ)(pr. name of a place . . רצה

בַּתַּרְשִׁישׁ[y] pref. בַּ for בְּהַ)(noun masc. sing. . רשש

בְּתוֹרָתוֹ[z] ו pref. בְּ)(noun fem. sing. with suff. 3 pers. sing. masc. from תּוֹרָה dec. 10; ו bef. lab. ירה

בִּתְשׂוּמֶת[a] pref. בְּ bef. (:))(noun fem. sing. . שום

בְּתִשְׁעָה pref. בְּ)(num. card. masc. from תֵּשַׁע fem. תשע

בָּתַת Root not used; Arab. *to cut; to mark out, define.*

בַּת com. dec. 8d, *bath,* a measure for liquids, the tenth part of an homer.

בַּת Chald. dec. 5a, idem.

בָּתָה fem. (for בַּתָּה) *excision, desolation,* Is. 5. 6.

בַּתָּה fem. dec. 10, *clefts, fissures,* Is. 7. 19.

בְּתֵת pref. בְּ)(contr. for [תֶּנֶת § 17. r. 9], Kal inf. construct dec. 8b. . . . נתן

בְּתִתּוֹ[b] pref. id.)(id., suff. 3 pers. sing. masc. . נתן

בְּתִתִּי pref. id.)(id., suff. 1 pers. sing. . . נתן

בְּתִתֵּךְ[c] ו pref. id.)(id., suff. 2 pers. s. fem.; ו bef. (:) נתן

בְּתִתְּךָ pref. id.)(id., suff. 2 pers. sing. masc. . נתן

בְּתִתָּם[d] pref. id.)(id., suff. 3 pers. pl. masc. . נתן

ג

גֵּא[e] adj. masc. sing. [for גֵּאֶה] . . . גאה

גָּאָה[f] I. *to grow up, to increase,* of a plant, of water.—II. *to be lifted, exalted, majestic.*

גֵּא adj. masc. *proud,* Is. 16. 6.

גֵּאֶה adj. masc. dec. 9b. (§ 38. Nos. 1 & 2).—I. *lifted up, high.*—II. *proud, haughty.*

גֵּאָה fem. *pride, haughtiness,* Pr. 8. 13.

גַּאֲוָה fem. (constr. גַּאֲוַת; no pl.)—I. *exaltation, majesty.*—II. *ornament, splendour.*—III. *pride, arrogance.*

גְּאוּאֵל (*majesty of God*) pr. name m. Nu. 13. 15.

גָּאוֹן masc. dec. 3a.—I. *excellency, majesty.*—II. *ornament, splendour.*—III. *pride, arrogance.*

גֵּאוּת fem.—I. *a rising up, ascending,* Is. 9. 17.—II. *majesty.*—III. *ornament, splendour.*—IV. *pride, arrogance.*

גַּאֲיוֹן adj. masc. *proud,* Ps. 123. 4. Kheth; Keri גְּאֵי יוֹנִים *proud oppressors.*

גֵּוָה fem. (contr. for גַּאֲוָה).—I. *exaltation,* Job 22. 29.—II. *pride, arrogance.*

גֵּוָה Chald. *pride,* Da. 4. 34.

גָּאֹה[g] Kal inf. abs. . . . . . גאה

גֵּאָה[h] noun fem. sing. . . . . גאה

גֵּאֶה adj. masc. sing. dec. 9b. (§ 38. Nos. 1 & 2) גאה

גָּאוּ[i] Kal pret. 3 pers. pl. . . . . גאה

גְּאוּאֵל pr. name masc. . . . . גאה

גַּאֲוָה noun fem. sing. dec. 10. . . . גאה

גְּאוּלַי[k] Kal part. p. pl. masc., suff. 1 pers. sing., from [גָּאוּל] dec. 3a. . . . . גאל

[a] Eze. 16. 40. [b] Ps. 139. 21. [c] Eze. 7. 14. [d] Ps. 150. 3. [e] Pr. 22. 26. [f] Da. 11. 17. [g] Da. 4. 27. [h] Ge. 15. 10. [i] Ca. 2. 17. [k] Pr. 28. 8. [l] Ge. 15. 10. [m] Le. 22. 12. [n] 2 Ch. 15. 14. [o] Je. 32. 23. [p] Je. 34. 19. [q] Je. 34. 18. [r] Da. 2. 39. [s] Ju. 9. 31. [t] Je. 8. 5. [u] Da. 2. 49. [x] Eze. 21. 26. [y] Ca. 5. 14. [z] Je. 44. 23. [a] Le. 5. 21. [b] Le. 20. 4. [c] Eze. 16. 34. [d] Eze. 43. 8. [e] Is. 16. 6. [f] Ex. 15. 1, 21. [g] Ex. 15. 1. [h] Pr. 8. 13. [i] Eze. 47. 5. [k] Is. 63. 4.

גְּאוּלֵי id. pl., construct state . . . . . גאל

גֹּאֲלָיו[a] וְ Kal part. act. pl. masc., suff. 3 pers. sing. masc. from גֹּאֵל dec. 7b. . . . גאל

גְּאוּלִים Kal part. act. masc. pl. of [גָּאוּל] dec. 3a. . גאל

גָּאוֹן[aa] וְ' noun masc. sing. dec. 3a. . . גאה

גְּאוֹן id., construct state . . . . . גאה

גְּאוֹנוֹ וּ' id., suff. 3 pers. sing. masc.; וּ bef. (:) . גאה

גְּאוֹנַיִךְ[b] id. pl., suff. 2 pers. sing. fem. [for ־ַיִךְ] . גאה

גְּאוֹנֶךָ[c] / גְּאוֹנְךָ[d] } id., suff. 2 pers. sing. masc. . . . גאה

גְּאוֹנָם[e] id., suff. 3 pers. pl. masc. . . . . גאה

גֵּאוּת[f] וְ'[g] noun fem. sing., constr. of גַּאֲוָה (no pl.) גאה

גֵּאוּת noun fem. sing. . . . . . גאה

גַּאֲוָתוֹ[h] וְ' noun fem. sing. suff. 3 pers. sing. masc. from גַּאֲוָה (no pl.) . . . גאה

גַּאֲוָתִי[i] id., suff. 1 pers. sing. . . . . גאה

גַּאֲוָתֶךָ[k] id., suff. 2 pers. sing. masc. [for ־ָתְךָ] . גאה

גַּאֲוָתֵךְ[l] id., suff. 2 pers. sing. fem. . . . גאה

גֵּאָיוֹת[m] n. com. with pl. fem. term., irr. of גַּיְא (§ 45) גיא

גֵּאִים adj. m., pl. of גֵּאֶה d. 9b. (§ 38. Nos. 1 & 2) גאה

I. גָּאַל[n] וְ' I. *to redeem, ransom, recover*, by paying back the value for.—II. *to retribute, to avenge*; part. גֹּאֵל *redeemer, avenger, nearest kinsman*, to whom was assigned the right of redemption and the duty of avenging the death of any one. Niph. *to be redeemed, ransomed.*

II. גָּאַל. Niph. *to be polluted, stained*, Zep. 3. 1. Pi. *to pollute*, Mal. 1. 7. Pu. *to be polluted*, Mal. 1. 7, 12. Hiph. *to soil, stain*, Is. 63. 3. Hithpa. *to defile oneself*, Da. 1. 8.

גֹּאַל masc. *pollution*, only Ne. 13. 29. גָּאֳלֵי comp. dec. 6f.

גְּאֻלָּה fem. dec. 10.—I. *redemption, purchase.*—II. *duty, right of redemption.*—III. *price of redemption.*—IV. *thing redeemed*, Ru. 4. 6.—V. *relationship*, Eze. 11. 15.

יִגְאָל (*He* (God) *will redeem* him) pr. name of several men.

גָּאוֹל[o] Kal inf. abs. . . . . . גאל

גְּאַל[p] / גְּאָל[q] } id. imp. masc. sing. . . . גאל

גֹּאֵל id. part. act. masc. sing. dec. 7b. . . גאל

גְּאָלֶהָ[r] id. imp. m. s. (גְּאַל) suff. 3 p. s. f. (§ 16. r. 11) גאל

גְּאֻלָּה noun fem. sing. dec. 10. . . . גאל

גְּאָלוֹ וּ Kal pret. 3 pers. sing. masc., suff. 3 pers. sing. masc.; וּ bef. (:) . . . גאל

גֹּאֲלוֹ[u] וְ' id. part. act. sing. masc. with suff. 3 pers. sing. masc. from גּוֹאֵל dec. 7b. . . גאל

גָּאֳלֵי[x] noun m. pl. constr. from [גֹּאַל] comp. dec. 6f. גאל

גֹּאֲלִי[y] Kal part. act. sing. masc., suff. 1 pers. sing. from גּוֹאֵל dec. 7b. . . . . גאל

גֹּאַלְךָ[z] / גֹּאֲלֶךָ[a] } id. s., suff. 2 pers. sing. m. (§ 36. rem. 3) גאל

גֹּאֲלֵךְ[b] וְ' id., suff. 2 pers. sing. fem. . . . גאל

גֹּאַלְכֶם[c] id., suff. 2 pers. pl. masc. (§ 36. rem. 3) . גאל

גְּאָלָם Kal pret. 3 pers. sing. m., suff. 3 pers. pl. m. גאל

גֹּאֲלָם id. part. act. sing. masc., suff. 3 pers. pl. masc. from גּוֹאֵל dec. 7b. . . . . גאל

גֹּאֲלֵנוּ id. id., suff. 1 pers. pl. . . . . גאל

גֵּאַלְנוּךָ[d] Piel pret. 1 pers. pl., suff. 2 pers. sing. masc. גאל

גְּאָלֵנִי[e] וּ' Kal imp. sing. masc. (גְּאַל), suff. 1 pers. sing. (§ 16. rem. 10); וּ bef. (:) . גאל

גָּאַלְתָּ[f] / גָּאָלְתָּ } id. pret. 2 pers. sing. masc. (§ 8. rem. 7) גאל

גְּאֻלַּת[g] noun fem. sing., constr. of גְּאֻלָּה dec. 10. . גאל

גְּאֻלָּתוֹ[h] id., suff. 3 pers. sing. masc. . . . גאל

גָּאַלְתִּי[i] וְ Kal pret. 1 pers. sing.; acc. shifted by conv. וְ (§ 8. rem. 7) . . . . גאל

גְּאֻלָּתִי[k] noun m. sing., suff. 1 p. s. from גְּאֻלָּה dec. 10. גאל

גְּאַלְתִּיךָ Kal pret. 1 pers. sing., suff. 2 pers. sing. m. גאל

גְּאַלְתִּיךְ[l] וּ id. id., suff. 2 pers. fem. sing.; וּ bef. (:) . גאל

גְּאֻלָּתֶךָ[m] n. f. s., suff. 2 p. s. m. [for ־ָתְךָ] fr. גְּאֻלָּה d. 10. גאל

גְּאֹנוֹ[n] n. m. sing., suff. 3 pers. s. m. from גָּאוֹן d. 3a. גאה

גַּב[o] / גַּב[p] } noun masc. sing. dec. 8d. . . . גבב

גָּבָא Root not used; Arab. *to gather together.*

גֶּבֶא masc. dec. 6a.—I. *cistern*, Is. 30. 14.—II. *marsh, pool*, Eze. 47. 11.

גַּבָּא noun masc. sing., emph. of גַּב dec. 5c. . גבב

גְּבָאָיו[q] וּ noun masc. pl., suff. 3 pers. sing. masc. from גֶּבֶא dec. 6; וּ bef. (:) . . . גבא

גָּבַב Root not used; in the deriv.—I. i.q. כָּפַף *to be curved.*—II. i.q. נָקַב *to dig.*

גַּב masc. dec. 8d. (pl. גַּבִּים, ־וֹת).—I. *a back.*—II. *boss* of a shield or buckler, Job 15. 26.—III. *defence, mound*, Job 13. 12.—IV. *vault.*—V. *the*

1 Ki. 16. 11. Eze. 16. 56. Is. 14. 11. Ex. 15. 7. Zep. 2. 10.
f Pr. 29. 23. g Is. 13. 11. h Je. 48. 29. i Is. 13. 3. k De. 33. 29.
l Zep. 3. 11. m Eze. 31. 12. n Le. 25. 25. o Le. 27. 13, 19, 31. p Ruth 4. 4.
q Ruth 4. 6. r Ps. 69. 19. s Je. 31. 11. t Le. 25. 25. u Is. 44. 6.
x Ne. 13. 29. y Job 19. 25. z Is. 44. 24. a Is. 48. 17. aa Pr. 8. 13.
b Is. 54. 8. c Is. 43. 14. d Mal. 1. 7. e Ps. 119. 154.
f Ex. 15. 13. g Le. 25. 32. h Le. 25. 26, 29, 29, 51, 52.
i E.. 6. 6. k Ruth 4. 6. l Ruth 3. 13. m Eze. 11. 15.
n Is. 2. 10. o Eze. 16. 24. p Eze. 43. 13. q Eze. 47. 11.

rim or *curvature* of a wheel.—VI. *arch of the eye-brow*, Le. 14. 9.

גַּב Chald. masc. dec. 5 a, *back*, Da. 7. 6.

גֹּב Chald. masc. dec. 5 c, *pit*, *den*.

גַּבַּי (*tax-gatherer* Chald. גַּבֵּב *to raise a tax*) pr. name masc. Ne. 11. 8.

גִּבְּתוֹן (*hilly*, from a form גִּבָּה i. q. Chald. גִּבְּבָא *hill*) pr. name of a town of the Philistines in the tribe of Dan.

גָּבַהּ [a] ק׳ I. *to be high, lofty*.—II. *to be lifted up, exalted.*—III. *to be proud, arrogant.* Hiph. *to make high, to raise*; הַמַּגְבִּיהִי לָשָׁבֶת *who maketh high to dwell*, i. e. dwelleth on high; יַגְבִּיהוּ עוֹף *they fly on high.*

גָּבָהּ adj. masc. dec. 4 a, *high, lofty, proud.*

גָּבֹהַּ, גָּבוֹהַּ masc. dec. 3 a. (constr. גְּבֹהַּ), גְּבֹהָה fem. d. 10. adj.—I. *high, tall.*—II. *proud, arrogant.*

גֹּבַהּ masc. dec. 6 c. (§ 35. rem. 5.)—I. *height.*—II. *majesty*, Job 40. 10.—III. *pride, arrogance*; גֹּבַהּ אַף *height of nose*, i. e. *insolence.*

גַּבְהוּת fem. *pride, arrogance*, Is. 2. 11, 17.

יָגְבְּהָה (*elevation*) pr. name of a town in the tribe of Gad.

גָּבֹהַּ adj. masc. sing. dec. 3 a. . . . . גבה

גְּבֹהַּ [b] id., construct state . . . . גבה

גֹּבַהּ ק׳, [c] ק׳ noun masc. sing. dec. 6 c. (§ 35. rem. 5); for ָ see lett. ו . . . . גבה

גְּבַהּ [d] ק׳ adj. masc. sing., constr. of [גָּבָהּ] dec. 4 a; ו before (:) . . . . . גבה

גָּבְהָא [e] Kal pret. 3 pers. s. fem. [for גָּבְהָה § 8. r. 3.] גבה

גְּבֹהָה adj. fem. sing. dec. 10, from גָּבֹהַּ masc. . . גבה

גָּבְהוֹ noun masc. sing. suff. 3 pers. sing. masc. from גֹּבַהּ dec. 6 c. (§ 35. rem. 5) . . גבה

גָּבְהוּ Kal pret. 3 pers. pl. . . . גבה

גַּבְהוּת [f] noun fem. sing. . . . . . גבה

גְּבֹהוֹת [g] adj. fem., pl of גְּבֹהָה dec. 10, fr. גָּבֹהַּ masc. גבה

גָּבְהֵי [h] n. m., pl. constr. of גֹּבַהּ d. 6 c. (§ 35. r. 5) גבה

גְּבֹהִים [i] [k] ק׳ adj. masc., pl. of גָּבֹהַּ dec. 3 a; ו bef. (:) גבה

גַּבֵּהֶם [l] ק׳ noun m. pl. [for גַּבֵּיהֶם] suff. 3 pers. pl. masc. from גַּב dec. 8 d. . . . גבב

גָּבַהְתָּ [m] Kal pret. 2 pers. sing. masc. . . גבה

גָּבוֹהַּ [n] ק׳ adj. masc. sing. dec. 3 a. . . . גבה

גְּבוּל ק׳ noun masc. sing. dec. 1 a; ו bef. (:) . גבל

גְּבוּלָהּ [o] ק׳ id., suff. 3 pers. sing. fem.; ו id. . . גבל

גְּבוּלוֹ id., suff. 3 pers. sing. masc. . . גבל

גְּבוּלוֹת [p] noun fem., pl. of [גְּבוּלָה] dec. 10. . . גבל

גְּבוּלִי [q] noun masc. s., suff. 1 pers. s. fr. גְּבוּל d. 1 a. גבל

גְּבוּלֶיהָ id. pl., suff. 3 pers. sing. fem. . . ל

גְּבוּלָיִךְ [r] id. pl. suff. 2 pers. sing. fem. [for ־לַיִךְ] . ל

גְּבוּלֶיךָ id. pl. with suff. 2 pers. sing. masc. . ל

גְּבוּלֶךָ, גְּבֻלְךָ [s] id. sing., suff. 2 pers. sing. masc. . . ל

גְּבוּלֵךְ id. sing., suff. 2 pers. sing. fem. . . ל

גְּבֻלְכֶם [t] id. sing., suff. 2 pers. pl. masc. . . ל

גְּבוּלָם id. sing., suff. 3 pers. pl. masc. . . ל

גְּבוּלָן [u] id. sing., suff. 3 pers. fem. pl. . . . ל

גְּבוּלֹת noun fem., pl. of [גְּבוּלָה] dec. 10. . ל

גִּבּוֹר ק׳ adj. masc. sing. dec. 1 b. . . . ר

גְּבוּרָה ק׳ noun fem. sing. dec. 10; ו bef. (:) . ר

גְּבוּרוֹת pl. of the preced. . . . . בר

גִּבּוֹרַי [x] adj. m. pl., suff. 1 pers. sing. fr. גִּבּוֹר d. 1 b. בר

גִּבּוֹרֵי [y] ק׳ id. pl., constr. state . . . בר

גִּבּוֹרֶיהָ id. pl., suff. 3 pers. sing. fem. . . . בר

גִּבּוֹרֵיהוּ [z] id. pl., suff. 3 pers. sing. masc. (§ 4. rem. 5) בר

גִּבּוֹרֵיהֶם [a] ק׳ id. pl., suff. 3 pers. pl. masc. . . בר

גִּבּוֹרָיו [b] id. pl., suff. 3 pers. sing. masc. . . בר

גִּבּוֹרֶיךָ id. pl., suff. 2 pers. sing. masc. . . בר

גִּבּוֹרִים id. pl., absolute state . . . בר

גִּבּוֹרָם [c] id. sing., suff. 3 pers. pl. masc. . . בר

גְּבוּרְתָּא [d] ו Ch. noun fem. sing., emph. of [גְּבוּרָא] dec. 8 a; ו bef. (:) . . . . בר

גְּבוּרָתוֹ ק׳ noun fem. sing., suff. 3 pers. s. m. from גְּבוּרָה dec. 10; ו id. . . . . בר

גְּבוּרֹתָו [e] id. pl., suff. 3 pers. sing. masc. (§ 4. rem. 1) בר

גְּבוּרָתִי [f] id. sing., suff. 1 pers. sing. . . . בר

גְּבוּרֹתָיו [g] id. pl., suff. 3 pers. sing. masc. . . בר

גְּבוּרֹתֶיךָ ו id. pl., suff. 2 pers. sing. masc.; ו bef. (:) בר

גְּבוּרָתֶךָ id. sing. with suff. 2 pers. sing. masc. for ־רָתְךָ . . . . . בר

גְּבוּרָתֵךְ [h] ו id. sing., suff. 2 pers. sing. fem.; ו bef. (:) בר

גְּבוּרָתְךָ [i] ו id. sing., suff. 2 pers. sing. masc.; ו id. בר

גְּבוּרַתְכֶם [k] id. sing., suff. 2 pers. pl. masc. . . בר

גְּבוּרָתָם [l] ק׳ id. sing., suff. 3 pers. pl. masc.; ו bef. (:) בר

גָּבַח Root not used; Samar. *to be high*, used in the Arab. of the forehead.

גִּבֵּחַ masc. *bald in the forehead*, Le. 13. 41.

גַּבַּחַת fem. dec. 13 a.—I. *baldness in the forehead* Le. 13. 42, 43.—II. trop. *bareness thread-bare* Le. 13. 15.

גִּבֵּחַ [m] noun masc. sing. . . . . . בח

גַּבַּי pr. name masc. . . . . . בב

גַּבֵּי [n] noun masc. pl. constr. from גַּב dec. 8 d. . בב

[a] Is. 52. 13. [b] 1 Sa. 16. 7. [c] Job 40. 10. [d] Eze. 31. 3. [e] Eze. 31. 5. [f] Is. 2. 11, 17. [g] Da. 8. 3. [h] Job 11. 8. [i] Is. 5. 15. [k] Ec. 5. 7. [l] Eze. 10. 12. [m] Eze. 31. 10. [n] Ps. 138. 6. [o] Eze. 43. 13. [p] Ps. 74. 17. [q] 1 Ch. 4. 10. [r] Eze. 27. 4. [s] Ex. 7. 27. [t] Jos. 1. 4. [u] 1 Sa. 7. 14. [x] Is. 13. 3. [y] 1 Ch. 11. 26. [z] Na. 2. 4. [a] Je. 46. 5. [b] Je. 26. 21. [c] 1 Sa. 17. 51. [d] Da. 2. 20, 23. [e] Job 26. 14. [f] Je. 16. 21. [g] Ps. 145. 12. [h] Is. 3. 25. [i] Ps. 145. 11. [k] Is. 30. 15. [l] Je. 23. 10. [m] Le. 13. 41. [n] Job 15. 26.

[a] גַּבִּי id. sing., suff. 1 pers. sing. . . . . גבב
[b] גַּבֵּי defect. for גּוֹבֵי n. m. pl. or collect. of גּוֹב גוב
[c] גַּבֹּהּ Ch. K. גַּבָּה noun masc. sing., suff. 3 pers. sing. fem. from גַּב dec. 5a. . . . גבב
[d] גַּבֵּיהֶם noun. m. pl., suff. 3 pers. pl. m. fr. גַּב d. 8d. גבב
[e] גַּבֵּיהֶן וְ׳ id., suff. 3 pers. pl. fem. . . . . גבב
[f] גַּבֵּיכֶם id., suff. 2 pers. pl. masc. . . . . גבב
גֵּבִים noun masc., pl. of [גֵּב] dec. 1a, also pr. n. גוב
[g] גְּבִיעַ noun masc. sing., constr. of גָּבִיעַ dec. 3a. גבע
[h] גְּבִיעִי id., suff. 1 pers. sing. . . . . גבע
גְּבִיעֶיהָ id. pl., suff. 3 pers. sing. fem. . . . גבע
[ll] גְּבִיעִים id. pl. abs. state . . . . גבע
[i] גְּבִיר noun masc. sing. . . . . . גבר
[k] גָּבִישׁ וְ noun masc. sing. . . . . . גבש
[l] גַּבֵּךְ noun m. s., suff. 2 pers. s. f. fr. גַּב d. 8d. גבב

גָּבַל I. *to bound, limit.*—II. *to set a boundary.*—III. with בְּ *to border upon.*

גְּבַל (*mountain*, coll. with the Arab.) pr. n. of a Phenician city, Eze. 27. 9.—Gent. n. גִּבְלִי 1 Ki. 5. 32.

גְּבָל (id.) pr. n. of a mountainous tract in the south of Idumea, Ps. 83. 8.

גְּבוּל, גְּבֻל masc. d. 1a.—I. *bound, limit, border.*—II. *a limited space, territory, margin, edge,* Eze. 43. 13, 17.

גְּבוּלָה, גְּבֻלָה fem. dec. 10.—I. *bound, border.*—II. *territory.*

גַּבְלֻת f. *a bordering, edging,* Ex. 28. 22; 39, 15.

מִגְבָּלָה fem. id. only מִגְבָּלוֹת, Ex. 28. 14.

גְּבַל pr. name of a region . . . . . גבל
גְּבָל pr. name of a place . . . . . גבל
גְּבֻל וּ׳ defect. for גְּבוּל n. m. s. d. 1a; וּ bef. (:) גבל
[m] גָּבְלוּ Kal pret. 3 pers. pl. . . . . גבל
גְּבֻלוֹ noun m. s., suff. 3 p. s. m. fr. גְּבוּל d. 1a. גבל
גְּבֻלְךָ / גְּבוּלְךָ } id., suff. 2 pers. sing. masc. . . . גבל
[n] גְּבֻלְכֶם id., suff. 2 pers. pl. masc. . . . . גבל
[o] גְּבֻלֹת noun fem., pl. of [גְּבוּלָה] dec. 10. . גבל
גַּבְלֻת noun fem. sing. [for גַּבְלוּת] . . . גבל
[p] גְּבֻלָתוֹ n. f. s., suff. 3 pers. s. m. fr. [גְּבוּלָה] d. 10. גבל

גָּבַן Root not used; Syr. *to coagulate, to be condensed.*

גְּבִינָה f. *cheese,* Job 10. 10. Also the two foll.

[q] גִּבֵּן masc. *hunchbacked,* Lev. 21. 20. . . גבן
[r] גַּבְנֻנִּים masc. pl. [of גַּבְנֹן dec. 8c] *heights, summits,* Ps. 68. 16, 17. . . . . גבן

גָּבַע Root not used; cogn. גָּבַהּ, גָּבַהּ, גָּבַב *to be high.*

גֶּבַע (*hill,* comp. גִּבְעָה) pr. name of a Levitical city in the tribe of Benjamin.

גִּבְעָא (id.) pr. name masc., 1 Ch. 2. 49.

גִּבְעָה fem. dec. 12b.—I. *a hill.*—II. pr. name of a city in the tribe of Judah, Jos. 15. 57.—III. more frequently with the art. הַגִּבְעָה pr. name of a city in the tribe of Benjamin, more fully גִּבְעַת בִּנְיָמִין, גִּבְעַת בְּנֵי ב׳, called also גִּבְעַת שָׁאוּל comp. 1 Sa. 11. 4, with 10. 26, as the birthplace of Saul, and גִּבְעַת הָאֱלֹהִים 1 Sa. 10. 5, comp. ver. 10. Gent. n. גִּבְעָתִי 1 Ch. 12. 3.—IV. גִּבְעַת פִּינְחָס pr. name of a city in the mount of Ephraim, Jos. 24. 33.

גִּבְעַת (*hill*) pr. name of a town in the tribe of Judah, Jos. 18. 28.

גִּבְעוֹן (*hill-city*) pr. name of a city in the tribe of Benjamin.—Gent. n. גִּבְעֹנִי.

גָּבִיעַ masc. dec. 3a.—I. *cup, goblet.*—II. *the cup* or *bell* of a flower, as an ornament of the sacred candlestick.

מִגְבָּעָה fem. only pl. מִגְבָּעוֹת *mitres* or *bonnets* of the common priests, probably of a *conic* form.

גָּבַע / גֶּבַע } וָ׳ pr. n. of a place; (§ 35. r. 2) for וָ see lett. ו גבע
גִּבְעָא pr. name masc. . . . . גבע
גִּבְעָה וְ׳׳ noun fem. sing. dec. 12b; also pr. name of a place . . . . . גבע
גִּבְעוֹן pr. name of a man and a place . . גבע
גִּבְעוֹנָה pr. name of a place (גִּבְעוֹן) with parag. ה . גבע
גְּבָעוֹת וּ׳ n. fem. pl. abs. fr. גִּבְעָה d. 12b; וּ bef. (:) גבע
גִּבְעוֹת id. pl., constr. state . . . . גבע
[t] גִּבְעוֹתֶיךָ id. pl., suff. 2 pers. sing. masc. . . גבע
גְּבִעִים noun masc., pl. of גָּבִיעַ׳ dec. 3a. . . גבע
גִּבְעֹל only Ex. 9. 31, הַפִּשְׁתָּה גִּבְעֹל *the flax was in the flower* (comp. גָּבִיעַ, ל being added as in כַּרְמֶל, חַרְגֹּל). Luther: *the flax had knots.* But the word is probably made up of the two roots גבע and גבל.
גִּבְעֹנָה pr. name of a place (גִּבְעוֹן) with parag. ה . גבע
גִּבְעַת noun fem. s., constr. of גִּבְעָה dec. 12.b, also in compos. with pr. n., as גִּבְעַת בִּנְיָמִין, &c. גבע
גִּבְעַת pr. name of a place . . . . גבע
גִּבְעֹת noun fem. pl. constr. of גִּבְעָה dec. 12b. . גבע
גִּבְעָתָה pr. name of a place (גִּבְעָה) with parag. ה גבע
[u] גִּבְעָתָהּ n. f. s., suff. 3 pers. s. f. from גִּבְעָה dec. 12b. גבע
[x] גִּבְעָתִי id., suff. 1 pers. sing. . . . . גבע

[a] Ps. 129. 3. [b] Am. 7. 1. [c] Da. 7. 6. [d] 1 Ki. 7. 33. [e] Eze. 1. 18. [f] Job 13. 12. [g] Ge. 44. 2. [h] Ge. 44. 2. [i] Ge. 27. 29, 37. [k] Job 28. 18. [l] Eze. 16. 31, 39. [ll] Ex. 25. 34. [m] De. 19. 14. [n] De. 11. 24. [o] De. 32. 8. [p] Is. 28. 25. [q] Le. 21. 20. [r] Ps. 68. 16, 17. [s] Is. 40. 4. [t] Eze. 35. 8. [u] Is. 31. 4. [x] Eze. 34. 26.

גָּבַר [a] וְ׳ (pl. גָּבְרוּ, גָּבֵרוּ).—I. *to be* or *become strong, powerful, mighty*, constr. abs.; with עַל, מִן *to be stronger than, to prevail against*.—II. *to increase*, of water; גָּבַר חַיִל *to increase in strength*. Pi. *to make strong, strengthen*. Hiph.—I. i. q. Kal No. I. constr. with לְ, Ps. 12. 5.—II. *to confirm*, Da. 9. 27. Hithp.—I. *to show oneself strong*, with עַל, Is. 42. 13.—II. *to behave oneself stoutly, insolently*, with אֶל against any one.

גֶּבֶר masc. dec. 6a.—I. *man*, i. q. אִישׁ.—II. *husband*.—III. *warlike-man, warrior*.—IV. *each, every one*; לַגְּבָרִים, לִגְבָרִים *man by man*.—V. pr. name masc., 1 Ki. 4. 19.

גְּבַר Chald. masc. *a man*, pl. גֻּבְרִין, emph. גֻּבְרַיָּא (as if from a sing. גּוּבַר).

גְּבַר masc. id. Ps. 18. 26.

גִּבָּר Chald. dec. 1b.—I. *hero*, Da. 3. 20.—II. pr. name of a city, Ezr. 2. 20.

גִּבּוֹר, גִּבֹּר masc. dec. 1b.—I. adj. *strong, mighty, valiant*.—II. subst. *warrior, hero, chief*; גִּבּוֹר חַיִל *a valiant warrior, hero*; also *one mighty in wealth*.

גְּבוּרָה fem. dec. 10.—I. *strength, power, might*.—II. *valour, courage*.—III. *mighty acts*.

גְּבוּרָא Chald. fem. id. only emph. גְּבוּרְתָּא (dec. 8a) Da. 2. 20, 23.

גְּבִיר masc. *master, lord*, Ge. 27. 29, 37.

גְּבִירָה fem. *mistress, lady, queen*.

גְּבֶרֶת fem. dec. 13, *mistress*.

גַּבְרִיאֵל (*man of God*) pr. name of an archangel.

גָּבֶר in pause for גֶּבֶר (q. v.) . . . . גבר

גְּבַר Heb. and Chald. noun masc. sing. גבר

גֶּבֶר וְ׳ noun masc. s. dec. 6a; also pr. name masc. גבר

גִּבָּר pr. name of a place . . . . . גבר

גִּבֹּר (for גִּבּוֹר) adj. masc. sing. dec. 1b. . גבר

גָּבְרוּ, גָּבֵרוּ [b] } Kal pret. 3 pers. pl. (§ 8. rem. 1) . גבר

גִּבָּרֵי [c] Chald. noun m., pl. constr. from [גִּבָּר] dec. 1. גבר

גִּבֹּרֵי adj. masc. pl. constr. from גִּבּוֹר dec. 1b. . גבר

גֻּבְרַיָּא [d] וְ׳ Ch. n. m. pl. emph. [as if from גּוּבַר] see גְּבַר גבר

גַּבְרִיאֵל pr. name masc. . . . . . . גבר

גִּבֹּרֶיהָ [e] וְ adj. m. pl., suff. 3 p. s. f. from גִּבּוֹר dec. 1b. גבר

גִּבֹּרָיו [f] וְ id., suff. 3 pers. sing. masc. . . גבר

גְּבָרִים [g] noun masc., pl. of גֶּבֶר dec. 6. . . גבר

גִּבֹּרִים adj. masc., pl. of גִּבּוֹר dec. 1b. . . גבר

גֻּבְרִין [h] Chald. n. m. pl. abs. [as if from גּוּבַר] see גְּבַר גבר

גְּבֶרֶת [i], גְּבָרֶת [k] } noun fem. sing. dec. 13a. (see the foll.) . גבר

גְּבִרְתָּהּ [l] id., suff. 3 pers. sing. fem. . . . . גבר

גִּבַּרְתִּי [m] וְ Piel pret. 1 pers. sing. . . . . גבר

גְּבִרְתִּי [n] noun fem. s., suff. 1 p. s. from גְּבֶרֶת dec. 13a. גבר

גְּבוּרָתִי [kk] noun fem. s., suff. 1 p. s. from גְּבוּרָה dec. 10. גבר

גִּבַּרְתִּים [o] וְ Piel pret. 1 pers. sing., suff. 3 pers. pl. m. גבר

גְּבִרְתֵּךְ [p] noun f. s., suff. 2 p. s. f. from גְּבֶרֶת dec. 13a. גבר

גָּבַשׁ Root not used; Arab. *to congeal*; Chald. גְּבַשׁ *to gather together*.

גָּבִישׁ masc. *crystal*, (prop. *ice*), Job 28. 18.

אֶלְגָּבִישׁ masc. *hail*, אֶל supposed to be i. q. אל the article in the Arab.

מַגְבִּישׁ (*gathering*) pr. name of a place or person, Ezr. 2. 30.

גַּבֹּת [q] noun m. with pl. fem. term. from גַּב dec. 8d. גבב

גַּבֹּתָם [r] וְ id., suff. 3 pers. pl. masc. . . גבב

גִּבְּתוֹן pr. name of a place . . . . גבב

גָּג masc. dec. 8a.—I. *roof* of a house.—II. *top* of an altar.

גַּג id., construct state . . . . . גג

גַּגּוֹ id., suff. 3 pers. sing. masc. . . . גג

גַּגּוֹת id. pl. fem. . . . . . . גג

גַּגּוֹתֶיהָ [s] id. pl., suff. 3 pers. sing. fem. . . גג

גַּגּוֹתֵיהֶם [t], גַּגֹּתֵיהֶם [u] } id. pl., suff. 3 pers. pl. masc. . . גג

גָּד pr. name of a man and a tribe . . גדד

גַּד noun masc. sing. . . . . . גדד

גְּדָבְרַיָּא Chald. noun masc. pl. emph. *treasurers*, Da. 3. 2, 3, comp. גִּזְבָּר.

גָּדַד prop. *to cut*, hence *to press upon*, with עַל Ps. 94. 21. Hithpo.—I. *to cut oneself, to make incisions*.—II. *to press* or *crowd together*.

גְּדַד Chald. *to cut* or *hew down*, Da. 4. 11, 20.

גָּד masc.—I. *good fortune*.—II. pr. name of a son of Jacob, and the tribe descended from him.—Gent. noun גָּדִי *Gadite*.

גַּד masc.—I. *coriander seed*.—II. (*fortuna*,) pr. name of an idol, Is. 65. 11.

גִּדְגָּד (*cleft, chink*,) pr. name of a station of the Israelites in the desert, De. 10. 7; called חֹר הַגִּדְגָּד (*cavern of the cleft*,) Nu. 33. 32.

גַּדָּה (*fortune*) see חֲצַר גַּ׳.

גְּדוּד masc. dec. 1b. (pl. ־ִים, ־וֹת.)—I. *a cutting*, Je. 48. 37.—II. *furrow*, Ps. 65. 11.—III. *troop*, or *detachment of an army*.

[a] Ex. 17. 11, 11. [b] 2 Sa. 1. 23. [c] Da. 3. 20. [d] Da. 3. 23. [e] Je. 51. 57. [f] 2 Ch. 32. 3. [g] Je. 41. 16. [h] Da. 3. 8, 12, 24, 25. [i] Is. 47. 7. [k] Is. 47. 5. [kk] Is. 33. 13. [l] Ge. 16. 4, ect. [m] Zec. 10. 6. [n] Ge. 16. 8. [o] Zec. 10. 12. [p] Ge. 16. 9. [q] Le. 14. 9. [r] Eze. 1. 18. [s] Is. 15. 3. [t] Je. 32. 29. [u] Je. 19. 13.

גָּדִי.—I. gent. noun of גָּד q. v.—II. pr. name masc., 2 Ki. 15. 14.

גַּדִּי (*fortunate*) pr. name masc., Nu. 13. 11.

גַּדִּיאֵל (*fortune of God*) pr. name m., Nu. 13. 10.

מְגִדּוֹ, מְגִדּוֹן (*place of troops*) pr. name of a city of Manasseh situated within the borders of Issachar.

גְּדֻדֹת[a] noun masc. with pl. f. term. from גְּדוּד dec. 1 a. גדד

גָּדָה Root not used; Arab. *to pluck out*, or *off*; Syr. *to leap*.

גָּדָה fem. dec. 11 a, *banks of a river*.

גְּדִי masc. dec. 6 i, *a kid*; גְּדִי עִזִּים *kid of the goats*.

גִּדְיָה fem. *banks of a river*, 1 Ch. 12. 15, Kheth.

גְּדִיָּה fem. dec. 10, *a female kid*, Ca. 1. 8.

גַּדָּה pr. name in compos. חֲצַר גַּדָּה . . חצר

גְּדוּ[b] Chald. Peal imp. pl. masc. . . . . גדד

גְּדוּד noun masc. sing. dec. 1 a. . . . גדד

גְּדוּדֶהָ[c] id. pl., suff. 3 pers. s. fem. [for ׳דֶיהָ] . גדד

גְּדוּדֵי[d] ׳גְּ id. pl. construct state; ּגְ before (:) . גדד

גְּדוּדָיו[e] id. pl., suff. 3 pers. s. masc. . . גדד

גְּדוּדִים id. pl., absolute state . . . . גדד

גָּדוֹל ׳ןְ adj. masc. sing. dec. 3 a. . . . גדל

גְּדוֹל[f] id., construct state . . . . גדל

גְּדָל־ ּגְ id. with Mak., Kh. גְּדוֹל, K. גְּדָל (§ 32. r. 7) גדל

גְּדוֹלָה[g] ׳גְּ adj. f. s. dec. 10, from גָּדוֹל m.; ּגְ bef. (:) גדל

גְּדוּלָּה[h] ּגְ noun fem. sing. dec. 10; ּגְ id. . גדל

גְּדוֹלֶיהָ[i] adj. m. pl., suff. 3 pers. s. f. from גָּדוֹל dec. 3 a. גדל

גְּדוֹלִים id. pl., absolute state . . . גדל

גְּדוֹלָם id. sing., suff. 3 pers. pl. masc. . . גדל

גְּדוֹלֹת id. fem., pl. of ׳לָה dec. 10, from גָּדוֹל masc. גדל

גְּדוּלָּתוֹ[k] noun f. s., suff. 3 p. s. m. from ׳לָּה dec. 10. גדל

גְּדוּעָה[l] Kal part. pass. sing. fem. . . . גדע

גְּדוּפָה[m] ּגְ noun fem. sing.; ּגְ before (:) . . גדף

גְּדוֹר ּגְ pr. name of a man and a place; ּגְ id. . גדר

גְּדוֹתָיו n. f. pl., suff. 3 p. s. m. from [גָּדָה] dec. 11 a. גדה

גָּדִי ׳ןְ pr. name masc., or patronym. of גָּד . גדד

גַּדִּי pr. name masc. . . . . . גדד

גְּדִי[n] ׳גְּ noun masc. sing. dec. 6 i; ּגְ before (:) גדה

גֶּדִי pr. name, see עֵין גֶּדִי . . . . עין

גַּדִּיאֵל pr. name masc. . . . . . גדד

גְּדָיֵי[o] noun masc. pl., constr. from גְּדִי dec. 6 i. . גדה

גְּדָיִים[p] id. pl., absolute state . . . גדה

גָּדִישׁ noun masc. sing. . . . . . גדש

גְּדִיֹתָיו[q] Kh. גְּדִיֹתָיו [pl. of גִּדְיָה], K. גְּדוֹתָיו (q. v.) גדה

גְּדִיֹּתַיִךְ[r] noun fem. pl., suff. from [גְּדִיָּה] dec. 10. גדה

גָּדַל (with suff. גִּדְּלַנִי, Job 31. 18; fut. יִגְדַּל).—I. Arab. & Syr. *to twist*, only in the deriv. גָּדִיל q. v.—II. *to be* or *become great, to grow*.—III. *to be great, exalted*. Pi.—I. *to make great, to cause to grow*, of hair, plants; of children *to educate*.—II. *to exalt, to extol*. Pu. *to be brought up*, Ps. 144. 12. Hiph.—I. *to make great*; הִגְדִּיל פֶּה *to boast*; הִ׳ חַסְדּוֹ עִם פְּ׳ *to show one great kindness*; with an inf. הִ׳ לַעֲשׂוֹת *to do great things*; in a bad sense, *to act proudly*, and so ellipt. הִגְדִּיל with עַל of the pers.; 1 Sa. 20. 41, עַד הִגְדִּיל [לִבְכּוֹת] *until he wept greatly*; הִ׳ בְּפֶה *to boast*.—II. *to lift up*, Ps. 41. 10. Hithpa. *to show oneself great*.

גָּדֵל adj. masc. dec. 5 a, *becoming great*, Ge. 26. 13; 1 Sa. 2. 26; *great*, Eze. 16. 26.

גָּדִיל masc. only pl. גְּדִלִים.—I. *fringes*, De. 22. 12. —II. *platted chain-work*, 1 Ki. 7. 17.

גָּדוֹל masc. dec. 3 a. (with Mak. ־גְּדָל § 32. rem. 7), גְּדוֹלָה fem. dec. 10.—I. adj. *great*, in extent, number, quantity, age, dignity, &c. עוֹד הַיּוֹם גָּדוֹל *it is yet great* [*high*] *day*, i. e. early, (French *grand jour*;) הַכֹּהֵן הַגָּדוֹל *the high-priest*.—II. subst. *greatness*, Ex. 15. 16; pl. גְּדֹלוֹת *great things*.

גְּדֻלָּה, גְּדוּלָּה, גְּדוּלָה fem. dec. 10.—I. *great deed* or *act*.—II. *greatness, majesty, magnificence*.

גֹּדֶל masc. dec. 6 c. (suff. ׳גָּדְ, גָּדְלוֹ § 35. rem. 8).—I. *greatness*.—II. *majesty, magnificence*.—III. *pride*.

גִּדֵּל (*over-grown*, comp. § 26. No. 9) pr. name of two different men.

גְּדַלְיָהוּ, גְּדַלְיָה (*great is the Lord*) pr. name of several men, especially of the governor of Judea, appointed by Nebuchadnezzar.

גִּדַּלְתִּי (*I extol* Him) pr. name masc. 1 Ch. 25. 4, 29.

יִגְדַּלְיָה (*the Lord be extolled*) pr. n. m. Je. 35. 4.

מִגְדָּל masc. dec. 2 b. (pl. ־ִים, ־וֹת).—I. *tower*. —II. *pulpit*, Ne. 8. 4.—III. *bed* in a garden, Ca. 5. 13.—IV. in compos. with pr. names, as מִגְדַּל־אֵל (*tower of God*) a fortress in the tribe of Naphtali, Jos. 19. 38; מִגְדַּל־גָּד (*tower of God*) a town in the tribe of Judah, Jos. 15. 37; מִגְדַּל עֵדֶר (*tower of the flock*) a village near Bethlehem.

מִגְדֹּל, מִגְדּוֹל masc.—I. *tower*, 2 Sa. 22. 51. Keri.—II. pr. name of a city in Egypt.

גָּדֵל ׳ןְ adj. masc. sing. dec. 5 a. . . . . גדל

גַּדֵּל[s] Piel inf. absolute . . . . גדל

גָּדֹל adj. masc. sing. for גָּדוֹל dec. 3 a. . . גדל

גְּדֹל id., construct state . . . . גדל

גִּדֵּל
גִּדֵּל[t] } Piel pret. 3 pers. sing. masc. (§ 10. rem. 1) גדל

[a] Je. 48. 37. [b] Da. 4. 11, 20. [c] Ps. 65. 11. [d] 2 Ki. 13. 20. [e] Job 19. 12. [f] Eze. 17. 3. [g] Ec. 9. 13. [h] Est. 6. 3. [i] Na. 3. 10. [k] Est. 1. 4. [l] Is. 15. 2. [m] Eze. 5. 15. [n] 1 Sa. 16. 20. [o] Ge. 27. 9, 16. [p] 1 Sa. 10. 3. [q] 1 Ch. 12. 15. [r] Ca. 1. 8. [s] Nu. 6. 5. [t] Is. 49. 21

גִּדֵּל pr. name masc. . . . . . גדל

גֹּדֶל noun masc. sing. dec. 6c. . . . גדל

גָּדְלָה Kal pret. 3 pers. sing. fem. . . . גדל

גְּדֹלָה [a] 'וּ adj. fem. s. dec. 10, from גָּדוֹל m.; וּ bef. (:) גדל

[b] גִּדְּלָה Piel pret. 3 p. s. f. [for גִּדְּלָה comp. § 8. r. 7] גדל

גָּדְלוּ Kal pret. 3 pers. pl. . . . . גדל

[c] גָּדְלוֹ noun m. s., suff. 3 p. s. m. from גֹּדֶל dec. 6c. גדל

[d] גַּדְּלוּ Piel imp. pl. masc. . . . . גדל

גִּדְּלוֹ id. pret. 3 pers. sing. masc., suff. 3 pers. s. m. גדל

[e] גִּדְּלוֹ for גִּדְּלוֹ q. v. (§ 35. rem. 8) . . . גדל

[f] גִּדְּלוּהוּ Piel pret. 3 pers. pl., suff. 3 pers. sing. masc. גדל

גְּדֹלוֹת adj. fem., pl. of גְּדוֹלָה dec. 10, from גָּדוֹל m. גדל

[g] גְּדֻלּוֹת noun fem., pl. of גְּדֻלָּה dec. 10, see גְּדוּלָּה . גדל

[h] גְּדֻלּוֹתֶיךָ Kh. גְּדֻלּוֹתֶיךָ, K. גְּדוּלָּתְךָ noun fem. pl. or s., suff. 2 p. s. m. from גְּדוּלָּה d. 10; וּ bef. (:) גדל

גְּדֹלֵי adj. masc. pl. construct from גָּדוֹל dec. 3a. גדל

[k] גִּדְלֵי adj. masc. pl. construct from גָּדֵל dec. 5a. גדל

גְּדַלְיָה 'וּ pr. name masc.; וּ before (:) . . גדל

גְּדַלְיָהוּ 'וּ pr. name masc.; וּ id. . . . גדל

[l] גְּדֹלָיו [m] 'וּ adj. m. pl., suff. from גָּדוֹל dec. 3a; וּ id. גדל

גְּדִלִים noun masc., pl. of [גָּדִיל] dec. 3a. . גדל

גְּדֹלִים adj. masc., pl. of גָּדוֹל dec. 3a. . . גדל

[n] גָּדְלְךָ n. m. s., suff. 2 pers. s. m. from גֹּדֶל dec. 6c. גדל

[o] גַּדֶּלְךָ Piel inf. (גַּדֵּל), suff. 2 pers. sing. masc. (§ 15. rem. 16, & § 36. rem. 3) . גדל

[p] גִּדְּלַנִי Kal pret. 3 pers. sing. masc. (גָּדֵל), suff. 1 pers. sing. (comp. § 8. rem. 1) . . גדל

גִּדַּלְתָּ id. pret. 2 pers. sing. masc. . . . גדל

[q] גְּדֻלַּת noun f. s., constr. of לָּה' dec. 10, see גְּדוּלָּה גדל

גְּדֹלֹת adj. f., pl. of גְּדוֹלָה dec. 10, from גָּדוֹל masc. גדל

[r] גִּדַּלְתּוֹ Piel pret. 2 pers. sing. m., suff. 3 pers. s. m. גדל

גִּדַּלְתִּי id. pret. 1 pers. sing. . . . . גדל

גִּדַּלְתִּי pr. name masc. . . . . . גדל

גָּדַלְתִּי וְ Kal pret. 1 pers. sing.; acc. shifted to ult. by conversive וְ (§ 8. rem. 7) . . גדל

[s] גְּדֻלָּתִי noun f. s., suff. 1 p. s. from גְּדֻלָּה see גְּדוּלָּה גדל

גָּדַע I. *to cut off* or *down*.—II. *to cut* or *break asunder*. Niph. *to be cut off*. Pi. *to break, break in pieces*. Pu. *to be cut down*, Is. 9. 9.

גִּדְעֹם (*a cutting down*) pr. name of a town in the tribe of Benjamin, Ju. 20. 45.

גִּדְעוֹן (*cutter*) pr. name of a judge in Israel, Ju. chap. 6—8.

גִּדְעֹנִי (id.) pr. name masc. Nu. 1. 11; 2. 22.

[t] גִּדֵּעַ, גִּדַּע } Piel pret. 3 pers. sing. masc. (§ 15. rem. 1) גדע

[u] גֻּדְּעוּ Pual pret. 3 p. pl. [for גֻּדְּעוּ comp. § 8. r. 7] גדע

גִּדְעוֹן 'וְ pr. name masc. . . . . גדע

[v] גְּדֻעִים Kal part. pass. pl. masc. from [גָּדוּעַ] dec. 3a. גדע

[w] גָּדַעְתִּי וְ Kal pret. 1 pers. sing.; acc. shifted to ult. by conversive וְ (§ 8. rem. 7) . . גדע

גִּדְעֹם pr. name of a place . . . . גדע

גִּדְעֹנִי pr. name masc. . . . . . גדע

גָּדַף. Pi. *to reproach, revile, blaspheme*.

גִּדּוּף masc. dec. 2b, only pl. (וֹת, ־ִים) *reproaches*.

גְּדוּפָה fem. *reproach*, Eze. 5. 15.

גִּדְּפוּ Piel pret. 3 pers. pl. . . . . גדף

[b] גִּדּוּפֵי 'וְ noun m. pl. constr. from [גִּדּוּף] dec. 1b. גדף

גִּדַּפְתָּ וְ Piel pret. 2 pers. sing. masc. . . גדף

גָּדַר *to wall, fence up*.

גָּדֵר com. dec. 5b.—I. *wall, fence*.—II. *fenced place*, Ezr. 9. 9.

גֶּדֶר (*wall*) pr. name of a Canaanitish city, Jos. 12. 13; i. q. בֵּית גָּדֵר.

גְּדֵרָה fem. dec. 11c. (§ 42. rem. 4)—I. *wall*.—II. *walled* or *fenced place*; גִּדְרוֹת צֹאן *sheep folds*.—III. pr. name of a city in the tribe of Judah, Jos. 15. 36. Gent. noun גְּדֵרָתִי, 1 Ch. 12. 4.

גֶּדֶרֶת fem. *wall, fence*, Eze. 42. 12.

גְּדֵרוֹת (*folds*) pr. name of a town in the tribe of Judah.

גְּדֵרֹתַיִם (*two folds*) pr. name of a town in the tribe of Judah, Jos. 15. 36.

גְּדֵרִי Gent. noun of בֵּית גָּדֵר q. v. 1 Ch. 27. 28.

גְּדוֹר (*wall*) pr. n.—I. of a town in the tribe of Judah, Jos. 15. 58—II. of a man, 1 Ch. 8. 31; 9. 37.

גָּדֵר 'וְ n. com. s. d. 5b. (pr. n. in compos. see בֵּית) גדר

[c] גֶּדֶר [d] 'וְ id. construct state; also pr. name . גדר

גְּדֹר pr. name masc. . . . . . גדר

גֹּדֵר Kal part. act. sing. masc. dec. 7b. . . גדר

[e] גְּדֵרָה [f] 'וּ n. f. s. dec. 11c. (§ 42. rem. 4); וּ bef. (:) גדר

[g] גְּדֵרוֹ noun m. s., suff. 3 p. s. m. from גָּדֵר dec. 5b. גדר

[h] גִּדְרוֹת [i] 'וְ noun fem. pl. constr. from גְּדֵרָה dec. 11c. גדר

גְּדֵרוֹת וּ id. pl. abs. pr. name of a place; וּ before (:) גדר

[k] גְּדֵרֶיהָ noun m. pl., suff. 3 pers. s. f. from גָּדֵר dec. 5b. גדר

[l] גְּדֵרַיִךְ id., suff. 2 pers. sing. fem. [for ־ַיִךְ] . גדר

[m] גִּדְרֹת [n] 'וְ noun fem. pl. constr. from גְּדֵרָה dec. 11c. (§ 42. rem. 4) . . . . גדר

---

[a] Ne. 7. 4. [b] Is. 51. 18. [c] De. 5. 24. [d] Ps. 34. 4. [e] Ps. 150. 2. [f] Eze. 31. 4. [g] 1 Ch. 17. 21. [h] Ps. 145. 6. [i] 2 Ki. 10. 6. [k] Eze. 16. 26. [l] 2 Ki. 10. 11. [m] Jon. 3. 7. [n] De. 3. 24. [o] Jos. 3. 7. [p] Job 31. 18. [q] Est. 10. 2. [r] Jon. 4. 10. [s] Ecc. 2. 9. [t] Ps. 71. 21. [u] La. 2. 3. [x] 2 Ch. 34. 7. [y] Is. 9. 9. [z] Is. 10. 33. [a] 1 Sa. 2. 31. [b] Zep. 2. 8. [c] Eze. 42. 10. [d] Pr. 24. 31. [e] Ho. 2. 8. [f] 1 Ch. 4. 23. [g] Is. 5. 5. [h] 1 Sa. 24. 4. [i] Zep. 2. 6. [k] Ps. 80. 13. [l] Mi. 7. 11. [m] Nu. 32. 16. [n] Nu. 32. 36.

[a]גְּדֵרֹת וּ id. pl., absolute state; וּ before (:) . גדר
גָּדַרְתִּי וְ Kal pret. 1 pers. sing.; acc. shifted to ult. by conversive וְ (§ 8. rem. 7) . . גדר
[b]גְּדֵרֹתָיו n. f. pl., suff. 3 p. s. m., from גְּדֵרָה (§ 42. r. 4) גדר
גְּדֵרֹתָיִם וּ pr. name of a place; וּ before (:) . . גדר

גָּדַשׁ Root not used; Chald. *to heap up*.
גָּדִישׁ masc.—I. *sepulchral mound*, Job 21. 32.—II. *stack of corn*.

גֵּה prob. for זֶה *this*, Eze. 47. 13.

[גָּהָה] *to heal, cure*, Ho. 5. 13. Hence
גֵּהָה fem. *healing, cure*, Pr. 17. 22. . . גהה

[גָּהַר] *to bow, bend down oneself*.
[c]גֵּו noun masc. sing. (§ 36. rem. 2) . . גוה
[d]גּוֹא Chald. noun m. s., constr. of [גַּו] irr. (§ 45) גוה
[e]גּוֹאֵל Kal part. act. sing. masc. dec. 7b. . גאל
[f]גֹּאֲלִי וְ id. with suff. 1 pers. sing. . . גאל

[גּוּב] I. Arab. *to cut, cleave*, only in the derivv. Hence —II. *to plough*, 2 Ki. 25. 12, Kheth.
גֵּב masc. dec. 1a.—I. *board, plank*, 1 Ki. 6. 9.—II. *well, cistern*, Je. 14. 3.—III. *locust*, Is. 33. 4.
גֵּבִים (*cisterns*, or *locusts*) pr. name of a place near Jerusalem, Is. 10. 31.
גּוֹב, גֹּב masc.—I. *locust*, pl. or collect. גֹּבַי, גּוֹבַי *locust*, Am. 7. 1; Na. 3. 17.—II. pr. name of a place, 2 Sa. 21. 18, 19, otherwise unknown.
[g]גּוֹבַי [for גֹּבַי] noun masc. pl. or collect. [of גּוֹב] גוב
גּוֹג pr. name.—I. of a Reubenite, 1 Ch. 5. 4.—II. of a prince of the land of Magog.
מָגוֹג pr. name.—I. of a son of Japheth, Ge. 10. 2.—II. of an unknown region, perhaps *Scythia*.

[גּוּד] *to press upon*, cogn. גָּדַד.

גָּוָה & גָּוַן Root not used; cogn. גָּבַהּ, גָּבַב *to be rising, convex*.
גֵּו masc. dec. 8e, *a back*.
גַּו Chald. masc. irr. (§ 68).—I. *middle, midst*. —II. prep. *in, into*.
גֵּו masc. dec. 1a.—I. *back*.—II. *middle, midst*, Job 30. 5.
גֵּוָה fem. *body*, Job 20. 25.

גְּוִיָּה fem. dec. 10.—I. *body, person*.—II. *dead body, corpse, carcase*, of men and animals.
גּוֹי masc. dec. 1a. (with suff. גּוֹיִ; pl. גּוֹיִם § 3. rem. 1) prop. a body of men, hence—I. *a people, nation*, generally of foreign nations; but also of Israel, Is. 1. 4; Ge. 12. 2; in the pl. foreign, heathen nations.—II. metaph. applied to locusts, Joel 1. 6, to other animals, Zep. 2. 14.
גֵּוָה [h]וְ'' noun fem. sing. [for גַּאֲוָה] . . גאה

[גּוּז] *to pass over*, Ps. 90. 10; perhaps causat. Nu. 11. 31.
[i]גֹּזְזַי Kal part. act. s. m., suff. 1 p. s. fr. [גֹּזֶה] d. 9a. גזה
[k]גּוֹזֵל Kal part. act. sing. masc. dec. 7b. . גזל
[l]גּוֹזָל וְ noun masc. sing. dec. 2b. . . גזל
[m]גּוֹזָלָיו id. pl. with suff. 3 pers. sing. masc. . גזל
גּוֹזָן pr. name of a place . . . . גזה
[n]גֵּוִי n. m. s. with suff. 1 p. s. from גֵּו (§ 36. r. 2) גוה
גּוֹי וְ' noun masc. sing. dec. 1a. . . גוה
[o]גּוֹיִ id. with suff. 1 pers. sing. (§ 3. rem. 1) . גוה
[p]גְּוִיּוֹת noun fem., pl. of גְּוִיָּה dec. 10. . . גוה
גּוֹיֵי noun masc. pl. constr. of גּוֹי d. 1a. (§ 3. r. 1) גוה
[q]גּוֹיֶךָ id. sing., suff. 2 pers. sing. masc. [for גּוֹיְךָ] גוה
[r]גּוֹיֵךְ וְ' id. sing. (Kh. גּוֹיֵךְ), or pl. (K. גּוֹיַיִךְ), suff. 2 pers. sing. fem. . . . גוה
גּוֹיִם [s]וְ' id., pl., absolute state . . גוה
[t]גְּוִיַּת noun fem. sing. constr. of גְּוִיָּה dec. 10. . גוה
[x]גְּוִיֹּת id. pl. [for גְּוִיּוֹת] . . . . גוה
[y]גְּוִיָּתוֹ [z]וּ' id. sing., suff. 3 pers. sing. masc.; וּ bef. (:) גוה
[a]גְּוִיֹּתֵיהֶם id. pl., suff. 3 pers. pl. masc. . . גוה
[b]גְּוִיֹּתֵיהֶנָה id., suff. 3 pers. pl. fem. (§ 4. rem. 6) . גוה
[c]גְּוִיֹּתֵינוּ id., suff. 1 pers. pl. . . . גוה
[d]גְּוִיָּתֵנוּ id. sing., suff. 1 pers. pl. . . . גוה
[e]גֵּוְךָ n. m. s., suff. 2 p. s. m. [for גֵּוְךָ, from גֵּו] d. 8d. גוה
[f]גֵּוֶךָ noun m. s., suff. 2 pers. sing. masc. from גֵּו גוה
[g]גֵּוֵךְ n. m. s., suff. 2 pers. s. fem. fr. [גַּו] dec. 8d. גוה
[h]גֵּוֵךְ noun masc. sing., suff. 2 pers. sing. fem. from גֵּו (§ 36. rem. 2) . . . . גוה
[i]גּוֹלִי Kh. גּוֹל, K. גִּיל Kal inf. abs. . . גיל
[k]גּוֹל Kal imp. sing. masc. for גֹּל . . . גלל
גּוֹלָה n. f. s., or (Is. 49. 21) fem. of the foll. dec. 10. גלה
גּוֹלֶה Kal part. act. sing. masc. dec. 9a. . . גלה
גּוֹלָן pr. name of a place . . . . גלה
[l]גֵּוָם n. m. s., suff. 3 pers. pl. m. from [גַּו] dec. 8d. גוה
[hh]גּוּמָּץ noun masc. sing. . . . . גמץ
גּוּנִי וְ' (*coloured*, Chald. גַּוַּן to colour, dye) pr. name masc.—I. Ge. 46. 24, and patronym. Nu. 26. 48.—II. 1 Ch. 5. 15.

[a] Nu. 32. 24. [b] Ps. 89. 41. [c] Job 30. 5. [d] Da. 3. 26. [e] Is. 59. 20. [f] Ps. 19. 15. [g] Na. 3. 17. [h] Job 33. 17. [i] Ps. 71. 6. [k] Pr. 28. 24. [l] Ge. 15. 9. [m] De. 32. 11. [n] Is. 50. 6. [o] Zep. 2. 9. [p] Ps. 110. 6. [q] Ps. 106. 5. [r] Eze. 36. 13. [s] Eze. 36. 14, 15. [t] Zec. 8. 22. [u] 1 Sa. 31. 12. [x] 1 Sa. 31. 12. [y] 1 Sa. 31. 10. [z] Da. 10. 6. [a] Eze. 1. 23 [b] Eze. 1. 11. [c] Ne. 9. 37. [d] Ge. 47. 18. [e] 1 Ki. 14. 9. [f] Is. 38. 17. [g] Eze. 23. 35. [h] Is. 51. 23. [hh] Ec. 10. 8. [i] Pr. 23. 24. [k] Ps. 37. 5. [l] Ne. 9. 26.

גָּוַע *to expire, to die.*

גֹּוֵעַ[a] ו̣ Kal part. act. sing. masc. . . . . גוע

גָּוְעוּ[b] Kal pret. 3 pers. pl., [גָּוְעוּ § 8. rem. 7] גוע

גָּוַעְנוּ id. pret. 1 pers. pl. . . . . . גוע

גּוֹעֵר[c] Kal part. act. sing. masc. . . . . נער

גּוּף Kal not used; *to be hollow*, cogn. נָבַב, גָּפַף. Hiph. *to shut*, Ne. 7. 3.

גּוּפָה fem. dec. 10, *dead body, corpse*, 1 Ch. 10. 12.

גּוּפַת[d] noun fem. sing. constr. of [גּוּפָה] dec. 10. גוף

גּוּפֹת[e] pl. of the preceding . . . . גוף

[גּוּר] I. *to sojourn, dwell* for a time, as a stranger, const. with בְּ, עִם, acc. Part. גָּר *dwelling;* גָּרֵי בֵיתִי *sojourners of my house*, i. e. servants; גָּרַת בֵּיתָהּ *her inmate.*—II. *to fear*, with מִפְּנֵי, מִן.—III. *to congregate, come together*, with עַל, אֶת against any one. Hithpal.—I. *to sojourn*, 1 Ki. 17. 20.—II. *to congregate*, Ho. 7. 14.

גֵּר masc. dec. 1 a, *sojourner, stranger, foreigner.*

גֵּיר masc. id. only 2 Ch. 2. 16.

גֵּרוּת fem. *place of sojourning, dwelling*, Je. 41. 17.

גּוּר i. q. גּוּר *lion's whelp*, only pl. ־ִים, ־וֹת, Je. 51. 38; Na. 2. 13.

גּוּר masc. dec. 1 a.—I. *a lion's whelp.*—II. *the whelp of a jackal*, La. 4. 3.—III. מַעֲלֵה־גוּר (*ascent of whelps*) pr. name of a place, 2 Ki. 9. 27.

גּוּר בַּעַל (*dwelling of Baal*) pr. name of a town in Arabia, 2 Ch. 26. 7.

יָגוּר (*He shall dwell* there) pr. name of a town in the tribe of Judah, Jos. 15. 21.

מָגוֹר masc. *fear, terror;* pl. La. 2. 22. מְגוּרַי (§ 32. rem. 5).

מָגוּר masc. dec. 3 a.—I. *sojourning.*—II. *dwelling, residence*, Ps. 55. 16.

מְגוֹרָה fem. dec. 10, *fear*, Pr. 10. 24.

מְגוּרָה fem. dec. 10.—I. *granary.*—II. *fear, terror.*

מַמְּגֻרָה fem. (denom. of מְגוּרָה) only pl., *garners, storehouses*, Joel 1. 17.

גּוֹר[f] Kal inf. absolute . . . . . גור

גּוּר n. m. s. or pr. n. in compos. גּוּר בַּעַל, מַעֲלֵה גוּר גור

גּוּר[g] Kal imp. sing. masc. . . . . . גור

גּוּרוּ[h] ו̣׳ id. imp. pl. masc. . . . . . גור

גּוּרִי[k] ו̣ id. imp. sing. fem. . . . . . גור

גּוּרֶיהָ[l] n. m. pl., suff. 3 pers. s. fem. fr. גּוּר dec. 1 a. גור

גּוּרֵיהֶן[m] id., suff. 3 pers. pl. fem. . . . . גור

גּוֹרָל ו̣׳ noun masc. sing. dec. 2 b. . . . רל

גּוֹרַל id. sing., construct state . . . . רל

גּוֹרָלוֹ[n] id., suff. 3 pers. sing. masc. . . . רל

גּוֹרָלוֹת id., pl. fem. term. . . . . . רל

גּוֹרָלִי[o] id. sing., suff. 1 pers. sing. . . . רל

גּוֹרָלְךָ[p] id., suff. 2 pers. sing. masc. . . . רל

גּוֹרָלֵךְ id., suff. 2 pers. sing. fem. . . . רל

גּוֹרָלָם id., suff. 3 pers. pl. masc. . . . . רל

גְּוֹרֹנֵךְ[q] ו K. גְּרוֹנֵךְ noun masc. sing., suff. 2 pers. sing. fem., from גָּרוֹן dec. 3 a; ו bef. (:) . רה

גָּז[r] Kal pret. 3 pers. sing. masc. . . . . זז

גֵּז noun masc. sing. dec. 8 b. . . . . זז

[גִּזְבָּר] masc. *treasurer*, Ezr. 1. 8, pl. גִּזְבְּרִין see the foll.

גִּזַּבְרַיָּא[s] Ch. id. pl. emph. as if from [גִּזְבָּר] see גִּזְבָּר

גָּזָה *to cut, cut off*, only part. Ps. 71. 6, for which comp. Eze. 16. 4.

גָּזִית fem. *a cutting, hewing*, hence אַבְנֵי גָ׳ and simply גָּזִית *hewn stones.*

גִּזָּה (for גִּיזָה *quarry*) only in the Gen. n. גִּזוֹנִי 1 Ch. 11. 34, comp. the forms שִׁילֹה, גִּלֹה, שִׁילֹנִי, גִּילֹנִי.

גּוֹזָן (id. after the form גֻּלָה גוֹלָן) pr. name of a region of Mesopotamia on the river Chaboras, whither Shalmaneser carried away part of the ten tribes.

גָּזוּל[t] ו̣׳ Kal part. pass. sing. masc. . . . . זל

[גָּזַז] *to shear, to cut off*, hair, wool, &c. Niph. *to be cut off*, Na. 1. 12.

גֵּז masc. dec. 8 b, prop. *a shearing, cutting*, hence —I. *the fleece.*—II. *young grass after mowing.*

גִּזָּה fem. dec. 10, *fleece*, Ju. 6. 37—40. Also

גָּזֵז (*barber*) pr. name masc. 1 Ch. 2. 46. . זז

גֹּזֵז[u] Kal part. act. sing. masc. dec. 7 b. . . זז

גֹּזְזֵי[v] id. pl. construct state . . . . . זז

גֹּזְזֶיהָ[y] id. pl., suff. 3 pers. sing. fem. . . . זז

גֹּזְזִים id. pl., absolute state . . . . . זז

גָּזִּי[z] } id. imp. s. fem. (§ 18. r. 4); for ו̣ see ו̣ זז
גֹּזִּי[a] }

גִּזֵּי[b] noun masc. pl. constr. from גֵּז dec. 8 b. . זז

גָּזִית[c] ו̣׳ noun fem. sing. . . . . . זה

גָּזַל, גָּזֵל (§ 8. rem. 7).—I. *to strip off*, Mi. 3. 2.—II. *to pluck, snatch away.*—III. *to spoil, rob* any one. Niph. *to be taken away*, Pr. 4. 16.

[a] Ps. 88. 16. [b] La. 1. 19. [c] Na. 1. 4. [d] 1 Ch. 10. 12. [e] 1 Ch. 10. 12. [f] Is. 54. 15. [g] Ge. 26. 3. [h] Job 19. 29. [i] Ps. 22. 24. [k] 2 Ki. 8. 1. [l] Eze. 19. 2. [m] La. 4. 3. [n] 1 Ch. 26. 14. [o] Ps. 16. 5. [p] Pr. 1. 14. [q] Je. 2. 25. [r] Ps. 90. 10. [s] Ezr. 7. 21. [t] De. 28. 29. [u] 1 Sa. 25. 4. [v] Ge. 38. 12. [y] Is. 53. 7. [z] Je. 7. 29. [a] Mi. 1. 16. [b] Am. 7. 1. [c] Is. 9. 9.

גּוֹזָל masc. (no vowel change) *young pigeon*, Ge. 15. 9; De. 32. 11. Also the three following:

גָּזֵל masc. *rapine, plunder* . . . . . גזל

גֶּזֶל וְ' masc. id. Eze. 18. 18; Ecc. 5. 7. . גזל

גְּזֵלָה [a] וְ' fem. dec. 10, idem. . . . גזל

גָּזְלוּ [b] [c] וְ' } Kal pret. 3 pers. pl. (§ 8. rem. 7) . גזל
גָּזָלוּ [d] וְ'

[e] גְּזֵלוֹת noun fem., pl. of גְּזֵלָה dec. 10. . . גזל

[f] גֹּזְלֵי Kal part. act. pl. constr. m. from גּוֹזֵל d. 7b. גזל

[g] גְּזֵלַת noun fem. sing., constr. of גְּזֵלָה dec. 10. גזל

[h] גָּזַלְתִּי Kal pret. 1 pers. sing. . . . . גזל

גָּזַם Root not used; Arab. *to cut, crop off*.

גָּזָם masc. a species of *locust*. Also

גַּזָּם (*devourer*) pr. name m. Ezr. 2. 48; Ne. 7. 51. גזם

גָּזַע Root not used; Arab. *to cut down*.

גֶּזַע masc. dec. 6a. (suff. גִּזְעוֹ; § 35. rem. 5) *stock* or *trunk* of a tree.

[i] גִּזְעוֹ noun masc. sing., suff. 3 pers. sing. masc. from גֶּזַע (§ 35. rem. 5) dec. 6a. . . . גזע

[k] גִּזְעָם id., suff. 3 pers. pl. masc. . . . גזע

[l] **גָּזַר** I. *to cut off* or *down*, 2 Ki. 6. 4.—II. *to cut in two parts, to divide*.—III. *to decide, decree*. Niph.—I. *to be cut off, separated*, with מִן.—II. *to perish*.—III. *to be decided, decreed*, with עַל, Est. 2. 1.

גְּזַר Chald. *to decide, decree*, part. גָּזְרִין *soothsayers*. Ithpe. *to be cut out*, Da. 2. 34, 45.

גֶּזֶר masc. dec. 6a.—I. *piece, part*.—II. pr. name of a Levitical city on the west of mount Ephraim.

גְּזֵרָה fem. *separation, solitude*, Le. 16. 22.

גְּזֵרָא Ch. fem. d. 8a, *decision, decree*, Da. 4. 14, 21.

גִּזְרָה fem. (no pl. abs.)—I. *form, figure* of a man, La. 4. 7.—II. *a separate place* or *side-chamber* in the temple, Eze. 42. 1, sq.

גִּזְרִי pr. name of a people in the neighbourhood of Philistia, 1 Sa. 27. 8. Keri.

מַגְזֵרָה fem. dec. 11b, *axe*, 2 Sa. 12. 31.

גֶּזֶר } pr. name of a place (§ 35. rem. 2) . גזר
גָּזֶר

גֶּזְרָה id. with loc. ה [for גֶּזְרָה] . . . גזר

[m] גְּזֵרָה noun fem. sing. . . . . גזר

[n] גִּזְרוּ } Kal imp. pl. masc. (§ 8. rem. 12) . גזר
[o] גְּזָרוּ

גָּזְרַיָּא וְ Ch. Peal part. act. pl. emph. m. fr. [גְּזַר] d. 2b. גזר

גָּזְרִין Ch. id. pl., absolute state . . . גזר

[p] גְּזֵרַת וּ Ch. n. f., constr. of [גְּזֵרָא] d. 8a; וּ bef. (:) גזר

[q] גִּזְרָתָם noun fem. sing., suff. 3 pers. pl. masc. from גִּזְרָה (no pl.) . . . . . גזר

[r] גִּזַּת noun fem. sing. constr. of גִּזָּה dec. 10. . גזז

[s] גְּחוֹן noun masc. sing. dec. 3a. . . . גחן

גִּחוֹן pr. name of a stream see גִּיחוֹן . . גיח

גֵּחֲזִי וְ' pr. name masc., see גֵּיחֲזִי וְ' . . גיא

[t] גֹּחִי Kal part. act. m., suff. 1 p. s. fr. [גּוֹחַ §21. r. 2] גיח

[u] גֹּחִי וְ id. imp. sing. fem.; for וְ see lett. וְ . גיח

גָּחַל Root not used; Arab. *to burn*.

גַּחֶלֶת fem. (of the form קְטֶלֶת; dag. f. impl.; with suff. גַּחַלְתִּי, pl. גֶּחָלִים (§ 42. No. 3 note) constr. גַּחֲלֵי, suff. גֶּחָלָיו) *coal, burning coal*; metaph. for *lightning*.

[w] גַּחֲלֵי וְ n. f. with pl. m. term. constr. st. fr. גַּחֶלֶת (q.v.) גחל

[y] גֶּחָלֶיהָ id. pl., suff. 3 pers. sing. fem. . . גחל

[z] גֶּחָלָיו id. pl., suff. 3 pers. sing. masc. . . גחל

גֶּחָלִים id. pl., absolute state . . . . גחל

[a] גַּחֶלֶת id. sing. absolute state . . . גחל

[b] גַּחַלְתִּי id. sing., suff. 1 pers. sing. . . . גחל

גַּחַם pr. name of a son of Nahor, Ge. 22. 24.

גָּחַן Root not used; Syr. and Chald. *to incline, to bend*.

גָּחוֹן masc. dec. 3a, *the belly* of any reptile.

[c] גְּחֹנְךָ noun m. s., suff. 2 pers. s. m. fr. גָּחוֹן d. 3a. גחן

גַּחַר } pr. name masc. Ezr. 2. 47; Ne. 7. 49.
גָּחַר

גֵּי noun com. sing., constr. of גַּיְא irr. (§ 45) also in compos. with pr. n. as הָעֲבָרִים &c. גיא

גָּיָא Root not used; i. q. גוה Arab. *to flow together*.

גַּיְא ,גָּיְא ,גֵּי ,גַּיְא com. irr. constr. גֵּיא and גֵּי pl. see § 46.—I. *valley, a low plain*.—II. pr. n. הַגַּיְא a station of the Israelites in mount Pisgah. גֵּי בְנֵי הִנֹּם, גֵּי הִנֹּם and גֵּיא בֶן־הִנֹּם— (*valley of the son* or *sons of Hinnom*) a valley on the south-east quarter of Jerusalem, also called הַגַּיְא Je. 2. 23.— גֵּי חֲרָשִׁים (*valley of artists*) place in the borders of Judah. גֵּי יִפְתַּח־אֵל (*a valley God does open*) in the northern part of Zebulun, Jos. 19. 14, 27. —גֵּי מֶלַח (*valley of salt*) near the Dead sea.— גֵּי הָעֲבָרִים (*valley of passengers*) on the sea of Galilee, Eze. 39. 11.—גֵּי הַצְּבֹעִים (*valley of hyænas*) in the tribe of Benjamin, 1 Sa. 13. 18.—גֵּי צְפָתָה

[a] Eze. 18. 16. [b] Ju. 21. 23. [c] Mi. 2. 2. [d] Eze. 22. 29. [e] Eze. 18. 12. [f] Mi. 3. 2. [g] Is. 3. 14. [h] Ps. 69. 5. [i] Job 14. 8. [k] Is. 40. 24. [l] Hab. 3. 17. [m] Le. 16. 22. [n] 1 Ki. 3. 26. [o] 1 Ki. 3. 25. [p] Da. 4. 21. [q] La. 4. 7. [r] Ju. 6. 37. [s] Le. 11. 42. [t] Ps. 22. 10. [u] Mi. 4. 10. [w] Ps. 18. 13, 14. [y] Eze. 24. 11. [z] Is. 44. 19. [a] Is. 47. 14. [b] 2 Sa. 14. 7. [c] Ge. 3. 14.

(*valley near Zephath*) in the plains of Judah, 2 Ch. 14. 9.

גֵּיחֲזִי (*valley of vision*) and גֵּחֲזִי pr. name of the servant of Elisha.

גַּיְא[a] noun com. sing. irr. (§ 45) . . . . גיא

גֵּיא ו' id. constr. state (abs. Zec. 14. 4), also in compos. with pr. n. as גֵּיא מֶלַח &c. . גיא

גָּיא[b] id. absolute state . . . . גיא

גֵּיאוֹתֶיךָ[c] ו id. pl., suff. 2 pers. sing. masc. . . גיא

גִּיד Root not used; Arab. *to bind*. Hence

גִּיד[d] [e]ו' m. d. 1 a, *sinew, nerve*; perhaps *band*, Is. 48. 4. גיד

גִּידֵי[f] id. pl., constr. state . . . . גיד

גִּידִים[g] [h]ו' id. pl., absolute state . . . גיד

[גִּיחַ & גּוּחַ] I. *to break* or *burst forth*, spoken of water, of an infant from the womb.—II. trans. *to bring forth*. Hiph. *to rush forth*, Ju. 20. 33.

גּוּחַ or גִּיחַ Ch. Aph. *to rush forth*, Da. 7. 2.—Hence the two following—

גִּיחַ (*a breaking forth*) pr. n. of a place, 2 Sa. 2. 24. גיח

גִּיחוֹן (*stream*) pr. name *Gihom*.—I. one of the four rivers of Eden, Ge. 2. 13.—II. an aqueduct near Jerusalem also called שִׁלֹחַ . . גיח

גֵּיחֲזִי pr. name masc. . . . . גיא

גֵּיִים[i] Kh., גּוֹיִם K. n. m., pl. of גּוֹי d. 1 a. (comp. § 3. r. 1) גוה

[גִּיל & גּוּל] prop. *to move in a circle*, hence *to exult, rejoice*; perh. *to tremble*, Ho. 10. 5. Hence the two following—

גִּיל [k]ו', ו' ו'' m. d. 1, prop. *a circle*, hence—I. *generation, age* (comp. דּוֹר) Da. 1. 10.—II. *exultation, rejoicing*.

גִּילָה[l] fem. dec. 10, *exultation, rejoicing*.

גִּילוּ[m] ו' Kal imp. pl. masc. . . . . גיל

גִּילִי [n]ו' id. imp. sing. fem. . . . גיל

גִּילִי[o] noun m. sing., suff. 1 pers. s. fr. גִּיל d. 1 a. גיל

גִּילַת[p] noun fem. sing., constr. of גִּילָה dec. 10. . גיל

גִּינַת pr. name masc. . . . . גנן

[גִּיר] masc. *burnt lime-stone*, Is. 27. 9; Chald. *plaster of lime*, Da. 5. 5.

גִּירָא[q] Ch. id., emph. state . . . . גיר

גִּישׁ ו masc. *clod*, Job 7. 5, Kheth., גּוּשׁ Keri.

גֵּישָׁן ו pr. name masc. 1 Ch. 2. 47.

גַּל[r] / גָּל } noun masc. sing. dec. 8 d. . . . גלל

גַּל[s] Piel imp. sing. masc. ap. [for גַּלֵּה] . . גלה

גַּל[t] Kal imp. sing. masc. (§ 18. rem. 4) . . גלל

גֹּל Kal inf. or imp. sing. masc. . . . גלל

גָּלֵא[u] ו'' Ch. Peal part. act. sing. m. R. גְּלָא see גלה

גלב Root not used; Arab. *to scrape, to shave*.

גַּלָּב masc. d. 1 b. (§ 30. No. 3), *barber*, Eze. 5.

גִּלְבֹּעַ pr. name of a region . . .

גִּלְגָּל pr. name of a place . . . .

גַּלְגַּל ו noun masc. sing. dec. 8 e. . . גלל

גַּלְגַּל[y] noun masc. sing., constr. of גַּלְגָּל dec. 2 b. . גלל

גַּלְגִּלּוֹהִי[z] Ch. noun masc. pl., suff. 3 pers. sing. masc. from גַּלְגַּל dec. 5. (§ 61) . . גלל

גַּלְגִּלָּיו[a] [b]ו' noun masc. pl., suff. 3 pers. sing. masc. from גַּלְגַּל dec. 8 e. . . . . גלל

גֻּלְגָּלְתּוֹ n. f. s., suff. 3 pers. s. m. fr. גֻּלְגֹּלֶת d. 13 c. גלל

גִּלְגַּלְתִּיךָ[c] ו Pilp. pret. 1 p. s., suff. 2 p. s. m. (§ 6. No. 4) גלל

[גֶּלֶד] masc. dec. 6 a, *skin*; only

גִּלְדִּי[d] noun m. sing., suff. 1 pers. sing. [fr. גֶּלֶד] גלד

גָּלָה I. *to make bare, open, to uncover*; גָּלָה אֹזֶן פ' *uncover the ear of any one*, i. e. to inform hi privately; גָּ' סוֹד *to disclose, reveal a secret*.—II. *to lay bare*, a city or country, i. e. *to emigrat to go* or *be carried into captivity*.—III. trop. *pass away, disappear*. Niph. I. *to be uncovered*.—II. *to be discovered, revealed*.—III. *to be carrie away*, Is. 38. 12. Pi. I. *to make naked, to un cover*.—II. with עֶרְוָה *to have carnal intercour with*.—III. *to disclose, reveal*. Pu. I. *to be un covered*, Na. 2. 8.—II. part. *open, plain*, Pr. 2 5. Hiph. *to lead away captive*. Hoph. pas Hithp. I. *to uncover oneself*, Ge. 9. 21.—II. *to dis close oneself*, Pr. 18. 2.

גְּלָא Ch. *to reveal*. Aph. *to carry into captivit*

גִּלֹה (*captivity*) pr. name of a city in the moun tains of Judah.—Gent. n. גִּילֹנִי 2 Sa. 15. 12.

גּוֹלָה fem. dec. 10.—I. *captivity*.—II. collec *captives, a company of exiles*.

גּוֹלָן (*captivity*) pr. name of a city in Manasse

גָּלוּ Ch. fem. dec. 8 c, *captivity*.

גָּלוּת fem. dec. 1 b.—I. *captivity*.—II. collec *captives*.

[a] 1 Sa. 17. 52. [b] Is. 40. 4. [c] Eze. 35. 8. [d] Ge. 32. 33. [e] Is. 48. 4. [f] Job 40. 17. [g] Eze. 37. 6, 8. [h] Job 10. 11. [i] Ge. 25. 23. [k] Ps. 65. 13. [l] Is. 65. 18. [m] Joel 2. 23. [n] Is. 49. 13. [o] Ps. 43. 4. [p] Is. 35. 2. [q] Da. 5. 5. [r] Ge. 31. 46. [s] Ps. 119. 18, 22. [t] Ps. 119. 22. [u] Da. 2. 22. [x] Da. 2. 29. [y] Is. 28. 28. [z] Da. 7. 9. [a] Je. 47. 3. [b] Is. 5. 28. [c] Je. 51. 25. [d] Job 16. 15.

גִּלָּיוֹן masc. dec. 3c.—I. *a tablet*, Is. 8. 1.—II. pl. *mirrors*, Is. 3. 23.

גָּלְיַת (*exile, captive*) pr. name of the Philistine giant slain by David.

יָגְלִי (*exiled*) pr. name masc. Nu. 34. 23.

גְּלָה [a] [b]'ו Ch. for גְּלָא (q. v.) . . . . . גלה

גָּלֹה Kal inf. absolute . . . . . גלה

גְּלֵה [c] ·ו id. imp. sing. masc.; ·ו bef. (:) . . . גלה

גִּלָּה [d] 'ו Piel pret. 3 pers. sing. masc. . . . גלה

גִּלֹה ו pr. name of a place . . . . גלה

גֹּלָה [e] fem. of the following . . . . גלה

גֹּלֶה [f] 'ו Kal part. act. sing. masc. dec. 9a. . . גלה

גַּלָּהּ [g] ו noun masc. sing., suff. 3 pers. sing. fem. from [גַּל] dec. 8c. . . . . . גלל

גָּלוּ [h] 'ו Kal pret. 3 pers. pl. . . . . . גלה

גִּלּוּ Piel pret. 3 pers. pl. . . . . . . גלה

גֹּלּוּ Kal imp. pl. masc. . . . . . גלל

גָּלוּי id. part. pass. sing. masc. dec. 3a. . . גלה

גְּלוּי [i] ·ו id. constr. state; ·ו bef. (:) . . . גלה

גִּלּוּלֵי noun masc. pl. constr. from [גִּלּוּל] dec. 1b. גלל

גִּלּוּלֶיהָ [k] id. pl., suff. 3 pers. sing. fem. . . . גלל

גִּלּוּלֵיהֶם id., suff. 3 pers. pl. masc. . . . . גלל

גִּלּוּלֵיהֶן [l] id., suff. 3 pers. pl. fem. . . . . גלל

גִּלּוּלָיו id., suff. 3 pers. sing. masc. . . . . גלל

גִּלּוּלֵיכֶם id., suff. 2 pers. pl. masc. . . . . גלל

גִּלּוּלֵיכֶן [m] id., suff. 2 pers. pl. fem. . . . . גלל

גִּלּוּלִים id. pl., absolute state . . . . . גלל

גָּלוֹן Kh. גָּלוֹן, K. גּוֹלָן pr. name of a place . . . גלה

גָּלוּת noun fem. sing. dec. 1b. . . . . . גלה

גְּלוֹת Kal inf. constr. . . . . . . גלה

גֻּלּוֹת noun fem., pl. of גֻּלָּה dec. 10. . . . גלל

גָּלוּתָא Ch. noun fem. sing. emph. of [גָּלוּ] dec. 8c. גלא

גָּלוּתִי [n] ו noun f. s., suff. 1 pers. s. fr. גָּלוּת d. 1b. גלה

גַּלּוֹתִי [o] Kal pret. 1 pers. sing. . . . . . גלל

גָּלַח. Pi.—I. *to shave*, the head, beard; intrans. *to shave oneself*.—II. trop. *to devastate*, Is. 7. 20. Pu. *to be shaven*. Hithpa. *to shave oneself*.

גִּלַּח ו Piel pret. 3 pers. sing. masc. . . . . גלח

גֻּלָּח [p] Pual pret. 3 p. s. m. [for גֻּלַּח comp. § 8. r. 7] גלח

גִּלְּחָה [q] ו Piel pret. 3 pers. sing. fem. . . . . גלח

גִּלְּחוֹ [r] ו id. pret. 3 pers. s. m., suff. 3 pers. s. m. גלח

גִּלַּחְתִּי [s] id. pret. 1 pers. sing. . . . . . גלח

גַּלִּי [t] Piel imp. sing. fem. . . . . . גלה

גְּלֵא [u] גְּלִי [x] } Ch. Peal part. pass. sing. m. R. גְּלָא see גלה

גַּלֵּיהֶם noun m. pl., suff. 3 pers. pl. m. fr. גַּל d. 8d. גלל

גַּלָּיו id. with suff. 3 pers. sing. masc. . . . גלל

גִּלָּיוֹן [y] noun masc. sing. dec. 3c. . . . . גלה

גַּלֶּיךָ [z] 'ו noun m. pl., suff. 2 p. s. m. fr. גַּל d. 8d. גלל

גְּלִיל [a] noun masc. sing., constr. of גָּלִיל dec. 3a. גלל

גְּלִילוֹת noun f., pl. of גְּלִילָה d. 10; also pr. name גלל

גְּלִילֵי constr. of the following . . . . . גלל

גְּלִילִים noun masc. pl. absolute from גָּלִיל dec. 3a. גלל

גַּלִּים noun masc., pl. of גַּל dec. 8d, also pr. name of a place . . . . . . גלל

גֹּלִים [b] Kal part. act. masc., pl. of גֹּלֶה dec. 9a. . גלה

גִּלִּיתָ [c] [d]'ו id. pret. 2 pers. sing. masc. . . . גלה

גִּלְיַת גָּלְיַת } pr. name masc. . . . . . גלה

גִּלִּית [e] [f]'ו Piel pret. 2 pers. sing. fem. . . . גלה

גָּלִיתָה [g] Kal pret. 2 pers. sing. masc. . . . גלה

גָּלִיתִי [h] 'ו id. pret. 1 pers. sing. . . . . גלה

גִּלִּיתִי גִּלֵּיתִי [i] } Piel pret. 1 pers. sing. (§ 24. rem. 11) . גלה

גִּלִּיתִי ו id.; acc. shifted to ult. by conv. ו (comp. § 8. rem. 7) . . . . . . גלה

[גָּלַל] I. *to roll*, e. g. stones.—II. metaph. with מֵעַל *to roll away, remove* from any one, e. g. reproach; גֹּל עַל ,אֶל יְהוָֹה *commit to the Lord*, as one's ways or works. Niph. נָגֹל—I. *to roll along*, Am. 5. 24. —II. *to be rolled together*, Is. 34. 4. Poal גּוֹלֵל with בְּ *to be rolled about in*, Is. 9. 4. Hithpo.—I. i. q. Po. 2 Sa. 20. 12.—II. *to roll, rush in*, with עַל *upon* Ge. 43. 18. Pilp. גִּלְגֵּל (§ 6. No. 4) *to roll down* any one, with מִן, Je. 51. 25. Hithpalp. (§ 6. No. 4) i. q. Hithpo. Job 30. 14. Hiph. הֵגֵל *to roll away*, Ge. 29. 10.

גָּלָל masc. dec. 4a.—I. *dung*, 1 Ki. 14. 10.—II. prop. *circumstance, cause*, as a prep. בִּגְלַל *because of*.—III. pr. name masc. of two persons.

גְּלָל Ch. *heaviness, weight* אֶבֶן גְּ' *heavy stone*.

גֵּלֶל masc. dec. 6. (suff. גֶּלְלוֹ' § 35. r. 3) *dung*.

גִּלֲלַי pr. name masc. Ne. 12. 36.

גִּלּוּל masc. dec. 1b, only in pl. *idols*.

גָּלִיל masc. dec. 3a.—I. adj. *rolling, turning*,

---

[a] Da. 2. 28. [b] Da. 2. 47. [c] Eze. 12. 3. [d] Le. 20. 18.
[e] Is. 49. 21. [f] 1 Sa. 22. 8. [g] Zec. 4. 2. [h] Am. 1. 5.
[i] Nu. 24. 4, 16. [k] Je. 50. 2. [l] Eze. 23. 37. [m] Eze. 23. 49.
[n] Is. 45. 13. [o] Jos. 5. 9. [p] Ju. 16. 22. [q] De. 21. 12.
[r] 2 Sa. 14. 26. [s] Ju. 16. 17. [t] Is. 47. 2. [u] Da. 2. 19.
[x] Da. 2. 30. [y] Is. 8. 1. [z] Job 38. 11.
[a] Is. 8. 23. [b] Am. 6. 7. [c] 1 Ch. 17. 25.
[d] Eze. 12. 3. [e] Is. 57. 8. [f] Ruth 3. 4.
[g] 2 Sa. 7. 26. [h] 1 Sa. 20. 12, 13. [i] Je. 49. 10.

1 Ki. 6. 34.—II. *ring*.—III. *circuit, tract of country*; הַגְּלִילָה ,הַגָּלִיל, a district with twenty towns in the tribe of Naphtali, *Galilee*.

גְּלִילָה fem. dec. 10, *circuit, region*.

גַּל masc. dec. 8 d.—I. *heap* of stones.—II. *spring, fountain*.—III. pl. *waves, billows*.

גַּלְבֹּעַ (*boiling fountain*, comp. בּוּעַ) pr. name of a mountain in the tribe of Issachar.

גַּלְעֵד (*heap of testimony*) pr. name of a heap of stones raised by Jacob and Laban, Ge. 31. 47, 48.

גֹּל masc. dec. 8 c, *an oil-bowl* or *cup*, Zec. 4. 2.

גֻּלָּה fem. dec. 10.—I. *spring, fountain*.—II. *an oil-bowl* or *cup*.—III. *bowl* or *globe*, as an ornament on the capitals of columns.

גַּלְגַּל masc. dec. 8 e.—I. *wheel*.—II. *whirlwind*.—III. *chaff*.

גַּלְגַּל Ch. masc. dec. 5. (§ 61), *wheel*, Da. 7. 9.

גִּלְגָּל masc.—I. *wheel*, Is. 28. 28.—II. pr. name of a place between Jericho and Jordan.

גֻּלְגֹּלֶת fem. dec. 13 c, *scull*; in counting men it is used for *head* or *poll*.

מְגִלָּה fem. d. 10, *volume, roll, book*. Chald. id.

גָּלָל ו׳ pr. name masc. . . . . . גלל

גְּלָל Ch. noun masc. sing. . . . . גלל

גֹּלֵל[a] וְ Kal part. act. sing. masc. . . . גלל

גָּלֲלוּ[b] וְ id. pret. 3 pers. pl. [for גָּלְלוּ] . . גלל

גִּלְלֵי[c] noun m. pl. constr. fr. [גֵּלֶל] d. 6. (§ 35. r. 3) גלל

גִּלֲלַי pr. name masc. . . . . . . גלל

גִּלּוּלֵיהֶם[d] n. m. pl., suff. 3 p. pl. m. fr. [גִּלּוּל] d. 1 b. גלל

[גָּלַם] *to wrap together*, 2 Ki. 2. 8.

גְּלוֹם masc. dec. 1 a, *mantle, cloak*, Eze. 27. 24.

גֹּלֶם masc. dec. 6 c, *embryo*, prop. *an unformed mass*, as it were wrapt up together, Ps. 139. 16.

גַּלְמוּד masc. adj.—I. *sterile barren*.—II. *famished*. Made up of גמד and גלד Arab. *to be hard*. (Gesen.)

גַּלְמוּדָה[e] וְ fem. of the prec.

גָּלְמִי[f] noun m. s., suff. 1 pers. s. fr. [גֹּלֶם] d. 6 c. גלם

גָּלַע. Hithpa. *to grow warm, become angry, irritated*, with בְּ of the thing or cause.

גַּלְעֵד pr. name of a place . . . . גלל

גִּלְעָד (*hard, rough*, coll. with the Arab.) pr. name.—I. of several men; especially a son of Machir grandson of Manasseh. Hence patronym. גִּלְעָדִי. — II. with the art. הַגִּלְעָד a region beyond Jordan.

גִּלְעָדָה pr. name (גִּלְעָד II) with parag. ה

גִּלְעָדִים gent. noun, pl. of גִּלְעָדִי fr. גִּלְעָד q. v.

[גָּלַשׁ] prob. i. q. שָׁלַג *to be white*, hence *to shine*, Ca. 4. 1; 6. 5. Eng. Ver. "appear".

גָּלֻת[g] וְ noun fem. sing. dec. 1 b, for גָּלוּת . גלה

גֻּלֹּת[h] noun fem. sing., constr. of גֻּלָּה dec. 10. . גלל

גֻּלֹּת[i] ו׳ pl. of the prec. . . . . . גלל

גָּלְתָה[k] Kal pret. 3 pers. sing. fem. . . . גלה

גִּלְּתָה[l] ו׳[m] Piel pret. 3 pers. sing. fem. . . גלה

גֻּלְּתָה[n] Pual pret. 3 pers. sing. fem. . . . גלה

גַּלְתִּי[o] ו׳ Kal pret. 1 pers. sing.; acc. shifted to ult. by conv. וְ (comp. § 8. rem. 7) . ניל

גַּם ו׳ conj. . . . . גמם

גָּמָא Pi. *to drink in, to swallow*, Job 39. 24. Hiph. *to give to drink*, Ge. 24. 17. Hence

גֹּמֶא ו׳[p] masc. *reed, paper reed, papyrus*; תֵּבַת גֹּמֶא *an ark of papyrus* . . . גמא

גֹּמֶד masc. a kind of *measure of length*, Ju. 3. 16.

גַּמָּדִים וְ masc., pl. *bold warriors*, Eze. 27. 11. גמד Arab. *to cut off*; Syr. *to be bold*. Others take it as a pr. name of a people.

גָּמוּל[q] Kal part. p. masc. sing. dec. 3 a. (pr. name in compos. see בֵּית) . . . גמל

גְּמוּל ו׳[r] noun masc. sing. dec. 1 a; וּ bef. (:) . גמל

גְּמוּלֵי[s] Kal part. p. pl. constr. m. from גָּמוּל dec. 3 a. גמל

גְּמוּלָיו[t] n. m. pl., suff. 3 pers. s. m. from גְּמוּל d. 1 a. גמל

גְּמוּלֵךְ[u] id. sing., suff. 2 pers. sing. fem. . . גמל

גְּמוּלָם[x] id. sing., suff. 3 pers. pl. masc. . . גמל

גִּמְזוֹ (*place of sycomores* Arab. נמיז Chald. נמזוז sycomore) pr. name of a town in the tribe of Judah, 2 Ch. 28. 18.

גְּמִיר[y] Chald. Peal part. pass. sing. masc. . . גמל

גָּמַל I. *to retribute, to recompense*, good or evil, with acc., עַל ,לְ.—II. generally *to do, show* good or evil to any one.—III. *to mature, ripen* fruit; intrans. *to become ripe*.—IV. *to wean* a child.

גָּמָל com. dec. 8. (pl. גְּמַלִּים § 37. No. 2) *camel*.

גָּמוּל (*weaned*) pr. name masc. 1 Ch. 24. 17.

גְּמוּל masc. dec. 1 a.—I. *retribution, recompense*.—II. any *act* done or shown to any one, good or evil.

[a] Pr. 26. 27. [b] Ge. 29. 3, 8. [c] Eze. 4. 15. [d] De. 29. 16. [e] Is. 49. 21. [f] Ps. 139. 16. [g] Ob. 1. 20. [h] Ec. 12. 6. [i] 1 Ki. 7. 41. [k] La. 1. 3. [l] Le. 20. 18. [m] Is. 26. 21. [n] Na. 2. 8. [o] Is. 65. 19. [p] Is. 35. 7. [q] Is. 11. 8. [r] Pr. 12. 14. [s] Is. 28. 9. [t] Ps. 103. 2. [u] Ps. 137. 8. [x] Ps. 28. 4. [y] Ezr. 7. 12.

גְּמוּלָה fem. dec. 10, *retribution, recompense;* especially *benefit.*

גְּמַלִּי (*camel-owner*) pr. name masc. Nu. 13. 12.

גַּמְלִיאֵל (*benefit of God*) pr. name masc.

תַּגְמוּל masc. dec. 1 b, *benefit, kindness,* Ps. 116. 12.

גָּמָל [a] n. com. s., pl. גְּמַלִּים d. 8 a. (§ 37. Nos. 2 & 3) . גמל

גְּמֹל [b] Kal imp. sing. masc. . . . . . גמל

גֹּמֵל id. part. act. sing. masc. dec. 7 b. . . גמל

גְּמָלָהּ [c] id. inf. with suff. 3 pers. sing. fem. . . גמל

גָּמְלוּ [hh] id. pret. 3 pers. pl. . . . . . גמל

גְּמֻלוֹ [d] וּ n. m. s., suff. 3 p. s. m. fr. גְּמוּל d. 1 a; וּ bef. (:) . גמל

גְּמָלוּךָ [e] Kal pret. 3 pers. pl. with suff. 2 pers. sing. m. גמל

גְּמֻלוֹת noun fem., pl. of גְּמוּלָה dec. 10. . . גמל

גְּמַלִּי pr. name masc. . . . . . גמל

גַּמְלִיאֵל pr. name masc. . . . . . גמל

גְּמַלֵּיהֶם ו׳ noun com. pl., suff. 3 pers. pl. masc. from גָּמָל dec. 8 a. (§ 37. No. 2); וּ bef. (:) . גמל

גְּמַלָּיו [f] id. pl., suff. 3 pers. sing. masc. . . גמל

גְּמַלֶּיךָ [g] id. pl., suff. 2 pers. sing. masc. . . גמל

גְּמַלִּים ו׳ id. pl., absolute state; וּ bef. (:) . גמל

גֹּמְלִים Kal part. act. masc., pl. of גֹּמֵל dec. 7 b. . גמל

גְּמָלֵךְ [h] id. inf. with suff. 2 pers. sing. fem. . . גמל

גְּמָלְךָ [i] id. pret. 3 pers. sing. m., suff. 2 pers. sing. m. גמל

גְּמֻלְךָ [k] n. m. s., suff. 2 pers. s. m. from גְּמוּל d. 1 a. גמל

גְּמֻלְכֶם [l] id., suff. 2 pers. pl. masc. . . . גמל

גְּמָלָם [ll] Kal pret. 3 pers. sing. m., suff. 3 pers. pl. m. גמל

גָּמַלְנוּ [m] id. pret. 1 pers. pl. . . . . גמל

גְּמָלָנוּ [n] id. pret. 3 pers. sing. masc., suff. 1 pers. pl. גמל

גְּמָלַתְהוּ [o] id. pret. 3 pers. sing. fem., suff. 3 pers. sing. m. גמל

גְּמָלַתּוּ [p] id. id. with dag. euph. . . . . גמל

גָּמַלְתִּי [q] id. pret. 1 pers. sing. . . . . גמל

גְּמַלְתִּיךָ [r] id. id., suff. 2 pers. sing. masc. . . גמל

גְּמַלְתַּנִי [s] id. pret. 2 pers. sing. masc., suff. 1 pers. sing. גמל

גָּמַם Root not used; Arab. *to heap up, increase;* intrans. *to be heaped up.*

גַּם conj.—I. *also;* גַּם—גַּם *both—and;* הִיא גַּם הִיא *she also herself.* A pronoun repeated for the sake of emphasis has the nominative form though the preceding is in the oblique case בָּרְכֵנִי גַם־אָנִי *bless me, me also,* Ge. 27. 34; אֶת־דָּמְךָ גַּם־אָתָּה *thy blood, thine also.*—II. *yea, truly,* especially at the beginning of a sentence; גַּם־כִּי *although.*—III. *yet, nevertheless.*

מְגַמָּה fem. dec. 10, *troop, host,* Hab. 1. 9. Others *desire, longing.*

גָּמַץ Root not used; Chald. *to dig.*

גּוּמָּץ masc. *a pit,* Ec. 10. 8.

גָּמַר I. *to bring to an end, to complete,* with בַּעַד, עַל.—II. intrans. *to come to an end, to fail.*

גְּמִר Ch. id. part. pass. *perfect, skilled,* Ezr. 7. 12.

גֹּמֶר (*perfection*) pr. name—I. of a son of Japheth, and applied to his posterity.—II. of the wife of the prophet Hosea, Ho. 1. 3.

גְּמַרְיָהוּ, גְּמַרְיָה (whom *the Lord makes perfect*) pr. name of two different men.

גֹּמֶר pr. name of a man and a people . . גמר

גֹּמֵר [t] Kal part. act. sing. masc. . . . . גמר

וּ גְּמַרְיָה / ו׳ גְּמַרְיָהוּ } pr. name masc.; וּ bef. (:) . . גמר

גַּן noun com. sing. dec. 8 d. . . . גנן

[גָּנַב] I. *to steal;* trop. *to carry away,* as a storm does the chaff.—II. *to deceive,* especially with לֵב. Niph. *to be stolen,* Ex. 22. 11. Pi. i. q. Kal. Pu.—I. *to be stolen.*—II. *to be brought secretly,* with אֶל of the person, Job 4. 12. Hithpa. *to steal oneself away,* 2 Sa. 19. 4.

גַּנָּב masc. dec. 1 b. (§ 30. rem. 3) *a thief.*

גְּנֵבָה fem. dec. 10, *a thing stolen,* Ex. 22. 2, 3.

גְּנֻבַת (*theft*) pr. name masc. 1 Ki. 11. 20.

גַּנָּב [u] וְ׳ noun masc. sing. dec. 1 b. . . . גנב

גָּנֹב [x] וְ׳ [y] Kal inf. abs. . . . . גנב

גֹּנֵב [z] וְ׳ [a] id. part. act. sing. masc. . . . גנב

גֻּנַּב [b] וְ Pual pret. 3 pers. sing. masc. . . . גנב

גֻּנֹּב [c] id. inf. abs. . . . . . גנב

גָּנְבוּ Kal pret. 3 pers. pl. . . . . גנב

גְּנָבוּךָ [d] id., suff. 2 pers. s. masc. . . . גנב

גַּנָּבִים noun masc., pl. of גַּנָּב dec. 1 b. . . גנב

גָּנַבְתָּ [e] Kal pret. 2 pers. sing. masc. . . . גנב

גְּנֻבַת pr. name masc. . . . . . גנב

גְּנָבַתּוּ id. Kal pret. 3 pers. s. fem., suff. 3 pers. s. m. גנב

גָּנַבְתִּי [f] וְ id. pret. 1 pers. sing.; acc. shifted to ult. by וְ conv. (§ 8. rem. 7) . . . גנב

גְּנֻבְתִי [g] וּ׳ [h] id. part. pass. fem. sing. [גְּנֻבָה] with parag. י (comp. § 8. rem. 19); וּ bef. (:) . גנב

גֻּנַּבְתִּי [i] Pual pret. 1 pers. sing. . . . . גנב

גְּנָבָתַם [k] Kal pret. 3 pers. sing. fem., suff. 3 pers. pl. m. גנב

גָּנוּב [l] id. part. pass. sing. masc. dec. 3 a. . גנב

---

[a] Is. 21. 7, etc. [b] Ps. 119. 17. [c] 1 Sa. 1. 23. [d] Pr. 19. 17. [e] Ge. 50. 17. [f] Ge. 24. 20. [g] Ge. 24. 14, 46. [h] 1 Sa. 1. 23. [i] Pr. 3. 30. [k] Ob. 1. 15. [l] Joel 4. 4, 7. [m] Ge. 50. 15. [n] Is. 63. 7. [o] Pr. 31. 12. [p] 1 Sa. 1. 24. [q] Ps. 7. 5. [r] 1 Sa. 24. 18. [s] 1 Sa. 24. 18. [t] Ps. 57. 3. [u] Ho. 7. 1. [x] Ex. 22. 11. [y] Ho. 4. 2. [z] De. 24. 7. [a] Ex. 21. 16. [b] Ex. 22. 6. [c] Ge. 40. 15. [d] 2 Sa. 19. 42. [e] Ge. 31. 30. [f] Pr. 30. 9. [g] Ge. 31. 39. [h] Ge. 31. 39. [hh] Is. 3. 9. [i] Ge. 40. 15. [k] Ge. 31. 32. [l] Ge. 30. 33. [ll] Is. 63. 7.

[a] גְּנוּבִים id. id. pl., absolute state . . . גנב

[b] גָּנוֹן Kal inf. abs. . . . . . גנן

גַּנּוֹת noun fem., pl. of גַּנָּה dec. 10. . . גנן

[c] וְגַנּוֹתִי Kal pret. 1 pers. sing.; acc. shifted to ult. by conv. וְ (comp. § 8. rem. 7) . גנן

[d] גַּנּוֹתֵיכֶם n. fem. pl., suff. 2 pers. pl. m. from גַּנָּה d. 10. גנן

גָּנַז Root not used; *to cover; to collect*, cogn. כָּנַס.

גֶּנֶז masc. only pl. com. גִּנְזֵי, *treasures;* Eze. 27. 24. perhaps *chests* in which precious things are stored.

גְּנַז Chald. masc. dec. 3 b, *treasure.*

גַּנְזַךְ masc. dec. 8 d, *treasury,* 1 Ch. 28. 11.

גִּנְזֵי noun masc. pl. constr. from [גֶּנֶז] dec. 6 a. . גנז

[e] גִּנְזֵי Chald. id. from [גְּנַז] dec. 3 b. . . גנז

גִּנְזַיָּא Chald. id. pl., emph. st. . . . גנז

[f] וְגַנְזַכָּיו n. m. pl., suff. 3 p. s. m. from [גַּנְזַךְ] d. 8. גנז

[g] גַּנִּי noun com. sing., suff. 1 pers. s. from גַּן d. 8 d. גנן

[h] גַּנִּים id. pl., absolute state . . . גנן

[גָּנַן] prop. *to cover,* whence *to protect,* const. with אֶל, עַל. Hiph. id. with בְּעַד ,עַל.

גַּן com. dec. 8 d, *garden.*

גַּנָּה and גִּנָּה fem. dec. 10, id.

גִּינַת (*garden* for גִּנַּת dag. forte resolved in Yod) pr. name masc. 1 Ki. 16. 21, 22.

גִּנְּתוֹן (*gardener*) pr. name masc., also written גִּנְּתוֹי comp. Ne. 12. 4, with ver. 16.

מָגֵן masc. dec. 8 b, pl. מָגִנִּים, וֹת (§ 37. rem. 4), *shield;* trop. *prince.*

מְגִנָּה fem. dec. 10, with לֵב *veiling, covering of the heart,* La. 3. 65.

גִּנַּת noun fem. sing., constr. of [גִּנָּה] dec. 10. . גנן

גַּנָּתוֹ n. fem. s., suff. 3 pers. s. m. from גַּנָּה d. 10. גנן

גִּנְּתוֹי } pr. name masc. . . . . . גנן
גִּנְּתוֹן

[k] גַּע Kal imp. sing. masc. . . . . נגע

[גָּעָה] *to low,* as an ox or cow.

גֹּעָה (*lowing*) pr. name of a place near Jerusalem, Je. 31. 39.

[l] גָּעוֹ Kal inf. abs. (§ 24. rem. 2) . . . געה

[גָּעַל] *to loathe, abhor.* Niph. *to be cast away,* 2 Sa. 1. 21. Hiph. *to cast* the young, i.e. suffer abortion, Job 21. 10.

גַּעַל (*loathing*), pr. name masc. Ju. 9. 26, 28, 30.

גֹּעַל masc. *a loathing,* Eze. 16. 5.

גַּעַל pr. name masc. . . . . . געל

[m] וְגָעֲלָה Kal pret. 3 pers sing. fem. . . . געל

[n] גָּעֲלוּ id. pret. 3 pers. pl. . . . . געל

[o] גֹּעֶלֶת id. part., act. sing. fem. (§ 8. rem. 19) . געל

[p] גְּעַלְתִּים id. pret. 1 pers. sing., suff. 3 pers. pl. masc. געל

[q] **גָּעַר** *to rebuke, reprove,* const. with בְּ.

גְּעָרָה fem. dec. 11 c. (constr. גַּעֲרַת § 42. rem. 1) *rebuke, reproof.*

מִגְעֶרֶת fem. *rebuke,* or *curse,* De. 28. 20.

[r] גְּעַר Kal imp. sing. masc. . . . . גער

[s] גֹּעֵר id. part. act. sing. masc. . . . גער

גְּעָרָה noun fem. sing. (constr. גַּעֲרַת) dec. 11 c. . גער

גָּעַרְתָּ Kal pret. 2 pers. sing. masc. . . . גער

גַּעֲרַת n. fem. s., constr. of גְּעָרָה d. 11 c. (§ 42. r. 1) גער

[t] גַּעֲרָתוֹ id., suff. 3 pers. sing. masc. . . . גער

[u] וְגָעַרְתִּי Kal pret. 1 pers. sing.; acc. shifted to ult. by conv. וְ (§ 8. rem. 7) . . . גער

[x] גַּעֲרָתְךָ noun fem. sing., suff. 2 pers. sing. masc. from גְּעָרָה dec. 11 c. (§ 42. rem. 1) . . גער

[גָּעַשׁ] *to shake, tremble.* Pu. *to be shaken,* Job 34. 20. Hithpa. *to be moved, shaken, agitated.* Hithpo. *to stagger, reel.*

גַּעַשׁ (*quaking*) pr. name of one of the mountains of Ephraim.

גָּעַשׁ pr. name of a mountain [for גַּעַשׁ] . . געש

גֹּעָתָה pr. name of a place [גֹּעָה] with paragogic ה געה

וְגַעְתָּם pr. name masc. . . . . . נגע

[y] גַּפֵּי noun fem. pl. constr. from [גַּף] dec. 8 d. . גפף

[z] גַּפַּיהּ Chald. K. גַּפַּהּ, Kh. גַּפֵּיהּ, noun fem. pl., suff. 3 pers. sing. fem. from [גַּף] dec. 5 d. . גפף

[a] גַּפִּין [b] וְ Chald. id. pl., absolute state . . גפף

גָּפַן Root not used; i. q. כָּפַן ,גָּבַן *to be bent, curved.* Hence

[c] גֶּפֶן } noun com. dec. 6 a, *vine;* גֶּ' שָׂדֶה }
[d] וְ, גָּפֶן } *the wild vine* . . . } גפן

[e] גַּפְנָהּ id., suff. 3 pers. sing. fem. . . . גפן

גַּפְנוֹ id., suff. 3 pers. sing. masc. . . . גפן

[f] גַּפְנִי id., suff. 1 pers. sing. . . . . גפן

[g] גַּפְנְךָ id., suff. 2 pers. sing. masc. . . . גפן

גַּפְנָם id., suff. 3 pers. pl. masc. . . . גפן

גָּפַף Root not used; i. q. גָּבַב *to be bent, curved.*

גַּף masc. dec. 8 d.—I. *back,* i. e. *hillock,* Pr. 9. 3. —II. *body, person,* only בְּגַפּוֹ *by himself, alone,* Ex. 21. 3, 4.

---

[a] Pr. 9. 17. [b] Is. 31. 5. [c] 2 Ki. 19. 34. etc. [d] Am. 4. 9. [e] Ezr. 7. 20. [f] 1 Ch. 28. 11. [g] Ca. 4. 16. [h] Ca. 4. 15. [i] Job 8. 16. [k] Ps. 144. 5. [l] 1 Sa. 6. 12. [m] Le. 26. 30. [n] Eze. 16. 45. [o] Eze. 16. 45. [p] Le. 26. 44 [q] Is. 17. 13. [r] Ps. 68. 31. [s] Mal. 2. 3. [t] Is. 66. 15. [u] Mal. 3. 11. [x] Ps. 104. 7. [y] Pr. 9. 3. [z] Da. 7. 4. [a] Da. 7. 6. [b] Da. 7. 4. [c] Is. 24. 7. [d] Joel 2. 22. [e] Ho. 2. 14. [f] Joel 1. 7. [g] Je. 5. 17.

גַּף Chald. fem. dec. 3a, *wing*, Da. 7. 4, 6.

אֲגַף masc. only pl. אֲגַפִּים, prop. *wings*, poet. for *armies, hosts*.

גֹּפֶר masc. the name of a tree; prob. the *pitch-pine*, Ge. 6. 14, גֹּפֶר i. q. כָּפַר *to cover over*.

גָּפְרִית וְ' fem. *brimstone*.

גָּר [a] וְ' Kal pret. 3 pers. sing. masc, part. act. . . . גור

גֵּר וְ' noun masc. sing. dec. 1a. . . . . גור

גֵּר [hh] defect. [for גֵּיר] noun masc. sing. . . גיר

גֵּרָא וְ' pr. name masc. . . . . . גרר

גָּרָב masc. *scurf, scurvy*.

גָּרֵב (*scurvied*) pr. name—I. masc. 2 Sa. 23. 38.—II. of a hill near Jerusalem, Je. 31. 39.

גַּרְגְּרִים [b] noun masc. pl. [of גַּרְגַּר, § 36. rem. 5] . גרר

גַּרְגְּרֹתֶיךָ noun fem. pl. [גַּרְגְּרוֹת], suff. 2 pers. s. m. גרר

[גִּרְגָּשִׁי] pr. name of a Canaanitish nation.

גָּרַד. Hithpa. *to scrape oneself*, Job 2. 8.

גָּרָה Kal not used; prob. to produce a *grating* sound, whence גָּרוֹן. Pi. *to excite, stir up* strife. Hithpa. *to excite oneself*, especially *to contention, war*; with בְּ *to contend with*.

גָּרוֹן noun dec. 3a, *the throat*.

תִּגְרָה fem. dec. 10, *strife, contention*, Ps. 39. 11.

גֵּרָה [c] וְ' noun fem. sing. [for גְּרָה] . . . גרר

גָּרוּ [d] Kal pret. 3 pers. pl. . . . . גור

גֵּרוֹ [e] noun m. s., suff. 3 pers. s. m. from גֵּר dec. 1a. גור

גָּרוֹן [kk] noun masc. sing. dec. 3a . . . גרה

גְּרוֹנִי [f] id. suff. 1 pers. sing. . . . . גרה

גְּרוֹנֶךָ [g] id., suff. 2 pers. sing. masc. . . . גרה

גְּרוּשָׁה [h] וּ' Kal part. pass. s., fem. of [גָּרוּשׁ]; וּ bef. (:) גרש

גְּרֹתָיו [i] n. pl. fem., suff. 3 pers. s. m. from [גּוֹר] d. 1a. גור

גָּרַז. Niph. *to be cut off*, Ps. 31. 23.

גִּרְזִי (*inhabitant of a sterile land*) pr. name of a Canaanitish nation subdued by David, 1 Sa. 27. 8. Kheth., גִּזְרִי Keri. Also the two following—

גְּרִזִים always with הַר (*mount of the Gerisites*) pr. name of a mountain near Shechem in the tribe of Ephraim, opposite mount Ebal.

גַּרְזֶן [k] masc. *an axe*.

גֵּרֵי [l] construct of the following . . . גור

גָּרִים וְ' Kal part. act. masc., pl. of גָּר dec. 1a. גור

גֵּרִים noun masc., pl. of גֵּר dec. 1a. . . . גור

גֵּרֵךְ וְ id. sing., suff. 2 pers. sing. masc. . . גור

גָּרַל Root not used; Arab. *to be gritty, stony*.

גָּרֹל adj. with Mak. ־גְּרָל *harsh angry*, Pr. 19. 19. Kheth., ־גְּדָל Keri.

גּוֹרָל masc. dec. 2b. (pl. גּוֹרָלוֹת).—I. *lot*, prop. the stone by which the lot was determined; הִפִּיל גּוֹרָל *to cast lots*, so also with the verbs עָלָה יָצָא גּוֹרָל ;נָתַן ,הֵטִיל ,הִשְׁלִיךְ ,יָדַד ,יָרָה *the lot fell*, constr. with עַל ,אֶל ,לְ of the person.—II. *lot, portion, inheritance*.

גְּרָל־ [m] Kh., גְּדָל K. adj. m. s., constr. of גָּרֹל or גָּדֹל, with Mak. [for גְּרֹל or גְּדֹל § 32. r. 7.]

גֹּרָלוֹת noun masc. with pl. fem. term., absolute state from גּוֹרָל dec. 2b. . . . . גרל

גֶּרֶם, גָּרֶם [n] (§ 35. rem. 2) masc. dec. 6a.—I. *bone*.—II. *strength*, חֲמוֹר גָּרֶם *strong ass*, Ge. 49. 14.—III. *substance, body*, 2 Ki. 9. 13. אֶל־גֶּרֶם הַמַּעֲלוֹת *upon the steps themselves*, the very steps, comp. עֶצֶם. Prof. Lee, *frame-work*.

גְּרַם Chald. masc. dec. 3a, *bone*, Da. 6. 25.

גָּרַם *to gnaw a bone*, Zep. 3. 3, *they shall not gnaw* לַבֹּקֶר *in the morning*, i. e. they shall leave nothing to gnaw. Pi. id. Nu. 24, 8. Meton. of sherds, *to gnaw*, lick them clean, Eze. 23. 34.

גַּרְמִי (*bony*) pr. name, masc. 1 Ch. 4. 19.

גָּרְמוּ [o] Kal pret. 3 pers. pl. . . . . גרם

גַּרְמֵיהוֹן [mm] Chald. noun masc. pl., suff. 3 pers. pl. masc. from [גְּרַם] dec. 3a. . . . . גרם

גְּרָמָיו [p] noun masc. pl., suff. 3 pers. sing. masc. from גֶּרֶם dec. 6. . . . . גרם

גֹּרֶן fem. dec. 6c, pl. גְּרָנוֹת, construct גָּרְנוֹת (גרן Arab. *to make smooth, level*).—I. *a level place at the gate of the city*, the *forum* of the Hebrews, 1 Ki. 22. 10; 2 Ch. 18. 9.—II. *threshing-floor*. Meton. for the grain itself, Job 39. 12.

גֹּרְנָה [q] id. with paragogic ה . . . . גרן

גָּרְנוֹת [r] id. pl., construct state . . . . גרן

גָּרְנִי [s] id. sing., suff. 1 pers. sing. . . . גרן

גָּרְנְךָ [t] וְ id. sing., suff. 2 pers. sing. masc. . . גרן

גְּרוֹנָם [u] noun masc. sing., suff. 3 pers. pl. masc. from גָּרוֹן dec. 3a. . . . . גרה

[גָּרַס] *to be broken, crushed*, Ps. 119. 20. Hiph. *to crush*, La. 3. 16.

גֶּרֶשׂ masc. dec. 6a. (suff. גִּרְשִׂי,) something *crushed, bruised*, perhaps *corn*.

---

[a] Is. 11. 6. [b] Is. 17. 6. [c] Le. 11. 26. [d] Ex. 6. 4. [e] De. 1. 16. [f] Ps. 69. 4. [g] Eze. 16. 11. [h] Le. 21. 7. [hh] Is. 27. 9. Na. 2. 13. [k] De. 20. 19. [kk] Is. 3. 16. Job 19. 15. [m] Pr. 19. 19. [mm] Da. 6. 25. [n] 2 Ki. 9. 13. [o] Zep. 3. 3. [p] Job 40. 18. [q] Mi. 4. 12. [r] Ho. 9. 1. [s] Is. 21. 10. [t] Job 39. 12. [u] Ps. 5. 10.

גָּרְסָה[a] Kal preter. 3 pers. sing. fem. . . גרס

[גָּרַע] fut. יִגְרַע.—I. *to take away* the beard.—II. *to detract, to withold,* construed with מִן; *to reserve,* with אֶל.—II. *to diminish,* with acc. Niph. *to be detracted, diminished, lessened.* Pi. *to draw off,* Job 36. 27.

מִגְרָעָה fem. only pl. absolute מִגְרָעוֹת *narrowed rests, rebatements,* in building, 1 Ki. 6. 6.

גְּרֻעָה[b] Kal part. pass. sing. fem. from [גָּרוּעַ] masc. גרע

[גָּרַף] I. *to carry, sweep away,* Ju. 5. 21.—II. in the deriv. *to grasp, gripe,* Germ. *greifen.*

אֶגְרוֹף masc. *fist,* Ex. 21. 18; Is. 58. 4.

מֶגְרָפָה fem. dec. 11a, *clod,* Joel 1. 17; so Gesenius and others before him. Prof. Lee, *furrow.*

גְּרָפָם[c] Kal pret. 3 pers. s. m., suff. 3 pers. pl. masc. גרף

[גָּרַר] *to drag, draw away.* Niph.—I. *to be dragged, carried away,* so נִגָּרוֹת Job 20. 28, which some derive from נָגַר.—II. *to ruminate, to chew the cud,* Le. 11. 7. Po. *to be sawed,* 1 Ki. 7. 9. Hithpo. *to sweep away with itself,* Je. 30. 23.

גֵּרָא (*grain* i. q. גֵּרָה) pr. name of several men, especially of a son of Benjamin, Ge. 46. 21.

גֵּרָה fem.—I. *the cud.*—II. *a grain, gerah,* a weight equal to the twentieth part of a shekel.

גְּרָר pr. name of a city of the Philistines, formerly the residence of their kings; נַחַל גְּרָר *valley of Gerar,* Ge. 26. 17.

גַּרְגַּר masc. only pl. גַּרְגְּרִים (§ 36. rem. 5) *berries,* Is. 17. 6.

גַּרְגְּרוֹת fem. pl. (perhaps from a sing. גַּרְגֶּרֶת) *throat, neck.*

מְגֵרָה fem. dec. 10, *a saw.*

גְּרָר pr. name of a place . . . . גרר

גְּרָרָה id. with paragogic ה . . . גרר

[גָּרַשׁ] I. *to cast out* or *up,* Is. 57. 20; hence *to drive out, expel, divorce.*—II. *to plunder, spoil,* Eze. 36. 5. Pi. *to drive out, expel,* with מִן of the place. Niph.—I. *to be cast out.*—II. *to be agitated, tossed,* Is. 57. 20.

גֶּרֶשׁ masc. *produce, fruit,* De. 33. 14.

גְּרֻשָׁה fem. dec. 10, *expulsion,* Eze. 45. 9.

גֵּרְשׁוֹן (*expulsion*) pr. name of a son of Levi. Patronym. גֵּרְשֻׁנִּי.

מִגְרָשׁ masc. dec. 2b, pl. מִגְרָשִׁים, once מִגְרָשׁוֹת (prop. from מִגְרֶשֶׁת).—I. inf. see the root No. II. and analyt. order.—II. *pasture,* a place whither cattle is driven to graze.—III. *any lands surrounding a city* or *edifice.*

גָּרֵשׁ Piel inf. (Ge. 20. 10), or imp. sing. masc. . גרש

גֶּרֶשׁ[d] noun masc. sing. . . . . גרש

גֶּרֶשׂ[e] noun masc. sing., suff. גַּרְשָׂהּ, dec. 6a, see . גרס

גֹּרֵשׁ[f] Kal part. act. sing. masc. . . . גרש

גֵּרְשָׁה[g] וְ Piel pret. 3 pers. sing. fem. . . . גרש

גֹּרְשׁוּ[h] Pual pret. 3 pers. pl. . . . גרש

גֵּרְשׁוֹם pr. name masc. see גֵּרְשֹׁם

גֵּרְשׁוֹן pr. name masc. . . . . גרש

גֵּרְשׁוּנִי[i] Piel pret. 3 pers. pl., suff. 1 pers. sing. . גרש

גֵּרְשֹׁם (*a stranger there,* see Ex. 2. 22, or *expulsion.* R. גרשׁ) pr. name.—I. of a son of Moses by Zipporah.—II. of a son of Levi.—III. Ju. 18. 30.—IV. Ezr. 8. 2.

גֵּרַשְׁתָּ[k] Pi. pret. 2 pers. sing. masc. . . גרש

גֵּרַשְׁתִּי[l] וְ id. pret. 1 pers. sing.; acc. shifted by conv. וְ (comp. § 8. rem. 7) . . . גרש

גֵּרַשְׁתִּיהוּ[m] id. id., suff. 3 pers. sing. masc. . גרש

גֵּרַשְׁתִּיו[n] וְ id. id., suff. 3 pers. sing. masc. . גרש

גְּרֻשֹׁתֵיכֶם[o] n. fem. pl., suff. 2 pers. pl. m. fr. [גְּרֻשָׁה] d. 10. גרש

גֵּרַשְׁתָּמוֹ[p] וְ Piel pret. 2 pers. sing. masc., suff. 3 pers. pl. גרש

גַּרְתָּה[q] Kal pret. 2 pers. sing. masc. (§ 8. rem. 5) גור

גַּרְתִּי id. pret. 1 pers. sing. . . . גור

גַּשׁ[r], גֶּשׁ־[s] } Kal imp. sing. masc. (§ 17. rem. 2) . נגש

גְּשָׁה־ id. id. with paragogic ה . . נגש

גֹּשׁוּ[t], וּ', גְּשׁוּ } id. imp. pl. masc. (§ 17. rem. 2); וּ bef. (:) נגש

גְּשׁוּר (*bridge,* Chald. גְּשׁוּרָא) pr. name of a district in Syria; whence gent. n. גְּשׁוּרִי *Geshurite,* —I. De. 3. 14; Jos. 12. 5; 13. 13; 1 Ch. 2. 23.—II. Jos. 13. 2; 1 Sa. 27. 8.

גְּשׁוּרָה id. with paragogic ה.

גְּשִׁי[u] id. imp. sing. fem. (§ 17. rem. 2) . נגש

גָּשַׁם. Hiph. *to cause to rain,* Je. 14. 22.

גֶּשֶׁם masc. dec. 6a. (pl. c. גִּשְׁמֵי, but in pause גָּשֶׁם § 35. rem. 5).—I. *rain, heavy shower.*—II. pr. name masc., also called גַּשְׁמוּ comp. Ne. 6. 1, 2, with ver. 6.

גֹּשֶׁם masc. dec. 6c, id. Eze. 22. 24.

גְּשֵׁם Ch. m. dec. 3, (suff. גִּשְׁמֵהּ, גֶּשְׁמְהוֹן) *body.*

גָּשֶׁם in pause, Seg. n. as if from גֶּשֶׁם (§ 35. rem. 5) גשם

---

a Ps. 119. 20. b Je. 48. 37. c Ju. 5. 21. d De. 33. 14. e Le. 2. 14. f Ex. 34. 11. g Ex. 23. 28. h Ex. 12. 39. i 1 Sa. 26. 19. k Ge. 4. 14. l Ex. 33. 2. m Ez. 31. 11. n Nu. 22. 11. o Eze. 45. 9. p Ex. 23. 31. q Ge. 21. 23. r 2 Sa. 1. 15. s Ge. 19. 9. t Je. 46. 3. u Ruth 2. 14.

גֶּשֶׁם 'ו noun masc. sing. (pl. c. גִּשְׁמֵי) dec. 6a; also pr. name. masc. . . . . . נשם

גִּשְׁמַהּ[a] Chald. noun masc., suff. 3 pers. sing. fem. from [גְּשֵׁם] dec. 3b. . . . . נשם

גִּשְׁמֵהּ Chald. id., suff. 3 pers. sing. masc. . . נשם

גִּשְׁמָהּ[b] noun masc. sing., suff. 3 pers. sing. fem. from [גֶּשֶׁם] dec. 6c. (§ 35. rem. 8) . . נשם

גַּשְׁמוּ וְ pr. name masc., see גֶּשֶׁם . . . נשם

גִּשְׁמֵי[c] noun masc. pl. construct from גֶּשֶׁם dec. 6a. נשם

גִּשְׁמֵיהוֹן[d] Chald. noun masc. pl. (Kh. גִּשְׁמֵיהוֹן) or sing. (K. גִּשְׁמְהוֹן), suff. 3 pers. pl. masc. from [גְּשֵׁם] comp. dec. 3c. . . . . נשם

גִּשְׁמֵיהֶם[e] n. m. pl., suff. 3 pers. pl. m. from גֶּשֶׁם dec. 6. נשם

גִּשְׁמֵיכֶם[f] id. pl., suff. 2 pers. pl. masc. . . . . נשם

גְּשָׁמִים[g] id. pl., absolute state . . . . נשם

גֹּשֶׁן 'ו pr. name.—I. of a region in Egypt inhabited by the Israelites during their bondage.—II. a city in the tribe of Judah.

גֹּשְׁנָה id. with paragogic ה

גִּשְׁפָּה וְ (*flattery*, coll. with the Syr.) pr. name masc. Ne. 11. 21.

גִּשֵּׁשׁ. Pi. *to feel, grope*, Is. 59. 10.

גִּשְׁתּוֹ[h] Kal inf. (גֶּשֶׁת) suff. 3 pers. sing. masc. dec. 13a. . . . . . נגש

גַּת 'ו fem. dec. 8e.—I. *wine-press*, or rather *the vat*, in which grapes were trodden.—II. pr. name—of a city of the Philistines, the birth-place of Goliah. —גַּת חֵפֶר (*wine-press of the well*) a city in Zebulun.—גַּת רִמּוֹן (*press of the pomegranate*) a city in the tribe of Dan, Jos. 19. 45.

גִּתִּי gent. noun from גַּת No. II.—Hence fem. גִּתִּית, the name of a musical instrument.

גִּתַּיִם (*two wine-presses*) pr. name of a city in the tribe of Benjamin, Ne. 11. 33.

גִּתָּה pr. name of a place (גַּת) with paragogic ה נת

גִּתָּה־חֵפֶר pr. name of a place (גַּת חֵפֶר) with parag. ה נת

גִּתּוֹת[i] noun fem., pl. of גַּת dec. 8e. . . . נת

גִּתַּיִם pr. name of a place [for גִּתַּיִם] . . . נת

גִּתַּיְמָה id. with paragogic ה . . . . . נת

גֶּתֶר וְ pr. name of a region in Syria, Ge. 10. 23.

ד

דָּא Chald. pron. demon. fem. *this*; דָּא לְדָא *one against the other, together.*

[דָּאַב] prop. *to flow, melt*; hence *to pine away, to languish.*

דְּאָבָה fem. *anxiety, distress*, Job 41. 14.

דְּאָבוֹן masc. dec. 3. (§ 32. rem. 2) *languor, fainting*, De. 28. 65.

דָּאֲבָה Kal pret. 3 pers. sing. fem. . . . . דאב

דְּאָבָה[k] noun fem. sing. . . . . . . דאב

דַּאֲבוֹן[l] וְ n. m. s., constr. of [דְּאָבוֹן] d. 3. (§ 32. r. 2) דאב

דָּאַג וְ *to be anxious, uneasy, afraid*, const. with acc., מִן, לְ.

דֹּאֵג (*solicitous*) pr. name of an Edomite, the chief of Saul's herdsmen, and betrayer of David and Ahimelech; also called דּוֹיֵג, comp. 1 Sa. 21. 8, with 22. 18, 22.

דְּאָגָה fem. *anxiety, alarm, dread.*

דָּאג[ee] noun masc. sing., see דָּג . . . . דגה

דֹּאֵג pr. name masc. . . . . . . דאג

דֹּאֵג[m] Kal part. act. sing. masc. dec. 7b. . . דאג

דְּאָגָה noun fem. sing. . . . . . . דאג

דֹּאֲגִים[n] Kal part. act. masc., pl. of דֹּאֵג dec. 7b. . דאג

דָּאַגְתְּ[o] id. pret. 2 pers. sing. fem. . . . . דאג

[דָּאָה] *to fly.*

דָּאָה fem. Le. 11. 14, the name of a bird, *kite* or *glede*, so Vulg. milvus.

דָּאְנִין[p] Ch. Kh. דָּאְנִין, K. דָּיְנִין Peal part. act. m. pl. [of דָּאן dec. 1, or דָּיִן dec. 2b] . . דון

דֹּאר pr. name of a place, see דּוֹר . . . דור

דָּאְרֵי[q] 'ו Ch. constr. of the following . . . דור

דָּאְרִין Ch. Kh. דָּאְרִין, K. דָּיְרִין Peal part. act. m. pl. [of דָּאר dec. 1, or דָּיֵר dec. 2b] . . דור

דֹּב[r] 'ו ,'ו noun masc. sing. dec. 8c; for וְ see lett. וְ . . . . . . דבב

דָּבָא Root not used; Arab. *to rest*; Chald. *to cause to flow in*, comp. דָּאַב, דָּבַב.

דֹּבֶא masc. dec. 6c, once De. 33. 25, *rest*, poet. for death; or *affluence, resource, means.*

דָּבְאֶךָ[t] noun masc. sing., suff. 2 pers. sing. masc. [for דָּבְאֲךָ from דֹּבֶא] dec. 6c. . . דבא

[a] Da. 7. 11. [b] Eze. 22. 24. [c] Eze. 34. 26. [d] Da. 3. 28. [e] Ps. 105. 32. [ee] Ne. 13. 16. [f] Le. 26. 4. [g] Ezr. 10. 13. [h] Ge. 33. 3. [i] Ne. 13. 15. [k] Job 41. 14. [l] De. 28. 65. [m] Je. 38. 19. [n] Je. 42. 16. [o] Is. 57. 11. [p] Ezr. 7. 25. [q] Da. 4. 32. [r] Pr. 28. 15. [s] Is. 11. 7. [t] De. 33. 25.

[דָּבַב] to go softly, to creep along, only of wine to flow softly, Ca. 7. 10.

דֹּב, דּוֹב masc. dec. 8c, *bear*. Ch. id. Da. 7. 5.

דִּבָּה fem. dec. 10, *slander, evil report*.

דָּבָה Root not used; i. q. דָּבַב, דָּבָא to flow.

דִּבְיוֹן masc., only pl. דִּבְיוֹנִים 2 Ki. 6. 25, Keri, *doves' dung*; perhaps properly for דִּב יוֹנִים *what flows from pigeons*.

דִּבָּה noun fem. sing. dec. 10. . . . דבב

דְּבוֹרָה ו׳ pr. name fem.; וּ bef. (:) . . . דבר

[דְּבַח] Ch. *to sacrifice*. Ezr. 6. 3, i. q. Heb. זָבַח.

דְּבַח Ch. m. d. 3b, *a sacrifice*, Ezr. 6. 3.

מַדְבַּח masc. dec. 2a, *altar*, Ezr. 7. 17.

דָּבְחִין[a] Ch. Peal part. act. m., pl. of [דְּבַח] d. 2a. דבח

דִּבְחִין[b] Ch. noun masc., pl. of [דְּבַח] dec. 2b. . דבח

דֻּבִּים[c] noun masc., pl. of דֹּב dec. 8c. . . . דבב

דְּבִיר[d] ו׳ noun masc. s., also pr. name; וּ bef. (:) דבר

דָּבַךְ Root not used; i. q. דָּבַק to cleave, adhere.

נִדְבָּךְ Chald. masc. d. 1, *a row, layer of stones*, Ezr. 6. 4.

דָּבַל Root not used; Arab. *to press together*.

דְּבֵלָה fem., constr. דְּבֶלֶת (§ 42. rem. 5), pl. דְּבֵלִים, *a cake of dried figs*.

דִּבְלָה (*cake*) pr. name of a city in the northern borders of Palestine, Eze. 6. 14.

דִּבְלַיִם (*two cakes*) pr. name masc. Ho. 1. 3.

דִּבְלָתַיִם (id.) Nu. 33. 46, & בֵּית ד׳ Je. 48. 22, pr. name of a city in Moab.

דְּבֵלָה[e] noun fem. sing., constr. דְּבֶלֶת (§ 42. r. 5) דבל

דְּבֵלִים id. with pl. masc. term. . . . דבל

דִּבְלָיִם pr. name masc. . . . . דבל

דְּבֶלֶת[f] noun fem. sing., constr. of דְּבֵלָה (§ 42. r. 5) דבל

דִּבְלָתָה pr. name of a place (דִּבְלָה) with parag. ה דבל

דִּבְלָתַיִם pr. name of a place . . . . דבל

דִּבְלָתָיְמָה id. with parag. ה . . . . דבל

דָּבַק[g] ו׳ [also דָּבֵק comp. Job 29. 10; 41. 15]—I. *to cleave, adhere*.—II. *to reach, overtake*. Const. with אַחֲרֵי, אֶל, לְ, בְּ. Pu. *to cleave together*, with בְּ. Hiph. I. *to make adhere*.—II. *to follow close, to pursue*, with אַחֲרֵי.—III. *to overtake*; causat. De. 28. 21. Hoph. part. *cleave fast*, Ps. 22. 16.

דְּבֵק Chald. *to adhere*, Da. 2. 43.

דָּבֵק m. d. 5a, f. דְּבֵקָה, adj. *cleaving, adhering*.

דֶּבֶק masc. dec. 6a.—I. *soldering* of metals, Is. 41. 7.—II. *a joint* in armour.

דָּבֵק adj. masc. sing. dec. 5a. . . . דבק

דָּבְקָה[h], דָּבְקָה } Kal pret. 3 pers. sing. fem. (§ 8. rem. 1a) דבק

דְּבֵקָה[i] adj. fem. sing. from דָּבֵק masc. . דבק

דָּבְקוּ[k], דָּבְקוּ[l] } ו׳[m] Kal pret. 3 pers. pl. (§ 8. rem. 1) . דבק

דָּבְקִין[n] Ch. Peal part. act. m., pl. of [דְּבֵק] d. 2b. דבק

דָּבַקְתִּי[o] Kal pret. 1 pers. sing. . . . דבק

דְּבַקְתֶּם[p] וּ id. pret. 2 pers. pl. masc.; וּ bef. (:) . דבק

[דָּבַר] *to speak*; primarily *to range in order, to connect*; whence, in the derivatives, *to lead, guide, drive, to subdue, destroy*. Pi. I. *to speak*, const. with the acc. of that which is spoken, as דִּבֶּר דְּבָרִים *to speak words*; to speak *to* or *with* any one, with אֶל, לְ, עִם, (rarely) אֵת, בְּ; *concerning* any one, with עַל, אֶל, בְּ; *against* any one, with עַל, בְּ; *by* any one, with בְּ פִּ׳; דִּבֶּר עַל-לֵב *to speak kindly to any one*; דִּבֶּר אֶל-, עַל-לִבּוֹ *to speak to one's own heart*, i. e. to think; for which also בְּלִבּוֹ, עִם לִבּוֹ; דִּבֶּר טוֹבוֹת אֵת, אֶל- *to speak kindly with* any one; דִּבֶּר שָׁלוֹם עִם, אֵת *to speak friendly with* any one; דִּבֶּר מִשְׁפָּט עִם, אֵת *to litigate, contend with* any one; דִּבֶּר שִׁיר *to sing a song*.—II. *to destroy*, 2 Ch. 22. 10. Pu. *to be spoken*. Niph. *to speak together*, comp. נִלְחַם. Hiph. *to subdue*. Hithpa. *to speak with*; part. מִדַּבֵּר (for מִתְדַּבֵּר) *speaking*.

דָּבָר masc. dec. 4a.—I. *word, speech, command*; אִישׁ, בַּעַל דְּבָרִים *a man of words*, i. e. eloquent man; עֲשֶׂרֶת הַדְּבָרִים *the ten commandments*.—II. *thing, matter, affair*; דִּבְרֵי הַיָּמִים *chronicles*; דְּבַר יוֹם בְּיוֹמוֹ *the thing* (i. e. duty) *of the day in its day*; דִּבְרֵי הָאֲתֹנוֹת *the matter about the asses*.—III. *something*; אֵין, לֹא דָבָר *nothing*; כָּל-דָּבָר *every thing*.—IV. *cause, suit at law*; בַּעַל דְּבָרִים *one who has law-suits*.—V. *cause, reason*; עַל דְּבַר, עַל דִּבְרֵי *because of*.

דֶּבֶר m. d. 6a, (in pause דָּבֶר) *plague, pestilence*.

דִּבֵּר m., with Mak. דִּבֶּר־ *word*, Je. 5. 13; Ho. 1. 2.

דֹּבֶר m. d. 6c, *pasture*, whither flocks are driven.

דַּבֶּרֶת fem. *words, sayings*, only De. 33. 3. יִשָּׂא מִדַּבְּרוֹתֶיךָ *he shall receive of thy sayings*; but it may better be regarded as a participle of Hithp. *things spoken by thee*, i. e. thy sayings, precepts.

דִּבְרָה fem. (no pl.) with parag. *Yod* דִּבְרָתִי.—

[a] Ezr. 6. 3. [b] Ezr. 6. 3. [c] 2 Ki. 2. 24. [d] 1 Ki. 6. 19. [e] 1 Sa. 30. 12. [f] 2 Ki. 20. 7. [g] Ge. 2. 24. [h] Job 29. 10. [i] 2 Ch. 3. 12. [k] Job 41. 15. [l] 2 Sa. 20. 2. [m] De. 28. 60. [n] Da. 2. 43. [o] Ps. 119. 31. [p] Jos. 23. 12.

I. *manner, mode, order*, Ps. 110. 4.—II. *cause, law-suit*, Job 5. 8.—III. *cause, reason;* עַל־דִּבְרַת *because of.*

דִּבְרָא Chald. fem. dec. 8a, *cause, reason.*

דִּבְרִי (perhaps for דִּבְרִיָּה *promise of the Lord*, דָּבָר = דְּבַר) pr. name masc. Le. 24. 11.

דָּבְרַת & דָּבְרַת, 1 Ch. 6. 57, (*pasture*, comp. דֹּבֶר) pr. name of a Levitical city in the tribe of Issachar, Jos. 19. 12; 21. 28.

דֹּבְרֶת fem. dec. 13a, *float, raft*, 1 Ki. 5. 23.

דְּבֹרָה, דְּבוֹרָה fem. d. 10. (pl. דְּבֹרִים).—I. *a bee.* —II. pr. name of a prophetess who judged Israel.— III. pr. name of the nurse of Rebekah, Ge. 35. 8.

דְּבִיר masc.—I. *oracle, seat of the oracle*, that part of the temple from whence the Lord *spoke* and issued his orders and directions, and where the ark of the covenant was placed, comp. 1 Ki. 6. 19, also called *Holy of Holies.*—II. pr. name of the king of Eglon, Jos. 10. 3.—III. pr. name of a city in the tribe of Judah.

מִדְבָּר masc. d. 2b.—I. *a large plain*, in which cattle are driven for pasture.—II. *a desert* or *wilderness.*—III. *speech*, Ca. 4. 3.

דָּבָר־[a] Kh. דָּבָר q. v., K. הַדָּבָר (q. v.) . . דבר

דָּבָר ו' noun masc. sing. dec. 4a. . . דבר

דֶּבֶר[b] noun sing. masc. d. 6a, for דֶּבֶר (§ 35. r. 2) דבר

דַּבֵּר ו' Piel inf., or imp. sing. masc. . . דבר

דַּבֶּר־ ו' id. with Mak. . . . . דבר

דָּבֻר[c] Kal part. pass. sing. masc. [defect. for דָּבוּר] דבר

דֶּבֶר ו', [d]וָ noun masc. s. d. 6a; for וָ see lett. ו דבר

דְּבַר pr. name, see לוֹ דְבַר . . . דבר

דְּבַר ו' n. m. s., constr. of דָּבָר d. 4a; וּ bef. (:) דבר

דְּבִר pr. name of a place, defect. for דְּבִיר . דבר

דִּבֶּר Piel pret. 3 pers. sing. masc. . . דבר

דִּבֵּר ו' id. id. (§ 10. rem. 1) or *inf.* (§ 10. rem. 2); or perhaps *subst.* (Ho. 1. 2) . . . דבר

דֹּבֵר ו' Kal part. act. sing. masc. dec. 7b. . דבר

דְּבִרָה pr. name of a place (דְּבִיר) with parag. ה דבר

דִּבְרָה pr. name fem. . . . . דבר

דִּבְּרָה Piel pret. 3 pers. sing. fem. . . דבר

דַּבְּרוֹ[e] id. inf. (דַּבֵּר), suff. 3 pers. sing. masc. d. 7b. דבר

דַּבְּרוּ[f] ו' / דַּבֵּרוּ } id. imp. pl. masc. (comp. § 8. rem. 7) דבר

דְּבָרוֹ noun m. s., suff. 3 pers. s. m. fr. דָּבָר d. 4a. דבר

דִּבְּרוֹ[g] Piel pret. 3 pers. sing. m., suff. 3 pers. s. m. דבר

דִּבְּרוּ / ו' דִּבֵּרוּ } id. pret. 3 pers. pl. (comp. § 8. rem. 7) דבר

דֹּבְרוֹת[h] noun fem., pl. of [דֹּבֶרֶת] dec. 13. . . דבר

דַּבֵּ֑רִי[i] Pi. imp. sing. fem. in pause for the foll. (comp. § 8. rem. 7) . . . דבר

דַּבְּרִי id. imp. sing. fem. (Ju. 5. 12); or inf. (דַּבֵּר) with suff. 1 pers. sing. dec. 7b. . . דבר

דְּבָרַי / ו' דְּבָרָי } noun masc. pl., suff. 1 pers. sing. for דָּבָר dec. 4a; וּ before (:) . . . דבר

דְּבָרִי id. sing., suff. 1 pers. sing. . . . דבר

דִּבְרֵי ו' id. pl., construct state . . . דבר

דִּבְרִי pr. name masc. . . . . דבר

דֹּבְרֵי Kal part. act. m. pl. constr. from דֹּבֵר d. 7b. דבר

דְּבָרֶיהָ noun m. pl., suff. 3 p. s. fem. from דָּבָר d. 4a. דבר

דִּבְרֵיהֶם id. pl., suff. 3 pers. pl. masc. . . דבר

דְּבָרָיו ו' id. id., suff. 3 pers. sing. masc.; וּ bef. (:) דבר

דְּבָרָיו id. sing., suff. 3 pers. sing. masc. (K. דְּבָרוֹ), Kh. דְּבָרָיו (q. v.) . . . . דבר

דְּבָרַיִךְ[k] id. pl. with suff. 2 pers. sing. fem. [for דְּבָרַיִךְ] דבר

דְּבָרֶיךָ[l] ו' id. pl., suff. 2 pers. sing. masc.; וּ bef. (:) דבר

דְּבָרֶיךָ[m] noun m. pl., suff. 2 p. s. m. from דֶּבֶר dec. 6a. דבר

דְּבָרֶיךָ Kh. דְּבָרֶיךָ q. v., K. דְּבָרְךָ (q. v.) . דבר

דִּבְרֵיכֶם n. m. pl., suff. 2 pers. pl. m. from דָּבָר d. 4a. דבר

דְּבָרִים ו' id. pl., absolute state; וּ before (:) . דבר

דְּבֹרִים[n] n. fem. with pl. m. term. from דְּבוֹרָה dec. 10. דבר

דֹּבְרִים[o] Kal part. act. masc., pl. of דֹּבֵר dec. 7b. דבר

דַּבֶּרְךָ[p] Piel inf. (דַּבֵּר), suff. 2 p. s. m. d. 7b. (§ 16. r. 15) דבר

דְּבָרְךָ / דְּבָרֶךָ } noun masc. sing., suff. 2 pers. sing. masc. from דָּבָר dec. 4a. . . . דבר

דַּבֶּרְכֶם Piel inf. (דַּבֵּר), suff. 2 p. pl. m. d. 7b. (§ 16. r. 15) דבר

דְּבָרֵנוּ[q] noun m. sing., suff. 1 pers. pl. fr. דָּבָר d. 4a. דבר

דִּבַּרְנוּ Piel pret. 1 pers. sing. . . . דבר

דָּבְרַת, דָּבְרַת pr. name of a place . . . דבר

דִּבַּרְתָּ Piel pret. 2 pers. sing. masc. . . דבר

דִּבַּרְתָּ ו' id. id.; acc. shifted to ult. by conv. וְ (§ 8. r. 7) דבר

דִּבַּרְתְּ[r] ו' id. pret. 2 pers. sing. fem. . . . דבר

דִּבְרַת noun fem., constr. of [דִּבְרָה; no vowel change] דבר

דֹּבְרֹת[s] Kal part. act. pl. fem. from דֹּבֵר masc. . דבר

דִּבַּרְתִּי Piel pret. 1 pers. sing. . . . דבר

דִּבַּרְתִּי ו' id. id.; acc. shifted to ult. by conv. וְ (§ 8. r. 7) דבר

דִּבַּרְתִּי[t] id. pret. 2 pers. sing. fem., Kh. דִּבַּרְתִּי, K. דִּבַּרְתְּ (§ 8. rem. 5) . . . . דבר

דִּבְרָתִי[u] noun fem. sing. with parag. י from [דִּבְרָה; no vowel change] . . . . דבר

דִּבְרָתִי[v] id. with suff. 1 pers. sing. . . . דבר

דִּבַּרְתֶּם ו' Piel pret. 2 pers. pl. masc. . . דבר

דְּבַשׁ ו' masc. dec. 6b. (§ 35. rem. 10), *honey.*

יִדְבָּשׁ (*sweet as honey*) pr. name masc. 1 Ch. 4. 3.

[a] Je. 40. 3. [b] Hab. 3. 5. [c] Pr. 25. 11. [d] Eze. 14. 21. [e] Ge. 37. 4. [f] Ju. 19. 30. [g] De. 18. 21, 22. [h] 1 Ki. 5. 23. [i] 2 Sa. 14. 12. [k] 1 Ki. 1. 14. [l] 2 Sa. 7. 28. [m] Ho. 13. 14. [n] Ju. 14. 8. [o] Nu. 36. 5. [p] Ex. 4. 10. [q] Jos. 2. 14, 20. [r] 2 Sa. 14. 3. [s] Nu. 27. 7. [t] Je. 3. 5. [u] Ps. 110. 4. [v] Job 5. 8.

דְּבָשׁ[a] וּ/ id. in pause; וּ bef. (:)
דִּבְשִׁי[b] id. with suff. 1 pers. sing. . . . דבשׁ
דַּבֶּשֶׁת fem.—I. *the bunch* or *hump* of a camel, Is. 30. 6.
—II. pr. name of a place, Jos. 19. 11.
דִּבַּת[c] וְ/ noun fem. sing. constr. of דִּבָּה dec. 10. . דבב
דִּבָּתְךָ[d] וְ id., suff. 2 pers. sing. masc. . . . דבב
דִּבָּתָם[e] id., suff. 3 pers. pl. masc. . . . דבב
דָּג[f] noun masc. sing. dec. 2a. . . . דגה

[דָּגָה] *to multiply, be increased*, Ge. 48. 16.
דָּג masc. dec. 2a, *fish;* once, with the mater lectionis, דָּאג Ne. 13. 16.
דָּגָה fem. dec. 11a, *a fish;* mostly collect. *fish.*
דָּגוֹן (*large fish*) pr. name of an idol of the Philistines worshipped at Ashdod.
דָּגָן masc. dec. 4a, *corn, grain;* meton. for *bread*, La. 2. 12.

דָּגָה[g] noun fem. sing. dec. 11a. . . . דגה
דָּגוּל[h] Kal part. pass. sing. masc. . . . דגל
דָּגוֹן pr. name of an idol (and pr. name in compos. with בֵּית q. v.) . . . דגה
דְּגֵי וּ/ n. m. pl. constr. from דָּג dec. 2a; וּ bef. (:) דגה
דָּגִים[i] id. pl., absolute state . . . דגה

[דָּגַל] I. *to be marked, signalized*, Ca. 5. 10.—II. (denom. of דֶּגֶל) *to set up a banner*, Ps. 20. 6. Niph. *to be furnished with banners*, Ca. 6. 4, 10. Hence
דֶּגֶל masc. dec. 6a, *flag banner, standard.*
דִּגְלוֹ[k] וְ/א id., suff. 3 pers. sing. masc. . . . דגל
דָּגָן וְ/ noun masc. sing. dec. 4a. . . . דגה
דָּגוֹן pr. name, see בֵּית דָּגוֹן, see . . . בית
דְּגַן[l] וּ id. constr. state; וּ bef. (:) . . . דגה
דְּגָנִי[m] id., suff. 1 pers. sing. . . . דגה
דְּגָנְךָ[n] / דְּגָנֶךָ } id., suff. 2 pers. sing. masc. . . . דגה
דְּגָנֵךְ[o] id., suff. 2 pers. sing. fem. . . . דגה
דְּגָנָם id., suff. 3 pers. pl. masc. . . . דגה

[דָּגַר] *to hatch, brood over eggs.*
דָּגַר[u] Kal pret. 3 pers. sing. masc. [for דָּגַר § 8. r. 7] דגר
דָּגְרָה[p] וְ id. pret. 3 pers. sing. fem. . . . דגר
דְּגַת[q] noun fem. sing., constr. of דָּגָה dec. 11a. . דגה
דְּגָתָם id., suff. 3 pers. pl. masc. . . . דגה

[דַּד] masc. dec. 8d, *the breast;* only in the dual, *breasts.*
דֹּד noun masc. sing. defect. for דּוֹד dec. 1a. . דוד

[דָּדָה]. Hithpa. *to proceed softly, gently, submissively.*
דֹּדוֹ n. m. s., suff. 3 pers. s. m. from דּוֹד dec. 1a. דוד
דֹּדִי[r] id., suff. 1 pers. sing. . . . דוד
דֹּדָי pr. name masc. Kheth. דֹּדַי, K. דּוֹדוֹ . . דוד
דַּדֵּי[s] noun masc. pl. constr. from [דַּד] dec. 8d. דד
דַּדֶּיהָ[t] id., suff. 3 pers. sing. fem. . . . דד
דּוֹדֵיהֶן[w] noun m. pl., suff. 3 p. pl. fem. from דּוֹד d. 1a. דוד
דַּדַּיִךְ[x] n. m. pl., suff. 2 pers. s. fem. fr. [דַּד] d. 8d. דד
דֹּדֶיךָ[y] n. m. pl., suff. 2 pers. s. m. from דּוֹד dec. 1a. דוד
דֹּדַיִךְ[z] id., suff. 2 pers. sing. fem. . . . דוד
דֹּדִים id. pl., absolute state . . . דוד
דֹּדְךָ[a] id. sing., suff. 2 pers. sing. masc. . . . דוד
דְּדָן וּ/ pr. name of a people and a region in the north of Arabia.
דְּדָנֶה וּ id. with parag. ה; וּ bef. (:)
דֹּדָנִים וְ pr. name of a people descended from Javan, Ge. 10. 4, written רוֹדָנִים in 1 Ch. 1. 7.
דְּדָנִים gen. n., pl. of דְּדָנִי from דְּדָן
דֹּדָתוֹ n. fem. s., suff. 3 p. s. m. from [דּוֹדָה] d. 10. דוד
דֹּדָתְךָ[b] id., suff. 2 pers. sing. masc. . . . דוד

דְּהַב[c] וּ/ Chald. masc. dec. 3a, i. q. Heb. זָהָב *gold.*
מַדְהֵבָה fem. Is. 14. 4, *gold-making*, i. e. *exactress of gold;* others, *place of gold.*
דְּהָב[d] וּ id. in pause; וּ bef. (:) . . . דהב
דַּהֲבָא[e] וְ/ / דַּהֲבָה[f] וְ/ } Chald. id. emph. st.; וּ id. . . דהב
דֶּהָוֵא pr. name of a people who were colonised in Samaria, Ezr. 4. 9, Keri דֶּהָיֵא

[דָּהַם]. Niph. *to be overwhelmed, overcome*, Je. 14. 9.

[דָּהַר]. *to move quickly*, spoken of a horse, *to prance*, Na. 3. 2.
דַּהֲרָה fem. only pl. דַּהֲרוֹת *prancings*, Ju. 5. 22.
תִּדְהָר masc. the name of a tree; Vulg. ulmus, *the elm*, Is. 41. 19; 60. 13.
דֹּהֵר[g] Kal part. act. sing. masc. . . . דהר
דַּהֲרוֹת[h] noun fem., pl. of [דַּהֲרָה] . . . דהר
דּוֹאֵג pr. name masc., see דֹּאֵג . . . דאג

[דּוּב]. Hiph. *to cause to waste*, or *pine away*, Le. 26. 16.
דִּיבוֹן (*a pining, wasting away*) pr. name—I. of a city in the borders of Moab built by the Gadites. —II. of a city in the tribe of Judah, Ne. 11. 25, called דִּימוֹנָה in Jos. 15. 22.

[a] 1 Sa. 14. 26. [b] Ca. 5. 1. [c] Eze. 36. 3. [d] Pr. 25. 10. [e] Ge. 37. 2. [f] Jon. 2. 1. [g] De. 4. 18. [h] Ca. 5. 10. [i] Job 40. 31. [k] Ca. 2. 4. [l] Ps. 78. 24. [m] Ho. 2. 11. [n] De. 11. 14. [o] Is. 62. 8. [p] Is. 34. 15. [q] Eze. 29. 4, 4, 5. [r] Je. 32. 8, 9, 12. [s] Eze. 23. 3, 8. [t] Pr. 5. 19. [u] Je. 17. 11. [w] Nu. 36. 11. [x] Eze. 23. 21. [y] Ca. 1. 2, 4. [z] Ca. 4. 10, 10. [a] Je. 32. 7. [b] Le. 18. 14. [c] Ezr. 7. 16. [d] Ezr. 7. 15. [e] Da. 5. 23. [f] Ezr. 7. 18, etc. [g] Na. 3. 2. [h] Ju. 5. 22.

דּוֹבֵב[a] Kal part. act. sing. masc. . . . דבב

דּוֹבְרֵי[b] Kal part. act. pl. c. masc. from דֹּבֵר dec. 7 b. דבר

[דּוּג, דִּיג] to fish, Je. 16. 16.

דַּיָּג, דַּוָּג masc. dec. 1 b, fisher. Also

דּוּגָה[c] fem. a fishing, Am. 4. 2, סִירוֹת דּוּגָה fishing-hooks . . . . . . דוג

דַּוָּגִים[d] noun masc., pl. of [דַּוָּג] dec. 1 a. . . דוג

דוד Root not used;—I. Syr. to disturb, agitate.—II. i. q. יָדַד to love.

דּוּד masc.—I. pot, boiler, or cauldron, pl. דְּוָדִים (§ 35. rem. 13).—II. basket, pl. דּוּדִים.

דּוֹד, דֹּד masc.—I. love, but only in the plural.—II. for concr. beloved, friend.—III. uncle, father's brother.

דָּוִד, דָּוִיד (beloved; passive form § 26. No. 5) pr. name of the son of Jesse, king of Israel.

דֹּדָה, דּוֹדָה fem. dec. 10, aunt.

דּוֹדוֹ (His, sc. God's, beloved, comp. דּוֹד) pr. name masc. of several persons.

דּוֹדָוָהוּ (love of the Lord, for דּוֹדְיָהוּ) pr. name masc. 2 Ch. 20. 37.

דּוּדַי masc. only pl. דּוּדָאִים (§ 35. rem. 15 note).—I. baskets, comp. דּוּד, Je. 24. 1.—II. mandrakes, the apples of the Madragora (Atropa Mandragora of Linn.)

דּוֹדַי (beloved) pr. name masc. 1 Ch. 27. 4.

דָּוִד ו׳ pr. name masc. . . . . דוד

דּוֹד noun masc. sing. dec. 1 a. . . . דוד

דּוּדָאֵי constr. of the following: . . . דוד

דּוּדָאִים[e] noun masc., pl. of [דּוּדַי § 35. rem 15 note] דוד

דּוֹדָהּ[f] noun masc. sing., suff. 3 pers. sing. fem. from דּוֹד dec. 1 a. . . . . דוד

דּוֹדוֹ id., suff. 3 pers. sing. masc. . . . דוד

דּוֹדוֹ pr. name masc. . . . . . דוד

דּוֹדָוָהוּ pr. name masc. . . . . . דוד

דּוֹדַי pr. name masc. . . . . . דוד

דּוֹדַי[g] n. m. pl., suff. 1 pers. sing., from דּוֹד d. 1 a. דוד

דּוֹדִי ו׳ id. sing., suff. 1 pers. sing. . . . דוד

דּוֹדִים[h] id. pl., absolute state . . . . דוד

דּוֹדֵךְ id. sing., suff. 2 pers. sing. fem. . . דוד

דּוֹדָנִים ו pr. name, see דֹּדָנִים

[דָּוָה] to be languid, sick, in the verb only used of the female periodical sickness, Le. 12. 2.

דָּוֶה masc., דָּוָה fem. adj.—I. sick, specially of a woman in the menses.—II. sad, unhappy.

דַּוָּי masc. sick, faint.

דְּוַי masc. pl. com. דְּוָיֵי (comp. § 38. rem. 2).—I. sickness, Ps. 41. 4.—II. something sickening, loathsome, Job 6. 7.

מַדְוֶה masc. dec. 9 a, sickness, disease.

דָּוָה fem. of the following . . . . דוה

דָּוֶה[i] adj. masc. sing. . . . . . דוה

דּוּחַ. Hiph. I. to cast out, expel, Je. 31. 54.—II. to cleanse, wash away.

דַּוָּי adj. masc. sing. . . . . . דוה

דְּוַי[k] noun masc. sing. [for דְּוָי] . . . דוה

דּוֹיֵג pr. name masc. for דֹּאֵג (q. v.) . . דאג

דָּוִיד pr. name masc., see דָּוִד . . . דוד

[דּוּךְ] to pound, bray in a mortar, Nu. 11. 8.

מְדֹכָה fem. mortar, Nu. 11. 8.

[דּוּכִיפַת] fem. the name of an unclean bird; Vulg. upupa, the hoopoe, Le. 11. 19; De. 14. 18.

דום Root not used, i. q. דָּמַם to be silent, still.

דּוּמָה fem.—I. silence, death. Meton. place of the dead, the grave.—II. pr. name of a tribe and district in Arabia.

דּוּמִיָּה fem.—I. silence, quietness, Ps. 22. 3; adv. silently, Ps. 39. 3.—II. silent resignation sc. to the will of God; Ps. 62. 2, ד׳ נַפְשִׁי my soul is silent resignation, i. e. is perfectly resigned; Ps. 65. 2. לְךָ דֻמִיָּה תְהִלָּה to thee silent resignation is praise, i. e. redounds to thy praise, or is that by which thou art to be praised.

דּוּמָם masc.—I. silence, dumbness, Hab. 2. 19.—II. adv. in silence, silently.

דּוֹם Kal imp. sing. masc. for דֹּם . . . דמם

דּוֹמֶה[l] Kal part. act. sing. masc. . . . דמה

דּוּמָה noun fem. sing. . . . . . דום

דּוּמָה ו׳ pr. name of a tribe and region . . דום

דּוֹמִּי[m] Kal imp. sing. fem. for דֹּמִּי . . . דמם

דּוּמִיָּה noun fem. sing. from [דּוּמִי] m. (§ 39. No. 2) דום

דּוּמָם[n] ו׳ adv. with the term. ָ־ם, comp. יוֹמָם, חִנָּם &c. דום

דּוֹמַמְתִּי[o] ו Poel pret. 1 pers. sing. . . . דמם

דּוּמֶשֶׂק pr. name, see דַּמֶּשֶׂק

[דּוּן] & [דִּין] pret. דָּן; imp. דִּין; fut. יָדוֹן & יָדִין.—I. to rule, govern, perhaps so in 1 Sa. 2. 10; Zec. 3. 7.—II. to judge.—III. to plead, defend the cause of any one.—IV. to judge, punish, with acc. בְּ.—V. to contend, strive, with עִם, Ec. 6. 10; Ge. 6. 3.

---

[a] Ca. 7. 10. [b] Ps. 63. 12. [c] Am. 4. 2. [d] Eze. 47. 10. [e] Ge. 30. 14. [f] Ca. 8. 5. [g] Ca. 7. 13. [h] Ca. 5. 1. [i] La. 5. 17. [k] Ps. 41. 4. [l] Ca. 2. 9. [m] Ps. 62. 6. [n] La. 3. 26. [o] Ps. 131. 2.

with ver. 5.—II. 2 Ch. 17. 8.—III. Ne. 10. 17, called אֲדֹנִיקָם (*lord of the enemy*, part. of קום) in Ezr. 2. 13. Comp. Ezr. 8. 13; Ne. 7. 18.

אֲדֹנִירָם (*the Lord is exalted*, part. of רום) pr. name of an officer under David, called also אֲדוֹרָם, comp. 1 Ki. 4. 6, with 12. 18, and again הֲדֹרָם, 2 Ch. 10. 18.

יָדוֹן (*He judges*) pr. name of a man, Ne. 3. 7.

מָדוֹן masc. pl. מְדָנִים or מְדוֹנִים (§ 32. rem. 8, & 35. rem. 13) only in Kheth.—I. *contention, strife*; אִישׁ מָדוֹן *man of contention*, pass. i. e. a man contended with, Je. 15. 10. (see also R. מדה); Kh. אִישׁ, אֵשֶׁת מִדְוָנִים act. *contentious man, woman*; K. מִדְיָנִים.—II. *object of strife*, Ps. 80. 7.—III. pr. name of a city of the Canaanites.

מִדְיָן masc. dec. 2 b.—I. *contention, strife*, see the preceding.—II. pr. name of a son of Abraham by Keturah and the tribe descended from the same.—Gent. noun מִדְיָנִי, pl. ־ִים, fem. ־ִית *Midianite*.

מְדִינָה fem. dec. 10, prop. *jurisdiction*, hence—I. *province*.—II. *region, country*.

מְדִינָא Chald. fem. dec. 8, id.

מְדָן masc.—I. *contention, strife*, only pl. מְדָנִים—II. pr. name of a son of Abraham by Keturah.

מְדָנִי gent. noun contr. for מִדְיָנִי (comp. מִדְיָן and מְדָן) *Midianite*, Ge. 37. 36, comp. ver. 28.

דּוֹנַגa noun masc sing. . . . . דנג

דּוֹפֵקb Kal part. act. sing. masc. . . . דפק

[דּוּץ] *to leap, exult*, Job 41. 14.

דּוּק Root not used; Chald. and Syr. *to look round, look out*; Arab. conj. IV. *to surround*.

דָּיֵק masc. *watch-tower*; but on account of the word סָבִיב with which it occurs, others understand it to signify, *a wall* or *line of circumvallation*. LXX. περίτειχος *a surrounding wall*.

[דּוּר] I. *to dwell*, Ps. 84. 11.—II. in the deriv., according to the Arab., *to move in a circle, go round*.

דּוּר Chald. *to dwell*.

דּוּר masc.—I. *a circle*, Is. 29. 3.—II. *a ball*, Is. 22. 18.—III. *a round pile* of bones, Eze. 24. 5.

דּוֹר, דֹּר masc. dec. 1 a, pl. ־ִים & וֹת, prop. *revolution*, hence,—I. *age, generation*; דֹּר וָדוֹר *age and age*, i. e. for ever; so likewise דּוֹר דּוֹרִים; בְּכָל־דּוֹר וָדוֹר *throughout all ages or generations*. So מִדֹּר דֹּר, עַד דֹּר וָדֹר, לְדֹר וָדֹר, לְדֹר דֹּר—

לֹא־יָדוֹן רוּחִי בָאָדָם לְעֹלָם *my spirit shall not always strive with man*, sc. in testifying against him, but judgment must ensue. Niph. *to contend, strive together*, 2 Sa. 19. 10.

דּוּן Chald. *to judge*, Ezr. 7. 25.

דּוּן masc. *judgment*, Job 19. 29, שַׁדּוּן K. *that* there is *a judgment*, Kh. שַׁדִּין.

דִּין masc. dec. 1 a.—I. *judgment*.—II. *cause for judgment*; עָשָׂה דִין, דָּן דִּין *to defend a cause*.—III. *controversy, strife*, Pr. 22. 10.

דִּין Chald. masc. dec. 1 a.—I. *judgment*.—II. meton. *tribunal, court of judgment*.—III. *justice, right*.—IV. *punishment*, Ezr. 7. 26.

דַּיָּן masc. (construct דַּ֫יַּן § 30 rem. 1.)—I. *a judge*, 1 Sa. 24. 16.—II. *defender*, Ps. 68. 6.; Chald. Ezr. 7. 25.

דִּינָה (*judged*) pr. name of the daughter of Jacob.

דִּינָיֵא Chald. masc. pl. pr. name of a people of Assyria, Ezr. 4. 9.

דָּן (*judge*) pr. name.—I. of a son of Jacob and the tribe descended from him. Gent. noun דָּנִי, *Danite*.—II. of a city in the north of Palestine, called also לַיִשׁ & לֶשֶׁם.

דָּנִאֵל, דָּנִיֵּאל (*judge of God*) pr. name of the celebrated Hebrew prophet at the court of Babylon.

אָדוֹן masc. dec. 3 a, *master, lord*. Pl. אֲדֹנִים *lords*; more frequently used as a Plur. excellentiæ, *lord*; אֲדֹנֵי הָאָרֶץ *lord of the land*; אֲדֹנִים קָשֶׁה *a hard master*; אִם־אֲדוֹנִים אָנִי *If I am Lord*. Note others derive this and the following word from אדן, whence is אֶדֶן *a base*.

אֲדֹנָי, once אֲדוֹנָי (Ju. 13. 8) *Lord, the Lord*, exclusively applied to God. Grammarians disagree about the termination ־ָי, which some regard as a pl. form for ־ַי i. q. ־ִים, to distinguish it from אֲדֹנַי *my lords*; others, as the suff. of 1 pers. with pl. nouns, prop. denoting *my Lord*, the force of the possessive pronoun being neglected. Others again regard it as an adjective termination, whence אֲדֹנַי *ruling, governing*, and in the same way explain שַׁדַּי *Almighty*.

אֲדֹנִי־בֶזֶק (*lord of Bezek*) pr. name of a king of the Canaanitish city *Bezek*, Ju. 1. 5, 6, 7.

אֲדֹנִי־צֶדֶק (*lord of righteousness*) pr. name of a Canaanitish king of Jerusalem, Jos. 10. 1, 3.

אֲדֹנִיָּהוּ (*the Lord is my Lord*) pr. name.—I. of a son of David, called also אֲדֹנִיָּה, comp. 1 Ki. 1. 8,

a Ps. 68. 3. b Ca. 5. 2.

II. *habitation*, Is. 38. 12; meton. for *sepulchre* Ps. 49. 20.—III. pr. name of a city, see נָפָה.

דּוּרָא Chald. pr. name of a valley in Babylonia, Da. 3. 1.

מְדוֹר Chald. masc. dec. 1 a, *habitation*.

מְדָר Chald. masc. dec. 1 a, id. Da. 2. 11.

מְדוּרָה fem. dec. 10, *pile of fuel*.

תְּדִירָא Chald. fem. *revolution*, hence בִּתְדִירָא *continually*, Da. 6. 17.

דּוֹר ן׳, ו׳ noun masc. sing. dec. 1 a; also pr. name for ן see lett. ו . . . . דור

דּוֹר[a] noun masc. sing. . . . . . דור

דּוֹרָא pr. name of a place. . . . . דור

דּוֹרוֹ[b] noun m. s., suff. 3 pers. s. m. from דּוֹר dec. 1 a. דור

דּוֹרוֹת[c] id. fem. with pl. term. . . . . דור

דּוֹרוֹתֵינוּ[d] id. pl., suff. 1 pers. pl. . . . . דור

דּוֹרִי[e] id. sing., suff. 1 pers. sing. . . . דור

דּוֹרִים id. pl., absolute state . . . . דור

דֹּרֵךְ[f] ן Kal part. act. sing. masc. dec. 7 b. . דרך

דּוֹרֵשׁ Kal part. act. sing. masc. dec. 7 b. . . דרש

[דּוּשׁ, דִּישׁ] ו׳ I. *to tread down, tread under foot*.—II. *to tread out corn, to thresh*.—III. metaph. Am. 1. 3.

דּוּשׁ Chald. *to thresh*, Da. 7. 23.

דַּיִשׁ masc. *threshing-time*, Le. 26. 5.

דִּישׁוֹן masc.—I. a species of *gazelle* or *antelope*, De. 14. 5.—II. pr. name; (*a*) of a son of Seir and of a region called after his name; (*b*) of a grandson of Seir.

דִּישָׁן pr. name of the third son of Seir and a region called after him.

מְדוּשָׁה fem. dec. 10, *a threshing*, Is. 21. 10.

דּוּשִׁי[g] ן Kal imp. sing. fem.; for ן see lett. ו . דוש

דּוּשָׁם[h] id. inf. [דּוּשׁ], suff. 3 pers. sing. masc. dec. 1 a. דוש

דְּוֹתָהּ[i] Kal inf. [דְּוֹת], suff. 3 pers. sing. fem. dec. 1 a. דוה

[דָּחָה] *to push, thrust, drive*; part. דְּחוּיָה *thrust down*. Niph. *to be thrust down*. Pu. id., Ps. 36. 13.

דַּחֲוָא Chald. fem. only pl. דַּחֲוָן Da. 6. 19, a sort of *musical instrument*.

דֶּחִי masc. only in pause דֶּחִי (§ 35. rem. 14) *stumbling, falling*.

מִדְחֶה masc. *fall, ruin*, Pr. 26. 28.

דָּחֹה[k] Kal inf. absolute . . . . דחה

דֹּחֶה[l] Kal part. act. sing. masc. . . . . דחה

דֹּחוּ[m] Pual pret. 3 pers. pl. [for דֻּחוּ] . . רחה

דַּחֲוָן[n] ן Chald. noun masc., pl. of [דַּחֲוָא] d. 8 a. דחה

דְּחוּפִים[o] ן׳ ו׳[p] Kal part. p. pl. of [דָּחוּף] dec. 3 a; ו bef. (:) דחף

דָּחַח. Niph. *to be thrust down*, Je. 23. 12.

דְּחִיל[q] Chald. Peal part. p. sing. masc. . . . דחל

דְּחִילָה[r] Chald. fem. of the preceding . . . דחל

דְּחִיתַנִי[s] Kal pret. 2 pers. sing. masc., suff. 1 pers. sing. דחה

[דְּחַל] Chald. *to fear, be afraid*; part. pass. *fearful, terrible*. Pa. *to terrify*, Da. 4. 2.

דָּחֲלִין ן Ch. Peal part. act. m., pl. of [דָּחֵל] dec. 2 b. דחל

דֹּחַן ן masc. *millet*, Eze. 4. 9.

[דָּחַף] *to impel, urge, hasten*. Niph. *to urge oneself, to hasten*.

מַדְחֵפָה fem. *ruin, destruction*, Ps. 140. 12.

[דָּחַק] *to press upon*; part. דֹּחֵק *oppressor*.

דֹּחֲקֵיהֶם[t] ן Kal part. act. pl., suff. 3 pers. pl. masc. from [דֹּחֵק] dec. 7 b. . . . דחק

דִּי ן׳ Chald.—I. relat. pron. *who, which, what*, i. q. Heb. אֲשֶׁר; דִּי אִנּוּן *which they* i. e. which; דִּי מְדָרְהוֹן *whose dwelling*; דִּי תַמָּה *where*.—II. a sign of the genitive; after the emphatic state שַׁלִּיטָא דִּי מַלְכָּא *the captain of the king*; after the construct state, נְהַר דִּי נוּר *a stream of fire*; pleon. after suff. as שְׁמֵהּ דִּי אֱלָהָא for שֵׁם דִּי אֱלָהָא *the name of God*.—III. conj. *that*; *so that*; *because that*; כְּדִי *when*; מִן דִּי *from the time when, after*; עַד דִּי *until*.

דִּי זָהָב (*of gold*) pr. name of a place in the desert of Sinai, De. 1. 1.

דָּי[u] [in pause for דַּי] noun m. dec. 8 d, constr. דֵּי (§ 37. rem. 6).—I. *sufficiency, what is sufficient*, hence adverbially, *enough*; דֵּי חֲלֵב *enough of milk*; דֵּי שֶׂה *as much as is sufficient for a lamb*; כְּדֵי גְאֻלָּתוֹ *sufficient for its redemption*; דַּיֶּךָ, דַּיָּם *sufficient for thee, them*.—II. in the construct state it is sometimes affixed to the prepositions בְּ, כְּ, מִן, as בְּדֵי *for*; *whenever*; כְּדֵי *as*; *according to*; מִדֵּי *as often as, whenever*; *from*. Etymo. doubtful.

דֵּי[x] ן׳ ו׳ id. construct state. . . . . די

דִּיגוּם[y] ן Kal pret. 3 pers. pl., suff. 3 pers. pl. masc. R. דיג see . . . . . דוג

[a] Eze. 24. 5. [b] Is. 53. 8. [c] Is. 51. 9. [d] Jos. 22. 27. [e] Is. 38. 12. [f] Job 9. 8. [g] Mi. 4. 13. [h] Am. 1. 3. [i] Le. 12. 2. [k] Ps. 118. 13. [l] Ps. 35. 5. [m] Ps. 36. 13. [n] Da. 6. 19. [o] Est. 3. 15. [p] Est. 8. 14. [q] Da. 2. 31. [r] Da. 7. 7, 19. [s] Ps. 118. 13. [t] Ju. 2. 18. [u] Mal. 3. 10. [x] Pr. 27. 27. [y] Je. 16. 16.

דִּיבוֹן } וְ' דִּיבֹן } pr. name of a place. . . . דוב

דָּיָה Root not used; prob. i. q. Chald. דְּהָא *to be dark, obscure.*

דַּיָּה fem. dec. 10, *the black vulture.*

דְּיוֹ masc. *ink*, Je. 36. 18.

דַּיּוֹת[a] noun fem., pl. of דַּיָּה dec. 10. . . דיה

דַּיֶּךָ[b] noun masc. sing., suff. 2 pers. sing. masc. [for דַּיְךָ] from דַּי dec. 8d. (§ 37. rem. 6) די

דַּיָּם id., suff. 3 pers. pl. masc. . . . . די

דִּימוֹן } דִּימוֹנָה } וְ pr. name, see דִּיבוֹן . . . דוב

דַּיָּן[c] וְ noun m. s., constr. of [דַּיָּן] R. דִּין see דון

דִּין וְ'[d], וְ'[e] noun masc. sing. dec. 1a; Chald. (Da. 4. 34) dec. 1; for וְ see lett. ו, see . דון

דִּין[f] וְ Kal imp. sing. masc. R. דִּין see . דון

דִּינָא[g] } דִּינָה[i] } וְ'[h] Chald. n. m. s. emph. of דִּין dec. 1a, see דון

דִּינָה pr. name fem. R. דִּין, see . . . דון

דִּינוּ[k] Kal imp. pl. masc. R. דִּין see . . דון

דִּינִי[hh] וְ noun m. s., suff. 1 p. s. fr. דִּין d. 1a, see דון

דִּינָיֵא Chald. pr. name of a people. R. דִּין see דון

דַּיָּנִין[m] וְ Ch. noun m., pl. of דַּיָּן d. 1a. דון

דִּינֵךְ[n] noun m. s., suff. 2 p. s. f. fr. דִּין d. 1a, see דון

דִּיפַת וְ pr. n. according to some copies, see רִיפַת

דָּיֵק noun masc. sing. . . . . . דוק

דַּיִשׁ[o] noun masc. sing. . . . . . . דוש

דִּישׁוֹן וְ' pr. name masc. . . . . . דוש

דִּישֹׁן[p] וְ noun masc. sing., also pr. name masc. . דוש

דָּךְ Chald. pron. demon., fem. of דֵּךְ . . . דך

דַּךְ[q] } דָּךְ[r] } וְ adj. masc. sing. dec. 8d; for וְ see lett. ו דכך

דֵּךְ Chald. pron. demon. masc. *this.* Fem. דָּךְ

דִּכֵּן Chald. i. q. דֵּךְ *this.*

דָּכָא Pi.—I. *to break in pieces, to bruise.*—II. *to trample upon.* Pu.—I. *to be broken, bruised.*—II. *to be contrite.* Niph. part. *broken, contrite,* Is. 57. 15. Hithp. הִדַּכָּא (for הִתְדַּכָּא) *to be broken in pieces.* Hence

דַּכָּא adj. masc. pl. c. דַּכְּאֵי (§ 30. rem. 1).—I. *bruised, crushed.*—II. *contrite, humble.*

דִּכָּא[s] Piel pret. 3 pers. sing. masc. . . . דכא

דַּכְּאוֹ[t] id. inf. [דַּכֵּא], suff. 3 pers. sing. m. d. 7b. דכא

דֻּכְּאוּ[u] Pual pret. 3 pers. pl. . . . . דכא

דַּכְּאֵי[x] adj. m. pl. constr. fr. דַּכָּא d. 2b. (§ 30. r. 1) דכא

דִּכִּאתָ[y] Piel pret. 2 pers. sing. masc. . . . דכא

[דָּכָה] *to be bruised, crushed,* Ps. 10. 10. Niph. *to be broken, crushed;* of the heart, *to be contrite.* Pi. *to break in pieces.*

דֳּכִי masc. dec. 6k, *a beating, dashing,* Ps. 93. 3.

דָּכָה[z] וְ Kh. וְדָכָה, K. יִדְכֶּה Kal pret. or fut. 3 pers. sing. masc. . . . . . דכה

דָּכוּ[a] Kal pret. 3 pers. sing. masc. . . . דוך

דַּכָּיו[ll] adj. m. pl., suff. 3 pers. s. m. fr. דַּךְ d. 8d. דכך

דֳּכְיָם[b] noun masc. sing., suff. 3 pers. pl. masc. fr. [דֳּכִי] dec. 6k. . . . . . . דכה

דִּכִּיתָ[c] Piel pret. 2 pers. sing. masc. . . . דכה

דִּכִּיתָנוּ[d] id., suff. 1 pers. pl. . . . . . דכה

דָּכַךְ Root not used; i. q. דָּכָה, דּוּךְ q. v.

דַּךְ adj. masc. dec. 8d, *afflicted, oppressed, poor;* Pr. 26. 28 יִשְׂנָא דַכָּיו *hateth its afflicted,* i. e. those to whom it had caused affliction.

דַּכָּה fem. *a crushing, bruising,* De. 23. 2 פְּצוּעַ דַּכָּה *mutilated by crushing.*

דִּכֵּן Chald. pron. demon. com. . . . . . דך

[דְּכַר] Chald. Root not used in the Holy Scriptures; i. q. זָכַר *to remember.*

דְּכַר Chald. masc. dec. 3b, prop. i. q. זָכָר *male,* only by way of eminence, *a ram.*

דִּכְרוֹן Ch. m. d. 1, *memorial, record,* Ezr. 6. 2.

דָּכְרָן Chald. masc. dec. 1, id. Ezr. 4. 15.

דִּכְרוֹנָה[e] Ch. n. m., emph. of [דִּכְרוֹן] dec. 1a. . דכר

דִּכְרִין וְ'[f] Chald. noun m., pl. of [דְּכַר] dec. 3b. דכר

דָּכְרָנַיָּא[g] Ch. noun m. pl. emph. fr. [דָּכְרָן] dec. 1b. דכר

דַּל } דָּל[i] } וְ'[h], וְ', וְ' adj. & subst. masc. sing. dec. 8d; for וְ see lett. ו . . . . } דלל

דַּל[k] noun masc. sing. . . . . . . דלה

[דָּלַג] *to leap, skip,* Zep. 1. 9. Pi. id. const. with acc., עַל.

דָּלָה[l] *to draw,* as water from a well. In the deriv. also *to hang down.* Pi. *to draw up,* as from a prison, *to deliver,* Ps. 30. 2.

דַּל masc. *door,* Ps. 141. 3, comp. דֶּלֶת.

דָּלָה fem. dec. 11a, *door, gate.* Du. דְּלָתַיִם, constr. דַּלְתֵי *double doors, folding doors* or *gates;* metaph. דַּלְתֵי שָׁמַיִם *the doors of heaven* i. e. the clouds; דַּ' פָּנִים *the doors of the face,* i. e. the jaws.

דֶּלֶת fem. of דַּל (§ 44. rem. 1) with suff. דַּלְתּוֹ id.—Pl. דְּלָתוֹת, constr. דַּלְתוֹת (ת being treated as if radical, comp. קֶשֶׁת, also § 44. rem. 5)—I.

[a] Is. 34. 15. [b] Pr. 25. 16. [c] Ps. 68. 6. [d] Job 36. 17. [e] Est. 1. 13. [f] Pr. 31. 9. [g] Da. 7. 10. [h] Da. 7. 22, 26. [i] Ezr. 7. 26. [k] Je. 21. 12. [l] Ps. 9. 5. [m] Ezr. 7. 25. [n] Je. 30. 13. [o] Le. 26. 5. [p] De. 14. 5. [q] Ps. 10. 18. [r] Ps. 74. 21. [s] Ps. 143. 3. [t] Is. 53. 10. [u] Je. 44. 10. [x] Ps. 34. 19. [y] Ps. 89. 11. [z] Ps. 10. 10. [a] Nu. 11. 8. [b] Ps. 93. 3. [c] Ps. 51. 10. [d] Ps. 44. 20. [e] Ezr. 6. 2. [f] Ezr. 6. 9. [g] Ezr. 4. 15. [h] Zep. 3. 12. [hh] Ps. 9. 5. [i] Pr. 28. 11. [k] Ps. 141. 3. [l] Ex. 2. 19. [ll] Pr. 26. 28.

doors, gates.—II. leaves or valves of gates.—III. leaves or columns of a roll or book, Je. 36. 23.

דְּלִי masc. bucket, Is. 40. 15.

דֳּלִי masc. id. Nu. 24. 7, see מִדָּלְיָו analyt. order.

דְּלָיָהוּ, דְּלָיָה (whom the Lord has delivered) pr. name m. of several persons.

דָּלִית f. only pl. דָּלִיּוֹת (§ 39, 4. rem. 1) boughs, branches.

דָּלֹה[a] Kal inf. abs. . . . . . . דלה

דַּלּוּ Kal pret. 3 pers. pl. . . . . . דלל

דַּלּוֹנוּ[b] id. pret. 1 pers. pl. . . . . . דלל

דַּלּוֹת[cc] adj. fem., pl. of דַּלָּה dec. 10, from דַּל masc. דלל

דִּלּוֹתִי Piel pret. 1 pers. sing. . . . . דלל

[דָּלַח] to trouble or disturb water by trampling in it, Eze. 32. 2, 13.

דְּלָיָה ו׳ pr. name masc.; וּ bef. (:) . . . . דלה

דְּלָיָהוּ וּ pr. name masc.; וּ id. . . . . דלה

דַּלְיוּ[c] Piel imp. pl. m., R. דלה (§ 24. r. 13 note) or דלל

דָּלִיּוֹתָיו ו׳[d] noun fem. pl., suff. 3 pers. sing. masc. [fr. דָּלִית § 39, 4. rem. 1] . . . . דלה

דְּלִילָה pr. name fem. . . . . . . דלל

דַּלִּים ו׳[e] adj. masc., pl. of דַּל dec. 8d. . . . דלל

דָּלִיֹּתָיו defect. for דָּלִיּוֹתָיו (q. v.) . . . . דלה

דִּלִּיתָנִי[f] Piel pret. 2 pers. sing. masc., suff. 1 pers. s. דלה

[דָּלַל] pret. דַּלּוּ and דַּלּוּ (§ 18. rem. 13); imp. דַּלְיוּ (but see § 24. r. 13 note).—I. to hang down.—II. to be languid, be weakened, feeble. Niph. to be brought low, be reduced.

דַּל m. pl. דַּלִּים, f. דַּלּוֹת adj. low, weak, poor.

דַּלָּה fem. dec. 10.—I. thin thread, spoken of the threads or thrums which tie the web to the weaver's beam, Is. 38. 12.—II. hair or locks of the head, Ca. 7. 6.—III. lowness, weakness, poverty.

דְּלִילָה (languishing, languid) pr. name fem. a paramour of Samson.

דָּלְלוּ[g] Kal pret. 3 pers. pl. . . . . . דלל

דִּלְעָן וְ (place of gourds, Chald. דְּלַעַת a gourd) pr. name of a city in the tribe of Judah, Jos. 15. 38.

[דָּלַף] I. to drop, drip, Ec. 10. 18.—II. to shed tears, to weep.

דֶּלֶף masc. rain-drop, Pr. 19. 13; 27. 15.

דַּלְפוֹן (weeper?) pr. name of a son of Haman, Est. 9. 7.

יִדְלָף (shedding tears) pr. name of a son of Nahor, Ge. 22. 22.

דֶּלֶף[h] ו׳[i] noun sing. masc. . . . . . דלף

דָּלְפָה Kal pret. 3 pers. sing. fem. . . . . דלף

דַּלְפוֹן pr. name masc. . . . . . . דלף

[דָּלַק] fut. יִדְלַק.—I. to burn, consume, const. with בְּ.—II. applied metaph. to the affections of the mind; Pr. 26. 23 שְׂפָתַיִם דֹּלְקִים burning lips, i. e. professing ardent love; to burn with anguish, Ps. 10. 2; const. with אַחֲרֵי to pursue ardently. Hiph. to kindle, inflame.

דְּלַק Chald. to burn, Da. 7. 9.

דַּלֶּקֶת fem. burning fever, De. 28. 22.

דָּלִק[k] Chald. Peal part. act. sing. masc. . . . דלק

דָּלְקוּ וְ[l] Kal pret. 3 pers. pl. . . . . . דלק

דֹּלְקִים[m] Kal part. act. masc., pl. of [דֹּלֵק] dec. 7b. דלק

דְּלָקֻנוּ[n] Kal pret. 3 pers. pl., suff. 1 pers. pl. . דלק

דָּלַקְתָּ[o] Kal pret. 2 pers. sing. masc. . . . דלק

דַּלַּת[p] ו׳[q] noun fem. sing., constr. of דַּלָּה dec. 10. דלל

דֶּלֶת[r] noun fem. sing. (q. v.) . . . . . דלה

דַּלְתוֹת id. pl., constr. of the foll. (§ 44. rem. 1) דלה

דְּלָתוֹת ו׳[ff] id. pl. abs. st. (§ 44. r. 5) ת treated as if radical; וּ bef. (:) . . . . . . דלה

דַּלְתוֹתֵיהֶם וְ id. pl., suff. 3 pers. pl. masc. . . . דלה

דַּלְתוֹתָיו ו׳[u] id. pl., suff. 3 pers. sing. masc. . . דלה

דַּלְתֵי ו׳ id. du., constr. of [דְּלָתַיִם] dec. 11a. (for דַּ comp. § 44. rem. 1) . . . . . . דלה

דְּלָתַי[t] id. du., suff. 1 pers. sing. . . . . דלה

דְּלָתֶיהָ id. du., suff. 3 pers. sing. fem. . . . דלה

דְּלָתֶיךָ[y] id. du., suff. 2 pers. sing. masc. . . . דלה

דְּלָתֶךָ[z] id. du. (Kh. דְּלָתֶיךָ; K. דְּלָתְךָ sing., suff. 2 pers. sing. masc. . . . . . . דלה

דְּלָתַיִם ו׳[a] / דְּלָתָיִם וּ[b] } id. du., absolute state; וּ bef. (:) . . . דלה

דַּלְתֹתַי[c] id. pl., suff. 1 pers. sing. from דֶּלֶת (q. v.) דלה

דַּלְתֹתָיו id. pl., suff. 3 pers. sing. masc. . . . דלה

דָּם ו׳, וְ noun masc. sing. d. 2a; for וָ see lett. ו אדם

דַּם ו׳ id., constr. state . . . . . . אדם

דֹּם[d] Kal imp. sing. masc. . . . . . . דמם

I. דָּמָה to be or become like, to resemble, const. with אֶל, לְ. Niph. to become like, to resemble, const. with כְּ,

[a] Ex. 2. 19. [b] Ps. 79. 8. [c] Pr. 26. 7. [cc] Ge. 41. 19. [d] Eze. 17. 7. [e] 2 Sa. 3. 1. [f] Ps. 30. 2. [ff] 2 Ch. 4. 9. [g] Is. 19. 6. [h] Pr. 27. 15. [i] Pr. 19. 13. [k] Da. 7. 9. [l] Ob. 1. 18. [m] Pr. 26. 23. [n] La. 4. 19. [o] Ge. 31. 36. [p] 2 Ki. 24. 14. [q] Ca. 7. 6. [r] Ca. 8. 9. [s] 2 Ch. 4. 9. [t] 2 Ch. 4. 22. [u] 2 Ch. 3. 7. [x] Job 31. 32. [y] Zec. 11. 1. [z] Is. 26. 20. [a] Eze. 38. 11. [b] Job 38. 10. [c] Pr. 8. 34. [d] Eze. 24. 17.

also with acc. Pi.—I. *to liken, compare,* with אֶל, לְ. —II. *to imagine think, meditate;* 2 Sa. 21. 5 דִּמָּה לָנוּ *meditated against us,* sc. destruction. Hithp. fut. 1 pers. אֶדַּמֶּה (for אֶתְדַּמֶּה) *to become like,* Is. 14. 14.

II. [דָּמָה] I. *to be dumb, silent, quiet.*—II. meton. *to reduce to silence, to destroy.* Niph. *to be destroyed, cut off.*

דְּמָה Chald. *to be like, similar.*

דָּם masc. *likeness, similitude,* so according to some in Eze. 19. 10.

דְּמוּת fem. dec. 1a.—I. *similitude, likeness.*—II. *model, pattern,* 2 Ki. 16. 10.—III. adv. *as, like,* Is. 13. 4; so כִּדְמוּת Ps. 58. 5.

דְּמִי, דֳּמִי masc. *silence, quiet, rest.*

דִּמְיוֹן masc. dec. 1b, *likeness,* Ps. 17. 12.

דָּמָהּ noun m. s., suff. 3 pers. s. fem. fr. דָּם d. 2a. . אדם

דָּמֵה[a] Ch. Peal part. act. sing. masc. (§ 47. rem. 4) דמה

דְּמֵה[b] ו׳[c] Kal imp. sing. masc.; וּ bef. (:) . דמה

דִּמָּה[d] Piel pret. 3 pers. sing. masc. . . דמה

דָּמוֹ וְ׳ n. m. s., suff. 3 pers. s. m. from דָּם d. 2a. אדם

דָּמוּ[e] Kal pret. 3 pers. pl. . . . . דמה

דַּמּוּ Kal pret. 3 pers. pl. [for דָּמְמוּ] . . דמם

דִּמּוּ[f] Piel pret. 3 pers. pl. . . . . דמה

דֹּמּוּ[g] וְ׳ Kal imp. pl. masc. . . . . . דמם

דְּמוּת וּ׳ noun fem. sing. dec. 1a; וּ bef. (:) . דמה

דֹּמִּי[h] וָ Kal imp. sing. fem.; for וָ see lett. ו . דמם

דָּמִי וְ׳[i] n. m. s., suff. 1 pers. s. from דָּם dec. 2a. אדם

דֳּמִי noun masc. sing. . . . . . דמה

דְּמֵי וּ׳[k] n. m., pl. constr. of דָּם dec. 2a; וּ bef. (:) אדם

דָּמְיָה[l] Chald. Peal part. sing. fem., of דָּמֵה masc. (§ 47. rem. 4) . . . . . דמה

דֻּמִיָּה[m] defect. for דּוּמִיָּה noun fem. sing. . דום

דָּמֶיהָ n. m. pl., suff. 3 pers. s. fem. from דָּם d. 2a. אדם

דְּמֵיהֶם id., suff. 3 pers. pl. masc. . . . אדם

דָּמָיו וְ׳[n] id., suff. 3 pers. sing. masc. . . אדם

דָּמֶיךָ[o] id. (Kh. דָּמֶיךָ, suff. 2 pers. sing. masc., K. דָּמְךָ (q. v.) . . . . . אדם

דָּמַיִךְ[p] id., suff. 2 pers. sing. fem. . . . אדם

דַּמִּים pr. name, see אֶפֶס דַּמִּים . . . אפס

דָּמִים וְ׳ noun masc., pl. of דָּם dec. 2a. . . אדם

דָּמִינוּ[q] Kal pret. 1 pers. pl. . . . . דמה

דִּמִּינוּ[r] Piel pret. 1 pers. pl. . . . . דמה

דִּמְיֹנוֹ[s] noun masc. sing., suff. 3 pers. sing. masc. from [דִּמְיוֹן] dec. 1b. . . . דמה

דָּמִיתָ[t] Kal pret. 2 pers. sing. masc. . . דמה

דִּמִּיתָ[u] Piel pret. 2 pers. sing. masc. . . . דמה

דָּמִיתִי וְ׳[x] Kal pret. 1 pers. sing. . . . דמה

דִּמִּיתִי Piel pret. 1 pers. sing. . . . . דמה

דִּמִּיתִיךְ[y] id., suff. 2 pers. sing. fem. . . . דמה

דָּמְךָ noun m. s., suff. 2 pers. s. m. from דָּם d. 2a. אדם

דָּמֵךְ id., suff. 2 pers. sing. fem. . . . אדם

דִּמְכֶם[z] id., suff. 2 pers. pl. masc. . . . אדם

[דָּמַם] fut. יִדֹּם pl. יִדְּמוּ (§ 18. rem. 14).—I. *to be dumb, silent, quiet;* דּוֹם לַיהוָֹה, לֵאלֹהִים *be silent toward the Lord God,* i. e. submit quietly to Him.—II. *to rest, cease, leave off.*—III. *to stand still,* Jos. 10.12,13. Po. *to silence, quiet,* Ps. 131. 2. Hiph. *to reduce to silence, to destroy, cut off,* Je. 8. 14. Niph. fut. יִדַּמּוּ, תִּדַּמִּי.—I. *to be destroyed, cut off, to perish.*—II. *to be laid waste.*

דְּמָמָה fem. *silence, stillness.*

דֻּמָה fem. *destruction, desolation,* for concr. *desolate,* Eze. 27. 32. But it may be rendered with Prof. Lee, כְּדֻמָה בְּתוֹךְ הַיָּם *as silence in the midst of the sea.*

דָּמָם וְ׳[a] id., suff. 3 pers. pl. masc. . . . אדם

דְּמָמָה noun fem. sing. . . . . . דמם

דֹּמֶן[b] masc. *dung, manure.*

דִּמְנָה (*dunghill*) pr. name of a town in the tribe of Zebulun, Jos. 21. 35.

מַדְמֵן (id.) pr. name of a town in Moab, Je. 48. 2.

מַדְמֵנָה fem.—I. *dunghill,* Is. 25. 10.—II. pr. name of a town in the tribe of Benjamin, Is. 10.31.

מַדְמַנָּה (*dunghill*) pr. name of a town in the tribe of Judah, Jos. 15. 31.

דִּמְנָה pr. name of a place . . . . דמן

[דָּמַע] *to weep, shed tears,* Je. 13. 17.

דֶּמַע masc. dec. 6a. (§ 35. rem. 5) prop. *tear,* collect. *tears;* metaph. for the *juice* of grapes and olives, &c. Ex. 22. 28.

דִּמְעָה fem. dec. 12b, *tear,* collect. *tears.*

דָּמֹעַ[c] וְ Kal inf. abs. . . . . דמע

דִּמְעָה noun fem. sing. dec. 12b. . . . דמע

דִּמְעֲךָ[d] וְ noun masc. sing., suff. 2 pers. sing masc. from [דֶּמַע] dec. 6a. (§ 35. rem. 5) . דמע

דִּמְעַת[e] noun fem. sing., constr. of דִּמְעָה dec. 12b. דמע

דִּמְעָתָהּ[f] וְ id., suff. 3 pers. sing. fem. . . דמע

דִּמְעָתִי id., suff. 1 pers. sing. . . . . דמע

דִּמְעָתֶךָ id., suff. 2 pers. sing. masc. [for תְךָ] . דמע

[a] Da. 3. 25. [b] Ca. 2. 17. [c] Ca. 8. 14. [d] 2 Sa. 21. 5. [e] Eze. 31. 8. [f] Ju. 20. 5. [g] Ps. 4. 5. [h] Je. 47. 6. [i] Je. 51. 35. [k] 2 Ki. 9. 7. [l] Da. 7. 5. [m] Ps. 65. 2. [n] Ho. 12. 15. [o] 2 Sa. 1. 16. [p] Eze. 16. 9. [q] Is. 9. 1. [r] Ps. 48. 10. [s] Ps. 17. 12. [t] Eze. 31. 2, 18. [u] Ps. 50. 21. [x] Ho. 4. 5. [y] Ca. 1. 9. [z] Ge. 9. 5. [a] Ju. 9. 24. [b] Ps. 83. 11. [c] Je. 13. 17. [d] Ex. 22. 28. [e] Ec. 4. 1. [f] La. 1. 2.

דַּמֶּשֶׂק } sometimes דּוּמֶּשֶׂק, דַּרְמֶשֶׂק (Syriac orthography) pr. name—I. *Damascus*,
וְ' דַּמֶּשֶׂק } the metropolis of Syria on the river Chrysorrhoas.—II. concrete for *Damascene*, Ge. 15. 2.

דְּמֶשֶׁק (in many MSS. דְּמֶשֶׂק) *damask*, silk cloth made at Damascus, Am. 3. 12.

דָּמְתָה[a] Kal pret. 3 pers. sing. fem. . . . דמה

[דֵּן] Chald. emph. דְּנָה pron. demonstr. com. gen. *this, that*; כְּדְנָה *like this, such; as this, thus*; עַל דְּנָה *thereupon, therefore*; אַחֲרֵי דְנָה *afterwards.*

דָּן וְ' pr. name of a man and a tribe (see also וְדָן lett. ו) . . . . . . דון

דָּן Kal pret. 3 p. s. m. (Je. 22. 16); or part. act. דון

דָּנִאֵל defect. for דָּנִיֵּאל (q. v.) . . . דון

דָּנַג Root not used; whence

דּוֹנַג masc. *wax.*

דַּנָּה וְ pr. name of a town in the tribe of Judah, Jos. 15. 49.

דְּנָה [b]וּ' Chald. pron. demon. com. emph. of [דֵּן] דן

דִּנְהָבָה pr. name of a town in Edom, Ge. 36. 32; 1 Ch. 1. 43.

דָּנוּ[c] Kal pret. 3 pers. pl. . . . . . דון

דָּנִיֵּאל וְ' pr. name masc. . . . . . דון

דָּנַנִּי[d] Kal pret. 3 p. sing. masc., suff. 1 pers. sing. דון

דַּע[e] וְ } Kal, or (Da. 6. 16) Ch. Peal, imp. sing.
דַּע וְ' } masc. (§ 20. rem. 1) . . . } ידע

דֵּעָה noun fem. sing. dec. 10, from דֵּעַ masc. ידע

דְּעָה[f] Kal imp. sing. masc. (דַּע) with parag. ה (§ 20. rem. 1 & 3) . . . . . . ידע

דָּעֵהוּ[g] id., suff. 3 pers. sing. masc. (comp. § 16. r. 12) ידע

דְּעוּ וּ' id. imp. pl. masc.; וּ bef. (:) . . . ידע

דְּעוּאֵל (*invocation of God*; דעה Arab. *to invoke*) pr. name masc., called also רְעוּאֵל, comp. Nu. 7. 42, with 2. 14.

דֵּעוֹת noun fem., pl. of דֵּעָה dec. 10. . . ידע

דְּעִי וּ' Kal imp. sing. fem.; וּ bef. (:) . . ידע

דֵּעִי noun masc. sing. from דֵּעַ dec. 1 a. (§ 36. r. 2) ידע

דֵּעִים[h] id. pl., absolute state . . . ידע

[דָּעַךְ] *to go out, be extinguished*, as a light; trop. *to be destroyed.* Niph. *to become extinct*, of water *to be dried up*, Job 6. 17. Pu. *to be quenched, destroyed*, Ps. 118. 12.

דָּעֲכוּ[i] Kal pret. 3 pers. pl. . . . . דעך

דֹּעֲכוּ[k] Pual pret. 3 pers. pl. . . . . דעך

דַּעַת וְ' } Kal inf. constr. (§ 20. r. 3) or subst.
דָּעַת וְ', וְ' } fem. dec. 13 a; for וְ see lett. ו } ידע

דַּעְתִּי[m] id. inf., suff. 1 p. s. [for דַּעְתִּי comp. § 35. r. 5] ידע

דַּעְתְּךָ[n] id. subst., suff. 2 pers. sing. masc. . . ידע

דַּעְתֵּךְ[o] וְ id. id., suff. 2 pers. sing. fem. . . ידע

דַּעְתָּם[p] וְ id. id., suff. 3 pers. pl. masc. . . ידע

דָּפָה Root not used; Arab. *to thrust, push.* Hence

דֳּפִי [for דָּפְי § 35. rem. 14] *stroke, ruin, destruction*, Ps. 50. 20. . . . . . . דפה

[דָּפַק] I. *to beat, knock*, Ca. 5. 2.—II. *to drive, overdrive*, Ge. 33. 13. Hithp. *to knock*, Ju. 19. 22.

דָּפְקָה (*cattle-driving*) pr. name of a station of the Israelites in the desert, Nu. 33. 12.

דְּפָקוּם[q] וּ Kal pret. 3 pers. pl. with suff. 3 pers. pl. masc.; וּ bef. (:) . . . . דפק

דַּק }
דָּק } Kal pret. 3 pers. masc. or adj. masc. sing. דקק

דַּקָּה adj., fem. of the preceding . . . . דקק

דָּקוּ[r] Chald. Peal pret. 3 pers. pl. masc. [for דְּקוּ] דקק

דַּקּוֹת[s] וְ' adj. fem., pl. of דַּקָּה d. 10, from דַּק masc. דקק

דִּקְלָה (i. q. Chald. דִּקְלָא *palm-tree*) pr. name of a district in Arabia, Ge. 10. 27.

[דָּקַק] pret. דַּק, fut. יָדֹק.—I. *to beat* or *grind small.*—II. intrans. *to be beaten* or *ground small*, Ex. 32. 20; De. 9. 21. Hiph. הֵדַק *to beat small, break in pieces*; inf. הָדֵק adv. *very small, fine*, and so לְהָדֵק (§ 18. r. 10). Hoph. *to be ground small*, Is. 28. 28.

דְּקַק Ch. *to be beaten, broken in pieces*, Da. 2. 35. Aph. הַדֵּק, fut. תַּדִּק, תַּדֵּק *to beat* or *grind small.*

דַּק, fem. דַּקָּה adj.—I. *small, thin, fine*, hence as a subst. *small dust.*—II. *slender, thin, withered.*

דֹּק masc. *thin, fine cloth*, Is. 40. 22.

[דָּקַר] *to thrust through, to pierce.* Niph. *to be thrust through*, Is. 13. 15. Pu. *to be thrust through*; metaph. by want, La. 4. 9.

דֶּקֶר (*a stabbing*) pr. name masc. 1 Ki. 4. 9.

מַדְקְרוֹת fem. pl. constr. (fr. מַדְקָרָה or מַדְקֵרָה) *piercings* of the sword, Pr. 12. 18.

דֶּקֶר pr. name masc. . . . . . דקר

דָּקְרוּ[t] Kal pret. 3 pers. pl. [for דָּקְרוּ § 8. r. 7] . דקר

דְּקָרֻהוּ[x] וּ id. id., suff. 3 pers. sing. masc.; וּ bef. (:) דקר

דָּקְרֵנִי וְ id. imp. sing. masc., suff. 1 pers. sing. . דקר

דְּקָרֻנִי[y] וּ id. pret. 3 pers. pl., suff. 3 p. s. m.; וּ bef. (:) דקר

[a] Ca. 7. 8. [b] Da. 5. 25. [c] Je. 5. 28. [d] Ge. 30. 6. [e] Ec. 11. 9. [f] Pr. 24. 14. [g] Pr. 3. 6. [h] Job 37. 16. [i] Is. 43. 17. [k] Ps. 118. 12. [l] Ps. 119. 66. [m] De. 9. 24. [n] Job 10. 7. [o] Is. 47. 10. [p] Is. 44. 25. [q] Ge. 33. 13. [r] Da. 2. 35. [s] Ge. 41. 6, 23. [t] Ge. 41. 3. [u] Zec. 12. 10. [x] Zec. 13. 3. [y] 1 Sa. 31. 4.

דַּקֹּת[a] ׀ adj. fem., pl. of דַּקָּה d. 10, from דַּק m. ׀ דקק
דָּר ׀ Chald. noun masc. sing. . . . ׀ דור
דַּר[b] ׀ noun masc. sing. . . . . ׀ דרר
דֹּר ׀ defect. for דּוֹר (q. v.) . . . ׀ דור

דָּרָא Root not used; Arab. *to excite evil.*

דְּרָאוֹן masc., constr. דִּרְאוֹן (§ 32. Nos. 1 & 2) *abhorrence, contempt*, Da. 12. 2. Also—

דֵּרָאוֹן (for דִּרְאוֹן) m. *abhorrence*, Is. 66. 24.

דָּרַב Root not used; Arab. *to be pointed.*

דָּרְבוֹן only in pl. דָּרְבֹנוֹת *goads*, Ec. 12. 11.

דָּרְבָן masc. *goad*, 1 Sa. 13. 21.

דָּרַג Root not used; Arab. *to ascend by steps.*

מַדְרֵגָה fem. *steep place, precipice*, Ca. 2. 14; Eze. 38. 20.

דַּרְדַּע ׀ (*pearl of wisdom*; דַּר Arab. *pearl*) pr. name masc. 1 Ki. 5. 11, called דָּרַע 1 Ch. 2. 6.

דַּרְדַּר ׀ noun masc. sing. . . . ׀ דרר
דְּרוּכָה[c] ׀ Kal part. pass. fem. sing. dec. 10, [from דָּרוּךְ masc.] . . . . ׀ דרך
דָּרוֹם ׀ [d] noun masc. sing. [for דִּרוֹם] . . ׀ דרר
דְּרוֹר ׀ [e] noun masc. sing.; וּ bef. (:) . . ׀ דרר
דְּרוּשָׁה[f] ׀ Kal part. pass. fem. sing. (see the foll.) ׀ דרש
דְּרוּשִׁים[g] ׀ id. masc., pl. of [דָּרוּשׁ] dec. 3 a. . ׀ דרש
דֹּרוֹת ׀ defect. for דּוֹרוֹת (q. v.) . . . ׀ דור

דָּרְיָוֶשׁ ׀ pr. name *Darius*.—I. *Darius* the Mede, i. e. Cyaxares, comp. Da. 6. 1.—II. *Darius* Hystaspis, king of Persia, comp. Hag. 1. 1. —III. *Darius* Nothus, king of Persia, Ne. 12. 22.

דָּרַךְ [h] fut. יִדְרֹךְ *to tread*, with the acc.; with עַל *to tread upon* any thing; with בְּ *to tread*, e. g. a way; hence *to tread in* or *upon, to enter*; with מִן *to tread forth, come forth, out of* a place; metaph. *to tread down* enemies; דָּרַךְ כּוֹכָב מִיַּעֲקֹב — דָּרַךְ גַּת *to tread the wine-press*; דָּ׳ יַיִן, זַיִת, *to tread the grapes, the olives*; דָּ׳ קֶשֶׁת *to bend the bow*; and meton. דָּ׳ חִצִּים *to bend the arrows*, for, the bow. Hiph.—I. *to cause to tread, go, walk, to lead.*—II. i. q. Kal *to tread* a way, *to walk* in it; *to tread* a threshing-floor; metaph. *to tread* or *bend* the tongue, like a bow; *to tread down* enemies.

דֶּרֶךְ com. dec. 6 a, with suff. דַּרְכִּי (Du. דְּרָכַיִם as if from דָּרֶךְ).—I. *a going, way, journey*; דֶּרֶךְ יוֹם *a day's journey*; עָשָׂה דֶרֶךְ *to make one's way*.—II. *way, path*; דֶּרֶךְ הַמֶּלֶךְ *the king's highway*; הָלַךְ לְדַרְכּוֹ *to go one's way*; הָלַךְ דֶּרֶךְ כָּל־הָאָרֶץ *to go the way of all the earth*, i. e. to die. —III. *mode, manner, custom*; כְּדֶרֶךְ כָּל־הָאָרֶץ *after the manner of all the earth*, i. e. all mankind.

מִדְרָךְ masc. *place trodden upon, footing*, De. 2. 5.

דֶּרֶךְ, דָּרֶךְ ׀ n. com. sing. d. 6 a. (§ 35. r. 2); for וְ see lett. ו ׀ דרך
דֹּרֵךְ[i] ׀ Kal part. act. sing. masc. dec. 7 b. ׀ דרך
דָּרְכָה[m] ׀ Kal pret. 3 pers. sing. fem. . . ׀ דרך
דַּרְכָּהּ[n] ׀ noun com. s., suff. 3 p. s. f. from דֶּרֶךְ d. 6 a. ׀ דרך
דַּרְכּוֹ[o] ׀ id., with suff., Kh. כּוֹ׳ 3 pers. s. m., K. כָּיו׳ 1 pers. sing. . . . . ׀ דרך
דְּרָכָו ׀ id. pl., suff. 3 p. sing. masc. K. כָּיו׳ (§ 4. r. 1) ׀ דרך
דָּרְכוּ ׀ [p] Kal pret. 3 pers. pl. . . . ׀ דרך
דַּרְכּוֹ ׀ [q] n. com. s., suff. 3 p. s. m. from דֶּרֶךְ d. 6 a. ׀ דרך
דְּרֻכוֹת[r] ׀ Kal part. pass. fem., pl. from דְּרוּכָה (q. v.) ׀ דרך
דַּרְכֵי ׀ noun com. pl. constr. from דֶּרֶךְ dec. 6 a. ׀ דרך
דַּרְכִּי ׀ id. sing., suff. 1 pers. sing. . . . ׀ דרך
דְּרָכַי, דְּרָכָי ׀ id. pl., suff. 1 pers. sing. . . . ׀ דרך
דֹּרְכֵי ׀ Kal part. act. pl. constr. m. from דֹּרֵךְ s. ׀ דרך
דְּרָכֶיהָ ׀ n. com. pl., suff. 3 pers. s. f. from דֶּרֶךְ d. 6 a. ׀ דרך
דַּרְכֵיהֶם ׀ id. pl., suff. 3 pers. pl. m. . . ׀ דרך
דְּרָכָיו ׀ id. pl., suff. 3 pers. sing. masc.; וּ bef. (:) ׀ דרך
דְּרָכַיִךְ, דְּרָכָיִךְ ׀ id. pl., suff. 2 pers. sing. fem. . . ׀ דרך
דְּרָכֶיךָ ׀ id. pl., suff. 2 pers. sing. masc.; וּ bef. (:) ׀ דרך
דַּרְכֵיכֶם ׀ id. pl., suff. 2 pers. pl. masc. . . ׀ דרך
דְּרָכַיִם[s] ׀ id. dual, absolute state (as if from דָּרֶךְ) ׀ דרך
דְּרָכִים ׀ id. pl., absolute state . . . ׀ דרך
דֹּרְכִים[u] ׀ Kal part. act. masc., pl. of דֹּרֵךְ dec. 7 b. ׀ דרך
דְּרָכֵינוּ[v] ׀ noun com. pl., suff. 1 pers. pl. from דֶּרֶךְ d. 6 a. ׀ דרך
דַּרְכְּךָ ׀ id. sing., suff. 2 pers. sing. masc. for כְּךָ׳ ׀ דרך
דַּרְכֵּךְ ׀ id. sing., suff. 2 pers. sing. fem. . . ׀ דרך
דְּרָכֶךָ ׀ id. pl., suff. 2 pers. s. masc. defect. for כֶיךָ׳ ׀ דרך
דַּרְכְּכֶם[w] ׀ id. sing., suff. 2 pers. pl. masc. . . ׀ דרך
דַּרְכָּם ׀ id. sing. suff., 3 pers. pl. masc. . . ׀ דרך
דַּרְכְּמוֹנִים, דַּרְכְּמֹנִים ׀ masc. pl. *darics*, a Persian coin.
דַּרְכֵּנוּ ׀ n. com. s., suff. 1 pers. pl. from דֶּרֶךְ d. 6 a. ׀ דרך
דָּרַכְתָּ[x] ׀ Kal pret. 2 pers. sing. masc. . . ׀ דרך
דָּרַכְתִּי ׀ id. pret. 1 pers. sing. . . . ׀ דרך
דַּרְמֶשֶׂק, דַּרְמֶשֶׂק ׀ pr. name, see דַּמֶּשֶׂק.

[a] Ge. 41. 4. [b] Est. 1. 6. [c] Is. 21. 15. [d] De. 33. 23. [e] Ps. 84. 4. [f] Is. 62. 12. [g] Ps. 111. 2. [h] Mi. 1. 3. [i] Is. 35. 8. [k] Is. 59. 8. [l] Am. 4. 13. [m] Jos. 14. 9. [n] Job 28. 23. [o] 2 Sa. 22. 33. [p] Ps. 37. 14. [q] Ps. 37. 23. [r] Is. 5. 28. [s] Pr. 31. 3. [t] Pr. 28. 6, 18. [u] Ne. 13. 15. [v] La. 3. 40. [y] Ju. 18. 6. [z] Hab. 3. 15.

[דְּרָע] Chald. i. q. Heb. זְרוֹעַ *the arm*, Da. 2. 32.

אֶדְרָע Chald. id. with prosthetic א Ezr. 4. 23.

אֶדְרֶעִי, in pause אֶדְרֶעִי (*strong, mighty*; Simonis, for אֶדֶר רְעִי *large pasture*) pr. name.—I. of the metropolis of Bashan, afterwards belonging to the tribe of Manasseh.—II. of a town in the tribe of Naphtali, Jos. 19. 37.

דָּרַע ן pr. name, for דַּרְדַּע, see דַּרְדַּע.

דְּרָעוֹהִי[a] ו Chald. n. com. pl., suff. 3 pers. sing. masc. from [דְּרָע] dec. 1a. . . . . דרע

דַּרְקוֹן pr. name masc. Ezr. 2. 56.

דָּרַר Root not used; Arab. *to fly round*, cogn. דּוּר, *to radiate; to flow freely.*

דַּר m. Est. 1. 6, *pearl*; others, *mother of pearl*, or some kind of alabaster resembling it.

דְּרוֹר m.—I. *swallow*.—II. *a spontaneous flowing*, Eze. 30. 23.—III. *liberty*.

דָּרוֹם m. (for דַּרּוֹם) *the south*, the southern quarter. Poet. for *the south* wind, Job 37. 17.

דַּרְדַּר m. *brambles*; others, *weeds*, as growing luxuriantly.

דָּרַשׁ fut. יִדְרֹשׁ.—I. *to seek unto, visit* or *frequent*, e. g. a place, const. with the acc. of the place or person, with אֶל, לְ.—II. *to seek, search for*, with an acc. of the thing; with אַחַר *to seek after*.—III. *to ask, inquire*, especially *to inquire of* or *consult* an oracle, the Lord; *to inquire about* any thing, with acc., לְ; with עַל of the person of whom, and the thing *about* which inquiry is made (2 Ch. 31. 9); with מֵאֵת, מֵעִם, also בְּ of the person *through* whom God is consulted.—IV. *to ask for, demand back, require*, with the acc. of the thing and with מֵאֵת, מִיַּד, מֵעִם, מִן of person; דָּרַשׁ דָּם, מֵעִם, מִיַּד *to require the blood of any one*, i. e. to punish bloodshed.—V. *to seek, apply oneself unto, to promote*; דָּרַשׁ שְׁלוֹם פ׳ *to promote the welfare of any one*; דָּרְשָׁה צֶמֶר *applieth herself to wool*; hence *to care for, regard*. Niph.—I. *to be sought for*, 1 Ch. 26. 31.—II. pass. of Kal No. III., with לְ.—III. pass. of Kal No. IV., Ge. 42. 22.

מִדְרָשׁ m. d. 2b, *commentary*, 2 Ch. 13. 22; 24. 27.

דָּרָשׁ[b] Kal pret. 3 pers. s. m. for דָּרַשׁ (§ 8. r. 7) דרשׁ

דָּרוֹשׁ id. inf. absolute . . . . . דרשׁ

דְּרָשׁ־ id. imp. sing. masc. for דְּרֹשׁ (§ 8. rem. 18) דרשׁ

דְּרֹשׁ[c] id. inf. constr. . . . . . דרשׁ

דֹּרֵשׁ ן id. part. act. sing. masc. dec. 7b. . דרשׁ

דָּרְשָׁה[d] id. pret. 3 pers. sing. fem. . . . דרשׁ

דְּרָשֻׁהוּ[e] id. pret. 3 pers. pl., suff. 3 pers. sing. masc. דרשׁ

דָּרְשׁוּ, דָּרָשׁוּ } ן׳ id. pret. 3 pers. pl. (§ 8. rem. 7) . דרשׁ

דָּרְשׁוֹ[f] id. inf., suff. 3 pers. sing. masc. . . דרשׁ

דִּרְשׁוּ ן׳ id. imp. pl. masc. . . . . . דרשׁ

דְּרָשׁוּהוּ[g] ו id. pret. 3 p. pl., suff. 3 p. s. m.; ו bef. (:) דרשׁ

דְּרָשׁוּם[h] id. id., suff. 3 pers. pl. masc. . . דרשׁ

דְּרָשׁוּנִי[i] id. id., suff. 1 pers. pl. . . . . דרשׁ

דִּרְשׁוּנִי[k] id. imp. pl. masc., suff. 1 pers. sing. . דרשׁ

דֹּרְשֵׁי[l] ן׳ id. part. act. pl. c. masc. from דֹּרֵשׁ d. 7b. דרשׁ

דֹּרְשָׁיו id. id., suff. 3 pers. sing. masc. . . דרשׁ

דֹּרְשֶׁיךָ[m] id. id., suff. 2 pers. sing. masc. . . דרשׁ

דָּרַשְׁנוּ[ll] id. pret. 3 pers. pl. . . . . . דרשׁ

דְּרַשְׁנֻהוּ id. id., suff. 3 pers. sing. masc. . . דרשׁ

דָּרַשְׁתָּ id. pret. 2 pers. sing. masc. . . . דרשׁ

דָּרַשְׁתָּ ן id. id.; acc. shifted by conv. ן (§ 8. r. 7) דרשׁ

דָּרַשְׁתִּי, דָּרַשְׁתִּי[n] } id. pret. 1 pers. sing. . . . . דרשׁ

דָּרַשְׁתִּי[o] ן id. id.; acc. shifted by conv. ן (§ 8. r. 7) דרשׁ

דְּרַשְׁתִּיךָ[p] id. pret., suff. 2 pers. sing. masc. . . דרשׁ

דֹּרֹתֵיכֶם[q] noun masc. with pl. fem. term. and suff. 2 pers. pl. masc. from דּוֹר dec. 1a. . דור

דֹּרֹתֵינוּ[r] id. with suff. 1 pers. pl. . . . . דור

דָּשׁ[s] Kal pret. 3 pers. sing. masc. . . . דושׁ

[דָּשָׁא] *to spring, sprout forth*, Joel 2. 22. Hiph. *to send forth grass*, Ge. 1. 11.

דֶּשֶׁא masc. *tender grass, young herbage.*

דָּשָׁא[t] Kal part. fem. sing. [for דָּשָׁה from דָּשׁ masc.] דושׁ

דֶּשֶׁא noun masc. sing. . . . . . דשא

דָּשְׁאוּ[u] Kal pret. 3 pers. pl. . . . . דשא

דָּשֵׁן ן *to grow fat*, De. 31. 20. Pi.—I. *to make fat*, Pr. 15. 30.—II. *to anoint*, Ps. 23. 5.—III. *to regard as fat*, an offering, i. e. accept it, Ps. 20. 4.—IV. denom. of דֶּשֶׁן *to remove the ashes*. Pu. *to be made fat, be abundantly satisfied*. Hothpa. הֻדַּשַּׁן for הָתְדַּשַּׁן (§ 6. No. 10 note) *to be besmeared with fat*, Is. 34. 6.

דָּשֵׁן adj. masc. dec. 5a.—I. *fat*, of soil; of trees, *full of sap*.—II. *rich, opulent*, Ps. 22. 30.

דֶּשֶׁן masc. dec. 6a. (with suff. דִּשְׁנִי).—I. *fatness, fat*; trop. *fertility*.—II. *ashes*, especially those from the victims consumed upon the altar.

דָּשֵׁן[x] adj. masc. sing. dec. 5a. . . . דשן

a Da. 2. 32. b 2 Ch. 17. 4. c De. 22. 2. d Pr. 31. 13. e Zep. 1. 6. f 2 Ch. 26. 5. g Ps. 78. 34. h Je. 8. 2. i Is. 65. 10. k Am. 5. 4. l Ps. 69. 33. ll 2 Ch. 14. 6. m Ps. 9. 11. n Ps. 34. 5. o Eze. 34. 10, 11. p Ps. 119. 10. q Le. 23. 43. r Jos. 22. 28. s 1 Ch. 21. 20. t Je. 50. 11. u Joel 2. 22. x Is. 30. 23.

דֶּשֶׁן, דֶּשֶׁן[a] וְ } noun masc. sing. dec. 6a. (§ 35. rem. 2, but comp. דִּשְׁנִי); for וָ see lett. ו } דשן

דִּשֹׁן וְ' pr. name masc., for דִּישׁוֹן . . . דוש

דִּשְּׁנוּ[b] וְ Piel pref. 1 pers. pl. . . . דשן

דִּשְׁנֵי[c] adj. masc. pl., constr. of דָּשֵׁן dec. 5a. . דשן

דִּשְׁנִי[d] noun m. s., suff. 1 pers. s. from דֶּשֶׁן dec. 6a. דשן

דְּשֵׁנִים[e] adj. masc., pl. of דָּשֵׁן dec. 5a. . . דשן

דִּשַּׁנְתָּ[f] Piel pret. 2 pers. sing. masc. . . דשן

דַשְׁתִּי[g] וְ Kal. pret. 1 pers. sing.; acc. shifted to ult. by conv. וְ (§ 8. rem. 7.) . . . דוש

דָּת וְ'[h] fem. dec. 1. (but also דַּת construct, and דָּתְכוֹן) Heb. & Chald.—I. *law, statute*.—II. *edict, decree*. דְּתָבָר Chald. masc. *judge* or *lawyer*, pl. emph. דְּתָבְרַיָּא Da. 3. 2, 3.

[דֶּתֶא] Chald. masc. emph. דִּתְאָא *tender grass*, i. q. Heb. דֶּשֶׁא, Da. 4. 12, 20.

דָּתָא וְ' Chald. noun fem. emph. of דָּת dec. 1b. דת

דְּתָבְרַיָּא[i] Chald. noun masc. pl. emph. of [דְּתָבָר] . דת

דָּתוֹ[k] וְ' noun fem. s., suff. 3 pers. s. m. fr. דָּת dec. 1a. דת

דָּתֵי Heb. & Chald. id. pl. construct state . דת

[דֹּתַיִן] (*two wells*, Chald. דּוֹת *a well*) Ge. 37. 17, contracted דֹּתָן 2 Ki. 6. 13, pr. name of a place in the north of Samaria.

דֹּתַיְנָה id. with local ה

דָּתֵיהֶם[l] וְ noun fem. pl., suff. 3 pers. pl. masc. from דָּת dec. 1a. . . . . . דת

דַּתְכוֹן[m] Chald. id. sing., suff. 2 pers. pl. m. dec. 1b. דת

דָּתָן וְ' pr. name of one of the conspirators with Korah.

ה

הַ· (followed by dag. forte) before letters not guttural, as הַסּוּס;—הָ (Pattah lengthened into Kamets) before the gutturals and ר; but invariably so before א and ר, as הָרֹאשׁ, הָאִישׁ, הָרֶגֶל, הָאָשָׁם; before ה and ח only in the monosyllabic words, הָהָר (הָהָרָה), הָחַי (הָהֵנָּה, הָהֵמָּה) הָהֵם Ge. 6. 19; before ע not having kamets for its vowel, as הָעִיר, הָעֶבֶד, or having kamets in a monosyllabic, or dissyllabic word with the accent on the penult, as הָעָם, הָעָיִן;—הַ (not followed by dag. forte) before ה and ח where dag. is said to be implied (*dag. forte implicitum, occultum*), as הַהוּא, הַהֹלֵךְ, הַחֹשֶׁךְ, הַחֲזִיר; before ע only in הָעֹזְבִים, הָעֹזֶבֶת, Pr. 2. 13, 17, הַעַרְקִי Ge. 10. 17, כַּעִוְּרִים Is. 59. 10. in which the best copies agree;—הֶ (dag. forte impl.) before a guttural having kamets, especially before ח, as הֶחָכָם, הֶחָלָל, הֶחָג, הֶחָי; before ה and ע only in polysyllabic words, as הֶהָרִים, הֶהָרִיוֹתֶיהָ, הֶעָנָן, הֶעָרִים; the Hebrew article.

I. prop. pron. demonstr. *this*; הַיּוֹם *this day*; הַפַּעַם *this time*.—II. for the definite article *the*.—III. for the indefinite article, *a*; הַיּוֹם *on a day, once*. Comp. our expression, "on a certain day; a certain man," in which there is both definiteness and indefiniteness.—IV. for the vocative; הַמֶּלֶךְ *O king*.—V. pron. relat. *who, which*, הֶהָלְכוּא *who had gone*, Jos. 10. 24; הֶעָלֶיהָ *that which is above her*, 1 Sa. 9. 24.

הֲ before letters not guttural; rarely followed by dag. forte, like the article, especially before sheva (comp. הַלְּבֶן Ge. 17. 17, הַכְּתֹנֶת 37. 32); הַ before gutturals, as הַאֵלֵךְ; הֶ before gutturals having kamets, as הֶאָנֹכִי, הֶחָזָק; a sign of interrogation.

I. of direct interrogation; Job 2. 3, הֲשַׂמְתָּ לִבְּךָ אֶל־עַבְדִּי אִיּוֹב *hast thou considered my servant Job?*—II. in indirect interrogation, *whether*, De. 13. 4, *to know* הֲיִשְׁכֶם אֹהֲבִים אֶת־יְהוָֹה *whether ye love the Lord.*

הָא Chald. interj. *lo! behold!* Da. 3. 25.

הֵא Heb. & Chald. id. Ge. 47. 23; Eze. 16. 43; Da. 2. 43.

הָאָב[n] pref. הָ for הַ·) noun masc. sing. irr. (§ 45) אב

הָאֲבֵדָה[o] pref. id.) noun fem. sing. dec. 10. . אבד

הָאֹבְדוֹת[p] pref. id.) Kal part. act. fem. pl. from אֹבֶדֶת dec. 13a. (§ 8. rem. 19) . . אבד

הָאֹבְדִים[q] pref. id.) id. masc., pl. of אֹבֵד dec. 7b. . אבד

הָאֹבֶדֶת[r] pref. id.) id. fem. sing. dec. 13a. . אבד

הַאֲבַדְתָּ, הֶאֱבַדְתָּ[s] וְ } Hiph. pret. 2 pers. sing. masc.; acc. shifted by conv. וְ (§ 8. rem. 7, & § 13. rem. 10) } אבד

הַאֲבַדְתִּי וְ id. pret. 1 pers. sing.; acc. shifted to ult. by conv. וְ (comp. id.) . . . אבד

הַאֲבַדְתִּיךָ[t] וְ id. id., suff. 2 pers. sing. masc. (comp. id.) אבד

הַאֲבַדְתִּיךְ[u] וְ id. id., suff. 2 pers. sing. fem. (comp. id.) אבד

הַאֲבַדְתָּם[x] וְ id. id. 2 pers. sing. masc., suff. 3 pers. pl. masc. (comp. id.) . . . אבד

[a] Ps. 63. 6. [b] Nu. 4. 13. [c] Ps. 22. 30. [d] Ju. 9. 9. [e] Ps. 92. 15. [f] Ps. 23. 5. [g] Ju. 8. 7. [h] Da. 7. 25. [i] Da. 3. 2, 3. [k] Est. 4. 11. [l] Est. 3. 8. [m] Da. 2. 9. [n] Eze. 18. 4, 20. [o] Le. 5. 23. [p] 1 Sa. 9. 20. [q] Is. 27. 13. [r] Eze. 34. 4, 16. [s] Job 14. 19. [t] Eze. 25. 7. [u] Zep. 2. 5. [x] De. 9. 3.

הָאָבוֹת וְ' pref. הָ for הַ)(noun masc. with fem. term. from אָב irr. (§ 45) . . . . אב

הָאֹבוֹת pref. id.)(noun masc. with pl. fem. term. from אוֹב dec. 1a. . . . . אוב

הָאֲבַטִּחִים[a] pref. id.)(noun m., pl. of [אֲבַטִּיחַ] dec. 1a. בטח

הָאָבִיב pref. id.)(name of a month. . . אבב

הַאֲבִיד[b] Hiph. inf. construct . . . אבד

הֶאֱבִיד[c] וְ id. pret. 3 pers. sing. masc. . אבד

הַאֲבִידוֹ[d] id. inf., suff. 3 pers. sing. masc. dec. 1b. אבד

הָאֶבְיוֹן[e] pref. הָ for הַ·)(adj. noun m. s. dec. 1b. . אבה

הָאֲבִיּוֹנָה[f] pref. id.)(noun fem. sing. . . אבה

הָאֶבְיוֹנִים[g] וְ pref. id.)(adj. masc., pl. of אֶבְיוֹן dec. 1a. אבה

הַאֶבְכֶּה[h] pref. הַ interr. for הֲ)(Kal fut. 1 pers. sing. בכה

הָאֵבֶל pref. הָ for הַ·)(n. m. s. dec. 6b. (§ 35. rem. 6) אבל

הָאֻבָל[i] pref. id.)(noun masc. sing. dec. 2b. . יבל

הֶאֱבַלְתִּי[k] Hiph. pret. 1 pers. sing. . . . אבל

הָאֶבֶן וְ' pref. הָ for הַ·)(n. fem. s. (suff. אַבְנוֹ) dec. 6a. אבן

הָאַבְנֵט[l] pref. id.)(noun masc. sing. dec. 1a. . בנט

הָאֲבָנִים וְ' pref. id.)(noun fem., pl. from אֶבֶן (suff. אַבְנוֹ) dec. 6a. . . . . אבן

הָאָבְנָיִם pref. id.)(noun fem., dual of [אֹבֶן] dec. 6c. אבן

הָאֵבֶר[m] pref. id.)(noun masc. sing. . . אבר

הָאֲגָגִי pref. id.)(gent. noun masc. from אֲגַג . אגג

הָאֲגַמִּים[n] pref. id.)(noun masc. pl. of אֲגַם dec. 8. אגם

הָאַגָּנוֹת[o] pref. id.)(noun masc. with pl. fem. term. from אַגָּן dec. 1b. . . . . אגן

הָאִגֶּרֶת[p] pref. id.)(noun fem. sing. dec. 13a. . אגר

הָאֲדוֹמִי pref. id.)(gent. noun masc. from אֱדוֹם . אדם

הָאָדוֹן pref. id.)(noun masc. sing. dec. 3a. . דון

הָאַדִּירִים pref. id.)(adj. masc., pl. of אַדִּיר dec. 1b. אדר

הָאָדָם [q]וְ' pref. id.)(noun. masc. sing. . . אדם

הָאָדֹם[r] pref. id.)(adj. masc. sing., pl. אֲדֻמִּים dec. 8c. (§ 37. Nos. 2 & 3) . . . . . אדם

הָאֲדָמָה וְ' pref. id.)(n. fem. s. dec. 11c. (§ 42. r. 1) אדם

הָאֲדֹמִי pref. id.)(gent. noun masc. from אֱדֹם . אדם

הָאָדֹן pref. id.)(noun masc. sing. dec. 3a. . דון

הָאֲדֹנִים pref. id.)(id. pl. absolute . . . דון

הָאֲדָנִים[s] וְ pref. id.)(noun masc. pl. (constr. אַדְנֵי) from [אֶדֶן] dec. 6a. . . . . אדן

הַאֵדַע[t] pref. הַ interr. הֲ)(Kal fut. 1 pers. sing. ידע

הַאִדָּרֹשׁ[u] pref. id.)(Niph. inf. absolute [for הַהִדָּרֹשׁ] דרש

הָאַדֶּרֶת[x] pref. הָ for הַ·)(n. fem. s. (suff. אַדַּרְתּוֹ) d. 13a. אדר

הָאַהֲבָה pref. id.)(noun fem. sing. dec. 10. . אהב

הָאֲהוּבָה[y] pref. id.)(Kal part. pass. fem. from אָהוּב m. אהב

הָאֵהֶל[z] Kheth. הָאֵהֶל q. v., Keri הָאֵלֶּה (q. v.) . אלה

הָאֹהֶל [a]וְ' pref. הָ for הַ·)(n. m. s. d. 6. (§ 35. r. 9) אהל

הָאֹהֱלָה pref. id.)(id. with local ה . . . אהל

הָאָהֳלִי[b] pref. id.)(id., suff. 1 pers. sing. . . אהל

הָאוּדִים[c] pref. id.)(noun masc., pl. of אוּד dec. 1a. . אוד

הָאוֹיֵב pref. id.)(Kal part. act. sing. masc. dec. 7b. איב

הָאֱוִיל[d] pref. id.)((prim. adj.), noun m. sing. dec. 1a. אול

הַאוֹכַל[e] pref. הַ interr. for הֲ)(Kal fut. 1 pers. sing. אכל

הַאוּכַל[f] pref. id.)(Hoph. fut. 1 pers. sing. . . יכל

הָאוּלָם וְ' pref. הָ for הַ·)(noun masc. sing., dec. 8a. אול

הָאָוֶן[g] pref. id.)(noun masc. sing. dec. 6g. און

הַאוֹסִיף[h]
הַאֹסִף[i] } pref. הַ interr. for הֲ)(Hiph. fut. 1 pers. s. יסף

הָאֹפִים[k] pref. הָ for הַ·)(Kal part. act., pl. of אֹפֶה d. 9a. אפה

הָאוֹפַן
הָאוֹפָן וְ' } pref. id.)(noun masc. sing. dec. 8a & d. אפן

הָאוֹפַנִּים[l] וְ' pref. id.)(id. pl., absolute state . . אפן

הָאוֹצָר pref. id.)(noun masc. sing. dec. 2b. . אצר

הָאֹצָרוֹת[m] pref. id.)(id. with pl. fem. term., constr. st. אצר

הָאוֹר[n] וְ' pref. id.)(noun masc. sing. dec. 1a. . אור

הָאֹרֵב[o] וְ pref. id.)(Kal part. act., pl. of אוֹרֵב d. 7b. ארב

הָאוּרִים pref. id.)(noun masc., pl. of [אוּר] dec. 1a. אור

הָאֲוַרְנָה pref. id.)(Kh. אוֹרְנָה, K. אֲרַוְנָה pr. name m. ארן

הָאוֹת pref. id.)(noun com. sing. dec. 1a. . אוה

הַאוֹתִי[p] pref. הַ interr. for הֲ)(as if from [אוֹת] with suff. 1 pers. sing., see אֵת sign of the accu. את

הָאֵזוֹב[q]
הָאֵזוֹב[r] } pref. הָ for הַ·)(noun masc. sing. . . אזב

הָאֵזוֹר pref. id.)(noun masc. sing. . . אזר

הֶאֱזִין[s] וְ
הֶאֱזִין[t] } Hiph. pret. 3 pers. sing. masc. (§ 13. r. 10) אזן

הַאֲזִינָה id. imp. sing. masc. with parag. ה . אזן

הַאֲזִינוּ וְ' id. imp. pl. masc. . . . . אזן

הֶאֱזִינוּ id. pret. 3 pers. pl. masc. . . . אזן

הַאֲזִינִי[u] וְ id. imp. sing. fem. (comp. § 13. rem. 10) אזן

הַאֶזְכֶּה[x] pref. הַ interr. הֲ)(Kal fut. 1 pers. sing. זכה

הָאָזֶל pref. הָ for הַ)([for אָזֵל] pr. name see אֶבֶן אבן

הַאְזֵנָּה Hiph. imp. pl. fem. [for הַאְזֵנְנָה § 17. rem. 9. & § 25. rem.) . . . . אזן

הָאָזְנִי pref. הָ for הַ·)(pr. name masc. . . אזן

הֶאֶזְנִיחוּ[y] וְ Hiph. pret. 3 pers. pl.; a mixed form from the Chald. אַזְנִיחוּ, and Heb. הִזְנִיחוּ . זנח

הַאֲזַנְתָּ[z] וְ id. pret. 2 pers. sing. masc., acc. shifted to ult. by conv. וְ (§ 8. rem. 7. & § 13. rem. 10) אזן

הָאזִקִּים[a] [for הָאֲזִקִּים pref. הָ; noun masc. pl. of [אֲזֵק] dec. 8b. . . . . זקק

הָאֶזְרָח pref. הָ for הַ·)(noun masc. sing. dec. 2b. זרח

הָאֶזְרָחִי pref. id.)(patronym. masc., from אֶזְרָח . זרח

---

[a] Nu. 11. 5. [b] 2 Ki. 10. 19. [c] Nu. 24. 19. [d] De. 28. 51. [e] De. 15. 7, 9. [f] Ec. 12. 5. [g] Is. 41. 17. [h] Zec. 7. 3. [i] Da. 8. 3, 6. [k] Eze. 31. 15. [l] Ex. 39. 29. [m] Eze. 17. 3. [n] Ex. 8. 1. [o] Is. 22. 24. [p] Est. 9. 26. [q] Ge. 4. 1. [r] Ge. 25. 30. [s] Ex. 38. 17. [t] 2 Sa. 19. 36. [u] Eze. 14. 3. [x] Jos. 7. 24. [y] De. 21. 15, 16. [z] 1 Ki. 7. 45. [a] Nu. 3. 25. [b] Jos. 7. 21. [c] Is. 7. 4. [d] Pr. 27. 22. [e] Ps. 50. 13. [f] 2 Sa. 12. 23. [g] Ps. 125. 5. [h] Ju. 20. 23. [i] Ju. 20. 28. [k] Ge. 40. 2. [l] 1 Ki. 7. 32. [m] 1 Ch. 9. 26. [n] Ec. 12. 2. [o] Jos. 8. 19. [p] Je. 5. 22. [q] Le. 14. 6, 51. [r] 1 Ki. 5. 13. [s] Ps. 77. 2. [t] De. 1. 45. [u] Is. 1. 2. [x] Mi. 6. 11. [y] Is. 19. 6. [z] Ex. 15. 26. [a] Je. 40. 4.

הָאָח interj. of joy or scorn, *aha!*

הָאָח[a] pref. הָ for הַ·) noun fem. sing. . . אחח

הָאֶחָד[b] Kh. הָאֶחָד q. v. K. אֶחָד (q. v.) . . אחד

הָאֶחָד וְ' pref. הָ for הַ·) num. card. masc. irr. (§ 45) אחד

הָאַחֲוָה[c] pref. id.) noun fem. sing. . . אח

הָאָחֻז[d] pref. id.) Kal part. p. s. m. for אָחוּז dec. 3a. אחז

הֵאָחֲזוּ וְ Niph. imp. pl. masc. . . . . אחז

הָאֲחֻזוֹת[e] pref. הָ for הַ·) Kal part. pass. fem. pl. from אָחוּז masc. dag. f. euph. . . . . אחז

הָאֲחֹחִי pref. id.) patronym. masc. from אֲחוֹחַ . אחח

הַאֶחְיֶה[f] pref. הַ interr. for הֲ) Kal fut. 1 pers. sing. חיה

הַאֲחֵיכֶם[g] pref. id.) noun masc. pl., suff. 2 pers. pl. masc. from אָח irr. (§ 45) . . אח

הָאֲחִירָמִי pref. הָ for הַ·) patronym. m. from אֲחִירָם (q.v.) אח

הָאַחֵר pref. id.) adj. masc. sing. irr. (§ 45) . אחר

הָאַחֲרוֹן[h] וְ' pref. id.) adj. masc. sing. dec. 1b. . אחר

הָאַחֲרוֹנִים וְ' / הָאַחֲרֹנִים וְ' } pref. id.) id. pl. . . . אחר

הָאַחֶרֶת pref. id.) adj. fem. s. from אַחֵר m. irr. (§ 45) אחר

הָאֲחַשְׁדַּרְפְּנִים[i] וְ'[k] pref. id.) noun masc. pl. of [אֲחַשְׁדַּרְפַּן] אחשדר'

הָאֲחַשְׁתָּרִי pref. id.) pr. name masc. . . אחשת'

הָאֲחַשְׁתְּרָנִים[l] pref. id.) noun masc., pl. of [אֲחַשְׁתְּרָן] אחשתר'

הָאַחַת וְ' / הָאֶחָת } pref. id.) num. card. fem. [for אַחֶדֶת] from אֶחָד m. for (ַ) comp. אָח § 45) אחד

הָאָטָד pref. id.) pr. name of a place . . אטד

הָאָטָד pref. id.) noun masc. sing. . . . אטד

הָאִטִּים[m] pref. id.) noun masc., pl. of אַט dec. 8e. . אטט

הָאֲטֻמוֹת[n] pref. id.) Kal part. pass. pl. fem. from [אָטוּם] masc. . . . . . אטם

הָאִי pref. id.) noun m. sing. dec. 8f. (§ 37. No. 4) אוה

הָאֹיֵב[o] defect. for הָאוֹיֵב (q. v.) . . . איב

הָאַיָּה pref. הָ for הַ·) noun fem. sing. . . אוה

הָאִיִּים pref. id.) n. m., pl. of אִי dec. 8f. (§ 37. r. 4) איה

הָאַיָּל[p] pref. id.) noun masc. sing. dec. 1b. . אול

הָאַיִל / הָאָיִל } pref. id.) noun masc. sing. dec. 6h. . אול

הָאַיָּלִים pref. id.) noun masc., pl. of אַיָּל dec. 1b. . אול

הָאֵילִים / הָאֵלִים } pref. id.) noun masc., pl. of אַיִל dec. 6h. אול

הָאֵימִים pref. id.) pr. name of a people . . אים

הַאֵין pref. הַ interr. for הֲ) adv., prop., noun masc. sing. constr. of אַיִן dec. 6h. . . און

הָאִיִּן[q] pref. הָ for הַ·) noun masc., pl. of אִי dec. 8f. (§ 37. No. 4) . . . . . אוה

הַאֵינְךָ[r] pref. הַ interr. for הֲ) adv. (suff. 2 pers. sing. masc. for אַיִן) dec. 6h. . . און

הָאִיעֶזְרִי pref. הָ for הַ·) patronym. m. from אֲבִיעֶזֶר (q.v.) ב

הָאֵיפָה pref. id.) noun fem. sing. dec. 10. . יף

הֵאִיר[s] וְ Hiph. pret. 3 pers. sing. masc. . . ור

הָאִירָה id. imp. sing. masc. with parag. ה . ור

הֵאִירָה[t] id. pret. 3 pers. sing. fem. . . . ור

הֵאִירוּ id. pret. 3 pers. pl. . . . . ור

הָאִישׁ וְ' noun masc. sing. dec. 1a. . . . יש

הַאִיתָךְ[u] Chald. pref. הַ interr. for הֲ) adv., (אִיתַי) with suff. 2 pers. sing. masc. . . ית

הַאַכֶּה[x] pref. הַ id.) Hiph. fut. 1 pers. sing. . כה

הֶאָכוֹל[y] pref. הֶ interr. for הֲ, הַ) Kal inf. abs. . כל

הָאֲכִילָה[z] pref. הָ for הַ·) noun fem. sing. . . כל

הַאֲכִילֵהוּ[a] Hiph. imp. sing. masc., suff. 3 pers. sing. m. כל

הַאֲכִילֻהוּ[b] וְ id. imp. pl. masc., suff. 3 pers. sing. masc. כל

הָאֹכֵל וְ' pref. הָ for הַ·) Kal part. act. s. m. d. 7b. כל

הָאֹכֶל pref. id.) noun masc. sing. dec. 6c. . כל

הֵאָכֹל Niph. inf. abs. . . . . . כל

הַאֲכִלֻהוּ[c] וְ Hiph. imp. pl. masc., suff. 3 pers. sing. m. כל

הָאֹכְלִים pref. הָ for הַ·) Kal part. act. masc., pl. of אֹכֵל dec. 7b. . . . כל

הָאֹכֶלֶת pref. id.) id. sing. fem. (§ 8. rem. 19) כל

הֶאֱכַלְתִּי[d] / וְהַאֲכַלְתִּי[e] } Hiph. pret. 1 pers. sing. (§ 13. r. 9 & 10) כל

הֶאֱכַלְתִּיךָ[f] / וְהַאֲכַלְתִּיךְ[g] } id. id., suff. 2 pers. s. m. & fem. (§ 13. rem. 9 & 10) . . . כל

וְהַאֲכַלְתִּים[h] id. id., suff. 3 pers. pl. masc. (§ 13. r. 9 & 10) כל

הֶאֱכַלְתָּם[i] id. pret. 2 pers. sing. masc., suff. 3 pers. pl. m. כל

הָאֵל[k] וְ' pref. הָ for הַ·) noun masc. sing. dec. 1a. ול

הָאֵל pref. id.) pron. demon. pl. com. . לה

הַאֵל[l] pref. הַ interr. for הֲ) noun masc. sing. d. 1a. ול

הָאֶל־[m] pref. id.) prep. see אֶל . . ל

הָאַלְגּוּמִּים[n] by transpos. for אַלְמֻגִּים q. v.

הָאָלָה pref. הָ for הַ·) noun fem. sing. dec. 10. לה

הָאָלָה pref. id.) noun fem. sing. . . . לל

הָאֵלָה pref. id.) pr. name of a valley . . ול

הָאֵלָה pref. id.) noun fem. sing. . . . אלה

הָאֵלֶּה pref. id.) pron. demon. pl. com. . . אל

הַאֱלֹהֵי[o] pref. הַ interr. for הֲ) constr. of the following אלה

הָאֱלֹהִים וְ' pref. הָ for הַ· art. / הַאֱלֹהִים[p] pref. הַ interr. for הֲ } noun masc., pl. of אֱלוֹהַּ dec. 1a. . אלה

הָאַלּוֹן[q] pref. הָ for הַ·) noun masc. sing. dec. 1b. . אלל

הָאָלוֹת pref. id.) noun fem., pl. of אָלָה dec. 10. אלה

הָאֱלִי pref. id.) gent. noun, see בֵּית הָאֱלִי . בית

---

[a] Je. 36. 22, 23. [b] 1 Ki. 4. 7. [c] Zec. 11. 14. [d] Nu. 31. 47. [e] Ec. 9. 12.
[f] 2 Ki. 8. 8, 9. [g] Nu. 32. 6. [h] Is. 8. 23. [i] Est. 8. 9. [k] Est. 9. 3.
[l] Est. 8. 10, 14. [m] Is. 19. 3. [n] Eze. 41. 16. [o] Je. 15. 11. [p] De. 12. 22.
[q] Eze. 26. 18. [r] Je. 7. 17. [s] Ex. 25. 37. [t] Eze. 43. 2.
[u] Da. 2. 26. [x] 2 Ki. 6. 21. [y] 2 Sa. 19. 43. [z] 1 Ki. 19. 8.
[a] Pr. 25. 21. [b] 2 Ch. 18. 26. [c] 1 Ki. 22. 27. [d] Ex. 16. 32.
[e] Is. 49. 26. [f] Eze. 16. 19. [g] Is. 58. 14. [h] Je. 19. 9.
[i] Ps. 80. 6. [k] Is. 5. 16. [l] Job 8. 3. [m] Is. 36. 12.
[n] 2 Ch. 9. 11. [o] Le. 23. 23. [p] 2 Ki. 7. 5. [q] Ge. 35. 8.

Word	Analysis	Root
הָאַלְיָה[a]	וְ״ pref. הָ for הַ·)(noun fem. sing. .	אלה
הָאֱלִיל[b]	pref. id.)(noun masc. sing. dec. 1a. .	אלל
הָאֱלִילִים[c] הָאֱלִלִם[d]	וְ׳ } pref. id.)(id. pl., absolute state .	אלל
הָאֵלִים[e]	pref. id.)(noun masc., pl. of אַיִל dec. 6h.	אול
הַאֵלֵךְ	pref. הַ interr. for הֲ)(Kal fut. 1 pers. sing.	ילך
הָאֻלָם[f]	pref. הָ for הַ·)(noun masc. sing. dec. 8a. .	אול
הָאַלְמֻגִּים[g]	pref. id.)(noun masc. pl., see אַלְגֻּמִּים	
הָאַלְמָנָה[h]	וְ pref. id.)(noun fem. sing. dec. 11a. .	אלם
הָאֵלֹנִי	pref. id.)(patronym. m. from אֵלוֹן .	אול
הָאֶלֶף[i] הָאָלֶף	} pref. id.)(noun m. s. d. 6a. (§ 35. r. 2)	אלף
הָאֲלָפִים[k]	וְ״ pref. id.)(id. pl., absolute state .	אלף
הָאֶלְקֹשִׁי	pref. id.)(gent. noun masc., see אֶלְקֹשִׁי	
הָאָלֹת[l]	pref. id.)(n. f., pl. of אָלָה d. 10. (§ 42. r. 2)	אלה
הָאֵם[m]	וְ״ pref. id.)(noun fem. sing. dec. 8b. .	אם
הַאִם	pref. הַ interr. for הֲ)(particle .	אם
הָאָמָה	pref. הָ for הַ·)(noun fem. sing. irr. (§ 45)	אמה
הָאַמָּה[o]	וְ׳ pref. id.)(noun fem. sing. dec. 10. .	אמם
הָאֲמָהוֹת[p] הָאֲמָהֹת[q]	} pref. id.)(n. f. pl. abs. of אָמָה irr. (§ 45)	אמה
הָאָמוֹן[r]	pref. id.)(noun masc. sing. .	אמה
הָאֱמוּנָה[t]	וְ״ pref. id.)(noun fem. sing. dec. 10.	אמן
הֶאָמוּר[u]	pref. הֶ interr. for הֲ)(Kal part. pass. s. m.	אמר
הָאֵמִים	pref. הָ for הַ·)(pr. name of a people .	אים
הָאֻמִּים[x]	pref. id.)(noun masc., pl. of אֹם dec. 6c.	אמם
הֶאֱמִין	Hiph. pret. 3 pers. sing. masc. . .	אמן
הַאֲמִינוּ[y]	Hiph. imp. pl. masc. . . .	אמן
הֶאֱמִינוּ[z]	וְ״ Hiph. pret. 3 pers. pl. . . .	אמן
הַאֲמִינוֹן	pref. הַ interr. bef. (ـ:))(pr. n. m., see אַמְנוֹן	אמן
הָאֱמֹרִי[a]	וְ pref. הָ for הַ·)(noun masc. sing. . .	אמר
הֶאֱמִירְךָ[b]	Hiph. pret. 3 pers. s. m., suff. 2 pers. s. m.	אמר
הָאֲמֵלָלִים[c]	pref. הָ for הַ·)(adj. masc., pl. of [אֲמֵלָל]	אמל
הָאֹמֵן[d]	pref. id.)(Kal part. act. sing. masc. .	אמן
הֶאֱמִן[e]	וְ Hiph. pret. 3 pers. masc. sing. . .	אמן
הָאֹמְנוֹת[f]	pref. הָ for הַ·)(n. f., pl. of [אֹמְנָה] d. 10.	אמן
הָאֱמֻנִים[g]	pref. id.)(Kal part. p. masc., pl. of [אָמוּן] dec. 3a.	אמן
הָאֹמְנִים[i]	וְ״ pref. id.)(id. part. act. m., pl. of אֹמֵן d. 7b.	אמן
הַאֻמְנָם	pref. הַ interr. for הֲ)(adv. formed from אֹמֶן and the term. ם ָ—	אמן
הֶאֱמַנְתִּי[k] הֶאֱמָנְתִּי	} Hiph. pret. 1 pers. sing. (§ 8. rem. 7)	אמן
הֶאֱמַנְתֶּם	id. pret. 2 pers. pl. masc. . .	אמן

Word	Analysis	Root
הָאֲמֻצִּים[l]	וְ pref. הָ for הַ·)(adj. m., pl. of [אָמֹץ] dec. 8c. (§ 37. No. 3) . . .	אמץ
הַאֹמֵר[m]	pref. הַ interr. for הֲ)(Kal. inf. constr. .	אמר
הָאֹמֵר	pref. הָ for הַ·)(id. part. act. masc. dec. 7b.	אמר
הֶאָמַר[n]	pref. הֶ interr. for הֲ, הַ)(id. pret. 3 p. s. m.	אמר
הַאָמֹר[o]	pref. id.)(id. inf. absolute . .	אמר
הָאֹמְרָה	pref. הָ for הַ·)(id. part. act., f. of אֹמֵר m.	אמר
הָאֹמְרוֹת[p]	pref. id.)(id. pl. d. 10, or from אֹמֶרֶת d. 13a.	אמר
הָאֱמֹרִי	וְ׳ pref. id.)(gent. noun masc. . .	אמר
הָאֹמְרִים	pref. id.)(Kal part. m. pl. of אֹמֵר dec. 7b.	אמר
הֶאֱמַרְתָּ[q]	Hiph. pret. 2 pers. sing. masc. . .	אמר
הָאֱמֶת / הַאֱמֶת[r]	וְ׳ pref. הָ for הַ· / pref. הַ interr. for הֲ } noun f. s. (suff. אֲמִתּוֹ } § 37. No. 3) d. 13a.	אמן
הַאֱנוֹשׁ[s]	pref. id.)(noun masc. s. (comp. אִישׁ § 45)	אנש
הֵאָנַח[t]	Niph. inf. constr.	אנח
הַאֲנִי[u]	pref. הַ interr. for הֲ)(pron. pers., 1 p. sing.	אני
הָאֳנִיָּה[x]	וְ pref. הָ art. for הַ·)(noun fem. sing. d. 10.	אנה
הֶאָנֹכִי	pref. הֶ interr. for הֲ, הַ)(pron. pers. 1 p. s.	אנך
הָאֲנָפָה[y]	וְ״[z] pref. הָ for הַ·)(noun fem. sing. .	אנף
הֵאָנֵק[a]	Niph. inf. constr. . . .	אנק
הָאֲנָקָה[b]	וְ pref. הָ for הַ·)(noun fem. sing. dec. 11c.	אנק
הָאֲנָשִׁים	וְ׳ n. m. pl., as if from אֱנָשׁ dec. 6, see אֱנוֹשׁ	אנש
הָאֵסוּר[ii]	pref. הָ for הַ·)(noun masc. sing. dec. 3b. .	אסר
הָאֲסוּרִים[c]	pref. id.)(Kh. אֲסוּרִים Kal part. p. pl. of אָסוּר d. 3a, K. אֲסִירִים (q. v.) . .	אסר
הָאָסִיף[d]	pref. id.)(noun masc. sing. . .	אסף
הָאֲסִירִים[e]	pref. id.)(Kh. אֲסִירִים noun m., pl. of אָסִיר dec. 3a, K. אֲסוּרִים (q. v.) . .	אסר
הָאָסִף[f]	defect. for הָאָסִיף (q. v.) . .	אסף
הָאֹסֵף[g]	pref. הָ for הַ·)(Kal part. act. s. m. dec. 7b.	אסף
הֵאָסֵף[h]	וְ״ Niph. inf. constr., or imp. sing. masc.	אסף
הֵאָסֹף[i]	id. inf. absolute . . .	אסף
הֵאָסְפוּ	id. imp. pl. masc. . . .	אסף
הֵאָסְפִי[k]	id. imp. sing. fem. . . .	אסף
הָאֲסֻפִּים[l]	pref. הָ for הַ·)(noun m., pl. of [אָסֹף] d. 8c. (§ 37. No. 3) . . .	אסף
הָאסַפְסֻף[m]	וְ pref. id., for הָאֲסַפְסֻף)(noun masc. sing.	אסף
הֵאָסְרוּ[n]	Niph. imp. pl. masc. . . .	אסר
הַאֶעֱלֶה	pref. הַ interr. for הֲ)(Kal fut. 1 pers. sing.	עלה
הָאַף[o] הָאָף	} pref. הָ for הַ·)(n. m. s. d. 8d. (§ 37. No. 3)	אנף
הַאַף	pref. הַ interr. for הֲ)(conj. . .	אף
הָאֵפֶר	pref. הָ for הַ·)(noun masc. sing. .	אפר
הָאֵפָה	pref. id.)(noun masc. sing. d. 10, for אֵיפָה	איף
הָאֹפֶה[p]	וְ pref. id.)(Kal part. act. masc. sing. d. 9a.	אפה
הָאֵפוֹד	pref. id.)(noun masc. sing. . .	אפד

[a] Ex. 29. 22. [b] Zec. 11. 17 etc. [c] Is. 2. 18, & 19. 3. [d] Le. 19. 4. [e] 2 Ch. 29. 22. [f] Eze. 40. 49. [g] 1 Ki. 10. 12. [h] 1 Ki. 17. 20. [i] 1 Sa. 17. 18. [k] Is. 30. 24. [l] Nu. 5. 23. [m] De. 22. 6, 7. [n] De. 22. 6. [o] Ex. 26. 13. [p] 2 Sa. 6. 22. [q] Ge. 31. 33. [r] Je. 52. 15. [s] Je. 7. 28. [t] Is. 11. 5. [u] Mi. 2. 7. [x] Ps. 117. 1. [y] 2 Ch. 20. 20, 20. [z] Ex. 4. 8. [a] Is. 17. 9. [b] De. 26. 18. [c] Ne. 3. 34. [d] Nu. 11. 12. [e] Ge. 15. 6. [f] 2 Ki. 18. 16. [g] La. 4. 5. [h] 2 Ki. 10. 1. [i] 2 Ki. 10. 5. [k] Ps. 119. 66. [l] Zec. 6. 7. [m] Job 34. 18. [n] Job 34. 31. [o] Eze. 28. 9. [p] Am. 4. 1. [q] De. 26. 17. [r] Ge. 42. 16. [s] Job 4. 17. [t] Eze. 21. 11. [u] Is. 66. 9. [x] Jon. 1. 4. [y] Le. 11. 19. [z] De. 14. 18. [a] Eze. 24. 17. [b] Lev. 11. 30. [c] Ge. 39. 22. [d] Ex. 34. 22. [e] Ju. 16. 21, 25. [f] Ex. 23. 16. [g] Nu. 19. 10. [h] De. 32. 50. [i] 2 Sa. 17. 11. [ii] Je. 37. 15. [k] Je. 47. 6. [l] 1 Ch. 26. 15. [m] Nu. 11. 4. [n] Ge. 42. 16. [o] Is. 3. 21. [p] Ge. 40. 1, 5.

הָאֹפִים pref. id.)(Kal part. act. m., pl. of אֹפֶה d. 9a. אפה

הַאֶפֶס[a] pref. הַ interr. for הֲ)(prop. subst. used adverbially . . . . . אפס

הֶאָפֵס[b] pref. הֶ id. for הֲ, הַ)(Kal pret. 3 pers. s. m. אפס

הָאֲפֵר[c] pref. הָ for ·הַ)(noun masc. sing . . אפר

הָאֵפֶר pref. id.)(noun masc. sing. . . . אפר

הָאֶפְרֹחִים[d] pref. id.)(noun m., pl. of [אֶפְרוֹחַ] d. 1b. פרח

הָאֶפְרָתִי pref. id. (interr.))(gent. noun masc. . אפר

הָאֵצֶל pref. id.)(pr. name, see בֵּית הָאֵצֶל . . בית

הָאֹצָרוֹת pref. id.)(noun masc. with pl. fem. term., abs. from אוֹצָר dec. 2b. . . אצר

הָאֹצְרִים[e] pref. id.)(Kal part. act. m., pl. of [אֹצֵר] d. 7b. אצר

הַאֲקַדְּמֶנּוּ[f] pref. הַ interr. for הֲ)(Piel fut. 1 pers. sing., suff. 3 pers. sing. masc. . . . קדם

הָאֵר וְ׳ Hiph. imp. sing. masc. . . . אור

הָאֲרִאֵיל[g] וְ pref. הָ for ·הַ)(K. אֲרִיאֵל noun m. sing. ארה

הָאַרְאֵלִי pref. id.)(pr. name masc. . . . ארה

הָאֹרֵב וְ׳ prf. id.)(Kal part. act. sing. masc. dec. 7b. ארב

הָאַרְבֶּה pref. id.)(noun masc. sing. . . . רבה

הָאַרְבִּי pref. id.)(gent. noun from אֲרָב . . ארב

הָאֹרְבִים[h] pref. id.)(Kal part. act. m., pl. of אֹרֵב d. 7b. ארב

הָאַרְבַּע pref. id.)(pr. name, see קִרְיַת הָ׳ under . קרה

הָאַרְבָּעִים pref. id.)(num. card. masc., pl. of אַרְבַּע (§ 31. rem. 5) . . . . . רבע

הָאֹרֶג[i] pref. id.)(noun masc. sing. . . ארג

הָאַרְגֹּב pref. id.)(pr. name of a region . . רגב

הָאַרְגָּז[k] pref. id.)(noun masc. sing. . . רגז

הָאַרְגָּמָן[hh] וְ׳ pref. id.)(noun masc. sing. see אַרְגָּמָן.

הַאֵרֵד[l] pref. הַ interr. for הֲ)(Kal fut. 1 pers. sing. ירד

הָאַרְדִּי pref. הָ for ·הַ)(gent. noun from אַרְדְּ . ארד

הָאַרְוָדִי pref. id.)(gent. noun from אַרְוַד . . רוד

הָאֲרוֹדִי pref. id.)(gent. noun from אֲרוֹד . . ארד

הָאֲרוּרָה[m] pref. הָ for ·הַ)(Kal part. pass., f. of אָרוּר m. ארר

הָאָרֶז / הָאֶרֶז } pref. id.)(noun masc. sing., dec. 6a. (§ 35. rem. 2) . . . . } ארז

הָאֲרָזִים pref. id.)(id. pl., absolute state . . ארז

הָאֹרֵחַ[n] pref. id.)(Kal part. act. sing. masc. . ארח

הַאֹרַח[o] pref. הַ interr. for הֲ)(noun com. sing. d. 6. (§ 35. rem. 5 & 9) . . . . . ארח

הָאֲרִי pref. הָ for ·הַ)(noun masc. sing. dec. 6i. ארה

הָאַרְיֵה[p] וְ׳ pref. id.)(id. with parag. ה; also pr. n. m. ארה

הָאֲרָיוֹת[q] pref. id.)(id. pl., absolute state . ארה

הֶאֱרִיךְ[r] Hiph. pret. 3 pers. sing. masc. . . ארך

הֶאֱרִיכוּ id. pret. 3 pers. pl. . . . . ארך

הַאֲרִיכִי[s] id. imp. sing. fem. . . . . ארך

הָאֹרֶךְ[t] pref. הָ for ·הַ)(noun masc. sing. dec. 6c. ארך

הָאַרְכִּי pref. id.)(gent. noun from אֶרֶךְ . . ארך

הָאֲרַמִּי pref. id.)(gent. noun from אֲרַם . . . רם

הָאֲרַמִּיָּה pref. id.)(id. fem. . . . . רם

הָאָרוֹן pref. id.)(noun com. sing. dec. 3a. . . רה

הַאֲרַכְתָּ[u] וְ Hiph. fut. 2 pers. sing. masc.; acc. shifted by conv. וְ (§ 8. rem. 7, & § 13. rem. 10) רך

הַאֲרַכְתִּי[x] וְ id. pret. 1 pers. sing.; acc. id. . . רך

הַאֲרַכְתֶּם[y] וְ id. pret. 2 pers. pl. masc. . . . רך

הָאָרֹן defect. for הָאָרוֹן (q. v.) . . . רה

הָאַרְנֶבֶת pref. הָ for הַ)(noun fem. sing. . . נב

הָאָרֶץ וְ׳ pref. id.)(noun fem. sing. with the art. for אֶרֶץ (§ 35. rem. 2) dec. 6a. . . רץ

הַאֶרְצֶה[z] pref. הַ interr. for הֲ)(Kal fut. 1 pers. sing. צה

הָאֲרָצוֹת / הָאֲרָצֹת } pref. הָ for ·הַ)(noun fem., pl. of אֶרֶץ (with suff. אַרְצִי) dec. 6a. . } רץ

הָאֲרָרִי pref. id.)(gent. noun for (הָ)הֲרָרִי . הרר

הָאֵשׁ וְ׳ pref. id.)(noun com. sing. dec. 8b. . שׁ

הַאִשׁ[a] pref. הַ interr. for הֲ)(adv. used for the subst verb . . . . . שׁ

הָאֶשְׁבֵּלִי pref. הָ for ·הַ)(patronym. from אַשְׁבֵּל q. v.

הָאַשְׁדּוֹדִי וְ pref. id.)(gent. noun from אַשְׁדּוֹד . שדד

הָאַשְׁדּוֹדִים וְ׳ pref. id.)(id. pl. . . . שדד

הָאֲשֵׁדוֹת[b] וְ pref. הָ for ·הַ)(noun masc. pl. abs. from [אֲשֵׁדָה] dec. 11c. (§ 42. rem. 4) . אשד

הָאִשָּׁה וְ׳ pref. id.)(noun fem. sing. [for אִנְשָׁה], dec. 10. (comp. § 45) . . . אנש

הָאִשֶּׁה[c] pref. id.)(noun masc. sing. dec. 9a. . . אשׁ

הָאַשּׁוּרִי pref. id.)(gent. noun, see אַשּׁוּרִי . . אשר

הַאַשִּׂיגֶנּוּ[d] pref. הַ interr. for הֲ)(Hiph. fut. 1 pers. sing., suff. 3 pers. sing. masc. . . שׂג

הַאֲשִׁימֵם[e] Hiph. imp. sing. masc., suff. 3 pers. pl. m. . אשם

הָאֶשְׁכּוֹל[f] pref. הָ for ·הַ)(noun masc. s., pl. אֶשְׁכֹּלוֹת (§ 36. rem. 6) . . . . שכל

הָאֵשֶׁל pref. id.)(noun masc. sing. . . . אשל

הָאָשָׁם וְ׳ pref. id.)(noun masc. sing. dec. 4c. . אשם

הָאַשְׁמֹרֶת[g] pref. id.)(noun fem. sing. . . . שמר

הָאֶשְׁנָב[h] pref. id.)(noun masc. sing. dec. 8a. . . שנב

הָאַשְׁפּוֹת[i] pref. id.)(written fully for הָאַשְׁפֹּת (q. v.) שפת

הָאַשָּׁפִים[k] pref. id.)(noun masc., pl. of אַשָּׁף dec. 1b. אשף

הָאַשְׁפֹּת pref. id.)(noun m. s. fr. שְׁפֹת with prosth. א שפת

הָאַשְׁקְלוֹנִי pref. id.)(gent. noun from אַשְׁקְלוֹן . שקל

הַאֲשֶׁר[l] pref. הַ interr. for הֲ)(pron. relat. com. . אשר

הָאֲשֵׁרָה[ll] וְ׳ pref. הָ for ·הַ)(noun fem. sing. dec. 10. אשר

הָאֲשֵׁרוֹת pref. id.)(id. pl. . . . . אשר

הָאָשֵׁרִי pref. id.)(gent. noun from אָשֵׁר . אשר

הָאֲשֵׁרִים וְ׳ pref. id.)(id. with pl. fem. term. . אשר

הָאֶשְׁתָּאֻלִי וְ pref. id.)(gent. noun from אֶשְׁתָּאֹל . שאל

הָאֹת pref. id.)(defect. for הָאוֹת (q. v.) . אוה

---

[a] 2 Sa. 9. 3. [b] Ps. 77. 9. [c] 1 Ki. 20. 41. [d] De. 22. 6.
[e] Am. 3. 10. [f] Mi. 6. 6. [g] Eze. 43. 16. [h] Je. 51. 12.
[i] Ju. 16. 14. [k] 1 Sa. 6. 11, 15. [l] 1 Sa. 14. 37. [m] 2 Ki. 9. 34.
[n] Ju. 19. 17. [o] Job 22. 15. [p] 1 Ki. 13. 24, 28. [q] 2 Ki. 17. 25, 26.
[r] Pr. 19. 11. [s] Is. 54. 2. [t] 2 Ch. 3. 3, 4. [u] De. 22. 7.
[x] 1 Ki. 3. 14. [y] De. 5. 33. [z] Mal. 1. 13. [a] Mi. 6. 10.
[b] Jos. 10. 40. [c] Nu. 28. 3. [d] 1 Sa. 30. 8. [e] Ps. 5. 11.
[f] Nu. 13. 24. [g] Ju. 7. 19. [h] Ju. 5. 28. [hh] Ex. 39. 1.
[i] Ne. 3. 14. [k] Da. 1. 20. [l] 2 Ki. 6. 22. [ll] Ju. 6. 28.

הַאַתָּה pref. הַ interr. for הֲ)(pron. pers. 2 p. s. m. — אנת
הָאָתוֹן pref. הָ for הַ·)(noun fem. sing. dec. 3a. — אתן
הָאֹתוֹת pref. id.)(noun com., pl. of אוֹת d. 1. — אוה
הַאֹתִי[a] pref. הַ interr. for הֲ)(as if [אוֹת] with suff. 1 pers. sing. (§ 5) see sign of the acc. — את
הָאֹתִיּוֹת pref. הָ for הַ·)(Kal part. act. fem. pl. [as if from אֹתִי masc. § 24. rem. 4] — אתה
הָאַתִּיקִים[b] וְ pref. id.)(noun masc., pl. of אַתִּיק d. 1 b. — אתק
הַאַתֶּם[c] pref. הָ interr. for הֲ)(pers. pron. 2 m. pl., from אַתָּה sing. — אנת
הַאֶתֵּן[d] pref. הַ id.)(Kal fut. 1 pers. sing. — נתן
הָאֲתֹנוֹת וְ[e] pref. הָ for הַ·)(n. f., pl. of אָתוֹן d. 3a. — אתן
הָאֵתָנִים[f] וְ[g] pref. id.)((prim. adj.) n. m., pl. of אֵיתָן — יתן
הָאֲתֹנֹת[h] defect. for הָאֲתֹנוֹת (q. v.) — אתן
הָאֲתָרִים pref. הָ for הַ·)(pr. name of a place — אתר
הָאֹתֹת וְ[i] defect. for הָאֹתוֹת (q. v.) — אוה
הַב[k] Kal, or (Da. 5. 17) Peal, imp. sing. masc. — יהב
הֵב וְ see וָהֵב under lett. ו
הֲבָא[l] pref. הֲ)(Kal pret. 3 pers. sing. masc. — בוא
הַבָּא וְ pref. הַ)(id. part. sing. masc. dec. 1a. — בוא
הָבֵא וְ[m] Hiph. imp. sing. masc. — בוא
הַבָּאָה pref. הַ)(Kal part. sing. fem. dec. 10. — בוא
הַבָּאוֹת[n] pref. id.)(id. id. pl. — בוא
הֲבֵאוֹתִי[o] וְ Hiph. pret. 1 pers. s. Kh. וַהֲבֵאוֹתִי (comp. parad. קוּם), K. וְהֵבֵאתִי (§ 21. rem. 13) — בוא
הֲבֵאוֹתִיךָ[p] וַ id. id., suff. 2 pers. sing. masc. וַ bef. (-:) for וְ, conv. — בוא
הֲבֵאוֹתָם[q] וַ id. pret. 2 pers. sing. masc., suff. 3 pers. pl. masc.; וַ id. — בוא
הַבָּאִים וְ pref. הַ)(Kal part. pl. m. fr. בָּא d. 1a. — בוא
הִבְאִישׁ Hiph. pret. 3 pers. sing. masc. — באשׁ
הִבְאִישׁ[r] Kh. הִבְאִישׁ q. v., K. הֹבִישׁ (q. v.) — יבשׁ
הִבְאִישׁוּ[s] Hiph. pret. 3 pers. pl. — באשׁ
הַבְּאֵר pref. הַ)(noun fem. s. d. 1, but pl. בְּאֵרוֹת (§ 35. rem. 10) — באר
הַבֹּאר[t] pref. id.)(noun masc. s. d. 1a. [for בֹּאר] — באר
הַבְּאֵרֹת[u] pref. id.)(noun fem., pl. of בְּאֵר dec. 1a, (pl. c. בְּאֵרוֹת § 35. rem. 10) — באר
הַבְּאֵרֹתִי pref. id.)(gent. noun from בְּאֵרוֹת — באר
הַבְּאֵרֹתִים pref. id.)(id. pl. — באר
הַבְאֵשׁ[x] Hiph. inf. absolute — באשׁ
הִבְאַשְׁתֶּם[y] id. pret. 2 pers. pl. masc. — באשׁ
הֲבָאתָ[z] pref. הֲ)(Kal pret. 2 p. s. m. (§ 25. No. 2f) — בוא
הַבָּאֹת[a] defect. for הַבָּאוֹת (q. v.) — בוא
הֵבֵאתָ Hiph. pret. 2 pers. sing. masc. (§ 21. r. 13) — בוא
הֵבֵאתָ וְ id. id. acc. shifted by conv. וְ (§ 8. r. 7) — בוא

הֻבָאת[b] Hoph. pret. 3 pers. fem. sing. (§ 25. No. 2f) — בוא
הֲבֵאתָה[c] id. pret. 2 pers. s. m. (comp. id. & § 8. r. 5) — בוא
הֲבֵאתָהּ[d] וַ Hiph. pret. 2 pers. sing. masc. with suff. 3 p. s. fem. (§ 25. No. 2f); וַ for וְ conv. — בוא
הֲבֵאתוֹ[e] וַ id., suff. 3 pers. sing. masc.; וַ id. — בוא
הֵבֵאתִי id. pret. 1 pers. sing. — בוא
הֵבֵאתִי וְ id. id.; acc. shifted by conv. וְ (§ 8. r. 7) — בוא
הֲבֵאתִיהָ[f] id. id., suff. 3 pers. sing. fem. — בוא
הֲבֵאתִיו[g] id., suff. 3 pers. sing. masc. (see parad. קוּם) — בוא
הֲבֵאתִים[h] וַ, הֲבֵאתִים[i] וַ } id., suff. 3 pers. pl. masc.; וַ for וְ conv. (§ 25. No. 2f) — בוא
הֲבֵאתֶם וְ id. pret. 2 pers. pl. m.; וַ for וְ conv. — בוא
הֲבֵאתָנוּ[k] id. pret. 2 pers. sing. masc., suff. 1 pers. pl. — בוא
הַבֶּגֶד וְ[l] pref. הַ)(noun m. s., (suff. בִּגְדִי) d. 6a. — בגד
הַבְּגָדִים pref. id.)(id. pl., absolute state — בגד
הַבַּד pref. id.)(for בַּד' noun masc. sing. dec. 8d. — בדד
הַבְּדִיל pref. id.)(noun masc. sing. — בדל
הִבְדִּיל Hiph. pret. 3 pers. sing. masc. — בדל
הִבְדִּילָה[m] וְ id. 3 p.s.f.; acc. shifted by conv. וְ (§ 8. r. 7) — בדל
הִבְדִּילוֹ[n] וְ id. 3 pers. sing. masc., suff. 3 pers. s. m. — בדל
הִבְדִּילוּ[o] id. pret. 3 pers. pl. — בדל
הַבַּדִּים pref. הַ)(noun masc., pl. of בַּד dec. 8 d. — בדד
הַבְדֵּל[p] Hiph. inf. absolute — בדל
הִבָּדְלוּ[q] וְ Niph. imp. pl. masc. — בדל
הַבְּדֹלַח pref. הַ)(noun masc. sing. — בדל
הִבְדַּלְתָּ וְ Hiph. pret. 2 pers. s. m.; acc. shifted by conv. וְ (§ 8. rem. 7) — בדל
הִבְדַּלְתִּי[r] id. pret. 1 pers. sing. — בדל
הִבְדַּלְתָּם[s] id. pret. 2 p. sing. masc., suff. 3 pers. pl. masc. — בדל
הִבְדַּלְתֶּם[t] וְ id. pret. 3 pers. pl. masc. — בדל
הַבְּדֶרֶךְ[y] preff. בְּ, and הַ interr. f. הֲ)(noun com. sing. (suff. דַּרְכִּי) dec. 6a. — דרך
הָבָה Kal. imp. sing. masc. with parag. ה — יהב
הַבְהָבַי[z] n. m. pl., suff. 1 p. s. fr. [הַבְהָב] (§ 31. r. 5) — יהב
הִבְהִילֻנִי[aa] Hiph. pret. 3 pers. sing. m., suff. 1 pers. s. — בהל
הַבְּהֵמָה וְ pref. הַ)(noun fem. s. d. 12, constr. בֶּהֱמַת (§ 42. rem. 4 & 5, & § 44. rem. 3) — בהם
הַבֶּהָרֹת[a] pref. id.)(noun f. s. pl. בֶּהָרוֹת (§ 44. r. 5) — בהר
הָבוּ, הָבוּ[b] } Kal. imp. pl. masc. (§ 20. rem. 1) — יהב
הֲבוֹא[c] pref. הֲ)(Kal inf. absolute — בוא
הֲבִוֹאתִים[d] וַ Kh., transpos. for הֲבֵאוֹתִים, Hiph. pret. 1 p. sing., suff. 3 pers. pl. masc.; וַ for וְ conv. — בוא
הַבּוֹגֵד[e] pref. הַ)(Kal part. act. sing. masc. dec. 7b. — בגד
הַבּוֹגְדִים[f] pref. id.)(id. pl., absolute state — בגד

[a] Je. 7. 19. [b] Eze. 41. 16. [c] Ju. 6. 31. [d] Mi. 6. 7. [e] Job 1. 14. [f] 1 Ki. 8. 2. [g] Mi. 6. 2. [h] 1 Sa. 9. 3. [i] De. 7. 19. [k] Pr. 30. 15. [l] 1 Sa. 10. 22. [m] Hag. 1. 6. [n] Is. 41. 22. [o] Je. 25. 13. [p] Eze. 39. 2. [q] Je. 35. 2. [r] Is. 30. 5. [s] Ps. 38. 6. [t] 2 Sa. 23. 20. [u] Ge. 26. 15. [x] 1 Sa. 27. 12. [y] Ex. 5. 21. [z] Job 38. 16, 22. [a] Ge. 41. 35. [b] Ge. 33. 11. [c] Eze. 40. 4. [d] De. 21. 12. [e] 2 Sa. 14. 10. [f] Is. 37. 26. [g] Is. 48. 15. [h] Je. 25. 9. [i] Eze. 23. 22. [k] Ps. 66. 11. [l] Le. 13. 47, 58. [m] Ex. 26. 33. [n] De. 29. 20. [o] Eze. 22. 26. [p] Is. 56. 3. [q] Nu. 16. 21. [r] Ezr. 10. 11. [s] Nu. 8. 14. [t] Le. 20. 24, 25. [u] 1 Ki. 8. 53. [x] Le. 20. 25. [y] Eze. 20. 30. [z] Ho. 8. 13. [a] Le. 13. 23, 28. [aa] Job 23. 16. [b] Ho. 4. 18. [c] Ge. 37. 10. [d] Ne. 1. 9. [e] Is. 21. 2. [f] Ps. 25. 3.

Form	Analysis	Root
הַבּוּז[gg]	pref. הַ ⟩ noun masc. sing.	בוז
הַבּוּזִי	pref. id. ⟩ gent. noun, from בּוּז	בוז
הִבּוֹז[a]	וְ Niph. inf. absolute	בזז
הַבּוֹטֵחַ[b]	[c] וְ׳ pref. הַ ⟩ Kal part. act. sing. m. dec. 7 b.	בטח
הַבּוֹנֶה[d]	pref. id. ⟩ Kal part. act. sing. masc. dec. 7 b.	בנה
הַבּוֹנִים	[e] וְ׳ pref. id. ⟩ id. pl., absolute state	בנה
הִבּוֹק[f]	Niph. inf. absolute, for הִבֹּק	בקק
הַבּוֹר	וְ׳ pref. הַ ⟩ noun masc. sing. dec. 1 a.	באר
הַבַּז[g]	pref. id. ⟩ with dist. acc. for בַּז n. m. s. d. 6 e.	בזז
הַבִּזָּה[h]	pref. id. ⟩ noun fem. sing.	בזז
הַבָּזָק[i]	pref. id. ⟩ noun masc. sing.	בזק
הַבַּחוּרִים	[k] וְ׳ pref. id. ⟩ n. m., pl. of בָּחוּר [for בַּחוּר]	בחר
הַבֹּחֵר[l]	pref. id. ⟩ Kal part. act. masc. sing.	בחר
הַבַּחֲרוּמִי	pref. id. ⟩ gent. noun, from בַּחוּרִים	בחר
הַבֵּט / הַבֶּט־	[m] וְ׳ Hiph. imp. sing. masc. (§ 11. rem. 5)	נבט
הַבֹּטְחָה[n]	pref. הַ ⟩ Kal part. fem. sing. dec. 10.	בטח
הַבִּטָּחוֹן	pref. id. ⟩ noun masc. sing.	בטח
הַבֹּטְחִים	[o] וְ׳ pref. id. ⟩ Kal part. act. m., pl. of בֹּטֵחַ d. 7 b.	בטח
הִבְטַחְתָּ[p]	Hiph. pret. 2 pers. sing. masc.	בטח
הִבַּטְתָּ[q]	וְ Hiph. pret. 2 pers. sing. m.; acc. shifted by conv. וְ (§ 8. rem. 7)	נבט
הִבַּטְתֶּם[r]	id. pret. 2 pers. pl. masc.	נבט
הַבֶּטֶן / הַבָּטֶן	pref. הַ ⟩ noun fem. s. d. 6 a. (suff. בִּטְנִי, but comp. § 35. rem. 2)	בטן
הָבִי[s]	Kal imp. fem. sing.	יהב
הָבֵיא[t]	Hiph. imp. sing. masc. for הָבֵא	בוא
הָבִיא	id. inf. constr.	בוא
הֵבִיא	וְ׳ id. pret. 3 pers. sing. masc.	בוא
הָבִיאָה	[u] וְ׳ id. imp. sing. masc. with parag. ה	בוא
הֵבִיאָה	id. pret. 3 pers. sing. fem.	בוא
הֲבִיאָה[x]	וְ id. id.; acc. shifted by conv. ו (comp. § 8. r. 7)	בוא
הֱבִיאָהּ	וֶ id. pret. 3 pers. sing. masc., suff. 3 pers. sing. fem.; וֶ bef. (-:) conv.	בוא
הָבִיאוּ	וְ׳ id. imp. 2 pers. pl. masc.	בוא
הָבִיאוֹ[y]	Kh. הָבִיאוּ (q. v.), K. הָבִיאִי (q. v.)	בוא
הֱבִיאוֹ	Hiph. pret. 3 pers. s. m., suff. 3 pers. s. m.	בוא
הֵבִיאוּ	וְ׳ id. pret. 3 pers. pl.	בוא
הֱבִיאוּהוּ[z]	id. id., suff. 3 pers. sing. masc.	בוא
הֱבִיאוּךְ[a]	id. id., suff. 2 pers. sing. fem.	בוא
הֱבִיאוּם	וֶ׳ id. id., suff. 3 pers. pl. m.; וֶ bef. (-:) conv.	בוא
הֲבִיאוֹתִיהוּ[b]	וַ id. pret. 1 pers. sing., suff. 3 pers. sing. masc.; וַ bef. (-:) conv.	בוא
הֲבִיאוֹתִיךָ[c]	וַ id. id., suff. 2 pers. sing. masc.; וַ id.	בוא
הֲבִיאוֹתִים	וַ id. id., suff. 3 pers. pl. masc.; וַ id.	בוא
הָבִיאִי	id. imp. sing. fem.	בוא
הֲבִיאֲךָ[d]	id. inf. (הָבִיא), suff. 2 pers. sing. masc. d. 3 a.	בוא
הֱבִיאֲךָ[e]	וֶ׳ id. pret. 3 pers. sing. masc., suff. 2 pers. sing. masc.; וֶ bef. (-:) conv.	בוא
הֲבִיאֲכֶם[f]	id. inf. (הָבִיא) with suff. 2 p. pl. m. d. 3 a.	בוא
הֱבִיאָם[g]	וֶ id. pret. 3 pers. pl., suff. 3 pers. pl. masc.; וֶ before (-:) conv.	בוא
הֱבִיאַנִי	id. pret. 3 pers. sing. masc., suff. 1 pers. sing.	בוא
הֲבִיאֹנוּם[h]	id. pret. 1 pers. pl., suff. 3 pers. pl. masc.	בוא
הֲבֵיאתָ[i]	id. pret. 2 pers. sing. masc. (§ 21. rem. 13)	בוא
הֵבֵאתָ[k]	וְ id. id.; acc. shifted by וְ conv.	בוא
הֲבֵיאתִי[l]	וְ id. pret. 1 pers. sing.; acc. id.	בוא
הֲבִיאֹתִיהָ[m]	id. id., suff. 3 p. sing. fem. (comp. parad. קום)	בוא
הֲבִיאֹתִיו[n]	וַ׳ id. id., suff. 3 p. sing. masc.; וַ bef. (-:) conv.	בוא
הֲבִיאֹתֶם[o]	וַ id. pret. 2 pers. pl. masc.; וַ id.	בוא
הֲבִיאֹתָנוּ[p]	id. pret. 2 pers. sing. masc., suff. 1 pers. pl.	בוא
הֲבִיאֹתַנִי	id. id., suff. 1 pers. sing.	בוא
הַבֵּיט[q]	Hiph. imp. sing. masc. for הַבֵּט	נבט
הַבִּיט[r]	וּ׳ id. inf. construct	נבט
הַבִּיטָה[s]	Kh. הַבֵּיט q. v., K. הַבִּיטָה (q. v.)	נבט
הִבִּיט	[u] וְ׳ Hiph. pret. 3 pers. sing. masc.	נבט
הַבִּיטָה	[x] וְ׳ id. imp. sing. masc. with ה paragogic	נבט
הַבִּיטוּ	וְ׳ id. imp. pl. masc.	נבט
הִבִּיטוּ	וְ id. pret. 3 pers. pl.	נבט
הָבִין	Hiph. inf. construct	בין
הֵבִין	id. pret. 3 pers. sing. masc.	בין
הָבִינוּ	id. imp. pl. masc.	בין
הֵבִינוּ	id. pret. 3 pers. pl.	בין
הֲבִינוֹתֶם[y]	id. pret. 2 pers. pl. masc.	בין
הֲבִינֵנִי	id. imp. sing. masc., suff. 1 pers. sing.	בין
הַבֵּיצִים[z]	pref. הַ ⟩ n. fem. with pl. m. term. [fr. בֵּיצָה]	בוץ
הַבִּירָה	pref. id. ⟩ noun fem. sing.	ביר
הֹבִישׁ	Hiph. pret. 3 pers. sing. masc.	יבשׁ
הֹבִישָׁה	id. pret. 3 pers. sing. fem.	יבשׁ
הֹבִישׁוּ	[a] וְ׳ id. pret. 3 pers. pl., or imp. pl. masc.	יבשׁ
הֱבִישׁוֹתָ[b]	Hiph. pret. 2 pers. sing. masc. (§ 21. rem. 14)	בושׁ
הֱבִישְׁתָה[c]	id. (§ 8. rem. 5)	בושׁ
הַבַּיִת / הַבָּיִת	[d] וְ׳ / וְ׳ pref. הַ ⟩ noun masc. sing. irr. (§ 45)	בית
הַבַּיְתָה / הַבָּיְתָה	pref. id. ⟩ id. with paragogic ה	בית
הַבִּיתָן[e]	pref. id. ⟩ noun masc. sing. dec. 2 b.	בית
הַבָּכָא[f]	pref. id. ⟩ noun masc. sing. dec. 4 a.	בכא
הַבְּכָאִים	pref. id. ⟩ id. pl., absolute state.	בכא
הַבְּכוֹר	pref. id. ⟩ noun masc. sing. dec. 1 a.	בכר
הַבִּכּוּרִים[g]	pref. id. ⟩ noun masc., pl. of [בִּכּוּר] dec. 1 b.	בכר
הַבֹּכִים	pref. id. ⟩ pr. name of a place.	בכה

[a] Is. 24. 3. [b] Ps. 86. 2. [c] Ps. 32. 10. [d] Am. 9. 6. [e] Ne. 4. 12. [f] Is. 24. 3. [g] Nu. 31. 32. [h] 2 Ch. 28. 14. [i] Eze. 1. 14. [k] Am. 8. 13. [l] Zec. 3. 2. [m] Ps. 84. 10. [n] Je. 49. 4. [o] Am. 6. 1. [p] Je. 28. 15. [q] 1 Sa. 2. 32. [r] Is. 22. 11. [s] Ruth 3. 15. [t] 1 Sa. 20. 40. [u] Ge. 27. 4. [x] Le. 15. 29. [y] Is. 16. 3. [z] 2 Ch. 28. 27. [a] Eze. 27. 26. [b] Eze. 17. 20. [c] Eze. 38. 16. [d] 2 Sa. 3. 13. [e] Ju. 18. 3. [f] Le. 23. 14, 15. [g] Le. 17. 5. [h] Nu. 32. 17. [i] Is. 43. 23. [k] 2 Ki. 9. 2. [l] Nu. 14. 31. [m] 2 Ki. 19. 25. [n] Ge. 43. 9. [o] 1 Sa. 16. 17. [p] Nu. 16. 14. [q] Ps. 142. 5. [r] Hab. 2. 15. [s] Hab. 1. 13. [t] La. 5. 1. [u] Nu. 21. 9. [x] La. 1. 11. [y] Is. 40. 21. [z] De. 22. 6. [a] Zec. 10. 5, 11. [b] Ps. 44. 8. [c] Ps. 53. 6. [d] 2 Ch. 34. 8. [e] Est. 7. 7, 8. [f] Ps. 84. 7. [g] Nu. 28. 26. [gg] Ps. 123. 4.

הַבְּכִירָה pref. id.)(adj. fem. sing. from [בָּכִיר] m. . בכר

הַבֶּכֶר pref. id.)(noun masc. sing. dec. 1 a. . בכר

הַבִּכְרָה[a] וְ׳ pref. id.)(noun fem. sing. dec. 10. . בכר

הַבִּכְרוֹת[b] pref. id.)(noun fem., pl. of [בִּכְרָה] dec. 10. בכר

הַבִּכְרִי pref. id.)(gent. noun from בֶּכֶר . בכר

הַבִּכֻּרִים[c] defect. for הַבִּכּוּרִים (q. v.) . . . בכר

הֶבֶל וְ׳ masc. dec. 6. (with suff. הֶבְלִי, pl. c. הַבְלֵי § 35. rem. 4)—I. *breath, vapour, mist,* comp. Ps. 62. 10; Is. 57. 13, הבלא Syr. and Chald. *breath, vapour.* —II. *vanity, something vain, foolish.*—III. *idols.*—IV. adv. *in vain, vainly.*—V. pr. name of the second son of Adam.

הֲבֵל masc. *vanity,* Ec. 1. 2; 12. 8.

הָבַל, fut. יֶהְבַּל, prop. *to become a vapour* (so Sym. on Ps. 62. 11, Μὴ γίνεσθε Ατμὶς) hence *to be* or *become vain, to act vainly, foolishly, sinfully.* Hiph. *to cause to act vainly,* Je. 23. 16.

הָבֶל id. in pause (§ 35. rem. 2) . . . . הבל

הֲבֵל noun masc. sing. . . . . . הבל

הֶבְלוֹ[d] noun masc. sing., suff. 3 pers. sing. masc. from הֶבֶל d. 6. (§ 35. rem. 4) . . הבל

הַבְלֵי id. pl., construct state . . . . הבל

הֶבְלִי[e] id. sing. suff. 1 pers. sing. . . . . הבל

הֲבָלִים[f] וַ׳ id. pl. absolute state; וַ before (ֲ) . הבל

הַבְּלִיַּעַל[g] / הַבְּלִיַּעַל pref. הַ)(noun masc. sing. compd. of בְּלִי & יַעַל see . . . בלה

הֶבְלֶךָ[h] noun masc. sing., suff. 2 pers. sing. masc. [for הֶבְלְךָ] from הֶבֶל (q. v.) . . הבל

הַבַּלְעִי pref. הַ)(gent. noun from בֶּלַע . . בלע

הַבָּמָה pref. id.)(noun fem. sing. dec. 10 (pl. c. בָּמֳתֵי); also pr. name . . . . בום

הַבָּמוֹת וְ׳ pref. id.)(id. pl., absolute state . בום

הַבְּמַחֲנִים preff. בְּ, and הַ interr. for הֲ)(noun masc., pl. of מַחֲנֶה dec. 9a. . . . . חנה

הַבָּמָתָה pref. הַ)(noun fem. sing. with paragogic ה from בָּמָה (q. v.) . . . . . בום

הָבֵן וְ׳[i] Hiph. imp. sing. masc. R. בון, see . בין

הַבֵּן וְ׳[m] pref. הַ / הֲבֵן[n] pref. הֲ } noun masc. sing. irr. (§ 45) בנה

הֲבִנְהָרִים preff. בִּ bef. (ְ), and הֲ)(noun masc., pl. of נָהָר dec. 4. . . . . נהר

הַבָּנוּי[p] pref. הַ)(Kal part. p. sing. masc. dec. 3a. בנה

הַבְּנוּיָה[q] pref. id.)(fem. of the prec. . . . בנה

הַבָּנוֹת pref. id.)(noun fem., pl. of בַּת irr. (§ 45) בנה

[הָבְנִי] masc. pl. הָבְנִים, (Kh. הוֹבְנִים) *ebony,* Eze. 27. 15, from הבן perhaps i. q. אבן *to be hard.*

הַבִּנְיָה[r] וְ pref. הַ)(noun fem. sing. . . . בנה

הַבָּנִים וְ׳ pref. id. / הֲבָנִים[s] pref. הֲ } noun masc. pl. [as if from בָּן dec. 2] see בֵּן (§ 45) . } בנה

הַבֵּנַיִם[t] pref. הַ)(noun masc., du. of [בַּיִן] dec. 6 h. בין

הַבֹּנִים pref. id.)(Kal part. act. masc., pl. of בֹּנֶה dec. 9a. . . . . . בנה

הַבִּנְיָן וְ׳[u] pref. id.)(noun masc. sing. . . בנה

הַבְּסוֹד[x] preff. בְּ, and הַ interr. for הֲ)(n. m. s. dec. 1. יסד

הַבֹּסֶר[y] pref. הַ art.)(noun masc. sing. . . בסר

הַבְּעַד[z] pref. הַ interr. for הֲ)(prep., with suff. בַּעֲדִי (§ 35. rem. 10) . . . . . בעד

הַבַּעַל / הַבָּעַל } pref. הַ art.)(noun masc. sing. dec. 6d, also pr. name . . . } בעל

הַבְּעָלִים pref. id.)(id. pl., absolute state, pr. name . בעל

הִבְעַרְתִּי[a] וְ Hiph. pret. 1 pers. sing.; acc. shifted by conv. וְ (§ 8. rem. 7) . . . . בער

הַבְּעֵרָה[b] pref. הַ)(noun fem. sing. . . . בער

הַבֵּץ[c] pref. id.)(noun masc. sing. . . . בוץ

הַבָּצוּר[d] pref. id.)(Kh. בָּצוּר part. pass., K. בָּצִיר adj. masc. dec. 3a. . . . . . בצר

הַבְּצָלִים[e] pref. id.)(noun masc., pl. of [בָּצָל] dec. 6. בצל

הַבֶּצַע[f] pref. id.)(noun masc. sing. for בֶּצַע (q. v.) בצע

הַבָּצֵק[g] pref. id.)(noun masc. sing. dec. 5a. . בצק

הַבַּצָּרוֹת[h] pref. id.)(noun fem., pl. of בַּצָּרָה dec. 10. בצר

הַבְּצֻרוֹת וְ׳[i] pref. id.)(Kal part. p. fem., pl. of בְּצוּרָה d. 10. בצר

הַבַּקְבֻּק[k] pref. id.)(noun masc. sing. . . . בקק

הָבְקְעָה[l] Hoph. pret. 3 pers. sing. fem. . . . בקע

הַבִּקְעָה pref. הַ)(noun fem. sing. dec. 12b. . בקע

הַבָּקָר וְ׳ pref. id.)(noun com. sing. dec. 4a. . בקר

הַבֹּקֶר וְ׳[qq] pref. id.)(noun masc. sing., d. 6c. (§ 35. r. 9) בקר

[הָבַר] prop. *to cut, divide,* so in the Arab., whence הֹבְרֵי שָׁמַיִם *they who divide the heavens, astrologers,* Is. 47. 13.

הַבָּר[m] pref. הַ)(noun masc. sing. . . . ברר

הִבָּֽרַאֲךָ[n] Niph. inf. [הִבָּרֵא] suff. 2 pers. sing. m. d. 7 b. ברא

הִבָּֽרַאֲךְ[o] id. id. & verbal suff. (§ 3. r. 2) 2 p. s. in pause ברא

הִבָּֽרְאָם[p] id. with suff. 3 pers. pl. masc. . . ברא

הֲבְרָב־[q] preff. בְּ, & הֲ interr.)(for רֹב n. m. s. d. 8 c. רבב

הַבָּרָד וְ׳[r] pref. הַ)(noun masc. sing. . . ברד

הַבְּרֻדִּים[s] וְ pref. id.)(adj. masc., pl. of [בָּרֹד] dec. 8 c. (§ 37. Nos. 2 & 3) . . . . ברד

הַבֹּרָה[t] pref. id.)(noun masc. sing. with parag. ה from בּוֹר dec. 1a. . . . . באר

הָבֵרוּ[u] Hiph. imp. masc. pl. [for הָבֵרּוּ] . . ברר

[a] 1 Ch. 5. 2. [b] Je. 24. 2. [c] Le. 23. 20. [d] Ec. 6. 12. [e] Ec. 7. 15. [f] Ec. 5. 6. [g] 2 Sa. 16. 7. [h] Ec. 9. 9, 9. [i] Nu. 13. 19. [k] 1 Sa. 9. 13. [l] Da. 9. 23. [m] Eze. 18. 19. [n] Je. 31. 20. [o] Hab. 3. 8. [p] Ju. 6. 28. [q] Ps. 122. 3. [r] Eze. 41. 13. [s] Je. 49. 1. [t] 1 Sa. 17. 4, 23. [u] Eze. 41. 12. [x] Job 15. 8. [y] Je. 31. 30. [z] Job 22. 13. [a] Na. 2. 14. [b] Ex. 22. 5. [c] 1 Ch. 4. 21. [d] Zec. 11. 2. [e] Nu. 11. 5. [f] 1 Sa. 8. 3. [g] Ex. 12. 39, etc. [h] Je. 14. 1. [i] De. 28. 52. [k] Je. 19. 10. [l] Je. 39. 2. [m] Je. 23. 28. [n] Eze. 28. 13. [o] Eze. 28. 15. [p] Ge. 5. 2. [q] Job 23. 6. [qq] Da. 8. 26. [r] Ex. 9. 29, 33, 34. [s] Zec. 6. 6. [t] Ge. 37. 24. [u] Je. 51. 11.

הִבָּרוּ[a] Niph. imp. pl. masc. [for הִבָּרְרוּ] . . ברר
הֹבְרֵו[b] Kh. הָבְרוּ Kal pret., K. הֹבְרֵי part. act. pl. constr. הבר
הַבְּרוּרִים pref. הַ (Kal part. p. m., pl. of בָּרוּר d. 3a. ברר
הַבְּרֹשִׁים[c] ן pref. id. (noun masc., pl. of בְּרוֹשׁ dec. 1a. ברש
הַבֹּרוֹת[d] pref. id. (noun masc. with pl. fem. term. from בּוֹר dec. 1a. . . . . . . באר
הַבַּרְזֶל [e] ן' pref. id. (noun masc. sing. . . ברזל
הַבַּרְחֻמִי pref. id. (gent. noun by transp. for בַּחֲרֻמִי from בַּחוּרִים . . . . . . בחר
הַבְּרִיאָה pref. id. (adj. fem. sing. d. 10, from בָּרִיא m. ברא
הַבְּרִיאֹות[f] [g] ן' pref. id. (id. pl. . . . . . ברא
הַבִּרְיָה pref. id. (noun fem. sing. . . . ברה
הַבְּרִיחַ [h] ן' pref. id. (noun masc. sing. dec. 1a. . ברח
הִבְרִיחוּ[i] Hiph. pret. 3 pers. pl. masc. . . . ברח
הַבְּרִיחִם pref. הַ (noun masc., pl. of בְּרִיחַ dec. 1a. ברח
הַבֵּרִים pref. id. (gent. noun pl. from בְּאֵר or בְּאֵרוֹת באר
הַבְּרִיעִי pref. id. (patronym. of בְּרִיעָה q. v. ברה
הַבְּרִית [k] ן' pref. id. (noun fem. sing. dec. 1a. ברה
הַבְרָכָה[l] pref. הֲ interr. f. הֲ } noun fem. sing. dec. 11c. ברך
הַבְּרָכָה pref. הַ art. }
הַבְּרֵכָה pref. id. (noun fem. sing. dec. 10. . . ברך
הַבְּרָכוֹת[m] pref. id. (noun fem., pl. of בְּרָכָה dec. 11c. ברך
הַבִּרְכַּיִם pref. id. (noun fem. du. of בֶּרֶךְ dec. 6a. ברך
הַבַּרְקֳנִים[n] pref. id. (noun masc. pl. [of בַּרְקָן] . . ברק
הַבֵּרֹתִי pref. id. (gent. noun from בְּאֵרוֹת . . באר
הֹבִישׁוּ[o] Hiph. pret. 3 pers. pl. for הוֹבִישׁוּ . יבש
הַבְּשׂוֹר pref. הַ (pr. name of a river . . . בשׂר
הִבְשִׁילוּ[p] Hiph. pret. 3 pers. pl. . . . בשל
הַבֹּשֶׂם pref. הַ (noun masc. sing. . . . . בשׂם
הַבְּשָׂמִים [q] ן' pref. id. (noun masc., pl. of בֶּשֶׂם dec. 6. בשׂם
הַבָּשָׁן ן' pref. id. (pr. name of a region . . בשן
הַבָּשָׂר ן' pref. id. (noun masc. sing. dec. 4a. . בשׂר
הַבֹּשֶׁת[r] ן pref. id. (noun fem. sing. dec. 13c. . בוש
הַבַּת[s] } pref. id. (noun masc. sing. dec. 8d. בתת
הַבַּת [t] ן' }
הַבַּת pref. id. } noun fem. sing. irr. (§ 45) בנה
הֲבַת[u] pref. הֲ }
הַבְּתוּלָה pref. הַ (noun fem. sing. dec. 10. . . בתל
הַבְּתוּלוֹת } pref. id. (id. pl. . . . . . . בתל
הַבְּתוּלֹת }
הַבַּתּוֹת[x] pref. id. (noun fem., pl. of [בַּתָּה] dec. 10. בתת
הַבָּתִּים pref. id. (noun masc. pl. irr. of בַּיִת (§ 45) בית
הַבַּתִּים[y] pref. id. (noun masc., pl. of בַּת dec. 8d. . בתת
הַבִּתְרוֹן pref. id. (pr. name of a place . . . בתר
הֵגֵא pr. name masc. Est. 2. 3, called הֵגַי ver. 8, 15.
הַגֵּאָיוֹת pref. הַ (noun com. pl. of גַּיְא, גַּי irr. (§ 45) גיא

הַגֹּאֵל[z] pref. id. (Kal part. act. masc. sing. dec. 7b. גאל
הַגְּאֻלָּה pref. id. (noun fem. sing. dec. 10. . . גאל
הַגָּבֹהַ[a] ן pref. id. (adj. masc. sing. dec. 3a. . גבה
הַגֹּבַהּ[b] ן pref. id. (noun m. sing. d. 6c. (§ 35. r. 5) גבה
הַגְבֵּהַ Hiph. inf. abs. or imp. sing. masc. . . גבה
הַגְּבֹהָה[c] ן pref. הַ (adj. fem. sing. d. 10, from גָּבֹהַּ m. גבה
הַגְּבֹהוֹת pref. id. (id. pl. . . . . . גבה
הַגְּבֹהִים [d] ן' pref. id. (adj. masc., pl. of גָּבֹהַּ dec. 3a. גבה
הַגְּבֹהֹת[e] pref. id. (id. pl. fem. . . . . גבה
הִגְבַּהְתִּי[f] Hiph. pret. 1 pers. sing. . . . גבה
הַגְּבֻלֹ[g] Kh. הַגְּבוּל q. v., K. הַגָּדוֹל (q. v.) . גבל
הַגְּבוּל [h] ן' pref. הַ (noun masc. sing. dec. 1a. . גבל
הַגִּבּוֹר pref. id. ((prim. adj.) noun m. sing. dec. 1b. גבר
הַגְּבוּרָה[i] ן pref. id. (noun fem. sing. dec. 10. . גבר
הַגִּבֹּרִים ן' pref. id. (noun masc., pl. of גִּבּוֹר dec. 1b. גבר
הַגֵּבִים pref. id. (pr. name of a place . . גבב
הַגָּבִיעַ pref. id. (noun masc. sing. dec. 3a. . . גבע
הִגְבִּיר[k] ן Hiph. pret. 3 pers. masc. sing. . . גבר
הַגְּבִירָה [l] ן' pref. הַ (noun fem. sing. from גְּבִיר m. גבר
הַגְבֵּל[m] Hiph. imp. sing. masc. . . . . . גבל
הַגְּבֻל defect. for הַגְּבוּל (q. v.) . . . גבל
הַגִּבְלִי pref. הַ (gent. n. from גְּבַל (comp. § 35. r. 10) גבל
הַגִּבְלִים ן pref. id. (id. pl. . . . . . גבל
הִגְבַּלְתָּ[n] ן Hiph. pret. 2 pers. sing. masc.; acc. shifted by conv. ן (§ 8. rem. 7) . . גבל
הַגִּבְעָה pref. הַ (n. fem. sing. d. 12b; also pr. name גבע
הַגִּבְעוֹנִי pref. id. (gent. noun from גִּבְעוֹן . . גבע
הַגְּבָעוֹת ן' pref. id. (noun fem., pl. of גִּבְעָה d. 12b. גבע
הַגִּבְעֹנִי pref. id. (gent. noun from גִּבְעוֹן . . גבע
הַגִּבְעֹנִים ן' pref. id. (id. pl. . . . . גבע
הַגִּבְעָתָה pref. id. (pr. name (גִּבְעָה) with parag. ה גבע
הַגִּבְעָתִי pref. id. (gent. noun from גִּבְעָה . . גבע
הַגֶּבֶר pref. id. (noun masc. sing. dec. 6. . . גבר
הַגִּבֹּר[o] pref. id. (noun masc. sing. dec. 1b. . גבר
הַגִּבֹּרִים [p] ן' pref. id. (id. pl., absolute state . . גבר
הַגְּבָרִים pref. id. (noun masc. pl. of גֶּבֶר dec. 6. גבר

הָגַג Root not used; Syr. *to imagine*, cogn. הָגָה.
הָגִיג masc. dec. 3a.—I. *musing, meditati*[on] Ps. 5. 2.—II. *meditation, prayer*, 39. 4.

הַגֻּנָּה[q] Kh. הַגַּג q. v., K. הַגָּנָּה (q. v.) . . .
הַגַּג pref. הַ (noun masc. sing. dec. 8a. . .
הַגָּגָה pref. id. (id. with parag. ה . . .
הַגַּגּוֹת[r] pref. id. (id. with pl. fem. term. . .
הַגַּד pref. id. (pr. name of a river . . גד
הַגֵּד ן' Hiph. inf. or imp. sing. masc. . . גד

[a] Is. 52. 11. [b] Is. 47. 13. [c] Na. 2. 4. [d] Ge. 37. 20. [e] Jos. 6. 24. [f] Ge. 41. 7, 20. [g] Ge. 41. 4. [h] Ex. 26. 28. [i] 1 Ch. 8. 13. [k] 2 Ki. 17. 38. [l] Ge. 27. 38. [m] De. 28. 2. [n] Ju. 8. 7, 16. [o] Je. 8. 9. [p] Ge. 40. 10. [q] 1 Ch. 9. 29. [r] Je. 8. 24. [s] Eze. 45. 11. [t] Eze. 45. 11. [u] Ge. 17. 17. [x] Is. 7. 19. [y] Eze. 45. 14, 14. [z] Ruth 4. 6, 8. [a] Eze. 21. 31. [b] 2 Ch. 3. 4. [c] Da. 8. 3. [d] Is. 10. 33. [e] De. 28. 52. [f] Eze. 17. 24. [g] Jos. 15. 47. [h] Eze. 43. 17. [i] 1 Ch. 29. 11. [k] Da. 9. 27. [l] Je. 29. 2. [m] Ex. 19. 23. [n] Ex. 19. 12. [o] De. 10. 17. [p] 1 Ch. 29. 24. [q] 1 Sa. 9. 26. [r] Zep. 1. 5.

הַגֵּד־ [a] וְ id. imp. sing. masc. (§ 11. rem. 5) . נגד
הֻגַּד [b] וְ Hoph. pret. 3 pers. sing. masc. . נגד
הֻגֵּד id. inf. abs. . . . . . . נגד
הַגִּדְגָּד pr. name in compos. חֹר הַגִּדְגָּד . . גדד
הַגֻּדְגֹּדָה pref. הַ (pr. name of a place . . גדד
הַגִּדוּ [c] Hiph. imp. pl. m. for הַגִּידוּ (comp. § 11. r. 5) נגד
הַגְּדוּד pref. הַ (noun masc. sing. dec. 1 a. . גדד
הַגָּדוֹל וְ pref. id. (adj. masc. sing. dec. 3 a. . גדל
הַגְּדוֹלָה [d] וְ pref. id. (id. fem., dec. 10. . . גדל
הַגְּדוּלָּה pref. id. (noun fem. sing. dec. 10. . . גדל
הַגְּדוֹלִים pref. id. (adj. masc., pl. of גָּדוֹל dec. 3 a; also pr. name masc. . . . . . גדל
הַגְּדוֹר pref. id. (pr. name of a place . . גדר
הַגָּדִי וְ pref. id. (patronym. of גָּד . . גדד
הַגְּדִי pref. id. (noun masc. sing. dec. 6 i. . גדה
הִגְדִּיל [e] וְ Hiph. pret. 3 pers. sing. masc. . גדל
הִגְדִּילוּ [f] id. pret. 3 pers. pl. . . . . גדל
הַגָּדֹל defect. for הַגָּדוֹל (q. v.) . . . גדל
הִגְדִּל [g] defect. for הִגְדִּיל (q. v.) . . . גדל
הַגְּדֹלָה pref. הַ (adj. fem. sing. dec. 10, from גָּדוֹל m. גדל
הַגְּדֻלָּה [h] pref. id. (noun fem. sing. dec. 10. . גדל
הַגְּדֹלוֹת pref. id. (adj. fem., pl. of גְּדוֹלָה dec. 10, from גָּדוֹל masc. . . . . . גדל
הַגְּדֻלּוֹת [i] pref. id. (noun fem., pl. גְּדֻלָּה dec. 10. . גדל
הַגְּדֹלִים pref. id. (adj. masc., pl. of גָּדוֹל dec. 3 a. . גדל
הַגְּדֹלֹת pref. id. (id. fem. pl. of גְּדֹלָה dec. 10. . גדל
הִגְדַּלְתָּ Hiph. pret. 2 pers. sing. masc. . . גדל
הִגְדַּלְתִּי id. pret. 1 pers. sing. . . . . גדל
הַגְּדֵרָה וְ prf. הַ (pr. name of a place . . גדר
הַגְּדֵרוֹת pref. id. (pr. name of a place . . גדר
הַגְּדֵרִי pref. id. (gent. noun from בֵּית־גָּדֵר q. v. . בית
הַגְּדֶרֶת [k] pref. id. (noun fem. sing. . . . גדר
הַגְּדֵרָתִי pref. id. (gent. noun from גְּדֵרָה . . גדר
הִגַּדְתָּ Hiph. pret. 2 pers. sing. masc. . . נגד
הִגַּדְתָּ וְ id. id.; acc. shifted by conv. וְ (§ 8. r. 7) נגד
הִגַּדְתָּה [l] id. id. written fully (§ 8. rem. 5) . . נגד
הִגַּדְתִּי וְ id. pret. 1 pers. sing. . . . נגד
הִגַּדְתֶּם [oo] וְ id. pret. 2 pers. pl. masc. . . . נגד

[הָגָה] fut. יֶהְגֶּה—I. *to murmur,* applied to the *cooing* of doves, the *lamenting* or *sighing* of men, the *growling* of the lion over his prey.—II. poet. *to utter, speak.*—III. *to meditate.* Po. *to utter, speak,* Is. 59. 13. Hiph. *to mutter,* spoken of enchanters, Is. 8. 19.

הֶגֶה masc. I. *a muttering* of thunder, Job 37. 2.—II. *murmuring, sighing,* Eze. 2. 10.—III. *meditation, thought,* Ps. 90. 9; Prof. Lee, *murmur.*

הָגוּת fem. (construct state) *meditation, thought,* Ps. 49. 4.

הִגָּיוֹן masc. dec. 3 c. (constr. הֶגְיוֹן § 32. rem. 3) —I. *murmur* or *sound* of the harp.—II. *meditation, thought.*

II. [m] הָגָה *to separate, to take away.*

הָגֹה [n] Kal inf. abs. . . . . . . הגה
הֶגֶה [o] [p] וְ, [q] וְ, noun masc. sing. (for וְ see lett. ו הגה
הֹגָה [r] Hiph. pret. 3 pers. sing. masc. . . יגה
הָגוֹ [s] Kal inf. abs. [for הָגֹה § 24. rem. 2] . הגה
הֹגוֹ [t] וְ Poel inf. abs. [for הֹגֵה comp. § 24. r. 2] הגה
הַגּוֹאֵל pref. הַ (Kal part. act. masc. dec. 7 b. . גאל
הַגּוֹי [u] וְ pref. הַ } noun masc. sing. dec. 1 a. . גוה
הַגּוֹי [w] pref. הַ
הַגּוֹיִם [y] וְ pref. הַ (id. pl. abs. [for גּוֹיִים comp. § 3. r. 1] גוה
הַגּוֹלָה pref. id. (noun fem. sing. . . . גלה
הַגּוּנִי pref. id. (gent. noun [for גּוּנִיִּי] from גּוּנִי . גון
הַגּוֹרָל pref. id. (noun masc. sing. dec. 2 b. . גרל
הַגִּזְבָּר [z] pref. id. (noun masc. sing. . . . גזבר
הָגוּת [a] וְ noun fem. sing. . . . . . הגה
הַגִּזָּה [b] pref. הַ (noun fem. sing. dec. 10. . . גזז
הַגִּזוֹנִי pref. id. (gent. noun from גִּזָּה . . גזה
הַגְּזֵלָה [ss] pref. id. (noun fem. sing. dec. 10. . גזל
הַגָּזָם [c] וְ pref. id., (noun masc. sing. . . . גזם
הַגְּזֵרָה [d] וְ pref. id. (noun fem. sing. (no pl.) . גזר
הַגְּזָרִים [e] pref. id. (noun masc., pl. of [גֶּזֶר] dec. 6. גזר
הַגֶּחָלִים [f] pref. id. (n. f., pl. of גַּחֶלֶת, d. 13 a. (suff. גַּחַלְתִּי) גחל
הֵגֶי } pr. name m. Est. 2. 8, 15, called הֵגָא v. 3.
הֵגַי
הַגַּיְ [g] וְ } pref. הַ (noun com. sing. irr. (§ 45) . גיא
הַגַּיְא [h]
הַגַּיְא וְ
הַגֵּאָיוֹת [k] pref. id. (id. pl. abs. Kh. הַגֵּאָיוֹת, K. הַגֵּאָיוֹת (q. v.) . . . . . . גיא
הֲגִיגִי [l] noun m. s., suff. 1 p. s. from [הָגִיג] d. 3 a. הגג
הַגֵּיד [m] Hiph. inf. absolute . . . . נגד
הִגִּיד וְ id. pret. 3 pers. sing. masc. . . נגד
הַגִּידָה id. imp. sing. masc. with parag. ה . , נגד
הִגִּידָה [n] וְ id. pret. 3 pers. sing. fem. . . נגד
הִגִּידָהּ [o] id. pret. 3 pers. sing. masc., suff. 3 pers. s. f. נגד
הַגִּידוּ [p] וְ id. imp. pl. masc. . . . . . נגד
הִגִּידוּ וְ id. pret. 3 pers. pl. . . . . נגד
הַגִּידִי id. imp. sing. fem. . . . . . נגד
הִגָּיוֹן noun masc. sing. dec. 3 c. (§ 32. rem. 3) הגה

[a] Jos. 7. 19. [b] De. 17. 4. [c] Ps. 9. 12. [d] Is. 27. 1. [e] Da. 8. 4. [f] Ps. 38. 17. [g] 1 Sa. 12. 24. [h] 1 Ch. 29. 11. [i] 1 Ch. 17. 19. [k] Eze. 42. 12. [l] Ju. 14. 16. [m] Is. 27. 8. [n] Is. 59. 11. [o] Ps. 90. 9. [oo] Ge. 45. 13. [p] Job 37. 2. [q] Eze. 2. 10. [r] 2 Sa. 20. 13. [s] Pr. 25. 4, 5. [ss] Le. 5. 23. [t] Is. 59. 13. [u] Je. 27. 11. [w] Ge. 20. 4. [y] Is. 60. 12. [z] Ezr. 1. 8. [a] Ps. 49. 4. [b] Ju. 6. 37, 38, 38. [c] Joel 2. 25. [d] Eze. 41. 13, 14. [e] Ge. 15. 17. [f] Pr. 6. 28. [g] Jos. 8. 11. [h] 1 Ch. 4. 39. [i] 1 Sa. 17. 3. [k] 2 Ki. 2. 16. [l] Ps. 5. 2. [m] Je. 36. 16. [n] 2 Sa. 17. 17. [o] Is. 45. 21. [p] Je. 31. 10.

הֶגְיוֹן[a]	וְ id. constr. state	הגה
הֶגְיוֹנָם[b]	וְ id. with suff. 3 pers. pl. masc. . .	הגה
הַגִּילֹנִי	pref. הַ) gent. noun from גִּלֹה . .	גלה
הֲגִינָה[c]	adj. fem. sing. from [הָגִין] masc. . .	הגן
הִגִּיעַ	Hiph. pret. 3 pers. sing. masc. . .	נגע
הִגִּיעוּ	[d] וְ' id. pret. 3 pers. pl.	נגע
הַגִּיעֵנוּ[e]	id. inf. (הַגִּיעַ) with suff. 1 pers. pl. dec. 1b.	נגע
הַגֵּירִים[f]	pref. הַ) noun masc., pl. of [גֵּיר] d. 1a.	גור
הַגִּישָׁה	Hiph. imp. sing. masc. with parag. ה .	נגש
הִגִּישָׁהּ[g]	וְ id. pret. 3 pers. sing. m., suff. 3 pers. s. f.	נגש
הַגִּישׁוּ	[h] וְ' id. imp. pl. masc.	נגש
הִגִּישׁוּ[i]	id. pret. 3 pers. pl.	נגש
הִגִּישׁוֹ[k]	וְ id. pret. 3 pers. s. m., suff. 3 pers. s. m.	נגש
הָגִיתָ[l]	וְ Kal pret. 2 pers. sing. masc. . . .	הגה
הָגִיתִי[m]	[n] וְ' id. pret. 1 pers. sing. . . .	הגה
הַגֵּל[o] / הַגָּל	pref. הַ) noun masc. sing. dec. 8d. .	גלל
הַגְּלָבִים[p]	pref. id.) n. m. pl. [of גַּלָּב d. 1b. § 30. r. 1]	גלב
הַגִּלְבֹּעַ	pref. id.) pr. n. of a region, see גִּלְבֹּעַ	
הַגַּלְגַּל	pref. id.) noun masc. dec. 8e. . .	גלל
הַגִּלְגָּל	וְ' pref. id.) pr. n. of a place (and in compos. with בֵּית q. v.)	גלל
הַגִּלְגָּלָה	pref. id.) id. with parag. ה . .	גלל
הַגֻּלְגֹּלֶת[q]	pref. id.) noun fem. sing. dec. 13c. . .	גלל
הָגְלָה[r]	Hoph. pret. 3 pers. sing. masc. . . .	גלה
הַגֹּלָה	pref. הַ) noun fem. sing.	גלה
הַגֻּלָּה[s]	pref. id.) noun fem. sing. dec. 10. . .	גלל
הֶגְלָה / וְ' [t] הִגְלָה	Kal pret. 3 pers. sing. masc. (§ 11. rem. 1)	גלה
הָגְלוּ	Hoph. pret. 3 pers. pl.	גלה
הִגָּלוּ[u]	Niph. imp. pl. masc.	גלה
הִגְלוּ[v]	Hiph. pret. 3 pers. pl.	גלה
הַגָּלוּי[y]	pref. הַ) Kal part. p. masc. dec. 3a. .	גלה
הַגִּלּוּלִים	pref. id.) noun masc., pl. of [גִּלּוּל] dec. 1b.	גלל
הַגֻּלּוֹת[z]	וְ pref. id.) noun fem., pl. of גֻּלָּה dec. 10.	גלל
הַגְלוֹת[a]	Hiph. inf. const. dec. 1b.	גלה
הַגְלוֹתָם[b]	id. with suff. 3 pers. pl. masc. . .	גלה
הַגְלִי	Ch. Aph. pret. 3 sing. masc. (§ 47. rem. 4)	גלא
הַגָּלִיל	pref. הַ) pr. name of a region	גלל
הַגָּלִילָה	pref. id.) id. with parag. ה . .	גלל
הַגְּלִילָה[c]	pref. id.) noun fem. sing. dec. 10. . .	גלל
הַגִּלְיֹנִים[d]	pref. id.) noun masc., pl. of גִּלָּיוֹן dec. 3c.	גלה
הִגְלִיתָ[e]	Hiph. pret. 2 pers. sing. m. (§ 24. rem. 14)	גלה
הִגְלֵיתִי[f]	id. pret. 1 pers. sing. . . .	לה
הִגְלִיתֶם[g]	id. pret. 2 pers. pl. masc. (§ 24. rem. 14)	לה
הַגָּלָל[h]	pref. הַ art.) noun masc. dec. 4a.	לל
הַגְּלָלִים	pref. id.) noun masc., pl. of [גָּלוּל] d. 1b.	לל
הִגְלָם[i] / וְ הֶגְלָם[k]	Hiph. pret. 3 pers. s. m., suff. 3 pers. sing. masc. (§ 11. rem. 1) . .	לה
הַגִּלֹנִי	pref. הַ) gent. noun from גִּלֹה . .	לה
הַגִּלְעָד	וְ' pref. id.) pr. name of a region, see גִּלְעָד	
הַגִּלְעָדָה	pref. id.) id. with parag. ה	
הַגִּלְעָדִי	pref. id.) gent. noun from גִּלְעָד q. v.	
הָגְלָת[l] / הָגְלָתָה[m]	Hoph. pret. 3 pers. fem. s. (§ 24. r. 14)	לה
הִגְלֵתִי[n]	וְ Hiph. pret. 1 pers. sing.; acc. shifted by conv. וְ (comp. § 8. rem. 7) .	לה
הֲגַם	pref. הֲ interr.) conj. . . .	מם
הַגְּמוּל[o]	pref. הַ art.) noun masc. sing. dec. 1a. .	מל
הַגְּמוּלָה[p]	pref. id.) noun fem. sing. dec. 10. .	מל
הַגְמִיאִינִי[q]	Hiph. imp. sing. fem., suff. 1 pers. sing. .	מא
הַגָּמָל	pref. הַ) n. m. s. d. 8a. (§ 37. Nos. 2 & 3)	מל
הִגָּמֵל[aa]	Niph. inf. constr.	מל
הַגְּמַלִּים	[r] וְ' pref. ה) n. m., pl. of גָּמָל d. 8a. (§ 37. Nos. 2 & 3)	מל

הגן Root not used; Chald. הַגּוֹן *suitable, convenient.*
הָגִין m. adj. *convenient, commodious,* Eze. 42. 1

הַגָּן	pref. הַ) noun com. sing. for גַּן dec. 8d. .	נן
הַנֶּגֶב	pref. id.) noun masc. sing. dec. 1b. .	נב
הֲגָנֹב[s]	pref. הֲ) Kal inf. absolute . .	נב
הַגֹּנֵב[t]	pref. הַ) Kal part. act. sing. masc. .	נב
הַגְּנֵבָה[u]	pref. id.) noun fem. sing. dec. 10. . .	נב
הַגַּנּוֹת[x]	pref. id.) noun fem., pl. of גַּנָּה dec. 10.	נן
הִגַּעַתְּ[y]	Hiph. pret. 2 pers. sing. fem. . .	נע
הִגַּעְתִּיהוּ[z]	וְ id. pret. 1 pers. sing., suff. 3 pers. s. m.	נע
הִגַּעְתֶּם[a]	וְ id. pret. 2 pers. pl. masc. . .	נע
הַגָּפֶן	pref. הַ) noun com. sing. (suff. גַּפְנִי) d. 6a.	פן
הַגְּפָנִים[b]	וְ pref. id.) id. pl., absolute state .	פן

הָגָר (*flight,* coll. with the Arab.) pr. name of the hand-maid of Sarah, the mother of Ishmael.
הַגְרִי (*fugitive*), pl. הַגְרִיאִים, הַגְרִים pr. n. of an Arabian people.

הַגָּר	pref. id.) Kal part. sing. masc. dec. 1a.	ור
הַגֵּר	וְ' pref. id.,) noun masc. sing. dec. 1a. .	ור
הַגִּרְגָּשִׁי	וְ' pref. id.) pr. name of a people, see גִּרְגָּשִׁי	
הַגֵּרָה	pref. id.) noun fem. sing. [for גֵּרָה]	רר

[a] Ps. 19. 15. [b] La. 3. 62. [c] Eze. 42. 12. [d] Ec. 12. 1. [e] 1 Sa. 14. 9. [f] 2 Ch. 2. 16. [g] Le. 2. 8. [h] Is. 45. 21. [i] 2 Sa. 17. 29. [k] Ex. 21. 6. [l] Jos. 1. 8. [m] Ps. 143. 5. [n] Ps. 77. 13. [o] Ge. 31. 46. [p] Eze. 5. 1. [q] 2 Ki. 9. 35. [r] Est. 2. 6. [s] Zec. 4. 3. [t] 2 Ki. 24. 14. [u] Is. 49. 9. [v] 2 Ki. 17. 28, etc. [y] Je. 32. 11, 14. [z] 2 Ch. 4. 12. [aa] Ge. 21. 8. [a] Je. 24. 1. [b] Am. 1. 6. [c] Eze. 47. 8. [d] Is. 3. 23. [e] 2 Ki. 17. 26. [f] Je. 29. 4, 7, 14. [g] 2 Ki. 17. 27. [h] 1 Ki. 14. 10. [i] 1 Ch. 8. 7. [k] Je. 20. 4. [l] Je. 13. 19. [m] Est. 2. 6. [n] Am. 5. 27. [o] Joel 4. 4. [p] 2 Sa. 19. 37. [q] Ge. 24. 17. [r] Ge. 32. 8. [s] Je. 7. 9. [t] Zec. 5. 3. [u] Ex. 22. 3. [x] Is. 66. 17. [y] Est. 4. 14. [z] Eze. 13. 14. [a] Ex. 12. 22. [b] Ca. 2. 13.

הַגִּרְזִי וְ pref. id.)(pr. n. Kh. R. גרז, K. גִּזְרִי' R. — גזר
הַגַּרְזֶן [b]וְ' pref. id.)(noun masc. sing. — גרז
הַגְּרִי pr. name masc. — הגר
הַגָּרִים [c]וְ' pref. id.)(Kal part. masc., pl. of גָּר d. 1 a. — גור
הַגֵּרִים[d] [e]וְ' pref. id.)(noun masc., pl. of גֵּר dec. 1 a. — גור
הַגְּרִים וְ pref. id.)(pr. n. of a people, pl. of הַגְּרִי — הגר
הַגַּרְמִי pref. id.)(pr. name masc. — גרם
הַגּוֹרָלוֹת[f] וְ pref. id.)(n. m. with pl. f. term. fr. גּוֹרָל d. 2 b. — גרל
הַגִּרֵם[g] וְ Hiph. imp. 2 p. s. m. [הַגֵּר] suff. 3 p. pl. m. — נגר
הַגֹּרֶן pref. id.)(noun sing. fem., dec. 6 c. — גרן
הַגֳּרָנוֹת pref. הַ)(pl. absolute (§ 35. rem. 9) — גרן
הִגַּרְתִּי[h] וְ Hiph. pret. 1 p. s. acc. shifted by conv. וְ — נגר
הַגֵּרְשֻׁנִּי pref. הַ)(patronym. of גֵּרְשׁוֹן — גרש
הַגִּישָׁה[i] Hiph. imp. sing. masc. with parag. ה — נגש
הַגִּישׁוּ[k] id. imp. pl. masc. — נגש
הֻגְּשׁוּ[l] Hoph. pret. 3 p. pl. (some copies have הֻגָּשׁוּ) — נגש
הַגְּשׁוּרִי pref. הַ)(pr. name of a people, see גְּשׁוּר
הַגֶּשֶׁם / הַגָּשֶׁם } pref. id.)(noun masc. sing. dec. 6 a. (§ 35. rem. 2, but pl. c. גִּשְׁמֵי) — גשם
הַגֹּשֶׁן pref. id.)(pr. name of a region — גשן
הִגַּשְׁתֶּם[m] Hiph. pret. 2 pers. pl. masc. — נגש
הַגִּתִּי pref. הַ)(gent. noun from גַּת — גת
הַגִּתִּים pref. id.)(id. pl. — גת
הַגִּתִּית pref. id.)(noun fem. sing. from גִּתִּי = גַּת — גת
הֵד[n] noun masc. sing. — הדד
הַדָּאָה[o] pref. id.)(noun fem. sing. — דאה
הַדֹּב[p] pref. id.)(noun masc. sing. dec. 8 c. — דבב
הִדְבִּיקֻהוּ Hiph. pret. 3 pers. pl., suff. 3 pers. sing. masc. — דבק
הִדְבִּיקַתְהוּ id. pret. 3 pers. sing. fem., suff. 3 pers. s. m. — דבק
הַדְּבִיר pref. הַ)(noun masc. sing. — דבר
הַדְּבָקִים[q] pref. id.)(noun masc., pl. of דֶּבֶק dec. 6. — דבק
הַדְּבֵקִים[r] pref. id.)(adj. masc., pl. of דָּבֵק dec. 5 b. — דבק
הִדְבַּקְתִּי[s] Hiph. pret. 1 pers. sing. — דבק
הִדְבַּקְתִּי[t] וְ id. acc. shifted by וְ conv. (comp. § 8. rem. 7) — דבק

[הַדָּבָר] Chald. masc. the title of a certain officer in the court of Babylon, Eng. Ver. *counsellor*. Etymology uncertain.

הַדָּבָר וְ' pref. הַ / הֲדָבָר[y] pref. הֲ } noun masc. sing. dec. 4 a. — דבר
הַדֶּבֶר [z]וְ' / הַדָּבֶר[a] [b]וְ' } pref. הַ)(noun masc. sing. dec. 6 a. (§ 35. rem. 2) — דבר
הַדֹּבֵר[c] וְ pref. id.)(noun masc. sing. — דבר
הַדֹּבֵר pref. id.)(Kal part. act. masc. dec. 7 b. — דבר
הַדָּבְרוֹ[d] pref. id.)(noun masc. sing., suff. 3 pers. sing. masc. from דֹּבֶר dec. 6 f. — דבר

הַדֹּבְרוֹת[e] pref. id.)(Kal part. act. fem., pl. from דֹּבֵר m. — דבר
הַדָּבְרַי[f] Ch. noun m. pl., suff. 1 pers. s. [from הַדָּבָר] — הדבר
הַדָּבְרֵי[g] וְ Chald. id. pl., construct state — הדבר
הַדָּבְרַיָּא[h] Chald. id. pl., emph. state — הדבר
הַדְּבָרִים [i]וְ' pref. הַ)(noun masc., pl. of דָּבָר dec. 4 a. — דבר
הַדֹּבְרִים[k] וְ pref. id.)(Kal part. act. m., pl. of דֹּבֵר d. 7 b. — דבר
הַדְּבֹרִים[l] pref. id.)(n. fem. with pl. m. term. fr. דְּבֹרָה — דבר
הַדָּבְרַת pref. id.)(pr. name of a place — דבר
הַדְּבַשׁ[ee] pref. id.)(for דְּבַשׁ' noun masc., (with suff. דִּבְשִׁי) dec. 6 (§ 35. rem. 10) — דבש
הַדָּג[m] pref. id.)(noun masc. sing. dec. 2 a. — דגה
הַדָּגָה [n]וְ' pref. id.)(noun fem. sing. dec. 11 a. — דגה
הַדָּגִים pref. id.)(noun masc., pl. of דָּג dec. 2 a. — דגה
הַדָּגָן [o]וְ' pref. id.)(noun masc. sing. dec. 4 a. — דגה

הָדַד Root not used; Arab. *to break; to give forth a heavy sound.*

הֵד masc. *a shouting*, Eze. 7. 7.

הֵידָד masc. *a shouting*, of those who tread the grapes, or of an attacking army.

הֲדַד pr. name—I. of a Syrian idol, see בֶּן־הֲדַד.—II. of a son of Ishmael, 1 Ch. 1. 30.—III. of a king of Edom.—IV. of an Idumean, 1 Ki. 11. 14—25, called אֲדַד in ver. 17.

הֲדַדְעֶזֶר (whose *help is Hadad*, see the prec.) pr. name of a king of Syria, also called הֲדַרְעֶזֶר, comp. 2 Sa. 8. 3 sq. with chaps. 10, 16, 19.

הֲדַדְרִמּוֹן (*Hadad, Rimmon,* two Syrian idols) pr. name of a town near Megiddo, Zec. 12. 11.

הַדַּי pr. name masc. 2 Sa. 23. 30, for which חוּרַי in 1 Ch. 11. 32.

הֲדַד / וַהֲדַד } pr. name masc. — הדד
הֲדַדְעֶזֶר / הֲדַדְעָזֶר } pr. name masc. — הדד
הֲדַדְרִמּוֹן pr. name of a place. — הדד

הָדָה *to thrust, put forth* the hand, Is. 11. 8; Arab. *to lead, direct.*

יֶהְדַּי (for יְהֺדָיָה whom *the Lord directs*) pr. name masc. 1 Ch. 2. 47.

הֹדֹה[p] noun m. s., suff. 3 pers. s. m. from הוֹד dec. 1. — הוד

[הֹדּוּ] (for הִנְדּוּ) pr. name *Hindustan, India,* Est. 1. 1; 8. 9.

הֹדוּ[q] (for הוֹדוּ) Hiph. imp. pl. masc. — ידה
הַדּוֹב[r] pref. הַ)(for דֹּב' noun masc. sing. dec. 8 c. — דבב

---

[a] Is. 10. 15. [b] 1 Ki. 6. 7. [c] 2 Ch. 15. 9. [d] 1 Ch. 22. 2. [e] 2 Ch. 30. 25.
[f] Ne. 10. 35. [g] Je. 18. 21. [h] Mi. 1. 6. [i] Ge. 27. 25. [k] 1 Sa. 13. 9.
[l] 2 Sa. 3. 34. [m] Am. 5. 25. [n] Eze. 7. 7. [o] Le. 11. 14. [p] Am. 5. 19, etc.
[q] 2 Sa. 1. 6. [r] Ju. 20. 42. [s] 1 Ki. 22. 34; & 2 Ch. 18. 33. [t] De. 4. 4.
[u] Je. 13. 11. [x] Eze. 29. 4. [y] 2 Sa. 7. 7. [z] Je. 32. 24. [a] Je. 21. 7.
[b] Eze. 7. 15. [c] Je. 5. 13. [d] Mi. 2. 12. [e] Ps. 31. 19. [ee] Ju. 14. 9.
[f] Da. 4. 33. [g] Da. 3. 27. [h] Da. 6. 8. [i] 1 Ch. 4. 22.
[k] Ps. 119. 20. [l] De. 1. 44. [m] Jon. 2. 1. [n] Ex. 7. 18, 21.
[o] Ne. 5. 11. [p] Je. 22. 18. [q] Ps. 107. 1. [r] 1 Sa. 17. 34, 36.

הַדּוּדַי[a] וְ pref. הַ ⟩⟨ noun masc., pl. דּוּדִים and דְּוָדִים (§ 35. rem. 12 & 13) . . דוד

הַדּוּדָאִים[b] pref. id. ⟩⟨ n. m. pl. [of דּוּדַי § 35. r. 15 note] דוד

הַדָּוָה[c] וְ pref. id. ⟩⟨ adj. fem. sing. from דָּוֶה masc. דוה

הַדּוּכִיפַת[d] וְ pref. id. ⟩⟨ noun fem. sing. . . . דוכ

הַדּוֹלֵג[f] pref. id. ⟩⟨ Kal part. act. sing. masc. . . דלג

הֲדוֹם noun masc. sing. . . . . . הדם

הָדוּר[g] Kal part. p. sing. masc. dec. 3 a. . . . הדר

הַדּוֹר pref. הַ ⟩⟨ noun masc. sing. dec. 1 a. . . . דור

הֲדוּרִים[h] וַ Kal part. p. masc., pl. of הָדוּר; וַ bef. (-:) הדר

הֲדוֹרָם pr. name of a people . . . . . הדר

הַדְּחוּיָה[i] pref. הַ ⟩⟨ Kal part. pass. fem. [fr. דָּחוּי m.] דחה

הִדַּחְתִּי Hiph. pret. 1 pers. sing. . . . . נדח

הִדַּחְתִּי[k] וְ id. acc. shifted by וְ conv. (§ 8. rem. 7) נדח

הִדַּחְתִּיו[l] וְ id. id., suff. 1 pers. sing. . . . נדח

הִדַּחְתִּיךָ[m] id. id., suff. 2 pers. sing. masc. . . נדח

הִדַּחְתִּים id. id., suff. 3 pers. pl. masc. . . . נדח

הִדַּחְתֶּם[n] id. pret. 2 pers. s. m., suff. 3 pers. pl. masc. נדח

הִדַּחְתֶּם[o] id. pret. 2 pers. pl. masc. . . . נדח

הֲדַי pr. name masc. . . . . . . הדד

הַדַּיָּגִים[p] pref. הַ ⟩⟨ noun masc., pl. of [דַּיָּג] dec. 1 a. . דוג

הַדַּיָּה[q] וְ pref. id. ⟩⟨ noun fem. sing. dec. 10. . . דיה

הִדִּיחַ[r] וְ Hiph. pret. 3 pers. sing. masc. . . . נדח

הִדִּיחוּ[s] id. pret. 3 pers. pl. . . . . . נדח

הַדִּיחִי[t] id. inf. (הַדִּיחַ) suff. 1 pers. sing. dec. 1 b. . נדח

הִדִּיחֲךָ[u] id. pret. 3 pers. sing. masc., suff. 2 pers. s. m. נדח

הִדִּיחָם[x] id. pret. 3 pers. sing. m., suff. 3 pers. m. pl. נדח

הַדִּיחֵמוֹ[y] id. imp. sing. masc., suff. 3 pers. pl. masc. נדח

הֱדִיחֻנוּ[z] Hiph. pret. 3 pers. sing. masc., suff. נוּ or נִי 1 pers. pl. or sing. . . . . . דוח

הוֹדִיעֵנִי[a] Hiph. imp. sing. masc., suff. 1 pers. sing. ידע

[הָדַךְ] *to throw down, tread down*; only in the foll. form.

הֲדֹךְ[b] וַ Kal. imp. sing. masc.; וַ before (-:) . הדך

הַדַּל[c] וְ[d] pref. הַ ⟩⟨ noun masc. sing. dec. 8 a. . דלל

הַדַּלִּים[e] pref. id. ⟩⟨ id. pl., absolute state . . . דלל

הַדְלֵק[f] Hiph. inf. absolute . . . . . דלק

הַדֶּלֶת / הַדָּלֶת } וְ[g] pref. הַ ⟩⟨ noun fem. sing. see דֶּלֶת . דלה

הַדְּלָתוֹת pref. id. ⟩⟨ id. pl. absolute (§ 44. rem. 5), ת treated as if radical . . . דלה

הָדַם Root not used; Arab. *to level with the ground*; Syr. and Chald. (הַדֵּם) *to cut in pieces*.

הַדָּם Chald. *piece*, Da. 2. 5; 3. 29.

הֲדֹם m. *footstool*, everywhere followed by רַגְלַיִם.

הָאָדָם[h] וְ pref. הַ ⟩⟨ noun masc. sing. dec. 2 a. . אדם

הַאָדָם pref. הֲ interr. ⟩⟨ id., construct state . אדם

הֲדֹם[i] elsewhere הֲדוֹם, noun masc. sing. . . הדם

הַדָּמִים pref. הַ ⟩⟨ noun masc., pl. of דָּם dec. 2 a. דמם

הַדָּמַיִן Chald. noun masc., pl. of [הַדָּם] dec. 1 a. . הדם

הֲדִמָּנוּ[k] Hiph. pret. 3 pers. sing. masc. [הֵדַם], suff. 1 pers. pl. . . . . . . דמם

הַדָּנִי pref. הַ ⟩⟨ gent. noun from דָּן . . דין

הֲדַס וַ[l] masc. (pl. הֲדַסִּים) *myrtle*. Hence

הֲדַסָּה (myrtle) pr. name, the former name of Esther, Est. 7. 2. . . . . . הדס

הַדַּעַת / הַדָּעַת } pref. הַ ⟩⟨ noun fem. sing. dec. 13 a. . ידע

[הָדַף] fut. יֶהְדֹּף (§ 13. rem. 5) *to push, thrust, repulse*.

הֲדָפוֹ Kal pret. 3 pers. sing. m., suff. 3 pers. s. m. הדף

הֲדַפְתִּיךָ[m] וַ Hiph. pret. 1 pers. s. & suff.; וַ for וְ conv. הדף

הָדֵק[n] Hiph. inf., used adverbially . . . דקק

הֵדַק[o] וְ[p] Hiph. pret. 3 pers. sing. m. (§ 18. r. 10) דקק

הַדִּקוּ[q] Ch. Aph. pret. 3 pers. pl. m. (§ 47. rem. 1 & 5) דקק

הַדַּקּוֹת[r] pref. הַ ⟩⟨ adj., fem. of דַּקָּה dec. 10, fr. דַּק m. דקק

הֲדִקּוֹת[s] וַ Hiph. pret. 2 pers. sing. fem.; וַ bef. (-:) דקק

הֲדִקֹּת[t] defect for הֲדִקּוֹת (q. v.) . . . דקק

הַדֶּקֶת[u] וְ Chald. Aph. pret. 3 pers. sing. fem. (§ 47. rem. 4, & § 49. rem. 1) . . . דקק

I. [הָדַר] i. q. Chald. הֲדַר *to turn*, whence part. pass הֲדוּרִים *uneven, crooked places*, Is. 45. 2, Rabbin הֲדוּרִין id., see Buxtorf.

II. [הָדַר] fut. יֶהְדַּר (§ 13. rem. 5).—I. *to adorn, decorate* Is. 63. 1.—II. *to honour, reverence, respect*. Niph *to be honoured, respected*, La. 5. 12. Hithp. *to show oneself glorious*, Pr. 25. 6.

הַדַּר Chald. Pa. *to honour*.

הָדָר masc. dec. 4 c.—I. *ornament, splendour*.—II. *honour*, Ps. 149. 9.

הֶדֶר masc. *ornament, splendour*, Da. 11. 20.

הֲדַר Ch. m. dec. 3 a, *honour*, Da. 4. 27, 33; 5. 18

הֲדַר pr. name masc. see הֲדַד.

הֲדָרָה or הֶדְרָה fem. only construct הַדְרַת *ornament, splendour, beauty*.

הֲדוֹרָם pr. name of an Arab tribe descende from Joktan, Ge. 10. 27.

הָדָר וְ[i] noun masc. sing. dec. 4 c. . . . הדר

הֲדַר וַ[k] id. construct state; וַ bef. (-:) . . הדר

---

[a] Je. 24. 2. [b] Ca. 7. 14. [c] Le. 15. 33. [d] Le. 11. 19. [e] De. 14. 18. [f] Zep. 1. 9. [g] Is. 63. 1. [h] Is. 45. 2. [i] Ps. 62. 4. [k] Je. 27. 10. [l] Joel 2. 20. [m] Je. 46. 28. [n] Da. 9. 7. [o] 2 Ch. 13. 9. [p] Is. 19. 8. [q] De. 14. 13. [r] 2 Sa. 15. 14. [s] Je. 50. 17. [t] Je. 27. 15. [u] De. 30. 1. [x] Je. 16. 15. [y] Ps. 5. 11. [z] Je. 51. 34. [a] Job 13. 23. [b] Job 40. 12. [c] Ju. 6. 15. [d] Ex. 30. 15. [e] Je. 39. 10. [f] Eze. 24. 10. [g] Ge. 19. 6. [h] De. 12. 27. [i] Ps. 110. 1. [k] Je. 8. 14. [l] Is. 41. 19. [m] Is. 22. 19. [n] Ex. 30. 36. [o] 2 Ki. 23. 15. [p] 2 Ch. 34. 4. [q] Da. 6. 25. [r] Ge. 41. 7. [s] Mi. 4. 13. [t] Ge. 41. 24. [u] Da. 2. 34, 45. [x] Pr. 20. 29.

הֶדֶר[a] noun masc. sing. . . . . הדר

הַדָּרְבָן[b] pref. הַ)(n. m. fr. [דָּרְבָ] with the term ־ָן דרב

הַדְרָא[c] וְ Chald. noun m. s., emph. of [הֲדַר] d. 3a. הדר

הֲדָרָהּ[de] וְ' n. m. s., suff. 3 pers. s. fem. fr. הָדָר dec. 4c. הדר

הַדָּרוֹם pref. הַ)(noun masc. sing. [for דָּרוֹם] . דרר

הַדְּרוֹר[f] pref. id.)(noun masc. sing. . . . דרר

הַדֹּרוֹת[g] pref. id.)(noun masc. with pl. fem. term. from דּוֹר dec. 1a. . . . . דור

הֲדָרִי[h] noun m. s., suff. 1 pers. s. fr. הָדָר dec. 4 c. הדר

הַדְרִי[i] Chald. noun masc. sing., suff. 1 pers. sing. from [הֲדַר] dec. 3a. . . . הדר

הִדְרִיךְ[k] וְ Hiph. pret. 3 pers. sing. masc. . דרך

הַדְרִיכָהּ[l] id. id. (or inf. § 11. rem. 4), suff. 3 pers. s. fem. דרך

הִדְרִיכֻהוּ id. pret. 3 pers. pl., suff. 3 pers. sing. masc. דרך

הַדְרִיכֵנִי id. imp. sing. masc., suff. 1 pers. sing. . דרך

הֲדָרְךָ, הֲדָרֶךָ[m] } וְ, וַ noun masc. sing., suff. 2 pers. sing. masc. from הָדָר dec. 4c; וַ bef. (ֲ) } הדר

הֲדָרֵךְ[n] n. m. s., suff. 2 pers. s. fem. fr. הָדָר dec. 4c. הדר

הַדֶּרֶךְ, הַדָּרֶךְ } pref. הַ)(noun com. sing., dec. 6a. (§ 35. rem. 2) . . . . } דרך

הַדֹּרֵךְ pref. id.)(Kal part. act. sing. masc. dec. 7b. דרך

הֲדַרְכִּי[o] pref. הֲ interr.)(noun com. sing., suff. 1 pers. sing. from דֶּרֶךְ dec. 6a. . . . דרך

הַדְּרָכַי[p] pref. הַ interr. for הֲ)(id. pl., suff. 1 pers. s. דרך

הַדְּרָכִים[q] pref. הַ art.)(id. pl., absolute state . דרך

הִדְרַכְתִּיךָ[r] Hiph. pret. 1 pers. sing., suff. 2 pers. s. m. דרך

הֲדֹרָם pr. name of a people . . . . הדר

הֲדַדְעֶזֶר, הֲדַרְעֶזֶר } pr. name masc., see הֲדַדְעֶזֶר . . . הדד

הַדֹּרֵשׁ[s] pref. הַ)(Kal part. act. sing. masc. dec. 7b. דרש

הָדַרְתָּ[t] וְ Kal pret. 2 pers. sing. masc.; acc. shifted to ult. by וְ conv. (§ 8. rem. 7) . . הדר

הַדַּרְתְּ[u] Chald. Pael pret. 2 pers. s. m. (§ 47. rem. 2) הדר

הַדְרַת[x] noun fem. sing. constr. [of הֲדָרָה or הַדְרָה from הָדָר or הֶדֶר masc. dec. 11 or 12] . הדר

הַדְּרֵת[y] וְ Chald. Pael pret. 1 pers. sing. . . הדר

הַדֶּשֶׁן[z], הַדָּשֶׁן } וְ'[a] pref. הַ)(noun m. s. dec. 6a. (with suff. דִּשְׁנִי, though pause דָּשֶׁן § 35. r. 2) } דשן

הֻדַּשְּׁנָה[b] Hoph. pret. 3 pers. sing. fem. . . דשן

הַדָּת[c] וְ'[d] pref. הַ)(noun fem. sing. dec. 1a. . דת

הָהּ interj. expressive of grief, *Ah!* Eze. 30. 2.

הַהֶבֶל pref. הַ)(noun m. s. dec. 6. (§ 35. rem. 4) הבל

הַהַגְרִאִים pref. id.)(pl. of the following . . הגר

הַהַגְרִי pref. id.)(pr. name of a people . הגר

הַהַגְרִיאִים pref. id.)(id. pl. . . . . הגר

הַהֲדַסִּים[e] pref. id.)(noun masc., pl. of הֲדַס dec. 8 d. הדס

הַהוּא pref. id. (interr. Nu. 23. 19))(pers. pron. 3 pers. sing. masc. . . . הוא

הַהִוא pref. id.)((read *hee*) id. 3 p. s. f. (§ 1. r. 3) הוא

הַהוֹד[f] וְ pref. id.)(noun masc. sing. dec. 1a. . הוד

הַהֹלֵךְ[g] pref. id.)(Kal part. act. sing. masc. dec. 7b. הלך

הַהִיא pref. id.)(pron. pers. 3 pers. sing. fem. see הוּא . . . . . הוא

הַהֵיטֵב[h] pref. הַ interr. for הֲ)(Hiph. inf. abs. (used adverbially) . . . . יטב

הַהֵיכָל וְ' pref. הַ art.)(noun com. sing. dec. 2b. היכל

הַהֵימִיר[i] pref. הַ interr. for הֲ)(Hiph. pret. 3 p. s. m. ימר

הַהִין pref. הַ art.)(noun masc. sing. . . הין

הֶהָיְתָה[k] pref. הֶ interr. bef. הָ, for הֲ)(Kal pret. 3 pers. sing. fem. . . . . . היה

הֶהֵכִין[l] pref. הַ relat. art.)(Hiph. pret. 3 pers. s. m. כון

הַהֹלֵךְ pref. הַ id.)(Kal part. act. sing. m. d. 7b. הלך

הֶהָלְכוּא[m] pref. הֶ id., bef. הָ for הַ)(Kal pret. 3 pers. pl., (§ 8. rem. 4) . . . . הלך

הַהֹלְכִים pref. הַ id.)(Kal part. act. m., pl. of הֹלֵךְ d. 7b. הלך

הַהֹלֶכֶת pref. id.)(id. fem. sing. dec. 13a. . הלך

הַהֹלְכֹת[n] pref. id.)(id. pl. . . . . הלך

הַהֻלָּלָה[o] pref. id.)(Hoph. pret. 3 pers. sing. fem. [for הֻלְּלָה comp. § 8. rem. 7] . . . הלל

הָהֵם pref. הָ for הַ)(pron. pers. 3 pers. pl. masc. הם

הָהֵמָּה pref. id.)(id. with ה parag. . . הם

הֶהָמוֹן[p] Kh. הֶהָמוֹן q. v., K. הָמוֹן (q. v.) . המה

הֶהָמוֹן[q] וְ'[q] pref. הֶ bef. הָ for הַ)(noun m. s. d. 3a. המה

הֶהָמֵת[r] pref. id. interr.)(Hiph. inf. absolute . מות

הָהֵנָּה pref. הָ for הַ)(pers. pron. 3 pers. pl. fem., ה parag. . . . . . . הן

הַהַסְכֵּן[s] pref. הַ interr. for הֲ)(Hiph. inf. abs. . סכן

הַהֲפוּכָה[ff] pref. הַ art.)(Kal part. p. s. f. [fr. הָפוּךְ m.] הפך

הָהְפַּךְ[t] Hoph. pret. 3 pers. sing. masc. . . הפך

הַהֲפֵכָה[u] pref. הַ)(noun fem. sing. . . הפך

הַהֹפְכִי[w] pref. id.)(Kal part. act. sing. masc. with parag. י (§ 8. rem. 19) . . . הפך

הַהֹפְכִים[y] pref. id.)(id. pl. dec. 7b. . . הפך

הַהִצִּילוּ[z] pref. הַ interr. for הֲ)(Hiph. pret. 3 pers. pl. נצל

הַהַצֵּל[z] pref. id.)(id. inf. absolute . . . נצל

הַהִצְלִיחַ[a] pref. id.)(Hiph. pret. 3 pers. sing. masc. צלח

הַהִקְדִּישׁ[b] pref. id.)(Hiph. pret. 3 pers. sing. masc. קדש

הָהָר וְ' pref. הָ for הַ)(with the art. for הַר noun masc. dec. 8. (§ 37. rem. 7) הרר

הָהַרְאֵל[c] וְ pref. הַ)(noun masc. sing. see אֲרִיאֵל . ארה

הַהֲרֵגָה pref. הַ)(noun sing. fem. . . הרג

a Da. 11. 20. b 1 Sa. 13. 21. c Da. 5. 18. de La. 1. 6. Is. 5. 14. f Eze. 46. 17. g Is. 41. 4. h Mi. 2. 9. i Da. 4. 27, 33. k Is. 11. 15. l Je. 51. 33. m Ps. 45. 4. n Eze. 27. 10. o Eze. 18. 25. p Eze. 18. 29. q Eze. 21. 26. r Pr. 4. 11. s Eze. 14. 10. t Le. 19. 32. u Da. 5. 23. x Pr. 14. 28. y Da. 4. 31. z Le. 1. 16. a Je. 31. 40. b Is. 34. 6. c Est. 4. 8. d Est. 3. 15, etc. e Zec. 1. 8, 10, 11. f 1 Ch. 29. 11. ff La. 4. 6. g Hab. 1. 6. h Jon. 4. 4, 9. i Je. 2. 11. k Joel 1. 2. l 2 Ch. 29. 36. m Jos. 10. 24. n 1 Sa. 25. 42. o Eze. 26. 17. p 2 Ki. 7. 13. q 1 Sa. 14. 19. r Je. 26. 19. s Nu. 22. 30. t Job 30. 15. u Ge. 19. 29. w Ps. 114. 8. y Am. 5. 7. z 2 Ki. 18. 33. a Ge. 24. 21. b 1 Ch. 26. 28. c Eze. 43. 15.

הָהָ֫רָה pref. הָ for ·הַ)(noun masc. sing. with parag. ה [for הַרָה] from הַר (§ 37. rem. 7) . הרר

הַהֲרוּגִים[a] pref. הַ)(Kal part. p. m., pl. of [הָרוּג] d. 3a. הרג

הַהֲרוּס[b] pref. הָ bef. הָ for הַ)(Kal part. pass. . הרס

הֶהָרוֹתֶיהָ[c] pref. id.)(adj. pl. fem., suff. 3 pers. sing. fem., fr. הָרָה [fr. הָרֶה masc.; § 42. r. 2] הרה

הֶהָרִים[d] וְ pref. id.)(noun masc., pl. of הַר dec. 8. (§ 37. rem. 7) . . . . . הרר

הַהֵרִימוּ[e] pref. הַ art. relat.)(Hiph. pret. 3 pers. pl. רום

הַהַרְמוֹנָה[f] pref. הַ art.)(noun masc. sing. with parag. ה [from הַרְמוֹן] . . . . הרם

הַהֶרֶס[g] pref. id.)(noun masc. sing. . . הרס

הַהֲרָרִי pref. id.)(pr. name of a people . . הרר

הֶהָשֵׁב[h] pref. הֶ interr. bef. הָ f. הַ, הֲ)(Hiph. inf. abs. שוב

הַהֹשִׁיב[i] pref. הַ art. relat.)(Hiph. pret. 3 pers. s. m. ישב

הַהֹשִׁיבוּ[k] pref. id.)(id. pret. 3 pers. pl. . . ישב

הוֹ[l] interj. . . . . . . הוי

הוּא וְ, וְ׳ masc., הִיא fem., pron. 3 pers. sing. (pl. הֵם, הֵן, see their places).—I. *he, she,* neut. *it.*—II. *this, that, same;* הַהוּא, הַהִיא *this, that, the same.*—Chald. id.

הִוא וְ id. fem. (§ 1. rem. 3).

הֲוָא Chald. Peal pret. 3 pers. sing. masc. see . הוה

הֱוֵא[m] Kal imp. sing. masc. see . . . הוה

הוֹאִיל Hiph. pret. 3 pers. sing. masc. . . . יאל

הוֹאִילוּ[n] id. pret. 3 pers. pl. . . . . יאל

הוֹאֵל } id. imp. sing. masc. . . . יאל
הוֹאֶל־ }

הוֹאַלְנוּ[o] id. pret. 1 pers. pl. . . . . יאל

הוֹאַלְתָּ[p] id. pret. 2 pers. sing. masc. . . יאל

הוֹאַלְתִּי[q] id. pret. 1 pers. sing. . . . . יאל

הוּבָא וְ׳ Hoph. pret. 3 pers. sing. masc. . . בוא

הוּבְאוּ[r] id. pret. 3 pers. pl. . . . . בוא

הוּבַד[s] וְ Ch. Hoph. pret. 3 pers. s. m. (§ 47. r. 9) אבד

הוֹבִישׁ Hiph. pret. 3 pers. sing. masc. . . יבש

הוֹבִישָׁה id. pret. 3 pers. sing. fem. . . . יבש

הוֹבִישׁוּ id. pret. 3 pers. pl. . . . . בוש

הָובְנִים[t] וְ Kh. הוֹבְנִים K. הָבְנִים noun masc. pl. [of הָבְנִי or הוֹבְנִי] . . . . . . הבן

הוֹבַשְׁתָּ Hiph. pret. 2 pers. sing. masc. . . יבש

הוֹבַשְׁתִּי[u] id. pret. 1 pers. sing. . . . . יבש

הוֹבַשְׁתִּי[x] וְ id.; acc. shifted by וְ conv. (comp. § 8. r. 7) יבש

הוֹגָה Hiph. pret. 3 pers. sing. masc. . . יגה

הוֹגָהּ[y] id. with suff. 3 pers. sing. fem. (§ 25. No. 2e) . . . . . יגה

הוֹגַעְנוּ[z] Hiph. pret. 1 pers. pl. [for הוֹגַעְנוּ § 7. r. 8] יגע

הוֹגַעְתִּיךָ[a] id. pret. 1 pers. sing., suff. 2 pers. sing. m. יגע

הוֹגַעְתֶּם[b] id. pret. 2 pers. pl. masc. . . . יגע

הוֹגַעְתַּנִי[c] id. pret. 2 pers. sing. masc. suff. 1 pers. sing. יגע

הוֹד[d] וְ, וְ׳, masc. dec. 1a.—I. *glory, majesty.*—II. *beauty, brightness.*—III. pr. name masc. 1 Ch. 7. 37. Root not defined, the lexicographers fluctuating between נָהַד, יָהַד, הוּד.

הוֹדִיָּה (*majesty of the Lord*) pr. name of several Levites.

הוֹדַוְיָהוּ, הוֹדַוְיָה (for הוֹדוֹ יָהּ *the Lord is his glory*) pr. name masc. of several persons.

הוֹדוֹ id., suff. 3 pers. sing. masc. . . . הוד

הוֹדוּ וְ׳ Hiph. pret. 3 pers. pl., or imp. pl. masc. ידה

הוֹדַוְיָה וְ׳ pr. name masc. . . . . . הוד

הוֹדוֹת[e] וְ׳ Hiph. inf. constr. . . . . ידה

הוֹדִי[f] וְ noun m. s., suff. 1 pers. s. fr. הוד d. 1a. הוד

הוֹדִיָּה pr. name masc. . . . . . הוד

הוֹדַיְוָהוּ Kh. הוֹדַוְיָהוּ K., pr. name masc. . . הוד

הוֹדִינוּ[g] Hiph. pret. 1 pers. pl. . . . ידה

הוֹדִיעַ[h] Hiph. pret. 3 p. s. m., or inf. constr. Ge. 41. 39. ידע

הוֹדִיעוּ id. pret. 3 pers. pl., or imp. pl. masc. . ידע

הוֹדִיעֲךָ[i] id. inf. (הוֹדִיעַ), suff. 2 pers. sing. m. d. 1b. ידע

הוֹדַע אֹתָם[k] id. imp. sing. masc., suff. 3 pers. pl. masc. ידע

הוֹדִיעֵנוּ[l] id. id., suff. 1 pers. pl. . . . . ידע

הוֹדִיעֻנוּ[m] id. imp. pl. masc., suff. 1 pers. pl. . ידע

הוֹדִיעַנִי[n] id. pret. 3 pers. sing. masc., suff. 1 pers. s. ידע

הוֹדִיעֵנִי וְ׳ id. imp. sing. masc., suff. 1 pers. sing. . ידע

הוֹדְךָ } noun masc. sing., suff. 2 pers. sing. masc. from הוד dec. 1a. . . . } הוד
הוֹדֶךָ }

הוֹדַע Hiph. imp. sing. masc.; or (Le. 4. 23, 28) Hoph. pret. 3 pers. sing. masc. [for הוּדַע] ידע

הוֹדַע[o] וְ׳[p] Ch. Aph. pret. 3 pers. s. m. (§ 47. r. 4 & 9) ידע

הִוָּדְעִי[q] Niph. inf., suff. 1 pers. sing. fr. [הִוָּדַע § 36. rem. 5] dec. 7b. . . . . ידע

הוֹדְעָךְ[r] Chald. Aph. pret. 3 pers. sing. masc. suff. 2 pers. sing. masc. (§ 47. rem. 4 & 9) . ידע

הוֹדַעְנָא[s] וְ Chald. id. pret. 1 pers. pl. . . . ידע

הוֹדַעְנִי[t] Hiph. pret. 3 pers. sing. m., suff. 1 pers. s. ידע

הוֹדַעְתָּ[u] } id. pret. 2 pers. sing. masc. (comp. § 8. rem. 7) . . . . } ידע
הוֹדַעְתָּ }

הוֹדַעְתָּ[x] וְ id. id.; acc. shifted by conv. וְ (comp. id.) ידע

הוֹדַעְתָּהּ[y] וְ id. id., suff. 3 pers. sing. fem. . . ידע

הוֹדַעְתִּי id. pret. 1 pers. sing. . . . . ידע

הוֹדַעְתִּי וְ id. id.; acc. shifted by conv. וְ (comp. § 8. r. 7) ידע

[a] Est. 9. 11. [b] 1 Ki. 18. 30. [c] 2 Ki. 15. 16. [d] Zec. 6. 1. [e] Ezr. 8. 25. [f] Am. 4. 3. [g] Is. 19. 18. [h] Ge. 24. 5. [i] Ezr. 10. 14. [k] Ezr. 10. 17. [l] Am. 5. 16. [m] Job 37. 6. [n] Job 6. 28. [o] Jos. 7. 7. [p] 1 Ch. 17. 27. [q] Ge. 18. 27, 31. [r] Ge. 43. 18. [s] Da. 7. 11. [t] Eze. 27. 15. [u] Eze. 17. 24. [x] Je. 51. 36. [y] La. 1. 5. [z] Mal. 2. 17. [a] Is. 43. 23. [b] Mal. 2. 17. [c] Is. 43. 24. [d] Job 40. 10. [e] 1 Ch. 25. 3. [f] Da. 10. 8. [g] Ps. 75. 2. [h] Ps. 98. 2. [i] De. 8. 3. [k] Eze. 20. 4. [l] Job 37. 19. [m] 1 Sa. 6. 2. [n] Je. 11. 18. [o] Da. 2. 15, 17, 45. [p] Da. 2. 28. [q] Je. 31. 19. [r] Da. 2. 29. [s] Ezr. 4. 14. [t] Ex. 33. 13. [u] Job 26. 3. [x] Ex. 18. 20. [y] Eze. 22. 2.

הוֹרַעְתִּיךָ[a] id. id., suff. 2 pers. sing. masc. . . ידע

הוֹרַעְתָּם[b] וְ id. pret. 2 pers. s. m., suff. 3 pers. pl. m. ידע

הוֹרַעְתֶּם[c] וְ id. pret. 2 pers. pl. masc. . . ידע

הוֹרַעְתָּנָא[d] Chald. Aph. pret. 2 pers. sing. masc., suff. 1 pers. pl. (§ 47. rem. 4 & 9) . . . ידע

הוֹרַעְתַּנִי Heb. & Ch. Hiph. or Aph. pret. 2 pers. sing. masc., suff. 1 pers. sing. (§ 4. rem. 4 & 9) ידע

[הָוָה] imp. הֱוֵה, הֱוֵא fut. יְהוּא (§ 24. rem. 3e & 20).—I. (Arab. *to breathe*) *to exist, to be.*—II. in the deriv. *to desire*, comp. הַוָּה.—III. *to fall, descend*, Job 37.6.

הֲוָה, הֲוָא Chald. *to be.* Fut. יֶהֱוֵא, יֶהֱוֵה, with the pref. ל, לֶהֱוֵא, לֶהֱוֵה, pl. לֶהֱוֹן, לֶהֶוְיָן, see analyt. order.

הַוָּה fem. dec. 10.—I. *desire, lust.*—II. *fall, calamity, destruction*, for which twice is found הַיָּה in Kheth. Job 6. 2; 30. 13.

הֹוָה fem. *fall, calamity.*

יְהֹוָה the most sacred name of God, expressive of His *eternal, Self-existence*, first communicated to the Hebrews, Ex. 3. 14, comp. chap. 6. 3. This name appears to be composed of יְהוֹ (fut. of הָוָה, like יְהִי from הָיָה) and וָה (preterite by aphæresis for הָוָה), the verb *to be* being twice repeated as in Ex. 3. 14. If we supply אֲשֶׁר between these words we obtain nearly the same sense as expressed there in the words אֶהְיֶה אֲשֶׁר אֶהְיֶה. The Jews who (from an early date) believed this name incommunicable, substituted, in the pronunciation, the consonants of אֲדֹנָי, the vowels being alike in both words (with the exception of simple and composite Sheva), and according to these the punctuators suited the vowels of the prefixes when coming to stand before יְהֹוָה, as לַיהוָֹה, בַּיהוָֹה, מֵיהוָֹה according to לַאדֹנָי, בַּאדֹנָי, מֵאֲדֹנָי. Where, however, יְהֹוָה is already preceded by אֲדֹנָי, to avoid repetition, they furnished it with the vowels of אֱלֹהִים, in order that it be pronounced with its consonants, so that אֲדֹנָי יֱהֹוִה is to be read אֲדֹנָי אֱלֹהִים. The punctuators seem to intimate the originality of the vowels of יְהֹוָה by not pointing Yod with Hhateph-Pattah (יֲהֹוָה) to indicate the reading of אֲדֹנָי just as they point it with Hhateph-Segol to indicate the reading of אֱלֹהִים. We could, moreover, not account for the abbreviated forms יְהוֹ, יוֹ prefixed to so many proper names, unless we consider the vowels of יְהֹוָה original.

יָהּ i. q. יְהֹוָה from which it may be an abbreviation, and that probably from the first two letters, Kamets being added to assist the enunciation. When affixed to proper names the Mappik in ה is omitted, as אֵלִיָּה; the form is also sometimes prolonged to יָהוּ=יְהוֹ (comp. יְהֹוָה), as אֵלִיָּהוּ.

יְהוֹאָחָז (*the Lord holds* him) pr. name—I. of a king of Israel, son of Jehu, comp. 2 Ki. 13. 1—9.—II. of a king of Judah, son of Josiah, comp. 2 Ki. 23. 31—34, also called יוֹאָחָז comp. 2 Ch. 36. 1 with 2.

יְהוֹאָשׁ (*the Lord has bestowed* him, R. אוּשׁ coll. with the Arab, *to give*) pr. name.—I. of a king of Judah, son of Ahaziah, written also יוֹאָשׁ, comp. 2 Ki. 12. 1 with 20.—II. of a king of Israel, son of Jehoahaz, called also יוֹאָשׁ, comp. 2 Ki. 13. 10 with 9.

יְהוֹזָבָד (*the Lord has bestowed* him) pr. name of several men.

יְהוֹחָנָן (*the Lord has graciously bestowed* him) pr. name of several men, especially a commander under Jehoshaphat, comp. 2 Ch. 17. 15.

יְהוֹיָדָע (whom *the Lord knows*, i. e. cares for) pr. name of several men, especially of a priest of great authority, comp. 2 Ki. 11. 4.

יְהוֹיָכִין (*the Lord will establish* him, R. כּוּן) pr. name of a king of Judah, son of Jehoiakim, comp. 2 Ki. 24. 6, 8, sq.; also written יוֹיָכִין Eze. 1. 2, יְכָנְיָה comp. Est. 2. 6, יְכָנְיָהוּ Je. 24. 1, Kh., כָּנְיָהוּ, comp. Je. 22. 24.

יְהוֹיָקִים (*the Lord will establish* him, R. קוּם) pr. name of a king of Judah, son of Josiah.

יְהוֹיָרִיב, יוֹיָרִיב (*the Lord will defend his cause*) pr. name of a distinguished priest at Jerusalem.

יְהוֹנָדָב, יוֹנָדָב (*the Lord liberally bestowed* him) pr. name of two different men.

יְהוֹנָתָן, יוֹנָתָן (whom *the Lord has given*) pr. name of several men, especially of a son of Saul, the friend of David.

יְהוֹעַדָּה (whom *the Lord adorns*) pr. name masc. 1 Ch. 8. 36, called יַעְרָה chap. 9. 42.

יְהוֹעַדָּן (*the Lord* is her *ornament*) pr. name fem. 2 Ki. 14. 2.

יְהוֹצָדָק, יוֹצָדָק (*the Lord is righteous*) pr. name of the father of Joshua the high-priest.

יְהוֹרָם, יוֹרָם (*the Lord is exalted*) pr. name m. —I. of a king of Judah, son of Jehoshaphat, comp. 2 Ki. 8. 16—24.—II. of a king of Israel, son of Ahab, comp. 2 Ki. chap. 3.

[a] Pr. 22. 19. [b] De. 4. 9. [c] Jos. 4. 22. [d] Da. 2. 23.

יְהוֹשֶׁבַע (*the Lord* is her *oath*) pr. name of a daughter of king Joram, 2 Ki. 11. 2.

יְהוֹשֻׁעַ, יְהוֹשׁוּעַ (*the Lord* is his *salvation*) pr. name of several men, especially—I. of the minister of Moses afterwards his successor, called also יֵשׁוּעַ, הוֹשֵׁעַ.—II. of a high-priest contemporary with Zerubbabel, called also יֵשׁוּעַ.

יְהוֹשָׁפָט (whom *the Lord judges*) pr. name.—I. of a king of Judah son of Asa, comp. 1 Ki. 22. 41—51.—II. of the recorder of king David, comp. 2 Sa. 8. 16.—III. 1 Ki. 4. 17.—IV. 2 Ki. 9. 2, 14.

יוֹאָב (*the Lord* is *his father*) pr. name of several men, especially of the chief military officer of David.

יוֹאָח (*the Lord* is his *friend*) pr. name of several men, especially—I. of a recorder of Hezekiah, comp. 2 Ki. 18. 18.—II. of a recorder of king Josiah, 2 Ch. 34. 8.

יוֹאֵל (*the Lord* is his *God*) pr. name of several men, especially—I. of a prophet, Joel 1. 1.—II. of a son of Samuel, 1 Sa. 8. 2.—III. of a son of king Uzziah, 1 Ch. 6. 21.

יוֹאָשׁ pr. name of several men, contr. for יְהוֹאָשׁ (q. v.) for which it often stands.

יוֹכֶבֶד (*the Lord has bestowed* him) pr. name of several Levites.

יוֹזָכָר (whom *the Lord remembers*) pr. name of the murderer of king Joash, 2 Ki. 12. 22, written also זָבָד in 2 Ch. 24. 26.

יוֹחָא (perhaps transp. for יוֹאָח q. v.) pr. name masc. of two different persons.

יוֹחָנָן (contr. for יְהוֹחָנָן q. v.) pr. name of several men.

יוֹיָדָע (contr. for יְהוֹיָדָע q. v.) pr. name masc.

יוֹיָקִים (*the Lord will establish* him) pr. name masc. Ne. 12. 10.

יוֹיָרִיב (contr. for יְהוֹיָרִיב q.v.) pr. n. m. Ne. 11. 5.

יוֹכֶבֶד (*the Lord* is her *glory*) pr. name of the mother of Moses.

יוֹנָתָן (contr. for יְהוֹנָתָן q.v.) pr. name masc. of several persons.

יוֹעֵד (*the Lord* is his *witness*) pr. n. m. Ne. 11. 7.

יוֹעֶזֶר (*the Lord* is his *helper*) pr. n. m. 1 Ch. 12. 6.

יוֹעָשׁ (whom *the Lord succours*, see עוּשׁ) pr. n. masc. of two different persons.

יוֹקִים (contr. for יוֹיָקִים) pr. n. m. 1 Ch. 4. 22.

יוֹרָם (contr. for יְהוֹרָם q. v.) pr. name masc. 2 Sa. 8. 10, for which הֲדוֹרָם 1 Ch. 18. 10.

יוֹתָם (*the Lord is perfect* R. תָּמַם) pr. name.—I. of a son of Gideon, Ju. 9. 5.—II. of a king of Judah, son of Uzziah, comp. 2 Ki. 15. 32—38.

הֲוָה Ch. Peal pret. 3 pers. sing. masc. . . . הוה

הֱוֵה[a] Kal imp. sing. masc. . . . . . הוה

הֹוָה noun fem. sing. . . . . . . הוה

הֹוֶה Kal part. act. sing. masc. . . . . הוה

הוֹהָם (perh. for יְהוֹהָם *Lord of multitude*) pr. name of a king of Hebron, Jos. 10. 3.

הֲווֹ [b]וֲ׳ Ch. Peal pret. 3 pers. pl. m.; וַ bef. (-:) הוה

הֱווֹ[c] Ch. id. imp. pl. masc. . . . . הוה

הַוּוֹת noun fem., pl. of [הַוָּה] dec. 10. . . הוה

הוּחַדָּה Hoph. pret. 3 pers. sing. fem. . . . חדד

הוֹחִילִי[d] Hiph. imp. sing. fem. . . . . יחל

הוּחַל[e] Hoph. pret. impers. . . . . חלל

הוֹחִלִי defect. for הוֹחִילִי (q. v.) . . . יחל

הוֹחַלְתִּי
הוֹחָלְתִּי[f] } Hiph. pret. 1 pers. sing. (comp. § 8. r. 7) יחל

הוֹחַלְתִּי[g] וְ id.; acc. shifted by conv. וְ (comp. id.) . יחל

הוּטְלוּ[h] Hoph. pret. 3 pers. pl. . . . טול

הוֹי interj.—I. of threatening, *ho! wo!* with acc., אֶל, עַל, לְ.—II. of grief, *alas!*—III. of exhortation, *ho!*

הוֹ interj. expressive of grief, *alas!* Am. 5. 16.

הֱוֵי[i] Kal imp. sing. masc. . . . . הוה

הוֹיֹדֵעַ[k] transpos. for הַיּוֹדֵעַ, pref. הַ art.; Kal part. act. m. ידע

הֹוִיָה[l] Kal part. act. sing. fem., [from הוֹיֶה masc.] היה

הֲוַיְתָ[m] Ch. Peal. pret. 2 pers. sing. masc. . . הוה

הֲוֵית Ch. id. pret. 1 pers. sing. . . . . הוה

[הוּךְ] Ch. fut. יְהָךְ, inf. מְהָךְ (§ 54. rem. 1) *to go.*

הוּכָּה[n] Hoph. pret. 3 p. s. m. for הֻכָּה (comp. הוּלֶּדֶת) נכה

הוֹכַח[o] Hiph. imp. sing. masc. . . . . יכח

הוֹכֵחַ [p]וְ׳ id. inf. absolute . . . . יכח

הוֹכִחַ[q] וְ id. pret. 3 pers. sing. masc. . . . יכח

הוּכַח[r] וְ Hoph. pret. 3 pers. sing. masc. . . יכח

הוֹכִיחַ וְ Hiph. pret. 3 pers. sing. masc. . . יכח

הוּכַן וְ׳ Hop. pret. 3 pers. sing. masc. . . . כון

הוֹלִד[s] defect. for הוֹלִיד (q. v.) . . . ילד

הִוָּלְדָהּ[t] Niph. inf., [הִוָּלֵד] suff. 3 pers. s. f. d. 7b. ילד

הִוָּלְדוֹ[u] id., suff. 3 pers. sing. masc. . . . ילד

הוֹלִדוּ[uu] defect. for הוֹלִידוּ (q.v.) . . . ילד

הוֹלַדְתָּ[y] Hiph. pret. 2 pers. sing. masc. . . ילד

הוּלֶּדֶת[z] Hoph. inf. constr. for הֻלֶּדֶת (§ 20. rem. 16. & § 10. rem. 5) . . . . ילד

הוֹלִיד וְ׳ Hiph. pret. 3 pers. sing. masc. . . ילד

הוֹלִיד[a] וְ id. inf. absolute . . . . . ילד

---

[a] Ge. 27. 29. [b] Da. 2. 35. [c] Ezr. 4. 22. [d] Ps. 42. 6. [e] Ge. 4. 26. [f] Job 32. 11. [g] Job 32. 16. [h] Je. 22. 28. [i] Is. 16. 4. [k] Je. 29. 23. [l] Ex. 9. 3. [m] Da. 2. 31, 34. [n] Ps. 102. 5. [o] Pr. 9. 8. [p] Job 13. 3. [q] Ge. 21. 25. [r] Job 33. 19. [s] Is. 30. 33. [t] Nu. 26. 58. [u] Ho. 2. 5. [uu] Eze. 47. 22. [x] Ec. 7. 1. [y] Ge. 48. 6. [z] Eze. 16. 4, 5. [a] Is. 59. 4.

הוֹלִידָהּ[a] וְ id. pret. 3 pers. sing. m., suff. 3 pers. s. f. ילד

הוֹלִידוֹ id. inf., (הוֹלִיד) suff. 3 pers. sing. m. d. 1 b. ילד

הוֹלִידוּ[b] [c]וְ׳ id. pret. 3 pers. pl. masc. or imp. pl. m. ילד

הוֹלִיךְ[d] Hiph. pret. 3 pers. sing. masc. . . . ילך

הוֹלִיכוֹ[e] וְ id., suff. 3 pers. sing. masc. . . . ילך

הוֹלִיכְךָ[f] id., suff. 2 pers. sing. masc. . . . ילך

הוֹלִיכָם[g] id., suff. 3 pers. pl. masc. . . . ילך

הָוֹלֵךְ[h] Kh. הוֹלֵךְ q. v.; K. הָלוֹךְ Kal inf. absolute הלך

הוֹלֵךְ[i] וְ׳ Kal part. act. sing. masc. dec. 7 b. . הלך

הוֹלֵךְ[k] וְ Hiph. imp. sing. masc. . . . ילך

הוֹלְכוֹת[l] Kal part. f., pl. of הֹלְכָה or הֹלֶכֶת d. 10, or 13 a. הלך

הוֹלְכִים[m] id. masc., pl. of הוֹלֵךְ dec. 7 b. . הלך

הוֹלַכְתִּי וְ Hiph. pret. 1 pers. s.; acc. shifted by conv. וְ (comp. § 8. rem. 7) . . . ילך

הוּלָּלוּ[n] Pual pret. 3 pers. pl. [for הֻלְּלוּ comp. § 8. rem. 7. & § 10. rem. 5] . . . הלל

הוֹלֵלוֹת[o] וְ׳ noun fem., pl. of [הוֹלֵלָה] dec. 10. . הלל

הוֹלֵלוּת[p] noun fem. sing. . . . הלל

הוֹלְלִים[q] Kal part. act. masc., pl. of [הוֹלֵל] dec. 7 b. הלל

הוֹלֶם[r] noun m. [for הֹלֶם], or rather part. act. and acc. drawn back (§ 8. rem. 19) . . . הלם

[הוּם] *to move, confound, perturbate,* De. 7. 23. Niph. (fut. תֵּהֹם) *to be moved, excited.* Hiph. *to be tumultuous.*

מְהוּמָה f. d.10, *confusion, consternation.*

תְּהוֹם m. d.1, pl. וֹת—I. *wave, billow.*—II. *the deep, ocean.*

הוֹמָה[s] fem. of the following . . . . המה

הוֹמֶה[t] Kal part. act. sing. masc. . . . המה

הוֹמִיָּה id. fem., (comp. § 24. rem. 4) . . המה

הוֹמָם וְ pr. name masc. . . . . המם

הוּמַת[u] [x]וְ׳ Hoph. pret. 3 pers. sing. masc. [for הוּמַת comp. § 8. r. 7] . . . מות

הוֹן Kal not used; Arab. *to be light, easy.* Hiph. *to make light of, regard as a light thing,* De. 1. 41.

הוֹן m. d. 1 a, prop. ease, commodity; hence, *wealth, plenty.* Adv. *plenty,* Pr. 30. 15, 16.

הִין masc. *a hin,* a liquid measure containing twelve לֹג.

הוֹן וְ׳ & [y]וָ׳ noun m. s. d. 1 a; for וָ see lett. ו . הון

הוֹנָה[z] Hiph. pret. 3 pers. sing. masc. (§ 25. No. 2 e) ינה

הוֹנוֹ[a] noun masc. sing. from הוֹן dec. 1 a. הון

הוֹנוּ[b] Hiph. pret. 3 pers. sing. masc. (§ 25. No. 2 e) ינה

הוּנַח[c] Hoph. pret. 3 pers. sing. masc. . . נוח

הוֹנַיִךְ[d] noun m. pl. suff. 2 pers. s. f. from הוֹן d. 1 a. הון

הוֹנֵךְ[e] id. sing., suff. 2 pers. sing. fem. . . הון

הוּנַף[f] Hoph. pret. 3 pers. sing. masc. . . נוף

הוּסַד Hoph. pret. 3 pers. sing. masc. . . יסד

הִוָּסְדָהּ[g] Niph. inf. from [הִוָּסֵד] suff. 3 pers. s. f. d. 7 b. יסד

הוֹסַפְתָּ[h] Hiph. pret. 2 pers. sing. masc. . . יסף

הוּסְפַת[i] Ch. Hoph. pret. 3 pers. s. f. (§ 47. rem. 9) יסף

הוֹסַפְתִּי וְ Hiph. pret. 1 pers. sing.; acc. shifted by conv. וְ (comp. § 8. rem. 7) . . יסף

הוּסַר Hoph. pret. 3 pers. sing. masc. . סור

הִוָּסְרוּ[k] Niph. imp. pl. masc. . . . . יסר

הִוָּסְרִי[l] id. imp. sing. fem. . . . . יסר

הוּעַד[m] וְ Hoph. pret. impers. . . . עוד

הוֹעִיל Hiph. pret. 3 pers. sing. masc. or inf. constr. יעל

הוֹעִיל[n] וְ id. inf. absolute . . . יעל

הוֹפִיעַ [o]וְ׳ Hiph. pret. 3 pers. m. or imp. sing. masc. יפע

הוֹפִיעָה[p] id. imp. sing. masc. with parag. ה . יפע

הוֹפַעְתָּ[q] id. pret. 2 p. s. m. [for הוֹפַעְתָּ comp. § 8. r. 7] יפע

הוֹצֵא[r] Kh. הוֹצֵא q. v., K. הַיְצֵא i. q. הוֹצֵא (§ 20. No. 1) יצא

הוֹצֵא [s]וְ׳ Hiph. imp. sing. masc. . . . יצא

הוֹצֵא[t] וְ Hiph. pret. 3 pers. sing. masc. (for הוֹצִיא) יצא

הוּצָאָה[u] Hoph. pret. 3 p. s. f. (הוּצְאָה comp. § 8. r. 7) יצא

הוֹצָאִי[x] [defect. for הוֹצִיאִי] Hiph. inf., suff. 1 p. s. d. 1 b. יצא

הוֹצִאֲךָ id. pret. 3 pers. sing. masc., suff. 2 pers. s. m. יצא

הוֹצֵאתָ id. pret. 2 pers. sing. masc. (§ 25. No. 2 d) יצא

הוֹצֵאתָ וְ id. id.; acc. shifted by conv. וְ (comp. § 8. r. 7) יצא

הוֹצֵאת[y] וְ id. pret. 2 pers. sing. fem. . . . יצא

הוֹצֵאתוֹ[z] וְ id. pret. 2 pers. sing. masc., suff. 3 p. s. m. יצא

הוֹצֵאתִי id. pret. 1 pers. sing. . . . יצא

הוֹצֵאתִי וְ id. id.; acc. shifted by conv. וְ (comp. § 8. r. 7) יצא

הוֹצֵאתִיהָ[a] id. suff. 3 pers. sing. fem. . . . יצא

הוֹצֵאתִיךָ id., suff. 2 pers. sing. masc. . . יצא

הוֹצֵאתִים[b] [c]וְ׳ id., suff. 3 pers. pl. masc. . . . יצא

הוֹצֵאתֶם[d] [e]וְ׳ id. pret. 2 pers. pl. masc. . . יצא

הוֹצֵאתָנוּ[f] id. pret. 2 pers. sing. masc., suff. 1 pers. pl. יצא

הוֹצֵאתָנִי[g] / וְ הוֹצֵאתַנִי } id. pret. 2 pers. sing. masc., suff. 1 p. s. יצא

הוֹצִיא וְ׳ id. pret. 3 pers. sing. m.; or inf. constr.; or (Is. 43. 8) imp. sing. masc. . . יצא

הוֹצִיאִי[h] Kh. id., K. הוֹצִיאִי (q. v.) . . . יצא

הוֹצִיאָהּ[i] Hiph. imp. sing, masc., suff. 3 pers. sing. fem. יצא

הוֹצִיאָה[k] id. imp. sing. masc. with parag. ה . . יצא

הוֹצִיאֻהוּ[l] וְ id. pret. 3 pers. pl. masc., suff. 3 pers. s. m. יצא

הוֹצִיאוּ וְ׳ id. pret. 3 pers. pl., or imp. pl. masc. . יצא

[a] Is. 55. 10. [b] Le. 25. 45. [c] Je. 29. 6. [d] 2 Ki. 24. 15. [e] Pr. 16. 29. [f] De. 8. 2. [g] Is. 48. 21. [h] Jos. 6. 13. [i] Pr. 28. 26. [k] Nu. 17. 11. [l] Ne. 6. 17. [m] Ge. 37. 25. [n] Ps. 78. 63. [o] Ec. 7. 25. [p] Ec. 10. 13. [q] Ps. 5. 6. [r] Is. 41. 7. [s] 1 Ki. 1. 41. [t] Je. 4. 19. [u] 2 Ki. 11. 2. [x] De. 21. 22. [y] Pr. 19. 14. [z] Eze. 18. 12, 16. [a] Pr. 28 8. [b] Eze. 22. 7, 29. [c] La. 5. 5. [d] Eze. 27. 33. [e] Eze. 27. 27. [f] Ex. 29. 27. [g] Ex. 9. 18. [h] 1 Ki. 10. 7. [i] Da. 4. 33. [k] Ps. 2. 10. [l] Je. 6. 8. [m] Ex. 21. 29. [n] Je. 23. 32. [o] Job 37. 15. [p] Ps. 80. 2. [q] Job 10. 3. [r] Ge. 8. 17. [s] Ex. 3. 10. [t] De. 22. 14, etc. [u] Eze. 38. 8. [x] Je. 34. 13. [y] 1 Ki. 17. 13. [z] Ne. 9. 7. [a] Zec. 5. 4. [b] Eze. 20. 14. [c] Eze. 34. 13. [d] Ex. 16. 3. [e] De. 22. 24. [f] De. 9. 28. [g] Job 10. 18. [h] Je. 7. 22. [i] Eze. 24. 6. [k] Ps. 142. 8. [l] 1 Ki. 21. 10.

הוֹצִיאוּהָ id. imp. pl. masc., suff. 3 pers. sing. fem. . יצא
הוֹצִיאִי[a] id. inf. with suff. 1 pers. s. d. 1 b, or imp. s. f. יצא
הוֹצִיאֲךָ id. pret. 3 pers. sing. m., suff. 2 pers. s. m. יצא
הוֹצִיאָם id. id., suff. 3 pers. pl. masc. . . יצא
הוֹצִיאֵם[b] id. imp. sing. masc., suff. 3 pers. pl. masc. . יצא
הוֹצִיאָנוּ id. pret. 3 pers. sing. masc., suff. 1 pers. pl. יצא
הוֹצִיאַנִי וְ id. id., suff. 1 pers. sing. . . . יצא
הוֹצִיאֵנִי[d] וְ'[c] id. imp. sing. masc., suff. 1 pers. sing. . יצא
הַוֹּצִיתִיהָ[f] וְ Kh. הוֹצִיתִיהָ', K. הַצִּיתוּהָ' Hiph. pret. 1 p. sing. or imp. pl. masc., suff. 3 pers. sing. fem. (§ 20. rem. 16) . . . יצת
הוּצַק[g] Hoph. pret. 3 pers. sing. masc. . . יצק
הוּקַם Hoph. pret. 3 pers. sing. masc. . . . קום
הוֹקַע[h] וְ Hiph. imp. sing. masc. . . . . יקע
הוֹקַעֲנוּם[i] וְ id. pret. 1 pers. pl., suff. 3 pers. pl. masc. יקע
הוֹרֵג Kal part. act. sing. masc. dec. 7 b. . . הרג
הוֹרָגְנוּ[k] Pual pret. 1 pers. pl. [for הֹרַגְנוּ ,הֹרֵ'] . הרג
הוֹרֵד Hiph. imp. sing. masc. . . . . ירד
הוּרַד וְ' Hoph. pret. 3 pers. sing. masc. . . ירד
הוֹרִדִי[l] Hiph. pret. 3 pers. sing. masc. for הוֹרִיד ירד
הוֹרִדֵהוּ[m] וְ Hiph. imp. sing. masc., 3 pers. sing. masc. ירד
הוֹרִדֻהוּ[n] id. pret. 3 p. pl. m. or imp. pl. m., suff. id. [for הוֹרִידוּהוּ] . . . . . ירד
הוֹרִדוּ וְ id. pret. 3 pers. pl. masc. [for הוֹרִידוּ] . ירד
הוֹרִדְנוּ[o] id. pret. 1 pers. pl. . . . . . ירד
הוֹרַדְתָּ[p] וְ Hiph. pret. 2 pers. s. m.; acc. shifted by וְ conv. (comp. § 8. rem. 7) . . . . ירד
הוּרַדְתָּ[q] וְ Hoph. pret. 2 p. s. m.; acc. id. (comp. id.) ירד
הוֹרַדְתִּי וְ Hiph. pret. 1 pers. s.; acc. id. (comp. id.) ירד
הוֹרַדְתִּיךְ[r] וְ id. with suff. 2 pers. sing. fem. . . ירד
הוֹרַדְתִּים וְ id. with suff. 3 pers. sing. masc. . ירד
הוֹרַדְתֶּם וְ id. pret. 2 pers. pl. masc. . . . ירד
הוֹרַדְתִּנוּ[s] id. pret. 2 pers. sing. fem., suff. 1 pers. pl. [for הוֹרַדְתִּינוּ § 16. rem. 5] . . . ירד
הוֹרֵהוּ[t] Hiph. pret. 3 p. s. m., suff. 3 p. s. m. (§ 25. No. 2 e) ירה
הוֹרוּנִי[u] id. imp. pl. masc.; suff. 1 pers. sing. . . ירה
הוֹרַי[y] Kal part. act. pl. m., suff. 1 p. s. fr. [הוֹרָה] 9 a. הרה
הוֹרִיד[z] וְ Hiph. pret. 3 pers. sing. masc. . . ירד
הוֹרִידוּ וְ' id. pret. 3 p. pl. m., or (Ge. 43. 11) imp. pl. m. ירד
הוֹרִידִי[a] id. imp. sing. fem. . . . . . ירד
הוֹרִידֵמוֹ[b] וְ id. imp. sing. masc., suff. 3 pers. pl. . ירד
הוֹרִישׁ[c] וְ Hiph. inf. absolute . . . . ירש
הוֹרִישׁ וְ' id. pret. 3 pers. sing. masc. . . . ירש
הוֹרִישׁוֹ[aa] id. pret., or inf. with suff. 3 pers. sing. masc. ירש
הוֹרִישׁוּ id. pret. 3 pers. pl. masc. . . . ירש
הוֹרִישָׁם[d] id. inf., suff. 3 pers. pl. masc. . . . ירש

הוֹרֵיתִי וְ Hiph. pret. 1 pers. sing.; acc. shifted to ult. by conv. וְ (§ 8. rem. 7) . . . ירה
הוֹרֵיתִיךָ[e] וְ id., suff. 2 pers. sing. masc. . . . ירה
הוּרַם[f] Hoph. pret. 3 pers. sing. masc. [for הוּרַם] רום
הוֹרֵנִי Hiph. imp. sing. masc., suff. 1 pers. sing. ירה
הוּרַק[g] Hoph. pret. 3 pers. sing. masc. . . רוק
הוֹרֵשׁ וְ Hiph. inf. abs. . . . . . . ירש
הוֹרַשְׁתָּ id. pret. 2 pers. sing. masc. . . . ירש
הוֹרַשְׁתִּים[h] וְ id. pret. 1 pers. sing., suff. 3 pers. pl. masc. ירש
הוֹרַשְׁתָּם[i] וְ id. pret. 2 pers. sing. m., suff. 3 pers. pl. m. ירש
הוֹרַשְׁתֶּם וְ id. pret. 2 pers. pl. masc. . . . ירש
הוֹרַשְׁתָּנוּ[k] id. pret. 2 pers. sing. masc., suff. 1 pers. pl. ירש
הוֹרָתִי[l] Kal part. act. sing. fem., suff. 1 pers. sing. [from הוֹרָה dec. 10, from הוֹרֶה masc.] . הרה
הוֹרָתָם[m] id., suff. 3 pers. pl. masc. . . . . הרה
הוֹרֵתָנִי[n] Hiph. pret. 2 pers. sing. masc., suff. 1 pers. sing. (for תַּנִי' § 2. rem. 1) . . . ירה
הוֹשֵׁב[o] Hiph. imp. sing. masc. . . . . ישב
הוּשַׁב[p] Hoph. pret. 3 pers. sing. masc. . . . שוב
הוֹשְׁבוֹתִים[q] וְ Hiph. pret. 1 p. s., suff. 3 p. pl. m. mixed form of פ״י & ע״ו, as הֲשִׁיבוֹתִים & הוֹשַׁבְתִּים ישב
הוֹשַׁבְתִּי[r] Hiph. pret. 1 pers. sing. . . . . ישב
הוֹשַׁבְתִּי וְ id. id. acc. shifted by וְ conv. (§ 8. rem. 7) ישב
הוֹשַׁבְתִּיךְ[s] וְ id. id., suff. 2 pers. sing. fem. . . . ישב
הוֹשַׁבְתִּים[t] וְ id., suff. 3 pers. pl. masc. . . . ישב
הוּשַׁבְתֶּם[u] וְ Hoph. pret. 3 pers. pl. masc. . . . ישב
הוֹשִׁיבוּ[x] וְ Hiph. imp. pl. masc. . . . . ישב
הוֹשִׁיבַנִי id. pret. 3 pers. sing. masc., suff. 1 pers. sing. ישב
הוֹשִׁיעַ וְ'[y] Hiph. pret. 3 pers. sing. masc.; or inf. constr. ישע
הוֹשִׁיעָה וְ' id. pret. 3 pers. sing. fem.; or imp. sing. masc. with parag. ה . . . ישע
הוֹשִׁיעוֹ[z] id. pret. 3 pers. sing. m., suff. 3 pers. sing. m. ישע
הוֹשִׁיעֵם[a] וְ' id. id., suff. 3 pers. pl. masc. . . . ישע
הוֹשִׁיעֵנוּ וְ'[b] id. imp. sing. masc., suff. 1 pers. pl. . ישע
הוֹשִׁיעֵנִי וְ'[c] id. id., suff. 1 pers. sing. . . . ישע
הוֹשָׁמָע (for יְהוֹשָׁמָע) pr. name masc. 1 Ch. 3. 18.
הוֹשַׁע Hiph. imp. sing. masc. . . . . ישע
הוֹשַׁע[d] וְ id. pret. 3 pers. sing. masc., for הוֹשִׁיעַ . ישע
הוֹשֵׁעַ וְ id. inf. abs. . . . . . . ישע
הוֹשֵׁעַ וְ' pr. name masc. . . . . . ישע
הוֹשַׁעָה[ff] defect. for הוֹשִׁיעָה (q.v.) . . . ישע
הוֹשַׁעְיָה pr. name masc. . . . . . ישע
הִוָּשְׁעוּ[e] וְ Niph. imp. pl. masc. . . . . ישע
הוֹשִׁעֵנִי[f] וְ Hiph. imp. sing. masc., suff. 1 pers. sing. ישע
הוֹשַׁעְתָּ[gg] id. pret. 2 pers. sing. masc. . . . ישע
הוֹשַׁעְתָּ וְ id. id. acc. shifted by וְ conv. (§ 8. rem. 7) ישע

[a] Je. 11. 4. Jos. 2. 3.
[b] Ge. 19. 5.
[c] Eze. 42. 15.
[d] Ps. 25. 17.
[e] 1 Ki. 22. 34.
[f] 2 Sa. 14. 30.
[g] Ps. 45. 3.
[h] Nu. 25. 4.
[i] 2 Sa. 21. 6.
[k] Ps. 44. 23.
[l] 2 Ki. 16. 17.
[m] Eze. 32. 18.
[n] Ge. 39. 1; 44. 21.
[o] Ge. 43. 22.
[p] 1 Ki. 2. 9.
[q] Eze. 31. 18.
[r] Eze. 26. 20.
[s] Joel 4. 2.
[t] Jos. 2. 18.
[u] 2 Ki. 12. 3.
[x] Job 6. 24.
[y] Ge. 49. 26.
[z] Am. 3. 11.
[a] La. 2. 18.
[b] Ps. 59. 12.
[c] Ju. 1. 28.
[d] Ju. 2. 23.
[e] Ex. 4. 12.
[f] Ex. 29. 27.
[g] Je. 48. 11.
[h] Jos. 14. 12.
[i] De. 9. 3.
[k] 2 Ch. 20. 11.
[l] Ca. 3. 4.
[m] Ho. 2. 7.
[n] Ps. 119. 102.
[o] Ge. 47. 6.
[p] Ge. 42. 28.
[q] Zec. 10. 6.
[r] Le. 23. 43.
[s] Eze. 26. 20.
[t] Ho. 11. 11.
[u] Is. 5. 8.
[x] 1 Ki. 21. 10.
[y] 1 Sa. 9. 16.
[z] Ps. 34. 7.
[a] Is. 63. 9.
[aa] Nu. 32. 21.
[b] Je. 2. 27.
[c] Ps. 71. 2.
[d] Zec. 12. 7.
[e] Is. 45. 22.
[f] 2 Ki. 16. 7.
[ff] 2 Sa. 14. 4.
[gg] Job 26. 2.

Word	Analysis	Root
הוֹשַׁעְתִּי	וְ id. pret. 1 pers. sing.; acc. id.	ישע
[a]הוֹשַׁעְתִּיךָ	וְ id. id., suff. 2 pers. sing. masc.	ישע
[b]הוֹשַׁעְתִּים	וְ id. id., suff. 3 pers. pl. masc.	ישע
[c]הוֹשַׁעְתֶּם	id. pret. 2 pers. pl. masc.	ישע
הוֹשַׁעְתָּנוּ	id. pret. 2 pers. sing. masc., suff. 1 pers. pl.	ישע
[d]הַוֹּשַׁר	Kh. הוֹשַׁר, K. הַיְשַׁר Hiph. imp. sing. masc. (§ 20. No. 1)	ישר
הֲוָת[e] / הֲוָת[f]	וַ Chald. Peal pret. 3 pers. sing. fem.; וֲ bef. (-:)	הוה
[g]הַוַּת	[h] וְ noun sing. fem. constr. of [הַוָּה] dec. 10.	הוה
הַוֹּת	id. pl. (for הַוּוֹת).	הוה
[i]הוֹתֵב	וְ Ch. Aph. pret. 3 pers. sing. m. (§ 47. r. 4)	יתב
הוֹתִיר	pr. name masc.	יתר
[aa]הוֹתִיר	Hiph. pret. 3 pers. sing. masc.; or inf. constr.	יתר
[k]הוֹתִירְךָ	וְ id., suff. 2 pers. sing. masc.	יתר
[l]הוּתַל	Hoph. pret. 3 pers. sing. masc.	תלל
[m]הוֹתֵר	Hiph. imp. sing. masc.	יתר
הוֹתֵר	וְ id. inf. abs.	יתר
[n]הוֹתִרָה	id. pret. 3 pers. sing. fem. [for הוֹתִירָה]	יתר
[o]הוֹתִרְךָ	וְ id. with suff. 2 pers. sing. masc.	יתר
הוֹתַרְתִּי	וְ id. pret. 1 pers. sing.; acc. on ult. by conv. וְ (§ 8. rem. 7)	יתר
הַזֹּאת / הֲזֹּאת	pref. הַ / pref. הֲ } pron. demon. sing. fem. see	זה
[p]הַזֹּאתָה	pref. הַ) id., Kheth. 'זֹאתָה id. with parag. ה, K. זֹאת, see	זה
הַזָּב	[q] וְ' pref. id.) Kal part. act. sing. masc.	זוב
הַזְּבוּלֹנִי	pref. id.) gent. n. from זְבוּלוּן	זבל
הַזֶּבַח[r] / הַזָּבַח	וְ' pref. id.) n. m. s. dec. 6a. (with suff. זִבְחִי but see § 35. rem. 2)	זבח
[s]הַזֹּבֵחַ	pref. id.) Kal part. act. sing. masc. dec. 7b.	זבח
הַזְּבָחִים	[u] וְ' pref. id.) noun masc., pl. of זֶבַח dec. 6. comp. הַזָּבַח	זבח
הַזֹּבְחִים	pref. id.) Kal part. act. m., pl. of זֹבֵחַ d. 7b.	זבח
[x]הַזֵּדוֹן	pref. id.) noun masc. sing. dec. 3a.	זדה
[y]הַזֵּדִים	pref. id.) adj. masc., pl. of זֵד dec. 1a.	זוד

[הָזָה] *to dream, to talk in one's dream*, Is. 56. 10; Prof. Lee, *to nod, doze*.

Word	Analysis	Root
[z]הַזֵּה	Hiph. imp. sing. masc.	נזה
הַזֶּה / הֶזֶּה	pref. הַ / pref. הֶ } & : pron. demon. sing. masc.	זה
הִזָּה	וְ Hiph. pret. 3 pers. sing. masc.	נזה
הַזָּהָב	וְ' prf. הַ) noun masc. sing. dec. 4a.	זהב
[a]הִזְהִיר	וְ Hiph. pret. 3 pers. sing. masc.	זהר
[b]הִזָּהֵר	Niph. imp. sing. masc.	זהר
[c]הִזְהִירוֹ	וְ Hiph. pret. 3 pers. sing. masc., suff. 3 pers. sing. masc., K. 'רוֹ	זהר
הִזְהַרְתָּ	id. pret. 2 pers. sing. masc.	זהר
הִזְהַרְתָּ / [d]הִזְהַרְתָּה	וְ id. id.; acc. shifted by conv. וְ (§ 8. rem. 7, comp. 5)	זהר
[e]הִזְהַרְתּוֹ	id. id., suff. 3 pers. sing. masc.	זהר
[ff]הִזְהַרְתֶּם	וְ id. pret. 2 pers. pl. masc.	זהר
הַזּוּזִים	pref. הַ) pr. name of a people	זוז
הַזּוֹנָה	pref. id.) fem. of the following, dec. 10.	זנה
[f]הַזּוֹנֶה	pref. id.) Kal part. act. sing. masc. dec. 9a.	זנה
[g]הַזּוּרֶה	וְ pref. id.) Kal part. pass. [זוּר] with term. ־ֶה [for זוּרָה] comp. לָנֶה	זור
הַזֹּחֶלֶת	pref. id.) pr. name, see אֶבֶן	אבן
[h]הֵזִידוּ	Hiph. pret. 3 pers. pl. masc.	זוד
[i]הַזֵּידוֹנִים	pref. הַ) noun masc., pl. of [זֵידוֹן] dec. 1b.	זוד
[k]הִזִּיל	Hiph. pret. 3 pers. sing. masc.	נזל
[l]הִזִּילוּהָ	Hiph. pret. 3 pers. pl. masc. with suff., 3 pers. sing. fem., Chald. inflexion (§ 18. rem. 14)	זלל
[m]הֹזִים	Kal part. act. masc., pl. of [הֹזֶה] dec. 9a.	הזה
הַזִּיפִים	pref. הַ) gent. noun pl. [of זִיפִי from זִיף]	זוף
[n]הִזִּיר	וְ Hiph. pret. 3 pers. sing. masc.	נזר
[o]הַזִּירוֹ	id. inf., suff. 3 pers. sing. m. from הַזִּיר d. 1b.	נזר
הַזַּיִת	pref. הַ) noun masc. sing. dec. 6h.	זית
[p]הִזֵּיתָ	וְ Hiph. pret. 2 pers. sing. masc. (§ 24. rem. 14); acc. shifted by וְ conv. (§ 8. rem. 7)	נזה
הַזֵּיתִים	pref. הַ) noun masc., pl. of זַיִת dec. 6h.	זית
[q]הִזַּכּוּ	Hithp. imp. pl. masc. [for הִתְזַכּוּ]	זכה
[zz]הֲזִכּוֹתִי	וַ Hiph. pret. 1 pers. sing.; וַ before (-:)	זכך
[u]הַזְכִּיר	Hiph. inf. construct	זכר
[v]הִזְכִּיר	id. pret. 3 pers. sing. masc.	זכר
הַזְכִּירוּ	id. imp. pl. masc.	זכר
[w]הַזְכִּירֵנִי	id. imp. sing. masc. with 1 pers. sing.	זכר
הַזָּכָר	pref. הַ) noun masc. sing. dec. 4a.	זכר
[u]הַזִּכָּרוֹן	pref. id.) noun masc. sing. dec. 3c.	זכר
הַזְּכָרִים	pref. id.) noun masc., pl. of זָכָר dec. 4a.	זכר
[x]הַזְכַּרְכֶם	Hiph. inf. [הַזְכַּר Chald. form.] 2 pers. pl. m.	זכר
[y]הִזָּכֶרְכֶם	Niph. inf. [הִזָּכֵר] suff. 2 pers. s. m. dec. 7b.	זכר
[z]הַזִּכְרֹנוֹת	pref. הַ) noun masc. with pl. fem. term. from זִכָּרוֹן dec. 3c.	זכר
[b]הִזְכַּרְתַּנִי	וְ Hiph. pret. 2 pers. sing. masc., suff. 1 pers. s.	זכר
[c]הַזַּלְזַלִּים	pref. הַ) noun masc., pl. of [זַלְזַל] dec. 8d.	זלזל
[d]הַזָּלִים	pref. id.) Kal part. act., pl. of [זָל] dec. 1a.	זול
הַזִּמָּה	pref. id.) noun fem. sing. dec. 10.	זמם
הַזְּמוֹרָה	pref. id.) noun fem. sing. dec. 10.	זמר
[e]הַזָּמִיר	pref. id.) noun masc. sing.	זמר
[f]הִזְמִנְתּוּן	Chald. Kh. הַזְמִנְתּוּן, K. הִזְדַּמִּנְתּוּן Aph. or	

[a] 1 Ch. 19. 12. [b] Ho. 1. 7. [c] Ju. 12. 2. [d] Ps. 5. 9. [e] Ezr. 4. 24. [f] Da. 2. 35.
[g] Mi. 7. 3. [h] Pr. 10. 3. [i] Ezr. 4. 10. [k] De. 30. 9. [l] Is. 44. 20. [m] Ps. 79. 11.
[n] Ruth 2. 18. [o] De. 28. 11. [p] Je. 26. 6. [q] Le. 15. 33. [r] Le. 7. 17. [s] Eze. 40. 42.
[t] 1 Sa. 2. 15. [u] 2 Ch. 7. 1. [x] Eze. 7. 10. [y] Je. 43. 2. [z] Nu. 8. 7. [a] Eze. 33. 3.
[b] Ec. 12. 12. [c] 2 Ki. 6. 10. [d] Ex. 18. 20. [e] Eze. 3. 18, 20, 21. [f] Eze. 6. 9. [g] Is. 29. 5.
[h] Ne. 9. 10, 16, 29. [i] Ps. 124. 5. [k] Is. 48. 21. [l] La. 1. 8. [m] Is. 56. 10. [n] Nu. 6. 12.
[o] Nu. 6. 6. [p] Ex. 29. 21. [q] Is. 1. 16. [r] Is. 49. 1. [s] Is. 43. 26. [t] 2 Sa. 18. 18.
[u] Nu. 5. 18. [x] Eze. 21. 29. [y] Eze. 21. 29. [z] Est. 6. 1. [zz] Job 9. 30. [aa] Je. 44. 7.
[b] Ge. 40. 14. [c] Is. 18. 5. [d] Is. 46. 6. [e] Ca. 2. 12. [f] Da. 2. 9. [ff] 2 Ch. 19. 10.

Ithpa. [for אִתְ׳, הִתְזַמִּנְתּוּן § 47. rem. 4] pret. 2 pers. pl. masc. . . . . זמן

הַזָּנָב[a] pref. הַ (noun masc. sing. dec. 4a. . . זנב

הַזְּנָבוֹת[b] pref. id. (id. pl. absolute (construct זַנְבוֹת § 33. rem. 1) . . . . זנב

הַזְנֵה[c] Hiph. inf. absolute . . . . זנה

הִזְנוּ[d] וְ׳[e] id. pret. 3 pers. pl. . . . זנה

הַזֹּנוֹת וְ׳[f] Kal part. act. fem., pl. of זוֹנָה dec. 10, from זוֹנֶה masc. . . . . זנה

הִזְנִיחַ[g] Hiph. pret. 3 pers. sing. masc. . . זנח

הִזְנִיחָם[h] id. with suff. 3 pers. pl. masc. . . זנח

הַזֹּנִים[i] pref. הַ (Kal part. act. m., pl. of זוֹנֶה dec. 9a. זנה

הִזְנֵיתָ[k] Hiph. pret. 2 pers. sing. masc. (§ 24. rem. 14) זנה

הַזָּעַם[l] pref. הַ (noun masc. sing. dec. 6d. (for זַעַם § 35. rem. 2) . . . . זעם

הַזְעֶק־[m] Hiph. imp. sing. m. [for הַזְעֵק § 11. rem. 5] זעק

הַזְּעָקָה[n] pref. הַ (noun fem. s. dec. 11c. (§ 42. rem. 1) זעק

הַזִּפִים pref. id. (gent. noun pl. [of זִיפִי fr. זִיף] . זוף

הַזָּקָן pref. id. (noun com. sing. dec. 4a. . זקן

הַזָּקֵן pref. id. (adj. and subst. masc. sing. dec. 5a. זקן

הַזְּקֵנִים וְ׳ pref. id. (id. pl. absolute . . זקן

הַזָּר וְ pref. id. (Kal part. act. sing. m. dec. 1a. זור

הַזְּרוֹעַ[o] pref. id. (noun com. sing. dec. 1a. . זקן

הַזַּרְחִי pref. id. (patronym. of זֶרַח . . . זרח

הַזָּרִים[p] pref. id. (Kal part. act. m., pl. of זָר dec. 1a. זור

הַזֶּרַע, הַזָּרַע } pref. id. (noun masc. sing. dec. 6a. (§ 35. rem. 2 & 5) . . } זרע

הַזְּרֹעַ וְ׳[q] pref. id. (noun com. sing. dec. 1a. . זרע

הַזְּרֹעִים[r] pref. id. (noun masc. pl. [of זֵרוֹעַ] . . זרע

הַזֹּרְעִים[s] pref. id. (Kal part. act. m., pl. of זֹרֵעַ dec. 7b. זרע

הַזֹּרֵק[t] pref. id. (Kal part. act. sing. masc. . זרק

הִזַּרְתֶּם[u] וְ Hiph. pret. 2 pers. pl. masc. . . נזר

הָחְבְּאוּ[x] Hoph. pret. 3 pers. pl. [הָחְבְּאוּ comp. § 8. rem. 7] . . . . . חבא

הֶחְבְּאַתָה[y] Hiph. pret. 3 pers. sing. fem. with parag. ה (§ 11. rem. 1) . . . . חבא

הֶחְבִּיאָה[z] id. pret. 3 pers. sing. fem. . . . חבא

הֶחְבִּיאָנִי[zz] id. pret. 3 pers. sing. masc., suff. 1 pers. sing. (§ 11. rem. 1, & § 2. rem. 1) . . חבא

הַחֶבֶל[a] pref. הַ (noun m. s. dec. 6. (§ 35. rem. 4) חבל

הַחֹבֵל[b] pref. id. (noun masc. sing. dec. 7b. . חבל

הַחֹבְלִים[c] pref. id. (Kal part. act. m., pl. of חֹבֵל d. 7b. חבל

הַחֶבְרִי pref. id. (patronym. of חֶבֶר . . . חבר

הַחֶבְרֹנִי pref. id. (patronym. of חֶבְרוֹן . . חבר

הַחֹבֶרֶת pref. id. (noun fem. sing. . . . חבר

הַחֲבִתִּים[d] pref. id. (noun masc., pl. of [חֲבִת] dec. 8b. חבת

הֶחָג וְ׳[e] pref. הֶ bef. חָ for הַ (noun m. s. dec. 8a. חגג

הֶחָגָב pref. id. (noun masc. sing. dec. 4c. . חגב

הֶחָגוּר[f] pref. id. (Kal part. p. sing. masc. dec. 3a. חגר

הַחַגִּי pref. הַ (patronym. [for חַגִּיִּי] from חַגִּי . חגג

הֶחָדֵל[g] וְ pref. הֶ bef. חָ for הַ (adj. masc. s. dec. 5a. חדל

הֶחָדַלְתִּי[h] pref. id. interr. (Kal pret. 1 pers. sing. (The form seems to be an error of the transcribers, and to stand for הֶחֳדַלְתִּי, like הַחֲרֵבוֹת for הֶחֳרֵבוֹת. Some codices have הֶחֱדַלְתִּי, Hiph. without the interr. ה) חדל

הַחֶדֶר pref. הַ (noun masc. dec. 6. (§ 35. rem. 4) חדר

הַחַדְרָה pref. id. } id. with paragogic ה . חדר

הֶחָדְרָה pref. הֶ bef. חָ for הַ } id. with paragogic ה . חדר

הַחֹדֶרֶת[i] pref. הַ (Kal part. act. sing. fem. . חדר

הַחֹדֶשׁ וְ׳[k] pref. id. (noun masc. sing. dec. 6c. . חדשׁ

הֶחָדָשׁ pref. הֶ bef. חָ for הַ (adj. masc. sing. dec. 4c. חדשׁ

הַחֲדָשָׁה pref. הַ (fem. of the prec. . . . חדשׁ

הַחֲדָשִׁים[l] pref. id. (adj. masc., pl. of חָדָשׁ dec. 4c. חדשׁ

הֶחֳדָשִׁים[m] pref. הֶ bef. חָ for הַ (n. m., pl. of חֹדֶשׁ d. 6c. חדשׁ

הַחוֹחַ pref. הַ (noun masc. sing. dec. 1a. . חוח

הַחוֹחִים[n] pref. id. (id. pl., also once חֲוָחִים׳ (§ 35. r. 13) חוח

הַחוּט[o] וְ pref. id. (noun masc. sing. . . חוט

הַחוֹטֶא[p] וְ pref. id. (Kal part. act. sing. masc. for חוֹטֵא § 23. rem. 9. . . . . חטא

הַחִוִּי וְ׳ pref. id. (pr. name of a people . חוה

הַחֲוִילָה pref. id. (pr. name of a country, see חֲוִילָה

הַחוֹל[q] pref. id. (noun masc. sing. . . . חול

הַחוֹלָה[r] pref. id. (fem. of the foll., dec. 10. . חלה

הַחוֹלֶה[s] pref. id. (Kal part. act. masc. sing. . חלה

הַחוֹמָה pref. id. (noun fem. sing. dec. 10. . חמה

הַחֲוֹנִי[t] Chald. Aph. imp. pl. masc., suff. 1 pers. sing. חוה

הַחוֹנִים[u], הַחוֹנִם[x] וְ } pref. הַ (Kal part. act. masc., pl. of חוֹנֶה dec. 9a. . . . } חנה

הַחוֹסֶה[y] וְ pref. id. (Kal part. act. sing. m., dec. 9a. חסה

הַחוֹסִים pref. id. (id. pl., absolute state - . . . חסה

הַחוּפָמִי pref. id. (patronym. of חוּפָם, see חֻפִּים . חפף

הַחוּץ pref. id. (noun masc. sing. dec. 1a. . חוי

הַחוּצָה pref. id. (id. with paragogic ה . . חוץ

הַחוֹר[ee] pref. id. (noun masc. sing. dec. 1a. . חור

הַחֹזֶה pref. id. (noun masc. sing. dec. 9a. . חזה

הֶחָזֶה pref. הֶ bef. חָ for הַ (noun masc. dec. 9b. חזה

הֶחָזוֹן pref. id. (noun masc. sing. dec. 3a. . חזה

הֶחָזוֹת[z] pref. id. (n. m. with pl. f. term. from חָזֶה חזה

הַחִזָּיוֹן[a] pref. הַ (noun masc. sing., dec. 3c. . חזה

הַחֹזִים וְ׳[b] pref. id. (Kal part. act. masc. or subst., pl. of חֹזֶה dec. 9a. . . . חזה

[a] Is. 9. 14. [b] Ju. 15. 4. [c] Ho. 4. 18. [d] Ho. 4. 10, 18. [e] Ex. 34. 16. [f] 1 Ki. 22. 38. [g] 2 Ch. 29. 19. [h] 2 Ch. 11. 14. [i] Le. 20. 5. [k] Ho. 5. 3. [l] Da. 8. 19. [m] 2 Sa. 20. 4. [n] Is. 15. 8. [o] Da. 11. 6. [p] Eze. 7. 21. [q] De. 7. 19. [r] Da. 1. 12. [s] Ps. 126. 5. [t] Le. 7. 14. [u] Le. 15. 31. [x] Is. 42. 22. [y] Jos. 6. 17. [z] Jos. 6. 25. [zz] Is. 49. 2. [a] 2 Sa. 8. 2. [b] Jon. 1. 6. [c] Zec. 11. 14. [d] 1 Ch. 9. 31. [e] 2 Ch. 7. 9. [ee] Ca. 5. 4. [f] Ju. 18. 17. [g] Eze. 3. 27. [h] Ju. 9. 9, 11, 13. [i] Eze. 21. 19. [k] Est. 9. 22. [l] Is. 66. 22. [m] Ne. 10. 34. [n] Ca. 2. 2. [o] Ec. 4. 12. [p] Is. 65. 20. [q] Pr. 27. 3. [r] Eze. 34. 4, 16. [s] Mal. 1. 13. [t] Da. 2. 6. [u] Na. 3. 17. [x] Nu. 2. 12. [y] Is. 57. 13. [z] Le. 9. 20, 21. [a] 2 Sa. 7. 17. [b] Eze. 13. 16.

Word	Analysis	Root
הֶחֱזִין וְ	Hiph. pret. 3 pers. sing. masc. . . .	חזק
הֶחֱזִיקָה וְ׳	id. pret. 3 pers. sing. fem. . .	חזק
[a]הַחֲזִיקוּ	id. imp. pl. masc.	חזק
הֶחֱזִיקוּ וְ׳	id. pret. 3 pers. pl. masc. . . .	חזק
[b]הַחֲזִיקִי [c]וְ׳	id. imp. sing. fem. . . .	חזק
[d]הַחֲזִקִי	id. inf. (הַחֲזִיק § 11. rem. 4, comp. § 13. rem. 9) with suff. 1 pers. sing. .	חזק
[e]הֶחֱזִיקֵךְ	id. pret. 3 pers. sing. m., suff. 2 pers. s. fem.	חזק
[f]הֶחֱזִיקַתְהוּ	id. pret. 3 pers. sing. fem., suff. 3 pers. s. m.	חזק
הַחֲזִיר	pref. הַ)(noun masc. sing. . . .	חזר
הַחֲזֵק	Hiph. imp. sing. masc. . . .	חזק
הֶחָזָק	pref. הֶ bef. חָ for הַ)(adj. masc. sing. dec. 4 a & c (§ 33. rem. 1) . . .	חזק
הַחֲזָקָה [g]וְ׳	pref. הַ)(fem. of the prec. . .	חזק
[h]הֶחֱזַקְתָּ וְ	Hiph. pret. 3 pers. sing. masc. . .	חזק
הֶחֱזַקְתִּי [i]וְ׳	id. pret. 1 pers. sing. . . .	חזק
[k]הַחֲזַקְתִּי וְ	id. id. acc. shifted by conv. וְ (§ 8. rem. 7, and § 13. rem. 10)	חזק
[l]הֶחֱזַקְתִּיךָ	id. id. suff. 2 pers. sing. masc. . .	חזק
[m]הֶחֱזִקַתְנוּ	id. pret. 3 pers. sing. fem., suff. 1 pers. pl.	חזק
[n]הֶחֱזַקְתְנִי	id. id., suff. 1 pers. sing. . . .	חזק
[o]הַחַטָּאָה	pref. הַ)(noun fem. sing. [from חַטָּא masc.]	חטא
הַחַטָּאִים	pref. id.)(noun masc., pl. of [חַטָּא] dec. 1 b.	חטא
הַחַטָּאת וְ׳	pref. id.)(noun fem. sing. (§ 39. No. 4, & § 44. rem. 5) . .	חטא
[p]הַחֹטֵאת	pref. הַ id.)(Kal part. act. fem. s. [for חֹטֵאת § 23. rem. 4] . . .	חטא
[q]הַחִטָּה וְ	pref. id.)(noun fem. sing. (pl. חִטִּים) .	חטה
[r]הַחֲטִי	Hiph. inf. constr. for הַחֲטִיא (§ 23. rem. 7)	חטא
[s]הֶחֱטִי, הֶחֱטִיא	id. pret. 3 pers. sing. masc. (§ 23. rem. 7)	חטא
[t]הֶחֱטִיאוּ	id. pret. 3 pers. pl.	חטא
הֶחֱטִיאָם וְ	id. pret. 3 pers. s. m., suff. 3 pers. pl. m.	חטא
הַחִטִּים [u]וְ׳	pref. הַ)(n. f. with pl. m. term. from חִטָּה	חטה
[x]הֶחָי	pref. הֶ for הַ } adj. masc. sing. dec. 8d. (§ 37. rem. 6)	חיי
הַחַי [y]וְ׳	pref. הַ dag. impl. } adj. masc. sing. dec. 8d. (§ 37. rem. 6)	חיי
הֶחָי	pref. הֶ bef. חָ for הַ } adj. masc. sing. dec. 8d. (§ 37. rem. 6)	חיי
הַחִידָה	pref. הַ)(noun fem. sing. dec. 10. .	חוד
הַחַיָּה	pref. id.)(adj. (Le. 14. 6, 7, 51) or subst. fem. dec. 10, from חַי masc. . . .	חיי
הֶחֱיָה	Hiph. pret. 3 pers. sing. masc. . . .	חיה
[z]הַחְיֵה וְ	id. inf. absolute	חיה
[a]הַחֲיוּ	id. imp. pl. masc.	חיה
הַחַיּוֹת [b]וְ׳	pref. הַ)(noun fem. pl. of חַיָּה dec. 10.	חיי
הַחַיִּים	pref. id.)(adj. and subst. masc., pl. of חַי dec. 8d. (§ 37. rem. 6) . . .	חיי

Word	Analysis	Root
[c]הַחֲיֵינִי וְ	Hiph. imp. sing. masc., suff. 1 pers. sing.	חיה
[d]הֶחֱיֵיתִי	id. pret. 1 pers. sing.	חיה
[e]הַחִיִּיתֶם	pref. הַ interr. for הֲ)(Piel. pret. 2 pers. pl. m.	חיה
הַחֵיל וְ׳	pref. הַ art. } noun m. s. dec. 6h.	חול
הֶחָיִל	pref. הֶ id. bef. חָ for הַ } noun m. s. dec. 6h.	חול
הַחֵילִים	pref. הַ)(id. pl., abs. state (§ 35. rem. 12)	חול
[f]הַחִיצוֹן	pref. id.)(adj. masc. sing. . . .	חוץ
הַחִיצוֹנָה, הַחִיצֹנָה	pref. id.)(fem. of the prec. . . .	חוץ
[g]הַחֵיק וְ	pref. id.)(noun masc. sing. dec. 1a. .	חוק
[h]הֵחִישׁוּ	Hiph. pret. 3 pers. pl.	חוש
[i]הַחֲיִתֶם [k]וְ׳	Hiph. pret. 2 pers. pl. masc. (§ 13. r. 10)	חיה
[l]הֶחֱיִתָנוּ	id. pret. 2 pers. sing. masc., suff. 1 pers. pl.	חיה
הַחֲכִילָה	pref. הַ)(pr. name of a hill . .	חכל
הֶחָכָם	pref. הֶ bef. חָ for הַ)(adj. masc. dec. 4c. .	חכם
הַחָכְמָה [m]וְ׳	pref. הַ)(noun fem. sing. (no pl. abs.)	חכם
[n]הַחֲכָמוֹת	pref. id.)(adj. fem., pl. of חֲכָמָה dec. 11c. from חָכָם masc.	חכם
הַחֲכָמִים [o]וְ׳	pref. id.)(noun m., pl. of חָכָם dec. 4c.	חכם
הָחֵל	Hiph. inf., or imp. sing. masc. . .	חלל
[p]הַחֵל	pref. הַ)(noun masc. sing. dec. 1a. .	חול
[q]הַחֹל	pref. הַ)(noun masc. sing. . . .	חלל
הֵחֵל	Hiph. pret. 3 pers. sing. masc.; or (Eze. 20. 9, 14, 22) Niph. inf. for [הֵחֵל § 18. rem. 14]	חלל
הַחֵלֶב	pref. הַ)(noun masc. sing. dec. 6d. .	חלב
הֶחָלָב	pref. הֶ bef. חָ for הַ)(noun masc. dec. 4c.	חלב
הַחֲלָבִים [r]וְ׳	pref. הַ)(noun masc., pl. of חֵלֶב dec. 6. (§ 35. rem. 6)	חלב
[s]הַחֹלֶד	pref. id.)(noun masc. sing. . .	חלד
[t]הַחַלָּה	pref. id.)(noun fem. sing. dec. 10. .	חלל
[u]הֵחֵלָּה	Hiph. pret. 3 pers. sing. fem. . .	חלל
הֵחֵלּוּ	id. pret. 3 pers. pl. . . .	חלל
[x]הֶחֱלוּ	Hiph. pret. 3 pers. pl. . . .	חלה
הַחֲלוֹם	pref. הַ)(noun masc. sing. dec. 1a. .	חלם
הַחַלּוֹן	pref. id.)(noun com. sing. dec. 1b. .	חלל
[y]הַחַלּוֹנִים [z]וְ׳	pref. id.)(id. pl. . . .	חלל
הֶחָלוּץ וְ׳	pref. הֶ bef. חָ for הַ)(Kal part. p. masc. dec. 3a.	חלץ
הַחִלּוֹתָ	Hiph. pret. 2 pers. sing. masc. [for הַחִלּוֹתָ by Chaldaism, § 18. rem. 14 note]	חלל
[a]הַחֳלִי	pref. הַ for חֳלִי (§ 35. r. 14) n. m. s. dec. 6k.	חלה
[b]הֶחֱלִי	Hiph. pret. 3 pers. sing. masc. for הֶחֱלָה (§ 24. rem. 17)	חלה
[c]הַחֲלִיפוּ וְ	Hiph. imp. pl. masc. . . .	חלף

[a] Je. 51. 12. [b] Na. 3. 14. [c] Ge. 21. 18. [d] Je. 31. 32. [e] Mi. 4. 9. [f] Je. 50. 43. [g] Is. 27. 1. [h] Le. 25. 35. [i] 1 Sa. 17. 35. [k] Eze. 30. 25. [l] Is. 41. 9. [m] Je. 6. 24. [n] Je. 8. 21. [o] Am. 9. 8. [p] Eze. 18. 4, 20. [q] Ex. 9. 32. [r] Je. 32. 35. [s] 2 Ki. 13. 6. [t] 2 Ki. 17. 21. [u] 1 Ch. 21. 23. [x] Ge. 6. 19. [y] Ec. 7. 2. [z] Jos. 9. 20. [a] Nu. 31. 18. [b] Eze. 1. 14. [c] Is. 38. 16. [d] Nu. 22. 33. [e] Nu. 31. 15. [f] Eze. 44. 1. [g] Eze. 43. 17. [h] Ju. 20. 37. [i] Ju. 8. 19. [k] Jos. 2. 13. [l] Ge. 47. 25. [m] Job 28. 12, 20. [n] Je. 9. 16. [o] Ec. 9. 1. [p] Ob. 1. 20. [q] Le. 10. 10. [r] 2 Ch. 35. 14. [s] Le. 11. 29. [t] Le. 24. 5. [u] Ju. 20. 40. [x] Ho. 7. 5. [y] Joel 2. 9. [z] Eze. 41. 16. [a] 2 Ch. 21. 15. [b] Is. 53. 10. [c] Ge. 35. 2.

Word	Analysis	Root
הַחֲלִיפוֹת[a]	pref. הַ)(noun fem., pl. of [חֲלִיפָה] dec. 10.	חלף
הֶחֱלִיק[b]	Hiph. pret. 3 pers. sing. masc. . . .	חלק
הֶחֱלִיקָה	id. pret. 3 pers. sing. fem. . . .	חלק
הָחֳלֵיתִי	Hoph. pret. 1 pers. sing.	חלה
הֶחֱלֵיתִי[c]	Hiph. pret. 1 pers. sing.	חלה
הֶחָלָל[d]	pref. הֶ bef. חָ for הַ)(adj. masc. dec. 4c.	חלל
הַחֲלָלִים	pref. הַ)(id. pl., absolute state . .	חלל
הַחִלָּם[e]	Hiph. inf. [הַחֵל, for הַהֵל, by Chaldaism § 18. rem. 14], suff. 3 pers. sing. masc. .	חלל
הַחֲלֹמוֹת	pref. הַ)(noun masc. with pl. fem. term. from חֲלוֹם dec. 1a.	חלם
הַחַלָּמִישׁ[f]	pref. id.)(noun m. s. (constr. חַלְמִישׁ) dec. 3c.	חלמש
הַחַלֹּנוֹת	וְ[g] pref. id., & וְ)(n. com., pl. of חַלּוֹן dec. 1b.	חלל
הֶחֱלִף[h]	וְ Hiph. pret. 3 pers. sing. masc. . .	חלף
הֵחָלְצוּ[i]	Niph. imp. pl. masc.	חלץ
הַחֵלֶק[k]	pref. הַ)(noun masc. sing. dec. 6d. .	חלק
הֶחָלָק	pref. הֶ before חָ for הַ)(adj. masc. sing. .	חלק
הַחֶלְקָה	pref. הַ)(noun fem. sing. dec. 12b. .	חלק
הַחֶלְקִי	pref. id.)(patronym. of חֵלֶק . . .	חלק
הַחֲלָקִים	pref. id.)(noun masc., pl. of חֵלֶק dec. 6. (§ 35. rem. 6)	חלק
הַחַלָּשׁ[l]	pref. id.)(noun masc. sing.	חלש
הַחִלֹּתִי	Hiph. pret. 1 pers. sing.; [for הַהִלֹּתִי, by Chaldaism § 18. rem. 14] . .	חלל
הַחֶמְדָּה[m]	pref. הַ)(noun fem. sing. (no pl.) .	חמד
הַחֲמֻדֹת[n]	pref. id.)(Kal part. p. pl. fem. from [חָמוּד]	חמד
הַחַמָּה	pref. id.)(noun fem. sing. dec. 10. .	חמם
הַחֵמָה[o]	וְ pref. id.)(noun fem. s. dec. 11b for [יְחֵמָה]	יחם
הַחֹמָה	pref. id.)(noun fem. sing. dec. 10. .	חמה
הֶחָמוּלִי	pref. הֶ bef. חָ for הַ)(gent. noun from חָמוּל	חמל
הַחֲמוֹר	וְ pref. id.)(noun masc. sing. dec. 1a. .	חמר
הַחֲמוֹרִים[p]	pref. id.)(id. pl., absolute state . .	חמר
הַחֹמוֹת[q]	pref. id.)(noun fem., pl. of חוֹמָה dec. 1a.	חמה
הַחֹמֶט[r]	וְ pref. id.)(noun masc. sing. . .	חמט
הַחֲמִישִׁי[s]	וְ pref. id.)(adj. ord. masc. from חָמֵשׁ .	חמש
הַחֲמִישִׁית	pref. id.)(fem. of the prec. . .	חמש
הַחַמָּנִים	וְ pref. id.)(noun masc., pl. of [חַמָּן] dec. 1b.	חמם
הֶחָמָס	pref. הֶ bef. חָ for הַ)(noun masc., dec. 4c.	חמס
הַחֲמֹר	pref. הַ)(noun masc. sing. dec. 1a. .	חמר
הַחֵמָר[t]	וְ pref. id.)(noun masc. sing. . .	חמר
הַחֹמֶר	pref. id.)(noun masc. sing. dec. 6c. .	חמר
הַחֲמֹרִים	pref. id.)(noun masc., pl. of חֲמוֹר dec. 1a.	חמר
הַחֹמֶשׁ	pref. id.)(noun masc. sing. . .	חמש
הַחֲמִשָּׁה[u]	pref. id.)(num. card. masc., from חָמֵשׁ fem.	חמש
הַחֲמִשִּׁי	pref. id.)(adj. ord. masc. from חָמֵשׁ	מש
הַחֲמִשִּׁים	pref. id.)(num. card., com., pl. of חָמֵשׁ	מש
הַחֲמֻשִׁים[x]	pref. id.)(Kal part. p. m., pl. of [חָמוּשׁ] d. 3a.	מש
הַחֲמִשִׁית	pref. id.)(adj. ord., fem. of חֲמִשִׁי	מש
הַחֲמַת[y]	pref. id.)(noun masc. sing., constr. חֵמֶת	מת
הַחֲמָתִי	pref. id.)(gent. noun from חֲמָת .	מה
הַחֹמֹתַיִם[z] / הַחֹמֹתַיִם	pref. id.)(noun fem., du. of חוֹמָה dec. 10.	מה
הַחֵן[a]	pref. id.)(noun masc. sing. dec. 8b. .	נן
הַחֲנֻטִים[b]	pref. id.)(noun masc., pl. of [חֲנֹט] .	נט
הַחֲנֻיוֹת[c]	pref. id.)(noun f., pl. of [חָנוּת, comp. מַלְכֻיוֹת, from ־כוּת]	נה
הַחֹנִים	וְ pref. id.)(Kal part. act. m., fr. חֹנֶה d. 9a.	נה
הַחֲנִית / הַחֲנִית[e]	וְ[d] / Kh. pref. id.)(noun fem. sing. dec. 1. .	נה
הַחֲנִיתִים[f]	pref. id.)(id. pl., absolute state . .	נה
הַחֲנֹכִי	pref. id.)(patronym. of חֲנוֹךְ . .	נך
הַחִנָּם[g]	pref. הַ interr. for הֲ)(adv., from חֵן and the term. ־ָם	נן
הַחֶסֶד	וְ pref. הַ art.)(n. m. s. (suff. חַסְדִּי) d. 6a.	סד
הַחֲסָדִים[h]	pref. הַ id.)(id. pl., absolute state .	סד
הֶחָסוּת[i]	וְ pref. הֶ bef. חָ for הַ)(noun fem. sing. .	סה
הַחֲסִידָה	וְ[k] pref. הַ)(noun fem. sing. . .	סד
הֶחָסִיל	וְ[l] pref. הֶ bef. חָ for הַ)(noun masc. sing. .	סל
הַחֹסִים[m]	pref. הַ)(Kal part. act. m., pl. of חֹסֶה d. 9a.	סה
הֶחְסִיר[n]	Hiph. pret. 3 pers. sing. masc. (§ 13. rem. 9)	סר
הֶחָסֹן[o]	pref. הֶ bef. חָ for הַ)(adj. masc. sing. .	סן
הֶחֱסַנּוּ[p]	Hiph. pret. 1 pers. pl.	סן
הֶחְפִּיר[q]	Hiph. pret. 3 pers. sing. masc. (§ 13. rem. 9)	פר
הַחֵפֶץ	pref. הַ)(noun masc. sing. dec. 6. (§ 35. r. 6)	פץ
הֶחָפֵץ	pref. הֶ bef. חָ for הַ)(adj. masc. dec. 5c. .	פץ
הֶחָפֹץ[r]	pref. הֶ id. interr.)(Kal inf. absolute .	פץ
הַחֲפֵצִים[s]	pref. הַ art.)(adj. masc., pl. of חָפֵץ dec. 5c.	פץ
הַחֵפֶר	pref. id.)(pr. n., see גַּת חֵפֶר . . .	ת
הַחֶפְרִי	pref. id.)(patronym. of חֵפֶר . .	פר
הַחָפְשׁוּת[t] / הַחָפְשִׁית[u]	pref. id.)(noun fem. sing.; Kh. ־שׁוּת .	פש
הַחֹצֵב[x]	pref. id.)(Kal part. act. sing. masc. dec. 7b.	צב
הַחִיצוֹנָה	pref. id.)(adj. fem. sing. from חִיצוֹן masc.	וץ
הַחֵצִי[y] / הַחֲצִי	וְ[z] pref. id.)(noun masc. sing. dec. 6i, (suff. חֶצְיוֹ § 35. rem. 14) . .	צה
הַחִצִּי[a]	pref. id.)(Kh. הַחֵצִי q.v., K. הַחִצִּים (q.v.)	צץ
הַחֶצְיוֹ[b]	וְ pref. id.)(n. m. s., suff. 3 p. s. m. fr. חֵצִי	צה
הַחִצִּים	pref. id.)(noun masc., pl. of חֵץ dec. 8b. .	צץ
הֶחָצֵר[c]	pref. הֶ bef. חָ for הַ)(noun masc. s. dec. 3a.	צר
הַחִצֹנָה[d]	defect. for הַחִיצוֹנָה q. v.	וץ

[a] Ju. 14. 19. [b] Ps. 36. 3. [c] Mi. 6. 13. [d] De. 21. 2, 3, 6. [e] Ge. 11. 6. [f] De. 8. 15. [g] Eze. 41. 16. [h] Ge. 31. 7. [i] Nu. 31. 3. [k] Am. 7. 4. [l] Joel 4. 10. [m] Is. 2. 16. [n] Ge. 27. 15. [o] Jer. 25. 15. [p] 2 Sa. 16. 2. [q] Ca. 5. 7. [r] Le. 11. 30. [s] 2 Sa. 3. 4. [t] Ge. 11. 3. [u] Ge. 14. 9. [x] Ju. 7. 11. [y] Ge. 21. 15, 19. [z] Je. 39. 4. [a] Pr. 31. 30. [b] Ge. 50. 3. [c] Je. 37. 16. [d] 1 Sa. 18. 10. [e] 1 Sa. 26. 22. [f] 2 Ch. 23. 9. [g] Job 1. 9. [h] Ge. 32. 11. [i] Is. 30. 3. [k] De. 14. 18. [l] Joel 2. 25. [m] 2 Sa. 22. 31. [n] Ex. 16. 18. [o] Is. 1. 31. [p] Da. 7. 22. [q] Is. 33. 9. [r] Eze. 18. 23. [s] Ne. 1. 11. [t] 2 Ch. 26. 21. [u] 2 Ki. 15. 5. [x] Is. 10. 15. [y] 1 Ki. 3. 25, 25. [z] 1 Ki. 16. 21. [a] 1 Sa. 20. 28. [b] Jos. 8. 33. [c] Nu. 11. 5. [d] Eze. 42. 9.

הַחֲצֹצְרוֹ	וְ pref. הַ)(noun fem., pl. of חֲצֹצְרָה dec. 10.	חצר
הֶחָצֵר	[a] וְ' pref. הֶ bef. חָ for הַ)(noun com. s. d. 5c.	חצר
הַחֶצְרוֹנִי	pref. הַ)(patronym. of חֶצְרוֹן	חצר
הַחֲצֵרוֹת	pref. id.)(noun com., pl. of חָצֵר dec. 5c.	חצר
הַחֲצֵרִים	pref. id.)(id. with pl. masc. term.	חצר
הַחֶצְרֹנִי	pref. id.)(patronym. of חֶצְרוֹן	חצר
הַחֲצֵרֹת [b]	pref id.)(noun com., pl. of חָצֵר dec. 5c.	חצר
הַחֻקָּה [ss]	pref. id.)(noun fem. sing. d. 10, from חֹק m.	חקק
הַחֻקִּים	וְ' pref. id.)(noun masc., pl. of חֹק dec. 8c.	חקק
הַחֹקְקִים [c]	pref. id.)(Kal part. act. m., pl. of [חֹקֵק] d. 7b.	חקק
הַחֵקֶר [d]	pref. הַ interr. for הֲ)(n. m., pl. חִקְרֵי dec. 6b.	חקר
הָחֳרֵב [e]	Hoph. inf. absolute	חרב
הַחֶרֶב	וְ' pref. הַ)(noun fem. sing. dec. 6a.	חרב
הֶחָרֵב [f]	pref. הֶ bef. חָ for הַ)(adj. masc. sing.	חרב
הֶחָרֶב	pref. id.)(in pause for הַחֶרֶב (q. v. § 35. r. 2)	חרב
הֶחָרָבָה	pref. id.)(noun fem. sing.	חרב
הָחֳרָבָה [g]	Hoph. pret. 3 pers. sing. fem.	חרב
הֶחֳרָבוֹת	[h] וְ' pref. הֶ bef. חָ for הַ)(n. f., pl. of חָרְבָּה d. 12c.	חרב
הֶחֳרֵבוֹת [i]	pref. id.)(adj. fem., pl. of חָרֵב ; הֶחֳרָבוֹת stands for הַחֲרֵבוֹת, comp. הֶחֱדַלְתִּי	חרב
הָחָרְבַת [k]	Ch. Hoph. pret. 3 pers. sing. fem.	חרב
הֶחֱרַבְתִּי [l]	Hiph. pret. 1 pers. sing.	חרב
הַחֲרַבְתִּי [m]	וְ id.; acc. shifted by conv. וְ (§ 8. rem. 7, & § 13. rem. 10)	חרב
הַחַרְגֹּל [n]	pref. הַ)(noun masc. sing.	חרגל
הַחֲרָדָה [o]	pref. id.)(noun fem. sing., (constr. חֶרְדַּת) dec. 11c. (§ 42. rem. 1)	חרד
הַחֲרֹדִי	pref. id.)(gent. noun from חֲרוֹד	חרד
הַחֲרֵדִים [p]	[q] וְ' pref. id.)(adj. masc., pl. of חָרֵד dec. 5c.	חרד
הַחֲרַדְתִּי [r]	וְ Hiph. pret. 1 pers. sing.; acc. shifted by conv. וְ (§ 8. rem. 7, & § 13. rem. 10)	חרד
הֶחֱרָה [s]	Hiph. pret. 3 pers. sing. masc.	חרה
הַחֲרוּפִי	pref. הַ)(Kh. חֲרוּפִי, K. חֲרִיפִי gent. n. see חָרִיף	חרף
הֶחָרוּץ [t]	pref. הֶ bef. חָ for הַ)(noun masc. sing. dec. 3a.	חרץ
הַחֲרוֹרִי	once 1 Ch. 11. 27, for הַחֲרֹדִי (q. v.)	חרד
הַחַרְטֻמִּים [u] } הַחַרְטֻמִּם	pref. הַ)(noun m., pl. of [חַרְטֹם] d. 8c.	חרט
הַחֹרִי	pref. id.)(pr. name of a people	חור
הֶחֱרִיב [x]	Hiph. pret. 3 pers. sing. masc.	חרב
הֶחֱרִיבוּ	id. pret. 3 pers. pl.	חרב
הֶחֱרִיד [y]	Hiph. pret. 3 pers. sing. masc.	חרד
הַחֲרִיטִים [z]	וְ pref. הַ)(noun masc., pl. of [חָרִיט] d. 3a.	חרט
הַחֹרִים	pref. id.)(pr. name of a people, pl. of חֹרִי	חור
הַחֹרִים [a]	pref. id.)(noun masc., pl. of חוֹר dec. 1a.	חור
הַחֹרִים	[b] וְ' pref. id.)(noun m., pl. of חֹר dec. 1a.	חרר
הֶחֱרִים	[c] וְ' Hiph. pret. 3 pers. sing. masc.	חרם
הַחֲרִימוּ [d]	id. imp. pl. masc.	חרם
הֶחֱרִימוּ	id. pret. 3 pers. pl.	חרם
הַחֲרִימוּהָ [e]	וְ id. imp. pl. masc., suff. 3 pers. sing. fem.	חרם
הַחֲרִימָם	id. inf. (הַחֲרִים), suff. 3 pers. pl. m. dec. 1b.	חרם
הֶחֱרִימָם	id. pret. 3 pers. sing. masc., suff. 3 p. pl. m.	חרם
הֶחֱרִישׁ	וְ Hiph. pret. 3 pers. sing. masc.	חרשׁ
הַחֲרִישׁוּ	id. imp. pl. masc.	חרשׁ
הֶחֱרִישׁוּ [f]	וְ id. pret. 3 pers. pl. masc.	חרשׁ
הַחֲרִישִׁי [g]	id. imp. sing. fem.	חרשׁ
הַחֲרַכִּים [h]	pref. הַ)(noun masc., pl. of [חָרָךְ] dec. 8a.	חרך
הַחֲרֵם	[i] וְ' Hiph. inf. or (De. 13. 16) imp. sing. m.	חרם
הַחֵרֶם	pref. הַ)(noun masc. s. d. 6. (§ 35. rem. 6)	חרם
הֶחֱרִם	Hiph. pret. 3 pers. sing. masc.	חרם
הַחָרְמָה	pref. הַ)(pr. name of a place	חרם
הֶחֱרַמְנוּ [k]	Hiph. pret. 1 pers. pl.	חרם
הַחֲרַמְתָּה [l]	וְ id. pret. 2 pers. sing. masc.; acc. shifted by conv. וְ (§ 8. rem. 7, & § 13. rem. 10)	חרם
הֶחֱרַמְתִּי [m]	id. pret. 1 pers. sing.	חרם
הַחֲרַמְתִּי [zz]	וְ id. id.)(acc. shifted by conv. וְ (§ 8. rem. 7, & § 13. rem. 10)	חרם
הַחֲרַמְתִּים [n]	וְ id. id. with suff. 3 pers. pl. masc.	חרם
הֶחֱרַמְתֶּם [o] } הַחֲרַמְתֶּם [p]	וְ id. pret. 2 pers. pl. masc. (§ 13. rem. 10)	חרם
הַחֹרֹנִי	pref. הַ)(gent. noun of חֹרֹנַיִם	חור
הֶחָרֶס [q]	pref. הֶ bef. חָ for הַ)(n. m. s. (for חֶרֶס § 35. r. 2)	חרס
הַחַרְסָה [r]	pref. הַ)(id. with parag. ה	חרס
הַחַרְסוּת	pref. id.)(pr. n. of a gate, Kh. סוּת', K. סִית'	חרס
הַחֹרֶף	pref. id.)(noun masc. sing. dec. 6c.	חרף
הַחֲרֵשׁ	Hiph. inf. abs., or imp. sing. masc.	חרשׁ
הַחֹרֵשׁ [s]	pref. הַ)(Kal part. act. sing. masc. dec. 7b.	חרשׁ
הַחֹרֶשׁ [t]	pref. id.)(noun masc. sing. dec. 6c.	חרשׁ
הֶחָרָשׁ	וְ' pref. הֶ bef. חָ)(noun masc. sing. dec. 1b. for [חָרָשׁ § 30. rem. 1]	חרשׁ
הֶחֱרִשׁ [u]	וְ' Hiph. pret. 3 pers. sing. masc.	חרשׁ
הַחֲרָשִׁים [x]	pref. הַ)(noun masc., pl. of [חֶרֶשׁ] dec. 6a.	חרשׁ
הַחֵרְשִׁים	pref. id.)(adj. m., pl. of חֵרֵשׁ d. 7b. [for חֵרְשִׁים	חרשׁ
הֶחֱרַשְׁתִּי	[y] וְ' Hiph. pret. 1 pers. sing.	חרשׁ
הַחֹשְׁבִים	pref. הַ)(Kal part. act. m., pl. of חֹשֵׁב d. 7b.	חשׁב
הֶחֱשׁוּ [z]	Hiph. pret. 3 pers. pl.	חשׁה
הֶחְשִׁיךְ [a]	Hiph. pret. 3 pers. sing. masc. (§ 13. rem. 9)	חשׁך
הֶחֱשֵׁיתִי	Hiph. pret. 1 pers. sing. (§ 24. rem. 14)	חשׁה
הַחֹשֶׁךְ	[b] וְ' pref. הַ)(noun masc. sing. dec. 6c.	חשׁך
הַחֲשַׁכְתִּי [c]	וְ Hiph. pret. 1 pers. sing.; acc. on ult. by conv. וְ (§ 8. rem. 7, & § 13. rem. 10)	חשׁך
הַחַשְׁמַל [d]	pref. הַ)(noun masc. sing.	חשׁמל
הַחַשְׁמַלָה [e]	pref. id.)(id. with parag. ה	חשׁמל

[a] Eze. 10. 4. [b] Ex. 8. 9. [c] Is. 10. 1. [d] Job 11. 7. [e] 2 Ki. 3. 23. [f] Je. 33. 12. [g] Eze. 26. 2. [h] Eze. 36. 10. [i] Eze. 36. 35, 38. [k] Ezr. 4. 15. [l] Zep. 3. 6. [m] Je. 51. 36. [n] Le. 11. 22. [o] 2 Ki. 4. 13. [p] Is. 66. 5. [q] Ezr. 10. 3. [r] 2 Sa. 17. 2. [s] Ne. 3. 20. [t] Joel 4. 14, 14. [u] Ex. 8. 15. [x] Eze. 19. 7. [y] Ju. 8. 12. [z] Is. 3. 22. [a] 1 Sa. 14. 11. [b] 1 Ki. 21. 11. [c] Is. 11. 15. [d] Je. 51. 3. [e] Je. 50. 26. [f] 2 Ki. 18. 36. [g] 2 Sa. 13. 20. [h] Ca. 2. 9. [i] Je. 50. 21. [k] 1 Sa. 15. 15. [l] 1 Sa. 15. 18. [m] 1 Sa. 15. 20. [n] Je. 25. 9. [o] Jos. 2. 10. [p] 1 Sa. 15. 3. [q] Ju. 8. 13. [r] Ju. 14. 18. [s] Is. 28. 24. [ss] Ex. 13. 10. [t] Is. 17. 9. [u] Nu. 30. 12, 15. [x] Ne. 11. 35. [y] Ps. 50. 21. [z] 2 Ki. 2. 3, 5. [zz] Mi. 4. 13. [a] Am. 5. 8. [b] Ex. 14. 20. [c] Am. 8. 9. [d] Eze. 1. 4. [e] Eze. 8. 2.

הַחֹשֶׁן	pref. הַ)(noun masc. sing. . . .	חשן
הַחֻשָׁתִי	pref. id.)(patronym. of חוּשָׁה . . .	חוש
הֶחָתוּם	pref. הֶ before חָ for הַ)(Kal part. p. sing. masc. dec. 3a. . . .	חתם
הַחֲתוּמִים[a]	pref. הַ)(id. pl., absolute state	חתם
הַחִתִּי	וְ' pref. id.)(gent. noun from חֵת	חתת
הַחִתִּים	pref. id.)(id. pl. . . .	חתת
הֶחְתִּים[b]	Hiph. pret. 3 pers. sing. masc. (§ 13. r. 9)	חתם
הָחְתֵּל[c]	וְ Hoph. inf. absolute (§ 11. rem. 11)	חתל
הַחֹתֶמֶת[d]	pref. הַ)(noun fem. sing., from חוֹתָם masc.	חתם
הַחִתֹּתָ[e]	Hiph. pret. 2 pers. sing. masc. [for הַחְתּוֹתָ by Chaldaism § 18. rem. 14 note] .	חתת
הַחִתֹּתִי[f]	וְ id. pret. 1 pers. sing., contr. [for הַחְתַּתְתִּי regular, for הַחִתּוֹתִי irr.] (§ 18. r. 13)	חתת
הַט	Hiph. imp. s. m., ap. for הַטֵּה (§ 25. No. 2b)	נטה
הַטֹּבָה	pref. הַ)(adj. & subst. f. d. 10, from טוֹב m.	טוב
הַטֹּבוֹת	pref. id.)(id. adj. pl. . . .	טוב
הַטַּבָּח[g]	pref. id.)(noun masc. sing. dec. 1b. .	טבח
הַטַּבָּחִים	pref. id.)(id. pl., absolute state . .	טבח
הַטֹּבִים[h]	pref. id.)(adj. masc., pl. of טוֹב dec. 1a. .	טוב
הֵטַבְנוּ[i]	וְ Hiph. pret. 1 pers. sing. . . .	יטב
הָטְבָּעוּ הָטְבְּעוּ[k]	} Hoph. pret. 3 pers. sing. (comp. § 8. r. 7)	טבע
הַטַּבָּעוֹת	pref. הַ)(pl. of the foll. (§ 44. rem. 5) .	טבע
הַטַּבַּעַת	pref. id.)(n. f. s. (with suff. טַבַּעְתּוֹ) d. 13a.	טבע
הַטַּבָּעֹת	pref. id.)(id. pl. absolute state (§ 44. r. 5)	טבע
הַטֹּבֹת[l]	pref. id.)(adj. f., pl. of טֹ֫בָה d. 10, fr. טוֹב m.	טוב
הֵטִבֹתִי[m]	וְ Hiph. pret. 1 pers. sing.; acc. shifted by conv. וְ (comp. § 8. rem. 7) . . .	טוב
הַטֵּה	Hiph. imp. sing. masc.	נטה
הִטָּה	id. pret. 3 pers. sing. masc. . . .	נטה
הִטָּהוּ[n]	id. id., suff. 3 pers. sing. masc. . .	נטה
הַטָּהוֹר	וְ' pref. הַ)(adj. masc. sing. dec. 3a. . .	טהר
הַטְּהוֹרָה	pref. הַ)(id. fem., dec. 10. . . .	טהר
הַטָּהֹר	defect. for הַטָּהוֹר (q. v.) . . .	טהר
הַטָּהֳרָה[o]	pref. הַ)(noun f. s. (constr. טָהֳרַת; no pl.)	טהר
הַטְּהֹרָה	defect. for הַטְּהוֹרָה (q. v.) . . .	טהר
הִטַּהֲרוּ[p]	[q]וְ' Hithpa. pret. 3 pers. pl., or imp. pl. masc. [for הִתְטַהֲרוּ]	טהר
הִטֶּהָרוּ[r]	וְ' id. pret. in pause, (§ 14. rem. 3) . .	טהר
הִטַּהַרְנוּ[s]	id. pret. 1 pers. sing., dag. impl. (§ 14. r. 1)	טהר
הַטּוּ	[u]וְ' Hiph. imp. pl. masc. (§ 25. No. 2b) .	נטה
הִטּוּ	id. pret. 3 pers. pl.	נטה
הַטּוֹב	וְ' pref. הַ)(adj. and subst. masc. dec. 1a. .	טוב
הֲטוֹב	pref. הֲ)(Kal pret. impers., or (Ju. 11. 25) inf. absolute (§ 21. rem. 2) . .	טוב

הַטּוֹבָה הֲטוֹבָה[x]	pref. הַ pref. הֲ } adj. or subst., fem. of טוֹב masc., dec. 10. . . .	טוב
הַטּוֹבִים הֲטוֹבִים[y]	pref. הַ pref. הֲ } id. masc., pl. of טוֹב dec. 1a.	טוב
הִטּוֹחַ[z]	Niph. inf. constr.	טוח
הַטּוּר	וְ' pref. הַ)(noun masc. sing. dec. 1a.	טור
הַטֹּחַ[a]	defect. for הַטּוֹחַ (q. v.) . . .	טוח
הַטָּחִים[b]	pref. הַ)(Kal part. act. m., pl. of [טָח] d. 1a.	טוח
הַטַּחֲנָה[ff]	pref. id.)(noun fem. sing. . . .	טחן
הַטֹּחֲנוֹת[ll]	pref. id.)(Kal part. act. fem. pl. [of טֹחֲנָה or טֹחֶנֶת]	טחן
הַטִּי[c]	[d]וְ' Hiph. imp. sing. fem. (§ 25. No. 2b) .	נטה
הֵיטִבָה[e]	Hiph. imp. sing. masc. with parag. ה	יטב
הֵיטִיבוּ[f]	id. imp. pl. masc. . . .	יטב
הֵטִיבוּ[g]	Hiph. imp. pl. masc. . . .	טוב
הֲטִיבוֹתָ[h]	Hiph. pret. 2 pers. sing. masc. . .	טוב
הֵיטִיבִי[i]	Hiph. imp. sing. fem. . . .	יטב
הֵטִיבֹתָ	Hiph. pret. 2 pers. sing. masc. . .	טוב
הַטִּיחַ[k]	pref. הַ)(noun masc. sing. . . .	טוח
הֵטִיל[l]	Hiph. pret. 3 pers. sing. masc. . .	טול
הֲטִילֻנִי[m]	וַ id. imp. pl. masc., suff. 1 pers. sing. .	טול
הִטִּיפוּ[n]	וְ Hiph. pret. 3 pers. pl. . . .	נטף
הַטִּירוֹת[o]	pref. הַ)(noun fem., pl. of [טִירָה] dec. 10.	טור
הִטֵּיתִי[p]	Hiph. pret. 1 pers. sing. (§ 25. No. 2b) .	נטה
הִטִּיתֶם	id. pret. 2 pers. pl. masc. . . .	נטה
הַטַּל[q] הַטָּל	} pref. הַ)(noun masc. sing. dec. 8d.	טלל
הַטְּלֻאִים[r]	וְ Kal part. p., pl. of טָלוּא dec. 3a. .	טלא
הַטְּלֻאֹת[s]	וְ id. pl. fem.	טלא
הֵטַלְתִּי	וְ Hiph. pret. 1 p. s. [for הֵטִילוֹתִי § 21. r. 13]	טול
הַטָּמֵא	pref. הַ)(adj. masc. s. d. 5a. (constr. טְמֵא)	טמא
הַטְּמֵאָה	pref. id.)(id. fem. dec. 10. . .	טמא
הַטֻּמְאָה	pref. id.)(noun fem. sing. dec. 10. .	טמא
הֻטַּמָּאָה[t]	[for הִתְטַמְּאָה] Hothpa. pret. 3 pers. sing. fem. (§ 6. No. 10 note) . . .	טמא
הַטְּמֵאִים	pref. הַ)(adj. masc., pl. of טָמֵא dec. 5a.	טמא
הִטָּמֵן[u]	וְ Niph. imp. sing. masc. . . .	טמן
הַטֶּנֶא[x]	pref. הַ)(noun m. s. (suff. טַנְאֲךָ) dec. 6a.	טנא
הִטְעוּ[y]	Hiph. pret. 3 pers. pl. masc. . .	טעה
הַטַּף[z] וְ' הַטָּף וְ'	} pref. הַ)(noun masc. sing. dec. 8d.	טפף
הַטִּפוּ[a]	וְ Hiph. imp. pl. masc. . . .	נטף
הַטְּפָחוֹת[b]	pref. הַ)(noun masc. with pl. fem. term. from טֶפַח dec. 6. (§ 35. rem. 5) . .	טפח
הַטְרִיפֵנִי[c]	Hiph. imp. sing. masc., suff. 1 pers. sing.	טרף
הֲטֶרֶם[qq]	pref. הֲ)(adv.	טרם

[a] Ne. 10. 2. [b] Le. 15. 3. [c] Eze. 16. 4. [d] Ge. 38. 25. [e] Is. 9. 3. [f] Je. 49. 37. [g] 1 Sa. 9. 24. [h] Joel 4. 5. [i] Nu. 10. 29, 32. [k] Je. 38. 22. [l] Ge. 41. 26. [m] Eze. 36. 11. [n] Is. 44. 20. [o] Ne. 12. 45. [p] Ezr. 6. 20. [q] Ge. 35. 2. [r] 2 Ch. 30. 18. [s] Nu. 8. 7. [t] Jos. 22. 17. [u] Jos. 24. 23. [x] Nu. 13. 19. [y] Am. 6. 2. [z] Le. 14. 43. [a] Le. 14. 48. [b] Eze. 13. 15. [c] Ge. 24. 14. [d] Ps. 45. 11. [e] Ps. 125. 4. [f] De. 5. 28. [ff] Ec. 12. 4. [g] Ho. 10. 1. [h] 2 Ch. 6. 8. [i] Is. 23. 16. [k] Eze. 13. 12. [l] Jon. 1. 4. [ll] Ec. 12. 3. [m] Jon. 1. 12. [n] Am. 9. 13. [o] Eze. 46. 23. [p] Pr. 5. 13. [q] Ex. 16. 13, 14. [qq] Ex. 10. 7. [r] Ge. 30. 35. [s] Ge. 30. 35. [t] De. 24. 4. [u] Is. 2. 10. [x] De. 26. 4. [y] Eze. 13. 10. [z] Ge. 47. 12. [a] Eze. 21. 2, 7. [b] 1 Ki. 7. 9. [c] Pr. 30. 8.

הַטְּרֵפָה[a] pref. הַ)(noun fem. sing. . . . . טרף

הַטַּתּוּ[b] [for הִטַּתְהוּ] Hiph. pret. 3 pers. sing. fem., suff. 3 pers. sing. masc. (§ 25. No. 2 b) נטה

הִי[c] וְ n. m. s. by syncope [for נְהִי]; for וְ see lett. ו נהה

הִוא[d] וְ & וְ[e] Kh. הִיא q. v., K. הוּא (q. v.) הוא

הִיא וְ &[f] וְ p. pron. 3 p. s. f. see הוּא; for וְ see lett. ו הוא

הֲיֹאבֶה[g] pref. הֲ)(Kal fut. 3 pers. sing. masc. . אבה

הֲיֵאָכֵל[h] pref. id.)(Niph. pret. 3 pers. sing. masc. אכל

הֲיֹאמַר[i] pref. id.)(Kal fut. 1 pers. sing. (§ 19. r. 1) אמר

הַיְאֹר pref. הַ)(noun masc. sing. dec. 1 a. . . יאר

הַיְאֹרָה[k] pref. id.)(id. with parag. ה יאר

הַיָּאִרִי pref. id.)(patronym. of יָאִיר . . אור

הַיְאֹרִים[l] pref. id.)(noun masc., pl. of יְאֹר dec. 1 a. יאר

הַיְאִתוֹן[m] pref. הָ)(Kh. הַיְאֵתוֹן, K. הָאִיתוֹן noun m. s. אתה

הַיְבוּסִי וְ pref. הַ)(gent. noun from יְבוּס . . בוס

הַיֹּבֵל pref. הַ)(noun masc. sing. dec. 7 b. . יבל

הֵיבֵל[n] וְ Ch. Aph. pret. 3 pers. sing. masc. . . יבל

הַיֹּבְלִים[o] pref. הַ)(noun masc., pl. of יוֹבֵל dec. 7 b. יבל

הַיְבֻסִי pref. id.)(gent. noun from יְבוּס . . בוס

הַיַּבֹּק pref. id.)(pr. name of a stream . . בקק

הַיַּבָּשָׁה pref. id.)(noun fem. sing. . . . יבש

הַיְבֵשׁוֹת[p] pref. id.)(adj. f., pl. of יְבֵשָׁה d. 10, fr. יָבֵשׁ m. יבש

הֲיִגְאֶה[q] pref. הֲ)(Kal fut. 1 pers. sing. . . גאה

הֲיַגִּיד[r] pref. id.)(Hiph. fut. 3 pers. sing. masc. נגד

הַיָּד וְ[s] pref. הַ)(noun com. sing. dec. 2 a. . יד

הֲיַד pref. הֲ)(id. constr. state . . . די

הֵידָד noun masc. sing. . . . . . הדד

הֲיָדֹעַ pref. הֲ)(Kal inf. absolute . . . ידע

הַיָּדוֹת pref. הַ)(noun fem., pl. of יָד dec. 2 a. . יד

הֻיְּדוֹת[t] noun fem. pl. [of הֻיְּדָה] ידה

הַיָּדַיִם[u] / הַיָּדָיִם[v] וְ} pref. הַ)(noun com., du. of יָד dec. 2 a. יד

הֲיָדֹעַ[x] pref. הֲ)(Kal inf. absolute . . . . ידע

הַיֹּדְעִים[a] pref. הַ)(Kal part. act. m., pl. of יֹדֵעַ d. 7 b. ידע

הַיִּדְּעֹנִי[b] pref. id.)(noun masc. sing. dec. 1. . . ידע

הַיִּדְּעֹנִים pref. id.)(id. pl., absolute state . . ידע

הֲיָדַעְתָּ pref. הֲ)(Kal pret. 2 pers. sing. masc. . ידע

הֲיְדַעְתֶּם pref. ה interr. f. הֲ)(id. pret. 2 pers. pl. m. ידע

הַיָּדֹת[c] defect. for הַיָּדוֹת (q. v.) . . . . יד

הָיָה וְ, fut. יִהְיֶה (תִּהְיֶה § 24. r. 20), apoc. יְהִי (r. 3 e); inf. c. הֱיוֹת (once הֱיֹה r. 20), with pref. בִּהְיוֹת, לִהְיוֹת (§ 14. r. 13)—I. *to be, to exist*; הָיָה לְ *to be to, belong to*; *to serve for*; before an inf. *to be about* to do any thing.—II. *to become*; הָיָה לְ *to become*; *to be for*; הָיָה כְּ *to become as*.—III. *to fall out, happen, come to pass* (comp. הָוָה No. III); וַיְהִי וְ, וַיְהִי כִּ *and it came to pass that*. Niph.—I. *to become, to be brought to pass*, with לְ.—II. *to fall*, Dan. 2. 1, שְׁנָתוֹ נִהְיְתָה עָלָיו his *sleep had fallen upon him*; Dan. 8. 27, נִהְיֵיתִי וְנֶחֱלֵיתִי *I fell and was sick*, i. e. I fell sick. Gesenius in both passages, *to be done for, be ended*, or *be over*. הַוָּה *calamity*, see הָוָה

הֱיֵה וְ Kal imp. sing. m., or inf. abs.; וֶ bef. (ֵ:) היה

הָיֹה id. inf. absolute . . . . . . היה

הָיָה[d] וְ Kh. הָיָה, K. הָיוּ Kal pret. 3 p. s. or pl. m. היה

הַיְּהֻדִיָּה pref. הַ)(fem. of the foll. . . . ידה

הַיְּהוּדִי pref. id.)(gent. noun from יְהוּדָה . . ידה

הַיְּהוּדִיִּים וְ / הַיְּהוּדִים וְ} pref. id.)(id. pl., Kh. יְהוּדִיִּים . ידה

הַיהוָה[e] pref. הַ interr. for הֲ)(the name of God, *the Eternal*, see under the root . הוה

הֲיִהְיֶה[f] pref. הֲ)(Kal fut. 3 pers. sing. masc. . היה

הֲיֵהָפֵךְ[g] pref. id.)(Kal fut. 3 pers. sing. masc. . הפך

הָיוּ[h] וְ Kh. הָיוּ q. v. K. הָיָה (q. v.) . . היה

הָיוֹ Kal inf. absolute, for הָיֹה (§ 24. rem 2) . היה

הָיוּ וְ id. pret. 3 pers. pl. . . . . היה

הֱיוּ id. imp. pl. masc. . . . . . היה

הָיוּ וְ Kh. הָיוּ q. v., K. יִהְיוּ q. v. . . היה

הֱיוּ וֶ Kal imp. m. pl. (§ 13. r. 13); וֶ bef. (ֱ) for וְ היה

הַיּוֹבֵל pref. הַ)(noun masc. sing. dec. 7 b. . . יבל

הַיֹּבְלִים[k] pref. id.)(id. pl., absolute state . . יבל

הֲיוֹרִדְךָ[i] pref. הֲ)(Hiph. fut. 3 p. s. m., suff. 2 p. s. m. ירד

הֲיִוָּדַע[m] pref. id.)(Niph. fut. 3 pers. sing. masc. ידע

הֲיוּחַל[n] pref. id.)(Hoph. fut. 3 pers. sing. masc. חול

הֲיוּכַל[o] pref. id.)(Hoph. fut. 3 pers. sing. masc. יכל

הַיּוּלָּד[p] pref. הַ)(Pual pret. 3 pers. sing. masc., (§ 10. rem. 5), or part [for מְיוּלָּד, rem. 6] . ילד

הַיּוֹם וְ pref. id.)(noun com. s., pl. יָמִים (§ 45) יום

הַיָּוֵן[q] pref. id.)(n. m. s., constr. יְוַן—(§ 34. r. 1) יון

הַיּוֹנָה pref. id.)(Kal part. act. s. f. from [יוֹנֶה] m. ינה

הַיּוֹנָה pref. id.)(noun fem. sing. dec. 10, see יוֹנָה

הַיְּוָנִים pref. id.)(patronym., pl. of יְוָנִי fr. יָוָן q. v.

הַיְהוֹנָתָן pref. הַ)(pr. name masc., see יְהוֹנָתָן . הוה

הַיּוֹצֵא וְ[r] pref. הַ)(Kal part. act. sing. masc. d. 7 b. יצא

הַיּוֹצְאִים[s] pref. id.)(id. pl. absolute . . . יצא

הַיּוֹצֵאת וְ[t] pref. id.)(id. f. s. [for יוֹצֵאת § 23. r. 4] יצא

הַיּוֹצֵר pref. id.)(Kal part. act. sing. masc. dec. 7 b. יצר

הַיֹּצְרִים[u] pref. id.)(id. pl., absolute state . . יצר

הַיֹּצֵאת[x] contr. for הַיּוֹצֵאת (q. v.) . . . יצא

הַיֹּרְדוֹת[y] pref. הַ)(Kal part. act. f., pl. of יוֹרְדָה or יוֹרֶדֶת dec. 10, or 13 a. (§ 8. rem. 19) . ירד

הַיּוֹרִים[z] pref. id.)(Kal part. act. m., pl. of יוֹרֶה d. 9 a. ירה

---

[a] Ex. 22. 12. [b] Pr. 7. 21. [c] Eze. 2. 10. [d] Job 31. 11. [e] 1 Ki. 17. 15. [f] Eze. 23. 43. [g] Job 39. 9. [h] Job 6. 6. [i] Is. 45. 9. [k] Ex. 1. 22. [l] Ex. 8. 1. [m] Eze. 40. 15. [n] Ezr. 5. 14. [o] Jos. 6. 13. [p] Eze. 37. 4. [q] Job 8. 11. [r] Ps. 30. 10. [s] De. 7. 19. [t] Ne. 12. 8. [u] 2 Ki. 9. 35. [x] Eze. 7. 17. [y] Ge. 27. 22. [z] Je. 40. 14. [a] Je. 44. 15. [b] 1 Sa. 27. 8. [c] Ge. 47. 24. [d] Je. 50. 6. [e] Je. 8. 19. [f] 2 Ki. 7. 2, 19. [g] Je. 13. 23. [h] Eze. 47. 12. [i] Je. 18. 23. [k] Jos. 6. 4, 8, 13. [l] Ps. 30. 10. [m] Ps. 88. 13. [n] Is. 66. 8. [o] Ps. 78. 19. [p] Ju. 13. 8. [q] Ps. 40. 3. [r] Je. 21. 9. [s] Zec. 6. 8. [t] Am. 5. 3. [u] 1 Ch. 4. 23. [x] De. 28. 57. [y] Ne. 3. 15. [z] 1 Ch. 10. 3.

הַיּוֹרֵשׁ[a] pref. הַ)(Kal part. act. masc. dec. 7b. ירשׁ

הַיּוֹשֵׁב pref. id.)(Kal part. act. masc. dec. 7b. ישׁב

הַיֹּשְׁבִים [b]וְ״ pref. id.)(id. pl., absolute state ישׁב

הַיּוֹשֶׁבֶת pref. id.)(id. fem. s. d. 13a. (§ 8. rem. 19) ישׁב

הֱיוֹת Kal inf. constr., dec. 1a. היה

הֱיוֹתָהּ[c] id., suff. 3 pers. sing. fem. היה

הֱיוֹתוֹ[d] id., suff. 3 pers. sing. masc. היה

הֱיוֹתִי[e] id., suff. 1 pers. sing. היה

הֱיוֹתֵךְ[f] id., suff. 2 pers. sing. fem. היה

הֱיוֹתְךָ[g] id., suff. 2 pers. sing. masc. היה

הֱיוֹתְכֶם[h] id., suff. 2 pers. pl. masc. היה

הֱיוֹתָם id., suff. 3 pers. pl. masc. היה

הֱיוֹתֵנוּ[i] id., suff. 1 pers. pl. היה

הַיּוֹתֵר[k] pref. הַ)(noun masc. sing. יתר

הֲיִזְבָּחוּ[l] pref. הֲ)(Kal fut. 3 p. s. m. (for יִזְבְּחוּ § 8. r. 15) זבח

הַיִּזְרָח pref. הַ)(patronym. for אֶזְרָחִי q. v. זרח

הַיִּזְרְעֵאלִי pref. id.)(gent. noun from יִזְרְעֵאל (q. v.) זרע

הַיִּזְרְעֵאלִית
הַיִּזְרְעֵלִית } pref. id.)(fem. of the preceding זרע

הַיְחֻבְּרְךָ[m] pref. הַ interr. for הֲ)(Pual fut. 3 pers. sing. masc., suff. 2 p. s. m. [for יְחֻבַּרְךָ § 10. r. 5] חבר

הַיָּחִיד[n] pref. הַ art.)(adj. masc. sing. dec. 3a. יחד

הֲיִחְיֶה[o] pref. הֲ)(Kal fut. 3 pers. sing. masc. חיה

הַיְחַיּוּ[p] pref. הַ interr. for הֲ)(Piel fut. 3 p. m. pl. חיה

הַיַּחְלְאֵלִי pref. הַ art.)(patronym. of יַחְלְאֵל q. v. יחל

הַיַּחְצְאֵלִי pref. id.)(gent. noun from יַחְצְאֵל q. v. חצה

הַיַּחַשׂ[q] pref. id.)(noun masc. sing. יחשׂ

הֲיַחְתֶּה[r] pref. הֲ)(Kal fut. 3 pers. sing. masc. חתה

הֵיטִב[s] וְ Hiph. pret. 3 pers. sing. masc. יטב

הֵיטֵב id. inf. absolute, used also adverbially יטב

הֵיטִבְךָ[t] וְ id. pret. 3 pers. sing. masc., suff. 2 p. s. m. יטב

הֵיטַבְתָּ[u] id. pret. 2 pers. sing. masc. יטב

הֵיטַבְתְּ[x] id. pret. 2 pers. sing. fem. יטב

הֵיטֵיב id. inf. absolute יטב

הֵיטִיב id. pret. 3 pers. sing. masc. יטב

הֵיטִיבָה[y] id. imp. sing. masc. with opt. ה יטב

הֵיטִיבוּ [z]וְ״ id. pret. 3 pers. pl. masc. or imp. pl. m. יטב

הֲיִטְמָא[a] pref. הֲ)(Kal fut. 3 pers. sing. masc. טמא

הֱיִי[b] Kal imp. fem. sing. היה

הַיִּיטַב[c] pref. הַ interr. for הֲ)(Kal fut. 3 pers. s. m. יטב

הַיָּיִן
הַיַּיִן } וְ' pref. הַ)(noun masc. sing. dec. 6h. יין

הָיִינוּ וְ' Kal pret. 3 pers. pl. היה

הָיִיתָ וְ' id. pret. 2 pers. sing. masc. היה

הָיִית [d]וְ'
הָיִיתְ[e] וְ } id. pret. 2 pers. sing. fem. היה

הָיִיתָה[f] Kh. תָה' q. v., K. הָיִיתָ q. v. היה

הָיִיתָה[g] וְ Kal pret. 2 pers. sing. masc. (§ 8. rem. 5) היה

הָיִיתִי וְ' id. pret. 1 pers. sing. היה

הָיִיתִי[h] id. pret. 2 pers. sing. fem. Kh. תִי', K. הָיִית, (§ 8. rem. 5) היה

הֱיִיתֶם
הֱיִיתֶם וְ } id. pret. 2 pers. pl. masc. (§ 13. rem. 13) היה

הֵיךְ[k] וְ' Chald. i. q. אֵיךְ *how?*

הֲיָכוֹל[l] pref. הֲ)(Kal inf. absolute יכל

הַיָּכִינִי pref. הַ)(patronym. of יָכִין כון

הֵיכָל [m]וְ״ masc. dec. 2b.—I. *a large splendid building, a palace.*—II. *the temple* of the Lord at Jerusalem.
הֵיכַל Chald. dec. 2a.—I. *palace.*—II. *temple*, Da. 5. 2, 3, 5.

הֵיכַל [n]וְ״ id., construct state היכל

הֲיָכֹל[o] pref. הֲ)(Kal inf. absolute יכל

הַיְכִל[p] Chald. pref. הַ interr. for הֲ)(Peal pret. 3 pers. sing. masc. (§ 47. rem. 6) יכל

הֵיכְלָא Chald. noun m. s., emph. of [הֵיכַל] dec. 2a. היכל

הַיְכַלּוּ[q] pref. הַ interr. for הֲ)(Piel pret. 3 pers. pl. כלה

הֵיכָלוֹ noun m. s., suff. 3 pers. s. m. fr. הֵיכָל dec. 2a. היכל

הֵיכָלוֹת[r] id. with pl. fem. term., absolute state היכל

הֵיכְלֵי[s] id. pl. masc., construct state היכל

הֵיכָלֶךָ id. sing., suff. 2 pers. sing. masc. [for הֵיכָלְךָ] היכל

הֲיִכְרֹת[t] pref. הֲ)(Kal fut. 3 pers. sing. masc. כרת

הַיֶּלֶד
הַיֶּלֶד } pref. הַ)(noun masc. sing. dec. 6a. (pl. c. יַלְדֵי & יִלְדֵי § 35. rem. 4) ילד

הַיַּלְדָּה[u] [x]וְ״ pref. id.)(noun fem. sing. dec. 12a. ילד

הַיֹּלְדָהּ[y] וְ pref. id.)(Kal part. act. sing. masc. (יוֹלֵד) suff. 3 p. sing. fem. dec. 7b. ילד

הַיַּלְדוּת[z] pref. id.)(noun fem. sing. dec. 1b. ילד

הַיֹּלְדוֹת[a] pref. id.)(Kal part. act. fem., pl. of יֹלֶדֶת dec. 13a. (§ 8. rem. 19) ילד

הַיְלָדִים וְ' pref. id.)(noun masc. pl. from יֶלֶד dec. 6a. (§ 35. rem. 2; pl. c. יִלְדֵי & יַלְדֵי rem. 4) ילד

הַיִּלֹּדִים pref. הַ)(noun masc., pl. of יִלּוֹד dec. 1b. ילד

הַיֹּלֶדֶת[b] pref. id.)(Kal part. act. s. f. d. 13a. (§ 8. r. 19) ילד

הַיָּלוּד[c] pref. id.)(Kal part. p. sing. masc. dec. 3a. ילד

הַיִּלּוֹד pref. id.)(noun masc. sing. dec. 1b. ילד

הַיְּלוּדִים[d] pref. id.)(Kal part. p. m., pl. of יָלוּד dec. 3a. ילד

הֵילִיכִי[e] Hiph. imp. sing. fem. ילך

הֵילִילוּ וְ' Hiph. imp. pl. masc. ילל

[a] 2 Sa. 14. 7. [b] 2 Ch. 30. 25. [c] Is. 48. 16. [d] Eze. 34. 12. [e] Jon. 4. 2. [f] Is. 60. 15. [g] Ju. 18. 19, 19. [h] Je. 44. 8. [i] 1 Sa. 25. 16. [k] 1 Sa. 15. 15. [l] Ne. 3. 34. [m] Ps. 94. 20. [n] Zec. 12. 10. [o] Job 14. 14. [p] Ne. 3. 34. [q] Ne. 7. 5. [r] Pr. 6. 27. [s] 1 Sa. 25. 31. [t] De. 30. 5. [u] Je. 1. 12. [x] Ruth 3. 10. [y] Ps. 51. 20. [z] Je. 35. 15. [a] Hag. 2. 13. [b] Ge. 24. 60. [c] Le. 10. 19. [d] Is. 62. 3. [e] 2 Sa. 14. 2. [f] 2 Sa. 5. 2. [g] Ju. 11. 6. [h] Eze. 16. 31. [i] 1 Ch. 13. 12. [k] Da. 10. 17. [l] 2 Ch. 32. 13. [m] Is. 44. 28. [n] Ezr. 3. 6. [o] Nu. 22. 38. [p] Da. 6. 21. [q] Ne. 3. 34. [r] Ho. 8. 14. [s] Ps. 45. 9. [t] Job 40. 28. [u] Ge. 34. 4. [x] Joel 4. 3. [y] Da. 11. 6. [z] Ec. 11. 10. [a] Je. 16. 3. [b] Le. 12. 7. [c] 1 Ki. 3. 26, 27. [d] 1 Ch. 14. 4. [e] Ex. 2. 9.

הֵילִילִי[a] id. imp. sing. fem. . . . . . ילל
הֲיֵלֵךְ[b] pref. הֲ χ Kal fut. 3 pers. sing. masc. . ילך
הֲיֵלְכוּ[c] pref. id. χ id. fut. 3 pers. pl. . . ילך
הֵילֵל[d] noun masc. sing. . . . . . הלל
הֵילֵל[e] וְ' Hiph. imp. sing. masc. . . . ילל
הֵילִל[g] וְ id. pret. 3 pers. sing. masc. . . ילל
הַיֶּלֶק[h] / הַיָּלֶק } pref. הַ χ noun masc. sing. (§ 35. rem. 2) ילק
הַיָּם וְ' pref. id. / הַיָּם[i] pref. הַ } noun masc. sing. dec. 8a. . ים
הַיָּמָּה pref. הַ χ id. with paragogic ה . . ים
הַיָּמִים וְ' pref. id. χ noun masc. pl. [as if for יָם, see יוֹם § 45] . . . יום
הַיַּמִּים[k] pref. הַ χ noun masc., pl. of יָם dec. 8a. . ים
הַיָּמִין[l] pref. id. χ noun masc. with Chald. pl. term. see הַיָּמִים . . . . יום
הַיָּמִין pref. id. χ noun masc. sing. dec. 3a. . . ימן
הַיָּמִינִי pref. id. χ patronym. of יָמִין . . ימן
הַיְמִינִי pref. id. χ gent. noun fr. בִּנְיָמִין q. v. . בנה
הַיְמִינִי[m] pref. id. χ adj. masc. sing. . . ימן
הַיְמִינִי[n] Kh. הַיְמִינִי q. v., K. הַיְמָנִי (q. v.) . ימן
הֵימִינִי[o] Hiph. imp. sing. fem. . . . ימן
הֲיִמָּלֵט[p] pref. הֲ χ Niph. fut. 3 pers. sing. masc. . מלט
הַיָּמִם[q] defect for הַיָּמִים (q. v.) . . . יום
הַיֵּמִם[r] pref. הַ χ noun masc. pl. [of יֵם q. v.]
הֵימָם וְ pr. name masc. . . . . המם
הֵימָן וְ' pr. name masc. . . . . אמן
הֵימַן[s] Chald. Aph. pret. 3 pers. sing. masc. (§ 53) אמן
הַיִּמְנָה pref. הַ χ pr. name masc. . . . ימן
הַיְמָנִי[t] pref. id. χ adj. masc. sing. (from יָמִין) . ימן
הַיְמָנִית pref. id. χ fem. of the prec. . . . ימן
הֲמִישֵׁנִי[u] וַ Kh. וְהֵימִשֵׁנִי Hiph. imp. sing., suff. 1 pers. sing. from יָמַשׁ, K. וַהֲמִשֵׁנִי id. from מוש
הִין[x] וְ' noun masc. sing. . . . . הון
הֲיִנְהַק[y] pref. הֲ χ Kal fut. 3 pers. sing. masc. . נהק
הֲיִנְטוֹר[z] pref. id. χ Kal fut. 3 pers. sing. masc. . נטר
הֵינִיקָה[a] Hiph. pret. 3 pers. sing. fem. . . ינק
הַיֹּנֵק[b] pref. הַ χ Kal part. act. sing. masc. dec. 7b. ינק
הֵינִקֵהוּ[c] וְ Hiph. imp. sing. fem., suff. 3 pers. sing. masc. ינק
הַיַּנְשׁוּף pref. הַ χ noun masc. sing. . . . נשף
הֲיַסְגִּרוּ[d] pref. הֲ χ Hiph. fut. 3 pers. pl. [def. for יַסְגִּירוּ] סגר
הֲיַסְגִּרֻנִי[e] pref. id. χ id. with suff. 1 pers. sing. . סגר
הַיְסוֹד pref. הַ χ noun masc. sing. dec. 1a. . יסד
הַיְסֻפַּר pref. הַ interr. for הֲ χ Pual fut. 3 pers. sing. masc. . . . . . ספר

הַיֹּסֵר[f] pref. הַ χ Kal part. act. sing. masc. . יסר
הַיְעוּצָה[g] pref. הַ χ Kal part. p. sing. fem. [fr. יָעוּץ m.] יעץ
הֲיַעֲזֹב[h] pref. הֲ χ Kal fut. 3 pers. sing. masc. . עזב
הֲיַעַזְבוּ[i] pref. id. χ id. pret. 3 pers. pl. m. . . עזב
הַיָּעִים pref. הַ χ noun masc. pl. [of יָע, no vowel change] . . . . יעה
הֲיַעֲלֶה[k] pref. הֲ χ Kal fut. 3 pers. sing. masc. . יעל
הַיְּעֵלִים[l] pref. הַ χ noun masc., pl. of [יָעֵל] dec. 5a. יעל
הֲיַעֲמֹד[m] pref. הֲ χ Kal fut. 3 pers. sing. masc. . עמד
הֲיַעַמְדוּ[n] pref. id. χ id. fut. 3 pers. pl. . . עמד
הַיַּעֲנָה pref. הַ χ noun fem. sing. . . . יען
הַיָּעֵף[o] pref. id. χ adj. masc. sing. dec. 5a. . עוף
הַיְּעֵפִים[p] pref. id. χ id. pl., absolute state . עוף
הַיֹּעֲצִים[q] וְ pref. id. χ Kal part. act. m., pl. of יֹעֵץ dec. 7b. . . . . יעץ
הַיַּעַר / הַיָּעַר } pref. id. χ noun masc. sing. (§ 35. rem. 2) dec. 6d. . . . . } יער
הַיַּעְרָה[r] pref. id. χ id. with paragogic ה . . יער
הַיְּעָרִים pref. id. χ id. pl., absolute state . . יער
הֲיַעֲרֹךְ[s] pref. הֲ χ Kal fut. 3 pers. sing. masc. . ערך
הֲיַעֲשֶׂה[t] pref. id. χ Kal fut. 3 pers. sing. masc. עשה
הַיָּפָה pref. הַ χ adj. fem. sing. dec. 11a, from יָפֶה m. יפה
הַיָּפוֹת[u] pref. id. χ id. pl., absolute state . יפה
הַיֳּפִי[x] pref. id. χ noun masc. sing. dec. 6k. [for יְפִי § 35. rem. 14] . . . . יפה
הֲיִפָּלֵא[y] pref. הֲ χ Niph. fut. 3 pers. sing. masc. . פלא
הֲיִפְּלוּ[z] pref. id. χ Kal fut. 3 pers. pl. m. . . נפל
הַיַּפְלֵטִי pref. הַ χ patronym. of יַפְלֵט . . . פלט
הַיֹּצֵא וְ' pref. id. χ Kal part. act. masc. s. dec. 7b. יצא
הַיֹּצְאִים pref. id. χ id. pl., absolute state . . יצא
הַיֹּצֵאת [a]וְ' pref. id. χ id. fem. sing. [for יֹצֵאת § 23. rem. 4; § 8. rem. 19] . . . יצא
הַיִּצְהָר וְ' pref. id. χ noun masc. sing. dec. 2b. . צהר
הַיִּצְהָרִי pref. id. χ patronym. of יִצְהָר . . צהר
הַיָּצוּעַ[b] pref. id. χ Kh. יָצוּעַ Kal part. pass., K. יָצִיעַ noun masc. dec. 3a. . . . יצע
הֲיִצְלַח[c] / הֲיִצְלָח[d] } pref. הֲ χ Kal fut. 3 pers. sing. masc. (§ 8. rem. 15) . . . } צלח
הַיֹּצֵר pref. הַ χ Kal part. act. sing. masc. dec. 7b. יצר
הַיִּצְרִי pref. id. χ patronym. of יֵצֶר . . . יצר
הַיֶּקֶב / הַיָּקֶב[e] } pref. id. χ noun masc. sing. dec. 6a. (§ 35. rem. 2; but pl. c. יִקְבֵי) } יקב
הַיְקָבִים pref. id. χ id. pl., absolute state . . יקב
הֲיִקְבַּע[f] pref. הֲ χ Kal fut. 3 pers. sing. masc. . קבע
הֲיִקְדָּשׁ[g] pref. id. χ Kal fut. 3 pers. sing. masc. (for יִקְדַּשׁ § 8. rem. 15) . . . קדש

[a] Je. 49. 3.
[b] Ex. 16. 4.
[c] Am. 3. 3.
[d] Is. 14. 12.
[e] Zec. 11. 2.
[f] Eze. 21. 17.
[g] Je. 47. 2.
[h] Joel 1. 4.
[i] Job 7. 12.
[k] Ne. 9. 6.
[l] Da. 12. 13.
[m] 2 Ch. 3. 17.
[n] Eze. 4. 6.
[o] Eze. 21. 21.
[p] Eze. 17. 15.
[q] Nu. 6. 5.
[r] Ge. 36. 24.
[s] Da. 6. 24.
[t] 1 Ki. 7. 21.
[u] Ju. 16. 26.
[x] Le. 19. 36.
[y] Job 6. 5.
[z] Je. 3. 5.
[a] Ge. 21. 7.
[b] Nu. 11. 12.
[c] Ex. 2. 9.
[d] 1 Sa. 23. 12.
[e] 1 Sa. 23. 11.
[f] Ps. 94. 10.
[g] Is. 14. 26.
[h] Je. 18. 14.
[i] Ne. 3. 34.
[k] Am. 3. 5.
[l] 1 Sa. 24. 3.
[m] Eze. 22. 14.
[n] Est. 3. 4.
[o] 2 Sa. 16. 2.
[p] Ju. 8. 15.
[q] Eze. 11. 2.
[r] Jos. 17. 15.
[s] Job 36. 19.
[t] Je. 16. 20.
[u] Am. 8. 13.
[x] Pr. 31. 30.
[y] Ge. 18. 14.
[z] Je. 8. 4.
[a] 1 Ch. 27. 1.
[b] 1 Ki. 6. 6, 10.
[c] Eze. 17. 15.
[d] Eze. 15. 4.
[e] Hag. 2. 16.
[f] Mal. 3. 8.
[g] Hag. 2. 12.

הַיְקוּם	pref. הַ)(noun masc. sing. . . .	קום
הֻיְקַּח	pref. הֲ)(Hoph. fut. 3 p. s. m. (§ 17. r. 8)	לקח
הַיְקָר[a]	pref. הַ)(noun masc. sing. dec. 1 a. .	יקר
הַיְקָרִים[b]	pref. id.)(adj. masc., pl. of יָקָר dec. 4 a. .	יקר
הֲיִקְרְךָ[c]	pref. הֲ)(Kal fut. 3 p. s. m., suff. 2 p. s. m.	קרה
הַיָּרֵא	pref. הַ)(adj. masc. sing. d. 5 a. (§ 34. r. 1)	ירא
הֲיַרְבֶּה[d]	pref. הֲ)(Hiph. fut. 3 pers. sing. masc. .	רבה
הֲיֵרֵד[e]	pref. id.)(Kal fut. 3 pers. sing. masc. .	ירד
הַיֹּרֵד	pref. הַ)(Kal part. act. sing. masc. dec. 7 b.	ירד
הַיֹּרְדִים	ו'[f] pref. id.)(id. pl., absolute state .	ירד
הַיַּרְדֵּן	ו' pref. id.)(pr. name of a river . .	ירד
הַיַּרְדֵּנָה	pref. id.)(id. with parag. ה . . .	ירד
הַיֹּרֶדֶת[g]	pref. id.)(id. fem. sing. dec. 13 a. . .	ירד
הַיֹּרֶה[h]	pref. id.)(Kal part. act. sing. masc. dec. 9 a.	ירה
הַיָּרֵחַ	ו' pref. id.)(noun masc. sing. dec. 5 a. .	ירח
הַיְרַחְמְאֵלִי	pref. id.)(patronym. of יְרַחְמְאֵל (q. v.) .	רחם
הַיֹּרִים[i]	pref. id.)(Kal part. act. m., pl. of יֹרֶה d. 9 a.	ירה
הַיְרִיעָה	pref. id.)(noun fem. sing. dec. 10. .	ירע
הַיְרִיעֹת	pref. id.)(id. pl.	ירע
הַיָּרֵךְ[k]	pref. id.)(noun fem. sing. dec. 5 a. .	ירך
הֲיָרֹעַ[l]	pref. הֲ)(Kal fut. 3 pers. sing. masc. .	רעע
הֲיִרְצֶה[m]	pref. id.)(Kal fut. 3 pers. sing. masc. .	רצה
הַיְרֻצוּן[n]	pref. הַ interr. for הֲ)(Kal fut. 3 pers. pl., with parag. ן	רוץ
הֲיִרְצְךָ[o]	pref. הֲ)(Kal fut. 3 pers. sing. masc., (יִרְצֶה) suff. 2 pers. sing. masc. . . .	רצה
הַיָּרָק[p]	pref. הַ)(noun masc. sing. dec. 4 a. .	ירק
הַיַּרְקוֹן	pref. id.)(pr. name, see מֵי הַיַּרְקוֹן . .	מוא
הַיֹּרֵשׁ[q]	pref. id.)(Kal part. act. sing. masc. dec. 7 b.	ירש
הַיְרֻשָּׁה[r]	pref. id.)(noun fem. sing. dec. 10. .	ירש
הֲיֵשׁ	pref. הֲ)(adv., with suff. יֶשְׁךָ, יֶשְׁכֶם, comp. dec. 7 a.	ישה
הֲיִשָּׂא[s]	pref. id.)(Kal fut. 3 pers. sing. masc.	נשא
הֲיִשְׁאַג[t]	pref. id.)(Kal fut. 3 pers. sing. masc.	שאג
הַיֹּשֵׁב	ו'[u] pref. הַ)(Kal part. act. sing. m. d. 7 b.	ישב
הַיֹּשְׁבָה[x]	pref. id.)(id. fem. dec. 10.	ישב
הַיֹּשְׁבִי[y]	pref. id.)(id. m., with parag. י (§ 8. r. 19)	ישב
הַיָּשֻׁבִי	pref. id.)(patronym. of יָשׁוּב	שוב
הַיֹּשְׁבִים	ו' pref. id.)(Kal part. act. m., pl. of יֹשֵׁב d. 7 b.	ישב
הַיֹּשֶׁבֶת[z]	pref. id.)(id. sing. fem. dec. 13 a. (§ 8. r. 19)	ישב
הַיֹּשַׁבְתִּי[a]	pref. id.)(id. id. Kh. יֹשַׁבְתִּי with parag. י comp. § 8. rem. 19; K. יֹשֶׁבֶת . .	ישב
הֲיָשׁוּב[b]	pref. הֲ)(Kal fut. 3 pers. sing. masc.	שוב
הַיִּשְׁוִי	pref. הַ)(pr. name masc. . . .	שוה
הַיְשׁוּעָה	pref. id.)(noun fem. sing. dec. 10. .	ישע
הַיְשִׁימוֹן	pref. id.)(noun masc. sing.	ישם

הַיְשִׁמוֹת	pref. id.)(pr. name, see בֵּית הַיְ' . .	בית
הַיְשִׁמֹן	pref. id.)(noun masc. sing. . .	ישם
הֲיִשְׁכֶם[c]	pref. הֲ)(adv. (יֵשׁ) with suff. 2 pers. pl. m.	ישה
הֲיְשֻׁלַּם[d]	pref. הֲ)(Pual pret. 3 pers. sing. masc.	שלם
הַיִּשְׁמְעֵאלִי	pref. id.)(patronym. of יִשְׁמָעֵאל (q. v.)	שמע
הַיִּשְׁמְעֵאלִים	pref. id.)(pl. of the prec. . .	שמע
הֲיִשְׁמְעוּ[e]	pref. הֲ)(Kal fut. 3 pers. pl. m. .	שמע
הַיִּשְׁמְעֵלִי	pref. הַ)(patronym. & contr. of יִשְׁמָעֵאל (q. v.)	שמע
הַיְשִׁמֹת	pref. id.)(pr. name, see בֵּית הַיְ' .	בית
הַיְשָׁנָה	pref. id.)(adj. fem. sing., from יָשָׁן masc. .	ישן
הַיָּשָׁר	ו' pref. id.)(adj. & subs. masc. sing. dec. 4 a.	ישר
הַיִּשְׂרְאֵלִי	pref. id.)(gent. noun from יִשְׂרָאֵל (q. v.)	שרה
הַיִּשְׂרְאֵלִית	pref. id.)(fem. of the prec. . .	שרה
הַיְשָׁרָה[f]	ו'[g] pref. id.)(adj. fem. sing. fr. יָשָׁר masc.	ישר
הָיִת	ו'[h] Kal pret. 2 pers. sing. masc. . .	היה
הָיָת[i]	ו id. pret. 3 pers. sing. fem. Kh. הָיָת (§ 24. rem. 1) K. הָיְתָה	היה
הַיָּתֵד	ו'[k] pref. הַ)(noun fem. sing. dec. 5 a.	יתד
הַיְתַד[l]	pref. id.)(id., constr. state .	יתד
הַיְתֵדֹת[m]	pref. id.)(id. pl., abs. state fem. term.	יתד
הָיְתָה ו' הָיְתָה	Kal pret. 3 pers. sing. fem. (§ 8. rem. 7)	היה
הָיִתָה[n]	ו id. pret. 2 pers. sing. masc. (§ 8. rem. 5)	היה
הַיָּתוֹם	ו noun masc. sing. dec. 3 a. . .	יתם
הַיָּתִי[o]	ו Kh.; K. הַוָּתִי noun fem. sing., suff. 1 pers. sing. from [הַוָּה or הָיָה] dec. 10.	הוה
הֵיתִי[p]	Ch. Aph. pret. 3 pers. sing. masc. (§ 56. rem. 2, comp. § 47. rem. 4) . . .	אתה
הֵיתִיו[q]	ו'[r] Ch. id. pret. 3 pers. pl. masc. . .	אתה
הֵיתָיוּ[s]	Ch. Hoph. pret. 3 pers. pl. m. (§ 56. r. 2)	אתה
הֵיתָיִת[t]	ו Chald. id. pret. 3 pers. sing. fem.	אתה
הֱיִתֶם[u] ו הֱיִתֶם[x]	Kal pret. 2 pers. pl. masc., ו bef. (:) for ו (§ 13. rem. 13, & § 24. rem. 7)	היה
הֲיִתֵּן[y]	pref. הֲ)(Kal fut. 3 pers. sing. masc.	נתן
הֲיִתְפָּאֵר[z]	pref. id.)(Hithpa. fut. 3 pers. sing. masc.	פאר
הַיִּתְרִי	pref. הַ)(patronym. of יֶתֶר . .	יתר
הַיְתָרִים[a]	pref. id.)(noun masc., pl. of יֶתֶר (suff. יִתְרוֹ) dec. 6 a.	יתר
הַיֹּתֶרֶת	pref. id.)(noun fem. sing. . .	יתר
הַךְ	ו' Hiph. imp. sing. masc., apoc. for הַכֵּה (§ 25. No. 2 b) . . .	נכה
הַכְּאֵב[b]	pref. הַ)(noun masc. sing. dec. 1 a. .	כאב
הִכְאַבְתִּיו[c]	Hiph. pret. 1 pers. sing., suff. 3 pers. sing. m	כאב
הַכְאוֹת[d]	Hiph. inf. construct . . .	כאה
הַכָּבֵד	pref. הַ)(adj. and subst. masc. sing. dec. 5, constr. כְּבֵד & כָּבֵד (§ 34. rem. 2)	כבד

[a] Zec. 11. 13. [b] La. 4. 2. [c] Nu. 11. 23. [d] Job 40. 27. [e] 1 Sa. 23. 11. [f] Jos. 3. 16.
[g] Ec. 3. 21. [h] Pr. 26. 18. [i] 2 Ch. 35. 23. [k] Ge. 32. 33. [l] Je. 15. 12. [m] Mi. 6. 7.
[n] Am. 6. 12. [o] Mal. 1. 8. [p] De. 11. 10. [q] Mi. 1. 15. [r] Je. 32. 8. [s] Mal. 1. 8, 9.
[t] Am. 3. 4. [u] Le. 15. 6. [x] Na. 3. 8. [y] Ps. 123. 1. [z] Ca. 8. 13. [a] Eze. 27. 3.
[b] Je. 3. 1. [c] De. 13. 4. [d] Je. 18. 20. [e] Ju. 3. 4. [f] Mi. 3. 9. [g] 1 Sa. 12. 23.
[h] 2 Sa. 15. 33. [i] 2 Ki. 9. 37. [k] Ju. 4. 22. Ju. 16. 14. [m] Ex. 38. 20.
[n] 2 Sa. 10. 11. [o] Job 6. 2. [p] Da. 5. 13. [q] Da. 5. 3, 23. [r] Da. 6. 17, 25.
[s] Da. 3. 13. [t] Da. 6. 18. [u] De. 31. 27. [x] 1 Sa. 12. 14. [y] Am. 3. 4.
[z] Is. 10. 15. [a] Ju. 16. 9. [b] Job 2. 13. [c] Eze. 13. 22. [d] Eze. 13. 22.

Form	Analysis	Root
הַכָּבֹד[a]	pref. הַ)(noun masc. sing. dec. 3a.	כבד
הַכְבֵּד[b]	[c]וְ' Hiph. inf., or imp. sing. masc.	כבד
הִכָּבֵד[d]	Niph. imp. sing. masc.	כבד
הִכָּבְדִי[e]	id. inf. (הִכָּבֵד), suff. 1 pers. sing. dec. 7b.	כבד
הִכְבַּדְתְּ[f]	Hiph. pret. 2 pers. sing. fem.	כבד
הִכְבַּדְתִּי[g]	id. pret. 1 pers. sing.	כבד
הִכְבַּדְתִּים[h]	וְ id. id., suff. 3 pers. pl. masc.	כבד
הַכָּבוֹד	[i]וְ' noun masc. sing. dec. 3a.	כבד
הַכְּבוּדָּה[k]	pref. הַ)([for כְּבֻדָּה] adj. fem. sing. from כָּבֹד (§ 39. No. 3, dec. 8)	כבד
הִכְבִּיד	Hiph. pret. 3 pers. sing. masc.	כבד
הִכְבִּידוּ	id. pret. 3 pers. pl.	כבד
הִכַּבֵּס[l]	Hothpael inf. construct [for הָתְכַּבֵּס § 6. rem. 10, note]	כבס
הַכֶּבֶשׂ	pref. הַ)(noun masc. sing. dec. 6.	כבשׂ
הַכִּבְשָׂה[m]	pref.)(noun fem. sing. dec. 12b.	כבשׂ
הַכְּבָשִׂים	pref. id.)(noun masc., pl. of כֶּבֶשׂ dec. 6.	כבשׂ
הַכִּבְשָׁן	pref. id.)(noun masc. sing.	כבשׁ
הַכַּדִּים[n]	pref. id.)(noun com. pl. abs. from כַּד dec. 8d.	כדד
הַכֵּה	Hiph. inf., or imp. sing. masc. (§ 25. No. 2b)	נכה
הִכָּה	וְ' id. pret. 3 pers. sing. masc.	נכה
הֻכָּה	[o]וְ' Hoph. pret. 3 pers. sing. m. (§ 25. No. 2b)	נכה
הַכֻּהוּ[p]	Hiph. imp. pl. masc., (הַכּוּ) suff. 3 pers. sing. masc. (§ 25. No. 2b)	נכה
הִכָּהוּ	וְ' id. pret. 3 pers. s. m., suff. 3 pers. s. m.	נכה
הִכֻּהוּ	id. pret. 3 pers. pl., (הִכּוּ) suff. 3 pers. s. m.	נכה
הַכֹּהֵן	וְ' pref. הַ)(noun masc. sing. dec. 7b.	כהן
הַכְּהֻנָּה	pref. id.)(noun fem. sing. dec. 10.	כהן
הַכְּהֻנּוֹת[q]	pref. id.)(id. pl.	כהן
הַכֹּהֲנִים	וְ' pref. id.)(noun masc., pl. of כֹּהֵן dec. 7b.	כהן
הַכּוּ[r]	[s]וְ' Hiph. imp. pl. masc. (§ 25. No. 2b)	נכה
הִכּוּ	וְ' id. pret. 3 pers. pl.	נכה
הֻכּוּ[t]	Hoph. pret. 3 pers. pl. (§ 25. No. 2b)	נכה
הַכּוֹכָבִים	[u]וְ' pref. הַ)(noun masc., pl. of כּוֹכָב dec. 2b. [for כָּבְכָּב]	כבב
הַכּוּם[x]	Hiph. imp. pl. masc., suff. 3 pers. pl. masc. (§ 25. No. 2b)	נכה
הִכּוּם	id. pret. 3 pers. pl., suff. 3 pers. pl. masc.	נכה
הִכּוֹן[y]	Niph. imp. sing. masc.	כון
הָכוֹנוּ[z]	וְ Kh. הִכּוֹנוּ' Niph., K הָכִינוּ' Hiph. imp. pl. m.	כון
הִכּוּנִי	[a]וְ' Hiph. pret. 3 pers. pl., suff. 1 pers. sing. (§ 25. No. 2b)	נכה
הַכּוֹס	pref. הַ)(noun fem. sing. dec. 1a.	כוס
הַכּוּשִׁי	pref. id.)(gent. noun from כּוּשׁ	כושׁ
הַכּוּשִׁים	pref. id.)(pl. of the preceding	כושׁ
הַכּוֹת	[b]וְ' Hiph. inf. const. dec. 1. (§ 25. No. 2b)	נכה

Form	Analysis	Root
הַכּוֹתְךָ[c]	id., suff. 2 pers. sing. masc. [for הַכְּוֹתְךָ]	נכה
הַכּוֹתֶרֶת	pref. הַ)(n. f. s., pl. כֹּתָרוֹת (§ 44. rem. 5)	כתר
הֲכָזֶה[d]	preff. כָּ (q. v.) & הֲ)(pron. demon. m. sing.	זה
הַכְזוֹנָה[e]	preff. הַ interr. for הֲ, & כְּ)(Kal part. act. fem. dec. 10, from זוֹנֶה masc.	זנה
הַכֹּחַ[f]	וְ pref. הַ)(noun masc., dec. 1a.	כחח
הִכְחַדְתִּיו[g]	וְ Hiph. pret. 1 pers. sing., suff. 3 pers. s. m.	כחד
הֹכַחְתָּ[h]	Hiph. pret. 2 pers. sing. masc. [for הוֹכַחְתָּ]	יכח
הֹכַחְתִּיו[i]	וְ id. pret. 1 pers. sing., suff. 3 pers. sing. m.	יכח
הֲכִי	pref. הֲ)(conj.	כי
הֲכַיּוֹצֵר[k]	preff. הֲ & כַּ for כְּהַ)(Kal part. act. s. m. d. 7b.	יצר
הַכִּיּוֹר	pref. הַ)(noun masc. sing. dec. 1b.	כור
הֹכִיחַ[l]	Hiph. pret. 3 pers. sing. masc. [for הוֹכִיחַ]	יכח
הָכִיל[m]	Hiph. inf. constr.	כול
הֲכִימֵי[n]	preff. הֲ, & כְ, f. כִּי, כִּימֵי')(n. m. pl., constr. of יָמִים, irr. of יוֹם (§ 45)	יום
הָכִין[o]	וְ' Hiph. inf. constr., used as an absolute	כון
הֵכִין	id. pret. 3 pers. sing. masc.	כון
הֱכִינָהּ[p]	id. id., suff. 3 pers. sing. fem.	כון
הָכִינוּ	וְ' id. imp. pl. masc.	כון
הֲכִינוֹ[q]	id. inf. (הָכִין), suff. 3 pers. sing. m. dec. 3a.	כון
הֱכִינוֹ	id. pret. 3 pers. sing. masc., suff. 3 pers. s. m.	כון
הֵכִינוּ	[r]וְ' id. pret. 3 pers. pl.	כון
הֲכִינוֹנוּ[s]	id. pret. 1 pers. pl.	כון
הֲכִינוֹתָ	[t]וַ' id. pret. 2 pers. sing. masc.; וַ bef. (-:)	כון
הֲכִינוֹתִי	וַ' id. pret. 1 pers. sing.; וַ id.	כון
הַכֵּנִי[u]	Hiph. imp. s. m. suff. 1 p. s. (§ 25. No. 2b)	נכה
הֱכִינַנִי[x]	Hiph. pret. 3 pers. sing. masc., suff. 1 pers. s.	כון
הֲכִינֹתָה[y]	וַ id. pret. 2 p. s. m. (comp. § 8. r. 5); וַ bef. (-:)	כון
הֲכִינֹתִי[z]	וַ id. pret. 1 pers. sing.; acc. shifted by conv. וַ for וְ (§ 8. rem. 7)	כון
הַכִּיֹּר	pref. הַ)(noun masc. sing. dec. 1b.	כור
הִכִּיר[a]	Hiph. pret. 3 pers. sing. masc.	נכר
הִכִּירֻהוּ[b]	id. pret. 3 pers. pl. (הִכִּירוּ), suff. 3 p. s. m.	נכר
הִכִּירוֹ[c]	id. pret. 3 pers. sing. masc., suff. 3 p. s. m.	נכר
הִכִּירוּ	id. pret. 3 pers. pl.	נכר
הַכִּיֹּרוֹת הַכִּיֹּרֹת	pref. הַ)(n. m. with pl. f. term. fr. כִּיּוֹר d. 1b.	כור
הִכִּיתָ וְהִכִּיתָ	Hiph. pret. 2 pers. sing. m. (§ 24. r. 14); acc. shifted by conv. וְ (§ 8. r. 7)	נכה
הִכִּיתָה[d] וְהִכִּיתָה	id. id. (§ 8. rem. 5)	נכה
הִכִּיתוֹ[e]	id. id., suff. 3 pers. sing. masc.	נכה
הִכֵּיתִי וְהִכֵּיתִי	id. pret. 1 pers. sing. (§ 24. rem. 14); acc. shifted by conv. וְ (§ 8. rem. 7)	נכה
הֻכֵּיתִי[f]	Hoph. pret. 1 pers. sing. (§ 25. No. 2b)	נכה

[a] Ge. 31. 1. [b] Is. 6. 10. [c] Ex. 8. 11. [d] 2 Ki. 14. 10. [e] Eze. 39. 13. [f] Is. 47. 6. [g] Ex. 10. 1. [h] Je. 30. 19. [i] 1 Ch. 29. 12. [k] Ju. 18. 21. [l] Le. 13. 55, 56. [m] 2 Sa. 12. 6. [n] Ju. 7. 16, 19, 20. [o] Ex. 22. 1. [p] 2 Ki. 9. 27. [q] 1 Sa. 2. 36. [r] 2 Sa. 13. 28. [s] Eze. 9. 5. [t] 1 Sa. 5. 12. [u] Ec. 12. 2. [x] 2 Ki. 10. 25. [y] Am. 4. 12. [z] 2 Ch. 35. 4. [a] Ge. 34. 30. [b] 2 Ki. 3. 24. [c] Mi. 6. 13. [d] Is. 58. 5. [e] Ge. 34. 31. [f] Le. 11. 30. [g] Ex. 23. 23. [h] Ge. 24. 14. [i] 2 Sa. 7. 14. [k] Je. 18. 6. [l] Ge. 24. 44. [m] Je. 6. 11. [n] Job 10. 5. [o] Jos. 4. 3. [p] Job 28. 27. [q] Na. 2. 4. [r] Ex. 16. 5. [s] 1 Ch. 29. 16. [t] 2 Ch. 19. 3. [u] 1 Ki. 20. 35, 37. [x] 1 Ki. 2. 24. [y] Eze. 4. 3. [z] 2 Sa. 7. 12. [a] De. 33. 9. [b] Job 2. 12. [c] Ge. 27. 23. [d] Je. 5. 3. [e] 2 Sa. 18. 11. [f] Zec. 13. 6.

Form	Analysis	Root
הִכִּית	id., suff. 2 p. s. f. (§ 24. r. 14, § 25. & No. 2b)	נכה
הִכִּיתָם	וְ id. pret. 2 pers. sing. m., suff. 3 p. pl. m.	נכה
הִכִּיתֶם	וְ' id. pret. 2 pers. pl. masc.	נכה
הִכִּיתָנוּ	id. pret. 2 pers. sing. masc. suff. 1 pers. pl.	נכה
הִכִּיתַנִי	id. id., suff. 1 pers. sing.	נכה
הִכְּךָ[f]	וְ id. pret. 3 pers. sing. m., suff. 2 pers. s. m.	נכה
הַכִּכָּר	pref. הַ)(noun masc. s. dec. 2b; [for כִּרְכָּר]	כרר
הַכֹּל[f] / הַכֹּל[g]	וְ' pref. הַ / pref. הַ } noun masc. sing. dec. 8c.	כלל
הַכֶּלֶא	pref. הַ)(noun masc. sing. (suff. כִּלְאוֹ) d. 6a.	כלא
הַכֶּלֶב / הַכֶּלֶב	pref. id. / pref. הַ } noun masc. s. (pl. c. כַּלְבֵי) d. 6a.	כלב
הַכְּלָבִים	וְ' pref. הַ)(id. pl., absolute state	כלב
הַכְּלִי[i] / הַכְּלִי	pref. id.)(noun masc. sing. irr. (§ 45; comp. § 35. rem. 14)	כלה
הַכְּלִיא[k]	pref. id.)(noun masc. s. Kh. כְּלִיא, K. כְּלוּא	כלא
הַכְּלָיוֹת	pref. id.)(n. f., pl. abs. from [כִּלְיָה] d. 12b.	כלה
הַכֵּלִים	וְ pref. id.)(noun masc. pl. [as if from כֶּלֶה], see כְּלִי (§ 45)	כלה
הַכְלִים	Hiph. inf. constr.	כלם
הַכְּלָיוֹת[m]	וְ' pref. הַ)(n. f. pl. abs. fr. [כִּלְיָה] d. 12b.	כלה
הִכָּלֵם[o]	וְ' Niph. inf. constr.	כלם
הִכְלִמוֹ	Hiph. pret. 3 pers. s. m., suff. 3 pers. s. m.	כלם
הָכְלְמוּ	וְ Hoph. pret. 3 pers. pl.	כלם
הִכָּלְמוּ	וְ Niph. imp. pl. masc.	כלם
הָכְלָמְנוּ	Hoph. pret. 1 pers. pl.	כלם
הֶכְלַמְנוּם	Hiph. pret. 1 p. pl., suff. 3 p. pl. m. (§ 11. r. 1)	כלם
הִכָּם[u]	וְ' Hiph. pret. 3 pers. s. m. (הִכָּה) suff. 3 pers. pl. masc. (§ 25. No. 2b)	נכה
הַכְּמוֹת	preff. הֲ interr. for. הַ, & כְּ)(noun masc. sing. constr. of מָוֶת dec. 6g.	מות
הַכְּמַכַּת	preff. id.)(noun f. s. contr. of מַכָּה dec. 10.	נכה
הַכְּמָרִים	pref. הַ)(n. m. pl. [of כֹּמֶר § 35. rem. 9]	כמר
הָכֵן	וְ' Hiph. imp. sing. masc.; or (Jos. 3. 17) inf. abs. as an adv.	כון
הִכּוֹן[z]	Niph. imp. sing. masc.	כון
הֻכַּן[a]	וְ Hoph. pret. 3 pers. sing. masc. for הוּכַן	כון
הֲכִנוּ[b]	Hiph. pret. 1 pers. pl. [for הֵכַנּוּ § 25. rem.]	כון
הַכִּנּוֹר[c]	pref. הַ)(noun masc. sing. dec. 1b.	כנר
הִכַּנִי[d] / הִכַּנִי[e]	וְ / וְ } Hiph. pret. 3 pers. sing. masc. (הִכָּה), suff. 1 pers. sing. (§ 25. No. 2b)	נכה
הַכִּנִּים[f]	pref. הַ)(noun masc., pl. of כֵּן dec. 6b.	כנן
הִכְנִיעַ[g]	Hiph. pret. 3 pers. sing. masc.	כנע
הַכְנִיעֵהוּ	Hiph. imp. sing. masc., suff. 3 pers. sing. m.	כנע

Form	Analysis	Root
הַכִּנָּם	pref. הַ)(n. m. collect., fr. כֵּן and the term. ־ָם	כנן
הִכָּנְעוֹ[i]	Niph. inf. (הִכָּנַע) suff. 3 pers. sing. masc. (§ 36. rem. 5)	כנע
הַכְּנַעֲנִי	וְ' pref. הַ)(gent. noun from כְּנַעַן	כנע
הַכְּנַעֲנִים	pref. id.)(id. pl.	כנע
הַכְּנַעֲנִית	pref. id.)(id. s. fem.	כנע
הִכְנַעְתִּי[k]	וְ Hiph. pret. 1 pers. sing.	כנע
הַכָּנָף[l]	וְ'[m] pref. הַ)(noun fem. sing. dec. 4c.	כנף
הַכְּנָפַיִם[n] / הַכְּנָפַיִם[o]	} pref. id.)(id. dual, abs. state; Kh. כְּנָפִים	כנף
הֲכִנֹתִי[p]	Hiph. pret. 1 pers. sing.	כון
הַכִּסֵּא[q]	pref. הַ)(noun masc. sing.	כסא
הַכִּסֵּא	pref. id.)(noun masc. sing. dec. 7b.	כסא
הִכָּסוֹת[r]	Niph. inf. constr.	כסה
הַכְּסִיל	וְ' pref. הַ)(noun masc. sing. dec. 1a.	כסל
הַכְּסִילִים	pref. id.)(id. pl., absolute state	כסל
הַכְּסָלוֹת	וְ pref. id.)(pr. name of a place	כסל
הַכְּסָלִים	pref. id.)(n. m., pl. of כֶּסֶל (suff. כִּסְלוֹ) d. 6a.	כסל
הַכֻּסֶּמֶת[s]	וְ pref. id.)(noun fem. sing., pl. כֻּסְּמִים	כסם
הַכֶּסֶף / הַכֶּסֶף	} וְ' pref. id.)(noun m. s. (suff. כַּסְפִּי) d. 6a.	כסף
הִכְעִיס	Hiph. pret. 3 pers. sing. masc.	כעס
הִכְעִיסוֹ[t]	id. id., suff. 3 pers. sing. masc.	כעס
הִכְעִיסוּ[u]	id. pret. 3 pers. pl.	כעס
הַכְעִיסֵנִי	id. inf., suff. 1 pers. sing. dec. 1b.	כעס
הַכַּעַס[x]	pref. הַ)(noun masc. sing. dec. 6d.	כעס
הַכְעִסוּנִי[y]	Kh. הַכְעִסוּנִי q. v.; K. הַכְעִסֵנִי Hiph. inf., suff. 1 pers. sing.	כעס
הִכְעִסוּנִי[z]	Hiph. pret. 3 pers. pl., suff. 1 pers. sing.	כעס
הַכְּעָסִים[a]	pref. הַ)(noun masc., pl. of כַּעַס dec. 6d.	כעס
הַכְעִסֵנִי[b]	defect. for הַכְעִיסֵנִי (q. v.)	כעס
הִכְעַסְתָּ[c]	Hiph. pret. 2 pers. sing. masc.	כעס
הִכְעַסְתִּי[d]	וְ id. pret. 1 p. s.; acc. shifted by conv. וְ (§ 8. r. 7)	כעס
הַכַּף[e] / הַכַּף[f]	pref. הַ / pref. הַ } noun fem. sing. dec. 8d.	כפף
הַכְּפוּפִים[g]	pref. הַ)(Kal part. pass. m., pl. of [כָּפוּף] d. 3a.	כפף
הַכַּפּוֹת	וְ' pref. id.)(noun fem., pl. of כַּף dec. 8d.	כפף
הַכְּפִיר[h]	וְ pref. id.)(noun masc. sing. dec. 1a.	כפר
הַכְּפִירָה	וְ pref. id.)(pr. name of a place	כפר
הַכְּפִירִים[i]	pref. id.)(noun masc., pl. of כְּפִיר dec. 1a.	כפר
הִכְפִּישַׁנִי[k]	Hiph. pret. 3 pers. sing. masc., suff. 1 pers. s.	כפש
הַכֹּפֶר[l]	pref. הַ)(noun masc. sing. dec. 6c.	כפר
הַכְּפָרִים	pref. id.)(noun masc., pl. of [כָּפָר] d. 1b.	כפר
הַכַּפֹּרֶת	pref. id.)(noun fem. sing.	כפר
הַכַּפֹּת[m]	defect. for הַכַּפּוֹת (q. v.)	כפף
הַכַּפְתּוֹר[n]	pref. הַ)(noun masc. sing. dec. 1b.	כפתר

De. 7. 2. Je. 37. 10. Je. 14. 19. Nu. 22. 28. 1 Ki. 20. 36. Ec. 3. 20. Is. 28. 24.
[h] 1 Sa. 17. 43. [i] Is. 56. 12. [k] 1 Sa. 17. 49. [l] Je. 6. 15. [m] Le. 9. 19. [n] Je. 3. 3. [o] Je. 8. 12.
[p] 1 Sa. 20. 34. [q] Je. 14. 11. [r] Eze. 36. 32. [s] 1 Sa. 25. 15. [t] 1 Sa. 25. 7. [u] Je. 5. 6. [v] 2 Sa. 3. 33.
[y] Is. 27. 7. [z] Eze. 38. 7. [a] Na. 2. 6. [b] 2 Ch. 29. 19. [c] 1 Sa. 16. 23. [d] 1 Sa. 17. 9. [e] Ge. 32. 12.
[f] Ex. 8. 14. [g] 2 Ch. 28. 19. [h] Job 40. 12. [i] 2 Ch. 33. 19. [k] 1 Ch. 17. 10. [l] Nu. 15. 38. [m] 2 Ch. 3. 11, 12.
[n] Eze. 17. 3. [o] Ec. 10. 20. [p] Ex. 23. 20. [q] Pr. 7. 20. [r] Eze. 24. 8. [s] Ec. 2. 14. [t] Ex. 9. 32.
[t] 2 Ki. 23. 26. [u] Ne. 3. 37. [x] 1 Ki. 21. 22. [y] Je. 25. 7. [z] Je. 8. 19. [a] 2 Ki. 23. 26.
[b] 2 Ki. 22. 17. [c] 1 Ki. 21. 22. [d] Eze. 32. 9. [e] Nu. 7. 86. [f] Ju. 8. 6, 15. [g] Ps. 145. 14.
[h] Is. 31. 4. [i] Ps. 104. 21. [k] La. 3. 16. [l] Ca. 1. 14. [m] Nu. 4. 7. [n] Am. 9. 1.

הַכְּצַעֲקָתָהּ[a] preff. הֲ interr. f. הַ, & כְּ)(noun f. s., suff. 3 pers. s. f. from צְעָקָה d. 11c. (§ 42. r. 1) צעק

הָכַר. Hiph. *to amaze, stun,* so תַּהְכְּרוּ (for תַּהְכִּירוּ § 11. rem. 7) Job 19. 13, which Prof. Lee takes as Kal in the sense of *contemning.*

הַכֵּר Hiph. inf., or imp. s. m. [for הַכִּר § 11. r. 5] נכר
הַכָּר[b] pref. הַ)(noun masc. sing. dec. 1a. כרר
הַכְּרֻבִים[c] וְ' pref. id.)(noun masc., pl. of כְּרוּב d. 1a. כרב
הִכִּרֻהוּ[d] Hiph. pret. 3 pers. pl. (הִכִּירוּ) suff. 3 p. s. m. נכר
הַכְּרוּב pref. הַ)(noun masc. sing. dec. 1a. כרב
הַכְּרוּבִים pref. id.)(id. pl., absolute state כרב
הַכְרִזוּ[e] וְ Ch. Aph. imp. pl. masc. (§ 47. rem. 4) כרז
הַכָּרִי[f] pref. הַ)(noun masc., prop. participle [כָּר] either with the adj. design. ִי, or כָּרִי is the pl. for כָּרִים כור
הַכָּרִי[g] Kh. הַכָּרִי q. v., K. הַכְּרֵתִי (q. v.) כרת
הַכָּרִים[h] pref. הַ)(n. m., pl. of כַּר dec. 8. (§ 37. r. 7) כרר
הִכְרִיעַ[i] Hiph. pret. 3 pers. sing. masc. כרע
הַכְרִיעֵהוּ[k] id. imp. sing. masc. suff. 3 pers. sing. masc. כרע
הַכְרִית[l] Hiph. inf. constr. כרת
הִכְרִית id. pret. 3 pers. sing. masc. כרת
הִכְרִיתָה[m] וְ id. pret. 3 pers. sing. fem. כרת
הִכְרִיתוּ[n] וְ'[o] id. pret. 3 pers. pl. כרת
הַכְרִיתְךָ[p] id. inf. (הַכְרִית), suff. 2 pers. sing. m. d. 1b. כרת
הַכֶּרֶם / הַכָּרֶם pref. הַ)(noun masc. sing. (and pr. name in compos. see בַּיִת) d. 6a. (§ 35. r. 2) כרם
הַכַּרְמִי pref. id.)(patronym. [for כַּרְמִיִּי from כַּרְמִי כרם
הַכְּרָמִים pref. id.)(n. m., pl. of כֶּרֶם d. 6a. (suff. כַּרְמִי) כרם
הַכַּרְמֶל[q] וְ' pref. id.)(noun masc. sing. (with suff. 'מִלּוֹ dec. 8. § 37. rem. 3 & 5) כרם
הַכַּרְמֶלָה pref. id.)(pr. n. of a region (כַּרְמֶל) with parag. ה כרם
הַכַּרְמְלִי pref. id.)(gent. noun of the prec. (§ 37. r. 5) כרם
הַכַּרְמְלִית pref. id.)(fem. of the prec. כרם
הַכְרֵעַ[r] Hiph. inf. absolute כרע
הַכְּרָעַיִם[s] / הַכְּרָעַיִם[t] וְ'[u] pref. הַ)(noun f. du. from [כֶּרַע] d. 4a. כרע
הִכְרַעְתִּנִי[x] Hiph. pret. 2 p. s. f. [for 'תִּינִי] suff. 1 p. s. כרע
הָכְרַת[y] Hoph. pret. 3 pers. sing. masc. כרת
הַכָּרַת[z] noun fem. s. constr. [of הַכָּרָה § 42. No. 3] נכר
הַכֹּרֵת[a] pref. הַ)(Kal part. act. sing. masc. dec. 7b. כרת
הִכָּרֵת[b] Niph. inf. constr. כרת
הַכְּרֵתִי וְ' pref. הַ)(noun masc. sing. כרת
הִכְרַתִּי Hiph. pret. 1 pers. sing. [for הִכְרַתְתִּי § 25. r.] כרת
הִכְרַתִּי וְ id.; acc. shifted by conv. וְ (§ 8. rem. 7) כרת
הִכְרַתִּיו[c] וְ id., suff. 3 pers. sing. masc. כרת

הִכְרַתִּיךָ[d] וְ id., suff. 2 pers. sing. masc. כרת
הַכֶּשֶׂב[e] pref. הַ)(noun masc. sing. dec. 6. כשב
הַכְּשָׂבִים[f] וְ'[g] pref. id.)(id. pl., absolute state כשב
הַכַּשְׂדִּים pref. id.)(pr. name of a people, pl. of כַּשְׂדִּי כשד
הִכְשִׁיל[h] Hiph. pret. 3 pers. sing. masc. כשל
הַכְשֵׁיר[i] Hiph. inf. absolute כשר
הַכֻּשִׁית pref. הַ)(gent. noun, fem. of כּוּשִׁי from כּוּשׁ כוש
הִכְשַׁלְתֶּם[k] Hiph. pret. 2 pers. pl. masc. כשל
הַכְּתָב pref. הַ)(noun m. sing. dec. 1a. (§ 30. No. 3) כתב
הַכְּתֻבִים pref. id.)(Kal part. p. m., pl. of כָּתוּב d. 3a. כתב
הַכֹּתְבִים[l] pref. הַ)(id. part. act. m., pl. of כֹּתֵב d. 7b. כתב
הֻכְּתָה Hoph. pret. 3 pers. sing. fem. (§ 25. No. 2b) נכה
הַכֹּתוֹ[m] Hiph. inf. (הַכּוֹת), suff. 3 pers. sing. masc. dec. 1b. (§ 25. No. 2b) נכה
הַכָּתוּב pref. הַ)(Kal part. p. sing. masc. dec. 3a. כתב
הַכְּתוּבָה pref. id.)(id. fem. dec. 10. כתב
הַכְּתוּבוֹת[n] pref. id.)(id. fem. pl. כתב
הַכְּתוּבִים pref. id.)(id. masc. pl. dec. 3a. כתב
הַכֹּתִי Hiph. inf. (הַכּוֹת), suff. 1 pers. sing. dec. 1a. (§ 25. No. 2b) נכה
הִכִּתִיו[o] וְ id. pret. 1 pers. sing., suff. 3 pers. sing. m. נכה
הִכִּתִיךָ[p] וְ id. id., suff. 2 pers. sing. masc. נכה
הַכֶּתֶם[q] pref. הַ)(noun masc. sing. כתם
הַכָּתְנֹת[r] pref. id.)(n. f. pl. constr. from כְּתֹנֶת d. 13c. כתן
הַכְּתֹנֶת pref. הַ art. or interr.)(noun fem. sing. כתן
הַכֻּתֹּנֶת pref. הַ art.)(noun fem. sing. dec. 13c. כתן
הַכָּתֵף pref. id.)(noun fem. sing. dec. 5b. כתף
הַכְּתֵפוֹת[s] pref. id.)(id. pl., absolute state כתף
הַכֹּתָרוֹת[t] / הַכֹּתֶרֶת וְ'[u] pref. הַ id.)(noun fem., pl. [as if from כֹּתָרָה] see the following כתר
הַכֹּתֶרֶת pref. id.)(noun fem. sing. (§ 44. rem. 5) כתר

הַל particle of interrogation, De. 32. 6.

הָלָא. Niph. *to be removed, cast away,* Mi. 4. 7.
הָלְאָ only with paragogic ה, הָלְאָה adv.—I. of space, *farther, farther off, beyond;* מִשָּׁם וָהָלְאָה *from thence and farther;* מֵהָלְאָה לְ *farther off than, beyond.*—II. of time *farther, forward, onward.*

הֲלֹא pref. הֲ)(adv. of negation לא
הָלְאָה וְ' adv. [הָלְאָ with parag. ה]; for וָ see lett. ו הלא
הַלְאוֹת[x] Hiph. inf. constr. לאה
הַלְאֵל preff. הֲ interr. for הֲ, & לְ)(noun m. s. d. 1a. אול
הֶלְאָנִי[y] Hiph. pret. 3 pers. sing. masc. (§ 11. rem. 1) לאה
הֶלְאַת[z] id. pret. 3 pers. sing. fem. (§ 24. rem. 14) לאה

[a] Ge. 18. 21. [b] Eze. 45. 14. [c] Eze. 10. 3. [d] Ge. 42. 8. [e] Da. 5. 29. [f] 2 Ki. 11. 19.
[g] 2 Sa. 20. 23. [h] 1 Sa. 15. 9. [i] Ps. 78. 31. [k] Ps. 17. 13. [l] Je. 44. 8.
[m] Le. 26. 22. [n] Ju. 4. 24. [o] Jos. 7. 9. [p] Is. 48. 9. [q] Is. 29. 17.
[r] Ju. 11. 35. [s] Le. 9. 14. [t] Le. 8. 21. [u] Le. 1. 13. [x] Ju. 11. 35.
[y] Joel 1. 9. [z] Is. 3. 9. [a] Is. 14. 8. [b] Nu. 15. 31. [c] Eze. 14. 8.
[d] Eze. 25. 7. [e] Le. 4. 35. [f] Le. 1. 10. [g] Ge. 30. 40. [h] La. 1. 14.
[i] Ec. 10. 10. [k] Mal. 2. 8. [l] Je. 32. 12. [m] De. 1. 4. [n] 2 Ch. 34. 24.
[o] 1 Sa. 17. 9, 35, 35. [p] 1 Sa. 17. 46. [q] La. 4. 1. [r] Ex. 39. 27. [s] 1 Ki. 7. 30.
[t] 2 Ch. 4. 12, 13. [u] 2 Ch. 4. 12. [x] Is. 7. 13. [y] Job 16. 7. [z] Eze. 24. 12.

הֲלֶאְתִךָ[a] id. pret. 1 pers. sing., suff. 2 pers. sing. masc. לאה
הַלֵּב[b] pref. הַ) noun masc. sing. dec. 8b. . לבב
הַלְּבָבִי pref. id.) noun masc. sing. dec. 5b. . . לבב
הַלְּבִבוֹת[d] pref. id.) noun fem., pl. of [לְבִיבָה] dec. 10. לבב
הַלְּבוֹנָה וְ' pref. id.) noun fem. sing. dec. 10. . לבן
הַלְּבוּשׁ pref. id.) noun masc. sing. dec. 1a. . לבש
הֲלָבֹז[e] preff. הֲ & לָ (q. v.)) Kal inf. constr. . בזז
הִלְבִּינוּ[f] Hiph. pret. 3 pers. pl. . . . . לבן
הִלְבִּישָׁה[g] id. pret. 3 pers. sing. fem. . . . לבש
הִלְבִּישׁוּ[h] id. pret. 3 pers. pl. . . . . לבש
הִלְבִּישַׁנִי[i] id. pret. 3 pers. sing. masc., suff. 1 pers. sing. לבש
הַלָּבָן[rr] pref. הַ) adj. masc. sing. dec. 4a. . לבן
הַלְבֶן[k] preff. הַ interr. for הֲ, & לְ) noun masc., constr. of בֵּן irr., (§ 45) . . . בנה
הַלְּבָנָה pref. הַ) noun fem. sing. . . . לבן
הַלְּבֵנָה[yy] pref. id.) n. fem. sing. dec. 11c, (§ 42. No. 1) לבן
הַלְּבֹנָה[l] pref. id.) noun fem. sing. dec. 10. . . לבן
הַלְּבָנוֹן וְ' pref. id.) pr. name of a mountain . לבן
הַלִּבְנִי pref. id.) pr. name masc. . . . לבן
הַלְּבָנִים[m] וְ pref. הַ) adj. masc., pl. of לָבָן dec. 4a. לבן
הַלְּבֵנִים pref. id.) noun fem. with pl. masc. term. from לְבֵנָה dec. 11c. (§ 42. rem. 1) לבן
הַלָּבֻשׁ[n] pref. id.) Kal part. p. s. m. d. 3a. (for לָבוּשׁ לבש
הַלְבֵּשׁ[o] וְ Hiph. inf. abs. . . . . . לבש
הַלְבִּשׁוּ[p] וְ Ch. Aph. pret. 3 pers. pl. masc. . לבש
הִלְבִּשׁוּ[q] וְ Hiph. pret. 3 pers. pl. . . . לבש
הַלֹּבְשִׁים[r] pref. הַ) Kal part. act. m., pl. of לֹבֵשׁ d. 7b. לבש
הִלְבַּשְׁתָּ וְ Hiph. pret. 2 pers. sing. masc.; acc. shifted by conv. וְ (§ 8. rem. 7) . . . לבש
הִלְבַּשְׁתִּיו[s] וְ id. pret. 1 pers. sing., suff. 3 pers. sing. m. לבש
הִלְבַּשְׁתָּם וְ id. pret. 2 pers. sing. m., suff. 3 pers. pl. m. לבש
הֲלִדְרֹשׁ[t] preff. הֲ, & לְ bef. (:)) Kal inf. constr. דרש
הֻלֶּדֶת[u] Hoph. inf. constr. (§ 20. rem. 16) . ילד
הֲלֹה[x] pref. הֲ) adv. of negation, Kh. for לֹא' לא
הַלַּהַב pref. הַ) noun masc. sing. dec. 6d. . להב
הַלְהוֹכֵחַ[y] preff. הַ interr. for הֲ, & לְ) Hiph. inf. constr. יכח
הֲלָהֵן[z] pref. הֲ) adv. see לָהֵן (§ 5. rem. 3) להן
הַלְהָרְגֵנִי[a] preff. הַ interr. for הֲ, & לְ) Kal inf., suff. 1 p. s. הרג
הֲלוֹא וְ'[b] pref. הֲ) adv. of negation, more frequently הֲלֹא לא
הַלּוּבִים וְ pref. הַ) gent. noun pl. . . . לוב
הַלּוּחִית pref. id.) pr. name of a place . . לוח
הַלּוֹחֵשׁ pref. id.) pr. name masc. . . . לחש

הַלּוֹט[c] pref. id.) Kal part. act., or noun masc. sing. לוט
הַלֵּוִי וְ' pref. id.) patronym. [for לְוִיִּי] from לֵוִי לוה
הַלְוִיִּם וְ' pref. id.) id. pl. dec. 8f. . . לוה
הִלְוִיתָ[d] וְ Hiph. pret. 2 pers. sing. masc. . . לוה
הָלוֹךְ Kal inf. absolute . . . . הלך
הִלּוּלִים noun masc., pl. of [הִלּוּל] dec. 1b. . . הלל
הֲלוּמֵי[e] Kal part. p. pl. construct masc. from [הָלוּם] dec. 3a. . . . . . . הלם
הַלָּז pron. demon. com. gend. sing., apoc. fr. הַלָּזֶה לזה
הֲלָזֶה[f] preff. הֲ & לָ) pron. demon. masc. sing. . זה
הַלָּזֶה pron. demon. masc. sing. . . . לזה
הַלֵּזוּ[g] pron. demon. fem. sing. . . . לזה
הַלֻּחוֹת pref. הַ) noun masc. with pl. fem. term. from לוּחַ dec. 1a. . . . . לוח
הַלְּחִי / הַלֶּחִי } pref. id.) noun fem. sing. dec. 6i, (§ 35. rem. 14) . . } לחה
הַלְּחָיַיִם[h] וְ pref. id.) id. dual, absolute state . לחה
הַלֶּחֶם / הַלָּחֶם } pref. הַ) noun com. s. dec. 6a. (§ 35. rem. 2) לחם
הִלָּחֵם[i] וְ'[k] Niph. imp. sing. masc. . . . לחם
הִלָּחֶם[l] וְ id. id.; acc. shifted bef. monos. (§ 9. rem. 3) לחם
הִלָּחֲמוֹ[m] id. inf., suff. 3 pers. sing. masc. . . לחם
הִלָּחֲמוּ וְ id. imp. pl. masc. . . . . לחם
הַלַּחְמִי gen. noun, see בֵּית הַלַּחְמִי בית
הַלַּחַץ[n] pref. הַ) noun masc. sing. dec. 6d. . לחץ
הַלֹּחֲצִים[o] pref. id.) Kal part. act. masc., pl. of [לֹחֵץ] dec. 7b. . . . . . לחץ
הַלְּחָשִׁים[p] וְ pref. id.) noun masc., pl. of לַחַשׁ dec. 6d. לחש
הַלֻּחֹת[q] וְ' pref. id.) noun masc., with pl. fem. term. from לוּחַ dec. 1a. . . . לוח
הַלְּטָאָה[r] וְ pref. id.) noun fem. sing. . . לטא
הֵלִיד defect. for הוֹלִיד (q. v.) . . . ילד
הֲלַיהוָֹה[s] pref. הַל interr. particle & יְהוָֹה (q. v.) others read הַ לַיהוָֹה, הֲלַיהוָֹה, הַל יְהוָֹה . הוה
הַלְיוֹעֵץ[t] preff. הַ interr. for הֲ, & לְ) Kal part. act. sing. masc. dec. 7b. . . . יעץ
הֵלִיכוּ[u] Hiph. imp. pl. masc. [for הוֹלִיכוּ] . . ילך
הֲלִיכוֹת noun fem., pl. of [הֲלִיכָה] dec. 10. הלך
הֲלִיכוֹתֶיךָ[x] id. suff. 2 pers. sing. masc. . . . הלך
הֲלִיכַי[y] n. m. pl., suff. 1 pers. s. from [הָלִיךְ] dec. 3a. הלך
הֲלִיכֹת[z] defect. for הֲלִיכוֹת (q. v.) . . . הלך
הַלַּיְלָה / הַלַּיְלָה }[a] וְ' pref. הַ) noun masc. sing. with parag. ה from לַיִל dec. 6h. . . } ליל

[a] Mi. 6. 3. [b] Je. 17. 9. [c] De. 20. 8. [d] 2 Sa. 13. 8, 10. [e] Eze. 38. 13. [f] Joel 1. 7. [g] Ge. 27. 16. [h] 2 Ch. 28. 15. [i] Is. 61. 10. [k] Ge. 17. 17. [l] Le. 6. 8. [m] Zec. 6. 6. [n] Eze. 9. 3. [o] Zec. 3. 4. [p] Da. 5. 29. [q] Est. 6. 9. [r] Zep. 1. 8. [rr] Ge. 30. 37. [s] Is. 22. 21. [t] Eze. 20. 3. [u] Ge. 40. 20. [x] De. 3. 11. [y] Job 6. 26. [yy] Ge. 11. 3. [z] Ruth 1. 13, 13. [a] Ex. 2. 14. [b] 2 Sa. 15. 35. [c] Is. 25. 7, 7. [d] De. 28. 12. [e] Is. 28. 1. [f] Is. 58. 5. [g] Eze. 36. 35. [h] De. 18. 3. [i] Ex 17. 9. [k] 1 Sa. 18. 17. [l] Ju. 9. 38. [m] Zec. 14. 3. [n] Ex. 3. 9. [o] 1 Sa. 10. 18. [p] Is. 3. 20. [q] Ex. 32. 16. [r] Le. 11. 30. [s] De. 32. 6. [t] 2 Ch. 25. 16. [u] 2 Ki. 17. 27. [x] Ps. 68. 25. [y] Job 29. 6. [z] Job 6. 19. [a] Job 3. 3.

וַ׳ הָלַךְ [h] / וְ׳ הָלַךְ } Kal pret. 3 pers. sing. masc. (comp. § 8. rem. 7) . . . הלך

וְ הֲלָךְ Chald. noun masc. sing.; וְ before (-:) . הלך

וְ׳ הָלֹךְ Kal inf. absolute . . . . . הלך

וְ הַלֵּךְ [i] Piel imp. sing. masc. . . . . הלך

הֲלֹךְ [k] Kal inf. construct . . . . . הלך

הֵלֶךְ noun masc. sing. . . . . . הלך

הֹלֵךְ Kal part. act. sing. masc. dec. 7b. . הלך

הָלְכָה [l] / וְ׳ הָלָכָה [m] } Kal pret. 3 pers. sing. fem. (§ 8. rem. 7) הלך

הֹלְכָה [n] id. part. act. sing. fem. dec. 10, from הֹלֵךְ m. הלך

הָלְכוּ / וְ׳ הָלָכוּ } id. pret. 3 pers. pl. (§ 8. rem. 7) . הלך

הִלְכוּ [o] id. imp. pl. masc. . . . . . הלך

הִלְּכוּ Piel pret. 3 pers. pl. . . . . . הלך

הֹלְכוֹת [p] Kal part. act. fem., pl. of הֹלֶכֶת or הֹלְכָה dec. 13a, or 10. . . . . . הלך

וְ׳ [r] הֹלְכֵי [q] construct of the following . . . הלך

וְ׳ [s] הֹלְכִים Kal part. act. masc., pl. of הוֹלֵךְ dec. 7b. הלך

וְ הָלַכְנוּ [t] / הָלָכְנוּ } Kal pret. 1 pers. pl. (§ 8. rem. 7) . הלך

הַלָּלֶכֶת [u] preff. הַ & לְ (see lett. ל)) (Kal inf. constr. כפף

וְ׳ [y] הָלַכְתָּ [w] / הָלַכְתָּ } Kal pret. 2 pers. sing. masc. (§ 8. rem. 7) הלך

וְ הָלַכְתָּ id. id.; acc. shifted by conv. וְ . . הלך

הָלַכְתְּ [x] / וְ׳ הָלַכְתְּ [a] } id. pret. 2 pers. sing. fem. . . . הלך

הֹלְכֹת [b] id. part. act. fem., pl. of הֹלֶכֶת or הֹלְכָה dec. 13a, or 10. . . . . . הלך

הָלַכְתְּי [c] id. pret. 2 pers. sing. fem. Kh. הָלַכְתִּי, K. הָלַכְתְּ (§ 8. rem. 5 & 7) . הלך

וְ׳ [e] הָלַכְתִּי [d] / הָלָכְתִּי } id. pret. 1 pers. sing. (§ 8. rem. 7) הלך

וְ הָלַכְתִּי id. id.; acc. shifted by conv. וְ . . . הלך

הִלַּכְתִּי [f] / הִלַּכְתִּי } Piel pret. 1 pers. sing. (comp. § 8. rem. 7) הלך

הֹלַכְתִּי [g] K. הֹלֶכֶת Kal part. act. sing. fem., Kh. הֹלַכְתִּי id. with parag. י (comp. § 8. rem. 19) . הלך

וְ הֹלַכְתִּיהָ [h] Hiph. pret. 1 pers. sing., suff. 3 pers. s. fem. ילך

וַ׳ הֲלַכְתֶּם Kal pret. 2 pers. pl. masc.; וֲ for וְ conv. הלך

[הָלַל] I. *to shine*, Job 29. 3.—II. *to boast, glory*; הוֹלְלִים *boasters, proud*. Pi.—I. *to praise, celebrate*. const.

הֵילִילוּ [a] Hiph. imp. pl. masc. . . . . . ילל

הַלֵּילוֹת [b] pref. הַ) (noun masc. with pl. fem. term. from לַיִל dec. 6h. . . . . ליל

הֵילִילִי [c] Kh. הֵילִילִי q. v., K. הֵילִילוּ (q. v.) . . ילל

הֵילִילִי [d] Hiph. imp. sing. fem. . . . . ילל

הֲלִינֹתֶם [e] Hiph. pret. 2 pers. pl. masc. . . . לון

הֱלִיצֻנִי [f] Hiph. pret. 3 pers. pl. [הֱלִיצוּ], suff. 1 pers. s. לוץ

הַלְיָרְשֵׁנוּ [g] preff. הַ interr. for הֲ, & לְ) (Piel inf. [יָרֵשׁ], suff. 1 pers. pl. dec. 7b. . . . ירש

הָלַךְ, [& יָלַךְ] fut. יֵלֵךְ ,וַיֵּלֶךְ (from יָלַךְ), poet. יַהֲלֹךְ; imp. לֵךְ ,לְכוּ (from יָלַךְ), also הִלְכוּ; inf. הָלוֹךְ; constr. לֶכֶת, with suff. לֶכְתִּי (from יָלַךְ).—I. *to go, walk, proceed*, const. with עַל ,לְ ,אֶל, acc., rarely בְּ, of the place whither one goes. But also with the acc. *to go through* or *over*; with בְּ *to go with*, i. e. lead, bring; with אֵת ,עִם (אֵת) *to accompany; to have intercourse with*; with אַחֲרֵי *to go after, to follow*.—II. *to go, walk, live*.—III. *to go away, depart*; especially with the dative לֵךְ לְךָ, הָלַךְ לוֹ.—IV. *to flow, run*, of liquids.—V. *to go on, continue*; הָלֵךְ וְגָדֵל *going on and growing*, i. e. waxing greater; הוֹלֵךְ וְסֹעֵר *going on raging*, i. e. continuing tempestuous; הָלוֹךְ וָשׁוֹב *going on and returning*, i. e. continually returning. Niph. נֶהֱלַךְ *to pass away, disappear*, Ps. 109. 23. Pi. i. q. Kal Nos. I, II, III; part. מְהַלֵּךְ *a wanderer*. Hiph. הוֹלִיךְ, once הֵילִיךְ (from יָלַךְ) part. pl. מַהְלְכִים (§ 11. rem. 8).—I. *to cause to go, to lead, conduct*.—II. *to lead away, to remove*, Ps. 125. 5.—III. *to cause to flow*. Hithp. הִתְהַלֵּךְ.—I. *to go, walk about*; part. מִתְהַלֵּךְ *a wanderer*, Pr. 24. 34.—II. *to walk, live*.—III. *to flow*, of wine, Pr. 23. 31.

הֲלַךְ Chald. Pa. *to go, walk*, Da. 4. 26. Aph. id.

הֵלֶךְ masc.—I. *a going, travelling*, used as a concrete, *traveller*, 2 Sa. 12. 4.—II. *a flowing, stream*, 1 Sa. 14. 26.

הֲלָךְ Chald. masc. *way-tax, toll*.

הֲלִיךְ masc. *a going, step*, Job 29. 6.

הֲלִיכָה fem. dec. 10.—I. *a going*.—II. *way*.—III. *caravan*, Job 6. 19.

מַהֲלָךְ masc. dec. 2b.—I. *a walk*.—II. *way, journey*.

תַּהֲלוּכָה fem. dec. 10, *procession*, Ne. 12. 31.

[a] Is. 13. 6; 23. 6. [b] Is. 21. 8. [c] Je. 48. 20. [d] Is. 14. 31. [e] Nu. 14. 29. [f] Ps. 119. 51. [g] Ju. 14. 15. [h] 1 Sa. 6. 8. [i] Ec. 11. 9. [k] Nu. 22. 14. [l] Is. 46. 2. [m] Na. 3. 10. [n] Je. 3. 6. [o] Je. 51. 50. [p] 2 Ch. 9. 21. [q] Je. 6. 28. [r] Ju. 5. 6, 10. [s] 2 Sa. 15. 11. [t] Ge. 34. 17. [u] Is. 58. 5. [w] 1 Ki. 13. 9. [y] Ex. 17. 5. [x] Eze. 23. 31. [a] Eze. 16. 47. [b] Ex. 2. 5. [c] Je. 31. 21. [d] Ge. 35. 3. [e] Ju. 4. 8. [f] Ps. 38. 7. [g] 2 Ki. 4. 23. [h] Hos. 2. 16.

with an acc., הַלְלוּ־יָהּ *praise ye the Lord*; but also with לְ, בְּ (Ps. 44. 9). Hence II.—*to praise, commend.* Pu. *to be praised*; מְהֻלָּל *praised, worthy to be praised.* Po. *to make foolish, to shame.* Hiph.—I. *to cause to shine.*—II. *to shine*, Job 31. 26. Hithpa.—I. *to be praised*, Pr. 31. 30. —II. *to boast oneself*, with בְּ, עִם (Ps. 106. 5) of that in which one glories. Hithpo. *to be* or *become mad.*

הִלֵּל (*apt to praise*, i. e. devout, comp. § 26. No. 8) pr. name masc. Ju. 12. 13, 15.

הִלּוּלִים masc. pl. (of הִלּוּל) *praises*, meton. *days of praise, festivals of thanksgiving.*

הֵילֵל masc. *the morning star, Lucifer*, Is. 14. 12. Others take it as the imp. of יָלַל *wail, lament.*

הוֹלֵלָה fem. only pl. הוֹלֵלוֹת, *folly.*

הוֹלֵלוּת fem. id. Ec. 10. 13.

יְהַלֶּלְאֵל (*he shall praise God*) pr. name of two men, 1 Ch. 4. 16; 2 Ch. 29. 12.

מַהֲלָל masc. dec. 2 b, *praise, commendation*, Pr. 27. 21.

מַהֲלַלְאֵל (*praise of God*) pr. name of two men, Ge. 5. 12; Ne. 11. 4.

תְּהִלָּה fem. dec. 10.—I. *praise.*—II. *an object of praise.*—III. *song of praise, hymn, psalm*; pl. תְּהִלִּים *the* (book of) *Psalms.*—IV. *praise, glory.*

תָּהֳלָה fem. *folly, sin.*

הַלֵּל ו Piel inf. constr. . . . . . הלל
הִלֵּל[a] id. pret. 3 pers. sing. masc. . . . הלל
הַלְּלָאוֹת pref. הַ ‖ noun pl. absolute fem. [from לוּלִי § 35. rem. 15 note] . . . . . לול
הַלְלוּ Piel. imp. pl. masc. [for הַלְּלוּ § 10. rem. 7] הלל
הַלְלוּהוּ id., suff. 3 pers. sing. masc. . . . הלל
הִלְלוּ[b] ו id. pret. 3 pers. pl. . . . . הלל
הִלְלוּךָ[c] id. id., suff. 2 pers. sing. masc. [for הִלְּלוּךָ § 10. rem. 7] . . . . . . הלל
הֹלֵלוֹת[d] noun fem., pl. of [הוֹלֵלָה] dec. 10. . הלל
הַלְלִי Piel imp. sing. fem. [for הַלְּלִי § 10. rem. 7] הלל
הִלַּלְנוּ[e] id. pret. 1 pers. pl. . . . . . הלל
הִלַּלְתִּיךָ[f] id. pret. 1 pers. sing., suff. 2 pers. sing. masc. הלל
הִלַּלְתֶּם[g] ו id. pret. 2 pers. pl. masc. . . . הלל

[הָלַם] fut. יַהֲלֹם.—I. *to strike, beat.*—II. *to beat in pieces*, Is. 16. 8.

הֲלֹם adv. *hither*; עַד־הֲלֹם *thus far.*

הֶלֶם (*blow*) pr. name masc. 1 Ch. 7. 35

הַלְמוּת fem. *a hammer*, Ju. 5. 26.

יַהֲלֹם masc. the name of a gem, which the versions variously render by the *diamond, emerald*, and the *jasper.*

מַהֲלֻמוֹת fem. pl. (of מַהֲלֻמָּה) *beatings, blows.*

הֲלֹם adv. . . . . הלם
הֲלֹם[h] ו Kal inf. constr.; ו bef. (-:) . . . הלם
הֶלֶם pr. name masc. . . . . . . הלם
הָלְמָה[i] ו Kal pret. 3 pers. sing. fem. . . הלם
הָלְמוּ id. pret. 3 pers. pl. . . . . הלם
הֲלָמוּנִי[k] id. id. with suff. 1 pers. sing. . . הלם
הַלְמַעַנְךָ[l] pref. הַ interrog. for הֲ ‖ prep. לְמַעַן with suff. 2 pers. sing. masc. [prop. pref. לְ & subst. מַעַן] . . . . . ענה
הַלְמֵּתִים[m] preff. הַ, & לְ for לַה ‖ Kal part. masc., pl. of מֵת dec. 1 a. . . . . . מות
הֲלָנוּ[n] pref. הֲ ‖ prep. לְ with suff. 1 pers. pl. (§ 5. parad.) . . . . . . ל
הֲלָנֶצַח[o] preff. הֲ, & לְ (see lett. ל) ‖ noun masc. sing. (suff. נִצְחִי) dec. 6 a (§ 35. rem. 5) . נצח
הַלָּעַג[p] pref. הַ ‖ noun masc. sing. dec. 6 d. . לעג
הַלְעוֹלָם preff. הַ interr. for הֲ, & לְ ‖ n. m. s. dec. 2 b. עלם
הַלְעִיטֵנִי[q] Hiph. imp. sing. masc., suff. 1 pers. sing. לעט
הַלְעוֹלָמִים[r] preff. הַ interr. for הֲ, & לְ ‖ noun masc., pl. of עוֹלָם dec. 2 b. . . . . עלם
הַלַּפִּידִים[s] } pref. הַ ‖ noun masc. sing. dec. 1 b. . לפד
הַלַּפִּדִם[t] }
הִלָּקַח[u] Niph. inf. construct (§ 36. rem. 5) . לקח
הִלָּקְחוֹ[x] id., suff. 3 pers. sing. masc. . . לקח
הַלֹּקְחִים[y] pref. הַ ‖ Kal part. act. m., pl. of לֹקֵחַ dec. 7. לקח
הַלָּקֶשׁ[z] pref. id. ‖ noun m. s. for לֶקֶשׁ (§ 35. r. 2) לקש
הֲלָרָשָׁע[pp] preff. הֲ, & לְ for לַה· לְהָ ‖ adj. m. dec. 4 a. רשע
הַלָּשׁוֹן[a] pref. הַ ‖ noun com. sing. dec. 3 a. . לשן
הַלִּשְׁכָּה[b] ו׳ pref. id. ‖ noun fem. sing. dec. 12 b. . לשך
הַלְּשָׁכוֹת[c] ו׳ pref. id. ‖ id. pl., absolute state . לשך
הַלִּשְׁכוֹת pref. id. ‖ id. pl., construct state . . לשך
הֲלִשְׁלֹל[d] preff. הֲ, & לְ for לִ ‖ Kal inf. construct . שלל
הַלָּשֹׁן[e] pref. הַ ‖ noun com. sing. dec. 3 a. . . לשן
הַלְּשֹׁנוֹת[f] ו pref. id. ‖ id. pl. . . . . לשן

הֵם, ו׳, ו׳[g], with parag. ה, הֵמָּה pers. pron. 3 pers. pl. masc. *they*; with the article הָהֵם, הָהֵמָּה *these.* Comp. הוּא (§ 1. rem. 6)

הִמּוֹ, הִמּוֹן Chald. *they.*

[a] Ps. 10. 3. [b] Is. 62. 9. [c] Is. 64. 10. [d] Ec. 1. 17. [e] Ps. 44. 9. [f] Ps. 119. 164. [g] Joel 2. 26. [h] 1 Sa. 14. 16. [i] Ju. 5. 26. [k] Pr. 23. 35. [l] Job 18. 4. [m] Ps. 88. 11. [n] Jos. 5. 13. [o] 2 Sa. 2. 26. [p] Ps. 123. 4. [pp] 2 Ch. 19. 2. [q] Ge. 25. 30. [r] Ps. 77. 8. [s] Eze. 1. 13. [t] Ex. 20. 18. [u] 1 Sa. 4. 19, 21. [x] 1 Sa. 21. 7. [y] Je. 23. 31. [z] Am. 7. 1. [a] Ec. 10. 11. [b] Eze. 40. 46. [c] Eze. 42. 5. [d] Eze. 38. 13. [e] Jos. 15. 2. [f] Is. 66. 18. [g] Nu. 16. 16.

הֵמּוֹ[a] Kh. for הֵם (q. v.) . . . . . הם

הֵמָּה[b] וְ Kh. הֵם q. v., K. הֵמָּה (q. v.) . . הם

הַמֹּאָבִי pref. הַ) gent. noun from מוֹאָב q. v.

הַמֹּאֲבִיָּה pref. id.) id. fem.

הַמֹּאֲבִים וְ pref. id.) id. pl. masc.

הַמְאָדָּמִים pref. id.) Pual part. masc., pl. of מְאָדָּם (§ 10. rem. 5) . . . . . אדם

הַמֵּאָה pref. id.) noun fem. sing. dec. 11 b. (also proper name) . . . . . . מאה

הַמָּאוֹר pref. id.) noun masc. sing. dec. 2 b. . אור

הַמֵּאוֹת וְ' pref. id.) noun fem. pl. of מֵאָה dec. 11 b. מאה

הַמְאַזְּרֵנִי pref. id.) Piel part. sing. masc. [מְאַזֵּר] suff. 1 pers. sing. dec. 7 b. . . . אזר

הַמֵּאָיוֹת pref. id.) Kh. מֵאָיוֹת (as if from מֵאָיָה), K. מֵאוֹת', noun fem., pl. of מֵאָה dec. 11 b. מאה

הַמַּאֲכִלְךָ pref. id.) Hiph. part. sing. masc. (מַאֲכִיל) suff. 2 pers. sing. masc. dec. 1 b. . . אכל

הַמַּאֲכֶלֶת pref. id.) noun fem. sing., pl. מַאֲכָלוֹת' (§ 44. rem. 5) . . . . . אכל

הַמַּאֲמִין pref. id.) Hiph. part. sing. masc. dec. 1 b. . אמן

הַמֵּאֲנִים pref. id.) adj. masc., pl. of [מֵאֵן] dec. 7 b. מאן

הָמָאֹס[h] pref. הָ) Kal inf. absolute . . . מאס

הַמְאַסֵּף וְ pref. הַ) Piel part. sing. masc. dec. 7 b. אסף

הַמַּאֲרָב / הַמַּאֲרָב[l] וְ'[k] } pref. id.) noun masc. sing. dec. 2 b. . ארב

הַמְּאֵרָה pref. id.) noun fem. sing. d. 10 [for מְאָרָה] ארר

הַמְאָרְרִים pref. id.) Piel part. m., pl. of [מְאָרֵר] dec. 7 b. ארר

הַמְאֹרָשָׂה pref. id.) Pual part. fem. [of מְאֹרָשׂ] ארשׂ

הַמְּאֹרֹת[m] pref. id.) noun masc. with pl. fem. term. from מָאוֹר dec. 3 a. . . . . אור

הַמָּאתַיִם / הַמָּאתָיִם וְ } pref. id.) noun fem. dual of מֵאָה, [for מָאתַיִם] } מאה

הַמִּבְדָּלוֹת pref. id.) noun fem. pl. . . . בדל

הַמָּבוֹא[g] pref. id.) noun masc. sing. dec. 3 a. . בוא

הַמְּבוֹא[r] Kh. הַמָּבוֹא q. v., K. הַמֵּבִיא Hiph. part. sing. masc. dec. 3 b. . . . . . בוא

הַמַּבּוּל וְ' pref. הַ) noun masc. sing. . . יבל

הַמְּבוֹנִים pref. id.) Kh. הַמְּבוֹנִים noun masc. [pl. of מָבוֹן], K. הַמְּבִינִים (q. v.) . . . בין

הַמַּבּוּעַ[u] pref. id.) noun masc. sing. dec. 1 b. . נבע

הַמֵּבִי[x] וְ / הַמֵּבִיא[y] וְ } Hiph. part. masc. sing. dec. 3 b. (comp. § 25. No. 2 f) . . . } בוא

הַמְּבִיאִים pref. הַ) id. pl., absolute state . . בוא

הַמַּבִּיטִ[a] pref. id.) Hiph. part. sing. masc. . . נבט

הַמֵּבִין pref. id.) Hiph. part. sing. masc. dec. 3 b. בין

הַמְּבִינִים[b] וְ'[c] pref. id.) id. pl., absolute state . . בין

הַמְּבִינָתֵךְ[d] preff. הַ & מִ) noun fem. s., suff. 2 pers. s. m. from בִּינָה dec. 10. . . . . בין

הַמִּבְּלִי[e] preff. id.) adv. . . . . בלה

הַמַּבְלִיג[f] pref. הַ) Hiph. part. sing. masc. . . בלג

הֲמִבַּלְעֲדֵי preff. הֲ & מִ) adv., compound. from בַּל, and עֲדֵי (pl. constr. of עַד) . . . בלה

הַמַּבְעֵר[g] pref. הַ) Hiph. part. sing. masc. [for מַבְעִיר] בער

הַמִּבְצָר pref. id.) noun masc. sing. dec. 2 b. . בצר

הַמְבַקְשִׁים וְ'[h] pref. id.) Piel part. masc., pl. of מְבַקֵּשׁ dec. 7 b. (קְ f. קֵ § 10. rem. 7) . . בקשׁ

הַמְבַשְּׁלִים[i] pref. id.) Piel part. m., pl. of [מְבַשֵּׁל] d. 7 b. בשׁל

הַמְבַשֵּׂר[k] pref. id.) Piel part. act. sing. masc. . בשׂר

הַמְבַשְּׂרוֹת[l] pref. id.) id. f., pl. of מְבַשֶּׂרֶת dec. 13 a. בשׂר

הַמַּגְבִּיהִי[m] pref. id.) Hiph. part. sing. masc. with parag. ׳ (comp. § 8. rem. 19) . . . . גבה

הַמִּגְבָּעֹת[n] pref. id.) noun fem. pl. [of מִגְבָּעָה] . נבע

הַמַּגְדִּילִים[o] pref. id.) Hiph. part. m., pl. of [מַגְדִּיל] d. 1 b. גדל

הַמִּגְדָּל וְ'[p] pref. id.) noun masc. sing. dec. 2 b. . גדל

הַמִּגְדָּלוֹת[q] / הַמִּגְדָּלִים } pref. id.) id. pl., absolute state . גדל

הַמָּגוֹג pref. id.) pr. name of a region . . גוג

הַמַּגִּיד pref. id.) Hiph. part. sing. masc. dec. 1 b. נגד

הַמְּגִלָּה pref. id.) noun fem. sing. dec. 10. . גלל

הַמָּגְלִים[r] pref. id.) Hoph. part. masc. pl. of [מָגְלֶה] 9 a. (comp. § 11. rem. 10) . . . גלה

הַמָּגֵן pref. id.) noun masc. sing. dec. 8 b. . גנן

הַמָּגִנּוֹת[s] / הַמָּגִנִּים[t] } pref. id.) id. pl. (§ 37. rem. 4) . גנן

הַמְּגֹעֶרֶת[u] pref. id.) noun fem. sing. . . גער

הַמַּגֵּפָה וְ'[x] pref. id.) noun fem. sing. dec. 10. . נגף

הַמְדַבֵּר pref. id.) Piel part. sing. masc. dec. 7 b. דבר

הַמִּדְבָּר pref. id. } noun masc. sing. dec. 2 b. דבר

הַמִּדְבָּר[y] pref. הַ } . . . דבר

הַמִּדְבָּרָה pref. הַ) id. with parag. ה . . . דבר

הַמְדַבְּרִים pref. id.) Piel part. m., pl. of מְדַבֵּר d. 7 b. דבר

הַמִּדָּה pref. id.) noun fem. sing. dec. 10. . מדד

הַמְּדוּרָה[z] pref. id.) noun fem. sing. dec. 10. . דור

הַמָּדִי pref. id.) gent. noun from מָדַי q. v.

הַמְּדִינָה pref. id.) noun fem. sing. dec. 10, R. דִּין see דון

הַמְּדִינוֹת וְ'[a] pref. id.) id. pl. . . . . דון

הַמִּדְיָנִי pref. id.) gent. noun from מִדְיָן R. דִּין see דון

הַמִּדְיָנִים pref. id.) id. pl. masc. . . . דון

הַמִּדְיָנִית pref. id.) id. sing. fem. . . . דון

הַמְּדָנִים וְ pref. id.) id. pl. masc. contr. for מִדְיָנִים דון

הַמַּדָּע[b] וְ pref. id.) noun masc. sing. dec. 2 b. . ידע

הַמַּדְרֵגָה[c] pref. id.) noun fem. sing. dec. 10. . דרג

[a] Ne. 2. 13. [b] 2 Sa. 21. 9. [c] Ex. 39. 34. [d] Ps. 18. 33. [e] De. 8. 16. [f] Is. 28. 16. [g] Je. 13. 10. [h] Je. 14. 19. [i] Jos. 6. 9, 13. [k] 2 Ch. 13. 13. [l] Ju. 9. 35. [m] Ge. 1. 16. [n] Nu. 3. 46. [o] Eze. 45. 15. [p] Jos. 16. 9. [q] 1 Ch. 9. 19. [r] Eze. 42. 9. [s] Ge. 7. 6. [t] 2 Ch. 35. 3. [u] Ec. 12. 6. [x] 2 Sa. 5. 2. [y] 1 Ch. 11. 2. [z] Ne. 10. 32. [a] Ps. 104. 32. [b] Ne. 8. 9. [c] Ne. 8. 3. [d] Job 39. 26. [e] Ex. 14. 11 [f] Am. 5. 9. [g] De. 22. 25, 27. [g] Ex. 22. 5. [h] 1 Sa. 25. 26. [i] Eze. 46. 24. [k] 1 Sa. 4. 17. [l] Ps. 68. 12. [m] Ps. 113. 5. [n] Ex. 39. 28. [o] Ps. 35. 26. [p] Ne. 3. 25, 26. [q] 2 Ch. 32. 5. [r] Je. 40. 1. [s] 2 Ch. 23. 9. [t] Ne. 4. 10. [u] De. 28. 20. [x] Nu. 17. 15. [y] Je. 2. 31. [z] Eze. 24. 9. [a] Ec. 2. 8. [b] 2 Ch. 1. 12. [c] Ca. 2. 14.

הַמַּדְרֵגוֹת[a] pref. הַ)(id. pl. . . . . . דרג
הַמְּדָתָא pref. id.)(pr. name masc., see מְדָתָא

[הָמָה] fut. יֶהֱמֶה to make a *humming* noise.—I. spoken of the sounds of certain animals, *to growl, to howl, to coo, to mourn*; trop. of men *to sigh*.—II. of the noise of a tumultuous crowd, of water, *to bustle, to be turbulent, to roar, rage*; of the harp *to hum*; applied to the emotion of the soul, such as anguish, sorrow, *to be agitated, disquieted*; to the commotion of the inward parts, Is. 16. 11, *my bowels sound* (moan) *like a harp*.

הָם or הֵם only pl. Eze. 7. 11, i. q. הָמוֹן *riches*.

הָם or הָם pr. name of an unknown region, Ge. 14. 5.

הָמוֹן masc. dec. 3 a.—I. *noise, sound*, of singing, rain, a multitude.—II. *multitude, crowd*.—III. *multitude of possession, riches, wealth*.—IV. *emotion of the mind, disquietude*, Is. 63. 15.

הֲמוֹנָה (*multitude*) the mystical name of a city, Eze. 39. 16.

הֶמְיָה f. *sound* of the harp, constr. הֶמְיַת Is. 14. 11.

הֵמָּה 'וְ pers. pron. masc. pl. (הֵם) with parag. ה . הם
הֹמֶה[b] Kal part. act. sing. masc. . . . המה
הַמְּהַגִּים[c] וְ pref. הַ)(Hiph. part. m. pl. of [מְהַגֶּה] d. 9 a. הגה
הַמְּהוּמָה pref. id.)(noun fem. sing. dec. 10. . . המה
הַמְהַלֵּךְ[d] pref. id.)(Piel part. sing. masc. dec. 7 b. הלך
הַמְהַלְּכִים[e] pref. id.)(id. pl., absolute state . . הלך
הַמְהַלְלִים[f] וְ pref. id.)(Piel part. masc. pl. of [מְהַלֵּל] dec. 7 b. (לְ for לֵ § 10. rem. 7) . . הלל
הַמַּהְפֶּכֶת[g] / הַמַּהְפֶּכֶת } pref. id.)(noun fem. s. (comp. § 35. r. 2) הפך
הָמוּ 'וְ Kal pret. 3 pers. pl. . . . . המה
הִמּוֹ Ch. pers. pron. 3 pers. masc. pl. . . . הם
הַמּוֹאָבִי pref. הַ)(gent. noun from מוֹאָב q. v.
הַמּוֹאֲבִיָּה pref. id.)(id. fem.
הַמּוֹאָבִים וְ pref. id.)(id. pl. masc.
הַמּוֹאָבִית pref. id.)(id. sing. fem.
הַמּוּבָא pref. id.)(Hoph. part. sing. masc. dec. 1 b. בוא
הַמּוֹט[h] pref. id.)(noun masc. sing. dec. 1 a. . . מוט
הַמּוֹטָה[i] pref. id.)(noun fem. sing. dec. 10. . . מוט
הַמּוֹכֵר[k] 'וְ[l] Kal part. act. sing. masc. dec. 7 b. . מכר
הִמּוֹל Niph. inf. absolute . . . . מול
הַמּוֹלְדִים[m] pref. הַ)(Hiph. part. act. m., pl. of מוֹלִיד d. 1 b. ילד
הֲמוּלָּה[n] noun fem. sing. . . . . . המל
הַמּוֹלִיד[o] pref. הַ)(Hiph. part. sing. masc. dec. 1 b. . ילד

הַמּוֹלִיךְ[p] pref. id.)(Hiph. part. sing. masc. dec. 1 b. ילך
הַמּוֹלִיכֲךָ[q] pref. id.)(id., suff. 2 pers. sing. masc. . ילך
הַמּוּמָתִים[r] pref. id.)(Hoph. part. masc., pl. of מוּמָת מות
הָמוֹן noun masc. sing. dec. 3 a. . . . . המה
הֲמוֹן 'וְ[s] id., constr. state; וּ bef. (-:) . . . המה
הִמּוֹן Ch. pers. pron. masc. pl. . . . . הם
הֲמוֹנָהּ 'וְ[t] noun masc. sing., suff. 3 pers. sing. fem. from הָמוֹן dec. 3 a.; וַ before (-:) . . המה
הֲמוֹנָה pr. name of a place . . . . המה
הֲמוֹנֹה / הֲמוֹנוֹ 'וְ[u] } noun masc. sing., suff. 3 pers. sing. m. from הָמוֹן dec. 3 a; וַ bef. (-:) . } המה
הֲמוֹנֶיהָ[x] id. pl., suff. 3 pers. sing. fem. . . . המה
הֲמוֹנֵךְ[y] id. sing., suff. 2 pers. sing. m. [for הֲמוֹנְךָ] המה
הַמְנוֹכָא[z] וְ Ch. in other copies, Kh. הַמְנוֹכָא׳, (read נוּ׳); K. הַמְנִיכָא׳, noun masc. sing. emph. [of הַמְנִיךְ or הַמְנוּךְ] . . . מנך
הַמּוּסָרִים[a] pref. הַ)(Hoph. part. m., pl. of מוּסָר d. 2 b. סור
הַמּוֹעֵד 'וְ[b] pref. id.)(noun masc. sing. dec. 7 b. . יעד
הַמּוּעָדָה[c] pref. id.)(noun fem. sing. . . . יעד
הַמּוֹפֵת 'וְ[d] pref. id.)(noun masc. sing. dec. 7 b. . יפת
הַמֹּפְתִים[e] וְ pref. id.)(id. pl., absolute state . . יפת
הַמּוּצָאִים pref. הַ)(Hoph. part. masc. pl. [of מוּצָא] . יצא
הַמּוֹצִיא pref. id.)(Hiph. part. sing. masc. dec. 1 b. יצא
הַמּוֹצִיאֲךָ pref. id.)(id., suff. 2 pers. sing. masc. . יצא
הַמּוּקָעִים[f] pref. id.)(Hoph. part. masc. pl. [of מוּקָע] יקע
הַמּוֹר[g] pref. id.)(noun masc. sing. d. 1 a, for מֹר׳ מרר
הַמּוֹרָא[h] pref. id.)(noun m. s. (suff. מוֹרַאֲכֶם) d. 2 b. ירא
הַמּוֹרְאִם[i] pref. id.)(Kh. מֹרְאִם׳ for K. מוֹרִים׳ Hiph. part. masc., pl. of מוֹרֶה . . . ירה
הַמּוֹרְדִים[k] pref. id.)(Kal part. act. m., pl. of [מוֹרֵד] d. 7 b. מרד
הַמּוֹרֶה[l] pref. id.)(subst.; prop. Hiph. part. masc. dec. 9 a; also pr. name . . . ירה
הַמּוֹרִיָּה pref. id.)(pr. name of a hill, see מֹרִיָּה
הַמּוֹרִיגִים[m] וְ for הַמֹּרִגִּים (q. v.) dag. f. resolved in י מרג
הַמּוֹרִים pref. הַ)(Hiph. part. m., pl. of מוֹרֶה d. 9 a. ירה
הַמּוֹרַשְׁתִּי pref. id.)(gent. noun from מוֹרֶשֶׁת גַּת q. v. ירש
הַמּוּשָׁב pref. id.)(Hoph. part. sing. masc. . . ישב
הַמּוּשִׁי pref. id.)(patronym. [for מוּשִׁיִּי] from מוּשִׁי מוש
הַמּוֹשִׁיעַ[n] pref. id.)(Hiph. part. sing. masc. dec. 1 b. ישע
הַמּוֹשֵׁל[o] pref. id.)(Kal part. act. sing. masc. dec. 7 b. משל
הַמּוֹשְׁלִים[p] pref. id.)(id. pl., absolute state . משל
הַמָּוֶת 'וְ[q] pref. id.)(noun masc. sing. dec. 6 g. . מות
הֹמוֹת[r] Kal part. act. f., pl. of הוֹמָה d. 10, fr. הוֹמֶה m. המה
הַמָּוְתָה[s] pref. הַ)(noun masc. s. (מָוֶת) with parag. ה מות
הַמִּזְבַּח pref. id.)(constr. of the following זבח
הַמִּזְבֵּחַ 'וְ pref. id.)(noun masc. sing. dec. 7 c. . זבח

[a] Eze. 38. 20. [b] Pr. 20. 1. [c] Is. 8. 19. [d] Ps. 104. 3. [e] Ec. 4. 15. [f] 2 Ch. 23. 12. [g] Je. 20. 3. [h] Nu. 4. 10, 12. [i] Je. 28. 10, 12. [k] Eze. 7. 13. [l] Eze. 7. 12. [m] Je. 16. 3. [n] Je. 11. 16. [o] Is. 66. 9. [p] Je. 2. 6. [q] De. 8. 15. [r] 2 Ch. 22. 11. [s] Ps. 65. 8. [t] Is. 5. 14. [u] Is. 5. 13. [x] Eze. 32. 20. [y] Eze. 32. 12. [z] Da. 5. 7, 16, 29. [a] 1 Sa. 21. 7. [b] Ju. 20. 38. [c] Jos. 20. 9. [d] De. 13. 3. [e] De. 34. 11. [f] 2 Sa. 21. 13. [g] Ca. 4. 6. [h] De. 34. 12. [i] 2 Sa. 11. 24. [k] Eze. 2 3. [l] Joel 2. 23. [m] 1 Ch. 21. 23. [n] 1 Sa. 14. 39. [o] Ec. 10. 4. [p] 2 Ch. 23. 20. [q] De. 30. 19. [r] Eze. 7. 16. [s] Ps. 116. 15.

הַמִּזְבֵּחָה pref. ה)(id. with parag. ה . . . זבח

הַמִּזְבְּחוֹת / הַמִּזְבְּחֹת [a] וְ׳ } pref. id.)(id. pl. . . . . זבח

הַמָּזֶג[b] pref. id.)(noun masc. s. [for מֶזֶג § 35. r. 2] מזג

הַמְּזוּזָה[c] [d] וְ׳ pref. id.)(noun fem. sing. dec. 10. . זוז

הַמְּזוּזוֹת[e] / הַמְּזוּזֹת[f] [g] וְ׳ } pref. id.)(id. pl. . . . . זוז

הַמָּזוֹן[h] pref. id.)(noun masc. sing. . . זון

הַמַּזְכִּיר pref. id.)(Hiph. part. sing. masc. dec. 1 b. זכר

הַמַּזְכִּירִים pref. id.)(id. pl., absolute state זכר

הַמַּזְלֵג[k] [l] וְ׳ pref. id.)(noun masc. sing. . . זלג

הַמִּזְלָגוֹת[m] / הַמִּזְלָגֹת [m] וְ׳ } pref. id.)(n. f., pl. of [מִזְלָגָה] d. 11 a. זלג

הַמְזַמְּרוֹת וְ׳ pref. id.)(noun f., pl. of [מְזַמֶּרֶת] d. 13 a. זמר

הַמְּזִמָּתָה pref. id.)(noun f. s. (מְזִמָּה) with parag. ה זמם

הַמִּזְרָח pref. id.)(noun masc. sing. dec. 2 b. . זרח

הַמִּזְרָק[g] pref. id.)(noun masc. sing. dec. 2 b. . זרק

הַמִּזְרָקוֹת / הַמִּזְרָקֹת וְ׳ } pref. id.)(id. pl., absolute state . זרק

הַמַּחֲבָאִים pref. id.)(noun masc., pl. of [מַחֲבָא] d. 1 b. חבא

הַמַּחֲבַת[i] pref. id.)(noun fem. sing. contr. [for מַחֲבֶתֶת] חבת

הַמַּחֲוִים pref. id.)(gent. noun pl. . . . . חוה

הַמַּחֲזִיק[k] pref. id.)(Hiph. part. sing. masc. dec. 1 b. חזק

הַמְחַטֵּא[n] pref. id.)(Piel part. sing. masc. . . חטא

הַמְחַכֶּה[x] pref. id.)(Piel part. sing. masc. dec. 9 a. חכה

הַמְחַכִּים pref. id.)(id. pl., absolute state . . חכה

הַמַּחֲלָה[z] pref. id.)(noun fem. sing. . . . חלה

הַמְּחֹלִי pref. id.)(gent. noun [for מְחֹלִיִי] from מְחֹלִי חלה

הַמְּחֹלוֹת וְ pref. id.)(noun fem., pl. of ־לָה dec. 10. חול

הַמְּחֻלָּל[b] pref. id.)(Pual part. sing. masc. . חלל

הַמְחֹלְלוֹת pref. id.)(Pilel part. f., pl. of [מְחֹלֶלֶת] d. 13 a. חול

הַמַּחֲלָצוֹת pref. id.)(noun fem., pl. of [מַחֲלָצָה] . חלץ

הַמַּחְלְקוֹת pref. id.)(pl. of the foll. (§ 44. rem. 5) . חלק

הַמַּחֲלֹקֶת pref. id.)(noun f. s. (suff. מַחֲלֻקְתּוֹ) d. 13 c. חלק

הַמְּחֹלָתִי pref. id.)(gent. noun from אָבֵל מְחוֹלָה q. v. אבל

הַמַּחֲנֶה [f] וְ׳ pref. id.)(noun com. sing. dec. 9 a. . חנה

הַמַּחֲנוֹת pref. id.)(id. with pl. fem. term. . . חנה

הַמַּחֲנַיִם[g] pref. id.)(id. du., or perh. pl. of a s. מַחֲנַי (§ 38. r. 2) חנה

הַמַּחֲנֹת defect. for הַמַּחֲנוֹת (q. v.) . . . חנה

הַמַּחְצֶבֶת pref. הַ)(Hiph. part. sing. fem. . . חצב

הַמֶּחֱצָה[h] pref. id.)(noun sing. fem. dec. 10. . חצה

הַמְחֻקֶּה[i] pref. id.)(Pual part. sing. masc. . חקק

הַמַּחֲרֶבֶת pref. id.)(Hiph. part. sing. fem. from מַחֲרִיב masc. (§ 39. No. 4 d) . . חרב

הַמָּחֳרָת[l] pref. id.)(noun fem. sing. (const. ־רַת) מחר

הַמַּחֲשָׁבֹת[m] pref. id.)(n. f., pl. abs. fr. מַחֲשָׁבָה (q. v.) חשב

הַמַּחְתָּה pref. id.)(noun fem. sing. dec. 10. . חתה

הַמַּחְתּוֹת / הַמַּחְתֹּת וְ׳ } pref. id.)(id. pl. . . . . חתה

הַמַּטֶּה וְ׳ pref. id.)(noun masc. sing. dec. 9 a. . נטה

הַמִּטָּה pref. id.)(noun fem. sing. dec. 10. . נטה

הַמְטַהֵר[n] pref. id.)(Piel part. sing. m. (§ 14. rem. 1) טהר

הַמִּטַּהֵר[o] pref. id.)(Hithp. part. s. m. d. 7 b. [for מִתְטַהֵר] טהר

הַמִּטַּהֲרִים[p] וְ pref. id.)(id. pl., abs. state (comp. § 14. r. 1) טהר

הַמַּטּוֹת pref. id.)(n. m. with pl. f. term. fr. מַטֶּה d. 9 a. נטה

הַמִּטּוֹת pref. id.)(noun fem., pl. of מִטָּה dec. 10. נטה

הַמַּטִּים[q] וְ pref. id.)(Hiph. part. masc., pl. of מַטֶּה dec. 9 a (§ 25. No. 2 b) . . נטה

הִמְטִיר Hiph. pret. 3 pers. sing. masc. . . מטר

הַמַּטְעַמִּים[r] pref. ה)(noun m., pl. of [מַטְעָם] d. 8 a. טעם

הַמִּטְפָּחוֹת[s] וְ pref. id.)(pl. abs. of the following טפח

הַמִּטְפַּחַת[t] pref. id.)(noun masc. f., pl. ־פָּחוֹת (§ 44. r. 5) טפח

הַמָּטָר[u] pref. id.)(noun masc. sing. dec. 4 a. . מטר

הַמַּטָּרָה pref. id.)(noun fem. sing. . . . נטר

הִמְטַרְתִּי[x] וְ Hiph. pret. 1 pers. sing.; acc. shifted by conv. וְ (comp. § 8. rem. 7) . . מטר

הַמַּטְרִי pref. הַ)(pr. name masc. . . . מטר

הַמַּטֹּת pref. id.)(n. m. with pl. f. term. fr. מַטֶּה d. 9 a. נטה

הֹמִיָּה Kal part. act. sing. fem. (§ 24. rem. 4) . המה

הֹמִיּוֹת[y] id. pl. of the preceding . . . המה

הַמְיַחֲלִים pref. הַ)(Piel part. m., pl. of מְיַחֵל d. 7 b. (§ 14. r. 1) יחל

הַמְיַלֶּדֶת pref. id.)(Piel part. act. fem. sing. dec. 13 a. ילד

הַמְיַלְּדֹת[z] pref. id.)(pl. of the preceding . . ילד

הַמַּיִם / הַמָּיִם וְ׳ } pref. הַ)(noun masc. pl. [of מַי § 38. rem. 2; comp. § 45] . . } מי

הַמַּיְמָה[a] / הַמָּיְמָה[b] } pref. id.)(id. pl. with loc. ה מי

הַמִּיָּמֶיךָ[c] preff. הַ & מִ)(noun masc. pl. (יָמִים), suff. 2 pers. sing. masc. irr. of יוֹם (§ 45) . יום

הֵמִיר[d] Hiph. pret. 3 pers. sing. masc. . . מור

הֲמִיִּרְאָתְךָ[e] preff. הֲ & מִ)(noun fem. sing., suff. 2 pers. sing. masc. from יִרְאָה (no pl.) . . ירא

הַמִּישֹׁר pref. הַ)(noun masc. sing. . . . ישר

הַמְיַשְּׁרִים[a] pref. id.)(Piel part. m., pl. of [מְיַשֵּׁר] d. 7 b. ישר

הָמִית[f] Hiph. inf. constr. dec. 3 a. . . . מות

הֵמִית [g] וְ׳ id. pret. 3 pers. sing. masc. . . מות

הֶמְיַת[h] noun fem. sing., const. of [הֶמְיָה] dec. 10. המה

הֲמִיתוֹ Hiph. inf. (הָמִית), suff. 3 pers. s. m. d. 3 a. מות

הָמִיתוּ[i] וְ id. imp. pl. masc. . . . מות

---

[a] Nu. 3. 31.
[b] Ca. 7. 3.
[c] Ex. 21. 6.
[d] Is. 57. 8.
[e] Ju. 16. 3.
[f] Ex. 12. 7, 22, 23.
[g] 1 Ki. 7. 5.
[h] 2 Ch. 11. 23.
[i] Is. 62. 6.
[k] 1 Sa. 2. 14.
[l] 1 Sa. 2. 13.
[m] 2 Ch. 4. 16.
[n] 1 Ch. 28. 17
[nn] Nu. 31. 36.
[o] Je. 52. 18.
[p] Je. 11. 15.
[q] Nu. 7. 85.
[r] 1 Sa. 23. 23.
[s] Le. 2. 5.
[t] Ju. 16. 26.
[tt] Pr. 9. 15.
[u] Le. 6. 19.
[x] Da. 12. 12.
[y] Job 3. 20.
[z] Ex. 15. 26.
[a] 1 Sa. 18. 6.
[b] Eze. 36. 23.
[c] Ju. 21. 23.
[d] Is. 3. 22.
[e] 1 Ch. 27. 1, 2.
[f] Ju. 8. 11.
[g] Ca. 7. 1.
[h] Is. 51. 9.
[i] 1 Ki. 6. 35.
[k] Is. 51. 10.
[l] Nu. 11. 32.
[m] Je. 29. 11.
[n] Le. 14. 11.
[o] Le. 14. 7, 8, &c.
[p] Is. 66. 17.
[q] Ps. 125. 5.
[r] Ge. 27. 17.
[s] Is. 3. 22.
[t] Ruth 3. 15.
[u] Ex. 9. 34.
[x] Am. 4. 7.
[y] Pr. 1. 21.
[z] Ex. 1. 17, 19, 21.
[a] Ex. 8. 16.
[b] Ex. 7. 15.
[c] Job 38. 12.
[d] Je. 2. 11.
[e] Job 22. 4.
[f] Le. 20. 4.
[g] Ex. 21. 29.
[h] Is. 14. 11.
[i] 1 Sa. 22. 17.

הֵמִיתוּ id. pret. 3 pers. pl. . . . . . מות

[a] וַהֲמִתִיו Kh. [for וַהֲמִתִּיו, id. for וַהֲמַתִּיו] Hiph. pret. 1 pers. s., suff. 3 p. s. m. (§ 25. r. 1) מות

[b] וֶהֱמִיתְךָ id. pret. 3 p. s. m., suff. 2 p. s. m.; וְ for וַ conv. מות

[c] הֱמִיתָם id. id. with 3 pers. pl. masc. . . . מות

[d] הֲמִיתֵנִי id. imp. sing. masc., suff. 1 pers. sing. . מות

[e] הֱמִיתַתְהוּ id. pret. 3 pers. sing. fem., suff. 3 pers. s. m. מות

הַמְכַבֵּד pref. הַ interr. for הֲ)(Piel part. s. m. d. 7b. כבד

[f] הַמַּכְבֵּר pref. הַ art.)(noun masc. sing. . . כבר

הַמַּכָּה pref. id.)(noun fem. sing. dec. 10. . נכה

הַמַּכֶּה pref. id.)(Hiph. part. sing. masc. dec. 9a. (§ 25. No. 2b) . . . . . נכה

[g] הַמֻּכָּה pref. id.)(fem. of the following . . נכה

[h] הַמֻּכֶּה pref. id.)(Hoph. part. sing. masc. dec. 9a. (§ 25. No. 2b) . . . . . נכה

[i] הַמַּכֵּהוּ pref. id.)(Hiph. part. sing. masc., suff. 3 pers. sing. m. from מַכֶּה dec. 9a. (§ 25. No. 2b) נכה

[k] וְהֻמְּכוּ Hoph. pret. 3 p. pl. [for הוּמְכוּ § 18. r. 14] מכך

[l] הַמִּכְוָה pref. הַ)(noun fem. sing. dec. 10. . כוה

[m] הַמְּכוֹנָה pref. id.)(noun fem. sing. dec. 10. . כון

[n] הַמְּכוֹנוֹת pref. id.)(pl. of the preceding . . כון

[o] הַמַּכּוֹת pref. id.)(noun fem., pl. of מַכָּה dec. 10. . נכה

הַמַּכִּים pref. id.)(Hiph. part. masc., pl. of מַכֶּה dec. 9a (§ 25. No. 2b, or subs. 2 Ki. 8. 29; 9. 15. נכה

[p] הַמֵּכִין pref. id.)(Hiph. part. sing. masc. . . כון

הַמָּכִירִי pref. id.)(patronym. of מָכִיר . . מכר

הַמִּכְמֶתֶת pref. id.)(pr. name of a place, see מִכְמְתָת

[q] הַמְּכֹנָה pref. id.)(noun fem. sing. dec. 10. . כון

הַמְּכֹנוֹת וְ'[r] pref. id.)(pl. of the preceding . כון

[s] הַמֶּכֶס pref. id.)(noun m. sing. (suff. מִכְסָם) dec. 6a. כסס

הַמְכַסֶּה וְ'[t] pref. הַ art., or interr. for הֲ)(Piel part. sing. masc. dec. 9a. . . . . כסה

[u] הַמַּכְעִסִים pref. הַ art.)(Hiph. part. m., pl. of [מַכְעִים] d. 1b. כעס

הַמַּכְפֵּלָה pref. id.)(pr. name of a place . . כפל

[x] הִמָּכְרוֹ Niph. Inf. [הִמָּכֵר], suff. 3 pers. s. m. dec. 7b. מכר

[y] הַמֹּכֶרֶת pref. הַ)(Kal part. act. sing. fem., from מֹכֵר m. מכר

הַמְּכֵרָתִי pref. id.)(gent. noun from מְכֵרָה . כור

[z] וְהַמַּכְשֵׁלָה pref. id.)(noun fem. sing. dec. 10. . כשל

[a] וְהַמַּכְשֵׁלוֹת pref. id.)(pl. of the preceding . כשל

[b] הַמִּכְשֹׁלִים pref. id.)(noun masc., pl. of מִכְשׁוֹל dec. 1b. כשל

[c] וְהַמִּכְתָּב pref. id.)(noun masc. sing. dec. 2b. . כתב

הַמַּכְתֵּשׁ pref. id.)(noun masc. sing. (also pr. name) כתש

המל Root not used; Arab. *to rain continually*.

הֲמוּלָּה, הֲמֻלָּה fem. probably *noise*, *bustle*, *tumult*.

[d] וְהַמָּלֵא pref. הַ)(adj. masc. sing. dec. 5a, const. מְלֵא (§ 34. rem. 1) . . . . מלא

הַמְלֵאָה pref. id.)(id. fem.; or subst. (De. 22. 9) d. 10. מלא

[e] וְהַמְּלֵאוֹת pref. id.)(id. pl. . . . . מלא

[f] הַמְלֵאִים pref. id.)(id. pl. masc. . . . מלא

הַמִּלֻּאִים pref. id.)(noun masc., pl. of [מִלּוּא] dec. 1b. מלא

וְהַמַּלְאָךְ pref. id.)(noun masc. sing. dec. 2b. . לאך

וְ'הַמְּלָאכָה pref. id.)(noun fem. sing., constr. מְלֶאכֶת, with suff. מְלַאכְתְּךָ (§ 42. rem. 5) . לאך

הַמַּלְאָכִים pref. id.)(noun masc., pl. of מַלְאָךְ dec. 2b. לאך

[g] הַמְּלָאכִים Kh. הַמַּלְאָכִים q. v., K. הַמְּלָכִים (q. v.) . מלך

[h] הַמֶּלְבּוּשׁ pref. הַ)(noun masc. sing. dec. 1b. . לבש

[i] הַמַּלְבִּשְׁכֶם pref. id.)(Hiph. part. m. s. from [מַלְבִּשׁ, § 11. rem. 8,] suff. 2 pers. pl. masc., dec. 7b. לבש

[k] הֲמֻלָּה noun fem. sing. . . . . . המל

[zz] הִמֹּלוּ Niph. imp. pl. masc. . . . . מול

הַמִּלּוֹא pref. הַ)(noun masc. sing. . . . מלא

הַמְּלוּכָה pref. id.)(noun fem. sing. . . . מלך

הַמָּלוֹן pref. id.)(noun masc. sing. dec. 3a. . . לון

[l] הַמֶּלַח, הַמֶּלַח } pref. id.)(noun masc. sing. K. מֶלַח . מלח

[m] וְהָמְלֵחַ Hoph. inf. abs. . . . . . מלח

[n] הַמַּלָּחִים pref. הַ)(noun masc., pl. of [מַלָּח] dec. 1b. מלח

[o] הַמְּלָחִים וְ pref. id.)(noun masc. pl. . . . מלח

[p] הַמִּלְחָמוֹת pref. id.)(id. pl. abs. state. . . לחם

וְ'הַמִּלְחָמָה pref. id.)(noun fem. sing. dec. 11b; with suff. מִלְחַמְתּוֹ' from מִלְחֶמֶת' 13a. (§ 42. rem. 5) . לחם

[q] הָמְלַחַתְּ Hoph. pret. 2 pers. sing. fem. (§ 11. rem. 10) מלח

הִמָּלֵט Niph. inf. or imp. sing. masc. . . . מלט

[r] הִמָּלְטִי id. imp. sing. fem. . . . . . מלט

[s] וְהִמְלִיט Hiph. pret. 3 pers. sing. masc. . . מלט

[t] וְהִמְלִיטָה id. pret. 3 pers. sing. fem. . . . מלט

הִמְלִיךְ Hiph. pret. 3 pers. sing. masc. . . מלך

[u] הִמְלִיכוּ id. pret. 3 pers. pl. . . . . . מלך

[x] הַמֵּלִיץ pref. הַ)(Hiph. part. sing. masc. dec. 3b. . ליץ

[y] הֲמָלֹךְ pref. הֲ)(Kal inf. abs. . . . . מלך

[z] הָמְלַךְ Hoph. pret. 3 pers. sing. masc. . . . מלך

הַמֶּלֶךְ pref. הַ וְ' ; [a] הַמֶּלֶךְ pref. הַ } noun masc. sing. dec. 6a. . מלך

הַמֹּלֶךְ pref. הַ)(pr. name of an idol . . . מלך

הַמֹּלֵךְ pref. id.)(Kal part. act. sing. masc. . . מלך

[b] וְ'הַמַּלְכָּה pref. id.)(noun fem. sing. dec. 12a. . מלך

[a] 1 Sa. 17. 35. [b] Is. 65. 15. [c] Je. 41. 8. [d] 1 Sa. 20. 8. [e] 2 Ch. 22. 11. [f] 2 Ki. 8. 15.
[g] Nu. 25. 15, 18. [h] Nu. 25. 14. [i] Is. 9. 12. [k] Job 24. 24. [l] Le. 13. 24, 28. [m] 1 Ki. 7. 27, 28, &c.
[n] Je. 27. 19. [o] Zec. 13. 6. [p] Ps. 147. 8. [q] 1 Ki. 7. 34, 34, 35. [r] 2 Ki. 25. 16. [s] Nu. 31. 37.
[t] Le. 9. 19. [u] Is. 65. 3. [x] Le. 25. 50. [y] Na. 3. 4. [z] Is. 3. 6. [zz] Je. 4. 4.
[a] Zep. 1. 3. [b] Eze. 21. 20. [c] Ex. 32. 16. [d] 2 Ki. 4. 4. [e] Ge. 41. 7.
[f] Is. 51. 20. [g] 2 Sa. 11. 1. [h] 2 Ki. 10. 22. [i] 2 Sa. 1. 24. [k] Eze. 1. 24.
[l] 2 Ki. 14. 7. [m] Eze. 16. 4. [n] Jon. 1. 5. [o] Je. 38. 12. [p] 1 Ch. 26. 27.
[q] Eze. 16. 4. [r] Zec. 2. 11. [s] Is. 31. 5. [t] Is. 66. 7. [u] Ho. 8. 4.
[x] Ge. 42. 23. [y] Ge. 37. 8. [z] Da. 9. 1. [a] Mi. 4. 9. [b] Est. 7. 6.

הַמַּלְכָּה[a] pref. הַ (noun fem. sing. defect. for מְלוּכָה' מלך
הַמַּלְכֻיּוֹת pref. id. (noun fem. sing. d. 1 b. (pl. מַלְכֻיּוֹת מלך
הַמַּלְכִּיאֵ pref. id. (patronym. of מַלְכִּיאֵל (q. v.) . מלך
הַמְּלָכִים ו' pref. id. (noun masc., pl. of מֶלֶךְ dec. 6 a. מלך
הַמֹּלֶכֶת pref. id. (pr. name fem. . . . מלך
הִמְלַכְתָּ, וְהִמְלַכְתָּ } Hiph. pret. 2 pers. sing. masc.; acc. shifted by conv. וְ (comp. § 8. rem. 7) } מלך
הִמְלַכְתִּי id. pret. 1 pers. sing. . . . . . מלך
הִמְלַכְתִּיךָ id. id., suff. 2 pers. sing. masc. . . מלך
הִמְלַכְתַּנִי[b] ו' id. pret. 2 pers. sing. masc., suff. 1 pers. sing. מלך
הַמְלַמֵּד pref. הַ (Hiph. part. sing. masc. dec. 7 b. . למד
הַמֶּלְצַר[c] pref. id. (noun masc. sing. . . . מלצר
הַמַּלְקוֹחַ pref. id. (noun masc. sing. dec. 1 b. . . לקח
הַמַּלְקָחַיִם ו' pref. id. (noun m. du. of [מֶלְקָח] d. 2 b. לקח
הַמְלַקְּקִים pref. id. (Piel part. masc., pl. of [מְלַקֵּק] dec. 7 b. (§ 10. rem. 7) . . . . לקק
הַמֶּלְתָּחָה pref. id. (noun fem. sing. . . . . לתח

הָמַם' — I. *to put in motion, to drive*, Is. 28. 28.—II. *to put to the rout, disperse, defeat.*—III. *to destroy.*

הוֹמָם (*defeat*) pr. name masc. 1 Ch. 1. 39; for which הֵימָם Ge. 36. 22.

הֲמָמָם[d] ו' Kal pret. 3 p. s. m. [הָם], suff. 3 p. pl. m. הום
הַמְּמוֹתִים pref. הַ (Kh. מְמוֹתִים' noun masc. pl. [of מָמוֹת dec. 3 a], K. מוּמָתִים', Hoph. part. pl. of מוּמָת . . . . . מות
הַמִּמְכָּר pref. id. (noun masc. sing. dec. 2 b. . . מכר
הַמְמַלְּאִים[e] ו' pref. id. (Piel part. masc., pl. of מְמַלֵּא dec. 7 b. (§ 10. rem. 7) . . . . מלא
הַמְמַלְּטִים pref. id. (Piel part. m., pl. מְמַלֵּט d. 7 b. מלט
הַמַּמְלִיךְ pref. id. (Hiph. part. sing. masc. . . מלך
הַמַּמְלָכָה ו' pref. id. (noun fem. dec. 11 a. (c. מַלְכֶת', suff. מַלְכְתּוֹ' dec. 13 a. § 42. rem. 5) . מלך
הַמַּמְלָכוֹת pref. id. (id. pl., absolute state . . מלך
הַמַּמְלְכוֹת pref. id. (id. pl., constr. state . . מלך
הֲמָמָם' Kal pret. 3 pers. sing. masc., suff. 3 p. pl. m. המם
הֲמִמֶּנּוּ[f] pref. הֲ (prep. (מִן), suff. 3 p. s. m. (§ 5 parad.) מנן
הֲמָמָנוּ[g] Kal pret. 3 pers. sing. masc., suff. Kh. מָנוּ' 1 pers. pl., K. מַנִי' 1 pers. sing. . . המם
הֲמִמֶּנִּי[h] pref. הֲ (prep. (מִן), suff. 1 p. s. (§ 5 parad.) מנן
הַמַּמְעִיט[i] ו' pref. הַ (Hiph. part. sing. masc. . . מעט
הַמֶּמְשָׁלָה pref. id. (noun. fem. sing., constr. שֶׁלֶת', suff. שַׁלְתּוֹ' (§ 42. rem. 5) . . . משל
הַמִּמְשָׁלִים pref. id. (noun masc., pl. of מִמְשָׁל d. 2 b. משל

[הָמַן] i. q. הָמָה *to make a noise, to rage*, Eze. 5. 7.

הָמָן ו' (*magnificent*, Gesen.) pr. name of a Persian at the court of Ahasuerus, who plotted the entire extirpation of the Jews, Est. 3. 1 seq.

הַמָּן[j] ו' pref. הַ (noun masc. sing. . . . מן
הֲמִן pref. הֲ (prep., with suff. מִמְּךָ, מִמֶּנִּי, מִנִּי &c. (§ 5 parad.) . . . . . מנן
הָמָן וְ pr. name masc. . . . . . . אמן
הַמְנָאֶפֶת[k] pref. הַ (Piel part. f., fr. מְנָאֵף m. [for מְנָאֶפֶת'] נאף
הַמְנַגֵּן[l] pref. id. (Piel part. sing. masc. . . . נגן
הַמְנַדִּים[m] pref. id. (Piel part. m., pl. of [מְנַדֶּה] d. 9 a. נדה
הַמָּנָה[n] pref. id. (noun fem. sing. dec. 11 a, pl. with suff. מְנוֹתֶיהָ (§ 42. rem. 2) . . . מנה
הַמָּנֶה[o] pref. id. (noun masc. sing. dec. 9 b. . . מנה
הֲמֹנֹה[p] n. m. s., suff. 3 pers. s. m. fr. הָמוֹן dec. 3 a. המה
הַמִּנְהָג[q] וְ pref. הַ (noun masc. sing. dec. 2 b. . נהג
הַמִּנְהָרוֹת[r] pref. id. (noun fem. pl. [of מִנְהָרָה] . נהר
הַמְּנוּחָה pref. id. (noun fem. sing. dec. 10. . . נוח
הַמְנוּכָא וְ Ch. Kh. הַמְנִיכָא, K. הַמְנוּכָא, noun masc. emph. of [הַמְנִיךְ or הַמְנוּךְ] Da. 5. 7, 16, 29.
הַמְּנוֹרָה pref. הַ (noun fem. sing. dec. 10. . . נור
הַמֻּנָּח[s] pref. id. (Hoph. part. masc. sing. . . נוח
הַמִּנְחָה ו' pref. id. (noun fem. sing. dec. 12 b. . מנח
[הַמְנִיךְ] Ch. see הַמְנוּכָא
הֲמֹנִים[t] noun masc. pl. of הָמוֹן dec. 3 a. . . המה
הֲמָנְכֶם[u] Kal inf., suff. 2 p. s. m. [fr. הָמַן § 32. r. 7] המן
הַמִּנְעוּל[v] pref. הַ (noun masc. sing. dec. 1 b. . נעל
הַמְּנַקִּיּוֹת[w] pref. id. (n. f. pl. [fr. מְנַקִּית comp. § 39. r. 1 note] נקה
הַמְּנֹרָה[x] ו' pref. id. (noun fem. sing. dec. 10. . נור
הַמְּנֹרוֹת pref. id. (id. pl. . . . . . נור
הַמְנַשֶּׁה pref. id. (pr. name of a tribe . . . נשה
הַמְנַשִּׁי ו' pref. id. (patronym. of the preceding . נשה

הָמַס Root not used; whence

הֲמָסִים Is. 64. 1, coll. with the Arab., according to Gesenius, after the Jewish commentators and Schultens, *brushwood*. Prof. Lee, *slight noises: As the kindling of fire* (excites) *slight noises*, &c. (?). Others, *melting*, מֶסֶם—הָמַס

הַמַּס, הַמַּס } pref. הַ (noun masc. sing. dec. 8 b, contr. from מֶכֶס . . . . } כסס
הִמָּס[y] Niph. inf. constr., used as an abs. . . מסס
הַמַּסְגֵּר[z] ו' pref. הַ (noun m. sing. (prop. Hiph. part.) סגר
הַמִּסְגְּרוֹת pref. id. (pl. of the following . . סגר
הַמִּסְגֶּרֶת pref. id. (noun fem. s. (suff. גַּרְתּוֹ') d. 13 a. סגר
הַמִּסְדְּרוֹנָה[aa] pref. id. (n. m. s. [מִסְדְּרוֹן] with loc. ה . סדר
הִמְסוּ[bb] Hiph. pret. 3 pers. pl. . . . . מסס

[a] 1 Sa. 10. 25.
[b] 1 Ki. 3. 7.
[c] 1 Sa. 8. 22.
[d] 1 Sa. 15. 11.
[e] 2 Ch. 1. 11.
[f] 2 Ch. 1. 9.
[g] 2 Ch. 1. 8.
[h] Da. 1. 11, 16.
[i] Ju. 7. 6, 7.
[k] 2 Ki. 10. 22.
[l] Is. 28. 28.
[m] De. 7. 23.
[n] 2 Ki. 11. 2.
[o] Eze. 7. 13.
[p] Is. 65. 11.
[q] 2 Sa. 19. 6.
[r] Eze. 17. 16.
[s] Je. 25. 26.
[t] 2 Ch. 15. 6.
[u] 1 Ki. 20. 33.
[x] Je. 51. 34.
[y] Je. 32. 27.
[z] Nu. 11. 32.
[a] Ex. 16. 17, 18.
[b] Mi. 4. 8.
[c] 1 Ch. 26. 6.
[d] Nu. 11. 7.
[e] Eze. 16. 32.
[f] 2 Ki. 3. 15.
[g] Am. 6. 3.
[h] 1 Sa. 9. 23.
[i] Eze. 45. 12.
[k] 2 Ki. 9. 20.
[l] Ju. 6. 2.
[m] Joel 4. 14.
[n] Eze. 5. 7.
[o] Ca. 5. 5.
[p] Nu. 4. 7; Je. 52. 19.
[q] Nu. 3. 31.
[qq] Eze. 29. 19.
[r] 2 Sa. 17. 10.
[s] Je. 24. 1.
[t] Ju. 3. 23.
[u] De. 1. 28.
[uu] Eze. 41. 11.

הַמַּסְוֶה[a] pref. הַ)(noun masc. sing. . . . . סוה

הַמַּסּוֹת[b] pref. id.)(noun fem., pl. of מַסָּה dec. 10. נסה

הִמְסִיו[c] Hiph. pret. 3 pers. pl., [by Chaldaism for הִמְסוּ § 24. rem. 17] . . . מסה

הֲמָסִים[d] noun masc. pl. [of הֶמֶס] dec. 6. . . . המס

הַמָּסָךְ וְ'[e] pref. הַ)(noun masc. sing. (constr. מְסַךְ § 37. rem. 4) . . . . . סכך

הַמַּסֵּכָה[f] וְ' prf. id.)(noun fem. sing. dec. 10. . נסך

הַמַּסֵּכוֹת[g] וְ pref. id.)(pl. of the preceding . נסך

הַמְסֻכָּן[h] pref. id.)(Pual part. sing. masc. . . סכן

הַמִּסְכֵּן[i] pref. id.)(noun masc. sing. . . סכן

הַמִּסְכְּנוֹת pref. id.)(noun fem. pl. fr. [מִסְכְּנֶת'] dec. 13. סכן

הַמַּסֶּכֶת[k] pref. id.)(n. f. s. [for מַסֶּכֶת' comp. § 35. r. 2] נסך

הַמְסֻלָּאִים[l] pref. id.)(Pual part. masc. pl. [of מְסֻלָּא] סלא

הַמְסִלָּה pref. id.)(noun fem. sing. dec. 10. . סלל

הַמְסִלּוֹת[m] pref. id.)(pl. of the preceding . . סלל

הַמִּסְפֵּד pref. id.)(noun masc. sing. d. 7c. (§ 36. r. 1) ספד

הַמִּסְפָּחוֹת[n] pref. id.)(noun fem., pl. of [מִסְפָּחָה'] d. 11a. ספח

הַמִּסְפַּחַת[o] pref. id.)(noun masc. sing. . . ספח

הַמִּסְפָּר[p] pref. id.)(noun masc. sing. dec. 2b. . . ספר

הַמַּסֹּת[q] pref. id.)(noun fem., pl. of מַסָּה dec. 10. נסה

הַמַּסְתִּיר[r] pref. id.)(Hiph. part. sing. masc. . סתר

הַמַּעְבָּרוֹת[s] וְ pref. id.)(n. f. pl. abs. fr. [מַעְבָּרָה'] d. 11a. עבר

הַמַּעְבְּרוֹת pref. id.)(n. f. pl. abs. fr. [מַעְבֶּרֶת'] d. 13. עבר

הַמַּעְגָּלָה[t] pref. id.)(noun fem. sing. dec. 11a. . עגל

הַמְעֵד[u] Hiph. imp. sing. m. (with gutt. for הַמְעֵד) מעד

הַמָּעוֹז pref. הַ)(for מָעֹז', noun masc. sing. dec. 8c. (suff. מָעֻזִּי' § 37. rem. 4) . . . עזז

הַמְּעוּנִים וְ pref. id.)(gent. noun pl., see מָעוֹן . עון

הַמְעַט pref. הַ art. & interr.)(subst., adj. & adv.; pl. מְעַטִּים . . . . . מעט

הַמַּעֲטִירָה[v] pref. הַ art.)(Hiph. part. sing. fem. . עטר

הַמַּעֲטָפוֹת[w] וְ pref. id.)(noun fem., pl. [of מַעֲטָפָה'] עטף

הַמְעַטְּרֵכִי[x] pref. id.)(Piel part. sing. masc. suff. 2 pers. sing. fem. (§ 2. rem. 2) . . . . עטר

הִמְעַטְתִּים[a] וְ Hiph. pret. 1 pers. s., suff. 3 pers. pl. m. מעט

הִמְעִיטָה[b] וְ id. pret. 3 pers. sing. fem. . . . . מעט

הַמְּעִיל pref. הַ)(noun masc. sing. dec. 1a. . מעל

הַמַּעְיָנוֹת[c] pref. id.)(noun m. pl. abs. fr. מַעְיָן dec. 2b. עין

הַמְּעִינִים[d] pref. id.)(Kh. מְעִי', K. מְעוּ', noun masc. pl. of מָעִין or מָעוֹן dec. 3a. . . עון

הַמַּעֲכָתִי וְ' pref. id.)(gent. noun fr. מַעֲכָה מעך

הַמַּעַל[e] pref. id.)(noun masc. sing. dec. 6d. . . מעל

הַמַּעֲלָה pref. id.)(noun fem. sing. dec. 10. . עלה

הַמַּעֲלֶה pref. id.)(Hiph. part. sing. masc. dec. 9a. עלה

הַמַּעֲלוֹת pref. id.)(noun fem., pl. of מַעֲלָה dec. 10. ה

הַמַּעַלְךָ pref. id.)(Hiph. part. sing. masc. (מַעֲלֶה), suff. 2 pers. sing. masc. dec. 9a. . . ה

הַמַּעֲלָם[f] pref. id.)(id. with (verbal) suff. 3 pers. pl. m. ה

הַמַּעֲמִיקִים[g] pref. id.)(Hiph. part. m., pl. [מַעֲמִיק] d. 1b. ק

הֲמֵעִמָּךְ[h] preff. הֲ, & f. מִ· מֵ)(prep. (עִם) with suff. 2 pers. sing. masc. . . . . ם

הַמְעֻנָּגָה[i] וְ pref. הַ)(Pual part. sing. fem. . .

הַמַּעֲרָב[k] pref. id.)(noun masc. sing. . . . ב

הַמְּעָרָה וְ' pref. id.)(noun fem. sing. dec. 10. .

הַמְּעָרוֹת[l] pref. id.)(pl. of the preceding . .

הַמַּעֲרָכָה pref. id.)(noun fem. sing. dec. 11a. . ך

הַמַּעֲרֶכֶת
הַמַּעֲרָכֶת } pref. id.)(noun fem. sing., see מַעֲרָכָה ך

הַמְעָרַת[m] pref. הַ interr. for הֲ)(noun fem. sing., constr. of מְעָרָה dec. 10. . . . . . ר

הַמַּעֲשֶׂה pref. הַ art.)(noun masc. sing. dec. 9a. . ה

הַמַּעֲשִׂים pref. id.)(id. pl., absolute state . ה

הַמְעֻשָּׁקָה[n] pref. id.)(Pual part. sing. fem. . . ק

הַמַּעֲשֵׂר וְ'[o] pref. id.)(noun m. s. d. 7c. (§ 36. r. 1) ר

הַמְעַשְּׂרִים[p] pref. id.)(Piel part. m., pl. of [מְעַשֵּׂר] d. 7b. ר

הַמַּעְתִּיק[q] pref. id.)(Hiph. part. sing. masc. . ק

הַמִּפְקָד pref. id.)(pr. name of a gate . . ד

הַמֻּפְקָדִים pref. id.)(Hoph. part. masc., pl. of [מֻפְקָד] ד

הַמִּפְשָׂעָה[r] pref. id.)(noun fem. sing. . . . ע

הַמַּפְתֵּחַ pref. id.)(n. m. s. constr. מַפְתֵּחַ (§ 36. r. 1) ח

הַמֹּפְתִים וְ' pref. id.)(noun masc., pl. of מוֹפֵת d. 7b.

הַמִּפְתָּן pref. id.)(noun masc. sing. dec. 2b.

הַמֵּץ[s] pref. id.)(Kal part. act. sing. m. (§ 21. r. 2)

הִמָּצֵא[t] Niph. inf. used as an absolute . א

הַמֹּצְאוֹת[u] pref. הַ)(Kal part. act. fem., pl. of מֹצֵאת [for מֹצֶאת § 23. rem. 4] . . . א

הַמֹּצְאִים[x] pref. id.)(id. m., pl. of מוֹצֵא (§ 23. rem. 9) א

הַמְצָאתַנִי[y] pref. הַ interr. for הֲ)(Kal pret. 2 pers. sing. masc., suff. 1 pers. sing. . . א

הַמַּצָּב[z] pref. הַ art.)(noun masc. sing. (suff. מַצָּבְךָ' § 31. rem. 5) . . .

הַמַּצְבִּא pref. id.)(Hiph. part. sing. m. [for מַצְבִּיא] א

הַמַּצָּבָה[a] pref. id.)(noun fem. sing. . . .

הַמַּצֵּבָה[b] pref. id.)(noun fem. sing. dec. 11b. (constr. מַצֶּבֶת, suff. מַצַּבְתָּהּ dec. 13a, § 42. rem. 5)

הַמַּצֵּבוֹת pref. id.)(id. pl., absolute state

הַמִּצְבָיָה pref. id.)(pr. name of a place, see מְצֹבָיָה

הַמַּצֵּבֹת pref. id.)(noun fem., pl. of מַצֵּבָה (q. v.)

הַמְּצָדוֹת[c] וְ"[d] pref. id.)(noun masc. with pl. fem. term. fr. מְצָד dec. 1a. . . .

[a] Ex. 34. 34, 35. [b] De. 29. 2. [c] Jos. 14. 8. [d] Is. 64. 1. [e] Nu. 3. 31. [f] Ju. 18. 17, 18. [g] 2 Ch. 34. 3, 4. [h] Is. 40. 20. [i] Ec. 9. 15, 16. [k] Ju. 16. 13, 14. [l] La. 4. 2. [m] Ju. 20. 32. [n] Eze. 13. 18. [o] Le. 13. 7, 8. [p] 1 Ch. 27. 24. [q] De. 7. 19. [r] Is. 8. 17. [s] Je. 51. 32. [t] 1 Sa. 17. 20. [u] Ps. 69. 24. [x] Is. 23. 8. [y] Is. 3. 22. [z] Ps. 103. 4. [a] Eze. 29. 15. [b] Le. 26. 22. [c] 2 Ch. 32. 4. [d] 1 Ch. 4. 41. [e] Jos. 22. 16, 31. [f] Is. 63. 11. [g] Is. 29. 15. [h] Job 34. 33. [i] Je. 6. 2. [k] Da. 8. 5. [l] Ju. 6. 2. [m] Je. 7. 11. [n] Is. 23. 12. [o] 2 Ch. 31. 12. [p] Ne. 10. 38. [q] Job 9. 5. [r] 1 Ch. 19. 4. [s] Is. 16. 4. [t] Ex. 22. 3. [u] Jos. 2. 23. [x] Nu. 15. 33. [y] 1 Ki. 21. 20. [z] 1 Sa. 14. [a] 1 Sa. 14. [b] Ge. 31. 51 [c] Ju. 6. 2. [d] Je. 48. 41.

הַמַּצָּה	וְ pref. הַ)(pr. name of a place . .	יצא
הַמְּצוּדָה	pref. id.)(noun fem. sing. dec. 10. .	צוד
הַמִּצְוָה	וְ pref. id.)(noun fem. sing. dec. 10. .	צוה
הַמָּצוֹר [a]	pref. id.)(noun masc. sing. dec. 3a. (with suff. מְצוֹרֵךְ § 32. rem. 5) . .	צור
הַמְּצוּרוֹת [b]	pref. id.)(noun fem., pl. of מְצוּרָה dec. 10.	צור
הַמְּצוֹרָע [c]	pref. id.)(Pual part. masc. sing. .	צרע
הַמַּצּוֹת	pref. id.)(noun fem., pl. of מַצָּה dec. 10.	מצץ
הַמִּצְוֹת	pref. id.)(noun fem., pl. of מִצְוָה dec. 10.	צוה
הִמְצִיאוּ [u]	Hiph. pret. 3 pers. pl.	מצא
הַמַּצִּיל [d]	pref. הַ)(Hiph. part. sing. masc. .	נצל
הַמֵּצִיק [e]	pref. id.)(Hiph. part. sing. masc. dec. 3b.	צוק
הַמְּצִיקִים [f]	וְ pref. id.)(id. pl., absolute state . .	צוק
הִמְצִיתִךְ [g]	Hiph. pret. 1 pers. sing., suff. 2 pers. sing. masc. [for הִמְצֵאתִיךָ § 23. rem. 11] .	מצא
הַמַּצְמִיחַ [h]	pref. הַ)(Hiph. part. sing. masc. . .	צמח
הַמִּצְנֶפֶת / הַמִּצְנֶפֶת	pref. הַ art.)(noun fem. s. (comp. § 35. r. 2)	צנף
הַמַּצָּע [yy]	pref. id.)(noun masc. sing. (comp. § 20. r. 16)	יצע
הַמְצַפֶּה [i]	pref. id.)(Piel part. sing. masc. dec. 9a.	צפה
הַמִּצְפָּה	וְ pref. id.)(pr. name of a place . .	צפה
הַמִּצְפֶּה [k]	וְ pref. id.)(n. m. s., also pr. name of a place	צפה
הַמְצַפְצְפִים [l]	pref. id.)(Pilpel (§ 6. No. 4) part. m., pl. of מְצַפְצֵף dec. 7b.	צפף
הַמִּצְפָּתָה	pref. id.)(pr. name of a place (מִצְפָּה) with parag. ה	צפה
הַמֵּצַר [m]	pref. id.)(n. m. s. (pl. מְצָרִים, dec. 8. § 37. r. 7)	צרר
הַמְּצֻרוֹת	pref. id.)(noun fem., pl. of מְצוּרָה dec. 10.	צור
הַמְּצָרִים [n]	pref. id.)(noun m. pl. of מֵצַר d. 8. (§ 37. r. 7)	צרר
הַמִּצְרִים	pref. id.)(gent. noun, pl. of מִצְרִי, fr. מִצְרַיִם	מצר
הַמִּצְרִית	pref. id.)(id. fem.	מצר
הַמִּצְרִיֹּת	pref. id.)(id. pl. fem. (§ 39. No. 4. r. 1 note)	מצר
הַמְּצֹרָע [o]	pref. id.)(Pual part. sing. masc. . .	צרע
הַמְּצֹרָעִים [p]	pref. id.)(id. pl., absolute state . .	צרע
הָמֵק [q]	Hiph. inf. absolute	מקק
הַמְקַבְּרִים [r]	pref. הַ)(Piel part. masc., pl. of מְקַבֵּר d. 7b.	קבר
הַמַּקֶּבֶת [s]	pref. id.)(noun fem. sing. . . .	נקב
הַמַּקְדִּישׁ	pref. id.)(Hiph. part. sing. masc. dec. 1b.	קדש
הַמִּקְדָּשׁ	pref. id.)(noun masc. sing. dec. 2b. .	קדש
הַמְקֻדָּשׁ [t]	pref. id.)(Pual part. masc. sing. dec. 2b.	קדש
הַמִּקְדָּשִׁים	pref. id.)(id. pl., absolute state .	קדש
הַמָּקוֹם	pref. id.)(noun com. sing. dec. 3a. . .	קום
הַמְּקוֹמוֹת, הַמְּקֹמֹת	pref. id.)(pl. of the preceding .	קום
הַמַּקָּחוֹת [u]	pref. id.)(n. f. pl. [of מַקָּחָה, comp. § 17. r. 8]	לקח
הַמַּקְטִירִים [x]	pref. id.)(Hiph. part. pl. masc. .	קטר
הַמְקַטְּרוֹת [y]	pref. id.)(Piel part. f., pl. of [מְקַטֶּרֶת] d. 13a.	קטר
הַמְקַטְּרִים	pref. id.)(Piel part. m., pl. of [מְקַטֵּר] d. 7b.	קטר
הַמַּקְלוֹת [z]	pref. id.)(noun masc. with pl. fem. term. from מַקֵּל dec. 7b (§ 36. rem. 1) .	מקל
הַמִּקְלָט	pref. id.)(noun masc. sing. dec. 2b. .	קלט
הַמְקַלֵּל [a]	pref. id.)(Piel part. sing. masc. dec. 7b. .	קלל
הַמְּקֹמוֹת [b]	וְ noun com., pl. of מָקוֹם dec. 3a. .	קום
הַמְקַנֵּא [c]	pref. interr. for הֲ)(Piel part. sing. masc.	קנא
הַמַּקְנֶה [d]	pref. הַ art.)(Hiph. part. masc. sing. [for מַקְנִיא § 23. rem. 11] . . .	קנא
הַמִּקְנָה [e]	pref. id.)(noun fem. sing. dec. 10. .	קנה
הַמִּקְנֶה	pref. id.)(noun masc. sing. dec. 7b. .	קנה
הַמִּקְצוֹעַ / הַמִּקְצֹעַ [f]	pref. id.)(noun masc. sing. dec. 1b. .	קצע
הַמִּקְצֹעֹת	pref. id.)(pl. of the preceding .	קצע
הַמְּקֵרָה [g]	pref. id.)(noun fem. sing. . .	קרר
הַמְקָרֶה [h]	pref. id.)(Piel part. sing. masc., or (Ec. 10. 18) subst. [for מְקָרֶה] . . .	קרה
הַמַּקְרִיב	pref. id.)(Hiph. part. masc. sing. dec. 1b. .	קרב
הַמְקֻשָּׁרוֹת [i]	pref. id.)(Pual part. fem. pl. [of מְקֻשָּׁרָה]	קשר

הָמַר Root not used; Arab. *to flow, stream.* מַהֲמֹרוֹת pl. fem. *streams, floods,* Ps. 140. 11.

הַמַּר [k]	pref. הַ)(adj. masc. sing. dec. 8 (§ 37. rem. 7)	מרר
הָמֵר [l]	וְ [m] Hiph. inf. absolute . .	מור or מרר
הַמֹּר	pref. הַ)(noun masc. sing. dec. 1a. .	מרר
הֵמַר	Hiph. pret. 3 pers. sing. masc. (§ 18. rem. 10)	מרר
הַמַּרְאָה	pref. הַ)(noun fem. sing. dec. 10. .	ראה
הַמַּרְאֶה	pref. id.)(noun masc. sing. dec. 9a. .	ראה
הַמַּרְבֶּה	pref. id.)(Hiph. part. sing. masc. dec. 9a.	רבה
הַמַּרְגִּיז [n]	pref. id.)(Hiph. part. sing. masc. dec. 1b. .	רגז
הַמֹּרִגִּים [o]	וְ pref. id.)(noun masc. pl. of מוֹרַג dec. 8e.	מרג
הַמְרַגְּלִים [p]	pref. id.)(Piel part. m., pl. of [מְרַגֵּל] dec. 7b.	רגל
הַמַּרְגֵּעָה [q]	pref. id.)(noun fem. sing. . . .	רגע
הַמַּרְדּוּת [r]	pref. id.)(noun fem. sing. . .	מרד
הַמֹּרְדִים [s]	pref. id.)(Kal part. act. masc., pl. of [מוֹרֵד] dec. 7b.	מרד
הִמְרוּ	Hiph. pret. 3 pers. pl. . . .	מרה
הַמָּרוֹם [t]	pref. הַ)(noun masc. sing. dec. 3a. .	רום
הַמֵּרוֹץ [u]	pref. id.)(noun masc. sing. . .	רוץ
הַמְּרוּצָה [x]	pref. id.)(noun fem. sing. [for מְרֻצָה]	רצץ
הַמֶּרְחָק	pref. id.)(noun masc. sing., pl. חַקִּים' dec. 8a (and pr. name in compos. see בֵּית)	רחק
הַמֶּרִי	pref. id.)(noun masc. sing. dec. 6i (for מֶרְיִ § 35. rem. 14) . . .	מרה
הַמֹּרִיָּה	pref. id.)(pr. name of a hill, see מֹרִיָּה	
הַמָּרִים [y]	pref. id.)(adj. m., pl. of מַר dec. 8e (§ 37. r. 7)	מרר

[a] Eze. 5. 2. [b] 2 Ch. 11. 11. [c] 2 Ki. 5. 11. [d] Ju. 8. 34. [e] Is. 51. 13, 13. [f] Is. 29. 7. [g] 2 Sa. 3. 8. [h] Ps. 147. 8. [i] Is. 21. 6. [k] 2 Ch. 20. 24. [l] Is. 8. 19. [m] Ps. 118. 5. [n] La. 1. 3. [o] Le. 14. 2. [p] 2 Ki. 7. 8. [q] Zec. 14. 12. [r] Eze. 39. 15. [s] Ju. 4. 21. [t] Eze. 48. 11. [u] Ne. 10. 32. [x] 1 Ki. 13. 2. [y] 2 Ch. 30. 14. [z] Ge. 30. 37, 38, 39, 41.

[a] Le. 24. 14, 23. [b] 2 Ch. 33. 19. [c] Nu. 11. 29. [d] Eze. 8. 3. [e] Je. 32. 11, 12, 14, 16. [f] Ne. 3. 19, 20. [g] Ju. 3. 20, 24. [h] Ps. 104. 3. [i] Ge. 30. 41. [k] Hab. 1. 6. [l] Le. 27. 10, 33. [m] Zec. 12. 10. [n] Job 9. 6. [o] 2 Sa. 24. 22. [p] Jos. 6. 22, 23. [q] Is. 28. 12. [r] 1 Sa. 20. 30. [s] Eze. 20. 38. [t] Is. 24. 21. [u] Le. 9. 13. [u] Ec. 9. 11. [x] Je. 22. 17. [y] Nu. 5. 18, 19, 23, 24. [yy] Is. 28. 20.

הַמֹּרִיב pref. הַ)(Kal part. act. masc., pl. of מֹרֶה dec. 9a. . . . . . . מרה
הַמְּרִיק pref. id.)(Hiph. part. masc., pl. of [מֵרִיק] dec. 3b. . . . . . . רוק
הַמֶּרְכָּב pref. id.)(noun masc. sing. dec. 2b. . . רכב
הַמֶּרְכָּבָה pref. id.)(noun fem. sing. dec. 11a (constr. ׳כֶּבֶת, suff. ׳כַּבְתּוֹ 13a (§ 42. rem. 5) . רכב
הַמַּרְכָּבוֹת pref. id.)(pr. name, in compos. ׳בֵּית הַמַּרְ בית
הַמֵּרֹנֹתִי pref. id.)(gent. noun, see מֵרֹנֹתִי
הַמַּרְעֶה pref. id.)(noun masc. sing. dec. 9a. . רעה
הַמְרַצֵּחַ pref. id.)(Piel part. sing. masc. dec. 7b. . רצח
הַמַּרְצֵעַ pref. id.)(noun masc. sing. . . . רצע
הַמָּרָק [h]וְ׳ pref. id.)(noun masc. sing. dec. 4a. . מרק
הַמֶּרְקָחָה pref. id.)(noun fem. sing. . . . . רקח
הַמִּרְקַחַת pref. id.)(noun fem. sing. . . . . רקח
הַמְּרָרִי pref. id.)(patronym. [for ׳מְרָרִי] from מְרָרִי מרר
הַמִּרְשַׁעַת pref. id.)(noun fem. sing. . . . . רשע
הַמֹּרַשְׁתִּי pref. id.)(gent. noun from מוֹרֶשֶׁת גַּת (q. v.) ירש
הַמַּשָּׂא pref. id.)(noun masc. sing. dec. 1b. . נשא
הַמַּשְׂאֵת וְ pref. id.)(noun fem. sing. [for ׳שֶׂאֶת] constr. מַשְׂאַת, pl. מַשְׂאוֹת . . . נשא
הַמַּשְׁבִּיעַ pref. id.)(Hiph. part. sing. masc. . . שבע
הַמַּשְׁבִּיר pref. id.)(Hiph. part. sing. masc. . . שבר
הַמִּשְׁבְּצוֹת / הַמִּשְׁבְּצִים pref. id.)(noun fem., pl. of [׳בֶּצֶת] dec. 13a. . . . . . שבץ
הַמִּשְׂגָּב pref. id.)(noun masc. sing., constr. ׳גַּב, suff. ׳גַּבִּי dec. 8a. . . . . . שגב
הַמְשֻׁגָּע pref. id.)(Pual part. sing. masc. . . שגע
הַמַּשּׁוֹר pref. id.)(noun masc. sing. . . . נשר
הַמְשׁוֹרֵר pref. id.)(Pilel part. sing. masc. dec. 7b. . שיר
הַמְשֹׁרְרִים וְ pref. id.)(id. pl., absolute state . שיר
הִמָּשַׁח Niph. inf. constr. . . . . . משח
הַמִּשְׁחָה pref. הַ)(noun fem. sing. (no pl.) . משח
הַמְּשֻׁחִים pref. id.)(Kal part. p. m., pl. of מָשׁוּחַ dec. 3a. משח
הֶמַּשְׁחִית pref. הֶ)(Hiph. part. sing. masc. dec. 1b. שחת
הַמַּשְׁחִית [a]וְ׳ pref. הַ)(Hiph. part. & subst. m. s. dec. 1b. שחת
הַמַּשְׁחִיתִים pref. id.)(id. pl., absolute state . . שחת
הַמְשַׂחֲקוֹת pref. id.)(Piel (§ 14. rem. 1) part. fem., pl. of מְשַׂחֶקֶת dec. 13a. . . . . . שחק
הַמָּשִׁיחַ pref. id.)(noun masc. sing. dec. 3a. . משח
הִמְשִׁילָם וְ Hiph. pret. 3 pers. s. m., suff. 3 pers. pl. m. משל
הַמִּשְׁכָּב pref. הַ)(noun masc. sing. dec. 2b. . שכב
הַמַּשְׂכִּיל pref. id.)(Hiph. part. sing. masc. dec. 1b. . שכל
הַמַּשְׂכִּילִים [f]וְ׳ pref. id.)(id. pl., absolute state . שכל
הַמִּשְׁכָּן pref. id.)(noun masc. sing. dec. 2b. . שכן
הַמָּשָׁל pref. id.)(noun masc. sing. dec. 4a. . משל

הַמְשֵׁל[g] Hiph. inf. absolute . . . . משל
הַמְשֹׁל[h] pref. הַ interr. for הֲ)(Kal inf. constr. . משל
הַמֹּשֵׁל[i] pref. הַ art.)(Kal part. act. sing. m. dec. 7b. משל
הַמְשַׁלֵּחַ[k] [l]וְ׳ pref. id.)(Piel part. sing. masc. dec. 7b. שלח
הַמְשַׁלְּחִים[m] pref. id.)(id. pl., absolute state . . שלח
הַמֹּשְׁלִים[n] pref. id.)(Kal part. act. m., pl. of מֹשֵׁל d. 7b. משל
הַמְשֻׁלָּשׁ[o] pref. id.)(Pual part. sing. masc. . . שלש
הַמְשַׂמֵּחַ[p] pref. id.)(Piel part. sing. masc. dec. 7b. שמח
הַמִּשְׁמָר pref. id.)(noun masc. sing. dec. 2b. . שמר
הַמִּשְׁנֶה pref. id.)(noun masc. sing. dec. 9a. . שנה
הַמִּשְׁנִים[q] [r]וְ׳ pref. id.)(id. pl., absolute state . . שנה
הַמִּשְׁעֶנֶת pref. id.)(noun fem. sing. dec. 13a. . שען
הַמִּשְׁפָּחָה [s]וְ׳ pref. id.)(noun fem. sing. dec. 11a (constr. ׳פַּחַת, suff. ׳פַּחְתּוֹ, 13a, § 42. r. 5) שפח
הַמִּשְׁפָּחוֹת pref. id.)(id. pl., absolute state . . שפח
הַמִּשְׁפָּט pref. id.)(noun masc. sing. dec. 2b. . שפט
הַמִּשְׁפָּטִים וְ׳ pref. id.)(id. pl., absolute state . שפט
הַמַּשְׁפִּילִי[t] pref. id.)(Hiph. part. sing. masc. with paragogic י (compare § 8. rem. 19) . . שפל
הַמִּשְׁפְּתַיִם[u] / הַמִּשְׁפְּתָיִם[x] pref. id.)(noun masc., du. of [מִשְׁפָּת] dec. 2b. . . . . שפת
הַמַּשְׁקֶה[y] pref. id.)(Hiph. part. sing. masc. dec. 9a. . שקה
הַמַּשְׁקוֹף[z] pref. id.)(noun masc. sing. . . שקף
הַמַּשְׁקִים pref. id.)(Hiph. part. m., pl. of ׳קֶה dec. 9a. שקה
הַמִּשְׁקָל[a] pref. id.)(noun masc. sing. dec. 2b. . שקל
הַמִּשְׂרָה[b] pref. id.)(noun fem. sing. . . . שרה
הַמִּשְׁרָעִי וְ pref. id.)(gent. noun see מִשְׁרָעִי
הַמְשֹׁרְרִים וְ׳ pref. id.)(Pilel part. m., pl. מְשׁוֹרֵר dec. 1b. שיר
הַמְשָׁרֵת[c] pref. id.)(noun masc. sing. . . . שרת
הַמְשָׁרְתִים [d]וְ׳ pref. id.)(Piel part. masc., pl. of מְשָׁרֵת dec. 7b. . . . . . . שרת
הַמִּשְׁתֶּה pref. id.)(noun masc. sing. dec. 9a. . . שתה
הַמִּשְׁתַּחֲוִים pref. id.)(Hithpalel (§ 24. rem. 25) part. masc., pl. of ׳וֶה dec. 9a. . . שחה
הַמִּשְׁתַּכֵּר[e] וְ pref. הַ)(Hithp. part. sing. masc. [for מִתְשַׁכֵּר § 12. rem. 3] . . . שכר
הָמֵת וְ׳ Hiph. inf. absolute . . . . מות
הַמֵּת וְ׳ pref. הַ)(Kal part. s. m. dec. 1a (§ 21. r. 2) מות
הֲמֵת[f] pref. הֲ)(id. pret. 3 pers. sing. masc. . מות
הַמִּתְאַבְּלִים[g] pref. הַ)(Hithpa. part. m., pl. of ׳בֵּל d. 7b. אבל
הַמִּתְאַוִּים pref. id.)(Hithpa. part. m., pl. of ׳וֶּה d. 9a. אוה
הַמְתֹאָר[h] pref. id.)(Pual part. sing. masc. . . תאר
הַמִּתְבָּרֵךְ[i] pref. id.)(Hithpa. part. sing. masc. . . ברך
הַמֵּתָה[k] pref. id.)(Kal part. s. f., from מֵת m. (§ 21. r. 2) מות
הֵמַתָּה וְ Hiph. pret. 2 p. s. m. [for ׳הֵמַתְּ § 21. r. 13] מות
הֱמִתֻהוּ[l] id. pret. 3 pers. pl. (הֵמִיתוּ) suff. 3 p. s. m. מות

[?]u. 20. 10. [?]ec. 4. 12. [?]e. 15. 9. [?]ze. 34. 18. [?]Ki. 6. 32. [?]e. 15. 17. [?]u. 6. 20.
[h] Ju. 6. 19. [i] Eze. 24. 10. [k] 1 Ch. 9. 30. [l] 2 Ch. 24. 7. [m] Ju. 20. 40. [n] Ps. 103. 5. [o] Ge. 42. 6.
[p] Ex. 28. 25. [q] Ex. 28. 14. [r] Je. 48. 1. [s] 2 Ki. 9. 11. [t] Is. 10. 15. [u] 1 Ch. 6. 18. [x] 2 Ch. 23. 13.
[y] Nu. 3. 3. [z] Eze. 9. 8. [a] 1 Sa. 14. 15. [b] 1 Sa. 6. 5. [c] 1 Sa. 18. 7. [d] Da. 11. 39.
[e] Am. 5. 13. [f] Da. 12. 3, 10. [g] Job 25. 2. [h] Ju. 9. 2. [i] Ge. 24. 2; Eze. 16. 44. [k] Ps. 104. 10.
[l] Le. 16. 26. [m] 2 Ch. 32. 31. [n] Nu. 21. 27. [o] Ec. 4. 12. [p] Ju. 9. 13. [q] 1 Ch. 15. 18.
[r] 1 Sa. 15. 9. [s] Jos. 7. 14. [t] Ps. 113. 6. [u] Ge. 49. 14. [x] Ju. 5. 16. [y] Ge. 40. 5.
[z] Ex. 12. 7, 22, 23. [a] Ezr. 8. 34. [b] Is. 9. 5, 6. [c] 2 Sa. 13. 9. [d] 2 Ch. 23. 6. [e] Hag. 1. 6.
[f] 2 Sa. 12. 19. [g] Is. 66. 10. [h] Jos. 19. 13. [i] Is. 65. 16. [k] Zec. 11. 9. [l] Je. 26. 19.

הַמִּתְהַלְּכִים[a] pref. הַ ⟩ Hithpa. part. m., pl. of 'הַלֵּךְ d. 7 b. הלך

הַמִּתְהַלֵּל[b] pref. id. ⟩ Hithpa. part. sing. masc. dec. 7 b. הלל

הַמִּתְהַלְלִים[c] pref. id. ⟩ id. pl., absolute state (§ 10. r. 7) הלל

הַמִּתְהַפֶּכֶת[d] pref. id. ⟩ Hithpa. part. s. f., fr. מִתְהַפֵּךְ m. הפך

הֻמְתוּ[e] Hoph. pret. 3 pers. pl. [for הוּמְתוּ] . מות

הַמִּתְחַבְּאִים[f] pref. הַ ⟩ Hithpa. part. m., pl. of 'חַבֵּא d. 7 b. חבא

הַמִּתְחַזְּקִים[g] pref. id. ⟩ Hithpa. part. masc., pl. 'חַזֵּק dec. 7 b. (§ 10. rem. 7) . . . חזק

הֵמַתִּי וְ Hiph. pret. 1 p. s. [for 'הֵמַתְתִּי § 21. r. 13]; acc. shifted by conv. וְ (comp. § 8. rem. 7) מות

הַמֹּתִי[h] וְ Kal pret. 1 pers. sing. acc. shifted (v. id.) המם

הֲמִתִּיהָ[i] וַ Hiph. pret. 1 pers. s., suff. 3 pers. s. fem. [for הֲמִתִּיהָ § 21. rem. 13]; וַ for וְ conv. מות

הַמִּתְיַחְשִׂים[k]
הַמִּתְיַחֲשִׂים[l] } pref. הַ ⟩ Hithpa. (§ 14. rem. 1) part. masc., pl. of ['יַחֵשׂ] dec. 7 b. . } יחש

הַמֵּתִים וְ[m] pref. id. ⟩ Kal part. m., pl. of מֵת d. 1 a (§ 21. rem. 2) . . . . . מות

הַמְתֻכָּן[n] pref. id. ⟩ Pual part. sing. masc. . . תכן

הֲמִתֶּם[o] וַ[p] Hiph. pret. 2 pers. pl. masc. [for 'הֲמִיתֹתֶם § 21. rem. 13]; וַ for וְ conv. . . מות

הֲמִתֶּן[q] וַ id. pret. 2 p. pl. f. [for הֲמִיתֹתֶן § 21. r. 13]; וַ id. מות

הַמִּתְנַבֵּא[r] pref. הַ ⟩ Hithpa. part. sing. masc. dec. 7 b. נבא

הַמִּתְנַבְּאוֹת[s] pref. id. ⟩ id. fem. pl. of ['בֵּאת='בְּאֶת] נבא

הַמִּתְנַדֵּב[t] pref. id. ⟩ Hithpa. part. sing. masc. dec. 7 b. נדב

הַמִּתְנַדְּבִים pref. id. ⟩ id. pl., absolute state . נדב

הַמִּתְנִי pref. id. ⟩ gent. noun . . . . מתן

הֱמִיתָנִי[u] וַ Hiph. pret. 3 pers. sing. masc. [הֵמִית], suff. 1 pers. sing. (§ 2. r. 1); וַ for וְ conv. מות

הַמִּתְנַשֵּׂא[x] וְ pref. הַ ⟩ Hithpa. part. sing. masc. . נשא

הַמְתַעֲבִים[y] pref. id. ⟩ Piel (§ 14. rem. 1) part. masc., pl. of 'מְתַעֵב dec. 7 b. . . . . תעב

הַמַּתְעִים[z] pref. id. ⟩ Hiph. part. masc., pl. of מַתְעֶה d. 9 a. תעה

הַמִּתְפָּרְצִים[a] pref. id. ⟩ Hithpa. part. m., pl. of ['פָּרֵץ] d. 7 b. פרץ

הַמִּתְקַדְּשִׁים[b] pref. id. ⟩ Hithpa. part. m., pl. of ['קַדֵּשׁ] d. 7 b. קדש

הַמִּתְקַשְּׁרִים[c] pref. id. ⟩ Hithpa. part. m., pl. of ['קַשֵּׁר] d. 7 b. קשר

הֵן, הֶן־, 'וְ—I. interj. *behold! lo!*—II. *whether*, of an indirect inquiry, Je. 2. 10.—III. *if*.

הֵן Ch.—I. *lo! surely*, Da. 3. 17.—II. *whether*, Ezr. 5. 17.—III. *if*; הֵן—הֵן *whether—or*, Ezr. 7. 26.

הֵנָּה adv. of place.—I. *hither*; הֵנָּה וָהֵנָּה *hither and thither*; מִמְּךָ וָהֵנָּה *from thee and hither*, i. e. on this side of thee; עַד־הֵנָּה *hitherto*, also spoken of time.—II. *here, in this place*, Ge. 21. 29; הֵנָּה וָהֵנָּה *here—there*, Da. 12. 5; הֵנָּה—הֵנָּה *here and there*, 1 Ki. 20. 40.

הִנֵּה, הִנֵּה interj. *behold! lo!* usually expressive of readiness to hear and to obey; with suff. הִנְנִי, הִנֵּנִי, הִנֶּנִּי, *behold me! lo, I am here!* הִנְנִי מֵבִיא *behold, I bring, am about to*, or *will bring*; (note Is. 28. 16 הִנְנִי יִסַּד, where אֲשֶׁר is to be supplied: *behold me, who has laid* for *have laid*, &c.); 2 pers. הִנְּךָ, הִנֵּךְ &c. see analyt. order.

הֵן only with the prefixes, מֵהֵן, כָּהֵן, בָּהֵן pers. pron. 3 p. pl. f. *they*, comp. הוּא (§ 1. r. 6). As a separate pronoun it invariably takes parag. ה, as הֵנָּה, with prefixes, בָּהֵנָּה, מֵהֵנָּה; כָּהֵנָּה *as they are* i. e. such; כָּהֵנָּה וְכָהֵנָּה *such and such things*, 2 Sa. 12. 8.

הֵן[d] Kh. הֵן q. v., K. הִנֵּה q. v. interj. . . הן

הַנֶּאֱהָבִים[e] pref. הַ ⟩ Niph. part. masc., pl. of [נֶאֱהָב] אהב

הַנֶּאֱכֶלֶת[f] pref. id. ⟩ Niph. part. s. fem. (fr. נֶאֱכָל m.) אכל

הַנֶּאֱמָן[g] pref. id. ⟩ Niph. part. sing. masc. dec. 2 b. אמן

הַנֶּאֱמָנִים[h] pref. id. ⟩ id. pl., absolute state . . אמן

הַנֶּאֱנָחִים[i] pref. id. ⟩ Niph. part. masc., pl. of נֶאֱנָח . אנח

הַנֶּאֱנָקִים[k] וְ pref. id. ⟩ Niph. part. masc. pl. [of נֶאֱנָק] אנק

הַנֹּאֵף[l] pref. id. ⟩ Kal part. act. sing. masc. . נאף

הַנֹּאֶפֶת[m] וְ pref. id. ⟩ id. fem. [for 'נֹאֶפֶת comp. § 35. r. 2] נאף

הַנִּבָּא[n] pref. id. ⟩ Niph. pret. 3 pers. sing. masc. נבא

הִנָּבֵא 'וְ Niph. imp. sing. masc. . . . נבא

הִנַּבְאוּ[o] Hithp. imp. pl. masc. [for הִתְנַבְּאוּ § 12. r. 3] נבא

הַנִּבָּאִים[p] pref. הַ ⟩ Niph. part. m., pl. of נִבָּא dec. 1 b. נבא

הַנְּבִאִים pref. id. ⟩ noun masc., pl. of נָבִיא dec. 3 a. נבא

הַנִּבְּאִים pref. הַ ⟩ Niph. part. masc. pl. [of נִבָּא § 23. rem. 6, comp. rem. 9] . . . נבא

הַנִּבְדָּל[q] pref. id. ⟩ Niph. part. sing. masc. . . בדל

הִנַּבֵּאתִי[r] וְ Hithpa. pret. 1 p. s. [for הִתְנַבֵּאתִי § 12. r. 3] נבא

הַנְּבוּאָה[s] 'וְ pref. הַ ⟩ noun fem. sing. dec. 10. . נבא

הַנָּבִיא 'וְ pref. id. ⟩ noun masc. sing. dec. 3 a. . נבא

הַנְּבִיאָה pref. id. ⟩ noun fem. sing. . . . . נבא

הַנְּבִיאִים 'וְ pref. id. ⟩ noun masc., pl. of נָבִיא dec. 3 a. נבא

הַנְּבִיאִים[u] Kh. הַנְּבִיאִים K. הַנְּבִאִים (q. v.) . . נבא

הַנֶּבֶל[x]
הַנֵּבֶל[y] } pref. הַ ⟩ noun masc. sing. (§ 35. rem. 2) נבל

הַנָּבָל[z] pref. id. ⟩ noun masc. sing. dec. 6 b. . . נבל

הַנְּבָלָה pref. id. ⟩ noun fem. sing. . . . נבל

הַנְּבֵלָה pref. id. ⟩ noun fem. sing. (constr. נִבְלַת, suff. נִבְלָתוֹ, once נִבְלָתִי § 42. rem. 4) . . נבל

הַנְּבָלוֹת[a] pref. id. ⟩ adj. fem. pl. from נָבָל masc. נבל

הַנְּבָלִים[b] pref. id. ⟩ n. m., pl. of 'נֵבֶל d. 6 b, or נָבָל d. 4 a. נבל

הַנִּבְנֶה[c] pref. id. ⟩ Niph. part. sing. masc. . . בנה

הַנִּבְשָׁן וְ pref. id. ⟩ pr. name of a place . . בשן

---

[a] 1 Sa. 25. 27. [b] Je. 9. 23. [c] Ps. 97. 7. [d] Ge. 3. 24. [e] 2 Sa. 21. 9. [f] 1 Sa. 14. 22. [g] 1 Ch. 11. 10. [h] Ex. 23. 27. [i] Ho. 2. 5. [k] Ezr. 2. 62. [l] Ne. 7. 64. [m] Ec. 9. 5. [n] 2 Ki. 12. 12. [o] Nu. 17. 6. [p] 2 Sa. 13. 28. [q] Ex. 1. 16. [r] Je. 29. 27. [s] Eze. 13. 17 [t] 2 Ch. 17. 16. [u] 2 Sa. 14. 32. [x] 1 Ch. 29. 11. [y] Mi. 3. 9. [z] Mi. 3. 5. [a] 1 Sa. 25. 10. [b] Is. 66. 17. [c] 2 Ch. 24. 26. [d] Is. 54. 16. [e] 2 Sa. 1. 23. [f] Le. 11. 47. [g] De. 7. 9. [h] Is. 55. 3. [i] Eze. 9. 4. [k] Eze. 9. 4. [l] Le. 20. 10. [m] Le. 20. 10. [n] 1 Ch. 25. 2, 3. [o] Je. 23. 13. [p] Eze. 13. 2. [q] Ezr. 6. 21. [r] Eze. 37. 10. [s] Ne. 6. 12. [t] 2 Ch. 15. 8. [u] 1 Ch. 25. 1. [x] Am. 6. 5 [y] Ps. 108. 3. [z] Ps. 57. 9. [a] Job 2. 10. [b] Is. 22. 24; Eze. 13. 3. [c] 1 Ch. 22. 19.

הַנֶּגֶב	ו׳ pref. הַ)(noun masc. dec. 6. (§ 35. r. 3)	נגב
הַנֶּגְבָּה	pref. הַ art.)(id. with parag. ה	נגב
הַנֹּגַהּ[a]	pref. id.)(noun masc. s. d. 6c. (§ 35. r. 5)	נגה
הַנָּגִיד	pref. id.)(noun masc. sing. dec. 3a	נגד
הֲנִגְלֹה[b]	pref. הֲ)(Niph. inf. absolute	גלה
הַנִּגְלוּ[c]	pref. id.)(id. pret. 3 pers. pl.	גלה
הַנִּגְלוֹת[d]	וְ pref. הַ)(id. part. fem., pl. of לֶה׳ d. 10. [from לֶה׳ masc.]	גלה
הַנֶּגַע / הַנָּגַע	ו׳[e] pref. id.)(noun masc. sing. dec. 6a. (§ 35. rem. 2&5; but with suff. נִגְעִי)	נגע
הַנֹּגֵעַ[f]	ו׳ pref. id.)(Kal part. act. sing. masc. d. 7b.	נגע
הַנֹּגְעִים[g]	pref. id.)(id. pl., absolute state	נגע
הַנֹּגַעַת[h]	pref. id.)(id. fem. sing. dec. 13 a.	נגע
הַנֶּגֶף[i] / הַנָּגֶף	pref. id.)(noun masc. sing. (§ 35. rem. 2)	נגף
הַנִּגָּרִים[k]	pref. id.)(Niph. part. masc. pl. [of נִגָּר]	נגר
הַנֹּגֵשׂ[l]	pref. id.)(Kal part. act. sing. masc. d. 7b.	נגשׂ
הַנִּגָּשִׂים[m]	pref. id.)(Niph. part. masc. pl. [of נִגָּשׂ]	נגשׂ
הַנֹּגְשִׂים[n]	ו׳[o] pref. id.)(Kal part. act. m., pl. of נֹגֵשׂ d. 7b.	נגשׂ
הַנְּדָבָה[p]	pref. id.)(noun fem. sing. dec. 11c	נדב
הַנִּדְבָּרִים[q]	pref. id.)(Niph. part. masc. pl. [of נִדְבָּר]	דבר
הַנִּדָּה	pref. id.)(noun fem. sing. dec. 10.	נדה
הַנִּדָּחָה	וְ pref. id.)(Niph. part. sing. f. fr. נִדָּח m.	נדח
הַנִּדָּחִים[r]	וְ pref. id.)(id. m., pl. of נִדָּח dec. 2b. (suff. נִדָּחוֹ § 15. rem. 2)	נדח
הַנִּדַּחַת[s]	pref. id.)(id., sing. fem.	נדח
הַנֹּדֵר[t]	pref. id.)(Kal part. act. sing. masc.	נדר
הֵנָּה	ו׳ pers. pron. 3 pers. f. pl. (הֵן) with parag. ה	הן
הֵנָּה	ו׳ adv. (הֵן) with parag. ה; for וָ see lett. ו	הן
הִנֵּה	ו׳ adv. or demon. interj., (הֵן) with parag. ה	הן
הִנֵּה[u]	id., bef. dag. f. conj. (נָּא)	הן
הִנֵּהוּ[v]	וְ Kh., הִנֵּה with suff. 3 pers. sing. masc. K. הִנֵּה הוּא׳	הן
הֲנִהְיָה[x]	pref. הֲ)(Niph. pret. 3 pers. sing. masc.	היה
הַנַּהֲלָאָה[y]	וְ pref. הַ)(Niph. part. sing. f. (§ 13. r. 6)	הלא
הַנַּהֲלֹלִים[z]	pref. id.)(noun masc., pl. of [נַהֲלֹל] d. 1b.	נהל
הַנָּהָר	ו׳[a] pref. id.)(noun masc. sing. dec. 4a.	נהר
הַנְּהָרוֹת	pref. id.)(id. pl. abs. (constr. נַהֲרוֹת)	נהר
הַנֶּהֱרָסוֹת[b]	ו׳ pref. id.)(Niph. part. fem., pl. of [נֶהֱרָסָה]	הרס
הַנְּהָרֹת[c]	defect. for הַנְּהָרוֹת (q. v.)	נהר
הִנּוֹ	ו׳[d] demon. interj. (הִנֵּה) with suff. 3 p. s. m.	הן
הַנּוֹגֵעַ	ו׳ pref. הַ)(Kal part. sing. masc. dec. 7b.	נגע
הַנָּוָה[e]	pref. id.)(adj. fem. sing. d. 11a, fr. נָוֶה m.	נוה
הַנָּוֶה	pref. id.)(noun masc. sing. dec. 9b.	נוה
הַנּוֹטֶה[f]	pref. id.)(Kal part. act. sing. masc. dec. 9a.	נטה
הַנּוֹטֵעַ[g]	pref. id.)(Kal part. act. sing. masc. dec. 7b.	נטע
הַנּוֹלָד[h]	ו׳[i] pref. id.)(Niph. part. sing. masc. d. 2b.	ילד
הַנּוֹלָדִים	pref. id.)(id. pl., absolute state	ילד
הַנּוֹעָדִים	pref. id.)(Niph. part. masc. pl. [of נוֹעָד]	יעד
הַנּוֹצָה[k]	pref. id.)(noun fem. sing.	נצה
הַנּוֹרָא[l]	ו׳ pref. id.)(Niph. part. sing. masc.	ירא
הַנּוֹרָאֹת[rr]	pref. id.)(id. fem., pl. abs. fr. נוֹרָאָה d. 11c.	ירא
הַנּוֹשָׁבוֹת[m]	pref. id.)(Niph. part. fem. pl. [of שָׁבָה׳, in use only שֶׁבֶת׳]	ישב
הַנֹּשֵׂא[n]	וְ pref. id.)(Kal part. act. sing. masc. d. 7b.	נשׂא
הַנֹּתֵן	pref. id.)(Kal part. act. sing. masc. dec. 7b.	נתן
הַנּוֹתָר	ו׳ pref. id.)(Niph. part. sing. masc.	יתר
הַנּוֹתָרוֹת[o]	pref. id.)(id. f. pl. [of תָרָה׳; in use only תֶרֶת׳]	יתר
הַנּוֹתָרִים	ו׳[p] pref. id.)(id. masc., pl. of נוֹתָר׳	יתר
הַנּוֹתֶרֶת[q] / הַנֹּתֶרֶת	וְ׳ pref. id.)(id. f. s. & pl., comp. הַנּוֹתָרוֹת	יתר
הַנָּזִיד	pref. id.)(noun m. sing. dec. 3a. R. זיד see	זוד
הַנָּזִיר[r]	pref. id.)(noun masc. sing. dec. 3a.	נזר
הַנֵּזֶר	pref. id.)(noun masc. sing. dec. 6b.	נזר
הִנָּזֵר[zz]	Niph. inf., abs.	נזר
הַנֶּזֶם[s]	pref. הַ)(noun masc. s. (suff. נִזְמָהּ) d. 6a.	נזם
הַנְּזָמִים[t]	pref. id.)(id. pl., absolute state	נזם
הַנְּזִרִים[u]	pref. id.)(noun masc., pl. of נָזִיר dec. 3a.	נזר
הַנַּח[x]	ו׳ Hiph. imp. masc. sing. ap. for הַנִּיחַ (§ 21. rem. 24, comp. rem. 19)	נוח
הֵנַח[y]	id. pret. 3 p. s. m. for הֵנִיחַ (see the prec.)	נוח
הֲנָחָה[z]	וַ noun fem. sing.; וַ bef. (-:)	נוח
הַנִּחוּ[a]	Hiph. imp. pl. masc. (§ 21. rem. 24)	נוח
הַנְחִילוֹ[b]	Hiph. inf., suff. 3 pers. sing. masc. dec. 1b.	נחל
הַנְּחִילוֹת[c]	pref. הַ)(noun f. pl. [of נְחִילָה for נְחִלָּה]	חלל
הִנְחִיתָם[d]	Hiph. pret. 2 pers. s. m., suff. 3 pers. s. m.	נחת
הַנַּחַל / הַנָּחַל	ו׳[e] pref. הַ)(noun m. s. d. 6d. (§ 35. r. 2)	נחל
הַנַּחֲלָה[f]	pref. id.)(noun fem. sing. dec. 12d.	נחל
הַנַּחְלוֹת[ff]	pref. id.)(Niph. part. f., pl. of נַחְלָה (§ 13. r. 7)	חלה
הַנְּחָלִים	pref. id.)(noun masc., pl. of נַחַל dec. 6 d.	נחל
הַנֶּחֱלָמִי, הַנֶּחְלָמִי	pref. id.)(patronym.	חלם
הַנְּחָלֹת[g]	pref. id.)(noun fem., pl. of נַחֲלָה dec. 12d.	נחל
הָנְחַלְתִּי[h]	Hoph. pret. 1 pers. sing.	נחל
הִנְחַלְתִּי / הִנְחַלְתִּי[i]	וְ Hiph. pret. 1 pers. sing. acc. shifted by conv. וְ (comp. § 8. rem. 7)	נחל
הִנְחַלְתֶּם[k]	וְ id. pret. 2 pers. pl. masc.	נחל
הִנָּחֵם	ו׳ Niph. imp. sing. masc. or inf. constr.	נחם
הַנֶּחָמִים[l]	pref. הַ)(Niph. part. pl. [for נִחָמִים Chaldaism for נֶחְמִים § 18. rem. 14]	חמם

[a] Eze. 1. 28. [b] 1 Sa. 2. 27. [c] Job 38. 17. [d] De. 29. 28. [e] Le. 13. 55. [f] Le. 15. 7. [g] Je. 12. 14.
[h] Nu. 19. 22. [i] Nu. 17. 11. [k] 2 Sa. 14. 14. [l] Is. 9. 3. [m] Ex. 19. 22. [n] Ex. 5. 6. [o] Ex. 5. 13.
[p] Ezr. 1. 4. [q] Eze. 33. 30. [r] Is. 27. 13. [s] Eze. 34. 4, 16. [t] Le. 27. 8. [u] Ge. 19. 2. [v] De. 4. 32.
[y] Mi. 4. 7. [z] Is. 7. 19. [a] Ge. 2. 14. [b] Ex. 36. 35, 36. [c] Ex. 8. 1. [d] Nu. 23. 17. [e] Je. 6. 2.
[f] Is. 40. 22. [g] Je. 11. 17. [h] Ge. 21. 3. [i] Ezr. 10. 3. [k] Eze. 17. 3. [l] Eze. 1. 22. [m] Eze. 12. 20.
[n] Le. 15. 10. [o] Je. 34. 7. [p] 1 Sa. 30. 9. [q] Le. 10. 12. [r] Nu. 6. 13, 18, 19 20, 21. [rr] De. 10. 21.
[s] Ge. 24. 30, 47. [t] Ge. 35. 4. [u] Am. 2. 12. [x] Ho. 4. 17. [y] 1 Ki. 8. 9. [z] Est. 2. 18. [zz] Zec. 7. 3.
[a] 2 Sa. 16. 11. [b] De. 21. 16. [c] Ps. 5. 1. [d] Ne. 9. 12. [e] 2 Ki. 3. 17. [f] De. 12. 9. [ff] Eze. 34. 4, 21.
[g] Jos. 19. 51. [h] Job 7. 3. [i] Zec. 8. 12. [k] 1 Ch. 28. 8. [l] Is. 57. 5.

הַנֶּחֱמָדִים	pref. הַ)(Niph. part. masc., pl. of נֶחֱמָד	חמד
הִנֶּחָמְתִּי	וְ Hithpa. pret. 1 pers. sing. [for הִתְנַחַמְתִּי, § 14. r. 3, & § 42. No. 3 note; see אָח § 45]	נחם
הִנְחַנִי[c]	Hiph. pret. 3 pers. sing. m., suff. 1 pers. s.	נחה
הַנֶּחֱרִים	pref. הַ)(Niph. part. m., pl. of [נֶחֱרָה] d. 9a.	חרה
הַנָּחָשׁ	[d] וְ' pref. id.)(noun masc. sing. dec. 4a.	נחש
הַנְּחָשִׁים	pref. id.)(id. pl., absolute state	נחש
הַנֶּחֱשָׁלִים	pref. id.)(Niph. part. pl. [of נֶחֱשָׁל]	חשל
הַנְּחֹשֶׁת	[g] וְ' pref. id.)(noun fem. sing. (with suff. נְחָשׁ & נְחֻשׁ) dec. 13c.	נחש
הַנְחַת[h]	Hiph. imp. sing. masc. [with gutt. for הַנְחֵת]	נחת
הָנְחַת[i]	Chald. Hoph. pret. 3 pers. sing. masc.	נחת
הִנַּחְתָּ[k]	וְ Hiph. pret. 2 pers. sing. masc. (§ 21. rem. 24); acc. shifted by conv. וְ (§ 8. rem. 7)	נוח
הִנַּחְתּוֹ[l]	וְ id. id., suff. 3 pers. sing. masc.	נוח
הֲנִחֹתִי	וַ id. pret. 1 pers. sing.; acc. shifted by וַ for וְ conv. (§ 8. rem. 7)	נוח
הִנַּחְתִּי	וְ id. id. (§ 21. rem. 24)	נוח
הִנַּחְתִּיו[m]	וְ id. id., suff. 3 pers. sing. masc.	נוח
הִנַּחְתָּם[n]	וְ id. pret. 2 pers. s. m., suff. 3 pers. pl. m.	נוח
הִנַּחְתֶּם	וְ id. pret. 2 pers. pl. masc.	נוח
הַנְּטוּיָה	pref. הַ)(Kal part. p. fem. d. 10, fr. נָטוּי m.	נטה
הַנְּטוֹפָתִי	pref. id.)(gent. noun fr. נְטֹפָה	נטף
הַנְּטִיפוֹת	וְ pref. id.)(noun fem., pl. of [נְטִיפָה] dec. 10.	נטף
הַנְּטִישׁוֹת	pref. id.)(noun fem., pl. of [נְטִישָׁה] dec. 10.	נטש
הֲנֹטֵעַ[q]	pref. הֲ)(Kal part. sing. masc. [for נֹטֵעַ comp. § 15. rem. 1]	נטע
הַנְּטִפוֹת[r]	noun fem., pl. of [נְטִיפָה] dec. 10.	נטף
הַנְּטֹפָתִי	pref. הַ)(gent. noun fr. נְטֹפָה	נטף
הֵנִיא	Hiph. pret. 3 pers. sing. masc.	נוא
הָנִיחַ[s]	Hiph. inf. constr. dec. 3a.	נוח
הֵנִיחַ וְ' / הִנִּיחַ וְ'	id. pret. 3 pers. sing. masc. (§ 21. rem. 24)	נוח
הַנִּיחָה	id. imp. m. s. with parag. ה (v.i. & § 11. r. 5)	נוח
הֻנִּיחָה[t]	וְ Hoph. pret. 3 pers. sing. fem. (§ 21. r. 24)	נוח
הָנִיחוּ[u] / הַנִּיחוּ	Hiph. imp. masc. pl. (§ 21. rem. 24)	נוח
הִנִּיחוֹ[z]	וְ id. pret. 3 pers. sing. masc., suff. 3 pers. s. m.	נוח
הֵנִיחוּ[a] / הִנִּיחוּ	וְ' id. pret. 3 pers. pl. (§ 21. rem. 24)	נוח
הִנִּיחֵךְ[b]	וְ id. id., suff. 2 pers. sing. fem.	נוח
הֲנִיחוֹתִי[c]	וַ id. pret. 1 pers. sing.; וַ for וְ conv.	נוח
הַנִּיחֹחַ[cc]	pref. הַ)(noun masc. sing. dec. 1b.	נוח
הֲנִיחִי[xx]	Hiph. inf. (הָנִיחַ), suff. 1 pers. sing. dec. 3a.	נוח
הִנִּיחָם	וְ id. pret. 3 p. s. m., suff. 3 p. pl. m. (§ 21. r. 24)	נוח
הֲנִיחֹתִי[aa]	וַ id. pret. 1 p. s.; acc. shifted by וַ for וְ conv.	נוח

הַנָּס[e]	pref. הַ)(Kh. נִיס' adj., K. נָס' Kal part. act. m.	נוס
הֵנִיס[f]	Hiph. pret. 3 pers. sing. masc.	נוס
הֵנִיף	וְ' Hiph. pret. 3 pers. sing. masc.	נוף
הָנִיפוּ[g]	id. imp. masc. pl.	נוף
הֲנִיפוֹתִי[h]	id. pret. 1 pers. sing.	נוף
הֲנִיפְכֶם[i]	id. inf. (הָנִיף), suff. 2 pers. pl. masc. dec. 3a.	נוף
הֵנִיעָה	Hiph. pret. 3 pers. sing. fem.	נוע
הֲנִיעֻמוֹ[k]	id. imp. masc. sing., suff. 3 pers. pl.	נוע
הֵנִיקוּ[l]	Hiph. pret. 3 pers. pl.	ינק
הִנָּךְ	interj. demon. (הֵן=הִנֵּה), suff. 2 pers. s. fem.	הן
הִנְּךָ וְ' / הִנֶּךָ[m]	id., suff. 2 pers. sing. masc. (§ 2. rem. 2)	הן
הַנִּכְבָּד[n]	pref. הַ)(Niph. part. sing. masc. dec. 2b, & 8a (§ 37. rem. 5)	כבד
הִנְּכָה[o]	full form for הִנְּךָ q. v. (§ 2. rem. 2)	הן
הַנִּכְחָדוֹת[p] / וְהַנִּכְחֶדֶת[q]	pref. הַ)(Niph. part. fem. sing. & pl. (§ 44. rem. 5)	כחד
הַנִּכְלָמוֹת[r]	pref. id.)(Niph. part. fem. pl. [of נִכְלָמָה]	כלם
הַנִּכְלָמִים[s]	pref. id.)(id. masc., pl. of נִכְלָם	כלם
הִנְּכֶם	וְ interj. demon. (הֵן=הִנֵּה), suff. 2 pers. s. m.	הן
הַנֵּכָר	pref. הַ)(noun masc. sing. (§ 33. rem. 3)	נכר
הַנָּכְרִי[t]	וְ' pref. id.)(adj. masc. sing. [from נֵכָר with adj. term. ִי—], pl. נָכְרִים	נכר
הַנָּכְרִיּוֹת	pref. id.)(fem., pl. of נָכְרִיָּה	נכר
הַנִּכְשָׁל[u]	pref. id.)(Niph. part. sing. masc.	כשל
הֲנִלְוָה[x]	pref. id.)(Niph. pret. 3 pers. sing. masc., for נִלְוָה (§ 24. rem. 18)	לוה
הַנִּלְוִים	pref. id.)(id. part. m., pl. of [נִלְוֶה] dec. 9a.	לוה
הַנִּלְחָם	pref. id.)(Niph. part. sing. masc.	לחם
הַנִּלְחָמִים	pref. id.)(id. pl., absolute state	לחם
הֲנֵלֵךְ	pref. הֲ)(Kal fut. 1 pers. pl.	ילך
הַנִּלְכָּד[y]	pref. הַ)(Niph. part. sing. masc.	לכד
הִנָּם	וְ' interj. demon. (הֵן=הִנֵּה), suff. 3 pers. pl. m.	הן
הִנֹּם	pr. name masc. see גַּי	
הַנִּמְהָר[z]	וְ pref. הַ)(Niph. part. sing. masc.	מהר
הַנְּמוּאֵלִי	pref. id.)(patronym. of נְמוּאֵל q. v.	
הַנִּמְכָּרִים[a]	pref. id.)(Niph. part. masc. pl. [of נִמְכָּר]	מכר
הַנִּמְלָט[b]	וְ' pref. id.)(Niph. part. sing. masc.	מלט
הַנְּמָלִים[c]	pref. id.)(noun fem. with pl. masc. term. from נְמָלָה	נמל
הֲנִמְצָא[d]	pref. הֲ)(Kal fut. 1 pers. pl.	מצא
הַנִּמְצָא	וְ' pref. הַ)(Niph. part. sing. masc. dec. 1b.	מצא
הַנִּמְצָאָה	pref. id.)(id. fem., dec. 11a.	מצא
הַנִּמְצְאוּ[e]	pref. id.)(id. pret. 3 pers. pl.	מצא
הַנִּמְצָאוֹת[f]	pref. id.)(id. part. fem., pl. of נִמְצָאָה' dec. 11a.	מצא

a Ps. 19. 11. b Eze. 5. 13. c Ge. 24. 48. d Ge. 3. 1. e Nu. 21. 6. f De. 25. 18.
g 1 Ch. 29. 2. h Joel 4. 11. i Da. 5. 20. k De. 14. 28. l De. 26. 10. m Je. 27. 11.
n Nu. 17. 19. o Ju. 8. 26. p Is. 18. 5. q Ps. 49. 9. r Is. 3. 19. s Is. 14. 3.
t Nu. 19. 9. u Zec. 5. 11. cc Ge. 8. 21. y Is. 28. 12. z De. 26. 4. a Zec. 6. 8.
b Eze. 16. 30. c 1 Ch. 22. 9. xx Eze. 24. 13. e Je. 48. 44. f Ex. 9. 20. g Is. 13. 2.
h Job 31. 21. i Le. 23. 12. k Ps. 59. 12. l La. 4. 3. m Ps. 139. 8. n De. 28. 58.
o 2 Ki. 7. 2. p Zec. 11. 16. q Zec. 11. 9. r Eze. 16. 27. s 2 Sa. 19. 4. t De. 29. 21.
u Zec. 12. 8. x Is. 56. 3. y Jos. 7. 15. z Hab. 1. 6. a Ne. 5. 8. aa 2 Sa. 7. 11.
b 1 Ki. 19. 17. c Pr. 30. 25. d Ge. 41. 38. e 1 Ch. 29. 17. f Ju. 20. 48.

הַנִּמְצָאִים[a] / הַנִּמְצְאִים — pref. הַ)(id. masc., pl. of נִמְצָא [or נִמְצֵא § 23. rem. 6] — מצא
הַנִּמְצָאֹת[b] — pref. id.)(id. fem., pl. of נִמְצָאָה dec. 11a. — מצא
הִנֵּנוּ[c] / הִנֶּנּוּ / וְ' הִנְנוּ — interj. demon. (הֵן=הִנֵּה), with suff. 1 pers. pl. (§ 2 note) — הן
הִנֵּנִי, הִנֶּנִּי, הִנְנִי — id. with suff. 1 pers. sing. — הן
הַנָּם — pref. הַ)(Kal part. act. sing. masc. dec. 1a — נום
הַנֵּס[d] — pref. id.)(noun masc. sing. dec. 8b — נסס
הֲנִסָּה — pref. הֲ)(Piel pret. 3 pers. sing. masc. — נסה
הַנְּסוֹגִים[ss] — pref. הַ)(Niph. part. masc. pl. of נָסוֹג dec. 3a — סוג
הַנְּסוּכָה[e] — pref. הַ)(Kal part. p. fem. sing. [fr. נָסוּךְ m.] — נסך
הַנָּסֶךְ[f] — pref. id.)(noun m. s. for נֶסֶךְ (§ 35. rem. 2) — נסך
הַנֵּסֶךְ[g] — וְ pref. id.)(noun masc. sing. dec. 6b. — נסך
הַנִּסְפֶּה[h] — pref. id.)(Niph. part. sing. masc. — ספה
הַנִּסְתָּרִים[i] — וְ pref. id.)(Niph. part. masc., pl. of נִסְתָּר — סתר
הַנִּסְתָּרֹת[k] — pref. id.)(id. fem. pl. [of נִסְתָּרָה] — סתר
הֵנַע — pr. name of a city in Mesopotamia
הַנּוֹעָדִים — pref. הַ)(Niph. part. masc. pl. [of נוֹעָד] — יעד
הַנֵּעָה — pref. id.)(pr. name of a place — נוע
הַנְּעוּרִים[l] — pref. id.)(noun masc., pl. of [נְעוּר] dec. 1a. — נער
הֲנִעוֹתִי[m] — וַ Hiph. pret. 1 pers. sing.; acc. shifted by וַ for וְ conv. (comp. § 8. rem. 7) — נוע
הַנֶּעֱזָבוֹת[n] — pref. הַ)(Niph. part. fem. pl. [of נֶעֱזָב=זָבָה'] — עזב
הַנְּעִימִים[o] — וְ'[p] pref. id.)(adj. m., pl. of נָעִים dec. 3a. — נעם
הַנָּעַל[q] — pref. id.)(n. f. s. dec. 6d. for נַעַל (§ 35. r. 2) — נעל
הַנְעֵל — Chald. Aph. pret. 3 pers. s. m. for [אַעֵל=הַעֵל § 47. rem. 4] dag. f. resolved in נ, comp. § 52. rem. 2 — עלל
הַנַּעֲמִי — pref. הַ)(patronym. [for נַעֲמָנִי] from נַעֲמָן — נעם
הַנַּעֲמָתִי — pref. id.)(gent. noun from נַעֲמָה — נעם
הַנַּעֲצוּץ[r] — pref. id.)(noun masc. sing. dec. 1b. — נעץ
הַנַּעֲצוּצִים[s] — pref. id.)(id. pl., absolute state — נעץ
הַנָּעַר / וְ' הַנַּעַר — pref. הַ)(noun masc. sing. dec. 6d. (§ 35. rem. 2) — נער
הַנַּעֲרָ[t] — וְ' pref. id.)(Kh. נַעַר' com. gen., K. נַעֲרָה (q.v.) — נער
הַנַּעֲרָה — וְ' pref. id.)(noun fem. sing. dec. 12d. — נער
הַנְּעָרוֹת[u] — pref. id.)(id. pl., absolute state — נער
הַנְּעָרִים — pref. id.)(noun masc., pl. of נַעַר dec. 6d. — נער
הַנְּעֹרֶת[x] — pref. id.)(noun fem. sing. — נער
הֲנַעֲשֶׂה[y] — pref. הֲ)(Kal fut. 1 pers. pl. — עשה
הַנַּעֲשׂוֹת[z] — pref. הַ)(Niph. part. f., pl. of [נַעֲשָׂה=נַעֲשֶׂה' m.] — עשה
הַנְּפִילִים[zz] — pref. id.)(noun masc., pl. of [נָפִיל] dec. 3a. — נפל
הַנָּפֶל[a] — pref. id.)(noun m. s. for נֵפֶל' (§ 35. rem. 2) — נפל
הַנֹּפֵל — pref. id.)(Kal part. act. sing. masc. dec. 7b. — נפל

הַנְּפִלִים — noun masc., pl. of [נָפִיל] dec. 3a. — ל
הַנֹּפְלִים — וְ'[b] pref. הַ)(Kal part. act. masc., pl. of נֹפֵל dec. 7b. — ל
הַנֹּפֶלֶת[c] — pref. id.)(id. fem. sing. (§ 8. rem. 19) — ל
הַנְפֵק — Chald. Aph. pret. 3 pers. sing. masc. (§ 47. rem. 4, & § 51. rem. 1) — ק
הַנְפִּקוּ[d] — Chald. id. pret. 3 pers. pl. masc. — ק
הַנֶּפֶשׁ / וְ' הַנֶּפֶשׁ — pref. הַ)(noun com. sing. (suff. נַפְשִׁי) dec. 6a (§ 35. rem. 2) — ש
הַנְּפָשׁוֹת — pref. הַ art.)(id. pl., absolute state — ש
הַנָּפֶת[e] — pref. id.)(n. f. s. [for נֶפֶת' comp. § 35. r. 2] — ף
הֵנַפְתָּ[f] / וְ הֲנַפְתָּ[g] — Hiph. pret. 2 pers. s. m. (§ 21. r. 13 & 14); acc. shifted by conv. וְ (§ 8. rem. 7) — ף
הַנֵּץ — pref. הַ)(noun masc. sing. — ץ
הַנִּצָּב — pref. id.)(Niph. part. or subst. masc. — ב
הַנִּצָּבָה[h] — pref. id.)(id. part. fem. sing. — ב
הַנִּצָּבוֹת[i] — pref. id.)(id. fem., pl. absolute — ב
הַנִּצָּבִים — pref. id.)(id. masc., pl. of נִצָּב — ב
הַנִּצֶּבֶת[k] — pref. id.)(id. fem. sing. — ב
הֵנֵצוּ — Hiph. pret. 3 pers. pl. (§ 21. rem. 13 & 14) — ץ
הַנָּצוּר[l] — וְ pref. הַ)(Kal part. p. masc. dec. 3a. — ר
הַנֵּצַח[m] — וְ pref. id.)(noun masc. sing. dec. 6e. — ח
הַנִּצָּיבִים[n] — pref. id.)(Kh. נְצִיבִים' pl. of נְצִיב, K. הַנִּצָּבִים (q. v.) — ב
הִנָּצֵל[o] — וְ'[p] Niph. imp. masc. sing. — ל
הַנִּצְמָדִים[q] — pref. הַ)(Niph. part. masc. pl. [of נִצְמָד] — מד
הַנִּצָּנִים[r] — pref. id.)(noun masc. pl. [of נִצָּן] — ץ
הַנֶּקֶב — pref. id.)(pr. name of a place — ב
הַנִּקְבָּצִים[s] — pref. id.)(noun masc., pl. of נִקְבָּץ dec. 2b. — בץ
הַנְּקֻדּוֹת[t] — pref. id.)(adj. fem. pl. of [נְקֻדָּה] dec. 10, from נָקֹד masc. (§ 26. No. 21) — ד
הִנָּקֵה[u] — Niph. inf. absolute — ה
הַנִּקְהָלִים[x] — pref. הַ)(Niph. part. masc. pl. [of נִקְהָל] — הל
הַנָּקִי — pref. id.)(adj. masc. sing., pl. נְקִיִּים dec. 8f, (§ 37. No. 4) — קה
הִנָּקִי[y] — Niph. imp. sing. fem. — קה
הֲנָקֵל — pref. הֲ)(Niph. pret. 3 pers. sing. masc. — לל
הֲנִקַלָּה[z] — pref. הַ interr. for הֲ)(id. part. fem. sing. — לל
הַנִּקְלֶה[a] — וְ pref. הַ art.)(Niph. part. sing. masc. — לה
הִנָּקֵם[b] — וְ Niph. imp. sing. masc.; acc. Milêl before monos. (§ 9. rem. 3) — קם
הִנָּקְמוּ[c] — id. imp. pl. masc. — קם
הַנִּקְרָא[d] — pref. הַ)(Niph. part. sing. masc. dec. 1b — רא
הַנִּקְרָאִים[e] — pref. id.)(id. pl., absolute state — רא
הַנִּרְאָה — pref. id.)(Niph. pret. 3 pers. sing. masc. — אה
הַנִּרְאֶה — pref. id.)(id. part. sing. masc. — אה

[a] Ezr. 8. 25. [b] Ge. 19. 15. [c] Job 38. 35. [d] Nu. 21. 9. [e] Is. 25. 7. [f] Nu. 4. 7. [g] Eze. 45. 17. [h] Is. 13. 15. [i] De. 7. 20. [k] De. 29. 28. [l] Ps. 127. 4. [m] Am. 9. 9. [n] Eze. 36. 4. [o] Pr. 23. 8. [p] 2 Sa. 1. 23. [q] Deu. 25. 10. [r] Is. 55. 13. [s] Is. 7. 19. [t] Ge. 24. 16. [u] Est. 2. 9. [x] Ju. 16. 9. [y] 2 Sa. 17. 6. [z] Eze. 9. 4. [a] Ec. 6. 3. [b] Ju. 8. 10. [c] Am. 9. 11. [d] Da. 5. 3. [e] Jos. 17. 11. [f] Ex. 20. 25. [g] Ex. 29. 24, 26, etc. [h] Zec. 11. 16. [i] 1 Sa. 4. 20. [k] 1 Sa. 1. 26. [l] Eze. 6. 12. [m] 1 Ch. 29. 11. [n] 2 Ch. 8. 10. [o] Pr. 6. 5. [p] Pr. 6. 3. [q] Nu. 25. 5. [r] Ca. 2. 12. [s] Je. 40. 15. [ss] Zep. 1. 6. [t] Ge. 30. 35. [u] Je. 25. 29. [x] Eze. 38. 7. [y] Nu. 5. 19. [z] 1 Sa. 18. 23. [zz] Nu. 13. 33. [a] Is. 3. 5. [b] Je. 15. 15. [c] Je. 50. 15. [d] Is. 43. 7. [e] Is. 48. 1.

הַנֵּרוֹת [a] וְ' pref. הַ)(n. m. with pl. f. term. from נֵר d. 1 a. נור
הַנִּרְצָחָה [b] pref. id.)(Niph. part. sing. f. [from נִרְצָח m.] רצח
הַנֵּרֹת [c] וְ' defect. for הַנֵּרוֹת (q. v.) . . . נור
הַנֹּשֵׂא [d] [e] וְ' pref. הַ)(Kal part. act. sing. masc. dec. 7 b נשא
הִנָּשֵׂא Niph. imp. sing. masc. . . . . נשא
הִנָּשְׂאוּ [f] וְ id. imp. pl. masc. . . . . נשא
הַנִּשָּׂאוֹת [g] pref. הַ)(id. part. fem. pl. [of נִשָּׂאָה, in use נִשֵּׂאת] . . . . נשא
הַנִּשָּׂאִים [h] וְ pref. id.)(id. part. m., pl. of נִשָּׂא dec. 1 b נשא
הַנֹּשְׂאִים [i] וְ' pref. id.)(Kal part. act. masc., pl. of נֹשֵׂא dec. 7 b . . . . . נשא
הַנְּשׂוּאִים [k] pref. id.)(id. part. p., pl. of [נָשׂוּא] dec. 3 a נשא
הַנְּשֻׂאִים / וְהַנְּשֻׂאִם [l] defect. for הַנְּשׂוּאִים (q. v.) . . . נשא
הַנִּשְׁאָר וְ' pref. הַ)(Niph. part. sing. masc. dec. 2 b שאר
הַנִּשְׁאָרָה pref. id.)(id. part. sing. fem. . . שאר
הַנִּשְׁאָרוֹת [m] וְ" pref. id.)(id. pl., absolute state . שאר
הַנִּשְׁאָרִים וְ' pref. id.)(id. masc., pl. of נִשְׁאָר . שאר
הַנִּשְׁאֶרֶת [n] / הַנִּשְׁאָרֶת [o] pref. id.)(id. fem. sing. (comp. § 35. r. 2) שאר
הַנִּשְׁבָּע [q] וְ' pref. id.)(Niph. part. sing. masc. . שבע
הַנִּשְׁבָּעִים [r] וְ' pref. id.)(id. pl., absolute state . שבע
הַנִּשְׁבֶּרֶת [s] / וְהַנִּשְׁבֶּרֶת pref. id.)(Niph. part. sing. fem. from נִשְׁבָּר masc. (comp. § 35. rem. 2) שבר
הַנָּשֶׁה [t] pref. id.)(noun masc. sing. . . נשה
הַנֹּשֶׁה [u] וְ pref. id.)(Kal part. sing. masc. dec. 9 a . נשה
הַנָּשׁוּב [v] pref. הַ)(Kal fut. 1 pers. sing. . . שוב
הַנָּשׁוּךְ [w] pref. הַ)(Kal part. p. sing. masc. . . נשך
הַנִּשְׁחָתוֹת [qq] pref. id.)(Niph. part. fem. pl. [of נִשְׁחָתָה] שחת
הַנָּשִׂיא וְ' pref. id.)(noun masc. sing. dec. 3 a . נשא
הַנְּשִׂיאִים וְ', הַנְּשִׂאִם pref. id.)(id. pl., absolute state נשא
הַנָּשִׁים וְ' pref. id.)(noun fem. with pl. masc. term. by aphaer. for אֲנָשִׁים see אִשָּׁה (§ 45) אנש
הַנֹּשֵׁךְ [a] pref. הַ)(Kal part. act. sing. masc. dec. 7 b . נשך
הַנְּשָׁכוֹת [b] pref. id.)(noun fem. pl. absolute from נְשָׁכָה dec. 12 b, for לִשְׁכָּה q. v. . . לשך
הַנִּשְׁכָּחִים [c] pref. id.)(Niph. part. masc. pl. [of נִשְׁכָּח] שכח
הַנֹּשְׁכִים [d] pref. id.)(Kal part. act. m., pl. of נֹשֵׁךְ d. 7 b נשך
הַנְּשָׁמָה pref. id.)(noun fem. sing. dec. 11 c . נשם
הַנְּשַׁמָּה [e] pref. id.)(Niph. part. f. s. d. 10, [from נָשָׁם m.] שמם
הַנְּשַׁמּוֹת [f] [g] וְ' pref. הַ)(id. pl. . . . . . שמם
הֲנִשְׁמַע pref. הֲ)(Niph. pret. 3 pers. sing. masc. . שמע
הַנִּשְׁמַעַת [h] pref. הַ)(id. part. sing. fem. from נִשְׁמָע m. שמע
הַנֶּשֶׁק [i] / וְהַנָּשֶׁק [k] pref. הַ)(noun masc. sing. (§ 35. rem. 2) נשק
הַנִּשְׁקָף pref. id.)(Niph. part. sing. masc. . . שקף

הַנִּשְׁקָפָה [l] pref. id.)(id. fem. . . . . . שקף
הַנֶּשֶׁר [m] / הַנָּשֶׁר pref. id.)(noun masc. sing. dec. 6 a, (§ 35. rem. 2) but pl. c. נִשְׁרֵי . . נשר
הַנִּשְׁתְּוָן [n] pref. id.)(noun masc. sing. . . . נשת
הַנְּתָחִים pref. id.)(noun masc., pl. of נֵתַח dec. 6 a נתח
הַנְּתוּנִים [o] pref. id.)(Kh. 'נְתוּ', K. 'נְתִי', noun masc., pl. of [נָתוּן or נָתִין] dec. 3 a . . נתן
הַנְּתִינִים וְ' pref. id.)(noun masc., pl. of [נָתִין] d. 3 a נתן
הַנִּתָּן [p] pref. id.)(Niph. part. masc. sing. . . נתן
הַנֹּתֵן pref. id.)(Kal part. act. masc. sing. dec. 7 b נתן
הִנָּתֹן Niph. inf. absolute . . . . נתן
הַנֹּתְנִים [q] pref. הַ)(Kal part. masc., pl. of נֹתֵן d. 7 b נתן
הַנְּתֻצִים [r] pref. id.)(Kal part. p. m., pl. of [נָתוּץ] d. 3 a נתץ
הַנֶּתֶק [s] pref. id.)(noun masc. sing. . . . נתק
הָנְתְּקוּ [t] Hoph. pret. 3 pers. pl. . . . . נתק
הַנּוֹתָר [u] וְ pref. הַ)(Niph. part. sing. masc. for נוֹתָר יתר
הַס / הָס Kal imp. sing. masc. apoc. [for הַסֵּה] . הסה
הָסֵב Hiph. imp. sing. masc. . . . . סבב
הֵסֵב [x] וְ' id. pret. 3 pers. sing. masc. . . . סבב
הַסֹּבֵב [y] pref. הַ)(Kal part. act. sing. masc. dec. 7 b סבב
הַסֹּבְבִים pref. id.)(id. pl., absolute state . . סבב
הֵסַבּוּ [z] Hiph. pret. 3 pers. pl. masc. . . . סבב
הָסֵבִּי [a] id. imp. sing. fem. . . . . . סבב
הַסָּבִיב [b] pref. הַ)(noun masc. sing. dec. 3 a . . סבב
הָסֵבִיב [c] full form for הָסֵב (q. v.) . . . סבב
הַסַּבָּל [d] pref. הַ)(noun masc. sing. dec. 1 b . . סבל
הַסַּבָּלִים [e] pref. id.)(id. pl., absolute state . . סבל
הֲסִבֹּתָ [f] / וַהֲסִבֹּתָ [g] Hiph. pret. 2 pers. sing. masc.; acc. shifted by וְ, for וַ, conv. (comp. § 8. r. 7) סבב
הֻסַּג [h] וְ Hoph. pret. 3 pers. sing. masc. . . נסג
הִסְגִּיר וְ' Hiph. pret. 3 pers. sing. masc. . . סגר
הַסְגִּירוֹ [i] id. inf. (הַסְגִּיר), suff. 3 pers. sing. masc. d. 1 b סגר
הִסְגִּירוֹ [k] וְ id. pret. 3 pers. sing. masc., suff. 3 pers. sing. masc. . . . . . . סגר
הַסְגִּירָם [l] id. inf. (הַסְגִּיר), suff. 3 pers. pl. m., d. 1 b סגר
הִסְגִּירָם [m] id. pret. 3 pers. sing. m., suff. 3 pers. pl. m. סגר
הַסְּגָנִים וְ' pref. הַ)(noun masc. pl. [of סָגָן or סֶגֶן] סגן
הִסָּגֵר [n] Niph. imp. sing. masc. . . . . סגר
הִסְגַּרְתִּי [o] וְ Hiph. pret. 1 pers. sing.; acc. shifted by conv. וְ (comp. § 8. rem. 7) . . סגר
הִסְגַּרְתַּנִי [p] id. pret. 2 pers. sing. masc., suff. 1 pers. sing. סגר
הַסְּדִינִים [q] וְ pref. הַ)(noun masc. pl. of סָדִין dec. 3 a סדן

הָסָה. Pi. imp. apoc. הַס *hist! hush! be silent*; adv. *silently*. Hiph. *to silence, still*, Nu. 13. 30.

[a] 2 Ch. 4. 21. [b] Ju. 20. 4. [c] 1 Ki. 7. 49. [d] Le. 11. 25. [e] Le. 11. 28, 40. [f] Ps. 24. 7. [g] Is. 2. 14.
[h] Is. 2. 13. [i] Ne. 4. 11. [k] Is. 46. 3. [l] Ex. 35. 27. [m] Zec. 12. 14. [n] Zec. 11. 9. [o] Jos. 13. 2.
[p] Ex. 10. 5. [q] Is. 65. 16. [r] Zep. 1. 5. [s] Eze. 30. 22. [t] Ge. 32. 33, 33. [u] 2 Ki. 4. 1. [v] Ezr. 9. 14.
[y] Nu. 21. 8. [z] Jos. 22. 32. [a] Ge. 49. 17. [b] Ne. 12. 44. [c] Job 28. 4. [d] Mi. 3. 5. [e] Eze. 36. 34, 35, 36.
[f] Je. 33. 10. [g] Eze. 36. 35. [h] Je. 41. 56. [i] 2 Ki. 10. 2. [k] Ne. 3. 19. [l] Ca. 6. 10. [m] De. 28. 49.
[n] Ezr. 4. 7 & 7. 11. [o] Ezr. 8. 17. [p] 2 Ki. 22. 7. [q] 2 Ch. 11. 16. [r] Je. 33. 4. [s] Le. 13. 31-37. [t] Ju. 20. 31.
[u] Ex. 12. 10. [x] Ezr. 6. 22. [y] Ge. 2. 11. [z] 1 Sa. 5. 9, 10. [a] Ca. 6. 5. [b] 1 Ch. 11. 8. [c] 2 Ki. 8. 21.
[d] Ne. 4. 4. [e] 2 Ch. 34. 13. [f] 1 Ki. 18. 37. [g] Eze. 7. 22. [h] Is. 59. 14. [i] 1 Sa. 23. 20. [k] Le. 13. 5, 26, 54.
[l] Am. 1. 9. [m] De. 32. 30. [n] Eze. 3. 24. [o] Am. 6. 8. [p] Ps. 31. 9. [q] Is. 3. 23. [qq] Eze. 20. 44.

הַסַּהַר[a]	pref. הַ) noun masc. sing.	סהר
הַסֹּהַר[b]	pref. id.) noun masc. sing. . . .	סהר
הַסּוּ[c]	Piel imp. pl. masc.	הסה
הַסּוֹבֵב	pref. הַ) Kal part. act. sing. masc. dec. 7b	סבב
הַסּוֹכֵךְ	pref. id.) Kal part. act. sing. masc. dec. 7b	סכך
הַסּוּס	[d] וְ pref. id.) noun masc. sing. dec. 1a .	סוס
הַסּוּסִים	[e] וְ pref. id.) id. pl., absolute state .	סוס
הַסּוּף[f]	pref. id.) noun masc. sing. . . .	סוף
הַסּוֹפְדִים[g]	pref. id.) Kal part. act. m., pl. of [סוֹפֵד] d. 7b	ספד
הַסּוֹפֵר	pref. id.) Kal part. act. sing. masc. dec. 7b	ספר
הָסוּרִים[h]	for הָאֲסוּרִים, pref. הָ) Kal part. p. masc., pl. of אָסוּר dec. 3a	אסר
הַסּוֹרְרִים[i]	pref. הַ) Kal part. act. m., pl. of סוֹרֵר d. 7b	סרר
הַסְּחָבוֹת[k] הַסְּחָבוֹת[l]	pref. id.) noun fem. pl. [of סְחָבָה or סְחָבָה]; K. סְחָבוֹת . .	סחב
הַסֹּחֲרִים[m]	וְ pref. id.) Kal part. act. m., pl. of סֹחֵר d. 7b	סחר
הַסֵּךְ[n]	וְ Hiph. inf. absolute (§ 11. rem. 2) . .	נסך
הַסִּינִי	pref. הַ) pr. name of a people . .	סין
הֹסִיף[o]	Hiph. pret. 3 pers. sing. masc. for הוֹסִיף .	יסף
הָסִיר[p]	Hiph. inf. constr.	סור
הַסִּיר	pref. הַ) noun com. sing. dec. 1a . .	סיר
הֵסִיר	וְ Hiph. pret. 3 pers. sing. masc. . .	סור
הֵסִירָה[q]	וְ id. pret. 3 pers. s. f.; acc. shifted (§ 11. r. 9)	סור
הֱסִירָהּ[r]	id. pret. 3 pers. sing. m., suff. 3 pers. sing. f.	סור
הָסִירוּ	[s] וְ id. imp. pl. masc.	סור
הֵסִירוּ	[t] וְ id. pret. 3 pers. sing. masc. . . .	סור
הַסִּירוֹת	pref. הַ) noun com. with pl. fem. term. d. 1a	סיר
הֲסִירוֹתִי	Hiph. pret. 1 pers. sing.	סור
הָסִירִי[u]	id. imp. sing. fem.	סור
הַסִּירִים[x]	pref. הַ) noun com., pl. of סִיר dec. 1a .	סיר
הֲסִירְךָ[y]	Hiph. inf. (הָסִיר), suff. 2 pers. sing. m. d. 3a	סור
הֲסִירְכֶם[z]	id., suff. 2 pers. pl. masc. . . .	סור
הַסִּירֹת[a]	noun com. with pl. f. term. from סִיר dec. 1a	סיר
הֲסִירֹתָ[b]	וַ Hiph. pret. 2 pers. sing. m.; וַ for וְ conv.	סור
הֲסִירֹתִי[c] הֲסִרֹתִי[d]	id. pret. 1 pers. sing.; acc. shifted by וְ, וַ for וְ conv. (comp. § 9. rem. 11)	סור
הֱסִיתוּךָ[e]	Hiph. pret. 3 pers. pl., suff. 2 pers. sing. masc. (§ 21. rem. 24)	סות
הֱסִיתְךָ[f] הֱסִיתְךָ[hh]	id. pret. 3 pers. sing. masc., suff. 2 pers. sing. masc. (§ 21. rem. 14) .	סות
הַסֵּךְ[g]	וְ Hiph. inf., or imp. sing. masc. .	נסך
הֵסַכּוּ[h]	וְ id. pret. 3 pers. pl.	נסך
הַסֻּכּוֹת	pref. הַ) noun fem. pl. of סֻכָּה dec. 10. .	סכך
הַסֹּכֵךְ[i]	pref. id.) Kal part. act. sing. masc. d. 7b	סכך
הַסָּכָל[k]	וְ pref. id.) noun masc. sing. dec. 4a .	סכל
הַסֶּכֶל[l]	pref. id.) noun masc. sing. . . .	סכל
הַסִּכְלוּת[m]	[n] וְ pref. id.) noun fem. sing. . . .	כל
הִסְכַּלְתָּ[o]	Hiph. pret. 2 pers. sing. masc. . .	כל
הִסְכַּלְתִּי[p]	id. pret. 1 pers. sing. . . .	כל
הַסֹּכֵן[q]	pref. הַ) Kal part. act. sing. masc. . .	כן
הַסְכֶּן־[r]	Hiph. imp. sing. masc., for הַסְכֵּן (§ 11. rem. 5)	כן
הִסְכַּנְתָּה[s]	id. pret. 2 pers. sing. masc. . . .	כן
הִסְכַּנְתִּי[t]	id. pret. 1 pers. sing.	כן
הַסְכֵּת[u]	Hiph. imp. sing. masc.	כת
הַסֻּכֹּת[x]	pref. הַ) noun fem., pl. of סֻכָּה dec. 10.	כך
הַסַּל	pref. id.) noun masc. sing. dec. 8d . .	לל
הַסֹּלֵחַ[y]	pref. id.) Kal part. act. sing. masc. .	לח
הַסְּלִחוֹת[z]	וְ pref. id.) pl. of the following . .	לח
הַסְּלִיחָה[a]	pref. id.) noun fem. sing. dec. 10. .	לח
הַסַּלִּים[b]	pref. id.) noun masc., pl. of סַל dec. 8d .	לל
הַסֹּלְלוֹת	pref. id.) noun fem., pl. of סֹלְלָה dec. 10.	לל
הַסֶּלַע הַסָּלַע	pref. id.) noun masc. sing. dec. 6a (suff. סַלְעִי § 35. rem. 5) . . .	לע
הַסְּלָעִים	pref. id.) id. pl., absolute state .	לע
הַסָּלְעָם[c]	pref. id.) noun masc. sing. . . .	לעם
הַסֹּלֶת	pref. id.) noun com. sing. dec. 6c . .	לת
הַסְּמָדַר[d]	pref. id.) noun masc. sing. . . .	מדר
הַסַּמִּים	pref. id.) noun masc., pl. of [סַם] dec. 8d	מם
הַסֶּמֶל	pref. id.) noun masc. sing. . . .	מל
הַסְּנָאָה	pref. id.) pr. name of a place . .	נא
הַסְּנָאָה	pref. id.) pr. name fem. . . .	נא
הַסְּנֶה[e]	[f] וְ pref. id.) noun masc. sing. . .	נה
הַסְּנוּאָה	pref. id.) pr. name fem. . . .	נא
הַסְּעִפִּים[g]	pref. id.) n. f. with pl. m. term. [fr. סְעַפָּה]	עף
הַסַּעַר[h]	pref. id.) noun masc. sing. dec. 6d . .	ער
הַסְּעָרָה	pref. id.) noun fem. sing. dec. 11c .	ער
הַסַּף, הַסָּף	pref. id.) noun masc. sing. dec. 8e	ספף
הַסִּפּוֹת[i] הַסִּפִּים	וְ pref. id.) id. with pl. masc. & fem. .	ספף
הַסְּפִינָה[k]	pref. id.) noun fem. sing. . . .	ספן
הַסַּפִּיר[l]	pref. id.) noun masc. sing. dec. 1b .	ספר
הַסֵּפֶל[m]	pref. id.) noun masc. sing. . . .	ספל
הַסִּפֻּן[n]	pref. id.) noun masc. sing. . . .	ספן
הַסֵּפֶר	pref. id.) noun masc. sing. dec. 6b .	ספר
הַסְּפָר[o]	pref. id.) noun masc. sing. . . .	ספר
הַסֹּפֵר	pref. id.) Kal part. act. sing. masc. .	ספר
הַסְּפַרְוִים	וְ pref. id.) gent. noun pl. fr. סְפַרְוַיִם .	ספר
הַסְּפָרִים	pref. id.) noun m., pl. of סֵפֶר dec. 6b	ספר
הַסֹּפֶרֶת	pref. id.) pr. name masc. . . .	ספר
הֹסַפְתִּי[oo]	וְ Hiph. fut. 1 pers. sing. . . .	יסף

[a] Ca. 7. 3. [b] Ge. 39. 20-23 & 40. 3, 5. [c] Ne. 8. 11. [d] Est. 6. 9. [e] 2 Ki. 10. 2. [f] Ex. 2. 5.
[g] Ec. 12. 5. [h] Ec. 4. 14. [i] Ps. 66. 7. [k] Je. 38. 11. [l] Je. 38. 12. [m] 2 Ch. 9. 14. [n] Je. 44. 17.
[o] 2 Ki. 24. 7. [p] Eze. 21. 31. [q] De. 21. 13. [r] 2 Ch. 15. 16. [s] Jos. 24. 14. [t] 2 Ch. 30. 14. [u] 1 Sa. 1. 14.
[x] Ec. 7. 6. [y] 2 Sa. 5. 6. [z] Jos. 7. 13. [a] Ex. 38. 3. [b] 1 Ki. 2. 31. [c] 2 Ki. 23. 27. [d] Eze. 11. 19.
[e] Je. 38. 22. [f] Job 36. 16. [g] Nu. 28. 7. [h] Je. 32. 29. [i] Na. 2. 6. [k] Ec. 10. 14. [l] Ec. 10. 6.
[m] Ec. 2. 13. [n] Ec. 7. 25. [o] Ge. 31. 28. [p] 1 Sa. 26. 21. [q] Is. 22. 15. [r] Job 22. 21. [s] Ps. 139. 3.
[t] Nu. 22. 30. [u] De. 27. 9. [x] De. 16. 13. [y] Ps. 103. 3. [z] Da. 9. 9. [a] Ps. 130. 4. [b] Ge. 40. 18.
[c] Le. 11. 22. [d] Ca. 7. 13. [e] Ex. 3. 2, 2, 3, 4. [f] Ex. 3. 2. [g] 1 Ki. 18. 21. [h] Jon. 1. 12. [hh] 1 Sa. 26. 19.
[i] 1 Ki. 7. 50. [k] Jon. 1. 5. [l] Ex. 24. 10. [m] Ju. 6. 38. [n] 1 Ki. 6. 15. [o] 2 Ch. 2. 16. [oo] 2 Ki. 20. 6.

הַסִּקוּ[a] Ch. Aph. pret. 3 pers. pl. masc. (§ 47. r. 4) נסק
הֻסַּק[b] וְ Ch. Hoph. pret. 3 pers. sing. masc. . נסק
הָסֵר[c] וְ Hiph. inf. abs., or imp. sing. masc. . סור
הָסִרוּ[d] [e]וְ id. imp. pl. masc. for הָסִירוּ . סור
הַסַּרְדִּי pref. הַ)(patronym. of סֶרֶד . . סרד
הַסִּרָה pref. id.)(pr. name of a well . סור
הַסִּרוֹת[f] defect. for הַסִּירוֹת (q. v.) . . סיר
הַסִּרְיֹנֹת[g] pref. הַ)(noun m. s. pl. of סִרְיוֹן see שִׁרְיוֹן שרה
הַסָּרִיס pref. id.)(noun masc. sing., (§ 32. rem. 2) סרס
הַסָּרִיסִים[h] וְ pref. id.)(id. pl., absolute state . סרס
הַסְּרָנִים pref. id.)(noun masc., pl. of [סֶרֶן] dec. 6a (pl. c. סַרְנֵי) . . . סרן
הַסְּרִסִים[i] defect. for הַסָּרִיסִים (q. v.) . . סרס
הַסַּרְפָּד[k] pref. הַ)(noun masc. sing. . . . סרפד
הֲסִרֹתִי[l] / וַהֲסִרֹתִי } Hiph. pret. 1 pers. sing.; acc. shifted by conv. וְ (§ 8. rem. 7) . } סור
הֵסַתָּה[m] id. pret. 3 pers. sing. fem. [for הֵסִיתָה § 21. rem. 13] . . . . סות
הַסְּתָו[n] pref. הַ)(K. סְתָיו noun masc. sing. . סתה
הִסְתּוֹפֵף[o] Hithpoel inf. [for הִתְסוֹפֵף § 12. rem. 3] . ספף
הִסְתִּיר Hiph. pret. 3 pers. sing. masc. . . סתר
הִסְתִּירוּ[p] id. pret. 3 pers. pl. . . . . סתר
הִסְתִּירַנִי[q] id. pret. 3 p. s. m., suff. 1 pers. s. (§ 2. r. 1) סתר
הַסְתֵּר id. inf. abs., or imp. sing. masc. . . סתר
הִסָּתֵר[r] Niph. imp. sing. masc. . . . . סתר
הִסְתַּרְתָּ Hiph. pret. 2 pers. sing. masc. . . סתר
הִסְתַּרְתִּי / וְהִסְתַּרְתִּי[s] } id. pret. 1 pers. sing.; acc. shifted by conv. וְ (comp. § 8. rem. 7) . } סתר
הָעֶבֶד pref. הָ art. for הַ / הֶעֶבֶד[t] pref. הֶ interr. for הֲ } noun m. s. (suff. עַבְדִּי) dec. 6a (§ 35. r. 2) } עבד
הָעֹבֵד[u] וְ pref. הָ for הַ)(Kal part. act. sing. masc. dec. 7b . . . . עבד
הָעֲבֹדָה pref. id.)(noun fem. sing. dec. 10. . עבד
הָעֲבָדִים pref. id.)(n. m., pl. of עֶבֶד d. 6a (suff. עַבְדִּי) עבד
הָעֹבְדִים[x] pref. id.)(Kal part. act. m., pl. of עֹבֵד d. 7b. עבד
הֶעֱבַדְתִּיךָ[y] / וְהַעֲבַדְתִּיךָ[z] } Hiph. pret. 1 pers. sing., suff. 2 pers. sing. masc., (§ 13. rem. 10) . } עבד
הֶעֱבַדְתָּנִי[a] id. pret. 2 pers. sing. masc., suff. 1 pers. s. עבד
הָעֲבוֹדָה[b] full form for הָעֲבֹדָה (q. v.) . . . עבד
הָעֲבוֹט[aa] pref. הָ for הַ)(noun masc. sing. dec. 1a. עבט
הַעֲבֵט[c] וְ Hiph. inf. abs. . . . . עבט
הַעֲבַטְתָּ[d] וְ id. pret. 2 pers. sing. masc., [for הֶעֱ] § 13. rem. 10] acc. shifted by conv. וְ . עבט
הֶעֱבִיד[e] Hiph. pret. 3 pers. sing. masc. . . עבד
הֶעָבִים pref. הֶ bef. עָ for הַ)(noun masc., pl. of עָב dec. 1. (except constr. once עַב) . . עוב

הֶעָבִים[f] וְ pref. הָ for הַ)(noun m., pl. of [עָב] d. 8c. עבב
הַעֲבִיר[g] Hiph. inf. constr. dec. 1b. . . . עבר
הֶעֱבִיר וְ id. pret. 3 pers. sing. masc. . . עבר
הֶעֱבִירוּ [h]וְ id. pret. 3 pers. pl. masc. . . עבר
הַעֲבִירוּנִי[i] id. imp. pl. masc., suff. 1 pers. sing. . עבר
הֶעֱבִירַנִי[k] וְ id. pret. 3 pers. sing. masc., suff. 1 pers. s. עבר
הַעֲבֵר[l] / הַעֲבֶר־ [m]וְ } id. imp. sing. masc. (§ 11. rem. 5) . עבר
הָעֵבֶר[n] pref. הָ for הַ)(noun masc. sing. dec. 6b עבר
הָעֹבֵר pref. id.)(Kal part. act. sing. masc. dec. 7b עבר
הָעֶבְרָה pref. id.)(noun fem. sing. . . . עבר
הָעִבְרִי pref. id.)(gent. noun from עֵבֶר . עבר
הָעִבְרִיָּה[o] [p]וְ pref. id.)(id. fem. . . . עבר
הָעִבְרִיּוֹת[q] pref. id.)(id. pl. fem. . . . . עבר
הָעִבְרִיִּים[r] pref. id.)(id. pl. masc. comp. dec. 8f . עבר
הָעֲבָרִים pref. id.)(pr. name of a place . . עבר
הָעִבְרִים [s]וְ pref. id.)(gent. noun, pl. of עִבְרִי, fr. עֵבֶר עבר
הָעֹבְרִים pref. id.)(Kal part. act. m., pl. of עֹבֵר d. 7b עבר
הָעִבְרִיֹּת pref. id.)(gent. n. f., pl. of עִבְרִיָּה, fr. עִבְרִי m. עבר
הַעֲבִרֵנוּ[t] Hiph. inf. (הַעֲבִיר), suff. 1 pers. pl. dec. 1b עבר
הֶעֱבַרְתָּ[u] / וְהַעֲבַרְתָּ } id. pret. 2 pers. sing. masc. (§ 13. rem. 12 & 10) . . . } עבר
הֶעֱבַרְתִּי[x] / וְהַעֲבַרְתִּי } id. pret. 1 pers. sing. (§ 13. rem. 10) עבר
הֶעֱבַרְתֶּם וְ id. pret. 2 pers. pl. masc. (comp. id.) . עבר
הָעֲבֹתִים[y] / הָעֲבֹתֹת } pref. הָ for הַ)(noun com., pl. of עֲבֹת dec. 1a . . . } עבת
הָעֵגֶל pref. id.)(noun masc. sing. d. 6. (§ 35. r. 6) עגל
הָעֲגָלָה pref. id.)(noun fem. sing. dec. 12b עגל
הָעֶגְלָה [z]וְ pref. id.)(noun fem. sing. dec. 11c, with suff. עֶגְלָתוֹ (§ 42. rem. 1) . . עגל
הָעֲגָלוֹת / הָעֲגָלֹת } pref. id.)(id. pl. absolute, constr. עֶגְלוֹת עגל
הָעֵד[a] pref. id.)(noun masc. sing. dec. 1a . . עוד
הָעֵד וְ Hiph. inf. abs., or imp. sing. masc. . עוד
הֵעִד[b] id. pret. 3 pers. sing. masc. for הֵעִיד עוד
הָעֵדָה pref. הָ for הַ)(noun f. s. dec. 11b (c. עֲדַת) יעד
הָעֵדוּת pref. id.)(noun fem. sing., (pl. suff. עֵדְוֹתֶי, once עֵדוֹתֶי) . . . . עוד
הַעֲדִיו[c] Ch. Aph. pret. 3 pers. pl. masc. (§ 47. r. 4) עדה
הָעֵדִים pref. הָ for הַ)(noun masc., pl. of עֵד d. 1a עוד
הָעַדֻלָּמִי pref. id.)(gent. noun from עֲדֻלָּם . עדל
הָעֹדֵף pref. id.)(Kal part. act. sing. masc. d. 7b עדף
הֶעְדִּיף[d] Hiph. pret. 3 pers. sing. masc. (§ 13. r. 9) עדף
הָעֹדְפִים[e] pref. הָ for הַ)(Kal part. act. masc., pl. of עֹדֵף dec. 7b . . . . . עדף

[a] Da. 3. 22. [b] Da. 6. 24. [c] Ec. 11. 10. [d] Ge. 35. 2. [e] Je. 4. 4. [f] Je. 52. 18. [g] Je. 46. 4. [h] Je. 29. 2. [i] Je. 34. 19. [k] Is. 55. 13. [l] 2 Sa. 7. 15. [m] 1 Ki. 21. 25. [n] Ca. 2. 11. [o] Ps. 84. 11. [p] Is. 59. 2. [q] Is. 49. 2. [r] Je. 36. 19. [s] De. 31. 17. [t] Je. 2. 14. [u] Eze. 48. 19. [x] Eze. 34. 27. [y] Is. 43. 23. [z] Je. 17. 4. [a] Is. 43. 24. [b] 2 Ch. 35. 10. [c] De. 15. 8. [d] De. 15. 6. [e] Eze. 29. 18. [f] Eze. 41. 26 [g] Jos. 7. 7. [h] Nu. 8. 7. [i] 2 Ch. 35. 23. [k] Eze. 37. 2. [l] Ps. 119. 37, 39. [m] Ec. 11. 10. [n] 1 Sa. 26. 13. [o] De. 15. 12. [p] Je. 34. 9. [q] Ex. 1. 16. [r] Ex. 3. 18. [s] 1 Sa. 14. 21. [t] De. 2. 30. [u] Jos. 7. 7. [x] Zec. 3. 4. [y] Ju. 15. 14. [z] 1 Sa. 6. 14. [a] De. 19. 18. [aa] De. 24. 11, 13. [b] Ge. 43. 3. [c] Da. 5. 20. [d] Ex. 16. 18. [e] Nu. 3. 46, 48, 49.

הָעֲדֶפֶת[u]	pref. הָ for הַ χ id. fem. sing.	עדף
הָעֵדֶר[a]	pref. id. χ noun m. sing. dec. 6. (§ 35. r. 6)	עדר
הָעֲדָרִים	pref. id. χ id. pl., absolute state	עדר
הָעֵדֹת	pref. id. χ noun f., pl. abs. of עֵדָה d. 11 b	יעד
הָעֵדֹת	defect. for הָעֵדוֹת (q. v.)	עוד
הַעִדֹתָה[b]	Hiph. pret. 2 pers. sing. masc., for הַעִידֹתָ (§ 8. rem. 5. & § 21. rem. 14 & 24)	עוד
הַעִדֹתִי	id. pret. 1 pers. sing. (§ 14. rem. 24)	עוד
הַעוֹד	pref. הַ interr. for הֲ χ adv., d. 1 a (§ 1 note)	עוד
הַעוֹדָם[c]	pref. id. χ id., suff. 3 pers. sing. masc.	עוד
הַעוֹדֶנּוּ	pref. id. χ id., (verbal) suff. 3 pers. sing. m.	עוד
הַעֲוֵה[d]	Hiph. inf. absolute	עוה
הֶעֱוָה[e]	id. pret. 3 pers. sing. masc.	עוה
הֶעֱווּ[f]	id. pret. 3 pers. pl.	עוה
הָעַוִּים	ו pref. הָ for הַ· χ gent. noun pl. fr. עַוָּא	עוה
הֶעֱוִינוּ[g]	ו׳ Hiph. pret. 1 pers. pl. (§ 24. rem. 14)	עוה
הֶעֱוֵיתִי	id. pret. 1 pers. sing.	עוה
הָעוֹלָה	pref. הָ for הַ· χ subs., or (1 Ch. 26. 16) Kal part. fem. (of עוֹלֶה) dec. 10.	עלה
הָעוֹלֶה[h]	ו pref. id. χ Kal part. act. sing. masc. dec. 9 a	עלה
הָעוֹלֹת[i]	pref. id. χ noun fem., pl. of עֹלָה dec. 10.	עלה
הָעֹלִים	pref. id. χ Kal part. act. masc., pl. of עוֹלֶה dec. 9 a	עלה
הָעוֹלָם	pref. id. χ noun masc. sing. dec. 2 b	עלם
הֶעָוֹן	pref. הֶ bef. עָ for הַ χ noun masc. s. d. 3 a	עוה
הָעוֹף	ו׳ pref. הָ for הַ· χ noun masc. sing.	עוף
הָעֹפֶרֶת[k]	pref. id. χ noun fem. sing.	עפר
הָעוּץ	pref. id. χ pr. name of a region	עוץ
הָעוֹר	pref. id. χ noun masc. sing. dec. 1 a	עור
הָעִוֵּר[l]	pref. id. χ adj. masc. sing. dec. 7 b	עור
הָעִוְרִים[m]	ו״ pref. id. χ id. pl. absolute state	עור
הָעֵזוּ[o]	Hiph. imp. pl. masc.	עוז
הֵעֵז[p]	Hiph. pret. 3 pers. sing. masc.	עזז
הָעֹזְבִים[q]	pref. הָ χ Kal part. act. m., pl. of עֹזֵב dec. 7 b	עזב
הָעֹזֶבֶת[r]	pref. id. χ id. fem. sing.	עזב
הֵעֵזָה[s]	Hiph. pret. 3 p. s. f. [for הֵעֵזָּה § 18. r. 15 note]	עזז
הָעִזוּ[t]	Hiph. imp. pl. masc.	עוז
הָעֲזוּבָה[u]	pref. הָ for הַ· χ noun fem. sing. dec. 10.	עזב
הָעָזִּיאֵלִי	pref. id. χ patronym. from עֻזִּיאֵל (q. v.)	עזז
הָעִזִּים	pref. id. χ noun fem. pl. of עֵז dec. 8 b	עזז
הָעֲזַנְיָה[x]	ו׳y pref. id. χ noun fem. sing.	עזנ
הָעֶזֶר / הָעֵזֶר / הָעֶזֶר	pref. id. χ pr. name, see אֶבֶן עֶזֶר	אבן
הָעֲזָרָה	ו׳ pref. id. χ noun fem. sing.	עזר
הָעֶזְרִי	pref. id. χ patronym., see אֲבִיעֶזֶר	אב
הָעַזָּתִי	pref. id. χ gent. noun from עַזָּה	עזז
הָעֲטוּפִים[z]	pref. id. χ Kal part. p. m., pl. of [עָטוּף] d. 3 a	עטף
הֶעֱטִית[a]	Hiph. pret. 2 pers. sing. masc. (§ 24. rem. 14)	עטה
הָעֲטַלֵּף[qq]	ו׳ pref. הָ for הַ· χ noun masc. sing. dec. 1 b	עטלף
הָעֲטֻפִים[b]	defect. for הָעֲטוּפִים (q. v.)	עטף
הָעֲטָרָה[c]	pref. הָ for הַ· χ noun fem. sing., constr. עֲטֶרֶת (§ 42. rem. 5)	עטר
הָעֲטָרוֹת[d]	ו pref. id. χ id. pl., abs. state (§ 44. rem. 5)	עטר
הָעַי / הָעָי	ו׳ ו׳ pref. id. χ pr. name of a place	עוה
הֵעִיד	Hiph. pret. 3 pers. sing. masc.	עוד
הָעִידוּ[e]	ו id. imp. pl. masc.	עוד
הֵעִידוּ[f]	id. pret. 3 pers. pl.	עוד
הַעִידֹתָ[g]	Hiph. pret. 2 pers. sing. masc. for הַעִידוֹתָ (§ 21. rem. 24)	עוד
הַעִידֹתִי	id. pret. 1 pers. sing.	עוד
הָעִיזוּ[h]	Hiph. imp. pl. masc.	עוז
הֵעִיזוּ[i]	id. pret. 3 pers. pl.	עוז
הָעַיִט[k] / הַעַיִט[l]	pref. הָ for הַ· / pref. הַ dag. impl. } noun masc. sing. dec. 6 h	עיט
הָעַיִן / הָעָיִן	pref. הָ for הַ· χ noun fem. sing. dec. 6 h	עין
הָעַיְנָה[m]	pref. id. χ id. with paragogic ה	עין
הָעֵינוֹת[n]	pref. id. χ id. pl. abs., constr. עֵינוֹת (§ 35. r. 12)	עין
הַעֵינֵי	pref. הַ interr. for הֲ χ id. du., constr. state	עין
הָעִיר[o]	Kh. הָעִיר q. v., K. חָצֵר (q. v.)	חצר
הָעִיר	ו׳ pref. הָ for הַ· χ noun fem. sing. irr., pl. עָרִים (§ 45)	עור
הֵעִיר	Hiph. pret. 3 pers. sing. masc.	עור
הָעִירָה[p]	id. imp. sing. masc. with parag. ה (§ 11. r. 5)	עור
הָעִירָה	pref. הָ for הַ· χ noun fem. sing. (עִיר) with paragogic ה, irr. (§ 45)	עור
הָעִירוּ[q]	Hiph. imp. pl. masc.	עור
הַעִירֹתִי[r]	id. pret. 1 pers. s., for הַעִירוֹתִי (§ 21. r. 24)	עור
הָעֲיָרִים[s]	ו pref. הָ for הַ· χ noun masc. pl. of עַיִר dec. 6 h (§ 35. rem. 12)	עיר
הַעִירֹתִיהוּ[t]	Hiph. pret. 1 pers. sing., suff. 3 pers. sing. masc. for הַעִי׳ (§ 21. rem. 24)	עור
הָעַכְבָּר	ו pref. הָ for הַ· χ noun masc. sing. dec. 2 b	עכב
הָעֲכָסִים[u]	pref. id. χ noun masc., pl. of עֶכֶס dec. 6 a	עכס
הַעַל	pref. הַ interr. χ prep., pl. c. עֲלֵי, suff. עֲלֵיהֶם &c. (§ 31. rem. 5)	עלה
הַעַל[x]	ו׳ Hiph. imp. s. m., ap. for הַעֲלֵה (§ 24. r. 17)	עלה
הָעֹל	pref. הָ for הַ· χ noun masc. sing. dec. 8 c	עלל
הֻעַל[y]	Chald. Hoph. pret. 3 pers. sing. masc. [for הֻעַל comp. § 14. rem. 1]	עלל

[a] Je. 13. 20. [b] Ex. 19. 23. [c] Ex. 4. 18. [d] Je. 9. 4. [e] 2 Sa. 19. 20. [f] Je. 3. 21. [g] Ps. 106. 6. [h] Is. 24. 18. [i] Eze. 45. 17. [k] Zec. 5. 8. [l] De. 28. 29. [u] Ex. 26. 12. [m] 2 Sa. 5. 6, 8. [n] Is. 42. 18. [o] Ex. 9. 19. [p] Pr. 21. 29. [q] Pr. 2. 13. [qq] Le. 11. 19. De. 14. 18. [r] Pr. 2. 17. [s] Pr. 7. 13. [t] Je. 6. 1. [u] Is. 6. 12. [x] Le. 11. 13. [y] De. 14. 12. [z] La. 2. 19. [a] Ps. 89. 46. [b] Ge. 30. 42. [c] Eze. 21. 31. [d] Zec. 6. 14. [e] Am. 3. 13. [f] Ne. 9. 26. [g] Ne. 9. 34. [h] Je. 4. 6. [i] Is. 10. 31. [k] Ge. 15. 11; Je. 12. 9. [l] Je. 12. 9, 9. [m] Ge. 24. 16, 45. [n] 2 Ch. 32. 3. [o] 2 Ki. 20. 4. [p] Ps. 35. 23. [q] Joel 4. 9. [r] Is. 41. 25. [s] Is. 30. 24. [t] Is. 45. 13. [u] Is. 3. 18. [x] Ex. 33. 12. [y] Da. 5. 13.

הַעֲלָה וְ pref. הָ for הַ·)(subst. or part. fem. (from עֹלֶה masc.) dec. 10 . . . עלה

הַעֲלֵה[a] Hiph. inf. absolute . . . . עלה

הָעֹלֶה[b] וְ pref. הָ for הַ·)(Kal part. act. m. dec. 7b עלה

הֶעָלֶה[c] [d] וְ pref. הֶ bef. עָ for הַ)(noun m. s. dec. 9b עלה

הֶעֱלָה[e] } Hiph. pret. 3 pers. s. m. (§ 13. rem. 12) עלה
וְ הֶעֱלָה

הָעֳלָה Hoph. pret. 3 pers. sing. masc. [for הָעֳלָה § 13. rem. 12] . . . . עלה

הַעֲלֵהוּ[f] וְ Hiph. imp. sing. masc., suff. 3 pers. s. m. עלה

הַעֲלוּ id. imp. pl. masc. . . . . . עלה

הֵעָלוּ[g] Niph. imp. pl. masc. . . . . עלה

הֶעֱלוּ וְ Hiph. pret. 3 pers. pl. . . . . עלה

הֻעֲלוּ[h] Hoph. pret. 3 p. pl. [for הָעֳלוּ comp. § 14. r. 1] עלל

הֶעֱלוּךָ[i] וְ Hiph. pret. 3 pers. pl., suff. 2 pers. s. m. עלה

הַעֲלוֹת[k] וְ id. inf. constr.; in 2 Ch. 24. 14, perhaps subst. (with the art. הָ), pl. of עֲלִי . . עלה

הָעֹלוֹת וְ pref. הָ for הַ·)(noun fem., pl. of עֹלָה d. 10. עלה

הֵעָלוֹת Niph. inf. constr. . . . . . עלה

הַעֲלוֹתִי Hiph. inf. (הַעֲלוֹת), suff. 1 pers. sing. dec. 1b עלה

הַעֲלִי[m] וְ Hiph. imp. sing. fem. . . . . עלה

הָעֲלִיָּה pref. הָ for הַ·)(noun fem. sing. dec. 10. עלה

הֶעָלֶיהָ[o] וְ pref. הֶ art. relat. before עָ for הַ)(prep. (עַל), suff. 3 pers. sing. fem. . . . עלה

הָעֶלְיוֹן pref. הָ for הַ·)(adj. masc. sing. dec. 1b . עלה

הָעֶלְיוֹנָה pref. id.)(id. fem. dec. 10. . . . עלה

הָעֶלְיוֹנֹת[p] pref. id.)(id. fem. pl. . . . . עלה

הָעֲלִיּוֹת[q] וְ pref. id.)(noun fem., pl. of עֲלִיָּה dec. 10. עלה

הָעַלִּיזָה[r] pref. id.)(adj. fem. sing. from [עַלִּיז] masc. עלז

הָעֲלִילִיָּה[s] pref. id.)(noun fem. sing. . . . . עלל

הָעֹלִים pref. id.)(Kal part. act. m., pl. עֹלֶה dec. 9a עלה

הֶעְלִים[t] Hiph. pret. 3 pers. sing. masc. [for הֶעֱלִים § 13. rem. 9] . . . . . עלם

הֶעְלִימוּ[u] id. pret. 3 pers. pl. . . . . . עלם

הֶעֱלִיתָ[x] } Hiph. pret. 2 pers. sing. masc. (§ 24. rem. 14) . . . . } עלה
הֶעֱלִיתָ

הֶעֱלִית[y] וְ } id. id. acc. shifted (§ 13. rem. 10, comp. § 8. rem. 7) . . . } עלה
וְ הֶעֱלִית

הֶעֱלִית[z] id. pret. 2 pers. sing. fem. . . . . עלה

הֶעֱלִיתִי } id. pret. 1 pers. sing. (§ 13. rem. 10, comp. § 9. rem. 11) . . . } עלה
וְ הֶעֱלִיתִי

הֶעֱלִיתִיהוּ[a] וְ id. id., suff. 3 pers. sing. masc. (§ 13. r. 10) עלה

הֶעֱלִיתִיךָ וְ id. id., suff. 2 pers. sing. masc. . . עלה

הֶעֱלִיתִים[b] וְ id. id., suff. 3 pers. pl. masc. . . עלה

הֶעֱלִיתֶם וְ id. pret. 2 pers. pl. masc. . . . עלה

הֶעֱלִיתָנוּ id. pret. 2 pers. sing. masc., suff. 1 pers. pl. עלה

הֶעֱלִיתֻנוּ id. pret. 2 pers. pl. masc., suff. 1 pers. pl. עלה

הֶעֶלְךָ[c] id. pret. 3 pers. sing. masc., suff. 2 pers. sing. masc. (§ 24. rem. 21) . . . עלה

הָעֹלָם[d] pref. הָ for הַ·)(noun masc. sing. dec. 2b (for עוֹלָם) . . . . . עלם

הָעֶלֶם[ll] pref. id.)(noun m. s. (for עֶלֶם § 35. rem. 2) עלם

הַעְלֵם[e] Hiph. inf. absolute (§ 13. rem. 10) . עלם

הָעַלְמָה pref. הָ for הַ·)(noun fem. sing. dec. 12a . עלם

הֶעֱלָנוּ Hiph. pret. 3 pers. sing. masc., suff. 1 pers. pl. (§ 24. rem. 21) . . . . עלה

הַעֲלֵנִי[f] Chald. Aph. imp. s. m., suff. 1 pers. s. [for אַעֲלְנִי; comp. § 47. rem. 4, & § 14. rem. 1] עלל

הָעֹלֹת[g] pref. הָ for הַ·)(Kal part. act. fem., pl. of עֹלָה, from עֹלֶה masc. . . . . עלה

הֶעֶלְתָה[h] וְ Hiph. pret. 3 pers. sing. fem. [for הֶעֶלְתָה = הֶעֱלָתָה; § 13. rem. 10] . . . . עלה

הָעַלְתָה[i] Hoph. pret. 3 pers. sing. fem. [for הָעָלְתָה § 13. rem. 12] . . . . . עלה

הֵעָלֹתוֹ[k] Niph. inf. (הֵעָלוֹת), suff. 3 pers. s. m. dec. 1b עלה

הַעֲלֹתִי Hiph. inf. (הַעֲלוֹת), suff. 1 pers. sing. dec. 1b עלה

הֶעֱלִתִיךָ[l] id. pret. 1 pers. sing., suff. 2 pers. sing. masc. עלה

הַעֲלִתֶם[pp] וְ id. pret. 2 pers. pl. masc. (§ 13. rem. 10) עלה

הֶעֱלָתַם[m] id. pret. 3 pers. sing. fem., suff. 3 pers. pl. masc. (§ 24. rem. 21c) . . . עלה

הָעָם וְ pref. הָ for הַ·)(with the art. for עַם, noun com. dec. 8d (§ 45) . . . . עמם

הָעַמֻּד[n] pref. id.)(noun masc. s. dec. 1b (for עַמּוּד) עמד

הָעֹמֵד pref. id.)(Kal part. act. sing. masc. dec. 7b עמד

הַעֲמֵד[o] Hiph. imp. sing. masc. . . . . . עמד

הֶעֱמִדָהּ[p] וְ Hiph. pret. 3 pers. s. m., suff. 3 pers. s. fem. עמד

הָעֹמְדוֹת pref. הָ for הַ·)(Kal part. act. fem., pl. עֹמֶדֶת dec. 13a (from עֹמֵד masc. § 8. rem. 19) עמד

הָעַמֻּדִים pref id.)(noun masc. pl. (for עַמּוּדִים) from עַמּוּד dec. 1b . . . . . עמד

הָעֹמְדִים pref. id.)(Kal part. act. m., pl. of עֹמֵד dec. 7b עמד

הֶעֱמַדְנוּ[q] וְ Hiph. pret. 1 pers. pl. . . . . עמד

הֶעֱמַדְתָּ } וְ id. pret. 2 pers. s. m. (§ 13. r. 10, & § 8. r. 5) עמד
הֶעֱמַדְתָּ
הֶעֱמַדְתָּה[r]

הֶעֱמַדְתִּי id. pret. 1 pers. sing. . . . . עמד

הֶעֱמַדְתִּיהוּ[s] וְ id. id., suff. 3 pers. sing. masc. (§ 13. r. 10) עמד

הֶעֱמַדְתִּיךָ[t] id. id., suff. 2 pers. sing. masc. . . . עמד

הָעַמּוּד pref. הָ for הַ·)(noun masc. sing. dec. 1b עמד

[a] Eze. 23. 46. [b] Je. 48. 44. [c] Job 13. 25. [d] Je. 8. 13. [e] Hab. 1. 15.
[f] Ge. 22. 2. [g] Nu. 16. 24. [h] Da. 5. 15. [i] Eze. 32. 3. [k] 1 Ch. 23. 31.
[l] 2 Ch. 31. 3. [m] 1 Sa. 28. 11. [n] 1 Sa. 28. 8. [o] 1 Sa. 9. 24. [p] Eze. 42. 5.
[q] 2 Ch. 3. 9. [r] Zep. 2. 15. [s] Je. 32. 19. [t] 2 Ki. 4. 27. [u] Eze. 22. 26.
[x] Ex. 32. 7. [y] Ex. 40. 4. [z] Is. 57. 6. [a] Ju. 11. 31. [b] Je. 27. 22.
[c] Ne. 9. 18. [d] 1 Ch. 16. 36. [e] Le. 20. 4. [f] Da. 2. 24. [g] Ge. 41. 27.
[h] 1 Sa. 2. 19. [i] Na. 2. 8. [k] Ex. 40. 37. [l] Mi. 6. 4. [ll] 1 Sa. 17. 56.
[m] Jos. 2. 6. [n] Je. 52. 21. [o] Is. 21. 6. [p] Nu. 5. 16. [pp] Ge. 50. 25.
[q] Ne. 10. 33. [r] Ps. 30. 8. [s] 1 Ch. 17. 14. [t] Ex. 9. 16.

הָעַמּוּדִים [a]	וְ״ pref. הָ for ·הַ)(id. pl., absolute state .	עמד
הָעַמּוֹנִי	pref. id.)(gent. noun from עַמּוֹן .	עמם
הָעַמּוֹנִים	pref. id.)(id. pl. masc. . .	עמם
הָעַמּוֹנִית	pref. id.)(id. sing. fem. . . .	עמם
הַעֲמִיד [b]	וְ Hiph. inf. absolute . . .	עמד
הֶעֱמִיד	וְ׳ id. pret. 3 pers. sing. masc. . .	עמד
הַעֲמִידָהּ [c]	וְ id. inf. sing. masc., suff. 3 pers. sing. fem.	עמד
הֶעֱמִידוֹ [d]	וְ id. pret. 3 pers. sing. m., suff. 3 pers. s. m.	עמד
הָעַמִּים	pref. הָ for ·הַ)(n. com., pl. of עַם d. 8d (§ 45)	עמם
הֶעֱמִים [e] הֶעֱמִים [f]	Hiph. pret. 3 pers. sing. masc. (§ 13. r. 9)	עמם
הֶעְמִיק [g]	Hiph. pret. 3 pers. sing. masc. .	עמק
הֶעְמִיקוּ	id. pret. 3 pers. pl.	עמק
הֶעָמָל [h]	pref. הֶ bef. עָ for הַ)(noun masc. sing. dec. 4c	עמל
הָעֲמָלֵק	pref. הָ for ·הַ)(pr. name of a people .	עמלק
הָעֲמָלֵקִי	וְ׳ pref. id.)(gent. noun from the preceding	עמלק
הָעַמֹּנִי	pref. id.)(gent. noun from עַמּוֹן . .	עמם
הָעַמֹּנִים	וְ pref. id.)(id. pl. masc. . . .	עמם
הָעַמֹּנִית	pref. id.)(id. sing. fem. . . .	עמם
הָעֲמֻסִים [i]	pref. הָ for ·הַ)(Kal part. pass. masc., pl. of [עָמוּס] dec. 3a	עמס
הַעֲמֵק [k]	Hiph. imp. sing. masc.	עמק
הָעֵמֶק	pref. הָ for ·הַ)(noun masc. sing. dec. 6b (and pr. name in compos. see בֵּית)	עמק
הָעֲמֻקָּה [l]	pref. id.)(adj. fem. sing. dec. 10, from עָמֹק masc. (comp. § 37. No. 3c) . .	עמק
הֶעֱמִקוּ [m]	Hiph. pret. 3 pers. pl. for הֶעֱמִיקוּ .	עמק
הָעֲמָקִים	וְ״ [n] pref. הָ for ·הַ)(n. m., pl. of עֵמֶק d. 6b	עמק
הָעֹמֶר	וְ׳ [o] pref. id.)(noun masc. sing. dec. 6c	עמר
הָעֳמָרִים [p]	pref. id.)(id. pl., absolute state .	עמר
הָעַמְרָמִי	pref. id.)(patronym. of עַמְרָם .	עמם
הָעֲנָבִים [q]	pref. id.)(noun masc., pl. of עֵנָב dec. 4b	ענב
הֶעָנֹג [r]	וְ pref. הֶ bef. עָ for ·הַ)(adj. masc. sing. .	ענג
הָעֲנֻגָּה [s]	וְ pref. הָ for ·הַ)(id. fem. (comp. § 37. No. 3c)	ענג
הָעֹנֶה [t]	pref. id.)(Kal part. act. sing. masc. dec. 9a	ענה
הָעֲנוֹק	pref. id.)(pr. name masc. . .	ענק
הֶעָנִי	pref. הֶ bef. עָ for הַ)(adj. m. d. 8 (§ 37. No. 4)	ענה
הָעֲנִיִּים [u]	pref. הָ for ·הַ)(id. pl., absolute state	ענה
הָעֹנִים [x]	pref. id.)(Kal part. act. m., pl. of עֹנֶה d. 9a	ענה
הָעִנְיָן	pref. id.)(noun masc. sing. dec. 2b .	ענה
הַעֲנֵיק [y]	Hiph. inf. absolute	ענק
הֶעָנָן	וְ׳ pref. הֶ bef. עָ for הַ)(noun masc. sing. d. 4c	ענן
הָעֲנָק	pref. הָ for ·הַ)(pr. name masc. .	ענק
הָעֲנָקוֹת [z]	pref. id.)(noun masc., with pl. fem. term. from עֲנָק . . .	ענק
הָעֲנָקִים	pref. id.)(pr. name of a people, pl. of עֲנָק	ענק
הָעַנְּתוֹתִי הָעַנְתֹתִי	pref. id.)(pr. name of a place . .	ענה
הָעֹפֶל	pref. id.)(noun masc. sing. dec. 6c .	עפל
הָעֶפְנִי	וְ pref. id.)(gent. noun . .	עפן
הֶעָפָר	וְ״ [a] pref. הֶ bef. f. עָ הַ)(noun masc. s. d. 4c	עפר
הָעֹפֶרֶת [b]	pref. הָ for ·הַ)(noun fem. sing. (for עֹפֶרֶת, comp. § 35. rem. 2) . . .	עפר
הָעֵץ	pref. id.)(noun m. s. d. 7 (§ 36. r. 2 & 4)	עצה
הָעֶצֶב [c]	pref. הָ)(noun masc. sing. dec. 6 .	עצב
הָעֲצַבִּים [d]	pref. הָ for ·הַ)(id. pl., absolute state .	עצב
הָעֲצַבִּים	pref. id.)(noun masc., pl. of [עָצָב] dec. 8a	עצב
הָעֵצָה	pref. id.)(noun fem. sing. d. 11b [for יְעָצָה]	יעץ
הֶעָצֶה [e]	pref. הֶ bef. עָ for הַ)(noun masc. sing. .	עצה
הָעֲצוּמִים [f]	pref. הָ for ·הַ)(adj. masc., pl. of עָצוּם d. 3a	עצם
הָעֵצִים	וְ׳ pref. id.)(n. m., pl. of עֵץ (§ 36. r. 2 & 4)	עצה
הֶעָצֵל [g]	pref. הֶ bef. עָ for הַ)(adj. masc. sing.	עצל
הָעֲצָמוֹת [h] הָעֲצָמִים	וְ׳ pref. הָ for ·הַ)(noun fem., pl. of עֶצֶם (suff. עַצְמִי) dec. 6a .	עצם
הָעֶצְנוֹ	pref. id.)(Kh. עֶצְנוֹ, K. עֶצְנִי, gent. noun; but see under the R. . .	עצן
הֶעָקֹב [k]	pref. הֶ bef. עָ for הַ)(noun masc. sing. .	עקב
הָעֲקֻדִּים [l]	pref. הָ for הַ)(adj. masc., pl. of עָקֹד dec. 8c (§ 37. Nos. 2 & 3) . .	עקד
הָעֶקְרוֹנִי	וְ pref. id.)(gent. noun from עֶקְרוֹן .	עקר
הָעֶקְרֹנִים	pref. id.)(id. pl. . . .	עקר
הָעָרֶב	in pause for הָעֶרֶב q. v. (§ 35. rem. 2) .	ערב
הַעֲרֵב [m]	וְ Hiph. inf. absolute . .	ערב
הָעֶרֶב	וְ״ [n] pref. הָ for ·הַ)(noun masc. sing. (du. עַרְבַּיִם) dec. 6a, also pr. name . .	ערב
הֶעָרֹב	pref. id.)(noun masc. sing. . .	ערב
הָעֹרֵב [o]	pref. id.)(noun masc. sing. dec. 7b	ערב
הֶעָרֹב [p]	pref. הֶ bef. עָ for הַ)(noun masc. sing. .	ערב
הָעֲרָבָה	וְ׳ pref. הָ for ·הַ)(noun fem. sing. dec. 11c, § 42. r. 1 (and pr. n. in compos. see בֵּית)	ערב
הָעֵרָבוֹן [q]	pref. id.)(noun masc. sing. .	ערב
הָעַרְבִי	pref. id.)(gent. n. fr. עֲרָב (comp. § 35. r. 10)	ערב
הָעַרְבִיאִים הָעַרְבִיִּים וְהָעַרְבִים	pref. id.)(id. pl., Kh. עַרְבִיִּים (§ 37. No. 4, also rem. 5) . . .	ערב
הָעֲרָבִים [r]	pref. id.)(n. m., pl. of עֲרָב d. 6a (comp. the foll.)	ערב
הָעַרְבַּיִם הָעַרְבָּיִם	pref. id.)(id. du., absolute state .	ערב
הָעֹרְבִים [s]	[t] וְ pref. id.)(noun masc., pl. of עֹרֵב dec. 7b	ערב
הָעֲרָבָתָה [u]	pref. id.)(noun f. s. (עֲרָבָה) with parag ה	ערב
הָעַרְבָתִי	pref. id.)(gent. n. fr. עֲרָבָה (comp. § 42. r. 1)	ערב
הֶעֱרָה	Hiph. pret. 3 pers. sing. masc.	ערה

[a] Je. 52. 21. [b] Ne. 7. 3. [c] Eze. 24. 11. [d] Le. 27. 8. [e] 2 Ch. 10. 11. [f] 1 Ki. 12. 11. [g] Is. 30. 33. [h] Ec. 2. 20. [i] Is. 46. 3. [k] Is. 7. 11. [l] Eze. 23. 32. [m] Je. 49. 8, 30. [n] Mi. 1. 4. [o] Ex. 16. 36. [p] Ruth 2. 15. [q] Ge. 40. 11. [r] De. 28. 54. [s] De. 28. 56. [t] Ge. 35. 3. [u] Is. 41. 17. [x] Je. 44. 20. [y] De. 15. 14. [z] Ju. 8. 26.

[a] Ne. 4. 4. [b] Nu. 31. 22. [c] Je. 22. 28. [d] Ps. 127. 2. [e] Le. 3. 9. [f] Is. 8. 7. [g] Pr. 10. 26. [h] Eze. 24. 10. [i] Eze. 24. 5. [k] Is. 40. 4. [l] Ge. 30. 35. [m] 1 Sa. 17. 16. [n] 2 Ch. 31. 3. [o] Ge. 8. 7. [p] Ex. 8. 17, 20, 25, 27. [q] Ge. 38. 18, 20. [r] Is. 15. 7. [s] 1 Ki. 17. 4. [t] 1 Ki. 17. 6. [u] Jos. 18. 18.

הָעֲרוּפָה[a] pref. הָ for הַ·)(Kal part. p. s. f. [fr. עָרוּף m.] — ערף
הָעֵרִי pref. id.)(pr. name masc. — עור
הֶעֱרִיךְ[b] [c]וְ' Hiph. pret. 3 pers. sing. masc. — ערך
הֶעֱרִיכוֹ[d] וְ id., suff. 3 pers. sing. masc. — ערך
הֶעָרִים וְ' pref. הֶ bef. עָ for הַ)(noun fem., prop. pl. (f עָר see עִיר (§ 45) — עיר
הָעֲרֻכוֹת[e] pref. הָ for הַ·)(Kal part. p. fem., pl. of עֲרוּכָה dec. 10 (from עָרוּךְ masc.) — ערך
הָעֹרְכִים[f] pref. id.)(id. part. act. m., pl. of עֹרֵךְ d. 7b — ערך
הָעֶרְכְּךָ[g] pref. id.)(noun masc. sing., suff. 2 pers. sing. masc. from עֵרֶךְ dec. 6 (§ 35. rem. 6) — ערך
הֵעָרֵל[h] וְ Niph. imp. sing. masc. — ערל
הֶעָרֵל pref. הֶ bef. עָ for הַ)(noun masc. sing. d. 5c — ערל
הָעֲרָלוֹת[i] pref. הָ for הַ)(n. f., pl. of עָרְלָה d. 12c (p. n.) — ערל
הָעֲרֵלִים pref. id.)(noun masc., pl. of עָרֵל dec. 5c — ערל
הָעֲרֵמָה[k] pref. id.)(noun fem. sing. dec. 10. — ערם
הָעֲרֵמוֹת pref. id.)(id. pl. — ערם
הָעֵרָנִי pref. id.)(gent. noun from עֵרָן — עור
הָעַרְעָר[l] pref. id.)(adj. masc. sing. — ערר
הָעֲרֹעֵרִי pref. id.)(gent. noun from עֲרוֹעֵר — ערר
הָעֲרָפֶל[m] [n]וְ' pref. id.)(noun masc. sing. — ערפל
הָעַרְקִי pref. id.)(gent. noun — ערק
הָעֹרְקִים[o] pref. id.)(Kal part. act. m., pl. of [עֹרֵק] d. 7b — ערק
הָעֹשֵׂה[p] pref. id.)(constr. of the following — עשה
הָעֹשֶׂה pref. id.)(Kal part. act. sing. masc. dec. 9a — עשה
הָעֹשׂוֹ[q] pref. id.)(id., suff. 3 pers. sing. masc. — עשה
הֶעָשׂוּ[r] } pref. הֶ bef. עָ for הַ)(Kal part. p. masc. sing. (§ 24. rem. 4) — עשה
הֶעָשׂוּי }
הָעֲשׂוּיָה[s] pref. הָ for הַ·)(id. fem. dec. 10. — עשה
הָעֲשׂוּיִם[t] pref. id.)(id. pl. absolute masc. dec. 3a — עשה
הֵעָשׂוֹתוֹ[ss] Niph. inf. fr. (הֵעָשׂוֹת) suff. 3 p. s. m. d. 1b — עשה
הָעֲשִׂיָה[u] defect. for הָעֲשׂוּיָה (q. v.) — עשה
הָעֹשִׂים pref. הָ for הַ·)(Kal part. act. masc., pl. of עֹשֶׂה dec. 9a — עשה
הֶעָשִׁיר pref. הֶ bef. עָ for הַ)(noun masc. sing. d. 3a — עשר
הָעֲשִׂירִי pref. הָ for הַ·)(adj. ord. masc. from עֶשֶׂר — עשר
הָעֲשִׂירִית[x] pref. id.)(id. fem. — עשר
הֶעָשָׁן pref. הֶ bef. עָ for הַ)(noun masc. sing. d. 4c — עשן
הָעֲשֵׁנִים[y] pref. הָ for הַ·)(adj. masc., pl. of עָשֵׁן d. 5c — עשן
הָעֹשֶׁק pref. id.)(noun masc. sing. — עשק
הָעֹשְׁקוֹת[zz] pref. id.)(Kal part. act. fem. pl. [of עֹשְׁקָה or עֹשֶׁקֶת § 8. rem. 19] — עשק
הָעֲשׁוּקִים[z] pref. id.)(id. part. p., pl. of עָשׁוּק dec. 3a; or noun masc. pl. — עשק
הָעֹשֶׁר [a]וְ' pref. id.)(noun masc. sing. dec. 6c — עשר
הֶעָשֹׂר pref. הֶ bef. עָ for הַ)(num. card. masc. sing. — עשר

הָעֶשְׂרֵה pref. הָ for הַ·)(id. masc. sing. — עשר
הָעֲשִׂרִי pref. id.)(adj. ord. masc. from עֶשֶׂר — עשר
הָעֶשְׂרִים pref. id.)(num. com. gen., pl. of עֲשָׂרָה — עשר
הָעֲשִׂירִית[b] pref. id.)(adj. ord., fem. of עֲשִׂירִי m. fr. עֶשֶׂר — עשר
הֶעֱשַׁרְתְּ[c] Hiph. pret. 2 pers. sing. fem. — עשר
הֶעֱשַׁרְתִּי[d] id. pret. 1 pers. sing. — עשר
הָעֹשֹׂת[e] pref. הָ for הַ·)(Kal part. act. fem., pl. of עֹשָׂה dec. 10, (from עֹשֶׂה masc.) — עשה
הָעַשְׁתָּרוֹת וְ' pref. id.)(pr. name, pl. of עַשְׁתֹּרֶת q. v.
הָעַשְׁתְּרָתִי pref. id.)(gent. noun from the preceding
הָעֵת [f]וְ' pref. הָ art. f. הַ· } noun com. sing. d. 8b — עדה
הַעֵת pref. הַ interr. f. הֲ } [for עֵדֶת]
הָעַתֻּדִים[g] } pref. הָ for הַ·)(noun masc., pl. [עַתּוּד] dec. 1b — עתד
הָעַתּוּדִים[h] }
הָעֲתִידִים[i] pref. id.)(adj. masc., pl. of עָתִיד dec. 3a — עתד
הָעִתִּים [k]וְ' pref. id.)(noun com., pl. of עֵת, see הָעֵת — עדה
הֶעְתִּיקוּ Hiph. pret. 3 pers. pl. [for הֶעֱתִיקוּ, § 13. r. 9] — עתק
הַעְתִּירוּ [l]וְ' Hiph. imp. pl. m. [for הַעֲתִירוּ § 13. r. 9] — עתר
הֵעָתֶר־[m] וְ Niph. imp. sing. masc. (§ 9. rem. 3) — עתר
הַעְתַּרְתִּי[n] וְ Hiph. pret. 1 pers. sing. (§ 13. r. 9 & 10, comp. § 8. rem. 2) — עתר
הַעְתַּרְתֶּם[o] וְ id. pret. 2 pers. pl. masc. — עתר
הַפְּאֵרִים[p] pref. הַ)(noun masc., pl. of פְּאֵר, pl. c. פַּאֲרֵי (§ 35. rem. 12) — פאר
הַפֵּאֹת pref. id.)(noun fem., pl. of פֵּאָה dec. 11b — פאה
הֲפֻגוֹת[q] noun fem., pl. of [הֲפוּגָה] dec. 10. — פוג
הִפְגִּיעַ[r] Hiph. pret. 3 pers. sing. masc. — פגע
הִפְגִּעוּ[s] id. pret. 3 pers. pl. — פגע
הִפְגַּעְתִּי[t] id. pret. 1 pers. sing. — פגע
הַפֶּגֶר[u] pref. הַ)(noun masc. s. (pl. c. פִּגְרֵי) d. 6a — פגר
הַפְּגָרִים pref. id.)(id. pl., absolute state — פגר
הָפְדֵּה[x] וְ Hoph. inf. absolute — פדה
הֶפְדָּהּ[y] וְ Hiph. pret. 3 pers. sing. masc., suff. 3 pers. sing. fem. (§ 11. rem. 1) — פדה
הַפֹּדְךָ[z] וְ pref. הַ)(Kal part. act. masc., suff. 2 pers. sing. masc. from (פֹּדֶה) dec. 9a — פדה
הַפִּדְיוֹם[a] pref. id.)(noun masc. sing. — פדה
הַפְּדֻיִם[b] pref. id.)(Kh. פְּדֻיִם' defect. for the preced., K. פְּדוּיִם' noun pl. [of פְּדוּי] — פדה
הַפֶּדֶר pref. id.)(noun m. s. [for פֶּדֶר § 35. r. 2] — פדר
הַפֶּה[c] pref. id.)(noun m. s. irr. § 45 [for פֵּאָה] — פאה
הָפוֹךְ[d] Kal inf. absolute — הפך
הַפּוּךְ pr. name, in compos. קֶרֶן הַפּוּךְ — קרן
הֲפוּכָה[e] Kal part. pass., fem. of הָפוּךְ masc. — הפך
הַפּוֹנֶה pref. הַ)(Kal part. act. sing. masc. dec. 9a — פנה
הַפּוּנִי pref. id.)(patronym. of פּוּן — פון

[a] De. 21. 6. [b] 2 Ki. 23. 35. [c] Le. 27. 8, 12. [d] Le. 27. 14. [e] Jos. 2. 6. [f] Is. 65. 11. [g] Le. 27. 23. [h] Hab. 2. 16. [i] Jos. 5. 3. [k] Ruth 3. 7. [l] Ps. 102. 18. [m] Ex. 20. 21. [n] De. 5. 22. [o] Job 30. 3. [p] Eze. 17. 15. [q] Job 40. 19. [r] Job 41. 25. [s] Ne. 3. 16. [t] 2 Ki. 23. 4. [u] Nu. 28. 6. [x] Je. 32. 1. [y] Is. 7. 4. [z] Ec. 4. 1, 1. [a] 1 Ch. 29. 12. [b] Eze. 29. 1. [c] Eze. 27. 33. [d] Ge. 14. 23. [e] Le. 18. 29. [f] Ezr. 10. 13. [g] Ge. 31. 10, 12. [h] Zec. 10. 3. [i] Job 3. 8. [k] 1 Ch. 29. 30. [l] Ex. 10. 17. [m] 2 Ch. 33. 19. [n] Ex. 8. 25. [o] Eze. 35. 13. [p] Is. 3. 20. [q] La. 3. 49. [r] Is. 53. 6. [s] Je. 36. 25. [ss] Eze. 43. 18. [t] Je. 15. 11. [u] Am. 8. 3. [x] Le. 19. 20. [y] Ex. 21. 8. [z] De. 13. 6. [zz] Am. 4. 1. [a] Nu. 3. 49. [b] Nu. 3. 51. [c] 1 Ki. 19. 18. [d] Pr. 12. 7. [e] Ho. 7. 8.

הַפּוֹצֶה[a] pref. הַ)(Kal part. act. sing. masc. . . פצה
הַפּוּר[b] pref. id.)(noun masc. sing. dec. 1a . פור
הַפּוּרִים[c] pref. id.)(id. pl., absolute state . . פור
הַפּוֹשְׁעִים[d] וְ pref. id.)(Kal part. act. masc., pl. of פֹּשֵׁעַ dec. 7b . . . . פשע
הַפּוּתִי וְ pref. id.)(patronym. from פּוּת . פות
הָפֵחַ[e] Hiph. inf. absolute . פחח
הַפַּח[f] pref. הַ)(noun masc. sing., pl. פַּחִים dag. forte impl. (§ 37. rem. 7) . . פחח
הַפַּחַד pref. id.)(noun masc. s. (suff. פַּחְדּוֹ) d. 6d פחד
הַפֶּחָה pref. id.)(noun masc. sing. irr. (§ 45) . פחה
הַפַּחוֹת[g] וְ' pref. id.)(id. pl. absolute . פחה
הִפְחִיד[h] Hiph. pret. 3 pers. sing. masc. . . פחד
הַפַּחַת pref. הַ)(noun masc. sing. dec. 6d . פחת
הִפַּחְתִּי[i] Hiph. pret. 1 pers. sing. [for הִפְחַתִּי comp. § 8. rem. 7] . . נפח
הַפְּחָתִים[k] pref. הַ art.)(noun masc., pl. of פַּחַת d. 6d פחת
הִפַּחְתֶּם[l] וְ Hiph. pret. 2 pers. sing. masc. . . נפח
הָפִיחִי[m] Hiph. imp. sing. fem. . . פוח
הִפִּיל[n] וְ' Hiph. pret. 3 pers. sing. masc. . . נפל
הַפִּילַגְשִׁים pref. הַ)(for פִּלַגְ' (note to § 18. rem. 12) noun fem., pl. of פִּילֶגֶשׁ d. 6 (§ 35. r. 16) פלגש
הִפִּילָה[o] Hiph. pret. 3 pers. sing. fem. . . נפל
הַפִּילוּ[p] id. imp. pl. masc. . . נפל
הִפִּילוֹ[q] וְ id. pret. 3 pers. s. m., suff. 3 pers. s. m. נפל
הִפִּילוּ[r] וְ' id. pret. 3 pers. sing. masc. . . נפל
הֵפִיץ וְ Hiph. pret. 3 pers. sing. masc. . . פוץ
הֲפִיצוֹתִי[s] וַ id. pret. 1 pers. sing.; acc. shifted by וַ for וְ conv. (comp. § 8. r. 7, & § 11. r. 9) פוץ
הֲפִיצוֹתִיךָ[t] id. id., suff. 2 pers. sing. masc. . . פוץ
הֲפִיצוֹתִים[u] וַ id. id., suff. 3 pers. pl. masc. . . פוץ
הֲפִיצוֹתֶם[x] id. pret. 2 pers. pl. masc. . . פוץ
הֱפִיצְךָ[y] וֶ'[z] id. pret. 3 pers. sing. masc., suff. 2 pers. sing. masc.; וֶ for וְ conv. . . . פוץ
הֱפִיצָם[a] id. id., suff. 3 pers. pl. masc. . . פוץ
הֵפִיר Hiph. pret. 3 pers. sing. masc. . . פור

הָפַךְ וְ' fut. יַהֲפֹךְ (1 pers. אֶהֱפֹךְ § 13. rem. 5)—I. *to turn, turn over.* Intrans. *to turn back.*—II. *to overturn, overthrow, ruin.*—III. *to convert, change,* const. with לְ. Intrans. *to change, be changed.*—IV. *to pervert.* Niph. נֶהְפַּךְ (§ 13. rem. 7)—I. *to turn oneself, to turn back;* with בְּ *to turn against,* with לְ, עַל *to, upon* any one.—II. *to be overthrown, ruined.*—III. *to be changed,* with לְ. Hoph. הָהְפַּךְ (§ 13. rem. 11) *to be turned,* with עַל *upon,* Job 30. 15. Hithp.—I. *to turn oneself.*—II. *to be changed,* Job 38. 14.—III. *to roll oneself, to tumble* Ju. 7. 13.

הֶפֶךְ, הֵפֶךְ masc. *reverse, contrary,* Eze. 16. 34.

הֹפֶךְ masc. *perverseness,* Is. 29. 16; which, however, may be taken as an infinitive.

הֲפֵכָה fem. *overthrow,* Ge. 19. 29.

הֲפַכְפַּךְ masc. *turning, crooked,* Pr. 21. 8.

מַהְפֵּכָה fem. dec. 10, *overthrow, destruction.*

מַהְפֶּכֶת f. *stocks, imprisonment;* בֵּית מַ' *prison house.*

תַּהְפֻּכָה fem. dec. 10, *perverseness, perversion.*

הֲפֹךְ Kal imp. sing. masc. . . . . הפך
הֶפֶךְ noun masc. sing. . . . . הפך
הֹפֵךְ[b] וְ Kal part. act. sing. masc. dec. 7b . הפך
הָפְכָה[c] Kal pret. 3 pers. sing. fem. . . הפך
הָפְכוּ[d] id. pret. 3 pers. pl. . . . הפך
הָפְכִּי[e] id. inf., suff. 1 pers. sing. . . הפך
הַפְכְּכֶם[f] noun m. s., suff. 2 pers. pl. m. fr. [הֹפֶךְ] d. 6c הפך
הֲפָכָם[g] Kal pret. 3 pers. s. m., suff. 2 pers. pl. m. הפך
הֲפַכְפַּךְ[h] adj. masc. sing. . . . . הפך
הָפַכְתָּ Kal pret. 2 pers. sing. masc. . . הפך
הָפַכְתִּי[i] / וְהָפַכְתִּי id. pret. 1 pers. sing.; acc. shifted by וְ conv. (§ 8. rem. 7) . . הפך
הֲפַכְתֶּם[k] וַ'[l] id. pret. 2 pers. pl. masc. וַ for וְ conv. הפך
הִפִּל[m] וְ Hiph. pret. 3 pers. sing. masc., for הִפִּיל . נפל
הַפְלֵא[n] וְ'[o] Hiph. inf. absolute . . . פלא
הִפְלָא[p] / הִפְלִא[q] וְ Hiph. pret. 3 pers. sing. m. (§ 23. r. 9) פלא
הַפְּלָאוֹת[r] pref. הַ)(noun m., pl. of פֶּלֶא (suff. פִּלְאֲךָ) dec. 6a . . . . פלא
הַפַּלְאִי pref. id.)(patronym. of פַּלּוּא . . פלא
הַפְלֵה[s] Hiph. imp. sing. masc. . . . פלה
הַפִּלֶהָ[t] Hiph. imp. sing. masc., suff. 3 pers. sing. f. נפל
הִפְלָה[u] וְ'[x] Hiph. pret. 3 pers. sing. masc. . פלה
הִפִּלֻהוּ[y] Hiph. pret. 3 pers. pl. (הִפִּילוּ) suff. 3 pers. s. m. נפל
הַפְּלוֹנִי pref. הַ)(patronym. of פַּלּוּן . . פלה
הַפְּלֵטָה pref. id.)(noun fem. sing. dec. 10. . פלט
הַפַּלְטִי pref. id.)(pr. name masc. . . . פלט
הִפְלִיא Hiph. pret. 3 pers. sing. masc. . . פלא
הַפָּלִיט pref. הַ)((prim. adj.) subst. masc. s. dec. 3a פלט
הַפְּלֵיטָה pref. id.)(noun fem. sing. dec. 10. . פלט
הִפְלֵיתִי[z] וְ Hiph. pret. 1 pers. sing.; acc. shifted by conv. וְ (comp. § 8. r. 7, & § 11. r. 9) . פלה
הִפַּלְנוּ[a] Hiph. pret. 1 pers. sing. . . . נפל

[a] Ps. 144. 10. [b] Est. 9. 26. [c] Est. 9. 28. [d] Eze. 20. 38. [e] Is. 42. 22. [f] Ps. 124. 7. [g] Est. 3. 12. [h] Job 4. 14. [i] Job 31. 39. [k] 2 Sa. 17. 9. [l] Mal. 1. 13. [m] Ca. 4. 16. [n] Da. 11. 12. [o] Pr. 7. 26. [p] 1 Sa. 14. 42. [q] De. 25. 2. [r] Je. 22. 7. [s] Eze. 22. 15, etc. [t] Je. 30. 11. [u] Je. 9. 15. [x] Eze. 34. 21. [y] De. 30. 3. [z] De. 28. 64. [a] Ge. 11. 9. [b] Am. 5. 8. [c] Le. 13. 10. [d] Ps. 78. 9. [e] Ge. 19. 21. [f] Is. 29. 16. [g] Job 9. 5. [h] Pr. 21. 8. [i] Am. 4. 11. [k] Am. 6. 12. [l] Je. 23. 36. [m] Est. 9. 24. [n] Is. 29. 14. [o] 2 Ch. 2. 8. [p] De. 28. 59. [q] Is. 28. 29. [r] Da. 12. 6. [s] Ps. 17. 7. [t] Jos. 13. 6. [u] Ps. 4. 4. [x] Ex. 9. 4. [y] 2 Ch. 32. 21. [z] Ex. 8. 18. [a] Ne. 10. 35.

הַפַּלֻּאִי pref. הַ)(patronym. of פַּלּוּא . . . פלה
הַפְּלִשְׁתִּי pref. id.)(gent. noun from פְּלֶשֶׁת . . פלש
הַפְּלִשְׁתִּים וְ׳ pref. id.)(id. pl. . . . . פלש
הַפְּלֵתִי וְ׳ pref. id.)(noun masc. sing. . . פלת
הִפַּלְתִּי } Hiph. pret. 1 pers. sing.; acc. shifted by conv. וְ (comp. § 8. rem. 7) . } נפל
הִפַּלְתִּי וְ }
הִפַּלְתִּיו וְ id., suff. 3 pers. sing. masc. . . נפל
הִפַּלְתִּים[a] וְ id., suff. 3 pers. pl. masc. . . נפל
הִפַּלְתָּם[b] id. pret. 2 pers. sing. masc., suff. 3 pers. pl. m. נפל
הַפִּנָּה pref. הַ)(noun fem. sing. dec. 10. . פנן
הַפֹּנֶה pref. id.)(Kal part. act. masc. dec. 9a . פנה
הִפְנָה[c] Hiph. pret. 3 pers. sing. masc. . . פנה
הָפְנוּ[d] Hoph. pret. 3 pers. pl. . . . . פנה
הִפְנוּ Hiph. pret. 1 pers. pl. . . . פנה
הַפֹּנוֹת[e] pref. הַ)(Kal part. act. fem. pl. of [פֹּנָה] dec. 10 from פֹּנֶה masc. . . . פנה
הַפִּנּוֹת pref. id.)(noun fem., pl. of פִּנָּה dec. 10. פנן
הֶפָּנָיו[f] pref. הֶ)(noun masc. pl., suff. 3 pers. sing. masc. from [פָּנֶה] dec. 9b . . . פנה
הַפָּנִים pref. הַ)(id. pl., absolute state . . פנה
הַפִּנִּים[g] pref. id.)(noun masc., pl. of [פֵּן] dec. 8b . פנן
הַפְּנִימִי pref. id.)(adj. masc. sing. dec. 1b . פנם
הַפְּנִימִיּוֹת[h] pref. id.)(id. fem., pl. of ׳מִית (comp. § 39. No. 4, rem. 1 note) . . . . פנם
הַפְּנִימִים pref. id.)(id. masc. pl. . . . פנם
הַפְּנִימִית pref. id.)(id. fem. sing., see הַפְּנִימִיּוֹת . פנם
הִפְנְתָה[k] Hiph. pret. 3 pers. sing. fem. . . פנה
הַפִּסְגָּה pref. הַ)(pr. name of a place . . . פסג
הַפָּסַח } pref. id.)(noun masc. sing. dec. 6 (§ 35 rem. 2 & 5) . . . . } פסח
הַפֶּסַח }
הַפִּסֵּחַ[l] pref. id.)(adj. masc. sing. dec. 7b . . פסח
הַפְּסָחִים[m] pref. id.)(noun masc., pl. of פֶּסַח dec. 6 (§ 35. rem. 5) . . . . פסח
הַפִּסְחִים[n] וְ׳ pref. id.)(adj. masc., pl. of פִּסֵּחַ dec. 7b פסח
הַפְּסִילִים וְ׳[o] pref. id.)(noun m., pl. of [פָּסִיל] dec. 3a פסל
הַפַּסִּים pref. id.)(noun masc., pl. of [פַּס] dec. 8d . פסס
הַפָּסֶל[p] } pref. id.)(noun masc. sing., dec. 6a (§ 35. rem. 2, but with suff. פִּסְלִי) } פסל
הַפֶּסֶל }
הַפְּסִלִים[q] וְ pref. id.)(noun m., pl. of [פָּסִיל] dec. 3a פסל
הַפָּעַם } pref. id.)(noun m. s. dec. 6d (§ 35. r. 2) פעם
הַפַּעַם }
הַפַּעֲמֹנִים[r] pref. id.)(noun masc., pl. of פַּעֲמֹן dec. 1b . פעם
הַפְּעוֹר pref. id.)(pr. name of a mountain . פער
הָפֵץ[s] Hiph. imp. sing. masc. . . . . פוץ
הֱפִיצֻהוּ[t] וַ id. pret. 3 pers. pl. [הֱפִיצוּ], suff. 3 pers. sing. masc.; וֶ before (ְ:) . . פוץ

הֲפִצוֹתִים[u] id. pret. 1 pers. sing., suff. 3 pers. pl. masc. פוץ
הַפְּצִירָה[x] pref. הַ)(noun fem. sing. . . . פצר
הַפְצַר[y] Hiph. inf. used as a subst. . . . פצר
הֲפִצֹתִי[zz] וַ Hiph. pret. 1 pers. sing.; acc. shifted by וַ for וְ conv. (comp. § 8. rem. 7) . פוץ
הֲפִצֹתֶם[z] id. pret. 2 pers. pl. masc. . . . פוץ
הָפְקַד Hoph. pret. 3 pers. sing. masc. . . פקד
הַפְקֵד Hiph. imp. sing. masc. . . . . פקד
הִפָּקֵד[a] Niph. inf. constr. used as an abs. . פקד
הַפְּקֻדָּה[b] pref. הַ)(noun fem. sing. dec. 10. . . פקד
הִפְקְדוּ[c] Hiph. pret. 3 pers. pl. [for הִפְקִידוּ] . פקד
הַפִּקָּדוֹן[d] pref. הַ)(noun masc. sing. . . . פקד
הַפְּקֻדִים pref. id.)(Kal part. p. m., pl. of [פָּקוּד] dec. 3a פקד
הַפְּקֻדֹּת[e] pref. id.)(noun fem., pl. of פְּקֻדָּה dec. 10. . פקד
הִפְקַדְתּוֹ[f] Hiph. pret. 2 pers. s. m., suff. 3 pers. s. m. פקד
הִפְקַדְתִּי[g] } id. pret. 1 pers. sing.; acc. shifted by conv. וְ (comp. § 8. rem. 7) . } פקד
הִפְקַדְתִּי[h] וְ }
הִפְקַדְתִּיךָ[i] id. id., suff. 2 pers. sing. masc. . . פקד
הַפָּקִיד[k] pref. הַ)(noun masc. sing. dec. 3a . . פקד
הִפְקִיד וְ׳[l] Hiph. pret. 3 pers. sing. masc. . . פקד
הַפְקִידוּ[qq] וְ id. imp. pl. masc. . . . . פקד
הַפְּקָעִים[m] pref. הַ)(n. m., pl. of [פֶּקַע § 35. r. 5] dec. 6 פקע
הַפָּר pref. id.)(with the art. for פַּר, noun masc. dec. 8. (§ 37. rem. 7) . . . פרר
הָפֵר וְ׳[n] Hiph. inf. abs. or imp. sing. masc. . פרר
הֵפַר } id. pret. 3 pers. sing. m. (§ 18. rem. 10) פרר
הֵפֵר וְ׳ }
הִפָּרֶד־[o] } Niph. inf. or imp. sing. masc., with Mak. or bef. monos. [for הִפָּרֵד § 9. rem. 3] } פרד
הִפָּרֶד[p] }
הַפֶּרֶד וְ׳[q] pref. הַ)(noun m. s. (suff. פִּרְדּוֹ) dec. 6a פרד
הַפִּרְדָּה[r] pref. id.)(noun fem. sing. dec. 10. . פרד
הַפַּרְדֵּס[s] pref. id.)(noun masc. sing. dec. 1b . . פרדס
הַפָּרָה[t] וְ׳ pref. id.)(noun fem. sing. dec. 10 [for פַּרָּה] from פַּר masc. (comp. § 37. rem. 7) also pr. name . . . . . פרר
הֵפֵרָה[u] Hiph. pret. sing. masc. with parag. ה . פרר
הֵפֵרוּ id. pret. 3 pers. pl. . . . . פרר
הַפַּרְוָרִים[x] pref. הַ)(Kh. פַּרְוָרִים׳, K. פַּרְזִים׳, noun masc., pl. of פַּרְוָרִי or פַּרְזִי . . . פרז
הַפְּרוּצָה[zz] pref. id.)(Kal part. pass. fem. [of פָּרוּץ m.] פרץ
הַפָּרוֹת pref. id.)(noun fem., pl. of פָּרָה dec. 10, from פַּר masc. (comp. § 37. rem. 7) . פרר
הַפְּרָזוֹת[cc] pref. id.)(noun fem. pl. [of פְּרָזָה] . פרז
הַפְּרָזִי pref. id.)(noun masc. sing. . . . פרז
הַפְּרִזִּי וְ׳ pref. id.)(pr. name of a people . פרז
הַפֶּרַח[y] וְ pref. id.)(n. m. s. (suff. פִּרְחָהּ) d. 6a (§ 35. r. 5) פרח
הֲפָרְחָה[hh] pref. הֲ)(Kal pret. 3 pers. sing. fem. . פרח

[a] Je. 19. 7. [b] Ps. 73. 18. [c] Je. 48. 39. [d] Je. 49. 8. [e] Eze. 46. 19. [f] Job 13. 8.
[g] Zec. 14. 10. [h] 2 Ch. 4. 22. [i] 1 Ch. 28. 11. [k] Je. 49. 24. [l] Mal. 1. 13. [ll] Eze. 29. 12.
[m] 2 Ch. 30. 17. [n] 2 Sa. 5. 6, 8. [o] 2 Ch. 34. 3, 4. [p] Ju. 18. 20, 30. [q] 2 Ch. 33. 19. [qq] Jos. 10. 18.
[r] Ex. 39. 25. [s] Job 40. 11. [t] Job 18. 11. [u] Eze. 11. 16. [x] 1 Sa. 13. 21. [zz] 2 Ch. 32. 5.
[y] 1 Sa. 15. 23. [z] Je. 23. 2. [a] 1 Ki. 20. 39. [b] Ho. 9. 7. [c] Je. 36. 20. [cc] Est. 9. 19.
[d] Le. 5. 23. [e] Je. 52. 11. [f] 1 Sa. 29. 4. [g] Is. 62. 6. [h] Lev. 26. 16. [hh] Ca. 6. 11.
[i] Je. 1. 10. [k] Ne. 12. 42. [l] 2 Ch. 12. 10. [m] 1 Ki. 7. 24. [n] Ps. 85. 5.
[o] Ge. 13. 14. [p] Ge. 13. 9. [q] 2 Sa. 18. 9. [r] 1 Ki. 1. 33. [s] Ne. 2. 8.
[t] Nu. 19. 5, 6, 9, 10. [u] 1 Ki. 15. 19. [x] Est. 9. 19. [y] 2 Ch. 4. 21.

הִפְרַחְתִּי[a]	וְ Hiph. pret. 1 pers. sing.	פרח
הַפֹּרְטִים[b]	pref. id.)(Kal part. act. m., pl. of [פֹּרֵט] d. 7b	פרט
הִפְרִיד[c]	Hiph. pret. 3 pers. sing. masc.	פרד
הַפָּרִים[d]	pref. הַ)(noun m. pl. of פַּר, d. 8 (§ 37. r. 7)	פרר
הַפֻּרִים[e]	pref. id.)(noun masc., pl. of פּוּר dec. 1a	פור
הִפְרִיסָה[f]	Hiph. pret. 3 pers. sing. fem.	פרס
הִפְרִיסוּ[g]	id. pret. 3 pers. pl.	פרס
הִפְרִיעַ[h]	Hiph. pret. 3 pers. sing. masc.	פרע
הִפְרֵיתִי[i]	וְ Hiph. pret. 1 pers. sing.; acc. shifted by conv. וְ (§ 8. rem. 7)	פרה
הַפָּרֹכֶת	pref. הַ)(noun fem. sing.	פרך
הֲפֵרָם[k]	Hiph. pret. 3 p. s. m. (הֵפֵר), suff. 3 p. pl. m.	פרר
הִפְרַנִי[l]	Hiph. pret. 3 pers. sing. masc. [הִפְרָה], suff. 1 pers. sing. (§ 24. rem. 21)	פרה
הַפֶּרֶם[m]	וְ'[n] pref. הַ)(noun masc. sing.	פרם
הַפַּרְסָה	pref. id.)(noun fem. sing. dec. 12a	פרס
הַפַּרְסִי	pref. id.)(gent. noun from פָּרַס	
הַפִּרְעָתוֹנִי, הַפִּרְעָתֹנִי	pref. id.)(gent. noun from פִּרְעָתוֹן	פרע
הַפֹּרֵץ[o]	pref. id.)(Kal part. act. sing. masc.	פרץ
הַפַּרְצִי	pref. id.)(patronym. of פֶּרֶץ	פרץ
הַפְּרֻצִים[p]	pref. id.)(Kal part., pl. of [פָּרוּץ] dec. 3a	פרץ
הַפֶּרֶק[q]	pref. id.)(noun masc. sing.	פרק
הַפַּרְשְׁדֹנָה[r]	pref. id.)(noun m. s. [פַּרְשְׁדוֹן] with loc. ה	פרשד
הַפָּרָשִׁים	וְ'[s] pref. id.)(n. m., pl. of פָּרָשׁ (§ 30. Nos. 2 & 3)	פרש
הֵפַרְתָּה[t]	וְ Hiph. pret. 2 pers. sing. masc. (§ 8. r. 5) R. either פָּרַר (comp. § 18. rem. 13) or	פור
הִפְרֵתִי[u]	וְ Hiph. pret. 1 pers. sing.; acc. shifted by conv. וְ (comp. § 8. rem. 7)	פרה
הַפַּרְתְּמִים	pref. id.)(noun masc. pl.	פרתם
הַפְשֵׁט[x]	וְ Hiph. imp. pl. masc.	פשט
הִפְשִׁיט[y]	וְ'[z] id. pret. 3 pers. sing. masc.	פשט
הִפְשִׁיטוּ[a]	וְ'[b] id. pret. 3 pers. pl.	פשט
הִפְשִׁיטוּךָ[c]	וְ id. id., suff. 2 pers. sing. masc.	פשט
הַפֶּשַׁע[d]	וְ'[e] pref. הַ)(noun masc. sing. (suff. פִּשְׁעִי) dec. 6a (§ 35. rem. 5)	פשע
הַפֹּשְׁעִים	pref. id.)(Kal part. act. m., pl. of פֹּשֵׁעַ d. 7b	פשע
הַפִּשְׁתָּה[f]	וְ pref. הַ)(noun fem. sing., (with suff. פִּשְׁתִּי)	פשת
הַפִּשְׁתִּים[g]	pref. id.)(id. pl., with masc. term.	פשת
הַפִּתּוֹת[h]	וְ pref. id.)(noun masc. with pl. fem. term. [from פַּת] comp. פָּתְהֶן	פות
הַפָּתַח[i], הַפֶּתַח	וְ'[k] pref. הַ)(noun masc. sing. dec. 6a (§ 35. rem. 2, 5, but with suff. פִּתְחוֹ)	פתח
הַפֶּתְחָה[l]	pref. id.)(id. with parag. ה (§ 35. rem. 18)	פתח
הַפְּתָחִים[m]	pref. id.)(id. pl., absolute state	פתח
הַפְּתִילִים[n]	וְ pref. id.)(noun masc., pl. of [פָּתִיל] d. 3a	פתל

הֲפִתִּיתָ[o]	וַ pref. הֲ)(Piel pret. 2 p. s. m.; וַ bef. (-:) for וְ	פתה
הַצֹּאן, הֲצֹאן[p]	וְ' pref. הַ; pref. הֲ)(noun com. sing. dec. 1a	צאן
הַצֹּאִים[q]	pref. הַ)(adj. masc. sing. from [צוֹא]	צא
הַצֶּאֱצָאִים[r]	pref. id.)(noun masc., pl. of [צֶאֱצָא] d. 1b	צא
הֹצֵאתִי[s]	וְ Hiph. pret. 1 pers. sing., acc. shifted by conv. וְ (comp. § 8. rem. 7)	יצא
הַצָּב[t]	וְ pref. הַ)(noun masc. sing. dec. 8a	צבב
הֻצַּב[u]	וְ Hoph. pret. 3 pers. sing. masc.	נצב
הַצָּבָא	pref. הַ)(n. m. s. d. 4a, constr. צְבָא (§ 33. r. 2)	צבא
הַצֹּבְאוֹת[v]	pref. id.)(Kal part. act. fem. pl. [of צֹבְאָה or צֹבֵאת]	צבא
הַצְּבָאוֹת	pref. id.)(n. m. with pl. f. term. fr. צָבָא d. 4a	צבא
הַצֹּבְאִים	pref. id.)(Kal part. act. m., pl. of [צֹבֵא] d. 7b	צבא
הַצֹּבְאֹת[y]	defect. for הַצֹּבְאוֹת (q. v.)	צבא
הַצֹּבֵבָה	pref. הַ)(pr. name fem.	צבב
הַצְּבִי, הַצֶּבִי[bb]	pref. id.)(noun masc. sing. dec. 6i (§ 35. rem. 14 & 15)	צבה
הַצְּבָיִים, הַצְּבָיִם[z]	pref. id.)(id. pl. also pr. name, see פֹּכֶרֶת הַ'	צבה
הַצְּבֹעִים	pref. id.)(pr. name of a valley	צבע
הִצַּבְתָּ	Hiph. pret. 2 pers. sing. masc.	נצב
הַצְּבָתִים[a]	pref. הַ)(noun masc. pl. of [צֶבֶת] dec. 6	צבת
הַצֵּג[b]	Hiph. inf. absolute (§ 20. rem. 16)	יצג
הִצַּגְתִּיהָ[c]	וְ id. pret. 1 pers. sing., suff. 3 pers. sing. fem.	יצג
הִצַּגְתִּיו[d]	וְ id., suff. 3 pers. sing. masc.	יצג
הַצָּד[e]	pref. הַ)(Kal part. act. sing. masc.	צוד
הַצְדָא[f]	Ch. pref. הַ interr. for הֲ)(noun masc. sing.; or for אַצְדָא, see under R.	צדה
הַצִּדִּים	pref. הַ art.)(pr. name of a place	צדד
הַצַּדִּיק	pref. id.)(adj. masc. sing. dec. 1b	צדק
הַצְדִּיקוּ[g]	Hiph. imp. pl. masc.	צדק
הִצְדִּיקוּ[h]	וְ id. pret. 3 pers. pl.	צדק
הַצַּדִּיקִים, הַצַּדִּיקִם	pref. הַ)(adj. masc., pl. of צַדִּיק dec. 1b	צדק
הַצֶּדֶק	pref. id.)(noun masc. sing. (suff. צִדְקִי) d. 6c	צדק
הַצְּדָקָה	pref. id.)(noun fem. sing. dec. 11c	צדק
הִצְדַּקְתִּיו[i]	וְ Hiph. pret. 1 pers. sing., suff. 3 pers. s. m.	צדק
הַצָּהֹב[k]	pref. הַ)(adj. masc. sing.	צהב
הַצָּהֳרַיִם[l], הַצָּהֳרָיִם	pref. id.)(noun fem., du. of צֹהַר dec. 6f	צהר
הִצּוּ[m]	Hiph. pret. 3 pers. pl. (§ 25. No. 2)	נצה
הֲצוֹם[n]	pref. הֲ)(Kal inf. absolute	צום
הַצּוֹמוֹת	pref. הַ)(n. m., with pl. f. term. fr. צוֹם d. 1a	צום
הַצּוּר	pref. id.)(noun masc. sing. dec. 1a	צור
הִצְטַיַּדְנוּ[o]	Hithp. pret. 1 p. s. [for הִתְצַ' = הִטְצַיַּדְנוּ § 12. r. 3]	צוד

[a] Eze. 17. 24. [b] Am. 6. 5. [c] Ge. 30. 40. [d] Nu. 8. 12. [e] Est. 9. 29, 31, 32. [f] Le. 11. 6. [g] De. 14. 7. [h] 2 Ch. 28. 19. [i] Ge. 17. 20, &c. [k] Nu. 30. 13. [l] Ge. 41. 52. [m] Le. 11. 13. [n] De. 14. 12. [o] Mi. 2. 13. [p] Ne. 4. 1. [q] Ob. 14. [r] Ju. 3. 22. [s] Is. 22. 7. [t] 2 Sa. 15. 34. [u] Ge. 17. 6. [x] Nu. 20. 26. [y] Job 19. 9. [z] Le. 1. 6. [a] Mi. 3. 3. [b] Eze. 16. 39. [c] Eze. 23. 26. [d] Da. 9. 24. [e] Da. 8. 13. [f] Ex. 9. 31. [g] Le. 13. 59. [h] 1 Ki. 7. 50. [i] Ge. 19. 11. [k] Eze. 41. 3. [l] Ge. 19. 6. [m] 1 Ki. 7. 5. [n] Ge. 38. 25. [o] Pr. 24. 28. [p] Nu. 11. 22. [q] Zec. 3. 4. [r] Is. 22. 24. [s] Je. 51. 44. [t] Le. 11. 29. [u] Na. 2. 8. [v] 1 Sa. 2. 22. [y] Ex. 38. 8. [z] 2 Sa. 2. 18. [a] Ruth 2. 16. [b] De. 28. 56. [bb] Da. 8. 9. [c] Ho. 2. 5. [d] Ge. 43. 9. [e] Ge. 27. 33. [f] Da. 3. 14. [g] Ps. 82. 3. [h] De. 25. 1. [i] 2 Sa. 15. 4. [k] Le. 13. 36. [l] 2 Sa. 4. 5. [m] Nu. 26. 9. [n] Zec. 7. 5. [o] Jos. 9. 12.

הֵצִיב[a] Hiph. pret. 3 pers. sing. masc. . . . נצב
הִצִּיבוּ[b] id. pret. 3 pers. pl. . . . . . נצב
הַצִּיבִי[c] id. imp. sing. fem. . . . . . נצב
הַצִּיגוּ[d] וְ Hiph. imp. pl. masc. (§ 20. rem. 16) . יצג
הִצִּיגָנוּ[e] id. pret. 3 pers. sing. masc., Kh. נוּ◌ָ 1 pers. pl., K. נִי◌ָ 1 pers. sing. . . . יצג
הִצִּיגַנִי[f] וְ id. pret. 3 pers. sing. m., suff. 1 pers. sing. יצג
הַצִּידֹנִי וְ pref. הַ)(gent. noun from צִידוֹן . . צוד
הַצִּידֹנִים pref. id.)(id. pl. absolute . . . צוד
הַצִּיּוֹן[g] pref. id.)(noun masc. sing. dec. 1b . צוה
הַצִּיל[h] Hiph. inf. constr. . . . . . נצל
הִצִּיל וְ id. pret. 3 pers. sing. masc. . . . נצל
הַצִּילָה id. imp. sing. masc. with parag. ה (§ 11. r. 5) נצל
הַצִּילוּ[i] וְ id. imp. masc. pl. . . . . . נצל
הִצִּילוֹ[k] id. pret. 3 pers. sing. m., suff. 3 pers. s. m. נצל
הִצִּילוּ[l] וְ id. pret. 3 pers. pl. . . . . נצל
הִצִּילָם[m] וְ id. pret. 3 pers. s. m., suff. 3 pers. pl. m. נצל
הַצִּילֵנוּ וְ id. imp. sing. masc., suff. 1 pers. pl. . נצל
הִצִּילָנוּ id. pret. 3 pers. sing. masc., suff. 1 pers. pl. נצל
הַצִּילֵנִי וְ id. imp. sing. masc., suff. 1 pers. sing. נצל
הִצִּילָנִי id. pret. 3 pers. s. m., suff. 1 p. s. (§ 2. r. 1) נצל
הַצִּינֹק[o] pref. הַ)(noun masc. sing. . . . צנק
הֵצִיץ[p] Hiph. pret. 3 pers. sing. masc. . . . צוץ
הַצִּיץ pref. הַ)(pr. name of a place . . צוץ
הֵצִיקָה[q] Hiph. pret. 3 pers. sing. fem. . . . צוק
הֲצִיקוֹתִי[r] וַ id. pret. 1 pers. sing.; acc. shifted by וַ for וְ conv. (comp. § 8. rem. 7) . . צוק
הֱצִיקַתְהוּ[s] id. pret. 3 pers. sing. fem., suff. 3 pers. s. m. צוק
הֱצִיקַתְנִי[t] id. id., suff. 1 pers. sing. . . . צוק
הִצִּית[u] Hiph. pret. 3 pers. sing. m. (§ 20. rem. 16) יצת
הִצִּיתוּ[x] וְ id. pret. 3 pers. pl. . . . . יצת
הַצֵּל[y] pref. הַ)(noun masc. sing. dec. 8b . . צלל
הַצֵּל וְ Hiph. inf., or imp. sing. masc. . . נצל
הַצָּלָה[z] וְ noun fem. sing. . . . . . נצל
הַצְלַח[a] Ch. Aph. pret. 3 pers. sing. masc. (§ 47. r. 4) צלח
הַצְלַח וְ Hiph. imp. sing. masc. . . . . צלח
הַצַּלַּחַת[b] pref. הַ)(noun fem. sing. . . . צלח
הִצְלַחְתָּ[c] וְ Hiph. pret. 2 pers. sing. masc.; acc. shifted by וְ conv. (comp. § 8. rem. 7) . . צלח
הִצְלִיחַ וְ id. pret. 3 pers. sing. masc. . . . צלח
הַצְלִיחָה[d] וְ[e] id. imp. sing. m. with parag. ה (§ 11. r. 5) צלח
הִצְלִיחָה[f] וַ id. pret. 3 pers. sing. fem. . . . צלח
הַצְלִיחוּ וְ id. imp. pl. masc. . . . . . צלח
הִצְלִיחוֹ[g] id. pret. 3 pers. sing. m., suff. 3 pers. s. m. צלח

הַצְּלָלִים pref. הַ)(noun masc., pl. of [צֵלֶל] dec. 6b צלל
הַצְּלֶלְפּוֹנִי pref. id.)(pr. name masc., see צְלֶלְפּוֹנִי . צלל
הִצַּלְנוּ[h] Hiph. pret. 1 pers. pl. . . . . נצל
הִצַּלַנִי[i] id. pret. 3 pers. sing. masc. (הִצִּיל), suff. 1 p.s. נצל
הַצֵּלָע pref. הַ)(noun fem. s. d. 4c (§ 33. No. 2. & r. 3) צלע
הַצֹּלֵעָה pref. id.)(Kal part. act., fem. of צֹלֵעַ . צלע
הַצְּלָעוֹת[k] וְ / הַצְּלָעֹת[m] pref. id.)(noun fem. pl. abs. fr. צֵלָע dec. 4c (§ 33. No. 2) . . צלע
הַצְּלָצַל[n] pref. הַ)(n. m. s. [for צְלָצַל] see under R. צלל
הִצַּלְתָּ / הִצַּלְתָּ[o] וְ Hiph. pret. 2 pers. sing. masc.; acc. shifted by conv. וְ (comp. § 8. r. 7) נצל
הִצַּלְתִּי וְ id. pret. 1 pers. sing.; acc. shifted, see the preceding . . . . . נצל
הִצַּלְתִּיךָ[p] וְ id. id., suff. 2 pers. sing. masc. . . נצל
הִצַּלְתִּים[q] וְ id. id., suff. 3 pers. pl. masc. . . נצל
הִצַּלְתֶּם[r] וְ id. pret. 2 pers. pl. masc. . . . נצל
הַצָּמֵא[s] pref. הַ)(adj. masc. sing. dec. 5a . . צמא
הַצְּמֵאָה[t] pref. id.)(id. fem. . . . . . צמא
הַצְּמִדִים[u] pref. id.)(noun masc., pl. of צָמִיד dec. 3a צמד
הַצֹּמֵחַ[x] pref. id.)(Kal part. act. sing. masc. . צמח
הַצְּמִידִים[y] וְ pref. id.)(noun masc., pl. of צָמִיד d. 3a צמד
הִצְמִיחָהּ[z] וְ Hiph. pret. 3 pers. s. m., suff. 3 p. s. f. צמח
הַצְמִיתֵם[a] Hiph. imp. sing. masc., suff. 3 pers. pl. masc. צמת
הַצֶּמֶר pref. הַ)(noun masc. s. (suff. צַמְרִי) d. 6a צמר
הַצְּמָרִי pref. id.)(pr. name of a people . . צמר
הִצְמַתָּה[b] Hiph. pret. 2 p. s. m. [for הִצְמַתְּ § 25. rem.] צמת

הֹצֶן masc. *armament, force,* Eze. 23. 24.
הַצִּנָּה pref. הַ)(noun fem. sing. dec. 10. . . צנן
הַצָּנִיף[c] pref. id.)(noun masc. sing. dec. 3a . צנף
הַצְּנִיפוֹת[d] וְ pref. id.)(id. pl. with fem. term. . צנף
הַצְנֵעַ[e] וְ Hiph. inf. absolute (§ 11. rem. 2) . צנע
הַצְּעָדָה[u] pref. id.)(noun fem. sing. (no vowel change) צעד
הַצְּעָדוֹת[f] וְ pref. id.)(id. pl. absolute . . צעד
הַצָּעִיף[g] pref. הַ)(noun masc. sing. dec. 3a . צעף
הַצָּעִיר וְ pref. id.)(adj. masc. sing. dec. 3a . צער
הַצְּעִירָה[h] וְ pref. id.)(id. fem. dec. 10. . . צער
הַצְּעָקָה[i] pref. הַ)(noun fem. sing. dec. 11c, constr. צַעֲקַת (§ 42. rem. 1) . . . צעק
הַצַּעֲקָתוֹ[k] pref. הֲ)(id., suff. 3 pers. sing. masc. . צעק
הַצְּעִרָה[l] defect. for הַצְּעִירָה (q. v.) . . . צער
הַצֹּעֲרִים[m] pref. הַ)(Kal part. act. masc., pl. of [צֹעֵר] dec. 7b . . . . . צער
הַצֹּפֶה וְ pref. id.)(Kal part. act. sing. masc. d. 9a צפה

a 1 Ki. 16. 34. b Je. 5. 26. c Je. 31. 21. d Am. 5. 15. e Je. 51. 44. f Job 17. 6. g 2 Ki. 23. 17.
h Ge. 37. 22. i Ps. 82. 4. k Ex. 18. 9. l Nu. 35. 25. m Ps. 34. 18. n Is. 19. 20. o Je. 29. 26.
p De. 11. 4. q Ju. 16. 16. r Is. 29. 2. s Ju. 14. 17. t Job 32. 18. u Je. 11. 16. x Je. 32. 29.
y 2 Ki. 20. 9, 10, 11. z Est. 4. 14. a Da. 3. 30; 6. 29. b 2 Ki. 21. 13. c 1 Ch. 22. 11. d Ps. 118. 25. e Ne. 1. 11.
f Da. 8. 12. g 2 Ch. 26. 5. h 1 Sa. 30. 22. i 1 Sa. 17. 37. k Eze. 41. 8. l Eze. 41. 6. u 1 Ch. 14. 15.
m 1 Ki. 7. 3. n De. 28. 42. o Ps. 86. 13. p 2 Sa. 12. 7. q Eze. 34. 27. r Jos. 2. 13.
s Is. 29. 8. t De. 29. 18. u Ge. 24. 30. x Ex. 10. 5. y Ge. 24. 47. z Is. 55. 10.
a Ps. 54. 7. b Ps. 73. 27. c Zec. 3. 5. d Is. 3. 23. e Mi. 6. 8. f Is. 3. 20.
g Ge. 24. 65. h Ge. 19. 38. i 1 Sa. 4. 14. k Job 27. 9. l 1 Sa. 9. 21. m Zec. 13. 7.

הַצָּפוֹן[a]	וְ' pref. הַ)(noun com. sing. dec. 3a .	צפן
הַצָּפוֹנָה	pref. id.)(id. with loc. ה . . .	צפן
הַצְּפוֹנִי	pref. id.)(patronym. of צְפוֹן, see צִפְיוֹן .	צפה
הַצְּפוֹנִי[b]	pref. id.)(adj. masc. sing. . .	צפן
הַצִּפּוֹר	pref. id.)(noun com. s., pl. צִפֳּרִים (§ 30. r. 2)	צפר
הַצֹּפִים[c]	pref. id.)(Kal part. act. m., pl. of צוֹפֶה d. 9a	צפה
הַצְפִּינוֹ[d]	Hiph. inf., suff. 3 pers. sing. masc. dec. 1b	צפן
הַצָּפִיר[e]	וְ pref. הַ)(noun masc. sing. dec. 3a .	צפר
הַצְּפִירָה[f]	pref. id.)(noun fem. sing. dec. 10. .	צפר
הַצַּפִּית[g]	pref. id.)(noun fem. sing. . .	צפה
הַצִּפְעֹות[h]	וְ pref. id.)(noun f., pl. of [צְפִיעָה] d. 10.	צפע
הַצִּפֹּר	pref. id.)(n. com. s., pl. צִפֳּרִים (§ 20. r. 2)	צפר
הַצְפַרְדֵּעַ[i]	pref. id.)(noun masc. sing. dec. 7b .	צפר
הַצְפַרְדְּעִים	pref. id.)(id. pl., absolute state .	צפר
הַצְּפִרָה[k]	defect. for הַצְּפִירָה (q. v.) . . .	צפר
הַצֶּפֶת[l]	וְ pref. הַ)(noun masc. sing. . .	צפת
הַצָּר[m] / הַצָּר[n]	pref. id.)(noun masc. sing. dec. 8 (§ 37. rem. 7)	צרר
הָצֵר[o]	Hiph. inf. constr.	צרר
הַצֻּר[p]	pref. הַ)(for צוּר' noun masc. sing. dec. 1a	צור
הֵצַר[q]	וְ Hiph. pret. 3 pers. sing. m. (§ 18. r. 10)	צרר
הַצְּרֵדָה	pref. הַ)(pr. name of a place . .	צרד
הַצָּרָה[r]	pref. id.)(noun fem. sing. dec. 10, fr. צַר masc., (comp. § 37. rem. 7) . .	צרר
הַצָּרוּעַ[s]	וְ' pref. id.)(Kal part. pass. sing. masc. .	צרע
הַצָּרוֹת[t]	pref. id.)(noun fem., pl. of צָרָה dec. 10, fr. צַר masc. (comp. § 37. rem. 7) .	צרר
הַצֳּרִי[u]	pref. id.)(noun masc. sing. . . .	צרה
הַצְּרִיחַ[x]	pref. id.)(noun masc. sing. dec. 1a .	צרח
הַצָּרִים	pref. id.)(Kal part. act. m., pl. of [צָר] d. 1a	צור
הַצֹּרִים	וְ pref. id.)(gent. noun fr. צוֹר . .	צור
הַצֻּרִים	[y] וְ' pref. id.)(noun masc., pl. of צוּר dec. 1a	צור
הַצִּרְעָה	pref. id.)(noun fem. sing. . .	צרע
הַצָּרְעִי	pref. id.)(gent. noun fr. צָרְעָה . .	צרע
הַצָּרַעַת / הַצָּרָעַת	[z] וְ' pref. id.)(noun fem. s. (suff. צָרַעְתּוֹ) dec. 13a	צרע
הַצָּרְעָתִי	pref. id.)(gent. noun fr. צָרְעָה . .	צרע
הַצֹּרְפִי	pref. id.)(pr. name masc. . .	צרף
הַצֹּרְפִים[b]	pref. id.)(Kal part. act. m., pl. of צֹרֵף d. 7b	צרף
הַצֹּרֵר[c]	pref. id.)(Kal part. act. sing. masc. dec. 7b	צרר
הֲצֵרֹתִי	וַ Hiph. pret. 1 pers. sing. [for הֲצִרוֹתִי]	צרר
הִצַּתִּי	וְ Hiph. pret. 1 pers. sing. [for הִצַּתְּתִּי § 20. rem. 16, & § 25. rem.] . .	יצת
הַקָּאָת[d]	[e] וְ' pref. הַ)(n.f.s. without the art. קָאַת, see R.	קוא
הֱקִיאַתוֹ[f]	וַ Hiph. pret. 3 pers. sing. masc., suff. 3 pers. s. m. (§ 21. r. 13); acc. shifted (§ 8. r. 7)	קוא
הַקֻּב[g]	pref. הַ)(noun masc. sing. . . .	קבב
הַקֵּבָה[h]	וְ pref. id.)(noun fem. sing. for נֵקֵבָה .	נקב
הַקֻּבָּה[i]	pref. id.)(noun fem. sing. . . .	קבב
הַקְּבוּרָה[k]	pref. id.)(noun fem. sing. dec. 10. .	קבר
הִקָּבְצוּ	Niph. imp. pl. masc.	קבץ
הַקֶּבֶר[l]	pref. הַ)(noun masc. sing. dec. 6a .	קבר
הַקְּבָרִים	pref. id.)(id. pl., absolute state . .	קבר
הַקָּדוֹשׁ	pref. id.)(adj. masc. sing. dec. 3a .	קדש
הַקְּדוֹשִׁים[m]	pref. id.)(id. pl., absolute state . .	קדש
הַקַּדַּחַת[n]	pref. id.)(noun fem. sing. . .	קדח
הַקָּדִים	pref. id.)(noun masc. sing. . . .	קדם
הַקָּדִימָה[o]	pref. id.)(id. with parag. ה . .	קדם
הִקְדִּימַנִי[p]	Hiph. pret. 3 pers. sing. masc. suff. 1 pers. s.	קדם
הִקְדִּישׁ	Hiph. pret. 3 pers. sing. masc. . .	קדש
הִקְדִּישׁוּ	[q] וְ' id. pret. 3 pers. pl. masc. . .	קדש
הַקֶּדֶם[r]	pref. הַ)(noun masc. sing. (pl. c. קַדְמֵי) d. 6a	קדם
הַקַּדְמוֹנָה[s]	pref. id.)(adj. fem. sing. [from קַדְמוֹן masc.]	קדם
הַקַּדְמוֹנִי	pref. id.)(adj. masc. sing. dec. 1b .	קדם
הַקַּדְמֹנִי	pref. id.)(pr. name masc. . . .	קדם
הַקֹּדְרִים[t]	pref. id.)(Kal part. act. m., pl. of קֹדֵר d. 7b	קדר
הִקְדַּרְתִּי[u]	וְ Hiph. pret. 1 pers. sing.; acc. shifted by conv. וְ (§ 8. rem. 7) . . .	קדר
הַקָּדֵשׁ[x]	pref. הַ)(noun masc. sing. dec. 5a .	קדש
הַקְדֵּשׁ[y]	Hiph. inf. absolute (§ 11. rem. 2) . .	קדש
הַקֹּדֶשׁ	[z] וְ' pref. הַ)(noun masc. sing. dec. 6c .	קדש
הַקְּדֵשָׁה[a]	pref. id.)(noun fem. s. d. 10, from קָדֵשׁ m.	קדש
הַקְּדֵשׁוֹת[b]	pref. id.)(id. pl.	קדש
הַקֳּדָשִׁים	וְ' pref. id.)(noun masc., pl. of קֹדֶשׁ dec. 6c	קדש
הַקְּדֵשִׁים	pref. id.)(noun masc., pl. of קָדֵשׁ dec. 4a	קדש
הַקְדִּשֵׁם[c]	וְ Hiph. imp. sing. masc., suff. 3 pers. pl. m.	קדש
הִקְדַּשְׁנוּ[d]	וְ id. pret. 1 pers. pl. (comp. § 8. rem. 7)	קדש
הִקְדַּשְׁתִּי / הִקְדַּשְׁתִּי[e]	וְ id. pret. 1 pers. sing.; acc. shifted by conv. וְ (comp. § 8. rem. 7) . .	קדש
הִקְדַּשְׁתִּיךָ[f]	id. id., suff. 2 pers. sing. masc. . .	קדש
הַקְהִילוּ[g]	Hiph. imp. pl. masc.	קהל
הִקְהִילוּ[h]	id. pret. 3 pers. pl.	קהל
הַקָּהָל	וְ' pref. הַ)(noun masc. sing. dec. 4a .	קהל
הַקְהֵל / הַקְהֶל־[k]	[i] וְ' Hiph. imp. sing. masc. (§ 11. rem. 5)	קהל
הִקְהַלְתָּ[l] / הִקְהַלְתָּ[m]	וְ id. pret. 2 pers. sing. masc.; acc. shifted by conv. וְ (comp. § 8. rem. 7) .	קהל
הַקְּהָתִי / הַקְּהָתִי	pref. הַ)(gent. noun from קְהָת or קֳהָת	קהת
הַקְּהָתִים / הַקְּהָתִים	pref. id.)(pl. of the preceding . .	קהת

[a] Eze. 40. 19. [b] Joel 2. 20. [c] 1 Sa. 14. 16. [d] Ex. 2. 3. [e] Da. 8. 5, 21. [f] Eze. 7. 7. [g] Is. 21. 5. [h] Is. 22. 24. [i] Ex. 8. 2. [k] Eze. 7. 10. [l] 2 Ch. 3. 15. [m] Est. 7. 4; Zec. 8. 10. [n] Nu. 10. 9. [o] 2 Ch. 28. 22. [p] 1 Ch. 11. 15. [q] De. 28. 52, 52. [r] Ge. 42. 21. [s] Le. 14. 3. [t] Le. 13. 45. [u] Is. 65. 16. [x] Je. 8. 22. [y] Ju. 9. 49, 49. [z] Na. 1. 6. [a] 2 Ch. 26. 19. [b] Ne. 3. 32. [c] Nu. 10. 9. [d] Le. 11. 18. [e] De. 14. 17. [f] Pr. 25. 16. [g] 2 Ki. 6. 25. [h] De. 18. 3. [i] Nu. 25. 8. [k] 2 Ch. 26. 23. [l] 2 Ki. 23. 17. [m] 2 Ch. 35. 3. [n] Le. 26. 16. [o] Eze. 40. 6. [p] Job 41. 3. [q] Is. 29. 23. [r] Ge. 10. 30. [s] Eze. 47. 8. [t] Job 6. 16. [u] Eze. 32. 7. [x] 1 Ki. 22. 47. [y] Ju. 17. 3. [z] Da. 9. 26. [a] Ge. 38. 21. [b] Ho. 4. 14. [c] Je. 12. 3. [d] 2 Ch. 29. 19. [e] 2 Ch. 7. 16. [f] Je. 1. 5. [g] De. 31. 28. [h] Nu. 1. 18. [i] Nu. 20. 8. [k] De. 4. 10. [l] Eze. 38. 13. [m] Nu. 8. 9.

הַקֹּהֶלֶת pref. הַ (noun fem. sing. . . . . קהל
הַקּוֹל וְ׳[aa] pref. id. (noun masc. sing. dec. 1a . קול
[a]הֲקוֹלְךָ pref. הֲ (id., suff. 2 pers. sing. masc. . קול
[b]הַקֹּלֹת pref. הַ (id. pl. . . . . קול
[c]הַקּוֹמָה pref. id. (noun fem. sing. dec. 10. . קום
[d]הַקּוֹמִים pref. id. (Kal part. act. masc., pl. of [קוֹם, for קָם § 21. rem. 2] . . . . קום
הַקֹּנֶה pref. id. (Kal part. act. sing. masc. dec. 9a קנה
[e]הַקֹּסֵם pref. id. (Kal part. act. sing. masc. dec. 7b קסם
[f]הַקֹּסְמִים וְ pref. id. (id. pl., absolute state . . קסם
הַקּוֹץ pref. id. (pr. name masc. . . . קוץ
[g]הַקֹּצֵר pref. id. (Kal part. act. sing. masc. dec. 7b קצר
הַקֹּצְרִים pref. id. (id. pl., absolute state . קצר
הַקֹּרֵא pref. id. (Kal part. act. sing. masc. dec. 7b קרא
[h]הַקּוֹרָה pref. id. (noun fem. sing. dec. 10. . קרה
[i]הַקְטֵיר וְ Hiph. inf. absolute . . . קטר
הִקְטִיר וְ׳ id. pret. 3 pers. sing. masc. . . קטר
[k]הִקְטִירוֹ וְ id. id., suff. 3 pers. sing. masc. . קטר
[l]הִקְטִירוּ וְ׳[m] id. pret. 3 pers. pl. . . . קטר
הִקְטִירָם וְ id. pret. 3 pers. sing. masc., suff. 3 p. pl. m. קטר
הַקָּטָן pref. הַ (adj. masc. sing. (suff. קְטַנָּם) dec. 8a (§ 37. Nos. 2 & 3), also pr. name . קטן
הַקָּטֹן וְ׳[n] pref. id. (adj. & subst. masc. sing. d. 3a קטן
הַקְּטַנָּה pref. id. (adj. f. s. d. 10, fr. קָטָן m. (§ 37. No. 3) קטן
[o]הַקְּטַנּוֹת pref. id. (id. pl. . . קטן
הַקְּטַנִּים וְ׳[p] pref. id. (id. pl. masc. from קָטָן dec. 8a קטן
[q]הַקֹּטְפִים pref. id. (Kal part. act. m., pl. of [קֹטֵף] d. 7b קטף
[r]הַקְטֵר Hiph. imp. sing. masc. . . . קטר
[s]הַקִּטֵּר pref. הַ (noun sing. masc. . . . קטר
הַקְּטֹרֶת וְ׳[t] pref. id. (noun fem. sing. dec. 13c . קטר
[u]הִקְטַרְתָּ וְ Hiph. pret. 2 pers. sing. masc.; acc. shifted by conv. וְ (comp. § 8. rem. 7) . . קטר
[x]הָקֵים Hiph. inf. absolute . . . . קום
[y]הֲקֵים וַ׳[z] Ch. Aph. pret. 3 pers. sing. masc. (§ 47. rem. 4); וַ bef. (-:) קום
הָקִים Hiph. inf. constr. . . . . קום
הֵקִים וְ׳ id. pret. 3 pers. sing. masc. . . קום
[a]הֲקִימֵהּ Ch. Aph. pret. 3 pers. sing. masc., suff. 3 pers. sing. masc. (§ 47. rem. 4) . . קום
[b]הָקִימוּ Hiph. imp. pl. masc. . . . קום
הֲקִימוֹ id. inf. (הָקִים), suff. 3 pers. sing. masc. d. 3a קום
[c]הֲקִימוּ וַ Ch. Aph. pret. 3 pers. pl. masc. (§ 47. rem. 4); וַ bef. (-:) . . . קום
הֵקִימוּ וְ׳[d] Hiph. pret. 3 pers. pl. . . . קום
הֲקִימוֹתִי וַ id. pret. 1 p. s.; acc. shifted by וַ for וְ conv. קום

[a]הֲקִימֵנִי וַ id. imp. sing. m., suff. 1 pers. s.; וַ bef. (-:) קום
[f]הֲקֵימֶת Chald. Aph. pret. 1 pers. sing. (§ 47, rem. 4, & § 54. rem. 4) . . . . קום
[g]הֲקֵימְתָּ Ch. id. pret. 2 pers. sing. masc. . . קום
[h]הֲקִימַת Ch. id. pret. 3 pers. sing. fem. . . קום
[i]הֳקִימַת Ch. Hoph. pret. 3 pers. sing. fem. . קום
[k]הֲקִימוֹתִי / הֲקִמֹתִי וַ } Hiph. pret. 1 pers. sing.; acc. shifted by conv. וְ (comp. § 8. rem. 7) . קום
הַקַּיִן pref. הַ (pr. name of a place . . קין
[l]הַקִּינָה pref. id. (noun fem. sing. dec. 10. . קין
[m]הַקִּינוֹת pref. id. (id. pl. . . . . קין
הַקֵּינִי pref. id. (pr. name of a people . . קין
הַקֵּינִים pref. id. (gent. noun, pl. of קֵינִי, see קֵינִי קין
[n]הַקֵּיף Hiph. inf. absolute . . . . נקף
[o]הִקִּיף id. pret. 3 pers. sing. masc. . . . נקף
[p]הִקִּיפָה id. pret. 3 pers. sing. fem. . . . נקף
הִקִּיפוּ וְ׳[q] id. pret. 3 pers. pl. . . . נקף
[r]הַקִּיפוּהָ וְ id. imp. pl. masc., suff. 3 pers. sing. fem. נקף
[s]הִקִּיפוּנִי id. pret. 3 pers. pl., suff. 1 pers. sing. נקף
[t]הַקַּיִץ / [u]הַקָּיִץ וְ } pref. הַ (noun masc. sing. dec. 6h . קיץ
הֵקִיץ וְ׳[x] Hiph. pret. 3 pers. sing. masc. . . קוץ
הָקִיצָה וְ׳[y] id. imp. s. m. with paragogic ה (§ 11. r. 5) קוץ
הָקִיצוּ id. imp. pl. masc. . . . . קוץ
הַקִּיצוֹנָה pref. הַ (adj. fem. s. [fr. קִיצוֹן for קִצּוֹן m.] קצץ
[z]הֲקִיצוֹתָ וַ Hiph pret. 2 pers. sing. m. (וַ for וְ conv. קוץ
[a]הֲקִיצוֹתִי id. pret. 1 pers. sing. (§ 21. rem. 14) קוץ
הַקִּיצֹנָה defect for הַקִּיצוֹנָה (q. v.) . . קצה
הֲקִיצֹתִי Hiph. pret. 1 pers. sing. (§ 21. rem. 14) . קוץ
[b]הַקִּיקָיוֹן pref. הַ (noun masc. sing. . . קיק
הַקִּיר וְ׳[c] pref. id. (noun masc. sing. dec. 1a . קיר
הַקִּירוֹת pref. id. (id. pl. . . . . קיר
[d]הַקַּל pref. id. (adj. masc. sing. dec. 8a . קלל
הָקֵל וְ׳[e] Hiph. imp. sing. masc. . . . קלל
הַקֹּל וְ׳[f] pref. הַ (for קוֹל, noun masc. sing. d. 1a קול
[g]הֵקַל Hiph. pret. 3 pers. sing. masc. (§ 18. r. 10) קלל
[h]הֲקַלּוּ pref. הֲ (Kal pret. 3 pers. pl. . . קלל
[i]הֵקַלּוּ Hiph. pret. 3 pers. pl. (§ 18. rem. 10) . קלל
[k]הַקֹּלוֹת pref. הַ (noun masc. with pl. fem. term. from קוֹל dec. 1a . . . . קול
[l]הַקָּלִיא pref. id. (noun masc. sing. for קָלִי . קלה
[m]הֲקֹלֵךְ pref. הֲ (noun masc. sing., suff. 2 pers. sing. masc. from קוֹל dec. 1a . . . קול
הַקְּלָלָה וְ׳ pref. הַ (noun fem. sing. dec. 11c . קלל
[n]הַקְּלָלוֹת pref. id. (id. pl., absolute state . . קלל

---

[a] 1 Sa. 26. 17. [b] Ex. 20. 18. [c] Is. 10. 33. [d] 2 Ki. 16. 7. [e] Jos. 13. 22. [f] Zec. 10. 2. [g] Je. 9. 21.
[h] 2 Ki. 6. 5. [i] 1 Ki. 9. 25. [k] Le. 3. 11. [l] 2 Ch. 29. 7. [m] Le. 3. 5. [n] Ge. 42. 32. [o] Eze. 16. 61.
[p] 2 Ch. 36. 18. [q] Job 30. 4. [r] 2 Ki. 16. 15. [s] Je. 44. 21. [t] Ex. 30. 37. [u] Ex. 29. 13, 18, 25. [x] Je. 44. 25.
[y] Da. 3. 2, 3, 5, 7. [z] Da. 6. 2. [a] Da. 5. 11. [b] Je. 51. 12. [c] Ezr. 6. 18. [d] Nu. 10. 21. [e] Ps. 41. 11.
[f] Da. 3. 14. [g] Da. 3. 12, 18. [h] Da. 7. 5. [i] Da. 7. 4. [k] 1 Sa. 15. 13. [l] 2 Sa. 1. 17. [m] 2 Ch. 35. 25.
[n] Jos. 6. 3. [o] Job 19. 6. [p] Is. 15. 8. [q] 2 Ch. 23. 7. [r] Ps. 48. 13. [s] Ps. 22. 17. [aa] Ezr. 3. 13.
[t] Am. 3. 15. [u] 2 Sa. 16. 2. [x] Is. 29. 8, 8. [y] Ps. 35. 23. [z] Pr. 6. 22. [a] Ps. 3. 6.
[b] Jon. 4. 6, 7, 9, 10. [c] Eze. 43. 8. [d] Je. 46. 6. [e] Ex. 18. 22. [f] Ge. 27. 22; 45. 16. [g] Is. 8. 23.
[h] Ge. 8. 8. [i] Eze. 22. 7. [k] Ex. 9. 29, 33. [l] 1 Sa. 17. 17. [m] 1 Sa. 24. 17. [n] De. 28. 15, 45.

הַקֶּ֫לַע[a] pref. הַ)(for קֶ֫לַע n. m. s. d. 6a (§ 35. r. 5) קלע

הַקַּלָּעִים[b] pref. id.)(noun masc. pl. [of קַלָּע] קלע

הַקְּלֹקֵל pref. id.)(adj. masc. sing. קלל

הַקֹּלֹת[c] וְ pref. הַ)(noun masc. with pl. fem. term. from קוֹל dec. 1a קול

הֲקִלֹּתַנִי[d] Hiph. pret. 2 pers. sing. masc., suff. 1 pers. s. קלל

הָקֵם[e] וְ׳ Hiph. inf. absolute, or imp. sing. masc. קום

הֻקַם[f] Hoph. pret. 3 pers. sing. masc. for הוּקַם (§ 21. rem. 24) קום

הַקָּמָה[g] pref. הַ)(noun fem. sing. dec. 10. קום

הַקָּמַח[h] pref. id.)(noun masc. sing. קמח

הַקָּמִים pref. id.)(Kal part. act. m., pl. of קָם dec. 1a קום

הֲקֵמֹנוּ[i] וַ Hiph. pret. 1 pers. pl. (§ 21. rem. 14); וַ for וְ conv. קום

הֲקֵמֹתָ וַ id. pret. 2 pers. sing. masc.; acc. shifted by וַ for וְ conv. (§ 8. rem. 7) קום

הֲקִמֹתוֹ[k] וַ׳ id. id., suff. 2 pers. sing. masc. (§ 21. rem. 14); וַ for וְ conv. קום

הֲקִמֹתִי / הֲקֵמֹתִי } id. pret. 1 pers. sing.; acc. shifted by וַ for וְ, conv. (comp. § 8. rem. 7) קום

הַקִּנְאָה[m] pref. הַ)(noun fem. sing. dec. 12b קנא

הַקְּנָאֹת[n] pref. id.)(id. pl., absolute state קנא

הַקָּנֶה pref. id.)(noun masc. sing. dec. 9b קנה

הַקֹּנֶה[o] pref. id.)(Kal part. act. sing. masc. dec. 9a קנה

הַקְּנִזִּי pref. id.)(pr. name of a people קנז

הַקֵּינִי pref. id.)(pr. name of a people קין

הַקָּנִים pref. id.)(noun masc., pl. of קָנֶה dec. 9b קנה

הִקְנַנִי[p] Hiph. pret. 3 pers. s. m. [הִקְנָה], suff. 1 pers. s. קנה

הַקֶּסֶם[q] pref. הַ)(noun masc. sing. dec. 6. קסם

הַקֹּסְמִים[r] וְ׳ pref. id.)(Kal part. act. masc., pl. of קֹסֵם dec. 7b קסם

הַקֶּשֶׁת[s] pref. id.)(noun fem. sing. קשה

הַקְּעָרָה[u] pref. id.)(noun fem. sing., constr. קַעֲרַת dec. 11c (§ 42. rem. 1 & 3) קער

הַקְּעָרֹת[v] pref. id.)(id. pl., absolute state קער

הַקֵּף[y] Hiph. inf. absolute נקף

הַקֹּפְאִים[z] pref. הַ)(Kal part. act. m., pl. [קֹפֵא] dec. 7b קפא

הִקַּפְתֶּם[a] וְ Hiph. pret. 2 pers. pl. masc. נקף

הַקֵּץ pref. הַ / הַקֵּץ[b] pref. הַ } noun masc. sing. dec. 8b קצץ

הַקָּצֶה pref. הַ)(noun masc. sing. dec. 9b קצה

הִקְצוּ[c] Hiph. pret. 3 pers. pl. קצה

הַקְּצוּבוֹת[d] pref. הַ)(Kal part. p. pl. fem. [fr. קָצוּב m.] קצב

הַקָּצוֹר[e] pref. הַ)(Kal inf. absolute קצר

הַקְּצָוֹת[f] pref. הַ)(noun fem. pl. absolute from קְצָת comp. מְנָת (§ 45) קצה

הַקְצוֹת[g] Hiph. inf. construct קצה

הַקָּצִיר pref. הַ)(noun masc. sing. dec. 3a קצר

הַקֶּצֶף[h] pref. id.)(noun m. s. dec. 6 (suff. קִצְפְּךָ ,קֶצֶף) קצף

הִקְצַפְתָּ[i] Hiph. pret. 2 pers. sing. masc. קצף

הִקְצַפְתֶּם[k] id. pret. 2 pers. pl. masc. קצף

הַקָּצַר[l] pref. הַ)(Kal pret. 3 pers. sing. masc. קצר

הַקֹּצְרִים pref. הַ)(Kal part. act. m., pl. of קוֹצֵר d. 7b קצר

הִקְצַרְתָּ[m] Hiph. pret. 2 pers. sing. masc. קצר

הֹקַר[n] Hiph. imp. sing. m. [for הוֹקַר, comp. הַשְׁמַע] יקר

הַקֹּרֵא[o] pref. הַ)(noun masc. sing. קרא

הַקְּרֻאִים pref. id.)(Kal part. p. m., pl. of קָרוּא d. 3a קרא

הַקָּרֵב pref. id.)(adj. masc. sing. dec. 5a קרב

הַקָּרֹב[p] וְ׳ pref. id.)(adj. masc. sing. dec. 3a קרב

הַקֶּרֶב[q] וְ׳ pref. id.)(noun m. s. (suff. קִרְבִּי) dec. 6a קרב

הַקְרֵב[r] וְ׳ Hiph. imp. sing. masc. קרב

הִקְרֵב[s] id. pret. 3 pers. sing. masc. for הִקְרִיב קרב

הַקְּרֹבָה[t] pref. הַ)(adj. fem. s. dec. 10, from קָרוֹב m. קרב

הַקְרְבוּהִי[u] Chald. Aph. pret. 3 pers. pl. masc., suff. 3 pers. sing. masc. (§ 47. rem. 4) קרב

הַקְּרֹבוֹת[x] וְ׳[y] pref. הַ)(adj. fem., pl. of קְרוֹבָה dec. 10, from קָרוֹב masc. קרב

הַקְּרֵבִים pref. id.)(adj. masc., pl. of קָרֵב dec. 5a קרב

הַקְּרֹבִים pref. id.)(adj. masc., pl. of קָרוֹב dec. 3a קרב

הַקָּרְבָּן[z] pref. id.)(noun masc. sing. see קָרְבָּן קרב

הִקְרַבְתָּ וְ Hiph. pret. 2 pers. sing. masc.; acc. shifted by conv. וְ (§ 8. rem. 7) קרב

הִקְרַבְתִּיו[a] וְ id. pret. 1 pers. sing., suff. 3 pers. s. m. קרב

הִקְרַבְתָּם[b] וְ id. pret. 2 pers. s. m., suff. 3 pers. pl. m. קרב

הִקְרַבְתֶּם וְ id. pret. 2 pers. pl. masc. קרב

הַקַּרְדֻּמּוֹת[c] pref. הַ)(noun masc., with pl. fem. term. from [קַרְדֹּם] dec. 8c (§ 37. No. 3) קרדם

הַקְרֵה[d] Hiph. imp. sing. masc. קרה

הֵקֵרָה[e] Hiph. pret. 3 p. s. f. (as if fr. קרר § 21. r. 22) קור

הִקְרָה[f] Hiph. pret. 3 pers. sing. masc. קרה

הַקְּרוּאִים pref. הַ)(Kal part. p. m., pl. of [קָרוּא] d. 3a קרא

הַקָּרוֹב[g] וְ pref. id.)(adj. masc. sing. dec. 3a קרב

הַקְּרוֹבָה[h] pref. id.)(id. fem. dec. 10. קרב

הַקְּרוֹבִים pref. id.)(id. pl. masc. dec. 3a קרב

הַקֹּרוֹת[i] pref. id.)(noun fem., pl. of קוֹרָה dec. 10. קרה

הַקֶּרַח[k] / הַקָּרַח[l] } pref. הַ)(noun masc. sing. (§ 35. rem. 2) קרח

הַקָּרְחִי pref. id.)(patronym. of קֹרַח קרח

הַקָּרְחִים pref. id.)(pl. of the preceding קרח

הַקְּרִיאָה[m] pref. id.)(noun fem. sing. קרא

הַקְרִיב[n] Hiph. inf. constr. dec. 1b קרב

הִקְרִיב וְ׳ id. pret. 3 pers. sing. masc. קרב

---

[a] 1 Sa. 25. 29. [b] 2 Ki. 3. 25. [c] Ex. 9. 34. [d] 2 Sa. 19. 44. [e] Ge. 38. 8. [f] 2 Sa. 23. 1. [g] Ex. 22. 5.
[h] 1 Ki. 17. 14, 16. [i] Mi. 5. 4. [k] Ps. 89. 44. [l] 2 Ki. 9. 2. [m] Eze. 8. 3, 5. [n] Nu. 5. 25, 29. [o] Le. 25. 28.
[p] Zec. 13. 5. [q] Eze. 21. 27. [r] Mi. 3. 7. [s] Eze. 13. 9. [t] Eze. 9. 11. [u] Nu. 7. 85. [v] Nu. 4. 7.
[y] Jos. 6. 11. [z] Zep. 1. 12. [a] 2 Ki. 11. 8. [b] Job 16. 3. [c] Le. 14. 41. [d] Ca. 4. 2. [e] Is. 50. 2.
[f] Ex. 38. 5. [g] Le. 14. 43. [h] Nu. 17. 11. [i] De. 9. 7. [k] De. 9. 8. [l] Mi. 2. 7. [m] Ps. 89. 46.
[n] Pr. 25. 17. [o] 1 Sa. 26. 20. [p] Est. 1. 14. [q] Le. 1. 13. [r] Le. 9. 2. [s] Nu. 7. 19.
[t] De. 21. 3. [u] Da. 7. 13. [x] Eze. 22. 5. [y] Je. 48. 24. [z] Eze. 40. 43. [a] Je. 30. 21.
[b] Eze. 43. 24. [c] Ju. 9. 48. [d] Ge. 24. 12. [e] Je. 6. 7. [f] Ge. 27. 20. [g] Eze. 6. 12.
[h] Le. 21. 3. [i] 2 Ch. 3. 7. [k] Job 38. 29. [l] Eze. 1. 22. [m] Jon. 3. 2. [n] Nu. 9. 7.

הִקְרִיבָהּ[a]	וְ id. id., suff. 3 pers. sing. fem. . . .	קרב
הִקְרִיבָה[b]	וְ'[c] id. pret. 3 pers. sing. fem. . . .	קרב
הַקְרִיבֵהוּ[d]	id. imp. sing. masc., suff. 3 pers. sing. masc.	קרב
הַקְרִיבוֹ[e]	id. inf., suff. 3 pers. sing. masc. dec. 1b	קרב
הַקְרִיבוּ[f]	וְ Chald. Aph. pret. 3 pers. pl. m. (§ 47. r. 4)	קרב
הִקְרִיבוֹ	וְ Hiph. pret. 3 pers. s. m., suff. 3 pers. s. m.	קרב
הִקְרִיבוּ	וְ' id. pret. 3 pers. pl.	קרב
הִקְרִיבֶם[g]	id. id., suff. 3 pers. pl. masc. (for ן fem. § 2. rem. 5)	קרב
הַקִּרְיָה	pref. הַ)(noun fem. sing. dec. 10. .	קרה
הַקְּרִיּוֹת	pref. id.)(pr. name of a city . .	קרה
הִקְרִיחוּ[h]	וְ Hiph. pret. 3 pers. pl.	קרח
הִקְרִיתֶם[i]	וְ Hiph. pret. 2 pers. pl. masc. . .	קרה
הַקֶּרֶן[k]	וְ'[l] pref. הַ)(noun fem. s. (suff. קַרְנִי) dec. 6a	קרן
הַקְּרָנוֹת	pref. id.)(id. pl. absolute state .	קרן
הַקְּרָנַיִם[m] הַקְּרָנָיִם[n]	וְ'[o] } pref. id.)(id. du. [as if from קָרָן] .	קרן
הַקְּרָסִים[p]	pref. id.)(noun m. pl., c. קַרְסֵי fr. [קֶרֶס] d. 6a	קרס
הַקַּרְקַע[q] הַקַּרְקָע[r]	} pref. הַ art.)(noun masc. sing. . .	קרקע
הַקַּרְקָעָה	pref. id.)(pr. name (קַרְקַע) with parag. ה .	קרקע
הַקֶּרֶשׁ הַקָּרֶשׁ	} pref. הַ)(noun masc. sing. (suff. קַרְשֶׁךָ) dec. 6a (§ 35. rem. 2) . . }	קרש
הַקְּרָשִׁים	pref. id.)(id. pl., absolute state .	קרש
הַקֹּרֹת[s]	pref. id.)(Kal part. act. fem. pl. [of קֹרָה, from קֹרֶה masc.]	קרה
הַקִּשֻּׁאִים[t]	pref. id.)(noun masc., pl. of [קִשֻּׁא] dec. 1b	קשא
הַקְשֵׁב[u]	Hiph. imp. sing. masc. . . .	קשב
הִקְשַׁבְתָּ[x]	id. pret. 2 pers. sing. masc. . .	קשב
הִקְשַׁבְתִּי[y]	id. pret. 1 pers. sing. . . .	קשב
הַקָּשָׁה	pref. הַ)(adj., fem. of the following, dec. 11a	קשה
הַקָּשֶׁה	pref. id.)(adj. masc. sing. dec. 9b	קשה
הִקְשָׁה	Hiph. pret. 3 pers. sing. masc. .	קשה
הִקְשׁוּ	id. pret. 3 pers. pl. . . .	קשה
הַקְּשָׂוֹת[z]	וְ'[a] pref. הַ)(n. fem., pl. of [קְשָׂוָה] dec. 12a	קשה
הִקְשִׁיב	וְ'[b] Hiph. pret. 3 pers. sing. masc. .	קשב
הַקְשִׁיבָה	וְ'[c] id. imp. s. m. with parag. ה (§ 11. rem. 5)	קשב
הַקְשִׁיבוּ	וְ' id. imp. pl. masc. . . .	קשב
הִקְשִׁיבוּ	id. pret. 3 pers. pl.	קשב
הַקְשִׁיבִי	id. imp. sing. fem.	קשב
הִקְשִׁיחַ[d]	Hiph. pret. 3 pers. sing. masc. . .	קשח
הִקְשִׁיתָ[e]	Hiph. pret. 2 pers. sing. masc. . .	קשה
הַקֶּשֶׁר[f]	pref. הַ)(noun m. sing. (suff. קִשְׁרוֹ) dec. 6c	קשר
הַקְּשֻׁרִים[g]	וְ pref. id.)(Kal part. p. m., pl. of [קָשׁוּר] d. 3a	קשר
הַקֹּשְׁרִים	pref. id.)(id. part. act. m., pl. of [קֹשֵׁר] dec. 7b	קשר
הַקִּשֻּׁרִים[h]	וְ pref. id.)(noun masc., pl. of [קִשֻּׁר] dec. 1b	קשר

הַקֶּשֶׁת	pref. id.)(noun com. sing. (with suff. קַשְׁתִּי comp. dec. 13a)	קוש
הַקְּשָׁתוֹת[i]	וְ pref. id.)(id. pl. abs., constr. קַשְּׁתוֹת ת treated as if radical . . .	קוש
הַר	וְ' noun masc. sing. dec. 8 (§ 37. rem. 7), and pr. name in compos. הַר הֶרֶס . .	הרר
הֹר	pr. name of a mountain . . .	הרר
הָרָא	וְ pr. name of a region	הרר
הָרָאָה[k]	וְ pref. הָ for הַ·)(noun fem. sing. .	ראה
הֶרְאָה[l]	וְ Hiph. pret. 3 pers. sing. masc. .	ראה
הָרֹאֶה הָרֹאֶה[m]	pref. f. הַ· הָ / pref. הָ } Kal part. act. sing. masc. dec. 9a	ראה
הֶרְאָה	וְ'[n] Hiph. pret. 3 p. s. m. [for הִרְ' § 11. rem. 1]	ראה
הֵרָאֵה[o]	Niph. imp. sing. masc.	ראה
הָרְאוּבֵנִי	וְ' pref. הָ for הַ·)(patronym. רְאוּבֵן	ראה
הָרֹאוֹת	pref. id.)(Kal part. act. fem., pl. of רֹאָה dec. 10, from רֹאֶה masc. .	ראה
הֵרָאוֹת[p]	Niph. inf. constr. dec. 1b . .	ראה
הַרְאוֹתְךָה[q]	Hiph. inf. (הַרְאוֹת), suff. 2 pers. sing. masc. (§ 3. rem. 2, comp. § 2. rem. 2) .	ראה
הַרְאוֹתָם[r]	id. with suff. 3 pers. masc. pl. .	ראה
הָרְאֻיוֹת[s]	pref. הָ for הַ·)(Kal part. p. fem. pl. [of רְאֻיָה from רָאוּי] masc. . . .	ראה
הָרֹאִים	pref. id.)(id. part. act. m., pl. of רֹאֶה dec. 9a	ראה
הַרְאִינִי[t]	Hiph. imp. sing. fem., suff. 1 pers. sing. .	ראה
הָרִאישׁוֹן[u]	Kh. הָרִאישׁוֹן, pref. הָ for הַ)(adj. masc. sing.; K. הָרִאשׁוֹן (q. v.) . . .	ראש
הֲרָאִיתָ	pref. הֲ)(Kal pret. 2 pers. sing. masc.	ראה
הָרְאֵיתָ[x]	Hoph. pret. 2 pers. sing. masc. . .	ראה
הִרְאִיתָ[y]	Hiph. pret. 2 pers. sing. masc. (§ 24. rem. 14)	ראה
הִרְאֵיתִי[z]	וְ id. pret. 1 pers. sing.; acc. shifted by conv. וְ (comp. § 8. rem. 7) . . .	ראה
הֶרְאִיתִךָ[a]	id. id., suff. 2 p. s. m. (§ 11. r. 1, & § 24. r. 14)	ראה
הִרְאִיתִים[b]	id. id., suff. 3 pers. pl. masc. (§ 24. rem. 14)	ראה
הַרְּאִיתֶם[c]	pref. הַ interr. for הֲ)(Kal pret. 2 pers. pl. masc. (for הַרְאִיתֶם, comp. הַכְּתֹנֶת) .	ראה
הִרְאִתִם[d]	Hiph. pret. 1 pers. sing., suff. 3 pers. pl. masc. (§ 24. rem. 14) for 'תִים . .	ראה
הִרְאִיתַנוּ[e]	id. pret. 2 pers. sing. masc., suff., Kh. 'תָנוּ 1 pers. pl., K. 'תַנִי 1 pers. sing.	ראה
הִרְאִיתַנִי[f]	id. pret. 2 p. s. m., suff. 1 p. s. (§ 24. rem. 14)	ראה
הֶרְאֲךָ[g]	id. pret. 3 pers. sing. masc., suff. 2 pers. sing. masc. (§ 11. rem. 1, & § 24. rem. 21)	ראה
הֶרְאָם	id. id., suff. 3 pers. pl. masc. (§ 11. rem. 1)	ראה
הֶרְאָנוּ	id. id., suff. 1 pers. pl. . . .	ראה
הַרְאֵנוּ	id. imp. sing. masc., suff. 1 pers. pl.	ראה

[a] Le. 2. 8. [b] Ju. 5. 25. [c] Nu. 15. 27. [d] Mal. 1. 8. [e] Le. 7. 16. [f] Ezr. 6. 17. [g] Nu. 17. 3. [h] Eze. 27. 31. [i] Nu. 35. 11. [k] Da. 8. 8. [l] Da. 8. 21. [m] Da. 8. 20. [n] Da. 8. 6. [o] Da. 8. 3. [p] Ex. 26. 11, 33. [q] 1 Ki. 7. 7. [r] 1 Ki. 6. 16. [s] Ge. 42. 29. [t] Nu. 11. 5. [u] Job 33. 31. [x] Is. 48. 18. [y] Je. 8. 6. [z] Ex. 37. 16. [a] 1 Ch. 28. 17. [b] Is. 21. 7. [c] Ps. 86. 6. [d] Job 39. 16. [e] 2 Ki. 2. 10. [f] 2 Sa. 15. 12. [g] Ge. 30. 42. [h] Is. 3. 20. [i] Ne. 4. 10. [k] De. 14. 13. [l] Le. 13. 49. [m] Eze. 8. 6. [n] Ec. 2. 24. [o] 1 Ki. 18. 1. [p] Le. 13. 14. [q] Eze. 40. 4. [r] Jos. 5. 6. [s] Est. 2. 9. [t] Ca. 2. 14. [u] Job 15. 7. [x] Ex. 26. 30. [y] Ps. 60. 5. [z] Na. 3. 5. [a] De. 34. 4. [b] Is. 39. 4. [c] 1Sa. 10. 24; 17. 25. 2 Ki. 6. 32. [d] 2 Ki. 20. 15. [e] Ps. 71. 20. [f] Je. 11. 18. [g] De. 4. 36.

הָרְאֵנִי[a] id. id., suff. 1 pers. sing. . . . ראה

הֶרְאַנִי[b] / הֶרְאַנִי ו' } id. pret. 3 pers. sing. masc. (§ 11. rem. 1) suff. 1 pers. sing. (§ 2. rem. 1) . } ראה

הָרֹאשׁ[c] ו' ו' pref. הָ f. הַ· / הָרֹאשׁ[d] pref. הָ } noun masc. sing., irr., pl. רָאשִׁים (§ 45) . } ראש

הָרָ֫אשׁ[e] pref. הָ for הַ·)(Kal part. masc. sing. Kh. (§ 21. rem. 1); K. רָשׁ id. dec. 1a . רוש

הָרָאשִׁים ו' ו'[f] pref. id.)(noun m., pl. of ראשׁ irr. (§ 45) ראש

הָרִאשָׁה[g] pref. id.)(noun fem. sing. . . . ראש

הָרִאשׁוֹן pref. id.)(adj. masc. sing. dec. 1b . ראש

הָרִאשׁוֹנָה pref. id.)(id. fem. dec. 10. . ראש

הָרִאשֹׁנִים pref. id.)(id. pl. masc. . . . . ראש

הָרִאשֹׁן[h] defect. for הָרִאשׁוֹן (q. v.) . . ראש

הָרִאשֹׁנָה defect. for הָרִאשׁוֹנָה (q. v.) . . ראש

הָרִאשֹׁנוֹת pref. הָ for הַ·)(adj. fem., pl. of רִאשׁוֹנָה dec. 10 from רִאשׁוֹן masc. . . ראש

הָרִאשֹׁנִים pref. id.)(id. masc., pl. of רִאשׁוֹן dec. 1b . ראש

הָרִאשֹׁנִית[i] pref. id.)(adj. fem. sing. [from רִאשֹׁנִי masc.] ראש

הָרֹאֹת pref. id.)(Kal part. act. fem., pl. of רֹאָה, from רֹאֶה masc. . . . ראה

הָרְאֵתָ[k] Hoph. pret. 2 pers. sing. masc. . . ראה

הֵרָאֹתוֹ[l] Niph. inf. (הֵרָאוֹת), suff. 3 pers. s. m. dec. 1b ראה

הַרְאֹתְךָ[m] Hiph. inf. (הַרְאוֹת), suff. 2 pers. s. m. dec. 1b ראה

הָרָב / הָרָב[n] } pref. הָ for הַ·)(adj. masc. sing. dec. 8d . רבב

הָרֹב[o] pref. הָ)(noun masc. sing. dec. 8c . רבב

הֲרֹב[p] pref. id.)(Kal inf. abs. R. רוב see ריב

הֶרֶב[q] Hiph. imp. s. m. apoc. from הַרְבֵּה (§ 24. r. 17) רבה

הָרַבָּה ו pref. הָ for הַ·)(pr. name of a place רבב

הַרְבֵּה ו' ו'[r] / הַרְבֵּה ו' } Hiph. inf. abs. (§ 24. rem. 15) . רבה

הֶרְבֹּה[s] Kh. הַרְבֵּה q. v., K. הֶרֶב (q. v.) . . רבה

הִרְבָּה ו' Hiph. pret. 3 pers. sing. masc. . . רבה

הַרְבּוּ id. imp. pl. masc. . . . . . רבה

הִרְבּוּ id. pret. 3 pers. pl. . . . . רבה

הַרְבּוֹת id. inf. constr. (§ 24. rem. 15) . . רבה

הַרְבִּי[t] id. imp. sing. fem. . . . . רבה

הָרַבִּים ו'[u] pref. הָ for הַ·)(adj. m., pl. of רַב d. 8d רבב

הִרְבִּינוּ[x] Hiph. pret. 1 pers. pl. (§ 24. rem. 14) . רבה

הָרְבִיעִי ו' pref. הָ for הַ·)(adj. ord. m. s. [fr. אַרְבַּע, רֶבַע] רבע

הָרְבִיעִית / הָרְבִיעִת } pref. id.)(id. fem. . . . . רבע

הָרַבִּית ו pref. id.)(pr. name of a place . . רבב

הִרְבֵּית[y] Hiph. pret. 2 pers. sing. fem. . . . רבה

הִרְבִּיתָ ו'[z] id. pret. 2 pers. sing. masc. (§ 24. r. 14) רבה

הִרְבֵּיתִי id. pret. 1 pers. sing. . . . רבה

הִרְבֵּיתִי ו id. id.; acc. shifted by conv. ו (§ 8. r. 7, & § 11. rem. 9) . . . רבה

הִרְבֵּיתָךְ[a] ו id. id., suff. 2 pers. sing. m. (§ 24. rem. 14) רבה

הִרְבֵּיתֶם[b] id. pret. 2 pers. pl. masc. . . . רבה

הָרִבְלָה pref. הָ for הַ·)(pr. name of a place . רבל

הִרְבֶּךָ / הִרְבְּךָ[c] } ו / ו Hiph. pret. 3 pers. sing. masc., suff. 2 pers. sing. masc. (§ 24. rem. 20) . } רבה

הָרְבִעִי pref. הָ for הַ·)(for רְבִיעִי, adj. ord. masc. sing. [from אַרְבַּע, רֶבַע] . . . רבע

הָרְבִעִית pref. id.)(id. fem. . . . . רבע

הָרֹבֵץ[d] pref. id.)(Kal part. act. sing. masc. dec. 7b רבץ

הִרְבַּתָה[e] Hiph. pret. 3 pers. sing. fem. . . . רבה

הִרְבִּתִים[f] ו id. pret. 1 pers. sing. with suff. 3 pers. masc. pl. (§ 24. rem. 14) . . . רבה

הָרַג ו' *to kill, slay,* in general, man, beast or plant; by the sword, pestilence, viper, or grief. Constr. with acc., לְ, בְּ. Niph. *to be killed, slain.* Pu. id.

הֶרֶג m. *a slaying, slaughter.*

הֲרֵגָה f. id.; צֹאן הַהֲרֵגָה *sheep for the slaughter.*

הָרָג Kal pret. 3 p. s. m. for הָרַג (comp. § 8. r. 7) הרג

הָרֹג id. inf. absolute . . . . הרג

הֲרֹג[g] id. inf. constr. . . . . . הרג

הֶרֶג ו'[h] noun masc. sing. . . . . הרג

הֹרָג[i] Pual pret. 3 pers. sing. masc. [for הֹרַג] הרג

הֹרֵג Kal part. act. sing. masc. dec. 7b . . הרג

הֲרֵגָה[k] noun fem. sing. . . . . . הרג

הָרְגוּ / הָרָגוּ ו'[l] } Kal pret. 3 pers. pl. (§ 8. rem. 7) . הרג

הֲרָגוֹ[m] id. pret. 3 pers. sing. m., suff. 3 pers. s. m. הרג

הִרְגוּ[n] / הִרְגוּ ו'[o] } id. imp. pl. masc. (§ 8. rem. 12) . הרג

הֲרָגוּם[p] וַ'[q] id. pret. 3 pers. pl., suff. 3 pers. pl. masc.; וַ bef. (-:) . . . . . הרג

הֲרָגוּנִי[r] וַ id. id., suff. 1 pers. sing.; וַ id. . . הרג

הַרְגִּזוּ[s] Ch. Aph. pret. 3 pers. pl. masc. (§ 47. r. 4) רגז

הִרְגַּזְתַּנִי[t] Hiph. pret. 2 pers. sing. m., suff. 1 pers. s. רגז

הֲרֻגֵי[u] Kal part. p. pl. constr. m. from [הָרוּג] d. 3. הרג

הֲרֻגָיו[x] id. pl., suff. 3 pers. sing. masc. . . הרג

הִרְגִּיז[y] וְ'[z] Hiph. pret. 3 pers. sing. masc. . . רגז

הֲרֻגִים[a] Kal part. pass. masc., pl. of [הָרוּג] dec. 3. הרג

הֹרְגִים[b] id. part. act. masc., pl. of הֹרֵג dec. 7b . הרג

הַרְגִּיעַ[c] Hiph. inf. constr. (§ 11. rem. 4) . . רגע

הִרְגִּיעָה[d] id. pret. 3 pers. sing. fem. . . . רגע

הֹרְגֶךָ[e] Kal part. act., suff. 2 pers. sing. masc. [for הֹרֶגְךָ] from הֹרֵג dec. 7b . . . הרג

---

[a] Ex. 33. 18. [b] Eze. 11. 25. [c] 1 Sa. 13. 18, 18. [d] 2 Sa. 3. 8. [e] 2 Sa. 12. 4. [f] Ju. 9. 44. [g] Zec. 4. 7. [h] Ex. 12. 15. [i] Je. 25. 1. [k] De. 4. 35. [l] Le. 13. 7. [m] Ex. 9. 16. [n] Nu. 35. 8. [o] Job 11. 2. [p] Ju. 11. 25; Job 40. 2. [q] Ju. 20. 38. [r] Ge. 22. 17. [s] Ps. 51. 4. [t] Is. 23. 16. [u] Is. 8. 7. [x] Ezr. 10. 13. [y] Na. 3. 16. [z] 1 Ch. 4. 10.

[a] Ge. 48. 4. [b] Eze. 11. 6. [c] De. 30. 5. [d] Eze. 29. 3. [e] 1 Sa. 1. 12. [f] Je. 30. 19. [g] Ju. 8. 20. [h] Est. 9. 5. [i] Is. 27. 7. [k] Je. 12. 3. [l] Ge. 12. 12. [m] Ge. 4. 25. [n] Nu. 31. 17. [o] Ex. 32. 27. [p] Jos. 9. 26. [q] 1 Ch. 7. 21. [r] Ge. 20. 11. [s] Ezr. 5. 12. [t] 1 Sa. 28. 15. [u] Je. 18. 21. [x] Is. 27. 7. [y] Is. 23. 11. [z] Je. 50. 34. [a] Is. 14. 19. [b] 2 Ki. 17. 25. [c] Je. 50. 34. [d] Is. 34. 14. [e] Eze. 28. 9.

הָרַגְלָיִם[a] | pref. הָ for הַ·) noun fem., du. of רֶגֶל dec. 6a . . . . . רגל
וְהָרַגְלַיִם[b] }

הֲרָגָם[c] Kal pret. 3 pers. sing. m., suff. 3 pers. pl. m. הרג

וַהֲרַגְנֻהוּ[d] וַ Kal pret. 1 p. pl., suff. 3 p. s. m.; וַ for וְ conv. הרג

וַהֲרַגְנוּם[e] וַ id. id., suff. 3 pers. pl. masc.; וַ id. . הרג

וַהֲרָגָנִי וַ id. pret. 3 pers. sing. masc., suff. 1 pers. sing. (§ 2. rem. 1); וַ id. . . . הרג

וַהֲרָגֻנִי[f] וַ id. pret. 3 pers. pl., suff. 1 pers. sing.; וַ id. הרג

הָרְגֵנִי[g] id. imp. sing. m., suff. 1 pers. s. (§ 8. r. 12) הרג

הֵרָגְעִי[h] Niph. imp. sing. fem. . . . . רגע

הַרְגִּשׁוּ[i] Ch. Aph. pret. 3 pers. pl. masc. (§ 47. r. 4) רגש

הָרַגְתָּ | Kal pret. 2 pers. sing. masc. (§ 8. rem. 7) הרג
הָרָגְתָּ }

וְהָרַגְתָּ[k] וְ id. id.; acc. shifted by conv. וְ . . הרג

הֲרָגַתְהוּ[l] id. pret. 3 pers. sing. fem., suff. 3 pers. sing. masc. [for 'גַתְהוּ' § 16. rem. 3] . . הרג

הָרַגְתִּי | id. pret. 1 pers. sing.; acc. shifted by conv. וְ (§ 8. rem. 7) . . הרג
וְהָרַגְתִּי[m] }

הֲרַגְתִּיךְ[n] id. id., suff. 2 pers. sing. masc. . . הרג

הֲרַגְתִּיךְ[o] id. id., suff. 2 pers. sing. fem. . . הרג

הֲרַגְתִּים[p] id. id., suff. 3 pers. pl. masc. . . . הרג

וַהֲרָגָתַם[q] וַ id. pret. 3 pers. sing. fem., suff. 3 pers. pl. masc.; וַ for וְ conv. . . . הרג

הֲרַגְתֶּם[r] id. pret. 2 pers. pl. masc. . . . הרג

הֲרַגְתָּנִי[s] id. pret. 2 p. s. m., suff. 1 p. s. [for 'תַּנִי' § 2. r. 1] הרג

הָרֹדֵד[t] pref. הָ for הַ·) Kal part. act. sing. masc. רדד

וְהָרְדִידִים[u] וְ pref. id.) noun masc., pl. of [רְדִיד] d. 3a רדד

הָרֹדִים pref. id.) Kal part. act. m., pl. of רֹדֶה d. 9a רדה

הִרְדִּיפֻהוּ[w] Hiph. pret. 3 pers. pl., suff. 3 pers. sing. m. רדף

הָרֹדְפִים pref. הָ for הַ·) Kal part. a. m., pl. of רֹדֵף d. 7b רדף

וְהָרָה[y] וְ fut. תַּהֲרֶה apoc. תַּהַר—I. *to conceive, become pregnant,* const. with לְ to or by whom.—II. *to conceive in mind, devise.* Pu. הֹרָה *to be conceived,* Job 3. 3. Po. *to devise,* Is. 59. 13.

הָרָה adj. only fem. הָרָה, constr. הָרַת, pl. with suff. הָרוֹתֶיהָ (§ 42. rem. 2) *pregnant, with child.*

הָרִי id. only pl. fem. הָרִיּוֹתָיו Ho. 14. 1.

הֵרָיוֹן masc. *conception, pregnancy.*

הֵרֹן dec. 1b (§ 30. 2 note) id. Ge. 3. 16.

הָרָה adj. fem. s. comp. § 42. r. 2 [from הָרֶה m.] הרה

הָרֹה[z] Kal inf. absolute . . . . הרה

הָהָרָה[a] noun masc. (הַר) with loc. ה [dag. f. impl. for הַהָרָה, § 37. r. 7, comp. § 42. No 3 note] הרר

הֹרָה[b] Pual pret. 3 pers. sing. masc. [for הֹרָה] הרה

הִרְהִיבֻנִי[c] Hiph. pret. 3 pers. pl., suff. 1 pers. sing. . רהב

הָרְהָטִים[d] pref. הָ for הַ·) noun masc., pl. of [רַהַט] dec. 6d . . . . . רהט

וְהַרְהֹרִין[e] וְ Ch. noun masc., pl. of [הַרְהֹר] dec. 1. הרר

הֲרוֹאֶה[f] pref. הֲ) Kal part. act. sing. masc. dec. 9a ראה

הָרוֹ[g] Kal inf. absolute for הָרֹה (§ 24. rem. 2) . הרה

הֹרוֹ[h] Poel inf. absolute (§ 6. No. 1, & § 24. r. 2) הרה

וְהָרוֹג[i] וְ Kal inf. absolute . . . . הרג

הֲרוּגֶיהָ Kal part. p. pl., suff. 3 pers. sing. fem. fr. [הָרוּג] dec. 3a . . . . . הרג

הֲרוּגִים[k] id. pl., absolute state . . . הרג

הָרוֹדֵף[l] pref. הָ for הַ) Kal part. act. sing. m. d. 7b רדף

הָרָוָה[m] pref. id.) adj. fem. sing. fr. רָוֶה masc. . רוה

הִרְוָה[n] Hiph. pret. 3 pers. sing. masc. . . רוה

וְהָרוּחַ וְ' pref. הָ for הַ) noun com. sing. dec. 1a רוח

הָרְוָחָה[o] pref. id.) noun fem. sing., (suff. 'רַוְחָתִי') dec. 11c. (§ 42. rem. 1) . . . רוח

הָרוּחֹת pref. id.) noun com. with pl. fem. term. fr. רוּחַ dec. 1a . . . . רוח

הִרְוֵיתִי[p] Hiph. pret. 1 pers. sing. . . . רוה

הִרְוִיתָנִי[q] id. pret. 2 pers. sing. masc. (§ 24. rem. 14), suff. 1 pers. sing. (§ 2. rem. 1) . רוה

הִרְוַנִי[r] id. pret. 3 pers. sing. masc. (הִרְוָה), suff. 1 pers. sing. (§ 24. rem. 21) . . רוה

הָרוֹפֵא[s] pref. הָ for הַ·) Kal part. act. s. m. d. 7b רפא

הָרוֹצֵחַ[t] pref. id.) Kal part. act. sing. masc. . רצח

הָרוֹת[u] adj. fem., pl. of הָרָה, dec. 11a (§ 42. rem. 2) fr. הָרֶה masc. . . . . הרה

וְהָרֹחַב[x] וְ pref. הָ for הַ·) noun masc. sing. dec. 6f רחב

הַרְחֶב־[y] Hiph. imp. sing. masc. (§ 11. rem. 2) . רחב

הִרְחִב[z] Hiph. pret. 3 pers. sing. masc. for הִרְחִיב רחב

הָרְחָבָה וְ'[a] pref. הָ for הַ·) adj. fem., constr. רַחֲבַת dec. 11c (§ 42. rem. 1) from רָחָב masc. רחב

הָרְחֹבוֹת[b] pref. id.) noun fem., pl. of רְחוֹב dec. 1a רחב

הִרְחִבִי[c] defect. for הִרְחִיבִי (q. v.) . . רחב

הִרְחַבְתָּ[d] Hiph. pret. 2 pers. sing. masc. . . רחב

הִרְחַבְתְּ[e] id. pret. 2 pers. sing. fem. . . . רחב

וְהִרְחַבְתִּי[f] וְ id. pret. 1 pers. sing.) acc. shifted by conv. וְ (§ 8. rem. 7) . . . רחב

הָרְחוֹב[g] pref. הָ for הַ·) noun fem. sing. dec. 1a רחב

הָרָחוֹק[h] pref. id.) adj. masc. sing. dec. 3a . רחק

הָרְחוֹקִים[i] וְ'[k] pref. id.) id. pl., absolute state . . רחק

הָרְחוֹת[l] noun com., pl. of רוּחַ, (for רוּחוֹת) רוח

הַרְחִיב[m] Hiph. inf. constr. . . . רחב

הִרְחִיב id. pret. 3 pers. sing. masc. . . רחב

הִרְחִיבָה[n] id. pret. 3 pers. sing. fem. . . . רחב

---

[a] Is. 7. 20. [b] 2 Ki. 9. 35. [c] Ps. 78. 34. [d] Ju. 16. 2. [e] Ne. 4. 5. [f] 1 Ki. 12. 27. [g] Nu. 11. 15.
[h] Je. 47. 6. [i] Da. 6. 7, 12, 16. [k] Le. 20. 16. [l] Ju. 9. 54. [m] Ex. 22. 23. [n] 1 Sa. 24. 12. [o] Nu. 22. 29.
[p] Ho. 6. 5. [q] Am. 9. 4. [r] Ju. 8. 18. [s] 1 Sa. 24. 19. [t] Ps. 144. 2. [u] Is. 3. 23. [v] Ju. 20. 43.
[y] Ps. 7. 15. [z] Job 15. 35. [a] Ge. 14. 10. [b] Job 3. 3. [c] Ca. 6. 5. [d] Ex. 2. 16. [e] Da. 4. 2.
[f] 2 Sa. 15. 27. [g] Is. 59. 4. [h] Is. 59. 13. [i] Est. 9. 16. [k] Is. 10. 4. [l] Jos. 8. 20. [m] De. 29. 18.
[n] Is. 55. 10. [o] Ex. 8. 11. [p] Je. 31. 25. [q] Is. 43. 24. [r] La. 3. 15. [s] Is. 30. 33. [t] Ps. 147. 3.
[t] Jos. 20. 6. [u] Am. 1. 13. [x] Eze. 42. 2. [y] Ps. 81. 11. [z] Is. 30. 33. [a] Eze. 23. 32.
[b] Pr. 26. 13. [c] Mi. 1. 16. [d] Ps. 4. 2. [e] Is. 57. 8. [f] Ex. 34. 24. [g] Ne. 8. 1, 3.
[h] Eze. 6. 12. [i] Is. 46. 12. [k] Est. 9. 20. [l] Je. 49. 36. [m] Am. 1. 13. [n] Is. 5. 14.

הִרְחִיבוּ[a] id. pret. 3 pers. pl. . . . . רחב
הַרְחִיבִי[b] id. imp. sing. fem. . . . . רחב
הָרֵחַיִם[c] pref. הָ for הַ·) noun masc. dual . . רח
הִרְחִיק Hiph. pret. 3 pers. sing. masc. . . . רחק
הַרְחִיקֵהוּ[d] id. imp. sing. masc., suff. 3 pers. sing. masc. רחק
הִרְחִיקוּ id. pret. 3 pers. pl. . . . . רחק
הַרְחִיקָם[e] id. inf., suff. 3 pers. pl. masc. dec. 1b . רחק
הָרְחֵלִים[f] pref. הָ for הַ·) noun fem., with pl. masc. term. fr. רָחֵל dec. 5a . . . . רחל
הָרְחָם[g] pref. id.) noun masc. sing. . . . רחם
הָרְחָמָה[h] pref. id.) id. with parag. ה . . . רחם
הָרַחֲמִים pref. id.) noun masc. pl. [for רְחָמִים see § 35. rem. 16] from רַחַם dec. 6d . . . רחם
הָרַחְצָה pref. id.) noun fem. sing. . . . רחץ
הַרְחֵק[i] / הַרְחֵק } Hiph. inf. absolute (§ 11. r. 2), or imp. s. m. רחק
הָרְחֹקוֹת[k] וְ'' pref. הָ for הַ·) adj. fem., pl. of רְחֹקָה dec. 10, fr. רָחוֹק masc. . . . . רחק
הָרְחֹקִים וְ' pref. id.) id. masc., pl. of רָחוֹק dec. 3a . רחק
הָרְחֹקֹת[l] defect. see הָרְחוֹקוֹת . . . . רחק
הִרְחַקְתָּ[m] Hiph. pret. 2 pers. sing. masc. . . . רחק
הִרְחַקְתִּים[n] id. pret. 1 pers. sing., suff. 3 pers. pl. masc. רחק
הֲרָרַי[p] / הֲרָרִי } noun masc. pl., suff. 1 pers. sing. fr. הַר dec. 8. (§ 37. rem. 7) . . . } הרר
הֲרָרֵי id. pl., constr. state . . . . . הרר
הָרִיב pref. הָ for הַ·) noun masc. sing. dec. 1a . רוב
הָרָיו noun masc. pl., suff. 3 pers. sing. masc. fr. הַר dec. 8. (§ 37. rem. 7) . . . הרר
הֵרָיוֹן[q] noun masc. sing. . . . . . הרה
הָרִיּוֹתָיו[r] וְ adj. fem. pl., suff. 3 pers. sing. masc. fr. [הָרִי] masc. . . . . . הרה
הֲרִיחוֹ[s] וַ Hiph. inf. (הָרִיחַ), suff. 3 pers. sing. masc. dec. 3a; וַ before (-:) . . . . רוח
הָרִים noun masc. pl. [for הֲרָרִים] fr. הַר dec. 8. (§ 37. rem. 7) . . . . הרר
הָרִים[t] וְ''[u] Hiph. inf. constr. used also as an abs. רום
הֵרִים וְ' id. pret. 3 pers. sing. masc. . . . רום
הֻרִים[x] Kh. הֵרִים q. v.; K. הוּרַם Hoph. pret. 3 p. s. m. רום
הָרִימָה[y] Hiph. imp. s. m. with parag. ה (§ 11. r. 5) רום
הָרִימוּ וְ'[z] id. imp. pl. masc. . . . . רום
הֵרִימוּ id. pret. 3 pers. pl. . . . . רום
הֲרִימוֹתָ / הֲרִימוֹתָה[a] } id. pret. 2 pers. sing. masc. (§ 8. rem. 5) רום
הֲרִימוֹתִי[b] id. pret. 1 pers. sing. . . . . רום
הָרִימִי[c] id. imp. sing. fem. . . . . רום
הֲרִימֹתִי[d] id. pret. 1 pers. sing. . . . . רום

הֲרִימֹתִיךָ[e] id. id., suff. 2 pers. sing. masc. . . . רום
הָרִינוּ[f] Kal pret. 1 pers. pl. . . . . הרה
הָרִיעוּ וְ[g] Hiph. imp. pl. masc. . . . . רוע
הֵרִיעוּ id. pret. 3 pers. pl. . . . . רוע
הָרִיעִי[h] id. imp. sing. fem. . . . . רוע
הֲרִיעֹתֶם[i] וַ id. pret. 2 pers. pl. masc.; וַ for וְ conv. רוע
הָרִיפוֹת[k] pref. הָ for הַ·) noun fem. pl. . . רוף
הֵרִיקוּ וְ Hiph. pret. 3 pers. pl. . . . רוק
הֲרִיקוֹתִי וַ id. pret. 1 pers. sing.; acc. shifted by וַ for וְ conv. (§ 8. rem. 7, & § 11. rem. 5) . רוק
הֹרִישׁ[l] Hiph. pret. 3 pers. sing. masc. for הוֹרִישׁ ירשׁ
הָרִית[m] וְ Kal pret. 2 pers. sing. fem. . . . הרה
הָרִיתִי[n] id. pret. 1 pers. sing. . . . . הרה
הָרַךְ[o] pref. הָ for הַ·) adj. masc. sing. dec. 8d רכך
הֵרַךְ[p] Hiph. pret. 3 pers. sing. masc. (§ 18. rem. 10) רכך
הָרֶכֶב / הָרָכֶב } pref. הָ for הַ·) noun masc. sing. dec. 6 (§ 35. rem. 2, but with suff. רִכְבִּי) } רכב
הַרְכֵּב[q] Hiph. imp. sing. masc. . . . . רכב
הָרֵכָבִים pref. הָ for הַ·) gent. noun from רֵכָב . רכב
הִרְכַּבְתָּ[r] Hiph. pret. 2 pers. sing. masc. . . . רכב
הִרְכַּבְתִּיךָ[s] וְ id. pret. 1 pers. sing., suff. 2 pers. sing. m. רכב
הִרְכַּבְתֶּם[t] וְ id. pret. 2 pers. pl. masc. . . . רכב
הָרַכָּה[u] pref. הָ for הַ·) adj. fem. s. dec. 10, from רַךְ m. רכך
הִרְכִּיבֻהוּ[x] וְ Hiph. pret. 3 pers. pl., suff. 3 pers. sing. m. רכב
הָרֹכְלִים וְ'[y] pref. הָ for הַ·) Kal part. act. masc., pl. of רֹכֵל dec. 7b . . . . רכל
הָרְכוּשׁ pref. id.) noun masc. sing. dec. 1b . רכשׁ
הַרְכֶם[z] noun masc. sing., suff. 2 pers. pl. masc. from הַר dec. 8. (§ 37. rem. 7) . . . הרר
הָרְכָסִים[a] וְ pref. הָ art. for הַ·) n. m. pl. of [רֶכֶס] d. 6 רכס
הָרְכֻשׁ[b] pref. הָ for הַ·) noun masc. sing. . רכשׁ
הָרְכֻשׁ[c] וְ'[d] pref. id.) noun m. sing. for רְכוּשׁ dec. 1a רכשׁ

הָרַם Root not used; *to be high*, cogn. רוּם, אָרַם.
הֹרָם (*height*; or *mountaineer*, from הֹר with the ending ־ָם) pr. name of a king of Canaan, 1 Ch. 4. 8.
הָרֻם (*high*) pr. name masc. 1 Ch. 4. 8.
הַרְמוֹן masc. *palace*, Am. 4. 3.

הָרָם pr. name, see בֵּית הָרָם . . . . בית
הָרֵם / הָרֶם[e] } Hiph. imp. sing. masc., acc. drawn back before monos. (לָךְ) comp. § 11. rem. 5 } רום
הָרֻם pr. name masc. . . . . . הרם
הֹרָם pr. name masc. . . . . . . הרם
הָרָמָה וְ' pref. הָ for הַ·) pr. name of a place . רום
הָרָמָה[f] pref. id.) Kal part. act. sing., fem. of רָם . רום
הֵרֹמּוּ[g] Niph. imp. pl. masc. [for הִרֹּמּוּ] . . רמם

[a] Ps. 25. 17. [b] Is. 54. 2. [c] Ex. 11. 5. [d] Job 11. 14. [e] Joel 4. 6. [f] Ca. 6. 6.
[g] Le. 11. 18. [h] De. 14. 17. [i] Job 13. 21. [k] Je. 48. 24. [l] Eze. 22. 5. [m] De. 20. 15.
[n] Ps. 88. 9, 19. [o] Eze. 11. 16. [p] Is. 65. 9. [q] Ruth 4. 13. [r] Ho. 14. 1. [s] Is. 11. 3.
[t] Ps. 75. 7. [u] Eze. 21. 31. [x] Da. 8. 11. [y] Ps. 74. 3. [z] Jos. 4. 5. [a] Is. 37. 23.
[b] Ps. 89. 20. [c] Is. 40. 9, 9. [d] Ge. 39. 15. [e] 1 Ki. 16. 2. [f] Is. 26. 18. [g] Joel 2. 1.
[h] Zec. 9. 9. [i] Jos. 6. 10. [k] Pr. 27. 22. [l] 2 Ch. 28. 3. [m] Ju. 13. 3. [n] Nu. 11. 12.
[o] De. 28. 54. [p] Job 23. 16. [q] 2 Ki. 13. 16. [r] Ps. 66. 12. [s] Is. 58. 14. [t] 1 Ki. 1. 33.
[u] De. 28. 56. [x] Est. 6. 9. [y] Ne. 3. 31, 32. [z] Ps. 11. 1. [a] Is. 40. 4. [b] Est. 8. 10, 14.
[c] Ge. 14. 16. [d] Ge. 14. 21. [e] 2 Ki. 6. 7. [f] Eze. 17. 22. [g] Nu. 17. 10.

הָֽרִמּוֹן [a] וְ pref. הָ for הַ)(noun masc. sing. dec. 1 b, also pr. name . . . רמם
הָֽרִמּוֹנִים [b] וְ pref. id.)(id. pl., absolute state . רמן
הָֽרְמָחִים [c] [d] וְ pref. id.)(noun masc., pl. of רֹמַח dec. 6 (§ 35. rem. 9 & 5) . . רמח
הָֽרָמִים pref. id.)(Kal part. act. masc., pl. of רָם dec. 1 a רום
הָֽרַמִּים pref. id.)(הָֽאֲרַמִּים gent. noun, pl. of אֲרַמִּי from אֲרָם . . . . ארם
הָֽרְמָּכִים [e] pref. id.)(noun masc., pl. of [רַמָּךְ] dec. 1 b רמך
הָֽרִמֹּנִים noun masc., pl. of רִמּוֹן dec. 1 b . רמם
הָֽרֶמֶשׂ pref. הָ for הַ)(noun masc. sing. רמשׂ
הָֽרֹמֵשׂ pref. id.)(Kal part. act. sing. masc. . רמשׂ
הָֽרֹמֶשֶׂת pref. id.)(id. fem. . . . רמשׂ
הָֽרָמָתָה pref. id.)(pr. name of a place (רָמָה) with parag. ה רום
הָֽרָמָתִי pref. id.)(gent. n. from the preceding . רום
הֲרֵמֹתָ [f] וַ Hiph. pret. 2 pers. sing. masc.; acc. shifted by וַ for וְ conv. . . . רום
הֲרִימֹתִי [g] id. pret. 1 pers. sing. . . . רום
הֲרִמֹתִיךָ [h] id. id., suff. 2 pers. sing. masc. . . רום
הֲרֵמֹתֶם [i] וַ id. pret. 2 pers. pl. masc.; וַ for וְ conv. רום
הָֽרָמָתַיִם pref. הָ for הַ)(pr. name of a place רום
הָרָן וְ pr. name m. (and in compos. with בֵּית q.v.) הרר
הָֽרִנָּה pref. הָ for הַ)(noun fem. sing. dec. 10 רנן
הֹרָנִי [k] Hiph. pret. 3 pers. sing. masc. [הוֹרָה], suff. 1 pers. sing. (§ 24. rem. 21, & § 25. No. 2 e) ירה
הֹרֵנִי [l] id. imp. sing. masc., suff. 1 pers. sing. . ירה
הַרְנִינוּ [m] וְ Hiph. imp. pl. masc. . . . רנן
הֵרֹנֵךְ [n] וְ noun m. s., suff. 2 p. s. f. from [הֵרֹן] dec. 1 b הרה

הָרַס [o] fut. יַהֲרֹס, יֶהֱרֹס (§ 13. rem. 4)—I. *to break, pull down, destroy.*—II. intrans. *to break through,* with לְ Ex. 19. 21, 24. Niph. *to be broken, torn down, destroyed.* Pi. *to break, pull down, destroy.*
הֶרֶס masc. *destruction,* Is. 19. 18.
הֲרִיסָה fem. dec. 10, *a ruin,* Am. 9. 11.
הֲרִיסוּת fem. dec. 1 b, *destruction,* Is. 49. 19.

הָרָֽס [p] Kal pret. 3 pers. sing. m. for הָרַס (§ 8. rem. 7) הרס
הָרֹס [q] Piel inf. absolute . . . . הרס
הֲרָס־ [r] Kal imp. sing. masc. [for הֲרֹס § 8. rem. 18] הרס
הֹרֵס [s] Kal part. act. sing. masc. . . הרס
הֲרָסֶהָ [t] וַ id. imp. sing. masc., suff. 3 pers. sing. fem. הרס
הָרָסוּ [u] / וְ הָרָסוּ } id. pret. 3 pers. pl. (§ 8. rem. 7) . הרס
הָרַסְתָּ [v] וְ id. pret. 2 pers. sing. masc.; acc. shifted by conv. וְ (§ 8. rem. 7) . . . הרס
הָרַסְתִּי וְ id. pret. 1 pers. sing.; acc. id. . הרס

הֲרִסֹתָיו [y] וַ n. fem. pl., suff. 3 p. s. m. from [הֲרִיסָה] d. 10 הרס
הֲרִסֻתֵךְ [z] noun fem. sing., suff. 2 pers. sing. fem. from [הֲרִיסוּת] dec. 1 b . . . הרס
הָרָע [a] וְ / הָרָע [b] וְ } pref. הָ for הַ)(noun masc. sing. dec. 8 (§ 37. rem. 7) . רעע
הָרֵעַ [c] וְ Hiph. inf. abs. and constr. . . רעע
הָרֵעַ [d] pref. הָ for הַ)(noun masc. sing. dec. 1 a . רעה
הֵרַע [e] וְ id. pret. 3 pers. sing. masc. (§ 18. rem. 10) רעע
הָֽרָעָב וְ pref. הָ for הַ)(noun masc. sing. dec. 4 a רעב
הָֽרָעֵב [f] pref. id.)(adj. masc. sing. dec. 5 a . רעב
הָֽרָעָה pref. id.)(noun fem. sing. dec. 10 [for רָעָה], from רַע masc. (§ 37. rem. 7) . . רעע
הָֽרֹעֶה pref. id.)(Kal part. act. sing. masc. dec. 9 a רעה
הָרָעָה [g] Kh. הָרָעָה q. v., K. הָרַע (q. v.) . . רעע
הֵרֵעוּ Hiph. pret. 3 pers. pl. . . . רעע
הֵרֵעוּ [h] וְ id., as if from רעע, see . . . רוע
הָֽרָעוֹת וְ pref. הָ for הַ)(noun fem., pl. of רָעָה dec. 10 [for רָעָה], from רַע masc. (§ 37. rem. 7) רעע
הֲרֵעוֹתָ [i] Hiph. pret. 2 pers. sing. masc. [for הֲרֵעוֹתָ] רעע
הֲרֵעוֹתִי [k] id. pret. 1 pers. sing. . . . רעע
הָֽרָעִים pref. הָ for הַ)(adj. masc., pl. [for רָעִים] from רַע dec. 8 (§ 37. rem. 7) . רעע
הָֽרֹעִים [l] וְ pref. id.)(Kal part. act. m., pl. of רֹעֶה dec. 9 a רעה
הִרְעִים [m] Hiph. pret. 3 pers. sing. masc. . רעם
הַרְעִיפוּ [n] Hiph. imp. pl. masc. . . . רעף
הָרְעֲלוּ [o] Hoph. pret. 3 p. pl. [for הָרְעֲלוּ comp. § 8. r. 7] רעל
הָֽרְעָלוֹת [p] וְ pref. הָ for הַ)(noun masc. with pl. fem. term. from רַעַל dec. 6 d . . . רעל
הַרְעִמָהּ [q] Hiph. inf. [הַרְעִים], suff. 3 pers. sing. fem. [for הַרְעִימָהּ] . . . רעם
הָרַעַשׁ [r] / הָרָעַשׁ } pref. הָ for הַ)(noun masc. sing. (§ 35. rem. 2) . . . רעשׁ
הִרְעַשְׁתָּה [s] Hiph. pret. 2 pers. s. m. (comp. § 8. rem. 5) רעשׁ
הִרְעַשְׁתִּי [t] / וְ הִרְעַשְׁתִּי [u] } id. pret. 1 pers. sing.; acc. shifted by conv. וְ (§ 8. rem. 7) . . רעשׁ
הֲרֵעֹת וְ defect. for הֲרֵעוֹת (q. v.) . . רעע
הֲרֵעֹתָ [y] / הֲרֵעֹתָה [z] } Hiph. pret. 2 pers. sing. masc. [for הֲרֵעוֹתָ; for תָה see § 8. rem. 5] . . רעע
הֲרֵעֹתִי id. pret. 1 pers. sing. . . . רעע
הֲרֵעֹתֶם id. pret. 2 pers. pl. masc. . . . רעע
הֲרֵעֹתֶם [a] וַ Hiph. pret. 2 pers. pl. masc. (§ 21. rem. 14); וַ for וְ conv. . . . רוע
הֶרֶף Hiph. imp. s. m., apoc. for הַרְפֵּה (§ 24. r. 17) רפה
הָֽרָפָא pref. הָ for הַ)(pr. name masc. . . רפא
הָֽרֹפֵא [b] pref. id.)(Kal part. act. sing. masc. dec. 7 b רפא
הֵרָפֵא [c] Niph. inf. construct . . . רפא

a Hag. 2. 19. b 1 Ki. 7. 20. c Je. 46. 4. d Ne. 4. 10. e Est. 8. 10. f Nu. 31. 28.
g Ge. 14. 22. h 1 Ki. 14. 7. i Nu. 18. 26. k Job 30. 19. l Job 34. 32. m Ps. 32. 11.
n Ge. 3. 16. o La. 2. 2, 17. p Is. 14. 17. q Ex. 23. 24. r Ps. 58. 7. s Je. 45. 4.
t 2 Sa. 11. 25. u 1 Ki. 19. 10, 14. v Ju. 6. 25. y Am. 9. 11. z Is. 49. 19. a 2 Sa. 14. 17.
b Ps. 51. 6. c 1 Ch. 21. 17. d Pr. 17. 17; 19. 6. e Jos. 24. 20. f Is. 29. 8.
g Je. 18. 10. h 1 Sa. 17. 20. i 1 Ki. 17. 20. k 1 Ch. 21. 17. l Je. 2. 8.
m Ps. 29. 3. n Is. 45. 8. o Na. 2. 4. p Is. 3. 19. q 1 Sa. 1. 6.
r Am. 1. 1. s Ps. 60. 4. t Eze. 31. 16. u Hag. 2. 7. v Ge. 41. 27.
y Nu. 11. 11. z Ex. 5. 22. a Nu. 10. 9. b Ps. 103. 3. c Je. 15. 18.

הָרְפָאִים וְ' pref. הָ for הַ· X gent. noun, pl. of רְפָאִי . רפא

הָרְפָאִים[a] pref. id. X noun masc. pl. [of רָפָא] . רפה

הָרֹפְאִים[b] pref. id. X Kal part. act. m., pl. of רֹפֵא dec. 7b רפא

הָרָפָה pref. id. X pr. name masc. . . . . רפה

הָרָפֶה[c] pref. הָ X adj. masc. sing. dec. 9b . . רפה

הַרְפֵּה Hiph. imp. sing. masc. . . . . רפה

הַרְפּוּ[d] id. imp. pl. masc. . . . . רפה

הָרִפוֹת[e] defect. for הָרִי' (q. v.) . . . . רוף

הָרֵץ[f] וְ Hiph. imp. sing. masc. . . . . רוץ

הָרָצוּץ pref. הָ for הַ· X Kal part. p. sing. m. dec. 3a רצץ

הָרֹצֵחַ pref. id. X Kal part. act. sing. masc. . רצח

הֲרָצַחְתָּ[g] pref. הֲ X Kal pret. 2 pers. sing. masc. . רצח

הָרָצִים / הָרָצִין[h] pref. הָ for הַ· X Kal part. act. masc., pl. of רָץ dec. 1a . . רוץ

הָרִצְפָּה וְ'[i] pref. id. X noun com. s. (constr. רִצְפַּת) רצף

הָרֹצְצוֹת[k] pref. id. X Kal part. act. fem. pl. [of רֹצְצָה or רֹצֶצֶת] . . . . רצץ

הִרְצָת[l] וְ Hiph. pret. 3 pers. s. fem. (§ 24. rem. 14) רצה

הָרֵק[m] וְ Hiph. imp. sing. masc. . . . רוק

הָרֵק[n] pref. הָ X adv. . . . . רקק

הָרַקּוֹן וְ pref. הָ for הַ· X pr. name of a place . רקק

הָרַקּוֹת[o] pref. id. X adj. fem., pl. [רַקָּה] d. 10, fr. רַק m. רקק

הָרֵקוֹת[p] pref. id. X adj. fem., pl. of רֵקָה dec. 10, from רֵק [or רֵיק] masc. . . . רוק

הָרֹקַח[q] pref. id. X noun masc. sing. . . . רקח

הַרְקַח[r] וְ Hiph. inf. absolute, or imp. רקח

הָרַקָּחִים[s] pref. הָ for הַ· X n. m., pl. of [רַקָּח] dec. 1b רקח

הָרֵקִים[t] pref. id. X adj. m., pl. of רֵק [or רֵיק] dec. 1a רוק

הָרָקִיעַ pref. id. X noun masc. sing. dec. 3a . רקע

הָרִקְמָה[u] pref. id. X noun fem. sing. dec. 12b . רקם

[הַר, הָרָר] masc. with suff. הֲרָרִי ,הֲרָרִי ; pl. c. הַרְרֵי, with suff. הֲרָרֶיהָ (comp. dec. 4 & 6) *mountain*, mostly poetic.

הֲרָרִי ,הָרָרִי (*mountaineer*) gent. noun of the inhabitants of the hill-country of Ephraim or Judah, 2 Sa. 23. 11, 33; also written אֲרָרִי in verse 33.

הַר masc. with the art. הָהָר, with ה local הָרָה ,הָהָרָה, pl. הָרִים (§ 37. rem. 7)—I. *mountain.*—II. *mountainous tract.*—III. pr. name הַר חֶרֶס (*mount of the sun*) a city of the Samaritans, Ju. 1. 35.

הֹר הָהָר, הוֹר pr. name —I. of a mountain in Edom where Aaron was buried.—II. of a mountain in Palestine, Nu. 34. 7, 8.

הֲרָא (*mountainous*) pr. name of a region in Syria, 1 Ch. 5. 26.

הָרָן (*mountaineer*) pr. name.—I. of a brother of Abraham, Ge. 11. 26, 27.—II. 1 Ch. 23. 9; see also בַּיִת

הַרְאֵל (*mount of God*) put for the altar of burnt-offering, Eze. 43. 15, elsewhere אֲרִיאֵל, see under ארה

הרר Root not used; Chald. Palp. *to think.*

הַרְהֹר Chald. masc. *thought,* Da. 4. 2.

הֲרָרִי pr. name of a people . . . . הרר

הֲרָרִי[x] noun m. s. with suff. 1 pers. s. fr. [הָרָר] d. 4c הרר

הַרְרֵי noun masc. pl. constr. fr. [הֶרֶר] dec. 6a הרר

הָרָשׁוּם[y] pref. הָ for הַ· X Kal part. p. masc. sing. רשם

הִרְשִׁיעַ[z] Hiph. pret. 3 pers. sing. masc. . רשע

הִרְשִׁיעוּ וְ id. pret. 3 pers. pl. . . . רשע

הָרָשָׁע וְ'[a] pref. הָ for הַ· X adj. masc. sing. dec. 4a . רשע

הָרֶשַׁע[b] / הָרֶשַׁע pref. id. X noun masc. sing. dec. 6 (§ 35. rem. 2 & 5, yet with suff. רִשְׁעִי) . רשע

הָרְשָׁעָה[c] pref. id. X adj. fem. sing. from רָשָׁע masc. . רשע

הָרִשְׁעָה[d] pref. id. X noun fem. sing. dec. 10. . רשע

הָרְשָׁעִים וְ'[e] pref. id. X adj. masc. pl. of רָשָׁע dec. 4a רשע

הִרְשַׁעְנוּ / הִרְשָׁעְנוּ[f] וְ Hiph. pret. 1 pers. pl. (comp. § 8. rem. 7) רשע

הָרֶשֶׁת[g] / הָרָשֶׁת[h] pref. הָ for הַ· X noun fem. sing. dec. 13a (comp. § 35. r. 2, yet with suff. רִשְׁתִּי) ישת

הָרַת[i] adj. fem. sing. constr. of הָרָה dec. 11a (but see § 42. rem. 2) from הָרֶה masc. . הרה

הָרְתָה[k] Kal pret. 3 pers. s. fem. [for הָרְתָה § 8. r. 7] הרה

הָרַתּוֹק[l] pref. הָ for הַ· X noun masc. sing. dec. 1b . רתק

הָרוֹתֵיהֶם[m] וְ adj. fem. pl., suff. 3 pers. pl. masc. from הָרָה (§ 42. rem. 2) from הָרֶה masc. . הרה

הֹרְתִיךָ[n] Hiph. pret. 1 pers. sing., suff. 2 pers. s. m. ירה

הַשֵּׂא[o] Hiph. inf. absolute . . . . נשא

הַשֹּׁאֲבֹת[p] pref. הַ X Kal part. act. fem. pl. [of שֹׁאֲבָה or שֹׁאֶבֶת] from שֹׁאֵב masc. . . שאב

הַשָּׁאוּלִי pref. id. X patronym. of שָׁאוּל . . שאל

הַשָּׁאטוֹת[q] / הַשָּׁאטִים[r] pref. id. X Kal part. act. fem. & masc. pl. [of שָׁאט שָׁאטָה § 21. rem. 1] . שוט

הִשְׁאִיר וְ'[s] Hiph. pret. 3 pers. sing. masc. שאר

הִשְׁאִירוּ[t] id. pret. 3 pers. pl. . . . שאר

הַשְּׁאֵלָה[u] pref. הַ X noun fem. sing., (suff. שְׁאֵלָתִי & שֵׁלָה) dec. 10 & 11 (§ 42. rem. 4) . שאל

הַשֹּׁאֲלִים[x] pref. id. X Kal part. act. m., pl. of שֹׁאֵל d. 7b שאל

הֲשָׁאַלְתִּי[y] pref. הֲ X Kal pret. 1 pers. sing. . . שאל

---

a Job 26. 5. b Ge. 50. 2, 2. c Nu. 13. 18. d Ps. 46. 11. e 2 Sa. 17. 19.
f 1 Sa. 17. 17. g 1 Ki. 21. 19. h 2 Ki. 11. 13. i Eze. 40. 18. k Am. 4. 1.
l Le. 26. 34. m Ps. 35. 3. n Nu. 12. 2. o Ge. 41. 20, 27. p Ge. 41. 27.
q Ca. 8. 2. r Eze. 24. 10. s Ne. 3. 8. t 2 Sa. 6. 20. u Eze. 17. 3.
x Je. 17. 3. y Da. 10. 21. z 2 Ch. 20. 35. a Eze. 18. 21. b Ec. 3. 16.
c Eze. 3. 18, 19. d Zec. 5. 8. e Is. 57. 20. f Da. 9. 5. g Pr. 1. 17.
h Ex. 27. 4, 5 i Je. 20. 17. k Ge. 16. 4. l Eze. 7. 23. m 2 Ki. 8. 12.
n Pr. 4. 11. o Je. 4. 10. p Ge. 24. 11. q Eze. 16. 37. r Eze. 28. 24, 26.
s Joel 2. 14. t Jos. 11. 14. u 1 Sa. 2. 20. x 1 Sa. 8. 10. y 2 Ki. 4. 28.

הִשְׁאִלְתִּיהוּ[a]	Hiph. pret. 1 pers. sing., suff. 3 pers. sing. masc. (§ 11. rem. 1) . . .	שאל
הַשַּׁאֲנַנִּים	pref. הַ)(adj. masc., pl. of שַׁאֲנָן dec. 8a	שאן
הַשֹּׁאֲפִים	pref. id.)(Kal part. act. m. pl. of שׁוֹאֵף d. 7b	שאף
הַשְּׁאֵרִית	pref. id.)(noun fem. sing. dec. 1b .	שאר
הִשְׁאַרְנוּ	Hiph. pret. 1 pers. pl. . . .	שאר
הִשְׁאַרְתִּי	וְ Hiph. pret. 1 pers. sing.; acc. shifted by conv. וְ (comp. § 8. rem. 7) . .	שאר
הַשֵּׁאת[ee]	pref. הַ)(noun fem. sing. . . .	שאה
הִשֵּׁאתָ[c]	Hiph. pret. 2 pers. sing. masc. (§ 25, No. 2a)	נשא
הָשָׁב[d]	in pause for הָשֵׁב (q. v.)	שוב
הַשָּׁב[e]	pref. הַ)(Kal pret. 3 pers. sing. masc. .	שוב
הָשֵׁב	וְ' Hiph. inf. absolute, or imp. sing. masc. .	שוב
הַשָּׁבָה	pref. הַ relat. art.)(Kal pret. 3 pers. sing. fem.	שוב
הֲשִׁבֵהוּ[f]	Hiph. imp. sing. masc., suff. 3 pers. sing. m.	שוב
הֵשִׁבוּ[g]	id. pret. 3 pers. pl., for הֵשִׁיבוּ . .	שוב
הֱשִׁבוֹם[h]	וֶ id. id., suff. 3 pers. pl. masc.; וֶ bef. (ֱ)	שוב
הַשָּׁבוּעַ[i]	pref. הַ)(noun masc. sing., irr. constr. שְׁבוּעַ, pl. שָׁבֻעִים (§ 32. rem. 1) . .	שבע
הַשְּׁבוּעָה	pref. id.)(noun fem. sing. dec. 10. .	שבע
הֲשִׁבוֹתִי	וַ Hiph. pret. 1 pers. sing., suff. 3 pers. pl. masc.; וַ for וְ conv. . . .	שוב
הוֹשְׁבוֹתִים	וְ Hiph. pret. 1 pers. sing., suff. 3 pers. pl. masc., after the analogy of ע״וּ, for הוֹשַׁבְתִּים	ישב
הַשָּׁבֶט	pref. הַ)(noun com. sing. [for שֵׁבֶט § 35. rem. 2] see under שֵׁבֶט . . .	שבט
הַשֵּׁבֶט	וְ'' pref. id.)(noun com. sing., dec. 6b .	שבט
הַשְּׁבָטִים	pref. id.)(id. pl., absolute state .	שבט
הַשֶּׁבִי[m] / הַשְּׁבִי	pref. id.)(noun masc. sing. dec. 6i (§ 35. rem. 14)	שבה
הַשִּׁבְיָה	pref. id.)(noun fem. sing. . . .	שבה
הַשָּׁבִים	pref. id.)(Kal part. act. m., pl. of שָׁב d. 1a	שוב
הַשְּׁבִיסִים	וְ pref. id.)(noun masc. pl. fr. [שָׁבִים] d. 3a	שבס
הִשְׂבִּיעַ	וְ' Hiph. pret. 3 pers. sing. masc. . .	שבע
הִשְׂבִּיעַ[o]	וְ[p] Hiph. pret. 3 pers. sing. masc. .	שבע
הִשְׁבִּיעוֹ[q]	Hiph. pret. 3 pers. s. m., suff. 3 pers. s. m.	שבע
הַשְּׁבִיעִי	pref. הַ)(adj. ord. masc. sing. from שֶׁבַע	שבע
הַשְּׁבִיעִית	pref. id.)(fem. of the preceding . .	שבע
הִשְׁבִּיעֶךָ	Hiph. pret. 3 pers. sing. masc., suff. 2 pers. sing. masc. [for בִּיעֲךָ׳] . . .	שבע
הִשְׂבִּיעַנִי	id., suff. 1 pers. sing. . . .	שבע
הִשְׁבִּיעַנִי	Hiph. pret. 3 pers. s. masc., suff. 1 pers. s.	שבע
הַשְּׁבִיעִת	וְ"[n] defect. for עִית׳ (q. v.) . . .	שבע
הִשְׁבִּית[r]	וְ' Hiph. pret. 3 pers. sing. masc. . .	שבת
הַשְׁבִּיתוּ	id. imp. pl. masc.	שבת
הִשְׁבִּיתוּ	וְ id. pret. 3 pers. pl. . . .	שבת
הַשְּׂבָכָה	pref. הַ)(noun fem. sing. (no vowel change)	שבך
הַשְּׂבָכוֹת	וְ' pref. id.)(id. pl., absolute state . .	שבך
הַשִּׁבֳּלִים[a]	pref. id.)(noun fem. with pl. masc. term. from שִׁבֹּלֶת (§ 44. No. 2) . .	שבל
הֲשִׁבֵנִי[b]	[c]וַ Hiph. imp. sing. masc., suff. 1 pers. sing.; וַ bef. (ֲ)	שוב
הֱשִׁבַנִי[d]	וֶ id. pret. 3 pers. sing. masc., suff. 1 pers. sing.; וֶ for וְ conv. . . .	שוב
הַשָּׂבָע[e]	וְ'[f] pref. הַ)(noun masc. sing. . .	שבע
הַשְׂבֵּעַ	Hiph. inf. absolute	שבע
הַשֶּׁבַע[g]	pref. הַ)(num. card. fem. sing. . .	שבע
הִשָּׁבֵעַ[h]	וְ Niph. inf. absolute	שבע
הִשָּׁבַע[i]	id. inf. constr.	שבע
הַשְּׁבֻעָה	וְ'[k] pref. הַ)(noun fem. sing. dec. 10. .	שבע
הַשִּׁבְעָה[l]	pref. id.)(num. card., masc. of שֶׁבַע fem.	שבע
הִשָּׁבְעָה	Niph. imp. s. m. with parag. ה (comp. § 8. r. 11)	שבע
הִשָּׁבְעוּ	id. imp. pl. masc.	שבע
הַשָּׁבֻעוֹת	pref. הַ)(noun masc., with pl. fem. term. abs., from שָׁבוּעַ, (§ 32. rem. 1) . .	שבע
הַשְּׁבִעִי	defect. for הַשְּׁבִיעִי q. v. . . .	שבע
הַשָּׁבֻעִים[m]	pref. הַ)(n. m., pl. of שָׁבוּעַ, c. שְׁבֻעַ (§32. r. 1)	שבע
הַשִּׁבְעִים[n]	וְ pref. id.)(num. card. com. gen., pl. of שֶׁבַע f.	שבע
הִשְׁבַּעַתְּ[o]	Hiph. pret. 2 pers. sing. fem. . .	שבע
הִשְׁבַּעְתִּי[p]	וְ id. pret. 1 pers. sing.; acc. shifted by conv. וְ (comp. § 8. rem. 7) . . .	שבע
הִשְׁבַּעְתִּי	Hiph. pret. 1 pers. sing. . . .	שבע
הִשְׁבַּעְתִּיךָ[q]	id. id., suff. 2 pers. sing. masc. . .	שבע
הִשְׁבַּעְתָּנוּ	id. pret. 2 pers. sing. masc., suff. 1 pers. pl.	שבע
הַשָּׁבָץ[r]	pref. הַ)(noun masc. sing. . . .	שבץ
הַשֶּׁבֶר / הַשֵּׁבֶר	וְ / וְ"[u] pref. id.)(noun masc. sing., dec. 6a (§ 35. rem. 2, yet with suff. שִׁבְרוֹ)	שבר
הַשְּׁבָרִים[x]	pref. id.)(id. pl., absolute state . .	שבר
הָשְׁבַּרְתִּי[y]	Hoph. pret. 1 pers. sing. . . .	שבר
הַשַּׁבָּת	וְ'[z] pref. הַ)(noun com. sing. dec. 8 a, but pl. שַׁבָּתוֹת, c. שַׁבְּתוֹת	שבת
הִשְׁבַּתָּ	Hiph. pret. 2 p. s. m. [for הִשְׁבַּתְתָּ § 25 rem.]	שבת
הַשֶּׁבֶת	pref. הַ)(n. f. s. for שֶׁבֶת (comp. § 35. r. 2)	ישב
הֲשֵׁבֹתָ	וַ Hiph. pret. 2 pers. s. m. (§ 21. r. 13 & 14); acc. shifted by וַ for וְ conv. (comp. § 8. r. 7)	שוב
הֲשֵׁבֹתוֹ[a]	וַ, id., suff. 3 pers. sing. masc.; וַ for וְ conv.	שוב
הַשַּׁבָּתוֹת[b]	pref. ה)(noun com., pl. abs. see הַשַּׁבָּת	שבת
הֲשֵׁבֹתִי	וַ Hiph. pret. 1 pers. sing.; acc. shifted by וַ for וְ conv. (comp. § 8. rem. 7) .	שוב
הִשְׁבַּתִּי / הִשְׁבַּתִּי	וְ Hiph. pret. 1 p. s. [for הִשְׁבַּתְתִּי § 25. r.]; acc. shifted by conv. וְ (comp. § 8. r. 7)	שבת
הֲשֵׁבֹתִיךָ	וַ Hiph. pret. 1 pers. sing., suff. 2 pers. s. m.	שוב

[a] 1 Sa. 1. 28. [b] De. 2. 34. [c] Je. 4. 10. [d] Is. 42. 22. [e] Ge. 43. 18. [f] 1 Ki. 13. 18.
[g] 1 Sa. 6. 21. [h] 2 Ch. 12. 11. [i] Da. 9. 27. [k] Zec. 10. 6. [l] 1 Ki. 11. 32. [m] Ne. 1. 2.
[n] Is. 3. 18. [o] Ps. 107. 9. [p] Is. 58. 11. [q] 2 Ch. 36. 13. [r] Ge. 50. 6. [s] Ge. 50. 5.
[t] La. 3. 15. [u] Ex. 23. 11. [x] Ruth 4. 14. [y] Is. 30. 11. [z] Jos. 22. 25. [a] Ge. 41. 7, 24, 26, 27. [ee] La. 3. 47.
[b] Je. 31. 18. [c] Ge. 37. 14. [d] 2 Sa. 15. 25. [e] Ge. 41. 30, 31, 34, 47, 53.
[f] Ec. 5. 11. [g] De. 15. 9. [h] Je. 7. 9. [i] Nu. 30. 3. [k] Da. 9. 11.
[l] Je. 15. 9. [m] Da. 9. 26. [n] Nu. 3. 46. [o] Eze. 27. 33. [p] Eze. 32. 4.
[q] 1 Ki. 2. 42. [r] 2 Sa. 1. 9. [s] La. 3. 47. [t] Ge. 43. 2. [u] Is. 51. 19.
[x] Jos. 7. 5. [y] Je. 8. 21. [z] Am. 8. 5. [a] De. 22. 2. [b] Ne. 10. 34.

הִשְׁבַּתִּיךְ[a]	וְ Hiph. pret. 1 pers. sing., suff. 2 pers. sing. fem. [for בַּתְּתִּיךְ' § 25. rem.] .	שבת
הֲשִׁבֹתִים	וַ Hiph. pret. 1 p.s., suff. 3 p.pl.m.; וַ for וְ conv.	שוב
הִשְׁבַּתִּים[b]	וְ Hiph. pret. 1 pers. sing., suff. 3 pers. pl. masc. [for בַּתְּתִּים' § 25. rem.] .	שבת
הֹשַׁבְתִּים[c]	וְ Hiph. pret. 1 pers. sing., suff. 3 pers. pl. m.	ישב
הֲשֵׁבֹתָם[d]	וַ Hiph. pret. 2 pers. sing. masc., suff. 3 pers. pl. masc. (§ 21. rem. 14); וַ for וְ conv. .	שוב
הֲשֵׁבֹתֶם	id. pret. 2 pers. pl. masc. . . .	שוב
הִשְׁבַּתֶּם[e]	וְ Hiph. pret. 2 p. pl. m. [for הִשְׁבַּתְתֶּם § 25. r.]	שבת
הִשְׁבַּתְנוּ[f]	וְ id. pret. 1 pers. pl.	שבת
הַשֵּׂג[g]	Hiph. inf. absolute	נשג
הַשֹּׁגֶגֶת[h]	pref. הַ)(Kal part. act. s. f. (from שֹׁגֵג m.)	שגג
הִשְׁגּוּ[i]	Hiph. pret. 3 pers. pl.	שגה
הִשְׁגִּיחַ[k]	Hiph. pret. 3 pers. sing. masc. . . .	שגח
הַשֹּׁגִים[l]	pref. הַ)(Kal part. act. m., pl. of שֹׁגֶה d. 9a	שגה
הַשֵּׁגָל[m]	וְ pref. id.)(noun fem. sing. . . .	שגל
הִשִּׂגָנוּ[n]	וְ Hiph. pret. 3 pers. sing. masc., suff. 1 p. pl.	נשג
הִשַּׂגְתָּם[o]	וְ id. pret. 2 pers. s. m., suff. 3 pers. pl. m.	נשג
הַשַּׁד[p]	pref. הַ)(noun masc. sing.	שדד
הַשֹּׁדֵד[q]	pref. id.)(Kal part. sing. masc. dec. 7b .	שדד
הַשָּׂדֶה	pref. id.)(noun masc. sing. dec. 9b .	שדה
הַשְּׁדוּדָה[r]	pref. id.)(Kal part. pass. fem. of שָׁדוּד m.	שדד
הַשִּׂדִּים	pref. id.)(pr. name of a valley . .	שדד
הַשְּׁדֵמוֹת[s]	pref. id.)(n. f., pl. of שְׁדֵמָה d. 11 (§ 42. r. 4)	שדם
הַשְּׂדֵרוֹת	pref. id.)(noun fem., pl. of [שְׂדֵרָה] d. 10, see	סדר
הַשָּׂדֹת[t]	pref. id.)(n. m. with pl. f. term., abs. st., fr. שָׂדֶה d. 9b	שדה
הַשֶּׂה	pref. id.)(noun com. sing. irr. (§ 45) .	שיה
הִשָּׁהּ[u]	Hiph. pret. 3 p.s.m., suff. 3 p.s.f. (§ 25. No. 2b)	נשה
הַשֹּׁהַם	pref. הַ)(noun masc. sing.	שהם
הַשַּׂהֲרֹנִים[v]	וְ' pref. id.)(noun m., pl. of שַׂהֲרֹן d. 1b, see	סהר
הַשָּׁוְא	pref. id.)(noun masc. sing. . . .	שוא
הַשּׁוֹבֵבָה[w]	pref. id.)(adj. fem. sing. . . .	שוב
הַשּׁוֹדֵד[a]	וְ pref. id.)(Kal part. act. masc., dec. 7b .	שדד
הַשּׁוֹדְדִים[b]	pref. id.)(id. pl., absolute state . .	שדד
הַשּׁוּחִי	pref. id.)(patronym. of שׁוּחַ . . .	שוח
הַשּׁוּחָמִי	pref. id.)(patronym. of שׁוּחָם . .	שוח
הַשּׁוֹטֵף[c]	pref. id.)(Kal part. act. sing. masc. dec. 7b	שטף
הַשֹּׁוטֵר[d]	pref. id.)(Kal part. act. sing. masc. dec. 7b	שטר
הַשּׁוּלַמִּית	pref. id.)(pr. name fem., perhaps gent. noun	שלם
הַשּׁוּמִים[e]	pref. id.)(noun masc., pl. of [שׁוּם] dec. 1a	שום
הַשּׁוּנִי	pref. id.)(patronym. for שׁוּנִיִּי from שׁוּנִי .	שון
הַשּׁוּנַמִּית	pref. id.)(gent. noun, f. of שׁוּנַמִּי, fr. שׁוּנֵם	שון
הַשּׁוֹעֵר[f]	pref. id.)(noun masc. sing. dec. 7b .	שער
הַשֹּׁעֲרִים	וְ' pref. id.)(id. pl., absolute state .	שער
הַשּׁוֹפֵט[g]	pref. id.)(Kal part. act. sing. masc. d. 7b	שפט
הַשּׁוּפָמִי	pref. id.)(patronym. fr. שְׁפוּפָם . .	שפף
הַשּׁוֹפָר	pref. id.)(noun masc. sing. dec. 2b .	שפר
הַשּׁוֹפָרוֹת	pref. id.)(id. pl., absolute state .	שפר
הַשּׁוּק[h]	pref. id.)(noun fem. sing. dec. 1a	שוק
הַשּׁוֹר	וְ' pref. id.)(noun masc. sing., suff. שׁוֹרוֹ, pl. שְׁוָרִים (§ 35. rem. 13) . .	שור
הֵשַׁח	Hiph. pret. 3 pers. sing. masc. (§ 18. r. 10)	שחח
הַשַּׁחַד	pref. הַ)(noun masc. sing. . . .	שחד
הַשֹּׁחֶה[k]	pref. id.)(Kal part. act. sing. masc. .	שחה
הַשְּׁחוּטָה[l] / הַשְּׁחֻטָה[m]	pref. id.)(Kal part. pass. fem. sing., fr. שָׁחוּט masc. . .	שחט
הַשֻּׁחִי	pref. id.)(patronym. of שׁוּחַ . .	שוח
הַשְּׁחִין	pref. id.)(noun masc. sing. . .	שחן
הַשְׁחִית[n]	Hiph. inf. constr.	שחת
הִשְׁחִית[o]	וְ' id. pret. 3 pers. sing. masc. . .	שחת
הַשְׁחִיתָהּ	וְ id. imp. sing. masc., suff. 3 pers. sing. f.	שחת
הִשְׁחִיתוּ[p]	וְ' id. pret. 3 pers. pl. masc. . .	שחת
הַשְׁחִיתֶךָ[q]	id. inf., suff. 2 pers. s. m. d. 1b [for חִיתְךָ]	שחת
הַשְׁחִיתָם[r]	id., suff. 3 pers. pl. masc. . . .	שחת
הַשַּׁחַף	pref. הַ)(noun masc. s. [for שַׁחַף § 35. r. 2]	שחף
הַשַּׁחֶפֶת[s]	pref. id.)(noun fem. sing. . . .	שחף
הַשַּׁחַק[t]	pref. id.)(noun masc. sing. . . .	שחק
הַשַּׁחַר / הַשָּׁחַר	pref. id.)(noun masc. sing. dec. 6d (§ 35. rem. 2)	שחר
הַשַּׁחֲרוּת[u]	וְ pref. id.)(noun fem. sing. . . .	שחר
הַשְּׁחֹרִים[v]	pref. id.)(adj. masc., pl. of שָׁחֹר dec. 3a	שחר
הַשַּׁחַת[y]	pref. id.)(n. m. s. for שַׁחַת' (comp. § 35. r. 2)	שחת
הַשְׁחֵת[z]	Hiph. inf. absolute (§ 11. rem. 2)	שחת
הִשְׁחַתִּי[a]	וְ Hiph. pret. 1 p. s. [for הִשְׁחַתְתִּי § 25. r.]	שחת
הִשְׁחַתֶּם[b]	וְ id. pret. 2 pers. pl. m. [for הִשְׁחַתְתֶּם v. i.]	שחת
הַשִּׁטָּה	pref. הַ)(pr. name in compos. בֵּית הַשִּׁטָּה	בית
הַשָּׁטִים[c]	pref. id.)(Kal part. act. m., pl. of [שָׁט] d. 1a	שוט
הַשִּׁטִּים	pref. id.)(pr. name of a place (pl. of שִׁטָּה)	שטה
הַשָּׂטָן[d]	וְ' pref. id.)(noun masc. sing. . .	שטן
הַשֶּׁטֶף[e]	pref. id.)(noun masc. sing. . .	שטף
הַשֹּׁטְרִים	pref. id.)(Kal part. act. m., pl. of שֹׁטֵר d. 7b	שטר
הִשִּׁיא[f]	Hiph. pret. 3 pers. sing. masc. . .	שא
הִשִּׁיאוּ	וְ Hiph. pret. 3 pers. pl. . . .	שא
הִשִּׁיאוּךָ[g]	Hiph. pret. 3 pers. pl., suff. 2 pers. sing. m.	שא
הִשִּׁיאֲךָ[h]	id. pret. 3 p. s. m., suff. 2 p. s. m. [for הִשִּׁיאֲךָ]	שא
הִשִּׁיאַנִי[i]	id. id., suff. 1 pers. sing. . . .	שא
הָשֵׁב[k]	Hiph. imp. sing. masc.	שוב
הָשִׁיב	id. inf. constr.	שוב
הֵשִׁיב	וְ' id. pret. 3 pers. sing. masc. . .	שוב
הָשִׁיבָה	id. imp. masc. s. with parag. ה (§ 11. r. 5)	שוב
הֲשִׁיבֵהוּ[l]	וַ id. id., suff. 3 pers. sing. masc.; וַ bef. (-:)	שוב

[a] Eze. 16. 41. [b] Eze. 34. 10. [c] Je. 32. 37. [d] 1 Ki. 8. 34. [e] Ex. 5. 5. [f] Ne. 4. 5. [g] 1 Sa. 30. 8. [h] Nu. 15. 28. [i] Ps. 73. 12. [k] Ps. 33. 14. [l] Ps. 119. 21. [m] Ne. 2. 6. [n] 2 Sa. 15. 14. [o] Ge. 44. 4. [p] Is. 51. 19. [q] Je. 6. 26. [r] Ps. 137. 8. [s] Je. 31. 40. [t] Ex. 8. 9. [u] Job 39. 17. [v] Ju. 8. 21, 26. [y] Is. 3. 18. [z] Je. 31. 22; 49. 4. [a] Is. 21. 2. [b] Je. 51. 48. [c] 2 Ch. 32. 4. [d] 2 Ch. 26. 11. [e] Nu. 11. 5. [f] 2 Ch. 31. 14. [g] Ju. 2. 18, 19. [h] 1 Sa. 9. 24. [i] Ex. 21. 32. [k] Is. 25. 11. [l] Le. 14. 51. [m] Le. 14. 6. [n] Is. 65. 8. [o] Ge. 6. 12. [p] Ju. 2. 19. [q] De. 10. 10. [r] 2 Ki. 13. 23. [s] Le. 26. 16. [t] Je. 48. 27. [u] Ec. 11. 10. [v] Zec. 6. 6. [y] Ps. 49. 10. [z] De. 31. 29. [a] Je. 51. 20. [b] De. 4. 25. [c] Eze. 27. 26. [d] Zec. 3. 1. [e] Da. 11. 22. [f] Je. 49. 16. [g] Ob. 7. [h] Ob. 3. [i] Ge. 3. 13. [k] 2 Ki. 8. 6. [l] 1 Ki. 22. 26.

הֲשִׁיבֻהוּ[a] וַ id. imp. pl. masc., suff. 3 pers. sing. masc.; וַ id. . . . . . . שוב

הָשִׁיבוּ וְ' id. imp. pl. masc. . . . . שוב

הֱשִׁיבוֹ[b] id. pret. 3 pers. sing. m., suff. 3 pers. s. m. שוב

הֵשִׁיבוּ וְ' id. pret. 3 pers. pl. . . . . . שוב

הֹשִׁיבוּ וְ'[c] Hiph. pret. 3 pers. pl., or imp. pl. masc. ישב

הֱשִׁיבוּם וַ Hiph. pret. 3 pers. pl. (הֵשִׁיבוּ), suff. 3 pers. pl. masc. וַ before (ְ:) . . . . שוב

הֲשִׁיבוֹתָ[e] id. pret. 2 pers. sing. masc. (§ 21. rem. 14) שוב

הֲשִׁיבוֹתִי וַ id. pret. 1 pers. sing.; וַ bef. (ֲ) . . . שוב

הֲשֵׁיבוֹתָם וַ id. pret. 2 pers. sing. masc., suff. 3 pers. pl. masc. (§ 21. rem. 14); וַ id. . שוב

הֱשִׁיבְךָ[h] וַ / הֱשִׁיבֶךָ[i] וַ } id. pret. 3 pers. sing. m. (הֵשִׁיב), suff. 2 pers. sing. m. וַ, וֶ for וְ conv. } שוב

הֲשִׁיבֵנוּ id. imp. sing. masc., suff. 1 pers. pl. שוב

הֲשִׁיבֹנוּ[k] id. pret. 1 pers. pl. . . . . . . שוב

הֲשִׁיבֵנִי וַ'[l] id. inf., or imp. s. masc., suff. 1 pers. sing.; וַ bef. (ֲ) . . . . . שוב

הֱשִׁיבַנִי id. pret. 3 pers. sing. masc., suff. 1 pers. s. שוב

הֲשִׁיבֹתִי וַ id. pret. 1 pers. sing; acc. shifted by וַ, for וְ conv. (comp. § 8. rem. 7) . שוב

הֲשִׁיבֹתִיךָ[m] וַ id. id., suff. 2 pers. sing. masc.; וַ bef. (ֲ) . שוב

הֲשִׁיבֹתִים וַ id. id., suff. 3 pers. pl. masc.; וַ id. . שוב

הֲשֵׁבֹתֶם וַ id. pret. 2 pers. pl. m. (§ 21. r. 14); וַ id. שוב

הִשִּׂיג[p] וְ Hiph. pret. 3 pers. sing. masc. . . . נשג

הִשִּׂיגָה[q] וְ'[r] id pret. 3 pers. sing. fem. . . . נשג

הִשִּׂיגוֹ וְ id. pret. 3 pers. sing. masc., suff. 3 pers. sing. masc. . . . . . . נשג

הִשִּׂיגוּ id. pret. 3 pers. pl. . . . . . . נשג

הִשִּׂיגוּהָ[t] id. id., suff. 3 pers. sing. fem. . . . נשג

הִשִּׂיגוּךָ[u] וְ id. id., suff. 2 pers. sing. masc. . . נשג

הִשִּׂיגוּנִי[x] id. id., suff. 1 pers. sing. . . . . נשג

הִשִּׂגֶךָ[y] וְ defect. for יגוּךָ (q. v.) . . . . . נשג

הַשִּׁיחִם[z] pref. הַ)(noun masc., pl. of שִׁיחַ dec. 1a . שיח

הַשִּׁיחוֹר pref. id.)(pr. name of a river . . שחר

הַשִּׁילוֹנִי / הַשִּׁלֹנִי } pref. id.)(gent. noun fr. שִׁילֹה . . . שלה

הָשִׂימִי[a] Hiph. imp. sing. fem. fr. שִׂים or . . . שום

הֵשִׁיקוּ[b] וְ'[c] Hiph. pret. 3 pers. pl. . . . . שוק

הִשִּׁיקוּ[d] וְ Hiph. pret. 3 pers. pl. . . . . נשק

הַשִּׁיר וְ'[e] pref. הַ)(noun masc. sing. dec. 1a . שיר

הַשִּׁירָה pref. id.)(noun fem. sing. dec. 10 . . שיר

הֵשִׁירוּ[f] Hiph. pret. 3 pers. pl. . . . . . . שור

הַשִּׁירִים[g] pref. הַ)(noun masc., pl. of שִׁיר dec. 1a שור

הַשְׁכֵּב[h] Hiph. inf. absolute (§ 11. rem. 2) . . שכב

הַשֹּׁכֵב וְ'[k] pref. הַ)(Kal part. act. masc. dec. 7b שכב

הָשְׁכַּב[l] וְ Hoph. pret. 3 pers. sing. masc. (§ 11. rem. 10) . . . . שכב

הַשְׁכְּבָה[m] וְ id. imp. sing. masc. with parag. ה . שכב

הַשֹּׁכְבִים[n] pref. הַ)(Kal part. act. m., pl. of שֹׁכֵב dec. 7b שכב

הִשְׁכַּבְתִּים[o] וְ Hiph. pret. 1 pers. sing., suff. 3 pers. pl. m. שכב

הַשְּׁכוּנֵי[p] pref. id.)(Kal part. pass. pl. constr. from [שָׁכוּן] dec. 3a . . . . . שכן

הֲשָׁכַח[q] pref. הֲ)(Kal pret. 3 pers. sing. masc. . שכח

הַשְׁכַּחוּ וְ Chald. Aph. pret. 3 pers. pl. masc. (§ 47. rem. 4, & § 49. No. 4) . . . שכח

הַשְּׁכֵחִים[oo] pref. הַ)(adj. masc., pl. of [שָׁכֵחַ] dec. 5a שכח

הַשְׁכַּחְנָא[r] Ch. Aph. pret. 1 p. pl. (§ 47. r. 4, & § 49. No. 4) שכח

הַשְׁכַּחַת[s] Chald. id. pret. 1 pers. sing. . . . שכח

הֲשְׁכַחְתֶּם[t] pref. הֲ interr. for הֲ)(Kal pret. 2 pers. pl. m. שכח

הִשְׁכִּיבָה[u] Hiph. pret. 3 pers. sing. fem. . . . שכב

הַשְׂכֵּיל[x] וְ Hiph. inf. abs. . . . . . . שכל

הִשְׂכִּיל[y] וְ'[z] id. pret. 3 pers. sing. masc. . . . שכל

הַשְׂכִּילוּ[a] id. imp. pl. masc. . . . . . . שכל

הִשְׂכִּילוּ id. pret. 3 pers. pl. . . . . . שכל

הַשְׁכֵּים Hiph. inf. abs. used adverbially . . שכם

הִשְׁכִּים וְ id. pret. 3 pers. sing. masc. . . . שכם

הִשְׁכִּימוּ[b] id. pret. 3 pers. pl. . . . . . שכם

הַשְּׂכִירָה[c] pref. הַ)(noun fem. sing. . . . . שכר

הַשְׁכִּירֻהוּ[d] Hiph. imp. pl. masc., suff. 3 pers. sing. masc. שכר

הַשְׂכֵּל וְ'[e] Hiph. inf. absolute (§ 11. rem. 2) . שכל

הִשְׂכַּלְתִּי[f] id. pret. 1 pers. sing. . . . . . שכל

הַשְׁכֵּם וְ'[g] Hiph. inf. abs. (§ 11. rem. 2), or imp. s. m. שכם

הִשְׁכַּמְתֶּם וְ id. pret. 2 pers. pl. masc. . . . שכם

הַשִּׁכְמִי pref. הַ)(patronym. of שֶׁכֶם . . . שכם

הַשֹּׁכֵן pref. id.)(Kal part. act. sing. masc. dec. 7b שכן

הַשְּׁכֵנוֹת[h] pref. id.)(fem. pl. [of שְׁכֵנָה from שָׁכֵן masc.] comp. מִשְּׁכֶנְתָּהּ . . . . . שכן

הַשְּׁכֵנִים[i] pref. id.)(Kal part. act. m., pl. of שָׁכֵן dec. 7b שכן

הִשְׁכַּנְתִּי[k] וְ Hiph. pret. 1 pers. sing.; acc. shifted by וְ conv. (comp. § 8. rem. 7) . . שכן

הַשֵּׁכָר[l] pref. הַ)(noun masc. sing. . . . שכר

הִשְׂכַּרְתִּי[m] וְ Hiph. pret. 1 pers. sing.; acc. shifted by וְ conv. (comp. § 8. rem. 7) . . . . שכר

הִשְׂכַּרְתִּים[n] וְ id., suff. 3 pers. pl. masc. . . . שכר

הֲשִׁכֹּתִי[o] וַ Hiph. pret. 1 pers. sing.; acc. shifted by וַ for conv. וְ (comp. § 8. rem. 7, & § 11. rem. 5) שכך

הַשָּׁלֵו[p] pref. הַ)(noun masc. sing. . . . שלה

הַשְּׁלַבִּים[q] pref. id.)(noun masc., pl. of [שָׁלָב] dec. 8d (§ 37. No. 3) . . . . . שלב

הַשֶּׁלֶג / וְהַשָּׁלֶג[r] } ה pref. id.)(noun masc. sing. (§ 35. rem. 2) שלג

---

[a] 2 Ch. 18. 25. [b] 1 Ki. 13. 20, 23, 26. [c] 1 Ki. 21. 9, 12. [d] 1 Ki. 14. 28. [e] Ps. 85. 4. [f] Am. 1. 8. [g] 2 Ch. 6. 25. [gg] Am. 1. 8.
[h] Ge. 40. 13. [i] De. 28. 68. [k] Ge. 44. 8. [l] Job 13. 22. [m] 2 Ki. 19. 28. [n] Je. 12. 15. [o] 1 Sa. 6. 7. [oo] Is. 65. 11.
[p] Le. 26. 5. [q] Le. 25. 49. [r] Le. 25. 26. [s] De. 19. 6. [t] La. 1. 3. [u] De. 28. 15, 45. [x] Ps. 40. 13.
[y] De. 28. 2. [z] Ge. 21. 15. [a] Eze. 21. 21. [b] Joel 4. 13. [c] Joel 2. 24. [d] Eze. 39. 9. [e] 2 Ch. 29. 28.
[f] Ho. 8. 4. [g] Ca. 1. 1. [h] 2 Sa. 8. 2. [i] De. 22. 22, 29. [k] Le. 14. 47. [l] Eze. 32. 32. [m] Eze. 32. 19.
[n] Am. 6. 4. [o] Ho. 2. 20. [p] Ju. 8. 11. [q] Ps. 77. 10. [r] Da. 6. 6. [s] Da. 2. 25. [t] Je. 44. 9.
[u] 1 Ki. 3. 20. [x] Je. 3. 15. [y] 1 Ch. 28. 19. [z] Je. 23. 5. [a] Ps. 2. 10. [b] Zep. 3. 7. [c] Is. 7. 20.
[d] Je. 48. 26. [e] Da. 1. 17. [f] Ps. 119. 99. [g] Je. 26. 5. [h] Ruth 4. 17. [i] Je. 25. 24. [k] Eze. 32. 4.
[l] Is. 28. 7. [m] Je. 51. 57. [n] Je. 51. 39. [o] Nu. 17. 20. [p] 2 Sa. 6. 7. [q] 1 Ki. 7. 28, 29. [r] Is. 55. 10.

הַשְּׁלָו pref. הַ)(K. 'שְׁלָיו, noun masc. sing., pl. שַׂלְוִים, dec. 6 (§ 35. rem. 16) . . . שלו

הַשָּׁלוֹם וְ' pref. id.
הֲשָּׁלוֹם pref. הֲ } (prim. adj.) noun masc. sing. dec. 3a . . . שלם

הַשְּׁלוֹשָׁה pref. הַ)(num. card. m. s. from שָׁלֹשׁ fem. שלש

הַשָּׁלִשִׁים pref. id.)(Kh. שְׁלוֹשִׁים q. v.; K. 'שָׁלִישִׁים, noun masc. pl. of שָׁלִישׁ dec. 1b . שלש

הַשְּׁלוֹשִׁים pref. id.)(num. card. com. gen., pl. of שָׁלֹשׁ fem. שלש

הַשֶּׁלַח[a]
הַשֶּׁלַח } pref. id.)(noun masc. sing. dec. 6 (§ 35. rem. 5 & 2, but with suff. שִׁלְחוֹ) שלח

הַשֶּׁלַח pref. id.)(pr. name of a pool . . שלח

הַשִּׁלֹחַ pref. id.)(pr. name of a pool . . שלח

הַשֹּׁלֵחַ pref. id.)(Kal part. act. sing. masc. dec. 7b שלח

הַשֻּׁלְחָן וְ' pref. id.)(noun masc. sing. dec. 2b . שלח

הַשֻּׁלְחָנוֹת pref. id.)(id. pl. absolute (constr. שֻׁלְחֲנוֹת) שלח

הִשְׁלַחְתִּי וְ Hiph. pret. 1 pers. sing.; acc. shifted by onv. וְ (comp. § 8. rem. 7) . . שלח

הַשְׁלְטֵהּ[b] וְ Ch. Aph. 3 p. s. m., suff. 3 p. s. m. (§ 47. r. 4) שלט

הַשְּׁלָטִים pref. id.)(noun masc., pl. of שֶׁלֶט dec. 6a (pl. c. שִׁלְטֵי) . . . . . שלט

הַשְׁלְטָךְ[c] וְ Ch. Aph. pret. 3 pers. sing. masc., suff. 2 pers. sing. masc. (§ 47. rem. 4) . . שלט

הַשַּׁלִּיט pref. id.)((prim. adj.) noun m. sing. dec. 1b שלט

הִשְׁלִיטוֹ[d] וְ Hiph. pret. 3 pers. sing. m., suff. 3 pers. s. m. שלט

הִשְׁלִיךְ וְ' Hiph. pret. 3 pers. sing. masc. . . שלך

הִשְׁלִיכָה[e] id. pret. 3 pers. sing. fem. . . . . שלך

הַשְׁלִיכֵהוּ id. imp. sing. masc., suff. 3 pers. sing. masc. שלך

הַשְׁלִיכוּ id. imp. pl. masc. . . . . שלך

הִשְׁלִיכוּ [f] וְ' id. pret. 3 pers. pl. . . . שלך

הַשְׁלִיכוֹ[g] id. inf. with suff. 3 p. s. m. [for הַשְׁלִיכוֹ § 11. r. 4] שלך

הַשְׁלִיכִי[h] וְ id. imp. sing. fem. . . . . שלך

הִשְׁלִיכָם id. pret. 3 pers. sing. masc., suff. 3 pers. pl. m. שלך

הִשְׁלִימָה Hiph. pret. 3 pers. sing. fem. . . . שלם

הִשְׁלִימוּ[i] id. pret. 3 pers. pl. . . . . שלם

הַשָּׁלִישׁ[k] pref. הַ)(noun masc. sing. dec. 1b . שלש

הַשְּׁלִישִׁי [uu] וְ prf. id.)(adj. ord. masc. sing. from שָׁלֹשׁ . שלש

הַשְּׁלִישִׁית וְ'
הֲשְּׁלִישִׁת[l] } pref. id.)(id. fem. . . . . שלש

הַשָּׁלָךְ pref. id.)(noun masc. sing. . . . שלך

הַשְׁלֵךְ וְ' Kal inf. abs. (§ 11. rem. 2), or imp. sing. m. שלך

הָשְׁלַךְ[m] וְ Hoph. pret. 3 pers. sing. masc. (§ 11. rem. 10) שלך

הָשְׁלְכָה[n] id. pret. 3 pers. s. fem. [for הָשְׁלְכָה § 11. rem. 10, comp. § 8. rem. 7] . . . שלך

הַשְׁלִכֵהוּ[o] Hiph. imp. s. m., suff. 3 p. s. m. [for הַשְׁלִיכֵהוּ] לך

הִשְׁלִכוּ[p] defect. for הִשְׁלִיכוּ (q. v.) . . . לך

הָשְׁלְכוּ[q] וְ Hoph. pret. 3 pers. pl. (§ 11. rem. 10) לך

הָשְׁלַכְתָּ[r] id. pret. 2 pers. sing. masc. . . לך

הִשְׁלַכְתָּ
הִשְׁלַכְתָּ[s] וְ } Hiph. pret. 2 pers. sing. masc.; acc. shifted by conv. וְ (comp. § 8. rem. 7) לך

הִשְׁלַכְתּוֹ[t] וְ id. id.)(with suff. 3 pers. sing. masc. . לך

הָשְׁלַכְתִּי [u] Hoph. pret. 1 pers. sing. . . . לך

הִשְׁלַכְתִּי [x]
הִשְׁלַכְתִּי וְ } Hiph. pret. 1 pers. sing.; acc. shifted by conv. וְ (comp. § 8. rem. 7) . לך

הִשְׁלַכְתִּיךְ[y] id. id., suff. 2 pers. sing. masc. . . לך

הִשְׁלַכְתֶּנָה[z] וְ id. pret. 2 pers. pl. fem. (§ 8. rem. 6) . לך

הַשָּׁלָל pref. הַ)(noun masc. sing. dec. 4a . לל

הַשֹּׁלְלִים [a] pref. id.)(Kal part. act. m., pl. of [שֹׁלֵל] dec. 7b לל

הַשְׁלֵם[b] Chald. Aph. imp. sing. masc. (§ 47. rem. 4) לם

הַשִּׁלֻּם[c] pref. הַ)(noun masc. sing. dec. 1b . לם

הָשְׁלְמָה[d] Hoph. pret. 3 pers. sing. fem. . . לם

הַשְׁלְמַהּ[e] וְ Ch. Aph. 3 p. s. m., suff. 3 p. s. f. (§ 47. rem. 4) לם

הַשִּׁלֵּמִי pref. הַ)(patronym. of שִׁלֵּם . . . לם

הַשְּׁלָמִים וְ' pref. id.)(noun masc. pl. (c. שַׁלְמֵי) from שֶׁלֶם dec. 6a . . . . לם

הַשֵּׁלָנִי pref. id.)(patronym. of שֵׁלָה . . . אל

הַשִּׁלֹנִי pref. id.)(gent. noun from שִׁילֹה . לה

הַשָּׁלֹשׁ[f] pref. id.)(num. card. fem. sing. . . לש

הַשְּׁלֹשָׁה pref. id.)(id. masc. . . . . לש

הַשְּׁלִשִׁי [g] וְ' pref. id.)(adj. ord. masc. sing. (for שְׁלִישִׁי) לש

הַשָּׁלֹשִׁי[h] pref. id.)(Kh. הַשְּׁלִשִׁי q. v., K. הַשְּׁלֹשָׁה (q. v.) לש

הַשָּׁלִשִׁי[i] pref. id.)(abbreviated for the following . לש

הַשָּׁלִשִׁים[k] וְ pref. id.)(noun masc., pl. of שָׁלִישׁ dec. 1b לש

הַשְּׁלֹשִׁים pref. id.)(num. card. com. gen., pl. of שָׁלֹשׁ fem. לש

הַשְּׁלִשִׁים [l] pref. id.)(adj. ord. m., pl. of שְׁלִישִׁי from שָׁלֹשׁ לש

הַשְּׁלִשִׁית וְ' pref. id.)(id. fem. sing. . . . לש

הָשֵׁם pr. name masc. 1 Ch. 11. 34, for which יָשֵׁן in 2 Sa. 23. 32.

הַשָּׂם pref. הַ relat. art.)(Kal part. act. sing. masc. dec. 1a, from שִׂים or . . . ים

הַשֵּׁם pref. הַ art.)(noun masc. sing. dec. 7a . ם

הַשְּׂמֹאול[m]
הַשְּׂמֹאל } pref. id.)(noun m. sing. dec. 1a (ו in otio) מאל

הַשְּׂמָאלִי pref. id.)(adj. masc. sing. . . . מאל

הַשְּׂמָאלִית pref. id.)(id. fem. . . . . מאל

הַשְׁמֵד Hiph. inf. abs. (§ 11. rem. 2), or imp. sing. m. מד

הִשָּׁמֵד[n] Niph. inf. constr. used as an abs. . . מד

---

[a] Ne. 4. 11. [b] Da. 2. 48. [c] Da. 2. 38. [d] Ec. 5. 18. [e] 2 Sa. 11. 21. [f] Eze. 43. 24. [g] Je. 52. 3. [h] Je. 7. 29. [i] Jos. 10. 1. [k] 2 Ki. 7. 2, 17, 19. [l] De. 26. 12. [m] Da. 8. 11. [n] Eze. 19. 12. [o] 2 Ki. 9. 25, 26. [p] 2 Ki. 24. 20. [q] Je. 22. 28. [r] Is. 14. 19. [s] Eze. 5. 4. [t] Je. 51. 63. [u] Ps. 22. 11. [uu] Eze. 10. 14. [x] Je. 7. 15. [y] Eze. 28. 17. [z] Am. 4. 3. [a] Zec. 2. 12. [b] Ezr. 7. 19. [c] Ho. 9. 7. [d] Job 5. 23. [e] Da. 5. 26. [f] De. 19. 9. [g] 2 Sa. 3. 3. [h] 2 Sa. 23. 18. [i] 2 Sa. 23. 8. [k] 2 Ki. 10. 25 [l] 1 Ki. 6. 8. [m] 1 Ch. 6. 29. [n] De. 4. 26.

הִשְׁמִדוֹ[a]	Kal pret. 3 pers. sing. masc. (הִשְׁמִיד), suff. 3 pers. sing. masc. (comp. § 11. rem. 4)	שמד
הִשָּׁמֶדְךָ[b]	Niph. inf. (הִשָּׁמֵד), suff. 2 p. s. m. pause d. 7 b	שמד
הִשָּׁמֶדְךָ[c]	id. with suff. 2 pers. sing. masc. (comp. § 16. rem. 15, & § 36. rem. 3) . . .	שמד
הַשְׁמִדְךָ[d]	Hiph. inf. with suff. 2 p. s. m. (for הַשְׁ' § 11. r. 4)	שמד
הִשָּׁמְדָם	Niph. inf. (הִשָּׁמֵד), suff. 3 pers. pl. m. dec. 7 b	שמד
הַשְׁמִדָם[e]	Hiph. inf., suff. 3 p. s. m. (for הַשְׁ' § 11. rem. 4)	שמד
הִשְׁמַדְתִּי[pp] / וְהִשְׁמַדְתִּי	id. pret. 1 pers. sing.; acc. shifted by conv. וְ (comp. § 8. rem. 7) .	שמד
וְהִשְׁמַדְתִּיו[f]	וְ id. id., suff. 3 pers. sing. masc. . .	שמד
הַשָּׁמָה[g]	pref. הַ relat. art.)(Kal pret. 3 pers. sing. fem.	שום
הָשַּׁמָּה[h]	Hoph. inf. [הָשַׁם for הוּשַׁם § 18. r. 14] with suff. 3 p. s. fem. הָ— for הּ— (§ 3. rem. 3)	שמם
וְהָשַּׁמּוּ[i]	וְ id. imp. pl. masc. [הוּשַׁמּוּ=הָשַׁמּוּ, compare the preceding]	שמם
הֵשַׁמּוּ	Hiph. pret. 3 pers. pl. (§ 18. rem. 10) .	שמם
הַשְּׁמוּעָה	pref. הַ)(noun fem. sing. dec. 10 . .	שמע
הֲשִׁמּוֹתָ[k]	Hiph. pret. 2 pers. sing. masc. . . .	שמם
וַהֲשִׁמּוֹתִי	וַ id. pret. 1 pers. sing.; acc. shifted by וַ, for וְ conv. (compare § 8. rem. 7) .	שמם
וַהֲשִׁמּוֹתִיהוּ[l]	וַ id. id. with suff. 3 pers. sing. masc. .	שמם
הַשִּׂמְחָה	pref. הַ)(noun fem. sing. dec. 12 b .	שמח
הַשְּׂמֵחִים	pref. id.)(adj. masc., pl. of שָׂמֵחַ dec. 5 a .	שמח
הִשְׂמַחְתָּ[m]	Hiph. pret. 2 pers. sing. masc. . . .	שמח
הַשְּׁמִטָּה	pref. הַ)(noun fem. sing.	שמט
הַשְׁמֵיד[n]	Hiph. inf. absolute	שמד
הִשְׁמִיד	id. pret. 3 pers. sing. masc. . . .	שמד
הַשְׁמִידוֹ[o]	id. inf., suff. 3 pers. sing. masc. dec. 1 b .	שמד
הִשְׁמִידוֹ	id. pret. 3 pers. s. m. suff. id.; or (De. 28. 48) inf. for הַשְׁ' (§ 11. rem. 4) . .	שמד
הִשְׁמִידוּ[p]	id. pret. 3 pers. pl.	שמד
הִשְׁמִידוּם[q]	id. id., suff. 3 pers. pl. masc. . . .	שמד
וְהִשְׁמִידְךָ	וְ id. pret. 3 pers. sing. m., suff. 2 pers. sing. m.	שמד
הַשְׁמִידָם[r]	id. inf., suff. 3 pers. pl. masc. dec. 1 b .	שמד
הִשְׁמִדָם[s]	defect. for הִשְׁמִידוּם (q. v.) . . .	שמד
הַשְּׁמִידָעִי	pref. הַ)(patronym. of שְׁמִידָע q. v.	שם
הַשְׂמִילִי	Hiph. imp. sing. fem. [for הַשְׂמְאִילִי]	שמאל
הַשָּׁמַיִם / וְהַשָּׁמָיִם	pref. הַ)(noun masc., pl. of [שָׁמַי], pl. c. שְׁמֵי, with suff. שָׁמֶיךָ (§ 38. r. 2)	שמה
הַשָּׁמַיְמָה / הַשָּׁמָיְמָה	pref. id.)(id. with paragogic ה . .	שמה
הַשְּׁמִינִי	pref. id.)(adj. ord. masc. sing. for שְׁמֹנֶה	שמן
הַשְּׁמִינִית / הַשְּׁמִנִית[t]	pref. id.)(id. fem.	שמן
הִשְׁמִיעַ[u]	וְ' Hiph. pret. 3 pers. sing. masc.	שמע
הַשְׁמִיעוּ	וְ' id. imp. pl. masc.	שמע

הִשְׁמִיעוּ[v]	וְ'[z] id. pret. 3 pers. pl. . . .	שמע
הַשְׁמִיעוּהָ[a]	וְ id. imp. pl. masc., suff. 3 pers. sing. fem. .	שמע
הִשְׁמִיעֲךָ[b]	id. pret. 3 pers. sing. m., suff. 2 pers. s. m.	שמע
הַשְׁמִיעֻנוּ[c]	id. imp. pl. masc. (הַשְׁמִיעוּ), suff. 1 pers. pl.	שמע
הִשְׁמִיעָנוּ[d]	id. pret. 3 pers. sing. masc., suff. 1 pers. pl.	שמע
הַשְׁמִיעִנִי[e]	id. imp. sing. fem., suff. 1 pers. sing. .	שמע
הַשְׁמִיעֵנִי[f]	id. imp. sing. masc., (§ 11. r. 5) suff. 1 pers. s.	שמע
הַשִּׂמְלָה	pref. הַ)(noun fem. sing. dec. 12 b . .	שמל
הַשְׁמֵם[g]	Hiph. inf. abs. (uncontracted form § 18. r. 13)	שמם
הַשָּׁמֵם[h]	pref. הַ)(adj. masc. sing.	שמם
הַשֹּׁמְמוֹת[i]	pref. id.)(Kal part. act. fem. pl. [of שֹׁמֶמֶת dec. 13 a, in use only שׁוֹמֵמָה comp. § 42. r. 5.]	שמם
הַשֶּׁמֶן / וְהַשָּׁמֶן[k]	pref. הַ)(noun masc. sing. dec. 6 a (§ 35. rem. 2) . .	שמן
הַשְׁמֵן[l]	Hiph. imp. sing. masc. . . .	שמן
הַשְּׁמֵנָה[m]	וְ' pref. הַ art., or interr. for הֲ)(adj. fem. sing. from שָׁמֵן masc. . . .	שמן
הֲשָׁמַע[n]	pref. הֲ)(Kal pret. 3 pers. sing. masc. .	שמע
הַשֹּׁמֵעַ	pref. הַ)(Kal part. act. sing. masc. dec. 7 b	שמע
הַשְּׁמָעָה	pref. id.)(pr. name masc. . . .	שמע
הַשְּׁמֻעָה[o]	וְ' pref. id.)(for שְׁמוּעָה, noun fem. s. dec. 10.	שמע
הַשִּׁמְעִי	pref. id.)(patronym. for שִׁמְעִיִּי from שִׁמְעִי	שמע
הַשֹּׁמְעִים	pref. id.)(Kal part. act. m., pl. of שֹׁמֵעַ d. 7 b	שמע
הַשִּׁמְעֹנִי	pref. id.)(patronym. of שִׁמְעוֹן .	שמע
הִשְׁמַעְתָּ[p]	Hiph. pret. 2 pers. sing. masc. . .	שמע
וְהִשְׁמַעְתִּי	וְ id. pret. 1 pers. sing. . . .	שמע
הִשְׁמַעְתִּיךָ	id. id., suff. 2 pers. sing. masc. . .	שמע
הַשֹּׁמֵר[q] / הַשֹּׁמֵר[r]	pref. הַ / pref. הַ Kal part. act. sing. masc. dec. 7 b .	שמר
הִשָּׁמֶר[s] / הִשָּׁמֵר	Niph. imp. sing. masc. (§ 9. rem. 3) .	שמר
הִשָּׁמְרוּ / הִשָּׁמֵרוּ[t]	id. imp. pl. masc. (comp. § 8. rem. 7) .	שמר
הִשָּׁמְרִי[u]	id. imp. sing. fem.	שמר
הַשֹּׁמְרִים / הַשֹּׁמְרִים[x]	pref. הַ / pref. הַ Kal part. act. masc., pl. of שֹׁמֵר dec. 7 b . .	שמר
הַשֹּׁמְרֹנִי	pref. הַ)(patronym. of שִׁמְרוֹן .	שמר
הַשֹּׁמְרֹנִים	pref. id.)(gent. noun from שֹׁמְרוֹן .	שמר
הַשֶּׁמֶשׁ / וְהַשֶּׁמֶשׁ	pref. id.)(noun masc. sing. dec. 6 a (§ 35. rem. 2, but with suff. שִׁמְשֵׁךְ)	שמש
הַשִּׁמְשִׁי	pref. id.)(gent. noun, see בֵּית הַשִּׁמְשִׁי .	בית
הֲשַׂמְתָּ	pref. הֲ)(Kal pret. 2 pers. sing. m. fr. שִׂים or	שום
וַהֲשִׁמֹּתִי	וַ Hiph. pret. 1 pers. sing.; acc. shifted by וַ for וְ conv. (comp. § 8. rem. 7) .	שמם
הַשּׁוּמָתִי	וְ pref. הַ)(patronym. of שׁוּמָה q. v. .	שום
הַשֵּׁן	pref. id.)(noun com. sing. dec. 8 b .	שנן
הַשִּׂנְאָה[y]	pref. id.)(noun fem. sing. (no pl.) .	שנא

[a] 1 Ki. 15. 29. [b] De. 28. 24, 45, 51, 61. [c] De. 28. 20. [d] De. 7. 24. [e] Jos. 11. 14. [f] Eze. 14. 9. [g] Is. 51. 10. [h] Le. 26. 34, 35. 2 Ch. 36. 21. [i] Job 21. 5. [k] Job 16. 7. [l] Eze. 14. 8. [m] Ps. 89. 43. [n] Am. 9. 8. [o] Jos. 23. 15. [p] Ps. 106. 34. [pp] Am. 2. 9. [q] 2 Ch. 20. 10. [r] Jos. 11. 20. [s] De. 2. 23. [t] Eze. 21. 21. [u] Le. 25. 22. [x] Is. 30. 30. [y] Je. 48. 4. [z] Eze. 27. 30. [a] Je. 5. 20. [b] De. 4. 36. [c] Is. 41. 22. [d] Ju. 13. 23. [e] Ca. 2. 14; 8. 13. [f] Ps. 143. 8. [g] Mi. 6. 13. [h] Da. 9. 17. [i] Eze. 36. 4. [k] 1 Ch. 9. 29. [l] Is. 6. 10. [m] Ne. 9. 35. [n] De. 4. 33. [o] 1 Sa. 2. 24. [p] Ps. 76. 9. [q] Ps. 146. 6. [r] Ge. 4. 9. [s] Is. 7. 4. [t] Je. 9. 3. [u] Ju. 13. 4. [x] Ju. 2. 22. [y] 2 Sa. 13. 15.

הַשָּׁנָה pref. הַ)(noun fem. sing. dec. 11a . . שנה
[a] הַשְּׂנוּאָה [b] וְ pref. id.)(Kal part. pass. s. f. fr. [שָׂנוּא] m. שנא
[c] הִשָּׁנוֹת Niph. inf. constr. . . . . שנה
הַשָּׁנִי pref. הַ)(noun m. s., constr. שְׁנֵי, pl. שָׁנִים שנה
הַשֵּׁנִי pref. id.)(adj. ord. masc. sing. from שְׁנַיִם . שנה
הַשָּׁנִים pref. id.)(noun fem. with pl. masc. term. from שָׁנָה dec. 11a . . . . שנה
הַשְּׁנַיִם pref. id.)(num. card. masc. dual, constr. שְׁנֵי & שְׁנֵים . . . . . שנה
[d] הַשִּׁנַּיִם pref. id.)(noun com., dual of שֵׁן dec. 8b שנן
הַשְּׁנַיִם pref. id.)(num. card. m. constr. of שְׁנַיִם du. שנה
הַשֵּׁנִית [e] וְ pref. id.)(adj. ord., fem. of שֵׁנִי, used also adverbially . . . . . שנה
הַשּׁוּנַמִּית pref. id.)(gent. noun, fem. of שׁוּנַמִּי fr. שׁוּנֵם שון
[f] הַשְּׁסוּעָה pref. id.)(Kal part. pass. s. f. [from שָׁסוּעַ m.] שסע
[g] הָשַׁע Hiph. imp. sing. masc. ap. for הַשְׁעֵה; it stands for הַשַׁע (like הַעַל from עָלָה § 24. rem. 17) comp. the lengthened vowel in יֵרֶב for יִרְבֶּה, יֵכַהּ for יִכְהֶה . שעה
[h] הָשַׁע Hiph. imp. sing. masc. [for הָשֵׁעַ comp. imp. הָבֵר § 15. rem. 1, & § 18. rem. 10] . שעע
הַשָּׂעִיר [i] וְ pref. הַ)(noun masc. sing. dec. 3a . שער
[k] הַשְּׂעִירִם pref. id.)(id. pl., absolute state . שער
הַשְּׂעִירָתָה pref. id.)(pr. name of a place [שְׂעִירָה] with paragogic ה . . . . . שער
הַשַּׁעַלְבֹנִי pref. id.)(gent. noun, see שַׁעַלַבִּים . שעלב
[l] הַשְׁעֲנוּ וְ Hiph. imp. pl. masc. . . . . שען
הַשַּׁעַר / וְהַשָּׁעַר pref. הַ)(noun com. sing. dec. 6d (§ 35. rem. 2) . . . . . שער
[m] הַשֹּׁעֵר pref. id.)(noun masc. sing. dec. 7b . שער
[n] הַשַּׁעְרָה pref. id.)(noun com. sing. with paragogic ה from שַׁעַר dec. 6d . . . . שער
[o] הַשְּׂעֹרָה pref. id.)(noun fem. sing. (no pl. abs.) . שער
הַשָּׁעֲרָה in pause for הַשַּׁעֲרָה (q. v. comp. § 35. r. 5) שער
[p] הַשְּׂעֹרָה וְ pref. הַ)(noun fem. sing. dec. 10 . שער
הַשְּׁעָרִים pref. id.)(noun com., pl. of שַׁעַר dec. 6d שער
הַשְּׂעֹרִים וְ pref. id.)(noun fem. with pl. masc. term. from שְׂעֹרָה . . . . . שער
[q] הַשֹּׁעָרִים pref. id.)(adj. masc. pl. [of שֹׁעָר] . שער
הַשֹּׁעֲרִים pref. id.)(noun masc., pl. of שֹׁעֵר dec. 7b . שער
[r] הַשָּׁפוּךְ pref. id.)(Kal part. pass. sing. masc. . שפך
[s] הָשְׁפּוֹת contr. for הָאַשְׁפּוֹת (q. v.) . . . שפת
הַשִּׁפְחָה pref. הַ)(noun fem. sing. dec. 12b . שפח
הַשְּׁפָחוֹת pref. id.)(id. pl., absolute state . . שפח
הַשֹּׁפֵט [t] וְ pref. id. / [u] הַשֹּׁפֵט pref. הַ)(Kal part. act. sing. masc. dec. 7b . . . שפט

הַשֹּׁפְטִים [x] וְ pref. הַ)(id. pl., absolute state . . שפט
[y] הַשְׁפִּיל Hiph. inf. construct . . . . שפל
[z] הִשְׁפִּיל [a] וְ id. pret. 3 pers. sing. masc . . שפל
[b] הַשְׁפִּילֵהוּ וְ id. imp. sing. masc., suff. 3 pers. sing. m. שפל
[c] הַשְׁפִּילוּ id. imp. pl. masc. . . . . שפל
[d] הִשְׁפִּילוּ id. pret. 3 pers. pl. . . . . שפל
[e] הִשָּׁפֵךְ Niph. inf. construct. . . . . שפך
[f] הַשֹּׁפְכִים pref. הַ)(Kal part. act. m., pl. of שֹׁפֵךְ d. 7b שפך
[g] הַשְּׁפָלָה pref. id.)(adj. masc. sing. with paragogic ה, from שָׁפָל dec. 4a . . . שפל
הַשְּׁפֵלָה וְ pref. id.)(noun fem. sing. dec. 10 . שפל
[h] הַשְׁפֵּלְתְּ Aph. pret. 2 pers. sing. masc. (§ 47. rem. 4) שפל
[i] הִשְׁפַּלְתִּי Hiph. pret. 1 pers. sing. . . . שפל
הַשִּׁפְמִי pref. הַ)(gent. noun from שְׁפָם . . שפה
הַשָּׁפָן pref. id.)(noun masc. sing., pl. שְׁפַנִּים dec. 8a (§ 37. Nos. 2 & 3) . . . שפן
הַשֹּׁפָר pref. id.)(noun masc. sing. dec. 2b . שפר
[k] הַשְּׂפָתַיִם וְ pref. id.)(noun masc., du. of [שָׂפָת] dec. 8a (§ 37. rem. 2 & 3) . . . שפת
הַשַּׂק pref. id.)(noun masc. sing. dec. 8d . שקק
[l] הַשָּׁקֵד pref. id.)(noun masc. sing. dec. 5a . שקד
הִשְׁקָה וְ Hiph. pret. 3 pers. sing. masc. . . שקה
[m] הִשְׁקָהּ וְ id. id., suff. 3 pers. s. fem. (§ 24. rem. 21) שקה
[n] הַשְׁקֵהוּ id. imp. sing. masc., suff. 3 pers. sing. masc. שקה
[o] הַשְׁקוּ id. imp. pl. masc. . . . . שקה
[p] הִשְׁקוּ וְ id. pret. 3 pers. pl. . . . . שקה
[q] הַשִּׁקּוּץ pref. הַ)(noun masc. sing. dec. 1b . שקץ
[r] הַשִּׁקּוּצִים pref. id.)(id. pl., absolute state . . שקץ
[s] הַשְׁקוֹת וְ Hiph. inf. constr. . . . . שקה
הַשְׁקֵט [t] וְ Hiph. inf. (§ 11. rem. 2), or imp. sing. m. שקט
[u] הַשֹּׁקְטִים pref. הַ)(Kal part. act. m., pl. of שֹׁקֵט d. 7b שקט
[x] הַשֹּׁקַיִם pref. id.)(noun fem. with du. masc. term. from שׁוֹק dec. 1a . . . . שוק
[y] הִשְׁקִינוּ וְ Hiph. pret. 1 pers. sing. (§ 24. rem. 14) . שקה
הַשְׁקִינִי id. imp. sing. fem. . . . . שקה
הִשְׁקִיף Hiph. pret. 3 pers. sing. masc. . . שקף
[z] הַשְׁקִיפָה id. imp. sing. m. with parag. ה (§ 11. r. 5) שקף
הִשְׁקִיתָ וְ / [a] הִשְׁקִיתָה וְ Hiph. pret. 1 p. s. (§ 24. r. 14, & § 8. r. 5); acc. shifted by וְ conv. (comp. § 8. r. 7) שקה
[b] הִשְׁקִיתִי וְ id. pret. 1 pers. sing. . . שקה
[c] הִשְׁקִיתִים וְ id. id., suff. 3 pers. pl. masc. (§ 24. r. 14) שקה
[d] הִשְׁקִיתָנוּ id. pret. 2 pers. s. m., suff. 1 pers. s. (v. id.) שקה
הַשָּׁקֶל / [e] וְהַשָּׁקֶל pref. הַ)(noun masc. sing. dec. 6a (§ 35. rem. 2, but pl. c. שִׁקְלֵי) . . שקל
[f] הַשִּׁקְמִים וְ pref. id.)(noun fem. with pl. masc. term. [from שִׁקְמָה] . . . שקם

[a] De. 21.16, 17. [b] De. 21.15. [c] Ge. 41.32. [d] 1 Sa. 2.13. [e] 2 Sa. 16.19. [f] De. 14.7. [g] Ps. 39.14. [h] Is. 6.10. [i] Le. 16.10. [k] Le. 16.7, 8. [l] Ge. 18.4. [m] 2 Sa. 18.26. [n] De. 25.7. [o] Ju. 20.16. [p] Ex. 9.31. [q] Je. 29.17. [r] Ps. 79.10. [s] Ne. 3.13. [t] Mi. 7.3. [u] Ge. 18.25. [x] De. 19.17. [y] Eze. 21.31. [z] Is. 25.12. [a] Is. 25.11. [b] Job 40.11. [c] Je. 13.18. [d] Job 22.29. [e] Eze. 16.36. [f] La. 4.13. [g] Eze. 21.31. [h] Da. 5.22. [i] Eze. 17.24. [k] Eze. 40.43. [l] Ec. 12.5. [m] Nu. 5.27. [n] Pr. 25.21. [o] Ge. 29.7. [p] Ge. 29.3. [q] Da. 11.31. [r] 2 Ch. 15.8. [s] Est. 1.7. [t] Is. 7.4. [u] Eze. 38.11. [x] De. 28.35. [y] Ge. 29.8. [z] De. 26.15. [a] Je. 25.15. [b] Eze. 32.6. [c] Je. 9.14. [d] Ps. 60.5. [e] Eze. 45.12. [f] 1 Ch. 27.28.

הַשֶּׁ֫קֶץ[pp] וְ pref. הַ)(noun masc. sing. . . . שקץ

הַשִּׁקֻּצִים defect. for הַשִּׁקּוּצִים (q. v.) . . שקץ

הַשֶּׁ֫קֶר / הַשָּׁ֫קֶר[b] } pref. הַ)(noun masc. sing. dec. 6a (§ 35. rem. 5, but pl. & suff. שִׁקְרֵיהֶם) . } שקר

הַשֹּׁ֫קֶת[c] pref. id.)(n. f. s., pl. שְׁקָתוֹת (§ 35. r. 9 note) שקה

הִשְׁקְתָה[d] Hiph. pret. 3 p. s. f. [for הִשְׁקָתָה comp. § 8. r. 7] שקה

הִשְׁקִתֶם וְ defect. for הִשְׁקִיתֶם (q. v.) . . שקה

הַשּׁוּר / הַשֹּׁר } pref. הַ)(noun masc. sing. dec. 8 (§ 37. rem. 7) . . . } שור

הַשָּׁרָב[f] pref. id.)(noun masc. sing. . . . שרב

הַשַּׁרְבִיט pref. id.)(noun masc. sing. . . שבט

הַשְּׂרִגִים[h] pref. id.)(noun masc. pl. of [שָׂרִיג] dec. 1b שרג

הַשָּׂרִיד pref. id.)(noun masc. sing. . . שרד

הַשָּׁרוֹן וְ' pref. id.)(pr. name of a region . ישר

הַשָּׁרוֹנִי pref. id.)(gent. noun from the preceding . ישר

הַשִּׁרְיוֹן[i] pref. id.)(noun masc. sing. dec. 1b שרה

הַשָּׁרוֹת[k] וְ pref. id.)(Kal part. act. fem., pl. [שָׁרָה] dec. 10, from שָׁר masc. . . שיר

הַשֵּׁרוֹת[l] וְ pref. id.)(noun fem., pl. of [שֵׁרָה] dec. 10. שרר

הַשְּׂרִידִים[m] וְ pref. id.)(noun masc., pl. of שָׂרִיד dec. 3a שרד

הַשָּׁרִים[n] pref. id.)(Kal part. act. m., pl. of שָׁר d. 1a שיר

הַשָּׂרִים וְ' pref. id.)(noun m., pl. of שַׂר d. 8 (§ 37. r. 7) שרר

הַשִּׁרְיָן pref. id.)(noun masc. sing. . . . שרה

הַשִּׁרְיֹנִים וְ pref. id.)(noun masc., pl. of שִׁרְיוֹן dec. 1b שרה

הַשְּׁרֵמוֹת pref. id.)(Kheth.; K. שְׁדֵמוֹת' noun fem., pl. of שְׁדֵמָה dec. 11 (§ 42. rem. 4) . . שדם

הַשֹּׂרֵף וְ pref. id.)(Kal part. act. sing. masc. d. 7b שרף

הַשְּׂרֵפָה pref. id.)(noun fem. sing. dec. 10. . שרף

הַשְּׂרָפִים pref. id.)(noun masc., pl. of שָׂרָף dec. 4a שרף

הַשְּׂרֻפִים[q] pref. id.)(Kal part. p. m. pl. of [שָׂרוּף] d. 3a שרף

הַשֶּׁ֫רֶץ[r] / הַשָּׁ֫רֶץ } pref. id.)(noun masc. sing. (§ 35. rem. 2) שרץ

הַשֹּׁרֵץ pref. id.)(Kal part. act. sing. masc. . שרץ

הַשֹּׁרֶ֫צֶת[s] pref. id.)(id. fem. (§ 8. rem. 19) . שרץ

הַשָּׁרֵת[t] pref. id.)(noun masc. sing. . . שרת

הַשֵּׁשׁ pref. id.)(noun masc. sing. . . . שוש

הַשִּׁשָּׁה[u] pref. id.)(num. card. masc. sing. from שֵׁשׁ f. שש

הַשִּׁשִּׁי וְ'[x] pref. id.)(adj. ord. masc. from שֵׁשׁ . שש

הַשִּׁשִּׁית pref. id.)(id. fem. . . . . שש

הַשָּׁתוֹת[y] pref. id.)(n. m. with pl. f. term. fr. [שָׁת] d. 1a שות

הִשְׁתַּחֲוָה[z] וְ [for הִתְשׁ' § 12. r. 3] Hithpalel pret. 3 pers. s. m., 3rd. rad. doubled for חָוָה' (§ 24. r. 25) שחה

הִשְׁתַּחֲווּ וְ' id. pret. 3 pers. pl., or, imp. pl. masc. שחה

הִשְׁתַּחֲוִי[a] וְ id. imp. sing. fem. . . . . שחה

הִשְׁתַּחֲוִיתָ וְ id. pret. 2 pers. sing. masc. . . שחה

הִשְׁתַּחֲוֵיתִי[b] וְ' id. pret. 1 pers. sing. . . . שחה

הִשְׁתַּחֲוִיתֶם וְ id. pret. 2 pers. pl. masc. . . . שחה

הַשְּׁתִי[c] pref. הַ)(noun masc. sing. . . . שתה

הַשְּׁתִיָּה[d] וְ pref. id.)(noun fem. sing. . . . שתה

הַשֹּׁתִים pref. id.)(Kal part. act. m., pl. of שֹׁתֶה d. 9a שתה

הִשְׁתַּכַּח[e] וְ' Ch. Ithp. [for הִתְשׁ' § 12. r. 3, for אִתְשְׁ' § 47. rem. 4] pret. 3 p. s. m. (§ 48. r. 4) שכח

הִשְׁתַּכַּחַת Ch. id. pret. 3 pers. sing. fem. . . שכח

הִשְׁתַּכַּחְתָּ[f] וְ id. pret. 2 pers. sing. masc. . . שכח

הַשֻּׁתַלְחִי pref. הַ)(patronym. of שׁוּתֶלַח (q. v.)

הִשְׁתַּנֵּית[g] וְ [for הִתְשׁ' § 12. r. 3] Hithpa. pret. 2 p. s. f. שנה

הִשְׁתַּעַשְׁעוּ[h] [for הִתְשׁ' § 12. rem. 3] Hithpalp. imp. pl. masc. (§ 6. No. 4) . . . שעה

הִשְׁתָּרֵר[i] [for הִתְשָׂרֵר § 12. rem. 3] Hithpa. inf. abs. שרר

הַתָּא[k] וְ' pref. הַ)(noun masc. sing. dec. 1a . תוה

הִתְאַבֵּל[m] Hithpa. pret. 3 pers. sing. masc. . אבל

הִתְאַבְּלִי[n] id. imp. sing. fem. . . . . אבל

הַתַּאֲוָה pref. הַ)(pr. name, see קִבְרוֹת הַתַּ' . קבר

הִתְאַוָּה[o] Hithpa. pret. 3 pers. sing. masc. . . אוה

הִתְאַוּוּ[p] id. pret. 3 pers. pl. . . . אוה

הִתְאַוֵּיתִי[q] id. pret. 1 pers. sing. . . . אוה

הִתְאַוִּיתֶם[r] וְ id. pret. 2 pers. pl. masc. (§ 24. rem. 14) אוה

הַתָּאוֹת[s] pref. הַ)(n. m. with pl. f. term. for תָּא d. 1a תוה

הִתְאַזָּר[t] Hiph. pret. 3 p. s. m. [for הִתְאַזֵּר § 12. r. 1] אזר

הִתְאַזְּרוּ[u] id. imp. pl. masc. . . . . אזר

הִתְאַחֲדִי[x] Hithpa. imp. sing. fem., (§ 14. rem. 1) . אחד

הַתָּאִים[y] pref. הַ)(noun masc., pl. of תָּא dec. 1a תוה

הֲתַאֲמִין[z] pref. הֲ)(Hiph. fut. 2 pers. sing. masc. . אמן

הִתְאַמֵּץ Hithpa. pret. 3 pers. sing. masc. . . אמץ

הַתְּאֵנָה וְ' pref. הַ)(noun fem. sing. dec. 10. . תאן

הַתְּאֵנִים pref. id.)(id. pl., absolute state . תאן

הִתְאַנַּף Hithpa. pret. 3 pers. sing. masc. . . אנף

הִתְאַפְּקוּ[a] Hithpa. pret. 3 p. pl. m. [for אַפְּקוּ' § 12. r. 1] אפק

הִתְאֹשָׁשׁוּ[b] וְ Hithpal. imp. pl. m. [for אֹשְׁשׁוּ' § 21. r. 20] איש

הִתְבָּאֲשׁוּ[c] Hithpa. pret. 3 pers. pl. . . . באש

הַתֵּבָה pref. הַ)(noun fem. sing. dec. 10. . תבה

הֲתָבוֹא[d] pref. הֲ)(Kal fut. 3 pers. sing. fem. . . בוא

הַתְּבוּאָה[e] pref. הַ)(noun fem. sing. dec. 10. . בוא

הַתְּבוּנָה[f] pref. id.)(noun fem. sing. d. 10. R. בּוּן, see בין

הִתְבּוֹנָן[g] Hithpal. pret. 3 pers. sing. masc., [for בּוֹנֵן' § 21. rem. 20] R. בון or . בין

הִתְבּוֹנֵן[h] וְ id. imp. sing. masc. . . . בין

הִתְבּוֹנָנוּ[i] id. pret. 3 pers. pl. [for בּוֹנְנוּ' § 21. rem. 20] בין

הִתְבּוֹנְנוּ[k] וְ' id. imp. pl. masc. . . . . בין

הִתְבּוֹנַנְתָּ[l] וְ id. pret. 2 pers. sing. masc. . . בין

הֲתִבְטַח[m] pref. הֲ)(Kal fut. 2 pers. sing. masc. . בטח

הַתֶּ֫בֶן[o] וְ'[p] pref. הַ)(noun masc. sing. . . . תבן

---

[a] 2 Ki. 23. 24. [b] Je. 7. 4. [c] Ge. 24. 20. [d] Ge. 24. 46. [e] Je. 23. 15. [f] Is. 35. 7. [g] Est. 5. 2.
[h] Ge. 40. 12. [i] 1 Sa. 17. 5. [k] 2 Ch. 35. 25. [l] Is. 3. 19. [m] Jos. 10. 20. [n] 2 Ch. 35. 25. [o] Ne. 4. 10.
[p] Je. 31. 40. [q] Nu. 17. 4. [r] Le. 11. 31. [s] Le. 11. 46. [t] Nu. 4. 12. [u] Ex. 28. 10. [x] 2 Sa. 3. 5.
[y] Ps. 11. 3. [z] Eze. 46. 2. [a] Ps. 45. 12. [b] 2 Sa. 16. 4. [c] Le. 13. 52, 56, 58, 59. [d] Est. 1. 8.
[e] Ezr. 6. 2. [f] Da. 5. 27. [g] 1 Ki. 14. 2. [h] Is. 29. 9. [i] Nu. 16. 13. [k] Eze. 40. 13. [l] Eze. 40. 7, 12.
[m] 1 Sa. 15. 35. [n] 2 Sa. 14. 2. [o] Pr. 21. 26. [p] Nu. 11. 4. [q] Je. 17. 16. [r] Nu. 34. 10. [s] Eze. 40. 12.
[t] Ps. 93. 1. [u] Is. 8. 9. [x] Eze. 21. 21. [y] Eze. 40. 7, 16. [z] Job 39. 12. [a] Is. 63. 15. [b] Is. 46. 8.
[c] 1 Ch. 19. 6. [d] 2 Sa. 24. 13. [e] Le. 25. 21, 22. [f] 1 Ki. 7. 14. [g] Is. 1. 3. [h] Job 37. 14. [i] Is. 52. 15.
[k] Je. 9. 16. [l] Je. 2. 10. [m] Ps. 37. 10. [n] Job 39. 11. [o] Ex. 5. 13. [p] 1 Ki. 5. 8. [pp] Is. 66. 17.

הַתַּבְנִית[a] pref. הַ)(noun fem. sing. dec. 1b . . . בנה

הִתְבּוֹנַנְתָּ[b] Hithpal. pret. 2 pers. sing. masc., R. בון or בין

הִתְבַּקְּעוּ[c] Hithpa. pret. 3 pers. pl. [for בִּקְּעוּ § 12. r. 1] בקע

הִתְבָּרֵךְ[d] וְ Hithpa. pret. 3 pers. sing. masc. . . ברך

הִתְבָּרְכוּ[e] וְ / הִתְבָּרֲכוּ[f] וְ } id. pret. 3 pers. pl. . . . ברך

הִתְגַּדִּלְתִּי[g] וְ Hithpa. pret. 1 pers. sing. . . . גדל

הִתְגְּזֶרֶת[h] Ch. Ithpe. pret. 3 pers. sing. fem. (§47. rem. 4, & § 49. rem. 1) . . . . גזר

הִתְגַּלְגָּלוּ[i] Hithpalp. (§ 6. No. 4) pret. 3 pers. pl. [for גִּלְגְּלוּ comp. § 12. rem. 1] . . גלל

הִתְגַּלָּה[k] וְ Hithpa. pret. 3 pers. sing. masc. [for גִּלָּה § 12. rem. 1] . . . . . גלה

הִתְגַּלֹּתוֹ[l] id. inf. [fr. הִתְגַּלֵּה], suff. 3 pers. sing. m. גלה

הִתְגַּלַּע[m] Hithpa. inf. constr. . . . . גלע

הִתְגֹּעֲשׁוּ[n] וְ Hithpo. pret. 3 pers. pl. . . . געש

הִתְגָּר[o] וְ Hithpa. imp. sing. masc., ap. [for גָּרֵה § 24. rem. 12] . . . גרה

הִתְגָּרִית[p] id. pret. 2 pers. sing. fem. . . . גרה

הֲתֵדַע[q] pref. הֲ)(Kal fut. 2 pers. sing. masc. ידע

הַתֹּהוּ[r] pref. הַ)(noun masc. sing. . . . תהה

הִתְהַלֵּךְ וְ Hithpa. pret. 3 pers. sing. m., or imp. m. הלך

הִתְהַלֶּךְ־ id. pret. 3 pers. sing. masc. (§ 12. rem. 4) הלך

הִתְהַלְּכוּ וְ id. pret. 3 pers. pl., or imp. pl. masc. הלך

הִתְהַלַּכְנוּ id. pret. 1 pers. pl. . . . . הלך

הִתְהַלַּכְתָּ id. pret. 2 pers. sing. masc. [for הִלַּכְתָּ comp. § 8. rem. 7] . . . . הלך

הִתְהַלָּכְתִּי[s] / הִתְהַלַּכְתִּי[t] וְ } id. pret. 1 pers. sing. (comp. id.) . הלך

הִתְהַלְלוּ Hithpa. imp. pl. masc. [for הַלְלוּ § 10. r. 7] הלל

הִתְהֹלָלוּ[u] וְ Hithpo. pret. 3 pers. pl. [for הֹלְלוּ comp. § 8. rem. 7, & § 12. rem. 1] הלל

הִתְהֹלְלוּ[x] וְ id. imp. masc., or pret. 3 pers. pl. . הלל

הַתָּו[y] pref. הַ)(noun m. s. [for תָּוֶה], with suff. תָּוִי תוה

הַתּוֹדָה[z] וְ[a] pref. id.)(noun fem. sing. dec. 10. . ידה

הִתְוַדָּה וְ Hithpa. pret. 3 pers. s. m. (§ 20. No. 1) ידה

הִתְוַדּוּ וְ id. pret. 3 pers. pl. . . . ידה

הַתּוֹדֹת[b] pref. הַ)(noun fem., pl. of תּוֹדָה dec. 10. ידה

הִתְווּ[c] Hiph. pret. 3 pers. pl. . . . תוה

הִתְוִיתָ[d] וְ id. pret. 2 pers. sing. masc. (§ 24. rem. 14) תוה

הַתָּוֶךְ pref. הַ)(noun masc. sing. dec. 6g . תוך

הַתּוֹלָעִי pref. id.)(patronym. of תּוֹלָע . . תלע

הַתּוֹלַעַת[e] / הַתֹּלַעַת[f] } pref. id.)(noun fem. sing., (suff. תּוֹלַעְתָּם) dec. 13a . . . . } תלע

הַתּוֹעֵבָה pref. id.)(noun fem. sing. dec. 11b . תעב

הַתּוֹעֵבוֹת / הַתּוֹעֵבֹת } pref. id.)(id. pl., absolute state . תעב

הַתּוֹעֲבֹת[g] pref. id.)(id. pl., constr. state . . תעב

הַתּוֹקֵעַ[h] וְ pref. הַ)(Kal part. act. sing. masc. d. 7b תקע

הַתּוֹר[i] pref. id.)(noun masc. sing. dec. 1a . תור

הֲתוֹרִדֵנִי[k] pref. הֲ)(Hiph. fut. 2 pers. sing. masc., suff. 1 pers. sing. . . . . ירד

הַתּוֹרָה וְ' pref. הַ')(noun fem. sing. dec. 10. . ירה

הַתּוֹרֹת[l] וְ'[m] pref. id.)(id. pl. . . . ירה

הַתּוֹשָׁבִים[n] pref. id.)(noun masc., pl. of תּוֹשָׁב dec. 1b except constr. תּוֹשַׁב (§ 31. rem. 1) . ישב

הֵתַז[o] Hiph. pret. 3 pers. sing. masc. [for הֵתֵז § 8. rem. 10] as if fr. תזז, see . תיז

הִתְחַבְּאוּ[p] Hithpa. pret. 3 pers. pl. . . . חבא

הִתְחַבְּרוּת[q] (prop. Hithp. inf.) subst. fem. sing. . חבר

הִתְחוֹלֵל[r] וְ Hithp. imp. sing. masc. . . . חול

הִתְחַזֵּק Hithpa. pret. 3 pers. sing. masc., or imp. masc. (§ 12. rem. 1) . . . חזק

הִתְחַזְּקוּ[s] id. imp. pl. masc. . . . . חזק

הִתְחַזַּקְתִּי id. pret. 1 pers. sing. . . . חזק

הִתְחַזַּקְתֶּם[t] וְ id. pret. 2 pers. pl. masc. . . חזק

הֲתִחְיֶינָה[u] pref. הֲ)(Kal fut. 3 pers. pl. fem. . חיה

הִתְחָל[x] וְ Hithpa. imp. s. m. ap. [for חַלֵּה § 24. r. 12] חלה

הַתְּחִלָּה[y] pref. הַ)(noun fem. sing. dec. 10. . חלל

הִתְחַלְּקוּ[z] וְ Hithpa. pret. 3 pers. pl. . . . חלק

הַתַּחְמָס pref. הַ)(noun masc. sing. . . . חמס

הַתַּחֲנִי pref. id.)(patronym. of תַּחַן . . . חנה

הַתְּחִנָּה[a] וְ pref. id.)(noun fem. sing. dec. 10. . חנן

הִתְחַנְּנוּ וְ Hithpa. pret. 3 pers. pl. . . . חנן

הִתְחַנַּנְתָּה[b] id. pret. 2 pers. sing. masc. (§ 8. rem. 5) חנן

הִתְחַנַּנְתִּי[c] id. pret. 1 pers. sing. . . . חנן

הִתְחַפֵּשׂ Hithpa. pret. 3 pers. sing. masc., or imp. m. חפש

הִתְחָרַךְ[d] Ch. Ithpa. pret. 3 pers. sing. m. (§ 47. r. 4) חרך

הַתַּחַשׁ[e] pref. הַ)(noun masc. sing. dec. 6d . תחש

הַתְּחָשִׁים[f] pref. id.)(id. pl. absolute state . . תחש

הַתַּחַת pref. הַ)(adv. . . . . . תוח

הַתַּחְתּוֹן[g] pref. הַ)(adj. masc. sing. . . . תוח

הַתַּחְתּוֹנָה pref. id.)(id. fem., dec. 10. . . תוח

הִתְחַתֵּן[h] Hithpa. inf., or imp. sing. masc. . חתן

הִתְחַתְּנוּ[i] וְ id. imp. pl. masc. . . . חתן

הִתְחַתַּנְתֶּם[k] וְ id. pret. 2 pers. pl. masc. . . חתן

הֲתִיב[l] Ch. Aph. pret. 3 pers. sing. m. (§ 47. r. 4) תוב

הֲתִיבוּנָא[m] Ch. id. pret. 1 pers. pl. . . . תוב

הֵתָיוּ[n] Hiph. imp. masc. pl. [for הֵאֱתָיוּ § 25. No. 2c, & § 24. rem. 5] . . . אתה

---

[a] 1 Ch. 28. 19. [b] Job 38. 18. [c] Jos. 9. 13. [d] De. 29. 18. [e] Ge. 22. 18. [f] Ge. 26. 4; Je. 4. 2. [g] Eze. 38. 23. [h] Da. 2. 34. [i] Job 30. 14. [k] Le. 13. 33. [l] Nu. 6. 19. [m] Pr. 17. 14. [n] Je. 25. 16. [o] De. 2. 24. [p] Je. 50. 24. [q] Job 37. 15, 16. [r] 1 Sa. 12. 21. [s] Jos. 18. 8. [t] Ps. 35. 14. [u] Je. 25. 16. [x] Je. 46. 9. [y] Eze. 9. 6. [z] Le. 7. 12. [a] Ne. 12. 38. [b] Ne. 12. 40. [c] Ps. 78. 41. [d] Eze. 9. 4. [e] Le. 14. 52. [f] Le. 14. 6, 51. [g] 1 Ki. 14. 24. [h] Ne. 4. 12. [i] Ca. 2. 12. [k] 1 Sa. 30. 15. [l] Ex. 18. 20. [m] Le. 26. 46. [n] Le. 25. 45. [o] Is. 18. 5. [p] 1 Sa. 14. 11. [q] Da. 11. 23. [r] Ps. 37. 7. [s] 1 Sa. 4. 9. [t] Nu. 13. 20. [u] Eze. 37. 3. [x] 2 Sa. 13. 5. [y] Ne. 11. 17. [z] Jos. 18. 5. [a] 1 Ki. 8. 54. [b] 1 Ki. 9. 3. [c] 1 Ki. 8. 59. [d] Da. 3. 27. [e] Nu. 4. 25. [f] Ex. 39. 34. [g] 1 Ch. 7. 24; 2 Ch. 8. 5. [h] 1 Sa. 18. 22, 23. [i] Ge. 34. 9. [k] Jos. 23. 12. [l] Da. 2. 14. [m] Ezr. 5. 11. [n] Is. 21. 14; Je. 12. 9.

הִתְיַחֵשׂ Hithpa. inf. constr. used as a noun (§ 14. r. 1) יחש
הִתְיַחְשׂוּ id. pret. 3 pers. pl. . . . . יחש
הִתְיַחְשָׂם וְ id. inf., suff. 3 pers. plur. masc. dec. 7 b יחש
[a] הֲתֵיטְבִי pref. הֲ)(Kal fut. 2 pers. s. m. (§ 20. r. 14) יטב
[b] הִתִּיכוּ Hiph. pret. 3 pers. pl. . . . נתך
[c] הַתִּיכוֹן pref. הַ)(adj. masc. sing. . . . תוך
[e] הַתִּיכוֹנָה וְ' pref. id.)(id. fem. dec. 10. . . תוך
[f] הַתִּיכֹן defect. for 'כוֹן (q. v.) . . . תוך
הַתִּיכֹנָה defect. for הַתִּיכוֹנָה (q. v.) . . . תוך
[g] הַתֵּימָן pref. הַ)(noun masc. sing. . . . ימן
הַתֵּימָנִי pref. id.)(patronym. of תֵּימָן . . ימן
הִתְיַצֵּב וְ' Hithpa. imp. sing. masc. . . . יצב
הִתְיַצְּבָה id. id. with parag. ה [for 'יַצֵּבָה comp. § 8. rem. 7, & § 12. rem. 1] . . . יצב
הִתְיַצְּבוּ וְ' id. pret. 3 pers. pl., or imp. pl. masc. יצב
הַתִּיצִי pref. הַ)(gent. noun fr. תִּיץ q. v.
[i] הַתִּיקֵנוּ Hiph. inf., suff. 1 pers. pl. dec. 1 b נתק
הַתִּירוֹשׁ וְ' pref. הַ)(noun masc. sing. dec. 1 b . ירש
הַתְּיָשִׁים pref. id.)(noun masc., pl. of תַּיִשׁ dec. 6 h (§ 35. rem. 12) . . . . . תיש
הֲתָךְ pr. name of a eunuch at the court of Ahasuerus, Est. 4. 5.
[k] הִתְכַּבֵּד Hithpa. imp. sing. masc. . . . כבד
[l] הִתְכַּבְּדִי id. imp. sing. fem. . . . . כבד
הַתִּכְלֶת pref. הַ)(noun fem. sing. . . . תכל
[m] הִתַּכְתִּי וְ Hiph. pret. 1 pers. sing. m. acc. shifted by וְ conv. (comp. § 8. rem. 7) . . . נתך
[n] הָתֵל Hiph. inf. constr. . . . . תלל
[o] הֵתֶל id. pret. 3 pers. sing. masc.; for הֵתֵל acc. shifted before monos. (בִּי) תלל
הַתְּלָאָה pref. הַ)(noun fem. sing. . . . לאה
[p] הֲתַלְבִּישׁ pref. הֲ)(Hiph. fut. 2 pers. sing. masc. . לבש
[q] הֲתֻלִים noun m., pl. of [הֲתֹל] d. 8 c. (§ 37. Nos. 3 & 4) תלל
הֲתֵלֵךְ pref. הֲ)(Kal fut. 2 pers. sing. masc. . ילך
[r] הֲתֵלְכִי pref. id.)(id. fut. 2 pers. sing. fem. . ילך
[s] הַתֹּלַעַת defect. for הַתּוֹלַעַת (q. v. comp. § 35. r. 2) תלע
[t] הֵתַלְתָּ Hiph. pret. 2 pers. s. m. (comp. § 18. r. 16) תלל
[u] הָתֵם Hiph. imp. sing. masc., or inf. . תמם
[x] הִתְמֹגָגוּ Hithpal. pret. 3 pers. pl. (for 'מוֹגְגוּ comp. § 8. rem. 7, & § 12. rem. 1] . . מוג
[y] הִתַּמְּהוּ וְ Hithpa. imp. pl. masc. [for הִתְתַּמְּהוּ, comp. § 12. rem. 3] . . . . . תמה
הִתְמַהְמְהוּ וְ' Hithpalp. imp. pl. m. (§ 6. No. 4) . מהה
הִתְמַהְמְהָם id. inf. ('מַהְמֵהַּ), suff. 3 pers. pl. m. d. 7 b מהה
הִתְמַהְמָהְנוּ id. pret. 1 p. pl. [for 'מַהְמַהְנוּ comp. § 8. r. 7] מהה

[d] הִתְמַהְמָהְתִּי id. pret. 1 p. s. [for 'מַהְמַהְתִּי comp. id.] מהה
[e] הֲתַמּוּ pref. הֲ)(Kal pret. 3 pers. pl. . . תמם
[f] הֵתַמּוּ Hiph. pret. 3 pers. pl. (§ 18. rem. 10) . תמם
[g] הַתַּמּוּז pref. הַ)(pr. name of an idol see תַּמּוּז
[h] הִתְמוֹטְטָה Hithpal. pret. 3 pers. sing. fem. . מוט
הַתְּמוּרָה pref. הַ)(noun fem. sing. dec. 10. . מור
[i] וַהֲתִמּוֹתִי Hiph. pret. 1 pers. sing.; acc. shifted by וְ, for וְ conv. (comp. § 8. rem. 7) . תמם
הַתָּמִיד pref. הַ)(noun masc. sing. . תמד
הַתָּמִים pref. id.)(noun masc., pl. of תֹּם dec. 8 c . תמם
[k] הִתְמַכֵּר Hithpa. pret. 3 pers. sing. masc. . . מכר
[l] הִתְמַכֶּרְךָ id. inf. ['מַכֵּר], suff. 2 pers. sing. masc. dec. 7 b (comp. § 16. rem. 15, & § 36. rem. 3) . מכר
[m] וְהִתְמַכַּרְתֶּם וְ id. pret. 2 pers. pl. masc. . . מכר
[n] הַתְמַלֵּא pref. הַ interr. for הֲ)(Piel fut. 2 pers. s. m. מלא
[o] הִתְמְלִי Ch. Ithpe. pret. 3 pers. sing. m. (§ 47. r. 4) מלא
[p] הֲתִמְלֹךְ pref. הֲ)(Kal fut. 2 pers. sing. masc. מלך
הַתֵּמָנִי pref. הַ)(patronym. of תֵּימָן . . ימן
הַתִּמְנִי pref. id.)(gent. noun from תִּמְנָה . . מנה
[q] הַתִּמֹּרָה pref. id.)(noun fem. sing. dec. 10. . תמר
[r] הַתִּמֹּרוֹת pref. id.)(id. pl. . . . . תמר
הַתְּמָרִים pref. id.)(noun masc., pl. of תָּמָר dec. 4 a תמר
[s] וְהַתִּמֹּרִים וְ pref. id.)(noun fem. with pl. masc. term. from תִּמֹּרָה dec. 10. . . . תמר
[t] הִתְנַבִּי וְ Chald. Ithpa. pret. 3 pers. s. m. (§ 47. r. 4) נבא
[u] וְהִתְנַבִּיתָ וְ Hithpa. pret. 2 pers. sing. masc. . נבא
[x] הִתְנַגְּשׁוּ Hithpa. imp. masc. pl. . . . . נגש
[y] הִתְנַדֵּב Hithpa. inf. constr. dec. 7 b . . נדב
[z] הִתְנַדַּבוּ Chald. Ithpa. pret. 3 pers. pl. m. (§ 47. rem. 4) נדב
הִתְנַדְּבוּ Hithpa. pret. 3 pers. pl. . . . נדב
[a] הִתְנַדָּבוּת Chald. prop. Ithpa. inf., used as a subst. . נדב
[b] הִתְנַדְּבָם Hithpa. inf. ('נַדֵּב), suff. 3 pers. pl. m. d. 7 b נדב
[c] הִתְנַדַּבְתִּי id. pret. 1 pers. sing. . . . . נדב
[d] הִתְנוּ Hiph. pret. 3 pers. pl. . . . . תנה
[e] וְהִתְנוֹדְדָה וְ Hithpal. pret. 3 pers. sing. fem. . נוד
הַתְּנוּפָה pref. הַ)(noun fem. sing. dec. 10. . נוף
הַתַּנּוּרִים pref. id.)(noun masc., pl. of תַּנּוּר dec. 1 b תנר
[f] הִתְנַחֵל Hithpa. inf. constr. (§ 14. rem. 1) נחל
[g] וְהִתְנַחֲלוּם וְ id. pret. 3 pers. pl., suff. 3 pers. pl. masc. נחל
וְהִתְנַחַלְתֶּם וְ id. pret. 2 pers. pl. masc. . . נחל
[h] הַתַּנִּים pref. הַ)(noun masc. sing., for 'תַּנִּין as several MSS. have it . . . . . תנן
הַתַּנִּין pref. id.)(noun masc. sing. dec. 1 b, also pr. name . . . . . תנן
[i] הַתַּנִּינִם pref. id.)(id. pl., absolute state . . תנן
[k] הִתְנַעֲרִי Hithpa. imp. sing. fem. (§ 14. rem. 1) . נער

[a] Na. 3. 8. [b] 2 Ki. 22. 9. [c] Eze. 47. 16. [d] Ju. 7. 19. [e] 1 Ki. 6. 6. [f] Ex. 26. 28; 36. 33. [g] Zec. 6. 6. [h] Job 33. 5. [i] Jos. 8. 6. [k] Na. 3. 15. [l] Na. 3. 15. [m] Eze. 22. 20. [n] Ex. 8. 25. [o] Ge. 31. 7. [p] Job 39. 19. [q] Job 17. 2. [r] Ge. 24. 58. [s] De. 28. 39. [t] Ju. 16. 10, 13, 15. [u] Eze. 24. 10. [x] Na. 1. 5. [y] Hab. 1. 5. [z] Is. 29. 9. [a] Ju. 19. 8. [b] Ju. 3. 26. [c] Ge. 43. 10. [d] Ps. 119. 60. [e] 1 Sa. 16. 11. [f] 2 Sa. 20. 18. [g] Eze. 8. 14. [h] Is. 24. 19. [i] Eze. 22. 15. [k] 1 Ki. 21. 25. [l] 1 Ki. 21. 20. [m] De. 28. 68. [n] Job 40. 31. [o] Da. 3. 19. [p] Je. 22. 15. [q] Eze. 41. 19, 19. [r] 1 Ki. 6. 32. [s] Eze. 41. 20. [t] Ezr. 5. 1. [u] 1 Sa. 10. 6. [x] Is. 45. 20. [y] Ezr. 1. 6. [z] Ezr. 7. 15. [a] Ezr. 7. 16. [b] 1 Ch. 29. 9. [c] 1 Ch. 29. 17. [d] Ho. 8. 9. [e] Is. 24. 20. [f] Nu. 32. 18. [g] Is. 14. 2. [h] Eze. 29. 3. [i] Ge. 1. 21. [k] Is. 52. 2.

הִתְנַפָּלְתִּי[a] Hithpa. pret. 1 pers. sing. [for 'נִפַּלְתִּי comp. § 8. rem. 7] . . . . . נפל

הִתְנַשֵּׂא[b] Hithpa. inf. constr. . . . . . נשא

וְ הַתִּנְשָׁמֶת / הַתִּנְשֶׁמֶת[c] } pref. הַ ⅹ noun fem. sing. (comp. § 35. rem. 2) . . . . } נשם

הַתֹּעֵבָה[d] pref. id. ⅹ noun fem. sing. dec. 11 b . . תעב

הַתֹּעֵבוֹת pref. id. ⅹ id. pl. absolute (constr. תּוֹעֲבוֹת) תעב

הִתְעַבָּר[e] Hithpa. pret. 3 pers. sing. m. (§ 12. rem. 1) עבר

הִתְעַבַּרְתָּ[f] id. pret. 2 pers. sing. masc. . . . עבר

הִתְעַבְתְּ[g] Hiph. pret. 2 pers. sing. fem. . . . תעב

הִתְעָה[h] Hiph. pret. 3 pers. sing. masc. . . . תעה

הִתְעוּ[i] וְ'[k] id. pret. 3 pers. pl. . . . . תעה

הַתְּעוּדָה[l] pref. הַ ⅹ noun fem. sing. . . . . עוד

הִתְעוּם[m] Hiph. pret. 3 pers. pl., suff. 3 pers. pl. masc. תעה

הֲתָעוּף[n] pref. הֲ ⅹ Kh. 'תָּעוּף Kal fut. 3 pers. sing. fem.; K. 'תָּעִיף Hiph. fut. 2 pers. sing. m. עוף

הִתְעוֹרְרִי[o] Hithpal. imp. sing. fem. . . . . עור

הִתְעַוְּתוּ[p] וְ Hithpa. pret. 3 pers. pl. . . . . עות

הִתְעִיבוּ[q] וְ'[r] Hiph. pret. 3 pers. pl. . . . . תעב

הַתְּעָלָה pref. הַ ⅹ noun fem. sing. dec. 10 (§ 42. r. 2) עלה

הִתְעַלֵּל[s] Hithpa. pret. 3 pers. sing. masc. . . עלל

הִתְעַלְּלוּ וְ id. pret. 3 pers. pl. . . . . . עלל

הִתְעַלַּלְתְּ[t] id. pret. 2 pers. sing. fem. . . . . עלל

הִתְעַלַּלְתִּי[u] id. pret. 1 pers. sing. . . . . . עלל

הִתְעַלַּמְתָּ[x] וְ Hithpa. pret. 2 pers. sing. masc.; acc. shifted by conv. וְ (comp. § 8. rem. 7) עלם

הִתְעַמֶּר־[y] וְ Hithpa. pret. 3 pers. sing. masc. [for 'עִמֵּר § 12. rem. 4] . . . . . . עמר

הִתְעַנַּג[z] וְ Hithpa. imp. sing. masc. (§ 12. rem. 1) ענג

הִתְעַנְּגוּ[a] וְ id. pret. 3 pers. pl. . . . . . ענג

הִתְעַנַּגְתֶּם[b] וְ id. pret. 2 pers. pl. masc. . . . ענג

הִתְעַנָּה[c] Hithpa. pret. 3 pers. sing. masc. . . ענה

הִתְעַנִּי[d] וְ id. imp. sing. fem. . . . . . ענה

הִתְעַנִּיתָ[e] id. pret. 2 pers. sing. masc. . . . ענה

הִתְעָרֵב Hithpa. imp. sing. masc., Milêl bef. monos. [for 'עָרֵב § 12. rem. 4] . . . . ערב

הִתְעָרְבוּ[f] וְ id. pret. 3 pers. sing. . . . . ערב

הַתַּעֲרֻבוֹת pref. הַ ⅹ noun fem., pl. of [תַּעֲרֻבָה] dec. 10. ערב

הִתְעֹרַרְתִּי[g] וְ Hithpal. pret. 1 pers. sing. . . . עור

הִתְעַשְּׁקוּ[h] Hithpa. pret. 3 pers. pl. . . . . עשק

הִתְעַתְּדוּ[i] Hithpa. pret. 3 pers. pl. . . . . עתד

הִתְעֵתֶם[k] Keri 'עֵיתֶם, Hiph. pret. 2 pers. pl. masc. תעה

הַתֹּף[l] pref. הַ ⅹ noun masc. sing. dec. 8 c . . תפף

הִתְפָּאֵר[m] Hithpa. imp. sing. masc. . . . . פאר

הַתִּפְאֶרֶת[n] וְ pref. הַ ⅹ noun fem. sing. dec. 13 a . פאר

הַתַּפּוּחַ[o] pref. id. ⅹ noun masc. sing. dec. 1 b . . פח

הֲתִפּוֹל[p] pref. הֲ ⅹ Kal fut. 3 pers. sing. fem. . . פל

הִתְפּוֹרְרָה[q] Hithpo. pret. 3 pers. sing. fem. . . פרר

הַתְּפִלָּה pref. הַ ⅹ noun fem. sing. dec. 10. . . פלל

הִתְפַּלֵּל וְ' Hithpa. pret. 3 pers. sing. m., or imp. s. m. פלל

הִתְפַּלֶּל־[r] id. imp. with Mak. (§ 12. rem. 4) . . פלל

הִתְפַּלְלוּ[s] וְ' id. imp. pl. m., or pret. comp. 1 Ki. 8. 33. פלל

הִתְפַּלַּלְתָּ id. pret. 2 pers. sing. masc. . . . . פלל

הִתְפַּלַּלְתִּי[t] id. pret. 1 pers. s. ['פִּלַּלְתִּי comp. § 8. r. 7] פלל

הִתְפַּלַּלְתֶּם[u] וְ id. pret. 2 pers. pl. masc. . . . פלל

הִתְפַּלְּשׁוּ[x] וְ Hithpa. imp. pl. masc. . . . . פלש

הִתְפַּלְּשִׁי[y] וְ id. imp. sing. fem. . . . . . פלש

הִתְפַּלָּשְׁתִּי[z] id., Kh. 'לַּשְׁתִּי, pret. 2 pers. sing. fem., K. 'לָּשִׁי in pause for הִתְפַּלְּשִׁי q. v. . . פלש

הָתְפָּקְדוּ Hothpa. pret. 3 pers. pl. [for 'פֻּקְּדוּ § 6. No. 10 note, § 12. rem. 5] . . . . פקד

הִתְפָּקְדוּ[a] Hithpa. pret. 3 p. pl. [for 'פַּקְּדוּ § 12. r. 5] פקד

הִתְפָּרְדוּ[b] וְ Hithpa. pret. 3 pers. pl. . . . . פרד

הִתְפָּרָקוּ[c] / הִתְפָּרְקוּ[d] } Hithpa. pret. 3 pers. pl. (comp. § 8. r. 7, & § 12. rem. 1) . . . . . } פרק

הַתֹּפֶת pref. הַ ⅹ noun fem. sing. . . . . תוף

הִתְפַּתְּחוּ[e] Kh. 'חוּ, Hithpa. imp. pl. masc.; K. 'חִי, s. f. פתח

הֲתָצוּד[f] pref. הֲ ⅹ Kal fut. 2 pers. sing. masc. . צוד

הֲתֹצִיא[g] pref. id. ⅹ Hiph. fut. 2 pers. sing. masc. . צא

הֲתִצְלַח[h] pref. id. ⅹ Kal fut. 3 pers. sing. fem. [for 'תִּצְלַח § 8. rem. 15] . . . . צלח

הֲתַצְלִחַ[i] pref. id. ⅹ Hiph. fut. 3 pers. sing. fem. . צלח

הִתְקַבְּצוּ Hithpa. pret. 3 pers. pl., or imp. pl. masc. קבץ

הִתְקַדְּרוּ[k] Hithp. pret. 3 pers. pl. . . . . קדר

הִתְקַדֶּשׁ־[l] Hithpa. pret. 3 pers. sing. masc. [for 'קַדֵּשׁ § 12. rem. 4] . . . . קדש

הִתְקַדְּשׁוּ / וְ'[m] הִתְקַדָּשׁוּ } id. pret. 3 pers. pl., or imp. pl. masc. (comp. § 8. rem. 7, & § 12. rem. 1) } קדש

הִתְקַדִּשְׁתִּי[n] וְ id. pret. 1 pers. sing.; acc. shifted by וְ conv. (§ 8. rem. 7, & § 12. rem. 2) . קדש

הִתְקַדִּשְׁתֶּם וְ id. pret. 2 pers. pl. masc. (§ 12. rem. 2) . קדש

הַתִּקְוָה[o] pref. הַ ⅹ noun fem. sing. dec. 10. . . קוה

הַתְּקוּעָה[p] pref. id. ⅹ Kal part. pass. s. f. fr. [תָּקוּעַ] m. תקע

הַתְּקוֹעִי pref. id. ⅹ gent. noun from תְּקוֹעַ . . תקע

הַתְּקוֹעִים pref. id. ⅹ id. pl. . . . . . . תקע

הַתְּקוֹעִית pref. id. ⅹ id. sing. fem. . . . . תקע

הִתְקוֹשְׁשׁוּ[q] Hithpo. imp. pl. masc. . . . . קשש

הִתְקַלְקְלוּ[r] Hithpalp. (§ 6. No. 4) pret. 3 pers. pl. [for 'קִלְקְלוּ comp. § 8. rem. 7] . . . קלל

a De. 9. 25. b Eze. 17. 14. c Le. 11. 18. d Je. 44. 4. e Ps. 78. 62. f Ps. 89. 39. g Eze. 16. 52.
h Ho. 4. 12. i Ge. 20. 13. k Is. 19. 13, 14. l Ruth 4. 7. m Je. 50. 6. n Pr. 23. 5. o Is. 51. 17.
p Ec. 12. 3. q Ps. 14. 1. r Ps. 53. 2. s 1 Sa. 6. 6. t Nu. 22. 29. u Ex. 10. 2. x De. 22. 1, 4.
y De. 24. 7. z Ps. 37. 4. a Ps. 37. 11. b Is. 66. 11. c 1 Ki. 2. 26. d Ge. 16. 9. e 1 Ki. 2. 26.
f Ezr. 9. 2. g Job 31. 29. h Ge. 26. 20. i Job 15. 28. k Je. 42. 20. l Ex. 15. 20. m Ex. 8. 5.
n 1 Ch. 29. 11. o Ca. 8. 5. p Am. 3. 5. q Is. 24. 19. r Je. 37. 3. s Je. 29. 7. t 1 Sa. 1. 27.
u Je. 29. 12. x Je. 25. 34. y Je. 6. 26. z Mi. 1. 10. a Ju. 20. 15, 17. b Ps. 22. 15. c Ex. 32. 24.
d Eze. 19. 12. e Is. 52. 2. f Job 38. 39. g Job 38. 32. h Eze. 17. 10. i Ju. 18. 5. k 1 Ki. 18. 45.
l Is. 30. 29. m 2 Ch. 35. 6. n Eze. 38. 23. o Zec. 9. 12. p Is. 22. 25. q Zep. 2. 1. r Je. 4. 24.

הַתְּקֵם[a] Hiph. imp. sing. masc., [הַתִּיק § 11. rem. 5] suff. 3 pers. pl. masc. . . . . נתק

הָתְקְנַת[b] Ch. Hoph. (by Hebraism) pret. 1 pers. sing. [for הָתְקְנֵת] . . . . . . תקן

הַתְּקֹעִי pref. הַ ꞉ gent. noun from תְּקוֹעַ . . . תקע

הַתְּקֹעִים pref. id. ꞉ id. pl. . . . . . . תקע

הַתְּקֹעִית pref. id. ꞉ id. sing. fem. . . . . . תקע

הִתְקַצֵּף[c] וְ Hithpa. pret. 3 pers. sing. masc. (§ 12. r. 1) קצף

הֲתִקְשָׁר־[d] pref. הֲ ꞉ Kal fut. 2 pers. sing. masc. (for תִּקְשֹׁר § 8. rem. 18) . . . . . קשר

הַתְקַשֵּׁר[e] pref. הַ interr. for הֲ ꞉ Piel fut. 2 pers. s. m. קשר

הִתְקַשְּׁרוּ[f] Hithpa. pret. 3 pers. pl. . . . . . קשר

הַתֵּר[g] Hiph. inf. absolute . . . . . . נתר

הִתְרַגֶּזְךָ Hithpa. inf. [הִתְרַגֵּז], suff. 2 pers. sing. masc. dec. 7 b (comp. § 16. rem. 15, & § 36. r. 3) רגז

הַתְּרוּמָה[h] וְ pref. הַ ꞉ noun fem. sing. dec. 10. . . רום

הִתְרוֹמַמְתָּ[i] Ch. Ithpal. pret. 2 pers. sing. masc. . . רום

הַתְּרוּעָה pref. הַ ꞉ noun fem. sing. dec. 10. . . . רוע

הִתְרֹעֲעִי[k] Hithpal. imp. sing. fem. (for רוֹעֲעִי comp. § 8. rem. 7, & § 21. rem. 20) . . . רוע

הִתְרְחִצוּ[l] Ch. Ithpe. pret. 3 pers. pl. m. (§ 47. r. 1 & 4) רחץ

הִתְרָחַצְתִּי[m] Hithpa. pret. 1 pers. sing. . . . . רחץ

הַתָּרִים pref. הַ ꞉ Kal part. act. m., pl. of [תָּר] d. 1 a תור

הֲתָרִים[n] pref. הֲ ꞉ Hiph. fut. 2 pers. sing. masc. . . רום

הַתֹּרִים pref. הַ ꞉ noun masc., pl. of תּוֹר dec. 1 a . תור

הֲתַרְעִישֶׁנּוּ[o] pref. הֲ ꞉ Hiph. fut. 2 pers. sing. masc., suff. 3 pers. sing. masc. . . . . . . רעשׁ

הַתַּרְעֵלָה[p] pref. הַ ꞉ noun fem. sing. . . . . רעל

הִתְרֹעֲעָה[q] Hithpo. pret. 3 pers. sing. fem. . . . רעע

הַתְּרָפִים pref. הַ ꞉ noun masc. pl. . . . . תרף

הִתְרַפִּיתָ[r] Hithpa. pret. 2 pers. sing. masc. (comp. § 24. rem. 14) . . . . . . רפה

הִתְרַפֵּס[s] Hithpa. imp. sing. masc. . . . . רפס

הַתִּרְשָׁתָא pref. הַ ꞉ a title, see תִּרְשָׁתָא

הַתִּשְׁבִּי pref. id. ꞉ gent. noun from תִּשְׁבֶּה . . שבה

הִתְשׁוֹטַטְנָה[t] וְ Hithpal. imp. pl. fem. . . . . שוט

הַתְּשׁוּעָה pref. id. ꞉ noun fem. sing. dec. 10. . . ישע

הֲתַשְׁחִית[u] pref. הֲ ꞉ Hiph. fut. 2 pers. sing. masc. . שחת

הַתְשַׂחֶק־[x] pref. הַ interr. for הֲ ꞉ Piel fut. 2 pers. sing. m. [for תְּשַׂחֵק § 10. r. 14, & § 14. r. 1] שחק

הֲתָשִׂים[y] pref. הֲ ꞉ Kal fut. 2 p. s. m., from שִׂים see שום

הַתְּשִׁיעִי pref. הַ art. ꞉ adj. ord. masc. sing. from תֵּשַׁע תשע

הַתְּשִׁיעִית
הַתְּשִׁיעִת[z] } pref. id. ꞉ id. fem. . . . . . תשע

הֲתִשְׁכַּח pref. הֲ ꞉ Kal fut. 3 pers. sing. fem. . . שכח

הַתְשַׁלַּח[a] pref. הַ interr. for הֲ ꞉ Piel fut. 2 pers. sing. m. שלח

הֲתִשְׁמֹר[b] pref. הֲ ꞉ Kal fut. 2 pers. sing. masc. . . שמר

הַתְּשֻׁעָה[c] defect. for הַתְּשׁוּעָה (q. v.) . . . . ישע

הַתְּשִׁעִי defect. for תְּשִׁיעִי (q. v.) . . . . . תשע

הַתְּשִׁעִית defect. for תְּשִׁיעִית (q. v.) . . . . תשע

הֲתִשְׁפּוֹט
הֲתִשְׁפֹּט[d] } pref. הֲ ꞉ Kal fut. 2 pers. sing. masc. (§ 8. rem. 18) . . . . . } שפט

הָתַת cogn. חָתַת q.v., hence Po. *to break in upon*, תְּהוֹתְתוּ, Ps. 62. 4; Prof. Lee, *to attack unjustly*. Others derive it from הוּת in the sense of *prating*, *talking*.

הֲתִתֵּן[e] pref. הֲ ꞉ Kal fut. 2 pers. sing. masc. . . נתן

הֲתִתְּנֵם pref. id. ꞉ id., suff. 3 pers. pl. masc. . . נתן

ו

וְ, conjunctive or copulative Vav, *and*; וּ before a consonant with simple Sheva, as וּלְכֹל; or before the labials ב, מ, פ, being homogeneous with it in the pronunciation, as וּבֵין ,וּמִן ,וּפַר; וָ sometimes before הָ and חָ, as וָהָיוּ ,וָחָיוּ (comp. § 13. rem. 1 & 13); before יְ, Yod becoming quiescent, as יְהִי, with ו prefixed וִיהִי (for וַיְהִי); וַ ,וֶ ,וָ before the composite Shevas, taking the corresponding short vowel, as וַעֲמֹד, (contr. וַאדֹנִי for וַאֲדֹנִי), וָאֱכֹל ,וָחֳלִי, and sometimes by contraction, as וֵאלֹהִים for וֶאֱלֹהִים (comp. § 13. rem. 2 & 5), וֶהְיֵה for וֶהֱיֵה; וָ (va) immediately before the tone-syllable, but only at the end of a sentence, especially when short words are connected in pairs, as וְקֹר וָחֹם וְקַיִץ וָחֹרֶף וְיוֹם וָלַיְלָה, but on the contrary זֶרַע וְקָצִיר Ge. 8. 22.

As a connective particle, the manner and nature of its connection is to be collected from the series of the discourse. Its principal uses are as follow—I. simply copulative, *and*, *also*, serving to connect words and phrases.—II. adversative, *but*; *yet*; *otherwise*.—III. *for*, *since*, *because*.—IV. eventual, *that*; וַיְהִי—וְ *it came to pass that*.—V. final, *that*, *to the end that*.—VI. concessive, *though*.—VII. *then*, comp. Ge. 3. 5.—VIII. exegetical, *even*, where properly the *relative* may be expressed instead, Ge. 49. 25. מֵאֵל אָבִיךָ וְיַעְזְרֶךָּ *from the God of thy father, even he*, or *who*, *will help thee*; Ps. 68. 10.

[a] Je. 12. 3. [b] Da. 4. 33. [c] Is. 8. 21. [d] Job 39. 10. [e] Job 38. 31. [f] 2 Ch. 24. 25. [g] Is. 58. 6. [h] Mal. 3. 8. [i] Da. 5. 23. [k] Ps. 60. 10. [l] Da. 3. 28. [m] Job 9. 30. [n] Job 38. 34. [o] Job 39. 20. [p] Is. 51. 17, 22. [q] Is. 24. 19. [r] Pr. 24. 10. [s] Pr. 6. 3. [t] Je. 49. 3. [u] Ge. 18. 28. [x] Job 40. 29. [y] Job 40. 26. [z] Le. 25. 22. [a] Job 38. 35. [b] De. 8. 2. [c] 2 Sa. 19. 3. [d] Eze. 22. 2, 2. [e] Job 39. 19.

נַחֲלָתְךָ וְנִלְאָה *thine inheritance even when weary,* or *which is weary;* 1 Sa. 28. 3. בְּרָמָה וּבְעִירוֹ *in Ramah, even in his own city.*—IX. וְ—וְ *both—and; whether—or.*

וַ, before guttural **וָ**, a letter which, prefixed to the forms of the Future, gives to them the sense of the Imperfect; hence called by grammarians *Conversive Vav*, e. g. יִקְטֹל *he will slay,* וַיִּקְטֹל *he slew.* It, nevertheless, frequently includes also the *copulative* power, comp. Ge. 3. 12, she gave me of the tree, וָאֹכֵל *and I did eat.*

NOTE.—*All forms beginning with Vav (the few following excepted) will be found in the alphabetical order of the analysis according to the letter which next follows Vav in each form.*

וְדָן *Vedan*, pr. name of a place in Arabia, Eze. 27. 19. So according to J. D. Michaelis, who judges the letter ו here to be radical, and collated with the Arab., to signify *two rivers;* Spicileg. Geogr. Hebr. p. 247.

וָהֵב (*gift.* Arab. وهب *to give*) *Vaheb*, pr. name of a place, Nu. 21. 14.

[וָו] masc. dec. 1 a, *hook* or *pin*, used for suspending the curtain in the tabernacle.

וָוֵי id. pl., construct state.

וָוֵיהֶם id. pl., suff. 3 pers. pl. masc.

וָוִים id. pl., absolute state, Ex. 38. 28.

וָזַר Root not used; Arab. *to be loaded,* act. *to commit crime;* hence the following:

וָזָר masc. *laden with guilt, guilty,* Pr. 21. 8, see the preceding R.

וַיְזָתָא (*pure* coll. with the Pers.) pr. name of a son of Haman, Est. 9. 9.

וָלַד Root not used; i. q. יָלַד *to bear, to bring forth;* whence the two following:

וָלָד masc. *a child, offspring,* Ge. 11. 30; and וָלֶד id. 2 Sa. 6. 23. Keri . . . . ולד

וַנְיָה pr. name masc. Ezr. 10. 36.

וָפְסִי pr. name masc. Nu. 13. 14.

וַשְׁנִי pr. name masc. 1 Ch. 6. 13.

וַשְׁתִּי (*beauty,* coll. with the Pers.) pr. name of the queen of Ahasuerus.

ז

זְאֵב ז׳ masc. dec. 1 a.—I. *a wolf.*—II. pr. name of a prince of Midian.

זְאֵבֵי[a] id. pl., construct state . . . . זאב

זָאֲנִין[b] Chald. Kh. זָאֲעִין, K. זָיְעִין, Peal part., pl. of [זָאַע or זָיַע] dec. 2 a . . . . זוע

זֹאת ז׳ pron. demon. fem. sing., see . זה

זָב Kal pret. 3 pers. sing. masc. (Le. 15. 2), or part. act. sing. masc. . . . . זוב

זָבַב Root not used; Arab. ذبذب *to rove up and down in the air.*

זְבוּב masc. dec. 1 a, *a fly;* זְבוּבֵי מָוֶת *deadly* (i. e. venomous) *flies.* See also בַּעַל.

[זָבַד] *to give, endow,* Ge. 30. 20.

זֶבֶד masc. *gift, dowry,* Ge. 30. 20.

זָבָד (*gift*) pr. name of several men; for which once יוֹזָכָר comp. 2 Ch. 24. 26, with 2 Ki. 22. 22.

זָבוּד (*given*) pr. name masc. 1 Ki. 4. 5.

זַבּוּד (id.) pr. name masc. Ezr. 8. 14. Khethib.

זְבוּדָּה (id. fem.) pr. name fem. 2 Ki. 23. 36. Keri; Kh. זְבִידָה.

זַבְדִּי (*giver,* for זְבַדְיָה *gift of the Lord,* Gesen.) pr. name of several men; for which once זִמְרִי comp. Jos. 7. 1, with 1 Ch. 2. 6.

זַבְדִּיאֵל (*gift of God*) pr. name masc. Ne. 11. 14.

זְבַדְיָה, זְבַדְיָהוּ (*gift of the Lord*) pr. name of several men.

זָבָד ז׳ pr. name masc. . . . . . זבד

זֶבֶד[c] noun masc. sing. . . . . . זבד

זַבְדִּי וְ׳ זַבְדִּיאֵל, זְבַדְיָה, זְבַדְיָהוּ ,וּ׳ & זְבַדְיָה & וּ׳ pr.n.m. זבד

זְבָדַנִי[d] Kal pret. 3 pers. sing. masc., suff. 1 pers. sing. זבד

זָבָה[e] Kal part. act. fem. dec. 10, from זָב masc. זוב

זָבָהּ[f] defect. for זוֹבָהּ (q. v.) . . . . זוב

זְבוּב pr. name, see בַּעַל זְבוּב.

זְבוּבֵי[g] noun masc. pl. constr. from זְבוּב׳ dec. 1 a זבב

זַבּוּד וְ pr. name masc. . . . . . זבד

---

[a] Zep. 3. 3. [b] Da. 5. 19: 6. 27. [c] Ge. 30. 20. [d] Ge. 30. 20. [e] Le. 15. 19. [f] Le. 15. 19. [g] Ec. 10. 1.

זְבִידָּה[a] Kh. זְבִידָה, K. זְבוּדָּה pr. name fem. . זבד

זְבוּלוּן, וּ׳ זְבוּלֻן } pr. name of a man and a tribe; וּ bef. (:) זבל

זָבַח[a] [b] וְ׳ *to slaughter* or *kill* animals, especially for sacrifice. Pi. *to sacrifice.*

זֶבַח masc. with suff. זִבְחִי dec. 6a (§ 35. rem. 5).—I. prop. *a slaughtering*, meton. *the flesh of slaughtered animals*, i. e. *a repast, banquet.*—II. *sacrifice*; זֶבַח הַיָּמִים *a yearly sacrifice*; זֶבַח מִשְׁפָּחָה *a family sacrifice.*—III. pr. name of a king of Midian.

מִזְבֵּחַ masc. dec. 7c, pl. מִזְבְּחוֹת, *altar.*

זָבַח [c] וְ׳ in pause for זֶבַח (§ 35. rem. 2) q. v.; for וָ see lett. ו . . . . . . זבח

זְבַח[d] Kal imp. sing. masc. . . . זבח

זֶבַח [e] וָ׳, [f] וְ׳ noun masc. sing. (suff. זִבְחִי) dec. 6. (§ 35. rem. 5) also pr. name; for וָ see ו זבח

זְבֹחַ[g] Kal inf. constr. . . . . זבח

זִבַּח[h] Piel pret. 3 pers. sing. masc. . . . זבח

זֹבֵחַ [i] וְ׳ Kal part. act. sing. masc. dec. 7b . זבח

זָבְחוּ וְ id. pret. 3 pers. pl. . . . . זבח

זִבְּחוּ[k], זִבֵּחוּ[l] } Piel pret. 3 pers. pl. (comp. § 8. rem. 7) זבח

זִבְחוֹ[m] noun masc. sing., suff. 3 pers. sing. masc. from זֶבַח dec. 6. (§ 35. rem. 5) . . זבח

זִבְחוּ Kal imp. pl. masc. . . . . זבח

זִבְחֵי noun m. pl. constr. from זֶבַח d. 6. (§ 35. r. 5) זבח

זִבְחִי id. sing., suff. 1 pers. sing. . . . זבח

זֹבְחֵי Kal part. act. m., pl. constr. from זֹבֵחַ dec. 7. זבח

זִבְחֵיהֶם [n] וְ׳ noun masc. pl., suff. 3 pers. pl. masc. from זֶבַח dec. 6. (§ 35. rem. 5) . . זבח

זְבָחֶיךָ [o] וּ׳ id., suff. 2 pers. sing. masc.; וּ bef. (:) זבח

זִבְחֵיכֶם וְ׳ id., suff. 2 pers. pl. masc. . . זבח

זְבָחִים וּ׳ id. pl., absolute state; וּ before (:) . זבח

זֹבְחִים Kal part. act. masc., pl. of זֹבֵחַ dec. 7b . זבח

זְבָחֵימוֹ[p] noun masc. pl., suff. 3 pers. pl. masc. from זֶבַח dec. 6. (§ 35. rem. 5) . . . זבח

זִבְחֲכֶם[uu] id. sing., suff. 2 pers. pl. masc. . . זבח

זְבַחְנוּ[q] וְ Kal pret. 1 pers. pl. . . . . זבח

זָבַחְתָּ וְ id. pret. 2 pers. sing. masc.; acc. shifted by conv. וְ (§ 8. rem. 7) . . . . זבח

זָבַחְתִּי[r] id. pret. 1 pers. sing. . . . . זבח

זְבַחְתֶּם[s] וּ id. pret. 2 pers. pl. masc.; וּ for וְ conv. זבח

זַבַּי pr. name masc. Ezr. 10. 28; Ne. 3. 20. Keri; for which זַכַּי Ezr. 2. 9; Ne. 7. 14.

זְבִינָא pr. name masc. . . . . . זבן

[זָבַל] *to dwell*, Ge. 30. 20. יִזְבְּלֵנִי *shall dwell with me.*

זְבֻל, זְבוּל masc. dec. 1a.—I. *habitation.*—II. pr. name masc. Ju. 9. 28.

זְבֻלוּן, זְבוּלֻן, זְבוּלוּן (*habitation*) pr. name of a son of Jacob and the tribe descended from him. Gen. noun זְבוּלֹנִי.

זְבֻל וּ׳ noun masc. sing. for זְבוּל dec. 1a, also pr. name; וּ before (:) . . . . זבל

זְבֻלָה[yy] id. with parag. ה . . . . . זבל

זְבֻלוּן וּ׳ defect. for זְבוּלוּן (q. v.) . . . זבל

[זְבַן] Chald. *to buy, gain*, Da. 2. 8.

זְבִינָא (*bought*) pr. name masc. Ezr. 10. 43.

זָבְנִין[t] Ch. Peal part. act. masc., pl. of [זָבֵן] dec. 2b זבן

זָבַת Kal part. act. f., constr. of זָבָה d. 10, fr. זָב m. זוב

זָג[u] masc. *the skin of the grape*, Nu. 6. 4, so called from its transparency. זוג Chald. זגג Samar. *to be pure*, from either of which roots it may be derived.

זֵד[x] adj. masc. sing. dec. 1a . . . . זוד

זָדָה[y] Kal pret. 3 pers. sing. fem. . . . זוד

זָדוּ[z] id. pret. 3 pers. pl. masc. . . . . זוד

זָדוֹן noun masc. sing. dec. 3a, as if from זדה, (§ 32. rem. 6) see . . . . . זוד

זְדוֹן id. construct state . . . . . זוד

זֵדִים adj. masc., pl. of זֵד dec. 1a . . . זוד

זְדֹנְךָ[a] noun m. s., suff. 2 pers. s. m. from זָדוֹן (q. v.) זוד

זֶה וְ׳ masc.; fem. זֹאת (for זֹאַת from a masc. זא=זה), rarely זֹה, once זֹאתָה (with demonstr. ה) Je. 26. 6, Kheth.; com. זוּ, & pl. אֵלֶּה, אֵל.—I. pron. demonstr. *this*; when put after the subst. it usually has the article, as הַבַּיִת הַזֶּה *this house*; when put before it without an article, it is usually the predicate of the proposition, זֶה הַדָּבָר *this* (is) *the thing*; זֶה—זֶה *this—that, the one—the other*; זֶה אֶל זֶה *one to the other*, Is. 6. 3.—With emphasis, *this same, very*; Ju. 5. 5. זֶה סִינַי *this very Sinai*, comp. Jos. 9. 12; Ps. 48. 15; 104. 25; also by way of contempt, comp. Ex. 32. 1; 1 Sa. 10. 27;—with the interrogative pronouns, מִי זֶה *who is this?* מַה־זֶּה *what is this? how then?* לָמָּה זֶה *why then?*—II. rarely for the relative, e. g. Ps. 104. 8. מְקוֹם זֶה יָסַדְתָּ *the place which thou hast founded.*—III. adv. of place, *here*; מִזֶּה *hence*; מִזֶּה וּמִזֶּה *hence and thence*; of time, *now*; זֶה פַעֲמַיִם *now twice.*—IV. with prefixes;—בָּזֶה

[a] 1 Ki. 8. 63. [b] 1 Ki. 13. 2. [c] Je. 7. 22. [d] Ps. 50. 14. [e] Je. 17. 26. [f] 2 Ki. 5. 17. [g] 1 Sa. 15. 15. [h] 2 Ch. 33. 22. [i] Mal. 1. 14. [k] Ho. 12. 12. [l] Ps. 106. 38. [m] Le. 7. 16. [n] Is. 56. 7. [o] Is. 43. 23. [p] De. 32. 38. [q] Ex. 8. 23. [r] Eze. 39. 19. [s] Ex. 8. 24. [t] Da. 2. 8. [u] Nu. 6. 4. [uu] Le. 19. 6. [x] Pr. 21. 24. [y] Je. 50. 29. [yy] Hab. 3. 11. [z] Ex. 18. 11. [a] 1 Sa. 17. 28.

in this place, here, comp. No. III; of time, *then* Est. 2. 13; but בָּזֶה (Ec. 7. 18), בְּזֹאת, בָּזֹאת *in, on, by this,* &c., comp. בְּ—; כָּזֶה, כָּזֹאת *like this, such; thus,* and so כָּזֹאת Ge. 45. 23; כָּזֹה וְכָזֶה, כָּזֹאת וְכָזֹאת *thus and thus, so and so;*—לָזֹאת *therefore,* Je. 5. 7; but לְזֹאת *to this, at this,* comp. לְ.

זוּ i. q. זֶה comp. Nos. I, II.

הַלָּזֶה masc. and apocopated הַלָּז com. gen. *this.*

הַלֵּזוּ id. Eze. 36. 35.

זֹה pron. demon. fem. sing. see the preceding.

זָהָב וְ masc. dec. 4a.—I. *gold,* after numerals שֶׁקֶל is to be supplied, עֲשָׂרָה זָהָב *ten* (shekels) *of* gold. —II. metaph. *brightness,* or *fair weather,* Job 37. 22.

זְהַב } id., construct state; וּ before (:) for וּזְהַב זהב
וּזְהַב[a]

זְהָבוֹ id., suff. 3 pers. sing. masc. . . זהב

זְהָבִי[b] וּ id., suff. 1 pers. sing.; וּ before (:) . זהב

זְהָבֵךְ[c] } וּ id., suff. 2 pers. sing. masc.; וּ id. . זהב
זְהָבְךָ[d]

זְהָבָם[e] וּ id., suff. 3 pers. pl. masc.; וּ id. . . זהב

זָהָה Root not used; Arab. *to shine, be bright, beautiful.*

זִיו Chald. masc. (for זְהִיו) dec. 1a, *brightness, splendour;* pl. *healthy complexion,* Da. 5. 6, 9, 10.

זִו. (*beauty,* especially of flowers) name of the second month of the Hebrew year, from the new moon of April to that of May, 1 Ki. 6. 1, 37.

זְהִירִין[f] וּ Chald. Peal part. pass. masc., pl. of [זְהִיר] dec. 1a; וּ before (:) . . . . זהר

זָהַם. Pi. *to loathe, abhor,* Job 33. 20.

זַהַם (*loathing*) pr. name masc. 2 Ch. 11. 19.

זָהַם pr. name masc. [for זַהַם § 35. rem. 2] . זהם

זִהֲמַתּוּ[g] וְ Piel pret. 3 pers. sing. fem., suff. 3 pers. sing. masc. [for זִהֲמַתְהוּ] . . . זהם

זָהַר. Hiph.—I. *to enlighten, to teach.*—II. *to admonish, warn,* with the acc. of the pers., and מִן of thing from which, or the pers. on whose part, one warns.—III. *to shine,* Da. 12. 3. Niph. *to be admonished, to receive admonition.*

זְהַר Chald., part. pass., *admonished, cautioned,* Ezr. 4. 22.

זֹהַר masc. *brightness, splendour.*

זֹהַר[h] noun masc. sing. . . . . זהר

זִו[i] name of a month . . . . זהה

זוֹ[k] pron. demon. fem. sing. . . . זה

זוּ pron. demon. com. gen. sing. . . . זה

[זוּב] I. *to flow.*—II. *to overflow, abound with.*—III. *to waste away, expire,* La. 4. 9.

זוֹב masc. dec. 1a, *flux, issue* of blood, &c.

זוֹב[l] noun masc. sing. dec. 1a . . . זוב

זוֹבָהּ[m] id., suff. 3 pers. sing. fem. . . . זוב

זוֹבוֹ[n] id., suff. 3 pers. sing. masc. . . . זוב

זוֹבֵחַ[o] Kal part. act. sing. masc. dec. 7b . זבח

[זִיד, זוּד] I. *to boil, seethe,* Ge. 25. 29.—II. *to act insolently, proudly, wickedly* against any one, const. with עַל, אֶל. Niph. part. נָזִיד *something sodden, pottage.*

זוּד Chald. Aph. *to act proudly, wickedly,* Da. 5. 20.

זֵד adj. dec. 1a, *proud, haughty.*

זֵידוֹן adj. m. *overflowing, overwhelming,* Ps. 124. 5.

זָדוֹן masc. dec. 3a (as if from זָדָה § 32. rem. 6) *insolence, pride, haughtiness.*

זָוָה Root not used; Arab. זוי *to hide, conceal.*

זָוִית fem. pl. זָוִיּוֹת (§ 39. No. 4. rem. 1) *corner, angle* of a building, &c.

מָזֶו masc. only pl. מְזָוִים (comp. dec. 6) *garners,* Ps. 144. 13.

זִיז זוּז Root not used; Chald. זוז *to move, move about;* hence perhaps *to abound,* comp. שָׁרַץ.

זוּזִים pr. name of a people on the borders of Palestine, Ge. 14. 5.

זִיז masc. *abundance, wealth;* זִיז שָׂדַי *wealth of the field,* for *beasts* pasturing there.

זִיזָא (*abundance*) pr. name of two different men, 1 Ch. 4. 37; 2 Ch. 11. 20.

זִיזָה (id.) pr. name masc. 1 Ch. 23. 11; for which זִינָא in ver. 10.

יָזִיז (*he moves,* or, *motion*) pr. name masc. 1 Ch. 27. 31.

מְזוּזָה fem. dec. 10, *door post,* on which the door moves.

זוֹחֵת pr. name masc. 1 Ch. 4. 20.

[זוּל] *to shake, pour out,* Is. 46. 6.

זוּלָה fem. dec. 10 (prop. *a removing*) constr. זוּלַת as a prep. *besides, except;* with suff. זוּלָתִי *besides me,* &c. with paragogic Yod, זוּלָתִי

---

[a] Ge. 2. 12. [b] Joel 4. 5. [c] 1 Ki. 20. 3, 5. [d] Is. 30. 22. [e] Zep. 1. 18. [f] Ezr. 4. 22. [g] Job 33. 20. [h] Eze. 8. 2. [i] 1 Ki. 6. 1, 37. [k] Ho. 7. 16, & Ps. 132. 12. [l] Le. 15. 25. [m] Le. 15. 26. [n] Le. 15. 2, 3, 33. [o] Is. 66. 3.

[a]זוֹלֵל [b]וְ׳ Kal part. act. sing. masc. dec. 7 b . זלל

[c]זוֹלְלָה id. fem. sing. . . . . . . זול

[d]זוֹלְלִים id. masc. pl., absolute state . . . זלל

[e]זוּלַת prop. noun fem., constr. of [זוּלָה] dec. 10, only as a prep. . . . . . זול

[f]זוּלָתָהּ id., suff. 3 pers. sing. fem. . . . זול

זוּלָתִי id. with paragogic ׳, or suff. 1 pers. sing. זול

זוּלָתְךָ / זוּלָתֶךָ } id., suff. 2 pers. sing. masc. . . זול

זוּן. Hoph. *to be fed, fattened,* Je. 5. 8.

זוּן Chald. Ithpe., or Ittaph. (§ 47. rem. 10) *to be nourished, fed,* Da. 4. 9.

מָזוֹן masc. *food, meat.*

מָזוֹן Chald. masc. id. Da. 4. 9, 18.

זוֹנָה fem. of the following, dec. 10 . . זנה

[g]זוֹנֶה Kal part. act. sing. masc. dec. 9 a . . זנה

[h]זוּנָּה Pual pret. 3 pers. s. m. [for זֻנָּה § 10. r. 5] זנה

[i]זוֹנוֹת Kal part. act. fem., pl. of זוֹנָה (q. v.) . זנה

[זוּעַ]. I. *to move, move oneself,* Est. 5. 9.—II. *to be agitated, to shake,* Ec. 12. 3. Pilp. (§ 6. rem. 4) *to agitate, vex,* Hab. 2. 7.

זוּעַ Ch. *to be moved, to tremble.*

זְוָעָה & transp. זַעֲוָה fem.—I. *agitation, disquiet.* —II. *terror,* Is. 28. 19.

זַעֲוָן (*unquiet*) pr. name of a man.

זִיעַ (*motion*) pr. name masc. 1 Ch. 5. 13.

[k]זְוָעָה noun fem. sing. . . . . . . זוע

זוּף Root not used; prob. i. q. זוּב *to flow.*

זֶפֶת fem. *pitch.*

זִיף (*flux*) pr. name—I. of a town and desert in the tribe of Judah. Gent. noun זִיפִי.—II. of a man, 1 Ch. 4. 16.

[l]זוֹקֵף וְ Kal part. act. sing. masc. . . . זקף

I. **[זוּר]** I. *to press, to press* or *squeeze out.*—II. intrans. *to be pressed out,* Is. 1. 6, זֹרוּ (§ 21. rem. 2), which others take as Pu. of זָרָה to be *sprinkled upon.*

II. **[זוּר]** pret. pl. זָרוּ, and זֹרוּ (Ps. 58. 4. § 21. rem. 2).— I. *to be loathsome* (Arab. זאר *to loathe*) Job 19. 17, *my breath is loathsome* (others, *estranged,* see the following) *to my wife.*—II. (cogn. סוּר) *to turn aside, depart,* hence *to be strange, a stranger;* part. זָר *a stranger, barbarian, enemy;* fem. זָרָה *a strange woman, a harlot.* Niph. *to turn, to recede, fall off,* Is. 1. 4. Hoph. *to become estranged,* Ps. 69. 9.

זָרָא fem. (for זָרָה) *loathsomeness,* Nu. 11. 20.

מָזוֹר masc. dec. 3 a, *compression of a wound by bandages,* meton. for *the wound itself.* In Ob. 7, according to some, *a net,* from the Aram. מְזַר *to spread.*

[m]זוֹרֵחַ Kal part. act. sing. masc. . . . זרח

זוֹרֵעַ Kal part. act. sing. masc. . . . זרע

זָחַח. Niph. *to be removed, displaced,* Ex. 28. 28; 39. 21.

[זָחַל] I. *to creep, crawl.*—II. *to fear,* Job 32. 6.

זֹחֶלֶת only in the pr. name אֶבֶן הַזּ׳ *stone of the serpent,* as would appear from this etymology, but see אֶבֶן

[n]זֹחֲלֵי Kal part. act. pl. c. masc. from [זָחַל] dec. 7 b זחל

[o]זָחַלְתִּי id. pret. 1 pers. sing. . . . . זחל

[p]זִיוֵהּ וְ Chald. noun masc. sing., suff. 3 pers. sing. masc. from [זִיו] dec. 1 . . . . זהה

[q]זִיוֹהִי [r]וְ׳ Chald. id. pl., suff. 3 pers. sing. masc. זהה

[s]זִיוַי וְ Chald. id. pl., suff. 1 pers. sing. . . זהה

[t]זִיוִי וְ Chald. id. sing., suff. 1 pers. sing. . זהה

[u]זִיוָיךְ וְ id. pl., suff. 2 pers. sing. masc. . . זהה

זִיז וְ noun masc. sing. . . . . . זוז

זִיזָא וְ׳ pr. name, masc. . . . . . זוז

זִיזָה וְ pr. name, masc. . . . . . זוז

זִינָא pr. name, masc., see זִיזָא . . . זוז

זִיעַ וְ pr. name, masc. . . . . . זוע

זִיף וְ׳ pr. name of a place . . . . זוף

זִיפָה וְ׳ id. with loc. ה . . . . . זוף

[v]זִיקוֹת noun fem. pl. [for זִנְקוֹת, זְקוֹת] . . זנק

[y]זַיִת / זָיִת } masc. dec. 6 h.—I. *olive-tree;* זֵית שֶׁמֶן *oil-olive;* שֶׁמֶן זַיִת *olive-oil;* הַר הַזֵּיתִים *Mount of Olives,* near Jerusalem.—II. *olive,* the fruit; עֵץ הַזַּיִת *an olive-tree.* The etymology is not defined.

זֵיתָן (Eng. *Oliver*) pr. name masc. 1 Ch. 7. 10.

זֵתָם (id.) pr. name masc. 1 Ch. 23. 8; 26. 22.

[z]זֵית id., construct state . . . . . זית

[a]זֵיתֵיהֶם id. pl., suff. 3 pers. pl. masc. . . . זית

זֵיתֵיכֶם וְ id. pl., suff. 2 pers. pl. masc. . . זית

זֵיתִים וְ׳ id. pl., absolute state . . . . זית

[b]זֵיתְךָ / [c]זֵיתֶךָ } id. sing., suff. 2 pers. sing. masc. . . זית

זֵיתָן וְ pr. name masc. . . . . . זית

---

a De. 21. 20. b Pr. 23. 21. c La. 1. 11. d Pr. 28. 7. e 2 Ki. 24. 14. f 1 Sa. 21. 10. g Ps. 73. 27. h Eze. 16. 34. i Pr. 29. 3. k Is. 28. 19. l Ps. 145. 14. m Ec. 1. 5. n De. 32. 24. o Job 32. 6. p Da. 2. 31. q Da. 5. 6. r Da. 5. 9. s Da. 7. 28. t Da. 4. 33. u Da. 5. 10. v Is. 50. 11. y Ju. 15. 5. z De. 8. 8, etc. a Ne. 5. 11. b De. 24. 20. c De. 28. 40.

[a] ו׳ זַךְ / זָךְ } adj. masc. sing. . . . . זכך

[זָכָה] *to be pure*, in a moral sense. Pi. *to cleanse, purify*. Hithp. הִזַּכָּה (§ 12. rem. 3) *to cleanse oneself*, Is. 1. 16.

זָכוּ Chald. fem. *purity, innocence*, Da. 6. 23.

זַכָּה adj. sing. fem. of זַךְ . . . . . זכך

[b] זָכוּ Chald. noun fem. sing. . . . . . זכה

זַכּוּ Kal pret. 3 pers. pl. . . . . . זכך

[c] זְכוּכִית ו noun fem. sing.; ו before (:) . . . זכך

זָכוֹר Kal inf. absolute, used also as an imp. . זכר

[d] זָכוּר id. part. pass. sing. masc. . . . . זכר

זַכּוּר ו׳ pr. name masc. . . . . . זכר

[e] זְכוֹר id. imp. sing. masc. . . . . . זכר

[f] זְכוּרֵהּ noun masc. sing., suff. 3 pers. sing. fem. from [זָכוּר] dec. 3a . . . . זכר

זְכוּרְךָ id., suff. 2 pers. sing. masc. . . . . זכר

זַכַּי pr. name masc. for זַכַּי . . . . . זכך

זִכִּיתִי Piel. pret. 1 pers. sing. . . . . זכה

[זָכַךְ] *to be clean, clear, pure*, physically and morally. Hiph. *to cleanse*, Job 9. 30.

זַךְ masc. זַכָּה fem. adj. *clean, pure*, physically of things; morally of the heart, *innocent, upright*.

זְכוּכִית fem. *glass* or *crystal*, Job 28. 17.

זַכַּי (*innocent*) pr. name of a man.

זָכַר *to remember, recollect, call to mind*. Niph.—I. *to be remembered, recollected, called to mind*, with the acc., rarely לְ, בְּ.—II. (from זָכָר) *to be born a male*, Ex. 34. 19. Hiph.—I. *to bring to remembrance*.—II. *to mention, make mention of*.—III. *to offer a memorial-offering*, Is. 66. 3.—IV. *to record*, מַזְכִּיר *a recorder*.

זָכָר masc. dec. 4a, *male*, spoken of men and of animals.

זֵכֶר, זֶכֶר m. dec. 6c.—I. *remembrance, memory*. —II. *memorial*.

זָכוּר m. d. 3a, *male*, spoken of men and animals.

זַכּוּר (*mindful*) pr. name of several men.

זִכְרִי (*renowned*) pr. name of several men.

זְכַרְיָה, זְכַרְיָהוּ (whom *the Lord remembers*) pr. name—I. of a king of Israel, son of Jeroboam.—II. of the well-known prophet Zechariah son of Berachia, comp. Zec. 1. 1, 7.—III. of a prophet son of Jehoiada, comp. 2 Ch. 24. 20, sq. — IV. of a cotemporary with Isaiah, Is. 8. 2.—V. of a prophet under Uzziah, 2 Ch. 26. 5;—also of several other men.

אַזְכָּרָה fem. dec. 10, *a memorial-offering*.

זָכָר noun masc. sing. dec. 4a; or (Ps. 9. 13) in pause for זָכַר q. v. . . . . . זכר

זָכֶר ו pr. name masc. for זֶכֶר (§ 35. rem. 2); for ו see lett. ו . . . . . זכר

זָכֹר Kal inf. absolute, used also as an imp. . זכר

זֵכֶר noun masc. sing. dec. 6b . . . . זכר

[g] ו׳ זְכֹר / זְכָר־ } Kal imp. sing. masc. (§ 8. rem. 18); ו bef. (:) . . . . . זכר

[h] זָכְרָה id. pret. 3 pers. sing. fem. . . . . זכר

זָכְרָה id. imp. sing. m. with parag. ה (§ 8. r. 11) זכר

[i] ו׳ זָכְרוּ id. pret. 3 pers. pl. . . . . זכר

[k] זִכְרוּ / זְכֹרוּ } id. imp. pl. masc. (§ 8. rem. 11) . . זכר

זִכְרוֹ noun masc. s., suff. 3 p. s. m. from זֵכֶר d. 6b זכר

[l] ו׳ זִכָּרוֹן noun masc. sing. dec. 3c . . . זכר

זִכְרוֹן id., constr. state . . . . . . זכר

[m] זִכְרוֹנֵךְ id., suff. 2 pers. sing. fem. . . . זכר

זִכְרִי ו׳ pr. name masc. . . . . . זכר

[n] זִכְרִי noun masc. sing., suff. 1 p. s. from זֵכֶר d. 6b זכר

ו׳ זְכַרְיָה / ו זְכַרְיָהוּ } pr. name masc.; ו bef. (:) . . . זכר

[o] זִכְרְךָ / [q] זִכְרֶךָ [p] ו׳ } noun masc. sing., suff. 2 pers. sing. masc. from זֵכֶר dec. 6b . . . . זכר

[r] ו׳ זִכְרָם id., suff. 3 pers. pl. masc. . . . זכר

[s] זִכָּרֹן defect. for זִכָּרוֹן (q. v.) . . . . זכר

[t] זָכַרְנוּ Kal pret. 1 pers. pl. . . . . . זכר

[u] זְכָרָנוּ id. pret. 3 pers. sing. masc., suff. 1 pers. pl. זכר

זָכְרֵנִי id. imp. sing. masc., suff. 1 pers. sing. . זכר

[x] זִכְרֹנֵיכֶם n. m. pl., suff. 2 p. pl. m. from זִכָּרוֹן d. 3c זרר

זָכַרְתָּ ו Kal pret. 2 pers. sing. masc.; acc. shifted by ו conv. (§ 8. rem. 7) . . . . זכר

[y] זָכַרְתְּ / [z] ו׳ זָכַרְתְּ } id. pret. 2 pers. sing. fem. (§ 8. rem. 7) זכר

זָכַרְתִּי / זָכַרְתִּי } id. pret. 1 pers. sing. (§ 8. rem. 7) . זכר

זָכַרְתִּי ו id. id.; acc. shifted by conv. ו . . זכר

[a] זָכַרְתִּי id. pret. 2 pers. sing. fem., Kh. זָכַרְתִּי, K. זָכַרְתְּ (§ 8. rem. 5) . . . . . זכר

[b] זְכַרְתִּיךָ id. id., suff. 2 pers. sing. masc. . . זכר

[c] זְכַרְתָּם id. pret. 2 pers. sing. m., suff. 3 pers. pl. m. זכר

זְכַרְתֶּם ו id. pret. 2 pers. pl. masc.; ו for ו conv. זכר

[d] זְכַרְתַּנִי / [e] ו זְכַרְתַּנִי } id. pret. 2 pers. sing. masc., suff. 1 pers. sing.; ו bef. (:) . . . . זכר

[a] Pr. 21. 8. [b] Da. 6. 23. [c] Job 28. 17. [d] Ps. 103. 14. [e] Ps. 132. 1. [f] De. 20. 13. [g] Ec. 12. 1. [h] La. 1. 7, 9. [i] Eze. 6. 9. [k] Ne. 4. 8. [l] Ne. 2. 20. [m] Is. 57. 8. [n] Ex. 3. 15. [o] Ps. 135. 13. [p] Ps. 102. 13. [q] Ps. 6. 6. [r] Est. 9. 28. [s] Ex. 28. 12. [t] Nu. 11. 5. [u] Ps. 115. 12. [x] Job 13. 12. [y] Is. 17. 10. [z] Eze. 16. 61. [a] Eze. 16. 22, 43. [b] Ps. 63. 7. [c] Ps. 88. 6. [d] 1 Sa. 1. 11. [e] Ge. 40. 14.

זָלַג Root not used; Arab. דלח *to draw out*; Aram. סְלֵק Aph. *to bring up*.

מַזְלֵג masc. *fork*, 1 Sa. 2. 13, 14.

מִזְלָגָה fem. dec. 11 a, id.

זְלֻוּת[a] noun fem. sing. . . . . . זלל

[זָלַל] prop. i. q. זול *to shake* or *pour out* (Arab. זלזל *to shake*), whence part. זוֹלֵל—I. *squanderer, prodigal*. —II. *vile, debased*. Niph. *to be shaken, to quake*. Hiph. *to debase*, La. 1. 8.

זֻלּוּת fem. Ps. 12. 9, *vileness, baseness*; others, *trembling, terror*.

זַלְזַלִּים masc. pl. *twigs, branches of the vine*, Is. 18. 5, comp. תַּלְתַּלִּים R. תָּלַל.

זַלְעָפָה[b] fem. dec. 11 a, *violent heat*, spoken of a poisonous wind called *Samoom*, of famine, of anger. Comp. זָעַף.

זַלְעֲפוֹת[c] id. pl., constr. state

זַלְעָפוֹת[d] id., pl. absolute for זַלְ׳

זִלְפָּה (*a dropping* דָּלַף=זָלַף *to drop, trickle down*) pr. name of the hand-maid of Leah.

זִמָּה noun fem. sing. dec. 10, also pr. name masc. זמם

זְמוֹרָה[e] noun fem. sing. dec. 10. . . . זמר

זַמּוֹתָ[f] Kal pret. 2 pers. sing. masc. . . . זמם

זִמּוֹת[g] noun fem., pl. of זִמָּה dec. 10. . . זמם

זִמֹּתַי[h] id. with suff. 1 pers. pl. . . . . זמם

זַמְזֻמִּים pr. name of a race of giants, De. 2. 20.

זָמִיר[i] noun masc. sing. dec. 1 a, pl. זְמִרוֹת . . זמר

זְמִירָה pr. name masc. . . . . . זמר

זָמַם pret. זַמֹּתִי ,זַמֹּתִי (§ 18. rem. 13); fut. pl. יָזְמוּ (rem. 15) *to devise, purpose, intend, think*, especially *to intend evil*, with לְ *against* any one.

זָמָם masc. dec. 4 a, *device, project*, Ps. 140. 9.

זִמָּה fem. dec. 10.—I. *device, plan, purpose*, for evil.—II. *wickedness, sin*, especially with reference to unchastity.—III. pr. name of a man.

מְזִמָּה fem. dec. 10.—I. *device, machination, contrivance*, in a bad sense.—II. *thought, consideration, discretion*, in a good sense.

זָמֵם[k] Kal pret. 3 pers. sing. m. for זָמַם (§ 8. r. 7) זמם

זֹמֵם[l] id. part. act. sing. masc. . . . . זמם

זָמְמָה[m] id. pret. 3 pers. sing. fem. . . . זמם

זָמָמוּ[n] id. pret. 3 pers. pl. [for זָמְמוּ § 8. rem. 7] זמם

זְמָמוֹ[o] noun m. s., suff. 3 p. s. m., from [זָמָם] d. 4 a זמם

זָמַמְתִּי[p] Kal pret. 1 pers. sing. . . . . זמם

זָמַן. Pu. *to be appointed, fixed, determined*.

זְמַן Ch. Pa. *to appoint, determine*, Da. 2. 9 Kheth., which according to Keri is Hithp. הִזְדַּמִּן *to agree together*.

זְמָן masc. dec. 8 a, *time*, especially *a stated, appointed time*.

זְמָן (Da. 2. 16), elsewhere זְמַן Ch. dec. 3 a.—I. *time, appointed time*.—II. זִמְנִין תְּלָתָה *three times*, Da. 6. 11.

זְמָן Heb. & Ch. noun masc. s., (suff. זְמַנָּם) d. 8 a זמן

זְמַן[q] Ch. noun masc. sing. dec. 3 b . . . זמן

זִמְנָא ר׳[r] Ch. id., emph. state . . . . זמן

זִמְנַיָּא[s] וְ Ch. id. pl., emph. state . . . זמן

זִמְנִין[t] וְ׳[u] Ch. id. pl., absolute state . . . זמן

[זָמַר] *to cut, prune*, Le. 25. 3, 4. Niph. *to be pruned*, Is. 5. 6. Pi. (prop. *to divide*, with reference to rhythmical numbers, hence) *to sing hymns, praises*, with לְ or the acc. of the person celebrated, with בְּ of the instrument for accompaniment.

זְמָר Ch. dec. 1 a, *song, music*, Da. 3. 5, 7, 10, 15.

זַמָּר Ch. dec. 1 a, *singer*, Ezr. 7. 24.

זֶמֶר masc. a species of *gazelle*, De. 14. 5.

זִמְרָה fem. (no pl.) *song, praise, music*; Ge. 43. 11 זִמְרַת הָאָרֶץ *the song of the land*, i. e. the most celebrated produce; others, *fruit cut off*.

זִמְרִי (*pruner*, or *singer*) pr. names of several men, especially—I. of a king of Israel, comp. 1 Ki. 16. 9, seq.—II. of a chief of the tribe of Simeon, Nu. 25. 14.

זִמְרָן (id.) pr. name of a son of Abraham by Keturah, and of a tribe descended from him

זִמְרָת fem. i. q. זִמְרָה *song, praise*.

זְמוֹרָה fem. dec. 10, *branch, bough*.

זָמִיר masc. *pruning-time*, Ca. 2. 12.

זָמִיר masc. *song, praise*, pl. זְמִרוֹת

זְמִירָה (*song*) pr. name masc. 1 Ch. 7. 8.

מִזְמוֹר masc. *song, hymn, psalm*.

מְזַמֶּרֶת fem. only pl. מְזַמְּרוֹת (dec. 13) *snuffers*; others, *psalteries*.

מַזְמֵרָה fem. dec. 11 b, *pruning-instruments*.

זֶמֶר[x] וְ noun masc. sing. [for זֶמֶר § 35. rem. 2]; for וְ see lett. ו . . . . זמר

זְמָרָא[y] Ch. noun masc., emph. of [זְמָר] dec. 1 a זמר

זַמְּרָה[z] Piel inf. with fem. term. (§ 10. rem. 2) . זמר

זִמְרָה noun fem. sing. dec. 10. . . . זמר

---

[a] Ps. 12. 9. [b] Ps. 119. 53. [c] La. 5. 10. [d] Ps. 11. 6. [e] Nu. 13. 23. [f] Pr. 30. 32. [g] Is. 32. 7. [h] Job 17. 11. [i] Is. 25. 5. [k] La. 2. 17. [l] Ps. 37. 12. [m] Pr. 31. 16. [n] Ps. 31. 14. [o] Ps. 140. 9. [p] Zec. 8. 14, 15. [q] Da. 7. 12. [r] Da. 7. 22. [s] Da. 2. 21. [t] Da. 7. 25. [u] Da. 6. 11. [x] De. 14. 5. [y] Da. 3. 5, 7, 10, 15. [z] Ps. 147. 1.

זַמְּרוּ[a] וְ׳ } Piel imp. pl. masc. (comp. § 8. rem. 7) זמר
זַמֵּרוּ

זְמִרוֹת noun masc. with pl. f. term. from זָמִיר d. 1a זמר

זִמְרִי וְ׳ pr. name masc. . . . . . זמר

זַמָּרַיָּא[b] Ch. noun masc. pl. emph. from זַמָּר d. 1a זמר

זְמִרֵיהֶם[c] וּ noun fem. with pl. masc. term. & suff. 3 pers. pl. m. fr. זְמוֹרָה d. 10; וּ bef. (:) . זמר

זִמְרָן pr. name masc. . . . . . זמר

זִמְרָת וְ noun fem. sing. . . . . זמר

זִמְרַת[d] וְ noun fem. sing., constr. of ־ְרָה (no pl.) זמר

זְמֹרַת[e] וּ n. f. s., constr. of זְמוֹרָה d. 10; וּ bef. (:) זמר

זְמִרֹת[f] defect. for זְמִרוֹת (q. v.) . . זמר

זִמַּת noun fem. sing., constr. of זִמָּה dec. 10. . זמם

זַמֹּתִי[g] Kal pret. 1 pers. sing. . . . זמם

זַמֹּתִי[h] Piel inf. [זַמּוֹת § 18. rem. 3] suff. 1 p. sing. זמם

זִמָּתֵךְ[i] וְ׳ noun f. s., suff. 2 p. s. f. from זִמָּה d. 10. זמם

זִמַּתְכֶנָה[k] id. with suff. 3 pers. pl. fem. (§ 3. rem. 5) זמם

זַן[l] for זַן masc., pl. זְנִים (§ 36. r. 5) *sort, kind, manner;* מִזַּן אֶל־זַן *of all kinds.*

זַן Ch. masc. id. only pl. constr. זְנֵי Da. 3. 5, 7, 10, 15.

זָנָב[m] וְ׳ masc. dec. 4, pl. זְנָבוֹת, constr. זַנְבוֹת, *tail* of an animal. Pi. *to cut off* or *smite the rear of an army.*

זְנָבוֹ[n] id., suff. 3 pers. sing. masc. . . . זנב

זַנְבוֹת[o] id. pl., constr. state (§ 33. rem. 1) . זנב

זִנַּבְתֶּם[p] וְ Piel pret. 2 pers. pl. masc. . . . זנב

זָנָה[q] וְ *to commit whoredom, play the harlot;* frequently also *to commit spiritual whoredom* or *idolatry;* const. with acc. בְּ ,אֶל ,אַחֲרֵי of the person with whom, with מִן ,מֵאַחֲרֵי ,מִתַּחַת ,תַּחַת ,מֵעַל of the person against whom, it is committed. Part. fem. זוֹנָה *harlot.* Pu. זוּנָּה pass. Eze. 16. 34. Hiph.—I. *to cause to commit whoredom.*—II. intrans. *to commit whoredom.*

זְנוּנִים masc. dec. 1a, only pl. זְנוּנִים *whoredom;* frequently applied to *idolatry.*

זְנוּת fem. dec. 1a, *whoredom,* only trop. of idolatry.

תַּזְנוּת fem. dec. 1b, the same.

זָנֹה[r] Kal inf. absolute . . . . זנה

זֹנָה fem. of the following, dec. 10. . . זנה

זֹנֶה[s] Kal part. act. sing. masc. dec. 9a . . זנה

זָנוּ[t] [u] וְ׳ id. pret. 3 pers. pl. . . . זנה

זָנוֹחַ וְ׳ pr. name of a man and a place . . זנח

זְנוּנֵי noun masc. pl. constr. from [זְנוּן] dec. 1a זנה

זְנוּנֶיהָ[x] id. pl., suff. 3 pers. sing. fem. . . זנה

זְנוּנַיִךְ[y] id. pl., suff. 2 pers. sing. fem. . . זנה

זְנוּנִים id. pl., absolute state . . . זנה

זְנוּת noun fem. sing. dec. 1a . . . זנה

זְנֻת defect. for זְנוּת (q. v.) . . . זנה

זְנוּתָהּ[z] noun f. s., suff. 3 pers. s. f. fr. זְנוּת d. 1a זנה

זְנוּתֵיכֶם[a] id. pl. [זְנוּתִים], suff. 2 pers. pl. masc. . זנה

זְנוּתֵךְ id. sing., suff. 2 pers. sing. fem. . . זנה

זְנוּתָם[b] id. sing., suff. 3 pers. pl. masc. . . זנה

זָנַח I. prop. *to be stinking, illsavoured,* hence *to be abominable,* Ho. 8. 5.—II. meton. *to reject* as abominable, with מִן *to thrust away, cast off.* Hiph. —I. *to stink,* Is. 19. 6.—II. *to reject, cast off.*

זָנוֹחַ (*marshy* place) pr. name of a place in the tribe of Judah.

זָנֹחַ pr. name of a place for זָנוֹחַ . . . זנח

זָנַחְתָּ Kal pret. 2 pers. sing. masc. . . . זנח

זְנַחְתִּים[c] id. pret. 1 pers. sing., suff. 3 pers. pl. masc. זנח

זְנַחְתָּנוּ id. pret. 2 pers. sing. masc., suff. 1 pers. pl. זנח

זְנַחְתָּנִי[d] id. id. with suff. 1 pers. sing. (§ 2. rem. 1) זנח

זְנֵי[e] Ch. noun masc. pl. constr., fr. זַן (q. v.)

זְנִים[f] וּ noun masc., pl. of זַן q. v.; וּ bef. (:)

זֹנִים Kal part. act. m., pl. of זֹנֶה dec. 9a . זנה

זָנִית[g] id. pret. 2 pers. sing. masc. . . . זנה

זָנִית[h] id. pret. 2 pers. sing. fem. . . . זנה

זָנַק Kal not used; Syr. *to cast, dart forth.*—Pi. *to leap, spring forth,* De. 23. 22.

זֵק masc. (for זֶנֶק § 37. No. 3b) only pl. זִקִּים, *arrows,* Pr. 26. 18.

זִיקָה fem. (for זִקָּה comp. § 18. rem. 12 note) only pl. זִיקוֹת *burning arrows, fiery darts,* Is. 50. 11.

זָנְתָה[i] וְ׳ Kal pret. 3 pers. sing. fem. . . זנה

זָע[k] Kal pret. 3 pers. sing. masc. . . . זוע

זְעוּם[l] Kal part. pass. masc., constr. of [זָעוּם] d. 3a זעם

זְעוּמָה[m] fem. of the preceding . . . זעם

זַעֲוָן וְ pr. name masc. . . . . זוע

זְעֵיר noun masc. sing. . . . . זער

זְעֵירָה[n] Ch. adj. fem. from זְעֵיר masc. . . זער

זָעַךְ i. q. דָּעַךְ, only Niph. *to be extinguished, extinct,* Job 17. 1; Professor Lee, *to be swift.*

זָעַם וְ׳, fut. יִזְעֹם, & יִזְעַם Pr. 24. 24 (§ 8. r. 13).—I. *to*

---

[a] Ps. 98. 4. [b] Ezr. 7. 24. [c] Na. 2. 3. [d] Am. 5. 23. [e] Is. 17. 10. [f] Is. 24. 16. [g] Je. 4. 28. [h] Ps. 17. 3. [i] Eze. 23. 29. [k] Eze. 23. 49. [l] Ps. 144. 13. [m] Ju. 15. 4. [n] Job 40. 17. [o] Is. 7. 4. [p] Jos. 10. 19. [q] De. 31. 16. [r] Ho. 1. 2. [s] Ho. 4. 15. [t] Ju. 2. 17. [u] Ex. 34. 15, 16. [x] Ho. 2. 4. [y] Eze. 23. 29. [z] Je. 3. 9. [a] Nu. 14. 33. [b] Eze. 43. 9. [c] Zec. 10. 6. [d] Ps. 43. 2. [e] Da. 3. 5, 7, 10, 15. [f] 2 Ch. 16. 14. [g] Ho. 9. 1. [h] Je. 3. 1. [i] Is. 23. 17. [k] Est. 5. 9. [l] Pr. 22. 14. [m] Mi. 6. 10. [n] Da. 7. 8.

be angry, indignant, with acc., עַל.—II. *to be insolent,* Ps. 7. 12, וְאֵל זֹעֵם בְּכָל־יוֹם *and God* (judges) *the insolent continually.* Niph. *to be made angry, sullen,* Pr. 25. 23.—III. part. pl. *cursed.*

זַעַם masc. dec. 6d, with suff. זַעְמִי, זַעַמְךָ.—I. *anger, indignation.*—II. *insolence,* Ho. 7. 16.

זָעַם } noun masc. sing. dec. 6d (§ 35. r. 2); } זעם
זַעַם [a] וְ׳ } for וָ see lett. ו . . . }

זֹעֵם[b] Kal part. act. sing. masc. . . . זעם

זֹעֲמָה[c] id. imp. sing. m. with parag. ה, [for זְעָמָה § 16. rem. 9] . . . . זעם

זַעְמוֹ noun masc. sing., suff. 3 pers. sing. masc. from זַעַם dec. 6d [for זַעֲמוֹ § 35. rem. 5] זעם

זַעְמִי id., suff. 1 pers. sing. [for זַעֲמִי v. id.] . זעם

זַעַמְךָ[d] }
זַעְמֶךָ } id., suff. 2 pers. sing. masc. (v. id.) . זעם

זָעַמְתָּה[e] Kal pret. 2 pers. sing. masc. (§ 8. rem. 5) . זעם

[זָעַף] I. *to be angry, enraged.*—II. to be *sullen, sad, gloomy.* Hence the two following—

זָעֵף masc. adj. *angry, indignant.*

זַעַף masc. dec. 6d (with suff. זַעְפּוֹ § 35. rem. 5). —I. *anger, rage.*—II. metaph. *raging of the sea,* Jon. 1. 15.

זֹעֲפִים Kal part. act. masc., pl. of [זֹעֵף] dec. 7b זעף

[זָעַק] fut. יִזְעַק, imp. זְעַק, inf. זְעֹק, *to cry, call out,* especially from pain, for help, with אֶל, לְ of the person implored; with לְ, עַל of the cause of suffering. Niph. *to be called together;* hence, *to come together, to assemble.* Hiph.—I. *to cry out,* Job 35. 9.—II. *to proclaim.*—III. *to call together, to assemble.*

זְעִק Ch. (§ 47. rem. 6) *to cry out,* Da. 6. 21.

זַעַק masc. dec. 6d, *cry, outcry,* Is. 30. 19.

זְעָקָה fem. dec. 11c, constr. זַעֲקַת (comp. § 42. rem. 1) *cry, outcry,* especially from pain, for help.

זְעַק[f] Kal imp. sing. masc. . . . . זעק

זְעִק[g] Ch. Peal pret. 3 pers. sing. masc. (§ 47. r. 6) זעק

זָעָקָה[h] וְ Kal pret. 3 pers. s. f. [for זָעֲקָה § 8. r. 7] זעק

זְעָקָה[i] וּ׳ noun fem. s. d. 11c (§ 42. r. 1); וּ bef. (:) זעק

זָעֲקוּ וְ׳ Kal pret. 3 pers. pl. . . . . זעק

זַעֲקוּ וְ id. imp. pl. masc. . . . . זעק

זַעֲקִי[k] id. imp. sing. fem. . . . . זעק

זְעָקִי[l] וּ Kal imp. sing. fem., or pl. masc., Kh. זְעָקִי, K. זְעָקוּ in pause for זַעֲקִי or זַעֲקוּ (comp. § 8. rem. 12) . . . . זעק

זַעֲקֵךְ[m] [for זַעֲקְךָ] noun masc. sing., suff. 2 pers. sing. masc. fr. [זַעַק] dec. 6d . . זעק

זַעֲקַת noun f. s., constr. of זְעָקָה d. 11c (§ 42. r. 1) זעק

זָעַקְתִּי[n] Kal pret. 1 pers. sing. . . . זעק

זַעֲקָתָם[o] וְ׳ noun fem. sing., suff. 3 pers. pl. masc. fr. זְעָקָה dec. 11c (§ 42. rem. 1) . . זעק

זְעַקְתֶּם[p] וּ Kal pret. 2 pers. pl. masc. וּ for וְ conv. זעק

זָעַר Root not used; i. q. צָעַר *to be little.*

זְעֵיר masc. *a little.*

זְעֵיר Ch. *small, little,* Da. 7. 8.

מִזְעָר masc. *littleness, smallness,* of time and number; מְעַט מִזְעָר *little of smallness,* i. e. very little; אֱנוֹשׁ מִזְעָר *very few men.* Others take this word as an adverb.

זִפִּים gent. noun, pl. of זִיפִי fr. זִיף . . זוף

זִפְרֹנָה pr. name of a city in the north of Palestine [זִפְרוֹן] with loc. ה, Nu. 34. 9.

זִקִּים[q] noun masc., pl. of [זֵק for זֵנֶק] dec. 8b (§ 36. No. 3b) . . . . . זנק

זְקֵינֵינוּ[r] adj. pl. masc., suff. 1 pers. pl. fr. זָקֵן dec. 5a זקן

זְקִיף[s] וּ Ch. Peal part. pass. sing. masc.; וּ bef. (:) זקף

זָקָן com. dec. 4a.—I. *beard.*—II. *the chin.*

זָקֵן *to be* or *grow old.* Hiph. *to grow old, be old.*

זָקֵן masc. dec. 5a, adj. *old, aged,* hence as a subst. *an old, aged man;* זְקֵנִים *elders, chiefs* of tribes, families or cities; fem. זְקֵנוֹת *old, old women.*

זֹקֶן masc. *old age,* Ge. 48. 10.

זִקְנָה fem. constr. זִקְנַת (no pl.) *old age.*

זְקֻנִים masc. pl. dec. 1a, *old age;* בֶּן־זְ׳ *son of old age,* i. e. born when the father was old.

זָקֵן וְ׳ Kal pret. 3 pers. sing. masc. or adj. sing. masc. dec. 5a . . . . . זקן

זְקַן constr. of זָקָן (Ps. 133. 2) or זָקֵן (Ge. 24. 2) זקן

זָקְנָה[t] Kal pret. 3 pers. sing. fem. . . זקן

זִקְנָה noun fem. sing. (no pl.) . . . זקן

זְקָנוֹ noun masc. sing., suff. 3 pers. sing. masc. fr. זָקָן dec. 4a . . . . . זקן

זְקֵנוֹת[u] וּ adj. f., pl. of זְקֵנָה fr. זָקֵן masc.; וּ bef. (:) זקן

זְקֵנַי[x] וּ id. pl. masc., suff. 1 pers. pl. fr. זָקֵן dec. 5a; וּ id. . . . . זקן

זְקָנִי[ll] וּ noun masc. sing., suff. 1 pers. sing. from זָקָן dec. 4a; וּ id. . . . . זקן

זִקְנֵי וְ׳ adj. pl. constr. masc. fr. זָקֵן dec. 5a . זקן

[a] Ps. 78. 49. [b] Ps. 7. 12. [c] Nu. 23. 7. [d] Ps. 102. 11. [e] Zec. 1. 12. [f] Eze. 21. 17. [g] Da. 6. 21. [h] 2 Sa. 13. 19. [i] Je. 50. 46. [k] Is. 14. 31. [l] Je. 48. 20. [ll] Ezr. 9. 3. [m] Is. 30. 19. [n] Ps. 142. 6. [o] Est. 9. 31. [p] 1 Sa. 8. 18. [q] Pr. 26. 18. [r] Jos. 9. 11. [s] Ezr. 6. 11. [t] Pr. 23. 22. [u] Zec. 8. 4. [x] La. 1. 19.

זְקֵנֶיהָ[a] id. pl., suff. 3 pers. sing. fem. . . . זקן
זְקֵנָיו[b] 'וּ id. pl., suff. 3 pers. sing. masc.; וּ bef. (:) זקן
זְקֵנֶיךָ id. pl., suff. 2 pers. sing. masc. . . . זקן
זִקְנֵיכֶם[c] 'וְ id. pl., suff. 2 pers. pl. masc. . . . זקן
זְקֵנִים 'וּ id. pl., abs. state; וּ bef. (:) . . . זקן
זְקָנִים noun masc., pl. dec. 1a . . . זקן
זְקָנְךָ noun masc. sing., suff. 2 pers. sing. masc. [for זְקַנְךָ] from זָקָן dec. 4a . . . זקן
זְקַנְכֶם id., suff. 2 pers. pl. masc. . . . זקן
זְקָנָם id., suff. 3 pers. pl. masc. . . . זקן
זָקַנְתָּ[d] Kal pret. 2 pers. sing. masc. . . . זקן
זִקְנַת[e] noun fem. sing., constr. of זִקְנָה (no pl.) זקן
זָקַנְתָּה[f] Kal pret. 2 pers. sing. masc. (§ 8. rem. 5) זקן
זִקְנָתָהּ[g] n. fem. s., suff. 3 pers. s. fem. from זִקְנָה (no pl.) זקן
זִקְנָתוֹ[h] id., suff. 3 pers. sing. masc. . . . זקן
זָקַנְתִּי Kal pret. 1 pers. sing. . . . זקן

[זָקַף] *to set upright, erect, raise up.*

זְקַף Ch. *to lift up, hang up,* a criminal, Ezr. 6. 11.

זֹקֵף[i] Kal part. act. sing. masc. . . . זקף

[זָקַק] I. *to pour out,* Job 36. 27.—II. *to fuse, refine,* as gold.—III. in the deriv. i. q. Chald. זְקַק *to join, bind together.* Pi. זִקֵּק *to refine, purify* gold, Mal. 3. 3. Pu. *to be refined,* spoken of wine, metals.

זֵק masc. only pl. זִקִּים *bonds, fetters, chains.*

אָזֵק masc. only pl. אֲזִקִּים id.

וְזִקַּק[k] Piel pret. 3 pers. sing. masc. (§ 10. rem. 1) זקק
זָר' וְ see the Root . . . וזר
זָר 'וְ Kal part. act. sing. masc. dec. 1a . . . זור
זֵר noun masc. sing. dec. 1a . . . זרר

זָרַב Kal not used; Syr. *to compress,* hence Pu. *to become straitened, narrow,* Job 6. 17. Others, *to become warm,* זָרַב=צָרַף, שָׂרַף, סָרַף.

זְרֻבָּבֶל 'וּ (for זְרוּבָבֶל *scattered in Babylon;* or זְרוּעַ בָּבֶל *sown* (i. e. begotten) *in Babylon*) pr. name of a leader of the first colony of Jews returning from the Babylonish captivity, comp. Ezr. 2. 2.

זֶרֶד, זָרֶד } pr. name of a valley and of a stream in the land of Moab, Chald. זְרַד *to prune*

[זָרָה] I. *to spread, scatter, disperse.*—II. *to winnow.* Niph. *to be scattered.* Pi. זֵרָה.—I. *to scatter, disperse.*—II. *to sift, discern.* Pu.—I. *to be spread,* Pr. 1. 17; others, *to be besprinkled,* and so in Is. 1. 6.—II. *to be scattered,* Job 18. 15; here also according to some, זֹרוּ Ps. 58. 4, comp. זוּר.

זֶרֶת fem. *a span,* a measure.

מִזְרֶה masc. *winnowing fan.*

מְזָרֶה masc. prop. *scatterer,* only pl. מְזָרִים (dec. 9) Job 37. 9, poet. for *the north winds;* so according to Kimchi. Others take it as the name of a constellation, comp. מַזָּרוֹת.

זָרָה[m] Kal pret. 3 pers. sing. fem. . . . זור
זָרָה id. part. act. fem. dec. 10, from זָר masc. זור
זְרֵה[n] Kal imp. sing. masc. . . . זרה
זֹרֶה[o] Kal part. act. masc.; Is. 30. 24, according to some Pu. part. [for מְזֹרֶה § 10. rem. 6] זרה
זָרוּ Kal pret. 3 pers. pl. . . . זור
זֵרוּ[p] Piel pret. 3 pers. pl. . . . זרה
זֹרוּ[q] Kal pret. 3 pers. pl. § 21. rem. 2, (less likely to be taken as Pu. of R. זרה) . . . זור
זֵרוּהָ[r] וְ Piel pret. 3 pers. pl., suff. 3 pers. sing. fem. זרה
זֵרוּעַ[pp] noun masc. sing. dec. 1b [for זֵרוּעַ] . זרע
זְרוֹעַ 'וּ noun com. sing. dec. 1a; וּ bef. (:) . זרע
זְרוּעָה[s] Kal part. pass. fem. from זָרוּעַ masc. . זרע
זְרֹעוֹ n. com. s., suff. 3 p. s. m., from זְרוֹעַ dec. 1a זרע
זְרֹעוֹת[t] id. with pl. fem. term. . . . זרע
זְרֹעִי id. sing., suff. 1 pers. sing. . . זרע
זֵרוּעֶיהָ[u] noun m. pl., suff. 3 pers. s. f. from זֵרוּעַ (q. v.) זרע
זְרוֹעֲךָ, זְרוֹעֶךָ[x] 'וּ } noun com. sing., suff. 2 pers. sing. masc. from זְרוֹעַ dec. 1a; וּ bef. (:) . זרע
זְרוֹעָם[y] וּ id., suff. 3 pers. pl. masc.; וּ before (:) . זרע
זְרֹעֹתָי[z] id. pl., suff. 1 pers. sing. [for 'עֹתַי] . זרע
זְרוֹעֹתֶיהָ[a] id. pl., suff. 3 pers. sing. fem. . . זרע
זְרֹעֹתָיו id. pl., suff. 3 pers. sing. masc. . . זרע
זְרוֹעֹתֵיכֶם[b] id. pl., suff. 2 pers. pl. masc. . . זרע
זְרֹעֹתָם[c] id. pl., suff. 3 pers. pl. masc. . . זרע
זָרוֹת Kal part. act. fem., pl. of זָרָה d. 10, from זָר m. זור
זַרְזִיף[d] noun masc. sing. . . . זרף
זַרְזִיר[e] noun masc. sing. . . . זור

זָרַח[f] 'וְ fut. יִזְרַח, inf. זְרֹחַ *to rise,* as the sun, light glory, leprosy, and in the deriv. also of plants.

זֶרַח masc. with suff. זַרְחֵךְ (§ 35. rem. 5).—I. *rising,* Is. 60. 3.—II. pr. name of a son of Judah by Tamar, and of others. Patronym. זַרְחִי.

זְרַחְיָה (whom *the Lord brings to light*) pr. name —I. of a man, called also יִזְרַחְיָה, comp. 1 Ch. 5. 32 with 7. 3.—II. Ezr. 8. 4.

אֶזְרָח masc. dec. 2b.—I. *a native tree,* growin

[a] Ju. 8. 14. [b] Is. 24. 23. [c] De. 5. 20. [d] 1 Sa. 8. 5. [e] 1 Ki. 11. 4. [f] Jos. 13. 1. [g] Ge. 24. 36. [h] 1 Ki. 15. 23. [i] Ps. 146. 8. [k] Mal. 3. 3. [l] Pr. 21. 8. [m] Job 19. 17. [n] Nu. 17. 2. [o] Ru. 3. 2. [p] Zec. 2. 2, 4. [pp] Le. 11. 37. [q] Ps. 58. 4; Is. 1. 6. [r] Is. 51. 2. [s] Je. 2. 2. [t] Ps. 37. 17. [u] Is. 61. 11. [x] Ca. 8. 6. [y] Ps. 44. 4. [z] Ps. 18. 35. [a] Pr. 31. 17. [b] Eze. 13. 20. [c] Ho. 7. 15. [d] Ps. 72. 5. [e] Pr. 30. 31. [f] Ps. 112. 4.

in its own soil, Ps. 37. 35.—II. *a native*, one born in the country.

אֶזְרָחִי patronym. *Ezrahite*, a descendant of אֶזְרָח.

יִזְרָח 1 Ch. 27. 8, with the art., for אֶזְרָחִי.

יִזְרַחְיָה (whom *the Lord brings to light*) pr. name m.—I. 1 Ch. 7. 3, see זְרַחְיָה.—II. Ne. 12. 42.

מִזְרָח masc. dec. 2b, *the east*, prop. *the sunrising*; also adv. *eastward*. With local ה, מִזְרָחָה *towards the east, eastward.*

זָרַח[a] Kal pret. 3 pers. sing. m. for זָרַח (§ 8. rem. 7) זרח

זָרַח וְ׳, זֶרַח וְ׳ } pr. name masc. (§ 35. rem. 2); for וְ see lett. ו . . . . } זרח

זָרְחָה [b] וְ׳ id. pret. 3 pers. sing. fem. . . זרח

זְרַחְיָה וּ׳ pr. name masc.; וּ before (:) . . זרח

זַרְחֵךְ[c] noun masc. sing., suff. 2 pers. sing. fem. from זֶרַח dec. 6a (§ 35. rem. 5) . . . זרח

זָרַיִךְ[d] Kal part. masc. pl., suff. 2 pers. sing. fem. [for זָרַיִךְ] from זָר dec. 1a . . . זור

זָרִים [e] וְ׳ id. pl., absolute state . . . זור

זֵרִיתָ[f] Piel pret. 2 pers. sing. masc. . . . זרה

זֵרִיתִי וְ id. pret. 1 pers. sing.; acc. shifted by conv. וְ (comp. § 8. rem. 7) . . . . זרה

זֵרִיתִיךָ[g] וְ id. id., suff. 2 pers. sing. masc. . . . זרה

זֵרִיתִים וְ id. id., suff. 3 pers. pl. masc. . . . זרה

זֵרִיתָנוּ[h] id. pret. 2 pers. sing. masc. with suff. 1 pers. pl. זרה

[זָרַם] *to flow, pour*, hence with an acc. *to overwhelm*, Ps. 90. 5. Po. *to pour down*, Ps. 77. 18.

זֶרֶם masc. *a violent shower, storm*; זֶרֶם בָּרָד *shower of hail*; זֶרֶם קִיר *a shower* (prostrating) *walls*.

זִרְמָה fem. constr. זִרְמַת (no pl.) *effusion, emission*, Eze. 23. 20.

זֶרֶם[i], זָרֶם[k] וְ׳ } noun masc. sing. (§ 35. rem. 2); for וְ see lett. ו . . . . } זרם

זֵרָם[m] וְ Piel pret. 3 pers. s. m. [זֵרָה], suff. 3 p. pl. m. זרה

זֹרְמוּ[n] Pual pret. 3 pers. pl. . . . . . זרם

זִרְמַת[o] וְ noun fem. sing. constr. [of זִרְמָה; no pl.] זרם

זְרַמְתָּם[p] Kal pret. 2 pers. sing. m., suff. 3 pers. pl. m. זרם

זִרְמָתָם[q] noun fem. sing., suff. 3 pers. pl. masc. [from זִרְמָה; no pl.] . . . . . זרם

זָרַע[r] prop. *to spread, to scatter*, and so perhaps Zec. 10. 9, cogn. זָרָה, hence—I. *to sow*; with an acc. of the seed sown, and the field sown upon; זֹרֵעַ זֶרַע *yielding seed*.—II. *to plant*, Is. 17. 10.—III. metaph. of good, evil, &c. Niph.—I. *to be sown*, of seed, a field.—II. trop. *to be propagated*, as a name, Na. 1. 14; of a woman conceiving, Nu. 5. 28. Pu. *to be sown*, Is. 40. 24. Hiph.—I. *to bear, yield seed*, as a plant, Ge. 1. 11, 12.—II. *to conceive*, of a woman, Le. 12. 2.

זֶרַע masc. dec. 6a (once constr. זְרַע § 35. r. 5, 7) —I. *seed*.—II. *seedtime*.—III. *issue, progeny*.

זְרַע Ch. *seed*, Da. 2. 43.

זְרוֹעַ com. dec. 1a, pl. ־ִים, ־וֹת.—I. *arm*.—II. *foreleg*, of an animal.—III. *strength, power, might*.

זֵרוּעַ masc. (for זְרוּעַ) dec. 1b, *a sowing, what is sown*, as garden herbs.

זֵרֹעַ m. only pl. זֵרֹעִים *legumes, vegetables*, Da. 1. 12.

זֵרְעֹן masc. only pl. זֵרְעֹנִים (dec. 3c) id. Da. 1. 16.

אֶזְרוֹעַ dec. 1b, i. q. זְרוֹעַ *the arm*.

יִזְרְעֶאל, יִזְרְעֵאל (*God planteth*) pr. name—I. of a city in the tribe of Issachar, comp. Jos. 19. 18; afterwards the residence of king Ahab and his successors; עֵמֶק י׳ the valley Jezreel near the city. Gent. noun יִזְרְעֵאלִי; fem. יִזְרְעֵאלִית, יִזְרְעֵלִית.—II. of a city in the tribe of Judah, Jos. 15. 56; 1 Sa. 29. 1.—III. pr. name of several men.

מִזְרָע masc. dec. 2b, *things sown, crop*, Is. 19. 7

זָרַע in pause for זֶרַע (q. v. § 35. rem. 2) . זרע

זֵרֻעַי Kal part. pass. sing. masc. [for זָרוּעַ] . זרע

זָרַע וְ׳, וְ׳[t] n. m. s., suff. זַרְעוֹ, dec. 6a (§ 35. r. 5) זרע

זְרַע[u] Kal imp. sing. masc. . . . . . זרע

זְרֹעַ defect. for זְרוֹעַ (q. v.) . . . . זרע

זֹרֵעַ[x] וְ׳[y] Kal part. act. sing. masc. dec. 7b . זרע

זַרְעָהּ[z] noun masc. sing., suff. 3 pers. sing. fem. from זֶרַע dec. 6a (§ 35. rem. 5) . . זרע

זָרְעוּ[a] Kal pret. 3 pers. pl. . . . . . זרע

זַרְעוֹ וְ׳ noun masc. sing., suff. 3 pers. sing. masc. from זֶרַע dec. 6a (§ 35. rem. 5) . זרע

זְרֹעוֹ וּ׳ defect. for זְרוֹעוֹ (q. v.); וּ before (:) . זרע

זִרְעוּ Kal imp. pl. masc. . . . . . זרע

זֹרָעוּ[b] Pual pret. 3 p. pl. [for זֹרְעוּ comp. § 8. r. 7] זרע

זְרֹעוֹת[c] וּ׳ n. com. with pl. f. term. from זְרוֹעַ d. 1a זרע

זְרֹעוֹתָיו[d] id. pl., suff. 3 pers. sing. masc. . . זרע

זַרְעִי noun masc. sing., suff. 1 pers. sing. from זֶרַע dec. 6a (§ 35. rem. 5) . . . זרע

זְרֹעֵי[e] noun com. pl. constr., from זְרוֹעַ dec. 1a . זרע

זְרֹעִי[f] id. sing., suff. 1 pers. sing. . . . . זרע

זֹרְעֵי[g] וְ׳[h] Kal part. act. pl. c. masc., from זֹרֵעַ d. 7b זרע

זְרֹעַי[i] וּ noun com. pl., suff. 1 pers. sing. from זְרוֹעַ dec. 1a; וּ bef. (:) . . . . . זרע

זְרֹעָיו[k] id., suff. 3 pers. sing. masc. . . . זרע

[a] Is. 60. 1. [b] Mal. 3. 20. [c] Is. 60. 3. [d] Is. 29. 5. [e] Joel 4. 17. [f] Ps. 139. 3. [g] Eze. 22. 15. [h] Ps. 44. 12. [i] Is. 32. 2. [k] Hab. 3. 10. [l] Is. 30. 30. [m] 1 Ki. 14. 15. [n] Ps. 77. 18. [o] Eze. 23. 20. [p] Ps. 90. 5. [q] Eze. 23. 20. [r] Ju. 6. 3. [s] Ps. 97. 11. [t] Je. 35. 9. [u] Ec. 11. 6. [x] Ge. 1. 29, 29. [y] Pr. 11. 18. [z] Ge. 3. 15. [a] Je. 12. 13. [b] Is. 40. 24. [c] Eze. 30. 24, 25. [d] Ju. 15. 14. [c] Ge. 49. 24. [f] Is. 63. 5. [g] Is. 32. 20. [h] Job 4. 8. [i] Is. 51. 5. [k] 2 Ki. 9. 24.

זְרֻעֵיכֶם[a] ן noun com. pl., suff. 2 pers. pl. masc. from זֶרַע dec. 6a (§ 35. rem. 5) . . זרע

זְרֹעִים[b] ׳ו noun com. pl. abs. fr. זְרוֹעַ d. 1 a; ׳ו bef. (:) זרע

זַרְעֲךָ[c] ׳ן noun masc. sing., suff. 2 pers. sing. masc. from זֶרַע dec. 6a (§ 35. rem. 5) זרע

זַרְעֶךָ[d] ׳ן (see above) זרע

זַרְעֵךְ[e] ׳ן id., suff. 2 pers. sing. fem. . . זרע

זְרֹעֲךָ[f] ׳ו defect. for זְרוֹעֲךָ (q. v.) . . . זרע

זַרְעֲכֶם noun masc. sing., suff. 2 pers. pl. masc. from זֶרַע dec. 6a (§ 35. rem. 5) . . זרע

זַרְעָם ׳ן id., suff. 3 pers. pl. masc. . . . זרע

זְרֹעָם[g] defect. for זְרוֹעָם (q. v.) . . . זרע

זֵרְעֹנִים[h] noun masc., pl. of [זֵרָעוֹן] comp. dec. 3c . זרע

זְרֹעֹת[i] for זְרוֹעוֹת noun com. with pl. fem. term. from זְרוֹעַ dec. 1 a . . . . . זרע

זָרַעְתִּי[k] ן Kal pret. 1 pers. sing.; acc. shifted by conv. ן (§ 8. rem. 7) . . . . . זרע

זְרֹעֹתַי[l] noun com. pl., suff. 1 pers. sing., see זְרֹעֹת זרע

זְרַעְתִּיהָ[m] ׳ו Kal pret. 1 p. s., suff. 3 p. s. f.; ׳ו for ן conv. זרע

זְרֹעֹתָיו[n] ׳ו noun com. pl., suff. 3 pers. sing. masc., see זְרֹעֹת; ׳ו bef. (:) . . . . . זרע

זְרַעְתֶּם[o] ׳ו Kal pret. 2 pers. pl. masc.; ׳ו for ן conv. זרע

זָרַף Root not used; Arab. *to flow.*

זַרְזִיף masc. *a copious rain*, Ps. 72. 6.

זָרַק[p] ׳ן[q] *to scatter, sprinkle*, spoken of dust, ashes, water, blood. Intrans. *to be sprinkled*, Ho. 7. 9. Pu. *to be sprinkled*, Nu. 19. 13, 20.

מִזְרָק masc. dec. 2 b, pl. וֹת ,ִ—ים, *dish* or *basin*, used for sprinkling.

זֹרַק[r] Pual pret. 3 pers. sing. masc. . . . זרק

זְרֹק[s] ׳ו Kal imp. sing. masc.; ׳ו bef. (:) . . זרק

זָרְקָה[t] id. pret. 3 pers. sing. fem. . . . . זרק

זָרְקוּ[u] ן id. pret. 3 pers. pl. . . . . זרק

זְרָקוֹ[x] ׳ו id. pret. 3 pers. sing. masc., suff. 3 pers. sing. masc.; ׳ו for ן conv. . . . זרק

זֹרְקִים[y] id. part. act. masc., pl. of זֹרֵק׳ dec. 7b . זרק

זָרַקְתָּ[z] ן id. pret. 2 pers. sing. masc.; acc. shifted by conv. ן (§ 8. rem. 7) . . . . זרק

זָרַקְתִּי[a] ן id. pret. 1 pers. sing.; acc. id. . . . זרק

I. **זָרַר**. Po. *to sneeze*, 2 Ki. 4. 35, comp. Chald. זְרִיר a sneezing.

II. **זָרַר** Root not used; Arab. *to bind, fasten together.*

זֵר masc. dec. 1 a, *wreath, crown, border.* This may also be suitably derived from צוּר=זוּר

זַרְזִיר masc. *bound together, girded*, once Prov. 30. 31 זַרְזִיר מָתְנַיִם *girded about the loins*; Prof. Lee, *compact of loins*; an epithet, according to some, of *the war-horse*, which used to be ornamented with girths and buckles round the loins. Simonis understands here the *Zebra*, from its stripes; some of the Rabbins, *the greyhound.*

זֶרֶשׁ ׳ן (*gold*, coll. with Pers., Gesenius; Simon., *the star of Venus*) pr. name of the wife of Haman, Est. 6. 13.

זָרֶת[b] ן noun fem. sing. (§ 35. rem. 2); for ן see lett. ו . . . . . זרה

זָרֶת ׳ן (see above) זרה

זֵרְתִים[c] ן defect. for זֵרִיתִים (q. v.) . . . זרה

זַתּוּא pr. name masc. comp. Ezr. 2. 8, Ne. 7. 13.

זֵתָם ׳ן pr. name masc. . . . . . זית

זֵתַר (*star*, comp. אֶסְתֵּר) pr. name of a eunuch of Ahasuerus, Est. 1. 10.

ח

חָבָא Kal not used; i. q. חָבָה *to hide, conceal.* Niph. *to be hid, concealed, to conceal oneself*, const. with בְּ, אֶל of the place; followed by an inf. with לְ, as נַחְבֵּאתָ לִבְרֹחַ *thou fleddest secretly.* Pu. *to be made to hide oneself*, Job 24. 4. Hiph. *to hide, conceal.* Hoph. *to be hid*, Is. 42. 22. Hithp. *to hide oneself, to lie hid.*

מַחֲבֵא masc. a *hiding-place*, Is. 32. 2.

מַחֲבֹא masc. id. only pl. מַחֲבֹאִים 1 Sa. 23. 23.

חֻבְּאוּ[d] Pual pret. 3 pers. pl. . . . . חבא

[חָבַב] *to love, cherish*, De. 33. 3.

חֹב masc. dec. 8c, *bosom, lap*, Job 31. 33. Also

חֹבָב (*beloved*) pr. name of the father-in-law of Moses . . . . חבב

חֹבֵב[e] Kal part. act. sing. masc. . . . חבב

[חָבָה] *to hide oneself*, Is. 26. 20. Niph. id. 1 Ki. 22. 25; 2 Ki. 7. 12.

חוֹבָה (*hiding-place*) pr. name of a place northward of Damascus, Ge. 14. 15.

[a] 1 Sa. 8. 15. [b] Da. 11. 31. [c] Ge. 17. 9. [d] De. 30. 19. [e] Is. 54. 3. [f] 1 Sa. 2. 31. [g] Is. 33. 2. [h] Da. 1. 16. [i] De. 33. 27. [k] Je. 31. 27. [l] 2 Sa. 22. 35. [m] Ho. 2. 25. [n] Da. 10. 6. [o] Hag. 1. 6. [p] Ex. 24. 6. [q] Le. 17. 6. [r] Nu. 19. 13, 20. [s] Eze. 10. 2. [t] Ho. 7. 9. [u] Le. 1. 5, 11. [x] Ex. 9. 8. [y] 2 Ch. 30. 16. [z] Ex. 29. 16, 20. [a] Eze. 36. 25. [b] 1 Sa. 17. 4. [c] Je. 49. 32, 36. [d] Job 24. 4. [e] De. 33. 3.

חֲבַיָּה, חֳבַיָּה (whom *the Lord protects*) pr. name masc. Ezr. 2. 61; Ne. 7. 63.

חֶבְיוֹן masc. *a covering, veil,* Hab. 3. 4.

יְחֻבָּה (*hidden, protected*) pr. name masc. 1 Ch. 7. 34 Kheth., וְחֻבָּה Keri.

נַחְבִּי (*hidden*) pr. name masc. Nu. 13. 14.

[a]חֲבוּלָה Ch. noun fem. sing. . . . . . חבל

חָבוֹר וְ pr. name of a river . . . . חבר

[b]חֲבוּר Kal part. p. masc., constr. of [חָבוּר] d. 3a חבר

[c]חַבּוּרָה [d]וְ noun fem. sing. dec. 10. . . . חבר

[e]חַבּוּרֹתַי id. pl. with suff. 1 pers. pl. [for ־תֵי] חבר

[f]חָבוּשׁ Kal part. pass. sing. masc. dec. 3a . חבשׁ

חֲבוֹשׁ id. imp. sing. masc. . . . . . חבשׁ

[g]חֲבוּשִׁים id. part. pass. masc., pl. of חָבוּשׁ dec. 3a . חבשׁ

[חָבַט] fut. יַחְבֹּט (§ 13. rem. 5).—I. *to beat off,* as fruit from a tree.—II. *to beat out, thresh.* Niph. *to be beaten out,* Is. 28. 27.

[h]חֹבֵט Kal part. act. sing. masc. . . . . חבט

[i]חֲבִי Kal imp. sing. fem. . . . . . חבה

חֲבַיָּה, חֳבַיָּה } pr. name masc. . . . . . חבה

[k]חֶבְיוֹן noun masc. sing. . . . . . חבה

I. [חָבַל] fut. יַחְבֹּל, יַחֲבֹל (§ 13. rem. 5).—I. *to twist, to bind,* only part. pl. חֹבְלִים *binders, bands;* a mystical name given to a shepherd's staff representing the union of *brotherhood,* Zec. 11. 7, 14.—II. *to bind by a pledge,* with an acc. of the pers., comp. Job 22. 6. Meton. *to take as a pledge,* with an acc. of the thing. Pi. *to writhe, to be in pain, to travail,* as a woman in labour.

חֵבֶל masc. dec. 6, pl. חֲבָלִים, constr. חֶבְלֵי (§ 35. rem. 6).—I. *writhing, pang, the throes* of child-bearing.—II. *pains* generally, Job 21. 16.

חֶבֶל masc. dec. 6, with suff. חַבְלִי; pl. חֲבָלִים, constr. חַבְלֵי, חֶבְלֵי (§ 35. rem. 4).—I. *cord, rope.*—II. *measuring-line.*—III. *a portion measured out,* whence generally, *a district, tract, region.*—IV. *gin, snare.*—V. *company, band of men,* 1 Sa. 10. 5, 10.

חֲבֹל masc. *a pledge, deposit.*

חֲבֹלָה fem. dec. 10, id. Eze. 18. 7.

חִבֵּל masc. *mast of a ship,* Pr. 23. 34.

חֹבֵל masc. dec. 7b, *ship-man, sailor.*

תַּחְבֻּלָה, תַּחְבּוּלָה fem. dec. 10, only in the pl.—I. *guidance, direction, management.*—II. *wise counsel.*—III. *cunning devices,* Pr. 12. 5.

II. [חָבַל] prop. to corrupt, destroy; hence, *to act corruptly, perversely, wickedly,* Ne. 1. 7; Job 34. 31. Niph. *to be destroyed, to perish,* Pr. 13. 13. Pi. *to corrupt, destroy, lay waste.* Pu. *to be destroyed*

חַבֵּל Ch. Pa.—I. *to injure, hurt,* Da. 6. 23.—II. *to corrupt, destroy.* Ithpa. *to be destroyed.*

חֲבָל Ch. masc. *hurt, harm,* Da. 3. 25.

חֲבָל Ch. masc. dec. 1a, *hurt, damage,* Ezr. 4. 22.

חֲבוּלָה fem. *fault, crime,* Da. 6. 23.

[l]חֲבַל Kal pret. 3 pers. sing. m. [for חָבַל § 8. r. 7] חבל

[m]חֲבֹל id. inf. absolute . . . . . חבל

[n]חֲבָל Ch. noun masc. sing. dec. 1a . . . חבל

[o]חֲבָל וַ Ch. noun masc. sing.; וּ bef. (-:) . חבל

חֲבֹל Kal inf. constr., or noun masc. . . חבל

[p]חֶבֶל noun masc. sing. dec. 6 (§ 35. rem. 6) . חבל

חֶבֶל וְ n. m. s., pl. c. חַבְלֵי & חֶבְלֵי d. 6 (§ 35. r. 4) חבל

[q]חִבֵּל [r]וְ noun m. s., or Piel pret. 3 pers. sing. m. חבל

[s]חֹבֵל Kal part. act. sing. masc. dec. 7b . . חבל

[t]חֻבַּל וְ Pual pret. 3 pers. sing. masc. . . חבל

[u]חֲבָלָא Ch. noun masc. sing., emph. of חֲבָל dec. 1a חבל

[x]חֻבָּלָה Pual pret. 3 pers. sing. fem. [for חֻבְּלָה comp. § 8. rem. 7] . . . . . . חבל

[y]חִבְּלָה Piel pret. 3 pers. sing. fem. . . . חבל

חַבְלֵהוּ Kal imp. sing. masc. [חֲבֹל] with suff. 3 pers. sing. masc. (comp. § 16. rem. 10) . . חבל

[z]חַבְלוֹ noun m. s., suff. 3 p. s. m. from חֶבֶל (q. v.) חבל

[a]חַבְּלוּהִי וְ Ch. Pael imp. pl. masc., suff. 3 pers. s. m. חבל

[b]חַבְּלוּנִי Ch. id. pret. 3 pers. pl. m., suff. 1 pers. sing. חבל

[c]חַבְלֵי noun masc. pl. constr. from חֶבֶל (q. v.) . חבל

חֶבְלֵי noun masc. pl. const. from חֵבֶל, or חֶבֶל (§ 35. rem. 6 & 4) . . . . . חבל

[d]חֹבְלֵי noun m. pl. constr. from חֹבֵל dec. 7b . חבל

[e]חֶבְלֵיהֶם noun masc. pl., suff. 3 pers. pl. masc. from חֵבֶל dec. 6d (§ 35. rem. 6) . . . . חבל

[f]חֲבָלָיו noun m. pl., suff. 3 p. s. m. from חֶבֶל (q. v.) חבל

[g]חֲבָלָיִךְ id., suff. 2 pers. sing. fem. [for חֲבָלַיִךְ] . חבל

[h]חֹבְלָיִךְ [i]וְ noun masc. pl., suff. 2 pers. sing. fem. [for חֹבְלַיִךְ] from חֹבֵל dec. 7b . . . חבל

חֲבָלִים וַ n. m. pl. of חֵבֶל or חֶבֶל (q. v.); וּ bef. (-:) חבל

[k]חֲבֻלִים Kal part. p. masc., pl. of [חָבוּל] dec. 3a חבל

[l]חֹבְלִים id. part. act. masc., pl. of חֹבֵל dec. 7b . חבל

[m]חָבַלְנוּ id. pret. 1 pers. pl. . . . . חבל

[n]חֲבֹלָתוֹ noun fem. sing., suff. 3 pers. sing. masc. from [חֲבֹלָה] dec. 10 . . . . . חבל

[a] Da. 6. 23. [b] Ho. 4. 17. [c] Ex. 21. 25. [d] Is. 1. 6. [e] Ps. 38. 6. [f] Jon. 2. 6. [g] Ju. 19. 10. [h] Ju. 6. 11. [i] Is. 26. 20. [k] Hab. 3. 4. [l] Eze. 18. 16. [m] Ex. 22. 25. [n] Da. 6. 24. [o] Da. 3. 25. [p] Is. 66. 7. [q] Pr. 23. 34. [r] Ec. 5. 5. [s] De. 24. 6. [t] Is. 10. 27. [u] Ezr. 4. 22. [x] Job 17. 1. [y] Ca. 8. 5. [z] Job 18. 10. [a] Da. 4. 20. [b] Da. 6. 23. [c] Jos. 17. 5. [d] Eze. 27. 29. [e] Job 39. 3. [f] Is. 33. 20. [g] Is. 33. 23. [h] Eze. 27. 8, 23. [i] Eze. 27. 27. [k] Am. 2. 8. [l] Zec. 11. 7. [m] Ne. 1. 7. [n] Eze. 18. 7.

חִבְּלָתֶךָ[a] Piel pret. 3 pers. sing. fem., suff. 2 pers. sing. masc. [for חִבְּלַתְךָ § 16. rem. 3] . חבל

חֲבַצֶּלֶת[b] fem. the name of a flower, according to the ancient versions, *a lily*, or *a narcissus*; according to Gesenius, *the meadow saffron*, an autumnal flower resembling saffron, springing from a *bulbous* root; the gutt. ח is prefixed to בֶּצֶל (bulb) as in חַשְׁמַנִּים from שָׁמֵן. Fürst suggests, חֲבַצֶּל from חָמַץ=חָבַץ *to have a pungent fragrance*, or *to be bright, splendid*, with the termination, ־ֶל as in כַּרְמֶל, עֲרָפֶל &c.

חֲבַצִּנְיָה pr. name masc. Je. 35. 3.

[חָבַק] I. *to embrace*.—II. *to fold the hands*, as a slothful person, Ec. 4. 5. Pi. *to embrace*.

חִבֻּק masc. *a folding of the hands*, spoken of the sluggard.

חֲבַקּוּק (*embrace*) pr. name of the prophet, Hab. 1. 1; 3. 1.

חִבֻּק[c] noun masc. sing. . . . . . חבק

חֹבֶק[d] Kal part. act. sing. masc. . . . . חבק

חִבְּקוּ Piel pret. 3 pers. pl. . . . . . חבק

חֲבַקּוּק pr. name masc. . . . . . חבק

חֹבֶקֶת[e] Kal part. act., fem. of חֹבֵק . . . חבק

[חָבַר] I. *to be bound, joined together, to consociate*.—II. *to charm, bind with a spell*. Pi. *to join, attach*. Pu. *to be joined together*. Hiph. *to join* or *connect* sentences, with בְּ of the object and עַל of the person, Job 16. 4. Hithp. *to join oneself* to any one.

חָבֵר masc. dec. 5 c, *associate, companion*.

חֲבֶרֶת fem. *a female companion*, only חֲבֶרְתְּךָ (§ 44. rem. 3) Mal. 2. 14.

חֲבַר Chald. masc. dec. 3 a, *companion*, Da. 2. 13, 17, 18.

חַבְרָה Chald. fem. dec. 8 a (§ 64) *female associate*, hence *fellow, other*, Da. 7. 20.

חַבָּר masc. *associate, companion*, only pl. חַבָּרִים Job 40. 30.

חָבוֹר (perhaps *strong*, כָּבַר=חָבַר) pr. name of a river in Mesopotamia.

חַבּוּרָה fem. dec. 10, *stripe, bruise, scar*.

חַבֻרָה fem. dec. 10, id. Is. 53. 5.

חֶבֶר masc. dec. 6.—I. *association, company*.—II. *incantation*, Is. 47. 9, 12.—III. pr. name of several men, written חֵבֶר in Nu. 26. 45.—Patronym. חֶבְרִי

חֶבְרָה fem. *association, company*, Job 34. 8.

חֶבְרוֹן (*alliance*) pr. name.—I. of a town in the tribe of Judah.—II. of several men.—Patronym. חֶבְרֹנִי

חֹבֶרֶת fem. *a joining, junction*.

חֲבַרְבֻּרָה fem. dec. 10, *stripe, streak* of the leopard, Je. 13. 23.

מַחְבֶּרֶת fem. dec. 13 a, with suff. ־בַּרְתּוֹ, *a joining, seam*.

מְחַבְּרָה fem. dec. 13.—I. *beam, brace*, for joining a building, 2 Ch. 34. 11.—II. *iron cramps*, 1 Ch. 22. 3.

חָבֵר noun masc. sing. dec. 5 c . . . חבר

חֶבֶר, וְחֶבֶר, חֶבֶר[f] noun m. s. dec. 6 (Ho. 6. 9); also pr. name m. (§ 35. rem. 2); for וְ see ו . חבר

חֵבֶר pr. name masc. . . . . . חבר

חִבֵּר[g] Piel pret. 3 pers. sing. masc. (§ 10. rem. 1) חבר

חֹבֵר[h] וְ Kal part. act. sing. masc. . . . חבר

חֻבָּר[i] וְ[k] Pual pret. 3 pers. sing. masc. [for חֻבַּר comp. § 8. rem. 7] . . . . חבר

חֲבַרְבֻּרֹתָיו[l] noun fem. pl., suff. 3 pers. sing. masc. from [חֲבַרְבֻּרָה] dec. 10. . . . חבר

חָבְרוּ[m] Kal pret. 3 pers. pl. . . . . חבר

חֲבֵרָו[n] noun masc. pl., suff. 3 pers. sing. masc. (K. ־רָיו § 4. rem. 1) from חָבֵר dec. 5 c חבר

חֲבֵרוֹ[o] id. sing., suff. 3 pers. sing. masc. . . חבר

חַבְרוֹהִי[p] וְ[q] Chald. noun masc. pl., suff. 3 pers. sing. masc. from [חֲבַר] dec. 3 a . . . חבר

חֶבְרוֹן וְ pr. name of a man and a place . . חבר

חֶבְרוֹנָה id. of a place with paragogic ה . . חבר

חַבּוּרוֹת[r] noun fem., pl. of חַבּוּרָה dec. 10. . . חבר

חֹבְרוֹת[s] Kal part. act. fem., pl. of [חֹבֶרֶת] dec. 13 a חבר

חַבְרֵי[t] וְ noun masc. pl. constr. from חָבֵר dec. 5 c חבר

חֲבֵרָיו[u] id. pl., suff. 3 pers. sing. masc. . . חבר

חֲבָרַיִךְ[v] noun masc. pl., suff. 2 pers. sing. fem. from חֶבֶר dec. 6 . . . . . חבר

חֲבֵרֶיךָ[y] noun masc. pl., suff. 2 pers. sing. masc. from חָבֵר dec. 5 c . . . . . חבר

חַבָּרִים[x] noun masc., pl. of [חַבָּר] dec. 1 b . . חבר

חֲבָרִים[a] noun masc., pl. of חֶבֶר dec. 6 . . חבר

חֲבֵרִים noun masc., pl. of חָבֵר dec. 5 c . . חבר

חֶבְרֹנָה pr. name of a place (חֶבְרוֹן) with parag. ה . חבר

חִבַּרְתָּ[b] וְ Piel pret. 2 pers. sing. masc.; acc. shifted by conv. וְ (comp § 8. rem. 7) . . חבר

חֹבְרֹת defect. for חוֹבְרוֹת (q. v.) . . . חבר

חַבְרָתַהּ[c] Chald. noun fem. sing., suff. 3 pers. sing. fem. [from חַבְרָה § 65] dec. 8 a . . . חבר

[a] Ca. 8. 5. [b] Ca. 2. 1. [c] Pr. 6. 10; 24. 33. [d] Ec. 4. 5. [e] 2 Ki. 4. 16. [f] Ho. 6. 9. [g] Ex. 36. 10. [h] De. 18. 11. [i] Ex. 39. 4. [k] Ex. 28. 7. [l] Je. 13. 23. [m] Ge. 14. 3. [n] Eze. 37. 16, 19. [o] Ec. 4. 10. [p] Da. 2. 17. [q] Da. 2. 13, 18. [r] Pr. 20. 30. [s] Eze. 1. 11. [t] Is. 1. 23. [u] Is. 44. 11. [v] Is. 47. 9. [y] Ca. 1. 7. [x] Job 40. 30. [a] Ps. 58. 6. [b] Ex. 26. 6, 9, 11. [c] Da. 7. 20.

[a]חֲבֶרְתֶּךָ noun fem. sing., suff. 2 pers. sing. masc. from [חֲבֶרֶת] dec. 13 (§ 44. rem. 3) . חבר

[חָבַשׁ] fut. יַחֲבֹשׁ, יַחְבֹּשׁ (§ 13. rem. 4, 5)—I. *to bind, bind round* or *about*, as with ropes; or as a head-dress; *to bind up*, as a wound, const. with לְ.—II. *to gird* or *saddle* a beast.—III. *to restrain, subdue, govern.* Pi.—I. *to bind up*, with לְ, Ps. 147. 3.—II. *to restrain, stop*, Job 28. 11. Pu. *to be bound up*, as a wound.

[b]חֲבֹשׁ Kal inf. constr. . . . . . חבשׁ

[c]חִבֵּשׁ Piel pret. 3 pers. sing. masc. . . . חבשׁ

[d]חֹבֵשׁ Kal part. act. sing. masc. . . . חבשׁ

[e]חֻבָּשָׁה Pual pret. 3 pers. sing. fem. . . . חבשׁ

[f]חִבְשׁוּ Kal imp. pl. masc. . . . . . חבשׁ

[g]חֻבָּשׁוּ Pual pret. 3 pers. pl. [for חֻבְּשׁוּ § 8. rem. 7] חבשׁ

חֲבֻשִׁים Kal part. pass. masc., pl. of חָבוּשׁ dec. 3a חבשׁ

[h]חָבַשְׁתָּ וְ id. pret. 2 pers. sing. masc.; acc. shifted by conv. וְ (§ 8. rem. 7) . . . חבשׁ

[i]חֲבַשְׁתֶּם id. pret. 2 pers. pl. masc. . . . חבשׁ

חָבַת Root not used; i. q. Arab خبز *to bake bread.*

חֲבִת masc. only pl. חֲבִתִּים (dec. 8b) 1 Ch. 9. 31, *baked cakes* or *pastry.* Others, *pans*, Arab. خبت *to be low* or *flat.*

מַחֲבַת fem. (for מַחֲבֶתֶת *a baking* or *frying-pan.*

[k]חָג Kal pret. 3 pers. sing. masc. . . . חוג

חַג noun masc. sing. dec. 8a . . . . חגג

חַג וְ id. constr. state, and, followed by לְ, abs. st. חגג

חָגָב masc. dec. 4c.—I. *locust.*—II. pr. name masc. Ezr. 2. 46. Hence

חֲגָבָא, חֲגָבָה } (*locust*) pr. name masc. Ne. 7. 48; Ezr. 2. 45.

[חָגַג] i. q. חוּג Syr. and Chald. to move in a circle, hence—I. *to dance*, 1 Sa. 30. 16.—II. *to keep* or *celebrate a feast.*—III. *to reel, to be giddy*, Ps. 107. 27.

חָג masc. dec. 8a, חַג constr., and, when followed by לְ, abs. (comp. Ex. 12. 14; 13. 6).—I. *festival, feast.*—II. meton. *a festival sacrifice.*

חָגָּא fem. (for חָגָּה, as seven of Dr. Kennicott's codices read) *commotion, tremor, fear*, Is. 19. 17.

חַגַּי (i. q. חַגִּי) pr. name of the prophet, Hag. 1. 1.

חַגִּי (*festive*, or perhaps for חַגִּיָּה q. v.) pr. name of a son of Gad; patronym. חַגִּי for חַגִּיִּי Nu. 26. 15.

חַגִּיָּה (*feast of the Lord*) pr. name masc. 1 Ch. 6. 15.

חַגִּית (*festive*) pr. name of one of the wives of David.

[m]חֹגְגִים וְ Kal part. act. masc., pl. of חוֹגֵג dec. 7b . חגג

חָגָה Root not used; prob. i. q., חָקָה *to cut, hew.*

חֲגָוִים masc. pl., only in constr. חַגְוֵי *chinks, clefts* of rocks. Others, *refuges*, Arab. حجا to take refuge.

[n]חַגָּהּ noun masc. sing., suff. 3 pers. sing. fem. from חַג dec. 8a . . . . . חגג

חָגוּר Kal part. pass. sing. masc. dec. 3a . . חגר

[o]חֲגוֹר וְ id. imp. sing. masc., or noun m. s. dec. 1a חגר

[p]חֲגוֹרָה noun fem. sing. dec. 10 . . . חגר

[q]חֲגוֹרֵי adj. masc. pl. constr. from [חָגוֹר] dec. 3a חגר

[r]חֲגוּרִים Kal part. pass. masc., pl. of חָגוּר dec. 3a . חגר

חַגַּי pr. name masc. . . . . . חגג

[s]חַגִּי noun m. s., suff. 1 pers. sing. fr. חַג dec. 8a חגג

חַגִּי וְ pr. name masc. . . . . . חגג

[t]חָגִּי Kal imp. sing. fem. (§ 18. rem. 4) . . חגג

חַגִּיָּה pr. name masc. . . . . . חגג

[u]חַגַּיִךְ noun masc. pl., suff. 2 pers. sing. fem. from חַג dec. 8a . . . . . . חגג

חַגֵּיכֶם id. pl., suff. 2 pers. pl. masc. . . . חגג

[x]חַגִּים id. pl., absolute state . . . . חגג

חַגִּית pr. name fem. . . . . . חגג

חָגְלָה וְ (*partridge*, Syr. ܚܓܠܐ) pr. name fem.; see also בֵּית חָ׳

[y]חַגֵּנוּ noun m. s., suff. 1 pers. pl. from חַג dec. 8a חגג

[חָגַר] fut. יַחְגֹּר (§ 13. rem. 5).—I. *to bind about, to gird, gird up, gird on*, with the acc. of the part girded, or acc. of the thing girded on and עַל of the part girded (Ps. 45. 4); with double acc. of the person and the thing; with בְּ of the thing girded on.—II. *to gird oneself.*—III. *to be straitened*, 2 Sa. 22. 46; or perh. *dismayed*, comp. חָרַג.

חָגוּר masc. dec. 3a, adj. *girded.* Eze. 23. 15.

חֲגוֹר masc. dec. 1a, *girdle.*

חֲגוֹרָה fem. dec. 10.—I. *girdle.*—II. *apron*, Ge. 3. 7.

מַחֲגֹרֶת fem. *cincture*, Is. 3. 24.

חֲגֹר Kal imp. sing. masc. . . . . . חגר

חֹגֵר id. part. act. sing. masc. . . . . חגר

[z]חֲגֹרָה וְ defect. for חֲגוֹרָה q. v.; וַ before (ֳ) . חגר

[a]חָגְרָה Kal pret. 3 pers. sing. fem. . . . חגר

[a] Mal. 2. 14. [b] Is. 30. 26. [c] Job 28. 11. [d] Is. 3. 7. [e] Eze. 30. 21. [f] 1 Ki. 13. 13, 27. [g] Is. 1. 6. [h] Ex. 29. 9. [i] Eze. 34. 4. [k] Job 26. 10. [l] 2 Ch. 7. 13. [m] 1 Sa. 30. 16. [n] Ho. 2. 13. [o] Pr. 31. 24. [p] Is. 3. 24. [q] Eze. 23. 15. [r] Ju. 18. 16. [s] Ex. 23. 18. [t] Na. 2. 1. [u] Na. 2. 1. [x] Is. 29. 1. [y] Ps. 81. 4. [z] 2 Ki. 3. 21. [a] Pr. 31. 17.

חֲגָרוּ ו׳ id. pret. 3 pers. pl. . . . . חגר

חֲגֹרוֹ[a] noun masc. sing., suff. 3 pers. sing. masc. from חֲגוֹר dec. 1a . . . חגר

חִגְרוּ[b] ו׳ Kal imp. pl. masc. . . . . . חגר

חִגְרִי[c] id. imp. sing. fem. . . . . חגר

חֲגֻרִים id. part. pass. pl. masc. (for חֲגוּרִים) from חָגוּר dec. 3a . . . . חגר

חֲגֹרְנָה[d] id. imp. pl. fem. . . . . . חגר

חָגַרְתָּ[e] וְ id. pret. 2 pers. sing. masc.; acc. shifted by conv. וְ (§ 8. rem. 7) . . . חגר

חֲגֹרַת[f] id. part. pass. fem., const. of [חֲגוּרָה] d. 10, from חָגוּר masc. . . . . חגר

חֲגֹרֹת[g] noun fem., pl. of חֲגוֹרָה dec. 10. . . חגר

חַגֹּתֶם וְ Kal pret. 2 pers. pl. masc. . . . חגג

חַד Ch. and once Heb. (Eze. 33. 30) num. masc. אחד

חֲדָא Ch. fem. of the preceding . . . אחד

[חָדַד] fut. יָחַד (§ 18. rem. 6)—I. *to be sharp, sharpened*, Pr. 27. 17.—II. *to be fierce*, Hab. 1. 8. Hiph. *to sharpen*, Pr. 27. 17. Hoph. *to be sharpened*, Eze. 21. 14, 15, 16.

חַד adj. fem. חַדָּה *sharp*.

חֲדַד (*sharpness*) pr. name of a son of Ishmael.

חַדּוּד masc. dec. 1b, *sharp point*, Job 41. 22.

חָדִיד (*sharp*) pr. name of a town in the tribe of Benjamin.

חֲדַד pr. name masc. . . . . . חדד

[חָדָה] fut. apoc. יִחַד (§ 24. rem. 3) *to rejoice, be glad*. Pi. *to make glad*, Ps. 21. 7. Hiph. *to make glad*, in this sense, according to some, יַחַד (§ 24. r. 16) Pr. 27. 17, but see חָדַד.

חֶדְוָה fem. constr. חֶדְוַת (no pl.) *joy, gladness*.

חֶדְוָה Ch. fem. id. Ezr. 6. 16.

יַחְדִּיאֵל (whom *God gladdens*) pr.n.m. 1 Ch. 5. 24.

יֶחְדְּיָהוּ (whom *the Lord gladdens*) pr. name masc.—I. 1 Ch. 24. 20.—II. 1 Ch. 27. 30.

חַדָּה adj. fem. from [חַד] masc. . . . חדד

חֲדָה Ch. i. q. חֲדָא (q. v.) . . . אחד

חַדּוּ[h] וְ Kal pret. 3 pers. pl. tone shifted (§ 18. r. 2) חדד

חַדּוּדֵי[i] noun masc. pl. constr. fr. [חַדּוּד] dec. 1b. חדד

חֶדְוָה[k] וְ noun fem. sing. dec. 10. . . . חדה

חֲדוֹהִי[l] Ch. noun masc. pl., suff. 3 pers. sing. masc. [fr. חֲדִי q. v.]

חַדּוֹן pr. name, see אֲסַר חַדּוֹן . . . אסר

חֶדְוַת[m] noun fem. sing., const. of חֶדְוָה dec. 10. . חדה

[חֲדִי] Ch. masc. i. q. Heb. חָזֶה *the breast*, only Da. 2. 32.

חָדִיד pr. name of a place . . . . חדד

חָדַל ו׳ pret. pl. חָדֵלוּ (from חָדֵל), fut. יֶחְדַּל, יֶחְדָּלוּ (§ 13. rem. 5)—I. *to cease, leave off, fail*.—II. *to forbear, decline, omit*.—Const. with מִן, rarely with an acc.; followed by a verb in the inf. with לְ, rarely without it.

חָדֵל adj. masc. dec. 5c.—I. *ceasing to be, frail*, Ps. 39. 5.—II. *forbearing* to do anything, Eze. 3. 27.—III. *forsaken*, Is. 53. 3.

חֶדֶל masc. *ceasing, frailty*, Is. 38. 11, יֹשְׁבֵי חָדֶל *inhabitants of frailty*, i. e. of this frail, transitory world. Eng. vers. "world," as a transposition for חֶלֶד. Gesenius, *place of rest, hades*. Prof. Lee, *leisure*.

חַדְלָי (*forsaken; or idler*) pr. name masc. 2 Ch. 28. 12.

חֲדַל[n] adj. masc. sing. dec. 5c . . . חדל

חָדֶל[o] noun masc. sing. [for חֶדֶל § 35. rem. 2] חדל

חֲדַל, חֲדָל } Kal imp. sing. masc. (§ 8. rem. 12) . חדל

חֲדַל[p] וַ adj. masc. sing., constr. of חָדֵל dec. 5c; וַ bef. (-:) . . . . . חדל

חָדְלוּ, חָדֵלוּ } Kal pret. 3 pers. pl. (§ 8. rem. 7) . חדל

חֲדָלוּ[bb], חִדְלוּ } Kal imp. pl. masc. (§ 8. rem. 12) . חדל

חַדְלָי pr. name masc. for חַדְלָי . . . חדל

חָדַלְנוּ[q] Kal pret. 1 pers. pl. . . . . חדל

חָדַלְתָּ[r] וְ id. pret. 2 pers. sing. masc. acc. shifted by conv. וְ (§ 8. rem. 7) . . . . חדל

חַדּוֹן pr. name masc., see אֲסַר חַדּוֹן . . אסר

חָדַק Root not used; Arab. *to sting, to be sharp*.

חֵדֶק, חֶדֶק masc. a species of *thorn*.

חָדֶק[s] noun masc. sing. [for חֵדֶק § 35. rem. 2] חדק

חִדֶּקֶל, חִדָּקֶל } pr. name, as is supposed, of the river Tigris, Ge. 2. 14; Da. 10. 4. Jewish interpreters suppose it compounded of חַד *sharp*, and קַל *light, swift*; but nearly the same idea may be obtained by deriving it from חֶדֶק=חַדֶק, with the termination ־ֶל (like כַּרְמֶל) with dagesh euphon.

[חָדַר] *to enclose, besiege, beset*, Eze. 21. 19.

חֶדֶר masc. dec. 6, constr. חֲדַר, with suff. חֶדְרוֹ, pl. c. חַדְרֵי (§ 35. rem. 4 & 7) *chamber, inner*

a 1 Sa. 18. 4. b 2 Sa. 3. 31. bb Zec. 11. 12. c Je. 6. 26. d Je. 49. 3. e Ex. 29. 9. f Joel 1. 8. g Ge. 3. 7. h Hab. 1. 8. i Job 41. 22. k 1 Ch. 16. 27 l Da. 2. 32. m Ne. 8. 10. n Ps. 39. 5. o Is. 38. 11. p Is. 53. 3. q Je. 44. 18. r Ex. 23. 5. s Pr. 15. 19.

apartment; חֶדֶר בְּחֶדֶר *chamber within a chamber,* i. e. the innermost, most secluded chamber. Metaph. חַדְרֵי תֵימָן *the remotest parts of the south,* Job 9. 9, once simply הַחֶדֶר ch. 37. 9; חַדְרֵי בֶטֶן *inner parts of the body;* חַדְרֵי מָוֶת *tombs.*

חֲדַר pr. name masc. . . . . . חדר

חֶדֶר noun masc. sing., (constr. חֲדַר § 35. rem. 7, comp. rem. 4) . . . . חדר

חַדְרֵי [a] וְ׳ id. pl., constr. state . . . חדר

חֲדָרָיו [b] [c] וַ׳ id. pl., suff. 3 pers. sing. masc.; וּ bef. (-:) חדר

חֲדָרִים [d] id. pl., absolute state . . . חדר

חַדְרָךְ pr. name of a region near Damascus, Zec. 9. 1

חָדַשׁ. Pi. *to make new, to renew, restore.* Hithp. *to be renewed,* Ps. 103. 5.

חָדָשׁ masc. dec. 4c, fem. חֲדָשָׁה, pl. חֲדָשׁוֹת, adj. *new, recent, fresh.*

חֹדֶשׁ masc. dec. 6c.—I. *new moon.*—II. *month;* חֹדֶשׁ יָמִים *a month of days,* i. e. a complete month.—III. pr. name fem. 1 Ch. 8. 9; matronym. חָדְשִׁי, 2 Sa. 24. 6.

חָדָשׁ adj. masc. sing. dec. 4c . . . חדשׁ

חַדֵּשׁ Piel imp. sing. masc. . . . . חדשׁ

חֹדֶשׁ noun masc. sing. dec. 6c, also pr. name fem. חדשׁ

חָדְשָׁהּ [e] id., suff. 3 pers. sing. fem. . . . חדשׁ

חֲדָשָׁה וַ׳ adj. fem. sing., from חָדָשׁ masc., also pr. name; וּ before (-:) . . . חדשׁ

חִדְּשׁוּ [f] וְ Piel pret. 3 pers. pl. . . . חדשׁ

חָדְשׁוֹ [g] noun masc. sing. with suff. 3 pers. sing. masc. from חֹדֶשׁ dec. 6c . . חדשׁ

חֲדָשׁוֹת [h] [i] וַ׳ adj. fem., pl. of חֲדָשָׁה, fr. חָדָשׁ masc. חדשׁ

חָדְשֵׁי [k] noun masc. pl. constr. from חֹדֶשׁ dec. 6c חדשׁ

חָדְשִׁי pr. name, see תַּחְתִּים חָדְשִׁי . . . תוח

חֳדָשָׁיו noun m. pl., suff. 3 p. s. m. from חֹדֶשׁ dec. 6c חדשׁ

חָדְשֵׁיכֶם id. pl., suff. 2 pers. pl. masc. . . . חדשׁ

חֲדָשִׁים adj. masc., pl. of חָדָשׁ dec. 4c . . חדשׁ

חֳדָשִׁים noun masc., pl. of חֹדֶשׁ dec. 6c . . חדשׁ

חָדְשֵׁכֶם defect. for חָדְשֵׁיכֶם q.v. . . חדשׁ

חֲדַת Ch. adj. masc. *new,* Ezr. 6. 4.

חֲדַתָּה pr. name, see חָצוֹר חֲדַתָּה . . . חצר

חַדְתָּה [l] Kal pret. 2 pers. sing. masc. (§ 8. rem. 5) . חוד

חוּב. Pi. חִיֵּב *to render guilty, to forfeit,* Da. 1. 10. Hence

חוֹב masc. *debt,* Eze. 18. 7. . . . . חוב

חוֹבָה pr. name of a place . . . . חבה

חוֹבֵר [m] Kal part. act. sing. masc. . . . חבר

חֹבְרוֹת [n] id. fem., pl. of [חֹבֶרֶת] dec. 13a . . חבר

[חוּג] *to draw a circle, to circumscribe,* Job 26. 10.

חוּג masc. *circle, sphere.*

מְחוּגָה fem. *compass, compasses,* Is. 44. 13.

חוּג [o] וְ׳ noun masc. sing. . . . חוג

חוֹגֵג [p] Kal part. act. sing. masc. dec. 7b . . חגג

חוּד *to propose a riddle, problem.*

חִידָה fem. dec. 10.—I. *riddle, enigma.*—II. *proverb, parable;* hence, *a sublime, spiritual discourse,* comp. Ps. 49. 5; 78. 2.

אֲחִידָא Ch. fem. dec. 8a, *riddle, enigma,* Da. 5. 12.

חוּד [q] Kal imp. sing. masc. . . . . חוד

חוּדָה [r] id. with parag. ה . . . . חוד

חָוָה Kal not used; cogn. חָיָה *to breathe, to live,* (comp. חַוָּה); *to breathe out,* hence Pi. *to declare, shew.*

חַוָּה Chald. Pa. *to declare, shew.* Aph. id.

חַוָּה fem. dec. 10.—I. *life,* but only as a pr. name of the first woman, *Eve,* Ge. 3. 20; 4. 1.—II. pl. חַוּוֹת *villages;* from the idea of *living, dwelling;* others compare it with the Arab. חוי *to assemble.*

חִוִּי (*villager*) pr. name of a people of Canaan, *Hivite,* collect. *Hivites.*

אַחֲוָה f. dec. 10, *declaration, argument,* Job 13. 17.

אַחֲוָיָה Chald. fem. dec. 8a, *declaration, explanation,* Da. 5. 12.

יְחִוְאֵל (whom *God preserves alive*) pr. name masc. 2 Ch. 29. 14. Kheth.

מַחֲוִים pr. name of a people, 1 Ch. 11. 46. אֱלִיאֵל הַמַּ׳ *Eliel of the Mahavites.*

חַוָּה pr. name fem. . . . . . . חוה

חוּז Root not used; Arab. חאז *to collect,* conj. VII. *to decline, recede.*

מָחוֹז masc. dec. 3a, *haven,* Ps. 107. 30.

חוֹזֵה [s] noun masc., constr. of חֹזֶה dec. 9a . חזה

חוֹזָי pr. name masc. for חוֹזַי . . . חזה

חוֹחַ וְ׳ masc. pl. חֲוָחִים, חוֹחִים (§ 35. rem. 13).—I. *thorn, thorn-bush.*—II. *fish-hook,* Job 40. 26.—III. *a hook* or *ring* used for fastening prisoners, 2 Ch. 33. 11.

חָח masc. with suff. חַחִי, pl. חַחִים (§ 37. r. 7).—I. *a hook* or *ring* put into the nose of animals.—II. *a nose-ring,* worn as an ornament, Ex. 35. 22.

[a] Job 9. 9. [b] Ca. 1. 4. [c] 1 Ch. 28. 11. [d] Pr. 24. 4. [e] Ho. 2. 13. [f] Is. 61. 4. [g] 1 Ki. 5. 7. [h] Is. 48. 6. [i] Is. 42. 9. [k] 1 Ch. 27. 1. [l] Ju. 14. 16. [m] Ps. 58. 6. [n] Eze. 1. 11. [o] Job 22. 14. [p] Ps. 42. 5. [q] Eze. 17. 2. [r] Ju. 14. 13. [s] 2 Ch. 35. 15. [t] Is. 34. 13.

חוט Ch. Aph. *to fasten, join together*, Ezr. 4. 12. Hence

[a]חוּט ו׳ masc.—I. *a thread*.—II. *cord, line*, Jos. 2. 18. חוט

חוֹטֵא ו׳ } Kal part. act. sing. masc. dec. 7b (§ 23. rem. 9) . . . חטא
[b]חוֹטֵא ו }

חֲוִילָה ו׳ pr. name—I. of a son of Joktan, Ge. 10. 29, and of a gold country, *Havilah*, Ge. 2. 11. —II. of a son of Cush, Ge. 10. 7, and of a district in southern Arabia.

[c]חוֹכֵי Kal part. act. pl. c. m. from [חוֹכֶה] dec. 9a חכה

[d]**חוּל** [& חִיל] fut. יָחוּל, יָחִיל apoc. וַיָּחֶל, וַתָּחֵל, וַתָּחֹל imp. חוּלִי, חִילוּ. According to Gesenius, coll. with the Arab., prop. *to turn about, twist, whirl*, and intrans. *to be turned, twisted, whirled*, hence—I. *to dance*, Ju. 21. 21.—II. *to be hurled, fall upon*, with בְּ, עַל.—III. *to writhe, to be in pain*.—IV. *to bear, bring forth*, Is. 54. 1.—V. *to tremble*.—VI. *to be strong, firm, durable*.—VII. *to wait, stay, delay*, i. q. יָחַל. Hiph. *to shake*, Ps. 29. 8. Hoph. *to be brought forth*, Is. 66. 8. Pil.—I. *to dance*, Ju. 21. 23. —II. *to bear, bring forth*, Job 39. 1; causat. Ps. 29. 2; metaph. *to create, form*.—III. *to tremble*, Job 26. 5.—IV. *to wait*, Job 35. 14. Pul. *to be born*. Hithpal.—I. *to whirl, precipitate itself*, Je. 23. 19.—II. *to writhe* with pain, Job 15. 20.—III. *to wait*, Ps. 37. 7. Hithpalp. (§ 6. No. 4) *to be pained, grieved*, Est. 4. 4.—Comp. Gesenius' Manuale.

חוֹל masc. *sand*; חוֹל הַיָּם *sand of the sea*, used as the image of multitude, or of *weight*.

חוּל (*pain*) pr. name of a son of Aram, Ge. 10. 23; 1 Ch. 1. 17.

חַיִל masc. dec. 6h, pl. חֲיָלִים (§ 35. rem. 12).—I. *strength, might, valour*; עָשָׂה חַיִל *to do valiantly*. —II. *forces, army, host*; אַנְשֵׁי, בְּנֵי חַיִל *men of the host*, i. e. soldiers; שַׂר הַחַיִל *captain of the host*, i. e. general.—III. *wealth, riches*; עָשָׂה חַיִל *to acquire riches*.—IV. *virtue, integrity*.

חֵיל Chald. masc. dec. 3d.—I. *strength*, spoken of the voice, Da. 3. 4.—II. *forces, army*.

חֵיל, חֵל masc. dec. 1a.—I. *host, army*.—II. *fortification*, or perhaps, *the space before it, the out-work*.

חִיל m.—I. *pain*.—II. *trembling, fear*, Ex. 15. 14.

חִילָה fem. *pain*, Job 6. 10.

חֵילָה fem. *fortification*, i. q. חֵיל, Ps. 48. 14, where others read חֵילָהּ, from חֵיל.

חֵילָם (*strength*; or *strength of the people*, for חֵיל עָם) pr. name of a city near the Euphrates, 2 Sa. 10. 16, for which in ver. 17, it is חֶלְאָם Khethib.

חִילֵן pr. name of a city in the tribe of Judah, 1 Ch. 6. 43, supposed to be the same as חֹלוֹן q. v.

חֹלֹן, חֹלוֹן (*sandy*; Simonis, *stay, sojourn*, comp. R. No. VII) pr. name—I. of a city in the tribe of Judah, Jos. 15. 51; 21. 15.—II. of a city in Moab, Je. 48. 21.

חֵלֹן (*strong*) pr. name masc. Nu. 1. 9; 2. 7.

חַלְחָלָה fem.—I. *pain*. Is. 21. 3.—II. *trembling, terror*.

חַלְחוּל (*trembling, terror*) pr. name of a city in the tribe of Judah, Jos. 15. 58.

מָחוֹל masc. dec. 3a.—I. *dance, dancing*.—II. pr. name masc. 1 Ki. 5. 11.

מְחוֹלָה fem. dec. 10, *dance, dancing*.

[e]חוּל ו׳ Kal inf. absolute; also pr. name masc. . חול

חוֹל noun masc. sing. . . . . . חול

[f]חוֹלָה fem. of the following, dec. 10. . . חלה

[g]חוֹלֶה Kal part. act. sing. masc. dec. 9a . חלה

חוּלִי id. imp. sing. fem. . . . . חול

[h]חוֹלָלְתְּ Pulal pret. 2 pers. sing. masc. [for חוֹלַלְתָּ comp. § 8. rem. 7] . . . . . . חול

חוֹלָלְתִּי id. pret. 1 pers. sing. [for חוֹלַלְתִּי v. id.] חול

[i]חוֹלֵם Kal part. act. sing. masc. dec. 7b . חלם

[k]חוֹלֵק Kal part. act. sing. masc. . . חלק

[l]חוֹלֵשׁ Kal part. act. sing. masc. . . . חלש

[m]חוֹלַת Kal part. act. fem., constr. of חוֹלָה dec. 10, from חוֹלֶה masc. . . . . . חלה

חוּם Root not used; i. q. Arab. חמם *to be black*. Hence—

חוּם ו׳ adj. m. *black*, Ge. 30. 32, 33, 35, 40. . חום

[n]חוֹמָה ו׳ noun fem. sing. dec. 10. . . חמה

חוֹמוֹת id. pl. . . . . חמה

חוֹמוֹתַיִךְ id. pl., suff. 2 pers. sing. fem. . . חמה

[o]חוֹמֵץ ו Kal part. act. sing. masc. . . חמץ

[p]חוֹמַת ו׳ noun fem. sing., constr. of חוֹמָה dec. 10. חמה

חוֹמֹת id. pl. . . . . חמה

חוֹמָתָהּ id. sing., suff. 3 pers. sing. fem. . . חמה

חוֹמֹתֶיהָ id. pl., suff. 3 pers. sing. fem. . . חמה

חוֹמֹתַיִךְ id. pl., suff. 2 pers. sing. fem. . . חמה

חוֹנֵן Kal part. act. sing. masc. . . . חנן

[חוּס] fut. תָּחוֹס, יָחֹס, יָחוּס (§ 21. rem. 3) *to pity, spare, grieve for*, const. with עַל of the thing; frequently spoken of the eye as that from which the pity proceeds, comp. Ge. 45. 20; De. 7. 16.

[q]חוּסָה ו׳ Kal imp. sing. masc. with parag. ה . חוס

[a] Jos. 2. 18. [b] Ec. 9. 18. [c] Is. 30. 18. [d] Eze. 30. 16. [e] Eze. 30. 16. [f] Ec. 5. 12, 15. [g] Ne. 2. 2. [h] Job 15. 7. [i] De. 13. 4. [k] Pr. 29. 24. [l] Is. 14. 12. [m] Ca. 2. 5. [n] La. 2. 8. [o] Ps. 71. 4. [p] Ne. 1. 3. [q] Joel 2. 17. [r] Ne. 13. 22.

חוֹסֵי Kal part. act. pl. c. masc. from חוֹסֶה d. 9a חסה

חוֹסִים[a] id. pl., absolute state . . . . חסה

חוֹף noun masc. sing. [for חֹף] . . . חפף

חָוַץ Root not used; Syr. Pa. *to surround.*

חוּץ masc. dec. 1a, pl. חוּצוֹת.—I. *an open place round about* or *without the house,* and generally for *the street.*—II. *out-field* or *lands,* without the city. —III. adv. *out of doors, without, abroad;* חוּצָה, הַחוּצָה *abroad, without;* בַּחוּץ *without, in the street, in the open air;* לַחוּצָה, לַחוּץ id.; מִחוּץ *from without, out of doors, without,* מִחוּץ לָעִיר *without the city,* מִחוּצָה לַשַּׁעַר *without the gate,* אֶל־מִחוּץ לַמַּחֲנֶה *without the camp;* חוּץ מִן *except, besides,* Ec. 2. 25.

חַיִץ masc. *wall,* Eze. 13. 10.

חִיצוֹן masc. חִיצוֹנָה fem. adj. *outer, exterior;* hence, *civil,* in opposition to *sacred,* 1 Ch. 26. 29; לַחִיצוֹן *without.*

חוּץ noun masc. dec. 1a, used also as an adv. . חוץ

חוּצָה[b] וְ id. with parag. ה; for וְ see lett. ו . . חוץ

חוּצוֹת[c] וְ id. with pl. fem. term. . . . חוץ

חוּצוֹתֶיהָ[d] id. pl., suff. 3 pers. sing. fem. . . חוץ

חוּצוֹתָיִךְ[e] id. pl., suff. 2 pers. sing. fem. [for תַיִךְ] . חוץ

חוּצוֹתָם[f] id. pl., suff. 3 pers. pl. masc. . . חוץ

חָוַק Root not used; i. q. Arab. חאג *to surround;* prob. derived from חָבַק *to embrace,* ב being softened into ו.

חוֹק masc. i. q. חֵיק *the bosom,* Ps. 74. 11 Khethib.

חֵיק, חֵק masc. dec. 1a.—I. *the bosom.*—II. *the feelings, affections.*—III. *bosom* or *lap* of a garment.—IV. *the hollow place* or *the inside* of a chariot, 1 Ki. 22. 35; also of an altar where the fire is kept, Eze. 43. 13, 14, 17.

חוֹקְךָ[g] noun masc. sing., suff. 2 pers. sing. masc., Kh. חוֹקְךָ, K. חֵיקְךָ from חוֹק or חֵיק . חוק

חוּקֹק pr. name of a place, see חֻקֹּק . . . חקק

חוֹקֵר[h] Kal part. act. sing. masc. . . . חקר

[חָוַר] fut. יֶחְוַר (§ 13. rem. 5) *to become white, pale,* Is. 29. 22.

חוּר, חֻר masc. *white, linen,* Est. 1. 6; 8. 15.

חוֹר masc. id. only pl. חֹרַי (poet. for חֹרִים) Is. 19. 9.

חִוָּר Ch. masc. *white,* Da. 7. 9.

חוּרַי (*linen-weaver*) pr. name masc. 1 Ch. 5. 14.

חֹרִי masc. *white bread,* Ge. 40. 16.

חוּרָם (*free-born, noble,* חָרַר=חוּר q. v.) pr. name —I. of a king of Tyre, 2 Ch. 2. 2, elsewhere חִירָם. —II. of a Tyrian artificer, 2 Ch. 4. 11; 1 Ki. 7. 13; called חִירוֹם 1 Ki. 7. 40, and חִירָם 2 Ch. 4. 11 Kh. As pr. names of the same person are considered, חוּרָם אָבִיו, חוּרָם אָבִי (*my father* or *his father is noble*) 2 Ch. 2. 12 (where the pref. לְ is to be taken as the accusative) and chap. 4. 16.—III. 1 Ch. 8. 5.

חִירָה (*nobility,* comp. חוּרָם) pr. name masc. Ge. 38. 1, 12.

חָוַר Root not used; prob. i. q. כּוּר *to dig, bore.*

חוֹר, חֹר masc. dec. 1a.—I. *hole,* Is. 11. 8; 42. 22. —II. pr. name of several men, espec. (a) of a king of Midian; (b) of the husband of Miriam the sister of Moses.

חוֹר, חֹר masc. dec. 1a, *cavern, aperture, hole.*

הוֹרִי more frequently חֹרִי (*dweller of caverns*) pr. name—I. *Horite,* collect. *Horites,* a Canaanitish people.—II. *Hori* pr. name masc. (a) Ge. 36. 22; (b) Nu. 13. 5.

חַוְרָן (*place of caverns*) pr. name of a country beyond Jordan, Eze. 47. 16, 18.

חֹרוֹן (*cavern*) pr. name, see בֵּית חֹרוֹן

חֹרֹנַיִם (*two caverns*) pr. name of a city of the Moabites.—Gent. noun חֹרֹנִי

חִוָּר[i] Ch. adj. masc. sing. . . . . חור

חוּר[k] וְ & [l] וְ noun masc. sing., also pr. name masc.; for וְ see lett. ו . . . . חור

חוֹרֵב pr. name of a place . . . . חרב

חוֹרוֹן pr. name, see בֵּית חוֹרוֹן R. . . . בית

חוֹרָי[m] for [חוֹרַי], poet. for חוֹרִים noun masc., pl. of חוֹר dec. 1. . . . . . חור

חוּרִי pr. name masc. . . . . חור

חוּרַי pr. name masc., see הִדַּי R. . . . הדד

חוּרַי pr. name masc. . . . . . חור

חוֹרִים[n] noun masc., pl. of [חֹר] dec. 1a . . חרר

חוּרָם וְ pr. name masc. . . . . . חור

חַוְרָן pr. name of a region . . . . חור

חוֹרֹן pr. name in compos. בֵּית חוֹרוֹן . . בית

חוֹרְפֶיךָ[o] Kal part. act. pl. masc., suff. 2 pers. sing. masc. from [חוֹרֵף] dec. 7b . . . חרף

חוֹרֵשׁ[p] Kal part. act. sing. masc dec. 7b . . חרשׁ

[חוּשׁ] I. *to hasten, make haste.*—II. *to be incited, ardent,* Job 20. 2.—III. (as in Syr.) *to feel, to enjoy,* Ec. 2. 25. Hiph.—I. *to hasten, accelerate.*—II. *to*

[a] Ps. 17. 7. [b] Nu. 35. 4. [c] Pr. 8. 26. [d] Eze. 11. 6. [e] Eze. 26. 11. [f] Zep. 3. 6. [g] Ps. 74. 11. [h] Job 28. 3. [i] Da. 7. 9. [k] Est. 1. 6. [l] Est. 8. 15. [m] Is. 19. 9. [n] Ec. 10. 17. [o] Ps. 69. 10. [p] Am. 9. 13.

hasten, make haste.—III. *to be excited, confused, confounded,* Is. 28. 16.

חוּשָׁה (*haste*) whence patronym. חֻשָׁתִי *Hushathite.*

חוּשַׁי (*hastening*) pr. name of a friend of David.

חוּשִׁים (*hastening*) pr. name of several men.

חוּשָׁם (*haste*) pr. name of a king of Edom, 1 Ch. 1. 45.

חִישׁ adj. masc. *hastily,* Ps. 90. 10.

חוֹשֵׁב Kal part. act. sing. masc. dec. 7 b . . . חשב

חוּשָׁה Kal imp. sing. m. with parag. ה (§ 21. rem. 5) חוש

חוּשָׁה pr. name masc. . . . . . . חוש

חוּשַׁי } וְ׳ pr. name masc. . . . . . . חוש
חוּשָׁי

[a]חוּשִׁי Kal inf., suff. 1 pers. sing. dec. 1 a . . חוש

חוּשִׁים pr. name masc. . . . . . חוש

חוֹשֵׂךְ וְ׳ Kal part. act. sing. masc. . . . חשך

חוּשָׁם pr. name masc. . . . . . . חוש

חַוֹּת noun fem., pl. of [חַוָּה] dec. 10. . . . חוה

[b]חַוֹּתֵיהֶם id. with suff. 3 pers. pl. masc. . . . חיה

[c]חוֹתָם n. m. s. (no vowel change), also pr. name m. חתם

[d]חוֹתֵם Kal part. act. sing. masc. . . . . חתם

[e]חֲזָא Ch. Peal pret. 3 pers. sing. masc. see . . חזה

חֲזָאֵל וְ׳ pr. name masc.; וַ bef. (-:) . . . . חזה

חָזָה fut. יֶחֱזֶה apoc. תַּחַז (§ 24. rem. 3 d).—I. *to see, behold,* especially a *vision,* and applied to a *prophecy* or *revelation* received in a vision.—II. *to look, gaze upon,* with בְּ.—III. *to look out, choose, select.*—IV. *to see, perceive;* hence perhaps metaph. *to feel, experience,* Job 8. 17.

חֲזָא, חֲזָה Ch. (§ 55) *to see.*

חָזֶה masc. dec. 9 b, pl. חָזוֹת, *the breast* of animals.

חֹזֶה masc. dec. 9 a.—I. part. act. *a seer, prophet.*—II. *league, agreement,* Is. 28. 15, comp. חָזוּת

חוֹזַי (*seer*) pr. name masc. 2 Ch. 33. 19.

חֲזוֹ (*vision*) pr. name masc. Ge. 22. 22.

חֵזֵו Ch. masc. emph. חֶזְוָא dec. 3 c.—I. *vision, sight.*—II. *look, appearance,* Da. 7. 20.

חָזוֹן masc. dec. 3 a.—I. *vision, sight.*—II. *revelation.*

חָזוּת fem. dec. 3 a, *vision, revelation,* 2 Ch. 9. 29.

חֲזוֹת Ch. dec. 1 a, *appearance, view,* Da. 4. 8, 17.

חָזוּת fem. dec. 1 b (§ 33. No. 3).—I. *appearance, conspicuity,* קֶרֶן חָזוּת *a conspicuous* (Eng. Vers. *notable*) *horn,* Da. 8. 5, 8.—II. *vision, revelation.*—III. *league, agreement,* Is. 28. 18; חָזָה i. q. חזו Arab. Conj. III. *to consent.* IV. *to enter into an agreement.*

חֶזְיוֹן (*vision*) pr. name masc. 1 Ki. 15. 18.

חִזָּיוֹן masc., dec. 3 c, constr. חֶזְיוֹן (§ 32. rem. 3).—I. *vision, sight.*—II. *revelation.*

חֲזָאֵל (whom *God beholds*), חֲזָהאֵל (2 Ki. 8. 8, 15) pr. name of a king of Syria.

חֲזִיאֵל (*vision of God*) pr. name masc. 1 Ch. 23. 9.

חֲזָיָה (whom *the Lord beholds,* comp. חֲזָאֵל) pr. name masc. Ne. 11. 5.

יַחֲזִיאֵל (*he shall see God*) pr. name masc. of several persons.

יַחְזְיָה (*he shall see the Lord*) pr. name masc. Ezr. 10. 15.

מַחֲזֶה masc. dec. 9 a, *vision.*

מֶחֱזָה fem. *window,* 1 Ki. 7. 4, 5.

מַחֲזִיאוֹת (*visions*) pr. name masc. 1 Ch. 25. 4, 30.

[f]חֲזָה Ch. for חֲזָא (q. v.) . . . . . חזה

חָזֶה Ch. Peal part. act. sing. masc. dec. 6 a (§ 62) חזה

[g]חֲזֵה Ch. id. part. pass. (§ 55 note) . . . חזה

חֲזֵה [h]וְ׳ Kal imp. sing. masc.; or noun masc constr. of חָזֶה dec. 9 b; וַ bef. (-:) . . . חזה

חֹזֵה noun masc., constr. of the following . . חזה

חֹזֶה Kal part. act. masc. (Eze. 12. 27); or subst dec. 9 a . . . . חזה

חֲזָהאֵל pr. name masc., see חֲזָאֵל . . . . חזה

חָזוּ Kal pret. 3 pers. pl. . . . . . חזה

חֲזוֹ pr. name masc. . . . . . . חזה

חֲזוּ Kal imp. pl. masc. . . . . . חזה

[i]חֶזְוֵהּ וְ Ch. noun masc. sing., suff. 3 pers. sing. fem. from [חֵזֵו] dec. 3 c . . . . חזה

[k]חֶזְוֵי וְ׳ Ch. id. pl., constr. state . . . . חזה

חָזוֹן noun masc. sing. dec. 3 a . . . . חזה

חֲזוֹן id., constr. state . . . . . . חזה

חָזוּת noun fem. sing. dec. 1 b (§ 33. No. 3) . חזה

[l]חֲזוֹתֵהּ וּ Ch. noun fem. sing., suff. 3 pers. sing. fem. from [חֲזוֹ=חֲזוֹת] dec. 9 b . . . חזה

[m]חָזוּתְכֶם וְ noun fem. sing., suff. 2 pers. pl. masc. from חָזוּת dec. 1 b (§ 33. No. 3) . . . חזה

חָזַז Root not used; Arab. *to pierce through.*

חֲזִיז masc. dec. 1 a, *lightning*

חֲזִיאֵל וַ pr. name masc.; וַ bef. (-:) . . . חזה

חֲזָיָה pr. name masc. . . . . . . חזה

[n]חֶזְיוֹן constr. of the foll.; (§ 32. rem. 3) also pr. n. חזה

[o]חִזָּיוֹן noun masc. sing. dec. 3 c . . . . חזה

[p]חֲזִיזִים noun masc., pl. of חֲזִיז dec. 1 a . . . חזז

[q]חֹזִים Kal part. act., pl. of חֹזֶה dec. 9 a . . חזה

[a] Job 20. 2. [b] Nu. 32. 41. [c] Ex. 28. 21. [d] Eze. 28. 12. [e] Da. 4. 20. [f] Da. 7. 1. [g] Da. 3. 19. [h] Le. 10. 15. [i] Da. 7. 20. [k] Da. 4. 6. [l] Da. 4. 8, 17. [m] Is. 28. 18. [n] Job 33. 15. [o] Is. 22. 1, 5. [p] Zec. 10. 1. [q] Eze. 22. 28.

[a] חָזַיִן Ch. Peal part. act., pl. of חָזֵה dec. 6a (§ 62) חזה

[b] חֶזְיֹנוֹת noun masc. with pl. fem. term. from חִזָּיוֹן dec. 3c (§ 32. rem. 3) . . . . חזה

חֲזִיר noun masc. sing. . . . . . . חזר

חֵזִיר pr. name masc. . . . . . חזר

חָזִיתָ Kal pret. 2 pers. sing. masc. . . . חזה

[c] חָזִית id. pret. 2 pers. sing. fem. . . . . חזה

חֲזַיְתָ Ch. Peal pret. 2 pers. sing. masc. . . חזה

חֲזֵית Ch. id. pret. 1 pers. sing. . . . . חזה

[d] חֲזַיְתָה Ch. id. pret. 2 pers. sing. masc., (§ 47. r. 2) חזה

[e] חֲזֵיתוּן Ch. id. pret. 2 pers. pl. masc. . . . חזה

[f] חָזִיתִי Kal pret. 1 pers. sing. . . . . חזה

[g] חֲזִיתִךָ id. id., suff. 2 pers. sing. masc. . . . חזה

חֲזִיתֶם [h] וַ׳ id. pret. 2 pers. pl. masc.; וַ bef. (ֲ) . חזה

חָזַק fut. יֶחֱזַק, יֶחְזַק (§ 13. rem. 5).—I. *to be* or *become strong, firm, fast;* perhaps trans. *to strengthen,* Eze. 30. 21. Const. with מִן *to be stronger than, to prevail over;* with עַל id.—II. *to be confirmed, established.*—III. *to be hardened, obstinate,* spoken of the heart.—IV. *to be strong* upon any one, i. e. *to be urgent, to press upon,* with עַל; once with acc. Je. 20. 7. Pi.—I. *to make strong, firm, to strengthen;* חִזַּק יָד *to strengthen the hand,* i. e. to encourage, help, assist.—II. *to harden,* spoken of one's own heart, the face i.e. to become obstinate, perverse.—III. *to heal, restore.* Hiph.—I. *to take hold of, to seize,* with לְ, עַל, בְּ; hence, *to hold, retain; to hold, contain,* 2 Ch. 4. 5.—II. *to hold fast, adhere to,* with עַל of the person.—III. *to make firm, strong, to strengthen,* hence, *to repair;* intrans. *to be strong, powerful.*—IV. *to help, assist* with בְּ. Hithpa.—I. *to be strengthened, confirmed, established.* Also *to strengthen oneself, to gather strength, take courage.*—II. *to show oneself strong, courageous,* with לִפְנֵי against any one; with בְּ, עִם for any one, i. e. to help, assist him.

חָזָק masc. dec. 4c (pl. c. חִזְקֵי), חֲזָקָה fem. adj. —I. *strong, mighty.*—II. *firm, hard,* of the heart, forehead, i. e. obstinate, daring.

חָזֵק masc. adj. *strong, powerful, waxing strong.*

חֵזֶק masc. dec. 6b, *strength,* Ps. 18. 2.

חֹזֶק masc. dec. 6c, *strength, might.*

חֶזְקָה fem. constr. חֶזְקַת (no pl.) strictly an inf. (§ 8. rem. 10).—I. *a being* or *becoming strong,* בְּחֶזְקָתוֹ *when he became strong, gained strength.* —II. *an urging on, impelling,* Is. 8. 11.

חָזְקָה fem.—I. *force, vehemence;* בְּחָזְקָה *with force, vehemently, greatly.*—II. *a strengthening, repairing,* 2 Ki. 12. 13.

חִזְקִי (*strong*) pr. name masc. 1 Ch. 8. 17.

חִזְקִיָּה, חִזְקִיָּהוּ (*strength of the Lord*) pr. name masc. of several persons, especially of Hezekiah king of Judah, who is likewise called יְחִזְקִיָּה, יְחִזְקִיָּהוּ (whom *the Lord shall strengthen,* for יְחַזְּקִיָּהוּ=יְחַזְקִיָּהוּ comp. יְחֶזְקֵאל).

יְחֶזְקֵאל (whom *God shall strengthen,* for יְחֶזְקֵאל =יְחַזֵּק אֵל, comp. אֲכָלְךָ § 24. rem. 21) pr. name masc. Ezekiel the prophet, son of Buzi a priest.

חִזְקִיָּה see יְחִזְקִיָּה

יְחִזְקִיָּהוּ pr. name of a man at the time of Ahaz, 2 Ch. 28. 12.

[i] חָזָק Kal pret. 3 pers. sing. m. for חָזַק (§ 8. r. 7) חזק

חָזָק וְ׳ adj. masc. sing. dec. 4c (pl. c. חִזְקֵי) . חזק

[k] חֲזָק [l] וַ׳ id. imp. sing. masc. (§ 8. rem. 12); חזק

[m] חֲזַק וַ׳ bef. (ֲ) . . . . . חזק

[n] חָזֵק וְ adj. masc. sing. . . . . . חזק

חַזֵּק Piel inf. const.; or imp. sing. masc. . . חזק

[o] חִזַּק id. pret. 3 pers. sing. masc. . . חזק

[p] חֹזֶק noun masc. sing. dec. 6c . . . חזק

[q] חָזָקָה / חָזְקָה Kal pret. 3 pers. sing. fem. (§ 8. rem. 7) חזק

חֲזָקָה adj. fem. sing. from חָזָק masc. . . חזק

חַזְּקֵהוּ וְ Piel imp. sing. masc., suff. 3 pers. sing. m. חזק

חָזְקוּ [r] וַ׳ Kal pret. 3 pers. pl. . . . . חזק

[s] חֲזָקוֹ id. pret. 3 pers. sing. masc., suff. 3 p. s. m. חזק

[t] חַזְּקוּ Piel imp. pl. masc. . . . . . חזק

חִזְקוּ Kal imp. pl. masc. . . . . . חזק

חִזְּקוּ וַ׳ Piel pret. 3 pers. pl. . . . . חזק

[u] חַזְּקִי / [x] חַזְּקִי Piel imp. sing. fem., (comp. § 8. rem. 12) חזק

[y] חִזְקֵי [z] וְ׳ noun masc. pl. c., fr. חָזָק d. 4 (§33. r.1) חזק

[a] חִזְקִי וְ׳ noun masc. sing., suff. 1 pers. sing. fr. [חֵזֶק] dec. 6b; also pr. name masc. . חזק

חִזְקִיָּה / חִזְקִיָּהוּ וְ׳ pr. name masc. . . . . . חזק

חֲזָקִים adj. masc., pl. of חָזָק dec. 4c (§ 33. rem. 1) חזק

[b] חַזְּקֵנִי וְ Piel imp. sing. masc., suff. 1 pers. sing. חזק

[c] חָזַקְתָּ וְ Kal pret. 2 pers. sing. masc.; acc. shifted by conv. וְ (§ 8. rem. 7) . . חזק

[d] חִזַּקְתִּי Piel pret. 1 pers. sing. . . . . חזק

חִזַּקְתִּי וְ id. id.; acc. shifted by conv. וְ (§ 8. r. 7) חזק

[e] חֲזַקְתֶּם וַ Kal pret. 2 pers. pl. masc.; וַ for וְ conv. חזק

[a] Da. 3. 27; 5. 23. [b] Joel 3. 1. [c] Is. 57. 8. [d] Da. 2. 41, 41. [e] Da. 2. 8. [f] Job 15. 17. [g] Ps. 63. 3. [h] Eze. 13. 8. [i] 2 Ch. 26. 15. [k] Is. 41. 6. [l] Da. 10. 19. [m] Hag. 2. 4, 4. [n] Ex. 19. 19; 2 Sa. 3. 1. [o] Ps. 147. 13. [p] Hag. 2. 22. [q] Eze. 3. 14. [r] 2 Sa. 16. 21. [s] 2 Ch. 28. 20. [t] Is. 35. 3. [u] Is. 54. 2. [x] Na. 3. 14. [y] Eze. 3. 7. [z] Eze. 2. 4. [a] Ps. 18. 2. [b] Ju. 16. 28. [c] 1 Ki. 2. 2. [d] Ho. 7. 15. [e] Jos. 23. 6.

חִזַּקְתֶּם[a] Piel pret. 2 pers. pl. masc. . . . חזק

חֲזַקְתַּנִי[b] Kal pret. 2 pers. sing. masc., suff. 1 pers. s. חזק

חִזַּקְתָּנִי[c] Piel pret. 2 pers. sing. masc., suff. 1 pers. sing. (§ 2. rem. 1) . . . . חזק

חָזַר Root not used; Arab. *to have small eyes;* but this may merely be a denom. of the following noun. Chald. *to return.*

חֲזִיר masc. *hog, swine.*

חֵזִיר (*swine*) pr. name of a man, 1 Ch. 24. 15; Ne. 10. 21.

יַחְזֵרָה (whom God *shall bring back*) pr. name masc. 2 Ch. 9. 12.

חָח[d] noun masc. sing., irr. see the following . חוח

חַחִי id. with suff. 1 pers. sing., dag. f. impl. (§ 37. rem. 7) . . . . חוח

חַחִיִּים[e] id. pl., Kh. חַחִיִּים [fr. חַחִי], K. חַחִים . חוח

חַחִים id. pl. absolute state . . . . חוח

חָטָא fut. יֶחֱטָא.—I. *to miss* a scope or aim, but only in Hiphil q. v.—II. *to miss one's step,* i. e. *to stumble, fall,* Pr. 19. 2.—III. *to miss,* opp. to מָצָא *to find,* so perhaps Pr. 8. 36; Job 5. 24.—IV. *to sin;* with לְ, בְּ or עַל *by, against.*—V. *to forfeit,* with acc. Pi.—I. *to suffer the loss of anything,* Ge. 31. 39.—II. *to offer as a sin-offering;* hence *to expiate, cleanse, free from sin.* Hiph.—I. *to miss* a scope or aim, Ju. 20. 16.—II. *to cause, induce to sin.*—III. *to declare guilty, to condemn,* Is. 29. 21. Hithp.—I. *to miss oneself* as it were, *to be at his wit's end, be astounded,* Job 41. 17.—II. *to purify oneself.*

חֵטְא masc. with suff. חֶטְאוֹ, pl. c. חֲטָאֵי (§ 35. rem. 6), *failure, sin.*

חַטָּא masc. d. 1 b (§ 30. No. 4, & r. 1) *sinner.*

חֲטָאָה fem.—I. *sin.*—II. *sin-offering,* Ps. 40. 7.

חַטָּאָה fem. of חַטָּא.—I. *sinner,* Am. 9. 8.—II. *sin.*

חַטָּאָה Ch. fem. *sin,* Ezr. 6. 17, Keri.

חַטַּאת (for חַטָּאַת § 39. No. 4) fem. constr. חַטַּאת (for חַטָּאַת from חַטָּאָה comp. § 23. r. 2) with suff. חַטָּאתִי, pl. חַטָּאוֹת (§ 44. rem. 5) constr. חַטֹּאות (for חַטְּאוֹת comp. § 23. rem. 2).—I. *sin.*—II. *sin-offering.*—III. *idols,* as the cause of sin.—IV. *punishment for sin.*

חֲטָי Ch. masc. *sin,* with suff. חֲטָיָךְ.

חַטָּת fem. *sin,* Nu. 15. 24, for חַטָּאת.

חֲטֹא[f] Kal inf. constr. . . . . . חטא

וְחִטֵּא[g] Piel pret. 3 pers. sing. masc. . . חטא

חֵטְא noun masc. sing. dec. 6 (§ 35. rem. 6) . חטא

חֹטֵא[h], חֹטֶא[i] Kal part. act. masc. s. dec. 7 b (§ 23. r. 9) חטא

חָטְאָה, חָטָאָה[k] וְ'[l] id. pret. 3 pers. sing. fem. (§ 8. r. 7) חטא

חֲטָאָה וְ'[m] noun fem. sing.; וּ bef. (-:) . . חטא

חַטָּאָה[n] וְ'[o] noun fem. sing. from חַטָּא masc. . . חטא

חָטְאוּ, חָטָאוּ Kal pret. 3 pers. pl. (§ 8. rem. 7) . חטא

חֲטָאָו[p] noun masc. pl., suff. 3 pers. sing. masc. [for חֲטָאָיו] from חֵטְא dec. 6 (§ 35. rem. 6) חטא

חֶטְאוֹ id. sing., suff. 3 pers. sing. masc. . . חטא

וְחִטְּאוֹ[q] Piel pret. 3 pers. sing. masc., suff. 3 pers. sing. masc. . . . . חטא

וְ'חִטְּאוּ[r] id. pret. 3 pers. pl. . . . חטא

וְ'חַטָּאוֹת[s] noun fem. pl. absolute from חַטָּאת, (§ 39. No. 4 d, & § 44. rem. 5) . . חטא

וְ'חַטֹּאות[t] id. pl., const. state [for חַטְּאוֹת] . חטא

חַטֹּאותַי[u] id. pl., suff. 1 pers. sing. [for חַטְּאוֹתַי] . חטא

חַטֹּאותֶיךָ id. pl., suff. 2 pers. sing. masc. . . חטא

וְ'חַטֹּאותֵיכֶם[v] id. pl., suff. 2 pers. pl. masc. . . חטא

וְחַטֹּאותֵינוּ[y] id. pl., suff. 1 pers. pl. . . . חטא

חַטֹּאותָם id. pl., suff. 3 pers. pl. masc. . . חטא

חֲטָאַי[x], חֲטָאָי[a] noun masc. pl., suff. 1 pers. sing. fr. חֵטְא dec. 6 (§ 35. rem. 6) . . . חטא

חַטָּאֵי[b] noun masc. pl. constr. fr. [חַטָּא] dec. 1 b חטא

חֲטָאֵי[c] וְ'[d] noun masc. pl. constr. fr. חֵטְא dec. 6 (§ 35. rem. 6) . . . . . חטא

וְחוֹטְאִי[e] Kal part. act. sing. masc. (חֹטֵא) suff. 1 pers. sing. dec. 7 b . . . . חטא

וְחַטָּאֶיהָ[f] noun masc. pl., suff. 3 pers. sing. fem. from [חַטָּא] dec. 1 b . . . . חטא

חֲטָאֵיכֶם[g] noun masc. pl., suff. 2 pers. pl. masc. fr. חֵטְא dec. 6 (§ 35. rem. 6) . . . חטא

חֲטָאִים[h] id. pl., absolute state . . . . חטא

וְ'חַטָּאִים noun masc. pl. of [חַטָּא] dec. 1 b . חטא

חֹטְאִים[i] Kal part. act. m., pl. of חֹטֵא d. 7 b (§ 23. r. 4) חטא

חֶטְאָם[k] noun masc. sing., suff. 3 pers. pl. masc. fr. חֵטְא dec. 6 (§ 35. rem. 6) . . . חטא

חָטָאנוּ Kal pret. 1 pers. pl. . . . . חטא

חָטָאתָ id. pret. 2 pers. sing. masc. . . . חטא

וְחָטָאת[l] id. pret. 3 pers. sing. fem. (§ 23. rem. 1) חטא

וְ'חַטָּאת[m] noun fem. sing. (§ 39. No. 4 d, & § 44. rem. 5, and note the following) . . חטא

וְ'חַטַּאת id., constr. state, [for חַטָּאַת fr. חַטָּאָה] חטא

---

[a] Eze. 34. 4. [b] Je. 20. 7. [c] Da. 10. 19. [d] Ex. 35. 22. [e] Eze. 29. 4. [f] Eze. 3. 21. [g] Le. 14. 52. [h] Is. 1. 4. [i] Ec. 8. 12. [k] La. 1. 8. [l] Le. 5. 15. [m] Ps. 40. 7. [n] Is. 5. 18. [o] Ex. 34. 7. [p] La. 3. 39. [q] Nu. 19. 19. [r] Eze. 43. 22. [s] Job 13. 23. [t] 1 Ki. 16. 13. [u] Ps. 25. 18. [x] Eze. 21. 29. [y] Is. 59. 12. [z] Ge. 41. 9. [a] Is. 38. 17. [b] Am. 9. 10. [c] 2 Ki. 10. 29. [d] Eze. 23. 49. [e] Pr. 8. 36. [f] Is. 13. 9. [g] Is. 1. 18. [h] Ec. 10. 4. [i] 1 Sa. 14. 33. [k] Le. 20. 20. [l] Ex. 5. 16. [m] Eze. 45. 23.

חַטֹּאת id. pl. constr., comp. חַטָּאוֹת . . חטא

חִטֵּאתָ וְ Piel pret. 2 p. s. m. acc. shifted (comp. § 8. r. 7) חטא

חַטָּאתוֹ [a] וְ׳ noun fem. sing., suff. 3 pers. sing. masc. fr. חַטָּאת (q. v.) . . . . חטא

חַטֹּאתָו id. pl., suff. (K. ־ָתִיו׳ § 4. r. 1) 3 pers. s. m. חטא

חֲטֹאתוֹ [b] Kal inf. (חֲטֹאת § 23. rem. 26), suff. 3 pers. sing. masc. . . . . . . חטא

חָטָאתִי וְ׳ Kal pret. 1 pers. sing. . . . חטא

חַטָּאתִי וְ׳ n. fem. sing., suff. 1 pers. sing. fr. חַטָּאת (q. v. & חַטָּאוֹת) . . . . חטא

חַטֹּאתֶיהָ id. pl., suff. 3 pers. sing. fem. . . . חטא

חַטֹּאתֵיהֶם id. pl., suff. 3 pers. pl. masc. . . . חטא

חַטֹּאתָיו [c] id. pl., suff. 3 pers. sing. masc. . . . חטא

חַטֹּאתַיִךְ / חַטֹּאתָיִךְ } id. pl. with suff. 2 pers. sing. fem. . . חטא

חַטֹּאתֶיךָ [g] וְ׳ id. pl., suff. 2 pers. sing. masc. . . חטא

חַטֹּאתֵיכֶם id. pl., suff. 2 pers. pl. masc. . . . חטא

חַטֹּאתֵינוּ [h] וְ׳ id. pl., suff. 1 pers. pl. . . . חטא

חַטָּאתְךָ [i] וְ׳ id. sing., suff. 2 pers. sing. masc. . . חטא

חַטַּאתְכֶם id. sing., suff. 2 pers. pl. masc. . . . חטא

חַטָּאתָם וְ׳ id. sing., suff. 3 pers. pl. masc. . . חטא

חַטֹּאתָם id. pl., suff. 3 pers. pl. masc. . . . חטא

חֲטָאתֶם [k] וְ׳ Kal pret. 2 pers. pl. masc.; וְ for וְ conv. חטא

חַטָּאתֵנוּ [l] noun fem. sing., suff. 1 pers. pl. from חַטָּאת (q. v. & חַטָּאוֹת) . . . . חטא

חַטֹּאתֵנוּ [m] id. pl., suff. 1 pers. pl. . . . חטא

[חָטַב] I. *to cut* or *hew* wood.—II. *to stripe, mark with stripes*, only part. pass. חֲטֻבוֹת *striped, variegated*, Pr. 7. 16. Pu. *to be hewn out*. Ps. 144. 12.

חֲטֻבוֹת [n] Kal part. pass. pl. fem. from [חָטוּב] masc. חטב

חֹטְבֵי [o] וְ׳ [p] id. part. act. pl. c. m. from חוֹטֵב׳ dec. 7 b חטב

חִטָּה fem. *wheat*; pl. חִטִּים, חִטִּין, constr. חִטֵּי *grains of wheat*.

חִנְטָה Chald. fem. only pl. חִנְטִין id., dag. forte resolved in נ

חַטּוּשׁ pr. name masc. of several persons.

חֲטִיטָא (*a digging*, R. חטט Aram. *to dig*) pr. name m.

חֲטָיָךְ [q] וַ Chald. noun masc. sing., suff. 2 pers. sing. m. [from חֲטָי]; K. חֲטָאָךְ id. from חֲטָא חטא

חַטִּיל (*waving*, Arab. حطل *to wave to and fro*) pr. name masc.

חִטִּים [r] וְ׳ noun fem. with pl. m. term. fr. חִטָּה (q. v.) חטה

חִטִּין [s] id. with the Chald. term. . . . חטה

חֲטִיפָא pr. name masc. . . . . חטף

[חָטַם] prop. *to muzzle*, hence *to restrain oneself*, with לְ *towards* any one. Is. 48. 9.

חָטַף fut. יַחְטֹף (§ 13. rem. 5) *to catch, seize*.

חֲטִיפָא (*a catching*) pr. name masc.

חֲטַפְתֶּם [t] וַ Kal pret. 2 pers. pl. masc.; וַ for וְ conv. חטף

חֹטֶר masc. *stick, rod*, Pr. 14. 3; Is. 11. 1.

חָי וְ׳ / חַי [u] וְ׳, וְ׳ } Kal pret. 3 pers. sing. masc.; or, adj. or subst. m. dec. 8 d (§ 37. rem. 6) } חיי

חֵי וְ׳ id. adj. or subst., construct state . חיי

חַיָּא [x] Chald. adj. masc. sing., emph. of חַי׳ dec. 5 a חיי

חִיאֵל pr. name masc. . . . . חיה

חִיַּבְתֶּם [y] וְ Piel pret. 2 pers. pl. masc. . . . חוב

חִידָה noun fem. sing. dec. 10. . . . חוד

חִידוֹת id. pl. . . . . . חוד

חִידָתִי id. sing., suff. 1 pers. sing. . . . חוד

חִידָתְךָ [z] id. sing., suff. 2 pers. sing. masc. . . חוד

חִידֹתָם [a] וְ id. pl., suff. 3 pers. pl. masc. . . חוד

חָיָה [b] וְ׳ fut. יִחְיֶה; ap. יְחִי (§ 24. rem. 3 e); inf. c. חֲיוֹת, with pref. לִחְיוֹת, imp. with pref. וֶחְיֵה, וִחְיוּ (§ 13. rem. 1 & 13).—I. *to live*.—II. *to revive*.—III. *to be* or *become strong, vigorous, to be restored*, with מִן, *from* sickness. Pi.—I. *to make alive, to give life, to quicken*.—II. *to preserve alive, to let live*.—III. *to revive, strengthen, comfort, refresh*. Hiph. הֶחֱיָה.—I. *to preserve alive, to let live*.—II. *to restore to life*.

חֲיָא, חֲיָה Chald. *to live*, only imp. חֱיִי. Aph. *to preserve alive*, Da. 5. 19.

חָיֶה adj., only pl. fem. חָיוֹת *lively, strong*, Ex. 1. 19.

חֵיוָא, חֵיוָה Chald. fem. dec. 8 a, *living creature, animal, beast*.

יְחִיאֵל (*God liveth*) pr. name masc. of several persons. Patronym. יְחִיאֵלִי.

חִיאֵל (by aphær. for יְחִיאֵל) pr. name masc. 1 Ki. 16. 34.

יְחִיָּה (*the Lord liveth* for יְחִיָּהוּ) pr. name masc. 1 Ch. 15. 24, elsewhere called יְחִיאֵל comp. ver. 18.

מִחְיָה fem. dec. 10.—I. *preservation of life*.—II. *means of living, food*.—III. *indication, sign, mark*, (from חָיָה i. q. חָוָה *to show*), Le. 13. 10, 24. According to others, *stroke, mark, spot*, fr. מָחָה q. v.

חָיָה [c] וְ Kal pret. 3 pers. sing. fem. in pause for חָיְתָה (§ 18. rem. 15 note) . . . חיי

חָיֹה Kal inf. absolute . . . . חיה

[a] 2 Ki. 21. 17. [b] Eze. 33. 12. [c] Is. 40. 2. [d] Ne. 9. 2. [e] 1 Ki. 16. 19. [f] Is. 44. 22. [g] Is. 43. 25. [h] Eze. 33. 10. [i] Is. 6. 7. [k] De. 20. 18. [l] Je. 16. 10. [m] 2 Ch. 28. 13 [n] Pr. 7. 16. [o] Jos. 9. 21, 27. [p] Jos. 9. 23. [q] Da. 4. 24. [r] 2 Sa. 17. 28. [s] Eze. 4. 9. [t] Ju. 21. 21. [u] 2 Sa. 12. 22. [x] Da. 6. 21, 27. [y] Da. 1. 10. [z] Ju. 14. 13. [a] Pr. 1. 6. [b] Ec. 6. 6. [c] Ex. 1. 16.

חַיָּה ן׳ noun fem. sing. dec. 10, from חַי masc. . חיי

[a]חִיָּה Piel pret. 3 pers. sing. masc. . . חיה

חֲיֵה ן Kal imp. s. m. [for וֶחְיֵה § 13. rem. 1 & 13] חיה

חָיוֹ Kal inf. absolute for חָיֹה (§ 24. rem. 2) חיה

[b]חָיוּ ן׳ id. pret. 3 pers. pl. . . . . . חיה

חַיּוֹ Khethib; K. חַיָּיו (q. v. comp. § 4. rem. 1) חיי

[c]חִיּוּ Piel pret. 3 pers. pl. . . . . . . חיה

חֲיוּ ן Kal imp. pl. masc.; ן before (:) for ן (§ 13. rem. 1 & 13) . . . . . חיה

[d]חֵיוָא } Chald. noun fem. sing. dec. 8a (§ 55 note) . . . . . } חיה

[e]חֵיוְתָה

[f]חֵיוָן Chald. id. pl., absolute state . . . חיה

[g]חָיוֹת adj. fem. pl. [of חָיָה, from חָיֶה masc.] . חיה

חַיּוֹת adj. (Le. 14. 4) or subst. fem., pl. of חַיָּה dec. 10, from חַי masc. . . . . חיי

[h]חַיּוּת noun fem. sing. . . . . . . חיי

חֵיוַת Chald. noun fem. sing., constr. of חֵיוָא dec. 8a חיה

[i]חֵיוָתָא Chald. id. pl., emph. state . . . חיה

חֵיוְתָא Chald. id. sing., emph. state . . . חיה

[k]חֲיוֹתָם Kal inf., suff. 3 pers. pl. masc. dec. 1a . חיה

[חָיִי] pret. חַי, *to live.*

חַי, masc. dec. 8d constr. חֵי, pl. חַיִּים (§ 37. rem. 6); fem. חַיָּה.—I. adj.—1. *living, alive.*—2. *lively, vigorous.*—3. *reviving,* כָּעֵת חַיָּה *when this time* or *season revives,* i. e. the coming spring, or, according to others, at this very time next year. Others who render this, *according to the time of life,* or (as Prof. Lee) *as at the season, period of a vigorous woman,* taking עֵת in the constr. state, have overlooked the article in כָּ; for we should then expect כְּעֵת־חַיָּה.—4. *live, raw,* of flesh.—II. subst. *life,* Le. 25. 36, וְחֵי אָחִיךָ עִמָּךְ *that the life of thy brother be with thee,* i. e. preserved with thee; חֵי פַרְעֹה *by the life of Pharaoh,* which others take as an adjective, *as Pharaoh liveth.*—III. pl. חַיִּים.—1. *life.*—2. *living, substance,* Pr. 27. 27.

חַי Chald. masc. dec. 5a.—I. adj. *living, alive.*—II. subst. pl. חַיִּין *life.*

חַיָּה fem. dec. 10 (comp חַי).—I. *living thing, animal, beast.*—II. *tribe, people, band, troop.*—III. *life.*

חַיּוּת fem. *life,* 2 Sa. 20. 3.

חַיַּי } noun masc. pl., suff. 1 pers. sing. from חַי dec. 8d (§ 37. rem. 6) . . } חיי

[l]חַיָּי ן׳

חַיֵּי id. pl., construct state . . . . חיי

[m]חַיִּי Kal imp. sing. fem. . . . . . יה

חֲיִי Chald. Peal imp. sing. masc. . . . . יה

חַיַּיָּא Chald. adj. m. pl. emph. from חַי׳ dec. 5a יי

[n]חַיֶּיהָ noun masc. pl., suff. 3 pers. sing. fem. from חַי dec. 8d (§ 37. rem. 6) . . . יי

[o]חַיֵּיהוּ Piel imp. sing. masc. [חַיֵּה], suff. 3 pers. sing. masc. (§ 24. rem. 21b) . . . . יה

חַיֵּיהֶם noun masc. pl., suff. 3 pers. pl. masc. from חַי dec. 8d (§ 37. rem. 6) . . . יי

חַיָּיו id., suff. 3 pers. sing. masc. . . . . יי

חַיֶּיךָ id., suff. 2 pers. sing. masc. . . . . יי

[p]חַיָּיְכִי id., suff. 2 pers. s. fem. [for חַיַּיִךְ § 4. rem. 3] יי

[q]חַיֵּיכֶם id., suff. 2 pers. pl. masc. . . . . יי

חַיִּים ן׳ id. pl., absolute state, adj. and subst. . יי

[r]חַיֵּינוּ id. pl., suff. 1 pers. pl. . . . . . יי

[s]חָיִיתָ ן Kal pret. 2 pers. sing. masc. . . . יה

[t]חֲיִיתֶם ן id. pret. 2 pers. pl. masc.; ן for ן conv. (§ 13. rem. 1 & 13) . . . . יה

חִיִּיתַנִי } Piel pret. 2 pers. sing. masc., suff. 1 pers. sing. (§ 2. rem. 1) . . } יה

[u]חִיִּיתַנִי

[x]חַיֶּךָ defect. for חַיֶּיךָ (q. v.) . . . . . יי

חֵיל } noun masc. sing. dec. 6h (§ 35. rem. 12), Chald. dec. 3d . . . } ול

חַיִל ן׳

חֵיל ן׳ id. constr. st.; or (Na. 3. 8) abs. dec. 1a ול

חִיל noun masc. sing. . . . . . ול

[y]חֵילָהּ noun masc. sing., suff. 3 pers. sing. fem. from חַיִל dec. 6h . . . . . ול

חֵילוֹ ן׳ id., suff. 3 pers. sing. masc. . . ול

חִילוּ Kal imp. pl. masc. R. חִיל, see . . ול

חֵילִי noun m. s., suff. 1 pers. s. from חַיִל dec. 6h ול

[z]חֵילֵיהֶם id. pl., suff. 3 pers. pl. masc. . . ול

חֲיָלִים [a]ן׳ id. pl., abs. st. (§ 35. rem. 12); ן bef. (-:) ול

חֵילֵךְ id. sing., suff. 2 pers. sing. masc. [for חֵילְךָ] ול

[b]חֵילֵךְ [c]ן׳ id. sing., suff. 2 pers. sing. fem. . ול

חֵילְךָ id. sing., suff. 2 pers. sing. masc. . . ול

חֵילָם [d]ן׳ id. s., suff. 3 pers. pl. m.; also pr. name ול

חִילֵן pr. name of a place . . . . ול

[e]חִין ן noun masc. sing. . . . . . נן

חַיֵּנִי Piel imp. sing. masc. [חַיֵּה], suff. 1 pers. sing. (§ 24 rem. 21) . . . . יה

[zz]חַיִץ noun masc. sing. . . . . . וץ

[f]חִיצוֹנָה adj. fem. sing. from חִיצוֹן masc. . . וץ

חֵיק [g]ן׳ noun masc. sing. dec. 1a . . . וק

[h]חֵיקָהּ id., suff. 3 pers. sing. fem. . . . וק

חֵיקוֹ id., suff. 3 pers. sing. masc. . . . וק

[i]חֵיקִי id., suff. 1 pers. sing. . . . . וק

[a] Ps. 22. 30. [b] Nu. 14. 38. [c] Ju. 21. 14. [d] Da. 4. 13. [e] Da. 7. 5, 7. [f] Da. 7. 3. [g] Ex. 1. 19. [h] 2 Sa. 20. 3. [i] Da. 7. 12, 7, 17. [k] Jos. 5. 8. [l] Ps. 88. 4. [m] Eze. 16. 6. [n] Pr. 31. 12. [o] Hab. 3. 2. [p] Ps. 103. 4. [q] De. 32. 47. [r] Is. 38. 20. [s] De. 30. 16. [t] Ps. 119. 93. [u] Ps. 30. 4. [x] 2 Sa. 11. 11. [y] Zec. 9. 4. [z] Is. 30. 6. [zz] Eze. 13. 10. [a] Ec. 10. 10. [b] Eze. 26. 12. [c] Eze. 27. 11. [d] Mi. 4. 13. [e] Job 41. 4. [f] 2 Ch. 33. 14. [g] Eze. 43. 13. [h] De. 28. 56. [i] Ps. 35. 13.

חֵיקֶךָ id., suff. 2 pers. sing. masc. [for חֵיקְךָ] . חוק

חֵיקָם id., suff. 3 pers. pl. masc. . . . חוק

חִירָה ו׳ pr. name masc. . . . . . חור

חִירוֹם pr. name masc., see חוּרָם . . . חור

חִירָם pr. name masc. see חוּרָם . . . חור

חִירָם Kh. חִירָם, K. חוּרָם (q. v.) . . . חור

חִישׁ[a] adv., R. חִישׁ, see . . . . . חוש

חִישָׁה[b] Kh. חִישָׁה, K. חוּשָׁה, Kal imp. sing. masc. with paragogic ה. R. חִישׁ or . . חוש

חַיַּת ו׳ noun fem. sing., constr. of חַיָּה dec. 10, from חַי masc. . . . . . חיי

חָיְתָה ו Kal pret. 3 pers. sing. fem. . . . חיה

חָיִתָה[c] ו id. pret. 2 pers. sing. masc. (§ 24. rem. 7, & § 8. rem. 5) . . . . . חיה

חַיָּתוֹ ו׳ noun fem. sing., suff. 3 pers. sing. masc. from חַיָּה dec. 10. . . . . . חיי

חַיְתוֹ ו׳[d] id. constr. with paragogic ו . . . חיי

חַיָּתִי[e] id., suff. 1 pers. sing. . . . . חיי

חַיָּתְךָ[f] id., suff. 2 pers. sing. masc. . . . חיי

חַיָּתָם ו׳ id., suff. 3 pers. pl. masc. . . . חיי

חִיִּתַנִי[g] Piel pret. 3 pers. sing. fem., suff. 1 pers. sing. [for חִיְּתַנִי] . . . . . חיה

חֵךְ ו noun masc. sing. [for חֵנֶךְ § 37. No. 3b] dec. 8b . . . . . . חנך

[חָכָה] *to wait*, Is. 30. 18, with לְ. Pi. id. with acc. & לְ.

חִכָּה[h] noun fem. sing. . . . . . חנך

חַכֵּה־[i] Piel imp. sing. masc. . . . . חכה

חִכָּהּ[k] noun masc. sing., suff. 3 pers. sing. fem. from חֵךְ [for חֵנֶךְ § 37. No. 3b] dec. 8b . חנך

חִכָּה[l] Piel pret. 3 pers. sing. masc. . . . חכה

חַכּוּ[m] id. imp. pl. masc. . . . . . חכה

חִכּוֹ noun masc. sing., suff. 3 pers. sing. masc. from חֵךְ [for חֵנֶךְ § 37. No. 3b] dec. 8b חנך

חִכּוּ[n] Piel pret. 3 pers. pl. . . . . חכה

חִכִּי noun masc. sing., suff. 1 pers. sing. from חֵךְ [for חֵנֶךְ § 37. No. 3b] dec. 8b . . חנך

חַכִּימֵי Chald. noun masc. pl. c. from [חַכִּים] dec. 1a חכם

חַכִּימַיָּא[o] ו׳[p] id. pl., emph. state . . . . חכם

חַכִּימִין[q] id. pl., absolute state . . . . חכם

חִכִּינוּ[r] ו Piel pret. 1 pers. pl. . . . . חכה

חִכִּיתִי[s] ו id. pret. 1 pers. sing. . . . . חכה

חִכֶּךָ / חִכְּךָ[t] noun m. sing., suff. 2 pers. sing. m. from חֵךְ [for חֵנֶךְ § 37. No. 3b] dec. 8b } חנך

חִכֵּךְ[u] ו id., suff. 2 pers. sing. fem. . . . חנך

חכל Root not used; signification uncertain. Hence the four following.

חֲכִילָה pr. name of a hill in the wilderness of Ziph, 1 Sa. 23. 19; 26. 1, 3. For the signification compare the three following.

חֲכַלְיָה pr. name masc. Ne. 10. 2 . . . . חכל

חַכְלִילִי adj. Ge. 49. 12. Eng. Vers. *red;* and so Schultens. LXX. χαροποιοί *cheerful*. Some of the other Greek Versions, καθαροί *bright;* θερμοί *glowing;* διάπυροι *fiery*. Prof. Lee, *refreshed*. Gesenius, *dim*. Vulg. pulchriores *more beautiful* (than wine), evidently confounding it with כָּחַל . . . . . חכל

חַכְלִלוּת fem. Pr. 23. 29. Eng. Vers. *redness*. Gesenius, *dimness*. Prof. Lee, *fierceness*, comp. the preceding . . . . . . חכל

חָכַם[v] fut. יֶחְכַּם (§ 13. rem. 5) *to be* or *become wise*. Pi. *to make wise, to teach*. Pu. *to be made wise, to be taught*. Hiph. i. q. Pi. Ps. 19. 8. Hithp.—I. *to show oneself wise*, Ec. 7. 16.—II. *to act wisely, cunningly*, Ex. 1. 10.

חָכָם masc. dec. 4c, חֲכָמָה fem. dec. 11c, constr. חַכְמַת (§ 42. rem. 1) adj.—I. *wise, intelligent*.—II. *knowing, skilful, skilled*.

חַכִּים Chald. masc. dec. 1, adj. *wise, wise man, magician*.

חָכְמָה fem. constr. חָכְמַת, with suff. חָכְמָתִי (no pl.).—I. *wisdom*.—II. *skill, dexterity*.

חָכְמָה Chald. fem. dec. 8a, *wisdom*.

חָכְמוֹת fem. (secondary form of חָכְמוֹת) *wisdom*.

חַכְמוֹת fem. id. Pr. 14. 1.

חַכְמֹנִי (*wise*) pr. name masc. 1 Ch. 11. 11; 27. 32, for which in the parallel passage, 2 Sa. 23. 8, it is תַּחְכְּמֹנִי.

חָכָם ו׳ adj. masc. sing. dec. 4c . . . . חכם

חֲכַם ו / חֲכַם ו׳[w] id. imp. sing masc.; or, constr. of חָכָם (q. v.) . . . . } חכם

חָכְמָה[x] Kal pret. 3 pers. sing. fem. . . . חכם

חָכְמָה ו׳ noun. fem. sing. (no pl. abs.); Chald. (Da. 5. 11, 14) dec. 8a . . . . חכם

חֲכָמָה adj. fem. sing., dec. 11c (§ 42. rem. 1) from חָכָם masc. . . . . . . חכם

חָכְמוּ[a] Kal pret. 3 pers. pl. . . . . חכם

חַכְמוּ[b] ו id. imp. pl. masc. for [חֲכָמוּ] from sing. חֲכַם חכם

חַכְמוֹנִי pr. name masc. . . . . . חכם

חָכְמוֹת noun fem. sing. [for חָכְמוֹת] . . . חכם

חַכְמוֹת[c] noun fem. sing. [for חַכְמוֹת] . . . חכם

חַכְמוֹת[d] adj. fem. pl. c. from חֲכָמָה dec. 11c (§ 42. rem. 1) from חָכָם masc. . . . חכם

[a] Ps. 90. 10. [b] Ps. 71. 12. [c] Je. 38. 17. [d] Ge. 1. 24. [e] Ps. 143. 3. [f] Ps. 68. 11. [g] Ps. 119. 50. [h] Is. 19. 8. [i] Hab. 2. 3. [k] Pr. 5. 3. [l] Job 32. 4. [m] Zep. 3. 8. [n] Ps. 106. 13. [o] Da. 5. 15. [p] Da. 2. 13. [q] Da. 2. 27. [r] 2 Ki. 7. 9. [s] Is. 8. 17. [t] Ho. 8. 1. [u] Ca. 7. 10. [v] Pr. 23. 15. [w] Is. 3. 3. [x] Zec. 9. 2. [a] De. 32. 29. [b] Pr. 8. 33. [c] Pr. 14. 1. [d] Ju. 5. 29.

חַכְמֵי[a] וְ' id. pl. c. masc. from חָכָם dec. 4c . . חכם

חֲכָמֶיהָ וְ' id. pl., suff. 3 pers. sing. fem.; וַ bef. (-:) חכם

חֲכָמָיו id. pl., suff. 3 pers. sing. masc. . . חכם

חֲכָמַיִךְ[b] id. pl., suff. 2 pers. sing. fem. . . חכם

חֲכָמֶיךָ id. pl., suff. 2 pers. sing. masc. . . חכם

חֲכָמִים[c] וְ' id. pl., absolute state; וַ before (-:) . חכם

חָכַמְתָּ[d] Kal pret. 2 pers. sing. masc. . . . חכם

חָכְמַת וְ' noun fem. s. constr. of חָכְמָה (no pl. abs.) חכם

חַכְמַת[e] adj. fem. sing., constr. of חֲכָמָה (§ 42. rem. 1) dec. 11c from חָכָם masc. . . . חכם

חָכְמְתָא[f] Ch. noun fem. sing., emph. of חָכְמָה dec. 8a חכם

חָכְמָתוֹ[g] וְ' noun fem. sing., suff. 3 pers. sing. masc. from חָכְמָה (no pl. abs.) . . . חכם

חָכַמְתִּי[h] Kal pret. 1 pers. sing. . . . חכם

חָכְמָתִי[i] noun fem. sing., suff. 1 pers. sing. from חָכְמָה (no pl. abs.) . . . . חכם

חָכְמָתְךָ, חָכְמָתֶךָ[k] } id., suff. 2 pers. sing. masc. . . חכם

חָכְמָתֵךְ[l] id., suff. 2 pers. sing. fem. . . . חכם

חָכְמַתְכֶם[m] id., suff. 2 pers. pl. masc. . . . חכם

חָכְמָתָם id., suff. 3 pers. pl. masc. . . . חכם

חִכְּתָה[n] Piel pret. 3 pers. sing. fem. . . . חכה

חַל־[o] Piel imp. s. m. apoc. [for חַלֵּה § 24. rem. 12] חלה

חֵל[p] [q]וְ' defect. for חֵיל, noun masc. sing. dec. 1; for וָ see lett. ו . . . . חול

חֹל noun masc. sing. . . . . . חלל

[חָלָא] to be sick, 2 Ch. 16. 12.

חֶלְאָה fem. dec. 10.—I. *rust*; others, *scum, froth.*—II. pr. name fem. 1 Ch. 4. 5, 7.

תַּחֲלוּא masc. only pl. תַּחֲלוּאִים *diseases.*

חֶלְאָה pr. name fem. . . . . . חלא

חֳלָאִים[r] noun masc., pl. of חֳלִי dec. 6. (§ 35. rem. 15) חלה

חֶלְאמָה Keri חֵלָמָה pr. name of a place (חֵילָם) with local ה . . . . . חול

חֶלְאָתָהּ[s], וְ' חֶלְאָתָהּ[t] } noun fem. sing., suff. 3 pers. sing. fem. from [חֶלְאָה] dec. 10. (§ 3. rem. 3) } חלא

חלב Root not used; probably *to be fat.*

חָלָב masc. dec. 4c, *milk.*

חֲלֵב masc. id. only in the constr. חֲלֵב.

חֵלֶב, חֵלֶב masc. dec. 6, with suff. חֶלְבּוֹ (§ 35. rem. 6).—I. *fat, fatness*; hence *the best* of any thing.—II. pr. name masc. 2 Sa. 23. 29, compare חֶלְדַּי.

חֶלְבָּה (*fatness, fertility*) pr. name of a city in the tribe of Asher, Ju. 1. 31.

חֶלְבּוֹן (*fat, fertile*) pr. name of a city in Syria, Eze. 27. 18.

חֶלְבְּנָה fem. *galbanum*, an odoriferous gum, Ex. 30. 34.

אַחְלָב (*fatness, fertility*) pr. name of a place in the tribe of Asher, Ju. 1. 31.

חָלָב וְ' noun masc. sing. dec. 4c . . . חלב

חֲלֵב[u] וַ' noun masc. sing. constr. of [חָלָב] dec. 5c חלב

חֵלֶב וְ' n. m. s. dec. 6. (§ 35. rem. 6), also pr. n. m. חלב

חֶלְבָּה pr. name of a place . . . . חלב

חֶלְבָּהּ[x] noun masc. sing., suff. 3 pers. sing. fem., from חֵלֶב dec. 6. (§ 35. rem. 6) . . . חלב

חֶלְבְּהֶן[y] id., suff. 3 pers. pl. fem. (§ 3. rem. 5) . חלב

חֶלְבּוֹ id., suff. 3 pers. sing. masc. . . . חלב

חֶלְבּוֹן pr. name of a place . . . . חלב

חֲלָבִי[z] noun m. s., suff. 1 pers. s. from חָלָב dec. 4c חלב

חֶלְבֵי n. m. pl. constr. from חֵלֶב dec. 6. (§ 35. rem. 6) חלב

חֲלָבֵךְ[a] noun masc. sing., suff. 2 pers. sing. fem. from חָלָב dec. 4c . . . . . חלב

חֶלְבָּם[b], חֶלְבָּמוֹ[c] } noun masc. sing., suff. 3 pers. pl. masc. from חֵלֶב dec. 6. (§ 35. rem. 6) . } חלב

חֶלְבְּנָה[d] וְ noun fem. sing. . . . . חלב

חלד Root not used; Rabb. *to hide, cover;* Syr. *to dig;* Arab. *to endure.*

חֶלֶד masc. dec. 6, with suff. חֶלְדִּי (§ 35. rem. 3) —I. *time, duration of life, lifetime.*—II. *world.*

חֹלֶד masc. *a mole*, Le. 11. 29.

חֻלְדָּה (*mole*) pr. name of a prophetess, 2 Ki. 22. 14; 2 Ch. 34. 22.

חֶלְדַּי pr. name masc.—I. 1 Ch. 27. 15, called חֵלֶד chap. 11. 30, and חֵלֶב 2 Sa. 23. 29.—II Zec. 6. 10, for which חֵלֶם in ver. 14

חֶלֶד n. m. sing. for חֶלֶד dec. 6. (§ 35. rem. 2 & 3) חלד

חֵלֶד pr. name masc. . . . . . חלד

חֻלְדָּה pr. name fem. . . . . . חלד

חֶלְדַּי pr. name masc. . . . . . חלד

חֶלְדִּי[e] וְ noun masc. sing., suff. 1 pers. sing. from חֶלֶד dec. 6. (§ 35. rem. 3) . . חלד

I. חָלָה I. *to be weak, feeble.*—II. *to be sick, diseased.*—III *to be pained*, Pr. 23. 35; hence, *to be grieved* 1 Sa. 22. 8, with עַל. Niph. נֶחֱלָה, part. fem

[a] 2 Ch. 2. 13. [b] Eze. 27. 8. [c] Pr. 29. 8. [d] Pr. 9. 12. [e] Ex. 35. 25. [f] Da. 2. 20, 21, 23. [g] 1 Ki. 11. 41. [h] Ec. 2. 15. [i] Ec. 2. 9. [k] Eze. 28. 5, 17. [l] Is. 47. 10. [m] De. 4. 6. [n] Ps. 33. 20. [o] 1 Ki. 13. 6. [p] La. 2. 8. [q] Is. 26. 1. [r] Ca. 7. 2. [s] Eze. 24. 6. [t] Eze. 24. 6, 11, 12. [u] De. 32. 14. [x] Le. 4. 31, 35. [y] Le. 8. 16, 25. [z] Ca. 5. 1. [a] Eze. 25. 4. [b] Nu. 18. 17. [c] Ps. 17. 10. [d] Ex. 30. 34. [e] Ps. 39. 6.

נַחְלָה (see analyt. order).—I. *to be exhausted, wearied*, Je. 12. 13.—II. *to become* or *be sick*; part. *sore, very sore*, מַכָּה נַחְלָה *a sore* (hardly curable) *wound*.—III. *to be grieved*, Am. 6. 6, with עַל. Pi. חִלָּה.—I. *to make sick, to afflict* with disease, De. 29. 21, with בְּ; חַלּוֹתִי הִיא *this makes me sick*, Ps. 77. 11.—II. *to weaken, soften down, appease*. Always fully חִלָּה פְּנֵי פ׳ *to appease the face* (i. e. anger) *of* any one; חִלָּה פְּנֵי יְהוָֹה *to appease the face* (anger) *of the Lord*, i. e. to seek his mercy, hence generally, *to beseech, supplicate*. Pu. *to be made weak*, Is. 14. 10. Hiph.—I. *to make sick*, Mi. 6. 13; intrans. *to become sick*, Ho. 7. 5.—II. *to afflict, grieve*, Pr. 13. 12. Hoph. *to be wounded*, 1 Ki. 22. 34. Hithp.—I. *to fall sick*, 2 Sa. 13. 2.—II. *to feign sickness*, 2 Sa. 13. 5, 6.

חֳלִי masc. dec. 6k—I. *sickness, disease*.—II. *affliction, grief*, Ec. 5. 16.—III. *calamity*, Ec. 6. 2.

מַחֲלֶה masc. dec. 9a, *sickness, disease*.

מַחֲלָה fem. (of the preceding) id.

מַחְלָה (*disease*) pr. name fem. of two different persons.

מַחְלוֹן (*sick*) pr. name masc. Ru. 1. 2, 4, 9.

מַחֲלוּי masc. pl. מַחֲלֻיִים, *disease*, 2 Ch. 24. 25.

מַחְלִי (*sick*) pr. name masc. of two different persons.

מָחֲלַת fem. the name of a certain musical instrument, Ps. 53. 1; 88. 1.

מָחֲלַת pr. name—I. of a daughter of Ishmael, the wife of Esau, Ge. 28. 9.—II. of the wife of Rehoboam, 2 Ch. 11. 18.

II. חָלָה Root not used; Syr. חלי *to be sweet, pleasant*, Pa. *to adorn*.

חֲלִי masc. dec. 6, pl. חֲלָאִים (§ 35. rem. 15) *ornament, necklace*.

חֶלְיָה fem. id., only חֶלְיָתָהּ Ho. 2. 15.

חָלָה[a] } Kal pret. 3 pers. sing. fem.; acc. shifted by וְ conv. (comp. § 8. rem. 7) } חול
וְחָלָה[b]

חַלָּה[c] noun fem. sing. dec. 10. . . . חלל

חִלָּה Piel pret. 3 pers. sing. masc. . . . חלה

חֹלֶה[d] וְ Kal part. act. sing. masc. . . חלה

חָלוּ[e] id. pret. 3 pers. pl. [for חָלוּ, comp. § 8. rem. 7] חלה

חָלוּ[f] } Kal pret. 3 pers. pl.; acc. shifted by וְ conv. (comp. § 8. rem. 7) . } חול
וְחָלוּ[g]

חַלּוּ[h] Piel imp. pl. masc. . . . . חלה

חָלוּ[i] וְ id. pret. 3 pers. pl. . . . . חלה

חֲלוֹם noun masc. sing. dec. 1a . . . . חלם

חַלּוֹן[k] noun com. sing. dec. 1b . . . . חלל

חֹלוֹן pr. name of a place . . . . חול

חַלּוֹנָיו[l] וְ noun masc. pl., suff. 3 pers. sing. masc. (§ 4. rem. 1) dec. 1b . . . . חלל

חַלּוֹנוֹת[m] וְ id. with pl. fem. term. . . . חלל

חַלּוֹנָי[n] id. pl. masc. poetic for חַלּוֹנִים (comp. חוֹרַי) חלל

חַלּוֹנֵי[o] id. pl. construct state . . . . חלל

חַלּוֹנִים וְ id. pl. absolute state . . . . חלל

חֲלוֹף[p] noun masc. sing. . . . . . חלף

חָלוּץ[q] Kal part. pass. masc. dec. 3a . . . חלץ

חֲלוּץ id., construct state . . . . חלץ

חֲלוּצֵי id. pl., construct state . . . . חלץ

חֲלוּצִים id. pl., abs. state . . . . . חלץ

חֲלוּשָׁה[r] noun fem. sing. . . . . . חלש

חַלּוֹת noun fem., pl. of חַלָּה dec. 10. . . חלל

חַלּוֹתִי[s] Piel inf., suff. 1 pers. sing.; acc. Milêl bef. monos. (הִיא) comp. § 3. rem. 1. . . חלה

[חֲלַח] pr. name of a province in the kingdom of Assyria whither the ten tribes were transported, 2 Ki. 17. 6; 18. 11; 1 Ch. 5. 26.

חַלְחוּל pr. name of a place . . . . חול

חַלְחָלָה[t] וְ noun fem. sing. . . . . חול

חָלַט Hiph. *to make declare* or *confirm*, 1 Ki. 20. 33.

חֲלִי[u] וְ noun masc. sing. pl. חֲלָאִים dec. 6i (§ 35. rem. 15); also pr. name Jos. 19. 25. . חלה

חֳלִי } noun masc. sing. dec. 6k (§ 35. rem. 14); וָ bef. (ֹ) for וְ . . } חלה
חֳלִי[x] וָ

חָלְיוֹ[y] וְ id., suff. 3 pers. sing. masc. . . . חלה

חָלִיל[z] וְ noun masc. sing. dec. 3a . . . חלל

חָלִילָה adv.; חָלִיל with parag. ה . . . חלל

חֳלָיִם[a] וָ noun masc., pl. of חֳלִי dec. 6k [for חֳלָיִים], וָ bef. (ֹ) for וְ . . . . חלה

חִלִּינוּ[b] Piel pret. 1 pers. pl. . . . . חלה

חֳלָיֵנוּ[c] noun masc. pl., suff. 1 pers. pl. from חֳלִי dec. 6k [for חֳלָיֵינוּ] . . . . חלה

חֲלִיפוֹת noun fem., pl. of [חֲלִיפָה] dec. 10. . . חלף

חֲלִיפָתִי[d] id. sing., suff. 1 pers. sing. . . . חלף

חֲלִיצוֹתָם[e] noun fem. pl., suff. 3 pers. pl. masc. from [חֲלִיצָה] dec. 10. . . . . חלץ

חָלִית[f] Kal pret. 2 pers. sing. fem. . . . חלה

חֻלֵּית[g] Pual pret. 2 pers. sing. fem. . . . חלה

[a] Is. 54. 1; 66. 8. Mi. 1. 12.
[b] Ho. 11. 6.
[c] Nu. 15. 20.
[d] Mal. 1. 8.
[e] Je. 5. 3.
[f] La. 4. 6.
[g] De. 2. 25.
[h] Mal. 1. 9.
[i] Job 11. 19.
[k] Ge. 8. 6.
[l] Eze. 40. 22.
[m] Ex. 40. 16, 29, 33.
[n] Je. 22. 14.
[o] 1 Ki. 6. 4.
[p] Pr. 31. 8.
[q] Nu. 32. 21, 29.
[r] Ex. 32. 18.
[s] Ps. 77. 11.
[t] Na. 2. 11.
[u] Pr. 25. 12.
[x] Ec. 6. 2.
[y] Ec. 5. 16.
[z] 1 Sa. 10. 5. Is. 5. 12.
[a] De. 28. 59.
[b] Da. 9. 13.
[c] Is. 53. 4.
[d] Job 14. 14.
[e] Ju. 14. 19.
[f] Is. 57. 10.
[g] Is. 14. 10.

[a] חֲלִיתָהּ וְ noun fem. s., suff. 3 pers. s. f. [from חֲלְיָה] חלה

חָלִיתִי וְ׳ Kal pret. 1 pers. sing. . . . . חלה

חִלִּיתִי Piel pret. 1 pers. sing. . . . . חלה

חָלַךְ Root not used; Arab. *to be black*, trop. *sad, wretched.*

חֵלְכָה (for חֵלְכָא) adj. masc. pl. חֵלְכָּאִים *wretched, poor.*

[b] חֵלְכָּאִים pl. of the following . . . . חלך

[c] חֵלְכָה noun masc. sing., with suff. 2 pers. sing. masc. (§ 3. rem. 2), from חֵל, R. חול, or rather, adj. masc. [for חֵלְכָא=חֵלְכָה] . . חלך

[d] חָלַל I. *to be pierced, wounded*, Ps. 109. 22.—II. according to the Arab. *to open, to loose*. Pi.—I. *to wound*. Eze. 28. 9.—II. *to make common, to profane, pollute, defile.*—III. *to violate, break*, a covenant.—IV. *to play the pipe* or *flute*, from חָלִיל, 1 Ki. 1. 40. Pu. *to be wounded*, Eze. 32. 26; *to be profaned*, 36. 23. Poel *to pierce, wound*. Poal, pass. Is. 53. 5. Niph. נִחַל dag. f. impl., inf. הֵחֵל (for הִחָּל § 18. rem. 14) *to be profaned, defiled*. Hiph. הֵחֵל.—I. *to loose, set free*, Ho. 8. 10.—II. *to profane, defile, violate.*—III. *to open, begin.*—IV. *to begin to be*, Ge. 9. 20. Hoph. *to be begun*, Ge. 4. 26.

חָלָל masc. dec. 4 c, חֲלָלָה adj.—I. *pierced, wounded, slain.*—II. *profane, common*, Eze. 21. 30; *polluted*, by prostitution, Le. 21. 7, 14.

חָלִיל masc. dec. 3 a.—I. *pipe.*—II. adj. *profane*, only in the form חָלִלָה, חָלִילָה used to express detestation of a thing, *profane! fie! far be it!* followed by לְ of the pers. and inf. with מִן, as חָ׳ לְךָ מֵעֲשׂוֹת אִם *far be it from thee to do*, &c.; and the finite verb is added in a solemn declaration, comp. Ps. 95. 11; חָ׳ לִי מֵיְהוָה אִם־אֶעֱשֶׂה lit. *profane be it to me from the Lord* (i.e. God forbid) *that I should do.*

חֹל masc. *profane, common.*

חַלָּה fem. dec. 10, *cake*, as being perforated with holes, used chiefly in sacred rites.

חַלּוֹן com. dec. 1 b, pl. ־ִים, וֹת, *window*; prop. a hole or opening for admitting the light.

נְחִילָה fem. (for נְחִלָּה perforated) *a pipe, flute*, only pl. נְחִילוֹת Ps. 5. 1, comp. חָלִיל.

מְחִלָּה fem. dec. 10, *cave, cavern*, Is. 2. 19.

תְּחִלָּה fem. dec. 10, *beginning*; בַּתְּחִלָּה *at the first, formerly, before.*

חָלָל adj. masc. sing. dec. 4 c . . . . חלל

[e] חַלֵּל Piel inf. constr. . . . . . חלל

חִלֵּל id. pret. 3 pers. sing. masc. . . . חלל

[f] חֹלֵל Pilel inf. constr. . . . . . חול

[g] חֲלָלָה וַ adj. fem. sing. from חָלָל masc.; וַ bef. (-:) חלל

חָלִלָה defect. for חָלִילָה (q. v.) . . . חלל

[h] חֹלְלָה Pilel pret. 3 pers. sing. fem. . . . חול

[i] חִלְּלוּהוּ Piel pret. 3 pers. pl., suff. 3 pers. sing. masc. חלל

[k] חִלְּלוֹ id. pret. 3 pers. sing. masc., suff. 3 p. s. m. חלל

[l] חִלְּלוּ וְ׳ / חִלֵּלוּ וְ׳ } id. pret. 3 pers. pl. (comp. § 8. rem. 7) חלל

[m] חִלְּלוּהָ וְ id. id., suff. 3 pers. sing. fem. . . חלל

[n] חִלְּלוּהָ וְ id. id., suff., Kh. ־לוּהָ׳ 3 pers. sing. fem., K. ־לוּהוּ׳ 3 pers. sing. masc. . . חלל

חַלְלֵי adj. masc. pl. constr. from חָלָל dec. 4 c חלל

[o] חֲלָלֶיהָ id. pl., suff. 3 pers. sing. fem. . . . חלל

[p] חַלְלֵיהֶם וְ׳ id. pl., suff. 3 pers. pl. masc. . . חלל

[q] חֲלָלָיו id. pl., suff. 3 pers. sing. masc. . . . חלל

[r] חֲלָלַיִךְ id. pl., suff. 2 pers. sing. fem. . . . חלל

[s] חֲלָלֶיךָ id. pl., suff. 2 pers. sing. masc. . . . חלל

חַלְלֵיכֶם id., suff. 2 pers. pl. masc. . . . חלל

חֲלָלִים id., pl. absolute state . . . . חלל

[t] חֲלָלֵינוּ id., suff. 1 pers. pl. . . . . חלל

[u] חַלְּלָם Piel inf. (חַלֵּל), suff. 3 pers. pl. masc. d. 7 b חלל

[x] חִלַּלְתְּ id. pret. 2 pers. sing. f. [for חִלַּלְתְּ § 8. r. 7] חלל

חִלַּלְתָּ / [y] וְחִלַּלְתָּ } id. pret. 2 pers. sing. masc.; acc. shifted by conv. וְ (comp. § 8. rem. 7) . חלל

[z] חִלַּלְתִּי id. pret. 1 pers. sing. . . . . חלל

[a] חִלַּלְתֶּם id. pret. 2 pers. pl. masc. . . . חלל

חָלַם fut. יַחֲלֹם.—I. *to be fat, stout, strong*, Job 39. 4.—II. *to dream.* Hiph.—I. *to make strong, restore to health*, Is. 38. 16.—II. *to cause to dream*, Je. 29. 8.

חֲלוֹם masc. pl. וֹת, *a dream.*

חֵלֶם Ch. masc.—I. *a dream.*—II. pr. name masc. Zec. 6. 14, see חֶלְדַּי.

חַלָּמוּת fem. Job 6. 6, Eng. Vers. "egg;" so the Jewish commentators, who consider חַלָּמוּת i. q. חֶלְבּוֹן=חֶלְמוֹן the yolk of an egg, hence רִיר חַ׳ *slime of a yolk*, i. e. the white of an egg. Others *purslain*, a herb proverbial among the Arabs for its insipidity. Prof. Lee, *cheese.*

אַחְלָמָה the name of a precious stone; according

---

[a] Ho. 2. 15. Ps. 10. 10. Ps. 10. 14. [d] Ps. 109. 22. [e] Am. 2. 7. [f] Job 39. 1. [g] Le. 21. 7, 14. [h] Job 26. 13. [i] Eze. 36. 21. [k] De. 20. 6. [l] Je. 31. 5. [m] Eze. 7. 22. [n] Eze. 7. 21. [o] Je. 51. 47. [p] Is. 34. 3. [q] Eze. 35. 8. [r] Is. 22. 2. [s] Ps. 69. 27. [t] Ju. 16. 24. [u] Je. 16. 18. [x] Eze. 22. 8. [y] Le. 19. 12. [z] Is. 47. 6. [a] Eze. 36. 22, 23.

to the LXX, *the amethyst.* Some suppose it to be the *emerald.* Ex. 28. 19; 39. 12.

נֶחֱלָמִי *Nehelamite,* patronym. otherwise unknown, Je. 29. 24, 31, 32.

חַלָּמִישׁ masc., constr. חַלְמִישׁ dec. 3c, *a hard stone, flint.*

חֵלֶם Ch. noun masc. sing. dec. 3c . . . חלם

חֹלֵם Kal part. act. sing. masc. dec. 7b . . . חלם

חֶלְמָא [a] ו׳ Ch. noun masc. sing., emph. of חֵלֶם
חֶלְמָה [b] dec. 3c . . . . חלם

חֲלֹמוֹ noun m. s., suff. 3 p. s. m. from חֲלוֹם d. 1a חלם

חַלָּמוּת noun fem. sing. . . . . . חלם

חֲלֹמוֹת ו׳ noun m. with pl. f. term. from חֲלוֹם d. 1a חלם

[d] חֶלְמִי Ch. n. m. s., suff. 1 pers. s. from חֵלֶם d. 3c חלם

[e] חֶלְמִין Ch. id. pl., abs. state . . . חלם

[f] חַלָּמִישׁ noun masc. sing., constr. חַלְמִישׁ dec. 3c חלמש

[g] חֶלְמָךְ Ch. noun masc. sing., suff. 2 pers. sing. masc. from חֵלֶם dec. 3c . . . . חלם

[h] חָלַמְנוּ
[i] חָלָמְנוּ Kal pret. 1 pers. pl. (§ 8. rem. 7) . . חלם

[k] חָלָמְתָּ id. pret. 2 pers. sing. masc. [for חָלַמְתָּ v. id.] חלם

חָלַמְתִּי
חָלָמְתִּי id. pret. 1 pers. sing. (v. id.) . . חלם

חֲלֹמֹתָיו noun masc., with pl. fem. term. & suff. 3 pers. sing. masc. from חֲלוֹם dec. 1a . . . חלם

חֲלֹמֹתֵיכֶם id., suff. 2 pers. pl. masc. . . . . חלם

חֲלֹמֹתֵינוּ id., suff. 1 pers. pl. . . . . . חלם

חֵלֶן pr. name masc., see חֵלוֹן . . . . חול

חֹלֹן ו׳ pr. name of a place . . . . חול

[m] חַלְנוּ Kal pret. 1 pers. pl. . . . . . חול

חָלַף [n] ו׳ fut. יַחֲלֹף.—I. *to pass by, pass on, pass away; to pass beyond* a law, *to transgress,* Is. 24. 5.—II. *to pass through,* only trans. *to pierce.*—III. *to rush upon, to assail.*—IV. *to revive, to flourish,* of a plant; of the spirit. Pi. *to change,* as a garment. Hiph.—I. *to change.*—II. *to renew, to cause to flourish.* Intrans. *to revive, to flourish again.*

חֲלַף Ch. *to pass,* Da. 4. 13, 20, 29.

חֵלֶף masc.—I. *exchange,* only as a prep. *instead of, for,* Nu. 18. 21, 31.—II. pr. name of a place in the tribe of Naphtali, Jos. 19. 33.

חֲלוֹף masc. *a passing away* or *perishing,* Pr. 31. 8, בְּנֵי חֲלוֹף *those who are about to perish.* Others, *children left behind,* i. e. orphans.

חֲלִיפָה fem. dec. 10.—I. *change, alternation;* חֲלִיפוֹת בְּגָדִים *changes* (i. e. suits) *of raiment.*—II. *reinforcement,* or *relief of guard,* Job 10. 17; where Gesenius renders חֲלִיפוֹת וְצָבָא (by Hendiadys) *changes and hosts* i. e. hosts continually succeeding each other.—III. חֲלִיפוֹת adv. *by courses, alternately,* 1 Ki. 5. 28.

מַחֲלָף masc. only pl. מַחֲלָפִים Ezr. 1. 9, *slaughtering-knives;* Syr. חלפא knife.

מַחְלָפָה fem. dec. 11a, only in the pl. *braided locks,* Ju. 16. 13, 19.

[o] חָלָף ו Kal pret. 3 pers. s. m. (for חָלַף § 8. r. 7) חלף

[p] חֵלֶף noun masc. sing. . . . . . חלף

[q] חָלְפָה ו Kal pret. 3 pers. sing. fem. . . . חלף

חָלְפוּ id. pret. 3 pers. pl. . . . . . חלף

חֲלִפוֹת defect. for חֲלִיפוֹת (q. v.) . . . חלף

[r] חָלַפְתָּ ו Kal pret. 2 pers. sing. masc.; acc. shifted by ו conv. (§ 8. rem. 7) . . . חלף

חֲלִפֹת defect. for חֲלִיפוֹת (q. v.) . . . חלף

חָלַץ fut. יַחֲלֹץ.—I. *to draw out,* La. 4. 3.—II. *to draw* or *pull off,* as a shoe; חֲלוּץ נַעַל *barefoot.*—III. *to disengage oneself, to withdraw,* with מִן Ho. 5. 6.—IV. part. חָלוּץ *ready, prepared* for war, *armed;* חֲלוּץ צָבָא *host ready, prepared for action;* חֲלֻצֵי מוֹאָב *the arrayed* (troops) *of Moab.* Niph.—I. *to be drawn out, delivered.*—II. *to get ready, to arm oneself.* Pi.—I. *to draw out,* Le. 14. 40, 43.—II. *to deliver.*—III. *to strip, spoil,* Ps. 7. 5. Hiph. *to make easy, pliant and flexible,* as the bones in their sockets or joints, Is. 58. 11. Others, *to make strong.* LXX. πιανθήσεται *shall be fat.*

חֶלֶץ masc. dec. 4c, only dual חֲלָצַיִם *the loins,* prob. as the seat of strength and activity, comp. Hiph. of the verb.

חֶלֶץ, חֵלֶץ (*deliverance*) pr. name masc. of two different persons.

חֲלִיצָה fem. dec. 10, *spoil, booty.*

מַחֲלָצָה fem. dec. 11, *costly dress, mantle.*

חֶלֶץ
חֵלֶץ ו׳ pr. name masc. (§ 35. rem. 2) . . חלץ

חָלֶץ pr. name masc., see חֶלֶץ . . . חלץ

[t] חִלֵּץ Piel pret. 3 pers. sing. masc. . . . חלץ

[u] חָלְצָה ו Kal pret. 3 pers. sing. fem. . . . חלץ

[x] חַלְּצָה Piel imp. sing. masc. with parag. ה (comp. § 8. rem. 11) . . . . . הלץ

[a] Da. 4. 4, 5. [b] Da. 4. 15. [c] Job 6. 6. [d] Da. 4. 6. [e] Da. 5. 12. [f] Ps. 114. 8. [g] Da. 2. 28. [h] Ge. 41. 11. [i] Ge. 40. 8. [k] Ge. 37. 10. [l] Ge. 41. 12. [m] Is. 26. 18. [n] Is. 8. 8. [o] Ps. 90. 6. [p] Nu. 18. 21, 31. [q] Ju. 5. 26. [r] 1 Sa. 10. 3. [s] Ho. 5. 6. [t] Le. 14. 43. [u] De. 25. 9. [x] Ps. 6. 5.

חָלְצוּ[a] Kal pret. 3 pers. pl. . . . חלץ

חָלְצוּ[b] Khethib for חֲלָצָיו (q. v. & § 4. rem. 1) . חלץ

חִלְּצוּ[c] וְ Piel pret. 3 pers. pl. masc. . . חלץ

חֲלָצַי defect. for חֲלוּצֵי (q. v.) . . . חלץ

חֲלָצָיו noun m. du., suff. 3 p. s. m. fr. [חָלָץ] d. 4c חלץ

חֲלָצֶיךָ id. id., suff. 2 pers. sing. masc. . . חלץ

חֲלָצַיִם[d] id. du., absolute state [for חֲלָצַיִם] . . חלץ

חַלְּצֵנִי[e] וְ/וּ Piel imp. sing. m. [חַלֵּץ] suff. 1 pers. s. חלץ

חִלַּצְתָּ[g] id. pret. 2 pers. sing. masc. . . חלץ

חֲלִצָתוֹ[h] noun fem. sing., suff. 3 pers. sing. masc. fr. [חֲלִיצָה] dec. 10. . . . . חלץ

חָלַק fut. יַחֲלֹק.—I. *to be smooth;* metaph. *flattering.*—II. *to divide, distribute, apportion,* especially by lot, with לְ to, עִם with any one, with בְּ of the thing.—III. *to spoil,* 2 Ch. 28. 21. Niph.—I. *to be divided, distributed.*—II. *to divide oneself,* Ge. 14. 15. Pi.—I. *to divide, distribute, apportion.*—II. *to disperse.* Pu. *to be divided, distributed.* Hiph.—I. *to make smooth, flattering.*—II. *to take a portion,* Je. 37. 12. Hithp. *to divide among themselves,* Jos. 18. 5.

חָלָק adj. masc.—I. *smooth, without hair; bare, bald,* of a mountain.—II. *flattering,* Pr. 26. 28.—III. *slippery, deceitful, false,* Eze. 12. 24.

חֲלָק Ch. dec. 1 a, *portion, lot,* Da. 4. 12, 20.

חֵלֶק masc. dec. 6, with suff. חֶלְקִי (§ 35. r. 6).—I. *smoothness, bareness,* spoken of a bare, unwooded place, Is. 57. 6.—II. *flattery,* Pr. 7. 21.—III. *part, portion, lot of land.*—IV. pr. name masc. Patronym. חֶלְקִי Nu. 26. 30.

חֲלַק adj. masc. *smooth,* 1 Sa. 17. 40.

חֶלְקָה fem. dec. 12 b.—I. *smoothness,* Ge. 27. 16.—II. *slippery place,* Ps. 73. 18.—III. metaph. *flattery.*—IV. *portion, part.*

חֲלַקָּה fem. only pl. חֲלַקּוֹת *flatteries,* Da. 11. 32.

חֲלֻקָּה fem. d. 10, *division, partition,* 2 Ch. 35. 5.

חֶלְקַי (*smooth*) pr. name masc. Ne. 12. 15.

חִלְקִיָּה, חִלְקִיָּהוּ (*portion of the Lord*) pr. name masc. of several persons, especially—I. of a high priest in the reign of Josiah, 2 Ki. 22. 8, 12.—II. of the father of Jeremiah the prophet, Je. 1. 1.—III. of the father of Eliakim, comp. 2 Ki. 18. 18, 26.

חֲלַקְלַק only pl. fem. חֲלַקְלַקּוֹת.—I. *slippery places.*—II. *flatteries, hypocrisy,* Da. 11. 21, 24.

מַחֲלֹקֶת fem. dec. 13 c.—I. *course, division, class.*—II. pr. n. of a place, 1 Sa. 23. 28, סֶלַע הַמַּחְלְקוֹת, *rock of smoothness,* i. e. slipping away, escape.

מַחְלְקָא Ch. fem. dec. 8 a, *course, division,* Ezr. 6. 18.

חָלָק[i] וְ/וּ adj. masc. sing. . . . . . חלק

חֲלָק[k] Ch. noun masc. sing. dec. 1 a . . חלק

חַלֵּק[l] Piel imp. sing. masc. . . . חלק

חֵלֶק וְ noun masc. sing. dec. 6 (§ 35. rem. 6), also pr. name masc. . . . . חלק

חֻלַּק[m] וְ[n] Pual pret. 3 pers. sing. masc. . . חלק

חֲלָקֵהּ[o] Ch. noun masc. sing., suff. 3 pers. sing. masc. from חֲלָק dec. 1 a . . . . חלק

חֶלְקָה וְ* noun fem. sing. dec. 12 b *Am. 4. 7. . חלק

חָלְקוּ Kal pret. 3 pers. pl. . . . . חלק

חֶלְקוֹ noun masc. sing., suff. 3 pers. sing. masc. from חֵלֶק dec. 6 (§ 35. rem. 6) . . חלק

חִלְּקוּ[p] Piel pret. 3 pers. pl. [for חִלְּקוּ, comp. § 8. rem. 7] . . . . . חלק

חִלְקוּ[q] Kal imp. pl. masc. . . . . חלק

חֲלָקוֹת noun fem., pl. abs. from חֶלְקָה dec. 12 b חלק

חַלְּקֵי[r] noun masc. pl. constr. from [חַלָּק] . חלק

חֶלְקַי for חֶלְקִי pr. name masc. for חִלְקִיָּה q. v.

חֶלְקִי וְ/וּ noun masc. sing., suff. 1 pers. sing. from חֵלֶק dec. 6 (§ 35. rem. 6) . . חלק

חִלְקִיָּה וְ, חִלְקִיָּהוּ } pr. name masc. . . . חלק

חֶלְקֵיהֶם[s] noun masc. pl., suff. 3 pers. pl. masc. from חֵלֶק dec. 6 (§ 35. rem. 6) . . חלק

חֲלָקִים id. pl., absolute state . . . חלק

חֶלְקֵךְ[u] id. sing., suff. 2 pers. sing. fem. . . חלק

חֶלְקְךָ[x], חֶלְקֶךָ } id. sing. with suff. 2 pers. sing. masc. . חלק

חֲלַקְלַקּוֹת[y] וַ noun pl. fem. from [חֲלַקְלַק]; וּ bef. (-:) חלק

חֶלְקָם noun masc. sing., suff. 3 pers. pl. masc. fr. חֵלֶק dec. 6 (§ 35. rem. 6) . . חלק

חִלְּקָם[z] Piel pret. 3 pers. sing. masc. [חִלֵּק] suff. 3 pers. pl. masc. . . . . חלק

חֶלְקַת, חֶלְקָת } pr. name of a place and in compos. חֶלְקַת הַצֻּרִים, see חֶלְקָה . . } חלק

חֶלְקַת noun fem. sing., constr. of חֶלְקָה dec. 12 b . חלק

חֲלֻקַּת[a] וַ noun fem. sing., constr. of [חֲלֻקָּה] d. 10. חלק

חִלְּקָתָהּ[b] Piel pret. 3 pers. sing. fem., suff. 3 pers. s. f. חלק

חֶלְקָתִי[c] noun fem. s., suff. 1 p. s. from חֶלְקָה d. 12 b חלק

חֶלְקָתָם[d] id., suff. 3 pers. pl. masc. . . חלק

---

[a] La. 4. 3. [b] Job 31. 20. [c] Le. 14. 40. [d] Is. 32. 11. [e] Ps. 140. 2. [f] Ps. 119. 153. [g] Ps. 116. 8. [h] 2 Sa. 2. 21. [i] Pr. 5. 3. [k] Ezr. 4. 16. [l] Jos 13. 7. [m] Is. 33. 23. [n] Zec. 14. 1. [o] Da. 4. 12, 20. [p] Joel 4. 2. [q] Jos. 22. 8. [r] 1 Sa. 17. 40. [s] Ps. 73. 26. [t] Ho. 5. 7. [u] Is. 57. 6. [x] Ps. 50. 18. [y] Ps. 35. 6. [z] La. 4. 16. [a] 2 Ch. 35. 5. [b] Is. 34. 17. [c] Je. 12. 10. [d] Job 24. 18.

[a]חִלַּקְתָּם וְ Piel pret. 2 pers. s. m., suff. 3 pers. pl. m. חלק
[b]חִלַּקְתֶּם וְ id. pret. 2 pers. pl. masc. . . . חלק

[חָלַשׁ] I. fut. יַחֲלֹשׁ *to overthrow, discomfit.*—II. fut. יֶחֱלַשׁ, (§ 8. rem. 13) *to be weak, feeble,* Job 14. 10.

חַלָּשׁ masc. *weak,* Joel 4. 10.

חֲלוּשָׁה fem. *overthrow, defeat,* Ex. 32. 18.

חַלַּת 'וְ noun fem. sing,, constr. of חַלָּה dec. 10. חלל
[c]חַלֹּת 'וְ pl. of the preceding . . . חלל
[d]חַלֹּתִי Kal pret. 1 pers. sing. . . . . חול

[חָם] masc. irr. with suff. חָמִיךְ (§ 45) *father-in-law.*

חָמוֹת fem. with suff. חֲמוֹתֵךְ *mother-in-law.*

חֲמִיטַל, חֲמוּטַל (*father-in-law of dew,* comp. אֲבִיטַל) pr. name of the wife of king Josiah.

[e]חָם 'וְ adj. masc. sing. dec. 8a, also pr. name m. חמם
[f]חַם 'וְ Kal pret. 3 pers. sing. masc. . . . חמם
[cc]חֹם 'וְ noun masc. sing. . . . . . חמם

חָמָא Root not used; Arab. *to curdle, coagulate.*

חֶמְאָה fem. constr. חֶמְאַת (comp. מַחֲמָאוֹת.—I. *curdled milk.* Eng. Vers. "butter," which modern interpreters reject as hardly known to the orientalists.—II. *cheese,* Pr. 30. 33.

חֵמָה Job 29. 5, for חֶמְאָה q. v.

מַחֲמָאוֹת fem. pl. *milky* (i. e. sweet) *words,* Ps. 55. 22; but Kimchi and others prefer to read here מֵחֶמְאוֹת *than cream* or *butter,* as the pl. of חֶמְאָה (dec. 12b).

[g]וַחֲמָא, [h]חֲמָא } Ch. noun fem. sing; וְ bef. (־:) . . . יחם
חֶמְאָה 'וְ noun fem. sing. (no pl.) . . . חמא
[i]חֶמְאַת id., constr. state . . . . חמא

חָמַד fut. יַחְמֹד, 'יַחְ (§ 13. rem. 5) *to desire, delight in* in a good sense; also in a bad sense, *to covet;* part. חָמוּד *desired,* hence *something desirable, delightful, pleasant.* Niph. part. נֶחְמָד (§ 13. r. 7) *desirable, pleasant.* Pi. *to desire, delight in,* Ca. 2. 3.

חֶמֶד masc. *desirableness;* שְׂדֵי חֶמֶד *desirable, pleasant fields;* בַּחוּרֵי חֶמֶד *pleasant, comely young men.*

חֶמְדָּה fem. constr. חֶמְדַּת (no pl.)—I. *desire.*—II. *object of desire;* חֶמְדַּת כָּל־הַגּוֹיִם *the* (object of) *desire of all nations,* i. e. the Messiah, Hag. 2. 7.—III. *desirableness, pleasantness;* 'אֶרֶץ ח *pleasant land;* 'כְּלֵי ח *desirable, precious vessels.*

חֲמֻדוֹת ,חֲמוּדוֹת fem. pl. *desirable, precious things,* applied to vessels and other valuables; 'לֶחֶם ח *desirable, pleasant, delicate food;* 'אִישׁ ח *man beloved* (of God).

חֶמְדָּן (*pleasant*) pr. name masc. Ge. 36. 26; for which חַמְרָן 1 Ch. 1. 41.

מַחְמָד masc. constr. מַחְמַד, pl. מַחֲמַדִּים d. 8a (§ 37. No. 3c).—I. *desire,* also *object of desire;* hence pl. *things desirable, precious, costly.*—II. pl. *loveliness,* Ca. 5. 16.

מַחְמוֹד masc. pl. מַחֲמֻדִּים d. 8c (§ 37. No. 3c) *precious, costly things,* La. 1. 7, 11.

חֶמֶד noun masc. sing. . . . . חמד
חֶמְדָּה noun fem. sing. (no pl.) . . . חמד
[k]חָמְדוּ [l]'וְ Kal pret. 3 pers. sing. . . . חמד
חֲמֻדוֹת noun fem. pl. [fr. חֲמוּדָה] . . . חמד
חֶמְדָּן pr. name masc. . . . . חמד
חֶמְדַּת noun fem. sing., constr. of דָּה' (no pl.) . חמד
[m]חֶמְדָּתִי id., suff. 1 pers. sing. . . . חמד
[n]חִמַּדְתִּי Piel pret. 1 pers. sing. . . . חמד
[o]חֶמְדָּתֵךְ noun fem. sing., suff. 2 pers. sing. fem. fr. חֶמְדָּה (no pl.) . . . . חמד
[p]חֶמְדָּתָם id., suff. 3 pers. pl. masc. . . . חמד
[q]חֲמַדְתֶּם Kal pret. 2 pers. pl. masc. . . . חמד

חָמָה Root not used; Arab. חמא *to guard, to surround with a wall.*

חוֹמָה fem. dec. 10, *a wall;* dual חוֹמֹתַיִם *double walls.*

חֲמָת (*fortress*) pr. name *Hamath,* a large city in Syria near the northern boundary of Palestine. Gent. noun חֲמָתִי *Hamathite,* Ge. 10. 18.

יַחְמַי (for יַחְמְיָה whom *the Lord guards, defends*) pr. name masc. 1 Ch. 7. 2.

[r]חַמָּה noun fem. sing. dec. 10. . . . חמם
חֵמָה 'וְ noun fem. sing. dec. 11b [for יְחֵמָה] . יחם
חֹמָה defect. for חוֹמָה (q. v.) . . . חמה
חַמּוּאֵל pr. name masc. . . . . חמם
[s]חֲמוּדוֹ Kal part. p. masc., suff. 3 pers. sing. masc. from [חָמוּד] dec. 3a . . . חמד
חֲמוּדוֹת noun fem. pl. [of חֲמוּדָה] . . . חמד
[t]חֲמוּדֵיהֶם וְ Kal part. p. pl. masc., suff. 3 pers. pl. masc. from [חָמוּד] dec. 3a . . . חמד
חֲמֻדֹת defect. for חֲמוּדוֹת (q. v.) . . . חמד
חֲמוּטַל pr. name fem. . . . . חם
חָמוּל וְ pr. name masc. . . . . חמל
חַמּוֹן 'וְ pr. name of a place . . . חמם

[a] Eze. 5. 1. [b] Eze. 47. 21. [c] Ex. 29. 2. [d] Is. 23. 4. [e] Jos. 9. 12. [cc] Ge. 8. 22. [f] Ps. 39. 4. [g] Da. 3. 13. [h] Da. 3. 19. [i] De. 32. 14. [k] Pr. 1. 22. [l] Mi. 2. 2. [m] Je. 12. 10. [n] Ca. 2. 3. [o] Eze. 26. 12. [p] Da. 11. 8. [q] Is. 1. 29. [r] Job 30. 28. [s] Ps. 39. 12. [t] Is. 44. 9.

חָמוֹץ[a] adj. masc. sing. . . . . חמץ

חֲמוּץ[b] Kal part. p. masc., constr. of [חָמוּץ] dec. 3a חמץ

חַמּוּקֵי[c] noun masc. pl. constr. from [חַמּוּק] dec. 1b חמק

חֲמוֹר וְ' noun masc. sing. dec. 1a, also pr. name; וַ before (-:) . . . . . חמר

חֲמוֹרֵיכֶם[d] id. pl., suff. 2 pers. pl. masc. . . . חמר

חֲמוֹרִים[e] וְ' id. pl. absolute state; וַ before (-:) . חמר

חֲמוֹת[f] noun fem. pl. abs. from חֵמָה dec. 11b . יחם

חֹמוֹת[g] noun fem., pl. of חוֹמָה dec. 10. . . חמה

חֲמוֹתָהּ noun fem. sing., suff. 3 pers. sing. fem. from [חָמוֹת] dec. 3a . . . . . חם

חַמּוֹתִי[h] Kal pret. 1 pers. sing. (§ 18. rem. 1) . חמם

חֲמוֹתֵךְ noun masc. sing., suff. 2 pers. sing. fem. from [חָמוֹת] dec. 3a . . . . . חם

[חֹמֶט] masc. kind of *lizard*, Le. 11. 30. Hence

חֻמְטָה וְ (*place of lizards*) pr. name of a city in Judah, Jos. 15. 54 . . . חמט

חָמִיהָ noun masc. sing., suff. 3 pers. sing. fem. from [חָם irr. § 45] . . . . . חם

חֲמִיטַל Kh. חֲמִיטַל, K. חֲמוּטַל q. v. . . חם

חָמִיךְ[i] n. m. s., suff. 2 pers. s. f. [from חָם irr. § 45] חם

חַמִּים[k] adj. masc., pl. of חַם dec. 8a . . . חמם

חָמִיץ[l] adj. masc. sing. . . . . . חמץ

חֲמִישִׁי adj. ord. masc. sing. from חָמֵשׁ . . חמש

חֲמִישִׁית fem. of the preceding dec. 1b . . . חמש

חֲמִישִׁיתוֹ, חֲמִישִׁתוֹ[m] וְ' } id. with suff. 3 pers. sing. masc. . חמש

חָמַל fut. יַחְמֹל (§ 13. rem. 5).—I. *to pity, have compassion*, with עַל of the person.—II. *to spare, save*, with אֶל.—III. *to spare, withhold*, with inf. and לְ, with עַל.

חָמוּל (*spared*) pr. name masc.—Patronym. חָמוּלִי Nu. 26. 21.

חֶמְלָה fem. constr. חֶמְלַת (no pl.) *mercy, clemency*.

מַחְמָל masc. dec. 2b, *object of tender affection*, Eze. 24. 21.

חָמָל Kal pret. 3 pers. s. m. for חָמַל (comp. § 8. r. 7) חמל

חָמַלְתָּ id. pret. 2 pers. sing. masc. [for חָמַלְתָּ § 8. rem. 7] . . . . . חמל

חָמַלְתִּי וְ id. pret. 1 pers. s.; acc. shifted (§ 8. r. 7) חמל

חֲמַלְתֶּם[o] id. pret. 2 pers. pl. masc. . . . . חמל

[חָמַם] fut. יֵחַם, וַיֵּחַם, יָחֹם (§ 18. rem. 6) *to be or grow warm*; כְּחֹם הַיּוֹם *in the heat of the day*, at noon; impers. יֵחַם, חַם לוֹ *it is warm to him, he becomes warm*. Niph. part. *burning, inflamed*, Is. 57. 5. Pi. *to warm, hatch*, Job 39. 14. Hithp. *to warm oneself*, Job 31. 20.

חָם masc. dec. 8a.—I. adj. *warm, hot*.—II. pr. name of a son of Noah.—III. *Ham* poet. for Egypt, comp. Ps. 78. 51; 105. 23, 27.

חֹם masc. *warmth, heat*.

חַמָּה fem. dec. 10.—I. *heat, glow*, Ps. 19. 7.—II. *the sun*.

חַמּוּאֵל (*warmth of God*) pr. name m. 1 Ch. 4. 26.

חַמּוֹן (*sunny*) pr. name—I. of a town in the tribe of Asher, Jos. 19. 28.—II. of a town in the tribe of Naphtali, 1 Ch. 6. 61.

חַמָּן masc. dec. 1b, only pl. (חַמָּנִים) *images dedicated to the sun, sun-images*.

חַמַּת (*hot bath*) pr. name of a city in the tribe of Naphtali, Jos. 19. 35.

חַמּוֹת דֹּאר (*hot baths of Dor*) pr. name of a city of refuge in the tribe of Naphtali, Jos. 21. 32.

חַמָּנֵיכֶם noun masc. pl., suff. 2 pers. pl. masc. from [חַמָּן] dec. 1b . . . . . חמם

חַמָּנִים[p] וְ id. pl., absolute state . . . חמם

[חָמַס] fut. יַחְמֹס (§ 13. rem. 5).—I. *to do violence* to any one, *to injure, wrong, oppress*; חָמַס תּוֹרָה *to violate the law*.—II. *to tear away with violence*, La. 2. 6.—III. *to shake off* as the tree its fruit, Job 15. 33.

חָמָס masc. dec. 4c, *violence, wrong, injury*; meton. *what is obtained by violence* or *wrong, ill-gotten wealth*, Am. 3. 10.

תַּחְמָס masc. a species of unclean bird, Le. 11. 16; De. 14. 15. According to Bochart, *the male ostrich*. Vulg. noctua, *night-hawk*.

חָמָס וְ' noun masc. sing. dec. 4c . . . . חמס

חֲמַס[q] וְ' id. construct state; וַ before (-:) . . חמס

חֹמֵס[r] Kal part. act. sing. masc. . . . . חמס

חָמְסוּ id. pret. 3 pers. pl. . . . . . חמס

חֲמָסוֹ[s] noun masc. sing., suff. 3 pers. sing. masc. from חָמָס dec. 4c . . . . חמס

חֲמָסִי id., suff. 1 pers. sing. . . . . חמס

חֲמָסִים id. pl., absolute state . . . . חמס

חָמֵץ[t] fut. יֶחְמַץ (§ 13. rem. 4, 5).—I. *to be sour, to be leavened*, of bread.—II. part. חָמוּץ, metaph. *splendid*, of the dazzling scarlet colour, Is. 63. 1.—III. i. q. חָמַס, part. חוֹמֵץ *a violent man*, Ps. 71. 4.

[a] Is. 1. 17. [b] Is. 63. 1. [c] Ca. 7. 2. [d] 1 Sa. 8. 16. [e] 1 Ch. 5. 21. [f] Pr. 22. 24. [g] Je. 51. 58. [h] Is. 44. 16. [i] Ge. 38. 13. [k] Job 37. 17. [l] Is. 30. 24. [m] Nu. 5. 7. [n] Mal. 3. 17. [o] 1 Sa. 23. 21. [p] Is. 27. 9. [q] Hab. 2. 8, 17. [r] Pr. 8. 36. [s] Ps. 7. 17. [t] Ex. 12. 39.

Hiph. part. מַחְמֶצֶת *soured, leavened.* Hithp. *to be embittered, provoked to anger,* Ps. 73. 21.

חָמֵץ masc. *what is leavened, fermented.*

חָמוֹץ masc. *violent man, oppressor,* Is. 1. 17, which others take in a passive sense, *oppressed.* Vulg. oppressors.

חָמִיץ masc. adj. *salted, seasoned,* Is. 30. 24. Prof. Lee, "a salt, sour plant of the desert much relished by the camels."

חֹמֶץ masc. *vinegar.*

חָמֵץ noun masc. sing. . . . . . חמץ

חֹמֶץ[a] וְ׳ noun masc. sing. . . . . חמץ

חֲמִצָתוֹ[b] Kal inf. [חֲמִצָה § 8. rem. 10] suff. 3 pers. sing. masc. . . . . . חמץ

חָמַק *to turn oneself, withdraw, depart,* Ca. 5. 6. Hithp. *to wander about,* Je. 31. 22.

חַמּוּק masc. only pl. (חַמּוּקִים) Ca. 7. 2. Eng. Vers., "joints." Others, *circuits.* Prof. Lee, *surroundings, clothings;* and as some think, a kind of *drawers* worn by the women of the east.

חָמַר[c] fut. יֶחְמַר (§ 13. rem. 4, 5).—I. *to rise, ferment,* Ps. 75. 9; others, *to be red.*—II. metaph. *to be agitated,* Ps. 46. 4.—III. fut. יַחְמֹר (§ 13. rem. 5) *to daub, cover with bitumen,* Ex. 2. 3; denom. from חֵמָר. Poalal (§ 6. No. 3).—I. *to become excited, troubled.*—II. *to become red, inflamed,* Job 16. 16.

חֵמָר masc. bitumen or asphaltus, a glutinous matter issuing from the earth, which springs in a *turbid effervescence* near Babylon, also near the Dead Sea and at its bottom.

חֶמֶר masc. *wine.*

חֲמַר Chald. masc. dec. 3a, id.

חֹמֶר masc. dec. 6c.—I. *a fermenting, foaming,* of waters, Hab. 3. 15; but comp. the following significations.—II. *clay, cement; mire, mud.*—III. *a heap,* Ex. 8. 10.—IV. *measure of capacity,* containing ten Baths.

חֲמוֹר, חֲמֹר masc.—I. *an ass.*—II. i. q. חֹמֶר *a heap,* Ju. 15. 16.—III. pr. name masc. comp. Ge. 33. 19.

חֲמֹרָה fem. dec. 10, *a heap,* Ju. 15. 16.

חַמְרָן pr. name masc. 1 Ch. 1. 41, called חֶמְדָּן in Ge. 36. 26.

יַחְמוּר masc. *goat* or *gazelle* of a brown or reddish colour.

חָמֶר[d] in pause for חֶמֶר (q. v. § 35. rem. 2) . חמר

חֲמַר Chald. noun masc. sing. dec. 3a . . חמר

חֵמָר noun masc. sing. dec. 1a . . . . חמר

חֵמָר[e] noun masc. sing. . . . . חמר

חֶמֶר[f] noun masc. sing. . . . . חמר

חֹמֶר[g] וְ׳ noun masc. sing. dec. 6c . . חמר

חַמְרָא[h] Chald. noun masc. s., emph. of חֲמַר dec. 3a חמר

חֲמֹרוֹ וְ׳ noun masc. sing. dec. 1a; וַ before (-:) חמר

חֲמֹרֵיהֶם[i] וְ׳ id. pl., suff. 3 pers. pl. masc. . . חמר

חֲמָרִים[k] noun masc., pl. of חֹמֶר dec. 6c . . חמר

חֲמֹרִים וְ׳ noun masc., pl. of חֲמוֹר dec. 1a; וַ bef. (-:) חמר

חֲמֹרֵינוּ[l] id. pl., suff. 1 pers. pl. . . . . חמר

חֲמֹרְךָ[m] } וְ׳ id. sing., suff. 2 pers. sing. masc.;
חֲמֹרֶךָ[n] } [o] וְ׳ וַ before (-:) . . . . } חמר

חֲמֹרִם[p] defect. for חֲמֹרִים (q. v.) . . . . חמר

חֳמַרְמְרָה[q] Kh. ׳מָרָה Poalal pret. 3 pers. sing. fem.; K. ׳מְרוּ (q. v.) . . . . חמר

חֳמַרְמְרוּ[r] }
חֳמַרְמָרוּ[s] } id. pret. 3 pers. pl. (§ 6. rem. 3; § 8. r. 7) חמר

חַמְרָן pr. name masc. . . . . . חמר

חֲמֹרָתָיִם[t] for [׳תַיִם] noun fem., dual of [חֲמֹרָה] dec. 10. חמר

חָמַשׁ only part. pass. חֲמֻשִׁים *brave, ready* for battle. Arab. *to be fat, stout; strong, courageous.*

חֹמֶשׁ masc. *the belly, abdomen.*

חָמֵשׁ וְ׳ constr. חֲמֵשׁ fem., חֲמִשָּׁה constr. חֲמֵשֶׁת masc. (§ 39. No. 4. rem. 1) num. card. *five;* חֲמִשִּׁים *fifty,* (with suff. חֲמִשֶּׁיךָ), ׳שַׂר חֲ *a captain of fifty,* sc. soldiers.

חִמֵּשׁ Piel (denom. of חָמֵשׁ) *to fifth, exact the fifth part,* Ge. 41. 34.

חֹמֶשׁ masc. *fifth part,* Ge. 47. 26.

חֲמִשִׁי, חֲמִישִׁי masc., ־ִית fem. adj. ordinal, *fifth;* חֲמִישִׁית *fifth part.*

חֲמֵשׁ וְ׳ constr. of the preceding . . . . חמש

חִמֵּשׁ[u] וְ Piel pret. 3 pers. sing. masc. . . . חמש

חֲמִשָּׁה וְ׳ num. card. masc. sing. from חָמֵשׁ fem.; וַ before (-:) . . . . . . חמש

חֲמִשֵּׁיהֶם[ll] id. pl. com. gen. (חֲמִשִּׁים) suff. 3 pers. pl. m. חמש

חֲמִשָּׁיו וְ׳ id. pl., suff. 3 pers. sing. masc.; וַ bef. (-:) חמש

חֲמִשֶּׁיךָ id. pl., suff. 2 pers. sing. masc. . . . חמש

חֲמִשִּׁים וְ׳ id. pl., absolute state; וַ before (-:) . חמש

חֲמֻשִׁים[x] וְ׳ Kal part. p. masc., pl. of [חָמוּשׁ] dec. 3a חמש

חֲמִשִׁית adj. ord. fem. s. for חֲמִישִׁית from חֲמִישִׁי m. חמש

חֲמִישִׁתוֹ id. with suff. 3 pers. sing. masc. . . . חמש

חֲמֵשֶׁת וְ׳ num. card. masc., constr. of חֲמִשָּׁה (§ 39. rem. 1) from חָמֵשׁ fem. . . . חמש

---

[a] Nu. 6. 3. [b] Ho. 7. 4. [c] Ps. 75. 9. [d] De. 32. 14. [e] Ge. 14. 10. [f] Is. 27. 2. [g] Ho. 3. 2. [h] Da. 5. 1, 2, 4, 23. [i] Ge. 44. 3. [k] Nu. 11. 32. [l] Ge. 43. 18. [ll] 2 Ki. 1. 14. [m] Ex. 23. 12. [n] De. 28. 31. [o] De. 5. 14. [p] Ex. 8. 10. [q] Job 16. 16. [r] La. 1. 20. [s] La. 2. 11. [t] Ju. 15. 16. [u] Ge. 41. 34. [x] Ex. 13. 18.

[a] חֲמִשְׁתּוֹ adj. ord. fem. (חֲמִישִׁית) suff. 3 pers. masc. from חֲמִשִּׁי masc. . . . . חמש
[b] חֲמִשְׁתָּיו וַ id. pl. [חֲמִישִׁיתִים], suff. 3 pers. sing. masc. (§ 4. rem. 3); וּ before (-:) . . חמש

[חֵמֶת] masc. constr. חֵמַת, *skin-bottle*.

חֲמָת / חֲמָת וְ׳ } pr. name of a place; וַ id. . . חמה
[c] חֵמַת וְ׳ n. fem. s., constr. of חֵמָה dec. 11b; וַ id. יחם
חַמּוֹת pr. name in compos. חַמּוֹת דֹּאר . . חמם
[d] חֵמַת וְ noun masc. sing., constr. of חֵמֶת׳ . . חמת
[e] חֵמֹת noun fem. pl. abs. from חֵמָה dec. 11b . יחם
חֲמָתָה pr. name of a place (חֲמָת) with paragogic ה חמה
[f] חֲמָתוֹ וְ׳ noun fem. sing., suff. 3 pers. sing. masc. from חֵמָה dec. 11b; וּ before (-:) . . יחם
חֲמָתִי וְ׳ id., with suff. 1 pers. sing. . . יחם
חֹמֹתַיִךְ noun fem. pl., suff. 2 pers. sing. masc. from חוֹמָה dec. 10. . . . . חמה
חֲמָתֶךָ / [g] חֲמָתְךָ וְ׳ } noun fem. sing., suff. 2 pers. sing. m. from חֵמָה dec. 11b; וַ bef. (-:) } יחם
[h] חֲמָתָם id., suff. 3 pers. pl. masc. . . . יחם
[i] חֵן וְ׳ noun masc. sing. dec. 8b . . . חנן
חֵנָדָד pr. name masc. . . . . חנן

חָנָה fut. יַחֲנֶה, apoc. יִחַן (§ 24. rem. 3).—I. *to decline*, of the day, Ju. 19. 9.—II. *to let oneself down, encamp, pitch one's tent*; const. with עַל *to encamp against*; with לְ *about* any one, sc. for his defence.—III. *to dwell*, Is. 29. 1.

חָנוּת fem. only pl. חֲנֻיוֹת (comp. מַלְכֻיּוֹת from מַלְכוּת) Je. 37. 16, *vaults, cells*. Prof. Lee, *wells*.

חֲנִית fem. dec. 1a, pl. חֲנִיתִים & חֲנִיתוֹת, *spear, lance*.

מַחֲנֶה com. (fem. Ge. 32. 9) dec. 9a, pl. מַחֲנִים, מַחֲנוֹת, du. מַחֲנַיִם (comp. § 38. rem. 1).—I. *camp, encampment*.—II. *troop, host, army*.—III. *swarm*, of locusts; *drove*, of cattle.

מַחֲנֵה־דָן (*camp of Dan*) pr. name of a place in the tribe of Judah, Ju. 18. 12.

מַחֲנַיִם (*two troops*) pr. name of a town beyond Jordan.

תַּחַן (*encampment*) pr. name masc. Patronym. תַּחֲנִי Nu. 26. 35.

תַּחֲנָה fem. dec. 10, *place of encampment*, 2 Ki. 6. 8.

[k] חֲנֵה וַ Kal imp. sing. masc.; וּ before (-:) . חנה
חַנָּה וְ׳ pr. name fem. . . . . חנן
חֹנָה fem. of the following . . . . חנה
חֹנֶה Kal part. act. sing. masc. dec. 9a . . חנה
[l] חָנוּ וְ׳ id. pret. 3 pers. pl. . . . חנה
חֲנוּ id. imp. pl. masc. . . . חנה
[m] חִנּוֹ noun m. s., suff. 3 pers. s. m. from חֵן dec. 8b חנן
חֲנוֹךְ וְ׳ pr. name of a man and a city . חנך
[n] חָנוֹן Kal inf. abs. (§ 18. rem. 13) . . חנן
חָנוּן pr. name masc. . . . . חנן
חַנּוּן וְ׳ adj. masc. sing., also pr. name masc. . חנן
[o] חָנּוּנוּ Kal imp. pl. m., suff. 1 pers. pl. (§ 18. rem. 4) חנן
[p] חָנוֹף Kal inf. abs. . . . . חנף
[q] חַנּוֹת Kal inf. constr. (§ 18. rem. 3); or noun fem., [pl. of חַנָּה] . . . . חנן
[r] חֲנוֹת Kal inf. construct dec. 1a . . . חנה
[s] חַנּוֹתִי וְ Kal inf. (§ 18. rem. 3), or noun fem. pl., [of חַנָּה] suff. 1 pers. sing. (§ 4. rem. 2) . חנן

[חָנַט] I. *to embalm*, Ge. 50. 2, 26.—II. *to ripen* fruit, Ca. 2. 13.

חֲנֻטִים masc. pl. *an embalming*, Ge. 50. 3; which others take as a part. pass. *embalmed bodies*.

[t] חָנְטָה Kal pret. 3 pers. sing. fem. . . . חנט
חִנְטִין Ch. noun fem. pl. [of חִנְטָא for חִטָּא], comp. חטה
חַנִּיאֵל וְ׳ pr. name masc. . . . . חנן
[u] חֲנִיכָיו noun masc. pl., suff. 3 pers. sing. masc. from [חָנִיךְ] dec. 3a . . . חנך
חֹנִים Kal part. act. masc., pl. of חֹנֶה dec. 9a . חנה
[x] חֲנִינָה noun fem. sing. . . . . חנן
חֲנִית וְ׳ noun fem. sing. dec. 1a; וּ before (-:) . חנה
חֲנִיתוֹ וְ׳ id., suff. 3 pers. sing. masc. . . חנה
[y] חֲנִיתוֹתֵיהֶם וַ id. pl., suff. 3 pers. pl. masc. . חנה
חָנִיתִי וְ Kal pret. 1 pers. sing. . . . חנה
[z] חֲנִיתֶךָ noun fem. sing., suff. 2 pers. sing. masc. [for חֲנִיתְךָ] from חֲנִית dec. 1a . . חנה
[a] חֲנִיתֹתֵיהֶם וַ id. pl., suff. 3 pers. pl. masc.; וּ before (-:) חנה

[חָנַךְ] fut. יַחְנְכוּ (§ 13. rem. 5).—I. *to instruct, initiate*, Pr. 22. 6.—II. *to consecrate, dedicate*, as a house, temple.

חֲנוֹךְ (*initiated*) pr. name—I. of a son of Cain; also of a city named after him, Ge. 4. 17, 18.—II. of the father of Methuselah, Ge. 5. 18—24.—III. of a son of Reuben. Patronym. חֲנֹכִי.—IV. Ge. 25. 4.

חָנִיךְ masc. dec. 3a, *trained*, Ge. 14. 14.

חֲנֻכָּה fem. dec. 10, *consecration, dedication*.

חֲנֻכָּא Chald. fem. dec. 8a, id.

חֵךְ masc. dec. 8b (for חֵנֶךְ § 37. No. 3, Syr.

[a] Le. 27. 27. [b] Le. 5. 24. [c] Est. 7. 10. [d] Ge. 21. 14. [e] Ps. 76. 11. [f] Est. 1. 12. [g] Da. 9. 16. [h] Job 6. 4. [i] Pr. 3. 22. [k] 2 Sa. 12. 28. [l] Nu. 1. 52. [m] Ge. 39. 21. [n] Is. 30. 19. [o] Ju. 21. 22. [p] Je. 3. 1. [q] Ps. 77. 10. [r] Ju. 19. 9. [s] Job 19. 17. [t] Ca. 2. 13. [u] Ge. 14. 14. [x] Je. 16. 13. [y] Is. 2. 4. [z] Hab. 3. 11. [a] Mi. 4. 3.

(חִנְּכָא).—I. *palate*, as the seat of taste.—II. metaph. Pr. 8. 7, as the *seat of perception*.

חַכָּה fem. *hook, angle.*

חֲנֹךְ[a] 'וְ Kal imp. sing. masc.; also pr. name; וַ id. חנך

חֹנֶךָ[b] Kal part. act. masc. sing. [חֹנֶה], suff. 2 pers. sing. masc. (§ 2 rem. 2) dec. 9a . . חנה

חֲנֻכָּה[c] noun fem. sing. dec. 10. . . . חנך

חֲנָכוֹ[d] Kal pret. 3 pers. sing. m., suff. 3 pers. sing. m. חנך

חֲנֻכַּת noun fem. sing., constr. of חֲנֻכָּה dec. 10; Chald. (Ezr. 6. 16) dec. 8a . . . חנך

חִנָּם adv.; from חֵן with the term. ־ָם . חנן

חֲנַמְאֵל pr. name masc. Je. 32. 7, 9.

[חֲנָמַל] *host*, Ps. 78. 47. Gesenius conjectures, *ants*; Prof. Lee, *a kind of locust*.

חָנַן[e] fut. יָחֹן, יֶחֱנַן (§ 18. rem. 13).—I. *to be gracious, merciful, compassionate* to any one, const. with an acc.—II. *to give graciously, to bestow in mercy and kindness.* Niph. נֵחַן (§ 18. rem. 8 & 14) *to be pitiable*, Je. 22. 23. Pi. *to make gracious, pleasant*, Pr. 26. 25. Po. i. q. Kal No. 1. Hoph. *to be favoured, to find favour.* Hithp. *to implore, supplicate favour, mercy*, const. with לְ, אֶל, לִפְנֵי.

חֲנַן Chald. *to show favour, mercy*, Da. 4. 24. Hithpa. *to implore favour*, Da. 6. 12.

חָנָן (*merciful*) pr. name masc. of several persons, comp. בֵּית חָ'.

חָנוּן (*favoured*) pr. name—I. of a king of the Ammonites.—II. Ne. 3. 30.—III. Ne. 3. 13.

חַנּוּן adj. masc. *gracious, merciful, compassionate.*

חֲנִינָה fem. *grace, favour*, Je. 16. 13.

חֲנַנְאֵל (which *God has graciously given*) pr. name of a tower in Jerusalem.

חֲנָנִי (*gracious*; or for חֲנַנְיָה q. v.) pr. name masc. of several persons, especially—I. of a prophet, the father of Jehu.—II. of a brother of Nehemiah.

חֲנַנְיָה (whom *the Lord has graciously given*) pr. name—I. of a false prophet, comp. Je. 28. 1.—II. of a companion of Daniel, Da. 1. 6, 7, &c.

חֲנַנְיָהוּ (id.) pr. name masc.—I. 2 Ch. 26. 11.—II. 1 Ch. 25. 23.—III. Je. 36. 12.

חֵן masc. dec. 8b.—I. *grace, favour*; נָשָׂא, מָצָא חֵן בְּעֵינֵי פ' *to find, obtain favour in the eyes of* any one i. e. with him; נָתַן אֶת־חֵן פ' בְּעֵינֵי פ' *to procure one the favour of another*, Ex. 3. 21; רוּחַ חֵן *the spirit of grace*, i. e. the spirit of God predisposing the heart of man to seek reconciliation with God, Zec. 12. 10.—II. *grace, elegance, beauty.*—III. pr. name masc. Zec. 6. 14.

חִין masc. (for חֵן, like אִישׁ from אֱנָשׁ) *grace, beauty*, Job 41. 4. Others compare it with an Arab. root חִין. Prof. Lee, *destruction*; Schultens, *fitness.*

חֵנָדָד (for חֵן הֲדַד *favour of Hadad*, comp. הֲדַד) pr. name of a man.

חַנִּיאֵל (*grace of God*) pr. name masc.—I. Nu. 34. 23.—II. 1 Ch. 7. 39.

חִנָּם adv.—I. *gratis, freely, for nothing.*—II. *in vain.*—III. *for nothing, undeservedly.*

חַנּוֹת fem. dec. 10.—I. *grace, favour*, Ps. 77. 10.—II. *supplication, prayer for favour*, Job 9. 17.—III. pr. name of the mother of Samuel, comp. 1 Sa. 1. 2, &c.

חַנָּתֹן (*favoured place*) pr. name of a place in Zebulun, Jos. 19. 14.

תְּחִנָּה fem. dec. 10.—I. *favour, mercy.*—II. *supplication, prayer for favour, mercy.*—III. pr. name masc. 1 Ch. 4. 12.

תַּחֲנוּן masc. dec. 1b, pl. ־ִים, ־וֹת, *supplication, prayer for mercy.*

חָנָן 'וְ pr. name m. (and in compos. with בֵּית q.v.) חנן

חֹנֵן Kal part. act. sing. masc. . . . חנן

חֲנַנְאֵל pr. name masc. . . . . חנן

חֲנָנוּ[f] Kal pret. 3 pers. pl. [for חָנְנוּ § 8. rem. 7, & § 18. rem. 13] . . . . חנן

חָנֵּנוּ id. imp. s. m. [חֹן], suff. 1 pers. pl. (§ 18. r. 4) חנן

חֲנָנִי pr. name masc. . . . . חנן

חַנַּנִי[g] Kal pret. 3 pers. sing. m. [חַן], suff. 1 pers. sing. חנן

חָנֵּנִי 'וְ id. imp. s. m. [חֹן], suff. 1 p. s. (§ 18. rem. 4) חנן

חָנֻּנִי[h] id. imp. pl. m., suff. 1 pers. sing. (§ 18. rem. 4) חנן

חֲנַנְיָה, חֲנַנְיָהוּ 'וְ } pr. name masc.; וַ before (־:) . . חנן

חָנְנֵנִי[i] uncontracted (like קָטְלֵנִי) for חָנֵּנִי q. v. . חנן

חָנֵס pr. name of a city in Egypt, Is. 30. 4.

[חָנֵף] fut. יֶחֱנַף.—I. *to be* or *become profaned, polluted, or defiled.*—II. *to be profane, ungodly*, Je. 23. 11.—III. trans. *to profane, pollute*, Je. 3. 9. Hiph. *to profane, pollute; to seduce to apostacy*, Da. 11. 32.

חָנֵף masc. dec. 5c, *profane, ungodly.*

Note.—The sense of *hypocrite* ascribed to this word (and that of *hypocrisy* in the following), is not recognised by modern lexicographers, though it is so rendered by Aqu. and Symm., and this word is

[a] Pr. 22. 6. [b] Ps. 53. 6. [c] Ne. 12. 27. [d] De. 20. 5. [e] Ge. 33. 5. [f] La. 4. 16. [g] Ge. 33. 11. [h] Job 19. 21. [i] Ps. 9. 14.

so used by the Rabbis. Syr. חַנְפָא *heathen, ungodly man,* אֶחַנְפֵּי *to apostatize from the true religion.*

חֹנֶף masc. *profaneness, wickedness,* Is. 32. 6; Eng. Vers. *hypocrisy.*

חֲנֻפָּה fem. id. Je. 23. 15.

חָנֵף noun masc. sing. dec. 5c . . . . חנף
[a] חֹנֶף noun masc. sing. . . . . . חנף
[b] חָנְפָה Kal pret. 3 pers. sing. fem. . . . חנף
[c] חֲנֻפָּה noun fem. sing. . . . . . חנף
[d] חָנֵפוּ Kal pret. 3 pers. pl. [for חָנְפוּ § 8. rem. 7] חנף
[e] חַנְפֵי וְ noun masc. pl. constr. from חָנֵף dec. 5c חנף
[f] חֲנֵפִים id. pl., absolute state . . . . חנף

חָנַק. Niph. *to strangle oneself,* 2 Sa. 17. 23. Pi. *to strangle,* Na. 2. 13.

מַחֲנָק masc. dec. 2b, *strangling, suffocation, death,* Job 7. 15.

[g] חַנֹּתִי וְ Kal pret. 1 pers. sing.; acc. shifted by conv. וְ (§ 8. rem. 7) . . . חנן
[h] חֲנֹתֵנוּ Kal inf. (חֲנוֹת) suff. 1 pers. pl. dec. 1a . חנה

חָסַד Kal not used; in the derivatives it has the signification of *kindness and benignity.* Pi. as in the Aram. *to reproach, disgrace,* Pr. 25. 10. Hithp. *to show oneself kind, merciful.*

חָסִיד masc. dec. 3a.—I. *kind, benevolent, gracious, merciful.*—II. *pious, godly, holy.*

חֲסִידָה fem. *stork,* prop. *the pious,* from its affection towards its young.

חֶסֶד masc. with suff. חַסְדִּי dec. 6a.—I. *kindness, mercy;* עָשָׂה חֶסֶד with אֵת, עַל, לְ, עִם *to show kindness to* any one; נָטָה חֶסֶד לְ *to procure kindness, favour for* any one.—II. *grace, beauty,* Is. 40. 6. — III. *reproach, disgrace,* comp. Pi.—IV. pr. name masc. 1 Ki. 4. 10.

חֲסַדְיָה (whom *the Lord loves*) pr. name masc. 1 Ch. 3. 20.

[i] חֶסֶד וָ׳ / חָסֶד וְ׳, וָ׳ } noun masc. sing. (suff. חַסְדִּי) d. 6a; for וָ see lett. ו } חסד
חֲסָדָו id. pl., suff. (K. דָיו׳ § 4. rem. 1) 3 pers. sing. masc. . . . . . חסד
[k] חַסְדּוֹ וְ׳ id. sing., suff. 3 pers. sing. masc. . חסד
חַסְדִּו id. sing., suff., Kh. דוֹ׳ 3 pers. sing. masc., K. דִּי׳ 1 pers. sing. . . . . חסד
[m] חֲסָדַי id. pl., suff. 1 pers. sing. . . . חסד
חַסְדֵי id. pl., constr. state . . . . חסד
חַסְדִּי וְ׳ id. sing., suff. 1 pers. sing. . . . חסד

חֲסַדְיָה וָ pr. name masc.; וָ bef. (-:) . . . חסד
[n] חֲסָדָיו וַ׳ noun masc. pl., suff. 3 pers. sing. masc. from חֶסֶד dec. 6a; וַ bef. (-:) . . חסד
[o] חֲסָדֶיךָ וַ׳ / [p] חֲסָדֶךָ } id. pl., suff. 2 pers. sing. masc. (§ 4. rem. 1); וַ id. . . . } חסד
חַסְדְּךָ / חַסְדֶּךָ } id. sing., suff. 2 pers. sing. masc. . חסד
חַסְדֵּךְ id. sing., suff. 2 pers. sing. fem. . חסד
[q] חַסְדְּכֶם וְ id. sing., suff. 2 pers. pl. masc. . . חסד
[r] חַסְדָּם id. sing., suff. 3 pers. pl. masc. . . חסד

[חָסָה] fut. יֶחְסֶה, יֶחֱסֶה (§ 13. rem. 5) prop. *to flee* (cogn. חוּשׁ) for shelter, refuge; hence, *to trust, confide in,* const. with בְּ.

חָסוּת fem. *trust, confidence,* Is. 30. 3.

חֹסָה (*confiding, confident*) pr. name of a man.

אַחְסְבַּי (prob. for אֶחֱסֶה בְּיָהּ *I will trust in the Lord*) pr. name masc. 2 Sa. 23. 34.

מַחְסֶה, מַחֲסֶה masc. dec. 9a, *shelter, refuge.*

[s] חָסָה וְ Kal pret. 3 pers. sing. masc.; acc. Milêl before monos. . . . . חסה
[t] חָסָה Kal pret. 3 pers. sing. fem. . . . חוס
חֹסָה וְ׳ pr. name masc. . . . . חסה
[u] חֹסֶה וְ Kal part. act. masc. dec. 9a . . חסה
[x] חָסוּ וְ׳[y] id. pret. 3 pers. pl. . . . . חסה
[z] חֲסוּ id. imp. pl. masc. . . . . . חסה
[a] חָסוֹר וְ Kal inf. absolute . . . . חסר
[b] חֹסֵי Kal part. act. masc. pl. c. from חֹסֶה dec. 9a; acc. Milêl before monos. . . חסה
חָסִיד וְ׳[c] adj. masc. sing. dec. 3a . . . חסד
חֲסִידָה noun fem. sing., prop. fem. of חָסִיד . חסד
חֲסִידָו Khethib for חֲסִידָיו (§ 4. rem. 1) . חסד
[d] חֲסִידַי noun masc. pl., suff. 1 pers. sing. [for דֵי׳] from חָסִיד dec. 3a . . . חסד
[e] חֲסִידֶיהָ וַ id., suff. 3 pers. sing. fem.; וַ bef. (-:) . חסד
חֲסִידָיו id., suff. 3 pers. sing. masc. . . חסד
חֲסִידֶיךָ וַ׳ id., suff. 2 pers. sing. masc.; וַ before (-:) חסד
[f] חֲסִידְךָ Kh. id. (דֶיךָ׳), K. דְךָ׳ sing., suff. 2 pers. sing. masc. . . . . . .
חֲסִידִים id. pl., absolute state . . . חסד
[g] חֲסִידֶךָ id. sing., suff. 2 pers. sing. m. [for חֲסִידְךָ] חסד
[h] חָסָיָה Kal pret. 3 pers. sing. fem. (§ 24. rem. 5) . חסה
[i] חָסָיוּ id. pret. 3 pers. pl. (v. id.) . . חסה
[k] חָסִיל וְ׳[l] noun masc. sing. . . . . חסל
[m] חֲסִין adj. masc. sing. . . . . חסן
[n] חַסִּיר Ch. adj. masc. sing. . . . . חסר
חָסִיתִי Kal pret. 1 pers. sing. . . . . חסה

[a] Is. 32. 6. [b] Is. 24. 5. [c] Je. 23. 15. [d] Je. 23. 11. [e] Job 36. 13. [f] Is. 33. 14. [g] Ex. 33. 19. [h] Nu. 10. 31. [i] Pr. 21. 21. [k] Ps. 66. 20. [l] Ps. 59. 11. [m] Ne. 13. 14. [n] Is. 63. 7. [o] Ps. 25. 6. [p] Ps. 119. 41. [q] Ho. 6. 4. [r] Jon. 2. 9. [s] Ps. 64. 11. [t] Eze. 16. 5. [u] Pr. 14. 32. [x] Ps. 37. 40. [y] Zep. 3. 12. [z] Ju. 9. 15. [a] Ge. 8. 5. [b] Na. 1. 7. [c] Ps. 145. 17. [d] Ps. 50. 5. [e] Ps. 132. 16. [f] Ps. 16. 10. [g] De. 33. 8. [h] Ps. 57. 2. [i] De. 32. 37. [k] 1 Ki. 8. 37. [l] 2 Ch. 6. 28. [m] Ps. 89. 9. [n] Da. 5. 27.

[חָסַל] *to crop off, to devour*, De. 28. 38.

חָסִיל masc. the name of a species of *locust*.

[חָסַם] fut. יַחְסֹם (§ 13. rem. 5) *to stop*, Eze. 39. 11; *to stop, bind up, muzzle*, De. 25. 4.

מַחְסוֹם masc. *a muzzle*, Ps. 39. 2.

חֹסֶמֶת[a] וְ Kal part. act. fem. sing. . . . חסם

חָסַן Kal not used; Syr. & Chald. *to be strong*. Niph. *to be laid up, hoarded*, Is. 23. 18.

חֲסַן Ch. Aph. or Hiph. (§ 47. rem. 9) *to possess, have in possession*, Da. 7. 18, 22.

חֱסֵן Ch. masc. dec. 3 b, *might, power*.

חָסֹן adj. masc. *strong, powerful*.

חֹסֶן masc. *riches, wealth, abundance*.

חֲסִין adj. masc. *strong, mighty*, Ps. 89. 9.

חָסֹן[b] וְ adj. masc. sing. . . . . חסן

חֹסֶן noun masc. sing. . . . . . . חסן

חִסְנָא[c] Ch. noun masc. sing., emph. of [חֱסֵן] d. 3 b חסן

חִסְנִי[d] Ch. id. with suff. 1 pers. sing. . . . חסן

חָסַף Kal not used; prob. i. q. חָשַׂף *to peel, scale*; hence quadril. part. pass. מְחֻסְפָּס (§ 6. No. 7) *scaled off, having the form of scales*, Ex. 16. 14.

חֲסַף Ch. masc. dec. 3 a, *sherds, earthen ware*, Da. 2. 33, 34, 35, 41, 42, 43, 45.

חֲסַף[e] / חֲסַף[f] } Ch. noun masc. sing. dec. 3 a . . חסף

חַסְפָּא[g] וְ[h]' id., emph. state . . . . . חסף

[חָסֵר] fut. יֶחְסַר, יַחְסְרוּ (§ 13. rem. 5, 6).—I. *to want, lack, be without* any thing.—II. *to be in want, suffer need*.—III. *to fail, be diminished*.—IV. *to fail, be wanting*. Pi. *to cause to want, lack*, with מִן of the thing. Hiph.—I. *to cause to want, cause to fail*, Is. 32. 6.—II. intrans. *to want, lack*, Ex. 16. 18.

חָסֵר adj. masc. dec. 5 c.—I. *wanting, lacking, destitute*, with מִן; חֲסַר־לֵב *lacking understanding*.—II. subst. *want, lack*, Pr. 10. 21.

חֶסֶר masc. *want, poverty*.

חֹסֶר masc. id. חֹסֶר כֹּל *want of every thing*; חֹסֶר לֶחֶם *want of bread*.

חַסִּיר Ch. *wanting, deficient*, Da. 5. 27.

חַסְרָה pr. name masc. 2 Ch. 34. 22, for which חַרְחַס in 2 Ki. 22. 14.

חֶסְרוֹן masc. *want, poverty*, Ec. 1. 15.

מַחְסֹר, מַחְסוֹר masc. dec. 1 b, *want, need, poverty*; אִישׁ מַ׳ *poor man*.

חָסֵר adj. masc. sing. dec. 5 c . . . . חסר

חֲסַר וְ׳, id., constr. state; וְ bef. (-:) . . . חסר

חֶסֶר[i] noun masc. sing. . . . . . . חסר

חֹסֶר[k] וְ noun masc. sing. . . . . . חסר

חַסְרָה pr. name masc. . . . . . . חסר

חָסֵרוּ[l] Kal pret. 3 pers. pl. [for חָסְרוּ § 8. rem. 7] חסר

חֶסְרוֹן[m] וְ noun masc. sing. . . . . . חסר

חָסַרְנוּ[n] Kal pret. 1 pers. sing. . . . . חסר

חָסַרְתָּ[o] id. pret. 2 pers. sing. masc. . . . חסר

חַסְתָּ[p] Kal pret. 2 pers. sing. masc. . . . חוס

חַף[q] adj. masc. sing. . . . . . . חפף

חָפָא Kal not used; i. q. חָפָה. Pi. *to act secretly, clandestinely*, 2 Ki. 17. 9.

[חָפָה] *to cover, veil*. Pi. *to overlay*, as with gold, silver. Pu. *to be covered, protected*, Is. 4. 5, with עַל. Niph. נֶחְפָּה (§ 13. rem. 7) *to be overlaid*, Ps. 68. 14.

חִפָּה[r] Piel pret. 3 pers. sing. masc. . . . חפה

חֻפָּה[s] noun fem. sing. dec. 10. . . . . חפף

חָפוּ וְ׳' Kal pret. 3 pers. pl. . . . . חפה

חָפוּי[u] id. part. pass. sing. masc. dec. 3 a . . חפה

חֲפוּי[w] וַ id., constr. state; וַ bef. (-:) . . . חפה

[חָפַז] fut. יַחְפֹּז (§ 13. rem. 5).—I. *to start up* (cogn. קָפַץ) especially in *haste* and *alarm*.—II. *to be alarmed, perplexed*. Niph. נֶחְפַּז (§ 13. rem. 7) *to take to flight, to flee in alarm*.

חִפָּזוֹן masc. *haste, hurry*.

חֻפִּים / חֻפָּם } pr. name masc. . . . . חפף

[חֹפֶן] m. only dual חָפְנַיִם (d. 8 c) *the hollow hands, the fists*.

חָפְנִי (*fighter*, comp. Lat. pugnus & pugnator) pr. name of one of the sons of Eli.

חָפְנִי pr. name masc. . . . . . . חפן

חָפְנֵי[y] noun masc. du. constr. from [חֹפֶן] dec. 6 c חפן

חָפְנָיו[z] id. du., suff. 3 pers. sing. masc. . . חפן

חָפְנֶיךָ[a] id. du., suff. 2 pers. sing. masc. . . חפן

חָפְנֵיכֶם[b] id. du., suff. 2 pers. pl. masc. . . . חפן

חָפְנָיִם[c] id. du., absolute state . . . . חפן

[חָפַף] I. i. q. חָפָה *to cover, protect*, De. 33. 12, with עַל.—II. Arab. *to scrape, wipe, wash off*, comp. deriv. חַף, חוֹף.

[a] Eze. 39. 11. [b] Am. 2. 9. [c] Da. 2. 37. [d] Da. 4. 27. [e] Da. 2. 33. [f] Da. 2. 41, 42 [g] Da. 2. 35, 43, 45. [h] Da. 2. 34. [i] Pr. 28. 22. [k] Am. 4. 6. [l] Ne. 9. 21. [m] Ec. 1. 15. [n] Je. 44. 18. [o] De. 2. 7. [p] Jon. 4. 10. [q] Job 33. 9. [r] 2 Ch. 3. 5, 9 [s] Is. 4. 5. [t] Je. 14. 3. [u] 2 Sa. 15. 30. [w] Est. 6. 12. [y] Eze. 10. 7. [z] Le. 16. 12. [a] Eze. 10. 2. [b] Ex. 9. 8. [c] Ec. 4. 6.

חַף adj. masc. *clean, pure, faultless*, Job 33. 9.

חוֹף masc. *coast, shore* of the sea.

חֻפָּה fem. dec. 10.—I. *a covering, defence*, Is. 4. 5; but see Pu. of חָפָה.—II. *bridal chamber.*—III. pr. name masc. 1 Ch. 24. 13.

חֻפִּים (*coverings*) pr. name masc.—I. Ge. 46. 21.—II. 1 Ch. 7. 12, 15.

[a]חֹפֵף Kal part. act. sing. masc. . . . חפף

חָפֵץ fut. יֶחְפַּץ, יַחְפֹּץ (§ 13. rem. 4, 5).—I. *to bend, incline*, Job 40. 17.—II. intrans. *to incline, to be favourably disposed towards* any one, or any thing, *to delight in, be pleased with*, const. with בְּ, also acc.; followed by an inf. *to will, to desire, to be pleased* to do anything.

חָפֵץ masc. dec. 5c (pl. c. חֲפֵצֵי § 34. rem. 2) adj. *willing, desiring, delighting*; אִם חָפֵץ אַתָּה *if thou art willing*; חָפֵץ רֶשַׁע *delighting in wickedness*; נֶפֶשׁ חֲפֵצָה *a willing mind.*

חֵפֶץ masc. dec. 6, with suff. חֶפְצִי (§ 37. r. 6).—I. *delight, pleasure.*—II. *wish, will*, Job 31. 16.—III. *preciousness*; אַבְנֵי חֵפֶץ *precious stones*, and simply חֲפָצִים *precious things.*—IV. *business, concern, affair.*

חֶפְצִי־בָהּ (*my delight is in her*) pr. name—I. of the mother of king Manasseh, 2 Ki. 21. 1.—II. a symbolic name of Zion, Is. 62. 4.

חָפֵץ Kal pret. 3 pers. s. m.; or adj. masc. d. 5c חפץ

חֵפֶץ [b]'וְ noun masc. sing. dec. 6 (§ 35. rem. 6) חפץ

[c]חָפֵצָה Kal pret. 3 pers. s. f. [for חָפְצָה § 8. r. 7] חפץ

[d]חֲפֵצָה adj. fem. sing. from חָפֵץ masc. . . חפץ

חֶפְצָהּ noun masc. sing., suff. 3 pers. sing. fem. from חֵפֶץ dec. 6 (§ 35. rem. 6) . . חפץ

חֶפְצוֹ id., suff. 3 pers. sing. masc. . . חפץ

חֲפֵצֵי adj. masc. pl. c. from חָפֵץ d. 5c (§ 34. r. 2). חפץ

חֶפְצִי noun masc. sing., suff. 1 pers. sing. from חֵפֶץ dec. 6 (§ 35. rem. 6) . . חפץ

[e]חֶפְצֵיהֶם id. pl., suff. 3 pers. pl. masc. . . . חפץ

[f]חֲפָצֶיךָ id. pl. suff. 2 pers. sing. masc. . . חפץ

[g]חֲפָצִים id. pl., absolute state . . . חפץ

[h]חֲפֵצִים adj. m., pl. of חָפֵץ dec. 5c . . חפץ

[oo]חֲפָצֶךָ noun masc. pl., suff. 2 pers. sing. masc. [for חֲפָצֶיךָ § 4. r. 1] fr. חֵפֶץ d. 6 (§ 35. r. 6) חפץ

[i]חֶפְצְךָ id. sing., suff. 2 pers. sing. masc. . . חפץ

[k]חֶפְצָם id. sing., suff. 3 pers. pl. masc. . . חפץ

[l]חֲפָצְנוּ Kal pret. 1 pers. s. [for חָפַצְנוּ § 8. rem. 7] חפץ

חָפַצְתָּ id. pret. 2 pers. sing. masc. . . . חפץ

חָפַצְתִּי, חָפָצְתִּי } Kal pret. 1 pers. sing. (§ 8. rem. 7) . חפץ

[m]חֲפַצְתֶּם id. pret. 2 pers. pl. masc. . . . חפץ

[n]**חָפַר** fut. יַחְפֹּר (§ 13. rem. 5).—I. *to dig*, as a pit, well.—II. *to search out, explore, investigate, espy.*

חֵפֶר (*pit, well*) pr. name—I. of a city of Canaan.—II. of several men; (*a*) Nu. 26. 32; Jos. 17. 2, from which patronym. חֶפְרִי Nu. 26. 32; (*b*) 1 Ch. 11. 36; (*c*) 1 Ch. 4. 6.

חֲפָרַיִם (*two wells*) pr. name of a town in the tribe of Issachar, Jos. 19. 19.

חֲפֹר פֵּרוֹת (with pref. לַחְפֹּר פֵּ׳, comp. § 13. rem. 1, 2, 5) Is. 2. 20, *a mole* or *rat*; lit. *digger of holes*, חֲפֹר constr. of חָפֹר *digger*, פֵּרוֹת for פְּאֵרוֹת (comp. בּוֹר for בְּאוֹר) *holes*, from פאר Arab. *to dig*. Modern lexicographers, however, agree in reading it as one word (according to three codices by Dr. Kennicott) חֲפַרְפֵּרוֹת pl. *moles*, as a form derived from the conj. Pealal (§ 6. No. 3).

[חָפֵר] fut. יֶחְפַּר (§ 13. rem. 5) *to blush, be ashamed, confounded*. Hiph.—I. *to put to shame, cause disgrace.*—II. intrans. *to be ashamed.*

חֵפֶר pr. name of a man and a place . . חפר

[o]חֹפֵר Kal part. act. sing. masc. . . . חפר

[p]וְחָפְרָה, [q]וְחָפְרָה [r]'וְ } id. pret. 3 pers. sing. fem. (§ 8. rem. 7) חָפֵר

[s]חָפְרוּ, וְחָפְרוּ '} id. pret. 3 pers. pl. (§ 8. rem.7) . חָפֵר

[t]חֲפָרוּהָ id. id., suff. 3 pers. sing. fr. . . חָפַר

חָפְרַע pr. name of a king of Egypt, Pharaoh Hophra, Je. 44. 30.

[u]וְחָפַרְתָּ id. pret. 2 pers. sing. masc. (§ 8. r. 5) }
[x]וְחָפַרְתָּה acc. shifted by conv. וְ (§ 8. r. 7) } חפר

[y]חָפַרְתִּי id. pret. 1 pers. sing. . . . חפר

[חָפַשׂ] fut. יַחְפְּשׂוּ (§ 13. rem. 5) *to search out, explore, investigate*. Niph. נֶחְפַּשׂ (§ 13. rem. 7) *to be sought out*, Ob. 6. Pi. *to search, search out, search through*. Pu. *to be sought, sought out*. Hithp. *to disguise oneself.*

חֵפֶשׂ masc. *device, purpose*, Ps. 64. 7.

חָפַשׁ Kal not used; Arab. *to stretch out, to prostrate*; intrans. *to lie prostrate*. In the Heb. only Pu. *to be set free, to be freed*, Le. 19. 20.

[a] De. 33. 12. [b] Is. 53. 10. [c] Is. 66. 3. [d] 1 Ch. 28. 9. [e] Ps. 111. 2. [f] Pr. 3. 15. [g] Pr. 8. 11. [h] Mal. 3. 1. [i] 1 Ki. 5. 22, etc. [k] Ps. 107. 30. [l] Job 21. 14. [m] Je. 42. 22. [n] Job 39. 29. [o] Ec. 10. 8. [oo] Is. 58. 13. [p] Je. 15. 9. [q] Je. 50. 12. [r] Is. 24. 23. [s] Ge. 26. 32. [t] Nu. 21. 18. [u] Job 11. 18. [x] De. 23. 14. [y] Ge. 21. 30.

חֹפֶשׁ masc. *a spreading*, Eze. 27. 20. Here we may refer, with Fürst, Ps. 88. 6, בַּמֵּתִים חָפְשִׁי *my couch, bed, is among the dead*; but see חָפְשִׁי.

חֻפְשָׁה fem. *freedom*, Le. 19. 20.

חָפְשִׁי adj. masc. (pl. חָפְשִׁים) *free*, from servitude, taxes; Ps. 88. 6, *free among the dead*, i. e. from the evils of life; but according to others, *prostrate*, i. e. weak, *among the dead*, comp. also חֹפֶשׁ.

חָפְשִׁית, חָפְשׁוּת fem. *freedom*, from business, בֵּית חָ׳ *house of retirement*; others, *sick-house*, comp. the Root.

[a]חֹפֶשׁ	noun masc. sing.	חפשׁ
[b]חֹפֵשׂ	Kal part. act. sing. masc. . . .	חפשׂ
[c]חֹפֶשׁ	noun masc. sing.	חפשׁ
[d]חֻפָּשָׁה	Pual pret. 3 pers. sing. fem. [for חֻפְּשָׁה comp. § 8. rem. 7] . . .	חפשׁ
[e]חֻפְשָׁה	noun fem. sing.	חפשׁ
[f]חַפְּשׂוּ	Piel imp. pl. masc.	חפשׂ
[g]חִפְּשׂוּ	וְ id. pret. 3 pers. pl.	חפשׂ
חָפְשִׁי	adj. masc. sing.; or perh. (Ps. 88. 6) subst. masc. with suff. 1 pers. s. fr. חֹפֶשׁ d. 6c	חפשׁ
חָפְשִׁים	id. pl. absolute state	חפשׁ
[h]חִפַּשְׂתִּי	וְ Piel pret. 1 pers. sing.; acc. shifted by conv. וְ (comp. § 8. rem. 7) . .	חפשׂ
חֵץ	וְ׳ noun masc. sing. dec. 8b . .	חצץ

[i]חָצַב fut. יַחְצֹב, inf. חֲצֹב (from חָצֵב middle A § 8. rem. 13).—I. *to cut, hew, hew out*, as stone, wood; part. חֹצֵב *a hewer*.—II. trop. *to kill, destroy*, Ho. 6. 5. Niph. *to be engraven*, Job 19. 24. Pu. *to be hewn out*, Is. 51. 1. Hiph. *to cut in pieces*, Is. 51. 9.

מַחְצֵב masc. *a hewing* of stone, אַבְנֵי מַ׳ *hewn stones*.

חֹצֵב	id. part. act. sing. masc. dec. 7b . .	חצב
[k]חָצְבָה	Kal pret. 3 pers. sing. fem. . . .	חצב
[l]חֹצְבִי	id. part. act. sing. masc. with parag. י (§ 8. rem. 19) dec. 7b	חצב
חֹצְבִים	id. pl., absolute state . . .	חצב
חָצַבְתָּ	id. pret. 2 pers. sing. masc. . . .	חצב
[m]חָצַבְתִּי	id. pret. 1 pers. sing.	חצב
[n]חֻצַּבְתֶּם	Pual pret. 2 pers. pl. masc. . . .	חצב

[o]חָצָה fut. יֶחֱצֶה, *to divide*, into two, also several parts; לֹא־יֶחֱצוּ יְמֵיהֶם *they shall not halve their days*, i. e. shall not live half their life. Niph. *to be divided*.

חֲצוֹת fem. only constr. חֲצוֹת, *middle, midst*.

חֵצִי masc. dec. 6, with dist. acc. חֶצִי, with suff. חֶצְיוֹ (§ 35. rem. 14).—I. *half, part, portion*.—II. *middle, midst*, Ju. 16. 3.—III. *an arrow*.

חֲצִי הַמְּנֻחוֹת (*midst of resting places*) pr. name masc. 1 Ch. 2. 52; patronym. חֲצִי הַמְּנַחְתִּי ver. 54.

יַחְצִיאֵל, יַחְצְאֵל (whom *God assigns a portion*) pr. name masc. Ge. 46. 24; 1 Ch. 7. 13. Gent. noun יַחְצְאֵלִי Nu. 46. 26.

מֶחֱצָה fem. dec. 10, *a half*, Nu. 31. 36, 43.

מַחֲצִית fem. dec. 1b—I. *a half*.—II. *the middle*, Ne. 8. 3.

[p]חוּצָה	noun masc. sing. (חוּץ) with parag. ה d. 1a	חוץ
[q]חָצוּ	וְ Kal pret. 3 pers. pl.	חצה
[r]חִצָּו	noun masc. pl. suff. (K. חִצָּיו § 4. rem. 1) 3 pers. sing. masc. fr. חֵץ dec. 8b .	חצץ
חִצּוֹ	id. sing., suff. 3 pers. sing. masc. .	חצץ
חֲצוּבִים	Kal part. pass. masc., pl. of [חָצוּב] dec. 3a	חצב
[t]חֲצֹצְרֹת	noun fem., pl. of חֲצֹצְרָה dec. 10. .	חצר
חָצוֹר	וְ׳ pr. n. of a place, also in compos. חָ׳ חֲדַתָּה	חצר
[u]חֲצוֹת	[x]וְ׳ noun fem. sing., constr. of [חָצוֹת] d. 3a	חצה
חֻצוֹת	[y]וְ׳ noun m. with pl. f. term. fr. חוּץ d. 1a	חוץ
חֲצִי	וְ׳ noun masc. sing., dec. 6i (suff. חֶצְיוֹ § 35. r. 14), & pr. name in compos. חֲ׳ הַמְּנֻחוֹת	חצה
חֶצִי	וְ id. with dist. acc. (§ 35. r. 14); וְ see ו	חצה
[z]חִצַּי	noun masc. pl., suff. 1 pers. sing. fr. חֵץ d. 8b	חצץ
חִצֵּי	id. pl., constr. state	חצץ
[a]חִצִּי	id. sing., suff. 1 pers. sing. . .	חצץ
[b]חֶצְיָהּ	noun masc. sing., suff. 3 pers. sing. fem. fr. חֲצִי dec. 6i (§ 35. rem. 14) . .	חצה
חֶצְיוֹ	[c]וְ׳ id. with suff. 3 pers. sing. masc. .	חצה
חִצָּיו	[d]וְ׳ noun masc. pl., suff. 3 pers. sing. masc. from חֵץ dec. 8b	חצץ
חִצֶּיךָ	[e]וְ׳ id. pl., suff. 2 pers. sing. masc. .	חצץ
[f]חֶצְיָם	וְ׳ noun masc. sing., suff. 3 pers. pl. masc. fr. חֲצִי dec. 6i (§ 35. rem. 14) . .	חצה
חִצִּים	וְ׳ noun masc., pl. of חֵץ dec. 8b . .	חצץ
[g]חֶצְיֵנוּ	noun masc. sing., suff. 1 pers. pl. fr. חֲצִי dec. 6i (§ 35. rem. 14) . . .	חצה
חָצִיר	noun masc. sing. dec. 3a . . .	חצר
חֲצִיר	id., constr. state	חצר
[h]חָצִיתָ	וְ Kal pret. 2 pers. sing. masc. . .	חצה
חִצָּם	noun masc. sing., suff. 3 pers. pl. masc. from חֵץ dec. 8b	חצץ

[חֹצֶן, חֵצֶן] masc. dec. 6b&c, *the bosom, folds of a garment covering the breast*.

---

[a] Ps. 64. 7. [b] Pr. 20. 27. [c] Eze. 27. 20. [d] Le. 19. 20. [e] Le. 19. 20. [f] 2 Ki. 10. 23. [g] 1 Ki. 20. 6. [h] 1 Sa. 23. 23. [i] Is. 5. 2. [k] Pr. 9. 1. [l] Is. 22. 16. [m] Ho. 6. 5. [n] Is. 51. 1. [o] Nu. 31. 42. [p] Is. 33. 7. [q] Ex. 21. 35. [r] Ps. 58. 8. [s] Zec. 9. 14. [t] Nu. 10. 2. [u] Ps. 119. 62. [x] Job 34. 20. [y] 1 Ki. 20. 34. [z] De. 32. 23, 42. [a] Job 34. 6. [b] Ne. 3. 38. [c] Zec. 14. 4. [d] Nu. 24. 8. [e] Eze. 39. 3. [f] Zec. 14. 8. [g] 2 Sa. 18. 3. [h] Nu. 31. 27

חֶצְנוֹ[a] וְ noun masc. sing., suff. 3 pers. sing. masc. fr. [חֵצֶן] dec. 6b . . . חצן

חָצְנִי[b] noun masc. sing., suff. 1 pers. sing. fr. חֹצֶן' dec. 6c . . . . . חצן

חֲצַף Ch. Aph. *to urge, hasten.*

[חָצַץ] i. q. חָצָה *to divide*, Pr. 30. 27, *the locusts have no king*, וַיֵּצֵא חֹצֵץ כֻּלּוֹ *yet they all go forth dividing* into many parts, sc. the prey for themselves. Others, חֹצֵץ (intrans.) *divided*, i. e. in divisions; Prof. Lee (coll. with the Arab.), *rushing on*, i. e. making the attack as an army. Pi. part. מְחַצְּצִים Ju. 5. 11, *those who divide*, sc. the booty, spoil. Others, *archers*, from חֵץ. Pu. *to be cut off in the midst*, Job 21. 21.

חָצָץ masc. dec. 4 c.—I. *small stones, gravel-stones.*—II. *arrow*, trop. for lightning, Ps. 77. 18.

חֵץ masc. d. 8b.—I. *arrow;* בַּעֲלֵי חִצִּים *archers.*—II. trop. *lightning.*—III. perhaps *the iron point of a spear*, 1 Sa. 17. 7, Kheth.

חַצְצוֹן־תָּמָר, חֲצַצֹן־תָּמָר (*pruning of the palm*) pr. name of a place in the desert of Judah, renowned for its palm-trees, Ge. 14. 7; 2 Ch. 20. 2.

חָצָץ[c] noun masc. sing. dec. 4c . . . . חצץ

חֹצֵץ[d] Kal part. act. sing. masc. . . . חצץ

חֻצָּצוּ[e] Pual pret. 3 pers. pl. [for חֻצְצוּ comp. § 8. r. 7] חצץ

חֲצָצֶיךָ[f] noun masc. pl., suff. 2 pers. sing. masc. fr. חָצָץ dec. 4c . . . . חצץ

חֲצֹצְרָה[g] noun fem. sing. dec. 10. . . . חצר

חֲצֹצְרוֹת וְ' id. pl.; וַ bef. (-:) . . . . חצר

חָצֵר Root not used; Arab. (*a*) *to enclose;* (*b*) *to be green;* (*c*) *to be present;* conj. X. *to call together, convoke.*

חָצֵר com. dec. 5c, pl. ־ִים, ־וֹת.—I. *enclosure, area, court.*—II. *village, hamlet.*—III. in the following pr. names of towns or villages—חֲצַר־אַדָּר (*village of Addar*) in the tribe of Judah, Nu. 34. 4; called simply אַדָּר Jos. 15. 3.—חֲצַר גַּדָּה (*village of fortune*) in the tribe of Judah, Jos. 15. 27.—חֲצַר סוּסִים, חֲ' סוּסָה (*village of horses*) in the tribe of Simeon, Jos. 19. 5; 1 Ch. 4. 31.—חֲ' עֵינוֹן, חֲ' עֵינָן (*village of fountains*) in the north of Palestine.—חֲצַר שׁוּעָל (*village of foxes*) in the tribe of Simeon.—חָצֵר הַתִּיכוֹן (*middle village*) on the border of Syria, Eze. 47. 16.—חֲצֵרוֹת a station of the Israelites in the desert.

חָצוֹר (*village, town*) pr. name—I. of a town in Naphtali.—II. of a town in Benjamin, Ne. 11. 33.—III. of a region in Arabia, Je. 49. 28.

חָצוֹר חֲדַתָּה (*new-town*) pr. name of a town in the tribe of Judah, Jos. 15. 25.

חָצִיר masc.—I. *enclosure, court*, Is. 34. 13.—II. *grass; leeks*, Nu. 11. 5.

חֶצְרוֹן (*enclosed, protected*) pr. name—I. of a son of Reuben.—II. of a son of Perez.—Patronym. חֶצְרֹנִי Nu. 26. 6.

חֶצְרַי (id.) pr. name masc. 2 Sa. 23. 35, Keth., Keri חֶצְרוֹ, and so in 1 Ch. 11. 37.

חֲצֹצְרָה fem. (pl. חֲצֹצְרֹת, חֲצֹ') *a trumpet.* Hence denom.

חֲצֹצֵר (§ 6. No. 11) *to blow the trumpet*, only in the part. מְחַצְצְרִים Kheth.; but the Keri has it everywhere מַחְצְרִים Hiph. (§ 11. rem. 8), except in 2 Ch. 5. 13, where it is מְחַצְּרִים Piel (§ 10. rem. 7).—Pilel id. 2 Ch. 5. 12, מְחַצְרְרִים Kheth. (§ 6. No. 2); but Keri מַחְצְרִים Hiph.

חֲצַרְמָוֶת (*court of death*) pr. name of a district in Arabia, Ge. 10. 26.

חָצֵר [h] וְ/וּ' noun com. sing. dec. 5c, also pr. name חצר

חֲצַר וְ' id., constr. state, and in compos. with pr. name, חֲ' אַדָּר &c. וַ before (-:) . . חצר

חָצֹר pr. name of a place . . . חצר

חָצֹרָה[i] pr. name (חָצֹר) with paragogic ה . . חצר

חֶצְרַיְ Kh. חֶצְרוֹ q. v., K. חֶצְרוֹן q. v. . . חצר

חֶצְרוֹ pr. name masc., see חֶצְרַי under . . חצר

חֶצְרוֹן וְ' pr. name of a man and a place . . חצר

חֲצֵרוֹת noun masc. with pl. fem. term., absolute state from חָצֵר dec. 5c; also pr. name . חצר

חַצְרוֹת id. pl. fem. construct state . . . חצר

חֲצֵרוֹתָי[k] וַ id. pl. suff. 1 pers. s. [for ־ַי'תָ]; וַ bef. (-:) חצר

חֲצֵרַי id. pl. masc., suff. 1 pers. sing. [for ־ַי'] חצר

חַצְרֵי[l] id. pl. masc. construct state . . . חצר

חַצְרֶיהָ וְ' id. pl. masc., suff. 3 pers. s. fem.; וַ bef. (-:) חצר

חַצְרֵיהֶם[m] וְ' id. pl. masc., suff. 3 pers. pl. masc. . חצר

חַצְרֵיהֶן וְ id. pl. masc., suff. 3 pers. pl. fem. . . חצר

חֲצֵרֶיךָ[n] id. pl. masc., suff. 2 pers. sing. masc. . חצר

חֲצֵרִים id. pl. masc. absolute state . . . חצר

חֲצַרְמָוֶת pr. name masc. . . . . חצר

חֶצְרֹן וְ' pr. name masc. . . . . חצר

חֲצֵרֹת וַ pr. name of a place; וַ before (-:) . חצר

חֲצֵרֹתָיו[o] noun masc. with pl. fem. term. and suff. 3 pers. sing. masc. from חָצֵר dec. 5c . חצר

חֵקִ[p] defect. for חֵיק (q. v.) . . . . חוק

חֹק וְ' ; חָק־[q] וְ' } noun masc. sing. dec. 8c (§ 37. rem. 2) חקק

[a] Ps. 129. 7. [b] Ne. 5. 13. [c] Pr. 20. 17. [d] Pr. 30. 27. [e] Job 21. 21. [f] Ps. 77. 18. [g] Ho. 5. 8. [h] 1 Ki. 7. 12. [i] Je. 36. 20. [k] 1 Ch. 28. 6. [l] Ne. 12. 28. [m] 1 Ch. 4. 33. [n] Ps. 65. 5. [o] Ps. 100. 4. [p] Pr. 5. 20. [q] Le. 10. 13, 14.

חָקָה Kal not used; i. q. חָקַק. Pu. part.—I. *engraven, carved,* 1 Ki. 6. 35.—II. *portrayed, painted,* Eze. 8. 10; 23. 14. Hithp. *to draw oneself a mark or furrow,* Job 13. 27.

חֻקֶּהָ[a] Kal imp. sing. masc., suff. 3 pers. sing. fem. חקק

חֻקָּה noun fem. sing. dec. 10, from חֹק masc. . חקק

חֻקּוֹ[b] Kheth. for חֻקָּיו (q. v. § 4. rem. 1) חקק

חֻקּוֹ[c] noun m. s., suff. 3 pers. s. m. fr. חֹק dec. 8c חקק

חֲקוּפָא (*bent,* coll. with the Arab.) pr. name masc. Ezr. 2. 51; Ne. 7. 53.

חַקּוֹתָ[d] וְ Kal pret. 2 pers. sing. masc.; acc. shifted by conv. וְ (comp. § 8. rem. 7) . . חקק

חֻקּוֹת noun fem., pl. of חֻקָּה dec. 10. . . חקק

חֻקּוֹתַי וְ' id. pl., suff. 1 pers. sing. . . חקק

חֻקַּי[e], חֻקַּי וְ' } noun masc. pl., suff. 1 pers. sing. from חֹק dec. 8c . . . . } חקק

חֻקֵּי[f] id. pl., construct state . . . חקק

חֻקִּי id. sing., suff. 1 pers. sing. . . . חקק

חֻקָּיו וְ' id. pl., suff. 3 pers. sing. masc. . . חקק

חֻקֶּיךָ וְ' id. pl., suff. 2 pers. sing. masc. . . חקק

חֻקִּים[g] וְ' id. pl. absolute state . . . חקק

חָקְךָ[h] id. sing., suff. 2 pers. sing. masc. . . חקק

חָקֵּךְ[i] id. sing., suff. 2 pers. sing. fem. . . חקק

חָקְכֶם[k] id. sing., suff. 2 pers. pl. masc. . . חקק

חֻקָּם[l] id. sing., suff. 3 pers. pl. masc. . . חקק

[חָקַק] I. *to engrave, inscribe.*—II. *to portray.*—III. part. חֹקֵק *legislator,* Ju. 5. 9. Pu. part. *what is prescribed, a law, statute,* Pr. 31. 5. Hoph. *to be engraven, inscribed,* Job 19. 23. Po. *to decide, decree;* part. (*a*) *lawgiver;* (*b*) *judge, ruler.*

חֵקֶק masc. dec. 6b (§ 35. rem. 6).—I. *impression, imagination,* Ju. 5. 15.—II. *decree,* Is. 10. 1.

חֹק masc. dec. 8c.—I. *something fixed* or *appointed;* לֶחֶם חֻקִּי *the bread appointed for me.*—II. *appointed portion of labour, a task.*—III. *appointed time.*—IV. *limit, bound.*—V. *statute, law.* —VI. *custom, privilege.*

חֻקָּה fem. dec. 10.—I. *statute, law.*—II. *custom, right, privilege.*

חֻקֹּק (*trench*) pr. name of a town on the borders of Asher and Naphtali, Jos. 19. 34; written חוּקֹק 1 Ch. 6. 60.

חֻקֹּקָה pr. name of a place (חֻקֹּק) with paragogic ה חקק

חִקְקֵי noun masc. pl. constr. from [חֵקֶק] dec. 6b חקק

חֹקְקִי[m] Kal part. act. s. m. with parag. י (§ 8. r. 19) חקק

חֲקֻקִים[n] id. part. pass. masc. pl. of [חָקוּק] dec. 3a חקק

[חָקַר] fut. יַחְקֹר (§ 13. rem. 5) *to search, search out, explore, examine, try.* Niph. נֶחְקַר (§ 13. rem. 7) *to be searched out.* Pi. *to search out,* Ec. 12. 9.

חֵקֶר masc. dec. 6b (§ 35. rem. 6).—I. *searching, investigation, examination;* לֹא ,אֵין חֵקֶר *unsearchable.*—II. *deliberation,* Ju. 5. 16.—III. *secret, inmost part,* Job 38. 16.

מֶחְקָר masc. dec. 2b, *inmost part,* Ps. 95. 4.

חֲקֹר Kal inf. construct . . . . . חקר

חֵקֶר[o] וְ' noun masc. sing. dec. 6b . . . חקר

חִקֵּר[p] וְ Piel pret. 3 pers. sing. masc. . . חקר

חֹקֵר[q] Kal part. act. sing. masc. . . . חקר

חֲקָרָהּ[r] id. pret. 3 pers. sing. m., suff. 3 pers. s. fem. חקר

חֲקָרוֹ[s] וַ id. id., suff. 3 pers. sing. m.; וַ for וְ conv. חקר

חִקְרוּ[t] id. imp. pl. masc. . . . . חקר

חִקְרֵי[u] noun masc. pl. constr. from חֵקֶר dec. 6b חקר

חֲקַרְנוּהָ[w] Kal pret. 1 pers. pl. suff. 3 pers. sing. fem. חקר

חָקְרֵנִי[y] id. imp. sing. masc., suff. 1 pers. sing. . חקר

חָקַרְתָּ[z] וְ id. pret. 2 pers. sing. masc.; acc. shifted by conv. וְ (§ 8. rem. 7) חקר

חֲקַרְתַּנִי[a] id. id., suff. 1 pers. sing. . . . חקר

חֻקַּת noun fem., constr. of חֻקָּה dec. 10. . חקק

חֻקֹּת[b] id. pl. for חֻקּוֹת . . . . חקק

חֻקֹּתַי[c] וְ, חֻקֹּתַי וְ' } id. pl., suff. 1 pers. sing. . . חקק

חֻקֹּתָיו וְ' id. pl., suff. 3 pers. sing. masc. . . חקק

חֲקַתִּיךְ[d] Kal pret. 1 pers. sing., suff. 2 pers. sing. fem. חקק

חֹר noun masc. sing. dec. 1a . . . חור

חֹר noun masc. sing. [for חוּר] dec. 1a . חור

חָרָא Root not used; Arab. *to ease oneself, to ease nature.*

חֲרָא masc. dec. 4c, *excrement, dung,* Is. 36. 12 Kheth.; 2 Ki. 18. 27 חֲרֵיהֶם Kheth. for חֲרָאֵיהֶם; 2 Ki. 6. 25 חֲרֵי יוֹנִים Kheth. (dove's dung) for חַרְאֵי יוֹנִים

מַחֲרָאָה fem. dec. 10, *a sink, privy,* 2 Ki. 10. 27 Kheth.

הַרְאֵיהֶם[e] K. צוֹאָתָם noun fem. s. with suff. R. יצא; Kh. חֲרָאֵיהֶם noun m. pl. with suff. [fr. חֲרָא] חרא

[חָרֵב, חָרַב] inf. חֲרֹב, fut. יֶחֱרַב.—I. *to be dried up, to be dry.*—II. *to be desolate, waste, ruined.*—III. trans. *to waste, destroy,* Je. 50. 21. Niph. *to be laid waste, to be ruined.* Pu. *to be dried up,* Ju. 16. 7, 8. Hiph.—I. *to dry up,* Is. 50. 2.—II. *to lay waste, to destroy, ruin.* Hoph. *to be laid waste, destroyed, ruined.*

---

[a] Is. 30. 8. [b] Job 14. 5 [c] Pr. 8. 29. [d] Eze. 4. 1. [e] Ps. 50. 16. [f] Ex. 18. 16. [g] Ne. 9. 14. [h] Le. 10. 13, 14. [i] Eze. 16. 27. [k] Ex. 5. 14. [l] Ge. 47. 22. [m] Is. 22. 16. [n] Eze. 23. 14. [o] Pr. 25. 27. [p] Ec. 12. 9. [q] Je. 17. 10. [r] Job 28. 27. [s] Pr. 18. 17. [t] Ju. 18. 2. [u] Ju. 5. 16. [w] Job 5. 27. [y] Ps. 139. 23. [z] De. 13. 15. [a] Ps. 139. 1. [b] Je. 31. 35. [c] 1 Ki. 11. 34. [d] Is. 49. 16. [e] Is. 36. 12.

חָרֵב Chald. Hoph. *to be laid waste, destroyed,* Ezr. 4. 15.

חָרֵב adj. fem. חֲרֵבָה.—I. *dry.*—II. *desolate, waste.*

חֶרֶב fem. dec. 6a, with suff. חַרְבִּי, pl. חֲרָבוֹת.—I. *sword.*—II. for other *cutting instruments.*—III. *dryness, drought,* De. 28. 22.

חֹרֵב, חוֹרֵב (*dry, desert*) pr. name of one of the summits of Sinai.

חֹרֶב masc.—I. *dryness, drought, heat.*—II. *desolation.*

חָרָבָה fem. (for חֲרֵבָה, after the form יַבָּשָׁה) *the dry land.*

חָרְבָּה fem. dec. 12c, *desolation, desolate places, ruins.*

חֲרָבוֹן m. dec. 3 (pl. c. חַרְבֹנֵי) *drought,* Ps. 32. 4.

חַרְבוֹנָא, חַרְבוֹנָה pr. name of a Persian eunuch, Est. 1. 10; 7. 9.

חָרֵב in pause for חֶרֶב (q. v. § 35. rem. 2) . חרב
חָרֵב adj. masc. sing. . . . . חרב
חָרֹב[a] Kal inf. absolute . . . . חרב
חֲרֹב[b] id. imp. sing. masc. . . . . חרב
חֶרֶב וְ' noun fem. sing. dec. 6a (suff. חַרְבִּי) . חרב
חֹרֵב pr. name of a place . . . חרב
חֹרֶב noun masc. sing. . . . . חרב
חָרָבָה[c] noun fem. sing. . . . . חרב
חָרְבָּה וְ'[d] noun fem. sing. dec. 12c . . חרב
חֲרֵבָה וַ'[e] adj. fem. sing. from חָרֵב masc. . חרב
חֹרֵבָה pr. name of a place (חֹרֵב) with paragogic ה חרב
חָרְבוּ[f] וְ'[g] Kal pret. 3 pers. pl. . . . חרב
חַרְבּוֹ וְ' noun fem. sing., suff. 3 pers. sing. masc. from חֶרֶב dec. 6a . . . . חרב
חִרְבוּ[h] Kal imp. pl. masc. . . . . חרב
חֹרָבוּ[i] Pual pret. 3 pers. pl. [for חֹרְבוּ] . חרב
חֲרָבוּ[k] Kal imp. pl. masc. (§ 8. rem. 12) . חרב
חַרְבוֹנָא, חַרְבוֹנָה } pr. name masc. . . . חרב
חַרְבוֹת[l] noun fem., pl. constr. from חֶרֶב dec. 6a חרב
חֲרָבוֹת id. pl., absolute state . . . חרב
חֳרָבוֹת noun fem. pl. abs., from חָרְבָּה dec. 12c . חרב
חָרְבוֹת וְ'[m] id. pl., constr. state . . . חרב
חָרְבוֹתֶיהָ[n] וְ id. pl. suff. 3 pers. sing. fem. . . חרב
חַרְבוֹתָם noun fem. pl., suff. 3 pers. pl. masc. from חֶרֶב dec. 6a . . . . חרב
חַרְבִּי וְ' id. sing., suff. 1 pers. sing. . . . חרב
חֳרָבִי[o] Kal imp. sing. fem. for חִרְבִי (חֲרָבִי) a mixed form from middle A and O, חָרֵב and חָרֹב=חֲרַב (comp. § 8. rem. 11 & 12) חרב

חַרְבְּךָ, חַרְבֶּךָ } noun fem. sing., suff. 2 pers. sing. masc. from חֶרֶב dec. 6a . . . . } חרב
חַרְבְּכֶם id., suff. 2 pers. pl. masc. . . . חרב
חַרְבָּם[p] id., suff. 3 pers. pl. masc. . . . חרב
חָרְבֹתֶיהָ[q] n. fem. pl., suff. 3 p. s. fem. from חָרְבָּה dec. 12c חרב
חַרְבֹתֵיהֶם n. fem. pl., suff. 3 pers. pl. m. from חֶרֶב dec. 6a חרב
חָרְבֹתָיו[r] n. fem. pl., suff. 3 p. s. m. from חָרְבָּה dec. 12c חרב
חָרְבֹתַיִךְ[s] id., suff. 2 pers. sing. fem. . . . חרב

[חָרַג] (coll. with the Arab.) *to be straitened, troubled,* Ps. 18. 46. Others, *to tremble, fear.*

[חַרְגֹּל] masc. *locust,* Le. 11. 22.

חָרַד[t] וְ fut. יֶחֱרַד.—I. *to tremble, to be timid, fearful,* with לְ, עַל; Ge. 42. 28. וַיֶּחֶרְדוּ אִישׁ אֶל־אָחִיו *and they turned trembling to one another.*—II. with אֶל *to care for, be concerned about* any one, 2 Ki. 4. 13.—III. *to hasten,* with מִן *from* a place, Ho. 11. 10, 11. Hiph. *to make afraid, terrify.*

חָרֵד adj. masc. dec. 5c.—I. *trembling, fearful, timid.*—II. *fearing, reverencing.*

חֲרָדָה fem. dec. 11c (constr. חֶרְדַּת § 42. rem. 1).—I. *trembling, terror, fear.*—II. *care, concern,* 2 Ki. 4. 13.—III. pr. name of a station of the Israelites in the desert, Nu. 33. 24.

חֲרוֹד (*trembling*) pr. name of a place in the mountain of Gilboa, Ju. 7. 1. Gent. n. חֲרֹדִי 2 Sa. 23. 25.

חָרֵד וְ' adj. masc. sing. dec. 5c . . . חרד
חֲרֹד pr. name of a place . . . . חרד
חָרְדָה[u] Kal pret. 3 pers. sing. fem. . . . חרד
חֲרָדָה n. fem. s., constr. חֶרְדַּת, dec. 11c (§ 42. rem. 1) חרד
חָרְדוּ וְ' Kal pret. 3 pers. pl. . . . . חרד
חִרְדוּ[x] id. imp. pl. masc. . . . . חרד
חֲרָדוֹת[y] noun fem., pl. abs. from חֲרָדָה (q. v.) . חרד
חָרַדְתְּ[z] Kal pret. 2 pers. sing. fem. . . . חרד
חֶרְדַּת[a] noun fem. sing. constr. of חֲרָדָה (q. v.) חרד

חָרָה וְ' fut. יֶחֱרֶה, ap. יִחַר (§ 24. rem. 3d) *to burn, be kindled; to become hot, angry, wroth;* חָרָה אַפּוֹ with עַל, אֶל, בְּ *his anger was kindled against;* חָרָה לוֹ or בְּעֵינָיו *he was angry, it grieved him.* Niph. נֶחֱרָה *to be angry, wroth,* with בְּ, Is. 41. 11; 45. 24. Hiph. הֶחֱרָה, fut. ap. יַחַר (§ 24. r. 16).—I. *to cause to burn, to kindle,* as anger, Job 19. 11.—II. *to become ardent, zealous, to do with zeal,* Ne. 3. 20. Tiph. (§ 6. No. 5) *to emulate, rival.* Hithpa. *to fret oneself, be vexed.*

[a] Is. 60. 12. [b] Je. 50. 21. [c] Eze. 30. 12. [d] Eze. 29. 9. [e] Le. 7. 10. [f] Ge. 8. 13. [g] Is. 19. 6. [h] Je. 50. 27. [i] Ju. 16. 7, 8. [k] Je. 2. 12. [l] Jos. 5. 2, 3. [m] Is. 5. 17. [n] Is. 44. 26. [o] Is. 44. 27. [p] Ps. 37. 15. [q] Is. 51. 3. [r] Ezr. 9. 9. [s] Is. 49. 19. [t] Is. 19. 16. [u] Is. 10. 29. [x] Is. 32. 11. [y] Eze. 26. 16. [z] 2 Ki. 4. 13. [a] Pr. 29. 25.

חָרוֹן masc. dec. 3a.—I. *heat, ardour*, Ps. 58. 10. Prof. Lee, *angry person*.—II. *anger, wrath*, fully חֲרוֹן אַף *heat of anger, burning wrath*.

חֳרִי masc. *heat, glow*, only in the phrase, חֳרִי אַף *heat of anger, burning wrath*.

תַּחְרָא masc. *coat of mail*; Eng. Vers. "habergeon." Comp. Tiph. of the Root.

[a] חָרָה [b] וְ' Kal fut. 3 pers. sing. fem. [for חָרָּה] . . . חרר

[c] חָרֹה Kal inf. abs. . . . . . חרה

חַרְהֲיָה, חַרְהֲיָה } pr. name masc. . . . . חרר

[d] חָרוּ Kal pret. 3 pers. pl. [for חָרְרוּ] . . . חרר

חָרוּל noun m. sing., pl. חֲרֻלִּים dec. 8 (§ 37. No. 3c) חרל

חֲרוּמַף pr. name masc. . . . . . . חרם

חָרוֹן noun masc. sing. dec. 3a . . . . חרה

חֲרוֹן וְ' id. construct state; וַ before (ֲ) . . . חרה

חֹרֹן pr. name in compos. בֵּית חוֹרוֹן, see . . בית

[e] חֲרוֹנִי id., suff. 1 pers. sing. . . . . חרה

[f] חֲרוֹנֶיךָ id. pl., suff. 2 pers. sing. masc. . . חרה

חֹרֹנַיִם pr. name of a place . . . . . חור

חָרוּץ וְ' Kal part. pass., adj. or subst. masc. dec. 3a חרץ

חָרוּץ n. m. sing. for [חֲרוּץ] dec. 1b; also pr. n. m. חרץ

חֲרוּצִים id. pl., absolute state . . . . חרץ

[g] חֲרוּצִים Kal part. pass. masc., pl. of חָרוּץ dec. 3a חרץ

[h] חֲרוּשָׁה Kal part. pass. sing. fem. from [חָרוּשׁ] masc. חרש

[i] חָרוּת Kal part. pass. sing. masc. . . . חרת

חָרַז Root not used; Syr. *to put in order, dispose regularly*.

חָרוּז masc. only pl. חֲרוּזִים, Ca. 1. 10, *strings of pearls, coral*, or the like. Sept. ὁρμίσκοι collars, necklaces.

חַרְחוּר pr. name masc. . . . . . . חרר

חַרְחַס pr. name masc. see חַסְרָה . . . . חסר

חָרַט Root not used; Syr. *to engrave*.

חָרִיט masc. *pocket, purse*.

חֶרֶט masc.—I. *graving tool*, Ex. 32. 4.—II. *writing style*, Is. 8. 1.

חַרְטֹם masc. dec. 8c, only pl. חַרְטֻמִּים *sacred writers, persons skilled in the hieroglyphics*, mentioned very early among the Egyptians, Ge. 41. 8, 24; and in aftertimes applied to *the wise men* among the Babylonians, Da. 1. 20; 2. 2. LXX. ἐξηγηταὶ *interpreters* of mysteries; ἐπαοιδοί *enchanters*; φαρμακοί *sorcerers, magicians*.

חַרְטֹם Chald. masc. dec. 5c, id.

[k] חֲרִטִים noun masc., pl. of [חָרִיט] dec. 3a . . חרט

[l] חַרְטֹם Chald. noun masc. sing., dec. 5c . . חרט

חַרְטֻמֵּי Heb. id. pl., construct state, dec. 8c . חרט

[m] חַרְטֻמַּיָּא Chald. id. pl., emph. st. dec. 5c . . חרט

חַרְטֻמִּין Chald. id. pl., absolute state . . חרט

[n] חֳרִי noun masc. sing. . . . . . חרה

[o] חֹרֵי noun masc. pl. constr. from חוֹר dec. 1a . חור

חֹרֵי noun masc. pl. constr. from חֹר dec. 1a . חרר

חֹרִי noun masc. sing.; also pr. name . . חור

[p] חֹרֶיהָ noun m. pl., suff. 3 p. s. fem. from חֹר dec. 1a חרר

[q] חֲרָיֵהֶם K. צוֹאָתָם n.f.s., suff. 3 p. pl. from צוֹאָה d. 10, R. יָצָא; Kh. חֲרֵיהֶם for חֲרָאֵיהֶם, see חֲרָא' חרא

[r] חֹרָיו n. m. pl., suff. 3 pers. s. m. from חוֹר dec. 1a חור

[oo] חֲרֵייוֹנִים K. דִּבְיוֹנִים, see R. דבה; Kh. חֲרֵי יוֹנִים see R. חרא

חָרִיף pr. name masc. . . . . . חרף

[s] חֲרִיצֵי noun masc. pl. constr. from [חָרִיץ] dec. 3a חרץ

[t] חָרִישׁ noun masc. sing. dec. 3a . . . חרש

[u] חֲרִישׁוֹ id., suff. 3 pers. sing. masc. . . חרש

[x] חֲרִישִׁית adj. fem. sing. [from חֲרִישִׁי masc.] . חרש

[חָרַךְ] perhaps i. q. כָּרַךְ to wrap round; hence, *to enclose* or *catch in a net* or *toil*, Pr. 12. 27, LXX. ἐπιτεύξεται *shall obtain*. Others, *to burn, singe, roast*, as in the Chald.

חֲרַךְ Chald. Ithpa. *to be singed*, Da. 3. 27.

חָרָךְ masc. dec. 4c, only Ca. 2. 9. חֲרַכִּים *lattices* of windows, from their *reticulate* form.

חָרַל Root not used; perhaps i. q. חָרַר *to burn*.

חָרוּל masc. pl. חֲרֻלִּים (§ 37. No. 3c) *nettle, nettles*, Job 30. 7; Zep. 2. 9; Pr. 24. 31.

[y] חֲרֻלִּים noun masc., pl. of חָרוּל (q. v.) . . חרל

חָרַם in Kal only part. pass. חָרֻם *flat-nosed, mutilated in the nose*. Arab. to cut, tear off; to shut up; to prohibit. Hiph. הֶחֱרִים.—I. *to devote to destruction*.—II. *to devote to God, to consecrate*. Hoph. הָחֳרַם.—I. *to be devoted to destruction*.—II. *to be consecrated*, Ezr. 10. 8.

חֳרֵם (*devoted*) pr. name of a town in the tribe of Naphtali, Jos. 19. 38.

חָרִם (*flat-nosed*) pr. name of a man.

חֵרֶם, חֶרֶם masc. dec. 6, with suff. חֶרְמִי (§ 35. rem. 6).—I. *a net*.—II. metaph. *allurement*, Ec. 7. 26. —III. *devotion to destruction*; אִישׁ חֶרְמִי *a man devoted by me to destruction*.

חָרְמָה (*devoted to destruction*) pr. name of a city of the Canaanites.

[a] Job 30. 30. [b] Eze. 24. 11. [c] 1 Sa. 20. 7. [d] Is. 24. 6. [e] Eze. 7. 14. [f] Ps. 88. 17. [g] Job 14. 5. [h] Je. 17. 1. [i] Ex. 32. 16. [k] 2 Ki. 5. 23. [l] Da. 2. 10. [m] Da. 4. 4, 6. [n] De. 29. 23. [o] Job 30. 6. [oo] 2 Ki. 6. 25. [p] Is. 34. 12. [q] 2 Ki. 18. 27. [r] Na. 2. 13. [s] 1 Sa. 17. 18. [t] Ge. 45. 6. [u] 1 Sa. 8. 12. [x] Jon. 4. 8. [y] Pr. 24. 31.

חֶרְמוֹן pr. name of a ridge or spur of Anti-Libanus, pl. חֶרְמֹנִים several summits or ridges belonging to the same.

חֲרוּמַף (for חֲרוּם אַף *flat-nosed*) pr. name masc. Ne. 3. 10.

חָרִם pr. name masc. . . . . . . חרם
חָרֻם[a] Kal part. pass. sing. masc. . . . . חרם
חָרֵם pr. name of a place . . . . . חרם
חֵרֶם } noun masc. sing. dec. 6 (suff. חֶרְמִי } חרם
וְ חֵרֶם[b] } § 35. rem. 6) . . . . } חרם
חָרְמָה וְ' pr. name of a place . . . . חרם
חֶרְמוֹ[c] noun masc. sing., suff. 3 pers. sing. masc. from חֵרֶם dec. 6 (§ 35. rem. 6) . . . חרם
חֶרְמוֹן וְ' pr. name of a mountain . . . . חרם
חֶרְמוֹנִים וְ id. pl. . . . . חרם
חֶרְמִי noun masc. sing., suff. 1 pers. sing. from חֵרֶם dec. 6 (§ 35. rem. 6) . . . . חרם
חֲרָמִים[d] וְ'[e] id. pl., absolute state; וַ bef. (-ָ) . . חרם

חֶרְמֵשׁ וְ' masc. *sickle*, De. 16. 9; 23. 26.
חָרָן וְ' pr. name of a man and a place . . חרר
חֹרֹן pr. name, see בֵּית חוֹרוֹן . . . . בית
חָרָנָה pr. name of a place (חָרָן) with parag. ה . חרר
חֹרֹנַיִם pr. name of a place . . . . . חרר
חֲרֹנְךָ[f] noun m. s., suff. 2 pers. s. m. from חָרוֹן d. 3 a חרה
חַרְנֶפֶר וְ pr. name masc. . . . . . . נחר

חָרַס Root not used; prob. *to be dry, hot*; which signification seems to lie in the syllable חַר, comp. חָרַר, חָרָה; Arab. *to scratch; to be scratched, be rough.*

חֶרֶס masc.—I. *the sun*, Ju. 8. 13; 14. 18; עִ'ר הַחֶרֶס mystical name of a city in Egypt, Is. 19. 18; where others read הַהֶרֶס.

חַרְסוּת fem. *pottery* (comp. חֶרֶשׂ); שַׁעַר הַחַרְסוּת *pottery-gate*, one of the gates of Jerusalem, Je. 19. 2 Kheth., חַרְסִית Keri.

חֶרֶס pr. name, see הַר חֶרֶס under the Root הרר

[חָרַף] fut. יֶחֱרַף (prim. to pluck, to gather fruit, comp. חֹרֶף autumn; hence)—I. *to pass the autumn, winter*, Is. 18. 6.—II. *to reproach, scorn.* Pi. *to reproach, scorn*; חֵרֵף נַפְשׁוֹ *to scorn*, i. e. *expose one's life.* Niph. part. נֶחֱרֶפֶת *abandoned* i. e. *exposed*, sc. to a man, Le. 19. 20.

חֲרוּפִי or חֲרִיפִי patronym. of an unknown חֲרִיף 1 Ch. 12. 5.

חָרִיף (*autumnal rain*, coll. with the Arab.) pr. name masc. Ne. 7. 24; 10. 20; called Ezr. 2. 18 יוֹרָה (*autumnal rain*).

חָרֵף (*plucking of*) pr. name masc. 1 Ch. 2. 51.

חֹרֶף masc. dec. 6 c, *autumn*, frequently including *the winter.*

חֶרְפָּה fem. dec. 12 b.—I. *reproach, contempt.*—II. *object of reproach.*

חָרִף pr. name masc. . . . . . . חרף
חָרֵף pr. name masc. . . . . . . חרף
חֵרֵף Piel pret. 3 pers. sing. masc. . . . חרף
חֹרֶף וְ noun masc. sing. dec. 6 c; for וָ see lett. ו חרף
חֶרְפָּה וְ'[g] noun fem. sing. dec. 12 b . . . חרף
חֵרְפוּ Piel pret. 3 pers. pl. . . . . . חרף
חֵרְפוּךָ[h] id., suff. 2 pers. sing. masc. . . . חרף
חֵרְפוּנִי id., suff. 1 pers. sing. . . . . חרף
חֶרְפּוֹת[i] וְ noun fem. pl. constr. from חֶרְפָּה d. 12 b חרף
חָרְפִּי[k] noun masc. sing. suff. 1 pers. sing. from חֹרֶף dec. 6 c . . . . חרף
חֹרְפִי Kal part. act. sing. masc. suff. 1 pers. sing. from [חֹרֵף] dec. 7 b . . . . חרף
חֵרַפְתָּ Piel pret. 2 pers. sing. masc. . . . חרף
חֶרְפַּת וְ' noun fem. sing., const. of חֶרְפָּה dec. 12 b חרף
חֶרְפָּתוֹ וְ'[l] id., suff. 3 pers. sing. masc. . . . חרף
חֵרַפְתִּי[m] Piel pret. 1 pers. sing. . . . . חרף
חֶרְפָּתִי noun f. s., suff. 1 pers. s. from חֶרְפָּה d. 12 b חרף
חֶרְפָּתֵךְ[n] id., suff. 2 pers. sing. fem. . . . חרף
חֶרְפָּתְךָ[o] id., suff. 2 pers. sing. masc. . . . חרף
חֶרְפָּתָם id., suff. 3 pers. pl. masc. . . . חרף
חֵרַפְתֶּם[p] Piel pret. 2 pers. pl. masc. . . . חרף
חֶרְפָּתֵנוּ noun fem. sing., suff. 1 pers. pl. from חֶרְפָּה dec. 12 b . . . . חרף

חָרַץ[q] fut. יֶחֱרַץ.—I. *to cut in, to wound, lacerate*, only part. pass. חָרוּץ *slightly wounded, lacerated*, Le. 22. 22.—II. *to sharpen, point*, only Ex. 11. 7 not a dog *shall sharpen* or *point* his tongue.—III. *to decide, determine.*—IV. *to be sharp, active, quick*, 2 Sa. 5. 24. Niph. part. נֶחֱרֶצֶת, נֶחֱרָצָה *decided, determined, decreed.*

חָרוּץ masc. dec. 3 a.—I. *ditch, trench*, Da. 9. 25.—II. *sharpened, pointed*, Is. 41. 15; as a subst., *a threshing-sledge*, furnished underneath with *teeth* of stone or iron; pl. חֲרוּצוֹת.—III. *what is decided, decision, judgment*, Joel 4. 14.—IV. *gold.*

חָרוּץ masc. dec. 1 b (for חַרּוּץ § 32. No. 3).—I. *active, diligent.* Prof. Lee, *sharpened, instructed, prudent.*—II. pr. name masc. 2 Ki. 21. 19.

חָרִיץ masc. dec. 3 a.—I. *a piece cut off, a slice,*

[a] Le. 21. 18. [b] Zec. 14. 11. [c] Hab. 1. 17. [d] Eze. 26. 5, 14. [e] Ec. 7. 26. [f] Ex. 15. 7. [g] Ps. 15. 3. [h] Ps. 79. 12. [i] Ps. 69. 10. [k] Job 29. 4. [l] Da. 11. 18, 18. [m] 1 Sa. 17. 10. [n] Is. 47. 3. [o] Ps. 74. 22. [p] Ju. 8. 15. [q] Jos. 10. 21.

1 Sa. 17. 18.—II. *threshing-sledge*, comp. חָרוּץ No. II.

חַרְצָן masc. dec. 8a, only pl. חַרְצַנִּים (sharp) *sour grapes*, Nu. 6. 4.

[חֲרַץ] Ch. m. d. 3a, *loin, loins*, Da. 5. 6; comp. Heb. חָלָץ.

חָרַצְב Root not used; coll. with the Arab. *to bind fast a cord.* Hence

חַרְצֻבּוֹת pl. fem. [fr. חַרְצֹב dec. 8c].—I. *tight bonds*, Is. 58. 6.—II. *pains, pangs*, Ps. 73. 4 . חרצב

חַרְצֵהּ[a] Ch. noun masc. sing., suff. 3 pers. sing. m. fr. [חֲרַץ] dec. 3a . . . . חרץ

חָרֻצִים[b] defect. for (חָרוּצִים q. v.) . . . חרץ

חָרַצְתְּ[c] Kal pret. 2 pers. s. m. [for חָרַצְתָּ § 8. rem. 7] חרץ

[d]חָרַק fut. יַחֲרֹק, *to grind, gnash* the teeth.

חָרֹק[e] Kal inf. absolute . . . . חרק

חֹרֵק[f] וְ id. part. act. sing. masc. . . . חרק

[חָרַר] I.—*to burn, glow.*—II. *to be dried up*, Job 30. 30. Niph. נָחַר & נִחַר (dag. f. impl. § 18. rem. 14), fut. יֵחַר (for יִחַר) *to be burned, scorched; to be dried up.* Pilp. (§ 6. No. 4) *to kindle*, as contention, Pr. 26. 21.

חֲרֵרִים masc. pl. (fr. חָרֵר dec. 4c) *dry, parched places*, Je. 17. 6.

חֹר masc. dec. 1a, only pl. (חוֹרִים חֹרִים) *nobles, free-born.*

חָרָן (*parched, scorched*) pr. name—I. of a city of Mesopotamia.—II. of a man, 1 Ch. 2. 46.

חַרְחֻר masc.—I. *inflammation, burning fever*, De. 28. 22.—II. pr. name of a man.

חַרְהֲיָה (*he was burning, hot*) pr. n. m. Ne. 3. 8.

חֲרֵרִים[g] noun masc., pl. of [חָרֵר] dec. 5c . חרר

חָרַשׂ Root not used; i. q. חָרַם *to scratch, to be rough.*

חֶרֶשׂ masc. dec. 6a (pl. c. חַרְשֵׂי) *sherd, potsherd*; כְּלִי חֶרֶשׂ *earthen vessel.*

חֲרֶשֶׂת *sherd*, see קִיר חֲרֶשֶׂת, R. קוּר.

[חָרַשׁ] fut. יַחֲרֹשׁ.—I. *to plough, till.*—II. *to engrave*, Je. 17. 1.—III. *to form, work, fabricate.* Metaph. *to devise, machinate evil.*—IV. fut. יֶחֱרַשׁ (prop. to be blunted, dull) *to be dumb, silent, deaf.* Niph. *to be ploughed.* Hiph.—I. *to fabricate, devise evil*, 1 Sa. 23. 9.—II. *to keep silent, be silent, quiet;* with לְ of the thing, to permit it silently, with אֶל to conceal it; with מִן of the person, to hear him silently, also to desist from him, with acc. to permit silently, also to pass anything in silence, to conceal it. Hithpa. *to keep still*, Ju. 16. 2.

חָרָשׁ masc. dec. 1b, but constr. חָרַשׁ (§ 30. No. 4, & rem. 1).—I. *engraver*, Ex. 28. 11.—II. *worker, artificer*, in wood, stone, metal, Eze. 21. 36; חָרָשֵׁי מַשְׁחִית *forgers of destruction.*

חֵרֵשׁ masc. (for חִרֵּשׁ § 26. No. 9) d. 7b, *deaf.*

חֶרֶשׁ masc.—I. *artificial, cunning work* (see גֵּי חֲרָשִׁים).—II. adv. *silently*, Jos. 2. 1.—III. pr. name masc. 1 Ch. 9. 15.

חֹרֵשׁ masc. *cutting instrument*, Ge. 4. 22.

חֹרֶשׁ masc. dec. 6c, *wood, forest* (Chald. חֲרַשׁ to be entangled).

חַרְשָׁא (Chald. *enchanter, magician*) pr. name masc.—I. Ezr. 2. 52.—II. Ne. 7. 54.

חֲרֹשֶׁת fem.—I. *sculpture*, Ex. 31. 5; 35. 33.—II. pr. name of a city in the north of Palestine.

חָרִישׁ masc. dec. 3a.—I. *a ploughing, tilling the land*; also, *time of ploughing.*

חֲרִישִׁי fem. חֲרִישִׁית adj. *silent, still, gentle*, Jon. 4. 8.

מַחֲרֵשָׁה, מַחֲרֶשֶׁת fem., with suff. מַחֲרַשְׁתּוֹ, מַחֲרֵשָׁתוֹ, pl. מַחֲרֵשׁוֹת, two kinds of *cutting instruments*, perhaps *the plouhgshare* and *the coulter.*

חָרָשׁ [h]וְ' noun masc. sing. [for. חָרָשׁ] dec. 1b . חרש

חָרַשׁ id. constr. state (§ 30. rem. 1) . . חרש

חָרֶשׁ in pause for חֶרֶשׁ (q. v. § 35. rem. 2) . חרש

חֵרֵשׁ [i]וְ' noun masc. sing. dec. 7b . . חרש

חֶרֶשׁ[k] noun m. (used as an adv.) pl. חֲרָשִׁים subst. חרש

חֶרֶשׁ noun masc. sing. (pl. c. חַרְשֵׁי) dec. 6a . חרש

חֹרֵשׁ Kal part. act., or (Ge. 4. 22) n. m. s. d. 7b חרש

חֹרֶשׁ[l] וְ noun masc. sing. dec. 6c . . חרש

חַרְשָׁא pr. name masc. (see תֵּל חַרְשָׁא) . . חרש

חֹרְשָׁה[m] noun masc. sing. (חֹרֶשׁ) with parag. ה . חרש

חָרְשׁוּ[n] Kal pret. 3 pers. pl. . . . . חרש

חֹרְשׁוֹת[o] id. part. act. fem. pl. [of חֹרְשָׁה or חֹרֶשֶׁת] חרש

חָרָשֵׁי וְ' noun masc. pl. constr. fr. חָרָשׁ (q. v.) חרש

חַרְשֵׁי[p] noun masc. pl. constr. fr. חֶרֶשׁ dec. 6a . חרש

חֹרְשֵׁי[q] Kal part. act. pl. const. masc. fr. חֹרֵשׁ d. 7b חרש

חֲרָשֶׂיהָ[r] noun m. pl., suff. 3 pers. s. f. fr. חֶרֶשׂ d. 6a חרש

חָרָשִׁים וְ' noun masc. pl. absolute fr. חָרָשׁ (q. v.) חרש

חֲרָשִׁים noun masc. pl. absolute fr. חֶרֶשׁ dec. 6 . חרש

חֵרְשִׁים[s] [t]וְ' noun masc. pl. abs. from חֵרֵשׁ (q. v.) חרש

חֹרְשִׁים[u] Kal part. act. masc., pl. of חֹרֵשׁ dec. 7b . חרש

[a] Da. 5. 6. [b] Pr. 13. 4. [c] 1 Ki. 20. 40. [d] Job 16. 9. [e] Ps. 35. 16. [f] Ps. 37. 12. [g] Je. 17. 6. [h] 1 Sa. 13. 19. [i] Is. 42. 19. [k] Jos. 2. 1. [l] Eze. 31. 3. [m] 1 Sa. 23. 16. [n] Ps. 129. 3. [o] Job 1. 14. [p] Is. 45. 9. [q] Job 4. 8. [r] Eze. 23. 34. [s] Is. 35. 5. [t] Is. 43. 8. [u] Ps. 129. 3.

חֲרֶשֶׁת
חֲרֶשֶׁת } pr. name in compos. קִיר חֲרֶשֶׂת . . קור

חֲרֹשֶׁת pr. name in compos. חֲ׳ הַגּוֹיִם . . חרש

חֲרַשְׁתֶּם Kal pret. 2 pers. pl. masc. . . חרש

[חָרַת] *to cut in, engrave*, Ex. 32. 10.

חֲרֶת (for חֶרֶת § 35. r. 2) pr. name of a wood in the tribe of Judah, 1 Sa. 22. 5.

חָשׁ [a] וְ׳ Kal pret. 3 pers. sing. masc. . . חוש

חָשַׁב וְ׳ fut. יַחְשָׁב־, יַחְשֹׁב (§ 13. rem. 5).—I. *to think, purpose, intend* to do anything, with לְ before the inf. of the action; usually in a bad sense, *to invent, devise*, with אֶל, עַל of the person, and acc. of the thing; in a good sense with לְ *to care for*, part. חֹשֵׁב *deviser, artificer*, especially a weaver in figures of various colours, *a damask-weaver*.—II. *to think, regard, count as*, with acc. and לְ Ge. 38. 15, בְּ Job 19. 11; absolute *to esteem, value*.—III. *to impute, reckon* to any one what does not properly belong to him. Niph. נֶחְשַׁב (§ 13. rem. 7).—I. *to be computed, reckoned, counted*, with לְ, עַל.—II. *to be regarded, counted as*, with בְּ, לְ, כְּ.—III. *to be imputed* to any one, with לְ. Pi.—I. *to compute, reckon*, with אֵת, עִם.—II. *to think upon, consider*.—III. *to think, purpose; to devise, plan;* metaph. *to be about* to do or suffer, Jon. 1. 4. Hithp. *to reckon oneself*, with בְּ Nu. 23. 9.

חֲשַׁב Ch. *to regard, count*, Da. 4. 32.

חַשּׁוּב (*considerate*) pr. name masc. of two different persons.

חֲשֻׁבָה (*esteemed*) pr. name masc. 1 Ch. 3. 20.

חֵשֶׁב masc. *the belt* or *girdle of the ephod*, prob. so called from its being richly embroidered.

חֶשְׁבּוֹן masc.—I. *result of an account* or *computation*, Ec. 7. 27.—II. *intelligence, understanding*.—III. pr. name of a city formerly the residence of an Amorite king, afterwards assigned to the Levites in the borders of Reuben and Gad.

חִשָּׁבוֹן masc. only pl. חִשְּׁבֹנוֹת.—I. *warlike engines*, 2 Ch. 26. 15.—II. *artifices, devices*, Ec. 7. 29.

חֲשַׁבְדָּנָה (for חֹשֵׁב בַּדָּנָה *thought in judgment*) pr. name masc. Ne. 8. 4.

חֲשַׁבְיָהוּ, חֲשַׁבְיָה (whom *the Lord esteems*) pr. name of several Levites.

חֲשַׁבְנְיָה, חֲשַׁבְנָה (?) pr. name masc. of several persons.

מַחֲשָׁבָה, מַחֲשֶׁבֶת, with suff. מַחֲשַׁבְתּוֹ, pl. מַחֲשָׁבוֹת, constr. מַחְשְׁבוֹת (comp. dec. 12 & 13, & § 42. rem. 5).—I. *thought, counsel, design, project*.—II. *work of art* or *skill*.

חֵשֶׁב וְ׳ noun masc. sing. . . . . . חשב

חִשֵּׁב וְ Piel pret. 3 pers. sing. masc. (§ 10. r. 1) . חשב

חֹשֵׁב וְ׳ Kal part. act. sing. masc. dec. 7 b . חשב

חֲשַׁבְדָּנָה וְ pr. name masc. . . . . חשב

חֲשָׁבָהּ [b] Kal pret. 3 pers. sing. m., suff. 3 pers. s. f. חשב

חֲשֻׁבָה וְ pr. name masc. . . . . חשב

חִשְּׁבָה [c] Piel pret. 3 pers. sing. fem. . . . חשב

חָשְׁבוּ [d]
חָשְׁבוּ } Kal pret. 3 pers. pl. (§ 8. rem. 7) . חשב

חֶשְׁבּוֹן [e] וְ׳ noun masc. sing., also pr. name . חשב

חֹשְׁבֵי [f] וְ׳ Kal part. act. pl. constr. m. fr. חֹשֵׁב d. 7 b חשב

חֲשַׁבְיָה
חֲשַׁבְיָהוּ } וְ׳ pr. name masc.; וַ bef. (-:) . . חשב

חֹשְׁבִים Kal part. act. masc., pl. of חֹשֵׁב dec. 7 b חשב

חֲשַׁבְנָה pr. name masc. . . . . . חשב

חֲשַׁבְנֻהוּ Kal pret. 1 pers. pl., suff. 3 pers. sing. masc. חשב

חִשְּׁבֹנוֹת noun m. with pl. fem. term. fr. [חִשָּׁבוֹן] dec. 3 c חשב

חֲשַׁבְנְיָה pr. name masc. . . . . . חשב

חָשַׁבְתָּ [g]
חָשַׁבְתָּ [h] וְ } Kal pret. 2 pers. sing. masc.; acc. shifted by conv. וְ (§ 8. rem. 7) . } חשב

חָשַׁבְתָּה [i] id., full form for חָשַׁבְתָּ (§ 8. rem. 5) . חשב

חָשַׁבְתִּי [k] id. pret. 1 pers. sing. . . . . חשב

חִשַּׁבְתִּי Piel pret. 1 pers. sing. . . . חשב

חֲשַׁבְתֶּם [l] Kal pret. 2 pers. pl. masc. . . . חשב

[חָשָׁה] fut. יֶחֱשֶׁה *to be silent, still, quiet*. Hiph.—I. *to silence, still, quiet*.—II. *to be silent, still, quiet*.

חַשּׁוּב וְ׳ pr. name masc. . . . . . חשב

חֲשׂוּפָא pr. name masc. . . . . . חשף

חֲשׂוּפָה [m] Kal part. pass. fem. [from חָשׂוּף] . . חשף

חֲשׂוּפֵי [n] וַ id. sing. masc. pl. const. dec. 3 a; וַ bef. (-:) חשף

חֲשׁוּקֵיהֶם וַ noun m. pl., suff. 3 pers. pl. m. [fr. חָשׁוּק] חשק

[חֲשַׁח] Chald.—I. *to be needed, necessary*, Ezr. 6. 9.—II. *to have need, occasion*, Da. 3. 16.

חַשְׁחוּ Chald. fem. dec. 8 c, *need, what is needful*, Ezr. 7. 20.

חַשְׁחוּת [o] Chald. noun fem. s., constr. of [חַשְׁחוּ] dec. 8 c חשח

חַשְׁחִין [p] Chald. Peal part. act. pl. masc. [for חָשְׁחִין from חֲשַׁח § 58. rem. 1] . . . חשח

חַשְׁחָן [q] Chald. id. pl. fem. [for חָשְׁחָן v. id.] . חשח

חֲשִׁיבִין [r] Chald. Peal part. pass. m., pl. of [חֲשִׁיב] d. 1 a חשב

חֻשִׁים pr. name masc. . . . . . חוש

חֻשִׁים [s] Kal part. pass. masc., pl. of [חוּשׁ] . . חוש

[a] De. 32. 35. [b] Ge. 50. 20. [c] Jon. 1. 4. [d] Ps. 10. 2. [e] Ec. 7. 27. [f] Ex. 35. 35. [g] Job 35. 2. [h] Eze. 38. 10. [i] 2 Sa. 14. 13. [k] Je. 18. 8. [l] Ge. 50. 20. [m] Eze. 4. 7. [n] Is. 20. 4. [o] Ezr. 7. 20. [p] Da. 3. 16. [q] Ezr. 6. 9. [r] Da. 4. 32. [s] Nu. 32. 17.

חָשַׂךְ fut. יַחְשֹׂךְ ,אֶחְשֹׂךְ ,אֶחֱשָׂךְ (§ 13. rem. 5).—I. *to hold back, restrain,* const. with acc., מִן of the thing *from* which.—II. *to save, preserve, deliver,* const. id.—III. *to withhold,* const. id.—IV. *to spare, keep back.* Niph.—I. *to be restrained,* Job 16. 6. —II. *to be reserved,* Job 21. 30.

חָשַׁךְ fut. יֶחְשַׁךְ (§ 13. rem. 5).—*to be* or *become obscure, dark.* Hiph.—I. *to darken, make dark, obscure.* —II. *to cause darkness,* Ps. 139. 12; Je. 13. 16.

חָשֹׁךְ adj. masc., pl. חֲשֻׁכִּים (§ 37. No. 3c) *obscure, mean,* Pr. 22. 29.

חֹשֶׁךְ masc. dec. 6c.—I. *darkness.*—II. *calamity, misery.*—III. *ignorance,* Job 37. 19.

חֲשׁוֹךְ Chald. masc. dec. 1a, *darkness,* Da. 2. 22.

חֲשֵׁכָה ,חֲשֵׁיכָה fem., constr. חֶשְׁכַת (comp. dec. 11, and § 42. rem. 4), pl. חֲשֵׁכִים, *darkness.*

חֶשְׁכָה fem. *darkness,* Mi. 3. 6.

מַחְשָׁךְ masc. pl. מַחֲשַׁכִּים (dec. 8a, § 37, No. 3c).—I. *darkness.*—II. *dark place.*

חָשָׂךְ[a] Kal pret. 3 pers. s. m. for חָשַׂךְ (§ 8. rem. 7) חשך
חֲשֹׂךְ[b] Kal imp. sing. masc. . . . . חשך
חוֹשֵׂךְ[c] ן Kal part. act. sing. masc. . . . חשך
חֹשֶׁךְ ן noun masc. sing. dec. 6c . . . חשך
חֲשֵׁכָה[d] ן[e] noun fem. sing., dec. 11 (§ 42. rem. 4) חשך
חָשְׁכָה[f] ן Kal pret. 3 pers. sing. fem. . . . חשך
חָשָׂכוּ[g] / חָשְׂכוּ[h] } Kal pret. 3 pers. pl. (§ 8. rem. 7) . חשך
חָשְׁכוּ[i] ן[k] Kal pret. 3 pers. pl. . . . . חשך
חָשְׁכִּי noun m. s., suff. 1 pers. s. from חֹשֶׁךְ dec. 6c חשך
חֲשֵׁכִים[l] noun fem. with pl. m. term. fr. חֲשֵׁכָה (q. v.) חשך
חֲשֻׁכִּים[m] adj. m., pl. of [חָשֹׁךְ] dec. 8c (§ 37. No. 2 & 3) חשך
חָשַׂכְתָּ Kal pret. 2 pers. sing. masc. . . . חשך
חֶשְׁכַת[n] noun fem. sing. constr. of חֲשֵׁכָה dec. 11. (§ 42. rem. 4) . . . . חשך
חָשַׂכְתִּי[o] Kal pret. 1 pers. sing. . . . . חשך

חָשַׁל Niph. part. *debilitated, enfeebled,* De. 25. 18.

חֲשַׁל Chald. *to beat small, pound,* Da. 2. 40.

חָשֵׁל[p] ן Chald. Peal part. act. sing. masc. . חשל

חָשַׁם Root not used; Arab. *to be fat; to be rich, opulent.*

חָשֻׁם (*rich*) pr. name of a man.

חֶשְׁמוֹן (*fat soil*) pr. name of a town in the tribe of Judah, Jos. 15. 27.

חַשְׁמֹנָה (id.) pr. name of a station of the Israelites in the desert, Nu. 33. 29.

חַשְׁמַן masc. only pl. חַשְׁמַנִּים Ps. 68. 32, *rich, opulent, noble.* Michaelis takes it as a pr. name, *Hushmoneans,* the inhabitants of Ashmunein, a city in Egypt.

חֻשָׁם ן pr. name masc. . . . . חשם
חֻשָׁם pr. name masc., see חוּשָׁם . . . חוש
חֻשִׁם pr. name masc., see חוּשִׁים . . . חוש
חַשְׁמַל[q] masc. *a kind of polished brass,* comp. Re. 1. 15. According to others, *a mixed metal of gold and silver,* supposing that the LXX. meant the same in rendering it ἤλεκτρον (not *amber*). The Hebrew word is supposed to be compounded of נְחָשׁ *brass* (dropping the initial נ) and מַל from מְלַל Chald. *to rub, polish,* or מַלָּא=מַל Chald. *gold.*
חֶשְׁמוֹן ן pr. name masc. . . . . חשם
חַשְׁמַנִּים[r] noun masc., pl. of [חַשְׁמָן] dec. 8a . חשם

חָשַׁן Root not used; Arab. *to be beautiful; to adorn.* Hence

חֹשֶׁן masc. prop. *ornament,* spoken of the *breast-plate* of the high-priest. LXX. once περίστηθιον *a breast-plate,* elsewhere λογίον or λογεῖον *oracle.* . . . . חשן

חָשַׂף fut. יֶחֱשֹׂף.—I. *to strip, make bare, uncover.*—II. *to uncover,* i. e. remove the covering, Is. 47. 2.—III. *to draw, draw off,* as water.

חֲשׂוּפָא (*bare, naked*) pr. name of a man.

חָשִׂיף masc. dec. 3a, *flock, a small separated flock,* 1 Ki. 20. 27.

מַחְשֹׂף masc. *a making bare,* Ge. 30. 37.

חָשׂוֹף[s] Kal inf. absolute . . . . . חשף
חֲשֻׂפָא pr. name masc., see חֲשׂוּפָא . . . חשף
חֲשָׂפָהּ[t] Kal pret. 3 pers. sing. masc., suff. 3 pers. s. f. חשף
חֲשִׂפֵי[u] noun masc. pl. constr. from [חָשִׂיף] dec. 3a חשף
חֶשְׂפִּי[y] Kal imp. sing. fem. (§ 13. rem. 3) . . חשף
חָשַׂפְתִּי id. pret. 1 pers. sing. . . . . חשף

חָשַׁק I. *to be attached, to cleave to* any one from affection, with בְּ.—II. *to desire, be pleased* to do anything, with לְ before the inf. of the action. Pi. *to connect, join together,* Ex. 38. 28. Pu. pass. of Piel.

חֵשֶׁק masc. dec. 6b, *desire, delight.*

חֲשֻׁקִים ,חֲשׁוּקִים masc. pl. (of חָשׁוּק) *the poles*

---

[a] Is. 14. 6. [b] Ps. 19. 14. [c] Pr. 11. 24. [d] Ge. 15. 12. [e] Is. 8. 22. [f] Mi. 3. 6. [g] Je. 14. 10. [h] Job 30. 10. [i] La. 5. 17. [k] Ec. 12. 3. [l] Is. 50. 10. [m] Pr. 22. 29. [n] Ps. 18. 12. [o] Job 38. 23. [p] Da. 2. 40. [q] Eze. 1. 27. [r] Ps. 68. 32. [s] Is. 52. 10. [t] Joel 1. 7. [u] Joel 1. 7. [x] 1 Ki. 20. 27. [y] Is. 47. 2.

or *rods* which connected the pillars of the court of the tabernacle, and from which the curtains were suspended.

חֲשֻׁקִים masc. pl. (of חָשׁוּק) *spokes of a wheel*, 1 Ki. 7. 33.

חֵשֶׁק noun masc. sing. dec. 6b . . . חשק
חִשֵּׁק[a] וְ Piel pret. 3 pers. sing. masc. (§ 10. rem. 1) חשק
חָֽשְׁקָה[b] Kal pret. 3 pers. sing. fem. . . . חשק
חִשְׁקִי[c] noun m. s., suff. 1 pers. s. from חֵשֶׁק dec. 6b חשק
חֲשֻׁקֵיהֶם וַ defect. for חֲשׁוּ׳ (q. v.) . . . חשק
חֲשֻׁקֵיהֶם[d] וְ noun m. pl., suff. 3 pers. pl. m. [fr. חָשׁוּק] חשק
חָשַׁקְתָּ[e] / חָשַׁקְתָּ[f] וְ } Kal pret. 2 pers. sing. masc.; acc. shifted by conv. וְ (§ 8. rem. 7) . . } חשק

חָשַׁר Root not used; Arab. *to collect*.

חַשְׁרָה fem. dec. 11 (§ 42. rem. 1) *a collection of waters*, 2 Sa. 22. 12.

חִשֻּׁרִים masc. pl. (of חִשּׁוּר) *the nave of a wheel*, 1 Ki. 7. 33.

חִשֻּׁרֵיהֶם[g] וְ noun m. pl., suff. 3 pers. pl. m. [from חִשּׁוּר] חשר
חַשְׁרַת[h] noun fem. sing. constr. [of חַשְׁרָה or חֲשֵׁרָה] חשר

חֲשַׁשׁ וַ masc. *dried grass, hay*, Is. 5. 24; 33. 11.

חַשְׁתִּי[i] Kal pret. 1 pers. sing. . . . . חוש
חַת[k] [for חַת] noun masc. sing. dec. 8d & e . חתת
חַת[l] Kal pret. 3 pers. sing. masc. . . . חתת
חֵת pr. name masc. . . . . . . חתת

[חָתָה] fut. יַחְתֶּה (§ 13. rem. 5) *to take, lay hold of, seize*, spoken especially of taking *fire, coals*.

מַחְתָּה fem. dec. 10.—I. *fire-shovel* or *fire-pan*.—II. *censer*.—III. *snuff-dishes*; others, *snuffers*.

מַחַת (*taking, removal*) pr. name of a man.

חַתָּה[m] / חַתָּה וְ } Kal pret. 3 pers. sing. fem. (comp. § 8. rem. 7); for וְ see lett. ו . . } חתת
חֹתֶה[n] Kal part. act. sing. masc. . . . . חתה
חַתּוּ[pp] / חַתּוּ וָ } Kal pret. 3 pers. pl. (comp. § 8. rem. 7); for וָ see lett. ו . . . } חתת
חֹתּוּ[o] וָ id. imp. pl. masc.; וָ id. . . . חתת
חִתּוּל[p] noun masc. sing. . . . . חתל
חָתוֹם[q] וְ Kal inf. absolute . . . . חתם
חָתוּם id. part. pass. sing. masc. dec. 3a . . חתם
חֲתוֹם[r] id. imp. sing. masc. . . . . חתם
חַתְחַתִּים[s] וְ adj. masc., pl. of [חַתְחַת] dec. 8d . . חתת
חַתִּים adj. masc. pl. of [חַת] dec. 8d . . חתת
חִתִּית gent. noun, fem. of חִתִּי from חֵת . . חתת
חִתִּית[tt] noun fem. sing. dec. 1b . . . חתת

חִתִּיּוֹת gent. noun fem., pl. of חִתִּית from חִתִּי masc., see חֵת . . . . . חתת
חִתִּיתוֹ[t] noun fem. sing., suff. Kh. ׳תוֹ 3 pers. sing. masc., K. ׳תִי 1 pers. s., from חִתִּית d. 1b חתת
חִתִּיתָם id., suff. 3 pers. pl. masc. . . . חתת

חָתַךְ Kal not used; Chald. *to cut, divide*. Niph. *to be determined*, Da. 9. 24.

חִתְּכֶם[u] וְ noun masc. sing., suff. 2 pers. pl. masc. from [חַת] dec. 8d . . . חתת

חָתַל. Pu. & Hoph. *to be bandaged, swaddled*, Eze. 16. 4.

חֲתֻלָּה fem. dec. 10, *bandage, swaddling band*, Job 38. 9.

חִתּוּל masc. *bandage* for a wound, Eze. 30. 21.

חֶתְלוֹן (*covered place*) pr. name of a town in Syria.

חֶתְלֹן pr. name of a place . . . . חתל
חֻתַּלְתְּ[x] Pual pret. 2 pers. sing. fem. [חֻתַּלְתְּ], comp. § 8. rem. 7] . . . חתל
חֲתֻלָּתוֹ[y] n. f. s., suff. 3 p. s. m. from [חֲתֻלָּה] d. 10 חתל

[חָתַם] fut. יַחְתֹּם (§ 13. rem. 5).—I. *to seal, seal up*, with the acc.; with בְּ of the seal-ring, also בְּעַד; rarely with בְּ, בְּעַד of the object, comp. Job 9. 7; 33. 16; 37. 7.—II. *to make an end of, finish*, Da. 9. 24.

חֲתַם Ch. *to seal, seal up*, Da. 6. 18.

חוֹתָם m. (no vowel change).—I. *seal, signet*.—II. pr. name masc. of two persons, 1 Ch. 7. 32; 11. 14.

חֹתֶמֶת fem. *seal, signet*, Ge. 38. 25.

חֲתֹם[z] וַ Kal imp. sing. masc.; וַ bef. (ֲ) . חתם
חָתֻם[a] id. part. pass. sing. masc. for חָתוּם . חתם
חֹתָם[b] defect. for חוֹתָם (q. v.) . . . חתם
חַתְמַהּ[c] וְ Ch. Peal pret. 3 pers. sing. masc., suff. 3 pers. sing. fem. . . . . . חתם
חִתְּמוּ[d] Piel pret. 3 pers. pl. . . . . חתם
חִתְמוּ[e] וְ Kal imp. pl. masc. . . . . חתם
חֲתֻמִים[f] וַ id. part. p. masc., pl. of חָתוּם dec. 3a . חתם
חֹתָמְךָ[g] noun masc. sing., suff. 2 pers. sing. masc. from חוֹתָם (no vowel change) . . חתם

[חָתַן] *to marry, give in marriage*, only part. חֹתֵן *father-in-law, the wife's father*; fem. חֹתֶנֶת *mother-in-law, the wife's mother*. Hithpa. *mutually to give and take daughters in marriage, to contract affinity by marriage*, with אֵת, בְּ, לְ.

[a] Ex. 38. 28. [b] Ge. 34. 8. [c] Is. 21. 4. [d] 1 Ki. 7. 33. [e] Is. 38. 17. [f] De. 21. 11. [g] 1 Ki. 7. 33. [h] 2 Sa. 22. 12. [i] Ps. 119. 60. [k] Job 41. 25. [l] Je. 50. 2. [m] Je. 48. 1. [n] Pr. 25. 22. [o] Is. 8. 9, 9. [p] Eze. 30. 21. [pp] Je. 50. 36. [q] Je. 32. 44. [r] Is. 8. 16. [s] Ec. 12. 5. [tt] Eze. 32. 23, 27. [t] Eze. 32. 32. [u] Ge. 9. 2. [x] Eze. 16. 4. [y] Job 38. 9. [z] Da. 12. 4. [a] Job 14. 17. [b] Ex. 28. 11. [c] Da. 6. 18. [d] Job 24. 16. [e] Est. 8. 8. [f] Da. 12. 9. [g] Ge. 38. 18.

חָתָן masc. dec. 4c.—I. *bridegroom, spouse*; Ex. 4. 25 חֲתַן דָּמִים *bridegroom of blood*, i.e. saved and become again her husband through her son's blood of circumcision, which Moses (as the intended mediator between God and Israel) had neglected and, on account of it, almost lost his life.—II. *son-in-law*.—III. *relative by marriage*, 2 Ki. 8. 27.

חֲתֻנָּה fem. dec. 10, *marriage*, Ca. 3. 11.

חָתָן noun masc. sing. dec. 4c . . . חתן
חֲתַן [a] וְ id. constr. state; ן bef. (-:) . . . חתן
חֹתֵן Kal part. act. sing. masc. dec. 7b . . חתן
חֲתָנוֹ [b] noun m. s., suff. 3 pers. s. m. from חָתָן d. 4c חתן
חֹתְנוֹ Kal part. act. sing. masc. (חֹתֵן) suff. 3 pers. sing. masc. dec. 7b . . . חתן
חֲתָנָיו [c] noun m. pl., suff. 3 p. s. m. from חָתָן d. 4c חתן
חֹתֶנְךָ [d] Kal part. act. sing. masc. (חֹתֵן) suff. 2 pers. sing. masc. (§ 36. rem. 1) . . . חתן
חֲתֻנָּתוֹ [e] noun fem. sing., suff. 3 pers. sing. masc. from [חֲתֻנָּה] dec. 10 . . . . חתן
חֹתַנְתּוֹ [f] Kal part. act. sing. fem. [חֹתֶנֶת], suff. 3 pers. sing. masc. dec. 13a, from חֹתֵן masc. . חתן

[חָתַף] *to catch, seize*, Job 9. 12.

חֶתֶף masc. *prey, rapine*, Pr. 23. 28.

חָתַר [g] fut. יַחְתֹּר (§ 13. rem. 15).—I. *to dig, break through*.—II. *to row*, Jon. 1. 13.

מַחְתֶּרֶת fem. *a digging through, breaking in*.

חֲתָר־ Kal imp. sing. masc. [for חֲתֹר § 8. rem. 18] חתר
חָתַרְתִּי [h] id. pret. 1 pers. sing. . . . חתר

[חָתַת] fut. יֵחַת, יֵחַתּוּ (§ 18. rem. 6).—I. *to be broken*, Is. 7. 8; 51. 6.—II. *to be terrified, dismayed, confounded*. Const. with מִפְּנֵי, מִן. Niph. *to be dismayed*, Mal. 2. 5. Pi.—I. *to be broken in pieces, be shivered*, Je. 51. 56.—II. *to terrify, dismay*, Job 7. 14. Hiph.—I. *to break in pieces*, Is. 9. 3.—II. *to terrify, confound, confuse*.

חֲתַת masc.—I. *terror, dismay*, Job 6. 21.—II. pr. name masc. 1 Ch. 4. 13.

חַת masc. dec. 8e.—I. adj. *broken*, 1 Sa. 2. 4.—II. *terrified, dismayed*, Je. 46. 5.—III. subst. *terror, dread*.

חֵת (*terror*) pr. name of the second son of Canaan, Ge. 10. 15, &c. Gent. noun חִתִּי pl. חִתִּים.

חִתָּה fem. dec. 10, *terror, fear*, Ge. 35. 5.

חִתִּית fem. dec. 1b, *terror, dread*.

חַתְחַת adj. masc. dec. 8d, *terrified, dismayed*, Ec. 12. 5.

מְחִתָּה fem. dec. 10.—I. *destruction, ruin*.—II. *terror, fear*.

חֲתַת [i] noun masc. sing., also pr. name masc. . חתת
חִתַּת [k] noun fem. sing., constr. of [חִתָּה] dec. 10 חתת
חִתְּתָה [l] Piel pret. 3 pers. sing. fem. . . חתת
חִתַּתַּנִי [m] וְ id. pret. 2 pers. sing. masc. [for חִתַּתָּ § 25. rem.], suff. 1 pers. sing. . . . חתת

ט

טְאֵב Ch. *to be glad*, Da. 6. 24.
טֵאטֵאתִיהָ [n] וְ Pilp. (§ 6. No. 4) pret. 1 pers. sing., suff. 3 pers. sing. fem. . . . . . טוא
טָב Ch. adj. masc. sing. . . . . טוב
טָבְאַל, טָבְאֵל } pr. name masc. . . . . טוב
טֹבוּ Kal pret. 3 pers. sing. (§ 21. rem. 2) . טוב
טָבוּחַ [o] Kal part. pass. sing. masc. . . . טבח
טְבוּלִים [p] noun masc., pl. of [טָבוּל] dec. 3a . טבל
טַבּוּר noun masc. sing. . . . . טבר
טֹבוֹת [q] וְ defect. for טוֹבוֹת (q. v.) . . . טוב

[טָבַח] *to slaughter*, especially animals, but also of men, *to slay, kill*.

טַבָּח masc. dec. 1b.—I. *a cook*, 1 Sa. 9. 23, 24.—II. *executioner*, or *guard*; for princes anciently employed their own *guards* as *executioners*.

טַבָּח Ch. masc. dec. 1a, *executioner*, or *guard*, see Heb. טַבָּח.

טַבָּחָה fem. *a cook*, 1 Sa. 8. 13.

טֶבַח masc. dec. 6a (with suff. טִבְחָהּ; but in pause טָבַח § 35. rem. 1 & 5).—I. *slaughter* of animals, but also of men.—II. *animals slaughtered, meat*.—III. pr. name masc. Ge. 22. 24.

טִבְחָה fem. (no pl.) i. q. טֶבַח.

טִבְחַת pr. name of a city in Syria, 1 Ch. 18. 8; but written בֶּטַח in 2 Sa. 8. 8.

מַטְבֵּחַ masc. *slaughter*, Is. 14. 21.

טֶבַח [r] וְ noun masc. sing. dec. 6a (suff. טִבְחָהּ § 35. rem. 5) also pr. name . . טבח

[a] 1 Sa. 22. 14. [b] Ju. 19. 5. [c] Ge. 19. 14. [d] Ex. 18. 6. [e] Ca. 3. 11. [f] De. 27. 23. [g] Job 24. 16. [h] Eze. 12. 7. [i] Job 6. 21. [k] Ge. 35. 5. [l] Je. 51. 56. [m] Job 7. 14. [n] Is. 14. 23. [o] De. 28. 31. [p] Eze. 23. 15. [q] Ge. 41. 22. [r] Is. 34. 6.

טְבֹחַ[a] [b]ו׳ Kal inf., or imp. sing. masc.; וּ bef. (:) טבח
טָבְחָה[c] id. pret. 3 pers. sing. fem. . . . טבח
טִבְחָה[d] noun fem. sing. (no pl.) . . . טבח
טִבְחָהּ[e] noun masc. sing., suff. 3 pers. sing. fem. from טֶבַח dec. 6 a (§ 35. rem. 5) . . . טבח
טְבָחוֹ[f] וּ Kal pret. 3 pers. sing. masc., suff. 3 pers. sing. masc.; וּ for וְ conv. . . . טבח
טַבָּחַיָּא[g] Ch. noun masc. pl. emph. from טַבָּח׳ dec. 1 a טבח
טַבָּחִים Heb. id. pl. abs. dec. 1 b . . . טבח
טָבַחְתָּ[h] Kal pret. 2 pers. sing. masc. . . . טבח
טָבַחְתִּי[i] id. pret. 1 pers. sing. . . . . טבח
טִבְחָתִי[k] noun f. s., suff. 1 pers. s. from טִבְחָה (no pl.) טבח
טֹבִיָּה וְ pr. name masc. . . . . . טוב
טֹבִים [l]וְ׳ adj. masc., pl. of טוֹב dec. 1 a . . . טוב
טְבַלְיָהוּ pr. name masc. . . . . . טבל

טָבַל וְ I. *to dip, immerse.*—II. *to stain,* Ge. 37. 31. Arab. *to dye with colours.* Niph. pass. Jos. 3. 15.

טָבוּל masc. prop. *something dyed;* hence, *coloured head-bands, turbans,* Eze. 23. 15. Others compare this word with the Ethiop. טבלל to wrap, wind round.

טְבַלְיָהוּ (whom *the Lord has purified*) pr. name masc. 1 Ch. 26. 11.

טֹבֵל[m] וְ id. part. act. masc. sing. . . . טבל
טָבַלְתְּ[n] וְ id. pret. 2 pers. sing. fem. . . . טבל
טְבַלְתֶּם[o] וּ id. pret. 2 pers. pl. masc.; וּ for וְ conv. . טבל

[טָבַע] I. *to sink,* as in water, mud.—II. *to sink, enter in, penetrate,* 1 Sa. 17. 49. Pu. *to sink, be immersed,* Ex. 15. 4. Hoph. *to be sunk, settled.*

טַבַּעַת fem. with suff. טַבַּעְתּוֹ, pl. טַבָּעוֹת (§ 44. rem. 5).—I. *seal, seal-ring.*—II. *any ring.*

טַבָּעוֹת (*rings,* or *impressions*) pr. name of a man, Ezr. 2. 43.

טָבְעוּ Kal pret. 3 pers. pl. . . . . טבע
טֻבְּעוּ[p] Pual pret. 3 pers. pl. . . . . טבע
טַבָּעוֹת pr. name masc. . . . . . טבע
טַבָּעוֹת pl. of the following, see טַבַּעַת
טַבַּעַת[q] [r]וְ׳ n. f. s. d. 13 a, but pl. טַבָּעוֹת (§ 44. r. 5) טבע
טַבָּעֹת id. pl. abs. state . . . . . טבע
טַבְּעֹת id. pl., constr. state . . . . . טבע
טַבַּעְתּוֹ id. sing., suff. 3 pers. sing. masc. . . . טבע
טָבַעְתִּי[s] Kal pret. 1 pers. sing. . . . . טבע
טַבְּעֹתֵיהֶם[t] } noun fem. pl., suff. 3 pers. pl. masc. (§ 4. rem. 2) from טַבַּעַת dec. 13 a . } טבע
טַבְּעֹתָם[u]

טבר Root not used; hence

טַבּוּר masc. *high, eminent place.* Comp. Chald. טוּר.

טַבְרִמֹּן pr. name masc. . . . . . טוב
טַבָּת (*celebrated* i. q. Syr. טביבא) pr. name of a town in the tribe of Ephraim, Ju. 7. 22.
טֹבַת adj. fem. s., constr. of טוֹבָה d. 10, fr. טוֹב m. טוב
טֵבֵת *Tebeth,* the tenth month of the Hebrew year, Est. 2. 16.
טֹבֹת[x] וְ׳ adj. or subst. f., pl. of טוֹבָה from טוֹב m. טוב
טֹבָתָם[y] וְ id. subst. sing., suff. 3 pers. pl. masc. . טוב
טָהוֹר adj. masc. sing. dec. 3 a . . . . טהר
טְהוֹר[z] id. const. state . . . . . טהר
טְהָר־[a] Kh. טָהוֹר q. v., K. טְהָר־ (q. v.) . . טהר
טְהוֹרָה adj. fem. sing. dec. 10, from טָהוֹר masc. . טהר
טְהוֹרִים id. pl. masc. dec. 3 a . . . . טהר

טָהֵר וְ *to be* or *become clean, pure,* in a physical and moral sense. Pi. טִהַר (§ 14. rem. 1).—I. *to cleanse, purify.*—II. *to pronounce* or *declare clean.* Pu. *to be cleansed,* Eze. 22. 24. Hithp. הִטַּהֵר, הִטָּהֵר (for הִתְטַהֵר § 12. rem. 3; § 14. rem. 1) *to cleanse* or *purify oneself.*

טָהוֹר masc. dec. 3 a (טְהָר־ § 32. rem. 7), טְהוֹרָה fem. dec. 10, adj. *clean, pure,* in a physical and moral sense.

טֹהַר masc. dec. 6 f.—I. *brightness, clearness, splendour.*—II. *purification,* Le. 12. 4, 6.

טָהֳרָה fem. constr. טָהֳרַת (no pl.).—I. *purity* of heart, 2 Ch. 30. 19.—II. *cleansing, purification.*

טַהֵר[b] Piel inf. constr. (§ 14. rem. 1) . . טהר
טִהַר וְ Piel pret. 3 pers. sing. masc. (§ 14. rem. 1) טהר
טְהָר[c] וּ Kal imp. sing. masc. [for טְהַר]; וּ bef. (:) טהר
טְהָר־[d] וּ with Mak. for טָהוֹר q. v. (§ 32. rem. 7) טהר
טָהֲרָה * } וְ Kal pret. 3 pers. sing. fem. (§ 8. rem. 1 a & 7) *Le. 12. 8. . . } טהר
טָהֲרָה[e] [f]וְ׳
טָהֳרָה[g] noun fem. sing. dec. 10 . . . טהר
טָהֳרָהּ[h] noun m. s., suff. 3 p. s. fem. from טֹהַר׳ dec. 6 f טהר
טְהֹרָה [i]וּ׳ adj. fem. s. dec. 10, from טָהוֹר m.; וּ bef. (:) טהר
טִהֲרוֹ וְ Piel pret. 3 pers. sing. masc., suff. 3 pers. sing. masc. (§ 14. rem. 1) . . . טהר
טִהֲרוּ וְ id. pret. 3 pers. pl. . . . . טהר
טְהֹרוֹת adj. fem., pl. of טְהֹרָה dec. 10, from טָהוֹר m. טהר
טַהֲרִי Piel inf., (טַהֵר § 14. rem. 1) suff. 1 p. s. dec. 7 b טהר
טְהֹרִים[k] וּ adj. masc., pl. of טָהוֹר dec. 3 a; וּ bef. (:) טהר
טִהַרְנוּ[l] Piel pret. 1 pers. pl., (§ 14. rem. 1) . . טהר
טַהֲרֵנִי[m] id. imp. sing. masc., suff. 1 pers. sing. . טהר
טָהַרְתְּ[n] Kal pret. 2 pers. sing. fem. . . . טהר

[a] Eze. 21. 15. [b] Ge. 43. 16. [c] Pr. 9. 2. [d] Ps. 44. 23. [e] Pr. 9. 2. [f] Ex. 21. 37. [g] Da. 2. 14. [h] La. 2. 21. [i] 1 Sa. 25. 11. [k] 1 Sa. 25. 11. [l] 1 Ki. 2. 32. [m] De. 33. 24. [n] Ru. 2. 14. [o] Ex. 12. 22. [p] Ex. 15. 4. [q] Nu. 31. 50. [r] Ex. 35. 22. [s] Ps. 69. 3. [t] Ex. 26. 29. [u] Ex. 36. 34. [x] Ge. 6. 2. [y] De. 23. 7. [z] Hab. 1. 13. [a] Pr. 22. 11. [b] Eze. 39. 12. [c] 2 Ki. 5. 10, 13. [d] Job 17. 9. [e] Le. 15. 28. [f] Le. 12. 7. [g] Le. 12. 4, 5. [h] Le. 12. 4, 6. [i] Nu. 5. 28. [k] Pr. 15. 26. [l] 2 Ch. 29. 18. [m] Ps. 51. 4. [n] Eze. 24. 13.

טִהַרְתְּ[a] וְ Piel pret. 2 pers. sing. fem. (§ 14. rem. 1); acc. shifted by conv. וְ (comp. § 8. rem. 7) טהר

טָהֳרַת[b] noun fem. sing., constr. of טָהֳרָה (no pl.) טהר

טָהֳרָתוֹ id., suff. 3 pers. sing. masc. . . טהר

טָהַרְתִּי[c] / טָהֳרְתִּי[d] } וְ Kal pret. 1 pers. sing. (§ 8. rem. 7) . טהר

טִהַרְתִּי[e] וְ Piel pret. 1 pers. sing. (§ 14. rem. 1); acc. shifted by וְ conv. (comp. id.) . . טהר

טִהַרְתִּיךְ[f] id., suff. 2 pers. sing. fem. . . . טהר

טִהַרְתִּים וְ id., suff. 3 pers. pl. masc. . . טהר

טְהַרְתֶּם וּ Kal pret. 2 pers. pl. masc.; וּ for conv. וְ טהר

טָוָא Root not used; Syr. *to fast.*

טְוָת Chald. *a fasting,* Da. 6. 19.

טוּא Kal not used; probably *to remove* or *be removed,* cogn. זוּעַ. Pilp. טֵאטֵא (§ 6. No. 4) *to remove dirt* or *mire, to sweep away,* Is. 14. 23.

מַטְאֲטֵא masc. *besom,* Is. 14. 23.

טִיט masc. *mire, mud.* Talmud. טִיאוּט *a sweeping out.*

טוֹב וְ׳ pl. טֹבוּ (§ 21. rem. 2).—I. *to be good, well, agreeable, pleasant;* impers. טוֹב לִי *it is well with me;* טוֹב בְּעֵינַי *it pleases me;* it is also followed by אֶל. עַל.—II. *to be cheerful, joyful.* Hiph.—I. *to do well, act rightly.*—II. *to do good,* Eze. 36. 11.—III. *to make fair, beautiful,* Ho. 10. 1.—IV. *to make cheerful,* Ec. 11. 9.

טוֹב masc. dec. 1a, טוֹבָה fem. dec. 10, adj.—I. *good, agreeable, pleasant.*—II. *goodly, fair, beautiful.*—III. *happy, prosperous.*—IV. *cheerful, joyful.*—V. adv. *well, rightly.* Subst. (masc. and fem.).—I. *good,* what is *good.*—II. *goodness,* Ps. 16. 2; 65. 12.—III. *wealth,* Ec. 5. 10.—IV. *prosperity, happiness,* Ps. 106. 5. טוֹב pr. name of a region beyond Jordan.

טוֹב אֲדֹנִיָּה pr. name masc. 2 Ch. 17. 8.

טוּב masc. dec. 1a.—I. *goodness.*—II. concr. *the good, the best.*—III. *wealth.*—IV. *beauty.*—V. *prosperity, happiness.*—VI. *cheerfulness.*

טוֹבִיָּהוּ, טוֹבִיָּה (*the Lord is good*) pr. name masc. of several persons.

טָב Chald. *good, pleasing.*

טָבְאֵל in pause טָבְאָל (*God is good*) pr. name masc.—I. Is. 7. 6.—II. Ezr. 4. 7.

טַבְרִמּוֹן (*Rimmon is good*) pr. name of the father of Benhadad, king of Syria, 1 Ki. 15. 18.

טוֹב וְ׳, וְ׳, adj. or subst. masc. sing. dec. 1a, also pr. name; for וְ see lett. ו . . . טוב

טוּב noun masc. sing. dec. 1a . . . טוב

טוֹבָה וְ׳ adj. or subst. fem. dec. 10, from טוֹב masc. טוב

טוּבָהּ[g] וְ׳[h] n. m. s., suff. 3 p. s. fem. from טוּב dec. 1a טוב

טוּבוֹ id., suff. 3 pers. sing. masc. . . . טוב

טוֹבוֹת adj. or subst. fem., pl. of טוֹבָה (q. v.) . טוב

טוּבִי noun m. s., suff. 1 pers. sing. from טוּב dec. 1a טוב

טוֹבֵי וְ adj. masc. pl. constr. from טוֹב dec. 1a . טוב

טוֹבִיָּה / טוֹבִיָּהוּ } וְ׳ pr. name masc. . . . . טוב

טוֹבִים וְ׳ adj. masc., pl. of טוֹב dec. 1a . . טוב

טוּבְךָ noun m. s., suff. 2 p. s. m. from טוּב dec. 1a טוב

טוּבָם[i] noun masc. sing., suff. 3 pers. pl. masc. from טוּב dec. 1a . . . . . טוב

טוּבָם[k] noun m. s., suff. 3 p. pl. m. from טוּב dec. 1a טוב

טוֹבַת וְ׳[l] adj. fem. sing., constr. of טוֹבָה dec. 10, from טוֹב masc. . . . טוב

טוֹבָתִי[nn] id. (subst.), suff. 1 pers. sing. . . טוב

טוֹבֹתָיו[m] id. (subst.) pl., suff. 3 pers. sing. masc. . טוב

טוֹבָתֶךָ[oo] id. (subst.) s., suff. 2 pers. s. m. [for טוֹבָתְךָ] טוב

טוֹבָתָם[n] וְ id. id., suff. 3 pers. pl. masc. . . טוב

[טָוָה] *to spin,* Ex. 35. 25, 26.

מַטְוֶה masc. *yarn,* Ex. 35. 25.

טָווּ[o] Kal pret. 3 pers. pl. . . . . טוה

[טוּחַ] *to besmear, daub, plaster* or *cover over,* as a wall; metaph. the eyes, so as not to see. Niph. pass. Le. 14. 43, 48.

טֻחוֹת fem. pl. (of טֻחָה) *the inward parts, the reins,* Job 38. 36; Ps. 51. 8.

טִיחַ masc. *a plastering,* Eze. 13. 12.

טוֹחֵן[p] Kal part. act. sing. masc. . . . טחן

טוּל Hiph. *to throw, cast, to cast out* or *forth.* Hoph. *to be cast down, out* or *forth.* Pilp. (§ 6. No. 4) *to cast forth with violence,* Is. 22. 17.

טַלְטֵלָה fem. *a casting forth,* Is. 22. 17.

טוּף Root not used; Arab. *to surround, bind round.*

טוֹטָפוֹת fem. pl. (for טָפְטָפוֹת, like כּוֹכָב for כָּבְכָּב) *frontlets, phylacteries.*

טוּר וְ׳ masc. dec. 1a, *series, order, range, row.*

טִירָה fem. dec. 10.—I. *row* or *range* of buildings or chambers, Eze. 46. 23.—II. *castle* or *palace.*

[a] Nu. 8. 6, 15. [b] 1 Ch. 23. 28. [c] 2 Ki. 5. 12. [d] Pr. 20. 9. [e] Eze. 37. 23. [f] Eze. 24. 13. [g] Ne. 9. 36. [h] Je. 2. 7. [i] Mi. 7. 4. [k] Job 21. 16. [l] Est. 2. 7. [m] Ne. 6. 19. [n] Ezr. 9. 12. [nn] Ps. 16. 2. [o] Ex. 35. 25, 26. [oo] Ps. 65. 12. [p] Ju. 16. 21.

יְטוּר (*castle*) pr. name of a son of Ishmael and of a people descended from him.

[טוּר] Ch. masc. dec. 1a, *mountain*, Da. 2. 35, 45. Targ. טַוָּר, cogn. טַבּוּר q. v.

[a] טוֹרֵד Kal part. act. sing. masc. . . . טרד

טוּרֵי noun masc. pl. constr. from טוּר dec. 1a טור

טוּרִים id. pl., absolute state . . . טור

[טוּשׁ] *to fly swiftly*, Job 9. 26.

[b] טְוָת Chald. noun fem. sing. . . . . טוא

[c] טָח וְ Kal pret. 3 pers. sing. masc. . . טוח

[d] טַח id. id. as if from R. טחח (§ 21. rem. 2) see טוח

טָחָה Kal not used; Arab. *to expand; perhaps to impel, drive, shoot*, cogn. דָּחָה, דָּחַף, דָּחַק. Pilel part. (§ 6. No. 2, & § 24. r. 22) מְטַחֲוֵי קֶשֶׁת *extenders* or *shooters of the bow*, i. e. *bowmen, archers*, Ge. 21. 16.

[e] טָחוּ Kal pret. 3 pers. pl. . . . . טוח

[f] טָחוֹן Kal inf. abs. . . . . . טחן

[g] טְחוֹן noun masc. sing. . . . . טחן

[h] טָחֵי construct of the following: . . טוח

[i] טָחִים Kal part. masc., pl. of [טָח] dec. 1a . טוח

[טָחַן] *to bruise; grind with a hand-mill;* Is. 3. 15, *to grind the face of the poor*, i. e. to oppress him.

טְחוֹן masc. *hand-mill*, La. 5. 13.

טַחֲנָה fem. id. Ec. 12. 4.

[k] טָחֲנוּ וְ Kal pret. 3 pers. pl. . . . טחן

[l] טַחֲנִי וְ id. imp. sing. fem. . . . טחן

טָחַר Root not used; Syr. *to pant, to strain hard in discharging the fæces.*

טְחֹרִים masc. pl. (of טְחֹר dec. 1a) *tumors* in the anus, *hemorrhoids*, in Keri, for Kheth. עפלים.

[m] טְחֹרֵי Keri, noun masc. pl. constr. from [טְחוֹר] dec. 1. Kh. עֲפֹלֵי (q. v.) . . . טחר

[n] טְחֹרֵיהֶם Keri, id., suff. 3 pers. pl. masc., Kh. עֲפֹלֵיהֶם טחר

[o] טַחְתֶּם Kal pret. 2 pers. pl. masc. . . . טוח

[p] טִיט וְ noun masc. sing.; for וְ see lett. ו . טוא

[טִין] Ch. masc. *clay, potter's clay*, only in the following form.

[q] טִינָא Ch. noun masc. sing. emph. of [טִין] dec. 1a טין

[r] טִירוֹתֵיהֶם n. fem. pl., suff. 3 p. pl. m. from [טִירָה] dec. 10. טור

[s] טִירַת id. sing., construct state . . . טור

[t] טִירָתָם id. sing., suff. 3 pers. pl. masc. . . . טור

[u] טִירֹתָם id. pl., suff. 3 pers. pl. masc. (§ 4. rem. 2) טור

טָל, [uu] וְ טַל } noun masc. sing. dec. 8d . . טלל

טָלָא only part. pass. טָלוּא *patched*, i. e. *spotted*. Pu. part. *patched, clouted*, Jos. 9. 5.

[x] טְלֻאוֹת Kal part. pass. pl. fem. from טָלוּא masc. טלא

[y] טְלָאִים noun m., pl. of [טְלִי] dec. 6i (§ 35. rem. 15) טלה

[z] טְלֻאִים וּ Kal part. p. m., pl. of טָלוּא dec. 3a; וּ bef. (:) טלא

טָלָה Root not used; Syr. *to be fresh, young*.

טָלֶה masc. dec. 9b, *young lamb*.

טְלִי masc. only pl. טְלָאִים (§ 35. rem. 15).—I. *lambs*, Is. 40. 11.—II. pr. name of a place in the tribe of Judah, 1 Sa. 15. 4, supposed to be the same which is called טֶלֶם in Jos. 15. 24.

[a] טָלֶה וְ noun masc. sing. dec. 9b . . . טלה

[b] טְלֵה id., construct state . . . . טלה

[c] טָלוּא וְ Kal part. pass. sing. masc. dec. 3a . טלא

[d] טַלְטֵלָה noun fem. sing. . . . . טול

[e] טַלֶּךָ noun masc. sing., suff. 2 pers. sing. masc. [for טַלְּךָ] from טַל dec. 8d . . . טלל

טָלַל Root not used; Arab.—I. *to moisten*.—II. *to shade, to cover*. Pi. *to cover, to roof*, Ne. 3. 15.

טְלַל Ch. Aph. *to take shade*, Da. 4. 9.

טַל masc. dec. 3c, *dew*. Chald. id.

טָלַם Root not used; Arab. *to oppress*.

טֶלֶם (*oppression*) pr. name of a city in the tribe of Judah, Jos. 15. 24, comp. also טְלָיִ R. טָלָה.

טַלְמוֹן (*oppressed*) pr. name masc. Ezr. 2. 42; Ne. 7. 45, &c.

[f] טַלָּם noun m. s. with suff. 3 p. pl. m. from טַל dec. 8d טלל

טֶלֶם וְ pr. name of a city . . . . טלם

טַלְמוֹן, טַלְמֹן } pr. name masc. . . . . טלם

טָמֵא וְ *to be unclean, defiled*, with בְּ *with* anything.

טָמֵא masc. dec. 5a (constr. טְמֵא § 34. rem. 1), טְמֵאָה fem. dec. 10, adj. *unclean, defiled*; טְמֵאַת הַשֵּׁם *infamous*.

טֻמְאָה Mi. 2. 10, & טֻמְאָה fem. dec. 10.—I. *uncleanness, pollution*.—II. concr. *an unclean thing*.

[g] טָמֵא וְ adj. masc. sing. dec. 5a . . . טמא

[a] Pr. 27. 15. [b] Da. 6. 19. [c] Le. 14. 42. [d] Is. 44. 18. [e] Eze. 22. 28. [f] De. 9. 21. [g] La. 5. 13. [h] Eze. 13. 11. [i] Eze. 13. 10. [k] Nu. 11. 8. [l] Is. 47. 2. [m] 1 Sa. 6. 4, 17. [n] 1 Sa. 6. 11. [o] Eze. 13. 12, 14. [p] Is. 57. 20. [q] Da. 2. 41, 43. [r] Eze. 25. 4. [s] Ca. 8. 9. [t] Ps. 69. 26. [uu] Job 29. 10. [u] Nu. 31. 10. [x] Eze. 16. 16. [y] Is. 40. 11. [z] Ge. 30. 39. [a] Is. 65. 25. [b] 1 Sa. 7. 9. [c] Ge. 30. 32, 33. [d] Is. 22. 17. [e] Is. 26. 19. [f] Zec. 8. 12. [g] Le. 13. 45; Is. 52. 1.

טַמֵּא Piel inf. constr. used also as an abs. . . טמא
טְמֵא adj. m. s., constr. of טָמֵא dec. 5a (§ 34. rem. 1) טמא
טִמֵּא וְ' Piel pret. 3 pers. sing. masc. . . . טמא
טָמְאָה וְ Kal pret. 3 pers. sing. fem. . . . טמא
[a] טֻמְאָה noun fem. sing. . . . . . טמא
טְמֵאָה adj. fem. sing. dec. 10, from טָמֵא masc. טמא
טֻמְאָה noun fem. sing. dec. 10. . . . טמא
[b] טָמְאוּ וְ Kal pret. 3 pers. pl. . . . . טמא
[c] טַמְּאוּ Piel imp. pl. masc. . . . . . טמא
[d] טִמְּאוֹ וְ id. pret. 3 pers. s. m., suff. 3 pers. s. m. טמא
טִמְּאוּ [e] וְ id. pret. 3 pers. pl. . . . . טמא
[f] טִמְּאוּהָ id. id., suff. 3 pers. sing. fem. . . טמא
[g] טֻמְאוֹתֵיכֶם n. f. pl., suff. 2 p. pl. m. fr. טֻמְאָה d. 10. טמא
טְמֵאִים [h] ו'ו adj. masc., pl. of טָמֵא d. 5a; וּ bef. (:) טמא
[i] טָמֵאת Kal pret. 2 pers. sing. fem. (§ 23. rem. 1) טמא
[k] טְמֵאַת adj. fem. sing., constr. of טְמֵאָה, fr. טָמֵא m. טמא
[l] טִמֵּאת Piel pret. 2 pers. sing. fem. . . . טמא
טֻמְאָתָהּ noun fem. sing., suff. 3 pers. sing. fem. fr. טֻמְאָה dec. 10. . . . . . טמא
טֻמְאָתוֹ וְ' id., suff. 3 pers. sing. masc. . . . טמא
[m] טֻמְאָתֵךְ id., suff. 2 pers. sing. fem. . . . טמא
[n] טִמֵּאתֶם [o] ו'ו Piel pret. 2 pers. pl. masc. . . . טמא
[p] טֻמְאֹתָם noun fem. pl., suff. 3 pers. pl. masc. from טֻמְאָה dec. 10. . . . . טמא

טָמָה. Niph. *to be unclean, despised,* Job 18. 3, but comp. § 23. rem. 11.

טָמוּן Kal part. pass. sing. masc. dec. 3a . . טמן
[q] טְמוּנָה id. fem. sing. . . . . . טמן
[r] טְמוּנֵי id. pl. constr. masc. . . . . . טמן

טָמַן I. *to hide, conceal,* especially in the earth.—II. *to hide, reserve,* with לְ for any one. Niph. *to hide oneself,* Is. 2. 10. Hiph. *to hide,* 2 Ki. 7. 8.

מַטְמוֹן masc. dec. 1b, (pl. c. מַטְמֹנֵי § 30. r. 4) *store, treasure.*

[s] טָמְנֵהוּ וְ Kal imp. sing. masc., suff. 3 pers. sing. m. טמן
[t] טָמְנוּ, טָמְנוּ } Kal pret. 3 pers. pl. (§ 8. rem. 7) . טמן
[u] טְמֻנִים id. part. pass. masc., pl. of טָמוּן dec. 3a טמן
[x] טָמְנֵם id. imp. sing. masc., suff. 3 pers. pl. masc. טמן
[y] טָמַנְתִּי id. pret. 1 pers. sing. [for טָמַנְתִּי § 8. r. 7] טמן
[z] טְמַנְתִּיו id. id., suff. 3 pers. sing. masc. . . טמן
[a] טְמַנְתָּם וּ id. pret. 2 pers. sing. masc., suff. 3 pers. pl. masc.; וּ for וְ, conv. . . . טמן

[טֶנֶא] masc. dec. 6a, *basket,* De. 26. 2, 4; 28. 5, 17.

[b] טַנְאֲךָ id. with suff. 2 pers. sing. masc. . . . טנא

טָנַף. Pi. *to soil, pollute,* Ca. 5. 3.

טָעָה Kal not used; i. q. תָּעָה. Hiph. *to cause to err, to seduce,* Eze. 13. 10.

טָעַם [c] I. *to taste.*—II. metaph. *to perceive, discriminate.*

טְעֵם Ch. Aph. *to cause to taste,* i. e. *make to eat, to feed.*

טַעַם masc. dec. 6d.—I. *taste.*—II. *discernment, judgment.*—III. *decree, edict,* Jon. 3. 7.

טְעֵם Ch. masc. *edict, decree.*

טְעֵם Ch. masc. dec. 3a.—I. *taste,* Da. 5. 2.—II. *discernment, judgment.*— III. *decree, edict;* בְּעֵל טְעֵם *master of the decrees,* an officer under the Persian government, as *Master of the rolls.*

מַטְעָם masc. only pl. מַטְעַמִּים, מַטְעַמּוֹת *dainty meat.*

טַעַם, טָעַם [d] ו'ו } noun masc. sing. dec. 6d (suff. טַעְמוֹ § 35. rem. 5) . . . . } טעם
[e] טָעֹם Kal inf. absolute . . . . טעם
טְעֵם [f] ו'ו Ch. noun masc. sing. dec. 3a; וּ bef. (:) טעם
טַעְמָא, [g] טַעְמָא } Ch. id., emph. state . . . . טעם
[h] טָעֲמָה Kal pret. 3 pers. sing. fem. . . . טעם
[i] טַעֲמוּ id. imp. pl. masc. . . . . . טעם
טַעְמוֹ [k] ו'ו noun masc. sing., suff. 3 pers. sing. masc. from טַעַם dec. 6d (§ 35. rem. 5) . טעם
[l] טַעְמֵךְ id., suff. 2 pers. sing. fem. (§ 35. rem. 5) טעם
[m] טָעַמְתִּי Kal pret. 1 pers. sing. . . . . טעם

[טָעַן] I. *to load,* as beasts of burden, Ge. 45. 17.—II. Pu. *to be thrust through,* Is. 14. 19.

[n] טַעֲנוּ Kal imp. pl. masc. . . . . . טען
טַף [o] ו'ו וְ' n. masc. sing. dec. 8d; for וְ see lett. ו טפף
[p] טָפוֹף וְ Kal inf. absolute . . . . טפף

טָפַח. Pi.—I. *to spread out, to extend,* Is. 48. 13.—II. denom. of טֶפַח *to stroke with the palm of the hand, to caress* or *dandle,* La. 2. 22. Eng. Vers. "swaddle," from the idea of *spreading out,* which is perhaps to be preferred; comp. מִטְפַּחַת.

טֶפַח masc. dec. 6a (§ 35. r. 5).—I. *palm, hand-breadth,* a measure.—II. pl. *coping stones of a building,* 1 Ki. 7. 9.

טֹפַח masc. *hand-breadth,* a measure.

---

[a] Mi. 2. 10. [b] Le. 15. 18. [c] Eze. 9. 7. [d] Le. 13. 8, 11, 15, 20. [e] Eze. 43. 8. [f] Eze. 36. 18. [g] Eze. 36. 25, 29 [h] Le. 11. 35. [i] Eze. 22. 4. [k] Eze. 22. 5, 10. [l] Eze. 5. 11. [m] Eze. 22. 15. [n] Eze. 33. 26. [o] Is. 30. 22. [p] Le. 16. 16. [q] Jos. 7. 22. [r] De. 33. 19. [s] Je. 13. 4. [t] Ps. 9. 16. [u] Jos. 7. 21. [x] Job 40. 13. [y] Je. 43. 10. [z] Je. 13. 7. [a] Je. 43. 9. [b] De. 28. 5, 17. [c] 1 Sa. 14. 24. [d] Job 12. 20. [e] 1 Sa. 14. 43. [f] Da. 2. 14. [g] Ezr. 5. 5. [h] Pr. 31. 18. [i] Ps. 34. 9. [k] Ex. 16. 31. [l] 1 Sa. 25. 33. [m] 1 Sa. 14. 29, 43. [n] Ge. 45. 17. [o] Je. 40. 7. [p] Is. 3. 16.

טִפֻּחִים masc. pl. (of טִפֻּח) *a nursing of children*, La. 2. 20, comp. the Root.

מִטְפַּחַת fem. pl. מִטְפָּחוֹת (§ 44. rem. 5) *upper garment, mantle, cloak*.

טֶפַח noun masc. sing. dec. 6 (§ 35. rem. 5) . טפח

טֹפַח ׳וְ noun masc. sing.; for וְ see lett. ו . . טפח

טִפְּחָה[a] Piel pret. 3 pers. sing. fem. . . . . טפח

טְפָחוֹת[b] noun masc. with pl. fem. term. fr. טֶפַח d. 6 (§ 35. rem. 5) . . . . טפח

טְפֻחִים[c] noun masc. pl. [from טִפֻּח] . . . . טפח

טִפַּחְתִּי[d] Piel pret. 1 pers. sing. . . . . טפח

טַפְּכֶם ׳וְ noun masc. sing., suff. 2 pers. pl. masc. from טַף dec. 8d . . . טפף

[טָפַל] *to devise, contrive, forge* (Talm. *to join, to sew on*). Prof. Lee, *to cover, conceal*.

טָפְלוּ[e] Kal pret. 3 pers. pl. . . . . טפל

טֹפְלֵי[f] id. part. act. pl. c. masc. fr. [טֹפֵל] dec. 7b טפל

טַפָּם[g] ׳וְ noun masc. sing., suff. 3 pers. pl. masc. from טַף dec. 8d . . . . טפף

טַפֵּנוּ[h] ׳וְ id. with suff. 1 pers. pl. . . . טפף

טִפְסָר׳[i] masc. *general, chief*.

טַפְסְרַיִךְ[k] ׳וְ id. pl., suff. 2 pers. sing. fem.

[טָפַף] *to trip, mince*, Is. 3. 16.

טַף masc. dec. 8d, *little ones, little children*.

[טְפַר] Chald. masc. dec. 3b.—I. *nail* of a man, Da. 4. 30. —II. *claw* of an animal, Da. 7. 19.

טִפְרַיהּ׳[l] ׳וְ Ch. noun masc. pl., suff. 3 pers. sing. fem. from [טְפַר] dec. 3b . . . . טפר

טִפְרוֹהִי׳[m] ׳וְ Ch. id., suff. 3 pers. sing. masc. . . טפר

טָפַשׁ *to be fat*, only metaph. *to be stupid*, Ps. 119. 70.

טֹפַת pr. name fem. . . . . . . נטף

טָרַד only part. act. *beating, tempestuous*, of rain, comp. Chald. טְרַד; others, *continual* i.e. *continual dropping*.

טְרַד Chald. *to thrust forth, to drive out*.

מַטְרֵד (*expeller*) pr. name masc. Ge. 36. 39.

טֹרֵד[n] Kal part. act. sing. masc. . . טרד

טָרְדִין[o] Ch. Peal part. act. masc., pl. of [טָרֵד] d. 2b טרד

טרה Root not used; Arab. *to be fresh, new*.

טָרִי adj. fem. טְרִיָּה, *fresh, moist*.

טָרַח. Hiph. *to load, burden*, Job 37. 11.

טֹרַח masc. dec. 6c (§ 35. rem. 5) *burden, trouble*

טָרְחֲכֶם[p] noun masc. sing., suff. 2 pers. pl. masc. from טֹרַח׳ dec. 6c (§ 35. rem. 5) . טרח

טְרִיד Ch. Peal part. pass. sing. masc. . . טרד

טְרִיָּה adj. fem. sing. [from טָרִי masc.] . טרה

טְרִים[q] noun masc. (for טוּרִים) pl. of טוּר dec. 1a טור

טֶרֶם[r] ׳וְ׳׳ adv. *not yet*; conj. בְּטֶרֶם *when not yet, before that*; טֶרֶם, מִטֶּרֶם id.

טְרוֹם *not yet*, Ru. 3. 14. Khethib.

טָרַף׳[s] ׳וְ fut. יִטְרֹף, יִטְרָף *to tear in pieces, to rend*. Niph. pass. Pu. id. Hiph. *to feed, provide for*, Pr. 30. 8.

טָרָף adj. masc. *fresh, new*, Ge. 8. 11. Others, *plucked off*.

טֶרֶף masc. dec. 6a (with suff. טַרְפּוֹ).—I. *prey*.—II. *food, provision*.—III. *leaf*, Eze. 17. 9, from the idea of *freshness*, comp. טָרָף.

טְרֵפָה fem. *any thing torn* by wild beasts.

טָרָף׳[t] ׳וְ Kal pret. 3 pers. s. m. for טָרַף (§ 8. r. 7) טרף

טָרָף[u] adj. masc. sing. . . . . טרף

טָרֹף Kal inf. absolute . . . טרף

טֶרֶף, טָרֶף[x] ׳וְ } noun masc. sing. dec. 6a (§ 35. r. 2) טרף

טֹרַף[y], טֹרָף[z] } Pual pret. 3 pers. s. m. (comp. § 8. r. 7) טרף

טֹרֵף Kal part. act. sing. masc. dec. 7b . טרף

טְרֵפָה׳ ׳וּ noun fem. sing.; וּ bef. (:) . . . טרף

טַרְפּוֹ[a] noun masc. sing., suff. 3 pers. sing. masc. from טֶרֶף dec. 6a . . . טרף

טַרְפֵּי[b] id. pl., constr. state . . . טרף

טֹרְפֵי[c] Kal part. act. pl. c. masc. fr. טֹרֵף dec. 7b טרף

טַרְפֵּךְ[d] noun masc. sing., suff. 2 pers. sing. fem. fr. טֶרֶף dec. 6a . . . . טרף

טַרְפְּלָיֵא Ch. pr. name of a people, Ezr. 4. 9.

---

[a] Is. 48. 13. [b] Ps. 39. 6. [c] La. 2. 20. [d] La. 2. 22. [e] Ps. 119. 69. [f] Job 13. 4. [g] Nu. 16. 27. [h] Nu. 14. 3. [i] Je. 51. 27. [k] Na. 3. 17. [l] Da. 7. 19. [m] Da. 4. 30. [n] Pr. 19. 13. [o] Da. 4. 22, 29. [p] De. 1. 12. [q] 1 Ki. 7. 20. [r] 1 Sa. 3. 7. [s] Job 16. 9. [t] Ho. 6. 1. [u] Ge. 8. 11. [x] Am. 3. 4. [y] Ge. 44. 28. [z] Ge. 37. 33. [a] Is. 31. 4. [b] Eze. 17. 9. [c] Eze. 22. 27. [d] Na. 2. 14.

י

[יָאַב] *to desire, long for,* with לְ. Ps. 119. 131

יְאַבֵּד[a] יְאַבֶּד־[b] } Piel fut. 3 pers. sing. masc. (§ 10. rem. 4) — אבד

יְאַבֵּד וְ id. with conj. וְ [for וִיאַבֵּד ,וְיְאַבֵּד] . — אבד

יֹאבַד יֹאבֵד } Kal fut. 3 pers. sing. masc. (§ 19. rem. 1) — אבד

יֵאבְדוּ[c] Chald. Peal fut. 3 pers. pl. masc. (§ 53) . — אבד

יְאָבְדוּ[d] Kh. יֹאבֵדוּ q. v., K. וְאָבְדוּ (q. v.) . — אבד

יֹאבֵדוּ וְ' / יֹאבְדוּ וַ"ּ, וְ' } Kal fut. 3 pers. pl. masc. (§ 19. rem. 1); ·וַ conv. . . — אבד

יְאַבְּדוּם וַ Piel fut. 3 pers. pl. masc., suff. 3 pers. pl. masc.; וַ id. . . . . . — אבד

יְאַבְּדֵם וַ id. fut. 3 pers. sing. m., suff. 3 pers. pl. m. — אבד

יֹאבֶה Kal fut. 3 pers. sing. masc. (§ 25. No. 2c) — אבה

יֹאבוּ[e] id. fut. 3 pers. pl. masc. . . . — אבה

יַאֲבֶל־[f] וַ Hiph. fut. 3 pers. sing. masc. ap. [for יַאֲבִל § 11. rem. 7]; ·וַ conv. . . — אבל

יֵאָבֵק[g] וַ Niph. fut. 3 pers. sing. masc.; ·וַ id. . — אבק

יַאֲבֶר־[h] Hiph. fut. 3 pers. sing. masc. ap. [for יַאֲבִר § 11. rem. 7] . . . . — אבר

יָאֲבְתִּי[i] Kal pret. 3 pers. s. [for יָאַבְתִּי § 8. rem. 7] — יאב

יַאְדִּימוּ[k] Hiph. fut. 3 pers. pl. m. (§ 13. rem. 5 & 9) — אדם

יַאְדִּיר[l] וְ Hiph. fut. 3 pers. s. m. (§ 13. rem. 5 & 9) — אדר

[יָאָה] *to be suitable, becoming,* with לְ. Je. 10. 7.

יֶאְהַב יֶאֱהַב יֶאֱהָב וַיֶּ' } Kal fut. 3 pers. sing. masc. (§ 8. rem. 15, & § 13. rem. 5); ·וַ conv. . — אהב

יֶאֱהָבֶהָ וַ id., suff. 3 pers. sing. fem. (§ 16. rem. 12) — אהב

יֶאֱהָבֵהוּ[m] וַ id., suff. 3 pers. sing. masc. (v. id.) . — אהב

יֶאֱהָבוֹ[n] וַ id., suff. 3 pers. sing. masc., Kh. 'בוֹ, K. 'בֵהוּ — אהב

יֶאֱהָבֶךָ[o] וְ id., suff. 2 pers. s. m. for ['הָבְךָ] (§ 2. r. 2) — אהב

יֶאֱהָבַנִי[p] id. with suff. 1 pers. sing. (§ 16. rem. 12) . — אהב

יַאֲהִיל[q] Hiph. fut. 3 pers. sing. masc. . . — אהל

יֶאֱהַל[r] וַ Kal fut. 3 pers. sing. masc.; ·וַ conv. . — אהל

יְאוֹר noun masc. sing. dec. 1a . . . — יאר

יְאוֹרֵי id. pl., constr. state . . . . — יאר

יֹאוֹשִׁיָּהוּ Kh., יֹאשִׁיָּהוּ K. (q. v.) . . . — אשה

יַאֲזִין Hiph. fut. 3 pers. sing. masc. . . — אזן

יַאֲזִינוּ[s] id. fut. 3 pers. pl. masc. . . . — אזן

יַאֲזַנְיָה יַאֲזַנְיָהוּ וְ } pr. name masc. . . . . — אזן

יַאַזְרֵנִי[t] Kal fut. 3 pers. sing. masc. [יֶאֱזוֹר comp. תֶּאֱזוֹר § 13. rem. 4], suff. 1 pers. s. (§ 13. rem. 6) — אזר

יֹאחֵז[u] וְ' / יֹאחֶז[x] וַ } Kal fut. 3 pers. sing. masc., acc. shifted by conv. ·וַ (§ 19. rem. 2) . — אחז

יֶאֱחֹז וַ id., with moveable א (§ 19. rem. 4); ·וַ id. — אחז

יֵאָחֲזוּ[y] וַ Niph. fut. 3 pers. pl. masc.; ·וַ id. . — אחז

יֹאחֲזוּ[z] וַ Kal fut. 3 pers. pl. masc.; ·וַ id. . . — אחז

יֹאחֲזוּהוּ[a] וַ id. id., suff. 3 pers. sing. masc.; ·וַ id. . — אחז

יֹאחֲזוּךְ[b] id. id., suff. 2 pers. sing. fem. . . — אחז

יֹאחֵזוּן[c] id. id. with parag. ן (§ 8. rem. 17) . — אחז

יֹאחֲזוּנִי[d] id. id., suff. 1 pers. sing. . . . — אחז

יֹאחֲזֵמוֹ[e] id. fut. 3 pers. sing. masc., suff. 3 pers. pl. m. — אחז

יְאַחֵר Piel fut. 3 pers. sing. masc. (§ 14. rem. 1) — אחר

יַאְטֵם[f] Hiph. fut. 3 pers. sing. masc. ap. [יַאֲטֵם, § 13. rem. 9, fr. יַאֲטִים] . . . — אטם

יָאִיצוּ[g] וַ Hiph. fut. 3 pers. pl. masc.; ·וַ conv. . — אוץ

יָאִיר וְ' pr. name masc. . . . . — אור

יָאִיר Hiph. fut. 3 pers. sing. masc. . . — אור

יָאִירוּ[h] id. fut. 3 pers. pl. masc. . . . — אור

יַאֲכִילֵהוּ[i] וַ Hiph. fut. 3 pers. sing. masc., suff. 3 pers. sing. masc.; ·וַ conv. . . . — אכל

יֵאָכֵל וַיֵּ'[k] Niph. fut. 3 pers. sing. masc.; ·וַ id. — אכל

יֵאכֻל[l] Chald. Peal fut. 3 pers. sing. masc. (§ 53) — אכל

יֹאכַל וְ' / יֹּאכַל וַ / יֹּאכַל וַ / יֹאכֵל } Kal fut. 3 pers. sing. masc.; acc. shifted by conv. ·וַ, but not so with distinctive accent (§ 19. rem. 1) . . — אכל

יֹאכְלֻהוּ id. fut. 3 pers. pl. masc., suff. 3 pers. s. m. — אכל

יֵאָכֵלוּ / יֵאָכְלוּ[m] } Niph. fut. 3 pers. pl. masc. (comp. § 8. rem. 15) . . . . . — אכל

יֹאכֵלוּ וַיּ', וְ'[n] / יֹאכְלוּ וַיּ', וְ' } Kal pret. 3 pers. pl. masc. (§ 19. rem. 1); ·וַ conv. . . — אכל

יֹאכְלוּהָ[o] וְ'[p] id., suff. 3 pers. sing. fem. . . — אכל

יַאֲכִלוּם[q] וַ Hiph. fut. 3 pers. pl. masc. [יַאֲכִיל], suff. 3 pers. pl. masc.; ·וַ conv. . . — אכל

יֹאכְלוּם[r] Kal fut. 3 pers. pl. masc., suff. 3 pers. pl. m. — אכל

יֹאכֵלוּן[s] / יֹאכְלוּן[t] } id. fut. 3 pers. pl. masc. with parag. ן (§ 8. rem. 17) . . . — אכל

יַאֲכִלְךָ[u] וַ Hiph. fut. 3 pers. sing. masc. [יַאֲכִיל], suff. 2 pers. sing. masc.; ·וַ conv. . . — אכל

יֹאכְלֵם וַיּ'[x] / יֹאכְלֵמוֹ[y] } Kal fut. 3 pers. sing. masc., suff. 3 pers. pl. masc.; ·וַ id. . . . — אכל

---

[a] Ec. 9. 18. [b] Pr. 29. 3. [c] Je. 10. 11. [d] Je. 6. 21. [e] Eze. 3. 7. [f] La. 2. 8. [g] Ge. 32. 25. [h] Job 39. 26. [i] Ps. 119. 131. [k] Is. 1. 18. [l] Is. 42. 21. [m] 1 Sa. 16. 21. [n] 1 Sa. 18. 1. [o] Pr. 9. 8. [p] Ge. 29. 32. [q] Job 25. 5. [r] Ge. 13. 12, 18. [s] Ps. 135. 17. [t] Job 30. 18. [u] Job 18. 9. [x] 2 Sa. 6. 6. [y] Ge. 47. 27. [z] Ju. 1. 6; 12. 6. [a] Ju. 16. 21. [b] Je. 13. 21. [c] Is. 13. 8. [d] Job 30. 16. [e] Ex. 15. 15. [f] Ps. 58. 5. [g] Ge. 19. 15. [h] Nu. 8. 2. [i] Ps. 81. 17. [k] Nu. 12. 12. [l] Da. 4. 30. [m] Le. 11. 13. [n] 2Ki. 4. 41, 42, 43. [o] Le. 6. 9. [p] Pr. 30. 17. [q] 2 Ch. 28. 15. [r] Eze. 44. 29. [s] De. 18. 1. [t] De. 4. 28. [u] De. 8. 3. [x] Ps. 78. 45. [y] Ex. 15. 7.

[a] יֹאכְלֶנָּה	id., suff. 3 pers. sing. fem. (§ 2. rem. 3)	אכל
[b] יַאֲכִלֵנוּ	Hiph. fut. 3 pers. s. m., [יַאֲכִיל] suff. 1 pers. pl.	אכל
יֹאכְלֶנּוּ	Kal fut. 3 pers. sing. masc., suff. 3 pers. sing. masc. (§ 2. rem. 3)	אכל
[c] יַּאֲכִלֵנִי	וַ Hiph. fut. 3 p. s. m., [יַאֲכִיל] suff. 1 p. s.; ·וַ conv.	אכל

I. יָאַל. Niph. נוֹאַל *to be foolish, to act foolishly.*

II. יָאַל. Hiph. הוֹאִיל.—I. *to begin, undertake.*—II. *to be willing, contented.*

[d] יֹאֶל, [e] יֹאֶל	וַ, וַ Hiph. fut. 3 pers. s. m. ap. [fr. יוֹאִיל]; acc. drawn back by conv. ·וַ (§ 20. rem. 9)	יאל
יֹאֶלְ	וַ Hiph. fut. 3 pers. sing. masc. ap. [for יֹאלֶה § 25. No. 2c, comp. § 19. rem. 8]	אלה
[g] יְאַלֵּף	Piel fut. 3 pers. sing. masc.	אלף
יַאֲמִין	Hiph. fut. 3 pers. sing. masc.	אמן
יַאֲמִינוּ	וַיַּ id. fut. 3 pers. pl. masc.; ·וַ conv.	אמן
[h] יַאֲמֵן	וַיַּ id. fut. 3 pers. sing. masc. ap. fr. יַאֲמִין	אמן
יֵאָמֵן, [k] יֵאָמֵן	וְ, [i] וְ Niph. fut. 3 pers. sing. masc. (§ 9. rem. 3)	אמן
יֵאָמְנוּ	וְ id. fut. 3 pers. pl. masc.	אמן
יַאֲמֵץ	וַ Hiph. fut. 3 pers. sing. m. ap. [fr. יַאֲמִיץ]	אמץ
[m] יְאַמֵּץ, [o] יְאַמֶּץ־	וְ, [n] וַ Piel fut. 3 pers. sing. masc.; (§ 10. rem. 4); וַ conv.	אמץ
[p] יֶאֱמָץ	Kal fut. 3 pers. sing. masc. [for יֶאֱמַץ, comp. § 8. rem. 15]	אמץ
[q] יְאַמְּצֵהוּ	וַ the foll. with suff. 3 pers. sing. m.; וַ conv.	אמץ
[r] יְאַמְּצוּ	וַ Piel fut. 3 pers. pl. masc.; וַ id.	אמץ
יֶאֱמְצוּ	וַ Kal fut. 3 pers. pl. masc.; ·וַ id.	אמץ
יֹאמֶר	וְ Kh. וַיֹּאמֶר or וַיֵּאָמֶר 2 Sa. 1. 8, & Ne. 7. 3, וַיֵּאָמֵר or וַיֹּאמַר Ne. 5. 9, & Zec. 4. 2, Kal or Niph. fut. 3 pers. sing. masc. (§ 19. rem. 2, & § 9. rem. 4 & 5); Keri. וָאֹמַר Kal fut. 1 pers. s. with וָ, for ·וַ, conv. (§ 19. rem. 2b)	
יֵאָמֵר, יֵאָמֵר, [u] יֵאָמֶר	[t] וַיֵּ Niph. fut. 3 pers. sing. m. (§ 9. rem. 4 & 3)	אמר
יֵאמַר	[w] וְ Chald. Peal fut. 3 pers. sing. masc. (§ 53)	אמר
יֹאמַר, יֹאמַר, יֹאמֶר	וְ, וַ, וַ Kal fut. 3 pers. sing. m. (§ 19. rem. 1 & 2)	אמר
[y] יֹאמְרוּ	וַ Kh. for וַיֹּאמְרוּ (q. v.)	אמר
יֹאמְרוּ, יֹאמְרוּ	וַיֹּ, וְ Kal fut. 3 pers. pl. masc. (§ 19. rem. 1); ·וַ conv.	אמר
יֹאמְרוּ	וַ Kh. מְרוּ q. v., K. מַר (q. v.)	אמר
[z] יְאֻנֶּה	Pual fut. 3 pers. sing. masc.	אנה

[a] יֵאָנַח	Niph. fut. 3 pers. sing. masc.; Milêl before monos. (comp. § 9. rem. 4)	אנח
[b] יֵאָנְחוּ	וְ id. fut. 3 pers. pl. masc.; ·וְ conv.	אנח
[c] יֶאֱנַף	Kal fut. 3 pers. sing. masc.	אנף
[d] יֶאֱנֹק	Kal fut. 3 pers. sing. masc. (§ 13. rem. 4)	אנק
[e] יֵאָנֵשׁ	וַ Niph. fut. 3 pers. sing. masc.; [for יֵאָנֵשׁ § 9. rem. 4]; ·וַ conv.	אנש
יֵאָסֵף, יֵאָסֵף	וַיֵּ, וְ Niph. fut. 3 pers. sing. masc. (§ 9. rem. 3); ·וְ id.	אסף
[f] יֹאסֶף	וַ for וַיּוֹסֶף Hiph. fut. 3 pers. sing. masc., with conv. ·וַ for יוֹסֶף, ap. fr. יוֹסִיף	יסף
יֶאֱסֹף	וַיֶּ Kal fut. 3 p. s. m. (§ 13. rem. 4); ·וַ conv.	אסף
[g] יַאַסְפֶהָ	וַ id. with suff. 3 pers. sing. fem. (§ 13. rem. 6)	אסף
[h] יַאַסְפֵהוּ	וַיַּ, [i] וְ id. with suff. 3 pers. sing. masc. (v. id.)	אסף
יַאַסְפוּ	וַ id. fut. 3 pers. pl. masc. (v. id.); ·וַ conv.	אסף
יֵאָסְפוּ, יֵאָסְפוּ	[k] וַיֵּ, וְ Niph. fut. 3 pers. pl. masc. (comp. § 8. rem. 15); ·וַ id.	אסף
[l] יֵאָסֵפוּן	id. with parag. ן (comp. § 8. rem. 17)	אסף
[m] יַאַסְפְךָ	Kal fut. 3 pers. sing. masc. [יֶאֱסֹף] suff. 2 pers. sing. masc. (§ 13. rem. 4 & 6)	אסף
[n] יַאַסְפֵם	וַ id., suff. 3 pers. pl. masc. (v. id.); ·וַ conv.	אסף
[o] יַאַסְפֵנִי	id. with suff. 1 pers. sing. (v. id.)	אסף
[p] יֵאָסֵר	Niph. fut. 3 pers. sing. masc.	אסר
[q] יֶאְסֹר, [r] יֶאְסֹר	וַיֶּ, וַ Kal fut. 3 pers. sing. masc. (§ 13. rem. 4 & 5); ·וַ conv.	אסר
יַאַסְרֵהוּ	וַ id. id., suff. 3 pers. sing. masc. (§ 13. rem. 6)	אסר
יַאַסְרֻהוּ, [s] יַאַסְרוּהוּ	וַ, וַ id. fut. 3 pers. pl. masc., suff. 3 pers. sing. masc. (v. id.); ·וַ conv.	אסר
[t] יַאַסְרוּם	וַ id. id., suff. 3 p. pl. m. (ם for ן fem. § 2. rem. 5)	אסר
[u] יַאַסְרוּנִי, [x] יַאַסְרֵנִי	id. id., suff. 1 pers. sing. (v. id.)	אסר
[y] יֶאְפֹּד	וַ Kal fut. 3 p. s. m. (§ 13. rem. 5); ·וַ conv.	אפד
[z] יֹאפוּ	[a] וַיֹּ Kal fut. 3 p. pl. m. (§ 25. No. 2c); ·וַ id.	אפה
[b] יָאצֶל	וַ Hiph. fut. 3 pers. sing. masc. ap. with conv. ·וַ [for יָאצִל, יָאצֶל § 19. rem. 8]	אצל
[c] יֵאָצֵר	Niph. fut. 3 pers. sing. masc.	אצר

[d] יְאֹר, יְאוֹר masc. dec. 1 a, *river*, especially the Nile; pl. יְאֹרִים *streams*, especially the artificial *canals* of the Nile.

יָאֵר, יָאֵר	וַ Hiph. fut. 3 p. s. m. ap. (§ 21. rem. 18) for יָאִיר	אור
[e] יֵאֹר	וַ [for יֵאוֹר] Niph. fut. 3 pers. s. m.; ·וַ conv.	אור
[f] יֶאֱרֹב	[g] וַיֶּ Kal fut. 3 p. s. m. (§ 13. rem. 4); ·וַ id.	ארב
יֶאֶרְבוּ, יֶאֱרֹבוּ	וַ id. fut. 3 pers. pl. masc. (§ 8. rem. 15)	ארב

[a] Le. 6. 11, 19. [b] Nu. 11. 4, 18. [c] Eze. 3. 2. [d] Job 6. 9. [e] 1 Sa. 17. 39. [f] 1 Sa. 14. 24. [g] Job 15. 5. [h] Job 15. 31. [i] 1 Ch. 17. 24. [k] 1 Ki. 8. 26. [l] Ge. 42. 20. [m] Am. 2. 14. [n] 2 Ch. 36. 13. [o] Is. 44. 14. [p] Ge. 25. 23. [q] 2 Ch. 24. 13. [r] 2 Ch. 11. 17. [s] 2 Ch. 13. 18. [t] Jos. 2. 2. [u] Is. 4. 3. [w] Da. 4. 32. [y] 1 Sa. 12. 10. [z] Pr. 12. 21. [a] Pr. 29. 2.

[b] Ex. 2. 23. [c] Ps. 2. 12. [d] Je. 51. 52. [e] 2 Sa. 12. 15. [f] 1 Sa. 18. 29. [g] 2 Sa. 11. 27. [h] 1 Sa. 14. 52. [i] Hab. 1. 15. [k] Is. 43. 9. [l] Ps. 104. 22. [m] Is. 58. 8. [n] 2 Ch. 29. 4. [o] Ps. 27. 10. [p] Ge. 42. 19. [q] 1 Ki. 20. 14. [r] Ge. 42. 24. [s] Ju. 16. 21. [t] 1 Sa. 6. 10. [u] Ju. 16. 11. [x] Ju. 16. 7. [y] Le. 8. 7. [z] Eze. 46. 20. [a] Ex. 12. 39. [b] Nu. 11. 25. [c] Is. 23. 18. [d] Eze. 29. 9. [e] 2 Sa. 2. 32. [f] Ps. 10. 9. [g] Ju. 9. 43.

[a] יֶאֶרְגוּ Kal fut. 3 pers. pl. masc. [for יֶאֶרְגוּ, from sing. יֶאֱרֹג § 8. rem. 15, & § 13. rem. 4] ארג
יְאֹרֵי noun masc. pl., constr. from יְאֹר dec. 1 a . יאר
[b] יְאֹרִי id. sing., suff. 1 pers. sing. . . . יאר
יְאֹרֵיהֶם id. pl., suff. 3 pers. pl. masc. . . . יאר
[c] יְאֹרָיו id. pl., suff. 3 pers. sing. masc. . . . יאר
יַאֲרִיךְ Hiph. fut. 3 pers. sing. masc. . . . ארך
[d] יְאֹרֶיךָ noun m. pl., suff. 2 pers. s.m. from יְאֹר dec. 1 a יאר
[e] יַאֲרִיכוּ [f] וַ״, וְ״ Hiph. fut. 3 pers. pl. masc.; ·וַ conv. ארך
[g] יַאֲרִיכוּן, [h] יַאֲרִכֻן } id. with paragogic ן . . . . ארך
יְאֹרִים noun masc. pl. abs. from יְאֹר dec. 1 a . יאר
וַ יַּאֲרִכוּ 1 Ki. 8. 8, defect. for יַאֲרִיכוּ (q.v.) . ארך
[i] יֶאֶרְכוּ Kal fut. 3 pers. pl. masc. . . . ארך
[k] יַאֲרִכֻן defect. for יַאֲרִיכוּן (q. v.) . . . ארך

יָאַשׁ Kal not used; Arab. *to despair, despond.* Niph. נוֹאַשׁ id., with מִן *to despair of, desist from,* 1 Sa. 27. 1; part. *desperate;* neut. *there is no hope, it is in vain.* Pi. *to render hopeless,* Ec. 2. 20.

יֹאָשׁ pr. name masc. for יְהוֹאָשׁ, יוֹאָשׁ (q. v.) . הוה
יֹאשִׁיָּה, יֹאשִׁיָּהוּ } pr. name masc. . . . . אשה
יֶאְשַׁם [l] וַ״ Kal fut. 3 pers. sing. masc. (§ 13. rem. 5); ·וַ conv. . . . אשם
יֶאְשְׁמוּ, יֶאְשָׁמוּ [m] וַ״, וְ״ } id. fut. 3 pers. pl. masc. (v. id. & § 8. rem. 15); ·וַ conv. . אשם
[n] יְאֻשַּׁר Kh. Pual fut. 3 pers. sing. masc.; K. וְאִשַּׁר pret. 3 pers. sing. masc. . . אשר
[o] יְאַשְּׁרֻהוּ Piel fut. 3 pers. pl. masc., suff. 3 pers. sing. m. אשר
וַ יְאַשְּׁרוּהָ id., suff. 3 pers. sing. fem.; וַ conv. . אשר
[p] וַ יֵּאת Kal fut. 3 pers. sing. masc. ap. [for יֵאֶת from יֶאֱתֶה, with conv. ·וַ, § 24. rem. 16, see § 19. rem. 3, & § 25. No. 2 c] . אתה
[q] יָאֲתָה Kal pret. 3 p. s. fem. [for יָאֲתָה § 8. rem. 7] יאה
יֶאֱתֶה Kal fut. 3 pers. sing. masc. . . . . אתה
[r] יֵאֹתוּ [s] וַ״ Niph., or Kal (comp. יֵבוֹשׁ from בּוֹשׁ) fut. 3 pers. pl.; וַ conv. . . . . אות
יֶאֱתָיוּ Kal fut. 3 pers. pl. masc. (§ 24. rem. 5) אתה
[t] וַ יֶּאֱתָיוּן id. with parag. ן; ·וַ conv. (v. id. & comp. § 8. rem. 17) . . . . . אתה
[u] וַ יֶּאֱתָיֻנִי id. with suff. 1 pers. sing. (§ 5. rem. 24); ·וַ id. אתה
יְאָתְרַי pr. name masc. 1 Ch. 6. 6.
וַ יָּבֵא Hiph. fut. 3 pers. s. m. ap. fr. יָבִיא; ·וַ conv. בוא
יָבֹא וַ״, וְ״ Kal fut. 3 pers. sing. masc. (§ 21. rem. 3, & § 25. No. 2); ·וַ conv. . . . בוא
יָבִא Hiph. fut. 3 pers. sing. masc. defect. for יָבִיא בוא

[x] יָבֹאº Kh. יָבֹא q. v.; K. וּבָא Kal pret. 3 pers. s. masc.; וּ for וְ conv. . . . בוא
וַ יְבִאֶהָ Hiph. fut. 3 pers. sing. masc. (יָבִיא), suff. 3 pers. sing. fem.; וַ conv. . . . בוא
[y] וַ יְבִאֵהוּ id. id., suff. 3 pers. sing. masc. . . בוא
[z] וַ יְבִאֻהוּ id. fut. 3 pers. pl. m. (יָבִיאוּ), suff. 3 p. s. m. בוא
[ff] וַ יָּבִאוּ id. fut. 3 pers. pl. masc. defect. for יָבִיאוּ בוא
יָבֹאוּ וַ״, וְ״ Kal fut. 3 pers. pl. masc. (§ 21. rem. 3, & § 25. No. 2 f); ·וַ conv. . . . בוא
וַ יָּבֹאוֹ Kh. יָבֹאוֹ q. v., K. יָבֹא (q. v.) . . בוא
[a] יָבֹאוּ Kh. יָבֹאוּ q. v., K. וּבָאוּ Kal pret. 3 pers. pl.; וּ for וְ conv. . . . . . בוא
[b] וַ יְבִאוּם Hiph. fut. 3 pers. pl. masc. (יָבִיאוּ), suff. 3 pers. pl. masc.; וַ conv. . . . בוא
[c] יְבֹאוּן Kal fut. 3 pers. pl. masc. with parag. ן (§ 21. rem. 3, & § 25. No. 2 f) . . . בוא
[kk] יְבֹאוּנִי id. fut. 3 pers. pl. m. with suff. 1 pers. s. (v. id.) בוא
יַבְאִישׁ Hiph. fut. 3 pers. sing. masc. . . . באשׁ
וַ יְבִאֵם Hiph. fut. 3 pers. sing. masc. (יָבִיא), suff. 3 pers. pl. masc.; וַ conv. . . . בוא
[e] וַ יְבִאֵנוּ id. with suff. 1 pers. pl. . . . בוא
וַ יְבִאֵנִי id. with suff. 1 pers. sing. . . . בוא
[f] יְבֹאֻנִי וִ for וִיבֹאֻנִי, defect. for יְבוֹאוּנִי (q. v.) . בוא
[g] יְבֹאֶנּוּ Kal fut. 3 pers. s. m. (יָבוֹא), suff. 3 pers. s. m. (§ 21. rem. 3, & § 25. No. 2 f, & § 2. rem. 3) בוא
וַ יִּבְאַשׁ Kal fut. 3 pers. sing. masc.; ·וַ conv. . באשׁ

יָבַב Pi. *to call aloud, to cry out,* Ju. 5. 28.
יוֹבָב (*crier;* Simonis, for יָאוֹב אָב, *desire of the father*) pr. name—I. of a descendant of Joktan and a people descended from him.—II. of a king of Edom.—III. of a king of the Canaanites, Jos. 11. 1.—IV. 1 Ch. 8. 9.—V. ibid. ver. 18.

[h] יִבְגֹּד Kal fut. 3 pers. sing. masc. . . . בגד
[i] יִבְגְּדוּ וַ״ id. fut. 3 pers. pl. masc.; ·וַ conv. . בגד
יַבְדִּיל Hiph. fut. 3 pers. sing. masc. . . . בדל
[k] יַבְדִּילוּ [l] וַ״ id. fut. 3 pers. pl. masc.; ·וַ conv. . בדל
[m] וַ יַּבְדִּילֵם id. fut. 3 pers. sing. masc., suff. 3 pers. pl. masc.; ·וַ id. . . . . בדל
[n] יַבְדִּילַנִי id. id., suff. 1 pers. sing. for לְנִי . בדל
וַ יַּבְדֵּל id. fut. 3 pers. s. m. ap. fr. יַבְדִּיל; ·וַ conv. בדל
[o] יִבָּדֵל [p] וַ״ Niph. fut. 3 pers. sing. masc.; ·וַ id. בדל
וַ יִּבָּדְלוּ id. fut. 3 pers. pl. masc.; ·וַ id. . בדל
[q] וַ יְבַהֲלוּהוּ Hiph. fut. 3 pers. pl. masc., suff. 3 pers. sing. masc.; ·וַ id. . . . . בהל
[r] וַ יִּבָּהֵל Niph. fut. 3 pers. sing. masc.; ·וַ id. . בהל
[s] וַ יְבַהֵל Piel fut. 3 pers. s. m. (§ 14. r. 1); וַ id. בהל

---

a Is. 59. 5. b Eze. 29. 3. c Eze. 29. 3. d Eze. 29. 4, 5, 10. e De. 25. 15. f 2 Ch. 5. 9. g Ex. 20. 12. h De. 5. 16. i Eze. 12. 22. k De. 6. 2. l Ho. 13. 1. m Eze. 6. 6. n Ps. 41. 3. o Ps. 72. 17. p Is. 41. 25. q Je. 10. 7. r Ge. 34. 22. s 2 Ki. 12. 9. t Is. 41. 5. u Job 3. 25. x Pr. 18. 17. y Ex. 22. 12. z Eze. 19. 9. a Ju. 6. 5. b Jos. 7. 23. c Ps. 95. 11. d Ps. 119. 77. e De. 26. 9. f Ps. 119. 41. ff 1 Ki. 5. 8. g Pr. 28. 22. h Mal. 2. 15. i Is. 33. 1. k Eze. 39. 14. kk Ps. 119. 77. l Ne. 13. 3. m 2 Ch. 25. 10. n Is. 56. 3. o Ezr. 10. 8. p 1 Ch. 23. 13. q 2 Ch. 26. 20. r Ju. 20. 41. s Est. 2. 9.

[a]יְבַהֲלֻהוּ	id. fut. 3 pers. pl. masc., suff. 3 pers. s. m.	בהל
[b]יַבְהִלוּ	וַ Hiph. fut. 3 pers. pl. masc.; וַ· conv.	בהל
יִבָּהֲלוּ	וְ Niph. fut. 3 pers. pl. masc.	בהל
[c]יְבַהֲלוּךְ	Ch. Pael fut. 3 pers. pl. masc., suff. 2 pers. sing. masc. (comp. § 14. rem. 1)	בהל
[d]יִבָּהֲלוּן	Niph. fut. 3 pers. pl. masc. with parag. ן (comp. § 8. rem. 17)	בהל
[e]יְבַהֲלוּנֵּהּ	Ch. Pael fut. 3 pers. pl. masc., suff. 3 pers. sing. masc. (§ 50)	בהל
[f]יְבַהֲלָךְ	Ch. id. fut. 3 pers. s. m., suff. 2 pers. s. m.	בהל
[g]יְבַהֶלְךָ	וִ Piel fut. 3 pers. sing. m. [יְבַהֵל § 14. r. 1], suff. 2 pers. s. m. with conj. וְ [וִי, וִיבַהֵל]	בהל
[h]יְבַהֲלֵמוֹ	id., suff. 3 pers. pl. masc.	בהל
[i]יְבַהֲלֻנֵּהּ	Ch. Pael fut. 3 pers. pl. masc., suff. 3 pers. sing. masc. (§ 50)	בהל
יְבַהֲלֻנַּנִי	Ch. id., suff. 1 pers. sing.	בהל
[k]יָבוֹ	וַ Kheth., for וַיָּבֹא K. (q. v.)	בוא
יָבוֹא	וַיָּ, וְ Kal fut. 3 p. s. m. (§ 21. r. 3); וַ· conv.	בוא
יָבוֹאוּ	וַיָּ, וְ id. fut. 3 pers. pl. masc. ·וַ id.	בוא
[m]יְבוֹאֶנּוּ	id. fut. 3 pers. sing. masc., suff. 1 pers. pl.	בוא
[n]יְבוֹאֶנּוּ	id. id., suff. 3 pers. sing. masc.	בוא
[o]יָבוּז	Kal fut. 3 pers. sing. masc.	בוז
יָבוּזוּ	id. fut. 3 pers. pl. masc.	בוז
[p]יָבוֹל	וַ Kal fut. 3 pers. sing. masc. Kheth. יָבוֹל (§ 18. rem. 2) K. יָבֹל; וַ· conv.	בלל
יִבּוֹל	Kal fut. 3 pers. sing. masc. (§ 17. rem. 3)	נבל
יְבוּל	noun masc. sing. dec. 1 a	יבל
יְבוּלָהּ, [q]יְבוּלָהּ	id., suff. 3 pers. sing. fem., with cop. וְ [וִי, וִיבוּלָה]	יבל
[r]יְבוּלָם	id., suff. 3 pers. pl. masc.	יבל
[s]יְבוֹנְנֵהוּ	Pilel fut. 3 pers. sing. m., suff. 3 pers. s. m.	בין
יָבוּס	Kal fut. 3 pers. sing. masc.	בוס
יְבוּס	pr. name of a place	בוס
יְבוּסִי	gent. noun from the preceding	בוס
[t]יָבוֹשׁ	Kal inf. abs.	יבש
[u]יֵבוֹשׁ	וְ Kal fut. 3 pers. sing. masc. (§ 21. rem. 6)	בושׁ
יֵבֹשׁוּ	id. fut. 3 pers. pl. masc.	בושׁ
יִבֶז	וַ Kal fut. 3 p. s. m. ap. [for יִבְזֶה]; וַ· conv.	בזה
[x]יִבְזֵהוּ	וַ id. id., suff. 3 pers. sing. masc.; וַ· id.	בזה
[y]יִבְזֻהוּ	וַ id. fut. 3 pers. pl. masc., suff. 3 pers. s. m.	בזה
[z]יָבֹזּוּ	וַיָּ, וְ Kal fut. 3 pers. pl. masc.; וַ· conv.	בזז
[a]יָבוּזוּ	Kal fut. 3 pers. pl. masc.	בוז
[b]יִבְזוּ	וַ Kal fut. 3 pers. pl. masc.; וַ· conv.	בזה
[c]יְבֻזּוּם	Kal fut. 3 pers. pl. masc. (יָבֹזּוּ), suff. 3 pers. pl. masc. (§ 18. rem. 5)	בזז
[d]יְבַזּוֹר	Kal fut. 3 pers. sing. masc. (§ 8. rem. 18)	בזר
[e]יִבָּחֵן	Niph. fut. 3 pers. sing. masc.	בחן
[f]יִבְחָן	Kal fut. 3 pers. sing. m. [fr. יִבְחַן § 8. r. 15]	בחן
[g]יִבָּחֲנוּ	וְ Niph. fut. 3 pers. pl. masc.	בחן
[h]יִבְחָנֵהוּ	Kal fut. 3 pers. sing. masc.	בחן
יִבְחָר	וְ pr. name masc.	בחר
יִבְחַר, וַיִּ יִבְחַר	Kal fut. 3 pers. sing. masc. (§ 8. rem. 15); וַ· conv.	בחר
[i]יְבֻחַר	Kheth. Pual fut. 3 pers. sing. m. (dag. impl. comp. § 14. r. 1) R. בחר; K. יְחֻבַּר id., R.	חבר
[k]יִבְחָרוּ	וְ Kal fut. 3 pers. pl. masc.	חבר
[l]יִבְחָרֶךָ	וַ id. fut. 3 pers. sing. masc. (יִבְחַר), suff. 2 pers. sing. masc. (§ 16. r. 12, & § 2. r. 2)	חבר
יַבֵּט	וַ Hiph. fut. 3 pers. sing. masc., ap. fr. יַבִּיט; וַ· conv.	נבט
[m]יְבַטֵּא	[n]וַיְ Piel fut. 3 pers. sing. masc.; וַ id.	בטא
יַבְטַח	[o]וַיַּ Hiph. fut. 3 pers. sing. masc. ap. fr. יַבְטִיחַ; וַ· id.	בטח
[p]יִבְטַח, [q]וַיִּ יִבְטַח	Kal fut. 3 pers. sing. masc. (§ 8. rem. 15); וַ· id.	בטח
יִבְטְחוּ	וַיִּ, וְ id. fut. 3 pers. pl. masc.; וַ· id.	בטח
[r]יָבִיא	וַ for וַיָּבֵא, ap. from יָבִיא (q. v.)	בוא
יָבִיא	[s]וַיָּ Hiph. fut. 3 pers. sing. masc.; וַ· conv.	בוא
[t]יְבִיאֶהָ	וַ, וְ id. id., suff. 3 pers. sing. fem.	בוא
יְבִיאֵהוּ	וַ id. id., suff. 3 pers. sing. masc.	בוא
יְבִיאֻהוּ	וַ id. fut. 3 pers. pl. masc. (יָבִיאוּ), suff. 3 pers. sing. masc.	בוא
יָבִיאוּ	וַיָּ id. fut. 3 pers. pl. masc.	בוא
[u]יְבִיאוּם	וַ id. id., suff. 3 pers. pl. masc.	בוא
[x]יְבִיאוּן	id. id. with parag. ן	בוא
[y]יְבִיאוּנִי	id. id., suff. 1 pers. sing.	בוא
יְבִיאֲךָ	id. fut. 3 pers. s. m. (יָבִיא), suff. 2 p. s. m.	בוא
[z]יְבִיאֵם	וַ id. id., suff. 3 pers. pl. masc.	בוא
[a]יְבִיאֶנָּה	id. id., suff. 3 pers. sing. fem. (§ 2. rem. 3)	בוא
יְבִיאֶנּוּ	id. id., suff. 3 pers. sing. masc. (v. id.)	בוא
יְבִיאֵנִי	וַ id. id., suff. 1 pers. sing.	בוא
יַבִּיט	Hiph. fut. 3 pers. sing. masc.	נבט
יַבִּיטוּ	id. fut. 3 pers. pl. masc.	נבט
יָבִין	pr. name masc.	בין
[mm]יָבִין	Hiph. or Kal, fut. 3 pers. s. masc. R. בון or	בין
[b]יְבִינֵהוּ	וַ Hiph. fut. 3 pers. sing. masc., suff. 3 pers. sing. masc. R. בון see	בין
יָבִינוּ	[c]וַיָּ Kal fut. 3 pers. pl. masc.; וַ· conv.	בין
יַבִּיעַ	Hiph. fut. 3 pers. sing. masc.	נבע
יַבִּיעוּ	id. fut. 3 pers. pl. masc.	נבע
[d]יַבִּיעוּן	id. id. with parag. ן	נבע

[a] Da. 11. 44. [b] Est. 6. 14. [c] Da. 5. 10. [d] Ps. 104. 29. [e] Da. 5. 6. [f] Da. 4. 16. [g] Job 22. 10. [h] Ps. 2. 5. [i] Da. 4. 16. [k] 1 Ki. 12. 12. [l] Eze. 33. 31. [m] Is. 28. 15. [n] Job 15. 21. [o] Pr. 23. 9. [p] Ju. 19. 21. [q] De. 32. 22. [r] Ps. 78. 46. [s] De. 32. 10. [t] Zec. 11. 17. [u] Is. 29. 22. [x] 1 Sa. 17. 42. [y] 1 Sa. 10. 27. [z] Ps. 109. 11. [a] Ca. 8. 1. [b] Ne. 2. 19. [c] Zep. 2. 9. [d] Da. 11. 24. [e] Job 34. 36. [f] Ps. 11. 5. [g] Ge. 42. 16. [h] Ps. 11. 4. [i] Ec. 9. 4. [k] 1 Ki. 18. 23. [l] Is. 49. 7. [m] Le. 5. 4. [mm] Is. 28. 9. [n] Ps. 106. 33. [o] Je. 29. 31. [p] Pr. 28. 1. [q] Ps. 52. 9. [r] Eze. 40. 3. [s] Ne. 8. 2. [t] Ex. 35. 5. [u] 1 Ch. 9. 28. [x] Ex. 18. 26. [y] Ps. 43. 3. [z] Nu. 27. 17. [a] Le. 4. 32. [b] Is. 40. 14. [c] Ne. 8. 8. [d] Ps. 59. 8.

יָבִישׁ pr. name of a place, see יָבֵשׁ . . . . יבשׁ

יָבֵישָׁה id. with parag. ה . . . . יבשׁ

יֵבְךְּ וַ Kal fut. 3 pers. sing. masc. ap. [fr. יִבְכֶּה § 24. rem. 3]; וַ conv. . . . בכה

יִבְכּוּ וַיִּ׳ id. fut. 3 pers. pl. masc. . . בכה

[a]יִבְכָּיוּן id. id. with parag. ן (§ 24. r. 5, & § 8. r. 17) בכה

[b]יְבַכֵּר Piel fut. 3 pers. sing. masc. . . . בכר

[c]יְבֻכַּר Pual fut. 3 pers. sing. masc. . . . בכר

יָבַל Kal not used; Arab. *to flow, run*. Hiph. הוֹבִיל *to lead, bring, bring forth, carry*. Hoph. pass.

יְבַל Ch. Aph. *to bring*, Ezr. 5. 14; 6. 5.

יָבָל masc. dec. 4a.—I. *stream, river*.—II. pr. name of a son of Lamech, Ge. 4. 20.

יַבָּל, fem. יַבֶּלֶת (§ 39. No. 4) *flowing, running*, as a sore, Le. 22. 22.

יוֹבֵל masc. dec. 7b.—I. *protracted sound*, hence קֶרֶן הַיּוֹבֵל *the horn* by which the like *sound* is produced; in the same sense pl. שׁוֹפְרוֹת יוֹבְלִים, הַיּוֹבְלִים; ellipt. יוֹבֵל for the instrument, Ex. 19. 13.—II. שְׁנַת הַיּוֹבֵל and ellipt. יוֹבֵל, *the year of jubilee*, celebrated every fiftieth year and so called from *the sounding of trumpets* on the tenth day of the seventh month, by which it was announced to the people, comp. Le. 25. 9.

יוּבַל masc.—I. *river*, Je. 17. 8.—II. pr. name of a son of Lamech, Ge. 4. 21.

יְבוּל masc. dec. 1a.—I. *produce, increase* of the earth.—II. *provision, wealth*, Job 20. 28.

בּוּל masc. (for יְבוּל).—I. *produce, increase*, Job 40. 20; בּוּל עֵץ *trunk of wood*, Is. 44. 19.—II. the name of the eighth Hebrew month, answering to our October, 1 Ki. 6. 38.

אֻבָל, אוּבָל masc. *river, canal*, Da. 8. 2, 3, 6.

מַבּוּל masc. *inundation, deluge*.

תֵּבֵל fem. (for תֵּיבֵל).—I. *the world, the earth*, especially the inhabited part of it.—II. *the world, the inhabitants of the world*.

תֻּבַל, תּוּבַל (*diffusion, propagation*) pr. name of a son of Japheth, used meton. for his descendants, a people of Asia Minor.

תּוּבַל קַיִן (*propagation of Cain*) pr. name of the third son of Lamech by Zillah, Ge. 4. 22.

יָבָל pr. name masc. . . . . . יבל

[d]יְבַלֵּא Ch. Pael fut. 3 pers. sing. masc. R. בְּלָא see בלה

[e]יִבְלֶה Kal fut. 3 pers. sing. masc. . . . בלה

[f]יְבוּלָהּ וְ noun masc. sing. with suff. from יְבוּל dec. 1a, with conj. וְ [for וִיבוּלָהּ, וִי׳] . יבל

יְבַלּוּ Piel fut. 3 pers. pl. masc. . . . בלה

יִבְלוּ Kal fut. 3 pers. pl. masc. . . . בלה

יִבֹּלוּ Kal fut. 3 pers. pl. masc. [§ 17. rem. 3, for יִבְּלוּ § 8. rem. 15] . . . . נבל

[bb]יֹבִלוּהָ Hiph. fut. 3 pers. pl. masc. (יוֹבִיל) suff. 3 pers. sing. masc. . . . . . יבל

[g]יִבֹּלוּן Kal fut. 3 pers. pl. masc. with parag. ן (§ 17. rem. 3, & § 8. rem. 17) . . . נבל

יִבְלֵי noun masc. pl. constr. from [יָבָל] dec. 4a יבל

[h]יֹבִלֵנִי Hiph. fut. 3 pers. s. m. [יוֹבִיל] suff. 1 pers. s. יבל

[i]יְבַלַּע Piel fut. 3 pers. sing. masc. . . . בלע

[k]יִבְלַע, [l]וַיִּבְלַע Kal fut. 3 pers. sing. masc. (comp. § 8. rem. 15); וַ conv. . . . בלע

[m]יְבֻלַּע, [n]יְבֻלָּע Pual fut. 3 pers. sing. masc. (comp. § 8. rem. 15) . . . בלע

[o]יִבְלָעֻהוּ Kal fut. 3 pers. pl. masc. (יִבְלְעוּ from sing. יִבְלַע), suff. 3 pers. sing. m. (§ 16. r. 12) בלע

[p]יְבַלְּעֵם Piel fut. 3 pers. s. m. (יְבַלַּע), suff. 3 pers. pl. m. בלע

יִבְלְעָם וְ׳ pr. name of a place . . . בלע

[q]יִבְלָעֶנָּה Kal fut. 3 pers. sing. masc. (יִבְלַע), suff. 3 pers. sing. fem. (§ 16. rem. 12) . . בלע

יְבַלְּעֶנּוּ Piel fut. 3 pers. s. m. (יְבַלַּע), suff. 3 pers. s. m. בלע

[r]יַבֶּלֶת (prop. adj.) subst. fem. sing. [from יַבָּל m.] יבל

[יָבָם] masc. dec. 4a, *brother-in-law, husband's brother*, who when the husband died without issue, was obliged to marry the widow, to raise up seed to him. Hence

Pi. יִבֵּם *to marry the brother's wife*.

יְבֵמֶת fem. dec. 13b, *a sister-in-law, a brother's wife*; also *the wife of a husband's brother*.

[s]יַבֵּם וְ Piel imp. sing. masc. . . . יבם

[t]יִבְּמָהּ וְ id. pret. 3 pers. s. m., suff. 3 p. s. f.; וְ conv. יבם

[u]יְבָמָהּ noun m. s., suff. 3 pers. s. fem. fr. [יָבָם] dec. 4a יבם

[x]יַבְּמִי Piel inf. [יַבֵּם], suff. 1 pers. sing. dec. 7b . יבם

[y]יְבָמִי noun m. s., suff. 1 pers. s. fr. [יָבָם] dec. 4a יבם

[z]יְבִמְתּוֹ noun f. s., suff. 3 pers. s. m. fr. [יְבֵמֶת] d. 13b יבם

[a]יְבִמְתֵּךְ id., suff. 2 pers. sing. fem. . . . יבם

יַבְנְאֵל וְ׳ pr. name of a place . . . . בנה

יַבְנֵה pr. name of a place . . . . בנה

יָבֵן וְ, יָבֶן וַ Kal fut. 3 pers. sing. masc., ap. fr. יָבִין; acc. drawn back by וַ conv. . . בין

[b]יִבֶן וְ, וַיִּ׳ Kal fut. 3 pers. sing. masc., ap. fr. יִבְנֶה; וַ id. . . . בנה

[a] Job 31. 38. Is. 33. 7. [b] Eze. 47. 12. [c] Le. 27. 26. [d] Da. 7. 25. [e] Job 13. 28. [f] De. 32. 22. [g] Ps. 37. 2. [h] Ps. 108. 11. [i] Pr. 19. 28. [k] Job 20. 18. [l] Ex. 7. 12. [m] Job 37. 20. [n] 2 Sa. 17. 16. [o] Ho. 8. 7. [p] Ps. 21. 10. [q] Is. 28. 4. [r] Le. 22. 22. [s] Ge. 38. 8. [t] De. 25. 5. [u] De. 25. 5. [x] De. 25. 7. [y] De. 25. 7. [z] De. 25. 7, 9. [a] Ru. 1. 15. [b] Ezr. 1. 3. [bb] Is. 23. 7.

יִבָּנֶה	Niph. fut. 3 pers. sing. masc. . . .	בנה
יִבְנֶה[a]	וַיִּ׳, וְיִ׳ Kal fut. 3 pers. sing. masc. . .	בנה
יִבְנֵהוּ[b]	וַיִּ׳[c] id. id., suff. 3 pers. sing. m. (§ 24. r. 21)	בנה
יִבְנוּ	וַיִּ׳ id. fut. 3 pers. pl. masc. . . .	בנה
יִבְנוֹן[d]	Chald. Peal fut. 3 pers. pl. masc. . .	בנה
יִבְנְיָה / וְ יִבְנִיָּה	pr. name masc.	בנה
יִבְנֵם[e]	Kal fut. 3 pers. sing. masc. (יִבְנֶה), suff. 3 pers. pl. masc. (§ 24. rem. 21) .	בנה
יִבְנֶנּוּ[f]	id. with suff. 3 pers. sing. masc. (v. id.) .	בנה
יִבְעֵא[g]	Chald. Peal fut. 3 pers. sing. masc. . .	בעא
יְבַעוֹן[oo]	Chald. Pael fut. 3 pers. pl. masc. (dag. forte impl. comp. § 14. rem. 1) . . .	בעא
יִבְעַט[h]	וַ Kal fut. 3 pers. sing. masc.; ·ִ· conv. .	בעט
יִבְעָל[i]	Kal fut. 3 pers. sing. masc. . . .	בעל
יִבְעָלוּךְ[k]	id. fut. 3 pers. pl. [יִבְעֲלוּ], suff. 2 pers. sing. fem. (§ 16. rem. 12) . . .	בעל
וַ יַבְעֵר / וַיַּ׳[m] יַבְעֶר־[l]	Hiph. fut. 3 pers. sing. masc. apoc. (§ 11. rem. 7); ·ַ· conv. .	בער
יְבַעֵר[n]	Piel fut. 3 pers. sing. masc. (§ 14. rem. 1)	בער
יִבְעַר[o] / וַיִּ׳[p] יִבְעָר	Kal fut. 3 pers. sing. masc. (comp. § 8. rem. 15) . . .	בער
יְבַעֲרוּ[q]	Piel fut. 3 pers. pl. masc. (§ 14. rem. 1) .	בער
יִבְעֲרוּ[r]	Kal fut. 3 pers. pl. masc.	בער
יְבַעֲתֻהוּ	Piel fut. 3 pers. pl. m. (§ 14. rem. 1), suff. 3 pers. sing. masc.	בעת
יְבַעֲתוּנִי[s] / יְבַעֲתֻנִי[t]	id. with suff. 1 pers. sing. . . .	בעת
יְבַצַּע[u]	Piel fut. 3 pers. sing. masc. . . .	בצע
יִבְצָע[x]	Kal fut. 3 pers. sing. masc. [for יִבְצַע, comp. § 8. rem. 15]	בצע
יִבְצָעוּ[y]	id. fut. 3 pers. pl. masc. [for יִבְצְעוּ v. id.]	בצע
יְבַצְּעֵנִי[z] / וִ יבַצְּעֵנִי[a]	Piel fut. 3 pers. sing. masc., suff. 1 pers. sing. with cop. וְ [for וִיבַצְּעֵנִי, וִיְ׳]	בצע
יִבָּצֵר	Niph. fut. 3 pers. sing. masc. . . .	בצר
יִבְצֹר[b]	Kal fut. 3 pers. sing. masc. . . .	בצר
יִבְצְרוּ[c]	וַ id. fut. 3 pers. pl. masc.; ·ִ· conv. .	בצר
יַבֹּק	pr. name of a torrent	בקק
יִבָּקַע[d] / יִבָּקֵעַ[e]	Niph. fut. 3 pers. sing. masc. (§ 15 rem. 1)	בקע
יְבַקַּע[f]	וַיְ׳[g] Piel fut. 3 pers. sing. masc. . .	בקע
יִבְקַע	וַ Kal fut. 3 pers. sing. masc.; ·ִ· conv. .	בקע
יִבָּקְעוּ[h]	וַ Niph. fut. 3 pers. pl. masc.; ·ִ· id. .	בקע
יְבַקְּעוּ[i]	וַ Piel fut. 3 pers. pl. masc.; ·ַ id. . .	בקע
יִבְקְעוּ	וַ Kal fut. 3 pers. pl. masc.; ·ִ· id. .	בקע
יְבֻקָּעוּ[k]	Pual fut. 3 p. pl. m. [for יְבֻקְּעוּ comp. § 8. r. 15]	בקע

יִבְקָעוּהָ[l]	וַ Kal fut. 3 pers. pl. masc. (יִבְקְעוּ fr. sing. יִבְקַע), suff. 3 pers. sing. fem. (§ 16. r. 12)	בקע
יְבֹקְקוּ[m]	וְ Poel fut. 3 p. pl. m.; with cop. וְ [for וִיבֹ׳, וִיְ׳]	בקק
יְבַקַּר[n]	Chald. Pael fut. 3 pers. sing. m. (§ 49. r. 4)	בקר
יְבַקֵּר	Piel fut. 3 pers. sing. masc. . . .	בקר
יְבַקֵּשׁ / וַיְ׳ יְבַקֶּשׁ־	Piel fut. 3 pers. sing. masc. (§ 10. rem. 4); ·ַ conv. . . .	בקש
יְבֻקַּשׁ[o]	וִ׳[p] Pual fut. 3 pers. sing. masc.; ·ִ id.	בקש
יְבַקְשֵׁהוּ[q]	וַ Piel fut. 3 pers. sing. masc. (יְבַקֵּשׁ), suff. 3 pers. sing. masc. (§ 10. rem. 7); ·ַ id.	בקש
יְבַקְשֻׁהוּ	וַ id. id. fut. 3 pers. pl. masc., suff. 3 pers. s. m.	בקש
יְבַקְשׁוּ / וַיְ׳ יְבַקֵּשׁוּ	id. id. fut. 3 pers. pl. masc. (comp. § 8. rem. 15, & § 10. rem. 7); ·ַ conv.	בקש
יְבַקְשׁוּ	וִ id. id. with cop. וְ [for וִיבַקְשׁוּ, וִיְ׳] .	בקש
יִבְרָא[r]	וַיִּ׳ Kal fut. 3 pers. sing. masc.; ·ִ· conv. .	ברא
יִבָּרֵאוּן[s]	Niph. fut. 3 pers. pl. masc. with parag. ן (comp. § 8. rem. 17)	ברא
יִבְרַח / וַיִּ׳ יִבְרַח[u]	Kal fut. 3 pers. sing. masc. (comp. § 8. rem. 15); ·ִ· conv. .	ברח
יִבְרְחוּ[x]	וַיִּ׳ id. fut. 3 pers. pl. masc. . .	ברח
יַבְרִיחַ[y]	Hiph. fut. 3 pers. sing. masc. . . .	ברח
יַבְרִיחוּ[z]	וַ id. fut. 3 pers. pl. masc.; ·ַ· conv. .	ברח
יַבְרִיחֶנּוּ[a]	id. fut. 3 pers. sing. masc., suff. 3 pers. s. m.	ברח
יַבְרֵךְ[b]	וַ Hiph. fut. 3 pers. sing. masc. ap. [fr. יַבְרִיךְ]; ·ַ· conv. . . .	ברך
יִבְרַךְ[c]	וַ Kal fut. 3 pers. sing. masc.; ·ִ· id. .	ברך
יְבָרֵךְ / וִ יְבָרֵךְ / וַ יְבָרֶךְ	Piel fut. 3 pers. sing. masc. with cop. וְ [for וִיבָרֵךְ, וִיְ׳]; acc. drawn back by conv. ·ַ (§ 14. rem. 2) . .	ברך
יְבֹרַךְ / יְבֹרָךְ	Pual fut. 3 pers. sing. masc. (comp. § 8. rem. 15)	ברך
וַ יְבָרְכֵהוּ / וַ יְבָרְכֵהוּ	Piel fut. 3 pers. sing. masc., suff. 3 pers. sing. masc.; ·ַ conv. . .	ברך
יְבָרְכוּ[d] / וַ יְבָרֲכוּ / וִ יְבָרְכוּ / וִ יְבָרְכוּ[e]	id. fut. 3 pers. pl. masc.; ·ַ conv.; with cop. וְ [for וִיבָרְכוּ, וִיְ׳]	ברך
יְבָרְכוּכָה[f]	id. id., suff. 2 pers. sing. masc. (§ 2. rem. 2)	ברך
יְבֶרֶכְיָהוּ	pr. name masc.	ברך
יְבָרֶכְךָ / יְבָרֶכְךָ[g] / וִ יְבָרֶכְךָ[h]	Piel fut. 3 pers. sing. masc., suff. 2 pers. sing. masc. (§ 2. rem. 2); with cop. וְ [for וִיבָ׳, וִיבָרֶכְךָ] .	ברך
וַ יְבָרְכֵם / וַ יְבָרְכֵם	id. id., suff. 3 pers. pl. masc.; ·ַ conv.	ברך
יְבָרְכֶנְהוּ[i]	id. id. with epenth. נ (§ 16. rem. 13) & suff. 3 pers. sing. masc. . . .	ברך

a Ps. 69. 36. b Job 20. 19. c 1 Ki. 6. 38. d Ezr. 6. 7. e Ps. 28. 5. f Ne. 3. 14, 15. g Da. 6. 8, 13.
h De. 32. 15. i Is. 62. 5. k Is. 62. 5. l Ex. 22. 4. m Ju. 15. 5. n 1 Ki. 14. 10. oo Da. 4. 33.
o Is. 62. 1. p La. 2. 3. q Eze. 39. 10. r Je. 10. 8. s Ps. 18. 5. t 2 Sa. 22. 5.
u Is. 10. 12. x Job 27. 8. y Joel 2. 8. z Is. 38. 12. a Job 6. 9. b Ps. 76. 13.
c Ju. 9. 27. d Is. 58. 8. e Job 32. 19. f Ps. 78. 15. g Ge. 22. 3. h Ex. 14. 21.
i 1 Sa. 6. 14. k Ho. 14. 1. l 2 Ch. 21. 17. m Je. 51. 2. n Ezr. 4. 15. o Je. 50. 20.
p Est. 2. 23. q 1 Sa. 23. 14. r Nu. 16. 30. s Ge. 1. 21, 27. t Ps. 104. 30. u Job 20. 24.
x Je. 52. 7. y Pr. 19. 26. z 1 Ch. 12. 15. a Job 41. 20. b Ge. 24. 11. c 2 Ch. 6. 13.
d Ps. 62. 5. e Ne. 9. 5. f Ps. 145. 10. g Job 1. 11; 2. h Ge. 49. 25. i Ps. 72. 15.

[a]יְבָרְכֵנוּ / [b]וִיבָרְכֵנוּ } id. id. with suff. 1 pers. pl.; with cop. וִ [for וִיבָ׳, וִיבָרְכֵנוּ] ברך

[c]יְבָרְכֵנִי וַ id. id. with suff. 1 pers. sing.; וַ conv. ברך

יָבֵשׁ וְ fut. יִיבַשׁ, *to be* or *become dry, to dry up.* Pi. *to make dry, to dry up.* Hiph.—I. *to dry up;* (*b*) intrans. *to be dried up.*—II. cogn. בּוֹשׁ *to make ashamed,* 2 Sa. 19. 6; (*b*) intrans. *to be ashamed, to be put to shame, be disgraced;* (*c*) *to act shamefully,* Ho. 2. 7.

יָבֵשׁ masc. dec. 5a, adj. יְבֵשָׁה fem. dec. 10.—I. *dry.*—II. pr. name of a town in Gilead, written also יָבֵישׁ.—III. pr. name of a man, 2 Ki. 15. 10, 13, 14.

יַבֶּשֶׁת, יַבָּשָׁה fem. *dry land.*

יַבֶּשֶׁת Chald. fem. id. emph. יַבֶּשְׁתָּא, Da. 2. 10.

יָבֵשׁ adj. masc. dec. 5a, also pr. name . . יבשׁ
[d]יָבוֹשׁ Kal inf. absolute . . . . יבשׁ
[e]יָבֵשׁ [f]וַיִּ׳ id. fut. 3 pers. s. m. for יִיבַשׁ; ·וַ conv. יבשׁ
יָבֵשָׁה pr. name of a place (יָבֵשׁ) with parag. ה יבשׁ
[g]יַבָּשָׁה noun fem. sing. . . . . יבשׁ
[h]יְבֵשָׁה adj. fem. sing. dec. 10, from יָבֵשׁ masc. יבשׁ
[i]יָבְשָׁה Kal pret. 3 pers. sing. fem. . . יבשׁ
[k]יַבְּשֵׁהוּ וְ Piel imp. masc. s., with suff. 3 pers. s. m. יבשׁ
[l]יָבְשׁוּ / יָבֵשׁוּ } וְ Kal pret. 3 pers. pl. (§ 8. rem. 7) . יבשׁ
יֵבֹשׁוּ וַיֵּ׳, וְ׳ Kal fut. 3 p. pl. m. (§ 21. r. 6); ·וַ conv. בושׁ
[m]יִבְשׁוּ [n]וְ׳, [o]וַיִּ׳ Kal fut. 3 pers. pl. masc. [for יִיבְשׁוּ § 8. rem. 15]; ·וַ conv. . . . . יבשׁ
[p]יְבֵשׁוֹת adj. fem., pl. of יְבֵשָׁה dec. 10, fr. יָבֵשׁ masc. יבשׁ
[q]יְבֵשִׁים וִ id. masc., pl. of יָבֵשׁ d. 5a [for וִיבֵ׳, וִיבֵ׳] יבשׁ
[r]יְבַשְּׁלוּ וַי׳ Piel fut. 3 pers. pl. masc.; וַ conv. . בשׁל
יִבְשָׂם וְ pr. name masc. . . . . בשׂם
[s]יְבַשְּׂרוּ Piel fut. 3 p. pl. m. [יְבַשְּׂרוּ] comp. § 8. r. 15] בשׂר
[t]יַבֶּשֶׁת וְ noun fem. sing. . . . . יבשׁ
[u]יְבֹשֶׁת Kal inf. constr. (§ 20. rem. 3) . . יבשׁ
[y]יַבֶּשְׁתָּא Ch. noun fem. sing., emph. of יַבֶּשֶׁת . יבשׁ
[z]יְבַתֵּר וַ Piel fut. 3 pers. sing. masc.; וַ conv. . בתר
[a]יִגְאֶה וְ Kal fut. 3 pers. sing. masc.; ·וְ id. . גאה
יִגָּאֵל Niph. fut. 3 pers. sing. masc. . . גאל
יִגְאָל וְ׳ pr. name masc. . . . . גאל
[b]יִגְאַל / יִגְאָל } Kal fut. 3 pers. sing. masc. (comp. § 8. rem. 15) . . . גאל
[c]יִגְאָלֻהוּ id. fut. 3 p. pl. m., suff. 3 p. s.m. (§ 16. r. 12) גאל
יְגֹאֲלוּ וַ Pual fut. 3 pers. pl. masc.; וְ׳ conv. . גאל
יִגְאָלֵךְ Kal fut. 3 pers. sing. masc. (יִגְאַל), suff. 2 pers. sing. fem. (§ 16. rem. 12) . . גאל

[d]יִגְאָלֵם וַ id., suff. 3 pers. pl. masc. (v. id.) . גאל
[e]יִגְאָלֶנָּה id., suff. 3 pers. sing. f. (v. id. & § 2. r. 3) . גאל
[f]יִגְאָלֶנּוּ id. with suff. 3 pers. sing. masc. (v. id.) . גאל

[יָגַב] i. q. גּוּב *to plough, till;* part. pl. יֹגְבִים *ploughmen,* 2 Ki. 25. 12, Keri, Je. 52. 16.

יָגֵב masc. dec. 5a, *field,* Je. 39. 10.

[g]יִגְבַּהּ וַיִּ׳ Kal fut. 3 pers. sing. masc.; ·וַ conv. . גבה
יָגְבְּהָה וְ pr. name of a place . . . גבה
[h]יִגְבְּהוּ / יִגְבָּהוּ } וְ Kal fut. 3 pers. pl. masc. (§ 8. r. 15); ·וַ conv. . . . גבה
[k]יִגְבּוֹל Kal fut. 3 pers. sing. masc. (§ 8. rem. 18) גבל
[l]יַגְבִּיהַּ Hiph. fut. 3 pers. sing. masc. . . גבה
[m]יַגְבִּיהֶהָ וְ id. id., suff. 3 pers. sing. fem. . . גבה
[n]יַגְבִּיהוּ id. fut. 3 pers. pl. masc. . . . גבה
[o]יֹגְבִים וְ noun m. pl. of יָגֵב d. 5c [for וְיֹגְ׳, וְיֹגְ׳] יגב
[p]יְגַבֵּר Piel fut. 3 pers. sing. masc. . . . גבר
[q]יִגְבַּר Kal fut. 3 pers. sing. masc. . . . גבר
[r]יִגְבְּרוּ וַ id. fut. 3 pers. pl. masc.; ·וַ conv. . גבר
[s]יָגֵד Kal fut. 3 pers. sing. masc. [for יָגוּד] . גוד
יַגֵּד / יַגֶּד־ } וְ / וַיַּ׳, וְ Hiph. fut. 3 pers. sing. masc. ap. (§ 11. rem. 7); ·וַ conv. . נגד
יֻגַּד וַ Hoph. fut. 3 pers. sing. masc.; ·וַ conv. נגד
[t]יַגִּדֶהָ וְ Hiph. fut. 3 pers. sing. masc. (יַגִּיד), suff. 3 pers. sing. fem. . . . . נגד
יַגִּדוּ וַיַּ׳ id. fut. 3 pers. pl. masc.; ·וַ conv. . נגד
יַגְדִּיל Hiph. fut. 3 pers. sing. masc. . . גדל
[u]יַגְדִּילוּ וַ id. fut. 3 pers. pl. masc.; ·וַ conv. . גדל
[x]יְגַדְּךָ וְ Piel fut. 3 pers. sing. masc., suff. 2 pers. sing. masc. [for יַגֶּדְךָ § 16. rem. 16] נגד
[y]יְגַדֵּל / [a]יְגַדֵּל } [z]וַיְ׳, וְ Piel fut. 3 pers. sing. masc.; וַ conv., with cop. וִ (וִי׳, וִיגַדֵּל for וִיגַדֵּל וְ) גדל
[b]יִגְדַּל / יִגְדָּל } וַיִּ׳, וְ׳, וַיִּ׳ Kal fut. 3 pers. sing. masc. (comp. § 8. rem. 15); ·וַ conv. . גדל
[c]יְגַדְּלֵהוּ וַ Piel fut. 3 pers. sing. masc. (יְגַדֵּל), suff. 3 pers. sing. masc.; וַ id. . . גדל
[d]יְגַדְּלוּ id. fut. 3 pers. pl. masc. . . . גדל
[e]יִגְדְּלוּ / יִגְדָּלוּ } וַ Kal fut. 3 pers. pl. masc. (§ 8. rem. 15); ·וַ conv. . . . גדל
יִגְדַּלְיָהוּ pr. name masc. . . . . גדל
[f]יְגַדַּע וַ Piel fut. 3 pers. sing. masc.; וַ conv. . גדע
[g]יְגַדְּעוּ וַ id. fut. 3 pers. pl. masc. . . . גדע

יָגָה Niph. נוּגָה (§ 20. rem. 5) *to be afflicted, grieved.* Pi. *to afflict, grieve,* La. 3. 33.

[a] Ps. 67. 7, 8. [b] Ps. 67. 2. [c] Ge. 30. 27. [d] Eze. 17. 10. [e] Is. 19. 7. [f] Ps. 102. 5. [g] Is. 44. 3. [h] Nu. 11. 6. [i] Ge. 8. 14. [k] Na. 1. 4. [l] Joel 1. 12. [m] Job 18. 16. [n] Job 12. 15. [o] Is. 40. 24. [p] Eze. 37. 2. [q] Nu. 6. 3. [r] Eze. 46. 20, 24. [s] 2 Ch. 35. 13. [t] Is. 60. 6. [u] Ps. 95. 5. [x] Ge. 8. 7. [y] Da. 2. 10. [z] Ge. 15. 10. [a] Job 10. 16. [b] Ru. 3. 13. [c] Job 3. 5. [d] Ps. 106. 10. [e] Le. 27. 13. [f] Le. 25. 48, 49. [g] Pr. 18. 12. [h] Job 36. 7. [i] Eze. 31. 14. [k] Jos. 18. 20. [l] Job 39. 27. [m] 2 Ch. 33. 14. [n] Job 5. 7. [o] Je. 39. 10. [p] Ec. 10. 10. [q] 1 Sa. 2. 9. [r] Ge. 7. 18, 24. [s] Ge. 49. 19. [t] Je. 9. 11. [u] Zep. 2. 8, 10. [x] De. 32. 7. [y] Is. 44. 14. [z] 1 Ch. 29. 25. [a] 1 Ki. 1. 37, 47. [b] Ge. 48. 19. [c] 2 Ch. 1. 1. [d] Ho. 9. 12. [e] Ru. 1. 13. [f] 2 Ch. 14. 2. [g] 2 Ch. 31. 1.

Hiph. הוֹגָה.—I. *to afflict, grieve.*—II. *to remove,* 2 Sa. 20. 13.

יָגוֹן masc. dec. 3a, *affliction, grief, sorrow.*

תּוּגָה fem. dec. 10, *sorrow, grief, vexation.*

וַיַּגֶּה[a] Piel fut. 3 pers. sing. masc. [for וַיְיַגֶּה § 20. rem. 8]; וַ· conv. . . . . יגה

יִגַּהּ[b] Kal fut. 3 pers. sing. masc. . . . . נגה

יִגְהֶה[c] Kal fut. 3 pers. sing. masc. . . . . גהה

וַיִּגְהַר Kal fut. 3 pers. sing. masc.; וַ· conv. . גהר

יָגוֹדּוּ[d] Kal fut. 3 pers. pl. masc. [for יָגֹדּוּ § 18. rem. 2] גדד

יְגוּדֶנּוּ Kal fut. 3 p. s. m., suff. 3 p. s. m. or 1 p. pl. (§ 2. r. 3) גוד

יָגוֹל[e] Kh. יָגוּל, K. יָגִיל Kal fut. 3 pers. sing. masc. R. גול or . . . . . . גיל

וְיָגוֹן noun masc. sing. dec. 3a . . . יגה

יִגְוַע[f], וַיִּגְוַע[g] } Kal fut. 3 pers. sing. masc. (§ 8. rem. 15); וַ· conv. . . . } גוע

יִגְוָעוּ[h], וְיִגְוָעוּ[i] } Kal fut. 3 pers. pl. masc. (§ 8. rem. 15) גוע

יִגְוָעוּן[k] id. with parag. ן (§ 8. rem. 17) . . גוע

יָגוֹר[l] adj. or part. sing. masc. (§ 26. No. 3, § 8. rem. 1, § 9. rem. 20) . . . . יגר

וְיָגוּר Kal fut. 3 pers. sing. masc.; also pr. name גור

יָגוּרוּ id. fut. 3 pers. pl. masc. . . . גור

יְגוֹרֵם[m] Kal fut. 3 pers. sing. masc. [יָגֹר], suff. 3 pers. pl. masc. [for יְגֹרֵּם=יְגָרֵם § 18. rem. 5] גרר

וַיָּגָז[n] Kal fut. 3 pers. sing. masc. with conv. וַ· [for יָגֹז § 18. rem. 5] . . . . גזז

וַיָּגָז[o] Kal fut. 3 pers. sing. masc. with conv. וַ· [for יָגֹז ap. from יָגוּז] . . . . גוז

יִגְזֹל[p] וַיִּ' Kal fut. 3 pers. sing. masc.; וַ· conv. גזל

יִגְזְלוּ[q] וַיִּ'[r] id. fut. 3 pers. pl. masc.; וַ· id. . גזל

וַיִּגְזֹר[s] Kal fut. 3 pers. sing. masc.; וַ· id. . . גזר

וַיִּגְזְרוּ[t] id. fut. 3 pers. pl. masc.; וַ· id. . . גזר

יִגַּח[u], יִגַּח[x] } Kal fut. 3 pers. sing. m. (comp. § 8. rem. 15) נגח

יַגִּיד[y], יַגִּיד } according to some copies . . Hiph. fut. 3 pers. sing. masc. . . } נגד

וְיַגִּידָה[z] id. id., suff. 3 pers. sing. fem. . . נגד

יַגִּידוּ וַיַּ', וְ' id. fut. 3 pers. sing. masc.; וַ· conv. נגד

יַגִּיהַּ Hiph. fut. 3 pers. sing. masc. . . נגה

יָגִיחַ[a] Kal fut. 3 pers. sing. masc. . . . גיח

יָגִיל[b] Kh. יָגִיל q.v., K. יָגֵל ap. from יָגִיל (§ 22. r. 3) גיל

יָגִיל[c] וְ[d] Kal fut. 3 pers. sing. masc. . . . גיל

יָגִילוּ id. fut. 3 pers. pl. masc. . . . גיל

יְגִילוּן[e] id. id. with parag. ן . . . . גיל

וַיַּגַּע[f] וְ' Hiph. fut. 3 pers. sing. masc. . . נגע

יְגִיעַ noun masc. sing. dec. 1a . . . יגע

יְגִיעָהּ id., suff. 3 pers. sing. fem. . . . יגע

יַגִּיעוּ[g] וַיַּ' Hiph. fut. 3 pers. pl. masc.; וַ· conv. נגע

יְגִיעוֹ[h] noun masc. sing., suff. 3 pers. sing. masc. from יְגִיעַ dec. 1a . . . . יגע

יְגִיעִי[i] id. pl. with suff. 1 pers. sing. . . יגע

יְגִיעֵי[k] adj. masc. pl. constr. from [יָגִיעַ] dec. 3a יגע

יְגִיעֲךָ[l], יְגִיעֶךָ[m] } noun masc. sing., suff. 2 pers. sing. masc. from יְגִיעַ dec. 1a . . } יגע

יְגִיעֵךְ[n] id. with suff. 2 pers. sing. fem. . יגע

וִיגִיעֲכֶם[o] id., suff. 2 pers. pl. masc. with cop. וְ [for וִי', וִיגִ'] . . . . יגע

וִיגִיעָם[p] id., suff. 3 pers. pl. masc. comp. preceding יגע

יַגִּיעֶנָּה[q] Hiph. fut. 3 pers. s. m., suff. 3 pers. sing. fem. נגע

יָנִיפוּ[r] Hiph. fut. 3 pers. pl. masc. . . נוף

יַגִּירֻהוּ[s] Hiph. fut. 3 pers. pl. m. [יַגִּירוּ], suff. 3 p. s. m. נגר

יַגִּשׁוּ[u] וַיַּ' Hiph. fut. 3 pers. pl. masc.; וַ· conv. . נגש

יָגֵל, וְיָגֵל[x] } Kal fut. 3 pers. sing. masc., ap. from יָגִיל (§ 22. rem. 3) . . . } גיל

וַיָּגֶל[y] Hiph. fut. 3 pers. sing. masc. with conv. וַ [for יָגֵל § 18. rem. 11] . . . גלל

וַיְגַל Piel fut. 3 pers. s. m. ap. for יְגַלֶּה; וַ conv. גלה

וַיֶּגֶל Hiph. fut. 3 pers. sing. masc. ap. [fr. יַגְלֶה] גלה

יִגֶל[z] וַיִּ', וְ'[a] Kal fut. 3 p. s. m. ap. fr. יִגְלֶה; וַ· conv. גלה

וְיִגָּל[b] Niph. fut. 3 pers. sing. masc. . . גלל

וְיַגְלֶהָ[c] Hiph. fut. 3 pers. sing. masc., suff. 3 pers. sing. fem. (§ 24. rem. 21) . . . גלה

יִגָּלֶה[d] Niph. fut. 3 pers. sing. masc. . . גלה

יְגַלֶּה[e] Piel fut. 3 pers. sing. masc. . . . גלה

יִגְלֶה Kal fut. 3 pers. sing. masc. . . . גלה

יִגָּלוּ[f] וַיִּ' Niph. fut. 3 pers. pl. masc.; וַ· conv. גלה

יְגַלּוּ[g] Piel fut. 3 pers. pl. masc. . . . גלה

יִגְלוּ[h] Kal fut. 3 pers. pl. masc. . . . גלה

וַיַּגְלוּם[i] Hiph. fut. 3 p. pl. m., suff. 3 p. pl. m.; וַ· conv. גלה

יְגַלַּח, וַיְגַלַּח } וַ' Piel fut. 3 pers. sing. masc. (§ 15. rem. 1); וַ conv. . . } גלח

יְגַלְּחוּ id. fut. 3 p. pl. m. [for יְגַלְּחוּ comp. § 8. rem. 15] גלח

וַיְגַלְּחֵם[k] id. fut. 3 p. s. m., suff. 3 pers. pl. m.; וַ conv. גלח

יְגַלְּחֶנּוּ[l] id. id., suff. 3 pers. sing. masc. (§ 2. rem. 3) גלח

יָגְלִי pr. name masc. . . . . . גלה

וַיַּגְלֵם Hiph. fut. 3 pers. sing. masc. [יַגְלֶה], suff. 3 pers. pl. masc. (§ 24. rem. 21) . . גלה

וְיִגְלֹם[m] Kal fut. 3 pers. sing. masc.; וַ· conv. . גלם

[a] La. 3. 33. [b] Job 18. 5. [c] Ho. 5. 13. [d] Ps. 94. 21. [e] Pr. 23. 24. [f] Ge. 6. 17. [g] Job 34. 15.
[h] Zec. 13. 8. [i] Job 36. 12. [k] Ps. 104. 29. [l] Je. 22. 25; 39. 17. [m] Pr. 21. 7. [n] Job 1. 20. [o] Nu. 11. 31.
[p] Eze. 18. 7. [q] Job 24. 9, 19. [r] Ju. 9. 25. [s] Is. 9. 19. [t] 2 Ki. 6. 4. [u] Ex. 21. 31. [x] Ex. 21. 28, 31.
[y] Ec. 10. 20. [z] Is. 44. 7. [a] Job 40. 23. [b] Ps. 21. 2. [c] Zep. 3. 17. [d] Hab. 1. 15. [e] Ps. 89. 17.
[f] Da. 12. 12. [g] Ps. 107. 18. [h] Ps. 109. 11. [i] Ho. 12. 9. [k] Job 3. 17. [l] De. 28. 33.
[m] Job 39. 11. [n] Eze. 23. 29. [o] Is. 55. 2. [p] Ps. 78. 46. [q] Is. 26. 5. [r] Ne. 7. 3.
[s] Ps. 63. 11. [t] Is. 41. 22. [u] 2 Ch. 29. 23. [x] Ps. 16. 9. [y] Ge. 29. 10. [z] Job 20. 28.
[a] Job 36. 15. [b] Am. 5. 24. [c] 2 Ki. 16. 9. [d] 1 Sa. 3. 7. [e] De. 23. 1. [f] 2 Sa. 22. 16.
[g] Job 20. 27. [h] Am. 6. 7. [i] 1 Ch. 8. 6. [k] 1 Ch. 19. 4. [l] Nu. 6. 9. [m] 2 Ki. 2. 8.

יִגְמָא־[a] Piel fut. 3 pers. s. m. [for יְגַמֵּא § 10. rem. 4] גמא

יִגָּמֵל[b] / יִגָּמֵל[c] וְ Niph. fut. 3 pers. sing. masc. (§ 9. rem. 3 & 4); וַ conv. גמל

יִגְמֹל[d] וְ Kal fut. 3 pers. sing. masc.; וַ id. גמל

יִגְמְלֵנִי id. with suff. 1 pers. sing. גמל

יִגְמֹר[e] / יִגְמָר־[f] Kal fut. 3 pers. sing. masc. (§ 8. rem. 18) גמר

יָגֵן Kal fut. 3 pers. sing. masc. גנן

יִגָּנֵב[g] Niph. fut. 3 pers. sing. masc. גנב

יִגְנֹב[h] וַיִּ Kal fut. 3 pers. sing. masc.; וַ conv. גנב

יְגַנֵּב[k] וַ Piel fut. 3 pers. sing. masc.; וַ id. גנב

יְגֻנַּב[l] Pual fut. 3 pers. sing. masc. [for יְגֻנַּב comp. § 8. rem. 15] גנב

יִגְנְבוּ[m] Kal fut. 3 pers. pl. masc. גנב

יִגְנוֹב[n] Kal fut. 3 pers. sing. masc. (§ 8. rem. 18) גנב

[יָגַע] fut. יִיגַע.—I. *to labour, toil.*—II. *to be wearied, fatigued with labour*, with בְּ. Pi. *to weary, fatigue.* Hiph. *to weary, be troublesome.*

יְגַע masc. *labour*, meton. *earnings*, Job 20. 18.

יָגֵעַ adj. masc. dec. 5a, *weary, fatigued, exhausted.*

יָגִיעַ adj. masc. dec. 3a, id. Job 3. 17.

יְגִיעַ masc. dec. 1a.—I. *labour, toil.*—II. *fruit of labour, earnings, gain, wealth.*

יְגִיעָה fem. dec. 10, *labour, exertion*, Ec. 12. 12.

יְגָע[o] noun masc. sing. יגע

יָגֵעַ[p] וְ[q] adj. masc. sing. dec. 5a יגע

יַגַּע וַ Hiph. fut. 3 pers. s. m. ap. fr. יַגִּיעַ; וַ conv. נגע

יִגַּע וַיִּ, וְ[r] Kal fut. 3 pers. sing. masc.; וַ id. נגע

יָגְעָה[s] Kal pret. 3 pers. sing. fem. יגע

יִגְעֶה[t] Kal fut. 3 pers. sing. masc. געה

יִגְעוּ[u] / יִגָעוּ[x] וְ / וְ[y] Kal fut. 3 pers. pl. masc. [for יִיגְעוּ, יִיגָעוּ § 20. rem. 2, & § 8. rem. 15] יגע

יִגְּעוּ Kal fut. 3 pers. pl. masc. נגע

יְגֵעִים[z] adj. masc., pl. of יָגֵעַ dec. 5a יגע

יַגְעִל[a] Hiph. fut. 3 pers. sing. masc. [for יַגְעִיל] געל

יָגַעְנוּ[b] Kal pret. 1 pers. pl. יגע

יִגְעַר[c] וַיִּ, וְ Kal fut. 3 pers. sing. masc.; וַ conv. גער

יִגְעֲשׁוּ[d] Pual fut. 3 pers. pl. masc. געש

יָגַעְתָּ Kal pret. 2 pers. sing. masc. יגע

יָגָעַתְּ[e] / יָגַעַתְּ Kal pret. 2 pers. sing. fem. (§ 8. rem. 15) יגע

יְגִעַת[f] noun fem. sing., constr. of [יְגִיעָה] dec. 10. יגע

יָגַעְתִּי Kal pret. 1 pers. sing. יגע

יִגֹּף וַיִּ Kal fut. 3 pers. sing. masc. (§ 17. r. 3); וַ conv. נגף

יִגְּפֵהוּ[g] / יִגְּפֶנּוּ[h] וְ id., suff. 3 pers. sing. masc. (§ 2. rem. 3, & § 8. rem. 14) נגף

[יָגֹר] 2 pers. יָגֹרְתָּ (§ 8. rem. 1) *to fear, be afraid*, with מִפְּנֵי.

יָגוֹר adj. masc. *fearing, afraid*, Je. 22. 25; 39. 17.

יְגַר Ch. masc. *heap of stones*, Ge. 31. 47.

יַגֵּר[i] וְ Hiph. fut. 3 pers. sing. masc. ap. [fr. יַגִּיר]; וַ conv. נגר

יָגָר וְ Kal fut. 3 pers. sing. masc. [with וַ conv. for יָגֹר, ap. fr. יָגוּר]. גור

יִגָּר[k] Niph. fut. 3 pers. sing. masc. [for יִגַּר] גרר

יְגָרֶה Piel fut. 3 pers. sing. masc. גרה

יְגֹרֵהוּ[l] Kal fut. 3 pers. sing. masc. [יָגֹר], suff. 3 pers. sing. masc. [for יְגֻרֵהוּ § 18. rem. 5] גרר

יְגֻרֶךָ[m] Kal fut. 3 pers. sing. masc. (יָגוּר), suff. 2 pers. sing. masc. גור

יְגָרֵם[n] Piel fut. 3 pers. sing. masc. גרם

יָגְרֶם[o] וְ Hiph. fut. 3 pers. sing. masc. ap. [from יַגְרִים]; וַ conv. גרם

יְגָרַע[p] Piel fut. 3 pers. sing. masc. גרע

יִגָּרַע[q] / יִגָּרֵעַ Niph. fut. 3 pers. sing. masc. (§ 15. rem. 1, comp. § 8. rem. 15) גרע

יִגְרַע[r] / יִגְרָע[s] Kal fut. 3 pers. sing. masc. (§ 8. rem. 15) גרע

יְגָרֵשׁ[t] / יְגָרֵשׁ וְ Piel fut. 3 pers. sing. masc. (§ 10. rem. 4); וְ conv. גרש

יְגָרְשֵׁהוּ[u] וְ id. id., suff. 3 pers. sing. masc.; וְ conv. גרש

יְגָרְשׁוּ[x] וְ id. fut. 3 pers. pl. masc.; וְ id. גרש

יְגֹרְשׁוּ[y] Pual fut. 3 pers. pl. masc. [for יְגֻרְשׁוּ comp. § 8. rem. 15] גרש

יִגְרְשׁוּ[z] וְ Kal fut. 3 pers. pl. masc.; וַ conv. גרש

יְגָרְשׁוּהָ[a] Piel fut. 3 pers. pl. masc., suff. 3 pers. s. f. גרש

יְגָרְשׁוּם[b] וְ id. id., suff. 3 pers. pl. masc. (for ן fem. § 2. rem. 5); וְ conv. גרש

יְגָרְשֵׁם[c] id. fut. 3 pers. sing. m., suff. 3 pers. pl. m. גרש

יָגֹרְתָּ[d] Kal pret. 2 pers. sing. masc. (§ 8. rem. 1) יגר

יָגֹרְתִּי id. pret. 1 pers. sing. (v. id.) יגר

יַגֵּשׁ[e] / יַגֶּשׁ[f] / יַגֶּשׁ־[g] וַיִּ / וְ / וְ Hiph. fut. 3 pers. sing. masc. ap. [for יַגִּישׁ § 11. rem. 6 & 7]; וַ conv. נגש

יִגַּשׁ[h] / יִגַּשׁ וַיִּ Kal fut. 3 pers. sing. masc. (§ 8. rem. 15); וַ conv. נגש

יִגֹּשׂ[i] Kal fut. 3 pers. sing. masc. (§ 17. rem. 3) נגש

יַגִּשׁוּ וְ Hiph. fut. 3 p. pl. m. (for יַגִּישׁוּ); וַ conv. נגש

[a] Job 39. 24. [b] Ge. 21. 8. [c] 1 Sa. 1. 22. [d] Nu. 17. 23. [e] Ps. 138. 8. [f] Ps. 7. 10. [g] Ex. 22. 11. [h] Ex. 21. 37. [i] Ge. 31. 20. [k] 2 Sa. 15. 6. [l] Job 4. 12. [m] Ob. 5. [n] Pr. 6. 30. [o] Job 20. 18. [p] 2 Sa. 17. 2. [q] De. 25. 18. [r] 2 Sa. 5. 8. [s] 2 Sa. 23. 10. [t] Job 6. 5. [u] Is. 40. 30. [x] Is. 65. 23. [y] Je. 51. 58. [z] Ec. 1. 8. [a] Job 21. 10. [b] La. 5. 5. [c] Zec. 3. 2. [d] Job 34. 20. [e] Is. 47. 15. [f] Ec. 12. 12. [g] 2 Ch. 13. 20. [h] 1 Sa. 26. 10. [i] Ps. 75. 9. [k] Le. 11. 7. [l] Hab. 1. 15. [m] Ps. 5. 5. [n] Nu. 24. 8. [o] La. 3. 16. [p] Job 36. 27. [q] Nu. 36. 3. [r] Ex. 21. 10. [s] Job 36. 7. [t] Ex. 11. 1. [u] Ps. 34. 1. [x] Ju. 11. 2. [y] Job 30. 5. [z] Is. 57. 20. [a] Zep. 2. 4. [b] Ex. 2. 17. [c] Ex. 6. 1. [d] De. 28. 60. [e] Job 40. 19. [f] Ju. 6. 19. [g] Ge. 27. 25. [h] Ps. 91. 7. [i] De. 15. 2.

יִגְּשׁוּ ^a^וַ'ִ } Kal fut. 3 pers. pl. masc. (§ 8. rem. } נגש
יִגְּשׁוּ וַ'ִ } 15); ·וַ conv. . . .

יָד וְ' com. dec. 2a (with grave suff. יֶדְכֶם § 31. rem. 3).—I. *hand*; followed by prepositions: the hand to be or go forth עִם, אֵת, (rarely) לְ *with* any one, i. e. *to assist, aid him*; followed by אֶל, לְ *upon* or *against* any one, i. e. *to trouble him*, and but seldom in a good sense; by עַל *upon* any one, i. e. *to strengthen and inspire him*; hence, Is. 8. 11 בְּחֶזְקַת הַיָּד with *the power of the hand*, i. e. *the power of inspiration*; נָתַן יָד *to give the hand*, as a pledge of agreement, also, of submission; פָּתַח יָד *to open the hand*, i. e. to give liberally; קָפַץ יָד *to shut the hand*, i. e. to be illiberal; Pr. 11. 21 יָד לְיָד *hand in hand*, i. e. throughout all generations, *ever*; this, however, is explained by others, "joining my hand to yours, I promise;" יָד לְפֶה *hand to mouth*, i. e. be silent.—II. *power, strength, might*; בְּאֶפֶס יָד, לֹא בְיָד *without human power*.—III. *care, protection*; תַּחַת יַד פְּ' *under the care of any one*.—IV. *part* (prop. handful); Da. 1. 20 עֶשֶׂר יָדוֹת עַל *ten parts above*, i. e. *ten times more*.—V. *side*, as of a river; רְחַב יָדַיִם *large on both sides*, i. e. spacious.—VI. *space, place*; אִישׁ עַל יָדוֹ *every one in his place*.—VII. *memorial, monument*.—VIII. pl. יָדוֹת *artificial hands* (different from du. יָדַיִם the human hands) as, (*a*) *tenons* of planks; (*b*) *axletrees* for wheels, 1 Ki. 7. 32, 33; (*c*) *the arms* of a throne, 1 Ki. 10. 19.—With prepositions; בְּיַד *with*; *by*; כְּיַד *according to the means of*; מִיַּד *from, out of*; עַל יַד, אֶל יַד, בְּעַד, לְיַד, יַד *at, on, by the side of*; עַל יַד, עַל יְדֵי *under the care* or *guidance of* any one.

יַד Ch. com. dec. 2a (with grave suff. יְדְהֹם § 58. rem. 3) *the hand*; *power*.

יַד וְ' id. constr.; also Chald. dec. 2a . . . יד
יָדְ^b^ Kh. יַד id., K. יְדֵי (q. v.) . . . . יד
^c^יַדָּא וַ Kh. יַדָּא Hiph. fut. 3 pers. sing. masc., ap. [from יַדִּיא] R. נדא, K. יַדַּח id. R. . נדח
^d^יֵדֶא וַ Kal fut. 3 pers. sing. masc., ap. from יִדְאֶה (§ 24. rem. 3); ·וַ conv. . . . . דאה
^e^יְדָא Ch. noun com. sing. emph. of יַד dec. 2a . יד
^f^יִדְאָג Kal fut. 3 pers. sing. masc. [for יִדְאַג § 8. rem. 15] . . . . . דאג
יִדְאֶה ^g^וְ' Kal fut. 3 pers. sing. masc. . . . דאה
יִדְאֲלָה וְ pr. name of a place in Zebulun, Jos. 19. 15.

יַדְבִּיקוּ וַ Hiph. fut. 3 pers. pl. masc.; ·וַ conv. . דבק
^h^יִדְּבֶנּוּ Kal fut. 3 pers. sing. masc., suff. 3 p. s. m. נדב
יַדְבֵּק ^k^וַ'ִ Hiph. fut. 3 pers. sing. masc. ap. [fr. יַדְבִּיק]; ·וַ conv. . . . . דבק
יִדְבַּק ^l^וַ'ִ Kal fut. 3 pers. sing. masc.; ·וַ id. . דבק
יְדֻבָּקוּ Pual fut. 3 pers. pl. masc. [for יְדֻבְּקוּ comp. § 8. rem. 15] . . . . . דבק
יַדְבְּקוּ וַ Hiph. fut. 3 pers. pl. for יַדְבִּיקוּ (§ 11. r. 7) דבק
^m^יִדְבְּקוּ Kal fut. 3 pers. pl. masc. . . . דבק
^n^יַדְבֵּר ^o^וַ'ִ Hiph. fut. 3 pers. sing. masc. ap. [from יַדְבִּיר]; ·וַ conv. . . . . . דבר
יְדַבֵּר } וַ'ִ } Piel fut. 3 pers. sing. masc. (§ 10. rem. } דבר
יְדַבֶּר־ } 4); וַ id. . . . .
יְדַבֵּרוּ } וַ'ִ }
יְדַבְּרוּ } וַ' } Piel fut. 3 pers. pl. masc.; וַ id. . דבר
^p^יְדַבְּרוּ וְ id. id. with conj. וְ [for וַ'ִ וִידַבְּרוּ] . דבר
^q^יְדַבְּרֵם וַ id. fut. 3 pers. sing. masc., suff. 3 pers. pl. masc.; וַ conv. . . . . . דבר
יִדְבָּשׁ וְ pr. name masc. . . . . . דבש
^r^יִדְגּוּ וַ Kal fut. 3 pers. pl. masc.; ·וַ conv. . דגה

I. [יָדַד] *to throw, cast*, Joel 4. 3; Na. 3. 10; Ob. 11.

II. [יָדַד] Root not used; i. q. דּוּד *to love*.

יְדִיד masc. dec. 3a.—I. *beloved, friend*.—II. adj. *lovely, pleasant*, Ps. 84. 2.—Pl. יְדִידוֹת *love*, שִׁיר יְדִידוֹת *a song of love*, Ps. 45. 1.

יְדִידָה (*beloved*) pr. name of the mother of king Josiah, 2 Ki. 22. 1.

יְדִידוּת fem. *love, object of love*, Je. 12. 7.

יְדִידְיָה (*beloved of the Lord*) a title of Solomon, 2 Sa. 12. 25.

יִדּוֹ (for יָדוֹן *loving*) pr. name masc.—I. 1 Ch. 27. 21.—II. Ezr. 10. 43.

יַדַּי (id.) pr. name masc. Ezr. 10. 43 Keri.

מֵידָד (*love*) pr. name masc. Nu. 11. 26, 27.

^s^יֻדַּד וְ Hoph. fut. 3 pers. sing. masc. . . נדד
^t^יִדֹּדוּן Kal fut. 3 pers. pl. masc. with parag. ן . נדד
^u^יְדִדוּת noun fem. sing. . . . . . ידד

[יָדָה] *to throw, cast*, Je. 50. 14. Pi. id. Hiph. הוֹדָה, fut. יוֹדֶה (§ 25. No. 2e).—I. *to confess openly and freely*.—II. *to give thanks, to praise*. Hithp. הִתְוַדָּה (§ 20. r. 1).—I. *to confess, make confession*.—II. *to praise*, with לְ 2 Ch. 30. 22.

יְדָא Ch. Aph. *to praise, celebrate*.

הֻיְּדוֹת pl. fem. *songs of praise, hymns*, Ne. 12. 8.

תּוֹדָה fem. dec. 10.—I. *confession*.—II. *praise*,

^a^ Ge. 45. 4. ^b^ 2 Ki. 12. 12. ^c^ 2 Ki. 17. 21. ^d^ Ps. 18. 11. ^e^ Da. 5. 5, 24. ^f^ Je. 17. 8. ^g^ Je. 49. 22. ^h^ Ex. 25. 2. ^i^ De. 28. 21. ^k^ Ge. 31. 23. ^l^ 2 Ki. 18. 6. ^m^ Nu. 36. 7, 9. ^n^ Ps. 47. 4. ^o^ Ps. 18. 48. ^p^ Ps. 73. 8. ^q^ 1 Sa. 8. 21. ^r^ Ge. 48. 16. ^s^ Job 20. 8. ^t^ Ps. 68. 13. ^u^ Je. 12. 7.

thanksgiving.—III. *a company of persons singing songs of praise, a choir of singers.*

יְדִיתוּן, יְדֻתוּן, יְדוּתוּן (*praising*) pr. name of a Levite skilled in music, whom David appointed one of the choristers.

יְדָיָה (*who praises the Lord*) pr. name masc.—I. 1 Ch. 4. 37.—II. Ne. 3. 10.

יְהוּדָה (*praised*) pr. name—I. of the fourth son of Jacob, also of the tribe descended from him, and ultimately applied to the kingdom and house of David, including Benjamin, in contradistinction to the other ten tribes or the kingdom of Israel.—II. pr. name masc. of several persons less known.

יְהוּד Ch. *Judah, the kingdom of Judah.*

יְהוּדִי pl. יְהוּדִים, יְהוּדִיִּים.—I. *a Jew, Jews;* fem. יְהוּדִיָּה *Jewess.*—II. pr. name masc. Je. 36. 14, 21.

יְהוּדִי Ch. *a Jew*, only pl. יְהוּדָאִין dec. 7.

יָהַד (denom. from יְהוּד) Hithpa. *to become a Jew*, Est. 8. 17.

יְהוּדִית.—I. adv. *Jewish, in the language of the Jews.*—II. pr. name fem. Ge. 26. 34.

יָדָהּ noun com. sing., suff. 3 pers. sing. fem. from יָד dec. 2a . . . . . יד

יְדֵהּ[a] Ch. n. com. s., suff. 3 p. s. m. from יַד d. 2a יד

יָדָו[b] וְ׳ noun com. du., suff. (K. יָדָיו § 4. rem. 1) 3 pers. sing. masc., from יָד dec. 2a . יד

יָדוֹ וְ׳ id. sing., suff. 3 pers. sing. masc. . . יד

יַדּוֹ Kh. יַדּוֹ, K. יַדִּי pr. name masc. . . ידד

יַדּוּ Kal pret. 3 pers. pl. . . . . ידד

יַדּוּ[c] וַ Piel fut. 3 pers. pl. masc. with ·וַ conv. [for וַיְיַדּוּ § 20. rem. 8] . . . . ידה

יְדוּ[d] Kal imp. pl. masc. . . . . ידה

יִדּוֹ pr. name masc. . . . . . ידד

יָדוֹ[e] וְ Kh. וְיָדוֹ q. v.; K. וִידֵי (q. v.) . . יד

יִדּוֹד[f] Kal fut. 3 p. s. m. (§ 17. rem. 1, & § 8. r. 18) נדד

יָדוֹן[g] וְ׳ Kal fut. 3 p. s. m.; also pr. n. (Ne. 3. 7) דון

יָדוֹעַ[h] Kal inf. abs. . . . . . . ידע

יַדּוּעַ וְ׳ pr. name masc. . . . . ידע

יְדוּעֵי[i] וִ [for וְיְדוּעֵי] Kal part. p. masc., constr. of [יָדוּעַ] dec. 3a; וִ conj., for וְ, bef. (:) ידע

יְדוּשֶׁנּוּ[pp] Kal fut. 3 pers. sing. masc. [יָדוּשׁ], suff. 3 pers. sing. masc. (§ 2. rem. 3) . . דוש

יָדוֹת[k] וְ׳ noun com. pl. abs. from יָד dec. 2a . יד

יְדוֹת[l] וִ id. pl. constr., with conj. וְ [for וְיְ׳, וִידוֹת] יד

יְדוּתוּן, וִידוּ׳ pr. name m., with conj. וְ [for וְיְדוּ׳, וִי׳] יד

יְדוֹתָם[m] noun com. pl. (יָדוֹת), suff. 3 pers. pl. masc. from יָד dec. 2a . . . . . יד

יַדַּח[n] וַ Hiph. fut. 3 pers. sing. masc. with gutt. [for יַדַּח ap. from יַדִּיחַ]; ·וַ conv. . . נדח

יִדַּח[o] Kal fut. 3 pers. sing. masc. . . . נדח

יִדָּחֶה[p] Niph. fut. 3 pers. sing. masc. . . . דחה

יִדָּחוּ[q] Niph. fut. 3 pers. pl. masc. [dag. f. implied in ח, for יִדַּחוּ] . . . . . דחח

יְדַחֲלִנַּנִי[r] וְ Ch. Pael fut. 3 pers. sing. masc., suff. 1 pers. sing. with conj. וְ [for וִיְדַ׳, וְיְדַ׳] דחל

יִדְחָקוּן[s] Kal fut. 3 p. pl. m. with parag. ן (§ 8. r. 17) דחק

יָדַי, יָדַי[t] וְ׳ noun com. du., suff. 1 pers. s. fr. יָד d. 2a (perh. for יָדַיִם in Eze. 13. 18) יד

יָדִי[u] וְ׳ id. sing., suff. 1 pers. sing. . . . יד

יְדַיָּ[x] Ch. n. com., du., suff. 1 pers. s. fr. יַד dec. 2a יד

יְדֵי, יְדֵי וִ noun com. du. constr. from יָד dec. 2a, with cop. וְ [for וְיְדֵי, וִידֵי] . . יד

יְדִיד[y] noun masc. sing., constr. of [יָדִיד] d. 3a ידד

יְדִידָה pr. name fem. . . . . ידד

יְדִידוֹת[z] adj. pl. fem. [from יָדִיד] . . . ידד

יְדִידְיָה pr. name masc. . . . . ידד

יְדִידֶיךָ noun masc. pl., suff. 2 pers. sing. masc. fr. [יָדִיד] dec. 3a . . . . ידד

יְדִידֹת[ss] noun fem. pl. fr. יָדִיד masc. . . . ידד

יְדָיָה pr. name masc. . . . . . ידה

יָדֶיהָ וְ׳ noun com. du., suff. 3 pers. sing. fem. fr. יָד dec. 2a . . . . . . יד

יְדֵיהוּ[a] id., suff. 3 pers. sing. masc. (§ 4. rem. 5) יד

יְדֵיהֶם, יְדֵיהֶם[b] וְ id., suff. 3 pers. pl. masc. with cop. וְ [for וְיְדֵי׳, וִידֵי׳] . . . יד

יְדֵיהֶן[c] id., suff. 3 pers. pl. fem. . . . יד

יָדָיו וְ׳ id., suff. 3 pers. sing. masc. . . . יד

יָדִיחַ[d] Hiph. fut. 3 pers. sing. masc. . . . דוח

יָדִיחוּ id. fut. 3 pers. pl. masc. . . . דוח

יַדִּיחוּ[e] וַ Hiph. fut. 3 pers. sing. masc.; וַ conv. נדח

יָדַיִךְ[f], יָדַיִךְ[g] וְ׳ noun com. dual, suff. 2 pers. sing. fem. from יָד dec. 2a . . . יד

יָדֶיךָ, יָדֶךָ id., suff. 2 pers. sing. masc.; Kh. יָדֶיךָ, K. יָדְךָ (q. v.) . . . . יד

יְדֵיכֶם id., suff. 2 pers. pl. masc. . . . יד

יָדַיִם, יָדָיִם וְ׳ id. dual, absolute state . . . יד

יָדִין Kal fut. 3 pers. sing. masc. R. דִּין see . דון

יָדֵינוּ noun com. du., suff. 1 pers. pl. fr. יָד d. 1a יד

יְדִיעַ Ch. Peal part. pass. sing. masc. . . ידע

יְדִיעֲאֵל & וִידִי׳ pr. name masc., with cop. וְ [for וְיְדִי׳, וִידִי׳] . . . . ידע

[a] Ezr. 6. 12. [b] Job 5. 18. [c] La. 3. 53. [d] Je. 50. 14. [e] Eze. 1. 8. [f] Na. 3. 7. [g] Ge. 6. 3. [h] Jos. 23. 13. [i] Is. 53. 3. [k] 2 Ch. 9. 18. [l] 1 Ki. 7. 32. [m] 1 Ki. 7. 33. [n] 2 Ch. 21. 11. [o] 2 Sa. 14. 14. [p] Pr. 14. 32. [pp] Is. 28. 28. [q] Je. 23. 12. [r] Da. 4. 2. [s] Joel 2. 8. [ss] Ps. 45. 1. [t] Ca. 5. 5. [u] 1 Sa. 24. 13, 14. [x] Da. 3. 15. [y] De. 33. 12. [z] Ps. 84. 2. [a] Hab. 3. 10. [b] Eze. 10. 12. [c] Eze. 23. 42. [d] Is. 4. 4. [e] De. 13. 14. [f] Zep. 3. 16. [g] Je. 2. 37.

ידיעו[a] Hiph. fut. 3 pers. pl. masc. . . . . ידע

ידיתון Kh. ידיתון for K. ידותון (q. v.) . . ידה

ידך } noun com. sing., suff. 2 pers. sing. masc. fr. יד dec. 2a . . . } יד

ידך[b] ו' }

ידך id., suff. 2 pers. sing. fem. . . . . יד

ידך[c] Ch. noun com. sing., suff. 2 pers. sing. masc. from יד dec. 2a . . . . . יד

ידכא[d] Pual fut. 3 pers. sing. masc. . . . דכא

ידכא[e] וְ Piel fut. 3 pers. sing. masc., with conj. וְ [for וְיְדַכֵּא ,וְ'] . . . . דכא

ידכאו[f] וְ } Hithpa. fut. 3 pers. pl. masc. (§ 12. rem. 3, comp. § 8. rem. 15) . } דכא

ידכאו[g] וְ }

ידכאו[h] Piel fut. 3 pers. pl. masc. . . . דכא

ידכאום[i] id. id., suff. 3 pers. pl. masc. . . . דכא

ידכאני[k] וְ id. fut. 3 pers. sing. masc., suff. 1 pers. sing. with conj. וְ [for וִידַכְּאֵנִי ,וְ'] . . דכא

ידכה[l] noun com. sing., suff. 2 pers. sing. masc. (§ 3. rem. 2) from יד dec. 2a . . . יד

ידכם id., suff. 2 pers. pl. m. [for יֶדְכֶם § 31. r. 3] יד

ידכם[m] id. dual, suff. 2 pers. pl. masc. for יְדֵיכֶם יד

ידל[o] וַ'} Niph. fut. 3 pers. sing. masc.; וַ conv. דלל

ידלג[p] Piel fut. 3 pers. sing. masc. . . . . דלג

ידליקם[q] Hiph. fut. 3 pers. sing. m., suff. 3 pers. pl. m. דלק

ידלנה[r] Kal fut. 3 pers. sing. masc., suff. 3 pers. sing. fem. (§ 2. rem. 3) . . . . דלה

ידלף pr. name masc. . . . . . דלף

ידלף[s] Kal fut. 3 pers. sing. masc. . . . דלף

ידלק[t] Kal fut. 3 pers. sing. masc. . . . דלק

ידם noun com. sing., suff. 3 pers. pl. masc. fr. יד dec. 2a . . . . . . יד

ידם[u] [x]וַ' ,וְ' Kal fut. 3 pers. sing. masc. [for יִדֹּם § 18. rem. 14] . . . . דמם

ידמה[y] Piel fut. 3 pers. sing. masc. . . . דמה

ידמה[z] Kal fut. 3 pers. sing. masc. . . . דמה

ידמו[a] } Niph. fut. 3 pers. pl. masc. (comp. § 8. rem. 15) . . . . } דמם

ידמו[b] }

ידמו[c] [d]וְ' Kal fut. 3 pers. pl. masc., Chald. form, (§ 18. rem. 14 & rem. 7 note) . דמם

ידנו [e]וְ' noun com. s., suff. 1 pers. pl. fr. יד d. 2a יד

ידע fut. יֵדַע, inf. c. דַּעַת (§ 20. r. 3).—I. *to know, perceive, discern, be aware of.*—II. *to know, be acquainted with;* part. יָדוּעַ *acquainted.*—III. *to know, recognize, acknowledge.*—IV. *to know carnally.*—V. *to regard, care for.* Niph. I. *to be* or *become known.*—II. *to be made to know,* Pr. 10. 9; Je. 31. 19. Pi. *to make to know, to appoint,* Job 38. 12. Pu. part. מְיֻדָּע *known, acquaintance, familiar.* Poel (§ 6. No. I), *to show, appoint,* 1 Sa. 21. 3. Hiph. הוֹדִיעַ, imp. הוֹדַע *to make known, show, inform, teach.* Hoph. *to be made known.* Hithp. הִתְוַדַּע (§ 20. rem. 1) *to make oneself known,* with אֶל.

יְדַע Ch. fut. יִנְדַּע (§ 52. r. 2) *to know, perceive, understand.* Aph. הוֹדַע *to make known, to show.*

יָדָע (*knowing*) pr. name masc. 1 Ch. 2. 28, 32.

יַדּוּעַ (*known*) pr. name masc.—I. Ne. 10. 22.—II. Ne. 12. 11, 22.

יְדַעְיָה (whom *the Lord knows*) pr. name masc. 1 Ch. 9. 10; 24. 7.

יְדִיעֲאֵל (*known of God*) pr. name of a son of Benjamin.

יִדְּעֹנִי masc. pl. יִדְּעֹנִים.—I. *wizard, soothsayer.*—II. *spirit of divination,* Le. 20. 27.

דֵּעַ masc. dec. 1a, *knowledge, opinion.*

דֵּעָה fem. pl. דֵּעוֹת, *knowledge.*

דַּעַת fem. dec. 13a (with suff. דַּעְתִּי).—I. *knowledge, the act of knowing.* בִּבְלִי דַעַת *without knowing, unawares.*—II. *intelligence, understanding, wisdom.*

מוֹדָע ,מֹדָע masc. *acquaintance, friend,* Ru. 2. 1; Pr. 7. 4.

מֹדַעַת fem. id. Ru. 3. 2.

מַדָּע ,מַדַּע masc. with suff. מַדָּעֲךָ.—I. *knowledge.*—II. *thought, mind,* Ec. 10. 20.

מַנְדַּע Ch. dec. 1a.—I. *knowledge.*—II. *intelligence, intellect,* Da. 4. 31, 33.

מַדּוּעַ (contr. for מָה יָדוּעַ) adv. interrog. *why? wherefore?*

ידע Ch. Peal part. act. sing. masc. (§ 49. No. 4) dec. 2a . . . . . . ידע

ידע וְ' pr. name masc. . . . . . ידע

ידע Kal pret. 3 pers. sing. m. for יָדַע (§ 8. r. 7) ידע

ידע [f]וְ' id. inf. abs. . . . . . ידע

ידע [g]וְ' } id. fut. 3 pers. sing. masc. (comp. § 8. rem. 15) . . . } ידע

ידע וְ' }

ידע וַ id. id.; acc. drawn back by conv. וַ (§ 20. rem. 1 & 3) . . . . . ידע

ידע[h] וְ } Hiph. fut. 3 pers. sing. masc. with gutt., [for יֹדַע] ap. from יוֹדִיעַ (§ 20. r. 9) } ידע

ידע[i] וַ }

ידע Ch. Peal pret. 3 pers. sing. masc. . . ידע

ידע וְ' Kal part. act. sing. masc. dec. 7b . ידע

---

[a] Job 32. 7. [b] 2 Ch. 6. 32. [c] Da. 3. 17. [d] Job 22. 9. [e] Ps. 72. 4. [f] Job 34. 25. [g] Job 5. 4. [h] Ps. 94. 5. [i] Job 4. 19. [k] Job 6. 9. [l] Ex. 13. 16. [m] Ps. 134. 2. [n] Is. 17. 4. [o] Ju. 6. 6. [p] Is. 35. 6. [q] Is. 5. 11. [r] Pr. 20. 5. [s] Ec. 10. 18. [t] Ps. 10. 2. [u] Ps. 30. 13; Am. 5. 13 [x] La. 3. 28. [y] Is. 10. 7. [z] Ps. 89. 7.

[a] 1 Sa. 2. 9. La. 2. 10. [b] Je. 49. 26; 50. 30. [c] Ex. 15. 16; Ps. 31. 18; [d] Job 29. 21. [e] Ge. 37. 27. [f] Je. 9. 23. [g] Job 21. 19. [h] Nu. 16. 5. [i] Ju. 8. 16.

יָדְעָה Kal pret. 3 pers. sing. fem. — ידע
[a]יְדָעָהּ id. pret. 3 pers. sing. m., suff. 3 pers. s. f. — ידע
[b]יְדָעֻהוּ id. pret. 3 pers. pl., suff. 3 pers. sing. masc. — ידע
יָדְעוּ, יָדָעוּ } וְ׳ id. pret. 3 pers. pl. (§ 8. rem. 7) — ידע
[c]יְדָעוֹ id. pret. 3 pers. sing. m., suff. 3 pers. s. m. — ידע
יֵדְעוּ וַיֵּ׳, וְ׳ id. fut. 3 pers. pl. masc.; וַ· conv. — ידע
[d]יֹדְעָו וְ id. part. act. pl. masc., suff. 3 pers. sing. masc. (K. יו׳ for ־ָיו § 4. rem. 1) — ידע
יְדָעוּךָ id. pret. 3 pers. pl., suff. 2 pers. sing. masc. — ידע
יְדָעוּם id. id., suff. 3 pers. pl. masc. — ידע
[e]יָדְעוּן id. id. with parag. ן (§ 8. rem. 4) — ידע
יֵדְעוּן id. fut. 3 pers. pl. m. with parag. ן (§ 8. rem. 17) — ידע
[f]יְדָעוּנִי id. pret. 3 pers. pl., suff. 1 pers. sing. — ידע
[g]יָדְעֵי Chald. Peal part. act. pl. constr. masc. from יָדַע dec. 2a — ידע
[h]יֹדְעַי וְ Kal part. act. pl. m., suff. 1 p. s. fr. יֹדֵעַ d. 7b — ידע
יֹדְעֵי וְ׳ id. pl. construct state — ידע
יְדַעְיָה pr. name masc. — ידע
[i]יֹדְעָיו Kal part. act. pl. m., suff. 3 p. m. s. fr. יֹדֵעַ dec. 7b — ידע
[k]יֹדְעִים וְ׳ id. pl., absolute state — ידע
[m]יְדֻעִים וִ Kal part. p. pl. abs. masc. from [יָדוּעַ] dec. 3a, with cop. וְ [for וִידוּעִים, וְיְדֻעִים] — ידע
[n]יָדְעִין Chald. Peal part. act. pl. abs. masc. from יָדַע (§ 49. No. 4) dec. 2a — ידע
יִדְעַךְ, [o]יִדְעָךְ } Kal fut. 3 pers. sing. masc. (§ 8. rem. 15) — דעך
[p]יְדָעֵם וְ Kal fut. 3 p. s. m., suff. 3 p. pl. m. (§ 16. r. 12) — ידע
[q]יָדַעְנוּ, יָדָעְנוּ } [r]וְ׳ Kal pret. 1 pers. pl. (§ 8. rem. 7) — ידע
[s]יְדָעָנוּ id. pret. 3 pers. sing. masc., suff. 1 pers. pl. — ידע
[t]יֵדָעֶנּוּ id. fut. 3 pers. sing. masc., suff. 3 pers. sing. masc. (§ 16. rem. 12, & § 2. rem. 3) — ידע
[u]יֹדְעֵנוּ id. part. act. s. m., suff. 1 p. pl. from יֹדֵעַ dec. 7b — ידע
[x]יְדַעֲנוּךָ id. pret. 1 pers. pl., suff. 2 pers. sing. masc. — ידע
[y]יְדַעֲנוּם id. id., suff. 3 pers. pl. masc. — ידע
[*]יִדְּעֹנִי וְ׳ noun masc. sing. dec. 1b *Le. 20. 27. — ידע
[z]יִדְּעֹנִים וְ id. pl. absolute state — ידע
יָדַעְתָּ, יָדָעְתָּ } Kal pret. 2 pers. sing. masc. (§ 8. rem. 7) — ידע
יָדַעְתָּ וְ id. id.; acc. shifted by conv. וְ (v. id.) — ידע
[a]יָדַעַתְּ, יָדַעַתְּ } וְ׳ id. pret. 2 pers. sing. fem. (v. id.) — ידע
יָדַעְתְּ Kh. יָדַעְתְּ q. v., K. יָדַעְתִּי q. v. — ידע
[b]יְדַעְתָּ Chald. Peal pret. 2 pers. sing. masc., [for יְדַעְתְּ § 47. rem. 2] — ידע

[c]יִדַּעְתָּ Keri, Piel pret. 2 p. s. m. (read יִדַּעְתָּ הַשַּׁחַר) — ידע
[d]יִדְעֵת Chald. Peal pret. 1 pers. sing. — ידע
יֹדַעַת Kal part. act. sing. fem. from יֹדֵעַ masc. (§ 8. rem. 19, & § 39. No. 4) — ידע
[e]יָדַעְתָּה full form for יָדַעְתָּ q. v. (§ 8. rem. 5) — ידע
[f]יִדַּעְתָּה Kh. יִדַּעְתָּה, full form for יִדַּעְתָּ (read יִדַּעְתָּה שַׁחַר comp. § 8. rem. 5) Piel pret. 2 p. s. m. — ידע
[g]יְדַעְתּוֹ Kal pret. 2 pers. sing. m., suff. 3 pers. sing. m. — ידע
יָדַעְתִּי, יָדָעְתִּי } id. pret. 1 pers. sing. (§ 8. rem. 7) — ידע
יָדַעְתִּי וְ id. id.; acc. shifted by וְ conv. (v. id.) — ידע
[h]יְדַעְתִּיהָ id. id., suff. 3 pers. sing. fem. — ידע
[i]יְדַעְתִּיו id. id., suff. 3 pers. sing. masc. — ידע
יְדַעְתִּיךָ id. id., suff. 2 pers. sing. masc. — ידע
[k]יְדַעְתִּים id. id., suff. 3 pers. pl. masc. — ידע
[l]יְדַעְתִּין id. id., suff. 3 pers. pl. fem. — ידע
יְדַעְתָּם id. pret. 2 pers. sing. masc., suff. 3 pers. pl. m. — ידע
יְדַעְתֶּם, יְדַעְתֶּם וְ } id. pret. 2 pers. pl. masc. with conv. וְ [for וִידַעְתֶּם, וְ׳] — ידע
[m]יְדַעְתֶּן, [n]יְדַעְתֶּן וְ } id. pret. 2 pers. pl. fem. with conv. וְ [for וִידַעְתֶּן, וְ׳] — ידע
יְדַעְתַּנִי id. pret. 2 p. s. m., suff. 1 p. s. [for ־תָּנִי § 2. r. 1] — ידע
[o]יִדְּפֶנּוּ Kal fut. 3 pers. sing. masc., suff. 3 pers. s. m. — נדף
יָדֶק וַ Hiph. fut. 3 pers. sing. masc. with conv. וַ [for יָדֵק § 18. rem. 11] — דקק
[p]יְדֻקֶּנּוּ Kal fut. 3 pers. sing. masc. [יָדֹק], suff. 3 pers. sing. masc. (§ 18. rem. 5, & § 2. rem. 3) — דקק
[q]יִדָּקֵר Niph. fut. 3 pers. sing. masc. — דקר
[r]יִדְקֹר וַ Kal fut. 3 pers. sing. masc.; וַ conv. — דקר
[s]יִדְקְרֵהוּ וַ id., suff. 3 pers. sing. masc.; וַ· id. — דקר
יִדֹּר, יִדֹּר } וַ Kal fut. 3 pers. sing. masc. (§ 8. rem. 13); וַ id. — נדר
[t]יִדְּרוּ וַ id. fut. 3 pers. pl. masc.; וַ id. — נדר
[u]יִדְרוֹן Ch. Kh. יִדְרוּן, Peal fut. 3 p. pl. m. (K. ־ָן׳) fem. — דור
[x]יִדְרוֹשׁ Kal fut. 3 pers. sing. m., for יִדְרֹשׁ (§ 8. rem. 18) — דרש
[y]יַדְרִיכֵם וַ Hiph. fut. 3 pers. sing. masc. [יַדְרִיךְ], suff. 3 pers. pl. masc.; וַ conv. — דרך
[z]יַדְרֵךְ id. fut. 3 pers. sing. masc. ap. [fr. יַדְרִיךְ] — דרך
יִדְרֹךְ Kal fut. 3 pers. sing. masc. — דרך
[a]יַדְרְכוּ וַ Hiph. fut. 3 pers. pl. masc., from the ap. יַדְרֵךְ, (§ 11. rem. 7); וַ· conv. — דרך
[b]יִדְרְכוּ [c]וַיִּ׳ Kal fut. 3 pers. pl. masc.; וַ· id. — דרך
[d]יִדְרְכוּן id. with parag. ן (§ 8. rem. 17) — דרך
[e]יַדְרִכֵנִי Hiph. fut. 3 pers. s. m. [יַדְרִיךְ], suff. 1 pers. s. — דרך
יִדְרֹשׁ [f]וְ׳, וַיִּ׳ Kal fut. 3 pers. sing. masc.; וַ· conv. — דרש
[g]יִדְרְשֵׁהוּ [h]וַיִּ׳ id., suff. 3 pers. sing. masc.; וַ· id. — דרש

---

[a] Ge. 24. 16; 1 Ki. 1. 4. [b] Da. 11. 38. [c] De. 34. 10; Job 28. 7. [d] Job 24. 1. [e] De. 8. 3, 16. [f] Je. 2. 8. [g] Ezr. 7. 25. [h] Job 19. 13. [i] Job 42. 11. [k] 2 Ki. 17. 26. [l] Job 34. 2. [m] De. 1. 13, 15. [n] Da. 5. 23. [o] Pr. 20. 20. [p] Ho. 14. 10. [q] Ge. 29. 5. [r] 1 Sa. 6. 9. [s] Is. 63. 16. [t] Je. 17. 9. [u] Is. 29. 15. [x] Ho. 8. 2. [y] Is. 59. 12. [z] 2 Ki. 21. 6. [a] Je. 50. 24. [b] Da. 5. 22. [c] Job 38. 12. [d] Da. 4. 6. [e] 2 Sa. 2. 26. [f] Job 38. 12. [g] De. 22. 2. [h] Eze. 11. 5. [i] Ge. 18. 19. [k] Pr. 30. 18. [l] Is. 48. 7. [m] Ge. 31. 6. [n] Eze. 13. 21, 23. [o] Job 32. 13. [p] Is. 28. 28. [q] Is. 13. 15. [r] Nu. 25. 8. [s] Ju. 9. 54. [t] Jon. 1. 16. [u] Da. 4. 9. [x] Job 39. 8. [y] Ps. 107. 7. [z] Ps. 25. 9. [a] Je. 9. 2. [b] 1 Sa. 5. 5. [c] Ju. 9. 27. [d] Ps. 11. 2. [e] Hab. 3. 19. [f] 2 Ch. 24. 22. [g] Job 3. 4. [h] 2 Ch. 1. 5.

יִדְרְשׁוּ / וַיִּדְרְשׁוּ[a] } Kal fut. 3 p. pl. m. (§ 8. rem. 15); ·ּוַ conv. דרשׁ

יִדְרְשׁוּהוּ[b] id. id., suff. 3 pers. sing. masc. . . דרשׁ

יִדְרְשׁוּן[c] id. id. with parag. ן (§ 8. rem. 17) . דרשׁ

יִדְרְשֶׁנּוּ[d] id. fut. 3 p. s. m., suff. 3 p. s. m. (§ 2. rem. 3) דרשׁ

יְדֻשָּׁן Pual fut. 3 p. s. m. [for יְדֻשַּׁן comp. § 8. rem. 15] דשׁן

יְדַשְּׁנֶה[e] Piel fut. 3 p. s. m. with parag. ה (§ 8. rem. 13) דשׁן

יָדֹת[f] וְ׳[g] noun com. pl. abs. from יָד dec. 2 a . יד

יְדֻתוּן וְ defect. for יְדוּתוּן q. v. . ידה

יְדֹתֶיהָ[h] noun com. pl., suff. 3 pers. sing. fem. from יָד dec. 2 a . . . . . . יד

יְדֹתָיו id. pl., suff. 3 pers. sing. masc. . . יד

יָהּ i. q. יְהוָֹה from which it is abbreviated . הוה

[יָהַב] imp. הַב, with ה parag. הָבָה, fem. הָבִי, pl. הָבוּ. —I. *to give.*—II. *to set, place.* הָבָה adv. *come, come on! go to!*

יְהַב Chald.—I. *to give.*—II. *to set, place.* Ithpe. *to be given, delivered over.*

יְהָב masc. *burden, trouble,* Ps. 55. 23; but which some take as a verb and render it, הַשְׁלֵךְ עַל־יְהוָֹה יְהָבְךָ *cast upon the Lord* what *he has given* or *laid upon thee,* i. e. thy lot, for אֲשֶׁר יָהַב לָךְ.

הַבְהָבִים masc. pl. *gifts,* Ho. 8. 13.

יָהֵב[i] Chald. Peal part. act. masc. dec. 2 b . יהב

יְהַב Chald. Peal pret. 3 pers. sing. masc. . יהב

יְהִב[zz] Chald. id. part. pass. sing. masc. (for יְהִיב) יהב

יְהַבוּ[bb] וִ id. pret. 3 pers. pl. masc. with conj. וְ [for וִי׳ וִיהַבוּ] . . . . . יהב

יָהֲבִין[k] Chald. id. part. act. masc., pl. of יָהֵב dec. 2 b יהב

יְהָבְךָ[l] Kal pret. 3 pers. sing. masc., suff. 2 pers. sing. m.; or rather noun m. [יְהָב] with suff., &c. יהב

יֶהְבְּלוּ וַ Kal fut. 3 pers. pl. m. [for יֶהְבְּלוּ § 8. rem. 15, & § 13. rem. 4 & 5]; ·ּוַ conv. . הבל

יְהַבְתְּ[m] Chald. Peal pret. 2 pers. sing. masc. . יהב

יֶהְגֶּה Kal fut. 3 pers. sing. masc. (§ 13. rem. 5) הגה

יֶהְגּוּ id. fut. 3 pers. pl. masc. (v. id.) . הגה

יְהֻד וִ pr. name of a place, for יְהוּד (וְ, for וְ cop.) ידה

יֶהְדַּי pr. name masc. for יֶהְדָּי . הדה

יֶהְדֳּף[n] Kal fut. 3 pers. sing. masc. (§ 13. rem. 5) הדף

יֶהְדְּפֻהוּ[o] id. fut. 3 pers. pl. m., suff. 3 pers. s. m. (v. id.) הדף

יֶהְדְּפֵם[p] id. fut. 3 pers. sing. masc., suff. 3 pers. pl. masc. (v. id. & § 8. rem. 14) . . הדף

יֶהְדָּפֶנּוּ[q] id. id., suff. 3 pers. s. m. (v. id. & § 2. rem. 3) הדף

יְהוּא[r] Kal fut. 3 pers. sing. masc. [for יְהוּ ap. for יֶהֱוֶה § 24. rem. 3] . . . . הוה

יֵהוּא וְ׳ (*he shall exist, live,* contr. for יְהִי הוּא=יְהִי)

pr. name of several men, especially—I. of a king of Israel, comp. 2 Ki. ch. 9.—II. of a prophet in Samaria, comp. 1 Ki. 16. 1.

יְהוֹאָשׁ, יְהוֹאָחָז pr. names masc. . . . הוה

יְהוֹבְדוּן[s] Ch. Aph. fut. 3 pers. pl. masc. (§ 53. No. 1) אבד

יְהוּד pr. name of a country . . ידה

יְהוּדָאִין Chald. gen. noun, pl. of [יְהוּדִי] dec. 7 . יהד

יְהוּדָה וִיהוּ׳ pr. name of a man and a tribe, with cop. וְ [for וִי׳, וִיהוּ׳] . . . ידה

יְהוֹדֶה[t] Hiph. fut. 3 pers. sing. masc. (§ 20. rem. 10) ידה

יְהוֹדוּךָ[u] id. fut. 3 pers. pl. m., suff. 2 pers. s. m. (v. id.) ידה

יְהוּדִי gent. noun from יְהוּדָה; also pr. name masc. ידה

יְהוּדָיֵא Chald. gen. m. pl. emph. from יְהוּדִי (§ 63) ידה

יְהוּדִים gent. noun., pl. of יְהוּדִי from יְהוּדָה . ידה

יְהוּדִית id. s. fem., used also as an adv.; or pr. n. f. ידה

יְהוֹדַע[x] Chald. Aph. fut. 3 pers. s. m. (§ 52 note) ידע

יְהוֹדְעוּן[y] Chald. id. fut. 3 pers. pl. masc. (v. id.) . ידע

יְהוֹדְעִנַּנִי[z] Chald. id. fut. 3 pers. s. m., suff. 1 p. s. (v. id.) ידע

יְהוֹדְעֻנַּנִי[a] Chald. id. fut. 3 pers. pl. m., suff. 1 p. s. (v. id.) ודע

יְהוָֹה, וַיהוָֹה the most sacred name of God, with the vowels of אֲדֹנָי except (ֲ), with וְ cop. וַיהוָֹה corresponds to the form וַאדֹנָי for וַאֲדֹנָי, see lett. ו, but see under יהוה הוה

יֱהוִֹה id. with the vowels of אֱלֹהִים, when אֲדֹנָי precedes . . . . . . הוה

יְהוֹזָבָד, וִיהוֹ׳ יְהוֹחָנָן, וִיהוֹ׳ & יְהוֹיָדָע, וִיהוֹ׳ & יְהוֹיָכִין, יְהוֹיָקִים, וִיהוֹיָרִיב pr. names masc. . . הוה

יְהוּכַל pr. name masc. . . . . יכל

יְהוֹלֵל Poel fut. 3 pers. sing. masc. . . הלל

יְהוֹנָדָב, וִיהוֹ׳ יְהוֹנָתָן, וִיהוֹ׳ & יְהוֹעַדָּה, יְהוֹעַדָּן, & יְהוֹצָדָק, וִיהוֹ׳ & יְהוֹרָם, וִיהוֹ׳ & יְהוֹשֶׁבַע, יְהוֹשׁוּעַ, יְהוֹשַׁבְעַת pr. names masc. . הוה

יְהוֹשִׁיעַ[b] Hiph. fut. 3 pers. sing. masc. (§ 20. r. 10) . ישׁע

יְהוֹשֻׁעַ וִיהוֹ׳ defect. יְהוֹשׁוּעַ (q. v.) . . הוה

יְהוֹשָׁפָט וִיהוֹ׳ pr. name of a man and a place, with cop. וְ [for וִי׳, וִיהוֹ׳] . . . הוה

יְהַחֲוֵה[c] Ch. Aph. fut. 3 pers. s. m. (§ 47. r. 4, & § 55 note) חוה

יְהִי[d] וַיְ׳, / וַיְהִי } Kal fut. 3 pers. s. m., ap. for יִהְיֶה (§ 24. rem. 3 e, comp. § 35. r. 14); וַ conv. היה

יְהִי וִ id. with conj. וְ [for וִי׳, וִיהִי] . . היה

יְהִיב[e] Chald. Peal part. pass. sing. masc. . יהב

יְהִיבוּ[f] וִ Chald. id. with the afformative of 3 pers. pl. masc. יְהִיבוּ, see § 47. rem. 11, with conj. וְ [for וִי׳, וִיהִיבוּ] . . . יהב

יְהִיבַת[g] / וִיהִיבַת } Chald. id., with the afformative 3 pers. sing. fem., comp. the preceding . } יהב

יָהְיָה[h] Kh. יִהְיֶה q. v., K. וְהָיָה Kal pret. 3 pers. s. m. היה

[a] Ju. 6. 29. [b] Ps. 119. 2. [c] Is. 58. 2. [d] De. 23. 22. [e] Ps. 20. 4. [f] Ex. 36. 22. [g] 1 Ki. 10. 19. [h] 1 Ki. 7. 35, 36. [i] Da. 2. 21. [k] Da. 6. 3. [l] Ps. 55. 23. [m] Da. 2. 23. [n] Pr. 10. 3. [o] Job 18. 18. [p] Jos. 23. 5. [q] Nu. 35. 20. [r] Ec. 11. 3. [s] Da. 2. 18. [t] Ne. 11. 17. [u] Ps. 45. 18. [x] Da. 2. 25. [y] Da. 2. 30. [z] Da. 7. 16. [zz] Da. 7. 14, 22. [a] Da. 4. 3. [b] 1 Sa. 17. 47; Ps. 116. 6. [bb] Da. 3. 28. [c] Da. 5. 12. [d] Eze. 16. 15. [e] Da. 7. 4, 6. [f] Ezr. 5. 14. [g] Da. 7. 12, 27. [h] Eze. 45. 5.

יְהִיֶה Kal fut. 3 pers. sing. masc. . . . היה
יִהְיֶה Kh. יִהְיֶה q. v., K. יְהִיו (q. v.) . . היה
יִהְיוּ וַיִּ, וְ׳ Kal fut. 3 pers. pl. masc.; ·וַ conv. היה
[a] יִהְיוּ וְ Kh. יִהְיוּ q. v., K. וְהָיוּ Kal pret. 3 pers. pl. היה
[b] יְהֵילִילוּ Hiph. fut. 3 pers. pl. masc. (§ 20. rem. 14) ילל
יָהִיר adj. masc. sing. . . . . . יהר
[c] יְהָךְ / [d] וְ יְהָךְ } Chald. Peal fut. 3 pers. sing. masc. (§ 54. rem. 1), with conj. וְ [for וְיִהָךְ] . הוך
[e] יָהֵל Hiph. fut. 3 pers. sing. masc. . . . הלל
[f] יַהֵל Piel fut. 3 pers. s. m. [for יְאַהֵל § 19. r. 10] אהל
[g] יָהֵלּוּ Hiph. fut. 3 pers. pl. masc. . . . הלל
[h] וַיִּ יַהֲלֹךְ Kal fut. 3 pers. sing. masc. . . . הלך
וַיְ׳ יְהַלֵּךְ Piel fut. 3 pers. sing. masc. . . . הלך
[k] יַהֲלְכוּ Kal fut. 3 pers. pl. m. [for יַהַלְכוּ § 8. r. 15] הלך
יְהַלֵּכוּ Piel fut. 3 pers. pl. m. [for יְהַלְּכוּ comp. id.] הלך
יְהַלֵּכוּן id. with parag. ן (§ 8. rem. 17, & § 10. r. 4) הלך
יְהַלֶּל־ Piel fut. 3 pers. s. m. [for יְהַלֵּל § 10. r. 4] הלל
[l] יְהֻלָּל Pual fut. 3 pers. sing. masc. . . . הלל
יְהַלֶּלְאֵל pr. name masc. . . . . . הלל
[m] וַ יְהַלְלֶהָ Piel fut. 3 pers. sing. masc., suff. 3 pers. sing. fem. (§ 10. rem. 7); וַ conv. . הלל
[n] וַ יְהַלְלוּ / וִי׳ יְהַלְלוּ } id. fut. 3 pers. pl. masc. (§ 10. rem. 7b); וַ id. . . . הלל
[o] וַ יְהַלְלוּהָ / [p] וְ יְהַלְלוּהָ } id. id., suff. 3 pers. sing. fem.; וַ conv.; with conj. וְ [for וִי׳, וִיהַ׳] הלל
יְהַלְלוּהוּ id. id., suff. 3 pers. sing. masc. . . הלל
[q] יְהַלְלוּךָ id. id., suff. 2 pers. sing. masc. . . הלל
[r] יְהַלְלֶךָּ / [s] יְהַלְלֶךָ } id. fut. 3 pers. sing. masc., suff. 2 pers. sing. masc. (§ 16. rem. 15, & § 2. r. 2) הלל
וְ יַהֲלֹם noun masc. sing. . . . . . הלם
[t] יַהַלְמוּן Kal fut. 3 pers. pl. masc. with parag. ן [for יַהַלְמוּן § 8. rem. 17, & § 13. rem. 5] . הלם
[u] יֶהֶלְמֵנִי id. fut. 3 pers. s. m., suff. 1 pers. s. (§ 13. r. 4) הלם
וַ יָּהָם Kal fut. 3 p. s. m. with conv. וַ [for וַיָּהָם] המם
יֶהֱמֶה Kal fut. 3 pers. sing. masc. . . . המה
וַיְ׳ יֶהֱמוּ id. fut. 3 pers. pl. masc.; ·וַ conv. . המה
יֶהֱמָיוּן id. id. with parag. ן (§ 8. rem. 17, & § 24. r. 5) המה
[x] וַ יְהֻמֹּם Kh. יְהֻמֵּם q.v. K. וַיָּהָם in pause for וַיָּהָם q.v. (§ 21. rem. 8) . . . . המם
וַ יְהֻמֵּם Kal fut. 3 pers. sing. masc. (יָהֹם), suff. 3 pers. pl. masc. (§ 18. rem. 5); ·וַ conv. המם
[y] וַ יַּהַס Hiph. fut. 3 pers. sing. masc. ap. [fr. יַהֲסֶה § 24. rem. 16]; ·וַ id. . . . הסה

[z] יְהַעְדּוֹן Ch. Aph. fut. 3 pers. pl. masc. (§ 47. r. 4) עדה
[a] וַיַּ יַהֲפֹךְ / [b] וַ יַהֲפָךְ־ } Kal fut. 3 pers. sing. masc. (§ 8. r. 18); ·וַ conv. . . . . } הפך
וַיֵּ יֵהָפֵךְ Niph. fut. 3 pers. sing. masc.; ·וַ id. הפך
[c] וַ יַהַפְכֵהוּ Kal fut. 3 pers. sing. masc., suff. 3 pers. sing. masc.; ·וַ id. . . . הפך
יַהַפְכוּ [d] וַיַּ, [e] וְ׳ id. fut. 3 pers. pl. masc.; ·וַ id. . הפך
[f] וַ יֵהָפְכוּ Niph. fut. 3 pers. pl. masc.; ·וַ id. . הפך
יַהַץ, יַהְצָה (*place trodden down*; coll. with the Arab.) pr. name of a city of Moab, afterwards reckoned to the tribe of Reuben.
יְהָקִים Ch. Aph. fut. 3 pers. sing. masc. (§ 47. rem. 4, & § 54. rem. 4) . . . . קום

יָהַר Root not used; prob. *to be high*, cogn. הָרָה, הָרַר. יָהִיר adj. masc. *elated, haughty, vain.*

וַיַּ יַהֲרֹג / [g] יַהֲרָג־ } Kal fut. 3 pers. sing. masc. (§ 8. rem. 18); ·וַ conv. . . . . } הרג
[h] יֵהָרֵג Niph. fut. 3 pers. sing. masc. . . . הרג
וַ יַהַרְגֵהוּ Kal fut. 3 pers. sing. masc., suff. 3 pers. sing. masc.; ·וַ conv. . . . הרג
[i] וַ יַהַרְגֻהוּ id. fut. 3 pers. pl. masc., suff. 3 pers. sing. masc.; ·וַ id. . . . . הרג
יַהַרְגוּ / וַ יַהַרְגוּ } id. fut. 3 pers. pl. masc. (§ 8. rem. 15); ·וַ id. . . . . } הרג
[ll] וַ יַהַרְגוּם id. id., suff. 3 pers. pl. masc.; ·וַ id. . הרג
וַ יַהַרְגֵם id. fut. 3 pers. sing. masc., suff. 3 pers. pl. masc.; ·וַ id. . . . . הרג
[k] יַהַרְגֻן id. fut. 3 pers. pl. masc. with parag. ן (§ 8. rem. 17) . . . . . הרג
[l] יַהַרְגֵנִי id. fut. 3 pers. sing. masc., suff. 1 pers. sing. הרג
[m] יַהַרְגֻנִי id. fut. 3 pers. pl. masc., suff. 1 pers. sing. הרג
[n] יַהֲרוֹס Kal fut. 3 pers. sing. masc. (§ 8. rem. 18) הרס
[o] יֵהָרֵס Niph. fut. 3 pers. sing. masc. . . הרס
[p] וְ יֶהֶרְסֶהָ Kal fut. 3 pers. sing. masc. [יַהֲרֹס], suff. 3 pers. sing. fem. (§ 13. rem. 4); ·וַ conv. הרס
[q] יֶהֶרְסוּ / [r] יַהַרְסוּ } id. fut. 3 pers. pl. masc. (v. id. & § 8. rem. 15) . . . } הרס
[s] יֵהָרְסוּן Niph. fut. 3 pers. pl. masc. with parag. ן (comp. § 8. rem. 17) . . הרס
[t] יֶהֶרְסֵךְ Kal fut. 3 pers. sing. masc. [יַהֲרֹס § 13. rem. 4], suff. 2 pers. sing. m. [for יֶהֶרָסְךָ] הרס
[u] יֶהֶרְסֵם id. id., suff. 3 pers. pl. masc. . . הרס
[x] יֶהֶרְסֶנָּה id. id., suff. 3 pers. sing. fem. (§ 2. rem. 3) הרס
[y] יְהַשְׁנֵא Ch. Aph. fut. 3 pers. sing. masc. (§ 47. r. 4) שנא
[z] יְהַשְׁפִּל Ch. Aph. fut. 3 pers. sing. masc. (§ 47. r. 4) שפל

[a] Jos. 19. 29. [b] Is. 52. 5. [c] Ezr. 5. 5; 7. 13. [d] Ezr. 6. 5. [e] Job 31. 26. [f] Is. 13. 20.
[g] Is. 13. 10. [h] Job 14. 20. [i] 1 Ki. 21. 27. [k] Job 41. 11. [l] Pr. 12. 8. [ll] 2 Sa. 4. 12.
[m] Pr. 31. 28. [n] Ge. 12. 15. [o] Ca. 6. 9. [p] Pr. 31. 31. [q] Ps. 84. 5.
[r] Pr. 27. 2. [s] Is. 38. 18. [t] Ps. 74. 6. [u] Ps. 141. 5. [x] 2 Sa. 22. 15.
[y] Nu. 13. 30. [z] Da. 7. 26. [a] La. 3. 3. [b] 1 Sa. 10. 9. [c] Ju. 7. 13.
[d] Job 12. 15. [e] 1 Sa. 25. 12. [f] Ex. 7. 20. [g] Job 5. 2. [h] La. 2. 20.
[i] 2 Ch. 24. 25. [k] Zec. 11. 5. [l] Ge. 4. 14. [m] Ge. 26. 7. [n] Job 12. 14.
[o] Je. 31. 40. [p] 1 Ch. 20. 1. [q] 2 Ki. 3. 25. [r] Ex. 19. 21, 24. [s] Ps. 11. 3.
[t] Is. 22. 19. [u] Ps. 28. 5. [x] Pr. 29. 4. [y] Ezr. 6. 11. [z] Da. 7. 24.

יְהַתְבוּן[a] Ch. Aph. fut. 3 pers. pl. masc. (§ 47. r. 4) — תוב

וַ יְהַתֵּל[b] Hiph. fut. 3 pers. sing. masc. uncontracted form [for יָהֵתֵל § 20. rem. 10 & 14, by Chaldaism for יָתֵל § 18. rem. 14]; וַ conv. — תלל

יְהַתֵּלוּ[c] id. fut. 3 pers. pl. masc. regular and uncontracted [for יְהָתֵלּוּ, in pause for יָתֵלּוּ, comp. § 18. rem. 15 note] — תלל

יוֹאָב וְ׳, יוֹאָח וְ׳ & יוֹאָחָז (see יְהוֹאָחָז), יוֹאֵל וְ׳ & pr. names masc. — הוה

וַיּוֹאֶל וַ Hiph. fut. 3 pers. sing. masc., with conv. וַ [for יוֹאֶל, ap. from יוֹאִיל] — יאל

יוּאָר[d] Hoph. fut. 3 pers. sing. masc. [for יוּאַר] — ארר

יוֹאָשׁ וְ׳ pr. name masc. — הוה

יוֹב וְ pr. name of a son of Issachar, Ge. 46. 13.

יוּבָא Hoph. fut. 3 pers. sing. masc. — בוא

יוּבָאוּ[e] id. fut. 3 pers. pl. masc. [for יוּבְאוּ comp. § 8. rem. 15] — בוא

יוֹבָב וְ׳ pr. name masc. — יבב

יוֹבִילוּ Hiph. fut. 3 pers. pl. masc. — יבל

יוּבָל pr. name masc. — יבל

יוּבָל / יוּבַל Hoph. fut. 3 pers. sing. masc.; or (Je. 17. 8) noun masc. sing. — יבל

יוֹבֵל noun masc. sing. dec. 7b — יבל

יוּבָלוּ[f] Hoph. fut. 3 pers. pl. masc. [for יוּבְלוּ comp. § 8. rem. 15] — יבל

יוֹבִלוּן[g] Hiph. fut. 3 pers. pl. masc. with ן parag. — יבל

יוֹבְלִים[h] noun masc., pl. of יוֹבֵל dec. 7b — יבל

יוֹבִלֵנִי[i] Hiph. fut. 3 pers. sing. masc., suff. 1 pers. sing. — יבל

יוֹדֶה[k] Hiph. fut. 3 pers. sing. masc. (§ 25. No. 2e) — ידה

יוֹדוּ וְ׳[l] id. fut. 3 pers. pl. masc. — ידה

יוֹדוּךָ id. id., suff. 2 pers. sing. masc. — ידה

יוֹדִיעַ Hiph. fut. 3 pers. sing. masc. — ידע

יוֹדִיעֶנּוּ[m] id., suff. 3 pers. sing. masc. (§ 2. rem. 3) — ידע

יוֹדֶךָּ[n] Hiph. fut. 3 pers. sing. masc. (יוֹדֶה § 25. No. 2e), suff. 2 pers. sing. masc. [for יוֹדְךָ, § 24. rem. 21] — ידה

יוֹדֻךָ[o] וְ id. fut. 3 pers. pl. masc., suff. 2 pers. s. m. — ידה

יִוָּדַע[p] וַיִּ׳ / יִוָּדֵעַ[q] Niph. fut. 3 pers. sing. masc. (§ 15. rem. 1); וַ conv. — ידע

יוֹדֵעַ Kal part. act. sing. masc. dec. 7b — ידע

יוֹדְעוֹ[r] id., suff. 3 pers. sing. masc. — ידע

יוֹדְעֵי id. pl., constr. state — ידע

יוֹדְעַיִךְ[s] id. pl., suff. 2 pers. sing. masc. — ידע

יוֹדְעִים id. pl., abs. state — ידע

יוֹדִעֵם[t] Hiph. fut. 3 pers. pl. (יוֹדִיעוּ), suff. 3 p. pl. m. — ידע

יוֹדַעְתִּי[u] Poel fut. 1 pers. sing. (§ 6. No. 1) — ידע

יוּדַק[x] Hoph. fut. 3 pers. sing. masc. [for יוּדַק] — דקק

יוּדַשׁ[y] Hoph. fut. 3 pers. sing. masc. — דוש

יוֹזָבָד וְ׳, יוֹזָכָר, וְיוֹחָא, יוֹחָנָן וְ׳ & pr. names masc. — הוה

יוּטָּה וְ pr. name of a place — נטה

יוּטַל[z] / יוּטָל[a] Hoph. fut. 3 pers. sing. masc. (comp. § 8. rem. 15) — טול

יוֹיָדָע וְ׳, יוֹיָרִיב וְ׳ &, יוֹיָקִים & יוֹיָכִין (see יְהוֹיָכִין), יוֹכֶבֶד pr. names masc. — הוה

יוֹכַח[b] וַ׳, וְ׳ / יוֹכִחַ Hiph. fut. 3 pers. sing. masc., apoc. יוֹכַח for יוֹכַח because of 3d rad. gutt., comp. יוֹשַׁע; וַ conv. — יכח

יוֹכִיחוּ[c] וְ id. fut. 3 pers. pl. masc. — יכח

יוֹכִיחֶךָ[d] id. fut. 3 pers. s. m., suff. 2 pers. s. m. [for יֹכִיחֲךָ] — יכח

יוֹכִיחֶנּוּ[e] id. id., suff. 3 pers. sing. masc. — יכח

יוֹכִיחֵנִי[f] וְ id. id., suff. 1 pers. sing. — יכח

יוּכַל / יוּכָל Hoph. fut. 3 pers. sing. masc. (comp. § 8. rem. 15) — יכל

יֻכְלוּ[g] Kh. יוּכְלוּ q. v., K. יָכְלוּ (q. v.) — יכל

יוּכְלוּ[h] Hoph. fut. 3 pers. pl. m. [for יֻאָכְלוּ § 19. r. 9] — אכל

יוּכָלוּ / יוּכָלוּ Hoph. fut. 3 pers. pl. masc. (comp. § 8. rem. 15) — יכל

יוּכְלוּן id. with parag. ן — יכל

יִוָּלֵד וַיִּ׳ / יִוָּלֶד[i] Niph. fut. 3 pers. sing. masc. (§ 9. rem. 3); וַ conv. — ילד

וַיּוֹלֵד[k] K. וַיּוֹלֶד, Kal part. act. sing. masc. dec. 7b — ילד

וַיּוֹלֶד וַ Hiph. fut. 3 pers. sing. masc. with conv. וַ for יוֹלֵד (§ 20. r. 9) ap. fr. יוֹלִיד; וַ conv. — ילד

יוּלַד[l] / יוּלָּד[m] Pual pret. 3 pers. sing. masc. (comp. § 8. rem. 7, for יֻלַּד § 10. rem. 5) — ילד

יוֹלֵדָה Kal part. act. sing. fem., from יוֹלֵד masc. — ילד

יִוָּלְדוּ[n] / וַיִּוָּלְדוּ[o] Niph. fut. 3 pers. pl. masc. (comp. § 8. rem. 15); וַ conv. — ילד

יוֹלֶדֶת[qq] וְ Kal part. act. fem. dec. 13a, from יוֹלֵד m. — ילד

יוֹלַדְתֵּךְ[p] id. with suff. 2 p. s. m. (§ 8. r. 19, & § 39. No. 4) — ילד

יוֹלַדְתְּכֶם[q] id., suff. 2 pers. pl. masc. — ילד

יוֹלִיד Hiph. fut. 3 pers. sing. masc. — ילד

יוֹלִיךְ Hiph. fut. 3 pers. sing. masc. — ילך

וַיּוֹלִיכֵהוּ וַ id. fut. 3 pers. pl. m., suff. 3 p. s. m.; וַ conv. — ילך

וַיּוֹלִיכֵם[r] וַיּ׳ id. fut. 3 pers. s. m., suff. 3 p. pl. m.; ו id. — ילך

יוֹלֵךְ[s] / וַיּוֹלֵךְ[u] id. fut. 3 pers. sing. masc. ap. and conv. (§ 20. rem. 9) for יוֹלִיךְ — ילך

וַיּוֹלִכֵנִי וַ id. with suff. 1 pers. sing.; וַ conv. — ילך

יוֹם וְ׳, וַ׳ masc. with suff. יוֹמִי (d. 1a), pl. יָמִים (as if fr. יָם d. 2a, § 45).—I. *a day*.—II. adv. *by day, in*

[a] Ezr. 6. 5. [b] 1 Ki. 18. 27. [c] Je. 9. 4. [d] Nu. 22. 6. [e] Je. 27. 22. [f] Job 21. 30. [g] Zep. 3. 10. [h] Jos. 6. 6. [i] Ps. 60. 11. [k] Ps. 6. 6. [l] Ps. 89. 6. [m] Is. 40. 13, 14. [n] Is. 38. 19. [o] Ps. 49. 19. [p] Est. 2. 22. [q] Pr. 10. 9. [r] 1 Sa. 10. 11. [s] Eze. 28. 19. [t] Eze. 44. 23. [u] 1 Sa. 21. 3. [x] Is. 28. 28. [y] Is. 28. 27. [z] Ps. 37. 24. [a] Pr. 16. 33. [b] Ho. 4. 4. [c] Ge. 31. 37. [d] Job 22. 4. [e] Job 5. 17. [f] Ps. 141. 5. [g] Jos. 15. 63. [h] Eze. 42. 5. [i] Is. 66. 8. [k] Pr. 23. 24. [l] Job 5. 7. [m] Ju. 18. 29. [n] Ps. 78. 6. [o] De. 23. 9. [p] Pr. 23. 25. [q] Je. 50. 12. [qq] Je. 31. 8. [r] Ps. 125. 5. [s] Ps. 106. 9. [t] De. 28. 36. [u] Ex. 14. 21.

the day time; יוֹם בְּיוֹם, יוֹם וָיוֹם, יוֹם יוֹם *day by day, every day, daily;* הַיּוֹם *this day, to day;* בְּיוֹם followed by an inf. *on the day that* or *when;*—בַּיּוֹם *in the day time,* Je. 36. 30; *on this day, immediately; on that day, lately,* Ju. 13. 10;—כַּיּוֹם, כְּהַיּוֹם *about this day, this time, now; at that time, then;* מִיּוֹם *from the time that, since.* Du. יוֹמַיִם *two days.*—Pl. יָמִים, poet. יְמוֹת (constr. of יָמוֹת). —I. *days, some days* or *time;* מִיָּמִים, מִקֵּץ יָמִים *after many days, some time after.*—II. *time, duration* generally; כָּל הַיָּמִים *at all times, always;* מִיָּמֶיךָ *as long as thou livest;* בָּא בַּיָּמִים *advanced in age;* חֹדֶשׁ יָמִים *a full month;* שְׁנָתַיִם יָמִים *two full years.*—III. *a definite time, as a year;* זֶבַח הַיָּמִים *yearly sacrifice;* מִיָּמִים יָמִימָה *from year to year, annually.*

יוֹם Chald. masc. dec. 1a, pl. יוֹמִין constr. יוֹמֵי, יוֹמָת, by Hebraism יְמֵי, *day, time, period.*

יוֹמָם adv.—I. *by day, in the day time;* בְּיוֹמָם id.—II. *daily,* Eze. 30. 16.

יוֹמוֹ id., suff. 3 pers. sing. masc. . . . . יום

יוֹמַיָּא Chald. id. pl. emph. state . . . . יום

יוֹמָיִם, יוֹמַיִם } id. du., absolute state . . . . יום

יוֹמִין Chald. id. pl., absolute state . . . יום

יוֹמְךָ[a] id. sing., suff. 2 pers. sing. masc. . . . יום

יוֹמָם ו׳ id. sing., suff. 3 pers. sing. masc.; or adv. with the term. ָם (comp. חִנָּם) . . יום

יוֹמָת[b] Chald. id. pl. constr. fem. . . . . יום

יוּמָת, יוּמַת } Hoph. fut. 3 pers. sing. masc. (comp. § 8. rem. 15) . . . . . } מות

יוֹמָת[c] Kh. יוּמָת q. v.; K. יָמוּת, Kal fut. 3 pers. s. m. מות

יוּמָתוּ, יוּמְתוּ } Hoph. fut. 3 pers. pl. masc. (comp. § 8. rem. 15) . . . . } מות

יָוַן Root not used; to which is ascribed the signification of *heat and fermentation,* comp. חָמַר, חֵמֶר, חֹמֶר

יָוֵן m. constr. יְוַן *mire, mud;* טִיט הַיָּוֵן *miry clay.*

יַיִן m. dec. 6h.—I. *wine.*—II. meton. *intoxication.*

יָוָן ו׳ pr. name of a son of Japheth, Ge. 10. 2, 4, the founder of the Greeks, *Ionians.* Patronym. יְוָנִי; בְּנֵי הַיְּוָנִים *Greeks.*

יוֹנָדָב ו׳ contr. for יְהוֹנָדָב q. v. . . . . הוה

יוֹנָה fem. dec. 10, pl. יוֹנִים.—I. *dove.*—II. *Jonah,* pr. name of a prophet.

יוֹנֶה[d] Hiph. fut. 3 pers. sing. masc. (§ 25. No. 2e) ינה

יוֹנוּ[e] id. fut. 3 pers. pl. masc. . . . . ינה

יוֹנִים[f] Keri, Kal part. act. m., pl. of [יוֹנֶה] dec. 9a ינה

יוֹנִים noun fem. with pl. masc. term. see . יוֹנָה

יוֹנֵק ו׳ Kal part. act. or subst. masc. dec. 7b . ינק

יוֹנְקֵי[g] ו id. pl. construct state . . . . ינק

יוֹנְקוֹתֶיהָ[h] id. pl. fem., suff. 3 pers. sing. fem. from [יוֹנֶקֶת] dec. 13a (§ 8. rem. 19, & § 39. No. 4) . ינק

יוֹנְקוֹתָיו[i] id. id., suff. 3 pers. sing. masc. . . ינק

יוֹנַקְתּוֹ ו׳[k] id. id. sing., suff. 3 pers. sing. masc. . ינק

יוֹנַת[l] noun fem. sing., constr. of . . . יוֹנָה

יוֹנָתִי id. with suff. 1 pers. sing. . . . . יוֹנָה

יוֹנָתָן ו׳ pr. name masc. . . . . . הוה

יוּסָּב[m] Hoph. fut. 3 pers. sing. masc. [for יוּסַב, יֻסַּב § 18. rem. 14. comp. § 10. rem. 5] . סבב

יוֹסִיף ו׳[n] Hiph. fut. 3 pers. sing. masc. . . . יסף

יוֹסִיפוּ ו׳[o], וַיּ׳ id. fut. 3 pers. pl. masc.; ·וַ conv. . יסף

יוֹסִפְיָה pr. name masc. . . . . . יסף

יָוֹסַף[p] Kh. יוֹסֵף q. v., K. יָסַף, Kal pret. 3 pers. s. m. יסף

יוֹסֵף ו׳ pr. name masc. . . . . . יסף

יוֹסֵף ו׳[q], יוֹסֶף וַיּ׳, ו } Hiph. fut. 3 pers. sing. masc., ap. and conv. (§ 20. r. 9) fr. יוֹסִיף } יסף

יוֹסֵף for יוֹסִיף q. v.; or perhaps (Is. 29. 14; 38. 5) for יוֹסֵף Kal part. act. (§ 9. rem. 7) . יסף

יוֹסִפוּ וַיּ׳[r] Hiph. fut. 3 pers. pl. masc.; ·וַ conv. יסף

יוֹסִפוּן[s] id. with parag. ן . . . . . יסף

יִוָּסֵר[t] Niph. fut. 3 pers. sing. masc., Milêl before penacute [for יִוָּסֵר § 9. rem. 3] . יסר

יוּסַר[u] Hoph. fut. 3 pers. sing. masc. . . . סור

יוֹעֵאלָה ו pr. name masc. 1 Ch. 12. 7.

יוֹעֵד pr. name masc. . . . . . הוה

יִוָּעֲדוּ וַ Niph. fut. 3 pers. pl. masc.; ·וַ conv. . יעד

יוֹעִדֵנִי[x] Hiph. fut. 3 pers. sing. masc., suff. 1 pers. sing. (§ 2. rem. 3) . . . . יעד

יוֹעֶזֶר ו pr. name masc. . . . . . הוה

יוֹעִידֵנִי[y] Hiph. fut. 3 pers. sing. masc., suff. 1 pers. s. יעד

יוֹעִיל Hiph. fut. 3 pers. sing. masc. . . . יעל

יוֹעִילוּ id. fut. 3 pers. pl. masc. . . . . יעל

יוֹעִילֻךְ[z] id. id., suff. 2 pers. sing. fem. . . . יעל

יוֹעִלוּ defect. for יוֹעִילוּ (q. v.) . . . . יעל

יוּעַם[a] Hoph. fut. 3 pers. sing. masc. . . . עמם

יִוָּעֵץ וַ Niph. fut. 3 pers. sing. masc.; ·וַ conv. . יעץ

יוֹעֵץ ו׳[b] Kal part. act. sing. masc. dec. 7b . יעץ

יִוָּעֲצוּ[c] וַיּ׳[d] Niph. fut. 3 pers. pl. masc.; ·וַ conv. . יעץ

יוֹעֲצָיו[e] ו Kal part. act. pl. masc., suff. 3 pers. sing. masc. from יוֹעֵץ dec. 7b . . . יעץ

יוֹעֲצִים id. pl., absolute state . . . . יעץ

יוֹעֲצֵךְ[f] id. sing., suff. 2 pers. sing. fem. . . יעץ

[a] Je. 50. 31. [b] Ezr. 4. 15, 19. [c] 2 Ki. 14. 6. [d] Eze. 18. 7. [e] Eze. 45. 8. [f] Ps. 123. 4. [g] Joel 2. 16. [h] Ps. 80. 12. [i] Ho. 14. 7. [k] Job 14. 7. [l] Ps. 56. 1. [m] Is. 28. 27. [n] Ec. 1. 18. [o] Pr. 9. 11. [p] 1 Sa. 27. 4. [q] 2 Sa. 24. 3. [r] Ge. 37. 5, 8. [s] 1 Ki. 19. 2. [t] Pr. 29. 19. [u] Le. 4. 35. [x] Je. 50. 44. [y] Job 9. 19. [z] Is. 57. 12. [a] La. 4. 1. [b] Is. 3. 3. [c] Is. 45. 21. [d] 2 Ch. 30. 23. [e] Ezr. 7. 28. [f] Mi. 4. 9.

יוֹעַצְתּוֹ[a]	id. fem. sing. [יוֹעֶצֶת], suff. 3 pers. sing. masc. dec. 13 a (§ 8. rem. 19, & § 39. No. 4) .	יעץ
יוֹעָשׁ	וְ' pr. name masc.	הוה
יוֹצֵא	Kal part. act. sing. masc. dec. 7 b . .	יצא
יוֹצֵא / יוֹצֵא	וַ / וַ Hiph. fut. 3 pers. sing. masc. ap. and defect. for יוֹצִיא; ·וַ conv. . .	יצא
יוֹצִאֶהָ[b]	וַ id. with suff. 3 pers. sing. fem.; ·וַ conv.	יצא
יוֹצְאוֹת	Kal part. act. fem., pl. יוֹצֵאת q. v. . .	יצא
יוֹצְאֵי	id. pl. constr. masc. from יוֹצֵא dec. 7 b .	יצא
יוֹצְאִים	id. id., absolute state	יצא
יוֹצִאֲךָ[c]	וַ Hiph. fut. 3 pers. sing. masc., (יוֹצִיא), suff. 2 pers. sing. masc.; ·וַ conv. . .	יצא
יוֹצֵאת	Kal part. act. sing. fem. [for יוֹצֵאֶת § 23. rem. 4, see § 8. rem. 19, & § 39. No. 4] .	יצא
יוֹצָדָק	pr. name masc., see יְהוֹצָדָק . .	הוה
יוֹצִיא	Hiph. fut. 3 pers. sing. masc. . .	יצא
יוֹצִיאֻהוּ[d]	וַ id. fut. 3 p. pl. m., suff. 3 p. s. m.; ·וַ conv.	יצא
יוֹצִיאוּ	וַיּ' id. fut. 3 pers. pl. masc.; ·וַ id. .	יצא
יוֹצִיאוּם[e]	id. id., suff. 3 pers. pl. masc. . . .	יצא
יוֹצִיאֵם	וַיּ' id. fut. 3 p. s. m., suff. 3 p. pl. m.; ·וַ conv.	יצא
יוֹצִיאֵנִי[f]	וַיּ' id. id., suff. 1 pers. sing.; ·וַ id. .	יצא
יוּצַק	Hoph. fut. 3 pers. sing. masc. . . .	יצק
יוּצַר[g]	Hoph. fut. 3 pers. sing. masc. . .	יצר
יוֹצֵר	Kal part. act. sing. masc. dec. 7 b . .	יצר
יוֹצְרוֹ[h]	וְ id., suff. 3 pers. sing. masc. . .	יצר
יוֹצְרִים[i]	id. pl., absolute state	יצר
יוֹקְשִׁים[k]	Kal part. act. masc., pl. of [יוֹקֵשׁ] dec. 7 b .	יקש
יוּקָשִׁים[l]	Pual part. pl. masc. (§ 10. rem. 6) .	יקש
יוֹר[m]	וַ Hiph. fut. 3 pers. sing. masc., ap. from יוֹרֶה (§ 25. No. 2 e); ·וַ conv. . . .	ירה
יוֹרֵא[n]	Hiph. or Hoph. fut. 3 pers. sing. masc. [for יוֹרֶה, or יוּרֶה comp. הוֹדַע § 20. rem. 12]	ירה
יוֹרֵד	Kal part. act. sing. masc. dec. 7 b . .	ירד
יוֹרֶד	וַ Hiph. fut. 3 pers. sing. masc with conv. ·וַ [for יוֹרֵד § 20. rem. 9, ap. fr. יוֹרִיד]	ירד
יוֹרְדוּ	וַ id. fut. 3 pers. pl. masc. (for יוֹרִידוּ); ·וַ conv.	ירד
יוֹרִדוּךָ[o]	id. id., suff. 2 pers. sing. masc. . .	ירד
יוֹרְדוֹת[p]	Kal part. act. fem., pl. of רֶדֶת' dec. 13 a. (§ 8. rem. 19, & § 30. No. 4) . .	ירד
יוֹרְדֵי	id. pl. constr. masc. from יוֹרֵד dec. 7 b. .	ירד
יוֹרְדִים	id. id., absolute state . . .	ירד
יוֹרִדֵם[q]	וַ Hiph. fut. 3 pers. sing. masc. [יוֹרִיד], suff. 3 pers. pl. masc.; ·וַ conv. . . .	ירד
יוֹרָה	pr. name masc.	ירה
יוֹרֶה	וְ' Hiph. fut. 3 p. s. m.; or, Kal part. or subst. m.	ירה
יוֹרֵהוּ[r]	וַ id. fut. 3 p. s. m., suff. 3 pers. s. m.; ·וַ conv.	ירה
יוֹרוּ	id. fut. 3 pers. pl. masc. . . .	ירה
יוֹרְךָ	id. id., suff. 2 pers. sing. masc. . .	ירה
יוֹרַי	וְ pr. name masc.	ירה
יוֹרִידוּ[s]	וַיּ' Hiph. fut. 3 pers. pl. masc.; ·וַ conv.	ירד
יוֹרִידֵנִי[t]	id. fut. 3 pers. sing. masc., suff. 1 pers. sing.	ירד
יוֹרִישׁ[u]	Hiph. fut. 3 pers. sing. masc. . .	ירש
יוֹרִישְׁךָ[x]	id., suff. 2 pers. sing. masc. . . .	ירש
יוּרָם[y]	Hoph. fut. 3 pers. sing. masc. [for יוּרַם]	רום
יוֹרָם	וְ' pr. name masc.	הוה
יוֹרֵנוּ	וְ Hiph. fut. 3 pers. sing. masc. (יוֹרֶה § 25. No. 2 e, & § 24. rem. 21), suff. 1 pers. pl.	ירה
יוֹרֶנּוּ	id. fut. 3 pers. sing. masc. (יוֹרֶה § 25. No. 2 e, & § 24. rem. 21), suff. 3 p. s. m. (§ 2. rem. 3)	ירה
יִוָּרֵשׁ[z]	Niph. fut. 3 pers. sing. masc. . .	ירש
יוֹרֵשׁ	Kal part. act. sing. masc. dec. 7 b . .	ירש
יוֹרֶשׁ	וַ Hiph. fut. 3 pers. sing. masc. with conv. ·וַ [for יוֹרֵשׁ, § 20. rem. 9] ap. from יוֹרִישׁ	ירש
יוֹרִשֶׁנָּה	id. fut. 3 p. s. m., suff. 3 p. s. fem. (§ 2. rem. 3)	ירש
יוּשַׁב	pr. name in compos. יוּשַׁב חֶסֶד . .	שוב
יוּשַׁב[a]	וַ Hoph. fut. 3 pers. sing. masc.; ·וַ conv. .	שוב
יוֹשֵׁב	[b] וְ' Kal part. act. sing. masc. dec. 7 b .	ישב
יוֹשֵׁב[c] / יוֹשֶׁב	וַ / וַ Hiph. fut. 3 pers. sing. masc. ap. and convers. (§ 20. rem. 9) for יוֹשִׁיב	ישב
יוֹשְׁבֵי	וְ' Kal part. act. pl. constr. m. from יוֹשֵׁב dec. 7 b	ישב
יוֹשְׁבֶיהָ	id. pl., suff. 3 pers. sing. fem. . .	ישב
יוֹשַׁבְיָה	pr. name masc.	ישב
יוֹשְׁבָיו[d]	Kal part. act. pl. masc., suff. 3 pers. sing. masc. from יוֹשֵׁב dec. 7 b	ישב
יוֹשְׁבִים	[e] וְ' id. pl., absolute state	ישב
יוֹשֶׁבֶת[u] / יוֹשֶׁבֶת	id. sing. fem. dec. 13 a (§ 8. rem. 19, & § 39. No. 4)	ישב
יוֹשֶׁבֶתְי	id. id. Kh. יוֹשַׁבְתִּי, K. יוֹשֶׁבֶת (comp. § 8. r. 5)	ישב
יוּשַׁר[f]	Hoph. fut. 3 pers. sing. masc. [for יוּשַׁד, comp. § 8. rem. 15]	שדד
יוֹשָׁה	וְיוֹשַׁוְיָה, וְ pr. names masc. . .	ישה
יוֹשֶׁט	וַ Hiph. fut. 3 pers. sing. masc. with conv. ·וַ [for יוֹשֵׁט] ap. fr. יוֹשִׁיט . . .	ישט
יוֹשִׁיבוּ[g]	[h] וַיּ' Hiph. fut. 3 pers. pl. masc.; ·וַ conv.	ישב
יוֹשִׁיבֵנִי[i]	וַ id. fut. 3 pers. sing. masc., suff. 1 pers. sing. Kh. 'בֵינִי, K. 'בֵנִי (§ 2. rem. 1)	ישב
יוֹשִׁיט[k]	Hiph. fut. 3 pers. sing. masc. . .	ישט
יוֹשִׁיעַ	Hiph. fut. 3 pers. sing. masc. . . .	ישע
יוֹשִׁיעוּ	id. fut. 3 pers. pl. masc. . . .	ישע
יוֹשִׁיעוּךָ[l]	id. id., suff. 2 pers. sing. masc. . .	ישע
יוֹשִׁיעוּם	[m] וְ, [n] וַיּ' id. id., suff. 3 pers. pl. m.; ·וַ conv.	ישע
יוֹשִׁיעֲךָ[o]	וְ id. fut. 3 pers. sing. m., suff. 2 pers. sing. m.	ישע
יוֹשִׁיעֻךְ[p]	וְ id. fut. 3 pers. pl. m., suff. 2 pers. sing. fem.	ישע
יוֹשִׁיעֵם[q]	וְ', וַיּ' id. fut. 3 p. s. m., suff. 3 p. pl. m.; ·וַ conv.	ישע

[a] 2 Ch. 22. 3. [b] Ex. 4. 6, 7. [c] De. 4. 37. [d] 2 Ki. 12. 12. [e] 1 Ch. 9. 28. [f] Mi. 7. 9. [g] Is. 54. 17. [h] Is. 45. 11. [i] Is. 30. 14. [k] Ps. 124. 7. [l] Ec. 9. 12. [m] 2 Ki. 13. 17. [n] Pr. 11. 25. [o] Eze. 28. 8. [p] Pr. 7. 27. [q] 1 Ki. 18. 40. [r] Ex. 15. 25. [s] Nu. 1. 51. [t] Ob. 3. [u] Jos. 2. 15. [u] Jos. 3. 10. [x] Ju. 11. 24. [y] Le. 4. 19. [z] Pr. 23. 21.

[a] Ex. 10. 8. [b] Is. 9. 8. [c] Ge. 47. 11. [d] 2 Ch. 34. 24, 27, 28. [e] 2 Ch. 18. 9. [f] Ho. 10. 14. [g] Is. 54. 3. [h] 2 Ch. 23. 20. [i] 1 Ki. 2. 24. [k] Est. 4. 11. [l] Je. 2. 28. [m] Ne. 9. 27. [n] Ju. 2. 16. [o] Ho. 13. 10. [p] Is. 47. 13. [q] Ps. 107. 13, 19.

יְוֹשִׁיעֵנוּ	וְ' id. id., suff. 1 pers. pl. . .	ישע
[a] יוֹשִׁעֶנּוּ	id. id., suff. 3 pers. sing. masc. (§ 2. rem. 3)	ישע
[b] יוֹשִׁיעֵנִי	[c] וְ' id. id., suff. 1 pers. sing. . .	ישע
יִוָּשֵׁעַ	Niph. fut. 3 pers. s. m. [for יִוָּשַׁע § 15. rem. 1]	ישע
[d] יוֹשַׁע, וַ יּוֹשַׁע	Hiph. fut. 3 p.s.m. def. for יוֹשִׁיעַ, ap. and conv. וַיּוֹשַׁע (§ 20. rem. 9) for יוֹשַׁע because of 3d rad. gutt., comp. יוֹכַח	ישע
[e] יוֹשִׁעֵךְ	id. with suff. 2 pers. sing. fem. . .	ישע
[f] יוֹשִׁעָן	וַ id. with suff. 3 pers. pl. fem. . .	ישע
יוֹשָׁפָט	וְ contr. for יְהוֹשָׁפָט q. v. . .	הוה
[g] יוּשַׁר	Hoph. fut. 3 pers. sing. masc. . .	שיר
[h] יוּשַׁת	Hoph. fut. 3 pers. sing. masc. . .	שית
[i] יוֹתִירִ	Hiph. fut. 3 pers. sing. masc. . .	יתר
יוֹתָם	וְ' pr. name masc. . .	הוה
יִוָּתֵר, [k] יִוָּתֵר	וַיִּ' Niph. fut. 3 pers. sing. masc. (§ 9. rem. 3); וַ conv. . .	יתר
[l] יוֹתֵר	וַיּ' Hiph. fut. 3 pers. sing. masc., ap. fr. יוֹתִיר; וַ id. . .	יתר
יוֹתֵר	Kal part., subst. or adv. . .	יתר
יִוָּתְרוּ	[m] וַיִּ' Niph. fut. 3 pers. pl. masc.; וַ conv. .	יתר
יוֹתִרוּ	וַ Hiph. fut. 3 pers. pl. masc.; וַ id. .	יתר
[n] יַז	וַ Hiph. fut. 3 pers. sing. masc. ap. fr. יַזֶּה (§ 25. No. 2b); וַ id. . .	נזה
[o] יִז, [p] יִז	וְ, וַ Kal fut. 3 pers. sing. masc., ap. fr. יִזֶּה (§ 25. No. 2b, comp. § 24. rem. 3)	נזה
[q] יָזֻבוּ	[r] וַיָּ' Kal fut. 3 pers. pl. masc.; וַ conv. .	זוב
[s] יִזְבַּח	וְ' Piel fut. 3 pers. sing. masc.; וַ id. bef. (:)	זבח
יִזְבַּח	וַ Kal fut. 3 pers. sing. masc.; וַ conv. .	זבח
[t] יִזְבָּחֵהוּ	וַ id., suff. 3 pers. sing. m. (§ 16. r. 12); וַ id.	זבח
יְזַבְּחוּ	Piel fut. 3 pers. pl. masc. [for יְזַבְּחוּ, comp. § 8. rem. 15] . .	זבח
יִזְבְּחוּ	וַיִּ', וְ' Kal fut. 3 pers. pl. masc.; וַ conv. .	זבח
[u] יִזְבְּלֵנִי	Kal fut. 3 pers. sing. masc., suff. 1 pers. sing.	זבל
[x] יָזֵד, [y] וַיָּזֶד	Hiph. fut. 3 pers. sing. masc. def. & ap. fr. יָזִיד, with conv. וַ (§ 21. rem. 17)	זוד
יַזֶּה	Hiph. fut. 3 pers. sing. masc. (§ 25. No. 2b)	נזה
[z] יִזֶּה	Kal fut. 3 pers. sing. masc. (§ 25. No. 2b)	נזה
[a] יַזְהִרוּ	Hiph. fut. 3 pers. pl. masc. . .	זהר
יְזוּאֵל	וְ Kh. וִיזוּאֵל, see K. יְזִיאֵל	
[b] יָזוּב	Kal fut. 3 pers. sing. masc. . .	זוב
יָזוּבוּ	וְ id. fut. 3 pers. pl. masc.; וַ conv. .	זוב
[c] יְזוֹרֵר	וְ Poel fut. 3 pers. sing. masc.; וְ id. .	זרר
[יְזִיאֵל]	(*assembly of God*; וזה Arab. to assemble) pr. name masc. 1 Ch. 12. 3.	
[d] יִזַּח	Niph. fut. 3 pers. sing. masc. . .	זחח
[e] יָזִיד	Hiph. fut. 3 pers. sing. masc. . .	זוד

[f] יְזִידוּן	id. fut. 3 pers. pl. masc. with parag. ן . .	זוד
יַזִּיָּה	וְ pr. name masc. . . .	נזה
יָזִיז	pr. name masc. . . .	זוז
[g] יַזִּיר	Hiph. fut. 3 pers. sing. masc. . .	נזר
[h] יְזַכֶּה	Piel fut. 3 pers. sing. masc. . .	זכה
יִזְכֶּה	Kal fut. 3 pers. sing. masc. . .	זכה
[i] יִזְכּוֹר	Kal fut. 3 pers. sing. masc. (§ 8. rem. 18)	זכר
[k] יַזְכִּיר	Hiph. fut. 3 pers. sing. masc. . .	זכר
[l] יַזְכִּירוּ	id. fut. 3 pers. pl. masc. . .	זכר
יִזָּכֵר	Niph. fut. 3 pers. sing. masc. . .	זכר
[m] יִזְכֹּר, יִזְכָּר־	וְ', וַיִּ' Kal fut. 3 pers. sing. masc. (§ 8. rem. 18); וַ conv. . .	זכר
[n] יִזְכְּרָהָ	וְ id., suff. 3 pers. sing. fem.; וַ id.	זכר
יִזָּכְרוּ	Niph. fut. 3 pers. pl. masc. . .	זכר
יִזְכְּרוּ	[o] וַיִּ' Kal fut. 3 pers. pl. masc.; וַ conv. .	זכר
[p] יִזְכְּרוּךָ	id., suff. 2 pers. sing. masc. . .	זכר
[q] יִזְכְּרוּנִי	id., suff. 1 pers. sing. . .	זכר
[r] יִזַּל	Kal fut. 3 pers. sing. masc. . .	נזל
יִזְּלוּ	id. fut. 3 pers. sing. masc. . .	נזל
יִזְלִיאָה	וְ pr. name masc. 1 Ch. 8. 18.	
[s] יָזֹמּוּ	Kal fut. 3 pers. pl. masc. [for יָזֹמּוּ § 18. rem. 15] . . .	זמם
[t] יִזָּמֵר	Niph. fut. 3 pers. sing. masc. . .	זמר
יְזַמְּרוּ, [u] יְזַמֵּרוּ	וְ, וִ Piel fut. 3 pers. pl. masc., with conj. וְ [for וִיזַ', וִיזַמְּרוּ] . .	זמר
[x] יְזַמֶּרְךָ	id. fut. 3 pers. sing. masc., suff. 2 pers. sing. masc. (§ 16. rem. 15) . .	זמר

יזן Kal not used; Arab. *to weigh, be heavy*.
Pu. part. מְיֻזָּנִים Je. 5. 8 Keri, *heavy, stout*.

[y] יֶזֶן	וְ Hiph. fut. 3 pers. sing. masc. ap. [from יַזְנֶה]; וַ conv. . .	זנה
[z] יְזַנֵּב	וְ Piel fut. 3 pers. sing. masc.; וְ id. bef. (:)	זנב
[a] יִזְנֶה	Kh. יִזְנֶה, K. יִזְנוּ, Kal fut. 3 p. s. or pl. m.	זנה
יִזְנוּ	וְ Kal fut. 3 pers. pl. masc.; וַ conv. .	זנה
יִזְנַח	Kal fut. 3 pers. sing. masc. . .	זנח
יַזַנְיָה, יַזַנְיָהוּ	וְ, וְ pr. name masc. with cop. וְ [for וְיַ', וְיַזַנְ'] see יַאֲזַנְיָהוּ under .	אזן
[b] יַזְנִיחֲךָ	Hiph. fut. 3 pers. sing. masc., suff. 2 pers. sing. masc. . . .	זנח
[c] יְזַנֵּק	Piel fut. 3 pers. sing. masc.	זנק

יזע Root not used; Arab. *to flow*.
יֶזַע masc. *sweat*, Eze. 44. 18.
זֵעָה fem. dec. 10, (for יְזֵעָה) id. Ge. 3. 19.

---

[a] Is. 46. 7. [b] Ps. 55. 17. [c] Ps. 57. 4. [d] Job 22. 29. [e] 2 Ki. 6. 27. [f] Ex. 2. 17. [g] Is. 26. 1. [h] Ex. 21. 30, 30. [i] De. 28. 54. [k] Zec. 13. 8. [l] Ex. 16. 19. [m] Jos. 18. 2. [n] Le. 8. 11, 30. [o] Is. 63. 3. [p] 2 Ki. 9. 33. [q] La. 4. 9. [r] Is. 48. 21. [s] Hab. 1. 16. [t] 1 Ki. 19. 21. [u] Ge. 30. 20. [x] Ex. 21. 14. [y] Ge. 25. 29. [z] Le. 6. 20. [a] Da. 12. 3. [b] Le. 15. 25. [c] 2 Ki. 4. 35. [d] Ex. 28. 28; 39. 21. [e] De. 18. 20. [f] De. 17. 13. [g] Nu. 6. 3, 5. [h] Ps. 119. 9. [i] Ho. 9. 9. [k] Is. 19. 17. [l] Is. 48. 1. [m] Ec. 11. 8. [n] 1 Sa. 1. 19. [o] Ps. 78. 35. [p] Is. 64. 4. [q] Zec. 10. 9. [r] Nu. 24. 7. [s] Ge. 11. 6. [t] Is. 5. 6. [u] Ps. 66. 4. [x] Ps. 30. 13. [y] 2 Ch. 21. 11. [z] De. 25. 18. [a] Eze. 23. 43. [b] 1 Ch. 28. 9. [c] De. 33. 22.

יַזְעִיקוּ[a] Hiph. fut. 3 pers. pl. masc. . . . . זעק

יִזְעָמוּהוּ[b] Kal fut. 3 pers. pl. masc. [יִזְעֲמוּ from sing. יִזְעַם], suff. 3 pers. sing. m. (§ 16. r. 12) זעם

יִזְעַף[c] וַיִּ[d] Kal fut. 3 pers. sing. masc.; ·וַ conv. . זעף

וַיַּזְעֵק Hiph. fut. 3 pers. sing. masc. ap. [fr. יַזְעִיק]; ·וַ id. . . . . . זעק

וַיִּזָּעֵק Niph. fut. 3 pers. sing. masc.; ·וַ id. . זעק

יִזְעַק[e] / וַיִּזְעַק } Kal fut. 3 pers. sing. masc. (§ 8. rem. 15); ·וַ id. . . . . . } זעק

וַיִּזָּעֲקוּ[f] Niph. fut. 3 pers. pl. masc.; ·וַ id. . . זעק

יִזְעֲקוּ[g] וַיִּ[h] / יִזְעָקוּ[i] וַיִּ, וְ[k] } Kal fut. 3 pers. pl. masc. (§ 8. rem. 15); ·וַ id. . . } זעק

וַיִּזְעָקוּךָ[l] id., suff. 2 pers. sing. masc. (§ 16. rem. 12); ·וַ id. . . . . . זעק

יָזֹקּוּ Kal fut. 3 pers. pl. masc. . . . . זקק

יַזְקִין Hiph. fut. 3 pers. sing. masc. . . . זקן

וַיִּזְקַן[m] Kal fut. 3 pers. sing. masc.; ·וַ conv. . זקן

וַיָּזַר[n] Kal fut. 3 pers. sing. masc. ap. (§ 21. r. 9) זור

וַיִּזֶר[o] Kal fut. 3 pers. sing. masc. ap. [fr. יִזְרֶה]; ·וַ conv. . . . . . . זרה

יְזֹרְבוּ[p] Pual fut. 3 pers. pl. masc. . . . . זרב

יְזֹרֶה[q] Pual fut. 3 pers. sing. masc. . . . . זרה

וַיִּזָּרוּ[r] Niph. fut. 3 pers. pl. masc.; ·וַ conv. . זרה

יְזָרוּ[s] Piel fut. 3 pers. pl. masc. . . . . זרה

יִזְרַח[t] / וַיִּזְרַח וַיִּ[u] } Kal fut. 3 pers. sing. masc. (§ 8. rem. 15); ·וַ conv. . . . } זרח

יִזְרַחְיָה וְ pr. name masc. . . . . זרח

יִזָּרַע[x] / יִזָּרֵעַ } Niph. fut. 3 pers. sing. masc. (§ 15. rem. 1) . . . . } זרע

יִזְרַע[y] / וַיִּזְרַע[z] } Kal fut. 3 pers. sing. masc. (§ 8. rem. 15); ·וַ conv. . . . } זרע

יִזְרְעֶאל / יִזְרְעֵאל } וְ pr. name of a man and a place . זרע

יִזְרְעֶאלָה id. with parag. ה . . . . זרע

וַיִּזְרָעֶהָ[a] Kal fut. 3 pers. sing. masc. (יִזְרַע), suff. 3 pers. sing. fem. (§ 16. r. 12); ·וַ conv. זרע

יִזְרְעוּ[b] / וַיִּזְרְעוּ[c] } id. fut. 3 pers. pl. masc. (§ 8. rem. 15); ·וַ id. . . . . . } זרע

וַיִּזְרֹק[d] וַיִּ Kal fut. 3 pers. sing. masc.; ·וַ id. . זרק

וַיִּזְרְקֵהוּ[e] id. id., suff. 3 pers. sing. masc.; ·וַ id. . זרק

וַיִּזְרְקוּ id. fut. 3 pers. pl. masc.; ·וַ id. . זרק

וַיְזָתָא see וַיְזָתָא under lett. ו.

יֵחָבְאוּ[f] וַיֵּ[g] Niph. fut. 3 pers. pl. masc.; ·וַ conv. חבא

יְחֻבָּה pr. name masc. . . . . . חבה

יַחֲבוֹשׁ[h] Kal fut. 3 pers. sing. masc. (§ 8. rem. 18) חבש

יַחְבֹּט[i] Kal fut. 3 pers. sing. masc. (§ 13. rem. 5) חבט

יֵחָבֶט[k] Niph. fut. 3 pers. sing. masc. bef. penacute [for יֵחָבֵט § 9. rem. 3] . . . חבט

וַיַּחְבִּיאֵם[l] Hiph. fut. 3 pers. sing. masc., suff. 3 pers. pl. masc.; ·וַ conv. . . . חבא

יֵחָבֶל[m] Niph. fut. 3 pers. sing. masc. bef. monos. [for יֵחָבֵל § 9. rem. 3] . . . חבל

יַחְבֹּל[n] Kal fut. 3 pers. sing. masc. . . . חבל

יְחַבֶּל־[o] Piel fut. 3 pers. s. m. [for יְחַבֵּל § 10. r. 4] חבל

יַחְבְּלוּ[p] / יַחְבֹּלוּ[q] } Kal fut. 3 pers. pl. masc. (§ 8. rem. 15, & § 13. rem. 5) . . . } חבל

וַיְחַבֵּק[r] / וַיְחַבֶּק־[s] } Piel fut. 3 pers. sing. masc. (§ 9. rem. 3) וַ conv. . . . . } חבק

וַיְחַבְּקֵהוּ[t] id., suff. 3 pers. sing. masc.; וַ id. . חבק

וַיְחַבֵּר[u] Piel fut. 3 pers. sing. masc.; וַ id. . חבר

וַיְחַבְּרֵהוּ[x] id., suff. 3 pers. sing. masc.; וַ id. . חבר

וַיַּחֲבֹשׁ / וַיַּחֲבָשׁ־[y] } Kal fut. 3 pers. sing. masc. (§ 8. r. 18) ·וַ id. . . . . } חבש

וְיַחֲבֹשׁ[z] id. id. in pause for [יַחֲבֹשׁ, יַחֲבֹשׁ § 8. r. 15, & § 13. rem. 5] . . . . חבש

וַיַּחַבְשׁוּ[a] / וַיַּחְבְּשׁוּ[b] } id. fut. 3 pers. pl. masc. (v. id.); ·וַ conv. חבש

וַיַּחְבְּשֵׁנוּ[c] id. fut. 3 pers. sing. masc., suff. 1 pers. pl. (v. id.); ·וַ id. . . . . חבש

וְיָחֹגּוּ[d] Kal fut. 3 pers. pl. masc. . . . חגג

וַיַּחְגֹּר[e] וַיַּ Kal fut. 3 pers. sing. masc. (§ 13. rem. 5); ·וַ conv. . . . . . חגר

יַחְגְּרֶהָ[f] id. id., suff. 3 pers. sing. fem. (v. id.) חגר

וַיַּחְגְּרוּ[g] וַיַּ, וְ[h] id. fut. 3 pers. pl. m. (v. id.); ·וַ conv. חגר

[יָחַד] fut. יֵחַד, *to be united, be one*, with אֶת ,בְּ. Pi. *to unite, join*, Ps. 86. 11.

יָחִיד masc. dec. 3 a, יְחִידָה fem. dec. 10.—I. *only, alone, only begotten.*—II. *solitary, forsaken.*—III. *only, most dear, darling.*

יַחַד masc.—I. *union*, 1 Ch. 12. 17.—II. adv. *together, in one place; wholly, entirely.*

יַחְדָּו ,יַחְדָּיו literally *union of them, they together*, (§ 4. rem. 1) hence—I. *together, in the same place.*—II. *together, at one time*, Ps. 4. 9.—III. *mutually, with one another.*

יַחְדּוֹ (for יַחְדּוֹן *united*) pr. name m. 1 Ch. 5.14.

יַחַת (for יַחֶדֶת *union*) pr. name masc. of several men.

יָחַד in pause for יַחַד adv. . . . . יחד

יֵחַד[i] Kal fut. 3 pers. sing. masc., middle A [for יָחֹד § 18. rem. 6] . . . . חדד

[a] Job 35. 9. [b] Pr. 24. 24. [c] Pr. 19. 3. [d] 2 Ch. 26. 19. [e] Is. 15. 5. [f] Jos. 8. 16. [g] Ho. 8. 2.
[h] Ex. 2. 23. [i] Mi. 3. 4. [k] Eze. 27. 30. [l] Ne. 9. 28. [m] 2 Ch. 24. 15. [n] Ju. 6. 38.
[o] Ex. 32. 20. [p] Job 6. 17. [q] Job 18. 15. [r] Eze. 36. 19. [s] Pr. 15. 7. [t] Job 9. 7.
[u] Ge. 32. 32. [x] Na. 1. 14. [y] Ec. 11. 4. [z] Ge. 26. 12. [a] Ju. 9. 45. [b] Ho. 8. 7.
[c] Ps. 107. 37 [d] Le. 7. 2; Is. 28. 25. [e] Le. 9. 12, 18. [f] Am. 9. 3. [g] Jos. 10. 16. [h] Job 34. 17.
[i] Is. 27. 12. [k] Is. 28. 27. [l] 1 Ki. 18. 4. [m] Pr. 13. 13. [n] De. 24. 6. [o] Ps. 7. 15.
[p] Job 24. 9. [q] Job 24. 3. [r] Ge. 48. 10. [s] Ge. 29. 13. [t] Ge. 33. 4. [u] Ex. 36. 10, 13, 16.
[x] 2 Ch. 20. 36. [y] 1 Ki. 13. 23. [z] Job 5. 18. [a] 1 Ki. 13. 27. [b] 1 Ki. 13. 13. [c] Ho. 6. 1.
[d] Ex. 5. 1. [e] Le. 16. 4. [f] Ps. 109. 19. [g] Eze. 44. 18. [h] 2 Sa. 22. 46. [i] Pr. 27. 17.

[a] יַחַד Hiph. fut. 3 pers. sing. masc. ap. R. חָדָה § 24. rem. 16); or it may be regarded as a Chaldaizing form of Hiph. fut. R. חָדַד, with implicit Dagesh in ח (§ 18. rem. 14) and Pattahh in the final syllable on account of this guttural letter [instead of יָחֵד], see § 18. rem. 6.

[b] יַחַד וְ׳ adv. . . . . יחד

[c] יַחֵד Piel imp. sing. masc. (§ 14. rem. 1) . יחד

[d] יַחְדָּו Kh. יַחַד q. v.; K. יַחְדָּו (q. v.) . יחד

[e] יִחַדְּ [f] וַיִּ׳ Kal fut. 3 pers. sing. masc., ap. [fr. יֶחְדֶּה § 24. rem. 4]; וַ conv. . . חדה

יַחְדָּו וְ׳ adv. . . . . יחד

יַחְדּוֹ pr. name masc. . . . . . יחד

יַחְדִּיאֵל וְ pr. name masc. . . . . . חדה

יֶחְדְּיָהוּ pr. name masc. . . . . . חדה

יַחְדָּיו adv. . . . . יחד

[g] יֶחְדַּל Kh. יֶחְדַּל q. v.; K. וַחֲדַל Kal imp. sing. masc.; וַ bef. (-:) . . . . חדל

[h] יֶחְדַּל וְ׳ / וַיֶּ׳ יֶחְדַּל Kal fut. 3 pers. sing. masc. (§ 13. r. 5, & § 8. rem. 15); וַ conv. . . חדל

יֶחְדָּלוּ / וַ יֶחְדָּלוּ id. fut. 3 pers. pl. masc. (§ 13. rem. 6, & § 8. rem. 15); וַ id. . . חדל

[k] יֶחְדָּלוּן id. id., parag. ן (§ 8. rem. 17) . . חדל

[l] יְחַדֵּשׁ וִ Piel fut. 3 pers. sing. masc.; וְ conv. . חדש

יְחוּאֵל Kh. יְחוּאֵל, K. יְחִיאֵל (q. v.) . . . חיה

יְחוּאֵל pr. name masc. . . . . . חוה

[m] יָחוֹגּוּ Kal fut. 3 pers. s. m. (for יָחֹגּוּ § 18. r. 2) חגג

[n] יְחַוֶּה־ Piel fut. 3 pers. sing. masc. . . . חוה

יָחוּל Kal fut. 3 pers. sing. masc. . . . . חול

[n] יְחוֹלֵל Pilel fut. 3 pers. sing. masc. . . . חול

[o] יְחֹלָלוּ Pulal fut. 3 pers. pl. masc. [for יְחוֹלְלוּ, comp. § 8. rem. 15] . . . . . חול

[p] יְחַוִּנַּהּ Ch. Pael fut. 3 pers. sing. masc., suff. 3 pers. sing. fem. . . . . . חוה

[q] יְחַוִּנַּנִי Ch. id. with suff. 1 pers. sing. . . . חוה

[r] יָחוּס Kal fut. 3 pers. sing. masc. . . . . חוס

[s] יְחוֹקְקוּ Poel fut. 3 pers. pl. masc. . . . . חקק

[t] יֶחֱוָרוּ Kal fut. 3 pers. pl. masc. [for יֶחֱוְרוּ comp. § 8. rem. 15] . . . . . חור

[u] יָחוּשׁ Kal fut. 3 pers. sing. masc. . . . . חוש

יֶחֱזֶה Kal fut. 3 pers. sing. masc. . . . . חזה

יֶחֱזוּ וַיֶּ׳ id. fut. 3 pers. pl. masc.; וַ conv. . . חזה

יַחֲזִיאֵל וְ׳ pr. name masc. . . . . . חזה

יַחְזְיָה וְ pr. name masc. . . . . . חזה

[x] יֶחֱזָיוּן Kal fut. 3 pers. pl. m. with parag. ן (§ 8. r. 17) חזה

יַחֲזִיק Hiph. fut. 3 pers. sing. masc. . . חזק

וַיַּחֲזִיקוּ id. fut. 3 pers. pl. masc.; וַ conv. . חזק

וַיַּחֲזֵק / וְיַחֲזֶק־ id. fut. 3 pers. sing. masc., ap. (§ 11. rem. 7) fr. יַחֲזִיק; וַ id. . . חזק

יְחַזֵּק וְ Piel fut. 3 pers. sing. masc.; וְ id. . חזק

[y] יֶחֱזַק וְ / [z] יֶחֱזַק וַיֶּ, וְ / [a] יֶחֱזָק [b] וַיֶּ Kal fut. 3 pers. sing. masc. (§ 13. rem. 5) וְ id. . . חזק

יְחֶזְקֵאל pr. name masc. . . . . חזק

[c] יְחַזְּקֵהוּ וְ Piel fut. 3 pers. sing. masc., suff. 3 pers. sing. masc.; וְ id. bef. (:) חזק

[d] יַחֲזִקוּ [e] וַיַּ׳ Hiph. fut. 3 pers. pl. masc. (for יַחֲזִיקוּ); וַ id. . . . . . . חזק

יְחַזְּקוּ וִ׳ Piel fut. 3 pers. pl. masc.; וְ id. . חזק

יֶחֶזְקוּ / [f] יֶחֶזְקוּ Kal fut. 3 pers. pl. masc. (§ 13. rem. 5) חזק

[g] יְחַזְּקוּם [h] וַיְ׳ Piel fut. 3 p. pl. m., suff. 3 p. pl. m.; וַ conv. חזק

יְחַזְּקֵם וְ id. fut. 3 pers. s. m., suff. 3 pers. pl. m.; וְ id. חזק

יְחַזְּקֵנִי וִ id. id., suff. 1 pers. sing. . . . חזק

יְחִזְקִיָּה, יְחִזְקִיָּהוּ & וִיחִזְ׳ pr. names masc. . חזק

יַחְזֵרָה pr. name masc. . . . . . חזר

[k] יַחֲטִא [l] וַיַּ׳ Hiph. fut. 3 p. s. m. [for יַחֲטִיא]; וַ conv. חטא

[m] יְחַטֵּא וְ Piel fut. 3 pers. sing. masc.; וְ id. . חטא

יֶחֱטָא Kal fut. 3 pers. sing. masc. . . . חטא

[n] יְחַטְּאֶהוּ וְ Piel fut. 3 pers. sing. masc., suff. 3 pers. sing. masc.; וְ id. . . . . . חטא

[o] יְחַטְּאוּ וְ id. fut. 3 pers. pl. masc.; וְ id. . . חטא

יֶחֶטְאוּ Kal fut. 3 pers. pl. masc. . . . . חטא

[p] יַחְטְבוּ Kal fut. 3 pers. pl. masc. (§ 13. rem. 5) חטב

[q] יַחֲטִיאוּ Hiph. fut. 3 pers. pl. masc. . . . חטא

[r] יַחְטֹף Kal fut. 3 pers. sing. masc. (§ 13. rem. 5) חטף

יְחִי וַיְ׳, וִי׳ / יְחִי וְ׳ / יְחִי וְ Kal fut. 3 pers. s. m., ap. fr. יִחְיֶה (§ 24. rem. 3e); וַ conv.; with וְ conj. וִיחִי [for וְיְחִי, וִיְחִי] חיה

יְחִיאֵל וִיחִ׳ (with cop. וְ) pr. name masc. . . חיה

יְחִיאֵלִי patronym. of יְחִיאֵל . . . . . חיה

[t] יָחִיד וְ׳ adj. masc. sing. dec. 3a . . . יחד

[u] יְחִידָה id. fem. dec. 10 . . . . . יחד

[x] יְחִידִים id. masc. pl. abs. dec. 3a . . . יחד

[y] יְחִידְךָ / [z] יְחִידְךָ id. id. sing. with suff. 2 pers. sing. masc. יחד

יְחִידָתִי id. fem. with suff. 1 pers. sing. dec. 10 . יחד

[a] יְחַיֶּהָ וַ Piel fut. 3 p. s. m., suff. 3 p. s. fem.; וַ conv. חיה

[b] יְחִיֶּה Kh. יְחִיֶה q. v.; K. וְחָיָה Kal pret. 3 pers. sing. masc.; וְ id. . . . . . חיה

יְחַיֶּה Piel fut. 3 pers. sing. masc. . . . חיה

---

[a] Pr. 27. 17. [b] Job 31. 38. [c] Ps. 86. 11. [d] Je. 48. 7. [e] Job 3. 6. [f] Ex. 18. 9.
[g] Job 10. 20. [h] Eze. 3. 27. [i] Job 14. 6. [k] Ex. 9. 29. [l] 2 Ch. 15. 8. [m] Ps. 107. 27.
[n] Ps. 29. 9. [o] Job 26. 5. [p] Da. 2. 11. [q] Da. 5. 7. [r] Je. 21. 7. [s] Pr. 8. 15.
[t] Is. 29. 22. [u] Ec. 2. 25. [x] Is. 26. 11. [y] Is. 39. 1. [z] Da. 11. 5, 5. [zz] Ps. 19. 3.
[a] 1 Ch. 28. 7. [b] 2 Ch. 27. 5. [c] Is. 41. 7. [d] Da. 11. 32. [e] 2 Sa. 2. 16.
[f] Is. 28. 22. [g] Je. 10. 4. [h] 2 Ch. 29. 34. [i] Da. 10. 18. [k] Ju. 20. 16.
[l] 2 Ki. 21. 11. [m] Le. 8. 15. [n] Le. 9. 15. [o] 2 Ch. 29. 24. [p] Eze. 39. 10.
[q] Ex. 23. 33. [r] Ps. 10. 9. [s] Is. 38. 21. [t] Pr. 4. 3. [u] Ju. 11. 34.
[x] Ps. 68. 7. [y] Ge. 22. 2, 12. [z] Ge. 22. 16. [a] 2 Sa. 12. 3. [b] Je. 21. 9; 38. 2.

יְחִיָּה וְ pr. name masc. [for יְחִיָּה] see יְחִיאֵל . חיה
יְחְיֶה Kal fut. 3 pers. sing. masc. . . חיה
יְחַיֵּהוּ[a] וְ Piel fut. 3 pers. sing. masc., suff. 3 pers. sing. masc., with conj. וְ [for וִיחַיֵּהוּ, וִי'] חיה
יְחַיּוּ id. fut. 3 pers. pl. masc. . . . חיה
יִחְיוּ [b]וְ', [c]וַיְ' Kal fut. 3 pers. pl. masc.; וַ· conv. חיה
יְחִיטוּ[d] Chald. Aph. fut. 3 pers. pl. masc. . חוט
יְחַיֵּנוּ[e] Piel fut. 3 p. s. m., suff. 1 p. pl. (§ 24. rem. 21) חיה
יָחִיל Kal, or Hiph. (Ps. 29. 8), fut. 3 pers. sing. masc. from חִיל or . . . . חול
יָחִיל[f] וְ adj. masc. sing. . . . . . יחל
יָחִילוּ [g]וַיָּ' Kal fut. 3 pers. pl. m.; וַ· conv., R. חִיל, see חול
יְחִילוּן[h] id. with parag. ן . . . . . חול
יְחַיֵּנוּ[i] Piel fut. 3 pers. pl. masc., suff. 1 pers. pl. [for יְחַיּוּנוּ] . . . . חיה
יָחִישׁ[k] Hiph. fut. 3 pers. sing. masc. . . חוש
יָחִישָׁה[l] id. with parag. ה (§ 8. rem. 13) . . חוש
יְחִיתַן[m] [for יְחִתֵּן] Hiph. fut. 3 pers. sing. masc. [יָחֵת], suff. 3 pers. pl. fem. (§ 18. rem. 12) . חתת
יְחַכֶּה[n] Piel fut. 3 pers. sing. masc. . . חכה
יְחַכֵּם[o] Piel fut. 3 pers. sing. masc. . . . חכם
יֶחְכָּם, יֶחְכַּם[p] [q]וְ', [r]וַיֶּ' } Kal fut. 3 pers. sing. masc. (§ 13. rem. 5, & § 8. rem. 15); וַ· conv. } חכם
יֶחְכָּמוּ[s] id. fut. 3 pers. pl. masc. [for יֶחְכְּמוּ v. id.] חכם
יְחַכְּמֵנוּ[t] Piel fut. 3 pers. s. m. [יְחַכֵּם], suff. 1 pers. pl. חכם

יָחַל Kal not used; *to wait*, cogn. חוּל. Pi. יִחַל (§ 14. rem. 1).—I. *to cause to wait, expect, hope*, with עַל.—II. *to wait, expect, hope*, with אֶל, לְ. Hiph. *to wait, expect*, with לְ. Niph. נוֹחַל, fut. יִיָּחֵל (§ 20. r. 6) id.

יָחִיל adj. masc. *waiting, expecting*, La. 3. 26.

יַחְלְאֵל (*hoping in God*) pr. name masc. Ge. 46. 14. Patronym. יַחְלְאֵלִי Nu. 26. 26.

תּוֹחֶלֶת fem. dec. 13a (with suff. תּוֹחַלְתִּי) *expectation, hope*.

יָחַל[u] וַ Kal fut. 3 pers. sing. masc. ap. [for יַחַל from יֶחֱלֶה § 24. rem. 3d]; וַ· conv. . . חלה
יָחֵל[x], יָחֶל וַ } Hiph. fut. 3 pers. sing. m. (§ 18. rem. 11) חלל
יָחֶל וַ Kal fut. 3 pers. sing. masc. with conv. וַ· [for יָחִל, ap. from יָחִיל § 22. r. 3] R. חִיל, see חול
יַחֵל[y] Piel imp. sing. masc. (§ 14. rem. 1) . יחל
יַחֵל[z] dag. forte impl. in ח [for יְחַלֵּל], Chald. form for יָחֵל q. v. (§ 18. rem. 14) . . חלל
יֵחָל[a] Niph. fut. 3 pers. sing. masc. [for יֵחַל, with gutt. for יִחַל] . . . . חלל

יְחַל וַ Piel fut. 3 pers. s. m. ap. [fr. יְחַלֶּה]; וַ conv. חלה
יֶחֱלָא[b] וַ Kal fut. 3 pers. sing. masc. [for יֶחֱלֶה § 24. rem. 19]; וַ· conv. . . . . חלה
יַחְלְאֵל וְ pr. name masc. . . . . יחל
יָחֵלּוּ[c] וַ Hiph. fut. 3 pers. pl. masc.; וַ· conv. . חלל
יִחֲלוּ, יִחֵלוּ[d] וְ, וְ } Piel pret. 3 pers. pl. (§ 14. rem. 1, & § 8. rem. 4) . . . . } יחל
יָחֻלוּ[e] Kal fut. 3 pers. pl. masc. [for יָחוּלוּ] . חול
יְחַלּוּ Piel fut. 3 pers. pl. masc. . . . חלה
יַחְלְטוּ[f] וַ Hiph. fut. 3 pers. pl. masc. [for יַחְלִיטוּ § 11. rem. 7]; וַ· conv. . . . חלט
יַחֲלִיף[g] Hiph. fut. 3 pers. sing. masc. . . חלף
יַחֲלִיפוּ id. fut. 3 pers. pl. masc. . . . חלף
יַחֲלִיפֶנּוּ[h] id. fut. 3 p. s. m., suff. 3 p. s. m. (§ 2. rem. 3) חלף
יַחֲלִיץ[i] Hiph. fut. 3 pers. sing. masc. . . . חלץ
יַחֲלִיקוּן[k] Hiph. fut. 3 pers. pl. m. with parag. ן . חלק
יְחַלֵּל[l] Piel fut. 3 pers. sing. masc. . . . חלל
יְחַלְלֻהוּ[m] id. fut. 3 pers. pl. m. (יְחַלְלוּ), suff. 3 pers. s. m. חלל
יְחַלְּלוּ, יְחַלֵּלוּ[n] וַ' } id. fut. 3 pers. pl. masc. (comp. § 8. rem. 15); וַ· conv. . . . } חלל
יְחַלְלֶנּוּ[o] id. fut. 3 p. s. m., suff. 3 p. s. m. (§ 2. rem. 3) חלל
יַחֲלֹם[p] וַיַּ' Kal fut. 3 pers. sing. masc.; וַ conv. . חלם
יַחַלְמוּ[q], יַחַלְמוּ[r] וַ } id. fut. 3 pers. pl. masc. (§ 13. rem. 5); וַ· id. . . . . } חלם
יַחֲלְמוּן[s] id. id. with parag. ן [for יַחַלְמוּן § 8. rem. 17] חלם
יִחַלְנוּ[t] Piel pret. 1 pers. pl. (§ 14. rem. 1) . יחל
יְחַלֵּף וַ Piel fut. 3 pers. sing. masc.; וַ conv. . חלף
יַחֲלֹף [u]וְ' Kal fut. 3 pers. sing. masc. . . חלף
יַחֲלֹפוּ[x] וְ id. fut. 3 pers. pl. masc. [for יַחַלְפוּ or יַחְלְפוּ § 13. rem. 5] . . . . חלף
יַחְלְפוּן[y] Chald. Peal fut. 3 pers. pl. masc. (§ 49. rem. 2) חלף
יְחַלֵּץ[z] Piel fut. 3 pers. sing. masc. . . חלץ
יֵחָלְצוּ[a] Niph. fut. 3 pers. pl. masc. [for יֵחָלְצוּ comp. § 8. rem. 7] . . . . . חלץ
יֵחָלְצוּן id. with parag. ן . . . . חלץ
יְחַלְּצֵם[b] וַ Piel fut. 3 pers. sing. masc. (יְחַלֵּץ), suff. 3 pers. pl. masc.; וַ conv. . . . חלץ
יְחַלְּצֵנִי id. with suff. 1 pers. sing. . . . חלץ
יַחֲלֹק Kal fut. 3 pers. sing. masc. . . . חלק
יֵחָלֵק, יֵחָלֶק[c] [ss]וַיֵּ' } Niph. fut. 3 pers. sing. masc. (§ 9. rem. 3); וַ· conv. . . . . } חלק
יְחַלֵּק, יְחַלֶּק־[d] וַ', וַ } Piel fut. 3 pers. sing. masc. (§ 10. rem. 4); וַ id. . . . . } חלק

[a] Ps. 41. 3. [b] Eze. 37. 9. [c] Eze. 37. 10. [d] Ezr. 4. 12. [e] Ho. 6. 2. [f] La. 3. 26. [g] Ju. 3. 25. [h] Is. 13. 8. [i] 2 Ki. 7. 4. [k] Is. 28. 16. [l] Is. 5. 19. [m] Hab. 2. 17. [n] Is. 30. 18. [o] Ps. 105. 22. [p] Pr. 21. 11. [q] Pr. 9. 9. [r] 1 Ki. 5. 11. [s] Job 32. 9. [t] Job 35. 11. [u] 2 Ki. 1. 2. [x] Ju. 10. 18; 13. 5. [y] Ps. 130. 7; 131. 3. [z] Nu. 30. 3. [a] Is. 48. 11. [b] 2 Ch. 16. 12. [c] Ho. 8. 10. [d] Job 29. 21. [e] 2 Sa. 3. 29. [f] 1 Ki. 20. 33. [g] Job 14. 7. [h] Le. 27. 10. [i] Is. 58. 11. [k] Ps. 5. 10. [l] Le. 21. 12, 15, 23. [m] Le. 22. 9. [n] Ps. 89. 32. [o] De. 20. 6. [p] Is. 29. 8, 8. [q] Job 39. 4. [r] Ge. 40. 5. [s] Joel 3. 1. [ss] Ge. 14. 15. [t] Ps. 33. 22. [u] Job 9. 11. [x] Ps. 102. 27. [y] Da. 4. 13, 20, 22, 29. [z] Job 36. 15. [a] Pr. 11. 9. [b] Ps. 34. 8. [c] Job 38. 24. [d] Jos. 18. 10.

וַיַּחְלְקוּ[a], יַחְלְקוּ[b] וַ} Kal fut. 3 pers. pl. masc. (§ 13. rem. 5, comp. § 8. rem. 15); ·וַ conv. . . חלק

יְחַלְּקוּ[c] וַ Piel fut. 3 pers. pl. masc.; וַ id. . . חלק

יַחְלְקוּם וַ Kal fut. 3 pers. pl. masc., suff. 3 pers. pl. masc. (§ 13. rem. 5); ·וַ id. . . חלק

יֵחָלְקֵם[d] וַ Niph. fut. 3 pers. sing. masc. (יֵחָלֵק), suff. 3 pers. pl. masc., others read יְחַלְּקֵם Piel, (§ 10. rem. 7) . . . . . חלק

יַחֲלשׁ[e] וַ, יַחֲלשׁ[f] וַ} Kal fut. 3 pers. sing. masc. (§ 8. rem. 13, comp. § 8. rem. 15); ·וַ conv. . . חלש

יִחַלְתִּי Piel pret. 1 pers. sing. (§ 14. rem. 1, comp. § 8. rem. 7) . . . . . . יחל

יִחַלְתָּנִי[g] id. fut. 2 pers. sing. masc., suff. 1 pers. sing. (§ 2. rem. 1) . . . . . יחל

[יָחַם] I. *to be hot, warm*, Eze. 24. 11.—II. *to be hot with anger*, De. 19. 6.—III. *to conceive*, Ge. 30. 38, 39. Pi.—I. *to be hot* (for sexual intercourse).—II. *to conceive*, Ps. 51. 7.

חֵמָה fem. dec. 11b.—I. *heat, anger, fury*.—II. *poison, venom*, De. 32. 33.

חֲמָא, חֵמָא Ch. fem. *heat, anger*, Da. 3. 13, 19.

יֵחַם[h], וַיֵּחַם} Kal fut. 3 pers. sing. masc. (§ 18. rem. 5) . . . חמם

יַחֵם[i] Piel inf. constr. (§ 14. rem. 1) . . . יחם

יֵחַם[k], יֵחָם[l]} Kal fut. 3 pers. sing. masc. (§ 18. rem. 6, comp. § 8. rem. 15) . . . חמם

יֵחַם[m] id., with dag. f. imp. in ח [for יֵחַם] a Chald. form (§ 18. rem. 14) . . . . חמם

יַחְמֹד[n] Kal fut. 3 pers. sing. masc. (§ 13. rem. 5) . חמד

יֵחַמּוּ[o], וַיֵּחַמוּ[p]} Kal fut. 3 pers. pl. masc. (§ 18. rem. 6, 14, & § 13. rem. 12); ·וַ conv. . חמם

יַחְמוֹל Kal fut. 3 pers. sing. masc. (§ 8. rem. 18, & § 13. rem. 5) . . . . . חמל

יַחְמוּר וְ noun masc. sing. . . . . . חמר

יַחְמַי וְ pr. name masc. . . . . . . חמה

יַחְמֹל וַ, וְ Kal fut. 3 pers. sing. masc. (§ 13. rem. 5); ·וַ conv. . . . . . חמל

יַחְמְלוּ[q] id. fut. 3 pers. pl. masc. [for יַחְמְלוּ v. id. & § 8. rem. 15] . . . . חמל

יֵחַמְנָה[r] וַ Kal fut. 3 pers. pl. fem. (§ 18. rem. 6, & § 8. rem. 16); ·וַ conv. . . . . חמם

יַחְמֹס[t] וַ, וְ Kal fut. 3 pers. sing. masc. (§ 13. rem. 5); ·וַ id. . . . . . חמס

יֶחְמָץ[u] Kal fut. 3 pers. sing. masc. [for יֶחְמַץ § 13. rem. 5, & § 8. rem. 15] . . . חמץ

יַחְמְרוּ[x] Kal fut. 3 pers. pl. masc. (§ 13. rem. 5) . חמר

יֶחֱמַתְנִי[y] Piel pret. 3 pers. sing. fem. suff. 1 pers. sing. [for יֶחֱמַתְנִי § 13. rem. 12] . . יחם

יָחֹן[z], וַיָּחֹן[a]} Kal fut. 3 pers. sing. masc. (§ 18. rem. 5) . . . . . חנן

יִחַן וַ Kal fut. 3 pers. sing. masc. ap. (§ 24. rem. 3); ·וַ conv. . . . חנה

יֻחַן Hoph. fut. 3 pers. sing. masc. [for יוּחַן] . חנן

יַחֲנוּ[b] וַ, וְ; וַיַּחֲנוּן[c]} Kal fut. 3 pers. pl. masc.; ן parag.; ·וַ conv. . . . חנה

יַחַנְטוּ[ee] וַ Kal fut. 3 pers. pl. masc.; ·וַ id. . חנט

יַחֲנִיף Hiph. fut. 3 pers. sing. masc. . . . חנף

יְחֻנְּךָ[d], וִיחֻנֶּךָּ[e]} Kal fut. 3 pers. sing. masc. (יָחֹן), suff. 2 pers. sing. masc. (§ 18. r. 5, & § 2. r. 2); with conj. וְ [for וִיחָנְּךָ, וְיְ] חנן

יַחֲנְכוּ וַ Kal fut. 3 pers. pl. m. (§ 13. r. 5); ·וַ conv. חנך

יַחַנְכֶנּוּ[f] id. fut. 3 pers. sing. masc., suff. 3 pers. sing. masc. (v. id. & § 2. rem. 3) . . חנך

יְחֹנַן[g] Piel fut. 3 pers. sing. masc. . . . חנן

יֶחֱנַן[h] Kal fut. 3 pers. sing. masc. (§ 18. rem. 13) חנן

יְחָנֵּנוּ[i], וִיחֻנֵּנוּ[k]} id. fut. 3 pers. s. m. (יָחֹן), suff. 1 pers. pl. (§ 18. r. 5), with conj. וְ [for וִיחָנֵּנוּ, וְיְ] חנן

יְחֹנְנוּ[l] Poel fut. 3 pers. pl. masc. [for יְחוֹנְנוּ comp. § 8. rem. 15] . . . . . חנן

יְחֻנֶּנּוּ[m] וִ, וְ[n] Kal fut. 3 pers. sing. masc. (יָחֹן), suff. 3 pers. sing. masc. (§ 2. rem. 3); וְ conv. חנן

יְחָנֵנִי[o] Kh. יְחָנֵנִי Kal fut. 3 pers. sing. masc. (יָחֹן), K. וְחָנֵנִי pret. 3 pers. sing. masc. [חָן, with וְ conv.], suff. 1 pers. sing. . . . חנן

יֵחָנֵק[p] וַ Niph. fut. 3 pers. s. m. (§ 9. r. 4); ·וַ conv. חנק

יָחֹס[q] Kal fut. 3 pers. sing. masc. (§ 21. rem. 7) חוס

יְחַסְּדְךָ[r] Piel fut. 3 pers. sing. masc., suff. 2 pers. sing. masc. (§ 16. rem. 15) . . . חסד

יֶחֱסֶה[s] Kal fut. 3 pers. sing. masc. . . . חסה

יֶחֱסוּ[t] id. fut. 3 pers. pl. masc. . . . חסה

יֶחֱסָיוּן[u] id. id. with parag. ן (§ 24. rem. 5) . חסה

יַחְסִיר[x] Hiph. fut. 3 pers. sing. masc. (§ 13. rem. 9) חסר

יַחְסְלֶנּוּ[y] Kal fut. 3 pers. sing. masc., suff. 3 pers. sing. masc. (§ 13. rem. 5) . . . . חסל

יֵחָסֵן[z] Niph. fut. 3 pers. sing. masc. . . . חסן

יַחְסְנוּן[a] וְ Chald. Aph. fut. 3 pers. pl. masc. (§ 49. rem. 2) . . . . . חסן

יֶחְסַר, יֶחְסָר} Kal fut. 3 pers. sing. masc. (§ 13. rem. 5, & § 8. rem. 15) . . . . חסר

יַחְסְרוּ[b] וְ, וַ id. fut. 3 pers. pl. masc. (§ 13. rem. 5); ·וַ conv. . . . . . . חסר

יַחְסְרוּן[kk] id. id. with parag. ן . . . . חסר

---

[a] Jos. 14. 5. [b] 1 Sa. 30. 24. [c] 1 Ki. 18. 6. [d] 1 Ch. 23. 6; 24. 3. [e] Ex. 17. 13. [f] Job 14. 10. [g] Ps. 119. 49. [h] Is. 44. 16. [i] Ge. 30. 41; 31. 10. [k] Ec. 4. 11. [l] De. 19. 6; 1 Ki. 19. 11. [m] 1 Ki. 1. 1. [n] Ex. 34. 24. [o] Ho. 7. 7. [p] Ge. 30. 39. [q] Is. 9. 18. [r] Ge. 30. 38. [s] Job 15. 33. [t] La. 2. 6. [u] Ex. 12. 34. [x] Ps. 46. 4. [y] Ps. 51. 7. [z] De. 28. 50. [a] 2 Ki. 13. 23. [b] Ex. 14. 2. [c] Ju. 11. 18. [d] Ge. 43. 29; Is. 30. 19. [e] Nu. 6. 25. [ee] Ge. 50. 2, 26. [f] De. 20. 5. [g] Pr. 26. 25. [h] Am. 5. 15. [i] Ps. 67. 2. [k] Mal. 1. 9. [kk] Ge. 18. 28. [l] Ps. 102. 15. [m] Is. 27. 11. [n] Job 33. 24. [o] 2 Sa. 12. 22. [p] 2 Sa. 17. 23. [q] Ps. 72. 13. [r] Pr. 25. 10. [s] Ps. 34. 9. [t] Is. 14. 32. [u] Ps. 36. 8. [x] Is. 32. 6. [y] De. 28. 38. [z] Is. 23. 18. [a] Da. 7. 18. [b] Ge. 8. 3.

יָחֵף[a] [b] וְ׳ *unshod, barefoot.*

יַחַף[c] וַ Piel fut. 3 pers. sing. masc. ap. [from יְחַפֶּה]; וַ conv. — חפה

יְחַפְּאוּ[d] וַ Piel fut. 3 pers. pl. masc.; וַ id. — חפא

יְחַפֵּהוּ[e] וַ Piel fut. 3 pers. sing. masc., suff. 3 pers. sing. masc. (§ 24. rem. 21); וַ id. — חפה

יַחְפּוֹז[f] Kal fut. 3 pers. sing. masc. (§ 8. rem. 18, & § 13. rem. 5) — חפז

יֵחָפֵזוּן[g] Niph. fut. 3 pers. pl. masc.; ן parag. [for יֵחָפְזוּן comp. § 8. rem. 17] — חפז

יַחְפִּיר[h] וְ Hiph. fut. 3 pers. sing. masc. (§ 13. r. 9) — חפר

יַחְפֹּץ / יַחְפֹּץ } Kal fut. 3 pers. sing. masc. (§ 13. rem. 4 & 5, & § 8. rem. 15) — חפץ

יַחְפְּצוּ / יַחְפְּצוּ[i] } id. fut. 3 pers. pl. masc. (v. id. & § 13. rem. 6) — חפץ

יַחְפְּצוּן[k] id. id. with parag. ן [for יַחְפְּצוּ § 8. r. 17] — חפץ

יַחְפֹּר[l] וַ Kal fut. 3 pers. sing. masc. (§ 13. rem. 5); ·ַ conv. — חפר

יַחְפְּרֵהוּ[m] וַ id. id., suff. 3 pers. sing. masc.; ·ַ id. — חפר

יַחְפְּרֻהוּ[n] וַ id. fut. 3 p. pl. m., suff. 3 p. s. m.; ·ַ id. — חפר

יַחְפְּרוּ[o] / יַחְפְּרוּ[//] וַיַּ׳, וְ׳ / וַיַּ׳ } id. fut. 3 pers. pl. masc. (§ 13. rem. 4, 5, 6, & § 8. rem. 15); ·ַ id. — חפר

יְחַפֵּשׂ וַ Piel fut. 3 pers. sing. masc.; וַ id. — חפשׂ

יְחֻפַּשׂ[p] Pual fut. 3 pers. sing. masc. — חפשׂ

יַחְפְּשׂוּ[q] Kal fut. 3 pers. pl. masc. (§ 13. rem. 5) — חפשׂ

יַחַץ וַ Kal fut. 3 pers. sing. masc. ap. (§ 24. rem. 3d); ·ַ conv. — חצה

יַחְצְאֵל / יַחְצִאֵל } pr. name masc. — חצה

יַחְצֹב[r] וַ Kal fut. 3 pers. sing. masc. (§ 13. rem. 5); ·ַ conv. — חצב

יֵחָצְבוּן[s] Niph. fut. 3 pers. pl. masc. with parag. ן — חצב

יֶחֱצֶה[t] Kal fut. 3 pers. sing. masc. — חצה

יֵחָצוּ[u] וַ Niph. fut. 3 pers. pl. masc.; ·ַ conv. — חצה

יֵחָצוּ[x] id. acc. drawn back before monos. — חצה

יֶחֱצוּ[y] Kal fut. 3 pers. pl. masc. — חצה

יֶחֱצוּהוּ[z] id. with suff. 3 pers. sing. masc. — חצה

יֶחֱצוּן[a] id. with parag. ן — חצה

יֶחֱצֵם[b] וַ id. fut. 3 pers. sing. masc., suff. 3 pers. pl. masc.; ·ַ conv. — חצה

יֻחָקוּ[c] וְ Hoph. fut. 3 pers. pl. masc. [for יֻחַקּוּ § 18. rem. 15 note] — חקק

יֵחָקֵר[d] Niph. fut. 3 pers. sing. masc. — חקר

יַחְקָר־[e] / יַחְקֹר[f] } Kal fut. 3 pers. sing. masc. (§ 13. rem. 5, & § 8. rem. 18) — חקר

יֵחָקְרוּ[g] וְ Niph. fut. 3 pers. pl. masc. — חקר

יַחְקְרוּ[h] Kal fut. 3 pers. pl. masc. [for יַחְקְרוּ § 13. rem. 5, & § 8. rem. 15] — חקר

יַחְקְרֶנּוּ[i] id. fut. 3 pers. sing. masc., suff. 3 pers. s. m. — חקר

[יָחַר] *to delay, tarry,* 2 Sa. 20. 5. Kheth.

יִחַר[k] וַ Niph. fut. 3 pers. s. m. [for יֵחַר]; ·ַ conv. — חרר

יַחַר[l] וַ Hiph. fut. 3 pers. sing. masc. ap. [from יַחֲרֶה § 24. rem. 16]; ·ַ id. — חרה

יִחַר וַיִּ׳ Kal fut. 3 pers. sing. masc. ap. (§ 24. rem. 3d); ·ַ id. — חרה

יֶחֱרַב[m] / יֶחֱרָב[n] וְ / וְ׳ } Kal fut. 3 pers. sing. masc. (§ 8. rem. 15); ·ַ id. — חרב

יֶחֶרְבוּ / יֶחֱרָבוּ[o] } id. fut. 3 pers. pl. masc. (v. id.) — חרב

יַחְרְגוּ[p] וְ Kal fut. 3 pers. pl. masc. (§ 13. rem. 5) — חרג

יֶחֱרַד[q] וַיֶּ׳ Kal fut. 3 pers. sing. masc.; ·ַ conv. — ירד

יֶחֶרְדוּ / יֶחֶרְדוּ[r] / יֶחֶרְדוּ[s] וַיֶּ׳, וְ׳ } id. fut. 3 pers. pl. masc. (§ 13. rem. 5, & § 8. rem. 15); ·ַ id. — חרד

יֶחֱרֶה Kal fut. 3 pers. sing. masc. — חרה

יֵחָרוּ[u] Niph. fut. 3 pers. pl. masc. [for יֵחַרּוּ] — חרר

יַחֲרוֹשׁ Kal fut. 3 pers. sing. masc. (§ 8. rem. 18) — חרשׁ

יַחֲרִימָהּ[x] וַ Hiph. fut. 3 pers. sing. masc., suff. 3 pers. sing. fem.; ·ַ conv. — חרם

יַחֲרִימוּ וַ id. fut. 3 pers. pl. masc. — חרם

יַחֲרִימֵם[y] וַ id. id., suff. 3 pers. pl. masc. — חרם

יַחֲרִישׁ Hiph. fut. 3 pers. sing. masc. — חרשׁ

יַחֲרִישׁוּ[z] וַיַּ׳ id. fut. 3 pers. pl. masc. — חרשׁ

יַחֲרֹךְ[a] Kal fut. 3 pers. sing. masc. — חרך

יַחֲרֵם וַ Hiph. fut. 3 pers. sing. masc. ap. [from יַחֲרִים]; ·ַ conv. — חרם

יַחֲרֵם[b] id. fut. 3 pers. sing. masc. def. [for יַחֲרִים] — חרם

יָחֳרַם[c] / יָחֳרָם } Hoph. fut. 3 pers. sing. masc. (comp. § 8. rem. 15) — חרם

יְחָרֵף / יְחָרֵף[d] וַ } Piel fut. 3 pers. sing. masc. (§ 10. rem. 4); וַ conv. — חרף

יֶחֱרַף[e] Kal fut. 3 pers. sing. masc. — חרף

יְחָרְפוּנִי[f] Piel fut. 3 pers. pl. masc., suff. 1 pers. sing. — חרף

יְחָרְפֵנִי[g] id. fut. 3 pers. sing. masc., suff. 1 pers. sing. — חרף

יֶחֱרַץ[h] Kal fut. 3 pers. sing. masc. — חרץ

יַחֲרֹק[i] Kal fut. 3 pers. sing. masc. — חרק

יַחַרְקוּ[k] וַ id. fut. 3 pers. pl. masc.; ·ַ conv. — חרק

יַחֲרֹשׁ / יַחֲרֹשׁ[l] } Kal fut. 3 pers. sing. masc. (§ 13. rem. 4) — חרשׁ

יַחֲרִשׁוּ[m] וַ Hiph. fut. 3 pers. pl. masc. (§ 13. rem. 9); ·ַ conv. — חרשׁ

---

a 2 Sa. 15. 30.
b Is. 20. 2, 3, 4.
c 2 Ch. 3. 7.
d 2 Ki. 17. 9.
e 2 Ch. 3. 5, 8.
f Job 40. 23.
g Ps. 104. 7.
h Pr. 13. 5.
i Ps. 68. 31.
k Is. 58. 2.
l Ge. 26. 18, 22.
m Ps. 7. 16.
n Job 3. 20.
o Job 39. 21.
p Pr. 28. 12.
q Ps. 64. 7.
r 2 Ch. 26. 10.
s Job 19. 24.
t Is. 30. 28.
u 2 Ki. 2. 8, 14.
x Eze. 37. 22.
y Ps. 55. 24.
z Job 40. 30.
a Ex. 21. 35.
b Ju. 9. 43.
c Job 19. 23.
d Je. 46. 23.
e Ps. 44. 22.
f Job 13. 9.
g Je. 31. 37.
h Eze. 39. 14.
i Pr. 28. 11.
k Eze. 15. 5.
l Job 19. 11.
// Ps. 34. 6; Job 6. 20.
m Ps. 106. 9.
n Ho. 13. 15.
o Eze. 6. 6.
p Ps. 18. 46.
q Job 37. 1.
r Ho. 11. 11.
s Ho. 11. 10.
t Eze. 26. 18.
u Eze. 24. 10.
x Jos. 10. 1.
y 1 Ch. 4. 41.
z Job 11. 3.
a Pr. 12. 27.
b Le. 27. 28.
c Ex. 22. 19.
d Ps. 74. 10.
e Job 27. 6.
f Ne. 6. 13.
g Ps. 55. 13.
h Ex. 11. 7.
i Ps. 112. 10.
k La. 2. 16.
l Ps. 50. 3.
m Je. 38. 27.

[יָחַשׂ] masc. *lineage, family*; סֵפֶר הַיַּחַשׂ *family register*, Ne. 7. 5.—Hithp. הִתְיַחֵשׂ *to enter one's name in the family register, to be enrolled*; inf. *registration.*

יַחְשָׁב־, יַחְשֹׁב } Kal fut. 3 pers. sing. masc. (§ 8. rem. 18, & § 13. rem. 5) . . . חשב

יֵחָשֵׁב Niph. fut. 3 pers. sing. masc. . . . חשב

יְחַשֵּׁב Piel fut. 3 pers. sing. masc. . . . חשב

יַחְשְׁבֶהָ וַ Kal fut. 3 pers. sing. masc., suff. 3 pers. sing. fem. (§ 13. rem. 5); וַ conv. . חשב

יַחְשְׁבוּ, יַחְשֹׁבוּ[a] } id. fut. 3 pers. pl. masc. (§ 8. rem. 15) חשב

יֵחָשְׁבוּ[b] Niph. fut. 3 pers. pl. masc. . . . חשב

יְחַשְּׁבוּ Piel fut. 3 pers. pl. masc. . . . חשב

יַחְשְׁבוּן[c] Kal fut. 3 pers. pl. masc.; parag. ן [for יַחְשְׁבוּן § 8. rem. 17] . . . חשב

יַחְשְׁבֵנִי[d] וַ[e] id. fut. 3 pers. sing. masc., suff. 1 pers. sing. (§ 13. rem. 4 & 5); וַ conv. . חשב

יֶחֱשׁוּ[f] וַ[g] Kal fut. 3 pers. pl. masc.; וַ id. חשה

יַחְשִׁיךְ[h], יַחְשֵׁךְ[i] } וַ[k] Hiph. fut. 3 pers. sing. masc. (§ 13. rem. 9); וַ id. . . . חשך

יֶחְשַׁךְ Kal fut. 3 pers. sing. masc. (§ 13. rem. 5) חשך

יֵחָשֵׁךְ[l], יֶחְשַׁךְ[m] } Niph. fut. 3 pers. sing. masc. (§ 9. rem. 3) חשך

יֶחְשְׁכוּ[n] Kal fut. 3 pers. pl. masc. (§ 13. rem. 5) . חשך

יֶחֱשֹׂף[o] וַ Kal fut. 3 pers. sing. masc.; וַ conv. . חשף

יַחַת, יַחַת } וְ pr. name masc. . . . . יחד

יֵחַת, יֵחַת } Kal fut. 3 pers. sing. masc. (§ 18. rem. 6, comp. § 8. rem. 7) . . . חתת

יֵחַת[p] Kal fut. 3 pers. sing. masc. [for יִנְחַת, יֵחַת] נחת

יֵחַתּוּ[q] id. fut. 3 pers. pl. masc. with euph. dag. [for יֵחֲתוּ, comp. יֵצְאוּ & § 8. rem. 3] . נחת

יֵחַתּוּ וַיֵּ[r] Kal fut. 3 pers. pl. masc. (§ 18. rem. 6) חתת

יַחְתּוֹם[s] Kal fut. 3 pers. sing. masc. (§ 13. rem. 5, & § 8. rem. 18) . . . חתם

יַחְתְּךָ[t] Kal fut. 3 pers. sing. masc. [יַחְתֶּה for יַחְתֶּה § 13. r. 5], suff. 2 pers. s. m. (§ 24. r. 21) חתה

יַחְתֹּם וַיֵּ[u] Kal fut. 3 pers. sing. masc. (§ 13. rem. 5); וַ conv. . . . . . . חתם

יְחִתֵּנִי[x] Hiph. fut. 3 pers. s. m. [יָחֵת], suff. 1 pers. s. חתת

יַחְתֹּף[y] Kal fut. 3 pers. sing. masc. (§ 13. rem. 5) חתף

יַחְתְּרוּ וַיֵּ[z] Kal fut. 3 pers. pl. masc. (§ 13. rem. 5); וַ conv. . . . . חתר

יַט[a] וַ Hiph. fut. 3 pers. sing. masc., ap. from יַטֶּה (§ 25, 2b); וַ id. . . . . נטה

יֵט, וַיֵּט, וְ[b] יֵט־[c] וַ Kal fut. 3 pers. sing. masc., ap. from יִטֶּה (§ 25, 2b, comp. § 24. rem. 3) נטה

יָטַב used only in the fut. תִּיטְבִי, יִטַב, יִיטַב.—I. *to be good, well*, with מִן *to be better*; יִיטַב לִי *it shall be well with me*; וַיִּיטַב בְּעֵינַי also with לְפָנֵי, לִי, *and it pleased me*.—II. *to be cheerful, joyful*, with לֵב. Hiph. הֵיטִיב.—I. *to make good, to do well*, followed by an inf., as הֵיטִיבוּ נַגֵּן *play well;* הֵיטַבְתָּ לִרְאוֹת *thou hast well* or *rightly seen*; with a subst. הֵיטִיב הַ׳ דְּרָכָיו *to make good one's way*. Inf. abs. הֵיטֵיב as an adv. *well, rightly*.—II. *to do good to* any one, with עִם, לְ, אֶל.—III. *to make cheerful*, Ju. 19. 22. —IV. *to adjust, dress*.—V. *to be pleasing to* any one, with אֶל, 1 Sa. 20. 13.

יְטַב Chald. id. with עַל *to seem good, be pleasing to* any one, Ezr. 7. 18.

יָטְבָה (*goodness*) pr. name of a place, 2 Ki. 21. 19.

יָטְבָתָה (id.) pr. name of a station of the Israelites in the desert.

מֵיטָב masc. dec. 2b, *the best, best part of* anything.

מְהֵיטַבְאֵל (*God does well*) pr. name—I. masc. Ne. 6. 10.—II. fem. Ge. 36. 39.

יִטַב[d] וְ defect. for יִיטַב (q. v.) . . . . יטב

יָטְבָה pr. name of a place . . . . יטב

יִטְבֹּל וַ Kal fut. 3 pers. sing. masc.; וַ conv. . טבל

יִטְבְּלוּ[e] וַ id. fut. 3 pers. pl. masc.; וַ id. . . טבל

יִטְבַּע[f] וַ id. fut. 3 pers. sing. masc.; וַ id. . . טבע

יָטְבָתָה pr. name of a place . . . . יטב

יַטֶּה[g] Hiph. fut. 3 pers. sing. masc. (§ 25, 2b) נטה

יִטֶּה[h] Kal fut. 3 pers. sing. masc. (§ 25, 2b) . נטה

יַטֵּהוּ וַ Hiph. fut. 3 pers. sing. masc. (יַטֶּה q. v.), suff. 3 pers. sing. masc.; וַ conv. . . נטה

יִטְהַר, וַיִּ[i] יִטְהָר } Kal fut. 3 pers. sing. masc. (§ 8. rem. 15); וַ id. . . . טהר

יְטַהֵר[k] וַ Piel fut. 3 pers. sing. m. (§ 14. r. 1); וַ id. טהר

יִטַּהֲרוּ[l] וַ Hithp. fut. 3 pers. pl. masc. [for יִתְטַהֲרוּ § 12. rem. 3]; וַ id. . . . . טהר

יְטַהֲרוּ וַ Piel fut. 3 pers. pl. m. (§ 14. rem. 1); וַ id. טהר

יַטּוּ וַיַּ Hiph. fut. 3 pers. pl. m. (§ 25, 2b); וַ id. נטה

יִטּוּ[m] וַ Kal fut. 3 pers. pl. masc. (§ 25, 2b); וַ id. נטה

יִטּוֹל[n] Kal fut. 3 pers. sing. masc. (§ 17. rem. 3) . נטל

יִטּוֹר[o] Kal fut. 3 pers. sing. masc. (§ 17. rem. 3) נטר

יְטוּר, יְטוּר } וְ pr. name masc., with cop. וְ [for וִיטוּר, וִי׳] טור

יָטוּשׁ[p] Kal fut. 3 pers. sing. masc. . . . טוש

יִטּוֹשׁ[q] Kal fut. 3 pers. sing. masc. (§ 17. rem. 3) נטש

יִטְחַן[r] וַ Kal fut. 3 pers. sing. masc.; וַ conv. . טחן

---

[a] Is. 13. 17. [b] De. 2. 11. [c] Ps. 35. 20. [d] Job 33. 10. [e] Job 19. 11. [f] Is. 62. 6. [g] Ps. 107. 29. [h] Ps. 139. 12. [i] Je. 13. 16. [k] Ps. 105. 28. [l] Job 16. 6. [m] Job 21. 30. [n] Job 3. 9. [o] Ps. 29. 9. [p] Je. 21. 13. [q] Job 21. 13. [r] 1 Sa. 17. 11. [s] Job 37. 7. [t] Ps. 52. 7. [u] Est. 8. 10. [x] Job 31. 34. [y] Job 9. 12. [z] Jon. 1. 13. [a] 2 Sa. 19. 15; Ezr. 9. 9. [b] Zep. 2. 13. [c] Ge. 26. 25; 1 Ch. 15. 1. [d] 1 Sa. 24. 5. [e] Ge. 37. 31. [f] Je. 38. 6. [g] Is. 31. 3. [h] Job 15. 29. [i] 2 Ki. 5. 14. [k] 2 Ch. 34. 5. [l] Ne. 12. 30. [m] 1 Sa. 8. 3. [n] Is. 40. 15. [o] Ps. 103. 9. [p] Job 9. 26. [q] Ho. 12. 15. [r] Ex. 32. 20.

יְטִיבְךָ[a]	וְ Hiph. fut. 3 pers. sing. masc. [יֵיטִיב], suff. 2 pers. s. m., with conj. וְ [for וִיטִיבְךָ ,וְי]	טוב
יְטִילוּ[b]	וַ Hiph. fut. 3 pers. pl. masc.; וַ· conv.	טול
יַטִּיפוּ[c]	Hiph. fut. 3 pers. pl. masc.	נטף
יַטִּיפוּן[d]	id. with parag. ן	נטף
יַטֶּךָּ[e]	Hiph. fut. 3 pers. sing. masc. (יַטֶּה), suff. 2 pers. sing. masc. (§ 25, 26, & § 2. r. 2)	נטה
יָטֶל	וַ Hiph. fut. 3 pers. sing. masc. ap. [fr. יָטֵל § 21. rem. 18, from יָטִיל]	טול
יֻטַּל[f]	Hoph. fut. 3 pers. sing. masc. [for יוּטַל § 21. rem. 24, comp. § 8. rem. 15)	טול
יְטִלֵהוּ[g]	וַ Hiph. fut. 3 pers. pl. masc. (יָטִיל), suff. 3 pers. sing. masc.; וַ conv.	טול
יְטַלְלֵנוּ[h]	וִ Piel fut. 3 pers. sing. masc. [יְטַלֵּל], suff. 3 pers. sing. masc. (§ 2. r. 3) with conj. וְ [for וִיטַל ,וְי]	טלל
יִטַּמָּא	Hithpa. fut. 3 pers. sing. masc. [for יִתְטַמָּא § 12. rem. 3]	טמא
יִטְמָא	Kal fut. 3 pers. sing. masc.	טמא
יְטַמְּאֵ[i]	וַ Piel fut. 3 pers. sing. masc.; וַ conv.	טמא
יְטַמְּאֵהוּ[k]	וַ id. with suff. 3 pers. sing. masc.; וַ id.	טמא
יִטְמָאוּ	in pause for יִטְמְאוּ (q. v.)	טמא
יְטַמְּאוּ	וִ׳ Piel fut. 3 pers. pl. masc.	טמא
יִטַּמְּאוּ	Hithpa. fut. 3 pers. pl. masc. [for יִתְטַמְּאוּ § 12. rem. 3]	טמא
יִטְמְאוּ[l]	וַ Kal fut. 3 pers. pl. masc.; וַ· conv.	טמא
יְטַמְּאֶנּוּ[m]	Piel fut. 3 pers. sing. masc., suff. 3 pers. s. m.	טמא
יִטְמֹן[n]	וַ Kal fut. 3 pers. sing. masc.; וַ· conv.	טמן
יִטְמְנֵהוּ[o]	וַ id. with suff. 3 pers. sing. masc.; וַ· id.	טמן
יַטְמִנוּ[p]	וַ Hiph. fut. 3 pers. pl. masc.; וַ· id.	טמן
יַטֶּנּוּ[q]	Hiph. fut. 3 pers. sing. masc. (יַטֶּה), suff. 3 pers. sing. masc. (§ 25, 2b, & § 2. r. 3)	נטה
יִטַּע	וַ׳ ,וְ׳ Kal fut. 3 pers. sing. masc.; וַ· conv.	נטע
יִטָּעֵהוּ[s]	וַ id. id., suff. 3 pers. sing. m. (§ 16. r. 12)	נטע
יִטְּעוּ	[u] וַ׳ id. fut. 3 pers. pl. masc.	נטע
יִטְעַם	Kal fut. 3 pers. sing. masc.	טעם
יִטְעֲמוּ[x]	id. fut. 3 pers. pl. masc.	טעם
יְטַעֲמוּן[y]	Ch. Pa. fut. 3 pers. pl. masc.	טעם
יְטַעֲמוּנֵּהּ[z]	Ch. id. with suff. 3 pers. sing. masc.	טעם
יִטְּפוּ[a]	Kal fut. 3 pers. pl. masc.	נטף
יַטְרִיחַ[bb]	Hiph. fut. 3 pers. sing. masc.	טרח
יִטָּרֵף	Niph. fut. 3 pers. sing. masc.	טרף
יִטְרַף[b] / יִטְרֹף[c] [d] וַ׳	Kal fut. 3 pers. sing. masc. (A & O § 8. r. 13, comp. r. 15); וַ· conv.	טרף
יִטֹּשׁ	וַ׳ Kal fut. 3 pers. s. m. (§ 17. r. 3); וַ· id.	נטשׁ
יִטְּשֵׁהוּ[e]	וַ id. fut. 3 p. pl. m., suff. 3 p. s. m.; וַ· id.	נטשׁ
יִטְּשֵׁנוּ[f]	Kal fut. 3 pers. sing. masc., suff. 1 pers. pl.	נטשׁ
יִיבַשׁ [g] וַ׳ / יִיבָשׁ [h] וַ	Kal fut. 3 pers. sing. masc. (comp. § 8. rem. 15); וַ· conv.	יבשׁ
יִיגַע[i]	Kal fut. 3 pers. sing. m. [for יִיגַע § 8. r. 15]	יגע
יִיגָעוּ[k] / יִיגָעוּ[l] וְ	id. fut. 3 pers. pl. masc. (v. id.)	יגע
יֵידַע[m]	Kal fut. 3 pers. sing. masc. (§ 20. rem. 15)	ידע
יֵיחֶל[n]	וַ Niph. fut. 3 pers. sing. masc. (§ 20. r. 6); acc. drawn back, conv. וַ· (§ 9. rem. 3)	יחל
יְיַחֵל[o]	Piel fut. 3 pers. sing. masc. (§ 14. rem. 1)	יחל
יּוֹחֶל[p]	וַ Kh. יְיַחֵל q. v.; K. יוֹחֶל Hiph. fut. 3 pers. sing. masc. ap. with conv. וַ· (§ 20. r. 9)	יחל
יְיַחֲלוּ[q]	Piel (§ 14. rem. 1) fut. 3 pers. pl. masc. [for יְיַחֲלוּ comp. § 8. rem. 15]	יחל
יְיַחֵלוּן[r]	id. with parag. ן (§ 10. r. 4, comp. § 8. r. 17)	יחל
יּוֹחֶר[s]	וַ Kh. יִיחַר Kal, K. יוֹחֶר Hiph. fut. comp. יּוֹחֶל	יחר
יִיטַב[t]	Ch. Peal fut. 3 pers. sing. masc.	יטב
יִּיטַב[u]	וַ Hiph. fut. 3 pers. sing. masc. ap. with conv. וַ· [for יֵיטֵב from יֵיטִיב]	יטב
יֵיטֵב	defect. for יֵיטִיב (q. v.)	יטב
יִיטַב	וַ׳ ,וְ׳ Kal fut. 3 pers. sing. masc.; וַ· conv.	יטב
יִּיטְבוּ[x]	וַ id. fut. 3 pers. pl. masc.; וַ· id.	יטב
יֵיטִיב[y] / יֵיטִיב[z] / יֵיטִיב	Hiph. fut. 3 pers. sing. m. (§ 20. r. 15)	יטב
יֵיטִיבוּ[a]	id. fut. 3 pers. pl. masc.	יטב
יְיֵלִיל	Hiph. fut. 3 p. s. m. [for יְהֵלִיל § 20. rem. 15]	ילל
יְיֵלִילוּ[b]	id. fut. 3 pers. pl. masc.	ילל
יַיִן וְ׳ / יָיִן וָ׳ ,וְ׳	noun masc. sing. dec. 6h	יון
יֵין[c] וְ׳	id., construct state	יון
יֵינָהּ[d]	id., suff. 3 pers. sing. fem.	יון
יֵינִי[e]	id., suff. 1 pers. sing.	יון
יֵינֵךְ[f]	id., suff. 2 pers. sing. fem.	יון
יֵינְךָ[g]	id., suff. 2 pers. sing. masc. [for יֵינְךָ]	יון
יֵינָם	id., suff. 3 pers. pl. masc.	יון
יִינַק[h]	Kal fut. 3 p. s. m. [for יִינַק comp. § 8. rem. 15]	ינק
יִינְקוּ[i]	id. fut. 3 pers. pl. masc. [for יִינְקוּ v. id.]	ינק
יְיַסְּדֶנָּה[k]	Piel fut. 3 pers. sing. masc. [יְיַסֵּד], suff. 3 pers. sing. fem. (§ 2. rem. 3)	יסד
יִיסַף[l]	Kal fut. 3 p. s. m. [for יִיסַף comp. § 8. rem. 15]	יסף
יְיַסֵּר[m]	Piel fut. 3 pers. sing. masc.	יסר
יִיעָדֶנָּה[n]	Kal fut. 3 pers. sing. masc. [יִיעַד], suff. 3 pers. sing. fem. (§ 16. rem. 12, & § 2. rem. 3)	יעד
יִיעַף[o]	Kal fut. 3 pers. sing. masc.	יעף

[a] Ec. 11. 9. [b] Jon. 1. 5. [c] Mi. 2. 6. [d] Mi. 2. 6. [e] Job 36. 18. [f] Job 41. 1. [g] Jon. 1. 15. [h] Ne. 3. 15. [i] 2 Ki. 23. 8. [k] 2 Ki. 23. 16. [l] Ps. 106. 39. [m] Le. 13. 44. [n] Ge. 35. 4. [o] Ex. 2. 12. [p] 2 Ki. 7. 8, 8. [q] Pr. 21. 1. [r] Da. 11. 45. [s] Is. 5. 2. [t] Is. 65. 22. [u] Ps. 107. 37. [x] Jon. 3. 7. [y] Da. 4. 22, 29. [z] Da. 5. 21. [a] Joel 4. 18. [b] Ge. 49. 27. [c] Ps. 7. 3. [d] Am. 1. 11. [e] Eze. 31. 12, 12. [f] 1 Ki. 8. 57. [g] Jon. 4. 7. [h] 1 Ki. 17. 7. [i] Is. 40. 28. [k] Is. 40. 31. [l] Hab. 2. 13. [m] Ps. 138. 6. [n] Ge. 8. 12. [o] Mi. 5. 6. [p] 1 Sa. 13. 8. [q] Is. 42. 4. [r] Is. 51. 5. [s] 2 Sa. 20. 5. [t] Ezr. 7. 18. [u] Ex. 1. 20. [x] Ge. 34. 18. [y] Job 24. 21. [z] 1 Ki. 1. 47. [a] Mi. 2. 7. [b] Ho. 7. 14. [bb] Job 37. 11. [c] De. 32. 38. [d] Pr. 9. 2. [e] Ca. 5. 1. [f] 1 Sa. 1. 14. [g] Ec. 9. 7. [h] Job 20. 16. [i] De. 33. 19. [k] Jos. 6. 26. [l] Ex. 30. 32. [m] De. 8. 5. [n] Ex. 21. 9. [o] Is. 40. 28.

ייעפו Kal fut. 3 pers. pl. masc. [for ייעפו comp. § 8. rem. 15] . . . . . יעף

ויּיף[a] Kal fut. 3 pers. sing. masc. ap. [from ייפה § 25, 2e]; וַ conv. . . . יפה

ויּפהו[b] Piel fut. 3 pers. s. m. [ייפה], suff. 3 pers. s. m. יפה

ויּיצר[c] Kal fut. 3 pers. sing. masc. with conv. וַ [for ייצר] . . . . . יצר

וייקץ } Kal fut. 3 pers. sing. masc.; וַ conv. . יקץ
וייקץ[d]

וייקר[e] } Kal fut. 3 pers. sing. masc. (§ 20. rem. 2); וַ id. . . . יקר
וייקר[f]

ויירא וַיּ' Kal fut. 3 pers. sing. m. (§ 25, 2d); וַ id. ירא

וייראו וַיּ', וְ'[g] } id. fut. 3 pers. pl. masc. (comp. § 8. rem. 15); וַ id. . ירא
וייראו וַיּ', וְ'

ייראוך id. id., suff. 2 pers. sing. masc. . . . ירא

וייראני[h] id. fut. 3 pers. sing. masc., suff. 1 pers. sing. ירא

יירה[i] Niph. fut. 3 pers. sing. masc. (§ 20. rem. 6) ירה

יירש[k] } Kal fut. 3 pers. sing. masc. (comp. § 8. rem. 15); וַ conv. . ירש
יירש וַיּ', וְ'

יירש[l] Piel fut. 3 pers. sing. masc. . . . ירש

ויירש[m] Kh. יירש q. v.; K. יורש q. v. . . ירש

יירשו } Kal fut. 3 pers. pl. masc. (comp. § 8. rem. 15); וַ conv. . ירש
יירשו וַיּ', וְ'[n]

יירשוה id. id., suff. 3 pers. sing. fem. (§ 16. rem. 12) ירש

יירשום[o] id. id., suff. 3 pers. pl. masc. (v. id.) ירש

יירשך[p] } id fut. 3 pers. sing. masc., suff. 2 pers. sing. masc. (v. id.) . . ירש
יירשך[q]

יירשם[r] id. id., suff. 3 pers. pl. masc. (v. id.) ירש

ויירשם[s] id. fut. 3 pers. pl. masc., suff. 3 pers. pl. masc. (v. id.); וַ conv. . ירש

ייישרו[t] Hiph. fut. 3 pers. pl. masc. (§ 20. No. 1b) ישר

ויישם[u] Kal fut. 3 pers. sing. masc. with conv. וַ [for ייישם] . . . . . ישם

ויישם[x] Kh. יישם q. v.; K. יושם Hoph. fut. 3 pers. sing. masc.; וַ conv. . . . שום

ויישן וַיּ' } Kal fut. 3 pers. sing. masc. (comp. § 8. rem. 15); וַ id. . . . ישן
ויישן[y]

יישר[z] } Piel fut. 3 pers. s. m. (comp. § 10. rem. 4) ישר
יישר[a]

ויישר[b] וַיּ' Kal fut. 3 pers. sing. masc.; וַ conv. . ישר

ויישרם[c] Kh. ויישרם Piel fut. 3 pers. s. m., suff. 3 pers. pl. m., for K. וַיְשִׁרֵם id. (§ 20. rem. 8); וַ id. ישר

ויך[d] in pause for יַךְ (q. v.) . . . נכה

יך[e] Kh. most probably an error of the copyists, for יד

ויך[f] וַיּ', וְ'[g] Hiph. fut. 3 pers. sing. masc., ap. from יַכֶּה (§ 25, 2b); וַ conv. . . נכה

יכאב[h] } Kal fut. 3 pers. sing. masc. (§ 8. rem. 15) כאב
יכאב[i]

יכאיב[k] Hiph. fut. 3 pers. sing. masc. . . כאב

יכבד Piel fut. 3 pers. sing. masc. . . . כבד

ויכבד Hiph. fut. 3 p. s. m. ap. [from יכביד]; וַ conv. כבד

יכבד } Kal fut. 3 pers. sing. masc. (comp. § 8. rem. 15); וַ id. . . כבד
ויכבד[l] וַיּ'[m]

יכבד Pual fut. 3 pers. s. m. [for יְכֻבַּד § 8. rem. 15] כבד

ויכבדו[n] } Piel fut. 3 pers. pl. masc., with conj. וְ [for וִיכַבְּדוּ ,וִי'] . . כבד
ויכבדו[o]

יכבדו Kal fut. 3 pers. sing. masc. . . כבד

יכבדונך[p] Piel fut. 3 pers. pl. m., suff. 2 pers. sing. m. כבד

יכבדנני[q] id. fut. 3 pers. sing. masc. with epenth. נ and suff. 1 pers. sing. (§ 16. rem. 13) . . כבד

יכבה Kal fut. 3 pers. sing. masc. . . כבה

ויכבו[r] Piel fut. 3 pers. pl. masc.; וַ conv. . כבה

יכבוש[s] Kal fut. 3 pers. sing. masc. (§ 8. rem. 18) כבש

ויכבישום[t] Kh. יכבישום Hiph., K. יכבשום Kal fut. 3 pers. pl. masc., suff. 3 pers. pl. masc. כבש

יכבנה[u] Piel fut. 3 p. s. m., suff. 3 p. s. fem. (§ 2. rem. 3) כבה

יכבס Piel fut. 3 pers. sing. masc. . . . כבס

ויכבסו id. fut. 3 pers. pl. masc.; וַ conv. . . כבס

יכבר[x] Hiph. fut. 3 pers. sing. masc. [for יַכְבִּיר] כבר

ויכה[y] the following with suff. 3 pers. sing. fem. (§ 24. rem. 21); וַ conv. . . . נכה

ויכה וַיּ'[z] Hiph. fut. 3 pers. sing. m. (§ 25. 2b); וַ id. נכה

יכהה[z] Kal fut. 3 pers. sing. masc. . . . כהה

ויכהו Hiph. fut. 3 pers. sing. masc., suff. 3 pers. sing. m. (§ 25. 2b, & § 24. rem. 21); וַ conv. נכה

ויכהו וַיּ'[a] id. fut. 3 p. pl. m. (יַכּוּ), suff. 3 p. s. m.; וַ id. נכה

ויכהן וְ'[b] Piel fut. 3 pers. sing. m. (§ 14. rem. 1); וַ id. כהן

ויכהנו[c] id. fut. 3 pers. pl. masc.; וַ id. . כהן

ויכו[d] וַיּ', וְ'[e] Hiph. fut. 3 p. pl. m. (§ 25, 2b); וַ id. נכה

ויכהו[f] id. fut. 3 pers. sing. masc. (יַכֶּה), suff. 3 pers. sing. masc. (§ 24. rem. 21); וַ id. . נכה

ויכו[g] Hoph. fut. 3 pers. pl. m. (§ 25, 2b); וַ id. נכה

ויכוה Hiph. fut. 3 pers. pl. masc., suff. 3 pers. sing. fem. (§ 25, 2b); וַ id. . . נכה

יכוך[h] id., suff. 2 pers. sing. masc. . . . נכה

יכול Kal pret. 3 pers. sing. masc. (§ 8. rem. 1), or (Nu. 13. 30) inf. absolute . . . יכל

ויכום Hiph. fut. 3 pers. pl. masc., suff. 3 pers. pl. masc. (§ 25, 2b); וַ conv. . . . נכה

יכון וְ'[i] Niph. fut. 3 pers. sing. masc. . . כון

יכוניה Kh. יכוניה, for K. יכניה q. v. . . כון

יכונן[k] Pilel fut. 3 pers. sing. masc. . . . כון

---

[a] Eze. 31. 7. [b] Je. 10. 4. [c] Ge. 2. 7. [d] Ge. 9. 24. [e] 1 Sa. 18. 30. [f] Ps. 72. 14. [g] Ge. 42. 35. [h] Mal. 2. 5. [i] Ex. 19. 13. [k] Is. 54. 3. [l] De. 28. 42. [m] Nu. 21. 32. [n] De. 10. 11. [o] De. 2. 12. [p] Ge. 15. 4. [q] Ge. 15. 4. [r] Ho. 9. 6. [s] De. 2. 21, 22. [t] Pr. 4. 25. [u] Ge. 50. 26. [x] Ge. 24. 33. [y] 1 Ki. 19. 5. [z] Pr. 3. 6. [a] Pr. 15. 21. [b] Nu. 23. 27. [c] 2 Ch. 32. 30. [d] 2 Ki. 15. 16. [e] 1 Sa. 4. 17. [f] Ho. 6. 1. [g] Ho. 14. 6. [h] Job 14. 22. [i] Pr. 14. 13. [k] Job 5. 18. [l] Is. 66. 5. [m] Ex. 9. 7. [n] Ju. 9. 9. [o] Ps. 86. 9. [p] Is. 25. 3. [q] Ps. 50. 23. [r] 2 Ch. 29. 7. [s] Mi. 7. 19. [t] Je. 34. 11. [u] Is. 42. 3. [x] Job 35. 16. [y] Jos. 10. 28, 30, 32. [z] Is. 42. 4. [a] 2 Sa. 4. 6, 7. [b] Is. 61. 10. [c] 1 Ch. 24. 2. [d] Mi. 4. 14. [e] Jos. 7. 3. [f] 2 Sa. 14. 6. [g] Ex. 5. 14. [h] 2 Ch. 25. 16. [i] Pr. 25. 5. [k] Is. 62. 7.

יְכוֹנְנֶהָ [a] וְ' id., suff. 3 pers. sing. fem.; וַ conv. . כון

יְכוֹנֶנּוּ [b] וַ' id., suff. 3 pers. sing. masc. [for יְכוֹנְנֶנּוּ § 21. rem. 21]; וַ id. . . . כון

יִכּוֹנָנוּ [c] וְ Hithpal. fut. 3 pers. pl. masc. [for יִתְכּוֹנְנוּ comp. § 12. rem. 3] . . . כון

יְכוֹנְנוּ [d] וַ Pilel fut. 3 pers. pl. masc.; וַ conv. . כון

יְכוֹנְנוּנִי [e] וַ id. with suff. 1 pers. sing.; וַ id. . כון

יְכַזֵּב, יְכַזֵּב [f] } Piel fut. 3 pers. sing. masc., with conj. וְ [for וִי', וִיכַזֵּב] . . . כזב

יְכַזְּבוּ id. fut. 3 pers. pl. masc. . . . כזב

יַכְזִיבֵנִי [g] Hiph. fut. 3 pers. sing. masc., suff. 1 pers. sing. כזב

יָכַח. Hiph. הוֹכִיחַ.—I. *to show, prove.*—II. *to reprove, reproach, rebuke, convict, correct,* with acc. אֶל, לְ, of the person, and בְּ, עַל of the thing.—III. *to punish, chasten.*—IV. *to decide, arbitrate,* with בֵּין; *to appoint, destine,* for any one, with לְ, Ge. 24. 14, 44.—V. *to contend, plead, reason,* Job 13. 3; 16. 21; 22. 4, with אֶל, לְ, acc. Hoph. *to be chastened,* Job 33. 19. Niph. נוֹכַח.—I. *to be convicted,* Ge. 20. 16.—II. *to contend, dispute.* Hithp. הִתְוַכַּח (§ 20. No. 1) *to contend,* Mi. 6. 2.

תּוֹכֵחָה fem. pl. תּוֹכֵחוֹת, *punishment, chastisement.*

תּוֹכַחַת fem. with suff. תּוֹכַחְתִּי, pl. תּוֹכָחוֹת (§ 44. r. 5).—I. *proof, argument.*—II. *reproof, admonition, correction.*—III. *punishment, chastisement.*

יַכְחֵד [h] וַ Hiph. fut. 3 pers. sing. masc. ap. [from יַכְחִיד]; וַ conv. . . . . כחד

יִכָּחֵד [i] Niph. fut. 3 pers. sing. masc. . . כחד

יַכְחִידֶנָּה [k] Hiph. fut. 3 pers. s. m., suff. 3 pers. s. fem. כחד

יְכַחֵשׁ [l] Piel fut. 3 pers. sing. masc. (§ 14. rem. 1) before monos. [for יְכַחֵשׁ § 10. rem. 4] . כחש

יִכָּחֲשׁוּ [m] וְ Niph. fut. 3 pers. pl. masc. . . כחש

יְכַחֲשׁוּ Piel fut. 3 pers. pl. masc. (§ 14. rem. 1) . כחש

יוֹכִיחֶךָ [zz] Hiph. fut. 3 pers. m. s. יוֹכִיחַ, suff. 2 p. m. s. יכח

יָכִיל Hiph. fut. 3 pers. sing. masc. . . כול

יְכָלְיָה Kh., for יְכָלְיָה K. (q.v.) . . . יכל

יְכִילֶנּוּ [n] Hiph. fut. 3 p. s. m. (יָכִיל), suff. 3 p. s. m. (§ 2. r. 3) כול

יָכִין וְ' pr. name of a man and a pillar . . כון

יָכִין Hiph. fut. 3 pers. sing. masc. . . . כון

יָבִין [o] Kh. id.; K. יָבִין Kal fut. 3 p. s. m. R. בִּין see בון

יָכִינוּ וַ Hiph. fut. 3 pers. pl. masc.; וַ conv. . כון

יַכִּיר Hiph. fut. 3 pers. sing. masc. . . נכר

יַכִּירֵהוּ [p] וַ id. id., suff. 3 pers. sing. fem.; וַ conv. . נכר

יַכִּירוּם [q] id. fut. 3 pers. pl. masc., suff. 3 pers. pl. m. נכר

יַכִּירֵנוּ [r] id. fut. 3 pers. sing. masc., suff. 1 pers. pl. נכר

יַכִּירֶנּוּ id. id., suff. 3 pers. sing. masc. . . נכר

יַכֶּכָּה, יַכְּכָה } Hiph. fut. 3 p. s. m. (יַכֶּה § 25. r. 6), suff. 2 p. s. m. [for יַכְּךָ & יַכֶּךָּ § 2. r. 2, & § 24. r. 21] } נכה

יָכֹל (§ 8. rem. 1) fem. יָכְלָה, 1 pers. יָכֹלְתִּי, with suff. יְכָלְתִּיו, inf. abs. יָכוֹל; Hoph. fut. יוּכַל.—I. *to be able* to do any thing; *can, could;* or *to be permitted* to do it, *may, might.*—II. *to be able to bear, to endure.*—III. *to prevail over, to overcome,* with לְ

יְכִל, יִכֻּל Chald. fut. יִכֻּל (§ 52), Hoph. fut. יוּכַל.—I. *to be able.*—II. *to prevail over, to overcome,* with לְ, Da. 7. 21.

יְהוּכַל, יוּכַל (*enabled, strong*) pr. name masc. Je. 37. 3; 38. 1.

יְכָלְיָהוּ, יְכָלְיָה (*the Lord has prevailed*) pr. name of the mother of King Uzziah, 2 Ki. 15. 2; 2 Ch. 26. 3.

יָכֹל Kal pret. 3 pers. sing. masc. (§ 8. rem. 1); or (1 Sa. 26. 25) inf. absolute . . יכל

יָכִל Chald. Peal part. act. sing. m. (§ 47. rem. 1) יכל

יֻכָל [s] וַ Hoph. fut. 3 pers. sing. masc. [for יוּכַל comp. § 8. rem. 15]; וַ conv. . . יכל

יְכַל וַ Piel fut. 3 pers. s. m., ap. from יְכַלֶּה; וַ id. כלה

יִכֶל [t] Kal fut. 3 pers. sing. masc., ap. from יִכְלֶה . כלה

יִכֻּל [u] Chald. Peal fut. 3 pers. s. m. (§ 52. rem. 2) יכל

יִכָּלֵא וַ Niph. fut. 3 pers. sing. masc.; וַ conv. כלא

יִכָּלְאוּ [x] וַ id. fut. 3 pers. pl. masc.; וַ id. . . כלא

יָכְלָה Kal pret. 3 pers. sing. fem. . . . יכל

יָכְלָה [y] וְ Chald. Peal part. sing., fem. of יָכִל (q. v.) יכל

יְכַלֶּה [z] Piel fut. 3 pers. sing. masc. . . כלה

יִכְלֶה [a] Kal fut. 3 pers. s. m. [for יִכְלָא § 23. rem. 11] כלא

יִכְלֶה [b] Kal fut. 3 pers. sing. masc. . . כלה

יְכַלֵּהוּ [c] וַ Piel fut. 3 pers. sing. masc., suff. 3 pers. sing. masc.; וַ conv. . . . כלה

יְכַלֻּהוּ [d] וַ id. fut. 3 pers. pl. masc. (יְכַלּוּ), suff. 3 pers. sing. masc.; וַ id. . . . . כלה

יָכְלוּ [e] וְ' Kal fut. 3 pers. pl. masc. . . יכל

יָכִלוּ Hiph. fut. 3 pers. pl. masc. [for יָכִילוּ] . כול

יָכְלוּ Kal pret. 3 pers. pl. for יָכְלוּ (§ 8. r. 1 & 7) יכל

יְכַלּוּ [f], יְכַלּוּ [g] } Piel fut. 3 pers. pl. masc.; וַ conv.; and with conj. וְ [for וִי', וִיכַלּוּ] . } כלה

יְכֻלּוּ [h] וַ Pual fut. 3 pers. pl. masc.; וַ conv. . כלה

יֻכְלוּ [i], יֻכְלוּ } Hoph. fut. 3 pers. pl. masc. (comp. § 8. rem. 15) . . . . } יכל

יִכְלוּ וַ' Kal fut. 3 pers. pl. masc.; וַ conv. . כלה

[a] Ps. 7. 13. [b] Job 31. 15. [c] Ps. 59. 5. [d] Ps. 107. 36. [e] Ps. 119. 73. [f] Nu. 23. 19. [g] Job 24. 25. [h] 2 Ch. 32. 21 [i] 2 Sa. 18. 13. [k] Job 20. 12. [l] Ho. 9. 2. [m] De. 33. 29. [n] Joel 2. 11. [o] Pr. 21. 29. [p] Ge. 37. 33. [q] Is. 61. 9. [r] Is. 63. 16. [s] Ho. 12. 5. [t] Job 33. 21. [u] Da. 3. 29. [x] Eze. 31. 15. [y] Da. 7. 21. [z] Is. 10. 18. [zz] Job 22. 4. [a] Ge. 23. 6. [b] Pr. 22. 8. [c] 1 Ki. 6. 9, 14. [d] Je. 10. 25. [e] Je. 38. 22. [f] Job 36. 11. [g] Eze. 43. 27. [h] Ge. 2. 1. [i] Je. 20. 11.

יְכַלְיָה, יְכָלְיָהוּ } pr. name masc. . . . . . יכל

[a]יְכַלְיוּן Kal fut. 3 p. pl. m. with parag. ן (§ 24. r. 5) כלה

[b]יַכְלִים Hiph. fut. 3 pers. sing. masc. . . כלם

יָכְלִין Chald. Peal part. masc., pl. of יְכִל (q. v.) יכל

[c]יְכַלְכֵּל וַ' Pilpel (§ 6. No. 4) fut. 3 p. s. m.; וַ conv. כול

[d]יְכַלְכְּלֻהוּ id. fut. 3 pers. pl. masc., suff. 3 pers. s. m. כול

[e]יְכַלְכְּלוּךָ id. id., suff. 2 pers. sing. masc. . . כול

[f]יְכַלְכְּלֶךָּ id. fut. 3 pers. s. m. (כַּלְכֵּל), suff. 2 pers. s. m. [for יְכַלְכֶּלְךָ comp. § 16. r. 15, & § 2. r. 2] כול

[g]יְכַלְכְּלוּךָ id. fut. 3 pers. pl. masc., suff. 2 pers. s. m. כול

[h]וַיְכַלְכְּלֵם id. fut. 3 p. pl. m., suff. 3 pers. pl. m.; וַ conv. כול

יִכָּלְמוּ וְ' Niph. fut. 3 pers. pl. masc. . . . כלם

[k]וְיָכֹלְתָּ Kal pret. 2 pers. sing. masc., acc. shifted by וְ conv. (for יָכֹלְתָּ § 8. rem. 1 & 7) יכל

[l]יְכִלְתָּ Chald. Peal pret. 2 pers. s. m. (§ 47. r. 6 & 2) יכל

יְכֹלֶת Kal inf. constr. (comp. § 8. r. 1, & § 20. r. 3) יכל

יָכֹלְתִּי id. pret. 1 pers. sing. . . . . יכל

[m]יְכָלְתִּיו id. id. with suff. 3 pers. sing. masc. . . יכל

[n]וַיַּכֵּם וַ' Hiph. fut. 3 pers. sing. masc. (יַכֶּה § 25, 2 b), suff. 3 p. pl. m. (§ 24. r. 21); וַ conv. נכה

וַיָּכֶן Hiph. fut. 3 pers. sing. masc. ap. and conv. from יָכִין . . . . . . כון

[o]יְכַנֶּה Piel fut. 3 pers. sing. masc. . . . כנה

יַכֵּנּוּ Hiph. fut. 3 pers. sing. masc. (יַכֶּה § 25, 2 b), suff. 3 pers. s. m. (§ 24. r. 21, & § 2. r. 3) נכה

יִכֹּנוּ וְ[p] Niph. fut. 3 pers. pl. masc. . . . כון

יְכָנְיָה, יְכָנְיָהוּ } pr. name masc. . . . . כון

[q]וַיַּכְנִיעֵם וַ' Hiph. fut. 3 pers. sing. masc., suff. 3 pers. pl. masc.; וַ conv. . . . . כנע

[r]וִיכוֹנְנֶךָ Pilel fut. 3 pers. sing. masc. (יְכוֹנֵן), suff. 2 pers. s. m. [for יְכוֹנֶנְךָ § 16. r. 15]; וַ id. כון

[s]יְכַנֵּס Piel fut. 3 pers. sing. masc. . . . כנס

וַיַּכְנַע Hiph. fut. 3 p. s. m. ap. [from יַכְנִיעַ]; וַ conv. כנע

וַיִּכָּנַע וַ' Niph. fut. 3 pers. sing. masc.; וַ id. . כנע

[t]וַיִּכָּנְעוּ, [u]וַיִּכָּנְעוּ } id. fut. 3 pers. pl. masc. (§ 15. rem. 1) וַ id. . . . . . כנע

[x]יִכָּנֵף Niph. fut. 3 pers. sing. masc. . . . כנף

וַיְכַס, יְכַסֶּה } Piel fut. 3 pers. sing. masc., ap. and full form; וַ conv. . . . . כסה

[y]יְכֻסֶּה Pual fut. 3 pers. sing. masc. . . . כסה

וַיְכַסֵּהוּ Piel fut. 3 p. s. m, suff. 3 p. s. m. (§ 24. r. 21) כסה

[z]וַיְכַסֻּהוּ id. fut. 3 pers. pl. masc., suff. 3 pers. s. m. נסה

[a]וַיְכַסּוּ וַ' id. fut. 3 pers. pl. masc.; וַ conv. . . כסה

[b]וַיְכֻסּוּ Pual fut. 3 pers. pl. masc.; וַ id. . . כסה

[c]יְכַסְיֻמוּ Kh. יְכַסּוּמוֹ Piel fut. 3 pers. pl. m., K. יְכַסֵּימוֹ 3 pers. s. m., suff. 3 pers. pl. (§ 24. r. 21 b) כסה

[d]יִכְסוֹף Kal fut. 3 pers. sing. masc. (§ 8. rem. 18) כסף

[e]יְכַסְיֻמוּ Piel fut. 3 pers. pl. masc. (§ 24. rem. 13), suff. 3 pers. pl. (§ 2. rem. 5) . . כסה

[f]יְכַסֵּךְ id. fut. 3 pers. sing. masc., suff. 2 pers. s. f. כסה

[g]יְכַסֶּךָּ id. id., suff. 2 pers. sing. masc. [for יְכַסְּךָ § 24. rem. 21, & § 2. rem. 2] . . כסה

[h]וְיִכְסְלוּ Kal fut. 3 pers. pl. m. [for יִכְסְלוּ § 8. r. 15] כסל

[i]יִכְסְמוּ id. fut. 3 pers. pl. masc. . . . כסם

[k]יְכַסֶּנָּה Piel fut. 3 pers. sing. masc. (יְכַסֶּה), suff. 3 pers. sing. fem. (§ 24. r. 21, & § 2. r. 3) כסה

יְכַסֶּנּוּ id. with suff. 3 pers. sing. masc. . . כסה

[l]יַכְעִיסֻהוּ defect. for יַכְעִיסוּהוּ (q. v.) . . כעס

[m]וַיַּכְעִסוּ Hiph. fut. 3 pers. pl. masc.; וַ conv. . כעס

[n]וַיַּכְעִיסוּהוּ id., suff. 3 pers. sing. masc.; וַ id. . כעס

וַיַּכְעֵס id. fut. 3 pers. s. m. ap. [from יַכְעִיס]; וַ id. כעס

וַיִּכְעַס Kal fut. 3 pers. sing. masc.; וַ id. . כעס

[o]וַיַּכְעִסוּ Hiph. fut. 3 pers. pl. m. (for יַכְעִיסוּ); וַ id. כעס

[p]יִכְפֶּה Kal fut. 3 pers. sing. masc. . . . כפה

וִיכַפֵּר, יְכַפֶּר־ } וְ' Piel fut. 3 pers. sing. masc. (§ 10. rem. 4); וַ conv. . . . כפר

יְכֻפַּר Pual fut. 3 pers. sing. masc. . . . כפר

[q]יְכַפְּרֶנָּה Piel fut. 3 pers. sing. masc. (יְכַפֵּר), suff. 3 pers. sing. fem. . . . . כפר

וַיַּכֵּר Hiph. fut. 3 p. s. m., ap. from יַכִּיר; וַ conv. נכר

[r]יִכָּרֶה Niph. fut. 3 pers. sing. masc. . . כרה

[s]וַיִּכְרֶה וַ'[t] Kal fut. 3 pers. sing. masc.; וַ conv. כרה

[u]וַיַּכִּרֵהוּ Hiph. fut. 3 pers. sing. masc. (יַכִּיר), suff. 3 pers. sing. masc.; וַ id. . . . נכר

[x]וַיִּכְרוּ וַ'[y] Kal fut. 3 pers. pl. masc.; וַ id. . כרה

יַכְרִית Hiph. fut. 3 pers. sing. masc. . . כרת

[z]וַיַּכִּרֵם Hiph. fut. 3 pers. sing. masc. (יַכִּיר), suff. 3 pers. pl. masc.; וַ conv. . . נכר

[a]יְכַרְסְמֶנָּה Piel fut. 3 pers. sing. masc. [יְכַרְסֵם], suff. 3 pers. sing. fem. (§ 7) . . כרסם

וַיִּכְרַע וַ' Kal fut. 3 pers. sing. masc.; וַ conv. כרע

[b]וַיִּכְרְעוּ וַ' id. fut. 3 pers. pl. masc.; וַ id. . כרע

[c]יִכְרָעוּן id. id. with parag. ן . . . . כרע

[d]וַיַּכְרֵת וְ', וַ' Hiph. fut. 3 pers. sing. masc., ap. from יַכְרִית; וַ conv. . . . . כרת

יִכָּרֵת Niph. fut. 3 pers. sing. masc. . . כרת

וַיִּכְרֹת, יִכְרָת־ } Kal fut. 3 pers. sing. masc. (§ 8. rem. 18); וַ conv. . . . . כרת

---

a Is. 31. 3. b Pr. 28. 7. c Ge. 47. 12. d 2 Ch. 2. 5. e 2 Ch. 6. 18. f Ps. 55. 23. g 1 Ki. 8. 27. h 2 Sa. 20. 3. i Ps. 69. 7. k Ex. 18. 23. l Da. 2. 47. m Ps. 13. 5. n Is. 49. 10. o Is. 44. 5. p Pr. 16. 3. q De. 9. 3. r De. 32. 6. s Ps. 147. 2. t Le. 26. 41. u 1 Ch. 20. 4. x Is. 30. 20. y Ec. 6. 4. z 1 Ki. 1. 1. a Hab. 2. 14.

b Ge. 7. 19, 20. c Ps. 140. 10. d Ps. 17. 12. e Ex. 15. 5. f Eze. 26. 10. g Hab. 2. 17. h Je. 10. 8. i Eze. 44. 20. k Eze. 30. 18. l De. 32. 10. m Ps. 106. 29. n Ps. 78. 58. o Ju. 2. 12. p Pr. 21. 14. q Pr. 16. 14. r Ps. 94. 13. s Ex. 21. 33. t 2 Ki. 6. 23. u 1 Ki. 18. 7. x Job 40. 30. y Ge. 26. 25. z Ge. 42. 7. a Ps. 80. 14. b 2 Ch. 7. 3. c Job 31. 10. d Ps. 109. 15.

יִלָּבֵט	Niph. fut. 3 pers. sing. masc. . . .	לבט
יַלְבִּינוּ[c]	Hiph. fut. 3 pers. pl. masc. . . .	לבן
וַיַּלְבֵּשׁ	וַ id. fut. 3 pers. sing. m. ap. [from יַלְבִּישׁ]; ·וַ conv.	לבש
וַיַּלְבִּשֵׁהוּ[d]	וַ id. fut. 3 pers. pl. masc., suff. 3 pers. sing. masc.; ·וַ id.	לבש
יִלְבַּשׁ / וַיִּלְבַּשׁ	Kal (or Peal, Da. 5. 7, §47. rem. 6) fut. 3 pers. sing. masc.; ·וַ id. . .	לבש
יִלְבְּשׁוּ[e]	Kh. יִלְבְּשׁוּ q. v.; K. וְלָבְשׁוּ Kal pret. 3 pers. pl.	לבש
יִלְבְּשׁוּ / וַיִּלְבְּשׁוּ[yy]	Kal fut. 3 pers. pl. masc. (§ 8. rem. 15); ·וַ conv.	לבש
וַיַּלְבִּשׁוּם[bb]	וַ Hiph. fut. 3 pers. pl. masc. [יַלְבִּישׁוּ], suff. 3 pers. pl. masc.; ·וַ id. . . .	לבש
וַיַּלְבִּשֵׁם	וַ id. fut. 3 pers. sing. masc. [יַלְבִּישׁ], suff. 3 pers. pl. masc.; ·וַ id. . . .	לבש
יִלְבָּשֵׁם[f]	Kal fut. 3 pers. sing. masc. (יִלְבַּשׁ), suff. 3 pers. pl. masc. (§ 16. rem. 12) . .	לבש
וַיִּלְבָּשֵׁנִי[g]	וַ id. with suff. 1 pers. sing.; ·וַ conv. .	לבש

יָלַד[h] fut. יֵלֵד, inf. c. לֵדָה, לֶדֶת, לַת.—I. *to bear, bring forth.*—II. *to beget*, as a father. Niph. נוֹלַד *to be born.* Pi. *to help to bring forth, to deliver*, Ex. 1. 16; part. מְיַלֶּדֶת *midwife.* Pu. יֻלַּד, יוּלַּד *to be born*; metaph. Ps. 90. 2. Hiph. הוֹלִיד —I. *to cause to bring forth.*—II. *to beget*; metaph. Job 38. 28. Hoph. *to be born*, inf. יוֹם הֻלֶּדֶת *the birthday of.* Hithp. *to declare* or *enrol one's genealogy* or *pedigree*, Nu. 1. 18.

יֶלֶד masc. dec. 6a (pl. c. יַלְדֵי once יִלְדֵי).—I. *lad, youth, child.*—II. *the young* of animals.

יַלְדָּה fem. dec. 12a, *a girl, maiden.*

יַלְדוּת fem. dec. 1b.—I. *birth*, Ps. 110. 3. Others, *youth, young men.*—II. *youth, childhood.*

יָלוּד masc. dec. 1b.—I. adj. *born.*—II. subst. *offspring, son.*

יָלִיד masc. dec. 3a.—I. adj. *born*; יְלִיד בַּיִת *one born in the house.*—II. subst. *son, child.*

מוֹלִיד (*genitor*) pr. name masc. 1 Ch. 2. 29.

מוֹלָדָה (*birth*) pr. name of a town in the tribe of Judah, afterwards yielded to Simeon.

מוֹלֶדֶת fem. dec. 13a (with suff. מוֹלַדְתִּי).—I. *birth, nativity.*—II. *birth-place.*—III. *offspring, progeny.*—IV. *family, relatives.*

תּוֹלָד (*family, race*) pr. name of a town in the tribe of Simeon, 1 Ch. 4. 29; called אֶלְתּוֹלַד Jos. 15. 30; 19. 4.

וַיִּכְרְתֻהוּ[a]	וַ Kal fut. 3 pers. pl. masc. (יִכְרְתוּ), suff. 3 pers. sing. masc.; ·וַ conv. . . .	כרת
יִכָּרֵתוּ / יִכָּרֵתוּ[b]	Niph. fut. 3 pers. sing. masc. (comp. § 8. rem. 15)	כרת
יִכְרֹתוּ / וַיִּכְרְתוּ	Kal fut. 3 pers. pl. masc. (§ 8. rem. 15); ·וַ conv.	כרת
יִכָּרֵתוּן	Niph. fut. 3 pers. pl. masc. with parag. ן [for יִכָּרְתוּן comp. § 8. rem. 17] . .	כרת
יִכָּשְׁלוּ[c]	Kh. יִכְשׁוּלוּ Kal (§ 8. rem. 14) K. יַכְשִׁילוּ Hiph. fut. 3 pers. pl. masc.	כשל
וַיַּכְשִׁלֻהוּ[d]	וַ Hiph. fut. 3 pers. pl. masc., suff. 3 pers. sing. masc.; ·וַ conv. . . .	כשל
יַכְשִׁילְךָ[e]	id. fut. 3 pers. sing. masc., suff. 2 pers. sing. masc.	כשל
יִכָּשֵׁלוּ[f]	Niph. fut. 3 pers. pl. masc. bef. monos. [for יִכָּשְׁלוּ § 9. rem. 3]	כשל
יִכָּשֵׁלוּ / יִכָּשֵׁלוּ	id. fut. 3 pers. pl. masc. (comp. § 8. rem. 15)	כשל
יִכָּשְׁלוּ[g]	Kh. יִכָּשְׁלוּ q. v.; K. וְכָשְׁלוּ Kal pret. 3 pers. pl.	כשל
וַיַּכְשִׁלוּם[h]	וַ Hiph. fut. 3 pers. pl. masc. [יַכְשִׁילוּ], suff. 3 pers. pl. masc.; ·וַ conv. . . .	כשל
יִכְשַׁר[i]	Kal fut. 3 pers. sing. masc. . . .	כשר
יֻכַּת[k]	Hoph. fut. 3 pers. sing. masc. [for יוּכַּת § 18. rem. 14]	כתת
יִכָּתֵב	וַיִּ, וְ[l] Niph. fut. 3 pers. sing. masc.; ·וַ conv.	כתב
יִכְתֹּב[m] / יִכְתָּב־[n]	וַיִּ, וַ Kal fut. 3 pers. sing. masc. (§ 8. rem. 18); ·וַ id.	כתב
יִכָּתֵבוּ	Niph. fut. 3 pers. pl. masc. [for יִכָּתְבוּ comp. § 8. rem. 15]	כתב
יִכְתְּבוּ	וְ[o], וַיִּ[p] Kal fut. 3 pers. pl. masc.; ·וַ conv.	כתם
וַיִּכְתְּבוּהָ[q]	וַ id. with suff. 3 pers. sing. fem.; ·וַ id. .	כתב
יִכָּתְבוּן[r]	וְ Niph. fut. 3 pers. pl. masc. with parag. ן .	כתב
וַיִּכְתְּבֵם[s]	וַיִּ Kal fut. 3 pers. sing. masc. (יִכְתֹּב), suff. 3 pers. pl. masc.; ·וַ conv. . . .	כתב
וַיַּכִּתוּ[t]	וַ Hiph. fut. 3 pers. pl. masc., Chald. form (§ 18. rem. 14); ·וַ id. . . .	כתת
יֻכַּתּוּ[u] / יֻכַּתּוּ	Hoph. fut. 3 pers. pl. masc. (§ 18. rem. 14)	כתת
וַיַּכְּתוּם[x]	וַ Hiph. fut. 3 pers. pl. masc., suff. 3 pers. pl. masc. (§ 18. rem. 14); ·וַ conv.	כתת
יַכְתִּירוּ[y] / יַכְתִּרוּ[z]	id. fut. 3 pers. pl. masc. . . .	כתר
וַיִּלְאוּ[a]	וַ Kal fut. 3 pers. pl. masc.; ·וַ conv. .	לאה
וַיַּלְאוּךָ[u]	וַ Hiph. fut. 3 pers. pl. masc., suff. 2 pers. sing. masc.; ·וַ id.	לאה
יִלָּבֵב[b]	Niph. fut. 3 pers. sing. masc. . . .	לבב

[a] Eze. 31. 12. [b] Zec. 13. 8. [c] Pr. 4. 16. [d] Ps. 64. 9. [e] 2 Ch. 25. 8. [f] Eze. 33. 12. [g] Na. 3. 3. [h] Je. 18. 15. [i] Ec. 11. 6. [k] Is. 24. 12. [l] Est. 1. 19. [m] Is. 44. 5. [n] Jos. 8. 32. [o] Jos. 18. 4. [p] Ex. 39. 30. [q] Jos. 18. 9. [r] Job 19. 23. [s] Is. 10. 19. [t] De. 1. 44. [u] Je. 12. 5. [u] Job 4. 20. [x] Nu. 14. 45. [y] Pr. 14. 18. [yy] Jon. 3. 5. [z] Ps. 142. 8. [a] Ge. 19. 11. [b] Job 11. 12. [bb] 2 Ch. 28. 15. [c] Is. 1. 18. [d] Zec. 3. 5. [e] Eze. 42. 14. [f] Ex. 29. 30. [g] Job 29. 14. [h] Ps. 7. 15.

תּוֹלְדוֹת fem. pl. c. (from תּוֹלָדָה or תּוֹלֶדֶת). —I. *birth*, Ex. 28. 10.—II. *generations, families.* —III. *family history, origin.*

יָלַד[a] Kal pret 3 pers. s. m. for יָלַד (§ 8. rem. 7) ילד

יָלֶד[b] Kh. for יָלַד q. v.; K. וָלָד [for וָלָד] noun masc. sing. ולד

יָלֹד[c] וְ Kal inf. absolute ילד

יֵלֵד[d] Kal fut. 3 pers. sing. masc., bef. monos. [for יֵלֵד § 20. rem. 4] ילד

יֶלֶד וְ׳ n. masc. s. (pl. c. יַלְדֵי, once יִלְדֵי) d. 6a ילד

יֹלֵד Kal part. act. sing. masc. dec. 7b ילד

יֻלַּד[e] according to most copies, &: } ילד
יֻלַּד Pual pret. 3 pers. sing. masc. }

יָלְדָה } Kal pret. 3 pers. sing. fem. (§ 8. rem. 7) ילד
יָלָדָה וְ׳ }

יֻלְּדָה[f] Pual pret. 3 pers. sing. fem. ילד

יָלְדוּ[g] וְ׳ } Kal pret. 3 pers. pl. (§ 8. rem. 7) ילד
יָלָדוּ וְ׳ }

יֵלְדוּ[h] וַ } Kal fut. 3 pers. pl. masc. (comp. § 8. rem. 15); ·וַ conv. ילד
יֵלֵדוּ }

יָלְדוּ[k] Kh. for יְלָדָיו (q. v. § 4. rem. 1) ילד

יְלָדוֹ[l] Kal pret. 3 pers. sing. masc., suff. 3 pers. sing. masc. ילד

יֻלָּדוּ[m] } Pual pret. 3 pers. pl. (comp. § 8. rem. 7) ילד
יֻלְּדוּ }

יֵלֵדוּן[n] Kal fut. 3 pers. pl. masc. with parag. ן [for יֵלְדוּן comp. § 8. rem. 17] ילד

יְלָדוֹת[o] וְ noun fem., pl. abs. [with cop. וְ, for וִילָדוֹת, וִי׳] from יַלְדָּה dec. 12a ילד

יְלָדַי noun masc. pl., suff. 1 pers. sing. from יֶלֶד (pl. c. יַלְדֵי & יִלְדֵי) dec. 6a ילד

יְלִידֵי[p] noun masc. pl. constr. from [יָלִיד] dec. 3a ילד

יַלְדֵי[q] וְ׳ } noun masc. pl. constr. from יֶלֶד dec. 6a ילד
יִלְדֵי[mm] }

יְלָדֶיהָ } id. pl., suff. 3 pers. sing. fem., with cop. וְ [for וִי׳ וִילָדֶיהָ] ילד
יְלָדֶיהָ וְ }

יַלְדֵיהֶם[r] וְ id. pl., suff. 3 pers. pl. masc. ילד

יַלְדֵיהֶן[s] וְ׳ id. pl., suff. 3 pers. pl. fem. ילד

יְלָדָיו id. pl., suff. 3 pers. sing. masc. ילד

יֹלְדָיו[t] Kal part. act. pl., suff. 3 pers. sing. masc. from יֹלֵד dec. 7b ילד

יְלָדִים } noun masc. pl. [with cop. וְ for וִי׳ וִילָדִים] from יֶלֶד dec. 6a ילד
יְלָדִים[u] וְ }

יְלִדְךָ[x] } Kal pret. 3 pers. sing. masc., suff. 2 pers. sing. masc. ילד
יְלִדְךָ[y] }

יְלִדְנוּ[z] id. pret. 1 pers. pl. ילד

יָלַדְתְּ[a] } id. pret. 2 pers. sing. fem. (§ 8. rem. 7) ילד
יָלַדְתְּ[b] וְ׳[c] }

יֹלֶדֶת וְ } id. part. act. sing. fem. dec. 13a (§ 39. No. 4. rem. 3) ילד
יֹלֶדֶת וְ׳[d] }

יְלָדַתּוּ[e] id. pret. 3 pers. sing. fem., suff. 3 pers. sing. masc. ילד

יָלַדְתִּי[f] } id. pret. 1 pers. sing. (§ 8. rem. 7) ילד
יָלָדְתִּי }

יָלַדְתִּי[g] Kh. יָלַדְתִּי & K. יָלַדְתְּ Kal pret. 2 pers. sing. fem. (§ 8. rem. 5) ילד

יֻלַּדְתִּי[h] Pual pret. 1 pers. sing. ילד

יְלִדְתִּיהוּ[i] Kal pret. 1 pers. sing. with suff. 3 pers. sing. masc. [for יְלַדְ׳ § 8. rem. 1b] ילד

יְלִדְתִּיךָ[k] id. id. with suff. 2 pers. sing. masc. (v. id.) ילד

יְלָדַתְךָ[l] } id. pret. 3 pers. s. fem., suff. 2 pers. sing. m. ילד
יְלָדַתְךָ[m] }

יַלְדֻתֶךָ[n] noun fem. sing., suff. 2 pers. sing. masc. from יַלְדוּת dec. 1b ילד

יֻלַּדְתֶּם[o] Pual pret. 2 pers. pl. masc. ילד

יְלָדַתְנִי[p] Kal pret. 3 pers. sing. fem., suff. 1 pers. sing. ילד

יְלִדְתָּנִי[q] id. pret. 2 pers. s. fem. (§ 8, rem. 1b, & § 16. rem. 5) with suff., Kh. נִי׳, K. נוּ׳, 1 p. s. or pl. ילד

יְלִדְתִּנִי[r] id. pret. 2 pers. sing. fem. with suff. 1 pers. s. ילד

יְלוּד id. part. p. sing. masc., constr. of יָלוּד׳ dec. 3a ילד

יִלָּוֶה[s] Niph. fut. 3 pers. sing. masc. לוה

יִלָּווּ[t] וְ id. fut. 3 pers. pl. masc. לוה

יַלְוְךָ[u] Hiph. fut. 3 pers. sing. masc. [יַלְוֶה], suff. 2 pers. sing. masc. (§ 24. rem. 21) לוה

יָלוֹן וְ pr. name masc. לון

יַלּוֹנוּ[x] וַ Kh. יִלּוֹנוּ׳ Niph. fut. 3 pers. pl. masc.; K. יַלִּינוּ Hiph. &c. (§ 21. rem. 24) לון

יִלְוֶנּוּ[y] Kal fut. 3 pers. sing. masc. [יִלְוֶה], suff. 3 pers. sing. masc. (§ 24. rem. 21) לוה

יָלֻזוּ[z] Kal fut. 3 pers. pl. masc. לוז

יְלַחֲכוּ } Piel fut. 3 pers. pl. masc. (§ 14. rem. 1, comp. § 8. rem. 15) לחך
יְלַחֲכוּ }

יִלָּחֵם } Niph. fut. 3 pers. sing. masc. (§ 9. rem. 3); ·וַ conv. לחם
יִלָּחֶם[a] וַיִּ׳ }

יִלָּחֲמוּ וַ id. fut. 3 pers. pl. masc.; ·וַ id. לחם

יִלְחָמוּנִי[b] וַ id. id., suff. 1 pers. sing.; ·וַ id. לחם

---

[a] Je. 17. 11. [b] 2 Sa. 6. 23. [c] Job 15. 35. [d] Pr. 27. 1. [e] Ge. 41. 50. [f] Ge. 24. 15. [g] Ex. 1. 19. [h] Ge. 20. 17. [i] Is. 65. 23. [k] Job 38. 41. [l] Job 38. 29. [m] Ps. 90. 2. [n] Ho. 9. 16. [o] Zec. 8. 5. [p] Nu. 13. 28. [q] Ho. 1. 2. [r] Job 21. 11. [s] Ge. 33. 6. [t] Zec. 13. 3, 3. [u] Ezr. 10. 1. [x] De. 32. 18. [y] Pr. 23. 22. [z] Is. 26. 18. [a] 1 Sa. 4. 20. [b] Ju. 13. 3. [c] Ju. 13. 3. [d] Is. 7. 14. [e] Ru. 4. 15. [f] 1 Ki. 3. 21. [g] Eze. 16. 20. [h] Je. 20. 14. [i] Nu. 11. 12. [k] Ps. 2. 7. [l] Ca. 8. 5. [m] Je. 22. 26. [mm] Is. 57. 4. [n] Ps. 110. 3. [o] Je. 22. 26. [p] Je. 20. 14. [q] Je. 2. 27. [r] Je. 15. 10. [s] Ge. 29. 34. [t] Nu. 18. 2. [u] De. 28. 44. [x] Ex. 16. 2; Nu. 14. 36. [y] Ec. 8. 15. [z] Pr. 3. 21. [a] Ne. 4. 14. [b] Ps. 109. 3.

יִלְחֲצוּ ו Kal fut. 3 pers. pl. masc.; ·וַ conv. . לחץ
יִלְחָצוּנ ו id. id., suff. 3 pers. pl. masc. (§ 16. rem. 12); ·וַ conv. . . . לחץ
יִלְחָצֵנִ id. fut. 3 pers. sing. masc. [יִלְחַץ], suff. 1 pers. sing. (§ 16. rem. 12) . . . לחץ
יָלֶט[d] ו Hiph. fut. 3 pers. sing. masc. ap. and conv. [from יָלִיט] . . . לוט
יִלְטוֹשׁ Kal fut. 3 pers. sing. masc. (§ 8. rem. 18) . לטש
יְלִיד } noun m. sing., constr. of [יָלִיד] dec. 3 a; ילד
יְלִיד[e] וִ } with cop. וִ [for וִיְ׳, וִילִיד] . ילד
יְלִידֵי id. pl., construct state . . . . ילד
יַלִּיזוּ[f] Hiph. fut. 3 p. pl. m., Chald. form (§ 21. r. 24) לוז
יָלִין Kal fut. 3 pers. sing. masc., R. לִין see . לון
יָלִינוּ וַיָּ׳ id. fut. 3 pers. pl. masc.; ·וַ conv. . לון
יִלּוֹנוּ[g] וַ׳ Kh. יַלִּינוּ Hiph. (§ 21. rem. 24), K. יִלּוֹנוּ Niph. fut. 3 pers. pl. masc. . . לון
יָלִיץ Hiph. fut. 3 pers. sing. masc. . . . לוץ

[יָלַךְ] *to go*, only fut. יֵלֵךְ, inf. constr. לֶכֶת, the rest being supplied from הָלַךְ q. v. Hiph. הוֹלִיךְ, fut. יוֹלִיךְ, see under הָלַךְ.

לֵכָה (*journey*, for יְלֵכָה) pr. name of a place in the tribe of Judah, 1 Ch. 4. 21.

יֵלֵךְ[h] וַיֵּ׳, וְ } Kal fut. 3 pers. sing. m. (§ 20. rem. 4) ילך
יֵלֶךְ }
יֵלֶךְ וַיֵּ׳ }
יֹלֵךְ[i] וַ } Hiph. fut. 3 p. s. m., ap. with conv. ·וַ for יוֹלִיךְ (§ 20. rem. 4) from יוֹלִיךְ . ילך
יֹלֵךְ וַ }
יִלָּכֵד וַיִּ׳ } Niph. fut. 3 pers. sing. masc. (§ 9. rem. 3); ·וַ conv. . . לכד
יִלָּכֵד[k] }
יִלְכֹּד וַ } Kal fut. 3 pers. sing. masc. (§ 8. rem. 18); ·וַ id. . . . . לכד
יִלְכָּד־[l] }
יִלְכְּדָהּ וַ id. id., suff. 3 pers. sing. fem.; ·וַ id. . לכד
יִלְכְּדָהָ וַ id. fut. 3 pers. pl. m., suff. 3 p. s. fem.; ·וַ id. לכד
יִלְכְּדֵהוּ וַ id. id., suff. 3 pers. sing. masc.; ·וַ id. . לכד
יִלָּכְדוּ[n] וַיִּ׳ } Niph. fut. 3 pers. pl. masc. (comp. § 8. rem. 15); ·וַ id. . . לכד
יִלָּכְדוּ[o] וְ }
יִלְכְּדוּ[p] } Kal fut. 3 pers. pl. masc. (§ 8. rem. 15); ·וַ id. . . . . . לכד
יִלְכְּדוּ[q] וַיִּ׳ }
יִלְכְּדוּהָ וַ id., suff. 3 pers. sing. fem.; ·וַ id. . . לכד
יִלָּכְדוּן Niph. fut. 3 pers. pl. masc. with parag. ן . לכד
יִלְכְּדֶנָּה Kal fut. 3 pers. sing. m., suff. 3 pers. sing. fem. לכד
יִלְכְּדֶנּוּ id. id., suff. 3 pers. sing. masc. . . לכד

יִלְכְּדֻנוּ[u] Kal fut. 3 pers. pl. masc. suff. 3 pers. sing. masc. . . . . לכד
יֵלְכוּ וַיֵּ׳, וְ׳ } Kal fut. 3 pers. pl. masc. (comp. § 8. rem. 15); ·וַ conv. . ילך
יֵלֵכוּ וַיֵּ׳, וְ׳ }
יֹלִכוּ[x] וַיּ׳ Hiph. fut. 3 p. pl. m. [for יוֹלִיכוּ]; ·וַ id. ילך
יִלְכּוֹד[y] Kal fut. 3 pers. sing. masc. (§ 8. rem. 18) לכד
יֵלֵכוּן id. fut. 3 pers. pl. masc.; ן parag. [for יֵלְכוּן comp. § 8. rem. 17] . . . . ילך

יָלַל. Hiph. הֵילִיל, fut. יְיֵלִיל, יְיֵלִיל (§ 20. rem. 15) *to wail, howl, lament*.

יְלֵל masc. *a howling*, De. 32. 10.

יְלָלָה fem. dec. 11 c, *a wailing, lamentation*.

תּוֹלָל masc. *he who causes to lament, an oppressor*, Ps. 137. 3.

יְלֵל[u] noun masc. sing. . . . . ילל
יְלָלָה[z] וְ noun fem. s. [with cop. וְ for וִילָלָה] dec. 11 c ילל
יִלְלַת[a] } id., construct state with cop. וְ [for וִילְלַת, וִילְלַת] . . . ילל
יִלְלַת[b] וְ }
יִלְלָתָהּ[c] id. with suff. 3 pers. sing. fem. . . ילל
יְלַמֵּד[d] וִ } Piel fut. 3 pers. sing. masc. (§ 10. rem. 4) with conj. וִ [for וִיְ׳, וִילַמֵּד] . למד
יְלַמֶּד־[e] }
יִלְמַד[f] וַיִּ׳ Kal fut. 3 pers. sing. masc.; ·וַ conv. . למד
יְלַמְּדָהּ[h] וִ Piel fut. 3 pers. sing. masc., suff. 3 pers. sing. fem. with conj. וִ [וִיְ׳, וִיל׳] . . למד
יְלַמְּדֵהוּ[i] וַ id. id., suff. 3 pers. sing. masc.; וַ conv. למד
יְלַמְּדוּ[k] וַיְ׳ Piel fut. 3 pers. pl. masc.; וַ id. . למד
יִלְמְדוּ[l] וַיִּ׳ Kal fut. 3 pers. pl. masc.; ·וַ id. . למד
יְלַמְּדוּן[m] Piel fut. 3 pers. pl. masc. with parag. ן [for יְלַמְּדוּן § 10. rem. 4, comp. § 8. rem. 17] למד
יִלְמְדוּן Kal fut. 3 pers. pl. masc. with parag. ן . למד
יָלֶן וַ Kal fut. 3 pers. sing. m. ap. from יָלִין R. לִין, or Hiph. (Ex. 17. 3) R. . . . לון
יִלֹּנוּ[n] וַ Kal fut. 3 pers. pl. masc.; ·וַ conv., R. לִין see לון
יִלֹּנוּ וַ Niph. fut. 3 pers. pl. masc.; ·וַ conv. . לון

יָלַע cogn. לוּעַ *to swallow, devour*, Pr. 20. 25. Gesenius, *to speak rashly, to utter at random*. Prof. Lee, *to retain*.

יָלַע[o] וַ Hiph. fut. 3 p. s. m. ap. [from יָלִיעַ]; וַ conv. לעג
יִלְעַג[p] } Kal fut. 3 pers. sing. masc. (§ 8. rem. 15) לעג
יִלְעַג־ }
יִלְעֲגוּ[q] id. fut. 3 pers. pl. masc. . . . לעג

Ju. 1. 34. Ps. 106. 42. Ps. 56. 2. 1 Ki. 19. 13. Le. 22. 11.
f Pr. 4. 21. g Ex. 16. 2. h Job 27. 21. i La. 3. 2. k Ec. 7. 26.
l Ju. 8. 14. m 2 Ch. 22. 4. n Je. 8. 9. o Ps. 59. 13. p Je. 5. 26.
q 2 Ch. 32. 18. r Job 36. 8. s Jos. 7. 14. t Jos. 7. 14. u De. 32. 10.
u Pr. 5. 22. x 1 Ki. 1. 38. y Am. 3. 5. z Zep. 1. 10.
a Zec. 11. 3. b Je. 25. 36. c Is. 15. 8, 8. d Ps. 25. 9.
e Job 21. 22. f De. 17. 19. g Eze. 19. 3, 6. h De. 31. 22.
i Is. 40. 14, 14. k 2 Ch. 17. 9, 9. l Ps. 106. 35. m De. 4. 10.
n Jos. 3. 1. o Nu. 3. 33. p Job 9. 23. q Ps. 80. 7.

[a] וַיִּלְעֲגוּ / [b] יַלְעִיגוּ } Hiph. fut. 3 pers. pl. masc.; ·וַ conv. — לעג

יָלַף Root not used; Arab. *to stick fast*. Hence
יַלֶּפֶת fem. *scab, scurf*, Le. 21. 20; 22. 22.

[c] וַיִּלָּפֵת Niph. fut. 3 pers. sing. masc.; ·וַ conv. — לפת
[d] וַיִּלְפֹּת Kal fut. 3 pers. sing. masc.; ·וַ id. — לפת
[e] יִלָּפְתוּ Niph. fut. 3 pers. pl. masc. — לפת

[f] **יֶלֶק** [g] וְ' masc. a species of winged *locust*.

[h] יָלֹק Kal fut. 3 pers. sing. masc. — לקק
[i] יָלֹקּוּ [k] וַ' id. fut. 3 pers. pl. masc.; ·וַ conv. — לקק
וַיְלַקֵּט Piel fut. 3 pers. sing. masc.; וַ id. — לקט
[l] יִלְקְטוּ [m] וַ' Kal fut. 3 pers. pl. masc.; ·וַ id. — לקט
[n] יִלְקֹטוּן id. with parag. ן [for יִלְקְטוּן § 8. rem. 17] — לקט
[o] יְלַקֵּשׁוּ Piel fut. 3 pers. pl. masc. [for יְלַקְּשׁוּ comp. § 8. rem. 15] — לקש

יָם וְ' masc. constr. יַם, יָם, dec. 8 a.—I. *a sea*; also *a great river*; הַיָּם הַגָּדוֹל, הַיָּם הָאַחֲרוֹן (the great, the hinder sea) the Mediterranean. Hence—II. *the west*; רוּחַ יָם *the west wind*; פְּאַת יָם *the western quarter*; יָמָּה *westward*.

יַם Chald. dec. 5 a, *a sea*, Da. 7. 2. 3.

יַם id. construct state (only in יַם־סוּף) — ים
[יֵם] masc. only pl. יֵמִם Ge. 36. 24, probably *hot springs*; Vulg. aquæ calidæ.
[p] יַמָּא Chald. noun masc. sing., emph. of [יַם] d. 5 a — ים
[q] יְמָאֵן וְ' Piel fut. 3 pers. sing. masc.; וַ conv. — מאן
[r] יְמָאֲנוּ וַ' id. fut. 3 pers. pl. masc.; וַ id. — מאן
[s] וַיִּמָּאֵס Niph. fut. 3 pers. sing. masc.; ·וַ id. — מאס
יִמְאַס / [ff] יִמְאָס וַ' } Kal fut. 3 pers. sing. masc. (§ 8. r. 15); ·וַ id. — מאס
[t] יִמָּאֲסוּ Niph. fut. 3 pers. pl. masc. — מסס
וַיִּמְאֲסוּ Kal fut. 3 pers. pl. masc.; ·וַ conv. — מאס
[u] יִמְאָסוּן id. id. with parag. ן [for יִמְאֲסוּן § 8. r. 17] — מאס
[x] וַיִּמְאָסְךָ id. fut. 3 pers. sing. masc., suff. 2 pers. sing. masc. (§ 16. rem. 12); ·וַ conv. — מאס
[y] יִמְאָסֵם [z] וַ' id. id., suff. 3 pers. pl. masc.; ·וַ id. — מאס
[a] יְמַגַּר Ch. Pael fut. 3 pers. sing. masc. — מגר
וַיָּמַד Kal fut. 3 pers. sing. masc., with conv. ·וַ [for יָמֹד] — מדד
יִמַּד Niph. fut. 3 pers. sing. masc. — מדד
[b] וַיְמַדֵּד Piel fut. 3 pers. sing. masc.; וַ conv. — מדד
[c] וַיְמֹדֵד Pil. (fr. מוּד) or Poel fut. 3 p. s. m.; וַ id. — מדד

[d] וַיְמַדְּדֵם Piel fut. 3 pers. sing. masc., suff. 3 pers. pl. masc.; וַ conv. — מדד
[e] וַיָּמֹדּוּ Kal fut. 3 pers. pl. masc.; ·וַ id. — מדד
[f] יִמַּדּוּ Niph. fut. 3 pers. pl. masc. — מדד
יָמָּה וָ', וְ' noun masc. sing. (יָם) with loc. ה, for וְ see lett. ו — ים
[g] יַמָּהּ id. with suff. 3 pers. sing. fem. dec. 8 a — ים
יְמַהֵר וְ' Piel fut. 3 p. s. m. (§ 14. r. 1); וַ conv. — מהר
[h] יְמַהֲרוּ וַ' / וִימַהֲרוּ } id. fut. 3 pers. pl. masc.; וַ conv., with conj. וְ for [וַיְמַ', וִיְמַ'] — מהר
[i] יִמְהָרֶנָּה Kal fut. 3 pers. sing. masc. [יִמְהַר], suff. 3 pers. sing. fem. (§ 16. rem. 12) — מהר
[k] יָמוֹ Kh. for יָמָיו (q. v.) — יום
יְמוּאֵל pr. name masc. Ge. 46. 10, and Ex. 6. 15; for which נְמוּאֵל Nu. 26. 12.
יִמּוֹט Niph. fut. 3 pers. sing. masc. — מוט
[u] יִמּוֹטוּ id. fut. 3 pers. pl. masc. — מוט
[l] יָמוּךְ Kal fut. 3 pers. sing. masc. — מוך
יִמּוֹל Niph. fut. 3 pers. sing. masc. — מול
[m] יְמוֹלֵל Pilel fut. 3 pers. sing. masc. — מול
יָמוּשׁ Kal fut. 3 pers. sing. masc. — מוש
יָמוּשׁוּ id. fut. 3 pers. pl. masc. — מוש
יָמוּת Kal fut. 3 pers. sing. masc. — מות
[n] יְמוֹת n. com. pl. constr. [of יָמוֹת] fr. יוֹם irr. (§ 45) — יום
[o] יָמֻת Kh. יָמוּת q. v.; K. יוּמַת Hoph. fut. 3 pers. sing. masc. — מות
יָמֻתוּ וַ' Kal fut. 3 pers. pl. masc.; ·וַ conv. — מות
[p] יְמֻתוּן id. with parag. ן — מות
[q] יִמַּח Niph. fut. 3 pers. sing. masc. [for יִמָּח ap. from יִמָּחֶה (§ 24. rem. 10) — מחה
[r] יִמַח וַ id., or, according to some copies, without dag. in מ, Kal fut. ap. from יִמְחֶה (§ 24. r. 3) — מחה
[s] יְמַחֵא Ch. Pael fut. 3 pers. s. m. (comp. § 14. r. 1) — מחא
יִמְחֲאוּ Kal fut. 3 pers. pl. masc. — מחא
יִמָּחֶה Niph. fut. 3 pers. sing. masc. — מחה
[t] יִמְחֶה Kal fut. 3 pers. sing. masc. — מחה
[u] יִמָּחוּ [x] וַ' Niph. fut. 3 pers. pl. masc. — מחה
[y] יִמְחַץ / יִמְחָץ } Kal fut. 3 pers. sing. masc. (§ 8. r. 15) — מחץ
[z] יִמְטָא Ch. Peal fut. 3 pers. sing. masc. — מטא
[a] יַמְטֵר [b] וַ', וְ' Hiph. fut. 3 pers. sing. masc. ap. [from יַמְטִיר]; ·וַ conv. — מטר
יָמַי / [c] יָמָי וְ' } noun com. pl. (יָמִים), suff. 1 pers. sing. irr. of יוֹם (§ 45) — יום
יְמֵי / וִימֵי } id. pl., constr. state, with cop. וְ (וִימֵי) [וִימֵי] — יום

---

[a] Ne. 2. 19. [b] Ps. 22. 8. [c] Ru. 3. 8. [d] Ju. 16. 29. [e] Job 6. 18. [f] Na. 3. 16. [g] Ps. 105. 34. [h] Ju. 7. 5. [i] 1 Ki. 21. 19. [k] 1 Ki. 22. 38. [l] Ex. 16. 5. [m] Ex. 16. 17, 21. [n] Ps. 104. 28. [o] Job 24. 6. [p] Da. 7. 3. [q] Ex. 22. 16. [r] Je. 25. 28. [s] Job 7. 5. [t] Ps. 58. 8. [u] Is. 31. 7. [x] 1 Sa. 15. 23, 26. [y] Ho. 9. 17. [z] Je. 33. 24. [a] Ezr. 6. 12. [b] 2 Sa. 8. 2. [c] Job 3. 6. [d] 2 Sa. 8. 2. [e] Ex. 16. 18. [f] Je. 31. 37. [ff] Job 8. 20. [g] Je. 51. 36. [h] Na. 2. 6. [i] Ex. 22. 15. [k] Je. 17. 11. [l] Le. 25. 25, 35, 39. [u] Ps. 82. 5. [m] Ps. 90. 6. [n] De. 32. 7. [o] 2 Ki. 14. 6 [p] Is. 51. 6. [q] Ps. 109. 13. [r] Ge. 7. 23. [s] Da. 4. 32. [t] 2 Ki. 21. 13 [u] Ps. 69. 29. [x] Ge. 7. 23. [y] Nu. 24. 8. [z] Da. 4. 8, 17. [a] Ps. 11. 6. [b] Job 20. 23. [c] Job 9. 25.

[a] יְמֶיהָ וְ׳ [b] id. pl., suff. 3 pers. sing. fem. . . יום
יְמֵיהֶם id. pl., suff. 3 pers. pl. masc. . . יום
יָמָיו id. pl., suff. 3 pers. sing. masc. . . יום
[c] יְמִיתוּ Hiph. fut. 3 pers. pl. masc. . . מות
[d] יִמּוֹטוּ Kh. יָמִיטוּ q. v.; K. יִמּוֹטוּ (q. v.) . מוט
[e] יָמַיִךְ noun com. pl. (יָמִים), suff. 2 pers. sing. fem. irr. of יוֹם (§ 45) . . . . . יום
יָמֶיךָ id. pl., suff. 2 pers. sing. masc. . . יום
יְמֵיכֶם id. pl., suff. 2 pers. pl. masc. . . יום
יָמִים וְ׳ [f] id. pl., absolute state . . . יום
יַמִּים noun masc., pl. absolute from יָם dec. 8a ים
[g] יָמַיִם noun com. du. (for יוֹמַיִם) fr. יוֹם (§ 45) יום
יָמִימָה id. pl. (יָמִים) with parag. ה יום
יְמִימָה (*dove*, coll. with the Arab.) pr. name of one of Job's daughters, Job 42. 14.
יָמִין וְ׳ pr. name masc. . . . ימן
יָמִין וְ׳ [h] noun masc. sing. dec. 3a . . . ימן
יְמִין id., constr. state . . . . ימן
[i] יְמִינָהּ וְ id., suff. 3 pers. sing. fem. with cop. וְ [for וְ׳, וִימִינָהּ] . . . . ימן
יָמֵינוּ noun com. pl. (יָמִים), suff. 1 pers. pl. irr. of יוֹם (§ 45) . . . . יום
יְמִינוֹ / וִ ימִינוֹ } noun m. s., suff. 3 pers. s. m. fr. יָמִין dec. 3a; with cop. וְ [for וְ׳, וִימִינוֹ] } ימן
יְמִינִי gent. noun from בִּנְיָמִין (q. v.) . . בנה
יְמִינִי / [k] וִ ימִינִי } noun masc. s., suff. 1 pers. s. fr. יָמִין dec. 3a, with cop. וְ [for וְ׳, וִימִינִי] } ימן
יְמִינְךָ וְ׳ [l] / יְמִינֶךָ וְ׳ [m] } id., suff. 2 pers. sing. mas.; with cop. וְ see preceding } ימן
[n] יְמִינָם / וִ ימִינָם } id., suff. 3 pers. pl. masc.; with cop. וְ see preceding } ימן
[o] יָמִיקוּ Hiph. fut. 3 pers. pl. masc. . . מוק
יָמִיר Hiph. fut. 3 pers. sing. masc. . . מור
[p] יָמִירוּ וַ id. fut. 3 pers. pl. masc.; וַ׳ conv. . מור
[q] יְמִירֶנּוּ id. fut. 3 pers. sing. masc., suff. 3 pers. sing. masc. (§ 2. rem. 3) . . . מור
יָמִישׁ Hiph. fut. 3 pers. sing. masc. . . מוש
[r] יְמִישׁוּן id. fut. 3 pers. pl. masc. with parag. ן . מוש
יָמִית Hiph. fut. 3 pers. sing. masc. . . מות
יְמִיתֵהוּ וַ id. id., suff. 3 pers. sing. masc.; וַ conv. מות
יְמִיתֻהוּ וַ id. fut. 3 p. pl. m., suff. 3 p. s. m.; וַ id. מות
[s] יְמִיתוּ וַ id. fut. 3 pers. pl. masc.; וַ׳ id. . מות
[t] יְמִיתוּהָ וַ id. id., suff. 3 pers. s. fem.; וַ id. מות
יְמִיתֵם וַ id. fut. 3 p. s. m., suff. 3 p. pl. m.; וַ id. מות
[u] יְמִיתֻנוּ id. fut. 3 pers. pl. masc., suff. 1 pers. pl. מות
[x] יִמַּךְ Niph. fut. 3 pers. sing. masc. . מכך
[uu] יָמֹכּוּ וַ Kal fut. 3 pers. pl. masc.; וַ׳ conv. . מכך

יִמָּכֵר Niph. fut. 3 pers. sing. masc. . . מכר
יִמְכֹּר וְ׳, וַ / [y] יִמְכָּר־ } Kal fut. 3 pers. sing. masc. (§ 8. r. 18) וַ׳ conv. } מכר
[z] יִמָּכְרוּ Niph. fut. 3 pers. pl. masc. . . מכר
[a] יִמְכְּרוּ וְ׳ [b] וַ Kal fut. 3 pers. pl. masc.; וַ׳ conv. . מכר
יִמְכְּרֵם וַ id. fut. 3 p. s. m., suff. 3 p. pl. m.; וַ׳ id. מכר
יָמָל וַ Kal fut. 3 pers. sing. masc. ap. and conv. [from יָמוּל] . . . . . מול
[c] יִמַּל וְ / [d] יִמָּל } Kal fut. 3 pers. sing. masc., Chald. form (§ 18. rem. 14); וַ׳ conv. } מלל
יִמָּלֵא וַ׳, וְ׳ Niph. fut. 3 pers. sing. masc.; וַ׳ id. מלא
יְמַלֵּא וְ׳ / [e] וִ ימַלֵּא } Piel fut. 3 pers. sing. masc.; וַ conv.; with conj. וְ [for וְ׳, וִימַלֵּא] } מלא
יִמְלָא pr. name masc. . . . . מלא
[f] יִמָּלְאוּ וְ Niph. fut. 3 pers. pl. masc. . . מלא
[g] יְמַלְּאוּ / וַ ימַלְּאוּ } Piel fut. 3 pers. pl. masc. (§ 10. rem. 7 comp. § 8. rem. 15); וַ conv. } מלא
יִמְלְאוּ וַ׳ Kal fut. 3 pers. sing. masc.; וַ׳ id. . מלא
[h] יְמַלְאוּם וַ Piel fut. 3 pers. pl. masc. (§ 10. rem. 7), suff. 3 pers. pl. masc. (ם for ן fem. § 2. rem. 5); וַ id. . . . . מלא
[i] יִמָּלְאוּן Niph. fut. 3 pers. pl. masc.; ן parag. . מלא
[k] יְמַלֶּה Piel fut. 3 pers. sing. m. for יְמַלֵּא (§ 23. r. 10) מלא
יִמְלָה pr. name masc., see יִמְלָא . . מלא
יִמְּלוּ Kal fut. 3 pers. pl. masc. [for יִמְלוּ § 18. rem. 14] . . . . מלל
[l] יִמֹּלוּ וַ Niph. fut. 3 pers. pl. masc.; וַ׳ conv. . מול
יִמְלוֹךְ Kal fut. 3 pers. sing. masc. (§ 8. rem. 18) . מלך
יִמָּלֵט וַ׳ Niph. fut. 3 pers. sing. masc.; וַ׳ conv. מלט
יְמַלֵּט / [m] וִ ימַלֵּט } Piel fut. 3 pers. sing. masc.; with conj. וְ [for וְ׳, וִימַלֵּט] } מלט
[n] יְמַלְּטֵהוּ id. id. with suff. 3 pers. sing. masc. . מלט
[o] יִמָּלְטוּ וַ / [p] יִמָּלֵטוּ } Niph. fut. 3 pers. pl. masc. (comp. § 8. rem. 15); וַ׳ conv. } מלט
[q] יְמַלְּטוּ וַ Piel fut. 3 pers. pl. masc.; וַ id. . מלט
[r] יַמְלִיכֶהָ וַ Hiph. fut. 3 pers. sing. masc., suff. 3 pers. sing. fem.; וַ׳ id. . . . מלך
[s] יַמְלִיכֻהוּ וַ id. fut. 3 p. pl. m., suff. 3 p. s. m.; וַ׳ id. מלך
[t] יַמְלִיכוּ וַ id. fut. 3 pers. pl. masc.; וַ׳ id. . מלך
יַמְלֵךְ וַ id. future, 3 pers. sing. masc., ap. [from יַמְלִיךְ], also pr. name . . . מלך
[u] יִמָּלֵךְ וַ Niph. fut. 3 pers. sing. masc.; וַ׳ conv. מלך
יִמְלֹךְ וַ׳ / [uu] יִמְלָךְ־ וַ׳ } Kal fut. 3 pers. sing. masc. (§ 8. rem. 18); וַ׳ id. } מלך

[a] Ge. 25. 24. [b] Is. 13. 22. [c] Ps. 55. 4. [d] Ps. 140. 11. [e] Eze. 22. 4. [f] 2 Ch. 15. 3. [g] Nu. 9. 22. [h] Ps. 89. 13. [i] Ju. 5. 26. [k] Is. 48. 13. [l] Ps. 18. 36. [m] Ps. 74. 11. [n] Ju. 7. 20. [o] Ps. 73. 8. [p] Ps. 106. 20. [q] Le. 27. 33. [r] Ps. 115. 7. [s] 2 Ki. 21. 23. [t] 2 Ch. 23. 15. [u] 2 Ki. 7. 4. [x] Ec. 10. 18. [y] Le. 25. 15. [z] Le. 25. 42. [a] Eze. 48. 14. [b] Ge. 37. 28. [c] Job 14. 2. [d] Job 18. 16. [e] Job 15. 2. [f] Pr. 3. 10. [g] Eze. 7. 19. [h] Ge. 26. 15; 1 Sa. 18. 27. [i] Eze. 32. 6. [k] Job 8. 21. [l] Ge. 34. 24. [m] Ps. 107. 20. [n] Ps. 41. 2. [o] Mal. 3. 15. [p] Da. 11. 41. [q] 2 Ki. 23. 18. [r] Est. 2. 17. [s] 2 Ch. 30. 1. [t] Ne. 5. 7. [u] Is. 32. 1. [uu] Ps. 106. 43.

יַמְלִכֵהוּ[a] וַ Hiph. fut. 3 pers. sing. masc., suff. 3 pers. sing. masc.; ·וַ conv. . . . . מלך

יַמְלִכוּ וַ defect. for יַמְלִיכוּ (q. v.) . . . מלך

יִמְלְכוּ[b] } Kal fut. 3 pers. pl. masc. (§ 8. rem. 15);
וַיִּמְלְכוּ[c] } ·וַ conv. . . . . . מלך

יְמַלֵּל[d] Piel fut. 3 pers. sing. masc. . . מלל

יְמַלִּל[e] Ch. Pael fut. 3 pers. sing. masc. (§ 47. r. 1 c) מלל

יָמַן. Hiph. הֵימִין.—I. *to take the right hand, turn to the right hand.*—II. *to use the right hand*, 1 Ch. 12. 2.

יָמִין masc. dec. 3a.—I. *the right*; יַד יְמִינוֹ *the hand of his right side*, i. e. *his right hand*; and also יַד omitted, *the right hand* (fem. gen.); יְמִין פְּ׳, מִיָּמִין, עַל יָמִין *on the right, at the right*; מִימִין פְּ׳, לִימִין פְּ׳, עַל or אֶל־יְמִין פְּ׳ *on the right hand, right side of any one*; אֶל־הַיָּמִין or עַל, and simply הַיָּמִין *towards the right*.—II. *the south*; מִיָּמִין *on the south of*.—III. pr. name masc. of several persons, especially of a son of Simeon, Ge. 46. 10. Patronym. יָמִינִי Nu. 26. 12.

יְמִינִי.—I. adj. *right, dexter*, only in Kheth. 2 Ch. 3. 17; Eze. 4. 6.—II. gent. noun for בֶּן־יְמִינִי *Benjamite* from בִּנְיָמִין, see R. בָּנָה.

יִמְנָה (*felicity*; coll. with the Arab.) pr. name of several persons, especially of a son of Asher, Ge. 46. 17.

יְמָנִי, fem. יְמָנִית adj. *right, dexter*.

תֵּימָן masc.—I. *the south*; תֵּימָנָה *towards the south*. Ellipt. (for רוּחַ הַתֵּימָן) *the south wind*.—II. pr. name of a grandson of Esau, and of a city and region in Idumea called *Teman* after him. Patronym. תֵּימָנִי.

תֵּימְנִי pr. name masc. 1 Ch. 4. 6.

יְמַן וַ Piel fut. 3 p. s. m., ap. [from יְמַנֶּה]; וַ conv. מנה

יִמָּנֶה[f] Niph. fut. 3 pers. sing. masc. . . מנה

יִמְנָה pr. name masc. . . . . . מנה

יִמְנוּ[g] וַ Kal fut. 3 pers. pl. masc.; ·וַ conv. . מנה

יִמָּנוּ[h] Niph. fut. 3 pers. pl. masc. . . . מנה

יִמָּנַע[i] וְ Niph. fut. 3 pers. sing. masc. . . מנע

יִמְנָע וְ pr. name masc. . . . . . מנע

יִמְנַע[k] Kal fut. 3 pers. sing. masc. . . . מנע

יִמָּנְעוּ[l] וַ Niph. fut. 3 pers. pl. masc.; ·וַ conv. . מנע

יִמְנָעֶנָּה[m] וְ Kal fut. 3 pers. sing. masc. (יִמְנַע), suff. 3 pers. sing. fem. (§ 16. rem. 12) . מנע

יִמְנָעֵנִי[n] id. with suff. 1 pers. sing. . . . מנע

יִמַּס } Niph. fut. 3 pers. sing. masc. (comp.
וַיִּ׳ יִמַּס } § 8. rem. 15); ·וַ conv. . . . מסס

יִמַּסּוּ[o] וַ id. fut. 3 pers. pl. masc.; ·וַ conv. . . מסס

יַמְסֵם[p] וְ Hiph. fut. 3 pers. sing. masc. [יַמְסֶה], suff. 3 pers. pl. masc. (§ 24. rem. 21) . מסה

יִמָּסְרוּ[q] וַ Niph. fut. 3 pers. pl. masc.; ·וַ conv. . מסר

יִמְעַט[r] }
יִמְעָט } Kal fut. 3 pers. sing. masc. (§ 8. rem. 15) מעט

יִמְעֲטוּ } Kal fut. 3 pers. pl. masc.; ·וַ conv. (v.
יִמְעָטוּ[s] וַ } id.) . . . . . . מעט

יַמְעִיט Hiph. fut. 3 pers. sing. masc. . . . מעט

יִמְעַל[t] וַיִּ׳[u] Kal fut. 3 pers. sing. masc.; ·וַ conv. . מעל

יִמְעֲלוּ וַ id. fut. 3 pers. pl. masc.; ·וַ id. . . מעל

יִמֶץ[x] וַ Kal fut. 3 pers. sing. masc. ap. [from יִמְצֶה]; ·וַ id. . . . . . מצה

יִמָּצֵא וַיִּ׳ Niph. fut. 3 pers. sing. masc.; ·וַ id. מצא

יִמְצָא וַיִּ׳ Kal fut. 3 pers. sing. masc.; ·וַ id. . מצא

יִמְצָאֶהָ וַ id. with suff. 3 pers. sing. fem.; ·וַ id. . מצא

יַמְצִאֵהוּ[y] Hiph. fut. 3 pers. sing. masc., suff. 3 pers. sing. masc. . . . . . . מצא

יִמְצָאֵהוּ[z] וַיִּ׳ Kal fut. 3 pers. sing. masc., suff. 3 pers. sing. masc.; ·וַ conv. . . . מצא

יִמְצָאֻהוּ[a] וַיִּ׳ id. fut. 3 p. pl. m., suff. 3 p. s. m.; ·וַ id. מצא

יַמְצִאוּ[b] וַ Hiph. fut. 3 pers. pl. masc.; ·וַ id. . מצא

יִמָּצְאוּ וַ Niph. fut. 3 pers. pl. masc.; ·וַ id. . מצא

יִמְצְאוּ } Kal fut. 3 pers. pl. masc. (§ 8.
יִמְצָאוּ[c] וַיִּ׳, וְיִ׳ } rem. 15); ·וַ id. . . . מצא

יִמָּצְאוּן[d] Niph. fut. 3 pers. pl. masc. with parag. ן . מצא

יִמְצָאוּנְהָ[e] Kal fut. 3 pers. pl. masc. with parag. נ & suff. 3 pers. sing. fem. (§ 16. rem. 14) מצא

יִמְצָאֲךָ[f] id. fut. 3 pers. sing. masc., suff. 2 pers. s. m. מצא

יִמְצָאֶכָּה[g] id. id., suff. 2 pers. sing. masc. (§ 2. rem. 2) מצא

יִמְצָאֵם וַ id. fut. 3 pers. sing. masc.; ·וַ conv. . מצא

יַמְצִאֶנּוּ[h] Hiph. fut. 3 pers. sing. masc., suff. 3 pers. sing. masc. (§ 2. rem. 3) . . . מצא

יִמְצָאֶנּוּ Kal fut. 3 pers. sing. masc., suff. 3 pers. sing. masc. (§ 2. rem. 3) . . . מצא

יִמְצָאֻנְנִי id. fut. 3 pers. pl. masc. with parag. נ & suff. 1 pers. sing. (§ 16. rem. 14) . מצא

יִמָּצֶה[i] Niph. fut. 3 pers. sing. masc. . . מצה

יִמָּצוּ[k] id. fut. 3 pers. pl. masc. . . . מצה

יִמְצוּ[l] Kal fut. 3 pers. pl. masc. . . . מצה

יִמַּקּוּ[m] } Niph. fut. 3 pers. pl. masc. (comp. § 8.
יִמַּקּוּ[n] } rem. 15) . . . . . מקק

יָמַר. Hiph. הֵמִיר *to change, exchange*, Je. 2. 11. Hithp. הִתְיַמֵּר *to change places* with any one, *to take his place* in anything, Is. 61. 6. Others, *to exercise dominion*. According to the Vulg., Chald. & Syr. *to boast oneself*, as if for הִתְאַמֵּר.

[a] 2 Sa. 2. 9. [b] Pr. 8. 15. [c] 1 Ki. 11. 24. [d] Ps. 106. 2. [e] Da. 7. 25. [f] Ge. 13. 16. [g] 2 Ki. 12. 11. [h] 2 Ch. 5. 6. [i] Job 38. 15. [k] Ps. 84. 12. [l] Je. 3. 3. [m] Job 20. 13. [n] 2 Sa. 13. 13. [o] Ju. 15. 14. [p] Ps. 147. 18. [q] Nu. 31. 5. [r] Pr. 13. 11. [s] Ps. 107. 39. [t] Pr. 16. 10. [u] 2 Ch. 26. 16. [x] Ju. 6. 38. [y] Job 37. 13. [z] De. 32. 10. [a] Job 20. 8. [b] Le. 9. 12, 18. [c] 1 Sa. 25. 8. [d] Ge. 18. 29, 32. [e] Je. 2. 24. [f] 1 Ki. 18. 12. [g] 1 Ki. 18. 10. [h] Job 34. 11. [i] Le. 5. 9. [k] Ps. 73. 10. [l] Ps. 75. 9. [m] Le. 26. 39. [n] Le. 26. 39.

יָמֵר[a] } Hiph. fut. 3 pers. sing. masc., ap. & } מור
יָמֵר[b] } defect. for יָמִיר . . . . }

יֵמַר[c] Kal fut. 3 pers. sing. masc. (§ 18. rem. 6) מרר

וַ יִּמְרֹד } Kal fut. 3 pers. sing. masc. (§ 8. rem. } מרד
וַ יִּמְרָד־ } 18); וַ· conv. . . . . }

וַ יִּמְרְדוּ[d] id. fut. 3 pers. pl. masc.; וַ· id. . . מרד

יַמְרֶה[e] Hiph. fut. 3 pers. sing. masc. . . . מרה

וְ יִמְרָה pr. name masc. . . . . מרה

וַיַּ׳ יַמְרוּ[f] Hiph. fut. 3 p. pl. masc. . . . מרה

יַמְרוּהוּ[g] id. id., suff. 3 pers. sing. masc. . . מרה

יֹמְרוּךָ[h] Kal fut. 3 pers. pl. masc., suff. 2 pers. sing.
masc. [for יֹאמְרוּךָ § 19. rem. 5] . . אמר

וַ יִּמְרְחוּ[i] Kal fut. 3 pers. pl. masc.; וַ· conv. . מרח

יִמָּרֵט[k] Niph. fut. 3 pers. sing. masc. . . . מרט

יַמְרִיצְךָ[l] Hiph. fut. 3 pers. sing. masc. with suff. 2 pers.
sing. masc. . . . . . . מרץ

וַ יְמָרְרֻהוּ[m] Piel fut. 3 pers. pl. masc., suff. 3 pers. sing.
masc.; וַ conv. . . . . . . מרר

וַ יְמָרְרוּ[n] id. fut. 3 pers. pl. masc.; וַ id. . . מרר

יָמַשׁ Kal not used; i. q. מָשַׁשׁ. Hiph. הֵימִישׁ *to let feel, grope*, Ju. 16. 26 Kheth.

וְ יָמֵשׁ[o] Hiph. fut. 3 pers. sing. masc. . . משש

וַ יְמֻשֵּׁהוּ[p] Kal fut. 3 pers. sing. masc. [יָמֹשׁ], suff.
3 pers. sing. masc.; וַ conv. . . . משש

יָמֻשׁוּ[q] defect. for יָמוּשׁוּ (q. v.) . . . מוש

יִמְשׁוֹךְ[r] Kal fut. 3 pers. sing. masc. (§ 8. rem. 18) משך

יִמְשׁוֹל[s] Kal fut. 3 pers. sing. masc. (§ 8. rem. 18) משל

וַיִּ׳ יִמְשַׁח[t] Kal fut. 3 pers. sing. masc.; וַ· conv. משח

וַ יִּמְשָׁחֵהוּ the foll. with suff. 3 pers. sing. masc.; וַ id. משח

יִמְשָׁחוּ[u] } Kal fut. 3 pers. pl. masc. (§ 8. rem. 15); } משח
וַ יִּמְשְׁחוּ } וַ· id. . . . . . }

וַ יִּמְשָׁחֲךָ[x] id. fut. 3 pers. sing. masc., suff. 2 pers. sing.
masc. (§ 16. rem. 12); וַ· id. . . משח

וַ יִּמְשָׁחֵם[y] id. id., suff. 3 pers. pl. masc.; וַ· id. . משח

וַ יִּמְשֹׁךְ[z] Kal fut. 3 pers. sing. masc.; וַ· id. . משך

יִמָּשֵׁכוּ[a] Niph. fut. 3 p. pl. m. [for יִמָּשְׁכוּ comp. § 8. r. 15] משך

וַ יִּמְשְׁכוּ Kal fut. 3 pers. pl. masc.; וַ· conv. . משך

יִמְשֹׁל } Kal fut. 3 pers. sing. masc. (§ 8. rem. 18) משל
יִמְשָׁל־ }

יִמְשְׁלוּ[b] } id. fut. 3 pers. pl. masc. (§ 8. rem. 15); } משל
וַיִּ׳ יִמְשָׁלוּ[c] } וַ· conv. . . . . }

יַמְשֵׁנִי Hiph. fut. 3 pers. sing. masc. [יַמְשֶׁה], suff.
1 pers. sing. (§ 24. rem. 21) . . משה

יְמֻשֵּׁנִי[d] Kal fut. 3 pers. s. m. [יָמֹשׁ], suff. 1 pers. s. משש

וַיְ׳ יְמַשֵּׁשׁ[e][f] Piel fut. 3 pers. sing. masc.; וַ conv. . ששׁ

יְמַשְׁשׁוּ id. fut. 3 pers. pl. masc. . . . ששׁ

וַ יָּמֶת Hiph. fut. 3 pers. sing. masc. ap. and conv.
from יָמִית . . . . . . ות

וַיָּ׳, וַ׳ יָמֹת[g][h] } Kal fut. 3 pers. sing. masc., ap. and } ות
וַ יָּמָת } conv. from יָמוּת (§ 21. rem. 8.) }

וַ יְמִתֵהוּ Hiph. fut. 3 pers. sing. masc. (יָמִית), suff.
3 pers. sing. masc.; וַ conv. . . ות

וַ יְמִתֻהוּ id. fut. 3 p. pl. (יָמִיתוּ), suff. 3 p. s. m.; וַ id. ות

וַיָּ׳ יָמֻתוּ Kal fut. 3 pers. pl. masc. for יָמוּתוּ; וַ· id. ות

יְמֻתוּן[k] id. with paragogic ן . . . . ות

וַ יִּמְתָּחֵם[l] Kal fut. 3 pers. sing. masc. [יִמְתַּח], suff.
3 pers. pl. masc. (§ 16. rem. 12); וַ· conv. תח

וַ יְמִתֵם[m] Hiph. fut. 3 pers. sing. masc. (יָמִית), suff.
3 pers. pl. masc.; וַ id. . . . ות

יְמִתֶנּוּ[n] id. with. suff. 3 pers. sing. m. (§ 2. rem. 3) ות

יִמְתְּקוּ[o] } Kal fut. 3 pers. pl. masc. (§ 8. rem. 15); } תק
וַ יִּמְתְּקוּ[p] } וַ· conv. . . . . . }

וַ יְמֹתְתֵהוּ[q] Pilel fut. 3 pers. sing. masc. [יְמֹתֵת], suff.
3 pers. sing. masc.; וַ id. . . . ות

וַ יִּנְאֲמוּ[r] Kal fut. 3 pers. pl. masc.; וַ· id. . אם

יִנְאַף[s] Kal fut. 3 pers. sing. masc. . . . אף

וַ יִּנְאָפוּ[t] id. fut. 3 pers. sing. masc. [for יִנְאֲפוּ § 8.
rem. 15]; וַ· conv. . . . אף

וַ יְנָאֲפוּ[u] Piel fut. 3 pers. pl. m. (§ 14. rem. 1); וַ id. אף

וְ יָנֵאץ[x] Hiph. fut. 3 pers. sing. masc. by Syriasm
[for יַנְאֵץ, comp. בֹּאר for בְּאֵר, מְלָאכָה
for מַלְאָכָה] . . . אץ

יְנָאֵץ[y] Piel fut. 3 pers. sing. masc. . . . אץ

וַ יִּנְאָץ[z] } Kal fut. 3 pers. sing. masc. (§ 8. rem. } אץ
וַיִּ׳ יִנְאַץ[a][b] } 15); וַ· conv. . . . }

יִנְאָצוּן[c] id. fut. 3 pers. pl. masc. with paragogic ן [for
יִנְאֲצוּן § 8. rem. 17] . . . אץ

יְנַאֲצֻנִי[d] Piel fut. 3 p. pl. m., suff. 1 p. s. (§ 14. r. 1) אץ

יִנְאָקוּ[e] Kal fut. 3 pers. pl. m. [for יִנְאֲקוּ § 8. r. 15] אק

וַיִּ׳ יִנָּבֵא[f] Niph. fut. 3 pers. sing. masc.; וַ· conv. בא

וַ יִּנָּבְאוּ[g] id. fut. 3 pers. pl. masc.; וַ· id. . . בא

וַ יְנַבֵּל[h] Piel fut. 3 pers. s. masc.; וַ id. . . בל

יְנַגֵּחַ[i] id. fut. 3 pers. sing. masc. . . . ח

וַ יְנַגַּע id. fut. 3 pers. sing. masc.; וַ conv. . ע

וַ יִּנָּגְעוּ[k] Niph. fut. 3 pers. pl. masc.; וַ· id. . . ע

יְנֻגָּעוּ[l] Pual fut. 3 pers. pl. m. [for יְנֻגְּעוּ § 8. r. 15] ע

יִנָּגֵף[m] } Niph. fut. 3 pers. sing. masc. (§ 9. } ף
וַ יִּנָּגֶף } rem. 3); וַ· conv. . . . }

וַ יִּנָּגְפוּ[n] } id. fut. 3 pers. pl. masc. (comp. § 8. } ף
וַ יִּנָּגְפוּ } rem. 15); וַ· id. . . . }

---

[a] Eze. 48. 14. [b] Ps. 15. 4. [c] Is. 24. 9. [d] Ne. 9. 26. [e] Jos. 1. 18. [f] Ps. 106. 43. [g] Ps. 78. 40.
[h] Ps. 139. 20. [i] Is. 38. 21. [k] Le. 13. 40, 41. [l] Job 16. 3. [m] Ge. 49. 23. [n] Ex. 1. 14. [o] Ex. 10. 21.
[p] Ge. 27. 22. [q] Je. 31. 36. [r] Job 21. 33. [s] Pr. 22. 7. [t] Le. 16. 32. [u] Am. 6. 6. [x] 1 Sa. 15. 17.
[y] Nu. 7. 1. [z] Ju. 20. 37. [a] Is. 13. 22. [b] De. 15. 6. [c] Ps. 106. 41. [d] Ge. 27. 12. [e] De. 28. 29.
[f] Ge. 31. 34. [g] De. 33. 6. [h] Ju. 6. 30. 1 Ki. 21. 10. [i] Ge. 5. 5, 8. [k] Nu. 16. 29. [l] Is. 40. 22. [m] Je. 52. 27.
[n] Nu. 35. 19. [o] Pr. 9. 17. [p] Ex. 15. 25. [q] 1 Sa. 17. 51. [r] Je. 23. 31. [s] Le. 20. 10, 10.
[t] Je. 5. 7. [u] Je. 29. 23. [x] Ec. 12. 5. [y] Ps. 74. 10. [z] De. 32. 19. [a] Pr. 15. 15.
[b] La. 2. 6. [c] Je. 33. 24. [d] Nu. 14. 11. [e] Job 24. 12. [f] Je. 26. 20. [g] Je. 28. 8.
[h] De. 32. 15. [i] De. 33. 17. [k] Jos. 8. 15. [l] Ps. 73. 5. [m] 2 Ch. 6. 24. [n] 2 Ch. 20. 22.

יְנַדְּהוּ[a] Hiph. fut. 3 p. pl. m. [יְנִדּוּ], suff. 3 p. s. m. — נדד
יָנֻדוּ[b] וַ Kal fut. 3 pers. pl. masc.; וַ־ conv. — נוד
יְנַדְּעוּן[c] Chald. Peal fut. 3 pers. pl. masc. [for יִדְּעוּן § 52. rem. 2] — ידע

[יָנָה] fut. יוֹנֶה (§ 25. No. 2e) *to oppress, vex.* Hiph. id.; with מִן *to dispossess, drive out.*

יְנַהֵג[d] וַ'[e] Piel fut. 3 pers. sing. masc. (§ 14. r. 1); וַ conv. — נהג
יִנְהַג[f] / וַיִּ' יִנְהָג[g] Kal fut. 3 pers. sing. masc. (§ 8. rem. 15); וַ־ id. — נהג
יְנַהֲגֵהוּ[h] וַ Piel fut. 3 pers. sing. masc. (§ 14. rem. 1) with suff. 3 pers. sing. masc.; וַ id. — נהג
יִנְהֲגוּ[i] / וַיִּ'[k] וְ'[l] יִנְהָגוּ Kal fut. 3 pers. pl. masc. (§ 8. rem. 15); וַ־ id. — נהג
יְנַהֶגְךָ[m] Piel fut. 3 pers. sing. masc. (§ 14. rem. 1), suff. 2 pers. sing. masc. — נהג
יְנַהֲגֵם[n] וַ'[o] id., suff. 3 pers. pl. masc.; וַ conv. — נהג
יְנַהֲגֵנוּ[p] id., suff. 1 pers. pl. — נהג
יִנָּהוּ[q] וַ Niph. fut. 3 pers. pl. masc.; וַ־ conv. — נהה
יְנַהֵל[r] Piel fut. 3 pers. sing. masc. (§ 14. rem. 1) — נהל
יְנַהֲלוּם[s] וַ id. fut. 3 pers. pl. masc., suff. 3 pers. pl. masc.; וַ conv. — נהל
יְנַהֲלֵם[t] וַ' id. fut. 3 pers. s. m., suff. 3 p. pl. m.; וַ id. — נהל
יְנַהֲלֵנִי[u] id. id., suff. 1 pers. sing. — נהל
יִנְהֹם וְ Kal fut. 3 pers. sing. masc. — נהם
יִנְהָקוּ[x] Kal fut. 3 pers. pl. m. [for יִנְהֲקוּ § 8. r. 15] — נהק
יִנְהֲרוּ[y] Kal fut. 3 pers. pl. masc. — נהר
יָנוּב Kal fut. 3 pers. sing. masc. — נוב
יְנוֹבֵב[z] Pilel fut. 3 pers. sing. masc. — נוב
יְנוּבוּן[a] Kal fut. 3 pers. pl. masc. with paragogic ן — נוב
יָנוּד Kal fut. 3 pers. sing. masc. — נוד
יִנְוֶה[b] Kal fut. 3 pers. sing. masc. — נוה
יָנוּחַ pr. name of a place — נוח
יָנוּחַ Kal fut. 3 pers. sing. masc. — נוח
יָנוֹחָה pr. name (יָנוֹחַ) with paragogic ה — נוח
יָנוּחוּ וַ'[c] Kal fut. 3 pers. pl. masc.; וַ־ conv. — נוח
יָנוּם Kal fut. 3 pers. sing. masc. — נום
יָנוּס Kal fut. 3 pers. sing. masc. — נוס
יָנוּסוּ וַ'[d] וְ' id. fut. 3 pers. pl. masc.; וַ־ conv. — נוס
יְנוּסוּן[e] id. id. with paragogic ן — נוס
יִנּוֹעַ[f] Niph. fut. 3 pers. sing. masc. — נוע
יָנוּעוּ[g] וְ'[h] Kal fut. 3 pers. pl. masc. — נוע
יִנּוֹעוּ[i] Niph. fut. 3 pers. pl. masc. — נוע
יְנוּעוּן[k] Kh. יְנוּעוּן Kal, K. יְנִיעוּן Hiph. fut. 3 pers. masc.; ן paragogic — נוע

יִנָּזֵר[l] וְ Niph. fut. 3 pers. sing. masc. — נזר
יִנָּזְרוּ וַ'[m] וְ'[n] id. fut. 3 pers. pl. masc.; וַ־ conv. — נזר
יָנַח וְ Kal or Hiph. fut. 3 pers. sing. masc. ap. from יָנִיחַ, יָנוּחַ (§ 21. rem. 9 & 19) — נוח
יַנַּח וַ Hiph. fut. 3 p. s. m. with 3rd rad. gutt. [for יַנִּחַ] ap. from יַנִּיחַ, Chald. form (§ 21. r. 24) — נוח
יַנִּחֵהוּ[o] וַ id. id., suff. 3 pers. sing. masc.; וַ־ conv. — נוח
יַנִּחֻהוּ[p] וַ id. fut. 3 pers. pl. m., suff. 3 pers. s. m.; וַ־ id. — נוח
יַנִּחוּם[q] וַ id. id., suff. 3 pers. pl. masc. (ם for ן fem. § 2. rem. 5); וַ־ id. — נוח
יַנְחוּנִי[r] Hiph. fut. 3 pers. pl. masc., suff. 1 pers. sing. — נחה
יַנְחִיל Hiph. fut. 3 pers. sing. masc. — נחל
יַנְחִילְךָ[s] id., suff. 2 pers. sing. masc. — נחל
יַנְחִל[t] defect. for יַנְחִיל (q. v.) — נחל
יִנְחַל Kal fut. 3 pers. sing. masc. — נחל
יִנְחֲלוּ / וַיִּ' יִנְחָלוּ Kal fut. 3 pers. pl. masc. (§ 8. rem. 15); וַ־ conv. — נחל
יִנְחָלוּהָ[u] id., suff. 3 pers. sing. fem. (§ 16. rem. 12) — נחל
יִנְחָלוּם[x] id., suff. 3 pers. pl. masc. — נחל
יַנְחִלֵם[y] Hiph. fut. 3 pers. s. m., suff. 3 pers. pl. m. — נחל
יַנְחִלֶנָּה[z] id., suff. 3 pers. sing. fem. — נחל
יַנְחֵם[a] וַיַּ' Hiph. fut. 3 pers. sing. masc. [יַנְחֶה], suff. 3 pers. pl. masc. (§ 24. rem. 21); וַ־ conv. — נחה
יִנָּחֵם / יִנָּחֶם וְ'[b] וַיִּ'[c] וְ Niph. fut. 3 pers. sing. masc. (§ 9. rem. 3); וַ־ id. — נחם
יְנַחֵם[d] וִ' Piel fut. 3 pers. s. m. (§ 14. rem. 1); וַ id. — נחם
יִנָּחֲמוּ וְ Niph. fut. 3 p. pl. masc.; וַ־ id. — נחם
יְנַחֲמוּ[e] וְ Piel fut. 3 pers. pl. masc. (§ 14. rem. 1); וַ id. — נחם
יְנַחֲמוּן[f] id. fut. 3 pers. pl. masc.; ן paragogic [for יְנַחֲמוּן comp. § 8. rem. 17] — נחם
יְנַחֲמֵנוּ[g] id. fut. 3 pers. sing. masc., suff. 1 pers. pl. — נחם
יְנַחֲמֻנִי[h] id. fut. 3 pers. pl. masc., suff. 1 pers. sing. — נחם
יַנְחֵנוּ[i] Hiph. fut. 3 pers. sing. masc. [יַנְחֶה], suff. 3 pers. sing. m. (§ 24. r. 21, & § 2. r. 3) — נחה
יַנְחֵנִי id. with suff. 1 pers. sing. — נחה
יְנַחֵשׁ[i] Piel fut. 3 pers. sing. masc. (§ 14. rem. 1) — נחש
יְנַחֲשׁוּ[k] / יְנַחֵשׁוּ[l] וְ Piel fut. 3 pers. pl. masc. (§ 14. r. 1. comp. § 8. rem. 15); וַ conv. — נחש
יִנָּטֶה[m] Niph. fut. 3 pers. sing. masc. — נטה
יִנָּטוּ[n] id. fut. 3 pers. pl. masc. — נטה
יְנַטְּלֵם[o] וַ Piel fut. 3 pers. sing. masc. [יְנַטֵּל], suff. 3 pers. pl. masc.; וַ conv. — נטל
יִנָּטְשׁוּ וַ Niph. fut. 3 pers. pl. masc.; וַ־ id. — נטש
יָנִי[p] / יָנִיא[q] Hiph. fut. 3 pers. sing. masc. (§ 25, 2 f) — נוא

[a] Job 18. 18. [b] Job 42. 11. [c] Da. 4. 14. [d] De. 4. 27. [e] Ps. 78. 26. [f] 2 Ki. 9. 20. [g] Is. 20. 4. [h] Ex. 14. 25. [i] Job 24. 3. [k] 1 Sa. 30. 22. [l] 1 Sa. 30. 2. [m] De. 28. 37. [n] Is. 49. 10. [o] Ps. 78. 52. [p] Ps. 48. 15. [q] 1 Sa. 7. 2. [r] Is. 40. 11. [s] 2 Ch. 28. 15. [t] Is. 49. 10. [u] Ps. 23. 2. [x] Job 30. 7. [y] Je. 51. 44. [z] Zec. 9. 17. [a] Ps. 92. 15. [b] Hab. 2. 5. [c] 1 Sa. 25. 9. [d] Ps. 68. 2. [e] Ps. 104. 7.
[f] Am. 9. 9. [g] Ps. 109. 10. [h] Ps. 107. 27. [i] Na. 3. 12. [k] Ps. 59. 16. [l] Eze. 14. 7. [m] Le. 22. 2. [n] Ho. 9. 10. [o] 1 Ki. 13. 29. [p] Ge. 19. 16. [q] Jos. 4. 8. [r] Ps. 43. 3. [s] De. 19. 3. [t] Eze. 46. 18. [u] Ps. 69. 37. [x] Zep. 2. 9. [y] 1 Sa. 2. 8. [z] De. 1. 38. [a] Ps. 78. 53. [b] Je. 26. 13. [c] Ge. 24. 67; Ps. 106. 45. [d] Job 29. 25. [e] Job 42. 11. [f] Zec. 10. 2. [g] Ge. 5. 29. [h] Ps. 23. 4. [i] Ge. 44. 5, 15. [k] 2 Ki. 17. 17. [l] 1 Ki. 20. 33. [m] Zec. 1. 16. [n] Je. 6. 4. [o] Is. 63. 9. [p] Ps. 141. 5. [q] Nu. 30. 9.

יָנִיאוּ[a] וַ Hiph. fut. 3 pers. pl. masc.; וַ· conv. . נוא
יָנִיד[b] וְ Hiph. fut. 3 pers. sing. masc. . . נוד
יָנִיחַ, יַנִּיחַ } Hiph. fut. 3 pers. sing. masc. (§ 21. rem. 24) . . . . } נוח
יַנִּיחֵהוּ[c] וַ id. id., suff. 3 pers. sing. masc.; וַ· conv. נוח
יַנִּיחֻהוּ וְ[d], וַיַּ[e]' id. fut. 3 pers. pl. masc., suff. 3 pers. sing. masc.; וַ· id. . . . . נוח
יַנִּיחוּ[f] וְ[g]', וַיַּ' id. fut. 3 pers. pl. masc.; וַ· id. . נוח
יַנִּיחוּם[h] וַ id. id., suff. 3 pers. pl. masc.; וַ· id. . נוח
יְנִיחֶךָּ[i] וְ id. fut. 3 pers. sing. masc. (יָנִיחַ), suff. 2 pers. sing. masc. in pause, and with conj. וְ [for וְיַנִּיחֲךָ ,וְיַ' § 2. rem. 2] . נוח
יַנִּיחֵם וַ id. fut. 3 pers. sing. masc. (יַנִּיחַ q. v.), suff. 3 pers. pl. masc.; וַ· conv. . . . נוח
יְנִיחֵנִי וַ id. fut. 3 pers. sing. masc. (יָנִיחַ), suff. 1 pers. sing.; וַ id. . . . . . נוח
יָנִים וְ Kh. יָנִים, K. יָנוּם pr. name masc. . נום
יִנּוֹן[k] Kh. יָנִין Hiph., K. יִנּוֹן Niph. fut. 3 pers. s. m. נין
יָנִיסוּ[l] Hiph. fut. 3 pers. pl. masc. . . נוס
יָנִיסוּ[m] וַ Kh. יָנִיסוּ q. v., K. יָנוּסוּ (q. v.) . נוס
יָנִיעַ[n] Hiph. fut. 3 pers. sing. masc. . . נוע
יָנִיעוּ[o] id. fut. 3 pers. pl. masc. . . . נוע
יְנִיעוּן[p] id. id. with parag. ן . . . . נוע
יְנִיפֵהוּ[q] וַ Hiph. fut. 3 pers. sing. masc. [יָנִיף], suff. 3 pers. sing. masc.; וַ conv. . . . נוף
יְנִיפֶנּוּ[r] id. with suff. 3 pers. sing. masc. (§ 2. r. 3) נוף
יְנִיקוֹתָיו[s] noun fem. pl., suff. 3 pers. sing. masc. fr. [יְנִיקָה] dec. 10 . . . . . ינק
יִנָּכֵר[t] Niph. fut. 3 pers. sing. masc. . . נכר
יְנַכְּרוּ[u] וְ[x]' Piel fut. 3 pers. pl. masc.; וַ conv. . נכר
יָנֹם, יָנֹם } Kal fut. 3 pers. sing. masc., ap. & conv. from יָנוּם (§ 21. rem. 8) . } נום
יָנֻסוּ[y] וְ', וַיָּ' id. fut. 3 pers. pl. m. defect. for יָנוּסוּ נוס
יְנַסּוּ וַ Piel fut. 3 pers. pl. masc.; וַ conv. נסה
יְנַסֵּךְ[z] וַ Piel fut. 3 pers. sing. masc.; וַ id. נסך
יְנַסֵּם[a] וַ Piel fut. 3 pers. sing. masc. [יְנַסֶּה], suff. 3 pers. pl. masc. (§ 24. rem. 21); וַ id. נסה
יָנַע[b] וַיָּ[c]' Kal or Hiph. fut. 3 pers. sing. masc. ap. and conv. (§ 21. rem. 9 & 19) . נוע
יְנִעוּ[d] וַ Hiph. fut. 3 p. pl. m. (for יְנִיעוּ); וַ· conv. נוע
יָנֻעוּ וַ Kal fut. 3 pers. pl. masc.; וַ· id. . נוע
יַנְעִלוּם[e] וַ Hiph. fut. 3 pers. pl. masc. [יַנְעִילוּ], suff. 3 pers. pl. masc.; וַ· id. . . . נעל
יִנְעַם Kal fut. 3 pers. s. m. [for יִנְעַם § 8. r. 15] נעם
יְנִעֵם[f] וַ Hiph. fut. 3 pers. sing. masc. [יָנִיעַ], suff. 3 pers. pl. masc.; וַ conv. . . נעם

יְנַעֵר[g] וַ[h]' Piel fut. 3 pers. s. m. (§ 14. r. 1); וַ id. ר
יִנָּעֲרוּ[i] וְ Niph. fut. 3 pers. pl. masc. . . ר
יָנֶף וַ Hiph. fut. 3 pers. sing. masc. ap. and conv. [from יָנִיף] . . . ף
יְנֹפֵף[k] Pilel fut. 3 pers. sing. masc. . . ף
יְנַפֵּצוּ[ss] Piel fut. 3 pers. pl. masc. [for יְנַפְּצוּ comp. § 8. rem. 15] . . . . ץ
יִנָּפֵשׁ[l], יִנָּפֵשׁ } וַ, וַיִּ', וְ' Niph. fut. 3 pers. s. masc. (§ 9. rem. 4); וַ· conv. . } ש
יִנָּצוּ וַיִּ' Niph. fut. 3 pers. pl. masc.; וַ· id. . ה
יִנָּצֵל Niph. fut. 3 pers. s. masc. . . ל
יִנָּצְלוּ, יִנָּצֵלוּ[o] } id. fut. 3 pers. pl. masc. (comp. § 8. rem. 15) . . . } ל
יְנַצְּלוּ[p] וַ' Piel fut. 3 pers. pl.; וַ· conv. . . ל
יִנְצְרֻהוּ[q] Kal fut. 3 pers. pl. masc., suff. 3 pers. sing. masc. (§ 17. rem. 3) . . . ר
יִנְצֹרוּ id. fut. 3 pers. pl. masc. [for יִנְצְרוּ § 8. rem. 15, see § 17. rem. 3] . ר

[יָנַק] fut. יִינַק, *to suck;* יוֹנֵק *a sucking child.* Hiph. הֵינִיק *to give suck, to suckle;* part. מֵינֶקֶת (§ 3 No. 4 d, with suff. מֵינִקְתּוֹ dec. 13 a) *a nurse;* pl. מֵינִיקוֹת.
יוֹנֵק masc. dec. 7 b, *a sucker, sprout, shoot.*
יוֹנֶקֶת fem. dec. 13 a (with suff. יוֹנַקְתּוֹ), id.
יְנִיקָה fem. dec. 10, id.

יִנְקֹב[r]־ Kal fut. 3 pers. sing. masc. [for יִנְקֹב § 8. rem. 18, see § 17. rem. 3] . . ב
יִנָּקֶה Niph. fut. 3 pers. sing. masc. . . ה
יְנַקֶּה Piel fut. 3 pers. sing. masc. . . ה
יְנִקֵהוּ[s] וַ Hiph. fut. 3 pers. sing. masc. [יֵינִיק], suff. 3 pers. sing. masc.; וַ· conv. . . ק
יֹנְקוֹתָיו[t] noun fem. pl. with suff. 3 pers. sing. masc. fr. יוֹנֶקֶת dec. 13 a, see יוֹנֵק masc. . ק
יֹנְקִים[u] וְ Kal part. act. or subst. masc., pl. of יוֹנֵק dec. 7 b . . . . . ק
יִנָּקֵם[x] Niph. fut. 3 pers. sing. masc. . . ם
יִנָּקְמוּ[y] וַ id. fut. 3 pers. pl. masc.; וַ· conv. . ם
יִנְקֹפוּ[z] Kal fut. 3 pers. pl. masc. [for יִנְקְפוּ § 8. rem. 15, see § 17. rem. 3] . . ף
יְנַקְּרוּ[a] וַ Piel fut. 3 pers. pl. masc.; וַ conv. ר
יְנַקֵּשׁ[b] Piel fut. 3 pers. sing. masc. . . ש
יְנַקְּשׁוּ[c] וַ id. fut. 3 pers. pl. masc.; וַ conv. ש
יָנַקְתְּ[d] וְ Kal pret. 2 pers. sing. fem.; וְ id. . ק
יְנַקְתֶּם[e] וְ id. pret. 2 pers. pl. masc. with conj. וְ [for וִינַקְתֶּם ,וְיִ'] . . . . ק

[a] Nu. 32. 9. [b] Je. 18. 16. [c] Ex. 16. 34. [d] Is. 46. 7. [e] Le. 24. 12. [f] Eze. 42. 13, 14. [g] Eze. 40. 42. [h] Jos. 6. 23. [i] Pr. 29. 17. [k] Ps. 72. 17. [l] De. 32. 30. [m] Ju. 7. 21. [n] Zep. 2. 15. [o] Ps. 22. 8. [p] Ps. 109. 25. [q] Le. 8. 29. [r] Le. 23. 11. [s] Eze. 17. 4 [t] Pr. 26. 24. [u] De. 32. 27. [x] Je. 19. 4. [y] Nu. 10. 35. [z] 1 Ch. 11. 18. [a] Da. 1. 14. [b] 2 Ki. 23. 18. [c] Is. 7. 2. [d] La. 2. 15. [e] 2 Ch. 28. 15. [f] Nu. 32. 13. [g] Ne. 5. 13. [h] Ex. 14. 27. [i] Job 38. 13. [k] Is. 10. 32. [l] Ex. 31. 17. [m] Ex. 23. 12. [n] 2 Sa. 16. 14. [o] Am. 3. 12. [p] Eze. 14. 14. [q] Ps. 61. 8. [r] Job 40. 24. [s] De. 32. 13. [ss] Je. 48. 12. [t] Eze. 17. 22. [u] Ps. 8. 3. [x] Ex. 21. 20. [y] Eze. 25. 15. [z] Is. 29. 1. [a] Ju. 16. 21. [b] Ps. 109. 11. [c] Ps. 38. 13. [d] Is. 60. 16. [e] Is. 66. 12.

[a]יִנָּשֵׂא [b]וַיִּ׳ Niph. fut. 3 pers. sing. masc.; וַ conv. . . . נשא

[c]יְנַשְּׂאֵהוּ וַ Piel fut. 3 pers. sing. masc. [יְנַשֵּׂא], suff. 3 pers. sing. masc.; וַ id. . . . נשא

[d]יִנָּשְׂאוּ, יִנָּשֵׂאוּ Niph. fut. 3 pers. pl. m. (comp. § 8. rem. 15) נשא

[e]יִנַּשְּׂאוּ Hithp. fut. 3 p. pl. m. [for יִתְנַשְּׂאוּ § 12. r. 3] נשא

יְנַשְּׂאוּהוּ Piel fut. 3 pers. pl. masc., suff. 3 pers. sing. m. נשא

[g]יְנַשְּׂאֵם וַ id. fut. 3 pers. sing. masc. [יְנַשֵּׂא], suff. 3 pers. pl. masc.; וַ conv. . . . נשא

[h]יִנָּשׂוּא Niph. fut. 3 pers. pl. m. [for יִנָּשְׂאוּ § 23. r. 11] נשא

[i]יַנְשׁוּף וְ noun masc. sing. . . . . . נשף

[k]יַנְשְׁכוּ וַ Piel fut. 3 pers. pl. masc.; וַ conv. . . נשך

[l]יְנַשֵּׁל וַ Piel fut. 3 pers. sing. masc.; וַ id. . . נשל

יְנַשֵּׁק, [m]יְנַשֶּׁק־ וַ Piel fut. 3 pers. sing. masc. (§ 10. rem. 4); וַ id. . . . . נשק

[n]יְנַתַּח וַ Piel fut. 3 pers. sing. masc.; וַ id. . . נתח

[o]יְנַתְּחֶהָ וַ id. id., suff. 3 pers. sing. fem.; וַ id. . . נתח

[p]יְנַתְּחֵהוּ וַ id. id., suff. 3 pers. sing. masc.; וַ id. . . נתח

[q]יְנַתְּחֻהוּ וְ id. fut. 3 pers. pl. masc., suff. 3 pers. sing. masc. and conj. וְ [for וַיְ׳, וַיְנַתְּחֻהוּ] . . נתח

יִנָּתֵן, וַיִּ׳ יִנָּתֶן Niph. fut. 3 pers. sing. masc. (§ 9. rem. 3) נתן

[r]יִנְתֶּן־ Chald. Peal fut. 3 pers. sing. m. (§ 51. rem. 2) נתן

[s]יֻנְתַּן־ Kh. יֻנְתַּן q.v., K. יֻתַּן־ Hoph. fut. 3 pers. s. m. נתן

[t]יִנָּתְנוּ וַיִּ״, וְיִ״ Niph. fut. 3 pers. pl. masc.; וַ conv. נתן

[x]יִנְתְּנוּן Chald. Peal fut. 3 pers. pl. m. (§ 51. rem. 2) נתן

[y]יְנַתֵּץ וַ Piel fut. 3 pers. sing. masc.; וַ conv. . . נתץ

יְנַתְּצוּ וַ id. fut. 3 pers. pl. masc.; וַ id. . . . נתץ

יִנָּתֵק Niph. fut. 3 pers. sing. masc. . . . . נתק

יְנַתֵּק [z]וַיְ׳ Piel fut. 3 pers. sing. masc.; וַ conv. . . נתק

[a]יִנָּתְקוּ, [b]וַ יִנָּתֵקוּ Niph. fut. 3 pers. pl. masc. (comp. § 8. rem. 15); וַ id. . . . . נתק

[c]יְנַתְּקֵם וַ Piel fut. 3 pers. sing. masc., suff. 3 pers. pl. masc.; וַ id. . . . . . נתק

[d]יִנָּתֵשׁ Niph. fut. 3 pers. sing. masc. . . . נתש

יִנָּתְשׁוּ id. fut. 3 pers. pl. masc. . . . . נתש

יִסֹּב, [e]וַ יִסֹּב Kal fut. 3 pers. sing. masc. (§ 21. rem. 8) סבב

יַסֵּב וַ Hiph. fut. 3 pers. sing. masc. Chald. form (§ 18. rem. 14); וַ conv. . . . סבב

יָסֹב וַיָּ׳ Kal fut. 3 pers. s. m. (§ 18. rem. 14); וַ id. סבב

[f]יְסֹבְבֶנְהוּ Poel fut. 3 pers. sing. masc. with epenth. נ (§ 16. rem. 13) & suff. 3 pers. sing. masc. סבב

[g]יְסֹבְבֵנִי id. fut. 3 pers. sing. m. with suff. 1 pers. sing. סבב

[h]יְסֻבֻּהוּ Kal fut. 3 pers. pl. masc. (יָסֹבּוּ), suff. 3 pers. sing. masc. (§ 18. rem. 5) . . . סבב

יַסֵּבּוּ וַ Hiph. fut. 3 pers. pl. masc. (§ 18. rem. 14); וַ conv. . . . . . סבב

[i]יָסֹבּוּ וַיָּ׳ Kal fut. 3 pers. pl. masc.; וַ id. . סבב

יִסַּבּוּ Niph. fut. 3 pers. pl. masc. . . . סבב

[k]יְסֻבְּכוּ Pual fut. 3 p. pl. m. [for יְסֻבְּכוּ comp. § 8. r. 15] סבך

[l]יִסְבֹּל Kal fut. 3 pers. sing. masc. . . . סבל

[m]יִסְבְּלֵהוּ id. fut. 3 pers. pl. masc., suff. 3 pers. sing. m. סבל

[n]יְסֻבֶּנּוּ Kal fut. 3 pers. sing. masc. (יָסֹב), suff. 3 pers. sing. masc. (§ 18. rem. 5) . . . סבב

[o]יְסֻבֵּנִי id. id., suff. 1 pers. sing. . . . . סבב

[p]יְסִבֵּנִי וַ Hiph. fut. 3 pers. sing. masc. [יָסֵב], suff. 1 pers. sing. (§ 18. rem. 11); וַ conv. . סבב

[q]יִסְבַּר וְ Chald. Peal fut. 3 pers. sing. masc. . . סבר

[r]יִסַּג Kal fut. 3 pers. sing. masc. . . . . נסג

[s]יִסְגָּד־ וַ id. fut. 3 pers. sing. masc. [for יִסְגֹּד § 8. rem. 18]; וַ conv. . . . . סגד

[t]יִסְגֻּד וְ Chald. Peal fut. 3 pers. sing. masc. . סגד

[u]יִסְגְּדוּ Kal fut. 3 pers. pl. masc. . . . . סגד

[x]יִסְגְּדוּן Chald. Peal fut. 3 pers. pl. masc. . . סגד

יִסֹּגוּ [y]וַיִּ׳, [z]וְיִ׳ Niph. fut. 3 pers. pl. masc.; וַ conv. סוג

[a]יִסְגּוֹד־ Kh. יִסְגּוֹד, K. יִסְגָּד־ Kal fut. 3 p. s. m. (§ 8. r. 18) סגד

[b]יַסְגִּיר וְ Hiph. fut. 3 pers. sing. masc. . . . סגר

[c]יַסְגִּירוּ id. fut. 3 pers. pl. masc. . . . . סגר

[d]יַסְגִּירֵנִי id. fut. 3 pers. sing. masc., suff. 1 pers. sing. סגר

[e]יִסָּגֵר Niph. fut. 3 pers. sing. masc. . . . סגר

[f]יַסְגֵּר וַ Hiph. fut. 3 p. s. m., ap. from יַסְגִּיר; וַ conv. סגר

[g]יִסְגֹּר [h]וַיִּ׳, וְיִ׳ Kal fut. 3 pers. sing. masc.; וַ id. . סגר

[i]יַסְגִּרוּ defect. for יַסְגִּירוּ (q. v.) . . . . סגר

יִסָּגְרוּ, [k]וַ יִסָּגֵרוּ Niph. fut. 3 pers. pl. masc. (comp. § 8. rem. 15); וַ conv. . . . סגר

[l]יִסְגְּרוּ וַ Kal fut. 3 pers. pl. masc.; וַ id. . . סגר

[m]יְסַגֶּרְךָ Piel fut. 3 pers. sing. masc. [יְסַגֵּר], suff. 2 pers. sing. masc. (§ 16. rem. 15) . . . סגר

[n]יַסְגִּרֶנּוּ Hiph. fut. 3 pers. sing. masc. (יַסְגִּיר), suff. 3 pers. sing. masc. (§ 2. rem. 3) . . סגר

יָסַד I. *to found, lay the foundation of* a building,—II. *to throw up*, as a heap, 2 Ch. 31. 7.—III. *to settle, establish.*—IV. *to ordain, decree.* Niph. נוֹסַד—I. *to be founded, established.*—II. *to sit together for consultation, to consult together, to plot.* Pi.—I. *to found.*—II. *to ordain, decree.* Pu. *to be founded.* Hoph. *to be founded*; part. מוּסָד *founded, secure.*
יְסוֹד masc. dec. 1 a, pl. ־ִם, ־וֹת *foundation, basis.*
סוֹד masc. dec. 1 a.—I. *assembly sitting together,* especially *for consultation.*—II. *consultation, de-*

[a] Is. 40. 4. [b] 2 Ch. 32. 23. [c] Est. 3. 1. [d] Pr. 30. 13. [e] Da. 11. 14. [f] Ezr. 1. 4. [g] Is. 63. 9. [h] Je. 10. 5. [i] Is. 34. 11. [k] Nu. 21. 6. [l] 2 Ki. 16. 6. [m] Ge. 29. 13. [n] 1 Ki. 18. 33. [o] Ju. 19. 29. [p] 1 Sa. 11. 7. [q] 1 Ki. 18. 23. [r] Da. 2. 16. [s] 2 Sa. 21. 6. [t] 2 Ch. 18. 14. [u] 1 Ch. 5. 20. [x] Ezr. 4. 13. [y] 2 Ch. 34. 7. [z] Ju. 16. 9. [a] Is. 33. 20. [b] Jos. 8. 16. [c] Ju. 16. 12. [d] Je. 31. 40. [e] Ju. 11. 18. [f] De. 32. 10. [g] Jon. 2. 4, 6. [h] Job 40. 22. [i] Job 16. 13. [k] Job 8. 17. [l] Is. 53. 11. [m] Is. 46. 7. [n] Je. 52. 21. [o] Ps. 49. 6. [p] Eze. 47. 2 [q] Da. 7. 25. [r] Mi. 2. 6. [s] Is. 11. 15. [t] Da. 3. 6, 10, 11. [u] Is. 46. 6. [x] Da. 3. 28. [y] Ps. 129. 5. [z] Ps. 78. 57. [a] Is. 44. 17. [b] Job 11. 10. [c] 1 Sa. 23. 12. [d] Job 16. 11. [e] Eze. 46. 2. [f] Ps. 78. 48, 62. [g] Job 12. 14. [h] Mal. 1. 10. [i] Jos. 20. 5. [k] Ne. 13. 19. [l] Ju. 9. 51. [m] 1 Sa. 17. 46. [n] Le. 13. 11.

liberation.—III. *familiar intercourse, intimacy.*—IV. *secret.*

סוֹדִי (*confidant, familiar*) pr. name m. Nu. 13. 10.

בְּסוֹדְיָה (*in the secret of the Lord*) pr. name masc. Ne. 3. 6.

יְסֻד masc. *beginning*, Ezr. 7. 9.

מוּסָד masc. dec. 2b, pl. ־ִם, וֹת *foundation, support, prop.*

יְסוּדָה fem. dec. 10, *foundation*, Ps. 87. 1.

מוּסָד masc. dec. 2b, *foundation*.

מוּסָדָה fem. dec. 11a.—I. *foundation*, Eze. 41. 8. —II. *appointment, decree*, Is. 30. 32.

מַסָּד masc. *foundation*, 1 Ki. 7. 9.

יִסַּד Piel pret. 3 pers. sing. masc. (§ 10. rem. 1). In Is. 28. 16, it is either Pi. pret. with אֲשֶׁר implied; or it is Kal fut. according to § 20. rem. 16 . . . . . יסד

יֹסֵד וְ Kal part. act. sing. masc. . . . . יסד

יְסֻד[a] noun masc. sing. . . . . . . יסד

יֻסַּד[b], יֻסָּד Pual pret. 3 pers. sing. masc. (comp. § 8. rem. 15) . . . . . יסד

יָסְדָה[c] Kal pret. 3 pers. sing. fem. . . . יסד

יְסָדָהּ id. pret. 3 pers. sing. m., suff. 3 pers. s. fem. יסד

יִסְּדָהּ[d] Piel pret. 3 pers. sing. masc. (יִסַּד q. v.), suff. 3 pers. sing. fem. . . . . יסד

יְסֹדוֹ[e] noun m. s., suff. 3 pers. s. m. from יְסוֹד dec. 1a יסד

יִסְּדוּ[f] [g]וְ׳ Piel pret. 3 pers. pl. masc. . . יסד

יְסֹדוֹתֶיהָ[h] noun masc. with pl. fem. term. & suff. 3 pers. sing. fem. from יְסוֹד dec. 1a . . יסד

יְסֹדֶיהָ[i] וְ id. with pl. masc. term. & suff. 3 pers. sing. fem. with cop. וְ [for וִיסֹדֶיהָ, וְי׳] . . יסד

יָסַדְתָּ Kal pret. 2 pers. sing. masc. . . יסד

יִסַּדְתָּ[k] Piel pret. 2 pers. sing. masc. . . . יסד

יְסַדְתּוֹ[l] Kal pret. 2 pers. sing. m., suff. 3 pers. sing. m. יסד

יְסֹדֹתֶיהָ[m] noun masc. with pl. fem. term. & suff. 3 pers. sing. fem. from יְסוֹד dec. 1a . . יסד

יְסַדְתִּיךְ[n] וִ Kal fut. 1 pers sing., suff. 2 pers. sing. fem. with conv. וְ [for וִיסַד׳, וְי׳] . . . יסד

יְסַדְתָּם id. pret. 2 pers. sing. m., suff. 3 pers. pl. m. יסד

יִסֹּב[o] Kal fut. 3 pers. s. m. Chald. form (§ 18 rem. 14) סבב

יְסוֹבְבֶהָ[p] Poel fut. 3 pers. pl. masc. [יְסוֹבְבוּ], suff. 3 pers. sing. fem. . . . . סבב

יְסוֹבְבוּ[q] וִ id. fut. 3 p. pl. m. with conv. וְ [for וַיְסוֹ׳, וְי׳] סבב

יְסוֹבְבֶנּוּ[r] id. fut. 3 p. s. m., suff. 3 p. s. m. (§ 2. rem. 3) סבב

יְסוֹד, וִיסוֹד[s] noun masc. sing. dec. 1a; with cop. וְ [for וִיסוֹד, וְי׳] . . . יסד

יְסוֹדָם id. with suff. 3 pers. pl. masc. . . יסד

יְסוּדָתוֹ[t] n. f. s., suff. 3 p. s. m. from [יְסוּדָה] dec. 10 יסד

יָסוּף[u] Kal fut. 3 pers. sing. masc. . . סוף

יָסוּר [x]וְ׳ Kal fut. 3 pers. sing. masc. . . סור

יִסּוֹר[y] noun masc. sing. (after the form גִּבּוֹר) . יסר

יָסוּרוּ [z]וַיָּ׳ Kal fut. 3 pers. pl. masc.; ־ַ conv. . סור

יְסוּרַי[a] Kh. noun masc. pl., suff. 1 pers. sing. from יְסוּר (comp. יָרִיב from רִיב); K. וְסוּרַי Kal part. pass. pl. & suff. 1 pers. sing. סור

יִסְחָבוּם[b] Kal fut. 3 pers. pl. masc. [יִסְחֲבוּ], suff. 3 pers. pl. masc. (§ 16. rem. 12) . . סחב

יִסַּח[c] Kal fut. 3 pers. sing. masc. . . . נסח

יִסְּחוּ[d] id. fut. 3 pers. pl. masc. . . . נסח

יִסָּחֲךָ[e] וְ id. fut. 3 pers. sing. masc., suff. 2 pers. sing. masc. (§ 16. rem. 12) . . . נסח

יִסְחָרוּ[f] וְ Kal fut. 3 pers. pl. masc. . . סחר

יַסִּיכוּ[g] וַ Hiph. fut. 3 pers. pl. masc.; ־ַ conv. נסך

יֹסִיף Hiph. fut. 3 pers. sing. masc. (§ 20. rem. 11) יסף

יֹסִיפוּ[h] וַיּ׳ id. fut. 3 pers. pl. masc.; ־ַ conv. . יסף

יָסִיר Hiph. fut. 3 pers. sing. masc. . . סור

יְסִירֵהוּ[i] וַ id. id., suff. 3 pers. sing. masc.; וַ conv. סור

יָסִירוּ [k]וַ, וְי׳, וַיְ׳ id. fut. 3 pers. pl. masc.; ־ַ id. . סור

יְסִירֶנָּה[l] id. fut. 3 pers. sing. masc. with suff. 3 pers. sing. fem. (§ 2. rem. 3) . . . סור

יָסִית Hiph. fut. 3 p. s. m., Chald. form (§ 21. r. 24) סות

יְסִיתֵהוּ[m] וַ id. id. [יָסִית], suff. 3 pers. sing. masc. . סות

יְסִיתְךָ id. id., suff. 2 pers. sing. masc. . . סות

יְסִיתֵם[n] וַ id. id., suff. 3 pers. pl. masc.; וַ conv. . סות

יָסֶךְ[o] וַיָּ׳ Hiph. fut. 3 p. s. m., with conv. ־ַ [for יָסִיךְ] סכך

יָסֶךְ[p] וַ Hiph. fut. 3 pers. sing. masc. ap. and conv. וַ [from יָסִיךְ] . . . סוך

יַסֵּךְ וַ Hiph. fut. 3 p. s. m. ap. [for יַסִּיךְ]; ־ַ conv. נסך

יֻסַּךְ Hoph. fut. 3 pers. sing. masc. R. נָסַךְ, or as a Chald. form (§ 18. rem. 14) from R. . סכך

יִסְכָּה pr. name of a sister of Lot, Ge. 11. 29.

יְסֻכֵּהוּ[q] the foll. (יָסֹכּוּ), suff. 3 pers. s. m. (§ 18. rem. 5) סכך

יָסֹכּוּ[r] וַ Kal fut. 3 pers. pl. masc.; ־ַ conv. . סכך

יִסְּכוּ[s] Kal fut. 3 pers. pl. masc. . . . נסך

יְסֻכוּם[t] וַ Kal fut. 3 pers. pl. masc. [יָסוּכוּ], suff. 3 pers. pl. masc.; וַ conv. . . . סוך

יִסְכּוֹן[u] Kal fut. 3 pers. sing. masc. (§ 8. rem. 18) . סכן

יְסַכֵּל[x] Piel fut. 3 pers. sing. masc. . . סכל

יִסָּכֶן[y] Niph. fut. 3 pers. sing. masc., before monos. [for יִסָּכֵן § 9. rem. 3] . . . סכן

יִסְכָּן[z], יִסְכָּן Kal fut. 3 pers. sing. masc. (§ 8. rem. 18) סכן

[a] Ezr. 7. 9. [b] Ezr. 3. 6. [c] Is. 48. 13. [d] 1 Ki. 16. 34. [e] Eze. 13. 14. [f] Zec. 4. 9. [g] Ezr. 3. 10. [h] Eze. 30. 4. [i] Mi. 1. 6. [k] Ps. 8. 3. [l] Hab. 1. 12. [m] La. 4. 11. [n] Is. 54. 11. [o] Zec. 14. 10. [p] Ps. 55. 11. [q] Ps. 57. 7, 15. [r] Ps. 32. 10. [s] 2 Ch. 24. 27. [t] Ps. 87. 1. [u] Est. 9. 28. [x] Job 15. 30. [y] Job 40. 2. [z] Ju. 18. 3, 15. [a] Je. 17. 13. [b] Je. 49. 20; 50. 45. [c] Pr. 15. 25. [d] Pr. 2. 22. [e] Ps. 52. 7. [f] Ge. 34. 21. [g] Eze. 20. 28. [h] 2 Sa. 7. 10. [i] 2 Ch. 36. 3. [k] Job 34. 20. [l] Le. 3. 4, 10, 15. [m] 2 Ch. 18. 2. [n] 2 Ch. 18. 31. [o] Ps. 91. 4. [p] 2 Sa. 12. 20. [q] Job 40. 22. [r] 1 Ki. 8. 7. [s] Ho. 9. 4. [t] 2 Ch. 28. 15. [u] Job 15. 3. [x] Is. 44. 25. [y] Ec. 10. 9. [z] Job 22. 2.

יְסַכְסֵךְ[a] Pilp. fut. 3 pers. sing. masc. (§ 6. No. 4) סכך

יִסָּכֵר[b] Niph. fut. 3 pers. sing. masc. . . סכר

יִסָּכְרוּ[qq] וַ id. fut. 3 pers. pl. masc.; ·וַ conv. . סכר

יָסֹלּוּ וְ Kal fut. 3 pers. pl. masc.; ·וְ id. . סלל

יִסְלַח Kal fut. 3 pers. sing. masc. . . . סלח

יְסַלֵּף[c] וִ[d]′ Piel fut. 3 pers. sing. masc.; וַ conv.; סלף

יְסַלֵּף וִ with conj. וְ [for וִיסַלֵּף ,וִי′] . סלף

יִסָּמֵךְ[e] וַיִּ′ Niph. fut. 3 pers. sing. masc.; ·וַ conv. . סמך

יִסְמֹךְ וְ Kal fut. 3 pers. sing. masc.; ·וְ id. . סמך

יִסָּמְכוּ[f] וְ Niph. fut. 3 pers. pl. masc.; ·וְ id. סמך

יִסְמְכוּ[g] וַיִּ′ Kal fut. 3 pers. pl. masc.; ·וַ id. . סמך

יִסְמַכְיָהוּ וְ pr. name masc. . . . . סמך

יִסְמְכֵנִי[h] Kal fut. 3 pers. sing. m. (יִסְמֹךְ), suff. 1 pers. s. סמך

יַסַּע[i] וַיִּ′ Hiph. fut. 3 pers. sing. masc.; ·וַ conv. נסע

יִסַּע[k] וַיִּ′ Kal fut. 3 pers. sing. masc.; ·וַ id. . נסע

יִסְעַד[l] Kal fut. 3 pers. s. m. [for יִסְעַד § 8. rem. 15] סעד

יִסְעָדֶךָ[m] id., suff. 2 pers. sing. masc. (§ 16. rem. 12, & § 2. rem. 3) . . . . . סעד

יִסְעָדֶנּוּ[n] id., suff. 3 pers. sing. masc. (v. id.) . סעד

יִסְעָדֵנִי[o] id., suff. 1 pers. sing. . . . . סעד

יַסִּעוּ[p] וַ Hiph. fut. 3 pers. pl. m. [for יַסִּיעוּ]; ·וַ conv. נסע

יִסְעוּ וַיִּ′, וְ′[q] Kal fut. 3 p. pl. m.; יִסְעוּ for יִסְעוּ on account of Sheva under ס, comp. § 10. rem. 7; ·וַ id. נסע

יִסְעוּ וַיִּ′

יִסָּעֵם[r] וַ id. fut. 3 pers. sing. masc., suff. 3 pers. pl. masc. (§ 16. rem. 12); ·וַ id. . . נסע

יִסָּעֵר[s] וַ Niph. fut. 3 pers. sing. masc.; ·וַ id. . סער

יְסֹעֵר[t] Poel fut. 3 pers. sing. masc. (§ 6. No. 1) סער

יִסְעֲרוּ[u] Kal fut. 3 pers. pl. masc. . . . סער

יָסַף וְ′ Kal and Hiph. (fut. יוֹסִיף ap. יוֹסֵף).—I. *to add*, with לְ, אֶל, עַל.—II. *to increase, enlarge*, with עַל, acc.—III. *to add to do, to do again* any thing, const. with an inf. with or without לְ, when it may generally be rendered by *again* or *more*; לֹא־יוֹסִיף לָקוּם *he shall rise no more*; וַיֹּסֶף שַׁלַּח אֶת־הַיּוֹנָה *and again he sent forth the dove*. Niph. נוֹסַף.—I. *to be added*, Nu. 36. 3, 4, with עַל.—II. *to join oneself*, Ex. 1. 10.—III. *to increase, grow*, Pr. 11. 24. Part. נוֹסָפוֹת, Is. 15. 9, *additions* sc. of calamities.

יְסַף Chald. Hoph. *to be added*, Da. 4. 33.

יוֹסֵף, once יְהוֹסֵף (*He shall add*, sc. the Lord, comp. Ge. 30. 24) pr. name—I. of a son of Jacob; applied also to the two tribes descended from his sons, Ephraim and Manasseh, and stands poetically for the kingdom of Israel or the ten tribes, of which the tribe of Ephraim was chief.—II. 1 Ch. 25. 2, 9. —III. Ne. 12. 14.—IV. Ezr. 10. 42.

יוֹסִפְיָה (whom *the Lord will increase*) pr. name masc. Ezr. 8. 10.

יָסַף[x] Kal pret. 3 pers. sing. m. for יָסַף (§ 8. rem. 7) יסף

יֹסֵף Hiph. fut. 3 pers. s. m. (§ 20. rem. 10) יסף

יֹסֶף וַ ap. and conv. from יוֹסִיף . יסף

יֹסֵף[y] וַ Kal fut. 3 pers. s. m. for וַיֶּאֱסֹף (§ 19. rem. 4) אסף

יִסָּפְדוּ Niph. fut. 3 pers. pl. masc. . . . ספד

יִסְפְּדוּ וַיִּ′ Kal fut. 3 pers. pl. masc.; ·וַ conv. . ספד

יָסְפָה[z] וְ′ Kal pret. 3 pers. sing. fem. . . יסף

יָסְפוּ[a] id. pret. 3 pers. pl. (§ 8. rem. 7) . יסף

יָסְפוּ וְ′

יָסֻפוּ[b] Kal fut. 3 pers. pl. masc. . . . סוף

יֹסִפוּ[c] וַיּ′ Hiph. fut. 3 pers. pl. masc. (for יוֹסִיפוּ § 20. rem. 11); ·וַ conv. . . . יסף

יִסְפּוֹק[d] Kal fut. 3 pers. sing. masc. (§ 8. rem. 18) ספק

יִסְפּוֹר[e] Kal fut. 3 pers. sing. masc. (§ 8. rem. 18) ספר

יְסֻפָּחוּ[f] Pual fut. 3 pers. pl. masc. [for יְסֻפְּחוּ comp. § 8. rem. 15] . . . ספח

יֹסְפִים[g] Kal part. act. pl. masc. from [יֹסֵף] dec. 7b יסף

יִסְפֹּן[h] וַ Kal fut. 3 pers. sing. masc.; ·וַ conv. . ספן

יָסַפְנוּ[i] Kal pret. 1 pers. pl. . . . יסף

יִסְפֹּק[k] וַ Kal fut. 3 pers. sing. masc.; ·וַ conv. ספק

יְסַפֵּר וִ′ Piel fut. 3 pers. sing. masc. (§ 10. rem. 4); ·וַ id. . . . ספר

יְסַפֶּר־[l] וַ

יְסֻפַּר[m] Pual fut. 3 pers. sing. masc. (comp. § 8. rem. 15) . . . . ספר

יְסֻפָּר[n]

יִסָּפֵר Niph. fut. 3 pers. sing. masc. . . ספר

יִסְפֹּר[o] וַיִּ′ Kal fut. 3 pers. sing. masc.; ·וַ conv. . ספר

יְסַפְּרֶהָ[p] וַ Piel fut. 3 pers. sing. masc. (יְסַפֵּר), suff. 3 pers. sing. fem.; וַ id. . . . ספר

יְסַפְּרוּ id. fut. 3 pers. plur. masc. (comp. § 8. rem. 15); וַ id. ספר

יְסַפֵּרוּ וַ′

יִסַפְּרוּ וִ id. with cop. וְ [for וִיסַפְּרוּ ,וִי′] . ספר

יִסָּפְרוּ[q] וַיִּ′ Niph. fut. 3 pers. pl. masc.; וַ conv. ספר

יִסְפְּרוּ[r] Kal fut. 3 pers. pl. masc. . . . ספר

יְסַפְּרוּם וַ Piel fut. 3 pers. pl. masc., suff. 3 pers. pl. masc.; וַ conv. . . . ספר

יִסְפְּרֵם[s] וַ Kal fut. 3 pers. sing. masc. (יִסְפֹּר), suff. 3 pers. pl. masc.; ·וַ id. . . . ספר

יָסַפְתָּ Kal pret. 2 pers. sing. masc.; acc. shifted by conv. וְ (§ 8. rem. 7) . . יסף

יָסַפְתָּ[t] וְ

יָסַפְתִּי[u] וְ id. pret. 1 pers. sing. acc. shifted (§ 8. r. 7) יסף

יִסָּכֵל Niph. fut. 3 pers. sing. masc. . . סכל

---

[a] Is. 9. 10. [b] Ps. 63. 12. [c] Job 12. 19. [d] Pr. 22. 12. [e] Ju. 16. 29. [f] 2 Ch. 32. 8. [g] Nu. 8. 12. [h] Ps. 3. 6. [i] Ps. 78. 26. [k] Is. 33. 20. [l] Ps. 104. 15. [m] Ps. 20. 3. [n] Ps. 41. 4. [o] Ps. 94. 18. [p] 1 Ki. 5. 31. [q] Ex. 14. 15. [r] Ju. 16. 3. [s] 2 Ki. 6. 11. [t] Ho. 13. 3. [u] Hab. 3. 14. [x] De. 5. 22. [y] 2 Sa. 6. 1. [z] Ge. 8. 12. [a] Nu. 11. 25. [b] Is. 66. 17. [c] De. 19. 20. [d] Job 34. 37. [e] Job 31. 4. [f] Job 30. 7. [g] De. 5. 25. [h] 1 Ki. 6. 9. [i] 1 Sa. 12. 19. [k] Nu. 24. 10. [l] 1 Ki. 13. 11. [m] Hab. 1. 5. [n] Ps. 22. 31. [o] Ps. 87. 6. [p] Job 28. 27. [q] 1 Ch. 23. 3. [qq] Ge. 8. 2. [r] Eze. 44. 26. [s] Ezr. 1. 8. [t] De. 19. 9. [u] Le. 26. 18, 21.

וַיְסַקֵּל[x] Piel fut. 3 pers. sing. masc.; וַ conv. . סקל
וַיְסַקְּלֵהוּ id., suff. 3 pers. sing. masc.; וַ id. . סקל
וַיִּסְקְלֻהוּ Kal fut. 3 pers. pl. m., suff. 3 p. s. m.; וַיִּ id. סקל
וַיִּסְקְלוּ id. fut. 3 pers. pl. masc.; וַיִּ id. . סקל
יִסְקְלֻנוּ id. id. with suff. 1 pers. pl. . . סקל

[יָסַר] fut. with suff. אֶסֳּרֵם (§ 20. rem. 16, & § 8. rem. 14); and Pi. יִסַּר.—I. *to chasten, correct, punish.*—II. *to admonish, exhort, instruct;* with מִן *to dehort from* any thing. Hiph. *to chasten,* Ho. 7. 12. Niph. נוֹסַר *to be admonished.* Nithp. נִוַּסַּר (§ 6. No. 10) id. Eze. 23. 48.

יִסּוֹר masc. (after the form גִּבּוֹר) *a corrector, reprover, censurer,* Job 40. 2. Others regard this word as a future of Kal.

מוּסָר masc. dec. 2b.—I. *chastisement, correction.*—II. *admonition, warning.*—III. *instruction, learning, doctrine.*

מוֹסָר masc. *admonition, instruction,* Job 33. 16.

וַיָּסַר Kal or Hiph. fut. 3 pers. sing. masc., ap. and conv. (§ 21. rem. 9 & 19) . סור
וְיָסֵר[f] Hiph. fut. 3 pers. sing. m., ap. from יָסִיר סור
יָסֹר[g] Kal inf. absolute (§ 8. rem. 8) . יסר
יָסַר Kal fut. 3 p. s. m. defect. for יָסוּר 2 Ki. 4. 8; or id. ap. Pr. 9. 4, 16 (§ 21. rem. 7) . סור
יַסֵּר Piel imp. sing. masc. . . . יסר
יַסֵּר[h] id. inf. absolute . . . . יסר
יִסַּר id. pret. 3 pers. sing. masc. (§ 10. rem. 1) יסר
יֹסֵר[i] Kal part. act. sing. masc. (§ 8. rem. 19) יסר
וַיְסִרֶהָ[k] Hiph. fut. 3 pers. sing. masc. (יָסִיר), suff. 3 pers. sing. fem.; וַ conv. . . סור
וַיְסִרֵהוּ[l] id. id., suff. 3 pers. sing. masc.; וַיְ id. סור
יָסֻרוּ[m] וַיָּ Kal fut. 3 p. pl. m. defect. for יָסוּרוּ; וַיָּ id. סור
וְיִסְּרוּ Piel pret. 3 pers. pl. . . . יסר
וְיִסְּרוֹ[n] id. pret. 3 pers. sing. m., suff. 3 pers. s. m. יסר
יִסְּרוּנִי[o] id. pret. 3 pers. pl., suff. 1 pers. sing. יסר
וַיְסִרֵם Hiph. fut. 3 pers. sing. masc. (יָסִיר), suff. 3 pers. pl. masc.; וַ conv. . . סור
יַסְּרֵנִי Piel imp. sing. masc., suff. 1 pers. sing. יסר
וְיִסְּרַנִי[q], יִסְּרַנִּי[r] id. pret. 3 pers. sing. masc., suff. 1 pers. sing. (§ 2. rem. 1) . . יסר
יִסַּרְתָּ id. pret. 2 pers. sing. masc. . . יסר
יִסְּרַתּוּ[s] id. pret. 3 pers. sing. fem., suff. 3 pers. s. m. יסר
יִסַּרְתִּי[t], וְיִסַּרְתִּי[u] id. pret. 1 pers. sing.; acc. shifted by conv. וְ (comp. § 8. rem. 7) . יסר

וְיִסַּרְתִּיךָ id. id., suff. 2 pers. sing. masc. . . יסר
יִסַּרְתַּנִי[x] id. pret. 2 pers. sing. masc., suff. 1 pers. sing. יסר
וַיָּסֶת Hiph. fut. 3 pers. sing. masc. ap. and conv. [from יָסִית] . . . . סות
וְיִסְתַּבֵּל[y] Hithpa. fut. 3 pers. sing. masc. [for יִתְסַבֵּל § 12. rem. 3] . . . סבל
יַסְתִּיר[z] Hiph. fut. 3 pers. sing. masc. . . סתר
יַסְתִּירֵנִי[a] id. with suff. 1 pers. sing. . . . סתר
יִסְתְּמוּ[b], וַיִּסְתְּמוּ[c] Kal fut. 3 pers. pl. masc. (§ 8. r. 15); וַיִּ conv. . . . סתם
וַיְסַתְּמוּם[d] Piel fut. 3 pers. pl. masc., suff. 3 pers. pl. masc.; וַ id. . . . . . סתם
יִסָּתֵר וַיִּ[e] Niph. fut. 3 pers. sing. masc.; וַיִּ id. סתר
יַסְתֵּר וַיַּ, וְ Hiph. fut. 3 pers. sing. masc. ap. [fr. יַסְתִּיר]; וַיַּ id. . . . . סתר
וְיִסָּתֵר[f] Kh. יִסָּתֵר q. v., K. נִסְתַּר (q. v.) . סתר
וַיַּסְתִּרוּ[g] Hiph. fut. 3 pers. pl. m.; וַיַּ conv. . סתר
יִסָּתְרוּ[h] Niph. fut. 3 pers. pl. masc. . . סתר
וַיַּסְתִּרֵם[i] Hiph. fut. 3 pers. sing. masc. (יַסְתִּיר), suff. 3 pers. pl. masc.; וַיַּ conv. . סתר
וַיַּעֲבֵר[k] Hiph. fut. 3 pers. sing. masc., ap. [fr. יַעֲבִיר]; וַיַּ id. . . . . . . עבר
יַעֲבֹד וַיַּ' Kal fut. 3 pers. sing. masc.; וַיַּ id. עבד
יֵעָבֵד[l] Niph. fut. 3 pers. sing. masc. . . עבד
וַיַּעַבְדֵהוּ[m] defect. for יַעַבְדוּהוּ (q. v.) . . עבד
וַיַּעֲבִדוּ[n] Hiph. fut. 3 pers. pl. masc.; וַיַּ conv. . עבד
יַעַבְדוּ[o] וַיַּ, וְ, יַעַבְדוּ[p] וְ[q] Kal fut. 3 pers. pl. masc. (§ 8. rem. 15); וַיַּ id. . . . עבד
יַעַבְדוּהוּ id. id., suff. 3 pers. sing. masc. . . עבד
יַעַבְדוּךָ id. id., suff. 2 pers. sing. masc. . . עבד
וַיַּעַבְדוּם id. id., suff. 3 pers. pl. masc. . . עבד
יַעַבְדוּנִי[r] id. id., suff. 1 pers. sing. . . . עבד
יַעַבְדֶנּוּ id. fut. 3 pers. sing. m., suff. 3 pers. s. m. עבד
וַיַּעַבְדֵם[s] id. id., suff. 3 pers. pl. masc.; וַיַּ conv. עבד
וְיַעַבְדֵנִי[t] id. id., suff. 1 pers. sing. . . . עבד
יַעַבְדֻנִי וְ' defect. for יַעַבְדוּנִי (q. v.) . . עבד
יַעֲבוֹר[u] Kh. יַעֲבוֹר q. v., K. יַעֲבִיר Hiph. fut. 3 pers. sing. masc. . . . . . עבר
יַעֲבוֹר[x] Kh. יַעֲבוֹר q. v., K. יַעֲבִר q. v. (§ 8. r. 18) עבר
יַעֲבוֹר וַיַּ' Kal fut. 3 pers. sing. masc. (§ 8. r. 18) עבר
יַעַבְטוּן[y] Piel fut. 3 pers. pl. masc. with parag. ן עבט
וַיַּעֲבִירֻהוּ[z] Hiph. fut. 3 pers. pl. masc., suff. 3 pers. sing. masc.; וַיַּ conv. . . . עבר
יַעֲבִירוּ[a] וַיַּ, וְ id. fut. 3 pers. pl. masc.; וַיַּ id. . עבר
וְיַעֲבִירוּ[b] Kh. וַיַּעֲבִירוּ q. v., K. הֶעֱבִירוּ q. v. . עבר
יַעֲבִירֻנִי[c] Hiph. fut. 3 pers. pl. masc., suff. 1 pers. s. עבר

2 Sa. 16. 6, 13.
Is. 5. 2.
1 Ki. 21. 13.
Jos. 7. 25.
Ex. 8. 22.
Job 9. 34.
[g] 1 Ch. 15. 22.
[h] Ps. 118. 18.
[i] Pr. 9. 7.
[k] 1 Ki. 15. 13.
[l] 1 Sa. 18. 13.
[m] Ex. 25. 15.
[n] Is. 28. 26.
[o] Ps. 16. 7.
[p] Je. 10. 24.
[q] Is. 8. 11.
[r] Ps. 118. 18.
[s] Pr. 31. 1.
[t] Ho. 7. 15.
[u] Le. 26. 28.
[x] Je. 31. 18.
[y] Ec. 12. 5.
[z] 1 Sa. 20. 2.
[a] Ps. 27. 5.
[b] 2 Ki. 3. 25.
[c] 2 Ch. 32. 4.
[d] Ge. 26. 18.
[e] 1 Sa. 20. 24.
[f] Pr. 22. 3.
[g] 2 Ki. 11. 2.
[h] Am. 9. 3.
[i] Je. 36. 26.
[k] 2 Ch. 34. 33.
[l] De. 21. 4.
[m] 1 Ch. 19. 19.
[n] Ex. 1. 13.
[o] Ex. 10. 7.
[p] Ge. 15. 14.
[q] Job 36. 11.
[r] Ps. 18. 44.
[s] 2 Ch. 33. 22.
[t] Ex. 4. 23.
[u] Ex. 48. 14.
[x] Is. 26. 20.
[y] Joel 2. 7.
[z] 2 Ch. 35. 24.
[a] Ne. 8. 15.
[b] 2 Sa. 19. 41.
[c] Ne. 2. 7.

וַיַּעֲבִירֵם[a] Hiph. fut. 3 pers. sing. masc., suff. 3 pers. pl. masc.; ·וַ conv. . . . . עבר

יַעְבֵּץ pr. name—I. of a man, 1 Ch. 4. 9, 10, which see for the signification.—II. of a place in the tribe of Judah, 1 Ch. 2. 55.

וַיַּעֲבֵר, וַיַּעֲבֶר } Hiph. fut. 3 pers. sing. masc., ap. from יַעֲבִיר (§ 11. rem. 7); ·וַ conv. . עבר

יַעֲבֹר, וַיַּ׳, וְ׳, יַעֲבָר־ } Kal fut. 3 pers. sing. masc. (§ 8. rem. 18); ·וַ id. . . . עבר

יֵעָבֵר[b] Niph. fut. 3 pers. sing. masc. . . עבר

וַיְעַבֵּר[c] Piel fut. 3 pers. sing. masc.; וַ conv. . עבר

וַיַּעֲבִרֵהוּ Hiph. fut. 3 pers. sing. masc., suff. 3 pers. sing. masc.; ·וַ id. . . . . עבר

יַעַבְרוּ, יַעֲבֹרוּ, וַיַּ׳, וְ׳[d] } Kal fut. 3 pers. pl. masc. (§ 8. rem. 15); ·וַ id. . . עבר

וַיַּעֲבִרוּ[e] Hiph. fut. 3 pers. pl. masc. for יַעֲבִירוּ ·וַ id. . . . . . . עבר

וַיַּעֲבִרוּם[f] id. with suff. 3 pers. pl. masc. (for ן fem. § 2. rem. 5); ·וַ id. . . . עבר

יַעַבְרוּם[g] Kal fut. 3 pers. plur. masc. (יַעֲבֹר), suff. 3 pers. pl. masc. . . . . . עבר

יַעֲבֹרוּן[h] id. id. with parag. ן [for יַעַבְרוּן § 8. r. 17] עבר

וַיַּעֲבִרֵם[i] defect. for יַעֲבִירֵם (q. v.) . . עבר

יַעַבְרֶנְהוּ Kal fut. 3 pers. sing. masc. (יַעֲבֹר) with epenth. נ & suff. 3 pers. s. m. (§ 16. r. 13) עבר

יַעַבְרֻנְהוּ[l] id. fut. 3 pers. pl. masc. with parag. ן & suff. 3 pers. sing. masc. (§ 16. rem. 14) . עבר

יַעַבְרֶנּוּ id. fut. 3 pers. sing. m., suff. 3 pers. s. m. עבר

וַיַּעֲבִרֵנִי Hiph. fut. 3 pers. sing. masc., suff. 1 pers. sing.; ·וַ conv. . . . . . עבר

וַיְעַבְּתוּהָ[m] Piel fut. 3 pers. pl. m., suff. 3 p. s. f.; וַ id. עבת

[יָעַד] fut. ייעַד.—I. *to appoint*, as a place, or time.—II. *to betroth*, Ex. 21. 8, 9. Niph. נוֹעַד.—I. *to meet with* any one *at an appointed place, by appointment*, with אֶל, לְ.—II. *to meet together at an appointed time and place, by appointment;* also generally *to come together*.—III. *to agree*, Am. 3. 3. Hiph. הוֹעִיד *to appoint for* any one, especially a time for trial, *to arraign*. Hoph. *to be fixed, set, directed*.

יֶעְדּוֹ pr. name masc. 2 Ch. 9. 29, Keth., Keri יֶעְדִּי.

עֵדָה fem. dec. 11 b.—I. *assembly, congregation*.—II. *a private party, a gang, faction*.—III. *family, household*.—IV. *swarm* of bees, Ju. 14. 8.

מוֹעֵד masc. dec. 7 b, מוֹעֲדִים, מוֹעֲדוֹת.—I. *a set time* or *season;* especially *festival days*.—II. *a coming together, assembly, congregation;* אֹהֶל מוֹעֵד *tabernacle of the congregation;* קְרִיאֵי מוֹעֵד *those called to the assembly*.—III. *place appointed*.—IV. *appointed sign, a signal*, Ju. 20. 38.

מוֹעָד masc. dec. 2 b, *assembly, host*, Is. 14. 31.

מוֹעָדָה f. d. 11 a, *festival, solemn feast*, 2 Ch. 8. 13.

מוּעָדָה fem. *appointment;* עָרֵי הַמּוּעָדָה *appointed cities* for refuge, Jos. 20. 9.

מוֹעַדְיָה (*festival of the Lord*) pr. name masc. Ne. 12. 17; called מַעַדְיָה v. 5, see R. עָדָה.

נוֹעַדְיָה (*with* whom *the Lord meets*) pr. name—I. masc. Ezr. 8. 33.—II. fem. Ne. 6. 14.

וַיָּעַד Hiph. fut. 3 pers. sing. masc., ap. & conv. (§ 21. rem. 19) . . . . . עוד

יְעָדָהּ Kal pret. 3 pers. sing. m., suff. 3 pers. s. f. יעד

יֶעְדֵּה[n] Ch. Peal fut. 3 pers. s. m. (comp. § 49. r. 2) עדה

וַיְעִדֻהוּ[o], וִיעִדֻהוּ[p] } Hiph. fut. 3 p. pl. m. [יָעִידוּ], suff. 3 p. s. m.; וַ conv.; וְ conj. [for וִי׳ וִיעִדֻהוּ] עוד

יְעָדוֹ[q] Kal pret. 3 pers. sing. m., suff. 3 pers. s. m. יעד

יֶעְדּוֹ Kh. יֶעְדִּי, K. יֶעְדּוֹ pr. name masc. . . יעד

יֵעָדֵר[r] Niph. fut. 3 pers. sing. masc. . . עדר

יְעַדֵּרוּ[s] Piel fut. 3 pers. pl. masc. . . . עדר

יֵעָדֵרוּן[t] Niph. fut. 3 pers. pl. masc.; ן parag. [for יֵעָדְרוּן comp. § 8. rem. 17] . . עדר

יָעָה וְ *to carry, sweep away*, Is. 28. 17.

יָע masc. (pl. יָעִים, with suff. יָעָיו) *shovel*.

יְעִיאֵל, יְעוּאֵל (*a carrying away of God*) pr. name masc. of several persons.

יְעוּאֵל, יְעוֹאֵל, וִיעְ׳ } pr. name masc., Kh. יְעִיאֵל . . יעה

יְעוֹדֵד[u] Pilel fut. 3 pers. sing. masc. . . עוד

יָעוֹז[x] Kal fut. 3 pers. sing. masc. for יָעֹז (§ 18. r. 2) עזז

יְעַוֶּל[y] Piel fut. 3 pers. sing. masc. . . . עול

יְעוֹלְלוּ[z] Poel fut. 3 pers. pl. masc. . . . עלל

יָעוּף Kal fut. 3 pers. sing. masc. . . . עוף

יְעוֹפֵף Pilel fut. 3 pers. sing. masc. . . . עוף

יָעוּץ pr. name masc. . . . . . עוץ

יָעוֹר Kh. יָעוּר, K. יָעִיר pr. name masc. . . עור

יְעוֹרֵר Piel fut. 3 pers. sing. masc. . . . עור

יֵעוֹר Niph. fut. 3 pers. s. m. (comp. conj. 1 gutt.) עור

יֵעוֹרוּ[a] id. fut. 3 pers. pl. masc. . . . . עור

יְעוּשׁ וִיעוּשׁ pr. name masc. . . . . עוש

יְעַוֵּת[uu] יְעַוֶּת־ Piel fut. 3 pers. sing. masc. . עות

יָעַז Kal not used; prob. i. q. עָזַז *to be strong, firm*. Niph. part. נוֹעָז *firm, obstinate*, Is. 33. 19.

---

[a] Ps. 78. 13. [b] Eze. 47. 5. [c] 1 Ki. 6. 21. [d] Job 34. 20. [e] 2 Sa. 19. 42. [f] Jos. 4. 8. [g] Je. 8. 13. [h] Ps. 104. 9. [i] Ge. 32. 24. [k] Je. 5. 22. [l] Je. 5. 22. [m] Mi. 7. 3. [n] Da. 7. 14. [o] 1 Ki. 21. 13. [p] 1 Ki. 21. 10. [q] 2 Sa. 20. 5. [r] Is. 5. 6. [s] 1 Ki. 5. 7. [t] Is. 7. 25. [u] Ps. 146. 9. [uu] Job 8. 3. [x] Da. 11. 12. [y] Is. 26. 10. [z] Je. 6. 9. [a] Joel 4. 12.

יָעֹז Kal fut. 3 pers. sing. masc. . . . עוז

יַעֲזֹב, יַעֲזָב־[a] וַיַּ׳, וַיַּ׳[b] Kal fut. 3 pers. sing. masc. (§ 8. rem. 18); ·וַ conv. . . . עזב

יַעַזְבֻהוּ[c] וַ id. fut. 3 p. pl. m., suff. 3 p. s. m.; ·וַ id. עזב

יַעֲזֹבוּ[d], יַעַזְבוּ[e] וַיַּ׳ id. fut. 3 pers. pl. masc. (§ 8. rem. 15); ·וַ id. . . . . עזב

יֵעָזְבוּ[f] Niph. fut. 3 pers. pl. masc. . . . . עזב

יַעַזְבֶךָּ Kal fut. 3 pers. sing. masc., suff. 2 pers. sing. masc. [for יַעַזְבְךָ § 2. rem. 3] . . עזב

יַעַזְבוּךָ[g] id. fut. 3 pers. pl. masc., suff. 2 pers. s. m. עזב

יַעַזְבֶנָּה[h] id. fut. 3 pers. sing. masc., suff. 3 pers. sing. fem. (§ 2. rem. 3) . . . . עזב

יַעַזְבֵנוּ[i] id. id., suff. 1 pers. pl. . . . . עזב

יַעַזְבֶנּוּ id. id., suff. 3 pers. sing. masc. . . עזב

יַעַזְבֵנִי[k] וַ id. id., suff. 1 pers. sing.; ·וַ conv. . עזב

יַעַזְבוּנִי[l] וַ id. fut. 3 pers. pl. m., suff. 1 pers. s.; ·וַ id. עזב

יַעֲזוֹב[m] id. fut. 3 pers. sing. masc. (§ 8. rem. 18) עזב

יַעֲזִיאֵל וְ, יַעֲזִיָּהוּ pr. names masc. . . . . עזה

יַעֲזֵיר pr. name of a place . . . . עזר

יְעַזְּקֵהוּ[n] וַ Piel fut. 3 pers. sing. masc. [יְעַזֵּק], suff. 3 pers. sing. masc.; וַ conv. . . עזק

יַעֲזָר־[o] וַיַּ׳[p] Kal fut. 3 pers. sing. masc. [for יַעֲזֹר § 8. rem. 18]; ·וַ id. . . . . עזר

יַעְזֵר וְ׳ pr. name of a place . . . עזר

יַעְזְרֶהָ[q] Kal fut. 3 pers. sing. masc. [יַעֲזֹר], suff. 3 pers. sing. fem. (§ 13. rem. 5 & 6) . עזר

יַעְזְרֵהוּ[r] וַ id. id., suff. 3 p. s. m. (§ 13. r. 5); ·וַ conv. עזר

יַעְזְרֻהוּ[s] וַ id. fut. 3 pers. pl. m., suff. 3 p. s. m.; ·וַ id. עזר

יַעְזֹרוּ, יַעְזְרוּ[t] וַ id. fut. 3 pers. pl. masc. (§ 13. rem. 5, & § 8. rem. 15); ·וַ id. . . עזר

יֵעָזְרוּ[u] וַיֵּ׳[x] Niph. fut. 3 pers. pl. masc.; ·וַ id. . עזר

יַעְזְרוּנִי[y] וְ Kal fut. 3 pers. pl. masc., suff. 1 pers. sing. (§ 13. rem. 5) . . . עזר

יַעְזְרֶךָּ[z] וְ[a] id. fut. 3 pers. sing. masc., suff. 2 pers. sing. masc. [for יַעְזָרְךָ v. id. & § 2. rem. 2] עזר

יַעְזְרֻכֶם[b] וְ id. fut. 3 pers. pl. masc., suff. 2 pers. pl. masc. (§ 13. rem. 5) . . . . . עזר

יַעְזְרֵם[c] וַ id. fut. 3 pers. sing. masc., suff. 3 pers. pl. masc.; ·וַ conv. . . . . עזר

יַעְזְרֻנִי[d] id. fut. 3 pers. pl. masc., suff. 1 pers. sing. עזר

[יָעַט] *to clothe, cover*, Is. 61. 10.

[יְעַט] Ch. i. q. Hebr. יָעַץ *to advise, counsel*, Ezr. 7. 14, 15. Ithp. *to consult together*, Da. 6. 8.

יְעֵטָא Ch. fem. *counsel, wisdom*, Da. 2. 14.

יָעַט[e] וַ Kal fut. 3 pers. sing. masc. ap. & conv. (§ 22. rem. 3) . . . . . עיט

יַעַט[f] וַ ap. for the following (§ 24. rem. 3) . עטה

יַעְטֶה Kal fut. 3 pers. sing. masc. (§ 13. rem. 5) עטה

יַעֲטֹהִי[g] Ch. defect. for יַעֲטוֹהִי (q. v.) . . . יעט

יַעֲטוּ[h] וְ׳[i] Kal fut. 3 pers. pl. masc. . . עטה

יַעֲטוֹהִי[k] וְ Ch. Peal part. pl. masc., suff. 3 pers. sing. m. [from s. יַעֵט for יָעֵט, comp. § 54. r. 1] יעט

יַעֲטוֹף[l] Kal fut. 3 pers. sing. masc. (§ 8. rem. 18) עטף

יְעָטָנִי[m] Kal pret. 3 p. s. m., suff. 1 p. s. (§ 2. r. 1) יעט

יַעֲטֹף[n], יַעְטֹף[o], יַעֲטָף־[p] Kal fut. 3 pers. sing. masc. (§ 13. rem. 5, & § 8. rem. 18) . . . עטף

יַעַטְפוּ[rr] id. fut. 3 pers. pl. masc. . . . עטף

יְעִיאֵל וִיעִי׳ pr. name masc. . . . . . יעה

יָעִיב[q] Hiph. fut. 3 pers. sing. masc. . . . עוב

יָעִידוּ[yy] וַ Hiph. fut. 3 pers. pl. masc. . . עוד

יְעִידֶנִּי[r] defect. for יוֹעִידֶנִּי (q. v. § 20. rem. 11) . יעד

יָעָיו[s] וְ noun masc. pl., suff. 3 pers. sing. masc. [from יָע] besides only in the abs. יָעִים יעה

יֹעִילוּ Hiph. fut. 3 p. pl. m. (for יוֹעִילוּ § 20. r. 11) יעל

יָעִיר Hiph. fut. 3 pers. sing. masc. . . . עור

יְעִירֶנּוּ[t] Kh. יְעִירֶנּוּ Hiph., K. יְעוּ׳ Kal fut. 3 pers. sing. masc., suff. 3 pers. sing. masc. . עור

יְעִירֵנִי[u] וַ Hiph. fut. 3 pers. sing. masc. (יָעִיר), suff. 1 pers. sing.; וַ conv. . . . עור

יְעִישׁ Kh. יְעִישׁ, K. יְעוּשׁ pr. name masc. . עוש

יַעְכָּן וְ pr. name masc. . . . . . עכן

יַעַכְרְךָ[x] Kal fut. 3 pers. sing. masc. [יַעְכֹּר], suff. 2 pers. sing. masc. (§ 13. rem. 5) . עכר

יָעַל Kal not used; prob. i. q. עָלָה q. v. Hiph. הוֹעִיל.—I. *to profit, help*, with לְ.—II. intrans. *to receive profit, to be benefited*.

יָעֵל masc. dec. 5a (pl. c. יַעֲלֵי).—I. *the mountain goat, wild goat, ibex*.—II. pr. name of a judge in Israel, Ju. 5. 6.—II. pr. name fem. Ju. 4. 17, 18; 5. 24.—III. צוּרֵי הַיְּעֵלִים (*rocks of the wild goats*) pr. name of a rock in the desert of Engedi, 1 Sa. 24. 3.

יַעֲלָה fem. dec. 10.—I. *wild she-goat, female ibex*, Pr. 5. 19.—II. pr. name of a man.

יַעַל[y], יַעַל וְ, וַיַּ׳[z], וְ׳, וַיַּ׳ Kal or Hiph. fut. 3 pers. s. m., ap. from יַעֲלֶה (§ 24. r. 3 & 16); ·וַ conv. עלה

יַעֲלָ[a] וַ Kh. יַעַל q. v., K. יַעֲלוּ (q. v.) . . עלה

יָעֵל pr. name fem. . . . . . יעל

---

[a] Ge. 2. 24.
[b] 1 Ch. 16. 37.
[c] 2 Ch. 29. 6.
[d] Jon. 2. 9.
[e] Ps. 89. 31.
[f] Is. 18. 6.
[g] Pr. 3. 3.
[h] Job 20. 13.
[i] 1 Ki. 8. 57.
[k] 1 Sa. 30. 13.
[l] 1 Sa. 8. 8.
[m] Job 6. 14.
[n] Is. 5. 2.
[o] Is. 50. 7, 9.
[p] 2 Sa. 21. 17.
[q] Ps. 46. 6.
[r] 2 Ch. 26. 7.
[rr] Ps. 65. 14.
[s] 2 Ch. 32. 3.
[t] 1 Ki. 1. 7.
[u] Da. 11. 34.
[x] 1 Ch. 5. 20.
[y] 2 Ch. 28. 23.
[yy] 2 Ch. 24. 19.
[z] Is. 44. 2.
[a] Ge. 49. 25.
[b] De. 32. 38.
[c] Ps. 37. 40.
[d] Ps. 119. 175.
[e] 1 Sa. 25. 14.
[f] Is. 59. 17.
[g] Ezr. 7. 14.
[h] Ps. 71. 13.
[i] Ps. 109. 29.
[k] Ezr. 7. 15.
[l] Is. 57. 16.
[m] Is. 61. 10.
[n] Ps. 102. 1.
[o] Job 23. 9.
[p] Ps. 73. 6.
[q] La. 2. 1.
[r] Je. 49. 19.
[s] Ex. 27. 3.
[t] Job 41. 2.
[u] Zec. 4. 1.
[x] Jos. 7. 25.
[y] 2 Ch. 36. 23.
[z] 1 Sa. 2. 6.
[a] Ezr. 3. 3.

יַעְלָא pr. name masc. for יַעֲלָה (q. v.) . . יעל

יֵעָלֶה[a] Niph. fut. 3 pers. sing. masc. . . עלה

יַעֲלָה pr. name masc. . . . . . יעל

וַיַּעֲלֵהוּ[b] Kh. יַעֲלֶה q. v., K. יַעֲלֵהוּ (q. v.) . . עלה

יַעֲלֶה, וְ, וַיַּ Kal or Hiph. fut. 3 pers. sing. masc. (comp. יַעַל); וַ conv. . . . . עלה

וַיַּעֲלֵהוּ Hiph. fut. 3 pers. sing. masc., suff. 3 pers. sing. masc.; וַ id. . . . . . עלה

וַיַּעֲלֻהוּ[c] id. fut. 3 pers. pl. masc., suff. 3 pers. sing. masc.; וַ id. . . . . . עלה

וַיֵּעָלוּ Niph. fut. 3 pers. pl. masc.; וַ id. . עלה

יַעֲלוּ, וְ, וַיַּ Kal or Hiph. fut. 3 pers. pl. m.; וַ id. עלה

וַיַּעֲלוּהוּ[d] Hiph. fut. 3 pers. pl. masc., suff. 3 pers. sing. masc.; וַ id. . . . . עלה

וַיַּעֲלֹז[e], וַיַּ[f] Kal fut. 3 pers. sing. masc.; וַ id. . עלז

יַעֲלֹזוּ / יַעְלֹזוּ[g] } id. fut. 3 pers. pl. masc. (§ 8. rem. 15, & § 13. rem. 5) . . . . } עלז

יַעֲלֵי[h] noun masc. pl. constr. from [יָעֵל] dec. 5 . יעל

יַעֲלִימוּ[i] Hiph. fut. 3 pers. pl. masc. (§ 13. rem. 9) עלם

יַעְלָם / וְיַעְלָם } pr. name masc. . . . . . עלם

וַיְעֹלְלֻהוּ[k] Poel fut. 3 pers. pl. masc., suff. 3 pers. sing. masc.; וַ conv. . . . . . עלל

וַיַּעֲלֵם / יַעֲלֵם[l] } Hiph. fut. 3 p. s. m. [יַעֲלֶה], suff. 3 p. pl. m. (§ 13. r. 9, & § 24. r. 21); וַ id. } עלה

יַעֲלֶנָּה[m] Kal fut. 3 pers. sing. masc. (יַעֲלֶה), suff. 3 pers. sing. fem. (§ 24. rem. 21, & § 2. r. 3) עלה

וַיַּעֲלֵנִי[n] Hiph. fut. 3 pers. sing. masc. (יַעֲלֶה), suff. 1 pers. sing. (§ 24. rem. 21); וַ conv. . עלה

יַעֲלֹם[o] Kal fut. 3 pers. sing. masc. . . . עלם

יְעַלְעוּ[p] Piel fut. 3 pers. pl. masc. (§ 10. rem. 7) . עלע

יַעֲלֹץ[q] Kal fut. 3 pers. sing. masc. . . . עלץ

יַעַלְצוּ / וְיַעְלְצוּ[r] } id. fut. 3 pers. pl. masc. (§ 13. rem. 5) . עלץ

יַעֲלַת[s] noun fem. sing. constr. [of יַעֲלָה] . . יעל

וַיַּעֲמֵד / וַיַּעֲמֶד־[t] } Hiph. fut. 3 pers. sing. masc., ap. from יַעֲמִיד (§ 11. rem. 7); וַ conv. . } עמד

יַעֲמֹד, וְ, וַיַּ / יַעֲמָד־ } Kal fut. 3 pers. sing. masc. (§ 8. rem. 18); וַ id. . . . } עמד

יָעֳמַד[u] Hoph. fut. 3 pers. sing. masc. . . . עמד

וַיַּעֲמִדֵהוּ Hiph. fut. 3 pers. sing. masc. (יַעֲמִיד), suff. 3 pers. sing. masc.; וַ conv. . . . עמד

יַעַמְדוּ / וַיַּעַמְדוּ[x], וְ, וַיַּ[y] } Kal fut. 3 p. pl. m. (§ 8. r. 15); וַ id. עמד

יַעֲמֹדוּ[z] Kh. יַעֲמֹדוּ q. v., K. עָמְדוּ (q. v.) . עמד

יַעֲמֹדְנָה[a] Kal fut. 3 p. pl. fem. for תַּעֲמֹדְנָה (§ 8. r. 16) עמד

יַעֲמוֹד, וַיַּ[b] id. fut. 3 pers. sing. masc. (§ 8. rem. 18); וַ conv. . . . . . . עמד

יַעֲמִיד[c], וְ[d] Hiph. fut. 3 pers. sing. masc. . . עמד

וַיַּעֲמִידֶהָ id. id., suff. 3 pers. sing. fem.; וַ conv. . עמד

וַיַּעֲמִידוּ id. fut. 3 pers. pl. masc.; וַ id. . . עמד

וְיַעֲמִידוּ[e] Kh. יַעֲמִידוּ q. v., K. יַעֲמִיד (q. v.) . עמד

וַיַּעֲמִידֵם Hiph. fut. 3 pers. sing. masc., suff. 3 pers. pl. masc.; וַ conv. . . . . עמד

וַיַּעֲמִידֵנִי, וַיַּ[f] id. with suff. 1 pers. sing.; וַ id. . עמד

יַעֲמֹל[g] Kal fut. 3 pers. sing. masc. . . עמל

יַעֲמֹס[h] / וַיַּעֲמָס־[i] } וַ Kal fut. 3 pers. sing. masc. (§ 8. rem. 18); וַ conv. . . . } עמס

יָעַן Root not used; Syr. *to be greedy, voracious.*

יָעֵן masc. dec. 5 a, *ostrich*, La. 4. 3.

יַעֲנָה fem. always בַּת הַיַּעֲנָה *the female ostrich*; pl. בְּנוֹת הַיַּעֲנָה.

יַעַן prep. and conj. . . . . . . ענה

וַיַּעַן Kal fut. 3 pers. sing. masc., ap. from יַעֲנֶה (§ 24. rem. 3); וַ conv. . . . . ענה

יַעֲנָה noun fem. sing. . . . . . . יען

יַעֲנֶה, וַיַּ[k] Kal fut. 3 pers. sing. masc.; וַ conv. ענה

יֵעָנֶה Niph. fut. 3 pers. sing. masc. . . . ענה

יְעַנֶּה[l] Piel fut. 3 pers. sing. masc. . . . ענה

וַיְעַנֶּהָ id., suff. 3 p. s. fem. (§ 24. r. 21); וַ conv. ענה

יַעֲנֵהוּ[m], וַיַּ Kal fut. 3 pers. sing. masc. (יַעֲנֶה), suff. 3 pers. sing. masc. (§ 24. rem. 21); וַ id. ענה

יַעֲנוּ, וַיַּ id. fut. 3 pers. pl. masc.; וַ id. . . ענה

יְעַנּוּ Piel fut. 3 pers. pl. masc. . . . ענה

יַעֲנוּכָה[n] Kal fut. 3 p. pl. m., suff. 2 p. s. m. (§ 2. r. 2) ענה

וַיְעַנּוּנוּ[o] Piel fut. 3 p. pl. m., suff. 1 p. pl.; וַ conv. ענה

וְיַעְנַי pr. name masc. . . . . . ענה

יַעַנְךָ Kal fut. 3 pers. sing. masc. (יַעֲנֶה), suff. 2 pers. sing. masc. (§ 24. rem. 21) . . ענה

וַיְעַנְּךָ[p] Piel fut. 3 pers. sing. masc. (יְעַנֶּה), suff. 2 pers. sing. masc. (§ 24. rem. 21); וַ conv. ענה

יַעֲנֵם[q], וַיַּ, וְ[r] Kal fut. 3 pers. sing. masc. (יַעֲנֶה), suff. 3 pers. pl. masc. (§ 24. rem. 21); וַ id. ענה

וַיְעַנֵּם[s] Piel fut. 3 pers. sing. masc. (יְעַנֶּה), suff. 3 pers. pl. masc. (§ 24. rem. 21); וַ id. . ענה

יַעֲנֶנָּה Kal fut. 3 pers. sing. masc. (יַעֲנֶה), suff. 3 pers. sing. fem. (§ 24. r. 21, & § 2. r. 3) ענה

יַעֲנֵנוּ[u] id., suff. 1 pers. pl. . . . . ענה

יַעֲנֶנּוּ id., suff. 3 pers. sing. masc. . . . ענה

[a] Ex. 40. 37. [b] 1 Sa. 7. 9. [c] Je. 39. 5. [d] Ju. 15. 13. [e] Ps. 96. 12. [f] Ps. 28. 7. [g] Ps. 149. 5. [h] Job 39. 1. [i] Le. 20. 4. [k] Ju. 20. 45. [l] De. 28. 61. [m] Is. 35. 9. [n] Ps. 40. 3. [o] Job 20. 18. [p] Job 39. 30. [q] 1 Ch. 16. 32. [r] Ps. 5. 12. [s] Pr. 5. 19. [t] 2 Ch. 11. 15. [u] Le. 16. 10. [x] 2 Sa. 2. 23. [y] Jos. 3. 13. [z] Eze. 47. 10. [a] Da. 8. 22. [b] Nu. 22. 26. [c] Pr. 29. 4. [d] Ne. 3. 14. [e] Ne. 3. 15. [f] Da. 8. 18. [g] Ec. 8. 17. [h] Ge. 44. 13. [i] Ps. 68. 20. [k] 2 Ki. 1. 10. [l] Job 37. 23. [m] Ps. 20. 7. [n] Je. 7. 27. [o] De. 26. 6. [p] De. 8. 3. [q] Ps. 99. 6. [r] Ps. 55. 20. [s] 2 Ch. 10. 13. [t] 2 Ki. 17. 20. [u] Ps. 20. 10.

יְעַנֵּנוּ[a] Piel fut. 3 pers. sing. masc. (יְעַנֶּה), suff. 3 pers. sing. masc. (§ 24. rem. 21, & § 2. r. 3) ענה

יַעֲנֵנִי וַיַּ׳ Kal fut. 3 pers. sing. masc. (יַעֲנֶה), suff. 1 pers. sing. (§ 24. rem. 21); וַ conv. ענה

יְעַנֵּנִי[b] וַ Piel fut. 3 pers. sing. masc. (יְעַנֶּה), suff. 1 pers. sing. (§ 24. rem. 21); וַ id. ענה

יֵעָנֵשׁ[c] Niph. fut. 3 pers. sing. masc. . . . ענש

יַעֲנֹשׁ[d] וַ Kal fut. 3 pers. sing. masc.; וַ conv. ענש

יְעֹעֵרוּ[e] Pilpel (§ 6. No. 4) fut. 3 pers. pl. masc. [for יְעַרְעֲרוּ ,יְעַרְעֲרוּ ר softened to ו] עור

[יָעַף] fut. יִיעַף *to be wearied, fatigued.* Arab. ועף *to run swiftly.* Hoph. part. מֻעָף Da. 9. 21, *wearied, faint*; others, *flying, swift.*

יָעֵף adj. masc. dec. 5a, *weary, fatigued.*

יְעָף masc. *flight, swift course,* Da. 9. 21.

תּוֹעָפוֹת fem. pl. (from תּוֹעָפָה dec. 11a).—I. *swiftness.*—II. *wealth, treasure.* Perhaps primarily, *brightness, splendour,* יָעַף=יָפַע *to be bright, to shine.*

וַיָּעַף[f] Kal fut. 3 p. s. m. ap. & conv. (§ 21. r. 9) עוף

יָעֵף[g] adj. masc. sing. dec. 5 . . . . יעף

וַיָּעָף / וַיָּעֹף[h] } Kal fut. 3 pers. sing. masc. ap. & conv. from יָעוּף (§ 21. rem. 8) עוף

וַיִּעַף[i] Kal fut. 3 pers. sing. masc. for יִיעַף (§ 20. rem. 2, & § 8. rem. 15); וַ conv. יעף

יָעֵפוּ[dd] וְ id. pret. 3 pers. pl. [for יָעֲפוּ § 8 r. 1 & 7] יָעֵף

יָעֻפוּ[k] Kal fut. 3 pers. pl. masc. . . . עוף

יִעֲפוּ[l] / וְיִעֲפוּ[m] } Kal fut. 3 pers. pl. masc. [for יִיעֲפוּ § 20. rem. 2, comp. § 8. rem. 15] יעף

וַיַּעְפִּלוּ[n] Hiph. fut. 3 pers. pl. masc. [for יַעְפִּילוּ, יַעֲפִּילוּ § 13. rem. 9]; וַ conv. עפל

יָעַץ fut. יִיעַץ.—I. *to counsel, advise,* with לְ; part. יוֹעֵץ *counsellor.*—II. *to take counsel, to decree,* with עַל ,אֶל *against* any one.—III. *to direct,* as the eye, Ps. 32. 8, with עַל *towards* any one, i. e. to care or provide for him.—IV. *to instruct,* Nu. 24. 14. Niph. נוֹעַץ.—I. *to be counselled, advised.*—II. *to consult, take counsel together,* with עִם ,אֶל ,אֵת. Hithp. *to consult together,* Ps. 83. 4.

עֵצָה fem. dec. 11b (for יְעָצָה).—I. *counsel, advice.*—II. *deliberation, purpose, plan;* בְּעֵצָה *advisedly.*

מוֹעֵצָה fem. dec. 11b, *counsel, device.*

יָעָץ Kal pret. 3 pers. sing. m. for יָעַץ (§ 8. rem. 7) יעץ

יֹעֵץ[o] id. part. act. sing. masc. dec. 7b . . יעץ

יֵעָצֵב Niph. fut. 3 pers. sing. masc. . . . עצב

יְעַצֵּבוּ[p] Piel fut. 3 p. pl. m. [for יְעַצְּבוּ comp. § 8. r. 15] עצב

יְעָצָהּ[q] Kal pret. 3 pers. sing. masc., suff. 3 pers. s. f. יעץ

יְעָצֻהוּ id. pret. 3 pers. pl., suff. 3 pers. sing. masc. יעץ

יָעָצוּ[r] id. pret. 3 pers. pl. . . . . יעץ

יֹעֲצֵי[s] וְ׳ id. part. act. pl. constr. from יוֹעֵץ dec. 7b יעץ

יַעֲצִיבוּהוּ[u] Hiph. fut. 3 pers. pl. m., suff. 3 pers. s. m. עצב

יֹעֲצָיו[x] וְ Kal part. act. pl., suff. 3 pers. sing. masc. from יוֹעֵץ dec. 7b . . . . יעץ

יֹעֲצַיִךְ[y] וְ id., suff. 2 pers. sing. fem. . . יעץ

יְעַצֵּם[z] וַ Piel fut. 3 pers. sing. masc.; וַ conv. . עצם

יַעֲצִמֵהוּ[a] וַ Hiph. fut. 3 p. s. m., suff. 3 p. s. m; וַ id. עצם

יַעַצְמוּ[b] וַ Kal fut. 3 pers. pl. masc.; וַ id. . עצם

יְעָצַנִי[c] Kal pret. 3 pers. sing. masc. with suff. 1 pers. sing. (§ 2. rem. 1) . . . יעץ

יַעֲצֹר / יַעֲצָר־[d] } Kal fut. 3 pers. sing. masc. (§ 8. rem. 18, & § 13. rem. 5) . . } עצר

יַעַצְרֵהוּ[e] וַ id., suff. 3 pers. sing. masc.; וַ conv. . עצר

יַעַצָרְכָה[f] id., suff. 2 pers. sing. masc. (§ 2. rem. 2) . עצר

יָעַצְתָּ Kal pret. 2 pers. sing. masc. . . יעץ

יָעַצְתִּי id. pret. 1 pers. sing. . . . . יעץ

יַעֲקֹב וְ׳ pr. name masc. . . . . . עקב

יַעְקֹב[g] Kal fut. 3 pers. sing. masc. (§ 13. rem. 5) . עקב

יַעֲקֹבָה וְ pr. name masc. . . . . . עקב

יְעַקְּבֵם[h] Piel fut. 3 pers. sing. masc., suff. 3 pers. pl. masc. (§ 10. rem. 7) . . . עקב

יַּעְקְבֵנִי[i] וַ Kal fut. 3 pers. sing. masc. (יַעְקֹב q. v.), suff. 1 pers. sing.; וַ conv. . . . עקב

יַּעֲקֹד[k] וַ Kal fut. 3 pers. sing. masc.; וַ id. . עקד

יַעֲקוֹב pr. name of a people, see יַעֲקֹב . . עקב

יַעֲקָן pr. name masc., see בְּנֵי יַעֲקָן . . . עקן

יְעַקֵּר וְ Piel fut. 3 pers. sing. masc.; וְ conv. . עקר

יְעַקֵּשׁוּ[l] Piel fut. 3 pers. pl. masc. [for יְעַקְּשׁוּ comp. § 8. rem. 15] . . . . . עקש

יַּעְקְשֵׁנִי[m] וַ Kal fut. 3 pers. sing. masc. [יַעְקֹשׁ], suff. 1 pers. sing. (§ 13. rem. 5); וַ conv. . עקש

יַעַר masc. dec. 6c (with suff. יַעְרִי, § 35. rem. 5; pl. יְעָרִים ,יְעָרוֹת).—I. *honeycomb,* Ca. 5. 1.—II. *thicket, wood, forest.*—III. pr. name of a town, Ps. 132. 6, prob. i. q. קִרְיַת יְעָרִים.

יַעְרָה fem.—I. *honeycomb,* only constr. יַעְרַת, 1 Sa. 14. 27.—II. pr. name masc. 1 Ch. 9. 42; called יְהוֹעַדָּה in chap. 8. 36.

יְעוֹר masc. *wood, forest,* Eze. 34. 25. Kheth.

יַעֲרֵי אֹרְגִים (*woods of the weavers*) pr. name masc. 2 Sa. 21. 19; but in the parallel passage, 1 Ch. 20. 5, it is יָעִיר, in Kheth. יָעוּר, or perhaps יְעוֹר, compare the preceding.

---

[a] Ps. 89. 23.
[b] Job 30. 11.
[c] Ex. 21. 22.
[d] 2 Ch. 36. 3.
[dd] Je. 51. 58, 64.
[e] Is. 15. 5.
[f] Ju. 4. 21; 1 Sa. 14. 28.
[g] Is. 50. 4.
[h] Is. 6. 6.
[i] Is. 44. 12.
[k] Hab. 1. 8.
[l] Hab. 2. 13.
[m] Is. 40. 30.
[n] Nu. 14. 44.
[o] Na. 1. 11.
[p] Ps. 56. 6.
[q] Is. 23. 9.
[r] Ps. 62. 5.
[s] Is. 19. 11.
[t] Job 3. 14.
[u] Ps. 78. 40.
[x] Ezr. 8. 25.
[y] Is. 1. 26.
[z] Is. 29. 10.
[a] Ps. 105. 24.
[b] Ex. 1. 7, 20.
[c] Ps. 16. 7.
[d] 2 Ch. 2. 5.
[e] 1 Ki. 17. 4.
[f] 1 Ki. 18. 44.
[g] Je. 9. 3.
[h] Job 37. 4.
[i] Ge. 27. 36.
[k] Ge. 22. 9.
[l] Mi. 3. 9.
[m] Job 9. 20.

יָעַר in pause for יַעַר (q. v.) . . . . יער

וְ יָעַר Hiph. fut. 3 pers. sing. masc., ap. & conv. from יָעִיר (§ 21. rem. 19) . עור

[a] וְ יָעַר (as above) עור

[b] יֶעֱרַב Kal fut. 3 pers. sing. masc. . . . ערב

[c] יֶעֶרְבוּ id. fut. 3 pers. pl. masc. . . . . ערב

יַעְרָה ו׳ pr. name masc. . . . . . יער

[d] יַעְרָהּ noun masc. sing., suff. 3 pers. sing. fem. from יַעַר dec. 6d (§ 35. rem. 5) . . יער

[e] יֵעָרֶה Niph. fut. 3 pers. sing. masc. . . ערה

[f] יְעָרֶה Piel fut. 3 pers. sing. masc. . . . ערה

[g] יַעְרוֹ noun masc. sing., suff. 3 pers. sing. masc. from יַעַר dec. 6d (§ 35. rem. 5) . . יער

יֵעֹרוּ Niph. fut. 3 pers. pl. masc. . . . עור

[h] וִ יְעָרוּ Piel fut. 3 pers. pl. masc. with conj. וְ [for וַיְ, וַיְעָרוּ] . . . . . ערה

[i] יְעָרוֹת noun masc. with pl. fem. term. abs., from יַעַר dec. 6d . . . . יער

יַעֲרֵי pr. name in compos. יַעֲרֵי אֹרְגִים . . יער

[k] יַעְרִי noun masc. sing., suff. 1 pers. sing. from יַעַר dec. 6d (§ 35. rem. 5) . . יער

[l] יַעֲרִיךְ Hiph. fut. 3 pers. sing. masc. . . . ערך

[m] יַעֲרִיכֶנּוּ id. with suff. 3 pers. sing. masc. . . ערך

יְעָרִים pr. name see קִרְיַת יְעָרִים . . . קרה

[n] יַעֲרִימוּ Hiph. fut. 3 pers. pl. masc. . . . ערם

[o] יַעֲרִיצוּ Hiph. fut. 3 pers. pl. masc. . . . ערץ

יַעֲרֹךְ וַיַּ׳ Kal fut. 3 pers. sing. masc.; ·וַ conv. ערך

[p] וְ יַעַרְכֶהָ id. id., suff. 3 pers. sing. fem. (§ 13. r. 5) ערך

יַעַרְכוּ וַ id. fut. 3 pers. pl. masc.; ·וַ conv. . ערך

[q] יַעַרְכוּנִי id. id. with suff. 1 pers. sing. . . ערך

יַעַרְכֶנָּה id. fut. 3 pers. sing. masc., suff. 3 pers. s. f. ערך

[r] יַעַרְכֶנּוּ id. id., suff. 3 pers. sing. masc. . . ערך

יַעְרִם Hiph. fut. 3 pers. sing. masc. (§ 13. rem. 5) ערם

יַעֲרֹף Kal fut. 3 pers. sing. masc. . . . ערף

[s] יַעַרְפוּ id. fut. 3 pers. pl. masc. . . . . ערף

יַעֲרֶשְׁיָה וְ (whom *the Lord makes fat*, i. e. *prosperous*; ערש Syr. *to fatten*) pr. n. m. 1 Ch. 8. 27.

יַעַשׂ וְ Kal fut. 3 pers. sing. m., ap. from יַעֲשֶׂה (§ 24. rem. 3); ·וַ conv. עשה

[t] יַעַשׂ וַיַּ׳, וְ׳ (as above) עשה

[u] יַעֲשׂ וַ Kh. q. v., K. יָעַט, Kal fut. 3 pers. sing. masc. [for יַעַט § 21. rem. 24] . . עיט

יַעֲשֶׂה וְ the following with suff. 3 pers. sing. fem. עשה

יַעֲשֶׂה וַיַּ׳ Kal fut. 3 pers. sing. masc.; ·וַ conv. עשה

[y] יַעֲשֶׂה Kh. יַעֲשֶׂה q. v., K. יַעַשׂ (q. v.) . . עשה

[z] יֵעָשֶׂה וְ׳ Niph. fut. 3 pers. sing. masc. . . עשה

[a] יַעֲשֵׂהוּ וַיַּ׳, וְ׳[b] Kal fut. 3 pers. sing. masc. (יַעֲשֶׂה), suff. 3 pers. s. m. (§ 24. r. 21); ·וַ conv. עשה

יַעֲשׂוֹ וְ Kh. יַעֲשׂוֹ, K. יַעֲשַׂי ,יַשַׁי pr. name masc. . עשה

יַעֲשׂוּ וַיַּ׳, וְ׳ Kal fut. 3 pers. pl. masc. ·וַ conv. עשה

[c] יֵעָשׂוּ Niph. fut. 3 pers. pl. masc. . . עשה

[d] יַעֲשׂוּהָ Kal fut. 3 pers. pl. m. with suff. 3 pers. s. f. עשה

יַעֲשׂוּן id. with parag. ן . . . . עשה

[e] וַ יַּעֲשׂוּנִי id. with suff. 1 pers. sing.; ·וַ conv. . עשה

יַעֲשִׂיאֵל וְ׳ pr. name masc. . . . . עשה

יַעֲשִׁיר Hiph. fut. 3 pers. sing. masc. . . . עשר

[f] וַ יַּעֲשִׁירוּ id. fut. 3 pers. pl. masc.; ·וַ conv. . עשר

[g] וְ יַעֲשֵׂם Kal fut. 3 pers. sing. masc. (יַעֲשֶׂה), suff. 3 pers. pl. masc. (§ 24. rem. 21) . עשה

יֶעְשַׁן Kal fut. 3 pers. sing. masc. (§ 13. rem. 5) עשן

יַעֲשֶׂנָּה Kal fut. 3 pers. sing. masc. (יַעֲשֶׂה), suff. 3 pers. sing. fem. (§ 24. rem. 21) . עשה

וְ יֶעֶשְׁנוּ Kal fut. 3 pers. pl. m. [for יֶעְשְׁנוּ § 8. r. 15] עשן

[h] יַעֲשֹׁק Kal fut. 3 pers. sing. masc. . . . עשק

[i] יַעַשְׁקֻנִי id. fut. 3 pers. pl. masc., suff. 1 pers. sing. עשק

[k] יַעֲשֵׁר defect. for יַעֲשִׁיר (q. v.) . . . עשר

[l] יֶעְשַׁר Kal fut. 3 pers. sing. masc. (§ 13. rem. 5) עשר

[m] יֶעְשָׁר Kal fut. 3 pers. sing. masc. (§ 13. rem. 5) עשר

[n] יַעְשְׁרֶנּוּ Hiph. fut. 3 pers. sing. m. [ap. יַעְשֵׁר], suff. 3 pers. sing. m. [for יַעֲשִׁירֶנּוּ § 16. r. 16] עשר

וַ יַּעְתֵּק Hiph. fut. 3 pers. sing. masc. ap. (§ 13. rem. 9); ·וַ conv. . . . . עתק

[o] יֶעְתַּק וְ׳[p] Kal fut. 3 pers. sing. masc. (§ 13. r. 5) עתק

[q] יֶעְתַּר וַיֶּ׳ Kal fut. 3 pers. sing. masc. (§ 13. rem. 5); ·וַ conv. . . . . . עתר

וְ יֵעָתֵר Niph. fut. 3 pers. sing. masc. (§ 9. rem. 3); ·וַ id. . . . . עתר

וַ יֵּעָתֶר (as above) עתר

[r] יְפָאֵר Piel fut. 3 pers. sing. masc. . . . פאר

וַ יָּפָג Kal fut. 3 p. s. m. ap. & conv. [from יָפוּג] פוג

[s] יַפְגִּיעַ Hiph. fut. 3 pers. sing. masc. . . פגע

וַ יִּפְגַּע Kal fut. 3 pers. sing. masc.; ·וַ conv. . פגע

יִפְגְּעוּ וַיִּ׳ id. fut. 3 pers. pl. masc.; ·וַ id. . . פגע

[u] יִפְגְּעוּן id. id. with parag. ן . . . . פגע

[x] יִפְגָּעֵנוּ id. fut. 3 pers. sing. masc., suff. 1 pers. pl. (§ 16. rem. 12) . . . . . פגע

[y] וַ יִּפְגְּשֵׁהוּ Kal fut. 3 pers. sing., suff. 3 pers. sing. masc.; ·וַ conv. . . . . פגש

[z] יְפַגְּשׁוּ Piel fut. 3 pers. pl. masc. . . . פגש

[a] וַ יִּפְגְּשׁוּם Kal fut. 3 pers. pl. masc., suff. 3 pers. pl. masc.; ·וַ conv. . . . . פגש

[b] יִפְגָּשְׁךָ id. fut. 3 pers. sing. masc. [יִפְגֹּשׁ], suff. 2 pers. sing. masc. (§ 16. rem. 12) . פגש

[c] יִפָּדֶה Niph. fut. 3 pers. sing. masc. . . . פדה

יִפְדֶּה Kal fut. 3 pers. sing. masc. . . . פדה

---

[a] Da. 11. 25. [b] Ps. 104. 34. [c] Ho. 9. 4. [d] Je. 46. 23. [e] Is. 32. 15. [f] Is. 3. 17. [g] Is. 10. 18, 19. [h] 2 Ch. 24. 11. [i] Ps. 29. 9. [k] Ca. 5. 1. [l] Le. 27. 14. [m] Le. 27. 8. [n] Ps. 83. 4. [o] Is. 29. 23. [p] Is. 44. 7. [q] Job 6. 4. [r] Le. 24. 8. [s] De. 33. 28. [t] Job 23. 13. [u] 2 Sa. 2. 6. [x] 1 Sa. 14. 32. [y] Ru. 1. 8. [z] Eze. 12. 25, 28. [a] Is. 44. 13. [b] Is. 46. 6. [c] Ge. 20. 9. [d] Mi. 2. 1. [e] Job 10. 8. [f] Je. 5. 27. [g] Ec. 6. 12. [h] Job 40. 23. [i] Ps. 119. 122. [k] Ps. 49. 17. [l] 1 Sa. 8. 15, 17. [m] Job 15. 29. [n] 1 Sa. 17. 25. [o] Job 14. 18. [p] Job 18. 4. [q] Job 33. 26. [r] Ps. 149. 4. [s] Ge. 45. 26. [t] Is. 53. 12. [u] Jos. 17. 10. [x] Ex. 5. 3. [y] Ex. 4. 24, 27. [z] Job 5. 14. [a] 2 Sa. 2. 13. [b] Ge. 32. 18. [c] Le. 27. 29.

[a] יִפְדּוּ וַ Kal fut. 3 pers. pl. masc.; ·וַ conv. . פדה

יִפְדְּיָה וְ pr. name masc. . . . . . פדה

יִפְדְּךָ וַ Kal fut. 3 pers. sing. masc., suff. 2 pers. sing. masc. (§ 24. rem. 21); ·וַ conv. . פדה

[יָפָה] fut. יִיפֶה, ap. יִיף, *to be fair, comely, beautiful.* Pi. *to beautify*, Je. 10. 4. Pu. יָפְיָפָה (§ 6. No. 9) *to be very beautiful.* Hithp. *to beautify oneself*, Je. 4. 30.

יָפֶה masc. dec. 9b, יָפָה fem. dec. 11a, adj.—I. *fair, comely, beautiful.*—II. *good, excellent*, Ec. 3. 11; 5. 17.

יָפוֹ, יָפוֹא pr. name *Joppa*, a maritime city in the territory of Dan.

יְפִי, יֳפִי, in pause יֹפִי, dec. 6k.—I. *beauty.*—II. *excellence, splendour.*

יְפֵה־פִיָּה adj. fem. *very beautiful*, Je. 46. 20.

יָפָה fem. of the following, d. 11a (§ 42. rem. 1) יפה

יָפֶה adj. masc. sing. dec. 9b . . . . יפה

יְפֵה, [b] יְפֵה וִ } id., constr. state, with cop. וְ [for וִיפֵה, וִיפֵה] . . . . . } יפה

יְפֵה־פִיָּה adj. fem. sing. see in its place under . יפה

יָפוֹ pr. name of a place . . . . יפה

יָפוּ Kal pret. 3 pers. pl. . . . . יפה

יָפוֹא pr. name of a place . . . . יפה

[c] יִפּוֹל Kh. יִפּוֹל, K. יִפָּל־ Kal fut. 3 pers. sing. masc. (§ 8. rem. 18) . . . . . נפל

יִפּוֹל Kal fut. 3 pers. s. m. (§ 8. r. 18, & § 17. r. 3) נפל

[d] יָפוּצוּ Kal fut. 3 pers. pl. masc. . . . פוץ

[e] יָפוֹת adj. fem., pl. abs. of יָפָה dec. 11a (§ 42. rem. 1) from יָפֶה masc. . . . . יפה

[f] יְפוֹת id. pl., constr. state . . . . יפה

[g] יָפֹזּוּ וַ Kal fut. 3 pers. pl. masc., ·וַ conv. . פזז

[h] יְפַזֵּר Piel fut. 3 pers. sing. masc. . . פזר

יָפַח Kal not used; i. q. פּוּחַ, נָפַח *to breathe.* Hithp. *to pant, sigh*, Je. 4. 31.

יָפֵחַ adj. masc. dec. 5a, *breathing, puffing out*, Ps. 27. 12.

[i] יָפֵחַ וְ׳ Kal fut. 3 p. sing. masc. ap. from יָפִיחַ . פוח

[k] יִפַּח וַ Kal fut. 3 pers. sing. masc.; ·וַ conv. . נפח

[l] יְפֵחַ וִ adj. masc. constr. [יְפֵחַ, with cop. וְ, for וִיפֵחַ, וִי׳] from יָפֵחַ dec. 5a . . יפח

[m] יִפְחָד Kal fut. 3 pers. s. m. [for יִפְחַד § 8. r. 15] פחד

[n] יִפְחָדוּ, [o] יִפְחֲדוּ } id. fut. 3 pers. pl. masc. (§ 8. rem. 15) פחד

[p] יַפְטִירוּ Hiph. fut. 3 pers. pl. masc. . . . פטר

[q] יִפְטַר וַ Kal fut. 3 pers. sing. masc.; ·וַ conv. . פטר

[r] יְפִי noun masc. sing. . . . . יפה

יֳפִי noun masc. sing. dec. 6k [for יְפִי, § 35. r. 14] יפה

יָפְיָהּ id., suff. 3 pers. sing. fem. . . . יפה

[s] יָפְיוֹ id., suff. 3 pers. sing. masc. . . יפה

יָפִיחַ וְ׳ Hiph. fut. 3 pers. sing. masc. . . . פוח

[t] יָפִיחוּ id. fut. 3 pers. pl. masc. . . . פוח

יָפְיֵךְ noun m. s., suff. 2 pers. s. f. fr. [יְפִי] d. 6k יפה

[u] יַפִּיל Hiph. fut. 3 pers. sing. masc. . . . נפל

יַפִּילוּ וַיַּ׳ id. fut. 3 pers. pl. masc.; ·וַ conv. . נפל

[oo] יַפִּילוּן id. id. with parag. ן . . . . נפל

[x] יַפִּילֵם וַ id. fut. 3 pers. sing. masc., suff. 3 pers. pl. masc.; ·וַ conv. . . . . . נפל

יָפִיעַ וְ׳ pr. name of a place . . . יפע

[y] יָפְיָפִיתָ Pu. pret. 2 pers. sing. masc. (§ 6. No. 9) יפה

[z] יָפִיץ Hiph. fut. 3 pers. sing. masc. . . פוץ

יְפִיצֵם וַ id., suff. 3 pers. pl. masc.; וַ conv. . פוץ

יָפִיק Hiph. fut. 3 pers. sing. masc. . . . פוק

[a] יָפִית Kal pret. 2 pers. sing. fem. . . . יפה

יַפֵּל וַ Hiph. fut. 3 pers. sing. masc., ap. fr. יַפִּיל נפל

[b] יִפֵּל, [c] יִפֶּל־ } Ch. Peal fut. 3 pers. sing. masc. . נפל

יִפֹּל וַיִּ׳, וְ׳, [d] יִפָּל־ וַיִּ׳ } Kal fut. 3 pers. sing. masc. (comp. § 8. rem. 18); ·וַ conv. . } נפל

יַפְלִא Hiph. fut. 3 pers. sing. masc. . . פלא

יִפָּלֵא [e] וַיִּ׳ Niph. fut. 3 pers. sing. masc.; ·וַ conv. פלא

[f] יַפְלֶה Hiph. fut. 3 pers. sing. masc. . . פלה

[g] יַפִּלוּ וַ defect. for יַפִּילוּ q. v. . . . . נפל

יִפְּלוּ, יִפְּלוּ וַיִּ׳ } Kal fut. 3 pers. pl. masc. (§ 8. r. 15); ·וַ conv. . . . . } נפל

יְפַלַּח [h] וַיְ׳ Piel fut. 3 pers. sing. masc.; וַ id. . פלח

יִפְלְחוּן Ch. Peal fut. 3 pers. pl. masc. . . . פלח

יַפְלֵט pr. name masc. . . . . פלט

[i] יְפַלְּטֵהוּ Piel fut. 3 pers. sing. masc. [יְפַלֵּט], suff. 3 pers. sing. masc. . . . . . פלט

[k] יְפַלְּטֵם [k] וַיְ׳ id., suff. 3 pers. pl. masc.; וַ conv. . פלט

[l] יַפְלִיט וְ Hiph. fut. 3 pers. sing. masc. . . פלט

[m] יְפַלֵּל וַ Piel fut. 3 pers. sing. masc.; וַ conv. . פלל

[n] יַפִּלֵם defect. for יַפִּילֵם (q. v.) . . . נפל

[o] יְפַלֵּס Piel fut. 3 pers. sing. masc. . . פלס

[p] יֶפֶן וַ Hiph. fut. 3 pers. sing. masc. ap. [from יַפְנֶה]; ·וַ conv. . . . . פנה

יִפֶן וַ, יִפְנֶה } Kal fut. 3 pers. sing. masc. ap. & full form; ·וַ id. . . . . } פנה

[a] 1 Sa. 14. 45. [b] Ge. 39. 6. [c] Pr. 22. 14. [d] Ps. 68. 2. [e] Job 42. 15. [f] Ge. 41. 2. [g] Ge. 49. 24. [h] Ps. 147. 16. [i] Hab. 2. 3. [k] Ge. 2. 7. [l] Ps. 27. 12. [m] Is. 19. 17. [n] Mi. 7. 17. [o] Is. 44. 11. [oo] Job 29. 24. [p] Ps. 22. 8. [q] 1 Sa. 19. 10. [r] Eze. 28. 7. [s] Zec. 9. 17. [t] Pr. 29. 8. [u] Ex. 21. 27. [x] Ps. 78. 55. [y] Ps. 45. 3. [z] Job 37. 11. [a] Ca. 7. 7. [b] Da. 3. 6, 10, 11. [c] Ezr. 7. 20. [d] 2 Sa. 2. 23. [e] 2 Sa. 13. 2. [f] Ex. 11. 7. [g] Jon. 1. 7. [h] 2 Ki. 4. 39. [i] Ps. 22. 9. [k] Ps. 37. 40. [l] Is. 5. 29. [m] Ps. 106. 30. [n] Ps. 140. 11. [o] Ps. 78. 50. [p] Ju. 15. 4.

יִפְנֶה pr. name masc. . . . . . פנה

וַיִּ֫פֶן, וַיִּפֶן Kal fut. 3 pers. pl. masc.; וַ conv. . פנה

[a] וַיִּפָּסֵחַ Niph. fut. 3 pers. sing. masc.; וַ id. . פסח

[b] וַיְפַסְּחוּ Piel fut. 3 pers. pl. masc.; וַ id. . . פסח

[c] וַיִּפְסֹל Kal fut. 3 pers. sing. masc.; וַ id. . . פסל

[d] וַיִּפְסְלוּ id. fut. 3 pers. pl. masc.; וַ id. . . פסל

יָפַע. Hiph. הוֹפִיעַ.—I. *to cause to shine*, Job 37. 15.—II. *to shine forth*.

פּוּעָה (for יְפוּעָה *splendid*) pr. name f. Ex. 1. 15.

יִפְעָה f. (no pl.) *brilliancy, beauty*, Eze. 28. 7, 17.

יָפִיעַ (*splendid*) pr. name—I. of a town in the tribe of Zebulon, Jos. 19. 12.—II. of a king of Lachish, Jos. 10. 3.—III. of a son of David, 2 Sa. 5. 15.

מֵפַעַת, מֵיפַעַת (*splendour*) pr. name of a Levitical city in the tribe of Reuben.

[e] יִפְעַל, יִפְעָל } Kal fut. 3 pers. sing. masc. (§ 8. rem. 15) פעל

[f] וַיִּפְעָלֵהוּ id., suff. 3 pers. sing. masc. (§ 16. r. 12); וַ conv. . . . . . . פעל

[g] יִפְעָתֶךָ noun fem. sing., suff. 2 pers. sing. masc. [for יְפָעָתְךָ, from יִפְעָה] . . . . יפע

[h] יָפִיץ, וַיָּפֶץ } Hiph. fut. 3 pers. sing. masc., ap. and conv. from יָפִיץ . . . . פוץ

[i] יִפְצֶה Kal fut. 3 pers. sing. masc. . . . . פצה

יָפֻצוּ, [k] וַיָּפֻצוּ, וְ Kal fut. 3 pers. pl. masc.; וַ conv. . פוץ

[l] יִפְצְחוּ Kal fut. 3 pers. pl. masc. . . . . . פצח

[m] יִפְצְחוּ Kh. יִפְצְחוּ q. v.; K. וּפִצְחוּ Kal imp. pl. m., וּ before labial . . . . . . פצח

[n] וַיְפַצֵּל Piel fut. 3 pers. sing. masc.; וַ conv. . פצל

[o] וַיְפַצְפְּצֵנִי Pilpel fut. 3 pers. sing. masc. [יְפַצְפֵּץ, § 6. No. 4], suff. 1 pers. sing.; וַ id. . פוץ

[p] יְפֹצֵץ Pilel fut. 3 pers. sing. masc. . . . . פוץ

וַיִּפְצַר Kal fut. 3 pers. sing. masc.; וַ conv. . פצר

וַיִּפְצְרוּ id. fut. 3 pers. pl. masc.; וַ id. . . פצר

וַיָּפֶק Hiph. fut. 3 pers. sing. masc. ap. and conv. from יָפִיק . . . . . . פוק

וַיַּפְקֵד, וְ, וַיִּ Hiph. fut. 3 pers. sing. masc. ap. fr. יַפְקִיד; וַ conv. . . . . . פקד

יִפָּקֵד, [q] וַיִּ, [r] יִפָּקֶד } Niph. fut. 3 pers. sing. masc. (§ 9. rem. 3); וַ id. . . . . פקד

יִפְקֹד, וְ, וַיִּ Kal fut. 3 pers. sing. masc.; וַ id. . פקד

[s] וַיַּפְקִדֵהוּ Hiph. fut. 3 pers. sing. masc., suff. 3 pers. sing. masc.; וַ id. . . . . פקד

[t] וַיַּפְקִדוּ id. fut. 3 pers. pl. masc.; וַ id. . . פקד

יִפָּקְדוּ, וַיִּפָּקְדוּ } Niph. fut. 3 pers. pl. masc. (comp. § 8. rem. 15); וַ conv. . . . פקד

[u] יִפְקְדוּ, [x] וַיִּפְקְדוּ } Kal fut. 3 pers. pl. masc. (§ 8. rem. 15); וַ id. . . . . פקד

[y] יִפְקְדֵם, וַיִּ id. fut. 3 p. s. m., suff. 3 p. pl. m.; וַ id. פקד

[z] יִפְקְדֵנִי id. id., suff. 1 pers. sing. . . . . פקד

יִפְקוֹד full form for יִפְקֹד q. v., (§ 8. rem. 18) פקד

[a] יַפְקִיד Hiph. fut. 3 pers. sing. masc. . . . פקד

וַיִּפְקַח Kal fut. 3 pers. sing. masc.; וַ conv. . פקח

[b] וַיַּפְקִידֵם Hiph. fut. 3 p. s. m., suff. 3 p. pl. m.; וַ id. פקד

יָפֵר, [c] וַיָּפֵר } Hiph. fut. 3 pers. sing. m. (§ 18. rem. 11.) פרר

[d] וַיֶּפֶר Hiph. fut. 3 pers. sing. masc. ap. [from יַפְרֶה]; וַ conv. . . . . . פרה

יִפָּרֵד Niph. fut. 3 pers. sing. masc. . . . פרד

[e] וַיַּפְרִדוּ Hiph. fut. 3 pers. pl. masc.; וַ conv. . פרד

[f] יִפָּרְדוּ, [g] וַיִּפָּרְדוּ } Niph. fut. 3 pers. pl. masc. (§ 8. rem. 15); וַ id. . . . . פרד

[h] יְפָרֵדוּ Piel fut. 3 p. pl. m. [for יְפָרְדוּ comp. § 8. r. 15] פרד

[i] יִפְרֶה Kal fut. 3 pers. sing. masc. . . . פרה

[k] יַפְרַח defect. for יַפְרִיחַ (q. v.) . . . . פרח

[l] וַיָּפֵרוּ Hiph. fut. 3 pers. pl. masc.; וַ conv. . פרר

יִפְרוּ, [m] וַ, [n] וַיִּ Kal fut. 3 pers. pl. masc.; וַ id. . פרה

יִפְרַח, יִפְרָח } Kal fut. 3 pers. sing. masc. (§ 8. rem. 15) פרח

[o] יִפְרְחוּ, [p] וְיִפְרָחוּ } id. fut. 3 pers. pl. masc. (§ 8. rem. 15) פרח

[q] יַפְרִיא Hiph. fut. 3 pers. sing. masc. . . . פרה

יַפְרִיד Hiph. fut. 3 pers. sing. masc. . . . פרד

[r] יַפְרִיחַ Hiph. fut. 3 pers. pl. masc. . . . פרח

[s] יַפְרִיחוּ id. fut. 3 pers. pl. masc. . . . . פרח

[t] יַפְרִיס Hiph. fut. 3 pers. sing. masc. . . . פרס

[u] וְיַפְרְךָ Hiph. fut. 3 pers. sing. masc. [יַפְרֶה], suff. 2 pers. sing. masc. (§ 24. rem. 21); וְ conv. פרה

[x] יִפְרֹם Kal fut. 3 pers. sing. masc. . . . פרם

[ff] יְפֵרֶנּוּ Hiph. fut. 3 pers. sing. masc. (יָפֵר), suff. 3 pers. sing. masc. [for יְפֵרֶהוּ] . . . פרר

[y] יִפְרְסוּ Kal fut. 3 pers. pl. masc. . . . . פרס

[z] יִפָּרַע Niph. fut. 3 pers. sing. masc. . . . פרע

[a] יִפְרָע Kal fut. 3 pers. s. m. [for יִפְרַע § 8. rem. 15] פרע

[b] וַיְפַרְפְּרֵנִי Pilp. fut. 3 pers. sing. masc., suff. 1 pers. sing. (§ 6. No. 4); וַ conv. . . . פרר

יִפְרֹץ, וַיִּ, [c] יִפְרָץ, וַיִּ } Kal fut. 3 pers. sing. masc. (§ 8. rem. 18); וַ id. . . . . פרץ

יִפְרְצוּ, וַיִּפְרְצוּ } id. fut. 3 pers. pl. masc. (§ 8. rem. 15); וַ id. . . . . פרץ

---

[a] 2 Sa. 4. 4. [b] 1 Ki. 18. 26. [c] Ex. 34. 4. [d] 1 Ki. 5. 32. [e] Ps. 7. 14, 16. [f] Is. 44. 12. [g] Eze. 28. 7, 17. [h] Job 38. 24. [i] Job 35. 16. [k] Nu. 10. 35. [l] Is. 55. 12. [m] Is. 49. 13. [n] Ge. 30. 37. [o] Job 16. 12. [p] Je. 23. 29. [q] 1 Sa. 20. 25, 27. [r] Pr. 19. 23. [s] Ge. 39. 4. [t] Je. 37. 21. [u] Je. 3. 16. [x] 1 Sa. 14. 17. [y] Zep. 2. 7. [z] 1 Sa. 20. 6. [a] Is. 10. 28. [b] 1 Ch. 26. 32. [c] Ne. 4. 9. [d] Ps. 105. 24. [e] 2 Ki. 2. 11. [f] Ge. 25. 23. [ff] Nu. 30. 14. [g] Ge. 13. 11. [h] Ho. 4. 14. [i] Is. 11. 1. [k] Job 14. 9. [l] Eze. 44. 7. [m] Is. 45. 8. [n] Ge. 47. 27. [o] Pr. 11. 28. [p] Ho. 14. 8. [q] Ho. 13. 15. [r] Pr. 14. 11. [s] Ps. 92. 14. [t] Le. 11. 5. [u] Ge. 28. 3. [x] Le. 21. 10. [y] Je. 16. 7. [z] Pr. 29. 18. [a] Le. 21. 10. [b] Job 16. 12. [c] Ex. 19. 24.

יִפְרְצֵנִי[a] Kal fut. 3 pers. sing. masc., suff. 1 pers. sing. פרץ
יְפָרֵק[b] Piel fut. 3 pers. sing. masc. . . פרק
יִפְרְקֵנִי[c] וַ Kal fut. 3 pers. sing. masc., suff. 1 pers. sing.; ·וַ conv. . . . . פרק
יַפְרִשׁ[d] Hiph. fut. 3 pers. sing. masc. . . פרשׁ
יְפָרֵשׂ[e] Piel fut. 3 pers. sing. masc. . . . פרשׂ
יִפְרֹשׂ וַיִּ׳, וְיִ׳[f] Kal fut. 3 pers. sing. masc.; ·וַ conv. פרשׂ
יִפְרְשֵׂהוּ וַ id., suff. 3 pers. sing. masc.; ·וַ id. . פרשׂ
יִפָּרְשׁוּ[g] Niph. fut. 3 pers. pl. masc. [for יִפָּרְשׂוּ, comp. § 8. rem. 15] . . . . . פרשׂ
יִפְרְשׂוּ[h] וַיִּ׳ Kal fut. 3 pers. pl. masc.; ·וַ conv. . פרשׂ
יִפְשֶׂה[i] Kal fut. 3 pers. sing. masc. . . . פשׂה
יְפַשְּׁחֵנִי[k] וַ Piel fut. 3 pers. s. m., suff. 1 pers. s.; וַ conv. פשׁח
יַפְשֵׁט[l] וַ Hiph. fut. 3 pers. sing. masc. ap. [from יַפְשִׁיט]; ·וַ id. . . . . . פשׁט
יִפְשַׁט[m] וַ Kal fut. 3 pers. sing. masc.; ·וַ id. . פשׁט
יַפְשִׁטוּ[n] וַ Hiph. fut. 3 pers. pl. masc.; ·וַ id. . פשׁט
יִפְשְׁטוּ[o] }
יִפְשֹׁטוּ[p] וַיִּ׳ } Kal fut. 3 pers. pl. masc. (§ 8. rem. 15); ·וַ id. . . } פשׁט
יַפְשִׁיטֻהוּ[q] וַ Hiph. fut. 3 p. pl. m., suff. 3 p. s. m.; ·וַ id. פשׁט
יַפְשִׁיטוּ[r] וַ id. fut. 3 pers. pl. masc.; ·וַ id. . . פשׁט
יִפְשַׁע[s] וַיִּ׳ Kal fut. 3 pers. sing. masc.; ·וַ id. . פשׁע
יִפְשְׁעוּ וַ id. fut. 3 pers. pl. masc.; ·וַ id. . . פשׁע

יָפַת Root not used; Arab. ופת *to be entire, perfect,* conj. III, *to arrive* (Lee).

מוֹפֵת masc. dec. 7 b.—I. *sign, wonder.*—II. *mark, intimation, portent.*

יֶפֶת וָ׳ pr. name masc. for יֶפֶת (comp. § 35. rem. 2) פתה
יַפְתְּ[t] Hiph. fut. 3 pers. sing. masc. ap. [from יַפְתֶּה § 24. rem. 16] . . . פתה
יִפְתְּ[u] וַ Kal fut. 3 pers. sing. masc. ap. (from יִפְתֶּה § 24. rem. 3); ·וַ conv. . . . פתה
יְפַת }
יְפַת וְ } adj. f. s. constr. [with cop. וְ, for וִיפַת, וִי׳] from יָפָה dec. 11a, from יָפֶה masc. } יפה
יְפֹת[x] }
יְפֹת[y] וְ } id. pl., construct state (comp. preceding) יפה
יֶפֶת וָ׳ pr. name masc.; for וָ see lett. וְ . פתה
יְפַתֶּה Piel fut. 3 pers. sing. masc. . . . פתה
יִפְתֶּה[z] Kal fut. 3 pers. sing. masc. . . פתה
יְפֻתֶּה Pual fut. 3 pers. sing. masc. . . . פתה
יְפַתּוּהוּ[a] וַ Piel fut. 3 p. pl. m., suff. 3 p. s. m.; וַ conv. פתה
יְפַתּוּךָ[b] id., suff. 2 pers. sing. masc. . . . פתה
יִפָּתַח[c] וַיִּ׳[d] }
יִפָּתֵחַ } Niph. fut. 3 pers. sing. masc. (§ 15. rem. 1); ·וַ conv. . . } פתח
יְפַתַּח[e] וַ׳ Piel fut. 3 pers. sing. masc.; ·וַ id. . פתח
יִפְתָּח pr. name masc. . . . . . פתח

יִפְתַּח וַיִּ׳, וְיִ׳[f] Kal fut. 3 pers. sing. masc.; ·וַ conv. פתח
יְפַתְּחֵהוּ[g] וַ Piel fut. 3 p. s. m., suff. 3 p. s. m.; וַ id. פתח
יִפָּתְחוּ[h] Niph. fut. 3 pers. pl. masc. . . פתח
יִפְתָּחוּ[i] וַ }
יִפְתְּחוּ[k] וַ } Kal fut. 3 pers. pl. masc. (§ 8. rem. 15); ·וַ conv. . . } פתח
יִפְתָּחוּם[l] id., suff. 3 pers. pl. masc. (§ 16. rem. 12) . פתח
יָפָתִי[m] adj. fem. sing., suff. 1 pers. sing. from יָפָה (§ 42. rem. 2), from יָפֶה masc. . יפה
יִפְתָּר־[n] וַ Kal fut. 3 pers. sing. masc. [for יִפְתֹּר § 8. rem. 18]; ·וַ conv. . . . פתר

יָצָא וְ׳ fut. יֵצֵא, imp. צֵא, inf. c. צֵאת (§ 25. No. 2d). —I. *to go out, go forth*; with מִן, also acc. of the place whence, with בְּ (rarely מִן) of the place through or by which one goes out.—II. *to come forth, to issue, descend,* of children, posterity.—III. *to escape,* as danger, with אֶת Ecc. 7. 18.—IV. *to rise,* as the sun, stars, &c.—V. *to shoot forth, spring up,* as plants; *to spring forth,* of water.—VI. *to go forth, be issued, published,* as a decree.—VII. *to go out, to end,* of a period of time. Hiph. הוֹצִיא.—I. *to cause to go, come out* or *forth, to lead, bring forth* or *out.*—II. *to cause to spring up, to yield,* as the earth plants.—III. *to cause to lay out,* as money, *to exact,* with עַל, 2 Ki. 15. 20.—IV. *to spread abroad, to publish,* with עַל, לְ of the person. —V. *to produce, make,* Is. 54. 16.—VI. *to take out, to separate,* Je. 15. 19. Hoph. *to be led, brought forth* or *out.*

יְצָא Chald. Shaph. שֵׁיצִא, שֵׁיצָא (§ 48) *to bring to an end, to finish.*

יָצִיא masc. dec. 3 a, *issued, proceeded,* 2 Ch. 32. 21.

צֵאָה fem. dec. 10 (for יְצָאָה) *excrement, ordure.*

צוֹא or צוֹאִי adj. masc. *filthy,* Zec. 3. 3, 4.

צֹאָה, צוֹאָה fem. dec. 10, *excrement, ordure, filth.*

צֶאֱצָאִים m. pl. (of צֶאֱצָא dec. 1, § 31. rem. 1).—I. *productions* of the earth.—II. *offspring, children.*

מוֹצָא masc. dec. 1 b (§ 31. rem. 1).—I. *a going out, an outgoing; a rising,* of the sun.—II. *the place of going* or *coming out,* applied to *a gate, fountain, the east* (where the sun rises).—III. *that which comes out,* i. e. *proceeds, is uttered,* as words, speech.—IV. *origin, race, breed,* 1 Ki. 10. 28.—V. pr. name masc. of two different persons.

מוֹצָאָה fem. dec. 10 (comp. § 31. rem. 1).—I *a going out, origin,* Mi. 5. 1.—II. *draught-house,* 2 Ki. 10. 27.

[a] Job 16. 14. [b] Zec. 11. 16. [c] Ps. 136. 24. [d] Pr. 23. 32. [e] Is. 25. 11. [f] Je. 49. 22. [g] Eze. 17. 21. [h] Nu. 4. 7, 11. [i] Le. 13. 35. [k] La. 3. 11. [l] Nu. 20. 28. [m] 1 Sa. 19. 24. [n] 1 Sa. 31. 9. [o] Eze. 26. 16. [p] Eze. 44. 19. [q] 1 Ch. 10. 9. [r] Ge. 37. 23. [s] Pr. 28. 21. [t] Ge. 9. 27. [u] Job 31. 27. [x] Ge. 41. 4. [y] Ge. 41. 18. [z] De. 11. 16. [a] Ps. 78. 36. [b] Pr. 1. 10. [c] Eze. 24. 27. [d] Eze. 33. 22. [e] Is. 28. 24. [f] Job 11. 5. [g] Ps. 105. 20. [h] Ne. 7. 3. [i] Ju. 3. 25. [k] Ge. 44. 11. [l] Ne. 13. 19. [m] Ca. 2. 10, 13. [n] Ge. 41. 12.

תּוֹצָאוֹת fem. pl. (of תּוֹצָאָה dec. 11a).—I. *termination, extremity.*—II. *deliverance, escape,* Ps. 68. 21.—III. *issue, result,* Pr. 4. 23.

יָצֹא Kal inf. absolute . . . . . יצא

יֵצֵא וַיֵּ', וְ' id. fut. 3 pers. sing. masc.; ·וַ conv. יצא

יֹצֵא וַ Hiph. fut. 3 pers. sing. masc., ap. from יוֹצִיא (§ 20. rem. 11); ·וַ id. . . יצא

יֹצֵא [a]וְ' Kal part. act. masc. dec. 7b . . יצא

יֹצֵא[b] [c]וַיֹּ' defect. for יוֹצִיא (q. v.) . . . יצא

יָצְאָה[d] יָצָאָה } וְ' Kal pret. 3 pers. sing. fem. (§ 8. rem. 7) יצא

יֹצִאֻהוּ[e] וַ Hiph. fut. 3 pers. pl. masc. (יוֹצִיאוּ), suff. 3 pers. sing. masc.; ·וַ conv. . . יצא

יָצְאוּ יָצָאוּ } וְ' Kal pret. 3 pers. pl. (§ 8. rem. 7) . יצא

יָצְאוֹ[f] Kh. יָצְאוֹ q. v., K. יְצָא (q. v.) . . יצא

יֵצְאוּ [h]וַיֵּ', [g]וְ' ; יֵצֵאוּ וַיֵּ', וְ' } Kal fut. 3 pers. pl. masc. (comp. § 8. rem. 15); ·וַ conv. . } יצא

יֵצְאוּ[k] Kh. יֵצְאוּ q. v., K. צְאוּ (q. v.) . . יצא

יֹצִאוּ[l] וְ' Hiph. fut. 3 pers. pl. for יוֹצִיאוּ; ·וַ conv. יצא

יֹצְאוֹת Kal part. act. fem., pl. of יֹצֵאת (§ 23. rem. 4) from יֹצֵא masc. . . . . . יצא

יֹצְאֵי id. pl. construct masc. dec. 7b . . יצא

יֹצְאִים id. id., absolute state . . . יצא

יֹצִאֲךָ[m] וַ Hiph. fut. 3 p.s.m. (יוֹצִיא), suff. 2 p.s.m.; וַ conv. יצא

יֹצִאֵנוּ[qq] וַ id. with suff. 1 pers. pl.; וַ id. . . יצא

יָצָאנוּ[n] [o]וְ' Kal pret. 1 pers. pl. . . . יצא

יְצָאֻנִי[p] id. pret. 3 pers. pl. with suff. 1 pers. sing. . יצא

יָצָאתָ וְ' id. pret. 2 pers. sing. masc. . . יצא

יָצָאת[q] וְ id. pret. 2 pers. sing. fem. . . . יצא

יֹצְאֹת[r] pl. of the following . . . . יצא

יֹצֵאת Kal part. act. fem. [for יֹצֵאת § 23. rem. 4] from יֹצֵא masc. . . . . . יצא

יָצָאתִי [s]וְ' id. pret. 1 pers. sing. . . . . יצא

יְצָאתֶם וִ } יְצָאתֶם וְ } id. pret. 2 pers. pl. masc., with conj. וְ [for וִיצָאתֶם, וְ'] . . . יצא

יָצַב Kal not used; i. q. נצב *to set, put, place.* Hithp. הִתְיַצֵּב.—I. *to set* or *place oneself,* const. with לִפְנֵי, עַל.—II. *to stand; to stand* before (לִפְנֵי) any one, i. e. to minister unto him.—III. *to stand firm,* as a conqueror, with בִּפְנֵי, לִפְנֵי, עִם.—IV. *to stand up* for any one, to assist him, with לְ of the person.

יַצֵּב Chald. Pa. *to certify,* Da. 7. 19.

יַצִּיב Chald. adj.—I. *firm, fixed, settled,* Da. 6. 13. —II. *certain, true;* מִן יַצִּיב *certainly,* Da. 2. 8.

יַצֵּב [t]וַיַּ', וְ' } יַצֶּב־ וַ } Hiph. fut. 3 pers. sing. masc., ap. from יַצִּיב (§ 11. r. 7); ·וַ conv. } נצב

יִצְבָּא Chald. Peal fut. 3 pers. sing. masc. . צבא

יִצְבְּאוּ[u] וַ Kal fut. 3 pers. pl. masc.; ·וַ conv. . צבא

יַצִּבוּ וַ Hiph. fut. 3 pers. pl. masc.; ·וַ id. נצב

יִצְבָּט־[y] וַ Kal fut. 3 pers. sing. masc. [for יִצְבֹּט § 8. rem. 18]; ·וַ id. . . . . צבט

יִצְבֹּר וַיִּ' Kal fut. 3 pers. sing. masc.; ·וַ id. צבר

יִצְבְּרוּ [x]וַיִּ', [z]וְ' id. fut. 3 pers. pl. masc.; ·וַ id. . צבר

יָצַג Kal not used; cogn. יָצַב, יָצַק. Hiph. הִצִּיג (§ 20. rem. 16).—I. *to set, put, place.*—II. *to establish,* Am. 5. 15.—III. *to let stay, to leave,* Ge. 33. 15. Hoph. הֻצַּג *to be left,* Ex. 10. 24.

יַצֵּג וַ Kal fut. 3 p. s. m. ap. [from יַצִּיג]; ·וַ conv. יצג

יֻצַּג[b] Hoph. fut. 3 pers. sing. masc. [for יֻצַּג comp. § 8. rem. 15] . . . . יצג

יַצִּגוּ[c] וַ Hiph. fut. 3 pers. pl. masc.; ·וַ conv. יצג

יַצִּגֵם[d] וַ id. fut. 3 pers. sing. masc., suff. 3 pers. pl. masc.; ·וַ id. . . . . יצג

יַצְדִּיק[e] Hiph. fut. 3 pers. sing. masc. . . צדק

יִצְדָּק יִצְדַּק } Kal fut. 3 pers. sing. masc. (§ 8. rem. 15) צדק

יִצְדְּקוּ[f] וְ } יִצְדָּקוּ[g] } id. fut. 3 pers. pl. masc. (§ 8. rem. 15) צדק

יַצְהִירוּ[h] Hiph. fut. 3 pers. pl. masc. . צהר

יִצְהָלוּ[i] Kal fut. 3 pers. pl. m. [for יִצְהֲלוּ § 8. r. 15] צהל

יִצְהָר וְ' noun masc. sing. dec. 2b, also pr. name m. צהר

יִצְהָרֶיךָ[k] וְ id. pl., suff. 2 pers. sing. masc. צהר

יִצְהָרֶךָ וְ id. sing., suff. 2 pers. sing. m. [for יִצְהָרְךָ] צהר

יְצַו[l] וַ' Pi. fut. 3 pers. sing. masc. ap. for יְצַוֶּה צוה

יְצַוּ[m] וַ Kh. יְצַו q. v., K. יְצַוּוּ (q. v.) . צוה

יָצוֹא Kal inf. absolute . . . . יצא

יָצוּד[n] Kal fut. 3 pers. sing. masc. . . צוד

יָצוּדוּ[o] id. fut. 3 pers. pl. masc. . . . צוד

יְצוּדֶנּוּ[p] id. fut. 3 pers. sing. masc., suff. 3 pers. s. m. צוד

יְצַוֶּה וַ' Piel fut. 3 pers. sing. masc.; וַ conv. . צוה

יְצֻוֶּה[q] Pual fut. 3 pers. sing. masc. . . צוה

יְצַוֵּהוּ וַ Piel fut. 3 pers. sing. masc., suff. 3 pers. sing. masc.; וַ conv. . . . צוה

יְצַוֵּהוּ[r] וַ Kh. יְצַוֵּהוּ q. v., K. יְצַוֶּה (q. v.) . צוה

יְצַוּוּ וַ Piel fut. 3 pers. pl. masc.; וַ conv. . צוה

יִצְוָחוּ[s] Kal fut. 3 pers. pl. m. [for יִצְוְחוּ § 8. rem. 15] צוח

יְצַוְּךָ[t] וִ Piel fut. 3 pers. s. m. (יְצַוֶּה), suff. 2 pers. s. m. (§ 24. r. 21); with conj. וְ [for וִיצַוְּךָ, וְ'] צוה

יָצֹם[u] וַ Kal fut. 3 pers. sing. masc. ap. [for יָצֹם, יָצוּם § 21. rem. 7 & 8]; ·וַ conv. . צום

[a] Je. 37. 4. [b] Job 28. 11. [c] Ju. 19. 25. [d] Is. 28. 29. [e] Ge. 19. 16. [f] Eze. 46. 9. [g] Je. 15. 1. [h] Ge. 34. 26. [i] Je. 46. 9. [k] Je. 50. 8. [l] 1 Ki. 10. 29. 2 Ki. 10. 26. [m] De. 5. 15. [n] Nu. 11. 20. [o] 1 Sa. 11. 3. [p] Je. 10. 20. [q] Je. 31. 4. [r] Ge. 24. 13. [s] 1 Sa. 17. 35. [t] De. 32. 8. [u] Pr. 15. 25. [x] Nu. 31. 7. [y] Ru. 2. 14. [z] Ge. 41. 35. [a] Ex. 8. 10. [b] Ex. 10. 24. [c] 2 Sa. 6. 17. [d] Ge. 47. 2. [e] Is. 53. 11. [f] Is. 43. 9. [g] Is. 45. 25. [h] Job 24. 11. [i] Je. 5. 8. [k] De. 7. 13. [l] De. 28. 8. [m] Ju. 21. 20. [n] Le. 17. 13. [o] Mi. 7. 2. [p] Ps. 140. 12. [q] Ex. 34. 34. [qq] Nu. 20. 16. [r] 2 Ki. 16. 15. [s] Is. 42. 11. [t] 1 Ch. 22. 12. [u] 1 Ki. 21. 27.

[a]יְצַוֵּם	וַ' Piel fut. 3 pers. sing. masc. (יְצַוֶּה), suff. 3 pers. pl. masc. (§ 24. rem. 21); וַ conv.	צוה
יָצ֫וּמוּ	וַ Kal fut. 3 pers. pl. masc.; ·וַ id. .	צום
[b]יְצַוֵּנוּ	וַ Piel fut. 3 pers. sing. masc. (יְצַוֶּה), suff. 1 pers. pl. (§ 24. rem. 21); וַ id. . .	צוה
[c]יָצוֹעַ	Kh. יָצוּעַ Kal part. p., K. יָצִיעַ noun m. s. d. 3a	יצע
[d]יְצוּעָי	Kal part. p. pl., suff. 1 p. s. from יָצוּעַ dec. 3a	יצע
[e]יְצוּעֵי	id. pl., construct state . . .	יצע
[f]יְצוּעִי	id. sing. with suff. 1 pers. sing. . .	יצע
[g]יָצוּק	Kal fut. 3 pers. sing. masc. . .	צוק
יָצוּק	[h]וְ' Kal part. pass. sing. masc. dec. 3a .	יצק
[i]יְצוּקִים	id. pl., absolute state . . .	יצק
יִצְחָק	וְ' pr. name masc.	צחק
[k]יִצְחָק [l]יִצְחַק־	וַ Kal fut. 3 pers. sing. masc. (§ 8. rem. 15, comp. § 35. rem. 17); ·וַ conv. .	צחק
[m]יְצַחֵק	וַ Piel fut. 3 pers. s. m. (§ 14. rem. 1); ·וַ id.	צחק
יִצְחַר	Kh. יִצְחָר, K. וְצֹחַר pr. name masc. . .	צחר
יִצְטַבַּע	Chald. Ithpa. fut. 3 pers. sing. masc. [for יִתְצַבַּע, comp. § 12. rem. 3] . .	צבע
[uu]יִצְטַיָּרוּ	וַ Hithpa. fut. 3 pers. pl. masc. [for יִתְצַיְּרוּ, § 12. rem. 3]; ·וַ conv. . . .	ציר
[n]יֹצִיאֻהוּ	וַ Hiph. fut. 3 pers. pl. masc., suff. 3 pers. sing. masc. [for יוֹצִיאוּהוּ, § 20. r. 11]; ·וַ id.	יצא
יֹצִיאוּ	וַ'' id. fut. 3 pers. pl. masc. (v. id.); ·וַ id.	יצא
יֹצִיאֵנוּ	וַ id. fut. 3 pers. s. m., suff. 1 pers. pl. (v. id.)	יצא
[o]יַצִּיב	Hiph. fut. 3 pers. sing. masc. . .	נצב
[p]יַצִּיב	[q]וְ' Chald. adj. masc. dec. 1 . . .	יצב
יַצִּיבָא	[r]וְ' id., emph. state	יצב
[s]יַצִּבֵנִי	וַ Hiph. fut. 3 pers. sing. masc., suff. 1 pers. sing.; ·וַ conv.	נצב
יַצִּינוּ	וַ Hiph. fut. 3 pers. pl. masc.; ·וַ id. .	יצג
יַצִּיל	Hiph. fut. 3 pers. sing. masc. . . .	נצל
[t]יַצִּילֶהָ	וַ id. id., suff. 3 pers. sing. fem.; ·וַ conv.	נצל
[u]יַצִּילֵהוּ	id. id., suff. 3 pers. sing. masc. . .	נצל
יַצִּילוּ	id. fut. 3 pers. pl. masc. . . .	נצל
[x]יַצִּילוּהָ	וַ id. id., suff. 3 pers. sing. fem.; ·וַ conv.	נצל
[y]יַצִּילְךָ [z]יַצִּילֶךָּ	id. fut. 3 pers. sing. masc., suff. 2 pers. sing. masc. (§ 2. rem. 2) . .	נצל
[a]יַצִּילֻךְ	id. fut. 3 pers. pl. masc., suff. 2 pers. s. fem.	נצל
יַצִּילֵם	id. fut. 3 pers. sing. masc., suff. 3 pers. pl. m.	נצל
[b]יַצִּילֶנָּה	id. id., suff. 3 pers. sing. fem. (§ 2. rem. 3)	נצל
יַצִּילֵנוּ	[c]וַ'' id. id., suff. 1 pers. pl. . . .	נצל
[d]יַצִּילֶנּוּ	id. id., suff. 3 pers. sing. masc. . .	נצל
יַצִּילֵנִי	id. id., suff. 1 pers. sing. . . .	נצל

[e]יַצִּיעַ	Hiph. fut. 3 pers. sing. masc. (§ 20. rem. 16)	יצע
יָצִיץ	Hiph. fut. 3 pers. sing. masc. . .	צוץ
יָצִיצוּ	[f]וְ', [g]וַ'' id. fut. 3 pers. pl. masc.; ·וַ conv. .	צוץ
[h]יָצִיק	Hiph. fut. 3 pers. sing. masc. . .	צוק
[i]יָצִיקוּ	id. fut. 3 pers. pl. masc. . . .	צוק
יַצִּיתוּ	וַ Hiph. fut. 3 p. pl. m. (§ 20. r. 16); ·וַ conv.	יצת
יַצֵּל	[k]וְ', וַ'' Kal fut. 3 pers. sing. masc. ap. from יַצִּיל; ·וַ id.	נצל
[l]יִצְלֶה	Kal fut. 3 pers. sing. masc. . . .	צלה
[m]יַצִּלֵהוּ	וַ Hiph. fut. 3 pers. sing. masc., suff. 3 pers. sing. masc.; ·וַ conv. . . .	נצל
יַצְלַח	וַ Hiph. fut. 3 p. s. m., ap. from יַצְלִיחַ; ·וַ id.	צלח
יִצְלָח יִצְלַח	Kal fut. 3 pers. sing. masc. (§ 8. rem. 15)	צלח
יַצְלִיחַ	Hiph. fut. 3 pers. sing. masc. . . .	צלח
יַצְלִיחוּ	[n]וְ', [o]וַ'' id. fut. 3 pers. pl. masc; ·וַ conv.	צלח
[p]יַצִּלֵם	וַ Hiph. fut. 3 p. s. m., suff. 3 p. pl. m.; ·וַ id.	נצל
יַצִּלֵנִי	[q]וְ', [r]וַ'' id. with suff. 1 pers. sing. .	נצל
[s]יָצֹם	וַ Kal fut. 3 pers. s. m., ap. and conv. fr. יָצוּם	צום
יִצְמָא	וַ Kal fut. 3 pers. sing. masc.; ·וַ conv. .	צמא
[t]יִצְמָאוּ	[u]וַ'' id. fut. 3 pers. pl. masc. [for יִצְמְאוּ § 8. rem. 15]	צמא
[x]יִצָּמֶד	וַ Niph. fut. 3 p. s. m. (§ 9. rem. 3); ·וַ conv.	צמד
[y]יִצָּמְדוּ	וַ id. fut. 3 pers. pl. masc.; ·וַ id. . .	צמד
[z]יָצֻמוּ	וַ'' Kal fut. 3 p. pl. m. def. for יָצוּמוּ; ·וַ id.	צום
[a]יַצְמַח	וַ Hiph. fut. 3 p. s. m. ap. from יַצְמִיחַ; ·וַ id.	צמח
יְצַמֵּחַ	Piel fut. 3 pers. sing. masc. . .	צמח
יִצְמָח [b]יִצְמַח	[c]וַ'' Kal fut. 3 pers. sing. masc. (§ 8. rem. 15); ·וַ conv. . . .	צמח
[d]יִצְמָחוּ	id. fut. 3 pers. pl. m. [for יִצְמְחוּ § 8. rem. 15]	צמח
יַצְמִיחַ	Hiph. fut. 3 pers. sing. masc. . .	צמח
[e]יַצְמִיתֵם	Hiph. fut. 3 pers. sing. m., suff. 3 pers. pl. m.	צמת
[f]יִצְנֹף	Kal fut. 3 pers. sing. masc. . . .	צנף
[g]יִצְנָפְךָ	id., suff. 2 pers. sing. masc. . .	צנף

[יָצַע] *to spread down, to strew*; only part. יָצוּעַ, (*a*) *bed, couch*; (*b*) *floor, story*, 1 Ki. 6. 5, 6, 10. Kh. Hiph. הִצִּיעַ (§ 20. rem. 16) *to spread down, to strew*. Hoph. יֻצַּע pass. of Hiph.

יָצִיעַ masc. *floor, story*, 1 Ki. 6. 5, 6, 10. Keri.

מַצָּע masc. *bed, couch*, Is. 28. 20.

יֻצַּע	Hoph. fut. 3 pers. sing. masc. (§ 20. r. 16)	יצע
[h]יִצְעָד	Kal fut. 3 pers. sing. m. [for יִצְעַד § 8. r. 15]	צעד
[i]יִצְעָדוּ	id. fut. 3 pers. pl. masc. [for יִצְעֲדוּ v. id.]	צעד
[k]יִצְעָן	Kal fut. 3 pers. sing. masc. [for יִצְעַן v. id.]	צען

[a] Job 37. 12. [b] De. 6. 24. [c] 1 Ki. 6. 5. [d] Job 17. 14. [e] 1 Ch. 5. 1. [f] Ge. 49. 4. [g] Job 28. 2; 29. 6. [h] Job 41. 16. [i] 2 Ch. 4. 3. [k] Ge. 17. 17. [l] Ge. 21. 6. [m] Ju. 16. 25. [n] 1 Ki. 21. 13. [o] Jos. 6. 26. [p] Da. 2. 8. [q] Da. 2. 45. [r] Da. 7. 16. [s] La. 3. 12. [t] 2 Sa. 23. 12. [u] Ps. 22. 9. [uu] Jos. 9. 4. [x] 1 Ch. 11. 14. [y] Ps. 91. 3. [z] Job 5. 19. [a] Is. 57. 13. [b] Ho. 2. 12. [c] Ezr. 8. 31. [d] Ps. 34. 20. [e] Is. 58. 5. [f] Ps. 72. 16. [g] Ps. 92. 8. [h] De. 28. 53, 55, 57. [i] Je. 19. 9. [k] 1 Sa. 7. 3. [l] Is. 44. 16. [m] Ge. 37. 21. [n] Je. 5. 28. [o] 2 Ch. 14. 6. [p] Ex. 18. 8. [q] 1 Sa. 26. 24. [r] Ex. 18. 4. [s] 2 Sa. 12. 16. [t] Is. 49. 10. [u] Job 24. 11. [x] Nu. 25. 3. [y] Ps. 106. 28. [z] Je. 14. 12. [a] Ge. 2. 9. [b] Job 5. 6. [c] Eze. 17. 6. [d] Job 8. 19. [e] Ps. 94. 23. [f] Le. 16. 4. [g] Is. 22. 18. [h] Pr. 7. 8. [i] Je. 10. 5. [k] Is. 33. 20.

יַצְעֵק[a] וַ Hiph. fut. 3 pers. sing. masc. ap. [from יַצְעִיק]; וַ conv. . . . צעק

יִצָּעֵק וַ Niph. fut. 3 pers. sing. masc.; וַ id. . צעק

יִצְעַק וַיִּ Kal fut. 3 pers. sing. masc.; וַ id. . צעק

יִצָּעֲקוּ וַ Niph. fut. 3 pers. pl. masc.; וַ id. . . צעק

יִצְעֲקוּ וַיִּ Kal fut. 3 pers. pl. masc.; וַ id. . צעק

יִצְעֲרוּ[b], יִצְעָרוּ[c] וְ } Kal fut. 3 pers. pl. masc. (§ 8. rem. 15) צער

יָצֵף[d] וַ Hiph. fut. 3 pers. sing. masc. ap. & conv. [from יָצִיף] . . . . . צוף

יִצֶף[e] Kal fut. 3 pers. sing. masc. ap. [from יִצְפֶּה] צפה

יְצַף וַ Piel fut. 3 pers. sing. masc. ap. [from יְצַפֶּה]; וַ conv. . . . . צפה

יְצַפֵּהוּ וַ id. id., suff. 3 pers. sing. masc.; וַ id. . צפה

יְצַפּוּ[f] וַ id. fut. 3 pers. pl. masc.; וַ id. . . צפה

יִצְפֹּינוּ[g] Kh. יַצְפִּינוּ Hiph., K. יִצְפּוֹנוּ, Kal fut. 3 pers. sing. masc. (§ 8. rem. 18) . . צפן

יְצַפֵּם[h] וַ Piel fut. 3 pers. sing. masc. [יְצַפֶּה], suff. 3 pers. pl. masc. (§ 24. rem. 21); וַ conv. צפה

יִצְפֹּן Kal fut. 3 pers. sing. masc. . . צפן

יִצְפְּנוּ, יִצְפֹּנוּ } id. fut. 3 pers. pl. masc. (§ 8. rem. 15) צפן

יִצְפְּנֵנִי[i] id. fut. 3 pers. sing. masc., suff. 1 pers. sing. צפן

יִצְפֹּר[k] וְ Kal fut. 3 pers. sing. masc. . . . צפר

יָצֵץ[l] וַ Hiph. fut. 3 pers. s. m. ap. & conv. fr. יָצִיץ צוץ

יָצַק[m] וַיִּ fut. יִצֹק, יִצַּק (§ 20. rem. 16), וַיִּצֶק; imp. צַק, יְצֹק; inf. צֶקֶת; *to pour, pour out*; intrans. *to be poured out*, 1 Ki. 22. 35; Job 38. 38; part. יָצוּק *poured out, cast*, of metal, and hence *hard, firm*. Pi. *to pour out*, 2 Ki. 4. 5 Kheth. Hiph. הִצִּיק *to put down, place, lay out*. Hoph. הוּצַק *to be poured out*; part. מוּצָק *cast, molten*, 1 Ki. 7. 23; מֻצָק *firm*, Job 11. 15.

יְצֻקָה fem. dec. 10, *casting* of metal 1 Ki. 7. 24.

מוּצָק masc. *something cast, a casting*.

מוּצָקָה fem. *a funnel*, pl. מוּצָקוֹת Zec. 4. 2.

מוּצֶקֶת fem. dec. 13 a, *a casting*, 2 Ch. 4. 3.

יִצֹּק[n] וַ, יִצֹק וַיִּ } Kal fut. 3 pers. sing. masc. (§ 20. rem. 16); וַ conv. . . . . . יצק

יְצֹק[o] id. imp. sing. masc. (§ 20. rem. 1) . . יצק

יַצִּקוּ[p] וַ Hiph. fut. 3 p. pl. m. (§ 20. r. 16); וַ conv. יצק

יִצְקוּ[q] וַ Kal fut. 3 pers. pl. masc.; וַ id. . יצק

יִצְקוּ[r] וְ id. imp. pl. masc. (§ 20. rem. 1) . . יצק

יְצֻקוֹת[s] Kal part. p. f. pl. [of יְצֻקָה] d. 10, fr. יָצוּק m. יצק

יְצֻקִים[t] id. masc., pl. of יָצוּק dec. 3a . . יצק

יְצָקָם id. pret. 3 pers. sing. m., suff. 3 pers. pl. m. יצק

יַצִּקֻם[u] וַ Hiph. fut. 3 pers. pl. masc. [יַצִּיקוּ], suff. 3 pers. pl. masc. (§ 20. rem. 16); וַ conv. יצק

יָצַקְתָּ וְ Kal pret. 2 pers. sing. masc.; acc. shifted by conv. וְ (§ 8. rem. 7) . . יצק

יָצַקְתְּ[x] וְ id. pret. 2 pers. sing. fem. . . . יצק

יָצַר[y] I. fut. יֵצַר, *to be straitened, to be distressed, anxious*; וַיֵּצֶר לוֹ *and he was distressed*.—II. fut. יִצֹר (§ 20. rem. 16), וַיִּצֶר, וַיִּיצֶר; (*a*) *to form, fashion, make*; part. יוֹצֵר *maker, creator, potter*; (*b*) *to devise, meditate*, with עַל *against* any one. Niph. נוֹצַר *to be formed, created*, Is. 43. 10. Pu. id. Ps. 139. 16. Hoph. הוּצַר id. Is. 54. 17.

יֵצֶר masc. dec. 6 b.—I. *something formed, form, frame*.—II. *imagination, thought*.—III. pr. name masc. Ge. 46. 24. Patronym. יִצְרִי Nu. 26. 49; also the pr. name of a man, 1 Ch. 25. 11.

יְצֻרִים masc. pl. (of יָצֻר dec. 1) *things formed, members*, Job 17. 7.

יָצָר[z] Kal pret. 3 pers. sing. masc. in pause for יָצַר יצר

יָצֶר[a] וַיָּ[b] Hiph. fut. 3 pers. sing. masc. with conv. וַ [for יָצֵר § 18. rem. 11] . . . צרר

יָצַר וַ Kal fut. 3 p. s. m., ap. & conv. (§ 21. r. 9) צור

יֵצֹר[c] Kal fut. 3 pers. sing. masc. . . צרר

יִצֶר[d], יִצֶר[e] וַיִּ } Kal fut. 3 pers. sing. masc. (§ 20. rem. 1 & 4); וַ conv. . . . יצר

יֵצֶר[f] וְ noun masc. s. dec. 6b, also pr. name m. יצר

יִצֶר[g] וַ Kal fut. 3 pers. sing. masc., defect. & with conv. וַ [for וַיִּיצֶר § 20. rem. 2] . יצר

יִצֹּר[h] Kal fut. 3 pers. sing. masc. . . . נצר

יֹצֵר וְ Kal part. act. sing. masc. dec. 7 b . יצר

יְצָרָהּ[k] id. pret. 3 pers. sing. masc., suff. 3 pers. s. f. יצר

יֹצְרָהּ[l] וְ id. part. act. s. m. (יֹצֵר), suff. 3 p. s. f. d. 7 b יצר

יִצְּרֵהוּ[m] id. fut. 3 pers. sing. masc. [יִצֹּר § 20. rem. 16], suff. 3 pers. sing. masc. . . יצר

יָצְרוּ[n] id. pret. 3 pers. pl. [for יָצְרוּ § 8. rem. 7] יצר

יָצֵרוּ[o] וַ Hiph. fut. 3 pers. pl. masc.; וַ conv. . צרר

יָצֻרוּ וַ Kal fut. 3 pers. pl. masc.; וַ id. . . צור

יִצְרוּ[p] Kal fut. 3 pers. pl. masc. . . . יצר

יִצְרוֹ noun m. s., suff. 3 p. s. m. from יֵצֶר dec. 6 b יצר

יִצְּרוּ[q] Kal fut. 3 pers. pl. masc. . . . נצר

יֹצְרוֹ[r] וְ Kal part. act. sing. masc. (יֹצֵר), suff. 3 pers. sing. masc. dec. 7 b . . . יצר

יֻצָּרוּ[s] Pual pret. 3 p. pl. [for יֻצְּרוּ comp. § 8. r. 7] יצר

יִצְּרוּנִי Kal fut. 3 pers. pl. masc., suff. 1 pers. sing. נצר

יֹצְרֵי[t] Kal part. act. pl. c. m. from יֹצֵר dec. 7 b . יצר

יֹצְרִי[u] id. sing. with suff. 1 pers. sing. . . יצר

---

[a] 1 Sa. 10. 17. [b] Je. 30. 19. [c] Job 14. 21. [d] 2 Ki. 6. 6. [e] Ge. 31. 49. [f] 2 Ch. 3. 10. [g] Ps. 56. 7. [h] Ex. 36. 36. [i] Ps. 27. 5. [k] Ju. 7. 3. [l] Nu. 17. 23. [m] Le. 2. 1. [n] 1 Ki. 22. 35. [o] Eze. 24. 3. [p] 2 Sa. 15. 24. [q] 2 Ki. 4. 40. [r] 1 Ki. 18. 34. [s] 1 Ki. 7. 30. [t] 1 Ki. 7. 24. [u] Jos. 7. 23. [x] 2 Ki. 4. 4. [y] Is. 44. 10. [z] Ge. 2. 8. [a] 1 Ki. 8. 37; 2 Ch. 6. 28. [b] 2 Ch. 28. 20. [c] Is. 11. 13. [d] Pr. 4. 12. [e] Job 20. 22. [f] Is. 29. 16. [g] Ge. 2. 19. [h] Pr. 3. 1. [i] Zec. 12. 1. [k] Is. 45. 18. [l] Is. 22. 11. [m] Is. 44. 12. [n] Ps. 95. 5. [o] Ne. 9. 27. [p] Job 18. 7. [q] Pr. 20. 28. [r] Is. 27. 11. [s] Ps. 139. 16. [t] Is. 44. 9. [u] Is. 49. 5.

יצרי[a] ו noun masc. pl., suff. 1 pers. sing. with cop. ו [for ויצרי, וי׳] from יצר dec. 1a . יצר

יצריח[b] Hiph. fut. 3 pers. sing. masc. . . . צרח

יצרך ו Kal part. act. sing. masc. (יצר), suff. 2 pers. sing. masc. dec. 7b (§ 36. rem. 3) . יצר

יצרנהו[c] Kal fut. 3 pers. sing. m. (יצר) with epenth. נ & suff. 3 pers. sing. masc. (§ 16. r. 13) נצר

יצרנו[d] noun masc. s., suff. 1 pers. pl. from יצר d. 6b יצר

יצרנו[e] Kal part. act. s. m. (יצר), suff. 1 p. pl. d. 7b יצר

יצרפו[f] ו Niph. fut. 3 pers. pl. masc. . . . צרף

יצרתה[g] id. pret. 2 pers. sing. masc. . . יצר

יצרתי id. pret. 1 pers. sing. . . . . יצר

יצרתיה[h] ו id. id., suff. 3 pers. sing. fem. with conj. ו [for ויצרתיה, וי׳] . . . . יצר

יצרתיו[i] id. id., suff. 3 pers. sing. masc. . . יצר

יצרתיך[k] id. id., suff. 2 pers. sing. masc. . . יצר

יצרתם[l] id. pret. 2 pers. sing. m., suff. 3 pers. pl. m. יצר

יצת only fut. יצת (§ 20. rem. 16).—I. *to set on fire, to kindle*, with ב Is. 9. 17.—II. *to be burned, consumed*. Niph. נצת.—I. *to be burned, consumed*. —II. *to burn* with anger, with ב *against* any one. Hiph. הוצית, הצית *to set on fire, to kindle*.

יצת[m] ו Hiph. fut. 3 pers. sing. masc. ap. & conv. (§ 11. rem. 7, & § 20. rem. 16) . . יצת

יצתו[n] Kal fut. 3 pers. pl. masc. with dag. euph. [for יצתו, in pause for יצתו, comp. יחתו, also § 8. rem. 3, 4, 7, & § 20. rem. 16] יצת

יצתי[o] Kal pret. 1 pers. sing. for יצאתי (§ 23. r. 1) יצא

יקא[p] ו Hiph. fut. 3 pers. sing. masc. ap. [from יקיא]; ו conv. . . . . קוא

יקאנו[q] ו id., suff. 3 pers. sing. masc. (§ 2. rem. 3) קוא

יקב[r] ו׳ masc. dec. 6a (with suff. יקבך).—I. *wine-vat*. —II. *wine-press*, i. e. *the trough* in which grapes are trodden out.

יקבי[s] noun masc. seg. [as if from יקב § 35. rem. 1 & 2] but see יקב . . . . יקב

יקב ו Kal fut. 3 pers. sing. masc.; ו conv. . נקב

יקבהו id. fut. 3 pers. pl. masc., suff. 3 pers. s. m. נקב

יקבי[u] noun masc. pl. constr. from יקב dec. 6a . יקב

יקביך[x] id. pl., suff. 2 pers. sing. masc. . . יקב

יקבים[y] id. pl., absolute state . . . . יקב

יקבלו[z] ו Piel fut. 3 pers. pl. masc.; ו conv. . קבל

יקבלון[a] ו Ch. Pael fut. 3 pers. pl. masc. with conj. ו [for ויקבלון, וי׳] . . . . קבל

יקבלם[b] ו Piel pret. 3 p. s. m., suff. 3 p. pl. m.; ו conv. קבל

יקבנו[c] Kal fut. 3 pers. sing. masc. [יקב], suff. 3 pers. sing. masc. (§ 8. r. 14, & § 2. r. 3) נקב

יקבץ, יקבץ[d] ו Kal fut. 3 pers. sing. masc. (§ 8. rem. 18); ו conv. . . . . קבץ

יקבץ Piel fut. 3 pers. sing. masc. . . . קבץ

יקבצו[e] ו׳, ו׳[f] Niph. fut. 3 pers. pl. masc.; ו conv. קבץ

יקבצו ו, ו׳ Kal fut. 3 pers. pl. masc.; ו id. . קבץ

יקבצך[g] Piel fut. 3 pers. sing. masc., suff. 2 pers. sing. masc. (§ 16. rem. 15) . . . קבץ

יקבצם[h] ו Kal fut. 3 p. s. m., suff. 3 p. pl. m.; ו conv. קבץ

יקבצנו[i] Piel fut. 3 p. s. m., suff. 3 p. s. m. (§ 2. r. 3) קבץ

יקבצנו[k] Kal fut. 3 p. s. m., suff. 3 p. s. m. (§ 2. r. 3) קבץ

יקבר[l] ו׳ Niph. fut. 3 pers. sing. masc.; ו conv. קבר

יקבר ו Kal fut. 3 pers. sing. masc.; ו id. . קבר

יקברהו ו id. fut. 3 p. pl. m., suff. 3 p. s. m.; ו id. קבר

יקברו Niph. fut. 3 pers. pl. masc. [for יקברו, comp. § 8. rem. 15] . . . . קבר

יקברו[m] ו׳ Kal fut. 3 pers. pl. masc.; ו conv. . קבר

[יקד] fut. יקד, ייקד *to burn*, as fire; part. pass. יקוד *burning mass* upon the hearth, Is. 30. 14. Hoph. הוקד *to be kindled, to burn*.

יקד Ch. id. Da. 3. 6, 11, 15, 17, 20, 21, 23, 26.

יקדא fem. dec. 8, *a burning*, Da. 7. 11.

יקוד masc. id. Is. 10. 16.

מוקד masc. dec. 7b.—I. *burning*, Is. 33. 14.— II. *firebrand*, Ps. 102. 4.

מוקדה fem. *hearth* where the burnt-offerings were consumed, Le. 6. 2.

יקד[n] Kal fut. 3 pers. sing. masc. (§ 20. rem. 2) . יקד

יקד[o] noun masc. sing. . . . . יקד

יקד ו Kal fut. 3 pers. sing. masc., Chald. form (§ 18. rem. 14); ו conv. . . . קדד

יקדו ו id. fut. 3 pers. pl. masc.; ו id. . . קדד

יקדיש[p] Hiph. fut. 3 pers. sing. masc. . . . קדש

יקדישו id. fut. 3 pers. pl. masc. . . . קדש

יקדמו[q] Piel fut. 3 pers. pl. masc. . . . קדם

יקדמונו[r] id. id., suff. 1 pers. pl. . . . קדם

יקדמוני[s] id. id., suff. 1 pers. sing. . . . קדם

יקדמנה id. 3 pers. sing. masc., suff. 3 pers. s. fem. קדם

יקדמני[t] id. id., suff. 1 pers. sing. . . . קדם

יקדמני[u] defect. for יקדמוני (q. v.) . . . קדם

יקדעם[pp] ו (*possessed of the people*, Syr. קדי *to possess*)

יקדש[x] ו Niph. fut. 3 pers. sing. masc.; ו conv. . קדש

יקדש[uu] defect. for יקדיש (q.v.) . . . קדש

[a] Job 17. 7. [b] Is. 42. 13. [c] De. 32. 10. [d] Ps. 103. 14. [e] Is. 64. 7. [f] Da. 12. 10. [g] Ps. 104. 26. [h] 2 Ki. 19. 25; Is. 37. 26. [i] Is. 43. 7. [k] Is. 44. 21. [l] Ps. 74. 17. [m] La. 4. 11. [n] Is. 33. 12; Je. 51. 58. [o] Job 1. 21. [p] Jon. 2. 11. [pp] Jos. 15. 56. [q] Job 20. 15. [r] Is. 5. 2. [s] Ho. 9. 2. [t] Nu. 18. 30. [u] Zec. 14. 10. [uu] Le. 27. 14. [x] Pr. 3. 10. [y] Job 24. 11. [z] 2 Ch. 29. 16, 22. [a] Da. 7. 18. [b] 1 Ch. 12. 18. [c] Is. 62. 2. [d] Ps. 41. 7. [e] Is. 60. 7. [f] 1 Ch. 13. 2. [g] De. 30. 4. [h] 2 Ch. 32. 6. [i] Je. 31. 10. [k] Pr. 28. 8. [l] Je. 22. 19. [m] Je. 19. 11. [n] Is. 10. 16. [o] Is. 10. 16. [p] Le. 27. 14, 18, 22, 26. [q] Ps. 89. 15. [r] Ps. 79. 8. [s] Ps. 18. 19. [t] Ps. 59. 11. [u] 2 Sa. 22. 19. [x] Nu. 20. 13.

וַיְקַדֵּשׁ וַ Piel fut. 3 pers. sing. masc.; וַ conv. . קדש

יִקְדַּשׁ / יִקְדָּשׁ[a] } Kal fut. 3 pers. sing. masc. (§ 8. rem. 15) קדש

וַיְקַדְּשֵׁהוּ וַ Piel fut. 3 pers. sing. masc. with suff. 3 pers. sing. masc.; וַ conv. . . . קדש

וַיְקַדְּשׁוּ[b] וַ defect. for יַקְדִּישׁוּ q. v. . . . קדש

יְקַדְּשׁוּ[c] / וַיְקַדְּשׁוּ[d] וַ } Piel fut. 3 pers. pl. masc. (comp. § 8. rem. 15); וַ conv. . . . קדש

וַיִּקְדְּשׁוּ[f] וַ Kal fut. 3 pers. pl. masc. [for יִקְדְּשׁוּ § 8. rem. 15]; וַ id. . . . קדש

וַיְקַדְּשֵׁם[g] וַ Piel fut. 3 pers. sing. masc., suff. 3 pers. pl. masc.; וַ id. . . . קדש

יֹקֶדֶת[h] Kal part. act. sing. fem. [from יֹקֵד masc. § 8. rem. 19] . . . . יקד

יָקִדְתָּא[i] Ch. Peal part. act. sing. fem. emph. [of יָקְדָא, from יָקֵד masc. § 47. rem. 1] . . יקד

יקה Root not used; Arab. *to venerate.*
 יָקֶה (*pious*) pr. name masc. Pr. 30. 1
 יְקוּתִיאֵל (*veneration of God*) pr. name masc. 1 Ch. 4. 18.

יקה Root not used; Arab. וקה *to obey.*
 יְקָהָה fem. dec. 11c (constr. יִקְּהַת with dag. forte euph. comp. § 33. rem. 1) *obedience,* Ge. 49. 10; Pr. 30. 17.

יָקֶה pr. name masc. . . . . . יקה

יַקְהִיל[k] / וַיַּקְהֵל[l] } Hiph. fut. 3 pers. sing. masc. . . קהל

וַיַּקְהֵל[m] וַ ap. from the preceding; וַ conv. . קהל

וַיִּקָּהֵל וַ Niph. fut. 3 pers. sing. masc.; וַ id. . קהל

וַיַּקְהִלוּ[n] וַ Hiph. fut. 3 pers. pl. masc.; וַ id. . קהל

וַיִּקָּהֲלוּ וַ Niph. fut. 3 pers. pl. masc.; וַ id. . קהל

יִקְּהַת[o] noun fem. sing. constr. of [יְקָהָה] dec. 11c, dag. forte euph. in ק . . . . יקה

וַיְקַו[p] וַ / יְקַוֶּה } Piel fut. 3 pers. sing. masc. ap. and full form; וַ conv. . . . קוה

יִקָּווּ[r] Niph. fut. 3 pers. pl. masc. . . . קוה

יְקַוּוּ Piel fut. 3 pers. pl. masc. . . . קוה

יָקוֹט[s] Kal fut. 3 pers. sing. m. [for יָקֹט § 18. r. 2] קטט

יָקוּם[t] וַיָּ Kal fut. 3 pers. sing. masc. . . . קום

יְקוּם Chald. Peal fut. 3 pers. sing. masc. . . קום

יִקּוֹם[u] Kal fut. 3 pers. sing. masc. (for יִקֹּם § 8. rem. 18, & § 17. rem. 3) . . . נקם

יָקוּמוּ וַיָּ Kal fut. 3 pers. pl. masc.; וַ conv. . קום

יְקוּמוּן id. with parag. ן; Chald. Da. 7. 10, 17 קום

יְקוֹמֵם[w] Pilel fut. 3 pers. sing. masc. . . . קום

יְקוֹמְמוּ[y] Pilel fut. 3 pers. pl. masc. [for יְקוֹמֵמוּ comp. § 8. rem. 15] . . . . . קום

וַיְקוֹנֵן[z] וַ Pilel fut. 3 pers. sing. masc.; וַ conv. . קון

יְקוֹסֵם[a] Poel fut. 3 pers. sing. masc. . . . קסם

יָקוֹשׁ[b] noun masc. sing. . . . . . יקש

יָקוּשׁ noun masc. sing. dec. 3a . . . . יקש

יְקוּשִׁים[c] id. pl., absolute state . . . . יקש

יְקוּתִיאֵל pr. name masc. . . . . . יקה

יִקַּח / יִקַּח[d] וַיִּ, וְ } Kal fut. 3 pers. sing. masc. (§ 17. rem. 8); וַ conv. . . . . לקח

יֻקַּח / יֻקַּח[e] } Hoph. fut. 3 pers. sing. masc. (§ 17. rem. 8) . . . . . לקח

יִקָּחֹ[f] Kh. יִקַּח q. v., K. יִקְחוּ (q. v.) . . לקח

יִקָּחֶהָ וַיִּ, וְ Kal fut. 3 pers. sing. masc. (יִקַּח), suff. 3 pers. sing. fem. (§ 16. rem. 12, & § 17. rem. 8); וַ conv. . . . . לקח

יִקָּחֵהוּ וַיִּ id. id., suff. 3 pers. sing. masc.; וַ id. לקח

וַיִּקָּחֻהוּ וַ id. fut. 3 pers. pl. m. with suff. 3 pers. s. m. לקח

יִקְחוּ / וַיִּקְחוּ וַיִּ, וְ } id. fut. 3 pers. pl. masc. (§ 8. rem. 15); וַ conv. . . . לקח

וַיִּקָּחוּם וַ id. id., suff. (יִקַּח), 3 p. pl. m. (§ 16. rem. 12) לקח

יִקָּחֲךָ[g] / יִקָּחֶךָּ[h] } id. fut. 3 pers. sing. masc., suff. 2 pers. sing. masc. (v. id.) . . . לקח

וַיִּקָּחֵם[i] וַ id. id., suff. 3 pers. pl. masc. (v. id.); וַ conv. לקח

יִקָּחֶנָּה[k] id. id., suff. 3 pers. s. fem. (v. id. & § 2. rem. 3) לקח

יִקָּחֶנּוּ[l] id. id., suff. 3 pers. sing. masc. (v. id.) . לקח

יִקָּחֵנִי[m] וַיִּ id. id., suff. 1 pers. sing. (v. id.); וַ conv. לקח

יַקְטִיר Hiph. fut. 3 pers. sing. masc. . . . קטר

וַיַּקְטִירוּ[n] וַ Kh. יַקְטִירוּ Hiph. fut. 3 pers. pl.; K. יְקַטְּרוּ (q. v.) . . . . . קטר

יַקְטִירֶנָּה[o] Hiph. fut. 3 pers. sing. masc., suff. 3 pers. sing. fem. (§ 2. rem. 3) . . . . קטר

יִקְטָל־[p] Kal fut. 3 pers. s. m. [for יִקְטֹל § 8. rem. 18] קטל

יִקְטְלֵנִי[q] id. with suff. 1 pers. sing. . . . קטל

יָקְטָן וְ pr. name masc. . . . . . קטן

יִקָּטֵף[r] Niph. fut. 3 pers. sing. masc. . . . קטף

וַיַּקְטֵר וַ Kal fut. 3 pers. s. m. ap. from יַקְטִיר; וַ conv. קטר

יְקַטֵּר[s] / יְקַטֵּר[t] וַ, וְ } Piel fut. 3 p. s. m.; וַ conv.; with וְ conj. [for וַיְקַטֵּר, וִיקַטֵּר] . . . . קטר

יְקַטְּרוּ / וַיְקַטְּרוּ } id. fut. 3 pers. pl. masc. (comp. § 8. rem. 15); וַ conv. . . . . קטר

יַקְטִרוּן[mm] Hiph. fut. 3 pers. pl. masc. with parag. ן קטר

יְקַטְּרוּן[u] Piel fut. 3 pers. pl. masc.; ן paragogic [for יְקַטְּרוּן comp. § 8. rem. 17] . . . קטר

יְקִידְתָּא[x] Chald. full form for יָקִדְתָּא (q. v.) . . יקד

יָקִים Hiph. fut. 3 pers. sing. masc. . . . קום

יָקִים וְ pr. name masc. . . . . . קום

[a] 1 Sa. 21. 6. [b] Jos. 20. 7. [c] Eze. 44. 24. [d] Eze. 44. 19. [e] 2 Ch. 29. 17. [f] Nu. 17. 3. [g] Job 1. 5. [h] Is. 65. 5. [i] Da. 3. 20, 23, 26. [k] 2 Ch. 5. 2. [l] Job 11. 10. [m] 1 Ki. 8. 1. [n] Nu. 20. 10. [o] Ge. 49. 10. [p] Job 3. 9. [q] Is. 5. 2, 7. [r] Ge. 1. 9. [s] Job 8. 14. [t] Ec. 12. 4. [u] De. 32. 43. [w] Mi. 2. 8. [y] Is. 61. 4. [z] 2 Ch. 35. 25. [a] Eze. 17. 9. [b] Ho. 9. 8. [c] Je. 5. 26. [d] Ge. 42. 16. [e] Ge. 18. 4. [f] 2 Ki. 20. 18. [g] Job 15. 12. [h] De. 30. 4. [i] Ge. 32. 24. [k] De. 20. 7. [l] Job 40. 24. [m] Eze. 8. 3; Am. 7. 15. [mm] 1 Sa. 2. 15, 16. [n] 2 Ch. 34. 25. [o] Ex. 30. 7, 8. [p] Job 24. 14. [q] Job 13. 15. [r] Job 8. 12. [s] 2 Ch. 25. 14. [t] Hab. 1. 16. [u] Ho. 11. 2. [x] Da. 3. 6, 11, 15, 17, 21.

יְקִים Chald. Aph. fut. 3 pers. sing. masc. . קום

[a]וַיְקִימֶהָ וַ Hiph. fut. 3 pers. sing. masc. (יָקִים), suff. 3 pers. sing. fem.; וַ conv. . . . . קום

[b]יְקִימוּ וַי' id. fut. 3 pers. pl. masc.; ·וְ id. . . קום

[c]יְקִימוּן id. id. with parag. ן . . . . קום

[d]יְקִימְךָ id. fut. 3 pers. s. m. (יָקִים), suff. 2 pers. s. m. קום

[e]יְקִימֶנָּה id. id., suff. 3 pers. sing. fem. (§ 2. rem. 3) קום

יְקִימֶנּוּ id. id., suff. 3 pers. sing. masc. (v. id.) . קום

[f]יְקִימֵנִי וַ id. id., suff. 1 pers. sing.; וַ conv. . קום

[g]יְקִיעֵם וַ Hiph. fut. 3 pers. pl. m., suff. 3 pers. pl. m. defect. [for יוֹקִיעוּם § 20. r. 2]; ·וְ id. יקע

[h]יַקִּיפוּ Hiph. fut. 3 pers. pl. masc. . . . נקף

יָקִיצוּ Hiph. fut. 3 pers. pl. masc. . . . קוץ

[i]יַקִּיר adj. masc. sing. . . . . . יקר

[k]יַקִּירָא Chald. adj. masc. sing., emph. of יַקִּיר dec. 1 יקר

[l]יַקִּירָה Chald. id. fem., absolute state . . יקר

[m]יָקֵל Hiph. fut. 3 pers. sing. masc. . . . קלל

[n]יִקָּלְהוּ Kh. יִקָּלְהוּ Niph. fut. 3 pers. pl. masc., transposed for K. יִקָּהֲלוּ (q. v.) . . קהל

[o]יֵקַלּוּ Kal fut. 3 pers. pl. m. [for יִקְלוּ § 18. rem. 6] קלל

[p]יִקַּלּוּ Niph. fut. 3 pers. pl. masc. . . . קלל

יְקַלֵּל, [q]יְקַלֵּל — Piel fut. 3 pers. sing. masc.; ·וְ conv.; with וְ conj. [for וִי', וִיקַלֵּל] קלל

[r]יְקֻלַּל Pual fut. 3 pers. sing. masc. [for יְקֻלַּל comp. § 8. rem. 15] . . . . . קלל

[s]יְקַלְלוּ וַיְ' Piel fut. 3 pers. pl. m. (§ 10. r. 7); וַ conv. קלל

[t]יְקַלֶּלְךָ id. fut. 3 pers. sing. masc. [יְקַלֵּל], suff. 2 pers. sing. masc. (§ 16. rem. 15) . . קלל

[u]יְקַלְלֵם וַ id. id., suff. 3 p. pl. m. (§ 10. rem. 7); וַ conv. קלל

[x]יְקַלַּע וַ Piel fut. 3 pers. sing. masc.; וַ id. . . קלע

[y]יְקַלְּעֶנָּה id., suff. 3 pers. sing. fem. . . . קלע

יָקֵם, וַיָּקֶם — Hiph. fut. 3 pers. sing. masc., ap. and conv. from יָקִים . . . . קום

[z]יָקֹם וַיָּ', וַ', [a]יָקֻם — Kal fut. 3 pers. sing. masc., ap. and conv. from יָקוּם (§ 21. r. 7 & 8) קום

[b]יִקֹּם Kal fut. 3 pers. sing. masc. (§ 17. rem. 3) . נקם

[c]יֻקַּם, יֻקָּם — Hoph. fut. 3 pers. sing. masc. (comp. § 8. rem. 15) . . . . נקם

יָקֻמוּ [d]וַיָּ', וַ' defect. for יָקוּמוּ (q. v.) . . קום

[e]יְקֻמוּן Chald. defect. for יְקוּמוּן (q. v.) . . קום

יְקַמְיָה pr. name m., with cop. וְ [for וִי', וִיקַמְיָה] קמה

[f]יְקִמֵנוּ defect. for יְקִימֵנוּ (q. v.) . . . קום

יְקַמְעָם יְקַמְעָם & יְקַמְ' pr. names masc. . . קמה

וַיִּקֶן וַ Kal fut. 3 pers. s. m. ap. from יִקְנֶה; ·וְ conv. קנה

יְקַנֵּא [g]וִי' Piel fut. 3 pers. sing. masc.; וַ id. . קנא

[h]יְקַנְאֻהוּ defect. for יְקַנְאוּהוּ (q. v.) . . . קנא

[i]יְקַנְאֻהוּ וַ the following with suff. 3 pers. sing. masc. קנא

וַיְקַנְאוּ וַ Piel fut. 3 pers. pl. m. (§ 10. rem. 7); וַ conv. קנא

יִקְנֶה Kal fut. 3 pers. sing. masc. . . . קנה

[k]יִקְנֵהוּ וַ id., suff. 3 pers. s. m. (§ 24. rem. 21); וַ conv. קנה

[l]יִקָּנוּ Niph. fut. 3 pers. pl. masc. . . . קנה

[m]יִקְנוּ Kal fut. 3 pers. pl. masc. . . . קנה

[n]יַקְנִיאוּהוּ Hiph. fut. 3 pers. pl. m., suff. 3 pers. sing. m. קנא

יְקוֹנֵן וַ Pilel fut. 3 pers. sing. masc.; וַ conv. . קון

[o]יְקַנֵּנוּ Piel fut. 3 pers. pl. masc. [for יְקַנְּנוּ comp. § 8. rem. 15] . . . . קנן

יָקְנְעָם pr. name of a place . . . . קנה

[p]יִקְסְמוּ, [q]וַיִּקְסְמוּ — Kal fut. 3 pers. pl. masc. (§ 8. rem. 15); ·וְ conv. . . . . קסם

יָקַע only fut. יֵקַע.—I. *to be dislocated*, Ge. 32. 26.—II. *to be alienated* from any one, with מֵעַל, מִן. Hiph. הוֹקִיעַ *to suspend, hang.* Hoph. *to be hanged*, 2 Sa. 21. 13.

[r]וַיַּקֵּף וַ Hiph. fut. 3 pers. sing. masc. ap. [from יַקִּיף]; ·וְ conv. . . . . נקף

יִקְפָּאוֹן Kh. יִקְפָּאוֹן Kal fut. 3 pers. pl. masc., ן parag. (§ 8. rem. 17); K. וְקִפָּאוֹן n. masc. sing. קפא

[s]וַיַּקִּפוּ וַ Hiph. fut. 3 pers. pl. masc.; ·וְ conv. . נקף

[u]יִקְפְּצוּ Kal fut. 3 pers. pl. masc. . . . קפץ

[x]יִקָּפְצוּן Niph. fut. 3 pers. pl. masc.; ן parag. . קפץ

יָקַץ only fut. יֵקַץ, וַיִּיקַץ, יִקַץ, יִיקַץ (§ 20. rem. 16), *to awake.*

וַיָּקֶץ וַ Kal fut. 3 p. s. m. ap. and conv. [fr. יָקוּץ] קוץ

[y]יִקַץ, [gg]וַיִּקַץ, [z]וַיִּקָץ — Kal fut. 3 pers. sing. masc., for יִיקַץ (§ 8. rem. 15, and § 20. rem. 2); ·וְ conv. . . . . יקץ

[a]וַיִּקְצָב־ וַ Kal fut. 3 pers. sing. masc. [for יִקְצֹב § 8 rem. 18]; ·וְ id. . . . . קצב

[b]יָקֻצוּ וַ Kal fut. 3 pers. pl. masc.; ·וְ id. . . קוץ

[c]יִקְצוּ וַ Kal fut. 3 p. pl. m. [for יִיקְצוּ § 20. rem. 2] יקץ

[d]יִקְצוֹר, יִקְצוֹר — Kh. יִקְצוֹר q. v., K. יִקְצָר־ with Mak. for Kal fut. 3 pers. sing. masc. (§ 8. rem. 18) קצר

[e]וַיַּקְצִיפוּ וַ Hiph. fut. 3 pers. pl. masc.; ·וְ conv. . קצף

[f]יַקְצִירוּ Kh. יַקְצִירוּ Hiph. fut. 3 pers. pl. masc., K. יִקְצֹרוּ (q. v.) . . . . קצר

[g]יַקְצִעַ Hiph. fut. 3 pers. sing. masc. . . . קצע

יִקְצֹף וַיִּ' Kal fut. 3 pers. sing. masc.; ·וְ conv. . קצף

וַיִּקְצְפוּ וַ id. fut. 3 pers. pl. masc.; ·וְ id. . . קצף

וַיְקַצֵּץ וַ Piel fut. 3 pers. sing. masc.; וַ id. . . קצץ

---

[a] Jos. 24. 26. [b] Nu. 1. 51. [c] Job 4. 4. [d] De. 28. 9. [e] Nu. 23. 19. [f] Job 16. 12.
[g] 2 Sa. 21. 9. [h] Ps. 17. 9. [i] Je. 31. 20. [k] Ezr. 4. 10. [l] Da. 2. 11. [m] 1 Sa. 6. 5.
[n] 2 Sa. 20. 14. [o] 1 Sa. 2. 30. [p] Is. 30. 16. [q] 2 Sa. 16. 11. [r] Is. 65. 20. [s] Ju. 9. 27.
[t] Pr. 30. 10. [u] 2 Ki. 2. 24. [x] 1 Sa. 17. 49. [y] 1 Sa. 25. 29. [z] Job 22. 28. [a] Ge. 27. 31.
[b] Jos. 10. 13. [c] Ge. 4. 15. [d] Jos. 18. 4. [e] Da. 7. 24. [f] Ho. 6. 2. [g] Joel 2. 18.
[h] De. 32. 16. [i] Eze. 31. 9. [k] Ge. 39. 1. [l] Je. 32. 15. [m] Je. 32. 44. [n] Ps. 78. 58.
[o] Ps. 104. 17. [p] Mi. 3. 11. [q] 2 Ki. 17. 17. [r] La. 3. 5. [s] Zec. 14. 6. [t] 2 Ki. 6. 14.
[u] Is. 52. 15. [x] Job 24. 24. [y] 1 Ki. 18. 27. [z] 1 Ki. 3. 15. [a] 2 Ki. 6. 6. [b] Ex. 1. 12.
[c] Hab. 2. 7. [d] Pr. 22. 8. [e] Ps. 106. 32. [f] Job 24. 6. [g] Le. 14. 41. [gg] Ju. 16. 20.

וַ יְקַצְּצוּ Piel fut. 3 pers. pl. masc.; וַ conv. . קצץ

יִקְצְרֻהוּ[a] Kal fut. 3 pers. pl. m., suff. 3 pers. sing. m. קצר

יִקְצֹרוּ id. fut. 3 pers. pl. m. [for יִקְצְרוּ § 8. rem. 15] קצר

יִקְצֹרוּן[b] id. with parag. ן (§ 8. rem. 17) . קצר

[יָקַר] fut. יִקַר, יֵיקַר, יִיקַר; (Arab. وقر *to be heavy*).—I. *to be dear, precious, esteemed.*—II. *to be estimated, prized*, Zec. 11. 13.—III. *to be honoured, respected*, 1 Sa. 18. 30. Hiph. הוֹקִיר *to make rare.*

יָקָר masc. dec. 4 a, יְקָרָה fem. dec. 11 c, adj.—I. *precious, dear.*—II. *splendid, beautiful.*—III. *honoured, respected*, Ec. 10. 1.—IV. *rare*, 1 Sa. 3. 1.—V. *quiet*, Pr. 17. 27.

יְקָר masc. dec. 1 a.—I. *preciousness*; כְּלִי יְקָר *precious vessel*; also *what is precious, precious thing.* —II. *splendour, glory, honour.*—III. *value, price*, Zec. 11. 13.

יְקָר Chald. dec. 1 b.—I. *costly things.*—II. *honour, glory.*

יַקִּיר adj. masc. *dear, beloved*, Je. 31. 20.

יַקִּיר Chald. adj. masc. dec. 1 a.—I. *hard, difficult*, Da. 2. 11.—II. *honourable, noble*, Ezr. 4. 10.

יָקָר adj. masc. sing. dec. 4 b . . . . יקר

וַיִּקֶר[c] וַ Kal fut. 3 pers. s. m., ap. fr. יִקְרֶה; וַ conv. קרה

וַיִּקָּר[d] וַ Niph. fut. 3 p. s. m., ap. from יִקָּרֶה; וַ id. קרה

וַיֵּקַר[e] וַ Kal fut. 3 pers. sing. masc. (§ 20. rem. 2) יקר

יְקָר / וִיקָר } noun masc. sing. dec. 1 a; with cop. וְ [for וִיְ', וִיקָר] . . } יקר

וַיִּקָּרֵא וַ, וַיִּ' Niph. fut. 3 pers. sing. masc.; וַ conv. קרא

וַיִּקְרָא וַיִּ' Kal fut. 3 pers. sing. masc.; וַ id. . קרא

וִיקָרָא וְ noun masc. sing. emph. [with cop. וְ, for וִיקָרָא ,וִיְ'] from יְקָר dec. 1 b . . יקר

וַיִּקְרָאֶהָ וַ Kal fut. 3 p. s. m., suff. 3 p. s. f.; וַ conv. קרא

וַיִּקְרָאֵהוּ[f] וַיִּ' id. id., suff. 3 pers. sing. masc. . . קרא

יִקְרָאֵהוּ id. fut. 3 pers. sing. masc. (יִקְרָא), suff. 3 pers. sing. masc. (§ 16. rem. 13) . . קרא

וַיִּקָּרְאוּ וַיִּ' Niph. fut. 3 pers. pl. masc.; וַ conv. . קרא

יִקְרָאוֹ[g] Kal fut. 3 pers. sing. masc. (יִקְרָא), suff. 3 pers. sing. masc. [for יִקְרָאֵהוּ comp. § 16. r. 12] קרא

וַיִּקְרְאוּ[h] / וַיִּקְרְאוּ[i] } id. fut. 3 pers. pl. masc. (§ 8. rem. 15); וַ conv. . . } קרא

וַיִּקְרָאֵם[k] וַ id. fut. 3 pers. sing. m., suff. 3 pers. pl. m. קרא

יִקְרָאֻנוּ id. id., suff. 3 pers. sing. masc. . . קרא

יִקְרָאֵנִי id. id., suff. 1 pers. sing. . . . קרא

יִקְרָאֻנְנִי[m] id. fut. 3 pers. pl. masc. with parag. נ and suff. 1 pers. sing. (§ 16. rem. 12 & 13) . קרא

יַקְרֵב[n] defect. for יַקְרִיב (q. v.) . . . . קרב

וַיַּקְרֵב וַ Hiph. fut. 3 p. s. m. ap. from יַקְרִיב; וַ conv. קרב

יִקְרַב / וַיִּקְרַב } Kal fut. 3 pers. sing. masc. (§ 8. rem. 15); וַ id. . . } קרב

וַיַּקְרִבוּ וַ defect. for וַיַּקְרִיבוּ (q. v.) . . קרב

יִקְרְבוּ[o] / וַיִּקְרְבוּ } Kal fut. 3 pers. pl. masc. (§ 8. rem. 15); וַ conv. . . } קרב

יָקְרָה[p] Kal pret. 3 pers. sing. fem. . . . יקר

יְקָרָה adj. fem. sing. dec. 11 c, from יָקָר masc. יקר

יְקָרָהּ[q] noun masc. sing., suff. 3 pers. sing. fem. from יְקָר dec. 1 a . . . . יקר

וִיקָרָה[r] וְ Chald. for וִיקָרָא (q. v.) . . . יקר

יִקָּרֶה[s] Niph. fut. 3 pers. sing. masc. . . קרה

יִקְרֶה[t] Kal fut. 3 pers. s. m., for יִקְרֶה (§ 24. r. 19 a) קרה

יִקְרֵה[u] Chald. Peal fut. 3 pers. sing. masc. [for יִקְרֵא § 55 note] . . . . . קרא

יִקְרֶה Kal fut. 3 pers. sing. masc. . . קרה

יָקְרוּ[x] Kal pret. 3 pers. pl. . . . . יקר

יִקְּרוּהָ[y] Kal fut. 3 pers. pl. masc., suff. 3 pers. s. fem. נקר

יִקְרוֹן[z] Chald. Peal fut. 3 pers. pl. masc. . . קרא

יְקָרוֹת adj. fem., pl. of יְקָרָה dec. 11 c, from יָקָר m. יקר

יִקָּרֵחַ[a] Niph. fut. 3 pers. sing. masc. . . . קרח

יִקְרְחָה[b] Keri יִקְרְחוּ, Kal fut. 3 pers. pl. masc. . קרח

יַקְרִיב Hiph. fut. 3 pers. sing. masc. . . . קרב

וַיַּקְרִיבוּ וַיַּ' id. fut. 3 pers. pl. masc. . . . קרב

יַקְרִיבֶנּוּ id. fut. 3 pers. sing. masc., suff. 3 pers. s. m. קרב

יִקְרֵךְ[c] Kal fut. 3 pers. sing. masc. (יִקְרֶה), suff. 2 pers. sing. fem. (§ 24. rem. 21) . . קרה

וַיִּקְרַם[d] וַ Kal fut. 3 pers. sing. masc.; וַ conv. . קרם

יִקְרֵנִי[e] Kal fut. 3 pers. sing. masc. (יִקְרֶה), suff. 1 pers. sing. (§ 24. rem. 21) . . קרה

יִקָּרֵעַ / וַיִּקָּרַע } Niph. fut. 3 pers. sing. masc. (§ 15. rem. 1); וַ conv. . . . } קרע

וַיִּקְרַע וַ Kal fut. 3 pers. sing. masc.; וַ id. . . קרע

וַיִּקְרָעֶהָ[g] וַיִּ'[h] id. id., suff. 3 pers. sing. f. (§ 16. r. 12) קרע

וַיִּקְרְעוּ וַ id. fut. 3 pers. pl. masc. . . . קרע

וַיִּקְרָעֵם וַ id. fut. 3 pers. sing. masc., suff. 3 pers. pl. masc. (§ 16. rem. 12) . . . קרע

יִקְרְצוּ[i] Kal fut. 3 pers. pl. masc. . . . קרץ

יָקַרְתָּ[k] Kal pret. 2 pers. sing. masc. . . . יקר

יְקָרֹת[l] adj. pl. absolute fem. from sing. יְקָרָה dec. 11 c, from יָקָר masc. . . . יקר

יִקְרַת[mm] id. sing., constr. state . . . יקר

יָקַרְתִּי[m] Kal pret. 1 pers. sing. . . . . יקר

[יָקֹשׁ] *to lay snares*; יָקֹשׁ *fowler*, Ps. 124. 7. Niph. נוֹקַשׁ *to be ensnared.* Pu. id. Ec. 9. 12.

יָקוּשׁ, יָקוֹשׁ masc. dec. 3 a, *fowler.*

---

[a] Job 4. 8. [b] Ru. 2. 9. [c] Ru. 2. 3. [d] Nu. 23. 4, 16. [e] Ps. 49. 9. [f] Is. 41. 2. [g] Je. 23. 6. [h] 2 Ki. 10. 20. [i] Jon. 3. 8. [k] 2 Ki. 19. 14. [l] Ge. 42. 4. [m] Pr. 1. 28. [n] Eze. 46. 4. [o] Nu. 18. 3. [p] 1 Sa. 26. 21. [q] Je. 20. 5. [r] Da. 5. 20. [s] Nu. 23. 3. [t] Da. 10. 14. [u] Da. 5. 7. [x] Ps. 139. 17. [y] Pr. 30. 17. [z] Da. 5. 15. [a] Je. 16. 6. [b] Le. 21. 5. [c] 1 Sa. 28. 10. [d] Eze. 37. 8. [e] Ec. 2. 15. [f] 1 Sa. 15. 27. [g] Je. 36. 23. [h] 1 Ki. 11. 30. [i] Ps. 35. 19. [k] Is. 43. 4. [l] 1 Ki. 7. 9. [m] Zec. 11. 13. [mm] Is. 28. 16.

יָקְשָׁן (*fowler*) pr. name of a son of Abraham by Keturah, Ge. 25. 2, 3.

מוֹקֵשׁ masc. dec. 7b (pl. ־ִים, ־וֹת), *snare, gin.*

יַקֶשׁ[a] וַ Hiph. fut. 3 pers. sing. masc., ap. [from יַקְשֶׁה]; וַ conv. . . . קשה

יִקֶשׁ[b] וַ Kal fut. 3 pers. s. m. ap. fr. יִקְשֶׁה; וַ id. קשה

יַקְשֵׁב[c] וַ Hiph. fut. 3 pers. s. m. ap. fr. יַקְשִׁיב; וַ id. קשב

יִקְשֶׁה Kal fut. 3 pers. sing. masc. . . קשה

יָקְשׁוּ[d] Kal pret. 3 pers. pl. . . . . יקש

יְקֹשׁוּן[e] Kal fut. 3 p. pl. m. (יָקוּשׁ § 21. r. 3) with parag. ן קוש

יַקְשׁוּ וַ Hiph. fut. 3 pers. pl. masc.; וַ conv. קשה

יַקְשִׁיב[f] Hiph. fut. 3 pers. sing. masc. . . . קשב

יָקְשָׁן וְ pr. name masc. . . . . . יקש

יִקְשֹׁר וַ / יִקְשָׁר־[g] וַ Kal fut. 3 pers. sing. masc. (§ 8. rem. 18); וַ conv. . . . קשר

יִקְשְׁרוּ וַ id. fut. 3 pers. pl. masc.; וַ id. . . קשר

יָקֹשְׁתִּי[h] Kal pret. 1 pers. sing. (§ 8. rem. 1) . . יקש

יָקְתְאֵל וְ (*subdued of God*; Arab. קתא *to serve*) pr. name—I. of a town in the tribe of Judah, Jos. 15. 38.—II. of a city in Arabia, 2 Ki. 14. 7.

יָרֵא וְ pret. יְרֵאתֶם ,יְרֵאתֶם (from יָרֵא § 23. rem. 1); fut. יִירָא ,יִרָא; inf. c. יְרֹא ,יִרְאָה (§ 8. rem. 10).—I. *to fear, be afraid*; with acc., מִפְּנֵי ,מִן of the person or thing feared; with לְ *to fear, be anxious for* any person or thing; with an inf. and לְ or מִן *to be afraid* to do anything; with פֶּן, *lest* any thing happen.—II. *to reverence, honour*, with אֶת, מִלִּפְנֵי. Niph. נוֹרָא *to be feared*, Ps. 130. 4. Part. נוֹרָא, (*a*) *fearful, dreadful, terrible*; (*b*) *awful, holy*; (*c*) *marvellous, wonderful*; נוֹרָאוֹת *marvellous deeds.* Pi. *to make afraid, to alarm.*

יָרֵא masc. dec. 5a (constr. יְרֵא § 34. rem. 1); יְרֵאָה fem. dec. 11c (constr. יִרְאַת Pr. 31. 30) adj. —I. *fearing, reverencing*; יָרֵא אָנֹכִי אֹתוֹ *I fear him*; יְרֵא אֱלֹהִים *fearing God.*—II. *fearful, timid*, De. 20. 8.

יִרְאָה fem. (no pl.)—I. inf. of the verb יָרֵא, *to fear*; hence לְיִרְאָה אֶת־שְׁמֶךָ *to fear thy name.*—II. subst. *fear, terror.*—III. *reverence, awe.*

יִרְאוֹן (*fearful*) pr. name of a city in the tribe of Naphtali, Jos. 19. 38.

מוֹרָא masc. dec. 2b.—I. *fear*, Ge. 9. 2.—II. *reverence, awe.*—III. *object of fear* or *reverence.*—IV. *fearful, stupendous act.*

תִּירְיָא (*fear*) pr. name masc. 1 Ch. 4. 16.

יָרֵא adj. masc. sing. dec. 5 (§ 34. rem. 1) . ירא

יֵרָא וַ Kal fut. 3 pers. sing. masc., ap. and conv. from יִרְאֶה (§ 24. rem. 3); or (2 Ki. 11. 4) Hiph., ap. from יַרְאֶה (§ 24. rem. 16) . ראה

יֵרָא[k] וְ׳, וַיֵּ׳ Niph. fut. 3 pers. sing masc. ap. from יֵרָאֶה; וַ conv. . . . ראה

יֵרֶא וְ׳ Kal fut. 3 p. s. m. ap. fr. יִרְאֶה (§ 24. r. 3c) ראה

יִרָא וַ id. fut. 3 pers. sing. masc. for יִירָא (§ 20. rem. 2); וַ conv. . . . . ירא

יִרְאֶ°[m] Kh. יֵרָא q. v., K. יִרְאֶה (q. v.) . ראה

יֵרָא°[n] וַ Kh. וַיֵּרָא q. v., K. וַיִּרְאֶה (q. v.) ראה

יְרָא Kal imp. sing. masc. . . . . ירא

יְרֵא / יְרֵא וְ adj. masc. sing., constr. of יָרֵא dec. 5; with cop. וְ [for וִירֵא ,וְיֵ׳] . ירא

יְרֹא[o] Kal inf. constr. . . . . ירא

יָרְאָה[p] / יָרְאָה Kal pret. 3 pers. sing. fem. (§ 8. rem. 1a & 7) . . ירא

יַרְאֶה[q] Hiph. fut. 3 pers. sing. masc. . . ראה

יֵרָאֶה Niph. fut. 3 pers. sing. masc. . . ראה

יִרְאֶהָ[r] וַ Kal fut. 3 pers. sing. masc. (יִרְאֶה), suff. 3 pers. sing. fem. (§ 24. rem. 21); וַ conv. ראה

יִרְאָה[s] וְ noun fem. sing. (no vowel change) . ירא

יִרְאֶה[t] וַיִּ׳, וְ׳ Kal fut. 3 pers. sing. masc.; וַ conv. ראה

יַרְאֵהוּ וַ Hiph. fut. 3 pers. sing. masc. (יַרְאֶה), suff. 3 pers. sing. masc. (§ 24. rem. 21); וַ id. ראה

יִרְאֵהוּ[u] וַ Kal fut. 3 pers. sing. masc. (יִרְאֶה), suff. 3 pers. sing. masc. (§ 24. rem. 21); וַ id. ראה

יִרְאֻהוּ[x] וַ id. fut. 3 pers. pl. m., suff. 3 p. s. m.; וַ id. ראה

יָרְאוּ וְ Kal pret. 3 pers. pl. . . . ירא

יֵרָאוּ[y] וְ׳, וַיֵּ׳ Niph. fut. 3 pers. pl. masc.; וַ conv. ראה

יְראוּ (read, yĕroo) Kal. imp. pl. masc. [for יְראוּ § 23. rem. 3] . . . . . ירא

יִרְאוּ / יִרְאוּ[z] וְ׳, וַיִּ׳ Kal fut. 3 pers. pl. masc. for יִירְאוּ (§ 20. r. 2, & § 8. r. 15); וַ conv. ירא

יִרְאוּ וְ׳, וַיִּ׳ Kal fut. 3 pers. pl. masc.; וַ id. . ראה

יִרְאוּ[a] וַ Kh. (§ 24. rem. 19, & § 23. rem. 3), K. יֹרוּ Hiph. fut. 3 pers. pl. masc. (§ 25. 2e) ירה

יִרְאוּהָ[b] Kal fut. 3 pers. pl. masc., suff. 3 pers. s. fem. ראה

יְרֵאוּהוּ[c] Kal pret. 3 pers. pl. (יָרְאוּ, from יָרֵא sing.), suff. 3 pers. sing. masc. (§ 16. rem. 1) ירא

יִירָאוּךָ[d] id. fut. 3 pers. pl. m. (יִירְאוּ, from יִירָא), suff. 2 p. s. m. (§ 16. rem. 12, & § 20. rem. 2) ירא

יְרֵאוּךָ[e] id. pret. 3 p. pl. (יָרְאוּ), suff. 2 p. s. m. (§ 16. r. 1) יָרֵא

יַרְאוּם[f] וַ Hiph. fut. 3 p. pl. m., suff. 3 p. pl. m.; וַ conv. ראה

יִרְאוּן[g] וְ Kal fut. 3 pers. pl. masc. with parag. ן [for יִירְאוּן § 20. rem. 2, & § 8. rem. 17] . ירא

יִרְאוּן[h] Kal fut. 3 pers. pl. masc. with parag. ן . ראה

---

[a] 2 Ch. 36. 13. [b] 2 Sa. 19. 44. [c] Mal. 3. 16. [d] Ps. 141. 9. [e] Is. 29. 21. [f] Is. 42. 23. [g] 2 Ki. 15. 30. [h] Je. 50. 24. [i] Ne. 7. 2. [k] Ex. 34. 3. [l] Le. 9. 6. [m] Je. 17. 8. [n] Job 42. 16. [o] Jos. 22. 25. [p] Ge. 18. 15. [q] Is. 30. 30. [r] Ge. 38. 15. [s] Eze. 1. 18. [t] 2 Ki. 6. 17. [u] Ju. 19. 3. [x] 2 Ki. 2. 15. [y] Da. 1. 13. [z] 2 Ki. 17. 28. [a] 2 Sa. 11. 24. [b] Nu. 14. 23. [c] Job 37. 24. [d] 1 Ki. 8. 40. [e] Ps. 119. 63. [f] Nu. 13. 26. [g] De. 13. 12. [h] De. 4. 28.

יִרְאוֹן וְ pr. name of a place . . . ירא

יְרֵאוּנִי[a] Kal pret. 3 p. pl. (יָֽרְאוּ, fr. יָרֵא sing.), suff. 1 pers. sing. (§ 16. rem. 1) . . ירא

יִרְאוּנִי Kal fut. 3 pers. pl. masc., suff. 1 pers. sing. ראה

יִרְאֵי adj. masc. pl. constr. from יָרֵא dec. 5 . ירא

יְרֵאָיו id. pl. with suff. 3 pers. sing. masc. . . ירא

יִרְאִיָּיה pr. name masc. . . . . ראה

יְרֵאֶיךָ adj. masc. pl., suff. 2 p. s. m. from יָרֵא dec. 5a ירא

יְרֵאִים id. pl., absolute state . . . . . ירא

יִרָאֲךָ[b] Kal fut. 3 pers. sing. masc. (יִירָא), suff. 2 pers. sing. masc. (§ 20. rem. 2) . . ירא

יַרְאֵם וַ Hiph. fut. 3 pers. sing. masc. (יַרְאֶה), suff. 3 pers. pl. masc. (§ 24. rem. 21); וַ conv. ראה

יִרְאֵם[c] וַ Kal fut. 3 pers. sing. masc. (יִרְאֶה), suff. 3 pers. pl. masc. (§ 20. rem. 21); וַ id. ראה

יִרְאֶנָּה id., suff. 3 pers. sing. fem. . . . ראה

יָרֵאנוּ[d] Kal pret. 1 pers. pl. (§ 23. rem. 1) יָרֵא

יַרְאֵנוּ[e] Hiph. fut. 3 pers. sing. masc. (יַרְאֶה), suff. 1 pers. pl. (§ 24. rem. 21) . . ראה

יַרְאֵנִי וַ׳ id. with suff. 1 pers. sing.; וַ conv. ראה

יִרְאֵנִי[f] וְ Kal fut. 3 pers. sing. masc. (יִרְאֶה), suff. 1 pers. sing. (§ 24. rem. 21); וַ id. . ראה

יֵרְאֻנִי[g] Piel pret. 3 pers. pl., suff. 1 pers. sing. . ירא

יִרְאֵנִי[h] Kal fut. 3 pers. sing. masc. (יִרְאֶה), suff. 1 pers. sing. (§ 24. rem. 21) . . . ראה

יָרֵאתָ[i] וְ׳ Kal pret. 2 pers. sing. masc. (§ 23. rem. 1) יָרֵא

יִרְאַת וְ noun f. s., constr. of יִרְאָה, or (Pr. 31. 30) adj. f. constr. of יְרֵאָה dec. 11 c, from יָרֵא m. ירא

יִרְאָתוֹ[k] id. with suff. 3 pers. sing. masc. . . ירא

יָרֵאתִי Kal pret. 1 pers. sing. (§ 23. rem. 1) יָרֵא

יִרְאָתִי[l] noun fem. s., suff. 1 p. s. from יִרְאָה (no pl.) ירא

יִרְאָתְךָ[m] וְ׳[n] id. with suff. 2 pers. sing. masc. . ירא

יְרֵאתֶם[o] Kal pret. 2 p. pl. m. as if from יָרֵא, comp. יְרֵאתֶם ירא

יִרְאָתָם[p] noun fem. sing. with suff. 3 pers. pl. masc. from יִרְאָה (q. v.) . . . . ירא

יְרֵאתֶם Kal pret. 2 pers. pl. masc. (§ 23. rem. 1) יָרֵא

יָרֵב[q] / יָרֵב וְ׳, וַ׳ Kal fut. 3 pers. sing. masc. ap. and conv. from יָרִיב . . . ריב

יֵרֶב[s] וַ׳ Kal fut. 3 pers. sing. masc., ap. from יִרְבֶּה; וַ conv. . . . . רבה

יֶרֶב / יַרְבֶּה וַ׳, וְ׳ Hiph. fut. 3 pers. sing. masc. ap. and full form; וַ id. . . רבה

יִרְבֶּה Kal fut. 3 pers. sing. masc. . . . רבה

יִרְבּוּ[u] וַ׳, וְ׳ id. fut. 3 pers. pl. masc.; וַ conv. רבה

יִרְבּוּן[x] / יִרְבְּיֻן[y] id. id. with parag. ן (§ 24. rem. 5) . רבה

יַרְבִּיצֵנִי[z] Hiph. fut. 3 pers. sing. masc., suff. 1 pers. sing. רבץ

יַרְבֶּךָ[a] וְ [for יַרְבְּךָ] Hiph. fut. 3 pers. sing. masc. (יַרְבֶּה), suff. 2 pers. s. m. (§ 24. rem. 21) רבה

יְרֻבַּעַל / יְרֻבַּעַל pr. name masc. R. רוב see . . . ריב

יָרָבְעָם וְ׳ pr. name masc. R. רוב, see . . ריב

יִרְבַּץ Kal fut. 3 pers. sing. m. [for יִרְבַּץ § 8. rem. 15] רבץ

יַרְבִּצוּ[b] Hiph. fut. 3 pers. pl. masc. . . . רבץ

יִרְבְּצוּ[c] / יִרְבָּצוּ[c] Kal fut. 3 pers. pl. masc. (§ 8. rem. 15) רבץ

יִרְבָּצוּן id. with parag. ן [for יִרְבְּצוּן § 8. rem. 17] רבץ

יָרָבְשֶׁת pr. name masc. R. רוב, see . . ריב

יִרְגַּז[d] / יִרְגַּז וַ׳[e] Kal fut. 3 pers. sing. masc. (§ 8. rem. 15); וַ conv. . . רגז

יִרְגְּזוּ / יִרְגָּזוּ וַ׳[oo] id. fut. 3 pers. pl. masc.; וַ id. . רגז

יִרְגְּזוּן[f] / יִרְגָּזוּן[g] id. with parag. ן (§ 8. rem. 17) . . רגז

יְרַגֵּל[h] וַ Piel fut. 3 pers. sing. masc.; וַ conv. . רגל

יְרַגְּלוּ וַ id. fut. 3 pers. pl. masc.; וַ id. . רגל

יִרְגְּמֻהוּ[i] וְ׳[k] Kal fut. 3 pers. pl. m., suff. 3 pers. sing. m. רגם

יִרְגְּמוּ וַ׳ id. fut. 3 pers. pl. masc.; וַ conv. . רגם

יֵרָגְנוּ וַ Niph. fut. 3 pers. pl. masc.; וַ id. . . רגן

יָרַד וְ׳ fut. יֵרֵד; imp. רֵד, רְדָה, יְרַד; inf. c. רֶדֶת.—I. *to go or come down, descend*; with לְ, אֶל, parag. ה, also acc. of the place *whither*.—II. *to go down, decline*, Ju. 19. 11, הַיּוֹם [יָ]רַד *the day was declining*.—III. *to flow, run down*, as the eye with tears; Is. 15. 3, יֹרֵד בַּבֶּכִי *melting in tears*.—IV. *to be cast down, to fall*. Hiph. הוֹרִיד.—I. *to cause to go down* or *descend*; *to send, bring, carry down*.—II. *to cast down*. Hoph. *to be brought down*.

יֶרֶד (*descent*) pr. name masc.—I. Ge. 5. 15.—II. 1 Ch. 4. 18.

יַרְדֵּן (*flowing, river*) pr. name, the river *Jordan* in Palestine flowing into the Dead Sea.

מוֹרָד masc. dec. 2b.—I. *descent, declivity*.—II. 1 Ki. 7. 29, מַעֲשֵׂה מוֹרָד *hanging work, festoons*. Others, *inlaid* or *inrun work*, the gold being *run down* into the engraved figures. Prof. Lee, *sloping*, i. e. in the manner of a declivity.

יָרָד[m] Kal pret. 3 pers. sing. m. for יָרַד (§ 8. rem. 7) ירד

יָרֶד[n] וַ Hiph. fut. 3 pers. sing. masc. conv. [for יָרֹד] רדד

יָרֶד pr. name masc. for יֶרֶד (§ 35. rem. 2) . ירה

יָרֹד[o] Kal inf. absolute . . . . ירד

יַרְדְּ[p] Hiph. fut. 3 pers. sing. masc. ap. [from יַרְדֶּה § 24. rem. 16] . . . רדה

[a] Mal. 3. 5. [b] Je. 10. 7. [c] 2 Ki. 2. 24. [d] Ho. 10. 3. [e] Ps. 4. 7. [f] 2 Sa. 1. 7. [g] 2 Sa. 14. 15. [h] Ex. 33. 20. [i] 2 Sa. 1. 14. [k] Ex. 20. 20. [l] Je. 32. 40. [m] Job 4. 6. [n] De. 2. 25. [o] Jos. 4. 24. [oo] Is. 5. 25. [p] Is. 29. 13. [q] Ho. 4. 4. [r] 1 Sa. 24. 16. [s] Ge. 1. 22; Ex. 1. 20. [t] Job 34. 37. [u] Pr. 4. 10. [x] Ps. 139. 18. [y] De. 8. 13. [z] Ps. 23. 2. [a] Ge. 28. 3. [b] Is. 13. 20. [c] Is. 11. 7; 14. 30. [d] Is. 28. 21. [e] 2 Sa. 19. 1. [f] Ex. 15. 14. [g] Hab. 3. 7. [h] 2 Sa. 19. 28. [i] Le. 20. 2. [k] 2 Ch. 24. 21. [l] Ps. 106. 25. [m] 2 Sa. 11. 13. [n] 1 Ki. 6. 32. [o] Ge. 43. 20. [p] Is. 41. 2.

וַיֵּרֶד[gg] Kal fut. 3 pers. sing. masc. . . . ירד

וַיֵּרַד, וַיֵּרֵד } id. with conv. ·וַ (§ 20. rem. 4) . . ירד

וַיֵּרְדְּ Kal fut. 3 pers. sing. masc., ap. [for יִרְדֶּה § 24. rem. 3]; ·וַ conv. . . . רדה

יֶרֶד pr. name masc. . . . . . . ירד

יֹרֵד Kal part. act. sing. masc. dec. 7b . . . ירד

וַיֹּרֶד[a] Hiph. fut. 3 pers. sing. masc. ap. & conv. [for יוֹרִד § 20. rem. 11] . . . ירד

יְרַד[b] Kal imp. s. m. (others, Piel fut. ap. from רדה) ירד

יָרְדָה[c], יָרֵדָה } id. pret. 3 pers. sing. fem. (§ 8. rem. 7) ירד

יֹרְדָה[d] id. part. act. sing., fem. of יֹרֵד . . . ירד

וַיִּרְדֵּהוּ[e] Kal fut. 3 pers. sing. masc. [יִרְדֶּה], suff. 3 pers. sing. masc. (§ 24. rem. 21); ·וַ conv. רדה

וַיֹּרִדֵהוּ Hiph. fut. 3 pers. sing. masc. [יוֹרִיד], suff. 3 pers. sing. masc. (§ 20. rem. 11); ·וַ id. ירד

וַיֹּרִדֻהוּ[f] id. fut. 3 pers. pl. m., suff. 3 pers. s. m.; ·וַ id. ירד

וְיָרְדוּ Kal pret. 3 pers. pl. . . . . ירד

וַיֵּרְדוּ id. fut. 3 pers. pl. masc.; ·וַ conv. . . ירד

יִרְדּוּ[g] וַיִּ, וְ[h] Kal fut. 3 pers. pl. masc. . . רדה

יֹרִדוּ Hiph. fut. 3 p. pl. m. [for יוֹרִידוּ § 20. rem. 11] ירד

יֹרְדוֹת[k] Kal part. act. fem., pl. of יֹרֶדֶת dec. 13a from יֹרֵד masc. (§ 8. rem. 19) . . . ירד

יֹרְדֵי id. pl. constr. masc. from יֹרֵד dec. 7b . . ירד

יֹרְדִים[kk] id. pl., absolute state . . . . ירד

וַיֵּרָדַם[nn] Niph. fut. 3 pers. sing. masc. [for יֵרָדֵם § 9. rem. 4]; ·וַ conv. . . . . רדם

וַיִּרְדֶּהָ[l] Kal fut. 3 pers. sing. masc. [יִרְדֶּה], suff. 3 pers. s. f. (§ 24. r. 21, & § 2. r. 3); ·וַ id. רדה

יַרְדֵּן pr. name of a river . . . . . ירד

יָרַדְנוּ וְ[m] Kal pret. 3 pers. pl. . . . . ירד

יִרְדֵּנּוּ[n] Kal fut. 3 pers. sing. masc. [יִרְדֶּה], suff. 3 pers. sing. masc. (§ 24. rem. 21) . . . רדה

יְרַדֵּף[o] Piel fut. 3 pers. s. m. [for יְרַדֵּף § 10. r. 4] רדף

יִרַדֹּף[p] mixed form of Kal & Piel fut., יְרַדֵּף & יִרְדֹּף רדף

יִרְדֹּף, יִרְדָּף־[q] וַיִּ } Kal fut. 3 pers. sing. masc. (§ 8. rem. 18); ·וַ conv. . . . . רדף

וַיִּרְדְּפֵהוּ[r] id. id., suff. 3 pers. sing. masc.; ·וַ id. . רדף

יִרְדְּפוֹ[s] id. id., suff. 3 pers. sing. masc. . . . רדף

יִרְדֹּפוּ, יִרְדְּפוּ[u] וַיִּ } id. fut. 3 pers. pl. masc. (§ 8. rem. 15); ·וַ conv. . . . . רדף

וַיִּרְדְּפוּם id. id., suff. 3 pers. pl. masc.; ·וַ id. . רדף

יִרְדְּפוּנִי[x] id. id., suff. 1 pers. sing. . . . רדף

יִרְדְּפֶךָּ[y] id. fut. 3 pers. sing. masc., suff. 2 pers. sing. masc. for יִרְדָּפְךָ (§ 8. rem. 15), יִרְדְּפֶךָּ רדף

וַיִּרְדְּפֵם[z] id. id., suff. 3 pers. pl. masc.; ·וַ conv. רדף

יָרַדְתָּ[a], יָרַדְתָּ, וְיָרַדְתָּ } Kal pret. 2 pers. sing. masc. acc. shifted by conv. וְ (§ 8. rem. 7) . . ירד

וְיֹרֶדֶת[b] id. part. act. fem. dec. 13a, from יֹרֵד masc. (§ 8. rem. 19) . . . . ירד

יָרַדְתִּי, וְיָרַדְתִּי } id. pret. 1 pers. sing. acc. shifted by conv. וְ (§ 8. rem. 7) . . . ירד

וְיָרַדְתְּ[c] id. pret. 2 p. s. f. Kh. תִּי', K. תְּ' (§ 8. r. 5) ירד

יָרָה fut. יִירֶה; inf. c. יְרוֹת, יְרֹה; imp. יְרֵה (§ 25. No. 2e, & § 24. rem. 2).—I. *to throw, cast; to shoot,* as an arrow; part. יוֹרִים *archers.*—II. *to cast, lay a foundation.*—III. *to sprinkle, to water,* Ho. 6. 3. Niph. *to be shot,* Ex. 19. 13. Hiph. הוֹרָה.—I. *to throw, cast; to shoot,* as arrows.—II. *to put forth,* as the finger, *to point out, show.*—III. *to teach, instruct;* with the acc. of the thing, also with a double acc.; with מִן, אֶל, בְּ *to instruct in* any thing.

יוֹרֶה masc. *the former* or *early rain,* falling in Judea about the beginning of November.

יוֹרָה (*former rain*) pr. name masc. Ezr. 2. 18.

יוֹרַי (for יוֹרְיָה whom *the Lord teaches*) pr. name masc. 1 Ch. 5. 13.

מוֹרֶה masc. dec. 9a, prop. Hiph. part.—I. *archer.*—II. *teacher.*—III. *former rain;* comp. יוֹרֶה.

תּוֹרָה fem. dec. 10.—I. *instruction, direction, precept.*—II. *law.*—III. *mode, manner,* 2 Sa. 7. 19.

תּוֹר masc. i. q. תּוֹרָה *mode, manner,* 1 Ch. 17. 17. תּוֹר, however, may stand for תֹּאַר, תאר *form, figure,* and hence perhaps *type,* comp. באר & בּוֹר, מְאוּם, מוּם.

יְרוּאֵל (*founded of God*) pr. name of a desert, 2 Ch. 20. 16.

יְרוּשָׁלַםִ, יְרוּשָׁלַיִם (*foundation of peace*) pr. name, *Jerusalem,* the royal city of Palestine on the confines of Judah and Benjamin; called שָׁלֵם Ge. 14. 18; Ps. 76. 3; in the Chald. יְרוּשְׁלֶם, יְרוּשְׁלֵם.

יְרִיאֵל (*established of God*) pr. name masc. 1 Ch. 7. 2.

יְרִיָּה, יְרִיָּהוּ (*established of the Lord*) pr. name masc. 1 Ch. 23. 19; 24. 23; 26. 31.

יָרַה only fut. תִּרְהוּ (for תִּירְהוּ) *to fear, be afraid,* Is. 44. 8.

יָרֹה[d] Kal inf. absolute . . . . ירה

יְרֵה[e] id. imp. sing. masc. . . . . ירה

---

[a] Pr. 21. 22. [b] Ju. 5. 13. [c] Is. 38. 8. [d] La. 1. 16. [e] Ju. 14. 9. [f] 1 Ki. 1. 53. [g] Je. 5. 31. [gg] 1 Sa. 17. 8. [h] Ge. 1. 26. [i] 1 Ki. 5. 23. [k] Pr. 5. 5. [kk] Ge. 28. 12. [l] La. 1. 13. [m] Ge. 44. 26. [n] Le. 25. 53. [nn] Jon. 1. 5. [o] Na. 1. 8. [p] Ps. 7. 6. [q] Jos. 23. 10. [r] Ju. 9. 40. [s] Ho. 8. 3. [t] Le. 26. 8, etc. [u] 2 Sa. 2. 28. [x] Ps. 23. 6. [y] Eze. 35. 6. [z] Is. 41. 3. [a] 1 Sa. 17. 28. [b] 1 Sa. 25. 20. [c] Ru. 3. 3. [d] Ex. 19. 13. [e] 2 Ki. 13. 17.

יִרְהֲבוּ[a]	Kal fut. 3 pers. pl. masc. . . .	רהב
יִרְהוּ[b]	the following with suff. 3 pers. sing. masc.	ירה
יִרוּ[ce] וַיּ׳	Hiph. fut. 3 pers. pl. masc. for יוֹרוּ, (§ 20. rem. 11, & § 25. No. 2a); ·וַ conv.	ירה
יְרוּאֵל	pr. name of a place	ירה
יָרוֹחַ	pr. name masc.	ירח
יִרְוַח[c]	וְ Kal fut. 3 pers. sing. masc. . .	רוח
יִרְוְיֻן[d]	Kal fut. 3 p. pl. m. with parag. ן (§ 24. r. 5)	רוה
יְרַוֻּךָ[e]	Piel fut. 3 pers. pl. m. [יְרַוּוּ], suff. 2 p. s. m.	רוה
יָרוּם	וְ[f]׳ Kal fut. 3 pers. sing. masc. . .	רום
יָרוּם[g]	Kh. יָרוּם q. v., K. וְרָם (q. v.) . .	רום
יָרוּמוּ	Kal fut. 3 pers. pl. masc. . . .	רום
יֵרוֹמּוּ[h]	וַיֵּ[i]׳ Niph. fut. 3 pers. pl. masc.; ·וַ conv.	רמם
יְרוֹמֵם[k]	Pilel fut. 3 pers. sing. masc. . .	רום
יְרוֹמְמוּהוּ[l]	וְ id. fut. 3 pers. pl. masc., suff. 3 pers. sing. masc. with cop. וְ [for וִירוֹ׳, וְיְ׳] . .	רום
יְרוֹמִמְךָ[m]	וְ id. fut. 3 p. s. m., suff. 2 p. s. m., see preced.	רום
יְרוֹמְמֵנִי[n]	id. id., suff. 1 pers. sing. . . .	רום
יָרוֹן[o]	Kal fut. 3 pers. sing. m. [for יָרֹן § 18. r. 12]	רנן
יֵרוֹעַ[p]	Niph. fut. 3 pers. sing. masc. . . .	רוע
יְרוֹפָפוּ[q]	Pulal fut. 3 pers. pl. masc. [for יְרוֹפְפוּ comp. § 8. rem. 15]	רוף
יָרוּץ[r]	Kal fut. 3 pers. sing. m. [for יָרֹץ § 18. r. 12]	רצץ
יָרוּץ	Kal fut. 3 pers. sing. masc. . . .	רוץ
יָרוּצוּ[pp]	וַיָּ[s]׳ id. fut. 3 pers. pl. masc.; ·וַ conv. .	רוץ
יְרוּצוּן[t]	id. with parag. ן	רוץ
יְרוֹצֵצוּ[u]	Pilel fut. 3 pers. pl. masc. [for יְרוֹצְצוּ comp. § 8. rem. 15]	רוץ
יָרוֹק[x]	noun masc. sing.	ירק
יְרוּשָׁא יְרוּשָׁה	pr. name fem.	ירש
יְרוּשָׁלַיְמָה	the following with loc. ה . . .	ירה
יְרוּשָׁלַםִ וִירוּ׳ יְרוּשָׁלָםִ וִירוּ׳	pr. name of a place; with cop. וְ [for וִירוּ׳, וְיְ׳] . .	ירה
יְרוּשְׁלֶם יְרוּשְׁלֵם	Chald. pr. name of a place . . .	ירה
יְרוּשָׁלֵמָה	pr. name m. (יְרוּשָׁלַםִ) with loc. ה, K. יְ׳לַיְמָה	ירה
יֵרָזֶה[y]	Niph. fut. 3 pers. sing. masc. . . .	רזה
יִרְזְמוּן[z]	Kal fut. 3 pers. pl. masc. with parag. ן .	רזם

יָרֵחַ ׳וְ masc. dec. 5a, *the moon.*

יֶרַח masc. dec. 6a (pl. c. יַרְחֵי; § 35. rem. 5).—I. *month, lunar month.*—II. pr. name of a descendant of Joktan, Ge. 10. 26.

יְרַח Chald. dec. 3a, *month.*

יָרוֹחַ (*moon*) pr. name masc. 1 Ch. 5. 14.

יָרַח	pr. name of a people and region, for יֶרַח (§ 35. rem. 2)	ירח
יָרַח[a] וַיָּרַח	Hiph. fut. 3 pers. sing. masc. ap. & conv. from יָרִיחַ (§ 21. rem. 19) .	רוח
יֶרַח	noun masc. sing. dec. 6a (§ 35. rem. 5) .	ירח
יְרֵחוֹ	pr. name of a place, see יְרִיחוֹ . .	רוח
יַרְחֵי[b]	n. m., pl. constr. from יֶרַח d. 6 (§ 35. r. 5)	ירח
יַרְחִיב	Hiph. fut. 3 pers. sing. masc. . . .	רחב
יַרְחִיבוּ[c]	וַ id. fut. 3 pers. pl. masc.; ·וַ conv. .	רחב
יְרָחִים	noun masc. pl. (constr. יַרְחֵי) from יֶרַח d. 6 (§ 35. rem. 5)	ירח
יַרְחִין[d]	Chald. noun masc., pl. of יְרַח dec. 3a .	ירח
יַרְחִיקֶנָּה[e]	Hiph. fut. 3 p. s. m., suff. 3 p. s. f. (§ 2. r. 3)	רחק
יְרֵחֵךְ[f]	וְ noun m. s., suff. 2 pers. s. m. with cop. וְ [for וְיְ׳, וִירֵחֵךְ § 35. r. 5] from יָרֵחַ d. 5	ירח
יְרַחֵם	Piel fut. 3 pers. sing. masc. (§ 14. rem. 1)	רחם
יְרֹחָם	pr. name masc.	רחם
יְרֻחָם[g] יְרֻחַם[h]	Pual fut. 3 pers. sing. masc. (§ 14. rem. 1, comp. § 8. rem. 15) . . .	רחם
יְרַחְמְאֵל	pr. name masc.	רחם
יְרַחֲמֵהוּ[i]	וְ Piel fut. 3 pers. sing. masc. (יְרַחֵם q. v.), suff. 3 p. s. m. with cop. וְ [for וִירַחֲמֵהוּ, וְיְ׳]	רחם
יְרַחֵמוּ	id. fut. 3 pers. pl. masc. [for יְרַחֲמוּ, comp. § 8. rem. 15]	רחם
יְרַחֲמֵם[k]	וַ id. fut. 3 p. s. m., suff. 3 p. pl. m.; וַ conv.	רחם
יְרַחֲמֶנּוּ[l]	id. id., suff. 3 pers. sing. masc. . .	רחם
יְרַחֲמֵנוּ[m]	id. id., suff. 1 pers. pl. . . .	רחם
יַרְחָע	pr. name of an Egyptian slave, 1 Ch. 2. 34, 35.	
יְרַחֵף[n]	Piel fut. 3 pers. sing. masc. (§ 14. rem. 1)	רחף
יִרְחָץ[o] וַיִּ׳ יִרְחַץ	Kal fut. 3 pers. sing. masc. (§ 8. rem. 15); ·וַ conv. . . .	רחץ
יִרְחֲצוּ[p] וַיִּ׳ יִרְחֲצוּ	Kal fut. 3 p. pl. m. (§ 8. r. 15); ·וַ id.	רחץ
יֵרָחֵק[q]	Kh., יֵרָתֵק K., Niph. fut. 3 pers. sing. masc. from רחק or	רתק
יִרְחַק	Kal fut. 3 pers. sing. masc. . . .	רחק
יְרַחֲקוּ[r]	Piel fut. 3 pers. pl. masc. (§ 14. rem. 1)	רחק
יִרְחֲקוּ[s]	Kal fut. 3 pers. pl. masc. . . .	רחק

יָרַט[t] I. *to cast down, precipitate,* Job 16. 11.—II. *to be perverse, destructive,* Nu. 22. 32.

יִרְטָבוּ[u]	Kal fut. 3 p. pl. m. [for יִרְטְבוּ § 8. r. 15]	רטב
יִרְטֵנִי[x]	or יִרְטֵנִי Kal fut. 3 pers. sing. masc., suff. 1 pers. sing. from רטה or . .	ירט
יְרֻטָּשׁוּ[y] יְרֻטָּשׁוּ	Pual fut. 3 pers. pl. masc. (comp. § 8. rem. 15) . . .	רטש
יְרִיאֵל	pr. name masc.	ירה

[a] Is. 3. 5. [b] Ps. 64. 5. [c] Job 32. 20. [d] Ps. 36. 9. [e] Pr. 5. 19. 2 Sa. 11. 20. 2 Ch. 35. 23.
[f] Ps. 18. 47. [g] Da. 11. 12. [h] Eze. 10. 17. [i] Eze. 10. 19. [k] Ho. 11. 7.
[l] Ps. 107. 32. [m] Ps. 37. 34. [n] Ps. 27. 5. [o] Pr. 29. 6. [p] Pr. 11. 15; 13. 20. [pp] Is. 55. 5.
[q] Job 26. 11. [r] Is. 42. 4. [s] Jos. 8. 19. [t] Joel 2. 4, 7. [u] Na. 2. 5.
[x] Job 39. 8. [y] Is. 17. 4. [z] Job 15. 12. [a] 1 Sa. 26. 19. [b] Job 7. 3.
[c] Ps. 35. 21. [d] Da. 4. 26. [e] Pr. 22. 15. [f] Is. 60. 20. [g] Pr. 28. 13.
[h] Ho. 14. 4. [i] Is. 55. 7. [k] 2 Ki. 13. 23. [l] Is. 27. 11 [m] Mi. 7. 19.
[n] De. 32. 11. [o] Le. 17. 16. [p] Ex. 40. 32. [q] Ec. 12. 6. [r] Eze. 43. 9.
[s] Job 5. 4. [t] Nu. 22. 32. [u] Job 24. 8. [x] Job 16. 11. [y] Ho. 14. 1.

יָרִיב וְ pr. name masc. . . . . . ריב
יָרִיב Kal fut. 3 pers. sing. masc. . . . ריב
[a] יָרִיבוּ וַ id. fut. 3 pers. pl. masc.; ·וַ conv. . . ריב
[b] יְרִיבוּן וַ id. id. with parag. ן; וַ id. . . . ריב
[c] יְרִיבַי / [d] יְרִיבַי } noun masc. pl., suff. 1 pers. sing. from [יָרִיב] dec. 3a . . . ריב
יְרִיבַי וְ pr. name masc. (יְרִיבַי) with cop. וְ [for וִירִיבַי, וְיְ] . . . ריב
[e] יְרִיבֶךָ noun masc. sing., suff. 2 pers. sing. masc. from [יָרִיב] dec. 3a . . . ריב
[f] יְרִבֻן defect. for יְרִיבוּן (q. v.) . . . . ריב
יְרִיָּה / יְרִיָּהוּ } pr. name masc. . . . . ירה
[g] יֹרִידוּ וַ Hiph. fut. 3 pers. pl. masc. for יוֹרִידוּ (§ 20. rem. 2); ·וַ conv. . . . ירד
[h] יֹרִידוּם וַ id., suff. 3 pers. pl. masc.; ·וַ id. . . ירד
[i] יָרִיחַ Hiph. fut. 3 pers. sing. masc. . . . רוח
יְרִיחֹה / יְרִיחוֹ } pr. name of a place [with cop. וְ for וִירִיחוֹ, וְיְ] . . . רוח
[k] יְרִיחוּן / [l] יְרִיחֻן } Hiph. fut. 3 pers. pl. masc. with parag. ן רוח
יָרִים Hiph. fut. 3 pers. sing. masc. . . . רום
[m] יְרִימֶהָ וַ id. id., suff. 3 pers. sing. fem.; וַ conv. . רום
יָרִימוּ id. fut. 3 pers. pl. masc. . . . רום
[n] יָרִימוּ Kh. יָרִימוּ q. v., K. יָרוּמוּ (q. v.) . . רום
יְרִימוֹת / ירימות } pr. name masc. [with cop. וְ, for וִירִ׳, וִירֵ׳, וְיְ׳] . . . ירם
יָרִיעַ Hiph. fut. 3 pers. sing. masc. . . . רוע
יָרִיעוּ וַיָּ id. fut. 3 pers. pl. masc.; ·וַ conv. . . רוע
יְרִיעוֹת / [o] יְרִיעוֹת וְ } noun fem., pl. of יְרִיעָה dec. 10, also pr. n. m. [with cop. וְ for וִירִיאוֹת, וְיְ] ירע
יְרִיעֹתַי id., suff. 1 pers. sing. [for ־תַי] . . . ירע
[p] יְרִיעוֹתֵיהֶם id., suff. 3 pers. pl. masc. . . . ירע
יְרִיעֹת defect. for יְרִיעוֹת (q. v.) . . . ירע
[q] יָרִיצוּ וַ Hiph. fut. 3 pers. pl. masc.; ·וַ conv. . . רוץ
[r] יָרִיק Hiph. fut. 3 pers. sing. masc. . . . רוק
יָרִיקוּ id. fut. 3 pers. pl. masc. . . . רוק
[s] יָרִיתִי וְ Kal pret. 1 pers. sing. . . . ירה

יָרֵךְ fem. dec. 5b.—I. *thigh*; יֹצְאֵי יָרֵךְ *the comers out of the thigh*, i. e. the descendants of; שׁוֹק עַל־יָרֵךְ *hip upon thigh*, i. e. wholly; סָפַק עַל־יָרֵךְ *to smite upon the thigh*, in token of distress.—II. of inanimate things; *the shank* of the candlestick in the tabernacle; *side* of a tent. Du. יְרֵכַיִם *both thighs*.

יַרְכָה fem., with suff. יַרְכָתוֹ dec. 11c (§ 39. No. 3. r. 3), *a side*, as of a country, Ge. 49. 13. Du. יַרְכָתַיִם, constr. יַרְכְּתֵי (strictly from יָרֵךְ=יַרְכָּה).—I. *hinder part, hinder side*, of a building.—II. *hindmost, innermost parts, recesses.*—III. *remotest parts*, as of the earth, the north.

יַרְכָא Chald. fem. dec. 8, *the thigh*, Da. 2. 32.

יֵרַךְ Kal fut. 3 pers. sing. masc. (§ 18. rem. 6) . רכך
יֶרֶךְ noun fem. sing., constr. of יָרֵךְ dec. 5b . ירך
יַרְכֵּב וַ Hiph. fut. 3 pers. sing. masc. ap. [from יַרְכִּיב]; ·וַ conv. . . . רכב
[u] יִרְכַּב וַיִּ Kal fut. 3 pers. sing. masc.; ·וַ id. . רכב
[t] יַרְכִּבֻהוּ וַ Hiph. fut. 3 pers. pl. masc. (יַרְכִּיבוּ), suff. 3 pers. sing. masc.; ·וַ id. . . רכב
[y] יַרְכִּבֵהוּ id. fut. 3 pers. s. m. [יַרְכִּיב], suff. 3 pers. s. m. רכב
יַרְכִּבוּ וַ id. fut. 3 pers. pl. m. for יַרְכִּיבוּ; ·וַ conv. רכב
יִרְכָּבוּ / [z] יִרְכְּבוּ וַ } Kal fut. 3 pers. pl. masc. (§ 8. rem. 15); ·וַ id. . . . רכב
[a] יַרְכִּבֵם וַ Hiph. fut. 3 pers. sing. masc., [יַרְכִּיב] suff. 3 pers. pl. masc.; ·וַ id. . . . רכב
יְרֵכָהּ noun fem. s., suff. 3 p. s. fem. from יָרֵךְ dec. 5b ירך
יְרֵכוֹ id., suff. 3 pers. sing. masc. . . . ירך
יְרֵכִי id., suff. 1 pers. sing. . . . ירך
[b] יַרְכִּיבֵהוּ וַ Hiph. fut. 3 p. s. m., suff. 3 p. s. m.; ·וַ conv. רכב
[c] יַרְכִּיבֻהוּ וַ id. fut. 3 pers. pl. m., suff. 3 p. s. m.; ·וַ id. רכב
[d] יַרְכִּיבוּ וַ id. fut. 3 pers. pl. masc.; ·וַ id. . רכב
[e] יְרֵכֶיךָ n. f. du., with suff. 2 p. s. m. from יָרֵךְ d. 5b ירך
[f] יְרֵכַיִם id. du., absolute state . . . ירך
יְרֵכֵךְ id. sing., suff. 2 pers. sing. fem. Nu. 5. 21. ירך
יִרְכְּסוּ [g] וְ, [h] וַיִּ Kal fut. 3 pers. pl. masc.; ·וַ conv. רכס
[i] יַרְכָּתֵהּ וְ Chald. noun fem. sing. with suff. 3 pers. sing. m. [from יַרְכָה] dec. 8a . . . ירך
[k] יַרְכָתוֹ וְ noun fem. sing., suff. 3 pers. sing. m. [from יַרְכָה comp. dec. 11c § 39. No. 3. rem. 3] ירך
יַרְכְּתֵי id. dual constr. [from יַרְכָה] . . ירך

יָרַם Root not used; Arab. ورم *to be high*, (§ 20. No. 1).

יַרְמוּת (*height*) pr. name—I. of a city in the tribe of Judah.—II. of a city assigned to the Levites in the tribe of Issachar, Jos. 21. 29; called רֶמֶת ch. 19. 21.

יְרֵמוֹת, יְרֵמוֹת, יְרִימוֹת (*heights*) pr. name masc. of several persons.

יְרֵמַי (*highlander*) pr. name masc. Ezr. 10. 33.

יָרֵם וְ / יָרֶם וַ } Hiph. fut. 3 pers. sing. masc., ap. and conv. from יָרִים . . . רום
[l] יָרֻם וְ / יָרָם וַ / [m] יָרֹם וַיָּ׳, [n] וְ } Kal fut. 3 pers. sing. masc., ap. and conv. from יָרוּם (§ 21. rem. 6 & 7) . . . רום

[a] Ge. 26. 20, 21. [b] Ju. 8. 1. [c] Je. 18. 19. [d] Ps. 35. 1. [e] Is. 49. 25. [f] Ex. 21. 18. [g] 2 Ki. 11. 19. [h] Jos. 10. 27. [i] Job 39. 25. [k] Ps. 115. 6. [l] De. 4. 28. [m] Ge. 31. 45. [n] Ps. 66. 7. [o] Is. 54. 2. [p] Je. 49. 29. [q] 2 Ch. 35. 13. [r] Hab. 1. 17. [s] Ge. 31. 51. [t] Jos. 18. 6. [u] Le. 15. 9. [x] 2 Ki. 23. 30. [y] De. 32. 13. [z] 2 Sa. 13. 29. [a] Ex. 4. 20. [b] Est. 6. 11. [c] 2 Ch. 35. 24. [d] 1 Ch. 13. 7. [e] Ca. 7. 2. [f] Ex. 28. 42. [g] Ex. 28. 28. [h] Ex. 39. 21. [i] Da. 2. 32. [k] Ge. 49. 13. [l] Nu. 24. 7. [m] 2 Sa. 22. 47. [n] Ex. 16. 20.

יֹרֵם[a] וְ, [b]וַיֹּ׳ Hiph. fut. 3 pers. sing. masc. (יוֹרֶה), suff. 3 pers. pl. m. (§ 25. No. 2e); ·וַ conv. ירה

יֵרֹמּוּ[c] וַ Niph. fut. 3 pers. pl. masc.; ·וַ id. . רמם

יְרֻמוּן[d] Kal fut. 3 pers. pl. masc. (יָרוּמוּ) with parag. ן רום

יַרְמוּת pr. name of a place . . . . ירם

יְרֵמוֹת וִירֵ׳ pr. name masc., see יְרִימוֹת . . ירם

יְרֵמַי pr. name masc. . . . . ירם

יִרְמְיָה וְ׳ / יִרְמְיָהוּ וְ׳ } pr. name masc. . . . . רמה

יִרְמֹס[e] [f]וְ׳ / יִרְמָס־[g] } Kal fut. 3 pers. sing. masc. (§ 8. rem. 18) רמס

יִרְמְסֵהוּ[h] וַ id. fut. 3 p. s. m., suff. 3 p. s. m.; ·וַ conv. רמס

יִרְמְסֻהוּ[i] וַ id. fut. 3 pers. pl. m., suff. 3 pers. s. m.; ·וַ id. רמס

יִרְמְסוּ[k] וַ id. fut. 3 pers. pl. masc.; ·וַ id. . רמס

יִרְמְסֶנָּה[l] וַ id. fut. 3 pers. sing. masc., suff. 3 pers. sing. fem. (§ 2. rem. 3); ·וַ id. . . . רמס

יָרֹנּוּ [ff]וַיָּ׳ Kal fut. 3 pers. pl. masc.; ·וַ id. . רנן

יֹרֵנִי[m] וַ Hiph. fut. 3 pers. sing. masc. (יוֹרֶה), suff. 1 pers. sing. (§ 25. No. 2e); ·וַ id. . ירה

יְרֻנַּן[n] Pual fut. 3 pers. sing. masc. [for יְרֻנַּן comp. § 8. rem. 15, & § 18. rem. 13] . רנן

יְרַנֵּנוּ / יְרַנְּנוּ } Piel fut. 3 pers. pl. masc. (comp. § 8. rem. 15) . . . . רנן

יְרַנְּנוּ[o] וְ id. with cop. וְ [for וִירַנְּנוּ ,וִי׳] . . רנן

[יָרַע] *to be fearful, distressed*, Is. 15. 4; perhaps primarily, *to tremble*.

יְרִיעָה fem. dec. 10, *a curtain, a hanging*, so called from its *tremulous motion*; so Gesenius, but compare Prof. Lee under יָרַע.

יְרִיעוֹת (*curtains*) pr. name fem. 1 Ch. 2. 18.

יָרַע[p] וַ Hiph. fut. 3 pers. sing. masc. ap. and conv. from יָרִיעַ (§ 21. rem. 19) . . רוע

יָרַע[q] וַ / יָרֵעַ[r] } Hiph. fut. 3 pers. sing. masc. (§ 18. rem. 11, comp. § 15. rem. 1) . } רעע

יֵרֹעַ[s] / יֵרַע } Kal fut. 3 pers. sing. masc. (§ 18. rem. 6) רעע

יֵרַע[t] [u]וַיֵּ׳ id. bef. penacute or by conv. ·וַ (v. id. comp. also rem. 5) . . . רעע

יֵרַע[v] Kal fut. 3 pers. sing. masc. ap. from יִרְעֶה (§ 24. rem. 3) . . . . . רעה

יִרְעָב[x] / יִרְעַב[y] } Kal fut. 3 pers. sing. masc. (§ 8. rem. 15) רעב

יִרְעָבוּ[z] id. fut. 3 pers. pl. masc. [for יִרְעֲבוּ v. id.] רעב

יַרְעִבֶךָ[a] וַ Hiph. fut. 3 pers. sing. masc., suff. 2 pers. sing. masc. [for יַרְעִיבְךָ]; ·וַ conv. . רעב

יָרְעָה[b] Kal pret. 3 pers. sing. fem. . . . ירע

יִרְעֶה Kal fut. 3 pers. sing. masc. . . רעה

יָרֵעוּ וַיָּ׳ Hiph. fut. 3 pers. pl. masc.; ·וַ conv. . רעע

יָרְעוּ וַ defect. for יָרִיעוּ (q. v.) . . . רוע

יֵרְעוּ[c] Kal fut. 3 pers. pl. masc. (as if from ירע comp. § 18. rem. 6) . . . רעע

יִרְעוּ וַיִּ׳ Kal fut. 3 pers. pl. masc.; ·וַ conv. . רעה

יִרְעוּךְ[d] id. fut. 3 pers. sing. m., suff. 2 pers. sing. fem. רעה

יִרְעוּן[e] id. id. with parag. ן . . . . רעה

יַרְעִיב[f] Hiph. fut. 3 pers. sing. masc. . . רעב

יַרְעֵם וַיַּ׳ Hiph. fut. 3 p.s.m., ap. [fr. יַרְעִים]; ·וַ conv. רעם

יַרְעֵם[g] וַ Hiph. fut. 3 pers. sing. masc. [יַרְעֶה], suff. 3 pers. pl. masc. (§ 24. rem. 21); ·וַ id. . רעה

יִרְעַם Kal fut. 3 pers. sing. masc. . . רעם

יִרְעֵם Kal fut. 3 pers. sing. masc. (יִרְעֶה), suff. 3 pers. pl. masc. (§ 24. rem. 21) . . . רעה

יִרְעֶנָּה[h] id. with suff. 3 pers. sing. fem. (§ 2. rem. 3) רעה

יְרֹעַע[i] Pulal fut. 3 p. s. m. [for יְרוֹעַע comp. § 8. rem. 15] רוע

יִרְעֲפוּ Kal fut. 3 pers. pl. masc. . . . רעף

יִרְעֲפוּן[k] id. with parag. ן . . . . . רעף

יִרְעֲצוּ[l] וַ Kal fut. 3 pers. pl. masc.; ·וַ conv. . רעץ

יִרְעַשׁ[m] Kal fut. 3 pers. sing. masc. . . . רעש

יִרְעֲשׁוּ [n]וְ׳, [o]וַיִּ׳ id. fut. 3 pers. pl. masc.; ·וַ conv. רעש

יֶרֶף[p] וַ Kal fut. 3 pers. sing. m. ap. from יִרְפֶּה; ·וַ id. רפה

יְרַפֵּא [q]וַ׳ Piel fut. 3 pers. sing. masc.; ·וַ id. . רפא

יִרְפָּא וַיִּ׳ Kal fut. 3 pers. sing. masc.; ·וַ id. . רפא

יִרְפְּאֵל pr. name of a place . . . . רפא

יֵרָפְאוּ[r] [s]וְ׳ Niph. fut. 3 pers. pl. masc. . . רפא

יְרַפְּאוּ[t] וַ Piel fut. 3 pers. pl. masc.; וַ conv. . רפא

יִרְפָּאֵם[u] וַ Kal fut. 3 pers. sing. m., suff. 3 pers. pl. m. רפא

יִרְפָּאֵנוּ[x] וְ id. with suff. 1 pers. pl. . . . רפא

יִרְפַּד[y] Kal fut. 3 pers. sing. masc. . . . רפד

יִרְפֶּה[z] Kal fut. 3 pers. sing. masc. . . . . רפה

יֵרָפוּ[a] וַ Niph. fut. 3 pers. pl. masc. [for יֵרָפְאוּ § 23. rem. 11]; ·וַ conv. . . . רפא

יְרַפּוּ[b] וַ Piel fut. 3 pers. pl. masc. for יְרַפְּאוּ (§ 23. rem. 11); וַ id. . . . . רפא

יִרְפּוּ [c]וַיִּ׳ Kal fut. 3 pers. pl. masc.; ·וַ id. . רפה

יַרְפְּךָ Hiph. fut. 3 pers. sing. masc. [יַרְפֶּה], suff. 2 pers. sing. masc. (§ 24. rem. 21) . רפה

יָרָץ[d] וַ / יָרָץ וַ / יָרֹץ[e] } Kal fut. 3 pers. sing. masc., ap. and conv. from יָרוּץ (§ 21. rem. 7 & 8) } רוץ

יֵרָצֶה Niph. fut. 3 pers. sing. masc. . . רצה

יִרְצֶה Kal fut. 3 pers. sing. masc. . . . רצה

יִרְצֵהוּ[f] וַ id. with suff. 3 pers. sing. masc.; ·וַ conv. רצה

---

[a] 2 Ki. 17. 27.
[b] Ps. 64. 8.
[c] Eze. 10. 15.
[d] Is. 49. 11.
[e] Eze. 26. 11.
[f] Ps. 7. 6.
[g] Is. 41. 25.
[h] Da. 8. 7.
[i] 2 Ki. 7. 17.
[k] 2 Ki. 7. 20.
[l] 2 Ki. 9. 33.
[m] Pr. 4. 4.
[n] Is. 16. 10.
[o] Ps. 67. 5.
[p] Jos. 6. 20.
[q] 1 Ki. 16. 25.
[r] Zep. 1. 12.
[s] Job 34. 24.
[t] 2 Sa. 20. 6.
[u] Ne. 2. 10.
[v] Job 20. 26.
[x] Pr. 6. 30.
[y] Is. 8. 21.
[z] Is. 49. 10.
[a] De. 8. 3.
[b] Is. 15. 4.
[c] Ne. 2. 3.
[d] Je. 2. 16.
[e] Zep. 2. 7.
[f] Pr. 10. 3.
[g] Ps. 78. 72.
[h] Ps. 80. 14.
[i] Is. 16. 10.
[k] Ps. 65. 12.
[l] Ju. 10. 8.
[m] Ps. 72. 16.
[n] Am. 9. 1.
[o] Is. 24. 18.
[p] Ex. 4. 26.
[q] 1 Ki. 18. 30.
[r] Eze. 47. 11.
[s] Eze. 47. 9.
[t] Je. 6. 14.
[u] Ps. 107. 20.
[x] Ho. 6. 1.
[y] Job 41. 22.
[z] Is. 5. 24.
[a] 2 Ki. 2. 22.
[b] Je. 8. 11.
[c] 2 Sa. 4: 1.
[d] 2 Sa. 18. 21.
[e] Job 16. 14.
[f] Job 33. 26.
[ff] Le. 9. 24.

וַיְרִצֻהוּ[a] וַ Hiph. fut. 3 pers. pl. masc. [יָרִיצוּ], suff. 3 pers. sing. masc.; וַ conv. . . רוץ

וַיָּרֻצוּ[b] וַ׳ וַיָּ Kal fut. 3 pers. pl. masc. for יָרוּצוּ; וַ· id. רוץ

יֵרָצוּ[c] Niph. fut. 3 pers. pl. masc. . . . רצה

יְרַצּוּ[d] Piel fut. 3 pers. pl. masc. . . . רצה

יִרְצוּ Kal fut. 3 pers. pl. masc. . . . רצה

יְרֻצוּן Kal fut. 3 pers. pl. m. with parag. ן for יְרוּצוּן רוץ

יִרְצַח Kal fut. 3 pers. sing. masc. . . רצח

יְרַצֵּחוּ[e]
יְרַצֵּחוּ[f] } Piel fut. 3 pers. pl. masc. (comp. § 8. rem. 15) . . . . } רצח

יִרְצֶךָּ[g] Kal fut. 3 pers. sing. masc. [יִרְצֶה], suff. 2 pers. sing. masc. (§ 24. rem. 21) for יִרְצְךָ רצה

וַיְרַצֵּץ[h] וַ Piel fut. 3 pers. sing. masc.; וַ conv. . רצץ

וַיְרֹצְצוּ[i] וַ Poel fut. 3 pers. pl. masc.; וַ id. . רצץ

יֶרֶק masc. dec. 4a, *greenness, verdure,* 2 Ki. 19. 26; Is. 37. 27; more frequently, *green herb, vegetable.*

יֶרֶק עֵשֶׂב יֶרֶק masc. *greenness, verdure, foliage; greenness of herb,* i. e. *green herb.*

יָרוֹק masc. *green herb,* Job 39. 8.

יֵרָקוֹן masc. *a yellowish livid paleness,* spoken—I. of a disease in corn, Eng. Vers. *mildew.*—II. of the human countenance when suddenly affrighted, Je. 30. 6.

יְרַקְרַק, pl. fem. יְרַקְרַקּוֹת.—I. adj. *greenish, yellowish,* Le. 13. 19; 14. 37.—II. *gold colour,* Ps. 68. 14.

יָרַק[k] *to spit,* const. with בִּפְנֵי *in the presence of.*

וַיָּרֶק[l] וַ Hiph. fut. 3 p. s. m. ap. and conv. from יָרִיק רוק

יָרֹק[m] Kal inf. absolute . . . . . ירק

יָרֹק[n] Kal fut. 3 pers. sing. masc. . . . רקק

יֶרֶק noun masc. sing. . . . . ירק

וִירַק וְ adj. masc. constr. [with cop. וְ for וְיָרַק, וְיִ׳] from יָרָק dec. 4a . . . . ירק

יִרְקָב[o]
יִרְקַב[p] } Kal fut. 3 pers. sing. masc. (§ 8. rem. 15) רקב

וְיָרְקָה[q] וְ Kal pret. 3 pers. sing. fem. . . . ירק

יְרַקְּדוּ[r] Piel fut. 3 pers. pl. masc. . . . רקד

יְרַקֵּדוּן id. with parag. ן [for יְרַקְּדוּן § 8. rem. 17] . רקד

וְיֵרָקוֹן[s] [t] וְ׳ noun masc. sing. . . . . . ירק

יִרְקַח[u] Kal fut. 3 pers. sing. masc. . . . רקח

וַיַּרְקִידֵם[x] וַ Hiph. fut. 3 pers. sing. masc., suff. 3 pers. pl. masc.; וַ· conv. . . . רקד

יָרְקְעָם pr. name of a place . . . . רקע

וַיְרַקְּעוּ[y] וַ Piel fut. 3 pers. pl. masc.; וַ conv. . רקע

וַיְרַקְּעוּם[z] וַ id. id., suff. 3 pers. pl. masc. (ם for ן fem. § 2. rem. 5) . . . . . רקע

יְרַקְּעֶנּוּ[a] Piel fut. 3 p. s. m., suff. 3 p. s. m. (§ 2. r. 3) רקע

יְרַקְרַק[b] adj. masc. sing. . . . . ירק

יְרַקְרַקֹּת[c] id. pl. fem. from [יְרַקְרַקָּה] dec. 10 . . ירק

יָרַשׁ[d] וְ׳ pret. pl. with suff. יְרֵשׁוּהָ, יְרֵשׁוּךָ (from יָרֵשׁ § 16. r. 1); fut. יִירַשׁ, יִרַשׁ; imp. רַשׁ, רֵשׁ, יְרַשׁ; inf. c. רֶשֶׁת.—I. *to take, seize upon; to take possession of.*—II. *to dispossess, to drive out.*—III. *to possess, hold in possession.*—IV. *to inherit;* part. יֹרֵשׁ *heir.* Niph. *to become poor.* Pi. יֵרֵשׁ.—I. *to take possession of,* De. 28. 42.—II. *to dispossess, impoverish,* Ju. 14. 15. Hiph. הוֹרִישׁ.—I. *to cause* or *make to possess, give for a possession,* with double acc.—II. *to take possession of.*—III. *to dispossess, to drive out.*—IV. *to make poor,* 1 Sa. 2. 7.—V. *to destroy,* Nu. 14. 12.

יְרֵשָׁה fem. *possession,* Nu. 24. 18.

יְרֻשָּׁה fem. dec. 10.—I. *possession.*—II. *heritage,* Je. 32. 8.

יְרוּשָׁה, יְרוּשָׁא (*possessed*) pr. name of the mother of King Jotham, 2 Ki. 15. 33; 2 Ch. 27. 1.

רֶשֶׁת fem. dec. 13a (with suff. רִשְׁתִּי), *net;* מַעֲשֵׂה רֶשֶׁת *net-work,* Ex. 27. 4.

מוֹרָשׁ masc. dec. 1b (but constr. מוֹרַשׁ, § 31. rem. 1), מוֹרָשָׁה fem. *possession.*

מוֹרֶשֶׁת גַּת (*possession of Gath*) pr. name of a town near Gath. Gent. noun מוֹרַשְׁתִּי.

תִּירֹשׁ, תִּירוֹשׁ masc. dec. 1b, *new wine, must.*

וַיֹּרֶשׁ וַ Hiph. fut. 3 pers. sing. masc. ap. and conv. from יוֹרִישׁ (comp. § 20. rem. 11) . ירשׁ

וְיִרַשׁ[e] וְ Kal fut. 3 p. s. m. for יִירַשׁ (§ 20. rem. 2) ירשׁ

רְשָׁה[f] id. imp. s. m. [רַשׁ] with parag. ה (§ 8. r. 12) ירשׁ

יְרֵשָׁה noun fem. sing. . . . . . ירשׁ

יְרֻשָּׁה noun fem. sing. dec. 10 . . . ירשׁ

וְיָרְשׁוּ וְ׳ Kal pret. 3 pers. pl. . . . . ירשׁ

וַיִּרְשׁוּ[g] וַיִּ׳ Kal fut. 3 pers. pl. masc. for יִירְשׁוּ (§ 20. rem. 2); וַ· conv. . . . . ירשׁ

וַיִּרָשׁוּהָ[h] וַ id. fut. 3 pers. pl. masc. (יִירְשׁוּ from יִירַשׁ), suff. 3 pers. sing. masc. (§ 16. rem. 12) . ירשׁ

וִירֵשׁוּהָ וְ id. pret. 3 pers. pl. (יָרְשׁוּ, fr. s. יָרֵשׁ § 16. r. 1), suff. 3 pers. s. m. with conj. וְ [for וְיָרֵשׁוּ, וְיִ׳] ירשׁ

וִירֵשׁוּךָ[i] וְ id. id., suff. 2 p. s. m. with cop. וְ, see prec. יָרֵשׁ

יֹרְשָׁיו[k] id. part. act. pl., suff. 3 p. s. m. fr. יוֹרֵשׁ d. 7b ירשׁ

יֹרְשִׁים[l] id. pl., absolute state . . . ירשׁ

יַרְשִׁיעַ Hiph. fut. 3 pers. sing. masc. . . . רשׁע

יַרְשִׁיעוּ[m] [n] וַיַּ׳ id. fut. 3 pers. pl. masc. . . רשׁע

יַרְשִׁיעֲךָ[o] id. fut. 3 pers. sing. masc., suff. 2 pers. s. m. רשׁע

---

[a] Ge. 41. 14. [b] Is. 40. 31; 59. 7. [c] Le. 22. 25. [d] Job 20. 10. [e] Ps. 94. 6.
[f] Ho. 6. 9. [g] 2 Sa. 24. 23. [h] 2 Ch. 16. 10. [i] Ju. 10. 8.
[k] Nu. 12. 14. [l] Ge. 14. 14. [m] Nu. 12. 14. [n] Le. 15. 8.
[o] Pr. 10. 7. [p] Is. 40. 20. [q] De. 25. 9. [r] Is. 13. 21.
[s] 1 Ki. 8. 37. [t] 2 Ch. 6. 28. [u] Ex. 30. 33. [x] Ps. 29. 6.
[y] Ex. 39. 3. [z] Nu. 17. 4. [a] Is. 40. 19. [b] Le. 13. 49.
[c] Le. 14. 37. [d] Je. 49. 1. [e] Ge. 22. 17. [f] De. 33. 23.
[g] Ob. 1. 20. [h] Jos. 21. 43. [i] Eze. 36. 12. [k] Je. 49. 2.
[l] De. 12. 2. [m] Ps. 94. 21. [n] Job 32. 3. [o] Job 15. 6.

[a]יַרְשִׁיעֻן Hiph. fut. 3 pers. pl. masc. with parag. ן . רשע
[b]יַרְשִׁיעֶנּוּ id. fut. 3 pers. sing. masc., suff. 3 pers. s. m. רשע
יַרְשִׁיעֵנִי id. id., suff. 1 pers. sing. . . . רשע
[c]יֹרִשֵׁם וַ Hiph. fut. 3 pers. sing. masc. (יוֹרִישׁ), suff. 3 pers. pl. masc. (§ 20. rem. 11); וַ conv. ירש
[d]יְרִשְׁנוּ [e]וִ' Kal pret. 1 pers. pl. . . . ירש
[f]יֹרִשֶׁנּוּ Hiph. fut. 3 pers. sing. masc. (יוֹרִישׁ), suff. 3 pers. sing. masc. (§ 20. rem. 11) . ירש
[g]יְרִשְׁנוּהָ וְ Kal pret. 1 pers. pl. (יָרַשְׁנוּ), suff. 3 pers. sing. fem. with conv. וְ [for וִ', וִירַשְׁנוּ'] . ירש
[h]יַרְשִׁעַ defect. for יַרְשִׁיעַ (q. v.) . . רשע
[i]יְרֹשֵׁשׁ Pilel fut. 3 pers. sing. masc. . . . רוש
[k]יָרַשְׁתָּ / וְיָרַשְׁתָּ } Kal pret. 2 pers. sing. masc., acc. shifted by conv. וְ (§ 8. rem. 7) . . ירש
יְרֻשַּׁת noun fem. sing., constr. of יְרֻשָּׁה dec. 10 . ירש
[l]יֹרֶשֶׁת Kal part. act., fem. of יוֹרֵשׁ (§ 8. rem. 19) ירש
יְרִשְׁתָּהּ וְ id. pret. 2 p. s. m. (יָרַשְׁתָּ), suff. 3 p. s. fem. (§ 8. r. 1b); with conv. וְ [for וְ', וִירַשְׁתָּהּ] ירש
[m]יְרֻשָּׁתוֹ noun fem. sing., suff. 3 pers. sing. fem. from יְרֻשָּׁה dec. 10 . . . . . ירש
[n]יְרֻשַּׁתְכֶם id., suff. 3 pers. pl. masc. . . . ירש
יְרִשְׁתֶּם וְ Kal pret. 2 pers. sing. masc. (יָרַשְׁתָּ), suff. 3 pers. pl. masc. (§ 8. rem. 1b); with conv. וְ [for וְ', וִירַשְׁתֶּם] . . יָרַשׁ
יְרִשְׁתֶּם וְ id. pret. 2 p. pl. m. with conv. וְ, see prec. יָרַשׁ
[o]יַרְתִּיחַ Hiph. fut. 3 pers. sing. masc. . . רתח
יֵשׁ / יֶשׁ־ } וְ', [p]וְ' [q]וְ' prop. subst., used as an adv., with suff. יֶשְׁךָ, יֶשְׁכֶם, יֶשְׁנוֹ (d. 7. § 36. r. 3) ישה
[r]יִשָּׂא defect. for יִשָּׂיא (q. v.) . . . נשא
יִשָּׂא וַיִּ' Kal fut. 3 p. s. m. (§ 25. No. 2a); וַ conv. נשא
יִשְׁאֲבוּ וַ Kal fut. 3 pers. pl. masc.; וַ id. . שאב
[s]יִשְׁאֲבוּן id. with paragogic ן . . . . שאב
יִשְׁאַג / יִשְׁאָג } Kal fut. 3 pers. sing. masc. (§ 8. rem. 15) שאג
[t]יִשְׁאֲגוּ / [u]יִשְׁאָגוּ } id. fut. 3 pers. pl. masc. (v. id.) . . שאג
[x]יִשָּׂאֶהָ וַ Kal fut. 3 pers. sing. m., suff. 3 pers. sing. fem. (§ 16. rem. 12, & § 25. No. 2a); וַ conv. נשא
יִשָּׂאֵהוּ [y]וַיִּ' id. id., suff. 3 pers. s. m. (v. id.); וַ id. נשא
[z]יִשָּׂאוּהָ [a]וַיִּ', וְ' id. fut. 3 pers. pl. masc., suff. 3 pers. sing. fem. (v. id.); וַ id. . . נשא
יִשָּׂאוּ / יִשְׂאוּ } וַיִּ' id. fut. 3 pers. pl. masc. (v. id. & § 8. rem. 15); וַ id. . . . נשא
יִשָּׂאוּם [b]וַיִּ' id. id., suff. 3 pers. pl. masc. (§ 16. rem. 12, & § 25. No. 2a); וַ id. . . נשא
יִשָּׁאוּן Niph. fut. 3 pers. pl. masc. with paragogic ן שאה

[c]יִשָּׂאוּנְךָ Kal fut. 3 pers. pl. m. parag. נ and suff. 2 pers. sing. m. (§ 16. rem. 12 & 14, & § 25. No. 2a) נשא
[d]יַשְׁאִיר Hiph. fut. 3 pers. sing. masc. . . . שאר
יַשְׁאִירוּ id. fut. 3 pers. pl. masc. . . . שאר
יַשִּׁאֲךָ Hiph. fut. 3 pers. sing. m., suff. 2 pers. s. m. נשא
[e]יִשָּׂאֲךָ Kal fut. 3 pers. sing. masc., suff. 2 pers. sing. masc. (§ 16. rem. 12, & § 25. No. 2a) . נשא
[f]יִשְׁאָל Kh. יִשְׁאַל q. v., K. וְשָׁאַל Kal pret. 3 p. s. m. שאל
[g]יִשְׁאַל / וַיִּ' יִשְׁאָל } Kal fut. 3 pers. sing. masc. (§ 8. rem. 15); וַ conv. . . . שאל
יִשְׁאָלֵהוּ וַ id., suff. 3 pers. s. m. (§ 16. r. 12); וַ id. שאל
[h]יְשַׁאֲלוּ Piel fut. 3 pers. pl. masc. . . . שאל
יִשְׁאֲלוּ / [k]וַיִּ', וְ' יִשְׁאָלוּ } Kal fut. 3 pers. pl. masc. (§ 8. rem. 15); וַ conv. . . . שאל
[l]יַשְׁאִלוּם וַ Hiph. fut. 3 pers. pl. masc. [יַשְׁאִיל], suff. 3 pers. pl. masc.; וַ id. . . . שאל
[m]יִשְׁאָלוּן Kal fut. 3 pers. pl. masc. with parag. ן (§ 8. rem. 17, comp. § 16. rem. 12) . שאל
יִשְׁאָלוּנִי id. id. with suff. 1 pers. sing. (v. id.) . שאל
יִשְׁאָלְךָ id. fut. 3 pers. sing. masc., suff. 2 pers. s. m. שאל
יִשְׁאֲלִנְכוֹן Chald. Peal fut. 3 pers. s. m., suff. 2 p. pl. m. שאל
[o]יִשָּׂאֵם וַ Kal fut. 3 pers. sing. masc., suff. 3 pers. pl. m. (§ 16. rem. 12, & § 25. No. 2a); וַ conv. נשא
[p]יִשָּׂאֻם וַ id. fut. 3 pers. pl. masc., suff. 3 pers. pl. masc. (v. id.) וַ id. . . . . נשא
[q]יִשָּׂאֶנָּה id. fut. 3 pers. sing. masc., suff. 3 pers. sing. fem. (v. id. & § 2. rem. 3) . . נשא
[r]יִשָּׂאֵנוּ id. fut. 3 pers. pl. m., suff. 1 pers. pl. (v. id.) נשא
[s]יִשָּׂאֵנִי id. fut. 3 pers. s. m., suff. 1 pers. s. (v. id.) נשא
[t]יִשְׁאַף Kal fut. 3 pers. sing. masc. . . . שאף
[u]יִשָּׁאֵר / [x]וַיִּשָּׁאֵר } Niph. fut. 3 pers. sing. masc. (§ 9. rem. 3); וַ conv. . . . . שאר
[y]יִשָּׁאֲרוּ [z]וַיִּ' id. fut. 3 pers. pl. masc.; וַ id. . . שאר

יָשַׁב וְ' fut. יֵשֵׁב; inf. c. שֶׁבֶת; imp. שֵׁב, שְׁבָה.—I. *to sit, sit down*; with עַל, בְּ of the place; וַתֵּשֶׁב לָהּ *and she sat down by herself*.—II. *to remain, stay, abide*.—III. *to dwell, dwell in, inhabit*; with עַל, בְּ of the place; part. יוֹשֵׁב *inhabitant*.—IV. *to be inhabited*, as a place, country. Niph. נוֹשַׁב, *to be inhabited*. Pi. *to set, place*, Eze. 25. 4. Hiph. הוֹשִׁיב.—I. *to cause to sit, to sit*.—II. *to cause to dwell; to let dwell*.—III. *to cause to be inhabited*. Hoph.—I. *to be made to dwell*, Is. 5. 8.—II. *to be inhabited*, Is. 44. 26.

[a] Ex. 22. 8. [b] Ps. 37. 33. [c] Jos. 13. 12. [d] De. 3. 12. [e] Nu. 13. 30. [f] Job 20. 15. [g] Eze. 35. 10. [h] Job 34. 29. [i] Je. 5. 17. [k] 1 Ki. 21. 19. [l] Nu. 36. 8. [m] De. 2. 12. [n] Jos. 1. 15. [o] Job 41. 23. [p] 2 Ki. 10. 15. [q] Ge. 47. 6. [r] Is. 36. 14. [s] Ru. 2. 9. [t] Je. 51. 38. [u] Je. 2. 15. [x] Ju. 9. 48. [y] 2 Ki. 4. 20. [z] Is. 46. 7. [a] 2 Ch. 24. 11. [b] 1 Ch. 23. 22. [c] Ps. 91. 12. [d] De. 28. 51. [e] 1 Ki. 18. 12. [f] Pr. 20. 4. [g] Ho. 4. 12. [h] 2 Sa. 20. 18. [i] Je. 50. 5. [k] Ex. 11. 2. [l] Ex. 12. 36. [m] Jos. 4. 6, 21. [n] Ezr. 7. 21. [o] 2 Sa. 5. 21. [p] Le. 10. 5. [q] Pr. 18. 14. [r] Is. 64. 5. [s] Job 32. 22. [t] Job 7. 2. [u] Is. 11. 11, 16. [x] Ge. 7. 23. [y] Eze. 36. 36. [z] Nu. 11. 26.

ישֵׁב בַּשֶּׁבֶת (*dwelling in quiet*) pr. name of one of David's chief officers, 2 Sa. 23. 8.

יֶשֶׁבְאָב (*father's dwelling*) pr. name masc. 1 Ch. 24. 13.

יִשְׁבּוֹ בְּנֹב (*his seat is in Nob*) pr. name m. 2 Sa. 21. 16. Kheth., K. יִשְׁבִּי בְּנֹב (*my seat is in Nob*).

יָשָׁבְקָשָׁה (for יֹשֵׁב בְּקָשָׁה *seat in a hard place*) pr. name masc. 1 Ch. 25. 4, 24.

שִׁיבָה fem. dec. 10, *abode, stay*, 2 Sa. 19. 33.

שֶׁבֶת fem. *a sitting, seat*, 2 Sa. 23. 7; 1 Ki. 10. 19.

יוֹשִׁבְיָה (whom *the Lord settles*) pr. name masc. 1 Ch. 4. 35.

מוֹשָׁב masc. dec. 2b (pl. c. מוֹשְׁבֵי, מוֹשָׁבוֹת).—I. *seat*.—II. *seat, dwelling, residence*.—III. *time of residing*, Ex. 12. 40.—IV. *inhabitants*, 2 Sa. 9. 12. —V. *site, situation*, 2 Ki. 2. 19.

תּוֹשָׁב masc. dec. 2 b (but comp. § 31. rem. 1) *settler, sojourner*.

יָשֵׁב Kal pret. 3 pers. sing. m. for יָשַׁב (§ 8. r. 7) — ישב

[a]יָשֵׂב וְ Kh. יָשֵׂב q.v.; K. יָשֵׂם ap. from יָשִׂים (q.v.) — שום

[b]יָשֵׁב, יָשֵׁב (וְ, וַ) Hiph. fut. 3 pers. sing. masc., ap. and conv. for יָשִׁיב — שוב

[c]יָשֹׁב Kal inf. absolute — ישב

יָשֵׁב, יָשָׁב־, יָשֹׁב (וַיָּ׳, וְ׳, וַיָּ׳) Kal fut. 3 pers. sing. masc. ap. & conv. (§ 21. rem. 7 & 8) — שוב

[d]יַשֵּׁב [e]וַיַּ׳ Hiph. fut. 3 pers. s. m. ap. [from יַשִּׁיב] — נשב

יֵשֵׁב [f]וַיֵּ׳ Kal fut. 3 pers. sing. masc., with conv. וַ in pause (§ 20. rem. 4) — ישב

יֵשֶׁב וַיֵּ׳ id. with Mak., bef. monos., or with conv. וַ — ישב

יִשְׁבְּ וַ Kal fut. 3 pers. sing. masc. ap. [from יִשְׁבֶּה § 24. rem. 3b]; וַ conv. — שבה

יֹשֵׁב [g]וְ Kal part. act. masc. dec. 7b (also pr. name in compos. יֹשֵׁב בַּשֶּׁבֶת) — ישב

[h]יֹשֵׁב וַ Hiph. fut. 3 pers. sing. masc. ap. & conv. [from יוֹשִׁיב, comp. § 20. rem. 11] — ישב

יִשְׁבּוֹ Kh. יֹשֵׁב q. v., K. יֹשְׁבִי (q. v.) — ישב

יֶשֶׁבְאָב pr. name masc. — ישב

[ii]יָשְׁבָה וְ׳ Kal pret. 3 pers. sing. masc. — ישב

[k]יְשִׁבֶהָ וַ Hiph. fut. 3 pers. sing. masc. (יָשִׁיב), suff. 3 pers. sing. fem.; וַ conv. — שוב

יְשִׁבֵהוּ וַ id. fut. 3 pers. pl. masc. (יָשִׁיבוּ). suff. 3 pers. sing. masc.; וַ id. — שוב

[l]יָשְׁבוּ, יָשָׁבוּ (וְ׳, וְ׳) Kal pret. 3 pers. pl. (§ 8. rem. 7) — ישב

[nn]יָשִׁבוּ וַיָּ׳, וְ Hiph. fut. 3 pers. pl. masc. (for יָשִׁיבוּ); וַ conv. — שוב

יָשֻׁבוּ וַיָּ׳, וְ Kal fut. 3 p. pl. m. (for יָשׁוּבוּ); וַ conv. — שוב

[m]יֵשְׁבוּ, יֵשֵׁבוּ (וַיֵּ׳, וַיֵּ׳, וְ) Kal fut. 3 pers. pl. masc. (comp. § 8. rem. 15, & § 20. rem. 4); וַ id. — ישב

[n]יִשְּׁבוּ וְ Piel pret. 3 pers. pl. — ישב

יִשְׁבּוּ וַ Kal fut. 3 pers. pl. masc; וַ conv. — שבה

[o]יִשְׁבּוֹ Kh. יִשְׁבּוֹ q. v., K. יִשְׁבִּי (q. v.) — ישב

[p]יְשִׁבוּם וְ Hiph. fut. 3 pers. pl. masc. (יָשִׁיבוּ), suff. 3 p. pl. m. with conj. וְ [for וִישִׁיבוּם, וְי׳] — שוב

יִשְׁבּוֹ וְ Kh. יִשְׁבּוֹ, K. יִשְׁבִּי pr. name masc. in compos. with בְּנֹב — ישב

יָשֻׁבוּן Kal fut. 3 p. pl. m. with parag. ן (for יָשׁוּבוּן) — שוב

[q]יִשְׁבּוֹר Kal fut. 3 pers. sing. masc. (§ 8. rem. 18) — שבר

[r]יִשְׁבּוֹת Kal fut. 3 pers. sing. masc. (§ 8. rem. 18) — שבת

יֹשְׁבוֹת Kal part. act. fem., pl. of יֹשֶׁבֶת dec. 13a, from יֹשֵׁב masc. (§ 8. rem. 19) — ישב

[s]יְשַׁבַּח Piel fut. 3 pers. sing. masc. — שבח

יִשְׁבַּח pr. name masc. — שבח

[t]יְשַׁבְּחוּנְךָ Piel fut. 3 pers. pl. masc. with parag. נ & suff. 2 pers. sing. masc. (§ 16. rem. 14) — שבח

[u]יְשַׁבְּחֶנָּה id. fut. 3 p. s. m., suff. 3 p. s. f. (§ 2. r. 3) — שבח

יֹשְׁבֵי וְ׳ Kal part. act. pl. c. from יֹשֵׁב dec. 7b — ישב

[x]יֹשְׁבִי Kh. יֹשְׁבִי, K. וּשְׁבִי Kal imp. sing. fem. (reg. or irreg. § 20. rem. 2); וּ bef. (:) for וְ — ישב

יָשֻׁבִי וְ pr. name in compos. יָשֻׁבִי לֶחֶם — שוב

יֹשְׁבֶיהָ וְ׳ Kal part. act. pl. masc., suff. 3 pers. sing. fem. from יֹשֵׁב dec. 7b — ישב

[y]יֹשְׁבֵיהֶם וְ id., suff. 3 pers. pl. masc. — ישב

יֹשְׁבֵיהֶן וְ id., suff. 3 pers. pl. fem. — ישב

[z]יֹשְׁבָיו id., suff. 3 pers. sing. masc. — ישב

יֹשְׁבִים [a]וְ׳ id. pl., absolute state — ישב

[b]יַשְׁבִּיעֵךְ Hiph. fut. 3 pers. sing. masc., suff. 2 p. s. f. — שבע

[c]יַשְׁבִּיעֵם id., suff. 3 pers. pl. masc. — שבע

[d]יַשְׁבִּית Hiph. fut. 3 pers. sing. masc. — שבת

[rr]יִשְׁבֵּם וַ Kal fut. 3 p. m. s. [יִשְׁבֶּה], suff. 3 p. pl. m. — שבה

יָשַׁבְנוּ [e]וְ׳ Kal pret. 1 pers. pl. — ישב

[f]יְשִׁבֵנִי [g]וַ׳ Hiph. fut. 3 p. s. m. (יָשִׁיב), suff. 1 p. s.; וַ conv. — שוב

יַשְׂבַּע וַ Hiph. fut. 3 pers. sing. masc. ap. [from יַשְׂבִּיעַ]; וַ id. — שבע

יִשָּׁבַע וַיִּ׳ Niph. fut. 3 pers. sing. masc.; וַ id. — שבע

יִשְׂבַּע, יִשְׂבָּע ([h]וְ׳, [i]וַיִּ׳) Kal fut. 3 pers. sing. masc. (§ 8. rem. 15); וַ id. — שבע

[k]יִשָּׁבְעוּ, יִשָּׁבֵעוּ ([l]וַיִּ׳, וַ) Niph. fut. 3 pers. pl. masc. (comp. § 8. rem. 15); וַ id. — שבע

[m]יְשַׂבְּעוּ Piel fut. 3 pers. pl. masc. [for יְשַׂבְּעוּ comp. § 8. rem. 15] — שבע

יִשְׂבְּעוּ, יִשְׂבָּעוּ ([n]וְ׳, [o]וַיִּ׳) Kal fut. 3 pers. pl. masc. (§ 8. rem. 15); וַ conv. — שבע

[a] Da. 11. 18. [b] Da. 11. 18, 19. [c] 1 Sa. 20. 5. [d] Ps. 147. 18. [e] Ge. 15. 11. [f] Ru. 4. 1. [g] Ps. 55. 20. [h] 2 Ki. 17. 6, 24. [i] Ju. 1. 27. [ii] La. 1. 1, 3. [k] 2 Ki. 14. 22. [l] Eze. 36. 35. [m] Ru. 4. 2. [n] Eze. 25. 4. [nn] De. 1. 22. [o] 1 Ch. 2. 55. [p] Je. 23. 22. [q] Is. 42. 3. [r] Ho. 7. 4. [rr] Je. 41. 10. [s] Ps. 145. 4. [t] Ps. 63. 4. [u] Pr. 29. 11. [x] Je. 48. 18. [y] Is. 42. 10. [z] 2 Ki. 22. 16, 19. [a] 2 Ch. 32. 10. [b] Ps. 147. 14. [c] Ps. 105. 40. [d] Pr. 18. 18, etc. [e] Ge. 34. 16. [f] 2 Sa. 15. 8. [g] Eze. 47. 1, 6. [h] Is. 44. 16. [i] 2 Ch. 24. 15. [k] Je. 5. 2. [l] Ezr. 10. 5. [m] Eze. 7. 19. [n] Ps. 22. 27. [o] Ho. 13. 6.

יִשְׂבְּעוּן[a] Kal fut. 3 pers. pl. masc. with parag. ן . שבע
יִשְׂבָּעֶךָּ[b] id. fut. 3 pers. sing. masc. (יִשְׂבַּע), suff. 2 pers. sing. masc. (§ 16. rem. 12) . שבע
יִשְׁבְּעָם 'וְ pr. name masc. . . . . שוב
יַשְׂבִּיעֵנִי[c] Hiph. fut. 3 pers. sing. masc., suff. 1 pers. s. שבע
וַיַּשְׂבִּעֵנִי[d] וַ Hiph. fut. 3 p. s. m., suff. 1 p. s.; ·וַ conv. שבע
יִשְׁבָּק 'וְ pr. name masc. . . . . שבק
יָשְׁבְּקָשָׁה pr. name masc. . . . . . ישב
יִשָּׁבֵר [e]'וַיִּ Niph. fut. 3 pers. sing. masc.; ·וַ conv. שבר
יְשַׁבֵּר 'וַ Piel fut. 3 pers. sing. masc.; וַ id. . שבר
יִשְׁבֹּר[f] [g]'וַיִּ Kal fut. 3 pers. sing. masc.; ·וַ id. . שבר
יְשַׁבְּרֵהוּ וַ id. fut. 3 p. s. m., suff. 3 p. s. m.; ·וַ id. שבר
יִשָּׁבְרוּ[h] וְ } Niph. fut. 3 pers. pl. masc. (comp. § 8. rem. 15); ·וַ id. . . . שבר
יִשָּׁבְרוּ[i] וַ
יִשְׁבְּרוּ [k]'וַיִּ Kal fut. 3 pers. pl. masc.; ·וַ id. . שבר
יְשַׁבְּרוּ[l] } Piel fut. 3 pers. pl. masc. (comp. § 8. rem. 15) . . . . . שבר
יְשַׁבְּרוּ[m]
יְשַׁבְּרוּ[n] וַ Piel fut. 3 pers. pl. masc.; וַ conv. . שבר
יִשְׁבְּרוּהוּ[o] Kal fut. 3 pers. pl. m., suff. 3 pers. s. m. שבר
יְשַׁבֵּרוּן[p] Piel fut. 3 pers. pl. masc.; parag. ן [for יְשַׁבְּרוּן § 10. rem. 4] . . . שבר
יָשַׁבְתָּ[q] וְ } Kal pret. 2 pers. sing. masc. (§ 8. r. 7) ישב
יָשַׁבְתָּ
יָשַׁבְתָּ וְ
יָשַׁבְתְּ[r] 'וְ id. pret. 2 pers. sing. fem. . . . ישב
יַשְׁבֵּת וַ Hiph. fut. 3 p. s. m. ap. from יַשְׁבִּית; ·וַ conv. שבת
יִשְׁבֹּת 'וַ, 'וַיִּ Kal fut. 3 pers. sing. masc.; ·וַ id. . שבת
יֹשֶׁבֶת[s] } Kal part. act. fem. dec. 13 a, from יֹשֵׁב masc. (§ 8. rem. 19) . . . ישב
יֹשֶׁבֶת
יֹשְׁבֹת pl. of the preceding. 1 Ki. 3. 17. . ישב
יָשַׁבְתָּה[t] וְ in full for יָשַׁבְתָּ q. v. (§ 8. rem. 5) ישב
יִשְׁבְּתוּ[u] } Kal fut. 3 pers. pl. masc. (§ 8. rem. 15); ·וַ conv. . . . . שבת
יִשְׁבְּתוּ[x] 'וַיִּ
יָשַׁבְתִּי [a]'וְ Kal pret. 1 pers. sing. . . . ישב
יֹשַׁבְתִּי[b] Kh. יֹשַׁבְתִּי, K. יֹשֶׁבֶת Kal part. act. fem. (§ 39. rem. 3, comp. § 8. rem. 5) . ישב
יְשַׁבְתֶּם } Kal pret. 2 pers. pl. masc., with conv. וְ [for וִישַׁבְתֶּם ,'וִי] . . . ישב
יְשַׁבְתֶּם וְ
יַשֵּׂג [c]'וְ, [d]'וַיַּ Hiph. fut. 3 pers. sing. masc., ap. for יַשִּׂיג; ·וַ conv. . . . . נשג
יִשְׂגֵּא Ch. Peal fut. 3 pers. sing. masc. . . שגא
יְשַׂגֵּב וַ Piel fut. 3 pers. sing. masc.; וַ conv. . שגב
יְשֻׂגַּב[e] Pual fut. 3 pers. sing. masc. [for יְשֻׂגַּב comp. § 8. rem. 15] . . . . שגב
יְשַׂגֶּבְךָ[f] Piel fut. 3 p. s. m., suff. 2 p. s. m. (§ 16. r. 15) שגב
יִשְׁגֶּה[g] Kal fut. 3 pers. sing. masc. . . . שגה
יִשְׁגֶּה Kal fut. 3 pers. sing. masc. . . . שגה

וַיַּשִּׂגוּ וַ Hiph. fut. 3 pers. pl. m. for וַיַּשִּׂיגוּ; ·וַ conv. נשג
יִשְׁגּוּ Kal fut. 3 pers. pl. masc. . . שגה
יַשְׂגִּיב[h] Hiph. fut. 3 pers. sing. masc. . שגב
יַשְׁגִּיחוּ[i] Hiph. fut. 3 pers. pl. masc. . . שגח
יִשְׁגָּלֶנָּה[k] Kh. Kal fut. 3 pers. sing. masc. [יִשְׁגַּל], suff. 3 pers. sing. fem. (§ 16. r. 12, & § 2. r. 3) שגל
וַיַּשִּׂגֵם[l] וַ Hiph. fut. 3 pers. sing. masc., suff. 3 pers. pl. masc. for וַיַּשִּׂיגֵם; ·וַ conv. . . נשג
יְשַׁדֵּד[m] } Piel fut. 3 pers. sing. masc., with conj. וְ [for וִישַׁדֵּד ,'וִי] . . . שדד
יְשַׁדֵּד[n] וְ
יְשַׁדֶּד[o] id. with Makkaph (§ 10. rem. 4) . שדד
יְשֹׁדֵד[p] Poel fut. 3 pers. sing. masc. . . שדד
יְשָׁדְדֵם[q] Kal fut. 3 pers. sing. masc. [יָשֹׁד], suff. 3 pers. pl. masc. [for the contracted form יְשָׁדֵּם § 18. rem. 13, comp. rem. 5] . שדד

יָשָׁה Root not used; *to be, exist, subsist; to be firm.* Comp. Prof. Lee under יֵשׁ; Arab. ושה *to help.*

יֵשׁ ,יֶשׁ־.—I. *substance, wealth,* Pr. 8. 21.—II. adv. *there is, there are;* with suff. יֶשְׁךָ *thou art.* יֶשְׁנוֹ *he is,* יֶשְׁכֶם *ye are;* יֵשׁ וָיֵשׁ *it is truly so,* יֶשׁ־לִי *I have;* יֶשׁ־אֲשֶׁר *there are those who.*

אִישַׁי ,יִשַׁי (*wealthy*) pr. name *Jesse,* the father of David.

יוֹשָׁה (*wealth*) pr. name masc. 1 Ch. 4. 34.

יוֹשַׁוְיָה (*whom the Lord establishes*) pr. name masc. 1 Ch. 11. 46.

מֵישָׁא (*wealth*) pr. name masc. 1 Ch. 8. 9.

תּוּשִׁיָּה fem.—I. *help, deliverance,* Job 6. 13; Pr. 2. 7; Mi. 6. 9. Others render these passages either by *wealth, wisdom* or *security.*—II. *purpose, enterprise,* Job 5. 12; Prof. Lee *wealth, abundance.*—III. *counsel, wisdom.*

יַשֶּׁה[r] Hiph. fut. 3 pers. sing. masc. . . נשה
וַיָּשֹׁב[s] וַ Kh. וַיָּשֹׁב for וַיֵּשֶׁב q. v., K. וַיָּשָׁב (q. v.) שוב
יָשׁוּב Kh. יָשׁוּב q. v., K. יָשִׁיב (q. v.) . . שוב
יָשׁוּב pr. name masc. . . . . . שוב
יָשׁוּב Kal fut. 3 pers. sing. masc. . . . שוב
יְשׁוֹבֵב[t] Pilel fut. 3 pers. sing. masc. . . שוב
יָשׁוּבוּ 'וַיָּ Kal fut. 3 pers. pl. masc.; ·וַ conv. . שוב
יְשׁוּבוּן id. with parag. ן . . . . . שוב
יָשׁוּד[u] Kal fut. 3 pers. sing. masc. . . . שוד
יְשַׁוֶּה[x] Piel fut. 3 pers. sing. masc. . . . שוה
יִשְׁוָה וְ pr. name masc. . . . . . שוה
יִשְׁווּ Kal fut. 3 pers. pl. masc. . . . . שוה
יְשׂוֹחֵחַ[y] Pilel fut. 3 pers. sing. masc. . . . שיח
יְשׁוֹחָיָה וְ pr. name masc. [for 'וִישׁ ,'וְיִ] . . שוח

---

[a] Ps. 104. 28. [b] Pr. 25. 17. [c] Job 9. 18. [d] Ge. 24. 37. [e] Je. 50. 23.
[f] Je. 19. 11. [g] Ge. 41. 56. [h] Da. 11. 22. [i] 2 Ch. 20. 37. [k] Ju. 7. 20.
[l] Ps. 145. 15. [m] Is. 38. 18. [n] 2 Ch. 31. 1. [o] Da. 11. 26. [p] Ps. 104. 27.
[q] De. 8. 12. [r] Je. 3. 2. [s] Eze. 23. 41. [t] Pr. 22. 10. [u] 2 Ki. 4. 13.
[x] De. 17. 14. [y] Ge. 8. 22. [z] Je. 31. 36. [a] Ca. 2. 3. [b] Je. 22. 23.
[c] Ps. 7. 6. [d] Ge. 31. 25. [e] Pr. 29. 25. [f] Ps. 20. 2. [g] Pr. 5. 23.
[h] Job 36. 22. [i] Is. 14. 16. [k] De. 28. 30. [l] Ge. 44. 6. [m] Job 39. 10.
[n] Is. 28. 24. [o] Ho. 10. 11. [p] Ho. 10. 2. [q] Je. 5. 6. [r] Job 11. 6.
[s] Eze. 18. 28. [t] Ps. 23. 3. [u] Ps. 91. 6. [x] Ho. 10. 1. [y] Is. 53. 8.

יְשׁוֹטְטוּ[a] Pilel fut. 3 pers. pl. masc. . . . . שוט

יִשְׁוִי וְ pr. name masc. . . . . . שוה

יָשׂוּם[b] Kal fut. 3 pers. sing. masc. . . . שום

יֵשׁוּעַ וְ (*he shall be a deliverance*, i. e. deliverer, for יְהִי־יָהּ שׁוּעַ comp. יֵהוּא) pr. name of several persons, and stands often for יְהוֹשׁוּעַ.

יְשׁוּעָה } noun fem. sing. dec. 10, with cop. וְ } ישע
וִישׁוּעָה[c] } [for וִי', וִישׁוּעָה] . . . }

יְשַׁוְּעוּ[d] } Piel fut. 3 pers. pl. masc. (comp. § 8. } שוע
יְשַׁוְּעוּ } rem. 15, & § 15. rem. 2) . }

יְשׁוּעוֹת noun fem., pl. of יְשׁוּעָה dec. 10 . ישע

יְשׁוּעַת id. sing., constr. state . . . . ישע

יְשׁוּעֹת id. pl. defect. for יְשׁוּעוֹת . . . . ישע

יְשׁוּעָתָה id. sing. with parag. ה . . . . ישע

יְשׁוּעָתָהּ[e] וְ id. sing., suff. 3 pers. sing. fem. [for וִי', וִישׁוּעָתָהּ] . . . . ישע

יְשׁוּעָתוֹ id. sing., suff. 3 pers. sing. masc. . . ישע

יְשׁוּעָתִי } id. sing., suff. 1 pers. sing. with cop. וְ } ישע
וִישׁוּעָתִי } [for וִי', וִישׁוּעָתִי] . }

יְשׁוּעָתֶךָ } id. sing., suff. 2 pers. sing. masc. . ישע
יְשׁוּעָתְךָ[f] }

יְשׁוּעָתֵנוּ id. sing., suff. 1 pers. pl. . . . . ישע

יְשׁוּפְךָ[g] Kal fut. 3 pers. sing. masc. [יָשׁוּף], suff. 2 pers. sing. masc. . . . . . שוף

יְשׁוּפֵנִי id. with suff. 1 pers. sing. . . . שוף

יָשׁוּר[h] Kal fut. 3 pers. sing. masc. . . . . . שור

יְשׁוּרֶנָּה id., suff. 3 pers. sing. fem. (§ 2. rem. 3) . שור

יְשׁוּרֶנּוּ[i] id., suff. 3 pers. sing. masc. (§ 2. rem. 3) . שור

יְשׁוֹרֵר[k] Pilel fut. 3 pers. sing. masc. . . . שיר

יְשֵׁיזִב[l] Chald. Peil fut. 3 pers. sing. masc. (§ 48) . שזב

[יֶשַׁח] masc. *emptiness of stomach, hunger*, Mi. 6. 14. So Gesenius, coll. with Arab. וחש *to be empty*. Others, *lowness, faintness*, יֶשַׁח=שָׁחַח q. v.

יָשֹׁחַ Kal fut. 3 pers. sing. masc. . . . שחח

וַיִּשַּׁח וְ Niph. fut. 3 pers. sing. masc.; וַ· conv. . שחח

יָשֹׁחוּ[m] וַיָּ'[n] Kal fut. 3 pers. pl. masc.; וַ· id. . שחח

יִשַּׁחוּ[o] וְ Niph. (dag. impl. in ח) fut. 3 pers. pl. m. שחח

יִשָּׁחֵט[p] Niph. fut. 3 pers. sing. masc. . . . שחט

יִשְׁחַט[q] וַיִּ'[r] } Kal fut. 3 pers. sing. masc. (§ 8. rem. } שחט
יִשְׁחָט וַיִּ' } 15); וַ· conv. . . }

יִשְׁחָטֵהוּ וַ id. id., suff. 3 p. s. m. (§ 16. r. 12); וַ· id. שחט

יִשְׁחֲטוּ } id. fut. 3 pers. pl. masc. (§ 8. rem. } שחט
יִשְׁחָטוּ וַיִּ' } 15); וַ· id. . . . }

יִשְׁחָטוּהוּ[s] וַ id. id., suff. 3 p. s. m. (§ 16. r. 12); וַ· id. שחט

יִשְׁחָטוּם וַ id. id., suff. 3 pers. pl. masc.; וַ· id. . שחט

יִשְׁחָטֵם וַ Kal fut. 3 pers. sing. masc., suff. 3 pers. pl. masc. (§ 16. rem. 12); וַ· conv. . . שחט

יַשְׁחִית Hiph. fut. 3 pers. sing. masc. . . . שחת

יַשְׁחִיתוּ וַיַּ' id. fut. 3 pers. pl. masc.; וַ· conv. . שחת

יַשְׁחִיתֶךָ id. fut. 3 p. s. m., suff. 2 p. s. m. [for 'חִיתְךָ] שחת

יַשְׁחֶנָּה[x] Hiph. fut. 3 pers. sing. masc. [יַשְׁחֶה], suff. 3 pers. sing. fem. (§ 24. r. 21, & § 2. r. 3) שחה

יֶשְׁחֲךָ[y] וְ noun masc. sing., suff. 2 pers. sing. masc. from [יֶשַׁח] dec. 6 (§ 35. rem. 3 & 5) . ישח

יִשְׂחָק } Kal fut. 3 pers. sing. masc. (§ 8. r. 15) שחק
יִשְׂחַק וַיִּ'[z] }

יְשַׂחֶק־[a] וְ Piel fut. 3 pers. sing. masc. [for יְשַׂחֵק § 14. r. 1 & 2] with conj. וְ [for וִי', וִישַׂ'] שחק

יְשַׂחֲקוּ[b] } id. fut. 3 pers. pl. masc., with conj. וְ } שחק
וִישַׂחֲקוּ[c] } [for וִי', וִישַׂחֲקוּ] . . . }

יִשְׂחָקוּ[d] Kal fut. 3 pers. pl. m. [for יִשְׂחֲקוּ § 8. r. 15] שחק

יְשַׁחֲרֻנְנִי Piel (§ 14. rem. 1) fut. 3 pers. pl. masc., with parag. נ & suff. 1 p. s. (§ 16. r. 14) שחר

וַיַּשְׁחֵת[e] } Hiph. fut. 3 pers. sing. masc. apoc. & } שחת
יַשְׁחֵת } defect. for יַשְׁחִית; וַ· conv. . }

וַיַּשְׁחִתוּ וַ id. fut. 3 p. pl. m., defect. for יַשְׁחִיתוּ; וַ· id. שחת

יָשַׁט. Hiph. הוֹשִׁיט *to stretch out, extend*, Est. 4. 11; 5. 2; 8. 4.

יֵשְׁטְ[f] Kal fut. 3 p. s. m. apoc. [fr. יִשְׁטֶה § 24. r. 3] שטה

יָשֻׁטוּ[g] וַ Kal fut. 3 p. pl. m. [for יָשׁוּטוּ]; וַ· conv. שוט

יִשְׁטוֹף[h] Kal fut. 3 pers. sing. masc. (§ 8. rem. 18) שטף

יִשְׁטְחוּ[i] וַ Kal fut. 3 pers. pl. masc.; וַ· conv. . שטח

יְשֹׁטְטוּ[k] Pilel fut. 3 pers. pl. masc. . . . שוט

יִשְׂטֹם[l] וַ Kal fut. 3 pers. sing. masc.; וַ· conv. . שטם

יִשְׂטְמֵהוּ[m] וַ id. fut. 3 p. pl. m., suff. 3 p. s. m.; וַ· id. שטם

יִשְׂטְמוּנִי[n] id. id., suff. 1 pers. sing. . . . שטם

יִשְׂטְמֵנוּ[o] id. fut. 3 pers. sing. masc., suff. 1 pers. pl. שטם

יִשְׂטְמֵנִי[p] וַ id. id., suff. 1 pers. sing.; וַ· conv. . שטם

יִשְׂטְנוּנִי Kal fut. 3 pers. pl. masc., suff. 1 pers. sing. שטן

יִשָּׁטֵף[q] Niph. fut. 3 pers. sing. masc. . . שטף

יִשְׁטֹף[r] וְ Kal fut. 3 pers. sing. masc.; וַ· conv. . שטף

יִשָּׁטְפוּ[s] Niph. fut. 3 pers. pl. masc. . . . שטף

יִשְׁטְפוּ } Kal fut. 3 pers. pl. masc. (§ 8. rem. 15) שטף
וְיִשְׁטְפוּ[t] }

יִשְׁטְפוּהָ[u] id., suff. 3 pers. sing. fem. . . . שטף

יִשְׁטְפוּךָ[x] id., suff. 2 pers. sing. masc. . . . שטף

יִשַׁי } pr. name masc. . . . . שה
וְיִשַׁי }

יַשִּׁיא[y] Hiph. fut. 3 pers. sing. masc. . . . שא

יַשִּׁיאוּ[z] id. fut. 3 pers. pl. masc. . . . . שא

[a] Am. 8. 12. [b] Ex. 4. 11. [c] Ps. 118. 15. [d] Job 38. 41. [e] Is. 63. 1. [f] Ps. 69. 30. [g] Ge. 3. 15. [h] Je. 5. 26. [i] Zep. 2. 14. [k] Da. 3. 17. [l] Ps. 10. 10. [ll] Job 34. 29. [m] Job 38. 40. [n] Ps. 107. 39. [o] Ec. 12. 4. [p] Nu. 11. 22. [q] Le. 17. 3. [r] Le. 8. 15, 19, 23. [s] Le. 9. 15. [t] Eze. 40. 41. [u] Ju. 12. 6. [x] Pr. 12. 25. [y] Mi. 6. 14. [z] Job 41. 21. [a] Ju. 16. 25. [b] Job 40. 20. [c] 2 Sa. 2. 14. [d] Ps. 52. 8. [e] 1 Ch. 20. 1. [f] Pr. 7. 25. [g] 2 Sa. 24. 8. [h] Da. 11. 26. [i] Nu. 11. 32. [k] Da. 12. 4. [l] Ge. 27. 41. [m] Ge. 49. 23. [n] Ps. 55. 4. [o] Ge. 50. 15. [p] Job 16. 9. [q] Le. 15. 12. [r] 1 Ki. 22. 38. [s] Da. 11. 22. [t] Je. 47. 2. [u] Ca. 8. 7. [x] Is. 43. 2. [y] Ps. 89. 23, e [z] Je. 29. 8.

יָשִׁ֫יב Kh. יָשִׁיב, K. יָשׁוּב pr. name masc. . . שׁוב
יָשִׁ֫יב Kh. יָשִׁיב q. v., K. יָשׁוּב (q. v.) . שׁוב
יָשִׁיב Hiph. fut. 3 pers. sing. masc. . . שׁוב
וַיְשִׁיבֶהָ[a] וַ id. id., suff. 3 pers. sing. fem.; וַ conv. . שׁוב
וַיְשִׁיבֵהוּ וַ id. id., suff. 3 pers. sing. masc.; וַ id. . שׁוב
וִישִׁיבֻהוּ[b] וְ id. fut. 3 pers. pl. masc., suff. 3 pers. sing. masc. with conj. וְ [for וְיְשִׁיבוּהוּ ,וְיְ׳] . שׁוב
יָשִׁיבוּ וַיְּ׳, וְ׳ id. fut. 3 pers. pl. masc.; ·ַ conv. . שׁוב
וַיֹּשִׁבוּם[c] וַ Hiph. fut. 3 pers. pl. masc. [יוֹשִׁיבוּ § 20. rem. 11], suff. 3 pers. pl. masc.; ·ַ id. ישׁב
יְשִׁיבוּנִי[d] Hiph. fut. 3 pers. pl. m. (יָשִׁיבוּ), suff. 1 p. s. שׁוב
וַיֹּשִׁבֵם[e] וַ Hiph. fut. 3 pers. sing. masc. [יוֹשִׁיב § 20. rem. 11], suff. 3 pers. pl. masc.; ·ַ conv. ישׁב
וַיֵּשְׁבֻם[f] וַ id. fut. 3 pers. pl. m., suff. 3 pers. pl. m. ישׁב
וַיְשִׁיבֵם[g] וַ Hiph. fut. 3 pers. sing. masc. (יָשִׁיב), suff. 3 pers. pl. masc.; וַ conv. שׁוב
יְשִׁיבֶנָּה id., suff. 3 pers. sing. fem. (§ 2. rem. 3) . שׁוב
יְשִׁיבֶנּוּ id., suff. 3 pers. sing. masc. (§ 2. rem. 3) שׁוב
יַשִּׂיג[h] Hiph. fut. 3 pers. sing. masc. . . . נשׂג
יַשִּׂיגוּ וַיְּ׳ id. fut. 3 pers. pl. masc.; ·ַ conv. . נשׂג
יַשִּׂיגוּן[i] id. id. with parag. ן . . . . נשׂג
יַשִּׂיגֵם[k] id. fut. 3 pers. sing. masc., suff. 3 p. pl. m. נשׂג
יִשִּׁיָּה וְ׳ / יִשִּׁיָּהוּ וְ pr. name masc. . . . . נשׁה
יְשֵׁיזְבִנָּךְ[l] Chald. Peil fut. 3 pers. sing. masc. (יְשֵׁיזִב), suff. 2 pers. sing. masc. (§ 48) . שׁזב
יְשֵׁיזְבִנְכוֹן Chald. id. with suff. 2 pers. pl. masc. . שׁזב
יָשִׂיחַ[n] Kal fut. 3 pers. sing. masc. . . . שׂיח
יָשִׂיחוּ[o] id. fut. 3 pers. pl. masc. . . . שׂיח
יָשִׂים Kal fut. 3 pers. sing. masc., R. שׂים see שׂום
יַשִּׁים[p] Hiph. fut. 3 pers. sing. masc. for יָשֵׁם, יַשֵּׁם (§ 18. rem. 12 & 14) . . . . שׁמם
וַיְשִׂימֶהָ[q] וַ Kal fut. 3 pers. sing. masc. (יָשִׂים, R. שׂים) with suff. 3 pers. sing. fem.; וַ conv., see שׂום
וַיְשִׂימֵהוּ וַ id. id. with suff. 3 pers. sing. masc.; וַ conv. שׂום
וַיְשִׂימֻהוּ[r] וַ id. fut. 3 p. pl. m. with suff. 3 p. s. m.; וַ id. שׂום
יָשִׂימוּ וַיְּ׳, וְ׳ id. fut. 3 pers. pl. masc.; ·ַ id. . שׂום
יִשְׂמָעֵאל pr. name masc. . . . . . שׁמע
יַשִּׁימָוֶת[s] Kh. יְשִׁימוֹת noun pl. R. ישׁם; K. יַשִּׁי מָוֶת see מָוֶת), יַשִּׁי for יַשִּׁיא (q.v. & § 23. r. 7) נשׁא
וַיְשִׂימְךָ[t] וַ Kal fut. 3 pers. sing. masc. (יָשִׂים, R. שׂים), suff. 2 pers. sing. masc.; וַ conv., see . שׂום
יְשִׂימֵם[u] id. with suff. 3 pers. pl. masc. . . שׂום
וַיְשִׂימֵנִי וַ id. with suff. 1 pers. sing.; ·ַ conv. . שׂום
וְיוֹשִׁיעֵנוּ[x] וְ Hiph. fut. 3 pers. sing. masc. (יוֹשִׁיעַ § 20. rem. 11), suff. 1 pers. pl. . . . ישׁע

יַשִּׁיק[y] Hiph. fut. 3 pers. sing. masc. . . . נשׂק
יָשִׁיר Kal fut. 3 pers. sing. masc. . . . שׁיר
יָשִׁירוּ וְ׳ id. fut. 3 pers. pl. masc. . . שׁיר
יָשִׁישׁ[a] noun masc. sing. dec. 3 a . . ישׁשׁ
יָשִׂישׂ[b] וְ׳ Kal fut. 3 pers. sing. masc. R. שִׂישׂ, see שׂושׂ
יָשִׂישׂוּ[c] וְ׳ id. fut. 3 pers. pl. masc. . . . שׂושׂ
יְשִׁישַׁי pr. name masc. . . . . . ישׁשׁ
יְשִׁישִׁים[d] / וִישִׁישִׁים[e] וְ noun masc. pl. [with cop. וְ, for וְיְשִׁישִׁים ,וַיְ׳], from יָשִׁישׁ dec. 3 a . . ישׁשׁ
יָשִׁית Kal fut. 3 pers. sing. masc. . . . שׁית
יָשִׁית[f] Kh. יָשִׁית q. v.; K. וְשִׁית Kal imp. sing. masc. שׁית
וִישִׁיתֵהוּ[g] וְ Hiph. fut. 3 pers. sing. m. (יָשִׁית) and suff. 3 p. s. m. with conj. וְ [for וְיָשִׁיתֵהוּ ,וַיְ׳] שׁית
יָשִׁיתוּ[h] וַיְּ׳ id. fut. 3 pers. pl. masc.; ·ַ conv. . שׁית
יְשִׁיתוּהוּ[k] id. id., suff. 3 pers. sing. masc. . . שׁית
יֶשְׁךָ adv. יֵשׁ with suff. 2 pers. sing. masc. comp. dec. 7 a (§ 36. rem. 3) . . . ישׁה
יִשֹּׁךְ Kal fut. 3 pers. s. m. [for יִשַּׁךְ § 8. rem. 15] נשׁך
יִשֹּׁךְ[l] id. middle O (§ 17. rem. 3) . . נשׁך
יִשְׁכַּב וַיְּ׳ / יִשְׁכָּב וַיְּ׳ Kal fut. 3 pers. sing. masc. (§ 8. rem. 15); ·ַ conv. . . . שׁכב
וַיַּשְׁכִּבֵהוּ[m] וַ Hiph. fut. 3 pers. sing. masc. (יַשְׁכִּיב), suff. 3 pers. sing. masc.; ·ַ id. . . . שׁכב
יִשְׁכְּבוּ / יִשְׁכָּבוּ וַיְּ׳ Kal fut. 3 pers. pl. masc. (§ 8. rem. 15); ·ַ id. . . . שׁכב
יִשְׁכְּבוּן / יִשְׁכָּבוּן[n] id. with parag. ן (§ 8. rem. 17) . . שׁכב
וַיָּשֹׁכּוּ[o] וַ Kal fut. 3 pers. pl. masc.; ·ַ conv. . שׁכך
יִשְׁכּוֹן[p] וַיְּ׳ Kal fut. 3 p. s. m. (§ 8. rem. 18); ·ַ id. שׁכן
יִשְׁכְּנוּ[q] id. fut. 3 pers. pl. masc. . . . שׁכן
יִשָּׁכַח[r] Niph. fut. 3 pers. sing. masc. . . שׁכח
יִשְׁכַּח[s] וַיְּ׳[t], וְ׳ Kal fut. 3 pers. sing. masc.; ·ַ conv. שׁכח
יִשְׁכָּחֵהוּ[u] וַיְּ׳[x] id. id., suff. 3 p. s. m. (§ 16. rem. 12); ·ַ id. שׁכח
יִשְׁכְּחוּ וַיְּ׳ id. fut. 3 pers. pl. masc.; ·ַ id. . שׁכח
יַשְׁכִּיב[y] Hiph. fut. 3 pers. sing. masc. . . שׁכב
וַיַּשְׁכִּיבֻהוּ[z] וַ id. fut. 3 p. pl. m., suff. 3 p. s. m.; ·ַ conv. שׁכב
יַשְׂכִּיל Hiph. fut. 3 pers. sing. masc. . . . שׂכל
יַשְׂכִּילוּ[a] וְ׳[b] id. fut. 3 pers. pl. masc. . . . שׂכל
וַיַּשְׁכִּימוּ וַ Hiph. fut. 3 pers. pl. masc.; ·ַ conv. . שׁכם
וַיַּשְׁכִּינוּ[c] וַ Hiph. fut. 3 pers. sing. masc.; ·ַ id. . שׁכן
וַיַּשְׁכֵּם וַ Hiph. fut. 3 p. s. m. ap. [from יַשְׁכִּים]; ·ַ id. שׁכם
יֶשְׁכֶם[d] adv. יֵשׁ with suff. 2 pers. pl. masc. (comp. הֲיִשְׁכֶם & § 36. rem. 3) . . . ישׁה
וַיַּשְׁכִּמוּ וַ defect. for יַשְׁכִּימוּ (q. v.) . . שׁכם
וַיַּשְׁכֵּן וַיְּ׳ Hiph. fut. 3 pers. sing. masc. apoc. [from יַשְׁכִּין]; ·ַ conv. . . . . שׁכן

[a] 2 Ch. 26. 2. [b] 2 Ch. 24. 11. [c] 2 Sa. 12. 8. [d] Job 20. 2. [e] Job 36. 7. [f] 1 Sa. 30. 21. [g] 2 Ch. 19. 4. [h] Le. 26. 5. [i] Is. 51. 11. [k] Ps. 69. 25. [l] Da. 6. 17. [m] Da. 3. 15. [n] Ps. 119. 23. [o] Ps. 69. 13. [p] Je. 49. 20; 50. 45. [q] Jos. 8. 28. [r] 2 Ki. 10. 27. [s] Ps. 55. 16. [t] 1 Ki. 10. 9. [u] De. 7. 15. [x] 1 Sa. 4. 3. [y] Is. 44. 15. [z] Ps. 138. 5. [a] Job 15. 10.

[b] Job 39. 21. [c] Ps. 68. 4. [d] Job 32. 6. [e] Job 29. 8. [f] Job 10. 20. [g] Ge. 41. 33. [h] Ps. 17. 11. [i] Je. 2. 15. [k] Ps. 84. 7. [l] Ec. 10. 11. [m] 1 Ki. 17. 19. [n] 1 Sa. 2. 22. [o] Ge. 8. 1. [p] Job 15. 28. [q] Ps. 102. 29. [r] Ps. 9. 19. [s] De. 4. 31. [t] Ho. 8. 14. [u] Job 24. 20. [x] Ge. 40. 23. [y] Job 38. 37. [z] 2 Ch. 16. 14. [a] De. 32. 29. [b] Is. 41. 20. [c] Jos. 18. 1. [d] Ge. 24. 49. [e] Ps. 7. 6.

יִשְׁכֹּן [a] | וַיִּ׳, וְ׳ } Kal fut. 3 pers. sing. masc. (§ 8. rem. 18); ·וַ conv. . . שׁכן
יִשְׁכָּן־ |

יִשְׁכֵנוּ [b] Kal fut. 3 pers. sing. masc. (comp. יִשַּׁךְ & וַיִּשַּׁךְ), suff. 3 pers. sing. masc. . . . נשׁך

יִשְׁכֹּנוּ [c] | } Kal fut. 3 pers. pl. masc. (§ 8. rem. 15); ·וַ conv. . . שׁכן
יִשְׁכְּנוּ [d] וַיִּ׳, וְ׳ [e] |

יִשְׁכְּנָן [f] Chald. Peal fut. 3 pers. pl. fem. . . . שׁכן

יִשְׁכָּר [g] וַ Kal fut. 3 pers. sing. masc. [for יִשְׁכַּר § 8. rem. 15]; ·וַ conv. . . . . שׁכר

יִשְׁכֹּר וַ Kal fut. 3 pers. sing. masc.; ·וַ id. . שׁכר

יְשַׁכְּרֵהוּ [h] וַ Piel fut. 3 pers. s. m., suff. 3 pers. s. m.; וַ id. שׁכר

יִשְׁכְּרוּ [i] וַיִּ׳ Kal fut. 3 pers. pl. masc.; ·וַ id. . שׁכר

יִשְׁכָּרוּ [k] וַ Kal fut. 3 pers. pl. masc.; ·וַ id. . . שׁכר

יִשְׁכָּרוּן [l] id. with parag. ן [for יִשְׁכְּרוּן § 8. rem. 17] שׁכר

יְשַׁכְּרֵנִי [m] וַ Kal fut. 3 pers. s. m., suff. 1 pers. s.; ·וַ conv. שׁכר

יִשַּׁל [n] Kal fut. 3 pers. sing. masc. . . . נשׁל

יִשֶׁל [o] Kal fut. 3 p. s. m. ap. [for יִשְׁלֶה § 24. rem. 3] שׁלה

יִשְׁלוּךָ [p] Kal fut. 3 pers. pl. masc. [יִשְׁלוּ], suff. 2 pers. sing. masc. (§ 18. rem. 5) . . . שׁלל

יְשַׁלַּח | וַיְ׳ } Piel fut. 3 pers. sing. masc.; וַ conv.; with conj. וְ [for וַיְשַׁלַּח, וִיְ׳] . שׁלח
יְשַׁלַּח [q] | וְ

יְשַׁלֵּחַ id. in pause (§ 15. rem. 1) . . . שׁלח

יְשֻׁלַּח [r] Pual fut. 3 pers. sing. masc. . . . שׁלח

יִשְׁלַח וַיִּ׳, וְ׳ Kal or (Chald.) Peal fut. 3 p. s. m.; ·וַ conv. שׁלח

יְשַׁלְּחֶהָ וַ Piel fut. 3 pers. s. m., suff. 3 pers. s. fem.; וַ id. שׁלח

יְשַׁלְּחֵהוּ וַ id., suff. 3 pers. sing. masc.; וַ id. שׁלח

יִשְׁלָחֵהוּ [s] וַ Kal fut. 3 pers. sing. masc. (יִשְׁלַח), suff. 3 pers. sing. masc. (§ 16. rem. 12); ·וַ id. שׁלח

יְשַׁלְּחוּ [t] | וַיְ׳ } Piel fut. 3 pers. pl. masc. (comp. § 8. rem. 15); וַ id. . שׁלח
יְשַׁלֵּחוּ [u] | וַ׳

יְשַׁלְּחוּ [y] וְ id. with conj. [for וַיְשַׁלְּחוּ, וִיְ׳] . שׁלח

יִשְׁלְחוּ [z] וַיִּ׳ Kal fut. 3 pers. pl. masc.; ·וַ conv. . שׁלח

יְשַׁלְּחוּהָ [a] וַ Piel fut. 3 p. pl. m., suff. 3 p. s. fem.; וַ id. שׁלח

יְשַׁלְּחוּם [b] וַ id., suff. 3 pers. pl. masc.; וַ id. . שׁלח

יִשְׁלָחֲךָ [c] וַיִּ׳ [d] Kal fut. 3 pers. sing. masc. (יִשְׁלַח), suff. 2 pers. sing. masc. (§ 16. rem. 12); ·וַ id. שׁלח

יְשַׁלְּחֵם [e] | וַ׳ } Piel fut. 3 p. s. m., suff. 3 p. pl. m.; וַ conv.; with conj. וְ [for וַיְשַׁלְּחֵם, וִיְ׳] . שׁלח
יְשַׁלְּחֵם [f] | וְ

יִשְׁלָחֵם וַ Kal fut. 3 pers. sing. masc. (יִשְׁלַח), suff. 3 pers. pl. masc. (§ 16. rem. 12); ·וַ conv. שׁלח

יְשַׁלְּחֵנוּ [g] וַ Piel fut. 3 pers. sing. m., suff. 1 pers. pl.; וַ id. שׁלח

יְשַׁלְּחֶנּוּ id., suff. 3 pers. sing. masc. . . שׁלח

יִשְׁלָחֶנּוּ [h] Kal fut. 3 pers. sing. masc. (יִשְׁלַח), suff. 3 pers. sing. masc. (§ 16. rem. 12) . . שׁלח

יְשַׁלְּחֵנִי וַ Kal fut. 3 pers. sing. masc., with suff. 1 pers. sing. (§ 16. rem. 10); ·וַ conv. . . שׁלח

יִשְׁלַט [i] Chald. Peal fut. 3 pers. sing. m. (§ 47. rem. 6 b) שׁלט

יִשְׁלֹט [k] וְ Kal fut. 3 pers. sing. masc. . . . שׁלט

יִשְׁלְטוּ [l] id. fut. 3 pers. pl. masc. . . . שׁלט

יִשְׁלָיוּ Kal fut. 3 pers. pl. masc. (§ 24. rem. 5) . שׁלה

יַשְׁלִיטֶנּוּ [m] Hiph. fut. 3 pers. sing. m., suff. 3 pers. sing. m. שׁלט

יַשְׁלִיךְ [n] Hiph. fut. 3 pers. sing. masc. . . שׁלך

יַשְׁלִיכֵהוּ [o] וַ id. id., suff. 3 pers. sing. masc.; ·וַ conv. שׁלך

יַשְׁלִיכוּ וַיַּ׳ id. fut. 3 pers. pl. masc.; ·וַ id. . שׁלך

יַשְׁלִיכוּם [p] | וַ } id. id., suff. 3 pers. pl. masc.; ·וַ id. . שׁלך
יַשְׁלִיכֵם [q] | וַ

יַשְׁלִים Hiph. fut. 3 pers. sing. masc. . . שׁלם

יַשְׁלִימוּ [ff] וַ id. fut. 3 pers. pl. masc.; ·וַ conv. . שׁלם

יַשְׁלֵךְ | וַיַּ׳, וְ } Hiph. fut. 3 pers. sing. masc., apoc. [from יַשְׁלִיךְ]; ·וַ conv. . שׁלך
יַשְׁלֵךְ־ [ll] | וְ

יַשְׁלִכֵהוּ וַ id. fut. 3 pers. pl. m., suff. 3 pers. s. m.; ·וַ id. שׁלך

יַשְׁלִכוּ וַ defect. for יַשְׁלִיכוּ (q. v.) . . שׁלך

יֻשְׁלְכוּ [r] Hoph. fut. 3 p. pl. m. [for יָשְׁלְכוּ comp. § 8. r. 15] שׁלך

יַשְׁלִכֵם [s] וַ Hiph. fut. 3 p. s. m., suff. 3 p. pl. m.; ·וַ conv. שׁלך

יַשְׁלֵם [t] | וַ } Hiph. fut. 3 pers. sing. masc., apoc. and defect. for יַשְׁלִים; ·וַ id. . . שׁלם
יַשְׁלֵם |

יִשְׁלָם [u] וַ Kal fut. 3 p. s. m. [for יִשְׁלַם § 8. r. 15]; ·וַ id. שׁלם

יְשַׁלֵּם | } Piel fut. 3 pers. sing. masc. (§ 10. rem. 4) שׁלם
יְשַׁלֶּם־ |

יְשֻׁלַּם | } Pual fut. 3 pers. sing. masc. (comp. § 8. rem. 15) . . . . שׁלם
יְשֻׁלָּם [x] |

יַשְׁלִמוּ [qq] וַ Hiph. fut. 3 pers. pl. masc.; ·וַ conv. . שׁלם

יְשַׁלְּמוּנִי [y] Piel fut. 3 pers. pl. masc., suff. 1 pers. sing. שׁלם

יְשַׁלֶּמְךָ [z] id. fut. 3 p. s. m., suff. 2 p. s. m. (§ 16. rem. 15) שׁלם

יְשַׁלְּמֶנָּה id. id., suff. 3 pers. sing. fem. (§ 2. rem. 3) שׁלם

יִשְׁלֹף [a] וַ Kal fut. 3 pers. sing. masc.; ·וַ conv. . שׁלף

יִשְׁלְפָהּ [b] וַ id., suff. 3 pers. sing. fem.; ·וַ id. . שׁלף

יְשַׁלְּשׁוּ [c] וַ Piel fut. 3 pers. pl. masc. [for יְשַׁלְּשׁוּ comp. § 8. rem. 15]; וַ id. . . . שׁלשׁ

יָשַׂם only fut. וַיִּישֶׂם.—I. *to put, place,* Ju. 12. 3. Kheth.—II. *to be put, placed,* Ge. 50. 26; 24. 33. Kheth.

יָשַׁם only fut. תֵּשַׁם, תִּישַׁמְנָה, *to be desolate, laid waste.*

יִשְׁמָא (for יְשִׁמָּה *desolation*) pr. name m. 1 Ch. 4.

יְשִׁימָה fem. only pl. יְשִׁימוֹת *desolations,* Ps. 55. Kheth. Compare בֵּית־הַיְשִׁימוֹת.

[a] Ge. 9. 27. [b] Ec. 10. 8. [c] Je. 49. 31. [d] Ps. 37. 29. [e] Ge. 25. 18. [f] Da. 4. 18.
[g] Ge. 9. 21. [h] 2 Sa. 11. 13. [i] Is. 46. 6. [k] Ge. 43. 34. [l] Is. 49. 26. [m] Ju. 18. 4.
[n] De. 28. 40. [o] Job 27. 8. [p] Hab. 2. 8. [q] Ex. 6. 11. [r] Pr. 17. 11. [s] Ge. 37. 14.
[t] Eze. 44. 20. [u] Je. 34. 10. [x] Job 21. 11. [y] Nu. 5. 2. [z] Ps. 125. 3. [a] Ju. 19. 25.
[b] 1 Sa. 6. 6. [c] Je. 42. 5. [d] 1 Sa. 15. 18. [e] Ex. 6. 1. [f] Job 12. 15. [ff] 1 Ch. 19. 19.
[g] Ge. 19. 13. [h] 1 Sa. 18. 5. [i] Da. 5. 7. [k] Ec. 2. 19. [l] Est. 9. 1. [ll] 2 Ki. 2. 21.
[m] Ec. 6. 2. [n] Is. 2. 20. [o] Da. 8. 7. [p] 2 Ch. 25. 12. [q] Jos. 10. 27. [qq] 2 Sa. 10. 19.
[r] Is. 34. 3. [s] De. 29. 27. [t] 1 Ki. 22. 45. [u] Job 9. 4. [x] Ps. 65. 2.
[y] Ps. 35. 12. [z] 1 Sa. 24. 20. [a] Ru. 4. 8. [b] 1 Sa. 17. 51. [c] 1 Ki. 18. 34.

יְשִׁימוֹן masc. *waste, desert.*

שִׁימוֹן (for יְשִׁימוֹן *desert*) pr. name m. 1 Ch. 4. 20.

שַׁמָּה (for יְשַׁמָּה *desolation*; Gesenius, *garlic*) pr. name whence patronym. שֻׁמָתִי 1 Ch. 2. 53.

וַיָּשֶׂם ,וַיָּשֶׂם וְ׳ ,וַ Kal fut. 3 pers. sing. masc., apoc. and conv. from יָשִׂים, R. שׂים see . שׂום

יָשֵׂם[a] defect. for יָשִׂים (q. v.) . . . שׂום

יֵשֵׁם Kal fut. 3 p. s. m., Chald. form (§ 18. rem. 14) שמם

יִשְׁמָא וְ pr. name masc. . . . ישם

וַיַּשְׁמֵד וַ Hiph. fut. 3 pers. sing. m., ap. from יַשְׁמִיד שמד

יִשָּׁמֵד Niph. fut. 3 pers. sing. masc. . . . שמד

וַיְשִׂמֶהָ[b] וַ Kal fut. 3 pers. sing. masc. (יָשִׂים R. שׂים), suff. 3 pers. sing. fem.; וַ conv., see . שׂום

וַיְשִׂמֵהוּ וַ id., suff. 3 pers. sing. masc.; וַ id. . שׂום

וַיָּשִׂמוּ וַ id. fut. 3 pers. pl. m. defect. for יָשִׂימוּ; וַ id. שׂום

יֵשַׁמּוּ Kal fut. 3 pers. pl. masc. . . . שמם

וַיְשַׂמַּח[c] וְ׳ ,וַ Piel fut. 3 pers. sing. masc.; וַ conv. שמח

יִשְׂמַח ,יִשְׂמָח[d] וְ׳ ,וַ׳ Kal fut. 3 pers. sing. masc. (§ 8. rem. 15); וַ id. . . שמח

יְשַׂמְּחוּ Piel fut. 3 pers. pl. masc. . . . שמח

יִשְׂמְחוּ ,יִשְׂמָחוּ וְ׳ ,וַ׳ Kal fut. 3 pers. pl. masc. (§ 8. rem. 15); וַ conv. . שמח

יְשַׂמְּחֶנָּה[e] Piel fut. 3 pers. sing. masc., suff. 3 pers. sing. fem. (§ 2. rem. 3) . . שמח

וַיְשִׂמְתוּהָ[f] וַ Kal fut. 3 pers. pl. masc., suff. 3 pers. sing. fem.; וַ conv. . . . שמם

יַשְׁמִיד Hiph. fut. 3 pers. sing. masc. . . שמד

יַשְׁמִידוּ[g] id. fut. 3 pers. pl. masc. . . . שמד

וַיַּשְׁמִידוּם[h] וַ id. id., suff. 3 pers. pl. masc.; וַ conv. שמד

יַשְׁמִידֵם[i] וַ׳[k] id. fut. 3 pers. sing. masc., suff. 3 pers. pl. masc.; וַ id. . . . שמד

וַיַּשְׁמִינוּ[l] וַ Hiph. fut. 3 pers. pl. masc.; וַ id. . שמן

יַשְׁמִיעַ Hiph. fut. 3 pers. sing. masc. . . שמע

יַשְׁמִיעוּ[m] וְ׳ ,וַ׳[n] id. fut. 3 pers. pl. masc.; וַ conv. . שמע

יַשְׁמִיעֻנוּ[p] id. id. with suff. 1 pers. pl. . שמע

יְשִׂמְךָ Kal fut. 3 pers. sing. masc. (יָשִׂים, R. שׂים), suff. 2 pers. sing. masc. (for יְשִׂימְךָ), see שׂום

וַיְשִׂמֵם[q] וַ id. with suff. 3 pers. pl. masc.; וַ conv. . שׂום

וַיַּשְׁמֵם[r] וַ Hiph. fut. 3 pers. sing. masc. [יַשֵׁם], suff. 3 pers. pl. masc.; וַ id. . . שמם

וַיִּשְׁמָן[s] וַ Kal fut. 3 pers. sing. masc.; וַ id. . שמן

יְשִׁמֹן[t] noun masc. sing. defect. for יְשִׁימוֹן . ישם

יְשִׂמֵנִי[u] Kal fut. 3 pers. sing. masc. (יָשִׂים, R. שׂים), suff. 1 pers. sing. (for יְשִׂימֵנִי), see שׂום

וַיְשַׁמַּע וַ Piel fut. 3 pers. sing. masc. וַ conv. . שמע

יִשָּׁמַע ,יִשָּׁמֵעַ[y] וַ׳ ,וְ׳[x] Niph. fut. 3 pers. sing. masc. (§ 15. rem. 1); וַ id. . . . שמע

יִשְׁמַע ,יִשְׁמָע וְ׳ ,וַ׳ Kal fut. 3 pers. sing. masc. (§ 8. rem. 15); וַ conv. . . שמע

יִשְׁמַע[z] Ch. Peal fut. 3 pers. sing. m. (§ 49. No. 4) שמע

יִשְׁמָעֵאל וְ pr. name masc. . . . . שמע

יִשְׁמְעֵאלִים וְ gent. noun pl. from the preceding . שמע

וַיִּשָּׁמְעוּ[a] וַ Niph. fut. 3 pers. pl. masc.; וַ conv. שמע

יִשְׁמְעוּ ,יִשְׁמָעוּ[b] וְ׳ ,וַ׳ Kal fut. 3 pers. pl. masc. (§ 8. rem. 15); וַ id. . . שמע

יִשְׁמָעוּן id. id. with parag. ן . . . . שמע

יִשְׁמַעְיָה ,יִשְׁמַעְיָהוּ וְ׳ pr. name masc. . . . . שמע

יִשְׁמָעֲךָ[c] וְ Kal fut. 3 pers. sing. masc. (יִשְׁמַע), suff. 2 pers. sing. m. (§ 16. r. 12, & § 2. r. 2) שמע

וַיַּשְׁמִעֵנוּ[d] וַ Hiph. fut. 3 pers. sing. masc. (יַשְׁמִיעַ), suff. 3 pers. pl. . . . . . שמע

יִשְׁמָעֵנִי Kal fut. 3 pers. sing. masc. (יִשְׁמַע), suff. 1 pers. sing. (§ 16. rem. 12) . שמע

יִשְׁמֹר ,יִשְׁמָר־[e] וְ׳ ,וַ׳ Kal fut. 3 pers. sing. masc. (§ 8. rem. 18); וַ conv. . . . שמר

יִשְׁמְרֵהוּ[f] id. id., suff. 3 pers. sing. masc. . . שמר

יִשְׁמְרוּ ,יִשְׁמָרוּ[g] וְ׳ ,וַ׳ id. fut. 3 pers. pl. masc. (§ 8. rem. 15); וַ conv. . . שמר

יִשְׁמְרַי וְ pr. name masc. . . . . שמר

יִשְׁמָרְךָ[h] ,יִשְׁמְרֶךָּ[i] וְ Kal fut. 3 pers. sing. masc., suff. 2 pers. sing. masc. . . . שמר

וַיִּשְׁמְרֵנוּ[k] וַ id. id., suff. 1 pers. pl.; וַ conv. . שמר

יִשְׁמְרֶנּוּ[l] id. id., suff. 3 pers. sing. masc. (§ 2. r. 3) שמר

יִשְׁמְרֵנִי[m] id. id., suff. 1 pers. sing. . . . שמר

יְשַׁמְּשׁוּנֵּהּ[n] Chald. Pael fut. 3 pers. pl. masc., suff. 3 pers. sing. masc. . . . . שמש

[יָשֵׁן ,יָשַׁן] fut. יִישַׁן.—I. *to fall asleep, to sleep.* Niph.—I. *to be dry,* Le. 26. 10.—II. *to grow old,* Le. 13. 11; De. 4. 25. Pi. *to make to sleep,* Ju. 16. 19.

יָשָׁן masc. dec. 4a, יְשָׁנָה fem. adj. *old.*

יָשֵׁן masc. dec. 5a (pl. c. יְשֵׁנֵי § 4. rem. 2), יְשֵׁנָה fem. adj.—I. *sleeping, asleep.*—II. pr. name masc. 2 Sa. 23. 32.

יְשָׁנָה (*old*) pr. name of a city in the tribe of Judah, 2 Ch. 13. 19.

שֵׁנָה fem. dec. 11b (once שֵׁנָא).—I. *sleep.*—II. *dream,* Ps. 90. 5.

שְׁנָא Chald. fem. dec. 9a, *sleep,* Da. 6. 19.

שְׁנַת fem. *sleep,* Ps. 132. 4.

יָשָׁן[o] וְ adj. masc. sing. dec. 4a . . . ישן

יָשֵׁן adj. masc. sing. dec. 5a, also pr. name m. ישן

יִשָּׁנֵא[p] Niph. fut. 3 pers. sing. masc. . . . שנא

[a] Job 23. 6. [b] 1 Sa. 30. 25. [c] La. 2. 17. [d] Ju. 9. 19. Pr. 12. 25. [f] 2 Ki. 9. 33. [g] 2 Sa. 14. 11. [h] De. 2. 12. [i] De. 9. 3. [k] De. 2. 21. [l] Ne. 9. 25. [m] Ne. 8. 15. [n] Je. 23. 22. [o] Ne. 12. 42. [p] Is. 43. 9. [q] 2 Ki. 13. 7. [r] 1 Sa. 5. 6. [s] De. 32. 15. [t] De. 32. 10. [u] 2 Sa. 15. 4. [x] 2 Ch. 30. 27. [y] 1 Sa. 1. 13. [z] Da. 3. 10. [a] 1 Sa. 17. 31. [b] Je. 6. 10. [c] Job 22. 27. [d] De. 30. 12, 13. [e] Ps. 107. 43. [f] Ps. 41. 3. [g] Eze. 43. 11. [h] Ps. 121. 7. [i] Nu. 6. 24. [k] Jos. 24. 17. [l] Ex. 21. 29, 36. [m] Job 29. 2. [n] Da. 7. 10. [o] Le. 26. 10. [p] Pr. 14. 17, 20.

יִשְׂנָא Kal fut. 3 pers. sing. masc. . . . . שׂנא

[a] יִשְׂנֵא Ch. Peal fut. 3 pers. sing. masc., see under שׁנה

[b] יִשְׁנֶא Kal fut. 3 pers. s. m. [for יִשְׁנֶה § 24. r. 19b] שׁנה

[c] יְשֻׁנָּא Pual fut. 3 pers. s. m. [for יְשֻׁנֶּה § 24. r. 19b] שׁנה

יִשְׂנָאֶהָ וַ Kal fut. 3 pers. sing. masc., suff. 3 pers. sing. fem.; וַ conv. . . . שׂנא

יִשְׂנְאוּ [d] וַיִּ id. fut. 3 pers. pl. masc.; וַ id. . שׂנא

[e] יִשְׂנָאֶךָ id. fut. 3 pers. sing. masc., suff. 2 pers. sing. masc. (§ 2. rem. 3) . . שׂנא

יְשָׁנָה pr. name of a place . . . . ישן

[f] יִשְׁנֶהָ וַ the foll. with suff. 3 pers. s. fem.; וַ conv. שׁנה

[g] יְשַׁנֶּה וִ Piel fut. 3 pers. sing. masc., with conj. וִ [for וִישַׁנֶּה, וִי] . . . . שׁנה

יְשֵׁנָה adj. fem. sing. from יָשֵׁן masc. . . ישן

[h] יְשַׁנּוֹ וַ Piel fut. 3 pers. sing. masc. (יְשַׁנֶּה), suff. 3 pers. sing. masc. (§ 24. r. 21); וַ conv. שׁנה

יֶשְׁנוֹ adv. יֵשׁ with epenth. נ and suff. 3 pers. sing. masc. (§ 36. rem. 3) . . . . ישׁה

יָשְׁנוּ וְ Kal pret. 3 pers. pl. . . . . . ישן

[i] יִשְׁנוּ id. fut. 3 pers. pl. m. [for יִישְׁנוּ § 20. r. 2] ישן

[k] יִשְׁנוּ [l] וַיִּ Kal fut. 3 pers. pl. masc.; וַ conv. . שׁנה

[m] יִשְׁנוֹן Chald. Peal fut. 3 pers. pl. masc., see under שׁנה

[n] יְשֵׁנִים adj. masc., pl. of יָשֵׁן dec. 4a . . ישן

יְשָׁנִים adj. masc., pl. of יָשָׁן dec. 5a . . ישן

[o] יְשַׁנֵּס וַ Piel fut. 3 pers. sing. masc.; וַ conv. . שׁנס

[p] יָשַׁנְתִּי Kal pret. 3 pers. sing. . . . . ישן

[q] יִשְׁסֶה Kal fut. 3 pers. sing. masc. . . . שׁסה

יָשֹׁסּוּ וַ Kal fut. 3 pers. pl. m.; וַ conv. . . שׁסס

[r] יִשַּׁסּוּ Niph. fut. 3 pers. pl. masc. . . . שׁסס

[s] יְשַׁסַּע וַ Piel fut. 3 pers. sing. masc.; וַ conv. . שׁסע

[t] יְשַׁסְּעֵהוּ וַ id., suff. 3 pers. sing. masc.; וַ id. . שׁסע

[u] יְשַׁסֵּף וַ Piel fut. 3 pers. sing. masc.; וַ id. . שׁסף

יָשַׁע. Hiph. הוֹשִׁיעַ fut. יוֹשִׁיעַ, apoc. יֹשַׁע.—I. *to deliver, save, set free,* with מִן, מִיַּד *from* any thing.—II. *to help, succour,* with acc., לְ. Niph. נוֹשַׁע.—I. *to be delivered, saved.*—II. *to be helped, succoured.* Part. נוֹשָׁע *aided, supported.*

יֵשַׁע, יֶשַׁע masc. dec. 6e (see § 35. rem. 6), *deliverance, freedom, safety, salvation.*

יְשׁוּעָה f. d. 10, *deliverance, help, safety, salvation.*

יִשְׁעִי (*salutary*) pr. name masc.—I. 1 Ch. 2. 31.—II. 1 Ch. 5. 24.—III. 1 Ch. 4. 20, 42.

יְשַׁעְיָהוּ (*salvation of the Lord*) pr. name masc.—I. *Isaiah,* the prophet under the reign of Uzziah, Jotham, Ahaz and Hezekiah.—II. 1 Ch. 25. 3, 15.—III. 1 Ch. 26. 25.

יְשַׁעְיָה (id.) pr. name masc.—I. 1 Ch. 3. 21.—II. Ezr. 8. 7.—III. Ezr. 8. 19.—IV. Ne. 11. 7.

הוֹשֵׁעַ (*deliverance*) pr. name—I. of the minister of Moses before he was called יְהוֹשׁוּעַ, *Joshua,* Nu. 13. 8, 16.—II. of a king of Israel.—III. of a prophet, Ho. 1. 1, 2.

הוֹשַׁעְיָה (whom *the Lord delivers*) pr. name masc. of several persons.

מוֹשָׁעוֹת fem. pl. (of מוֹשָׁעָה) *deliverances,* Ps. 68. 21.

מֵישַׁע (*deliverance*) pr. name of a king of Moab, 2 Ki. 3. 4.

מֵישָׁע (id.) pr. name masc. 1 Ch. 2. 42.

[x] יֶשַׁע noun masc. sing. dec. 6e . . . ישׁע

יֵשַׁע noun masc. sing. dec. 6e (§ 35. r. 5) . ישׁע

[y] יִשַׁע וַ Kal fut. 3 pers. s. m. ap. fr. יִשְׁעֶה; וַ conv. שׁעה

יֹשַׁע [z] וַ, וְ Hiph. fut. 3 pers. sing. masc., apoc. and conv. from יוֹשִׁיעַ (§ 20. rem. 11) . ישׁע

[a] יִשְׁעֶה Kal fut. 3 pers. sing. masc. . . . שׁעה

יִשְׁעוֹ noun masc. sing., suff. 3 pers. sing. masc. from יֵשַׁע dec. 6e . . . . ישׁע

יִשְׁעוּ Kal fut. 3 pers. pl. masc. . . . . שׁעה

[b] יְשֻׁעוֹת noun fem., pl. of יְשׁוּעָה dec. 10 . . ישׁע

יִשְׁעִי וְ pr. name masc. . . . . . ישׁע

יִשְׁעִי [c] וְ noun m. s., suff. 1 pers. s. from יֵשַׁע d. 6e ישׁע

יְשַׁעְיָה (וִישַׁע׳), יְשַׁעְיָהוּ (וִישַׁע׳) } pr. name masc. . . . . ישׁע

[d] יִשְׁעֲךָ וְ noun masc. sing., suff. 2 pers. sing. masc. from יֵשַׁע dec. 6 (§ 35. rem. 6) . . ישׁע

יִשְׁעֵךְ id., suff. 2 pers. sing. fem. . . . ישׁע

יִשְׁעֶךָ id., suff. 2 pers. sing. masc. [for יִשְׁעֲךָ] ישׁע

[e] יֹשִׁעֲכֶם וְ Hiph. fut. 3 pers. sing. masc. (יֹשַׁע § 20. rem. 11), suff. 2 pers. pl. m. [for יֹשִׁיעֲכֶם § 16. rem. 16 note] . . . ישׁע

[f] יִשָּׁעֵן וְ Niph. fut. 3 pers. sing. masc. . . שׁען

יִשָּׁעֵנוּ Niph. fut. 3 pers. pl. masc. [for יִשָּׁעֲנוּ comp. § 8. rem. 15] . . . . שׁען

יִשְׁעֵנוּ noun masc. s., suff. 1 pers. pl. fr. יֵשַׁע d. 6e ישׁע

[g] יֹשִׁעֵנוּ Hiph. fut. 3 pers. sing. masc. with suff. 1 pers. pl. [for יוֹשִׁיעֵנוּ] . . . . ישׁע

[h] יְשָׂעֲרֵהוּ וְ Piel fut. 3 pers. sing. masc. [יְשָׂעֵר § 14. rem. 1], suff. 3 pers. sing. masc. with cop. וְ [for וִישָׂעֲרֵהוּ, וִי] . . . שׂער

[i] יִשְׂעָרוּ Kal fut. 3 pers. pl. masc. . . . שׂער

[k] יִשְׂעָרֶנּוּ id. fut. 3 pers. sing. masc. [יִשְׂעַר], suff. 3 pers. sing. masc. (§ 16. rem. 12) . שׂער

[l] יְשַׁעֲשְׁעוּ Pilpel fut. 3 pers. pl. masc. (§ 6. No. 4) שׁעע

[a] Da. 7. 24. [b] La. 4. 1. [c] Ec. 8. 1. [d] Ge. 37. 4. [e] Pr. 9. 8. [f] Est. 2. 9. [g] Pr. 31. 5. [h] 1 Sa. 21. 14. [i] Pr. 4. 16. [k] Job 29. 22. [l] 1 Ki. 18. 34. [m] Da. 4. 13. [n] Ca. 7. 14. [o] 1 Ki. 18. 46. [p] Job 3. 13. [q] Ho. 13. 15. [r] Is. 13. 16. [s] 1 Sa. 24. 8. [t] Ju. 14. 6. [u] 1 Sa. 15. 33. [x] Ps. 20. 7. [y] Ge. 4. 4. [z] Pr. 20. 22. [a] Is. 17. 7, 8. [b] Ps. 53. 7. [c] Ps. 27. 1. [d] Ps. 85. 8. [e] Is. 35. 4. [f] Job 8. 15. [g] 1 Sa. 10. 27. [h] Job 27. 21. [i] Eze. 32. 10. [k] Ps. 58. 10. [l] Ps. 94. 19.

יְשֻׁעָתוֹ [a] noun f. s., suff. 3 pers. s. m. fr. יְשׁוּעָה d. 10 — ישע

יְשֻׁעָתִי [b] id. with suff. 1 pers. sing. — ישע

יְשֻׁעָתֶךָ [c] id., suff. 2 pers. sing. masc. — ישע

יָשְׁפֵה וְ masc. *jasper*, a variegated gem, Ex. 28. 20; 39. 13; Eze. 28. 13.

יִשְׁפָּה וְ pr. name masc. — שפה

יִשְׁפּוֹט Kal fut. 3 pers. sing. masc. (§ 8. rem. 18) — שפט

יִשְׁפּוֹטוּ [d] id. fut. 3 pers. pl. masc. (§ 8. rem. 14) — שפט

יִשְׁפֹּט [e] / יִשְׁפָּט־ [f] וַיִּ׳, וְ׳ id. fut. 3 pers. sing. masc. (§ 8. rem. 18); וַ־ conv. — שפט

יִשָּׁפְטוּ [g] Niph. fut. 3 pers. pl. masc. — שפט

יִשְׁפְּטוּ / יִשְׁפֹּטוּ Kal fut. 3 pers. pl. masc. (§ 8. rem. 15) — שפט

יִשְׁפְּטֵנִי [h] וְ id. fut. 3 pers. sing. masc., suff. 1 pers. s. — שפט

יַשְׁפִּיל [i] Hiph. fut. 3 pers. sing. masc. — שפל

יַשְׁפִּילֶהָ [k] / יַשְׁפִּילֶנָּה [l] id., suff. 3 pers. sing. fem. (§ 2. rem. 3) — שפל

יַשְׁפִּיקוּ [m] Hiph. fut. 3 pers. pl. masc. — שפק

יִשָּׁפֵךְ [n] וַיִּ׳ Niph. fut. 3 pers. sing. masc.; וַ־ conv. — שפך

יִשְׁפֹּךְ [o] וַיִּ׳, וְ׳ Kal fut. 3 pers. sing. masc.; וַ־ id. — שפך

יִשְׁפְּכוּ וַ id. fut. 3 pers. pl. masc.; וַ־ id. — שפך

יִשְׁפְּכֵם וַ id. fut. 3 pers. sing. masc., suff. 3 pers. pl. masc.; וַ־ id. — שפך

יִשְׁפַּל וַ Kal fut. 3 pers. sing. masc.; וַ־ id. — שפל

יִשְׁפָּלוּ id. fut. 3 pers. pl. m. [for יִשְׁפְּלוּ § 8. r. 15] — שפל

יִשְׁפָּן וְ pr. name masc. — שפה

יִשְׁפֹּק Kal fut. 3 pers. sing. masc. — שפק

יִשְׁפַּר [p] Chald. Peal fut. 3 pers. sing. m. (§ 47. r. 6 b) — שפר

יַשְׁקְ וַ Hiph. fut. 3 pers. sing. masc., apoc. and conv. from יַשְׁקֶה (§ 24. rem. 16) — שקה

יִשַּׁק [q] / יִשָּׁק [r] וַיִּ׳ Kal fut. 3 pers. sing. masc. (comp. § 8. rem. 15); וַ־ conv. — נשק

יִשְׁקֹד [s] וְ Kal fut. 3 pers. sing. masc.; וְ־ id. — שקד

יַשְׁקֶה [t] Hiph. fut. 3 pers. sing. masc. — שקה

יְשֻׁקֶּה [u] Pual fut. 3 pers. sing. masc. — שקה

יַשְׁקֻהוּ [x] וַ Hiph. fut. 3 pers. pl. masc., suff. 3 pers. sing. masc.; וַ־ conv. — שקה

יִשָּׁקֵהוּ וַ Kal fut. 3 pers. sing. masc. (יִשַּׁק), suff. 3 pers. sing. masc. (§ 16. rem. 12); וַ־ id. — נשק

יִשְׁקוּ [y] Kal fut. 3 pers. pl. masc. — שקק

יַשְׁקוּ Hiph. fut. 3 pers. pl. masc. — שקה

יִשְׁקוּ [z] וַ Kal fut. 3 pers. pl. masc. [for יִשְּׁקוּ comp. § 10. rem. 7]; וַ־ conv. — נשק

יִשְׁקוֹד [a] Kal fut. 3 pers. sing. masc. (§ 8. rem. 18) — שקד

יַשְׁקוּם [b] וַ Hiph. fut. 3 pers. pl. masc., suff. 3 pers. pl. masc.; וַ־ conv. — שקה

יִשָּׁקוּן [c] Kal fut. 3 pers. pl. masc. with parag. ן [for יִשְּׁקוּן § 8. rem. 17] — נשק

יַשְׁקוּנִי [d] Hiph. fut. 3 pers. pl. masc., suff. 1 pers. sing. — שקה

יַשְׁקִט [e] defect. for יַשְׁקִיט (q. v.) — שקט

יִשְׁקֹט [f] Kal fut. 3 pers. sing. masc. — שקט

יַשְׁקִיט [g] Hiph. fut. 3 pers. sing. masc. — שקט

יַשְׁקִיף [h] Hiph. fut. 3 pers. sing. masc. — שקף

יַשְׁקִיפוּ [i] וַ id. fut. 3 pers. pl. masc.; וַ־ conv. — שקף

יִשָּׁקֵל Niph. fut. 3 pers. sing. masc. — שקל

יִשְׁקֹל [k] וַיִּ׳ [l] Kal fut. 3 pers. sing. masc.; וַ־ conv. — שקל

יִשְׁקְלוּ [m] / יִשְׁקֳלוּ [n] וַ Kal fut. 3 pers. pl. masc. (§ 8. rem. 15); וַ־ id. — שקל

יִשְׁקְלֵנִי [o] id. fut. 3 pers. sing. masc., suff. 1 pers. sing. — שקל

יַשְׁקֵנוּ [p] וַ Hiph. fut. 3 pers. sing. masc. (יַשְׁקֶה), suff. 1 pers. pl. (§ 24. rem. 21); וַ־ conv. — שקה

יַשְׁקֵנִי id., suff. 1 pers. sing. — שקה

יִשָּׁקֵנִי [q] Kal fut. 3 pers. sing. masc. (יִשַּׁק), suff. 1 pers. sing. (§ 16. rem. 12) — נשק

יַשְׁקֵף וַ Hiph. fut. 3 pers. sing. masc., apoc. from יַשְׁקִיף; וַ־ conv. — שקף

יַשְׁקִפוּ [r] וַ id. fut. 3 pers. pl. masc.; וַ־ id. — שקף

יְשַׁקֵּר [s] Piel fut. 3 pers. sing. masc. — שקר

יְשַׁקְּרוּ [t] id. fut. 3 p. pl. m. [for יְשַׁקֵּרוּ comp. § 8. r. 15] — שקר

יָשַׁר fut. יִשַׁר, יִישַׁר (§ 20. rem. 16) *to be straight, even, right*; metaph. יָשַׁר בְּעֵינַי *it is right in my eyes*, i. e. is pleasing to me. Pi.—I. *to make straight, even*, the way; metaph. *to make one's way even*, i. e. to make successful, prosperous.—II. *to direct, lead*, an aqueduct.—III. *to esteem right, approve*, Ps. 119. 128. Pu. part. *smoothed, spread*, 1 Ki. 6. 35. Hiph. הַיְשִׁיר or הוֹשִׁיר (Kheth.) *to make even*, the way; of the eyes, *to look straight forwards*, Pr. 4. 25.

יָשָׁר masc. dec. 4, יְשָׁרָה fem. adj. *straight, even*, opp. to עִקֵּשׁ; metaph. *right, upright, righteous, true*, especially with לִפְנֵי, בְּעֵינֵי; יִשְׁרֵי לֵב, דֶּרֶךְ י׳ *upright in heart, walk*; neut. יָשָׁר *what is right*; סֵפֶר הַיָּשָׁר Eng. Ver. "book of Jasher." LXX. according to the Complutension edition, του βιβλιου του ευθους, *the right* or *correct book*, i. e. probably *the authentic record*; and as Josephus (Ant. lib. v. cap. 1. § 17) explains it by, *the writings laid up in the temple*.

יֵשֶׁר (*uprightness*, concr. *upright*) pr. name masc. 1 Ch. 2. 18.

[a] De. 32. 15. [b] Job 30. 15. [c] Ps. 35. 3. [d] Ex. 18. 26. [e] Ex. 5. 21. [f] 1 Ki. 7. 7. [g] Ps. 9. 20. [h] 1 Sa. 24. 16. [i] Ps. 75. 8. [k] Is. 26. 5. [l] Is. 26. 5. [m] Is. 2. 6. [n] 1 Ki. 13. 5. [o] Da. 11. 15. [p] Da. 4. 24. [q] Pr. 24. 26. [r] Ge. 41. 40. [s] Da. 9. 14. [t] Nu. 5. 26. [u] Job 21. 24. [x] 1 Sa. 30. 11. [y] Joel 2. 9. [z] 1 Sa. 20. 41. [a] Job 21. 32. [b] 2 Ch. 28. 15. [c] Ho. 13. 2. [d] Ps. 69. 22. [e] Job 34. 28. [f] Ru. 3. 18. [g] Pr. 15. 18. [h] La. 3. 50. [i] 2 Ki. 9. 32. [k] Ex. 22. 16. [l] Ge. 23. 16. [m] Is. 46. 6. [n] Zec. 11. 12. [o] Job 31. 6. [p] Je. 8. 14. [q] Ca. 1. 2. [r] Ge. 18. 16. [s] 1 Sa. 15. 29. [t] Is. 63. 8.

יֹשֶׁר masc. dec. 7c, *uprightness, rectitude, integrity*; Pr. 11. 24 מִיֹּשֶׁר *more than is right, meet.*

יְשַׂרְאֵלָה (*upright towards* or *with God*) pr. name masc. 1 Ch. 25. 14.

יִשְׁרָה or יְשָׁרָה f. *uprightness, integrity*, 1 Ki. 3. 6.

יְשֻׁרוּן masc. a periphrastic name of Israel, *the right, righteous*; or *the little righteous people*; if וּן be really a termination of diminutives.

שָׁרוֹן (for יְשָׁרוֹן *plain, level*) pr. name invariably הַשָּׁרוֹן, *Sharon*, the plain between Joppa and Cesarea.

מִישׁוֹר masc.—I. *a plain, a level country.*—II. *righteousness, equity*, Ps. 45. 7; adv. *righteously, justly*, Ps. 67. 5.

מֵישָׁר masc. only pl. מֵישָׁרִים.—I. *straightness*, of a way, Is. 26. 7; with pref. בְּ, לְ *straight, right.*—II. *righteousness, justice, truth*; adv. *righteously*; Ca. 1. 4, *truly, sincerely*, which others take as a concr. *righteous men.*—III. *agreement, concord*, Da. 11. 6.

יָשָׁר 'וְ adj. and subst. masc. sing. dec. 4a . ישר

יָשַׂר וַ Kal fut. 3 pers. sing. masc. apoc. & conv. (§ 21. rem. 9) . . . . . שור

יָשֹׁר[a] Kal fut. 3 pers. sing. masc. R. שׁרר, or id. apoc. from יָשׁוּר R. . . . שור

יִשַּׁר וַ[b] Kal fut. 3 pers. sing. masc. for יִישַׁר (§ 20. rem. 2); ·וַ conv. . . . . ישר

יְשַׁר[c] adj. masc. sing., constr. of יָשָׁר dec. 4a . ישר

יֵשֶׁר pr. name masc. . . . . . ישר

יֹשֶׁר 'וְ[d] noun masc. sing. dec. 6c; for וְ see lett. ו ישר

יִשְׂרָאֵל 'וְ pr. name of a man and a people . שרה

יְשַׂרְאֵלָה pr. name masc. . . . . . ישר

יִשְׂרְאֵלִית gent. noun, fem. of יִשְׂרְאֵלִי from יִשְׂרָאֵל . שרה

יְשֹׂרָגוּ[e] Pual fut. 3 pers. pl. masc. [for יְשֹׂרְגוּ comp. § 8. rem. 15] . . . . . . שרג

יָשְׁרָה Kal pret. 3 pers. sing. fem. . . . ישר

יְשָׁרָה adj. fem. sing. dec. 11c, from יָשָׁר masc. . ישר

יִשְּׁרֵהוּ[f] Piel pret. 3 pers. sing. masc., suff. 3 pers. sing. masc. [for יִשְּׁרֵהוּ § 10. rem. 7] . ישר

יָשֹׁרוּ[g] Kal fut. 3 pers. pl. masc. . . . . שרר

יָשְׁרוּ[h] Kal pret. 3 pers. pl. . . . . ישר

יַשְּׁרוּ[i] Piel imp. pl. masc. . . . . ישר

יָשְׁרוֹ[k] noun masc. sing., suff. 3 pers. sing. masc. from יֹשֶׁר dec. 6c . . . ישר

יְשֻׁרוּן, וִישֻׁרוּן[l] noun masc. s., with cop. וְ [for 'וִי, וִישֻׁרוּן] ישר

יְשָׁרוֹת[m] adj. fem., pl. of יְשָׁרָה dec. 11c, from יָשָׁר m. ישר

יִשָּׂרְטוּ[n] Niph. fut. 3 pers. pl. masc. [for יִשָּׂרְטוּ comp. § 8. rem. 15] . . . . . שרט

יִשְׂרְטוּ[o] Kal fut. 3 pers. pl. masc. . . . שרט

יִשְׁרֵי constr. of the following: . . . ישר

יְשָׁרִים, וִישָׁרִים adj. masc. pl. absolute [with cop. וְ, for 'וִי, וִישָׁרִים] from יָשָׁר dec. 4a . ישר

יַשֵּׁרְנָה וַ[p] [for תִּישַׁרְנָה § 8. rem. 16] Kal fut. 3 pers. pl. fem. (§ 20. rem. 16); ·וַ conv. . ישר

יִשָּׂרֵף Niph. fut. 3 pers. sing. masc. . . שרף

יִשְׂרֹף 'וַי Kal fut. 3 pers. sing. masc.; ·וַ conv. . שרף

יִשְׂרְפֶהָ וַ[q] id. with suff. 3 pers. sing. fem.; ·וַ id. . שרף

יִשָּׂרְפוּ 'וַי[dd] Niph. fut. 3 pers. pl. masc.; ·וַ id. . שרף

יִשְׂרְפוּ[r], 'וַי יִשְׂרְפוּ Kal fut. 3 pers. pl. masc. (§ 8. rem. 15); ·וַ id. . . . . שרף

יִשְׂרְפוּהָ וַ[s] id. id., suff. 3 pers. sing. fem.; ·וַ id. . שרף

יִשְׂרְפֵם וַ[t] id. fut. 3 pers. sing. masc., suff. 3 pers. pl. masc.; ·וַ id. . . . . . שרף

יִשְׁרֹץ[u] Kal fut. 3 pers. sing. masc. . . . שרץ

יִשְׁרְצוּ[x] 'וַי[y] id. fut. 3 pers. pl. masc.; ·וַ conv. . שרץ

יִשְׂרֹק 'וְ Kal fut. 3 pers. sing. masc. . . . שרק

יַשְׁרֵשׁ[z] Hiph. fut. 3 pers. sing. masc., ap. from יַשְׁרִישׁ שרש

יְשֹׁרָשׁוּ[a] Pual fut. 3 pers. pl. masc. [for יְשֹׁרְשׁוּ comp. § 8. rem. 15] . . . . שרש

יְשָׁרֶת וַ Piel fut. 3 pers. sing. masc.; acc. drawn back by conv. וַ . . . . . שרת

יְשָׁרְתֵהוּ וַ[b] id. id., suff. 3 pers. sing. masc.; וַ conv. שרת

יְשָׁרְתוּהוּ[c] id. fut. 3 pers. pl. masc., suff. 3 pers. s. m. שרת

יְשָׁרְתוּ id. fut. 3 pers. pl. masc. . . . שרת

יְשָׁרְתוּךָ וִ[d] id. id., suff. 2 pers. sing. masc. and conj. וְ [for 'וִי, וִישָׁרְתוּךָ] . . . . . שרת

יְשָׁרְתוּנֶךְ[e] id. id. with parag. נ (§ 16. rem. 14) and suff. 2 pers. sing. fem. (§ 2. rem. 2) . שרת

יִשַּׁרְתִּי[f] Piel pret. 1 p. s. [for יִשַּׁרְתִּי comp. § 8. r. 7] ישר

יְשָׁרְתֻנִי[g] Piel fut. 3 pers. s. m. (יְשָׁרֵת), suff. 1 p. s. שרת

יָשֵׁשׁ וְ masc. *old, aged man*, 2 Ch. 36. 17.

יָשִׁישׁ masc. dec. 3a, id.

יְשִׁישַׁי (*of aged*, sc. parents) pr. name masc. 1 Ch. 5. 14.

יְשִׁשׁוּם[h] Kal fut. 3 p. pl. m. [יְשׁוּשׁ], suff. 3 p. pl. m. שוש

יִשָּׂשכָר וְ pr. name masc. . . . . . שכר

יָשֶׁת[i], 'וַי יָשֶׁת[k] Kal fut. 3 pers. sing. masc., apoc. and conv. from יָשִׁית R. שית see . שות

יֵשְׁתְּ 'וַי, 'וְ Kal fut. 3 pers. sing. masc. apoc. from יִשְׁתֶּה, (§ 24. rem. 3); ·וַ conv. . . שתה

יִשָּׁתֶה[m] Niph. fut. 3 pers. sing. masc. . . שתה

יִשְׁתֶּה 'וַי[n] Kal fut. 3 pers. sing. masc.; ·וַ conv. שתה

[a] Job 33. 27. [b] 1 Sa. 18. 20, 26. [c] Pr. 29. 27. [d] Ps. 25. 21. [dd] 1 Ch. 14. 12. [e] Job 40. 17. [f] Job 37. 3. [g] Is. 33. 1. [h] 1 Ki. 9. 12. [i] Is. 40. 3. [k] Job 33. 23. [l] Is. 44. 2. [m] Eze. 1. 23. [n] Zec. 12. 3. [o] Le. 21. 5. [p] 1 Sa. 6. 12. [q] 1 Ki. 9. 16. [r] Eze. 23. 47. [s] 2 Ki. 10. 26. [t] 2 Ki. 23. 4. [u] Eze. 47. 9. [x] Ge. 1. 20. [y] Ex. 1. 7. [z] Is. 27. 6. [a] Job 31. 8. [b] 1 Ki. 19. 21. [c] Nu. 1. 50. [d] Nu. 18. 2. [e] Is. 60. 7, 10. [f] Ps. 119. 128. [g] Ps. 101. 6. [h] Is. 35. 1. [i] Job 9. 33. [k] Ps. 18. 12. [l] 1 Ki. 18. 18. [m] Le. 11. 34. [n] 1 Ki. 19. 8.

יִשְׁתָּהוּ[a] Kal fut. 3 pers. pl. masc., suff. 3 pers. s. m. שתה

יִשְׁתּוּ [b]וַיִּ׳, וְ׳ id. fut. 3 pers. pl. masc.; ·ַ conv. שתה

יִשְׁתַּוֵּה[c] Ch. Ithpael fut. 3 pers. sing. masc. [for יִתְשַׁוֵּה comp. § 12. rem. 3] . . שוה

יִשְׁתּוֹמֵם[d] [e]וַיִּ׳ Hithpoel fut. 3 pers. sing. masc. [for יִתְשׁוֹמֵם comp. § 12. rem. 3]; ·ַ conv. שמם

יִשְׁתּוֹן[f] וְ Ch. Peal fut. 3 pers. pl. masc. . . שתה

יִשְׁתָּחוּ / יִשְׁתַּחוּ } וַ / וַיִּ׳, וְ[g] } ap. fr. יִשְׁתַּחֲוֶה׳ (q. v.) . . שחה

יִשְׁתַּחֲוֻן [h]וְ, [i]וַיִּ׳ Kh. יִשְׁתַּחוּ ap. fr. יִשְׁתַּחֲווּ; K. יִשְׁתַּחֲווּ (q. v.) . . . . . שחה

יִשְׁתַּחֲוֶה [k]וַיִּ׳ [for יִתְשׁ׳ comp. § 12. rem. 3] Hithpalel fut. 3 pers. sing. masc., 3rd rad. doubled [for חֲוָה׳ comp. § 24. r. 2, 4, 22]; ·ַ conv. שחה

יִשְׁתַּחֲווּ וַיִּ׳, וְ׳ id. fut. 3 pers. pl. masc.; ·ַ id. . שחה

יִשְׁתָּיוּן[l] Kal fut. 3 pers. pl. m.; ן parag. (§ 24. r. 5) שתה

יִשְׁתַּכְּחוּ[m] וְ Hithpa. fut. 3 pers. pl. masc. [for יִתְשַׁכְּחוּ comp. § 12. rem. 3] . . . . שכח

יִשְׁתַּכְלְלוּן[n] Ch. Ishtaph. fut. 3 pers. pl. masc. (§ 48) כלל

יִשְׁתַּמְעוּן[o] וְ Ch. Ithpa. fut. 3 pers. pl. masc. [for יִתְשַׁמְעוּן comp. § 12. rem. 3] . . . שמע

יִשְׁתַּמֵּר[p] וְ Hithpa. fut. 3 p. s. m. [for יִתְשַׁמֵּר v. id.] שמר

יִשְׁתַּנֵּא[q] Ch. Ithpa. fut. 3 p. s. m. [for יִתְשַׁנֵּא v. id.] שנה

יִשְׁתַּנּוֹ[r] / יִשְׁתַּנּוֹן[s] } Ch. id. fut. 3 pers. pl. masc. . . שנה

יִשְׁתָּעֵר[t] וְ Hithpa. fut. 3 pers. sing. masc. [for יִתְשָׁעֵר comp. § 12. rem. 3] . . . שער

יִשְׁתֹּק[u] [x]וְ׳ Kal fut. 3 pers. sing. masc. . . שתק

יִשְׁתֹּקוּ[y] id. fut. 3 pers. pl. m. [for יִשְׁתְּקוּ § 8. r. 15] שתק

יִשְׁתַּקְשְׁקוּן[z] Hithpalp. (§ 6. No. 4) fut. 3 pers. pl. masc. with parag. ן [for יִתְשַׁק׳ comp. § 12. r. 3] שקק

יִשְׂתָּרְגוּ[a] Hithpa. fut. 3 pers. pl. m. [for יִתְשָׂרְגוּ v. id.] שרג

יִשָּׁתְרוּ[b] וַ Niph. fut. 3 pers. pl. masc.; ·ַ conv. . שתר

[יָת] Ch. i.q. Heb. אֵת sign of the acc., Da. 3. 12.

יֵתֵא[c] וַ Kal fut. 3 pers. sing. masc. [for יֶאֱתֶה § 24. rem. 20, for יֶאֱתֶה § 19. rem. 3] contr. for יֶאֱתֶה, comp. § 19. rem. 6, & § 25. No. 2c; acc. Milêl by conv. ·ַ . . . . אתה

יִתְאַבְּכוּ[d] וַ Hithpa. fut. 3 pers. pl. masc.; ·ַ conv. . אבך

יִתְאַבָּל[e] / וַ יִתְאַבֵּל } Hithpa. fut. 3 pers. sing. masc. (§ 12. rem. 1); ·ַ id. . . . } אבל

וַ יִתְאַבְּלוּ[f] / וַ יִתְאַבְּלוּ } id. fut. 3 pers. pl. masc.; ·ַ id. . . אבל

יִתְאַדָּם[g] Hithpa. fut. 3 pers. sing. masc. (§ 12. r. 1) אדם

יִתְאָו[h] וְ, [i]וַיִּ׳ ap. fr. the following . . . אוה

יִתְאַוֶּה[k] [l]וַיִּ׳ Hithpa. fut. 3 pers. sing. masc.; ·ַ conv. אוה

יִתְאַוּוּ[m] וַ id. fut. 3 pers. pl. masc.; ·ַ id. . . אוה

יִתְאוֹנֵן[n] Hithpo. fut. 3 pers. sing. masc. . . אנן

יִתְאַמְּצוּ[o] וַ Hithpa. fut. 3 pers. pl. masc.; ·ַ conv. . אמץ

יִתְאַמְּרוּ[p] Hithpa. fut. 3 pers. pl. masc. . . אמר

יִתְאַנַּף וַ Hithpa. fut. 3 p. s. m. (§ 12. r. 1); ·ַ conv. אנף

יִתְאַפַּק וַ Hithpa. fut. 3 pers. s. m. (§ 12. r. 1); ·ַ id. אפק

יְתָאֲרֵהוּ[q] Piel fut. 3 p. s. m. [יְתָאֵר], suff. 3 p. s. m. תאר

יְתָאֳרֵהוּ[r] doubtless a faulty reading for the preceding תאר

יְתִב[s] (§ 47. rem. 6) i. q. Heb. יָשַׁב.—I. *to sit*, Da. 7. 9, 10, 26.—II. *to dwell*. Aph. *to cause to dwell*, Ezr. 4. 10.

יִתְבּוֹלָל[t] Hithpo. fut. 3 pers. s. m. (comp. § 21. r. 20) בלל

יִתְבּוֹנָן Hithpal. fut. 3 pers. sing. masc. (§ 21. r. 20) בין

יִתְבּוֹנָנוּ[u] / וְ יִתְבּוֹנְנוּ[x] } id. fut. 3 pers. pl. masc. (§ 21. rem. 20) בין

יָתְבִין[y] Ch. Peal part. act. masc., pl. of [יָתֵב] d. 2b יתב

יִתְבְּנֵא Ch. Ithpe. fut. 3 pers. sing. m. R. בנא, see בנה

יִתְבַּקָּעוּ[z] Hithpa. fut. 3 pers. pl. masc. (§ 12. rem. 1) בקע

יִתְבַּקַּר[a] Ch. Ithpa. fut. 3 pers. sing. masc. . בקר

יִתְבָּרֵךְ[b] Hithpa. fut. 3 pers. sing. masc. . . ברך

יִתְבָּרְכוּ[c] וְ id. fut. 3 pers. pl. masc. . . . . ברך

יִתְבָּרְרוּ[d] Hithpa. fut. 3 pers. pl. masc. . . . ברר

יִתְבַּשֵּׂר[e] Hithpa. fut. 3 pers. sing. masc. . . בשר

יִתְבֹּשָׁשׁוּ[f] Hithpal. fut. 3 pers. pl. masc. (§ 21. rem. 20) בוש

יִתְגָּאָל[g] / יִתְגָּאַל[h] } Hithpa. fut. 3 pers. sing. masc. (§ 12. rem. 1) . . . . } גאל

יִתְגַּבָּר Hithpa. fut. 3 pers. sing. masc. (§ 12. r. 1) גבר

יִתְגַּבָּרוּ[i] id. fut. 3 pers. pl. masc. . . . גבר

יִתְגֹּדַד[k] Hithpo. fut. 3 pers. s. m. (comp. § 12. r. 1) גדד

יִתְגֹּדְדוּ[l] וַ id. fut. 3 pers. pl. masc.; ·ַ conv. . . גדד

יִתְגַּדָּל[m] / יִתְגַּדֵּל[n] } [o]וְ } Hithpa. fut. 3 pers. sing. masc. (§ 12. rem. 1) . . . . . } גדל

יִתְגּוֹדָדוּ[p] in pause & in full for יִתְגֹּדְדוּ (q. v.) . גדד

יִתְגּוֹרָרוּ[q] Hithpal. fut. 3 pers. pl. masc. (§ 21. r. 20) גור

יִתְגַּל[r] וַ Hithpa. fut. 3 pers. sing. masc. ap. [from יִתְגַּלֶּה]; ·ַ conv. . . . . גלה

יִתְגַּלָּע Hithpa. fut. 3 pers. sing. masc. . . גלע

יִתְגַּנֵּב[s] וַיִּ׳ Hithpa. fut. 3 pers. sing. masc.; ·ַ conv. גנב

יִתְגָּעֲשׁוּ[t] וַיִּ׳ Hithpa. fut. 3 pers. pl. masc.; ·ַ id. . געש

יִתְגֹּעֲשׁוּ[u] Hithpo. fut. 3 pers. pl. masc. . . . געש

יִתְגָּרֶה[x] Hithpa. fut. 3 pers. sing. masc. . . גרה

יִתְגָּרוֹ[y] וְ Kh. יִתְגָּרֶה׳ q. v., K. יִתְגָּרוּ (q. v.) . . גרה

יִתְגָּרוּ Hithpa. fut. 3 pers. pl. masc. . . גרה

---

[a] Is. 62. 9. [b] 2 Ki. 6. 22. [c] Da. 3. 29. [d] Ps. 143. 4. [e] Is. 59. 16. [f] Da. 5. 2. [g] Is. 44. 17. [h] Ge. 27. 29. [i] 1 Ki. 9. 9. [k] 1 Ki. 22. 54. [l] Ps. 78. 44. [m] Ec. 8. 10. [n] Ezr. 4. 13, 16. [o] Da. 7. 27. [p] Mi. 6. 16. [q] Da. 2. 9. [r] Da. 5. 10. [s] Da. 7. 28. [t] Da. 11. 40. [u] Pr. 26. 20. [x] Jon. 1. 11, 12. [y] Ps. 107. 30. [z] Na. 2. 5. [a] La. 1. 14. [b] 1 Sa. 5. 9. [c] De. 33. 21. [d] Is. 9. 17. [e] Eze. 7. 12, 27. [f] Ex. 33. 4. [g] Pr. 23. 31. [h] Ps. 45. 12. [i] 1 Ch. 11. 17. [k] 2 Sa. 23. 16. [l] Ec. 6. 2. [m] Ps. 106. 14. [n] La. 3. 39. [o] 2 Ch. 13. 7. [p] Ps. 94. 4. [q] Is. 44. 13. [r] Is. 44. 13. [s] Da. 7. 9, 10, 26. [t] Ho. 7. 8. [u] Is. 14. 16. [x] Ps. 107. 43. [y] Ezr. 4. 17. [z] Mi. 1. 4. [a] Ezr. 5. 17. [b] Is. 65. 16. [c] Ps. 72. 17. [d] Da. 12. 10. [e] 2 Sa. 18. 31. [f] Ge. 2. 25. [g] Da. 1. 8. [h] Da. 1. 8. [i] Job 36. 9. [k] Je. 16. 6. [l] 1 Ki. 18. 28. [m] Da. 11. 37. [n] Is. 10. 15. [o] Da. 11. 36. [p] Je. 5. 7. [q] Ho. 7. 14. [r] Ge. 9. 21. [s] 2 Sa. 19. 4. [t] Je. 46. 7. [u] Je. 46. 8. [x] Da. 11. 25. [y] Da. 11. 10.

יָתֵד [a] וְ com. dec. 5a.—I. *pin, peg, nail*; especially *a tent-pin* or *stake*.—II. *a pointed stake* or *paddle*, De. 23. 14.

יְתֵת (for יְתֶדֶת *pin, nail*) pr. n. m. Ge. 36. 40.

יְתַד [b] id., constr. state . . . . . יתד

יִתְדֹת id. pl., constr. state . . . . . יתד

יְתֵדֹתֶיהָ וְ id. pl. with suff. 3 pers. sing. fem. with cop. וְ [for וִיתֵדֹתֶיהָ ,וִי׳] יתד

יְתֵדֹתָיו id. pl., suff. 3 pers. sing. masc. . . . יתד

יְתֵדֹתַיִךְ [c] וְ id. pl. with suff. 2 pers. sing. fem. with cop. וְ [for וִיתֵדֹתַיִךְ ,וִי׳] יתד

יְתֵדֹתָם וְ id. pl., suff. 3 pers. pl. masc. with cop. וְ comp. preceding . . . . . יתד

יִתְהוֹלָלוּ [e] Hithpo. fut. 3 pers. pl. masc. . . . הלל

יָתְהוֹן [f] Chald. sign of the accusative (יָת) with suff. 3 pers. pl. masc. . . . . . ית

יִתְהַלָּךְ, וַיִּ׳ יִתְהַלֵּךְ [g], יִתְהַלֶּךְ־ [h] } Hithpa. fut. 3 pers. sing. masc. (§ 12. rem. 1 & 4); ·וַ conv. . . } הלך

יִתְהַלָּכוּ, וַיִּ׳ ,וְ׳ [i] יִתְהַלְּכוּ } id. fut. 3 pers. pl. masc. (§ 12. rem. 1); ·וַ id. . . . } הלך

יִתְהַלְּכוּן [k] id. with parag. ן [for יְהַלְּכוּן § 8. rem. 17, & § 12. rem. 4] . . . . הלך

יִתְהַלָּל, יִתְהַלֵּל } Hithpa. fut. 3 pers. sing. masc. (§ 12. rem. 1) . . . . . } הלל

וַיִּתְהֹלֵל [m] Hithpo. fut. 3 pers. sing. masc.; ·וַ conv. הלל

יִתְהַלָּלוּ, וְ יִתְהַלְלוּ } Hithpa. fut. 3 pers. pl. masc. (§ 12. rem. 1) . . . . } הלל

יִתְהוֹלָלוּ [n], יִתְהֹלָלוּ } Hithpo. fut. 3 pers. pl. masc. (comp. § 21. rem. 20) . . . . } הלל

וַיְתָו [o] Piel fut. 3 pers. sing. masc. ap. [from יְתַוֶּה § 24. rem. 12]; ·וַ conv. . . . תוה

יְתוּב [p] Chald. Peal fut. 3 pers. sing. masc. . . תוב

וַיִּתְוַדּוּ [q] Hithpa. fut. 3 p. pl. m. (§ 20. No. 1); ·וַ conv. ידה

יִתְוַכָּח [r] Hithpa. fut. 3 pers. sing. masc. (§ 12. rem. 1) יכח

יָתוֹם וְ׳ [s] noun masc. sing. dec. 3a . . . יתם

יְתוֹמִים, וִ יתוֹמִים [t] } id. pl. abs., with cop. וְ [for וִיתוֹמִים ,וִי׳] יתם

יְתוּר noun masc. sing. . . . . . תור

יִתְּזִין [u] Chald. Ithpe. or Ittaphal fut. 3 pers. sing. masc. (§ 47. rem. 10) . . . . זון

יָתַח Root not used; Arab. *to beat with a club*.

תּוֹתָח masc. *club*, Job 41. 21.

וַיִּתְחַבֵּא [v], וַיִּ׳ Hithpa. fut. 3 pers. sing. masc.; ·וַ conv. חבא

יִתְחַבְּאוּ [w], וַ יִּתְחַבְּאוּ [a] } id. fut. 3 pers. pl. masc. (§ 12. rem. 1); ·וַ id. . . } חבא

יִתְחַבְּרוּ [b] Hithpa. fut. 3 pers. pl. masc. (§ 12. rem. 1) חבר

וַ יִּתְחַזַּק, וַ יִּתְחַזֵּק } Hithpa. fut. 3 pers. sing. masc. (§ 12. rem. 1); ·וַ conv. . . . } חזק

יִתְחַזְּקוּ [c] id. fut. 3 pers. pl. masc. (v. id.) . . חזק

יִתְחַטָּא Hithpa. fut. 3 pers. sing. masc. . . . חטא

יִתְחַטָּאוּ [d], וַ יִּתְחַטְּאוּ [e] } id. fut. 3 pers. pl. masc. (comp. § 8. rem. 15); ·וַ conv. . . . } חטא

וַ יָּתַחַל [f] Kal fut. 3 pers. sing. masc. ap. [from יִתְחַלֶּה § 24. rem. 12]; ·וַ id. . . . חלה

יִתְחַמָּם [g] Hithpa. fut. 3 pers. sing. masc. (§ 12. rem. 1) חמם

יִתְחַמָּץ [h] Hithpa. fut. 3 pers. sing. masc. . . חמץ

וַ יִּתְחַנַּן [i], וַ יִּתְחַנֶּן־ [k] } Hithpa. fut. 3 pers. sing. masc. (§ 12. rem. 4); ·וַ conv. . . . } חנן

וַיִּ׳ יִתְחַפֵּשׂ [l] Hithpa. fut. 3 pers. sing. masc.; ·וַ id. חפש

וַ יִּתְחָרְשׁוּ [m] Hithpa. fut. 3 pers. pl. masc.; ·וַ id. . חרש

יִתְחַשָּׁב [n] Hithpa. fut. 3 pers. sing. masc. (§ 12. rem. 1) חשב

וַ יִּתְחַתֵּן Hithpa. fut. 3 pers. sing. masc.; ·וַ conv. חתן

יְתִיבוּן [o] Chald. Aph. fut. 3 pers. pl. masc. . . תוב

יִתְיְהֵב [p] Chald. Ithpe. fut. 3 pers. s. m. (§ 47. rem. 1 b) יהב

וְ יִתְיַהֲבוּן [q] Chald. id. fut. 3 pers. pl. masc. . . יהב

וַ יַּתִּיכוּ [r] Hiph. fut. 3 pers. pl. masc.; ·וַ conv. . נתך

וַ יִּתְיַלְדוּ [s] Hithpa. fut. 3 pers. pl. masc.; ·וַ id. . ילד

וְ יִתְיָעֲצוּ [t] Hithpa. fut. 3 pers. pl. masc. . . . יעץ

יִתְיַצֵּב, וַיִּ׳ וַ יִּתְיַצֵּב } Hithpa. fut. 3 pers. sing. masc. (§ 12. rem. 1); ·וַ conv. . . . } יצב

וַיִּ׳ ,וְ׳ [u] יִתְיַצְּבוּ id. fut. 3 pers. pl. masc.; ·וַ id. . יצב

וְ יֶתֶר pr. name masc. . . . . . יתר

יַתִּיר [x] Chald. adj. masc. sing. dec. 1 a . . . יתר

יַתִּירָא [y], יַתִּירָה } Chald. id., emph. st. . . . . יתר

וַ יַּתִּירֵהוּ [z] Hiph. fut. 3 p. s. m., suff. 3 p. s. m.; ·וַ conv. נתר

וַ יָּתִירוּ [a] Hiph. fut. 3 pers. pl. masc.; ·וַ id. . תור

וַ יִּתְּכוּ [b] Kal fut. 3 pers. pl. masc.; ·וַ id. . . נתך

יִתְכּוֹנָן [c] Hithpal. fut. 3 pers. sing. masc. (§ 21. rem. 20) כון

יִתְכַּחֲשׁוּ [d] Hithpa. fut. 3 pers. pl. masc. (§ 14. rem. 1) כחש

יִתָּכֵן Niph. fut. 3 pers. sing. masc. . . . תכן

יִתָּכְנוּ [e], יִתָּכֵנוּ [f] } id. fut. 3 pers. pl. masc. (comp. § 8. rem. 15) . . . . } תכן

וַ יִּתְכַּס Hithpa. fut. 3 p. s. m. ap. [fr. יִתְכַּסֶּה]; ·וַ conv. כסה

וַיִּ׳ [h] יִתְכַּסּוּ [g] id. fut. 3 pers. pl. masc. . . . כסה

יִתְכַּפֵּר [i] Hithpa. fut. 3 pers. sing. masc. . . . כפר

וְ יִתְלַבְּנוּ [k] Hithpa. fut. 3 pers. pl. masc. . . . לבן

וְ יִתְלָה pr. name of a place . . . . . תלה

[a] De. 23. 14. [b] Ju. 4. 21. [c] Ex. 39. 40. [d] Is. 54. 2. [e] Na. 2. 5. [f] Da. 3. 12. [g] Pr. 23. 31. [h] Ps. 39. 7. [i] Jos. 18. 4. [k] Ps. 12. 9. [l] Pr. 20. 14. [m] 1 Sa. 21. 14. [n] Je. 50. 38. [o] 1 Sa. 21. 14. [p] Da. 4. 31, 33, 33. [q] Ne. 9. 2. [r] Mi. 6. 2. [s] Ps. 94. 6. [t] Job 39. 8. [u] Da. 4. 9. [v] 1 Sa. 23. 23. [y] Ge. 3. 8. [z] Job 38. 30. [a] 1 Sa. 13. 6. [b] Da. 11. 6. [c] Eze. 7. 13. [d] Job 41. 17. [e] Nu. 8. 21. [f] 2 Sa. 13. 6. [g] Job 31. 20. [h] Ps. 73. 21. [i] 2 Ki. 1. 13. [k] Ho. 12. 5. [l] Job 30. 18. [m] Ju. 16. 2. [n] Nu. 23. 9. [o] Ezr. 5. 5. [p] Da. 4. 13. [q] Da. 7. 25. [r] 2 Ch. 34. 17. [s] Nu. 1. 18. [t] Ps. 83. 4. [u] Job 38. 14. [x] Da. 2. 31. [y] Da. 5. 12. [z] Ps. 105. 20. [a] Ju. 1. 23. [b] Job 3. 24. [c] Pr. 24. 3. [d] 2 Sa. 22. 45. [e] Eze. 18. 25. [f] Eze. 18. 29. [g] Is. 59. 6. [h] Jon. 3. 8. [i] 1 Sa. 3. 14. [k] Da. 12. 10.

[a] יִתָּלוּ — וַ Niph. fut. 3 pers. pl. masc.; ·וַ conv. — תלה

[b] יִתְלוּ — [c] וַיִּ, וְ Kal fut. 3 pers. pl. masc.; ·וַ id. — תלה

[d] יִתְלוֹנָן — Hithpal. fut. 3 pers. sing. m. (§ 21. rem. 20) — לון

[e] יִתְלַחֲשׁוּ — Hithpa. fut. 3 pers. pl. masc. (§ 14. rem. 1) — לחש

[f] יִתְלַכְּדוּ, [g] יִתְלַכָּדוּ — Hithpa. fut. 3 pers. pl. masc. (§ 12. rem. 1) — לכד

[h] יִתְלֵם — וַ Kal fut. 3 pers. sing. masc. (יִתְלֶה), suff. 3 pers. pl. masc. (§ 24. rem. 21); ·וַ conv. — תלה

[i] יִתְלֹנָן — וְ defect. for יִתְלוֹנָן (q. v.) — לון

[k] יִתְלַקְּטוּ — וַ Hithpa. fut. 3 pers. pl. masc.; ·וַ conv. — לקט

יָתַם Root not used; *to be lonely, bereaved.*

יָתוֹם masc. dec. 3a, *an orphan.*

יִתְמָה (*orphanage*) pr. name masc. 1 Ch. 11. 46.

אֶתָם (*solitary*) pr. name of a place in the boundary of the Arabian desert.

[l] יִתַּם — וְ Hiph. fut. 3 p. s. m. Chald. form (§ 18. r. 14) — תמם

[m] יִתֹּם — [n] וַיִּ Kal fut. 3 p. s. m. (§ 18. r. 14); ·וַ conv. — תמם

[o] יִתְמֹדֵד — וַ Hithpo. fut. 3 pers. sing. masc.; ·וַ id. — מדד

יִתְמָה — וְ pr. name masc. — יתם

יִתְמְהוּ, [p] יִתְמָהוּ — [q] וַיִּ, וְ Kal fut. 3 pers. pl. masc. (§ 8. rem. 15); ·וַ conv. — תמה

[r] יִתְמַהְמָהּ — וַיִּ Hithpalp. fut. 3 pers. sing. m. (§ 6. No. 4) — מהה

יִתַּמּוּ — Niph. fut. 3 pers. pl. masc. — תמם

[t] יִתַּמּוּ, [u] יִתַּמּוּ — וַ Kal fut. 3 pers. pl. masc., Chald. form (§ 18. rem. 14); ·וַ conv. — תמם

[x] יִתְמְחָא — Chald. Ithpe. fut. 3 pers. sing. masc. — מחא

[y] יְתֹמָיו — noun m. pl., suff. 3 p. s. m. from יָתוֹם dec. 3a — יתם

[z] יְתֹמֶיךָ — id. pl., suff. 2 pers. sing. masc. — יתם

יְתֹמִים — id. pl., absolute state — יתם

[a] יִתָּמֵךְ — Niph. fut. 3 pers. sing. masc. — תמך

[b] יִתְמֹךְ, [d] יִתְמָךְ־ — [c] וַיִּ Kal fut. 3 pers. sing. masc. (§ 8. rem. 18); ·וַ conv. — תמך

יִתְמְכוּ, יִתְמֹכוּ — id. fut. 3 pers. pl. masc. (§ 8. rem. 15) — תמך

[e] יִתְמַכְּרוּ — וַ Hithp. fut. 3 pers. pl. masc.; ·וַ conv. — מכר

[f] יִתְמַלְּאוּן — Hithpa. fut. 3 pers. pl. masc.; ן parag. (comp. § 8. rem. 17) — מלא

[g] יִתְמַלָּטוּ — Hithpa. fut. 3 pers. pl. masc. (§ 12. rem. 1) — מלט

[h] יִתְמֹלְלוּ — Hithpal. fut. 3 pers. pl. masc. (§ 21. rem. 20) — מול

יִתְמַרְמַר — [i] וְ, [k] וַיִּ Hithpalp. fut. 3 pers. sing. masc. (§ 6. No. 4); ·וַ conv. — מרר

יָתַן Root not used; Arab. *to be perennial, to flow constantly;* hence, *to be constant, stable, firm,* Gesenius.

אֵיתָן masc. (no vowel change).—I. adj. *perennial, constant;* subst. *perennity, constancy,* of streams.—II. *firm, strong, mighty;* subst. *firmness.* יֶרַח הָאֵיתָנִים *the month Ethanim,* the seventh month of the Hebrew year, otherwise called Tishri.—III. pr. name masc. 1 Ki. 5; Ps. 89. 1.

יִתֵּן, יִתֶּן־ — וַיִּ, וְ Kal fut. 3 pers. sing. masc. (§ 17. rem. 3); ·וַ conv. — נתן

יֻתַּן — [l] וַיֻּ Hoph. fut. 3 pers. sing. masc.; ·וַ id. — נתן

יִתְנַבֵּא — וַיִּ Hithpa. fut. 3 pers. sing. masc.; ·וַ id. — נבא

יִתְנַבְּאוּ — וַ id. fut. 3 pers. pl. masc.; ·וַ id. — נבא

[m] יִתְנַגָּח — Hithpa. fut. 3 pers. sing. masc. — נגח

[n] יִתְנַגְּפוּ — Hithpa. fut. 3 pers. pl. masc. — נגף

[o] יִתְנַדְּבוּ — וַ Hithpa. fut. 3 pers. pl. masc.; ·וַ conv. — נדב

יִתְּנָהּ — וַ Kal fut. 3 pers. sing. masc. (יִתֵּן), suff. 3 pers. sing. fem.; ·וַ id. — נתן

[p] יִתְּנָהּ — וְ Kh. יִתְּנָהּ Kal fut. 3 pers. pl. masc., suff. 3 pers. sing. fem.; K. יִתְּנֵהוּ (q. v.) — נתן

יִתְּנֵהוּ — וַ Kal fut. 3 pers. s. m., suff. 3 p. s. m.; ·וַ conv. — נתן

[q] יִתְּנֻהוּ — וַיִּ id. fut. 3 pers. pl. m., suff. 3 p. s. m.; ·וַ id. — נתן

[r] יְתַנּוּ — Piel fut. 3 pers. pl. masc. — תנה

[s] יִתְּנוּ, יִתְּנוּ — וַיִּ, וְ Kal fut. 3 pers. pl. masc. (§ 17. rem. 3, & § 8. rem. 15); ·וַ conv. — נתן

[t] יִתְנוּ — Kal fut. 3 pers. pl. masc. — תנה

[u] יִתְנוֹדְדוּ — Hithpo. fut. 3 pers. pl. masc. — נדד

[x] יִתְּנוּהוּ — וַ Kal fut. 3 pers. pl. m., suff. 3 p. s. m.; ·וַ conv. — נתן

[y] יִתְּנוּם — וַ id., suff. 3 pers. pl. masc.; ·וַ id. — נתן

[z] יִתְנֶחָם — וְ Hithpa. fut. 3 pers. s. m. (§ 14. rem. 1 & 3) — נחם

יִתְנִיאֵל — pr. name masc. — תנה

יִתֶּנְךָ — [a] וַיִּ Kal fut. 3 pers. sing. masc. (יִתֵּן), suff. 2 pers. sing. masc. (§ 17. rem. 3); ·וַ conv. — נתן

[b] יִתְנַכְּלוּ — וַ Hithpa. fut. 3 pers. pl. masc.; ·וַ id. — נכל

[c] יִתְנַכֵּר, [d] יִתְנַכֶּר־ — וַ Hithpa. fut. 3 pers. sing. masc. (§ 12. rem. 4); ·וַ id. — נכר

[e] יִתְּנֵם — וַיִּ Kal fut. 3 pers. sing. masc. (יִתֵּן), suff. 3 pers. pl. masc. (§ 17. rem. 3); ·וַ id. — נתן

[f] יִתְּנֻם — וַ id. fut. 3 p. pl. m., suff. 3 p. pl. m.; ·וַ id. — נתן

יִתְנָן — וְ pr. name of a city — תנה

[g] יִתְּנֶנָּה — Kal fut. 3 pers. sing. masc. (יִתֵּן), suff. 3 pers. sing. fem. (§ 17. rem. 3) — נתן

[h] יִתְּנִנַּהּ, [i] יִתְּנִנַּהּ — Chald. Peal fut. 3 pers. sing. masc. [יִנְתֵּן] with suff. 3 pers. sing. fem. — נתן

[k] יִתְּנֵנוּ — וַ Kal fut. 3 pers. sing. masc. (יִתֵּן), suff. 1 pers. pl. (§ 17. rem. 3); ·וַ conv. — נתן

יִתְּנֶנּוּ — id., suff. 3 pers. sing. masc. — נתן

יִתְּנֵנִי — id., suff. 1 pers. sing. — נתן

---

[a] Est. 2. 23. [b] Est. 9. 13. [c] Est. 5. 14. [d] Ps. 91. 1. [e] Ps. 41. 8. [f] Job 38. 30. [g] Job 41. 9.
[h] Jos. 10. 26. [i] Job 39. 28. [k] Ju. 11. 3. [l] 2 Ki. 22. 4. [m] Eze. 47. 12. [n] Ge. 47. 15. [o] 1 Ki. 17. 21.
[p] Job 26. 11. [q] Ge. 43. 33. [r] Hab. 2. 3. [s] Ge. 19. 16. [t] Ps. 102. 28. [u] De. 34. 8.
[x] Ezr. 6. 11. [y] Is. 9. 16. [z] Je. 49. 11. [a] Pr. 5. 22. [b] Pr. 29. 23. [c] Ge. 48. 17.
[d] Pr. 4. 4. [e] 2 Ki. 17. 17. [f] Job 16. 10. [g] Job 41. 11. [h] Ps. 58. 8. [i] Da. 11. 11.
[k] Da. 8. 7. [l] 2 Sa. 18. 9. [m] Da. 11. 40. [n] Je. 13. 16. [o] 1 Ch. 29. 6. [p] 2 Ki. 22. 5.
[q] 2 Ki. 12. 15. [r] Ju. 5. 11. [s] Je. 38. 20. [t] Ho. 8. 10. [u] Ps. 64. 9. [x] 2 Ch. 34. 17.
[y] 2 Ch. 35. 25. [z] Nu. 23. 19. [a] 2 Ch. 9. 8. [b] Ge. 37. 18. [c] Ge. 42. 7. [d] Pr. 20. 11.
[e] Mi. 5. 2. [f] Ex. 39. 18, 20. [g] Ge. 23. 9. [h] Da. 4. 22, 29. [i] Da. 4. 14. [k] Ju. 6. 13.

יִתְנְסַח[a] Chald. Ithpe. fut. 3 pers. s. m. (§ 49. r. 4) — נסח

יִתְנַצְּלוּ[b] וַ Hithpa. fut. 3 pers. pl. masc.; וַ conv. — נצל

יִתְנַשָּׂא[c] Hithpa. fut. 3 pers. sing. masc. (§ 12. rem. 1) — נשא

יִתַּע[d] וַ Hiph. fut. 3 pers. sing. masc. ap. [from יַתְעֶה comp. § 24. rem. 3]; וַ conv. — תעה

יִתְעֵב[e] וַ Hiph. fut. 3 pers. sing. masc. ap. [from יַתְעִיב]; וַ id. — תעב

יְתָעֵב[f] [g]וַ Piel fut. 3 pers. sing. masc.; וַ id. — תעב

יְתָעֲבוּ[h] id. fut. 3 pers. pl. masc. [for יְתָעֲבוּ comp. § 8. rem. 15] — תעב

יִתְעֲבֵד Chald. Ithpe. fut. 3 pers. sing. m. (§ 49. r. 2) — עבד

יִתְעַבָּר[i] וַ / יִתְעַבָּר[k] וַ Hithpa. fut. 3 pers. sing. masc. (§ 12. rem. 1); וַ conv. — עבר

יִתְעַדְּנוּ[l] וַ Hithpa. fut. 3 pers. pl. masc.; וַ id. — עדן

יַתְעוּ[m] וַ Hiph. fut. 3 pers. pl. masc.; וַ id. — תעה

יִתְעוּ Kal fut. 3 pers. pl. masc. — תעה

יַתְעוּם[n] וַ Hiph. fut. 3 pers. pl. masc., suff. 3 pers. pl. masc.; וַ conv. — תעה

יִתְעוֹפֵף[o] Hithpal. fut. 3 pers. sing. masc. — עוף

יִתְעַל[p] Hithpa. fut. 3 pers. s. m. ap. [from יִתְעַלֶּה] — עלה

יִתְעַלְּלוּ[q] וַ Hithpa. fut. 3 pers. pl. masc.; וַ conv. — עלל

יִתְעַלֶּם־[r] Hithpa. fut. 3 pers. sing. masc. (§ 12. rem. 4) — עלם

יִתְעַלָּף[s] וַ Hithpa. fut. 3 p. s. m. (§ 12. r. 1); וַ conv. — עלף

יַתְעֵם וַ Hiph. fut. 3 pers. sing. masc. [יַתְעֶה], suff. 3 pers. pl. masc. (§ 24. rem. 21); וַ id. — תעה

יִתְעַנָּג[t] Hithpa. fut. 3 pers. sing. masc. (§ 12. rem. 1) — ענג

יִתְעַנּוּ[u] Hithpa. fut. 3 pers. pl. masc. — ענה

יִתְעַצֵּב[x] וַ Hithpa. fut. 3 pers. sing. masc.; וַ conv. — עצב

יִתְעַצְּבוּ[y] וַ id. fut. 3 pers. pl. masc.; וַ id. — עצב

יִתְעָרָב[z] Hithpa. fut. 3 pers. sing. masc., acc. Milêl before monos. (comp. § 12. rem. 4) — ערב

יִתְעָרְבוּ[a] וַ id. fut. 3 pers. pl. masc.; וַ conv. — ערב

יִתְעֹרָר[b] Hithpal. fut. 3 pers. s. m. (comp. § 21. r. 20) — עור

יִתְעַשָּׁת[c] Hithpa. fut. 3 pers. sing. masc. — עשת

יִתְפָּאֵר[d] / יִתְפָּאָר[e] Hithpa. fut. 3 pers. sing. masc. (§ 12. rem. 1) — פאר

יִתְפַּלֵּל / יִתְפַּלֶּל־[f] וַיִּ׳, וְ׳ Hithpa. fut. 3 pers. sing. masc. (§ 12. rem. 4); וַ conv. — פלל

יִתְפַּלְּלוּ[g] / יִתְפַּלָּלוּ [h]וְ׳ id. fut. 3 pers. pl. masc. (§ 12. rem. 1, comp. § 10. rem. 7) — פלל

יִתְפַּלָּצוּן[i] Hithpa. fut. 3 pers. pl. masc.; ן parag. [for יִתְפַּלְּצוּן comp. § 8. rem. 17, & § 12. rem. 1] — פלץ

יִתְפַּלָּשׁוּ[k] Hithpa. fut. 3 pers. pl. masc. (§ 12. rem. 1) — פלש

יִתְפֹּצְצוּ[l] וַ Hithpal. fut. 3 pers. pl. masc.; וַ conv. — פוץ

יִתְפָּקֵד[m] וַ Hithpa. fut. 3 pers. s. m. (§ 12. r. 5); וַ id. — פקד

יִתְפָּקְדוּ[n] וַ Hithpa. fut. 3 pers. pl. masc. (§ 12. rem. 5) — פקד

יִתְפָּרָדוּ / יִתְפָּרְדוּ[o] Hithpa. fut. 3 pers. pl. masc. (§ 12. rem. 1) — פרד

יִתְפְּרוּ[p] וַ Kal fut. 3 pers. pl. masc.; וַ conv. — תפר

יִתְפָּרְקוּ[q] וַ Hithpa. fut. 3 pers. pl. masc.; וַ id. — פרק

יִתְפֹּשׂ[r] וַיִּ׳ Kal fut. 3 pers. sing. masc.; וַ id. — תפשׂ

יִתְפְּשֵׂהוּ[s] וַ id. id., suff. 3 pers. sing. masc.; וַ id. — תפשׂ

יִתָּפְשׂוּ[t] Niph. fut. 3 pers. pl. masc. — תפשׂ

יִתְפְּשׁוּ וַ Kal fut. 3 pers. pl. masc.; וַ conv. — פשה

יִתְפְּשׁוּם וַ id. id., suff. 3 pers. pl. masc.; וַ id. — פשה

יִתְפַּשֵּׁט[u] וַ Hithpa. fut. 3 pers. sing. masc.; וַ id. — פשט

יִתְפְּשֵׁם וַ Kal fut. 3 pers. sing. masc. (יִתְפּשׂ), suff. 3 pers. pl. masc.; וַ id. — פשה

יִתֹּץ[x] וַיִּ׳ Kal fut. 3 pers. s. m. (§ 17. r. 3); וַ id. — נתץ

יֻתַּץ[y] Hoph. fut. 3 pers. sing. masc. [for יֻנְתַּץ comp. § 8. rem. 15] — נתץ

יִתְּצֵהוּ וַ the following with suff. 3 pers. sing. masc. — נתץ

יִתְּצוּ[z] / יִתְּצוּ[a] וַ Kal fut. 3 pers. pl. masc. (§ 8. rem. 15); וַ conv. — נתץ

יִתָּצְךָ[b] id. fut. 3 pers. s. m. (יִתֹּץ), suff. 2 pers. s. m. — נתץ

יִתְּצֵנִי[c] id. id. with suff. 1 pers. sing. — נתץ

יִתְקַבְּצוּ[d] וַיִּ׳ Hithpa. fut. 3 pers. pl. masc.; וַ conv. — קבץ

יִתְקַדָּשׁוּ[e] / יִתְקַדְּשׁוּ וַיִּ׳ Hithpa. fut. 3 pers. pl. masc. (§ 12. rem. 1); וַ id. — קדש

יִתְקַלָּס[f] Hithpa. fut. 3 pers. sing. masc. (§ 12. r. 1) — קלס

יִתְקַלְּסוּ[g] [h]וַיִּ׳ id. fut. 3 pers. pl. masc.; וַ conv. — קלס

יִתָּקַע / יִתָּקֵעַ[i] Niph. fut. 3 pers. sing. masc. (§ 15. rem. 1) — תקע

יִתְקַע[k] / יִתְקַע וַ Kal fut. 3 pers. sing. masc. (§ 8. rem. 15); וַ conv. — תקע

יִתְקָעֶהָ[l] וַ id. id., suff. 3 pers. sing. fem. (§ 16. rem. 12); וַ id. — תקע

יִתְקָעֵהוּ[m] וַ id. id., suff. 3 pers. sing. masc.; וַ id. — תקע

יִתְקְעוּ[n] / יִתְקְעוּ וַיִּ׳ id. fut. 3 pers. pl. masc. (§ 8. rem. 15); וַ id. — תקע

יִתְקָעֵם[o] וַ id. fut. 3 pers. sing. masc., suff. 3 pers. pl. masc. (§ 16. rem. 12); וַ id. — תקע

יִתְקְפוֹ[p] Kal fut. 3 pers. sing. m., suff. 3 pers. s. m. — תקף

יִתְקְרֵי[q] Ch. Ithpe. fut. 3 pers. sing. masc. — קרא

יִתְקַשֵּׁר[r] וַ Hithpa. fut. 3 pers. sing. masc.; וַ conv. — קשר

[יָתַר] *to remain, be left,* only part. יוֹתֵר *the rest,* 1 Sa. 15. 15. Hiph. הוֹתִיר.—I. *to cause to abound,* with acc. of the pers. and בְּ of the thing.—II. *to let remain, leave.*—III. *to abound, excel,* Ge. 49. 4. Niph. נוֹתַר *to be left, remain;* part. *that which is left.*

[a] Ezr. 6. 11. [b] Ex. 33. 6. [c] Nu. 23. 24. [d] 2 Ch. 33. 9. [e] 1 Ki. 21. 26. [f] Ps. 5. 7. [g] Ps. 106. 40.
[h] Am. 5. 10. [i] Ps. 78. 21, 59. [k] De. 3. 26. [l] Ne. 9. 25. [m] Je. 23. 13, 32. [n] Am. 2. 4. [o] Ho. 9. 11.
[p] Je. 51. 3. [q] Ju. 19. 25. [r] Job 6. 16. [s] Jon. 4. 8. [t] Job 27. 10. [u] Ps. 107. 17. [x] Ge. 6. 6.
[y] Ge. 34. 7. [z] Pr. 14. 10. [a] Ps. 106. 35. [b] Job 17. 8. [c] Jon. 1. 6. [d] Is. 44. 23. [e] Ju. 7. 2.
[f] 1 Sa. 2. 25. [g] Is. 45. 14. [h] 2 Ch. 7. 14. [i] Job 9. 6. [k] Eze. 27. 30. [l] Hab. 3. 6. [m] Ju. 21. 9.
[n] Ju. 20. 15. [o] Ps. 92. 10. [p] Ge. 3. 7. [q] Ex. 32. 3. [r] Is. 3. 6. [s] 2 Ki. 16. 9. [t] Ps. 10. 2.
[u] 1 Sa. 18. 4. [x] Eze. 26. 9. [y] Le. 11. 35. [z] Eze. 26. 12. [a] 2 Ki. 10. 27. [b] Ps. 52. 7. [c] Job 19. 10.
[d] Is. 44. 11. [e] Ex. 19. 22. [f] Hab. 1. 10. [g] Eze. 22. 5. [h] 2 Ki. 2. 23. [i] Job 17. 3. [k] Zec. 9. 14.
[l] Ju. 3. 21. [m] Ex. 10. 19. [n] Nu. 10. 4. [o] 2 Sa. 18. 14. [p] Ec. 4. 12. [q] Da. 5. 12. [r] 2 Ki. 9. 14.

יֶתֶר, יוֹתֵר masc.—I. *abundance, profit*, Ec. 6. 8. —II. adv. (*a*) *more, further*; (*b*) *too much, over much*, Ec. 7. 16; (*c*) *besides*; יוֹתֵר שֶׁ׳ conj. *besides that*.

יֹתֶרֶת fem. *the great lobe of the liver*, followed by מִן הַ׳, עַל הַ׳ הַכָּבֵד.

יֶתֶר masc. dec. 6 a (with suff. יִתְרוֹ).—I. *abundance*; adv. *abundantly*.—II. *remainder, residue, rest*.—III. *excellence, pre-eminence*.—IV. *cord, string*.—V. pr. name masc. of several persons, especially of the father-in-law of Moses, elsewhere called יִתְרוֹ, Ex. 4. 18. Patronym. יִתְרִי.

יִתְרָא (*residue*) pr. name masc. 2 Sa. 17. 25, for יֶתֶר 1 Ki. 2. 5.

יִתְרָה fem. *remainder, residue, rest*, Is. 15. 7, constr. יִתְרַת Je. 48. 36.

יִתְרְעָם (*abundance of the people*) pr. name masc. 2 Sa. 3. 5; 1 Ch. 3. 3.

יַתִּיר (*excellent*) pr. name of a town in the tribe of Judah.

יַתִּיר Chald. masc. dec. 1 a, adj. *very great, excellent*; fem. יַתִּירָה *very, exceedingly*.

יִתְרוֹ (*pre-eminence*) pr. name of the father-in-law of Moses, called also יֶתֶר & חֹבָב.

יִתְרוֹן masc.—I. *gain, profit*.—II. *excellence, pre-eminence*, Ec. 2. 13.

יִתְרָן (id.) pr. name, 1 Ch. 7. 37, for יֶתֶר ver. 38.

מוֹתָר masc. dec. 2 b.—I. *abundance*.—II. *excellence*, Ec. 3. 19.

מֵיתָר masc. dec. 2 b, *string, cord*.

[a] יֹתֵר Hiph. fut. 3 pers. sing. m. ap. [from יוֹתִיר] תור

[b] יָתֶר in pause for יֶתֶר [as if from יָתַר § 35. rem. 5] but with suff. יִתְרוֹ . . . . יתר

[hh] וַיַּ׳ יַתֵּר Hiph. fut. 3 pers. sing. masc. ap. from יַתִּיר; וַ׳ conv. . . . נתר

[c] וְ יַתֵּר by Chaldaism for יָתֵר q. v. (§ 21. rem. 24); וַ׳ id. . . . . . . תור

[d] וְ יִתַּר Kal fut. 3 pers. sing. masc. . . . נתר

יַתִּר pr. name of a place for יַתִּיר . . . יתר

וְ׳ יֶתֶר noun masc. sing. (suff. יִתְרוֹ) dec. 6 a, also pr. name masc. . . . . . יתר

[e] וְ׳ יֶתֶר adv. comp. יוֹתֵר . . . . יתר

יִתְרָא pr. name masc. . . . . . יתר

וַ יִּתְרָאוּ Hithpa. fut. 3 pers. pl. masc.; וַ׳ conv. . ראה

[f] יִתְרָה noun fem. sing. (no pl.) . . . . יתר

יִתְרוֹ pr. name masc. . . . . . . יתר

[g] וְ, וַיָּ׳ יָתֻרוּ Kal fut. 3 pers. pl. masc.; וַ׳ conv. . תור

[h] וְ יִתְרוֹ } noun masc. sing., suff. 3 pers. sing. masc. (K. יִתְרִי suff. 1 pers. s.) fr. יֶתֶר d. 6 a } יתר
יִתְרוֹ

[k] וְ יִתְרוֹמֵם Hithpal. fut. 3 pers. sing. masc. . . רום

וְ׳ יִתְרוֹן noun masc. sing. . . . . . יתר

[l] יִתְרוֹעֲעוּ Hithpal. fut. 3 pers. pl. masc. . . . רוע

[m] יְתָרִים n. m., pl. of יֶתֶר d. 6 a (comp. the following) יתר

[n] וְ׳וּ יִתְרָם id. sing., suff. 3 pers. pl. masc. . . . יתר

[o] יִתְרְמֵא Ithpe. fut. 3 pers. sing. masc. R. רמא, see רמה

וְ יִתְרָן pr. name, see יֶתֶר . . . . . יתר

יִתְרְעָם pr. name masc. . . . . . . יתר

[p] יִתְרַצֶּה Hithpa. fut. 3 pers. sing. masc. . . . רצה

[q] וַ יִּתְרֹצְצוּ Hithpo. fut. 3 pers. pl. masc.; וַ׳ conv. . רצץ

[r] יִתְרַת noun fem. sing. constr. from יִתְרָה (no pl.) יתר

וְ׳ יֹתֶרֶת noun fem. sing. . . . . . . יתר

[s] יִתְּשָׂם Ch. Ithpe. fut. 3 pers. sing. masc. . . . שום

[u] וַ יִּתְּשֵׁם Kal fut. 3 pers. sing. masc. [יִתֹּשׁ], suff. 3 pers. pl. masc.; וַ׳ conv. . . . . . נתש

[kk] יִתְּשָׂמוּן Ch. Ithpe. fut. 3 p. pl. m. (comp. § 12. r. 3) שום

יֶתֶת pr. name masc. . . . . . . יתד

כ

כְּ everywhere with Sheva except in the following cases:—כִּ before a word beginning with Sheva, as כִּבְשַׂר for כְּבְשַׂר; before יְ, Yod becoming quiescent, as יְדֵי with כ pref. כִּידֵי for כְּיְדֵי;—כַּ, כֶּ, (כָּ) before the composites ־ֲ, ־ֱ, (־ֳ), as כַּאֲרִי, כֶּאֱסֹף (and contr. כַּאדֹנָיו for כַּאֲדֹנָיו), (and contr. כֵּאלֹהִים for כֶּאֱלֹהִים), but there is no example extant for Kamets-khatuph;—כַּ, כָּ, כֶּ, when displacing the article ה (q. v.), as כַּיּוֹם for כְּהַיּוֹם, כָּאוֹר for כְּהָאוֹר, כֶּחָצִיר for כְּהֶחָצִיר;—

כָּ rarely before the tone-syllable, as כָּזֹה, כָּזֶה, כָּאֵלֶּה, כָּהֵם, כָּזֹאת. For כ with suffixes see § 5.

I. adv. (*a*) *as*, of quality: כְּ—כְּ, כְּ—וּכְ, כְּ—כֵּן *as—so; so—as*, e. g. Is. 24. 2, כָּעָם כַּכֹּהֵן *as the people so the priest*; Ge. 44. 18, כָּמוֹךָ כְּפַרְעֹה *so thou* (art) *as Pharaoh* (is);—(*b*) relat. *how, in what way*, Ec. 11. 5;—(*c*) indef. *about, nearly, almost*, before words of measure, number or time; כְּאֵיפָה *about an ephah*; כְּעֶשֶׂר שָׁנִים *about ten years*; כָּעֵת מָחָר *about this time to-morrow*; hence,

[a] Pr. 12. 26. [b] Pr. 17. 7. [c] 2 Sa. 22. 33 [d] Job 37. 1. [e] Ec. 2. 15. [f] Is. 15. 7. [g] Nu. 13. 2, 21. [h] Is. 44 19. [hh] Job 6. 9. [i] Job 30. 11. [k] Da. 11. 36. [kk] Da. 2. 5. [l] Ps. 65. 14. [m] Ju. 16. 7, 8. [n] Ex. 23. 11. [o] Da. 3. 6, etc. [p] 1 Sa. 29. 4. [q] Ge. 25. 22. [r] Je. 48. 36. [s] Le. 9. 19. [t] Ezr. 4. 21. [u] De. 29. 27.

כְּיוֹם *about this day*, i. e. *to-day*, but not limited to any particular time of the day; כְּרֶגַע *in a moment*; especially with the inf. *when, as*; e. g. כְּדַבְּרָהּ *about* (the time of) *her speaking*, i. e. *when, as soon as she spoke*; Is. 10. 15, *as if*.—II. prep. (*a*) *as, like, as if*, of resemblance; כָּאֵלֶּה, כָּזֹאת, כָּזֶה *like this, these*, or *such*; כָּזֹאת וְכָזֹאת, כָּזֶה וְכָזֶה *thus and thus, so and so*;—(*b*) *according to, after*;—(*c*) noting intensity (so Gesenius; others, כְּ veritatis); Ne. 7. 2, כְּאִישׁ אֱמֶת *as a man of truth*, sc. can possibly be; 1 Sa. 10. 27, וַיְהִי כְּמַחֲרִישׁ *he was as quiet*, sc. as possible; Is. 1. 7, כְּמַהְפֵּכַת זָרִים *as an overthrow of strangers*, sc. can possibly make it; כִּמְעַט *very little*.—III. conj. i. q. כַּאֲשֶׁר *as, like as*, Is. 8. 23.

[כָּאַב] fut. יִכְאַב *to be pained, be in pain*; trop. *to be grieved*, with עַל Job 14. 22. Hiph.—I. *to cause pain, sadness*.—II. *to mar, destroy*, 2 Ki. 3. 19.

כְּאֵב masc. dec. 1 a, *pain*; trop. *grief, sorrow*.

מַכְאוֹב masc. dec. 1 b, pl. ־ִים, ־וֹת id.

[a] כָּאָב — [b] ו׳ pref. כְּ)(noun m. s., irr. (§ 45); וּ bef. (:) — אב

[c] כְּאֵב — ו׳ noun masc. sing. dec. 1 a; וּ id. — כאב

[d] כָּאָבוֹת — pref. כְּ)(noun masc. with pl. fem. term. fr. אוֹב dec. 1 a — אוב

כַּאֲבוֹתֵיכֶם — pref. כַּ bef. (־ֲ))(noun masc. pl., suff. 2 pers. pl. masc. fr. אָב irr. (§ 45) — אב

[e] כַּאֲבוֹתָם — pref. id.)(id., suff. 3 pers. pl. m. (§ 4. r. 2) — אב

כְּאֵבִי — [f] ו׳ noun masc. sing., suff. 1 pers. sing. from כְּאֵב dec. 1 a; וּ bef. (:) — כאב

[g] כְּאָבִיו — pref. כְּ)(noun masc. sing., suff. 3 pers. sing. masc. from אָב irr. (§ 45) — אב

[h] כֹּאֲבִים — Kal part. act. masc., pl. of כּוֹאֵב dec. 7 b — כאב

[i] כְּאַבִּיר — Kh. כְּאַבִּיר pref. כְּ, see אַבִּיר; K. כַּבִּיר adv. — כבר

[k] כַּאֲבֶל־ — pref. כַּ bef. (־ֲ))(adj. masc. sing., bef. Mak. [for אֲבֶל־], constr. of אָבֵל (§ 34. No. 2, & rem. 1) — אבל

[l] כְּאֵבֶל — pref. כְּ)(noun masc. sing. d. 6 (§ 35. r. 6) — אבל

[m] כָּאֶבֶן, [n] כָּאָבֶן — pref. כָּ f. כְּהַ·, כְּהָ; [o] כְּאֶבֶן — pref. כְּ q. v. } noun fem. sing. (suff. אַבְנוֹ) dec. 6 a (§ 35. rem. 2) — אבן

[p] כְּאַבְנֵי — pref. id.)(id. pl., constr. state — אבן

כָּאֲבָנִים — pref. כָּ for כְּהַ·, כְּהָ)(id. pl., absolute state — אבן

[q] כָּאָבָק — pref. id.; [r] כְּאָבָק — pref. כְּ } noun masc. sing. dec. 4 c — אבק

[s] כָּאַבִּירִים — pref. כָּ for כְּהַ·, כְּהָ)(adj. or subst. masc., pl. of אַבִּיר dec. 1 b — אבר

כְּאַבְשָׁלוֹם — ו׳ pref. כְּ)(pr. name masc.; וּ before (:) — אב

כַּאֲבֹתֵיכֶם — defect. for כַּאֲבוֹתֵיכֶם (q. v.) — אב

[u] כְּאַגְמֹן — pref. כְּ)(noun masc. sing. — אגם

כְּאָדָם — pref. id.)(noun masc. sing. — אדם

כְּאַדְמָה — pref. id.)(pr. name of a place — אדם

[x] כַּאדֹנָיו — pref. כַּ, contr. for כַּאֲדֹנָיו)(noun masc. pl., suff. 3 pers. sing. m. fr. אָדוֹן d. 3 a — דון

[y] כְּאַדֶּרֶת — pref. כְּ)(noun fem. s., (suff. אַדַּרְתּוֹ) d. 13 a — אדר

כָּאָה. Hiph. *to cause to despond*, as the heart, Eze. 13. 22. Niph. *to be dejected, faint-hearted*.

כָּאֶה masc. dec. 9 b, *desponding, dejected*, Ps. 10. 10, Keri.

[z] כְּאֹהֲבָם — pref. id.)(noun masc. sing., suff. 3 pers. pl. masc. from [אֹהַב] dec. 6 f — אהב

[a] כְּאַהֲבַת — pref. id.)(noun f. s., constr. of אַהֲבָה (no pl.) — אהב

[b] כָּאֹהֶל — pref. כָּ f. כְּהַ·, כְּהָ; [c] כְּאֹהֶל — pref. כְּ q. v. } noun masc. sing. d. 6 (§ 35. rem. 9) — אהל

[d] כְּאָהֳלֵי — pref. id.)(id. pl., constr. state — אהל

[e] כַּאֲהָלִים — pref. כַּ bef. (־ֲ))(noun masc. only in the pl. — אהל

[f] כְּאוֹב — pref. כְּ)(noun masc. sing. dec. 1 a — אוב

[g] כְּאוּד — pref. id.)(noun masc. sing. dec. 1 a — אוד

[h] כְּאוֹיֵב — pref. id.)(Kal part. act. sing. masc. dec. 7 b — איב

[i] כָּאוּלָם — pref. כָּ for כְּהַ·, כְּהָ)(noun masc. sing. (pl. c. אֵלַמֵּי) dec. 8 a — אול

[k] כְּאִוַּלְתּוֹ — pref. כְּ)(noun fem. sing., suff. 3 pers. sing. masc. from אִוֶּלֶת dec. 13 a — אול

כָּאוֹר — pref. כָּ f. כְּהַ·, כְּהָ; כְּאוֹר — [l] ו׳ pref. כְּ q. v. } noun m. sing. dec. 1 a; וּ bef. (:) — אור

[m] כָּאוֹרָה — pref. כָּ for כְּהַ·, כְּהָ)(noun fem. sing. — אור

[n] כָּאֵזוֹר — pref. id.)(noun masc. sing. — אזר

כָּאֶזְרָח — pref. id.; כְּאֶזְרָח — pref. כְּ } noun masc. sing. dec. 2 b — זרח

[o] כְּאֶזְרַח — pref. id.)(id., constr. state — זרח

כְּאָח — pref. id.)(noun masc. sing. irr. (§ 45) — אח

כְּאַחְאָב — pref. id.)(pr. name masc. — אח

כְּאֶחָב — ו׳ pref. id.)(pr. name masc.; וּ bef. (:) — אח

כְּאַחַד, כְּאֶחָד — [p] ו׳ pref. id.)(num. card. masc. constr. and abs., irr. (§ 45); וּ id. — אחד

כְּאָחִיו — pref. id.)(noun masc. sing., suff. 3 pers. sing. masc. from אָח (§ 45) — אח

[q] כְּאֶחָיו — pref. id.)(id. pl., suff. 3 pers. sing. masc. — אח

[r] כַּאֲחֵיכֶם — וְ pref. כַּ bef. (־ֲ))(id. pl., suff. 2 pers. pl. m. — אח

[s] כָּאַחֲרֹנָה — וְ pref. כָּ for כְּהַ·, כְּהָ)(adj. fem. sing. from אַחֲרוֹן masc. — אחר

כְּאַחַת — pref. כְּ)(num. card. [for אַחֶדֶת] fem. of אֶחָד irr. (§ 45) — אחד

---

[a] Job 31. 18. [b] Pr. 3. 12. [c] Is. 17. 11. [d] Job 32. 19. [e] Ps. 78. 8, 57. [f] Ps. 39. 3. [g] 2 Ki. 3. 2. [h] Ge. 34. 25. [i] Is. 10. 13. [k] Ps. 35. 14. [l] Am. 8. 10. [m] Ex. 15. 16. [n] Job 38. 30. [o] Eze. 10. 1. [p] Is. 27. 9. [q] Is. 5. 24. [r] Is. 29. 5. [s] Je. 50. 11. [t] 2 Ch. 30. 7. [u] Is. 58. 5. [x] Is. 24. 2. [y] Ge. 25. 25. [z] Ho. 9. 10. [a] Ho. 3. 1. [b] Is. 40. 22. [c] Is. 38. 12. [d] Ca. 1. 5. [e] Nu. 24. 6. [f] Is. 29. 4. [g] Am. 4. 11. [h] La. 2. 4, 5. [i] 1 Ki. 7. 8. [k] Pr. 26. 4, 5. [l] 2 Sa. 23, 4. [m] Ps. 139. 12. [n] Je. 13. 10. [o] Ex. 12. 48. [p] Ps. 82. 7. [q] Ge. 38. 11. [r] 2 Ch. 30. 7. [s] Da. 11. 29.

[g] כֶּאֱסֹף — [h] 'וְ pref. כְּ bef. (ֱ)) Kal inf. constr. . אסף
[i] כְּאַסְפֵּי — pref. כְּ) noun m. pl. constr. from אֹסֶף dec. 6c אסף
[k] כְּאַפִּי — pref. id.) noun masc. sing., suff. 1 pers. sing. from אַף dec. 8d (§ 37. No. 3b) . אנף
[l] כַּאֲפִיק — pref. כַּ bef. (ֲ)) n.m.s., constr. of [אָפִיק] d. 3a אפק
[m] כַּאֲפִיקִים — pref. כַּ id.) id. pl., abs. st. . . אפק
[n] כְּאַפְּךָ — pref. כְּ) noun masc. sing., suff. 2 pers. sing. masc. from אַף dec. 8d (§ 37. No. 3b) אנף
[o] כָּאֲפֵלָה — pref. כָּ for כְּהַ·, כְּהָ) noun fem. sing. dec. 10 אפל
[p] כְּאֶפֶס — וּ pref. כְּ) n. m. s. (du. אַפְסַיִם) dec. 6a; וּ bef. (:) אפס
[q] כָּאֵפֶר — pref. כָּ for כְּהַ·, כְּהָ) noun masc. sing. . אפר
כְּאֶפְרַיִם — pref. כְּ) pr. name masc. . . . אפר
[r] כַּאֹר — contr. for כִּיאוֹר (q. v.) . . . יאר
כָּאַרְבֶּה — pref. כָּ for כְּהַ·, כְּהָ) noun masc. sing. . רבה
כְּאַרְבַּע — pref. כְּ) num. card. fem. (§ 31. rem. 5) רבע
[s] כְּאַרְבָּעִים — pref. id.) id. pl. com. gen. . . רבע
[t] כְּאַרְבַּעַת — pref. id.) id. s. m., constr. of אַרְבָּעָה (§ 42. r. 5) רבע
[u] כָּאֹרֵג — pref. כָּ for כְּהַ·, כְּהָ) Kal part. a. m. dec. 7b ארג
[x] כָּאַרְגָּמָן — pref. כָּ id.) noun masc. sing. . . ארג
[y] כְּאֶרֶז — pref. כְּ) noun masc. sing. (pl. c. אַרְזֵי) dec. 6a ארז
[z] כָּאֲרָזִים — pref. כָּ f. כְּהַ·, כְּהָ } id. pl., abs. st. . ארז
[a] כַּאֲרָזִים — pref. כַּ bef. (ֲ) }
[b] כְּאֹרַח — וּ pref. כְּ) noun com. sing. dec. 6 (§ 35. rem. 5 & 9); וּ bef. (:) . . . ארח
[kk] כְּאֹרֵחַ — וּ pref. id.) Kal part. act. masc. dec. 7b; וּ id. ארח
[c] כָּאֲרִי — pref. כָּ for כְּהַ·, כְּהָ) n. m. s. d. 6i (§ 35. r. 14) ארה
[d] כָּארִים — Kal part. act. pl. masc. [for כָּרִים § 21. r. 1] כור
[e] כַּאֲרִי — 'וְ pref. כַּ bef. (ֲ)) n. m. s. d. 6i (§ 35. r. 14) ארה
כַּאֲרִיאֵל — pref. id.) n. m., compound. of אֲרִי & אֵל see R. ארה
כְּאַרְיֵה — pref. כְּ) noun masc. sing., אֲרִי, with parag. ה (§ 35. rem. 14) . . . ארה
[f] כְּאַרְכֶּן — pref. id.) noun masc. sing., suff. 3 pers. pl. fem. from אֹרֶךְ dec. 6c . . . ארך
כְּאַרְפָּד — pref. id.) pr. name of a place . רפד
כָּאָרֶץ — pref. כָּ f. כְּהַ·, כְּהָ } noun fem. sing. dec. 6a (§ 35. rem. 1d) . ארץ
כְּאֶרֶץ — pref. כְּ q. v. }
[g] כְּאַרְצְכֶם — pref. id.) id., suff. 2 pers. pl. masc. . ארץ
כָּאֵשׁ — pref. כָּ f. כְּהַ·, כְּהָ } noun com. sing. dec. 8b אשׁ
כְּאֵשׁ — pref. כְּ q. v. }
כְּאִשָּׁה — pref. id.) noun fem. sing. dec. 10 (comp. § 45) אנשׁ
[h] כְּאַשְׁכֹּלוֹת — pref. כְּ) noun masc. with pl. fem. term. from אֶשְׁכֹּל (§ 36. rem. 6, & § 44. rem. 5) שׁכל
[i] כָּאָשָׁם — [h] 'וְ pref. כָּ for כְּהַ·, כְּהָ) noun m. s. dec. 4c אשׁם
[l] כְּאָשֵׁם — pref. כְּ) adj. masc. sing. dec. 5c . אשׁם
כַּאֲשֶׁר — 'וְ pref. כַּ bef. (ֲ)) pref. כ forming an adv. with אֲשֶׁר (q. v.) . . . . אשׁר

כְּאִיּוֹב — pref. כְּ) pr. name masc. . . . איב
[a] כָּאַיִל — 'וְ pref. כָּ f. כְּהַ·, כְּהָ } noun m. sing. dec. 1b (§ 30. No. 3) אול
[b] כְּאַיִל — pref. כְּ q. v. }
[z] כָּאַיָּלוֹת — pref. כָּ for כְּהַ·, כְּהָ) noun fem., pl. of אַיָּלָה (§ 42. rem. 5) . . . אול
[c] כְּאֵילִים — pref. כְּ) n. m., pl. of אַיִל dec. 1b (§ 30. No. 3) אול
כְּאֵילִים — pref. id.) noun masc., pl. of אֵיל dec. 6h אול
כְּאַיִן — pref. id.) noun masc. sing. dec. 6h און
[d] כְּאַיִן — וּ pref. id.) id. constr. st. as an adv.; וּ bef. (:) און
[e] כְּאֵיפָה — pref. id.) noun fem. sing. dec. 10 . איף
[f] כָּאִישׁ — pref. כָּ f. כְּהַ·, כְּהָ } noun masc. sing. dec. 1a (but comp. § 45) אישׁ
כְּאִישׁ — pref. כְּ q. v. }
כְּאִישׁוֹן — pref. id.) noun masc. sing. . . אישׁ
[g] כֶּאֱכֹל — pref. כְּ bef. (ֱ)) Kal inf. constr. . . אכל
[h] כְּאָכְלָם — pref. כְּ Kal inf. with suff. 3 pers. pl. masc. אכל
כָּאֵל — pref. כָּ for כְּהַ·, כְּהָ) noun m. sing. dec. 1a אול
[i] כְּאֵלָה — pref. id.) noun fem. sing. . . . אול
כָּאֵלֶּה — 'וְ pref. כָּ, see lett. כ) pron. demon. com. pl. אל
[k] כְּאֵלָה — pref. כְּ) noun fem. sing. . . . אול
כְּאֵלֶּה — pref. id.) pron. demon. com. pl. . . אל
[l] כֵּאלֹהֵי — 'וְ pref. כֵּ, contr. for כֶּאֱלֹהֵי, noun masc. pl. constr. from אֱלוֹהַּ dec. 1a . . . אלה
כֵּאלֹהִים — pref. כֵּ id.) id. pl., abs. st. . . אלה
[m] כֵּאלֹהֵינוּ — pref. כֵּ id.) id., suff. 1 pers. pl. . אלה
[n] כָּאַלּוֹן — וְ pref. כָּ for כְּהַ·, כְּהָ) noun m. sing. dec. 2b אלל
[o] כָּאַלּוֹנִים — pref. כָּ id.) id. pl., abs. st. . . אלל
[p] כְּאִלֵּם — וּ pref. כְּ) adj. masc. sing. dec. 7b; וּ bef. (:) אלם
[q] כְּאַלְמָנָה — pref. id.) noun fem. sing. dec. 11a . אלם
[r] כְּאַלְמָנוֹת — pref. id.) id. pl., abs. st. . . . אלם
[s] כְּאַלֻּפִי — pref. id.) for אַלּוּף, noun masc. sing. dec. 1b אלף
[t] כְּאֶלֶף — pref. id.) noun m. s. dec. 6a (comp. the foll.) אלף
כְּאַלְפַּיִם — pref. id.) id. du., abs. st. . . . אלף
[u] כְּאִמָּהּ — pref. id.) noun fem. sing., suff. 3 pers. sing. masc. (§ 3. rem. 3) from אֵם dec. 8b . אם
[x] כְּאִמּוֹ — וּ pref. id.) id., suff. 3 pers. s. m.; וּ bef. (:) אם
[y] כֶּאֱמֹר — pref. כְּ bef. (ֱ)) Kal inf. constr. . . אמר
[z] כְּאִמְרָתֶךָ — { pref. כְּ) noun fem. sing., suff. 2 pers. sing. masc. from [אִמְרָה] dec. 12b } אמר
[a] כְּאִמְרָתְךָ
[b] כְּאַמָּתַיִם — וּ pref. כְּ) n. fem. du. of אַמָּה d. 10; וּ bef. (:) אם
[c] כָּאֳנִיּוֹת — pref. כָּ bef. (ֳ)) noun fem., pl. of אֳנִיָּה dec. 10 אנה
[d] כֶּאֱנָשׁ — Chald. pref. כְּ bef. (ֱ)) noun m. sing. dec. 1 אנשׁ
[e] כְּאַנְשֵׁי — pref. כְּ) noun masc. pl. constr. [as if from אֱנָשׁ] see אֱנוֹשׁ, & אִישׁ (§ 45) אנשׁ
[f] כַּאֲנָשִׁים — pref. כַּ bef. (ֲ)) id. pl., abs. st. . . אנשׁ

[a] Is. 35. 6. [b] Ps. 42. 2. [c] La. 1. 6. [d] Is. 59. 10. [e] Ru. 2. 17. [f] Ju. 8. 21. [g] Is. 5. 24.
[h] 2 Ki. 4. 40. [i] Is. 6. 13. [k] Is. 1. 30. [l] 2 Ch. 32. 17. [m] 1 Sa. 2. 2. [n] Is. 6. 13. [o] Am. 2. 9.
[p] Ps. 38. 14. [q] La. 1. 1. [r] La. 5. 3. [s] Zec. 9. 7. [t] Ju. 9. 49. [u] Eze. 16. 44. [x] 2 Ki. 3. 2.
[y] Jos. 6. 8. [z] Ps. 119. 41, 58. [a] Ps. 119. 76, 116, 170. [b] Nu. 11. 31. [c] Pr. 31. 14. [d] Da. 7. 4.
[e] Joel 2. 7. [f] Ju. 9. 36. [g] Is. 17. 5. [h] Is. 10. 14. [i] Mi. 7. 1. [k] Eze. 25. 14. [kk] Jer. 14. 8.
[l] Job 6. 15. [m] Ps. 126. 4. [n] Eze. 35. 11. [o] Pr. 4. 19. [p] Is. 41. 12. [q] Ps. 147. 16.
[r] Am. 8. 8. [s] Jos. 4. 13. [t] 1 Sa. 4. 2. [u] Is. 38. 12. [x] Ca. 7. 6. [y] Ps. 92. 13.
[z] Ca. 5. 14. [a] Nu. 24. 6. [b] Job 34. 11. [c] Is. 38. 13. [d] Ps. 22. 17. [e] Nu. 23. 24.
[f] Eze. 12. 11. [g] Is. 36. 17. [h] Ca. 7. 9. [i] Le. 7. 7. [k] Le. 6. 10. [l] 2 Sa. 14. 13.

כְּאֶתְמוֹל pref. כְּ)(adv. . . . . מול
כְּבֹא [a] ו׳ pref. כְּ)(Kal inf. defect. for בּוֹא (§ 21. rem. 3) dec. 1a; וּ bef. (:) . . בוא
כְּבֹאָהּ[b] pref. כְּ)(id., suff. 3 pers. sing. masc. . בוא
כְּבֹאִי[c] pref. id.)(id., suff. 1 pers. sing. . . בוא
כְּבֹאֲךָ pref. id.)(id., suff. 2 pers. sing. masc. . בוא
כְּבֹאֲכֶם pref. id.)(id., suff. 2 pers. pl. masc. . בוא
כְּבֹאָם pref. id.)(id., suff. 3 pers. pl. masc. . בוא
כְּבֹאָנָה[d] pref. id.)(id., suff. 3 pers. pl. fem. (§ 3. rem. 5) בוא

כָּבַב Root not used; Arab. and Ethiop. *to roll up*.

כַּבּוֹן (*cake*, Syr. כבונא) pr. name of a place in the tribe of Judah, Jos. 15. 40.

כּוֹכָב masc. dec. 2b (for כָּבְכָּב) *star*.

כַּבֶּגֶד pref. כַּ for כְּהַ } noun masc. sing. (suff. בִּגְדִי) dec. 6a . בגד
כְּבֶגֶד [e] ו׳ pref. כְּ q. v.

כָּבֵד ,וְ כָּבֵד[f] (Ge. chaps. 12. 13. 43. 47; Ex. 7. 18; Nu. 11; 2 Sa. 14; all of these, however, may be taken as adjectives) fut. יִכְבַּד.—I. *to be heavy*.—II. *to be weighty, honoured, respected, mighty*.—III. *to be* or *become vehement, violent, great*.—IV. *to be grievous, burdensome*, with עַל *upon* or *to any one*.—V. *to be dull*, of the senses, also of the mind. Niph.—I. *to be, become*, or *show oneself honoured, renowned, glorious*; part. נִכְבָּד *glorious*; נִכְבָּדוֹת *glorious things*.—II. *to be abounding*, Pr. 8. 24. Pi.—I. *to honour*.—II. *to make obdurate, to harden*, the heart, 1 Sa. 6. 6. Pu. *to be honoured*. Hiph.—I. *to make heavy, grievous*.—II. *to honour, make honourable*; intrans. *to acquire honour*, 2 Ch. 25. 19. Hithp.—I. *to show oneself honourable, boast oneself*, Pr. 12. 9.—II. *to multiply oneself, become numerous*, Na. 3. 15.

כָּבֵד masc. dec. 5a & b (§ 34. rem. 2).—I. adj. *heavy*; Is. 1. 4, כֶּבֶד עָוֹן *laden with iniquity*.—II. *abounding, numerous*.—III. *heavy, grievous, sore*.—IV. *difficult, arduous*.—V. *slow* of utterance, Ex. 4. 10.—VI. subst. *the liver*.

כָּבוֹד masc. dec. 3a.—I. *honour, glory*; adv. *unto glory*, Ps. 73. 24.—II. *splendour, majesty*.—III. *abundance, wealth*.—IV. *heart, mind, soul*.

כָּבֹד adj. only fem. כְּבוּדָּה (for כְּבֵדָה) *glorious, magnificent*; subst. *precious things*, Ju. 18. 21.

כֹּבֶד masc.—I. *weight*, Pr. 27. 3.—II. *vehemence, violence*, Is. 21. 15; 30. 27.—III. *abundance, multitude*, Na. 3. 3.

כְּבֵדֻת fem. *heaviness, difficulty*, Ex. 14. 25.

כָּבֵד[g] וְ adj. masc. sing. dec. 5a & b (§ 34. rem. 2) כבד
כָּבֵד[h] defect. for כָּבוֹד (q. v.) . . . כבד
כַּבֵּד Piel inf., or imp. sing. masc. . . כבד
כְּבַד[i] ו׳ } adj. m. sing. constr. of כָּבֵד dec. 5a & b (§ 34. rem. 2); וּ bef. (:) . . כבד
כְּבֵד[k]
כֹּבֶד ו׳ noun masc. sing. . . . . כבד
כְּבוֹד[l] ו׳ n. m. s., constr. of כָּבוֹד dec. 3a; וּ bef. (:) כבד
כָּבְדָה[m] } Kal pret. 3 pers. sing. fem. (§ 8. rem. 1a) כבד
כָּבֵדָה
כָּבְדוּ[n] id. pret. 3 pers. pl. . . . כבד
כַּבְּדוּ[o] Piel imp. pl. masc. . . . . כבד
כְּבֵדוֹ[p] noun masc. sing., suff. 3 pers. sing. masc. from כָּבֵד ו׳ dec. 5 (§ 34. rem. 2) . . כבד
כְּבוֹדוֹ n. m. s., suff. 3 pers. s. m. from כָּבוֹד d. 3a כבד
כִּבְּדוּ[q] Piel pret. 3 pers. pl. . . . . כבד
כַּבְּדוּהוּ[r] id. imp. pl. masc., suff. 3 pers. sing. masc. כבד
כִּבְּדוּנִי[s] id. pret. 3 pers. pl., suff. 1 pers. sing. . כבד
כְּבֵדִי[t] n. m. s., suff. 1 pers. s. fr. כָּבֵד d. 5 (§ 34. r. 2) כבד
כְּבֹדִי noun m. s., suff. 1 pers. s. from כָּבוֹד d. 3a כבד
כִּבְדֵי[u] וְ constr. of the foll. . . . כבד
כְּבֵדִים[x] adj. masc., pl. of כָּבֵד dec. 5 (§ 34. rem. 2) כבד
כַּבֶּדְךָ[y] Piel inf. (כַּבֵּד), suff. 2 pers. sing. masc. for [כַּבֶּדְךָ] dec. 7b (§ 16. r. 16, & § 36. r. 3) כבד
כְּבֹדֶךָ noun masc. sing., suff. 2 pers. sing. masc. [for כְּבוֹדְךָ] from כָּבוֹד dec. 3a . . כבד
כְּבֹדָם[z] id., suff. 3 pers. pl. masc. . . . כבד
כִּבַּדְנוּךָ[a] וְ Piel pret. 1 pers. pl., suff. 2 pers. sing. m. כבד
כַּבְּדֵנִי[b] id. imp. sing. masc. (כַּבֵּד), suff. 1 pers. s. כבד
כִּבַּדְתּוֹ[c] וְ id. pret. 2 p. s. m. [כִּבַּדְתָּ], suff. 3 p. s. m. כבד
כִּבַּדְתָּנִי[d] id. id., suff. 1 pers. sing. . . . כבד

[כָּבָה] *to be extinguished*. Pi. *to extinguish, to quench*.

כַּבְּהֵמָה pref. כַּ for כְּהַ)(noun f. s. d. 11 (§ 42. r. 5) בהם
כַּבְּהֵמוֹת[e] pref. id.)(id. pl., abs. st. . . . בהם
כָּבוּ[f] Kal pret. 3 pers. pl. . . . . כבה
כִּבּוּ[g] וְ Piel pret. 3 pers. pl. . . . כבה
כְּבוֹא ו׳ pref. כְּ)(Kal inf. c. (§ 21. rem. 3) dec. 1a; וּ bef. (:) . . . . בוא
כָּבוֹד ו׳ noun masc. sing. dec. 3a . . . כבד
כְּבוֹד ו׳ id. constr. state; וּ bef. (:) . . כבד
כְּבוֹדָהּ[h] id. with suff. 3 pers. sing. fem. . . כבד
כְּבוּדָּה adj. f. [for כְּבֵדָה, fr. כָּבֹד m. § 39. No. 3. d. 8] כבד
כְּבוֹדוֹ ו׳ noun masc. sing., suff. 3 pers. sing. masc. from כָּבוֹד dec. 3a; וּ bef. (:) . . כבד
כְּבוֹדִי ו׳ id., suff. 1 pers. sing.; וּ id. . . כבד
כְּבוֹדֶךָ[i] ו׳ id., suff. 2 pers. s. m. [for כְּבוֹדְךָ]; וּ id. כבד
כְּבוֹדֵךְ[k] id., suff. 2 pers. sing. fem. . . . כבד

[a] De. 23. 12. [b] 1 Ki. 14. 5. [c] Ge. 44. 30. [d] Ru. 1. 19. [e] Is. 64. 5. [f] Is. 24. 20. [g] Ge. 50. 10; 1 Sa. 4. 18. [h] Na. 2. 10. [i] Ex. 4. 10. [k] Is. 1. 4. [l] Pr. 25. 2, 2. [m] Ju. 20. 34. [n] Ge. 48. 10. [o] Is. 24. 15. [p] Pr. 7. 23. [q] 1 Sa. 6. 6. [r] Ps. 22. 24. [s] Is. 29. 13. [t] La. 2. 11. [u] Eze. 3. 5, 6. [x] Ex. 17. 12. [y] Nu. 22. 37. [z] Pr. 25. 27. [a] Ju. 13. 17. [b] 1 Sa. 15. 30. [c] Is. 58. 13. [d] Is. 43. 23. [e] Ps. 49. 13, 21. [f] Is. 43. 17. [g] 2 Sa. 14. 7. [h] Is. 66. 11. [i] Ps. 63. 3. [k] Is. 62. 2.

כְּבוֹדְכֶם[a] id., suff. 2 pers. pl. masc. . . . . כבד
כְּבוֹדָם id., suff. 3 pers. pl. masc. . . . . כבד
כָּבוּל pr. name of a place . . . . . כבל
כַּבּוֹן וְ pr. name of a place . . . . . כבב
כְּבוֹצֵר[b] pref. כְּ)(Kal part. act. sing. masc. dec. 7b בצר
כִּבְחֹן[c] pref. כְּ bef. (:))(Kal inf. constr. . . בחן
כַּבַּחֲצִי[d] preff. כְּ, & בְּ bef. (-:))(noun masc. sing. (with suff. חֶצְיוֹ) dec. 6i (§ 35. rem. 14) . חצה
כַּבִּיר adj. masc. sing. dec. 1b . . . . כבר
כְּבִיר[e] וּ noun masc. sing.; וּ bef. (:) . . כבר
כַּבִּירִים adj. masc., pl. of כַּבִּיר dec. 1b . . כבר
כְּבֵית וּ pref. כְּ)(noun masc. sing. constr. of בַּיִת irr. (§ 45); וּ bef. (:) . . . . בית
כְּבִכּוּרָהּ[f] pref. כְּ)(noun masc. sing., suff. 3 pers. sing. fem. from [בִּכּוּר] dec. 1b . . בכר
כְּבִכּוּרָה[g] pref. id.)(noun fem. sing. . . . . בכר
כִּבְכֹרָתוֹ[h] pref. כְּ bef. (:))(noun fem. sing., suff. 3 pers. sing. masc. from בְּכֹרָה dec. 10 . בכר

כָּבַל Root not used; prob. i. q. גָּבַל, חָבַל to twist, in the kindred dialects, to bind together.

כֶּבֶל masc. dec. 6a (pl. c. כַּבְלֵי) *fetter*, Ps. 105. 18; 149. 8.

כָּבוּל (*district*) pr. name—I. of a district in Galilee, 1 Ki. 9. 13.—II. of a town in the tribe of Asher, Jos. 19. 27.

כְּבַלַּע[i] pref. כְּ)(Piel inf. constr. . . . . בלע
כִּבְנוֹת pref. כְּ bef. (:))(noun fem. pl., constr. of בָּנוֹת, irr. of sing. בַּת (§ 45) . . . בנה
כִּבְנֵי pref. id.)(noun masc. pl., constr. of בָּנִים irr. of sing. בֵּן (§ 45) . . . בנה
כִּבְנֵיהֶם[k] pref. id.)(id. pl. with suff. 3 pers. pl. masc. בנה

[כָּבַס] *to wash*; only part. כּוֹבֵס *washer, fuller*. Pi. כִּבֵּס, כִּבֶּס (§ 9. rem. 4) *to wash*, as clothes; metaph. *to cleanse, purify*. Pu. *to be washed*, Le. 13. 58; 15. 17. Hothp. הֻכַּבֵּס (§ 6. No. 10 note) id. Le. 13. 55, 56.

כִּבֵּס, וְכִבֶּס } Piel pret. 3 pers. sing. masc. (§ 10. rem. 1) . . . . } כבס
כֻּבַּס וְ Pual pret. 3 pers. sing. masc. . . . כבס
כִּבְּסוּ וְ Piel pret. 3 pers. pl. . . . כבס
כַּבְּסִי[l] id. imp. sing. fem. . . . . כבס
כַּבְּסֵנִי[m] id. imp. sing. masc., suff. 1 pers. sing. . כבס
כִּבַּסְתֶּם[n] וְ id. pret. 2 pers. pl. masc. . . כבס

כָּבַע Root not used; i. q. גָּבַע *to be high*.

כּוֹבַע masc. (constr. כּוֹבַע, קוֹבַע, pl. כּוֹבָעִים) (§ 31. rem. 5) *a helmet*.

כַּבָּקָר pref. כַּ for כְּהַ)(noun com. sing. dec. 4a . בקר
כַּבֹּקֶר[o] pref. id.)(noun masc. sing. dec. 6c . בקר
כְּבַקָּרַת[p] pref. כְּ)(noun f. s., constr. of [בַּקָּרָה] d. 10 בקר

כָּבַר Kal not used; i. q. cogn. גָּבַל, חָבַל *to twist*; Arab. *to be great, powerful*. Hiph. *to multiply*, Job 35. 16; part. *abundance*, Job 36. 31, לְמַכְבִּיר *abundantly*.

כְּבָר.—I. adv. *already, formerly*.—II. pr. name of a river in Mesopotamia, called also חָבוֹר.

כְּבִיר masc. *quilt, mattrass*, 1 Sa. 19. 13, 16.

כַּבִּיר adj. masc. dec. 1b.—I. *great, mighty*; כַּבִּיר יָמִים *very old*.—II. *copious, numerous, many*.

כְּבָרָה fem. *a sieve*, Am. 9. 9.

כִּבְרָה fem. only constr. כִּבְרַת, an unknown measure of *length*.

מִכְבָּר masc. dec. 2b, *lattice-work* of brass.

מַכְבֵּר masc. *cloth of a coarse texture*, 2 Ki. 8. 15.

כַּבֹּר[q] pref. כַּ for כְּהַ)(noun masc. sing. dec. 1a . ברר
כְּבָר adv.; also pr. name of a river . . כבר
כְּבַר Ch. pref. כְּ)(noun masc. sing. dec. 2a . ברא
כְּבֹר pref. id.)(noun masc. sing. dec. 1a . ברר
כְּבָרִאשֹׁנָה preff. כְּ, & בְּ for בְּהָ, בְּהַ)(adj., f. of רִאשׁוֹן ראש
כִּבְרוֹשׁ[r] pref. כְּ bef. (:))(noun masc. sing. dec. 1a ברש
כַּבַּרְזֶל[s] pref. כַּ for כְּהַ)(noun masc. sing. . ברזל
כְּבֹרִי[t] pref. כְּ)(n. m. s., suff. 1 p. s. from בֹּר d. 1a ברר
כִּבְרִיחַ[u] pref. כְּ bef. (:))(noun masc. sing. dec. 1a ברח
כִּבְרִית[x] וּ pref. כְּ)(noun fem. sing.; וּ bef. (:) . ברר
כַּבְּרִית[y] pref. כַּ f. כְּהַ }
כִּבְרִית[z] pref. כְּ bef. (:) } noun fem. sing. dec. 1a . ברת
כְּבִרְכַּת pref. כְּ)(noun fem., constr. of בְּרָכָה d. 11c ברך
כִּבְרֵכַת[a] pref. כְּ bef. (:))(n. f., constr. of בְּרֵכָה d. 10 ברך
כְּבִרְכָתוֹ[b] pref. כְּ)(n. f. s., suff. 3 p. s. m. fr. בְּרָכָה d. 11c ברך
כַּבָּרָק[c] pref. כַּ for כְּהַ)(noun masc. sing. dec. 4a ברק
כַּבְּרָקִים[d] pref. id.)(id. pl., abs. st. . . . ברק
כִּבְרַת noun fem. constr. [of כִּבְרָה] . . . כבר

כֶּבֶשׂ וּ׳[e], וְ׳[f] masc. dec. 6a, *lamb*; by transp. כֶּשֶׂב, which, though of less frequent occurrence, may yet be the primary form, כָּסַף=כָּשַׂב *to be white*.

כַּבְשָׂה, כִּבְשָׂה fem. dec. 12b, *ewe-lamb*.

[כָּבַשׁ] I. *to trample, tread under foot*; metaph. *to disregard*, Mi. 7. 19.—II. *to subdue, subject*.—III. *to humble, force, ravish*, Est. 7. 8. Niph. pass. of

[a] Is. 10. 3. [b] Je. 6. 9. [c] Zec. 13. 9. [d] 1 Sa. 14. 14. [e] 1 Sa. 19. 13, 16. [f] Is. 28. 4. [g] Ho. 9. 10. [h] Ge. 43. 33. [i] Nu. 4. 20. [k] Ne. 5. 5. [l] Je. 4. 14. [m] Ps. 51. 4. [n] Nu. 31. 24. [o] Job 11. 17. [p] Eze. 34. 12. [q] Is. 1. 25. [r] Ho. 14. 9. [s] Le. 26. 19. [t] 2 Sa. 22. 25. [u] Pr. 18. 19. [x] Mal. 3. 2. [y] Je. 31. 32. [z] 2 Ch. 34. 32. [a] Na. 2. 9. [b] Ge. 49. 28. [c] Zec. 9. 14. [d] Na. 2. 5. [e] Eze. 46. 13. [f] Le. 9. 3.

Kal, Nos. II. & III. (Ne. 5. 5). Pi. *to subdue*, 2 Sa. 8. 11. Hiph. id. Je. 34. 11, Kheth.

כֶּבֶשׁ masc. *footstool*, 2 Ch. 9. 18.

כִּבְשָׁן masc. *smelting furnace*.

כֶּבֶשׂ[a] וְ noun masc. sing. . . . . כבשׂ
כִּבֵּשׁ[b] Piel pret. 3 pers. sing. masc. . . . כבשׁ
כִּבְשָׂה וְ noun fem. sing. from כֶּבֶשׂ masc. . . כבשׂ
כִּבְשָׂה[c] noun fem. sing. dec. 12b, from כֶּבֶשׂ masc. כבשׂ
כִּבְשֻׁהָ[d] וְ Kal imp. pl. masc., suff. 3 pers. sing. fem. כבשׁ
כָּבְשׁוּ[e] וְ id. pret. 3 pers. pl. . . . . כבשׁ
כְּבָשַׂי[f] noun m. pl., suff. 1 pers. s. from כֶּבֶשׂ d. 6 כבשׂ
כְּבָשִׂים וּ' id. pl., abs. st.; וּ bef. (:) . . כבשׂ
כֹּבְשִׁים[g] Kal part. act. masc., pl. of [כֹּבֵשׁ] dec. 7b כבשׁ
כְּבַשֵּׁל[h] pref. כְּ) Piel inf. constr. . . . בשׁל
כַּבֹּשֶׂם pref. כַּ for כְּהַ) noun masc. sing. . בשׂם
כִּבְשָׁן[i] noun masc. sing. . . . . כבשׁ
כִּבְשָׂר[k] וּ pref. כְּ) noun masc. sing. d. 4a; וּ bef. (:) בשׂר
כִּבְשַׂר pref. כְּ bef. (:)) id., constr. st. . . בשׂר
כִּבְשָׂרוֹ[l] pref. id.) id., suff. 3 pers. sing. masc. . בשׂר
כְּבָשֹׂת[m] noun fem. pl. abs., from כִּבְשָׂה dec. 12b כבשׂ
כְּבֹשֶׁת[n] pref. כְּ) noun fem. sing. dec. 13c בושׁ
כִּבְשַׂת[o] noun fem. sing., constr. of כִּבְשָׂה dec. 12b כבשׂ
כִּבְשֹׂת[p] id. pl., constr. state . . . . כבשׂ
כְּבַת[q] pref. כְּ) noun fem. s. [for בִּנְתְּ, בֶּנֶת § 45] בנה
כִּבְתוּלָה[r] pref. כִּ before (:)) noun fem. sing. dec. 10 בתל
כְּבַתְּחִלָּה[s] preff. כְּ, & בַּ for בְּהַ) noun f. sing. d. 10 חלל
כִּגְאוֹן[t] pref. כִּ bef. (:)) noun masc. sing., constr. of גָּאוֹן dec. 3a . . . . . גאה
כִּגְבֹהַּ pref. כְּ) noun masc. sing. d. 6c (§ 35. r. 5) גבה
כִּגְבֹהַּ[u] pref. כִּ bef. (:)) Kal inf. constr. . . גבה
כַּגִּבּוֹר[x] pref. כַּ f. כְּהַ } adj. or subst. masc. sing.
כְּגִבּוֹר pref. כְּ q. v. } dec. 1b . . . . גבר
כְּגִבּוֹרִים[y] pref. id.) id. pl., abs. st. . . . גבר
וְ כִּגְבוּרֹתֶיךָ[z] pref. כִּ bef. (:)) noun fem. pl., suff. 2 pers. sing. masc. from גְּבוּרָה dec. 10 . . גבר
כַּגְּבִנָה[a] וְ pref. כַּ for כְּהַ) noun fem. sing. . . גבן
כְּגֶבֶר[b] וּ' pref. כְּ) noun masc. sing. d. 6; וּ bef. (:) גבר
כְּגִבֹּרִים[c] defect. for כְּגִבּוֹרִים (q. v.) . . . גבר
כַּגְּבִרְתָּהּ[d] pref. כַּ for כְּהַ) noun fem. sing., suff. 3 pers. sing. fem. from גְּבֶרֶת dec. 13a . . גבר
כַּגָּדוֹל }
כַּגָּדֹל[e] } pref. id.) adj. masc. sing. dec. 3a . . גדל
כְּגֹדֶל pref. כְּ) noun masc. sing. dec. 6c . . גדל
כְּגוֹב[f] pref. id.) noun m. sing., pl. or collect. גּוֹבַי נוב
כְּגוֹי[g] pref. id.) noun masc. sing. dec. 1a . . גוה

כַּגּוֹיִם pref. כַּ for כְּהַ) id. pl., abs. st., for גּוֹיִים (comp. § 3. rem. 1) . . . . . גוה
כְּגוּרֵי[h] pref. כְּ) noun m. pl. constr. fr. [גּוּר] d. 1a גור
כִּנְחָלֵי[i] pref. id.) noun fem. with pl. masc. term., constr. of גֶּחָלִים, fr. גַּחֶלֶת (q. v.) . . . נחל
כְּגִילְכֶם[k] pref. כְּ) n. m. pl., suff. 2 p. pl. m. from גִּיל d. 1a ניל
כַּגַּלְגַּל[l] pref. כַּ for כְּהַ }) noun masc. sing. d. 8e;
וּכְגַלְגַּל[m] וּ pref. כְּ q. v. } וּ before (:) . . גלל
כְּגַלֵּי[n] pref. כְּ) noun m. pl. constr. from גַּל d. 8d גלל
כְּגַלִּים[o] pref. id.) id. pl., abs. st. . . . גלל
כְּגֶלְלוֹ[p] pref. id.) noun masc. sing., suff. 3 pers. sing. masc. from גֵּלֶל dec. 6 (§ 35. rem. 3) גלל
כַּגְּלָלִים[q] pref. כַּ for כְּהַ) id. pl., abs. st. . . גלל
כִּגְמוּל pref. כִּ bef. (:)) noun masc. sing. dec. 1a גמל
כַּגָּמֻל[r] pref. כַּ f. כְּהַ } Kal part. pass. sing. masc.
כְּגָמֻל[s] pref. כְּ q. v. } (for גָּמוּל) dec. 3a . } גמל
כַּגַּן[t] pref. כַּ f. כְּהַ }
כְּגַן pref. כְּ q. v. } noun com. sing. dec. 8d . גנן
כַּגַּנָּב pref. כַּ for כְּהַ) noun m. s. d. 1b (§ 30. r. 1) גנב
כְּגַנָּה וּ pref. כְּ) noun fem. sing. d. 10; וּ bef. (:) גנן
כְּגַנֹּת[u] pref. id.) id. pl. . . . . . גנן
כִּנְגֹעַת pref. id.) Kal inf. constr. . . . נגע
כַּגֶּפֶן[x] }
כַּגָּפֶן } pref. כַּ f. כְּהַ } noun com. sing. (suff. גַּפְנִי)
כְּגֶפֶן[y] pref. כְּ q. v. } dec. 6a (§ 35. rem. 2) } גפן
כַּגֵּר pref. כַּ for כְּהַ) n. m. s. dec. 1a (כְּגֵר Je. 14. 8) גור
כְּגֹרֶן[z] pref. כְּ) noun fem. sing. dec. 6c . גרן
כַּגֶּשֶׁם[a] pref. כַּ for כְּהַ) n. m. s. (pl. c. גִּשְׁמֵי) d. 6c גשם
כַּד noun com. sing. dec. 8d . . . . כדד

כְּדַב Chald. not used as a verb (in the Bible); i. q. Heb. כָּזַב *to lie, deceive*.

כִּדְבָה Chald. adj. m. d. 3b, *lying, false*, Da. 2. 9.

כְּדֹב[b] pref. כְּ) noun masc. sing. dec. 8c . דבב
כִּדְבָה[c] Chald. adj. fem. sing. [from כִּדְבָה masc.] כדב
כַּדֻּבִּים[d] pref. כַּ for כְּהַ) noun m., pl. of דֹּב d. 8c דבב
כַּדָּבָר pref. id.) noun masc. sing. dec. 4a . דבר
כְּדַבֵּר pref. כְּ) Piel inf. constr. dec. 7b . . דבר
כִּדְבַר pref. כִּ bef. (:)) n. m., constr. of דָּבָר d. 4a דבר
כְּדַבְּרָהּ[e] pref. כְּ) Piel inf. (דַּבֵּר), suff. 3 pers. sing. fem. dec. 7b . . . . . דבר
כְּדִבְרֵי[f] pref. id.) noun m. pl. constr. fr. דָּבָר d. 4a דבר
כִּדְבָרֶיךָ[g] pref. כִּ bef. (:)) id. pl. (Kh. כִּדְבָרֶיךָ), suff. 2 pers. sing. masc., K. כִּדְבָרְךָ id. sing. דבר
כְּדִבְרֵיכֶם pref. כְּ) id. pl., suff. 2 pers. pl. masc. . דבר

[a] 2 Ch. 9. 18. [b] 2 Sa. 8. 11. [c] 2 Sa. 12. 3. [d] Ge. 1. 28. [e] Zec. 9. 15. [f] Job 31. 20.
[g] Ne. 5. 5. [h] 1 Sa. 2. 13. [i] Ex. 9. 8. [k] Mi. 3. 3. [l] Ex. 4. 7. [m] Ge. 21. 29, 30.
[n] Je. 2. 26. [o] 2 Sa. 12. 4. [p] Ge. 21. 28. [q] 2 Sa. 12. 3. [r] Joel 1. 8. [s] Is. 1. 26.
[t] Na. 2. 3. [u] Ps. 103. 11. [x] Is. 42. 13. [y] Joel 2. 7. [z] De. 3. 24. [a] Job 10. 10.
[b] Je. 23. 9. [c] Zec. 10. 5. [d] Is. 24. 2. [e] De. 1. 17. [f] Na. 3. 17. [g] Is. 58. 2.
[h] Je. 51. 38. [i] Eze. 1. 13. [k] Da. 1. 10. [l] Ps. 83. 14. [m] Is. 17. 13. [n] Is. 48. 18.
[o] Ho. 12. 12. [p] Job 20. 7. [q] Zep. 1. 17. [r] Ps. 131. 2. [s] Ps. 131. 2. [t] La. 2. 6.
[u] Nu. 24. 6. [x] Ho. 14. 8. [y] Ps. 128. 3. [z] Je. 51. 33. [a] Ho. 6. 3. [b] Ho. 13. 8.
[c] Da. 2. 9. [d] Is. 59. 11. [e] Ge. 39. 10. [f] Is. 29. 11. [g] Ezr. 10. 12. [gg] Eze. 17. 10.

דמם כִּדְמָה[a] pref. כְּ) noun fem. sing. [from דֹּם masc.]
דמה כִּדְמוּת pref. כִּ bef. (:)) noun fem. sing. dec. 1 a
דמה כִּדְמוּתֵנוּ[b] pref. id.) id., suff. 1 pers. pl.
אדם כְּדְמֵי[c] וְ pref. id.) n. m. pl. constr. from דָּם d. 2 a
דמן כְּדֹמֶן pref. id.) noun masc. sing.
דמשק כְּדַמֶּשֶׂק pref. id.) pr. name of a place
דן כְּדְנָה[d] וְ' Chald. pref. כְּ bef. (:)) emph. or fem. of דֵּן pron. demonst.
דון כְּדָנִיֵּאל pref. כְּ) pr. name masc.
ידע כְּדַעְתְּכֶם[e] pref. id.) noun fem. sing., suff. 2 pers. pl. masc. from דַּעַת דֵּעָה dec. 13 a (§ 44. No. 1)
דקק כַּדַּק[f] pref. כַּ for כְּהַ) adj. or subst. masc. sing.
דקק כַּדֹּק[g] pref. id.) noun masc. sing.

כָּדַר Root not used; Arab. *to be agitated, troubled.*

כִּידוֹר masc. Job 15. 24, *tumult, warlike tumult.* Prof. Lee, *attack, onset.*

דרב כַּדָּרְבֹנוֹת[h] pref. id.) noun pl. fem.
דרר כִּדְרוֹר[i] pref. id.) noun masc. sing.
דרך כְּדֶרֶךְ[k] וְ' pref. כְּ) noun com. sing. (suff. דַּרְכִּי) dec. 6 a; וְ bef. (:)
דרך כְּדֹרֵךְ[l] pref. id.) Kal part. act. masc. dec. 7 b
דרך כִּדְרָכָו[m] / כִּדְרָכָיו } pref. כִּ bef. (:)) noun com. pl., suff. 3 pers. sing. masc. from דֶּרֶךְ dec. 6 a
דרך כִּדְרָכַיִךְ[n] / כִּדְרָכַיִךְ[o] } pref. id.) id. pl., suff. 2 pers. sing. fem.
דרך כְּדַרְכֵיכֶם[p] pref. id.) id. pl., suff. 2 pers. pl. masc.
דרך כְּדֹרְכִים[q] pref. id.) Kal part. act. m., pl. of דֹּרֵךְ d. 7 b
דרך כִּדְרָכֵינוּ[r] pref. כִּ bef. (:)) n. com. pl., suff. 1 p. fr. דֶּרֶךְ d. 6 a
דרך כְּדַרְכָּם[s] pref. כְּ) id. sing., suff. 3 pers. pl. masc.
כְּדָר־לָעֹמֶר / כְּדָרְלָעֹמֶר } (*handful of sheaves*; coll. with the Arab. by Simonis) pr. n. of a king of Elam, Ge. 14. 1, 9.
דשא כַּדֶּשֶׁא[t] pref. כַּ for כְּהַ) noun masc. sing.
דת כַּדָּת pref. id.) noun f. s. dec. 1 a; but comp. כְּדָת
דת כְּדָת Chald. and Heb. pref. כְּ) noun fem. sing. dec. 1 a (but comp. דָּתְכוֹן)
דת כְּדַת[u] pref. id.) id. constr. (but this reading is doubtful)

כֹּה וְ', וְ' adv.—I. *so, thus*; בְּכֹה—בְּכֹה *in this manner—in that manner*, 1 Ki. 22. 20.—II. of place, *here, hither*; עַד־כֹּה *yonder*, Ge. 22. 5; כֹּה—כֹּה *here—there, on this side—on the other side*, Nu. 11. 31; כֹּה וָכֹה *hither and thither*, Ex. 2. 12.—III. of time, *now*; עַד־כֹּה *until now, hitherto*, Ex. 7. 16; Jos. 17. 14; עַד־כֹּה וְעַד־כֹּה *till now and then*, i. e. *meanwhile*, 1 Ki. 18. 45.

דבר כַּדְּבָרִים pref. כַּ for כְּהַ) id. pl., abs. st.
דבר כִּדְבָרִים[a] pref. כִּ bef. (:)) noun fem. with pl. masc. term. from דְּבֹרָה' dec. 10
דבר כִּדְבָרֶךָ in pause for כִּדְבָרְךָ (q. v.)
דבר כִּדְבָרֵךְ[b] pref. כִּ bef. (:)) noun masc. sing., suff. 2 pers. sing. fem. from דָּבָר dec. 4 a
דבר כִּדְבָרְךָ pref. id.) id., suff. 2 pers. sing. masc.
דבר כְּדַבֶּרְכֶם[c] pref. כְּ) Piel inf. (דַּבֵּר) suff. 2 pers. pl. masc. dec. 7 b (§ 16. rem. 15, & § 36. rem. 3)
דבר כְּדָבְרָם[d] pref. id.) noun masc. sing., suff. 3 pers. pl. masc. from [דֹּבֶר] dec. 6 c
דבש כִּדְבַשׁ[e] pref. כִּ bef. (:)) noun masc. sing. (suff. דִּבְשִׁי) dec. 6 (§ 35. rem. 10)
דגה כִּדְגֵי[f] pref. id.) noun m. pl. constr. from דָּג dec. 2 a
דגה כַּדָּגִים[g] pref. כַּ for כְּהַ) id. pl., abs. st.
דגה כַּדָּגָן[h] pref. id.) noun masc. sing. dec. 4 a
דגה כִּדְגַת[i] pref. כִּ bef. (:)) n. fem., constr. of דָּגָה dec. 11 a

כָּדַד Root not used; i. q. כָּתַת *to beat, strike*; Arab. *to hammer, to toil; to draw out of a well.*

כַּד com. dec. 8 d, *earthen jar*, espec. for drawing water, *a pitcher*; but also for keeping meal, 1 Ki. 17. 12, 14, 16.

כִּידוֹד masc. dec. 1 b, Job 41. 11, *a spark*; Arab. כִּיד to strike fire.

כַּדְכֹּד masc. a *sparkling* or *flashing gem*, supposed to be *a ruby.*

כדד כַּדָּהּ[k] וְ' n. com. s., suff. 3 p. s. f. from כַּד dec. 8 d
דבב כְּדוֹב[m] pref. כְּ) for דֹּב', noun masc. sing. dec. 8 c
דוד כְּדָוִד pref. id.) pr. name masc.
דוד כְּדוֹד[n] pref. id.) noun masc. sing., pl. דּוֹדִים' and דְּוָדִים' (§ 35. rem. 13)
דוה כִּדְוֵי[o] pref. כִּ bef. (:)) noun masc. pl. constr. from דְּוַי (comp. § 38. rem. 2)
דוד כְּדָוִיד pref. כְּ) pr. name masc., see דָּוִד
דנג כַּדּוֹנַג[p] / כַּדּוֹנַג } pref. כַּ for כְּהַ) noun masc. sing.
דור כַּדּוּר pref. id.) noun masc. sing.
די כְּדֵי[q] וּ pref. כְּ) noun masc. sing. dec. 8 d (§ 37. rem. 6); וּ bef. (:)
די כְּדֵי pref. כְּ) id., constr. st.
די כְּדִי[r] וּ' Chald. pref. כְּ) (prim. pron. relat.) *conj.*, see דִּי; וּ bef. (:)
כדד כַּדִּים[t] וְ' noun com., pl. of כַּד dec. 8 d
כדד כַּדֵּךְ[u] id. sing., suff. 2 pers. sing. fem.
כדד כַּדְכֹּד[y] וְ' noun masc. sing.
אדם כָּאָדָם[z] pref. כַּ for כְּהַ) noun masc. sing. dec. 2 a

[a] Ps. 118. 12. [b] 1 Ki. 17. 13. [c] Ex. 12. 31. [d] Is. 5. 17. [e] Eze. 3. 3. [f] Hab. 1. 14. [g] Ec. 9. 12. [h] Nu. 18. 27. [i] Eze. 47. 10. [k] Ge. 24. 16, 18, 20, 46. [l] Ge. 24. 15, 45. [m] 2 Sa. 17. 8. [n] Job 41. 12. [o] Job 6. 7. [p] Ps. 22. 15. [q] Est. 1. 18. [r] Da. 5. 20. [s] 1 Ki. 18. 34. [t] Ju. 7. 16. [u] Ge. 24. 14. [x] Is. 54. 12. [y] Eze. 27. 16. [z] 2 Ki. 3. 22.

[a] Eze. 27. 32. [b] Ge. 1. 26. [c] Eze. 16. 36. [d] Ezr. 5. 7. [e] Job 13. 2. [f] Is. 40. 15. [g] Is. 40. 22. [h] Ec. 12. 11. [i] Pr. 26. 2. [k] Nu. 11. 31. [l] Is. 63. 2. [m] Je. 17. 10. [n] Eze. 7. 3, 8. [o] Eze. 24. 14. [p] Eze. 20. 44. [q] Je. 25. 30. [r] Zec. 1. 6. [s] Eze. 36. 19. [t] Is. 66. 14. [u] Est. 2. 12.

כָּה Chald. i. q. כֹּה, only Da. 7. 28, עַד־כָּה *hitherto, thus far.*

כְּהִגָּלוֹת[a] pref. כְּ) Niph. inf. constr. . . . גלה

כְּהִדּוֹשׁ[b] pref. id.) Niph. inf. constr. (§ 21. rem. 12) דושׁ

[כָּהָה] fut. יִכְהֶה, apoc. וַתֵּכַהּ (§ 24. rem. 3) *to become weak, languid, faint,* Is. 42. 4; of the eyes, *to become dull, dim.* Pi. כִּהָה.—I. intrans. *to become faint, timid,* Eze. 21. 12.—II. *to make timid, to admonish,* 1 Sa. 3. 13.

כֵּהֶה adj. only fem. כֵּהָה dec. 10.—I. *weak, faint,* of the mind, Is. 61. 3; *dull, dim,* of the eyes; פִּשְׁתָּה כֵהָה *dim wick* of a lamp about to go out, Is. 42. 3.—II. *faint, pale,* of spots of leprosy.

כֵּהָה fem. *weakening, relaxation, mitigation,* Na. 3. 19.

כָּהֹה[c] Kal inf. abs. . . . . . . כהה

כֵּהָה subst. or adj. fem. s. dec. 10 [from כֵּהֶה m.] כהה

כִּהָה[d] Piel pret. 3 pers. sing. masc. (comp. קֵהָה, נִהֲלָה) according to Gesenius, in an intrans. sense, *to become pale* . . . . כהה

כִּהָה[e] id. with dag. forte impl. (§ 14. rem. 1) . כהה

כְּהוֹלֵךְ[f] pref. כַּ for כְּהַ) Kal part. act. masc. dec. 7b הלך

כְּהוֹצִיאָם pref. כְּ) Hiph. inf. (הוֹצִיא), suff. 3 pers. pl. masc. dec. 1b . . . . . . יצא

כֵּהוֹת adj. fem., pl. of כֵּהָה dec. 10 [from כֵּהֶה m.] כהה

כְּהַזְכִּירוֹ[g] pref. כְּ) Hiph. inf. (הַזְכִּיר), suff. 3 pers. sing. masc. dec. 1b . . . . . זכר

כְּהַזְנוֹת[aa] pref. id.) Hiph. inf. constr. dec. 1b . . זנה

כֶּהָחָכָם[h] preff. כְּ, & הֶ bef. חָ for הַ) adj. m. dec. 4c חכם

כְּהַחַלֹּנוֹת[i] preff. כְּ, & הַ for הַ) noun com., pl. of חַלּוֹן dec. 1b . . . . . חלל

כְּהַיּוֹם preff. כְּ, & הַ) noun masc. dec. 1, pl. יָמִים irr. (§ 45) . . . . . . יום

כְּהַכּוֹתָם[k] pref. כְּ) Hiph. inf. (הַכּוֹת § 25. No. 2), suff. 3 pers. pl. masc. dec. 1b . . . . נכה

כְּהָכִין[l] pref. id.) Hiph. inf. constr. dec. 3a . . כון

כְּהִכָּנַע[m] pref. id.) Niph. inf. constr. dec. 7 (§ 36. r. 5) כנע

[כְּהַל] *to be able, can;* הַאִיתָךְ כָּהֵל לְ *canst thou?* &c.

כָּהֵל Chald. Peal part. act. dec. 2b . . . כהל

כָּהֲלִין[n] Chald. id. pl., abs. st. . . . . כהל

כָּהֶם[o] ו׳ pref. כָּ q. v.) pron. pers. masc. pl. . הם

כָּהֶם[p] prep. (כְּ) with suff. 3 pers. pl. m. (§ 5. parad.) כ

כָּהֵמָּה[q] pref. כָּ q.v.) pron. 3.m.pl. (הֵם) with parag. ה הם

כַּהֲמוֹת[r] pref. כַּ bef. (ֲ)) Kal inf. constr. . . המה

כְּהִמֵּס[s] pref. כְּ) Niph. inf. constr. (§ 18. rem. 7) . מסס

כְּהָמֵר[t] pref. id.) Hiph. inf. constr. . . . מרר

כָּהַן Kal not used; prob. i. q. כּוּן *to stand,* whence Pi. כִּהֵן (§ 14. rem. 1).—I. *to prepare, make ready, adjust* or *adorn* (comp. הֵכִין) Is. 61. 10.—II. *to minister, act* or *officiate as a priest.*

כֹּהֵן masc. dec. 7b (pl. כֹּהֲנִים).—I. *priest;* כֹּ׳ הַגָּדוֹל, כֹּ׳ הָרֹאשׁ *the high priest,* also called, כֹּ׳ הַמָּשִׁיחַ *the anointed priest.*—II. *minister of civil affairs,* 2 Sa. 8. 18, comp. 1 Ch. 18. 17; some refer here, 2 Sa. 20. 26; 1 Ki. 4. 5; Job 12. 19.

כַּהֵן, כָּהֵן (Ezr. 7. 13), Chald. masc. dec. 2b, *priest.*

כְּהֻנָּה fem. dec. 10, *priesthood, office of the priest.*

כָּהֵן[u] pref. כָּ) pron. 3 p. fem. pl. (comp. הוּא) הן

כִּהֵן[x] ו׳[y] Piel pret. 3 pers. sing. masc. (§ 14. rem. 1) כהן

כֹּהֵן ו׳ noun masc. sing. dec. 7b . . . כהן

כָּהֲנָא[z] Ch. n. m. s. emph. [of כַּהֵן for כָּהֵן] d. 2b כהן

כְּהִנָּבְאִי pref. כְּ) Niph. inf. (הִנָּבֵא), suff. 1 p. s. d. 7b נבא

כְּהִנָּדֹף[a] pref. id.) Kal inf. constr. (§ 9. rem. 2) . נדף

כָּהֵנָּה ו׳ pref. כָּ q. v.) pron. 3 p. fem. pl. (הֵן) with parag. ה (comp. § 5. parad.) . . . הן

כְּהֻנָּה noun fem. sing. dec. 10 . . . . כהן

כִּהֲנוּ ו׳ Piel pret. 3 pers. pl. (§ 14. rem. 1) . כהן

כָּהֲנוֹהִי[b] ו׳ Ch. n. m. pl., suff. 3 pers. s. m. fr. כָּהֵן d. 2b כהן

כֹּהֲנַי[c] noun m. pl., suff. 1 pers. s. from כֹּהֵן dec. 7b כהן

כֹּהֲנֵי id. pl., constr. st. . . . . . כהן

כָּהֲנַיָּא[d] ו׳ Ch. noun m. pl. emph. from [כָּהֵן] d. 2b כהן

כֹּהֲנֶיהָ ו׳ noun m. pl., suff. 3 p. s. f. from כֹּהֵן d. 7b כהן

כֹּהֲנֵיהֶם[e] ו׳[f] id. pl., suff. 3 pers. pl. masc. . . כהן

כֹּהֲנָיו ו׳ id. pl., suff. 3 pers. sing. masc. . . כהן

כֹּהֲנֶיךָ id. pl., suff. 2 pers. sing. masc. . . כהן

כֹּהֲנִים ו׳[g] id. pl., abs. st. . . . . כהן

כֹּהֲנֵינוּ id. pl., suff. 1 pers. pl. . . . כהן

כַּהֲנִיף[h] pref. כְּ) Hiph. inf. constr. dec. 3a . . נוף

כְּהֻנַּת noun fem. sing., constr. of כְּהֻנָּה dec. 10 כהן

כְּהֻנַּתְכֶם[i] id., suff. 2 pers. pl. masc. . . . כהן

כְּהֻנָּתָם[k] id., suff. 3 pers. pl. masc. . . . כהן

כְּהַעֲלוֹת[l] pref. כְּ) Hiph. inf. constr. dec. 1b . עלה

כְּהַפְנֹתוֹ[m] pref. id.) Hiph. inf., suff. 3 p. s. m. d. 1b פנה

כְּהָצֵר[n] וּ pref. כְּ) Hiph. inf. constr.; וּ bef. (:) צרר

כְּהָקִיר[o] pref. כְּ) Hiph. inf. constr. . . . קור

כְּהַר pref. id.) noun masc. sing. d. 8 (§ 37. r. 7) הרר

כְּהֶרֶג[p] pref. id.) noun masc. sing. . . . הרג

כַּהֲרִים[q] ו׳[r] pref. כְּ) Hiph. inf. constr. dec. 3a . רום

---

a 2 Sa. 6. 20. b Is. 25. 10. c Zec. 11. 17. d Le. 13. 6, 56. e 1 Sa. 3. 13.
f Is. 30. 29. g 1 Sa. 4. 18. h Ec. 8. 1. i Eze. 40. 25. k Eze. 9. 8.
l 2 Ch. 12. 1. m 2 Ch. 33. 23. n Da. 5. 8, 15. o 2 Sa. 24. 3. p 2 Ki. 17. 15.
q Je. 36. 32. r Is. 17. 12. s Ps. 68. 3. t Zec. 12. 10. u Eze. 18. 14.
x 1 Ch. 5. 36. y Ex. 40. 13. z Ezr. 7. 12, 21. a Ps. 68. 3. aa 2 Ch. 21. 13.
b Ezr. 7. 13. c La. 1. 19. d Ezr. 7. 16. Je. 33. 32.
f Je. 2. 26. g 2 Ch. 13. 10. h Is. 10. 15. Nu. 18. 1, 7.
k Nu. 3. 10. l Eze. 26. 3. m 1 Sa. 10. 9. n 2 Ch. 33. 12.
o Je. 6. 7. p Is. 27. 7. q Is. 10. 15. r 2 Ch. 5. 13.

כְּהָרִימִי[a] pref. כְּ bef. (-:))(id. with suff. 1 pers. sing. — רום

כְּהַרְרֵי[b] pref. כְּ)(n. m. pl. constr. from [הָרָר] d. 4c — הרר

כְּהַשְׁחִית[c] וּ pref. כְּ)(Hiph. inf. constr. d. 2b; וּ bef. (:) — שחת

כָּהֲתָה[d] Kal pret. 3 pers. sing. fem. . . . — כהה

כִּהֲתָה[e] וְ Piel pret. 3 pers. sing. fem. (§ 14. rem. 1) — כהה

כְּהִתְוַדֹּתוֹ[f] וּ pref. כְּ)(Hithpa. inf., suff. 3 pers. sing. masc. (§ 20. No. 1); וּ bef. (:) . . — ידה

כְּהִתּוּךְ[g] pref. כְּ)(noun masc. sing. . . . — נתך

כַּהֲתִימְךָ[h] pref. כַּ bef. (-:))(Hiph. inf., suff. 2 pers. sing. masc. [for הֲתִמְּךָ § 18. rem. 12] . — תמם

כְּהִתְכַּנֵּס[i] pref. כְּ)(Hithpa. inf. constr. . . — כנס

כְּהָתֵל[k] pref. id.)(Hiph. inf. constr. . . — תלל

כְּהָתֵם[l] pref. id.)(Hiph. inf. constr. . . — תמם

כְּהִתָּעוֹת[m] pref. id.)(Niph. inf. constr. . . — תעה

כְּהִתְפַּלֵּל[n] וּ pref. id.)(Hithpa. inf. constr. d. 7b; וּ bef. (:) — פלל

כּוֹאֵב[o] וְ Kal part. act. sing. masc. dec. 7b . . — כאב

כּוּב וְ (*thorn, paliurus*, Syr.) pr. name of an unknown country, Eze. 30. 5.

כּוֹבֵס Kal part. act. sing. masc. . . . . — כבס

כּוֹבַע[p] וְ, כּוֹבַע[q] וְ } noun masc. sing. (§ 31. rem. 5) . . — כבע

כּוֹבַע[r] וְ id. constr. st. . . . . . — כבע

כּוֹבָעִים[s] וְ id. pl., abs. st. . . . . . — כבע

כָּוָה. Niph. *to be burned, scorched.*

כִּי masc. (for כְּוִי § 27. No. VI, 4) *brand, mark burnt in*, Is. 3. 24.

כְּוִיָּה fem. *a burning, branding*, Ex. 21. 25.

מִכְוָה fem. dec. 10, *inflamed part* in the body, Le. 13. 24, 25, 28.

כָּוַן Root not used; prob. i. q. נָקַב, קָבַב *to hollow out.*

כַּו Chald. masc. dec. 5a, *window*, Da. 6. 11.

כּוֹחִי[t] in full for כֹּחִי (q. v.) . . . . — כחח

כְּוִיָּה[u] noun fem. sing. . . . . . — כוה

כַּוִּין[w] וְ Chald. noun masc., pl. of [כַּו] dec. 5a — כוו

כּוֹכָב[y] noun masc. sing. dec. 2b [for כָּבְכָּב] . — כבב

כּוֹכַב[z] id., constr. st. . . . . . — כבב

כּוֹכְבֵי id. pl., constr. st. . . . . — כבב

כּוֹכָבִים וְ׳ id. pl., abs. st. . . . . — כבב

[כּוּל] *to measure*, Is. 40. 12. Pilp. כִּלְכֵּל (§ 6. No. 4). —I. *to contain.*—II. *to sustain, hold out, endure.*—III. *to sustain, maintain, nourish.*—IV. *to maintain one's cause*, Ps. 55. 23. Polp. כָּלְכַּל *to be sustained, provided for*, 1 Ki. 20. 27. Hiph. הֵכִיל.—I. *to contain.*—II. *to sustain, hold out, endure.*

כַּלְכֹּל (*sustenance*) pr. name of a wise man, 1 Ki. 5. 11; 1 Ch. 2. 6.

כּוּלָּם[a] (for כֻּלָּם) n. m. s., suff. 3 p. pl. m. fr. כֹּל d. 8c — כלל

כּוּם Root not used; Arab. *to heap up.*

כִּימָה fem. *the constellation of the pleiades.*

כּוּמָז וְ noun masc. sing. . . . . . — כמז

[כּוּן] Kal not used; *to stand*, Arab. *to exist*, hence Pil. כּוֹנֵן.—I. *to set up, fix, confirm, establish.*—II. *to prepare, fashion, form.*—III. *to adjust, direct, aim*, with acc. and עַל *against*; abs. *to prepare, dispose, apply oneself*, Job 8. 8; Is. 51. 13. Pul.—I. *to be established*, Ps. 37. 33.—II. *to be prepared*, Eze. 28. 13. Hiph. הֵכִין.—I. *to set up, establish, strengthen.*—II. *to constitute, appoint*, with עַל *over.*—III. *to adjust, direct, aim*, with לְ *against.* —IV. *to prepare, make ready*; הֵכִין לֵב לְ *to prepare, set his heart, purpose* to do anything, or towards any one; so also abs. (without לֵב) comp. 1 Ch. 28. 2. Hoph.—I. *to be set up, established*, Is. 16. 5.—II. *to be prepared, ready.* Niph.—I. *to be set up, confirmed, fixed, established*; נְכוֹן הַיּוֹם *the fixed day*, i. e. full noon; שַׁחַר נָכוֹן *the fixed, steady dawn*, as opposed to the premature twilight in the East; metaph. *to be upright, right, sincere, true*; אֶל־נָכוֹן *truly, certainly.*—II. *to be suitable, becoming.*—III. *to be prepared, ready.* Hithpal. הִכּוֹנֵן, הִתְכּוֹנֵן.—I. *to be established.*—II. *to prepare oneself*, Ps. 59. 5.

כּוּן (*stability*) pr. name of a town in Syria, 1 Ch. 18. 8.

כֵּן.—I. adj. masc. dec. 1a, *upright, right, true, honest.*—II. adv. (*a*) *right, rightly, well*; (*b*) *so, thus*; כֵּן—כַּאֲשֶׁר *as—so*; כְּ—כֵּן *so—as*; (*c*) with prepositions, אַחֲרֵי־כֵן, אַחַר כֵּן *afterwards*; בְּכֵן *then, so*; לָכֵן *therefore*, לָכֵן אֲשֶׁר *because*; עַל־כֵּן *therefore, because*; עַד־כֵּן *till now, hitherto*, Ne. 2. 16.

כֵּן Chald. *so, thus.*

כַּוָּן masc. only pl. כַּוָּנִים *small cakes*; Chald. כַּוֵּן *to prepare.*

כִּיּוּן Am. 5. 26, according to Kimchi, *cake* (i. q. כַּוָּן). Others take it as a pr. name of an idol, called Ῥεμφὰν, Acts 7. 43, the planet Saturn. Vulg. *imaginem.*

אָכֵן adv.—I. *surely, certainly, truly.*—II. *but, yet.*

---

[a] Ge. 39. 18. [b] Ps. 36. 7. [c] 1 Ch. 21. 15. [d] De. 34. 7. [e] Eze. 21. 12. [f] Ezr. 10. 1. [g] Eze. 22. 22. [h] Is. 33. 1. [i] Is. 28. 20. [k] Job 13. 9. [l] Da. 8. 23. [m] Is. 19. 14. [n] Ezr. 10. 1. [o] Ps. 69. 30. [p] Eze. 38. 5. [q] Eze. 27. 10. [r] 1 Sa. 17. 5; Is. 59. 17. [s] 2 Ch. 26. 14. [t] Da. 11. 6. [u] Ex. 21. 25. [w] Da. 6. 11. [y] Nu. 24. 17. [z] Am. 5. 26. [a] Je. 31. 34.

יָכִין (*He shall establish*) pr. name—I. of a son of Simeon, Ge. 46. 10 (for which יָרִיב 1 Ch. 4. 24); Patronym. יָכִינִי Nu. 26. 12.—II. of one of the columns of the temple of Solomon, 1 Ki. 7. 21.

כָּנְיָהוּ, יְכָנְיָהוּ, יְכָנְיָה (whom *the Lord establishes*) pr. name of a king, see יְהוֹיָכִין.

מָכוֹן masc. dec. 3 a.—I. *place, habitation.*—II. *foundation, basis.*

מְכֹנָה, מְכוֹנָה fem. with suff. מְכֻנָתָהּ (comp. § 30. rem. 4; § 32. rem. 5; § 39. No. 3. rem. 1), pl. מְכֹנוֹת.—I. *place*, Ezr. 3. 3.—II. *base, stand.*—III. pr. name of a town in the tribe of Judah, Ne. 11. 28.

נָכוֹן (*established*) pr. name of a threshing-floor, 2 Sa. 6. 6.

תְּכוּנָה fem. dec. 10.—I.—*place, seat*, Job 23. 3.—II. *arrangement*, Eze. 43. 11.—III. *furniture, store*, Na. 2. 10.

כַּוָּנִים n. m. pl. of [כַּוָּן] d. 1 b (§ 30. No. III. & r. 1) כון

כּוֹנֵן ו' Pilel pret. 3 pers. sing. masc., or (Job 8. 8) imp. sing. masc. . . . כון

כּוֹנְנָה[a] id. imp. sing. masc. with parag. ה . . כון

כּוֹנְנָהּ[b] id. pret. 3 pers. sing. masc., suff. 3 pers. s. f. כון

כּוֹנְנֵהוּ[c] id. imp. sing. masc., suff. 3 pers. sing. masc. כון

כּוֹנְנוּ [for כּוֹנְנוּ from כּוֹנַן] Pulal pret. 3 pers. pl. כון

כּוֹנְנוּ Pilel pret. 3 pers. pl. . . . . כון

כּוֹנְנִיָהוּ ו' Kh. כּוֹנַנְיָהוּ, K. כָּנַנְיָהוּ (q. v.) . . כון

כּוֹנַנְתָּ, כּוֹנַנְתָּה[d] } Pilel pret. 2 pers. sing. masc. (comp. § 8. rem. 5, and rem. 7) . . } כון

כּוֹנַנְתָּהּ[e] id. id., suff. 3 pers. sing. fem. . . כון

כּוֹס f ו' fem. dec. 1 a.—I. *cup.*—II. *pelican.* The Root is doubtful; according to Gesenius, it stands for כֹּנֶס, from כָּנַס *to collect.* Others derive it from כָּסָה *to cover.* But the signification of the obsol. כּוּס may be i. q. כָּסָה *to cover*; whence *to hide, preserve.* Hence perhaps also

כִּיס masc. dec. 1 a, *bag, purse.*

כּוֹסֵהוּ[g] id. with suff. 3 pers. sing. masc. . . כוס

כּוֹסִי[h] i ו' id. with suff. 1 pers. sing. . . כוס

כּוֹסָם[k] id. with suff. 3 pers. pl. masc. . . כוס

[כּוּר] *to dig, pierce*, only Ps. 22. 17 (comp. § 21. rem. 1).

כָּרִי masc. (prop. *piercer, stabber*, hence) *an executioner, sheriff*, attached to a kind of body-guard.

כּוּר masc. *a furnace* for smelting metals.

כּוּר עָשָׁן (*smoking furnace*) pr. name of a city in the tribe of Simeon, 1 Sa. 30. 30, elsewhere called עָשָׁן

כִּיר masc. only du. כִּירַיִם Le. 11. 35, *pot* or *jar*, prob. consisting of *two* compartments.

כִּיּוֹר masc. dec. 1 b, pl. ־ִים, ־וֹת.—I. a *firepan* or *basin*, Zec. 12. 6.—II. *basin, wash-basin, laver.*—III. *chafingdish*, 1 Sa. 2. 14.—IV. *pulpit*, 2 Ch. 6. 13.

מְכֵרָה fem. dec. 10, *sword*, Ge. 49. 5.

מְכֵרָתִי gentile noun from מְכֵרָה, a place otherwise unknown, 1 Ch. 11. 36.

מְכוּרָה, מְכֹרָה fem. dec. 10, *place of origin* or *nativity.*

כּוּר ו' noun masc. sing. . . . . כור

כּוֹרִין ו' Chald. noun masc., pl. of כֹּר dec. 1 a . כרר

כּוֹרֶשׁ pr. name masc., see כֹּרֶשׁ.

כּוּשׁ ו' (*terror*; coll. with the Arab.) pr. name—I. of a son of Ham, Ge. 10. 6, and a country, *Ethiopia*, so called after him, and applied also to its inhabitants, *Ethiopians.*—II. of a Benjamite, Ps. 7. 1.

כּוּשִׁי masc.—I. gent. noun from כּוּשׁ No. 1, *a Cushite, Ethiopian*; pl. כּוּשִׁיִּים, כּוּשִׁים. Fem. כּוּשִׁית an *Ethiopian woman*, Nu. 12. 1.—II. pr. name, *Cushi*, father of the prophet Zephaniah, Zep. 1. 1.

כּוּשָׁן fem. i. q. כּוּשׁ *Ethiopia*, Hab. 3. 7.

כּוּשַׁן רִשְׁעָתַיִם (*Ethiopian of great wickedness*) pr. name of a king of Mesopotamia, Ju. 3. 8, 10.

כּוּשִׁי gent. noun masc. from the preced. . כוש

כּוּשִׁים ו' id. pl. . . . . . . כוש

כּוֹשֵׁל Kal part. act. sing. masc. . . . כשל

כּוּשָׁן pr. name of a country . . . . כוש

כּוּשַׁן pr. name in compos. כּוּ׳ רִשְׁעָתַיִם . כוש

כּוּת pr. n. of a region where the ten tribes were colonised after the depopulation of their kingdom, 2 Ki. 17. 30, called כּוּתָה in ver. 24.

כִּזְאֵב ו' pref. כְּ bef. (:))(pr. name masc. . . זאב

כִּזְאֵבִים[gg] pref. id.)(noun masc., pl. of זְאֵב dec. 1 a זאב

כָּזֹאת, כַּזֹּאת[m] ו' } pref. כָּ or כַּ q. v.)(pron. demon. fem. sing., see . . . . } זה

[כָּזַב] *to lie, speak falsehood*, Ps. 116. 11. Pi.—I. *to lie, deceive.*—II. metaph. *to deceive, fail* of water, Is. 58. 11. Hiph. *to convict of falsehood*, Job 24. 25. Niph. *to be proved false, fallacious.*

כָּזָב masc. dec. 4 a, *lie, falsehood.*

כְּזִבָא (*lying, false*) pr. name of a place, 1 Ch. 4. 22.

כָּזְבִּי (id.) pr. name of a Midianitish princess, Nu. 25. 15, 18.

[a] Ps. 90. 17. [b] Is. 45. 18. [c] Ps. 90. 17. [d] Ps. 8. 4. [e] Ps. 68. 10. [f] Ge. 40. 11. [g] Eze. 23. 31. [gg] Eze. 22. 27. [h] Ge. 23. 5. [i] Ps. 16. 5. [k] Ps. 11. 6. [l] Ezr. 7. 22. [m] Ge. 45. 23.

כֶּחָג[o] pref. כֶּ for כְּהֶ, bef. חָ for כְּהַ·)(n. m. s. d. 8a חגג
כַּחֲגָבִים pref. כַּ bef. (-:))(noun m., pl. of חָגָב d. 4c חגב

כָּחַד Pi. כִּחֵד (§ 14. rem. 1) *to keep back, conceal,* with acc. of the thing and לְ or מִן of the person. Hiph. —I. *to hide,* Job 20. 12.—II. *to destroy, bring to nought.* Niph.—I. *to be concealed.*—II. *to be destroyed.*

כִּחֵד[p] Piel pret. 3 pers. sing. masc. (§ 14. rem. 1) כחד
כַּחֲדָה[q] Chald. pref. כַּ bef. (-:))(num. adj. fem. of חַד, with pref. כְּ *adv.* . . . אחד
כִּחֲדוּ[r] / כִּחֵדוּ[s] } Piel pref. 3 p. pl. (§ 14. r. 1, comp. § 8. r. 7) כחד
כְּחֵדֶק[t] pref. כְּ)(noun masc. sing. . . . חדק
כִּחַדְתִּי Piel pret. 1 pers. sing. (§ 14. rem. 1) . כחד
כֹּחָהּ noun masc. s., suff. 3 pers. s. f. fr. כֹּחַ d. 1a כחח
כֹּחוֹ id. with suff. 3 pers. sing. masc. . . כחח
כֹּחוֹ[u] Kh. כֹּחוֹ q. v., K. כֹּחִי (q. v.) . . כחח
כַּחוּט[x] pref. כַּ f. כְּהַ / כְּחוּט[y] pref. כְּ q. v. } noun masc. sing. . . חוט
כַּחוֹטֵא[z] pref. כַּ for כְּהַ)(Kal part. act. masc. dec. 7b חטא
כַּחוֹל ו' pref. id. / וּכְחוֹל[a] pref. כְּ } noun masc. sing.; וּ bef. (:) . חול
כְּחוֹלָה[b] pref. id.)(Kal part. act. fem. d. 10, from חֹלֶה m. חלה
וּכְחוֹמָה[c] pref. id.)(noun fem. sing. d. 10; וּ bef. (:) חמה
וְכַחוּץ[d] pref. כַּ for כְּהַ·)(noun masc. sing. dec. 1a חוץ
כְּחוֹתָם pref. id.)(noun masc. sing. (no vowel change) חתם
כַּחֲזֵה[e] pref. id.)(noun m. sing., constr. of חָזֶה d. 9b חזה
כְּחֶזְיוֹן[f] pref. כְּ)(noun masc. sing., constr. of חִזָּיוֹן dec. 3c (§ 32. rem. 3) . . . חזה
וּכְחֶזְקָתוֹ pref. id.)(noun fem. sing. constr. [of חֶזְקָה, no pl.]; וּ bef. (:) . . חזק

כָּחַח Root not used; i. q. Syr. כחי *to pant,* then, *to exert oneself* (Gesenius).

כֹּחַ, once כּוֹחַ (Da. 11. 6) masc. dec. 1a.—I. *strength, vigour, power, ability.*—II. *substance, wealth, riches.*—III. a species of *lizard,* Le. 11. 30.

כַּחֲטָאֵינוּ[g] pref. כַּ bef. (-:))(noun masc. pl., suff. 1 pers. pl. from חֵטְא dec. 6 (§ 35. rem. 6) חטא
כַּחַטָּאת pref. כַּ for כְּהַ·)(n. f. s. (§ 39. No. 4, & § 44. r. 5) חטא
כְּחַטֹּאתֵיכֶם[h] pref. כְּ)(id. pl. (חַטֹּאת for חַטָּאת), suff. 2 pers. pl. masc. . . . חטא
כְּחֹטְבֵי[i] pref. id.)(Kal part. act. pl. c. from חֹטֵב d. 7b חטב
כֹּחִי noun m. sing., suff. 1 pers. sing. from כֹּחַ d. 1a כחח
כַּחַיִל[k] pref. כַּ for כְּהַ·)(noun masc. sing. dec. 6h חול
כְּחֵיל[l] pref. כְּ)(id. constr. st. . . . חול

כְּזִיב pr. name of a town in the tribe of Judah, Ge. 38. 5.

אַכְזָב adj. masc. *false, deceitful, failing.*

אַכְזִיב (*false, deceitful*) pr. name—I. of a town in the tribe of Asher.—II. of a town in the tribe of Judah.

כָּזָב noun masc. sing. dec. 4a . . . . כזב
כִּזֵּב[a] Piel pret. 3 pers. sing. masc. . . . כזב
כֹּזֵב[b] Kal part. act. sing. masc. . . . כזב
כֹּזֵבָא pr. name of a place . . . . כזב
וּכְזֶבַח pref. כְּ)(pr. name masc.; וּ bef. (:) . זבח
כָּזְבִּי pr. name fem. . . . . . כזב
כִּזְבֵיהֶם[c] noun masc. pl., suff. 3 pers. pl. masc. from כָּזָב dec. 4a . . . . . כזב
כְּזָבִים id. pl., abs. st. . . . . . כזב
כָּזֶה ו' / כָּזֹה { pref. כְּ (see lett. כ))(pron. demon. masc. and fem. sing. . . . } זה
כַּזָּהָב pref. כַּ for כְּהַ)(noun masc. sing. dec. 4a . זהב
כְּזֹהַר[d] pref. כְּ)(noun masc. sing. . . . זהר
כְּזָוִיּוֹת pref. id.)(noun fem. pl. [of זָוִית comp. § 39, 4. rem. 1] . . . . זוה
כַּזּוֹנָה[e] pref. כַּ for כְּהַ)(Kal part. act. fem. dec. 10, from זוֹנֶה masc. . . . . זנה
כְּזֹחֲלֵי[f] pref. כְּ)(Kal part. act. pl. c. masc. from [זֹחֵל] dec. 7b . . . . . זחל
כַּזַּיִת pref. כַּ f. כְּהַ / כְּזַיִת[g] pref. כְּ q. v. } noun masc. sing. dec. 6h . זית
כִּזְכֹּר[h] pref. כְּ bef. (:))(Kal inf. constr. . . זכר
וְכִזְמַנָּם[i] pref. id.)(noun masc. sing., suff. 3 pers. pl. masc. from זְמָן dec. 8a . . . זמן
כְּזִמָּתְכֶנָה[k] pref. כְּ)(noun fem. sing., suff. 2 pers. pl. fem. (§ 3. rem. 5) from זִמָּה dec. 10 . זמם

כָּזַר Root not used; Syr. *to be valiant, daring.*

אַכְזָר adj. masc.—I. *bold, daring,* Job 41. 2.—II. *cruel, fierce.*—III. *deadly* of poison, De. 32. 33. Vulg. insanabile, *incurable.*

אַכְזָרִי adj. masc. *fierce, cruel.*

אַכְזְרִיּוּת fem. *cruelty, fierceness,* Pr. 27. 4.

כִּזְרֹחַ pref. כְּ bef. (:))(Kal inf. constr. . . זרח
כְּזֶרֶם pref. כְּ)(noun masc. sing. . . . זרם
כְּזֶרַע[l] pref. id.)(noun masc. sing. (suff. זַרְעוֹ) dec. 6a (§ 35. rem. 5) . . . . זרע
כִּזְרַע[m] pref. כְּ bef. (:))(id. constr. st. (§ 35. rem. 7) זרע
כֹּחַ ו' noun masc. sing. dec. 1a . . . . כחח
כַּחֲבַצֶּלֶת[n] pref. כַּ bef. (-:))(noun fem. sing. [for חֲבַצֶּלֶת', comp. § 35. rem. 2] . . . . חבצל

[a] Mi. 2. 11. [b] Ps. 116. 11. [c] Am. 2. 4. [d] Da. 12. 3. [e] Eze. 16. 31. [f] Mi. 7. 17. [g] Ps. 52. 10. [h] Je. 17. 2. [i] Est. 9. 27. [k] Eze. 23. 48. [l] Ex. 16. 31. [m] Nu. 11. 7. [n] Is. 35. 1. [o] 1 Ki. 12. 32. [p] 1 Sa. 3. 18. [q] Da. 2. 35. [r] Job 15. 18. [s] Is. 3. 9. [t] Mi. 7. 4. [u] Ps. 102. 24. [x] Ju. 16. 12. [y] Ca. 4. 3. [z] Ec. 9. 2. [a] Ps. 78. 27. [b] Je. 4. 31. [c] Pr. 18. 11. [d] Is. 51. 23. [e] Nu. 18. 18. [f] Job 20. 8. [g] Ps. 103. 10. [h] Le. 26. 21. [i] Je. 46. 22. [k] 1 Ki. 20. 25. [l] Job 20. 18.

כֹּחֲךָ[a] / כֹּחֶךָ[b] / כֹּחֲכָה[c] } noun masc. sing., suff. 2 pers. sing. masc. from כֹּחַ dec. 1a (§ 3. rem. 2) . } כחח

כְּחַכֵּי[d] וּ pref. כְּ)(Piel inf. constr. by Chaldaism [for חַכֵּה § 24. rem. 20] . . . . חכה

כֹּחֲכֶם[e] noun m. s., suff. 2 pers. pl. m. from כֹּחַ d. 1a כחח

כְּחָכְמַת pref. כְּ)(noun fem. sing., constr. of חָכְמָה Chald. dec. 8a (no pl.) . . . . חכם

כְּחָכְמָתְךָ[f] pref. id.)(id. with suff. 2 p. s. m. for חָכְמָתְךָ חכם

[כָּחַל] *to blacken* or *paint* the eyes with stibium, a kind of powder, see פּוּךְ, Eze. 23. 40.

כַּחֵלֶב[g] pref. כַּ for כְּהַ / כְּחֵלֶב[h] pref. כְּ q. v. } noun masc. sing. dec. 6 (§ 35. rem. 6) . } חלב

כֶּחָלָב[i] pref. כֶּ for כְּהֶ, bef. חָ for כְּהַ)(n. m. dec. 4c חלב

כַּחֲלוֹם pref. כַּ bef. (-:))(noun masc. sing. dec. 1a חלם

כֶּחָלָל pref. כֶּ for כְּהֶ, bef. חָ for כְּהַ)(adj. m. s. d. 4c חלל

כְּחֹלְלִים[k] pref. כְּ)(Kal part. act. pl. of [חֹלֵל] dec. 7b חלל

כַּחֲלִילִים[l] pref. כַּ bef. (-:))(noun m., pl. of חָלִיל dec. 3a חלל

כַּחֲלֹמוֹ[m] pref. id.)(noun masc. sing., suff. 3 pers. sing. masc. from חֲלוֹם dec. 1a . . חלם

כְּחֹלְמִים[n] pref. כְּ)(Kal part. act. m., pl. of חֹלֵם dec. 7b חלם

כַּחַלָּמִישׁ[zz] pref. כַּ for כְּהַ)(noun masc. sing. (constr. חַלְּמִישׁ) dec. 3c . . . חלמש

כְּחֵלֶק וּ[o] pref. כְּ)(noun masc. sing. d. 6 (§ 35. r. 6) חלק

כַּחֲלַקְלַקּוֹת[p] pref. כַּ bef. (-:))(noun pl. fem. [from חֲלַקְלַק] חלק

כָּחַלְתְּ[q] Kal pret. 2 pers. sing. fem. . . . כחל

כְּחֹם pref. כְּ)(noun masc. sing. dec. 8c . . חמם

כֹּחָם[r] noun m. s., suff. 3 pers. pl. m. from כֹּחַ d. 1a כחח

כַּחַמָּה[s] pref. כַּ for כְּהַ)(noun fem. sing. dec. 10 חמם

כַּחֹמֶץ[t] pref. id.)(noun masc. sing. . . . חמץ

כַּחֹמֶר[u] וְ pref. id. / כְּחֹמֶר pref. כְּ } noun masc. sing. dec. 6c . חמר

כַּחֲמֵשֶׁת pref. כַּ bef. (-:))(num. card. masc. constr. of חֲמִשָּׁה (§ 39. No. 4. rem. 1) from חָמֵשׁ fem. חמש

כַּחֲמָתִי[x] וְ pref. id.)(noun fem. sing., suff. 1 pers. sing. from חֵמָה dec. 11b . . . . יחם

כַּחֶסֶד[y] pref. כַּ for כְּהַ)(noun masc. sing. dec. 6a חסד

כְּחַסְדְּךָ / כְּחַסְדֶּךָ } pref. כְּ)(id., suff. 2 pers. sing. masc. . חסד

כַּחֲצִי[z] pref. כַּ bef. (-:))(noun masc. sing. dec. 6i (suff. חֶצְיוֹ § 35. rem. 14) . . . חצה

כְּחִצִּים[a] pref. כְּ)(noun masc., pl. of חֵץ dec. 8b . חצץ

כַּחֲצִיר[b] pref. כַּ bef. (-:))(constr. of the foll. . חצר

כֶּחָצִיר pref. כֶּ for כְּהֶ, bef. חָ for כְּהַ)(noun m. d. 3a חצר

כַּחֲצֹת[c] pref. כַּ bef. (-:))(n. m. s., constr. of [חֲצוֹת] d. 3a חצה

כְּחֻקַּת[d] pref. כְּ)(noun fem. sing., constr. of חֻקָּה d. 10 חקק

כְּחֻקֹּתָם[e] pref. id.)(id. pl., suff. 3 pers. pl. masc. . חקק

כַּחֶרֶב[f] pref. כַּ f. כְּהַ / כְּחֶרֶב pref. כְּ q. v. } noun fem. sing. (suff. חַרְבִּי) dec. 6a . . . } חרב

כַּחֹרֶב[g] pref. id.)(noun masc. sing. . . . חרב

כַּחֶרֶשׂ[h] pref. כַּ for כְּהַ)(n. m. s. (pl. c. חַרְשֵׂי) d. 6a חרשׂ

כְּחֵרֵשׁ[i] pref. כְּ)(adj. s. m. d. 7b [for חֵרֵשׁ § 36. No. 1] חרשׁ

כָּחַשׁ[k] *to fail, waste away,* Ps. 109. 24. Pi. כִּחֵשׁ (§ 14. rem. 1).—I. *to deny;* with בְּ of the person and thing, *to disavow.*—II. *to lie, to speak falsehood,* with לְ.—III. *to fail, deceive, flatter.* Niph. *to feign, flatter,* De. 33. 29. Hithp. id. 2 Sa. 22. 45.

כַּחַשׁ masc. dec. 6d.—I. *leanness,* Job 16. 8.—II. *lie, falsehood, deceit.*

כֶּחָשׁ m. *a lying, false,* only pl. כֶּחָשִׁים Is. 30. 9.

כַּחַשׁ[l] / כַּחַשׁ[m] } noun masc. sing. dec. 6d . . כחש

כַּחֵשׁ[n] וְ Piel inf. abs. or constr. (§ 14. rem. 1) . כחש

כִּחֵשׁ[o] וְ / כִּחֶשׁ[p] וְ } id. pret. 3 pers. sing. masc. (§ 10. rem. 1) כחש

כִּחֲשׁוּ id. pret. 3 pers. pl. . . . . כחש

כַּחֲשִׁי[q] or כַּחְשִׁי, n. m. s., suff. 1 p. s. from כַּחַשׁ d. 6d כחש

כַּחֲשֵׁיכָה[r] pref. כַּ bef. (-:) noun fem. sing. dec. 10 . חשך

כֶּחָשִׁים[s] noun m. pl. [of כֶּחָשׁ for כַּחָשׁ, כַּחַשׁ [כַּחָשׁ] dec. 1b (§ 30. rem. 3, comp. also § 42. No. 3, note) כחש

כִּחַשְׁתִּי[t] וְ[u] Piel pret. 1 pers. sing. (§ 14. rem. 1) כחש

כֶּחָתָן[x] pref. כֶּ for כְּהֶ, bef. חָ for כְּהַ)(and . / כְּחָתָן[y] pref. כְּ q. v.)(noun masc. sing. dec. 4c } חתן

כַּחֶתֶף[z] pref. id.)(noun masc. sing. . . חתף

כְּטָהֳרַת[a] pref. id.)(n. fem. s., constr. of טָהֳרָה (no pl.) טהר

כַּטּוֹב pref. כַּ for כְּהַ)(adj. or subst. and / כְּטוֹב pref. כְּ q. v.)(inf. or adj. m. sing. dec. 1a } טוב

כְּטִיט pref. id.)(noun masc. sing. [for טְאִיט] טוא

כַּטַּל וְ pref. כַּ for כְּהַ / כְּטַל[b] וּ pref. כְּ q. v. } noun masc. sing. dec. 8a; וּ bef. (:) . . } טלל

כַּטָּמֵא[c] pref. כַּ for כְּהַ)(adj. masc. sing. dec. 4a (constr. טְמֵא § 34. rem. 1) . . טמא

כְּטֻמְאַת pref. כְּ)(noun f. s., constr. of טֻמְאָה d. 10 טמא

כְּטֻמְאָתָם[d] pref. id.)(id., suff. 3 pers. pl. masc. . טמא

כְּטַעַם[e] pref. id.)(n. m. s. d. 6d (suff. טַעְמוֹ § 35. r. 5) טעם

כִּי וְ particle.—I. supposed (by Gesenius and Fürst, but disputed by Prof. Lee) to be primarily a relative pron. i. q. אֲשֶׁר *which,* espec. in the passages

[a] Ju. 16. 6, 15. [b] Pr. 5. 10. [c] Pr. 24. 10. [d] Ho. 6. 9. [e] Le. 26. 20. [f] 1 Ki. 2. 6. [g] Ps. 119. 70. [h] Le. 4. 26. [i] Job 10. 10. [k] Ps. 87. 7. [l] Je. 48. 36. [m] Ge. 41. 12. [n] Ps. 126. 1. [o] 1 Sa. 30. 24. [p] Je. 23. 12. [q] Eze. 23. 40. [r] Pr. 20. 29. [s] Ca. 6. 10. [t] Pr. 10. 26. [u] Job 27. 16. [x] Eze. 25. 14. [y] Ge. 21. 23. [z] Eze. 16. 51. [a] Ps. 127. 4. [b] Ps. 129. 6. [c] Ex. 11. 4. [d] Nu. 9. 14. [e] 2 Ki. 17. 34. [f] Ps. 64. 4. [g] Is. 25. 5. [h] Ps. 22. 16. [i] Ps. 38. 14. [k] Ps. 109. 24. [l] Ho. 10. 13. [m] Na. 3. 1. [n] Zec. 13. 4. [o] Le. 5. 21. [p] Le. 5. 22; Job 8. 18. [q] Job 16. 8. [r] Ps. 139. 12. [s] Is. 30. 9. [t] Job 31. 28. [u] Pr. 30. 9. [x] Is. 61. 10. [y] Ps. 19. 6. [z] Pr. 23. 28. [zz] Is. 50. 7. [a] 2 Ch. 30. 19. [b] Pr. 19. 12. [c] Is. 64. 5. [d] Eze. 39. 24. Nu. 11. 8.

Ge. 3. 19 (כִּי מִמֶּנָּה); Ge. 4. 25 (כִּי הֲרָגוֹ); Is. 54. 6 (כִּי תִמָּאֵס); Is. 57. 20.—II. relat. conj. (*a*) *that*, especially after the verbs of seeing, knowing, hearing, believing, saying, &c. as מִי הִגִּיד לְךָ כִּי *who told thee that*, &c.; also after an adv. e. g. Job 12. 2, *no doubt that* (כִּי) *ye are the people*; הֲכִי *is it that? is it not that?* עַל כִּי, יַעַן כִּי *on account of, that, because;* עַד כִּי *until that;* אֶפֶס כִּי *except that;* תַּחַת כִּי, עֵקֶב כִּי *because that;* (*b*) *for, because;* כִּי—וְכִי *because*—and *because;* (*c*) *but*, preceded by a negation, comp. Ge. 24. 4; also, *nay but, nay for*, espec. after an interrogation including a negation though not expressed, comp. Job 31. 14; without a negation, *but yet, nevertheless;* (*d*) of time, *if; when; so, then*, comp. Nu. 22. 33.—III. כִּי אִם (*a*) *that if*, the אִם referring to a parenthetic clause, e. g. 1 Sa. 20. 9; *that since; for if; but if;* (*b*) *unless, except, if not; but; yet, nevertheless; that.*

כִּי[a] noun masc. sing. [for כְּוִי] — כוה
כִּי[b] Kh. כִּי q. v. K. כֹּה (q. v.) — כה
כַּיְאוֹר[c] pref. כַּ for כְּהַ) noun masc. sing. dec. 1a — יאר
כַּיְאֹר
כִּיאֹר pref. כְּ) n.m. יְאֹר with pref. כְּ [for כִּיְאֹר, כְּיְאֹר] — יאר
כִּיבוּסִי pref. id.) gent. n. יְבוּסִי (see preced.) fr. יְבוּס — בוס
כְּיָבִין pref. כְּ) pr. name masc. — בין

[כִּיד] masc. dec. 1a, *ruin, destruction*, Job 21. 20.

כִּידוֹן masc.—I. *spear*, or *javelin.*—II. גֹּרֶן כִּ׳ (*threshing-floor of spears*) pr. name of a place near Jerusalem, 1 Ch. 13. 9; for which גֹּרֶן נָכוֹן 2 Sa. 6. 6.

כְּיַד pref. כְּ) noun com. s., constr. of יָד d. 2a — יד
כִּידוֹ[d] noun m. s., suff. 3 pers. s. m. fr. כִּיד d. 1a — כיד
כִּידוֹדֵי[e] noun masc. pl. constr. from [כִּידוֹד] dec. 1b — כדד
בִּידוֹן[f] וְ׳ noun masc. sing. — כיד
כִּידֵי[g] pref. כְּ [for כְּיְדֵי, כְּיְ׳]) noun com. pl. constr. from יָד dec. 2a — יד
כִּידֹן [h] וְ noun masc. sing., also pr. name masc. — כיד
כַּיהוָֹה the most sacred name of God with the vowels of אֲדֹנָי; pref. כַּ bef. (-:) — הוה
כַּיּוֹלֵדָה pref. כַּ for כְּהַ) Kal part. act. s. f. of יוֹלֵד — ילד
כַּיּוֹם pref. id.) noun masc. sing. irr. (§ 45); ו bef. (:) — יום
כְּיוֹם [i] ו׳ pref. כְּ
כִּיּוּן[k] noun masc. sing. — כון
כַּיּוֹנָה pref. כַּ for כְּהַ) noun fem. sing. dec 10; ו bef. (:) — יונה
כְּיוֹנָה [l] ו׳ pref. כְּ q.v.

כְּיוֹנֵי[m] pref. כְּ) noun fem. pl., constr. st. — יונה
כַּיּוֹנִים וְ pref. כַּ f. כְּהַ) id. pl., abs. st. — יונה
כְּיוֹנִים[n] pref. כְּ q. v.
כַּיּוֹנֵק[o] pref. כַּ for כְּהַ) noun masc. sing. dec. 7b — ינק
כִּיּוֹר noun masc. sing. dec. 1b — כור
כְּיוֹרְדֵי[ff] pref. כְּ) Kal part. act. pl. c. m. fr. יוֹרֵד d. 7b — ירד
כִּיּוֹרִים[p] noun masc., pl. of כִּיּוֹר dec. 1b — כור
כְּיֹטוֹב[q] Kh. כִּי טוֹב q. v., K. כְּטוֹב (q. v.) — טוב
כְּיַיִן[r] pref. כְּ) noun masc. sing. dec. 6h — יון
כְּיֵין pref. כְּ) id., constr. st. — יון
כַּיֹּלֵדָה[s] pref. כַּ for כְּהַ) Kal part. act. s., f. of יוֹלֵד — ילד
כֵּילַפּוֹת[t] וְ noun pl. fem. — כלף
כַּיֶּלֶק[u] pref. כַּ f. כְּהַ) noun masc. s. (§ 35. r. 2) — ילק
כַּיָּלֶק
כְּיֶלֶק[x] pref. כְּ q. v.
כַּיָּם pref. כַּ for כְּהַ) noun masc. sing. dec. 8a — ים
כִּימָה [y] וְ׳ noun fem. sing. — כום
כִּימוֹת[z] pref. כְּ [for כְּיְמוֹת, כְּיְ׳]) n.m. with pl. f. term., constr. of יָמוֹת [as if fr. יָם] see יוֹם (§ 45) — יום
בִּימֵי [a] וְ׳ pref. כְּ [for כְּיְמֵי, כְּיְ׳]) id. pl. masc., constr. of יָמִים — יום
כְּיָמֶיךָ[b] ו pref. כְּ) id. pl. with suff. 2 p. s. m.; ו bef. (:) — יום
כַּיָּמִים pref. כַּ f. כְּהַ) id. pl. abs. masc. — יום
כְּיָמִים[c] pref. כְּ q. v.
כִּים noun masc. sing. dec. 1a — כום
כִּי עֵנִים[d] Kh. כִּי עֵנִים (pl. of עוֹנֶה q. v.); K. כַּיְעֵנִים, pref. כַּ for כְּהַ) noun m., pl. of [יָעֵן] d. 5a — יען
כִּיקוֹד[e] pref. כְּ [for כְּיְקוֹד, כְּיְ׳]) noun masc. sing. — יקד
כִּיקַר[f] pref. כְּ [for כְּיְקַר, כְּיְ׳]) adj. masc. sing., constr. of יָקָר dec. 4a — יקר
כְּיִרְאָתְךָ[g] ו pref. כְּ) noun fem. sing., suff. 2 pers. sing. masc. fr. יִרְאָה (no pl.); ו bef. (:) — ירא
כִּירוּשָׁלַם pref. כְּ [for כְּיְרוּ׳ כְּיְ׳]) pr. name of a place — ירה
כִּיֹּרוֹת[h] noun masc. with pl. f. term. fr. כִּיּוֹר dec. 1b — כור
כְּיָרֵחַ[i] pref. כְּ) noun masc. sing. dec. 4a — ירח
כְּיַרְחֵי[k] pref. id.) n. m. pl. c. fr. יֶרַח d. 6a (§ 35. r. 5) — ירח
בִּירַיִם[l] וְ noun masc., du. of [כִּיר] dec. 1a — כור
כַּיְרִיעָה[m] pref. כַּ for כְּהַ) noun fem. sing. dec. 10 — ירע
כִּירִיעוֹת[n] pref. כְּ [for כְּיְרִי׳, כְּיְ׳]) id. pl. — ירע
כְּיֶרֶק[o] [p] ו׳ pref. כְּ) noun masc. sing.; ו bef. (:) — ירק
כְּיָשֵׁן[q] pref. id.) adj. masc. sing. dec. 5a — ישן
כַּיָּשָׁר וְ pref. כַּ for כְּהַ) adj. m. s. d. 4a; ו bef. (:) — ישר
כְּיִשְׂרָאֵל pref. id.) pr. name of a people — שׂרה
כִּיתְרוֹן[r] transp. and contr. [for כְּיִתְרוֹן], noun masc. sing., יִתְרוֹן, with pref. כְּ — יתר
כַּכָּבוֹד[s] pref. כַּ for כְּהַ) noun masc. sing. dec. 3a — כבד

[a] Is. 3. 24. [b] 2 Sa. 12. 10. [c] Je. 46. 8. [d] Job 21. 20. [e] Job 41. 11. [f] Job 41. 21. [g] Ge. 27. 23. [h] Je. 50. 42. [i] Ho. 2. 17. [k] Am. 5. 26. [l] Ho. 11. 11. [m] Eze. 7. 16. [n] Ca. 5. 12. [o] Is. 53. 2. [p] 2 Ch. 4. 6. [q] Ju. 16. 25. [r] Job 32. 19. [s] Je. 22. 23. [t] Ps. 74. 6. [u] Na. 3. 15. [x] Je. 51. 27. [y] Job 9. 9. [z] Ps. 90. 15. [a] Job 7. 1. [b] De. 33. 25. [c] Ge. 29. 20. [d] La. 4. 3. [e] Is. 10. 16. [f] Ps. 37. 20. [ff] Pr. 1. 12. [g] Ps. 90. 11. [h] 1 Ki. 7. 38. [i] Ps. 89. 38. [k] Job 29. 2. [l] Le. 11. 35. [m] Ps. 104. 2. [n] Ca. 1. 5. [o] Ge. 9. 3. [p] Ps. 37. 2. [q] Ps. 78. 65. [r] Ec. 2. 13. [s] Eze. 3. 23.

כִּכְבוֹד[a] pref. כִּ bef. (:))(id., constr. st. . . . כבד
כִּכְבֵיהֶם[b] the foll. with suff. 3 pers. pl. masc. . . כבב
כְּכָבִים[c] וְ noun masc. pl. abs. from כּוֹכָב dec. 2b . כבב
כְּכֶבֶשׂ pref. כְּ)(noun masc. sing. dec. 6a . . כבש
כָּכָה וְ' adv. *thus*; contr. from כֹּה כָּה i. q. כֹּה כֹּה *so and so*. Others take it as the pref. כּ with suff., *hoc tibi*.
כַּכֹּהֵן pref. כַּ for כְּהַ)(noun masc. sing. dec. 7b . כהן
כְּכוֹכְבֵי pref. כְּ)(noun m. pl. constr. from כּוֹכָב d. 2b כבב
כַּכּוֹכָבִים[d] pref. כַּ for כְּהַ)(id. pl., abs. st. . . כבב
כְּכוֹס[ff] pref. כְּ)(noun fem. sing. dec. 1a . . . כוס
כְּכֹחִי[e] וְ' pref. id.)(noun m. sing. dec. 1a; וּ bef. (:) כחח
כְּכֹחָם[f] pref. id.)(id., suff. 3 pers. pl. masc. . כחח
כְּכִיּוֹר[g] pref. כְּ)(noun masc. sing. dec. 1b . . כור
כְּכֹכְבֵי defect. for כְּכוֹכְבֵי (q. v.) . . . . כבב
כַּכֹּל[h] pref. כַּ f. כְּהַ ; כְּכֹל וְ' pref. כְּ ; כְּכָל־ וּ' pref. id. } noun masc. sing. dec. 8c (§ 37. rem. 2); וּ bef. (:) } כלל
כַּכֶּלֶב[k] pref. כַּ f. כְּהַ ; כְּכֶלֶב[l] pref. כְּ q. v. } noun masc. sing. (pl. c. כַּלְבֵי) dec. 6a . . . } כלב
כַּכַּלָּה[m] n' וְ' pref. כַּ for כְּהַ, & וְ)(noun fem. sing. d. 10 כלל
כִּכְלוּב[o] pref. כִּ bef. (:))(noun masc. sing. . . כלב
כְּכַלּוֹת וְ' pref. כְּ)(Piel inf. constr. d. 1b; וּ bef. (:) כלה
כִּכְלוֹת[p] pref. כִּ bef. (:))(Kal inf. constr. . . . כלה
כְּכַלּוֹתְךָ[q] pref. כְּ)(Piel inf. (כַּלּוֹת), suff. 2 pers. s. m. כלה
כְּכַלּוֹתָם וּ pref. id.)(id., suff. 3 pers. pl. masc.; וּ bef. (:) כלה
כִּכְלֵי[r] pref. כִּ bef. (:))(pl. constr. of the foll. . כלה
כִּכְלִי pref. id.)(noun masc. sing. irr. (§ 45) . כלה
כְּכַלֹּת[s] pref. כְּ)(for כַּלּוֹת Piel inf. c. dec. 1b . כלה
כְּכַלֹּתוֹ pref. id.)(id., suff. 3 pers. sing. masc. . כלה
כְּכַלֹּתְךָ[t] pref. id.)(id., suff. 2 pers. sing. masc. . כלה
כָּכֶם pref. prep. כּ with suff. 3 p. pl. m. (§ 5 parad.) כ
כַּכִּנּוֹר[u] pref. כַּ for כְּהַ)(noun masc. sing. dec. 1b . כנר
כְּכַנְפֵי[x] pref. כְּ)(n. fem. pl. c. from כָּנָף d. 4a (§ 33. r. 1) כנף
כַּכֶּסֶף[y] z' וְ' pref. כַּ for כְּהַ)(noun masc. sing. dec. 6a (for כֶּסֶף § 35. rem. 2) . . . כסף
כְּכַף pref. כְּ)(noun fem. sing. dec. 8d . . כפף
כַּכְּפִיר a' וְ' pref. כַּ for כְּהַ ; כִּכְפִיר b' וְ' pref. כִּ bef. (:) } noun masc. sing. dec. 1a כפר
כַּכְּפִירִים[c] pref. כַּ for כְּהַ)(id. pl., abs. st. . . כפר
כַּכֹּפֶר[d] pref. id.)(noun masc. sing. dec. 1a . . כפר
כַּכְּפִרִים[e] defect. for כַּכְּפִירִים (q. v.) . . . כפר
כִּכָּר noun fem. sing. dec. 2b [for כִּרְכָּר] . . כרר
כִּכַּר וְ' id., constr. st. . . . . . כרר
כִּכְּרוֹת id. pl. fem. constr. [of כִּכָּרוֹת] . . . כרר

כִּכְּרֵי noun pl. masc. constr. (of כִּכָּרִים) . . כרר
כְּכָרִים[f] pref. כְּ)(n. m., pl. of כַּר dec. 8 (§ 37. rem. 7) כרר
כִּכָּרַיִם[g] noun fem. with du. masc. term. from כִּכָּר dec. 2b [for כִּרְכָּר] . . . . כרר
כִּכָּרִים id. pl., abs. st. . . . . . כרר
כִּכָּרַיִם[h] id. du. (see כִּכָּר under the Root) . . כרר
כַּכְּרִין[i] Chald. id. pl. abs. st. . . . . כרר
כִּכְרַכְמִישׁ pref. כְּ)(pr. name of a place . . . כרר
כַּכַּרְמֶל וּ' pref. כַּ for כְּהַ)(pr. name of a place; וּ bef. (:) כרם
כִּכְתָב[k] Ch. pref. כִּ bef. (:))(n. m., constr. of כְּתָב d. 1b כתב
כִּכְתָבָהּ pref. כְּ)(noun masc. sing., suff. 3 pers. sing. fem. from כְּתָב dec. 1 (§ 30. rem. 1) . כתב
כִּכְתָבָם pref. id.)(id. with suff. 3 pers. pl. masc. . כתב
כַּכָּתוּב pref. כַּ for כְּהַ)(Kal part. pass. s. m. d. 3a כתב
כָּל וְ Kal pret. 3 pers. sing. masc. . . . כול
כֹּל וְ' ; כָּל־ וְ' } noun masc. sing. dec. 8c, comp. § 37. rem. 2 (Chald. dec. 5) . . . } כלל

[כָּלָא] I. *to shut up, confine*; intrans. *to be shut up*, Hag. 1. 10.—II. *to restrain, withhold*, with מִן of the person or thing. Niph. *to be restrained.*

כֶּלֶא masc. dec. 6a (with suff. כִּלְאוֹ).—I. *prison*, and so when preceded by בֵּית.—II. *separation*, hence du. כִּלְאַיִם *separate* or *distinct species* of animals, seeds or materials for clothing, Le. 19. 19; De. 22. 9.

כְּלוּא masc. *prison*, Je. 37. 4; 52. 31, Keri, Kheth. כְּלִיא.

מִכְלָה masc. (for מִכְלָא) pl. c. מִכְלְאוֹת *fold* or *pen for flocks, sheepfold.*

כֶּלֶא[m] defect. for כְּלוּא (q. v.) . . . כלא
כֶּלֶא noun masc. sing. (suff. כִּלְאוֹ) dec. 6a . כלא
כֹּלָּא Ch. by Syriasm [for כָּלָּא], emph. of כֹּל (q. v.) כלל
כֻּלָּה[n] for כֻּלָּהּ q. v. (§ 3. rem. 3) . . כלל
כִּלְאָב pr. name of a son of David, 2 Sa. 3. 3. Etymon uncertain.
כָּלְאָה[o] Kal pret. 3 pers. sing. fem. . . . כלא
כְּלֵאָה וּ pref. כְּ)(pr. name fem.; וּ bef. (:) . לאה
כָּלְאוּ[p] Kal pret. 3 pers. pl. . . . . כלא
כְּלָאוֹ[q] id. pret. 3 pers. sing. masc., suff. 3 pers. s. m. כלא
כִּלְאוֹ noun m. s., suff. 3 p. s. m. from כֶּלֶא d. 6a כלא
כְּלָאִים[r] id. pl., abs. st. . . . . . כלא
כִּלְאַיִם ; כִּלְאַיִם[s] } id. dual, abs. st. . . . . כלא

[a] Is. 17. 3. [b] Eze. 32. 7. [c] Joel 4. 15. [d] Da. 12. 3. [e] Jos. 14. 11.
[f] Ezr. 2. 69. [g] Zec. 12. 6. [h] Job 24. 24. [i] Nu. 9. 3. [k] Ps. 59. 7, 15.
[l] Pr. 26. 11. [m] Is. 49. 18. [n] Is. 61. 10. [o] Je. 5. 27. [p] Ps. 71. 9.
[q] 2 Sa. 11. 19. [r] Eze. 12. 4, 7. [s] De. 20. 9. [t] Je. 51. 63. [u] Is. 16. 11.
[x] Zec. 5. 9. [y] Pr. 2. 4. [z] Mal. 3. 3. [a] Ho. 5. 14. [b] Ps. 17. 12.
[c] Is. 5. 29. [d] Ex. 16. 14. [e] Je. 51. 38. [f] Je. 51. 40. [ff] Ps. 102. 7.
[g] 2 Ki. 5. 23. [h] 2 Ki. 5. 23. [i] Ezr. 7. 22. [k] Ezr. 6. 18.
[l] Is. 40. 12. [m] Ps. 88. 9. [n] Eze. 36. 5. [o] Hag. 1. 10.
[p] Hag. 1. 10. [q] Je. 32. 3. [r] Is. 42. 22. [s] Le. 19. 19.

כְּלָאָם[a] Kal imp. sing. masc., suff. 3 pers. pl. masc. כלא

כְּלָאתִי[b] id. pret. 1 pers. sing. (§ 23. rem. 9) . כלא

כָּלַב Root not used; supposed to be onomatopoetic, as imitating the sound of striking, Eng. *clap*, hence *to bark*; Arab. *to plait, braid.*

כָּלֵב (*barker*) pr. name—I. of a contemporary of Joshua, patronym. כָּלִבִּי 1 Sa. 25. 3.—II. 1 Ch. 2. 18, 19, כְּלוּבַי in ver. 9.—III. 1 Ch. 2. 50.—IV. כָּלֵב אֶפְרָתָה of an unknown place, 1 Ch. 2. 24.

כֶּלֶב masc. dec. 6a (pl. c. כַּלְבֵי) *dog.*

כְּלוּב masc.—I. *fruit-basket*, Am. 8. 1, 2.—II. *bird-cage*, Je. 5. 27.—III. pr. name masc. of two different persons, 1 Ch. 4. 11; 27. 26.

כָּלֵב וְ׳ pr. name masc. . . . . כלב

כָּלֶב[c] / כֶּלֶב } noun masc. sing. dec. 6a (§ 35. rem. 2) כלב

כְּלֵב pref. כְּ) noun masc. sing. dec. 6b . לבב

כִּלְבַב pref. כִּ bef. (:)) n. m., constr. of לֵבָב d. 4b לבב

כִּלְבָבוֹ pref. id.) id., suff. 3 pers. sing. masc. . לבב

כִּלְבָבֶךָ pref. id.) id., suff. 2 pers. s. m. (for לְבָבְךָ׳) לבב

כָּלִבּוֹ[d] Kh. כְּלִבּוֹ appellative (*as his own heart*); K. כָּלִבִּי patronym. of כָּלֵב . . . כלב

כַּלְבוּשׁ pref. כַּ for כְּהַ) noun masc. sing. dec. 1a לבש

כַּלְבֵי[e] noun masc. pl. constr. from כֶּלֶב dec. 6a . כלב

כְּלִבִּי[f] pref. כְּ) n. m. s., suff. 1 p. s. from לֵב d. 8b לבב

כַּלָּבִיא[g] pref. כַּ f. כְּהַ / וְ׳ כְּלָבִיא pref. כְּ q.v. } noun masc. sing.; וּ bef. (:) לבא

כְּלָבֶיךָ[h] noun masc. pl., suff. 2 pers. sing. masc. from כֶּלֶב dec. 6a . . . . כלב

כְלִבְּךָ וּ pref. כְּ) noun masc. sing., suff. 2 pers. sing. masc. from לֵב dec. 8b; וּ bef. (:) . . לבב

כְּלָבִים noun m. pl. abs. (c. כַּלְבֵי) from כֶּלֶב d. 6a כלב

כַּלְּבָנָה[i] pref. כַּ for כְּהַ) noun fem. sing. . . לבן

כַּלְּבָנוֹן pref. id.) pr. name of a mountain . . לבן

כָּלָה וְ׳ fut. יִכְלֶה, תִּכְלָה apoc. יִכֶל, וַתֵּכֶל (§ 24. rem. 3).—I. *to be completed, finished, ended*; hence *to be accomplished, fulfilled.*—II. *to be spent, wasted, destroyed; to waste away, pine.* Pi. כִּלָּה.—I. *to complete, finish, end.*—II. *to waste, ruin, destroy*; also *to cause to languish; to cause to vanish.* Pu. כֻּלָּה, כֻּלָּה (§ 10. rem. 5) *to be completed, finished.*

כָּלֶה f. כָּלָה adj. *languishing, pining*, De. 28. 32.

כָּלָה fem.—I. *completion*, only as an adv. *entirely, wholly.*—II. *destruction.*

כְּלִי masc. dec. 6 i, but pl. כֵּלִים (see § 45) constr. כְּלֵי.—I. *vessel, utensil.*—II. *boat, skiff.*—III. *implement, tool.*—IV. *weapons, arms.*—V. *equipment, clothing, dress.*

כִּלְיָה fem. dec. 12b, only pl. (כְּלָיוֹת) *the reins, kidneys*; meton. *the inward, secret parts*, denoting *the secret workings and affections* of the soul.

כִּלָּיוֹן masc. dec. 3c.—I. *consumption, destruction*, Is. 10. 22.—II. a *pining, wasting* of the eyes, De. 28. 65.

כִּלְיוֹן (*a pining*) pr. name, Ru. 1. 2; 4. 9.

מִכְלָה f. only pl. מִכְלוֹת *perfection*, 2 Ch. 4. 21.

תִּכְלָה fem. *perfection*, Ps. 119. 96.

תַּכְלִית f.—I. *completeness, perfection.*—II. *end, extremity, boundary.*

כָּלָה וְ׳ Kal pret. 3 pers. sing. masc., or noun f. s. כלה

כַּלָּה וְ׳[k] noun fem. sing. dec. 10 . . כלל

כַּלֵּה וְ׳[oo] Piel inf., or imp. sing. masc. . . כלה

כְּלָה׳[l] Chald. pref. כְּ) for לָא׳ adv. . . לא

כִּלָּה וְ׳ Piel pret. 3 pers. sing. masc. . . כלה

כֻּלֹּה noun m. s., suff. 3 pers. s. m. from כֹּל d. 8c כלל

כֻּלֹה id. with suff. 3 pers. sing. masc. . . כלל

כְלֶהָבָה[m] וּ pref. כְּ) noun fem. sing., pl. לְהָבוֹת, constr. לַהֲ׳ dec. 11a (§ 42. No. 3 note); וּ bef. (:) להב

כָּלְּהוֹן[n] Chald. for כֻּלְּהֵ׳ (§ 37. rem. 2); noun masc. sing. with suff. (Kh. הוֹן׳, 3 pers. pl. (K. הֵן) 3 pers. pl. fem. from כֹּל (q. v.) . כלל

כֻּלָּהֶם[o] n. m. s., suff. 3 p. pl. m. (§ 3. r. 5) fr. כֹּל d. 8c כלל

כָּלוּ[p] Kal pret. 3 pers. pl. for כָּלְאוּ (§ 23. rem. 11) כלא

כָּלוּ Kal pret. 3 pers. pl. . . . . כלה

כַּלּוּ[q] Piel imp. pl. masc. . . . . כלה

כִּלּוּ id. pret. 3 pers. pl. . . . . כלה

כֻּלּוּ[r] Pual pret. 3 pers. pl. [for כֻּלּוּ § 10. rem. 5] כלה

כֻּלּוֹ וְ׳ noun m. s., suff. 3 p. s. m. from כֹּל d. 8c כלל

כָּלוּא[s] Kal part. pass. sing. masc. . . . כלא

כְּלוֹא[t] pref. כְּ) לוֹא for לֹא adv. (q. v.) . . ל

כְלוּב[u] וּ׳ noun m. s., also pr. name m.; וּ bef. (:) כלב

כְּלוּבַי pr. name masc., see כָּלֵב . . . כלב

כַּלֹּוֶה[x] pref. כַּ for כְּהַ) Kal part. act. sing. masc. לוה

כְּלוּהִי[y] Kh. כְּלוּהַי, K. כְּלוּהוּ pr. name masc. Ezr. 10. 35. Etymon uncertain.

כְּלוּלֹתַיִךְ[y] [for תַיִךְ׳] n. f. pl. [כְּלוּלֹת], suff. 2 p. s. f. כלל

[a] Nu. 11. 28. [b] Ps. 119. 101. [c] Pr. 26. 17. [d] 1 Sa. 25. 3. [e] Job 30. 1. [f] Je. 3. 15. [g] Is. 5. 29. [h] Ps. 68. 24. [i] Ca. 6. 10. [k] Joel 2. 16. [l] Da. 4. 32. [m] Ps. 83. 15. [n] Da. 7. 19. [o] 2 Sa. 23. 6. [oo] 1 Sa. 3. 12. [p] 1 Sa. 6. 10. [q] Ex. 5. 13. [r] Ps. 72. 20. [s] Je. 32. 2. [t] Ob. 1. 16. [u] Am. 8. 1, 2. [x] Is. 21. 2. [y] Je. 2. 2.

כִּלּוּם[a] Piel pret. 3 pers. pl., suff. 3 pers. pl. masc. כלה

כִּלּוּנִי[b] id. with suff. 1 pers. pl. . . . . כלה

כָּלוֹת[c] ׀ adj. f. pl. of [כָּלָה] d. 11a, [from כָּלֶה m.] כלה

כַּלּוֹת[d] Piel inf. constr. dec. 1b . . . . כלה

כְּלוֹת Kal inf. constr. dec. 1a . . . . . כלה

כַּלֹּתִי Piel inf. (כַּלּוֹת), suff. 1 pers. sing. dec. 1b כלה

כְּלוּלֹתַיִךְ ׳ו ׀ n. f. pl., suff. 2 pers. pl. m. fr. כְּלוּלָה d. 10 כלל

כַּלֹּתְךָ[f] Piel inf. (כַּלּוֹת), suff. 2 pers. sing. m. d. 1b כלה

כַּלֹּתָם id., suff. 3 pers. pl. masc. . . . . כלה

כְּלוֹתָם[g] Kal inf. (כְּלוֹת), suff. 3 pers. pl. m. dec. 1a כלה

[כֶּלַח] masc.—I. *old age, full age*, Job 5. 26; 30. 2.—II. pr. name of a city, Ge. 10. 11, 12.

כָּלַח[h] noun masc. sing. for כֶּלַח, (§ 35. rem. 2) . כלח

כִּלְחֹךְ[i] pref. כְּ bef. (:)) Kal inf. constr. . . . לחך

כַּלֶּחֶם[k] pref. כַּ f. כְּהַ } noun com. sing. (suff. לַחְמִי) dec. 6a . . . לחם

כְּלֶחֶם[l] pref. כְּ q. v. }

כֵּלַי[m] ׀ adj. or subst. masc. sing. [for נִכְלַי] . נכל

כֵּלֵינוּ noun m. pl., suff. 1 p. pl., irr. of כְּלִי (§ 45) כלה

כְּלֵי ׳ו id. pl. constr. st.; וּ bef. (:) . . . כלה

כְּלִי ׳ו } id. sing. abs. st. (§ 35. rem. 14); וּ id. . כלה

כֶּלִי }

כֵּלֶיהָ id. pl., suff. 3 pers. sing. masc. (§ 45) . כלה

כְּלֵיהֶם id. id., suff. 3 pers. pl. masc. . . . כלה

כֵּלָיו ׳ו ׀ id. id., suff. 3 pers. sing. masc. . . כלה

כִּלָּיוֹן[n] noun masc. sing. dec. 3c . . . . כלה

כִּלְיוֹן[o] ׀ id., constr. st.; also pr. name masc. . כלה

כְּלָיוֹת ׳ו ׳p ׀ noun fem. pl. abs. from [כִּלְיָה] dec. 12b; וּ bef. (:) . . . . כלה

כִּלְיוֹת id. pl., constr. st. . . . . . כלה

כִּלְיוֹתָי } id. pl. with suff. 1 pers. sing. . . כלה

כִּלְיוֹתַי ׳ו ׳q }

כֵּלֶיךָ noun m. pl., suff. 2 p. s. m. irr. of כְּלִי (§ 45) כלה

כֶּלְיְךָ[r] id. sing., suff. 2 pers. sing. masc. . . כלה

כְּלֵיכֶם[s] id. pl., suff. 2 pers. pl. masc. . . . כלה

כָּלִיל ׳ו ׀ adj. masc. sing. dec. 3a . . . . כלל

כַּלַּיִל[t] pref. כַּ for כְּהַ) noun masc. sing. dec. 6h לול

כְּלֵיל[u] pref. כְּ) id., constr. st. . . . . לול

כְּלִיל ׳ו[x] adj. m. s. constr. of כָּלִיל dec. 3a; וּ bef. (:) כלל

כַּלַּיְלָה[y] ׀ pref. כַּ for כְּהַ) noun masc. sing. (לַיִל q. v.) with parag. ה . . . . . . לול

כְּלִילַת adj. fem., constr. of [כְּלִילָה] d. 10, fr. כָּלִיל m. כלל

כֵּלִים ׳ו ׀ noun masc. pl. irr. of כְּלִי (§ 45) . . כלה

כָּלִינוּ[z] Kal pret. 1 pers. pl. . . . . . כלה

כִּלִּינוּ[a] Piel pret. 1 pers. pl. . . . . . כלה

כִּלִּיתָ[b] ׀ Piel pret. 2 pers. sing. masc.) acc. shifted by conv. ׀ (comp. § 8. rem. 7) . . כלה

כָּלִיתִי[c] Kal pret. 1 pers. sing. . . . . כלה

כִּלִּיתִי[d] Piel pret. 1 pers. sing. . . . . כלה

כִּלְיֹתַי[e] } noun fem. pl., suff. 1 pers. sing. from [כִּלְיָה] dec. 12b . . . . } כלה

כִּלְיֹתַי ׳ו[f] }

כִּלִּיתִי[g] } Piel pret. 1 pers. sing. acc. shifted by conv. ׀ (§ 11. r. 24; comp. § 8. r. 7) } כלה

כִּלִּיתִי ׀ }

כִּלִּיתִיךָ[h] ׀ id. id., suff. 2 pers. sing. masc. . . כלה

כִּלִּיתִים[i] id. id., suff. 3 pers. pl. masc. . . . כלה

כִּלִּיתָם[k] id. pret. 2 pers. sing. m., suff. 3 pers. pl. m. כלה

כְּלִיתֶם ׳ו[l] ׳m Kal pret. 2 pers. pl. masc.; וּ for ׀ conv. כלה

כִּלִּיתֶם[n] Piel pret. 2 pers. pl. masc. . . . . כלה

כֻּלֵּךְ } noun masc. sing., suff. 2 pers. sing. fem. from כֹּל dec. 8c (§ 3. rem. 2) . } כלל

כֻּלֵּךְ[o] }

כַּלְכֵּל[p] Pilpel inf. constr. (§ 6. No. 4) . . . כול

כַּלְכֹּל ׀ pr. name masc. . . . . . . כול

כִּלְכֵּל[q] Pilpel pret. 3 pers. sing. masc. (§ 6. No. 4) כול

כָּלְכְּלוּ[r] ׀ Pulpal. pret. 3 pers. pl. (§ 6. No. 4) . כול

כִּלְכְּלוּ ׀ Pilpel pret. 3 pers. pl. (§ 6. No. 4) . כול

כִּלְכְּלָם[s] ׀ id. pret. 3 pers. s. m., suff. 3 pers. pl. m. כול

כִּלְכַּלְתִּי ׀ id. pret. 1 pers. sing., acc. shifted by conv. ׀ (comp. § 8. rem. 7) . . . . . כול

כִּלְכַּלְתָּם[t] id. pret. 2 pers. sing. m., suff. 3 pers. pl. m. כול

כֻּלְּכֶם ׳ו[u] ׀ noun m. s., suff. 2 p. pl. m. fr. כֹּל d. 8c כלל

[כָּלַל] *to complete*, Eze. 27. 4, 11.

כְּלַל Chald. Shaph. שַׁכְלֵל (§ 48) *to complete, finish.* Ishtaph. *to be finished*, Ezr. 4. 13, 16.

כְּלָל (*perfection*) pr. name masc. Ezr. 10. 30.

כֹּל, כּוֹל (only Je. 33. 8), כָּל־ dec. 8c.—I. *the whole*, expressive of totality; הַכֹּל *the whole*; before a noun sing. with the art.; also without it, when the noun is in the constr. st. or it has suff., or being a pr. name, as כָּל־הָאָרֶץ *the whole earth*; כָּל־עֲדַת יִשְׂרָאֵל *the whole congregation of Israel*; כָּל־יִשְׂרָאֵל *the whole* (people) *of Israel*; בְּכָל־לְבָבְךָ *with thy whole heart*; כֻּלֹּה, כֻּלּוֹ *the whole of it.*—II. *all*, before noun pl., as כָּל־הַגּוֹיִם *all nations*; abs. כֹּל, הַכֹּל *all, they all*; כֻּלָּנוּ *all of us*, כֻּלְּכֶם *all of you*, &c.; before a noun sing. collective, כָּל־הַחַיָּה *all*

---

[a] 2 Ch. 8. 8. [b] Ps. 119. 87. [c] De. 28. 32. [d] Nu. 7. 1. [e] Ho. 4. 13, 14. [f] Eze. 4. 8. [g] Je. 44. 27. [h] Job 30. 2. [i] Nu. 22. 4. [k] Ps. 102. 10. [l] Ho. 9. 4. [m] Is. 32. 7. [n] Is. 10. 22. [o] De. 28. 65 [p] Ps. 7. 10. [q] Ps. 73. 21. [r] De. 23. 25. [s] Ge. 45. 20. [t] Is. 16. 3. [u] Is. 30. 29. [x] Eze. 28. 12. [y] Job 5. 14. [z] Ps. 90. 7. [a] Ps. 90. 9. [b] Eze. 4. 6. [c] Ps. 39. 11. [d] Nu. 25. 11. [e] Ps. 139. 13. [f] Job 19. 27. [g] Is. 49. 4. [h] Ex. 33. 5. [i] Eze. 22. 31. [k] Je. 5. 3. [l] Mal. 3. 6. [m] Eze. 13. 14. [n] Ex. 5. 14. [o] Is. 14. 29, 31. [p] Je. 20. 9. [q] 2 Sa. 19. 33. [r] 1 Ki. 20. 27. [s] 1 Ki. 18. 4. [t] Ne. 9. 21. [u] Is. 65. 12.

living things.—III. *every*, before a noun without the art., כָּל־אִישׁ *every man.*—IV. *any one, any thing;* כָּל־דָּבָר *any thing, whatever;* with אֵין, לֹא *not any, no.*—V. *of all kinds, sorts.*—VI. adv. *altogether*, Ps. 39. 6; כָּל־עַד *as long as*, Job 27. 3; כָּל־עֻמַּת שֶׁ *wholly as, just as*, Ec. 5. 15.

כֹּל, כָּל־ Chald. emph. כֹּלָּא, with suff. כָּלְּהוֹן (§ 61) i. q. Heb. כֹּל Nos. I, II, IV, VI.

כָּלִיל masc. dec. 3a.—I. adj. *complete, perfect;* fem. כְּלִילַת, adverb, *wholly, entirely.*—II. subst. (*a*) *the whole;* (*b*) *whole burnt-offering.*

כְּלוּלוֹת fem. pl. (of כְּלוּלָה) *bridal state*, Je. 2. 2; Eng. Ver. « espousals."

כַּלָּה fem. d. 10.—I. *bride, spouse.*—II. *daughter-in-law.*

מִכְלוֹל masc. *perfection*, Eze. 23. 12; 38. 4.

מִכְלָל masc. dec. 2b, id. Ps. 50. 2.

מַכְלֻלִים masc. pl. (of מִכְלוֹל) *splendid things*, of costly garments, Eze. 27. 24.

כְּלָל וּ pr. name masc.; וּ bef. (:) . . . כלל

כָּלְלוּ[a] Kal pret. 3 pers. pl. . . . . כלל

כָּלַם. Hiph. הִכְלִים, הֶכְלִים (§ 11. rem. 1).—I. *to put to shame, make ashamed.*—II. *to injure, hurt.* Hoph. pass. 1 Sa. 25. 15; Je. 14. 3. Niph. *to be put to shame;* also *to feel ashamed*, with בְּ, מִן on account of anything.

כְּלִמָּה fem. dec. 10, *shame, ignominy.*

כְּלִמּוּת fem. id. Je. 23. 40.

כִּלָּם[b] Piel pret. 3 pers. sing. masc. (כִּלָּה), suff. 3 pers. pl. masc. (§ 24. rem. 21) . . כלה

כֻּלָּם וְ' noun m. s., suff. 3 p. pl. m. from כֹּל d. 8c כלל

כִּלְמַד pr. name of a region or city, Eze. 27. 23.

כְּלִמָּה וּ' noun fem. sing. dec. 10; וּ bef. (:) . כלם

כַּלְּמוּדִים[c] pref. כַּ for כְּהַ) adj. or subst. masc. pl. of [לָמוּד] dec. 1b . . . . למד

כְּלִמּוֹת[d] noun fem., pl. of כְּלִמָּה dec. 10 . . כלם

כְּלִמּוּת[e] וּ noun fem. sing.; וּ bef. (:) . . כלם

כְּלִמַּת noun fem. sing., constr. of כְּלִמָּה dec. 10 . כלם

כְּלִמָּתִי[f] וּ' id., suff. 1 pers. sing.; וּ bef. (:) . כלם

כְּלִמָּתֵךְ id., suff. 2 pers. sing. fem. . . . כלם

כְּלִמָּתָם id., suff. 3 pers. pl. masc. . . . כלם

כְּלִמָּתֵנוּ[g] id., suff. 1 pers. pl. . . . . כלם

כַּלְנֵה, כַּלְנֶה, כַּלְנוֹ pr. name of a city on the river Tigris, Ge. 10. 10; Is. 10. 9; Am. 6. 2.

כֻּלָּנָה[h] noun masc. sing., suff. 3 pers. sing. fem. (§ 3. rem. 5) from כֹּל dec. 8c . . כלל

כַּלְנוֹ pr. name of a place, see כַּלְנֵה.

כִּלָּנוּ[i] Piel pret. 3 pers. sing. masc. (כִּלָּה), suff. 1 pers. pl. (§ 24. rem. 21) . . כלה

כֻּלָּנוּ[k] וְ' noun m. sing., suff. 1 pers. pl. from כֹּל d. 8c כלל

כַּלַּעֲנָה[l] pref. כַּ for כְּהַ) noun fem. sing. . . לען

כָּלַף Root not used; prob. *to strike*, comp. כָּלַב.

כֵּילַפּוֹת fem. pl. *hammers* or *axes*, Ps. 74. 6.

כְּלַפִּיד[m] וּ' pref. כְּ) noun masc. sing. d. 1b; וּ bef. (:) לפד

כְּלַפִּידֵי[o] pref. כְּ) id. pl., constr. st. . . לפד

כַּלַּפִּידִים[p] pref. כַּ for כְּהַ) id. pl., abs. st. . . לפד

כִּלְשׁוֹן[q] וְ' pref. כְּ bef. (:)) noun com. sing., constr. of לָשׁוֹן dec. 3a . . . . . לשן

כִּלְשׁוֹנוֹ pref. id.) id., suff. 3 pers. sing. masc. . לשן

כִּלְשׁוֹנָם וְ pref. id.) id., suff. 3 pers. pl. masc. . לשן

כִּלְשֹׁנוֹ[r] defect. for כִּלְשׁוֹנוֹ (q. v.) . . . לשן

כָּלָתָה[s] in pause for כָּלְתָה (q. v. § 8. rem. 7) . כלה

כַּלָּתָהּ n. fem. s., suff. 3 pers. s. fem. from כַּלָּה d. 10 כלל

כָּלְתָה Kal pret. 3 pers. sing. fem. . . . כלה

כִּלְּתָה[t] וְ Piel pret. 3 pers. sing. fem. . . . כלה

כַּלָּתוֹ[nn] וְ' n. fem. s., suff. 3 pers. s. m. from כַּלָּה d. 10 כלל

כַּלֹּתוֹ Piel inf. (כַּלּוֹת), suff. 3 pers. sing. masc. d. 1b כלה

כִּלַּתּוּ[y] וְ Piel pret. 3 pers. sing. fem., suff. 3 pers. sing. masc. (§ 24. rem. 21) . . כלה

כְּלֹתוֹ[z] Kal inf. (כְּלוֹת), suff. 3 pers. sing. masc. d. 1a כלה

כַּלֹּתֶיהָ[a] וְ' n. fem. pl., suff. 3 p. s. fem. from כַּלָּה d. 10 כלל

כַּלָּתֵךְ[b]
כַּלָּתְךָ[c] } id. sing., suff. 2 pers. sing. masc. . כלל

כַּלֹּתַיִךְ[d] id. id., suff. 2 pers. sing. fem. . . כלל

כַּלֹּתָם defect. for כַּלּוֹתָם (q. v.) . . . כלה

כְּלִתְנִי[e] Kal pret. 2 pers. sing. fem. with suff. 1 pers. sing. (§ 23. rem. 11) . . . כלא

כְּמַאֲכֹלֶת[f] pref. כְּ) noun fem. sing. . . . אכל

כְּמֵאמַר[g] Chald. pref. כְּ) noun masc. sing. . . אמר

כִּמְבוֹא[h] pref. כְּ bef. (:)) n. m. s., constr. of מָבוֹא d. 3a בוא

כִּמְבוֹאֵי[i] pref. id.) id. pl., constr. st. . . בוא

כְּמֵבִיא[k] pref. כְּ) Hiph. part. sing. masc. dec. 3b . בוא

כְּמַבְכִּירָה[l] pref. id.) Hiph. part. sing. fem. , . בכר

כְּמִבְנֵה[m] pref. id.) noun m. sing., constr. of [מִבְנֶה] d. 9a בנה

כִּמְבַשֵּׂר[n] pref. כְּ bef. (:)) Piel part. sing. masc. . בשר

כְּמִגְדַּל pref. כְּ) noun m. sing., constr. of מִגְדָּל d. 2b גדל

כַּמִּגְדָּלוֹת[o] pref. כַּ for כְּהַ) id. with pl. fem. term., abs. st. גדל

[a] Eze. 27. 4, 11. [b] La. 2. 22. [c] Is. 50. 4. [d] Mi. 2. 6. [e] Je. 23. 40. [f] Ps. 69. 20. [g] Je. 3. 25. [h] Ge. 42. 36; Pr. 31. 29. [i] 2 Sa. 21. 5. [k] 2 Sa. 19. 7. [l] Pr. 5. 4. [m] Is. 62. 1. [n] Zec. 12. 6. [nn] 1 Sa. 4. 19. [o] Da. 10. 6. [p] Na. 2. 5. [q] Est. 1. 22. [r] Ne. 13. 24. [s] Est. 8. 9. [t] Est. 3. 12. [u] 1 Ki. 17. 16 [x] Ho. 11. 6. [y] Zec. 5. 4. [z] 2 Ch. 8. 16. [a] Ru. 1. 6, 7, 8. [b] Le. 18. 15. [c] Ge. 38. 24. [d] Ru. 4. 15. [e] 1 Sa. 25. 33. [f] Is. 9. 18. [g] Ezr. 6. 9. [h] Eze. 33. 31. [i] Eze. 26. 10. [k] Ps. 74. 5. [l] Je. 4. 31. [m] Eze. 40. 2. [n] 2 Sa. 4. 10. [o] Ca. 8. 10.

כַּמַּגֵּפָה[a] pref. id.)(noun fem. sing. dec. 10 . נגף

כַּמִּדְבָּר pref. כַּ for כְּהַ)(noun masc. sing. dec. 2 b . דבר

כְּמַדּוֹ[b] pref. כְּ)(noun masc. sing., suff. 3 pers. sing. masc. from מַד dec. 8 d & e . . מדד

כַּמִּדּוֹת[c] pref. כַּ f. כְּהַ } noun fem., pl. of מִדָּה dec. 10 מדד
כְּמִדּוֹת[qq] pref. כְּ q. v. }

כַּמְּדָיָן pref. id.)(pr. name of a people . . דין

כְּמַדְקְרוֹת[d] pref. id.)(noun fem. pl. c. [from מַדְקָרָה or מַדְקֵרָה] dec. 11 . . . . דקר

כְּמִדַּת[e] pref. id.)(noun fem. s., constr. of מִדָּה d. 10 מדד

כָּמַהּ to long for, desire ardently, Ps. 63. 2.

כִּמְהָם (longing) pr. name masc.; written also כִּמְהָם (Kh.), and כִּמְהָן.

כַּמָּה } וְ'[f] pref. כַּ for כְּהַ)(pron. interrog. with the pref. adverbially . . } מה
כַּמֶּה }

כְּמָה[g] Chald. pref. כְּ)(pron. interrog. . . מה

כְּמוֹהוּ וְ' defect. for כְּמוֹהוּ (q. v.) . . . . מו

כִּמְהַלֵּךְ[h] pref. כְּ bef. (:))(Piel part. sing. masc. d. 7 b הלך

כִּמְהָם }
וְ כִּמְהָן } pr. name masc. . . . . כמה

כְּמַהְפֵּכַת pref. כְּ)(n. fem. s., constr. of [מַהְפֵּכָה] d. 10 הפך

כְּמַהֵר[i] pref. id.)(Piel inf. constr. (§ 14. rem. 1) מהר

כְּמֹהַר[k] pref. id.)(noun masc. sing. . . . מהר

כְּמוֹ וּ' adv., prep. or conj.; וּ bef. (:) . . מו

כָּמוֹהָ id., suff. 3 pers. sing. fem. (§ 5, parad.) . מו

כָּמוֹהוּ[l] id., suff. 3 pers. sing. masc. . . . מו

כְּמוֹהֶם id., suff. 3 pers. pl. masc. . . . . מו

כְּמוֹהָם Kh. כְּמוֹהָם, K. כִּמְהָם pr. name masc. . כמה

כָּמוֹךָ adv. or prep. (כְּמוֹ), suff. 2 p. s. m. (§ 5, parad.) מו

כְּמוֹכֶם[m] id., suff. 2 pers. pl. masc. . . . מו

כַּמּוֹכֵר[n] pref. כַּ for כְּהַ)(Kal part. act. sing. m. d. 7 b מכר

כָּמוֹנוּ[o] adv. (כְּמוֹ) with suff. 1 pers. pl. . . מו

כָּמוֹנִי id. (& prep.) with suff. 1 pers. sing. . . מו

כַּמּוֹפֵת[p] pref. כַּ f. כְּהַ } noun masc. sing. dec. 7 b . יפת
כְּמוֹפֵת[q] pref. כְּ q. v. }

כְּמוֹץ[xx] pref. כְּ)(noun masc. sing. . . . . מוץ

כְּמוֹצָא[r] וּ pref. כְּ)(n. m. s. d. 1 b (§ 31. r. 1); וּ bef. (:) יצא

כְּמוֹצֵא[s] pref. id.)(Kal part. act. sing. masc. dec. 7 b מצא

כְּמוֹצָאֵי[t] pref. id.)(n. m. pl. c. fr. מוֹצָא d. 1 b (§ 31. r. 1) יצא

כְּמוֹצֵאת[u] pref. id.)(Kal part. act. fem. [for צֵאת' § 23. rem. 4], from מוֹצֵא masc. . . מצא

כְּמוֹקֵד[x] pref. id.)(noun masc. sing. dec. 7 b . יקד

כְּמוֹשׁ (perhaps subduer כָּבַשׁ=כָּמַשׁ) pr. name of an idol of the Moabites and Ammonites; עַם כְּ' the Moabites, Nu. 21. 29.

כַּמָּוֶת pref. כַּ for כְּהַ)(noun masc. sing. dec. 6 g מות

כְּמוֹת pref. כְּ)(id., constr. st. . . . מות

כְּמוֹתוֹ[y] וּ pref. id.)(id. with suff. 3 pers. s. m.; וּ bef. (:) מות

כָּמַז Root not used; Arab. to gather or compress into a roundish form.

כּוּמָז masc. bracelet, prob. of gold beads, Ex. 35. 22; Nu. 31. 50.

כַּמִּזְרָק[z] pref. כַּ for כְּהַ)(noun masc. sing. dec. 2 b זרק

כַּמִּזְרָקִים[a] pref. id.)(id., pl. absolute . . . זרק

כְּמַחֲבֵא[b] pref. כְּ)(noun masc. sing. . . . חבא

כְּמַחְלְקֹתָם pref. id.)(noun fem. pl., suff. 3 pers. pl. masc. from מַחֲלֹקֶת dec. 13 c . . . חלק

כִּמְחֹלַת[c] pref. כְּ bef. (:))(noun fem. sing., constr. of [מְחֹלָה] dec. 10 . . . חול

כְּמַחֲנֵה[d] pref. כְּ)(noun m. s., constr. of מַחֲנֶה d. 9 a חנה

כְּמַחֲרִישׁ[e] pref. id.)(Hiph. part. sing. masc. dec. 1 b חרש

כִּמְטַחֲוֵי[f] pref. כְּ bef. (:))(Pilel (§ 6. No. 2) part. pl. c. [from מְטַחֲוֶה 3rd rad. ה doubled and changed to ו for מְטַחֲהֶה § 24. r. 25] טחה

כְּמָטָל[g] pref. id.)(noun masc. sing. . . . מטל

כְּמַטְמֹנִים[h] וְ pref. כְּ)(noun masc., pl. of מַטְמוֹן dec. 1 b (§ 30. rem. 4) . . . . טמן

כַּמָּטָר וְ'[i] pref. כַּ f. כְּהַ } noun masc. sing. dec. 4 a מטר
כְּמָטָר[k] pref. כְּ q. v. }

כַּמַּטָּרָא[l] pref. כַּ for כְּהַ)(for מַטָּרָה' noun fem. sing. נטר

כַּמַּיִם pref. id. }
כַּמָּיִם וְ'[m] pref. id. } noun masc. pl. [of מַי irr. § 45, comp. § 38. rem. 2] } מי
כְּמַיִם pref. כְּ }

כְּמוֹשׁ Kh. כְּמִישׁ, K. כְּמוֹשׁ q. v.

כְּמַכְאֹבִי[n] pref. id.)(n. m. s., suff. 1 p. s. fr. מַכְאוֹב d. 1 b באב

כָּמֹכָה[o] prep. (כְּמוֹ) with suff. 2 pers. sing. masc. (§ 5, parad. & § 3. rem. 2) . . מו

כְּמַכַּת[p] pref. כְּ)(noun fem. s. constr. of מַכָּה d. 10 נכה

כַּמִּכְתָּב[q] pref. כַּ for כְּהַ)(noun masc. sing. dec. 2 b . כתב

כַּמְּלֵאָה[r] וְ pref. id.)(noun fem. sing. dec. 10 . מלא

כִּמְלֹאות[s] with ו in otio, see כִּמְלֹאת . . . מלא

כְּמַלְאַךְ pref. כְּ)(noun m. s., constr. of מַלְאָךְ d. 2 b לאך

כְּמַלְאָכִי[t] pref. id.)(id. with suff. 1 pers. sing. לאך

כִּמְלֹאת pref. כְּ bef. (:))(Kal inf. constr. (§ 23. r. 2) מלא

כַּמַּלְוֶה[u] pref. כַּ for כְּהַ)(noun masc. sing. . . לוה

כַּמְּלוּנָה[x] pref. כַּ for כְּהַ } noun fem. sing. . . . לון
כִּמְלוּנָה[y] pref. כְּ bef. (:) }

כַּמִּלְחָמָה[z] pref. כַּ for כְּהַ)(noun fem. sing. (suff. מִלְחַמְתּוֹ § 42. rem. 5) . . . . . לחם

[a] Zec. 14. 15. [b] Ps. 109. 18. [c] Eze. 40. 28, 29, 35. [d] Pr. 12. 18. [e] Eze. 40. 21, 22. [f] Zec. 2. 6. [g] Da. 3. 33. [h] Pr. 6. 11. [i] Pr. 7. 23. [k] Ex. 22. 16. [l] Eze. 5. 9. [m] Job 12. 3. [n] Is. 24. 2. [o] Is. 14. 10. [p] 1 Ki. 13. 5. [q] Ps. 71. 7. [qq] 1 Ki. 7. 9, 11. [r] Is. 58. 11. [s] Ps. 119. 162. [t] Eze. 12. 4. [u] Ca. 8. 10. [x] Ps. 102. 4. [xx] Zeph. 2. 2. [y] 2 Ch. 24. 22. [z] Zec. 9. 15. [a] Zec. 14. 20. [b] Is. 32. 2. [c] Ca. 7. 1. [d] 1 Ch. 12. 22. [e] 1 Sa. 10. 27. [f] Ge. 21. 16. [g] Job 40. 18. [h] Pr. 2. 4. [i] Pr. 26. 1. [k] Ps. 72. 6. [l] La. 3. 12. [m] 2 Sa. 14. 14. [n] La. 1. 12. [o] Ex. 15. 11. [p] Is. 10. 26. [q] De. 10. 4. [r] Nu. 18. 27. [s] Je. 25. 12. [t] Is. 42. 19. [u] Is. 24. 2. [x] Is. 24. 20. [y] Is. 1. 8. [z] Ju. 20. 39.

כְּמֶלֶךְ pref. כְּ)(noun masc. sing. (suff. מַלְכִּי), d. 6a — מלך
כְּמָלְכוֹ[a] pref. id.)(Kal inf. with suff. 3 pers. sing. m. — מלך
כְּמַלְכֵי[b] pref. id.)(noun masc. pl. c. from מֶלֶךְ d. 6a — מלך
כְּמַלְקוֹשׁ[c] pref. id.)(noun masc. sing. . . — לקש
כִּמְלַקֵּט[d] pref. כִּ bef. (:))(Piel part. sing. masc. d. 7b — לקט

כָּמַן Root not used; Syr. & Arab. *to lay up*.
מִכְמָן masc. *treasure*, only pl. c. מִכְמַנֵּי (dec. 8a) Da. 11. 43

כַּמֹּן ו׳ masc. *cummin*, a herb, Is. 28. 25, 27.
כְּמִנְהַג[e] pref. כְּ)(noun m. s., constr. of מִנְהָג d. 2b — נהג
כָּמֹנוּ prep. (כְּמוֹ) with suff. 1 pers. pl. (§ 5, parad.) — מו
כִּמְנוֹר pref. כִּ bef. (:))(noun masc. sing. constr. of מָנוֹר dec. 3a, R. נור see . . . — ניר
כַּמִּנְחָה[f] [g]וְ׳ pref. כַּ for כְּהַ)(noun fem. sing. dec. 12b — מנח
כְּמִנְחַת pref. כְּ)(id. constr. st. . . . — מנח
כָּמֹנִי defect. for כָּמוֹנִי (q. v.) . . . — מו
כִּמְנַשֶּׁה וְ pref. כִּ bef. (:))(pr. name masc. — נשה

[כָּמַס] *to lay up, treasure up*, De. 32. 34.
מִכְמָס (*treasure*), also מִכְמָשׁ, מִכְמַשׁ pr. name of a city in the tribe of Benjamin, 1 Sa. 13. 2, 5; Ezr. 2. 27; Ne. 11. 31.
כָּמֻס[h] Kal part. pass. sing. masc. [for כָּמוּס] . — כמס
כִּמְסוֹס[i] pref. כִּ bef. (:) Kal inf. constr. . . — מסס
כְּמַסִּיגֵי[k] pref. כְּ)(Hiph. part. pl. c. m. fr. מַסִּיג d. 1b — נסג
כְּמִסְפַּד[l] pref. id.)(constr. of the following . . — ספד
כְּמִסְפֵּד[m] pref. id.)(noun masc. sing. dec. 7c . — ספד
כַּמִּסְפָּר[n] pref. כַּ for כְּהַ)(noun masc. sing. dec. 2b — ספר
כְּמִסְפַּר[o] pref. כְּ)(id. constr. st. . . . — ספר
כְּמִסְפָּרָם[p] pref. id.)(id., suff. 3 pers. pl. masc. . — ספר
כְּמַסְתִּר[q] וּ pref. id.)(Hiph. part. for מַסְתִּיר (§ 11. rem. 8); וּ bef. (:) . . . — סתר
כִּמְעוֹתָיו[r] pref. כִּ bef. (:))(noun masc. with pl. fem. term. and suff. from [מֵעַ] dec. 7a . — מע
כִּמְעַט / כִּמְעָט } pref. id.)(adj. masc. sing. (pl. מְעַטִּים) dec. 8d . . . . } — מעט
כַּמְּעִיל / כִּמְעִיל[s] pref. כַּ f. כְּהַ / pref. כִּ bef. (:) } noun masc. sing. dec. 1a — מעל
כִּמְעַלְלָיו[t] pref. כִּ)(noun masc. pl., suff. 3 pers. sing. masc. from [מַעֲלָל] dec. 2b . . — עלל
כְּמַעַלְלֵינוּ[u] וּ pref. id.)(id. pl., suff. 1 p. pl.; וּ bef. (:) — עלל
כְּמַעַר[x] pref. כְּ)(noun masc. sing. (with suff. מַעֲרֵךְ) — ערה
כַּמַּעֲשֶׂה[y] pref. כַּ for כְּהַ)(noun masc. sing. dec. 9a — עשה
כְּמַעֲשֵׂה וּ׳ pref. כְּ)(id. constr. st.; וּ bef. (:) . — עשה

כְּמַעֲשֵׂהוּ pref. id.)(id., suff. 3 pers. sing. masc. . — עשה
כְּמַעֲשֵׂיהֶם[z] pref. id.)(id. pl., suff. 3 pers. pl. masc. — עשה
כְּמַעֲשָׂיו[a] pref. id.)(id. pl., suff. 3 pers. sing. masc. — עשה
כְּמַעֲשֶׂיךָ pref. id.)(id. pl., suff. 2 pers. sing. masc. — עשה
כִּמְפְּנֵי[b] pref. id.)(noun masc. pl., constr. of פָּנִים, from [פָּנֶה] dec. 9b . . — פנה
כִּמְפַתֵּחַ[c] pref. כִּ bef. (:))(Piel part. sing. masc. . — פתח
כַּמֹּץ / כְּמֹץ pref. כַּ f. כְּהַ / ו׳ pref. כְּ q. v. } noun masc. sing.; וּ bef. (:) — מוץ
כְּמִצְבְּיֵהּ[d] וּ Chald. pref. id.)(Peal inf. [מִצְבָּא], suff. 3 pers. sing. masc. dec. 6a; וּ id. . — צבא
כַּמִּצְוָה[e] וְ pref. כַּ for כְּהַ)(noun fem. sing. dec. 10 — צוה
כְּמִצְוֹת[f] ו׳ pref. כְּ)(id. constr. st.; וּ bef. (:) . — צוה
כִּמְצַחֵק[g] pref. כִּ bef. (:))(Piel inf. constr. (§ 14. r. 1) — צחק
כַּמָּק[h] pref. כַּ for כְּהַ)(noun masc. sing. . — מקק
כִּמְקוֹם[i] pref. כִּ bef. (:))(noun com. sing., constr. of מָקוֹם dec. 3a . . . . . — קום
כְּמִקְרְבַהּ[k] וּ Chald. pref. כְּ)(Peal inf. [מִקְרַב], suff. 3 pers. sing. fem. dec. 2a; וּ bef. (:) . — קרב
כְּמִקְרֵה[l] pref. כְּ)(noun m. s., constr. of מִקְרֶה d. 9a — קרה

כָּמַר. Niph.—I. *to be burned, be black with burning*, La. 5. 10.—II. trop. *to be warmed, kindled*, of love, or compassion.—III. according to the derivatives, i. q. כָּבַר *to plait, braid*.
כֹּמֶר masc. only pl. (כְּמָרִים § 35. rem. 9) *idolatrous priests*.
כִּמְרִיר masc. dec. 1b, *blackness* or *heat*, trop. for *calamity*, Job 3. 5.
מִכְמָר, מַכְמֹר masc. dec. 2b, *a net, snare*, Ps. 141. 10; Is. 51. 20.
מִכְמֶרֶת f. d. 13a (with suff. ׳מַרְתּוֹ) *fishing-net*.
כְּמַר[m] pref. כְּ)(noun masc. sing. dec. 8 (§ 37. r. 7) — מרר
כַּמַּרְאֶה pref. כַּ for כְּהַ)(noun masc. sing. dec. 9a — ראה
כְּמַרְאֵה[n] ו׳ pref. כְּ)(id. constr. st.; וּ bef. (:) — ראה
כִּמְרַגְּלִים[o] pref. כִּ bef. (:))(Piel part. masc., pl. of [מְרַגֵּל] dec. 7b . . . . — רגל
כִּמְרִיבָה pref. id.)(pr. name of a place . . — ריב
כִּמְרִיבֵי[p] pref. id.)(Kal part. pl. c. m. from [מֵרִיב] d. 3b — ריב
כִּמְרִימֵי[q] pref. id.)(Hiph. part. pl. c. m. from מֵרִים d. 3b — רום
כְּמָרָיו[r] וּ noun masc. pl. (כְּמָרִים), suff. 3 pers. sing. m. — כמר
כִּמְרִירֵי[s] noun masc. pl. constr. from [כִּמְרִיר] dec. 1b — כמר
כְּמַרְעִיתָם[t] pref. כְּ)(noun fem. sing., suff. 3 pers. pl. masc. from מַרְעִית dec. 1b . . — רעה
כִּמְרֻצַת[u] pref. כִּ bef. (:))(n. fem. s., constr. of מְרוּצָה d. 10 — רוץ
כַּמֶּרְקָחָה[x] pref. כַּ for כְּהַ)(noun fem. sing. . . — רקח

---

a 1 Ki. 15. 29. b 2 Ki. 17. 2. c Ho. 6. 3. d Is. 17. 5. e 2 Ki. 9. 20. f Le. 5. 13. g Eze. 45. 25. h De. 32. 34. i Is. 10. 18. k Ho. 5. 10. l Zec. 12. 11. m Zec. 12. 10. n Nu. 15. 12. o 1 Ki. 18. 31. p Nu. 15. 12. q Is. 53. 8. r Is. 48. 19. s Job 29. 14. t Ho. 12. 3. u Zec. 1. 6. x 1 Ki. 7. 36. y 1 Ki. 7. 8. z Ex. 23. 24. a Ne. 6. 14. b Le. 26. 37. c 1 Ki. 20. 11. d Da. 4. 32. e 2 Ki. 17. 34. f 2 Ch. 30. 6. g Ge. 19. 14. h Is. 5. 24. i Je. 19. 13. k Da. 6. 21. l Ec. 2. 15. m Is. 40. 15. n Eze. 43. 3. o Ge. 42. 30. p Ho. 4. 4. q Ho. 11. 4. r Ho. 10. 5. s Job 3. 5. t Ho. 13. 6. u 2 Sa. 18. 27. x Job 41. 23.

כְּמַשָּׂא[a] pref. כְּ)(noun masc. sing. dec. 1b . נשא

כְּמֹשֶׁה pref. id.)(pr. name masc. . . משה

כְּמֵשִׁיב[b] pref. id.)(Hiph. part. sing. masc. dec. 3b שוב

כְּמִשְׁכַּב[c] pref. id.)(noun m. s., constr. of מִשְׁכָּב d. 2b שכב

כִּמְשֻׂכַת[d] pref. כְּ bef. (:))(noun fem. sing. constr. of [מְשׂוּכָה] dec. 10 . . . . שוך

כְּמָשְׁלוֹ[e] pref. כְּ)(Kal inf., suff. 3 pers. sing. masc. משל

כִּמְשֻׁלָּם[f] pref. כְּ bef. (:))(Pual part. sing. masc. . שלם

כְּמִשְׁלֹשׁ[g] pref. כְּ)(noun masc. sing. . . שלש

כְּמִשְׁפְּחוֹת[h] pref. id.)(noun fem. pl., constr. from מִשְׁפָּחָה dec. 11a (but comp. § 42. rem. 5) . שפח

וּכְמַשְׂמְרוֹת[i] וּ pref. id.)(for מַסְמְרוֹת noun masc. with pl. fem. term. from [מַסְמֵר] dec. 7b; וּ bef. (:) סמר

כַּמִּשְׁפָּט pref. כַּ f. כְּהַ } noun masc. sing. dec. 2b . שפט
כְּמִשְׁפָּט pref. כְּ q. v. }

כְּמִשְׁפַּט pref. id.)(id. constr. st. . . . שפט

וּכְמִשְׁפָּטוֹ[k] וּ' pref. id.)(id., suff. 3 pers. s. m.; וּ bef. (:) שפט

וּכְמִשְׁפְּטֵי וּ pref. id.)(id. pl., constr. st.; וּ id. שפט

וּכְמִשְׁפְּטֵיהֶן[l] וּ pref. id.)(id. pl., suff. 3 pers. pl. m.; וּ id. שפט

כְּמִשְׁפָּטֶיךָ[m] pref. כְּ)(id. pl., suff. 2 pers. sing. masc. שפט

כַּמִּשְׁפָּטִים[n] pref. כַּ for כְּהַ)(id. pl., abs. st. . . שפט

כְּמִשְׁפָּטֶךָ[o] pref. כְּ)(id. pl., suff. 2 p. s. m. for ־ֶיךָ (§ 4. r. 1) שפט

וּכְמִשְׁפָּטָם[p] וּ' pref. id.)(id. s., suff. 3 pers. pl. m.; וּ bef. (:) שפט

כְּמַשַּׁק[q] pref. כְּ)(noun masc. sing. constr. [of מַשָּׁק] שקק

כְּמִשְׁתֵּה[r] pref. id.)(noun m. s., constr. of מִשְׁתֶּה d. 9a שתה

כַּמֵּת[s] pref. כַּ f. כְּהַ } Kal part. sing. masc. dec. 1a
כְּמֵת[t] pref. כְּ q. v. } (§ 21. r. 2, & § 30. No. 3) } מות

כְּמִתְאֹנְנִים[u] pref. id.)(Hithpo. part. pl. m. fr. [מִתְאוֹנֵן] d. 7b אנן

כְּמֵתֵי pref. כְּ)(Kal part. pl. masc. constr. from מֵת dec. 1a (§ 21. rem. 2, & § 30. No. 3) . מות

כַּמֵּתִים[x] pref. כַּ for כְּהַ)(id. pl., abs. st. . מות

כְּמִתְלַהְלֵהַּ[y] pref. כְּ)(Hithpalp. part. sing. masc. (§ 6. r. 4) להה

כְּמִתְלַהֲמִים pref. id.)(Hithpa. (§ 14. rem. 1) part. masc., pl. of [מִתְלַהֵם] dec. 7b . להם

כְּמַתְּנַת[z] pref. id.)(n. fem. s., constr. of מַתָּנָה d. 11a נתן

כִּמְתַעְתֵּעַ[a] pref. כְּ bef. (:))(Pilp. part. sing. m. (§ 6. r. 4) תעע

כֵּן noun m.s. (suff. כַּנּוֹ, pl. כַּנִּים d. 8b, § 37. r. 1) כנן

כֵּן וְ'
כֵּן } adj. masc. sing. dec. 1a; or adv. . כון
כֵּן

כְּנֹאד[b] pref. כְּ)(noun masc. sing. dec. 1a . נאד

כְּנָבָל pref. id.)(pr. name masc. . . נבל

כִּנְבֹל[c] pref. כְּ bef. (:))(Kal inf. constr. . נבל

וּכִנְבֶלֶת[d] וּ pref. כְּ)(Kal part. act. sing. fem. (§ 8. rem. 19); וּ bef. (:) . . . נבל

כְּנֶגְדּוֹ[e] pref. id.)(prep. נֶגֶד with suff. 3 pers. sing. masc. dec. 6 (§ 35. rem. 3) . נגד

כַּנֹּגַהּ[f] pref. כַּ for כְּהַ)(noun masc. sing. (suff. נָגְהוֹ), dec. 6c (§ 35. rem. 5) . . . נגה

כְּנַגֵּן[g] pref. כְּ)(Piel inf. constr. . . . נגן

כְּנֶגַע[h] pref. id.)(n. m. s. (suff. נִגְעִי), d. 6a (§ 35. r. 5) נגע

כַּנֵּד[i] pref. כַּ for כְּהַ)(noun masc. sing. . נדד

כַּנִּדְגָּלוֹת[k] pref. id.)(Niph. part. fem. pl. [of נִדְגָּלָה, from נִדְגָּל masc.] . . . דגל

כְּנִדָּתָהּ[l] pref. כְּ)(n. fem. s., suff. 3 p. s. from נִדָּה d. 10 נדה

כָּנָה. Pi.—I. *to call by name.*—II. *to call by flattering names* or *titles*, i. e. to flatter, Job 32. 21, 22.

כְּנָוֹת כְּנָת fem. *companion, associate*, only pl. (§ 45) Ezr. 4. 7.

כְּנָת Chald. fem. id. pl. with suff. כְּנָוָתֵהּ, comp. the preceding.

כְּנֵמָא Chald. adv. (for כִּנְאמָא) *namely; hence, thus, in this manner.* Others take כְּ as a prefix and נֵמָא for נְאֵמָא (from נְאַם) *according to the saying*; or נֵמָא for נֵאמַר, נֵימַר, נֵימָא (from אמר) *as is said*, or *as we say.*

כַּנָּה[m] וְ noun fem. sing. . . . . כנן

כְּנַהֲמַת[n] pref. כְּ)(noun fem. sing., constr. of [נְהָמָה] dec. 11c (§ 42. rem. 1) . . . נהם

כַּנָּהָר pref. כַּ f. כְּהַ } noun masc. sing. dec. 4a נהר
כְּנָהָר[o] pref. כְּ q. v. }

כַּנְּהָרוֹת[p] וְ'[q] pref. כַּ for כְּהַ)(id. pl., abs. st. . נהר

כַּנֵּה וְ pr. name of a place, see כַּלְנֵה.

כַּנּוֹ[r] וְ' noun m. s., suff. 3 p. s. m. from כֵּן d. 8d & e כנן

כְּנוֹחַ[s] וּ' pref. כְּ)(Kal inf. constr. (§ 21. r. 3); וּ bef. (:) נוח

כְּנוֹס[t] pref. id.)(Kal inf. constr. (§ 21. r. 3), or imp. s. m. כנס

כְּנוֹעַ[u] pref. id.)(Kal inf. constr. (§ 21. rem. 3) נוע

כִּנּוֹר וְ' noun masc. sing. dec. 1b . . כנר

כִּנּוֹרוֹתֵינוּ[x] id. pl. fem., suff. 1 pers. pl. כנר

כִּנּוֹרַיִךְ[y] id. pl. masc., suff. 2 pers. sing. fem. . כנר

כְּנָוָתֵהּ[z] וּ Chald. noun. fem. sing., suff. 3 pers. sing. m. [from כְּנָת irr. § 45]; וּ bef. (:) . כנה

כְּנָוָתְהוֹן[a] וְ' Chald. id. with suff. 3 pers. pl. masc. . כנה

כְּנוֹתָו[b] Heb. id. pl., suff. 3 pers. sing. masc. . כנה

כַּנַּחַל[c] pref. כַּ for כְּהַ } noun masc. sing. dec. 6d;
וּכְנַחַל[d] וּ' pref. כְּ q. v. } וּ bef. (:) . . } נחל

כִּנְחָלִים[e] pref. כְּ bef. (:))(id. pl., abs. st. . נחל

כַּנָּחָשׁ pref. כַּ f. כְּהַ } noun masc. sing. dec. 4a נחש
כְּנָחָשׁ[f] pref. כְּ q. v. }

כַּנְּחֻשָׁה[g] pref. כַּ for כְּהַ)(adj. fem. sing. from נָחוּשׁ m. נחש

כִּנְטוֹת[h] pref. כְּ bef. (:))(Kal inf. c. dec. 1b נטה

כִּנְטוֹתוֹ[i] pref. id.)(id., suff. 3 pers. sing. masc. נטה

---

a Ps. 38. 5. b Ge. 38. 29. c Le. 15. 26. d Pr. 15. 19. e Da. 11. 4. f Is. 42. 19. g Ge. 38. 24. h Eze. 20. 32. i Ec. 12. 11. k Nu. 9. 14. l Eze. 42. 11. m Ps. 119. 156. n 2 Ki. 17. 34. o Ps. 119. 149. p 2 Ki. 17. 34. q Is. 33. 4. r 1 Sa. 25. 36. s Nu. 12. 12. t Ps. 31. 13. u Nu. 11. 1. x Is. 59. 10. y Pr. 26. 18. z De. 16. 17. a Ge. 27. 12. b Ps. 119. 83. c Is. 34. 4. d Is. 34. 4. e Ge. 2. 18, 20. f Is. 62. 1. g 2 Ki. 3. 15. h Le. 14. 35. i Ps. 33. 7. k Ca. 6. 4, 10. l Le. 12. 5. m Ps. 80. 16. n Is. 5. 30. o Is. 66. 12. p Ps. 78. 16.; Je. 46. 7. q Je. 46. 8. r Ex. 30. 18. s Ne. 9. 28. t Ec. 3. 5; Est. 4. 16. u Is. 7. 2. x Ps. 137. 2. y Eze. 26. 13. z Ezr. 5. 6. a Ezr. 4. 9, 17. b Ezr. 4. 7. c La. 2. 18. d Is. 66. 12. e Nu. 24. 6. f Pr. 23. 32. g Le. 26. 19. h Jos. 8. 19. i Ps. 109. 23.

[a]כִּנְטָעִים pref. id.)(noun masc., pl. of [נָטִיעַ] dec. 3a נטע

[b]כַּנִּי noun m. s., suff. 1 pers. s. from כֵּן d. 8d & e כנן

כָּנְיָהוּ pr. name masc., see יְהוֹיָכִין . . . הוה

[c]כֵּנִים adj. masc., pl. of כֵּן dec. 1a . . . . כון

כִּנִּים noun masc., pl. of כֵּן dec. 8b (§ 37. rem. 1) כנן

[d]כַּנֶּךָ id. sing., suff. 2 pers. sing. masc. [for כַּנְּךָ] כנן

[e]כְּנַלֹּתְךָ pref. כְּ)(contr. [for כְּהַנְלֹתְךָ], Hiph. inf., suff. 2 pers. sing. masc. . . . . נלה

[f]כְּנֵמָא ו׳ Chald. adv.; וּ bef. (:) . . . . כנה

[g]כִּנְמַר pref. כְּ)(noun masc. sing. dec. 5a . נמר

[h]כִּנְמַר Chald. pref. כְּ bef. (:))(noun masc. sing. . נמר

כְּנִמְרֹד pref. כְּ)(pr. name masc. . . . . מרד

כָּנַן Root not used; prob. i. q. כּוּן q. v. In the Arab. *to protect.*

כֵּן masc. dec. 8 (with suff. כַּנִּי § 37. rem. 1).—I. *place, station.*—II. *base, pedestal,* of the base or foot of the laver.

כֵּן masc. (in the sing. perhaps, Is. 51. 6) pl. כִּנִּים *lice;* Sept. σκνῖφες, Vulg. *sciniphes,* a species of small *gnats.*

כַּנָּה fem. *plant;* or *stock, root,* Ps. 80. 16.

כִּנָּם i. q. the preceding כִּנִּים *lice* or *gnats,* Ex. 8. 13, 14.

כְּנָנִי (*protector*) pr. name masc. Ne. 9. 4.

כְּנַנְיָהוּ (whom *the Lord protects*) pr. name masc.

כְּנַנְיָהוּ (id.) pr. name masc. called also כְּנַנְיָה comp. 1 Ch. 15. 22, with ver. 27.

כְּנָנִי pr. name masc. . . . . . . כנן

כְּנַנְיָה ו׳ / כְּנַנְיָהוּ ו׳ } pr. name masc.; וּ bef. (:) . . כנן

כֹּנַנְתִּי וְ Pilel pret. 1 pers. sing.; acc. shifted by conv. וְ (comp. § 8. rem. 7) . . כון

[כָּנַס] *to collect, gather together, assemble.* Pi. id. Hithp. *to collect oneself,* i. e. *to wrap oneself up,* Is. 28. 20.

מִכְנָס m. d. 2b, only in pl. or du. constr. מִכְנְסֵי *trowsers* or *drawers,* for the priests, comp. Hithp.

[i]כַּנֵּס וְ pref. כַּ for כְּהַ)(noun masc. sing. dec. 8b נסס

[k]כֹּנֵס Kal part. act. sing. masc. . . . . כנס

[l]כְּנִסְכָּהּ וּ pref. כְּ)(noun masc. sing., suff. 3 pers. sing. fem. from נֶסֶךְ dec. 6a; וּ bef. (:) . . נסך

[m]כְּנִסְכּוֹ וּ pref. id.)(id., suff. 3 pers. sing. masc.; וּ id. נסך

[n]כָּנַסְתִּי Kal pret. 1 pers. sing. . . . . כנס

[o]כִּנַּסְתִּי וְ Piel pret. 1 pers. sing.; acc. shifted by conv. וְ (comp. § 8. rem. 7) . . כנס

[p]כִּנַּסְתִּים וְ id. with suff. 3 pers. pl. masc. . . כנס

כָּנַע. Hiph. *to bow down, bring low, humble, subdue.* Niph.—I. *to be humbled, subdued.*—II. *to humble oneself, to submit,* with מִלִּפְנֵי, מִפְּנֵי, לִפְנֵי.

כִּנְעָה fem. dec. 11c, *bundle, package, bale,* from the idea of *folding together,* Je. 10. 17.

כְּנַעַן (*low*) pr. name—I. of a son of Ham.—II. of the land inhabited by his posterity.—III. *merchant* (comp. כְּנַעֲנִי No. II.); pl. with suff. כִּנְעָנֶיהָ (§ 35. r. 5).

כְּנַעֲנִי, fem. כְּנַעֲנִית, pl. masc. כְּנַעֲנִים gent. noun —I. *Canaanite,* inhabitant of Canaan, collect. *Canaanites.*—II. *merchant,* like כַּשְׂדִּי Chaldean, for *astrologer.*

[q]כִּנְעוּרֶיהָ pref. כְּ bef. (:))(n. m. pl. (נְעוּרִים), suff. 3 p. s. m. נער

כְּנַעַן ו׳ / כְּנָעַן ו׳ } pr. name of a man and a people; וּ bef. (:) . . . . . כנע

[r]כִּנְעָן noun masc. sing. (§ 35. rem. 5) . . כנע

כְּנַעֲנָה ו׳ pr. name masc.; וּ bef. (:) . . . כנע

כְּנַעֲנִי gent. noun from כְּנַעַן, also as an appellative כנע

[s]כִּנְעָנֶיהָ noun masc. pl., suff. 3 pers. sing. fem. from כִּנְעָן dec. 6 (§ 35. rem. 5) . . כנע

כְּנַעֲנִים gent. noun, pl. of כְּנַעֲנִי from כְּנַעַן . . כנע

[t]כְּנַעֲנִים noun masc., pl. of כְּנַעֲנִי (comp. § 35. rem. 5) כנע

[u]כַּנַּעַר pref. כַּ for כְּהַ)(noun masc. sing. dec. 6d נער

[x]כִּנְעָתֵךְ noun fem. sing., suff. 2 pers. sing. fem. [from כִּנְעָה or כְּנָעָה] . . . כנע

כָּנָף fem. dec. 4a (du. c. כַּנְפֵי, pl. c. כַּנְפוֹת § 33. rem. 1).—I. *wing* of a bird; עוֹף כָּנָף *bird of wing,* i. e. *winged bird;* בַּעַל כָּנָף *possessor of wings,* i. e. *bird.* Metaph. for *swiftness* כַּנְפֵי רוּחַ, כַּ׳ שַׁחַר *wings of the wind, morning;* as the means of protection, צֵל כְּנָפַיִם *shadow of wings.*—II. *wing* of an army, Is. 8. 8.—III. *extremity, extreme part, corner,* as of the earth.—IV. *skirt* of the loose flowing upper garment.—V. perhaps *pinnacle,* Da. 9. 28, *upon the pinnacle of abomination,* i. e. the temple filled with abominations.

כָּנַף. Niph. *to be removed to a distant part,* Is. 30. 20. Others, *to be hid,* or *hide oneself,* coll. with the Arabic.

כְּנַף ו׳ id. constr. st.; וּ bef. (:) . . . כנף

[y]כְּנָפָיו id. pl., suff. 3 pers. sing. masc. (§ 4. rem. 1) כנף

[z]כִּנְפוֹל pref. כְּ bef. (:))(Kal inf. constr. . . נפל

כַּנְפוֹת noun fem. pl. constr. [of כְּנָפוֹת] from כָּנָף dec. 4a (§ 33. rem. 1) . . . כנף

[a]כַּנְפֵי וְ׳ id. dual masc. constr. of כְּנָפַיִם . . כנף

[b]כְּנָפִי id. sing., suff. 1 pers. sing. . . . כנף

---

a Ps. 144. 12. b Ge. 41. 13. c Ge. 42. 11, 19. d Ge. 40. 13. e Is. 33. 1. f Ezr. 5. 11. g Ho. 13. 7. h Da. 7. 6. i Is. 30. 17. k Ps. 33. 7. l Ex. 29. 41. m Nu. 28. 8. n Ec. 2. 8. o Eze. 22. 21. p Eze. 39. 28. q Le. 22. 13. r Ho. 12. 8; Zep. 1. 11. s Is. 23. 8. t Job 40. 30. u 2 Sa. 18. 32. x Je. 10. 17. y Job 39. 26. z 2 Sa. 3. 34. a 2 Ch. 3. 11. b Eze. 16. 8.

כַּנְפֵיהֶם וְ' id. dual, suff. 3 pers. pl. masc. . . . כנף

כַּנְפֵיהֶן[a] id. dual, suff. 3 pers. pl. fem. . . . . כנף

כְּנָפָיו id. dual, suff. 3 pers. sing. masc. . . . כנף

כְּנָפֶיךָ id. dual, suff. 2 pers. sing. masc. . . . כנף

כְּנָפַיִם, כְּנָפָיִם } id. dual abs. st. . . . . . . כנף

כְּנָפֶךָ[b] id. sing., suff. 2 pers. sing. masc. [for כְּנָפְךָ] כנף

כִּנְפֹל[c] pref. כְּ) noun masc. sing. . . . . נפל

כִּנְפֹל[d] pref. כְּ bef. (:)) Kal inf. constr. . . . נפל

כְּנֶפֶשׁ[e] וּ' pref. כְּ) noun com. sing. d. 6a; וּ bef. (:) נפש

כְּנַפְשׁוֹ[f] pref. id.) id., suff. 3 pers. sing. masc. . נפש

כְּנַפְשְׁךָ pref. id.) id., suff. 2 pers. sing. masc. . נפש

כְּנֵצֶר[g] pref. id.) noun masc. sing. . . . . נצר

כְּנָקָף pref. id.) noun masc. sing. . . . . נקף

כָּנַר Root not used; prob. imitating a *tremulous and stridulous sound.*

כִּנּוֹר masc. dec. 1b (pl. ־ִים, ־וֹת) *harp* or *lyre.*

כִּנֶּרֶת, כִּנְּרוֹת, כִּנְּרוֹת pr. name of a city in the tribe of Naphtali, near the sea of Galilee, called יָם כִּנֶּרֶת Nu. 34. 11.

כִּנְּרוֹת, כִּנֲּרוֹת } pr. name of a place, כִּנֶּרֶת . . . כנר

כִּנֹּרוֹת וְ noun m. with pl. fem. term. fr. כִּנּוֹר d. 1b כנר

כִּנֹּרִי[h] id. sing., suff. 1 pers. sing. . . . . כנר

כִּנֶּרֶת, כִּנֶּרֶת } וְ pr. name of a place . . . . כנר

[כְּנַשׁ] Chald. *to collect, assemble,* Da. 3. 2. Ithpa. pass. Ge. 3. 3, 27.

כִּנְשֹׂא[i] pref. כְּ bef. (:)) Kal inf. constr. . . . נשא

כַּנֹּשֶׁה[k] pref. כַּ f. כְּהַ } Kal part. act. sing. masc. } נשה

כְּנֹשֶׁה[l] pref. כְּ q. v. } dec. 9a . . . . נשה

כַּנָּשִׁים pref. כַּ for כְּהַ) noun fem. with pl. masc. term. see אֱנוֹשׁ and אִישׁ (§ 45) . . אנש

כַּנֶּשֶׁף[m] pref. id.) noun masc. sing. (suff. נִשְׁפּוֹ) d. 6a נשף

כַּנֶּשֶׁר pref. id. } noun masc. sing. (pl. c. נִשְׁרֵי) } נשר

כְּנֶשֶׁר pref. כְּ } dec. 6c . . . . . נשר

כַּנְּשָׁרִים[n] pref. כַּ for כְּהַ) id. pl., abs. st. . . . נשר

כְּנִשְׁרִין[o] Chald. pref. כְּ) noun masc., pl. of [נְשַׁר] d. 3b נשר

כֵּס[p] noun masc. sing. . . . . . . כסא

כָּסָא Root not used; i. q. כָּסָה *to cover.*

כֶּסֶא, כֶּסֶה masc. *the new moon,* Pr. 7. 20; Ps. 81. 4; Arab. כשה *to cover with brightness* (Prof. Lee).

כִּסֵּא masc. dec. 7b (with suff. כִּסְאֲךָ § 36. rem. 3) pl. כִּסְאוֹת for כִּסְּאוֹת.—I. *seat,* of the high-priest, of a judge.—II. *throne, royal throne.*

כִּסֵּה masc. *throne,* 1 Ki. 10. 19; Job 26. 9.

כֵּס masc. id. Ex. 17. 16.

כִּסֵּא וְ' noun masc. sing. dec. 7b . . . . כסא

כִּסְאוֹ וְ' id., suff. 3 pers. sing. masc. . . . כסא

כִּסְאוֹת[q] id. pl. . . . . כסא

כִּסְאוֹתָם[r] id. pl., suff. 3 pers. pl. masc. . . . כסא

כִּסְאִי id. sing., suff. 1 pers. sing. . . . . כסא

כִּסְאֲךָ, כִּסְאֶךָ } id. sing., suff. 2 pers. sing. masc. (§ 36. r. 3) כסא

כְּסָבְאָם[s] וּ pref. כְּ) noun masc. sing. with suff. 3 pers. pl. masc. from סֹבֶא dec. 6e; וּ bef. (:) סבא

כַּסְדָּיאָ Chald. Kh. כַּסְדָּיאָ, K. כַּשְׂדָּאֵי gent. n., emph. of כַּסְדַּי dec. 7, see כַּשְׂדִּי . . . כשד

כִּסְדֹם pref. כְּ bef. (:)) pr. name of a place . סדם

[כָּסָה] *to cover, conceal.* Niph. *to be covered.* Pi. כִּסָּה.—I. *to cover,* with acc.; with לְ, עַל *to cover over* with acc. or עַל of the person covered, and acc. or בְּ of the covering. כְּסוּי חֲטָאָה *covered* (as to sin, i. e. *whose sin is covered, pardoned.*—II. *to put on, to cover oneself.*—III. *to cover, hide, conceal.* Intrans. Ps. 143. 9, *to thee I hide myself,* i. e. to thee I hasten or flee to hide myself. Pu. כֻּסָּה כֻּסָּה (§ 10. rem. 5) *to be covered,* with בְּ, also without it. Hithp. *to cover oneself,* with בְּ, also without it.

כָּסוּי masc. dec. 3a, *a covering,* Nu. 4. 6, 14.

כְּסוּת fem. dec. 10.—I. *a covering.*—II. *garment,* De. 22. 12.

סוּת fem. *clothing, garment,* Ge. 49. 11; but see Root סָוָה.

כֶּסֶת fem. only pl. כְּסָתוֹת, constr. כִּסְּתוֹת (ת treated as if radical, comp. דְּלָת) *cushions,* Eze. 13. 18, 20.

מִכְסֶה masc. dec. 9a, *a covering.*

מְכַסֶּה masc. dec. 9a (§ 38. rem. 1).—I. *covering.*—II. *the caul* which covers the intestines, Le. 9. 19.

כִּסָּה וְ' Piel pret. 3 pers. sing. masc. . . . כסה

כֶּסֶה[t] noun masc. sing. for כִּסֵּא (q. v.) . . . כסא

כֹּסֶה[u] וְ' Kal part. act. sing. masc. . . . . כסה

כִּסָּהוּ[x] וְ'[y] Piel pret. 3 pers. sing. m., suff. 3 pers. s. m. כסה

כִּסּוּ וְ Piel pret. 3 pers. pl. . . . . . כסה

כֻּסּוּ Pual pret. 3 pers. pl. [for כֻּסּוּ § 10. rem. 5] כסה

כַּסּוּחָה[z] pref. כַּ for כְּהַ) noun fem. sing. . . . סוח

כְּסוּחָה[a] Kal part. pass. sing. fem. [of כָּסוּחַ] . . כסח

[a] Eze. 1. 24, 25. [b] Ru. 3. 9. [c] Job 3. 16. [d] 2 Sa. 17. 9. [e] Eze. 18. 4. [f] 1 Sa. 18. 1, 3. [g] Is. 14. 19. [h] Job 30. 31. [i] Is. 18. 3. [k] Is. 24. 2. [l] Ex. 22. 24. [m] Is. 59. 10. [n] Is. 40. 31. [o] Da. 4. 30. [p] Ex. 17. 16. [q] Ps. 122. 5. [r] Eze. 26. 16. [s] Na. 1. 10. [t] Job 26. 9. [u] Pr. 12. 16, 23. [x] Nu. 17. 7. [y] Le. 17. 13. [z] Is. 5. 25. [a] Ps. 80. 17.

[a]כְּסוּחִים Kal part. pass. pl. masc. [of כָּסוּחַ] dec. 3a . כסח
[b]כְּסוּיֵי Kal part. p. or subst. m., constr. of [כָּסוּי] d. 3a כסה
[c]כִּסּוּךְ וְ Piel pret. 3 pers. pl., suff. 2 pers. sing. fem. כסה
[d]כָּסוֹם Kal inf. abs. . . . . . . כסם
[e]כַּסּוּנוּ Piel imp. pl. masc., suff. 1 pers. pl. . כסה
כַּסּוּס pref. כַּ f. כְּהַ } noun masc. sing. dec. 1a . סוס
כְּסוּס pref. כְּ q. v.
כְּסוּסַי pref. id.)(id. pl., suff. 1 pers. sing. . סוס
כְּסוּסֶיךָ pref. id.)(id. pl., suff. 2 pers. sing. masc. סוס
[f]כַּסּוּפָה וְ' pref. כַּ for כְּהַ)(noun fem. sing. dec. 10 סוף
[g]כְּסוּפוֹת pref. כְּ)(id. pl. . . . . . סוף
[h]כַּסּוֹת Piel inf. constr. . . . . כסה
כְּסוּת noun fem. sing. dec. 1a . . . . כסה
[i]כֹּסוֹת וְ noun fem., pl. of כּוֹס dec. 1a . כוס
[k]כְּסוּתָהּ noun f. s., suff. 3 pers. s. f. fr. כְּסוּת d. 1a כסה
[l]כְּסוּתֹה id., suff. 3 pers. sing. masc. . . . כסה
[m]כְּסוּתְךָ id., suff. 2 pers. sing. masc. . . כסה
[n]כְּסוּתָם id., suff. 3 pers. pl. masc. . . . כסה

[כָּסַח] *to cut off*, Is. 33. 12; Ps. 80. 17.
כְּסִיל וּ' noun m. s. d. 1a, also pr. name; וּ bef. (:) כסל
[o]כְּסִילוּת noun fem. sing. . . . . . . כסל
[p]כְּסִילֵיהֶם וּ noun masc. pl., suff. 3 pers. pl. masc. fr. כְּסִיל dec. 1a; וּ bef. (:) . . . . כסל
כְּסִילִים וּ' id. pl., abs. st.; וּ id. . . . . כסל
[q]כִּסִּינוּ וְ Piel pret. 1 pers. pl. . . . . כסה
כְּסִיסְרָא pref. כְּ)(pr. name masc., see סִיסְרָא.
[r]כַּסִּיר pref. כַּ for כְּהַ)(noun com. sing. dec. 1a . סיר
[s]כִּסִּיתָ וְ' Piel pret. 2 pers. sing. masc. . . כסה
[u]כִּסִּיתוֹ [x]וְ' id. id., suff. 3 pers. sing. masc. . כסה
כִּסִּיתִי
[y]כִּסֵּיתִי } וְ id. pret. 1 pers. sing. (§ 24. rem. 11) כסה
[z]כִּסִּיתִיךְ id. id., suff. 2 pers. sing. masc. . . כסה
[a]כְּסֻכָּה [b]וּ' noun fem. sing. dec. 1b; וּ bef. (:) . סכך

כָּסַל *to be foolish*, only fut. יִכְסָל Je. 10. 8. In the derivatives (according to Gesenius) *to be fat, strong*; hence *to be firm, confident*.

כֶּסֶל masc. dec. 6a (with suff. כִּסְלִי).—I. *loin*; כְּסָלִים *loins*.—II. *inward parts, viscera*, Ps. 38. 8.—III. *confidence, hope*.—IV. *folly*, Ec. 7. 25.

כִּסְלָה fem. (no vowel change).—I. *confidence, hope*, Job 4. 6.—II. *folly*, Ps. 85. 9.

כִּסְלֵו *Chislev*, the ninth month of the Hebrew year, beginning with the new moon of our December.

כְּסִיל masc. dec. 1a.—I. *fool*.—II. the constellation *Orion*.—III. pr. name of a city in Judah, Jos. 15. 30.

כְּסִילוּת fem. *folly*, Pr. 9. 13.

כְּסָלוֹן (*hope*) pr. name of a town in the borders of Judah, Jos. 15. 10.

כִּסְלוֹן (id.) pr. name masc. Nu. 34. 21.

כְּסֻלּוֹת (*hopes*) pr. name of a town in Issachar, Jos. 19. 18.

כִּסְלוֹת תָּבוֹר (*confidence of Tabor*) pr. name of a town at the foot of mount Tabor, Jos. 19. 12.

[c]כָּסֶל in pause, Seg. [as if from כֶּסֶל § 35. rem. 5] } כסל
כֶּסֶל noun masc. sing. (suff. כִּסְלוֹ), dec. 6a .
[d]כִּסְלֵו name of a month . . . . כסל
[e]כִּסְלוֹ noun m. s., suff. 3 pers. s. m. from כֶּסֶל d. 6a כסל
כְּסָלוֹן pr. name of a place . . . . כסל
כִּסְלוֹן pr. name masc. . . . . . כסל
כַּסְלֻחִים pr. name of a people, Ge. 10. 14; 1 Ch. 1. 12.
[f]כְּסָלַי noun m. pl., suff. 1 pers. sing. from כֶּסֶל d. 6a כסל
[g]כִּסְלִי id. sing., suff. 1 pers. sing. . . . כסל
[h]כִּסְלָם id. sing., suff. 3 pers. pl. masc. . . כסל
כִּסְלֹת pr. name in compos. כִּסְלֹת־תָּבֹר . . כסל
[i]כִּסְלָתֵךְ noun masc. sing., suff. 2 pers. sing. masc. [for כִּסְלָתְךָ from כִּסְלָה (no pl.) . . כסל

[כָּסַם] *to shave, poll* the head, Eze. 44. 20. Prof. Lee, *to adorn*.

כֻּסֶּמֶת fem. pl. כֻּסְּמִים, a kind of corn, *spelt*.

[k]כִּסָּמוֹ Piel pret. 3 pers. s. m. (כִּסָּה), suff. 3 p. pl. m. כסה
[l]כֻּסְּמִים וְ pl. abs. of the foll. . . . כסם
[m]כֻּסֶּמֶת וְ noun fem. sing. dec. 13 . . . כסם

[כָּסַס] *to number, reckon*, Ex. 12. 4.

מֶכֶס masc. (with suff. מִכְסָם) *tribute*.

מִכְסָה fem. only constr. מִכְסַת.—I. *number*, Ex. 12. 4.—II. *price*, Le. 27. 23.

מַס masc. (contr. from מֶכֶס) pl. מִסִּים, *tribute, tax*; מַס עֹבֵד *tribute-service*; הָיָה לָמַס *to become tributary*; שׂוּם, נָתַן לָמַס *to impose tribute, make tributary*; שָׂרֵי מִסִּים *tribute masters*.

מִסָּה fem. dec. 10, *tribute, offering*, De. 16. 10.

[כָּסַף] prop. as in the Chald. *to be pale, wan*; hence, *to desire greatly, to long after*, const. with לְ of the person. Niph.—I. *to be ashamed*, Zep. 2. 1.—II. *to long after*.

כֶּסֶף masc. dec. 6a (with suff. כַּסְפִּי).—I. *silver*;

[a] Is. 33. 12. [b] Ps. 32. 1; Nu. 4. 6, 14. [c] Eze. 26. 19. [d] Eze. 44. 20. [e] Ho. 10. 8. [f] Is. 5. 28; Pr. 1. 27. [g] Is. 21. 1. [h] Mal. 2. 13. [i] Is. 35. 5. [k] Ex. 21. 10. [l] Ex. 22. 26. [m] De. 22. 12. [n] Is. 50. 3. [o] Pr. 9. 13. [p] Is. 13. 10. [q] Ge. 37. 26. [r] Job 41. 23. [s] Ps. 85. 3. [t] De. 23. 14. [u] Ps. 104. 6. [x] Is. 58. 7. [y] Eze. 32. 7. [z] Is. 51. 16. [a] Is. 1. 8. [b] Job 27. 18. [c] Job 15. 27. [d] Ne. 1. 1. [e] Job 8. 14. [f] Ps. 38. 8. [g] Job 31. 24. [h] Ps. 78. 7. [i] Job 4. 6. [k] Ex. 15. 10. [l] Eze. 4. 9. [m] Is. 28. 25.

שֶׁקֶל כֶּסֶף *a shekel of silver;* with the numeral שֶׁקֶל is omitted, as עֶשְׂרִים כֶּסֶף *twenty shekels of silver.*—II. *money.*

כְּסַף Chald. masc. dec. 3a, *silver.*

כָּסִפְיָא pr. name of a country, according to others, of a town, Ezr. 8. 17.

כָּסֶף וְ' in pause for כֶּסֶף (q. v. § 35. rem. 5) — כסף

כְּסַף[a] / כְּסַף } Chald. noun masc. sing. dec. 3a — כסף

כֶּסֶף וְ', וְ' noun masc. sing. (suff. כַּסְפִּי), dec. 6a; for וָ see lett. ו — כסף

כַּסְפָּא וְ' Chald. noun m. sing., emph. of כְּסַף dec. 3a — כסף

כַּסְפּוֹ noun m. s., suff. 3 pers. s. m. from כֶּסֶף d. 6a — כסף

כַּסְפִּי id. with suff. 1 pers. sing. — כסף

כַּסְפֵּיהֶם[b] id. pl., suff. 3 pers. pl. masc. — כסף

כַּסְפֶּךָ / כַּסְפְּךָ } id. sing., suff. 2 pers. sing. masc. — כסף

כַּסְפֵּךְ[c] id. id., suff. 2 pers. sing. fem. — כסף

כַּסְפְּכֶם[d] id. id., suff. 2 pers. pl. masc. — כסף

כַּסְפָּם id. id., suff. 3 pers. pl. masc. — כסף

כַּסְפֵּנוּ id. id., suff. 1 pers. sing. — כסף

כַּסֵּפֶר[e] pref. כַּ for כְּהַ)(noun masc. sing. dec. 6b — ספר

כִּסְּתָה וְ' Piel pret. 3 pers. sing. fem. — כסה

כְּסָתוֹת[f] noun fem. pl. abs. from [כֶּסֶת] dec. 13a — כסה

כְּסְתוֹתֵיכֶנָה[g] id. pl., suff. 2 pers. pl. fem., ת retained as if radical, (comp. קֶשֶׁת, דֶּלֶת) — כסה

כִּסְּתִי[h] defect. for כִּסֵּיתִי (q. v.) — כסה

כִּסַּתְנִי[i] Piel pret. 3 pers. sing. f. (כִּסְּתָה), suff. 1 p. s. — כסה

כָּעָב pref. כָּ f. כְּהַ· כְּהָ / כְּעָב [k] וּ' pref. כְּ q. v. } noun com. s. d. 1a (once constr. עָב); וּ bef. (:) — עוב

כָּעֶבֶד[l] pref. כַּ f. כְּהָ / כְּעֶבֶד pref. כְּ q. v. } noun masc. sing. dec. 6a — עבד

כְּעַבְדִּי pref. id.)(id. with suff. 1 pers. sing. — עבד

כַּעֲבָדִים[m] pref. כַּ bef. (-:))(id. pl., abs. st. — עבד

כַּעֲבוֹדַת[n] pref. id.)(noun fem. s., constr. of 'דָה d. 10 — עבד

כַּעֲבוּר[o] pref. id.)(Kal inf. constr. — עבר

כַּעֲבֹת[p] וְ suff. id.; noun m. s., constr. of עֲבֹת d. 3a — עבת

כַּעֲבֹר[q] pref. id.)(Kal inf. constr. — עבר

כְּעָבְרָם[r] pref. כְּ)(id., suff. 3 pers. pl. masc. — עבר

כְּעֵגֶל[s] pref. id.)(noun masc. sing. d. 6 (§ 35. r. 6) — עגל

כְּעֶגְלָה[t] pref. id.)(noun fem. sing. dec. 10 — עגל

כְּעֶגְלֵי pref. id.)(noun masc. pl. constr. of עֵגֶל dec. 6 (§ 35. rem. 6) — עגל

כַּעֲדִי[u] pref. כַּ bef. (-:))(noun masc. sing. (suff. עֶדְיוֹ) dec. 6i (§ 35. rem. 14) — עדה

כְּעֵדֶן pref. כְּ)(pr. name of a place — עדן

כָּעֵדֶר[x] pref. כָּ f. כְּהַ· כְּהָ / כְּעֵדֶר pref. כְּ q. v. } noun masc. sing. dec. 6 (§ 35. rem. 6) — עדר

כַּעֲדָתוֹ[y] וְ pref. כַּ bef. (-:))(noun fem. sing., suff. 3 pers. sing. masc. from עֵדָה dec. 11b — יעד

כְּעָוֶל[z] pref. כְּ)(noun masc. sing. — עול

כַּעֲוֹן[a] pref. כַּ bef. (-:))(n. m. s. constr. of עָוֹן d. 3a — עוה

כַּעֲוֹנֹתֵנוּ[b] pref. id.)(id. pl., suff. 1 pers. pl. — עוה

כָּעוֹף[c] pref. כָּ f. כְּהַ·, כְּהָ / כְּעוֹף pref. כְּ q. v. } noun masc. sing. — עוף

כָּעֹפֶרֶת[d] pref. כָּ for כְּהַ·, כְּהָ)(noun fem. sing. — עפר

כְּעוּר[e] Chald. pref. כְּ)(noun masc. sing. — עור

כָּעֹרֵב[f] pref. כָּ for כְּהַ·, כְּהָ)(noun masc. sing. d. 7b — ערב

כַּעִוְרִים pref. כַּ for כְּהַ)(adj. masc., pl. of עִוֵּר d. 7b — עור

כַּעֲזוּבַת[g] pref. כַּ bef. (-:))(n. f. s., constr. of עֲזוּבָה d. 10 — עזב

כְּעֹטְיָה[h] pref. כְּ)(Kal part. act., fem. (§ 24. rem. 5) — עטה

כְּעֵין pref. id.)(noun fem. s. constr. of עַיִן d. 6h — עין

כְּעֵינֵי[i] Chald. pref. id.)(id. pl. constr. dec. 3d — עין

כְּעֵינֵי[k] pref. id.)(id. pl. constr. st. — עין

כְּעִיר pref. id.)(noun fem. sing. irr. (§ 45) — עור

כְּעֶכֶס[l] וּ pref. כְּ)(noun masc. sing. d. 6; וּ bef. (:) — עכס

כְּעַל pref. כְּ)(prep. עַל (prop. constr. of עָל) — עלה

כֶּעָלֶה[m] וְ'[n] pref. כֶּ for כְּהֶ bef. עָ for כְּהַ)(n. m. d. 9b — עלה

כָּעֹלָה[o] pref. כָּ for כְּהַ·, כְּהָ)(noun fem. sing. d. 10 — עלה

כַּעֲלוֹת pref. כַּ bef. (-:))(Kal inf. constr. dec. 1b — עלה

כַּעֲלִילוֹתַיִךְ[p] וְ pref. id.)(noun fem. pl., suff. 2 pers. sing. fem. from עֲלִילָה dec. 10 — עלל

כַּעֲלִילוֹתֵיכֶם[q] וְ pref. id.)(id., suff. 2 pers. pl. masc. — עלל

כַּעֲלִילוֹתָם[r] וְ pref. id.)(id., suff. 3 pers. pl. m. (§ 4. r. 2) — עלל

כְּעֹלְלִים[s] pref. כְּ)(noun masc., pl. of עוֹלֵל dec. 7b — עלל

כְּעֹלְלֹת[t] pref. id.)(constr. of the foll. — עלל

כְּעֹלֵלֹת[u] pref. id.)(noun fem. pl. dec. 11b — עלל

כָּעָם pref. כָּ f. כְּהַ·, כְּהָ / כְּעַם[x] pref. כְּ q. v. } noun masc. sing. dec. 8 (but comp. § 45) — עמם

כְּעָמְדוֹ[y] וּ pref. כְּ)(Kal inf., suff. 3 p. s. m.; וּ bef. (:) — עמד

כְּעַמּוּדֵי[z] pref. id.)(noun m. pl. constr. fr. עַמּוּד d. 1b — עמד

כְּעַמֵּי[a] pref. id.)(n. m. pl. c. fr. עַם d. 8a (comp. § 45) — עמם

כְּעַמִּי pref. id.)(id. sing., suff. 1 pers. sing. — עמם

כָּעַמִּים[b] pref. כָּ for כְּהָ, כְּהַ)(id. pl., abs. st. — עמם

כֶּעָמִיר[c] pref. כֶּ f. כְּהֶ bef. עָ f. כְּהַ dag. forte impl.)(& / כְּעָמִיר[d] וּ pref. כְּ q. v.)(noun masc. s.; וּ bef. (:) } — עמר

כְּעַמְּךָ / כְּעַמֶּךָ [e] וְ' } pref. id.)(noun masc. sing., suff. 2 p. sing. m. from עַם d. 8a (comp. § 45) — עמם

כְּעֵמֶק[f] pref. id.)(noun masc. sing. dec. 6b — עמק

כַּעֲמַר[g] Chald. כַּ bef. (-:))(noun masc. sing. — עמר

a Da. 2. 32. b Ge. 42. 25, 35. c Is. 1. 22. d Ge. 43. 23. e Is. 34. 4. f Ex. 13. 18. g Eze. 13. 20. h Eze. 31. 15. i Ps. 44. 16. k Job 30. 15. l Is. 24. 2. m Ec. 10. 7. n 1 Ch. 28. 15. o Pr. 10. 25. p Is. 5. 18. q 1 Ki. 18. 29. r 2 Ki. 2. 9. s Je. 31. 18. t Je. 50. 11. u Is. 49. 18. x Ps. 78. 52. y Nu. 17. 5. z Job 27. 7. a Eze. 14. 10. b Ps. 103. 10. c Ho. 9. 11. d Ex. 15. 10. e Da. 2. 35. f Ca. 5. 11. g Is. 17. 9. h Ca. 1. 7. i Da. 7. 8. k Ps. 123. 2. l Pr. 7. 22. m Is. 64. 5. n Pr. 11. 28. o Eze. 45. 25. p Eze. 24. 14. q Eze. 20. 44. r Eze. 36. 19. s Job 3. 16. t Mi. 7. 1. u Is. 24. 13. x Joel 2. 5. y Da. 11. 4. z Eze. 42. 6. a 2 Ch. 13. 9. b Ho. 9. 1. c Mi. 4. 12. d Je. 9. 21. e 2 Ch. 18. 3. f Is. 28. 21. g Da. 7. 9.

כַּעֲמֹרָה pref. id.)(pr. name of a place . . עמר

כְּעַן ꞉ Chald. adv. *now*; עַד כְּעַן *until now*. Hence a fem. form כְּעֶנֶת, contr. כְּעֶת adv. *so on, so forth*. Etymon doubtful.

כַּעֲנָבִים[a] pref. כַּ bef. (-:))(noun m., pl. of עֵנָב d. 4b ענב

כַּעֲנַן pref. id.)(constr. of the foll. . . ענן

כֶּעָנָן[b] [c]'וְ pref. כְּ f. כְּהָ bef. עָ f. ·כְּהַ)(n. m. s. d. 4c ענן

כַּעֲנָנִים[d] pref. כַּ bef. (-:))(id. pl., abs. st. . . ענן

כַּעֲנָקִים pref. id.)(noun m. pl. abs. from עֲנָק d. 4c ענק

כְּעֶנֶת ꞉ Chald. adv. see כְּעַן; ꞉ bef. (:).

כָּעַס[e]

וְ fut. יִכְעַס *to be vexed, irritated, provoked, angry*. Pi. כִּעֵס *to irritate, provoke*. Hiph. הִכְעִיס *to vex, grieve; to irritate, provoke to anger*.

כַּעַס masc. dec. 6d (with suff. כַּעְסוֹ, כַּעֲסוֹ § 35. r. 5).—I. *vexation, grief, sadness*.—II. *anger*; pl. כְּעָסִים *excitements to anger*, 2 Ki. 23. 26.

כַּעַשׂ masc. dec. 6d, id. only Job 5. 2; 6. 2; 10. 17; 17. 7.

כָּעָס[f] וְ Kal pret. 3 pers. s. m. for כָּעַס (§ 8. r. 7) כעס

כָּעַס[g] [h]'וָ } noun masc. sing. dec. 6d; for וְ see } כעס

כַּעַס [i]'וְ, 'וָ } lett. ו . . . . } כעס

כַּעְסוֹ[k] id., suff. 3 pers. s. m. [for כַּעֲסוֹ § 35. r. 5] כעס

כִּעֲסוּנִי[l] Piel pret. 3 pers. pl. (§ 14. r. 1), suff. 1 p. s. כעס

כַּעְסִי[m] וְ noun masc. sing., suff. 1 pers. sing. from כַּעַס dec. 6d [for כַּעֲסִי § 35. rem. 5] . כעס

כֶּעָסִים[n] וְ pref. כֶּ for כְּהֶ bef. עָ for כְּהַ; n. m. s. d. 3a עסס

כַּעַסְךָ[o] noun m. s., suff. 2 pers. s. m. from כַּעַס d. 6d כעס

כִּעֲסַתָּה[p] וְ Piel pret. 3 p. s. f. (§ 14. r. 1), suff. 3 p. s. f. כעס

כְּעַפְעַפֵּי[xx] pref. כְּ)(n. m. pl. constr. fr. [עַפְעַף] d. 8d עוף

כַּעֲפַר pref. כַּ bef. (-:))(constr. of the foll. . . עפר

כֶּעָפָר pref. כֶּ for כְּהֶ bef. עָ for כְּהַ & . . } עפר

כְּעָפָר[q] pref. כְּ)(noun masc. sing. dec. 4c . } עפר

כָּעֵץ pref. כָּ f. כְּהָ, ·כְּהַ } noun m. s. d. 7a (but } עצה

כְּעֵץ pref. כְּ q. v. } comp. § 36. r. 2 & 4) } עצה

כְּעֶצֶם[r] ꞉ pref. כְּ)(n. f. s. (suff. עַצְמִי) d. 6a; ꞉ bef. (:) עצם

כְּעָצְמוֹ[s] ꞉ pref. id.)(Kal inf., suff. 3 p. s. m.; ꞉ id. עצם

כַּעֲצָמִים[t] pref. כַּ bef. (-:))(noun fem. pl. of עֶצֶם (suff. עַצְמִי) dec. 6a . . . . עצם

כַּעֲצַת pref. id.)(noun f. s., constr. of עֵצָה d. 11b יעץ

כְּעֹרֵב pref. כְּ)(pr. name masc. . . . ערב

כָּעֲרָבָה pref. כָּ for כְּהָ, ·כְּהַ)(noun fem. sing. d. 11c ערב

כַּעֲרָבִי pref. כַּ bef. (-:))(gent. noun from עֲרַב . ערב

כַּעֲרָבִים[u] pref. id.)(n. m. pl. (c. עַרְבֵי) from עֶרֶב d. 6a ערב

כַּעֲרוּגַת[x] pref. id.)(n. f. s. constr. of [עֲרוּגָה] d. 10 ערג

כַּעֲרוֹעֵר[y] pref. id.)(adj. masc. sing. . . . ערר

כֶּעָרִים pref. כֶּ for כְּהֶ bef. עָ for כְּהַ)(noun fem., pl. of עָר see עִיר (§ 45) . . . עור

כְּעֶרְכּוֹ[z] pref. כְּ)(noun masc. sing., suff. 3 pers. sing. masc. from עֵרֶךְ dec. 6 (§ 35. rem. 6) . ערך

כְּעֶרְכִּי[a] pref. id.)(id. with suff. 1 pers. sing. . ערך

כְּעֶרְכְּךָ[b] pref. id.)(id., suff. 2 pers. sing. masc. . ערך

כְּעַרְעָר[c] pref. id.)(adj. masc. sing. . . . ערר

כְּעֹרֶף[ee] pref. id.)(noun masc. sing. dec. 6c . . ערף

כָּעָשׁ pref. כָּ for כְּהָ, ·כְּהַ)(noun masc. sing. . . עשש

כָּעַשׂ[kk] for כַּעַשׂ' noun masc. sing. dec. 6d . . כעס

כָּעֵשֶׂב pref. כָּ f. כְּהָ, ·כְּהַ } noun masc. sing. dec. 6 } עשב

כְּעֵשֶׂב pref. כְּ q. v. } (§ 35. rem. 6) . } עשב

כַּעְשִׂי[d] noun masc. sing., suff. 1 pers. sing. [for כַּעֲשִׂי § 35. rem. 5] from כַּעַשׂ' dec. 6d . כעס

כַּעַשְׂךָ[e] id. with suff. 2 pers. sing. masc. . . כעס

כֶּעָשָׁן[f] [g]'וְ pref. כֶּ for כְּהֶ bef. עָ for כְּהַ & . } עשן

כְּעָשָׁן[h] ꞉ pref. כְּ)(noun masc. s. d. 4c; ꞉ bef. (:) } עשן

כְּעֶשֶׁן[i] '꞉ pref. כְּ)(id. constr. st. (§ 33. r. 3); ꞉ id. עשן

כְּעֶשֶׂר[k] pref. id.)(num. card. fem. . . . עשׂר

כְּעֶשְׂרִים pref. id.)(id. pl. com. gen. (§ 35. rem. 16) עשׂר

כַּעֲשֶׂרֶת pref. כַּ bef. (-:))(id. sing. masc., constr. of עֲשָׂרָה (§ 42. rem. 5) . . . . עשׂר

כָּעֵת [l]'וְ pref. כָּ f. כְּהָ, ·כְּהַ } noun com. sing. } עדה

כְּעֵת[pp] '꞉ pref. כְּ q. v. } dec. 8b; ꞉ bef. (:) } עדה

כְּעֶת[m] ꞉ Chald. adv. see כְּעַן; ꞉ id.

כְּעַתּוּדִים[n] pref. כְּ)(noun masc., pl. of [עַתּוּד] dec. 1b עתד

כֵּף

masc. *a rock*, only pl. כֵּפִים, Je. 4. 29; Job 30. 6.

כָּף } noun fem. sing. dec. 8a . . . כפף

כַּף 'וְ } כפף

כְּפֶגֶר[o] pref. כְּ)(noun masc. s. (pl. c. פִּגְרֵי) d. 6a פגר

כִּפְגֹשׁ[r] pref. כִּ bef. (:))(Kal inf. constr. . . פגשׁ

[כָּפָה]

to cover, extinguish, cogn. כָּבָא, חָבָא, חָפָה, only metaph. of anger, *to appease*, Pr. 21. 14. Others, *to bend, to avert*, cogn. כָּפַף.

כַּפָּהּ noun f. s., suff. 3 pers. s. fem. fr. כַּף d. 8d כפף

כִּפָּה noun fem. sing. dec. 10 . . . כפף

כַּפָּו Kh. for כַּפָּיו (q. v. § 4. rem. 1) . . כפף

כַּפּוֹ noun fem. s., suff. 3 pers. s. m. fr. כַּף d. 8d כפף

כָּפוּל Kal part. pass. sing. masc. . . כפל

כְּפוּפִים[q] Kal part. pass. masc., pl. of [כָּפוּף] dec. 3a כפף

כְּפוֹר[r] [s]'꞉ noun masc. sing. dec. 1a; ꞉ bef. (:) . כפר

כְּפוֹרֵי[t] [u]'꞉ id. pl., constr. st.; ꞉ id. . . כפר

כַּפּוֹת 'וְ noun fem., pl. of כַּף dec. 8d . . כפף

כְּפַטִּישׁ[x] ꞉ pref. כְּ)(noun masc. sing.; ꞉ bef. (:) . פטשׁ

---

[a] Ho. 9. 10.
[b] Eze. 38. 9, 16.
[c] Is. 44. 22.
[d] Je. 4. 13.
[e] Ec. 5. 16.
[ee] 2 Ki. 17. 14.
[f] Ps. 112. 10.
[g] Ec. 1. 18.
[h] Pr. 21. 19.
[i] Pr. 27. 3.
[k] Pr. 12. 16.
[kk] Job 5. 2.
[l] De. 32. 21.
[m] 1 Sa. 1. 16.
[n] Is. 49. 26.
[o] Ps. 85. 5.
[p] 1 Sa. 1. 6.
[pp] Da. 9. 21.
[q] Ps. 18. 43.
[r] Ex. 24. 10.
[s] Da. 8. 8.
[t] Ec. 11. 5.
[u] Is. 44. 4.
[x] Ca. 5. 13.
[y] Je. 48. 6.
[z] 2 Ki. 23. 35.
[a] Ps. 55. 14.
[b] Le. 27. 12, 17.
[c] Je. 17. 6.
[d] Job 6. 2.
[e] Job 10. 17.
[f] Is. 51. 6.
[g] Pr. 10. 26.
[h] Ho. 13. 3.
[i] Ex. 19. 18.
[k] Ru. 1. 4.
[l] Ju. 13. 23.
[m] Ezr. 4. 17.
[n] Je. 50. 8.
[o] Is. 14. 19.
[p] Je. 41. 6.
[q] Ps. 146. 8.
[r] Ps. 147. 16.
[s] 1 Ch. 28. 17.
[t] Ezr. 1. 10.
[u] Ezr. 8. 27.
[x] Je. 23. 29.
[xx] Job. 41. 10.

כַּפַּי / כַּפָּי } noun fem. dual, suff. 1 pers. sing. from כַּף dec. 8 d . . . . } כפף

כַּפֵּי id. dual, constr. st. . . . . . כפף

כַּפִּי id. sing. with suff. 1 pers. sing. . . כפף

כְּפִי pref. כְּ) noun masc. sing., constr. of פֶּה, or (Je. 15. 19), with suff. 1 pers. s. irr. (§ 45) פאה

כַּפֶּיהָ[bb] וְ' noun f. du., suff. 3 pers. s. f. fr. כַּף d. 8 d כפף

כַּפֵּיהֶם[dd] id. dual, suff. 3 pers. pl. masc. . . כפף

כַּפָּיו וְ' id. dual, suff. 3 pers. sing. masc. . . כפף

כַּפֶּיךָ id. dual, suff. 2 pers. sing. masc. . . כפף

[a]כַּפַּיִךְ id. dual, suff. 2 pers. sing. fem. . . כפף

[b]כְּפִיךָ pref. כְּ) noun masc. sing., suff. 2 pers. sing. masc. from פֶּה irr. (§ 45) . . פאה

כַּפֵּיכֶם noun f. du., suff. 2 pers. pl. m. fr. כַּף d. 8 d כפף

כַּפַּיִם / כַּפָּיִם } id. dual, abs. st. . . . . . כפף

[c]כֵּפִים וְ noun masc. pl. [of כֵּף q. v.]

[d]כַּפֵּימוֹ noun fem. du., suff. 3 pers. pl. fr. כַּף d. 8 d כפף

[e]כַּפֵּינוּ id. dual, suff. 1 pers. pl. . . . כפף

[f]כָּפִיס וְ noun masc. sing. . . . . . כפס

כְּפִיר [g]וּ' noun masc. sing. dec. 1 a; וּ bef. (:) . כפר

כְּפִירָה pr. name of a place . . . . כפר

[h]כְּפִירֶיהָ noun m. pl., suff. 3 pers. s. f. fr. כְּפִיר d. 1 a כפר

[i]כְּפִירַיִךְ וּ id. pl., suff. 2 pers. sing. fem.; וּ bef. (:) כפר

כְּפִירִים id. pl., abs. st. . . . . . כפר

[k]כַּפְּךָ / [l]כַּפֶּךָ } noun fem. sing., suff. 2 pers. sing. masc. from כַּף dec. 8 d . . . } כפף

[m]כַּפֶּכָה id. with parag. ה (§ 3. rem. 2) . . כפף

[כָּפַל] *to double;* part. כָּפוּל *doubled.* Niph. *to be doubled,* Eze. 21. 19.

כֶּפֶל masc. dec. 6 a, *a doubling,* Job 41. 5, see רֶסֶן; dual כִּפְלַיִם *double,* twice as much, Is. 40. 2; *double, manifold,* Job 11. 6.

מַכְפֵּלָה (*a doubling*) pr. name of a place, perhaps a plain near Hebron.

[n]כְּפַלְגֵי pref. כְּ) noun m. pl. constr. fr. פֶּלֶג d. 6 a פלג

כְּפֶלַח pref. id.) noun masc. sing. . . . פלח

כִּפְלַיִם noun masc., dual of כֶּפֶל' dec. 6 a . . כפל

[o]כָּפַלְתָּ וְ Kal pret. 2 pers. sing. masc; acc. shifted by conv. וְ (§ 8. rem. 7) . . . . כפל

כַּפְּלִשְׁתִּים pref. כַּ for כְּהַ) gent. noun, pl. of פְּלִשְׁתִּי from פְּלֶשֶׁת . . . . . פלש

[כָּפַן] *to languish, be languid,* Eze. 17. 7.

כָּפָן masc. *hunger,* Job 5. 22; 30. 3.

[p]כָּפְנָה Kal pret. 3 pers. sing. fem. . . . . כפן

כָּפַס Root not used; Syr. *to connect, join.*

כָּפִיס masc. *cross beam, rafter,* Hab. 2. 11.

כַּפֶּסַח pref. כַּ for כְּהַ) noun m. s. d. 6 (§ 35. r. 5) פסח

[q]כְּפָעֳלָהּ pref. כְּ) noun masc. sing., suff. 3 pers. sing. fem. from פֹּעַל dec. 6 f . . . . פעל

[r]כְּפָעֳלוֹ pref. id.) id., suff. 3 pers. sing. masc. . פעל

כְּפָעֳלָם pref. id.) id., suff. 3 pers. pl. masc. . פעל

כְּפַעַם pref. id.) noun fem. sing. dec. 6 d . . פעם

[s]כָּפַף *to bend, bow down.* Intrans. *to be bowed down,* Ps. 57. 7. Niph. *to bow, humble oneself,* Mi. 6. 6.

כַּף fem. dec. 8 d.—I. *the hollow, palm of the hand;* often also for the *hand* itself; dual כַּפַּיִם, pl. כַּפּוֹת; in animals the *paw;* כַּף רֶגֶל, *the sole of the foot.*—II. *pan, spoon, dish;* כַּף הַקֶּלַע *the hollow, cavity of a sling;* כַּף הַיָּרֵךְ *the hollow of the thigh,* i. e. the socket of the hip-bone.—III. *handle* of a bolt, Ca. 5. 5.—IV. כַּפּוֹת תְּמָרִים *palm-branches,* Le. 23. 40.

כִּפָּה fem. dec. 10, *palm-branch;* also *branch* in general, Job 15. 32.

כָּפַר *to cover, overlay,* with pitch, *to pitch,* Ge. 6. 14. Pi. כִּפֶּר (§ 10. rem. 1).—I. *to cover over* sin, i. e. *to forgive, pardon* sin, const. with עַל, לְ, בְּעַד.—II. *to expiate* an offence, with עַל, בְּעַד, מִן; *to make atonement* for an offender, *to purify,* with עַל, בְּ, בְּעַד.—III. *to appease, pacify,* with acc. of the person; of calamity, *to avert,* with בְּ of the sacrifice. Pu.—I. pass. of Pi. No. II.—II. *to be abolished,* Is. 28. 18. Hithp. and Nithpa. (§ 6. No. 10) *to be expiated.*

כָּפָר masc. dec. 4 a, *village, hamlet.*

כְּפַר הָעַמּוֹנִי (*village of the Ammonites*) pr. name of a place in the tribe of Benjamin, Jos. 18. 24.

כְּפוֹר m. dec. 1 a.—I. *cup, bowl.*—II. *hoar frost.*

כְּפִיר masc. dec. 1 a.—I. *young lion.*—II. *village,* Ne. 6. 2.

כֹּפֶר masc. dec. 6 c.—I. *village,* 1 Sa. 6. 18.—II. *pitch,* Ge. 6. 14.—III. *cyprus-flower, Alhenna* of the Arabs, a shrub or low tree with fragrant whitish flowers growing in clusters like grapes (Gesenius), which when dried and reduced to powder is used by the women for colouring their eyebrows or nails.—IV. *ransom.*

כִּפֻּרִים masc. pl. (of כִּפּוּר) *atonement, expiation;* יוֹם הַכִּפֻּרִים *day of atonement.*

[a] La. 2. 19. [b] Job 33. 6. [bb] Pr. 31. 19. [c] Job 30. 6. [d] Job 27. 23. [dd] Le. 8. 28. [e] Ps. 44. 21. [f] Hab. 2. 11. [g] Is. 11. 6. [h] Eze. 38. 13. [i] Na. 2. 14. [k] Job 13. 21. [l] Job 40. 32. [m] Ps. 139. 5. [n] Is. 32. 2. [o] Ex. 26. 9. [p] Eze. 17. 7. [q] Je. 50. 29. [r] Pr. 24. 12, 29. [s] Ps. 57. 7.

כַּפֹּרֶת fem. *covering of the ark, the mercy-seat;* בֵּית הַכַּפֹּרֶת *the holy of holies,* where the ark of the covenant was placed, 1 Ch. 28. 11.

כַּפֵּר[a] וְ׳ Piel imp. sing. masc. . . . . כפר

כִּפֶּר וְ id. pret. 3 pers. sing. masc. (§ 9. rem. 1) כפר

כֹּפֶר noun masc. sing. dec. 6c . . . . כפר

כֻּפַּר[b] [c]וְ׳ Pual pret. 3 pers. sing. masc. . . כפר

כְּפֹר[d] וּ defect. for כְּפוֹר (q. v.) . . . כפר

כְּפַר וּ pr. name in compos. כְּ׳ הָעַמּוֹנִי . . כפר

כִּפְרֹאתָיו[e] pref. כְּ)(transp. for פֹּארֹתָיו (q. v.) . פאר

כְּפֶרֶד[u] pref. id.)(noun masc. sing. (suff. פִּרְדּוֹ) d. 6a פרד

כַּפְּרָהּ[f] Piel inf. (כַּפֵּר׳), suff. 3 pers. sing. fem. dec. 7b כפר

כְּפָרָה[g] pref. כְּ)(noun f. s. d. 10 [for פָּרָה] fr. פַּר m. פרר

כִּפְּרוּ[h] וְ Kh. וְכִפְּרוּ, K. יְכַפְּרוּ Piel pret. or fut. 3 p. pl. כפר

כָּפְרוֹ[i] noun m. s., suff. 3 pers. s. m. from כֹּפֶר d. 6c כפר

כְּפַרְזְלָא[k] ו׳ Chald. pref. כְּ)(noun masc. sing. emph. of פַּרְזֶל dec. 2a (§ 58. rem. 2); וּ bef. (:) פרזל

כְּפֹרַחַת[l] pref. כְּ)(Kal part. act. s. f. d. 13a, fr. פֹּרֵחַ m. פרח

כִּפְרִי[m] וְ׳ pref. כִּ bef. (:))(noun masc. sing. dec. 6i פרה

כְּפָרִים[n] noun masc., pl. of כֹּפֶר dec. 6c (§ 35. rem. 9) כפר

כְּפִרִים defect. for כְּפִירִים (q. v.) . . . כפר

כִּפֻּרִים[o] noun masc., pl. of [כִּפּוּר] dec. 1b . . כפר

כָּפְרֶךָ[p] noun m. s., suff. 2 p. s. m. from כֹּפֶר d. 6c כפר

כְּפַרְעֹה pref. כְּ)(pr. name masc., see פַּרְעֹה.

כְּפֶרֶץ pref. id.)(n. m. s. (pl. with suff. פְּרָצֵיהֶם׳) d. 6c פרץ

כִּפְרֹץ[q] וְ pref. כִּ bef. (:))(Kal inf. constr. . . פרץ

כְּפָרָשִׁים[r] וּ pref. כְּ)(noun masc., pl. of פָּרָשׁ dec. 1b (§ 30. No. 3); וּ bef. (:) . . . פרש

כִּפַּרְתָּ[s] וְ Kal pret. 2 pers. sing. masc.; acc. shifted by conv. וְ (§ 8. rem. 7) . . . כפר

כַּפֹּרֶת noun fem. sing. . . . . . כפר

כִּפַּרְתָּהוּ[t] וְ Piel pret. 2 pers. s. m., suff. 3 pers. s. m. כפר

כִּפַּרְתֶּם[u] וְ id. pret. 2 pers. pl. masc. . . . כפר

כָּפַשׁ. Hiph. *to cover over,* La. 3. 16.

כְּפֶשַׁע[x] pref. כְּ)(noun masc. sing. . . . פשע

כְּפִשְׁעֵיהֶם[y] וּ pref. id.)(noun m. pl., suff. 3 pers. pl. m. from פֶּשַׁע dec. 6a (§ 35. r. 5); וּ bef. (:) פשע

כַּפִּשְׁתָּה[z] pref. כַּ for כְּהַ)(noun fem. sing. . . פשת

כַּפִּשְׁתִּים[a] pref. id.)(id. with pl. masc. term. . . פשת

[כְּפַת] Chald. *to bind, fetter.* Pret. Peil, Da. 3. 21. Pa. id. Da. 3. 20, 23, 24.

כַּפֹּת[b] noun fem., pl. of כַּף dec. 8d . . . כפף

כִּפָּתוֹ[c] וְ noun f. s., suff. 3 p. s. m. from כִּפָּה d. 10 כפף

כְּפִתוּ[d] Chald. Peil pret. 3 pers. pl. masc. (§ 47. r. 6) כפת

כִּפְתֹחוֹ[e] וּ pref. כְּ)(Kal inf. [פְּתֹחַ], suff. 3 pers. sing. masc. (§ 16. rem. 10); וּ bef. (:) . . פתח

כְּפִתְחֵי[f] וּ pref. id.)(noun masc. pl. c. from פֶּתַח dec. 6a (§ 35. rem. 5); וּ id. . . . פתח

כְּפִתְחֵיהֶן[g] וּ pref. id.)(id. pl., suff. 3 p. pl. fem.; וּ id. פתח

כַּפְתּוֹר pr. name of a place . . . . כפתר

כַּפֹּתָיו[h] [i]וְ׳ noun f. pl., suff. 3 p. s. m. from כַּף d. 8d כפף

כְּפִתִּים[k] pref. כְּ)(noun fem., pl. of פַּת dec. 8d . פתת

כַּפְתֹּר וְ׳ masc. dec. 1b.—I. a *round* or *spherical knob,* an ornament on the golden candlestick; LXX. σφαιρωτήρ, and Vulg. sphærula; then the *knob* or *capital of a pillar,* Am. 9. 1; Zep. 2. 14. Etymon uncertain.—II. pr. name of a country; pl. כַּפְתֹּרִים of its inhabitants.

כְּפִתְרוֹן pref. כְּ)(noun masc. sing. dec. 1b . פתר

כַּפְתֹּרֶיהָ noun m. pl., suff. 3 p. s. m. from כַּפְתֹּר d. 1b כפתר

כַּפְתֹּרֵיהֶם id. pl. with suff. 3 pers. pl. masc. . כפתר

כַּפְתֹּרִים gent. noun, pl. of כַּפְתֹּרִי from כַּפְתֹּר . כפתר

כַּצֹּאן pref. כַּ for כְּהַ } noun com. sing. dec. 1b; } צאן
כְּצֹאן[l] [ll]וּ pref. כְּ q. v. } וּ bef. (:) . . }

כְּצֵאת pref. כְּ)(Kal inf. constr. dec. 1a [for צֵאת § 25, n. 2d, comp. § 23. rem. 2 & 4] . יצא

כְּצֵאתִי[m] pref. id.)(id. with suff. 1 pers. sing. . יצא

כִּצְבָאִים[n] וְ pref. כִּ bef. (:))(n. m., pl. of צְבִי (§ 35. r. 15) צבה

כִּצְבָאִים pref. id.)(pr. name of a place . צבה

כַּצְּבִי pref. כַּ f. כְּהַ } noun masc. sing. dec. 6i } צבה
כִּצְבִי pref. כִּ bef. (:) } (§ 35. rem. 14 & 15) }

כַּצַּדִּיק[o] pref. כַּ for כְּהַ)(noun masc. sing. dec. 1b צדק

כַּצִּדֹנִים pref. id.)(gent. noun, pl. of צִידֹנִי fr. צִידוֹן צוד

כְּצִדְקוֹ[p] pref. כְּ)(noun masc. sing. from צֶדֶק dec. 6a צדק

כְּצִדְקִי pref. id.)(id. with suff. 1 pers. sing. . צדק

כְּצִדְקִיָּהוּ pref. id.)(pr. name masc. . . . צדק

כְּצִדְקֶךָ[q] pref. id.)(noun masc. sing., suff. 2 pers. sing. masc. from צֶדֶק dec. 6a . . . צדק

כְּצִדְקָתוֹ pref. id.)(noun fem. sing., suff. 3 pers. sing. masc. from צְדָקָה dec. 11c . . . צדק

כְּצִדְקָתִי[r] pref. id.)(id. with suff. 1 pers. sing. . צדק

כַּצָּהֳרָיִם pref. כַּ for כְּהַ)(noun m., dual of צֹהַר d. 6f צהר

כְּצוּר pref. כְּ)(pr. name of a place . . . צור

כְּצוּרֵנוּ[s] pref. id.)(noun masc. sing., suff. 1 pers. pl. from צוּר dec. 1a . . . . צור

כְּצִיץ pref. id.)(noun masc. sing., pl. צִצִּים . צוץ

כְּצִירֵי[t] pref. id.)(noun m. pl. constr. from צִיר d. 1a ציר

כַּצֵּל pref. כַּ f. כְּהַ } noun masc. sing. dec. 6b . צלל
כְּצֵל pref. כְּ q. v. }

---

[a] De. 21. 8. [b] Ex. 29. 33. [c] Is. 28. 18. [d] Job 38. 29. [e] Eze. 31. 8. [f] Is. 47. 11. [g] Ho. 4. 16. [h] Eze. 43. 26. [i] Ps. 49. 8. [k] Da. 2. 40. [l] Ge. 40. 10. [m] Je. 32. 19. [n] Ca. 4. 13. [o] Le. 23. 28. [p] Is. 43. 3. [q] 2 Ch. 31. 5. [r] Joel 2. 4. [s] Ge. 6. 14. [t] Eze. 43. 20. [u] Eze. 45. 20. [x] 1 Sa. 20. 3. [y] Eze. 39. 24. [z] Is. 43. 17. [a] Ju. 15. 14. [b] Le. 23. 40. [c] Job 15. 32. [d] Da. 3. 21. [e] Ne. 8. 5. [f] Eze. 42. 12. [g] Eze. 42. 11. [h] Ex. 37. 16. [i] Ex. 25. 29. [k] Ps. 147. 17. [l] Is. 13. 14. [ll] Ps. 32. 9. [m] Ex. 9. 29. [n] 1 Ch. 12. 8. [o] Ge. 18. 25. [p] Ps. 7. 18. [q] Ps. 35. 24. [r] 2 Sa. 22. 21, 25. [s] De. 32. 31. [t] Is. 21. 3.

כְּצַלְמֻנָּע וּ pref. id.)(pr. name m., see צַלְמֻנָּע; וּ bef. (:)

כְּצֶמַח[a] pref. id.)(noun masc. sing. (suff. צִמְחָהּ) dec. 6 (§ 35. rem. 5) . . . צמח

כַּצֶּמֶר[b] / כַּצָּמֶר[c] pref. כַּ for כְּהַ)(noun masc. sing. (suff. צַמְרִי) dec. 6a (§ 35. rem. 2) [d]וְ' . צמר

כַּצִּנָּה[e] pref. id.)(noun fem. sing. dec. 10 . . צנן

כְּצִנַּת[f] pref. כְּ)(id. constr. st. . . . צנן

כִּצְעִרָתוֹ[g] pref. כְּ bef. (:))(noun fem. sing., suff. 3 pers. sing. masc. from [צְעִירָה] dec. 10 . צער

כַּצִּפּוֹר pref. כַּ for כְּהַ / כְּצִפּוֹר [h] וּ' pref. כְּ q. v. — noun com. sing., pl. צִפֳּרִים (§ 30. r. 1); וּ bef. (:) צפר

כְּצַפִּיחִת[i] pref. id.)(noun fem. sing. . . . צפח

כִּצְפִעֹנִי[k] וּ pref. id.)(noun masc. sing. d. 1b; וּ bef. (:) צפע

כַּצִּפֳּרִים[l] וְ pref. כַּ f. כְּהַ / כְּצִפֳּרִים[m] pref. כְּ q. v. — noun com., pl. of צִפּוֹר (§ 30. rem. 1) צפר

כְּצִפְּרִין[n] Ch. pref. id.)(n. com. pl. [f. צִפְּרִין fr. צְפַר] d. 2a צפר

כַּצַּר[o] pref. כַּ f. כְּהַ / כְּצָר[p] pref. כְּ q. v. — noun masc. sing. dec. 8 (§ 37. rem. 7) . . צרר

כִּצְרוֹר[q] pref. כְּ bef. (:))(n. masc. sing. dec. 1a . צרר

כְּצָרָיו[r] pref. כְּ)(noun masc. pl., suff. 3 pers. pl. masc. from צַר dec. 8c (§ 37. rem. 7) . . צרר

כִּצְרֹף[s] / כִּצְרֹף־[t] pref. כְּ bef. (:))(Kal inf. constr. (§ 8. rem. 18) . . . צרף

כְּקֶבֶר[u] pref. כְּ)(noun masc. sing. (suff. קִבְרִי) d. 6a קבר

כִּקְדֹחַ[x] pref. כְּ bef. (:))(Kal inf. constr. . . קדח

כְּקֶדֶם pref. כְּ)(noun masc. s. (pl. c. קַדְמֵי) d. 6a קדם

כְּקַדְמוֹתֵיכֶם[y] pref. id.)(noun masc. pl., suff. 2 pers. pl. masc. [from קַדְמָה no pl. abs.] . . קדם

כְּקוֹל pref. id.)(noun masc. sing. dec. 1a . קול

כַּקּוֹנֶה[z] pref. כַּ for כְּהַ)(Kal part. act. sing. m. d. 9a קנה

כְּקוֹץ[a] pref. כְּ)(noun masc. sing. dec. 1a . קוץ

כַּקָּטָן[b] pref. כַּ for כְּהַ)(adj. masc. sing. (pl. קְטַנִּים) dec. 8a (§ 37. No. 3) . . . קטן

כַּקָּטֹן pref. id.)(adj. masc. sing. dec. 3a . . קטן

כְּקִיטֹר[c] pref. כְּ)(noun masc. sing. . . . קטר

כְּקִיר[d] pref. id.)(noun masc. sing. dec. 1a . . קיר

כַּקֵּן[e] pref. כַּ for כְּהַ)(noun masc. sing. dec. 8b קנן

כְּקִנְאָתְךָ[f] וּ pref. כְּ)(noun fem. sing., suff. 2 pers. sing. masc. from קִנְאָה dec. 12b; וּ bef. (:) . קנא

כִּקְסֹם[g] pref. כְּ bef. (:))(Kh. קְסוֹם, K. קְסָם־, Kal inf. constr. (§ 8. rem. 18) . . קסם

כְּקֶצֶף[h] pref. כְּ)(n. m. s. d. 6 (suff. קִצְפִּי & קֶצְפְּךָ) קצף

כִּקְרֹא pref. כְּ bef. (:))(Kal inf. constr. . . קרא

כְּקָרְבְכֶם[i] pref. כְּ)(Kal inf., suff. 2 p. pl. m. (§ 16. r. 8) קרב

כְּקֹרַח pref. id.)(pr. name masc. . . . קרח

כַּקַּשׁ pref. כַּ f. כְּהַ / כְּקַשׁ pref. כְּ q. v. — noun masc. sing. קשש

כְּקֶשֶׁת pref. id.)(noun com. sing., suff. קַשְׁתִּי, pl. קְשָׁתוֹת, c. קַשְׁתוֹת, ת treated as if radical, comp. dec. 6a . . . . . קוש

כַּר noun masc. sing. dec. 8, § 37. rem. 7 (and pr. name in compos. with בֵּית q. v.) . כרר

כֹּר[k] noun masc. sing. (pl. כֹּרִים) dec. 1a . . כרר

כְּרָא Chald. Ithpe. *to be pained, grieved,* Da. 7. 15.

כִּרְאוּבֵן pref. כְּ bef. (:))(pr. name masc. . . ראה

כִּרְאוֹת וְ' pref. id.)(Kal inf. constr. . . . ראה

כִּרְאוֹתָהּ[l] pref. id.)(id., suff. 3 pers. sing. fem. . ראה

כִּרְאוֹתוֹ pref. id.)(id., suff. 3 pers. sing. masc. . ראה

כִּרְאוֹתָם [m]וְ' pref. id.)(id., suff. 3 pers. pl. masc. . ראה

כְּרֳאִי[n] pref. כְּ)(noun masc. s. [for רְאִי § 35. r. 14] ראה

כִּרְאִי[o] pref. כְּ bef. (:))(noun masc. sing. . ראה

כִּרְאֵים[xx] pref. id.)(noun masc. sing. dec. 1a . ראם

כָּרֹאשׁ[p] pref. כָּ f. כְּהַ·, כְּהָ / כְּרֹאשׁ[q] וּ pref. כְּ q. v. — noun masc. sing. irr. (§ 45); וּ bef. (:) ראש

כָּרִאשׁוֹן[r] pref. כָּ for כְּהַ·, כְּהָ)(adj. masc. sing. d. 1b ראש

כָּרִאשֹׁנָה pref. id.)(id. fem. dec. 10 . . ראש

כָּרִאשֹׁנִים pref. id.)(id. pl. masc. . . . ראש

כִּרְאֹת pref. כְּ bef. (:))(Kal inf. constr. d. 1b (for כִּרְאוֹת) ראה

כִּרְאֹתוֹ pref. id.)(id., suff. 3 pers. sing. masc. . ראה

כִּרְאֹתְכֶם* pref. id.)(id., suff. 2 pers. pl. m. *Jos. 3. 3. ראה

כָּרַב Root not used; whence

כְּרוּב masc. dec. 1a.—I. *cherub*, a certain symbolical figure described Eze. 1. 6 sq.; etymon uncertain.—II. pr. name masc. Ezr. 2. 59; Ne. 7. 61.

כְּרֹב[s] וּ' pref. כְּ)(noun masc. s. d. 8c; וּ bef. (:) רבב

כִּרְבִיבִים [t]וְ' pref. כְּ bef. (:))(noun masc. pl. . . רבב

כְּרֻבִים defect. for כְּרוּבִים (q. v.) . . . כרב

כִּרְבֵּל only part. pass. מְכֻרְבָּל *girded, clothed,* 1 Ch. 15. 27.

כַּרְבְּלָא Ch. fem. dec. 1a, *mantle, cloak,* Da. 3. 21.

כַּרְבְּלָתְהוֹן[u] וְ Chald. noun fem. pl., suff. 3 pers. pl. masc. from [כַּרְבְּלָא] dec. 9a . כרבל

כְּרֻבָּם[x] pref. כְּ)(noun masc. sing., suff. 3 pers. pl. masc. from רֹב dec. 8c . . . רבב

כְּרֶגַע pref. id.)(noun m. s. d. 6, for רֶגַע (§ 35. r. 5) רגע

כָּרָה I. *to dig*; trop. of plots and devices against any one; Ps. 40. 7 אָזְנַיִם כָּרִיתָ לִּי *mine ears hast thou digged,* i. e. *opened,* given me a listening ear. Niph. *to be dug,* Ps. 94. 13.—II. Kal *to buy, purchase.*—III. *to give a feast,* 2 Ki. 6. 23.

---

[a] Eze. 16. 7. [b] Ps. 147. 16. [c] Is. 1. 18. [d] Is. 51. 8. [e] Ps. 5. 13. [f] Ps. 25. 13. [g] Ge. 43. 33. [h] Pr. 6. 5. [i] Ex. 16. 31. [k] Pr. 23. 32. [l] Ec. 9. 12. [m] Is. 31. 5. [n] Da. 4. 30. [o] Is. 5. 28. [p] La. 2. 4. [q] Pr. 26. 8. [r] Job 19. 11. [s] Zec. 13. 9. [t] Ps. 66. 10. [u] Je. 5. 16. [x] Is. 64. 1. [y] Eze. 36. 11. [z] Is. 24. 2. [a] 2 Sa. 23. 6. [b] 2 Ch. 31. 15. [c] Ge. 19. 28. [d] Ps. 62. 4. [e] Is. 10. 14. [f] Eze. 35. 11. [g] Eze. 21. 28. [h] Ho. 10. 7. [i] De. 20. 2. [k] 1 Ki. 5. 2, 25. [l] Ge. 39. 13. [m] 2 Ch. 24. 11. [n] Na. 3. 6. [o] Job 37. 18. [p] Ho. 10. 4. [q] Job 24. 24. [r] Le. 9. 15. [s] Is. 63. 7. [t] De. 32. 2. [u] Da. 3. 21. [x] Ho. 4. 7. [xx] Ps. 92. 11.

כֵּרָה fem. dec. 11 b.—I. *well, cistern,* Zep. 2. 6. —II. *feast, banquet,* 2 Ki. 6. 23.

מִכְרֶה masc. dec. 9 a, *pit,* Zep. 2. 9.

[a] כֵּרָה noun fem. sing. . . . . . כרה

כֹּרֶה Kal part. act. sing. masc. . . . . כרה

כָּרוּ id. pret. 3 pers. pl. . . . . . כרה

כְּרוּב 'ו n. m. s. d. 1 a, also pr. name m.; ו bef. (:) . כרב

[b] כְּרוּבִים 'ו id. pl., abs. st.; ו id. . . . כרב

[c] כָּרוּהָ Kal pret. 3 pers. pl., suff. 3 pers. sing. fem. כרה

[d] כָּרוֹזָא ן Chald. noun m. s., emph., of [כָּרוֹז] d. 1 a כרז

כָּרוּחַ pref. כְּ f. כְּהַ, כְּהָ · כְּ } noun com. sing. dec. 1 a רוח

[e] כְּרוּחַ pref. כְּ q. v. }

[f] כָּרוֹת ן Kal inf. abs. . . . . . . כרת

[g] כָּרוּת ן id. part. pass. sing. masc. dec. 3 a . . כרת

[h] כְּרוּת ו id. constr. st.; ו bef. (:) . . . . כרת

כְּרַז Chald. Aph. *to cry out, proclaim,* Da. 5. 29.

כָּרוֹז Chald. masc. dec. 1 a, *herald,* Da. 3. 4.

[i] כְּרָחֵל ו pref. כְּ) (noun fem. sing. d. 5 a; ו bef. (:) רחל

כְּרָחֵל pref. id.) (pr. name fem. . . . . רחל

[k] כְּרַחֵם pref. id.) (Piel (§ 14. r. 1) inf. constr. d. 7 b רחם

[l] כְּרַחֲמָיו pref. id.) (noun masc. pl., suff. 3 pers. sing. masc. [for רַחֲמִים] from רַחַם (§ 35. r. 16) רחם

[m] כְּרַחֲמֶיךָ 'ו" pref. id.) (id., suff. 2 p. s. m.; ו bef. (:) רחם

[o] כִּרְחֹק pref. כְּ bef. (:)) (Kal inf. constr. . . . רחק

כְּרֵיחַ pref. כְּ) (noun masc. sing. dec. 1 a . . רוח

כָּרִים noun masc., pl. of כַּר dec. 8 (§ 37. rem. 7) כרר

כֹּרִים noun masc. pl. of כֹּר dec. 1 a . . . כרר

[p] כָּרִיתָ Kal pret. 2 pers. sing. masc. . . . כרה

כְּרִית pr. name of a brook . . . . . כרת

[q] כְּרִיתוּת noun fem. sing. dec. 1 b . . . . כרת

[r] כָּרִיתִי Kal pret. 1 pers. sing. . . . . כרה

[s] כְּרִיתֻת for כְּרִיתוּת, noun fem. sing. dec. 1 b . . כרת

[t] כְּרִיתֻתֶיהָ id. pl., suff. 3 pers. sing. masc. . . כרת

כָּרַךְ Root not used; Syr. and Chald. *to surround; to wrap round.*

תַּכְרִיךְ masc. *robe,* Est. 8. 15.

כַּרְכְּמִישׁ (*fortress of Camosh,* compounded of כַּרְךְ & כְּמִישׁ i. q. כְּמוֹשׁ the name of an idol) pr. name of a city on the Euphrates.

כַּרְכֹּב masc. dec. 8 c, *margin, border,* or *ledge* going round the inside of the altar. Vulg. arula, *hearth.* Ex. 27. 5; 38. 4.

[u] כְּרִכְבּ pref. כְּ for כְּהַ, כְּהָ) (n. m. s. (suff. כַּרְכֻּבּוֹ) d. 6 c רכב

[v] כַּרְכֻּבּוֹ noun m. s., suff. 3 pers. s. m. from כַּרְכֹּב d. 8 c כרכב

כַּרְכֹּם ן masc. *saffron,* Ca. 4. 14.

כַּרְכְּמִישׁ pr. name of a place . . . . . כרך

כַּרְכַּס ן pr. name of a eunuch of Ahasuerus, Est. 1. 10, coll. with the Persic *Eagle* (Gesenius).

כֶּרֶם 'ן masc. (fem. Is. 27. 2, 3) dec. 6 a, with suff. כַּרְמִי, *vineyard;* with זַיִת *an olive-yard,* Ju. 15. 5.

כֹּרֵם masc. dec. 7 b, *vine-dresser.*

כַּרְמִי (*vine-dresser*) pr. name masc.—I. Ge. 46. 9; Ex. 6. 14; also patronym. (for כַּרְמִיִּי) Nu. 26. 6.—II. Jos. 7. 1.

כַּרְמֶל masc. with suff. כַּרְמִלּוֹ (§ 37. No. 3) with ה loc. כַּרְמֶלָה.—I. *well-cultivated plain, garden, orchard, field;* גֶּרֶשׂ כַּ' *grits of the garden* or *of the best cultivated grounds,* Le. 2. 14.—II. pr. name *Carmel;* (*a*) a fruitful hill south of Asher on the Mediterranean; (*b*) a mountain and city westward from the Dead sea, Jos. 15. 55; 1 Sa. 15. 12; 25. 5; Gent. n. כַּרְמְלִי for ־ִית.

[y] כָּרֶם 'ןו id. in pause (§ 35. rem. 2) . . . כרם

[z] כְּרֻם pref. כְּ) (Kal inf. constr. (for רוּם') . . רום

[a] כַּרְמוֹ noun m. s., suff. 3 pers. s. m. from כֶּרֶם d. 6 a כרם

כַּרְמֵי id. pl., constr. st. . . . . . כרם

כַּרְמִי 'ן pr. name masc. . . . . . . כרם

כַּרְמִי noun m. sing., suff. 1 pers. sing. from כֶּרֶם d. 6 a כרם

[b] כְּרָמֶיהָ id. pl., suff. 3 pers. sing. masc. . . . כרם

כַּרְמֵיהֶם id. pl., suff. 3 pers. pl. masc. . . . כרם

[c] כַּרְמֵיכֶם 'ן id. pl., suff. 2 pers. pl. masc. . . . כרם

[d] כֹּרְמֵיכֶם ן n. m. pl., suff. 2 pers. pl. m. from [כֹּרֵם] d. 7 b כרם

כַּרְמִיל ן masc. *crimson,* 2 Ch. 2. 6, 13; 3. 14.

כְּרָמִים 'ו noun masc., pl. of כֶּרֶם (q. v.) dec. 6 a כרם

[e] כֹּרְמִים [f] 'ןו noun masc., pl. of [כֹּרֵם] dec. 7 b . כרם

כְּרָמֵינוּ ו noun masc. pl., suff. 1 pers. pl. from כֶּרֶם (q. v.) dec. 6 a; ו bef. (:) . . . כרם

[g] כַּרְמְךָ }
כַּרְמְךָ 'ן } id. sing., suff. 2 pers. sing. masc. . . כרם

כַּרְמֶל 'ן noun m. sing., d. 8 (§ 37. r. 3) also pr. name כרם

כַּרְמֶלָה id. with loc. ה (pr. name) . . . . כרם

[h] כַּרְמִלּוֹ 'ןו id., suff. 3 pers. sing. masc. . . . כרם

[i] כְּרֶמֶשׂ pref. כְּ) (noun masc. sing. . . . . רמש

כְּרָן ו (*harp,* Arab. כראן) pr. name m. Ge. 36. 26.

כָּרַס Root not used; prob. i. q. כָּרַשׂ *to be curved;* hence

[k] כָּרְסֵא Chald. noun fem. *seat, throne* . . . כרס

[l] כָּרְסָוָן Chald. id. pl. as if from כָּרְסוּ (comp. dec. 9) כרס

[m] כָּרְסְיֵהּ Chald. id. s., suff. 3 p. s. m. [as if from כָּרְסִי] כרס

---

[a] 2 Ki. 6. 23. [b] 1 Ki. 7. 29. [c] Nu. 21. 18. [d] Da. 3. 4. [e] Je. 18. 17. [f] Ne. 9. 8. [g] Le. 22. 24. [h] De. 23. 2. [i] Is. 53. 7. [k] Ps. 103. 13. [l] Is. 63. 7. [m] Ne. 9. 28. [n] Ne. 9. 27. [o] Ps. 103. 12. [p] Ps. 40. 7. [q] Is. 50. 1. [r] Ge. 50. 5. [s] De. 24. 1, 3. [t] Je. 3. 8. [u] 1 Ki. 20. 25. [x] Ex. 38. 4. [y] Nu. 16. 14. [z] Ps. 12. 9. [a] Ex. 22. 4. [b] Ho. 2. 17. [c] 1 Sa. 8. 15. [d] Is. 61. 5. [e] Joel 1. 11. [f] 2 Ch. 26. 10. [g] Le. 25. 3. [h] Is. 10. 18. [i] Hab. 1. 14. [k] Da. 5. 20. [l] Da. 7. 9. [m] Da. 7. 9.

[כִּרְסֵם] (§ 7) *to devour*, Ps. 80. 14.

כָּרַע fut. יִכְרַע, *to bend, bow, sink down*, of the knees, Is. 45. 23; of a person כָּרַע עַל־בִּרְכַּיִם *to bow down upon the knees*, i. e. *to kneel*; of an animal *bowing* the legs in order to lie down; of persons in token of reverence or worship, with לִפְנֵי, לְ before any one; as an indication of weakness, בִּרְכַּיִם כֹּרְעוֹת *sinking*, i. e. *feeble knees*, Job 4. 4, comp. Ju. 5. 27; hence of females in labour. Hiph. *to cause to bow down, to prostrate*. Meton. *to depress, afflict*.

כְּרָע fem. dec. 4a, only dual כְּרָעַיִם *the legs* or *leg bones*; also of the springing legs of the locust, Le. 11. 21.

כְּרֵעַ[a] pref. כְּ)(noun masc. sing. dec. 1a . רעה
כֹּרֵעַ[b] Kal part. act. sing. masc. dec. 7b . . כרע
כְּרֵעַ[c] וּ pref. כְּ)(noun masc. sing.; וּ bef. (:) . רעע
כְּרֹעֶה pref. id.)(Kal part. act. sing. masc. dec. 9a רעה
כָּרְעוּ Kal pret. 3 pers pl. . . . . כרע
כִּרְעוּת[d] Chald. כְּ bef. (:))(noun fem. sing. constr. of [רְעוּ] dec. 9b . . . . רעה
כֹּרְעוֹת[e] Kal part. act. f., pl. of [כֹּרַעַת] d. 13a fr. כֹּרֵעַ m. כרע
כְּרָעָיו[f] וּ noun fem. du., suff. 3 pers. s. m., see the foll. כרע
כְּרָעַיִם id. du. abs. from [כָּרָע] dec. 4a . כרע
כֹּרְעִים[f] Kal part. act. m., pl. of כֹּרֵעַ dec. 7b . כרע
כְּרָעָתוֹ[g] pref. כְּ)(noun fem. sing., suff. 3 pers. sing. m. from רָעָה dec. 10 [for רָעָה] from רַע m. רעע
כְּרַפְּאִי[h] pref. id.)(Kal inf., suff. 1 pers. sing. . רפא

כַּרְפַּס masc. *a fine white cotton cloth* or *linen*, Est. 1. 6.
כִּרְצוֹן[i] pref. כְּ bef. (:))(n. m. s., constr. of רָצוֹן d. 3a רצה
כִּרְצוֹנוֹ[k] pref. id.)(id., suff. 3 pers. sing. masc. . רצה
כִּרְצוֹנָם pref. id.)(id., suff. 3 pers. pl. masc. . רצה
כִּרְצֹנוֹ[l] defect. for כִּרְצוֹנוֹ (q. v.) . . . רצה
כָּרָקָב[m] וְ pref. כְּ f. כְּהַ·, כְּהָ } noun m. sing. d. 4a; }
כְּרָקָב[n] וּ[o] pref. כְּ q. v. } וּ bef. (:) . } רקב

כָּרַר. Pilp. כִּרְכֵּר (§ 6. No. 4) *to leap, dance*, 2 Sa. 6. 14, 16.

כַּר masc. pl. כָּרִים (§ 37. rem. 7).—I. *fatted lamb*, so called from its *leaping*.—II. meton. *pasture* where lambs feed, Ps. 65. 14; Is. 30. 23.—III. *battering-ram*, Eze. 4. 2; 21. 27.—IV. כַּר הַגָּמָל Ge. 31. 34, *camel's saddle*, "the *haudaj*, or *portable chamber*, in which the Eastern women ride on the backs of camels," (Prof. Lee).

כֹּר masc. dec. 1a, *a cor*, a measure of capacity, containing ten baths.

כּוֹר Chald. masc. id. Ezr. 7. 22.

כִּרְכָּרָה fem. only pl. כִּרְכָּרוֹת Is. 66. 20, *dromedaries*, from their agility and swiftness.

כִּכָּר masc. d. 2b (du. כִּכְּרַיִם, כִּכָּרַיִם pl. כִּכָּרוֹת).—I. *a circuit, circumjacent tract* of country.—II. *a cake* or *round loaf* of bread.—III. *a talent*, a weight of gold, silver or lead.

כִּכַּר Chald. masc. id. pl. כַּכְּרִין Ezr. 7. 22.

כָּרַשׁ Root not used; *to be curved*, cogn. קָרַס, כָּרַם.

כְּרֵשׁ masc. dec. 1a, *the belly*, Je. 51. 34.

כֹּרֶשׁ, כּוֹרֶשׁ (*sun*) pr. name, *Cyrus*, king of Persia.
כְּרֵשׁוֹ[p] noun m. s., suff. 3 pers. s. m. from [כְּרֵשׁ] d. 1a כרשׁ
כְּרִשְׁיוֹן[q] pref. כְּ)(noun masc. sing. . . . רשׁה
כַּרְשְׁנָא pr. name of a prince in the court of Ahasuerus, Est. 1. 14.
כָּרָשָׁע[r] pref. כְּ f. כְּהַ·, כְּהָ } adj. masc. sing. dec. 4a רשׁע
כְּרָשָׁע[s] pref. כְּ q. v. }

כָּרַת וְ pret. 1 & 2 pers. כָּרַתִּי, כָּרַתָּ (for כָּרַתְתִּי, &c. § 25. rem.) fut. יִכְרֹת.—I. *to cut, cut off, cut down*; כֹּרֵת עֵצִים *wood-cutter*; De. 23. 2, כְּרוּת שָׁפְכָה *cut off as to his privy members*, i. e. eunuch, and simply כָּרוּת Le. 22. 24.—II. *to cut off, destroy*.—III. כָּרַת בְּרִית (and sometimes ellipt. without בְּרִית) *to make a covenant, agreement*, from the ancient custom of *cutting up* victims on such occasions; const. with אֵת, עִם, לְ. Niph.—I. *to be cut off* or *down*.—II. *to be divided, separated*.—III. *to be destroyed*.—IV. *to perish, fail*. Pu. כָּרַת, כֹּרַת (§ 10. rem. 5) *to be cut off* or *down*. Hiph. *to cut off, destroy*; trop. to cut off, i. e. *to withdraw*, with acc. and מִן, 1 Sa. 20. 15. Hoph. *to be cut off, to perish*, Joel 1. 9.

כְּרֻתוֹת fem. pl. *hewn beams*.

כְּרִית (*a cutting*) pr. name of a brook which falls into Jordan below Beth-shan, 1 Ki. 17. 3, 5.

כְּרִיתוּת fem. dec. 1b, *separation, divorce*; with סֵפֶר, *bill of divorce*.

כְּרֵתִי pl. כְּרֵתִים.—I. pr. name of a portion of the Philistines residing on the south-west shore of Judea.—II. the title of a certain class of soldiers in the army of David, supposed to have been of Philistine origin. According to Gesenius, *executioners*, attached to David's body-guard; hence הַכְּרֵתִי וְהַפְּלֵתִי *executioners and couriers*.

כָּרַתָּ[t] וְ Kal pret. 2 pers. s. m. [for כָּרַתְתָּ § 25. r.] כרת

[a] Ps. 35. 14. [b] Est. 3. 5. [c] Ps. 28. 4. [d] Ezr. 7. 18. [e] Job 4. 4. [f] Est. 3. 2. [g] 2 Sa. 3. 39. [h] Ho. 7. 1. [i] Est. 1. 8. [k] Da. 11. 3, 16. [l] Da. 8. 4. [m] Ho. 5. 12. [n] Job 13. 28. [o] Pr. 12. 4. [p] Je. 51. 34. [q] Ezr. 3. 7. [r] Ge. 18. 25. [s] Job 27. 7. [t] De. 20. 20.

כָּרֹת[a] Kal inf. abs. . . . . . . כרת
כֹּרַּת[b] Pual pret. 3 pers. sing. masc. (§ 10. rem. 5) כרת
כָּרֹת[c] noun fem. pl. constr. from [כֵּרָה or כָּרָה] d. 11 כרה
כְּרֹת[d] Kal inf. constr. . . . . . כרת
כְּרָת־[e] id. imp. masc. sing. (for כְּרֹת § 8. rem. 18) כרת
כֹּרֵת id. part. act. sing. masc. d. 7 b . . כרת
כָּרְתָה[f] id. imp. sing. masc. with parag. ה (§ 8. r. 11) כרת
כֹּרָתָה[g] Pual pret. 3 p. s. f. [for כֹּרְתָה comp. § 8. r. 7] כרת
כָּרְתוּ[h] וְ Kal pret. 3 pers. pl. . . . כרת
כְּרָתוֹ[i] id. pret. 3 pers. sing. m., suff. 3 pers. s. m. כרת
כִּרְתוּ id. imp. pl. masc. . . . . . כרת
כְּרֻתוֹת[k] וְ[l] noun fem. pl.; or, Kal part. pass. fem., pl. [of כְּרוּתָה] from כָּרוּת masc. . . כרת
כָּרַתִּי / וְכָרַתִּי { Kal pret. 1 pers. sing. [for כָּרַתְתִּי § 25. rem.], acc. shifted by conv. וְ (§ 8. r. 7) } כרת
כֹּרְתֵי[m] id. part. act. pl. c. masc. fr. כֹּרֵת dec. 7 b כרת
כְּרֵתִים gent. noun, pl. of כְּרֵתִי . . . כרת
כֹּרְתִים[n] Kal part. act. masc., pl. of כֹּרֵת dec. 7 b כרת
כָּרַתְנוּ[o] id. pret. 1 pers. pl. . . . . כרת
כְּרֻתֹת defect. for כְּרֻתוֹת (q. v.) . . . כרת
כְּשַׁאֲוָה[p] pref. כְּ)(Kh. שַׁאֲוָה noun f. comp. נַאֲוָה, (K. שׁוֹאָה q. v.) . . . . . שאה
כִּשְׁאוֹל pref. כְּ bef. (:))(noun com. sing. dec. 1 a שאל
כִּשְׁאוֹן[q] pref. id.)(noun m. s., constr. of שָׁאוֹן d. 3 a שאה

כֶּשֶׂב וְ[r] masc. dec. 6 a, *lamb*, comp. כֶּבֶשׂ.
כִּשְׂבָּה fem. *ewe-lamb*, Le. 5. 6; comp. כִּבְשָׂה.

כְּשֶׁבָּא[s] preff. כְּ & שֶׁ)(Kal pret. 3 pers. sing. masc. בוא
כִּשְׂבָּה[t] noun fem. sing. from כֶּשֶׂב masc. . . כשב
כִּשְׁבִיּוֹת[u] pref. כְּ bef. (:))(Kal part. act. fem. pl. [of שְׁבוּיָה from שָׁבוּי masc.] . . שבה
כְּשָׂבִים[x] noun masc., pl. of כֶּשֶׂב dec. 6 . . כשב
כְּשֶׁבֶר[y] pref. כְּ)(noun masc. sing. dec. 6 b שבר
כְּשֶׁבֶת[z] pref. id.)(Kal inf. constr. (suff. שִׁבְתִּי) d. 13 a ישב
כְּשִׁבְתּוֹ pref. id.)(id. with suff. 3 pers. sing. masc. ישב
כִּשְׁגָגָה[a] pref. כְּ bef. (:))(noun fem. sing. dec. 11 c שגג

כֶּשֶׂד pr. name of a son of Nahor; the progenitor of the Chaldeans, Ge. 22. 22.

כַּשְׂדִּי, only pl. כַּשְׂדִּים (once כַּשְׂדִּיִּים Eze. 23. 14, Kh.).—I. Gent. noun *the Chaldeans*, the inhabitants of Babylon; אֶרֶץ כַּשְׂדִּים *Chaldea*; with ה loc. כַּשְׂדִּימָה to Chaldea.—II. meton. *Chaldeans* for *astrologers*, Da. 2. 2, 4.

כַּשְׂדַּי Ch. dec. 7, i. q. Heb. כַּשְׂדִּי Nos. I, II.

כְּשֹׁד[b] וְ pref. כְּ)(noun masc. sing.; וּ bef. (:) . שדד

כַּשְׂדָּאִין Chald. gent. noun, pl. of כַּשְׂדַּי dec. 7 . כשד
כִּשְׂדֵה[c] pref. כְּ bef. (:))(noun masc. sing., constr. of שָׂדֶה dec. 9 b . . . . שדה
כַּשְׂדָּי וְ Chald. for כַּשְׂדִּי, gent. noun sing. dec. 7 כשד
כַּשְׂדָּיָא Ch. Kh. כַּשְׂדָּיָא, K. כַּשְׂדָּאָה, id., emph. st. (§ 63) כשד
כַּשְׂדָּיֵא Ch. Kh. כַּשְׂדָּיֵא, K. כַּשְׂדָּאֵי, id. pl. emph. כשד
כַּשְׂדִּיִּים / וְכַשְׂדִּים { gent. noun, pl. of כַּשְׂדִּי, Kh. כַּשְׂדִּיִּים dec. 8 f (§ 37. rem. 5) } כשד
כַּשְׂדִּימָה id. with parag. ה . . . . . כשד

[כָּשָׂה] *to be covered with fat*, De. 32. 15.

כַּשֶּׂה[d] pref. כַּ f. כְּהַ / כְּשֶׂה[e] pref. כְּ q. v. { noun com. sing. irr. (§ 45) } שה
כְּשֶׁהָיָה[f] preff. כְּ & שֶׁ)(Kal pret. 3 pers. sing. masc. היה
כְּשֶׁהַסָּכָל[g] Kh. כְּשֶׁהַסָּכָל, preff. כְּ, שֶׁ & הַ)(n. m. s. d. 4 a סכל
כַּשּׁוֹאָה[h] pref. כַּ for כְּהַ)(noun fem. sing. dec. 10 שוא
כְּשׁוּב[i] וְ[k] pref. כְּ)(Kal inf. c. dec. 1 a; וּ bef. (:) שוב
כָּשׁוֹל[l] Kal inf. abs. . . . . . כשל
כַּשּׁוֹפָר[m] pref. כַּ for כְּהַ)(noun masc. sing. dec. 2 b שפר
כְּשׁוֹק[n] וְ pref. כְּ)(noun fem. sing. d. 1 a; וּ bef. (:) שוק
כְּשׁוֹר[o] pref. כְּ)(noun masc. sing. (§ 35. rem. 13) שור
כַּשּׁוֹשַׁנָּה[p] pref. כַּ f. כְּהַ / כְּשׁוֹשַׁנָּה[ff] pref. כְּ q. v. { noun fem. sing. dec. 10 } שוש
כִּשְׂחוֹק[q] pref. כְּ bef. (:))(noun masc. sing. . שחק
כַּשַּׁחַל pref. כַּ for כְּהַ)(noun masc. sing. . שחל
כְּשַׁחַק[r] וְ pref. כְּ)(noun masc. s. d. 6 d; וּ bef. (:) שחק
כַּשַּׁחַר[s] pref. כַּ f. כְּהַ / כְּשַׁחַר pref. כְּ q. v. { noun masc. sing. dec. 6 d } שחר
כֻּשִׁיִּים / וְכֻשִׁים { gent. noun, pl. of כּוּשִׁי (comp. dec. 8 f, § 37. rem. 5) from כּוּשׁ . } כוש
כְּשִׁיר[t] pref. id.)(noun masc. sing. dec. 1 a . שיר
כְּשִׁירַת[u] pref. id.)(noun f. s., constr. of שִׁירָה d. 10 שיר
כָּשִׂיתָ[x] Kal pret. 2 pers. sing. masc. . . כשה
כֻּשִׁית gent. noun, fem. of כּוּשִׁי from כּוּשׁ . כוש
כְּשַׁךְ[y] / כְּשֹׁךְ[z] { pref. כְּ)(Kal inf. constr. (§ 18. rem. 3) } שכך
כְּשֹׁכֵב[a] וְ pref. id.)(Kal part. act. s. m. d. 7 b; וּ bef. (:) שכב
כִּשְׁכַּב[ll] pref. כְּ bef. (:))(id. inf. constr. . . שכב
כַּשִּׁכּוֹר pref. כַּ for כְּהַ)(noun masc. sing. dec. 1 b. שכר
כְּשָׂכִיר[b] וְ pref. כְּ)(noun masc. sing. d. 3 a; וּ bef. (:) שכר
כִּשְׂכִיר[c] pref. כְּ bef. (:))(id. constr. st. . . שכר

כָּשַׁל וְ fut. יִכְשׁוֹל (Pr. 4. 16).—I. *to totter, stagger*; part. כֹּשֵׁל *feeble, weary*.—II. *to stumble*, with בְּ *against* any thing. Niph. *to totter, stumble* from weakness. Pi. *to cause to fall*, Eze. 36. 14. Kheth. Hiph.—I. *to*

---

[a] Ho. 10. 4.
[b] Eze. 16. 4.
[c] Zep. 2. 6.
[d] Je. 34. 8.
[e] 1 Sa. 11. 1.
[f] 2 Sa. 3. 12.
[g] Ju. 6. 28.
[h] Je. 22. 7.
[i] Je. 10. 3.
[k] 1 Sa. 5. 4.
[l] 1 Ki. 7. 2.
[m] Ps. 50. 5.
[n] Ne. 10. 1.
[o] Is. 28. 15.
[p] Pr. 1. 27.
[q] Is. 17. 12, 13.
[r] Le. 7. 23.
[s] Ec. 5. 14.
[t] Le. 5. 6.
[u] Ge. 31. 26.
[x] De. 14. 4.
[y] Is. 30. 14.
[z] Est. 1. 2.
[a] Ec. 10. 5.
[b] Joel 1. 15.
[c] Le. 27. 21.
[d] Is. 53. 7.
[e] Ps. 119. 176.
[f] Ec. 12. 7.
[ff] Ca. 2. 2.
[g] Ec. 10. 3.
[h] Eze. 38. 9.
[i] 2 Sa. 17. 3.
[k] 1 Sa. 17. 57
[l] Is. 40. 30.
[ll] 1 Ki. 1. 21.
[m] Is. 58. 1.
[n] Nu. 18. 18.
[o] Pr. 7. 22.
[p] Ho. 14. 6.
[q] Pr. 10. 23.
[r] Is. 40. 15.
[s] Is. 58. 8.
[t] Eze. 33. 32.
[u] Is. 23. 15.
[x] De. 32. 15.
[y] Je. 5. 26.
[z] Est. 2. 1.
[a] Pr. 23. 34.
[b] Job 7. 2.
[c] Le. 25. 53.

cause to totter, to make feeble, La. 1. 14.—II. *to cause to stumble and fall*; metaph. *to seduce*, Mal. 2. 8. Hoph. *to be made to stumble*, Je. 18. 23.

כַּשִּׁיל masc. *an axe*, Ps. 74. 6.

כִּשָּׁלוֹן masc. *fall, ruin*, Pr. 16. 18.

מִכְשׁוֹל m. d. 1 b.—I. *a cause of stumbling, a stumbling-block.*—II. in a moral sense, *cause of offence.*

מַכְשֵׁלָה fem. dec. 10.—I. *ruin*, Is. 3. 6.—II. *cause of offence*, Zep. 1. 3.

כַּשֶּׁלֶג, כַּשָּׁלֶג } pref. כַּ for כְּהַ)(noun masc. sing. (§ 35. rem. 2) . . . . . שלג
כָּשְׁלָה Kal pret. 3 pers. sing. fem. . . . כשל
כְּשִׁלֹה pref. כְּ)(pr. name of a place . . שלה
כָּשְׁלוּ, וְכָשְׁלוּ } Kal pret. 3 pers. pl. (§ 8. rem. 7) . . כשל
כְּשִׁלוֹ pref. כְּ)(pr. name of a place, see שִׁלֹה . שלה
[a] כִּשָּׁלוֹן noun masc. sing. . . . . . כשל
[b] כֹּשְׁלוֹת Kal part. act. pl. fem. from כּוֹשֵׁל masc. . כשל
[c] כְּשַׁלְּחוֹ pref. כְּ)(Piel inf. (שַׁלֵּח for שַׁלַּח), suff. 3 pers. sing. masc. dec. 7b (§ 36. rem. 5) . . שלח
[d] כַּשַּׂלְמָה pref. כַּ for כְּהַ)(noun fem. sing. dec. 12a . שלם
[e] כָּשַׁלְנוּ Kal pret. 1 pers. pl. . . . . . כשל
כִּשְׁלֹשִׁים, [f] כִּשְׁלשָׁם } pref. כִּ bef. (:))(num. card. com. gen., pl. of שָׁלשׁ fem. . . . . שלש
כִּשְׁלֹשֶׁת pref. כִּ bef. (:))(num. card. masc. constr. of שְׁלֹשָׁה (§ 42. rem. 5) from שָׁלשׁ fem. . שלש
[g] כָּשַׁלְתָּ, [h] וְכָשַׁלְתָּ } Kal pret. 2 pers. sing. masc., acc. shifted by conv. וְ (§ 8. rem. 7) . . כשל
כְּשֵׁם pref. כְּ)(noun masc. sing. dec. 7a . . שם
[i] כְּשֻׁם Chald. pref. כְּ)(n. masc. sing. irr. (§ 68) . שם
[k] כִּשְׁמוֹ pref. כִּ bef. (:))(noun masc. sing., suff. 3 pers. sing. masc. from שֵׁם 7a . . . . שם
[l] כִּשְׂמֹחַ pref. id.)(Kal inf. constr. . . . . שמח
[m] כְּשִׂמְחַת pref. כְּ)(noun fem. s., constr. of שִׂמְחָה d. 12b שמח
[n] כְּשִׂמְחָתְךָ pref. id.)(id. with suff. 2 pers. sing. masc. שמח
[o] כְּשָׁמִיר pref. id.)(noun masc. sing. dec. 3a . שמר
[p] כְּשִׁמְךָ pref. כְּ)(n. m. s., suff. 2 pers. s. m. fr. שֵׁם d. 7a שם
[q] כַּשֶּׁמֶן, [r] כַּשָּׁמֶן וְ } pref. כַּ for כְּהַ)(noun masc. sing. dec. 6a (§ 35. rem. 5) . . . . שמן
כְּשֵׁמַע pref. כְּ)(noun masc. sing. dec. 6e . שמע
[s] כִּשְׁמֹעַ וְ pref. כִּ bef. (:))(Kal inf. constr. . . שמע
[t u] כְּשָׁמְעוֹ וּ pref. כְּ)(id., suff. 3 pers. sing. masc.; וּ bef. (:) שמע
[x] כְּשָׁמְעִי וּ pref. id.)(id., suff. 1 pers. sing.; וּ id. . שמע
כְּשָׁמְעֶךָ pref. id.)(id., suff. 2 pers. sing. masc. . שמע
כְּשָׁמְעֲכֶם pref. כְּ)(id., suff. 2 pers. pl. masc. . . שמע

כְּשָׁמְעָם pref. כְּ)(id. suff. 3 pers. pl. masc. . . שמע
[x] כְּשֶׁמְעָתוֹ pref. id.)(id. with fem. term. [שְׁמְעָה], and suff. 3 pers. sing. masc. (§ 8. rem. 10) . שמע
[y] כְּשֹׁמְרֵי pref. כְּ)(Kal part. act. pl. c. fr. שֹׁמֵר d. 7b שמר
[z] כַּשֶּׁמֶשׁ pref. כַּ f. כְּהַ)(n. com. s. (suff. שִׁמְשֵׁךְ) d. 6c שמש
[a] כִּשְׁמֹת pref. id.)(n. m. with pl. f. term. abs. fr. שֵׁם d. 7a שם
[b] כְּשָׁנָה pref. כְּ)(noun fem. sing. dec. 11a . שנה
כִּשְׁנֵי pref. כִּ bef. (:))(id. pl. c.; or num. card. constr. of שְׁנַיִם (q. v.) . . . . שנה
כַּשָּׁנִים, [c] כְּשָׁנִים } pref. כַּ for כְּהַ; וּ pref. כְּ q. v. } id. pl. abs. st.; or (Is. 1. 18) pl. of שָׁנִי; וּ bef. (:) שנה
[d] כְּשַׁסַּע pref. כְּ)(Piel inf. constr. . . . שסע
[ff] כְּשָׁעָה pref. id.)(noun fem. sing. [emph. שַׁעְתָּא] . שעה
[e] כִּשְׂעִירִם pref. כִּ bef. (:))(noun masc. pl. under . שער
[f] כַּשֻּׁעָלִים pref. כְּ)(n. m., pl. of שׁוּעָל (no vowel change) שעל

כָּשַׁף. Piel, *to practise magic, use witchcraft*; part. מְכַשֵּׁף *magician, wizard*; f. מְכַשֵּׁפָה *sorceress, witch.*

כֶּשֶׁף m. d. 6, only pl. כְּשָׁפִים *incantations, sorceries.*

כַּשָּׁף masc. dec. 1 b, *magician*, Je. 27. 9.

אַכְשָׁף (*incantation*) pr. name of a city in Asher, Jos. 12. 20; 19. 25.

[g] כִּשֵּׁף וְ' Piel pret. 3 pers. sing. masc. . . . כשף
[h] כַּשִּׁפְחָה pref. כַּ for כְּהַ)(noun fem. sing. dec. 12b . שפח
[i] כְּשָׁפֶיהָ וּ noun masc. pl., suff. 3 pers. sing. masc. fr. [כֶּשֶׁף] dec. 6; וּ bef. (:) . . . . כשף
[k] כְּשָׁפַיִךְ id. pl. with suff. 2 pers. sing. fem. . כשף
[l] כַּשָּׁפֵיכֶם n. m. pl., suff. 2 pers. pl. m. fr. [כַּשָּׁף] d. 1b כשף
כְּשָׁפִים noun masc., pl. of [כֶּשֶׁף] d. 6 . . כשף
כַּשִּׁקְמִים pref. כַּ for כְּהַ)(noun fem. with pl. masc. term. [fr. שִׁקְמָה § 35. rem. 16] . שקם

[m] כָּשֵׁר וְ fut. יִכְשַׁר *to be right, proper, acceptable.* Hiph. *to give success*, Ec. 10. 10.

כּוֹשָׁרָה f. d. 10, *prosperity, success*, Ps. 68. 7.

כִּישׁוֹר masc. *distaff*, Pr. 31. 19.

כִּשְׁרוֹן masc. *prosperity, success.*

כִּשְׁרוֹן noun masc. sing. . . . . כשר
[n] כַּשִּׁרְיָן pref. כַּ for כְּהַ)(noun masc. sing. . . שרה
[o] כִּשְׂרֵפַת pref. כִּ bef. (:))(noun sing. fem., constr. of שְׂרֵפָה dec. 10 . . . . שרף
[p] כַּשֹּׁרֶשׁ וְ pref. כַּ for כְּהַ)(noun masc. sing. dec. 6c שרש
כְּשֵׁשׁ pref. כְּ)(num. card. fem. . . . שש
[q] כִּשְׁתִלֵי pref. כִּ bef. (:))(noun masc. pl. constr. [from שָׁתִיל or שְׁתִיל] . . . . שתל
[r] כְּשֶׁתִּפּוֹל preff. כְּ & שֶׁ)(Kal fut. 3 pers. sing. fem. . נפל
[s] כִּתְאֵנֵי pref. כִּ bef. (:))(constr. of the foll. . . תאן

a Pr. 16. 18. b Is. 35. 3. c Ex. 11. 1. d Ps. 104. 2. e Is. 59. 10. f 1 Sa. 9. 22. g Ho. 14. 2. h Ho. 4. 5. i Da. 4. 5. k 1 Sa. 25. 25. l Eze. 35. 14. m Is. 9. 2. n Eze. 35. 15. o Eze. 3. 9. p Ps. 48. 11. q Eze. 45. 25. r Ps. 109. 18. s 2 Ch. 15. 8. t Ge. 24. 30. u Ne. 1. 4. x Is. 30. 19. y Je. 4. 17. z Ps. 89. 37. a Ge. 26. 18. b 2 Ki. 17. 4. c Mal. 3. 4. d Ju. 14. 6. e De. 32. 2. f Eze. 13. 4. ff Da. 4. 16. g 2 Ch. 33. 6. h Is. 24. 2. i 2 Ki. 9. 22. k Is. 47. 9, 12. l Je. 27. 9. m Est. 8. 5. n Is. 59. 17. o 2 Ch. 21. 19. p Is. 53. 2. q Ps. 128. 3. r Ec. 9. 12. s Je. 24. 2.

כַּתְּאֵנִים [a] ו׳ pref. כַּ for כְּהַ)(noun fem. with pl. masc. term. from תְּאֵנָה dec. 10 . . . תאן

כְּתֹאַר [b] pref. כְּ)(noun masc. sing. dec. 6 f . תאר

כָּתַב ו׳ fut. יִכְתֹּב.—I. *to write, engrave,* with אֶל, לְ, עַל, בְּ, or acc. of the thing written upon; also with acc. of the thing written; כָּתַב סֵפֶר אֶל־ *to write a letter to* any one.—II. *to describe, write down.*—III. *to write, ordain, decree,* Is. 65. 6; Job 13. 26. Niph. *to be written down.* Piel *to write, decree,* Is. 10. 1.

כְּתַב Chald. *to write.*

כְּתָב m. d. 1a (§ 30. No. 3).—I. *a writing.*—II. *epistle, letter,* 2 Ch. 2. 10.—III. *register, record.*—IV. *scripture,* Da. 10. 21.

כְּתָב Chald. masc. dec. 1b.—I. *a writing.*—II. *precept, prescription,* Ezr. 6. 18; 7. 22.

כְּתֹבֶת f. *a writing, mark,* Le. 19. 28.

מִכְתָּב masc. dec. 2b.—I. *writing.*—II. *thing written, a writing, letter;* hence, *composition, ode,* Is. 33. 9.

כְּתָב [ii] ו׳ ו noun m. s. dec. 1a, Ch. dec. 1b; ו bef. (:) כתב

כְּתַב Chald. Peal pret. 3 pers. sing. masc. . כתב

כְּתֹב ו׳ ו } Kal imp. sing. masc. (§ 8. rem. 18); ו bef. (:) . . . . } כתב
כְּתָב־

כֹּתֵב [c] id. part. act. sing. masc. dec. 7 b . כתב

כְּתָבָא [d] ו׳ ו Ch. noun m. s., emph. of כְּתָב dec. 1b כתב

כָּתְבָא [e] Ch. Peal part. act. fem. dec. 10 [from כָּתֵב] כתב

כָּתְבָהּ [f] Kal imp. sing., suff. 3 pers. sing. fem. כתב

כְּתָבָה [g] Ch. n. m. s. (for כְּתָבָא), emph. of כְּתָב d. 1b כתב

כָּתְבוּ [h] Kal pret. 3 pers. pl. . . . . . כתב

כְּתַבוּ [i] Chald. Peal pret. 3 pers. pl. masc. . כתב

כִּתְבוּ [k] ו׳ Kal imp. pl. masc. . . . . . כתב

כִּתְּבוּ [l] Piel pret. 3 pers. pl. [for כִּתְּבוּ comp. § 8. r. 7] כתב

כִּתְבוּאַת [m] ו׳ pref. כְּ bef. (:))(n. f. s., constr. of תְּבוּאָה d. 10 בוא

כְּתָבוֹר pref. כְּ)(pr. name of a place . . תבר

כֹּתְבִים [n] ו Kal part. act. m., pl. of כֹּתֵב d. 7b . כתב

כְּתֻבִים defect. for כְּתוּבִים (q. v.) . . . . כתב

כָּתְבֵם Kal imp. sing. masc., suff. 3 pers. pl. masc. [ם for ן fem. in Pr. 7. 3, § 2. rem. 5] כתב

כְּתָבָם n. m. s., suff. 3 pers. pl. m. fr. כְּתָב dec. 1a כתב

כָּתְבָן [o] ו Chald. Peal part. act. fem., pl. of כָּתְבָא dec. 10 [from כָּתֵב masc.] . . כתב

כְּתֶבֶן [p] pref. כְּ)(noun masc. sing. . . . תבן

כְּתַבְנִית [q] pref. id.)(noun fem. sing. dec. 1b בנה

כָּתַבְתָּ [r] } Kal pret. 2 pers. sing. masc. (§ 8. rem. 7) . . . . . } כתב
כָּתָבְתָּ

כָּתַבְתָּ ו׳ id.; acc. shifted by conv. ו (§ 8. rem. 7) כתב

כְּתֹבֶת [s] ו noun masc. sing.; ו bef. (:) . . כתב

כָּתַבְתִּי } Kal pret. 1 pers. sing., acc. shifted by conv. ו (§ 8. rem. 7) . . } כתב
כָתַבְתִּי [t] ו׳

כְּתַבְתָּם ו id. pret. 2 pers. sing. masc., suff. 3 pers. pl. masc.; ו for ו conv. . . . כתב

כַּתֹּהוּ [u] pref. כַּ for כְּהַ)(Seg. noun for [תֹּהֶו] . תהה

כִּתְהֹמוֹת [x] pref. כְּ bef. (:))(noun com., pl. of תְּהוֹם d. 1a הום

כֹּתּוּ [y] Kal imp. pl. masc. . . . . . כתת

כְּתוֹא [z] pref. כְּ)(n. m. s. by transp. & contr. for תְּאוֹ תאה

כָּתוֹב [a] ו Kal inf. abs. . . . . . . כתב

כָּתוּב ו׳ id. part. pass. sing. masc. dec. 3a . כתב

כְּתוֹב־ [b] Kh. כְּתוֹב, K. כְּתָב־, Kal imp. sing. masc. (§ 8. rem. 18) . . . . . . כתב

כְּתוּבָה Kal part. p. sing. fem. dec. 10, fr. כָּתוּב m. כתב

כְּתוּבִים id. masc., pl. of כָּתוּב dec. 3a . . כתב

כְּתוֹלְדֹתָם [c] pref. כְּ)(noun fem. pl. (תּוֹלְדוֹת), suff. 3 pers. pl. masc. . . . . . . ילד

כַּתּוֹלָע [d] pref. כַּ f. כְּהַ)(n. m. s. (no vowel change) תלע

כְּתוֹעֲבוֹת pref. כְּ)(n. f. pl. constr. fr. תּוֹעֵבָה dec. 11b תעב

כְּתוֹעֲבוֹתֵיהֶן [e] ו pref. id.)(id., suff. 3 pers. pl. fem.; ו bef. (:) תעב

כְּתוֹעֲבֹת defect. for כְּתוֹעֲבוֹת (q. v.) . . תעב

כְּתוֹעֲפֹת pref. כְּ)(noun fem. pl. c. fr. [תּוֹעָפָה] d. 11a יעף

כְּתוֹר [f] pref. id.)(noun masc. sing. dec. 1a . . ירה

כַּתּוֹרָה ו pref. כַּ f. כְּהַ)(noun fem. sing. dec. 10 ירה

כְּתוֹרִין Ch. pref. כְּ)(noun masc., pl. of [תּוֹר] d. 1a תור

כְּתוֹרַת [g] pref. id.)(n. f. sing., constr. of תּוֹרָה d. 10 ירה

כְּתוֹרָתֶךָ [h] pref. id.)(id., suff. 2 pers. s. m. (for רָתְךָ) ירה

כְּתוֹשָׁב [nn] pref. id.)(noun masc. sing. dec. 1b (except constr. תּוֹשַׁב § 31. rem. 1) . . . ישב

כָּתוֹת [i] Kal inf. abs. . . . . . . כתת

כָּתוּת [k] ו id. part. pass. sing. masc. . . . כתת

כַּתּוֹתִי [l] ו id. pret. 1 pers. sing. . . . . כתת

כְּתִיב Ch. Peal part. pass. sing. masc. . . כתב

כִּתִּיִּים } gent. noun, pl. of כִּתִּי, K. כִּתִּים (§ 37. rem. 5) . . . . . } כתת
כִּתִּיִּם

כִּתִּים } id., Kh. כִּתִּים, K. כִּתִּיִּים (§ 37. rem. 5) כתת
כִּתִּיִּם

כְּתִימְרוֹת [m] pref. כְּ)(n. f. pl. constr. fr. [תִּימָרָה] dec. 11a תמר

כָּתִית noun masc. sing. . . . . . . כתת

כֹּתֶל masc. dec. 6 c, *wall,* Ca. 2. 9.

כְּתַל Ch. id. Da. 5. 5; pl. כֻּתְלַיָּא (from כּוּתַל) Ezr. 5. 8.

כִּתְלִישׁ (prob. for כְּתַל אִישׁ *wall of man*) pr. name of a town in Judah, Jos. 15. 40.

כְּתַל־ [n] Chald. noun masc. sing. . . . כתל

כִּתְלַג [o] Chald. pref. כְּ bef. (:))(noun masc. sing. תלג

[a] Je. 24. 8. [b] Ju. 8. 18. [c] Je. 36. 18. [d] Da. 5. 24. [e] Da. 5. 5. [f] Is. 30. 8. [g] Da. 5. 7, 15. [h] Ezr. 4. 6. [i] Ezr. 4. 8. [ii] Ezr. 4. 7. [k] Jos. 18. 8. [l] Is. 10. 1. [m] Nu. 18. 30. [n] Ne. 10. 1. [nn] Le. 25. 40. [o] Da. 5. 5. [p] Job 21. 18. [q] Is. 44. 13. [r] Ex. 32. 32. [s] Le. 19. 28. [t] Ex. 34. 1. [u] Is. 40. 23. [x] Ps. 78. 15. [y] Joel 4. 10. [z] Is. 51. 20. [a] Je. 32. 44. [b] Eze. 24. 2. [c] Ex. 28. 10. [d] Is. 1. 18. [e] Eze. 16. 47. [f] 1 Ch. 17. 17. [g] 2 Ch. 30. 16. [h] Ps. 119. 85. [i] Is. 30. 14. [k] Le. 22. 24. [l] Ps. 89. 24. [m] Ca. 3. 6. [n] Da. 5. 5. [o] Da. 7. 9.

כִּתְלִישׁ ‖ pr. name of a place . . . . כתל

כָּתְלֵנוּ[a] n. m. sing., suff. 1 pers. pl. fr. [כֹּתֶל] d. 6c כתל

כָּתַם Kal not used; *to shut up, hide*; cogn. חָסַם, חָתַם, חָטַם, hence Niph. Je. 2. 22, *to be shut, laid up*. Others, according to the Syr. *spotted, stained*; hence Eng. vers. " marked."

כֶּתֶם masc. *fine gold*; used only poetically for זָהָב.

מִכְתָּם m. in the superscription of several Psalms, prob. *a golden poem*.

כֶּתֶם[b] / כָּתֶם[c] } noun masc. sing. . . . . . כתם

כְּתֹם[d] pref. כְּ)(noun masc. sing. dec. 8c . . תמם

כְּתֹם־[e] pref. id.)(Kal inf. constr. for תֹּם dec. 8c (§ 18. rem. 3) . . . . תמם

כִּתְמוֹל pref. כְּ bef. (:))(adv. . . . . מול

כְּתֻמִּי[f] ‖ pref. כְּ)(noun masc. sing., suff. 1 pers. sing. fr. תֹּם dec. 8c; ו bef. (:) . תמם

כִּתְמֹל defect. for כִּתְמוֹל (q. v.) . . . מול

כְּתֻמָּם[g] pref. כְּ)(noun masc. sing., suff. 3 pers. pl. masc. fr. תֹּם dec. 8c . . . תמם

כַּתָּמָר[h] pref. כַּ)(for כְּהַ)(noun masc. sing. dec. 4a תמר

כְּתֹמֶר[i] pref. כְּ)(noun masc. sing. . . . תמר

כָּתַן Root not used; *to cover, hide*, cogn. כָּתַם.

כְּתֹנֶת, כֻּתֹּנֶת fem. dec. 13c (with suff. כֻּתָּנְתִּי, pl. כֻּתֳּנוֹת, constr. כָּתְנוֹת § 44. rem. 5) *an under garment, shirt*.

כַּתַּנּוּר pref. כַּ f. כְּהַ } noun masc. sing. dec. 1b } תנר
כְּתַנּוּר pref. כְּ q. v. } see . . }

כָּתְנוֹת[k] ‖' see כְּתֹנֶת defect. . . . כתן

כַּתַּנִּים pref. כַּ for כְּהַ)(n. m. pl. [of תַּן or תָּן] d. 8 תנן

כַּתַּנִּין[l] pref. id.)(noun masc. sing. dec. 1b . תנן

כְּתֹנֶת ‖' noun fem. sing.; ו bef. (:) . . . כתן

כָּתְנֹת[m] ‖ noun fem. pl. constr. fr. כְּתֹנֶת dec. 13c . כתן

כֻּתֳּנֹת id. pl., abs. st. . . . . . כתן

כֻּתָּנְתּוֹ id. sing., suff. 3 pers. sing. masc. . . כתן

כֻּתָּנְתִּי id. sing., suff. 1 pers. sing. . . . כתן

כֻּתָּנְתֶּךָ[n] id. sing., suff. 2 pers. sing. masc. . . כתן

כְּתוֹעֲבוֹת pref. כְּ)(n. f. pl. constr. fr. תּוֹעֵבָה d. 11b תעב

כְּתוֹעֲבֹתֵיהֶם[o] pref. id.)(id. pl., suff. 3 pers. pl. masc. . תעב

כְּתַעַר[p] pref. כְּ)(noun masc. sing. dec. 6d . . תער

כָּתֵף [q]‖' fem. dec. 5b (pl. כְּתֵפוֹת, constr. כִּתְפוֹת, with suff. כְּתֵפָיו).—I. *shoulder*.—II. trop. *side* of an edifice, of the sea, of a city or region.—III. pl. (*a*) *shoulder-pieces* of a garment; (*b*) *sides, jambs of doors* or *gates*, Eze. 41. 2, 26; (*c*) *shoulders* of an axle, 1 Ki. 7. 30, 34.

כֶּתֶף id. constr. st. . . . . . כתף

כְּתִפְאֶרֶת[r] pref. כְּ)(noun fem. sing. constr. d. 13a, abs. תִּפְאָרָה (§ 42. rem. 5) . . . פאר

כְּתַפּוּחַ[s] pref. id.)(noun masc. sing. dec. 1b . נפח

כַּתַּפּוּחִים[t] pref. כַּ for כְּהַ)(id. pl., abs. st. . . נפח

כְּתֵפוֹת[u] noun fem. pl. abs. fr. כָּתֵף dec. 5b . . כתף

כִּתְפוֹת [x]‖' id. pl., constr. st. . . . . כתף

כְּתֵפִי[y] id. sing., suff. 1 pers. sing. . . . כתף

כְּתֵפֶיהָ[z] id. pl., suff. 3 pers. sing. fem. . . כתף

כְּתֵפָיו id. id., suff. 3 pers. sing. masc. . . כתף

כְּתָפְשְׂכֶם[a] pref. כְּ)(Kal inf., suff. 2 pers. pl. masc. . תפשׂ

כְּתֵפֹת defect. for כְּתֵפוֹת (q. v.) . . . כתף

כְּתֹפֶת pref. כְּ)(pr. name of a place . . . תפת

כִּתְפֹת defect. for כִּתְפוֹת (q. v.) . . . כתף

כִּתְקֹעַ[b] ‖ pref. כְּ bef. (:))(Kal inf. constr. . . תקע

כָּתַר Piel.—I. *to surround, encompass* in a hostile manner.—II. *to wait*, as in Syr. & Chald. Job 36. 2. Hiph.—I. *to surround*, with בְּ.—II. intrans. *to be crowned with*, Pr. 14. 18. Prof. Lee, trans. *to comprehend*.

כֶּתֶר masc. *diadem, crown*, Est. 1. 11; 2. 17; 6. 8.

כֹּתֶרֶת fem. pl. כּוֹתָרוֹת (§ 44. rem. 5) *capital, chapiter* of a column.

כַּתַּר־[c] Piel imp. sing. masc. (comp. § 10. rem. 3) כתר

כֶּתֶר noun masc. sing. . . . . . כתר

כִּתְּרוּ[d] Piel pret. 3 pers. pl. . . . . כתר

כִּתְרוּמַת[e] pref. כְּ bef. (:))(n. f. s., constr. of תְּרוּמָה d. 10 רום

כִּתְּרוּנִי[f] Piel pret. 3 pers. pl., suff. 1 pers. sing. . כתר

כְּתָרוֹת[g] noun fem. pl. abs. [as if from כְּתָרָה dec. 11a], see כֹּתֶרֶת (§ 44. rem. 5) . . . כתר

כַּתֹּרֶן[h] pref. כַּ for כְּהַ)(noun masc. sing. dec. 6c תרן

כְּתִרְצָה pref. כְּ)(pr. name of a place . . רצה

כְּתַרְשִׁישׁ[i] pref. id.)(noun masc. sing. . . . רשש

כֹּתָרֹת ‖ / כֹּתֶרֶת ‖ } noun fem. pl. & sing. (§ 44. rem. 5) . כתר

[כָּתַשׁ] *to bruise, pound*, Pr. 27. 22.

מַכְתֵּשׁ masc.—I. *mortar*, Pr. 27. 22.—II. prob. *a hole in the shape of a mortar*, Ju. 15. 19.—III. pr. name of a valley near Jerusalem, Zep. 1. 11.

[כָּתַת] fut. יַכֹּת.—I. *to beat, hammer, forge*, Joel 4. 10.—II. *to beat, break in pieces*; Le. 22. 24 כָּתוּת

[a] Ca. 2. 9. [b] Pr. 25. 12. [c] Ca. 5. 11. [d] Ps. 78. 72. [e] Is. 18. 5. [f] Ps. 7. 9. [g] Is. 47. 9. [h] Ps. 92. 13. [i] Je. 10. 5. [k] Ne. 7. 72. [l] Je. 51. 34. [m] Ezr. 2. 69. [n] Is. 22. 21. [o] Ezr. 9. 1. [p] Ps. 52. 4. [q] Eze. 24. 4. [r] Is. 44. 13. [s] Ca. 2. 3. [t] Ca. 7. 9. [u] 1 Ki. 7. 34. [x] Eze. 41. 2. [y] Job 31. 22. [z] 1 Ki. 7. 44. [a] Jos. 8. 8. [b] Is. 18. 3. [c] Job 36. 2. [d] Ju. 20. 43. [e] Nu. 15. 20. [f] Ps. 22. 13. [g] 1 Ki. 7. 16. [h] Is. 30. 17. [i] Da. 10. 6.

one crushed, i. e. as to his testicles.—III. *to beat down, rout*, as enemies, Ps. 89. 24. Pi. כִּתֵּת i. q. Kal. Pu. *to be broken.*

כָּתִית masc. *beaten oil*, from olives beaten in a mortar.

כִּתִּי, only pl. כִּתִּיִּים, כִּתִּים gent. noun, *the Chittim*, according to Gesenius the inhabitants of *Cyprus*; and, in a wider sense, also those of the islands and coasts of the Mediterranean sea, especially the northern parts.

מְכִתָּה fem. dec. 10, *a breaking in pieces*, Is. 30. 14.

כִּתַּת [a]	[b] ו' Piel pret. 3 pers. sing. masc. (§ 10. r. 1)	כתת
כִּתְּתוּ	וְ id. pret. 3 pers. pl.	כתת
כֻּתְּתוּ [c]	וְ Pual pret. 3 pers. pl. . . .	כתת

ל

ל everywhere with Sheva except in the following cases;—לִ before a word which has Sheva under the first letter, as לִפְרִי for לְפְרִי;—before יְ, so that Yod becomes quiescent, as יְהוּדָה, with ל pref. לִיהוּדָה (for לְיְהוּדָה);—לַ, לֶ, לָ before the composites ֲ, ֱ, ֳ, as לַעֲמֹד (and contr. לַעְזוֹר, לַאדֹנִי, for לַעֲזוֹר, לַאֲדֹנִי), לֶאֱכֹל (and contr. לֶאֱהֹב, for לֶאֱהֹב, לֶאֱמֹר), לָחֳלִי, לָחֳדָשָׁיו;—לַ, לֶ, לָ, לְ when displacing the art. ה (q. v.), as לֶהָרִים for לְהֶהָרִים, לָאוֹר for לְהָאוֹר, לַדּוֹר for לְהַדּוֹר;—לָ frequently before the tone-syllable, as before several forms of the pronouns, and the infinitives of verbs, as לָזֶה, לָאֵלֶּה, לָקוּם, לָלֶכֶת; moreover before substantives, usually at the end of a sentence, and especially when short words are connected in pairs (comp. lett. וָ), comp. לָמָיִם Ge. 1. 6, לָנֶגַע De. 17. 8. For ל with suffixes see § 5.

Prep.—I. noting motion or direction *towards* any object, *to, unto, towards*, hence with verbs of motion, longing, and the like affections; but also of rest, delay, and condition, *at, on, in*, as לְפֶתַח אָהֳלוֹ *at the door of his tent*, לְעֵינֵי פ' *in the sight of any one*; of the time in which any thing is done, as לַבֹּקֶר וְלָעֶרֶב *in the morning and in the evening*, לִשְׁלֹשֶׁת הַיָּמִים *within three days*; with the plural, distribut., as לַבְּקָרִים *every morning*.—II. *into*, of the transition into another state, as נֶהְפַּךְ לְאֵבֶל *is turned into mourning*; הָיָה—לְ *to be, become, be made into* anything.—III. sign of the dative, after verbs of giving, assigning, &c.; also as dative *commodi* and *incommodi*, מִי יֵלֶךְ־לָנוּ *who shall go for us*; יֵשׁ לִי, הָיָה לִי *there is to me*, i. e. *I have*; frequently pleonastic with the verb, לֶךְ־לְךָ *get thee away*; דְּמֵה לְךָ *be thou like*, Ca. 2. 17; 8. 14.—IV. noting possession, *to, belonging to*, equivalent to the genitive, as מִזְמוֹר לְדָוִד *a psalm belonging to*, or *of David*; בֶּן לְיִשַׁי *a son of Jesse*; לַיהוָה הַיְשׁוּעָה *to the Lord belongs salvation*.—V. adverbs with לְ put before nouns take the force of prepositions: סָבִיב לְ *round about*, מִתַּחַת לְ *beneath, under*, &c.; with nouns it frequently serves for a periphrasis of the adv., as לָבֶטַח *securely*, לְבַד *separately*.—VI. by later writers לְ is also used for the accusative, comp. Je. 40. 2; 5. 2.—VII. *at*, noting occasion, e. g. לְשֵׁמַע *at the fame*, Ps. 18. 45.—VIII. *as to, in respect to*.—IX. *on account of, because*; לָכֵן, לָהֵן *therefore*.—X. *about, concerning*.—XI. *according to, after*, as לְמִינוֹ *after its kind*; also *as if, as though, like*.—XII. prefixed to the infinitive, it may be variously rendered, *to*; *till that*; *so that*; *because*; *when*; *as though*.

לְ Chald.—I. *to, unto, towards*; also before the infin.—II. as sign of the dative, accusative, and genitive.—III. conj. *that*, prefixed to the future.

לֹא וְ, וֹ rarely לוֹא, also לוֹ (15 times) adv. of negation.—I. *not*, noting an absolute negation of the verb, whether in the preterite or future; though also found with the future, indicating prohibition or dissuasion, i. q. אַל comp. Le. 19. 4; Pr. 22. 24, where both are used indiscriminately. In combination with substantives and adjectives it conveys a negative signification, e. g. לֹא עֵץ *not wood*, i. e. that which is not wood, a man, Is. 10. 15; לֹא חָסִיד *impious*, Ps. 43. 1.—II. *no, nay*, in answer to a question.—III. *without*, comp. 1 Ch. 2. 30; לֹא כֹל *no one, none*; לֹא דָבָר *nothing*.—IV. *not yet*, 2 Ki. 20. 4; Ps. 139. 16.—V. with prefixes; בְּלֹא (*a*) of time, *when not, before*; (*b*) *without*; (*c*) often ellipt. for בַּאֲשֶׁר לֹא *for that which not*.—הֲלֹא *is not? lo! surely!*—לְלֹא (*a*) *without*, 2 Ch. 15. 3; (*b*) ellipt. for לַאֲשֶׁר לֹא comp. Is. 65. 1.

[a] 2 Ch. 34. 7. [b] 2 Ki. 18. 4. [c] 2 Ch. 15. 6.

לָא, לָה (Da. 4. 32) Chald.—I. *not*.—II. *nothing*, Da. 4. 32.

לֹא דְבָר (*no pasture*) pr. name of a town in Gilead, 2 Sa. 17. 27; but לוֹ דְבָר in 2 Sa. 9. 4, 5, comp. לֹא.

לֹא עַמִּי (*not my people*) symbolical name given to the prophet Hosea, Ho. 1. 9.

לֹא רֻחָמָה (*not pitied*) symbolical name given to a daughter of Hosea.

לָא וְ' Chald. adv. . . . . . לא

לֹא Kh.; K. לוֹ pref. prep. לְ with suff. 3 p. s. m. ל

לֹא[a] [b]וְ' Kh. לֹא q. v., K. לוֹ (q. v.) . . לו

לאב Root not used; Arab. *to thirst*.

תַּלְאוּבָה fem. dec. 10, *thirst, drought*, Ho. 13. 5.

לְאָב pref. לְ)(noun masc. sing. irr. (§ 45) . אב

לְאַב[c] pref. id.)(id. constr. st. . . . אב

לְאַבֵּד וּ' pref. לְ)(Piel inf. constr. d. 7 b; וּ bef. (:) אבד

לָאֲבַדּוֹן[d] pref. לָ for לְהַ·, לְהָ)(noun masc. sing. . אבד

לְאַבְּדָם [e]וּ' pref. לְ)(Piel inf. (אַבֵּד), suff. 3 pers. pl. masc. dec. 7 b; וּ bef. (:) . . . אבד

לְאַבְּדֵנִי[f] pref. לְ)(id. with suff. 1 pers. sing. . . אבד

לְאָבוֹת pref. id.)(noun masc. with pl. fem. term. abs. from אָב irr. (§ 45) . . . אב

לַאֲבוֹתֵיהֶם[g] [h]וְ' pref. לַ bef. (-:))(id. pl., suff. 3 p. pl. m. אב

לַאֲבוֹתֵיכֶם pref. id.)(id. pl., suff. 2 pers. pl. masc. . אב

לַאֲבוֹתָם pref. id.)(id. pl., suff. 3 p. pl. m. (§ 4. r. 2) אב

לַאֲבִי[i] pref. id.)(id. sing., constr. st. . . אב

לְאָבִי pref. לְ)(id. sing., suff. 1 pers. sing. . . אב

לַאֲבִיגַיִל, וְ' לַאֲבִיגַל, לַאֲבִיגַ˚ל Kh., לַאֲבִיָּה, pref. לַ bef. (-:))(pr. names . . . אב

לְאָבִיהָ pref. id.)(noun masc. sing., suff. 3 pers. sing. fem. from אָב irr. (§ 45) . . . אב

לַאֲבִיהֶם[k] pref. לַ bef. (-:))(id., suff. 3 pers. pl. masc. אב

לְאָבִיו וּ' pref. לְ)(id., suff. 3 pers. s. m. וּ bef. (:) אב

לָאֶבְיוֹן pref. לָ for לְהַ·, לְהָ)(adj. masc. sing. d. 1 b אבה

לָאֶבְיוֹנִים pref. id.)(id. pl., absolute state . . אבה

לַאֲבִיטַל pref. לַ bef. (-:))(pr. name fem. . . אב

לְאָבִיךָ pref. לְ)(noun masc. sing., suff. 2 pers. sing. masc. from אָב irr. (§ 45) . . . אב

לַאֲבִימֶלֶךְ pref. לַ bef. (-:))(pr. name masc. . . אב

לְאָבִינוּ pref. לְ)(noun masc. sing., suff. 1 pers. pl. from אָב irr. (§ 45) . . . אב

לָאֶבְיֹנִים[l] pref. לָ for לְהַ·, לְהָ)(adj. m., pl. of אֶבְיוֹן d. 1 b אבה

לְאֶבְיֹנְךָ[m] וּ pref. לְ)(id. s., suff. 2 pers. s. m.; וּ bef. (:) אבה

לַאֲבִיר[n] pref. לַ bef. (-:))(noun masc. sing. constr. of [אָבִיר] dec. 3 a . . . אבר

לַאֲבִירָם וְ pref. id.)(pr. name masc. . . . אב

לְאֶבְיָתָר וּ' pref. לְ)(pr. name masc.; וּ bef. (:) . אב

לְאָבֵל pref. id.)(noun masc. sing. d. 6 (§ 35. r. 6) אבל

לַאֲבֵלֵי[o] pref. לַ bef. (-:))(adj. masc. pl. constr. from אָבֵל dec. 5 (§ 34. rem. 2) . . אבל

לַאֲבֵלָיו[p] וְ pref. id.)(id. pl., suff. 3 pers. sing. masc. אבל

לָאֶבֶן[q] וְ pref. לָ f. לְהַ·, לְהָ } noun fem. sing. dec. 6 a (§ 35. rem. 2) וּ bef. (:) . אבן
לְאָבֶן
לְאֶבֶן[r] וּ' } pref. לְ q. v.

לְאַבְנֵי[s] [t]וּ' pref. id.)(id. pl., constr. st.; וּ id. . אבן

לָאֲבָנִים[u] pref. לָ for לְהַ·, לְהָ)(id. pl., abs. st. . אבן

לְאַבְנֵר pref. לְ)(pr. name masc. . . . אב

לְאָבָק[x] pref. id.)(noun masc. sing. dec. 4 c . אבק

לְאַבְרָהָם, וּ' לְאַבְרָם, וּ' לְאַבְשָׁלוֹם, וּ' לְאַבְשָׁלֹם pref. לְ)(pr. names masc.; וּ bef. (:) . . אב

לַאֲבֹתֵיהֶם [y]וְ' pref. לַ bef. (:))(noun masc. pl., suff. 3 pers. pl. masc. from אָב irr. . . אב

לַאֲבֹתָיו pref. id.)(id., suff. 3 pers. sing. masc. . אב

לַאֲבֹתֶיךָ [z]וְ' pref. id.)(id., suff. 2 pers. sing. masc. אב

לַאֲבֹתֵיכֶם וְ' pref. id.)(id., suff. 2 pers. pl. masc. . אב

לַאֲבֹתֵינוּ וְ' pref. id.)(id., suff. 1 pers. pl. . . אב

לַאֲבֹתָם pref. id.)(id., suff. 3 pers. pl. m. (§ 4. r. 2) אב

לַאֲגֻדָּה[a] pref. id.)(noun fem. sing. dec. 10 . אגד

לַאֲגוֹרַת[b] pref. id.)(noun f. s. constr. of [אֲגוֹרָה] d. 10 גרר

לַאֲגַמִּים[c] } pref. לַ bef. (-:))(noun masc. sing., pl. אֲגַמִּים, constr. אַגְמֵי (§ 35. rem. 10) } אגם
לַאֲגַם

לְאֵידוֹ[d] pref. לְ)(noun masc. sing., suff. 3 pers. sing. masc. from אֵיד dec. 1 a . . . אוד

לֶאֱדוֹם pref. לֶ bef. (v:))(pr. name of a people . אדם

לַאֲדוֹן[e] pref. לַ bef. (-:))(constr. of the foll. . דון

לְאָדוֹן[f] וּ' pref. לְ)(noun masc. s. dec. 3 a; וּ bef. (:) דון

לַאֲדִיב[g] וְ pref. לַ contr. [for לְהַאֲדִיב] Hiph. inf. constr. (§ 11. rem. 3) . . . אדב

לְאַדִּירִים[h] pref. לְ)(adj. or subst. m., pl. of אַדִּיר d. 1 b אדר

לָאָדָם pref. לָ f. לְהַ·, לְהָ } noun masc. sing. also pr. name; וּ bef. (:) . } אדם
לְאָדָם וּ' pref. לְ, q. v. }

לָאֲדָמָה[i] pref. לָ for לְהַ·, לְהָ)(noun fem. sing. d. 11 c אדם

לְאַדְמַת pref. לְ)(id. constr. st. (§ 42. rem. 1) . אדם

לְאַדְמָתוֹ[k] pref. id.)(id., suff. 3 pers. sing. masc. . אדם

[a] 2 Sa. 19. 7. [b] 2 Sa. 18. 12. [c] Ge. 17. 4. [d] Job 26. 6. [e] Est. 9. 24. [f] Ps. 119. 95. [g] 1 Ki. 14. 15. [h] Je. 24. 10. [i] De. 22. 19, 29. [k] 1 Ki. 13. 11. [l] Est. 9. 22. [m] De. 15. 11. [n] Ps. 132. 2, 5. [o] Is. 61. 3. [p] Is. 57. 18. [q] Je. 2. 27. [r] Hab. 2. 19. [s] Is. 54. 12. [t] 2 Ch. 26. 14. [u] Je. 43. 10. [x] Ex. 9. 9. [y] 2 Ch. 6. 25. [z] Ex. 13. 11. [a] 2 Sa. 2. 25. [b] 1 Sa. 2. 36. [c] Is. 35. 7. [d] Job 36. 27. [e] Mi. 4. 13. [f] Ge. 45. 8, 9. [g] 1 Sa. 2. 33. [h] Ju. 5. 13. [i] Ps. 83. 11. [k] Ps. 146. 4.

לְאָדֹן pref. לְ q. v.)(noun masc. sing. dec. 6a [for אָדֹן § 35. rem. 2] . . . . . אדן
לַאדֹנָי pref. לְ, contr. [for לַאֲדֹנָי])(the name of God דון
לַאֲדֹנֵי[b] pref. לְ bef. (-:))(noun m. pl. c. fr. אָדוֹן d. 3a דון
לַאדֹנִי pref. לְ contr. [for לַאֲ׳])(id. s., suff. 1 p. s. דון
לַאדֹנֶיהָ[c] pre . לְ id.)(id. pl., suff. 3 pers. sing. fem. דון
לַאֲדֹנִיָּהוּ[i] pref. לְ bef. (-:))(pr. name masc. . . דון
לַאדֹנֵיהֶם pref. id.)(noun masc. pl., suff. 3 pers. pl. m. from אָדוֹן dec. 3a . . . . . דון
לַאדֹנָיו pref. לְ, contr. [for לַאֲ׳])(id. pl., suff. 3 p. s. m. דון
לַאדֹנֶיךָ[d] pref. לְ id.)(id. pl., suff. 2 pers. sing. masc. דון
לַאֲדֹנֵינוּ[i] pref. לְ bef. (-:))(id. pl., suff. 1 pers. pl. . דון
לַאֲדַרְכֹּנִים[f] pref. id.)(noun masc. pl. [of אֲדַרְכּוֹן] אדרכ׳
לְאַדְרַמֶּלֶךְ pref. לְ)(pr. name of an idol . . אדר

[לָאָה] fut. תִּלְאֶה, ap. וַתֵּלֶא (§ 24. rem. 3).—I. *to labour*, especially *in vain*, Ge. 19. 11.—II. *to be weary, faint*. Niph.—I. *to labour, exert oneself*, Je. 9. 4; espec. *to labour in vain*.—II. *to be weary, faint*.—III. *to be grieved, vexed*.—IV. *to dislike, loathe*, Ex. 7. 18. Hiph. הֶלְאָה (§ 11. rem. 1) *to make weary, to vex*.

לֵאָה (*wearied*) pr. name of Laban's elder daughter, wife of Jacob.

תְּלָאָה fem. *weariness, trouble, vexation*.

לֵאָה וְ׳ pr. name fem. . . . . . לאה
לֶאֱהֹב[g] pref. לְ bef. (-:) } Kal inf. constr. (§ 8. r. 10) אהב
לְאַהֲבָה וּ׳ pref. לְ q. v. }
לְאֹהֲבַי[h] } pref. לְ)(id. part. act. pl. masc., suff. 1 pers. sing. from אֹהֵב dec. 7b . } אהב
לְאֹהֲבַי[i] }
לְאֹהֲבֵי[k] pref. id.)(id. id. constr. st. . . . אהב
לְאֹהֲבָיו pref. id.)(id. id. with suff. 3 pers. pl. masc. אהב
לָאֹהֶל pref. לָ f. לַה׳ ,לָה } noun masc. sing. dec. 6c } אהל
לְאֹהֶל pref. לְ q. v. } (§ 35. rem. 9) . }
לְאָהֳלוֹ pref. id.)(id. sing., suff. 3 pers. sing. masc. אהל
לְאֹהָלָיו[l] pref. id.)(id. pl., suff. 3 pers. sing. masc. (א by Syr. § 35. rem. 9) . . אהל
לְאָהֳלִי[m] pref. id.)(id. sing., suff. 1 pers. sing. . אהל
לְאָהֳלֵיהֶם pref. id.)(id. pl., suff. 3 pers. pl. masc. אהל
לְאֹהָלָיו pref.id.)(id.pl.,suff.3p.s.m.(א by Syr. §35.r.9) אהל
לְאֹהָלֶיךָ pref. id.)(id. pl., suff. 2 pers. s. m. (א id.) אהל
לְאָהֳלֵיכֶם pref. id.)(id. pl., suff. 2 pers. pl. masc. . אהל
לְאָהֳלֶךָ[n] pref. id. [for אָהָלְךָ])(id. sing., suff. 2 pers. sing. masc. (א by Syr. § 39. rem. 9) . אהל

לְאַהֲרֹן וּ׳ pref. לְ)(pr. name masc.; וּ bef. (:) . אהר
לְאוֹבֵד[o] pref. id.)(Kal part. act. sing. masc. . . אבד
לְאוֹיֵב pref. id.)(Kal part. act. sing. masc. dec. 7b איב
לְאוֹיְבִים[p] pref. id.)(id. pl., abs. st. . . . איב
לֶאֱוִיל pref. לְ bef. (-:))(noun masc. sing. dec. 1a . אול
לָאוּלָם[q] pref. לָ f. לַה׳ ,לָה } noun masc. sing. (pl. c. } אול
לְאוּלָם[r] pref. לְ q. v. } אֵלַמֵּי) dec. 8a . }
לְאִוַּלְתִּי[s] pref. id.)(noun fem. sing., suff. 1 pers. sing. from אִוֶּלֶת dec. 13a . . אול
לְאוֹם[t] for לְאֹם, noun masc. sing. dec. 8c . לאם
לְאוּמִּי[u] וּ id., suff. 1 pers. sing. (§ 37. r. 2); וּ bef. (:) לאם
לְאֻמִּים[x] id. pl., abs. st. . . . . לאם
לָאָוֶן[y] pref. לְ)(noun masc. sing. dec. 6g . און
לְאוֹנָן pref. id.)(pr. name masc. . . . און
לָאוֹפַנִּים[z] pref. לָ for לַה׳ ,לָה)(noun m., pl. of אוֹפָן d. 8d אפן
לָאוֹצָר[a] pref. id.)(noun masc. sing. dec. 2b . אצר
לְאוֹצַר pref. לְ)(id., constr. st. . . . אצר
לָאֹצָרוֹת pref. לָ for לַה׳ ,לָה)(id. pl., abs. st. . אצר
לָאוֹר pref. id.)(noun masc. sing. dec. 1a . אור
לֵאוֹר[b] pref. לְ, contr. [for לְהֵאוֹר], Niph. inf. constr. (comp. § 9. rem. 6) . . . אור
לְאוֹר pref. לְ)(noun masc. sing. dec. 1a . . אור
לְאוֹרוֹ[c] pref. id.)(id., suff. 3 pers. sing. masc. . אור
לַאֲוֵרוֹת[d] pref. לְ bef. (-:))(noun fem. pl. [by transp. for אֲרָוֹת] i. q. אֻרְוֹת see אֻרְוָה . ארה
לְאוּרִיָּה, לְאוּרִיאֵל pref. לְ)(pr. names masc. . אור
לָאוּרִים pref. id.)(noun masc., pl. of [אוּר] dec. 1a אור
לְאוֹרֵךְ[e] pref. id.)(noun masc. sing., suff. 2 pers. sing. fem. from אוֹר dec. 1a . . אור
לָאוֹת pref. id.)(noun com. sing. dec. 1a [for אֹות] אוה
לְאַזְכָּרָה[f] pref. id.)(noun fem. sing. dec. 10 . זכר
לְאָזְנִי pref. id.)(pr. name masc. . . . אזן
לָאֶזְרָח pref. לָ for לַה׳ ,לָה)(noun masc. sing. d. 2b זרח
לְאֶזְרַח[g] וּ pref. לְ)(id. constr. st.; וּ bef. (:) . זרח
לְאָח[h] pref. לְ)(noun masc. sing. irr. (§ 45) אח
לְאַחְאָב וּ׳ pref. id.)(pr. name masc.; וּ bef. (:) . אח
לָאֶחָד pref. לָ f. לַה׳ ,לָה } num. card. sing. masc. } אחד
לְאֶחָד וּ׳ וּ pref. לְ q. v. } irr. (§ 45); וּ bef. (:) }
לְאַחַד[k] וּ׳ pref. id.)(id. constr. st.; וּ id. . אחד
לַאֲחָדִים[l] pref. לְ bef. (-:))(id. pl. abs. . אחד
לֶאֱחֹז[m] pref. לְ bef. (-:))(Kal inf. constr. . אחז
לְאָחוֹר pref. לְ)(noun masc. sing. dec. 3a אחר
לַאֲחוֹת[n] וּ pref. id.)(noun fem. s. irr. (§ 45); וּ bef. (:) אח

[a] Ex. 38. 27. [b] Ps. 136. 3. [c] Ex. 21. 4. [d] 1 Ki. 18. 8, 11, 14. [e] Ne. 8. 10. [f] Ezr. 8. 27. [g] Ec. 3. 8. [h] De. 5. 10. [i] Ex. 20. 6. [k] Ps. 119. 132, 165. [l] 2 Ki. 14. 12. [m] Job 19. 12. [n] Ju. 19. 9. [o] Pr. 31. 6. [p] Ps. 139. 22. [q] 1 Ki. 7. 8. [r] 2 Ch. 29. 17. [s] Ps. 69. 6. [t] Pr. 11. 26. [u] Is. 51. 4. [x] Is. 55. 4. [y] Am. 5. 5. [z] Eze. 10. 13. [a] Ne. 7. 70. [b] Job 36. 30. [c] Job 29. 3. [d] 2 Ch. 32. 28. [e] Is. 60. 3. [f] Le. 2. 7. [g] Nu. 9. 14. [h] Eze. 44. 25. [i] Ec. 4. 11. [k] Zec. 11. 7. [l] Eze. 37. 17. [m] Job 38. 13. [n] Eze. 44. 25.

לַאֲחוֹתֵיכֶם[a] וְ pref. לַ bef. (־ֲ) X id. pl., suff. 2 pers. pl. m. אח
לַאֲחוֹתֵךְ[b] pref. id. X id. sing., suff. 2 pers. sing. fem. אח
לַאֲחוֹתֵנוּ[c] pref. id. X id. sing., suff. 1 pers. pl. . . אח
לֶאֱחֹז[d] [e]וְ' pref. לֶ bef. (־ֱ) X Kal inf. constr. . . אחז
לְאָחָז pref. לְ X pr. name masc. . . . . אחז
לַאֲחֻזָּה pref. לַ bef. (־ֲ) X noun fem. sing. dec. 10 אחז
לַאֲחַזְיָהוּ pref. id. X pr. name masc. . . . אחז
לַאֲחֻזַּת וְ' pref. id. X noun fem. s., constr. of אֲחֻזָּה d. 10 אחז
לַאֲחֻזָּתוֹ pref. id. X id. with suff. 3 pers. sing. masc. אחז
לַאֲחֵי[f] pref. id. X noun m. pl. constr. from אָח irr. (§ 45) אח
לְאָחִי[g] pref. לְ X id. sing., suff. 1 pers. sing. . . אח
לְאַחַי pref. id. X id. pl., suff. 1 pers. sing. [for אַחַּי] dag. forte impl. in ח (§ 45) . . . אח
לַאֲחִיָּה pref. לַ bef. (־ֲ) X pr. name masc. . . . אח
לְאָחִיהָ[h] pref. לְ X noun masc. sing., suff. 3 pers. sing. fem. from אָח irr. (§ 45) . . . אח
לַאֲחֵיהֶם וְ' pref. לַ bef. (־ֲ) X id. pl., suff. 3 pers. pl. m. אח
לְאָחִיו וּ' pref. לְ X id. s., suff. 3 pers. s. m.; וּ bef. (:) אח
לְאֶחָיו וּ' pref. id. X id. pl., suff. 3 pers. sing. masc. (dag. forte impl. in ח § 45); וּ id. . . אח
לְאָחִיךָ [i]וּ' pref. id. X id. sing., suff. 2 pers. s. m.; וּ id. אח
לְאָחִיךְ[k] pref. id. X id. sing., suff. 2 pers. sing. fem. אח
לְאַחֶיךָ pref. id. X id. pl., suff. 2 pers. sing. masc. (dag. forte impl. in ח § 45) . . . אח
לַאֲחֵיכֶם pref. לַ bef. (־ֲ) X id. pl., suff. 2 pers. pl. masc. אח
לַאֲחִימֶלֶךְ pref. id. X pr. name masc. . . . . אח
לְאָחִינוּ[l] pref. לְ X noun masc. sing., suff. 1 pers. pl. from אָח irr. (§ 45) . . . . אח
לַאֲחִינֹעַם m., לַאֲחִירָם fem.; pref. לַ bef. (־ֲ) X pr. names אח
לְאַחֵר pref. לְ X adj. masc. sing., dag. forte impl. in ח, irr. (§ 45) . . . . אחר
לַאֲחֵרִים [m]וְ' pref. לַ bef. (־ֲ) X id. pl. abs. [as if from אָחֵר] אחר
לְאַחֲרִיתָהּ[n] pref. לְ X noun fem. sing., suff. 3 pers. sing. fem. from אַחֲרִית dec. 1 b . . . אחר
לְאַחֲרִיתוֹ[o] pref. id. X id., suff. 3 pers. sing. masc. . אחר
לְאַחֲרִיתֵךְ[p] pref. id. X id., suff. 2 pers. sing. fem. . אחר
לְאַחֲרִיתָם pref. id. X id., suff. 3 pers. pl. masc. . אחר
לְאָחֳרָן[q] Chald., pref. id. X adj. masc. sing. . . אחר
לָאַחֲרֹנָה pref. לָ for לְהַ·, לְהָ X adj. fem. from אַחֲרוֹן m. אחר
לְאַחֲרֹנִים[r] pref. id. X id. pl. masc. dec. 1 b . . אחר
לְאַחֶרֶת[s] pref. id. X adj. fem. from אַחֵר masc. (dag. forte impl. in ח § 45) . . . . אחר
לַאֲחַשְׁדַּרְפְּנֵי pref. לַ bef. (־ֲ) X constr. of the foll. אחשר'

לַאֲחַשְׁדַּרְפְּנַיָּא Chald., pref. id. X noun masc. pl., emph. from [אֲחַשְׁדַּרְפַּן] dec. 2 a . . אחשר'
לְאַחַת / לְאֶחָת pref. לְ X num. card. [for אַחְדַת], fem. of אֶחָד (§ 45) . . . אחד
לַאֲחֹתוֹ[t] וְ pref. לַ bef. (־ֲ) X noun fem. s., suff. 3 pers. sing. masc. from אָחוֹת irr. (§ 45) . אח
לְאֲחֹתִי[u] וּ pref. לְ X id. with dag. forte impl. in ח; וּ bef. (:) אח

לאט to vail, cover the face, 2 Sa. 19. 5.

לְאַט[y] / לָאט pref. לְ or לְ q. v. X subst. masc., with the prefix used adverbially . אטט
לְאִטִּי[x] pref. לְ X id. with suff. 1 pers. sing. dec. 8 e אטט
לְאֹיֵב[a] pref. id. X Kal part. act. sing. masc. dec. 7 b איב
לְאֹיְבֵי[b] pref. id. X id. pl., constr. st. . . . . איב
לְאֹיְבָיו pref. id. X id. pl., suff. 3 pers. sing. masc. איב
לְאֹיְבַיִךְ pref. id. X id. pl., suff. 2 pers. sing. fem. איב
לְאֹיְבֶיךָ[c] pref. id. X id. pl., suff. 2 pers. sing. masc. . איב
לְאֹיְבִים[d] pref. id. X id. pl., abs. st. . . . . איב
לְאֵיד[e] pref. id. X noun masc. sing. dec. 1 a . . אוד
לְאִיּוֹב pref. id. X pr. name masc. . . . איב
לְאִיזֶבֶל pref. id. X pr. name fem., see אִיזֶבֶל.
לָאִיִּים / לְאִיִּים[f] pref. לָ f. לְהַ·, לְהָ / pref. לְ q. v. noun masc., pl. of אִי dec. 8 (§ 37. No. 4) אוה
לָאַיִל[g] / לְאַיִל pref. לָ for לְהַ·, לְהָ X noun m. sing. d. 6 h אול
לָאֵילִים / לְאֵילִם pref. id. X id. pl., abs. st. . . . אול
לְאֵילָמָו[h] וּ pref. לְ X noun masc. pl., suff. 3 pers. sing. masc. from [אֵילָם] dec. 8 a; וּ bef. (:) אול
לְאָיִן[dd] pref. id. X for אַיִן', noun masc. sing. dec. 6 h אין
לְאֵין [i]וּ' pref. id. X id., constr. st. (adverbially); וּ bef. (:) אין
לָאֵיפָה pref. לָ for לְהַ·, לְהָ X noun fem. sing. dec. 10 אוף
לָאִישׁ / לְאִישׁ [k]וְ' pref. id. / וּ' pref. לְ noun masc. sing. dec. 1 a (but comp. § 45); וּ bef. (:) איש
לְאִישָׁהּ [l]וּ' pref. id. X id., suff. 3 pers. sing. fem. איש
לְאִישִׁי pref. id. X id., suff. 1 pers. sing. . . איש
לְאִישֵׁךְ[m] pref. id. X id., suff. 2 pers. sing. fem. . איש
לְאִיתִיאֵל pref. id. X pr. name masc. . . . . אית
לְאִיתָמָר וּ' pref. id. X pr. name masc.; וּ bef. (:) אוה
לְאֵיתָן pref. id. X pr. name masc. . . . . יתן
לְאֵיתָנוֹ[n] pref. id. X noun masc. sing., suff. 3 pers. sing. masc. from אֵיתָן (no vowel change) . יתן

[a] Ho. 2. 3. [b] Eze. 16. 52. [c] Ca. 8. 8. [d] 1 Ch. 13. 9. [dd] Is. 40. 23.
[e] Ec. 2. 3. [f] Nu. 27. 10. [g] 1 Ki. 2. 15. [h] Ge. 24. 53.
[i] De. 23. 21. [k] Ge. 20. 16. [l] Ru. 4. 3. [m] Da. 11. 4.
[n] Je. 5. 31. [o] Da. 11. 4. [p] Je. 31. 17. [q] Da. 5. 17.
[r] Ec. 1. 11. [s] Eze. 41. 24. [t] Ezr. 8. 36. [u] Le. 21. 3.
[x] Nu. 6. 7. [y] Job 15. 11. [z] Ge. 33. 14. [a] Je. 6. 25.
[b] 1 Sa. 25. 22. [c] De. 28. 31, 68. [d] La. 1. 2. [e] Pr. 17. 5.
[f] Da. 11. 18. [g] Nu. 29. 3. [h] Eze. 40. 25. [i] Is. 40. 29.
[k] Ju. 19. 24. [l] 1 Sa. 25. 19. [m] 2 Ki. 4. 26. [n] Ex. 14. 27.

לאך Root not used; Ethiop. *to send; to minister*.

מַלְאָךְ masc. dec. 2 b.—I. *messenger.*—II. *angel.*—III. perh. *priest*, Ec. 5. 5, comp. Mal. 2. 7.

מַלְאַךְ Chald. dec. 2 a, *angel*, Da. 3. 28; 6. 23.

מְלָאכָה fem. (for מַלְאָכָה), constr. מְלֶאכֶת, with suff. מְלַאכְתּוֹ; pl. c. מַלְאֲכוֹת (§ 42. rem. 5).—I. *work, business, labour.*—II. *acquisition, wealth, property*, Ex. 22. 7, 10; hence, *cattle*, comp. Ge. 33. 14.

מַלְאָכוּת fem. dec. 3 a, *message*, Hag. 1. 13.

מַלְאָכִי (*messenger*) pr. name, *Malachi*, the prophet, Mal. 1. 1.

לֶאֱכוֹל pref. לְ bef. (ֱ))(Kal inf. constr. (§ 8. r. 18) אכל

לֶאֱכוֹל־[a] Kh. לֶאֱכוֹל (q. v.), K. לֶאֱכָל־ (q. v. & § 8. r. 18) אכל

לְאַכְזָב[b] pref. לְ)(adj. masc. sing. כזב

לְאַכְזָר pref. id.)(adj. masc. sing. כזר

לְאַכְזָרִי[c] pref. id.)(adj. masc. sing. כזר

לָאֹכֵל[d] pref. לְ for לְהַ· ,לְהָ)(Kal part. act. s. m. d. 7 b אכל

לֶאֱכֹל ,לֶאֱכָל־[e] וְ pref. לְ bef. (ֱ))(id. inf. constr. (§ 8. rem. 18) אכל

לְאָכְלָה pref. לְ)(noun fem. sing. אכל

לְאָכְלוֹ[f] pref. id.)(Kal inf., suff. 3 pers. sing. masc. אכל

לְאָכְלוֹ[g] pref. id.)(noun masc. sing., suff. 3 pers. sing. masc. from אֹכֶל dec. 6 c אכל

לְאָכְלְכֶם[h] וּ pref. id.)(id. with suff. 2 p. pl. m.; וּ bef. (:) אכל

לָאֵל pr. name masc. אול

לָאֵל pref. לְ for לְהַ· ,לְהָ)(noun masc. sing. d. 1 a אול

לְאַל[i] pref. לְ)(noun masc. sing. (אַל elsewhere adv.) אלל

לְאֵל pref. id.)(noun masc. sing. dec. 1 a אול

לָאֵלֶּה pref. לְ for לְהַ· ,לְהָ)(pron. demon. com. pl. אל

לְאָלָה pref. לְ)(noun fem. sing. dec. 10 (§ 42. r. 2) אלה

לֶאֱלָהּ Chald., pref. לְ bef. (ֱ))(noun masc. s. d. 1 a אלה

לֶאֱלֹהַּ[k] וְ pref. id.)(noun masc. sing. dec. 1 a אלה

לָאֵלֶּה[l] וְ pref. לְ)(pron. demon. com. pl.; וּ bef. (:) אל

לֵאלָהָא[m] וְ Chald., pref. לְ, contr. [for לֶאֱלָ])(noun masc. sing., emph. of אֱלָהּ dec. 1 a אלה

לֵאלָהֲהוֹן[n] Ch. pref. id.)(id. with suff. 3 pers. pl. masc. אלה

לֵאלָהוּ[o] Ch. pref. id.)(noun masc. sing., suff. 3 pers. sing. masc. from אֱלוֹהַּ dec. 1 a אלה

לֵאלָהִי[p] Ch., pref. id.)(noun masc. sing., suff. 1 pers. sing. from אֱלָהּ dec. 1 a אלה

לֵאלֹהַי[q], לֵאלֹהָי pref. id.)(noun masc. pl., suff. 1 pers. pl. from אֱלוֹהַּ dec. 1 a אלה

לֵאלָהַיִּ[r] וְ Ch., pref. id.)(noun m. pl. c. from אֱלָהּ d. 1 a אלה

לֵאלֹהֵי pref. id.)(noun masc. pl. c. from אֱלוֹהַּ dec. 1 a אלה

לֵאלֹהֵיהֶם[s] וְ pref. id.)(id. pl., suff. 3 pers. pl. masc. אלה

לֵאלֹהֵיהֶן pref. id.)(id. pl., suff. 3 pers. pl. fem. אלה

לֵאלֹהָיו pref. id.)(id. pl., suff. 3 pers. sing. masc. אלה

לֵאלָהָיךְ[t] Ch., pref. id.)(noun masc. pl. (K. ךְ sing.), suff. 2 pers. sing. masc. from אֱלָהּ dec. 1 a אלה

לֵאלֹהֵיכֶם pref. id.)(noun masc. pl., suff. 2 pers. pl. masc. from אֱלוֹהַּ dec. 1 a אלה

לָאֱלֹהִים[u] pref. לְ f. לְהַ· ,לְהָ, לֵאלֹהִים pref. לְ, contr. [for לֶאֱלֹ] } id. pl. abs. st. אלה

לֵאלֹהֵינוּ pref. id.)(id. pl., suff. 1 pers. pl. אלה

לֶאֱלוֹהַּ[x] וְ pref. לְ bef. (ֱ))(id. sing. abs. אלה

לֶאֱלוּל[y] pref. id.)(name of a month אלל

לְאֵילוֹן pref. לְ)(pr. name masc. אול

לֶאֱלִילֶיהָ[z] וְ pref. לְ bef. (ֱ))(noun masc. pl., suff. 3 pers. sing. fem. from [אֱלִיל] dec. 1 a אלל

לֶאֱלִימֶלֶךְ ,לֶאֱלִיעֶזֶר ,לֶאֱלִיפַז, pref. לְ bef. (ֱ))(pr. n. m. אלה

לְאֶלְיָקִים ,לְאֶלְיָשִׁיב, pref. לְ)(pr. names masc. אלה

לֶאֱלִישָׁע ,לֶאֱלִיָּתָה, pref. לְ bef. (ֱ))(pr. names masc. אלה

לְאִלֵּם[a] pref. לְ)(adj. masc. sing. dec. 7 b אלם

לְאֵלָם[b] וּ pref. id.)(noun masc. sing. (pl. c. אֵלַמֵּי) dec. 8 a; וּ bef. (:) אול

לְאֵלַמָּו[c] וּ pref. id.)(noun masc. pl., suff. 3 pers. sing. masc. from [אֵילָם] dec. 8 a; וּ bef. (:) אול

לָאַלְמוֹת[d] pref. לְ for לְהַ· ,לְהָ)(id. with pl. fem. term. אול

לְאַלְמָנָה וְ pref. id.)(noun fem. sing. dec. 11 a אלם

לַאֲלֻמֹּתַי[e] pref. לְ bef. (ֲ))(noun fem. sing., suff. 1 pers. sing. from [אֲלֻמָּה] dec. 10 אלם

לְאֶלְנָתָן ,וּלְאֶלְעָזָר וּ, pref. לְ)(pr. n. m.; וּ bef. (:) אלה

לָאָלֶף pref. לְ f. לְהַ· ,לְהָ, לְאָלֶף[f], לְאֶלֶף } pref. לְ q. v. } noun masc. sing. dec. 6 a (§ 35. rem. 2) אלף

לְאַלְפֵי pref. id.)(id. pl., constr. st. אלף

לְאַלְפֵיהֶם[g] pref. id.)(noun masc. pl., suff. 3 pers. pl. masc. from אַלּוּף dec. 1 b אלף

לְאַלְפֵיכֶם[h] וּ pref. id.)(noun masc. pl., suff. 2 pers. pl. masc. from אֶלֶף dec. 6 a; וּ bef. (:) אלף

לָאֲלָפִים[i] pref. לְ f. לְהַ· ,לְהָ, וְלַאֲלָפִים pref. לְ bef. (ֲ) } id. pl., abs. st. אלף

לְאֹם[k] וּ[l] masc. dec. 8 c (with suff. לְאֻמִּי or לְאוּמִּי Is. 51. 4).—I. *people, nation.*—II. לְאֻמִּים pr. name of a people, Ge. 25. 3.

---

[a] Eze 44. 3. [b] Mi. 1. 14. [c] Pr. 5. 9. [d] Is. 55. 10. [e] Ge. 47. 24. [f] Eze. 33. 27. [g] Job 20. 21. [h] Ge. 47. 24. [i] Job 24. 25. [k] Da. 11. 38. [l] 1 Ch. 26. 12. [m] Da. 5. 23. [n] Da. 3. 28. [o] Hab. 1. 11. [p] Da. 3. 14. [q] Ps. 69. 4. [r] Da. 5. 4, 23. [s] Ex. 23. 32. [t] Da. 3. 18, 12. [u] Ex. 22. 19. [x] Da. 11. 38. [y] Ne. 6. 15. [z] Is. 10. 11. [a] Pr. 31. 8. [b] 1 Ki. 7. 12. [c] Eze. 40. 29, 33. [d] Eze. 40. 16. [e] Ge. 37. 7. [f] 1 Ch. 12. 14. [g] Ge. 36. 30. [h] 1 Sa. 10. 19. [i] Ex. 34. 7. [k] Pr. 14. 28. [l] Ge. 25. 23.

לְאֵם[a] [b] ו׳ וּ pref. לְ)(noun fem. sing. d. 8b; וּ bef. (:) . אם

לְאָמָה[u] pref. id.)(noun fem. sing. irr. (§ 45) . אמה

לְאִמָּהּ[c] [d] ו׳ pref. id.)(noun fem. sing., suff. 3 pers. sing. fem. from אֵם dec. 8b; וּ bef. (:) . אם

לְאִמּוֹ ו׳ pref. id.)(id., suff. 3 pers. sing. m.; וּ id. אם

לֶאֱמוּנָה pref. לֶ bef. (ֱ))(noun fem. sing. dec. 10 . אמן

לֵאמוֹר in full for לֵאמֹר (q. v. & § 8. rem. 18) . אמר

לְאַמּוֹת[e] pref. לְ)(noun fem., pl. of אַמָּה dec. 10 . אם

לְאִמִּי וּ pref. id.)(noun fem. sing., suff. 1 pers. sing. from אֵם dec. 8b; וּ bef. (:) . אם

לְאֻמִּים ו׳ pref. id.)(noun masc., pl. of לְאֹם dec. 8c, also pr. name; וּ id. . לאם

לְאַמְנוֹן ו׳ pref. id.)(pr. name masc.; וּ id. . אמן

לְאֹמֶנֶת[f] pref. id.)(Kal part. act. f. d. 13a, fr. אֹמֵן m. אמן

לַאֲמַצְיָהוּ pref. לַ bef. (ֲ))(pr. name masc. . אמץ

לֵאמֹר ו׳ pref. לֵ, contr. [for לֶאֱמֹר])(Kal inf. constr. אמר

לְאִמֵּר pref. לְ)(pr. name masc. . אמר

לָאֱמֹרִי pref. לָ for לְהַ· לְהָ)(pr. name of a people . אמר

לַאֲמָרַי[g] pref. לַ bef. (ֲ))(noun masc. pl., suff. 1 pers. sing. from [אֵמֶר] dec. 6b . אמר

לְאִמְרֵי pref. לְ)(id. pl., constr. st. . אמר

לַאֲמַרְיָה pref. לַ bef. (ֲ))(pr. name masc. . אמר

לְאִמְרַת[h] וּ pref. לְ)(noun fem. sing., constr. of [אִמְרָה] dec. 12b; וּ bef. (:) . אמר

לְאִמְרָתֶךָ[i]
לְאִמְרָתֶךָ[k] } pref. id.)(id. with suff. 2 pers. sing. masc. אמר

לֶאֱמֶת[l] pref. לֶ bef. (ֱ))(noun fem. sing. dec. 8 [for אֲמֶנֶת § 37. No. 3b] . אמן

לַאֲמָתְךָ
לַאֲמָתֶךָ[m] } ו׳ pref. לַ bef. (ֲ))(noun fem. sing., suff. 2 p. s. m. fr. אָמָה d. 11a, pl. irr. (§ 45) אמה

לְאִמֹּתָם[n] pref. לְ)(noun fem. pl., suff. 3 pers. pl. masc. from אֵם dec. 8b . אם

לְאַמֹּתָם[o] pref. id.)(noun fem. pl., suff. 3 pers. pl. masc. from אַמָּה dec. 10 . אמם

לֶאֱנוֹשׁ pref. לֶ bef. (ֱ))(n. m. s. irr. (see אִישׁ § 45) אנש

לְאַנְשֵׁי pref. לְ)(id. pl. constr. [prop. from [אֱנָשׁ] . אנש

לְאַנְשֵׁיהֶם וּ pref. id.)(id. pl., suff. 3 p. pl. m.; וּ bef. (:) אנש

לַאֲנָשָׁיו pref. לַ bef. (ֲ))(id. pl., suff. 3 pers. sing. m. אנש

לַאֲנָשֶׁיךָ[p] pref. id.)(id., suff. 2 pers. sing. masc. . אנש

לָאֲנָשִׁים[q] pref. לָ f. לְהַ· לְהָ }
לַאֲנָשִׁים [r] ו׳ וְ pref. לַ bef. (ֲ) } id. pl., abs. st. . אנש

לְאָסָא pref. לְ)(pr. name masc. . אסה

לֶאֱסוֹר[s] in full for לֶאֱסֹר (q. v. & § 8. rem. 18) . אסר

לָאֲסוּרִים[t] [w] ו׳ וְ pref. לָ bef. (ֲ))(Kal p. p. pl. m. fr אָסוּר d. 3a אסר

לֶאֱסוּרִין[x] וְ Chald., pref. לֶ bef. (ֱ))(noun masc., pl. of אֱסוּר dec. 1a . אסר

לְאָסָף pref. לְ)(pr. name masc. . אסף

לֶאֱסֹף pref. לֶ bef. (ֱ))(Kal inf. constr. dec. 6c . אסף

לָאֲסֻפִּים[y] וְ pref. לָ for לְהַ· לְהָ)(noun masc., pl. of [אָסֹף] dec. 8c (§ 37. No. 3c) . אסף

לְאֱסָר[z] וּ pref. לְ)(noun masc. sing., constr. of אֱסָר dec. 2b; וּ bef. (:) . אסר

לֶאְסֹר[a]
לֶאֱסֹר } pref. לֶ bef. (ֱ))(Kal inf. constr. (§ 13. rem. 2) . אסר

לֶאְסָרְךָ[b] pref. id.)(id. with suff. 2 pers. sing. masc. אסר

לְאֶסְתֵּר pref. לְ)(pr. name fem., see אֶסְתֵּר.

לָאֵפֹד[c] pref. לָ for לְהַ· לְהָ)(noun masc. sing. . אפד

לְאַפּוֹ[d] pref. לְ)(noun masc. sing., suff. 3 pers. sing. masc. from אַף dec. 8d (§ 37. No. 3b) . אנף

לָאֵפוֹד[e] pref. לָ f. לְהַ· לְהָ }
לְאֵפוֹד[f] pref. לְ q. v. } noun masc. sing. . אפד

לְאֹפוֹת[g] וּ pref. id.)(Kal part. act., pl. of [אֹפָה] dec. 10, from אֹפֶה masc.; וּ bef. (:) אפה

לְאַפֵּי[h] pref. id.)(noun masc. du. constr., from אַף dec. 8d (§ 37. No. 3b) . אנף

לְאַפִּי[i] pref. id.)(id. sing., suff. 1 pers. sing. . אנף

לְאַפָּיו pref. id.)(id. du., suff. 3 pers. sing. masc. אנף

לָאֲפִיקִים[k] pref. לָ f. לְהַ· לְהָ }
לַאֲפִיקִים pref. לַ bef. (ֲ) } noun masc., pl. of [אָפִיק] dec. 3a . אפק

לְאַפְסֵי[zz] pref. לְ)(noun m. du. constr. fr. אֶפֶס d. 6a אפס

לְאֵפֶר[l] pref. id.)(noun masc. sing. . אפר

לְאֶפְרַיִם
לְאֶפְרָיִם } pref. id.)(pr. name of a man and a tribe אפר

לְאָצֵל וּ pref. id.)(pr. name masc.; וּ bef. (:) . אצל

לָאֹצָרוֹת[m] וְ pref. לָ, for לְהַ· לְהָ)(noun masc. with pl. fem. term. abs. from אוֹצָר dec. 2b . אצר

לְאֹצְרוֹת ו׳ pref. לְ)(id. pl. constr. st.; וּ bef. (:) אצר

לְאֹצְרֹתָיו[dd] pref. id.)(id. pl., suff. 3 pers. sing. masc. . אצר

לְאַרְאֵלִי pref. id.)(pr. name masc., see אַרְאֵלִי ארה

לְאֹרֵב[n] pref. id.)(Kal part. act. sing. masc. dec. 7b ארב

לָאַרְבֶּה pref. לָ for לְהַ· לְהָ)(noun masc. sing. . רבה

לְאַרְבַּע pref. לְ)(num. card. fem. (§ 31. rem. 5) . רבע

לְאַרְבָּעָה pref. id.)(id. masc. (comp. § 42. rem. 5) רבע

לְאַרְבַּעַת[o] pref. id.)(id. id. constr. . רבע

לְאַרְבַּעְתָּם pref. id.)(id. id. with suff. 3 pers. pl. masc. רבע

לְאַרְבַּעְתָּן[p] pref. id.)(id. id. with suff. 3 pers. pl. fem. רבע

---

[a] 1 Ki. 2. 19. [b] Eze. 44. 25. [c] Ca. 6. 9. [d] Ge. 24. 53. [e] 2 Ch. 3. 11. [f] Ru. 4. 16. [g] Pr. 4. 20. [h] Ps. 119. 123. [i] Ps. 119. 154. [k] Ps. 119. 82. [l] Is. 42. 3. [m] 1 Ki. 1. 17. [n] La. 2. 12. [o] Ge. 25. 16. [p] Ju. 8. 15. [q] Ge. 19. 8. [r] 2 Sa. 3. 20. [s] Ju. 15. 10. [t] Is. 49. 9. [u] Ex. 21. 7. [w] Is. 61. 1. [x] Ezr. 7. 26. [y] 1 Ch. 26. 17. [z] Nu. 30. 13. [zz] Ps. 59. 14.

[a] Nu. 30. 3. [b] Ju. 15. 12. [c] Ex. 25. 7. [d] Ps. 78. 50. [dd] Is. 2. 7. [e] Ex. 35. 9, 27. [f] Ju. 8. 27. [g] 1 Sa. 8. 13. [h] 1 Sa. 25. 23. [i] Is. 13. 3. [k] Eze. 36. 6. [l] Eze. 28. 18. [m] 2 Ch. 8. 15. [n] 1 Sa. 22. 8, 13. [o] Eze. 1. 15. [p] Eze. 1. 10, 16, 18.

לַאֲרוֹד pref. לְ bef. (-:))(pr. name masc. . . ארד

לָאָרוֹן pref. לְ for לְהַ·, לְהָ)(noun masc. sing. d. 3a ארה

לַאֲרוֹן pref. לְ bef. (-:))(id. constr. st. . . ארה

לָאֶרֶז[a] pref. לְ)(noun masc. sing. (pl. c. אַרְזֵי) d. 6a ארז

לָאֹרַח[b] pref. לְ for לְהַ·, לְהָ)(noun com. sing. dec. 6 (§ 35. rem. 5 & 9) . . . . ארח

לְאֹרֵחַ[c] pref. id.)(Kal part. act. sing. masc. . ארח

לַאֲרִיאֵל[dd] pref. לְ bef. (-:))(compound noun masc. from אֲרִי & אֵל, see אֲרִיאֵל . . . ארה

לָאַרְיֵה[d] pref. לְ for לְהַ·, לְהָ)(n.m.s., אֲרִי, with parag. ה ארה

לְאַרְיוֹךְ pref. לְ)(pr. name masc. . . . ארה

לַאֲרָיוֹת[e] pref. לְ bef. (-:))(noun masc. with pl. fem. term. from אֲרִי dec. 6i (§ 35. rem. 14) . ארה

לְאֶרֶךְ[f] pref. לְ)(noun masc. sing. . . ארך

לְאֹרֶךְ pref. id.)(noun masc. sing. dec. 6c . ארך

לְאָרְכָּהּ[g] pref. id.)(id., suff. 3 pers. sing. fem. . ארך

לַאֲרָם pref. לְ bef. (-:))(pr. name of a people . ארם

לְאַרְנוֹן pref. לְ)(pr. name of a river . . רנן

לְאָרְנָן pref. id.)(pr. name masc. . . . ארן

לְאַרְעִית[h] Chald., pref. id.)(noun fem. sing., constr. of [אַרְעִי] dec. 8b . . . . ארע

לָאָרֶץ[i] וְ׳ pref. לְ f. לְהַ·, לְהָ } noun fem. sing. d. 6a (§ 35. rem. 2) ארץ
לְאֶרֶץ pref. לְ q. v.

לְאַרְצָהּ pref. id.)(id., suff. 3 pers. sing. masc. . ארץ

לְאַרְצוֹ pref. id.)(id., suff. 3 pers. sing. masc. . ארץ

לְאַרְצִי[hh] וּ pref. id.)(id., suff. 1 pers. sing.; וּ bef. (:) ארץ

לְאַרְצְךָ[k] } pref. id.)(id., suff. 2 pers. sing. masc. . ארץ
לְאַרְצֶךָ[l]

לְאַרְצֵךְ[m] וּ pref. id.)(id., suff. 2 pers. s. fem.; וּ bef. (:) ארץ

לְאַרְצָם[n] וּ pref. id.)(id., suff. 3 pers. pl. masc.; וּ id. ארץ

לְאַרְתַּחְשַׁסְתְּא } pref. id.)(pr. name masc., see אַרְתַּחְ׳
לְאַרְתַּחְשַׁשְׂתְּא

לָאֵשׁ pref. לְ f. לְהַ·, לְהָ } noun com. sing. dec. 8b אשׁ
לְאֵשׁ pref. לְ q. v.

לְאַשְׁבֵּל pref. id.)(pr. name masc. see אַשְׁבֵּל. . אשב

לְאַשְׁדּוֹד pref. id.)(pr. name of a place . שדד

לָאִשָּׁה[o] וְ׳ pref. לְ f. לְהַ·, לְהָ } noun fem. sing. irr. (§ 45); וּ bef. (:) אנשׁ
לְאִשָּׁה[p] וּ׳ pref. לְ q. v.

לְאַשּׁוּר וּ׳ pref. id.)(pr. name of a country; וּ id. . אשר

לְאַשְׁחוּר וּ pref. id.)(pr. name masc.; וּ id. . שחר

לְאִשַּׁי[q] pref. id.)(noun masc. pl., suff. 1 pers. sing. from אִשֶּׁה dec. 9a . . . . אשׁ

לַאֲשִׁישֵׁי[r] pref. לְ bef. (-:))(noun masc. pl. constr. from [אָשִׁישׁ] dec. 3a . . . אשׁשׁ

לְאַשְׁכְּלוֹתָי[s] pref. לְ)(noun masc. with pl. fem. term., abs. from אֶשְׁכֹּל (q. v.) . . שכל

לָאָשָׁם[t] וְ pref. לְ f. לְהַ·, לְהָ } noun masc. sing. d. 4c אשׁם
לְאָשָׁם pref. לְ q. v.

לְאַשְׁמָה pref. id.)(noun fem. sing. dec. 12a . אשׁם

לְאַשְׁמַת pref. id.)(id., constr. st. . . . אשׁם

לְאָשְׁפַיָּא[u] Chald., pref. id.)(noun masc. pl. emph. [as if from אָשַׁף dec. 2b] see אַשָּׁף . . אשׁף

לָאַשָּׁפִים[x] וְ pref. לְ for לְהַ·, לְהָ)(n. m., pl. of אַשָּׁף d. 1b אשׁף

לְאַשְׁפְּנַז pref. לְ)(pr. name masc., see אַשְׁפְּנַז.

לְאַשְׁקְלוֹן pref. id.)(pr. name of a place . . שקל

לַאֲשֶׁר וְ׳ pref. לְ bef. (-:))(pron. relat. com. s. & pl. אשׁר

לְאָשֵׁר וּ׳ pref. לְ)(pr. name of a tribe; וּ bef. (:) אשׁר

לָאֲשֵׁרָה[y] וְ׳ pref. לְ f. לְהַ·, לְהָ } noun fem. sing. dec. 10 אשׁר
לַאֲשֵׁרָה pref. לְ bef. (-:)

לְאַשְׁרוֹ[z] pref. id.)(noun masc. sing., suff. 3 pers. sing. masc. from [אָשׁוּר] dec. 3a . . אשׁר

לְאֵשֶׁת[a] pref. לְ)(noun fem. sing. d. 13b (comp. § 45) אישׁ

לְאִשְׁתּוֹ[b] וּ׳ pref. id.)(id., suff. 3 pers. s. m.; וּ bef. (:) אישׁ

לְאִשְׁתִּי[c] pref. id.)(id., suff. 1 pers. sing. . . אישׁ

לְאֹת[d] defect. for לְאוֹת (q. v.) . . . אוה

לָאָתוֹן[e] pref. לְ for לְהַ·, לְהָ)(noun fem. sing. dec. 3a אתן

לְאַתּוּן[f] Ch., pref. לְ)(noun m. s. dec. 1a [for אַתְנוּן] תנן

לְאַתּוּנָא[g] Ch., pref. id.)(id., emph. st. . . תנן

לְאֹתוֹת[h] pref. id.)(n. com., pl. of אוֹת d. 1a [for אֹת] אוה

לָאִתִּים[i] וְ pref. לְ for לְהַ·, לְהָ } noun masc. pl. [of אֵת § 37. rem. 5] את
לְאִתִּים pref. לְ q. v.

לָאֲתֹנוֹת[k] וְ pref. לְ bef. (-:))(noun f., pl. of אָתוֹן d. 3a אתן

לְאֶתְנַנָּהּ[l] pref. לְ)(noun masc. sing., suff. 3 pers. sing. (§ 3. rem. 3) fem. from אֶתְנָן dec. 8a . תנה

לְאַתְרֵהּ[m] Ch., pref. id.)(noun masc. sing., suff. 3 pers. sing. masc. from אֲתַר dec. 3a . . אתר

לְאֹתֹת[n] pref. id.)(defect. for אוֹתוֹת see לְאוֹתוֹת . אוה

לֵב (וְ׳, וְ׳) } noun masc. sing. dec. 8b (comp. § 36. rem. 3); for וָ see lett. ו לבב
לֶב־ (וְ׳)

לָבָא or **לָבָה** Root not used; most prob. onomatopoetic, imitating the sound of *lowing, roaring* (Gesenius). לָבִי.—I. pl. masc. לְבָאִים (§ 35. rem. 15) *lions*, Ps. 57. 5.—II. pl. fem. לְבָאוֹת, (*a*) *lionesses*, constr.

[a] Eze. 17. 23.
[b] Job 31. 32.
[c] 2 Sa. 12. 4.
[d] 1 Ki. 13. 26.
[dd] Is. 29. 2.
[e] 1 Ki. 7. 29.
[f] Je. 15. 15.
[g] Ge. 13. 17.
[h] Da. 6. 25.
[hh] Ge. 30. 25.
[i] Nu. 35. 33.
[k] 2 Sa. 7. 23.
[l] Ge. 32. 10.
[m] Is. 62. 4.
[n] De. 31. 4.
[o] 1 Sa. 28. 24.
[p] Is. 45. 10.
[q] Nu. 28. 2.
[r] Is. 16. 7.
[s] Ca. 7. 8.
[t] Le. 7. 37.
[u] Da. 5. 7.
[x] Da. 2. 2.
[y] 2 Ki. 23. 4, 7.
[z] Pr. 14. 15.
[a] Ju. 14. 15.
[b] Ge. 3. 21.
[c] Job 19. 17.
[d] Ex. 12. 13.
[e] Nu. 22. 29.
[f] Da. 3. 20.
[g] Da. 3. 19.
[h] Is. 8. 18.
[i] 1 Sa. 13. 21.
[k] 1 Sa. 9. 20
[l] Is. 23. 17.
[m] Ezr. 6. 5.
[n] Ge. 1. 14.

לְבָאוֹת Na. 2. 13; (b) בֵּית לְ׳ (*house of lionesses*) pr. name of a town in the tribe of Simeon, Jos. 19. 6.

לָבִיא *lion*; according to others, *lioness*.

לְבִיָּא fem. (for לְבִיָּה) *lioness*, Eze. 19. 2.

לְבֹא, לְבֹא } defect. for לָבוֹא, לְבוֹא (q. v.) . . בוא

לְבָאוֹת ו׳ pr. n. of a place (see also בֵּית לְבָ׳); וּ bef. (:) לבה

לַבָּא וְ pref. לַ f. לְהַ) Kal part. sing. masc. dec. 1a בוא

לַבָּאִים[a] pref. id.) id. pl., abs. st. . . . בוא

לְבָאִם[b] noun m., pl. of [לְבִי] dec. 6i (§ 35. rem. 15) לבה

לַבְּאֵר[c] pref. לַ f. לְהָ; לְהַ· } n. f. s. d. 1a (but pl. c. בְּאֵרֹת § 35. rem. 10) } באר

לִבְאֵר[d] pref. לְ bef. (:)

לֵבָב, לֵב masc. dec. 4d & 8b (pl. לְבָבוֹת, לְבָבִים).—I. *the heart*, in the physical sense; frequently for *life, the vital principle*. To *the heart* is ascribed, *thought, reasoning, understanding, will, judgment, design, affection, love, hatred, courage, fear, joy, sorrow*; חֲכַם לֵב *wise in heart*; חֲסַר לֵב *wanting in understanding, foolish*; אַנְשֵׁי לֵב *men of understanding*; also *men of courage*; בְּלֵב וָלֵב *with a double heart*, i. e. *deceitfully*.—II. *middle, midst*, inner part.

לְבַב, לֵב Chald. masc. dec. 3b & 5b, id.

לָבַב denom. Niph. *to become wise, acquire understanding*, Job 11. 12. Piel, Ca. 4. 9, *to encourage, embolden*; others, *to ravish the heart*.

לִבָּה fem. dec. 10, *the heart*.

לְבִיבָה f. d. 10, *cake, pancake*, 2 Sa. 13. 6, 8, 10.

לִבֵּב denom. Pi. *to make such cakes*, 2 Sa. 13. 6, 8.

לְבַב ו׳ Heb. & Chald., noun masc. sing., constr. of לֵבָב dec. 4d (Ch. d. 3b); וּ bef. (:) . לבב

לְבָבָהּ id., suff. 3 pers. sing. fem. . . . לבב

לִבְבֵהּ[e] וְ Chald., noun masc. sing., suff. 3 pers. sing. masc. from לְבַב dec. 3b . . . לבב

לִבְבֵהֶן[f] noun masc. pl., suff. 3 pers. pl. [for לִבְבֵיהֶן] from לֵבָב dec. 4b . . . . לבב

לְבָבוֹ ו׳ id. sing., suff. 3 pers. sing. masc.; וּ bef. (:) לבב

לְבָבוֹת[g] id. pl. abs. with fem. term. . . . לבב

לְבִבוֹת[h] noun fem., pl. of לְבִיבָה dec. 10 . . לבב

לְבָבִי[i] ו׳ n. m. sing., suff. 1 pers. sing. fr. לֵבָב d. 4b לבב

לְבָבְךָ, לְבָבֶךָ[k] וְ } id., suff. 2 pers. sing. masc.; וּ bef. (:) לבב

לְבָבֵךְ id., suff. 2 pers. sing. fem. . . . לבב

לִבְבָךְ Chald., noun masc. sing., suff. 2 pers. sing. masc. from לְבַב dec. 3b . . . לבב

לְבַבְכֶם n. m. s., suff. 2 pers. pl. masc. from לֵבָב d. 4b לבב

לְבָבֶל pref. לְ) pr. n. of a country [for בַּבְלֶל] בלל

לְבָבָם noun masc. sing., suff. 3 pers. pl. masc. from לֵבָב dec. 4b . . . . . לבב

לְבָבֵנוּ id. with suff. 1 pers. pl. . . . לבב

לִבַּבְתִּנִי[l] Piel pret. 2 pers. sing. fem., suff. 1 pers. sing. לבב

לְבַג[m] pref. לְ) see בַּג; K. לָבַז (q. v.)

לְבֶגֶד[n] pref. id.) noun masc. s. (suff. בִּגְדִי), d. 6a בגד

לִבְגֹּד[gg] pref. לְ bef. (:)) Kal inf. constr. . . בגד

לְבִגְדֵי[o] וּ pref. לְ) noun masc. pl. constr. from בֶּגֶד dec. 6a; וּ bef. (:) . . . בגד

לְבַד, לְבַד[p] ו׳ } pref. id.) noun masc. sing., with the pref. used adverbially; וּ id. . } בדד

לְבָדָד pref. id.) n. m. s. with the pref. used adverbially בדד

לְבַדָּהּ pref. id.) adv. לְבַד (q. v.), with suff. 3 p. s. f. בדד

לְבַדְּהֶן[q] pref. id.) id., suff. 3 pers. pl. fem. . בדד

לְבַדּוֹ pref. id.) id., suff. 3 pers. sing. masc. . בדד

לִבְדּוֹק[r] pref. לְ bef. (:)) Kal inf. constr. (§ 8. r. 18) בדק

לְבַדִּי pref. לְ) adv. לְבַד (q. v.), with suff. 1 pers. s. בדד

לַבַּדִּים pref. לַ f. לְהַ, לְבַדִּים pref. לְ q. v. } noun masc., pl. of בַּד dec. 8d בדד

לְבַדְּךָ, לְבַדֶּךָ } pref. id.) id. sing., suff. 2 pers. sing. masc., adverbially . . . } בדד

לְבַדְּכֶם pref. id.) id. sing., suff. 2 pers. pl. masc. בדד

לְבַדָּם pref. id.) id. sing., suff. 3 pers. pl. masc. בדד

לְבַדְּהֶנָה[s] pref. id.) id. s., suff. 3 pers. pl. f. (§ 3. r. 5) בדד

לְבֶדֶק[t] pref. id.) noun masc. s. (suff. בִּדְקֵךְ) d. 6a בדק

לִבָּהּ noun masc. sing., suff. 3 pers. sing. fem. from לֵב dec. 8b . . . . לבב

לַבֶּהָלָה[u] pref. לַ for לְהַ) noun fem. sing. dec. 10 . בהל

לְבַהֲלָם[x] וּ pref. לְ) Piel inf. [בַּהֵל § 14. r. 1], suff. 3 pers. pl. dec. 7b; וּ bef. (:) . . בהל

לְבַהֲלֵנִי[y] pref. id.) id. with suff. 1 pers. sing. . בהל

לַבְּהֵמָה ו׳, לִבְהֵמָה[z] pref. לַ f. לְהַ, pref. לְ bef. (:) } noun fem. sing. (§ 42. r. 5, & § 44. rem. 3) } בהם

לְבֶהֱמַת וּ pref. לְ) id. constr. st. (comp. § 42. r. 4); וּ bef. (:) . . . . . בהם

לִבְהֶמְתְּךָ[a], וְלִבְהֶמְתְּךָ[b] } pref. לְ bef. (:)) id., suff. 2 p. s. f. [prop. from בְּהֶמֶת § 42. r. 5, & § 44. r. 3] } בהם

לִבְהֶמְתָּם[c] pref. id.) id., suff. 3 pers. pl. masc. . בהם

לִבְהֶמְתֵּנוּ[d] pref. id.) id., suff. 1 pers. pl. . . בהם

לַבֹּהָרֶת[e] וְ pref. לַ for לְהַ) noun fem. sing., in pause for בַּהֶרֶת q.v. (§ 44. rem. 5) . . בהר

[a] Pr. 23. 30. [b] Ps. 75. 5. [c] Ge. 16. 14. [d] Ps. 55. 24. [e] Da. 5. 21. [f] Na. 2. 8. [g] 1 Ch. 28. 9. [gg] Is. 33. 1. [h] 2 Sa. 13. 6. [i] Ps. 73. 26. [k] Is. 7. 4. [l] Ca. 4. 9. [m] Eze. 25. 7. [n] Is. 59. 6. [o] Ex. 35. 21. [p] Ju. 8. 26. [q] Ge. 21. 28. [r] 2 Ch. 34. 10. [s] Ge. 21. 29. [t] 2 Ki. 12. 8. [u] Is. 65. 23. [x] 2 Ch. 32. 18. [y] 2 Ch. 35. 21. [z] Ps. 147. 9. [a] De. 11. 15. [b] Le. 25. 7. [c] Nu. 35. 3. [d] Jos. 21. 2. [e] Le. 14. 56.

לְבֵין[q] pref. לְ)(prep. [prop. constr. of [בַּיִן] dec. 6h — בין

לַבִּינָה pref. לְ for לְהַ)(noun fem. sing. dec. 10 — בין

וְ' לַבַּיִת / וְ' לַבָּיִת pref. לְ for לְהַ)(noun masc. sing. dec. 6m, pl. irr. בָּתִּים (§ 45) — בית

וּ' לְבֵית[s] pref. לְ)(id. constr. st. Heb. & Ch., also pr. name in compos., as לְבֵית־אֵל &c. — בית

לְבֵיתָהּ[r] pref. id.)(id., suff. 3 pers. sing. fem. — בית

לְבַיְתֵהּ Ch., pref. id.)(id., suff. 3 pers. sing. m. (§ 68) — בית

וּ' לְבֵיתוֹ pref. id.)(id. with suff. 3 p. s. m.; וּ bef. (:) — בית

לְבֵיתִי pref. id.)(id., suff. 1 pers. sing. — בית

וּ' לְבֵיתְךָ / לְבֵיתֶךָ[t] pref. id.)(id., suff. 2 pers. sing. masc.; וּ bef. (:) — בית

לְבֵיתֵךְ pref. id.)(id., suff. 2 pers. sing. fem. — בית

לִבְּךָ / וְ' לִבֶּךָ noun masc. sing., suff. 2 pers. sing. masc. from לֵב dec. 8b — לבב

לִבֵּךְ id., suff. 2 pers. sing. fem. — לבב

וְ לַבִּכּוּרִים[u] pref. לְ for לְהַ)(n. m., pl. of [בִּכּוּר] d. 1b — בכר

לִבְכּוֹת pref. לְ bef. (:))(Kal inf. constr. dec. 1b — בכה

לִבְכִי[x] / לְבֶכִי[y] pref. לְ, or לְ bef. (:))(noun masc. sing. dec. 6i (§ 35. rem. 14) — בכה

לִבְּכֶם noun m. s., suff. 2 pers. pl. m. from לֵב d. 8b — לבב

לְבַכֵּר[z] pref. לְ)(Piel inf. constr. — בכר

לְבֶכֶר pref. id.)(pr. name masc. — בכר

לַבְּכֹרָה[a] pref. לְ for לְהַ)(noun fem. sing. dec. 10 — בכר

וְ לִבְכֹּתָהּ[b] pref. לְ bef. (:))(Kal inf. [בְּכוֹת], suff. 3 pers. sing. fem. dec. 1b — בכה

לְבֵלְאשַׁצַּר pref. לְ)(pr. name masc., see בֵּלְשַׁאצַּר.

לְבִלְגָּה pref. id.)(pr. name masc. — בלג

לַבָּלָה[c] pref. לְ for לְהַ)(adj. f. s. d. 11a, from בָּלֶה m. — בלה

לִבְלוֹם[d] pref. לְ bef. (:))(Kal inf. constr. (§ 8. r. 18) — בלם

לְבַלּוֹת[e] pref. לְ)(Piel inf. constr. — בלה

לִבְלִי pref. לְ bef. (:))(adv. with & without the pref. — בלה

לְבֶלַע / לְבָלַע pref. לְ)(pr. name masc. (§ 35. rem. 2) — בלע

לִבְלֹעַ[f] pref. לְ bef. (:))(Kal inf. constr. — בלע

לְבַלְּעוֹ[g] pref. לְ)(Piel inf. (בַּלַּע'), suff. 3 pers. sing. masc. dec. 7b (§ 36. rem. 5) — בלע

לְבִלְעָם pref. id.)(pr. name masc. — בלע

לְבָלָק pref. id.)(pr. name masc. — בלק

לְבַלֹּתוֹ[h] pref. id.)(Piel inf. (בַּלּוֹת'), suff. 3 p. s. m. d. 1b — בלה

וּ' לְבִלְתִּי pref. id.)(adv., [בֶּלֶת] with parag. 'י; וּ bef. (:) — בלת

וְ' לִבָּם noun m. s., suff. 3 p. pl. m. from לֵב d. 8b — לבב

וְ' לִבּוֹ noun masc. sing., suff. 3 pers. sing. masc. from לֵב dec. 8b — לבב

וְ' לָבוֹא / לָבוֹא pref. לְ or לָ q. v.)(Kal inf. constr. (§ 21. rem. 2, & § 25. No. 2) dec. 1a — בוא

לְבוֹאָם pref. לְ)(id., suff. 3 pers. pl. masc. — בוא

לָבוּז in full for לָבֹז (q. v.) — בזז

לַבּוּז pref. לְ, see lett. ל)(noun masc. sing. — בוז

לְבוּל pref. לְ)(noun masc. sing. for יְבוּל — יבל

וּ' לְבוֹנָה pref. id.)(noun fem. s. d. 10; וּ bef. (:) — לבן

וְ לָבוּר[a] pref. לָ, see lett. ל)(Kal inf. constr. — בור

לָבוֹשׁ[b] Kal inf. abs. — לבש

לָבוּשׁ id. part. pass. sing. masc. dec. 3a — לבש

לְבוּשׁ id. id. constr.; or noun masc. sing. dec. 1a — לבש

לְבוּשָׁהּ noun masc. sing., suff. 3 p. s. f. fr. לְבוּשׁ d. 1a — לבש

לְבוּשֵׁהּ[c] Chald. id., suff. 3 pers. sing. masc. — לבש

לְבוּשׁוֹ id., suff. 3 pers. sing. masc. — לבש

לְבוּשִׁי id., suff. 1 pers. sing. — לבש

וּ לְבוּשֵׁיהוֹן[d] Ch. id. pl., suff. 3 pers. pl. m.; וּ bef. (:) — לבש

לְבוּשְׁכֶן[e] id. sing., suff. 2 pers. pl. fem. — לבש

לְבוּשָׁם[f] id. sing., suff. 3 pers. pl. masc. — לבש

לִבּוֹת noun fem., pl. of [לִבָּה] dec. 10 — לבב

וְ' לָבַז[g] pref. לְ (see lett. ל))(noun m. s. d. 8e — בזז

וְ' לָבֹז[h] pref. id.)(Kal inf. constr. — בזז

לְבַז pref. לְ)(noun masc. sing. dec. 8e — בזז

לְבִזָּה[yy] pref. id.)(noun fem. sing. — בזז

לִבְזֹה[i] pref. לְ bef. (:))(adj. m., constr. of בָּזֹה d. 3a — בזה

לְבֹזְזִים[k] pref. לְ)(Kal part. act. m., pl. of [בֹּזֵז] d. 7b — בזז

לְבֹזְזֵינוּ[l] pref. id.)(id. with suff. 1 pers. pl. — בזז

לִבְחִירַי[m] pref. לְ bef. (:))(adj. pl. masc., suff. 1 pers. pl. from בָּחִיר dec. 3a — בחר

לִבְחִירִי[n] pref. id.)(id. sing., suff. 1 pers. sing. — בחר

לָבַט Niph. *to stumble, fall*, Pr. 10. 8, 10; He. 4. 14.

לְבַטֵּא[o] pref. לְ)(Piel inf. constr. — בטא

לָבֶטַח pref. לָ, see lett. ל)(noun masc. with the pref. as an adv. — בטח

לְבַטָּלָא Chald., pref. id.)(Pael inf. — בטל

וְ' לִבִּי noun m. s., suff. 1 pers. s. from לֵב d. 8b — לבב

לָבִיא pref. לָ, contr. for לְהָבִיא, Hiph. inf. (comp. § 11. rem. 3) — בוא

לָבִיא noun masc. sing. — לבא

לְבִיָּא[p] [for לְבִיָּה] noun fem. sing. — לבה

וְ לֻבִים pr. name of a people, see לוּבִים — לוב

---

a Ec. 9. 1. b Hag. 1. 6. c Da. 7. 9. d Da. 3. 21. e 2 Sa. 1. 24. f Je. 10. 9. g Eze. 23. 46. h 2 Ch. 20. 25. i Is. 49. 7. k Is. 42. 24. l Is. 17. 14. m Is. 65. 15. n Ps. 89. 4. o Le. 5. 4. p Eze. 19. 2. q Is. 59. 2. r Pr. 31. 15, 21. s De. 26. 11. t 2 Sa. 11. 8; Ps. 93. 5. u Ne. 13. 31. x Is. 15. 2. y Is. 22. 12. yy Ne. 3. 36. z De. 21. 16. a 1 Ch. 5. 1. b Ge. 23. 2. c Eze. 23. 43. d Ps. 32. 9. e Ps. 49. 15. f Jon. 2. 1. g Job 2. 3. h 1 Ch. 17. 9.

לַבָּמָה[a] pref. לַ for לְהַ) (noun f. s. d. 10 (pl. c. (בָּמֳתֵי בום

לַבָּמוֹת[b] pref. id. } id. pl., abs. st. . . . בום
לְבָמוֹת pref. לְ }

[לָבַן] Kal not used.—I. *to be white.*—II. from לְבֵנָה, *to make bricks.* Hiph.—I. *to make white, clean,* Da. 11. 35.—II. intrans. *to become white.* Hithp. *to cleanse oneself,* Da. 12. 10.

לָבָן masc. dec. 4a.—I. adj. *white;* fem. לְבָנָה, pl. לְבָנוֹת.—II. pr. name of the father-in-law of Jacob.—III. pr. name of a place in the desert, De. 1. 1.

לָבֵן adj. masc. *white,* only constr. לְבֶן Ge. 49. 12 (§ 34. No. 2).

לְבָנָה fem.—I. *the moon,* from her whiteness. —II. pr. name masc. Ezr. 2. 45; called לְבָנָא Ne. 7. 48.

לְבֵנָה fem. dec. 10 (pl. (לְבֵנִים *brick* or *tile.*

לִבְנֶה masc. *the white poplar,* Ge. 30. 37; Ho. 4. 13.

לִבְנָה fem.—I. *whiteness, clearness;* only constr. לִבְנַת Ex. 24. 10.—II. pr. name of a city in the tribe of Judah.—III. pr. name of a station of the Israelites in the desert, Nu. 33. 20.

לְבֹנָה, לְבוֹנָה fem. dec. 10.—I. *frankincense.*— II. pr. name of a city near Shiloh, Ju. 21. 19.

לְבָנוֹן (*white*) pr. name, *Mount Lebanon,* on the confines of Syria and Palestine.

לִבְנִי (id.) pr. name of a son of Gershon; also patronym. for לִבְנִיִּי.

מַלְבֵּן masc. *brickkiln.*

לָבָן ןְ adj. masc. sing. d. 4a, also pr. name masc. לבן

לַבֵּן[c] pref. לַ f. לְהַ }
לְבֵן[d] וּ״ן pref. לְ q. v. } noun masc. sing. irr. (§ 45) בנה

לְבֶן־[e] וּ״ן pref. id.) (id. constr. before Mak. (also pr. name in composition) . . . בנה

לְבֶן־[f] וּ adj. masc. [for לְבֵן], constr. of לָבֵן dec. 5a (§ 34. No. 2); וּ bef. (:) . . . לבן

לִבָּן[g] noun m. s., suff. 3 p. pl. fem., from לֵב d. 8b לבב

לְבָנָא pr. name masc., see לְבָנָה . . . לבן

לִבְנֵא[h] Chald., pref. לְ (for (לְמִבְנֵא, Peal inf. . בנה

לְבָנָה pr. name masc. . . . . לבן

לְבָנָה adj. fem., pl. לְבָנוֹת, from לָבָן masc. . לבן

לִבְנֶה[i] noun masc. sing. dec. 11 (§ 42. rem. 4) . לבן

לְבֵנָה וּ״ noun fem. sing. dec. 10; וּ bef. (:) . לבן

לִבְנָה pr. name of a place . . . . לבן

לִבְנֶה[k] ןְ״ noun masc. sing. . . . . לבן

לִבֵּנוּ[l] noun m. sing., suff. 1 pers. pl. from לֵב d. 8b לבב

לִבְנוֹ ןְ pref. לְ bef. (:)) (noun masc. sing., suff. 3 pers. sing. masc. from בֵּן irr. (§ 45) . בנה

לְבָנוֹן וּ pr. name of a mountain; וּ bef. (:) . לבן

לְבָנוֹנָה id. with parag. ה . . . . לבן

לִבְנוֹת[m] pref. לְ) (n.f.pl., as if of בָּנָה, see בַּת irr. (§45) בנה

לְבָנוֹת[n] adj. pl., fem. of לְבָנָה, from לָבָן masc. . לבן

לִבְנוֹת ןְ pref. לְ bef. (:)) (Kal inf. constr. dec. 1a בנה

לִבְנוֹת pref. id.) (noun fem. pl., constr. of בָּנוֹת, irr. of בַּת (§ 45) . . . בנה

לִבְנוֹתֶיהָ[o] ןְ pref. id.) (id. pl., suff. 3 pers. sing. fem. בנה

לִבְנוֹתָיו[p] ןְ pref. id.) (id. pl., suff. 3 pers. sing. masc. בנה

לְבָנַי[q] וּ״ן pref. לְ) (noun masc. pl. (בָּנִים), suff. 1 pers. sing., irr. of בֵּן (§ 45); וּ bef. (:) בנה

לִבְנֵי ןְ pref. לְ bef. (:)) (id. pl., constr. st. . בנה

לִבְנִי pr. name masc. . . . . לבן

לִבְנִי וּ״ן pref. לְ bef. (:)) (noun masc. sing., suff. 1 pers. sing., from בֵּן irr. (§ 45) . בנה

לִבְנָיָהוּ[r] ןְ pref. id.) (pr. name masc., see בְּנָיָהוּ בנה

לִבְנֵיהֶם ןְ pref. id.) (noun masc. pl. (בָּנִים), suff. 3 pers. pl. masc. irr. of בֵּן (§ 45) . . בנה

לִבְנֵיהֶן[s] pref. id.) (id. pl., suff. 3 pers. pl. fem. . בנה

לְבָנָיו וּ pref. לְ) (id. pl., suff. 3 pers. s. m.; וּ bef. (:) בנה

לְבָנֶיךָ וּ pref. id.) (id. pl., suff. 2 pers. sing. m.; וּ id. בנה

לִבְנֵיכֶם pref. לְ bef. (:)) (id., suff. 2 pers. pl. masc. בנה

לַבֹּנִים ןְ pref. לַ for לְהַ) (Kal part. act. masc., pl. of בּוֹנֶה dec. 9a . . . . בנה

לְבָנִים וּ״ adj. m., pl. of לָבָן d. 4a; וּ bef. (:) לבן

לְבָנִים[t] pref. לְ) (noun masc. pl. irr. of בֵּן (§ 45) בנה

לְבֵנִים וּ״ן noun fem. with pl. masc. term. from לְבֵנָה dec. 11 (§ 42. rem. 4); וּ bef. (:) לבן

לְבִנְיָמִין pref. לְ) (pr. name of a tribe . . בנה

לַבִּנְיָמִינִי pref. לַ for לְהַ) (Kh. בִּנְיָמִינִי, K. בֶּן יְמִינִי, gent. noun of the preceding . . בנה

לְבִנְיָמִן וּ pref. לְ) (pr. n. of a man and a tribe; וּ bef. (:) בנה

לְבָנֵינוּ[u] וּ pref. id.) (noun masc. pl., suff. 1 pers. pl. irr. of בֵּן (§ 45); וּ id. . בנה

לְבִנְךָ[v] וּ״ } pref. לְ or לִ bef. (:)) (id. sing., suff.
לִבְנְךָ } 2 pers. sing. masc.; וּ id. . . } בנה

לְבִנֵךְ[w] ןְ pref. לְ bef. (:)) (id. s., suff. 2 pers. s. fem. בנה

לְבָנֹת[x] defect. for לְבָנוֹת (q. v.) . . . לבן

לִבְנַת pr. name, see שִׁיחוֹר לִבְנַת under . . שחר

---

[a] 2 Ch. 1. 3, 13. [b] 2 Ch. 11. 15. [c] Ps. 9. 1. [d] Eze. 44. 25. [e] Job 35. 8. [f] Ge. 49. 12. [g] Ex. 35. 26. [h] Ezr. 5. 3, 13. [i] Eze. 4. 1. [k] Ge. 30. 37. [l] Ho. 4. 13. [m] Eze. 16. 61. [n] Ge. 30. 37. [o] Eze. 16. 49. [p] Ge. 32. 1. [q] Ge. 31. 28. [r] 1 Ki. 20. 7. [s] 1 Ki. 17. 12. [t] Ge. 31. 43. [u] Zec. 1. 8. [v] Is. 38. 19. [w] Ex. 5. 16. [x] 1 Sa. 25. 8. [a] 1 Ki. 17. 13. [b] Le. 13. 38, 39.

לִבְנַת[a] noun fem. sing. constr. [of לְבֵנָה] . . לבן

לִבְנֹת[b] pref. לְ bef. (:)) Kal inf. constr. . בנה

לִבְנָתָהּ[c] noun fem. s. with suff. 3 p. s. fem. fr. לְבֵנָה d. 10 לבן

וְלִבְנֹתַי[d] / וְלִבְנֹתַי[e] pref. לְ bef. (:)) noun fem. pl. (בָּנוֹת), suff. 1 pers. pl. irr. of בַּת (§ 45) . בנה

לִבְנֹתָיו[f] pref. id.) id., suff. 3 pers. sing. masc. . בנה

וְלִבְנֹתֶיךָ[g] pref. id.) id., suff. 2 pers. sing. masc. . בנה

לְבַעֲבוּר preff. לְ, & בְּ bef. (-:)) in this form only as a conj. comp. בַּעֲבוּר . . . עבר

לְבֹעַז pref. לְ) pr. name masc. . . . בעז

לַבַּעַל / לַבָּעַל pref. לְ for לְהַ; לְבַעַל pref. לְ q. v. } noun masc. sing. dec. 6d (also pr. name) בעל

לִבְעָלֶיהָ[h] pref. לְ bef. (:)) id. pl., suff. 3 pers. s. fem. בעל

לְבַעֲלֵיהֶן[i] pref. לְ) id. pl., suff. 3 pers. pl. fem. . בעל

לִבְעָלָיו pref. לְ bef. (:)) id. pl., suff. 3 pers. sing. masc. בעל

לַבְּעָלִים pref. לְ for לְהַ) id. pl., abs. st. . . בעל

לְבַעֵר pref. לְ) Piel inf. constr. . . . בער

לְבַעֲרָם[k] pref. id.) id. [בַּעֵר § 14. rem. 1] with suff. 3 pers. pl. masc. dec. 7b . . . בער

לְבַעְשָׁא pref. id.) pr. name masc. . . . . בעש

לְבִצְעוֹ[l] pref. id.) noun masc. sing., suff. 3 pers. sing. masc. from בֶּצַע dec. 6 (§ 35. rem. 5) . בצע

לְבַצֵּר[m] pref. id.) Piel inf. constr. . . . בצר

לְבִצָּרוֹן[n] pref. id.) noun masc. sing. . . . בצר

לְבִקְעָה[o] pref. id.) noun fem. sing. dec. 12b . בקע

לְבִקְעָם[p] pref. id.) Kal inf. [בְּקֹעַ], suff. 3 pers. pl. masc. (§ 16. rem. 10) . . . בקע

לַבָּקָר[oo] וְ[ss] noun com. sing. dec. 4a . . . בקר

לַבֹּקֶר וְ' pref. לְ for לְהַ) noun m. s., d. 6c (§ 35. r. 9) בקר

לְבַקֵּר[q] וּ' pref. לְ) Piel inf. constr.; וּ bef. (:) . בקר

לְבַקָּרָה[r] Chald., pref. id.) Pael inf. (§ 47. rem. 5) בקר

לִבְקָרוֹ[s] pref. לְ bef. (:)) noun com. sing., suff. 3 pers. sing. masc. from בָּקָר dec. 4a . . בקר

לַבְּקָרִים / לִבְקָרִים[t] pref. לְ for לְהַ / pref. לְ bef. (:) } noun masc., pl. of בֹּקֶר dec. 6c (§ 35. rem. 9) בקר

לְבַקֵּשׁ וּ' pref. לְ) Piel inf. c. dec. 7b; וּ bef. (:) . בקש

לְבַקְשׁוֹ[u] pref. id.) id., suff. 3 p. s. m. (קְ for קּ § 10. r. 7) בקש

לְבַקֶּשְׁךָ[v] pref. id.) id., suff. 2 pers. sing. masc. . בקש

לְבַקְשֵׁנִי[y] pref. id.) id., suff. 1 pers. sing. . . בקש

לְבָר[z] Chald., pref. id.) noun masc. sing. dec. 2a ברא

לַבָּרָד[a] pref. לְ for לְהַ) noun masc. sing. . ברד

לְבָרוֹת[b] pref. לְ) Piel inf. constr., or subst. fem. sing. ברה

לַבַּרְזֶל[c] וְ[d] pref. לְ for לְהַ) noun masc. sing. . ברזל

לְבַרְזִלַּי pref. לְ) pr. name masc. . . . ברזל

לִבְרֹחַ pref. לְ bef. (:)) Kal inf. constr. . . ברח

לְבָרֵי[e] pref. לְ) adj. pl. constr. masc. fr. בַּר dec. 8 (§ 37. rem. 7) . . . . . ברר

לַבְּרִיחִם pref. לְ for לְהַ) noun m., pl. of בְּרִיחַ d. 1a ברח

לִבְרִיעָה pref. לְ bef. (:)) pr. name masc. . . ברע

לַבְּרִית[f] / לִבְרִית pref. לְ for לְהַ / pref. לְ bef. (:) } noun fem. sing. dec. 1a . ברה

לְבָרֵךְ וּ' pref. לְ) Piel inf. constr.; וּ bef. (:) . ברך

לִבְרָכָה pref. לְ bef. (:)) noun fem. sing. dec. 11c . ברך

לְבָרְכוֹ[g] pref. לְ) Kal inf. with suff. 3 pers. sing. m. ברך

וּלְבָרְכוֹ[h] pref. id.) Piel inf. (בָּרֵךְ), suff. 3 pers. sing. masc. dec. 7b; וּ bef. (:) . . ברך

לְבָרָם[i] pref. id.) Kal inf. [בַּר § 18. rem. 3], suff. 3 pers. pl. masc. dec. 8 (§ 37. rem. 7) . ברר

לְבָרָק pref. id.) noun m. s. dec. 4a; also pr. name m. ברק

וּלְבָרֵר[k] pref. id.) Piel inf. constr.; וּ bef. (:) . ברר

לָבַשׁ, וְ' & **לָבֵשׁ** (Ps. 93. 1) fut. יִלְבַּשׁ.—I. *to put on a garment, to be clothed.*—II. metaph. *to be clothed or covered,* with flocks, worms, glory, justice, &c. Part. pass. לָבוּשׁ *clothed.* Pu. part. *clothed.* Hiph. *to clothe, invest.*

לְבַשׁ Chald. fut. יִלְבַּשׁ id. Da. 5. 7, 16. Aph. *to clothe,* Da. 5. 29.

לְבוּשׁ masc. dec. 1a, *garment, vestment.* Chald. id. Da. 3. 21; 7. 9.

מַלְבּוּשׁ masc. dec. 1b, id.

תִּלְבֹּשֶׁת fem. id. Is. 59. 17.

לְבֻשׁ[l] defect. for לָבוּשׁ (q. v.) . . . לבש

לְבַשׁ Kal imp. sing. masc. . . . . לבש

לָבֻשׁ[m] participle or subst. defect. for לָבוּשׁ (q. v.) לבש

לָבְשָׁה Kal pret. 3 pers. sing. fem. . . . לבש

לָבְשׁוּ[n] וְ'[o] id. pret. 3 pers. pl. . . . לבש

לְבֻשׁוֹ defect. for לְבוּשׁוֹ (q. v.) . . . לבש

לִבְשׁוּ[p] Kal imp. pl. masc. . . . . לבש

לְבֻשֵׁי[q] id. part. pass. pl. constr. from לָבוּשׁ d. 3a לבש

לִבְשִׁי וְ'[r] id. imp. sing. masc. . . . לבש

וּלְבֵשָׁם[s] id. pret. 3 pers. sing. masc. (לָבֵשׁ § 16. r. 1), suff. 3 pers. pl. masc.; וּ bef. (:) לבש

---

a Ex. 24. 10. b Ge. 11. 8. c Le. 2. 2, 16. d Ge. 31. 28. e Ge. 31. 43. f Nu. 33. 2. g Nu. 18. 11, 19. h Ec. 5. 10. i Est. 1. 20. k 2 Ch. 4. 20. l Is. 56. 11. m Is. 22. 10. n Zec. 9. 12. o Is. 40. 4. p 2 Ch. 32. 1. q Ps. 27. 4. r Ezr. 7. 14. s 1 Sa. 11. 7. t Job 7. 18. u 1 Sa. 27. 4. x 1 Ki. 18. 10. y 1 Sa. 27. 1. z Da. 3. 25. a Ps. 78. 48. b La. 4. 10. c 1 Ch. 29. 2. d 1 Ch. 22. 14, 16. e Ps. 73. 1. f Ps. 74. 20. g 1 Sa. 13. 10. h 2 Sa. 8. 10; 1 Ch. 18. 10. i Ec. 3. 18. k Da. 11. 35. l Pr. 31. 21. m Eze. 10. 7; Is. 14. 19. n Ps. 65. 14. o Eze. 44. 19. oo 2 Ch. 35. 12. p Je. 46. 4. q Eze. 23. 6, 12. r 2 Sa. 14. 2. s Le. 16. 4. ss 1 Ki. 7. 29.

לַבְּשָׂמִים[a] pref. לְ for לְהַ } noun masc., pl. of בֶּשֶׂם } בשם
וְלִבְשָׂמִים[b] pref. לְ bef. (:) } dec. 6 . . . } בשם
לְבָשָׂר pref. לְ) noun masc. sing. dec. 4a . . בשר
לְבַשֵּׂר pref. id.) Piel inf. constr. . . . בשר
לִבְשָׂרִי[c] pref. לְ bef. (:)) noun masc. sing., suff. 1 pers. sing. from בָּשָׂר dec. 4a . . בשר
לָבָשְׁתָּ[d] Kal pret. 2 pers. sing. m. [for לָבַשְׁתָּ § 8. r. 7] לבש
לַבֹּשֶׁת pref. לְ for לְהַ } noun fem. sing. dec. 13c; } בוש
לִבֹשֶׁת[e] וּ[f] pref. לְ q. v. } וּ bef. (:) . . } בוש
לָבַשְׁתִּי[g] Kal pret. 1 pers. sing. . . . . לבש
לְבָשְׁתְּךָ[h] pref. לְ) noun fem. sing., suff. 2 pers. sing. masc. from בֹּשֶׁת dec. 13c . . בוש
לְבַת וּ[i] pref. id.) noun fem. sing. irr. (§ 45); also pr. name in compos.; וּ bef. (:) . . בנה
לְבִתּוֹ וּ[k] pref. id.) noun fem. sing., suff. 3 pers. sing. masc. from בַּת irr. (§ 45); וּ id. . בנה
לִבְתוּאֵל pref. לְ bef. (:)) pr. name masc., see בְּתוּאֵל
לִבְתוּלַת[l] pref. id.) noun f. s., constr. of בְּתוּלָה d. 10 בתל
לַבָּתִּים pref. לְ f. לְהַ } noun masc. pl. irr. of בַּיִת } בית
לְבָתִּים pref. לְ q. v. } (§ 45) . . . } בית
לְבִתֵּךְ[m] pref. id.) noun fem. sing., suff. 2 pers. sing. masc. from בַּת irr. (§ 45) . . בנה
לִבָּתֵךְ[n] noun fem. s., suff. 2 p. s. f. from [לִבָּה] d. 10 לבב
לִבֹּתָם[o] id. pl., suff. 3 pers. pl. masc. . . . לבב

לֹג masc. *a Log*, a measure for liquids, containing the twelfth part of a Hin, Le. 14. 10, 12, 15, 21, 24.

לִגְאוֹל[p] } pref. לְ bef. (:)) Kal inf. constr., Kh. לִגְאוֹל } גאל
לִגְאָול[q] } q. v., K. לִגְאָל־ id. with Mak. (§ 8. r. 18) } גאל
לְגָאוֹן pref. לְ) noun masc. sing. dec. 3a . גאה
לִגְאוֹן[r] pref. לְ bef. (:)) id. constr. st. . . גאה
לִגְאֵיוֹנִים[s] pref. לְ) Kh. לִגְאֲיוֹנִים noun masc. pl. [of גַּאֲיוֹן]; K. לִגְאֵי יוֹנִים pref. לְ bef. (:), גְּאֵי adj. pl. c. masc. from גֵּאֶה dec. 9 (§ 38. No. 1 & 2) and יוֹנִים (q. v.) . . גאה
לַגֵּאָיוֹת[t] וְ pref. לְ for לְהַ) noun com. pl. transp. [for גֵּיָאוֹת] from גַּיְא irr. (§ 45) . . גיא
לְגֹאֵל[u] pref. id.) Kal part. act. sing. masc. dec. 7b גאל
לִגְאָלֵךְ[x] pref. לְ) id. inf. with suff. 2 p. s. f. (§ 16. r. 8) גאל
לְגֹב[y] וּ Ch., pref. id.) noun m. s. d. 5c; וּ bef. (:) גבב
לְגֻבָּא[z] Chald., pref. id.) id. emph. st. . . גבב
לְגָבְהָה[a] pref. id.) Kal inf. constr. (§ 8. rem. 11) . גבה
לִגְבוּל pref. לְ bef. (:)) noun masc. sing. dec. 1a גבל

לִגְבוּלָם[b] pref. id.) id., suff. 3 pers. pl. masc. . גבל
לִגְבוּלֶתָהָ pref. id.) n. f. s., suff. 3 p. s. f. from [גְּבוּלָה] d. 10 גבל
וְלִגְבוּרָה[c] pref id.) noun fem. sing. dec. 10 . . גבר
לְגִבּוֹרֵי[d] pref. לְ) noun m. pl. constr. from גִּבּוֹר d. 1b גבר
לַגִּבּוֹרִים[e] pref. לְ for לְהַ) id. pl., abs. state . . גבר
לְגַבֵּי[f] pref. לְ) noun m. pl. constr. from גַּב d. 8d גבב
לְגֹבִים[ff] וּ pref. id.) Kh. לְגָבִים pl. of גֵּב R. גוב, K. לְיֹגְבִים q. v.
וְלַגְּבִירָה[g] pref. לְ for לְהַ) noun fem. sing. . גבר
לִגְבֻלֹתֶיהָ[h] defect. for לִגְבוּלֹתֶיהָ (q. v.) . . . גבל
לְגֶבַע pref. לְ) pr. name of a place . . גבע
לַגִּבְעָה pref. לְ for לְהַ) pr. name of a place . גבע
לַגִּבְעֹנִים pref. id.) gent. noun., pl. of גִּבְעֹנִי fr. גִּבְעוֹן גבע
וְלַגְּבָעוֹת pref. id.) noun f. pl. abs. fr. גִּבְעָה d. 12b גבע
לַגֶּבֶר[i] pref. id. } noun masc. sing. dec. 6 . . גבר
לְגֶבֶר pref. לְ } גבר
לְגֻבְרַיָּא[k] Chald., pref. id.) noun masc. pl. emph. [as if from גְּבַר] dec. 2b . . . . גבר
לַגְּבָרִים[l] pref. לְ f. לְהַ } noun masc., pl. of גֶּבֶר } גבר
לִגְבָרִים[m] pref. לְ bef. (:) } dec. 6a . . . } גבר
וּלְגֻבְרִין[n] וּ Ch., pref. לְ) noun m. pl. [as if from גְּבַר] dec. 2b; וּ bef. (:) . . . . גבר
לְגַגּוֹ[o] pref. לְ) noun masc. sing., suff. 3 pers. sing. masc. from גַּג dec. 8d . . . גג
לַגַּגּוֹת[p] pref. לְ for לְהַ) id. pl. fem. . . . גג
לְגַגֶּךָ[q] pref. לְ) id. s., suff. 2 pers. s. m. [for גַּגְּךָ] גג
לַגַּד[r] pref. לְ for לְהַ) noun masc. sing. . גדד
לְגָד וּ pref. לְ) pr. name of a tribe; וּ bef. (:) גדד
לִגְדוּד pref. לְ bef. (:)) noun masc. sing. dec. 1a גדד
לִגְדוּדָיו[s] pref. id.) id. pl., suff. 3 pers. sing. masc. גדד
לְגִדּוּפִים[t] pref. לְ) noun masc., pl. of גִּדּוּף dec. 1b גדף
לַגָּדִי וּ pref. לְ for לְהַ) pr. name of a tribe . גדד
לְגַדֵּל[u] pref. לְ) Piel inf. constr. dec. 7b . . גדל
לְגַדְּלָם[x] וּ pref. id.) id., suff. 3 pers. pl. m.; וּ bef. (:) גדל
וְלִגְדֻלָּתוֹ[y] pref. לְ bef. (:)) noun fem. sing., suff. 3 pers. sing. fem. from גְּדֻלָּה dec. 10 . גדל
לְגִדַּלְתִּי pref. לְ) pr. name masc. . . . גדל
לְגִדְעוֹן וּ pref. id.) pr. name masc.; וּ bef. (:) . גדע
וְלַגֹּדְרִים[z] pref. לְ for לְהַ) Kal part. act. masc., pl. of גֹּדֵר dec. 7b . . . . גדר
לְגֵו pref. לְ) noun masc. sing. dec. 1a . . גוה
לְגוֹא[a] Ch., pref. id.) n. m. s., constr. of גַּו irr. (§ 68) גוא
לְגוֹב[b] Chald. in full for לְגֹב (q. v.) . . גבב

[a] 1 Ch. 9. 30.
[b] 2 Ch. 32. 27.
[c] Ps. 102. 6.
[d] Ps. 104. 1.
[e] Is. 30. 3, 5.
[f] 1 Sa. 20. 30.
[g] Job 29. 14.
[h] 1 Sa. 20. 30.
[i] Eze. 44. 25.
[k] Le. 21. 2.
[l] La. 1. 15.
[m] De. 22. 17.
[n] Eze. 16. 30.
[o] Is. 44. 18.
[p] Ru. 4. 4, 6.
[q] Ru. 4. 6.
[r] Is. 60. 15.
[s] Ps. 123. 4.
[t] Eze. 36. 4, 6.
[u] Ru. 4. 3.
[x] Ru. 3. 13.
[y] Da. 6. 8, 25.
[z] Da. 6. 17, 20, 21.
[a] Zep. 3. 11.
[b] Je. 31. 17.
[c] Is. 28. 6.
[d] 2 Ch. 26. 12.
[e] Ec. 9. 11.
[f] Job 13. 12.
[ff] 2 Ki. 25. 12.
[g] Je. 13. 18.
[h] Nu. 34. 2, 12.
[i] La. 3. 27.
[k] Da. 3. 27; Ezr. 6. 8.
[l] Jos. 7. 14, 17, 18.
[m] 1 Ch. 23. 3.
[n] Da. 3. 20.
[o] Eze. 40. 13.
[p] Is. 22. 1.
[q] De. 22. 8.
[r] Is. 65. 11.
[s] Job 25. 3.
[t] Is. 43. 28.
[u] 1 Ch. 29. 12.
[x] Da. 1. 5.
[y] Ps. 145. 3.
[z] 2 Ki. 12. 13.
[a] Da. 3. 6, 11, 15, 21, 24.
[b] Da. 6. 8.

לְגוֹג pref. לְ)(pr. name masc. . . . . גוג

[a] לַגּוֹי pref. לַ for לְהַ } noun masc. sing. dec. 1a (§ 3. rem. 1) . . גוה
לְגוֹי pref. לְ q. v.

[b] לַגְּוִיָּה pref. לַ for לְהַ)(noun fem. sing. dec. 10 . גוה

[c] לְגוֹיֵהֶם pref. לְ)(noun masc. pl., suff. 3 pers. pl. masc. from גּוֹי dec. 1a (§ 3. rem. 1) . גוה

לַגּוֹיִם pref. לַ f. לְהַ } id. pl., abs. st. . . . גוה
לְגוֹיִם pref. לְ q. v.

לְגוּנִי pref. id.)(pr. name masc. . . . . גוני

[d] לִגְוֹעַ pref. לִ bef. (:))(Kal inf. constr. . . גוע

לָגוּר pref. לָ (see lett. ל))(Kal inf. constr. . גור

[e] לָגֹז pref. id. } Kal inf. constr. (§ 18. rem. 13) גזז
[f] לִגְזֹז pref. לִ bef. (:)

[ll] לְגֹזְזָי pref. לְ)(id. part. act. pl., suff. 1 pers. sing. from גֹּזֵז dec. 7b . . . . גזז

[g] וְלִגְזֹל pref. לִ bef. (:))(Kal inf. constr. . גזל

[h] לְגֹזֵר pref. לְ)(Kal part. act. sing. masc. . . גזר

[i] לִגְזָרִים pref. לִ bef. (:))(noun m. pl. of [גֶּזֶר] d. 6b גזר

[k] לְגֶחָלִים pref. לְ)(noun fem. pl. [as if from גְּחָלָה] see גַּחֶלֶת (§ 44. rem. 5, & § 42. No. 3 note) גחל

[l] לַגַּי pref. לַ for לְהַ)(noun com. sing. irr. (§ 45) גיא

[m] וְלַגֵּאָיוֹת pref. id.)(id. pl., Kh. גֵּיאָוֹת, K. by transp. גֵּאָיוֹת . . . . . גיא

[n] לְ֯גִּיד Kh. לַגִּיד contr. for K. לְהַגִּיד (q. v. & § 11. r. 3) נגד

לְגִיחוֹן pref. לְ)(pr. name of a river . . גיח

לְגֵיחֲזִי pref. id.)(pr. name masc. . . . גיא

[o] לַגַּל pref. לַ for לְהַ)(for גַּל noun masc. s. d. 8d גלל

[p] לַגַּלְגַּל pref. id.)(noun masc. sing. dec. 8e . . גלל

לַגִּלְגָּל pref. לַ)(pr. name of a place . . . גלל

לַגֻּלְגֹּלֶת pref. לַ for לְהַ)(noun fem. sing. dec. 13c גלל

לְגֻלְגְּלֹתָם pref. לְ)(id. pl., suff. 3 pers. pl. masc. . גלל

[q] לַגֹּלָה pref. לַ for לְהַ)(noun fem. sing. . . גלה

[r] לְגִלּוּלֵיהֶם pref. לְ)(n. m. pl., suff. 3 p. pl. m. fr. [גִּלּוּל] d. 1b גלל

לְגָלוֹת pref. id.)(noun fem. s. d. 1b (§ 32. No. 3) גלה

לְגַלּוֹת pref. id.)(Piel inf. constr. . . . גלה

[s] לְגָלוּתֵינוּ } pref. id.)(noun fem. sing., suff. 1 pers. pl. fr. גָּלוּת d. 1b (§ 32. No. 3; & § 4. r. 1) גלה
[t] לְגָלוּתֵנוּ

[u] לְגַלָּיו pref. id.)(n. m. pl., suff. 3 p. s. m. fr. גַּל d. 8d גלל

לְגַלִּים pref. id.)(id. pl., abs. st. . . . . גלל

לַגִּלְעָד pref. לַ f. לְהַ } pr. name of a man and a place, see גִּלְעָד.
לְגִלְעָד pref. לְ q. v.

לְגָמוּל pref. id.)(pr. name masc. . . . . גמל

וְלִגְמַלֵּיהֶם pref. לִ bef. (:))(noun masc. pl., suff. 3 pers. pl. masc. from גָּמָל dec. 8a (§ 37. No. 2) גמל

[x] לִגְמַלֶּיךָ pref. id.)(id., suff. 2 pers. sing. masc. . גמל

[y] לַגְּמַלִּים pref. לַ for לְהַ)(id. pl., abs. st. . . גמל

לְגַן pref. לְ)(noun com. sing. dec. 8d . . . גנן

[z] לַגַּנָּב pref. לַ for לְהַ)(noun masc. sing. dec. 1b גנב

לְגַנּוֹ pref. לְ)(n. com. s., suff. 3 p. s. m. fr. גַּן d. 8d גנן

[a] לְגַנִּי pref. id.)(id. with suff. 1 pers. sing. . גנן

לְגִנְּתוֹן pref. id.)(pr. name masc. . . . גנן

[b] לָגַעַת pref. לָ (see lett. ל))(Kal inf. constr. . נגע

[c] לַגֶּפֶן } pref. לַ f. לְהַ } noun com. sing. dec. 6a (§ 35. rem. 2) . גפן
[d] לַגָּפֶן
[e] לְגֶפֶן pref. לְ q. v.

[f] לְגָפְרִית pref. id.)(noun fem. sing. from גֹּפֶר masc. גפר

לַגֵּר וְ׳ pref. לַ for לְהַ)(noun masc. sing. dec. 1a גור

לְגַרְגְּרֹתֶיךָ pref. לְ)(n. f. pl., suff. 2 p. s. m. fr. [גַּרְגֶּרֶת] d. 13 גרר

[g] לִגְרוֹעַ pref. לִ bef. (:))(Kal inf. constr. . . גרע

[h] לְגֹרָלֶךָ pref. לְ)(n. m. s., suff. 2 p. s. m. fr. גּוֹרָל d. 2b גרל

לִגְרָר pref. לִ bef. (:))(pr. name of a place . גרר

[i] לְגָרֵשׁ pref. לְ)(Piel inf. constr. . . . גרש

לְגֵרְשׁוֹן pref. id.)(pr. name masc. . . . גרש

[k] לְגָרְשֵׁנוּ pref. id.)(Piel inf. (גָּרֵשׁ), suff. 1 p. pl. d. 7b גרש

לַגֵּרְשֻׁנִּי pref. לַ for לְהַ)(patronym. of גֵּרְשׁוֹן . גרש

לְגֶשֶׁם וּ pref. לְ)(pr. name masc.; וּ bef. (:) . גשם

לָגֶשֶׁת וְ׳ pref. לָ (see lett. ל))(Kal inf. constr. (suff. גִּשְׁתּוֹ) dec. 13a . . . . נגש

לְגַת pref. לְ)(pr. name of a place . . . גת

לַד וָלָד & וָ see under lett. ו.

לֹד pr. name of a town in the tribe of Benjamin.

[m] לְדָא Chald., pref. לְ)(pron. demon. sing. fem. . דא

[n] לְדַאֲבָה pref. id.)(noun fem. sing. . . . דאב

[o] לְדֹב Chald., pref. id.)(noun m. sing., comp. Heb. דֹּב דבב

[p] וְלַדְּבוֹרָה pref. לַ for לְהַ)(noun fem. s. (pl. דְּבֹרִים) d. 10 דבר

[pp] לַדְּבִיר וְ׳ pref. id.)(noun masc. sing. . . דבר

[q] לַדֶּבֶק pref. id.)(noun masc. sing. dec. 6a . . דבק

לְדָבְקָה וּ pref. לְ)(Kal inf. constr. (§ 8. r. 10); וּ bef. (:) דבק

לַדֶּבֶר pref. לַ for לְהַ)(noun masc. sing. dec. 4a דבר

[r] לַדָּבָר pref. לַ f. לְהַ } noun masc. sing. dec. 6 (§ 35. rem. 2); וּ bef. (:) . דבר
[s] לְדָבָר וּ pref. לְ q. v.

לְדֶבֶר pref. לְ)(noun masc. sing. dec. 4a . . דבר

לְדַבֵּר וּ׳ } pref. id.)(Piel inf. constr. (§ 10. rem. 4); וּ bef. (:) . . דבר
[t] לְדַבֶּר־

[a] Is. 26. 15. [b] Na. 3. 3. [c] Ge. 10. 31. [d] Nu. 17. 28. [e] Ge. 38. 13. [f] Ge. 31. 19. [g] Is. 10. 2. [h] Ps. 136. 13. [i] Ps. 136. 13. [k] Pr. 26. 21. [l] Mi. 1. 6. [m] Eze. 6. 3. [n] 2 Ki. 9. 15. [o] Is. 25. 2. [p] Eze. 10. 2. [q] Na. 3. 10. [r] Eze. 23. 39. [s] Eze. 33. 21. [t] Eze. 40. 1. [u] Eze. 26. 3. [x] Ge. 24. 19, 44. [y] Ge. 24. 31, 32. [z] Pr. 6. 30. [a] Ca. 5. 1. [b] 2 Sa. 14. 10. [c] Ju. 9. 12 [d] Ge. 49. 11. [e] Eze. 17. 6, 8. [f] Is. 34. 9. [g] Ec. 3. 14. [h] Da. 12. 13. [i] 1 Ch. 17. 21. [k] 2 Ch. 20. 11. [l] Eze. 44. 13. [ll] 1 Sa. 25. 11. [m] Da. 5. 6. [n] Je. 31. 12. [o] Da. 7. 5. [p] Is. 7. 18. [pp] 1 Ki. 6. 5, 22. [q] Is. 41. 7. [r] Ps. 78. 50. [s] Je. 28. 8. [t] Is. 32. 6.

Word	Analysis	Root
לְדָבָר	pref. לְ bef. (:))(n. m. s., constr. of דָּבָר d. 4a	דבר
לִדְבִר[a]	pref. id.)(for דְּבִיר, noun masc. sing., also pr. name of a place	דבר
לִדְבִרָה	pref. id.)(pr. name (דְּבִיר with loc. ה)	דבר
לִדְבָרוֹ[b]	ו׳ pref. id.)(n.m.s., suff. 3 p.s.m. fr. דָּבָר d. 4a	דבר
לְדִבְרֵי[d]	pref. לְ)(id. pl. constr. st.	דבר
לִדְבָרַי[e]	pref. לְ bef. (:))(id. pl., suff. 1 pers. sing.	דבר
לְדִבְרֵיהֶם[f]	pref. לְ)(id. pl., suff. 3 pers. pl. masc.	דבר
לִדְבָרֶיךָ[g]	pref. לְ bef. (:))(id. pl. (Kh. ׳רֶיךָ, K. ׳רְךָ sing., suff. 2 pers. sing. masc.	דבר
לְדִבְרֵיכֶם[h]	pref. לְ)(id. pl., suff. 2 pers. pl. masc.	דבר
לַדְּבָרִים[i]	pref. לְ for לְהַ)(id. pl., abs. st.	דבר
לִדְבָרְךָ[k]	pref. לְ bef. (:))(id. sing., suff. 2 pers. s. m.	דבר
לַדָּג[l]	pref. לְ for לְהַ)(noun masc. sing. dec. 2a	דגה
לְדָגוֹן	pref. לְ)(pr. name of an idol	דגה
לְדִגְלֵיהֶם[m]	pref. id.)(n.m.pl., suff. 3 p. pl. m. fr. דֶּגֶל d. 6a	דגל
לֵדָה[n]	Kal inf. constr. (§ 20. rem. 3)	ילד
לְדַוָּגִים[o]	pref. לְ)(Kh. noun masc. pl. [from דַּוָּג], K. ׳דַיָּגִים [from דַּיָּג] dec. 1b	דוג
לְדָוִד	pref. id.)(pr. name masc.	דוד
לְדוֹדִי	pref. id.)(noun m. s., suff. 1 p. s. fr. דּוֹד d. 1a	דוד
לְדוֹאֵג	pref. id.)(pr. name masc., K. דּוֹאֵג	דאג
לְדָוִיד	pref. id.)(pr. name masc., see דָּוִד	דוד
לְדוֹר[p] / לַדּוֹר[q] / לְדֹר	pref. לְ (see ל) / pref. לְ for לְהַ / pref. לְ (q. v.) } noun masc. sing. dec. 1a	דור
לָדוּשׁ[r]	pref. לְ (see lett. ל))(Kal inf. constr.	דוש
לִדְחוֹת[s]	pref. לְ bef. (:))(Kal inf. constr.	דחה
לָדִין	pref. לְ (see lett. ל))(Kal inf. constr. R. see דִּין	דון
לְדִינִי[t]	pref. לְ)(noun masc. sing. dec. 2b, R. דִּין see	דון
לְדִין[u]	pref. id.)(noun masc. sing. dec. 1a, R. דִּין see	דון
לַדָּךְ[w]	pref. לְ for לְהַ)(for דַּךְ, adj. masc. sing. d. 8d	דכך
לְדַכֵּא[y]	pref. לְ)(Piel inf. constr.	דכא
לַדָּל / לַדָּל[z]	pref. לְ for לְהַ)(adj. masc. sing. dec. 8d	דלל
לִדְלְיָהוּ	pref. לְ bef. (:))(pr. name masc.	דלה
לְדֹלְקִים[a]	pref. לְ)(Kal part. act. m., pl. of [דֹּלֵק] d. 7b	דלק
לַדֶּלֶת[b]	pref. id.)(noun fem. sing., comp. דֶּלֶת	דלה
לַדְּלָתוֹת[c]	pref. לְ for לְהַ)(id. pl. abs. (§ 44. rem. 5), ת treated as if radical	דלה
לְדַלְתוֹת	pref. לְ)(id. pl., constr. st. (§ 44. rem. 1)	דלה
לְדַלְתֵי[d]	pref. לְ)(noun fem., constr. of דְּלָתַיִם from [דָּלָה] dec. 11a (§ 44. rem. 1)	דלה
לַדָּם[e] / לְדָם	pref. לְ for לְהַ / pref. לְ q. v. } noun masc. sing. dec. 2a	אדם
לְדַם[f]	pref. id.)(id. constr. st.	אדם
לְדָמִים[g]	pref. id.)(id. pl., abs. st.	אדם
לְדָמָם[h]	pref. id.)(id. sing., suff. 3 pers. pl. masc.	אדם
לִדְמָמָה[i]	pref. לְ bef. (:))(noun fem. sing.	דמם
לְדֹמֶן	pref. לְ)(noun masc. sing.	דמן
לְדַמֶּשֶׂק / לְדַמָּשֶׂק	pref. id.)(pr. name of a place	דמשק
לְדָן	ו׳ pref. id.)(pr. name of a tribe; וּ bef. (:)	דון
לְדָנִיֵּאל	ו׳ pref. id.)(pr. name masc.; וּ id.	דון
לְדֵעָה[k]	pref. id.)(Kal inf. constr. (§ 20. rem. 3)	ידע
לָדַעַת[l]	pref. לְ (see lett. ל))(for דַּעַת׳ n. fem. s. d. 13a	ידע
לָדַעַת	וְ pref. id.)(Kal inf. constr. d. 13a (§ 20. r. 3)	ידע
לְדַעְתָּהּ[m]	pref. לְ)(id., suff. 3 pers. sing. fem.	ידע
לְדַעְתּוֹ[n]	pref. id.)(id., suff. 3 pers. sing. masc.	ידע
לְדַעְתִּי[o]	pref. id.)(n. fem. s., suff. 1 p. s. fr. דַּעַת d. 13a	ידע
לְדֹר	defect. for לְדוֹר (q. v.)	דור
לְדִרְאוֹן[p]	pref. לְ)(noun masc. sing. constr. [of דְּרָאוֹן § 32. Nos. 1 & 2]	דרא
לַדָּרוֹם[q]	pref. לְ for לְהַ)(noun masc. sing. [for דַּרְוֹם	דרר
לִדְרוֹשׁ	in full for לִדְרֹשׁ (q. v.)	דרש
לְדָרְיָוֶשׁ	pref. לְ)(pr. name masc., see דָּרְיָוֶשׁ.	
לְדַרְיוֹשׁ[r]	pref. id.)(Piel inf. [for דַּרוֹשׁ § 8. rem. 10]	דרש
לַדֶּרֶךְ / לַדָּרֶךְ[s] / לְדֶרֶךְ	pref. לְ f. לְהַ / pref. לְ q. v. } noun com. sing. dec. 6a (§ 35. rem. 2)	דרך
לְדַרְכָּהּ[t]	pref. id.)(id., suff. 3 pers. sing. fem.	דרך
לְדַרְכּוֹ	pref. id.)(id., suff. 3 pers. sing. masc.	דרך
לְדַרְכְּךָ[u]	pref. id.)(id., suff. 2 pers. sing. masc.	דרך
לְדַרְכְּכֶם	pref. id.)(id., suff. 2 pers. pl. masc.	דרך
לְדַרְכָּם	pref. id.)(id., suff. 3 pers. pl. masc.	דרך
לִדְרֹשׁ / לִדְרָשׁ־[x]	pref. לְ bef. (:))(Kal inf. constr. (§ 8. rem. 18)	דרש
לְדָרְשֵׁנִי[y]	pref. לְ)(id. with suff. 1 pers. sing.	דרש
לְדֹרֹת[z]	pref. id.)(noun masc., pl. of דּוֹר dec. 1a	דור
לְדֹרֹתָיו[a]	pref. id.)(id., suff. 3 pers. sing. masc.	דור
לְדֹרֹתֵיכֶם	pref. id.)(id., suff. 2 pers. pl. masc.	דור
לְדֹרֹתָם	pref. id.)(id., suff. 3 pers. pl. m. (§ 4. r. 2)	דור

[a] 1 Ki. 6. 16. [b] Ps. 106. 24. [c] Ps. 130. 5. [d] Job 16. 3. [e] Pr. 4. 20. [f] 2 Ch. 9. 6. [g] Ps. 119. 147. [h] Job 32. 11. [i] 1 Ki. 10. 7. [k] Ps. 119. 81, 114. [l] Jon. 2. 11. [m] Nu. 2. 17, 31, 34. [n] Je. 13. 21. [o] Je. 16. 16. [p] Is. 34. 10. [q] Ps. 22. 31. [r] Ho. 10. 11. [s] Ps. 140. 5. [t] 1 Sa. 24. 16. [u] De. 17. 8. [w] Ps. 9. 10. [y] La. 3. 34. [z] Job 5. 16. [a] Ps. 7. 14. [b] Eze. 41. 24. [c] Eze. 41. 24. [d] 1 Ki. 7. 50. [e] Nu. 35. 33. [f] Le. 16. 15. [g] Mi. 7. 2. [h] Pr. 1. 18. [i] Ps. 107. 29. [k] Ex. 2. 4. [l] Is. 32. 4. [m] Ge. 38. 26. [n] Is. 7. 15. [o] Pr. 22. 17. [p] Da. 12. 2. [q] Eze. 41. 11. [r] Ezr. 10. 16. [s] Jos. 9. 11. [t] 1 Sa. 1. 18. [u] 1 Ki. 19. 15. [x] Eze. 14. 7. [y] Je. 37. 7. [z] Ge. 9. 12. [a] Le. 25. 30.

לְדֻשׁ[a] defect. for לָדוּשׁ (q. v.) . . . . דוש

לְדַשְּׁנוֹ[b] pref. לְ) Piel inf. [דַּשֵּׁן], suff. 3 pers. sing. masc. dec. 7 b . . . . דשן

לֶדֶת Kal inf. const. dec. 13 a . . . ילד

לִדְתָּהּ[c] id. with suff. 3 pers. sing. fem. . . ילד

לְדָתָן pref. לְ) pr. name masc. . . . . דת

לִדְתָּנָה[d] Kal inf. (לֶדֶת), suff. 3 pers. pl. fem. dec. 13 a (§ 3. rem. 5) . . . ילד

לָהּ וְ' Heb. & Ch., pref. prep. לְ with suff. 3 pers. sing. fem. (§ 5, parad.) . . . ל

לֵהּ[e] וְ' Ch., pref. prep. לְ with suff. 3 pers. s. m. ל

לֹה[f] Kh. לֹה q. v.; K. לִי (q. v.) . . ל

לְהַאֲבִיד[g] וּ' pref. לְ) Hiph. inf. constr. d. 1 b; וּ bef. (:) אבד

לְהַאֲבִידוֹ pref. id.) id., suff. 3 pers. sing. masc. . אבד

לְהַאֲבִידֵנוּ[h] pref. id.) id., suff. 1 pers. pl. . . אבד

לְהָאִיר pref. id.) Hiph. inf. constr. . . . אור

לְהַאֲלֹתוֹ pref. id.) Hiph. inf. [הַאֲלוֹת], suff. 3 pers. sing. masc. dec. 1 b . . . אלה

לָהַב Root not used; Arab. *to burn, flame.*

לַהַב masc. dec. 6 d.—I. *flame.*—II. *glitter* of a sword or spear, i. e. *the blade* or *iron-head.*

לֶהָבָה fem. dec. 11 a (pl. לֶהָבוֹת, constr. לַהֲבוֹת § 42. No. 3 note), and לַהֶבֶת.—I. *flame.* —II. *iron-head* of a spear, 1 Sa. 17. 7.

לַבָּה fem. for לֶהָבָה *flame,* Ex. 3. 2.

לְהָבִים pr. name of a people, Ge. 10. 13; prob. *Libyans,* comp. לוּבִים.

שַׁלְהֶבֶת fem. *flame,* Job 15. 30; Ca. 8. 6, שַׁלְהֶבֶת־יָהּ *flame of the Lord,* i. e. intense flame.

לַהַב וְ' noun masc. sing. dec. 6 d . . . להב

לְהַבְאִישֵׁנִי[i] pref. לְ) Hiph. inf. [הַבְאִישׁ], suff. 1 pers. sing. dec. 1 b . . . . באש

לְהַבְדִּיל וּ' pref. id.) Hiph. inf. constr.; וּ bef. (:) בדל

לֶהָבָה וְ' noun fem. sing. d. 11 a (§ 42. No. 3 note) להב

לַהֲבוֹת[k] id. pl., constr. st. . . . . להב

לֶהָבוֹת[l] id. pl., abs. st. . . . . להב

לְהַבְזוֹת[m] pref. לְ) Hiph. inf. constr. . . . בזה

לְהָבִיא וּ' pref. id.) Hiph. inf. constr. d. 3 a; וּ bef. (:) בוא

לַהֲבִיאֲךָ[n] וְ'[o] pref. לַ bef. (-:)) id., suff. 2 pers. sing. m. בוא

לַהֲבִיאָם pref. id.) id., suff. 3 pers. pl. masc. . בוא

לְהַבִּיט[p] pref. לְ) Hiph. inf. constr. dec. 1 b נבט

לְהַבִּיטָם[q] pref. id.) id., suff. 3 pers. pl. masc. . נבט

לְהָבִים pr. name of a people . . . . להב

לְהָבִים[r] noun masc., pl. of לַהַב dec. 6 d . . להב

לְהָבִין pref. לְ) Hiph. inf. constr. dec. 3 a . בין

לַהֲבִינְךָ[s] pref. לַ bef. (-:)) id., suff. 2 pers. sing. masc. בין

לְהַבְלִי[t] pref. לְ for לְהַ) noun m. s. d. 6 a (§ 35. r. 4) הבל

לְהִבָּנוֹת pref. לְ) Niph. inf. constr. . . . בנה

לְהַבְקִיעַ[u] pref. id.) Hiph. inf. constr. . . בקע

לְהִבָּקַע[x] pref. id.) Niph. inf. constr. [for הִבָּקַע § 15. rem. 1] . . . . . בקע

לְהָבַר[y] pref. id.) Hiph. inf. constr. (§ 18. rem. 10) ברר

לְהַבְרוֹת[z] pref. id.) Hiph. inf. constr. . . ברה

לְהַבְרִיאֲכֶם[a] pref. id.) Hiph. inf. [הַבְרִיא], suff. 2 pers. pl. masc. dec. 1 b . . . . ברא

לַהֶבֶת[b] וְ'[c] noun fem. sing., pl. לֶהָבוֹת from לֶהָבָה (§ 42. No. 3 note, comp. rem. 5) . להב

לַהַג וְ masc. *study,* Ec. 12. 12.

לְהַגְּדוּד preff. לְ & הַ) noun masc. sing. dec. 1 a גדד

לְהַגְדִּיל[d] וּ'[e] pref. לְ) Hiph. inf. constr.; וּ bef. (:) גדל

לְהַגִּיד וּ'[ff] pref. id.) Hiph. inf. constr.; וּ id. . נגד

לְהִגָּלוֹת[f] pref. id.) Niph. inf. constr. . . גלה

לְהַגְלוֹת[g] וּ pref. id.) Hiph. inf. constr. d. 1 b; וּ bef. (:) גלה

לְהַגְלוֹתֵךְ[h] pref. id.) id. with suff. 2 pers. sing. fem. . גלה

לְהַגֵּרִים[i] וּ preff. לְ & הַ) n. m., pl. of גֵּר d. 1 a; וּ bef. (:) גור

לָהַד [for לַהַד] pr. name masc. 1 Ch. 4. 2.

לְהַדָּבְרוֹהִי[k] Chald., pref. לְ) noun masc. pl., suff. 3 pers. sing. masc. [from הַדָּבָר] . . . דבר

לַהֲדַדְעֶזֶר pref. לַ bef. (-:)) pr. name masc. . . הדד

לְהֹדוֹת וּ' defect. for לְהוֹדוֹת (q. v.) . . . ידה

לְהַדִּיחַ[l] pref. לְ) Hiph. inf. constr. dec. 1 b . נדח

לְהַדִּיחֲךָ[m] pref. id.) id., suff. 2 pers. sing. masc. . נדח

לְהֹדִיעַ[n] defect. for לְהוֹדִיעַ (q. v.) . . . ידע

לַהֲדֹם וְ'[o] pref. לַ bef. (-:)) noun masc. sing. . הדם

לַהֲדֹף[p] pref. id.) Kal inf. constr. . . . הדף

לְהָדְפָהּ[q] pref. לְ) id., suff. 3 pers. sing. fem. . הדף

לְהָדֵק[r] pref. id.) Hiph inf. constr. (§ 18. rem. 10) דקק

לַהֲדַרְעֶזֶר pref. לַ bef. (-:)) pr. n. m., see הֲדַדְעֶזֶר under הדד

לְהַדְרַת[s] pref. לְ) n. f. s. constr. [of הַדְרָה or הֲדָרָה] הדר

[לָהַהּ] fut. apoc. וַתֵּלַהּ (§ 24. rem. 3) *to be weary, faint,* Ge. 47. 13. Hithpalp. (§ 6. No. 3) part. מִתְלַהְלֵהַּ *insane, mad person,* Pr. 26. 18.

---

[a] 2 Ki. 13. 7. [b] Ex. 27. 3. [c] Ge. 38. 27. [d] Job 39. 2. [e] Da. 7. 14.
[f] Ju. 16. 18. [g] De. 28. 63. [h] Jos. 7. 7. [i] Ge. 34. 30. [k] Ps. 29. 7.
[l] Ps. 105. 32. [m] Est. 1. 17. [n] De. 4. 38. [o] Ex. 23. 20. [p] Jon. 2. 5.
[q] La. 4. 16. [r] Is. 13. 8. [s] Da. 10. 14. [t] Ps. 144. 4. [u] 2 Ki. 3. 26.
[x] Eze. 30. 16. [y] Je. 4. 11. [z] 2 Sa. 3. 35. [a] 1 Sa. 2. 29. [b] Eze. 21. 3.
[c] 1 Sa. 17. 7. [d] 1 Ch. 22. 5. [e] Am. 8. 5. [f] Is. 56. 1. [ff] Est. 4. 8.
[g] Je. 43. 3. [h] La. 4. 22. [i] Eze. 47. 22. [k] Da. 3. 24.
[l] Ps. 62. 5. [m] De. 13. 6, 11. [n] 1 Ch. 17. 19. [o] 1 Ch. 28. 2.
[p] De. 19. 9. [q] 2 Ki. 4. 27. [r] 2 Ch. 34. 7. [s] 2 Ch. 20. 21.

לֶהֱוֵא Ch., pref. לְ bef. (‥:))(contr. [for לִיהֱוֵא] preform. י omitted, Peal fut. 3 pers. sing. m. הוה

לְהוֹבָדָא[a] / לְהוֹבָדָה[b] } Chald., pref. לְ)(Aph. inf. constr. (§ 53. rem. 1, & § 47. rem. 5); [c]וּ' וּ bef. (:) אבד

לְהוֹדָיָה pref. id.)(K. הוֹדָיָה' (q. v.) הוד

לְהוֹדוֹת [d]וּ' pref. id.)(Hiph. inf. constr.; וּ bef. (:) ידה

לְהוֹדִיעַ pref. id.)(Hiph. inf. constr. dec. 1b ידע

לְהוֹדִיעֲךָ[e] pref. id.)(id., suff. 2 pers. sing. masc. ידע

לְהוֹדִיעָם pref. id.)(id., suff. 3 pers. pl. masc. ידע

לְהוֹדִיעֵנִי[f] pref. id.)(id., suff. 1 pers. sing. ידע

לְהוֹדָעָה[g] Chald., pref. id.)(Aph. inf. constr. (§ 47. r. 5) ידע

לְהוֹדָעוּתָךְ[h] Ch., pref. id.)(id., suff. 2 p. s. m. [fr. הוֹדָעוּת] ידע

לְהוֹדָעוּתַנִי / לְהוֹדָעֻתַנִי } Chald., pref. id.)(id., suff. 1 pers. sing. ידע

לֶהֱוֵה[i] Chald., pref. לְ bef. (‥:))(Peal fut. 3 pers. sing. masc., comp. לֶהֱוֵא הוה

לֶהֶוְיָן[k] Chald., pref. id.)(id. fut. 3 pers. pl. fem. הוה

לְהוֹכִיחַ[l] pref. לְ)(Hiph. inf. constr. יכח

לַהוֹלְלִים[m] pref. לַ for לְהַ)(Kal part. act., pl. of הוֹלֵל d. 7b הלל

לְהוֹם[n] Chald., pref. prep. ל with suff. 3 pers. pl. m. ל

לַהוֹן[o] pref. לַ for לְהַ)(noun masc. sing. dec. 1a הון

לֶהֱוֹן Chald., pref. לְ bef. (‥:))(Peal fut. 3 pers. pl. masc. comp. לֶהֱוֵא הוה

לְהוֹן Chald., pref. prep. ל with suff. 3 pers. pl. m. ל

לְהוֹנֹתָם[p] pref. לְ)(Hiph. inf. [הוֹנוֹת], suff. 3 pers. pl. masc. (§ 25. No. 2 e) ינה

לְהוֹסִיף pref. id.)(Hiph. inf. constr. יסף

לְהוֹעִיל pref. id.)(Hiph. inf. constr. יעל

לְהוֹצִאֵהוּ[q] pref. id.)(the foll. with suff. 3 pers. s. m. יצא

לְהוֹצִיא pref. id.)(Hiph. inf. constr. dec. 1b יצא

לְהוֹצִיאָם pref. id.)(id., suff. 3 pers. pl. masc. יצא

לְהוֹצִיאֵנוּ[r] pref. id.)(id., suff. 1 pers. pl. יצא

לְהוֹרְגִים[s] pref. id.)(Kal part. act. m., pl. of הֹרֵג d. 7b הרג

לְהוֹרִיד[t] pref. id.)(Hiph. inf. constr. ירד

לְהוֹרִישׁ pref. id.)(Hiph. inf. constr. dec. 1b ירש

לְהוֹרִישָׁם pref. id.)(id., suff. 3 pers. pl. masc. ירש

לְהוֹרֹת וּ' pref. id.)(Hiph. inf. constr. (§ 25. No. 2e) ירה

לְהוֹרֹתָם[u] pref. id.)(id., suff. 3 pers. pl. masc. ירה

לְהוֹשִׁיב[v] pref. id.)(Hiph. inf. constr. dec. 1b ישב

לְהוֹשִׁיבִי[x] pref. id.)(id. with parag. ישב

לְהוֹשִׁיעַ [y]וּ' pref. id.)(Hiph. inf. constr. d. 1b; וּ bef. (:) ישע

לְהוֹשִׁיעָהּ pref. id.)(id., suff. 3 pers. sing. fem. ישע

לְהוֹשִׁיעֲךָ[z] / לְהוֹשִׁיעֶךָ[a] } pref. לְ)(id., suff. 2 pers. sing. masc. ישע

לְהוֹשִׁיעֵנִי pref. id.)(id., suff. 1 pers. sing. ישע

לְהוֹשֵׁעַ pref. id.)(pr. name masc. ישע

לְהוֹתִיר pref. id.)(pr. name masc. יתר

לַהֲזָדָה[b] Ch., pref. לַ bef. (-:))(Aph. inf. (§ 21. r. 15, & § 47. rem. 4) זוד

לְהַזְהִיר pref. לְ)(Hiph. inf. constr. זהר

לְהִזָּהֵר[c] pref. id.)(Niph. inf. constr. זהר

לְהַזִּיר[d] pref. id.)(Hiph. inf. constr. dec. 1b נזר

לְהַזְכִּיר [e]וּ' pref. id.)(Hiph. inf. constr.; וּ bef. (:) זכר

לְהַזְנוֹתָהּ[f] pref. id.)(Hiph. inf. (הַזְנוֹת'), suff. 3 pers. sing. fem. dec. 1b זנה

לְהַזְעִיק[g] pref. id.)(Hiph. inf. constr. זעק

לְהֵחָבֵא[h] pref. id.)(Niph. inf. constr. חבא

לְהֵחָבֵה pref. id.)(Niph. inf. constr. חבה

לְהַחֲוָיָה Ch., pref. id.)(Aph. inf. constr. (§ 47. r. 4, & § 35. rem. 3) חוה

לְהַחוֹמָה[i] preff. לְ & הַ)(noun fem. sing. dec. 10 חמה

לְהַחֲזִיק pref. לְ)(Hiph. inf. constr. חזק

לְהַחֲטִיא[k] pref. id.)(Hiph. inf. constr. חטא

לְהַחֲיוֹת / לְהַחֲיֹת[l] } וּ' pref. id.)(Hiph. inf. constr. dec. 1b; וּ bef. (:) חיה

לְהַחֲיֹתוֹ[m] pref. id.)(id. with suff. 3 pers. sing. masc. חיה

לְהֵחַלּוֹ[n] pref. id.)(Niph. inf. [הֵחַל], suff. 3 pers. sing. masc. (§ 18. rem. 7) חלל

לְהַחֲרִיד pref. id.)(Hiph. inf. constr. חרד

לְהַחֲרִים[o] [p]וּ' pref. id.)(Hiph. inf. constr. d. 1b; וּ bef. (:) חרם

לְהַחֲרִימָם pref. id.)(id. with suff. 3 pers. pl. masc. חרם

[לָהַט] *to burn, flame,* only part. לֹהֵט *flaming.* Pi. לִהַט (§ 14. rem. 1) *to kindle, inflame.*

לַהַט masc. *flame, glittering,* Ge. 3. 24.

לְהָטִים masc. pl. (of לַהַט) *flames; hence dazzlings, delusions,* Ex. 7. 11. Others, take it to stand for לָטִים *enchantments* from לוּט; or suppose the signification of the Root לָהַט to be the same as לוּט.

לַהַט[q] noun masc. sing. להט

לִהַט[r] וְ Piel pret. 3 pers. sing. masc. (§ 14. r. 1) להט

לֹהֵט[s] Kal part. act. sing. masc. להט

לִהֲטָה[t] Piel pret. 3 pers. sing. fem. (§ 14. rem. 1) להט

לְהַטּוֹת pref. לְ)(Hiph. inf. constr. (§ 25. No. 2 b) נטה

[a] Da. 2. 24. [b] Da. 2. 12. [c] Da. 7. 26. [d] 1 Ch. 16. 4. [e] Pr. 22. 21. [f] 1 Sa. 28. 15. [g] Da. 5. 8. [h] Ezr. 5. 10. [i] Da. 4. 22. [k] Da. 5. 17. [l] Hab. 1. 12. [m] Ps. 75. 5. [n] Je. 10. 11. [o] Pr. 28. 22. [p] Eze. 46. 18. [q] Je. 39. 14. [r] Ex. 14. 11. [s] Je. 4. 31. [t] Ge. 37. 25. [u] Ex. 24. 12. [x] Ps. 113. 8. [y] 1 Sa. 25. 31. [z] Je. 15. 20. [a] Je. 30. 11. [b] Da. 5. 20. [c] Ec. 4. 13. [d] Nu. 6. 2. [e] 1 Ch. 16. 4. [f] Le. 19. 29. [g] 2 Sa. 20. 5. [h] 2 Ch. 18. 24. [i] Ne. 12. 38. [k] 1 Ki. 16. 19. [l] Ge. 50. 20. [v] 1 Sa. 2. 8. [m] Eze. 13. 22. [n] Le. 21. 4. [o] 2 Ch. 20. 23. [p] Da. 11. 44. [q] Ge. 3. 24. [r] Mal. 3. 19. [s] Ps. 104. 4. [t] Joel 1. 19.

לְהֵטִיב[a] defect. for לְהֵיטִיב (q. v.) . . . יטב

לְהֲטִים[b] Kal part. act. masc., pl. of לֹהֵט dec. 7 b — להט

לְהַטּוֹת[c] pref. לְ)(for הַטּוֹת', Hiph. inf. constr. (§ 25. No. 2 b) . . . . . נטה

לְהַטֹּתָהּ[d] pref. id.)(id. with suff. 3 pers. sing. fem. . נטה

לְהֵיבָלָה[e] וּ Ch., pref. id.)(Aph. inf. (§ 47. r. 4); וּ bef. (:) — יבל

לִהְיוֹת[f] וְ'ו pref. לְ bef. (:))(Kal inf. constr. dec. 1 a (§ 13. rem. 13) . . . . היה

לִהְיוֹתְכֶם[g] pref. id.)(id. with suff. 2 pers. pl. masc. — היה

לְהֵיטִבְךָ[h] pref. לְ)(the foll. with suff. 2 pers. sing. m. — יטב

לְהֵיטִיב וּ'ו[i] pref. id.)(Hiph. inf. constr. d. 1 b; וּ bef. (:) — יטב

לְהֵיטִיבִי[k] pref. id.)(id. with suff. 1 pers. sing. . יטב

לַהֵיכָל pref. לַ for לְהַ)(noun com. sing. dec. 2 b — היכל

לְהֵיכְלָא Chald., pref. לְ)(id., emph. of הֵיכַל dec. 2 a — היכל

לְהֵיכְלֵהּ[l] Chald., pref. id.)(id., suff. 3 pers. sing. m. — היכל

לְהֵיכְלֵיכֶם[m] pref. id.)(id. pl., suff. 2 pers. pl. masc. . היכל

לְהֵימָן pref. id.)(pr. name masc. . . . אמן

לְהֵינִיק[n] pref. id.)(Hiph. inf. constr. . . ינק

לִהְיֹת defect. for לִהְיוֹת (q. v.) . . . היה

לְהַיָּתִי[o] pref. לְ)(noun f. s., suff. 1 pers. s., see הַוָּה — הוה

לְהַיְתָיָה Ch., pref. id.)(Aph. inf. (§ 56. r. 2, & § 55. r. 3) — אתה

לִהְיֹתְךָ[p] וְ pref. לְ bef. (:))(Kal inf. (הֱיוֹת), suff. 2 pers. sing. masc. (§ 13. rem. 13) . . היה

לְהַכְבִּיד[q] pref. לְ)(Hiph. inf. constr. . . . כבד

לְהַכּוֹת[r] וּ'ו pref. id.)(Hiph. inf. constr. (§ 25. No. 2 b) — נכה

לְהַכְחִיד[s] וּ pref. id.)(Hiph. inf. constr.; וּ bef. (:) — כחד

לְהָכִיל[t] pref. id.)(Hiph. inf. constr. (§ 19. rem. 8) [contr. for הַאֲכִיל] . . . אכל

לְהָכִיל pref. id.)(Hiph. inf. constr. — כול

לְהָכִין וּ"ו pref. id.)(Hiph. inf. constr. d. 3 a; וּ bef. (:) — כון

לַהֲכִינָהּ[z] pref. לַ bef. (-:))(id. with suff. 3 pers. s. f. — כון

לְהַכִּירֵנִי[y] pref. לְ)(Hiph. inf. [הַכִּיר], suff. 1 p. s. f. d. 1 b — נכר

לְהַכְעִים pref. id.)(Hiph. inf. constr. dec. 1 b . כעס

לְהַכְעִיסוֹ pref. id.)(id., suff. 3 pers. sing. masc. . כעס

לְהַכְעִיסֵנִי / לְהַכְעִסֵנִי } pref. id.)(id., suff. 1 pers. sing. . . כעס

לְהַכְרִית ו׳ וּ pref. id.)(Hiph. inf. constr. d. 1 b; וּ bef. (:) — כרת

לְהַכְרִיתוֹ[z] pref. id.)(id., suff. 3 pers. sing. masc. — כרת

לְהַכְשִׁיל[a] וּ pref. id.)(Hiph. inf. constr. d. 1 b; וּ bef. (:) — כשל

לְהַכְשִׁילוֹ[b] pref. id.)(id., suff. 3 pers. sing. masc. — כשל

לְהַכֹּתָהּ[c] pref. id.)(Hiph. inf. הַכּוֹת, suff. 3 pers. sing. fem. dec. 1 b (§ 25. No. 2 b) . . נכה

לְהַכֹּתוֹ pref. לְ)(id., suff. 3 pers. sing. masc. . נכה

לְהַכֹּתְךָ[d] pref. id.)(id., suff. 2 pers. sing. masc. . נכה

לְהַכֹּתָם pref. id.)(id., suff. 3 pers. pl. masc. . נכה

לְהַלְבִּישׁ[xx] pref. id.)(Hiph. inf. constr. . . לבש

לְהַלָּז[e] pref. id.)(pron. demon. com. gen. sing., ap. for הַלָּזֶה (q. v.) . . . זה

לְהַלֶּחֶם[f] וְ Kh. וּלְהַלֶּחֶם preff. הַ art., לְ, & וּ bef. (:), K. וְהַלֶּחֶם, pref. הַ)(noun com. sing. d. 6 a — לחם

לְהִלָּחֵם / לְהִלָּחֶם } וּ'ו[g] pref. לְ)(Niph. inf. constr. (§ 9. rem. 3); וּ bef. (:) . . . לחם

לְהוֹלִיכוֹ[h] pref. id.)(Hiph. inf. [הוֹלִיךְ], suff. 3 p. s. m. d. 1 b — ילך

לַהֲלֹךְ pref. לַ bef. (-:))(Kal inf. constr. . . הלך

לַהֹלֵךְ[i] pref. לַ for לְהַ)(Kal part. act. m. dec. 7 b — הלך

לְהֹלְכֵי[k] pref. לְ)(id. pl., constr. st. . . . הלך

לַהֹלְכִים pref. לַ for לְהַ)(id. pl., abs. st. . . הלך

לְהַלֵּל וּ'ו pref. לְ)(Piel inf. constr.; וּ bef. (:) — הלל

לְהַלְמוּת[l] pref. id.)(noun fem. sing. . . . הלם

לָהַם Root not used; Arab. *to swallow greedily*. Hithpa. part. מִתְלַהֲמִים *dainties*, which are greedily swallowed, Pr. 18. 8; 26. 22.

לָהֶם וְ'ו pref. prep. לְ with suff. 3 p. pl. m. (§ 5, parad.) — ל

לְהֹם Ch., pref. prep. לְ with suff. 3 p. pl. m. for לְהוֹן — ל

לָהֵמָּה[m] pref. לְ (see lett. לְ))(pron. pers. masc. pl. (הֵם) with parag. ה . . . . הם

לְהִמּוֹל pref. לְ)(Niph. inf. constr. . . מול

לַהֲמוֹן[n] pref. לַ bef. (-:))(n. m. s., constr. of הָמוֹן d. 3 a — המה

לְהַמִּזְבֵּחַ[o] preff. לְ & הַ)(noun masc. sing. dec. 7 c . זבח

לְהַמְטִיר[p] pref. לְ)(Hiph. inf. constr. . . . מטר

לְהָמִין[q] pref. id.)(Hiph. inf. constr. . . ימן

לְהָמִית ר׳ו pref. id.)(Hiph. inf. constr. d. 3 a; וּ bef. (:) — מות

לַהֲמִיתוֹ ו׳[s] pref. לַ bef. (-:))(id., suff. 3 pers. sing. m. — מות

לַהֲמִיתֵךָ[t] pref. id.)(id., suff. 2 pers. s. m. [for הֲמִיתְךָ] — מות

לַהֲמִיתָם[u] pref. id.)(id., suff. 3 pers. pl. masc. . מות

לַהֲמִיתֵנוּ pref. id.)(id., suff. 1 pers. pl. . . מות

לַהֲמִיתֵנִי pref. id.)(id., suff. 1 pers. sing. . . מות

לְהִמֹּל[x] defect. for לְהִמּוֹל (q. v.) . . . מול

לְהִמָּלֵט pref. לְ)(Niph. inf. constr. . . . מלט

לְהַמְלִיךְ pref. id.)(Hiph. inf. constr. dec. 1 b — מלך

לְהַמְלִיכוֹ pref. id.)(id., suff. 3 pers. sing. masc. — מלך

לְהֻמָּם pref. id.)(Kal inf. [הֹם], suff. 3 p. pl. m. d. 8 c — המם

לְהָמָן pref. id.)(pr. name masc. . . . המן

---

[a] Je. 32. 41. [b] Ps. 57. 5. [c] Ex. 23. 2. [d] Nu. 22. 23. [e] Ezr. 7. 15. [f] Est. 8. 13; 2 Ch. 29. 11. [g] Eze. 36. 3. [h] De. 8. 16. [i] Je. 4. 22. [k] Je. 32. 40. [l] Da. 6. 19. [m] Joel 4. 5. [n] 1 Ki. 3. 21. [o] Job 30. 13. [p] De. 26. 19. [q] 2 Ch. 25. 19. [r] Is. 58. 4. [s] 1 Ki. 13. 34. [t] Eze. 21. 33. 2 Ch. 2. 8. [x] Je. 33. 2. [y] Ru. 2. 10. [z] Je. 51. 62. [a] 2 Ch. 25. 8. [b] 2 Ch. 28. 23. [c] Nu. 22. 25. [d] Je. 40. 14. [e] Da. 8. 16. [f] 2 Sa. 16. 2. [g] 2 Ch. 32. 8. [h] 2 Ch. 36. 6. [i] Je. 22. 10. [k] Pr. 2. 7. [l] Ju. 5. 26. [m] Je. 14. 16. [n] Job 39. 7. [o] 2 Ch. 29. 27. [p] Job 38. 26. [q] 2 Sa. 14. 19. [r] 1 Ki. 17. 18. [s] 1 Sa. 19. 11. [t] 1 Sa. 19. 2. [u] 1 Sa. 2. 25. [x] Ge. 34. 15. [xx] Est. 4. 4.

לְהִמָּנוֹת[a] pref. לְ)(Niph. inf. constr. . . . מנה

לַהֲמִתָם[b] defect. for לַהֲמִיתָם (q. v.) . . . מות

לָהֵן Chald., i. q. Heb. לָכֵן.—I. *therefore*.—II. *nevertheless, but, except.*

לָהֵן pref. prep. ל with suff. 3 pers. pl. fem. . ל

לְהִנָּבֵא pref. לְ)(Niph. inf. constr. dec. 7 b . נבא

לָהֵנָּה ו׳[c] pref. לָ (see lett. ל))(pron. pers. fem. pl. הן

לְהַנְזָקַת[d] Chald., pref. לְ)(Aph. inf. constr. [of הַנְזָקָה § 47. rem. 4] . . . . נזק

לְהַנְחִיל pref. id.)(Hiph. inf. constr. . . נחל

לְהִנָּחֵם pref. id.)(Niph. inf. constr. . . נחם

לְהַנְחֹתָם[e] pref. id.)(Hiph. inf. [הַנְחוֹת], suff. 3 pers. pl. masc. dec. 1 b . . . . נחה

לְהָנִיד[f] pref. id.)(Hiph. inf. constr. . . נוד

לְהָנִיחַ[g] pref. id.)(Hiph. inf. constr. . . . נוח

לְהַנִּיחוֹ[h] pref. id.)(Hiph. inf. [הַנִּיחַ], suff. 3 pers. sing. masc. (§ 21. rem. 24) . . נוח

לְהַנִּיחָם[i] pref. id.)(id., suff. 3 pers. pl. masc. dec. 1 b נוח

לְהָנִים[k] pref. id.)(Hiph. inf. constr. . . . נום

לְהָנִיף pref. id.)(Hiph. inf. constr. dec. 3 a . נוף

לְהַנְסָקָה[l] Chald., pref. id.)(Aph. inf. constr. (§ 47. r. 4) נסק

לְהַנְעָלָה[m] Chald., pref. id.)(Aph. inf. [for הַעָלָה] dag. forte resolved in נ . . . . עלל

לַהֲנָפָה[n] pref. לַ bef. (-:))(Hiph. inf. (§ 21. rem. 15) נוף

לְהִנָּצֵל pref. לְ)(Niph. inf. constr. . . נצל

לְהִנָּקֵם pref. id.)(Niph. inf. constr. . . . נקם

לְהַנְתִּיךְ[o] pref. id.)(Hiph. inf. constr. . . נתך

לְהִנָּתֵן pref. id.)(Niph. inf. constr. . . . נתן

לְהָסֵב pref. id.)(Hiph. inf. constr. . . סבב

לְהַסְגִּיר[p] pref. id.)(Hiph. inf. constr. . . . סגר

לְהֹסִיף[q] pref. id.)(Hiph. inf. constr. (for הוֹסִיף § 20. rem. 11) . . . . יסף

לְהָסִיר ו׳[r] pref. id.)(Hiph. inf. constr. d. 3 a; ו bef. (:) סור

לַהֲסִירָהּ[s] pref. לַ bef. (-:))(id. with suff. 3 pers. sing. fem. סור

לְהָסֵךְ[t] pref. לְ)(Hiph. inf. constr. . . . סכך

לְהַסֵּךְ[u] ו pref. id.)(Hiph. inf. constr. [for הַסִּיךְ § 11. r. 2] נסך

לְהִסָּתֵם[x] pref. id.)(Niph. inf. constr. . . סתם

לְהִסָּתֵר[y] pref. id.)(Niph. inf. constr. (§ 9. rem. 3) . סתר

לְהַעֲבִיד[z] pref. id.)(Hiph. inf. constr. . . עבד

לְהַעֲבִיר pref. id.)(Hiph. inf. constr. dec. 1 b . . עבר

לְהַעֲבִרוֹ[a] pref. id.)(id., suff. 3 pers. sing. masc. . עבר

לְהֵעָזֵר[b] pref. id.)(Niph. inf. constr. . . . עזר

לְהַעָלָה[c] Chald., pref. לְ)(Aph. inf. constr. [dag. impl. for הַעָלָה, comp. § 42. No. 3 note, & הַעָלָא § 47. rem. 4 & 5] . . . עלל

לְהַעֲלוֹת pref. id.)(Hiph. inf. constr. dec. 1 b . . עלה

לְהַעֲלוֹתָם[d] pref. id.)(id., suff. 3 pers. pl. masc. . עלה

לְהַעֲלֹת pref. id.)(defect. for לְהַעֲלוֹת (q. v.) . עלה

לְהַעֲלֹתוֹ[e] ו pref. id.)(id. with suff. 3 pers. s. m.; ו bef. (:) עלה

לְהָעָם[f] pref. id.)(noun com. s. d. 8 a (but comp. § 45) עמם

לְהַעֲמִיד ו׳ pref. id.)(Hiph. inf. constr. d. 1 b; ו bef. (:) עמד

לְהַעֲמִידוֹ pref. id.)(id. with suff. 3 pers. sing. masc. עמד

לְהַעֲצִבָהּ[g] pref. id.)(Hiph. inf. [הַעֲצִיב], suff. 3 p. s. f. d. 1 b עצב

לְהֵעָשׂוֹת[h] pref. id.)(Niph. inf. constr. . . . עשה

לְהַעֲשִׁיר pref. id.)(Hiph. inf. constr. . . עשר

לְהַפִּיל ו׳[i] pref. id.)(Hiph. inf. constr.; ו bef. (:) . נפל

לְהָפִיץ[k] pref. id.)(Hiph. inf. constr. dec. 3 a . פוץ

לַהֲפִיצֵנִי[l] pref. לַ bef. (-:))(id. with suff. 1 pers. sing. פוץ

לְהָפִיר[m] pref. לְ)(Hiph. inf. constr. for הָפֵר . . פרר

לַהֲפֹךְ[n] וְ pref. לַ bef. (-:))(Kal inf. constr. . הפך

לְהֶפֶךְ[o] pref. לְ)(noun masc. sing. . . . הפך

לְהָפְכָהּ[p] ו pref. id.)(Kal inf., suff. 3 p. s. f.; ו bef. (:) הפך

לְהַפְלִיא pref. id.)(Hiph. inf. constr. . . פלא

לְהַפִּצֵּץ preff. לְ & הַ)(pr. name masc. . . פצץ

לְהִפָּקֵד[q] pref. לְ)(Niph. inf. constr. . . פקד

לְהָפֵר pref. id.)(Hiph. inf. constr. . . . פרר

לְהַפְרְכֶם[r] pref. id.)(id. with suff. 2 pers. pl. masc. [for הֲפֵרְכֶם comp. § 36. rem. 3] . פרר

לְהַפְשִׁיט[s] pref. id.)(Hiph. inf. constr. . . . פשט

לְהִפָּתֵחַ[t] pref. id.)(Niph. inf. constr. . . פתח

לְהַצְדִּיק ו pref. id.)(Hiph. inf. constr.; ו bef. (:) . צדק

לְהַצְהִיל[u] pref. id.)(Hiph. inf. constr. . . צהל

לְהַצִּיב[x] ו׳[y] pref. id.)(Hiph. inf. constr.; ו bef. (:) . נצב

לְהַצִּיל ו׳[z] pref. id.)(Hiph. inf. constr. dec. 1 b; ו id. נצל

לְהַצִּילוֹ[a] pref. id.)(id., suff. 3 pers. sing. masc. . נצל

לְהַצִּילֶךָ[b] ו׳[c] } pref. id.)(id., suff. 2 pers. sing. masc.; ו bef. (:) . . . . } נצל
לְהַצִּילְךָ

לְהַצִּילָם pref. id.)(id., suff. 3 pers. pl. masc. . נצל

לְהַצִּילֵנִי pref. id.)(id., suff. 1 pers. sing. . . נצל

לְהַצָּלָה[d] Ch., pref. id.)(Aph. inf. constr. (§ 47. r. 4 & 5) נצל

לְהַצָּלוּתֵהּ[e] Ch., pref. id.)(id. inf. [הַצָּלוּת], suff. 3 pers. sing. masc. . . . . . . נצל

לְהַצִּלְךָ[f] defect. for לְהַצִּילְךָ (q. v.) . . . נצל

לְהַצְמִיחַ[g] ו pref. לְ)(Hiph. inf. constr.; ו bef. (:) צמח

---

[a] Ec. 1. 15. [b] De. 9. 28. [c] Zec. 5. 9. [d] Ezr. 4. 22. [e] Ne. 9. 19. [f] 2 Ki. 21. 8.
[g] Eze. 44. 30. [h] Nu. 32. 15. [i] Est. 3. 8. [k] Ju. 6. 11. [l] Da. 6. 24. [m] Da. 4. 3.
[n] Is. 30. 28. [o] Eze. 22. 20. [p] Am. 1. 6. [q] 2 Ch. 28. 13. [r] Est. 4. 4. [s] Je. 32. 31.
[t] 1 Sa. 24. 4. [u] Je. 44. 19, 25. [x] Ne. 4. 1. [y] Job 34. 22. [z] 2 Ch. 2. 17. [a] 1 Sa. 20. 36.
[b] 2 Ch. 26. 15. [c] Da. 5. 7. [d] Ju. 20. 38. [e] Ex. 3. 8. [f] 2 Ch. 10. 7. [g] Je. 44. 19.
[h] Est. 9. 1, 14. [i] Ps. 106. 27. [k] Eze. 20. 23. [l] Hab. 3. 14. [m] Zec. 11. 10. [n] 1 Ch. 19. 3.
[o] Eze. 16. 34. [p] 2 Sa. 10. 3. [q] Ju. 21. 3. [r] Le. 26. 15. [s] 2 Ch. 29. 34. [t] Is. 51. 14.
[u] Ps. 104. 15. [x] 1 Ch. 18. 3. [y] 1 Sa. 13. 21. [z] Je. 42. 11. [a] Ex. 3. 8. [b] Je. 1. 19
[c] Je. 15. 20. [d] Da. 3. 29. [e] Da. 6. 15. [f] Je. 1. 8. [g] Job 38. 27.

לְהִקָּבֵץ[a]	pref. לְ) (Niph. inf. constr. . .	קבץ
לְהַקְדִּישׁ	pref. id.) (Hiph. inf. constr. dec. 1 b .	קדשׁ
לְהַקְדִּישׁוֹ[b]	pref. id.) (id., suff. 3 pers. sing. masc. .	קדשׁ
לְהַקְדִּישֵׁנִי	pref. id.) (id., suff. 1 pers. sing. . .	קדשׁ
לְהִקָּהֵל[c]	pref. id.) (Niph. inf. constr. . .	קהל
לְהַקּוֹץ	preff. לְ & הַ) (pr. name masc. . .	קוץ
לְהַקְטִין[d]	pref. לְ) (Hiph. inf. constr. . .	קטן
לְהַקְטִיר	pref. id.) (Hiph. inf. constr. . . .	קטר
לְהָקִים	ו׳[e] pref. id.) (Hiph. inf. constr. d. 3 a; וּ bef. (:)	קום
לַהֲקִימוֹ	pref. לַ bef. (-:)) (id., suff. 3 pers. sing. masc.	סום
לְהָקֵל[f]	pref. לְ) (Hiph. inf. constr. . . .	קלל
לַהֲקָמוּתֵהּ[g]	Chald., pref. לַ bef. (-:)) (Aph. inf. [הֲקָמוּת], suff. 3 pers. sing. fem. (§ 47. rem. 4) .	קום
וּלְהַקַּרְדֻּמִּים[h]	preff. לְ & הַ) (noun masc., pl. of [קַרְדֹּם] dec. 8 c; וּ bef. (:)	קרדם
לְהַקְרִיב	pref. לְ) (Hiph. inf. constr. . . .	קרב
לְהַקְשִׁיב	pref. id.) (Hiph. inf. constr. . .	קשׁב
לַהֲקַת[i]	noun fem. sing. constr. [of לַהֲקָה by transp. for קְהָלָה] *assembly, company* . .	קהל
לְהַר	pref. לְ) (noun masc. sing. dec. 8 (§ 37. r. 7)	הרר
לְהֵרָאֹה	pref. id.) (Niph. inf. abs. (used as a constr.)	ראה
לְהַרְאוֹת	pref. id.) (Hiph. inf. constr. dec. 1 b .	ראה
לְהֵרָאוֹת	pref. id.) (Niph. inf. constr. . . .	ראה
לְהַרְבֵּה	pref. id.) (Hiph. inf. used adverbially (§ 24. r. 15)	רבה
לְהַרְבּוֹת	ו׳[k] pref. id.) (id. inf. constr.; וּ bef. (:) .	רבה
לַהֶרֶג[l]	pref. לַ for לְהַ) (noun masc. sing. . .	הרג
לַהֲרֹג	pref. לַ bef. (-:)) (Kal inf. constr. . .	הרג
לְהָרְגוֹ[m]	pref. לְ) (id. with suff. 3 pers. sing. masc.	הרג
לְהַרְגִּיעוֹ[n]	pref. id.) (Hiph. inf. [הַרְגִּיעַ], suff. 3 p. s. m. d. 1 b	רגע
לְהָרְגֶךָ / לַהֲרָגְךָ[o]	pref. id.) (Kal inf., suff. 2 pers. sing. masc. (§ 16. rem. 7) . .	הרג
לְהָרְגֵנוּ[p]	pref. לְ) (id. with suff. 1 pers. pl. . .	הרג
לַהֲרוֹג[q]	in full for לַהֲרֹג (q. v. § 8. rem. 18) . .	הרג
לַהֲרוֹס[r]	וְ in full for לַהֲרֹס (q. v. § 8. rem. 18) .	הרס
לְהָרִיחַ[s]	pref. לְ) (Hiph. inf. constr. . . .	רוח
לֶהָרִים	pref. לֶ for לְהֶ, bef. הָ for לְהַ) (noun masc. pl. of הַר dec. 8 d (§ 37. rem. 7) .	הרר
לְהָרִים	pref. לְ) (Hiph. inf. constr. . . .	רום
לְהָרִיעַ[t]	pref. id.) (Hiph. inf. constr. . .	רוע
לְהָרִיק[u]	pref. id.) (Hiph. inf. constr. . . .	רוק
לַהֲרֹס[x]	וְ pref. לַ bef. (-:)) (Kal inf. constr. .	הרס

לְהָרַע / לְהָרֵעַ ו׳[y]	pref. לְ) (Hiph. inf. constr. (comp. § 15. rem. 1); וּ bef. (:) .	רעע
לְהָרָפָא	preff. לְ, & הָ for הַ·) (pr. name masc. .	רפא
לְהֵרָפֵא[z]	pref. לְ) (Niph. inf. constr. . . .	רפא
לְהָרָפָה	preff. לְ, & הָ for הַ·) (pr. name masc. .	רפה
לְהֵרָפֵה[a]	pref. לְ) (Niph. inf. constr. for הֵרָפֵא (§ 23. r. 10)	רפא
לְהַרְרִי[b]	pref. id.) (n. m. s., suff. 1 p. s. fr. [הָרָר] d. 6 a	הרר
לְהַרְשִׁיעַ	pref. id.) (Hiph. inf. constr. . . .	רשׁע
לְהַשְׁאוֹת[c]	pref. id.) (Hiph. inf. constr. . .	שׁאה
לְהַשְׁאִיר[d]	pref. id.) (Hiph. inf. constr. . . .	שׁאר
לְהַשְׂבִּיעַ[e]	pref. id.) (Hiph. inf. constr. . .	שׂבע
לְהַשְׁבִּיעַ[f]	pref. id.) (Hiph. inf. constr. . . .	שׁבע
לְהַשְׁבִּית[g]	pref. id.) (Hiph. inf. constr. . .	שׁבת
לְהִשָּׁבֵעַ[h]	pref. id.) (Niph. inf. constr. (§ 15. rem. 1)	שׁבע
לְהִשָּׁבֵר[i]	pref. id.) (Niph. inf. constr. . . .	שׁבר
לַהְשׁוֹת[k]	contr. and defect. for לְהַשְׁאוֹת (q. v.) .	שׁאה
לְהַשְׁחִית	ו׳[l] pref. לְ) (Hiph. inf. constr. d. 1 b; וּ bef. (:)	שׁחת
לְהַשְׁחִיתָהּ	pref. id.) (id., suff. 3 pers. sing. fem. .	שׁחת
לְהַשְׁחִיתֶךָ[m]	pref. id.) (id., suff. 2 p. s. m. [for הַשְׁחִיתְךָ]	שׁחת
לְהַשְׁחִתוֹ[n]	pref. id.) (id., suff. 3 pers. sing. masc. .	שׁחת
לְהָשִׁיב	ו׳[o] pref. id.) (Hiph. inf. constr. d. 3 a; וּ bef. (:)	שׁוב
לְהֹשִׁיב[p]	defect. for לְהוֹשִׁיב (q. v.) . . .	ישׁב
לַהֲשִׁיבָהּ	pref. לַ bef. (-:)) (Hiph. inf. (הָשִׁיב), suff. 3 pers. sing. fem. dec. 3 a . . .	שׁוב
לַהֲשִׁיבוֹ[q]	pref. id.) (id., suff. Kh. בוֹ׳ 3 p. s. m., K. בָהּ׳ f.	שׁוב
לַהֲשִׁיבוֹ	pref. id.) (id., suff. 3 pers. sing. masc. .	שׁוב
לַהֲשִׁיבָם	pref. id.) (id., suff. 3 pers. pl. masc. .	שׁוב
לְהַשְׁכָּחָה[r]	Chald., pref. לְ) (Aph. inf. constr. (§ 47. r. 4)	שׁכח
לְהַשְׁכִּיחַ[s]	pref. id.) (Hiph. inf. constr. . . .	שׁכח
לְהַשְׂכִּיל	ו׳ pref. id.) (Hiph. inf. constr. d. 1 b; וּ bef. (:)	שׂכל
לְהַשְׂכִּילְךָ[t]	pref. id.) (id., suff. 2 pers. sing. masc. .	שׂכל
לְהַשְׂכִּילָם[u]	pref. id.) (id., suff. 3 pers. pl. masc. . .	שׂכל
לְהַשְׁלִיחַ[x]	pref. id.) (Hiph. inf. constr. . .	שׁלח
לְהַשְׁלִיךְ[y]	pref. id.) (Hiph. inf. constr. . . .	שׁלך
לְהַשְׁמָדָה[z]	Chald., pref. id.) (Aph. inf. constr. (§ 47. r. 4)	שׁמד
לְהִשָּׁמְדָם[a]	pref. id.) (Niph. inf. (הִשָּׁמֵד), suff. 3 pers. pl. masc. dec. 7 b	שׁמד
לְהַשְׁמִיד	ו׳ pref. id.) (Hiph. inf. constr. d. 1 b; וּ bef. (:)	שׁמד
לְהַשְׁמִידוֹ[b]	pref. id.) (id., suff. 3 pers. sing. masc. .	שׁמד
לְהַשְׁמִידָם	pref. id.) (id., suff. 3 pers. pl. masc. .	שׁמד
לְהַשְׁמִידֵנוּ[c]	pref. id.) (id., suff. 1 pers. pl. . .	שׁמד

a Ezr. 10. 7. b 1 Ch. 23. 13. c Est. 8. 11. d Am. 8. 5. e 2 Sa. 3. 10. f Jon. 1. 5.; Is. 23. 9.
g Da. 6. 4. h 1 Sa. 13. 21. i 1 Sa. 19. 20. k De. 28. 63. l Pr. 24. 11. m Ex. 21. 14.
n Je. 31. 2. o 1 Sa. 24. 11. p Ex. 5. 21. q Ec. 3. 3. r Je. 1. 10. s Ex. 30. 38.
t 2 Ch. 13. 12. u Is. 32. 6. x Je. 31. 28. y Je. 31. 28. z De. 28. 27, 35. a Je. 19. 11.
b Ps. 30. 8. c Is. 37. 26. d Ezr. 9. 8. e 1 Sa. 20. 17. f Job 38. 27.
g Ps. 8. 3. h Je. 12. 16. i Jon. 1. 4. k 2 Ki. 19. 25. l Je. 15. 3.
m 2 Ch. 25. 16. n 2 Ki. 18. 25. o Ge. 42. 25. p Ne. 13. 27. q Ju. 19. 3.
r Da. 6. 5. s Je. 23. 27. t Da. 9. 22. u Ne. 9. 20. x 2 Ki. 15. 37.
y Ec. 3. 5, 6. z Da. 7. 26. a Ps. 92. 8. b De. 9. 20. c De. 1. 27.

לְהַשְׂמִיל[a]	וּ pref. לְ) Hiph. inf. constr.; וּ bef. (:)	שׂמאל
לְהַשְׁמִיעַ	pref. id.) Hiph. inf. constr. . . .	שׁמע
לְהַשְׁמָעוּת[b]	pref. id.) noun fem. sing. (formed from Hiph.)	שׁמע
לְהַשְׁנָיָא[c] / לְהַשְׁנָיָה	Chald., pref. id.) Aph. inf. constr. (§ 47. rem. 4 & 5) . . .	שׁנה
לְהִשָּׁעֵן[d]	pref. id.) Niph. inf. constr. . . .	שׁען
לְהַשְׁפָּלָה[e]	Ch., pref. id.) Aph. inf. constr. (§47. r.4&5)	שׁפל
לְהַשְׁקוֹת	pref. id.) Hiph. inf. constr. . . .	שׁקה
לְהַשְׁקִיט[f]	pref. id.) Hiph. inf. constr. . . .	שׁקט
לְהַשְׁקֹתוֹ[g]	pref. id.) Hiph. inf. (הַשְׁקוֹת), suff. 3 pers. sing. masc. dec. 1 b . . .	שׁקה
לְהִשְׁתַּבֵּחַ	pref. id.) Hithpa. inf. constr. [for הִתְשַׁבֵּחַ § 12. rem. 3]	שׁבח
לְהִשְׁתַּגֵּעַ[h]	pref. id.) Hithpa. inf. constr. [for הִתְשַׁגֵּעַ § 12. rem. 3]	שׁגע
לְהִשְׁתַּחֲוֺת	ל' pref. id.) Hithpalel inf. c. [for הִתְשַׁחֲוֺת comp. § 12. r. 3, § 6. No. 2, & § 24. r. 25]	שׁחה
לְהִתְאַפֵּק[i]	pref. id.) Hithpa. inf. constr. .	אפק
לַהֲתָבוּתָךְ[k]	Ch., pref. לַ bef. (-:)) Aph. inf. [הֲתָבוּת], suff. 2 pers. sing. masc. (§ 47. rem. 4)	תוב
לְהִתְגֹּלֵל[l]	pref. לְ) Hithpoel inf. constr. . . .	גלל
לְהִתְגָּרֵד[m]	pref. id.) Hithpa. inf. constr. . . .	גרד
לְהִתְהַלֵּךְ	pref. id.) Hithpa. inf. constr. . . .	הלך
לְהִתְהַלֵּל[n]	pref. id.) Hithpa. inf. constr. . . .	הלל
לְהִתְחַזֵּק	pref. id.) Hithpa. inf. constr. . . .	חזק
לְהִתְחַלּוֹת[o]	pref. id.) Hithpa. inf. constr. . . .	חלה
לְהִתְחַנֶּן־[p]	pref. id.) Hithpa. inf. constr. (for חַנֵּן' § 12. rem. 4)	חנן
לְהִתְחַתֵּן	ל' וּ[q] pref. id.) Hithpa. inf. constr.; וּ bef. (:)	חתן
לְהִתְיַחֵשׂ	ל' וּ[r] pref. id.) Hithpa. inf. constr. (§ 14. rem. 1); וּ id.	יחשׂ
לְהִתְיַצֵּב	pref. id.) Hithpa. inf. constr. . . .	יצב
לַהֲתָךְ	pref. לַ bef. (-:)) pr. name masc. .	התך
לְהִתְמַהְמֵהַּ[s]	pref. לְ) Hithpalp. inf. constr. (§ 6. r. 4)	מהה
לְהִתְנַדֵּב[t] / לְהִתְנַדֶּב־[u]	pref. id.) Hithpa. inf. constr. (§ 12. rem. 4)	נדב
לְהִתְנוֹסֵס[v]	pref. id.) Hithpal. inf. fr. נוּס, or Hithpoel fr.	נסס
לְהִתְנַחֵם[y]	pref. id.) Hithpa. inf. constr. (§ 14. rem. 1)	נחם
לְהִתְנַכֵּל[z]	pref. id.) Hithpa. inf. constr. . . .	נכל
לְהִתְנַפֵּל[a]	וּ pref. id.) Hithpa. inf. constr.; וּ bef. (:)	נפל
לְהִתְעוֹלֵל[b]	pref. id.) Hithpoel inf. constr. . . .	עלל
לְהִתְעַלֵּם[c]	pref. id.) Hithpa. inf. constr. . . .	עלם
לְהִתְעַנּוֹת[d]	ל' וּ[e] pref. לְ) Hithpa. inf. constr.; וּ bef. (:)	ענה
לְהִתְפָּאֵר	pref. id.) Hithpa. inf. constr. . . .	פאר
לְהִתְפַּלֵּל	pref. id.) Hithpa. inf. constr. . . .	פלל
לְהִתָּפֵשׂ[f]	pref. id.) Niph. inf. constr. . . .	תפשׂ
לְהִתְקַדֵּשׁ[g]	pref. id.) Hithpa. inf. constr. . . .	קדשׁ
לְהִתְקְטָלָה[h]	Ch., pref. id.) Ithpeel inf. constr. (§47. r.4)	קטל
לְהִתְרוֹעֵעַ[i]	pref. id.) Hithpoel inf. constr. . . .	רעע
לְהִתְרַפֵּא	pref. id.) Hithpa. inf. constr. . . .	רפא

לוּ ,לֻא ,לוּא & ל' I. conj. *if.*—II. interj. *O if! O that! would that!*

לוּלֵא ,לוּלֵי (from לוּ *if* and לֵא ,לֵי, i. q. לֹא *not*) *if not, unless.*

לוֹ	ל' pref. prep. לְ with suff. 3 p.s. m. (§ 5, parad.)	ל
לוֹא	ל' more usually לֹא adv.	לא
לוּא	interj. & conj.	לו
לוּבִים	ל' gent. n. *Libyans*, inhabitants of the desert, west of Egypt; written לֻבִים Da. 11. 43, and לְהָבִים Ge. 10. 13	לוב
לוּד	ל pr. name—I. of a people descended from Shem, Ge. 10. 22, according to Josephus the Lydian in Asia Minor.—II. of a people in Africa; pl. לוּדִים.	
לוּדִיִּים / לוּדִים	ל' gent. n., pl. of לוּד; Kh. לוּדִיִּים, pl. of לוּדִי	לוד

[לָוָה] fut. יִלְוֶה.—I. *to be joined to, adhere to*, Ec. 8. 15.—II. *to borrow*; part. לֹוֶה *borrowing; borrower.* Niph. *to join oneself to* any one, const. with עַל ,עִם ,אֶל. Hiph. *to lend*, with acc. of the person, with double acc. of the person and thing, part. מַלְוֶה *lender.*

לֵוִי (*adhesion*, comp. Ge. 29. 34).—I. pr. name *Levi*, son of Jacob by Leah.—II. patronym. (for בְּנֵי לֵוִי), *Levite*, pl. לְוִיִּם, (& בְּנֵי לֵוִי) *Levites.*

לֵוִי Ch.m. dec. 7, *Levite.*

לִוְיָה fem. *garland, crown*, only constr. לִוְיַת Pr. 1. 9; 4. 9.

לֹיָה fem. (from masc. לוֹי after the form (נוֹי only pl. לֹיוֹת *wreaths, festoons*, in architecture, 1 Ki. 7. 29, 30, 36.

לִוְיָתָן masc.—I. *sea-monster*, generally.—II. *large serpent.*—III. *crocodile*, Job 40. 25, sq.

לְוָת Ch., prep. *by, with*, Ezr. 4. 12.

לֹוֶה	Kal part. act. sing. masc.	לוה

[a] 2 Sa. 14. 19. [b] Eze. 24. 26. [c] Ezr. 6. 12. [d] Is. 10. 20. [e] Da. 4. 34. [f] Ps. 94. 13. [g] Ge. 24. 19. [h] 1 Sa. 21. 16. [i] Ge. 45. 1. [k] Da. 3. 16. [l] Ge. 43. 18. [m] Job 2. 8. [n] Ps. 106. 5. [o] 2 Sa. 13. 2. [p] Est. 4. 8. [q] Ezr. 9. 14. [r] 2 Ch. 31. 18. [s] Ex. 12. 39. [t] 1 Ch. 29. 14. [u] 1 Ch. 29. 17. [v] Ps. 60. 6. [y] Ge. 37. 35. [z] Ps. 105. 25. [a] Ge. 43. 18. [b] Ps. 141. 4. [c] De. 22. 3. [d] Ezr. 8. 21. [e] Da. 10. 12. [f] Eze. 21. 28. [g] 2 Ch. 29. 34. [h] Da. 2. 13. [i] Pr. 18. 24.

[לוּז] *to turn aside, to decline, depart,* Pr. 3. 21. Niph. part. נָלוֹז *perverse;* also neut. *what is perverse,* Is. 30. 12. Hiph. i. q. Kal, Pr. 4. 21. Hence

לוּז 'ן masc.—I. *almond-tree,* Ge. 30. 37.—II. pr. name of a city, afterwards called בֵּית־אֵל, in the tribe of Benjamin.—III. pr. name of another city, Ju. 1. 26 . . . . לוז

לוּזָה pr. name (לוּז) with parag. ה . לוז

לוּחַ masc. dec. 1a (pl. לוּחוֹת, לֻחֹת).—I. *tablet* of stone or wood; trop. *tablet* of the heart, Pr. 3. 3; Je. 17. 1.—II. *leaf* or *valve* of a folding-door, Ca. 8. 9.—III. du. לֻחֹתַיִם Eze. 27. 5, *the boarding* or *deck* of a ship.

לוּחִית (*tabulata,* i. e. built of boards) pr. name of a city in Moab.

לוּחֹת noun m. with pl. fem. term. for לוּחַ dec. 1a לוח

[לוּט] *to wrap up, to cover, conceal;* part. בַּלָּאט, בַּלָּט (§ 21. rem. 1) *secretly;* pl. לָטִים *secret arts.* Hiph. *to wrap up, cover,* 1 Ki. 19. 13.

לֹט, לוֹט masc.—I. *veil, covering,* Is. 25. 7.—II. Ge. 37. 25; 43. 11, *ladanum,* a fragrant resinous gum. Vulg. *stacte,* the purest kind of myrrh, distilling from the trees of its own accord. Syr. *pistacia.*—III. pr. name *Lot,* nephew of Abraham.

לוֹטָן (*covering*) pr. name masc. Ge. 36. 20, 29.

לוֹט 'ן pr. name masc. . . . . . לוט

[a]לוּטָה Kal part. pass. sing. fem. [from לוּט masc.] לוט

לוֹטָן pr. name masc. . . . . . . לוט

לֵוִי 'ן pr. name masc., also patronym. [for לֵוִיִּי] לוה

לֵוָיֵא ן Chald., gent. n. pl. emph. from לֵוִי d. 7 (§ 63) לוה

[b]לָוִינוּ Kal pret. 1 pers. sing. . . . . לוה

לְוִיֵּנוּ gent. n. (לֵוִי) with suff. 1 pers. pl. dec. 8f . לוה

לִוְיַת noun fem. sing. [constr. of לִוְיָה] . לוה

לִוְיָתָן noun masc. sing. . . . . . לוה

לוּל Root not used; prob. *to wind, turn, move round,* cogn. גָּלַל.

לוּל masc. pl. לוּלִים *winding-stairs,* 1 Ki. 6. 8.

לֻלָי, only pl. לֻלָאוֹת, constr. לֻלְאֹת (§ 35. rem. 15 note) *loops* or *eyes* for hooks.

לוּלֵא conj. compounded of לוּ & לֹא . . . לו

לוּלֵי conj. compounded of לוּ & לִי . . . . לו

I. [לוּן & לִין] inf. (gerund.) לִין, לָלוּן; imp. לִין; fut. יָלִין, ap. וַיָּלֶן.—I. *to lodge, remain,* or *pass the night.*—II. *to abide, remain.* Hiph. *to let remain,* Je. 4. 14. Hithpal. *to lodge, remain.*

II. לוּן. Niph. fut. יִלּוֹן (§ 21. rem. 24) *to complain, murmur,* const. with עַל *against* any one. Hiph. הֵלִין, הִלִּין id.

יָלוֹן (*abiding*) pr. name masc. 1 Ch. 4. 17.

מָלוֹן masc. dec. 3a, *lodging-place, an inn.*

מְלוּנָה fem. *lodge, hovel, hut,* Is. 1. 8; 24. 20.

תְּלוּנָה fem. dec. 10, *a murmuring, complaining.*

[לוּעַ] *to swallow,* Ob. ver. 16.

לֹעַ masc. dec. 1a, *throat,* Pr. 23. 2.

[לוּץ] I. Arab. *to turn, twist;* also, *to speak in obscure sentences,* comp. Hiph.—II. Heb. *to mock, deride, scorn;* part. לֵץ (§ 21. rem. 2) *scorner, scoffer.* Hiph.—I. *to interpret;* only part. מֵלִיץ *interpreter;* also, *intercessor.*—II. *to mock, deride.* Pil. part. *scorners, scoffers,* Ho. 7. 5. Hithpal. *to show oneself a mocker,* Is. 28. 22.

לָצוֹן masc. *derision, scorn.*

מְלִיצָה fem.—I. *obscure saying, enigma,* Pr. 1. 6. —II. *satire,* Hab. 2. 6.

[לוּשׁ] *to knead.* Arab. *to be strong;* hence

לַיִשׁ masc.—I. *lion.*—II. pr. name of a man, 1 Sa. 25. 44; Kh. לוּשׁ, 2 Sa. 3. 15.—III. pr. name of a place in the north of Palestine.

לַיִשׁ Kh. לוּשׁ, K. לַיִשׁ (q. v.) pr. name masc. . לוש

[c]לוּשִׁי Kal imp. sing. fem. . . . . לוש

[d]לְוָתָךְ Chald., *prep.* [לְוָת] with suff. 2 pers. sing. m. לוה

לָזֹאת / לְזֹאת } pref. לָ or לְ q. v. { pron. demon. fem. sing., see . } זה

[e]לַזְּבוּב pref. לַ for לְהַ) noun masc. sing. dec. 1a . זבב

[f]לִזְבּוֹחַ pref. לְ bef. (:)) Kal inf. constr. (§ 8. r. 18) זבח

לִזְבוּלֻן 'ו pref. id.) pr. name of a tribe . . זבל

[g]לַזֹּבֵחַ ן pref. לַ for לְהַ) Kal part. act. sing. m. d. 7b זבח

לַזָּבַח pref. id. } in pause, Seg. n. as if fr. זָבַח (§ 35.
[h]לִזְבַח 'ו pref. לְ } r. 2) but see זֶבַח'; ו bef. (:) } זבח

[i]לְזַבֵּחַ pref. id.) Piel inf. constr. (§ 15. rem. 1) . זבח

לְזֶבַח 'ו pref. id.) n. m. s. (suff. זִבְחִי) d. 6a; ו bef. (:) זבח

[k]לִזְבֹּחַ 'ו pref. id.) Kal inf. constr. . . זבח

[a] 1 Sa. 21. 10. [b] Ne. 5. 4. [c] Ge. 18. 6. [d] Ezr. 4. 12. [e] Is. 7. 18. [f] 2 Ch. 11. 16. [g] Ec. 9. 2. [h] Jos. 22. 26, 29. [i] 1 Ki. 12. 32. [k] 1 Sa. 1. 3.

Word	Analysis	Root
לְזִבְחֵי[a]	pref. לְ)(noun masc. pl. constr. from זֶבַח dec. 6a (§ 35. rem. 5)	זבח
לָזָה	Root not used; prob. i. q. לוּז q. v. — לָזוּת fem. *perverseness*, Pr. 4. 24.	
לָזֶה	pref. לָ (see lett. ל))(pron. demon. masc. s.	זה
לַזָּהָב	pref. לַ f. לְהַ } noun masc. sing. dec. 4a;	זהב
לְזָהָב	וּ pref. לְ q. v. } וּ bef. (:)	זהב
לִזְהָבִי[b]	וְ pref. לְ bef. (:))(id. with suff. 1 pers. sing.	זהב
לְזוֹנָה	pref. לְ)(Kal part. act. s. f. d. 10, fr. זוֹנֶה m.	זנה
לְזַוְעָה	pref. id.)(Kh. זַוְעָה, K. by transp. זַעֲוָה n. f. s.	זוע
לְזוּת[c]	וּ noun fem. sing.; וּ bef. (:)	לזה
לַזַּיִת[d]	pref. לַ for לְהַ)(noun masc. sing. dec. 6h	זית
לְזֵיתֶךָ[e]	pref. לְ)(id., suff. 2 pers. sing. m. [for זֵיתְךָ]	זית
לַזָּכָר	pref. לַ for לְהַ)(noun masc. sing. dec. 4a	זכר
לְזֵכֶר	pref. לְ)(noun masc. sing. dec. 6b	זכר
לִזְכֹּר	pref. לְ bef. (:))(Kal inf. constr.	זכר
לְזִכָּרוֹן[f]	ו׳ pref. לְ)(noun masc. s. d. 3c; וּ bef. (:)	זכר
לְזֹכְרֵי[g]	וּ pref. id.)(Kal part. act. pl. c. masc. from [זֹכֵר] dec. 7b; וּ id.	זכר
לִזְכַרְיָה	וְ pref. לְ bef. (:))(pr. name masc.	זכר
לִזְכָרִים	pref. id.)(noun masc., pl. of זָכָר dec. 4a	זכר
לְזִכְּרֹן[h]	defect. for לְזִכָּרוֹן (q. v.)	זכר
לְזִכְרְךָ[i]	וּ pref. לְ)(noun masc. sing., suff. 2 pers. sing. masc. from זֵכֶר dec. 6b; וּ bef. (:)	זכר
לְזַמֵּר[k]	וּ pref. id.)(Piel inf. constr.; וּ id.	זמר
לְזָנָב[l]	pref. id.)(noun masc. sing. d. 4a (§ 33. r. 1)	זנב
לִזְנוּנִים[m]	pref. לְ bef. (:))(noun m. pl. [of זְנוּן] d. 1a	זנה
לִזְנוֹת / לִזְנֹת[n]	pref. id.)(Kal inf. constr.	זנה
לְזַעֲוָה	pref. לְ)(noun fem. sing., by transp. for זַוְעָה	זוע
לִזְעֹק[o]	וְ pref. לְ bef. (:))(Kal inf. constr.	זעק
לְזַעֲקָתִי[p]	pref. לְ)(noun fem. sing., suff. 1 pers. sing. from זְעָקָה dec. 11c (§ 42. rem. 1)	זעק
לְזֶפֶת[q]	pref. id.)(noun fem. sing.	זפת
לְזָקֵן[r]	pref. id.)(adj. or subst. masc. sing. dec. 5a	זקן
לְזִקְנֵי[s]	ו׳ וּ pref. id.)(id. pl. constr.; וּ bef. (:)	זקן
לִזְקֵנָיו[t]	pref. לְ bef. (:))(id. pl., suff. 3 pers. sing. m.	זקן
לִזְקֻנָיו[u]	pref. id.)(n. m. pl., suff. 3 p. s. m. fr. [זָקוּן] d. 1a	זקן
לַזְּקֵנִים[x]	pref. לַ f. לְהַ)(adj. or subst. m., pl. of זָקֵן d. 5a	זקן
לַזָּר[y] / לְזָר[z]	pref. id. / pref. לְ } Kal part. act. sing. masc. dec. 1a	זור
לְזָרָא[a]	pref. לְ)(noun fem. sing. [for זָרָה]	זור
לְזֵרוֹ	pref. id.)(n. m. s., suff. 3 p. s. m. fr. זֵר d. 1a	זרר
לִזְרוֹת[b]	pref. לְ bef. (:))(Kal inf. constr.	זרה
לְזָרוֹת[c]	וּ pref. לְ)(Piel inf. constr. dec. 1; וּ bef. (:)	זרה
לְזָרוֹתָהּ[d]	pref. id.)(id., suff. 3 pers. sing. fem.	זרה
לְזָרוֹתָם[e]	וּ pref. id.)(id., suff. 3 p. pl. m.; וּ bef. (:)	זרה
לְזֶרַח	pref. id.)(pr. name masc.	זרח
לַזַּרְחִי	pref. לַ for לְהַ)(patronym. of the preced.	זרח
לַזָּרִים[f] / לְזָרִים	pref. id. / pref. לְ } Kal part. act. masc., pl. of זָר dec. 1a	זור
לַזֹּרֵעַ[g]	pref. לַ for לְהַ)(Kal part. act. sing. m. d. 7b	זרע
לְזֶרַע[h] / לְזָרַע	pref. לְ)(noun masc. sing. dec. 6a (§ 35. rem. 5 & 7)	זרע
לִזְרֹעַ[i]	pref. לְ bef. (:))(Kal inf. constr.	זרע
לְזַרְעוֹ	ו׳ וּ pref. לְ)(noun masc. sing., suff. 3 pers. s. m. from זֶרַע d. 6 (§ 35. r. 5); וּ bef. (:)	זרע
לִזְרֹעוֹ[k]	pref. לְ bef. (:))(noun com. sing., suff. 3 pers. sing. masc. from זְרוֹעַ dec. 1a	זרע
לְזַרְעֲךָ / לְזַרְעֶךָ[l]	ו׳ / וּ } pref. לְ)(noun m. s., suff. 2 pers. s. m. from זֶרַע dec. 6 (§ 35. r. 5); וּ bef. (:)	זרע
לְזַרְעֲכֶם[m]	pref. id.)(id., suff. 2 pers. pl. masc.	זרע
לְזַרְעָם	וּ pref. id.)(id., suff. 3 p. pl. m.; וּ bef. (:)	זרע
לִזְרֹק[n]	וְ pref. לְ bef. (:))(Kal inf. constr.	זרק
לְזֶרֶשׁ	pref. לְ)(pr. name fem.	זרשׁ
לַח[o] / לַח	adj. masc. sing., pl. לַחִים (§ 37. rem. 7)	לחח
לְחֹבָב	pref. לְ)(pr. name masc.	חבב
לַחֲבוֹק[p]	pref. לַ bef. (-:))(Kal inf. constr. (§ 8. r. 18)	חבק
לְחַבֵּל	pref. לְ)(Piel inf. constr.	חבל
לְחַבָּלָה[q]	Chald., pref. id.)(Pael inf. constr. (§ 47. r. 5)	חבל
לַחֲבָלִים[r]	pref. לַ bef. (-:))(n. m., pl. of חֶבֶל d. 6 (§ 35. r. 4)	חבל
לַחֲבַקּוּק	pref. id.)(pr. name masc.	חבק
לְחַבֵּר[s]	pref. לְ)(Piel inf. constr.	חבר
לְחֶבֶר	pref. id.)(pr. name masc.	חבר
לְחֶבְרָה[t]	pref. id.)(noun fem. sing.	חבר
לְחֶבְרוֹן	pref. id.)(pr. name of a place	חבר
לַחֶבְרוֹנִי	pref. לַ for לְהַ)(gent. noun from the preced.	חבר
לְחַבֻּרָתִי[u]	pref. לְ)(n. f. s., suff. 1 p. s. fr. חַבּוּרָה d. 10	חבר
לַחֲבֹשׁ[x]	pref. לַ bef. (-:))(Kal inf. constr.	חבשׁ
לְחָבְשָׁהּ[y]	pref. לְ)(id., suff. 3 pers. sing. fem.	חבשׁ
לָחֹג[z]	ו׳ וְ pref. לָ (see lett. ל))(Kal inf. constr.	חגג

a Nu. 25. 2. b 1 Ki. 20. 7. c Pr. 4. 24. d Ju. 9. 8. e Ex. 23. 11. f Ex. 13. 9. g Ps. 103. 18. h Ex. 28. 12, 29. i Is. 26. 8. k Ps. 92. 2. l De. 28. 13, 44. m Ge. 38. 24. n Le. 20. 6. o 2 Sa. 19. 29. p Job 16. 18. q Is. 34. 9. r De. 28. 50. s Le. 9. 1. t Jos. 23. 2. u Ge. 21. 2. x Ru. 4. 9. y Pr. 6. 1. z Job 19. 15.

a Nu. 11. 20. b Je. 4. 11. c Eze. 20. 23. d Zec. 2. 4. e Ps. 106. 27. f Je. 3. 13. g Is. 55. 10. h Le. 18. 20. i Is. 28. 24. k Eze. 22. 6. l Ge. 28. 13. m Ex. 32. 13. n Eze. 43. 18. o Eze. 17. 24. p Ec. 3. 5. q Ezr. 6. 12. r Je. 38. 12. s Ex. 36. 18. t Job 34. 8. u Ge. 4. 23. x Is. 61. 1. y Eze. 30. 21. z Zec. 14. 16, 18, 19.

לְחַגָּא[a] pref. לְ) noun fem. sing. [for חָגָּה] . חגא
לְחַגִּי pref. id.) pr. name masc. . . חגג
לַחֲגֹר[b] וְ' pref. לַ bef. (ֲ)) Kal inf. constr. . חגר
לַחֹדֶשׁ pref. לַ for לְהַ) noun masc. sing. dec. 6c . חדש
לְחַדֵּשׁ[c] pref. לְ) Piel inf. constr. . . . חדש
לְחֹדֶשׁ pref. id.) noun masc. sing. dec. 6c . חדש
לְחָדְשֵׁי pref. id.) id. pl. constr. st. . . חדש
לְחֳדָשָׁיו[d] pref. לְ bef. (ֳ)) id. pl., suff. 3 p. s. masc. חדש
לֶחֳדָשִׁים וְ' pref. לֶ f. bef. חֳ f. לְהֶ f. לְהַ) id. pl. abs. st. חדש

לָחָה Root not used; hence
לְחִי fem. dec. 6i (§ 35 rem. 14 & 15).—I. *cheek.* —II. *jaw-bone.*—III. pr. name of a place on the borders of Philistia.

לֵחֹה[ll] n. m. s., suff. 3 pers. sing. masc. fr. [לֵחַ] d. 1a לחח
לַחוֹטֵא[e] וְ pref. לַ for לְהַ) Kal part. act. sing. m. d. 7b חטא
לָחוּל[f] pref. לָ (see lett. ל)) Kal inf. constr. . חול
לַחוֹמָה pref. לַ f. לְהַ) noun fem. sing. dec. 10 . חמה
לְחוֹמַת[g] וּ' [h] pref. לְ) id. constr. st.; וּ bef. (:) חמה
לְחוֹנֵן[i] pref. id.) Kal part. act. sing. masc. . חנן
לַחוֹסִים[k] pref. לַ f. לְהַ) Kal part. a., pl. of חוֹסֶה' d. 9a חסה
לְחוֹף pref. לְ) noun masc. sing. . . . חפף
לְחוּפָּם pref. id.) pr. name masc., see חֻפִּים . חפף
לַחוּץ[l] וְ' [m] pref. לַ for לְהַ) noun masc. sing. dec. 1a חוץ
לַחוּצָה[n] וְ pref. id.) id. with loc. ה . . חוץ
לְחוֹקְקֵי[o] pref. לְ) Kal part. act. pl. c. m. fr. [חֹקֵק] d. 7b חקק
לְחוּרָם pref. id.) pr. name masc. . . . חור
לְחוּשַׁי pref. id.) pr. name masc. . . . חוש
לְחֹת defect. [for לוּחוֹת], see לוּחַ . . לוח
לַחֲזָאֵל pref. לַ bef. (ֲ)) pr. name masc. . . חזה
לַחֲזוֹת[p] pref. id.) Kal inf. constr. . . חזה
לַחֲזִיז pref. id.) noun masc. sing. dec. 1a . . חזז
לַחֹזִים[q] וְ pref. לַ for לְהַ) noun m., pl. of חֹזֶה d. 9a חזה
לְחֵזִיר pref. לְ) pr. name masc. . . . חזר
לְחַזֵּק וּ' pref. id.) Piel inf. constr.; וּ bef. (:) . חזק
לְחֶזְקָה[r] pref. id.) noun fem. sing. . . . חזק
לְחֶזְקָהּ[s] pref. id.) Kal inf., suff. 3 pers. sing. fem. חזק
לְחִזְקִיָּה / לְחִזְקִיָּהוּ[t] } pref. id.) pr. name masc. . . חזק

לָחַח Root not used; Chald. & Ethiop. לחלח *to moisten.*
לַח m. pl. לַחִים (§ 37. rem. 7) adj. *moist, fresh.*
לֵחַ masc. dec. 1, *freshness, vigour,* De. 34. 7.

לַחֲטֹא pref. לַ bef. (ֲ)) Kal inf. constr. . . חטא
לְחַטֵּא[t] pref. לְ) Piel inf. constr. . . . חטא
לַחֲטָאָה[qq] pref. לַ bef. (ֲ)) noun fem. sing. . . חטא
לַחֲטָּאוֹת[u] וְ pref. לַ for לְהַ) noun fem., pl. abs. from חַטָּאת (q. v.) . . . . חטא
לְחַטֹּאותֵיכֶם[w] וּ pref. לְ) id. pl., suff. 2 p. pl. m.; וּ bef. (:) חטא
לַחַטָּאת[y] וְ'[z] pref. לַ f. לְהַ / לְחַטָּאת pref. לְ } id. s. abs. [for חַטָּאֶת § 39. No. 4 d] pl. חַטָּאוֹת (comp. prec. & § 44. r. 5) } חטא
לְחַטַּאת pref. id.) id. constr. st. [for חַטָּאַת, comp. § 23. rem. 2 & 4] prop. from חַטָּאָה חטא
לְחַטָּאתִי[a] וּ pref. id.) id. s., suff. 1 pers. s.; וּ bef. (:) חטא
לְחַטֹּאתָם[b] וּ' pref. id.) id., suff. 3 pers. pl. masc.; וּ id. חטא
לְחַטֹּאתֵנוּ[c] וּ pref. id.) id., suff. 1 pers. pl.; וּ id. חטא
לַחְטֹב[d] pref. לַ) Kal inf. constr. [for לַחֲטֹב comp. § 13. rem. 1 & 2] . . . . חטב
לַחֹטְבִים[e] pref. לַ for לְהַ) Kal part. act. masc., pl. of חוֹטֵב' dec. 7b . . . . חטב
לַחְטוֹף[f] pref. לַ) Kal inf. constr. [for לַחֲטֹף comp. § 13. rem. 1 & 2, & § 8. rem. 18] . חטף
לַחֲטִיא[g] pref. לַ contr. [for לְהַחֲטִיא]) Hiph. inf. constr. (§ 11. rem. 3) . . . חטא
לְחַטָּיָא[h] Chald., pref. לְ) Kh. for חַטָּאָה Keri n. f. s. חטא
לְחַטָּת[i] defect. for לְחַטָּאת (q. v.) . . . חטא
לַחַי רֹאִי pr. name, see בְּאֵר לַ' under . . . באר
לֶחָי[k] pref. לֶ for לְ, bef. חָ for לְהַ) adj. masc. sing. dec. 8a (for חַי § 37. rem. 6) חיי
לְחַי וּ Chald., pref. לְ) adj. m. s. d. 5a; וּ bef. (:) חיי
לְחִי / לֶחִי[m] } noun fem. sing. dec. 6i (suff. לֶחְיוֹ § 35. rem. 14), also pr. name . . } לחה
לַחַיָּה[n] וְ' pref. לַ for לְהַ) n. f. s. d. 10, from חַי m. חיי
לֶחֱיָהּ[o] noun f. s., suff. 3 pers. s. f. from לְחִי (q. v.) לחה
לְחָיֵיהֶם[p] id. du. [לְחָיִים § 35. rem. 15], suff. 3 p. pl. m. לחה
לְחָיָו[q] id. du. [לְחָיַיִם], suff. 3 p. s. m. (§ 4. r. 1 & 2) לחה
לֶחְיוֹ[r] id. sing., suff. 3 pers. sing. masc. (§ 35. r. 14) לחה
לְחַיּוֹת[s] וּ' pref. לְ) Piel inf. constr.; וּ bef. (:) . חיה
לִחְיוֹת[u] pref. לִ bef. (:)) Kal inf. constr. (§ 13. r. 13) חיה
לְחֵיוְתָא[x] Chald., pref. לְ) n. f. s., emph. of חֵיוָא d. 8a חוה
לְחַיּוֹתָם[y] וּ'[z] pref. id.) Piel inf. (חַיּוֹת), suff. 3 pers. pl. masc. dec. 1b; וּ bef. (:) . . חיה

[a] Is. 19. 17. [b] Is. 22. 12. [c] 2 Ch. 24. 4, 12. [d] Eze. 47. 12. [e] Ec. 2. 26. [f] Ju. 21. 21. [g] Je. 15. 20. [h] Ne. 2. 8. [i] Pr. 28. 8. [k] Ps. 31. 20. [l] Ps. 41. 7. [ll] De. 34. 7. [m] Eze. 41. 17. [n] 2 Ch. 32. 5. [o] Ju. 5. 9. [p] Ps. 27. 4. [q] Is. 30. 10. [qq] Ps. 109. 7. [r] 2 Ki. 12. 13. [s] Eze. 30. 21. [t] Le. 14. 49. [u] Ne. 10. 34. [w] Jos. 24. 19. [y] Le. 5. 8. [z] Le. 7. 37. [a] Job 10. 6. [b] 2 Ch. 7. 14. [c] Ex. 34. 9. [d] De. 19. 5. [e] 2 Ch. 2. 9. [f] Ps. 10. 9. [g] Ec. 5. 5. [h] Ezr. 6. 17. [i] Nu. 15. 24. [k] 1 Sa. 25. 6. [l] Da. 4. 31. [m] Ju. 15. 15. [n] Le. 25. 7. [o] La. 1. 2. [p] Ho. 11. 4. [q] Ca. 5. 13. [r] Job 40. 26. [s] Ge. 7. 3. [t] Eze. 13. 19. [u] Eze. 33. 12. [x] Da. 7. 6. [y] Jos. 9. 15. [z] Ps. 33. 19.

לְחָיַי[a] / לְחָיַי[b] וּ } noun fem. du., suff. 1 pers. sing. from לְחִי dec. 6 i; וּ bef. (:) } לחה

לְחָיֵי[c] id. pl., constr. st. . . . . לחה

לְחַיֵּי pref. לְ) noun masc. pl. c. from חַי dec. 8 d (§ 37. rem. 6), Chald. (Ezr. 6. 10) dec. 5 a חיי

לְחָיַיִךְ[d] noun fem. du., suff. 2 p. s. f. from לְחִי d. 6 i לחה

לַחַיִּים[e] pref. לַ f. לְהַ / לְחַיִּים pref. לְ q. v. } noun masc., pl. of חַי dec. 8 d (§ 37. rem. 6) . . } חיי

לְחֵיל[f] pref. id.) noun masc. sing. dec. 6 h . . חול

לְחֵיל pref. id.) id. constr. st. . . . . חול

לְחֵילָהּ[g] pref. id.) id., suff. 3 pers. sing. fem.; the general reading is חֵילָה noun fem. . חול

לְחֵילוֹ[h] וּ[i] pref. id.) id., suff. 3 pers. s. m.; וּ bef. (:) חול

לַחִים adj. masc., pl. of לַח (§ 37. rem. 7) . לחח

לַחִיצוֹן[i] וְ pref. לַ for לְהַ) adj. masc. sing. . . חוץ

לְחִירָם pref. לְ) pr. name masc., see חוּרָם . . חור

לְחַיַּת[k] וּ pref. id.) noun fem. sing., constr. of חַיָּה dec. 10, from חַי masc. . . חיי

לְחַיְתוֹ[l] pref. id.) id. constr. with parag. ו (for dag. omitted in יְ comp. § 10. rem. 7) . חיה

לְחַיֹּתוֹ[m] pref. id.) Piel inf. (חַיּוֹת), suff. 3 pers. sing. masc. dec. 1 a . . . . . חיה

לְחַיֹּתֵנוּ[n] pref. id.) id. with suff. 1 pers. pl. . חיה

[לָחַךְ] i. q. לָקַק only Nu. 22. 4, and Pi. לִחֵךְ (§ 14. r. 1) *to lick, lick up*, as an ox in feeding; *to lap up*, as a dog in drinking.

לִחֲכָה[o] Piel pret. 3 pers. sing. fem. [for לִחֲכָה, comp. § 7. rem. 8, & § 14. rem. 1] . . לחך

לְחִכִּי pref. לְ) noun masc. sing., suff. 1 pers. sing. from חֵךְ [for חִנְךְ] dec. 8 b . . חנך

לְחַכִּימֵי Ch., pref. id.) noun m. pl. c. fr. [חַכִּים] d. 1 a חכם

לְחַכִּימִין[p] Ch., pref. id.) id. pl., abs. state . חכם

לַחֲכַם pref. לַ bef. (-:)) constr. of the foll. . חכם

לֶחָכָם pref. לֶ f. לְהַ· לְהֶ / לְחָכָם pref. לְ q. v. } adj. masc. sing. dec. 4 c חכם

לְחִכָּם[q] pref. id.) noun masc. sing., suff. 3 pers. pl. masc. from חֵךְ [for חִנְךְ] dec. 8 b . חנך

לַחָכְמָה pref. לַ for לְהַ / לְחָכְמָה[r] וּ[s] pref. לְ q. v. } noun fem. sing. (no pl.) חכם

לַחֲכָמִים pref. לַ bef. (-:)) adj. m., pl. of חָכָם d. 4 c חכם

לְחָכְמָתִי[t] pref. לְ) noun fem. sing., suff. 1 pers. sing. from חָכְמָה (no pl.) . . . חכם

לְחָל pref. לְ) noun masc. sing. . . . . חלל

לַחֲלוֹף[u] pref. לַ bef. (-:)) Kal inf. constr. (§ 8. r. 18) חלף

לְחַלּוֹת[v] וּ pref. לְ) Piel inf. constr.; וּ bef. (:) . חלה

לַחְלַח pref. לַ for לְהַ) pr. name of a province . חלח

לָחֳלִי pref. לָ bef. (T:)) noun masc. sing. dec. 6 k חלה

לְחֵלְכָה[y] pref. לְ) adj. masc. sing. [for חֵלְכָא] . חלך

לְחַלֵּל[z] וּ pref. id.) Piel inf. constr. d. 7 b; וּ bef. (:) חלל

לְחַלְּלוֹ pref. id.) id. with suff. 3 pers. sing. masc. חלל

לְחֵלֶם pref. id.) pr. name masc. . . . חלם

לַחְלִק[a] pref. לַ, contr. & defect. [for לְהַחֲלִיק] Hiph. inf. constr. (§ 11. rem. 3) . . חלק

לַחֲלֹק[b] pref. לַ bef. (-:)) Kal inf. constr. . . חלק

לְחֵלֶק[c] pref. לְ) noun masc. sing. dec. 6 b (§ 35. rem. 6), also pr. name masc. . . חלק

לְחִלְקִיָּה pref. id.) pr. name masc. . . חלק

[לָחַם] fut. יִלְחַם.—I. *to eat, consume*, with acc., בְּ of the food; metaph. לְחֻמֵי רֶשֶׁף *consumed of fever*, Da 32. 24.—II. *to war, fight*, with לְ, אֶת of the person. Niph. נִלְחַם *to make* or *wage war, to fight* with בְּ, עִם, אֶל, עַל *against*, and לְ, עַל *for* whom.

לְחוּם or לָחוּם masc.—I. *eating, feasting*, with suff. לְחוּמוֹ Job 20. 23.—II. *flesh, body*, Zep. 1. 17 where the MSS. and editions differ between לְחֻמָם & לְחוּמָם.

לֶחֶם com. dec. 6 a (with suff. לַחְמִי).—I. *food meat*; applied also to *fruit*, Je. 11. 19; meton. *meal, feast*.—II. *bread*, as the principal part of the *food* of men; לֶ׳ הַמַּעֲרֶכֶת, לֶ׳ הַפָּנִים, *shew-bread* the bread *arranged* or *piled up* in the tabernacle in the *presence* of the Lord; שְׁתֵּי לֶ׳ *two loaves*, meton. *bread-corn*, Is. 28. 28; לֶ׳ אֲנָשִׁים *food necessary for men*; אַנְשֵׁי לַחְמְךָ *men who eat thy food*.

לְחֶם Chald. *meal, feast*, Da. 5. 1.

לָחֶם masc. (for לַחֶם, לָחֶם) *war*, only constr. לָחֶם Ju. 5. 8.

לַחְמִי pr. name masc. 1 Ch. 20. 5; see also under בַּיִת.

מִלְחָמָה and מִלְחֶמֶת fem. dec. 11 a, & 13 a (with suff. ׳חַמְתִּי, pl. ׳חָמוֹת § 42. rem. 5).—I. *a warring, fighting*, Is. 7. 1; hence, *fight, battle*.—II. *war*; עָשָׂה מִלְחָמָה (with אֶת, עִם) *to make*

a Job 16. 10. b Is. 50. 6. c Is. 30. 28. d Ca. 1. 10. e Is. 4. 3. f 2 Ch. 16. 8. g Ps. 48. 14. h Eze. 29. 18, 19. i 1 Ki. 6. 29, 30. k 1 Sa. 17. 46. l Ps. 79. 2. m Eze. 3. 18. n De. 6. 24. o 1 Ki. 18. 38. p Da. 2. 21. q Job 29. 10. r Job 13. 5. s 1 Ki. 10. 23. t Pr. 5. 1. u Is. 21. 1. v Zec. 8. 22. y Ps. 10. 8. z Le. 20. 3. a Je. 37. 12. b Ne. 13. 13. c Job 17. 5.

war with any one; אִישׁ מִ׳ *warrior, soldier*; כְּלֵי מִ׳ *weapons of war, arms*.—III. *event of war, victory*, Ec. 9. 11.

לָחֶם in pause for לֶחֶם (q. v. & § 35. rem. 2) . לחם

[a]לְחֶם noun masc. sing. constr. [of לָחֶם]; some MSS. read לְחֶם, others לֶחֶם . . לחם

[b]לְחַם Kal imp. sing. masc. . . . . . לחם

לֶחֶם וְ׳, [c]וְ׳ noun com. s. d. 6 a (and pr. name in compos. with בֵּית q. v.); for וָ see lett. ו לחם

[d]לְחֶם Chald. noun masc. sing. . . . . לחם

[e]לַחֹם pref. לְ)(noun masc. sing. dec. 8 c . חמם

[f]לֹחֵם Kal part. act. sing. masc. dec. 7 b . לחם

לַחְמָהּ noun com. s., suff. 3 pers. s. f. fr. לֶחֶם d. 6 a לחם

[g]לָחֲמוּ Kal pret. 3 pers. pl. . . . . לחם

[h]לַחֲמוּ id. imp. pl. masc. . . . . . לחם

לַחְמוֹ noun com. s., suff. 3 p. s. m. from לֶחֶם d. 6 a לחם

לְחָמוּל pref. לְ)(pr. name masc. . . . חמל

[i]לַחֲמוֹרִי pref. לַ bef. (-:))(noun masc. sing. dec. 1 a חמר

[k]לַחֲמוֹרֵיהֶם pref. id.)(id., suff. 3 pers. pl. masc. . חמר

[l]לַחֲמוֹרִים pref. id.)(id. pl., abs. st. . . . חמר

[m]לַחֲמוֹרֵינוּ pref. id.)(id. pl., suff. 1 pers. pl. . . חמר

[n]לְחוֹמֹת [o]וְ׳ pref. לְ)(n. f., pl. of חוֹמָה d. 10; וּ bef. (:) חמה

לַחֲמוֹתָהּ pref. לַ bef. (-:))(noun fem. sing., suff. 3 pers. sing. fem. from [חָמוֹת] dec. 3 a . חם

לַחְמִי pr. name masc. . . . . . . לחם

לַחְמִי [p]וְ׳ noun com. s., suff. 1 p. s. from לֶחֶם d. 6 a לחם

[q]לֹחֲמָי Kal part. act. pl. m., suff. 1 p. s. fr. לֹחֵם d. 7 b לחם

[r]לְחֻמֵי וּ id. part. pass. pl. constr. masc. from [לָחוּם] d. 3 a; Milêl bef. penacute (רֶשֶׁף); וּ bef. (:) לחם

[s]לֹחֲמִים id. part. act. masc., pl. of לֹחֵם dec. 7 b . לחם

[t]לַחְמְךָ וְ׳ / לַחְמֶךָ noun com. sing., suff. 2 pers. sing. masc. from לֶחֶם dec. 6 a . לחם

[u]לַחְמְכֶם id., suff. 2 pers. pl. masc. . . . לחם

[x]לְחֶמְלָה pref. לְ)(Kal inf. constr. with fem. term. (§ 8. rem. 10) . . . . חמל

לַחְמָם noun com. s., suff. 3 p. pl. m. from לֶחֶם d. 6 a לחם

[y]לַחְמָם pref. לַ, contr. [for לַחֲמֹם], Kal inf. constr. (after the form קְטֹל comp. § 13. rem. 2 & 13, & § 18. rem. 13) . . . חמם

[z]לְחֻמָם וּ for לְחוּמָם (as other copies read) n. m. s., suff. 3 p. pl. m. [fr. לְחוּם or לָחוּם]; וּ bef. (:) לחם

לַחְמֵנוּ noun m. s., suff. 1 pers. pl. from לֶחֶם dec. 6 a לחם

לַחְמָס וְ pr. n. of a place in the tribe of Judah, Jos. 15. 40.

[a]לֶחָמָס pref. לְ)(noun masc. sing. dec. 4 c . חמס

לַחֲמֹר pref. לַ for לְהַ)(noun masc. sing. dec. 6 c חמר

לַחֲמֹרוֹ pref. לַ bef. (-:))(noun masc. sing., suff. 3 pers. sing. masc. from חֲמוֹר dec. 1 a . חמר

[b]לַחֲמֹרֵיהֶם pref. id.)(id., suff. 3 pers. pl. masc. . חמר

[c]לַחֹמֶשׁ pref. לַ for לְהַ)(noun masc. sing. . חמש

[d]לַחֲמִשָּׁה pref. לַ bef. (-:))(num. card. m. from חָמֵשׁ f. חמש

[e]לַחֲמִשִּׁים pref. id.)(id. com. gen., pl. of חָמֵשׁ . דמש

[f]לַחֲמֵשֶׁת pref. id.)(id. masc. sing., constr. of חֲמִשָּׁה (§ 39. No. 4. rem. 1) . . . חמש

לְחֵן Chald. Root not used; Arab. *to be rancid, corrupt*; metaph. *to be obscene*.

לְחֵנָא Chald. fem. d. 8 a, *concubine*, Da. 5. 2, 3, 23.

לְחֵן וּ pref. לְ)(pr. name masc.; וּ bef. (:) . חנן

לְחַנָּה וּ pref. id.)(pr. name fem.; וּ id. . חנן

לַחֲנוֹךְ pref. לַ bef. (-:))(pr. name masc. . . חנך

לְחָנוּן pref. לְ)(pr. name masc. . . . חנן

[g]לַחֲנֹט pref. לַ bef. (-:))(Kal inf. constr. . . חנט

לַחֲנֻכַּת Heb. & Chald., pref. id.)(noun fem. sing., constr. of חֲנֻכָּה dec. 10, Chald. dec. 8 a . חנך

[h]לְחֶנְנָהּ pref. לְ)(Piel or Kal inf., suff. 3 pers. sing. fem. [for חַנְּנָהּ, comp. § 10. rem. 7; or for חַנְנָהּ, from חָנַן, § 16. rem. 10] . חנן

לַחֲנָנִי, וְ׳ לַחֲנַנְיָהוּ pref. לַ bef. (-:))(pr. names masc. חנן

[tt]לַחֲנַנְכֶם pref. id.)(Kal inf. [חָנַן], suff. 2 pers. pl. masc. (§ 16. rem. 10) . . . חנן

[i]לְחֵנָתֵהּ וּ Chald. noun. fem. sing., suff. 3 pers. sing. fem. from [לְחֵנָא] dec. 8 a; וּ bef. (:) . לחן

[zz]לְחֵנָתָךְ וּ Chald. id. with suff. 2 pers. sing. masc.; וּ id. לחן

[k]לַחֲנֹתְכֶם pref. לַ bef. (-:))(Kal inf. (חֲנוֹת), suff. 2 pers. pl. masc. dec. 1 a . . . חנה

לְחֶסֶד pref. לְ)(noun masc. sing. d. 6 a (see the foll.) חסד

לְחַסְדּוֹ וּ׳ pref. id.)(id., suff. 3 pers. s. m.; וּ bef. (:) חסד

[l]לְחַסְדֵי pref. id.)(id. pl., constr. st. . . חסד

לְחֹסָה וּ׳ pref. id.)(pr. name masc.; וּ bef. (:) . חסה

לַחֲסוֹת [m]וְ׳ pref. לַ bef. (-:))(Kal inf. constr. . חסה

[dd]לַחֲסִידָיו pref. id.)(adj. pl. m., suff. 3 p. s. m. fr. חָסִיד d. 3 a חסד

[n]לַחֲסִידֶךָ pref. id.)(id., suff. 2 pers. sing. fem. for חֲסִידְךָ חסד

[o]לֶחָסִיל pref. לֶ for לְהֶ, bef. חָ for לְהַ)(noun m. sing. חסל

[p]לַחֹסִים pref. לַ for לְהַ)(Kal part. m., pl. of חֹסֶה d. 9 a חסה

[q]לַחֲסַר pref. לַ bef. (-:))(adj. m. s., constr. of חָסֵר d. 5 c חסר

לְחֻפִּים, לְחֻפָּה pref. לְ)(pr. names masc. . . חפף

---

[a] Ju. 5. 8. [b] Ps. 35. 1. [c] Ge. 45. 23. [d] Da. 5. 1. [e] Hag. 1. 6. [f] Ps. 56. 2. [g] Pr. 4. 17. [h] Pr. 9. 5. [i] Pr. 26. 3. [k] Jos. 9. 4. [l] Ju. 19. 21. [m] Ju. 19. 19. [n] Ne. 4. 1. [o] Je. 1. 18. [p] Eze. 16. 19. [q] Ps. 35. 1. [r] De. 32. 24. [s] Ps. 56. 3. [t] Je. 5. 17. [tt] Je. 30. 18. [u] Le. 26. 5, 26. [x] Eze. 16. 5. [y] Is. 47. 14. [z] Zep. 1. 17. [zz] Da. 5. 23.

[a] Hab. 1. 9. [b] Ge. 43. 24. [c] Ge. 47. 26. [d] 1 Ch. 25. 22. [dd] Ps. 116. 15. [e] Ne. 6. 15. [f] 1 Sa. 6. 18. [g] Ge. 50. 2. [h] Ps. 102. 14. [i] Da. 5. 2, 3. [k] De. 1. 33. [l] 2 Ch. 6. 42. [m] Is. 30. 2. [n] Ps. 89. 20. [o] Ps. 78. 46. [p] Pr. 30. 5. [q] Pr. 15. 21.

לַחְפֹּר[a] pref. לַ contr. for [לַחְפֹּר], Kal inf. constr. (comp. § 13. rem. 2 & 9) . . . חפר

לַחְפֹּר[b] see חֲפֹר פֵּרוֹת under . . . חפר

לַחָפְשִׁי pref. לַ for לְהַ)(adj. masc. sing. dec. 1 b . חפש

לָחַץ fut. יִלְחַץ.—I. *to press, squeeze.*—II. *to oppress, afflict.* Niph. *to press oneself,* with אֶל *against,* Nu. 22. 25. Hence

לַחַץ[c] / לָחַץ } masc. dec. 6d (§ 35. rem. 2) *oppression, affliction* . . . . לחץ

לַחֵץ[d] pref. לַ f. לְהַ / לְחֵץ[e] pref. לְ q. v. } noun masc. sing. dec. 8b . חצץ

לַחְצֹב[f] pref. לַ)(Kal inf. constr. [for לַחְצֹב, comp. § 13. rem. 2 & 9] . . . חצב

לְחֹצְבֵי[g] וּ pref. לְ)(Kal part. act. pl. c. masc. from חֹצֵב dec. 7 b; וּ bef. (:) . . . חצב

לַחֹצְבִים[h] pref. לַ for לְהַ)(id. pl., abs. st. . . חצב

לָחֲצוּ[i] וְ[k] Kal pret. 3 pers. pl. . . . . לחץ

לַחְצוֹב[l] in full for לַחְצֹב (q. v. & § 8. rem. 18) חצב

לַחֲצִי / לַחֲצִי[m] } וְ pref. לַ bef. (-:) / pref. לַ for לְהַ } noun m. s. (suff. חֶצְיוֹ) dec. 6 (§ 35. rem. 14) חצה

לֹחֲצֵיהֶם[n] Kal part. act. pl. masc., suff. 3 pers. pl. masc. from [לֹחֵץ] dec. 7 b . . . לחץ

לֹחֲצָיו[o] id. pl. with suff. 3 pers. sing. masc. . . לחץ

לְחֶצְיוֹ[p] וּ pref. לְ)(noun m. sing., suff. 3 pers. sing. m. from חֵצִי dec. 6 (§ 35. r. 14); וּ bef. (:) חצה

לֹחֲצֵיכֶם[q] the foll. with suff. 2 pers. pl. masc. . לחץ

לֹחֲצִים Kal part. act. masc., pl. of [לֹחֵץ] dec. 7 b . לחץ

לַחֲצֵנוּ[r] וְ[s] noun masc. sing., suff. 1 pers. pl. from לַחַץ dec. 6d . . . . לחץ

לַחֲצַר וְ[t] pref. לַ bef. (-:))(constr. of the foll. . חצר

לֶחָצֵר וְ[u] pref. לֶ for לְהֶ, bef. חָ for לְהַ)(noun com. sing. dec. 5 c . . . . חצר

לְחַצְרוֹת[x] pref. לְ)(id. pl., constr. st. . . . חצר

לַחֲצֵרוֹתָיו[y] pref. id.)(id. pl., suff. 3 pers. sing. masc. חצר

לְחֶצְרוֹן pref. id.)(pr. name masc. . . חצר

לְחַצְתֶּם[z] וּ Kal pret. 2 pers. pl. masc.; וּ for וְ conv. לחץ

לְחֹק / לְחָק } pref. לְ)(noun masc. sing. dec. 8 c (§ 37. rem. 2) . . } חקק

לַחְקוֹר[a] in full for לַחְקֹר (q. v. & § 8. rem. 18) חקר

לְחֻקִּים[b] pref. לְ)(noun masc., pl. of חֹק dec. 8 c . חקק

לְחֵקֶר[c] pref. id.)(noun masc. sing. dec. 6 b . . חקר

לַחְקֹר[d] pref. לַ)(Kal inf. constr. [for לַחֲקֹר comp. § 13. rem. 2 & 9] . . . חקר

לְחָקְרָהּ[e] וּ pref. לְ)(Kal inf., suff. 3 p. s. fem.; וּ bef. (:) חקר

לְחֻקַּת pref. id.)(noun fem. s., constr. of חֻקָּה d. 10 חקק

לַחֶרֶב pref. לַ for לְהַ)(noun fem. s. (suff. חַרְבִּי) d. 6 a חרב

לַחֹרֶב[f] pref. id.)(noun masc. sing. . . . חרב

לֶחָרֶב pref. לֶ for לְהֶ, bef. חָ for לְהַ)(in pause for חֶרֶב (q. v. & § 35. rem. 2) . . . חרב

לְחֹרֶב[g] pref. לְ)(noun masc. sing. . . . חרב

לֶחָרָבָה[h] pref. לֶ for לְהֶ, bef. חָ for לְהַ)(noun fem. sing. חרב

לְחָרְבָּה pref. לְ)(noun fem. sing. dec. 12 c . חרב

לַחֲרָבוֹת[i] pref. לַ bef. (-:))(n. fem. pl. abs. fr. חֶרֶב d. 6 a חרב

לֶחֳרָבוֹת[k] וְ pref. לֶ for לְהֶ, לְהַ)(noun fem. pl. abs. from חָרְבָּה dec. 12 c . . . . חרב

לְחָרְבוֹת וּ[l] pref. לְ)(id. constr. st.; וּ bef. (:) . חרב

לַחֲרָדָה[m] pref. לַ bef. (-:))(noun fem. sing. dec. 11 c . חרד

לְחֶרְדַּת[n] pref. לְ)(id. constr. st. (§ 42. rem. 1) . חרד

לַחֲרוֹת[o] pref. לַ bef. (-:))(Kal inf. constr. . . חרה

לְחַרְחַר[p] pref. לְ)(Pilpel inf. constr. (§ 6. rem. 4) חרר

לַחַרְטֻמִּים[q] pref. לַ for לְהַ)(noun m., pl. of [חַרְטֹם] d. 6 c חרטם

לַחֹרִים[r] וְ pref. id.)(noun masc., pl. of חֹר dec. 1 a חרר

לְחָרִם pref. לְ)(pr. name masc. . . . חרם

לַחֵרֶם[s] / לְחֵרֶם } pref. לַ f. לְהַ / pref. לְ q. v. } noun masc. sing. dec. 6 b (§ 35. rem. 6) . } חרם

לְחֶרְמוֹ[t] pref. id.)(id., suff. 3 pers. sing. masc. . חרם

לְחֶרְמוֹן pref. id.)(pr. name of a ridge . . חרם

לַחֲרָמִים[u] pref. לַ bef. (-:))(noun masc., pl. of חֵרֶם dec. 6 b (§ 35. rem. 6) . . . . חרם

לַחֶרֶס[x] pref. לַ for לְהַ)(noun masc. sing. . . חרס

לְחָרֵף pref. לְ)(Piel inf. constr. . . . חרף

לְחֶרְפָּה וּ' pref. id.)(noun fem. sing. d. 12 b; וּ bef. (:) חרף

לַחֲרָפוֹת pref. לַ bef. (-:))(id. pl., abs. st. . . חרף

לַחֲרֹשׁ[y] וְ pref. id.)(Kal inf. constr. . . . חרש

לְחָרָשֵׁי pref. לְ)(noun masc. pl. constr. from חָרָשׁ (q. v.) dec. 1 b . . . . חרש

לֶחָרָשִׁים וְ[z] pref. לֶ for לְהֶ, לְהַ)(id. pl., abs. st. . חרש

לָחַשׁ. Pi. לִחֵשׁ (§ 14. rem. 1) *to whisper, mutter,* only part. pl. מְלַחֲשִׁים *whisperers, charmers,* Ps. 58. 6. Hithp. *to whisper among themselves,* 2 Sa. 12. 19 Ps. 41. 8.

לוֹחֵשׁ (*charmer*) pr. name m. Ne. 3. 12; 10. 25

---

a Jos. 2. 2, 3. b Is. 2. 20. c Is. 30. 20. d La. 3. 12. e Is. 49. 2.
f Je. 2. 13. g 2 Ki. 12. 13. h Ezr. 3. 7. i Ju. 10. 12. k Am. 6. 14.
l 1 Ch. 22. 2. m 1 Ki. 16. 21. n Ju. 2. 18. o Je. 30. 20. p Jos. 22. 7.
q Ju. 6. 9. r De. 26. 7. s Ps. 44. 25. t 1 Ki. 7. 12. u Ex. 38. 20.
x 1 Ch. 28. 12. y Ps. 96. 8. z 2 Ki. 6. 32. a Pr. 23. 30. b 2 Ch. 19. 10.
c Job 8. 8. d 1 Ch. 19. 3. e Ju. 18. 2. f Je. 36. 30. g Je. 49. 13.
h Ex. 14. 21. i Joel 4. 10. k Eze. 36. 4. l Je. 25. 9. m Is. 21. 4.
n 1 Sa. 14. 15. o 2 Sa. 24. 1. p Pr. 26. 21. q Da. 2. 2. r Ne. 2. 16.
s Is. 43. 28. t Hab. 1. 16. u Eze. 47. 10. x Job 9. 7. y 1 Sa. 8. 12. z Ezr. 3. 7.

לַחַשׁ masc. dec. 6d.—I. *a whispering*, of prayer, Is. 26. 16.—II. *incantation, charm.*—III. *amulet*, Is. 3. 20.

לָחַשׁ, לָחַשׁ[a] } noun masc. sing. dec. 6d (§ 35. rem. 2) — לחש

לַחְשֹׁב[b] וְ pref. לְ)(Kal inf. constr. [for לַחֲשֹׁב comp. § 13. rem. 2 & 13] — חשב

לְחֵשֶׁב pref. לְ)(noun masc. sing. — חשב

לְחֹשְׁבֵי[b] וּ pref. id.)(Kal part. act. pl. c. masc. from חֹשֵׁב dec. 7b; וּ bef. (:) — חשב

לַחֲשַׁבְיָה pref. לְ bef. (ֲ))(pr. name masc. — חשב

לַחֲשׂוֹף[c] וְ in full for לַחְשֹׂף (q. v. & § 8. rem. 18) — חשף

לַחֲשׁוֹת[d] pref. לְ bef. (ֲ))(Kal inf. constr. — חשה

לַחֹשֶׁךְ[e] f/ וְ pref. לְ f. לְהַ; לְחֹשֶׁךְ pref. לְ q. v. } noun masc. sing. dec. 6c — חשך

לַחֹשֶׁן וְ pref. לַ for לְהַ)(noun masc. sing. — חשן

לַחְשֹׂף[g] pref. לְ)(Kal inf. constr. [for לַחֲשֹׂף comp. § 13. rem. 2 & 13] — חשף

לֻחֹת for לוּחֹת, n. m. with pl. f. term. fr. לוּחַ d. 1a — לוח

לַחְתּוֹת[h] pref. לְ)(Kal inf. constr. [for לַחֲתוֹת comp. § 13. rem. 2 & 13] — חתה

לֻחֹתַיִם[i] noun masc. du. from לוּחַ dec. 1a — לוח

לַחְתֹּם[k] וְ pref. לְ)(Kal inf. constr. [for לַחֲתֹם § 13. rem. 2 & 13] — חתם

לְהָתֵם[l] וּ Kh. וּלְהַתֵּם q. v.; K. וּלְהָתֵם pref. לְ)(Hiph. inf. constr.; וּ bef. (:) — תמם

לְחֹתְנוֹ[m] pref. לְ)(Kal part. act. masc., suff. 3 pers. sing. masc. from חֹתֵן dec. 7b — חתן

לָט וְ noun masc. sing.; for וְ see lett. ו — לוט

לָטָא Root not used; Arab. *to adhere to the ground.*

לְטָאָה fem. a species of *poisonous lizard*, Le. 11. 30. Vulg. stellio, *a newt.*

לְטֹבָה defect. for לְטוֹבָה (q. v.) — טוב

לִטְבֹּחַ pref. לְ bef. (:))(Kal inf. constr. (§ 8. r. 18) — טבח

לַטָּבַח in pause for לַטֶּבַח (q. v.) — טבח

לַטַּבָּח[n] pref. לַ for לְהַ)(noun masc. sing. dec. 1b — טבח

לַטֶּבַח pref. id., לְטֶבַח[o] pref. לְ, לַטָּבַח[p] pref. id. } noun masc. sing. dec. 6a (with suff. טִבְחָה, but comp. § 35. rem. 2) — טבח

לְטִבְחָה[q] pref. id.)(noun fem. sing. (no pl.) — טבח

לְטַבָּחוֹת[r] וּ pref. id.)(n. f., pl. of [טַבָּחָה] d. 10; וּ bef. (:) — טבח

לְטָהוֹר pref. לְ q. v.; לַטָּהוֹר[s], לַטָּהֹר[t] וְ pref. לַ f. לְהַ } adj. masc. sing. dec. 3a — טהר

לְטֹהַר[u] pref. לְ (see lett. ל))(noun masc. sing. d. 6f — טהר

לְטַהֵר pref. לְ)(Piel inf. constr. (§ 14. r. 1) dec. 7b — טהר

לְטַהֲרָהּ[x] pref. id.)(id., suff. 3 pers. sing. fem. — טהר

לְטַהֲרוֹ[y] pref. id.)(id., suff. 3 pers. sing. masc. — טהר

לְטַהֲרָם pref. id.)(id., suff. 3 pers. pl. masc. — טהר

לְטָהֳרָתוֹ pref. id.)(n. f. s., suff. 3 p. s. m. fr. [טָהֳרָה] d. 10 — טהר

לַטּוֹב[z] וְ pref. לַ f. לְהַ; לְטוֹב pref. לְ q. v. } (prim. adj.) subst. masc. sing. dec. 1a — טוב

לַטּוֹבָה[a] pref. לַ f. לְהַ; לְטוֹבָה pref. לְ q. v. } (prim. adj.) subst. fem. sing. dec. 10 — טוב

לְטוֹבִיָּה וּ pref. id.)(pr. name masc.; וּ bef. (:) — טוב

לַטּוֹבִים[b] pref. לַ for לְהַ)(adj. masc., pl. of טוֹב d. 1a — טוב

לָטוּחַ[c] pref. לְ (see lett. ל))(Kal inf. constr. — טוח

לְטוֹטָפֹת[d] e/ וּ pref. לְ)(n. f. pl. [for טֹטָפֹת]; וּ bef. (:) — טוף

לְטוּר[f] Chald., pref. id.)(noun masc. sing. dec. 1a — טור

לְטוּשִׁם וּ pr. name of a people; וּ bef. (:) — לטש

לְטֹטָפֹת[g] defect. for לְטוֹטָפֹת (q. v.) — טוף

לְטִירוֹתָם[h] pref. לְ)(n. f. pl., suff. 3 p. pl. m. fr. [טִירָה] d. 10 — טור

לַטָּמֵא[i] k/ וְ pref. לַ for לְהַ)(adj. masc. sing. dec. 5a — טמא

לְטַמֵּא[l] pref. לְ)(Piel inf. constr. dec. 7b — טמא

לַטְּמֵאָה[m] pref. לַ for לְהַ)(adj. fem. sing. dec. 10 — טמא

לְטָמְאָה pref. לְ)(Kal inf. constr. (§ 8. rem. 10) — טמא

לְטַמְּאוֹ pref. id.)(Piel inf. (טַמֵּא), suff. 3 p. s. m. d. 7b — טמא

לִטְמוֹן pref. לְ bef. (:))(Kal inf. constr. — טמן

לְטָמְנוֹ[n] pref. לְ)(id. with suff. 3 pers. sing. masc. — טמן

לָטַעַת[o] pref. לְ (see lett. ל))(Kal inf. constr. (§ 20. r. 1) — נטע

לְטַפְּכֶם pref. לְ)(n. m. s., suff. 2 p. pl. m. fr. טַף d. 8d — טפף

לְטַפֵּנוּ[p] q/ וּ pref. id.)(id. with suff. 1 p. pl.; וּ bef. (:) — טפף

לְטֹרַח[ff] pref. לְ (see lett. ל))(n. m. s. d. 6c (§ 35. r. 5) — טרח

לַטָּרֶף pref. לַ for לְהַ)(noun masc. sing. dec. 6a (for טֶרֶף § 35. rem. 2) — טרף

לִטְרֹף[r], לִטְרָף־[s] } pref. לְ bef. (:))(Kal inf. constr. (§ 8. r. 18) — טרף

[לָטַשׁ] *to sharpen*; metaph. *to sharpen the eye*, i. e. to cast a *sharp, penetrating* look, Job 16. 9. Pu. part. *sharpened*, Ps. 52. 4.

לְטוּשִׁם (*sharpened, sharp*) pr. name of an Arabian people, Ge. 25. 3.

---

[a] Is. 26. 16. [b] Mal. 3. 16. [c] Is. 30. 14. [d] Ec. 3. 7. [e] Job 28. 3. [f] Ge. 1. 5. [g] Hag. 2. 16. [h] Is. 30. 14. [i] Eze. 27. 5. [k] Da. 9. 24. [l] Da. 9. 24. [m] Ex. 18. 8, 15. [n] 1 Sa. 9. 23. [o] Eze. 21. 20. [p] Eze. 21. 33. [q] Je. 12. 3. [r] 1 Sa. 8. 13. [s] Ec. 9. 2. [t] Le. 20. 25. [u] Ex. 24. 10. [x] Eze. 39. 14. [y] Le. 13. 59. [z] Is. 5. 20. [a] Ne. 2. 18. [b] Ps. 125. 4. [c] 1 Ch. 29. 4. [d] De. 11. 18. [e] Ex. 13. 16. [f] Da. 2. 35. [ff] Is. 1. 14. [g] De. 6. 8. [h] 1 Ch. 6. 39. [i] Nu. 19. 17. [k] Ec. 9. 2. [l] Le. 20. 25. [m] Le. 20. 25. [n] Je. 13. 6. [o] Ec. 3. 2. [p] Nu. 32. 16. [q] Ezr. 8. 21. [r] Ps. 17. 12. [s] Eze. 19. 3, 6.

לֹטֵשׁ[a] Kal part. act. sing. masc. . . . . לטשׁ

לִי ,וְ' pref. prep. לְ with suff. 1 p. s. (§ 5, parad.) ל

לִיו[b] Kh. לִי q. v.; K. לָנוּ id. with suff. 1 pers. pl. ל

לְיָאֵשׁ[c] pref. לְ)(Piel inf. constr. . . . . יאשׁ

לְיֹאשִׁיָּהוּ pref. id.)(pr. name masc. . . . . אשה

לַיַּבָּשָׁה[d] pref. לַ f. לְהַ } noun fem. sing. . . יבשׁ
לְיַבָּשָׁה[e] pref. לְ q. v. }

לְיֹגְבִים[f] וּ pref. id.)(Kal part. act. masc., pl. of [יֹגֵב] dec. 7 b; וּ bef. (:) . . . . יגב

לְיָד pref. id.)(noun com. sing. dec. 2 a . . . יד

לְיַד pref. id.)(id. constr. (used with the suff. as a prep.) . . . . . יד

לְיָדוֹ[g] pref. id.)(id. with suff. 3 pers. sing. masc. יד

לְיַדּוֹת[h] pref. id.)(Piel inf. constr. . . . . ידה

לִידוּתוּן pref. לְ [for לִידוּ'])(pr. name masc. . . ידה

לְיָדַי pref. לְ)(noun com. sing., suff. 1 pers. sing. from יָד dec. 2 a . . . . . יד

לִידִידוֹ[k] pref. לְ [for לִיְ', לִידִידוֹ])(noun masc. sing., suff. 3 pers. sing. masc. fr. [יָדִיד] d. 3 a ידד

לִידִידִי pref. id.)(id. with suff. 1 pers. sing. . ידד

לִידִיתוּן Kh. לִידִיתוּן, K. לִידוּתוּן (q. v.) . . . ידה

לְיֹדְעַי pref. לְ)(Kal part. act. pl. masc., suff. 1 pers. sing. from יֹדֵעַ dec. 7 b . . . ידע

לְיָדְעֵי[m] Ch., pref. id.)(Peal part. act. pl. c. masc. from יְדַע dec. 2 a . . . . . ידע

לִידַעְיָה וְ' pref. לְ [for לִידַעְ'])(pr. name masc. . ידע

לְיֹדְעֶיךָ[n] pref. לְ)(the following with suff. 2 pers. s. m. ידע

לַיֹּדְעִים[o] pref. לַ for לְהַ)(Kal part. act. masc., pl. of יֹדֵעַ dec. 7 b . . . . . ידע

לִידֻתוּן defect. for לִידוּתוּן (q. v.) . . . . ידה

לְיֵהוּא pref. לְ)(pr. name masc., see יֵהוּא.

לִיהוֹאָחָז pref. לְ [for לִיהוֹ'])(pr. name masc. . הוה

לִיהוּד Ch., pref. id.)(pr. name of a country . ידה

לִיהוּדָה וְ' pref. id.)(pr. name of a man and a tribe ידה

לַיְּהוּדִים וְ' pref. לַ for לְהַ)(gent. masc., pl. of יְהוּדִי from יְהוּדָה . . . . . ידה

לַיהוָה וְ' the most sacred name of God (יהוה), with the vowels of אֲדֹנָי, whence pref. לַ bef. (-:) הוה

לֵיהוִֹה וְ id. with the vowels of אֱלֹהִים hence with pref. לֵאלֹהִים (q. v.) . . . . הוה

לִיהוֹיָדָע, לִיהוֹיָקִים, לִיהוֹיָרִיב, לִיהוֹנָתָן ,וְ' לִיהוֹרָם, לִיהוֹשֻׁעַ, לִיהוֹשָׁפָט pref. לְ [for לִיהוֹ'])(pr. names m. הוה

לְיוֹאָב ,וּ' לְיוֹאָשׁ, pref. לְ)(pr. names m.; וּ bef. (:) הוה

לִיוֹיָרִיב וּ pref. לְ)(pr. name m. (see יְהוֹיָרִיב); וּ bef. (:) וה

לְיוֹלַדְתָּהּ[p] pref. id.)(Kal part. act. sing. fem., suff. 3 pers. sing. fem. from יֹלֶדֶת dec. 13 a . ילד

לְיוֹלַדְתּוֹ[q] pref. id.)(id. with suff. 3 pers. sing. masc. ילד

לַיּוֹם pref. לַ for לְהַ } noun m. s. d. 1, but pl. irr. } יום
לְיוֹם[r] וּ' pref. לְ q. v. } יָמִים (§ 45); וּ bef. (:) }

לִיהוֹנָדָב pref. id.)(pr. name masc. (see יְהוֹנָדָב) . וה

לְיוֹנָה pref. id.)(pr. name masc., see יוֹנָה.

לְיוֹנָתָן וּ pref. id.)(pr. name masc.; וּ bef. (:) . וה

לְיוֹסֵף וּ' pref. id.)(pr. name masc.; וּ id. . סף

לְיוֹעֲצַי וּ pref. id.)(Kal part. act. pl. c. masc. from יוֹעֵץ dec. 7 b; וּ id. . . עץ

לַיּוֹצֵא[u] וְ' pref. לַ for לְהַ)(Kal part. act. s. m. d. 7 b. צא

לְיוֹרָם pref. לְ)(pr. name masc. . . . . וה

לְיוֹרְשִׁים[x] pref. id.)(Kal part. act. m., pl. of יוֹרֵשׁ d. 7 b רשׁ

לַיּוֹשֵׁב[y] pref. לַ for לְהַ } Kal part. act. s. m. d. 7 b שׁב
לְיוֹשֵׁב pref. לְ q. v. }

לְיוֹשְׁבֵי pref. id.)(id. pl. constr. st. . . . שׁב

לְיוֹשְׁבָיו[z] וּ pref. id.)(id., suff. 3 pers. s. m.; וּ bef. (:) שׁב

לֵיוֹת[a] וְ' noun fem. pl. of [לְיָה] dec. 10 . . . וה

לְיוֹתָם pref. לְ)(pr. name masc. . . . . וה

לְיִזְרְעֶאל pref. id.)(pr. name of a place . . רע

לְיַחַד[b] pref. id.)(for יַחַד, adv. with and without pref. חד

לִיחִזְקֵאל pref. לְ [for לִיחִזְ'], לִיחִזְקִיָּה, לִיחִזְקִיָּהוּ, pr. names masc. . . . . . זק

לְיַחְלְאֵל pref. לְ)(pr. name masc. . . . . חל

לְיַחֲמֶנָּה[c] pref. id.)(Piel inf. (יִחֵם § 14. rem. 1), suff. 3 pers. sing. fem. . . . . חם

לְיַחְצְאֵל pref. id.)(pr. name masc. . . . . צה

לַיַּיִן[d] pref. לַ for לְהַ)(noun masc. sing. dec. 6 h ין

לְיָכִין pref. לְ)(pr. name masc. . . . . ון

לַיִל masc. dec. 6 h, most frequently with ה parag. לַיְלָה (pl. לֵילוֹת) *night*; trop. for *calamity, adversity*; adv. בַּלַּיְלָה, לַיְלָה, לֵילוֹת *by night*; הַלַּיְלָה *this night, to-night.*

לֵילְיָא Ch. m. *night*, only in the emph. st. לֵילְיָא

לִילִית fem. *screech-owl*, Is. 34. 14.

לֵיל noun masc. sing., constr. of לַיִל dec. 6 h . יל

לַיֶּלֶד[f] pref. לַ for לְהַ)(noun masc. sing. dec. 6 a, for יֶלֶד (§ 35. rem. 2) . . . לד

לַיְלָה וְ' } noun masc. sing. (לַיִל with parag. ה, } יל
לָיְלָה וָ', וְ' } dec. 6 h; for וָ see lett. ו . }

[a] Ge. 4. 22. [b] 2 Sa. 21. 4. [c] Ec. 2. 20. [d] Ge. 1. 10. [e] Ps. 66. 6. [f] Je. 52. 16. [g] Ex. 21. 13. [h] Zec. 2. 4. [i] Job 17. 3. [k] Ps. 127. 2. [l] Ps. 87. 4. [m] Da. 2. 21. [n] Ps. 36. 11. [o] Ec. 9. 11. [p] Ca. 6. 9. [q] Pr. 17. 25. [r] Ho. 9. 5. [s] Pr. 12. 20. [t] 2 Ch. 15. 5. [u] Zec. 8. 10. [x] Je. 8. 10. [y] Is. 28. 6. [z] Je. 19. 12. [a] 1 Ki. 7. 29, 30, 36. [b] 1 Ch. 12. 17. [c] Ge. 30. 41. [d] Mi. 2. 11. [e] Ex. 12. 42. [f] 2 Ki. 4. 26.

לֵילוֹת [a] וְ' id. with pl. fem. term. . . . ליל

לֵילְיָא Ch. noun masc. sing. emph. [of לֵילֵי] . ליל

לִילִית [zz] noun fem. sing. . . . . ליל

לַיָּם pref. לְ for לַה) noun masc. sing. dec. 8 a . ים

לְיַם [b] pref. לְ) id. constr. st. . . . . ים

לְיַמָּא [c] Ch., pref. id.) id. emph. st. dec. 5 a . ים

לַיָּמָּה [d] pref. לְ for לַה) id. with loc. ה . . ים

לִימֵי [e] pref. לְ [for לְיְ' לִימֵי]) constr. of the foll. . יום

לַיָּמִים pref. לְ for לַה } n. m. pl. [as if fr. יָם d. 2 a], see יוֹם (§ 45); וּ bef. (:) יום

לְיָמִים [f] וּ' pref. לְ q. v. }

לַיָּמִין [g] pref. לְ for לַה) noun masc. sing. dec. 3 a . ימן

לְיָמִין pref. לְ) pr. name masc. . . . . ימן

לִימִין pref. לְ [for לְיְ' לִימִין]) noun masc. sing., constr. of יָמִין dec. 3 a . . . . ימן

לִימִינוֹ pref. id.) id., suff. 3 pers. sing. masc. . ימן

לִימִינִי [h] pref. id.) id., suff. 1 pers. sing. . . ימן

לִימִינְךָ [cc] pref. id.) id., suff. 2 pers. sing. masc. . ימן

לְיִמְנָה pref. לְ) pr. name masc. . . . . ימן

לִין [i] וְ' Kal imp. sing. masc. R. לִין, see לון

לִינוּ [k] וְ' id. imp. pl. masc. . . . . . לון

לִינִי [l] id. imp. sing. fem. . . . . . לון

לְיַסֵּד pref. לְ) Piel inf. constr. . . . . יסד

לִיסּוֹד [m] } pref. לְ [for לִיסוֹד]) Kal inf. constr. (§ 8. rem. 18) . . . יסד

לִיסֹד [n] וְ }

לְיַסְּרָה [o] pref. לְ) Piel inf. [יַסֵּר] with fem. term. . יסר

לְיַסְּרֶךָּ [p] pref. id.) id. with suff. 2 p. s. m. (§ 2. r. 2) יסר

לִיעֻזְיָהוּ pref. id.) pr. name masc. . . . עזה

לַיְּעֵלִים [q] pref. לְ for לַה) noun masc., pl. of יָעֵל d. 5 יעל

לַיָּעֵף [r] pref. id.) adj. masc. sing. dec. 5 a . . יעף

לְיַעֲקֹב וּ' pref. לְ) pr. name masc.; וּ bef. (:) . עקב

לַיַּעַר pref. לְ f. לַה } noun masc. sing. dec. 6 d . יער

לְיַעַר pref. לְ q. v. }

לְיֶפֶת pref. id.) pr. name masc. . . . . פתה

לְיִפְתָּח pref. id.) pr. name masc. . . . . פתח

לְיַצָּבָא Chald., pref. id.) Pael inf. constr. . יצב

לַיִּצְהָרִי pref. לְ for לַה) patronym. of יִצְהָר . צהר

לְיִצְחָק וּ' pref. לְ) pr. name masc.; וּ bef. (:) . צחק

לְיֵצֶר pref. id.) noun masc. sing. dec. 6 b . . יצר

לְיֵצֶר pref. id.) pr. name masc. . . . . יצר

לְיֹצְרוֹ pref. id.) Kal part. act. masc., suff. 3 pers. sing. masc. from יוֹצֵר dec. 7 b . . . . יצר

לַיִּצְרִי pref. לְ for לַה) patronym. of יֵצֶר . . יצר

לִיקְדַת [u] Chald., pref. לְ [for לְיְ' לִיקְדַת]) noun fem. sing., constr. of [יְקֵדָא] dec. 8 a . . יקד

לִיקְהַת [x] pref. id.) n. f. s. constr. [of יְקָהָה or יִקְהָה] יקה

לְיָקִים pref. לְ) pr. name masc. . . . . קום

לְיָקְמְעָם pref. id.) pr. name of a place . . קמה

לִיקָר [y] וְ Chald., pref. לְ [for לִיקָר]) noun masc. sing., constr. of יְקָר dec. 1 b . . . יקר

לְיִרְאָה וּ' pref. לְ) Kal inf. constr. (§ 8. r. 10); וּ bef. (:) ירא

לְיִרְאֵי pref. id.) adj. pl. constr. masc. from יָרֵא d. 5 a ירא

לִירֵאָיו pref. לְ [for לְיְרֵ']) id. pl., suff. 3 pers. s. m. ירא

לִירֵאֶיךָ pref. id.) id. pl., suff. 2 pers. sing. masc. . ירא

לְיָרְאָם [z] pref. לְ) Piel inf. [יָרֵא], suff. 3 p. pl. m. d. 7 b ירא

לְיִרְאָנִי [a] pref. id.) id. with suff. 1 pers. sing. . ירא

לְיִרְאָתֶךָ [b] pref. id.) noun fem. sing., suff. 2 pers. sing. masc. from יִרְאָה (no pl.) . . . ירא

לִירָבְעָם pref. id.) pr. name masc. . . . ריב

לַיַּרְדֵּן pref. לְ f. לַה } pr. name of a river . . ירד

לְיַרְדֵּן pref. לְ q. v. }

לִירוֹא [c] pref. לְ [for לִירוֹא]) Kal inf. constr. [for יְרֹה § 24. rem. 18] . . . . ירה

לִירוּשָׁלַיִם וְ' } pref. לְ [for לִירוּ']) pr. name of a city . . . . ירה

לִירוּשָׁלַם וְ' }

לִירוּשְׁלֶם וְ' Ch. }

לִירוֹת pref. לְ [for לִירוֹת]) Kal inf. constr. . . ירה

לַיָּרֵחַ [d] וְ' pref. לְ for לַה) noun masc. sing. dec. 5 a ירח

לִירַח [e] Chald., pref. לְ [for לְיְ' לִירַח]) n. m. s. d. 3 a ירח

לִירַחְמְאֵל pref. id.) pr. name masc. . . . רחם

לִירְחָע pref. לְ) pr. name masc., see יַרְחָע.

לִירִיחוֹ pref. לְ [for לִירִי']) pr. name of a place רוח

לְיַרְכְּתֵי וּ pref. לְ) noun fem. du., constr. [from יֶרֶךְ = יַרְכָה m. § 39. No. 3. r. 3]; וּ bef. (:) ירך

לַיַּרְכָתַיִם pref. לְ f. לַה) id. du. abs. [fr. יָרֵךְ = יַרְכָה m.] ירך

לִירֵמוֹת pref. לְ [for לִירֵ']) pr. name masc. . . ירם

לְיִרְמְיָה }

לְיִרְמְיָהוּ } pref. לְ) pr. name masc. . . . רמה

לַיֵּרָקוֹן [f] pref. id.) noun masc. sing. . . . ירק

לִירֻשָּׁתוֹ [g] pref. לְ [for לִירֻשׁ']) noun fem. sing., suff. 3 pers. sing. fem. from יְרֻשָּׁה dec. 10 . ירש

לַיִשׁ [h] וְ' n. m. s., also pr. name; for וְ see lett. ו לוש

לְיֶשֶׁבְאָב pref. לְ) pr. name masc. . . . ישב

לְיֹשְׁבֵי וּ' pref. id.) constr. of the foll.; וּ bef. (:) ישב

לַיֹּשְׁבִים [i] pref. לְ for לַה) Kal part. act. masc., pl. of יוֹשֵׁב dec. 7 b . . . . . ישב

---

[a] Job 7. 3. [b] Jos. 4. 23. [c] Da. 7. 2. [d] Jos. 19. 11. [e] Job 33. 25. [f] Ge. 1. 14. [g] Ne. 12. 31. [h] Ps. 110. 1. [i] Ju. 19. 6, 9. [k] Ge. 19. 2. [l] Ru. 3. 13. [m] 2 Ch. 31. 7. [n] Is. 51. 16. [o] Le. 26. 18. [p] De. 4. 36. [q] Ps. 104. 18. [r] Is. 40. 29. [s] Da. 7. 19. [t] 1 Ch. 29. 13. [u] Da. 7. 11. [x] Pr. 30. 17. [y] Da. 4. 27, 33. [z] 2 Ch. 32. 18 [zz] Is. 34. 14. [a] Ne. 6. 19. [b] Ps. 119. 38. [c] 2 Ch. 26. 15. [cc] Ps. 45. 10. [d] De. 17. 3. [e] Ezr. 6. 15. [f] Je. 30. 6. [g] De. 3. 20. [h] Is. 30. 6. [i] Is. 23. 18.

לִישְׁבַּקְשָׁה pref. לְ)(pr. name masc. ישב

לַיְשָׁה, לָיְשָׁה } pr. name of a place (לַיִשׁ) with loc. ה לוש

לְיָשׁוּב pref. לְ)(pr. name masc. שוב

לְיִשְׁוִי pref. id.)(pr. name masc. שוה

לִישׁוֹן[a] pref. לְ [for לְיְ, לְיִשׁוֹן])(Kal inf. constr. ישן

לְיֵשׁוּעַ pref. לְ)(pr. name masc., see יֵשׁוּעַ.

לִישׁוּעָה pref. לְ [for לִיְשׁוּ])(noun fem. sing. dec. 10 ישע

לִישׁוּעָתֶךָ, לִישׁוּעָתְךָ[b] } pref. id.)(id., suff. 2 pers. sing. masc. ישע

לְיִשְׂחָק pref. לְ)(pr. name masc., see יִצְחָק under צחק

לְיִשַׁי pref. id.)(pr. name masc. ישה

לְיִשְׁמָעֵאל וּ pref. id.)(pr. name masc.; וּ bef. (:) שמע

לַיִּשְׁמְעֵאלִים pref. לַ for לְהַ)(patronym. pl. from the prec. שמע

לְיֶשַׁע[c] pref. לְ)(noun masc. sing. dec. 6 (§ 35. r. 6) ישע

לִישֻׁעָתָה[d] pref. לְ [for לְיְ, לִישׁ])(noun fem. sing. (יְשׁוּעָה) with parag. ה ישע

לְיִשְׂרָאֵל וּ' pref. לְ)(pr. name of a man and a people; וּ bef. (:) שרה

לְיִשְׁרֵי[e] וּ' pref. id.)(constr. of the foll.; וּ id. ישר

לַיְשָׁרִים pref. לַ for לְהַ } adj. pl. masc. from יָשָׁר dec. 4a. ישר
לִישָׁרִים[cc] וְ pref. לְ [f. לְיְשָׁ] }

לְיִשָּׂשכָר pref. לְ)(pr. name masc. שכר

לַיָּתֵד[f] pref. לַ for לְהַ)(noun fem. sing. dec. 5a יתד

לַיָּתוֹם pref. id.)(noun masc. sing. dec. 3a יתם

לִיתוֹמָיו[g] pref. לְ [for לְיְ, לִיתוֹ])(id. pl., suff. 3 p. s. m. יתם

לְיֶתֶר וּ pref. לְ)(noun masc. sing. (suff. יִתְרוֹ) dec. 6a; וּ bef. (:) יתר

לְיֶתֶר pref. id.)(pr. name masc. יתר

לָךְ וְ' pref. prep. ל with suff. 2 p. s. f. (§ 5, parad.) ל

לְךָ וְ', לָךְ וּ' } id. with suff. 2 pers. sing. m.; וּ bef. (:); וָ in pause ל

לֵךְ, לְךָ וְ' וּ', לֶךְ, לֵךְ וְ' } Kal imp. sing. masc. (§ 20. rem. 3); for וָ see lett. ו ילך

לְכָבוֹד וּ' pref. לְ)(noun masc. sing. d. 3a; וּ bef. (:) כבד

לִכְבוֹדִי[h] וְ pref. לְ bef. (:))(id. with suff. 1 pers. sing. כבד

לִכְבּוֹשׁ[i] in full for לִכְבֹּשׁ (q. v. & § 8. rem. 18) כבש

לְכַבּוֹת[k] pref. לְ)(Piel inf. constr. כבה

לַכֶּבֶשׂ pref. לַ for לְהַ)(noun masc. sing. dec. 6a כבשׂ

לִכְבֹּשׁ[l] pref. לְ bef. (:))(Kal inf. constr. כבש

לַכְּבָשִׂים וְ pref. לַ for לְהַ)(noun m., pl. of כֶּבֶשׂ d. 6a כבשׂ

לָכַד[m] וְ' I. *to take, catch.*—II. *to intercept*, Ju. 7. 24.—III. *to take, choose*, by lot, Jos. 7. 17. Niph. *to be taken, caught.* Hithp. *to take* or *catch hold on each other, to hang together*, Job 38. 30; 41. 9.

לֶכֶד masc. *capture*, Pr. 3. 26.

מַלְכֹּדֶת fem. dec. 13c, *snare, trap*, Job 18. 10.

לָכָד[n] Kal pret. 3 pers. sing. masc. for לָכַד (§ 8. r. 7) לכד

לֹכֵד[o] id. part. act. sing. masc. לכד

לְכָדָהּ[p] וְ id. imp. sing. masc., suff. 3 pers. sing. fem. לכד

לְכָדָהּ וּ id. pret. 3 pers. sing. masc., suff. 3 pers. sing. fem.; וּ for וְ conv. לכד

לְכָדֻהָ[q] וּ id. pret. 3 p. pl. [לָכְדוּ], suff. 3 p. s. f.; וּ id. לכד

לִכְדוּ[r] וְ id. imp. pl. masc. לכד

לְכָדוּהָ[s] וּ id. pret. 3 pers. pl., suff. 3 pers. sing. fem.; וּ for וְ conv. לכד

לָכָדְנוּ[t] id. pret. 1 pers. pl. [for לָכַדְנוּ § 8. rem. 7] לכד

לָכַדְתִּי[u] id. pret. 1 pers. sing. לכד

לֵכָה pr. name of a place ילך

לְכָה[w] וְ, לְכָה וּ' } Kal imp. sing. masc. with parag. ה (§ 20. rem. 3); וּ bef. (:) ילך

לְכָה[y] [x]וּ' pref. prep. ל with suff. 2 pers. sing. masc. (§ 5. rem. 3); וּ id. ל

לַכֹּהֵן pref. לַ for לְהַ)(noun masc. sing. dec. 7b כהן

לְכַהֵן pref. לְ)(Piel inf. constr. (§ 14. rem. 1) כהן

לְכֹהֵן וּ' pref. id.)(noun masc. sing. d. 7b; וּ bef. (:) כהן

לְכַהֲנוֹ[a] pref. id.)(Piel inf. [כַּהֵן § 14. rem. 1], suff. 3 pers. masc. dec. 7b כהן

לְכֹהֲנֶיהָ[b] pref. id.)(the foll. with suff. 3 pers. sing. fem. כהן

לַכֹּהֲנִים וּ' pref. לַ for לְהַ)(noun masc., pl. of כֹּהֵן d. 7b כהן

לְכֹהֲנֵינוּ[c] וּ pref. לְ)(id. with suff. 1 pers. pl.; וּ bef. (:) כהן

לִכְהֻנַּת[d] pref. לְ bef. (:))(n. f. s., constr. of כְּהֻנָּה d. 10 כהן

לְכוּ וְ', לְכוּ וּ' } Kal imp. pl. masc.; וּ bef. (:), וָ bef. pause ילך

לָכוֹד[e] וְ Kal inf. abs. לכד

לְכוֹכְבֵי[f] pref. לְ)(constr. of the foll. כבב

לַכּוֹכָבִים[ff] pref. לַ for לְהַ)(noun masc., pl. of כּוֹכָב dec. 2b [for כַּבְכָּב] כבב

לְכֹל[g] pref. לְ)(Kh. לְכוֹל, K. לְכָל־; noun masc. sing. [כֹּל] dec. 8c (§ 37. rem. 2) כלל

לְכוֹן[h] Chald., pref. prep. ל with suff. 2 pers. pl. m. ל

לְכֹרֶשׁ pref. לְ)(pr. name masc. כרש

לַכּוּשִׁי pref. לַ for לְהַ)(gent. noun from כּוּשׁ כוש

לְכֹחִי[i] pref. לְ)(noun masc. sing. dec. 1a כוח

[a] Ec. 5. 11. [b] Ps. 119. 123. [c] Hab. 3. 13. [d] Ps. 80. 3. [e] Ps. 97. 11. [f] Ju. 5. 26. [g] Ps. 109. 12. [h] Is. 43. 7. [i] Est. 7. 8. [k] Ca. 8. 7. [l] 2 Ch. 28. 10. [m] Da. 11. 15, 18. [n] Am. 3. 4. [o] Job 5. 13. [p] 2 Sa. 12. 28. [q] Je. 37. 8. [r] Ju. 7. 24. [s] Je. 34. 22. [t] De. 2. 35. [u] 2 Sa. 12. 27. [x] 1 Sa. 23. 27. [y] Is. 3. 6. [z] Ge. 27. 37; 2 Sa. 18. 22. [a] Ex. 28. 1, 3, 4. [b] Je. 1. 18. [c] Ne. 9. 32. [cc] Ps. 125. 4. [d] Ex. 40. 15. [e] Am. 3. 5. [f] Is. 14. 13. [ff] Ps. 147. 4. [g] Je. 33. 8. [h] Da. 3. 4. [i] Job 9. 19.

Word	Explanation	Root
לְכִי	Kh. לְכִי q. v., K. לָךְ (q. v.)	ל
לְכִי / לֵכִי / וּ' לְכִי	Kal imp. sing. fem.; וּ bef. (:)	ילך
לַכִּידוֹר[a]	pref. לַ for לְהַ) noun masc. sing.	כדר
וּלְכִילַי[b]	וּ pref. לְ) noun m. sing. [for נְכִילַי]; וּ bef. (:)	נכל
לַכִּיּר[c]	pref. לַ for לְהַ) noun masc. sing. dec. 1b	כור
לָכִישׁ	pr. name of a fortified city in the tribe of Judah.	
לָכִישָׁה	id. with parag. ה.	
לְכִכָּרִים	pref. לְ) n. f., pl. of כִּכָּר d. 2b [for כִּרְכָּר]	כרר
לַכֹּל	pref. לַ for לְהַ } noun masc. sing. dec. 8c (§ 37. rem. 2); וּ bef. (:)	כלל
וּ' לְכֹל / וּ' לְכָל־	pref. לְ q. v. } noun masc. sing. dec. 8c (§ 37. rem. 2); וּ bef. (:)	כלל
לְכַלֵּא[d]	pref. id.) Piel inf. constr. for לְכַלֵּה (§ 24. r. 19)	כלה
לְכָלָא[e]	Chald., pref. id.) noun masc. emph. by Syriasm [for כֻּלָּא] from כֹּל dec. 5c	כלל
לַכֶּלֶב[f]	pref. לַ for לְהַ) n. m. s. (pl. c. כַּלְבֵי) d. 6a	כלב
וּ' לְכָלֵב	pref. לְ) pr. name masc.; וּ bef. (:)	כלב
לְכֶלֶב[g]	pref. id.) noun masc. s. (pl. c. כַּלְבֵי) d. 6a	כלב
לְכַלָּה	pref. id.) noun fem. sing.	כלה
לְכַלֵּה	pref. id.) Piel inf. constr.	כלה
לְכֻלְּהֵנָה[h]	pref. id.) noun masc. sing., suff. 3 pers. pl. fem. (§ 3. rem. 5) from כֹּל dec. 8c	כלל
לִכְלוֹא[i]	pref. לְ bef. (:)) Kal inf. constr. (§ 8. r. 18)	כלא
לְכַלּוֹת	pref. לְ) Piel inf. constr.	כלה
לִכְלוֹת[k]	pref. לְ bef. (:)) Kal inf. constr.	כלה
לְכִלְיוֹן	pref. לְ) pr. name masc.	כלה
לְכַלְכֵּל[l]	m וּ' pref. id.) Pilp. (§ 6. No. 4) inf. constr. dec. 7b; וּ bef. (:)	כול
לְכַלְכֶּלְךָ[n] / לְכַלְכֶּלְךָ[o]	pref. id.) id. with suff. 2 pers. sing. masc.	כול
לְכֻלְּכֶם[p]	pref. id.) n. m. s., suff. 2 p. pl. m. fr. כֹּל d. 8c	כלל
לְכֻלָּם	pref. id.) id., suff. 3 pers. pl. masc.	כלל
לִכְלִמָּה	pref. לְ bef. (:)) noun fem. sing. dec. 10	כלם
לְכֻלָּנוּ	pref. לְ) n. m. s., suff. 1 p. pl. from כֹּל d. 8c	כלל
לְכַלָּתָהּ[q]	pref. id.) n. f. s., suff. 3 p. s. f. fr. כַּלָּה d. 10	כלל
לְכַלֹּתָם	r וּ' pref. id.) Piel inf. (כַּלּוֹת), suff. 3 pers. pl. masc. dec. 1b	כלה
לָכֶם	וּ' pref. prep. ל with suff. 2 p. pl. m. (§ 5, parad.)	ל
לְכֹם[s]	וּ Chald. id. with suff. 2 pers. pl. masc.	ל
לִכְמוֹשׁ	וּ' pref. ל bef. (:)) pr. name of an idol, see כְּמוֹשׁ	
לָכֵן	וּ' pref. לָ (see lett. ל)) adv.	כון
לֵכְןָ[t]	Kal imp. pl. f., for לֵכְנָה (comp. § 8. r. 16)	ילך
לָכֵנָה[u]	pref. prep. ל with suff. 2 pers. pl. fem. (§ 5, parad. & rem. 3)	ל
לֵכְנָה[x]	Kal imp. pl. fem.	ילך
לִכְנוֹס[y]	וּ' pref. ל bef. (:)) Kal inf. constr. (§ 8. r. 18)	כנס
לְכַנִּם[z]	pref. לְ) noun masc., pl. of כֵּן dec. 8b	כנן
לַכְּנַעֲנִי	pref. לַ for לְהַ) gent. noun from כְּנַעַן	כנע
לִכְנַעֲנִי[a]	pref. id.) noun masc. sing., pl. כְּנַעֲנִים	כנע
לִכְנַף[b]	pref. ל bef. (:)) noun f. s. d. 4a (§ 33. r. 1)	כנף
לַכִּסֵּא	pref. לַ f. לְהַ } noun masc. sing. dec. 7b	כסא
לְכִסֵּא	pref. לְ q. v. } noun masc. sing. dec. 7b	כסא
לְכִסְאוֹ[c]	וּ pref. id.) id., suff. 3 pers. s. m.; וּ bef. (:)	כסא
לַכִּסֵּה[d]	for לַכִּסֵּא (q. v.)	כסא
לְכַסּוֹת	pref. לְ) Piel inf. constr. dec. 1b	כסה
לִכְסִיל	pref. ל bef. (:)) noun masc. sing. dec. 1a	כסל
לְכִסְלָה[e]	pref. לְ) noun fem. sing. (no pl.)	כסל
לַכֶּסֶף	וּ' pref. לַ f. לְהַ } noun masc. sing. dec. 6a	כסף
לְכֶסֶף	pref. לְ q. v. } noun masc. sing. dec. 6a	כסף
לְכַסְפִּי[f]	וּ pref. id.) id., suff. 1 pers. sing.; וּ bef. (:)	כסף
לְכַסְפָּם[g]	pref. id.) id., suff. 3 pers. pl. masc.	כסף
לְכַסֹּת[h]	pref. id.) Piel inf. constr. dec. 1b	כסה
לְכַסֹּתוֹ[i]	pref. id.) id., suff. 3 pers. sing. masc.	כסה
לִכְעוֹס[k]	pref. ל bef. (:)) Kal inf. constr. (§ 8. r. 18)	כעס
לְכַף	pref. לְ) noun fem. sing. dec. 8d	כפף
לִכְפוֹר[l]	pref. ל bef. (:)) noun masc. sing. dec. 1a	כפר
לִכְפוֹרֵי[m]	וְ pref. id.) id. pl., constr. st.	כפר
לְכָפָן[n]	וּ pref. ל noun masc. sing.; וּ bef. (:)	כפן
לְכַפֵּר	וּ' pref. id.) Piel inf. constr. dec. 7b; וּ id.	כפר
לַכְּפִרִים[o]	pref. ל for לְהַ) noun m., pl. of כְּפִיר dec. 1a	כפר
לְכַפָּתָה[p]	Chald., pref. לְ) Pael inf. constr. (§ 47. r. 5)	כפת
לַכְּרֻבִים[q]	defect. for לַכְּרוּבִים (q. v.)	כרב
לַכְּרוּב	pref. ל f. לְהַ } noun masc. sing. dec. 1a	כרב
לִכְרוּב[r]	pref. ל bef. (:) } noun masc. sing. dec. 1a	כרב
לַכְּרוּבִים[s]	pref. לַ for לְהַ) id. pl., abs. st.	כרב
לִכְרוֹת	in full for לִכְרֹת (q. v. & § 8. rem. 18)	כרת
לַכָּרִי[t]	pref. לַ for לְהַ) noun masc. either sing. or pl. comp. הַכָּרִי	כור
לְכַרְמוֹ[u]	pref. לְ) noun masc. sing., suff. 3 pers. sing. masc. from כֶּרֶם dec. 6a	כרם
לְכַרְמִי	pref. id.) pr. name masc.	כרם
לְכַרְמִי[x]	pref. id.) noun masc. sing., suff. 1 pers. sing. from כֶּרֶם dec. 6a	כרם
לְכֹרְמִים	pref. id.) noun masc., pl. of [כֹּרֵם] dec. 7b	כרם

[a] Job 15. 24. [b] Is. 32. 5. [c] 1 Ki. 7. 30. [d] Da. 9. 24. [e] Da. 4. 9, 18. [f] Ex. 22. 30. [g] Ec. 9. 4. [h] 1 Ki. 7. 37. [i] Ec. 8. 8. [k] 2 Ch. 36. 22, etc. [l] 1 Ki. 4. 7. [m] Ru. 4. 15. [n] 1 Ki. 17. 9. [o] 1 Ki. 17. 4. [p] 1 Sa. 22. 7. [q] Ru. 2. 20. [r] Ex. 32. 12. [s] Ezr. 5. 3, 9; 7. 24. [t] Ru. 1. 12. [u] Eze. 13. 18. [x] Ru. 1. 8. [y] Ec. 2. 26. [z] Ex. 8. 12. [a] Pr. 31. 24. [b] 2 Ch. 3. 11, 12. [c] 1 Ki. 2. 33. [d] 1 Ki. 10. 19. [e] Ps. 85. 9. [f] 1 Ki. 20. 7. [g] Ho. 9. 6. [h] Nu. 4. 15. [i] Ex. 26. 13. [k] Ec. 7. 9. [l] 1 Ch. 28. 17. [m] 1 Ch. 28. 17. [n] Job 5. 22. [o] Na. 2. 12. [p] Da. 3. 20. [q] Eze. 10. 2, 7, 8. [r] Eze. 41. 18. [s] Eze. 10. 7. [t] 2 Ki. 11. 4. [u] Is. 5. 1. [x] Is. 5. 4, 5.

לַכְּרָמִים[a] pref. לַ for לְהַ)(noun m., pl. of כֶּרֶם d. 6a כרם
לְכַרְמְךָ[b] pref. לְ)(id. sing., suff. 2 pers. sing. masc. כרם
לַכַּרְמֶל pref. לַ for לְהַ)(pr. name of a place . כרם
לִכְרֹת, לִכְרָת־ pref. לִ bef. (:))(Kal inf. constr. (§ 8. rem. 18) . . . . כרת
לְכֹרְתֵי[c] pref. לְ)(Kal part. act. pl. c. fr. כֹּרֵת d. 7 b כרת
לַכַּשְׂדִּים וְ pref. לַ for לְהַ)(gent. noun, pl. of כַּשְׂדִּי כשד
לְכַשְׂדָּיֵא Ch., pref. id.)(Kh. כַּשְׂדָּיֵא, K. כַּשְׂדָּאֵי, gent. noun pl. emph. fr. כַּשְׂדַּי dec. 7 (§ 63) כשד
לֶכֶת, לֶכֶת Kal inf. constr. (suff. לֶכְתּוֹ) dec. 13a (§ 44. rem. 3) . . . ילך
לִכְתֹּב pref. לִ bef. (:))(Kal inf. constr. . כתב
לֶכְתּוֹ[d] Kal inf. (לֶכֶת), suff. 3 pers. sing. m. d. 13 (§ 44. rem. 3) . . . . ילך
לֶכְתִּי[e] id., suff. 1 pers. sing. . . . ילך
לֶכְתְּךָ[f] id., suff. 2 pers. sing. masc. . . . ילך
לֶכְתֵּךְ[g] id., suff. 2 pers. sing. fem. . . . ילך
לֶכְתָּם[h] id., suff. 3 pers. pl. masc. . . . ילך
לַכֶּתֶם[i] וְ pref. לַ for לְהַ)(noun masc. sing. . כתם
לַכָּתֵף[k] וְ׳ pref. id.)(noun fem. sing. dec. 5 b . כתף
לְכֶתֶף[l] pref. לְ)(id. constr. st. . . . כתף
לַכֹּתָרֹת[m], לַכֹּתֶרֶת[n] pref. לַ for לְהַ)(noun fem. pl. & sing. (§ 44. rem. 5) . . . כתר
לְלֹא[o] וּ׳ pref. לְ)(adv. (in 2 Ch. 15. 3, it forms a *prep*. with the pref.); וּ bef. (:) . לא
לְלֵאָה וּ׳ pref. id.)(pr. name fem.; וּ id. . . לאה
לֻלָאֹת noun pl. abs. fem. [fr. לוּלַי § 35. r. 15 note] לול
לֻלְאֹת id. pl., constr. st. . . . . לול
לִלְבָאֹתָיו[p] pref. לְ)(noun pl. fem. [לְבָאוֹת], suff. 3 pers. sing. masc. [fr. לְבִי § 35. rem. 15] . לבא
לַלֵּבָב[q] pref. לַ for לְהַ)(noun masc. sing. dec. 4 b לבב
לִלְבָבָם[r] pref. לִ bef. (:))(id., suff. 3 pers. pl. masc. לבב
לִלְבוֹנָה pref. id.)(pr. name of a city . . לבן
לִלְבוּשֶׁךָ pref. id.)(noun masc. sing., suff. 2 pers. sing. masc. [for לְבוּשְׁךָ] fr. לְבוּשׁ dec. 1a . לבש
לְלָבִיא[s] pref. לְ)(noun masc. sing. . . לבא
לְלָבָן וּ׳ pref. id.)(pr. name masc.; וּ bef. (:) . לבן
לְלָבָן[t] pref. id.)(adj. masc. sing. dec. 4 a . לבן
לַלְבֵּן[u] וְ pref. לַ, contr. [for לְהַלְבֵּן] Hiph. inf. constr. (§ 11. rem. 2 & 3) . . . לבן
לִלְבֹּן[x] pref. לִ bef. (:))(Kal inf. constr. . לבן
לִלְבְנָה pref. לְ)(pr. name of a place . . לבן

לִלְבֹּשׁ pref. לִ bef. (:))(Kal inf. constr. . . לבש
לְלֶדֶה pref. לְ)(Kal inf. with fem. term. (§ 20. r. 3) ילד
לָלֶדֶת pref. לָ (see lett. ל))(id. inf. constr. d. 13a ילד
לְלִדְתִּי[y] pref. לְ)(id. with suff. 1 pers. sing. . ילד
לְלֶהָבָה[z] pref. id.)(noun fem. sing. dec. 11 a . להב
לְלוֹא[a] in full for לְלֹא (q. v.) . . . . לא
לְלוֹט pref. לְ)(pr. name masc. . . . לוט
לַלֵּוִי pref. לַ for לְהַ, וּ׳ לְלֵוִי pref. לְ q. v. — pr. name masc., or gent. noun [for לֵוִיִּי] . לוה
לַלְוִיִּם וְ׳ pref. לַ for לְהַ)(pl. of the preceding . לוה
לָלוּן pref. לָ (see lett. ל))(Kal inf. constr. . לון
לִלְחוֹם[b] pref. לִ bef. (:))(Kal inf. constr. . . לחם
לַלֶּחֶם[c], וְ׳ לַלֶּחֶם[d] pref. לַ f. לְהַ; לְלֶחֶם[e], וְ׳ לְלֶחֶם[f] pref. לְ q. v. — noun com. s. d. 6a (§ 35. rem. 1); וּ bef. (:) לחם
לְלַחְמְךָ[g] pref. id.)(id. with suff. 2 pers. sing. masc. לחם
לִלְטוֹשׁ[h] pref. לִ bef. (:))(Kal inf. constr. (§ 8. r. 18) לטש
לְלַיְלָה[i] pref. לְ)(noun masc. sing. (לַיִל) with parag. ה dec. 6 h . . . . . ליל
לָלִין[k] pref. לָ (see lett. ל))(Kal inf. constr. R. לִין, see לון
לְלָכְדָהּ[l] pref. לְ)(Kal inf., suff. 3 pers. sing. fem. לכד
לְלָכְדֵנִי[m] pref. id.)(id. with suff. 1 pers. sing. . לכד
לְלָכִישׁ pref. id.)(pr. name of a place, see לָכִישׁ.
לָלֶכֶת[n], וְ׳ לָלֶכֶת pref. לָ (see lett. ל))(Kal inf. constr. dec. 13 (§ 44. rem. 3) . ילך
לְלַמֵּד[o] וּ׳ pref. לְ)(Piel inf. constr. d. 7 b; וּ bef. (:) למד
לְלַמְּדָם[p] וּ׳[q] pref. id.)(id., suff. 3 pers. pl. masc.; וּ id. למד
לְלַעַג וּ pref. id.)(noun masc. sing. dec. 6 d; וּ id. לעג
לְלַעְדָּן pref. id.)(pr. name masc. . . . לעד
לְלַעֲנָה pref. id.)(noun fem. sing. . . . לען
לַלֵּצִים pref. לַ for לְהַ)(Kal part. act. masc., pl. of לֵץ (§ 21. rem. 2) dec. 1a . . לוץ
לְלַקֵּט pref. לְ)(Piel inf. constr. . . . לקט
לִלְקֹט[r] וְ׳ pref. לִ bef. (:))(Kal inf. constr. . לקט
לְלִשְׁכַּת[s] pref. לְ)(noun f. s., constr. of לִשְׁכָּה d. 12b לשך
לְלֶשֶׁם pref. id.)(pr. name of a place . . לשם
לִלְשֹׁנוֹ[t] pref. לִ bef. (:))(noun com. sing., suff. 3 pers. sing. masc. from לָשׁוֹן dec. 3 a . לשן
לִלְשֹׁנֵנוּ[u] pref. id.)(id., suff. 1 pers. pl. . . לשן
לִלְשֹׁנֹתָם[x] pref. id.)(id. pl., suff. 3 pers. pl. masc. . לשן

[a] Ca. 7. 13. [b] Ex. 23. 11. [c] 2 Ch. 2. 9. [d] 1 Ki. 16. 31. [e] 1 Ki. 2. 8. [f] De. 2. 7. [g] Je. 2. 2. [h] 2 Sa. 17. 21. [i] Job 31. 24. [k] Ex. 27. 14. [l] Eze. 40. 41. [m] 1 Ki. 7. 17. [n] 1 Ki. 7. 17, 18, 31. [o] 2 Ch. 15. 3. [p] Na. 2. 13. [q] 1 Sa. 16. 7. [r] Ho. 7. 2. [s] Job 38. 39. [t] Le. 13. 16. [u] Da. 11. 35. [x] Ex. 5. 7, 14. [y] 1 Ki. 3. 18 [z] Is. 10. 17. [a] Is. 65. 1. [b] Pr. 23. 1. [c] Ge. 41. 55. [d] Je. 42. 14. [e] Eze. 4. 9. [f] 1 Ch. 23. 29. [g] Pr. 27. 27. [h] 1 Sa. 13. 20. [i] Ps. 19. 3. [k] Ge. 24. 23. [l] Je. 32. 24. [m] Je. 18. 22. [n] Ec. 1. 7. [o] Ezr. 7. 10. [p] Ju. 3. 2. [q] Da. 1. 4. [r] Ca. 6. 2. [s] Je. 35. 4. [t] Ge. 10. 5. [u] Ps. 12. 5. [x] Ge. 10. 20, 31.

Form	Analysis	Root
לָלֶ֫ת [a]	pref. לָ (see lett. ל)) Kal inf. constr., contr. from לֶ֫דֶת (§ 25. rem.)	ילד
לְמָא [b]	Chald., pron. i. q. Heb. מָה	מה
לִמְאֹד [c]	pref. לְ bef. (:)) noun masc. sing. dec. 1a	אוד
לְמֵֽאָדָם [d]	preff. לְ, & מֵ for מִ־) noun masc. sing.	אדם
לַמֵּאָה [e]	pref. לַ f. לְהַ } noun fem. sing. dec. 11b	מאה
לְמֵאָה	pref. לְ q. v. }	
לַֽמְאַהֲבַי [f]	pref. לַ for לְהַ) Piel (§ 14. rem. 1) part. pl., suff. 1 pers. sing. from [מְאַהֵב] dec. 7b	אהב
לִמְאוּמָה	pref. לְ bef. (:)) see מְאוּמָה under	מה
לַמָּאוֹר	pref. לַ f. לְהַ } noun masc. sing. dec. 3a	אור
לְמָאוֹר [g]	pref. לְ q. v. }	
לִמְאוֹר [h]	pref. לְ bef. (:)) id., constr. st.	אור
לִמְאוֹרֹת [i]	pref. id.) id. pl. with fem. term.	אור
לְמֵאוֹת	pref. לְ) noun f. pl. abs. from מֵאָה d. 11b	מאה
לְמֵאוֹת [k]	Kh. לְמֵאוֹת q. v.; K. לִמְאַת (q. v.)	מאה
לַֽמְאַחֲרִים [l]	pref. לַ for לְהַ) Piel (§ 14. rem. 1) part. pl. masc. from [מְאַחֵר] dec. 7b	אחר
לְמֵאִישׁ	preff. לְ, & מֵ f. מִ־) n. m. s. d. 1a (comp. § 45)	איש
לְמַאֲכָל	pref. לְ) noun masc. sing. dec. 2b	אכל
לְמֵאמַר [m]	Chald., pref. id.) Peal inf. constr. (§ 53)	אמר
לְמָאנֵי [n]	Chald., pref. id.) n. m. pl. constr. fr. [מָאן] d. 1a	מאן
לְמָאנַיָּא [o]	וּ Chald., pref. id.) id. pl., emph. st.; וּ bef. (:)	מאן
לַמָּאֹר [p]	defect. for לַמָּאוֹר (q. v.)	אור
לִמְאַת [q]	pref. לְ bef. (:)) n. f., constr. of מֵאָה d. 11b	מאה
לִמְבוֹא	pref. id.) noun m. s., constr. of מָבוֹא d. 3a	בוא
לַמַּבּוּל [r]	pref. לַ f. לְהַ } noun masc. sing. dec. 1b	יבל
לְמַבּוּל [s]	pref. לְ q. v. }	
לְמַבּוּעֵי [t]	pref. id.) noun m. pl. constr. fr. מַבּוּעַ d. 1b	נבע
לְמִבְטָח [u]	pref. id.) noun m. s. d. 2 & 8 (§ 37. r. 5)	בטח
לַמֵּבִין [x]	pref. לַ for לְהַ) Hiph. part. sing. m. d. 3b	בין
לְמִבַּיִת [y]	וּ preff. לְ & מִ) noun masc. sing., constr. of בַּיִת d. 6h, pl. irr. בָּתִּים (§ 45); וּ bef. (:)	בות
לְמִבֵּן	preff. id.) n. m. s., constr. of בֵּן irr. (§ 45)	בנה
לְמִבְנֵא	Chald., pref. לְ) Peal inf.	בנה
לְמִבְנְיָה [z]	Chald., pref. id.) id. emph. st. dec. 6a	בנה
לְמִבְעֵא [a]	Chald., pref. id.) Peal inf.	בעה
לְמִבְצָרֵי [b]	pref. id.) noun m. pl. constr. fr. מִבְצָר d. 2b	בצר
לְמַבָּרִאשׁוֹנָה [c]	pref. id.) compounded of מָה (q. v.) & בָּרִאשֹׁנָה (q. v.)	ראש
לְמִגָּדוֹל [d]	preff. לְ & מִ) adj. masc. sing. dec. 3a	גדל
לְמִגְדַּל	pref. לְ) noun m. s., constr. of מִגְדָּל d. 2b	גדל
לְמִגְדָּנוֹת [e]	וּ pref. לְ) n. f. pl. abs. [fr. מִגְדָּנָה]; וּ bef. (:)	מגד
לְמָגוֹר [f]	pref. id.) noun masc. s. d. 3a (§ 32. r. 5)	גור
לְמַגִּידֵי [g]	pref. id.) Hiph. part. pl. constr. m. fr. מַגִּיד d. 1b	נגד
לְמִגְלֵא [h]	Chald., pref. id.) Peal inf.	גלה
לְמָגִנִּים [i]	וּ pref. id.) noun masc., pl. of מָגֵן dec. 8b (§ 37. No. 3); וּ bef. (:)	גנן
לְמַגֵּפָה [k]	pref. id.) noun fem. sing. dec. 10	נגף
לְמִגְרָשׁ [l]	וּ pref. id.) noun masc. s. d. 2b; וּ bef. (:)	גרש

לָמַד [m] fut. יִלְמַד.—I. *to accustom oneself,* with אֶל Je. 10. 2.—II. *to learn,* with לְ and an inf.; with acc. Pi.—I. *to accustom,* Je. 9. 4.—II. *to teach,* with acc. of the pers.; with double acc.; with acc. of the thing and לְ of the pers.; with בְּ of the pers.; and with מִן Ps. 94. 12. Pu. *to be accustomed, trained, taught.*

לִמֻּד, לִמּוּד adj. masc. dec. 1b.—I. *accustomed,* Je. 2. 24.—II. *trained, taught;* hence, *a disciple.*

מַלְמָד masc. dec. 2b, *ox-goad,* Ju. 3. 31.

תַּלְמִיד masc. *learner, disciple,* 1 Ch. 25. 8.

Form	Analysis	Root
לָמֹד [n]	Kal inf. abs.	למד
לָמֹד [o]	pref. לָ (see lett. ל)) Kal inf. constr.	מדד
לַמֵּד	וְ Piel inf. constr. dec. 7b	למד
לִמֶּד־ [p]	id. pret. 3 pers. sing. masc. (§ 10. rem. 1)	למד
לֻמַּד [q]	Pual pret. 3 p. s. m. [for לֻמַּד comp. § 8. r. 7]	למד
לִמֻּד [r]	[defect. for לִמּוּד] adj. masc. sing. dec. 1b	למד
לַמִּדְבָּר [s]	pref. לַ f. לְהַ } noun masc. sing. dec. 2b	דבר
לְמִדְבָּר [t]	pref. לְ q. v. }	
לְמִדְבַּר	pref. id.) id. constr. st.	דבר
לַמְּדָהּ [u]	וְ Piel imp. sing. m. [לַמֵּד], suff. 3 pers. s. f.	למד
לָמְדוּ [x]	[y] וְ׳ Kal pret. 3 pers. pl.	למד
לִמְדוּ [z]	id. imp. pl. masc.	למד
לִמְּדוּ	Piel pret. 3 pers. pl.	למד
לִמְּדוּם [a]	id. with suff. 3 pers. pl. masc.	למד
לְמַדְחֵפֹת [b]	pref. לְ) noun fem. pl. [of מַדְחֵפָה]	רחף
לְמָדָי	pref. id.) pr. name of a country, see מָדַי.	
לְמַדַּי	pref. id.) for מַה־דַּי, comp. מָה & דַּי.	
לְמֻדֵי [c]	defect. for לִמּוּדֵי (q. v.)	למד
לְמַדָּיו	pref. לְ) noun masc. pl., suff. 3 pers. sing. masc. from מַד dec. 8d & c, &c.	מדד
לַמְּדִינוֹת [d]	pref. לַ for לְהַ) n. f., pl. of מְדִינָה d. 10. R. דִּין see	דון
לְמִדָּן	preff. לְ & מִ) pr. name of a tribe	דון

[a] 1 Sa. 4. 19. [b] Ezr. 6. 8. [c] 2 Ch. 16. 14. [d] Je. 51. 62. [e] Ju. 20. 10. [f] La. 1. 19. [g] Ex. 35. 28. [h] Ps. 90. 8. [i] Ge. 1. 15. [k] 2 Ch. 25. 9. [l] Pr. 23. 30. [m] Da. 2. 9. [n] Da. 5. 2. [o] Da. 5. 23. [p] Ex. 25. 6. [q] Ex. 38. 27. [r] Ps. 29. 10. [s] Ge. 9. 15. [t] Is. 35. 7. [u] Eze. 29. 16. [x] Pr. 8. 9. [y] Nu. 18. 7. [z] Ezr. 5. 9. [a] Da. 2. 18. [b] Da. 11. 39. [c] 1 Ch. 15. 13. [d] Est. 1. 5, 20. [e] 2 Ch. 21. 3. [f] Je. 20. 4. [g] Ju. 14. 19. [h] Da. 2. 47. [i] 2 Ch. 32. 27. [k] 1 Ch. 21. 17. [l] Eze. 48. 15. [m] Is. 26. 10. [n] Je. 12. 16. [o] Zec. 2. 6. [p] Ec. 12. 9. [q] Je. 31. 18. [r] Je. 2. 24. [s] 2 Ch. 20. 24. [t] Ps. 107. 33. [u] De. 31. 19. [x] Is. 26. 9. [y] De. 31. 13. [z] Is. 1. 17. [a] Je. 9. 13. [b] Ps. 140. 12. [c] Je. 13. 23. [d] Est. 2. 18.

לִמְדְנָה[a] וְ Piel imp. pl. fem. . . . . . למד
לַמְּדֵנִי וְ id. imp. sing. masc. [לַמֵּד], suff. 1 pers. s. למד
לְמִדַּת[b] pref. לְ) noun fem. s., constr. of מִדָּה d. 10 מדד
לָמַדְתִּי[c] Kal pret. 1 pers. sing. . . . . למד
לִמַּדְתִּי[d] Piel pret. 1 pers. sing. . . . . למד
לִמַּדְתְּ[e] id. pret. 2 p. s. f. Kh. לִמַּדְתִּי, K. לִמַּדְתְּ (§ 8. r. 5) למד
לִמַּדְתֶּם[f] וְ id. pret. 2 pers. pl. masc. . . . למד
לְמַדְתֶּם[g] וּ Kal pret. 2 pers. pl. m.; וּ bef. (:) for וְ conv. למד
לִמַּדְתַּנִי[h] id. pret. 2 pers. sing. masc., suff. 1 pers. sing. למד
לָמָּה וְ' (for לְהַמָּה, לַמָּה comp. כַּמָּה, בַּמָּה), & וְ' לָמָה & (chiefly bef. א, ה, ע, and the name יְהוָֹה) & לָמֶה & וְ' (three times) adv. interr., from the pref. לְ & מָה or מֶה q. v. . . . . . מה
לְמָה[i] Chald., adv. interr., from the pref. לְ & מָה q. v. מה
לִמְהוּמָן pref. לְ bef. (:)) pr. name masc. . . אמן
לִמְהָךְ[k] Chald., pref. id.) Peal inf. . . . הוך
לְמַהֲלֻמּוֹת[l] pref. לְ) noun fem., pl. of [מַהֲלֻמָּה] dec. 10 הלם
לְמַהֵר pref. id.) Piel inf. constr. (§ 14. rem. 1) . מהר
לָמוֹ[m] pref. prep. לְ with suff. 3 pers. pl. or sing. masc. (§ 5. rem. 2) . . . ל
לְמוֹ pref. לְ) parag. syl. forming one word with the pref. prepp. לְ, כְּ, בְּ without affecting the signification, see . . . . מו
לְמוֹאָב וּ' pref. id.) pr. name of a country, see מוֹאָב; וּ bef. (:).
לְמוּאל[n] pref. id.) prep., K. מוּל' (q. v.) . . מול
לְמוּאֵל, לְמוֹאֵל (*to God*, sc. dedicated; for לָאֵל, comp. לְמוֹ) title of king Solomon, Pr. 31. 1, 4.
לָמוּג[o] pref. לָ, (see lett. ל)) Kal inf. constr. . מוג
לִמּוּדֵי[p] adj. pl. constr. masc. from [לִמּוּד] dec. 2b למד
לְמוּדֵי[q] וְ Kal part. pass. pl. constr. masc. from [לָמוּד] dec. 3a; וּ bef. (:) . . . . למד
לִמּוּדִים[r] adj. pl. masc. from [לִמּוּד] dec. 2b . למד
לַמּוֹט pref. לַ for לְהַ) noun masc. sing. dec. 1a מוט
לַמּוֹכִיחַ[s] וְ pref. id.) Hiph. part. sing. masc. dec. 1b יכח
לַמּוֹכִיחִים[t] וְ pref. id.) id. pl. abs. . . . יכח
לְמוֹלַדְתֶּךָ[u] וּ / לְמוֹלַדְתְּךָ[x] וּ } pref. לְ) noun fem. sing., suff. 2 pers. s. m. from מוֹלֶדֶת d. 13a; וּ bef. (:) ילד
לְמוֹלַדְתֵּנוּ[y] וּ pref. id.) id., suff. 1 pers. pl.; וּ id. ילד
לְמוֹלִיךְ[z] pref. id.) Hiph. part. sing. masc. dec. 1b ילך
לַמּוּלֹת[a] pref. לַ for לְהַ) noun f., pl. of [מוּלָה] d. 10 מול

לְמוֹסְדוֹת[b] pref. לְ) noun masc. with pl. fem. term., abs. from [מוֹסָד] dec. 2b . . . יסד
לַמּוּסָר pref. לַ for לְהַ) noun masc. sing. dec. 2b יסר
לְמֹסְרַי[c] pref. לְ) n. m. pl., suff. 1 p. s. [fr. מוֹסֵר for מַאֲסָר] אסר
לַמּוֹעֵד pref. לַ f. לְהַ / לְמוֹעֵד pref. לְ q. v. } noun masc. sing. dec. 7b . יעד
לְמוֹעֲדָהּ[d] pref. id.) id. pl. constr. st. . . יעד
לַמּוֹעֲדוֹת[e] וְ' pref. לַ for לְהַ) id. pl. abs. fem. . יעד
לְמוֹעֲדֵי[f] וּ pref. לְ) id. pl. c. m. R. יעד, or Kal[bb] part. R. מעד
לְמוֹעַדְיָה pref. id.) pr. name masc. . . . יעד
לַמּוֹעֲדִים[g] וְ'[hh] pref. לַ f. לְהַ / לְמוֹעֲדִים[h] וּ' pref. לְ q. v. } noun masc., pl. of מוֹעֵד dec. 7b; וּ bef. (:) יעד
לְמוֹפֵת[k] וּ' pref. id.) noun masc. sing. d. 7b; וּ id. יפת
לְמוֹפְתִים[m] וּ pref. id.) id. pl., abs. st.; וּ id. . . יפת
לְמוֹצָאֵי[n] pref. id.) n. m. pl. constr. fr. מוֹצָא d. 1b (§ 31. r. 1) יצא
לְמוֹצָאֵיהֶם[o] pref. id.) id. pl., suff. 3 pers. pl. masc. יצא
לַמּוּצָק[p] pref. לַ for לְהַ) noun masc. sing. . יצק
לְמוֹקֵשׁ וּ' pref. לְ) noun masc. sing. d. 7b; וּ bef. (:) יקש
לַמּוֹרָא[q] pref. לַ f. לְהַ) n. m. s. d. 2b (§ 31. r. 1 & 3) ירא
לְמוֹרַג[r] pref. לְ) noun masc. s. (pl. מוֹרַגִּים) d. 8e מרג
לְמוֹרַשֵׁי[s] pref. id.) noun masc. sing. [constr. of מוֹרָשׁ, but see § 31. rem. 1] . . . . ירש
לְמוֹרָשָׁה pref. id.) noun fem. sing. . . . ירש
לְמוֹשָׁב pref. id.) noun masc. sing. dec. 2b ישב
לְמוֹשִׁיעַ[t] pref. id.) Hiph. part. sing. masc. dec. 1b ישע
לְמוֹשָׁעוֹת[u] pref. id.) noun fem. pl. [of מוֹשָׁעָה] . ישע
לָמוּת pref. לָ (see lett. ל)) Kal inf. constr. dec. 1a מות
לַמָּוֶת[x] וְ' pref. לַ f. לְהַ / לְמָוֶת[y] pref. לְ q. v. } noun masc. sing. dec. 6g מות
לְמוֹת[z] Chald., pref. id.) noun masc. sing. . מות
לְמוֹתוֹ[a] pref. id.) n. m. s., suff. 3 p. s. m. fr. מָוֶת d. 6g מות
לְמוֹתָם[b] pref. id.) id., suff. 3 pers. pl. masc. . מות
לְמוֹתַר[c] pref. id.) noun masc. sing. dec. 2b . יתר
לְמוֹתֵת[d] pref. id.) Pilel inf. constr. . . . מות
לְמֵזֵא[e] Chald., pref. id.) Peal inf. (§ 53 & 56, 2) אזא
לַמִּזְבֵּחַ וְ' pref. לַ for לְהַ) noun masc. sing. dec. 7c זבח
לְמִזְבַּח[f] וּ' pref. לְ) id., constr. st.; וּ bef. (:) . זבח
לַמִּזְבְּחוֹת[g] pref. לַ for לְהַ) id. pl. fem. . . . זבח
לְמָזוֹר[h] pref. לְ) noun masc. sing. dec. 3a . זור
לְמֵזַח[i] וּ pref. id.) noun masc. sing.; וּ bef. (:) . מזח

[a] Je. 9. 19. [b] Ne. 5. 4. [c] Pr. 30. 3. [d] De. 4. 5. [e] Je. 2. 33; 13. 21. [f] De. 11. 19. [g] De. 5. 1. [h] Ps. 71. 17. [i] Ezr. 4. 22; 7. 23. [k] Ezr. 7. 13. [l] Pr. 18. 6. [m] Ge. 9. 26, 27; Is. 44. 15; 53. 8; Ps. 28. 8. [n] Ne. 12. 38. [o] Eze. 21. 20. [p] Is. 54. 13. [q] 1 Ch. 5. 18. [r] Is. 50. 4. [s] Is. 29. 21. [t] Pr. 24. 25. [u] Ge. 31. 3. [x] Ge. 32. 10. [y] Ge. 43. 7. [z] Ps. 136. 16. [a] Ex. 4. 26. [b] Je. 51. 26. [bb] Job 12. 5. [c] Ps. 116. 16. [d] Ex. 13. 10. [e] 2 Ch. 8. 13. [f] 2 Ch. 2. 3. [g] Ne. 10. 34. [h] Ps. 104. 19. [hh] 2 Ch. 31. 3. [i] Ge. 1. 14. [k] Eze. 24. 24, 27. [l] De. 28. 46. [m] Is. 8. 18. [n] Is. 41. 18. [o] Nu. 33. 2. [p] Job 38. 38. [q] Ps. 76. 12. [r] Is. 41. 15. [s] Is. 14. 23. [t] Is. 63. 8. [u] Ps. 68. 21. [x] Ps. 118. 18. [y] 2 Sa. 15. 21. [z] Ezr. 7. 26. [a] Pr. 11. 19. [b] Ps. 73. 4. [c] Pr. 21. 5 [d] Ps. 109. 16. [e] Da. 3. 19. [f] 2 Ch. 26. 19. [g] Ho. 10. 1. [h] Je. 30. 13. [i] Ps. 109. 19.

לְמֵזֵיהּ[a] Chald., pref. לְ)(Peal inf. (מֵזֵא § 53 & 56, 2), suff. 3 pers. sing. masc. dec. 6a . אזא
לַמַּזָּלוֹת[b] וְ pref. לְ for לְהַ)(noun pl. fem. [from מַזָּל] מזל
לִמְזִמָּה[c] pref. לְ bef. (:))(noun fem. sing. dec. 10 זמם
לַמְזַמְּרוֹת pref. לְ)(noun f. pl. abs. fr. [מְזַמְּרָה] d. 11b זמר
לַמִּזְרָח וְ' pref. לְ for לְהַ)(noun masc. sing. dec. 2b זרח
לְמִזְרַח pref. לְ)(id., constr. st. . . . זרח
לַמִּזְרָחָה[d] pref. לְ for לְהַ)(id. with loc. ה . . זרח
לַמְחַבְּרוֹת[e] וְ' pref. id.)(noun f., pl. of [מְחַבֶּרֶת] d. 13a חבר
לַמַּחֲבַת[g] וְ pref. id.)(noun fem. sing. [for מַחֲבֶתֶת comp. § 25. rem.] . . . חבת
לְמָחוֹל[h] pref. id.)(noun masc. sing. dec. 3a . חול
לְמַחוֹת[i] pref. לְ [for לְהַמְחוֹת], Hiph. inf. constr. (§ 11. rem. 3); but see מָחָה . . מחה
לִמְחוֹת[k] pref. לְ bef. (:))(Kal inf. constr. . . מחה
לְמֶחֱזֵא[l] Chald., pref. לְ)(Peal inf. (§ 49. No. 2) . חזא
לְמַחֲזִיאוֹת pref. id.)(pr. name masc. . . . חזא
לְמַחֲזִיק[m] pref. id.)(Hiph. part. sing. masc. dec. 2b . חזק
לַמַּחֲזִיקִים[n] pref. לְ for לְהַ)(id. pl., abs. st. . . חזק
לְמִחְיָה[o] pref. לְ)(noun masc. sing. dec. 10 . . חיה
לִמְחַכֵּה[p] pref. לְ bef. (:))(Piel part. sing. masc., constr. of מְחַכֶּה dec. 9a . . . . חכה
לְמַחְלִי pref. לְ)(pr. name masc. . . . חלה
לַמַּחְלְקוֹת[q] וְ' pref. id.)(n.f., pl. of מַחֲלֹקֶת d. 13c; וּ bef. (:) חלק
לַמַּחֲנֶה' pref. לְ f. לְהַ } noun com. sing. dec. 9a . חנה
לְמַחֲנֶה[r] pref. לְ q. v. }
לְמַחֲנֵה pref. id.)(id., constr. st. . . . חנה
לְמַחֲנוֹת[s] pref. id.)(id. pl. fem. . . . חנה
לְמַחֲסֶה[t] וּ pref. id.)(noun masc. s. d. 9a; וּ bef. (:) חסה
לְמַחְסוֹר pref. id.)(noun masc. sing. dec. 1b . . חסר
לַמְחַצְּצְרִים[u] pref. לְ for לְהַ)(Kh. מְחַצְּצְרִים Peopel (§ 6. No. 7) K. מַחְצְרִים or מְחַצְּרִים Piel or Hiph. part. pl. masc. . . . חצר
לְמָחָר pref. לְ)(noun masc. or adv. . . מחר
לְמַחְרָאוֹת[x] pref. id.)(Kh. מַחֲרָאוֹת noun fem. pl. [of מַחֲרָאָה]; (K. מוֹצָאוֹת R. יצא) . חרא
לַמַּחֲרֵשׁוֹת[y] pref. לְ for לְהַ)(noun fem. pl. [of מַחֲרֵשָׁה] חרש
לַמָּחֳרָת[z] pref. id.)(noun fem. sing. . . . מחר
לְמָחֳרַת[a] pref. לְ)(id., constr. st. . . . מחר
לְמָחֳרָתָם[b] pref. id.)(adv (comp. אָמְנָם, רֵיקָם) . . מחר
לִמְחִתָּה[c] וְ[d] pref. לְ bef. (:))(noun fem. sing. dec. 10 חתת
לַמַּטֶּה pref. לְ for לְהַ)(noun masc. sing. dec. 9 a נטה

לְמַטָּה וְ' } pref. לְ)(prop. subst. [מַט] with loc. ה, as an adv.; וּ bef. (:) . . נטה
לְמָטָּה וּ[e] }
לְמַטֶּה וְ' pref. id.)(noun masc. s. d. 9a; וּ id. נטה
לְמַטֵּה וְ' pref. id.)(id., constr. st.; וּ id. . . נטה
לַמִּטַּהֵר[f] pref. לְ for לְהַ)(Hithpa. part. sing. masc. [for מִתְטַהֵר § 12. r. 3, & § 14. r. 1] d. 7 b. טהר
לְמַטּוֹת pref. לְ)(noun masc. with pl. fem. term. fr. מַטֶּה dec. 9 a . . . . . נטה
לְמַטְּעֵי[g] pref. id.)(noun m. pl. constr. fr. מַטָּע d. 1b נטע
לְמַטְעַמּוֹתָיו[h] } pref. id.)(noun pl. fem., suff. 3 pers. sing. masc. from [מַטְעָם] dec. 8 a } טעם
לְמַטְעַמֹּתָיו[i] }
לַמָּטָר pref. לְ for לְהַ)(noun masc. sing. dec. 4 a מטר
לִמְטַר[k] pref. לְ bef. (:))(id., constr. st. . . מטר
לְמַטָּרָה pref. לְ)(noun fem. sing. . . . נטר
לְמֵי pref. id.)(noun masc. pl., constr. of מַיִם [fr. מַי sing. irr. § 38. r. 2, & § 45] מים
לְמִי וְ' pref. id.)(pron. pers. interrog.; וּ bef. (:) . מה
לִמְיֻדָּעַי[l] pref. לְ bef. (:))(for יֻדָּ'; Pual part. pl. masc., suff. 1 pers. sing. [fr. מְיֻדָּע] . . ידע
לְמִיּוֹם preff. לְ & מִ)(noun masc. sing. dec. 1 a, pl. irr., יָמִים (§ 45) . . . . יום
לַמְיַחֲלִים[m] pref. לְ for לְהַ)(Piel (§ 14. rem. 1) part. masc., pl. of מְיַחֵל dec. 7b . . יחל
לְמִיכָה }
לְמִיכָיְהוּ וּ } pref. לְ)(pr. name masc., see מִיכָה; וּ bef. (:).
לְמִיכָיְהוּ }
לְמִיכַל וּ pref. id.)(pr. name f.; וּ bef. (:), see מִיכַל.
לַמְיַלְּדֹת[n] pref. לְ for לְהַ)(Piel part. fem., pl. of מְיַלֶּדֶת dec. 13 a . . . . . ילד
לְמַיִם[o] pref. לְ (see ל) } noun masc. pl. [of מַי irr. § 38. r. 2, & § 45] } מים
לַמַּיִם[p] } pref. לַ f. לְהַ
לַמָּיִם }
לָמָיִם[q] pref. לְ q. v. id. in pause for the preced.
לְמֵימֵי[r] pref. id.)(id. pl. constr. st. . . . מים
לְמִימֵי [for לְמִיְּמֵי] preff. לְ & מִ)(constr. of the foll. יום
לְמִיָּמִים[s] וּ preff. id.)(n.m.pl.irr. of יוֹם (§ 45); וּ bef. (:) יום
לְמִיָּמִן pref. לְ)(pr. name masc., see מִיָּמִן.
לְמִינָהּ pref. id.)(noun masc. sing., suff. 3 pers. sing. fem. from [מִין] dec. 1 a . . מון
לְמִינֵהוּ pref. id.)(id., suff. 3 pers. sing. masc. מון
לְמִינֵהֶם[t] pref. id.)(id. pl., suff. 3 p. pl. m. [for מִינֵיהֶם] מון
לְמִינוֹ pref. id.)(id. sing., suff. 3 pers. sing. masc. מון
לְמִישָׁאֵל וּ pref. id.)(pr. name m., see מִישָׁ'; וּ bef. (:)

[a] Da. 3. 19. [b] 2 Ki. 23. 5. [c] Ps. 139. 20. [d] 2 Ch. 31. 14. [e] 2 Ch. 34. 11. [f] 1 Ch. 22. 3. [g] 1 Ch. 23. 29 [h] Ps. 30. 12. [i] Pr. 31. 3. [k] 2 Ki. 14. 27. [l] Ezr. 4. 14. [m] Da. 11. 1. [n] Pr. 3. 18. [o] Ge. 45. 5. [p] Is. 64. 3. [q] 1 Ch. 28. 13. [r] 1 Ch. 12. 22. [s] 1 Ch. 9. 18. [t] Is. 4. 6. [u] 2 Ch. 5. 13. [x] 2 Ki. 10. 27. [y] 1 Sa. 13. 21. [z] Jon. 4. 7. [a] 1 Ch. 29. 21 [b] 1 Sa. 30. 17. [c] Je. 17. 17. [d] Je. 48. 39. [e] 1 Ch. 27. 23. [f] Le. 14. 4. [g] Mi. 1. 6. [h] Pr. 23. 3. [i] Pr. 23. 6. [k] De. 11. 11. [l] Ps. 31. 12. [m] Ps. 33. 18. [n] Ex. 1. 15, 18, 20. [o] Ge. 1. 6. [p] Je. 14. 3. [q] Jos. 7. 5. [r] Da. 12. 6, 7. [s] Ge. 1. 21.

לְמִישׁוֹר pref. לְ)(noun masc. sing. . . . ישר

לְמֵישָׁרִים[a] pref. id.)(noun masc., pl. of [מֵישָׁר], with the prefix as an *adv*. . . . ישר

לֶמֶךְ / וְ׳ לָמֶךְ } (§ 35. rem. 2) pr. name masc. *Lamech*.

לְמַכְאוֹבָהּ[b] pref. לְ)(noun masc. sing., suff. 3 pers. sing. fem. from מַכְאוֹב dec. 1 b . . . כאב

לְמַכְבִּיר[c] pref. id.)(Hiph. part. as a *subst*. . כבר

לְמִכְבַּר[d] pref. id.)(noun m. s., constr. of מִכְבָּר d. 2 b כבר

לְמַכֵּה[e] pref. id.)(Hiph. part. sing. masc., constr. of מַכֶּה dec. 9 a . . . . נכה

לְמַכֵּהוּ[f] pref. id.)(id. with suff. 3 pers. sing. masc. נכה

לַמְּכוֹנָה[g] pref. לַ for לְהַ)(noun fem. sing. dec. 10 . כון

לְמִיָּמִים[h] וּ preff. לְ & מִ)(noun masc. pl. abs. (as if from יָם dec. 2 a) see יוֹם (§ 45); וּ bef. (:) יום

לִמְכּוֹר[i] pref. לִ bef. (:))(Kal inf. constr. (§ 8. r. 18) מכר

לְמַכִּים[k] pref. לְ)(Hiph. part. masc., pl. of מַכֶּה d. 9 a נכה

לְמָכִיר וּ׳ pref. id.)(pr. name masc.; וּ bef. (:) . מכר

לְמִכְמַרְתּוֹ[l] pref. id.)(noun fem. sing., suff. 3 pers. sing. masc. from [מִכְמֶרֶת] dec. 13 a . . כמר

לְמִכְמָשׁ pref. id.)(pr. name of a place, see מִכְמָס כמס

לְמִכְנַשׁ[m] Ch., pref. id.)(Peal inf. . . . כנש

לְמָכְרָהּ[n] pref. id.)(Kal inf., suff. 3 pers. sing. fem. מכר

לִמְכַסֶּה[o] וְ pref. לִ bef. (:))(noun masc. sing. d. 9 a כסה

לְמִכְשׁוֹל[p] וּ׳ pref. לְ)(noun masc. sing. dec. 1 b . כשל

לַמְכַשְּׁפִים וְ pref. לַ for לְהַ)(Piel part. masc., pl. of מְכַשֵּׁף dec. 7 b . . . . כשף

לְמַלֵּא[dd] וּ׳ pref. לְ)(Piel inf. constr. d. 7 b; וּ bef. (:) מלא

לְמַלֹּאות with ו in otio for לְמַלֹּאת (q. v.) . מלא

לַמַּלְאָךְ pref. לַ for לְהַ)(noun masc. sing. dec. 2 b לאך

לַמְּלָאכָה / לִמְלָאכָה pref. לַ id. / pref. לִ bef. (:) } noun fem. sing., constr. מְלֶאכֶת (§ 42. rem. 5) } לאך

לְמַלְאֲכֵי[q] pref. לְ)(constr. of the following . לאך

לַמַּלְאָכִים[r] pref. לַ for לְהַ)(noun m., pl. of מַלְאָךְ d. 2 b לאך

לִמְלֶאכֶת pref. לִ bef. (:))(noun fem. sing. constr. of מְלָאכָה (§ 42. rem. 5) . . . לאך

לִמְלַאכְתּוֹ pref. id.)(id., suff. 3 pers. sing. m. d. 13 a לאך

לְמַלְאָם[s] וּ pref. לְ)(Piel inf. (מַלֵּא׳), suff. 3 pers. pl. masc. dec. 7 b; וּ bef. (:) . מלא

לְמַלֹּאת pref. id.)(Piel inf. with f. term. [for מַלֵּאת § 23. rem. 2 & 4] . . . מלא

לְמִלָּה[t] pref. id.)(noun fem. sing. d. 10 (pl. מִלִּים) מלל

לַמִּלֻּאִים[u] וְ pref. לַ for לְהַ)(noun m., pl. of [מִלּוּא] d. 1 b מלא

לִמְלוּכָה[x] pref. לִ bef. (:))(noun fem. sing. . . מלך

לִמְלוֹכִי pref. לְ)(Kh. (לְ)מַלּוּכִי, K. (לְ)מְלִיכוּ, see מַלּוּךְ מלך

לְמַלּוֹתִי pref. לְ)(pr. name masc. . . . מלל

לְמֶלַח[y] pref. id.)(noun masc. sing. . . . מלח

לִמְלֵחָה[z] pref. לִ bef. (:))(noun fem. sing. . מלח

לַמִּלְחָמָה / לְמִלְחָמָה pref. לַ f. לְהַ / pref. לְ q. v. } n. f. s. d. 11 a, with suff. מִלְחַמְתּוֹ fr. חֶמֶת׳ d. 13 a (§ 42. r. 5) } לחם

לְמִלִּין[a] pref. id.)(noun fem. with pl. masc. term. from מִלָּה dec. 10 . . . . מלל

לַמֶּלֶךְ וְ׳ pref. לַ for לְהַ)(noun masc. sing. dec. 6 a מלך

לַמֹּלֶךְ / וּלַמֹּלֶךְ pref. id. / וּ pref. לַ } pr. name of an idol; וּ bef. (:) מלך

לְמֶלֶךְ pref. id.)(noun masc. s. d. 6 a; Chald. d. 3 a מלך

לִמְלֹךְ pref. לִ bef. (:))(Kal inf. constr. . . מלך

לְמַלְכָּא Chald., pref. לְ)(noun masc. sing., emph. of מֶלֶךְ (§ 59) dec. 3 a . . . מלך

לְמַלְכָּהּ[b] וּ׳ pref. id.)(noun masc. sing., suff. 3 pers. sing. fem. from מֶלֶךְ dec. 6 a; וּ bef. (:) מלך

לְמַלְכּוֹ[c] pref. id.)(id. with suff. 3 pers. sing. masc. מלך

לְמָלְכוֹ pref. id.)(Kal inf., suff. 3 pers. sing. masc. מלך

לַמַּלְכוּת[d] / לְמַלְכוּת pref. לַ f. לְהַ / pref. לְ q. v. } noun fem. sing. dec. 10; Ch. constr. of מַלְכוּ dec. 8 c . } מלך

לְמַלְכוּתוֹ pref. id.)(id. with suff. 3 pers. sing. masc. . מלך

לְמַלְכֵי[e] וּ׳ pref. id.)(noun masc. pl. constr. from מֶלֶךְ dec. 6 a; וּ bef. (:) . . . מלך

לְמַלְכִּיאֵל, לְמַלְכִּיָּה pref. id.)(pr. name masc. . מלך

לַמְּלָכִים pref. לַ for לְהַ)(noun m. pl. of מֶלֶךְ d. 6 a מלך

לִמְלָכֵינוּ pref. לִ bef. (:))(id. pl., suff. 1 pers. pl. . מלך

לְמַלְכָּם וּ pref. לְ)(pr. name of an idol; וּ bef. (:) . מלך

לְמַלְכֵּנוּ[f] pref. id.)(noun masc. sing., suff. 1 pers. pl. from מֶלֶךְ dec. 6 a . . . . מלך

לְמַלְכַּת pref. id.)(n. fem. s., constr. of מַלְכָּה d. 12 a מלך

לִמְלֶכֶת pref. לִ bef. (:))(noun fem. sing. . מלך

לִמְלַמְּדַי[g] וְ pref. id.)(Piel part. pl. masc., suff. 1 pers. sing. from מְלַמֵּד dec. 7 b . . למד

לְמַלְקוֹשׁ[h] pref. לְ)(noun masc. sing. . . . לקש

לְמַמְלָכָה[i] pref. id.)(noun fem. sing., constr. לֶכֶת׳ with suff. לַכְתּוֹ׳ (§ 42. rem. 5) . מלך

לְמַמְלְכֹת[k] וּ׳[l] pref. id.)(id. pl. constr. st. מלך

לְמֵמַר[m] Chald., pref. id.)(for מֵאמַר׳ Peal inf. (§ 53) אמר

לְמֶמְשָׁלוֹת[n] pref. id.)(pl. of the foll. . . . משל

לְמֶמְשֶׁלֶת pref. id.)(noun fem. sing. dec. 13 a (used as the constr. of מֶמְשָׁלָה § 42. rem. 5) . משל

[a] Ca. 7. 10. [b] Je. 51. 8. [c] Job 36. 31. [d] Ex. 38. 5. [dd] Ex. 20. 29. [e] Ps. 136. 10. [f] La. 3. 30. [g] 1 Ki. 7. 30. [h] 1 Ch. 17. 10. [i] Ne. 10. 32. [k] Is. 50. 6. [l] Hab. 1. 16. [m] Da. 3. 2. [n] Ex. 21. 8. [o] Is. 23. 18. [p] 1 Sa. 25. 31. [q] 1 Ki. 20. 9. [r] 1 Sa. 11. 9. [s] Je. 33. 5. [t] Job 30. 9. [u] Le. 7. 37. [x] Eze. 16. 13. [y] Eze. 47. 11. [z] Ps. 107. 34. [a] Job 18. 2. [b] Jos. 10. 30. [c] 1 Sa. 2. 10. [d] Est. 4. 14. [e] 1 Ki. 10. 29. [f] Ps. 47. 7. [g] Pr. 5. 13. [h] Job 29. 23. [i] 2 Ch. 22. 9. [k] Is. 10. 10. [l] Je. 49. 28. [m] Ezr. 5. 11. [n] Ps. 136. 9.

לַמְמִתִים[a] pref. לַ for לְהַ)(Hiph. part. masc., pl. of מֵמִית dec. 3b . . . . מות

לְמָן ו Chald., pref. לְ)(pron. interrog.; ו bef. (:) מן

לְמִן [b]ו' pref. id.)(prep. (§ 5, parad.) . . מנן

לִמְנַאֲצַי[c] pref. לְ bef. (:))(Piel (§ 14. rem. 1), part. pl., suff. 1 pers. sing. from [מְנַאֵץ] dec. 7b נאץ

לְמָנָה pref. לְ)(noun f. s., d. 10 & 11a (§ 42. r. 2) מנה

לִמְנוּחָיְכִי[d] pref. לְ bef. (:))(noun masc. pl. with suff. 2 p. s. f. fr. מָנוֹחַ d. 3a (§ 30. r. 5 & § 4. r. 4) נוח

לִמְנוּחָתֶךָ[e] pref. id.)(noun fem. sing., suff. 2 pers. sing. masc. from מְנוּחָה dec. 10 . . נוח

לִמְנוֹרָה[f] pref. id.)(noun fem. sing. dec. 10 . נור

לִמְנוֹת pref. id.)(Kal inf. constr. . . . מנה

לַמֻּנָּח[g] pref. לַ for לְהַ)(Hoph. part. sing. masc. [Chald. form for מוּנָח § 21. rem. 24] . נוח

לַמִּנְחָה pref. id. } noun fem. sing. dec. 12b . מנח
לְמִנְחָה pref. לְ q. v. }

לִמְנֻחָה[h] pref. לְ bef. (:))(for מְנוּחָה, noun f. s. d. 10 נוח

וְלַמְנַחֲמִים[i] pref. לַ for לְהַ)(Piel (§ 14. rem. 1) pl. masc. from מְנַחֵם dec. 7b . . נחם

לְמִנְחַת[k] pref. לְ)(noun f. s., constr. of מִנְחָה d. 12b מנח

לְמִנְחֹתֵיכֶם[l] ו pref. id.)(id. pl., suff. 2 p. pl. m.; ו bef. (:) מנח

לַמְנִי[m] pref. לַ for לְהַ)(pr. name of an idol . מנה

לְמִנִּי[n] ו' pref. לְ)(prep. מִן with parag. י see (§ 5, parad.) . . . . . מנן

לְמִנְיָמִין pref. id.)(pr. name masc., see מִיָּמִין.

לְמִנְיַן[o] Chald., pref. id.)(noun masc. sing. . . מנה

לַמְנַצֵּחַ pref. לַ for לְהַ)(Piel part. sing. masc. d. 7b נצח

וְלִמְנֹרוֹת[p] ו' pref. לְ bef. (:))(noun f., pl. of מְנוֹרָה d. 10 נור

וְלִמְנַשֶּׁה ו' pref. id.)(pr. name of a tribe . נשה

לַמְנַשִּׁי pref. לַ for לְהַ)(gent. noun from the prec. נשה

לְמִנְתַּן[q] Chald., pref. לְ)(Peal inf. . . . נתן

לָמָס pref. לְ (see lett. ל))(noun masc. sing. dec. 8e, contr. from מֶכֶס . . . כסס

לַמָּס[r] pref. לַ for לְהַ)(noun masc. sing. . . מסס

לְמֶכֶס pref. לְ)(noun m. s. d. 8e, contr. from מֶכֶס כסס

לַמִּסְגְּרוֹת[s] pref. לַ for לְהַ)(noun f., pl. of מִסְגֶּרֶת d. 13a סגר

לְמִסְגַּרְתּוֹ pref. לְ)(id. sing., suff. 3 pers. sing. masc. סגר

לַמָּסָךְ[t] pref. לַ f. לְהַ } noun masc. sing. (constr. מְסַךְ § 37. rem. 4) . סכך
לְמָסָךְ[u] pref. לְ q. v. }

לִמְסֹךְ[x] pref. לְ bef. (:))(Kal inf. constr. . . מסך

לְמַסֵּכָה pref. לְ)(noun fem. sing. dec. 10 . נסך

לַמְסִלָּה pref. לַ for לְהַ } noun fem. sing. dec. 10 . סלל
לִמְסִלָּה[ll] pref. לְ bef. (:) }

וְלַמְּסְמְרוֹת[y] pref. לְ } noun pl. fem. and masc. [from מַסְמֵר] dec. 7b . סמר
לַמְּסַמְּרִים[z] pref. לַ f. לְהַ }

לְמַסַּע[a] [b]ו' pref. לְ)(noun masc. sing. dec. 2 (§ 31. rem. 5); ו bef. (:) . . . נסע

לְמַסְעֵיהֶם pref. id.)(id. pl., suff. 3 pers. pl. masc. . נסע

לְמַסָּעָיו[c] pref. id.)(id. pl., suff. 3 pers. sing. masc. נסע

וּלְמִסְפֵּד[d] ו pref. id.)(noun masc. s. dec. 7c; ו bef. (:) ספד

לְמִסְפַּר pref. id.)(noun m. s., constr. of מִסְפָּר dec. 2b ספר

לְמִסְפָּרָם pref. id.)(id. with suff. 3 pers. pl. masc. . ספר

לִמְסָר[e] pref. לְ bef. (:))(Kal inf. constr. [for מְסֹר § 8. rem. 18] . . . . מסר

לְמַסַּת[f] pref. לְ)(noun fem. s., constr. of מַסָּה d. 10 נסה

וּלְמִסְתּוֹר[g] ו pref. id.)(noun masc. sing.; ו bef. (:) סתר

לְמֶעְבַּד Chald., pref. id.)(Peal inf. (§ 49. No. 2) עבד

וְלַמֹּעֲדִים[pp] ו pref. לַ f. לְהַ } noun masc., pl. of מוֹעֵד dec. 7b; ו bef. (:) . יעד
וּלְמֹעֲדִים[h] ו pref. לְ q. v. }

לְמַעֲדַנִּים[i] pref. id.)(noun masc., pl. of [מַעֲדָן] dec. 8a עדן

לְמָעוֹז[k] [l]ו' pref. id.)(noun masc. sing. (suff. מָעֻזִּי § 37. rem. 4) dec. 8c . . . עזז

לְמָעוּזֵי[m] pref. id.)(id. pl., constr. st. (§ 37. rem. 2) עזז

לִמְעוֹל-[n] pref. לְ bef. (:))(Kh. לִמְעוֹל, K. לִמְעָל-, and } מעל
לִמְעוֹל[o] pref. id.)(Kal inf. constr. (§ 8. rem. 18) }

לִמְעוֹן pref. id.)(noun m. s., constr. of מָעוֹן dec. 3a עון

לְמַעֲזְיָהוּ pref. לְ)(pr. name masc. . . . עזה

וְלַמְעַט ו pref. לַ f. לְהַ } subst. and adj. masc. (pl. מְעַטִּים) dec. 8d . מעט
לִמְעַט pref. לְ bef. (:) }

לְמַעְיְנוֹ[p] pref. לְ)(noun masc. sing. (מַעְיָן) with parag. ו (comp. חַיְתוֹ) . . . . עין

לִמְעֹל } pref. לְ bef. (:))(Kal inf. constr. (§ 8. rem. 18) . . . . } מעל
לִמְעָל-[q] }

וּלְמַעְלָה ו' } pref. לְ)(subst. m. [מַעַל] with parag. ה, as an *adv.*; ו bef. (:) . } עלה
לְמַעְלָה ו' }

לְמַעֲלֵה pref. id.)(noun m. s., constr. of לָה' d. 9a עלה

לַמַּעֲלוֹת[r] pref. לַ for לְהַ)(noun f., pl. of מַעֲלָה' d. 10 עלה

לְמַעַן ו' *prep.*; prop. subst. masc. [מַעַן] with pref. לְ; ו bef. (:) . . . . . ענה

לַמַּעֲנֵהוּ[s] pref. לַ for לְהַ)(noun masc. sing., suff. 3 pers. sing. masc. from מַעֲנֶה dec. 9a . ענה

לְמַעֲנוֹתָם[t] pref. לְ)(Kh. מַעֲנוּתָם', K. מַעֲנִיתָם, noun f. s., suff. 3 pers. pl. m. [fr. מַעֲנוּת' or נִית'] ענה

[a] Job 33. 22. [b] 2 Sa. 7. 11. [c] Je. 23. 17. [d] Ps. 116. 7. [e] Ps. 132. 8. [f] 1 Ch. 28. 15. [g] Eze. 41. 11. [h] 2 Sa. 14. 17 [i] Ps. 69. 21. [k] Ezr. 9. 4. [l] Nu. 29. 39. [m] Is. 65. 11. [n] Mi. 7. 12, 12. [o] Ezr. 6. 17. [p] 1 Ch. 28. 15, 15. [q] Ezr. 7. 20. [r] Job 6. 14. [s] 1 Ki. 7. 32. [t] Ex. 26. 37. [u] Ps. 105. 39. [x] Is. 5. 22. [y] 2 Ch. 3. 9. [z] 1 Ch. 22. 3. [a] De. 10. 11. [b] Nu. 10. 2. [c] Ge. 13. 3. [d] Is. 22. 12. [e] Nu. 31. 16. [f] Job 9. 23. [g] Is. 4. 6. [h] Zec. 8. 19. [i] La. 4. 5. [k] Na. 1. 7. [l] Da. 11. 1. [ll] Ju. 21. 19. [m] Da. 11. 19. [n] 2 Ch. 36. 14. [o] 2 Ch. 28. 22. [p] Ps. 114. 8. [pp] 1 Ch. 23. 31. [q] Eze. 14. 13. [r] Ps. 121. 1. [s] Pr. 16. 4. [t] Ps. 129. 3.

לְמַעֲנִי prep. לְמַעַן [prop. subst. masc., מַעַן, with pref. לְ], suff. 1 pers. sing. . . . ענה
לְמַעַנְךָ[a] id. with suff. 2 pers. sing. masc. . . ענה
לְמַעַנְכֶם id. with suff. 2 pers. pl. masc. . . ענה
לְמַעֲצֵבָה[b] pref. לְ)(noun fem. sing. . . . עצב
לַמַּעֲרָב[c] וְ pref. לְ for לְהַ)(noun masc. sing. dec. 2b ערב
לְמַעֲשֵׂה pref. לְ)(noun m. s., constr. of מַעֲשֶׂה d. 9a עשה
לְמַעֲשֵׂהוּ[d] pref. id.)(id., suff. 3 pers. sing. masc. . עשה
לְמַעֲשַׂי[e] pref. id.)(id. pl., constr. st. . . . עשה
לַמַּעַשְׂרוֹת וְ pref. לְ for לְהַ)(noun masc. with pl. fem. term. from מַעֲשֵׂר dec. 7c . . . עשר
לְמִפְגָּע[f] pref. לְ)(noun masc. sing. . . . פגע
לִמְפִיבֹשֶׁת[qq] וְ pref. לְ bef. (:))(pr. name masc. . . פאה
לְמִפְלַגּוֹת[g] pref. לְ)(noun fem., pl. of [מִפְלַגָּה] dec. 10 פלג
לְמַפֵּלָה pref. id.)(noun fem. sing. . . . נפל
לְמִפְשַׁר[h] Chald., pref. id.)(Peal inf. . . . פשר
לִמְצֹא pref. לְ bef. (:))(Kal inf. constr. . . מצא
לְמֹצָאֵי[i] pref. לְ)(noun masc. pl. constr. from מוֹצָא dec. 1b (§ 31. rem. 1) . . . . יצא
לְמֹצְאֵי[k] pref. id.)(Kal part. act. pl. constr. masc. from מוֹצֵא' dec. 7b . . . . מצא
לְמֹצְאֵיהֶם[l] pref. id.)(id. pl. with suff. 3 pers. pl. masc. מצא
לַמַּצֵּבֶת[m] pref. לְ for לְהַ)(noun fem. sing. (suff. מַצַּבְתּוֹ) dec. 13a . . . . נצב
לַמָּצָד[n] pref. id.)(noun masc. sing. dec. 1 . . צוד
לִמְצַד[o] pref. id.)(id. constr. (by exception comp. § 30. No. 1) . . . . צוד
לִמְצָדָה[p] pref. לְ bef. (:))(for מְצוּדָה' noun f. s. d. 10 צוד
לִמְצוֹא[q] pref. id.)(Kal inf. constr. . . . מצא
לְמִצְוָה[r] pref. לְ)(noun fem. sing. dec. 10 . . צוה
לְמָצוֹר[s] pref. id.)(noun masc. sing. dec. 3a . . צור
לְמִצְוֺתַי[t] pref. id.)(noun fem. pl., suff. 1 pers. sing. from מִצְוָה dec. 10 . . . צוה
לְמִצְוֺתָיו[u] pref. id.)(id., suff. 3 pers. sing. masc. . צוה
לְמִצְוֺתֶיךָ pref. id.)(id., suff. 2 pers. sing. masc. . צוה
לַמִּצְעָר[x] pref. לְ for לְהַ)(noun masc. sing. dec. 2b צער
לַמִּצְפָּה pref. לְ)(pr. name of a place . . צפה
לְמִצְרַיִם / וּלְמִצְרָיִם } pref. id.)(pr. name of a country; (וּ bef. (:) . . . } מצר
לַמִּקְדָּשׁ pref. לְ f. לְהַ / לְמִקְדָּשׁ pref. לְ q. v. } noun masc. sing. dec. 2b . קדש
לְמִקְדָּשׁוֹ[y] pref. id.)(id., suff. 3 pers. sing. masc. קדש

לְמִקְדָּשַׁי[z] pref. לְ bef. (:))(Pu. part. pl. masc., suff. 1 pers. sing. from מְקֻדָּשׁ . . . קדש
וּלְמִקְוֵה[a] pref. לְ)(noun masc. sing., constr. of מִקְוֶה dec. 9a; וּ bef. (:) . . קוה
וְלַמָּקוֹם[b] pref. לְ for לְהַ)(noun com. sing. dec. 3a קום
לִמְקוֹמוֹ pref. לְ bef. (:))(id., suff. 3 pers. sing. masc. קום
לִמְקוֹמֶךָ[c] pref. id.)(id., suff. 2 pers. s. m. (for מְקוֹמְךָ) קום
לִמְקוֹמָם pref. id.)(id., suff. 3 pers. pl. masc. . קום
לְמִקָּטֹן preff. לְ & מִ)(adj. masc. sing. dec. 3a . קטן
לְמִקְּטַנָּם[d] preff. id.)(adj. masc. sing., suff. 3 pers. pl. masc. from קָטָן dec. 8a (§ 37. No. 3c) קטן
לְמִקְלָט pref. לְ)(noun masc. sing. dec. 2b . קלט
לִמְקֹמָהּ[e] pref. לְ bef. (:))(noun com. sing., suff. 3 pers. sing. fem. from מָקוֹם dec. 3a . . קום
לִמְקֹמוֹ pref. id.)(id., suff. 3 pers. sing. masc. . קום
לִמְקֹמֹתָם[f] pref. id.)(id. pl., suff. 3 pers. pl. masc. . קום
לְמִקְנָה[g] pref. לְ)(noun fem. sing. dec. 10 . קנה
וּלְמִקְנֵהוּ[uu] pref. id.)(noun masc. sing., suff. 3 pers. sing. masc. from מִקְנֶה dec. 9a; וּ bef. (:) קנה
לְמִקְנֵיהֶם[h] pref. id.)(id. pl., suff. 3 pers. pl. masc. . קנה
לְמִקְנֵנוּ[i] pref. id.)(id. sing., suff. 1 pers. pl. . קנה
לַמְקוֹנְנוֹת[k] pref. לְ for לְהַ)(Pil. part. pl. fem. [from מְקוֹנֶנֶת dec. 13, from מְקוֹנֵן masc.] . קון
וּלְמִקְצֵה[l] [for וּלְמִקְצֵה] preff. לְ & מִ)(noun masc. sing., constr. of קָצֶה dec. 9b; וּ bef. (:) קצה
לִמְקֻצְעֹת[m] pref. לְ bef. (:))(Pu. part. pl. constr. fem. from [מְקֻצָּעָה] dec. 11a . . קצע
וּלְמִקְצָת[n] preff. לְ & מִ)(noun fem. sing., pl. קְצָוֹת, comp. מְנָת (§ 45); וּ bef. (:) . קצה
לְמִקְרָא[o] pref. לְ)(noun masc. sing. dec. 1b (pl. c. מִקְרָאֵי § 31. rem. 1) . . . קרא
לְמִקְרָא[p] Chald., pref. id.)(Peal inf. . . . קרא
לְמָר[q] pref. id.)(for מַר adj. masc., pl. מָרִים, dec. 8 (§ 37. rem. 7) . . . . מרר
לְמַרְאֶה pref. id.)(noun masc. sing. dec. 9a . ראה
לְמַרְאֵה pref. id.)(id., constr. state . . ראה
לְםַרְבֵּה[r] pref. id.)(for מַרְבֵּה, noun masc. sing., constr. of מַרְבֶּה dec. 9a . . . רבה
וְלַמֻּרְבֶּכֶת[s] pref. לְ for לְהַ)(Hoph. part. sing. fem. [from מֻרְבָּךְ masc.] . . רבך
לְמַרְבֵּץ[t] pref. לְ)(noun masc. sing., constr. of מַרְבֵּץ dec. 7 (§ 36. rem. 1) . . רבץ
לְמַרְגִּיזֵי[u] pref. id.)(Hiph. part. pl. c. m. fr. מַרְגִּיז d. 1b רגז

[a] Da. 9. 19. [b] Is. 50. 11. [c] 1 Ch. 26. 16, 18. [d] Is. 54. 16. [e] Je. 1. 16. [f] Job 7. 20. [g] 2 Ch. 35. 12. [h] Da. 5. 16. [i] Ps. 107. 35. [k] Pr. 8. 9. [l] Pr. 4. 22. [m] 2 Sa. 18. 18. [n] 1 Ch. 12. 16. [o] 1 Ch. 12. 8. [p] Eze. 13. 21. [q] Ec. 8. 17. [r] 2 Ch. 19. 10. [s] 2 Ch. 11. 5. [t] Is. 48. 18. [u] Ex. 15. 26. [x] Is. 63. 18. [y] 2 Ch. 30. 8. [z] Is. 13. 3. [a] Ge. 1. 10. [b] Je. 7. 14. [c] 2 Sa. 15. 19. [d] Je. 31. 34. [e] Ge. 29. 3. [f] Ge. 36. 40. [g] Ge. 23. 18. [h] Jos. 14. 4. [i] Nu. 32. 16. [k] Je. 9. 16. [l] De. 4. 32. [m] Ex. 26. 23; 36. 28. [n] Da. 1. 18. [o] Nu. 10. 2. [p] Da. 5. 8, 16. [q] Is. 5. 20. [qq] Ne. 12. 44. [r] Is. 9. 6. [s] 1 Ch. 23. 29. [t] Eze. 25. 5. [u] Job 12. 6. [uu] Ge. 33. 17.

לִמְרֹד[a] pref. לְ bef. (:))(Kal inf. constr. . . מרד

לְמָרְדֳּכַי / לְמָרְדֳּכָי וּ' pref. לְ)(pr. name m., see מָרְדֳּכַי; וּ bef. (:)

לְמָרְדְּכֶם[b] pref. לְ bef. (:))(Kal inf., suff. 2 pers. pl. m. מרד

לִמְרוֹד[c] in full for לִמְרֹד (q. v. & § 8. rem. 18) . מרד

לַמָּרוֹם[d] pref. לַ f. לְהַ / לְמָרוֹם pref. לְ q. v. } noun masc. sing. dec. 3a . רום

לַמְרוֹת pref. לַ [f. לְהַמְרוֹת] Hiph. inf. constr. (§ 11. r. 3) מרה

לַמֶּרְחָב pref. לַ for לְהַ)(noun masc. sing. dec. 2b רחב

לְמֶרְחֲבֵי[e] pref. לְ)(id. pl., constr. st. . . . רחב

לְמֵרָחוֹק preff. לְ, & מֵ for מִ·)((prim. adj.) subst. masc. sing. dec. 3a . . . . . רחק

לְמָרְטָה[f] pref. לְ)(Kal inf. constr. (§ 8. rem. 10) . מרט

לְמֹרְטִים[g] pref. id.)(id. part. masc., pl. of [מֹרֵט] d. 7b מרט

לְמָרֵי pref. id.)(adj. pl. constr. masc. [for מָרֵי] from מַר dec. 8 (§ 37. rem. 7) . מרר

לִמְרָיוֹת pref. לְ bef. (:))(pr. name masc. . . מרה

לְמָרִים[h] pref. לְ)(noun masc. pl. abs. [for מָרִים] from מַר dec. 8 (§ 37. rem. 7) . מרר

לְמִרְיָם pref. id.)(pr. name fem. . . . מרה

לְמֶרְכָּבוֹ[i] pref. id.)(noun masc. sing., suff. 3 pers. sing. masc. from מֶרְכָּב dec. 2b . . . רכב

לְמַרְכְּבֹתָיו[k] pref. id.)(noun fem. pl., suff. 3 pers. sing. m. fr. מֶרְכָּבָה, constr. מֶרְכֶּבֶת (§ 42. r. 5) רכב

לְמִרְמָא Chald., pref. id.)(Peal inf. . . . רמה

לְמִרְמָה[l] pref. id.)(noun fem. sing. dec. 10 . רמה

לְמִרְמָס pref. id.)(noun masc. sing. dec. 2b . רמס

לְמִרְמַס[m] וּ' pref. id.)(id. constr. st.; וּ bef. (:) רמס

לְמֵרֵעַ preff. לְ, & מֵ for מִ·)(with dist. acc. for רַע, adj. masc. sing. dec. 8 (§ 37. rem. 7) . רעע

לְמֵרֵעֵהוּ[n] pref. לְ)(n. m. s., suff. 3 p. s. m. fr. [מֵרֵעַ] d. 1b רעה

לְמֵרֵעֶךָ[o] pref. id.)(id. with suff. 2 p. s. m. [for עֲךָ'] רעה

לִמְרָרִי pref. לְ bef. (:))(pr. name masc. . . מרר

לְמָרֵשָׁה pref. לְ)(pr. name of a place, see מָרֵאשָׁה ראש

לְמַשָּׂא וּ'[p] pref. id.)(noun masc. s. d. 1b; וּ bef. (:) נשא

לְמַשְּׂאוֹת[q] pref. id.)(Kal inf. with preformative מ in the manner of the Chald. and the ending וֹת after the verb ל״ה (§ 23. r. 3 & 9, & § 8. r. 10) נשא

לְמַשֻּׁאוֹת[r] defect. for לְמַשּׁוּאוֹת (q. v.) . . שוא

לְמִשְׁבַּק[s] Chald., pref. לְ)(Peal inf. . . שבק

לְמֹשְׁבֹתָם[ll] pref. id.)(noun masc., pl. fem., suff. 3 pers. pl. masc. from מוֹשָׁב dec. 2b . . ישב

לְמִשְׂגָּב pref. לְ)(noun masc. sing., dec. 8a (suff. מִשְׂגַּבִּי § 37. No. 3c) . . . . שגב

לְמַשֶּׂגֶת[t] pref. id.)(Hiph. part. sing. fem. . . נשג

לְמֹשֶׁה pref. id.)(pr. name masc. . . . . משה

לְמַשּׁוּאוֹת[u] pref. id.)(noun fem., pl. of [מַשּׁוּאָה] d. 10 שוא

לִמְשׁוּבָתִי[x] pref. לְ bef. (:))(noun fem. sing., suff. 1 pers. sing. from מְשׁוּבָה dec. 10 . . . שוב

לִמְשׁוֹךְ[y] pref. id.)(Kal inf. constr. (§ 8. rem. 18) משך

לִמְשׁוֹל[z] pref. id.)(Kal inf. constr. (§ 8. rem. 18) משל

לִמְשׁוּסָּה[a] pref. id.)(Kh. מְשׁוּסָּה, K. מְשִׁסָּה noun fem. sing. dec. 10 . . . . שסס

לִמְשֹׁחַ[b] וְ'[c] pref. id.)(Kal inf. constr. . . משח

לְמָשְׁחָה[d] pref. לְ)(id. with fem. term. (§ 8. rem. 10); noun fem. Nu. 18. 8 . . . משח

לְמַשְׁחִית pref. id.)(noun masc. sing. . . שחת

לְמָשְׁחֲךָ[e] pref. לְ bef. (:))(Kal inf. [מְשֹׁחַ], suff. 2 pers. sing. masc. (§ 16. rem. 10 & 11; but others read מְשַׁחֲךָ from מְשַׁח) . . משח

לְמֵשִׁיב[f] pref. לְ)(Hiph. part. sing. masc. dec. 3b שוב

לִמְשִׁיחַ[g] pref. לְ bef. (:))(n. m. s., constr. of מָשִׁיחַ d. 3a משח

לִמְשִׁיחוֹ pref. id.)(id., suff. 3 pers. sing. masc. משח

לִמְשִׁיחִי[h] pref. id.)(id., suff. 1 pers. sing. . משח

לְמִשְׁכָּבוֹ[i] pref. לְ)(noun masc. sing. dec. 2b . שכב

לְמִשְׁכַּב pref. id.)(id., constr. st. . . שכב

לְמַשְׂכִּיל[k] pref. id.)(Hiph. part. sing. masc. dec. 1b שכל

לַמִּשְׁכָּן pref. לַ for לְהַ)(noun masc. sing. dec. 2b שכן

לְמִשְׁכַּן pref. לְ)(id. constr. st. . . . שכן

לְמִשְׁכְּנוֹתָיו pref. id.)(id. pl. fem., suff. 3 pers. sing. m. שכן

לְמָשָׁל וּ'[l] pref. id.)(noun masc. s. d. 4a; וּ bef. (:) משל

לִמְשֹׁל[m] / לִמְשָׁל־[o] וְ'[n] pref. לְ bef. (:))(Kal inf. constr., or (Job 17. 6) subst. masc. (§ 8. r. 18) משל

לְמִשְׁלַח[pp] pref. לְ)(noun m. s., constr. of [מִשְׁלָח] d. 2b שלח

לִמְשָׁלִים[p] וְ pref. לְ bef. (:))(noun m., pl. of מָשָׁל d. 4a משל

לִמְשֻׁלָּם וְ pref. id.)(pr. name masc. . . . שלם

לִמְשֶׁלֶמְיָהוּ וְ pref. id.)(pr. name masc. . . שלם

לִמְשַׁמּוֹת[q] pref. id.)(noun fem., pl. of מְשַׁמָּה dec. 10 שמם

לְמַשְׁמִיעִים[r] pref. לְ)(Hiph. part. m., pl. of מַשְׁמִיעַ d. 1b שמע

לְמִשְׁמַע[s] pref. id.)(n. m. s., constr. of [מִשְׁמָע] d. 2b שמע

לְמִשְׁמָר[t] pref. id.)(noun masc. sing. dec. 2b . שמר

לְמִשְׁמָרוֹת pref. id.)(pl. of the foll. (§ 44. rem. 5) . שמר

לְמִשְׁמֶרֶת / לְמִשְׁמָרֶת } pref. id.)(noun fem. sing. (suff. מִשְׁמַרְתּוֹ') dec. 13a . . . שמר

[a] Jos. 22. 29. [b] Jos. 22. 16. [c] Ne. 6. 6. [d] Job 5. 11. [e] Hab. 1. 6. [f] Eze. 21. 16. [g] Is. 50. 6. [h] Nu. 5. 24, 27. [i] 1 Ki. 5. 6. [k] Is. 2. 7 [l] Ps. 24. 4. [m] Mi. 7. 10. [n] Is. 7. 25. [o] Ju. 15. 2. [p] Nu. 4. 24. [q] Eze. 17. 9. [r] Ps. 74. 3. [s] Da. 4. 23. [t] 1 Ch. 21. 12. [u] Ps. 73. 18. [x] Ho. 11. 7. [y] Ec. 2. 3. [z] Eze. 19. 14. [a] Is. 42. 24. [b] Ju. 9. 8. [c] Da. 9. 24. [d] Ex. 29. 29. [e] 1 Sa. 15. 1. [f] Ru. 4. 15. [g] 1 Sa. 24. 7. [h] Ps. 132. 17. [i] Ex. 21. 18. [k] Pr. 15. 24. [l] Je. 24. 9. [ll] Ge. 36. 43. [m] Job 17. 6. [n] Ge. 1. 18. [o] Joel 2. 17. [p] Eze. 14. 8. [pp] Is. 7. 25. [q] Je. 48. 34. [r] 1 Ch. 16. 42. [s] Is. 11. 3. [t] Ex. 16. 34. [u] Eze. 38. 7.

Word	Analysis	Root
לִמְשַׂנְאַי[aa]	וְ pref. לְ bef. (:))(Piel (§ 10. rem. 7) part. pl. m., suff. 1 pers. s. from [מְשַׂנֵּא] d. 7 b	שׂנא
לְמִשְׁנֶה	pref. לְ)(noun masc. sing. dec. 9 a .	שׁנה
לִמְשִׁסָּה[a] / לִמְשִׁסּוֹת[b]	וְ, [a] pref. לְ bef. (:))(noun fem. sing. & pl. dec. 10	שׁסס
לְמִשְׁעִי[c]	pref. לְ)(noun masc. sing. . .	משׁע
לְמִשְׁעָן[d]	pref. id.)(noun masc. sing. dec. 2 b . .	שׁען
לְמִשַּׁעַר[e]	preff. לְ & מִ)(noun com. sing. dec. 6 d	שׁער
לְמִשְׁפָּחָה[f]	וּ pref. לְ)(noun fem. sing. dec. 11 a (c. פַּחַת', suff. פַּחְתּוֹ' dec. 13 a, § 42. r. 5); וּ bef. (:)	שׁפח
לַמִּשְׁפָּחוֹת[g] / לְמִשְׁפָּחוֹת[h]	pref. לְ f. לְהַ / pref. לְ q. v. — id. pl., abs. st. . .	שׁפח
לְמִשְׁפְּחוֹת[k]	וּ, ו pref. id.)(id. pl., constr. st.; וּ bef. (:)	שׁפח
לְמִשְׁפְּחוֹתֵיהֶם[i] / לְמִשְׁפְּחוֹתָם	pref. id.)(id. pl., suff. 3 pers. pl. masc. (§ 4. rem. 2) . .	שׁפח
לְמִשְׁפַּחַת	pref. id.)(id. sing., constr. st. . .	שׁפח
לְמִשְׁפְּחֹת	pref. id.)(id. pl., constr. st. . .	שׁפח
לְמִשְׁפְּחֹתָו[m]	pref. id.)(id. pl., suff. 3 p. s. m. (§ 4. r. 1)	שׁפח
לְמִשְׁפְּחֹתֵיהֶם[n]	pref. id.)(id. pl., suff. 3 pers. pl. masc.	שׁפח
לְמִשְׁפַּחְתּוֹ[o]	וּ pref. id.)(id. sing., suff. 3 p. s. m.; וּ bef. (:)	שׁפח
לְמִשְׁפְּחֹתָיו	pref. id.)(id. pl., suff. 3 pers. sing. masc.	שׁפח
לְמִשְׁפְּחֹתֵיכֶם	pref. id.)(id. pl., suff. 2 pers. pl. masc.	שׁפח
לְמִשְׁפְּחֹתָם	pref. id.)(id. pl., suff. 3 pers. pl. m. (§4. r. 2)	שׁפח
לַמִּשְׁפָּט / לְמִשְׁפָּט	pref. לְ for לְהַ / וּ, [p] pref. לְ q. v. — noun masc. sing. dec. 2 b; וּ bef. (:) . .	שׁפט
לְמִשְׁפַּט[q]	pref. id.)(id., constr. st. . .	שׁפט
לְמִשְׁפָּטִי[r]	pref. id.)(id. with suff. 1 pers. sing. .	שׁפט
לִמְשֹׁפְטִי[s]	pref. לְ bef. (:))(Poel (§ 6. No. 1) part., suff. 1 pers. sing. from [מְשֹׁפֵט] dec. 7 b .	שׁפט
לְמִשְׁפָּטֶיךָ[t]	pref. לְ)(noun masc. pl., suff. 2 pers. sing. masc. from מִשְׁפָּט dec. 2 b . .	שׁפט
לְמִשְׁפָּטִים[u]	וּ pref. id.)(id. pl., abs. st.; וּ bef. (:)	שׁפט
לְמִשְׁפָּטֶךָ[x]	pref. id.)(id. sing., suff. 2 p. s. m. [for מִשְׁפָּטְךָ]	שׁפט
לְמִשְׁקֶלֶת[y]	pref. id.)(n. f. s. [for מִשְׁקֶלֶת comp. § 35. r. 2]	שׁקל
לְמִשְׁרֵא[z]	Chald., pref. id.)(Peal inf.	שׁרא
לַמְשֹׁרְרִים[a]	וְ pref. לְ for לְהַ)(Pilel part. masc., pl. of מְשׁוֹרֵר dec. 7 b	שׁיר
לָמֵת[b] / לָמֵת	pref. לְ & לָ q.v.)(Kal part. act. sing. masc. dec. 1 a (§ 21. rem. 2, & § 30. No. 3)	מות
לְמֵתֵא[c]	Chald., pref. לְ)(Peal inf. [for מֵאתֵא § 53. No. 1, & § 56. No. 2] . . .	אתא
לְמָתוֹק	pref. לְ)(adj. m. s. (pl. מְתוּקִים § 32. r. 5)	מתק
לְמִתַּחַת[d]	preff. לְ & מִ)((prop. noun masc.) as a *prep.*, with suff. תַּחְתִּי see תַּחַת . .	תוח
לְמָתַי[e]	pref. לְ)(adv. interrog.	מתה
לִמְתָעֵב[f]	pref. לְ bef. (:))(Piel part. sing. masc. .	תעב
לְמִתַּפְּרוֹת[g]	pref. id.)(Piel part. f. pl., of [מְתַפֶּרֶת] d. 13 a	תפר
לָן[h]	וְ Kal pret. 3 pers. sing. masc. . .	לון
לַנָא[i]	Chald., pref. prep. ל with suff. 1 pers. pl.	ל
לְנֶאֱמָנִים[l]	pref. לְ)(Niph. part. m., pl. of נֶאֱמָן dec. 2 b	אמן
לַנְּבִאִים[m] / לִנְבִאִים[n]	pref. לְ for לְהַ / pref. לְ bef. (:) — noun masc., pl. of נָבִיא dec. 3 a . . .	נבא
לִנְבוּכַדְנֶצַּר / לִנְבוּכַדְרֶאצַּר	pref. id.)(pr. name masc. .	נבא
לְנָבוֹן	pref. לְ)(Niph. part. sing. masc. dec. 3 a	בין
לְנָבוֹת	pref. id.)(pr. name masc. . . .	נוב
לְנֹבַח	pref. id.)(pr. name of a place	נבח
לִנְבֹּחַ[o]	pref. לְ bef. (:))(Kal inf. constr. . .	נבח
לַנָּבִיא / לְנָבִיא	pref. לְ f. לְהַ / pref. לְ q. v. — noun masc. sing. dec. 3 a .	נבא
לִנְבִיאַי[p]	וְ pref. לְ bef. (:))(id. pl., suff. 1 pers. sing.	נבא
לִנְבִיאֵי	pref. id.)(id. pl., constr. state . .	נבא
לִנְבִיאֵינוּ[q]	וְ pref. id.)(id. pl., suff. 1 pers. pl. .	נבא
לְנָבָל	pref. לְ)(noun masc. s. d. 4 a, also pr. name	נבל
לְנִבְלֵי[r]	pref. id.)(noun m. pl. constr. fr. נֵבֶל d. 6 b	נבל
לַנְּבֹנִים[s]	pref. לְ for לְהַ)(Niph. part. m., pl. of נָבוֹן d. 3 a	בין
לַנֶּגְבָּה[t]	pref. id.)(n. m. s. (נֶגֶב) with loc. ה (§ 35. r. 3)	נגב
לְנֶגֶד	pref. לְ)((prop. subst. masc.) as a *prep.*, dec. 6 (§ 35. rem. 3) . . .	נגד
לְנֶגְדּוֹ[u]	pref. id.)(id., suff. 3 pers. sing. masc.	נגד
לְנֶגְדִּי	pref. id.)(id., suff. 1 pers. sing. . .	נגד
לְנֶגְדֶּךָ	pref. id.)(id., suff. 2 pers. s. m. (for נֶגְדְּךָ)	נגד
לְנֶגְדְּכֶם[x]	pref. id.)(id., suff. 2 pers. pl. masc. .	נגד
לְנֶגְדָּם	pref. id.)(id., suff. 3 pers. pl. masc. .	נגד
לְנֹגַהּ	וּ, [y] pref. id.)(noun m. s. d. 6 c (§ 35. r. 5)	נגהּ
לִנְגֹהוֹת[z]	pref. לְ bef. (:))(noun f., pl. of [נְגֹהָה] d. 10	נגהּ
לִנְגּוֹעַ[a]	in full for לִנְגֹּעַ (q. v. & § 8. rem. 18) .	נגע
לְנָגִיד	[b] וּ pref. לְ)(noun m. s. dec. 3 a; וּ bef. (:)	נגד
לִנְגִיד[c]	pref. לְ bef. (:))(id., constr. st. .	נגד
לְנַגֵּן[d]	pref. לְ)(Piel inf. constr. . . .	נגן
לְנֶגַע[e] / לַנֶּגַע[f]	pref. לְ or לַ q. v.)(noun masc. sing. (suff. נִגְעוֹ) dec. 6 a (§ 35. rem. 5)	נגע

[a] 2 Ki. 21. 14. [b] Hab. 2. 7. [c] Eze. 16. 4. [d] Ps. 18. 19. [e] Zec. 14. 10. [f] Ju. 18. 19. [g] Jos. 7. 14. [h] Ne. 4. 7. [i] Jos. 21. 20, 34. [k] Nu. 3. 30. [l] Jos. 18. 21. [m] 1 Sa. 10. 21. [n] Ge. 8. 19. [o] Ju. 21. 24. [p] 1 Sa. 30. 25. [q] 2 Ch. 19. 8. [r] Ps. 35. 23. [s] Job 9. 15. [t] Ps. 119. 91. [u] 2 Ch. 19. 10. [x] Ps. 119. 43. [y] Is. 28. 17. [z] Da. 5. 16. [a] 2 Ch. 5. 13 [b] De. 14. 1. [c] Da. 3. 2. [d] 1 Ki. 7. 32. [e] Ex. 8. 5. [f] Is. 49. 7. [g] Eze. 13. 18. [h] Ge. 32. 22. [i] 2 Sa. 12. 16. [k] Ezr. 4. 14. [l] Job 12. 20. [m] Je. 23. 9. [n] Am. 2. 11. [o] Is. 56. 10. [p] Ps. 105. 15. [q] Ne. 9. 32. [r] La. 4. 2. [s] Ec. 9. 11. [t] 1 Ch. 26. 17. [u] Jos. 5. 13. [x] Is. 1. 7. [y] Is. 60. 19. [z] Is. 59. 9. [a] Job 6. 7. [aa] De. 32. 41. [b] 1 Ch. 5. 2. [c] Eze. 28. 2. [d] 1 Sa. 16. 17. [e] De. 17. 8. [f] Le. 13. 2.

לִנְגֹּעַ pref. לְ bef. (:))(Kal inf. constr. . . נגע

לִנְגֹּף[a] pref. id.)(Kal inf. constr. . . נגף

לִנְדָבָה pref. id.)(noun fem. sing. dec. 11 c . נדב

לַנֹּדֵד[b] pref. לַ for לְהַ)(Kal part. act. s. m. d. 7b נדד

לְנִדָּה וּ[c] pref. לְ)(noun fem. sing. d. 10; וּ bef. (:) נדד

לִנְדֹּחַ[d] pref. לְ bef. (:))(Kal inf. constr. . נדח

לְנָדִיב[e] pref. לְ)((prim. adj.) noun masc. sing. d. 3a נדב

לִנְדֹּר pref. לְ bef. (:))(Kal inf. constr. . . נדר

לְנֶדֶר[f] וּ pref. לְ)(noun masc. sing. d. 6b; וּ bef. (:) נדר

לִנְדָרַי[g] pref. לְ bef. (:))(id. pl., suff. 1 p. s. (for נְדָרַי) נדר

לִנְדָרֶיהָ[h] pref. id.)(id. pl., suff. 3 pers. sing. fem. . נדר

לָנֶה[i] וְ Kal pret. 3 pers. sing. fem. [for לָנָה, comp. הַזּוֹרֶה for הַזּוֹרָה] . . . לון

לַנָּהָר[k] pref. לַ for לְהַ)(noun masc. sing. dec. 4a נהר

לְנַהֲרֵי pref. לְ)(id. pl., constr. st. . . . נהר

לָנוּ[l] לְ, וְ pref. prep. לְ with suff. 1 pers. pl. (§ 5, parad.); וְ see lett. ו . . . ל

לַנּוּ[m] וְ Kal pret. 1 pers. pl. [for לַנְנוּ § 25. rem.] לון

לָנוּד pref. לְ (see lett. ל))(Kal inf. constr. . נוד

לִנְוֵה pref. לְ bef. (:))(noun m., constr. of נָוֶה d. 9b נוה

לָנוּחַ[n] pref. לְ (see lett. ל))(Kal inf. constr. . נוח

לְנוּחֶךָ[o] pref. לְ)(noun masc. sing., suff. 2 pers. sing. masc. from נוֹחַ (comp. § 30. rem. 4) . נוח

לָנוּם[p] pref. לְ (see lett. ל))(Kal inf. constr. . נום

לָנוּס pref. id.)(Kal inf. constr. . . . נוס

לָנוּעַ pref. id.)(Kal inf. constr. . . . נוע

לְנוֹעַדְיָה pref. לְ)(pr. name fem. . . . יעד

לַנּוֹתָרִים[q] pref. לַ for לְהַ)(Niph. part. m., pl. of נוֹתָר יתר

לִנְזִירִים[r] pref. לְ bef. (:))(noun m., pl. of נָזִיר d. 3a נזר

לְנֹחַ pref. לְ)(pr. name masc. . . . נוח

לְנָחוֹר pref. id.)(pr. name masc. . . . נחר

לַנַּחַל[s] pref. לַ f. לְהַ } noun masc. sing. dec. 6d נחל

לַנָּחַל[t] pref. לַ f. לְהַ }

לְנַחַל pref. לְ q. v. }

לְנַחֵל[u] pref. id.)(Piel inf. constr. (§ 14. rem. 1) נחל

לִנְחֹל pref. לְ bef. (:))(Kal inf. constr. . נחל

לְנַחֲלָה pref. לְ)(noun fem. sing. dec. 12 d . נחל

לְנַחֲלַת[x] pref. id.)(id., constr. st. . . נחל

לְנַחֲלָתוֹ pref. id.)(id., suff. 3 pers. sing. masc. . נחל

לְנַחֵם[y] pref. id.)(Piel (§ 14. r. 1) inf. constr. d. 7b נחם

לְנַחֲמוֹ וּ[z] pref. id.)(id., suff. 3 pers. s. m.; וּ bef. (:) נחם

לְנַחֲמֵנִי pref. לְ)(id., suff. 1 pers. sing. . . נחם

לְנָחָשׁ pref. id.)(noun masc. sing. dec. 4 a . נחש

לַנְּחֹשֶׁת[a] וְ[b] pref. לַ f. לְהַ } noun com. sing., dec. 13c נחש

לִנְחֹשֶׁת[c] pref. לְ bef. (:) }

לִנְחֻשְׁתַּיִם[d] pref. id.)(id. dual, abs. st. (§ 44. rem. 4) נחש

לִנְחֻשְׁתָּם[e] pref. id.)(id. sing., suff. 3 pers. pl. masc. נחש

לַנְחֹתָם[f] pref. לַ contr. for לְהַנְחֹתָם, Hiph. inf. with suff. 3 pers. pl. masc. (§ 11. rem. 3) . נחה

לִנְטוֹעַ וְ in full for לִנְטֹעַ (q. v. & § 8. rem. 18) נטע

לִנְטוֹת pref. לְ bef. (:))(Kal inf. constr. . נטה

לִנְטֹעַ[g] pref. id.)(Kal inf. constr. . . . נטע

לַנֹּטְרִים[h] pref. לַ f. לְהַ } Kal part. act. masc., pl. of נוֹטֵר dec. 7b . . } נטר

לְנֹטְרִים[i] pref. לְ q. v. }

לִנְטֹת[k] defect. for לִנְטוֹת (q. v.) . . . נטה

לְנִידָה[l] pref. לְ)(noun fem. sing. R. נוּד; or for נִדָּה, dag. forte resolved in Yod . . נדד

לֵנִים[m] Kal part. act. masc. pl. [of לֵן § 21. rem. 2, & § 30. No. 3] dec. 1a . . . לון

לְנִינִי[n] וּ pref. לְ)(noun masc. sing., suff. 1 pers. sing. from נִין dec. 1a; וּ bef. (:) . נון

לְנִיצוֹץ[o] pref. id.)(noun masc. sing. . . נצץ

לְנֶכְדִּי[p] וּ pref. id.)(noun masc. sing., suff. 1 pers. sing. fr. נֶכֶד dec. 6 (§ 35. r. 3); וּ bef. (:) נכד

לְנֹכַח pref. id.)((prop. subst. m.) as a *prep.* & *adv.* נכח

לַנָּכְרִי[q] pref. לַ f. לְהַ } adj. masc. sing. נכר

לְנָכְרִי[r] pref. לְ q. v. }

לְנָכְרִים[s] pref. id.)(id. pl., abs. st. . . . נכר

לְנִמְהֲרֵי[t] pref. id.)(Niph. part. pl. constr. masc. from [נִמְהָר] dec. 2b . . . . מהר

לִנְמוּאֵל pref. לְ bef. (:))(pr. name masc., see נְמוּאֵל

לָנֻם defect. for לָנוּם (q. v.) . . . . נום

לְנֵס pref. לְ)(noun masc. sing. dec. 8b . נסס

לְנַסּוֹת pref. id.)(Piel inf. constr. dec. 1b . נסה

לְנַסּוֹתוֹ[u] pref. id.)(id., suff. 3 pers. sing. masc. נסה

לַנֶּסֶךְ pref. לַ for לְהַ)(noun m. s. (suff. נִסְכִּי) d. 6a נסך

לִנְסֹךְ[x] וְ pref. לְ bef. (:))(Kal inf. constr. . . נסך

לְנַסָּכָה[y] Chald., pref. לְ)(Pael inf. constr. (§ 47. r. 5) נסך

לְנִסְכֵּיכֶם[z] וּ pref. id.)(noun masc. pl., suff. 2 pers. pl. masc. from נֶסֶךְ dec. 6a; וּ bef. (:) . נסך

לְנַסֹּתוֹ[a] pref. id.)(Piel inf. (נַסּוֹת), suff. 3 p. s. m. d. 1b נסה

לְנַסֹּתְךָ[b] pref. id.)(id., suff. 2 pers. sing. masc. נסה

---

[a] Ex. 12. 23. [b] Je. 49. 5. [c] Zec. 13. 1. [d] De. 20. 19. [e] Pr. 17. 7. [f] Le. 22. 23. [g] Ps. 61. 6. [h] Nu. 30. 13. [i] Zec. 5. 4. [k] 1 Ki. 14. 15. [l] Ezr. 4. 3. [m] Ju. 19. 13. [n] 2 Sa. 21. 10. [o] 2 Ch. 6. 41. [p] Is. 56. 10. [q] Ju. 21. 7, 16. [r] Am. 2. 11. [s] Jos. 15. 7. [t] Jos. 17. 9, 9. [u] Nu. 34. 29. [x] Eze. 35. 15. [y] Is. 61. 2. [z] Job 2. 11.

[a] 1 Ch. 29. 2. [b] 1 Ch. 22. 14, 16. [c] 2 Ki. 25. 16. [d] 2 Sa. 3. 34. [e] Je. 52. 20. [f] Ex. 13. 21. [g] Is. 51. 16. [h] Ca. 8. 11. [i] Ca. 8. 12. [k] Ex. 23. 2. [l] La. 1. 8. [m] Ne. 13. 21. [n] Ge. 21. 23. [o] Is. 1. 31. [p] Ge. 21. 23. [q] De. 23. 21. [r] De. 14. 21. [s] La. 5. 2. [t] Is. 35. 4. [u] 2 Ch. 32. 31. [x] Is. 30. 1. [y] Da. 2. 46. [z] Nu. 29. 39. [a] 1 Ki. 10. 1. [b] De. 8. 2.

לְנָעֳמִי ו׳ pref. לְ)(pr. name fem.; וּ bef. (:) . נעם

לְנַעֲמָן pref. id.)(pr. name masc. . . . נעם

לַנַּעַר / לַנַּעַר[a] ו׳ pref. לַ f. לְהַ; לְנַעַר[b] pref. לְ q. v. } noun masc. sing. dec. 6d נער

לַנַּעֲרָ[c] ו׳ pref. לַ for לְהַ)(Kh. נַעַר׳ com. gen. (q.v.); K. נַעֲרָה׳ noun fem. sing. dec. 12d . נער

לְנַעֲרוֹ pref. לְ)(noun masc. sing., suff. 3 pers. sing. masc. from נַעַר dec. 6a . . נער

לְנַעֲרוֹתֶיךָ pref. id.)(noun fem. pl., suff. 2 pers. sing. masc. from נַעֲרָה dec. 12d . . נער

לִנְעָרֶיהָ[d] pref. לִ bef. (:))(noun masc. pl., suff. 3 pers. sing. fem. from נַעַר dec. 6d . . נער

לַנְּעָרִים pref. לַ for לְהַ)(id. pl., abs. st. . . נער

לְנַעֲרַת[e] pref. לְ bef. (:))(noun fem. sing. . . נער

לְנַעֲרֹתֶיהָ[f] pref. לְ)(noun fem. pl., suff. 3 pers. sing. fem. from נַעֲרָה dec. 12d . . נער

לִנְפֹּל[g] וְ pref. לִ contr. [for לְהַנְפִּיל] Hiph. inf. constr. (§ 11. rem. 3, & § 17. rem. 6) . נפל

לִנְפֹּל pref. לִ bef. (:))(Kal inf. constr. (§ 17. r. 1) נפל

לְנִפְלְאֹתָיו[h] pref. לְ)(Niph. part. pl. fem., suff. 3 pers. sing. masc. from נִפְלָאָה dec. 11a, from נִפְלָא m. פלא

לְנֶפֶשׁ / לָנֶפֶשׁ[k] pref. לְ (see לָ); לַנֶּפֶשׁ[l] pref. לַ for לְהַ; לְנֶפֶשׁ[m] / לְנֶפֶשׁ pref. לְ q. v. } noun com. sing. dec. 6a (§ 35. rem. 2) נפש

לְנַפְשָׁהּ[n] pref. id.)(id., suff. 3 pers. sing. fem. . נפש

לְנַפְשׁוֹ pref. id.)(id., suff. 3 pers. sing. masc. . נפש

לְנַפְשִׁי pref. id.)(id., suff. 1 pers. sing. . . נפש

לְנַפְשְׁךָ / לְנַפְשֶׁךָ[o] } pref. id.)(id., suff. 2 pers. sing. masc. נפש

לְנַפְשֵׁךְ[p] pref. id.)(id., suff. 2 pers. sing. fem. . נפש

לְנַפְשְׁכֶם[q] pref. id.)(id., suff. 2 pers. pl. masc. . נפש

לְנַפְשָׁם pref. id.)(id., suff. 3 pers. pl. masc. . נפש

לְנַפְשֹׁתֵיכֶם pref. id.)(id. pl., suff. 2 pers. pl. masc. . נפש

לְנַפְשֹׁתֵינוּ[r] pref. id.)(id. pl., suff. 1 pers. pl. נפש

לְנַפְשֹׁתָם[s] pref. id.)(id. pl., suff. 3 pers. pl. m. (§ 4. r. 2) נפש

לְנָפֶת[t] pref. id.)(noun fem. sing. constr. of [נָפָה] dec. 10, also pr. name . . . נוף

לְנַפְתָּלִי ו׳ pref. id.)(pr. name of a tribe; וּ bef. (:) פתל

לָנֶצַח pref לָ (see lett. ל))(noun masc. sing. (suff. נִצְחִי) dec. 6a (§ 35. rem. 5) . . נצח

לְנַצֵּחַ pref. לְ)(Piel inf. constr. . . . נצח

לָנֶצַח[u] pref. id.)(noun masc. sing. dec. 6e . נצח

לִנְצֹר[x] pref. לִ bef. (:))(Kal inf. constr. . . נצר

לְנֹצְרֵי[y] pref. לְ)(id. part. pl. constr. m. from נֹצֵר d. 7b נצר

לַנְּקֵבָה[z] וְ׳ pref. לַ for לְהַ)(noun fem. sing. . נקב

לְנִקְבָּצָיו[a] pref. לְ)(Niph. part. pl. masc., suff. 3 pers. sing. masc. [from נִקְבָּץ] . קבץ

לְנָקִי[b] pref. id.)(adj. masc. (constr נְקִי, pl. נְקִיִּים) dec. 8 (§ 37. No. 4) . . . נקה

לִנְקֹם[c] pref. לִ bef. (:))(Kal inf. constr. . . נקם

לַנֵּרוֹת[d] pref. לַ for לְהַ)(noun masc. with pl. fem. term. from נֵר dec. 1a . . נור

לְנֹשֵׂא[e] pref. לְ)(Kal part. act. sing. masc. dec. 7b נשא

לְנִשְׁבְּרֵי pref. id.)(Niph. part. pl. constr. masc. from נִשְׁבָּר dec. 2b . . . שבר

לַנִּשְׁבֶּרֶת[f] וְ pref. לַ for לְהַ)(id. sing. fem. . שבר

לְנָשַׁי[g] pref. לְ)(noun fem. with pl. masc. term. (נָשִׁים), suff. 1 pers. s. see אִשָּׁה irr. (§ 45) אנש

לַנָּשִׂיא[h] וְ׳ pref. לַ f. לְהַ; לְנָשִׂיא[i] pref. לְ q. v. } noun masc. sing. dec. 3a נשא

לְנָשָׁיו[k] pref. id.)(noun fem. pl. (נָשִׁים), suff. 3 pers. sing. masc. see אִשָּׁה irr. (§ 45) . אנש

לִנְשֵׁיכֶם[l] וְ pref. לִ bef. (:))(id. with suff. 2 pers. pl. m. אנש

לַנָּשִׁים pref. לַ for לְהַ; לְנָשִׁים pref. לְ q. v. } id. pl., abs. st. . אנש

לְנַשֵּׁק[m] pref. id.)(Piel inf. constr. . . נשק

לִנְשֹׁק[n] pref. לִ bef. (:))(Kal inf. constr. [for נְשֹׁק, § 8. rem. 18, & § 17. rem. 1] . נשק

לִנְתִיבוֹת[o] pref. id.)(noun fem. pl. of נְתִיבָה dec. 10 נתב

לְנָתָן ו׳ pref. לְ)(pr. name masc.; וּ bef. (:) . נתן

לִנְתַנְאֵל וְ pref. לִ bef. (:))(pr. name masc. . נתן

לִנְתוֹץ וְ pref. id.)(Kal inf. constr. (§ 8. r. 18, & § 17. r. 1) נתץ

לִנְתוֹשׁ pref. id.)(Kal inf. constr. (§ 8. r. 18, & § 17. r. 1) נתש

לִנְתָחֶיהָ pref. id.)(noun masc. pl., suff. 3 pers. sing fem. from נֵתַח dec. 6e . . . נתח

לִנְתָחָיו pref. id.)(id. pl., suff. 3 pers. sing. masc. . נתח

לִנְתִיבָתִי[p] pref. id.)(noun fem. sing., suff. 1 pers. sing. from נְתִיבָה dec. 10 . . . נתב

לַנֶּתֶק[q] וְ pref. לַ for לְהַ)(n. m. s. (for נֶתֶק § 35. r. 2) נתק

לְנַתֵּר[r] pref. לְ)(Piel inf. constr. . . . נתר

לִסְבֹב[s] pref. לִ bef. (:))(Kal inf. constr. (§ 18. r. 13) סבב

לִסְבִיבוֹתֵינוּ pref. id.)(noun masc. with pl. fem. term. and suff. 1 pers. pl. from סָבִיב dec. 3a סבב

---

[a] Ju. 19. 19. [b] Pr. 1. 4. [c] De. 22. 26. [d] 1 Sa. 25. 19. [e] Is. 1. 31. [f] Pr. 31. 15. [g] Nu. 5. 22. [h] Ps. 111. 4. [i] Nu. 5. 2. [k] Le. 19. 28; Nu. 9. 10. [l] Pr. 16. 24. [m] Pr. 13. 19. [n] De. 21. 14. [o] Pr. 2. 10. [p] Is. 51. 23. [q] Je. 6. 6. [r] Jos. 9. 24. [s] Pr. 1. 18. [t] Jos. 12. 23. [u] Is. 34. 10. [x] Pr. 2. 8. [y] Ps. 25. 10. [z] Le. 12. 7. [a] Is. 56. 8. [b] Pr. 1. 11. [c] Eze. 24. 8. [d] Zec. 4. 2. [e] 1 Sa. 31. 4. [f] Eze. 34. 4, 16. [g] 1 Ki. 20. 7. [h] Eze. 45. 7. [i] Nu. 17. 21. [k] Ge. 4. 23. [l] Ge. 45. 19. [m] Ge. 31. 28. [n] 2 Sa. 20. 9. [o] Je. 6. 16. [p] Ps. 119. 105. [q] Le. 14. 54. [r] Le. 11. 21. [s] Nu. 21. 4.

לִסְבֹּל[a] pref. לְ bef. (:))(Kal inf. constr. . . . סבל

לְסִבְלֹתֵיכֶם[b] pref. לְ)(noun fem. pl., suff. 2 pers. pl. masc. [from סְבָלָה or סִבְלָה] . . סבל

לִסְגּוֹר[c] pref. לְ bef. (:))(Kal inf. constr. (§ 8. r. 18) סגר

לְסִגִים pref. לְ)(noun m. pl. abs. for סִיגִים fr. סִיג' סוג

לִסְגֻלָּתוֹ[d] pref. לְ bef. (:))(noun fem. sing., suff. 3 pers. sing. masc. from סְגֻלָּה dec. 10 . . סגל

לַסְּגָנִים[e] וְ pref. לְ for לְהַ)(noun masc. pl. [of סָגָן or סֶגֶן comp. § 35. rem. 12] . . . סגן

לְסוּג[f] pref. לְ)(Kh. סוּג'; K. סִיג, noun masc. sing. dec. 1a, comp. לְסִגִים . . . . סוג

לַסּוּס pref. לְ for לְהַ)(noun masc. sing. dec. 1a . סוס

לְסוּסָיו[g] pref. לְ)(id. pl., suff. 3 pers. sing. masc. סוס

לַסּוּסִים[h] pref. לְ for לְהַ)(id. pl., abs. st. . . סוס

לְסוֹפָא[i] Chald., pref. לְ)(noun masc. sing. dec. 1a . סוף

לָסוּר pref. לְ (see lett. ל))(Kal inf. constr. . סור

לִסְחֹב[k] pref. לְ bef. (:))(Kal inf. constr. . . סחב

לַסֹּחֵר[l] pref. לְ for לְהַ)(Kal part. act. sing. m. d. 7b סחר

לְסִיחוֹן
לְסִיחֹן } pref. לְ)(pr. name masc. . . . סוח

לְסִיסְרָא pref. id.)(pr. name masc., see סִיסְרָא

לַסִּיר[m] pref. id.)(noun com. sing. dec. 1a . . סיר

לִסְלוֹחַ[n]
לִסְלֹחַ[o] } pref. לְ bef. (:))(Kal inf. constr. (§ 8. rem. 18) . . . . } סלח

לְסַלַּי pref. לְ)(pr. name masc. . . . סלל

לְסַנְבַלַּט וּ' pref. id.)(pr. name masc., see סַנְבַלַּט

לְסֻסָתִי[p] pref. id.)(noun fem. sing., suff. 1 pers. sing. from [סוּסָה] dec. 10 . . . . סוס

לִסְפֹּד
לִסְפּוֹד[q] } pref. לְ bef. (:))(Kal inf. constr. (§ 8. r. 18) ספד

לְסֹלֶת[r] וּ pref. לְ)(noun com. sing. dec. 6c; וּ bef. (:) סלת

לְסַעֲדָהּ[s] וּ pref. id.)(Kal inf. [סְעַד], suff. 3 pers. sing. fem. (§ 16. rem. 10); וּ id. . . סעד

לִסְפּוֹת[t] pref. לְ bef. (:))(Kal inf. constr. . . ספה

לִסְפּוֹתָהּ[u] pref. id.)(id. with suff. 3 pers. sing. fem. . ספה

לַסַּפַּחַת[x] וְ pref. לְ for לְהַ)(noun fem. sing. . ספח

לְסַפֵּר[y] וּ' pref. לְ)(Piel inf. constr.; וּ bef. (:) ספר

לִסְפֹּר pref. לְ bef. (:))(Kal inf. constr. . . ספר

לְסָקְלוֹ[z] pref. לְ)(Kal inf., suff. 3 pers. sing. masc. . סקל

לְסֶרֶד pref. id.)(pr. name masc. . . . סרד

לְסָרִיסָיו[a] pref. id.)(noun masc. pl., suff. 3 pers. sing. masc. from סָרִיס d. 1b (but see § 32. r. 2) סרם

לַסָּרִיסִים[b] pref. לְ for לְהַ)(id. pl., abs. st. . . סרם

לְסַרְנֵי[c] pref. לְ)(noun m. pl. constr. from [סֶרֶן] d. 6a סרן

לְסַרְנֵיכֶם[d] וּ pref. id.)(id. pl., suff. 2 p. pl. m.; וּ bef. (:) סרן

לִסְתּוֹם[e] pref. לְ bef. (:))(Kal inf. constr. (§ 8. rem. 18) סתם

לַסְתִּר[f] pref. לְ)(contr. and defect. [for לְהַסְתִּיר] Hiph. inf. constr. (§ 11. rem. 3) . . סתר

לַעַב. Hiph. *to mock at, to deride*, 2 Ch. 36. 16.

לָעָב pref. לְ (see lett. ל))(noun com. sing. dec. 1a (except constr. once עָב) . . . עוב

לַעֲבֹד וְ' pref. לְ bef. (-:))(Kal inf. constr. . . עבד

לְעֶבֶד pref. לְ)(noun masc. sing. (suff. עַבְדִּי) dec. 6a, also pr. name in compos. עֶבֶד מֶלֶךְ' עבד

לְעֹבֵד וּ' pref. id.)(pr. name in compos. עֹבֵד אֱדֹם עבד

לַעֲבֹדָה pref. לְ bef. (-:))(noun fem. sing. dec. 10 . עבד

לְעָבְדָהּ[g] pref. לְ)(Kal inf., suff. 3 pers. sing. fem. . עבד

לְעָבְדוֹ וּ' pref. id.)(id., suff. 3 pers. s. m.; וּ bef. (:) עבד

לְעַבְדוֹהִי Chald., pref. id.)(noun masc. pl., suff. 3 pers. sing. masc. from עֲבַד dec. 3a . . עבד

לְעַבְדִּי pref. id.)(noun masc. sing., suff. 1 pers. sing. from עֶבֶד dec. 6a . . . . עבד

לְעֹבְדֵי pref. id.)(Kal part. act. pl. constr. masc. from עֹבֵד dec. 7b . . . עבד

לְעַבְדְּיָה וּ pref. id.)(pr. name masc.; וּ bef. (:) . עבד

לְעֹבְדֵיהֶם[h] pref. id.)(Kal part. act. pl., suff. 3 pers. pl. masc. from עֹבֵד dec. 7b . . עבד

לְעַבְדֵיהֶם[i] pref. id.)(noun masc. pl., suff. 3 pers. pl. masc. from עֶבֶד dec. 6a . . . עבד

לַעֲבָדָיו וְ' pref. לְ bef. (-:))(id. pl., suff. 3 pers. s. m. עבד

לְעַבְדָיךְ[k] Chald., pref. לְ)(noun masc. pl., suff. (K. ךְ'דָּ) 2 pers. sing. masc. from עֲבֵד dec. 3a . עבד

לַעֲבָדֶיךָ וְ' pref. לְ bef. (-:))(noun masc. pl., suff. 2 pers. pl. masc. from עֶבֶד dec. 6a . . עבד

לַעֲבָדִים pref. id.)(id. pl., abs. st. . . . עבד

לְעַבְדְּךָ
לְעַבְדֶּךָ וּ'[l] } pref. לְ)(id. sing., suff. 2 pers. sing. masc.; וּ bef. (-:) . . . } עבד

לְעָבְדָם pref. id.)(Kal inf., suff. 3 pers. pl. masc. עבד

לַעֲבֹדַת וְ'[m] pref. לְ bef. (-:))(noun fem. sing., constr. of עֲבוֹדָה dec. 10 . . . . עבד

לַעֲבֹדָתוֹ[n] וְ'[o] pref. id.)(id., suff. 3 pers. sing. masc. . עבד

לַעֲבֹדָתָם pref. id.)(id., suff. 3 pers. pl. masc. . עבד

לְעַבְדֻתָם[p] pref. לְ)(noun fem. sing., suff. 3 pers. pl. masc. from [עַבְדוּת] dec. 10 . . עבד

---

[a] Ge. 49. 15. [b] Ex. 5. 4. [c] Jos. 2. 5. [d] Ps. 135. 4. [e] Ne. 2. 16. [f] Eze. 22. 18. [g] De. 11. 4. [h] 1 Ki. 5. 8. [i] Da. 4. 8, 19. [k] Je. 15. 3. [l] Ge. 23. 16. [m] Eze. 11. 11. [n] Is. 55. 7. [o] 2 Ki. 24. 4. [p] Ca. 1. 9. [q] Je. 16. 5. [r] 1 Ch. 23. 29. [s] Is. 9. 6. [t] Nu. 32. 14. [u] Ps. 40. 15. [x] Le. 14. 56. [y] Ps. 26. 7. [z] 1 Sa. 30. 6. [a] 1 Sa. 8. 15. [b] Is. 56. 4. [c] Ju. 16. 18. [d] 1 Sa. 6. 4. [e] 2 Ch. 32. 3. [f] Is. 29. 15. [g] Ge. 2. 15. [h] Zec. 2. 13. [i] Zec. 2. 13. [k] Da. 2. 4. [l] Le. 25. 6. [m] 1 Ch. 26. 30. [n] 1 Ch. 23. 26. [o] Ps. 104. 23. [p] Ne. 9. 17.

לַעֲבוֹד[a] in full for לַעֲבֹד (q. v. & § 8. r. 18) . עבד
לַעֲבוֹדָה pref. לַ bef. (-:)) noun fem. sing. dec. 10 . עבד
לַעֲבוֹדַת pref. id.) id., constr. st. . . . עבד
לַעֲבוֹדָתָם pref. id.) id., suff. 3 pers. pl. masc. . עבד
לַעֲבוֹר[i] pref. id.) Kh. לַעֲבוֹר q. v., K. לַעֲבָר־ q. v. (§ 8. rem. 18) . . . . . עבר
לַעֲבוֹר in full for לַעֲבֹר (q. v. & § 8. rem. 18) . עבר
לַעֲבֹט[e] pref. לַ bef. (-:)) Kal inf. constr. . . עבט
לַעֲבִידַת Chald., pref. id.) noun fem. sing., constr. of [עֲבִידָא] dec. 8a . . . . . עבד
לַעֲבִיר[g] contr. for לְהַעֲבִיר (q. v. & § 11. rem. 3) . עבר
לַעֲבֹר / לַעֲבָר־[h] pref. לַ bef. (-:)) Kal inf. constr. (§ 8. rem. 18) . . . . . עבר
לְעֵבֶר[i] וְ pref. לְ) noun masc. sing. dec. 6 (§ 35. rem. 6), also pr. name masc.; וּ bef. (:) עבר
לְעֶבְרוֹ[i] pref. id.) id., suff. 3 pers. sing. masc. . עבר
לְעֹבְרֵי[k] pref. id.) Kal part. act. pl. c. masc. from עֹבֵר dec. 7b . . . . . עבר
לָעִבְרִים pref. f. לָ f. לְהַ·, לְהָ) gent. n., pl. of עִבְרִי fr. עֵבֶר עבר
לָעִבְרִים[l] pref. לָ for לְהָ) id. pl., abs. st. . . עבר
לְעָבְרְךָ[m] pref. לְ) Kal inf., suff. 2 pers. sing. masc. עבר

[לָעַג] fut. יִלְעַג, *to mock, deride, scorn.* Niph. *to stammer*, Is. 33. 19. Hiph. *to mock, deride*, with בְּ, עַל, לְ.

לָעֵג adj. masc. dec. 5 (only pl. c. לַעֲגֵי).—I. *stammering, stammerer*, Is. 28. 11; Gesenius, *speaking in a foreign* or *barbarous tongue.*—II. *mocker, jester*, Is. 28. 11 לַעֲגֵי מָעוֹג *cake jesters*, i. e. *parasites*, who act the part of jesters at the table.

לַעַג masc. dec. 6d, *scorn, derision, scoffing*; meton. *cause of derision*, Ho. 7. 16.

לַעַג noun masc. sing. dec. 6d . . . . לעג
לֹעֵג Kal part. act. sing. masc. . . . לעג
לָעֲגָה id. pret. 3 pers. sing. fem. . . . לעג
לַעֲגֵי[n] adj. pl. constr. masc. from [לָעֵג] dec. 5c . לעג
לְעֶגְלָה pref. לְ) pr. name fem. . . . עגל
לְעֶגְלוֹן pref. id.) pr. name of a man and a place . עגל
לְעֶגְלוֹת[o] pref. id.) noun f., pl. c. fr. עֲגָלָה (no pl. abs.) עגל
לַעֲגָלִים[p] [q] וְ pref. לַ bef. (-:)) noun masc., pl. of עֵגֶל dec. 6 (§ 37. rem. 6) . . . . עגל
לַעְגָם[r] noun masc. sing., suff. 3 pers. pl. masc. from לַעַג dec. 6d . . . . . לעג

[לָעַד] Root not used; Arab. *to put in order.*

לַעְדָּה (*order*) pr. name masc. 1 Ch. 4. 21.

לַעְדָּן (*put in order*) pr. name masc. of two different persons.

לָעַד / לָעֲדֵי[s] pref. לָ & לְ q. v.) prep. עַד, constr. עֲדֵי, with suff. עָדַי (§ 21. rem. 5) . עדה
לָעַד[t] וְ pref. id.) noun masc. s. d. 1a; וּ bef. (:) עוד
לָעֵדָה pref. לָ for לְהַ·, לְהָ) noun fem. sing. d. 11b יעד
לַעְדָּה וְ pr. name masc. . . . . . לעד
לְעֵדָה pref. לְ) noun fem. sing. dec. 10 . . עוד
לְעֵדְוֹתֶיךָ[u] וּ pref. id.) (read ēhdĕvō-) noun fem. pl., suff. 2 p. s. m. from עֵדוּת (q. v.); וּ bef. (:) עוד
לְעִדּוֹא pref. id.) Kh. עִדּיא, K. עִדּוֹא (q. v.) . עדד
לַעְדָּן pr. name masc. . . . . . לעד
לְעַדְרִיאֵל pref. לְ) pr. name masc. . . . עדר
לַעֲדֹר[x] וְ pref. לַ bef. (-:)) Kal inf. constr. . . עדר
לַעֲדָרִים pref. id.) n. m., pl. of עֵדֶר d. 6 (§ 37. r. 6) עדר
לַעֲדַת[y] pref. id.) noun f. s., constr. of עֵדָה d. 11b יעד
לָעֵדֻת[z] pref. לָ for לְהַ·, לְהָ) noun fem. sing. (pl. with suff. עֵדְוֹתֶיךָ) . . . עוד
לַעֲדָתָם[a] pref. לַ bef. (-:)) noun fem. sing., suff. 3 pers. pl. masc. from עֵדָה dec. 11b . יעד

[לָעָה] *to be rash*, in speaking, Job 6. 3.

לָעוּ[b] [for לָעוּ] Kal pret. 3 pers. pl. . . לעה
לָעוּ[c] וְ Kal pret. 3 pers. pl. . . . . לוע
לְעוֹג וּ pref. לְ) pr. name masc.; וּ bef. (:) . עוג
לָעוֹז[d] pref. לָ (see lett. ל)) Kal inf. c. R. עוז, or for עז (§ 18. rem. 2) R. . . . עזז
לְעָוֶל[e] pref. לְ) noun masc. sing. . . . עול
לָעוֹלָה[f] pref. לָ for לְהַ·, לְהָ) noun fem. sing. d. 10 עלה
לְעוֹלֶה[g] pref. id.) Kal part. act. sing. masc. dec. 9a עלה
לְעֹלָה[h] [i] וְ pref. לְ) noun fem. sing. dec. 10; וּ bef. (:) עלה
לְעוֹלְלֵיהֶם[k] pref. id.) noun masc. pl., suff. 3 pers. pl. masc. from עוֹלֵל dec. 7b . . . עלל
לְעוֹלָם[l] וְ pref. id.) noun masc. s. d. 2b; וּ bef. (:) עלם
לְעוֹלַת[m] וּ pref. id.) n. f. s., constr. of עוֹלָה d. 10; וּ id. עלה
לַעֲוֹן[n] pref. לַ bef. (-:)) n. m. s., constr. of עָוֹן d. 3a עוה
לַעֲוֹנוֹתֶיךָ[o] pref. id.) id. pl., suff. 2 pers. sing. masc. עוה
לַעֲוֹנִי pref. id.) id. sing., suff. 1 pers. sing. . עוה
לַעֲוֹנָם pref. id.) id. sing., suff. 3 pers. pl. masc. . עוה
לַעֲוֹנֵנוּ[p] pref. id.) id. sing., suff. 1 pers. pl. . עוה

[a] 2 Ch. 33. 16. [b] 2 Ch. 34. 13. [c] 2 Ch. 31. 16. [d] Na. 2. 1. [e] De. 24. 10. [f] Ezr. 6. 7. [g] 2 Sa. 19. 19. [h] 1 Ki. 18. 6. [i] Is. 47. 15. [k] Pr. 9. 15. [l] Is. 51. 23. [m] De. 29. 11. [n] Ps. 35. 16. [o] Ho. 10. 5. [p] 1 Ki. 12. 32. [q] 2 Ch. 11. 15. [r] Ho. 7. 16. [s] Zep. 3. 8. [t] Is. 19. 20. [u] Ne. 9. 34. [x] 1 Ch. 12. 33. [y] Nu. 19. 9. [z] Ex. 31. 7. [a] Ho. 7. 12. [b] Job 6. 3. [c] Ob. 1. 16. [d] Is. 30. 2. [e] Job 31. 3. [f] Eze. 40. 42. [g] Eze. 40. 40. [h] Jos. 22. 26, 28. [i] Eze. 45. 15. [k] Ps. 17. 14. [l] Ps. 119. 160. [m] Ne. 10. 34. [n] Nu. 14. 19. [o] Job 22. 5. [p] Ex. 34. 9.

Word	Analysis	Root
לְעוֹף[a]	pref. לְ for לְהַ·, לְהָ)(noun masc. sing.	עוף
לָעוּף[b]	pref. לָ (see lett. ל))(Kal inf. constr.	עוף
לָעוֹף ·ו	·ו pref. לָ)(noun masc. sing.; ו bef. (:)	עוף
לְעִוֵּר[c]	pref. לְ for לְהַ·, לְהָ)(adj. masc. sing. d. 7b	עור
לָעוּת[d]	pref. לָ (see lett. ל))(Kal inf. constr.	עות
לְעַוֵּת[e]	[f]·ו pref. לְ)(Piel inf. constr.; ו bef. (:)	עות

[לָעַז] *to speak in a barbarous* or *foreign tongue*, Ps. 114. 1. Syr. id.

Word	Analysis	Root
לֹעֵז[g]	Kal part. act. sing. masc.	לעז
לַעֲזָאזֵל[h]	pref. לַ bef. (-:))(see under עֲזָאזֵל.	
לַעֲזֹב[i]	pref. id.)(Kal inf. constr.	עזב
לְעֹזֵב[k]	pref. לְ)(id. part. act. sing. masc. dec. 7b	עזב
לְעָזְבֵךְ[l]	pref. id.)(id. inf., suff. 2 pers. sing. fem.	עזב
לְעַזָּה	pref. id.)(pr. name of a place	עזז
לַעְזוֹר לַעְזוֹר[m]	in full for לַעֲזֹר & לַעְזֹר (q. v. & § 8. r. 18)	עזר
לְעָזִיאֵלִי	pref. לְ for לְהַ, לְהָ)(patronym. of עֻזִּיאֵל q. v.	עזז
לְעֻזִּיָּה לְעֻזִּיָּהוּ	pref. לְ)(pr. name masc.	עזז
לַעְזִיר[n]	Kh. לַעְזִיר pref. לַ, for לְהַעְזִיר Hiph. inf. c. (§ 11. rem. 3); K. לַעְזוֹר (q. v.)	עזר
לַעְזֹר לַעְזֹר	pref. לַ bef. (-:))(Kal inf. constr. (comp. § 13. rem. 2 & 1)	עזר
לְעֵזֶר[o]	pref. לְ)(noun masc. sing. dec. 6 (§ 35. r. 6)	עזר
לְעֶזְרָא	pref. id.)(pr. name masc.	עזר
לַעֲזָרָה[p]	pref. לַ bef. (-:))(noun fem. sing.	עזר
לְעֶזְרָה	pref. לְ)(noun fem. sing. dec. 12b	עזר
לְעָזְרוֹ[q]	pref. id.)(Kal inf., suff. 3 pers. sing. masc.	עזר
לַעֲזַרְיָה ·ו לַעֲזַרְיָהוּ ·ו	pref. לַ bef. (-:))(pr. name masc.	עזר
לְעֹזְרַיִךְ[r]	pref. לְ)(Kal part. act. pl., suff. 2 pers. sing. masc. [for עֹזְרֶיךָ § 4. r. 1] from עֹזֵר d. 7b	עזר
לְעָזְרֵנוּ	pref. id.)(id. inf., suff. 1 pers. pl.	עזר
לְעָזְרֵנִי	pref. id.)(id. id., suff. 1 pers. sing.	עזר
לְעֶזְרַת[s]	pref. id.)(noun f. s., constr. of עֶזְרָה d. 12b	עזר
לְעֶזְרָתִי	pref. id.)(id. with suff. 1 pers. sing.	עזר
לְעַזָּתִים	pref. לְ f. לְהַ·, לְהָ)(gent. n., pl. of עַזָּתִי fr. עַזָּה	עזז

לְעַט. Hiph. *to give to eat*, Ge. 25. 30.

Word	Analysis	Root
לַעֲטַלֵּפִים[dd]	וְ pref. לְ for לְהַ·, לְהָ)(noun masc., pl. of עֲטַלֵּף dec. 1b (§ 36. No. 1)	עטלף
לַעֲטֶרֶת[t]	pref. לַ bef. (-:))(n. f. s., pl. עֲטָרוֹת (§ 44. r. 5)	עטר
לְעַי ·ו לְעָי	pref. לְ for לְהַ·, לְהָ)(pr. name of a place	עוה
לְעִי[u]	pref. לְ)(n. s. m., pl. עִיִּים d. 8 (§ 37. No. 4)	עוה
לָעַיִט	pref. id.)(noun m. s., constr. of עַיִט d. 6h	עיט
לְעִיִּים[x]	pref. id.)(noun m., pl. of עִי dec. 8 (§ 37. No. 4)	עוה
לְעֵילוֹם[y]	pref. id.)(noun masc. sing.	עלם
לָעַיִן[z] לָעַיִן[a]	pref. לְ for לְהַ·, לְהָ)(noun fem. sing. d. 6h	עין
לְעֵינַי לְעֵינָי	pref. לְ)(id. du., suff. 1 pers. sing.	עין
לְעֵינֵי ·ו	·ו pref. id.)(id. du. constr. st.; ו bef. (:)	עין
לְעֵינֵיהֶם	pref. id.)(id. du., suff. 3 pers. pl. masc.	עין
לְעֵינָיו	pref. id.)(id. du., suff. 3 pers. sing. masc.	עין
לְעֵינֶיךָ	pref. id.)(id. du., suff. 2 pers. sing. masc.	עין
לְעֵינֵיכֶם	pref. id.)(id. du., suff. 2 pers. pl. masc.	עין
לָעֵינַיִם[b] לָעֵינָיִם[c]	pref. לְ for לְהַ·, לְהָ — id. du., abs. st.	עין
לָעֵינַיִם	pref. לָ f. לְהַ (dag. f. impl.) — id. du., abs. st.	עין
לְעֵינַיִם[d]	pref. לְ q. v. — id. du., abs. st.	עין
לְעֵינֵינוּ	pref. id.)(id. du., suff. 1 pers. pl.	עין
לָעָיֵף[e]	pref. לְ for לְהַ·, לְהָ)(adj. masc. sing. dec. 5c	עיף
לַעֲיֵפָה[f]	pref. לַ bef. (-:))(id. fem.	עיף
לָעִיר לְעִיר	pref. לְ f. לְהָ pref. לְ q. v. — noun fem. sing. irr. (§ 45)	עור
לְעִירוֹ	pref. id.)(id. with suff. 3 pers. sing. masc.	עור
לָעֹלָה לְעֹלָה	pref. לְ f. לְהַ·, לְהָ pref. לְ q. v. — noun fem. sing. dec. 10	עלה
לַעֲלוֹז[g]	pref. לַ bef. (-:))(Kal inf. constr. (§ 8. rem. 18)	עלז
לַעֲלָוָן[h]	Ch., pref. id.)(noun fem. pl. abs. fr. [עֲלָו] d. 8c	עלה
לַעֲלוּקָה[i]	pref. id.)(noun fem. sing.	עלק
לַעֲלוֹת	pref. id.)(Kal inf. constr. dec. 1b	עלה
לָעֹלוֹת לְעֹלוֹת[k]	pref. לְ f. לְהַ·, לְהָ pref. לְ q. v. — noun fem., pl. of עוֹלָה dec. 10	עלה
לְעֵלִי	pref. id.)(pr. name masc.	עלה
לְעִלָּיָא[l]	ו Chald., pref. id.)(adj. masc. sing. emph. [of עִלַּי]; K. עִלָּאָה, dec. 7; ו bef. (:)	עלה
לְעֶלְיוֹן	pref. id.)(adj. masc. sing. dec. 1b	עלה
לָעֹלָם[m]	pref. לְ for לְהַ·, לְהָ)(noun masc. sing.	עלם
לְעֹלָם	pref. לְ)(noun masc. sing. dec. 2b	עלם
לְעָלְמַיָּא[n]	Chald., pref. id.)(noun masc. pl. emph. from עָלַם dec. 2a	עלם

a Le. 7. 26. b Pr. 26. 2. c Job 29. 15. d Is. 50. 4. dd Is. 2. 20. e La. 3. 36. f Am. 8. 5. g Ps. 114. 1. h Le. 16. 8, 10, 26. i Ge. 44. 22. k Pr. 15. 10. l Ru. 1. 16. m 2 Ch. 25. 8. n 2 Sa. 18. 3. o Is. 30. 5. p 2 Ch. 4. 9. q 1 Ch. 12. 22. r 1 Ch. 12. 18. s Ju. 5. 23. t Is. 28. 5. u Mi. 1. 6. x Ps. 79. 1. y 2 Ch. 33. 7. z Nu. 34. 11. a Eze. 12. 12. b Pr. 10. 26. c Ge. 3. 6. d Nu. 10. 31. e Is. 28. 12. f Is. 46. 1. g Is. 23. 12. h Ezr. 6. 9. i Pr. 30. 15. k 2 Ch. 31. 3. l Da. 4. 31. m 1 Sa. 20. 22. n Da. 2. 44.

לְעֹלָמִים[a] pref. לְ)(noun masc., pl. of עוֹלָם dec. 2b — עלם

לְעָלְמִין Ch., pref. id.)(noun m. pl. abs. from עָלַם d. 2a — עלם

לַעֲלֹת pref. לַ bef. (-:))(Kal inf. constr. — עלה

לְעֹלַת[b] pref. לְ)(noun fem. sing., constr. of עוֹלָה d. 10 — עלה

לְעֹלֹתֵיכֶם[c] pref. id.)(id. pl., suff. 2 pers. pl. masc. — עלה

לָעָם וְ pref. לְ f. לְהַ·, לְהָ
לְעָם
לְעָם[d] וּ pref. לְ q. v. } noun com. s. d. 8a (§ 45); וּ bef. (:) — עמם

לַעֲמֹד וְ pref. לַ bef. (-:))(Kal inf. constr. — עמד

לְעָמְדָהּ[e] pref. לְ)(id. with suff. 3 pers. sing. fem. — עמד

לָעַמֻּדִים[f] pref. לְ for לְהַ·, לְהָ)(noun masc. pl. (for עַמּוּדִים) from עַמּוּד dec. 1b — עמד

לְעַמּוֹ pref. לְ)(noun com. sing., suff. 3 pers. sing. masc. from עַם dec. 8d (§ 45) — עמם

לַעֲמוֹד in full for לַעֲמֹד (q. v. & § 8. rem. 18) — עמד

לָעַמּוּד pref. לְ f. לְהַ·, לְהָ
לְעַמּוּד[g] וּ pref. לְ q. v. } noun masc. sing. dec. 1b; וּ bef. (:) — עמד

לָעַמּוּדִים[h] pref. לְ for לְהַ·, לְהָ)(id. pl., abs. st. — עמד

לְעָמוֹק pref. לְ)(pr. name masc. — עמק

לְעֻמּוֹת[i] pref. id.)((prop., noun fem. pl. of עֻמָּה dec. 10) as a *prep.* — עמם

לְעַמֵּי[k] pref. id.)(n. com. pl. constr. fr. עַם d. 8a (§45) — עמם

לְעַמִּי pref. id.)(id. sing., suff. 1 pers. sing. — עמם

לַעֲמִיתֶךָ[l] pref. לַ bef. (-:))(noun fem. sing., suff. 2 pers. sing. masc. from עָמִית dec. 3a — עמה

לָעַמִּים[m] pref. לְ noun com., pl. of עַם dec. 8a (§ 45) — עמם

לְעַמֶּךָ[n]
לְעַמְּךָ[o] וּ } pref. id.)(id. sing., suff. 2 pers. sing. masc.; וּ bef. (:) — עמם

לְעַמֵּךְ[p] pref. id.)(id. sing., suff. 2 pers. sing. fem. — עמם

לֶעָמָל[q] pref. id.)(noun masc. sing. dec. 4c — עמל

לְעָמֵל[r] pref. id.)(adj. masc. sing. dec. 5c — עמל

לַעֲמָלֵק pref. לַ bef. (-:))(pr. name of a people — עמלק

לָעֵמֶק[s] pref. לְ for לְהַ·, לְהָ)(noun masc. sing. dec. 6b — עמק

לְעֵמֶק[t] pref. id.)(noun masc. sing. — עמק

לְעֵמֶק[u] pref. לְ)(noun masc. sing. dec. 6b — עמק

לַעֲמֹרָה pref. לַ bef. (-:))(pr. name of a place — עמר

לְעַמְרָם pref. לְ)(pr. name masc., see עַמְרָם — עמם

לָעַמְרָמִי pref. לְ for לְהַ·, לְהָ)(patronym. of the prec. — עמם

לַעֲמָשָׂא וְ pref. לַ bef. (-:))(pr. name masc. — עמש

לְעֻמַּת pref. id.)((prop. noun fem. sing., constr. of עֻמָּה dec. 10) *prep.* — עמת

לְעֻמָּתוֹ pref. id.)(id., suff. 3 pers. sing. masc. — עמת

לְעֻמָּתָם pref. לְ)(id., suff. 3 pers. pl. masc. — עמת

לַעַן Root not used; Arab. *to reject, detest;* also *to curse.* Hence

לַעֲנָה[x] וְ fem. *wormwood;* metaph. of *distress* — לען

לַעֲנְוֵי[y] pref. לְ)(adj. pl. constr. masc. fr. עָנָו d. 4c — ענה

לַעֲנוֹת pref. לַ bef. (-:))(Kal inf. constr. — ענה

לְעַנּוֹת[z] pref. לְ)(Piel inf. constr. dec. 1b — ענה

לְעַנֹּתוֹ[a] pref. id.)(id., suff. 3 pers. sing. masc. — ענה

לְעַנֹּתְךָ[b] pref. id.)(id., suff. 2 pers. s. m. [for עַנּוֹתְךָ] — ענה

לֶעָנִי pref. לֶ for לְהָ, bef. עָ for לְהַ; &
לֶעָנִי[c] pref. לְ)(adj. masc. s. d. 8 (§ 37. No. 4) } — ענה

לַעֲנִיִּים[d] וְ pref. לַ bef. (-:))(id. pl. abs. (Kh. עֲנִיִּים; K. עֲנָוִים (q. v.)) — ענה

לַעֲנִיֶּךָ[e] pref. id.)(id. sing., suff. 2 pers. sing. masc. — ענה

לַעֲנָשׁ[f] Chald., pref. id.)(noun masc. sing. — ענש

לַעֲנֹת[g] pref. לַ, contr. [for לְהֵעָנֹת], Niph. inf. constr. (§ 9. rem. 6) — ענה

לְעַנֹּת[h] pref לְ)(Piel inf. constr. — ענה

לָעֹפֶל pref. לְ for לְהַ·, לְהָ)(pr. name of a tower — עפל

לְעַפְעַפַּי[i] pref. id.)(noun masc. du., suff. 1 pers. sing. from [עַפְעַף] dec. 8d — עוף

לְעַפְעַפֶּיךָ[k] pref. id.)(id., suff. 2 pers. sing. masc. — עוף

לֶעָפָר pref. לֶ for לְהָ, bef. עָ for לְהַ; &
לְעָפָר pref. לְ)(noun masc. sing. dec. 4c } — עפר

לַעֲפַר[l] וְ pref. לַ bef. (-:))(id., constr. st. — עפר

לְעֹפֶר pref. לְ)(noun masc. sing. dec. 6c — עפר

לְעָפְרָה pref. id.)(pr. name of a place — עפר

לְעֶפְרוֹן pref. id.)(pr. name masc. — עפר

לָעֵץ pref. לְ f. לְהַ·, לְהָ
לְעֵץ pref. לְ q. v. } noun masc. sing. dec. 7a (§ 36. rem. 2 & 4) — עצה

לְעַצְּבוֹתָם[m] pref. id.)(noun fem. pl., suff. 3 pers. pl. masc. from עַצֶּבֶת q. v. — עצב

לַעֲצַבֵּי[n] pref. לַ bef. (-:))(noun masc. pl. constr. fr. [עָצָב] dec. 8a — עצב

לַעֲצַבֶּיהָ[o] וְ pref. id.)(id. with suff. 3 pers. sing. fem. — עצב

לָעֲצַבִּים[p] pref. לְ for לְהַ·, לְהָ)(id. pl., abs. st. — עצב

לְעֵצָה[q] pref. לְ)(noun fem. sing. dec. 11b — יעץ

לְעֶצְיוֹן pref. id.)(pr. name in compos. עֶצְיוֹן גֶּבֶר — עצה

לָעֵצִים pref. לְ for לְהַ·, לְהָ)(noun masc., pl. of עֵץ dec. 7a (§ 36. rem. 2 & 4) — עצה

לְעֶצֶם[r] pref. id.)(noun fem. sing. dec. 6a (for עֶצֶם § 35. rem. 2) — עצם

---

a Ec. 1. 10. b Nu. 28. 23. c Nu. 29. 39. d Je. 1. 18. e Eze. 17. 14. f Ex. 38. 17. g Je. 1. 18. h Ex. 38. 28. i Eze. 45. 7. k Ne. 10. 31. l Le. 25. 14. m Is. 2. 4. n Ex. 32. 12. o Ex. 8. 5. p Ru. 1. 10. q Job 5. 7. r Job 3. 20. s Ju. 1. 34. t Pr. 25. 3. u 2 Ch. 20. 26. x De. 29. 17. y Is. 11. 4. z Ps. 88. 1. a Ju. 16. 5, 19. b Ju. 16. 6. c Ps. 102. 1. d Pr. 3. 34. e De. 15. 11. f Ezr. 7. 26. g Ex. 10. 3. h Nu. 30. 14. i Ps. 132. 4. k Pr. 6. 4. l Ps. 22. 16. m Ps. 147. 3. n Ps. 106 38. o Is. 10. 11. p Ho. 14. 9. q Pr. 12. 15. r Pr. 16. 24.

לָעֲצָמוֹת[a]	pref. לְ for לְהַ·, לְהָ)(id. pl. abs. fem.	עצם
לְעַצְמוֹתֶיךָ[b]	pref. לְ)(id. pl. fem., suff. 2 pers. sing. m.	עצם
לַעֲצָמֶיהָ[c]	pref. לְ bef. (-:))(id. pl. m., suff. 3 pers. s. f.	עצם
לַעְצֹר[d]	pref. id.)(Kal inf. constr.	עצר
לַעֲצָתוֹ[e]	pref. id.)(noun fem. sing., suff. 3 pers. sing. masc. from עֵצָה dec. 11 b	יעץ
לַעֲצָתִי	pref. id.)(id. with suff. 1 pers. sing.	יעץ
לַעֲקוֹר[f]	pref. id.)(Kal inf. constr. (§ 8. rem. 18)	עקר
לְעֵקֶר[g]	pref. לְ)(noun masc. sing.	עקר
לְעֶקְרוֹן	pref. id.)(pr. name of a place	עקר
לְעָר	pref. id.)(pr. name masc.	עור
לָעָרֶב[h] וְ / לָעֶרֶב וְ	pref. לְ for לְהַ·, לְהָ)(noun com. sing. dec. 6a (§ 35. rem. 2)	ערב
לְעֹרֵב[i]	pref. id.)(noun masc. sing. dec. 7b	ערב
לַעֲרֹב[k]	pref. לְ bef. (-:))(Kal inf. constr.	ערב
לְעֹרוֹ[l]	pref. לְ)(noun masc. sing., suff. 3 pers. sing. masc. from עוֹר dec. 1a	עור
לַעֲרוֹב[m]	in full for לַעֲרֹב (q. v. & § 8. rem. 18)	ערב
לַעֲרוּגוֹת[n]	pref. לְ bef. (-:))(n. f., pl. of [עֲרוּגָה] dec. 10	ערג
לֶעָרֵי[o] וּ	pref. לְ)(noun fem. pl. constr. (prop. from עָר see עִיר § 45); וּ bef. (:)	עור
לְעֵרִי	pref. id.)(pr. name masc.	עור
לֶעָרֶיהָ[p]	pref. id.)(noun fem. pl., suff. 3 pers. sing. fem. (prop. from עָר see עִיר § 45)	עור
לְעָרֵיהֶם[q]	pref. id.)(id. with suff. 3 pers. pl. masc.	עור
לְעָרָיךְ[r]	Chald., pref. id.)(noun masc. pl., suff. 2 pers. sing. masc. from עָר dec. 1a	עיר
לֶעָרִים וְ	pref. לְ for לְהָ, bef. עָ for לְהַ·)(noun fem. pl. of עָר see עִיר (§ 45)	עור
לְעָרִיץ[s]	pref. id.)(noun masc. sing., pl. עָרִיצִים d. 1b	ערץ
לַעֲרֹךְ[t]	pref. לְ bef. (-:))(Kal inf. constr.	ערך
לְעֵרָן	pref. לְ)(pr. name masc.	עור
לַעֲרָפֶל[u]	pref. לְ bef. (-:))(noun masc. sing.	ערף
לַעֲרֹץ	pref. id.)(Kal inf. constr.	ערץ
לָעֹשֶׂה[x]	pref. לְ for לְהַ·, לְהָ)(Kal part. act. sing. masc. dec. 9a	עשה
לְעֹשֵׂה	pref. לְ)(id., constr. st.	עשה
לְעֹשֵׂהוּ[y]	pref. id.)(id. with suff. 3 pers. sing. masc.	עשה
לְעֵשָׂו	pref. id.)(pr. name masc.	עשה
לַעֲשׁוּקִים[z]	pref. לְ bef. (-:))(Kal part. pass. masc., pl. of עָשׁוּק dec. 3a	עשק
לַעֲשׂוֹת וְ	pref. id.)(Kal inf. constr. dec. 1b	עשה
לַעֲשֹׂתָם[a]	pref. לְ bef. (-:))(id., suff. 3 pers. pl. masc.	עשה
לְעֹשֵׂי	pref. לְ)(Kal part. act. pl. constr. masc. from עֹשֶׂה dec. 9a	עשה
לֶעָשִׁיר[b] / לְעָשִׁיר	pref. לְ f. לְהַ, לְהָ / pref. לְ q. v. } noun masc. sing. dec. 3a	עשר
לַעֲשֹׁק[c]	pref. לְ bef. (-:))(Kal inf. constr.	עשק
לְעֹשְׁקָי[d]	pref. לְ)(id. part. act. pl. masc., suff. 1 pers. sing. from עוֹשֵׁק dec. 7b	עשק
לְעָשְׁקָם	pref. id.)(id. inf., suff. 3 pers. pl. masc.	עשק
לַעְשֵׂר[e]	pref. לְ, contr. [for לְהַעֲשִׂר], Hiph. inf. constr. (§ 11. rem. 2 & 3)	עשר
לְעֶשֶׂר[f]	pref. לְ)(num. card. fem.	עשר
לְעֹשֶׁר	pref. id.)(noun masc. sing. dec. 6c	עשר
לְעֶשְׂרִים[g]	pref. id.)(card. num. com., pl. of עֶשֶׂר (§ 35. rem. 16)	עשר
לַעֲשׂת	pref. לְ bef. (-:))(Kal inf. constr.	עשה
לַעֲשֹׂתָהּ	pref. id.)(id., suff. 3 pers. sing. fem.	עשה
לַעֲשֹׂתוֹ	pref. id.)(id., suff. 3 pers. sing. masc.	עשה
לְעַשְׁתּוֹת[h]	pref. לְ)(noun fem., pl. of עֶשֶׁת dec. 6a	עשת
לְעַשְׁתֹּת[i]	pref. id.)(n. f. s. (a different reading of the prec.)	עשת
לְעַשְׁתֵּי עָשָׂר / לְעַשְׁתֵּי עֶשְׂרֵה	pref. id. / pref. id. { id. pl. constr. of עֶשֶׁת only in combination with the num. *ten*, making together *eleven* }	עשת
לַעֲשֹׂתְכֶם[k]	pref. לְ bef. (-:))(Kal inf. (עֲשׂוֹת), suff. 2 pers. pl. masc. dec. 1b	עשה
לַעֲשֹׂתָם	pref. id.)(id., suff. 3 pers. pl. masc.	עשה
לָעַשְׁתָּרוֹת[l] וְ	pref. לְ for לְהַ·, לְהָ)(pl. of the foll. (§ 44. rem. 5).	
לְעַשְׁתֹּרֶת	pref. לְ)(pr. name of an idol, see עַשְׁתֹּרֶת	
לְעֵת וּ / לְעֶת־	pref. id.)(noun com. sing. dec. 8b (§ 36. rem. 3); וּ bef. (:)	עדה
לָעַתּוּדִים[m] וְ	pref. לְ for לְהַ·, לְהָ)(n. m., pl. of [עַתּוּד] d. 1b	עתד
לְעִתּוֹת	pref. לְ)(noun com. with pl. fem. term. from עֵת dec. 8b	עדה
לָעִתִּים[n] / לְעִתִּים[o] וּ	pref. לְ f. לְהַ·, לְהָ / pref. לְ q. v. } id. with pl. masc. term.; וּ bef. (:)	עדה
לְעָתְנִיאֵל	pref. id.)(pr. name masc., see עָתְנִיאֵל	
לַפֵּאָה[p] / לְפֵאָה[q]	pref. לְ f. לְהַ / pref. לְ q. v. } noun fem. sing. dec. 11b	פאה
לְפָאֵר	pref. id.)(Piel inf. constr.	פאר
לִפְאַת[r] וְ	pref. לְ bef. (:))(n. f., constr. of פֵּאָה d. 11b	פאה
לִפְגֹּעַ[s]	pref. id.)(Kal inf. constr.	פגע

a Eze. 37. 5. b Pr. 3. 8. c Ju. 19. 29. d 2 Ch. 22. 9. e Ps. 106. 13. f Ec. 3. 2. g Le. 25. 47. h 1 Ch. 23. 30. i Job 38. 41. k Eze. 27. 9. l Ex. 22. 26. m Ju. 19. 9. n Ca. 6. 2. o Is. 44. 26. p Nu. 32. 33. q 2 Ch. 31. 1. r Da. 4. 16. s Eze. 36. 4. t Job 15. 20. u Je. 13. 16. x Nu. 15. 29. y Is. 29. 16. z Ps. 146. 7. a Ps. 103. 18. b Ec. 5. 11. c Ho. 12. 8. d Ps. 119. 121. e De. 26. 12. f 1 Ki. 7. 38. g 1 Ch. 25. 27. h Job 12. 5. i Job 12. 5. k De. 4. 14. l Je. 14. 19. ll Ju. 2. 13. m Eze. 34. 17. n 1 Ch. 12. 32. o Eze. 12. 27. p Ex. 27. 9. q Ne. 9. 22. r Ex. 38. 11, 12, 13. s 1 Sa. 22. 17.

לָפַד Root not used; prob. *to shine*, whence Gr. λάμπω (μ inserted after the first radical) and subst. λαμπάς, Chald. לַמְפַּד, Syr. לַמְפִּידָא *lamp*.

לַפִּיד masc. dec. 1 b.—I. *lamp, torch.*—II. *flame.*

לַפִּידוֹת (*lamps*) pr. name of the husband of the prophetess Deborah, Ju. 4. 4.

לִפְדּוֹת pref. לְ bef. (:))(Kal inf. constr. פדה

לַפִּדִים[a] [b]וְ׳ defect. for לַפִּידִים (q. v.) לפד

לָפֶה pref. לָ (see לְ) } noun masc. sing. irr. (§ 45) פאה
לְפֶה pref. לְ q. v. }

לְפֻוָּה pref. id.)(pr. name masc., see פֻּוָּה

לְפוֹטִיפַר pref. id.)(pr. name masc., see פּוֹטִי׳

לְפוּל pref. id.)(pr. name masc. פול

לְפוּקָה[c] pref. id.)(noun fem. sing. פוק

לְפָח[d] } pref. id.)(noun masc. sing., pl. פַּחִים
לְפַח } (§ 37. rem. 7) } פחח

לְפַחַד[e] pref. id.)(noun masc. sing. dec. 6 d פחד

לְפַחַת[mm] pref. לְ (see lett. ל))(Kal inf. constr. נפח

לְפֶחָתֶךָ[f] pref. לְ)(noun masc. sing. with fem. term. and suff. 2 pers. s. m. from פֶּחָה irr. (§ 45) פחה

לְפִי וּ׳ pref. id.)(noun masc. constr., or with suff. 1 p. s. from פֶּה irr. (§ 45); וּ bef. (:) פאה

לַפִּיד [g]וְ׳ noun masc. sing. dec. 1 b לפד

לַפִּידוֹת pr. name fem. לפד

לַפִּידִים[h] noun masc., pl. of לַפִּיד dec. 1 b לפד

לְפִיהוּ[i] pref. לְ)(noun masc. sing., suff. 3 pers. sing. masc. from פֶּה irr. (§ 45) פאה

לְפִיהֶם[k] pref. id.)(id., suff. 3 pers. pl. masc. פאה

לְפִיהֶן[l] pref. id.)(id., suff. 3 pers. pl. fem. פאה

לְפִיו pref. id.)(id., suff. 3 pers. sing. masc. פאה

לְפַלֵּא pref. id.)(Piel inf. constr. פלא

לִפְלַגּוֹת[m] pref. לְ bef. (:))(noun f., pl. of [פְּלַגָּה] d. 10 פלג

לִפְלֻגּוֹת[n] pref. id.)(noun fem., pl. of [פְּלֻגָּה] dec. 10 פלג

לְפַלּוּא pref. לְ)(pr. name masc. פלא

לְפָלְחַן[o] Chald., pref. id.)(noun masc. sing., constr. of [פָּלְחָן] dec. 1 b פלח

לְפַלְטִי pref. id.)(pr. name masc. פלט

לִפְלֵיטָה pref. לְ bef. (:))(noun fem. sing. dec. 10 פלט

לִפְלֵיטַת pref. id.)(id. constr. st. פלט

לְפִלְכּוֹ[p] pref. לְ)(noun masc. sing., suff. 3 pers. sing. masc. from פֶּלֶךְ dec. 6 a פלך

לַפַּלְמוֹנִי[q] pref. לַ for לְהַ)(by contr. for פְּלֹנִי אַלְמֹנִי see פלה

לַפְּלִשְׁתִּים pref. לַ for לְהַ)(gent. noun, pl. of פְּלִשְׁתִּי פלש

לְפִנָּה[r] pref. לְ)(noun fem. sing. dec. 10 פנן

לִפְנוֹת pref. לְ bef. (:))(Kal inf. constr. dec. 1 a פנה

לְפָנַי } pref. לְ)(noun masc. pl. (פָּנִים), suff. 1
לְפָנָי } pers. sing. from [פָּנֶה] dec. 9 b } פנה

לְפָנַי[s] [for לִפְנַי] adj. m. fr. the pl. constr. לִפְנֵי (q. v.) פנה

לִפְנֵי וְ׳ pref. לְ bef. (:))(noun masc. pl. constr. [from פָּנֶה], as a *prep.* פנה

לְפָנֶיהָ pref. לְ)(id., suff. 3 pers. sing. fem. פנה

לִפְנֵיהֶם וְ׳ pref. לְ bef. (:))(id., suff. 3 pers. pl. masc. פנה

לְפָנָיו וּ׳ pref. לְ)(id., suff. 3 pers. s. m.; וּ bef. (:) פנה

לְפָנֶיךָ וּ׳ pref. id.)(id., suff. 2 pers. sing. masc.; וּ id. פנה

לִפְנֵיכֶם pref. לְ bef. (:))(id., suff. 2 pers. pl. masc. פנה

לַפָּנִים[dd] pref. לַ)(id. pl. abs. פנה

לְפָנִים pref. לְ)(id. pl. abs. *adverbially* פנה

לִפְנִימָה pref. לְ bef. (:))(n. m. s. (פְּנִים) with loc. ה פנם

לְפָנֵינוּ pref. לְ)(noun masc. pl. (פָּנִים), suff. 1 pers pl. from [פָּנֶה] dec. 9 b פנה

לִפְנִנָּה pref. לְ bef. (:))(pr. name fem. פנן

לַפִּסֵּחַ[t] pref. לַ for לְהַ)(adj. masc. sing. dec. 7 b פסח

לַפְּסָחִים[u] pref. id.)(noun masc., pl. of פֶּסַח dec. 6 a פסח

לַפְּסִילִים[x] pref. id.)(noun masc., pl. of [פָּסִיל] d. 3 a פסל

לְפִסְלוֹ[y] pref. לְ)(n. m. s., suff. 3 p. s. m. fr. פֶּסֶל d. 6 a פסל

לַפְּסִלִים[z] וְ defect. for לַפְּסִילִים (q. v.) פסל

לְפָעֳלוֹ[a] pref. לְ)(n. m. s., suff. 3 p. s. m. fr. פֹּעַל d. 6 f פעל

לִפְעֻלּוֹת[b] pref. לְ bef. (:))(noun f., pl. of [פְּעֻלָּה] d. 10 פעל

לְפֹעֲלִי[c] וּ pref. לְ)(Kal part. act., suff. 1 pers. sing. from פֹּעֵל dec. 7 b; וּ bef. (:) פעל

לְפֹעֲלֵי pref. id.)(id. pl., constr. st. פעל

לְפָעֳלָם[d] pref. id.)(n. m. s., suff. 3 p. pl. m. fr. פֹּעַל d. 6 f פעל

לִפְעֻלָּתֵךְ[e] pref. לְ bef. (:))(noun fem. sing., suff. 2 pers. sing. fem. from [פְּעֻלָּה] dec. 10 פעל

לִפְעֻלֹּתֵכֶם[f] pref. id.)(id., suff. 2 pers. pl. masc. פעל

לְפַעֲמוֹ[g] pref. לְ)(Kal inf. [פְּעֹם], suff. 3 pers. sing. masc. (§ 16. rem. 10) פעם

לִפְעָמַי[h] pref. לְ bef. (:))(n. f. s., suff. 1 p. s. fr. פַּעַם d. 6 d פעם

לְפִצְעִי[i] pref. לְ)(noun masc. sing., suff. 1 pers. sing. from פֶּצַע dec. 6 a (§ 35. rem. 5) פצע

לִפְקֹד [k]וְ׳ pref. לְ bef. (:))(Kal inf. constr. פקד

לִפְקֻדָּה[l] pref. id.)(noun fem. sing. dec. 10 פקד

לְפִקָּדוֹן[m] pref. לְ)(noun masc. sing. פקד

לִפְקֻדֵיהֶם defect. for לִפְקוּדֵיהֶם (q. v.) פקד

[a] Ju. 15. 4. [b] Ju. 7. 16. [c] 1 Sa. 25. 31. [d] Ps. 69. 23. [dd] Pr. 27. 19. [e] Job 39. 22. [f] Mal. 1. 8. [g] Ge. 15. 17. [h] Job 41. 11. [i] Ec. 6. 7. [k] Job 29. 9. [l] Le. 25. 51. [m] Ju. 5. 16. [n] 2 Ch. 35. 5. [o] Ezr. 7. 19. [p] Ne. 3. 17. [q] Da. 8. 13. [r] Je. 51. 26. [s] 1 Ki. 6. 17. [t] Job 29. 15. [u] 2 Ch. 35. 7, 8, 9. [x] Is. 42. 8. [y] Is. 44. 17. [z] Ho. 11. 2. [a] Ps. 104. 23. [b] Ps. 17. 4. [c] Job 36. 3. [d] Job 37. 12. [e] Je. 31. 16. [f] 2 Ch. 15. 7. [g] Ju. 13. 25. [h] Ps. 57. 7. [i] Ge. 4. 23. [k] Ho. 12. 3. [l] 1 Ch. 23. 11. [m] Ge. 41. 36. [mm] Eze. 22. 20.

לִפְקֻדָּתָם[s] pref. לְ bef. (:))(noun fem. sing., suff. 3 pers. pl. masc. from פְּקֻדָּה dec. 10 . פקד

לִפְקוּדֵיהֶם[t] pref. id.)(Kal part. pass. pl. masc., suff. 3 pers. pl. masc. from [פָּקוּד] dec. 3a פקד

לְפִקּוּדֶיךָ[c] pref. לְ)(noun masc. pl., suff. 2 pers. sing. masc. from [פִּקּוּד] dec. 1b . . פקד

לְפֶקַח pref. id.)(pr. name masc. . . פקח

לִפְקֹחַ[d] pref. לְ bef. (:))(Kal inf. constr. . פקח

לַפָּר pref. לְ for לְהַ)(פַּר, with the art.; & }
לְפָר[e] pref. לְ)(noun masc. sing. d. 8 (§ 37. r. 7) } פרר

לַפַּרְבָּר[f] pref. לְ for לְהַ)(noun masc. sing. . פרבר

לִפְרוֹץ[g] pref. לְ bef. (:))(Kal inf. constr. (§ 8. r. 18) פרץ

לְפֹרְחוֹת[hh] pref. לְ)(Kal part. act. fem., pl. of פֹּרַחַת dec. 13, from פֹּרֵחַ masc. . . פרח

לְפִרְיוֹ[a] pref. id.)(n. m. s., suff. 3 p. s. m. fr. פְּרִי d. 6i פרה

לַפָּרִים pref. לְ for לְהַ)(noun masc. pl. [for פָּרִים] from פַּר dec. 8 (§ 37. rem. 7) . פרר

לַפָּרֹכֶת pref. id. }
לְפָרֹכֶת[i] pref. לְ } noun fem. sing. . . . פרך

לְפָרַס pref. id.)(pr. name of a country . פרס

לְפַרְעֹה pref. id.)(pr. name masc., see פַּרְעֹה.

לְפֶרֶץ pref. id.)(pr. name masc. . . פרץ

לִפְרֹשׂ[k] pref. לְ bef. (:))(Kal inf. constr. . פרש

לְפָרָשִׁים וּ pref. לְ)(noun masc., pl. of פָּרָשׁ dec. 1b (§ 30. rem. 1); וּ bef. (:) . . פרש

לְפֹרְשִׂים[l] pref. id.)(Kal part. act. m., pl. of פֹּרֵשׂ d. 7b פרשׂ

לְפַשֵּׁט pref. id.)(Piel inf. constr. . . . פשט

לְפֶשַׁע pref. id.)(n. m. s. (suff. פִּשְׁעִי) d. 6a (§ 35. r. 5) פשע

לִפְשֹׁעַ pref. לְ bef. (:))(Kal inf. constr. . פשע

לַפֹּשְׁעִים[m] וְ pref. לְ f. לְהַ)(id. part. a. m., pl. of פֹּשֵׁעַ d. 7b פשע

לְפִשְׁעֲכֶם pref. לְ)(noun masc. sing., suff. 2 pers. pl. masc. from פֶּשַׁע dec. 6a (§ 35. rem. 5) . פשע

לַפִּשְׁתִּים[n] pref. לְ for לְהַ)(noun fem. with pl. masc. term. from פִּשְׁתָּה dec. 10 . . פשת

[לָפַת] fut. יִלְפֹּת, *to embrace*, Ju. 16. 29. LXX περιέλαβε; Vulg. apprehendens. Targ. prehendit; Prof. Lee, intrans. *to turn towards*; const. with אֵת. Niph. —I. *to turn aside*, Job 6. 18.—II. *to turn oneself, turn round*, Ru. 3. 8.

לִפְתָאִים[o] pref. לְ bef. (:))(noun masc., pl. of [פְּתִי] dec. 6i (§ 35. rem. 15) . . . פתה

לְפֹתֶה[ll] וּ pref. לְ)(Kal part. act. sing. m.; וּ bef. (:) פתה

לַפֶּתַח[p] pref. לְ for לְהַ)(noun masc. sing. (suff. פִּתְחוֹ) dec. 6a (§ 35. rem. 5) . . פתח

לְפַתֵּחַ וְ[q] pref. לְ)(Piel inf. constr.; וּ bef. (:) . פתח

לְפֶתַח pref. id.)(n. m. s. (suff. פִּתְחִי) d. 6a (§ 35. r. 5) פתח

לִפְתֹּחַ pref. לְ bef. (:))(Kal inf. constr. . . פתח

לִפְתַחְיָה pref. id.)(pr. name masc., see פְּתַחְיָה . פתח

לְפֶתַע pref. לְ (noun masc.) only *adverbially* פתע

לִפְתֹּר[r] pref. לְ bef. (:))(Kal inf. constr. . . פתר

לְפַתֹּתְךָ[s] pref. לְ)(Piel inf. [פַּתּוֹת], suff. 2 p. s. m. d. 1b פתה

לֵץ וְ[t] Kal part. act. sing. masc. dec. 1a (§ 21. rem. 2, & § 36. rem. 2) . . . לוץ

לַצֹּאן[u] pref. לְ for לְהַ)(noun com. sing. dec. 1a צאן

לְצֹאנִי[x] pref. לְ)(id., suff. 1 pers. sing. . . צאן

לְצֹאנְךָ[y] pref. id.)(id., suff. 2 pers. s. m. (for צֹאנְךָ') צאן

לְצֹאנָם[z] pref. id.)(id., suff. 3 pers. pl. masc. . . צאן

לָצֵאת[a] וְ pref. לָ, when not followed by a genit., & }
לְצֵאת pref. לְ when followed by a genit.)(Kal inf. constr. dec. 1a (comp. § 23. rem. 4) } יצא

לְצֵאתָם pref. id.)(id. with suff. 3 pers. pl. masc. יצא

לַצָּבָא pref. לְ for לְהַ)(noun m. s. d. 4a (§ 33. r. 2) צבא

לְצִבָא pref. לְ)(pr. name masc. for צִיבָא . נצב

לִצְבָא[b] pref. לְ bef. (:))(noun masc. sing., constr. of צָבָא dec. 4a (§ 33. rem. 2) . צבא

לִצְבֹּא pref. id.)(Kal inf. constr. . . . צבא

לִצְבָאֲךָ[c] pref. id.)(n. m. s., suff. 2 p. s. m. fr. צָבָא d. 4a צבא

לְצִבְאֹתָם pref. לְ)(id. with pl. f. & suff. 3 pers. pl. m. צבא

לַצְבּוֹת[d] pref. לְ [for לְהַצְבּוֹת], Hiph. inf. constr. צבה

לִצְבִי pref. לְ bef. (:))(noun masc. sing. dec. 6i צבה

לְצִבְעוֹן pref. לְ)(pr. name masc. . . צבע

לְצַד[e] Chald., pref. id.)(noun masc. sing. . צדד

לְצָדוֹק וּ pref. id.)(pr. name masc.; וּ bef. (:) . צדק

לְצִדִּים[f] pref. id.)(noun masc., pl., of צַד dec. 8e צדד

לַצַּדִּיק pref. לְ f. לְהַ }
לְצַדִּיק[g] pref. לְ q. v. } adj. masc. sing. dec. 1b . צדק

לַצִּדֹנִים pref. לְ for לְהַ)(gent. n., pl. of צִידֹנִי fr. צִידוֹן צוד

לְצֶדֶק[h] pref. לְ)(noun masc. sing. (suff. צִדְקִי) d. 6a צדק

לִצְדָקָה pref. לְ bef. (:))(noun fem. sing. dec. 11c צדק

לְצִדְקִיָּהוּ pref. לְ)(pr. name masc. . . . צדק

לָצָו[i] pref. לָ (see lett. ל))(for צַו, noun masc. sing. צוה

לְצַוְּארֵי[k] pref. לְ)(noun m. pl. constr. from צַוָּאר d. 2b צור

לָצוּד[dd] pref. לָ (see lett. ל))(Kal inf. constr. . צוד

לְצוֹדֵד[l] pref. לְ)(Pilel inf. constr. . . . צוד

[a] 1 Ch. 24. 3. [b] 1 Ch. 23. 24. [c] Ps. 119. 40. [d] Is. 42. 7. [dd] Gen. 27. 5.
[e] Le. 4. 20. [f] 1 Ch. 26. 18. [g] Ec. 3. 3. [h] Ho. 10. 1.
[i] Le. 24. 3. [k] Le. 24. 12. [l] 1 Ch. 28. 18. [m] Is. 53. 12.
[n] Le. 13. 48. [o] Pr. 1. 4. [p] Ge. 4. 7. [q] 2 Ch. 2. 13.
[r] Ge. 41. 15. [s] 2 Sa. 3. 25. [t] Pr. 13. 1. [u] Ge. 47. 4.
[x] Eze. 34. 22. [y] Ex. 22. 29. [z] 1 Ch. 4. 39, 41. [a] Jos. 14. 11.
[b] Zep. 1. 5. [c] Ju. 8. 6. [d] Nu. 5. 22. [e] Da. 7. 25.
[f] Ju. 2. 3. [g] Pr. 9. 9. [h] Is. 32. 1. [hh] Eze. 13. 20.
[i] Is. 28. 10, 13. [k] Ju. 5. 30. [l] Eze. 13. 18. [ll] Pr. 20. 19.

לְצַוּוֹת[a] ו pref. לְ)(Piel inf. constr.; ו bef. (:) . צוה

לַצּוּלָה[b] pref. לַ for לְהַ)(noun fem. sing. . . צול

לָצוֹן noun masc. sing. . . . . לוץ

לָצוּר[c] pref. לָ (see lett. ל))(Kal inf. constr. . צור

לְצוֹר pref. לְ)(pr. name of a place . . צור

לְצוּר[d] ו׳ pref. id.)(noun m. sing. dec. 1a; ו bef. (:) צור

לַצּוֹרֵף[f] pref. לַ for לְהַ)(Kal part. act. masc. dec. 7b צרף

לְצַוֹּת defect. for לְצַוּוֹת (q. v.) . . . צוה

לִצְחִיחַ pref. לִ bef. (:))(noun m. s. Eze. 26. 4, 14. צחח

לְצַחֶק[e] / לְצַחֵק } pref. לְ Piel inf. constr. (§ 10. rem. 4, & § 14. rem. 1) . . . } צחק

לִצְחֹק[f] pref. לִ bef. (:))(noun masc. sing. . צחק

לְצִיבָא ו pref. לְ)(pr. name masc.; ו bef. (:) . נצב

לְצִידוֹן ו׳ pref. id.)(pr. name of a place; ו id. . צוד

לַצִּידֹנִים pref. לַ for לְהַ)(gent. n. pl. from the preced. צוד

לְצִיּוֹן ו׳ pref. לְ)(pr. name of a place; ו bef. (:) ציה

לְצִיִּים pref. id.)(noun masc. pl. [of צִיִּי] . . ציה

לֵצִים[g] ה׳ ו׳ Kal part. act. masc., pl. of לֵץ dec. 1a (§ 21. rem. 2, & § 36. rem. 2) . לוץ

לְצִיצִת[i] pref. לְ)(noun fem. sing. [for צִיצִית] . צוץ

לְצִיקְלַג pref. id.)(pr. name of a place, see צִיקְלַג.

לַצֵּל[k] pref. לַ f. לְהַ / לְצֵל[l] pref. לְ q. v. } noun masc. sing. dec. 8b צלל

לִצְלוֹת[m] pref. לִ bef. (:))(Kal inf. constr. . . צלה

לְצֶלֶם[n] ו׳ Ch., pref. לְ)(noun m. sing. d. 3a; ו bef. (:) צלם

לְצַלְמָא Chald., pref. id.)(id. emph. st. . . צלם

לְצַלְמָוֶת[o] pref. id.)(noun f. s. compd. of צֵל & מָוֶת, see צלל

לַצֵּלָע[p] pref. לַ for לְהַ)(noun fem. sing. dec. 4c (§ 33. No. 2, & rem. 3) . . . צלע

לְצֶלַע[q] pref. לְ)(noun m. s. (suff. צַלְעִי) d. 6a (§ 35. r. 5) צלע

לְצֶלַע[r] ו pref. id.)(noun fem. sing., constr. of צֵלָע (§ 33. rem. 3); ו bef. (:) . . צלע

לְצַלְעוֹ[s] pref. id.)(id., suff. 3 pers. sing. m. (§ 33. No. 2) צלע

לַצְּלָעוֹת[t] pref. לַ for לְהַ)(id. pl., abs. st. . צלע

לִצְלָפְחָד ו׳ pref. לִ bef. (:))(pr. name masc. see צְלָפְחָד

לְצִמָּאוֹן[u] pref. לְ)(noun masc. sing. . . . צמא

לִצְמָאִי[x] ו pref. לִ bef. (:))(noun masc. sing., suff. 1 pers. sing. from צָמָא d. 4a (§ 33. rem. 2) צמא

לִצְמָאָם[y] pref. id.)(id., suff. 3 pers. pl. masc. . צמא

לְצַמֵּחַ[z] pref. לְ)(Piel inf. constr. . . . צמח

לַצְּמִיתֻת[a] pref. לַ for לְהַ)(noun fem. sing. . צמת

לַצֶּמֶר[b] ו pref. לַ f. לְהַ)(for צֶמֶר, n. m. s. d. 6a (§ 35. r. 2) צמר

לְצַמָּתֵךְ pref. לְ)(noun f. s., suff. 2 p. s. f. fr. [צַמָּה] d. 10 צמם

לִצְמִתֻת[c] pref. לִ bef. (:))(noun fem. s., comp. לַצְּמִיתֻת צמת

לְצֹאנְכֶם[d] pref. לְ)(noun com. s., suff. 2 pers. pl. m. צֹנֶא dec. 7b, R. צנא, or by transp. for צֹאנְכֶם q.v. צאן

לִצְנִינִים[e] ו / לִצְנִנִים[f] ו } pref. לִ bef. (:))(noun masc. pl. [from צָנִין or צָ׳] . . . . } צנן

לִצְעֹק[g] pref. id.)(Kal inf. constr. . . . צעק

לְצֹפֶה[h] pref. לְ)(Kal part. act. sing. masc. dec. 9a צפה

לַצָּפוֹן pref. לַ for לְהַ)(noun masc. sing. dec. 3a צפן

לִצְפוֹן pref. לִ bef. (:))(pr. name masc., see צְפִיּוֹן צפה

לַצָּפוֹנָה[i] pref. לַ for לְהַ)(n. m. s. (צָפוֹן) with parag. ה צפן

לִצְפוּנָיו[k] pref. לִ bef. (:))(Kal part. pass. pl. masc., suff. 3 pers. sing. masc. from צָפוּן dec. 3a צפן

לְצִפּוֹר[l] pref. לְ)(noun com. s., pl. צִפֳּרִים (§ 30. r. 1) צפר

לִצְפִירַת[m] ו pref. לִ bef. (:))(noun fem., constr. of צְפִירָה dec. 10 . . . צפר

לְצָצִים[n] Pil. part. p. pl. m. [for מְלוֹצָצִים comp. § 10. r. 6] לוץ

לָצֶקֶת[o] pref. לָ (see lett. ל))(Kal inf. constr. . יצק

לְצֹר pref. לְ)(pr. name of a place, for צוֹר . צור

לְצָרָה[p] pref. id.)(noun fem. sing. dec. 10 [for צָרָה] from צַר masc. . . . צרר

לִצְרוֹף[q] pref. לִ bef. (:))(Kal inf. constr. (§ 8. r. 18) צרף

לְצָרַי[r] / לְצָרַי[s] } pref. לְ)(noun masc. pl., suff. 1 pers. sing. from צַר dec. 8 (§ 37. rem. 7) } צרר

לְצָרָיו pref. id.)(id. pl., suff. 3 pers. sing. masc. צרר

לְצָרֶיךָ[t] pref. id.)(id. pl., suff. 2 pers. sing. masc. צרר

לַצֹּרִים ו pref. לַ for לְהַ)(gent. n. pl. of צֹרִי from צוֹר צרר

לְצָרֵינוּ[u] pref. לְ)(noun masc. pl., suff. 1 pers. pl. from צַר dec. 8 (§ 37. rem. 7) . צרר

לְצָרַעַת[x] ו pref. id.)(noun fem. sing. dec. 13a; ו bef. (:) צרע

לַצֹּרֵף[y] pref. לַ for לְהַ)(Kal part. act. sing. masc. d. 7b צרף

לִצְרֹר[z] pref. לִ bef. (:))(Kal inf. constr. . . צרר

לַצְתָּ[a] ו Kal pret. 2 pers. sing. masc. . . לוץ

לִקְאַת[b] pref. לִ bef. (:))(n. f. s., constr. of קָאַת (q.v.) קוא

לָקֹב pref. לָ (see lett. ל))(Kal inf. constr. . קבב

לִקְבוֹר[c] in full for לִקְבֹּר (q. v. & § 8. rem. 18) . קבר

לְקֳבֵל / לָקֳבֵל[d] ו׳ } Chald., pref. לְ bef. (ֳ:) and contr. לָקֳ׳)(prep. . . . . } קבל

לְקָבְלָךְ[e] Chald., pref. לְ)(id. with suff. 2 pers. sing. m. קבל

לְקַבֵּץ[f] pref. id.)(Piel inf. constr. dec. 7b . קבץ

[a] Est. 4. 8. [b] Is. 44. 27. [c] 1 Sa. 23. 8. [d] Is. 8. 14. [e] Ex. 32. 6. [f] Eze. 23. 32. [g] Ps. 1. 1. [h] Pr. 1. 22. [i] Nu. 15. 39. [k] 2 Ki. 20. 10. [l] Is. 4. 6. [m] 1 Sa. 2. 15. [n] Da. 3. 5, 7, 10, 12, 14, 18. [o] Je. 13. 16. [p] Eze. 41. 9. [q] Ps. 38. 18. [r] Ex. 26. 20; 36. 25. [s] Job 18. 12. [t] Eze. 41. 6, 7. [u] Ps. 107. 33. [x] Ps. 69. 22. [y] Ne. 9. 15, 20. [z] Ju. 16. 22.

[a] Le. 25. 30. [b] Le. 13. 48. [c] Le. 25. 23. [d] Nu. 32. 24. [e] Nu. 33. 55. [f] Jos. 23. 13. [g] 2 Ki. 8. 3. [h] Eze. 33. 2. [i] 1 Ch. 26. 17. [k] Job 20. 26. [l] Eze. 39. 17. [m] Is. 28. 5. [n] Ho. 7. 5. [o] Ex. 38. 27. [p] Pr. 17. 17. [q] Da. 11. 35. [r] De. 32. 41. [s] 1 Ch. 12. 17. [t] Is. 64. 1. [u] Jos. 5. 13. [x] Le. 14. 55. [y] Pr. 25. 4. [z] Le. 18. 18. [a] Pr. 9. 12. [b] Ps. 102. 7. [c] Je. 19. 11. [d] Da. 5. 1. [e] Da. 2. 31. [f] Is. 66. 18. [ff] Ju. 17. 4.

לְקַבְּצִי[a] pref. לְ)(Kal inf., suff. 1 pers. sing. . קבץ

לַקֶּבֶר[b] pref. לְ for לְהַ)(noun m. s. (suff. קִבְרִי) d. 6 a קבר

לְקַבֵּר[c] pref. לְ)(Piel inf. constr. . . . קבר

לִקְבֹּר pref. לְ bef. (:))(Kal inf. constr. . . קבר

לְקָבְרָהּ[d] pref. לְ)(id., suff. 3 pers. sing. fem. . קבר

לְקָבְרוֹ[e] וּ pref. id.)(id., suff. 3 pers. s. m.; וּ bef. (:) קבר

לִקְבָרוֹת[f] pref. לְ bef. (:))(noun masc. with pl. fem. term. abs. from קֶבֶר dec. 6 a . . קבר

לְקִבְרֵי[g] pref. לְ)(id. pl. constr. masc. . . קבר

לִקְדוֹשׁ[h] וְ pref. לְ bef. (:))(adj. masc. sing., constr. of קָדוֹשׁ dec. 3 a . . . . קדשׁ

לִקְדוֹשִׁים[i] pref. id.)(id. pl., abs. st. . . קדשׁ

לַקָּדִים[k] וְ[l] pref. לְ for לְהַ)(noun masc. sing. with ה parag., קָדִימָה . . . קדם

לְקַדִּישֵׁי[m] וּ Chald., pref. לְ)(adj. pl. constr. masc. from קַדִּישׁ dec. 1 a; וּ bef. (:) . . קדשׁ

לְקַדְמִיאֵל pref. id.)(pr. name masc. . . . קדם

לְקַדְמַתְכֶן[n] pref. id.)(noun fem. sing., suff. 2 pers. pl. fem. from קַדְמָה (no pl. abs.) . . קדם

לְקַדְמָתָן[o] pref. id.)(id. with suff. 3 pers. pl. fem. . קדם

לְקָדְקֹד וּ pref. id.)(noun masc. sing. (suff. קָדְקֳדוֹ & קָדְקֹדוֹ § 36. rem. 6) . . . . קדד

לְקֵדָר pref. id.)(pr. name of a tribe . . קדר

לַקֹּדֶשׁ[p] וְ[q] pref. לְ for לְהַ)(noun masc. sing. dec. 6 c קדשׁ

לְקָדֵשׁ pref. לְ)(pr. name in compos. קָדֵשׁ בַּרְנֵעַ קדשׁ

לְקַדֵּשׁ וְ[r] pref. id.)(Piel inf. constr.; וּ bef. (:) קדשׁ

לְקֹדֶשׁ pref. id.)(noun masc. sing. dec. 6 c . קדשׁ

לְקָדְשׁוֹ[s] pref. id.)(id., suff. 3 pers. sing. masc. . קדשׁ

לְקַדְּשׁוֹ[t] pref. id.)(Piel inf. (קַדֵּשׁ), suff. 3 p. s. m. d. 7 b קדשׁ

לַקֳּדָשִׁים[x] וְ pref. לְ for לְהַ)(noun m., pl. of קֹדֶשׁ d. 6 c קדשׁ

לְקַדְּשָׁם[u] pref. לְ)(Piel inf. (קַדֵּשׁ) suff. 3 p. pl. m. d. 7 b קדשׁ

לַקָּהָל[x] pref. לְ f. לְהַ }

לְקָהָל[dd] pref. לְ q. v. } noun masc. sing. dec. 4 a . קהל

לִקְהַל pref. לְ bef. (:))(id., constr. st. . . קהל

לִקְהָת וְ pref. id.)(pr. name masc. . . . קהת

לָקָו[y] pref. לְ (see לְ) }

לָקָו[z] pref. לְ q. v. } noun masc. sing. (suff. קַוָּם) d. 8 a (§ 37. r. 4) קוה

לְקֹוָיו[a] pref. id.)([for קֹוָיו] Kal part. act. pl., suff. 3 pers. sing. masc. from קוֶֹה dec. 9 a . קוה

לָקוֹחַ Kal inf. abs. . . . . . . לקח

לְקוֹל pref. לְ)(noun masc. sing. dec. 1 a . קול

לְקוֹלִי pref. id.)(id., suff. 1 pers. sing. . . קול

לְקוֹלֵךְ[b] pref. id.)(id., suff. 2 pers. sing. fem. . קול

לַקּוּם (*fortress*; Arab. لقم *to stop the way*) pr. name of a town in the tribe of Naphtali, Jos. 19. 33.

לָקוּם pref. לְ (see lett. ל))(Kal inf. constr. d. 1 a קום

לַקּוֹצְרִים[c] pref. לְ for לְהַ)(Kal part. act. masc., pl. of קוֹצֵר dec. 7 b . . . . קצר

לָקַח וְ fut. יִקַּח (see more under § 17. rem. 8).—I. *to take, to take hold of*, with acc. of the pers., and בְּ *by*; לְ אִשָּׁה *to take a wife*.—II. *to take away*.—III. *to take possession of, seize, capture*.—IV. *to take, receive*. Niph. נִלְקַח *to be taken*. Pu. and Hoph. id. Hithpa. part. אֵשׁ מִתְלַקַּחַת *continuous fire*, prop. *taking hold of itself*.

לֶקַח masc. dec. 6 (with suff. לִקְחִי § 35. r. 5).—I. *captivating, persuasive speech*, Pr. 7. 21.—II. *doctrine, instruction*.

לִקְחִי (*captivating*) pr. name masc. 2 Ch. 19. 7.

מַלְקוֹחַ masc. dec. 1 b.—I. *spoil, booty*.—II. du. מַלְקוֹחַיִם *the jaws*, Ps. 22. 16.

מֶלְקָח, מַלְקָח masc. dec. 2 b, only du. מֶלְקָחַיִם.—I. *tongs*, for the fire, Is. 6. 6.—II. *snuffers*.

מִקָּח masc. *receiving, accepting*, 1 Ch. 19. 7.

מַקָּחוֹת f. pl. (fr. מַקָּחָה) *merchandise*, Ne. 10. 32.

לָקַח Kal pret. 3 pers. sing. m. for לָקַח (§ 8. r. 7) לקח

לָקֹחַ[d] id. inf. abs. . . . . . לקח

לֶקַח noun m. s. (suff. לִקְחִי) d. 6 a (§ 35. r. 5) לקח

קַח[e] וְ Kal imp. sing. masc.; וּ bef. (:) . . לקח

לֹקֵחַ[f] וְ id. part. act. sing. masc. dec. 7 b . לקח

לֻקַּח }

לֻקָּח[g] וְ } Pual pret. 3 pers. s. m. (comp. § 8. r. 7) לקח

לָקְחָה[h] וְ Kal pret. 3 pers. sing. fem. . . לקח

לְקָחָהּ[i] וּ id. pret. 3 pers. sing. masc., suff. 3 pers. sing. fem.; וּ bef. (:) . . . לקח

לִקְחָהּ[k] noun masc. sing., suff. 3 pers. sing. fem. fr. לֶקַח dec. 6 a (§ 35. rem. 5) . . לקח

לֻקְחָה־[l] Pual pret. 3 pers. s. f. [for לֻקְּחָה § 10. r. 7] לקח

לָקְחוּ[m] וְ }

לָקָחוּ וְ } Kal pret. 3 pers. pl. (§ 8. rem. 7) . לקח

לֻקָּחוּ[n] Pual pret. 3 pers. pl. . . . לקח

לְקָחוּם וּ Kal pret. 3 pers. pl., suff. 3 pers. pl. masc.; וּ for וְ conv. . . . . . לקח

לִקְחִי וְ pr. name masc. . . . . לקח

לְקָחִי Kal imp. fem. (1 Ki. 17. 11), or noun masc. with suff. 1 pers. s. fr. לֶקַח d. 6 a (§ 35. r. 5) לקח

[a] Zep. 3. 8.
[b] Job 10. 19.
[c] 1 Ki. 11. 15.
[d] 2 Ki. 9. 35.
[dd] Ps. 40. 11.
[e] 1 Ki. 13. 29.
[f] Job 21. 32.
[g] 2 Ch. 28. 27.
[h] Is. 58. 13.
[i] Ps. 16. 3.
[k] Eze. 41. 14.
[l] Eze. 40. 23.
[m] Da. 7. 22, 25.
[n] Eze. 16. 55.
[o] Eze. 16. 55.
[p] Ex. 31. 11.
[q] Eze. 41. 23.
[r] Je. 17. 24.
[s] Ps. 114. 2.
[t] Ne. 10. 34.
[u] Le. 8. 11.
[x] 2 Ch. 30. 24.
[y] Is. 28. 10, 13.
[z] Is. 28. 17.
[a] La. 3. 25.
[b] Ca. 8. 13.
[c] Ru. 2. 4.
[d] De. 31. 26.
[e] Eze. 37. 16.
[f] Pr. 11. 30.
[g] Je. 29. 22.
[h] Le. 12. 8.
[i] De. 25. 5.
[k] Pr. 7. 21.
[l] Ge. 2. 23.
[m] 1 Ki. 20. 6.
[n] Je. 48. 46.

לְקֻחֵי Kal part. act. pl. constr. m. fr. לֹקֵחַ dec. 7b — לקח

לְקֻחִים[a] id. part pass. pl. abs. from [לָקוּחַ] dec. 3a — לקח

לְקָחָם[b] id. pret. 3 pers. sing. masc., suff. 3 pers. pl. m. — לקח

לָקַחְנוּ וְ id. pret. 1 pers. pl. — לקח

לְקָחַנִי[c] id. pret. 3 pers. sing. masc., suff. 1 pers. sing. — לקח

לָקַחַת וְ pref. לְ (see lett. ל))(id., inf. constr. (קַחַת § 17. rem. 8) dec. 13a — לקח

לָקַחְתָּ, וְלָקַחְתָּ } id. pret. 2 pers. sing. masc.; acc. shifted by conv. וְ (§ 8. rem. 7) — לקח

לָקַחַתְּ[d] וְ[e] id. pret. 2 pers. sing. fem. — לקח

לֻקָּחְתָּ[f] Pual pret. 2 p. s. m. [for לֻקַּחְתָּ comp. § 8. r. 7] — לקח

לְקַחְתָּהּ pref. לְ)(Kal inf. (קַחַת) dec. 13a, § 17. rem. 8, with suff. 3 pers. fem. sing. — לקח

לְקַחְתּוֹ[g] pref. id.)(id., suff. 3 pers. sing. masc. — לקח

לָקַחְתִּי[h], לָקַחְתִּי, וְלָקַחְתִּי } id. pret. 1 pers. sing.; acc. shifted by conv. וְ (§ 8. rem. 7) — לקח

לְקַחְתִּיו[i] id. id., suff. 3 pers. sing. masc. — לקח

לְקַחְתִּיךָ[k] וּ id. id., suff. 2 pers. sing. m.; וּ for וְ conv. — לקח

לְקַחְתִּים[l] וּ id. id., suff. 3 pers. pl. masc.; וּ id. — לקח

לְקַחְתֵּךְ[m] pref. לְ)(id. inf. constr. (קַחַת § 17. rem. 8), suff. 2 pers. sing. fem. dec. 13a — לקח

לְקַחְתֶּם וּ id. pret. 2 pers. pl. masc.; וּ for וְ conv. — לקח

לְקַחְתָּנוּ[n] id. pret. 2 pers. sing. masc., suff. 1 pers. pl. — לקח

[לָקַט] *to collect, gather, glean.* Pi. id. Pu. *to be gathered together.* Hithp. id.

לֶקֶט masc. *a gleaning*, Le. 19. 9; 23. 22.

יַלְקוּט masc. *bag, scrip*, 1 Sa. 17. 40.

לֶקֶט וְ noun masc. sing. — לקט

לִקֵּטָה[o], וְלִקְּטָה[p] } Piel pret. 3 pers. sing. fem. (comp. § 8. rem. 7) — לקט

לָקְטוּ[q], וְלָקְטוּ[r] } Kal pret. 3 pers. pl. (§ 8. rem. 7) — לקט

לִקְטוּ id. imp. pl. masc. — לקט

לְקַטָּלָה[s] Chald., pref. לְ)(Peal inf. constr. (§ 47. r. 5) — קטל

לְקַטֵּר pref. id.)(Piel inf. constr. — קטר

לִקְטֹרֶת[t] וְ pref. לְ bef. (:))(noun fem. sing. dec. 13c — קטר

לִקַּטְתְּ[u] Piel pret. 2 pers. sing. fem. — לקט

לְקַיֵּם pref. לְ)(Piel inf. constr. — קום

לְקַיָּמָה[x] Chald., pref. id.)(Pael inf. constr. (§ 47. r. 5) — קום

לְקַיִן pref. id.)(pr. name masc. — קון

לְקִינָה pref. לְ)(noun fem. sing. dec. 10 — קון

לְקִיר pref. id.)(noun masc. sing. dec. 1a — קיר

לַקִּירוֹת[y] pref. לַ for לְהַ)(id. pl. — קיר

לְקִישׁ pref. לְ)(pr. name masc. — קוש

לְקֹלִ[z] pref. id.)(noun masc. sing. dec. 1a, for קוֹל — קול

לְקֹלִי[a] וּ pref. id.)(id., suff. 1 pers. sing.; וּ bef. (:) — קול

לַקַּלִּים[b] pref. לַ for לְהַ)(adj. pl. masc. from קַל d. 8d — קלל

לְקֹלֶךָ pref. לְ)(for לְקוֹלְךָ, noun masc. sing., suff. 2 pers. sing. masc. from קוֹל dec. 1a — קול

לְקַלֵּל pref. id.)(Piel inf. constr. dec. 7b — קלל

לִקְלָלָה וְ pref. לְ bef. (:))(noun fem. sing. dec. 11c — קלל

לְקַלְלוֹ[c] pref. לְ)(Piel inf. (קַלֵּל), suff. 3 pers. sing. masc. dec. 7b (§ 10. rem. 7) — קלל

לְקַלֶלְךָ[d] pref. id.)(id., suff. 2 pers. sing. masc. [for לְקַלֶּלְךָ § 2. rem. 2, & § 10. rem. 7] — קלל

לְקֹלָם pref. id.)(noun masc. sing., suff. 3 pers. pl. masc. from קוֹל dec. 1a — קול

לְקַלֵּס[e] pref. id.)(Piel inf. constr. — קלס

לְקֶלֶס[f] וּ pref. id.)(noun masc. sing.; וּ bef. (:) — קלס

לִקְמָצִים[g] pref. לְ bef. (:))(noun masc., pl. קֹמֶץ dec. 6c (§ 35. rem. 9) — מץ

לְקָנֶה[h] pref. לְ)(noun masc. sing. dec. 9b — נה

לַקֹּנֶה[i] pref. לַ for לְהַ)(Kal part. act. sing. m. d. 9a — נה

לִקְנוֹת וְ[k] pref. לְ bef. (:))(id. inf. constr. dec. 1b — נה

לְקִנְיָנָם[l] וּ pref. לְ)(noun masc. sing., suff. 3 pers. pl. masc. from קִנְיָן dec. 2b; וּ bef. (:) — נה

לִקְסָם־[m] pref. לְ bef. (:))([for קְסֹם § 8. rem. 18] Kal inf. constr. — סם

לַקֹּסְמִים[n] וְ pref. לַ for לְהַ)(id. part. act. masc., pl. of קֹסֵם dec. 7b — סם

לַקֵּץ pref. לַ for לְהַ; לְקֵץ וְ pref. לְ q. v. } noun masc. sing. dec. 8b; וּ bef. (:) — ץ

לְקַצְבֵי[o] pref. id.)(noun m. pl. constr. fr. קֶצֶב d. 6a — ב

לְקַצּוֹת[p] pref. id.)(Piel inf. constr. — ץ

לִקְצוֹת[q] pref. לְ bef. (:))(noun fem. pl. constr. from קָצָה dec. 11a — ה

לִקְצִין[r] וְ pref. לְ)(noun masc. s. d. 3a; וּ bef. (:) — ה

לַקָּצִיר[s] pref. לַ for לְהַ)(noun masc. sing. dec. 3a — ר

לִקְצָפָה[t] pref. לְ bef. (:))(noun fem. sing. — ף

לִקְצֹר[u] וְ[x] pref. id.)(Kal inf. constr. — ר

לִקְצָת[y] וְ Chald., pref. id.)(noun fem. sing., constr. of קְצָת dec. 1b — ה

[a] Pr. 24. 11. [b] Je. 27. 20. [c] Ge. 24. 7. [d] Eze. 22. 12. [e] 1 Ki. 14. 3. [f] Ge. 3. 19. [g] De. 24. 19. [h] Nu. 23. 20. [i] Ju. 17. 2. [k] Ge. 27. 45. [l] Am. 9. 3. [m] 1 Sa. 25. 40. [n] Ex. 14. 11. [o] Ru. 2. 17, 18. [p] Ru. 2. 16. [q] Ex. 16. 18. [r] Ex. 16. 22. [s] Da. 2. 14. [t] Ex. 40. 5. [u] Ru. 2. 19. [x] Da. 6. 8. [y] Eze. 41. 25 [z] Ex. 4. 8. [a] 2 Ki. 10. 6. [b] Ec. 9. 11. [c] Ne. 13. 2. [d] De. 23. 5. [e] Eze. 16. 31. [f] Je. 20. 8. [g] Ge. 41. 47. [h] Is. 35. 7. [i] Le. 25. 30. [k] 2 Ki. 12. 13. [l] Jos. 14. 4. [m] Eze. 21. 26. [n] 1 Sa. 6. 2. [o] Jon. 2. 7. [p] 2 Ki. 10. 32. [q] Job 28. 24. [r] Ju. 11. 6, 11. [s] Am. 4. 7. [t] Joel 1. 7. [u] Le. 19. 9. [x] 1 Sa. 8. 12, [y] Da. 4. 26,

[לָקַק] pret. לָקְקוּ, fut. יָלֹק *to lick, lap.* Pi. id. Ju. 7. 6, 7.

לָקְקוּ [a] Kal pret. 3 pers. pl. . . . . . לקק

לִקְרֹא pref. לְ bef. (:))(Kal inf. constr. . . . קרא

לִקְרַאת [ii] וְ pref. id.)(prep. [prop. noun fem. contr. for לִקְרָאַת, constr. of קְרָאָה] . . קרא

לִקְרָאתָהּ pref. id.)(id., suff. 3 pers. sing. fem. . קרא

לִקְרָאתוֹ pref. id.)(id., suff. 3 pers. sing. masc. . קרא

לִקְרָאתִי pref. id.)(id., suff. 1 pers. sing. . . קרא

לִקְרָאתֶךָ / לִקְרָאתְךָ [b] } pref. id.)(id., suff. 2 pers. sing. masc. . קרא

לִקְרַאתְכֶם pref. id.)(id., suff. 2 pers. pl. masc. . קרא

לִקְרָאתָם pref. id.)(id., suff. 3 pers. pl. masc. . קרא

לִקְרָאתֵנוּ pref. id.)(id., suff. 1 pers. pl. . . קרא

לַקְרָב [c] pref. לַ for לְהַ)(n. m. s. d. 1a (§ 30. No. 30) קרב

לְקָרְבָה [d] pref. לְ)(Kal inf. constr. (§ 8. rem. 10) . קרב

לְקָרְבַּן [e] pref. id.)(noun m. s., constr. of קָרְבָּן d. 2b קרב

לְקֻרְבַּן [f] וּ pref. id.)(noun masc., constr. of [קֻרְבָּן] dec. 2b; וּ bef. (:) . . . . . קרב

לִקְרוֹעַ [g] pref. לִ bef. (:))(Kal inf. constr. (§ 8. r. 18) קרע

לַקָּרוֹב [h] וְ pref. לַ for לְהַ)(adj. masc. sing. dec. 3a קרב

לִקְרוֹת [i] [k] וּ pref. לִ)(Piel inf. constr.; וּ bef. (:) . קרה

לַקָּרְחִי [l] וְ pref. לַ for לְהַ)(noun masc. sing. . . קרח

לְקֹרַח pref. לְ)(pr. name masc. . . . . קרח

לְקָרְחָה [m] וּ pref. id.)(noun fem. s. (no pl.); וּ bef. (:) קרח

לַקָּרְחִים pref. לַ for לְהַ)(patronym. pl. of קָרְחִי fr. קֹרַח קרח

לְקַרְנוֹת [n] וּ pref. לְ)(noun fem. pl. constr. (abs. קְרָנוֹת) from קֶרֶן dec. 6a; וּ bef. (:) . . קרן

לַקֶּרֶשׁ pref. לַ for לְהַ)(noun masc. sing. dec. 6a קרשׁ

לְקַרְשֵׁי pref. לְ)(id. pl., constr. st. . . . קרשׁ

לָקַשׁ Kal not used; Syr. *to be late.* Pi. *to glean, to gather the last fruits,* Job 24. 6.

לֶקֶשׁ masc. *latter grass, aftermath,* Am. 7. 1.

אֶלְקֹשִׁי gent. noun, *Elkoshite,* of the prophet Nahum from a place אֶלְקֹשׁ (more prob. from the Root קוּשׁ, אֵל being the art.) Na. 1. 1.

מַלְקוֹשׁ masc. *the latter rain,* which falls in Palestine in the months of March and April.

לְקֹשׁ pref. לְ)(noun masc. sing. . . . קשׁשׁ

לֶקֶשׁ [o] noun masc. sing. . . . . . לקשׁ

לִקְשֵׁה [p] pref. לִ bef. (:))(adj. m. s., constr. of קָשֶׁה d. 9b קשׁה

לְקֹשֵׁשׁ [q] pref. לְ)(Poel inf. constr. . . . קשׁשׁ

לְרֵא [r] pref. לְ [contr. for לִירֹא, לִירֹא], Kal inf. constr. ירא

לִרְאוּבֵן pref. לִ bef. (:))(pr. name of a tribe . ראה

לָרְאוּבֵנִי וְ pref. לָ for לְהַ· לְהָ)(gent. n. fr. the preced. ראה

לִרְאָוָה [s] pref. לִ)(Kal inf. constr. (§ 24. rem. 2) ראה

לֵרָאוֹת contr. for לְהֵרָאוֹת (q. v. & § 9. rem. 6) ראה

לִרְאוֹת וְ pref. לִ bef. (:))(Kal inf. constr. dec. 1a . ראה

לִרְאוֹתוֹ [t] pref. id.)(id., suff. 3 pers. sing. masc. . ראה

לִרְאוֹתֶךָ [u] pref. id.)(id., suff. 2 p. s. m. [for רְאוֹתְךָ] ראה

לְרֹאֵי [x] pref. לְ)(Kal part. a. pl. constr. m. fr. רֹאֶה d. 9a ראה

לָרֹאִים [y] pref. לָ for לְהַ· לְהָ)(id. pl., abs. st. . ראה

לְרֹאשׁ [z] pref. id. / לְרֹאשׁ pref. לְ } noun masc. sing. irr. (§ 45) . ראשׁ

לְרֹאשׁוֹ [a] pref. id.)(id., suff. 3 pers. sing. masc. . ראשׁ

לְרָאשֵׁי pref. id.)(id. pl., constr. st. . . ראשׁ

לְרֹאשִׁי pref. id.)(id. sing., suff. 1 pers. sing. ראשׁ

לְרָאשָׁיו וּ pref. id.)(id. pl., suff. 3 p. s. m.; וּ bef. (:) ראשׁ

לָרֵאשִׁית [b] pref. לָ for לְהַ· לְהָ)(noun fem. sing. d. 1a ראשׁ

לְרֹאשְׁךָ [c] / לְרֹאשֶׁךָ [d] } pref. לְ)(noun masc. sing., suff. 2 pers. sing. masc., from רֹאשׁ (§ 45) . ראשׁ

לָרִאשֹׁנָה pref. לָ for לְהַ· לְהָ)(adj., fem. of רִאשׁוֹן, used *adverbially* . . . . ראשׁ

לְרֹאשֵׁנוּ [e] pref. לְ)(n. m. s., suff. 1 p. pl. fr. רֹאשׁ (§ 45) ראשׁ

לָרִאשֹׁנִים [f] pref. לָ for לְהַ· לְהָ)(adj. m., pl. of רִאשׁוֹן (q. v.) ראשׁ

לִרְאֹת pref. לִ bef. (:))(Kal inf. constr. dec. 1a . ראה

לִרְאֹתָהּ [g] pref. id.)(id., suff. 3 pers. sing. fem. . ראה

לַרְאֹתְכֶם [h] pref. לַ (contr. for לְהַרְאֹתְכֶם § 11. rem. 3), Hiph. inf., suff. 2 pers. pl. masc. dec. 1b ראה

לִרְאֹתָם [i] pref. לִ bef. (:))(Kal inf. (רְאוֹת), suff. 3 pers. pl. masc. dec. 1a . . . . ראה

לָרֹב pref. לָ for לְהַ· לְהָ)(adj. masc. sing. d. 8d רבב

לָרִב [k] defect. for לָרִיב (q. v.) . . . ריב

לָרֹב pref. לָ (see lett. ל))(noun masc. dec. 8, used *adverbially*; or (Ge. 6. 1) Kal inf. constr. רבב

לָרְבָבָה [l] pref. לָ for לְהַ· לְהָ)(noun fem. sing. d. 11c רבב

לְרַבִּים pref. id. / לָרַבִּים pref. לָ } adj. masc., pl. of רַב dec. 8d . רבב

לְרִבְעָה [m] pref. id.)(Kal inf. constr. (§ 8. rem. 10) רבע

לְרִבְעָהּ [n] pref. id.)(Kal inf. [רְבֹעַ], suff. 3 pers. sing. fem. (§ 16. rem. 10) . . . רבע

לְרֵבֶץ [o] pref. id.)(noun masc. sing. dec. 6b . רבץ

לְרִבְקָה וּ pref. id.)(pr. name fem.; וּ bef. (:) . רבק

[a] 1 Ki. 21. 19. [b] Ge. 32. 7. [c] Ps. 144. 1. [d] Ex. 36. 2. [e] Le. 22. 27. [f] Ne. 13. 31. [g] Ec. 3. 7. [h] Is. 57. 19. [i] Ne. 2. 8. [ii] 1 Sa. 30. 21. [k] 2 Ch. 34. 11. [l] Je. 36. 30. [m] Is. 22. 12. [n] Je. 17. 1. [o] Am. 7. 1. [p] Job 30. 25. [q] Ex. 5. 12. [r] 1 Sa. 18. 29. [s] Eze. 28. 17. [t] 2 Sa. 13. 6. [u] 2 Sa. 13. 5. [x] Ec. 7. 11. [y] Is. 30. 10. [z] 2 Ch. 11. 22. [a] Ps. 21. 4. [b] Ne. 12. 44. [c] Pr. 1. 9. [d] Pr. 4. 9. [e] Ps. 66. 12. [f] Ec. 1. 11. [g] De. 28. 68. [h] De. 1. 33. [i] Ex. 14. 13. [k] Pr. 25. 8. [l] Ju. 20. 10. [m] Le. 20. 16. [n] Le. 18. 23. [o] Is. 65. 10.

לְרַבְרְבָנוֹהִי[a] Ch., pref. לְ) noun masc. pl., suff. 3 pers. sing. masc. from רַבְרְבָן dec. 1 . . רבב

לִרְגּוֹם[b] pref. לִ bef. (:)) Kal inf. constr. (§ 8. r. 18) רגם

לְרַגֵּל[c] וּ' pref. לְ) Piel inf. constr. d. 7 b; וּ bef. (:) רגל

לְרֶגֶל[d] וּ' pref. id.) noun com. sing. dec. 6 a; וּ id. רגל

לְרַגְלָהּ[e] pref. id.) id., suff. 3 pers. sing. fem. . רגל

לְרַגְּלָהּ[f] וּ pref. id.) Piel inf. (רַגֵּל'), suff. 3 pers. sing. fem. dec. 7 b; וּ bef. (:) . . . רגל

לְרַגְלוֹ[g] pref. id.) n. com. s., suff. 3 p. s. m. fr. רֶגֶל d. 6 a רגל

לְרַגְלַי[h] / לְרַגְלָי[i] } pref. id.) id. du., suff. 1 pers. sing. . רגל

לְרַגְלִי pref. id.) id. sing., suff. 1 pers. sing. . רגל

לְרַגְלָיו pref. id.) id. du., suff. 3 pers. sing. masc. רגל

לְרַגְלֶיךָ[k] pref. id.) id. du., suff. 2 pers. sing. masc. רגל

לְרַגְלֶךָ[l] pref. id.) id. s., suff. 2 pers. s. m. (for ךָ') רגל

לִרְגָעִים pref. לִ bef. (:)) n. m., pl. of רֶגַע d. 6 (§ 35. r. 5) רגע

לְרַד[m] pref. לְ) Kal inf. constr. (§ 18. rem. 3) . רדד

לִרְדֹּף pref. לִ bef. (:)) Kal inf. constr. . . רדף

לְרָדְפְךָ[n] pref. id.) id., suff. 2 pers. sing. masc. . רדף

לָרֶדֶת pref. לָ (see lett. ל)) Kal inf. constr. (suff. רִדְתִּי) dec. 13 a . . . . ירד

לָרוֹב[o] pref. id.) Kh. רוֹב' Kal inf. R. רוב; K. רִיב' id. R. ריב

לָרֹב[p] pref. id.) Kal inf. constr. (§ 18. rem. 2) רבב

לָרוֹב[q] pref. לָ) for רֹב', noun masc. sing. dec. 8 d רבב

לְרוֹזְנִים[r] וּ pref. id.) Kal part. act. masc., pl. of [רוֹזֵן] dec. 7 b; וּ bef. (:) . . . רזן

לָרוּחַ / לְרוּחַ } pref. לָ for לְהָ·, לְהַ· / וּ' pref. לְ q. v. } noun com. sing. dec. 1 a; וּ id. . רוח

לְרוּחוֹ[s] pref. id.) id. with suff. 3 pers. sing. masc. רוח

לְרְוָחָתִי[t] pref. id.) noun fem. sing., suff. 1 pers. sing. from רְוָחָה dec. 11 c (§ 42. rem. 1) . רוח

לָרְוָיָה[u] pref. לָ for לְהָ·, לְהַ·) noun fem. sing. . רוה

לָרוּם[x] pref. לָ (see lett. ל)) Kal inf. constr. or (Pr. 25. 3) subst. . . . . . . רום

לְרוֹמֵם[y] pref. לְ) Pilel inf. constr. . . . רום

לְרוֹמַמְתִּי pref. id.) pr. name in compos. רוֹ' עֶזֶר . רום

לָרוּץ pref. לָ (see lett. ל)) Kal inf. constr. . רוץ

לְרוֹקַע[rr] pref. לְ) Kal part. act., constr. of [רוֹקֵעַ] d. 7 c רקע

לְרָחְבָּהּ[z] וּ pref. id.) noun masc. sing., suff. 3 pers. sing. fem. from רֹחַב dec. 6 c; וּ bef. (:) . רחב

לִרְחַבְיָהוּ[s] pref. לִ bef. (:)) pr. name masc. . . רחב

לִרְחַבְעָם pref. id.) pr. name masc. . . . רחב

לִרְחוֹב[a] pref. לִ bef. (:)) noun fem. sing. dec. 1 a . רחב

לָרָחוֹק[b] pref. לָ for לְהָ·, לְהַ·) adj. masc. sing. d. 3 a רחק

לְרָחֵל pref. לְ) pr. name fem. . . . רחל

לְרַחֲמִים[c] וּ' pref. id.) noun masc. pl. [for רְחָמִים § 35. rem. 16] from רַחַם . . . . . רחם

לְרַחֶמְכֶם[d] pref. id.) Piel inf. (רַחֵם § 14. rem. 1), suff. 2 pers. pl. masc. dec. 7 b . . . . רחם

לִרְחֹץ pref. לִ bef. (:)) Kal inf. constr. . . רחץ

לְרָחְצָה pref. לְ) id. with fem. term. (§ 8. rem. 10) רחץ

לִרְחֹק[e] pref. לִ bef. (:)) Kal inf. constr. . . רחק

לְרָחְקָה[f] pref. לְ) id. with fem. term. (§ 8. rem. 10) רחק

לָרִיב pref. לָ (see lett. ל)) Kal inf. constr. . ריב

לָרִיב[g] / לְרִיב } וְ pref. לָ f. לְהָ / pref. לְ q. v. } noun masc. sing. dec. 1 a ריב

לְרִיבִי[h] pref. id.) id., suff. 1 pers. sing. . . ריב

לְרֵיחַ pref. id.) noun masc. sing. dec. 1 a . . רוח

לָרִיק / לָרִיק[i] } pref. לָ or לְ (see lett. ל) prim. adj. masc. as an *adv.* . . . . . } רוק

לָרֶכֶב[k] pref. לָ for לְהָ·, לְהַ·) noun masc. sing. d. 1 b רכב

לְרֹכֵב[l] pref. id.) Kal part. act. sing. masc. dec. 7 b רכב

לְרֶכֶב pref. לְ) noun masc. sing. (suff. רִכְבִּי) d. 6 a רכב

לִרְכֹּב pref. לִ bef. (:)) Kal inf. constr. . . רכב

לְרִכְבָּה[m] pref. לְ) noun fem. sing. . . . רכב

לְרַכָּבוֹ[n] pref. id.) noun masc. sing., suff. 3 pers. sing. masc. from רַכָּב dec. 1 b . . רכב

לְרִכְבּוֹ[o] וּ' pref. id.) noun masc. sing., suff. 3 pers. sing. masc. from רֶכֶב dec. 6 a; וּ bef. (:) רכב

לְרֹכְבוֹ[q] וּ pref. id.) Kal part. act. sing. masc. (רֹכֵב), suff. 3 pers. sing. masc. dec. 7 b; וּ id. רכב

לָרְכֻשׁ[r] / לָרְכֻשׁ } וְ pref. לָ for לְהָ·, לְהַ·) noun masc. sing. (§ 35. rem. 2) . . . } רכשׁ

לִרְכוּשָׁם[s] וְ pref. לִ bef. (:)) noun masc. sing., suff. 3 pers. pl. masc. from רְכוּשׁ dec. 1 a . רכשׁ

לָרִמָּה[u] pref. לָ for לְהָ·, לְהַ·) noun fem. sing. . רמם

לְרִמּוֹן pref. לְ) pr. name masc. . . . רמם

לְרַמּוֹתַנִי[x] pref. id.) Piel inf. [רַמּוֹת], suff. 1 pers. s. d. 1 b רמה

לִרְמָחִים[y] pref. לִ bef. (:)) noun masc., pl. of רֹמַח dec. 6 b (§ 35. rem. 5 & 9) . . רמח

לְרִנָּתִי[z] pref. לְ) noun fem. s., suff. 1 p. s. fr. רִנָּה d. 10 רנן

לָרֹס[a] pref. לָ (see lett. ל)) Kal inf. constr. . רסס

לָרַע / לָרָע } pref. לָ for לְהָ·, לְהַ·) subst. masc. sing. dec. 8 (§ 37. rem. 7) . . } רעע

---

[a] Da. 5. 1. [b] Nu. 14. 10. [c] 1 Ch. 19. 3. [d] Ge. 33. 14, 14. [e] 1 Sa. 25. 42. [f] 2 Sa. 10. 3. [g] Is. 41. 2. [h] Je. 18. 22. [i] La. 1. 13. [k] Ps. 110. 1. [l] De. 33. 3. [m] Is. 45. 1. [n] 1 Sa. 25. 29. [o] Ju. 21. 22. [p] 1 Ch. 4. 38. [q] Est. 10. 3. [r] Pr. 31. 4. [rr] Ps. 136. 6. [s] Pr. 25. 28. [t] La. 3. 56. [u] Ps. 66. 12. [x] Eze. 10. 16. [y] Ezr. 9. 9. [z] Ge. 13. 17. [a] 2 Ch. 29. 4. [b] Is. 57. 19. [c] Da. 1. 9. [d] Is. 30. 18. [e] Ec. 3. 5. [f] Eze. 8. 6. [g] 2 Ch. 19. 8. [h] Ps. 35. 23. [i] Job 39. 16. [k] 2 Ch. 18. 33. [l] Ps. 68. 5, 34. [m] Eze. 27. 20. [n] 1 Ki. 22. 34. [o] Je. 47. 3. [p] De. 11. 4. [q] Job 39. 18. [r] 1 Ki. 5. 8. [s] Mi. 1. 13. [t] Nu. 35. 3. [u] Job 17. 14. [x] 1 Ch. 12. 17. [y] Joel 4. 10. [z] Ps. 88. 3. [a] Eze. 46. 14.

לָרֹעַ[a] pref. לָ (see lett. ל))(noun masc. sing. . רעע

לְרָע / לָרָע } pref. לְ)(noun masc. sing. dec. 8. (§ 37. rem. 7) . . . רעע

לָרָעֵב pref. לָ for לְהַ·, לְהָ)(noun masc. sing. d. 4a רעב

לְרָעֵב[b] / לָרָעֵב[c] } pref. id. / pref. לָ } adj. masc. sing. dec. 5a . . רעב

לָרְעֵבִים[d] pref. לָ for לְהַ·, לְהָ)(id. pl., abs. st. . רעב

לִרְעָבָם[e] pref. לִ bef. (:))(noun masc. sing., suff. 3 pers. pl. masc. from רָעָב dec. 4a . . רעב

לְרָעָה[f] / לְרָעָה[g] } pref. לָ f. לְהַ·, לְהָ / וּ pref. לְ q. v. } n. fem. s. d. 10 [for רָעָה] from רַע m.; וּ bef. (:) רעע

לְרֹעֶה[h] pref. לְ)(Kal part. act. sing. masc. dec. 9a רעה

לְרֵעֵהוּ[i] pref. id.)(noun masc. sing., or (1 Sa. 30. 26) pl. for רֵעָיו, suff. 3 pers. sing. masc. (§ 4. rem. 5) from רֵעַ dec. 1a (§ 36. rem. 4) רעה

לִרְעוֹת pref. לִ bef. (:))(Kal inf. constr. dec. 1b . רעה

לִרְעוּתָהּ pref. id.)(noun fem. sing., suff. 3 pers. sing. fem. from רְעוּת dec. 1a . . . רעה

לְרֵעַי pref. לְ)(noun masc. sing., suff. 1 pers. sing. from רֵעַ dec. 1a (§ 36. rem. 4) . . רעה

לְרֵעֶיךָ pref. id.)(id. pl., or sing. (2 Sa. 12. 11; Pr. 3. 28, Kh. § 38. r. 1), suff. 2 p. s. m. from רֵעֶה d. 9a רעה

לָרֹעִים[k] pref. לָ for לְהַ·, לְהָ)(Kal part. act. masc. pl. of רֹעֶה dec. 9a . . . רעה

לְרֵעֲךָ / לְרֵעֶךָ } pref. לְ)(noun masc. sing., suff. 2 pers. sing. masc. from רֵעַ d. 1a (§ 36. r. 4) רעה

לְרַעַשׁ[l] pref. id.)(noun masc. sing. . . . רעש

לְרָעֹת[m] pref. id.)(noun fem., pl. of רָעָה d. 10, fr. רַע m. רעע

לְרָעָתוֹ[n] pref. id.)(id. sing., suff. 3 pers. sing. masc. רעע

לִרְפֹּא[o] / לִרְפּוֹא[p] } pref. לִ bef. (:))(Kal inf. constr. (§ 8. rem. 18) . . . . רפא

לְרָצוֹן pref. לְ)(noun masc. sing. dec. 3a . רצה

לִרְצוֹת[q] pref. לִ bef. (:))(Kal inf. constr. dec. 1a . רצה

לָרָצִים וְ'[r] pref. לָ for לְהַ·, לְהָ)(Kal part. act. masc., pl. of רָץ dec. 1a . . . . רוץ

לִרְצֹנוֹ[s] pref. לִ bef. (:))(noun masc. sing., suff. 3 pers. sing. masc. from רָצוֹן 3a . . . רצה

לִרְצֹנְכֶם pref. id.)(id., suff. 2 pers. pl. masc. . רצה

לְרַקָּחוֹת[t] pref. לְ)(noun fem., pl. of רַקָּחָה dec. 10 . רקח

לָרָקִיעַ[u] pref. לָ for לְהַ·, לְהָ)(noun masc. sing. dec. 3a רקע

לִרְקִיקֵי[x] וְ pref. לִ bef. (:))(noun masc. pl. constr. from רָקִיק dec. 3a . . . רקק

לְרִקְמוֹת[y] pref. לִ bef. (:))(n. f. pl. abs. from רִקְמָה d. 12b רקם

לָרָשׁ[z] וְ' pref. לָ for לְהַ·, לְהָ)(Kal part. act. m. d. 1a רוש

לְרָשָׁע / לָרָשָׁע } וְ' pref. id. / pref. לָ } adj. masc. sing. dec. 4a . רשע

לְרִשְׁעָה[a] pref. id.)(noun fem. sing. (no pl.) . רשע

לְרִשְׁעֵי[b] וּ pref. id.)(noun masc. pl. constr. from רֶשַׁע dec. 4a; וּ bef. (:) . . רשע

לָרְשָׁעִים[c] וְ' pref. לָ for לְהַ·, לְהָ)(id. abs. st. רשע

לָרְשָׁפִים[d] pref. id.)(noun masc. pl. (constr. רִשְׁפֵּי) from רֶשֶׁף dec. 6a . . . . רשף

לָרֶשֶׁת[e] / לָרֶשֶׁת } pref. לָ (see lett. ל))(Kal inf. constr. (suff. רִשְׁתּוֹ) dec. 13b . ירש

לְרִשְׁתָּהּ pref. לְ)(id., suff. 3 pers. sing. fem. . ירש

לְרִשְׁתּוֹ[f] pref. id.)(id., suff. 3 pers. sing. masc. . ירש

לְרִשְׁתְּךָ[g] pref. id.)(id., suff. 2 pers. sing. masc. ירש

לִשְׁאֹב pref. לִ bef. (:))(Kal inf. constr. . . שאב

לְשָׁאוּל וּ' pref. לְ)(pr. name masc.; וּ bef. (:) . שאל

לִשְׁאוֹל-[h] Kh. לִשְׁאוֹל q.v., K. לִשְׁאָל- q.v. (§ 8. rem. 18) שאל

לִשְׁאוֹל pref. לִ bef. (:))(n. m. s.; or Kal inf. see לִשְׁאֹל שאל

לִשְׁאוֹלָה[i] pref. id.)(id. with loc. ה . . . שאל

לִשְׁאֹל / לִשְׁאָל- } pref. id.)(Kal inf. constr. (§ 8. rem. 18) שאל

לִשְׁאָר pref. id.)(noun masc. sing. . . . שאר

לִשְׁאָרוֹ pref. id.)(noun masc. sing., suff. 3 pers. sing. masc. from שְׁאָר dec. 1a . . שאר

לִשְׁאֵרִית[k] וְ' pref. id.)(noun fem. sing. dec. 1b שאר

לָשֵׂאת וְ' pref. לָ (see lett. ל))(Kal inf. constr. (§ 25. No. 2a) . . . . נשא

לַשְּׂאֵת[l] וְ pref. לַ for לְהַ)(n. f. s. (suff. שְׂאֵתוֹ) d. 1a נשא

לַשְּׁבָאִים pref. לַ bef. (:))(gent. noun pl. from שְׁבָא שבא

לִשְׁבוּיִם[m] pref. id.)(Kal part. p. m., pl. of [שָׁבוּי] d. 3a שבה

לִשְׁבוּעָה[n] pref. id.)(noun fem. sing. dec. 10 . שבע

לִשְׁבוּרֵי[o] pref. id.)(Kal part. p. pl. constr. fr. שָׁבוּר d. 3a שבר

לַשֵּׁבֶט / לְשֵׁבֶט[p] } pref. לַ f. לְהַ)(n. m. s. [שֵׁבֶט § 35. r. 2] see שֵׁבֶט / וּ' pref. לְ)(noun com. sing. d. 6b; וּ bef. (:) שבט

לְשִׁבְטוֹ[q] pref. id.)(id., suff. 3 pers. sing. masc. שבט

לְשִׁבְטֵי pref. id.)(id. pl., constr. st. . . שבט

לְשִׁבְטֵיהֶם pref. id.)(id. pl., suff. 3 pers. pl. masc. שבט

לִשְׁבָטָיו pref. לִ bef. (:))(id. pl., suff. 3 pers. sing. m. שבט

לִשְׁבָטֶיךָ[r] pref. id.)(id. pl., suff. 2 pers. sing. masc. שבט

לְשִׁבְטֵיכֶם pref. לְ)(id. pl., suff. 2 pers. pl. masc. . שבט

[a] Ge. 41. 19. [b] Is. 58. 7, 10. [c] Eze. 18. 7, 16. [d] Ps. 146. 7. [e] Ne. 9. 15. [f] Pr. 6. 18. [g] Je. 28. 8. [h] Eze. 34. 23. [i] Ps. 139. 2. [k] Eze. 34. 2. [l] Job 41. 21. [m] Ex. 23. 2. [n] Ec. 5. 12. [o] Ho. 5. 13. [p] Ec. 3. 3. [q] Ps. 77. 8. [r] 2 Ki. 11. 4. [s] Le. 1. 3. [t] 1 Sa. 8. 13. [u] Ge. 1. 7, 8, etc. [x] 1 Ch. 23. 29. [y] Ps. 45. 15. [z] 2 Sa. 12. 3. [a] Eze. 5. 6. [aa] Es. 1. 19.

[b] Eze. 7. 21. [c] Ps. 75. 5. [d] Ps. 78. 48. [e] Ne. 9. 23. [f] 1 Ki. 21. 16, 18. [g] Ge. 28. 4. [h] 1 Ch. 18. 10. [i] Ps. 9. 18. [k] Is. 15. 9. [l] Le. 14. 56. [m] Is. 61. 1. [n] Is. 65. 15. [o] Ps. 147. 3. [p] Jos. 13. 33. [q] Ju. 21. 24. [r] De. 16. 18.

לִשְׁבִי / לַשְּׁבִי	pref. לְ for לְהַ)(noun masc. sing. dec. 6i (§ 35. rem. 14)	שבה
לְשָׁבֵי[a]	ו pref. לְ)(Kal part. act. pl. const. masc. from שָׁב dec. 1a (§ 30. No. 3); ו bef. (:)	שוב
לְשָׁבֵי[b]	ו Chald., pref. id.)(Peal part. act. pl. constr. masc. from [שָׁב] d. 1a (§ 30. No. 3); ו id.	שיב
לְשָׁבַיָּא[c]	Chald., pref. id.)(id. pl., emph. st.	שיב
לְשֹׁבֵיהֶם[d]	pref. id.)(Kal part. act. pl. masc., suff. 3 pers. pl. masc. from [שֹׁבֶה] dec. 9a	שבה
לַשְׁבִּית[e]	וְ pref. לַ contr. (for לְהַשְׁבִּית), Hiph. inf. constr.	שבת
לַשְּׂבָכָה	pref. לַ for לְהַ)(n. f. s., pl. שְׂבָכוֹת (no pl. c.)	שבך
לִשְׁבַנְיָה	pref. לִ bef. (:))(pr. name masc.	שבן
לְשֶׁבַע	pref. לְ (see lett. ל))(n. m. s. d. 6c (§ 35. r. 5)	שבע
לְשֶׁבַע[f]	pref. לְ)(num. card. fem.	שבע
לְשֶׁבַע[g]	pref. id.)(noun masc. sing. dec. 6c (§35. r.5)	שבע
לִשְׁבֹעַ	pref. לִ bef. (:))(Kal inf. constr.	שבע
לְשָׂבְעָה	pref. לְ)(noun fem. sing. (no pl.)	שבע
לִשְׁבֻעָה[h]	וְ defect. for לִשְׁבוּעָה (q.v.)	שבע
לְשִׁבְעָה	pref. id.)(num. card. masc. from שֶׁבַע fem.	שבע
לְשִׁבְעַת	pref. id.)(id. constr. state	שבע
לִשְׁבֹּר / לְשַׁבֵּר	pref. לִ bef. (:))(Kal inf. constr. (§ 8. rem. 18)	שבר
לְשִׁבְרֵךְ[i]	pref. לְ)(noun masc. sing., suff. (for ךְ') 2 pers. sing. masc. fr. שֶׁבֶר dec. 6 b	שבר
לְשִׁבְרֵךְ[k]	pref. id.)(id., suff. 2 pers. sing. fem.	שבר
לָשֶׁבֶת / לָשָׁבֶת	pref. לָ, when not followed by a Genitive, otherwise לָשֶׁבֶת (q. v.)	ישב
לַשַּׁבָּת[l]	pref. לַ for לְהַ)(noun com. sing. (suff. שַׁבַּתּוֹ, pl. שַׁבָּתוֹת)	שבת
לָשֶׁבֶת	pref. לָ)(Kal inf. constr. dec. 13 a	ישב
לְשִׁבְתּוֹ[m]	pref. id.)(id., suff. 3 pers. sing. masc.	ישב
לַשַּׁבָּתוֹת	pref. לַ for לְהַ)(noun com. pl. abs. (constr. שַׁבְּתוֹת) from שַׁבָּת (q. v.)	שבת
לְשִׁבְתִּי[n]	pref. לְ)(Kal inf. constr. (שֶׁבֶת), suff. 1 pers. sing. dec. 13 a	ישב
לְשִׁבְתְּךָ	pref. id.)(id., suff. 2 pers. sing. masc.	ישב
לְשִׁבְתֵּנוּ[o]	pref. id.)(id., suff. 1 pers. pl.	ישב
לִשְׁגָגָה[p]	pref. לִ bef. (:))(noun fem. sing. dec. 11 c	שגג
לִשְׁגוֹת[q]	pref. id.)(Kal inf. constr.	שגה

לְשַׁד[r] masc. dec. 8 d.—I. *moisture, vital power*, Ps. 32. 4 (Arab. לשד *to suck*).—II. לְשַׁד הַשָּׁמֶן *oil cake*, Nu. 11. 8.

לְשֹׁד[s]	pref. לְ)(noun masc. sing.	דד
לְשֹׁדְדִים[t]	pref. id.)(Kal part. act. m., pl. of שֹׁדֵד d. 7 b	דד
לְשָׂדֶה[u]	pref. id.)(noun masc. sing. dec. 9 b	דה
לְשָׂדֵהוּ[x]	pref. id.)(id., suff. 3 pers. sing. masc.	דה
לִשְׁדוֹד[y]	pref. לִ bef. (:))(Kal inf. constr.	דד
לְשַׁדַּי[z]	pref. לְ)(noun m. [שַׁד] with the pl. term. ַי	דד
לְשַׁדִּי[a]	noun m. s., suff. 1 pers. sing. fr. לְשַׁד d. 8 d	שד
לִשְׂדֵי[b]	pref. לִ bef. (:))(noun masc. pl. constr. fr. שָׂדֶה dec. 9 b	דה
לַשֵּׁדִים	pref. לַ for לְהַ)(noun m., pl. of [שֵׁד] d. 1a	וד
לְשַׁדְרַךְ	pref. לְ)(pr. name masc.	דר
לַשְּׂדֵרֹת[c]	pref. לַ for לְהַ)(noun fem., pl. of [שְׂדֵרָה] dec. 10, see	דר
לְשֶׂה[d] / לַשֶּׂה[e]	pref. לְ (see lett. ל) / pref. לַ for לְהַ } noun masc. sing. irr. (§ 45)	יה
לַשָּׁוְא	pref. id.)(noun masc. sing.	וא
לְשׁוֹאָה[f]	[g] ו' pref. לְ)(noun fem. s. d. 10; ו bef. (:)	וא
לָשׁוּב	ו' pref. לָ (see lett. ל))(Kal inf. constr.	וב
לְשׁוֹבֵב	pref. לְ)(Pilel inf. constr.	וב
לְשׁוֹבָל	pref. id.)(pr. name masc.	בל
לָשׂוּחַ[h]	pref. לָ (see lett. ל))(Kal inf. constr.	יח
לְשׁוֹחָם	pref. לְ)(pr. name masc.	יח
לָשׂוּם	ו' pref. לָ (see lett. ל))(Kal inf. constr.	ום
לָשׁוֹן[i]	ו' noun com. sing. dec. 3a	שן
לְשׁוֹן	ו' id. constr. st.; ו bef. (:)	שן
לְשׁוֹנָהּ[k]	id., suff. 3 pers. sing. fem.	שן
לְשׁוֹנוֹ	ו' id., suff. 3 pers. sing. masc.; ו bef. (:)	שן
לְשׁוֹנִי	ו' id., suff. 1 pers. sing.; ו id.	שן
לַשּׁוּנִי	pref. לְ)(pr. name masc., for שְׁאוּנִי	אן
לְשׁוֹנְךָ[l] / לְשׁוֹנֶךָ[m]	ו' noun com. sing., suff. 2 pers. sing. masc. from לָשׁוֹן dec. 3a; ו bef. (:)	שן
לְשׁוֹנֵךְ[n]	id., suff. 2 pers. sing. fem.	שן
לְשׁוֹנְכֶם[o]	id., suff. 2 pers. pl. masc.	שן
לְשׁוֹנָם	ו' id., suff. 3 pers. pl. masc.; ו bef. (:)	שן
לַשּׁוּנַמִּית	pref. לַ for לְהַ)(gent. noun, fem. of שׁוּנַמִּי from שׁוּנֵם	ן
לְשׁוֹנֵנוּ[p]	ו noun com. sing., suff. 1 pers. pl. from לָשׁוֹן dec. 3a; ו bef. (:)	שן
לְשַׁוְעָתִי[q]	pref. לְ)(noun fem. sing., suff. 1 pers. sing. from שַׁוְעָה (no pl.)	ע
לָשׁוֹר[r]	pref. לָ (see lett. ל))(Kh. שׁוּר Kal inf. R. שׁוּר, K. שִׁיר id. R.	ר

[a] Is. 59. 20. [b] Ezr. 6. 7. [c] Ezr. 5. 9. [d] Is. 14. 2. [e] Am. 8. 4. [f] Ge. 41. 36. [g] Pr. 13. 25. [h] Nu. 5. 21. [i] Na. 3. 19. [k] Je. 30. 12. [l] Is. 58. 13. [m] Ps. 68. 17. [n] 2 Sa. 7. 5. [o] Je. 35. 9. [p] Nu. 15. 24. [q] Pr. 19. 27. [r] Nu. 11. 8. [s] Job 5. 22. [t] Job 12. 6. [u] Ec. 5. 8. [x] Ne. 13. 10. [y] Je. 47. 4. [z] Job 22. 3. [a] Ps. 32. 4. [b] Ne. 12. 44. [c] 2 Ki. 11. 15. [d] Eze. 34. 17, 22. [e] Nu. 15. 11. [f] Ps. 63. 10. [g] Is. 10. 3. [h] Ge. 24. 63. [i] Pr. 25. 15. [k] Pr. 31. 26. [l] Ps. 52. 4. [m] Ps. 34. 14. [n] Ca. 4. 11. [o] Is. 59. 3. [p] Ps. 126. 2. [q] La. 3. 56. [r] 1 Sa. 18. 6.

Word	Analysis	Root
לֶשֶׁךְ	Root not used; prob. i. q. Arab. לשק, לצק *to be joined, to adhere to* (Lee).	
	לִשְׁכָּה fem. dec. 12b, *chamber*, espec. those *attached* to the sides of the temple; written also נִשְׁכָּה by interchange of the liquids.	
לִשְׁכַּב לִשְׁכָּב[f] וְ	pref. לְ bef. (:)) Kal inf. constr.	שכב
לִשְׁכָּה[g]	וְ[h] noun fem. sing. dec. 12b	לשך
לַשֶּׂכְוִי[i]	pref. לְ for לְהַ) noun masc. sing.	שכה
לִשְׁכּוֹן[k]	in full for לִשְׁכֹּן (q. v. & § 8. rem. 18)	שכן
לְשָׁכוֹת	noun fem. pl. abs. from לִשְׁכָּה dec. 12b	לשך
לִשְׁכוֹת	id., constr. st.	לשך
לְשִׂכִּים[l]	pref. לְ) noun masc., pl. of [שֵׂךְ] dec. 8b	שכך
לִשְׂכִירֶךָ[m]	וְ pref. לְ bef. (:)) noun masc. sing., suff. 2 pers. sing. masc. from שָׂכִיר dec. 3a	שכר
לְשֶׂכֶל[n]	pref. לְ) noun masc. sing. dec. 6b	שכל
לְשַׁכְלָלָה[o]	Chald., pref. id.) Shaph. inf. constr. (§ 48)	כלל
לְשַׂכְּלָם[p]	pref. id.) Piel inf. [שַׂכֵּל], suff. 3 pers. pl. masc. dec. 7b	שכל
לְשַׁכֵּן	pref. id.) Piel inf. constr.	שכן
לִשְׁכֹּן	pref. לְ bef. (:)) Kal inf. constr.	שכן
לְשִׁכְנוֹ[q]	pref. לְ) noun masc. sing. with suff. 3 pers. sing. masc. from [שֶׁכֶן] dec. 6a	שכן
לְשָׁכְנִי[r]	pref. id.) Kal inf., suff. 1 pers. sing.	שכן
לִשְׁכַנְיָה לִשְׁכַנְיָהוּ	pref. לְ bef. (:)) pr. name masc., see שְׁכַנְיָה	שכן
לִשְׁכֵנַי[s]	וְ pref. id.) noun masc. pl., suff. 1 pers. sing. from שָׁכֵן dec. 5a	שכן
לִשְׁכֵנָיו[t]	pref. id.) id., suff. 3 pers. sing. masc.	שכן
לִשְׁכֵנֵינוּ	pref. id.) id., suff. 1 pers. pl.	שכן
לַשֵּׁכָר[u]	וְ pref. לְ for לְהַ) noun masc. sing.	שכר
לִשְׂכֹּר[x]	pref. לְ bef. (:)) Kal inf. constr.	שכר
לְשָׁכְרָה[y]	pref. לְ) Kal inf. constr. (§ 8. rem. 10)	שכר
לְשִׁכֹּרָה[z]	pref. id.) noun fem. sing. from שִׁכּוֹר masc.	שכר
לְשִׁכָּרוֹן[a]	pref. id.) noun masc. sing.	שכר
לְשָׁכֹת[b]	noun fem., pl. of לִשְׁכָּה dec. 12b	לשך
לִשְׁכַּת	id. sing., constr. st.	לשך
לִשְׁכָּתָה[c]	id. sing. with parag. ה	לשך
לַשֶּׁלֶג[d]	pref. לְ for לְהַ) noun masc. sing.	שלג
לְשֵׁלָה	pref. לְ) pr. name masc.	שאל
לְשִׁלוֹ	pref. id.) pr. name of a place	שלה
לִשְׁלוֹט[e]	pref. לְ bef. (:)) Kal inf. constr. (§ 8. r. 18)	שלט
לַשּׁוֹר[a]	pref. לְ for לְהַ) noun masc. s. (§ 35. r. 13)	שור
לָשׂוּשׂ[b]	pref. לְ (see lett. ל)) Kal inf. constr.	שוש
לָשׁוֹת[c]	Kal part. act. fem. pl. [of לָשָׁה dec. 10, from לָשׁ masc.]	לוש
לְשׁוּתֶלַח	pref. לְ) pr. name masc., see 'שׁוּתֶ	
לִשְׁחוֹט[d]	in full for לִשְׁחֹט (q. v. & § 8. rem. 18)	שחט
לִשְׂחוֹק	pref. לְ bef. (:)) Kal inf. constr. (§ 8. rem. 18); or noun masc. sing.	שחק
לִשְׁחוֹת[e]	pref. id.) Kal inf. constr.	שחח
לִשְׁחֹט[f]	pref. id.) Kal inf. constr.	שחט
לִשְׁחִין[g]	pref. id.) noun masc. sing.	שחן
לְשַׂחֶק־[h]	pref. לְ) Piel (§ 14. rem 1) inf. constr. [for שַׂחֵק § 10. rem. 4]	שחק
לִשְׂחֹק[i]	pref. לְ bef. (:)) noun masc. sing.	שחק
לִשְׁחָקִים[k]	pref. id.) noun masc., pl. of 'שַׁחַק dec. 6d	שחק
לְשַׁחֵר[l]	pref. לְ) Piel inf. constr. (§ 14. rem. 1)	שחר
לַשַּׁחַת	pref. לְ for לְהַ) noun fem. sing. dec. 13a	שוח
לְשַׁחַת[m]	pref. id.) noun masc. sing.	שחת
לְשַׁחֵת	pref. לְ) Piel (§ 14. rem. 1) inf. constr. d. 7b	שחת
לְשַׁחֲתָהּ	pref. id.) id., suff. 3 pers. sing. fem.	שחת
לְשַׁחֶתְכֶם[n]	pref. id.) id., suff. 2 pers. pl. masc.	שחת
לְשֹׁטְטִם[o]	וּ pref. id.) Pilel inf. constr.; וּ bef. (:)	שוט
לְשָׂטָן	pref. id.) noun masc. sing.	שטן
לְשִׂטְנוֹ[p]	pref. id.) Kal inf. [שְׂטֹן], suff. 3 pers. sing. masc. (§ 16. rem. 10)	שטן
לַשֶּׁטֶף[q]	pref. לְ for לְהַ) noun masc. sing.	שטף
לְשֶׁטֶף[r]	pref. לְ) noun masc. sing.	שטף
לִשְׂטַר[s]	וְ Chald., pref. לְ bef. (:)) noun masc. sing.	שטר
לְשֹׁטְרָיו	וּ pref. לְ) the foll. with suff. 3 pers. sing. masc.; וּ bef. (:)	שטר
לְשֹׁטְרִים[t]	pref. id.) Kal part. act. m., pl. of שֹׁטֵר d. 7b	שטר
לְשֵׂיבָה[u]	pref. id.) noun fem. sing. dec. 10	שיב
לַשִּׂיד[x]	pref. לְ for לְהַ) noun masc. sing.	שיד
לְשֵׁיזָבוּתַהּ[y]	Chald., pref. לְ) Peel inf. [שֵׁיזָבוּת], suff. 3 pers. sing. fem. (§ 48)	שזב
לְשֵׁיזָבוּתָךְ[z]	Chald., pref. id.) id., suff. 2 pers. sing. m.	שזב
לְשֵׁיזָבוּתַנָא[a]	Chald., pref. id.) id., suff. 1 pers. pl.	שזב
לָשִׂיחַ[b]	pref. לְ (see lett. ל)) Kal inf. constr.	שיח
לְשִׂימוֹ[c]	וּ pref. לְ) Kh. 'שִׂימוֹ, K. 'שׂוּמוֹ, Kal inf. with suff. R. שִׂים or	שום
לָשִׁית[d]	pref. לְ (see lett. ל)) Kal inf. constr. d. 1a	שית
לַשַּׁיִת[e]	וְ pref. לְ for לְהַ) noun masc. sing. dec. 6m	שית

[a] Nu. 15. 11. [b] De. 30. 9. [c] Je. 7. 18. [d] Eze. 40. 39. [e] Is. 25. 11. [f] Ge. 22. 10.
[g] Ex. 9. 9. [h] Ps. 104. 26. [i] Je. 48. 39. [k] Job 37. 18. [l] Pr. 7. 15. [m] Job 17. 14.
[n] Eze. 5. 16. [o] Jos. 23. 13. [p] Zec. 3. 1. [q] Job 38. 25. [r] Ps. 32. 6. [s] Da. 7. 5.
[t] 1 Ch. 26. 29. [u] Job 41. 23. [x] Am. 2. 1. [y] Da. 6. 15. [z] Da. 6. 21. [a] Da. 3. 17.
[b] Ps. 119. 148. [c] Is. 10. 6. [d] Job 30. 1. [e] Is. 7. 23. [f] 2 Sa. 11. 11. [g] Ne. 13. 5.
[h] Eze. 40. 38. [i] Job 38. 36. [k] 2 Ch. 6. 1. [l] Nu. 33. 55. [m] Le. 25. 6. [n] Pr. 23. 9.
[o] Ezr. 5. 3, 9. [p] Eze. 36. 12. [q] De. 12. 5. [r] Ex. 29. 46. [s] Ps. 31. 12.
[t] Ps. 89. 42. [u] Mi. 2. 11. [x] 1 Ch. 19. 6. [y] Hag. 1. 6. [z] 1 Sa. 1. 13.
[a] Eze. 39. 19. [b] Eze. 45. 5. [c] 1 Sa. 9. 22. [d] Job 37. 6. [e] Est. 9. 1.

לְשָׁלוֹם — ו׳ pref. לְ)((prim. adj.) subst. m. s. d. 3 a; וּ bef. (:) — שלם
לִשְׁלוֹם[a] — ו׳ pref. לִ bef. (:))(id. constr. st. — שלם
לִשְׁלוֹמִים[b] — וְ pref. id.)(id. (adj.) pl., abs. st. — שלם
לִשְׁלוֹשׁ[c] — pref. לְ)(num. card. fem. comp. לִשְׁלשׁ — שלש
לִשְׁלְוְתָךְ[d] — Chald., pref. לִ bef. (:))(noun fem. sing., suff. 2 pers. sing. masc. from [שְׁלֵוָא] d. 8 a — שלה
לְשַׁלַּח / לְשַׁלֵּחַ[e] — ו׳ pref. לְ)(Piel inf. constr. dec. 7 (§ 15. rem. 1); וּ bef. (:) — שלח
לִשְׁלֹחַ — pref. לִ bef. (:))(Kal inf. constr. — שלח
לְשַׁלְּחָהּ[f] — pref. לְ)(Piel inf. (שַׁלַּח), suff. 3 p. s. f. d. 7 b — שלח
לְשַׁלְּחוֹ — pref. id.)(id. with suff. 3 pers. sing. masc. — שלח
לְשֹׁלְחָיו — pref. id.)(Kal part. act. pl. masc., suff. 3 pers. sing. masc. from שֹׁלֵחַ dec. 7 b — שלח
לְשֹׁלְחֶיךָ[g] — pref. id.)(id. with suff. 2 pers. sing. masc. — שלח
לְשַׁלְּחָם — pref. id.)(Piel inf. (שַׁלַּח), suff. 3 p. pl. m. d. 7 b — שלח
לְשֻׁלְחָן[h] — pref. id.)(noun masc. sing. dec. 2 b — שלח
לְשַׁלְּחֵנוּ[i] — pref. id.)(Piel inf. (שַׁלַּח), suff. 1 p. pl. d. 7 b — שלח
לְשֻׁלְחֲנוֹת[k] — pref. id.)(noun masc. with pl. fem. term., constr. of חָנוֹת׳ from שֻׁלְחָן dec. 2 b — שלח
לְשַׁלְּחֵנִי[l] — pref. id.)(Piel inf. (שַׁלַּח), suff. 1 p. s. d. 7 b — שלח
לְשֻׁלְחָנְךָ[m] — pref. id.)(n. m. s., suff. 2 p. s. m. fr. שֻׁלְחָן d. 2 b — שלח
לַשָּׁלָל[n] / לְשָׁלָל — pref. לַ for לְהַ / pref. לְ q. v. } noun masc. sing. dec. 4 a — שלל
לִשְׁלֹל — pref. לִ bef. (:))(Kal inf. constr. — שלל
לְשָׁלֹם — defect. for לְשָׁלוֹם (q. v.) — שלם
לְשַׁלֵּם[o] — pref. לְ)(Piel inf. constr. — שלם
לְשַׁלֻּם, לְשַׁלֵּם — pref. id.)(pr. names masc. — שלם
לִשְׁלֹמֹה — וְ׳ pref. לִ bef. (:))(pr. name masc. — שלם
לְשַׁלְּמוֹ — pref. לְ)(Piel inf. (שַׁלֵּם), suff. 3 p. s. m. d. 7 b — שלם
לִשְׁלֹמִי[p] — pref. id.)(id. with suff. 1 pers. sing. — שלם
לְשֶׁלֶמְיָהוּ — pref. id.)(pr. name masc. — שלם
לְשַׁלְמֵיכֶם[q] — וּ pref. id.)(the foll. with suff. 2 p. pl. m.; וּ bef. (:) — שלם
לִשְׁלָמִים — וְ׳ pref. לִ bef. (:))(n. m., pl. of שֶׁלֶם d. 6 a — שלם
לְשָׁלֹשׁ[r] — pref. לְ)(num. card. fem. — שלש
לִשְׁלֹשׁ[s] — וְ׳ pref. לִ bef. (:))(id., constr. st. — שלש
לִשְׁלֹשָׁה — pref. id.)(id. masc. from שָׁלֹשׁ fem. — שלש
לַשָּׁלִשִׁים[u] — וְ pref. לַ for לְהַ)(n. m., pl. of שָׁלִישׁ d. 1 b — שלש
לִשְׁלֹשֶׁת — pref. לִ bef. (:))(num. card. masc., constr. of שְׁלֹשָׁה (§ 42. rem. 5) — שלש
לִשְׁלָשְׁתָּם — pref. id.)(id. with suff. 3 pers. pl. m. d. 13 c — שלש

לֶשֶׁם — masc. — I. *ligure*, a precious stone, Ex. 28. 19; 39. 12.—II. pr. name of a city, Jos. 19. 47, elsewhere called לַיִשׁ & דָּן.

לְשֵׁם — ו׳ pref. לְ)(n. m. s. d. 7 a; also pr. n. m.; וּ bef. (:) — שם
לִשְׂמֹאלוֹ — pref. לִ bef. (:))(noun masc. sing., suff. 3 pers. sing. masc. from שְׂמֹאל dec. 1 a — שמאל
לַשְׁמִד[v] — contr. & defect. for לְהַשְׁמִיד (q. v. & § 11. r. 3) — שמד
לְשַׁמָּה — ו׳ pref. לְ)(noun fem. sing. d. 10; וּ bef. (:) — שמם
לִשְׁמוֹ[y] — pref. לִ bef. (:))(noun masc. sing., suff. 3 pers. sing. masc. from שֵׁם dec. 7 a — שם
לִשְׁמוּאֵל — pref. id.)(pr. name masc. — שמע
לִשְׂמוֹחַ[z] — וְ׳ in full for לִשְׂמֹחַ (q. v. § 8. rem. 18) — שמח
לִשְׁמוֹנָה — pref. לִ bef. (:))(num. card. m., from נָה׳ f. — שמן
לִשְׁמוֹעַ — in full for לִשְׁמֹעַ (q. v. & § 8. rem. 18) — שמע
לִשְׁמוּעָה[a] — pref. לִ bef. (:))(noun fem. sing. dec. 10 — שמע
לִשְׁמוֹר — וְ׳ in full for לִשְׁמֹר (q. v. & § 8. rem. 18) — שמר
לִשְׁמוֹת[b] — pref. לִ bef. (:))(noun masc. with pl. fem. term. constr. from שֵׁם dec. 7 a — שם
לִשְׂמֹחַ[c] — וְ׳[d] pref. id.)(Kal inf. constr. — שמח
לְשִׂמְחָה — ו׳ pref. לְ)(noun fem. sing. d. 12 b; וּ bef. (:) — שמח
לְשִׂמְחַת[e] — וּ pref. id.)(id. constr. st.; וּ id. — שמח
לִשְׁמִי — pref. לִ bef. (:))(noun masc. sing., suff. 1 pers. sing. from שֵׁם dec. 7 a — שם
לִשְׁמַיָּא[f] — Ch., pref. id.)(n. m. pl. emph. [from שְׁמַי׳] — שמה
לַשָּׁמַיִם / לַשָּׁמָיִם — pref. לַ for לְהַ)(noun masc. pl. constr. שְׁמֵי, suff. שָׁמֶיךָ, [from שְׁמַי׳ § 38. r. 2] — שמה
לְשָׁמִיר[g] — pref. id.)(noun masc. sing. dec. 3 a — שמר
לִשְׁמֶךָ / לְשִׁמְךָ — pref. לִ bef. (:) / ו׳ pref. לְ q. v. } noun m. s., suff. 2 pers. s. m. fr. שֵׁם d. 7 a; וּ bef. (:) — שם
לְשִׂמְלָתוֹ[h] — pref. id.)(noun fem. sing., suff. 3 pers. sing. masc. from שִׂמְלָה dec. 12 b — שמל
לְשַׁמָּמָה[i] — pref. id.)(noun fem. sing. — שמם
לִשְׁמָמָה — pref. לִ bef. (:))(noun fem. sing. dec. 11 c — שמם
לְשִׁמְמוֹת[k] — pref. לְ)(id. pl., constr. st. — שמם
לְשֶׁמֶן — ו׳[l] pref. id.)(n. m. s. (suff. שַׁמְנִי׳) d. 6 a; וּ bef. (:) — שמן
לַשְׁמָעַ[m] — contr. & defect. for לְהַשְׁמִיעַ (q. v. & § 11. r. 3) — שמע
לְשֵׁמַע — pref. לְ)(noun masc. sing. dec. 6 e — שמע
לִשְׁמֹעַ — וְ׳[n] pref. לִ bef. (:))(Kal inf. constr. — שמע
לְשִׁמְעוֹן — pref. לְ)(pr. name of a tribe — שמע
לַשִּׁמְעוֹנִי — pref. ל for לְהַ)(gent. noun from the preced. — שמע
לְשִׁמְעִי — ו׳ pref. לְ)(pr. name masc.; וּ bef. (:) — שמע
לִשְׁמַעְיָה — וְ׳ pref. לִ bef. (:))(pr. name masc., שְׁמַעְיָה.
לַשִּׁמְעֹנִי — pref. לַ for לְהַ)(gent. noun from שִׁמְעוֹן — שמע

a 2 Sa. 11. 7. b Ps. 69. 23. c 2 Ch. 9. 21. d Da. 4. 24. e Ne. 8. 12. f De. 22. 19. g Pr. 22. 21. h 1 Ch. 28. 16. i Ex. 13. 15. k 1 Ch. 28. 16. l 2 Sa. 13. 16. m Ps. 128. 3. n 2 Ki. 3. 23. o Pr. 22. 27. p Ps. 61. 9. q Nu. 29. 39. r 1 Ki. 10. 22. s Le. 25. 21. t 1 Sa. 13. 21. u 2 Ki. 10. 25. v Is. 23. 11. y Ps. 135. 3. z Ec. 3. 12; 8. 15. a Eze. 16. 56. b Nu. 26. 55. c Ps. 106. 5. d Ec. 5. 18. e Je. 15. 16. f Da. 4. 8, 17, 19, 31. g Is. 7. 23. h De. 22. 3. i Eze. 35. 7. k Je. 25. 12. l Ex. 35. 8, 28. m Ps. 26. 7. n De. 26. 17.

לִשְׁמֻעָתֵנוּ[a] pref. לְ bef. (:))(noun fem. sing., suff. 1 pers. pl. from שְׁמוּעָה dec. 10 . . שמע
לְשִׁמְצָה[b] pref. לְ)(noun fem. sing. . . . שמץ
לִשְׁמֹר וְ' pref. לְ bef. (:))(Kal inf. constr. . . שמר
לְשָׁמְרָהּ[c] וּ pref. לְ)(id., suff. 3 pers. sing. fem.; וּ bef. (:) שמר
לְשָׁמְרוֹ[d] pref. id.)(id., suff. 3 pers. sing. masc. . שמר
לְשֹׁמְרוֹן pref. id.)(pr. name of a place . . שמר
לְשֹׁמְרֵי וּ' pref. id.)(Kal part. act. pl. constr. masc. from שׁוֹמֵר dec. 7 b; וּ bef. (:) . שמר
לִשְׁמָרְךָ pref. לְ bef. (:))(id. inf., suff. 2 pers. sing. m. שמר
לְשָׁמְרָם[e] pref. לְ)(id. id., suff. 3 pers. pl. masc. . שמר
לְשִׁמְרֹן pref. id.)(pr. name masc. . . . שמר
לַשֶּׁמֶשׁ[f] } pref. לַ for לְהַ)(noun com. sing. (suff.
לַשָּׁמֶשׁ[g] וְ' } שִׁמְשְׁךָ) dec. 6 a (§ 35. rem. 2) } שמש
לְשִׁמְשׁוֹן pref. id.)(pr. name masc. . . . שמש

לָשַׁן Root not used; in Po. and Hiph. (only as denom. of לָשׁוֹן) *to slander*, Ps. 10. 8; Pr. 30. 10.
לָשׁוֹן com. dec. 3 a (pl. לְשֹׁנוֹת).—I. *tongue*; אִישׁ לְ' *slanderer*; כְּבַד לְ' *stammerer*; לְ' תַּהְפֻּכוֹת *perverse, deceitful tongue*.—II. *speech*, Job 15. 5.—III. *tongue, dialect*.—IV. applied to inanimate things; לְ' זָהָב *bar of gold*; לְ' אֵשׁ *flame of fire*.
לְשָׁן Chald., d. 1 a, *tongue, dialect*, Da. 3. 4, 29, &c.

לִשָּׁן[h] וְ Chald., noun com. sing. dec. 1 . . לשן
לִשְׂנֹא וְ'[i] pref. לְ bef. (:))(Kal inf. constr. . שנא
לְשֹׂנְאוֹ[k] pref. לְ)(Kal part. act. sing. masc., suff. 3 pers. sing. masc. from שׂוֹנֵא dec. 7 b . . שנא
לְשֹׂנְאַי pref. id.)(id. pl., suff. 1 pers. sing. . . שנא
לְשֹׂנְאֵי וּ pref. id.)(id. pl., constr. st.; וּ bef. (:) שנא
לְשֹׂנְאָיו[l] pref. id.)(id. pl., suff. 3 pers. sing. masc. שנא
לְשָׂנְאָיךְ[m] Chald., pref. id.)(Peal part. act. pl. masc., suff. 2 pers. sing. masc. from [שָׂנֵא] d. 2 b שנא
לַשָּׁנָה pref. לַ for לְהַ)(noun fem. sing. dec. 11 a שנה
לְשֹׁנוֹ defect. for לְשׁוֹנוֹ (q. v.) . . . לשן
לְשַׁנּוֹת[o] pref. לְ)(Piel inf. constr. . . שנה
לְשֹׁנוֹת noun com., pl. of לָשׁוֹן dec. 3 a . . לשן
לִשְׁנֵי pref. לְ bef. (:))(num. card. m., constr. of שְׁנַיִם שנה
לִשָּׁנַיָּא וְ Chald., noun com. pl. emph. from לִשָּׁן d. 1 לשן
לַשְּׁנִיאָה[p] pref. לַ for לְהַ)(adj. sing. fem. [of שָׂנִיא] שנא
לְשִׁנֵּיהֶם[q] pref. לְ)(n. com. du., suff. 3 p. pl. m. שֵׁן d. 8 b שנן
לִשְׁנֵיהֶם pref. לְ bef. (:))(num. card. masc. (שְׁנַיִם, c. שְׁנֵי), suff. 3 pers. pl. masc. . . שנה

לַשִּׁנַּיִם[r] pref. לַ for לְהַ)(noun com., du. of שֵׁן d. 8 b שנן
לְשָׁנִים[s] pref. לְ)(noun fem. with pl. masc. term. from שָׁנָה dec. 11 a . . . שנה
לִשְׁנַיִם[t] }
לִשְׁנַיִם וְ'[u] } num. card. masc. . . . . . שנה
לִשְׁנֵים pref. לְ bef. (:))(id. constr. (only with עָשָׂר to express *twelve*) . . . . שנה
לִשְׁנִינָה[v] וְ' pref. id.)(noun fem. sing. . . . שנן
לִשְׁנַת[y] pref. id.)(noun fem. sing., constr. of שָׁנָה d. 11 a שנה
לִשְׁנָתַיִם[z] pref. id.)(id. du., abs. st. . . . שנה
לָשַׁע [for לֶשַׁע] pr. name of a place, Ge. 10. 19.
לַשְּׂעִירִם[a] וְ } pref. לַ for לְהַ)(noun masc., pl. of
לַשְּׂעִרִם[b] } שָׂעִיר dec. 3 a . . . } שער
לִשְׁעָלִים[c] pref. לְ bef. (:))(noun m., pl. of [שֻׁעָל] d. 6 d שעל
לְשַׁעַר[d] pref. לְ (see lett. לְ) }
לַשַּׁעַר[e] } pref. לַ for לְהַ } noun com. sing. dec. 6 d
לַשָּׁעַר[f] } שער
לְשֵׂעָר[g] pref. id.)(noun masc. sing. dec. 4 b . . שער
לְשָׁעַר[h] וּ' pref. לְ)(noun com. sing. d. 6 d; וּ bef. (:) שער
לְשַׁעֲרֵי[i] pref. id.)(id. pl., constr. st. . . . שער
לְשֹׁעֲרֵי[k] pref. id.)(noun m. pl. constr. from שׁוֹעֵר d. 7 b שער
לַשְּׁעָרִים[l] pref. לַ for לְהַ)(noun com., pl. of שַׁעַר d. 6 d שער
לְשֹׁעֲרִים pref. לְ)(noun masc., pl. of שׁוֹעֵר dec. 7 b . שער
לִשְׂעֹרִים pref. לְ bef. (:))(pr. name masc. . . . שער
לִשְׁפּוֹט[m] in full for לִשְׁפֹּט (q. v. & § 8. rem. 18) . שפט
לִשְׁפּוֹךְ[n] in full for לִשְׁפֹּךְ (q. v. & § 8. rem. 18) . שפך
לִשְׁפוּפָם pref. לְ bef. (:))(pr. name masc. . . שפף
לְשִׁפְחָה pref. לְ)(noun fem. sing. dec. 12 b . . שפח
לִשְׁפָחוֹת וְ pref. לְ bef. (:))(id. pl., abs. st. . . שפח
לְשִׁפְחָתְךָ[o] וּ'[p] pref. לְ)(id. sing., suff. 2 p. s. m.; וּ bef. (:) שפח
לְ׳שְׁפָּט[q] Kh. לִשְׁפֹּט q. v.)(K. לְמִשְׁפָּט (q. v.) . שפט
לִשְׁפֹּט pref. לְ bef. (:))(Kal inf. constr. . . שפט
לְשֹׁפְטָיו וּ pref. לְ)(the foll. with suff. 3 pers. sing. m. שפט
לַשֹּׁפְטִים[r] וְ pref. לַ f. לְהַ } Kal part. act. masc., pl. of
לְשֹׁפְטִים[s] וּ pref. לְ } שׁוֹפֵט d. 7 b; וּ bef. (:) } שפט
לְשָׁפְטֵנוּ[t] pref. id.)(id. inf., suff. 1 pers. pl. . שפט
לִשְׁפִּים וּ' pref. id.)(pr. name masc.; וּ bef. (:) . שפף
לִשְׁפֹּךְ pref. לְ bef. (:) }
לִשְׁפָּךְ־[u] וְ' pref. id. } Kal inf. constr. (§ 8. rem. 18) שפך
לַשְׁפַנִּים[x] pref. לַ for לְהַ)(noun masc., pl. of שָׁפָן dec. 8 a (§ 37. No. 3 c) . . . שפן
לִשְׂפַת[y] pref. לְ bef. (:))(n. f. s., constr. of שָׂפָה d. 11 a שפה

[a] Is. 53. 1. [b] Ex. 32. 25. [c] Ge. 2. 15. [d] 1 Sa. 19. 11. [e] Jos. 10. 18. [f] Eze. 8. 16. [g] De. 17. 3. [h] Da. 3. 29. [i] 2 Sa. 19. 7. [k] De. 7. 10. [l] 2 Ch. 19. 2. [m] De. 7. 10. [n] Da. 4. 16. [o] Je. 2. 36. [p] De. 21. 15. [q] Ps. 124. 6. [r] Pr. 10. 26. [s] 2 Ch. 11. 17. [t] 1 Ki. 3. 25. [u] Jos. 6. 22. [x] Je. 24. 9. [y] 2 Ch. 15. 10. [z] 2 Sa. 13. 23. [a] 2 Ch. 11. 15. [b] Le. 17. 7. [c] 1 Ki. 20. 10. [d] Ex. 32. 27. [e] 1 Ch. 16. 42. [f] Eze. 40. 16, 44. [g] Le. 13. 36. [h] Ex. 27. 16. [i] Je. 22. 19. [k] 2 Ch. 23. 4. [l] Ju. 5. 11. [m] 1 Ch. 16. 33. [n] Je. 22. 17. [o] 2 Ki. 4. 2. [p] 2 Sa. 14. 6. [q] Eze. 44. 24. [r] 2 Ch. 1. 2. [s] 1 Ch. 26. 29. [t] 1 Sa. 8. 5, 6. [u] 1 Sa. 25. 31. [x] Ps. 104. 18. [y] Da. 12. 5.

לִשְׂפָתוֹ[a] pref. לְ bef. (:))(id. with suff. 3 pers. s. m. . שפה
לִשְׁקֹד[b] pref. id.)(Kal inf. constr. . . שקד
לִשְׁקוֹל[c] pref. id.)(Kal inf. constr. (§ 8. rem. 18) שקל
לִשְׁקָלִים[d] pref. id.)(noun masc. pl. (c. שִׁקְלֵי) from שֶׁקֶל dec. 6 a . . . . שקל
לַשֶּׁקֶר / לַשָּׁקֶר } pref. לַ for לְהַ)(noun masc. sing. (pl. suff. שִׁקְרֵיהֶם) d. 6 a (comp. § 35. r. 2) } שקר
וּלְשַׂר / לְשַׂר } ו׳ pref. לְ)(noun masc. sing. dec. 8 (§ 37. rem. 7); וּ bef. (:) . . } שרר
לְשֵׁרֵבְיָה pref. id.)(pr. name masc., see שֵׁרֵבְ׳
לְשָׂרָה ו׳ pref. id.)(pr. name fem.; וּ bef. (:) . שרר
לַשָּׁרוֹן pref. לַ for לְהַ)(pr. name of a region . ישר
לְשָׂרֵי ו׳ pref. לְ)(noun masc. pl. constr. fr. שַׂר dec. 8 (§ 37. rem. 7); וּ bef. (:) . שרר
לְשָׂרֶיהָ pref. id.)(id. pl. with suff. 3 pers. sing. fem. שרר
לִשְׂרָיָה pref. לְ bef. (:))(pr. name masc., see שְׂרָיָה שרה
לְשָׂרָיו[g] pref. לְ)(noun masc. pl., suff. 3 pers. sing. masc. from שַׂר dec. 8 (§ 37. rem. 7) . שרר
לַשָּׁרִים[h] pref. לַ for לְהַ)(Kal part. act. masc., pl. of שָׁר dec. 1 a (§ 30. No. 1) . . שיר
לַשָּׂרִים[i] / לְשָׂרִים[k] } וְ pref. id. / ו׳ pref. לְ q. v. } noun masc., pl. of שַׂר d. 8 e (§ 37. r. 7); וּ bef. (:) } שרר
לְשָׂרֵינוּ pref. id.)(id. pl. with suff. 1 pers. pl. . שרר
לְשָׂרֵךְ[m] pref. id.)(noun masc. sing., suff. 2 pers. sing. masc. from [שַׂר] dec. 8 c . . שרר
לְשָׁרֵךְ[n] pref. id.)(noun masc. sing., suff. 2 pers. sing. masc. from שׁוֹר (§ 35. rem. 13) . שור
לִשְׂרֹף pref. לְ bef. (:))(Kal inf. constr. . שרף
לִשְׂרֵפָה pref. id.)(noun fem. sing. dec. 10 . שרף
לְשָׂרְפוֹ[o] pref. לְ)(Kal inf., suff. 3 pers. sing. masc. שרף
לִשְׂרֵפַת[p] pref. לְ bef. (:))(noun fem. sing., constr. of שְׂרֵפָה dec. 10 . . . . שרף
לַשְּׂרֵקָה[q] וְ pref. לַ for לְהַ)(noun fem. sing. . . שרק
לִשְׂרֵקָה ו׳ pref. לְ bef. (:))(noun fem. sing. . שרק
לְשֹׁרְרָי[r] pref. לְ)(Kal part. act. pl., suff. 1 pers. sing. fr. [שׁוֹרֵר] dec. 7 b . . . . . שרר
לְשָׁרְשׁוֹ[s] Ch., pref. לְ bef. (:))(Kh. שָׁרְשׁוּ, K. שְׁרָשִׁי, noun fem. sing. . . . . . שרש
לְשָׁרֵת[t] / לְשָׁרֵת[u] } ו׳ pref. לְ)(Piel inf. constr. dec. 7 b (comp. § 10. rem. 3); וּ bef. (:) } שרת
לְשָׁרְתוֹ[x] ו׳ pref. id.)(id., suff. 3 pers. s. m.; וּ id. שרת
לְשָׁרְתָם pref. id.)(id., suff. 3 pers. pl. masc. . שרת

לְשָׁרְתֵנִי pref. לְ)(id., suff. 1 pers. sing. . . שרת
לְשֵׁשׁ[y] pref. id.)(num. card. f., pl. שִׁשִּׁים (com. gen.) שש
לְשֵׁשְׁבַּצַּר pref. id.)(pr. name masc., see שֵׁשְׁבַּצַּר
לְשִׁשָּׁה[z] pref. id.)(num. card. masc. (constr. שֵׁשֶׁת) from שֵׁשׁ fem. . . . . . שש
לְשָׂשׂוֹן pref. id.)(noun masc. sing. dec. 3 a . שוש
לְשָׁשָׁן ו׳ pref. id.)(pr. name masc.; וּ bef. (:) . שוש
לְשֵׁשֶׁת pref. id.)(num. card. masc., constr. of שִׁשָּׁה (§ 39. No. 4. rem. 1) from שֵׁשׁ fem. . שש
לְשֵׁת ו׳ pref. id.)(pr. name masc.; וּ bef. (:) . שית
לִשְׁתּוֹת ו׳ pref. לְ bef. (:))(Kal inf. constr. dec. 1 a שתה
לִשְׁתּוֹתָהּ[a] pref. id.)(id., suff. 3 pers. sing. fem. . שתה
לִשְׁתּוֹתָם pref. id.)(id., suff. 3 pers. pl. masc. . שתה
לִשְׁתֵּי pref. id.)(num. card. du., constr. of שְׁתַּיִם, fem. of שְׁנַיִם . . . . . שנה
לִשְׁתֵּיהֶן[b] pref. id.)(id. with suff. 3 pers. pl. masc. . שנה
לְשֹׁתָיו[c] pref. לְ)(Kal part. act. pl. masc., suff. 3 pers. sing. masc. from שֹׁתֶה dec. 9 a שתה
לִשְׁתֹּת defect. for לִשְׁתּוֹת (q. v.) . . . שתה
לְתַאֲבָה[d] pref. לְ)(noun fem. sing. . . תאב
לְתַאֲוָה[e] pref. id.)(noun fem. sing. dec. 10 . אוה
לַתְּאֵנָה[f] pref. לַ for לְהַ)(noun fem. sing. dec. 10 . תאן
לַתֵּבָה[g] pref. id.)(noun fem. sing. dec. 10 . תבה
לִתְבוּאַת[h] pref. לְ bef. (:))(noun fem. sing., constr. of תְּבוּאָה dec. 10 . . . . בוא
לַתְּבוּנָה[i] pref. לַ for לְהַ)(noun f. s. d. 10. R. בון see בין
לִתְבוּנָתוֹ pref. לְ bef. (:))(id., suff. 3 pers. sing. masc. בין
לִתְבוּנָתִי[k] pref. id.)(id., suff. 1 pers. sing. . . בין
לַתֶּבֶן / לְתֶבֶן[l] } pref. לַ f. לְהַ / pref. לְ q. v. } noun masc. sing. . . תבן
לְתַבְנִית[m] וּ pref. id.)(noun fem. sing. d. 1 b; וּ bef. (:) בנה
לְתֹהוּ[n] pref. id.)(Seg. noun [for תֹּהֶו] . . תהה
לִתְהִלָּה ו׳ pref. לְ bef. (:))(noun fem. sing. dec. 10 הלל
לְתוּגָה[o] pref. לְ)(noun fem. sing. dec. 10 . יגה
לְתוֹדָה[p] pref. id.)(noun fem. sing. dec. 10 . ידה
לְתוֹכַחְתִּי[q] pref. id.)(noun fem. sing., suff. 1 pers. sing. from תּוֹכַחַת dec. 13 a, pl. תּוֹכָחוֹת (§ 44. r. 5) יכח
לְתוֹלְדֹתָם pref. id.)(noun fem. pl. (תּוֹלְדוֹת q. v.), suff. 3 pers. pl. masc. . . . . ילד
לְתוֹלָע pref. id.)(pr. name masc. . . תלע
לְתוֹעֵבָה pref. id.)(noun fem. sing. dec. 11 b . תעב
לָתוּר ו׳ pref. לָ (see lett. ל))(Kal inf. constr. תור

a 1 Ki. 7. 24. b Pr. 8. 34. c Est. 4. 7. d 2 Ch. 3. 9. e 1 Ch. 11. 6. f Je. 1. 18. g 2 Ch. 17. 7. h 2 Ch. 9. 11. i Nu. 22. 40. k Ps. 45. 17. l Is. 32. 1. m Pr. 3. 8. n Ex. 22. 29. o Ju. 9. 52. p Is. 64. 10. q Ge. 49. 11. r Ps. 54. 7. s Ezr. 7. 26. t 2 Ch. 8. 14. u De. 17. 12. x 1 Ch. 15. 2. y Ex. 38. 26. z 1 Ch. 25. 23.

a Is. 51. 22. b Eze. 23. 13. c Is. 24. 9. d Ps. 119. 20. e Pr. 18. 1. f Ju. 9. 10. g Ge. 6. 16. h 2 Ch. 32. 28. i Pr. 2. 2, 3. k Pr. 5. 1. l Job 41. 19. m 1 Ch. 28. 18. n Is. 49. 4. o Pr. 17. 21. p Ps. 100. 1. q Pr. 1. 23.

לַתּוֹרָה[a] pref. לַ f. לְהַ } noun fem. sing. dec. 10 . ירה

לְתוֹרָה[b] pref. לְ q. v. } ירה

וּלְתוֹרָתוֹ[c] וּ pref. id.)(id., suff. 3 pers. s. m.; וּ bef. (:) ירה

וְלַתּוֹשָׁב[d] וְ pref. לַ for לְהַ)(noun m. s. d. 1 b (§ 31. r. 1) ישב

וּלְתוֹשָׁבְךָ[e] וּ pref. לְ)(id., suff. 2 pers. s. m.; וּ bef. (:) ישב

לְתוּשִׁיָּה[f] pref. id.)(noun fem. sing. . . . ישה

לתח Root not used; perh. *to spread out*, i. q. מָתַח, Sam. נתח (Gesenius).

מֶלְתָּחָה fem. *wardrobe, vestry*, 2 Ki. 10. 22.

לְתַחַן pref. לְ)(pr. name masc. . . . . חנה

לַתִּיכוֹנָה[g] pref. לַ for לְהַ)(adj. f. s. d. 10, fr. תִּיכוֹן m. תוך

וְלְתֵימָן[h] וְ pref. לְ)(noun masc. sing. (with parag. ה, תֵּימָנָה); וּ bef. (:) . . . ימן

לֶתֶךְ וְ masc. *measure*, of capacity, Ho. 3. 2.

לַתְּבוּנָה[k] pref. לַ for לְהַ)(noun fem. sing. dec. 10 . כון

לְתֵלִי[l] pref. לְ)(noun masc. sing. dec. 8 b . תלל

לְתֹלְדוֹתָם pref. id.)(n. m. pl. (תּוֹלְדוֹת), suff. 3 pers. pl. m. ילד

לְתֹלְדֹתָיו[m] pref. id.)(id. with suff. 3 pers. sing. masc. ילד

לְתֹלְדֹתָם defect. for לְתֹלְדוֹתָם (q. v.) . . ילד

לִתְלוֹת pref. לִ bef. (:))(Kal inf. constr. . . תלה

לְתַלְפִּיּוֹת[n] pref. לְ)(noun fem. pl. . . . . תלה

לַתֹּם[o] pref. לַ for לְהַ)(noun masc. sing. dec. 8 c . תמם

לְתֻמּוֹ pref. לְ)(id., suff. 3 pers. sing. masc. . תמם

וּלְתֻמִּים[p] וּ pref. id.)(id. pl., abs. st.; וּ bef. (:) . תמם

לְתֻמָּם[q] pref. id.)(id. sing., suff. 3 pers. pl. masc. תמם

לְתָמָר pref. id.)(pr. name fem. . . . תמר

לְתָמֶר[r] pref. id.)(noun masc. sing. dec. 4 a . תמר

לִתְנוּפָה[s] pref. לִ bef. (:))(noun fem. sing. dec. 10 . נוף

לְתַנּוֹת[t] pref. לְ)(Piel inf. constr. . . . תנה

לְתַנּוֹת[u] pref. id.)(noun fem., pl. of [תַּנָּה] dec. 10 . תנן

לְתַנִּים[x] pref. id.)(noun masc., pl. of [תַּן] dec. 8 d תנן

לְתַנִּין pref. id.)(noun masc. sing. dec. 1 b . תנן

לְתַנִּינִם[y] pref. id.)(id. pl., abs. st. . . . תנן

לתע Root not used; Arab. *to bite*.

מַלְתָּעָה fem. dec. 11 a, pl. *teeth*, Ps. 58. 7; by transp. מְתַלְּעוֹת Pr. 30. 14; Job 29. 17; Joel 1. 6.

וְלִתְעוּדָה[z] וְ pref. לִ bef. (:))(noun fem. sing. . . עוד

וּלְתִפְאֶרֶת[a] / וּלְתִפְאָרֶת } וּ pref. לְ)(noun fem. sing. dec. 13 a (comp. § 35. rem. 2); וּ bef. (:) } פאר

לְתִפְאַרְתֵּךְ[b] pref. id.)(id. with suff. 2 pers. sing. fem. . פאר

לִתְפּוֹר[c] pref. לִ bef. (:))(Kal inf. constr. (§ 8. r. 18) תפר

לַתְּפִלָּה[d] pref. לַ for לְהַ)(noun fem. sing. dec. 10 . פלל

לִתְפִלַּת pref. לִ bef. (:))(id., constr. st. . . פלל

לִתְפֹּשׂ pref. id.)(Kal inf. constr. . . . תפש

לְתָפְשָׂהּ[e] pref. לְ)(id., suff. 3 pers. sing. fem. . תפש

לְתָפְשָׂם[f] pref. id.)(id., suff. 3 pers. pl. masc. . תפש

לִתְקוֹעַ[g] pref. לִ bef. (:))(Kal inf. constr. (§ 8. r. 18) תקע

לִתְקוּפַת[h] pref. id.)(noun f. s., constr. of [תְּקוּפָה] d. 10 קוף

לְתַקֵּן[i] pref. לְ)(Piel inf. constr. . . . תקן

לִתְקֹן[k] pref. לִ bef. (:))(Kal inf. constr. . . תקן

וּלְתַקָּפָהּ[l] וּ Chald., pref. לְ)(Pael inf. constr. (§ 47. rem. 5); וּ bef. (:) . . . . תקף

לִתְקֻפוֹת[m] pref. לִ bef. (:))(noun f., pl. of תְּקוּפָה d. 10 קוף

לַתְּרוּמוֹת[n] pref. לַ for לְהַ)(noun f., pl. of תְּרוּמָה d. 10 רום

לִתְרוּמַת pref. לִ bef. (:))(id. sing., constr. st. . רום

לִתְרוּפָה[o] pref. id.)(noun fem. sing. . . . רוף

לְתֶרַע[p] pref. id.)(noun masc. sing. . . . תרע

וְלִתְשׁוּבַת[q] וְ pref. id.)(n. f. s., constr. of [תְּשׁוּבָה] d. 10 שוב

לִתְשׁוּעָה pref. id.)(noun fem. sing. dec. 10 . שוע

לִתְשׁוּעַת[r] pref. id.)(id., constr. st. . . . שוע

לִתְשׁוּעָתְךָ[s] pref. id.)(id. with suff. 2 pers. sing. masc. שוע

לַתְּשִׁיעִי[t] pref. לַ for לְהַ)(num. ord. masc., from תֵּשַׁע תשע

לְתִשְׁעָה[u] pref. לְ)(num. card. masc. from תֵּשַׁע fem. . תשע

לְתִשְׁעַת pref. id.)(id., constr. st. . . . תשע

וְלָתֵת / וְלָתֶת־ } וְ pref. לָ (see lett. ל))(Kal inf. constr. [for תֶּנֶת § 17. rem. 8] . } נתן

לְתִתָּהּ pref. לְ)(id. with suff. 3 pers. sing. f. d. 8 b נתן

לְתִתִּי pref. id.)(id., suff. 1 pers. sing. . . נתן

וּלְתִתְּךָ[x] וּ pref. id.)(id., suff. 2 pers. s. m.; וּ bef. (:) נתן

לְתִתָּם[y] pref. id.)(id., suff. 3 pers. pl. masc. . נתן

לְתִתֵּן[z] pref. id.)(Kal fut. 2 pers. sing. masc. (*that thou mayest put*), but some MSS. read לְתִתּוֹ inf. with suff. . . . נתן

וּלְתִתֵּנוּ[a] וּ pref. id.)(Kal inf. (תֵּת § 17. rem. 1), suff. 1 pers. pl. 8 b; וּ bef. (:) . . . נתן

[a] Ne. 8. 7.
[b] Is. 8. 20.
[c] Is. 42. 4.
[d] Nu. 35. 15. Le. 25. 6.
[f] Job 11. 6.
[g] Eze. 41. 7.
[h] Job 39. 26.
[i] Is. 43. 6.
[k] Na. 2. 10.
[l] Je. 49. 2.
[m] 1 Ch. 26. 31.
[n] Ca. 4. 4.
[o] Pr. 10. 29.
[p] Ezr. 2. 63.
[q] 2 Sa. 15. 11.
[r] Ca. 7. 8.
[s] Le. 14. 21.
[t] Ju. 11. 40.
[u] Mal. 1. 3.
[x] Job 30. 29.
[y] Ex. 7. 12.
[z] Is. 8. 20.
[a] 2 Ch. 3. 6.
[b] Is. 60. 19.
[c] Ec. 3. 7.
[d] Ne. 11. 17.
[e] De. 20. 19.
[f] 1 Sa. 23. 26.
[g] Ju. 7. 20.
[h] 2 Ch. 24. 23.
[i] Ec. 7. 13.
[k] Ec. 1. 15.
[l] Da. 6. 8.
[m] 1 Sa. 1. 20.
[n] Ne. 12. 44.
[o] Eze. 47. 12.
[p] Da. 3. 26.
[q] 2 Ch. 36. 10.
[r] La. 3. 26.
[s] Ps. 119. 81.
[t] 1 Ch. 25. 26.
[u] Ezr. 9. 8, 9.
[x] De. 26. 19.
[y] 2 Ch. 35. 12.
[z] 1 Ki. 6. 19.
[a] Ezr. 9. 8.

מ

מֵ, מִ· (before guttural) pref. prep. i. q. מִן q. v. Root מָנַן.

מְאַבְּדִים[a] Piel part. masc., pl. of [מְאַבֵּד] dec. 7 b . אבד

מֵאֲבוֹתָם pref. מֵ for מִ·)(noun masc., with pl. fem. term. & suff. 3 pers. pl. m. fr. אָב irr. (§ 45) אב

מַאֲבִיד[b] Hiph. part. sing. masc. . . . אבד

מֵאֲבִיהֶן[c] pref. מֵ for מִ·)(noun masc. sing., suff. 3 pers. pl. fem. from אָב irr. (§ 45) . . אב

מֹאֲבִיּוֹת gent. noun fem., pl. of מֹאֲבִיָּה, masc. מוֹאָבִי, from מוֹאָב q. v.

מֵאָבִיךָ[d] pref. מֵ for מִ·)(noun masc. sing., suff. 2 pers. sing. masc. from אָב irr. (§ 45) . . אב

מֵאָבִיךְ[e] pref. id.)(id., suff. 2 pers. sing. fem. . . אב

מֵאֲבִימֶלֶךְ pref. id.)(pr. name masc. . . . . אב

מֵאָבִינוּ pref. id.)(noun masc. sing., suff. 1 pers. pl. from אָב irr. (§ 45) . . . אב

מֵאֵבֶל[f] וּ pref. id.)(noun masc. sing. dec. 6 (§ 35. rem. 6); וּ bef. lab. . . . אבל

מֵאָבֵל pref. id.)(pr. name in compos. אָבֵל מְחוֹלָה אבל

מֵאֶבֶן[g] pref. id.)(noun fem. sing. dec. 6a (also pr. name in compos. אֶבֶן הָעֵזֶר) . . אבן

מֵאַבְנֵי[h] pref. id.)(id. pl. constr. . . . אבן

מַאֲבַסֶיהָ[i] noun masc. pl., suff. 3 pers. sing. fem. from [מַאֲבוּס] dec. 1 b . . . . אבס

מֵאַבְרָהָם pref. מֵ for מִ·)(pr. name masc. . . . אב

מֵאֹבֹת pref. id.)(pr. name of a place . אוב

מֵאֲבֹתַי[k] pref. id.)(noun masc. with pl. fem. term. and suff. 1 pers. sing. from אָב irr. (§ 45) אב

מֵאֲבֹתֶיךָ[l] pref. id.)(id., suff. 2 pers. sing. masc. . אב

מֵאֲבֹתֵיכֶם[m] pref. id.)(id., suff. 2 pers. pl. masc. . אב

מֵאֲגַג pref. id.)(pr. name masc. . . אגג

מְאֹד noun masc. sing. dec. 1 a, generally as an *adv.* אוד

מְאֹדוֹ[n] id. with suff. 3 pers. sing. masc. . . אוד

מֵאֱדוֹם pref. ·מִ for מִ·)(pr. name of a country . אדם

מֵאַדִּירֵי[o] pref. id.)(adj. pl. constr. m. from אַדִּיר d. 1 b אדר

מְאֹדֶךָ[p] [for מְאֹדְךָ] noun masc. sing., suff. 2 pers. sing. masc. from מְאֹד dec. 1 a . . אוד

מֵאָדָם pref. מֵ for מִ·)(noun masc. sing. . אדם

מְאָדָּם[q] Pual part. sing. masc. [for מְאֻדָּם § 10. r. 5] אדם

מֵאֲדָמָה[r] וּ pref. מֵ for מִ·)(noun fem. sing. dec. 11 c (§ 42. rem. 1); וּ bef. lab. . . אדם

מְאָדָּמִים Pual part. masc., pl. of מְאָדָּם (q. v.) . אדם

מֵאֲדֹנִי[s] pref. מֵ for מִ·)(noun masc. sing., suff. 1 pers. sing. from אָדוֹן dec. 3 a . . דון

מֵאֲדֹנָיו[t] pref. מֵ for מִ·)(id. pl., suff. 3 pers. sing. m. דון

מֵאָה וּ fem. constr. מְאַת dec. 11 b.—I. *a hundred*; qualifying other words either in apposition, as מֵאָה שָׁנָה, or in the state of construction, as מְאַת שָׁנָה *a hundred years*; more rarely this numeral follows, comp. 2 Ch. 3. 16; 4. 8; Ezr. 2. 69; du. מָאתַיִם (for מְאָתַיִם) *two hundred*; pl. מֵאוֹת (and in Kh. מְאָיוֹת) *hundreds.*—II. adv. *hundred times*, Pr. 17. 10; Ec. 8. 12.—III. *the hundredth*, sc. part, of money, &c., Ne. 5. 11.—IV. pr. name of a tower in Jerusalem, Ne. 3. 1; 12. 39.

מְאָה Chald. *hundred*; dual מָאתַיִן, Ezr. 6. 17.

מֵאַהֲבָה pref. מֵ for מִ·)(noun fem. sing. (no pl.) . אהב

מְאַהֲבַי, מְאַהֲבַי[u] } Piel (§ 14. rem. 1) part. pl. masc., suff. 1 pers. sing. from [מְאַהֵב] dec. 7 b } אהב

מְאַהֲבֶיהָ id. pl., suff. 3 pers. sing. fem. . . אהב

מְאַהֲבַיִךְ, מְאַהֲבָיִךְ[x] וּ } id. pl., suff. 2 pers. sing fem.; וּ bef. lab. אהב

מֵאַהֲבַת pref. מֵ for מִ·)(noun fem. sing., constr. of אַהֲבָה (no pl.) . . . . אהב

מֵאֹהֶל pref. id.)(noun masc. sing. d. 6 c (§ 35. r. 9) אהל

מֵאָהֳלוֹ[y] pref. id.)(id., suff. 3 pers. sing. masc. . אהל

מֵאָהֳלֵי[z] pref. id.)(id. pl., constr. st. . . אהל

מֵאָהֳלֵיהֶם[ii] pref. id.)(id. pl., suff. 3 pers. pl. masc. אהל

מֵאֹהָלֶיךָ[a] pref. id.)(id. pl., suff. 2 pers. sing. masc. אהל

מְאוּזָּל[nn] Pual part. sing. masc. [for מְאֻזָּל § 10. r. 5] אזל

מֵאוֹיֵב pref. מֵ for מִ·)(Kal part. act. s. m. d. 7 b איב

מֵאֹיְבַי[b] pref. id.)(id. pl., suff. 1 pers. sing. . איב

מֵאֹיְבֵיהֶם[c] pref. id.)(id. pl., suff. 3 pers. pl. masc. . איב

מַאֲוַיֵּי[d] noun masc. pl. constr. from [מַאֲוַי] dec. 8 d (§ 37. No. 4) . . . אוה

מְאוּם[e] Kh., see the foll.; K. מוּם (q. v.) . מום

מְאוּם[f] noun masc. sing. elsewhere contr. מוּם מאם

מְאוּמָה וּ compounded fr. מָה וּמָה; וּ bef. lab. . מה

מֵאוֹן[g] pref. מֵ for מִ·)(noun masc. sing. dec. 6 g און

מָאוֹס[h] [i] וּ Kal inf. abs.; וּ bef. lab. . . מאס

מֵאוּפָז pref. מֵ for מִ·)(pr. name of a place, see אוּפָז

מֵאוֹפִיר pref. id.)(pr. name of a country . אפר

מֵאוֹצָר[k] pref. id.)(noun masc. sing. dec. 2 b . אצר

מֵאוֹצְרוֹתָיו[l] pref. id.)(id. pl. fem., suff. 3 pers. s. m. אצר

מָאוֹר[m] noun masc. sing. dec. 3 a . . אור

מֵאוֹר[n] pref. מֵ for מִ·)(noun masc. sing. dec. 1 a אור

מְאוֹר[o] noun masc. sing., constr. of מָאוֹר dec. 3 a אור

[a] Je. 23. 1. [b] De. 8. 20. [c] Ge. 19. 36. [d] Job 15. 10. [e] 2 Sa. 6. 21. [f] Est. 9. 22. [g] Is. 62. 10. [h] Ge. 28. 11. [i] Je. 50. 26. [ii] Jos. 3. 14. [k] 1 Ki. 19. 4. [l] De. 30. 5. [m] Je. 16. 12. [n] 2 Ki. 23. 25. [nn] Eze. 27. 19. [o] Je. 25. 35. [p] De. 6. 5. [q] Na. 2. 4. [r] Job 5. 6. [s] Ge. 47. 18. [t] Job 3. 19. [u] Ho. 2. 7. [x] Je. 22. 22. [y] Job 18. 14. [z] Mal. 2. 12. [a] Job 22. 23. [b] Is. 1. 24. [c] 2 Ch. 20. 27. [d] Ps. 140. 9. [e] Da. 1. 4. [f] Job 31. 7. [g] Job 36. 10. [h] Is. 7. 15, 16. [i] La. 3. 45. [k] Pr. 15. 16. [l] Ps. 135. 7. [m] Ps. 74. 16. [n] Job 18. 18. [o] Pr. 15. 30.

מֵאוּר pref. מֵ for מִ·)(pr. name of a place . . אור
מְאוֹרֵי[a] noun masc. pl. constr. from מָאוֹר dec. 3a אור
מְאוּרַת[b] noun fem. sing., constr. of [מְאוּרָה] dec. 10 אור
מֵאוֹת noun fem., pl. of מֵאָה dec. 11 b . . מאה
מֵאוֹתוֹ[c] pref. מֵ for מִ·)(as if אוֹת with suff. 3 pers. sing. masc., see אֵת (§ 5, parag.) . . את
מֵאוֹתִי[d] pref. id.)(id., suff. 1 pers. sing. . . את
מֵאוֹתָךְ[e] pref. id.)(id., suff. 2 pers. sing. fem. . את
מֵאוֹתְךָ[f] pref. id.)(id., suff. 2 pers. sing. masc. . את
מֵאוֹתֹתֶיךָ[g] pref. id.)(noun com. pl., suff. 2 pers. sing. masc. from אוֹת dec. 1 a . . . אוה
מֵאָז וּ׳[h] pref. id.)(adv.; וּ bef. lab. . . אז
מֹאזְנֵי וּ׳ constr. of the foll.; וּ id. . . . אזן
מֹאזְנַיִם[i] noun masc. du. [for מֹאזֶן] dec. 7 b . אזן
מְאַזְּרֵי[k] Piel part. pl. constr. masc. fr. [מְאַזֵּר] d. 7 b אזר
מֵאָח pref. מֵ for מִ·)(noun masc. sing. irr. (§ 45) אח
מֵאַחַד pref. id.)(num. m., constr. of אֶחָד irr. (§ 45) אחד
מֵאָחוֹר[l] וּ׳[m] pref. id.)(noun masc. s. d. 3 a; וּ bef. lab. אחר
מְאַחֵז[n] Piel part. sing. masc. (§ 14. rem. 1) . אחז
מָאֳחָזִים[o] Hoph. part. masc. pl. [of מָאֳחָז] . אחז
מֵאֲחֻזַּת[p] וּ׳[q] pref. מֵ for מִ·)(noun fem. sing., constr. of אֲחֻזָּה dec. 10 ; וּ bef. lab. . . אחז
מֵאֲחֻזָּתוֹ pref. id.)(id., suff. 3 pers. sing. masc. . אחז
מֵאֲחֻזָּתָם[r] pref. id.)(id., suff. 3 pers. pl. masc. . אחז
מֵאַחַי[s] pref. id.)(n. m. pl., suff. 1 p. s. fr. אָח irr. (§ 45) אח
מֵאַחֵי pref. id.)(id. pl., constr. st. . . אח
מֵאֲחֵיהֶם pref. id.)(id. pl., suff. 3 pers. pl. masc. . אח
מֵאָחִיו[t] pref. id.)(id. sing., suff. 3 pers. sing. masc. אח
מֵאֶחָיו pref. id.)(id. pl., suff. 3 pers. sing. masc. אח
מֵאָחִיךָ[u] pref. id.)(id. sing., suff. 2 pers. sing. masc. אח
מֵאַחֶיךָ pref. id.)(id. pl., suff. 2 pers. sing. masc. אח
מֵאֲחֵיכֶם pref. id.)(id. pl., suff. 2 pers. pl. masc. אח
מֵאַחַר pref. id.)((prim. subst. masc.) as a *prep.* אחר
מֵאַחֲרַי[x] } pref. id.)(id. pl., suff. 1 pers. sing.; } אחר
וּ׳[y] מֵאַחֲרָי } וּ bef. lab. . . . . }
מֵאַחֲרֵי pref. id.)(id. pl., constr. st. . . . אחר
מְאַחֲרֵי Piel (§ 14. rem. 1) part. pl. constr. masc. from [מְאַחֵר] dec. 7 b . . . אחר
מֵאַחֲרֶיהָ[z] pref. מֵ for מִ·)(prep. (אַחַר) with pl. suff. 3 pers. sing. fem. . . . . אחר
מֵאַחֲרֵיהֶם pref. id.)(id. with suff. 3 pers. pl. masc. אחר
מֵאַחֲרָיו pref. id.)(id. with suff. 3 pers. sing. masc. אחר
מֵאַחֲרָיִךְ[a] pref. id.)(id., suff. 2 pers. sing. fem. . אחר
מֵאַחֲרֶיךָ pref. id.)(id., suff. 2 pers. sing. masc. . אחר
מֵאַחֲרֵיכֶם[b] pref. id.)(id., suff. 2 pers. pl. masc. . אחר
מֵאַחֶרֶת[c] pref. id.)(adj. f., pl. אֲחֵרוֹת, fr. אַחֵר m. irr. (§ 45) אחר

מֵאַחַת pref. מֵ for מִ·)(num. adj. [for אַחֶדֶת], fem. of אֶחָד (§ 45) . . . . אחד
מְאֹיְבַי } pref. id.)(Kal part. act. sing. masc. } איב
וּ׳[d] מֵאֹיְבָי } dec. 7 b ; וּ bef. lab. . . }
מֵאֹיְבִי pref. id.)(id. sing., suff. 1 pers. sing. . איב
מֵאֹיְבֵיהֶם pref. id.)(id. pl., suff. 3 pers. sing. masc. . איב
מֵאֹיְבֶיךָ[e] pref. id.)(id. pl., suff. 2 pers. sing. masc. איב
מֵאֹיְבֵיכֶם[f] pref. id.)(id. pl., suff. 2 pers. pl. masc. . איב
מֵאֹיְבִים[g] pref. id.)(id. pl., abs. st. . . . איב
מֵאִיֵּי[h] וּ׳[i] pref. id.)(n. m. pl. constr. fr. אִי d. 8 (§ 37. No. 4) אוה
מֵאַיִל[k] pref. id.)(noun masc. s. d. 1 b (§ 30. No. 3) אול
מֵאֵיל pref. id.)(noun m. s., constr. of אַיִל d. 6 h אול
מֵאֵילוֹת pref. id.)(pr. name of a place . . אול
מֵאֵילִים[l] pref. id.)(noun masc., pl. of אֵיל dec. 1 a . אול
מֵאֵילִם pref. id.)(pr. name of a place . . אול
מֵאֵילַת pref. id.)(pr. name of a place . . אול
מֵאַיִן וּ׳ pref. id.)(adv. of interr.; וּ bef. lab. . אי
מֵאַיִן[m] pref. id.)(noun masc. sing. dec. 6h . . אין
מֵאֵין וּ׳ pref. id.)(id. constr. as an *adv.*; וּ bef. lab. אין
מֵאִיר[n] Hiph. part. sing. masc. . . . אור
מְאִירוֹת[o] id. fem., pl. of [מְאִירָה] dec. 10 . . אור
מְאִירַת[p] id. id. sing., constr. st. . . . אור
מֵאִישׁ pref. מֵ for מִ·)(n. m. s. d. 1 a (comp. § 45) איש
מֵאִישָׁהּ[q] וּ׳[r] pref. id.)(id. suff. 3 p. s. f.; וּ bef. lab. איש
מֵאֵיתָן pref. id.)(pr. name of a place . . יתן
מַאֲכִילִ[s] Hiph. part. sing. masc. dec. 1 b . . אכל
מַאֲכִילָם[t] id., suff. 3 pers. pl. masc. . . . אכל
מַאֲכָל וּ׳[u] noun masc. sing. dec. 2 b ; וּ bef. lab. אכל
מַאֲכַל וּ׳ id., constr. st.; וּ id. . . . אכל
מֵאֲכֹל[x] pref. מֵ for מִ·)(Kal inf. constr. . . אכל
מַאֲכָלָהּ[y] noun m. s., suff. 3 pers. s. f. fr. מַאֲכָל d. 2 b אכל
מַאֲכָלוֹ[z] וּ id., suff. 3 pers. sing. masc.; וּ bef. lab. אכל
מַאֲכַלְכֶם[a] id., suff. 2 pers. pl. masc. . . . אכל
מַאֲכָלוֹת[mm] וּ noun fem. pl. abs. [as if from מַאֲכָלָה] see מַאֲכֶלֶת' (§ 44. rem. 5); וּ bef. lab. . אכל
מַאֲכָלְךָ[b] וּ n. m. s., suff. 2 p. s. m. fr. מַאֲכָל d. 2 b; וּ id. אכל
מַאֲכֶלֶת[c] noun fem. sing. . . . . אכל
מֵאֵל pref. מֵ f. מִ·)(n. m. s. d. 1 a, or constr. of אַיִל d. 6 h אול
מֵאָלָה[d] וּ pref. id.)(n. f. s. d. 10 (§ 42. r. 2); וּ bef. lab. אלה
מֵאֵלֶּה וּ׳ pref. id.)(pron. demon. pl. com. gen.; וּ id. אל
מֵאֱלֹהָי } pref. id.)(noun masc. pl., suff. 1 pers. } אלה
וּ׳[f] מֵאֱלֹהָי[e] } sing. from אֱלוֹהַּ dec. 1 a ; וּ id. }
מֵאֱלֹהֵי pref. id.)(id. pl., constr. st. . . אלה
מֵאֱלֹהָיו[g] pref. id.)(id. pl., suff. 3 pers. sing. masc. . אלה

---

[a] Eze. 32. 8.
[b] Is. 11. 8.
[c] 1 Ki. 22. 7; 2 Ki. 3. 11; 8. 8.
[d] Is. 54. 15.
[e] 1 Ki. 20. 25.
[f] 2 Sa. 24. 24.
[g] Ps. 65. 9.
[h] Ex. 5. 23.
[i] Is. 40. 15.
[k] Is. 50. 11.
[l] Is. 9. 11.
[m] 2 Sa. 10. 9.
[mm] Pr. 30. 14.
[n] Job 26. 9.
[o] 2 Ch. 9. 18.
[p] Nu. 35. 8.
[q] Eze. 48. 22.
[r] Eze. 46. 18.
[s] Ne. 1. 2.
[t] Ne. 4. 13.
[u] De. 15. 7.
[x] 2 Sa. 2. 22.
[y] Je. 3. 19.
[z] Jos. 8. 2.
[a] Ru. 1. 16.
[b] De. 29. 21.
[c] 2 Sa. 13. 16.
[d] 2 Sa. 22. 4.
[e] Ju. 11. 36.
[f] Nu. 10. 9.
[g] Ps. 68. 24.
[h] Eze. 27. 6, 7.
[i] Is. 11. 11.
[k] 1 Ki. 5. 3.
[l] Is. 1. 29.
[m] Is. 41. 24; Je. 30. 7.
[n] Pr. 29. 13.
[o] Is. 27. 11.
[p] Ps. 19. 9.
[q] Le. 21. 7.
[r] Ru. 1. 5.
[s] Je. 23. 15.
[t] Je. 9. 14.
[u] Ezr. 3. 7.
[x] Ps. 102. 5.
[y] Pr. 6. 8.
[z] Hab. 1. 16.
[a] Da. 1. 10.
[b] Eze. 4. 10.
[c] Is. 9. 4.
[d] Ps. 59. 13.
[e] 1 Ch. 11. 19.
[f] Is. 40. 27.
[g] Je. 51. 5.

מֵאֱלֹהֶיךָ pref. מֵ for מִ·)(id. pl., suff. 2 pers. sing. m. אלה
מֵאֱלֹהִים [a]'וּ pref. id.)(id. pl., abs. st.; וּ bef. lab. אלה
מֵאֱלֹהֵינוּ[b] pref. id.)(id. pl., suff. 1 pers. pl. . . אלה
מֵאֱלוֹהַּ[c] pref. id.)(id. sing., abs. . . . אלה
מֵאֵלוֹן pref. id.)(noun masc. sing. dec. 1b . אלל
מֵאָלוּשׁ pref. id.)(pr. name of a place . . אלש
מֵאֵלִיָּהוּ pref. id.)(pr. name masc. . . . אול
מַאֲלִיפוֹת[d] Hiph. part. f. pl. [of מַאֲלִיפָה fr. מַאֲלִיף m.] אלף
מְאַלְּמִים[e] Piel part. masc., pl. of [מְאַלֵּם] dec. 7b . אלם
מֵאָלֶף[f], מֵאָלֶף[g] } pref. מֵ for מִ·)(noun masc. sing. dec. 6a (§ 35. rem. 2) . . . . } אלף
מֵאַלְפֵי pref. id.)(id. pl., constr. st. . . . אלף
מֵאָלָתִי[h] pref. id.)(noun fem. sing., suff. 1 pers. sing. from אָלָה dec. 10 (§ 42. rem. 2) . אלה

מאם Root not used; hence
מְאוּם m. (for מְאוּם) Da. 1. 4; Job 31. 7, and מוּם (contr.) masc. dec. 1a, *spot, blemish,* in a physical and moral sense.

מַאֲמִינִים[i] Hiph. part. masc., pl. of מַאֲמִין dec. 1b . אמן
מְאַמֶּצְךָ[k] Piel part. sing. masc. [for מְאַמֵּץ] . אמץ
מַאֲמַצֵּי[l] noun masc. pl. constr. from [מַאֲמָץ] d. 8a אמץ
וּמַאֲמַר[m] 'וּ n. m. s., constr. of [מַאֲמָר] d. 2b; וּ bef. lab. אמר
מֵאמַר[n] וּ Chald. noun masc. sing. (§ 53. r. 1); וּ id. אמר
מֵאִמְרֵי pref. מֵ for מִ·; n. m. pl. constr. fr. [אֵמֶר] d. 6b אמר

מָאֵן. Pi. מֵאֵן *to refuse, to be unwilling.*
מָאֵן adj. masc. *refusing, unwilling.*
מֵאֵן masc. (for מְאֵן) d. 7b, *refusing,* Je. 13. 10.

[מָאן] Chald. masc. dec. 1a, *vessel.* Da. 5. 2, 3, 23; Ezr. 5. 14; 7. 19.

מָאֵן adj. masc. s.; or (Ex. 22. 16) Piel inf. abs. מאן
מֵאָ֯ן[o] pref. מֵ for מִ·)(Kh. מֵאָן see אָן, K. מֵאַיִן (q.v.) אי
מֵאֵן Piel pret. 3 pers. sing. masc. . . . . מאן
מֵאֲנָה id. pret. 3 pers. sing. fem. . . . מאן
מֵאֲנוּ id. pret. 3 pers. pl. . . . . מאן
מֵאֱנוֹשׁ pref. מֵ for מִ·)(n. m. s. irr. (see אִישׁ § 45) אנש
מָאנֵי[p] Chald. noun masc. pl. constr. fr. [מָאן] d. 1a מאן
מָאנַיָּא[q] 'וּ Chald. id. pl. emph.; וּ bef. lab. . מאן
מֵאֳנִיּוֹתֵיהֶם[r] pref. מֵ for מִ·)(noun fem. pl., suff. 3 pers. pl. masc. from אֳנִיָּה dec. 10 . . אנה
מֵאַנְקַת[s] pref. id.)(noun fem. sing., constr. of אֲנָקָה dec. 11c (§ 42. rem. 1) . . . אנק

מֵאַנְשֵׁי[t] 'וּ pref. מֵ for מִ·)(noun masc. pl. constr. [as if from אֱנֶשׁ], see אֱנוֹשׁ; וּ bef. lab. . אנש
מֵאַנְתָּ[u] Piel pret. 2 pers. masc. sing. . . . מאן
מֵאַנְתְּ[v] id. pret. 2 pers. sing. fem. . . . מאן
מֵאַנְתֶּם[y] id. pret. 2 pers. pl. masc. . . . מאן

***I.* מָאַס** fut. יִמְאַס.—I. *to reject.*—II. *to despise, lightly esteem,* with בְּ; inf. מָאוֹס La. 3. 45, *aversion, contempt.* Niph. *to be contemned, despised.*

***II.* מָאַס** Kal not used; i. q. מָסַס, Niph. *to melt, dissolve, waste away,* Ps. 58. 8; Job 7. 5.

מָאוֹס[z] Kal inf. abs. . . . . . . מאס
מֹאֵס[a] id. part. act. sing. masc. . . . . מאס
מָאָסוּ, מָאָסוּ } id. pret. 3 pers. pl. (§ 8. rem. 7) . . מאס
מָאָסְכֶם[b] id. inf., suff. 2 pers. pl. (§ 16. rem. 8) . מאס
מֹאֲסָם[c] id. id., suff. 3 pers. pl. masc. . . . מאס
מְאָסָם[d] id. pret. 3 pers. sing. m., suff. 3 pers. pl. m. מאס
מְאַסֵּף Piel part. sing. masc. dec. 7b . . אסף
מְאֻסָּף[e] Pual part. sing. masc. . . . . אסף
מְאַסְּפָיו[f] Piel part. pl. masc., suff. 3 pers. sing. masc. from מְאַסֵּף dec. 7b . . . אסף
וּמְאַסִּפְכֶם[g] וּ id., suff. 2 pers. pl. masc.; וּ bef. lab. . אסף
מָאַסְתָּ Kal pret. 2 pers. sing. masc. . . . מאס
מֹאֶסֶת[h] id. part. act. sing., fem. of מוֹאֵס . . מאס
מָאַסְתָּה id. pret. 2 pers. sing. masc. (§ 8. rem. 5) מאס
מָאַסְתִּי, וּמָאַסְתִּי[i] } id. pret. 1 pers. sing., acc. shifted by וּ for וְ conv. (§ 8. rem. 7) . } מאס
מְאַסְתִּיהוּ[k] id. id., suff. 3 pers. sing. masc. . . מאס
מְאַסְתִּיו[l] id. id., suff. 3 pers. sing. masc. . . מאס
מְאַסְתִּיךָ[m] id. id., suff. 2 pers. sing. masc. . . מאס
מְאַסְתִּים[n] id. id., suff. 3 pers. pl. masc. . . מאס
מְאַסְתֶּם id. pret. 2 pers. pl. masc. . . . מאס
מְאַסְתָּנוּ[o] id. pret. 2 pers. sing. masc., suff. 1 pers. pl. מאס
מֵאֶסְתֵּר pref. מֵ for מִ·)(pr. name fem., see אֶסְתֵּר
מֵאַף[p] pref. id.)(noun m. sing. d. 8d [for אֲנַף, אֶנֶף] אנף
מַאֲפֵה[q] noun masc. sing., constr. of [מַאֲפֶה] dec. 9a אפה
מֵאֹפֶה[r] pref. מֵ for מִ·)(Kal part. sing. masc. dec. 9a אפה
מֵאַפְּכֶם[s] pref. id.)(noun masc. sing., suff. 2 pers. pl. masc. from אַף dec. 8d [for אֶנֶף, אֲנַף] אנף
מַאֲפֵל[t] noun masc. sing. . . . . אפל
וּמֵאֹפֶל[u] וּ pref. מֵ for מִ·)(noun masc. s.; וּ bef. lab. אפל
מַאְפֵּלְיָה[x] n. m. (מַאֲפֵל q.v.) with the term. יָה for יָהּ (q.v.) אפל
מֵאֶפֶס[y] pref. מֵ for מִ·)(noun masc. sing. dec. 6a . אפס
מֵאַפְסֵי[z] pref. id.)(id. du., constr. st. . . אפס

[a] 2 Ch. 22. 7. [b] Ezr. 8. 23. [c] Job 4. 17. [d] Ps. 144. 13. [e] Ge. 37. 7. [f] Ps. 84. 11. [g] Ec. 7. 28. [h] Ge. 24. 41. [i] De. 1. 32. [k] Pr. 24. 5. [l] Job 36. 19. [m] Est. 9. 32. [n] Da. 4. 14. [o] 2 Ki. 5. 25. [p] Da. 5. 3; Ezr. 6. 5. [q] Ezr. 5. 14; 7. 19. [r] Eze. 27. 29. [s] Ps. 12. 6. [t] Ps. 59. 3. [u] Ex. 10. 3. [x] Je. 3. 3. [y] Ex. 16. 28. [z] La. 5. 22. [a] Is. 33. 15. [b] Is. 30. 12. [c] Am. 2. 4. [d] Ps. 53. 6. [e] Eze. 38. 12. [f] Is. 62. 9. [g] Is. 52. 12. [h] Eze. 21. 15, 18. [i] 2 Ki. 23. 27. [k] 1 Sa. 16. 7. [l] 1 Sa. 16. 1. [m] Is. 41. 9. [n] Le. 26. 44. [o] La. 5. 22. [p] Ps. 37. 8. [q] Le. 2. 4. [r] Ho. 7. 4. [s] Nu. 11. 20. [t] Jos. 24. 7. [u] Is. 29. 18. [x] Je. 2. 31. [y] Is. 40. 17. [z] Je. 16. 19.

מֵאֶפַע[a] pref. מֵ for ·מִ) [for אֶפַע] noun masc. sing. — אפע
מֵאֶפְרַיִם pref. id.) pr. name of a tribe . . — אפר
מֵאֲצִילֶיהָ[b] וּ pref. id.) noun masc. pl., suff. 3 pers. sing. fem. from [אָצִיל] dec. 3a; וּ bef. lab. . — אצל
מֵאֵצֶל pref. id.) (prop. subst. masc. dec. 6. § 35. rem. 6) as a *prep.* . . . — אצל
מֵאֶצְלוֹ pref. id.) id., suff. 3 pers. sing. masc. . — אצל
מֵאֶצְלִי[c] pref. id.) id., suff. 1 pers. sing. . . — אצל
מֵאֶצְלָם[d] pref. id.) id., suff. 3 pers. pl. masc. . — אצל
מֵאֹצְרוֹת[e] pref. id.) noun masc. with pl. fem. term., constr. of צָרוֹת׳ from אוֹצָר dec. 2b . — אצר
מֵאֹצְרוֹתָיו[f] pref. id.) id., suff. 3 pers. sing. masc. . — אצר
מֵאֹצְרֹתָיו[g] pref. id.) id., suff. 3 pers. sing. masc. . — אצר

מָאַר. Hiph. הַמְאִיר *to irritate, pain*; part. *painful.*

מֵאַרְבֶּה[h] pref. מֵ for ·מִ) noun masc. sing. . . . — רבה
מֵאֲרֻבָּה[i] pref. id.) noun fem. sing. dec. 10 . — ארב
מְאָרְבִים Piel part. masc., pl. of [מְאָרֵב] dec. 7b . — ארב
מֵאַרְבַּע pref. מֵ for ·מִ) num. card. fem. (§ 31. rem. 5) — רבע
מְאֵרוֹת[k] noun fem., pl. of מְאֵרָה׳ dec. 10 [for מְאֹרָה] — ארר
מֵאֲרִי[l] pref. מֵ for ·מִ) noun m. sing. d. 6i (§ 35. r. 14) — ארה
מֵאֲרָיוֹת[m] pref. id.) id. pl. abs. fem. . . — ארה
מַאֲרִיךְ[n] וּ׳ Hiph. part. sing. masc.; וּ bef. lab. . — ארך
מֵאֲרָם pref. מֵ for ·מִ) pr. name of a country . — ארם
מֵאַרְנוֹן } מֵאַרְנֹן } pref. id.) pr. name of a river . . — רנן
מֵאַרְעָא[o] Chald., pref. id.) noun fem. sing., emph. of [אֲרַע] dec. 3a . . . . — ארע
מֵאֶרֶץ } pref. id.) noun fem. sing. dec. 6a (§ 35.
מֵאָרֶץ וּ׳ } rem. 2); וּ bef. lab. . . } — ארץ
מֵאַרְצוֹ[p] וּ׳ pref. id.) id., suff. 3 pers. sing. masc.; וּ id. — ארץ
מֵאֲרָצוֹת[q] וּ pref. id.) id. pl., abs. st.; וּ id. . . — ארץ
מֵאַרְצוֹת[r] pref. id.) id. pl., constr. st. . . — ארץ
מֵאַרְצְךָ pref. id.) id. sing., suff. 2 pers. sing. masc. — ארץ
מֵאַרְצָם[s] pref. id.) id. sing., suff. 3 pers. pl. masc. . — ארץ
מְאֹרָשָׂה[t] Pual part. sing. fem. [of מְאֹרָשׂ] . . — ארש
מְאֵרַת[u] noun f. s., constr. of מְאֵרָה׳ d. 10 [for מְאֹרָה] — ארר
מְאֹרֹת[x] noun m. with pl. fem. term. from מָאוֹר d. 3a — אור
מֵאֵשׁ pref. מֵ for ·מִ) noun com. sing. dec. 8b . — אשׁ
מֵאַשְׁדּוֹד pref. id.) pr. name of a place . . — שׁדד
מֵאִשָּׁה pref. id.) noun fem. sing. dec. 10 [for אִנְשָׁה] — אנשׁ
מֵאַשּׁוּר וּ׳ pref. id.) pr. name of a country; וּ bef. lab. — אשׁר
מֵאִשָּׁי[y] pref. id.) noun masc. pl., suff. 1 pers. sing. from אִשֶּׁה dec. 9a . . . . — אשׁ
מֵאִשֵּׁי pref. id.) id. pl., constr. st. . . — אשׁ
מֵאַשְׁפֹּת pref. id.) noun masc. sing. . . . — שׁפת

מֵאַשְׁקְלוֹן pref. מֵ for ·מִ) pr. name of a place . — שׁקל
מֵאָשֵׁר וּ׳ pref. id.) pr. name of a man and a tribe; וּ bef. lab. . . . . . — אשׁר
מֵאֲשֶׁר וּ׳ pref. id.) pron. relat. of all genders and numbers; וּ id. . . . . . — אשׁר
מְאֻשָּׁר[z] Pual part. sing. masc. . . . . — אשׁר
מְאַשְּׁרֵי[a] Piel part. pl. constr. masc. fr. [מְאַשֵּׁר] d. 7b — אשׁר
מְאֻשָּׁרָיו[b] וּ Pual part. pl., suff. 3 p. s. m. fr. מְאֻשָּׁר; וּ bef. lab. — אשׁר
מְאַשְּׁרֶיךָ[c] the foll. with suff. 2 pers. sing. masc. . — אשׁר
מְאַשְּׁרִים[d] Piel part. masc., pl. of [מְאַשֵּׁר] dec. 7b . — אשׁר
מֵאֵשֶׁת pref. מֵ for ·מִ) noun fem. sing. dec. 13b . — אישׁ
מֵאִשְׁתַּם[e] Kh. מֵאֶשָׁתָם pref. מֵ for ·מִ) noun fem. sing., suff. 3 pers. pl. masc. from [אֶשָׁה] from אֵשׁ K. מֵאֵשׁ (q. v.) & תַּם 3 pers. sing. — תמם
מְאַת וּ׳ noun f. s., constr. of מֵאָה d. 11b; וּ bef. lab. — מאה
מֵאוֹת id. pl. abs. st. . . . . . — מאה
מֵאֵת וּ׳ pref. מֵ for ·מִ) prep. (אֵת), comp. dec. 8b; וּ bef. lab. . . . . . — את
מֵאִתּוֹ pref. id.) id., suff. 3 pers. sing. masc. . — את
מֵאֹתוֹ pref. id.) as if אוֹת with suff. 3 pers. sing. masc. see אֵת (§ 5, parad.) . . — את
מֵאֹתוֹת[f] וּ pref. id.) noun com., pl. of אוֹת dec. 1a [for אֹוֶת]; וּ bef. lab. . . . — אוה
מֵאִתִּי pref. id.) prep. אֵת with suff. 1 p. s. (comp. d. 8b) — את
מָאתַיִם וּ׳ } noun fem., by Syriasm [for מְאָתַיִם],
מָאתָיִם וּ׳ } du. of מֵאָה dec. 11b; וּ bef. lab. } — מאה
מָאתַיִן[g] Chald. [for מְאָתַיִן], noun fem., dual of מְאָת — מאה
מֵאִתָּךְ pref. מֵ for ·מִ) prep. אֵת with suff. in pause for מֵאִתְּךָ (q. v.), or (1 Ki. 2. 16, 20) 2 p. s. f. — את
מֵאִתָּךְ[h] pref. id.) id. with suff. 2 pers. sing. fem. — את
מֵאִתְּךָ pref. id.) id. with suff. 2 pers. sing. masc. — את
מֵאִתְּכֶם pref. id.) id. with suff. 2 pers. pl. masc. — את
מֵאֵתָם pref. id.) pr. name of a place . . — יתם
מֵאִתָּם pref. id.) prep. אֵת with suff. 3 pers. pl. masc. (comp. dec. 8b) . . . — את
מֵאֶתְמוֹל[i] } מֵאִתְּמוֹל[k] } pref. id.) *adv.* . . . . — מול
מֵאֶתְנַן[l] pref. id.) noun m. sing., constr. of אֶתְנָן d. 2b — תנה
מְבָא[m] defect. for מְבוֹא (q. v.) . . . — בוא
מְבֹאוֹ[n] defect. for מְבוֹאוֹ (q. v.) . . . — בוא
מְבִאֵי[o] וּ Hiph. part. pl. constr. masc. from מֵבִיא dec. 3b; וּ bef. lab. . . . . — בוא
מְבִאִים[p] id. pl. abs. (comp. מְבִיאִים) . . — בוא
מִבְּאֵר pref. מִ) pr. name in compos. בְּאֵר שֶׁבַע . — באר
מִבֹּאר[q] pref. id.) Kh. בְּאֵר׳ q. v., K. בֹּר (see מְבוֹר) — באר
מִבְּאֵרֹת pref. id.) pr. name in compos. בְּאֵרֹת בְּנֵי יַעֲקָן — באר

[a] Is. 41. 24. [b] Is. 41. 9. [c] 1 Ki. 3. 20. [d] Eze. 10. 16. [e] 2 Ch. 16. 2. [f] Je. 10. 13. [g] Je. 51. 16. [h] Je. 46. 23. [i] Ho. 13. 3. [k] Pr. 28. 27. [l] Ju. 14. 18. [m] 2 Sa. 1. 23. [n] Ec. 7. 15; 8. 12. [o] Je. 10. 11. [p] Eze. 36. 20. [q] Ps. 107. 3. [r] Eze. 39. 27. [s] De. 2. 5. [t] De. 22. 23. [u] Pr. 3. 33. [x] Ge. 1. 14. [y] Le. 6. 10. [z] Pr. 3. 18.

[a] Is. 9. 15. [b] Is. 9. 15. [c] Is. 3. 12. [d] Mal. 3. 15. [e] Je. 6. 29. [f] Je. 10. 2. [g] Ezr. 6. 17. [h] Is. 54. 10. Is. 30. 33. [k] 1 Sa. 10. 11. [l] Mi. 1. 7. [m] 2 Ki. 23. 11. [n] Ps. 50. 1. [o] Je. 17. 26; 33. 11. [p] Je. 17. 26; 33. 11. [q] 2 Sa. 23. 15, 16.

מִבָּבֶל pref. ·מִ)(pr. name of a place . . . בלל

מִבָּבֶלָה pref. id.)(id. with parag. ה . . בלל

מִבֹּגְדָה[a] pref. id.)(Kal part. act., fem. of בּוֹגֵד (§ 39. No. 3. rem. 4) . . . . . . בגד

מִבְּגָדַיִךְ[b] pref. id.)(noun masc. pl., suff. 2 pers. sing. fem. from בֶּגֶד dec. 6a . . . . בגד

מַבְדִּיל[c] Hiph. part. sing. masc. dec. 1 b . . . בדל

מַבְדִּילִים[d] id. pl., abs. st. . . . . . . בדל

מְבֹהָלִים[e] Pual part. masc. pl. [of מְבֹהָל] . . בהל

מִבַּהֲמוֹת[f] pref. ·מִ)(noun fem. pl., constr. of בְּהֵמוֹת, from בְּהֵמָה (§ 42. rem. 1 & 5) . . בהם

מָבוֹא[u] noun masc. sing. dec. 3a . . . . בוא

מְבוֹא id., constr. st. . . . . בוא

מִבּוֹא pref. ·מִ)(Kal inf. constr. (§ 25. No. 2f) בוא

מְבוֹאוֹ noun m. s., suff. 3 pers. s. m. fr. מָבוֹא d. 3a בוא

מְבוֹאֶךָ[g] Kh. מְבוֹאֶךָ id. with suff. [for מְבוֹאֲךָ] 2 pers. sing. masc.; K. מוֹבָאֶךָ from מוֹבָא d. 2b בוא

מְבוֹאֹת[h] noun masc. with pl. fem. term. fr. מָבוֹא d. 3a בוא

מְבוּכָה[i] ·וּ noun fem. sing. dec. 10; ·וּ bef. lab. . בוך

מְבוּכָתָם[k] id., suff. 3 pers. pl. masc. . . . בוך

מַבּוּל[l] noun masc. sing. . . . . . . יבל

מְבוּסָה ·וּ noun fem. sing.; ·וּ bef. lab. . . . בוס

מַבּוּעֵי[m] noun masc. pl. constr. from מַבּוּעַ' dec. 1b . נבע

מְבוּקָה[n] ·וּ noun fem. sing.; ·וּ bef. lab. . . . בוק

מִבּוֹר pref. ·מִ)(n. m. s. d. 1a, contr. for בְּאֹר=בּאר באר

מִבּוֹרֶךָ[o] pref. id.)(id., suff. 2 pers. s. m. [for בּוֹרְךָ] בור

מִבְחוֹר noun masc. sing. . . . . . . בחר

מִבַּחוּרֵיכֶם[p] ·וּ pref. id.)(noun masc. pl. (בַּחוּרִים, dag. forte impl. in ח), suff. 2 pers. pl. masc. from בָּחוּר [for בַּחוּר]; ·וּ bef. lab. . בחר

מִבַּחֻרִים pref. ·מִ)(pr. name of a place . . בחר

מְבֹהֶלֶת[q] Kh. Pual part. s. f. R. בחל, K. מְבֹהֶלֶת R. בהל

מִבְחָר pr. name masc. . . . . בחר

מִבְחַר ·וּ noun masc. sing., constr. of [מִבְחָר] dec. 2b; ·וּ bef. lab. . . . . . . בחר

מִבְחָרָיו[r] id. pl., suff. 3 pers. sing. masc. . . בחר

מִבְּחָרָיו[s] pref. ·מִ)(n. m. pl. [בְּחָרִים], suff. 3 p. s. m. בחר

מִבַּחֲרִים pref. id.)(pr. name of a place . . בחר

מִבְטָא[t] noun masc. sing. constr. (§ 31. rem. 1) בטא

מֶבְטָאהּ[u] noun masc. sing., suff. 3 pers. sing. fem. [for מִבְטָאהּ from מִבְטָא comp. אָח § 45] dec. 1b נבט

מִבֶּטַח ·וּ pref. ·מִ)(pr. name of a place; ·וּ bef. lab. בטח

מִבְטַח noun masc. sing., constr. of מִבְטָח', dec. 2b בטח

מִבְּטֹחַ[x] pref. ·מִ)(Kal inf. constr. . . . בטח

מִבְטֶחָה[y] noun masc. sing., suff. 3 pers. s. f. (§ 3. r. 3) from מִבְטָח d. 8 (§ 37. r. 7, comp. אָח § 45) בטח

מִבְטָחוֹ / מִבְטַחוֹ[z] } id., suff. 3 pers. sing. masc. . . בטח

מִבְטַחִי[a] / מִבְטָחִי[b] } id., suff. 1 pers. sing. . . . בטח

מִבְטַחִים[c] id. pl., abs. st. . . . . . . בטח

מִבְטַחֵךְ[d] id. sing., suff. 2 pers. sing. m. [for מִבְטַחֲךָ] בטח

מִבְטֶחָם[e] id. sing., suff. 3 pers. pl. m. (comp. אָח § 45) בטח

מַבְטִיחִי[f] Hiph. part. sing. masc., suff. 1 pers. sing. from [מַבְטִיחַ] dec. 1b . . . בטח

מַבָּטָם[g] noun masc. sing., suff. 3 pers. pl. masc. from [מַבָּט] dec. 1b . . . . נבט

מִבֶּטֶן / ·וּ מִבֶּטֶן } pref. ·מִ)(noun fem. sing. dec. 6a (§ 35. r. 2, but with suff. בִּטְנִי); ·וּ bef. lab. } בטן

מַבָּטֵנוּ[h] noun m. s., suff. 1 pers. pl. fr. [מַבָּט] d. 1b נבט

מִבִּטְנוֹ noun fem. s., suff. 3 pers. s. m. fr. בֶּטֶן d. 6a בטן

מֵבִי[i] Kh. for מֵבִיא Keri (q. v. & § 23. rem. 7) בוא

מֵבִיא Hiph. part. sing. masc. dec. 3b . . . בוא

מְבִיאֶיהָ[i] ·וּ id. pl., suff. 3 pers. sing. fem.; ·וּ bef. lab. בוא

מְבִיאִים[k] ·וּ id. pl. abs. st.; ·וּ id. . . . בוא

מְבִיאֲךָ[l] id. sing., suff. 2 pers. sing. masc. . . בוא

מֵבִין[m] ·וּ Hiph. part. sing. masc.; ·וּ bef. lab. . בין

מִבֵּין ·וּ pref. ·מִ)([prim. noun masc. sing., constr. of בַּיִן dec. 6a] *prep.*; ·וּ id. . . בין

מִבֵּינוֹת pref. id.)(id. with pl. fem. term. . . בין

מְבִינֵי[n] ·וּ constr. of the foll.; ·וּ bef. lab. . . בין

מְבִינִים Hiph. part. masc., pl. of מֵבִין dec. 3b . בון

מִבִּינָתִי[o] pref. ·מִ)(noun fem. sing., suff. 1 pers. sing. from בִּינָה dec. 10 . . . . בון

מִבִּינָתְךָ[p] pref. id.)(id., suff. 2 pers. sing. masc. . בון

מִבֵּיצֵיהֶם[q] noun fem. with pl. masc. term. (בֵּיצִים) and suff. 3 pers. pl. masc. [from בֵּיצָה sing.] . ביץ

מֵבִישׁ Hiph. part. sing. masc. . . . . בוש

מְבִישָׁה[r] id. part. sing. fem. . . . . . בוש

מִבַּיִת / מִבָּיִת } pref. ·מִ)(noun masc. sing. irr. (§ 45) . בית

מִבֵּית ·וּ pref. id.)(id. constr. st. (also pr. name in composition, as בֵּית אֵל &c.); ·וּ bef. lab. בית

מִבַּיְתָה[s] pref. id.)(id. with loc. ה . . . בית

מִבֵּיתוֹ pref. id.)(id., suff. 3 pers. sing. masc. . בית

מִבֵּיתִי[t] pref. id.)(id., suff. 1 pers. sing. . . בית

מִבֵּיתֶךָ[u] / מִבֵּיתְךָ[x] } pref. id.)(id., suff. 2 pers. sing. masc. . בית

מְבַכָּה[y] Piel part. sing. fem. dec. 10 [from מְבַכֶּה m.] בכה

מִבְּכוֹר pref. ·מִ)(noun masc. sing. dec. 1a . בכר

מְבַכּוֹת[z] Piel part. fem., pl. of מְבַכָּה dec. 10 [from מְבַכֶּה masc.] . . . . . . בכה

---

[a] Je. 3. 11. [b] Eze. 16. 16. [c] Ge. 1. 6. [d] Is. 59. 2. [e] Est. 8. 14. [f] Job 35. 11. [g] 2 Sa. 3. 25. [h] Eze. 27. 3. [i] Is. 22. 5. [k] Mi. 7. 4. [l] Ge. 9. 11. [u] Je. 38. 14. [m] Is. 49. 10. [n] Na. 2. 11. [o] Pr. 5. 15. [p] Am. 2. 11. [q] Pr. 20. 21. [r] Da. 11. 15. [s] Nu. 11. 28. [t] Nu. 30. 7, 9. [u] Zec. 9. 5. [x] Ps. 118. 8, 9. [y] Pr. 21. 22. [z] Job 18. 14. [a] Ps. 71. 5. [b] Job 31. 24. [c] Is. 32. 18. [d] Pr. 22. 19. [e] Je. 48. 13. [f] Ps. 22. 10. [g] Is. 20. 5. [h] Is. 20. 6. [i] Da. 11. 6. [k] Ne. 13. 15. [l] De. 8. 7. [m] Da. 8. 23. [n] Da. 1. 4. [o] Job 20. 3. [p] Pr. 23. 4. [q] Is. 59. 5. [r] Pr. 12. 4. [s] 1 Ki. 6. 15. [t] Ho. 9. 15. [u] 2 Sa. 12. 10, 11. [x] Ps. 50. 9. [y] Je. 31. 15. [z] Eze. 8. 14.

בעל מִבַּעֲלֵי[u] pref. ·מִ)(n. m. pl., suff. 3 p. s. m. fr. בַּעַל d. 6d

בעל מִבְּעָלָיו pref. id.)(id., suff. 3 pers. sing. masc. .

בער מְבַעֲרִים[v] Piel (§ 14. r. 1) part. m., pl. of [מְבַעֵר] d. 7b

בער מְבֹעֶרֶת[x] Pual part. sing. fem. [for מְבֹעֶרֶת] .

בעת מְבַעֲתֶךָ[a] [contr. for תְּךָ·, מְבַעֲתְתֶךָ] Piel part. sing. fem. [מְבַעֶתֶת], suff. 2 pers. sing. masc. comp. dec. 13 (§ 25 rem.)

בצר מִבְּצִיר[b] pref. ·מִ)(noun m. s., constr. of בָּצִיר d. 3a

בצק מִבְּצְקַת pref. id.)(pr. name of a place .

בצר מִבְצָר noun m. s. d. 2b; also pr. name of a place

בצר מִבְצַר[c] ו' id. constr. st.; ו bef. lab. . .

בצר מִבָּצְרָה pref. מִ)(pr. name of a place . .

בצר מִבְצָרוֹת[d] n. m. with pl. f. term., abs. fr. מִבְצָר d. 2b

בצר מִבְצְרֵי[e] id. pl. constr. masc. . . . .

בצר מִבְצְרֵיהֶם[f] id. id., suff. 3 pers. pl. masc. . .

בצר מִבְצָרָיו id. id., suff. 3 pers. sing. masc. . .

בצר מִבְצָרַיִךְ / מִבְצָרַיִךְ[g] } id. id., suff. 2 pers. sing. fem. . .

בצר מִבְצָרֶיךָ id. id., suff. 2 pers. sing. masc. . .

בצר מִבְצָרִים[h] id. pl., abs. st. . . . . .

בקע מְבֻקָּעָה[i] Pual part. sing. fem. [of מְבֻקָּע] . .

בקע מְבֻקָּעִים[k] ו id. part. masc. pl. [of מְבֻקָּע]; ו bef. lab.

בקע מִבִּקְעַת[l] pref. ·מִ)(noun f. s., constr. of בִּקְעָה d. 12b

בקר מִבֹּקֶר[m] pref. id.)(n. m. s. (pl. בְּקָרִים) d. 6c (§ 35. r. 9)

בקר מִבְּקָרוֹ[n] ו pref. id.)(noun com. sing., suff. 3 pers. sing. masc. from בָּקָר dec. 4a; ו bef. lab. .

בקר מִבְּקָרְךָ[o] pref. id.)(id., suff. 2 pers. sing. masc. .

בקש מְבַקֵּשׁ / מְבַקֶּשׁ־ ו' } Hiph. part. sing. masc. dec. 7b; ו bef. lab. . . . . .

בקש מְבַקְשֵׁי ו' id. pl. constr. [for מְבַקְּשֵׁי § 10. rem. 7]

בקש מְבַקְשֶׁיהָ[p] id. pl., suff. 3 pers. sing. fem.

בקש מְבַקְשָׁיו[q] id. pl., suff. 3 pers. sing. masc.

בקש מְבַקְשֶׁיךָ id. pl., suff. 2 pers. sing. masc.

בקש מְבַקְשִׁים id. pl., abs. st. . . . . .

ברח מַבְרִחַ[r] Hiph. part. sing. masc. [for מַבְרִיחַ] .

ברח מִבְרָחוֹ noun masc. pl., suff. 3 pers. sing. masc. (K. חָיו') from [מִבְרָח] dec. 2b .

ברה מִבְּרִיתֶךְ[s] pref. ·מִ)(n. f. s., suff. 2 p. s. f. fr. בְּרִית d. 1a

ברך מְבָרֵךְ Piel (Peal Da. 2. 20) part. sing. masc. d. 7b

ברך מְבֹרָךְ[u] ו' Pual part. sing. masc.; ו bef. lab. .

ברך מְבֹרָכָיו[x] id. pl., suff. 3 pers. sing. masc. .

ברך מְבָרְכֶיךָ[y] ו' Piel part. pl. masc., suff. 2 pers. sing. m. (for רְכֶיךָ') from מְבָרֵךְ d. 7b; ו bef. lab.

ברך מְבֹרֶכֶת[z] Pual part. sing., fem. of מְבֹרָךְ .

ברך מִבִּרְכָתְךָ[a] ו pref. ·מִ)(noun fem. sing., suff. 2 pers. sing. masc. from בְּרָכָה dec. 11c; ו bef. lab.

בכה מִבְּכִי[i] / מִבְּכִי } pref. ·מִ)(noun masc. sing. dec. 6i (§ 35. rem. 14) . . .

בכר מִבֶּכֶר pref. id.)(noun masc. sing. dec. 1a .

בכר מִבְּכֹרוֹת[b] pref. id.)(noun fem., pl. of בְּכֹרָה dec. 10

בהל מְבֹהָלִים[c] ו Kh. מְבֹהָלִים Piel part. pl. masc. R. בלה; K. מְבֹהָלִים Piel (dag. forte impl.) part. p. masc. R. . . . . .

בלה מִבְּלִי[d] ו' pref. ·מִ)((prim. subst. comp. Is. 38. 17) *adv.*; ו bef. lab.

בלג מַבְלִיגִיתִי[e] noun fem. s., suff. 1 p. s. fr. [מַבְלִיגִית] d. 1b

בלע מִבַּלַּע[f] pref. ·מִ)(Piel inf. constr. for בַּלַּע' (§ 15. r. 1)

בלה מִבַּלְעָדַי[g] ו' pref. id.)(the foll. with suff. 1 p. s.; ו bef. lab.

בלה מִבַּלְעֲדֵי pref. id.)(*adv.* compd. of בַּל, & עֲדֵי pl. constr. of עַד

בלע מְבַלְּעָיִךְ[h] Piel part. pl., suff. 2 pers. sing. fem. [from מְבַלֵּעַ, מְבַלֵּעַ § 15. rem. 1] dec. 7b .

בלע מְבֻלָּעִים[i] Pual part. masc. pl. [of מְבֻלָּע] .

בלק מִבָּלָק pref. ·מִ)(pr. name masc. .

בלק מְבֻלָּקָה[k] ו Pual part. sing. fem. [of מְבֻלָּק]; ו bef. lab.

בלה מִבִּלְתִּי pref. ·מִ)(adv. [בֶּלֶת] with parag. 'י .

בום מִבָּמוֹת ו pref. id.)(pr. name of a place; ו bef. lab.

בנה מִבֶּן ו' pref. id.)(n. m. s., constr. of בֵּן irr. (§ 45); ו id.

בנה מִבֶּן יָמִין pref. id.)(pr. n. of a tribe, for בִּנְיָמִין (q. v.)

בנה מִבָּנוֹת[l] ו pref. id.)(noun fem. pl. abs. irr. of בַּת (§ 45); ו bef. lab. . . . .

בנה מִבְּנוֹת pref. id.)(id., constr. st., or Kal inf. constr.

בנה מִבְּנוֹתֵינוּ[m] pref. id.)(id., suff. 1 pers. pl. . .

סבך מְבֻנַּי pr. name masc., see סִבְּכַי under .

בנה מִבְּנֵי ו' pref. ·מִ)(noun masc. pl., constr. of בָּנִים [as if from בָּן] see בֵּן irr. (§ 45) also pr. name in compos.; ו bef. lab. .

בנה מִבְּנֵיהֶם[n] pref. id.)(id., suff. 3 pers. pl. masc. .

בנה מִבָּנָיו pref. id.)(id., suff. 3 pers. sing. masc.

בנה מִבָּנֶיךָ[o] ו' pref. id.)(id., suff. 2 p. s. m.; ו bef. lab.

בנה מִבְּנֵיכֶם[p] pref. id.)(id., suff. 2 pers. pl. masc. .

בנה מִבָּנִים pref. id.)(id. pl., abs. st. .

בין מְבִנִים[q] pref. id.)(Kal part. act. masc. pl. [of בָּן]

בנה מִבִּנְיָמִן ו' pref. id.)(pr. name of a tribe; ו bef. lab.

בנה מִבְּנֹתֵיהֶם pref. id.)(noun fem. pl. (בָּנוֹת), suff. 3 pers. pl. masc. irr. of בַּת (§ 45) .

בנה מִבְּנֹתָיו[r] pref. id.)(id., suff. 3 pers. sing. masc.

בנה מִבְּנֹתֵינוּ[s] pref. id.)(id., suff. 1 pers. pl. . .

בעד מִבַּעַד pref. id.)((prop. subst. masc. dec. 6d) *prep.*

בער מַבְעִיר[t] Hiph. part. sing. masc. . . . .

בעל מִבַּעַל pref. ·מִ)(pr. name in compos., as בַּעַל גָּד &c.

בעל מִבַּעֲלָה pref. id.)(pr. name of a place .

---

[a] Je. 31. 16. [b] Ge. 4. 4. [c] Ezr. 4. 4. [d] Job 24. 7. [e] Je. 8. 18. [f] La. 2. 8. [g] Is. 44. 6. [h] Is. 49. 19. [i] Is. 9. 15. [k] Na. 2. 11. [l] Is. 56. 5. [m] Ju. 21. 7, 18. [n] Ps. 78. 4. [o] 1 Ch. 17. 11. [p] Am. 2. 11. [q] Je. 49. 7. [r] Ex. 34. 16. [s] Ne. 5. 5. [t] 1 Ki. 16. 3. [u] Ju. 9. 20; 2 Sa. 6. 2. [x] Pr. 3. 27. [y] Je. 7. 18. [z] Je. 36. 22. [a] 1 Sa. 16. 15. [b] Ju. 8. 2. [c] Is. 25. 12. [d] Da. 11. 15. [e] La. 2. 2. [f] 2 Ki. 8. 12. [g] Na. 3. 12. [h] Da. 11. 24. [i] Eze. 26. 10. [k] Jos. 9. 4. [l] Am. 1. 5. [m] Job 4. 20. [n] 2 Sa. 12. 4. [o] De. 12. 21. [p] Je. 2. 24. [q] Ezr. 8. 22. [r] Ex. 26. 28. [s] Eze. 17. 21. [t] Eze. 16. 61. [u] 1 Ch. 17. 27. [x] Ps. 37. 22. [y] Ge. 27. 29. [z] De. 33. 13. [a] 2 Sa. 7. 29.

מְבֻשָּׁל Pual part. sing. masc. . . . . בשל

מְבַשְּׁלוֹת[a] וּ noun f., pl. of [מְבַשֶּׁלֶת] d. 13; וּ bef. lab. בשל

מִבְשָׂם ו׳ pr. name of a place; וּ id. . . . בשם

מִבָּשָׁן pref. ·מִ) pr. name of a region . בשן

מְבַשֵּׂר Piel part. sing. masc. . . . . בשר

מִבְּשַׂר pref. ·מִ) noun m. s., constr. of בָּשָׂר d. 4 a בשר

מִבְּשָׂרוֹ pref. id.) id., suff. 3 pers. sing. masc. . בשר

מִבְּשָׂרִי[b] ו׳ pref. id.) id., suff. 1 pers. s.; וּ bef. lab. בשר

מִבְּשָׂרְךָ[c] } pref. id.) id., suff. 2 pers. sing. masc.; } בשר
מִבְּשָׂרֶךָ[d] וּ } וּ id. . . . . . }

מִבְּשַׂרְכֶם[e] pref. id.) id., suff. 2 pers. pl. masc. . בשר

מִבְּשָׂרָם pref. id.) id., suff. 3 pers. pl. masc. . בשר

מְבַשֶּׂרֶת[f] Piel part. sing. fem. dec. 13, from מְבַשֵּׂר m. בשר

מִבַּת[g] pref. ·מִ) noun f. s. irr. [for בֶּנֶת=בַּנְתְּ, § 45] בנה

מִבַּת־שׁוּעַ pref. id.) pr. name fem. . . . בנה

מִבָּתֵּיהֶם[h] pref. id.) noun masc. pl. (בָּתִּים), suff. 3 pers. pl. masc. irr. of בַּיִת (§ 45) . בית

מִבָּתֶּיךָ[i] וּ pref. id.) id., suff. 2 pers. s. m.; וּ bef. lab. בית

מִבָּתֵּיכֶם pref. id.) id., suff. 2 pers. pl. masc. . בית

מִבָּתֵּינוּ[k] pref. id.) id., suff. 1 pers. pl. . . בית

מָג masc. *magian, a Persian* or *Median priest*, only Je. 39. 3, רַב־מָג *chief of the magi.*

מִגְּאוֹן pref. ·מִ) noun m. s., constr. of גָּאוֹן d. 3 a גאה

מְגֹאָל[l] Pual part. sing. masc. . . . גאל

מִגֹּאֵל pref. ·מִ) Kal part. sing. masc. dec. 7 b . גאל

מִגֹּאֲלֵנוּ[m] pref. id.) id. (some read לֵינוּ׳ pl.), suff. 1 p. pl. גאל

מִגֶּבֶא[n] pref. id.) noun masc. sing. dec. 6 . . גבא

מִגָּבֹהַּ[o] pref. id.) adj. masc. sing. dec. 3 a . גבה

מִגְּבַהּ[p] pref. id.) adj. m. s., constr. of [גָּבָהּ] d. 4 a גבה

מִגְּבוּל pref. id.) noun masc. sing. dec. 1 a . גבל

מִגִּבּוֹר pref. id.) (prim. adj.) subst. masc. s. d. 1 b גבר

מִגְּבוּרָה[q] pref. id.) noun fem. sing. dec. 10 . גבר

מִגְּבוּרָתָם[r] pref. id.) id., suff. 3 pers. pl. masc. . גבר

מַגְבִּיהַּ[s] Hiph. part. sing. masc. . . . גבה

מִגְּבִירָה pref. ·מִ) noun fem. sing. . . . גבר

מַגְבִּישׁ pr. name of a place . . . . גבש

מִגְּבֻלִי pref. ·מִ) noun masc. sing. dec. 1 a, defect. for מִגְּבוּל (q. v.) . . . . גבל

מִגְּבֻלְכֶם[u] pref. id.) id., suff. 2 pers. pl. masc. . גבל

מִגְבָּלֹת[t] noun fem. pl. abs. [from מִגְבָּלָה] . . גבל

מִגָּבַע } pref. ·מִ) pr. name of a place (§ 35. } גבע
מִגֶּבַע } rem. 2) . . . . . }

מִגִּבְעוֹן pref. id.) pr. name of a place . . גבע

מִגְּבָעוֹת[qq] וּ׳ pref. id.) noun fem., pl. abs. from גִּבְעָה dec. 12 b; וּ bef. lab. . . . גבע

מִגְבָּעוֹת[y] וּ׳ noun f. pl. abs. [fr. מִגְבָּעָה]; וּ bef. lab. בע

מִגִּבְעַת pref. ·מִ) noun fem. sing., constr. of גִּבְעָה dec. 12 b, also pr. name . . . בע

מִגֶּבֶר[z] pref. id.) noun masc. sing. dec. 6 . בר

מִגִּבֹּרֵי[a] pref. id.) (prim. adj.) subst. masc. pl. constr. from גִּבּוֹר dec. 1 b . . . . בר

מִגַּבְּתוֹן pref. id.) pr. name of a place . . בב

מִגַּג[b] pref. id.) noun masc. s., constr. of גָּג d. 8 a ג

מָגַד Root not used; Arab. *to be honoured, to be noble excellent.*

מֶגֶד masc. dec. 6 a, *what is most precious, excellent, pleasant.*

מַגְדִּיאֵל (*noble of God*) pr. name of a prince o Edom.

מִגְדָּנוֹת fem. pl. (of מִגְדָּנָה) *choice, preciou things.*

מְגִדּוֹ ו׳ pr. name of a place; וּ bef. (:) . . דד

מִגָּדוֹל[c] pref. ·מִ) adj. masc. sing. dec. 3 a . . דל

מִגְּדוֹלָם[d] pref. id.) id., suff. 3 pers. pl. masc. . דל

מְגִדּוֹן pr. name of a place . . . . דד

מַגְדִּיאֵל pr. name masc. . . . גד

מְגָדָיו[e] noun m. pl., suff. 3 pers. sing. m. fr. מֶגֶד׳ d. 6 גד

מִגְדִּיל[f] Kh. מַגְדִּיל Hiph. part. s. m.; K. מִגְדּוֹל n. m. s. דל

מְגָדִים noun masc. pl. of מֶגֶד׳ dec. 6 . . גד

מִגָּדִישׁ[g] pref. ·מִ) noun masc. sing. . . רש

מַגְדִּל[h] defect. for מַגְדִּיל (q. v.) . . . דל

מִגְדָּל ו׳׳ noun m. sing. dec. 2 b . . . דל

מִגְדַּל ו׳ id. constr. st., and pr. name in compos. as מִגְדַּל־אֵל, &c.; וּ bef. lab. . . . דל

מִגְדֹּל pr. name of a place . . . . דל

מִגְדְּלוֹת[k] noun m. with f. pl. term., constr. fr. מִגְדָּל d. 2 b דל

מִגְדָּלֶיהָ id. with pl. m. term. and suff. 3 pers. sing. fem. דל

מְגַדְּלִים[l] Piel part. masc. pl. of [מְגַדֵּל] dec. 7 b . דל

מְגֻדָּלִים[m] Pual part. masc. pl. of [מְגֻדָּל] . . דל

מִגְדָּלִים ו׳ noun masc. pl. of מִגְדָּל d. 2 b; וּ bef. lab. דל

מִגְדְּלֹתַיִךְ[n] וּ id. with fem. term. and suff. 2 p. s. fem.; וּ id. דל

מִגְדָּנוֹת[o] וּ } noun fem. pl. abs. from [מִגְדָּנָה]; וּ id. גד
מִגְדָּנֹת[p] וּ }

מְגַדֵּף[q] ו׳׳ Piel part. sing. masc.; וּ id. . . דף

מִגִּדּוּפֹתָם[s] וּ pref. ·מִ) noun m. with pl. fem. term. and suff. 3 pers. pl. m. from [גִּדּוּף] d. 1 b; וּ id. דף

מַגֶּדֶת[t] Hiph. part. sing., f. of מַגִּיד (§ 39. No. 4 d) גד

מָגוֹג וּ pr. name masc.; וּ bef. lab. . . וג

מִגְּוִיָּה[u] pref. ·מִ) noun sing. fem. . . . וה

[a] Eze. 46. 23. [b] Ge. 2. 23. [c] Ec. 11. 10. [d] Is. 58. 7. [e] Eze. 36. 26. [f] Is. 40. 9. [g] 1 Ch. 2. 3. [h] Je. 18. 22. [i] Ex. 8. 5, 7. [k] Jos. 9. 12. [l] Mal. 1. 7, 12. [m] Ru. 2. 20. [n] Is. 30. 14. [o] Ec. 12. 5. [p] Ec. 7. 8. [q] Ec. 9. 16. [r] Eze. 32. 30. [s] Pr. 17. 19. [t] Nu. 21. 13. [u] Am. 6. 2. [x] Ex. 28. 14. [y] Ex. 28. 40. [z] Job 33. 17. [a] Ca. 3. 7. [b] Eze. 40. 13. [c] 2 Ch. 34. 30. [d] Jon. 3. 5. [e] Ca. 4. 16. [f] 2 Sa. 22. 51. [g] Ju. 15. 5. [h] Ps. 18. 51. [i] Ge. 11. 4. [k] Ca. 5. 13. [l] 2 Ki. 10. 6. [m] Ps. 144. 12. [n] Eze. 26. 9. [o] 2 Ch. 32. 23. [p] Ge. 24. 53. [q] Nu. 15. 30. [qq] Nu. 23. 9. [r] Ps. 44. 17. [s] Is. 51. 7. [t] Est. 2. 20. [u] Job 20. 25.

מִגּוֹי pref. מִ·)(noun masc. sing. dec. 1a (§ 3. r. 1) . גוה

מִגּוֹיִם[a] pref. id.)(id. pl. abs. (for גּוֹיִם' comp. § 3. r. 1) גוה

מִגְּוִיַּת[b] pref. id.)(noun fem. s., constr. of גְּוִיָּה d. 10 גוה

מְגוֹלָלָה[c] Poal part. sing. fem. [of מְגוֹלָל] . . גלל

מָגוֹר noun masc. sing., see § 32. rem. 5 (also pr. name in compos.) . . גור

מְגוּרוֹתַי[d] noun fem. pl., suff. 1 pers. s. from מְגוּרָה' d. 10 גור

מְגוּרַי noun m. pl., suff. 1 pers. s. from [מָגוּר] d. 3a גור

מְגוּרַי[e] noun m. pl., suff. 1 pers. s. fr. מָגוֹר (§ 32. r. 5) גור

מְגוּרֵי[f] Kal part. pass. pl. c. m. from [מָגוּר] dec. 3a מגר

מְגוּרֵי noun masc. pl. constr. from [מָגוּר] dec. 3a גור

מְגוּרֵיהֶם id. pl., suff. 3 pers. pl. masc. . . . גור

מְגוֹרַת[g] noun fem. sing., constr. of [מְגוֹרָה] dec. 10 גור

וּמְגוּרֹתָם[ll] וּ noun fem. pl., suff. 3 pers. pl. masc. (§ 4. rem. 2) from מְגוּרָה' dec. 10; וּ bef. lab. גור

וּמִגֵּז[h] וּ pref. מִ·)(noun masc. sing. dec. 8b; וּ id. גזז

מִגֹּזְלוֹ[i] pref. id.)(Kal part. act. sing. masc., suff. 3 pers. sing. masc. from גּוֹזֵל dec. 7b . גזל

מִגִּזְעוֹ[k] pref. id.)(noun masc. sing. (suff. גִּזְעוֹ) d. 6a גזע

מַגִּיד ו' Hiph. part. sing. masc. dec. 1b; וּ bef. lab. נגד

מְגִיחַ[l] Hiph. part. sing. masc. R. גוח or . גיח

מְגִיחָן[m] Chald. Aph. part. pl. fem. [from מְגִיחַ masc.] גוח

מַגִּיעַ Hiph. part. sing. masc. . . . . נגע

מַגִּיעֵי[n] id. pl., constr. st. . . . . נגע

וּמַגִּישׁ[o] וּ Hiph. part. sing. masc.; וּ bef. lab. . נגש

מַגִּישֵׁי[p] id. pl., constr. st. . . . . נגש

מַגִּישִׁים id. pl., abs. st. . . . . . נגש

מַגָּל noun masc. sing. . . . . . נגל

מְגַלֶּה Piel part. sing. masc. . . . . גלה

מְגִלָּה noun fem. sing. dec. 10 . . . גלל

מְגֻלָּה[q] Pual part. sing. fem. [from מְגֻלֶּה masc.] גלה

מִגֹּלָה pref. מִ·)(pr. name of a place . . גלה

מְגֻלְּחֵי[r] Pual part. pl. constr. masc. from [מְגֻלָּח] d. 2b גלח

מִגַּלִּים pref. מִ·)(pr. name of a place . . גלל

מִגִּלְעָד pref. id.)(pr. name of a region, see גִּלְעָד.

מְגִלַּת noun fem. sing., constr. of מְגִלָּה dec. 10 גלל

מִגָּמָל[s] pref. מִ·)(noun masc. sing. d. 8a (§ 37. No. 3c) גמל

מִגְּמַלֵּי[t] pref. id.)(id. pl., constr. st. . . גמל

מְגַמַּת[u] noun fem. sing., constr. of [מְגַמָּה] dec. 10 גמם

מָגַן. Pi. מִגֵּן—I. *to give over, deliver*, Ge. 14. 20; with double acc. Pr. 4. 9.—II. *to make one to* or *as* any thing, Ho. 11. 8, comp. נָתַן *to give, to make.* Others take it as denom. of מָגֵן shield (R. גָּנַן) (*a*) *to protect, surround*, Pr. 4. 9; Ho. 11. 8; (*b*) privat. *to deprive one of his shield, to disarm*, Ge. 14. 20, מִ' צָרֶיךָ בְּיָדֶךָ *disarmed thine enemies by thy hand.*

מָגֵן ו' noun masc. sing. (suff. מָגִנִּי) dec. 8b (§ 37. rem. 4); וּ bef. lab. . . . גנן

מִגַּן[v] pref. מִ·)(noun com. sing. dec. 8d . גנן

מִגֵּן[w] Piel pret. 3 pers. sing. masc. . . מגן

מְגַנְּבֵי[x] Piel part. pl. constr. masc. from [מְגַנֵּב] d. 7b גנב

מָגִנֵּי noun masc. pl. constr. from מָגֵן d. 8a (§ 37. r. 4) גנן

מָגִנִּי ו' id. sing., suff. 1 pers. sing.; וּ bef. lab. גנן

מָגִנֶּיהָ[a] id. pl., suff. 3 pers. sing. fem. . . גנן

מָגִנָּיו[b] id. pl., suff. 3 pers. sing. masc. . . גנן

מָגִנִּים [c] ו' id. pl., abs. st.; וּ bef. lab. . . גנן

מָגִנָּם[d] וּ id. sing., suff. 3 pers. pl. masc.; וּ id. . גנן

מָגִנֵּנוּ [e] ו' id. sing., suff. 1 pers. pl.; וּ id. . גנן

מְגִנַּת[f] noun fem. sing., constr. of [מְגִנָּה] dec. 10 גנן

מִגִּנַּת[g] pref. מִ·)(noun fem. sing., constr. of [גִּנָּה] d. 10 גנן

וּמִגְּעֶר־[h] וּ pref. id.)(Kal inf. constr. [for גְּעֹר § 8. rem. 18]; וּ bef. lab. . . . . גער

מִגַּעֲרַת[i] pref. id.)(n. f., constr. of גַּעֲרָה d. 11c (§ 42. r. 1) גער

מִגַּעֲרָתוֹ[k] pref. id.)(id., suff. 3 pers. sing. masc. גער

מִגַּעֲרָתְךָ pref. id.)(id., suff. 2 pers. sing. masc. . גער

מַגַּעַת[l] Hiph. part. sing., fem. of מַגִּיעַ (§ 39. No. 4d) נגע

מַגֵּפָה noun fem. sing. (constr. מַגֵּפַת) dec. 10 . נגף

מַגְפִּיעָשׁ pr. name masc. Ne. 10. 21.

מִגֶּפֶן pref. מִ·)(noun com. sing. (suff. גַּפְנוֹ) d. 6a גפן

מַגֵּפַת[m] noun fem. sing., constr. of מַגֵּפָה dec. 10 נגף

מַגֵּפֹתַי[n] id. pl. with suff. 1 pers. sing. . . נגף

מָגַר only part. pl. c. מְגוּרֵי *fallen, delivered up*, Eze. 21. 17. Pi. *to cast down, to overthrow*, Ps. 89. 45. מְגַר Ch. Pa. *to cast down, to overthrow*, Ezr. 6. 12. מִגְרוֹן (*precipice*) pr. name of a town in Benjamin, 1 Sa. 14. 2; Is. 10. 28.

מִגֵּרֶיהָ[o] pref. מִ·)(noun m. pl., suff. from גֵּר d. 1a. גור

מְגֻרֵיהֶם[p] noun m. pl., suff. 3 p. pl. m. from מָגוּר d. 3a גור

מְגוּרֶיךָ id. pl., suff. 2 pers. sing. masc. . . גור

מֻגָּרִים[q] Hoph. part. masc. pl. [of מֻגָּר] . . נגר

מִגֵּרְךָ[r] pref. מִ·)(noun masc. sing., suff. 2 pers. sing. masc. from גֵּר dec. 1a (§ 30. No. 3) . גור

וּמִגּוֹרָל[s] וּ pref. id.)(noun masc. sing. constr. of גּוֹרָל dec. 2b; וּ bef. lab. . . . . גרל

מִגֹּרֶן[t] pref. id.)(noun masc. sing. dec. 6c . גרן

מִגָּרְנְךָ[u] [x] ו' pref. id.)(id. with suff. 2 p. s. m.; וּ bef. lab. גרן

מְגֻרָעוֹת[y] noun fem. pl. abs. [from מְגֻרָעָה] . . גרע

מֶגְרְפֹתֵיהֶם[z] noun fem. pl., suff. 3 pers. sing. masc. from [מֶגְרָפָה] dec. 11a . . . גרף

[a] Eze. 38. 12. [b] Ju. 14. 9. [c] Is. 9. 4. [d] Ps. 34. 5. [e] La. 2. 22. [f] Eze. 21. 17.
[g] Pr. 10. 24. [h] Job 31. 20. [i] Ps. 35. 10. [k] Is. 11. 1. [l] Ju. 20. 33. [ll] Is. 66. 4.
[m] Da. 7. 2. [n] Is. 5. 8. [o] Mal. 2. 12. [p] Mal. 3. 3. [q] Pr. 27. 5.
[r] Je. 41. 5. [s] 1 Sa. 15. 3. [t] Ge. 24. 10. [u] Hab. 1. 9. [x] Ge. 3. 23.
[y] Ge. 14. 20. [z] Je. 23. 30. [a] Ho. 4. 18. [b] Job 15. 26. [c] 2 Ch. 32. 5.
[d] Ps. 115. 9, 10, 11. [e] Ps. 33. 20. [f] La. 3. 65. [g] Est. 7. 8. [h] Is. 54. 9.
[i] Ps. 80. 17. [k] Job 26. 11. [l] 2 Ch. 3. 11. [m] Zec. 14. 15. [n] Ex. 9. 14.
[o] Eze. 19. 3, 5. [p] Ex. 6. 4. [q] Mi. 1. 4. [r] De. 24. 14. [s] Nu. 36. 3.
[t] Hos. 13. 3. [u] De. 16. 13. [x] De. 15. 14. [y] 1 Ki. 6. 6. [z] Joel 1. 17.

מִגָּרָר pref. ·מִ) pr. name of a place . . גרר

מְגֹרָרוֹת[a] Pual part. f. pl. abs. [fr. מְגֹרָרָה, fr. מְגֹרָר m.] גרר

מִגְרָשׁ[b] וּ׳ noun masc. sing. dec. 2b; וּ bef. lab. . גרשׁ

מִגְרַשׁ id., constr. st. . . . . . . גרשׁ

מִגְרָשָׁהּ[c] Kal inf. [מִגְרַשׁ § 8. rem. 10], suff. 3 p. s. f. גרשׁ

מִגְרָשֶׁהָ defect. for מִגְרָשֶׁיהָ (q. v.) . . . גרשׁ

מִגַּרְשָׁהּ[d] pref. ·מִ) noun masc. sing., suff. 3 pers. sing. fem. from גֶּרֶשׁ dec. 6a . . . גרם

מִגְרָשׁוֹת[e] n. pl. f. abs. st. (prop. fr. מִגְרֶשֶׁת) see מִגְרָשׁ גרשׁ

מִגְרְשֵׁי[f] וּ׳ noun masc. pl. constr. from מִגְרָשׁ dec. 2b; וּ bef. lab. . . . . . גרשׁ

מִגְרָשֶׁיהָ[g] וּ׳ id., suff. 3 pers. sing. fem.; וּ id. . גרשׁ

מִגְרְשֵׁיהֶם וּ׳ id., suff. 3 pers. pl. masc.; וּ id. . גרשׁ

מִגְרְשֵׁיהֶן וּ׳ id., suff. 3 pers. pl. fem.; וּ id. . . גרשׁ

מִגָּרַת[h] וּ pref. ·מִ) Kal part. act. f., constr. of [גָּרָה] dec. 10, fr. גָּר m. (comp. § 30. No. 3); וּ id. גור

מִגַּרְתָּה[i] Piel pret. 2 pers. sing. masc. (comp. § 8. r. 5) מגר

מֻגָּשׁ[k] Hoph. part. sing. masc. . . . . נגשׁ

מִגְּשׁוּר pref. ·מִ) pr. name of a place, see גְּשׁוּר

מַגִּשִׁים[l] defect. for מַגִּישִׁים (q. v.) . . . נגשׁ

מַגְשִׁמִים[m] Hiph. part. masc., pl. of [מַגְשִׁים] dec. 1b . גשׁם

מִגֶּשֶׁת[n] pref. ·מִ) Kal inf. constr. (suff. גִּשְׁתּוֹ) d. 13b נגשׁ

מִגַּת } pref. id.) pr. name of a place . . . גת
מִגַּת

מִדְּאָנָה[o] pref. id.) noun fem. sing. . . . דאג

מַדְבְּחָה[p] Chald. noun masc. sing. [for מַדְבְּחָא] emph. of [מַדְבַּח] dec. 2a . . . . דבח

מֻדְבָּק[q] Hoph. part. sing. masc. (§ 11. rem. 10) . דבק

מְדַבֵּר[r] וּ׳ Piel part. sing. masc. dec. 7b; וּ bef. lab. דבר

מְדֻבָּר[s] Pual part. sing. masc. . . . . דבר

מִדָּבָר[t] pref. ·מִ) noun masc. sing. dec. 4a . . דבר

מִדֶּבֶר[u] וּ pref. id.) noun masc. sing. dec. 6 (for דֶּבֶר § 35. rem. 2); וּ bef. lab. . . . דבר

מִדַּבֵּר pref. id.) Piel inf. constr. . . . . דבר

מִדַּבֵּר[w] וּ׳ Hithpa. part. s. m. [for מִתְדַּבֵּר § 12. r. 3.] דבר

מִדְּבַר pref. ·מִ) noun masc. s.; constr. of דָּבָר d. 4a דבר

מִדְבָּר noun masc. sing. dec. 2b . . . . דבר

מִדְבַּר id., constr. st. . . . . . . דבר

מִדֶּבֶר[x] pref. ·מִ) noun masc. sing. dec. 6 . . דבר

מִדְבָּרָה noun masc. s. with parag. ה (מִדְבָּר) dec. 2b דבר

מִדְבָּרָהּ[y] id. with suff. 3 pers. sing. masc. . . דבר

מִדְבָּרָה[z] id. constr. with parag. ה, comp. מִדְבָּר . דבר

מְדַבְּרוֹת[a] Piel part. f. pl. of מְדַבֶּרֶת d. 13, fr. מְדַבֵּר m. דבר

מִדִּבְרֵי[b] pref. ·מִ) noun m. pl. constr. fr. דָּבָר d. 4a דבר

מִדִּבְרֵיהֶם[c] וּ׳ pref. id.) id., suff. 3 pers. pl. m.; וּ bef. lab. דבר

מִדְּבָרֶיךָ[d] וּ pref. id.) id. pl. (Kh. דְּבָרֶיךָ׳), or sing. (K. דְּבָרְךָ׳) with suff. 2 pers. sing. m.; וּ id. דבר

מְדַבְּרִים Piel part. masc., pl. of מְדַבֵּר dec. 7b . דבר

מִדְבָּרֵךְ[e] וּ noun masc. sing., suff. 2 pers. sing. fem. from מִדְבָּר dec. 2b; וּ bef. lab. . דבר

מְדַבֶּרֶת Piel part. sing. fem. from מְדַבֵּר masc. . דבר

מִדַּבְּרֹתֶיךָ[f] pref. ·מִ) noun f. pl., suff. 2 pers. s. m. fr. [דַּבָּרָה] d. 10; or Hithpa. part. pl. with suff, [fr. מִתְדַּבֶּרֶת=מִדַּבֶּרֶת § 12. r. 3] דבר

מִדְּבַשׁ pref. id.) noun masc. sing. d. 6 (§ 35. r. 10) דבשׁ

מָדַד

וּ׳ pret. מַדֹּתִי, מָדְדוּ.—Arab. *to extend,* hence—I. *to measure.*—II. metaph. *to apportion,* Is. 65. 7. Niph. *to be measured.* Pi. *to measure.* Po. מוֹדֵד id. Hab. 3. 6, but see מוּד. Hithpo. *to extend, stretch oneself,* 1 Ki. 17. 21.

מַד masc. dec. 8 (with suff. מִדּוֹ, מַדּוֹ, pl. מַדִּים, (מִדִּין).—I. *vestment, garment.*—II. *covering or carpet,* Ju. 5. 10.—III. *measure.*

מִדָּה fem. dec. 10.—I. *extension;* אִישׁ מ׳ *a man of extension, a tall man;* בֵּית מִדּוֹת *spacious house.* —II. *measure.*—III. *vestment, garment,* Ps. 133. 2. —IV. *tribute,* Ne. 5. 4.

מִנְדָּה, מִדָּה (dag. forte. resolved in נ) Chald. fem. dec. 8a, *tribute.*

מִדִּין (*measures*) pr. name of a town in the tribe of Judah, Jos. 15. 61.

מֵמַד masc. dec. 8d, *measure,* Job 38. 5.

מָדַד[g] Kal pret. 3 pers. sing. m. for מָדַד (§ 8. r. 7) מדד

מִדַּד[h] וּ noun masc. sing. constr. [of מִדָּד for מִנְדָּד]; וּ bef. lab. . . . נדד

מָדְדוּ וּ Kal pret. 3 pers. pl.; וּ id. . . . מדד

מְדָדוֹ וּ׳ id. pret. 3 pers. s. m., suff. 3 p. s. m.; וּ id. מדד

מָדָה

Root not used; i. q. מָדַד *to extend.*

מַדְוֶה masc. dec. 9a, *vestment, garment,* 2 Sa. 10. 4; 1 Ch. 19. 4.

מָדוֹן masc. *extension,* 2 Sa. 21. 20, אִישׁ מָ׳ *tall man,* comp. מַד under preced. root.

מִדָּה וּ׳ noun fem. sing. dec. 10; וּ bef. lab. . מדד

מִדָּה[k] וּ Chald. noun fem. sing. dec. 8a; וּ id. . מדד

מַדָּהּ[l] noun m. s., suff. 3 p. s. f. fr. [מַד] d. 8d & e מדד

מַדְהֵבָה[m] noun fem. s. (some prefer מַרְהֵבָה R. רהב) דהב

מִדַּהֲרוֹת[n] pref. ·מִ) n. f. pl. constr. [fr. דַּהֲרָה or דַּהֲרָה] דהר

מַדּוֹ noun m. s., suff. 3 p. s. m. from [מַד] d. 8e מדד

מִדּוֹד[o] pref. ·מִ) noun masc. sing. dec. 1a . . דוד

מִדּוּד[p] pref. id.) noun masc. sing. pl. דוּדִים׳ & דְּוָדִים׳ (§ 35. rem. 13) . . . דוד

מִדּוּדָאֵי[q] noun m. pl. constr. [fr. דּוּדַי § 35. r. 15, note] דוד

---

[a] 1 Ki. 7. 9. [b] Nu. 35. 2. [c] Eze. 36. 5. [d] Le. 2. 16. [e] Eze. 27. 28. [f] Nu. 35. 4. [g] Jos. 21. 40. [h] Ex. 3. 22. [i] Ps. 89. 45. [k] Mal. 1. 11. [l] 1 Ki. 5. 1. [m] Je. 14. 22. [n] Ex. 34. 30. [o] Jos. 22. 24. [p] Ezr. 7. 17. [q] Ps. 22. 16. [r] Ps. 87. 3. [s] Jos. 22. 24. [t] Eze. 12. 16. [tt] Est. 1. 22. [u] 2 Sa. 14. 13. [x] Ps. 91. 3, 6. [y] Is. 51. 3. [z] 1 Ki. 19. 15. [a] Is. 19. 18. [b] 1 Sa. 28. 20. [c] Eze. 2. 6. [d] Ps. 119. 161. [e] Ca. 4. 3. [f] De. 33. 3. [g] Eze. 42. 18. [h] Job 7. 4. [i] Eze. 42. 15, 20. [k] Ezr. 4. 20. [l] Job 11. 9. [m] Is. 14. 4. [n] Ju. 5. 22. [o] Ca. 5. 9. [p] Ps. 81. 7. [q] Ge. 30. 14.

מַדְוֵה[a] noun masc. sing., constr. of [מַדְוֶה] dec. 9a דוה

מַדּוּחִים[b] וּ noun m., pl. of [מַדּוּחַ] d. 1b; וּ bef. lab. נדח

מַדְוֵי[c] noun masc. pl. constr. from [מַדְוֶה] dec. 9a דוה

מַדְוֵיהֶם noun m. pl., suff. 3 p. pl. m. fr. [מֶדֶו] d. 6a מדה

מָדוֹן[d] וּ noun masc. sing., also pr. name; וּ bef. lab. דון

מְדָוְנִים[e] וּ id. pl. abs. Kh. מְדוֹנִים, or מְדָוְנִים=מִדְיָנִים comp. § 32. rem. 8, & § 35. rem. 13 (Keri. מִדְיָנִים q. v.); וּ id. . . דון

מַדּוּעַ[f] וּ adv. of interrog., compnd. of מָה (q. v.) & יָדוּעַ part. pass. see . . . . מה

מִדּוֹר[f] pref. ·מִ)(noun masc. sing. dec. 1a . דור

מִדּוּר[g] pref. id.)(Kal inf. constr. . . . . דור

מְדוֹרֵהּ[h] Chald. n. m. s., suff. 3 p. s. m. fr. [מְדוֹר] d. 1a דור

מִדּוֹת noun fem., pl. of מִדָּה dec. 10 . . מדד

מִדּוֹתֶיהָ[i] id., suff. 3 pers. sing. fem. . . . מדד

מִדּוֹתָיו[k] id., suff. 3 pers. sing. masc. . . . מדד

מֻדָּח[l] Hoph. part. sing. masc. . . . . נדח

מַדְחֶה[qq] noun masc. sing. . . . . . דחה

מִדֶּחִי pref. ·מִ)(noun m. s. [for דְּחִי § 35. r. 14] דחה

מָדַי / מָדָי וּ { *Media*; meton. *the Medes*. Gent. noun מָדִי *a Mede*, Da. 11. 1.—Chald. Gent. noun, מָדַי *Mede*. Da. 6. 1. }

מִדֵּי[m] וּ pref. ·מִ)(noun masc. sing. constr. of דַּי dec. 8 (§ 37. rem. 6); וּ bef. lab. . די

מָדָיָא Chald. Kh. מָדָיָא; K. מָדָאָה gent. noun, emph. of מָדַי dec. 7 . . . מדי

מִדִּיבֹן pref. ·מִ)(pr. name masc. . . . . דוב

מְדִיבֹת[n] וּ Hiph. part. fem. pl. [of מְדִיבָה from מֵדִיב masc.]; וּ bef. lab. . . . . דוב

מַדָּיו[o] וּ noun masc. pl., suff. 3 pers. sing. masc. from [מַד] dec. 8d; וּ id. . . . מדד

מַדַּיִךְ[p] id. pl., suff. 2 pers. sing. fem. dec. 8e . מדד

מָדְיָן[q] Kh. מָדְיָן R. מדד (q. v.); K. מָדוֹן (q. v.) דון

מִדְיָן וּ pr. name of a people and country; וּ bef. lab. דון

מִדִּין pr. name of a place . . . . . מדד

מִדִּין[r] noun m. pl. abs. [for מִדִּים from מַד] d. 8b מדד

מִדִּין[s] pref. ·מִ)(noun masc. s. d. 1a. R. דִּין see דון

מְדִינָה וּ noun fem. s. d. 10. R. דִּין; וּ bef. lab., see דון

מְדִינוֹת pl. of the preced. . . . . . דון

מִדְיְנֵי[t] noun m. pl. constr. fr. מִדְיָן d. 2b. R. דִּין see דון

מִדְיָנִים[u] id. pl., abs. st.; also gent. noun, pl. of מִדְיָנִי דון

מְדִינָן[x] וּ Chald. noun fem. pl. abs. from [מְדִינָא] dec. 8a. R. דִּין; וּ bef. lab., see . . דון

מְדִינַת Chald. id. sing., constr. st. R. דִּין see . דון

מְדִינָתָא[y] Chald. id. pl., emph. st. . . . . דון

מְדִינְתָּא Chald. id. sing., emph. st. . . . . דון

מְדֻכָּא[z] Pual part. sing. masc. . . . . דכא

מְדֻכָּאִים[a] id. pl., abs. st. . . . . . . דכא

מְדַלֵּג[b] Piel part. sing. masc. . . . . . דלג

מִדַּלָּה[c] pref. ·מִ)(noun fem. sing. dec. 10 . . דלל

מִדַּלּוֹת[d] וּ pref. id.)(id. pl.; וּ bef. lab. . . . דלל

מִדְּלִי[e] pref. id.)(noun masc. sing. . . . . דלה

מִדָּלְיָו[f] pref. id.)(noun masc. pl., suff. 3 pers. sing. masc. [from [דְּלִי]. The form דָּלְיָו (dol-yav) stands for דָּלְיָיו=דָּלָיו (comp. קָדָשָׁיו, & קָדָשָׁיו 2 Ch. 15. 18), and having taken the shorter form by dropping ָ under ל according to § 35. rem. 16, it has irregularly retained the Metheg. . . . . דלה

מִדְּלֹק[g] pref. id.)(Kal inf. constr. . . . . דלק

מִדֶּלֶת וּ pref. id.)(noun fem., constr. of דַּלָּה dec. 10; וּ bef. lab. . . . . . דלל

מִדַּלְתֵי pref. id.)(noun fem. du., constr. of דְּלָתַיִם from [דֶּלֶת] dec. 11a (§ 44. rem. 1) . דלה

מִדָּם pref. id.)(noun masc. sing. dec. 2a . . אדם

מִדַּם[h] וּ pref. id.)(id. constr. st.; וּ bef. lab. . אדם

מִדָּמָהּ pref. id.)(id., suff. 3 pers. sing. fem. . אדם

מִדָּמוֹ pref. id.)(id., suff. 3 pers. sing. masc. . אדם

מִדְּמֵי pref. id.)(id. pl., constr. st. . . . אדם

מִדָּמִים[i] pref. id.)(id. pl., abs. st. . . . אדם

מִדָּמְךָ[k] pref. id.)(id. sing., suff. 2 pers. sing. masc. אדם

מִדָּמָם pref. id.)(id. sing., suff. 3 pers. pl. masc. . אדם

מַדְמֵן pr. name of a place . . . . . דמן

מַדְמֵנָה וּ pr. name of a place; וּ bef. lab. . . דמן

מַדְמֵנָה[l] noun fem. sing., also pr. name of a place דמן

מִדִּמְעָה[m] pref. ·מִ)(noun fem. sing. dec. 12b . דמע

מִדַּמֶּשֶׂק / מִדַּמָּשֶׂק } pref. id.)(pr. name of a place, see דַּמֶּשֶׂק

מְדָן וּ pr. name masc.; וּ bef. lab. . . . . דון

מִדָּן pref. ·מִ)(pr. name of a tribe . . . דון

מִדָּנִאֵל pref. id.)(pr. name masc. . . . . דון

מְדָנִים noun masc., pl. of [מְדָן] dec. 1a . . דון

מְדָוְנִים[n] Kh. מְדָנִים q.v.; K. מְדוֹנִים pl. of מָדוֹן (q.v.) דון

מַדָּע[o] וּ noun masc. sing. dec. 1b; וּ bef. lab. . ידע

מַדָּע[p] וּ noun masc. sing.; וּ id. . . . . ידע

מַדֻּעַ[q] defect. for מַדּוּעַ (q. v.) . . . . מה

מֹדָע[r] וּ for [מוֹדָע] noun masc. sing.; וּ bef. lab. ידע

מִדַּעַת pref. ·מִ)(noun fem. sing. dec. 13a . . ידע

מִדַּעְתִּי[s] pref. id.)(id. with suff. 1 pers. sing. . . ידע

מֹדַעְתֵּנוּ[t] noun fem. sing., suff. 1 pers. pl. (§ 3. rem. 4) from [מוֹדַעַת] dec. 13a . . . ידע

מִדַּפְקָה pref. ·מִ)(pr. name of a place . . דפק

מַדְּקָה[u] וּ Ch. Aph. part. s. fem. [of מַדֵּק]; וּ bef. lab. דקק

[a] De. 28. 60. [b] La. 2. 14. [c] De. 7. 15. [d] Hab. 1. 3. [e] Pr. 18. 19. [f] Is. 34. 10. [g] Ps. 84. 11. [h] Da. 5. 21. [i] Eze. 48. 16. [k] Ps. 133. 2. [l] Is. 13. 14. [m] Is. 66. 23. [n] Le. 26. 16. [o] 1 Sa. 17. 38. [p] Je. 13. 25. [q] 2 Sa. 21. 20. [r] Ju. 5. 10. [s] Is. 10. 2. [t] Pr. 19. 13. [u] Pr. 18. 18. [x] Ezr. 4. 15. [y] Da. 3. 2, 3. [z] Is. 53. 5.

[a] Is. 19. 10. [b] Ca. 2. 8. [c] Is. 38. 12. [d] Je. 52. 15, 16. [e] Is. 40. 15. [f] Nu. 24. 7. [g] 1 Sa. 17. 53. [h] Le. 16. 18. [i] Ps. 51. 16. [k] Eze. 32. 6. [l] Is. 25. 10. [m] Je. 31. 16. [n] Pr. 6. 14. [o] 2 Ch. 1. 11. [p] 2 Ch. 1. 10. [q] Eze. 18. 19. [qq] Pr. 26. 28. [r] Pr. 7. 4. [s] Is. 48. 4. [t] Ru. 3. 2. [u] Da. 7. 7, 19.

מְדֻקָּרִים[a] וּ Pual part. masc., pl. of [מְדֻקָּר]; וּ bef. lab. דקר

מְדֹר[b] defect. for מְדוֹר (q. v.) . . . דור

מְדָרְהוֹן[c] Ch. n. m. s., suff. 3 pers. pl. m. from [מְדָר] d. 1 a דור

מִדָּרוֹם[d] pref. ·מִ) noun masc. sing. [for דָּרוֹם] . דרר

מַדְרִיכֵךְ[e] Hiph. part. s. [מַדְרִיךְ], suff. 2 pers. s. m. d. 2 b דרך

מְדָרָךְ[f] Chald. noun masc. sing., suff. 2 pers. sing. masc. from [מְדוֹר] dec. 1 a . . דור

מִדָּרֶךְ[g] in pause for מִדַּרְךָ (q. v. § 35. rem. 2) . דרך

מִדְרַךְ[h] noun masc. sing., constr. of [מִדְרָךְ] dec. 2 b דרך

מִדֶּרֶךְ pref. ·מִ) noun com. sing. dec. 6 a . דרך

מִדַּרְכּוֹ וּ' pref. id.) id., suff. 3 pers. sing. m.; וּ bef. lab. דרך

מִדַּרְכֵיהֶם pref. id.) id. pl., suff. 3 pers. pl. masc. . דרך

מִדְּרָכָיו pref. id.) id. pl., suff. 3 pers. sing. masc. דרך

מִדְּרָכֶיךָ[i] pref. id.) id. pl., suff. 2 pers. sing. masc. דרך

מִדַּרְכֵיכֶם pref. id.) id. pl., suff. 2 pers. pl. masc. דרך

מִדַּרְכֵּךְ[k] pref. id.) id. sing., suff. 2 pers. sing. fem. דרך

מִדַּרְכָּם [l]וּ' pref. id.) id. s., suff. 3 p. pl. m.; וּ bef. lab. דרך

מִדְרַשׁ[m] noun masc. sing., constr. of [מִדְרָשׁ] dec. 2 b דרש

מְדֻרָתָהּ[n] noun fem. s., suff. 3 pers. s. f. from מְדוּרָה' d. 10 דור

מִדֶּשֶׁן[o] pref. ·מִ) noun masc. sing. (suff. דִּשְׁנִי) d. 6 a דשן

מְדֻשָׁתִי[p] noun fem. s., suff. 1 pers. s. from [מְדוּשָׁה] d. 10 דוש

מִדַּת[q] [r]וּ' noun fem. sing., constr. of מִדָּה dec. 10, Chald. 8 a; וּ bef. lab. . . . מדד

מַדֹּתִי[s] וּ Kal pret. 1 pers. sing.; acc. shifted by וְ, for וְ, conv. (§ 8. rem. 7) . . מדד

מַדֹּתֶם[t] וּ id. pret. 2 pers. pl. masc.; וּ bef. lab. . מדד

מָה וּ' *every where* in pause, except before א and ר, as מָה־אֵלֶּה, מָה רְאִיתֶם; *rarely* before הֶ, הַ, הָ, עֵ, עָ;—מַה־, מַה· (followed by Dag. forte) before non-guttural letters, as מַה־שְּׁמוֹ (& contr. מַזֶּה, מַלָּכֶם, for מַה־זֶּה, מַה־לָּכֶם);—מַה (Dag. forte impl.) before the harsher gutturals, as מַה־הוּא;—מֶה before הָ, חָ, עָ (once עֶ 1 Sa. 20. 1), as מֶה עָשִׂיתָ, מֶה חָדֵל. This latter form stands also frequently before non-gutturals, chiefly at the beginning of a sentence. It is still more frequently found with prefixes, as לָמָּה כַּמָּה, בַּמֶּה.

Part.—I. pron. interrog. *what?* (of things) in a direct and indirect question, espec. with the verbs אָמַר, שָׁאַל; frequently also in the genit. after the constr. חָכְמַת מָה *wisdom, of what* (thing)?—מַה־לְּךָ *what wilt thou?* מַה־לִּי וָלָךְ *what have I to do with thee?*—II. pron. indefinite, *whatever, anything, something;* מַה שֶּׁ *that which.*—III. pron. relat. *what.*—IV. adv. of interrog.; (*a*) *why? wherefore?* (*b*) *how? in what manner?* (*c*) *how! how much!*—V. with prepositions; בַּמֶּה, בַּמָּה *in what? whereby? on what account?*—כַּמָּה, כַּמֶּה *how great? how long? how many? how often?*—לָמָּה, לָמָה (the latter usually before א, ה, ע, and the name יְהוָה), לָמָּה *wherefore? why?* לָמָּה זֶּה *why then?* שַׁלָּמָּה *that not, lest;* 1 Ch. 15. 13, לְמַבָּרִאשׁוֹנָה (for לְמַה־בָּ') *because that from the beginning;* 2 Ch. 30. 3, לְמַדַּי (for לְמַה־דַּי to what is enough) *sufficiently;*—עַד־מָה *till when? how long?*—עַל־מֶה, עַל־מָה *wherefore? why?*

מָא, מָה Chald.—I. *what?*—II. *what, whatever;* מָה דִּי *whatever* (it is) *which;* כְּמָה *how! how very!* דִּי לְמָה, לְמָה *wherefore?* or *lest, that not.*

מְאוּמָה (for מָה וּמָה i. e. whatever) *anything whatever, something;* with אַל, אֵין, לֹא *nothing.*

מַדּוּעַ adv. (for מַה־יָּדוּעַ) *why? wherefore? on what account?* also in indirect question.

מֵהָאֹרֵב[u] preff. מֵ for ·מִ, & הָ for ·הַ) Kal part. act. sing. masc. dec. 7 b . . . ארב

מֵהָאֹכֵל[w] preff. id.) Kal part. act. sing. masc. dec. 7 b אכל

מֵהָאֱלֹהִים preff. id.) noun masc., pl. of אֱלוֹהַּ dec. 1 a אלה

מֵהָאֲנָשִׁים[y] preff. id.) n. m. pl. (as if fr. אֱנֶשׁ d. 6) see אֱנוֹשׁ אנש

מֵהָאֲרִיאֵל[z] וּ preff. id.) for אֲרִיאֵל (q. v.); וּ bef. lab. ארה

מֵהָאָרֶץ preff. id.) with the art. (הָ) for אֶרֶץ noun fem. sing. dec. 6 a (§ 35. rem. 2) . ארץ

מֵהָאֵשׁ[a] preff. id.) noun com. sing. dec. 8 b . אשׁ

מֵהַבְּאֵר[b] preff. מֵ for ·מִ, & ·הַ) noun fem. sing. dec. 1 a (except pl. c. בְּאֵרֹת) . . . באר

מֵהָבִיא[c] pref. מֵ for ·מִ) Hiph. inf. constr. . . בוא

מֵהַבִּיט[d] pref. id.) Hiph. inf. constr. . . נבט

מֵהַבָּיִת[e], מֵהַבַּיִת[f] } preff. מֵ for ·מִ, & ·הַ) noun masc. sing. irr. (§ 45) . . . . } בית

מֵהֶבֶל pref. מֵ for ·מִ) noun m. sing. d. 6 (§ 35. r. 4) הבל

מַהְבִּלִים[g] Hiph. part. masc. pl. [of מַהֲבִיל § 13. r. 9] הבל

מֵהַבָּמָה preff. מֵ for ·מִ, & ·הַ) n. f. s. d. 10 (§ 36. r. 6) בום

מֵהַבֹּקֶר preff. id.) noun masc. sing. d. 6 c (§ 35. r. 9) בקר

מֵהַגְּבָעוֹת[h] preff. id.) noun fem. pl. abs. from גִּבְעָה d. 12 b גבע

מֵהַגְּדוּדִי[i] preff. id.) noun masc. sing. dec. 1 a . גדד

מֵהַגּוֹלָה[k] preff. id.) noun fem. sing. . . גלה

מֵהַגִּיד[l] pref. מֵ for ·מִ) Hiph. inf. constr. . . נגד

מֵהַגַּנּוֹת[n] preff. מֵ for ·מִ, & ·הַ) n. f., pl. of גַּנָּה' dec. 10 גנן

מֵהַגֵּר[m] וּ preff. id.) noun masc. s. d. 1; וּ bef. lab. גור

מֵהַגְּשָׁמִים[n] וּ preff. id.) n. m. pl. (c. גִּשְׁמֵי) fr. גֶּשֶׁם d. 6 a; וּ id. גשׁם

מֵהֹדּוּ pref. מֵ for ·מִ) pr. name of a country, see הֹדּוּ.

מְהַדֵּק[o] Ch. Aph. part. act. s. m. [for מַדֵּק § 47. r. 4] דקק

מֵהֲדַר וּ pref. מֵ for ·מִ) noun masc. sing., constr. of הָדָר dec. 4 c; וּ bef. lab. . . הדר

[a] Je. 51. 4. [b] Ex. 17. 16. [c] Da. 2. 11. [d] Job 37. 16. [e] Is. 48. 17. [f] Da. 4. 22, 29. [g] Job 24. 4. [h] De. 2. 5. [i] Is. 63. 17. Is. 1. 29. [k] Eze. 16. 27. [l] Ju. 2. 19. [m] 2 Ch. 24. 27. [n] Is. 30. 33. [o] Ps. 36. 9. [p] Is. 21. 10. [q] Ezr. 6. 8. [r] Ps. 39. 5. [s] Is. 65. 7. [t] Nu. 35. 5. [u] Jos. 8. 7. [w] Ju. 14. 14. [y] 1 Sa. 30. 22. [z] Eze. 43. 15. [a] Eze. 15. 7. [b] 2 Sa. 17. 21. [c] Ex. 36. 6. [d] Ex. 3. 6. [e] Eze. 43. 6. [f] Eze. 40. 7, 8. [g] Je. 23. 16. [h] Zep. 1. 10. [i] 2 Sa. 3. 22. [k] Ezr. 6. 21. [l] 1 Sa. 3. 15. [m] Eze. 14. 7. [n] Ezr. 10. 9. [o] Da. 2. 40.

מְהַדַּר[a] ·וּ Chald. Pael part. sing. masc.; ·וּ bef. lab. הדר

מָהַהּ. Hithpalp. הִתְמַהְמַהּ (§ 6. No. 4) *to delay, tarry, wait.*

מֵהָהָר[b] preff. מֵ for ·מִ, & הָ for ·הַ) noun masc. sing., with the art. for הַר, dec. 8 (§ 37. rem. 7) הרר

מְהוֹדֵא[c] Ch. Aph. part. s. m., for מוֹדֵא (§ 47. r. 4) ידה

מֵהוֹדְךָ[d] pref. מֵ for ·מִ) noun masc. sing., suff. 2 pers. sing. masc. from הוֹד dec. 1 a . . הוד

מְהוֹדְעִין Ch. Aph. part. masc., pl. of [מְהוֹדַע § 47. rem. 4] dec. 2 a . . . . . ידע

מָהוּל[e] Kal part. pass. sing. masc. . . . מהל

מְהוֹלָל[f] Poal part. sing. masc. . . . הלל

מְהוֹלָלַי[g] id. pl. with suff. 1 pers. sing. . . . הלל

מְהוּמָה[h] ·וּ' noun fem. sing. dec. 10; ·וּ bef. lab. . הום

מְהוּמוֹת[i] id. pl. comp. מְהוּמֹת . . . . הום

מְהוּמַת id. sing., constr. st. . . . . הום

מְהוּמֹת[k] id. pl. defect. (for מְהוּמוֹת) . . . הום

מֵהוֹנֶךָ[l] pref. מֵ for ·מִ) noun masc. sing., suff. 2 pers. sing. masc. from הוֹן dec. 1 a . הון

מֵהוֹשִׁיעַ[m] pref. id.) Hiph. inf. constr. . . . ישע

מֵהַחוּץ[n] preff. מֵ for ·מִ, & הַ) noun masc. dec. 1 a חוץ

מֵהָחֵל pref. מֵ for ·מִ) Hiph. inf. constr. . . חלל

מְהַחְצְפָה[o] Ch. Aph. part. s. f. [for מְחַצְפָה § 47. r. 4] חצף

מֵהֶחָצֵר[p] preff. מֵ f. ·מִ, & הֶ bef. חָ f. ·הַ) n. m. d. 5 c חצר

מְהַחֲתִין[q] Ch. Aph. (comp. § 14. rem. 1) part. masc., pl. of [מְהַחֵת § 47. rem. 4] dec. 2 b נחת

מֵהַיּוֹם preff. מֵ for ·מִ, & ·הַ) noun com. s. irr. (§ 45) יום

מִהְיוֹת pref. ·מִ) Kal inf. constr. dec. 1 a . . היה

מִהְיוֹתְךָ[r] pref. id.) id., suff. 2 pers. sing. masc. . היה

מִהְיוֹתָם[s] pref. id.) id., suff. 3 pers. pl. masc. . היה

מְהֵיטַבְאֵל pr. name masc. . . . . . ימב

מֵהֵיכָל[t] pref. מֵ for ·מִ) noun com. sing. dec. 2 b היכל

מֵהֵיכַל pref. id.) id., constr. st. . . . היכל

מֵהֵיכָלוֹ pref. id.) id., suff. 3 pers. sing. masc. . היכל

מֵהֵיכָלֶךָ[u] pref. id.) id., suff. 2 pers. sing. masc. . היכל

מֵהַיָּם[x] preff. מֵ for ·מִ, & ·הַ) noun masc. s. d. 8 a ים

מְהֵימַן[y] ·וּ' Ch. Aph. part. sing. masc. (§ 53 & 47. rem. 4); ·וּ bef. lab. . . . . אמן

מָהִיר adj. masc. sing. dec. 3 a . . . . מהר

מִהְיֹת defect. for מִהְיוֹת (q. v.) . . . . היה

מֵהַכֹּהֲנִים preff. מֵ for ·מִ, & ·הַ) noun masc., pl. of כֹּהֵן dec. 7 b . . . . . . כהן

מֵהַכּוֹת pref. מֵ f. ·מִ) Hiph. inf. constr. (§ 25. No. 2 b) נכה

מֵהַכּוֹתוֹ[z] pref. id.) id., suff. 3 pers. sing. masc. . נכה

מֵהָכִיל[a] pref. מֵ for ·מִ) Hiph. inf. constr. . . כול

מָהַל only part. pass. מָהוּל *adulterated*, of wine, Is. I. 22.

מֵהָלְאָה pref. מֵ for ·מִ) adv. . . . . הלא

מֵהַלְּבָנוֹן preff. מֵ for ·מִ, & ·הַ) pr. n. of a mountain לבן

מֵהַלְוִיִּם ·וּ preff. id.) patronym., pl. of לֵוִי d. 8 f; ·וּ bef. lab. לוה

מֵהֲלֹךְ־[b] pref. מֵ for ·מִ) Kal inf. constr. for הֲלֹךְ (§ 8. rem. 18) . . . . . הלך

מַהֲלַךְ noun masc. sing., constr. of [מַהֲלָךְ] dec. 2 b הלך

מְהַלֵּךְ[c] Chald. Pael part. sing. masc. . . . הלך

מֵהֲלֹךְ[d] pref. מֵ for ·מִ) Kal inf. constr. . . הלך

מַהְלְכִים[e] Hiph. part. masc. pl. [of מַהְלֵךְ ap. for מַהְלִיךְ § 11. rem. 8] dec. 7 b . . . הלך

מַהְלְכִין Chald. Aph. part. masc., pl. of [מַהְלֵךְ] d. 2 b הלך

מַהֲלָכְךָ[f] noun masc. sing., suff. 2 pers. sing. masc. from [מַהֲלָךְ] dec. 2 b . . . . . הלך

מְהֻלָּל ·וּ' Pual part. sing. masc.; ·וּ bef. lab. . הלל

מַהֲלַלְאֵל pr. name masc. . . . . . הלל

מַהֲלָלוֹ[g] noun m. s., suff. 3 pers. s. m. fr. [מַהֲלָל] d. 2 b הלל

מְהַלְלִים[h] ·וּ' Piel part. m., pl. of [מְהַלֵּל] d. 7 b; ·וּ bef. lab. הלל

מַהֲלֻמוֹת[i] ·וּ noun fem., pl. of [מַהֲלֻמָּה] dec. 10; ·וּ id. הלם

מָהֵם[k] Kh. contr. from מָה הֵם (q. v.) . הם & מה

מֵהֶם ·וּ' pref. prep. מֵ, bef. gutt. for ·מִ, with suff. 3 pers. pl. masc., see מִן (§ 5); ·וּ bef. lab. מנן

מֵהַמִּדְבָּר preff. מֵ for ·מִ, & ·הַ) noun masc. sing. d. 2 b דבר

מֵהֵמָּה[l] pref. מֵ for ·מִ) pron. pers. masc. pl. (הֵם) with parag. ה . . . . . הם

מֵהֶמְהֶם[m] pref. id.) noun masc. pl., suff. 3 pers. pl. masc. [for הֲמֵיהֶם from הֵם] . . המה

מֵהֲמוֹן[n] pref. id.) noun m. s., constr. of הָמוֹן d. 3 a המה

מֵהֲמוֹנָם[o] ·וּ'[p] pref. id.) id., suff. 3 pers. pl. m.; ·וּ bef. lab. המה

מֵהַמּוֹרִים[q] preff. מֵ for ·מִ, & ·הַ) Hiph. part. masc., pl. of מוֹרֶה dec. 9 a . . . . ירה

מֵהַמְטִיר[r] pref. מֵ for ·מִ) Hiph. inf. constr. . . מטר

מֵהַמֶּלֶךְ[s] preff. מֵ for ·מִ, & ·הַ) n. m. s. (suff. מַלְכִּי) d. 6 a מלך

מֵהָמָן pref. מֵ for ·מִ) pr. name masc. . . . המן

מֵהַמְּעָרָה[t] preff. מֵ for ·מִ, & ·הַ) noun fem. sing., constr. מְעָרַת, dec. 10 . . . . . עור

מֵהַמַּעֲרָכָה[u] preff. id.) noun fem. sing. dec. 11 a . ערך

מֵהֵן[x] pref. מֵ for ·מִ) pron. pers. fem. pl. . . הן

מֵהַנְּבִיאִים[y] preff. מֵ for ·מִ, & ·הַ) n. m., pl. of נָבִיא d. 3 a נבא

מֵהֵנָּה pref. מֵ for ·מִ) pron. pers. fem. pl. (הֵן) with parag. ה . . . . . הן

מֵהַנָּזִיר[z] preff. מֵ for ·מִ, & ·הַ) n. m. s. d. 3 a, R. זיר see זוד

[a] Da. 4. 34. [b] Jos. 2. 23. [c] Da. 2. 23. [d] Nu. 27. 20. [e] Is. 1. 22. [f] Ec. 2. 2. [g] Ps. 102. 9. [h] Pr. 15. 16. [i] 2 Ch. 15. 5. [k] Am. 3. 9. [l] Pr. 3. 9. [m] Is. 59. 1. [n] Eze. 41. 25. [o] Da. 2. 15. [p] Eze. 42. 9. [q] Ezr. 6. 1. [r] Is. 49. 6. [s] Hag. 2. 16. [t] Is. 66. 6. [u] Ps. 68. 30. [x] Is. 19. 5. [y] Da. 2. 45; 6. 5. [z] 2 Sa. 8. 13. [a] 1 Ki. 8. 64. [b] Ec. 6. 9. [c] Da. 4. 26. [d] Nu. 22. 16. [e] Zec. 3. 7. [f] Ne. 2. 6. [g] Pr. 27. 21. [h] 1 Ch. 23. 5. [i] Pr. 19. 29. [k] Eze. 8. 6. [l] Je. 10. 2; Ec. 12. 12. [m] Eze. 7. 11. [n] Ps. 37. 16. [o] Eze. 7. 11. [p] Is. 31. 4. [q] 1 Sa. 31. 3. [r] Is. 5. 6. [s] 2 Sa. 3. 37. [t] 1 Sa. 24. 8. [u] 1 Sa. 4. 12. [x] Eze. 16. 47, 52. [y] 1 Ki. 20. 41. [z] 2 Ki. 4. 40.

מְהַנְזְקַת[a] וּ Chald. Aph. part. sing. constr. [of מְהַנְזְקָא d. 8a, fr. מְהַנְזֵק m. § 47. r. 4]; וּ bef. lab. — נזק

מֵהַנַּחַל[b] preff. מֵ for ·מִ, & הַ) (noun masc. sing. d. 6d — נחל

מֵהַנְּעָרִים preff. id.) (noun masc., pl. of נַעַר dec. 6d — נער

מֵהַנֶּשֶׁף[c] preff. id.) (noun masc. sing. (suff. נִשְׁפּוֹ) d. 6a — נשף

מֵהַסֶּלַע[d] preff. id.) (noun masc. sing. (suff. סַלְעִי) dec. 6a (§ 35. rem. 5) . . . — סלע

מֵהִסְתַּפֵּחַ[e] pref. מֵ for ·מִ) (Hithpa. inf. constr. [for הִתְסַפֵּחַ' § 12. rem. 3] . . . — ספח

מֵהָעֵבֶר[f] preff. מֵ for ·מִ, & הָ for ·הַ) (noun masc. sing. dec. 6 (§ 35. rem. 6) . . — עבר

מְהַעְדֵּה[g] Chald. Aph. part. sing. masc. (§ 47. rem. 4) — עדה

מֵהָעֵדֶר[h] preff. מֵ for ·מִ, & הָ for ·הַ) (noun masc. sing. dec. 6 (§ 35. rem. 6) . . — עדר

מֵהָעוֹלָם[i] preff. id.) (noun masc. sing. dec. 2b — עלם

מֵהָעוֹף[k] preff. id.) (noun masc. sing. . . — עוף

מֵהָעֲזָרָה[l] וּ preff. id.) (noun fem. sing.; וּ bef. lab. . — עזר

מֵהָעִיר preff. id.) (noun fem. sing. irr. (§ 45) . — עור

מֵהַעֲלוֹת pref. מֵ for ·מִ) (Hiph. inf. constr. . . — עלה

מֵהָעָם preff. מֵ for ·מִ, and הָ for ·הַ) (noun com. sing. dec. 8a, also irr. עֲמָמִים (§ 45) . — עמם

מֵהָעַמּוֹנִים preff. id.) (gent. noun, pl. of עַמּוֹנִי fr. עַמּוֹן — עמם

מֵהֶעָרִים preff. מֵ id., & הֶ bef. עָ for ·הַ) (noun fem. pl. irr. of עִיר (§ 45) . . . — עור

מֵהַקָּדִים[m] preff. מֵ id., & ·הַ) (noun masc. sing. . — קדם

מֵהַקֹּדֶשׁ[n] preff. id.) (noun masc. sing. dec. 6c . — קדש

מְהָקִים[o] וּ Aph. part. sing. m. (§ 47. r. 4); וּ bef. lab. — קום

מֵהָקִיץ[p] pref. מֵ for ·מִ) (Hiph. inf. constr. . — קוץ

מְהֻקְצָעוֹת[q] Hoph. part. fem. pl. [of מְהֻקְצָעָה from מְהֻקְצָע masc.] . . . — קצע

מְהַקְרְבִין[r] Chald. Aph. (§ 47. rem. 4) part. masc., pl. of [מְהַקְרֵב] dec. 2b . . . — קרב

מֵהַקַּרְקַע[s] preff. מֵ for ·מִ, & ·הַ) (noun masc. sing. — קרקע.

I. [מָהַר] *to haste, hasten*, Ps. 16. 4. Pi. מִהֵר (§ 14. rem. 1) *to hasten, make haste, be quick;* מִהֲרוּ שָׁכְחוּ *they hasted, they forgot*, i. e. *they quickly forgot;* מִהֵר לִמְצֹא *he found quickly.* Niph. *to be hasty, rash*, Job 5. 13. Part. נִמְהָר (*a*) *hasty, rash, inconsiderate*, Is. 32. 4; (*b*) *impetuous*, Hab. 1. 6; (*c*) *timid*, with לֵב, Is. 35. 4.

מָהִיר adj. masc. dec. 3a, *quick, ready, skilful.*

מַהֵר masc.—I. adj. *hasty, speedy*, Zep. 1. 14.—II. adv. *quickly, speedily.*

מְהֵרָה fem. *haste, speed;* as an adv. *quickly, speedily.*

מַהֲרַי (*ready, skilful*) pr. name of one of David's captains.

II. [מָהַר] cogn. מוּר q. v. *to purchase* a wife, by a dowry or present to the father, Ex. 22. 15.

מֹהַר masc. *price* or *dowry*, tendered by the bridegroom to the parents of the bride.

מָהֹר[t] Kal inf. abs. . . . . . — מהר

מַהֵר[u] וּ Piel (§ 14. rem. 1) imp. sing. masc.; or *adv.*; or (Zep. 1. 14) adj.; וּ bef. lab. . — מהר

מֵהַר pref. מֵ for ·מִ) (noun m. sing. d. 8 (§ 37. r. 7) — הרר

מֵהַר pref. id.) (pr. name of a mountain . — הרר

מִהַר Piel pret. 3 pers. sing. masc. (§ 14. rem. 1) — מהר

מֹהַר[x] noun masc. sing. . . . — מהר

מְהִר[y] וּ adj. m. sing., constr. of מָהִיר d. 3a; וּ bef. lab. — מהר

מֵהָרֹאשׁ[z] preff. מֵ for ·מִ, and הָ for ·הַ) (noun masc. sing. irr. (§ 45) . . . . — ראש

מֵהַרְבֵּה[a] pref. מֵ for ·מִ) (Hiph. inf. abs. as an *adv.* (§ 24. rem. 15) . . . . — רבה

מֵהַרְבִּית[b] pref. id.) (id. inf. constr., Kh. בִּית׳, K. בַּת׳ — רבה

מַהֲרָה Piel imp. s. m. (מַהֵר § 14. r. 1) with parag. ה — מהר

מִהֲרָה[c] id. pret. 3 pers. sing. fem. . . . — מהר

מְהֵרָה noun fem. s. (Ps. 147. 15); used also *adverbially* — מהר

מָהָרוּ[d] Kal pret. 3 pers. pl. [for מָהֲרוּ § 8. rem. 7] — מהר

מַהֲרוּ Piel imp. pl. masc. (§ 14. rem. 1) . . — מהר

מִהֲרוּ id. pret. 3 pers. pl. . . . — מהר

מַהֲרַי pr. name masc. . . . — מהר

מַהֲרִי[e] Piel imp. sing. fem. . . . — מהר

מֵהֲרֵי[f] pref. מֵ for ·מִ) (noun masc. pl. constr. fr. הַר dec. 8 (§ 37. rem. 7) . . . — הרר

מֵהֵרָיוֹן[g] וּ pref. id.) (noun masc. sing.; וּ bef. lab. — הרה

מְהָרְסַיִךְ[h] Piel part. pl. masc., suff. 2 pers. sing. fem. from [מְהָרֵס] dec. 7b — הרס

מֵהָרַע[i] pref. מֵ for ·מִ) (Hiph. inf. constr. (§ 18. r. 10) — רעע

מֵהַרְרֵי pref. id.) (noun m. pl. constr. from [הָרָר] d. 4c — הרר

מֵהֲרָרֶיהָ[k] וּ pref. id.) (id., suff. 3 pers. s.; וּ bef. lab. — הרר

מִהַרְתָּ[l] Piel pret. 2 pers. sing. masc. (§ 14. rem. 1) — מהר

מִהַרְתְּ[m] id. pret. 2 pers. sing. fem. . . — מהר

מִהַרְתֶּם[n] וּ id. pret. 2 pers. pl. m.; וּ, bef. lab. for וְ, conv. — מהר

מִהַרְתֶּן[o] id. pret. 2 pers. pl. fem. . . . — מהר

מֵהַשְּׁבִי preff. מֵ for ·מִ, & ·הַ) (noun masc. sing. d. 6i — שבה

מֵהַשְׁחִית[p] pref. מֵ for ·מִ) (Hiph. inf. constr. dec. 1b — שחת

מֵהַשְׁחִיתָם[q] pref. id.) (id., suff. 3 pers. pl. masc. . — שחת

מֵהַשִּׁטִּים preff. מֵ for ·מִ, & ·הַ) (pr. name of a place, see שִׁטָּה.

מֵהַשְׂכִּיל[tt] pref. מֵ for ·מִ) (Hiph. inf. constr. . — שכל

[a] Ezr. 4. 15. [b] 1 Ki. 17. 4. [c] 1 Sa. 30. 17. [d] Ju. 1. 36. [e] 1 Sa. 26. 19. [f] 1 Sa. 14. 4. [g] Da. 2. 21. [h] 1 Sa. 17. 34. [i] Ps. 41. 14. [k] Ge. 6. 20. [l] Eze. 43. 14. [m] Eze. 42. 9. [n] Eze. 42. 14. [o] Da. 2. 21. [p] Ps. 73. 20. [q] Eze. 46. 22. [r] Ezr. 6. 10. [s] 1 Ki. 7. 7. [t] Ex. 22. 15. [tt] Is. 44. 18. [u] Zep. 1. 14. [x] Ge. 34. 12. [y] Is. 16. 5. [z] 2 Sa. 16. 1. [a] Je. 42. 2. [b] 2 Sa. 14. 11. [c] Je. 48. 16. [d] Ps. 16. 4. [e] Ge. 18. 6. [f] Nu. 33. 48. [g] Ho. 9. 11. [h] Is. 49. 17. [i] 1 Sa. 25. 34. [k] De. 8. 9. [l] Ge. 27. 20. [m] 1 Sa. 25. 34. [n] Ge. 45. 13. [o] Ex. 2. 18. [p] Ps. 106. 23. [q] Je. 13. 14.

מֵהַשָּׁלָל preff. מֵ for מִי, & הַ)(noun masc. s. d. 4a שלל

מֵהַשְּׁלֹשִׁים[a] preff. id.)(num. card. com., pl. of שָׁלֹשׁ fem. שלש

מֵהַשְּׂמֹאול preff. id.)(noun masc. sing. dec. 1a . שמאל

מֵהַשָּׁמַיִם[b] preff. id.)(noun masc. pl. [of שָׁמַי], constr. שְׁמֵי, suff. שָׁמֶיךָ (§ 38. rem. 2) . שם

מְהַשְׁנֵא[c] Chald. Aph. part. sing. masc. (§ 47. rem. 4) שנה

מֵהַשְׁפִּילְךָ[d] pref. מֵ for מִי)(Hiph. inf. (הַשְׁפִּיל), suff. 2 pers. sing. masc. dec. 1b . . שפל

מֵהִשְׂתָּרֵעַ[e] pref. id.)(Hithpa. inf. constr. [for הִתְשָׂרֵעַ § 12. rem. 3] . . . . שרע

מֵהִתְהַלֵּךְ[f] וּ pref. id.)(Hithpa. inf. constr.; וּ bef. lab. הלך

מֵהַתַּחְתֹּנוֹת[g] preff. מֵ for מִי, & הַ)(adj. pl. fem. from ־נָה dec. 10, from תַּחְתּוֹן masc. . תחת

וּ מֵהַתִּיכוֹנוֹת[h] / וּ מֵהַתִּיכֹנוֹת[i] } preff. id.)(adj. fem., pl. of ־נָה, dec. 10, from תִּיכוֹן masc.; וּ bef. lab. } תוך

מֵהִתְיַצֵּב pref. מֵ for מִי)(Hithpa. inf. constr. . יצב

מֵהַתְּלוֹת[k] noun fem., pl. of [מַהֲתַלָּה] dec. 10 . . תלל

מֵהִתְנַבּוֹת[l] pref. מֵ for מִי)(Hithpa. inf. c. as if from נבה (§ 23. rem. 11) . . . נבא

מֵהִתְעַנֵּג[m] pref. id.)(Hithpa. inf. constr. ענג

מֵהַתֹּפֶת preff. מֵ for מִי, & הַ)(pr. name of a place תוף

מוֹ (prob. i. q. מָה *what*) does not occur as a separate word, but is merely annexed to the prefixes כְּ, בְּ, לְ to make them independent words, the signification not being affected thereby. Hence

בְּמוֹ i. q. בְּ.—I. *in*, noting rest; *into, to*, noting motion, Job 37. 8.—II. *with*, Job 16. 4, 5.

כְּמוֹ, כָּמוֹ (the latter form only before light suffixes, comp. § 5) i. q. כְּ.—I. adv. *thus*, Ps. 73. 15.—II. prep. *as, like*; repeated, *as—so*.—III. conj. i. q. כַּאֲשֶׁר *when*.

לְמוֹ i. q. לְ *so, at; for; upon*. Only Job 27. 14; 29. 21; 38. 40; 40. 4.

מוֹאָב וּ (*water*, i. e. *progeny, of the father*; מוֹ i. q. מַי) pr. name—I. *Moab*, a descendant of Lot. —II. of the people descended from him, and the region between the Dead Sea and the river Arnon. Gent. noun מוֹאָבִי, fem. מוֹאָבִית, see also the foll.

מוֹאֲבִיָּה sing. / מוֹאֲבִיּוֹת pl. } gent. noun, fem. of מוֹאָבִי from מוֹאָב q. v.

מוֹאֵס[n] Kal part. act. sing. masc. . . . מאס

מוּבָאוֹת[o] Hoph. part. f., pl. [of מוּבָאָה fr. מוּבָא m.] בוא

מְבוֹאָיו[p] וּ noun masc. pl., suff. 3 pers. sing. masc. from [מוֹבָא] d. 1b (§ 31. r. 1); וּ bef. lab. בוא

מוּבָאִים Hoph. part. m., pl. of מוּבָא d. 1b (§ 31. r. 1) בוא

מוּבָס[q] Hoph. part. sing. masc. . . . בוס

[מוּג] *to melt, flow down, dissolve*, metaph. from fear; trans. *to cause to melt, despond*, Is. 64. 6. Niph. *to be dissolved, undone*, 1 Sa. 14. 16; metaph. *to melt away*, from fear. Pil. *to dissolve, soften*, Ps. 65. 11; metaph. *to cause to waste away*, Job 30. 22. Hithpal. *to flow down, to melt*, Am. 9. 13; metaph. *to despond*, from fear.

מוֹגַיִךְ[r] Hiph. part. pl. masc., suff. 2 pers. sing. fem. from [מוֹגֶה] dec. 9a . . . יגה

מוּד Kal not used; Arab. *to be moved*, cogn. מוט. Hence perhaps Pil. *to move, shake*, Hab. 3. 6, but see מָדַד.

תָּמִיד masc.—I. *continuance, perpetuity*; עֹלַת הַתָּמִיד *continual*, i. e. *daily burnt-offering*; for which simply הַתָּמִיד id.; לֶחֶם הַתָּמִיד *the continual bread*, i. e. the shew-bread.—II. adv. *constantly, continually, always*.

מוֹדֵא[s] וּ Ch. Aph. part. s. m. (§ 56. No. 3); וּ bf. lab. ידה

מוֹדֶה[t] וּ Hiph. part. s. m. (§ 25. No. 2e) d. 9a; וּ id. ידה

מוֹדִים[u] id. pl., abs. st. . . . . . ידה

מוֹדִיעִים[x] [y] וּ Hiph. part. masc., pl. of [מוֹדִיעַ] dec. 1b; וּ bef. lab. . . . . . ידע

מוֹדִיעֲךָ[z] id. sing., suff. 2 pers. sing. masc. . . ידע

מוֹדִיעָם[a] id. sing., suff. 3 pers. pl. masc. . . ידע

מוּזָנִים[b] K. מְיֻזָּנִים Pu. part. pl. m. R. יזן; Kh. מוּזָנִים Hoph. part. masc. pl. [of מוּזָן masc.] . זון

מוּזָר[c] Hoph. part. sing. masc. . . . זור

מוֹט[d] fut. יָמוּט *to totter, shake*; of the foot, *to slip, slide*; of the hand, *to be weak, to fail*, trop. of prosperity, Le. 25. 35. Niph. *to be moved, shaken*. Hiph. *to cause to fall* or *come down*, Ps. 55. 4; 140. 11. Kheth. Hithpa. i. q. Kal, Is. 24. 19.

מוֹט masc. dec. 1a.—I. *a tottering, shaking*.—II. *pole, staff*.—III. *yoke*, Na. 1. 13.

מוֹטָה fem. dec. 10.—I. *pole, staff*.—II. *yoke*.

מוֹט[e] noun masc. sing. dec. 1a . . . מוט

מוֹטָה[f] noun fem. sing. dec. 10 . . . מוט

מֹטֹת[g] pl. of the preced. . . . מוט

[מוּךְ] *to become reduced, to wax poor*.

מָכִי (*reduced, thin*) pr. name masc. Nu. 13. 15.

מוֹכִיחַ[h] וּ׳ Hiph. part. sing. masc. dec. 1b; וּ bef. lab. יכח

מוּכָן[i] Hoph. part. sing. masc. . . . כון

---

[a] 2 Sa. 23. 13. [b] 2 Ch. 7. 1. [c] Da. 2. 21. [d] Pr. 25. 7. [e] Is. 28. 20. [f] Job 1. 7; 2. 2. [g] Eze. 42. 5, 6. [h] Eze. 42. 5. [i] Eze. 42. 6. [k] Is. 30. 10. [l] 1 Sa. 10. 13. [m] De. 28. 56. [n] Pr. 15. 32. [o] Ps. 45. 15. [p] Eze. 43. 11. [q] Is. 14. 19. [r] Is. 51. 23. [s] Da. 6. 11. [t] Pr. 28. 13. [u] 1 Ch. 29. 13. [x] Is. 47. 13. [y] 2 Ch. 23. 13. [z] Da. 8. 19. [a] Je. 16. 21. [b] Je. 5. 8. [c] Ps. 69. 9. [d] Is. 24. 19. [e] Ps. 55. 23. [f] Is. 58. 6, 6, 9. [g] Je. 28. 13. [h] Pr. 9. 7. [i] Pr. 21. 31.

מֻוכָנִים[a] id. pl., abs. st. . . . . . כון

מֹוכְרִים[b] ו֙ Kal part. act. masc., pl. of מוֹכֵר׳ dec. 7 b; ו֙ bef. lab. . . . . . מכר

[מוּל] *to circumcise.* Niph. *to be circumcised, to circumcise oneself.* Pil. *to cut off,* Ps. 90. 6. Hiph. *to cut off, destroy,* Ps. 118. 10, 11, 12. Hithpal. *to be cut off, destroyed,* Ps. 58. 8; where others refer the verb to חָצִיץ, and render it, *to be blunted.*

מוּלָה ו֙ fem. dec. 10, *circumcision,* Ex. 4. 26.

מוּל [c] ו׳֙, once מֹל (De. 1. 1), contr. from מוֹאל׳ (Ne. 12. 38), for מוּאָל (compounded of מוֹ i. q. מָה *what, that which is,* & אֶל *towards, before;* hence, *that which is in front, opposite*) prep.—I. *over against, opposite.*—II. *before,* Ex. 18. 19.—III. with prepositions: אֶל־מוּל *over against, towards;*—מִמּוּל, (*a*) *from before;* (*b*) *before, opposite,* noting rest.

אֶתְמוֹל, אֶתְמוּל, אִתְּמוֹל (for אֶת־מוֹל) adv.—I. *before, formerly.*—II. *yesterday.*

תְּמוֹל (for אֶתְמוֹל) adv. *yesterday;* frequently coupled with שִׁלְשׁוֹם the day before yesterday.

מוּל[d] ו֙ *adv.*; ו֙ bef. lab. . . . . . מול

מוּלִי[e] Kal part. pass. sing. masc. dec. 1 a . . מול

מוֹלָדָה ו֙ pr. name of a place; ו֙ bef. lab. . . ילד

מוֹלְדוֹתַיִךְ[f] ו֙ pl. of the foll. with suff. 2 pers. s. f.; ו֙ id. ילד

מוֹלֶדֶת[g] noun fem. sing. dec. 13 a . . . . ילד

מוֹלַדְתָּהּ[h] id., suff. 3 pers. sing. fem. . . . . ילד

מוֹלַדְתּוֹ id., suff. 3 pers. sing. masc. . . . . ילד

מוֹלַדְתִּי id., suff. 1 pers. sing. . . . . . ילד

מוֹלַדְתְּךָ[i], ו֙ מוֹלַדְתֶּךָ[k] } id., suff. 2 pers. sing. masc.; ו֙ bef. lab. ילד

מוֹלַדְתֵּךְ[l] id., suff. 2 pers. sing. fem. . . . . ילד

מוֹלַדְתָּם[m] id., suff. 3 pers. pl. masc. . . . . ילד

מוֹלַדְתֵּנוּ[n] id., suff. 1 pers. pl. . . . . . ילד

מוֹלִיד pr. name masc. . . . . . . ילד

מוֹלִיךְ Hiph. part. sing. masc. dec. 1 b . . . ילך

מוֹלִיכָם[o] id., suff. 3 pers. pl. masc. . . . . ילך

מוֹלִכוֹת[p] id. pl. fem. [from מוֹלִיכָה] dec. 10 . . ילך

מוֹלִכֵךְ[q] id. sing. masc., suff. 2 pers. sing. fem. . ילך

מוֹלֵל[r] Kal part. act. sing. masc. . . . . . מלל

מוּם[s] ו׳֙ noun m. s. d. 1 a (for מאוּם); ו֙ bef. lab. מאם

מוּמוֹ[t] id., suff. 3 pers. sing. masc. . . . . . מאם

מוּמְכָן Kh. מוּמכן, K. מְמוּכָן q. v.

מוּמָם[u] noun masc. sing., suff. 3 pers. pl. masc. from מוּם (for מְאוּם) dec. 1 a . . . . . מאם

מוּמָת[x] Hoph. part. sing. masc. . . . . . מות

מוּן & מִין Root not used; signification uncertain, perhaps i. q. מָנָה *to appoint, define;* Fürst, *to devise, form, fashion,* cogn. Arab. מאן mentiri ementiri.

מִין masc. dec. 1 a, *species, sort, kind.*

תְּמוּנָה fem. dec. 10.—I. *image, likeness.*—II. *form, appearance.*

מוֹנֶה Kal part. sing. masc. . . . . . מנה

מוֹנַיִךְ[y] Hiph. part. pl., suff. 2 pers. sing. fem. from [מוֹנֶה] dec. 9 a . . . . . ינה

מוּסַב[z] noun masc. sing. . . . . . סבב

מוּסַבּוֹת[a], מוּסַבֹּת } Hoph. part. fem. pl. [of מוּסַבָּה dec. 10, from מוּסָב masc.] . . . } סבב

מוּסָּד[b] Hoph. part. sing. masc. (§ 20. rem. 16) . יסד

מוּסָד[c] noun masc. sing. dec. 2 b . . . . יסד

מוּסַד[d] id. constr. st. . . . . . . יסד

מוּסָדָה[e] noun fem. sing. dec. 11 a . . . . יסד

מוֹסְדוֹת noun masc. with pl. fem. term., constr. of מוֹסָדוֹת, from [מוֹסָד] dec. 2 b . . . יסד

מוֹסְדֵי[f] ו׳֙ id. pl. constr. masc.; ו֙ bef. lab. . . יסד

מוֹסִיפִים[g] Hiph. part. masc., pl. of [מוֹסִיף] dec. 1 b . יסף

מוּסָר[h] Hoph. part. sing. masc. . . . . . סור

מוּסָר ו׳֙ noun masc. sing. dec. 2 b; ו֙ bef. lab. . יסר

מוּסַר ו׳֙ id. constr. st.; ו֙ id. . . . . . יסר

מוֹסֵרָה pr. name of a place (מוֹסֵר) with loc. ה . אסר

מוֹסֵרוֹת noun masc. with pl. fem. term. abs. [from מוֹסֵר for מָאסֵר] dec. 7 b . . . . אסר

מוֹסְרוֹתֵיהֶם[i] ו֙ id. pl., suff. 3 pers. pl. masc.; ו֙ bef. lab. אסר

מוֹסְרוֹתֶיךָ[k] ו֙ id. pl., suff. 2 pers. sing. masc.; ו֙ id. . אסר

מוֹסְרוֹתַיִךְ[l] id. pl., suff. 2 pers. sing. fem. . . . אסר

מוֹסְרוֹתֵימוֹ[m] id. pl., suff. 3 pers. pl. masc. . . . אסר

מוֹסְרֵי[n] id. pl., constr. masc. . . . . . אסר

מוּסָרִי[o] noun m. s., suff. 1 pers. s. from מוּסָר d. 2 b יסר

מוֹסְרֵיכֶם[p] noun masc. pl., suff. 2 pers. pl. masc. [from מוֹסֵר for מָאסֵר] dec. 7 b . . . . אסר

מוּסָרְךָ[q] noun m. s., suff. 2 p. s. m. from מוּסָר d. 2 b יסר

מוֹסְרֹתַיִךְ[r] ו֙ defect. for מוֹסְרוֹתַיִךְ׳ (q. v.) . . . אסר

מוֹעֵד noun masc. sing. dec. 7 b . . . . יעד

מוֹעֲדָהּ[s] id., suff. 3 pers. sing. masc. . . . יעד

מוֹעֲדַי[t], מוֹעֲדַי[u] } id. pl., suff. 1 pers. sing. . . . יעד

מוֹעֲדֵי id. pl., constr. st. . . . . . יעד

מוֹעֲדֶיהָ[x] id. pl., suff. 3 pers. sing. fem. . . . יעד

---

[a] Eze. 40. 43. [b] Ne. 13. 16. [c] 1 Ki. 7. 5. [d] 1 Ki. 7. 5. [e] Je. 9. 24. [f] Eze. 16. 4. [g] Le. 18. 9, 11. [h] Est. 2. 10. 20. [i] Ge. 31. 13. [k] Ge. 48. 6. [l] Ru. 2. 11. [m] Eze. 23. 15. [n] Je. 46. 16. [o] Is. 63. 13. [p] Zec. 5. 10. [q] Je. 2. 17. [r] Pr. 6. 13. [s] Ca. 4. 7. [t] Pr. 9. 7. [u] De. 32. 5. [x] 1 Sa. 19. 11. [y] Is. 49. 26. [z] Eze. 41. 7. [a] Eze. 41. 24. [b] Is. 28. 16. [c] Is. 28. 16. [d] 2 Ch. 8. 16. [e] Is. 30. 32. [f] Ps. 18. 8. [g] Ne. 13. 18. [h] Is. 17. 1. [i] Ps. 107. 14. [k] Je. 30. 8. [l] Je. 2. 20. [m] Ps. 2. 3. [n] Is. 52. 2. [o] Pr. 8. 10. [p] Is. 28. 22. [q] Is. 26. 16. [r] Na. 1. 13. [s] Ho. 2. 13. [t] Le. 23. 2. [u] Eze. 44. 24. [x] Je. 8. 7.

מוֹעֲדֵיכֶם[a] וּ id. pl., suff. 2 pers. pl. masc.; וּ bef. lab. יעד
מוֹעֲדִים[b] id. pl., abs. st. . . . . יעד
מְוֹעָדִים[c] Hoph. part. masc. pl. [of מוּעָד] . יעד
מוֹעֲדֶךָ[d] noun masc. pl., suff. 2 pers. sing. masc. [for דֶיךָ' § 4. rem. 1] from מוֹעֵד dec. 7 b . יעד
מוֹעֲדֵנוּ[e] id. sing., suff. 1 pers. pl. . . . . יעד
מוּעֶדֶת[f] Kal part. fem. [for מוֹעֶדֶת]; or Pual part. fem. [for מְמֹעֶדֶת § 10. rem. 6] . מעד
מוֹעִיל[g] Hiph. part. sing. masc. . . . . יעל
מוּעָף[h] noun masc. sing. . . . . . עוף
מוּעָקָה[i] noun fem. sing. . . . . עוק
מוּפָז[k] Hoph. part. sing. masc. . . . . פזז
מֵוֹפַעַת Kh. מוֹ', K. מֵי', pr. name of a place . יפע
מוֹפֵת וּ' noun masc. sing. dec. 7 b; וּ bef. lab. . יפת
מוֹפְתִי id. pl., suff. 1 pers. sing. . . . יפת
מוֹפְתָיו[l] וּ id. pl., suff. 3 pers. sing. masc.; וּ bef. lab. יפת
מוֹפְתִים[m] וּ' id. pl. abs. . . . . . יפת
מוֹפֶתְכֶם[n] id. sing., suff. 2 pers. pl. masc. . . יפת

מוּץ to press, only part. מֵץ (§ 21. r. 2) oppressor, Is. 16. 4.
מֹץ, מוֹץ masc. chaff.
מִיץ masc. pressing, of cream to make butter, churning, Pr. 30. 33.

מוֹצָא וּ' noun m. s. d. 1 b, also pr. name; וּ bef. lab. יצא
מוֹצָא[o] Hiph. part. sing. masc. apoc. from מוֹצִיא יצא
מוֹצֵא[p] וּ Kal part. act. s. m. (§ 23. r. 9); וּ bef. lab. מצא
מוֹצָאוֹ[q] noun masc. sing., suff. 3 pers. sing. masc. from מוֹצָא dec. 1 b (§ 31. rem. 1) . יצא
מְוּצָאוֹת[r] Hoph. part. pl. f. [from מוּצָאָה from מוּצָא] m. יצא
מוֹצָאֵי n. m. pl. constr. for מוֹצָא d. 1 b (§ 31. r. 1) יצא
מְוֹצִאֵי[s] Hiph. part. pl. constr. from מוֹצִיא dec. 1 b יצא
מוֹצָאֵיהֶם[t] noun masc. pl., suff. 3 pers. pl. masc. from מוֹצָא dec. 1 b (§ 31. rem. 1) . . יצא
מוֹצָאֵיהֶן[u] id. pl., suff. 3 pers. pl. fem. . . . יצא
מוֹצָאָיו[x] וּ id. pl., suff. 3 pers. sing. masc.; וּ bef. lab. יצא
מוֹצָאִים[y] defect. for מוֹצִיאִים (q. v.) . . . יצא
מוֹצָאֲךָ[z] n. m. s., suff. 2 p. s. m. fr. מוֹצָא d. 1 b (§ 31. r. 1) יצא
מוּצֵאת[a] Hoph. part. sing. fem. [for מוּצָאת], pl. מוּצָאוֹת (§ 44. rem. 5) . . . יצא
מוֹצָאֹתָיו[b] וּ noun fem. pl., suff. 3 pers. sing. masc. [from מוֹצָאָה § 31. r. 1] d. 10; וּ bef. lab. יצא
מוֹצִיא[c] וּ[d] Hiph. part. sing. masc. dec. 1 b; וּ id. . יצא
מוֹצִיאוֹ[e] id., suff. 3 pers. sing. masc. . . . יצא
מוֹצִיאִי[f] וּ id., suff. 1 pers. sing.; וּ bef. lab. . . יצא
מוֹצִיאִים[g] וּ'[h] id. pl., abs. st.; וּ id. . . . יצא
מוֹצִיאָם[i] id. sing., suff. 3 pers. pl. masc. . . . יצא

מוּצָק Hoph. part. s. m., or (1 Ki. 7. 37) n. m. s. יצק
מוּצָק[k] noun masc. sing. . . . . . צוק
מוּצָק[l] noun masc. sing. . . . . . צוק
מֻצָּקוֹת[m] noun fem. pl. abs. [from מוּצָקָה] . . יצק

מוּק. Hiph. to mock, deride, Ps. 73. 8.

מוֹקְדָה[n] noun fem. sing. . . . . . יקד
מוֹקְדֵי[o] noun masc. pl. constr. from מוֹקֵד' dec. 7 b . יקד
מוֹקֵשׁ וּ'[p] noun masc. sing. dec. 7 b; וּ bef. lab. יקש
מוֹקְשֵׁי[q] id. pl., constr. st. . . . . . יקש
מוֹקְשִׁים[r] id. pl., abs. st. . . . . . יקש

מוּר. Niph. to be changed, altered, Je. 48. 11. Hiph.—I. to exchange, with בְּ of the thing for which.—II. to change, undergo change, Ps. 15. 4; 46. 3.
תְּמוּרָה fem. dec. 10.—I. exchange, transfer.—II. restitution, Job 20. 18.—III. equivalent, recompense.

מוֹרִי[s] noun m. s. (with suff. מוֹרִי) for מֹר (q. v.) מרר
מוֹרָא[t] noun masc. sing. dec. 2 b . . . . ירא
מוֹרְאָה[u] Kal part. act. fem. [of מוֹרֵא] R. מרא; or it stands for מוֹרָה, fem. of מוֹרֶה R. מרה
מוֹרָאוֹ[x] n. m. s., suff. 3 p. s. m. fr. מוֹרָא d. 2 b (§ 31. r. 3) ירא
מוֹרָאִי[y] id., suff. 1 pers. sing. . . . . ירא
מוֹרַאֲכֶם[z] וּ' id., suff. 2 pers. pl. masc.; וּ bef. lab. . ירא
מוֹרָד[a] noun masc. sing. dec. 2 b . . . ירד
מוֹרָה[b] וּ' noun masc. s. with fem. term.; וּ bef. lab. מרה
מוֹרָה[c] for מוֹרָא (q. v.) noun masc. sing. . . ירא
מוֹרֶה וּ' participial n. m. s. d. 9 a, also pr. n.; וּ bef. lab. ירה
מוֹרֶה וּ Kal part. sing. masc. dec. 9 a; וּ id. . מרה
מוֹרָט[d] וּ Pual part. sing. m. for מְמֹרָט (§ 10. r. 6) מרט
מוֹרַי[e] participial n. m. pl., suff. 1 p. s. fr. מוֹרֶה d. 9 a ירה
מוֹרִי[f] n. m. s., suff. 1 p. s. for [מֹרִי] fr. מֹר d. 1 a מרר
מוֹרִיד[g] Hiph. part. sing. masc. . . . . ירד
מוֹרֶיךָ[h] participial noun masc. pl., suff. 2 pers. sing. masc. from מוֹרֶה dec. 9 a . . ירה
מוֹרִישׁ Hiph. part. sing. masc. dec. 1 b . . ירש
מוֹרִישָׁם[i] id. with suff. 3 pers. pl. masc. . . . ירש
מוֹרָשָׁה noun fem. sing. . . . . . ירש
מוֹרָשֵׁי[k] noun masc. pl. constr. from [מוֹרָשׁ] dec. 1 b (exc. sing. constr. מוֹרַשׁ' § 31. rem. 1) ירש
מוֹרָשֵׁיהֶם[l] id. pl. with suff. 3 pers. pl. masc. . . ירש
מוֹרֶשֶׁת גַּת pr. name in compos. . . . ירש

I. **[מוּשׁ]** I. to move, withdraw, depart.—II. to remove, put away, Zec. 3. 9. Hiph.—I. to let remove, go or

[a] Is. 1. 14. [b] Da. 12. 7. [c] Je. 24. 1. [d] Ps. 74. 4. [e] Is. 33. 20. [f] Pr. 25. 19. [g] Je. 16. 19. [h] Is. 8. 23. [i] Ps. 66. 11. [k] 1 Ki. 10. 18. [l] Ps. 78. 43. [m] Joel 3. 3. [n] Eze. 12. 11. [o] Ps. 135. 7. [p] Ec. 7. 26. [q] Ps. 19. 7. [r] Je. 38. 22. [s] Nu. 14. 37. [t] Nu. 33. 2. [u] Eze. 42. 11. [x] Eze. 43. 11. [y] Je. 38. 23. [z] 2 Sa. 3. 25. [a] Ge. 38. 25. [b] Mi. 5. 1. [c] Ps. 68. 7. [d] Is. 54. 16; Pr. 10. 18. [e] Nu. 24. 8. [f] 2 Sa. 22. 49. [g] Ne. 6. 19. [h] 2 Ch. 9. 28. [i] Nu. 26. 22. [k] Is. 8. 23. [l] Job 36. 16. [m] Zec. 4. 2. [n] Le. 6. 2. [o] Is. 33. 14. [p] Am. 3. 5. [q] Ps. 18. 6. [r] Ps. 64. 6. [s] Ca. 5. 5, 5, 13. [t] Mal. 2. 5. [u] Zep. 3. 1. [x] Is. 8. 12. [y] Mal. 1. 6. [z] Is. 8. 13. [a] 1 Ki. 7. 29. [b] Ju. 16. 17. [c] Ps. 9. 21. [d] Is. 18. 2, 7. [e] Pr. 5. 13. [f] Ca. 5. 1. [g] 1 Sa. 2. 6. [h] Is. 30. 20, 20. [i] De. 9. 4, 5. [k] Job 17. 11. [l] Ob. 1. 17.

escape, hence *to withdraw,* Na. 3. 1; Mi. 2. 3.—II. *to withdraw, depart.*

II. [מְוּשׁ] i. q. מָשַׁשׁ *to feel, touch,* Ge. 27. 21. Hiph. id. Ps. 115. 7; Ju. 16. 26, Keri.

מֻשִׁי, מוּשִׁי (*tried*) pr. name masc.—Patronym. מוּשִׁי for מוּשִׁיִּי.

מוֹשָׁב noun masc. sing. dec. 2b . . . ישב
מוֹשַׁב ו׳ id., constr. st.; וּ bef. lab. . . . ישב
מוֹשָׁבוֹ id., suff. 3 pers. sing. masc. . . . ישב
[a] מוֹשְׁבוֹתֵיהֶם id. pl. fem., suff. 3 pers. pl. masc. . ישב
[b] מוֹשְׁבוֹתֵיכֶם id. id., suff. 2 pers. pl. masc. . ישב
[c] מוֹשְׁבוֹתָם id. id., suff. 3 pers. pl. masc. (§ 4. rem. 2) ישב
[d] מוֹשָׁבִי id. sing., suff. 1 pers. sing. . . . ישב
[e] מוֹשְׁבֵי id. pl. constr. st. . . . . ישב
[f] מוּשָׁבִים Hoph. part. masc., pl. of מוּשָׁב׳ . . שוב
מוֹשָׁבֶךָ noun masc. sing., suff. 2 pers. sing. masc. (for שִׁבְתְּךָ׳) from מוֹשָׁב dec. 2b . ישב
[g] מוֹשָׁבָם id., suff. 3 pers. pl. masc. . . . ישב
[h] מוֹשְׁבֹתֵיהֶם id. pl. fem., suff. 3 pers. pl. masc. . ישב
מוֹשְׁבֹתֵיכֶם id. id., suff. 2 pers. pl. masc. . . ישב
[i] מוֹשְׁבֹתָם id. sing., suff. 3 pers. pl. masc. (§ 4. rem. 2) ישב
מוּשִׁי ו׳ pr. name masc.; וּ bef. lab. . . . מוש
[k] מוֹשִׁיב Hiph. part. sing. masc. . . . . ישב
[l] מוֹשִׁיבִי id. constr. with parag. י . . . ישב
מוֹשִׁיעַ ו׳ Hiph. part. sing. masc. dec. 1b; וּ bef. lab. ישע
[m] מוֹשִׁיעוֹ id., suff. 3 pers. sing. masc. . . . ישע
מוֹשִׁיעִים id. pl., abs. st. . . . . ישע
[mm] מוֹשִׁיעֲךָ, [n] מוֹשִׁיעֶךָ } id. sing., suff. 2 pers. sing. masc. . . ישע
מוֹשִׁיעֵךְ id. sing., suff. 2 pers. sing. fem. . . ישע
[o] מוֹשִׁיעָם id. sing., suff. 3 pers. pl. masc. . . ישע
[p] מוֹשְׁכוֹת noun fem., pl. of [מוֹשֶׁכֶת] dec. 13 . משך
מוֹשֵׁל ו׳ Kal part. act. sing. masc. dec. 7b; וּ bef. lab. משל
*מוֹשִׁעֲךָ defect. for מוֹשִׁיעֲךָ (q.v.) *Je. 46. 27 . ישע

[מוּת] pret. מֵת, 1 pers. מַתִּי (§ 21. rem. 2, & § 25. rem.) —I. *to die,* both naturally and by violence; with מִפְּנֵי, בְּ of the cause; part. מֵת *a dead person.*— II. *to perish, be destroyed,* of a state. Pil. מוֹתֵת *to kill, slay.* Hiph. הֵמִית, 1 pers. הֵמַתִּי (§ 25. rem.), *to put to death, kill, slay.* Hoph. הוּמַת *to be put to death.*

מָוֶת masc. dec. 6g.—I. *death;* כְּלֵי מָוֶת *weapons of death;* אִישׁ מָוֶת, בֶּן־מָוֶת *guilty of death;* מִשְׁפַּט מָוֶת *sentence of death.*—II. *the grave.* חַדְרֵי מָוֶת, שַׁעֲרֵי מָוֶת *gates, chambers of hell.*— III. *pestilence.*—IV. *destruction, ruin.*

מוֹת Chald., masc. *death,* Ezr. 7. 26.

מוּת masc. id. Ps. 48. 15; מוּת לַבֵּן in the title of Ps. 9, signification not known; Gesenius (without sufficient ground) proposes the reading of עֲלָמוֹת *female voices* (see עַלְמָה) for the first passage, and עֹלָמוֹת *eternity,* for the second.

מָמוֹת masc. dec. 3a, only pl. מְמוֹתִים—I. *deaths,* Je. 16. 4; Eze. 28. 8.—II. as a concrete, *the dead, slain,* 2 Ki. 11. 2, Kheth.

תְּמוּתָה fem. *death;* only בְּנֵי־תְ׳ *condemned to death,* Ps. 79. 11; 102. 21.

מָוֶת וָ׳ noun masc. sing. dec. 6g; for וָ see lett. ו מות
מוֹת id. constr. st.; or Kal inf. abs. . . מות
[q] מוּת noun masc. sing. or inf., but see under the Root מות
[r] מוֹתָהּ noun m. s., suff. 3 pers. s. fem. from מָוֶת d. 6g מות
[s] מוּתָהּ Kal inf. (מוּת׳), suff. 3 pers. sing. fem. dec. 1a מות
[t] מוֹתוֹ noun m. s., suff. 3 pers. s. m. from מָוֶת d. 6g מות
[u] מוֹתֵי id. pl., constr. st. . . . . מות
מוֹתִי id. sing., suff. 1 pers. sing. . . . מות
[x] מוּתִי Kal inf. (מוּת), suff. 1 pers. sing. dec. 1a מות
[y] מוּתֵנוּ id. with suff. 1 pers. pl. . . . מות
[z] מוֹתָר noun masc. sing. dec. 2b . . . יתר
[a] מוֹתַר וּ id. constr. st.; וּ bef. lab. . . . יתר
[b] מוֹתְתֵנִי Pilel pret. 3 pers. s. m. [מוֹתֵת], suff. 1 pers. s. מות
[c] מוֹתְתֵנִי וּ id. imp. sing. masc. [מוֹתֵת], suff. 1 pers. sing.; וּ bef. lab. . . . . מות
[d] מִזְאֵבֵי pref. מִ)(noun m. pl. constr. from זְאֵב d. 1a זאב
[e] מִזֹּאת pref. id.)(pron. demon. fem. sing., see . זה
[f] מִזְּבוּל pref. id.)(noun masc. sing. dec. 1a . זבל
מִזְּבוּלֻן ו׳ pref. id.)(pr. name of a tribe; וּ bef. lab. זבל
[g] מְזַבֵּחַ Piel part. sing. masc. . . . . זבח
[h] מִזָּבַח pref. מִ)(Seg. noun in pause for זֶבַח [as if from זְבַח § 35. r. 2] but with suff. זִבְחִי זבח
מִזְבַּח ו׳ noun masc. sing., constr. of מִזְבֵּחַ dec. 7c זבח
מִזֶּבַח pref. מִ)(n. m. s. (suff. זִבְחִי) d. 6a (§ 35. r. 5) זבח
מִזְבֵּחַ noun masc. sing. dec. 7c . . . זבח
מִזְבְּחוֹ id. with suff. 3 pers. sing. masc. . . זבח
מִזִּבְחוֹ pref. מִ)(noun masc. sing., suff. 3 pers. sing. masc. from זֶבַח dec. 6a (§ 35. rem. 5) זבח
[k] מְזַבְּחוֹת וּ Piel part. fem. pl. [of מְזַבְּחָה or מְזַבַּחַת]; וּ bef. lab. . . . . . זבח
מִזְבְּחוֹת noun masc. with pl. fem. term. fr. מִזְבֵּחַ d. 7c זבח
מִזְבְּחוֹתֵיהֶם id., suff. 3 pers. pl. masc. . . . זבח
[l] מִזְבְּחוֹתֶיךָ id., suff. 2 pers. s. masc. . . . זבח
מִזְבְּחוֹתֵיכֶם id., suff. 2 pers. pl. masc. . . . זבח
[m] מִזְבְּחוֹתָם id., suff. 3 p. pl. m. K. חוֹתָם׳; Kh. חוֹתִים׳ with a double pl. comp. מְרַאֲשֹׁתַי, בָּמֳתֵי זבח

[a] Eze. 6. 14. [b] Eze. 6. 6. [c] 1 Ch. 6. 39. [d] Job 29. 7. [e] Eze. 34. 13. [f] Je. 27. 16. [g] Ge. 10. 30. [h] Eze. 37. 23. [i] 1 Ch. 4. 33. [k] Ps. 68. 7. [l] Ps. 113. 9. [m] Je. 14. 8. [n] Is. 43. 3. [o] Ps. 106. 21. [p] Job 38. 31. [q] Ps. 9. 1; 48. 15. [r] 2 Sa. 6. 23. [s] 1 Sa. 4. 20. [t] Ge. 27. 10, etc. [u] Eze. 28. 10. [x] 2 Sa. 19. 1. [y] Ex. 16. 3. [z] Pr. 14. 23. [a] Ec. 3. 19. [b] Je. 20. 17. [c] Ju. 9. 54. [d] Hab. 1. 8. [e] 2 Sa. 6. 22. [f] Is. 63. 15. [g] 1 Ki. 3. 3. [h] Pr. 21. 3. [i] Ex. 34. 15. [k] 1 Ki. 11. 8. [l] Ps. 84. 4. [m] 2 Ch. 34. 5. [mm] Jer. 30. 10.

מִזִּבְחוֹתָם id., suff. 3 pers. pl. masc. (§ 4. rem. 2) . זבח
מִזְבְּחִי id. sing., suff. 1 pers. sing. . . . זבח
מִזִּבְחֵי pref. ·מִ) (noun masc. pl. constr. from זֶבַח dec. 6a (§ 35. rem. 5) . . . זבח
מִזִּבְחִי[a] pref. id.) (id. sing. with suff. 1 pers. sing. . זבח
מְזַבְּחִים Piel part. masc., pl. of מְזַבֵּחַ dec. 7b . זבח
מִזְבַּחֲךָ } noun masc. sing., suff. 2 pers. sing.
מִזְבַּחֶךָ[b] } masc. from מִזְבֵּחַ dec. 7c . . } זבח
מִזְבְּחֹת[c] id. pl. fem. comp. מִזְבְּחוֹת . . . זבח
מִזְבְּחֹתָו[d] id. id., suff. 3 pers. sing. m. (K. תָיו' § 4. r. 1) זבח
מִזְבְּחוֹתֵיהֶם[e] id. id., suff. 3 pers. pl. masc. . . זבח
מִזְבְּחֹתָיו id. id., suff. 3 pers. sing. masc. . . זבח
מִזְבְּחוֹתֶיךָ[f] id. id., suff. 2 pers. sing. masc. . . זבח
מִזְבְּחֹתָם id. id., suff. 3 pers. pl. masc. (§ 4. rem. 2) . זבח
מִזְבְּחֹתָם[g] noun masc. with pl. fem. term. & suff. 3 pers. pl. m. (§ 4. r. 2) fr. זֶבַח d. 6a (§ 35. r. 5) זבח
מִזְּבֻל[h] defect. for זְבוּל (q. v.) . . . זבל
מִזְּבֻלֻן pref. ·מִ) (pr. name of a tribe, see זְבוּלוּן . זבל

מזג Root not used; i. q. מָסַךְ *to mix.*
מֶזֶג masc. *mixed wine*, Ca. 7. 3.

מִזֵּדִים[i] pref. ·מִ) (adj. masc., pl. of זֵד dec. 1a (§ 21. rem. 2, & § 30. No. 3) . . . זוד

מזה Root not used; i. q. מָצַץ, מָצָה *to suck, suck out.*
מָזֶה adj. masc. dec. 9b, *sucking*, only De. 32. 24, מְזֵי רָעָב *sucking famine*, i. e. *exhausted with famine.*

מַזֵּה[k] ·וּ Hiph. part. sing. masc., constr. of [מַזֶּה] dec. 9a (§ 25. No. 2a); ·וּ bef. lab. . . נזה
מַזֶּה[l] contr. for מַה־זֶּה see . . . . מה
מִזָּה ·וּ (*fear*; Root מזז i. q. מָסַס q. v.) pr. name masc. Ge. 36. 13, 17.
מִזֶּה ·וּ pref. ·מִ) (pron. demon. masc. sing., as an *adv.*; ·וּ bef. lab. . . . . זה
מִזָּהָב[m] ·וּ pref. id.) (noun masc. sing. d. 4a; ·וּ id. זהב
מִזְּהַב pref. id.) (id. constr. st. . . . . זהב
מִזְּהָבִי[n] pref. id.) (id. with suff. 1 pers. sing. . זהב
מִזּוֹב[o] pref. id.) (noun masc. sing. dec. 1a . . זוב
מִזּוֹבָהּ[p] pref. id.) (id., suff. 3 pers. sing. fem. . זוב
מִזּוֹבוֹ[q] pref. id.) (id., suff. 3 pers. sing. masc. . זוב
מְזוּזוֹת noun fem., pl. of מְזוּזָה' dec. 10 . . זוז
מְזוּזַת id. sing., constr. st. . . . . זוז
מְזוּזֹת[r] id. pl., defect. for מְזוּזוֹת . . . זוז
מְזוּזָתִי[s] id. sing., suff. 1 pers. sing. . . . זוז
מְזוּזֹתָם[t] ·וּ id. sing., suff. 3 pers. pl. masc.; ·וּ bef. lab. זוז
מְזוֹנֵנוּ[u] noun masc. pl., suff. 1 pers. pl. fr. [מָזוֹן] d. 6 זוה

מְזוֹלְלִ[x] pref. ·מִ) (Kal part. act. sing. masc. dec. 7b זלל
מָזוֹן[y] ·וּ Ch. & Heb. noun masc. sing.; ·וּ bef. lab. זון
מִזּוֹנָה[z] pref. ·מִ) (Kal part. act. s. f. d. 10, fr. זוֹנֶה m. זנה
מָזוֹר noun masc. sing. dec. 3a . . . . זור
מְזוֹרָה[a] [for מְזֹרָה] Pual part. sing. f. [of מְזֹרֶה m.] זרה
מְזֻזֹת[b] defect. for מְזוּזוֹת (q. v.) . . . . זוז

מָזִיחַ, מֵזַח masc. *a girdle*, Ps. 109. 19; Is. 23. 10.

מְזֵי[c] adj. pl. constr. masc. from [מָזֶה] dec. 9a מזה
מִזִּיו[d] pref. ·מִ) (noun masc. sing. . . . זוו
מְזִיחַ[e] ·וּ noun masc. sing.; ·וּ bef. lab. . . מזח
מְזִין[f] Hiph. part. sing. masc. [for מַאֲזִין § 19. r. 8] אזן
מַזְכִּיר Hiph. part. sing. masc. dec. 1b . . זכר
מִזֵּכֶר[g] pref. ·מִ) (noun masc. sing. dec. 4a . זכר
מַזְכֶּרֶת[h] Hiph. part. s., fem. of מַזְכִּיר (§ 39. No. 4d) זכר
מִזְלְגֹתָיו[i] ·וּ noun fem. pl., suff. 3 pers. sing. masc. from [מִזְלָגָה] dec. 11a; ·וּ bef. lab. . זלג
מְזִמָּה[k] ·וּ noun fem. sing. dec. 10; ·וּ id. . . זמם
מִזְמוֹר noun masc. sing. . . . . . זמר
מְזִמּוֹת[k] ·וּ noun fem., pl. of מְזִמָּה d. 10; ·וּ bef. lab. זמם
מְזִמּוֹתָיו[l] id. with suff. 3 pers. sing. masc. . . זמם
מְזֻמָּנוֹת[m] Pual part. f. pl. [of מְזֻמָּנָה from מְזֻמָּן m.] זמן
מְזֻמָּנִים id. masc., pl. of [מְזֻמָּן] dec. 2b . . זמן
מְזַמְּרוֹת[n] noun fem., pl. of [מְזַמֶּרֶת] dec. 13 . זמר
מַזְמְרוֹתֵיכֶם[o] ·וּ noun fem. pl., suff. 2 pers. pl. masc. from [מַזְמֵרָה] dec. 11b; ·וּ bef. lab. . . זמר
מִזִּמְרַת[p] pref. ·מִ) (noun f. s., constr. of זִמְרָה (no pl.) זמר
מְזִמָּתוֹ[q] noun f. s., suff. 3 p. s. m. from מְזִמָּה d. 10 זמם
מִזַּן[r] pref. ·מִ) (noun masc. s., pl. זְנִים (§ 36. r. 5) זן
מִזְּנוּנֵי[s] pref. id.) (noun m. pl. constr. fr. [זְנוּן] d. 1a זנה
מְזַעְזְעֶיךָ[t] Pilp. (§ 6. No. 4) part. pl. masc., suff. 2 pers. sing. masc. [from מְזַעְזֵעַ § 36. rem. 5] . זוע
מִזַּעַם[u] pref. ·מִ) (noun masc. sing. dec. 6d . . זעם
מִזַּעְפּוֹ[x] pref. id.) (noun masc. sing., suff. 3 pers. sing. masc. from זַעַף dec. 6d (§ 35. rem. 5) . זעף
מִזְּעֹק[ee] pref. id.) (Kal inf. constr. . . . זעק
מִזַּעֲקַת pref. id.) (noun fem. sing., constr. of זְעָקָה dec. 11c (§ 42. rem. 1) . . . זעק
מִזְעָר noun masc. sing. . . . . . זער
מִזָּקֵן[y] pref. ·מִ) (noun masc. sing. . . . זקן
מִזִּקְנֵי[z] ·וּ pref. id.) (adj. or subst. masc. pl. constr. from זָקֵן dec. 5a; ·וּ bef. lab. . . זקן
מִזְּקֵנִים pref. ·מִ) (id. pl., abs. st. . . . זקן
מְזֻקָּק Pual part. sing. masc. dec. 2b . . . זקק
מְזֻקָּקִים[a] id. pl., abs. st. . . . . . זקק
מִזְרֵה[b] constr. of the foll. . . . . . זרה

[a] Eze. 39. 19. [b] De. 33. 10. [c] Nu. 23. 1, 14, 29. [d] 2 Ki. 11. 18. [e] De. 7. 5. [f] 1 Ki. 19. 10, 14. [g] Ho. 4. 19. [h] Ps. 49. 15. [i] Ps. 19. 14. [k] Nu. 19. 21. [l] Ex. 4. 2. [m] Pr. 22. 1. [n] Eze. 16. 17. [o] Le. 15. 30. [p] Le. 15. 28. [q] Le. 15. 3, 13, 15. [r] Pr. 8. 34. [s] Eze. 43. 8. [t] Eze. 43. 8. [u] Ps. 144. 13. [x] Je. 15. 19. [y] Ge. 45. 23; Da. 4. 9, 18. [z] Eze. 16. 41. [a] Pr. 1. 17. [b] De. 6. 9. [c] De. 32. 24. [d] Is. 66. 11. [e] Job 12. 21. [ee] 1 Sa. 7. 8. [f] Pr. 17. 4. [g] Nu. 5. 3. [h] Nu. 5. 15. [i] Ex. 27. 3. [k] Job 21. 27. [l] Ps. 10. 4. [m] Ne. 13. 31. [n] 2 Ki. 12. 14. [o] Joel 4. 10. [p] Ge. 43. 11. [q] Je. 51. 11. [r] Ps. 144. 13. [s] Eze. 23. 11. [t] Hab. 2. 7. [u] Ho. 7. 16. [x] Jon. 1. 15. [y] Ge. 48. 10. [z] Je. 19. 1. [a] Is. 25. 6. [b] Je. 31. 10.

מְזָרֶה[a] Piel part. sing. masc. dec. 9 a . . זרה
מְזֹרוֹ[b] noun m. s., suff. 3 pers. s. m. from מָזוֹר d. 3 a זור
מִזְּרוֹעַ[c] pref. ·מִ (noun com. sing. dec. 1 a . . זרע
מַזָּרוֹת[d] noun pl. fem. . . . . . . מזר
מִזְרָח noun masc. sing. dec. 2 b . . . . זרח
מִזְרַח id., constr. st. . . . . . . זרח
מִזְרָחָה, מִזְרָחָה[e] וּ' } id. abs. & constr. with loc. ה ; וּ bef. lab. . . . . . } זרח
מַזְרִיעַ[f] Hiph. part. sing. masc. . . . . זרע
מִזֶּרֶם pref. ·מִ (noun masc. sing. . . . זרם
מִזֶּרַע[g] וּ' pref. id. (noun masc. sing. (suff. זַרְעוֹ) dec. 6 a (§ 35. rem. 5) ; וּ bef. lab. . זרע
מִזְרָע[h] noun masc. sing., constr. of [מִזְרָע] dec. 2 b זרע
מִזַּרְעוֹ[i] וּ' pref. ·מִ (noun masc., suff. 3 pers. sing. masc. from זֶרַע d. 6 a (§ 35. r. 5) ; וּ bef. lab. זרע
מִזַּרְעֲךָ[k] וּ' pref. id. (id., suff. 2 pers. sing. m. ; וּ id. זרע
מִזַּרְעָם[l] pref. id. (id., suff. 3 pers. pl. masc. . . זרע
מִזְרָק[m] noun masc. sing. dec. 2 b . . . זרק
מִזְרָקוֹת id. with pl. fem. term. abs. . . . זרק
מִזְרְקֵי id. pl. constr. masc. . . . . . זרק
מִזְרְקֹתָיו[n] id. with pl. f. term. & suff. 3 p. s. m. ; וּ bef. lab. זרק
מֹחַ[o] וּ noun masc. sing. ; וּ id. . . . . מחח

[מְחָא] *to strike, clap* the hands, exultingly. Pi. id. Eze. 25. 6.

מְחָא Ch. *to strike, smite.* Pa. id. with בְּיַד *to strike upon the hand,* i. e. *to hinder, restrain,* Da. 4. 32. Ithpe. *to be fastened* or *nailed to,* with עַל, Ezr. 6. 11.

מָחֵא[p] or מַחֵא Ch. by Syriasm [for מַחְיֵא] Aph. part. sing. masc. . . . . . חיה
מַחֲאֲךָ[q] Piel inf. [מַחֵא § 14. rem. 1], suff. 2 pers. sing. masc. dec. 7 b (§ 36. rem. 3) . . מחא
מֵחֲבָלִי[r] pref. מֵ for ·מִ (noun m. s. d. 6 (§ 35. r. 6) חבל
מֵחֲבָלַי[s] pref. id. (noun masc. sing. dec. 6 a (pl. c. חַבְלֵי & חֶבְלֵי § 35. rem. 4) . . . חבל
מְחַבְּלִים[t] Piel part. masc., pl. of [מְחַבֵּל] dec. 7 b . חבל
מֵחֲבֹק[u] pref. מֵ for ·מִ (Piel inf. constr. . . חבק
מֵחֶבְרוֹן pref. id. (pr. name of a place . . חבר
מֵחֲבֵרֶיךָ[x] pref. id. (n. m. pl., suff. 2 p. s. m. fr. חָבֵר d. 5 c חבר
מַחְבַּרְתּוֹ noun f. s., suff. 3 p. s. m. from מַחְבֶּרֶת d. 13 a חבר
מְחַבֵּשׁ[y] וּ Piel part. sing. masc. ; וּ bef. lab. . חבשׁ
מַחֲבַת noun fem. sing. [for מַחֲבֶתֶת] . . . חבת
מַחֲגֹרֶת[z] noun fem. sing. . . . . . חגר
מֵחֲדֹל[a] pref. מֵ for ·מִ (Kal inf. constr. . . חדל
מֵחֶדְרוֹ[b] pref. id. (noun masc. sing., suff. 3 pers. sing. masc. from חֶדֶר, dec. 6 a (§ 35. rem. 4) חדר

מֵחֲדָרִים[c] וּ pref. מֵ for ·מִ (id., pl., abs. st. ; וּ bef. lab. חדר
מֵחֹדֶשׁ[d] וּ pref. id. (noun masc. sing. dec. 6 c ; וּ id. חדשׁ

מָחָה[e] וּ' I. *to strike, wipe out* or *away.*—II. *to blot out destroy.*—III. with עַל *to strike upon, reach unto* Nu. 34. 11. Niph. (fut. ap. יִמַּח § 24. rem. 10) *to be blotted out, destroyed.* Pi. not used ; i. q. Arab. מחח to take out the marrow ; hence Pu part. מְמֻחָי (§ 38. rem. 1) *taken from the marrow* Is. 25. 6. Hiph. (fut. ap. תֶּמַח § 24. rem. 16) *to blot out, destroy.*

מֹחֶה, מָחָה, fem. מֹחָה (dec. 11 a) *destroying, corrupting,* Pr. 31. 3, לַמְחוֹת מְלָכִין *to* (women) *destroying kings.* לַמְחוֹת for לְמֹחוֹת, not for לְהַמֹּחוֹת, לַמֹּחוֹת, unless this is supposed to be one of the exceptions where the article stands with the noun in the constr. st.

מְחִי masc. *a striking,* of battering-rams, Eze. 26. 9.

מְחִיָּאֵל, מְחוּיָאֵל (*smitten of God*) pr. name masc. Ge. 4. 18.

מָחֹה[f] Kal inf. abs. . . . . . . מחה
מְחֵה[g] id. imp. sing. masc. . . . . . מחה
מֹחֶה[h] id. part. act. sing. masc. . . . . מחה
מְחוֹז[i] noun masc. sing., constr. of [מָחוֹז] dec. 3 a חוז
מִחוּט[k] pref. מִ (noun masc. sing. . . . חוט
מְחוּיָאֵל pr. name masc. . . . . . מחה
מֵחֲוִילָה pref. מֵ for ·מִ (pr. name of a region, see חֲוִילָה
מָחוֹל[l] וּ noun masc. sing. dec. 3 a, also pr. name; וּ bef. lab. . . . . . חול
מֵחוֹל pref. מֵ for ·מִ (noun masc. sing. . . חול
מְחוֹלָה see אָבֵל מְחוֹלָה under . . . אבל
מְחוֹלָל[m] Poal part. sing. masc. . . . . חלל
מְחוֹלֵל[n] Pilel part. sing. masc. . . . . חול
מְחוֹלֶלֶת[o] Poel part. sing. fem. [of מְחוֹלֵל masc.] . חלל
מְחוֹלֵנוּ[p] noun masc. sing., suff. 1 pers. pl. from מָחוֹל dec. 3 a . . . . . חול
מֵחוֹמַת[q] pref. מֵ for ·מִ (noun fem. sing., constr. of חוֹמָה dec. 10 . . . . . חמה
מְחוֹנֵן[r] וּ Poel part. sing. masc. ; וּ bef. lab. . חנן
מִחוּץ וּ' pref. ·מִ (noun fem. sing. dec. 1 a ; וּ id. חוץ
מִחוּצָה[s] וּ' pref. id. (id. with loc. ה ; וּ id. . . חוץ
מֵחוּצוֹת[t] וּ pref. מֵ for ·מִ (id. pl. ; וּ id. . . חוץ
מֵחַוֹּת[u] pref. id. (Piel inf. constr. . . . חוה
מַחֲזֵה noun masc. sing., constr. of [מַחֲזֶה] dec. 9 a חזה
מֶחֱזָה[x] וּ' noun fem. sing. ; וּ bef. lab. . . חזה

[a] Pr. 20. 8, 26. [b] Ho. 5. 13. [c] Job 35. 9. [d] Job 38. 32. [e] De. 3. 27. [f] Ge. 1. 11, 12. [g] Da. 1. 3. [h] Is. 19. 7. [i] 2 Sa. 4. 8. [k] Le. 18. 21. [l] Est. 9. 28. [m] Nu. 7. 13, 19, &c. [n] Ex. 27. 3. [o] Job 21. 24. [p] Da. 5. 19. [q] Eze. 25. 6. [r] Jos. 19. 29. [s] Jos. 19. 9. [t] Ca. 2. 15. [u] Ec. 3. 5. [x] Ps. 45. 8. [y] Ps. 147. 3. [z] Is. 3. 24. [a] 1 Sa. 12. 23. [b] Joel 2. 16. [c] De. 32. 25. [d] Est. 3. 7. [e] 2 Ki. 21. 13. [f] Ex. 17. 14. [g] Ps. 51. 3, 11. [h] Is. 43. 25. [i] Ps. 107. 30. [k] Ge. 14. 23. [l] Ps. 150. 4. [m] Is. 53. 5. [n] Pr. 26. 10. [o] Is. 51. 9. [p] La. 5. 15. [q] 1 Sa. 31. 12. [r] Pr. 14. 21. [s] Eze. 40. 40, 44. [t] Je. 7. 34. [u] Job 32. 6. [x] 1 Ki. 7. 4, 4, 5.

מֵחָזוֹן[a] pref. מֵ for מִ·)(noun masc. sing. dec. 3 a . . . חזה

מַחֲזִיאוֹת pr. name masc. . . . . . חזה

מֶחֶזְיוֹנוֹת[b] וּ' pref. מֵ for מִ·)(noun masc. with pl. fem. term. from חִזָּיוֹן dec. 3 c; וּ bef. lab. . חזה

מֵחֶזְיֹנוֹ[c] pref. id.)(id. sing., suff. 3 pers. sing. masc. . חזה

מַחֲזִיק[d] וּ' Hiph. part. sing. masc. d. 1 b; וּ bef. lab. . חזק

מַחֲזִיקֵי[e] id. pl. constr. st. . . . . . חזק

מַחֲזִיקִים[f] וּ' id. pl., abs. st.; וּ bef. lab. . . חזק

מֵחָזָק[g] pref. מֵ for מִ·)(adj. masc. sing. dec. 4 c (but pl. c. חִזְקֵי) . . . . . חזק

מְחַזֵּק[h] Piel part. sing. masc. dec. 7 b . . חזק

מַחֲזִקָהּ[i] Hiph. part. sing. masc. (מַחֲזִיק), suff. 3 pers. sing. fem. dec. 1 a . . . חזק

מְחַזְּקִים[k] Piel part. masc., pl. of מְחַזֵּק dec. 7 b . חזק

מַחֲזֶקֶת[l] Hiph. part. sing., f. of מַחֲזִיק (§ 39. No. 4 d) חזק

מָחַח Root not used; *to be marrowy.*

מֵחַ adj. masc. dec. 1 a.—I. *fat*, Ps. 66. 15.—II. *rich*, Is. 5. 17.

מֹחַ masc. *marrow*, Job 21. 24.

מֵחַטֹּא[m] pref. מֵ for מִ·)(Piel inf. constr. . . . חטא

מֵחֲטֹא[n] pref. id.)(Kal inf. constr. . . . . חטא

מֵחַטֹּאות[o] pref. id.)(noun fem. pl. constr. from חַטָּאת see מַחֲטָאת . . . . . חטא

מֵחֲטָאַי[p] pref. id.)(noun masc. pl., suff. 1 pers. sing. from חֵטְא dec. 6 (§ 35. rem. 6) . . חטא

מֵחַטַּאת[q] pref. id.)(noun fem. s. [for חַטָּאת] constr. of חַטָּאָה see חַטָּאת (§ 39. No. 4 d, & § 44. r. 5) חטא

מֵחַטֹּאת[r] pref. id.)(id. pl. [for חַטָּאוֹת], constr. of חַטָּאת חטא

מֵחַטָּאתוֹ pref. id.)(id. sing., suff. 3 pers. sing. masc. חטא

מֵחַטָּאתִי[s] וּ' pref. id.)(id. sing., suff. 1 p. s.; וּ bef. lab. חטא

מֵחַטָּאתָם[t] [u] וּ' pref. id.)(id., suff. 3 pers. pl. m.; וּ id. חטא

מֵחֹטֵב[x] pref. id.)(Kal part. act. sing. masc. . . חטב

מְחֻטָּבוֹת[y] Pual part. pl. f. [of מְחֻטָּבָה from מְחֻטָּב m.] חטב

מֵחֲטוֹ[z] / מֵחֲטוֹא[a] } pref. מֵ for מִ·)(Kal inf. constr. (§ 23. r. 2) חטא

מַחֲטִיאֵי[b] Hiph. part. pl. constr. m. from מַחֲטִיא d. 1 b חטא

מְחִידָא pr. name masc. . . . . . . חוד

מְחִי[c] וּ noun masc. sing.; וּ bef. lab. . . . מחה

מְחַיֶּה[d] [e] וּ' Piel part. sing. masc.; וּ id. . . . חיה

מִחְיָה noun masc. sing. dec. 10 . . . . חיה

מֵחַיָּי[f] pref. מֵ for מִ·)(noun masc. pl., suff. 1 pers. sing. from חַי dec. 8 d (§ 37. rem. 6) . חיי

מְחִייָאֵל וּ pr. name masc., see מְחוּיָאֵל; וּ bef. lab.

מֵחַיִּים pref. מֵ for מִ·)(n. m., pl. of חַי d. 8 d (§ 37. r. 6) חיי

מֵחַיִל[g] pref. id.)(noun masc. sing. dec. 6 h . . חול

מֵחִים[h] adj. masc. pl. [of מֵחַ] . . . . מחח

מֵחֵיק[i] וּ' pref. מֵ for מִ·)(noun m. s. d. 1 a; וּ bef. lab. חוק

מֵחֵיקָהּ[k] pref. id.)(id., suff. 3 pers. sing. fem. . . חוק

מֵחֵיקוֹ[l] pref. id.)(id., suff. 3 pers. sing. masc. . חוק

מְחִיר וּ' n. m. s. d. 1 a, also pr. name m.; וּ bef. lab. מחר

מְחִירָהּ[m] id., suff. 3 pers. sing. fem. . . . . מחר

מָחִיתָ[n] Kal pret. 2 pers. sing. masc. . . . מחה

מֵחַיַּת[o] וּ pref. מֵ for מִ·)(noun fem. sing., constr. of חַיָּה dec. 10, from חַי masc.; וּ bef. lab. . חיי

מִחְיַת[p] וּ' noun fem. s., constr. of מִחְיָה d. 10; וּ id. חיה

מָחִיתִי[q] וּ' Kal pret. 1 pers. sing.; וּ id. . . מחה

מִחְיָתְךָ[r] וּ n. f. s., suff. 2 p. s. m. fr. מִחְיָה d. 10; וּ id. חיה

מַחְכִּימַת[s] Hiph. part. constr. f. [of מַחְכִּימָה fr. מַחְכִּים m.] חכם

מֵחָכָם[t] pref. מֵ for מִ·)(adj. masc. sing. dec. 4 c . חכם

מְחֻכָּם[u] Hoph. part. sing. masc. . . . . חכם

מֵחָכְמָה pref. מֵ for מִ·)(noun fem. sing. (no pl.) . חכם

מְחֻכָּמִים[x] Hoph. part. masc., pl. of מְחֻכָּם . . חכם

מֵחָכְמַת[y] pref. מֵ for מִ·)(n. f. s. constr. of חָכְמָה (no pl.) חכם

מַחֵל[z] Hiph. part. sing. masc. . . . . חלל

מֵחָלָב pref. מֵ for מִ·)(noun masc. sing. dec. 4 c חלב

מֵחֵלֶב / מֵחֶלְבּ[a] } pref. id.)(noun masc. sing. dec. 6 (§ 35. rem. 6) . . . . . חלב

מֵחֶלְבְהֶן[b] וּ pref. id.)(id. pl., suff. 3 pers. pl. fem. [for ־בֵיהֶן § 4. rem. 1]; וּ bef. lab. . חלב

מֵחֶלֶד[c] pref. id.)(noun masc. sing. d. 6 (§ 35. r. 4) חלד

מֵחֶלְדִּי pref. id.)(pr. name masc. . . . חלד

מַחֲלָה noun fem. sing.; or (Pr. 13. 12) Hiph. part. fem. [of מַחֲלֶה masc.] . . . חלה

מַחְלָה pr. name fem. . . . . . . חלה

מַחֲלֵהוּ[d] noun m. s., suff. 3 p. s. m. from מַחֲלֶה d. 9 a חלה

מַחְלוֹן וּ' pr. name masc.; וּ bef. lab. . . . חלה

מַחְלִי pr. name masc. . . . . . חלה

מֵחֳלִי pref. מֵ for מִ·)(noun masc. sing. dec. 6 k . חלה

מֵחָלְיוֹ[e] pref. id.)(id., suff. 3 pers. sing. masc. . חלה

מַחֲלִיק[f] Hiph. part. sing. masc. . . . . חלק

מְחַלֵּל[g] Piel part. sing. masc. dec. 7 b . . חלל

מֵחַלְּלוֹ[h] pref. מֵ for מִ·)(Piel inf. (חַלֵּל), suff. 3 pers. sing. masc. dec. 7 b . . . . חלל

מֵחַלְלֵי[i] pref. id.)(adj. pl. constr. masc. fr. חָלָל d. 3 c הלל

מְחֻלְלֵי[k] Pual part. pl. constr. masc. from [מְחֻלָּל] dec. 2 b (§ 10. rem. 7) . . . חלל

מְחֹלְלֶיהָ[l] the foll. with suff. 3 pers. sing. f. (§ 10. r. 7) חלל

מְחַלְּלִים[m] וּ' Piel part. m., pl. of מְחַלֵּל d. 7 b; וּ bef. lab. חלל

מְחַלְלֶךָ[n] id. s., suff. 2 pers. s. m. [for מְחַלֶּלְךָ § 10. r. 7] חלל

---

a Mi. 3. 6. b Job 4. 13; 7. 14. c Zec. 13. 4. d 2 Sa. 3. 29. e Eze. 27. 9, 27. f Is. 56. 4, 6. g Ps. 35. 10. h Ex. 14. 17. i Da. 11. 6. k 2 Ki. 12. 8. l Ne. 4. 11. m Eze. 43. 23. n 1 Sa. 12. 23. o 2 Ki. 15. 9, 24. p Ps. 51. 11. q La. 4. 6. r 2 Ki. 13. 6. s Ps. 51. 4. t 2 Ch. 6. 26. u 1 Ki. 8. 35. x De. 29. 10. y Ps. 144. 12. z Ge. 20. 6. a Ps. 39. 2. b Is. 29. 21. c Eze. 26. 9. d Ne. 9. 6. e 1 Sa. 2. 6. f Jon. 4. 3, 8. g Ps. 84. 8. h Is. 5. 17. i Eze. 43. 14. k 1 Ki. 17. 19. l Ex. 4. 7. m Job 28. 15. n Ps. 9. 6. o Job 5. 22. p Le. 13. 10, 24. q Is. 44. 22. r Ju. 17. 10. s Ps. 19. 8. t Je. 18. 18. u Ps. 58. 6. x Pr. 30. 24. y 1 Ki. 5. 10. z Je. 25. 29. a Is. 34. 6, 6. b Ge. 4. 4. c Ps. 17. 14. d Pr. 18. 14. e Is. 38. 9. f Is. 41. 7. g Eze. 24. 21. h Is. 56. 2, 6. i La. 4. 9. k Eze. 32. 26. l Ex. 31. 14. m Ne. 13. 17. n Eze. 28. 9.

מְהֹלֲלֶךָ[a] Pilel part. sing. masc., suff. 2 pers. sing. masc. [for ־לֶלְךָ from מְהוֹלֵל dec. 7b . . חול

מְחַלֶּלֶת[b] Piel part. sing., fem. of מְחַלֵּל . . חלל

מַחֲלִמִים[c] Hiph. part. masc. pl. [of מַחֲלִם apoc. for מַחְלִים § 11. rem. 8] . . חלם

מֵחַלְמִישׁ[d] pref. מֵ for מִ·)(n. m. s., constr. of חַלָּמִישׁ d. 3c חלמש

מֵחֶלֶף pref. id.)(pr. name of a place . חלף

מַחְלְפוֹת[e] noun fem. pl. constr. from [מַחֲלָפָה] d. 11a חלף

מַחֲלָפִים[f] noun masc. pl. [of מַחֲלָף] . חלף

מַחֲלָצוֹת[g] noun fem., pl. of [מַחֲלָצָה] dec. 11a . חלץ

מֵחֲלָצֶיךָ pref. מֵ for מִ·)(noun masc. du. (חֲלָצַיִם), suff. 2 pers. sing. masc. from [חָלָץ] d. 4c חלץ

מֵחַלֵּק pref. id.)(Piel inf. constr. . . . חלק

מַחְלְקוֹת noun fem., pl. of מַחֲלֹקֶת dec. 13c . . חלק

מַחְלְקוֹתָם id., suff. 3 pers. pl. masc. . . . חלק

מַחֲלֹקֶת[h] id. sing., abs. st. . . . חלק

מֵחֶלְקַת[i] pref. מֵ for מִ·)(n. f., constr. of חֶלְקָה d. 12b חלק

מַחֲלֻקְתּוֹ[k] ו׳ noun fem. sing., suff. 3 pers. sing. masc. from מַחֲלֹקֶת dec. 13c; ו bef. lab. . חלק

מַחְלְקֹתָם[l] id. pl., suff. 3 pers. pl. masc. . . חלק

מַחֲלַת noun fem. sing., also pr. name fem. . חלה

מְחֹלֹת[m] ו noun fem., pl. of מְחֹלָה [for מְחוֹלָה] dec. 10; ו bef. lab. . חול

מַחֲמָאֹת[n] noun fem., pl. of [מַחֲמָאָה] dec. 11a . חמא

מַחְמַד noun masc. sing., constr. of [מַחְמָד] dec. 8a חמד

מַחֲמַדֵּי id. pl., constr. st. (§ 37. No. 3c) . חמד

מַחֲמַדַּי[o] ו id. pl., suff. 1 pers. sing.; ו bef. lab. חמד

מַחֲמַדֶּיהָ id. pl., suff. 3 pers. sing. fem. . . חמד

מַחֲמֻדֶּיהָ[p] noun masc. pl., suff. 3 pers. sing. fem. from [מַחְמֹד] dec. 8c (§ 37. No. 3c) . חמד

מַחֲמַדִּים[q] noun m., pl. of [מַחְמָד] d. 8a (§ 37. No. 3c) חמד

מַחֲמַדֵּינוּ[r] id. pl. with suff. 1 pers. pl. . חמד

מַחֲמוֹדֵיהֶם[s] K. ׳מַדֵּיהֶם id. pl. with suff., Kh. ׳מוֹדֵיהֶם [for ׳מֻדֵּיהֶם from [מַחְמֹד] dec. 8c . חמד

מַחְמַל[t] ו noun masc. sing., constr. of [מַחְמָל] dec. 2b; ו bef. lab. . חמל

מֵחָמָס[u] [w]ו׳ pref. מֵ for מִ·)(noun m. s. d. 4c; ו id. חמס

מֵחֲמַס pref. id.)(id., constr. st. . . חמס

מֵחֹמֶץ[y] pref. id.)(noun masc. sing. . . חמץ

מַחְמֶצֶת[z] noun fem. sing., formed from Hiph. part. חמץ

מֵחֹמֶר pref. מֵ for מִ·)(noun masc. sing. dec. 6c חמר

מֵחֲמֵשׁ[a] pref. id.)(num. card. fem., constr. of חָמֵשׁ חמש

מֵחֲמַת pref. id.)(pr. name of a place . . חמם

מֵחֲמַת ו pref. id.)(pr. name of a place; ו bef. lab. חמה

מֵחֲמַת[b] ו pref. מֵ for מִ·)(noun f. s., constr. of חֵמָה dec. 11b; ו bef. lab. . . . יחם

מֵחַמָּתוֹ[c] pref. id.)(noun fem. sing., suff. 3 pers. sing. masc. from חַמָּה dec. 10 . חמם

מַחֲנֵה ו׳ constr. of the foll., and pr. name in compos. מַחֲנֵה דָן; ו bef. lab. . . . חנה

מַחֲנֶה noun com. sing. dec. 9a . . חנה

מַחֲנֵהוּ id. with suff. 3 pers. sing. masc. . . חנה

מַחֲנוֹת id. pl. with fem. term. . . . חנה

מְחֵנִי[d] Kal imp. s. (מְחֵה), suff. 1 p. s. (§ 24. r. 21) מחה

מַחֲנֵיהֶם[e] ו׳ noun com. sing., suff. 3 pers. pl. masc. from מַחֲנֶה dec. 9a; ו bef. lab. . חנה

מַחֲנֶיךָ id. pl., suff. 2 pers. sing. masc. . חנה

מַחֲנֵיכֶם[f] id. pl., suff. 2 pers. pl. masc. . . חנה

מַחֲנַיִם / מַחֲנָיִם } pr. name of a place . . חנה

מַחֲנַיְמָה id. with parag. ה . . . חנה

מַחֲנֶךָ[g] defect. for מַחֲנֶיךָ (q. v.) . . חנה

מַחֲנַק[h] noun masc. sing., constr. of [מַחֲנָק] dec. 2b חנק

מֵחַנֵּק[i] ו Piel inf. constr.; ו bef. lab. . . חנק

מַחֲסֶה / מַחְסֶה[k] } noun masc. sing. dec. 9a . . חסה

מַחְסֵה[l] id., constr. st. . . . חסה

מַחְסֵהוּ[m] id., suff. 3 pers. sing. masc. . . חסה

מַחְסוֹם[n] noun masc. sing. . . . חסם

מַחְסוֹר noun masc. sing. dec. 1b . . חסר

מַחְסוֹרְךָ[o] id., suff. 2 pers. sing. masc. . . חסר

מַחְסִי / מַחֲסִי } noun masc. sing., suff. 1 pers. sing. from מַחֲסֶה dec. 9a (comp. § 35. rem. 5) } חסה

מַחְסֵיָה pr. name masc. . . . חסה

מַחְסֵנוּ[p] noun m. s., suff. 1 pers. pl. fr. מַחְסֶה d. 9a חסה

מְחֻסְפָּס[q] Pu. (§ 6. No. 7) part. sing. masc. . חסף

מְחַסֵּר[r] ו Piel part. sing. masc.; ו bef. lab. חסר

מַחְסֹרוֹ[s] noun masc. sing., suff. 3 pers. sing. masc. from מַחְסוֹר dec. 1b . . חסר

מַחְסֹרֶיךָ[t] ו id. pl., suff. 2 pers. sing. masc.; ו bef. lab. חסר

מַחְסֹרְךָ[u] ו id. sing., suff. 2 pers. sing. masc.; ו id. חסר

מַחְפִּיר[w] ו Hiph. part. sing. masc.; ו id. חפר

מֵחֵפֶץ[y] pref. מֵ for מִ·)(noun masc. sing. dec. 6 (§ 35. rem. 6) . . . חפץ

מְחֻפָּשׂ[z] Pual part. sing. masc. . . חפש

מֵחֻפָּתָהּ[a] pref. מֵ for מִ·)(noun fem. sing., suff. 3 pers. sing. fem. from חֻפָּה dec. 10 . חפף

מֵחֻפָּתוֹ[b] pref. id.)(id., suff. 3 pers. sing. masc. . חפף

מָחַץ[c] ו׳ I. *to dash, plunge*, as the foot in blood, Ps.

[a] De. 32. 18. [b] Le. 21. 9. [c] Je. 29. 8. [d] De. 32. 13. [e] Ju. 16. 13, 19. [f] Ezr. 1. 9. [g] Zec. 3. 4. [h] 1 Ch. 27. 4. [i] Pr. 6. 24. [k] 1 Ch. 27. 2, 4, 7, &c. [l] Eze. 48. 29. [m] Ex. 32. 19. [n] Ps. 55. 21. [o] Joel 4. 5. [p] La. 1. 7. [q] Ca. 5. 16. [r] Is. 64. 10. [s] La. 1. 11. [t] Eze. 24. 21. [u] 2 Sa. 22. 3. [w] Ps. 72. 14. [y] Am. 4. 5. [z] Ex. 12. 19, 20. [a] Nu. 31. 28. [b] Job 21. 20. [c] Ps. 19. 7. [d] Ex. 32. 32. [e] Ju. 8. 10. [f] Am. 4. 10. [g] De. 23. 15. [h] Job 7. 15. [i] Na. 2. 13. [k] Is. 25. 4. [l] Is. 28. 17. [m] Ps. 14. 5. [n] Ps. 39. 2. [o] Ju. 19. 20. [p] Is. 28. 15. [q] Ex. 16. 14. [r] Ec. 4. 8. [s] De. 15. 8. [t] Pr. 24. 34. [u] Pr. 6. 11. [w] Pr. 19. 26. [y] Job 31. 16. [z] Ps. 64. 7. [a] Joel 2. 16. [b] Ps. 19. 6. [c] Nu. 24. 17.

68. 24.—II. *to dash, break in pieces*; metaph. *to crush*, of wisdom, Job 26. 12.

מַחַץ masc. *contusion, bruise*, Is. 30. 26.

מְחַץ[a] Kal imp. sing. masc. . . . . מחץ
וּמַחַץ[b] וּ noun masc. sing.; וּ bef. lab. . . מחץ
מֵחֵץ[c] pref. מֵ for מִ)(noun masc. sing. dec. 8b חצץ
מַחְצֵב noun masc. sing. . . . . חצב
וּמָחֲצָה[d] וּ Kal pret. 3 pers. sing. fem.; וּ bef. lab. מחץ
וּמֵחֲצִי[e] ו' pref. מֵ for מִ)(noun masc. sing. dec. 6i (§ 35. rem. 14); וּ id. . . חצה
מֵחֶצְיוֹ[f] pref. id.)(id. with suff. 3 pers. sing. masc. . חצה
מַחֲצִית noun fem. sing. dec. 1b . . . חצה
וּמַחֲצִיתָהּ[g] ו' id., suff. 3 pers. sing. fem.; וּ bef. lab. . חצה
מַחֲצִיתוֹ[h] id., suff. 3 pers. sing. masc. . . . חצה
מְהַחְצְפָה[i] Chald. Aph. part. sing. masc. (§ 47. rem. 5) חצף
מְחַצְּצִים[k] Piel part. m., pl. of [מְחַצֵּץ] d. 7b (§ 10. r. 7) חצץ
מַחְצְצְרִים Kh. מַחֲצֹצְרִים part. pl. masc. (from חֲצֹצֵר § 6. No. 11); K. מַחְצְרִים Hiph. part. pl. [of מַחְצֵר for מַחְצִיר § 11. rem. 8] . חצר
מֵחֲצַר[l] pref. מֵ for מִ)(noun com. s., constr. of חָצֵר d. 5c, also pr. name in compos. חֲצַר עֵינָן' חצר
מֵחֲצֵרוֹת pref. id.)(pr. name of a place, see חָצֵר חצר
מַחְצְרְרִים[m] Kh. מַחֲצֹרְרִים Pilel part. pl. masc. [from מְחַצְרֵר § 6. No. 2]; for Keri see מַחְצְצְרִים חצר
מֵחֲצֵרֹת pref. מֵ for מִ)(pr. name of a place, see חָצֵר חצר
מָחַצְתָּ[n] Kal pret. 2 pers. sing. masc. . . . מחץ
מֶחֱצַת[o] noun f. s., constr. of מֶחֱצָה dec. 10 . חצה
מָחַצְתִּי[p] Kal pret. 1 pers. sing. . . . . מחץ

[מָחַק] *to strike, smite*, Ju. 5. 26.

מֵחֹק[q] defect. for מֵחִיק (q. v.) . . . . חוק
מָחֲקָה[r] Kal pret. 3 pers. sing. fem. . . . מחק
מְחֻקֶּה Pual part. sing. masc. . . . . חקה
מֵחֻקּוֹת[s] pref. מֵ for מִ)(noun fem., pl. of חֻקָּה dec. 10 חקק
מֵחֻקַּי[t] pref. id.)(noun masc. pl., suff. 1 pers. sing. from חֹק dec. 8c . . . חקק
מֵחֻקִּי[u] pref. id.)(id. sing., suff. 1 pers. sing. . . חקק
מֵחֻקֶּיךָ[x] pref. id.)(id. pl., suff. 2 pers. sing. masc. . חקק
מְחֹקֵק[y] [z]ו' Poel part. sing. masc., dec. 7b; וּ bef. lab. חקק
מְחֻקָּק[a] Pual part. sing. masc. . . . . חקק
מְחֹקְקִי Poel part. s. m. (מְחֹקֵק), suff. 1 pers. s. d. 7b חקק
מְחֹקְקִים[b] id. pl., abs. st. . . . . . חקק
מְחֹקְקֵנוּ[c] id. sing., suff. 1 pers. pl. . . . . חקק
מֶחְקְרֵי[d] noun masc. pl. constr. from [מֶחְקָר] dec. 1b חקר

מָחַר Root not used; prob. i. q. מָכַר *to sell*.

מְחִיר masc. dec. 1 a.—I. *price*.—II. *hire, wages*.—III. pr. name masc. 1 Ch. 4. 11.

מָחָר ו' I. *to-morrow*; יוֹם מָחָר, לְמָחָר id.; כָּעֵת מָחָר, מָחָר כָּעֵת הַזֹּאת *about this time to-morrow*; כָּעֵת מָחָר הַשְּׁלִשִׁית *this time the day after to-morrow*.—II. *in time to come, in future time*.

מָחֳרָת, constr. מָחֳרַת fem. *the morrow*; לְמָחֳרָת, מִמָּחֳרָת *the next day*; עַד־מִמָּחֳרָת *until the next day*; מִמָּחֳרַת הַשַּׁבָּת *the day after the sabbath*.

מָחֳרָתָם adv. *the day after*, 1 Sa. 30. 17.

מֵחֹר pref. מֵ for מִ)(pr. name in compos. חֹר הַגִּדְגָּד', see under . . . . גדד
מֵחֶרֶב pref. id.)(noun fem. sing. (suff. חַרְבִּי) d. 6a חרב
מֵחֹרֵב pref. id.)(pr. name of a mountain . חרב
מֵחֹרֶב pref. id.)(noun masc. sing. . . . חרב
מָחֳרָבוֹת[e] Hoph. part. pl. fem. [from מָחֳרָב=מָחֳרָבָה m.] חרב
מֵחָרְבוֹתֵיהֶם[f] pref. מֵ for מִ)(noun fem. pl., suff. 3 pers. pl. masc. from חָרְבָּה dec. 12c . . חרב
מֵחֲרָדָה pref. id.)(pr. name of a place . . חרד
מֵחֲרוֹן pref. id.)(noun m. sing., constr. of חָרוֹן d. 3a חרה
מֵחֹרֹנַיִם pref. id.)(pr. name of a place . . חור
מֵחָרוּץ [g]ו' pref. id.)(noun m. sing. d. 3a; וּ bef. lab. חרץ
מַחֲרִיב[h] Hiph. part. sing. masc. dec. 1b . . חרב
מַחֲרִיבַיִךְ[i] וּ id. pl., suff. 2 pers. sing. fem.; וּ bef. lab. חרב
מַחֲרִיד Hiph. part. sing. masc. . . . . חרד
מַחֲרִישׁ Hiph. part. sing. masc. dec. 1b . . חרשׁ
מֵחָרָן pref. מֵ for מִ)(pr. name of a place . חרר
מֵחֹרֹנַיִם pref. id.)(pr. name of a place . . חור
מְחָרֵף[k] Piel part. sing. masc. . . . . חרף
מֵחֹרֶף[l] ו' pref. מֵ for מִ)(noun masc. sing. dec. 6c . חרף
מֵחֶרְפַּת[m] pref. id.)(noun fem. sing., constr. of חֶרְפָּה dec. 12b (comp. § 35. rem. 6) . . חרף
מֵחַרְצַנִּים[n] pref. id.)(n. m., pl. of [חַרְצָן] d. 6a (§ 37. No. 3) חרץ
מַחֲרִשִׁים[o] Hiph. part. masc., pl. of מַחֲרִישׁ dec. 1b . חרשׁ
מֵחֲרֹשֶׁת pref. מֵ for מִ)(pr. n. in compos. חֲרֹשֶׁת הַגּוֹיִם' חרשׁ
מַחֲרַשְׁתּוֹ[p] noun fem. sing., suff. 3 pers. sing. masc. from [מַחֲרֶשֶׁת] dec. 13a . . . . חרשׁ
מַחֲרֵשָׁתוֹ[q] noun m. s., suff. 3 pers. s. m. [from מַחֲרֵשָׁה] חרשׁ
מְחַשֵּׁב[r] Piel part. sing. masc. . . . . חשׁב
מַחֲשָׁבָה noun fem. s. d. 11a, constr. מַחֲשֶׁבֶת (§ 42. r. 5) חשׁב
מֵחֶשְׁבּוֹן ו' pref. מֵ for מִ)(pr. name of a place; וּ bef. lab. חשׁב
מַחֲשָׁבוֹת noun masc., pl. of מַחֲשָׁבָה dec. 11a . חשׁב
מַחְשְׁבוֹת id. pl., constr. st. . . . . חשׁב
מַחְשְׁבוֹתַי[t] [s]ו' id. pl., suff. 1 pers. sing.; וּ bef. lab. חשׁב
מַחְשְׁבוֹתָיו וּ id. pl., suff. 3 pers. sing. masc.; וּ id. . חשׁב
מַחְשְׁבוֹתֵיכֶם id. pl., suff. 2 pers. pl. masc. . . חשׁב

[a] De. 33. 11. [b] Is. 30. 26. [c] Ps. 91. 5. [d] Ju. 5. 26. [e] Jos. 21. 27. [f] Zec. 14. 4. [g] Le. 6. 13, 13. [h] Ex. 30, 23. [i] Da. 3. 22. [k] Ju. 5. 11. [l] Je. 39. 14. [m] 2 Ch. 5. 12. [n] Hab. 3. 13. [o] Nu. 31. 43. [p] De. 32. 39. [q] Pr. 17. 23. [r] Ju. 5. 26. [s] Le. 18. 30. [t] Mal. 3. 7. [u] Job 23. 12. [x] Ps. 119. 118. [y] De. 33. 21. [z] Ge. 49. 10. [a] Pr. 31. 5. [b] Ju. 5. 14. [c] Is. 33. 22. [d] Ps. 95. 4. [e] Eze. 29. 12. [f] Ps. 109. 10. [g] Pr. 3. 14. [h] Ju. 16. 24. [i] Is. 49. 17. [k] Ps. 44. 17. [l] Pr. 20. 4. [m] Ne. 5. 9. [n] Nu. 6. 4. [o] 2 Sa. 19. 11. [p] 1 Sa. 13. 20. [q] 1 Sa. 13. 20. [r] Pr. 24. 8. [s] Is. 55. 8. [t] Is. 55. 9.

מַחְשְׁבוֹתֵינוּ[a] id. pl., suff. 1 pers. pl. . . . . חשב

מַחֲשָׁבֶת in pause for מַחֲשֶׁבֶת (q. v. & comp. § 35. r. 2) חשב

מַחֲשָׁבֹת pl. abs. of מַחֲשָׁבָה, see the following . חשב

מַחֲשֶׁבֶת noun fem. sing. dec. 13 a, used for the constr. of מַחֲשָׁבָה (§ 42. rem. 5) . . חשב

מַחְשְׁבֹת id. pl., constr. st. . . . . חשב

מַחֲשַׁבְתּוֹ id. sing., suff. 3 pers. sing. masc. . חשב

מַחְשְׁבֹתֵיהֶם [b] 'וּ id. pl., suff. 3 pers. pl. masc.; וּ bef. lab. חשב

מַחְשְׁבֹתָיו id. pl., suff. 3 pers. pl. masc. . . . חשב

מַחְשְׁבֹתֶיךָ [c] 'וּ id. pl., suff. 2 pers. sing. masc.; וּ bef. lab. חשב

מַחְשְׁבֹתָם id. pl., suff. 3 pers. pl. masc. (§ 4. rem. 2) חשב

מַחְשֶׁה[d] Hiph. part. sing. masc. dec. 9 a . . חשה

מַחְשִׁיךְ[e] Hiph. part. sing. masc. . . . חשך

מַחְשִׁים Hiph. part. masc., pl. of מַחְשֶׁה dec. 9 a חשה

מֵחֻשִׁים וּ pref. מֵ for ·מִ) (pr. name masc.; וּ bef. lab. חוש

מַחְשָׁךְ noun masc. sing. dec. 8 a, comp. מַחֲשַׁכֵּי חשך

מֵחֹשֶׁךְ[f] [g] 'וּ pref. מֵ for ·מִ) (n. m. s. d. 6 c; וּ bef. lab. חשך

מַחֲשַׁכֵּי[h] noun masc. pl. constr. from מַחְשָׁךְ dec. 8 a (§ 37. No. 3) . . . . . חשך

מֵחֶשְׁמוֹנָה pref. מֵ for ·מִ) (pr. name of a place . חשם

מַחְשֹׂף[i] noun masc. sing. . . . . חשף

מְחֻשָּׁקִים Pual part. pl. masc. [from מְחֻשָּׁק] . . חשק

מַחַת 'וּ pr. name masc.; וּ bef. lab. . . חתה

מְחָת[k] 'וּ Chald. Peal pret. 3 pers. sing. fem.; וּ id. מחא

מָחֲתָה[l] וּ Kal pret. 3 pers. sing. fem.; וּ id. . מחה

מַחְתָּה 'וּ noun fem. sing. dec. 10; וּ id. . . חתת

מַחְתּוֹת
מַחְתֹּת[m] } noun fem., pl. of מַחְתָּה dec. 10 . . חתה

מְחִתַּת noun fem. sing., constr. of מְחִתָּה dec. 10 חתת

מַחְתָּתוֹ noun fem. s., suff. 3 p. s. m., fr. מַחְתָּה d. 10 חתה

מַחְתֹּתֶיהָ[n] 'וּ id. pl., suff. 3 pers. sing. fem.; וּ bef. lab. חתה

מַחְתֹּתָיו[o] וּ id. pl., suff. 3 pers. sing. fem.; וּ id. חתה

מָט[p] Kal part. sing. masc. dec. 1 a (§ 30. No. 3) מוט

מְטָא[q], מְטָה[r] Chald. I. *to come on* or *to, to arrive at*; with עַל *to come upon* any one, *to happen* to him.—II. *to reach to*, Da. 4. 8, 17, 19.

מֵטִב[s] וּ defect. for מֵיטִיב (q. v.) . . . יטב

מַטְבֵּחַ[t] noun masc. sing. . . . . טבח

מִטִּבְחַת וּ pref. ·מִ) (pr. name of a place; וּ bef. lab. טבח

מֵטִבֵי[u] defect. for מֵיטִיבֵי (q. v.) . . . יטב

מִטַּבְּעֹתָו[x] pref. ·מִ) (noun fem. pl., suff. 3 pers. sing. masc. fr. טַבַּעַת (§ 44. rem. 5) . . טבע

מָטָה [y] 'וּ Kal pret. 3 pers. sing. fem.; וּ bef. lab. מוט

מַטָּה[z]
מָטָּה } prop. subst. (מַט) with loc. ה, as an *adv.* נטה

מַטֵּה 'וּ constr. of the following . . . נטה

מַטֶּה [a] 'וּ Hiph. part. or noun masc. sing. dec. 9 a; וּ bef. lab. . . . . נטה

מְטָה[b] Ch. Peal pret. 3 pers. sing. masc. . . מטא

מִטָּה noun fem. sing. dec. 10 . . . נטה

מֻטֶּה[c] noun masc. sing. . . . . . נטה

מַטֵּהוּ [d] 'וּ noun masc. sing., suff. 3 pers. sing. m. fr. מַטֶּה dec. 9 a; וּ bef. lab. . . נטה

מֹטֵהוּ[e] noun masc. sing., suff. 3 pers. sing. masc. fr. מוֹט dec. 1 a . . . . מוט

מְטַהֵר[f] וּ Piel part. sing. m. (§ 14. r. 1); וּ bef. lab. טהר

מְטֹהָרָה[g] Pual part. sing. fem. [fr. מְטֹהָר masc.] . טהר

מִטְּהָרוֹ[h] pref. ·מִ) (noun masc. sing. with suff. 3 pers. sing. masc. [for טָהֳרוֹ] fr. טֹהַר . . טהר

מִטַּהֲרִים[i] Hithpa. part. masc. pl. of מִטַּהֵר [for מִתְטַהֵר § 12. rem. 3] dec. 7 b . . . טהר

מָטוּ[k] Kal pret. 3 pers. pl. . . . . מוט

מְטוֹ[l] Ch. Peal pret. 3 pers. pl. masc. . . מטא

מִטּוּב pref. ·מִ) (noun masc. sing. dec. 1 a . טוב

מִטֹּב pref. id.) (noun masc. sing. dec. 1 a . טוב

מִטּוֹבָה[m] pref. id.) (noun fem. sing. d. 10, fr. טוֹב m. טוב

מַטְוֶה[n] noun masc. sing. . . . . טוה

מִטּוּרָא[o] Ch. pref. ·מִ) (noun masc. sing., emph. of טוּר dec. 1 a . . . . . טור

מַטּוֹת noun masc. with pl. f. term. fr. מַטֶּה d. 9 a נטה

מִטּוֹת noun fem., pl. of מִטָּה dec. 10 . . נטה

מֹטוֹת [p] 'וּ defect. for מוֹטוֹת (q. v.) . . מוט

מֻטּוֹת[q] noun fem., pl. of [מֻטָּה] dec. 10 . . נטה

מַטּוֹתָם[r] noun masc. with pl. fem. term. and suff. 3 pers. pl. masc. fr. מַטֶּה dec. 9 a . . נטה

מַטֵּי[s] וּ Hiph. part. pl. constr. masc. fr. מַטֶּה (§ 25. No. 2 b) dec. 9; וּ bef. lab. . נטה

מֵטִיב[t] וּ defect. for מֵיטִיב (q. v.) . . . יטב

מִטִּיט pref. ·מִ) (noun masc. sing. . . . טוא

מָטִים[u] וּ Kal part. act. masc., pl. of מָט dec. 1 a (§ 30. No. 3); וּ bef. lab. . . . מוט

מַטִּיף[x] Hiph. part. sing. masc. . . . נטף

מַטֵּךְ [y] 'וּ noun masc. sing., suff. 2 pers. sing. fem. fr. מַטֶּה dec. 9 a; וּ bef. lab. . . . נטה

מטל Root not used; Arab. *to forge iron.*
מְטִיל masc. dec. 3 a, *bar of iron*, Job 40. 18.

מִטַּל
מִטַּל[z] } pref. ·מִ) (noun masc. sing. dec. 8 d; 'וּ bef. lab. . . . . } טלל

מְטֻלָּאוֹת[a] וּ Pual part. pl. fem. [fr. מְטֻלָּא=מְטֻלָּאָה masc.]; וּ id. . . . . טלא

---

[a] Je. 18. 12. [b] Is. 66. 18. [c] Ps. 40. 6. [d] Is. 57. 11. [e] Job 38. 2. [f] Ps. 107. 14. [g] Is. 29. 18. [h] Ps. 74. 20. [i] Ge. 30. 37. [k] Da. 2. 34, 35. [l] Pr. 30. 20. [m] Nu. 16. 17. [n] Nu. 4. 9. [o] Ex. 27. 3. [p] Pr. 25. 26. [q] Da. 4. 25. [r] Da. 7. 13, 22. [s] Eze. 33. 32. [t] Is. 14. 21. [u] Pr. 30. 29. [x] Ex. 28. 28; 39. 21. [y] Le. 25. 35. [z] De. 28. 43. [a] Is. 10. 5. [b] Da. 7. 13, 22. [c] Eze. 9. 9. [d] Is. 10. 24, 26. [e] Na. 1. 13. [f] Mal. 3. 3. [g] Eze. 22. 24. [h] Ps. 89. 45. [i] Ne. 13. 22. [k] Ps. 46. 7. [l] Da. 6. 25. [m] Ec. 4. 8. [n] Ex. 35. 25. [o] Da. 2. 45. [p] Je. 27. 2. [q] Is. 8. 8. [r] Nu. 17. 21. [s] Mal. 3. 5. [t] Ps. 119. 68. [u] Pr. 24. 11. [x] Mi. 2. 11. [y] Ge. 27. 28. [z] Jos. 9. 5.

מְטַלְטֶלְךָ[a] Pilp. part. sing. masc. [מְטַלְטֵל], suff. 2 pers. sing. masc. dec. 7 b . . . . טול

מִטָּמֵא[b] pref. ·מִ) adj. masc. sing. dec. 5 a (constr. טְמֵא § 34. rem. 1) . . . . טמא

מְטֻמָּאָה[c] Pual part. sing. fem. [of מְטֻמָּא masc.] . טמא

מִטֻּמְאַת[d] pref. ·מִ) noun f. s., constr. of טֻמְאָה d. 10 טמא

מִטֻּמְאֹת[e] pref. id.) id. pl. constr. . . . . טמא

מִטֻּמְאָתָהּ[f] pref. id.) id. sing., suff. 3 pers. sing. fem. טמא

מִטֻּמְאָתוֹ[g] pref. id.) id. sing., suff. 3 pers. sing. masc. טמא

מִטֻּמְאָתֵךְ[h] pref. id.) id. sing., suff. 2 pers. sing. fem. טמא

מִטֻּמְאֹתָם[i] pref. id.) id. sing., suff. 3 pers. pl. masc. טמא

מַטְמוֹן[k] noun masc. sing. dec. 1 a . . . . טמן

מַטְמֹנֵי[l] ׳וּ id. pl. constr. (§ 30. rem. 4); ׳וּ bef. lab. טמן

מַטְמֹנִים[m] id. pl., abs. st. . . . . . טמן

מַטָּע[n] noun masc. sing. d. 2 b (except pl. c. מַטָּעֵי) נטע

מַטַּע[o] id., constr. st. . . . . . . נטע

מַטָּעָהּ id., suff. 3 pers. sing. fem. . . . נטע

מַטָּעָו[p] id. pl. with suff. Kh. ׳עָו 3 pers. sing. masc., K. ׳עַי 1 pers. sing. . . . . . נטע

מִטַּעַם[q] pref. ·מִ) noun masc. sing. dec. 6 d . טעם

מִטְּעֵם[r] ׳וּ Ch., pref. id.) noun m. s. d. 3 a; ׳וּ bef. lab. טעם

מַטְעַמִּים[s] noun m., pl. of [מַטְעָם] d. 8 a (§ 37. No. 2) טעם

מְטֹעֲנֵי[t] Pual part. pl. constr. masc. fr. [מְטֹעָן] d. 2 b טען

מִטַּף[u] pref. ·מִ) noun masc. sing. (for ׳טַף) d. 8 d טפף

מָטַר. Hiph. הִמְטִיר *to rain, cause* or *give rain;* applied to the sending of hail, lightning, fire and brimstone, manna; const. with acc. בְּ of the thing rained down, and עַל *upon* anything. Niph. *to be rained upon*, Am. 4. 7.

מָטָר masc. dec. 4 a (pl. c. מִטְרוֹת) *rain.*

מַטְרִי (*rain of the Lord*, for מַטְרִיָּה) pr. name masc. 1 Sa. 10. 21.

מָטָר ׳וּ noun masc. sing. dec. 4 a; ׳וּ bef. lab. . מטר

מְטַר[x] ׳וּ id., constr. st.; ׳וּ id. . . . . מטר

מַטְרֵד pr. name masc. . . . . . . טרד

מִטְרוֹת[y] noun masc. with pl. fem. term. constr. [of מְטָרוֹת] from מָטָר dec. 4 a . . . מטר

מִטֶּרֶם[z] pref. ·מִ) *adv.* . . . . . טרם

מִטֶּרֶף[a] pref. id.) noun masc. sing. (suff. טַרְפּוֹ) d. 6 a טרף

מְטָת[b] ׳וּ Chald. Peal pret. 3 pers. s. f.; ׳וּ bef. lab. מטא

מַטַּת[c] noun fem. sing., constr. of מִטָּה dec. 10 . נטה

מֹטֹת[d] defect. for מוֹטוֹת (q. v.) . . . . מוט

מִטָּתוֹ noun fem. s., suff. 3 pers. s. m. fr. מִטָּה d. 10 נטה

מִטָּתִי[e] id., suff. 1 pers. sing. . . . . . נטה

מִטָּתֶךָ[f] id., suff. 2 pers. sing. masc. [for מִטָּתְךָ] . נטה

מַטֹּתָם[g] defect. for מַטּוֹתָם (q. v.) . . . נטה

מֵי an obsol. sing. *water* (a trace of which is found in the pr. name אֲחוּמַי *brother of water*); pl. מַיִם, constr. מֵי and reduplicated מֵימֵי, with suff. מֵימֶיךָ (§ 38. rem. 2, & § 45).—I. *waters, water;* joined with the adj. and verb in the pl., with the latter sometimes also in the sing.; מֵי רֹאשׁ *juice of poppies;* מֵי רַגְלַיִם *water of the feet*, by euphemism for *urine.* Emblemat. of abundance, overwhelming danger, terror, arrogance.—II. in pr. names. מֵי זָהָב (*water*, i. e. *lustre of gold*) of a man, Ge. 36. 39.—מֵי הַיַּרְקוֹן (*water of a greenish yellow*) of a town in the tribe of Dan, Jos. 19. 46.—מֵי־נֶפְתּוֹחַ (*waters of opening*) of a fountain in the tribe of Judah, Jos. 15. 9; 18. 15.

מֵידְבָא (*water of rest*, see Root דָּבָא) pr. name of a city in the tribe of Reuben.

מִי ׳וְ״ ׳וּ pron. pers.—I. interrog. *who?* usually of persons, rarely of things, as מִי־שְׁמֶךָ *what is thy name?* put in the genitive, בַּת־מִי *whose daughter?* With prep. לְמִי *to whom?* מִמִּי *from whom, more than who?* אֶת־מִי *whom?* בְּמִי *by whom?*—II. without interrogation, *whoever, any one;* מִי אֲשֶׁר *whosoever.*

מֵי ׳וּ noun masc. pl., constr. of מַיִם, [from מֵי § 45]; also pr. n. in compos. as מֵי זָהָב, &c. מי

מֵאִתִּי[i] Kh. מֵאִתִּי & מִי אִתִּי, see מִי, K. מֵאִתִּי אתי את

מִיָּבֵשׁ pref. ·מִ) pr. name of a place . יבש

מִיָּגוֹן[k] pref. id.) noun masc. sing. dec. 3 a יגה

מִיגוֹנָם[l] pref. מִ [for ׳מִיְּגוֹ]) id., suff. 3 pers. pl. m. יגה

מִיגִיעוֹ[m] ׳וּ pref. id.) n. m. s. (יְגִיעַ), suff. 3 p. m. s. d. 1 a יגע

מִיַּד pref. ·מִ) noun com. sing. dec. 2 a . . יד

מִיַּד ׳וּ pref. id.) id. constr. st.; ׳וּ bef. lab. . יד

מֵידְבָא pr. name of a place . . . . מי

מֵידָד ׳וּ pr. name masc.; ׳וּ bef. lab. . . ידד

מִיָּדָהּ pref. ·מִ) n. com. s., suff. 3 p. s. f. fr. יָד d. 2 a יד

מִיָּדָיו[n] pref. id.) id. du. (יָדַיִם), suff. 3 pers. s. m. יד

מִיָּדוֹ pref. id.) id. sing., suff. 3 pers. sing. masc. יד

מִיָּדִי pref. id.) id. sing., suff. 1 pers. sing. . יד

מִידֵי pref. מִ [for מִיְּדֵי]) id. du., constr. of יָדַיִם יד

מִיָּדְךָ pref. ·מִ) id. sing., suff. 2 pers. sing. masc. יד

מִיָּדֵךְ pref. id.) id. sing., suff. 2 pers. sing. fem. יד

מִיָּדֶךָ[o] ׳וּ pref. id.) id. sing., suff. 2 p. s. m.; ׳וּ bef. lab. יד

מִיֶּדְכֶם pref. id.) id. sing., suff. 2 pers. pl. masc. [for יֶדְכֶם § 31. rem. 2] . . . . יד

מִיֶּדְכֶן[p] pref. id.) id. sing., suff. 2 pers. pl. fem. . יד

מִיָּדָם pref. id) id. sing., suff. 3 pers. pl. masc. יד

[a] Is. 22. 17. [b] Job 14. 4. [c] Eze. 4. 14. [d] Ezr. 6. 21. [e] Le. 16. 16, 19. [f] 2 Sa. 11. 4. [g] Le. 14. 19. [h] Eze. 24. 13. [i] Le. 15. 31. [k] Ge. 43. 23. [l] Is. 45. 3. [m] Je. 41. 8. [n] Eze. 34. 29. [o] Is. 61. 3. [p] Is. 60. 21. [q] Jon. 3. 7. [r] Ezr. 6. 14. [s] Ge. 27. 4, 7, 9, etc. [t] Is. 14. 19. [u] Ex. 12. 37. [x] Zec. 10. 1. [y] Job 37. 6. [z] Hag. 2. 15. [a] Ge. 49. 9. [b] Da. 4. 19, 21. [c] 2 Ki. 4. 21. [d] Le. 26. 13. [e] Ps. 6. 7. [f] Ex. 7. 28. [g] Ex. 7. 12. [h] Ex. 10. 8. [i] Is. 44. 24. [k] Est. 9. 22. [l] Je. 31. 13. [m] Ne. 5. 13. [n] Ex. 32. 19. [o] 1 Ch. 29. 14. [p] Eze. 13. 21, 23.

מִיָּדֵנוּ[a] pref. ·מִ)(id. sing., suff. 1 pers. pl. . יד

מְיֻדָּע[b] Kh. מְיֻדָּע Pual part. s. m.; K. מוֹדַע subst. ידע

מְיֻדָּעַי[c] ·וּ[d] id. pl. with suff. 1 pers. sing.; וּ bef. lab. ידע

מְיֻדָּעִי[e] וּ id. sing., suff. 1 pers. sing.; וּ id. . ידע

מְיֻדָּעָיו[f] וּ id. pl., suff. 3 pers. sing. masc.; וּ id. . ידע

מְיֻדַּעַת[g] Kh. מְיֻדַּעַת, K. מוּדַעַת Pu. or Hoph. part., fem. of מְיֻדָּע or מוּדָע . . . ידע

מֵיהוּדָה וּ pref. מֵ [for מִיְהוּ׳], pr. name of a man and a tribe; וּ bef. lab. . . . ידה

מֵיְהוָה וּ the most sacred name of God (יהוה) with the vowels of אֲדֹנָי, whence pref. מֵ bef. gutt. for ·מִ . . . . . הוה

מִיּוֹם וּ[h] pref. ·מִ)(noun masc. sing. dec. 1a, but pl. irr. יָמִים (§ 45); וּ bef. lab. . יום

מִיּוֹרְדֵי[i] pref. id.)(Kh. יוֹרְדֵי Kal part. pl. c. masc.; K. יְרִדִי inf. with suff. 1 pers. sing. . ירד

מִיּוֹשֵׁב[k] pref. id.)(Kal part. act. sing. masc. dec. 7b ישב

מִיּוֹשְׁבֵי[l] pref. id.)(id. pl., constr. st. . . ישב

מִיִּזְרְעֶאל pref. id.)(pr. name of a place . זרע

מִיחִים[m] according to some copies, see מְחִים . מחה

מְיַחֵל[n] Piel (§ 14. rem. 1) part. sing. masc. dec. 7b יחל

מִיָּחֵף[o] pref. ·מִ)(adj. masc. sing. . . . יחף

מֵיטַב וּ[p] noun masc. sing., constr. of [מֵיטָב] d. 2b יטב

מִיָּטְבָתָה pref. ·מִ)(pr. name of a place . . יטב

מֵיטִיב[q] Hiph. part. sing. masc. dec. 1b . . יטב

מֵיטִיבֵי[r] id. pl., constr. st. . . . . . יטב

מֵיטִיבִים[s] id. pl., abs. st. . . . . . . יטב

מִיָּיִן / מִיַּיִן } pref. ·מִ)(noun masc. sing. dec. 6h . יון

מִיֵּין[t] וּ pref. id.)(id. constr. st.; וּ bef. lab. . יון

מִיֵּינָהּ[u] pref. id.)(id. with suff. 3 pers. sing. fem. יון

מִיֵּינוֹ[x] pref. id.)(id., suff. 3 pers. sing. masc. . יון

מִיכָא pr. name masc., see מִיכָיָה.

מִיכָאֵל וּ (*who is like unto God?*) pr. name—I. *Michael* the archangel.—II. of several men.

מִיכָה (for מִיכָיָהוּ q. v.) pr. name masc.—I. *Micah*, the prophet.—II. 2 Ch. 34. 20, called מִיכָיָה in 2 Ki. 22. 12.—III. stands for מִיכָיְהוּ & מִיכָיָהוּ q. v.

מִיכָיָה (*who is like unto the Lord?*) pr. name masc. —I. Ne. 12. 35, for which מִיכָא Ne. 11. 17, 22.—II. Ne. 12. 41. See also מִיכָה.

מִיכָיָהּ pr. name m. Kh. מִיכָיָה, K. מִיכָה, Je. 26. 18.

מִיכָיָהוּ (i. q. מִיכָיָה q. v.) pr. name—I. masc. 2 Ch. 17. 7.—II. fem., wife of Rehoboam, 2 Ch. 13. 2.

מִיכָיְהוּ (id.) pr. name masc.—I. Ju. 17. 1, 4, called מִיכָה vers. 5, 8, 9, 10.—II. of a prophet, 1 Ki. 28. 8; 2 Ch. 18. 7, called מִיכָיְהוּ ver. 24, מִכָהוּ ver. 8, Kh.

מִיכַל noun masc. [constr. of מִיכָל dec. 2b] *a brook*, 2 Sa. 17. 20. Root uncertain.

מִיכַל / מִיכָל וּ } pr. name of the daughter of Saul, the wife of David.

מִילְדֵי[y] pref. ·מִ)(noun masc. pl. constr. fr. יֶלֶד d. 6a ילד

מִילִידֵי[z] pref. מִ [for מִיְלִידֵי], noun masc. pl. constr. from [יָלִיד] dec. 3a . . . . ילד

מַיִם וָ׳ / מָיִם וּ׳ &[a] וָ׳ } noun m. pl. [of מַי irr. § 38. r. 2, & §45]; וּ bef. lab., for וָ see lett. ו מי

מִיָּם וּ׳ pref. ·מִ)(noun masc. s. d. 8a; וּ bef. lab. ים

מִיַּם pref. id.)(id. constr. st. (only before סוּף) ים

מִיָּמַי[b] pref. id.)(noun masc. pl. (יָמִים), with suff. 1 pers. sing. irr. of יוֹם (§ 45) . . יום

מֵימַי[c] וּ[d] the foll. with suff. 1 pers. s.; וּ bef. lab. מי

מֵימֵי noun masc. pl. constr., a reduplicated form from מַיִם (§ 45) . . . . . מי

מִימֵי pref. מִ [for מִיְמֵי], noun m., pl. c. of יָמִים, irr. of יוֹם (§ 45) . . . . . יום

מֵימֶיהָ noun m. pl., suff. 3 p. s. f. irr. of מַיִם (§ 45) מי

מֵימֵיהֶם וּ[e] id., suff. 3 pers. pl. masc.; וּ bef. lab. מי

מֵימָיו id., suff. 3 pers. sing. masc. . . . מי

מִיָּמָיו[f] pref. ·מִ)(noun masc. pl. (יָמִים), suff. 3 pers. sing. masc. irr. of יוֹם (§ 45) . . יום

מֵימֶיךָ וּ[g] noun masc. pl. [מֵימִים], suff. 2 pers. sing. masc. irr. of מַיִם (§ 45); וּ bef. lab. מי

מִיָּמֶיךָ[h] pref. ·מִ)(the foll. with suff. 2 pers. sing. m. יום

מִיָּמִים pref. id.)(noun masc. pl., irr. of יוֹם (§ 45) יום

מִיַּמִּים pref. id.)(noun masc., pl. of יָם dec. 8a . ים

מִיֹּמָיִם[i] pref. id.)(n. m., du. of יוֹם d. 1a (comp. § 45) יום

מִיָּמִין (*at the right hand*) pr. name masc.—I. 1 Ch. 24. 9.—II. of another person, called also מִנְיָמִין, comp. Ne. 12. 5 with vers. 17, 41.

מִיָּמִין pref. ·מִ)(noun masc. sing. dec. 3a . ימן

מִימִין pref. מִ [for מִיְמִין], id., constr. st. . ימן

מֵימֵינוּ[k] noun masc. pl. [מֵימִים], suff. 1 pers. pl. irr. of מַיִם (§ 45) . . . . . מי

מִימִינוֹ pref. מִ [for מִיְמִי׳], noun masc. sing., suff. 3 pers. sing. masc. from יָמִין dec. 3a . ימן

מִימִינִי[l] pref. id.)(id. with suff. 1 pers. sing. . ימן

מַיְמִינִים[m] Hiph. part. m. pl. [of מַיְמִין § 20. r. 14] d. 1b ימן

מִימִינְךָ[n] pref. מִ [for מִיְמִי׳], noun masc. sing., suff. 2 pers. sing. masc. from יָמִין dec. 3a ימן

מִימִינֵךְ[o] pref. id.)(id., suff. 2 pers. sing. fem. . ימן

מִימִינָם[p] pref. id.)(id., suff. 3 pers. pl. masc. . ימן

---

[a] Ju. 13. 23. [b] Ru. 2. 1. [c] Ps. 88. 9, 19. [d] Job 19. 14. [e] Ps. 55. 14. [f] 2 Ki. 10. 11. [g] Is. 12. 5. [h] Le. 22. 27. [i] Ps. 30. 4. [k] Is. 49. 19. [l] Ju. 21. 9, 12. [m] Ps. 66. 15. [n] Ps. 69. 4. [o] Je. 2. 25. [p] Ex. 22. 4. [q] 1 Sa. 16. 17. [r] Pr. 30. 29. [s] Ju. 19. 22. [t] Da. 1. 5. [u] Je. 51. 7. [x] Ge. 9. 24. [y] Ex. 2. 6. [z] 1 Ch. 20. 4. [a] 2 Ki. 6. 22. [b] Job 27. 6. [c] 1 Sa. 25. 11. [d] Ho. 2. 7. [e] Eze. 12. 19. [f] 1 Ki. 1. 6. [g] Eze. 12. 18. [h] 1 Sa. 25. 28. [i] Ho. 6. 2. [k] La. 5. 4. [l] Ps. 16. 8. [m] 1 Ch. 12. 2. [n] Ps. 91. 7. [o] Eze. 16. 46. [p] Ex. 14. 22, 29.

מִיָּמִן וּ׳ pr. name masc., see מִיָּמִין; וּ bef. lab.
מִיָּנוֹחָה pref. ·מִ) pr. name of a place (יָנוֹחַ) with parag. ה . . . . . . נוח
מֵינִיקוֹת[a] Hiph. part. fem., pl. of [מֵינִיקָה] dec. 10 . ינק
מֵינִיקוֹתַיִךְ[b] id. pl. with suff. 2 pers. sing. fem. . ינק
מֵינֶקֶת id. sing. dec. 13a . . . . . ינק
מֵינִקְתּוֹ[c] id. sing., suff. 3 pers. sing. masc. . ינק
מְיֻסָּד[d] וּ Pual part. sing. masc.; וּ bef. lab. . . יסד
מִיסְּדוֹת[e] Kh. מֵיסְדוֹת, K. מוֹסְדוֹת, noun fem. pl. constr. from מוּסָדָה, or מֵיסָדָה dec. 11a יסד
מְיֻסָּדִים[f] Pual part. masc., pl. of מְיֻסָּד dec. 2b . יסד
מֵיסַךְ[g] Kh. מֵיסַךְ [for מֵסַךְ], K. מוּסַךְ, noun masc. sing., constr. [of סָךְ׳] . . . סכך
מְיַסְּרֶךָּ[h] [for מְיַסֶּרְךָ § 2. rem. 2]; Piel part. [מְיַסֵּר], suff. 2 pers. sing. masc. dec. 7b . יסר
מִיַּעֲקֹב pref. ·מִ) pr. name of a man and a people עקב
מִיָּעַר[i] / מִיַּעַר } pref. id.) noun masc. sing. dec. 6d . יער
מֵיפָעַת / מֵיפַעַת } pref. id.) pr. name of a place . . יפע
מִיץ[k] וּ׳ noun masc. sing.; וּ bef. lab. . . מוץ
מִיצִיאָיו[l] וּ pref. מִ [for מִיְּצִי׳], K. אֵי׳ adj. pl. constr. masc., Kh. אָו׳, with suff. 3 pers. sing. masc. from [יָצִיא] dec. 3a; וּ id. . . יצא
מֵיצָקֶת[m] Kh. מֵיצָקֶת, K. מוּצָקֶת, Hiph. part. s. fem. יצק
מִיְּקָבִים[n] pref. ·מִ) noun masc. pl. of יֶקֶב dec. 6a . יקב
מִיִּקְבֶךָ וּ pref. id.) id. sing., suff. 2 pers. sing. masc. for בְךָ׳; וּ bef. lab. . . . יקב
מִיָּקוּד[o] pref. id.) Kal part. pass. sing. masc. . יקד
מְיָרְאִים[p] Piel part. masc., pl. of [מְיָרֵא] dec. 7b . ירא
מִיִּרְאָתוֹ[q] pref. ·מִ) Kal inf. from (יִרְאָה), suff. 3 pers. sing. masc. (§ 8. rem. 10) . . . ירא
מִיִּרְאָתֶךָ[r] pref. id.) id. (subst.) with suff. 2 pers. sing. m. ירא
מִיַּרְדֵּן pref. id.) pr. name of a river . . ירד
מִירוּשָׁלֵם / מִירוּשָׁלַיִם וּ׳ } pref. מִ [for מִיְרוּ׳], pr. name of a place ירה
מִירִיחוֹ pref. id.) pr. name of a place . . רוח
מִיַּרְכּוֹתֵי[s] pref. ·מִ) Kh. יַרְכּוֹתֵי, K. יַרְכְּתֵי׳ see the foll. ירך
מִיַּרְכְּתֵי pref. id.) noun fem., du., constr. of יַרְכָּתַיִם [from יַרְכָּה § 39. No. 3. rem. 3] . ירך
מִיְּרֻשָּׁתֶךָ pref. id.) noun fem. sing., suff. 2 pers. sing. masc. from יְרֻשָּׁה dec. 10 . . . ירש
מֵישָׁא pr. name masc. . . . . . ישה
מִישָׁאֵל וּ׳ (*who is what God is?* comp. מִי, ·שֶׁ or ·שַׁ) pr. name m. of several persons, especially one of the companions of Daniel, Da. 1.6; 2.17.

מִיְּשְׁבֵי[u] defect. for מִיּוֹשְׁבֵי (q. v.) . . . ישב
מִישׁוּעָתִי[x] pref. מִ [for מִיְּשׁוּ׳], noun fem. sing., suff. 1 pers. sing. from יְשׁוּעָה dec. 10 . . ישע
מִישׁוֹר noun masc. sing. . . . . . ישר
מֵישַׁךְ Chald. pr. name masc. Da. 2.49; 3.12.
מִיְּשֵׁנֵי[y] pref. ·מִ) adj. pl. constr. masc. from יָשֵׁן dec. 5a (§ 34. rem. 2) . . . ישן
מֵישַׁע וּ׳ pr. name masc.; וּ bef. lab. . . ישע
מִיֶּשַׁע[z] pref. ·מִ) noun masc. sing. (suff. יִשְׁעִי) dec. 6a (§ 35. rem. 5) . . . ישע
מְיֻשָּׁר[a] Pual part. sing. masc. . . . . ישר
מִיֹּשֶׁר* pref. ·מִ) noun masc. sing. d. 6c *Pr. 11.24. ישר
מִישֹׁר defect. for מִישׁוֹר (q. v.) . . . ישר
מִיִּשְׂרָאֵל וּ׳ pref. ·מִ) pr. name of a people; וּ bef. lab. שׂרה
מֵישָׁרִים וּ׳ noun m. pl. [of מֵישָׁר], also *adverbially*; וּ id. ישר
מֵיתֶר וּ׳[b] noun masc. sing. (suff. יִתְרוֹ) dec. 6a; וּ id. יתר
מֵיתָרַי[c] noun masc. pl., suff. 1 pers. s. fr. [מֵיתָר] d. 2b יתר
מֵיתְרֵיהֶם וּ׳[d] id., suff. 3 pers. pl. masc.; וּ bef. lab. יתר
מֵיתָרָיו id., suff. 3 pers. pl. masc. . . . יתר
מֵיתָרַיִךְ[e] id., suff. 2 pers. sing. fem. . . . יתר
מָךְ וּ׳[f] Kal pret. 3 pers. sing. masc., or (Le. 27.8) part. sing. masc.; וּ bef. lab. . . מוך
מַכְאִב[g] Hiph. part. sing. masc. . . . כאב
מִכְּאֵב[h] pref. ·מִ) noun masc. sing. dec. 1a . כאב
מַכְאֹבוֹ[i] וּ noun masc. sing., suff. 3 pers. sing. masc. from מַכְאוֹב dec. 1b; וּ bef. lab. . . כאב
מַכְאֹבוֹת[k] id. with pl. fem. term. . . . כאב
מַכְאֹבִי id. sing., suff. 1 pers. sing. . . . כאב
מַכְאֹבָיו[l] id. pl. masc., suff. 3 pers. sing. masc. . כאב
מַכְאֹבִים[m] id. pl., abs. st. . . . . . כאב
מַכְאֹבֵינוּ[n] וּ id. pl., suff. 1 pers. pl.; וּ bef. lab. . כאב
מַכְאֹבֵךְ[o] id. sing., suff. 2 pers. sing. fem. . . כאב
מַכְאוֹב id. sing. abs. st. dec. 1b . . . כאב
מַכְאוֹבִי[p] וּ id. sing., suff. 1 pers. sing.; וּ bef. lab. . כאב
מַכְאוֹבִים[q] id. pl., abs. st. . . . . כאב
מְכֻבָּד[r] Pual part. sing. masc. . . . . כבד
מְכַבְּדוֹ[s] וּ Piel part. sing. masc. (מְכַבֵּד), suff. 3 pers. sing. masc. dec. 7b; וּ bef. lab. . כבד
מִכְּבֹדוֹ[t] pref. ·מִ) noun masc. sing., suff. 3 pers. sing. masc. from כָּבוֹד dec. 3a . . . כבד
מְכַבְּדַי[u] Piel part. pl. masc., suff. 1 p. s. fr. מְכַבֵּד׳ d. 7b כבד
מַכְבִּיד[x] וּ Hiph. part. sing. masc.; וּ bef. lab. . כבד
מְכַבְּדֶיהָ[y] Piel part. pl. masc., suff. 3 pers. sing. fem. from מְכַבֵּד dec. 7b . . . . כבד
מְכַבֶּה Piel part. sing. masc. . . . . כבה
מִכָּבוֹד pref. ·מִ) noun masc. sing. dec. 3a . . כבד

[a] Ge. 32. 16. [b] Is. 49. 23. [c] 2 Ch. 22. 11. [d] 1 Ki. 7. 10. [e] Eze. 41. 8. [f] Ca. 5. 15. [g] 2 Ki. 16. 18. [h] De. 8. 5. [i] Ps. 80. 14. [k] Pr. 30. 33. [l] 2 Ch. 32. 21. [m] 2 Ki. 4. 5. [n] Je. 48. 33. [o] Is. 30. 14. [p] Ne. 6. 9, 14. [q] 2 Sa. 3. 11. [r] Is. 63. 17. [s] 1 Ki. 6. 16. [t] 2 Ch. 20. 11. [u] Ju. 20. 15. [x] Ps. 22. 2. [y] Da. 12. 2. [z] Job 5. 4. [a] 1 Ki. 6. 35. [b] Le. 14. 17. [c] Je. 10. 20. [d] Nu. 3. 37; 4. 32. [e] Is. 54. 2. [f] Le. 25. 47. [g] Eze. 28. 24. [h] Is. 65. 14. [i] 2 Ch. 6. 29. [k] Is. 53. 3. [l] Ex. 3. 7. [m] Ec. 2. 23. [n] Is. 53. 4. [o] Je. 30. 15. [p] Ps. 38. 18. [q] Ps. 32. 10. [r] Is. 58. 13. [s] Pr. 14. 31. [t] Eze. 43. 2. [u] 1 Sa. 2. 30. [x] Hab. 2. 6. [y] La. 1. 8.

מַכְבֵּנָא (*circuit*, or *band*, Syr. כבן *to bind round*) pr. name of a town in Judah, 1 Ch. 2. 49.

מַכְבַּנַּי (*binder*) pr. name masc. 1 Ch. 12. 13.

מְכַבְּסִים[a] Piel part. masc., pl. of [מְכַבֵּס] dec. 7b . כבס

מִכְבָּר noun masc. sing. dec. 2b . . . כבר

מִכְבַּר id., constr. st. . . . . . . כבר

מִכַּדֵּךְ[b] pref. מִ)(noun com. sing., suff. 2 pers. sing. fem. from כַּד dec. 8d . . . כדד

מַכָּה ו׳ noun fem. sing. dec. 10; וּ bef. lab. . נכה

מַכַּת ו׳ constr. of the foll.; וּ id. . . . נכה

מַכֶּה Hiph. part. sing. masc. (§ 25. No. 2b) d. 9a נכה

מֻכֵּה[c] Hoph. part. sing. masc., constr. of [מֻכֶּה] d. 9a נכה

מַכֵּהוּ Hiph. part. sing. masc. (מַכֶּה § 25. No. 2b), suff. 3 pers. sing. masc. dec. 9a . . נכה

מִכַּהֵן pref. מִ)(Piel inf. constr. (§ 14. rem. 1) כהן

מִכֹּהֵן pref. id.)(noun masc. sing. dec. 7b . כהן

מִכּוֹכְבֵי[d] pref. id.)(noun m. pl. constr. fr. כּוֹכָב d. 2b כבב

מָכוֹן ו׳[e] noun masc. sing. dec. 3a; וּ bef. lab. . כון

מְכוֹן id., constr. st. . . . . . . כון

מִכּוּן וּ pref. מִ)(pr. name masc.; וּ bef. lab. . כון

מְכוֹנוֹ[f] noun m. s., suff. 3 pers. s. m. fr. מָכוֹן d. 3a כון

מְכוֹנֶיהָ[g] id. pl., suff. 3 pers. sing. fem. . . . כון

מְכוֹנֹתָיו[h] noun f. pl., suff. 3 pers. s. m. fr. מְכוֹנָה d. 10 כון

מִכּוֹר pref. מִ)(noun masc. sing. . . . כור

מְכוּרֹתָם[i] noun f. s., suff. 3 p. pl. m. fr. [מְכוּרָה] d. 10 מכר

מִכּוּשׁ ו׳ pref. מִ)(pr. name of a country; וּ bef. lab. כוש

מִכּוּשִׁים pref. id. gent. noun, pl. of כּוּשִׁי . . כוש

מַכּוֹת ו׳[k] noun fem., pl. of מַכָּה d. 10; וּ bef. lab. נכה

מִכְוַת[l] noun fem. sing., constr. of מִכְוָה dec. 10 כוה

מִכּוּתָה וּ pref. מִ)(pr. name of a region; וּ bef. lab. כות

מַכּוֹתֶהָ[m] / מַכּוֹתֶיהָ } noun fem. pl., suff. 3 pers. sing. fem. from מַכָּה dec. 10 . . . } נכה

מַכּוֹתָם[n] id. with suff. 3 pers. pl. masc. (§ 4. rem. 2) נכה

מִכֹּחַ[o] pref. מִ)(noun masc. sing. dec. 1a . . כחח

מִכֹּחֲכֶם[xx] וּ pref. id.)(id. with suff. 2 p. m. pl.; וּ bef. lab. כחח

מִכַּחַשׁ[p] וּ pref. id.)(noun masc. s. d. 6d; וּ bef. lab. כחש

מָכִי pr. name masc. . . . . . . מוך

מֻכֵּי[q] Hoph. part. pl. constr. masc. from מֻכֶּה (§ 25. No. 2b) dec. 9a . . . . . . נכה

מִכָיְהוּ defect. for מִיכָיְהוּ q. v.

מֻכִּים[r] Hoph. part. m., pl. of [מֻכֶּה] (§ 25. No. 2b) d. 9a נכה

מֵכִין Hiph. part. sing. masc. . . . . כון

מִכִּיס[s] pref. מִ)(noun masc. sing. dec. 1a . . כוס

מָכִיר pr. name masc. . . . . . . מכר

מַכִּיר[t] Hiph. part. sing. masc. dec. 1b . . . נכר

מַכִּירִים id. pl., abs. st. . . . . . . נכר

מַכִּירֵךְ[u] id. sing., suff. 2 pers. sing. fem. . . . נכר

[מָכַךְ] *to waste, pine away*, Ps. 106. 43. Niph. *to decay*, or *sink*, Ec. 10. 18. Hoph. *to decay, perish*, Job 24. 24.

מַכֵּךְ[v] Hiph. part. sing. masc. (מַכֶּה § 25. No. 2b), suff. 2 pers. sing. fem. dec. 9a . . נכה

מִכֹּל ו׳ / מִכָּל־ ו׳ } pref. מִ)(noun masc. sing. dec. 8c; וּ bef. lab. . . . . . } כלל

מְכַלֶּה Piel part. sing. masc. . . . . כלה

מִכְלוֹל noun masc. sing. . . . . . כלל

מְכַלּוֹת[w] Piel part. f. pl. [of מְכַלָּה d. 10] fr. מְכַלֶּה m. כלה

מִכְלוֹת[x] noun fem., pl. of [מִכְלָה] dec. 10 . . כלה

מִכְּלֵי ו׳[a] pl. constr. of the foll.; וּ bef. lab. . כלה

מִכְּלִי[b] pref. מִ)(noun m. s. d. 6i, pl. irr. כֵּלִים (§ 45) כלה

מַכְלִים[c] Hiph. part. sing. masc. . . . . כלם

מִכֵּלִים[d] pref. מִ)(noun m. pl. [prop. from כֶּלֶה=כֶּל] see כְּלִי (§ 45) . . . . . כלה

מִכֵּלֵינוּ[e] pref. id.)(id. pl. with suff. 1 pers. pl. . כלה

מִכִּלְיוֹתֵיהֶם[f] pref. id.)(noun masc. pl., suff. 3 pers. pl. masc. from [כִּלְיָה] dec. 12b . . . כלה

מְכַלְכֵּל[g] Pilp. part. sing. masc. (§ 6. No. 4) . כול

מִכְלַל[h] noun masc. sing., constr. of [מִכְלָל] dec. 2b כלל

מַכְלִם[i] defect. for מַכְלִים (q. v.) . . . כלם

מִכֻּלָּם[k] ו׳ pref. מִ)(noun masc. sing., suff. 3 pers. sing. masc. from כֹּל dec. 8c; וּ bef. lab. כלל

מִכְּלִמּוֹת[m] pref. id.)(noun fem., pl. of כְּלִמָּה dec. 10 כלם

מִכֻּלָּנוּ[n] pref. id.)(n. m. s., suff. 1 p. pl. fr. כֹּל d. 8c כלל

מַכֹּלֶת[o] noun fem. sing. contr. from מַאֲכֹלֶת . אכל

מִכֶּם pref. prep. מִ with suff. 2 p. pl. m. see מִן (§ 5) מנן

מִכְּמוֹשׁ pref. מִ)(pr. name of an idol, see כְּמוֹשׁ.

מִכְמָס pr. name of a place . . . . . כמס

מִכְמָר[p] noun masc. sing. . . . . . כמר

מִכְמֶרֶת[q] noun fem. sing. . . . . . כמר

מִכְמָשׁ / מִכְמָשׂ } pr. name of a place, see מִכְמָס . כמס

מִכְמְתָת pr. name of a town on the borders of Ephraim and Manasseh, Jos. 16. 6; 17. 7.

מַכְנַדְבַי pr. name masc. Ezr. 10. 40.

מִכְנְסֵי ו׳ noun fem. du. constr. [of מִכְנָסַיִם, from מִכְנָס] dec. 2b; וּ bef. lab. . . . כנס

מִכְּנַף[r] pref. מִ)(noun fem. s., constr. of כָּנָף d. 4a כנף

מִכִּנֶּרֶת pref. id.)(pr. name of a place . . כנר

מְכֻנָתָהּ[s] n. f. s., suff. 3 p. s. f. fr. מְכֹנָה see under the R. כון

מֶכֶס[t] noun masc. sing. (with suff. מִכְסָם) dec. 6a כסס

מִכִּסֵּא[u] pref. מִ)(noun masc. sing. d. 7b (§ 36. r. 3) כסא

מִכִּסְאוֹ[v] pref. id.)(id., suff. 3 pers. sing. masc. . כסא

---

[a] Mal. 3. 2. [b] Ge. 24. 17, 43. [c] Is. 53. 4. [d] Na. 3. 16. [e] 2 Ch. 6. 2.
[f] Ezr. 2. 68. [g] Ps. 104. 5. [h] Ezr. 3. 3. [i] Eze. 29. 14. [k] Pr. 20. 30.
[l] Le. 13. 24. [m] Je. 49. 17. [n] Ps. 64. 8. [o] Je. 48. 45. [p] Ps. 59. 13.
[q] Je. 18. 21. [r] Ex. 5. 16. [s] Is. 46. 6. [t] Ps. 142. 5. [u] Ru. 2. 19.
[v] Is. 14. 29. [w] Le. 26. 16. [x] 2 Ch. 4. 21. [a] 2 Ch. 36. 7. [b] Je. 48. 11.
[c] Ju. 18. 7. [d] Est. 1. 7. [e] 1 Sa. 9. 7. [f] Je. 12. 2. [g] Mal. 3. 2.
[h] Ps. 50. 2. [i] Job 11. 3. [k] Da. 1. 19. [l] Ps. 34. 20. [m] Is. 50. 6.
[n] 2 Ki. 9. 5. [o] 1 Ki. 5. 25. [p] Is. 51. 20. [q] Is. 19. 8. [r] Is. 24. 16.
[s] Zec. 5. 11. [t] Nu. 31. 28, 41. [u] 1 Ki. 1. 37. [v] Jon. 3. 6. [xx] Job 6. 22.

מְכַסְאוֹתָם[a] pref. ·מִ)(id. pl. f., suff. 3 p. pl. m. (§ 4. r. 2) כסא

מִכִּסְאֲךָ[b] pref. id.)(id. sing., suff. 2 p. s. m. (for כִּסְאֲךָ) כסא

מְכַסֶּה Piel part. sing. masc. . . . כסה

מִכְסֵה וּ' constr. of the foll.; וּ bef. lab. . . כסה

מִכְסֶה noun masc. sing. dec. 9a . . . כסה

מְכַסֵּהוּ id., suff. 3 pers. sing. masc. . . . כסה

מִכּוֹסוֹ[c] וּ pref. ·מִ)(noun fem. sing., suff. 3 pers. sing. masc. from כּוֹס dec. 1a; וּ bef. lab. . כוס

מְכַסּוֹת Piel part. f. pl. [of מְכַסָּה d. 10], fr. מְכַסֶּה m. כסה

מְכֻסּוֹת[d] Pual part. fem. pl. [of מְכֻסָּה dec. 10, from מְכֻסֶּה masc.] . . . . . כסה

מְכַסֶּיךָ[e] וּ noun masc. pl. (or sing. § 38. rem. 1), suff. 2 pers. sing. m. fr. מְכַסֶּה d. 9a; וּ bef. lab. כסה

מְכַסִּים[f] Piel part. masc. pl. of מְכַסֶּה dec. 9a כסה

מְכֻסִּים[g] Pual part. masc. pl. of [מְכֻסֶּה] dec. 9a . כסה

מְכַסֵּךְ[h] noun masc. sing., suff. 2 pers. sing. fem. from מְכַסֶּה dec. 9a . . . . כסה

מִכְסָם[i] וּ noun masc. sing., suff. 3 pers. pl. masc. from מֶכֶס; וּ bef. lab. . . . כסס

מִכֶּסֶף / מִכָּסֶף } pref. ·מִ)(noun masc. sing. dec. 6a (§ 35. rem. 2) . . . . . } כסף

מִכַּסְפִּי[k] וּ pref. id.)(id., suff. 1 pers. sing.; וּ bef. lab. כסף

מִכַּסְפָּם[l] pref. id.)(id., suff. 3 pers. pl. masc. . כסף

מִכְסַת[m] noun fem. sing., constr. of מִכְסָה dec. 10 כסס

מַכְעִיסִים Hiph. part. masc., pl. of [מַכְעִיס] dec. 1b כעס

מִכַּעַס pref. ·מִ)(noun masc. sing. dec. 6d . כעס

מַכְעִסִים defect. for מַכְעִיסִים (q. v.) . . . כעס

מִכַּעַשׂ[n] pref. ·מִ)(noun masc. sing. dec. 6d . כעשׂ

מִכַּף וּ' pref. id.)(noun fem. s. d. 8d; וּ bef. lab. כפף

מִכְּפִירִים[o] pref. id.)(noun masc., pl. of כְּפִיר dec. 1a כפר

מִכַּפֵּר[p] pref. id.)(Piel inf. constr. . . . כפר

מִכַּפְתּוֹר pref. id.)(pr. name of a region . . כפתר

מְכַפְּתִין[q] Chald. Pael part. m., pl. of [מְכַפֵּת] dec. 2b כפת

מִכַּפְתֹּר pref. ·מִ)(pr. name of a region . . כפתר

מָכַר וּ'[r] fut. יִמְכֹּר. I. *to sell.*—II. *to give in marriage,* for a price, Ge. 31. 15; Ex. 21. 7.—III. *to deliver, give up* into the power of another. Niph. I. *to be sold.*—II. *to be delivered up.* Hithp. I. *to be sold,* De. 28. 68.—II. *to sell oneself, give oneself up,* sc. to do evil.

מָכִיר (*sold*) pr. name—I. of a son of Manasseh; patronym. מָכִירִי Nu. 26. 29.—II. 2 Sa. 9. 4, 5; 17. 27.

מֶכֶר masc. dec. 6a (with suff. מִכְרָהּ).—I. *ware, merchandise,* Ne. 13. 16.—II. *price, value.*

מִכְרִי (*price of the Lord,* for מִכְרִיָּה) pr. name masc. 1 Ch. 9. 8.

מִמְכָּר masc. dec. 2b.—I. *sale.*—II. *thing sold.*—III. *ware, merchandise.*

מִמְכֶּרֶת fem. *sale,* Le. 25. 42.

מָכֹר[s] וּ'[t] Kal inf. abs.; וּ bef. lab. . . מכר

מֶכֶר[u] noun masc. sing. (suff. מִכְרָהּ) dec. 6a . מכר

מֹכֵר[x] Kal part. sing. masc. dec. 7b . . מכר

מְכֻרְבָּל[y] Pual part. sing. masc. (§ 7) . . כרבל

מָכְרָה[z] Kal pret. 3 pers. sing. fem. . . . מכר

מִכְרָה[a] id. imp. s. m. [מְכֹר] with parag. ה (§ 8. r. 11) מכר

מִכְרָהּ[b] noun masc. s., suff. 3 pers. s. f. fr. מֶכֶר d. 6a מכר

מְכֵרָה[c] וּ noun masc. sing., constr. of [מְכֵרָה] dec. 9a; וּ bef. lab. . . . . כרה

מַכָּרוֹ[d] noun masc. s., suff. 3 p. s. m. fr. [מַכָּר] d. 1b נכר

מָכְרוּ וּ'[e] Kal pret. 3 pers. pl.; וּ bef. lab. . . מכר

מְכָרוֹ[f] וּ' id. pret. 3 pers. sing. masc., suff. 3 pers. sing. masc.; וּ id. . . . . מכר

מְכֻרוֹתַיִךְ[g] noun fem. pl., suff. 2 pers. sing. masc. from [מְכוּרָה] dec. 10 . . . . כור

מְכָרוּם[h] וּ Kal pret. 3 pers. pl., suff. 3 pers. pl. masc.; וּ bef. lab. . . . . . מכר

מִכְרִי pr. name masc. . . . . . מכר

מִכְרִי[i] Kal imp. sing. fem. . . . . מכר

מֹכְרֵי[k] וּ id. part. pl. constr. masc. from מֹכֵר dec. 7b; וּ bef. lab. . . . . מכר

מֹכְרֵיהֶן[l] וּ id., suff. 3 pers. pl. fem.; וּ id. . . מכר

מַכָּרֵיכֶם[m] noun m. pl., suff. 2 p. pl. m. fr. [מַכָּר] d. 1b נכר

מְכַרְכֵּר[n] וּ' Pilp. part. sing. m. (§ 6. No. 4); וּ bef. lab. כור

מְכָרָם[o] Kal pret. 3 pers. sing. m., suff. 3 pers. pl. m. מכר

מִכְרָם id. inf. [מְכֹר § 16. rem. 10] with suff.; or (Nu. 20. 19) subst. masc. with suff. 3 pers. pl. masc. from מֶכֶר dec. 6a . . מכר

מִכַּרְמֶל pref. ·מִ)(pr. name of a place . . כרם

מְכָרָנוּ[p] Kal pret. 3 pers. s. m., with suff. 1 pers. pl. מכר

מִכְּרֹעַ[q] pref. ·מִ)(Kal inf. constr. . . . כרע

מָכַרְתִּי[r] / וּמָכַרְתִּי } Kal pret. 1 pers. sing.; acc. shifted by conv. וּ, bef. lab. for וְ (§ 8. rem. 7) } מכר

מְכֵרֹתֵיהֶם[s] noun fem. pl., suff. 3 pers. pl. masc. from [מְכֵרָה] dec. 10 . . . . כור

מְכֹרֹתַיִךְ[t] noun fem. pl., suff. 2 pers. sing. fem. from [מְכוֹרָה] dec. 10 . . . . כור

מְכַרְתֶּם Kal pret. 2 pers. pl. masc. . . . מכר

מִכַּשְׂדִּים pref. ·מִ)(gent. noun, pl. of כַּשְׂדִּי . כשׂד

מִכְשׁוֹל וּ' / מִכְשֹׁל[u] } noun masc. sing. dec. 1b; וּ bef. lab. . כשל

מֻכְשָׁלִים[x] Hoph. part. masc. pl. [of מֻכְשָׁל § 11. r. 10] כשל

[a] Is. 14. 9. [b] 1 Ki. 1. 47. [c] 2 Sa. 12. 3. [d] Eze. 41. 16. [e] Is. 14. 11. [f] Is. 11. 9. [g] 1 Ch. 21. 16. [h] Eze. 27. 7. [i] Nu. 31. 38, 39, 40. [k] Eze. 16. 17. [l] Hos. 13. 2. [m] Le. 27. 23. [n] Job 17. 7. [o] Ps. 35. 17. [p] Le. 16. 20. [q] Da. 3. 23, 24. [r] Le. 25. 25. [s] De. 14. 21. [t] De. 21. 14. [u] Ne. 13. 16. [x] Le. 25. 16. [y] 1 Ch. 15. 27. [z] Ru. 4. 3. [a] Ge. 25. 31. [b] Pr. 31. 10. [c] Zep. 2. 9. [d] 2 Ki. 12. 6. [e] Ex. 21. 35. [f] Ex. 21. 37. [g] Eze. 21. 35. [h] Joel 4. 8. [i] 2 Ki. 4. 7. [k] Ne. 13. 20. [l] Zec. 11. 5. [m] 2 Ki. 12. 8. [n] 2 Sa. 6. 14, 16. [o] De. 32. 30. [p] Ge. 31. 15. [q] 1 Ki. 8. 54. [r] Is. 50. 1. [s] Ge. 49. 5. [t] Eze. 16. 3. [u] Le. 19. 14. [x] Je. 18. 23.

מִכְשֹׁלִים [a] noun masc., pl. of מִכְשׁוֹל dec. 1b . . כשל

מְכַשֵּׁף [b] וּ } Piel part. sing. masc. & fem. dec. 7b (§ 39. No. 3. r. 4); וּ bef. lab. . } כשף
מְכַשֵּׁפָה [c]

מַכַּת noun fem. sing., constr. of מַכָּה dec. 10 . נכה

מִכְתָּב noun masc. sing. dec. 2b . . . כתב

מִכְתַּב id., constr. st. . . . . . כתב

מְכַתְּבִים [d] וּ Piel part. masc. pl. [of מְכַתֵּב] dec. 7b; וּ bef. lab. . . . . . כתב

מַכֹּתֶהָ [e] noun fem. pl., suff. 3 pers. sing. fem. from מַכָּה dec. 10, defect. for מַכּוֹתֶיהָ . . נכה

מַכָּתוֹ [f] id. sing., suff. 3 pers. sing. masc. . . נכה

מַכָּתִי [g] וּ [h] id. sing., suff. 1 pers. sing.; וּ bef. lab. . נכה

מַכְתִּיר [i] Hiph. part. sing. masc. . . . כתר

מַכָּתֶךָ [k] noun fem. s., suff. 2 pers. s. m. fr. מַכָּה d. 10 נכה

מַכָּתֵךְ [l] id., suff. 2 pers. sing. fem. . . . נכה

מַכֹּתְךָ [m] id. pl., suff. 2 p. s. m. [for מַכֹּתֶיךָ § 4. r. 2] נכה

מִכְתָּם noun masc. sing. . . . . כתם

מִכֶּתֶם [n] pref. מִ·)(noun masc. sing. . . . כתם

מִכֶּתֶף pref. id.)(noun fem. s., constr. of כָּתֵף d. 5b כתף

מָל [o] וּ [p] Kal pret. 3 pers. sing. masc.; וּ, bef. lab. for וְ, conv. . . . . מול

מֹל [q] Kal imp. sing. masc. . . . . . מלל

מָלֵא (and middle Kametz, מִלָאוֹ Est. 7. 5) fut. יִמְלָא.—I. *to be full, filled*, with the acc. of that *with* which anything is filled.—II. *to be fulfilled, completed*, of time.—III. trans. *to fill, make full*, with double acc. of the space filled and the thing filling it; Ex. 32. 29, מִלְאוּ יֶדְכֶם לַיהוָֹה *fill your hands*, i. e. to act fully, *for the Lord*, Est. 7. 5, אֲשֶׁר מְלָאוֹ לִבּוֹ *whose heart has filled him*, i. e. was filled with courage, was bold enough. Niph. I. *to be filled*, with acc., also לְ, מִן.—II. *to be fulfilled, completed*, of time, Ex. 7. 25; Job 15. 32. Pi. מִלֵּא (once מִלָּא).—I. *to fill*, with acc., double acc., less frequently עַל, בְּ, מִן; מִ׳ יָדוֹ לְכֹהֵן *to fill his hand*, i. e. give over to him, *the priesthood*; מִ׳ יָדוֹ לַיהוָֹה *to fill one's* (own) *hand*, i. e. be liberal, *towards the Lord*; מִ׳ יָדוֹ בַּקֶּשֶׁת *to fill his hand with the bow*, i. e. to seize the bow.—II. *to fulfil, complete*, of time, promise, desire.—III. *to fill up, complete*, as a number, words.—IV. ellipt. and adverbially מִ׳ [לָלֶכֶת] אַחֲרֵי יְהוָֹה *to follow the Lord fully*; מִ׳ הַקֶּשֶׁת *to* [bend] *the bow fully*, sc. with full strength; Je. 4. 5, קִרְאוּ מַלְאוּ *cry fully*, i. e. *aloud*.—V. *to fill in, insert, set*, as precious stones. Pu. part. *filled in, inserted, set*, of gems, Ca. 5. 14. Hithp. *to set themselves against*, with עַל, Job 16. 19.

מְלָא Ch. *to fill*, Da. 2. 35. Ithpe. pass. Da. 3. 19.

מָלֵא masc. dec. 5a (constr. מְלֵא § 34. rem. 1), מְלֵאָה fem. dec. 10; adj.—I. *filling*.—II. *filled, full*; מְלֵא יָמִים *full of days*, i. e. advanced in age; neut. *fulness*, מֵי מָלֵא *abundant water*.—III. adv. *in full, fully*.

מְלֹא, מְלוֹא, מְלוֹ masc. dec. 1a.—I. *fulness*; מְלֹא כַף *the fulness of the hand*, i. e. *handful*.—II. *multitude*.

מְלֵאָה f. d. 10, *fulness, plenty*, of grain and wine.

מִלּוֹא masc.—I. a certain part of the citadel of Jerusalem, called also בֵּית מִלּוֹא 2 Ki. 12. 21.—II. a castle of the Shechemites, Ju. 9. 6, 20.

מִלֻּאָה, מִלּוּאָה f. d. 10, *insertion, setting* of gems.

מִלֻּאִים, מִלּוּאִים masc. pl. (of מִלּוּא dec. 1b).—I. *consecration* to the priestly office; meton. *the sacrifice of consecration*.—II. *insertion, setting* of gems.

מִלֵּאת fem. *setting, bezel* of a ring; applied to the socket of the eye, Ca. 5. 12.

יִמְלָה, יִמְלָא (*He* (God) *will fill* him) pr. name masc. 1 Ki. 22. 8, 9.

מָלֵא וּ [r] adj. masc. dec. 5a (§ 34. r. 1); וּ bef. lab. מלא

מַלֵּא וּ [s] Piel imp. sing. masc.; וּ id. . . מלא

מְלֵא [t] adj. m. s., constr. of מָלֵא dec. 5a (§ 34. r. 1) מלא

מְלֹא וּ noun masc. sing. dec. 1a; וּ bef. lab. . מלא

מִלֵּא [u] Piel pret. 3 pers. sing. masc. . . . מלא

מִלֵּא וּ [x] id. pret. 3 pers. sing. masc.; וּ for וְ conv. מלא

מִלֹּא [gg] noun masc. sing. . . . . מלא

מִלֹּא pref. מִ·)(pr. name in compos., לֹא דְבָר . לא

מָלְאָה וּ [y] Kal pret. 3 pers. sing. fem.; וּ for וְ conv. מלא

מְלֵאָה [z] adj. fem. sing. dec. 10, from מָלֵא masc. . מלא

מִלֵּאָה pref. מִ·)(pr. name fem. . . . לאה

מְלֹאָה וּ defect. for מְלוֹאָה (q. v.) . . . מלא

מָלְאוּ [a] } Kal pret. 3 pers. pl. (§ 8. rem. 1 & 7); וּ for וְ conv. . . . } מלא
מָלְאוּ וּ

מַלְאוּ [b] וּ [c] Piel imp. pl. masc. (§ 10. r. 7); וּ bef. lab. מלא

מְלָאוֹ [d] Kal pret. 3 pers. sing. m., suff. 3 pers. sing. m. מלא

מִלְאוּ וּ id. imp. pl. masc.; or [for מִלְּאוּ] Piel pret. 3 pers. sing. masc. (§ 10. rem. 7); וּ bef. lab. מלא

מְלֹאִי וּ noun masc. sing., suff. 1 pers. sing. from מְלוֹא dec. 1a; וּ id. . . . מלא

[a] Je. 6. 21. [b] De. 18. 10. [c] Ex. 22. 17. [d] Is. 10. 1. [e] Je. 19. 8. [f] Is. 30. 26. [g] Je. 10. 19. [gg] 2 Ki. 12. 22. [h] Je. 15. 18. [i] Hab. 1. 4. [k] Na. 3. 19. [l] Je. 30. 12. [m] De. 28. 59. [n] Is. 13. 12. [o] Jos. 5. 4, 7. [p] De. 30. 6. [q] Jos. 5. 2. [r] De. 33. 23. [s] Eze. 10. 2. [t] Je. 6. 11. [u] Je. 51. 34. [x] Le. 21. 10. [y] Le. 19. 29. [z] Nu. 7. 14, 20, 26, &c. [a] Is. 1. 15. [b] Je. 4. 5. [c] Eze. 9. 7. [d] Est. 7. 5.

Form	Explanation	Root
מִלְאוּהָ[a]	[b]וּ' Piel pret. 3 pers. pl., suff. 3 pers. sing. fem. (§ 10. rem. 7); וּ bef. lab.	מלא
מִלְאוּךְ[c]	id. with suff. 2 pers. sing. fem.	מלא
מְלֵאוֹת[d]	adj. fem., pl. constr. of מְלֵאָה d. 10, fr. מָלֵא m.	מלא
מִלֻּאֵיכֶם[e]	noun m. pl., suff. 2 pers. pl. m. fr. [מִלּוּא] d. 1 b	מלא
מְלֵאִים	adj. masc., pl. of מָלֵא dec. 5 a (§ 34. rem. 1)	מלא
מִלֻּאִים	noun masc., pl. of [מִלּוּא] dec. 1 b	מלא
מַלְאָךְ	וּ' noun masc. sing. dec. 2 b; וּ bef. lab.	לאך
מַלְאַךְ	וּ' id., constr. st.; וּ id.	לאך
מַלְאֲכֵהּ	Chald. id., suff. 3 pers. sing. fem. dec. 2 a	לאך
מְלָאכָה	[f]וּ' noun fem. sing. dec. 11 c (comp. מַלְאֲכוֹת), constr. מְלֶאכֶת (§ 42. rem. 5); וּ bef. lab.	לאך
מַלְאָכוֹ[g]	noun masc. sing., suff. 3 pers. sing. masc. from מַלְאָךְ dec. 2 b	לאך
מַלְאֲכוֹת[h]	noun fem. pl. constr. [of מְלָאכוֹת] from מְלָאכָה (q. v.) dec. 11 c	לאך
מַלְאֲכוֹתֶיךָ[i]	id. pl. with suff. 2 pers. pl. masc.	לאך
מַלְאֲכֵי	noun masc. pl. constr. from מַלְאָךְ dec. 2 b	לאך
מַלְאָכִי	pr. name masc.	לאך
מַלְאָכִי	noun masc. s., suff. 1 pers. sing. fr. מַלְאָךְ d. 2 a	לאך
מַלְאָכָיו	[k]וּ' id. pl., suff. 3 pers. sing. masc.; וּ bef. lab.	לאך
מַלְאָכֶיךָ	id. pl., suff. 2 pers. sing. masc.	לאך
מַלְאָכִים	וּ' id. pl., abs. st.; וּ bef. lab.	לאך
מַלְאָכֵכֵה[l]	id. pl., suff. 2 pers. sing. fem. (§ 4. rem. 4)	לאך
מְלֶאכֶת	noun fem. sing. (used as the constr. of מְלָאכָה § 42. rem. 5) dec. 13 a	לאך
מְלַאכְתּוֹ	id., suff. 3 pers. sing. fem.	לאך
מְלַאכְתֶּךָ / מְלַאכְתְּךָ[m]	id., suff. 2 pers. sing. masc.	לאך
מִלְאֹם[n]	pref. מִ) noun masc. sing. (suff. לְאֻמִּי) d. 8 c	לאם
מִלֵּאנוּ[o]	Piel pret. 1 pers. pl.	מלא
מָלֵאתָ[p]	Kal pret. 2 pers. sing. masc.	מלא
מְלָאת[q]	וּ Chald. Peal pret. 3 pers. sing. fem.; וּ bef. lab.	מלא
מְלֵאֹת	defect. for מְלֵאוֹת (q. v.)	מלא
מְלֹאת	Kal inf. constr. (§ 23. rem. 2)	מלא
מִלֵּאתָ / וּ מִלֵּאתָ	Piel pret. 2 pers. sing. masc.; acc. shifted by conv. וּ, bef. lab. for וְ (§ 8. r. 7)	מלא
מְלֵאת[r]	noun fem. sing. [for מְלֵאֶת]	מלא
מִלֻּאַת[s]	noun fem. sing., constr. of [מִלּוּאָה] dec. 10	מלא
מָלֵאתִי	Kal pret. 1 pers. sing.	מלא
מְלֵאֲתִי[t]	adj. fem. constr. [מְלֵאַת], with parag. י from מְלֵאָה dec. 10, from מָלֵא masc.	מלא

Form	Explanation	Root
מִלֵּאתִי / וּ מִלֵּאתִי	Piel pret. 1 pers. sing.; acc. shifted by conv. וּ, bef. lab. for וְ (§ 8. rem. 7)	מלא
מִלֵּאתִיו[u]	id., suff. 3 pers. sing. masc.	מלא
מִלֵּאתִיךְ[x]	id., suff. 2 pers. sing. fem.	מלא
מִלֵּאתִים[y]	וּ Kh. מִלֵּאתִים, id., suff. 3 pers. pl. masc.; K. מִלֵּאתֶם (q. v.); וּ bef. lab.	מלא
מְלֵאָתֵךְ[z]	noun fem. sing., suff. 2 pers. sing. masc. from מְלֵאָה dec. 10 (§ 42. rem. 4)	מלא
מִלֵּאתֶם	Piel pret. 2 pers. pl. masc.	מלא
מִלֵּאתָנִי[a]	id. pret. 2 pers. s. m., suff. 1 pers. s. (§ 2. r. 1)	מלא
מִלֵּב	pref. ·מִ) noun masc. sing. dec. 8 b	לבב
מִלְּבָבְךָ[b]	pref. id.) noun masc. sing., suff. 2 pers. sing. masc. from לֵבָב dec. 4 b	לבב
מִלְּבַד	[c]וּ' preff. ·מִ & לְ) בַּד subst. masc., with the preff. לְ & ·מִ as an *adv.*; וּ bef. lab.	בדד
מִלִּבֹּד[d]	Kh. מִלְּבַד q. v.; K. מִלִּבּוֹ (q. v.)	לבב
מִלְּבַדּוֹ[e]	adv. מִלְּבַד (q. v.) with suff. 3 pers. sing. m.	בדד
מִלִּבְּהֶן[f]	pref. ·מִ) noun masc. sing., suff. 3 pers. pl. fem. (§ 3. rem. 5) from לֵב dec. 8 b	לבב
מִלִּבּוֹ	pref. id.) id., suff. 3 pers. sing. masc.	לבב
מִלְּבוֹא	preff. ·מִ & לְ) Kal inf. constr. (§ 25. No. 2 f)	בוא
מַלְבּוּשׁ	noun masc. sing. dec. 1 b	לבש
מַלְבּוּשַׁי[g]	id. pl., suff. 1 pers. sing.	לבש
וּ מַלְבּוּשֵׁיהֶם	וּ id. pl., suff. 3 pers. pl. masc.; וּ bef. lab.	לבש
מַלְבּוּשֵׁךְ[h]	וּ id. sing., suff. 2 pers. sing. fem.; וּ id.	לבש
מִלִּבִּי	pref. ·מִ) noun masc. sing., suff. 1 pers. sing. from לֵב dec. 8 b	לבב
מִלִּבֶּךָ[i] / מִלִּבְּךָ[k]	pref. id.) id., suff. 2 pers. sing. masc.	לבב
מִלִּבָּם[l]	[m]וּ' pref. id.) id., suff. 3 p. pl. m.; וּ bef. lab.	לבב
מַלְבֵּן[n]	noun masc. sing.	לבן
מִלִּבְנָה	pref. ·מִ) pr. name of a place	לבן
מִלְּבָנוֹן	pref. id.) pr. name of a mountain	לבן
מִלִּבְנֵיכֶם[o]	pref. id.) noun fem. with pl. m. term. & suff. 2 pers. pl. masc. fr. לְבֵנָה d. 11 (§ 42. r. 4)	לבן
וּ מַלְבֻּשֵׁיהֶם[p]	וּ defect. for מַלְבּוּשֵׁיהֶם (q. v.)	לבש
מְלֻבָּשִׁים[q]	Pual part. masc. pl. [of מְלֻבָּשׁ]	לבש
מִלֹּג[r]	pref. ·מִ) noun masc. sing.	לג
מִלֵּדָה[s]	pref. id.) Kal inf., or subst. fem. (§ 20. r. 3)	ילד
מִלֶּדֶת	pref. id.) id. inf. constr. dec. 13 a	ילד
מֹלְדֹתַיִךְ[t]	וּ defect. for מוֹלְדוֹתַיִךְ (q. v.)	ילד
מִלָּה[u]	[x]וּ' noun fem. sing. dec. 10, Chald. dec. 8 a	מלל
מָלוּ[y]	Kal pret. 3 pers. pl. for מָלְאוּ (§ 23. rem. 11)	מלא

[a] Ezr. 9. 11. [b] 2 Ki. 3. 25. [c] Is. 23. 2. [d] Eze. 36. 38. [e] Le. 8. 33.
[f] 2 Ch. 17. 13. [g] Ge. 24. 7, 40. [h] 1 Ch. 28. 19. [i] Ps. 73. 28. [k] Is. 30. 4.
[l] Na. 2. 14. [m] Jon. 1. 8. [n] Ge. 25. 23. [o] Jos. 9. 13. [p] Job 36. 17.
[q] Da. 2. 35. [r] Ca. 5. 12. [s] Ex. 28. 17. [t] Is. 1. 21. [u] Ex. 28. 3.
[x] Je. 51. 14. [y] Eze. 11. 6. [z] Ex. 22. 28. [a] Je. 15. 17. [b] De. 4. 9.
[c] Le. 23. 38. [d] 1 Ki. 12. 33. [e] De. 4. 35. [f] Eze. 13. 17. [g] Is. 63. 3.
[h] Eze. 16. 13. [i] Ec. 11. 10. [k] Ne. 6. 8. [l] Eze. 13. 2. [m] Job 8. 10.
[n] Na. 3. 14. [o] Ex. 5. 19. [p] 1 Ki. 10. 5. [q] 1 Ki. 22. 10. [r] Le. 14. 15.
[s] Ho. 9. 11. [t] Eze. 16. 3. [u] Ps. 139. 4. [x] Da. 2. 9. [y] Eze. 28. 16.

מָלוּ[a] Kal pret. 3 pers. pl. . . . . . מול

מָלוּ[b] defect. for מָלוּא (q. v.) . . . . מלא

מִלּוֹ pr. name in compos. לוֹ דְבָר see לֹא דְ׳ under לא

מִלּוֹא noun masc. sing. . . . . . מלא

מְלוֹא noun masc. sing. dec. 1 a . . . . מלא

מְלוֹאָהּ ו id., suff. 3 pers. sing. fem.; ו bef. lab. . מלא

מְלוֹאוֹ[oo] ו id., suff. 3 pers. sing. masc.; ו id. . . מלא

מִלֻּאִים[c] ו noun masc., pl. of [מִלּוּא] dec. 1 b; ו id. מלא

מַלְוֵה[d] constr. of the foll. . . . . . לוה

מַלְוֶה[e] [f]ו׳ ו Hiph. part. sing. masc. d. 9 a; ו bef. lab. לוה

מַלּוּחַ[g] noun masc. sing. . . . . . מלח

מַלּוּךְ pr. name masc. . . . . . . מלך

מְלוֹכָה[h] Kh. מְלוֹכָה, K. מָלְכָה Kal imp. sing. masc. with parag. ה (§ 8. rem. 12) . . . מלך

מְלוּכָה noun fem. sing. . . . . . מלך

מְלוֹכִי[i] Kh. מְלוֹכִי, K. מָלְכִי Kal imp. sing. fem. (§ 8. rem. 12) . . . . . מלך

מָלוֹן[k] noun masc. sing. dec. 3 a . . . . לון

מְלוֹן id., constr. st. . . . . . . לון

מִלּוּשׁ[l] pref. ·מִ)(Kal inf. constr. . . . . לוש

מְלוֹשְׁנִי[ss] Kh. מְלוֹשְׁנִי Poel part. (§ 6. No. 1), K. מְלָשְׁנִי for מְלַשְּׁנִי Piel part. (§ 10. r. 7 b), suff. 1 pers. sing. . . . . . לשן

מַלּוֹתִי pr. name masc. . . . . . . מלל

מָלַח Niph. *to pass away, vanish*, Is. 51. 6.

מְלָחִים masc. pl. (from מֶלַח) *decay, rottenness*, Je. 38 12, בְּלוֹיֵ מְ׳ *rotten rags.*

מֶלַח [m]וָ׳ masc. *salt;* יָם הַמֶּלַח *the salt sea*, i. e. the Dead Sea; בְּרִית מֶלַח *covenant of salt*, i. e. lasting covenant; salt as the emblem of perpetuity.

מְלַח Chald. masc. *salt.*

מָלַח *to salt*, Le. 2. 13. Pu. pass. Ex. 30. 35. Hoph. *to be salted, washed with salt water*, Eze. 16. 4.

מְלַח Chald. *to eat salt*, Ezr. 4. 14.

מַלָּח masc. dec. 1 a, *seaman, mariner.*

מַלּוּחַ masc. ἅλιμος, *sea-purslain*, a marine plant, the leaves of which are eaten by the poor, Job 30. 4.

מְלֵחָה fem. *salt, barren land.*

מְלַח [n]ו׳ Chald. noun masc. sing.; ו bef. lab. . מלח

מְלֵחָה noun fem. sing. . . . . . מלח

מַלָּחֵיהֶם[o] ו noun masc. pl., suff. 3 pers. pl. masc. fr. [מַלָּח] dec. 1 b; ו bef. lab. . . . מלח

מַלָּחַיִךְ[p] id. pl., suff. 2 pers. sing. fem. . . . מלח

מַלָּחִים[q] id. pl., abs. st. . . . . . מלח

מְלָחִים[r] noun masc. pl. of [מֶלַח] dec. 6 . . . מלח

מִלֶּחֶם pref. ·מִ)(noun com. sing. (suff. לַחְמִי) d. 6a לחם

מִלְחָמָה ו׳ ו noun f. s. d. 11 a (§ 42. r. 5); ו bef. lab. לחם

מִלַּחְמוֹ pref. ·מִ)(noun com. sing., suff. 3 pers. sing. masc. fr. לֶחֶם dec. 6 a . . . . לחם

מִלְחָמוֹת [t]ו׳ ו noun fem. pl. abs. fr. מִלְחָמָה dec. 11 a (§ 42. rem. 5); ו bef. lab. . . . לחם

מִלְחֲמוֹת [u]ו׳, מִלְחֲמֹת[x] } id. pl. constr.; ו id. . . . . לחם

מִלְחֶמֶת[y] noun fem. sing. dec. 13 a, see מִלְחָמָה . לחם

מִלְחַמְתָּהּ[z] id., suff. 3 pers. sing. fem. . . . לחם

מִלְחַמְתּוֹ id., suff. 3 pers. sing. masc. . . . לחם

מִלְחַמְתִּי[a] id., suff. 1 pers. sing. . . . . לחם

מִלְחֲמֹתָיו[b] id. pl., suff. 3 pers. sing. masc. . . . לחם

מִלְחֲמֹתֵינוּ[c] id. pl., suff. 1 pers. pl. . . . . לחם

מִלְחַמְתֶּךָ[d] id. sing., suff. for מִלְחַמְתְּךָ (q. v.) . . לחם

מִלְחַמְתֵּךְ[e] id. sing., suff. 2 pers. sing. fem. . . . לחם

מִלְחַמְתְּךָ[f] id. sing., suff. 2 pers. sing. masc. . . . לחם

מִלְחַמְתָּם id. sing., suff. 3 pers. pl. masc. . . . לחם

מִלְחֲמֹתֵנוּ[g] defect. for מִלְחֲמוֹתֵינוּ (q. v.) . . . לחם

מְלַחְנָא[h] Chald. Peal pret. 1 pers. pl. . . . מלח

מְלַחֲשִׁים[i] Piel (§ 14. r. 1) part. m., pl. of [מְלַחֵשׁ] d. 7 b לחש

מָלַט. Pi. מִלֵּט, מִלַּט (§ 10. rem. 1).—I. *to let escape* or *slip, to deliver.*—II. *to lay* eggs, Is. 34. 15. Hiph. I. *to deliver*, Is. 31. 5.—II. *to bring forth*, Is. 66. 7. Niph. *to be delivered; to deliver oneself, escape.* Hithp. *to escape*, Job 19. 20; 41. 11.

מֶלֶט masc. *mortar, cement*, Je. 43. 9.

מְלַטְיָה (whom *the Lord delivers*) pr. name masc. Ne. 3. 7.

מַלֵּט Piel inf. abs. & constr. . . . . מלט

מִלַּט־[k], מִלֵּט[yy] } ו id. pret. 3 pers. sing. masc. (§ 10. rem. 1); ו bef. lab. . . . . } מלט

מַלְּטָה[l] id. imp. sing. masc. with parag. ה . . מלט

מַלְּטוּ[m] [n]ו׳ ו id. imp. pl. masc.; ו bef. lab. . . מלט

מַלְּטוּנִי[o] ו id. id. with suff. 1 pers. sing.; ו id. . מלט

מַלְּטִי[p] ו id. imp. sing. fem.; ו id. . . . מלט

מְלַטְיָה pr. name masc. . . . . . מלט

[a] Jos. 5. 5, 7. [b] Eze. 41. 8. [c] 1 Ch. 29. 2. [d] Pr. 19. 17. [e] Pr. 22. 7. [f] Ps. 112. 5. [g] Job 30. 4. [h] Ju. 9. 8. [i] Ju. 9. 12. [k] Is. 10. 29. [l] Ho. 7. 4. [m] De. 29. 22. [n] Ezr. 7. 22. [o] Eze. 27. 9. [oo] 1 Ch. 16. 32. [p] Eze. 27. 27. [q] Eze. 27. 29. [r] Je. 38. 11. [s] Pr. 22. 9. [ss] Ps. 101. 5. [t] 1 Ch. 22. 8. [u] 2 Ch. 12. 15. [x] Nu. 21. 14. [y] 1 Sa. 13. 22. [yy] Eze. 33. 5. [z] Je. 50. 30. [a] 2 Ch. 35. 21. [b] 2 Ch. 27. 7. [c] 2 Ch. 32. 8. [d] Is. 41. 12. [e] Eze. 27. 10, 27. [f] 2 Sa. 11. 25. [g] 1 Sa. 8. 20. [h] Ezr. 4. 14. [i] Ps. 58. 6. [k] Ec. 9. 15. [l] Ps. 116. 4. [m] Je. 48. 6. [n] Je. 51. 6, 45. [o] Job 6. 23. [p] 1 Ki. 1. 12.

מִלְּטָנוּ[a] Piel pret. 3 pers. s. m. (מִלֵּט), suff. 1 pers. pl. — מלט

מְלֻטָּשׁ[b] Pual part. sing. masc. — לטש

מִלַּי [for מִלַּי] noun fem. with pl. masc. term. & suff. 1 pers. sing. from מִלָּה dec. 10 — מלל

מִלֵּי[c] Chald. noun fem. with pl. masc. term., constr. st. from מִלָּה [for מִלָּא] dec. 8a — מלל

מִלַּיָּא[d] Chald. id. pl., emph. st. — מלל

מִלֵּיהֶם[e] noun fem. with pl. masc. term. & suff. 3 pers. pl. masc. from מִלָּה dec. 10 — מלל

מִלֶּיךָ id. pl. with suff. 2 pers. sing. masc. — מלל

מִלֵּיל[f] pref. ·מִ)(noun m. sing., constr. of לַיִל d. 6h — ליל

מִלַּיְלָה[g] pref. id.)(id. abs. with parag. ה — ליל

מְלִילֹת[h] noun fem., pl. of [מְלִילָה] dec. 10 — מלל

מִלִּים[ll] וּ noun fem. with pl. masc. term. from מִלָּה dec. 10; וּ bef. lab. — מלל

מֻלִים[i] Kal part. pass. masc., pl. of מוּל dec. 1a — מול

מִלִּין[k] וּ Heb. & Chald. noun fem. with pl. masc. term. fr. מִלָּה d. 10, Chald. d. 8a; וּ bef. lab. — מלל

מַלִּינִים[l], מַלִּינִם } Hiph. part. masc. pl. [of מַלִּין], Chald. form (§ 21. rem. 24) — לון

מֵלִיץ[m] Hiph. part. sing. masc. dec. 3b — לוץ

מְלִיצָה וּ noun fem. sing.; וּ bef. lab. — לוץ

מְלִיצַי[n] Hiph. part. pl. m., suff. 1 p. s. fr. מֵלִיץ d. 3b — לוץ

מְלִיצֶיךָ[o] וּ id. pl. with suff. 2 pers. sing. m.; וּ bef. lab. — לוץ

מָלַךְ וּ' fut. יִמְלֹךְ.—I. *to reign, to be king*, with בְּ, עַל *over*.—II. *to be made king*. Hiph. *to make king*, with acc., also לְ. Hoph. *to be made king*, Da. 9. 1. Niph. *to consult, take counsel*, Ne. 5. 7; comp. מְלַךְ.

מֶלֶךְ masc. dec. 6a (with suff. מַלְכִּי).—I. *king*; applied to God, and also false gods.—II. pr. name masc., also with the art. הַמֶּלֶךְ.

מֶלֶךְ Chald. masc. dec. 3a, *king*.

מְלַךְ Chald. m. d. 3b, *advice, counsel*, Da. 4. 24.

מֹלֶךְ with the art. הַמֹּלֶךְ (*the king*) *Moloch*, pr. name of an idol of the Ammonites.

מַלְכָּה fem. dec. 12a, *queen*.

מַלְכָּא Chald. fem. dec. 8a, *queen*.

מִלְכָּה (*counsel*) pr. name of a daughter of Haran, Ge. 11. 29; 22. 20.

מַלּוּךְ (*counsellor*) pr. name masc. of several persons; for which also מַלּוּכִי Kh., but מְלִיכוּ Keri, comp. Ne. 12. 2, with ver. 14.

מַלְכוּ Chald. fem. dec. 8c.—I. *dominion, reign, rule*.—II. *kingdom, realm*.

מַלְכוּת fem. dec. 1b (pl. מַלְכֻיּוֹת).—I. *kingdom, dominion, reign, rule*.—II. *royalty, royal dignity*; בֵּית מַ׳ *royal palace*; לְבוּשׁ מַ׳ *royal garments*; also לְבוּשׁ omitted, Est. 5. 1.—III. *kingdom, realm*.

מַלְכִּיאֵל (*king of*, i. e. appointed by, *God*) pr. name masc. Ge. 46. 17.

מַלְכִּיָּה, מַלְכִּיָּהוּ (*king of the Lord*; see preced.) pr. name masc. of several persons.

מַלְכִּי־צֶדֶק (*king of righteousness*) name of a king of Salem (Jerusalem, comp. אֲדֹנִי־צֶדֶק) priest of the Most High God, Ge. 14. 18; Ps. 110. 4.

מַלְכִּירָם (*the king is exalted*; part. of רוּם) pr. name masc. 1 Ch. 3. 18.

מַלְכִּישׁוּעַ, מַלְכִּי־שׁוּעַ (*king of help* or *wealth*) pr. name of a son of Saul.

מַלְכָּם pr. name—I. i. q. מֹלֶךְ, מִלְכֹּם, an idol of the Moabites and Ammonites.—II. of a man, 1 Ch. 8. 9.

מִלְכֹּם pr. n., i. q. מֹלֶךְ, an idol of the Ammonites.

מְלֶכֶת fem. *queen*, only in the phrase מְלֶכֶת הַשָּׁמַיִם *the queen of heaven, the Astoreth*, Astarte of the Phenicians, i. e. the Diana or Venus.

מֹלֶכֶת (*queen*) pr. name fem. 1 Ch. 7. 18.

יַמְלֵךְ (whom *he*, sc. God, *shall cause to reign*) pr. name masc. 1 Ch. 4. 34.

מַמְלָכָה fem. constr. מַמְלֶכֶת, with suff. מַמְלַכְתִּי, pl. מַמְלָכוֹת (§ 42. rem. 5) i. q. מַלְכוּת q. v.

מַמְלָכוּת fem. dec. 3c, *kingdom, realm*.

מָלָךְ Kal pret. 3 pers. sing. masc. for מָלַךְ (§ 8. r. 7) — מלך

מָלֹךְ[p] id. inf. abs. — מלך

מֶלֶךְ, וּ', וְ noun masc. sing. dec. 6a, Chald. 3a, also pr. name; וּ bef. lab., for וְ see lett. ו — מלך

מְלֹךְ Kal inf. constr. — מלך

מְלָךְ־ id. with Mak., or (Ju. 9. 14) imp. sing. masc. (§ 8. rem. 18) — מלך

מֹלֵךְ[q] id. part. act. sing. masc. — מלך

מַלְכָּא וּ' Chald. noun m. sing., emph. of מֶלֶךְ d. 3a — מלך

מִלֶּכֶד[r] pref. ·מִ)(noun masc. sing. [for לֶכֶד] — לכד

מִלֹּכֵד[s] pref. id.)(Kal part. act. sing. masc. — לכד

מַלְכֻּדְתּוֹ[t] וּ noun fem. sing., suff. 3 pers. sing. masc. from [מַלְכֹּדֶת] dec. 13c; וּ bef. lab. — לכד

מַלְכָּה[u] Chald. in some copies for מַלְכָּא (q. v.) — מלך

מַלְכֵּהּ noun masc. s., suff. 3 pers. s. m. fr. מֶלֶךְ d. 6a — מלך

מִלְכָּה וּ' pr. name fem.; וּ bef. lab. — מלך

מָלְכוֹ[v] Kal inf., suff. 3 pers. sing. masc. — מלך

מָלְכוּ id. pret. 3 pers. pl. — מלך

---

[a] 2 Sa. 19. 10. [b] Ps. 52. 4. [c] Da. 5. 10. [d] Da. 7. 11, 16. [e] Ps. 19. 5. [f] Is. 21. 11. [g] Is. 21. 11. [h] De. 23. 26. [i] Jos. 5. 5. [k] Da. 7. 25. [l] Nu. 14. 27. [ll] Job 15. 3. [m] Job 33. 23. [n] Job 16. 20. [o] Is. 43. 27. [p] 1 Sa. 24. 21. [q] Je. 33. 21. [r] Pr. 3. 26. [s] Pr. 16. 32. [t] Job 18. 10. [u] Da. 4. 16. [v] 2 Ki. 25. 27.

מַלְכּוֹ noun masc. sing., suff. 3 pers. sing. masc. from מֶלֶךְ dec. 6a . . מלך

מַלְכוּ וּ Chald. noun fem. sing. dec. 8c; וּ bef. lab. מלך

מַלְכְוָת[a] Chald. id. pl., constr. st. . . . מלך

מַלְכוּת Ch. id. s. constr.; or Heb. n. f. (pl. מַלְכֻיוֹת) מלך

מַלְכוֹת[b] noun fem. pl. abs. from מַלְכָּה dec. 12a . מלך

מַלְכוּתָא[c] וּ Ch. noun fem. sing., emph. of מַלְכוּ d. 8c מלך

מַלְכְוָתָא Chald. id. pl., emph. st. . . . מלך

מַלְכוּתֵה[d] [e] וּ Chald. id. sing., emph. for מַלְכוּתָא (q. v.) מלך

מַלְכוּתָהּ[f] וּ id. sing., suff. 3 pers. sing. fem.; וּ bef. lab. מלך

מַלְכוּתֵהּ וּ Chald. noun fem. sing., suff. 3 pers. sing. masc. from מַלְכוּ dec. 8c; וּ bef. lab. . מלך

מַלְכוּתוֹ[g] וּ noun fem. sing., suff. 3 pers. sing. masc. from מַלְכוּת (pl. מַלְכֻיוֹת); וּ id. . . מלך

מַלְכוּתִי Ch. noun fem. s., suff. 1 pers. s. fr. מַלְכוּ d. 8c מלך

מַלְכוּתָךְ Chald. id., suff. 2 pers. sing. masc. . מלך

מַלְכוּתֶךָ[h] וּ / מַלְכֻתְךָ[i] } noun fem. sing., suff. 2 pers. sing. masc. fr. מַלְכוּת, (pl. מַלְכֻיוֹת); וּ bef. lab. } מלך

מַלְכוּתָם id., suff. 3 pers. pl. masc. . . . מלך

מַלְכִּי[k] Kal imp. sing. fem. (§ 8. rem. 12) . . מלך

מַלְכֵי וּ noun m. pl. constr. fr. מֶלֶךְ d. 6a; וּ bef. lab. מלך

מַלְכִּי id. sing., suff. 1 pers. sing. . . . מלך

מַלְכִּי וּ pr. name in compos. as מַלְכִּי צֶדֶק, &c.; וּ bef. lab.

מַלְכִּי[l] Ch. noun m. s., suff. 1 pers. s. fr. [מְלַךְ] d. 3b מלך

מַלְכַיָּא Chald. noun masc. pl. emph. from מֶלֶךְ dec. 3a מלך

מַלְכִּיאֵל וּ pr. names masc.; וּ bef. lab. also מַלְכִּיָּה, וּ . מלך

מְלָכֶיהָ noun m. pl., suff. 3 pers. s. fem. fr. מֶלֶךְ d. 6a מלך

מַלְכִּיָּהוּ pr. name masc., see מַלְכִּיָּה . . . מלך

מַלְכֵיהֶם וּ noun masc. pl., suff. 3 pers. pl. masc. from מֶלֶךְ dec. 6a; וּ bef. lab. . . . מלך

מַלְכֻיוֹת[m] noun fem., pl. of מַלְכוּת . . . מלך

מַלְכֵיכֶם[n] noun masc. pl., suff. 2 pers. pl. m. fr. מֶלֶךְ d. 6a מלך

מַלְכִים[o] Ch. n. m. pl. with Heb. term. for מַלְכִין (q. v.) מלך

מְלָכִים וּ noun masc., pl. of מֶלֶךְ dec. 6a; וּ bef. lab. מלך

מַלְכִין[p] וּ Ch. noun masc., pl. of מֶלֶךְ [or מְלַךְ] d. 3a מלך

מְלָכִין[q] noun masc. pl. with Chald. term. fr. מֶלֶךְ d. 6a מלך

מְלָכֵינוּ id. pl. with suff. 1 pers. pl. . . . מלך

מַלְכִּירָם וּ pr. name masc.; וּ bef. lab. . . . מלך

מִלָּכִישׁ pref. מִ) (pr. name of a place . . לכש

מַלְכִּישׁוּעַ וּ pr. name masc.; וּ bef. lab. . . מלך

מַלְכְּךָ noun m. s., suff. 2 pers. s. m. fr. מֶלֶךְ d. 6a מלך

מַלְכֵּךְ[r] id., suff. 2 pers. sing. fem. . . . מלך

מַלְכְּכֶם id., suff. 2 pers. pl. masc. . . . מלך

מַלְכֶּם[s] Kh., for K. מַה־לָּכֶם, see לָכֶם, & . . מה

מַלְכָּם pr. name masc. . . . . . מלך

מַלְכָּם noun m. s., suff. 3 pers. pl. m. fr. מֶלֶךְ d. 6a מלך

מִלְכֹּם pr. name masc. . . . . . מלך

מַלְכֵּנוּ noun masc. s., suff. 1 pers. pl. fr. מֶלֶךְ d. 6a מלך

מָלַכְתָּ[t] / וּמָלַכְתָּ { Kal pret. 2 pers. sing. masc.; acc. shifted by conv. וּ, bef. lab. for וְ (§ 8. r. 7) } מלך

מַלְכַּת וּ noun fem. sing., constr. of מַלְכָּה dec. 12a מלך

מִלֶּכֶת pref. מִ) (Kal inf. constr. . . . ילך

מֹלֶכֶת Kal part. act. sing. fem., from מֹלֵךְ masc. . מלך

מַלְכְּתָא[u] Ch. noun fem. sing., emph. of [מַלְכָּא] d. 8a מלך

מַלְכֻתוֹ defect. for מַלְכוּתוֹ (q. v.) . . . מלך

I. [מָלַל] *to speak*, Pr. 6. 23. Pi. *to speak, declare, announce.*

מַלֵּל Ch. Pa. *to speak*, with עִם *with* any one, Da. 6. 22; *to declare*, with acc.

מִלֲלַי (*eloquent*) pr. name masc. Ne. 12. 36.

מִלָּה fem. dec. 10 (pl. מִלִּים, מִלִּין).—I. *word, saying, discourse*; meton. *object of discourse*, Job 30. 9.—II. *thing*, Job 32. 11.

מִלָּה Ch. fem. dec. 8a (§ 64) pl. מִלִּין.—I. *word*, espec. *order, mandate*.—II. *thing*.

מַלּוֹתִי (*I spoke*, comp. גִּדַּלְתִּי, רוֹמַמְתִּי) pr. name masc. 1 Ch. 25. 4, 26.

II. [מָלַל] I. *to circumcise*, Jos. 5. 2.—II. intrans. fut. יִמַּל (§ 18. rem. 14) *to be cut off*, as grass, &c. Niph. *to be circumcised*, Ge. 17. 11; comp. also נָמַל. For Po. and Hithpo. which might properly be referred here, see מוּל.

מְלִילָה fem. dec. 10, *an ear of corn*, De. 23. 26.

מַלִּל[x] Ch. Peal pret. 3 pers. sing. masc. (§ 47. r. 1) מלל

מִלֵּל[y] Piel pret. 3 pers. sing. masc. . . . מלל

מִלֵּלוּ[z] id. pret. 3 pers. pl. [for מִלְּלוּ comp. § 8. r. 7] מלל

מִלֲלַי pr. name masc. . . . . . מלל

מְלַמֵּד Piel part. sing. masc. dec. 7b . . . למד

מְלֻמָּדָה Pual part. sing. fem. [of מְלֻמָּד] . . למד

מְלַמְּדַי[a] Piel part. pl., suff. 1 pers. s. fr. מְלַמֵּד d. 7b למד

מְלֻמְּדֵי Pual part. pl. constr. from [מְלֻמָּד] dec. 2b למד

מְלַמֶּדְךָ[b] Piel part. s. מְלַמֵּד, suff. 2 pers. s. m. d. 7b למד

מִלְמַטָּה[c] / מִלְמַטָּה { preff. מִ & לְ) (prop. subst. מַט with loc. ה as an *adv*. . . . } נטה

[a] Da. 7. 27. [b] Ca. 6. 8, 9. [c] Da. 7. 22, 27. [d] Da. 7. 24. [e] Da. 2. 44. [f] Est. 1. 19. [g] Ps. 103. 19. [h] 1 Sa. 20. 31. [i] Ps. 145. 11, 13. [k] Ju. 9. 10. [l] Da. 4. 24. [m] Da. 8. 22. [n] Je. 44. 21. [o] Ezr. 4. 13. [p] Ezr. 4. 20. [q] Pr. 31. 3. [r] Zec. 9. 9. [s] Is. 3. 15. [t] 2 Sa. 16. 8. [u] Da. 5. 10, 10. [x] Da. 6. 22. [y] Ge. 21. 7. [z] Job 33. 3. [a] Ps. 119. 99. [b] Is. 48. 17. [c] Ex. 27. 5.

מִלְמַעְלָה } preff. מִ & לְ) prop. subst. מַעַל with loc. ה as an *adv.*; וּ bef. lab. — עלה
וּ[kk] מִלְמַעְלָה }
מִלְמַעְלָה[a] preff. id.) n. m. s., constr. of מַעֲלָה d. 9 a — עלה
מַלְעִבִים[b] Hiph. part. masc. pl. [of מַלְעִיב] dec. 1 b . — לעב
מַלְעִגִים[c] וּ Hiph. part. m. pl. [of מַלְעִיג] d. 1 b; וּ bef. lab. — לעג
מִלְעֻמַּת[d] preff. מִ & לְ) prop. subst., constr. of עֻמָּה dec. 10, as a *prep.* . . . — עמת
מַלְּפֵנוּ[e] [for מְאַלְּפֵנוּ § 19. rem. 10] Piel part. sing. [מְאַלֵּף], suff. 1 pers. pl. dec. 7 b . . — אלף
מִלְּפָנַי } preff. מִ & לְ) the foll. with suff. 1 pers. sing. . . . . . — פנה
מִלְּפָנַי }
וּ[oo] מִלִּפְנֵי preff. מִ, & לְ bef. (:)) noun masc. pl. constr. fr. [פָּנֶה] d. 9 b, as a *prep.* or *adv.* — פנה
מִלְּפָנָיו preff. מִ & לְ) id., suff. 3 pers. sing. masc. — פנה
מִלְּפָנֶיךָ preff. id.) id., suff. 2 pers. sing. masc. . — פנה
מִלִּפְנֵיכֶם preff. מִ, & לְ bef. (:)) id., suff. 2 p. pl. m. — פנה
מִלְּפָנִים[f] וּ preff. מִ & לְ) id. pl. abs. *adverbially*; וּ bef. lab. — פנה
מִלִּפְנִים[g] preff. מִ, & לְ bef. (:)) noun masc. sing. — פנם
מִלְּפָנֵינוּ[h] preff. מִ & לְ) noun masc. pl., suff. 1 pers. pl. as an *adv.* comp. מִלְּפָנַי . . — פנה

מָלַץ Niph. *to be smooth, agreeable*, Ps. 119. 103.

מֶלְצַר only with the art. הַמֶּלְצַר, a certain officer in the Babylonian court; coll. with the Persic, according to some, *master of the wine, chief butler*; according to others, *treasurer*, Da. 1. 11. 16.

מָלַק וּ *to wring* or *pinch off*, Le. 1. 15; 5. 8.

וּ[i] מַלְקוֹחַ noun masc. sing. dec. 1 b; וּ bef. lab. . — לקח
מַלְקוֹחָי[k] id. du. [מַלְקוֹחַיִם], with suff. 1 pers. sing. — לקח
וּ מַלְקוֹשׁ noun masc. sing.; וּ bef. lab. . . — לקשׁ
וּ מֶלְקָחֶיהָ[l] noun masc. du. [מֶלְקָחַיִם], suff. 3 pers. sing. fem. from [מֶלְקָח] dec. 2 b; וּ id. — לקח
מְלַקְּטִים Piel part. masc., pl. of מְלַקֵּט dec. 7 b . — לקט
מִלָּשׁוֹן[m] pref. מִ) noun com. sing. dec. 3 a . . — לשׁן
מִלְּשׁוֹן* pref. id.) id., constr. st.* Jos. 15. 5. . — לשׁן
מִלִּשְׁכַּת[n] pref. id.) noun fem., constr. of לִשְׁכָּה d. 12 b — לשׁך
וּ[p] מִלַּת[o] Ch. noun fem. sing. constr. of מִלָּה [for מִלְאָה] dec. 8 a; וּ bef. lab. . . — מלל
וּ מִלְּתָא Ch. id., emph. st.; וּ id. . . — מלל
וּ מַלְתָּה[q] Kal pret. 2 pers. sing. masc. (§ 8. rem. 5); acc. shifted by וּ for וְ, conv. (§ 8. rem. 7) — מול
מִלְּתָה[r] Ch. for מִלְּתָא (q. v.) . . . . — מלל

וּ מִלָּתוֹ[s] noun fem. sing., suff. 3 pers. sing. masc. from מִלָּה dec. 10; וּ bef. lab. . . — מלל
מַלֹּתִי[t] Kal pret. 1 pers. sing. for מִלֵּאתִי (§ 23. r. 11) — מלא
מִלָּתִי noun fem. sing., suff. 1 pers. s. fr. מִלָּה d. 10 — מלל
וּ מַלְתֶּם[u] Kal pret. 2 pers. pl. masc.; וּ for וְ, conv. — מול
מַלְתְּעוֹת[x] noun fem. pl. constr. of [מַלְתָּעָה] dec. 11 a — לתע
מַמְאִיר[y] Hiph. part. sing. masc. . . . . — מאר
מְמָאֶרֶת id. fem. (§ 39. No. 4 d) . . . . — מאר
וּ מִמֶּגֶד[z] pref. מִ) noun masc. sing. dec. 6 . — מגד
מִמְּגִדּוֹ pref. id.) pr. name of a place . . — גדד
מִמִּגְדַּל pref. id.) n. m. s., constr. of [מִגְדָּל] d. 2 b — גדל
מִמִּגְדֹּל pref. id.) pr. name of a place . . — גדל
מִמָּגוֹר[a] pref. id.) noun masc. sing. (§ 30. rem. 4) . — גור
מַמְּגֻרוֹת[b] noun fem., pl. of [מַמְּגֻרָה] dec. 10 . — גור
וּ מִמִּדְבָּר pref. מִ) noun masc. s. d. 2 b; וּ bef. lab. — דבר
מִמִּדְבַּר pref. id.) id., constr. st. . . . — דבר
מְמַדֶּיהָ[c] noun m. pl., suff. 3 p. s. f. fr. [מֵמַד] d. 8 d — מדד
מִמְּדָן pref. מִ) pr. name of a country, R. דִּין see — דון
מִמְּדִינוֹת[d] pref. id.) n. f., pl. of מְדִינָה d. 10, R. דִּין see — דון
וּ[f] מְמַהֵר[e] Piel part. sing. m. (§ 14. r. 1); וּ bef. lab. — מהר
מְמַהֲרוֹת[g] id. fem., pl. of [מְמַהֶרֶת] dec. 13 . . — מהר
מִמּוֹאָב וּ pr. name of a people, see מוֹאָב; וּ bef. lab.
מְמוּכָן pr. name of a prince at the court of Ahasuerus, Est. 1. 14, 16, 21.
מִמּוּל pref. מִ) *prep.* (suff. מוּלִי) dec. 1 a . . — מול
וּ מִמּוֹלַדְתְּךָ[h] pref. id.) noun fem. sing., suff. 2 pers. sing. masc. from מוֹלֶדֶת d. 13 a; וּ bef. lab. — ילד
מִמּוּם[i] pref. id.) noun m. s. d. 1 a, for מְאוּם, מאום — מאם
מִמּוֹעֵד[k] pref. id.) noun masc. sing. dec. 7 b . — יעד
וּ[ll] מִמּוֹעֲצוֹתֵיהֶם[ss] pref. id.) noun fem. pl., suff. 3 pers. pl. masc. from מוֹעֵצָה dec. 11 b; וּ bef. lab. — יעץ
מִמּוֹצָא[m] pref. id.) noun masc. sing. d. 1 b (§ 31. r. 1) — יצא
מִמּוֹקְשֵׁי[n] pref. id.) noun m. pl. constr. fr. מוֹקֵשׁ d. 7 b — יקשׁ
מִמּוֹשְׁבֹתֵיכֶם[o] pref. id.) noun masc. with pl. fem. term. & suff. 2 pers. pl. masc. from מוֹשָׁב d. 2 b — ישׁב
מִמָּוֶת pref. id.) noun masc. sing. dec. 6 g . — מות
מְמוֹתֵי noun masc. pl. constr. from [מָמוֹת] dec. 3 a — מות
מְמוֹתֵת[p] Pilel part. sing. masc. . . . . — מות
מַמְזֵר masc. *bastard*; according to the Mishna (Jebamoth) the offspring of adultery or incest; De. 23. 3; Zec. 9. 6. Etymo. uncertain.
מִמִּזְרָח pref. מִ) noun masc. sing. dec. 2 b . — זרח
וּ[q] מִמִּזְרַח pref. id.) id. constr. st.; וּ bef. lab. — זרח
וּ מִמְּזָרִים[r] pref. id.) noun m., pl. of [מְזָרֶה] dec. 9 a — זרה
מְמֻחָיִם Pual (§ 14. rem. 1) part. masc. pl. [of מְמֻחֶה § 38. rem. 1] . . . . . — מחה

[a] Ju. 8. 13. [b] 2 Ch. 36. 16. [c] 2 Ch. 30. 10. [d] 1 Ki. 7. 20. [e] Job 35. 11.
[f] Is. 41. 26. [g] 1 Ki. 6. 29. [h] Ec. 1. 10. [i] Is. 49. 25. [k] Ps. 22. 16.
[l] Nu. 4. 9. [m] Ps. 120. 2. [n] Je. 36. 21. [o] Da. 2. 10, 23. [p] Da. 3. 28.
[q] Ex. 12. 44. [r] Da. 2. 5. [s] 2 Sa. 23. 2. [t] Job 32. 18. [u] De. 10. 16.
[x] Ps. 58. 7. [y] Eze. 28. 24. [z] De. 33. 13, 14, 15, 16. [a] Is. 31. 9.
[b] Joel 1. 17. [c] Job 38. 5. [d] Eze. 19. 8. [e] Mal. 3. 5. [f] Ge. 41. 32.
[g] Pr. 6. 18. [h] Ge. 12. 1. [i] Job 11. 15. [k] Zep. 3. 18. [kk] 1 Ki. 7. 11.
[l] Pr. 1. 31. [m] Ps. 75. 7. [n] Pr. 14. 27. [o] Le. 23. 17. [oo] 2 Ch. 32. 7.
[p] 1 Sa. 14. 13 [q] Is. 59. 19. [r] Job 37. 9. [s] Is. 25. 6. [ss] Ho. 11. 6.

מַמְחֲלִיק[a] pref. מִ·)(Hiph. part. sing. masc. . . חלק
מִמַּחֲנֵה pref. id.)(noun m. s., constr. of מַחֲנֶה d. 9a חנה
מִמַּחֲנוֹת[b] pref. id.)(id. with pl. fem. term. . חנה
מִמַּחֲנַיִם ׳וּ pref. id.)(pr. name of a place; וּ bef. lab. חנה
מִמַּחֲצִית ׳וּ pref. id.)(noun fem. sing. dec. 1b; וּ id. חצה
מִמַּחֲצִיתָם[c] pref. id.)(id., suff. 3 pers. pl. masc. . חצה
מִמַּחֲצַת[d] ׳וּ defect. for מִמַּחֲצִית (q. v.) . . חצה
מִמָּחֳרָת ׳וּ pref. מִ)(noun fem. sing.; וּ bef. lab. . מחר
מִמָּחֳרַת pref. id.)(id., constr. st. . . מחר
מִמַּחְשְׁבֹתֵיכֶם[e] pref. id.)(noun fem. pl., suff. 2 pers. pl. masc. from מַחֲשָׁבָה or מַחֲשֶׁבֶת . חשב
מִמְּחִתָּה[f] וּ pref. id.)(noun fem. sing. d. 10; וּ bef. lab. חתת
מִמַּטֵּה ׳וּ pref. id.)(constr. of the foll.; וּ id. נטה
מִמַּטֶּה pref. id.)(noun masc. sing. dec. 9a . . נטה
מִמַּטּוֹת[g] pref. id.)(id. with pl. fem. term. . . נטה
מַמְטִיר Hiph. part. sing. masc. . . . . מטר
מִמַּטְמוֹנִים[h] pref. מִ·)(noun masc. pl. of מַטְמוֹן dec. 1a טמן
מִמְּטַר[i] ׳וּ[k] pref. id.)(noun masc. s. d. 4a; וּ bef. lab. מטר
מִמֵּי ׳וּ[l] pref. id.)(noun masc. pl. constr. [from מַיִם § 38. rem. 2, & § 45] . . . מי
מִמִּי pref. id.)(pron. pers. interr. . . . . מי
מִמַּיִם pref. id.)(n. m. pl. [of מַי § 38. r. 2, & § 45] מי
מִמֵּימֵי pref. id.)(id. constr. st. (§ 45) . . . מי
מֵמִית[m] Hiph. part. sing. masc. dec. 3b . . מות
מְמִיתִים[n] id. pl., abs. st. . . . . מות
מִמְּךָ / מִמְּךָ } prep. מִן with suff. 2 pers. sing. m. (§ 5) מנן
מִמֵּךְ id. with suff. 2 pers. sing. fem. . . . מנן
מִמְּכוֹן pref. מִ·)(noun m. s., constr. of מָכוֹן d. 3a כון
מִמַּכּוֹתַיִךְ[o] וּ pref. id.)(noun fem. pl., suff. 2 pers. sing. fem. from מַכָּה dec. 10; וּ bef. lab. .. נכה
מִמִּכְלְאֹת[p] pref. id.)(n. f. pl. constr. fr. [מִכְלָאָה] d. 11a כלא
מִמִּכְלְאֹתֶיךָ[q] pref. id.)(id., suff. 2 pers. sing. masc. . כלא
מִמִּכְלָה[r] pref. id.)(id. sing. abs. [for מִכְלָאָה] . כלא
מִמִּכְמָשׂ pref. id.)(pr. name of a place, see מִכְמָס . כמס
מִמְכָּר noun masc. sing. dec. 2b . . . מכר
מִמְכַּר[s] id. constr. st. . . . . . מכר
מִמְכָּרוֹ[t] id. with suff. 3 pers. sing. masc. . . מכר
מִמְכָּרָיו[u] id. pl., suff. 3 pers. sing. masc. . . מכר
מִמְכֶּרֶת[x] noun sing. fem. . . . . מכר
מְמַלֵּא Piel part. sing. masc. dec. 7b . . . מלא
מִמְּלֹא[y] pref. מִ·)(noun masc. sing. dec. 1a . מלא
מִמְּלֹאָהּ pref. id.)(id., suff. 3 pers. sing. fem. . מלא
מְמֻלָּאִים[z] Pual part. masc. pl. [of מְמֻלָּא] . . מלא
מִמְּלַאכְתּוֹ[a] pref. מִ·)(noun fem. sing., suff. 3 pers. sing. masc. from מְלֶאכֶת (dec. 13a), constr. of מְלָאכָה (§ 42. rem. 5) . . לאך
מְמֻלָּח[b] Pual part. sing. masc. . . . . מלח
מִמִּלְחָמָה pref. מִ·)(noun fem. sing. dec. 11a, (suff. מִלְחַמְתּוֹ, from מִלְחֶמֶת dec. 13a, § 42. rem. 5) לחם
מְמַלֵּט[c] Piel part. sing. masc. dec. 7b . . מלט
מִמֻּלִי[d] pref. מִ·)(prep. (מוּל) with suff. 1 p. s. d. 1a מול
מִמֶּלֶךְ pref. id.)(noun masc. sing. dec. 6a . מלך
מִמְּלֹךְ pref. id.)(Kal inf. constr. . . . מלך
מַמְלָכָה ׳וּ noun fem. sing. dec. 11a, but constr. מַמְלֶכֶת (§ 42. rem. 5); וּ bef. lab. . מלך
מַמְלָכוֹת ׳וּ id. pl., abs. st.; וּ id. . . . מלך
מַמְלְכוֹת id. pl., constr. st. . . . . מלך
מַמְלְכוּת noun fem. sing. . . . . . מלך
מַמְלֶכֶת noun fem. sing., constr. of מַמְלָכָה (§ 42. r. 5) מלך
מַמְלַכְתּוֹ id., suff. 3 pers. sing. masc. (comp. dec. 13) מלך
מַמְלַכְתִּי[e] ׳וּ[f] id., suff. 1 pers. sing.; וּ bef. lab. for וְ מלך
מַמְלַכְתְּךָ ׳וּ[g] id., suff. 2 pers. sing. masc.; וּ id. . מלך
מְמַלֵּל[h] Ch. Pael part. sing. masc. . . . מלל
מְמַלִּל[i] Ch. id. part. sing. masc. . . . מלל
מְמַלְּלָא[k] Ch. id. part. sing. fem. . . . . מלל
מִמַּמְלָכָה[l] ׳וּ[m] pref. מִ·)(noun fem. sing., comp. מַמְלָכָה מלך
מִמֶּנָּה ׳וּ[n] prep. (מִן) with suff. 3 p.s.f. (§ 5); וּ bef. lab. מנן
מִמֶּנּוּ ׳וּ id. with suff. 3 pers. s. masc. or 1 pers. pl. מנן
מִמְּנוֹחַ[o] pref. מִ·)(noun m. s., constr. of מָנוֹחַ d. 3a נוח
מִמֶּנִּי prep. (מִן) with suff. 1 pers. sing. (§ 5) . מנן
מְמֻנִּים[p] Pual part. masc., pl. of [מְמֻנֶּה] dec. 9a . מנה
מִמְּנַשֶּׁה ׳וּ pref. מִ·)(pr. name of a tribe; וּ bef. lab. נשה
מִמַּסְגֵּר[q] pref. id.)((prop. Hiph. part.) subst. masc. s. סגר
מִמִּסְגְּרוֹתֵיהֶם[r] / מִמִּסְגְּרוֹתָם[s] / מִמִּסְגְּרֹתֵיהֶם[t] } pref. מִ·)(noun fem. pl., suff. 3 pers. pl. masc. (§ 4. rem. 2) fr. מִסְגֶּרֶת dec. 13a . } סגר
מִמַּסַּד[u] וּ pref. id.)(noun masc. sing.; וּ bef. lab. יסד
מִמְּסוּכָה[x] pref. id.)(noun fem. sing. [for מְשׂוּכָה] שוך
מִמְסָךְ noun masc. sing. . . . . . מסך
מִמְּסִלּוֹתָם[y] pref. מִ·)(noun fem. pl., suff. 3 pers. pl. masc. from מְסִלָּה dec. 10 . . . סלל
מִמּוֹסֵרוֹת pref. id.)(pr. name of a place, see מוֹסֵר אסר
מִמְּעוֹן ׳וּ[z] pref. id.)(noun masc sing., constr. of מָעוֹן dec. 3a (§ 32. rem. 5) . . . עון
מִמֵּעַי[a] pref. id.)(n. m. pl., suff. 1 p. s. fr. [מֵעַ] d. 7a מע
מִמְּעֵי pref. id.)(id. pl., constr. st. . . . מע
מִמֵּעַיִךְ[b] pref. id.)(id. pl., suff. 2 pers. sing. fem. מע
מִמֵּעֶיךָ pref. id.)(id. pl., suff. 2 pers. sing. masc. מע

[a] Pr. 28. 23. [b] 1 Sa. 17. 4. [c] Nu. 31. 29. [d] Nu. 31. 30, 42, 47. [e] Is. 55. 9. [f] Is. 54. 14. [g] Nu. 36. 8. [h] Job 3. 21. [i] 2 Sa. 23. 4. [k] Is. 4. 6. [l] Is. 48. 1. [m] 1 Sa. 2. 6. [n] 2 Ki. 17. 26. [o] Je. 30. 17. [p] Ps. 78. 70. [q] Ps. 50. 9. [r] Hab. 3. 17. [s] Le. 25. 25, 33. [t] Le. 25. 27, 28, 29, 50. [u] De. 18. 8. [x] Le. 25. 42. [y] Ec. 4. 6. [z] Ca. 5. 14. [a] Ex. 36. 4. [b] Ex. 30. 35. [c] 1 Sa. 19. 11. [d] Nu. 22. 5. [e] Ge. 20. 9. [f] 2 Sa. 3. 28. [g] 2 Sa. 7. 16. [h] Da. 7. 8. [i] Da. 7. 20. [k] Da. 7. 11. [l] Ps. 105. 13. [m] 1 Ch. 16. 20. [n] Je. 30. 7. [o] 1 Ch. 6. 16. [p] 1 Ch. 9. 29. [q] Ps. 142. 8. [r] Ps. 18. 46. [s] 2 Sa. 22. 46. [t] Mi. 7. 17. [u] 1 Ki. 7. 9. [x] Mi. 7. 4. [y] Ju. 5. 20. [z] Je. 25. 30. [a] 2 Sa. 16. 11. [b] Ge. 25. 23.

מִמַּעַיְנֵי[a] pref. ·מִ)(noun m. pl. constr. fr. מַעְיָן d. 2 b . עין
מִמַּ֫עַל / וּמִמַּ֫עַל } pref. id.)((prop. subst.) as an *adv.*; וּ bef. lab. . . . . עלה
מִמַּעֲלֵה[b] pref. id.)(noun m. s., constr. of מַעֲלֶה d. 9a . עלה
מִמַּעֲלֵי pref. id.)(Hiph. part. pl. constr. fr. מַעֲלֶה d. 9a . עלה
מִמַּעַלְלֵיהֶם pref. id.)(noun masc. pl., suff. 3 pers. pl. masc. fr. [מַעֲלָל] dec. 2 b . . עלל
וּמִמַּעֲמָדְךָ[c] pref. id.)(noun masc. sing., suff. 2 pers. sing. masc., from [מַעֲמָד] d. 2 b; וּ bef. lab. עמד
וּמִמַּעֲמַקֵּי[d] pref. id.)(constr. of the foll.; וּ id. . עמק
מִמַּעֲמַקִּים[e] pref. id.)(noun masc., pl. of [מַעֲמָק] d. 8 a . עמק
מִמְּעֹנוֹת[f] pref. id.)(noun fem., pl. of מְעֹנָה [or מְעוֹנָה] dec. 10 . . . . עון
מִמְּעֹנָתוֹ[g] pref. id.)(id. sing., suff. 3 pers. sing. masc. עון
מִמֹּעֲצוֹתֵיהֶם[h] defect. for מִמּוֹעֲצוֹתֵיהֶם (q. v.) . יעץ
וּמִמַּעֲרָב pref. ·מִ)(noun masc. s. d. 2 b; וּ bef. lab. ערב
וּמִמַּעֲרָבָה[i] pref. id.)(noun fem. sing. fr. מַעֲרָב; וּ id. ערב
מִמַּעֲרֵה[k] pref. id.)(noun m. s., constr. of [מַעֲרֶה] d. 9 a ערה
מִמַּעַרְוֹת[l] pref. id.)(Kh. מַעֲרוֹת [pl. c. of מַעֲרָה] R. ערה; K. מַעַרְכוֹת (q. v.) . . ערך
מִמַּעֲשָׂיו[m] prf. id.)(n. m. pl., suff. 3 p. m. s. fr. מַעֲשֶׂה d. 9 a עשׂה
מִמַּעֲשֵׂנוּ[n] pref. id.)(id. sing., suff. 1 pers. pl. . . עשׂה
מִמַּעְשְׂרוֹ[o] pref. id.)(noun masc. sing., suff. 3 pers. sing. masc. from מַעֲשֵׂר dec. 7 b . . עשׂר
וּמִמַּפְרִיסֵי[p] / וּמִמַּפְרִסֵי[q] } pref. id.)(Hiph. part. pl. constr. fr. מַפְרִים dec. 1 b; וּ bef. lab. . . פרס
מִמַּצָּב[r] pref. id.)(noun m. s., constr. of [מַצָּב] d. 2b נצב
מִמַּצָּבְךָ[s] pref. id.)(id., suff. 2 pers. s. m. [for מַצָּבְךָ] נצב
מִמְּצוֹא[t] pref. id.)(Kal inf. constr. . . מצא
מִמְּצוּקוֹתַי[u] pref. id.)(noun fem. pl., suff. 1 pers. sing. from מְצוּקָה dec. 10 . . . . צוק
מִמְּצוּקוֹתֵיהֶם[x] pref. id.)(id., suff. 3 pers. pl. masc. צוק
מִמִּצְוֹת[y] pref. id.)(noun fem., pl. of מִצְוָה dec. 10 צוה
מִמִּצְוֹתֶיךָ pref. id.)(id., suff. 2 pers. sing. masc. . צוה
מַמְצִיא[z] Hiph. part. sing. masc. . . . מצא
מִמְּצֻלוֹת[a] pref. ·מִ)(noun fem., pl. of מְצוּלָה dec. 10 צול
וּמִמִּצְפֶּה pref. id.)(pr. name of a place; וּ bef. lab. צפה
וּ · מִמְּצֻקוֹתֵיהֶם[b] defect. for מִמְּצוּקוֹ׳ (q. v.) . . צוק
מִמִּצְרַיִם / וּמִמִּצְרַיִם } pref. ·מִ)(pr. name of a country; וּ bef. lab. מצר
מִמַּקֵּדָה pref. id.)(pr. name of a place . . נקד
וּמִמִּקְדָּשִׁי[c] pref. id.)(noun masc. sing., suff. 1 pers. sing. from מִקְדָּשׁ dec. 2b; וּ bef. lab. . קדשׁ
מִמִּקְדָּשֶׁיךָ[d] pref. id.)(id. pl., suff. 2 pers. sing. masc. . קדשׁ
מִמַּקְהֵלוֹת pref. id.)(pr. name of a place . . קהל

מִמָּקוֹם[e] pref. ·מִ)(noun com. sing. dec. 3a . . קום
מִמְּקוֹם[f] וּ׳[g] pref. id.)(id. constr. st.; וּ bef. lab. . . קום
מִמְּקוֹמָהּ[h] pref. id.)(id., suff. 3 pers. sing. fem. . קום
מִמְּקוֹמוֹ pref. id.)(id., suff. 3 pers. sing. masc. . קום
מִמְּקוֹמְךָ pref. id.)(id., suff. 2 pers. sing. masc. . קום
מִמְּקוֹמְכֶם[i] pref. id.)(id., suff. 2 pers. pl. masc. . קום
מִמְּקוֹמָם[k] pref. id.)(id., suff. 3 pers. pl. masc. . . קום
מִמְּקוֹר[l] pref. id.)(noun m. sing., constr. of מָקוֹר d. 3a קור
מִמְּקֹמוֹ defect. for מִמְּקוֹמוֹ (q. v.) . . . קום
מִמִּקְנֵה[m] וּ׳ pref. ·מִ)(noun masc. sing., constr. of מִקְנֶה dec. 9a; וּ bef. lab. . . . קנה
מִמְּקֹר[n] defect. for מִמְּקוֹר (q. v.) . . . קור
מִמֹּקְשֵׁי defect. for מִמּוֹקְשֵׁי (q. v.) . . . יקשׁ
מַמְרֵא וּ׳ pr. name of a man and a place; וּ bef. lab. מרא
מֶמֶר[o] וּ noun masc. sing.; וּ id. . . . מרר
מִמַּרְאֵה וּ׳ pref. ·מִ)(noun masc. sing., constr. of מַרְאֶה dec. 9a; וּ id. . . . ראה
מִמָּרָה pref. id.)(pr. name of a place . . מרר
מִמָּרוֹם pref. id.)(noun masc. sing. dec. 3a . רום
מִמְּרוֹם[p] pref. id.)(id. constr. st. . . . רום
מִמְּרוֹמִים[q] pref. id.)(id. pl., abs. st. . . . רום
מַמְּרוֹרִים[r] noun masc. pl. [of מַמְרוֹר] . . מרר
מֶמְרָחָק noun masc. sing. (pl. מֶרְחַקִּים & מַרְ׳) d. 8a רחק
מְמֹרָט[s] Pual part. sing. masc. . . . . מרט
מַמְרִים Hiph. part. masc., pl. of [מַמְרֶה] dec. 9a מרה
מִמְּרֹרָתוֹ[t] pref. ·מִ)(noun fem. sing., suff. 3 pers. sing. fem. from [מְרֹרָה] dec. 10 . . מרר
מִמָּרֵשָׁה pref. id.)(pr. name of a place . . ראשׁ
מִמַּשָּׂא[u] pref. id.)(noun masc. sing. dec. 1b . נשׂא
מִמֵּישָׁא pref. id.)(pr. name of a place, see מֵישָׁא.
מִמַּשְׂאוֹת[x] pref. id.)(noun f., pl. of מַשְׂאֵת [for מַשְׂאֶת] נשׂא
מִמִּשְׁבְּצוֹת[y] pref. id.)(noun fem., pl. [מִשְׁבֶּצֶת] dec. 13 שׁבץ
מִמְשַׁח[z] noun masc. sing. . . . . משׁח
מְמֻשָּׁךְ[a] Pual part. sing. masc. . . . משׁך
מְמֻשָּׁכָה[b] id. part. sing. fem. . . . . משׁך
וּמִמִּשְׁכָּן[c] וּ׳ pref. ·מִ)(noun masc. sing. dec. 2b; וּ bef. lab. . . . . . שׁכן
מִמִּשְׁכַּן[d] pref. id.)(id. constr. st. . . . שׁכן
מְמַשֵּׁל[e] Piel part. 2 pers. sing. masc. . . משׁל
מִמְשָׁל[f] noun masc. sing., pl. מִמְשָׁלִים׳ . . משׁל
מַמְשְׁלוֹתָיו[g] the foll. with suff. 3 pers. sing. masc. . משׁל
מֶמְשֶׁלֶת[h] noun fem. sing. dec. 13a, used as the constr. of מֶמְשָׁלָה׳ (§ 42. rem. 5) . . משׁל
מֶמְשַׁלְתּוֹ id., suff. 3 pers. sing. masc. . . משׁל
וּמֶמְשַׁלְתְּךָ id., suff. 2 pers. sing. masc.; וּ bef. lab. . משׁל

a Is. 12.3. b Ju. 1.36. c Is. 22.19. d Ps. 69.15. e Ps. 130.1. f Ca. 4.8.
g Am. 3.4. h Ps. 5.11. i Is. 45.6. k Ju. 20.33. l 1 Sa. 17.23. m Ex. 5.4.
n Ge. 5.29. o Le. 27.31. p De. 14.7. q Le. 11.4. r Jos. 4.3. s Is. 22.19.
t Is. 58.13. u Ps. 25.17. x Ps. 107.6,13,19. y Le. 4.27. z Zec. 11.6. a Ps. 68.23.
b Ps. 107.28. c Eze. 9.6. d Ps. 68.36. e Est. 4.14. f 2 Ch. 6.21. g Ec. 8.10.
h Job. 9.6; Is. 13.13. i Jos. 3.3. k Job 6.17. l Ps. 68.27. m Ex. 9.6, 7 n Le. 12.7.
o Pr. 17.25. p Ps. 102.20. q Job 31.2. r Job 9.18. s 1 Ki. 7.45. t Job 20.25.
u Ho. 8.10. x Ge. 43.34. y Ps. 45.14. z Eze. 28.14. a Is. 18.2, 7. b Pr. 13.12.
c 1 Ch. 17.5. d 2 Ch. 29.6. e Eze. 21.5. f Da. 11.3, 5. g Ps. 114.2. h Je. 34.1.

מִמִּשְׁפַּחְתָּהּ[a] pref. מִ) noun fem. sing. dec. 11a, suff. דec. 13a, from פַּחַת' (§ 42. rem. 5) פַּחְתִּי' שׁפח

מִמִּשְׁפְּחוֹת[b] [c] וּ pref. id.) id. pl., constr. of מִשְׁפָּחוֹת שׁפח

מִמִּשְׁפַּחַת pref. id.) id. sing., dec. 13a . . . שׁפח

מִמִּשְׁפְּחֹת pref. id.) id. pl. constr. st. . . . שׁפח

מִמִּשְׁפַּחְתּוֹ pref. id.) id. sing., suff. 3 pers. sing. masc. שׁפח

מִמִּשְׁפַּחְתִּי[d] pref. id.) id. sing., suff. 1 pers. sing. שׁפח

מִמִּשְׁפְּחֹתָם[e] [f] וּ pref. id.) id. sing., suff. 3 pers. pl. masc.; וּ bef. lab. . . . שׁפח

מִמִּשְׁפָּט[g] וּ pref. id.) noun masc. sing. dec. 2b; וּ id. שׁפט

מִמִּשְׁפָּטֶיךָ[h] וּ pref. id.) id. pl., suff. 2 pers. sing. m.; וּ id. שׁפט

מִמְשַׁק[i] noun masc. sing., constr. of [מִמְשָׁק] dec. 2b משק

מִמַּשְׁקֵה[k] pref. מִ) noun m. s., constr. of מַשְׁקֶה d. 9a שׁקה

מִמַּשְׂרֵקָה pref. id.) pr. name of a place . . שׂרק

מְמַשֵּׁשׁ[l] Piel part. sing. masc. . . . . מישׁ

מִמִּשְׁתֵּה[m] pref. מִ) noun m. s., constr. of מִשְׁתֶּה d. 9a שׁתה

מְמֹתִים[n] defect. for מְמוֹתִים (q. v.) . . . מות

מִמְתִים[o] pref. מִ) noun m. pl. of [מַת] d. 7 (§ 36. r. 5) מתה

מִמִּתְכַּבֵּד[p] pref. מִ) Hithpa. part. sing. masc. . כבד

מִמַּתָּנָה וּ pref. id.) pr. name of a place; וּ bef. lab. נתן

מִמֻּתֵנוּ[q] pref. id.) Kal inf. (מוּת'), suff. 1 pers. pl. d. 1a מות

מִמָּתְנֵי pref. id.) noun m. du., constr. of [מֹתֶן] d. 6c מתן

מִמָּתְנָיו[r] וּ pref. id.) id. du., suff. 3 p. s. m.; וּ bef. lab. מתן

מִמָּתְנַיִם[s] pref. id.) id. du., abs. st. . . . מתן

מִמִּתְקָה pref. id.) pr. name of a place . . . מתק

מִמִּתְקוֹמְמַי[t] pref. id.) the foll. with suff. 1 pers. sing. קום

מִמִּתְקוֹמְמִים[u] pref. id.) Hithpal. part. masc. pl. [of מִתְקוֹמֵם] dec. 7b . . . קום

מַמְתַּקִּים noun masc., pl. of [מַמְתָּק] dec. 8a . מתק

מָן masc. once with suff. מַנְךָ Ne. 9. 20, (according to some MSS. מַנֶּךָ) *manna*, the *miraculous* food with which God fed the Israelites in the wilderness, described Ex. 16. 31; Nu. 11. 7. Etymo. uncertain. According to Ex. 16. 15, its name is derived from the words מָן הוּא *what is this?* (comp. Chald. מַן) or, *it is a portion*; from the Root מָנַן q. v.

מַן־ וּ Chald. [with Mak. for מָן] pron.—I. interrog. *who? what?*—II. relat. מַן־דִּי *whoever, whosoever.*

מַן[x] Piel imp. sing. masc. ap. [from מַנֵּה] . מנה

מִן וּ Heb. & Chald. *prep.* (§ 5) . . . מנן

מִן בְּהֵמָה[y] Kh. מִן בְּהֵ'; K. מֵהַבְּהֵמָה pref. מֵ for מִ see הַבְּהֵמָה.

מְנֵא[z] Chald. Peal part. pass. sing. masc. . . מנא

מִנֹּא pref. מִ) pr. name of a place . . . נא

מְנָאוֹת[a] noun fem., pl. of מְנָת irr. (§ 45) . . מנה

מְנָאֵף[b] Piel part. sing. masc. dec. 7b . . . נאף

מְנָאֲפִים id. pl., abs. st. . . . . . נאף

מְנָאֲפִים[c] id. id. dag. forte impl. (§ 14. rem. 1) . נאף

מְנָאֶפֶת[d] [e] וּ id. sing. fem. [for מְנָאֶפֶת]; וּ bef. lab. נאף

מִנֹּאָץ[f] [for מִתְנֹאָץ] Hithpoal (§ 6, No. 1) part. s. m. נאץ

מְנַאֲצַי[g] Piel part. pl., suff. 1 pers. s. fr. [מְנָאֵץ] d. 7b נאץ

מְנַאֲצַיִךְ[h] id. pl., suff. 2 p. s. f., dag. f. impl. (§ 14. r. 1) נאץ

מִנַּאֲקָתָם[i] pref. מִ) noun fem. sing., suff. 3 pers. pl. masc. from [נְאָקָה] dec. 11c (§ 42. r. 1) נאק

מִנָּבִיא [k] וּ pref. id.) noun masc. s. d. 3a; וּ bef. lab. נבא

מִנְּבִיאֵי[l] pref. id.) id. pl., constr. st. . . . נבא

מִנָּבָל pref. id.) pr. name masc. . . . נבל

מְנַבֵּל[m] Piel part. sing. masc. . . . . נבל

מִנִּבְלָתָהּ[n] pref. מִ) noun fem. sing., suff. 3 pers. sing. fem. from נְבֵלָה dec. 11c (§ 42. rem. 4) . נבל

מִנִּבְלָתָם[o] pref. id.) id. with suff. 3 pers. pl. masc. נבל

מִנֶּגֶב [p] וּ pref. id.) noun masc. sing. (§ 35. rem. 3); וּ bef. lab. . . . . . . נגב

מִנֶּגֶד pref. id.) (prop. noun masc. sing., dec. 6) as a *prep.* (§ 35. rem. 3) . . נגד

מִנֶּגְדּוֹ[q] pref. id.) id., suff. 3 pers. sing. masc. . נגד

מִנֶּגְדִּי[r] pref. id.) id., suff. 1 pers. sing. . . נגד

מִנָּגְהָהּ pref. id.) n. m. s. (suff. נָגְהָם) d. 6c (§ 35. r. 5) נגה

מְנַגֵּחַ[s] Piel part. sing. masc. . . . . נגח

מַנְגִּינָתָם[t] noun f. s., suff. 3 p. pl. m. fr. [מַנְגִּינָה] d. 10 נגן

מִנְּגִינָתָם[u] pref. מִ) noun fem. sing., suff. 3 pers. pl. masc. from נְגִינָה dec. 10 . . . נגן

מְנַגֵּן Piel part. sing. masc. . . . . . נגן

מֻנָּד[x] Hoph. part. sing. m. [for מוּגָּד § 21. r. 24] נגד

מִנְדָּה Ch. dag. forte resolved in נ for מִדָּה (q. v.) מדד

מְנֻדָּח[y] Pual part. sing. masc. . . . . נדח

מְנַדֵּיכֶם[z] Piel part. pl. masc., suff. 2 pers. pl. masc. from [מְנַדֶּה] dec. 9a . . . . נדה

מַנְדַּע[a] וּ Ch. noun masc. sing., dag. forte resolved in נ for מַדַּע dec. 2a; וּ bef. lab. ידע

מַנְדְּעָא[b] וּ Ch. id., emph. st.; וּ id. . . . ידע

מַנְדְּעִי[c] וּ Ch. id., suff. 1 pers. sing.; וּ id. ידע

מִנִּדְרֵיכֶם[d] pref. מִ) n. m. pl., suff. 2 p. pl. m. fr. נֶדֶר d. 6a נדר

מָנָה[e] I. *to separate, appoint.*—II. *to number.* Niph. *to be numbered.* Pi. *to appoint, constitute, destine*; with לְ *to appoint, assign.*

מְנָא, מְנָה Ch. *to number.* Pa. *to appoint, constitute.*

מָנֶה masc. dec. 9b, *Maneh*, a Hebrew weight,

---

[a] Je. 3. 14. [b] Jos. 21. 40. [c] 1 Ch. 6. 51. [d] Ge. 24. 40. [e] Ju. 18. 2. [f] Le. 25. 45.
[g] Is. 53. 8. [h] Ps. 119. 102, 120. [i] Zep. 2. 9. [k] Eze. 45. 15. [l] De. 28. 29. [m] Est. 7. 7.
[n] Je. 26. 15. [o] Ps. 17. 14. [p] Pr. 12. 9. [q] Ex. 14. 12. [r] Eze. 8. 2. [s] Ex. 28. 42.
[t] Ps. 59. 2. [u] Ps. 17. 7. [x] Ps. 61. 8. [y] 1 Ki. 18. 5. [z] Da. 5. 25, 26. [a] Ne. 12. 44.
[b] Is. 57. 3. [c] Ho. 7. 4. [d] Pr. 30. 20. [e] Ho. 3. 1. [f] Is. 52. 5. [g] Nu. 14. 23.
[h] Is. 60. 14. [i] Ju. 2. 18. [k] Je. 6. 13. [l] 1 Ki. 18. 13. [m] Mi. 7. 6. [n] Le. 11. 40.
[o] Le. 11. 25, 35, 37, 38. [p] Ju. 21. 19. [q] Ps. 10. 5. [r] Ca. 6. 5. [s] Da. 8. 4.
[t] La. 3. 63. [u] La. 5. 14. [x] 2 Sa. 23. 6. [y] Is. 8. 22. [z] Is. 66. 5.
[a] Da. 5. 12. [b] Da. 2. 21. [c] Da. 4. 31, 33. [d] Nu. 29. 39. [e] Nu. 23. 10.

consisting of 100 shekels; for smaller kinds, see Eze. 45. 12.

מָנוֹתֶהָ מָנָה fem. constr. מְנָת, but pl. with suff. (§ 42. rem. 2) *part, portion.*

מֹנֶה masc. only pl. מֹנִים *times,* Ge. 31. 7, 41, *ten times.*

מְנִי, the name of an idol, prob. the god of *destiny, fortune,* Is. 65. 11.

מְנָת fem. pl. מְנָאוֹת ,מְנָיוֹת (§ 45) *part, portion.*

מִנְיָן Ch. dec. 1 b, *number,* Ezr. 6. 17.

תִּמְנָה (*portion, possession*) pr. name—I. of a city in the tribe of Judah.—II. תִּמְנָתָה, prob. another city in the tribe of Dan. Gent. noun תִּמְנִי Ju. 15. 6.

תִּמְנַת־סֶרַח (*portion of abundance*) pr. name of a city in the tribe of Ephraim, Jos. 19. 50; 24. 30; called also (by transp.) תִּמְנַת חֶרֶס Ju. 2. 9.

מָנֶה[a] noun fem. sing. dec. 11a (§ 42. rem. 2) . מנה

מְנֵא[b] Ch. Peal pret. 3 pers. sing. masc. (§ 55. r. 1) מנה

מְנֵה[c] Kal imp. sing. masc. . . . . מנה

מִנָּה[d] Piel pret. 3 pers. sing. masc. . . . מנה

מִנַּהּ[e] ’וּ Ch. prep. מִן with suff. 3 p. s. f.; וּ bef. lab. מנן

מִנֵּהּ[f] ’וּ Ch. id. with suff. 3 pers. sing. m.; וּ id. מנן

מְנַהֲגוֹת[g] Piel (§ 14. rem. 1) part. fem. pl. [of מְנַהֶגֶת dec. 13, from מְנַהֵג masc.] . . . נהג

מִמֶּנּוּ[h], מִנֵּהוּ[i] } prep. מִן with suff. 3 pers. sing. masc. (§ 5) מנן

מִנְּהוֹן[k], מִנְּהֵין[l] ’וּ } Chald. prep. מִן with suff. 3 pers. pl. masc., K. הֵין fem.; וּ bef. lab. . } מנן

מְנַהֵל[m] Piel part. sing. masc. (§ 14. rem. 1) . נהל

מֵהֶם[n] prep. מִן with suff. 3 pers. pl. masc. (§ 5) מנן

מִנַּהֲמַת[o] pref. ·מִ)(noun fem. sing., constr. of [נְהָמָה] dec. 11c (§ 42. rem. 1) . . . . נהם

מִנָּהָר וּ pref. id.)(noun masc. s. d. 4a; וּ bef. lab. נהר

מִנְּהַר pref. id.)(id., constr. st. . . . נהר

מִנּוּ[p] Piel pret. 3 pers. pl. . . . . מנה

מְנוֹד[q] noun masc., constr. of [מָנוֹד] dec. 3a . נוד

מָנוֹחַ ’וּ noun m. s., dec. 3a, also pr. n.; וּ bef. lab. נוח

מְנוּחָה[r] ’וּ noun fem. sing. dec. 10; וּ id. . נוח

מְנוּחוֹת[s] id. pl. . . . . . . נוח

מְנוּחָתִי id. sing., suff. 1 pers. sing. . . . נוח

מִנָּוֹית pref. ·מִ)(Kh. נָוִית, K. נָיוֹת, pr. n. of a place נוה

מָנוֹן[t] noun masc. sing. . . . . . . נון

מָנוֹס ’וּ noun masc. sing. dec. 3a; וּ bef. lab. . נוס

מְנוּסִי וּ id. with suff. 1 pers. sing. (§ 32. r. 5); וּ id. נוס

מְנוֹרָה[u] ’וּ noun fem. sing. dec. 10; וּ id. . . נור

מְנֹרַת[x] ’וּ id., constr. st; וּ id. . . . . נור

מְנוֹשַׁי[y] pref. ·מִ)(Kal part. pl. masc., suff. 1 pers. sing. from נוֹשֶׁה dec. 9a . . . נשה

מָנוֹת noun fem. pl. abs. from מָנָה dec. 11a . מנה

מְנוֹתֶהָ[z] id. pl., suff. 3 pers. sing. fem. (§ 42. rem. 2) מנה

מִנְּזָרַיִךְ[a] noun m. pl., suff. 2 p. s. f. fr. [מִנְּזָר] d. 2b נזר

מנח

Root not used; Arab. *to give.*

מִנְחָה fem. dec. 12b.—I. *gift, present.*—II. *tribute.*—III. *an offering to God, a sacrifice,* Ge. 4. 3, 4, 5; especially a bloodless offering.

מִנְחָה Ch. fem. dec. 8a, id. Da. 2. 46; Ezr. 7. 17.

מֻנָּח[b] Hoph. part. sing. m. [for מוּנָּח § 21. r. 24] נוח

מְנֻחָה[c] defect. for מְנוּחָה (q. v.) . . . . נוח

מִנְחָה ’וּ noun fem. sing. dec. 12b; וּ bef. lab. . מנח

מַנְחִיל[d] Hiph. part. sing. masc. . . . . נחל

מִנְּחִירָיו[e] pref. ·מִ)(n. m. du. [נְחִירַיִם], suff. 3 p. pl. m. נחר

מִנַּחַל pref. id.)(noun masc. sing. dec. 6d . נחל

מִנַּחֲלָה[f] pref. id.)(noun fem. sing., dec. 12d . . נחל

מִנַּחֲלֵי[g] pref. id.)(noun m. pl. constr. fr. נַחַל d. 6d נחל

מִנַּחֲלִיאֵל וּ pref. id.)(pr. name masc.; וּ bef. lab. נחל

מִנַּחֲלַת[h] ’וּ pref. id.)(noun fem. sing., constr. of נַחֲלָה dec. 12d; וּ id. . . . . נחל

מִנַּחֲלָתוֹ[i] pref. id.)(id., suff. 3 pers. sing. masc. . נחל

מִנַּחֲלָתְךָ[k] pref. id.)(id., suff. 2 pers. sing. masc. . נחל

מִנַּחֲלָתָם[l] pref. id.)(id., suff. 3 pers. pl. masc. . נחל

מְנַחֵם Piel (§ 14. r. 1) part. s. m. d. 7b, also pr. n. נחם

מְנַחֲמַי[m] id. pl., constr. st. . . . . . נחם

מְנַחֲמִים id. pl., abs. st. . . . . . נחם

מְנַחֶמְכֶם[n] id. sing., suff. 2 pers. pl. masc. . . נחם

מְנַחֵשׁ[o] וּ Piel part. sing. masc. (§ 14. r. 1); וּ bef. lab. נחש

מָנַחַת ’וּ pr. name of a place; וּ id. . . . נוח

מִנְחַת ’וּ noun fem. sing., constr. of מִנְחָה dec. 12b (Chald. 8a); וּ id. . . . . מנח

מִנְחָתָהּ ’וּ id., suff. 3 pers. sing. fem.; וּ id. . . מנח

מִנְחָתְהוֹן[p] וּ Chald. noun fem. pl., suff. 3 pers. pl. masc. from מִנְחָה dec. 8a; וּ id. . . . מנח

מְנֻחָתוֹ noun fem. sing., suff. 3 pers. sing. masc. from מְנוּחָה dec. 10 . . . . . נוח

מִנְחָתוֹ ’וּ noun fem. sing., suff. 3 pers. sing. masc. from מִנְחָה dec. 12b; וּ bef. lab. . . מנח

מִנְחָתִי id., suff. 1 pers. sing. . . . . מנח

מִנְחֹתֶיךָ[q] id. pl., suff. 2 pers. sing. masc. . . מנח

מִנְחֹתֵיכֶם[r] וּ id. pl., suff. 2 pers. pl. masc.; וּ bef. lab. . מנח

מִנְחָתֶךָ[s], מִנְחָתְךָ[t] } id. sing., suff. 2 pers. sing. masc. . מנח

מִנְחָתָם ’וּ id. sing., suff. 3 pers. pl. masc.; וּ bef. lab. מנח

[a] 1 Sa. 1. 5. [b] Da. 5. 26. [c] 2 Sa. 24. 1. [d] Da. 1. 10, 11. [e] Da. 7. 24. [f] Da. 4. 9. [g] Na. 2. 8. [h] Job 4. 12. [i] Ps. 68. 24. [k] Da. 2. 33, 41, 42. [l] Da. 6. 3. [m] Is. 51. 18. [n] Job 11. 20. [o] Ps. 38. 9. [p] Job 7. 3. [q] Ps. 44. 15. [r] Je. 45. 3. [s] Ps. 23. 2. [t] Pr. 29. 21. [u] 1 Ch. 28. 15. [x] 2 Ch. 13. 11. [y] Is. 50. 1. [z] Est. 2. 9. [a] Na. 3. 17. [b] Eze. 41. 9. [c] Ge. 49. 15. [d] De. 12. 10. [e] Job 41. 12. [f] Eze. 48. 29. [g] 2 Sa. 23. 30; 1 Ch. 11. 32. [h] Nu. 36. 4. [i] Eze. 46. 17. [k] Je. 17. 4. [l] Jos. 2. 3. [m] Job 16. 2. [n] Is. 51. 12. [o] De. 18. 10. [p] Ezr. 7. 17. [q] Ps. 20. 4. [r] Am. 5. 22. [s] Le. 2. 13. [t] Le. 2. 13.

מַנִּי [a] וּ Chald. Pael pret. 3 pers. sing. masc.; וּ id. מנה

מַנִּי [b] Chald. id. imp. sing. masc. . . . . מנה

מֶנִּי prep. מִן with suff. 1 pers. sing. (§ 5) . מנן

מִנֵּי [c] (as if pl. constr. of מֵן) used poetically for the prep. מִן . . . . . . מנן

מִנִּי pr. name of a province . . . . מנן

מִנִּי [d] perh. for מִנִּים pl. of [מֵן] dec. 8b . מנן

מִנִּי [e] וּ prep. מִן with suff. 1 pers. sing., or parag. ׳ ; וּ bef. lab. . . . . . מנן

מְנָיוֹת noun fem., pl. of מְנָת irr. (§ 45) . . מנה

מֵנִיחַ / מְנִיחַ [f] } Hiph. part. sing. masc. (§ 21. rem. 24) נוח

מָנִים noun masc., pl. of מָנֶה dec. 9a . . מנה

מֹנִים [g] noun masc., pl. of [מֹנֶה] dec. 9a . . מנה

מִנְיָמִין [h] וּ pr. name masc. see מִיָּמִין; וּ bef. lab.

מֵנִיף Hiph. part. sing. masc. dec. 3b . . נוף

מְנִיפוֹ [i] id. with suff. 3 pers. sing. masc. . . נוף

מַנִּיתָ [i] Chald. Pael pret. 2 pers. sing. m. (§ 47. r. 2) מנה

מִנִּית pr. name of a place . . . . מנן

מָנִיתִי [k] וּ Kal pret. 1 pers. sing.; וּ for וְ conv. . מנה

מַנְךָ [l] וּ noun masc. sing., suff. 2 pers. sing. masc. from מַן q. v.; וּ bef. lab.

מִנָּךְ Chald., prep. מִן with suff. 2 pers. sing. masc. מנן

מִנִּכְסֵי [m] וּ Chald. noun masc. pl. constr. from [נְכַס] dec. 3b; וּ bef. lab. . . . . נכס

מִנָּכְרִיָּה pref. מִ) adj. fem. s. dec. 10, from נָכְרִי m. נכר

מִנְלָם [n] noun masc. sing., suff. 3 pers. pl. masc. from [מִנְלֶה] dec. 9a . . . . . נלה

מִנְּמֵרִים [o] noun masc., pl. of נָמֵר dec. 4a . . נמר

מָנַן Root not used; Arab. *to divide, apportion.*

מֵן masc.—I. *part, portion*; not used as a subst. in this sense, yet it is a primary form, of which the prep. מִן is the constr. st.—II. pl. מִנִּים Ps. 150. 4, for which מִנִּי Ps. 45. 9, *strings* of an instrument.

מִן, as a prefix מִ with dag. forte, sometimes also without it, when the next letter has sheva, especially when this letter is Yod, which then becomes quiescent (e. g. מִידֵי for מִיְּדֵי); before guttural מֵ, rarely מִ with dag. forte impl. (as מִהְיוֹת, מִחוּץ) poet. מִנֵּי, מִנִּי, with suff. מִמֶּנִּי (see § 5) prep.—I. *of*, noting a part taken *from* or *out of* a whole, both with reference to number and quantity; מִן הָעָם *some of the people*; מִן הַדָּם *some of the blood*; with a negation *nothing of*, comp. De. 16. 4; hence מֵאַיִן, מֵאֶפֶס *nothing at all.*—II. *from*, noting motion, departing, fleeing, trembling, fearing, derivation, distance, &c. Hence as marking cause and means; (*a*) *before, in the presence of*; (*b*) *by, through*; (*c*) *because, on account of*; (*d*) *according to*; (*e*) *about, concerning*; (*f*) *far from, away from*; (*g*) *without*; (*h*) *besides*; (*i*) מִן—אֶל, מִן—עַד *from—to*; *both—and.*—III. *out of, from*, after verbs of going or bringing out, delivering.—IV. *out of, of*, indicating the material of which anything is made.—V. *more than*, noting comparison.—VI. *at, in, on, by*, in specification of space and time; (*b*) *from, since, after*, of time; מִנְּעֻרַי *from my youth*; מִיָּמִים *after some time.*—VII. before an inf. (*a*) *because*; (*b*) *after that, since*; (*c*) *so that not, lest*; (*d*) *more than.*—VIII. with a finite verb, *so that not, lest*, De. 33. 11. Before other particles, see תַּחַת, פָּנִים, עִם, עַל, בַּעַד, בֵּין, אֵת, אַחַר.

מִן Ch. with suff. מִנִּי, מִנָּךְ, מִנֵּהּ, מִנַּהּ, מִנְּהוֹן —I. *part of*, comp. Da. 2. 33.—II. *from*, i. q. Heb. No. II; hence of time, Da. 3. 22.—III. *out of, from*, of the author and cause; hence, (*a*) *on account of, because of*, Da. 5. 19; (*b*) *according to*, Ezr. 6. 14; (*c*) מִן יַצִּיב, מִן קְשֹׁט *of a truth, truly, certainly.*—IV. *more than*, of comparison, Da. 2. 30.

מִנִּי (perh. *allotted*) pr. name of a region, Je. 51. 27.

מִנִּית (id.) pr. name of a place in Ammon, Ju. 11. 33; Eze. 27. 17.

מִנֵּס [p] pref. מִ) noun masc. sing. dec. 8b . נסס

מְנַסֶּה [q] Piel part. sing. masc. . . . . . נסה

מְנֻסַת [r] noun fem. sing., constr. of מְנוּסָה dec. 10 נוס

מִנִּסְתָּרוֹת [s] Niph. part. pl. abs. [fr. נִסְתָּרָה, fr. נִסְתָּר m.] סתר

מָנַע [t] I. *to restrain, hold back*, with מִן *from* any thing.—II. *to restrain, keep back, withhold, refuse*, with acc. of the thing, and מִן, rarely with לְ of the person. Niph. I. *to be restrained, hindered.*—II. *to be withheld* or *withdrawn*, Job 38. 15.

יִמְנָע (whom *He withholds*) pr. name masc. 1 Ch. 7. 35.

תִּמְנָע (*restraint*) pr. name—I. of the concubine of Eliphaz, the son of Esau.—II. of one of the tribes of Edom.

מְנַע [u] Kal imp. sing. masc. . . . . מנע

מֹנֵעַ id. part. sing. masc. . . . . מנע

מָנְעוּ [x] id. pret. 3 pers. pl. . . . . מנע

מַנְעוּלָיו [y] noun masc. pl., suff. 3 pers. sing. masc. from מַנְעוּל dec. 1b . . . . נעל

[a] Da. 2. 24, 49. [b] Ezr. 7. 25. [c] Is. 30. 11. [d] Ps. 45. 9. [e] Ec. 5. 11. [f] Jos. 1. 13. [g] Ge. 31. 7, 41. [h] Is. 10. 15. [i] Da. 3. 12. [k] Is. 65. 12. [l] Ne. 9. 20. [m] Ezr. 6. 8. [n] Job 15. 29. [o] Hab. 1. 8. [p] Is. 31. 9. [q] De. 13. 4. [r] Le. 26. 36. [s] Ps. 19. 13. [t] Ge. 30. 2. [u] Pr. 1. 15. [x] Je. 5. 25. [y] Ne. 3. 3.

Word	Analysis	Root
מִנְּעוּרַי / מִנְּעֻרַי	pref. מִ· (noun masc. pl., suff. 1 pers. sing. from [נְעוּר] dec. 1a	נער
מִנְּעוּרָיו[a]	pref. id. (id., suff. 3 pers. sing. masc.	נער
מִנְּעוּרַיִךְ[b] / מִנְּעֻרַיִךְ	pref. id. (id., suff. 2 pers. sing. fem.	נער
מִנְּעוּרֵינוּ	pref id. (id., suff. 1 pers. pl.	נער
מִנְעִי	Kal imp. sing. fem.	מנע
מְנָעֲךָ	id. pret. 3 pers. sing. masc., suff. 2 pers. sing. masc.	מנע
מַנְעָלָיו[c]	וּ' defect. for מַנְעוּלָיו (q. v.); וּ bef. lab.	נעל
מִנְעָלֶךָ[d]	[for מִנְעָלֵךְ] noun masc. sing., suff. 2 pers. sing. masc. from [מִנְעָל] dec. 2b	נעל
מְנָעַנִי[e]	Kal pret. 3 pers. sing. masc., suff. 1 pers. s.	מנע
מִנַּעַר	pref. מִ· (noun masc. sing. dec. 6d	נער
מִנֹּעַר	pref. id. (noun masc. sing.	נער
מִנְּעָרָי[f]	וּ pref. id. (the following with suff. 1 pers. sing.; וּ bef. lab.	נער
מִנַּעֲרֵי[g]	pref. id. (noun m. pl. constr. fr. נַעַר d. 6d	נער
מִנְּעֻרַי[h] / מִנְּעֻרָי[i]	pref. id. (noun masc. pl., suff. 1 pers. sing. from [נְעוּר] dec. 1a	נער
מִנְּעָרָיו	pref. id. (id., suff. 3 pers. sing. masc.	נער
מִנְּעֻרֵיכֶם[k]	pref. id. (id., suff. 2 pers. pl. masc.	נער
מִנְּעֻרֹתֵיהֶם[l]	pref. id. (noun fem. pl. [נְעוּרוֹת], suff. 3 pers. pl. masc.	נער
מָנַעְתָּ	Kal pret. 2 pers. sing. masc.	מנע
מָנַעְתִּי	id. pret. 1 pers. sing.	מנע
מִנֹּף	pref. מִ· (pr. name of a place, see נֹף.	
מְנֻפָּצוֹת[m]	Pual part. f. pl. [of מְנֻפָּצָה from מְנֻפָּץ m.]	נפץ
מִנֶּפֶשׁ[n]	pref. מִ· (noun com. sing. (suff. נַפְשִׁי) d. 6a	נפש
מִנַּפְתָּלִי	וּ' pref. id. (pr. name of a tribe; וּ bef. lab.	פתל
מְנַצְּחִים[o]	וּ' Piel part. masc., pl. of מְנַצֵּחַ d. 7b; וּ id.	נצח
מִנֵּצֶר	pref. מִ· (noun masc. sing.	נצר
מִנְּקִיקֵי[p]	וּ pref. id. (noun m. pl. constr. fr. [נָקִיק or נְקִיק]; וּ bef. lab.	נקק
מְנַקִּיֹּתָיו[q]	וּ' noun fem. pl., suff. 3 pers. sing. masc. [from מְנַקִּית § 39. rem. 1, note]	נקה
מֵנִקְתָּהּ[r]	Hiph. part. sing. fem. מֵינֶקֶת, suff. 3 pers. sing. f. d. 13a [fr. מֵינִיק m. § 39. No. 4d]	ינק
מֵנִקְתּוֹ[s]	id., suff. 3 pers. sing. masc.	ינק
מְנֹרָה	noun fem. sing. dec. 10	נור
מְנֹרוֹת[t]	id. pl.	נור
מְנֹרַת	id. sing., constr. st.	נור
מִנְּשׂוֹא[u]	pref. מִ· (Kal inf. constr.	נשׂא
מְנַשְּׂאִים	Piel part. masc., pl. of [מְנַשֵּׂא] dec. 7b	נשׂא
מְנַשֶּׁה	וּ' pr. name of a man and a tribe; וּ bef. lab.	נשה
מִנְּשֵׁי	pref. מִ· (constr. of the following	אנש
מִנָּשִׁים	pref. מִ· (noun fem. with pl. masc. term., for אֲנָשִׁים see אִשָּׁה (§ 45)	אנש
מִנְּשִׁיקוֹת[x]	pref. id. (noun fem., pl. of [נְשִׁיקָה] dec. 10	נשק
מִנִּשְׁמַת	pref. id. (noun f. s., constr. of נְשָׁמָה d. 11c	נשם
מִנֶּשֶׁק[y]	pref. id. (noun masc. sing.	נשק
מִנִּשְׁרֵי[z]	pref. id. (constr. of the following	נשר
מִנְּשָׁרִים	pref. id. (noun masc., pl. of נֶשֶׁר dec. 6a	נשר
מְנָת	[a] וּ' noun fem. sing. irr. (§ 45); וּ bef. lab.	מנה
מְנָת[b]	noun f. s., constr. of מָנָה d. 11a (§ 42. r. 2)	מנה
מִנְּתִיבָתָם[c]	pref. מִ· (n. f. s., suff. 3 p. pl. m. fr. נְתִיבָה d. 10	נתב
מַס	noun m. s. (pl. מִסִּים) d. 8b, contr. fr. מֶכֶס	כסס
מֵסַב[d]	prop. noun masc. sing. (with suff. מְסִבּוֹ) dec. 8d, as an *adv.*	סבב
מֵסֵב[e]	Hiph. part. sing. masc.	סבב
מְסִבּוֹת[f]	noun fem., pl. [of מְסִבָּה dec. 10]	סבב
מְסִבַּי[g]	noun m. pl., suff. 1 pers. s. fr. מֵסַב d. 8d	סבב
מְסִבֵּי[h]	וּ id. pl., constr. st.; וּ bef. lab.	סבב
מִסָּבִיב	pref. מִ· ((prop. noun masc. sing. dec. 3a) as an *adv.* or *prep.*	סבב
מִסְּבִיבוֹת[i]	וּ pref. id. (id. with pl. fem. term., as a *prep.*; וּ bef. lab.	סבב
מִסְּבִיבֹתָם[k]	pref. id. (id. (subst.) with pl. fem. term. and suff. 3 pers. pl. masc. (§ 4. rem. 1)	סבב
מִסֻּבְּכוֹ[l]	pref. id. (noun masc. sing., suff. 3 pers. sing. masc., dag. euph. [fr. סְבָךְ § 35. rem. 17]	סבך
מִסֵּבֶל[m]	pref. id. (noun masc. sing.	סבל
מְסֻבָּלִים[n]	Pual part. masc., pl. of מְסֻבָּל	סבל
מִסִּבְלֹתָם[o]	pref. מִ· (noun fem. pl., suff. 3 pers. pl. masc. [fr. סִבְלָה or סְבָלָה]	סבל
מְסִבֹּת	defect. for מוּסִבּוֹת (q. v.)	סבב
מַסְגֵּר[p]	noun masc. sing.	סגר
מִסְגְּרוֹת[q] / מִסְגְּרֹת[r]	וּ pl. of the foll.; וּ bef. lab. / וּ defect. for מִסְגְּרוֹת q. v.; וּ bef. lab. f. וְ	סגר
מְסֻגֶּרֶת[s]	וּ Pual part. sing. fem. [of מְסֻגָּר]; וּ bef. lab.	סגר
מִסְגֶּרֶת	noun fem. sing. (suff. 'גַּרְתּוֹ) dec. 13a	סגר
מִסְגְּרֹתֶיהָ[t]	וּ noun fem. pl., suff. 3 pers. sing. fem. fr. מִסְגֶּרֶת dec. 13a; וּ bef. lab.	סגר
מִסְגְּרֹתֵיהֶם[u]	וּ id., suff. 3 pers. pl. masc.; וּ id.	סגר
מְסֻדוֹת[x]	defect. for מוּסָדוֹת (q. v.)	יסד

מָסָה i. q. מָסַס, only Hiph. *to cause to flow down, dissolve, melt.*

Word	Analysis	Root
מַסָּה[y]	noun fem. sing. dec. 10	נסה
מְסוֹבְלִין[z]	Ch. Poal (§ 48) part. m., pl. of [מְסוֹבַל] d. 2a	סבל
מִסּוֹד[a]	pref. מִ· (noun masc. sing. d. 1a [for יְסוֹד]	יסד
מַסְוֶה[b]	noun masc. sing.	סוה

a Je. 48. 11. b Is. 47. 12. c Ne. 3. 6, 13, 14, 15. d De. 33. 25. e 1 Sa. 25. 34.
f Ne. 13. 19. g 2 Sa. 20. 11. h 1 Ki. 18. 12. i 1 Sa. 12. 2. k 2 Sa. 19. 8. l Je. 32. 30.
m Is. 27. 9. n Is. 10. 18. o 2 Ch. 2. 17. p Je. 16. 16. q Ex. 25. 29; 37. 16. r Ge. 24. 59.
s 2 Ki. 11. 2. t 2 Ch. 4. 7. u Ge. 4. 13. x Ca. 1. 2. y Job 20. 24. z La. 4. 19.
a 2 Ch. 31. 3. b Je. 13. 25. c Pr. 1. 15. d 1 Ki. 6. 29. e Je. 21. 4.
f Job 37. 12. g Ps. 140. 10. h 2 Ki. 23. 5. i Je. 17. 26. k Eze. 28. 26.
l Je. 4. 7. m Ps. 81. 7. n Ps. 144. 14. o Ex. 5. 5. p Is. 24. 22.
q 1 Ki. 7. 28. r 1 Ki. 7. 28. s Jos. 6. 1. t 1 Ki. 7. 35, 36. u 1 Ki. 7. 31.
x 2 Sa. 22. 16. y Ps. 95. 8. z Ezr. 6. 3. a Ps. 64. 3. b Ex. 34. 33.

מַסָּח[a] noun masc. sing. . . . . נסח

מִסְּחַר[b] pref. ·מִ) noun m. s., constr. of [סָחָר] d. 4a סחר

מִסְחַר[c] ·וּ n. m. s., constr. of [מִסְחָר] d. 2b; ·וּ bef. lab. סחר

מַסִּיג[d] Hiph. part. sing. masc. dec. 1b . . נסג

מֵסִיךְ[e] Hiph. part. sing. masc. [for מֵסֵךְ § 18. r. 12] סכך

מִסִּים[f] noun masc., pl. of מַס d. 8b, contr. from מֶכֶס כסס

מִסִּינַי pref. ·מִ) pr. name of a mountain . סין

מַסִּיעַ[g] Hiph. part. sing. masc. . . . נסע

מֵסִיר Hiph. part. sing. masc. . . . סור

מַסִּית Hiph. part. sing. masc. [for מֵסִית § 21. r. 24] סות

מָסַךְ[h] *to mix, mingle.*

מֶסֶךְ m. *mixture*, i. e. mixed or spiced wine, Ps. 75. 9.

מִמְסָךְ masc. id. Pr. 23. 30; Is. 65. 11.

מָסָךְ noun masc. sing. (§ 37. rem. 4) . . סכך

מְסַךְ ·וּ id. constr. st.; ·וּ bef. lab. . . סכך

מֶסֶךְ[i] noun masc. sing. . . . . מסך

מָסְכָה[k] Kal pret. 3 pers. sing. fem. . . מסך

מַסֵּכָה ·וּ noun fem. sing. dec. 10; ·וּ bef. lab. . נסך

מַסֵּכוֹת[l] ·וּ[m] id. pl.; ·וּ id. . . . . נסך

מִסֻּכּוֹת pref. ·מִ) pr. name of a place . . סכך

מְסֻכָּן noun masc. sing. . . . . . סכן

מִסְכְּנוֹת ·וּ[n] noun fem., pl. of [מִסְכְּנֶת] d. 13; ·וּ bef. lab. סכן

מַסֶּכֶת[o] noun fem. sing., constr. of מַסֵּכָה dec. 10 נסך

מִסֻּכֹּת pref. ·מִ) pr. name of a place . . סכך

מָסַכְתִּי Kal pret. 1 pers. sing. [for מָסַכְתִּי § 8. r. 7] מסך

מְסֻכָתֶךָ[p] [for כָתֵךְ noun fem. sing., suff. 2 pers. sing. masc. from [מְסֻכָּה] dec. 10 . סכך

מַסֵּכֹתָם[q] noun fem. sing., suff. 3 pers. pl. masc. from מַסֵּכָה dec. 10 . . . . . נסך

מִסַּל[r] ·וּ[r] pref. ·מִ) noun m. sing. d. 8a; ·וּ bef. lab. סלל

מְסִלָּה noun fem. sing. dec. 10 . . . סלל

מַסְלוּל[s] noun masc. sing. . . . . . סלל

מְסִלּוֹת noun fem., pl. of מְסִלָּה dec. 10 . . סלל

מִסֶּלַע[u] } pref. ·מִ) noun masc. sing. (suff. סַלְעִי dec. 6a, § 35. rem. 5) . . } סלע
מִסָּלַע

מְסַלֵּף[x] Piel part. sing. masc. . . . . סלף

מְסִלַּת noun fem. sing., constr. of מְסִלָּה dec. 10 סלל

מִסֹּלֶת[y] pref. ·מִ) noun com. sing. dec. 6c . . סלת

מִסָּלְתָּהּ[z] pref. id.) id., suff. 3 pers. sing. fem. . סלת

מְסִלֹּתַי[a] ·וּ noun fem. pl., suff. 1 pers. sing. from מְסִלָּה dec. 10; ·וּ bef. lab. . . . סלל

[מָסַס] i. q. מָסָה *to flow down, melt*; only trop. *to faint*, Is. 10. 18. Niph. נָמַס, in pause נָמָס & נָמֵס (§ 18. rem. 7).—I. *to melt, flow down*.—II. *to become weak, faint*, as the heart, of fear, grief, sorrow. Hiph. *to cause to faint, make faint-hearted*, De. 1. 28.

מָס masc. *faint, unhappy*, Job 6. 14.

תֶּמֶס masc. *a melting, wasting away*, Ps. 58. 9.

מַסָּע[b] noun masc. sing. . . . . נסע

מִסְעָד[c] noun masc. sing. . . . . סעד

מְסַעֲדִין[d] Chald. Pael part. masc., pl. of [מְסַעֵד] dag. forte impl. comp. § 14. rem. 1] dec. 2a . סעד

מַסְעֵי noun m. pl. constr. [for מַסְּעֵי] from מַסָּע d. 2b נסע

מַסְעֵיהֶם[e] id. pl., suff. 3 pers. pl. masc. [for מַסְּעֵיהֶם] נסע

מְסָעֵף[f] Piel part. sing. masc. . . . . סעף

מִסַּעַר[g] pref. ·מִ) for סַעַר, noun masc. sing. dec. 6d סער

מִסְפַּד constr. of the foll. . . . . . ספד

מִסְפֵּד ·וּ noun m. sing. d. 7c (§ 36. r. 1); ·וּ bef. lab. ספד

מִסְפְּדִי[h] id. with suff. 1 pers. sing. . . . ספד

מִסְפּוֹא ·וּ[i] noun masc. sing.; ·וּ bef. lab. . . ספא

מְסַפֵּחַ[k] Piel part. sing. masc. . . . . ספח

מִסְפַּחַת[l] noun fem. sing. . . . . . ספח

מִסְפְּחֹתֵיכֶם[m] noun fem. pl., suff. 2 pers. pl. masc. from [מִסְפָּחָה] dec. 11a . . . . ספח

מְסַפֵּר Piel part. sing. masc. dec. 7b . . ספר

מִסַּפֵּר[n] pref. ·מִ) Piel inf. constr. . . . ספר

מִסְפָּר[o] ·וּ noun m. s. d. 2b, also pr. name; ·וּ bef. lab. ספר

מִסְפַּר ·וּ id., constr. st.; ·וּ id. . . . ספר

מִסֵּפֶר[p] pref. ·מִ) noun masc. sing. dec. 6b . . ספר

מִסְפְּרֵי[q] noun masc. pl. constr. from מִסְפָּר dec. 2b ספר

מִסִּפְרִי[r] pref. ·מִ) noun masc. sing., suff. 1 pers. sing. from סֵפֶר dec. 6b . . . . ספר

מְסַפְּרִים Piel part. masc., pl. of מְסַפֵּר dec. 7b . ספר

מִסִּפְרְךָ[s] pref. ·מִ) noun masc. sing., suff. 2 pers. sing. masc. from סֵפֶר dec. 6b . . . ספר

מִסְפַּרְכֶם[t] noun m. s., suff. 2 pers. pl. m. fr. מִסְפָּר d. 2b ספר

מִסְפָּרָם id. with suff. 3 pers. pl. masc. . . ספר

מִסְפֶּרֶת pr. name masc. . . . . . ספר

[מָסַר] as in the Chald. *to deliver, offer*; hence *to teach*, Nu. 31. 16. Prof. Lee, *to stir up*. Niph. *to be delivered, given up*, Nu. 31. 5.

מֹסְרוֹת[u] ·וּ noun masc. with pl. fem. term., constr. st. [from מוֹסֵר for מַאְסֵר] dec. 7b; ·וּ bef. lab. אסר

מִסָּרִיסֵי[x] noun masc. pl. constr. from סָרִיס (§ 32. r. 2) סרס

מְסָרְפוֹ[y] ·וּ Piel part. sing. masc. [מְסָרֵף], suff. 3 pers. sing. masc. dec. 7b; ·וּ bef. lab. . סרף

מִסַּת[z] n. f., constr. of [מִסָּה] contr. fr. מֶכֶס=מִכְסָה כסס

[a] 2 Ki. 11. 6. [b] Pr. 3. 14. [c] 1 Ki. 10. 15. [d] De. 27. 17. [e] Ju. 3. 24. [f] Ex. 1. 11. [g] Ec. 10. 9. [h] Is. 19. 14. [i] Ps. 75. 9. [k] Pr. 9. 2. [l] 2 Ch. 28. 2. [m] 1 Ki. 14. 9. [n] 2 Ch. 32. 28. [o] Is. 30. 22. [p] Eze. 28. 13. [q] Nu. 33. 52. [r] Ex. 29. 23. [s] Le. 8. 26. [t] Is. 35. 8. [u] Ps. 78. 16. [x] Pr. 21. 12. [y] Le. 6. 8. [z] Le. 2. 2. [a] Is. 49. 11. [b] 1 Ki. 6. 7; Job 41. 18. [c] 1 Ki. 10. 12. [d] Ezr. 5. 2. [e] Ex. 40. 36, 38. [f] Is. 10. 33. [g] Ps. 55. 9. [h] Ps. 30. 12. [i] Ge. 24. 32. [k] Hab. 2. 15. [l] Le. 13. 6. [m] Eze. 13. 21. [n] Ps. 40. 6. [o] Nu. 23. 10. [p] Ps. 69. 29. [q] 1 Ch. 12. 23. [r] Ex. 32. 33. [s] Ex. 32. 32. [t] Nu. 14. 29. [u] Job 39. 5. [x] Est. 4. 5. [y] Am. 6. 10. [z] De. 16. 10.

מִסְתּוֹלֵל[a] Hithpoel part. s. m. [for מִתְסוֹלֵל § 12. r. 3.] סלל
מִסְתָּרָיו[b] the foll. with suff. 3 pers. sing. masc. . סתר
מִסְתָּרִים[c] noun masc., pl. of מִסְתָּר dec. 2b . סתר
מְסֻתֶּרֶת[d] [for תָּרֶת'] Pual part. s. fem. [of מְסֻתָּר m.] סתר
מְסַתְּרָתָא[e] וּ Chald. Pael part. pass. fem., emph. st. from מְסַתְּרָא d. 8a, fr. [מְסַתַּר] m.; וּ bef. lab. סתר
מִסְתַּתֵּר Hithpa. part. sing. m. [for מִתְסַתֵּר § 12. r. 3] סתר

מֵעַ masc. sing. not used; pl. מֵעִים, constr. מְעֵי (d. 7a), with suff. מֵעַי, מֵעֵיהֶם (§ 36. rem. 4).—I. *intestines, bowels.*—II. meton. *belly.*—III. *womb.*—IV. *viscera,* trop. for *heart, mind.*—V. pl. מֵעוֹת Is. 48. 19, *the bowels,* trop. of the sea.

מְעֵא Ch. masc. d. 2b, only pl. מְעִין *belly,* Da. 2. 32.

מָעַי (*compassionate*) pr. name masc. Ne. 12. 36.

מֵעֲבֹדָה[f] וּ pref. מֵ for מִ·) noun fem. s. d. 10; וּ bef. lab. עבד
מַעְבָּדוֹהִי[g] Chald. noun masc. pl., suff. 3 pers. sing. masc. from [מַעְבַּד] dec. 1a . . עבד
מֵעַבְדֵי pref. מֵ for מִ·) noun masc. pl. c. fr. עֶבֶד d. 6a עבד
מַעֲבָדֵיהֶם[h] noun m. pl., suff. 3 pers. pl. m. fr. [מַעֲבָד] d. 1b עבד
מֵעֲבָדָיו pref. מֵ for מִ·) noun masc. pl., suff. 3 pers. sing. masc. from עֶבֶד dec. 6a . עבד
מֵעֲבָדֶיךָ[i] וּ/ pref. id.) id., suff. 2 pers. s. m.; וּ bef. lab. עבד
מַעֲבִדִים[k] Hiph. part. masc., pl. of [מַעֲבִיד] dec. 1b עבד
מֵעַבְדְּךָ[l] pref. מֵ for מִ·) noun masc. sing., suff. (for דְךָ') 2 pers. sing. masc. from עֶבֶד dec. 6a עבד
מֵעָבְדֵנוּ[m] pref. id.) Kal inf., suff. 1 pers. pl. . עבד
מֵעֲבֹדַת[n] pref. id.) noun f. s., constr. of עֲבֹדָה d. 10 עבד
מֵעֲבֹדַתְכֶם[o] pref. id.) id., suff. 2 pers. pl. masc. . עבד
מֵעֲבֹדָתָם[p] pref. id.) id., suff. 3 pers. pl. m. (§ 4. r. 2) עבד
מֵעֲבוֹד[q] pref. id.) Kal inf. constr. (§ 8. rem. 18) עבד
מֵעֲבוֹדַת[r] pref. id.) noun f. s., constr. of עֲבוֹדָה d. 10 עבד
מֵעֲבוֹר[s] pref. id.) Kal inf. constr. (§ 8. rem. 18) עבר
מֵעֲבוּר[t] pref. id.) noun m. s., constr. of [עֲבוּר] d. 3a עבר
מַעֲבִיר Hiph. part. sing. masc. dec. 1b . עבר
מַעֲבַר noun masc. sing., constr. of [מַעֲבָר] dec. 2b עבר
מֵעֲבֹר pref. מֵ for מִ·) Kal inf. constr. . עבר
מֵעֵבֶר וּ/ pref. id.) noun masc. sing. dec. 6 (§ 35. rem. 6); וּ bef. lab. . . עבר
מֵעֹבֵר[u] pref. id.) Kal part. act. sing. masc. dec. 7b עבר
מַעְבָּרָה[x] noun fem. sing. dec. 11a . . עבר
מַעְבָּרוֹת[y] id. pl., abs. st. . . עבר
מַעְבְּרוֹת id. pl., constr. st. . . . עבר
מַעֲבִרִים[z] Hiph. part. masc., pl. of מַעֲבִיר dec. 1b . עבר
מֵעֲבָרִים pref. מֵ for מִ·) pr. name of a place עבר
מֵעֹבְרִים[a] pref. id.) Kal part. act. m., pl. of עֹבֵר d. 7b עבר

מֵעֶבְרֹנָה pref. מֵ for מִ·) pr. name of a place . עבר
מַעְגָּלוֹ[b] noun masc. sing. dec. 2b . . עגל
מַעְגַּל id., constr. st. . . . . עגל
מֵעֶגְלוֹנָה pref. מֵ for מִ·) pr. name of a place (עֶגְלוֹן) with parag. ה . . . . עגל
מַעְגָּלֶיךָ[c] וּ noun masc. pl., suff. 2 pers. sing. masc. from מַעְגָּל dec. 2b; וּ bef. lab. . עגל
מַעְגְּלֹתֶיהָ noun fem. pl., suff. 3 p. s. f. fr. מַעְגָּלָה d. 11a עגל
מַעְגְּלֹתָיו[d] id. with suff. 3 pers. sing. masc. . . עגל

[מָעַד] *to vacillate, totter.* Hiph. *to make to vacillate, totter,* Ps. 69. 24. Pu. *to be made to vacillate,* Pr. 25. 19, מוּעֶדֶת, for מְמֻעֶדֶת, מְמוּעֶדֶת (§ 10. r. 6). Gesenius takes this as a participle of Kal, for מוֹעֶדֶת *vacillating.*

מַעֲדֶה[e] Hiph. part. sing. masc. . . . עדה
מָעֲדוּ Kal pret. 3 pers. pl. . . . . מעד
מֹעֲדוֹ[f] noun masc. s., suff. 3 p. s. m. fr. מוֹעֵד d. 7b יעד
מֻעָדוֹת[g] Hoph. part. fem. pl. [of מוּעָדָה fr. מוּעָד m.] יעד
מֵעֵדֹתֶיךָ[h] pref. מֵ for מִ·) noun fem. pl., suff. 2 pers. sing. masc. from עֵדוּת (comp. Chald. d. 8c) עוד
מַעֲדַי pr. name masc. . . . . עדה
מֹעֲדֵי[i] defect. for מוֹעֲדֵי (q. v.) . . . יעד
מַעַדְיָה pr. name masc. . . . . עדה
מֵעֵדֶן pref. מֵ for מִ·) pr. name of a place . עדן
מַעֲדַנּוֹת[k] noun fem. pl. by transp. [for מַעֲנַדּוֹת] . ענד
מַעֲדַנֵּי[l] noun masc. pl. constr. from [מַעֲדָן] dec. 8a עדן
מֵעֶדְנַי[m] pref. מֵ for מִ·) noun masc. pl., suff. 1 pers. sing. from עֵדֶן dec. 6 (§ 35. rem. 6) . עדן
מַעֲדַנִּים[n] / מַעֲדַנֹּת[o] } noun masc., pl. of [מַעֲדָן] dec. 8a . עדן
מֵעֲדַת pref. מֵ for מִ·) noun fem. sing., constr. of עֵדָה dec. 11b . . . יעד
מֵעֵדֹתֶיךָ[p] pref. id.) noun fem. pl., suff. 2 pers. sing. masc. from עֵדָה dec. 10 . . עוד
מֵעַוָּא וּ pref. id.) pr. name of a place; וּ bef. lab. עוה
מָעוֹג noun masc. sing. . . . . עוג
מְעוֹדֵד[q] Pilel part. sing. masc. . . . עוד
מֵעוֹדִי[r] pref. מֵ for מִ·) adv. עוֹד with suff. 1 p. s. d. 1a עוד
מֵעוֹדְךָ[s] pref. id.) id. with suff. 2 pers. sing. masc. עוד
מְעוֹהִי[t] Chald. noun masc. pl., suff. 3 pers. sing. masc. from [מְעֵא] dec. 2b . . מע
מָעוֹז וּ/ noun masc. sing., for מָעֹז (suff. מָעֻזִּי) dec. 8c (§ 37. rem. 2 & 4); וּ bef. lab. . עזז
מָעוּזּוֹ id., suff. 3 pers. s. m. [for מָעֻזּוֹ § 37. r. 2] עזז
מָעוּזִּי[u] id., suff. 1 pers. sing. (v. id.) . . עזז
מָעוּזָּם[v] id., suff. 3 pers. pl. masc. (v. id.) . עזז

a Ex. 9. 17. b Je. 49. 10. c Is. 45. 3. d Pr. 27. 5. e Da. 2. 22. f Ex. 6. 9. g Da. 4. 34. h Job 34. 25. i Ex. 8. 7. k Ex. 6. 5. l Ps. 69. 18. m Ex. 14. 5. n 1 Ki. 12. 4. o Ex. 5. 11. p Ex. 6. 6. q Je. 40. 9. r 2 Ch. 10. 4. s La. 3. 44. t Jos. 5. 11, 12. u Zec. 7. 14; 9. 8. x Is. 10. 29. y Is. 16. 2. z 1 Sa. 2. 24. a Mi. 2. 8. b Ps. 140. 6. c Ps. 65. 12. d Pr. 5. 21. e Pr. 25. 20. f La. 2. 6. g Eze. 21. 21. h Ps. 119. 157. i Le. 23. 44. k Job 38. 31. l Ge. 49. 20. m Je. 51. 34. n Pr. 29. 17. o 1 Sa. 15. 32. p Ps. 119. 152. q Ps. 147. 6. r Ge. 48. 15. s Nu. 22. 30. t Da. 2. 32. u 2 Sa. 22. 33. v Ps. 37. 39.

Form	Analysis	Root
מָעוֹךְ	pr. name masc.	מעך
מָעוּךְ[a]	וּ Kal part. pass. sing. masc.; וּ bef. lab.	מעך
מְעוּכָה[b]	fem. of the preced.	מעך
מָעוֹל[c]	וּ Kal inf. abs. (§ 8. rem. 8); וּ bef. lab.	מעל
מֵעָוֶל	pref. מֵ for ·מִ)(noun masc. s. (§ 35. r. 11)	עול
מְעַוֵּל[d]	Piel part. sing. masc.	עול
מֵעוֹלֵל	pref. מֵ for ·מִ)(noun masc. sing. dec. 7b	עלל
מְעוֹלֵל[e]	Poel part. or subst. masc.	עלל
מֵעוֹלָם	וּ׳ pref. מֵ for ·מִ)(noun m. s. d. 2b; וּ bef. lab.	עלם
מָעוֹן	וּ׳ noun masc. sing. d. 3a, also pr. name; וּ id.	עון
מֵעָוֹן	pref. מֵ for ·מִ)(noun masc. sing. dec. 3a	עוה
מְעוֹן	noun masc. sing., constr. of מָעוֹן dec. 3a (also pr. name in compos. see בַּיִת)	עון
מְעוֹנָהּ[f]	id., suff. 3 pers. sing. fem.	עון
מְעוֹנוֹ[g]	id., suff. 3 pers. sing. masc.	עון
מְעוֹנֹתַי	וּ pr. name masc.; וּ bef. lab.	עון
מֵעֲוֹנוֹתֵיהֶם[h]	pref. מֵ for ·מִ)(noun masc. with pl. fem. and suff. 3 pers. pl. masc. from עָוֹן dec. 3a	עוה
מֵעֲוֹנוֹתֵינוּ[i]	pref. id.)(id. pl., suff. 1 pers. pl.	עוה
מֵעֲוֹנִי	וּ׳[k] pref. id.)(id. s., suff. 1 p. s.; וּ bef. lab.	עוה
מְעוֹנַי[l]	in full for מְעֹנַי (q. v.)	ענה
מְעוּנִים	pr. name of a people, see מָעוֹן	עון
מֵעֲוֹנֵינוּ[m]	pref. מֵ for ·מִ)(noun masc. pl. [עֲוֹנִים], suff. 1 pers. pl. from עָוֹן dec. 3a	עוה
מֵעֲוֹנֶךָ[n]	pref. id.)(id. sing., suff. 2 pers. sing. masc. (for עֲוֹנְךָ)	עוה
מְעוֹנֶךָ[o]	[for מְעוֹנְךָ] noun masc. sing., suff. 2 pers. sing. masc. from מָעוֹן dec. 3a	עון
מְעוֹנֵן[p]	Poel (§ 6. No. 1) part. sing. masc. dec. 7b	ענן
מֵעֲוֹנֵנוּ[q]	pref. מֵ for ·מִ)(noun masc. sing., suff. 1 pers. pl. from עָוֹן dec. 3a	עוה
מְעוֹנְנִים[r]	וּ Poel (§ 6. No. 1) part. masc., pl. of מְעוֹנֵן dec. 7b; וּ bef. lab.	ענן
מְעוֹנָתוֹ[s]	וּ noun fem. sing., suff. 3 pers. sing. masc. from מְעוֹנָה dec. 10; וּ id.	עון
מְעוֹנֹתָיו[t]	וּ id. pl., suff. 3 pers. sing. masc.; וּ id.	עון
מֵעֲוֹנֹתֵיהֶם[u]	וּ defect. for מֵעֲוֹנוֹתֵיהֶם (q. v.)	עוה
מְעוֹנֹתָם[x]	noun fem. pl., suff. 3 pers. pl. masc. (§ 4. rem. 1) from מְעוֹנָה dec. 10	עון
מֵעוֹף	וּ׳ pref. מֵ for ·מִ)(noun masc. s.; וּ bef. lab.	עוף
מְעוּף[y]	noun masc. sing., constr. of [מָעוּף] dec. 3a	עוף
מְעוֹפֵף	Pilel part. sing. masc.	עוף
מֵעוֹר[z]	pref. מֵ for ·מִ)(noun masc. sing. dec. 1a	עור
מְעוֹרֵיהֶם[a]	noun m. pl., suff. 3 p. pl. m. fr. [מָעוֹר] d. 3a	עור
מְעֻוָּת[b]	Pual part. sing. masc.	עות
מֵעַזֵּי[c]	וּ pref. מֵ for ·מִ)(adj. m. s. d. 8d; וּ bef. lab.	עזז
מָעוֹז[d]	noun masc. sing. (suff. מָעֻזִּי) d. 8c (§ 37. r. 4)	עזז
מֵעֲזֹב	pref. מֵ for ·מִ)(Kal inf. constr.	עזב
מָעֻזֹּה[e]	n. m. s., suff. 3 p. s. m. fr. מָעוֹז d. 8c (§ 37. r. 4)	עזז
מֵעַזָּה	pref. מֵ for ·מִ)(pr. name of a place	עזז
מָעֻזִּי	וּ׳[f] n. m. s., suff. 1 p. s. fr. מָעוֹז d. 8c (§ 37. r. 4)	עזז
מַעַזְיָה	pr. name masc.	עזה
מָעֻזִּים	noun masc., pl. of מָעוֹז dec. 8c (§ 37. rem. 4)	עזז
מָעֻזֵּךְ[g]	id. sing., suff. 2 pers. sing. fem.	עזז
מָעֻזְּכֶם[h]	id. sing., suff. 2 pers. pl. masc.	עזז
מָעֻזְּכֶן[i]	id. sing., suff. 2 pers. pl. fem.	עזז
מָעֻזָּם[k]	id. sing., suff. 3 pers. pl. masc.	עזז
מָעֻזְנֶיהָ[l]	id. pl., epenth. נ & suff. 3 p. s. f. (§ 4. r. 5)	עזז
מַעְזְרִים[m]	Hiph. part. masc. pl. [of מַעְזֵר § 11. rem. 8]	עזר

[מָעַט] *to be* or *become little, few.* Pi. id. Ec. 12. 3. Hiph. I. *to make small, few, to diminish.*—II. *to make* or *do little.*—III. *to give little.*

מְעַט, מְעָט, masc. pl. מְעַטִּים dec. 8.—I. *smallness, fewness;* hence, *a little, few;* מְעַט מַיִם *a little water;* מְתֵי מְעָט *men of fewness,* i. e. *a few men.*—II. adj. *small, few;* בֵּין רַב לִמְעָט *between many and few;* יִהְיוּ יָמָיו מְעַטִּים *let his days be few.*—III. adv. *a little;* of time, *for a little, a little while;* מְעַט מְעַט *by little and little.*—IV. כִּמְעַט lit. *as a little;* (*a*) *nearly, almost;* (*b*) *shortly, soon;* כִּמְעַט שֶׁ *little that,* i. e. *scarcely;* (*c*) intens. *very little;* of number, *very few;* לִמְעַט i. q. מְעַט Hag. 1. 9; 2 Ch. 29. 34.

מָעֹט, fem. מְעֻטָּה adj. Eze. 21. 20, *naked, drawn,* of a sword (Arab. מעט *smooth, bare*). Gesenius, *polished, sharp.*

Form	Analysis	Root
מְעָט מְעַט	noun masc. sing., also *adv.* (pl. מְעַטִּים) dec. 8d; וּ bef. lab. (וּ׳ at מְעַט)	מעט
מְעֹט[n]	Kal inf. constr.	מעט
מַעֲטֵה[o]	noun masc. sing., constr. of מַעֲטֶה dec. 9a	עטה
מְעֻטָּה[p]	adj. fem. [from מָעֹט masc. dec. 8] R. מעט; or Pual part. fem. [of מְעֻטֶּה masc.]	עטה
מִעֲטוּ[q]	Piel (§ 14. rem. 1) pret. 3 pers. sing. [for מִעֲטוּ, comp. § 8. rem. 7]	מעט
מְעַטִּים	adj. masc., pl. of מְעַט dec. 8d	מעט
מָעַי	pr. name masc.	מע
מֵעָי מֵעַי	noun masc. pl. [מֵעִים], suff. 1 pers. sing. [fr. מֵעַ § 36. r. 4]; וּ bef. lab. (וּ׳[r] at מֵעַי)	מע
מְעִי[s]	noun masc. sing. [for מַעֲוִי]	עוה
מֵעִיד[t]	Hiph. part. sing. masc.	עוד
מֵעֵיהֶם[u]	וּ noun masc. pl. [מֵעִים], suff. 3 pers. pl. masc. [from מֵעַ § 36. rem. 4]; וּ bef. lab.	מע

[a] Le. 22. 24. [b] 1 Sa. 26. 7. [c] 2 Ch. 28. 19. [d] Ps. 71. 4. [e] Is. 3. 12. [f] Zep. 3. 7. [g] 2 Ch. 36. 15. [h] Eze. 43. 10. [i] Is. 53. 5. [k] Job 10. 14. [l] Ps. 107. 41. [m] Da. 9. 13. [n] Job 11. 6. [o] Ps. 91. 9. [p] De. 18. 10. [q] Ezr. 9. 13. [r] Mi. 5. 11. [s] Ps. 76. 3. [t] Na. 2. 13. [u] Ps. 107. 17. [x] Ps. 104. 22. [y] Is. 8. 22. [z] Le. 13. 3. [a] Hab. 2. 15. [b] Ec. 1. 15.

[c] Ju. 14. 14. [d] Pr. 10. 29. [e] Da. 11. 10. [f] Je. 16. 19. [g] Is. 17. 10. [h] Ne. 8. 10. [i] Is. 23. 14. [k] Eze. 24. 25. [l] Is. 23. 11. [m] 2 Ch. 28. 23. [n] Le. 25. 16. [o] Is. 61. 3. [p] Eze. 21. 20. [q] Ec. 12. 3. [r] Ca. 5. 4. [s] Is. 17. 1. [t] De. 32. 46. [u] Eze. 7. 19.

מֵעָיו id. with suff. 3 pers. sing. masc. . . מע

מֵעִיִּים pref. מֵ for מִ·) (pr. name of a place . עוה

מֵעַיִךְ [a]ו׳ noun masc. pl., suff. 2 pers. sing. masc. [from מֵעַ § 36. rem. 4]; וּ bef. lab. . מע

מְעִיל ו׳ noun masc. sing. dec. 1 a; וּ id. . מעל

מְעִילוֹ[b] id., suff. 3 pers. sing. masc. . . . מעל

מְעִילִי[c] וּ id., suff. 1 pers. sing.; וּ bef. lab. . מעל

מְעִילֵיהֶם[d] id. pl., suff. 3 pers. pl. masc. . . מעל

מְעִילִים[e] id. pl., abs. st. . . . . מעל

מְעִילֶךָ id. sing., suff. 2 pers. sing. masc. . . מעל

מֵעֵילָם וּ pref. מֵ for מִ·) (pr. name of a province; וּ bef. lab. . . . . . עלם

מַעְיָן [f]ו׳ noun masc. sing. dec. 2 b; וּ id. . . עין

מַעְיַן id., constr. st. . . . . . . עין

מֵעֵין pref. מֵ for מִ·) (pr. name in compos. עֵין גֶּדִי׳ עין

מַעְיָנוֹ[g] noun m., suff. 3 pers. sing. m. fr. מַעְיָן d. 2 b עין

מַעְיָנוֹת id. pl. abs. fem. . . . . . עין

מַעְיְנוֹת[h] id. pl. constr. fem. . . . . . עין

מַעְיָנַי[i] id. pl. masc. (מַעְיָנִים), suff. 1 pers. sing. . עין

מַעְיְנֵי id. pl., constr. st. . . . . . עין

מֵעֵינַי pref. מֵ for מִ·) (noun fem. du. (עֵינַיִם), suff. 1 pers. sing. from עַיִן dec. 6 h . . עין

מֵעֵינֵי pref. id.) (id. du., constr. st. . . עין

מֵעֵינָיו[k] pref. id.) (id. du., suff. 3 pers. sing. masc. . עין

מֵעֵינַיִךְ[l] pref. id.) (id. du., suff. 2 pers. sing. fem. עין

מֵעֵינֶיךָ pref. id.) (id. du., suff. 2 pers. sing. masc. עין

מַעְיָנִים[m] noun masc., pl. of מַעְיָן dec. 2 b . . עין

מַעְיְנֹת[n] id. pl. constr. fem. . . . . . עין

מַעְיְנֹתֶיךָ[o] id. pl. fem., suff. 2 pers. sing. masc. . עין

מֵעִיק[p] Hiph. part. sing. masc. . . . . עוק

מֵעִיר Hiph. part. sing. masc. dec. 3 b . . עור

מֵעִיר pref. מֵ for מִ·) (Kal inf. constr. Ho. 7. 4; and perhaps (Job 24. 12) noun m. s. see עִיר עיר

מֵעִיר pref. id.) (noun fem. sing. irr., pl. עָרִים more usually עָרִים (§ 45) . . . עור

מֵעִירוֹ pref. id.) (id., suff. 3 pers. sing. masc. . עור

מֵעִירְךָ[q] pref. id.) (id., suff. 2 pers. sing. masc. . עור

מְעִירָם[r] Hiph. part. masc., pl. of מֵעִיר dec. 3 b . עור

[מָעַךְ] *to press*, 1 Sa. 26. 7; part. Le. 22. 24, מָעוּךְ *bruised, castrated*. Pu. *to be pressed*, Eze. 23. 3.

מָעוֹךְ (*oppression*) pr. name masc. 1 Sa. 27. 2; otherwise called מַעֲכָה, comp. 1 Ki. 2. 39.

מַעֲכָה, מַעֲכָת (id.) pr. name—I. of a region and city near Mount Hermon. Gent. מַעֲכָתִי.—II. of several persons, male and female.

מַעֲכָה ו׳ pr. name of a man and a region (and in compos. see בֵּית); וּ bef. lab. . . מעך

מֹעֲכוּ[s] Pual pret. 3 pers. pl. . . . מעך

מַעֲכָת וּ pr. name of a region, see מַעֲכָה; וּ bef. lab. מעך

מָעַל *to act perversely, treacherously, to be faithless*, with בְּ of the thing or person.

מַעַל masc. dec. 6 d, *perverseness, treachery, sin*, against God.

מְעִיל masc. dec. 1 a, *long and full upper garment*, worn by persons of dignity (men and women), *robe, mantle*.

מַעַל[t] } noun masc. sing. dec. 6 d (§ 35. rem. 2) . מעל
מָעַל }

מִמַּעַל pref. מֵ for מִ·) (adv. . . . עלה

מֵעַל ו׳ pref. id.) (prep. see עַל; וּ bef. lab. . עלה

מֵעַל[u] pref. id.) (Kh. מֵעַל q. v., K. מֵעֲלֵי see עֲלֵי עלה

מָעֲלָה וּ Kal pret. 3 pers. sing. fem.; וּ, for וְ conv. מעל

מַעֲלֵה constr. of the foll. . . . . עלה

מַעֲלֶה ו׳וּ Hiph. part. or subst. m. d. 9 a; וּ bef. lab. עלה

מַעֲלָה[y] id. part., fem. of the preced., dec. 10 . עלה

מַעְלָה[z] (וְ׳) } adv. [מַעַל] with loc. ה; for וְ see lett. ו עלה
מָעְלָה[z] (וְ׳) }

מָעֲלוּ Kal pret. 3 pers. pl. . . . . מעל

מַעֲלָיו[a] noun masc. pl., suff. 3 pers. sing. masc. (§ 4. rem. 1) fr. מַעֲלֶה dec. 9 a . . עלה

מַעֲלוֹ[b] ו׳ noun masc. sing., suff. 3 pers. sing. masc. fr. מַעַל dec. 6 d; וּ bef. lab. . . מעל

מֵעָלוֹ וּ pref. מֵ for מִ·) (noun masc. sing., suff. 3 pers. sing. masc. fr. עֹל dec. 8 c; וּ id. עלל

מְעִלוֹ[c] defect. for מְעִילוֹ (q. v.) . . . מעל

מַעֲלוֹת ו׳ noun fem., pl. of מַעֲלָה d. 10; וּ bef. lab. עלה

מֵעֲלוֹת pref. מֵ for מִ·) (Kal inf. constr. . . עלה

מֵעֹלוֹת[e] pref. id.) (noun f., pl. of עֹלָה or עוֹלָה d. 10 עלה

מַעֲלוֹתָו[f] noun fem. pl., suff. 3 pers. sing. masc. (§ 4. rem. 1) fr. מַעֲלָה׳ dec. 10 . . עלה

מֵעָלַי } pref. מֵ for מִ·) (prep. (עַל), pl. with suff. 1 pers. sing. (§ 31. rem. 5) . } עלה
מֵעָלָי }

מַעֲלַיִ[g] (or מַעֲלֵי) Ch. noun masc. pl. constr. [fr. מַעַל or מֶעָל] dec. 1 a . . . עלל

מֵעָלֶיהָ pref. מֵ for מִ·) (prep. (עַל) pl. with suff. 3 pers. sing. fem. (§ 31. rem. 5) . . עלה

מֵעֲלֵיהֶם pref. id.) (id., suff. 3 pers. pl. masc. . עלה

מֵעָלָיו[h] ו׳ pref. id.) (id., suff. 3 p. s. m.; וּ bef. lab. עלה

---

[a] Eze. 3. 3. [b] 1 Sa. 15. 27. [c] Ezr. 9. 3, 5. [d] Eze. 26. 16. [e] 2 Sa. 13. 18. [f] Joel 4. 18. [g] Ho. 13. 15. [h] Ge. 7. 11. [i] Ps. 87. 7. [k] Ju. 6. 21. [l] Ca. 4. 9. [m] Ps. 104. 10. [n] Ge. 8. 2. [o] Pr. 5. 16. [p] Am. 2. 13. [q] Da. 9. 16. [r] Joel 4. 7. [s] Eze. 23. 3. [t] Job. 21. 34; Nu. 5. 12. [u] 1 Ki. 20. 41. [x] Je. 50. 9. [y] Le. 11. 26. [z] De. 28. 43. [a] Eze. 40. 31, 34, 37. [b] Eze. 17. 20. [c] 2 Ch. 33. 19. [d] Job 1. 20; 2. 12. [e] Ho. 6. 6. [f] Am. 9. 6. [g] Da. 6. 15. [h] Pr. 14. 14.

מֵעֲלִיּוֹתָיו pref. מֵ for ·מִ)(noun fem. pl., suff. 3 pers. sing. masc. fr. עֲלִיָּה dec. 10 . . עלה

מֵעָלַיִךְ pref. id.)(prep. (עַל) pl. with suff. 2 pers. sing. fem. (§ 31. rem. 5) . . עלה

מֵעָלֶיךָ pref. id.)(id., suff. 2 pers. sing. masc. . עלה

מֵעֲלֵיכֶם pref. id.)(id., suff. 2 pers. pl. masc. . . עלה

וּמַעַלְלֵיכֶם Kh. מַעֲלִילֵיכֶם' noun masc. pl., suff. 2 pers. pl. masc. from [מַעֲלִיל] dec. 1 b; K. מַעַלְלֵיכֶם (q. v.); וּ bef. lab. . . עלל

מַעֲלִים Hiph. part. masc., pl. of מַעֲלֶה dec. 9 a עלה

מַעְלִים[c] [d]וּ' Hiph. part. sing. masc.; וּ bef. lab. . עלם

מֵעָלֵינוּ pref. מֵ for ·מִ)(prep. (עַל) pl. with suff. 1 pers. pl. (§ 31. rem. 5) . . . עלה

מַעַלְלֵי noun masc. pl. constr. fr. [מַעֲלָל] dec. 2 b עלל

מַעַלְלֵיהֶב[e] וּ' id. pl., suff. 3 pers. pl. masc.; וּ bef. lab. עלל

מַעַלְלֵיהֶם id. pl., suff. 3 p. pl. m.; K. כֶם' 2 p. pl. m. עלל

מַעֲלָלָיו[g] וּ' id. pl., suff. 3 pers. sing. m.; וּ bef. lab. עלל

מַעֲלָלֶיךָ[h] id. pl., suff. 2 pers. sing. masc. . . עלל

מַעֲלָלַיִךְ[i] וּ id. pl., suff. 2 pers. sing. fem.; וּ bef. lab. עלל

מַעַלְלֵיכֶם וּ' id. pl., suff. 2 pers. pl. masc.; וּ id. עלל

מַעֲלָלִים[k] id. pl., abs. st. . . . . עלל

מַעֲלָם[l] noun masc. sing., suff. 3 pers. pl. masc. fr. מַעַל dec. 6 d . . . . . . מעל

מֵעַלְמוֹן pref. מֵ for ·מִ)(pr. name of a place . עלם

מָעַלְנוּ[m] Kal pret. 1 pers. pl. . . . . מעל

מְעֻלֶּפֶת[n] Pual part. sing. fem. [of מְעֻלָּף] . . עלף

מַעֲלַת Hiph. part. sing. fem., constr. of מַעֲלָה dec. 10, from מַעֲלֶה masc. . . . . עלה

מָעַלְתָּ[o] Kal pret. 2 pers. sing. masc. . . . מעל

וּמַעֲלֹתָהוּ וּ noun fem. pl., suff. 3 pers. sing. masc. fr. מַעֲלָה dec. 10 (§ 4. rem. 1 & 2); וּ bef. lab. עלה

מְעַלְתֶּם Kal pret. 2 pers. pl. masc. . . . מעל

מֵעָם / וּמֵעָם[ee] וּ' } pref. מֵ for ·מִ)(noun com. s. (pl. עַמִּים) d. 8 d, & irr. עֲמָמִים (§ 45); וּ bef. lab. } עמם

מֵעִם[q] וּ' pref. id.)(prep. (§ 5); וּ id. . . עמם

מֵעֲמַד וּ noun m. sing., constr. of [מַעֲמָד] d. 1 b; וּ id. עמד

מָעֳמָד[r] Hoph. part. or subst. masc. sing. . . עמד

מֵעִמָּדִי pref. מֵ for ·מִ)(prep. [עִמָּד] with suff. 1 p. s. עמד

מַעֲמָדָם noun m. s., suff. 3 pers. pl. m. fr. [מַעֲמָד] d. 3 a עמד

מֵעַמּוֹ וּ pref. מֵ for ·מִ)(noun com. sing., suff. 3 pers. sing. masc. from עַם dec. 8 d (§ 45) . עמם

מֵעִמּוֹ pref. id.)(prep. (עִם) with suff. 3 p. s. m. (§ 5) עמם

מֵעַמֵּי pref. id.)(n. com. pl. constr. fr. עַם d. 8 d (§ 45) עמם

וּמֵעַמִּי וּ pref. id.)(id. sing., suff. 1 pers. s.; וּ bef. lab. עמם

מֵעִמִּי pref. מֵ for ·מִ)(prep. עִם with suff. 1 p. s. (§ 5) עמם

מַעֲמִיד[u] Hiph. part. sing. masc. . . . עמד

מֵעַמֶּיהָ pref. מֵ for ·מִ)(noun com. pl., suff. 3 pers. sing. fem. from עַם dec. 8 d (§ 45) . עמם

מֵעַמָּיו pref. id.)(id. pl., suff. 3 pers. sing. masc. . עמם

מֵעַמִּים[x] [y]וּ' pref. id.)(id. pl., abs. st.; וּ bef. lab. עמם

מֵעַמֶּךָ[z] / מֵעַמְּךָ } וּ pref. id.)(id. sing., suff. 2 pers. sing. masc.; וּ id. . . . . } עמם

מֵעִמָּךְ pref. id.)(prep. (עִם) with suff. 2 pers. sing. fem., or 2 pers. masc. in pause for the foll. עמם

מֵעִמְּךָ pref. id.)(id., suff. 2 pers. sing. masc. . עמם

מֵעִמָּכֶם[a] pref. id.)(id., suff. 2 pers. pl. masc. . עמם

מֵעֲמַל[b] pref. id.)(noun m. sing., constr. of עָמָל d. 4 c עמל

מֵעֲמָלֵקִי וּ' pref. id.)(gent. n. fr. עֲמָלֵק (q. v.); וּ bef. lab. עמם

מֵעִמָּנוּ pref. id.)(prep. (עִם) with suff. 1 pers. pl. (§ 5) עמם

מַעֲמָסָה[c] noun fem. sing. . . . . . עמס

מֵעֵמֶק pref. מֵ for ·מִ)(noun masc. sing. dec. 6 b עמק

מַעֲמַקֵּי[d] noun masc. pl. constr. from [מַעֲמָק] dec. 8 a עמק

מְעַמֵּר[e] Piel part. sing. masc. . . . . עמר

מַעֲנָה[f] noun fem. sing. dec. 10 . . . ענה

מַעֲנֵה / מַעֲנֶה } noun masc. sing. constr. & abs. dec. 9 a ענה

מְעֹנָה[g] noun fem. sing. dec. 10 . . . עון

מְעֻנֶּה[h] וּ Pual part. sing. masc.; וּ bef. lab. ענה

מֵעֲנוֹת[i] pref. מֵ for ·מִ)(Kal inf. constr. . . ענה

מֵעֲנִיִּי[k] pref. id.)(adj. masc., pl. עֲנִיִּים d. 8 (§ 37. r. 4) ענה

מֵעָנְיִי / מֵעָנְיִי[l] } pref. id.)(noun masc. sing. dec. 6 k (§ 35. rem. 14) . . . } ענה

מְעַנַּיִךְ Piel part. pl. masc. [מְעַנִּים], suff. 2 pers. sing. fem. from [מְעַנֶּה] dec. 9 a . ענה

מְעֹנְנִים[m] defect. for מְעוֹנְנִים (q. v.) . . . ענן

מֵעֲסִיס[n] pref. מֵ for ·מִ)(n. m. s., constr. of עָסִיס d. 3 a עסס

מֻעָף[o] Hoph. part. sing. masc. [for מוּעָף] . יעף

מֵעָפָר וּ' pref. מֵ for ·מִ)(noun m. s. d. 4 c; וּ bef. lab. עפר

מֵעֲפַר[p] pref. id.)(id., constr. st. . . . עפר

מַעַץ (anger, Gesenius) pr. name masc. 1 Ch. 2. 27.

מֵעֵץ [q]וּ' pref. מֵ for ·מִ)(noun masc. sing. dec. 7 b (§ 36. rem. 2 & 4); וּ bef. lab. . עצה

מֵעִצְּבוֹן[r] וּ pref. id.)(noun m. sing. constr. of עִצָּבוֹן' dec. 3 c; וּ id. . . . . . . עצב

מֵעָצְבְּךָ[s] pref. id.)(noun m. s., suff. 2 p. s. m. fr. עֹצֶב d. 6 c עצב

מַעֲצָד[t] noun masc. sing. עצד

מַעְצוֹר[u] noun masc. sing. עצר

מֵעֲצֵי[x] pref. מֵ for ·מִ)(noun m. pl. constr. fr. עֵץ d. 7 b עצה

מֵעֶצְיוֹן וּ' pref. id.)(pr. name in compos., see עֶצְיוֹן גֶּבֶר; וּ bef. lab. . . . . עצה

---

[a] Ps. 104. 13. [b] Zec. 1. 4. [c] Job 42. 3. [d] Pr. 28. 27. [e] Is. 3. 8. [ee] Is. 18. 7. [f] Je. 21. 12. [g] Ho. 4. 9. [h] De. 28. 20. [i] Je. 4. 18. [k] 1 Sa. 25. 3. [l] Eze. 39. 26. [m] Ezr. 10. 2. [n] Ca. 5. 14. [o] 2 Ch. 26. 18. [p] Eze. 43. 17. [q] 1 Sa. 18. 12. [r] 1 Ki. 22. 35; Ps. 69. 3. [s] Ex. 8. 4. [t] Ge. 31. 31. [u] 2 Ch. 18. 34. [x] Eze. 38. 8. [y] Is. 63. 3. [z] Ex. 8. 7. [a] 2 Sa. 15. 28. [b] Is. 53. 11. [c] Zec. 12. 3. [d] Is. 51. 10. [e] Ps. 129. 7. [f] 1 Sa. 14. 14. [g] De. 33. 27. [h] Is. 53. 4. [i] Job 32. 1. [k] Eze. 18. 17. [l] Ex. 3. 17. [m] De. 18. 14. [n] Ca. 8. 2. [o] Da. 9. 21. [p] Nu. 19. 17. [q] Ge. 2. 17. [r] Ge. 5. 29. [s] Is. 14. 3. [t] Is. 44. 12. [u] 1 Sa. 14. 6. [x] Ca. 3. 9.

מֵעַצְמוֹן pref. מֵ for ·מִ)(pr. name of a place . עצם
[a] מֵעַצְמוֹתָי pref. id.)(noun fem. pl. (עֲצָמוֹת), suff. 1 pers. sing. from עֶצֶם dec. 6a . . . עצם
[b] מֵעֲצָמַי pref. id.)(id. pl. m. (עֲצָמִים), suff. 1 pers. s. עצם
[c] מַעְצָר noun masc. sing. . . . . עצר
מֵעֹצֶר pref. מֵ for ·מִ)(noun masc. sing. . עצר
[d] מֵעֲצַת perh. constr. of עֵצָה R. . . . עצה
[e] מֵעֲצַת pref. מֵ for ·מִ)(n. f. s., constr. of עֵצָה d. 11b יעץ
[f] מֵעֲצָתוֹ pref. id.)(id. with suff. 3 pers. sing. masc. יעץ
[g] מַעֲקֶה noun masc. sing. . . . . . עקה
[h] מְעֻקָּל Pual part. sing. masc. . . . . עקל
מֵעֶקְרוֹן pref. מֵ for ·מִ)(pr. name of a place עקר
מֵעִקֵּשׁ pref. id.)(adj. masc. sing. dec. 7b . עקש
מְעַקֵּשׁ וּ Piel part. sing. masc.; וּ bef. lab. עקש
[k] מַעֲקַשִּׁים וּ noun masc., pl. of [מַעֲקָשׁ] dec. 8a; וּ id. עקש
[l] מְעָרַב Chald. Pael part. sing. masc. (§ 49. rem. 3) ערב
מֵעֶרֶב pref. מֵ for ·מִ)(n. com. s. (du. עַרְבַּיִם) d. 6a ערב
מַעֲרָבָה noun masc. sing. [מַעֲרָב] with parag. ה, d. 2b ערב
[m] מַעֲרָבַיִךְ וּ id. pl., suff. 2 pers. sing. fem.; וּ bef. lab. ערב
[n] מַעֲרָבֵךְ id. sing., suff. 2 pers. sing. fem. . . ערב
[o] מֵעַרְבֹת pref. מֵ for ·מִ)(noun fem. pl. constr. from עֲרָבָה dec. 11c (§ 42. rem. 1) . ערב
[p] מֵעֲרֻגוֹת pref. id.)(noun fem., pl. of [עֲרוּגָה] dec. 10 ערג
[q] מְעָרָה [r] וּ noun fem. s. (constr. מְעָרַת) d. 10; וּ bef. lab. עור
מֵעֲרוֹעֵר pref. מֵ for ·מִ)(pr. name of a place ערר
[s] מְעָרוֹת noun fem. plural, abs. of מְעָרָה dec. 10 (comp. § 39. No. 3) . . . עור
מֵעָרֵי pref. מֵ for ·מִ)(noun fem. pl. constr. prop. from עָר see עִיר (§ 45) . . . עור
מֵעָרֵיהֶם pref. id.)(id. pl., suff. 3 pers. pl. masc. . עור
מֵעָרָיו pref. id.)(id. pl., suff. 3 pers. sing. masc. . עור
[t] מַעֲרִיצְכֶם Hiph. part. or subst. masc. (מַעֲרִיץ), suff. 2 pers. pl. masc. dec. 1b . . ערץ
[u] מַעֲרֵךְ noun masc. sing., suff. 2 pers. sing. fem. from מַעַר [contr. from מַעֲרֶה] . . . ערה
מַעֲרָכָה noun fem. sing. dec. 11a . . . . ערך
[x] מַעֲרָכוֹת id. pl., abs. st. . . . . . ערך
מַעַרְכוֹת id. pl., constr. st. . . . . . ערך
[y] מַעַרְכֵי noun masc. pl. constr. from [מַעֲרָךְ] dec. 2b ערך
[z] מֵעֶרְכְּךָ pref. מֵ for ·מִ)(noun masc. sing., suff. 2 pers. sing. masc. from עֵרֶךְ dec. 6 (§ 35. rem. 6) ערך
[a] מַעֲרֶכֶת וּ noun fem. sing.; וּ bef. lab. . . ערך
מַעַרְכֹת noun fem. pl. constr. of מַעֲרָכָה . . ערך
[b] מֵעֲרֵלִים pref. מֵ for ·מִ)(adj. masc., pl. of עָרֵל d. 5b ערל
[c] מֵעֲרֵמוֹת pref. id.)(noun fem., pl. of עֲרֵמָה constr. עֲרֵמַת dec. 10 . . . . . ערם
[d] מַעֲרֻמֵּיהֶם noun m. pl., suff. 3 p. pl. m. fr. [מַעֲרֹם] d. 8c ערם

מֵעֲרֹעֵר pref. מֵ for ·מִ)(pr. name of a place . ערר
מַעֲרַת וּ pr. name of a place; וּ bef. lab. . . ערה
מְעָרַת noun fem. sing., constr. of מְעָרָה dec. 10 (comp. § 39. No. 3) . . . עור
מַעֲשֶׂה וּ / מַעֲשֶׂה } noun masc. sing. constr. & abs. dec. 9a; וּ bef. lab. . . . עשה
מַעֲשֵׂהוּ וּ id., suff. 3 pers. sing. masc.; וּ bef. lab. . עשה
[e] מֵעֹשֵׂהוּ pref. מֵ for ·מִ)(Kal part. act., suff. 3 pers. sing. masc. from עֹשֶׂה dec. 9a . . עשה
מֵעֲשׂוֹת pref. id.)(Kal inf. constr. dec. 1a . עשה
[f] מַעֲשַׂי / מַעֲשַׂי וּ } noun f. pl. with suff. 1 pers. s. fr. מַעֲשֶׂה dec. 9a (also pr. name); וּ bef. lab. עשה
מַעֲשֵׂי id. pl. constr. st. . . . . עשה
מַעֲשֵׂיָה וּ pr. name masc.; וּ bef. lab. . . עשה
[g] מַעֲשֶׂיהָ noun masc. pl., suff. 3 pers. sing. fem. from מַעֲשֶׂה dec. 9a . . . . . עשה
מַעֲשֵׂיָהוּ וּ pr. name masc., see מַעֲשֵׂיָה; וּ bef. lab. עשה
מַעֲשֵׂיהֶם [h] וּ noun masc. pl., suff. 3 pers. pl. masc. from מַעֲשֶׂה dec. 9a; וּ id. . . עשה
מַעֲשָׂיו id. pl., suff. 3 pers. sing. masc. . . עשה
מַעֲשֶׂיךָ id. pl., suff. 2 pers. sing. masc. . . עשה
[i] מַעֲשַׂיִךְ / מַעֲשַׂיִךְ } id. pl., suff. 2 pers. sing. fem. . . עשה
מַעֲשֵׂיכֶם id. pl., suff. 2 pers. pl. masc. . . . עשה
[k] מַעֲשִׂים id. pl., abs. st. . . . . עשה
[l] מַעֲשֵׂינוּ id. pl., suff. 1 pers. pl. . . . . עשה
[m] מַעֲשִׁיר וּ Hiph. part. sing. masc.; וּ bef. lab. . עשר
[n] מַעֲשֵׂךְ accord. to some copies for מַעֲשַׂיִךְ (q. v. & § 4. r. 1) עשה
מֵעֹשֶׁק pref. מֵ for ·מִ)(noun masc. sing. . עשק
מַעֲשַׁקּוֹת noun fem., pl. of [מַעֲשַׁקָּה] dec. 10 . עשק
מַעְשַׂר / מַעֲשֵׂר } noun masc. sing. constr. & abs., suff. מַעַשְׂרוֹ, dec. 7c . . . עשר
מַעְשַׂר וּ id., constr. st.; וּ bef. lab. . . עשר
[o] מֵעֹשֶׁר pref. מֵ for ·מִ)(noun masc. sing. dec. 6c עשר
מֵעֲשָׂרָה pref. id.)(num. card. masc., constr. עֲשֶׂרֶת, see עֶשֶׂר fem. . . . . עשר
מַעְשְׂרֹתֵיכֶם noun masc. with pl. fem. term. and suff. 2 pers. pl. masc. from מַעֲשֵׂר (q. v.) עשר
[p] מֵעֲשֹׂת pref. מֵ for ·מִ)(Kal inf. constr. 1a, see מֵעֲשׂוֹת עשה
[q] מֵעֲשֹׂתִי pref. id.)(id. with suff. 1 pers. sing. עשה
מֵעֵת וּ pref. id.)(noun com. sing. dec. 8b [for עֵדֶת]; וּ bef. lab. . . . . עדה
[r] מֵעַתָּה / מֵעָתָּה } pref. id.)(adv. . . . . עדה
מֹף pr. name, *Memphis*, a city of Egypt, Ho. 9. 6, otherwise called נֹף Is. 19. 13; Je. 2. 16.
מִפָּארָן pref. ·מִ)(pr. name of a place . פאר

[a] Job 7. 15. [b] Ge. 2. 23. [c] Pr. 25. 28. [d] Pr. 27. 9. [e] 2 Sa. 17. 14. [f] Ho. 10. 6. [g] De. 22. 8. [h] Hab. 1. 4. [i] Pr. 10. 9. [k] Is. 42. 16. [l] Da. 2. 41, 43. [m] Eze. 27. 33. [n] Eze. 27. 13, 17, 25, 27, 34. [o] De. 34. 1. [p] Eze. 17. 7. [q] 1 Sa. 24. 4. [r] Jos. 13. 4. [s] Is. 32. 14. [t] Is. 8. 13. [u] Na. 3. 5. [x] Le. 24. 6. [y] Pr. 16. 1. [z] Le. 27. 8, 18. [a] 2 Ch. 2. 3; 13. 11. [b] Eze. 32. 27. [c] Ne. 3. 34. [d] 2 Ch. 28. 15. [e] Job 4. 17. [f] Ec. 2. 4. [g] Pr. 31. 31. [h] Eze. 1. 16, 16. [i] Eze. 27. 16. [k] Ge. 20. 9. [l] Is. 26. 12. [m] 1 Sa. 2. 7. [n] De. 15. 10. [o] Pr. 22. 1. [p] Ge. 18. 25. [q] 2 Sa. 23. 17. [r] Ho. 2. 9.

מִפְּאַת ו' pref. מִ)(noun fem., constr. of פֵּאָה dec. 11 b; ו bef. lab. . . . פאה
מִפְגִּיעַ[a] Hiph. part. sing. masc. . . . פגע
מִפְּדוּת[b] pref. מִ)(noun fem. sing. . . . פדה
מִפַּדָּן pref. id.)(pr. name of a place . . פדן
מִפַּדַּן אֲרָם pref. id.)(pr. name of a place, פַּדַּן אֲ' . פדן
מִפֶּה[c] pref. id.)(noun masc. sing. irr. (§ 45) . פאה
מִפֹּה } pref. id.)(adv.; ו bef. lab. . . . פה
מִפּוֹ ו' }
מִפּוּנֹן pref. id.)(pr. name of a place . . פון
מִפַּז[d] ו' pref. id.)(noun masc. sing.; ו id. . . פזז
מְפַזֵּז[e] Piel part. sing. masc. . . . . פזז
מְפַזֵּר[f] Piel part. sing. masc. . . . . פזר
מְפֻזָּר[g] Pual part. sing. masc. . . . . פזר
מַפַּח[h] noun masc. sing., bef. penacute for מַפָּח . נפח
מַפֻּחַ[i] noun masc. sing. . . . . . נפח
מִפַּח pref. מִ)(noun m. s., pl. פַּחִים (§ 37. r. 7) פחח
מְפַחֵד[k] Piel part. sing. masc. (§ 14. rem. 1) . פחד
מִפַּחַד[l] } pref. מִ)(noun masc. sing. dec. 6 d (§ 35. rem. 2) . . . . } פחד
מִפַּחַד }
מִפַּחְדְּךָ[ff] pref. id.)(id., suff. 2 pers. s. m. (§ 35. r. 5) פחד
מִפִּי ו'[m] pref. id.)(noun masc. sing. constr., or with suff. 1 p. s. fr. פֶּה irr. (§ 45); ו bef. lab. פאה
מִפִּיבֹשֶׁת ו' noun masc.; ו id. . . . . פאה
מִפִּיהָ[n] pref. מִ)(noun masc. sing., suff. 3 pers. sing. fem. from פֶּה irr. (§ 45) . . . . פאה
מִפִּיהוּ[o] pref. id.)(id., suff. 3 pers. sing. masc. . . פאה
מִפִּיהֶם pref. id.)(id., suff. 3 pers. pl. masc. . . פאה
מִפִּיו pref. id.)(id., suff. 3 pers. sing. masc. . . פאה
מִפִּיךָ pref. id.)(id., suff. 2 pers. sing. masc. . . פאה
מִפִּיכֶם pref. id.)(id., suff. 2 pers. pl. masc. . . פאה
מַפִּיל ו'[p] Hiph. part. sing. masc. d. 1 b; ו bef. lab. נפל
מַפִּילִים[q] id. pl., abs. st. . . . . . נפל
מֻפִּים pr. name masc. Ge. 46. 21; called שְׁפוּפָם in Nu. 26. 39.
מִפִּינוּ[r] pref. מִ)(noun masc. sing., suff. 1 pers. pl. from פֶּה irr. (§ 45) . . . . פאה
מֵפִיץ[s] Hiph. part. s. m. dec. 3 b, subs. in Pr. 25. 18. פוץ
מְפִיקִים[t] Hiph. part. masc., pl. of [מֵפִיק] dec. 3 b פוק
מְפַכִּים[u] Piel part. masc., pl. of [מְפַכֶּה] dec. 9 a . פכה
מַפַּל[x] ו noun m. s., constr. of [מַפָּל] d. 2 b; ו bef. lab. נפל
מַפְלִא[y] ו Hiph. part. sing. masc. [for מַפְלִיא]; ו id. פלא
מִפְלְאוֹת[z] noun fem. pl. constr. from [מִפְלָאָה] dec. 11 a פלא
מַפָּלָה[a] noun fem. sing. . . . . . . נפל
מִפְלָט[b] noun masc. sing. . . . . . . פלט

מְפַלְטִי ו'[c] Piel part. sing. masc. [מְפַלֵּט], suff. 1 pers. sing. dec. 7 b; ו bef. lab. . . . פלט
מַפְּלֵי[d] noun masc. pl. constr. from [מַפָּל] dec. 2 b נפל
מְפַלֵּס[e] Piel part. sing. masc. . . . . פלס
מִפְלֶצֶת[f] } noun fem. sing. dec. 13 a (comp. § 35. rem. 2) . . . . } פלץ
מִפְלֶצֶת[g] }
מִפְלַצְתָּהּ id. with suff. 3 pers. sing. fem. . . . פלץ
מִפְלְשֵׂי[h] noun masc. pl. constr. from [מִפְלָשׂ] dec. 2 b פלס
מִפְּלִשְׁתִּים ו' pref. מִ)(gent. n., pl. of פְּלִשְׁתִּי; ו bef. lab. פלש
מַפֶּלֶת[i] noun fem. sing. dec. 13 a . . . . נפל
מַפַּלְתּוֹ[k] id., suff. 3 pers. sing. masc. . . . נפל
מַפַּלְתֵּךְ id., suff. 2 pers. sing. fem. . . . . נפל
מַפַּלְתֶּךָ[l] id., suff. 2 pers. sing. masc. for ־תְּךָ . . נפל
מֻפְנֶה[m] Hoph. part. sing. masc. . . . . פנה
מַפְנֶה[n] Hiph. part. sing. masc. . . . . פנה
מִפָּנַי } pref. מִ)(the foll. with suff. 1 pers. sing.; ו bef. lab. . . . } פנה
מִפָּנָי ו' }
מִפְּנֵי ו' pref. id.)(noun masc. pl., constr. of פָּנִים [from פָּנֶה] dec. 9 b; ו id. . . . פנה
מִפָּנֶיהָ[o] pref. id.)(id., suff. 3 pers. sing. fem. . . פנה
מִפְּנֵיהֶם ו'[p] pref. id.)(id., suff. 3 pers. pl. m.; ו bef. lab. פנה
מִפָּנָיו pref. id.)(id., suff. 3 pers. sing. masc. . פנה
מִפְּנִיִּים[q] pref. id.)(Kh., פְּנִינִים Keri (q. v.) . . פנן
מִפָּנֶיךָ ו'[r] pref. id.)(noun masc. pl. (פָּנִים), suff. 2 pers. sing. masc. [from פָּנֶה] dec. 9 b פנה
מִפְּנֵיכֶם pref. id.)(id. pl., suff. 2 pers. pl. masc. . פנה
מִפָּנִים[s] pref. id.)(id. pl., abs. st. . . . . פנה
מִפְּנִימָה pref. id.)(noun masc. sing. 'פְּנִים with loc. ה פנם
מִפָּנֵינוּ pref. id.)(noun masc. pl. (פָּנִים), suff. 1 pers. pl. [from פָּנֶה] dec. 9 b . . . . פנה
מִפְּנִינִים pref. id.)(noun masc. pl. abs. . . . פנן
מְפַנֵּק[t] Piel part. sing. masc. . . . . . פנק
מִפִּסֵּחַ[u] pref. מִ)(adj. masc. sing. dec. 7 b . . פסח
מִפֶּסֶל pref. id.)(Seg. noun m. sing. dec. 6 a, in pause for פָּסֶל (§ 35. rem. 2), but with suff. פִּסְלִי פסל
מִפְעֲלוֹת noun fem. pl. constr. from [מִפְעָלָה] dec. 11 a פעל
מִפֹּעֲלֵי[x] pref. מִ)(Kal part. act. pl. c. from פֹּעֵל d. 7 b פעל
מִפְעָלָיו[y] noun masc. pl., suff. 3 pers. sing. masc. from [מִפְעָל] dec. 2 b . . . . . פעל
מֵפַעַת ו pr. name for מֵיפַעַת (q. v.); ו bef. lab. . יפע
מַפֵּץ[z] noun masc. sing. . . . . . . נפץ
מַפָּצוֹ[a] noun m. s., suff. 3 pers. s. m. fr. [מַפָּץ] d. 2 b נפץ
מְפִצִים[b] ו Hiph. part. m., pl. of מֵפִיץ d. 3 b; ו bef. lab. פוץ
מְפַקֵּד[c] Piel part. sing. masc. . . . . . פקד

[a] Is. 59. 16. [b] Is. 50. 2. [c] Ezr. 9. 11. [d] Is. 13. 12. [e] 2 Sa. 6. 16. [f] Pr. 11. 24.
[g] Est. 3. 8. [h] Job 11. 20. [i] Je. 6. 29. [k] Pr. 28. 14. [l] Job 21. 9. [m] Is. 48. 3.
[n] Ho. 2. 19. [o] Mal. 2. 7. [p] Da. 9. 20. [q] Da. 9. 18. [r] Je. 44. 17. [s] Na. 2. 2.
[t] Ps. 144. 13. [u] Eze. 47. 2. [x] Am. 8. 6. [y] Ju. 13. 19. [z] Job 37. 16. [a] Is. 17. 1.
[b] Ps. 55. 9. [c] Ps. 18. 49. [d] Job 41. 15. [e] Pr. 5. 21. [f] 2 Ch. 15. 16. [ff] Ps. 119. 120.
[g] 1 Ki. 15. 13. [h] Job 37. 16. [i] Ju. 14. 8. [k] Eze. 31. 13, 16. [l] Eze. 32. 10.
[m] Eze. 9. 2. [n] Na. 2. 9. [o] Ho. 2. 4. [p] Eze. 2. 6. [q] Pr. 3. 15.
[r] Ge. 4. 14. [s] 2 Sa. 10. 9. [t] Pr. 29. 21. [u] Pr. 26. 7. [x] Ps. 59. 3.
[y] Pr. 8. 22. [z] Je. 51. 20. [a] Eze. 9. 2. [b] Je. 23. 1. [c] Is. 13. 4.

מְפַקֵּד noun masc. sing., constr. of מְפַקֵּד׳ dec. 2b — פקד

מְפֻקָּדִים[a] Hoph. part. m., pl. of [מֻפְקָד § 11. r. 10] d. 2b — פקד

מִפְּקוּדֵי[b] pref. ·מִ) (Kal part. pass. pl. constr. from [פָּקוּד] dec. 3a . . . — פקד

מִפְּקוּדֶיךָ[c] ׳ו pref. id.) (noun masc. pl., suff. 2 pers. sing. masc. from [פִּקּוּד] d. 1b; ו bef. lab. . — פקד

מֵפֵר Hiph. part. sing. masc. . . . — פרר

מְפֹרָד[d] ו Pual part. sing. masc.; ו bef. lab. . — פרד

מִפְּרִי[e] ׳ו pref. ·מִ) (noun masc. sing. dec. 6i; ו id. — פרה

מַפְרִיד Hiph. part. sing. masc. . . . — פרד

מִפִּרְיוֹ[f] pref. ·מִ) (noun masc. sing., suff. 3 pers. sing. masc. from פְּרִי dec. 6i . — פרה

מַפְרִים Hiph. part. sing. masc. dec. 1b . — פרם

מַפְרֵךְ[g] Hiph. part. s. m. [מַפְרֶה], suff. 2 p. s. m. d. 9a — פרה

מַפְרֶסֶת Hiph. part. s., fem. of מַפְרִים (§ 39. No. 4d) — פרס

מִפַּרְעֹה pref. ·מִ) (pr. name masc., see פַּרְעֹה. —

מִפְרָצָיו[h] noun m. pl., suff. 3 pers. s. m. fr. [מִפְרָץ] d. 2b — פרץ

מְפֹרֶצֶת[i] Pual part. sing. fem. [of מְפֹרָץ] . . — פרץ

מְפָרֵק[k] Piel part. sing. masc. . . . . — פרק

מַפְרַקְתּוֹ[l] noun fem. sing., suff. 3 pers. sing. masc. from [מַפְרֶקֶת] dec. 13a . . — פרק

מְפָרַשׁ[m] Chald. Pael part. pass. sing. masc. (§ 19. r. 3) — פרש

מְפֹרָשׁ[n] Pual part. sing. masc. . . . . — פרש

מִפְרְשֵׂי[o] noun masc. pl. constr. from [מִפְרָשׂ] dec. 2b — פרש

מִפְרָשֵׂךְ[p] id. sing., suff. 2 pers. sing. fem. . — פרשׂ

מַפְשִׁיטִים[q] Hiph. part. masc., pl. of [מַפְשִׁיט] dec. 1b — פשט

מִפֶּשַׁע pref. ·מִ) (noun masc. sing. dec. 6a (§ 35. r. 5) — פשע

מִפִּשְׁעֵיהֶם[r] ו pref. id.) (id. pl., suff. 3 p. pl. m.; ו bef. lab. — פשע

מִפְּשָׁעֵינוּ[s] pref. id.) (id. pl., suff. 1 pers. pl. . — פשע

מְפַשַּׁר[t] Chald. Pael part. act. sing. masc. . — פשר

מִפַּת[u] Keri pref. ·מִ) (noun fem. sing. dec. 8e . — פתת

מִפַּתְבַּג[x] pref. ·מִ) (noun m. s., constr. of [פַּתְבַּג] d. 2b — פתבג

מִפִּתּוֹ[y] pref. id.) (noun fem. sing., suff. 3 pers. sing. masc. from פַּת dec. 8e . . . — פתת

מִפְּתוֹר pref. id.) (pr. name of a place . — פתר

מַפְתֵּחַ[z] noun masc. sing. dec. 7b . . . — פתח

מְפַתֵּחַ[a] Piel part. sing. masc. . . . — פתח

מִפֶּתַח ׳ו pref. ·מִ) (noun masc. sing. (suff. פִּתְחוֹ dec. 6a (§ 35. rem. 5); ו bef. lab. . — פתח

מִפְתַּח[b] ו noun masc. sing., constr. of מַפְתֵּחַ (§ 36. rem. 1); ו id. . . . — פתח

מְפֻתָּחֹת[c] Pual part. fem. pl. [of מְפֻתָּחָה fr. מְפֻתָּח m.] — פתח

מִפֶּתִי[d] ׳ו pref. ·מִ) (noun masc. sing. dec. 6i [for פְּתִי § 35. rem. 15]; ו bef. lab. . — פתה

מְפַתֶּיהָ[e] Piel part. pl. masc., suff. 3 pers. sing. fem. from [מְפַתֶּה] dec. 9a . . . — פתה

מִפְתָּיו the foll. with suff. 3 pers. sing. masc. . — יפת

מֹפְתִים ו noun masc., pl. of מוֹפֵת d. 7b; ו bef. lab. — יפת

מִפְתַּן noun masc. sing., constr. of מִפְתָּן׳ dec. 2b — פתן

מִפַּתְרוֹס ו pref. ·מִ) (pr. name of a country, see פַּתְרוֹס.

מָצָא ׳ו fut. יִמְצָא.—I. *to come to, reach to, arrive at,* with עַד, Job 11. 7.—II. *to obtain, acquire.*—III. *to find, discover.*—IV. *to come upon* any one, *to befall, happen,* with acc., לְ of pers.—V. *to be sufficient, enough,* for anything, with לְ. Niph. נִמְצָא.—I. *to be obtained, acquired* by any one, with לְ.—II. *to be found.*—III. *to be present, at hand;* נִמְצָא מְאֹד *very present,* or *is readily found.* Hiph. הִמְצִיא.—I. *to cause to come to,* i. e. *to deliver, give up.*—II. *to cause to obtain.*—III. *to offer, present,* with אֶל Le. 9. 12, 13, 18.

מְצָא[f] [g]׳ו Kal imp. sing. masc.; ו bef. lab. . — מצא

מְצֹא[h] id. inf. constr. . . . . — מצא

מֹצָא[i] defect. for מוֹצָא (q. v.) . . — יצא

מָצְאָה [k]׳ו Kal pret. 3 pers. sing. fem.; ו bef. lab. — מצא

מְצָאָהּ [l]׳ו id. pret. 3 pers. sing. masc., suff. 3 pers. sing. fem.; ו id. . . . . — מצא

מְצָאֻהוּ[m] [n]׳ו id. pret. 3 pers. pl., suff. 3 p. s. m.; ו id. — מצא

מָצְאוּ / מָצָאוּ [o]׳ו } id. pret. 3 pers. pl. (§ 8. rem. 7); ו id. . . . } — מצא

מְצָאוֹ[p] id. pret. 3 pers. sing. masc., suff. 3 pers. sing. masc.; bef. monos. for מְצָאוֹ . — מצא

מֹצָאוֹ[q] defect. for מוֹצָאוֹ (q. v.) . . — יצא

מֹצְאוֹ[r] Kal part. sing. masc. fr. מוֹצֵא, suff. 3 pers. sing. masc. dec. 7b . . . — מצא

מִצְאוּ[s] ו id. imp. pl. masc.; ו bef. lab. . — מצא

מְצָאוּךָ ו id. pret. 3 pers. pl. with suff. 2 pers. sing. masc.; ו id. conv. . . . — מצא

מְצָאוּנִי id. id. with suff. 1 pers. sing. . . — מצא

מֹצָאֵי[t] ו defect. for מוֹצָאֵי (q. v.) . . — יצא

מֹצְאִי Kal part. act. sing. masc., suff. 1 pers. sing. fr. מוֹצֵא dec. 7b . . . . — מצא

מֹצְאֵיהֶם[u] id. pl., suff. 3 pers. pl. masc. . . — מצא

מִצֹּאן[x] pref. ·מִ) (noun com. sing. dec. 1a . — צאן

מְצֶאןָ[y] ו Kal imp. pl. f. (comp. § 8. r. 16); ו bef. lab. — מצא

מְצָאנֻהוּ[z] the following with suff. 3 pers. sing. masc. — מצא

מָצָאנוּ Kal pret. 1 pers. pl. . . . . — מצא

מְצָאָנוּ[a] ו id. pret. 3 pers. sing. masc., suff. 1 pers. pl.; ו for וְ, conv. . . . — מצא

מִצֹּאנוֹ[b] pref. ·מִ) (noun com. sing., suff. 3 pers. sing. masc. fr. צֹאן dec. 1a . . . — צאן

---

[a] 2 Ch. 34. 12. [b] Nu. 26. 64. [c] Ps. 119. 104, 110. [d] Est. 3. 8. [e] Ge. 3. 3. [f] Ge. 3. 6. [g] Ge. 48. 4. [h] Ju. 5. 17. [i] Ne. 1. 3. [k] 1 Ki. 19. 11. [l] 1 Sa. 4. 18. [m] Ezr. 4. 18. [n] Ne. 8. 8. [o] Job 36. 29. [p] Eze. 27. 7. [q] 2 Ch. 35. 11. [r] Le. 16. 16. [s] Is. 53. 5. [t] Da. 5. 12. [u] Da. 1. 5. [x] Da. 1. 5. [y] 2 Sa. 12. 3. [z] Is. 22. 22. [a] Zec. 3. 9. [b] Pr. 8. 6. [c] Ex. 39. 6. [d] Eze. 45. 20. [e] Ho. 2. 16. [f] 1 Sa. 20. 21, 36. [g] Pr. 3. 4. [h] Ps. 32. 6. [i] Da. 9. 25, etc. [k] Ex. 22. 5; Is. 34. 14. [l] De. 22. 23. [m] 2 Ki. 2. 17. [n] De. 31. 17. [o] 2 Ch. 32. 4. [p] Job 31. 29. [q] Ho. 6. 3. [r] Ge. 4. 15. [s] Je. 6. 16. [t] Ps. 107. 33. [u] Je. 50. 7. [x] Am. 6. 4. [y] Ru. 1. 9. [z] Job 37. 23. [a] 2 Ki. 7. 9. [b] 2 Sa. 12. 4.

מְצָאנֻהָ[a] Kal pret. 1 pers. pl., suff. 3 pers. sing. fem. — מצא
מְצָאֻנִי[b] defect. for מְצָאוּנִי (q. v.) . . . — מצא
מִצֹּאנֶךָ[c] וּ' pref. ·מִ)(noun com. sing., suff. 2 pers. sing. masc. from צֹאן dec. 1 a; וּ bef. lab. — צאן
מָצָאתָ Kal pret. 2 pers. sing. masc. . — מצא
וּמָצָאתָ id. id.; acc. shifted by conv. וְ, for וְ, but וּמָצָאתָ De. 4. 29, in pause (§ 8. r. 7) — מצא
מָצָאת[d] id. pret. 2 pers. sing. fem. . . — מצא
מֹצֵאת[e] id. part. sing. fem. (§ 23. r. 4) fr. מוֹצֵא m. — מצא
מְצָאתָהּ[f] וּ'[g] id. pret. 2 p. s. m., suff. 3 p. s. f.; וּ for וְ conv. — מצא
מִצֵּאתוֹ[h] וּ pref. ·מִ)(noun fem. sing., suff. 3 pers. sing. masc. fr. צֹאָה dec. 10; וּ bef. lab. — יצא
מָצָאתִי Kal pret. 1 pers. sing. . . . . — מצא
מְצָאתִיהָ id., suff. 3 pers. sing. fem. . . . — מצא
מְצָאתִיהוּ[i] / מְצָאתִיו[l] } id., suff. 3 pers. sing. masc. . . — מצא
מְצָאתִים[m] id. pret. 1 pers., or 2 pers. f., suff. 3 p. pl. m. — מצא
מִצֵּאתֵךְ[n] pref. ·מִ)(Kal inf. constr. צֵאת (§ 25, 2 d), suff. 2 pers. sing. fem. dec. 1 a . . — יצא
מְצָאָתַם[o] Kal pret. 3 pers. f. sing., suff. 3 pers. pl. m. — מצא
מְצָאתֶם וּ' id. pret. 2 pers. pl. masc.; וּ for וְ, conv. — מצא
מְצָאַתְנוּ[p] / מְצָאַתְנוּ } id. pret. 3 pers. sing. fem., suff. 1 pers. pl. . . . } — מצא
מַצַּב[q] וּ' noun m. s., constr. of מַצָּב d. 2 b; וּ bef. lab. — נצב
מֻצָּב[r] Hoph. part. sing. masc. . . . . — נצב
מִצְּבָא pref. ·מִ)(n. m. s., constr. of צָבָא d. 4 a (§ 33. r. 2) — צבא
מַצָּבָה[s] noun fem. sing. . . . . . — נצב
מַצֵּבָה וּ' n. f. s. (constr. מַצֶּבֶת) d. 11 b; וּ bef. lab. — נצב
מִצֹּבָה pref. ·מִ)(pr. name of a country . — נצב
מַצֵּבוֹת וּ'[t] noun f. pl. abs. fr. מַצֵּבָה d. 11 b; וּ bef. lab. — נצב
מַצְּבוֹת וּ'[u] id. pl., constr. st.; וּ id. — נצב
מַצֵּבוֹתֶיךָ וּ id. pl., suff. 2 p. s. m. (comp. § 42. r. 4); וּ id. — נצב
מַצֵּבוֹתָם[v] id. pl., suff. 3 pers. pl. masc. (v. id.) . — נצב
[מְצֹבָיָה] pr. name of a place otherwise unknown, 1 Ch. 11. 47, where it stands with the article as a gentile noun.
מְצַבְּעִין[w] Ch. Pael part. act. m., pl. of [מְצַבַּע] d. 2 a — צבע
מַצֶּבֶת noun fem. sing., constr. of מַצֵּבָה dec. 11 a — נצב
מַצֶּבֶת noun fem. sing. dec. 13 a . . . — נצב
מַצַּבְתָּהּ[a] id., suff. 3 pers. sing. fem. . . . — נצב
מַצְּבֹתֵיהֶם[b] / מַצְּבֹתָם וּ'[c] } noun fem. pl. (retaining (..) under צ, comp. §42. r. 4), suff. 3 p. pl. m. d. 10 (§ 4. r. 2) } — נצב
מִצַּד pref. ·מִ)(noun masc. sing. dec. 8 e . . — צדד
מְצֹדְדוֹת[d] Pilel part. f. pl. [of מְצוֹדֶדֶת d. 13, fr. מְצוֹדֵד m.] — צוד
מִצִּדָּהּ pref. ·מִ)(n. m. s., suff. 3 p. s. f. fr. צַד d. 8 e — צדד
מִצִּדּוֹ[e] pref. id.)(id., suff. 3 pers. sing. masc. . — צדד

מְצָדוֹת[f] noun masc. with pl. fem. term., abs. st., from מְצָד dec. 1 a (comp. § 30. No. 3) . — צוד
מִצִּדֶּיהָ pref. ·מִ)(n. m. pl., suff. 3 p. s. f. fr. צַד d. 8 b — צדד
מַצְדִּיק[g] Hiph. part. sing. masc. dec. 1 b . — צדק
מִצַּדִּיק[h] pref. ·מִ)(adj. masc. sing. dec. 1 b . — צדק
מַצְדִּיקֵי[i] וּ'[k] Hiph. part. pl. constr. masc. from מַצְדִּיק dec. 1 b; וּ bef. lab. . . — צדק
מַצְדִּיקִי[l] id. sing. with suff. 1 pers. sing. . — צדק
מִצִּדְּךָ[m] pref. ·מִ)(n. m. s., suff. 2 p. s. m. fr. צַד d. 8 e — צדד
מִצְּדָקָה[n] pref. id.)(noun fem. sing. dec. 11 c . — צדק
מִצִּדְקוֹ[o] pref. id.)(n. m. s., suff. 3 p. s. m. fr. צֶדֶק d. 6 a — צדק
מִצִּדְקָתוֹ pref. id.)(n. f. s., suff. 3 p. s. m. fr. צְדָקָה d. 11 c — צדק
מְצֻדַת noun fem. sing., constr. of מְצוּדָה dec. 10 — צוד
מְצֻדָתָהּ[p] וּ noun fem. sing., suff. 3 pers. sing. fem., from מְצוּדָה dec. 10; וּ bef. lab. . — צוד
מְצֻדָתִי[q] וּ noun f. s., suff. 1 p. s. fr. מְצוּדָה d. 10; וּ id. — צוד

[מָצָה] *to suck, drain, wring out.* Niph. pass.

מַצָּה noun fem. sing. dec. 10 . . . — מצץ
מַצָּה וּ'[r] noun fem. sing.; וּ bef. lab. . — נצה
מֻצְהָב[s] Hoph. part. sing. masc. (§ 11. rem. 10) . — צהב
מִצְהֲלוֹת[t] noun fem. pl., constr. from [מִצְהָלָה] dec. 11 a — צהל
מִצְהֲלוֹתַיִךְ[u] וּ id. pl., suff. 2 pers. sing. fem.; וּ bef. lab. — צהל
מִצָּהֳרָיִם[x] וּ pref. ·מִ)(noun f., du. of צֹהַר d. 6 f; וּ id. — צהר
מִצּוֹבָה וּ pref. id.)(pr. name of a country; וּ id. — נצב
מְצוֹד[y] noun masc. sing., constr. of [מָצוֹד] dec. 3 a — צוד
מְצוּדָה[z] וּ noun fem. sing. dec. 10; וּ bef. lab. — צוד
מְצוּדוֹ[a] וּ noun masc. sing., suff. 3 pers. sing. masc. from [מְצוֹד § 32. rem. 5 מָצוֹד]; וּ id. . — צוד
מְצוּדוֹת[b] noun fem., pl. of מְצוּדָה dec. 10 . — צוד
מְצוֹדִים[c] noun masc., pl. of [מָצוֹד] dec. 3 a . — צוד
מְצוּדָתִי וּ noun fem. sing., suff. 1 pers. sing. from מְצוּדָה dec. 10; וּ bef. lab. . . — צוד
מְצַוָּה[d] Piel part. sing., fem. of מְצַוֶּה . . — צוה
מְצַוֶּה וּ'[e] id. part. sing. masc. dec. 9 a; וּ bef. lab. — צוה
מִצְוָה / מִצְוֹות[f] וּ } noun fem. sing. & pl. dec. 10; וּ id. — צוה
מְצַוְּךָ[g] / מְצַוְּךָ / מְצַוְּךָ } Piel part. sing. masc., suff. 2 pers. sing. masc. (§ 2. rem. 2) from מְצַוֶּה dec. 9 a } — צוה
מְצוּלָה / מְצוּלוֹת[h] } noun fem. sing. & pl. dec. 10 . . — צול
מִצּוֹם[i] pref. ·מִ)(noun masc. sing. dec. 1 a . — צום
מִצּוֹעַר pref. id.)(pr. name of a place . . — צער
מָצוֹק[k] וּ'[l] noun masc. sing.; וּ bef. lab. . . — צוק

[a] Ps. 132. 6. [b] Ca. 5. 7. [c] De. 12. 21; 15. 14. [d] Is. 57. 10. [e] 2 Sa. 18. 22. [f] Ge. 38. 23. [g] De. 22. 3. [h] Pr. 30. 12. [i] Ge. 38. 22. [k] Ca. 5. 6. [l] Ca. 3. 1, 2. [m] Je. 2. 34. [n] Eze. 26. 18. [o] Ex. 18. 8. [p] Nu. 20. 14. [q] 2 Sa. 23. 14. [r] Is. 29. 3. [s] Zec. 9. 8. [t] 1 Ki. 14. 23. [u] Eze. 26. 11. [x] Mi. 5. 12. [y] Ho. 10. 2. [z] Da. 4. 22. [a] Is. 6. 13. [b] Ex. 23. 24. [c] De. 7. 5. [d] Eze. 13. 20. [e] 1 Sa. 6. 8. [f] Is. 33. 16. [g] Pr. 17. 15. [h] Job 36. 7. [i] Is. 5. 23. [k] Da. 12. 3. [l] Is. 50. 8. [m] Ps. 91. 7. [n] Is. 46. 12. [o] Eze. 3. 20. [p] Is. 29. 7. [q] 2 Sa. 22. 2. [r] Is. 58. 4. [s] Ezr. 8. 27. [t] Je. 8. 16. [u] Je. 13. 27. [x] Job 11. 17. [y] Pr. 12. 12. [z] Job 39. 28. [a] Job 19. 6. [b] Ps. 31. 3. [c] Ec. 7. 26. [d] Ge. 27. 8. [e] Is. 55. 4. [f] Ne. 9. 14. [g] De. 6. 2. [h] Zec. 10. 11. [i] Ps. 109. 24. [k] 1 Sa. 22. 2. [l] Ps. 119. 143.

מְצוּק[a] noun masc. sing. dec. 3a . . . צוק
מְצוּקָה וּ noun fem. sing. dec. 10; וּ bef. lab. . צוק
מָצוֹר pr. name of a country . . . מצר
מָצוֹר noun masc. sing. dec. 3a (§ 32. rem. 5) . צור
מְצוֹר[b] id., constr. st. . . . . . צור
מִצּוּר [c]וּ' pref. ·מִ)(noun masc. s. d. 1a; וּ bef. lab. צור
מְצוּרָה, מְצוּרוֹת } noun fem. sing. and pl. dec. 10 . . צור
מְצוּרֶךָ[d] noun masc. sing., suff. 2 pers. sing. masc. [for מְצוֹרְךָ] from מָצוֹר dec. 3a (§ 32. rem. 5) צור
מִצַּוְּרֹנַיִךְ[e] pref. ·מִ)(n. m. pl., suff. 2 p. s. f. fr. [צַוָּרוֹן] d. 3c צור
מְצוֹרָע[f] in full for מְצֹרָע (q. v.) . . . צרע
מַצּוֹת וּ' noun fem., pl. of מַצָּה dec. 10; וּ bef. lab. מצץ
מִצְוַת noun fem. sing., constr. of מִצְוָה dec. 10 צוה
מִצְוֹת [g]וּ' id. pl.; וּ bef. lab. . . . צוה
מִצְוָתוֹ[h] id. sing., suff. 3 pers. sing. masc. . . צוה
מִצְוֹתָו id. pl., suff. 3 pers. s. m. (for ־ָיו § 4. r. 1) צוה
מִצְוֹתָי, מִצְוֹתַי וּ' } id. pl., suff. 1 pers. sing.; וּ bef. lab. צוה
מִצְוֹתָיו וּ' id. pl., suff. 3 pers. sing. masc.; וּ id. צוה
מִצְוֹתֶיךָ [i]וּ' id. pl., suff. 2 pers. sing. masc.; וּ id. צוה
מִצְוָתְךָ id. sing., suff. 2 pers. sing. masc. . . צוה
מִצְוֹתֶךָ[k] defect. for מִצְוֹתֶיךָ (q. v. & § 4. rem. 1) . צוה

מֵצַח [l]וּ' masc. dec. 6e (pl. c. מִצְחוֹת), *forehead, brow, front.*

מִצְחָה fem. *greaves,* armour of the legs, only constr. מִצְחַת 1 Sa. 17. 6.

מִצְחוֹ id., suff. 3 pers. sing. masc. . . . מצח
מִצְחוֹת[m] id. with pl. fem. term., constr. st. . מצח
מִצְחֲךָ[n], מִצְחֵךְ[p] [o]וּ' } id. sing., suff. 2 pers. sing. m.; וּ bef. lab. מצח
מִצְחָם[q] id. sing., suff. 3 pers. pl. masc. . . מצח
מְצַחֵק Piel part. sing. masc. (§ 14. rem. 1) . צחק
מִצְחַת[r] וּ noun fem. sing. constr. [of מִצְחָה]; וּ bef. lab. מצח
מַצִּיב[s] Hiph. part. sing. masc. . . . נצב
מַצִּיג[t] Hiph. part. sing. masc. (§ 20. rem. 16) יצג
מִצֵּיד[u] pref. ·מִ)(noun m. sing., constr. of צַיִד d. 6h צוד
מִצֵּידוֹ[x] pref. id.)(id. with suff. 3 pers. sing. masc. צוד
מִצִּידוֹן pref. id.)(pr. name of a place . . צוד
מִצֵּידִי[y] pref. id.)(noun masc. sing., suff. 1 pers. sing. from צַיִד dec. 6h . . . . צוד
מִצֵּידָם[z] pref. id.)(id. with suff. 3 pers. pl. masc. צוד
מִצִּידֹן pref. id.)(pr. name of a place . . צוד
מִצִּידֹנִים pref. id.)(gent. n. pl. from the preced. . צוד
מִצִּיּוֹן וּ' pref. id.)(pr. name of a place; וּ bef. lab. ציה

מַצִּיל Hiph. part. sing. masc. . . . . נצל
מֵצִיץ[a] Hiph. part. sing. masc. . . . צוץ
מָצִית[b] [c]וּ' Kal pret. 2 pers. sing. fem.; וּ for וְ, conv. מצה
מַצִּית[d] Hiph. part. sing. masc. (§ 20. rem. 16) יצת
מַצִּל[e] וּ defect. for מַצִּיל (q. v.) . . . נצל
מֵצַל[f] Hiph. part. sing. masc. (§ 18. rem. 10) . צלל
מֻצָּל Hoph. part. sing. masc. . . . נצל
מְצַלֵּא[g] וּ Chald. Pael part. sing. masc. d. 6a; וּ bef. lab. צלא
מִצִּלּוֹ[h] pref. ·מִ)(noun masc. sing., suff. 3 pers. sing. masc. from צֵל dec. 8b . . . צלל
מְצִלּוֹת[i] noun fem., pl. of [מְצִלָּה] dec. 10 . צלל
מַצְלַח[k] וּ Ch. Aph. part. sing. masc. d. 2b; וּ bef. lab. צלח
מַצְלְחִין[l] וּ id. pl. abs.; וּ id. . . . . צלח
מַצְלִיחַ Hiph. part. sing. masc. . . . צלח
מְצַלַּיִן[m] וּ Ch. Aph. part. m., pl. of מְצַלֵּא d. 6a; וּ bef. lab. צלא
מִצַּלְמֹנָה pref. ·מִ)(pr. name of a place . . צלם
מִצַּלְעֹתָיו[n] pref. id.)(noun fem. pl., suff. 3 pers. sing. masc. from צֵלָע dec. 4b (§ 33. 2c & r. 3) צלע
מְצִלְתַּיִם[o], מְצִלְתַּיִם[p] וּ, [q]וּ' } noun fem. du. from [מְצֶלֶת] dec. 13b; וּ bef. lab. . . . } צלל
מִצִּמְאָה[r] pref. ·מִ)(noun fem. sing. . . . צמא
מְצֻמֶּדֶת[s] Pual part. sing. fem. [of מְצֻמָּד] . . צמד
מַצְמִיחַ[aa] Hiph. part. sing. masc. . . . צמח
מַצְמִיתַי[t] Hiph. part. pl. masc., suff. 1 pers. sing. from [מַצְמִית] dec. 1b . . . . צמת
מִצַּמֶּרֶת[u] pref. ·מִ)(noun fem. s. (suff. צַמַּרְתּוֹ) d. 13a צמר
מִצִּנִּים[x] pref. id.)(noun masc., pl. of [צֵן] dec. 8b צנן
מִצְנֶפֶת noun fem. sing. . . . . צנף
מִצְעֲדֵי noun masc. pl. constr. from [מִצְעָד] dec. 2b צעד
מִצְּעִירָה[y] noun fem. sing. compnd. of צְעִירָה & מִן . צער
מְצַעֵק[z] Piel part. sing. masc. (§ 14. rem. 1) . צעק
מִצְעָר noun masc. sing. . . . . צער
מִצֹּעַר pref. ·מִ)(pr. name of a place . . צער
מְצַפֶּה Piel part. sing. masc. dec. 9a . . . צפה
מְצֻפֶּה[a] Pual part. sing. masc. dec. 9a . . צפה
מִצְפֶּה[ff], מִצְפָּה } pr. name of a place . . . . צפה
מִצְפֶּה[b] noun masc. sing. dec. 9a . . . צפה
מִצָּפוֹן וּ' pref. מִ)(noun masc. sing. d. 3a; וּ bef. lab. צפן
מִצְּפוֹן pref. ·מִ)(id. constr. st. . . . צפן
מִצָּפוֹנָה[c] pref. id.)(id. abs. with parag. ה . . צפן
מִצְּפוֹנָה[d] pref. id.)(id. constr. with parag. ה . . צפן
מְצַפֶּיךָ[e] Piel part. pl. masc., suff. 2 pers. sing. masc. from מְצַפֶּה dec. 9a . . . צפה
מְצֻפִּים[f] Pual part. pl. masc. from מְצֻפֶּה dec. 9a . צפה

[a] 1 Sa. 14. 5. [b] Eze. 4. 7. [c] Ps. 81. 17. [d] Eze. 4. 8. [e] Ca. 4. 9. [f] 2 Ch. 26. 23. [g] Ne. 9. 13. [h] Nu. 15. 31. [i] Ps. 119. 166. [k] Ps. 119. 98. [l] Je. 3. 3. [m] Eze. 9. 4. [n] Eze. 3. 8. [o] Is. 48. 4. [p] Eze. 3. 9. [q] Eze. 3. 8. [r] 1 Sa. 17. 6. [s] 1 Sa. 15. 12. [t] Ju. 6. 37. [u] Ge. 27. 25, 31. [x] Ge. 27. 30. [y] Ge. 27. 19. [z] Jos. 9. 14. [a] Ca. 2. 9. [b] Is. 51. 17. [c] Eze. 23. 34. [d] Eze. 21. 3. [e] Da. 6. 28. [f] Eze. 31. 3. [g] Da. 6. 11. [h] Eze. 31. 12. [i] Zec. 14. 20. [k] Ezr. 5 8. [l] Ezr. 6. 14. [m] Ezr. 6. 10. [n] Ge. 2. 21. [o] 1 Ch. 15. 16. [p] Ne. 12. 27. [q] 1 Ch. 16. 42. [r] Je. 2. 25. [s] 2 Sa. 20. 8. [t] Ps. 69. 5. [u] Eze. 17. 22. [x] Job 5. 5. [y] Da. 8. 9. [z] 2 Ki. 2. 12. [a] Pr. 26. 23. [aa] Ps. 104. 14. [b] Is. 21. 8. [c] Jos 15. 10. [d] Ju. 21. 19. [e] Mi. 7. 4. [f] Ex. 26. 32. [ff] 1 Sa. 4. 13.

מִצְפֻּנָיו[a] n. m. pl., suff. 3 pers. s. m. [fr. מִצְפּוֹן § 3. r. 4] צפן

מְצַפְצֵף[b] וּ Pilp. (§ 6. No. 4) part. s. m. d. 7 b; וּ bef. lab. צפף

מָצַץ *to suck*, Is. 66. 11.

מַצָּה fem. dec. 10, *unleavened bread*, or *cake* (either from the idea of *pressing*, *extending by pressure*, or *sweetness* supposed to be contained in the root); חַלּוֹת מַצּוֹת *unleavened cakes;* חַג הַמַּצּוֹת *the feast of unleavened bread, the passover.*

מֻצָּק[c] Hoph. part. sing. masc. dec. 2 b (§ 20. r. 16) יצק

מֻצַּק[d] id. constr. st. . . . . . יצק

מְצֻקֵי[e] noun masc. pl. constr. from מָצוּק dec. 3 a . צוק

מָצַר Root not used; prob. *to shut;* Arab. *to limit, border.*

מָצוֹר (*fortified*, or *border*) pr. name, *Egypt;* יְאֹרֵי מ׳ the streams or canals of the Nile.

מִצְרַיִם pr. name—I. of one of the sons of Ham.—II. *Egypt;* frequently for *Egyptians.* Gent. n. מִצְרִי (fem. מִצְרִית, pl. מִצְרִים, fem. מִצְרִיּוֹת) *Egyptian.*

מִצָּר / מִצָּר[f] } pref. ·מִ)(noun masc. sing. dec. 8 (§ 37. rem. 7) . . . . } צרר

מִצֹּר pref. id.)(noun masc. sing. (Eze. 3. 9) also pr. name for צוֹר . . . . צור

מִצָּרָה pref. id.)(noun fem. sing. dec. 10 [for צָרָה] from צַר masc. . . . . צרר

מְצֵרָה[g] Hiph. part. sing. fem. [for מְצֵרָה fr. מֵצֵר m.] צרר

מִצָּרוֹת[h] pref. ·מִ)(noun fem., pl. of צָרָה dec. 10 [for צָרָה] from צַר masc. . . . צרר

מִצָּרַי[i] pref. id.)(noun masc. pl., suff. 1 pers. sing. from צַר dec. 8 (§ 37. rem. 7) . צרר

מְצָרֵי[k] וּ noun masc. pl. constr. from מֵצַר dec. 8 e (§ 37. rem. 7); וּ bef. lab. . . . צרר

מִצְרִי gent. noun masc. from מִצְרַיִם . . מצר

מִצָּרָיו pref. ·מִ)(noun masc. pl., suff. 3 pers. sing. masc. from צַר dec. 8 (§ 37. rem. 7) . צרר

מִצְרַיִם / וּ מִצְרָיִם } pr. name of a country; וּ bef. lab. . מצר

מִצְרַיְמָה / מִצְרָיְמָה } id. with parag. ה . . . מצר

מִצָּרֵינוּ pref. ·מִ)(noun masc. sing., suff. 1 pers. pl. from צַר dec. 8 (§ 37. rem. 7) . . צרר

מִצְרִית gent. noun, fem. of מִצְרִי from מִצְרַיִם . מצר

מְצֹרָע[l] וּ Pual part. sing. masc.; וּ bef. lab. . צרע

מִצָּרְעָה pref. ·מִ)(pr. name of a place . . צרע

מְצֹרָעִים[m] Pual part. masc., pl. of מְצֹרָע . . צרע

מְצֹרַעַת[n] / מְצֹרַעַת } id. sing. fem. . . . . . צרע

מִצָּרַעְתּוֹ[o] pref. ·מִ)(noun fem. sing., suff. 3 pers. sing. masc. from צָרַעַת [for צָרַעַת] dec. 13 a צרע

מַצְרֵף noun masc. sing. . . . . . צרף

מְצָרֵף[p] Piel part. sing. masc. . . . . צרף

מְצֹרָרִים[q] וּ Pual part. masc., pl. of מְצֹרָר; וּ bef. lab. צרר

מְצֻרֹת[r] defect. for מְצוּרוֹת (q. v.) . . . צור

מִצָּרָתוֹ[s] pref. ·מִ)(noun fem. sing., suff. 3 pers. sing. masc. from צָרָה dec. 10, from צַר masc. צרר

מִצָּרָתֵינוּ[t] pref. id.)(id. sing. (written in full) or pl. with suff. 1 pers. pl. (§ 4. rem. 3) . צרר

מַצֹּת defect. for מַצּוֹת (q. v.) . . . מצץ

מָצָתִי[u] Kal pret. 1 pers. s. for מָצָאתִי (§ 23. r. 1) מצא

מַצֻּתֶךָ[x] noun f. s., suff. 2 p. s. m. fr. [מַצּוּת] d. 1 b נצה

מַק[y] noun masc. sing. . . . . . מקק

מַקָּבוֹת[z] וּ noun fem., pl. of מַקָּבָה; וּ bef. lab. נקב

מַקְבִּילֹת Hiph. part. fem. pl. [of מַקְבִּילָה fr. מַקְבִּיל m.] קבל

מְקַבֵּץ Piel part. sing. masc. dec. 7 b . . קבץ

מִקַּבְצְאֵל pref. ·מִ)(pr. name of a place, see יְקַבְצְאֵל קבץ

מְקַבְּצָיו[a] וּ Piel part. pl. masc., suff. 3 pers. sing. masc. from מְקַבֵּץ dec. 7 b; וּ bef. lab. . קבץ

מְקַבְּצָם[b] id. sing., suff. 3 pers. pl. masc. . . קבץ

מְקֻבֶּצֶת[c] Pual part. sing. fem. [of מְקֻבָּץ § 39. No. 4] קבץ

מְקַבֵּר[d] Piel part. sing. masc. dec. 7 b . . קבר

מִקְּבֹר[e] pref. ·מִ)(Kal inf. constr. . . . קבר

מִקִּבְרוֹת pref. id.)(pr. n. in compos. קִבְרוֹת הַתַּאֲוָה קבר

מִקִּבְרֹתֵיכֶם[f] pref. id.)(noun masc. with pl. fem. term. and suff. 2 pers. pl. masc. fr. קֶבֶר d. 6 a קבר

מִקִּבְרֵיהֶם[g] pref. id.)(id. pl. masc., suff. 3 pers. pl. masc. קבר

מְקַבְּרִים Piel part. masc., pl. of מְקַבֵּר dec. 7 b . קבר

מִקִּבְרְךָ[h] pref. ·מִ)(n. m. s., suff. 2 p. s. m. fr. קֶבֶר d. 6 a קבר

מִקִּבְרֹת pref. id.)(pr. name in compos. קִבְרוֹת הַתַּאֲוָה קבר

מַקֶּבֶת[i] noun fem. sing. . . . . . נקב

מַקֵּדָה [k]וּ pr. name of a place; וּ bef. lab. . נקד

מִקְּדוֹשׁ[h] pref. ·מִ)(adj. masc. s., constr. of קָדוֹשׁ d. 3 a קדש

מִקֶּדֶם [l]וּ pref. id.)(noun masc. s. d. 6 a; וּ bef. lab. קדם

מִקַּדְמֵי[m] pref. ·מִ)(id. pl., constr. st. . . . קדם

מִקַּדְמַת[n] Chald. noun f. s., constr. of [קַדְמָא] dec. 8 a קדם

מְקַדֵּשׁ[tt] Piel part. sing. masc. dec. 7 b . . קדש

מִקָּדֵשׁ pref. ·מִ)(pr. name of a place . . קדש

מִקְדָּשׁ [o]וּ noun masc. sing. dec. 2 b; וּ bef. lab. קדש

מִקְדַּשׁ [p]וּ id., constr. st.; וּ id. . . . קדש

מִקֶּדֶשׁ pref. ·מִ)(pr. name of a place . . קדש

מִקֹּדֶשׁ pref. id.)(noun masc. sing. dec. 6 c . קדש

מִקְדָּשֶׁהָ[q] noun masc. sing., suff. 3 pers. sing. fem. from מִקְדָּשׁ dec. 2 b . . . . קדש

---

[a] Ob. 6. [b] Is. 10. 14. [c] Job 11. 15. [d] 1 Ki. 7. 16. [e] 1 Sa. 2. 8. [f] Ps. 32. 7. [g] Je. 48. 41; 49. 22. [h] Pr. 21. 23. [i] Is. 1. 24. [k] Ps. 116. 3. [l] 2 Sa. 3. 29. [m] 2 Ki. 7. 3. [n] Nu. 12. 10. [o] 2 Ki. 5. 3, 6, 7. [p] Mal. 3. 2, 3. [q] Jos. 9. 4. [r] Is. 29. 3. [s] Is. 46. 7. [t] 2 Ch. 20. 9. [tt] Eze. 37. 28. [u] Nu. 11. 11. [x] Is. 41. 12. [y] Is. 3. 24. [z] 1 Ki. 6. 7.

[a] Is. 62. 9. [b] Je. 32. 37. [c] Eze. 38. 8. [d] Je. 14. 16. [e] Ge. 23. 6. [f] Eze. 37. 12, 13. [g] Je. 8. 1. [h] Is. 14. 19. [i] Is. 51. 1. [k] Je. 51. 5. [l] Is. 46. 10. [m] Pr. 8. 23. [n] Ezr. 5. 11. [o] Eze. 45. 4. [p] Eze. 48. 21. [q] La. 1. 10.

מְקַדְּשׁוֹ[a] Piel part. sing. masc., suff. 3 pers. sing. masc. from מְקַדֵּשׁ dec. 7b . קדשׁ

מִקְדָּשׁוֹ / מִקְדָּשׁוֹ[b] } noun m. s., suff. 3 p. s. m. fr. מִקְדָּשׁ d. 2b [the latter form as if from מִקְדֵּשׁ d. 7b] } קדשׁ

מִקָּדְשֵׁי pref. מִ)(noun m. pl. constr. fr. קֹדֶשׁ d. 6c קדשׁ

מִקְדָּשַׁי noun masc. pl., suff. 1 p. s. fr. מִקְדָּשׁ d. 2b קדשׁ

מִקְדָּשִׁי ו׳ id. sing., suff. 1 pers. sing.; וּ bef. lab. . קדשׁ

מִקְדְּשֵׁי [c] ו׳ id. pl., constr. st.; וּ id. . . קדשׁ

מְקַדְּשֵׁיהֶם[d] Piel part. pl. masc., suff. 3 pers. pl. masc. from מְקַדֵּשׁ dec. 7b . . . . קדשׁ

מִקְדָּשֶׁיךָ[ss] noun masc. pl., suff. 2 pers. sing. masc. from מִקְדָּשׁ dec. 2b . . . . . קדשׁ

מִקְדְּשֵׁיכֶם[e] id. with suff. 2 pers. pl. masc. . קדשׁ

מַקְדִּשִׁים [f] ו׳ Hiph. part. masc., pl. of מַקְדִּישׁ dec. 1b קדשׁ

מִקְדָּשִׁים[g] noun masc., pl. of מִקְדָּשׁ dec. 2b . קדשׁ

מִקְּדֹשִׁים[h] pref. מִ)(adj. masc., pl. of קָדוֹשׁ dec. 3a . קדשׁ

מִקְדָּשְׁךָ / מִקְדָּשְׁךָ[k] } noun masc. sing., suff. 2 pers. sing. masc. from מִקְדָּשׁ dec. 2b . . } קדשׁ

מְקַדִּשְׁכֶם Piel part. sing. masc., suff. 2 pers. pl. masc. from מְקַדֵּשׁ dec. 7b . . . . קדשׁ

מְקַדְּשָׁם id. with suff. 3 pers. pl. masc. . . קדשׁ

מִקְדָּשָׁם[l] noun masc. s., suff. 3 p. pl. m. fr. מִקְדָּשׁ d. 2b קדשׁ

מְקַדִּשֵׁנוּ[m] id. with suff. 1 pers. pl. . . . קדשׁ

מִקְּהַל[n] pref. מִ)(noun m. s., constr. of קָהָל d. 4a קהל

מַקְהֵלֹתָה pref. id.)(pr. name of a place (קְהֵלָה), ה parag. קהל

מִקְוֵא[o] ו׳ for מִקְוֵה (q. v.); וּ bef. lab. . . קוה

מִקְוָה[p] וּ noun fem. sing. from מִקְוֶה masc.; וּ id. . קוה

מִקְוֵה / מִקְוֶה ו׳ } noun masc. sing. constr. & abs. dec. 9a; וּ id. . . . . } קוה

מִקּוֹל pref. מִ)(noun masc. sing. dec. 1a . קול

מִקּוֹלָם[q] pref. id.)(id., suff. 3 pers. pl. masc. קול

מָקוֹם ו׳ noun com. sing. dec. 3a; וּ bef. lab. קום

מְקוֹם ו׳ id., constr. st.; וּ id. . . קום

מְקוֹמָהּ id., suff. 3 pers. sing. fem. . . . קום

מְקוֹמוֹ id., suff. 3 pers. sing. masc. . . . קום

מְקוֹמִי id., suff. 1 pers. sing. . . . . קום

מְקוֹמֶךָ[r] / מְקוֹמְךָ[s] } id. with suff. 2 pers. sing. masc. . . קום

מְקוֹמָם id., suff. 3 pers. pl. masc. . . . קום

מְקוֹמֹתֵיכֶם[t] id. pl., suff. 2 pers. pl. masc. . . קום

מְקוֹמֹתָם[u] id. pl., suff. 3 pers. pl. masc. (§ 4. rem. 2) קום

מְקוֹר[x] [y] ו׳ noun masc. sing. dec. 3a; וּ bef. lab. . קור

מְקוֹר id., constr. st. . . . . . קור

מְקוֹרָהּ[z] id., suff. 3 pers. sing. fem. . . . . קור

מְקוֹרוֹ[a] id., suff. 3 pers. sing. masc. . . . קור

מְקוֹרֶךָ[b] id., suff. 2 pers. sing. masc. . . . קור

מִקַּח[c] וּ noun masc. sing., constr. of [מֶקַח] dec. 2b; וּ bef. lab. . . . . . לקח

מִקַּחַת pref. מִ)(Kal inf. constr. (§ 17. rem. 8) לקח

מִקֶּטֶב[d] pref. id.)(noun masc. sing. . . קטב

מַקְטִיר וּ Hiph. part. sing. masc. d. 1b; וּ bef. lab. . קטר

מַקְטִירוֹת[e] id. pl. fem. [from מַקְטִירָה] dec. 10 . קטר

מַקְטִירִים[f] id. pl. masc. dec. 1b . . . . קטר

מִקֶּטֶל[g] pref. מִ)(noun masc. s. [for קֶטֶל § 35. r. 2] קטל

מִקָּטֹן pref. id.)(adj. masc. sing. dec. 3a . קטן

מִקְּטַנֵּי[h] pref. id.)(adj. pl. masc. constr. from קָטָן dec. 8a (§ 37. No. 2) . . . קטן

מִקְּטַנָּם[i] pref. id.)(id. sing., suff. 3 pers. pl. masc. קטן

מִקְטַר[k] noun masc. sing., constr. of [מִקְטָר] dec. 2b קטר

מֻקְטָר[l] Hoph. part. sing. masc. (§ 11. rem. 10) קטר

מְקַטְּרוֹת[m] Piel part. f., pl. of מְקַטֶּרֶת d. 13 [fr. מְקַטֵּר m.] קטר

מַקְטְרִים וּ defect. for מַקְטִירִים q. v.; וּ bef. lab. . קטר

מְקַטְּרִים ו׳ Piel part. masc., pl. of [מְקַטֵּר] d. 7b; וּ id. קטר

מְקֻטֶּרֶת[n] Pual part. sing. fem. [of מְקֻטָּר § 39. No. 4] קטר

מִקְטֶרֶת[o] noun fem. sing. dec. 13a . . . קטר

מִקְטַרְתּוֹ[p] id., suff. 3 pers. sing. masc. . . קטר

מֵקִים [q] ו׳ Hiph. part. sing. masc. dec. 3b; וּ bef. lab. קום

מְקִימָהּ[r] id., suff. 3 pers. sing. fem. . . . קום

מְקִימִי[s] id. with parag. י (comp. § 8. rem. 19) . קום

מִקַּיִן pref. מִ)(pr. name masc. . . . קון

מַקִּיפִים[t] Hiph. part. masc., pl. of [מַקִּיף] dec. 1b נקף

מֵקִיץ[u] Hiph. part. sing. masc. . . . קוץ

מִקִּיר pref. מִ)(noun m. s. d. 1a (also pr. name) קיר

מַקֵּל masc. dec. 7b (constr. מַקַּל, מַקֵּל, with suff. מַקְלִי, מַקֶּלְכֶם § 36. rem. 1 & 3).—I. *shoot, twig*, Ge. 30. 37—39, 41; Je. 1. 11.—II. *staff, stick*; מַקֵּל יָד *a javelin*.—III. *mace*, badge of authority, Je. 48. 17. Root coll. with the Ethiop. *to shoot, sprout*.

מִקְלוֹת (*shoots*) pr. name masc. of two different persons.

מַקַּל[x] id. constr. st. . . . . . מקל

מִקַּל[y] pref. מִ)(for קַל, adj. masc. sing. dec. 8d קלל

מִקֹּל[z] defect. for מִקּוֹל (q. v.) . . . קלל

מַקְלֶה[a] Hiph. part. sing. masc. dec. 9a . . קלה

מַקְלוֹ[b] [c] ו׳ noun masc. sing., suff. 3 pers. sing. masc. [for מַקְּלוֹ] from מַקֵּל dec. 7b; וּ bef. lab. מקל

מַקְלוֹת[d] id. with pl. fem. term. [for מַקְּלוֹת] מקל

מִקֹּלוֹת[e] pref. מִ)(noun masc. with pl. fem. term. from קוֹל dec. 1a . . . . קול

מִקְלוֹת וּ pr. name masc.; וּ bef. lab. . . מקל

מִקְלָט noun masc. sing. dec. 2b . . . קלט

---

[a] Le. 21. 15.
[b] Nu. 18. 29.
[c] Am. 7. 9.
[d] Eze. 7. 24.
[e] Le. 26. 31.
[f] Ne. 12. 47.
[g] Eze. 21. 7.
[h] Job 5. 1.
[i] Is. 63. 18; Ps. 74. 7.
[k] Da. 9. 17.
[l] 2 Ch. 36. 17.
[m] Je. 17. 12.
[n] Ezr. 10. 8.
[o] 2 Ch. 1. 16, 16.
[p] Is. 22. 11.
[q] Is. 31. 4.
[r] Nu. 24. 11.
[s] Ec. 10. 4.
[t] Am. 4. 6.
[u] Ne. 12. 27.
[x] Zec. 13. 1.
[y] Pr. 25. 26.
[z] Je. 51. 36.
[a] Ho. 13. 15.
[b] Pr. 5. 18.
[c] 2 Ch. 19. 7.
[d] Ps. 91. 6.
[e] 1 Ki. 11. 8.
[f] 1 Ch. 6. 34.
[g] Ob. 1, 9.
[h] 1 Sa. 9. 21.
[i] Je. 6. 13.
[k] Ex. 30. 1.
[l] Mal. 1. 11.
[m] Je. 44. 15.
[n] Ca. 3. 6.
[o] 2 Ch. 26. 19.
[p] Eze. 8. 11.
[q] Je. 10. 20.
[r] Am. 5. 2.
[s] Ps. 113. 7.
[ss] Eze. 28. 18.
[t] 2 Ch. 4. 3.
[u] 1 Sa. 26. 12.
[x] Ge. 30. 37.
[y] Am. 2. 14.
[z] Je. 3. 9.
[a] De. 27. 16.
[b] 1 Sa. 17. 40.
[c] Ho. 4. 12.
[d] Zec. 11. 7.
[e] Ps. 93. 4.

מִקְלָט[a] id., constr. st. . . . . קלט

מִקְלָטוֹ id. with suff. 3 pers. sing. masc. . . קלט

מַקְלִי[b] noun masc. sing., suff. 1 pers. sing. [for מַקְלִי] from מַקֵּל dec. 7b . . . מקל

מַקֶּלְכֶם[c] וּ id., suff. 2 p. pl. m. (§ 36. r. 3); וּ bef. lab. מקל

מְקַלֵּל[d] וּ' Piel part. sing. masc. dec. 7b; וּ id. . קלל

מְקַלְלַוְנִי[e] or מְקַלְלַוְנִי id. with suff. 1 pers. sing., an anomalous form, perh. for מְקַלְלוּנִי a participle with the afformative of the plural. Ewald proposes מְקַלְלֵנִי, with epenth. נ. Gesenius takes it as a mixed form made up from two readings קִלְלוּנִי & מְקַלְלֵנִי *part.* and *pret.* . . . . קלל

מְקֻלָּלָיו[f] וּ Pual part. pl. masc. with suff. 3 pers. sing. fem. from [מְקֻלָּל] dec. 2b; וּ bef. lab. קלל

מְקַלְּלִים[g] Piel part. masc., pl. of מְקַלֵּל dec. 7b . קלל

מְקַלֶּלְךָ[h] / וּמְקַלֶּלְךָ[i] } id. sing., suff. 2 pers. sing. masc. (§ 10. rem. 7); וּ bef. lab. . . . } קלל

מִקְלְעוֹת[k] / מִקְלָעוֹת[l] } noun fem. pl. abs. and constr. [as if from מִקְלָעָה] see the foll. . . } קלע

מִקְלַעַת[m] id. sing. (§ 44. rem. 5) . . . . קלע

מְקוֹמָהּ[n] noun com. sing., suff. 3 pers. sing. fem. from מָקוֹם dec. 3a . . . . קום

מְקֹמוֹ id., suff. 3 pers. sing. masc. . . . קום

מְקֹמוֹת[o] id. pl. fem. . . . . . קום

מְקָמַי[p] וּ pref. ·מְ)(Kal part. pl. masc., suff. 1 pers. sing. fr. קָם d. 1a (§ 30. No. 3); וּ bef. lab. קום

מִקְנָהּ[q] pref. id.)(noun masc. sing., suff. 3 pers. sing. fem. from קָנֶה dec. 9b . . . קנה

מִקְנֵה / מִקְנֶה וּ' } noun masc. sing. constr. and abs. dec. 9a; וּ bef. lab. . . . } קנה

מִקְנֵהוּ וּ'[r] id., suff. 3 pers. sing. masc.; וּ id. . קנה

מִקְנֵהֶם id. pl., suff. 3 pers. pl. masc. for מִקְנֵיהֶם קנה

מִקְנַי וּ'[s] id. pl., suff. 1 pers. sing.; וּ bef. lab. . קנה

מִקְנֵיָהוּ וּ pr. name masc.; וּ id. . . . . קנה

מִקְנֵיהֶם וּ' noun masc. pl., suff. 3 pers. pl. masc. from מִקְנֶה dec. 9a; וּ id. . . . . קנה

מִקְנֵיךְ[u] id. sing. (§ 38. rem. 1), suff. 2 pers. pl. masc. קנה

מִקְנֵיכֶם וּ'[v] id. pl., suff. 3 pers. pl. masc.; וּ bef. lab. קנה

מִקְנְךָ id. sing., suff. 2 pers. sing. masc. . . קנה

מִקְנֵכֶם[y] וּ id. pl., suff. 3 pers. pl. masc. for מִקְנֵיכֶם; וּ bef. lab. . . . . . קנה

מִקְנֵנוּ id. sing., suff. 1 pers. pl. . . . קנה

מְקֻנַּנְתִּי[z] Kh. מְקֻנַּנְתִּי', K. מְקֻנֶּנֶת' Pual part. s. f. [for the Seg. מְקֻנֶּנֶת § 39. No. 4. r. 3, comp. § 8. r. 19] קנן

מִקְנַת וּ' noun f. s., constr. of מִקְנָה d. 10; וּ bef. lab. קנה

מִקְנָתוֹ id. with suff. 3 pers. sing. masc. . קנה

מִקְסַם וּ n. m. s., constr. of [מִקְסָם] d. 2b; וּ bef. lab. קסם

מִקְסֹם[a] pref. ·מִ)(Kal inf. constr. . . . קסם

מִקְּעִילָה pref. id.)(pr. name of a place, see קְעִילָה.

מַקִּפִים[b] defect. for מַקִּיפִים (q. v.) . . . נקף

מְקַפֵּץ[c] Piel part. sing. masc. . . . . קפץ

מִקֵּץ pref. ·מִ)(noun masc. sing. dec. 8b . קצץ

מִקְצָה pref. id.)(noun fem. sing. dec. 11a . קצה

מְקַצֶּה[d] Piel part. sing. masc. . . . קצה

מִקָּצֶה pref. ·מִ)(noun masc. sing. dec. 9b . קצה

מִקְצֵה וּ'[e] pref. id.)(id., constr. st.; וּ bef. lab. . קצה

מִקָּצֵהוּ pref. id.)(id. with suff. 3 pers. sing. masc. קצה

מִקְצוֹעֵי[f] noun masc. pl. constr. from מִקְצוֹעַ dec. 1b קצע

מִקְצוֹת pref. ·מִ)(noun fem. pl. constr. fr. קָצָה d. 11a קצה

מִקְצוֹתָם pref. id.)(id. with suff. 3 pers. pl. masc. קצה

מִקְצֵיהֶם[g] pref. id.)(n. m. pl., suff. 3 p. pl. m. fr. קָצֶה d. 9a קצה

מִקְצֹעֹת[h] noun masc. with pl. f. term. fr. מִקְצוֹעַ d. 1b קצע

וּמִקְצֹעֹתָיו[i] וּ id. with suff. 3 pers. sing. masc.; וּ bef. lab. קצע

מִקֶּצֶף[k] pref. ·מִ)(noun masc. sing. (suff. קִצְפִּי) d. 6a קצף

מִקְצֹף[l] pref. id.)(Kal inf. constr. . . . קצף

מִקִּצְפּוֹ[m] pref. id.)(n. m. s., suff. 3 p. s. m. fr. קֶצֶף d. 6a קצף

מַקְצִפִים[n] Hiph. part. masc. pl. [of מַקְצִיף] dec. 1b קצף

מְקֻצָּצִים[o] Pual part. masc. pl. [of מְקֻצָּץ] . . קצץ

מִקֹּצֶר[p] pref. ·מִ)(noun masc. sing. . . . קצר

מִקְצַת וּ pref. מִ [for מִקְּצַת])(noun fem. sing., pl. קְצוֹת comp. מְנָת (§ 45); וּ bef. lab. . קצה

מִקְצָתָם[q] וּ pref. id.)(id., suff. 3 pers. pl. masc.; וּ id. קצה

מקק. Niph. נָמַק.—I. *to be melted, to melt, flow, run.*—II. *to waste, consume away.* Hiph. הֵמַק *to cause to waste away,* Zec. 14. 12.

מַק masc. *rottenness,* Is. 3. 24.

מִקְרָא noun masc. sing. dec. 1b . . . קרא

מִקְרָאֶהָ[r] noun m. pl., suff. 3 pers. s. f. [for מִקְרָאֶיהָ] קרא

מִקְרָאֵי id. pl., constr. st. . . . . קרא

מְקֹרָאַי[s] Pual part. s., suff. 1 p. s. fr. [מְקֹרָא] d. 1b קרא

מִקְרָב defect. for מִקָּרוֹב (q. v.) . . . קרב

מִקְּרָב[t] pref. ·מִ)(noun masc. sing. dec. 1a . קרב

מִקֶּרֶב pref. id.)((prop. *subs.* m. s. d. 6a) as a *prep.* קרב

מִקִּרְבָּהּ pref. id.)(id., suff. 3 pers. sing. fem. . קרב

מִקִּרְבּוֹ pref. id.)(id., suff. 3 pers. sing. masc. . קרב

מִקִּרְבְּךָ / מִקִּרְבֶּךָ[u] } pref. id.)(id., suff. 2 pers. sing. masc. . קרב

מִקִּרְבֵּךְ[x] pref. id.)(id., suff. 2 pers. sing. fem. . קרב

מִקִּרְבְּכֶם[y] pref. id.)(id., suff. 2 pers. pl. masc. . קרב

---

a Jos. 21. 13, 21, 27, 32, 36. b Zec. 11. 10, 14. c Ex. 12. 11. d Pr. 20. 20. e Je. 15. 10. f Ps. 37. 22. g 1 Sa. 3. 13. h Ec. 7. 21. i Ge. 12. 3. k 1 Ki. 7. 31. l 1 Ki. 6. 29, 32. m 1 Ki. 6. 18. n Ge. 38. 21. o Ps. 103. 22. p 2 Sa. 22. 49. q Job 31. 22. r Job 1. 10. s Ex. 17. 3. t Nu. 20. 19. u Is. 30. 23. v Ge. 47. 16. y De. 3. 19. z Je. 22. 23.

a Mi. 3. 6. b 1 Ki. 7. 24. c Ca. 2. 8. d Pr. 26. 6. e Ge. 47. 2. f Eze. 46. 21. g Eze. 38. 2. h Eze. 46. 22. i Eze. 41. 22. k Je. 50. 13. l Is. 54. 9. m Je. 10. 10. n De. 9. 22. o Jud. 1. 7. p Ex. 6. 9. q Da. 1. 5. r Is. 4. 5. s Is. 48. 12. t Ps. 55. 19. u De. 18. 15. x Zep. 3. 11. y Jos. 7. 12, 13.

[a] מִקִּרְבָּם pref. ·מִ)(id., suff. 3 pers. pl. masc. . קרב

[b] מְקֹרָהּ defect. for מְקוֹרָהּ (q. v.) . . . קור

[c] מִקְרֶהָ noun masc. sing., suff. 3 pers. sing. fem. fr. מִקְרֶה dec. 9 a . . . . . קרה

[d] מִקְּרֵה pref. ·מִ)(noun m. s., constr. of [קָרֶה] d. 9 b קרה

מִקְרֶה [e] ו׳ noun masc. sing. dec. 9 a ; וּ bef. lab. קרה

מִקָּרוֹב pref. ·מִ)((prim. adj. masc. dec. 3 a) with the pref. as an *adv.* . . . . קרב

[f] מְקֹרָח Hoph. part. sing. masc. (§ 11. rem. 10) . קרח

מַקְרִיב Hiph. part. sing. masc. dec. 1 b . . קרב

[g] מַקְרִיבֵי id. pl., constr. st. . . . . . קרב

מַקְרִיבִם[h] id. pl., abs. st. . . . . . קרב

[i] מִקִּרְיָה pref. ·מִ)(noun fem. sing. (no pl.) . . קרה

מִקִּרְיַת pref. id.)(id., constr. st., also pr. name in compos. ק׳ יְעָרִים . . . . . קרה

[k] מַקְרִן Hiph. part. sing. masc. defect. [for מַקְרִין] קרן

[l] מִקַּרְנֵי ו pref. ·מִ)(noun fem. du., constr. of קַרְנַיִם from קֶרֶן dec. 6 a; וּ bef. lab. . . קרן

[m] מִקַּרְקַע pref. id.)(noun masc. sing. . . . קרקע

[n] מְקַרְקַר Pilpel (§ 6. rem. 4) part. sing. masc. . קור

[o] מַקְשֶׁה [p] ו׳ Hiph. part. sing. masc.; וּ bef. lab. . קשה

מִקְשָׁה noun fem. sing. . . . . . . קשה

[q] מִקְשֶׁה noun masc. sing. . . . . . קשה

[r] מוֹקְשׁוֹת ו noun masc. with pl. fem. term. fr. מוֹקֵשׁ dec. 7 b; וּ bef. lab. . . . . יקש

[s] מֹקְשֵׁי id. pl. constr. masc. . . . . . יקש

מַקְשִׁיב Hiph. part. sing. masc. dec. 1 b . . קשב

מַקְשִׁיבִים id. pl., abs. st. . . . . . קשב

[u] מֹקְשִׁים defect. for מוֹקְשִׁים (q. v.) . . . יקש

[x] מְקֹשֵׁשׁ, מְקֹשֶׁשֶׁת } Poel part. sing. masc. and fem. . קשש

[z] מִקֶּשֶׁת pref. ·מִ)(noun com. s., suff. קַשְׁתּוֹ, pl. קְשָׁתוֹת, ת treated as if radical, comp. d. 6 a . קוש

[a] מַר, מָר } וָ Kal pret. 3 pers. s. m.; or adj. m. d. 8 e (§ 37. rem. 7); for וָ see lett. ו } מרר

מֹר, מָר־[b] } noun masc. sing. (§ 37. rem. 2) . . מרר

I. מרא *to be rebellious*, cogn. מָרָה, only part. fem. מֹרְאָה Zep. 3. 1. Hiph. *to fly*, Job 39. 18 (Talm. מְרָא *to fly*; the primary idea may be that of *rising*).

II. מרא Root not used; Arab. *to be well fed, be fat*.

מְרִיא adj. masc. d. 1 a—I. *fattened, fat*, Eze. 39. 18. —II. *a fatling*, espec. *a fatted calf*.

מֻרְאָה fem. dec. 10, *crop*, of birds, Le. 1. 16.

מַמְרֵא (*fattening*; or *causing rebellion*) pr. name —I. of an Amorite, a confederate of Abraham, Ge. 14. 13, 24.—II. אֵלוֹנֵי מ׳ (*oaks of Mamre*) and simply מַמְרֵא, a place near Hebron.

[c] **מָרֵא** [d] ו׳ Ch. masc. (with suff. מָרְאִי Kh. מָרִי K.), *lord*.

[e] מָרָא adj. fem. for מָרָה (q. v.) . . . מרר

מְרֹאדַךְ pr. name in compos. מְרֹאדַךְ בַּלְאֲדָן see מְרֹדַךְ

[f] מַרְאֶהָ ו׳ noun masc. sing., suff. 3 pers. sing. fem. from מַרְאֶה dec. 9 a; וּ bef. lab. . ראה

מַרְאֵה ו׳ id., constr. st.; וּ id. . . . . ראה

מַרְאֶה [g] ו׳ Hiph. part. sing. m. (Ex. 25. 9; Eze. 40. 4) or subst. dec. 9 a; וּ id. . . . . ראה

[h] מָרְאֶה Hoph. part. sing. masc. . . . . ראה

מַרְאֵהוּ ו׳ noun masc. sing., suff. 3 pers. sing. masc. from מַרְאֶה dec. 9 a; וּ bef. lab. . ראה

מְרֹאוֹן pr. name in compos. שִׁמְרוֹן מְרֹאוֹן see . שמר

[i] מַרְאוֹת ו׳ noun masc. with pl. fem. term. from מַרְאֶה dec. 9 a; וּ bef. lab. . . . ראה

מֵרְאוֹת pref. מֵ for ·מִ)(Kal inf. constr. dec. 1 a ראה

[k] מָרְאִי Chald. Kh. מָרְאִי noun masc. sing. with suff. from מָרֵא dec. 2 b, K. מָרִי [from מָר] d. 1 מרא

מֵרֹאַי pref. מֵ for ·מִ)(Kal part. pl. masc., suff. 1 pers. sing. from רֹאֶה dec. 9 a . ראה

[l] מֵרְאִי pref. id.)(noun m. sing. (for רְאִי § 35. r. 14) ראה

מַרְאֵיהֶם ו׳ noun masc. pl., or sing. (§ 38. rem. 1), suff. 3 pers. pl. masc. from מַרְאֶה d. 9 a; וּ bef. lab. ראה

מַרְאֵיהֶן ו׳ id., suff. 3 pers. pl. fem.; וּ id. . . ראה

[m] מַרְאָיו id., suff. 3 pers. sing. masc. . . . ראה

[n] מַרְאַיִךְ id., suff. 2 pers. sing. fem. . . . ראה

[o] מַרְאֵךְ ו id., suff. 2 pers. sing. fem., Kh. מַרְאַיִךְ q. v., K. מַרְאֵךְ; וּ bef. lab. . . . . ראה

[p] מַרְאֵינוּ id., suff. 1 pers. pl. . . . . ראה

מֵרֹאשׁ [q] ו׳ pref. מֵ for ·מִ)(n. m. s. irr. (§ 45); וּ bef. lab. ראש

מָרֵאשָׁה ו pr. name of a place; וּ id. . . ראש

[r] מֵרֹאשׁוֹ pref. מֵ for ·מִ)(noun masc. sing., suff. 3 pers. sing. masc. from רֹאשׁ irr. (§ 45) . ראש

[s] מֵרִאשׁוֹן pref. id.)(adj. masc. sing. dec. 1 b . ראש

מֵרָאשֵׁי ו׳ pref. id.)(noun masc. pl. constr. from רֹאשׁ irr. (§ 45); וּ bef. lab. . . . ראש

מֵרֵאשִׁית [t] ו׳ pref. id.)(noun fem. sing. dec. 1 b; וּ id. ראש

[u] מֵרֵאשִׁיתוֹ pref. id.)(id. with suff. 3 pers. sing. masc. ראש

[x] מְרַאֲשֹׁתָו Kh., מְרַאֲשֹׁתָיו K. (q. v.) . . . ראש

[y] מְרַאֲשֹׁתוֹ defect. for מְרַאֲשֹׁתָיו (q. v.) . . . ראש

[z] מְרַאֲשֹׁתֵי pref. מֵ for ·מִ)(noun fem. with pl. m. term., constr. st. [from רַאֲשׁוֹתַיִם, see רַאֲשׁוֹת] ראש

מְרַאֲשֹׁתָיו n. f. pl. [מְרַאֲשׁוֹת], suff. 3 p. s. m., *adverbially* ראש

---

[a] Ju. 10. 16. [b] Le. 20. 18. [c] Ru. 2. 3. [d] De. 23. 11. [e] Ec. 3. 19. [f] Eze. 29. 18. [g] Nu. 16. 35. [h] Le. 21. 6. [i] Mi. 4. 10. [k] Ps. 69. 32. [l] Ps. 22. 22. [m] 1 Ki. 6. 15. [n] Is. 22. 5. [o] Pr. 29. 1. [p] Pr. 28. 14. [q] Is. 3. 24. [r] Ps. 141. 9. [s] 2 Sa. 22. 6. [t] Ca. 8. 13. [u] Ps. 140. 6. [x] Nu. 15. 32, 33. [y] 1 Ki. 17. 10, 12. [z] Is. 22. 3. [a] Je. 2. 19. [b] Ex. 30. 23. [c] Da. 5. 23. [d] Da. 2. 47. [e] Ru. 1. 20. [f] Le. 13. 4, 20, 25. [g] Nu. 12. 8. [h] Ex. 25. 40. [i] Eze. 1. 1; 43. 3. [k] Da. 4. 16, 21. [l] Job 33. 21. [m] Job 41. 1. [n] Ca. 2. 14. [o] Ca. 2. 14. [p] Da. 1. 13. [q] De. 33. 15. [r] Le. 13. 12. [s] Je. 17. 12. [t] Pr. 3. 9. [u] Ec. 7. 8. [x] 1 Sa. 26. 7, 11, 16. [y] Job 42. 12. [z] 1 Sa. 26. 12.

מֵרָאשֹׁתֵיכֶם[a] pref. מֵ for מִ·)(noun fem. pl., suff. 2 pers. pl. masc. [from רַאֲשָׁה] . ראשׁ

מַרְאֲשֹׁתֵיכֶם[b] noun fem. pl. [מַרְאֲשׁוֹת], suff. 2 pers. pl. m. ראשׁ

מֵרְאֹת[c] defect. for מֵרְאוֹת (q. v.) . . . . ראה

מַרְאָתוֹ[d] noun fem. sing., suff. 3 pers. sing. masc. [from מַרְאָה, no pl.] . . . . . מרה

מֵרַב pr. name fem. . . . . . רבב

מֵרֹב ו׳ pref. מֵ for מִ·)(noun m. s. d. 8c; וּ bef. lab. רבב

מֵרְבָבָה[e] pref. id.)(noun fem. sing. dec. 11c . רבב

מֵרִבְבוֹת[f] pref. id.)(id. pl., constr. of רְבָבוֹת . רבב

מְרֻבָּבוֹת[g] Pual part. fem. pl. [of מְרֻבָּבָה fr. מְרֻבָּב m.] רבב

מֵרִבְבֹת[h] defect. for מֵרִבְבוֹת (q. v.) . . רבב

מַרְבַדִּים noun masc., pl. of [מַרְבַד] dec. 8a . . רבד

מַרְבָּה[i] Hiph. part., fem. of the foll. . . . רבה

מַרְבֵּה[k] id. masc., constr. of the foll. . . . רבה

מַרְבֶּה Hiph. part., or (Is. 33. 23) subst. m. sing. d. 9a רבה

מִרְבָּה[l] noun masc. sing. . . . . . רבה

מַרְבִּים ו׳[m] Hiph. part. m., pl. of מַרְבֶּה d. 9a; וּ bef. lab. רבה

מֵרַבִּים[n] pref. מֵ for מִ·)(adj. masc., pl. of רַב d. 8d רבב

מַרְבִּיץ[o] Hiph. part. sing. masc. dec. 1b . . רבץ

מַרְבִּית noun fem. sing. dec. 1b . . . . רבה

מַרְבִּיתָם[p] id. with suff. 3 pers. pl. masc. . . רבה

מֵרֻבְּכֶם[q] pref. מֵ for מִ·)(noun masc. sing., suff. 2 pers. pl. masc. from רֹב dec. 8c . . . רבב

מֻרְבֶּכֶת Hoph. part. sing. fem. [of מֻרְבָּךְ § 39. No. 4] רבך

מְרֻבָּע[r] Pual part. sing. masc. . . . . רבע

מְרֻבָּעוֹת[s] [as if fr. מְרֻבָּעָה] as the pl. of the foll. (§ 44. r. 5) רבע

מְרֻבַּעַת[t] [for מְרֻבַּעַת] Pual part. sing. fem. of מְרֻבָּע רבע

מַרְבֵּץ[u] noun m. sing. d. 7b (constr. מַרְבַּץ § 36. r. 1) רבץ

מַרְבִּצִים[x] Hiph. part. masc. pl. of מַרְבִּיץ dec. 1b . רבץ

מַרְבֵּק noun masc. sing. . . . . . רבק

מֵרַבַּת pref. מֵ for מִ·)(pr. name of a place . רבת

מָרַג Root not used; whence

מוֹרַג masc. (pl. מוֹרִגִּים, מוֹרִיגִים, dag. resolved in Yod) *threshing-sledge*, a kind of dray, in which are inserted wooden rollers, and in these are fixed teeth of iron, stone, &c.

מַרְגּוֹעַ[y] noun masc. sing. . . . . . רגע

מֵרָגְזֶךָ[z] וּ pref. מֵ for מִ·)(noun masc. sing., suff. 2 pers. sing. masc. from רֹגֶז dec. 6c; וּ bef. lab. רגז

מַרְגִּיז[a] Hiph. part. sing. masc. . . . . רגז

מַרְגְּלוֹתָו[b] Kh. for מַרְגְּלֹתָיו (q. v.) . . . רגל

מְרַגְּלִים Hiph. part. masc. pl. of [מְרַגֵּל] dec. 7b רגל

מֵרֹגְלִים pref. מֵ for מִ·)(pr. name of a place . רגל

מַרְגְּלֹתָיו[c] ו׳[d] n. f. pl. [מַרְגְּלוֹת], suff. 3 p. s. m.; וּ bef. lab. רגל

מֵרִגְשַׁת[e] pref. מֵ for מִ·)(noun f. s. constr. [of רִגְשָׁה] רגשׁ

מָרַד fut. יִמְרֹד *to rebel, revolt, cause sedition*, with בְּ, עַל of the pers. against whom; מֹרְדֵי אוֹר *wh[o] rebel against the light*, are enemies of the light.

מְרַד Chald. *rebellion*, Ezr. 4. 19.

מֶרֶד masc.—I. *rebellion, defection*, Jos. 22. 22 —II. pr. name masc. 1 Ch. 4. 17, 18.

מָרָד Chald. adj. *rebellious*, only fem. מָרָדָא dec 8a, Ezr. 4. 12, 15.

מַרְדּוּת fem. *rebellion, contumacy*, 1 Sa. 20. 30.

נִמְרֹד (*rebel*, or, *let us rebel*) pr. name, *Nimrod*, the founder of Babylon, Ge. 10. 8, 9. אֶרֶץ נ׳ *Babylonia*, Mi. 5. 5.

מָרָד[f] Kal pret. 3 pers. sing. m. [for מָרַד § 8. r. 7] מרד

מֶרֶד / מָרֶד ו׳ } pr. name masc. (§ 35. r. 2); וּ bef. lab. . מרד

מְרַד[g] ו׳ Ch. Peal pret. 3 pers. sing. masc.; וּ id. מרד

מָרָדָא[qq] Ch. adj. fem. dec. 11 [fr. מָרָד masc.] . מרד

מֵרְדָה[h] pref. מֵ for מִ·)(Kal inf. constr. (§ 20. r. 3) ירד

מָרְדוּ[i] / מָרָדוּ[k] } Kal pret. 3 pers. pl. (§ 8. rem. 7) . מרד

מֹרְדִים[uu] id. part. masc., pl. of [מוֹרֵד] dec. 7b . מרד

מְרֹדָךְ pr. name, *Merodach*, an idol of the Babylonians, prob. the planet *Mars*. Je. 50. 2.

מְרֹאדַךְ בַּלְאֲדָן (*Merodach is his lord*) pr. name of a king of Babylon, Is. 39. 1.

מָרְדֳּכַי / מָרְדֳּכָי ו׳ } pr. name, *Mordecai*, a Jew of the tribe of Benjamin, living in Persia, who was the foster-father of Esther, and afterwards prime minister in the court of Ahasuerus, Est. 2. 5 seq.

מָרַדְנוּ[l] ו׳ / מָרָדְנוּ[m] } Kal pret. 1 pers. pl. (§ 8. rem. 7); וּ bef. lab. . . . . . } מרד

מְרַדֵּף[n] ו׳ Piel part. sing. masc.; וּ id. . . רדף

מֵרְדֹף pref. מִ)(Kal inf. constr. . . . רדף

מֻרְדָּף[o] noun masc. sing. . . . . . רדף

מֵרֹדְפַי[p] / מֵרֹדְפַי[r] [q]ו׳ } pref. מֵ for מִ·)(Kal part. act. pl., suff. 1 pers. sing. from רֹדֵף dec. 7b } רדף

מָרַדְתָּ Kal pret. 2 pers. sing. masc. . . . מרד

מֵרֶדֶת[s] pref. מֵ f. מִ·)(Kal inf. constr. (suff. רִדְתִּי) d. 13a ירד

מָרָדְתָּא[t] Ch. adj. f., emph. of מָרָדָא d. 11 [fr. מָרָד m.] מרד

מָרָה[u] I. *to rebel, be disobedient*, const. with בְּ, acc. II. i. q. מָרַר *to be bitter*, 2 Ki. 14. 26. Hiph. הִמְרָה.—I. *to resist, contend with*, const. with ...

[a] Eze. 36. 11. [b] Je. 13. 18. [c] Ge. 27. 1. [d] Le. 1. 16. [e] Ca. 5. 10. [f] Ps. 3. 7. [g] Ps. 144. 13. [h] De. 33. 2. [i] Ne. 9. 37. [k] Le. 11. 42. [l] Eze. 23. 32. [m] 1 Ch. 8. 40. [n] Ne. 7. 2. [o] Is. 54. 11. [p] 1 Ch. 12. 29. [q] De. 7. 7. [r] Eze. 45. 2. [s] 1 Ki. 7. 31. [t] Eze. 40. 47. [u] Zep. 2. 15. [x] Je. 33. 12. [y] Je. 6. 16. [z] Is. 14. 3. [a] Is. 14. 16. [b] Ru. 3. 14. [c] Ru. 3. 4, 7, 8. [d] Da. 10. 6. [e] Ps. 64. 3. [f] 2 Ch. 36. 13. [g] Ezr. 4. 19. [h] Ge. 46. 3. [i] Ge. 14. 4. [k] Eze. 2. 3. [l] Da. 9. 5. [m] Da. 9. 9. [n] Pr. 19. 7. [o] Is. 14. 6. [p] Ps. 142. 7. [q] Ps. 31. 16. [qq] Ezr. 4. 15. [r] Je. 15. 15. [s] Job 33. 24. [t] Ezr. 4. 12. [u] 1 Ki. 13. 26. [uu] Ne. 2. 19.

—II. *to be rebellious, disobedient*, with acc., בְּ.—III. *to embitter, grieve*, with the acc.

מוֹרָה masc. *a razor.* Its connection with the Root is not obvious.

מְרִי masc. dec. 6 i.—I. *rebellion, contumacy.*—II. *bitterness*, Job 23. 2.

מְרִי בַעַל (i. q. מְרִיב בַּעַל *contender against Baal*, see R. ריב) pr. name masc. 1 Ch. 9. 40.

מְרָיָה (*rebellion*) pr. name masc. Ne. 12. 12.

מְרָיוֹת (*rebellions*) pr. name masc. of several persons.

מִרְיָם (*rebellion*) pr. name fem. *Miriam.*—I. sister of Moses, a prophetess.—II. 1 Ch. 4. 17.

מְרָתַיִם (*double rebellion*) symbolical name for Babylon, Je. 50. 21.

יִמְרָה (*refractory*) pr. name masc. 1 Ch. 7. 36.

מָרָה ׳וּ adj. or subst. fem. sing. dec. 10 [for מָרָּה] from מַר masc.; also pr. name; וּ bef. lab. — מרר
מָרָה Kal pret. 3 pers. sing. fem. [for מָרָּה] . — מרר
מֹרֶה pr. name of a place . . . . — ירה
מֹרֶה[e] defect. for מוֹרֶה (q. v.) . . . — ירה
מֹרֶה[b] ׳וּ Kal part. act. sing. masc. d. 7 b; וּ bef. lab. — מרה
מָרוֹ[c] Kal inf. abs. [for מָרֹה § 24. rem. 2] . — מרה
מָרוּ[d] id. pret. 3 pers. pl. . . . . — מרה
מֵרוֹב in full for מֵרֹב (q. v. & § 18. rem. 2) . — רבב
מְרוּדַי[e] וּ noun masc. sing., suff. 1 pers. sing. from [מָרוּד] dec. 3 a; וּ bef. lab. . . — רוד
מְרוּדֶיהָ[e] וּ id. pl., suff. 3 pers. sing. fem.; וְ id. . — רוד
מְרוּדִים[f] id. pl., abs. st. . . . . — רוד
מַרְוֶה[g] וּ Hiph. part. sing. masc.; וּ bef. lab. . — רוה
מֵרוֹז pr. name of a place . . . . — ארז
מְרוֹחַ[h] adj. masc. sing., constr. of [מָרוֹחַ] dec. 3 a — מרח
מֵרוּחַ[k] ׳וּ pref. מֵ for מִ X n. com. s. d. 1 a; וּ bef. lab. — רוח
מְרֻוָּחִים[l] Pual part. masc. pl. [of מְרֻוָּח] . . — רוח
מֵרוּחֶךָ[m] pref. מֵ for מִ X noun com. sing., suff. 2 pers. sing. masc. [for רוּחֲךָ] from רוּחַ dec. 1 a — רוח
מְרוּטָה Kal part. pass. sing. fem. [from מָרוּט masc.] — מרט
מָרוֹם noun masc. sing. dec. 3 a . . . — רום
מֵרוֹם pr. name of a place . . . . — רום
מְרוֹם noun masc. sing., constr. of מָרוֹם dec. 3 a . — רום
מְרוֹמֵי[n] id. pl., constr. st. . . . . — רום
מְרוֹמִים[o] id. pl., abs. st. . . . . — רום
מְרוֹמָם[p] וּ Pulal part. sing. masc.; וּ bef. lab. . — רום
מְרוֹמֵם[q] ׳רוּ Heb. & Ch. Pilel part. s. m. d. 7 b; וּ id. — רום
מְרוֹמְמִי[s] id. with suff. 1 pers. sing. . . . — רום
מְרוּצַת[t] noun fem. sing., constr. of מְרוּצָה׳ dec. 10 — רוץ

מְרוּצָתָם[u] noun fem. sing., suff. 3 pers. pl. masc. . — רוץ
מָרוּק[x] Kal part. pass. sing. masc. . . . — מרק
מְרוּקֵיהֶן[y] noun m. pl., suff. 3 p. pl. f. fr. [מָרוּק] d. 1 a — מרק
מְרוֹרַת[z] noun fem. sing., constr. of מְרוֹרָה dec. 10 — מרר
מָרוֹת pr. name of a place . . . . — מרר
מִרְזַח[a] noun masc. sing. dec. 7 b . . . — רזח
מִרְזַח[b] id., constr. st. (§ 36. rem. 1) . . — רזח

[מָרַח] *to rub, bruise, crush*, Is. 38. 21, *and crush them over the ulcer*, i. e. apply them crushed, softened.

מְרוֹחַ masc. dec. 3 a, *bruised, crushed*, Le. 21. 20 מְרוֹחַ אָשֶׁךְ *crushed at the testicles.*

מֵרְחֹב[c] pref. מֵ for מִ X noun fem. sing. dec. 1 a . — רחב
מֵרְחָבָהּ[d] pref. id. X id. sing., suff. 3 pers. sing. fem. — רחב
מֵרְחֹבוֹת[e] pref. id. X id. pl. fem.; also pr. name . — רחב
וּמֵרָחוֹק[gg] pref. id. X adj. masc. sing. d. 3 a, as an *adv.* — רחק
מַרְחִיב[f] Hiph. part. sing. masc. . . . . — רחב
מֵרָחֶם in pause for מֵרֶחֶם (q. v. & § 35. rem. 2) — רחם
מֵרַחֵם[g] pref. מֵ for מִ X Piel inf. constr. (§ 14. r. 1) — רחם
מֵרֶחֶם pref. id. X noun masc. s. (suff. רַחְמָהּ) d. 6 a — רחם
מְרַחֵם[h] Piel part. sing. masc. (§ 14. rem. 1) dec. 7 b — רחם
מְרַחֲמֵךְ[i] id., suff. 2 pers. sing. fem. . . . — רחם
מְרַחֲמָם[k] id., suff. 3 pers. pl. masc. . . . — רחם
מְרַחֶפֶת[l] Piel (§ 14. r. 1) part. sing. f. [of מְרַחֵף m.] — רחף
מֶרְחָק defect. for מֵרָחוֹק (q. v.) . . . — רחק
מֶרְחָק noun masc. sing. dec. 8 a (see the foll.) . — רחק
מֶרְחַקֵּי[m] id. pl., constr. st. . . . . . — רחק
מֶרְחַקִּים id. pl., abs. st. . . . . . — רחק
מַרְחֶשֶׁת[n] noun fem. sing. . . . . . — רחש

[מָרַט] to make smooth.—I. of a sword, *to polish, sharpen.*—II. of the head, *to pluck out the hair, make it bald.* Niph. *to become bald*, Le. 13. 40, 41. Pu. I. *to be polished*, of metal, 1 Ki. 7. 45.—II. *to be sharpened, sharp*, of a sword.—III. Is. 18. 2, 7, part. מוֹרָט (for מְמֹרָט) *made bald, peeled*; but Gesenius (who thinks that that prophecy refers to the *Ethiopians*) takes it as a noun, *destruction*, and renders גּוֹי מוֹרָט *a destructive* nation.

מְרַט Chald. pret. pass. *to be plucked*, Da. 7. 4.

מֹרָטָה [for מְמֹרָטָה & dag. forte euph.] Pual part. sing., fem. of מְמֹרָט (§ 10. rem. 6) . — מרט
מָרֵי[o] ׳וּ adj. pl. constr. masc. from מַר dec. 8 e (§ 37. rem. 7); וּ bef. lab. . . — מרר
מְרִי, מְרִי ׳וּ } noun masc. s. d. 6 i (§ 35. r. 14), also pr. name in compos. מְרִי בַעַל; וּ id. } — מרה

[a] Pr. 6. 13. [b] 2 Ki. 14. 26. [c] La. 1. 20. [d] La. 3. 19. [e] La. 1. 7. [f] Is. 58. 7. [g] Pr. 11. 25. [h] Le. 21. 20. [i] Ps. 55. 9. [k] Job 4. 9. [l] Je. 22. 14. [m] Ps. 139. 7. [n] Ju. 5. 18. [o] Is. 33. 16. [p] Ne. 9. 5. [q] 1 Sa. 2. 7. [r] Da. 4. 34. [s] Ps. 9. 14. [t] 2 Sa. 18. 27. [u] Je. 23. 10. [x] 2 Ch. 4. 16. [y] Est. 2. 12. [z] Job 20. 14. [a] Je. 16. 5. [b] Am. 6. 7. [c] 2 Sa. 21. 12. [d] Ps. 55. 12. [e] Je. 9. 20. [f] De. 33. 20. [g] Is. 49. 15. [gg] Job 39. 25. [h] Ps. 116. 5. [i] Is. 54. 10. [k] Is. 49. 10. [l] Ge. 1. 2. [m] Is. 8. 9. [n] Le. 2. 7. [o] Ju. 18. 25. [p] 2 Sa. 17. 8.

מְרִיא[a] ‏וּ adj. masc. sing. dec. 1 a; וּ bef. lab. . מרא
מְרִיאֵי[b] id. pl., constr. st. . . . . . . מרא
מְרִיאֵיכֶם[c] id. pl., suff. 2 pers. pl. masc. . . . מרא
מְרִיאִים[d] id. pl., abs. st. . . . . . . מרא
מֵרִיב pref. מֵ for ·מִ) (noun masc. sing. dec. 1 a ריב
מְרִיב וּ' pr. name in compos. מְרִיב בַּעַל; וּ bef. lab. ריב
מְרִיבָה ‏וּ'[e] noun fem. sing. d. 10, also pr. name; וּ id. ריב
מְרִיבָו[f] Hiph. part. pl. masc., suff. 3 pers. sing. masc. (§ 4. rem. 1) fr. [מֵרִיב] dec. 3 b . ריב
מְרִיבוֹת[g] noun fem., pl. of מְרִיבָה dec. 10 ריב
מֵרִיבֵי pref. מֵ for ·מִ) (noun m. pl. c. fr. רִיב d. 1 a ריב
מְרִיבַת noun fem. sing., constr. of מְרִיבָה dec. 10 ריב
מֹרִיד[h] ‏וּ defect. for מוֹרִיד (q. v.); וּ bef. lab. ירד
מְרָיָה pr. name masc. . . . . . . מרה
מֹרִיָּה (for מֹרְאֶה יָהּ=מֹרְאָיָה *shown of the Lord*; or, *chosen of the Lord*, comp. Ge. 22. 14), pr. name, *Moriah*, a hill near Jerusalem where Isaac was to have been offered, and where afterwards the temple was built by Solomon.
מְרָיוֹת pr. name masc. . . . . . . מרה
מֵרֵיחַ[pp] pref. מֵ for ·מִ) (noun masc. sing. dec. 1 a רוח
מְרִיטוּ[i] Ch. part. p., or Peil, 3 pers. pl. m. (§ 47. r. 11) מרט
מֶרְיְךָ[k] noun masc. pl., suff. 2 pers. sing. masc. fr. מְרִי dec. 6 i (§ 35. rem. 14) . . מרה
מְרִים[l] Chald. Aph. part. sing. masc. (§ 54. rem. 5) רום
מָרִים[m] adj. masc., pl. of מַר dec. 8 (§ 37. rem. 7) מרר
מֵרִים וּ'[n] Hiph. part. sing. masc. d. 3 b; וּ bef. lab. רום
מִרְיָם וּ' pr. name fem.; וּ id. . . . . מרה
מְרִימָיו[o] Hiph. part. pl. m., suff. 3 p. pl. m. fr. מֵרִים d. 3 b רום
מָרִינוּ[p] ‏וּ Kal pret. 1 pers. pl.; וּ bef. lab. . מרה
מְרִיעִים[q] Hiph. part. masc. pl. [of מֵרִיעַ] dec. 3 b . רוע
מְרִיקִים[r] Hiph. part. masc. pl. [of מֵרִיק] dec. 3 b רוק
מְרִירִי[s] adj. masc. sing. . . . . . . מרר
מָרִיתָ[t] Kal pret. 2 pers. sing. masc. . . . מרה
מָרִיתִי id. pret. 1 pers. sing. . . . . . מרה
מְרִיתֶם וּ' id. pret. 2 pers. pl. masc.; וּ for וְ, conv. מרה
מֵרֹךְ[u] ‏וּ pref. מֵ for ·מִ) (noun masc. sing.; וּ bef. lab. רכך
מֹרֶךְ[x] noun masc. sing. . . . . . . רכך
מֶרְכָּבָה ‏וּ'[y] noun fem. sing. dec. 11 a, constr. מִרְכֶּבֶת', suff. מֶרְכַּבְתּוֹ (§ 42. rem. 5); וּ bef. lab. רכב
מֶרְכָּבוֹ[z] noun masc. sing., suff. 3 pers. sing. masc. from מֶרְכָּב' dec. 2 b . . . . . רכב
מַרְכָּבוֹת וּ' noun fem. pl. abs. from מֶרְכָּבָה dec. 11 (comp. § 42. rem. 5); וּ bef. lab. . רכב
מַרְכְּבוֹת id. pl., constr. st. . . . . . רכב
מַרְכְּבוֹתָיו id. pl., suff. 3 pers. sing. masc. . . רכב
מַרְכְּבֹת[a] id. pl., constr. st. for מַרְכְּבוֹת (q. v.) רכב

מֶרְכַּבְתּוֹ id. sing., suff. 3 pers. sing. masc. (from constr. מִרְכֶּבֶת dec. 13 a) . . . רכב
מַרְכְּבֹתֵיהֶם id. pl., suff. 3 pers. pl. masc. . . רכב
מַרְכְּבֹתָיו id. pl., suff. 3 pers. sing. masc. . . רכב
מַרְכְּבֹתֶיךָ id. pl., suff. 2 pers. sing. masc. . . רכב
מֵרְכוּשׁ[b] pref. מֵ for ·מִ) (noun masc. sing. dec. 1 a רכש
מֵרְכְסֵי[c] pref. id.) (noun masc. pl. constr. from [רֹכֶס] dec. 6 c (§ 35. rem. 9) . . . . רכס
מִרְמָה וּ' noun f. s. d. 10, also pr. name; וּ bef. lab. רמה
מֵרֹמוֹת pr. name of a place . . . . . רום
מִרְמוֹת[d] ‏וּ' noun fem., pl. of מִרְמָה dec. 10; וּ bef. lab. רמה
מְרֹמֵי[e] & מְרֹמִים defect. for מְרוֹמֵי, &c. (q.v.) . רום
מֵרֹמְמֻתֶךָ[f] pref. מֵ for ·מִ) (noun fem. sing., suff. 2 pers. sing. masc. from [רוֹמֵמוּת] dec. 3 b . רום
מֵרִמּוֹן pref. id.) (pr. name in compos. see רִמּוֹן פֶּרֶץ רמם
מִרְמָס[g] noun masc. sing. dec. 2 b . . . . רמס
מִרְמַס id. constr., also abs. Is. 10. 6 . . . רמס
מְרֵמוֹת pr. name masc. . . . . . . רום
מֵרֹנֹתִי gent. noun, 1 Ch. 27. 30; Ne. 3. 7.
מֶרֶס pr. name of a Persian prince, Est. 1. 14.
מֵרִסָּה pref. מֵ for ·מִ) (pr. name of a place . רסס
מַרְסְנָא pr. name of a Persian prince, Est. 1. 14.
מֵרָע[h] ‏וּ Hiph. part. in pause for מֵרַע (q.v.); וּ bef. lab. רעע
מֵרָע / מֵרַע[i] } pref. מֵ for ·מִ) (noun masc. sing. dec. 8 (§ 37. rem. 7) . . . . . } רעע
מֵרַע[k] Hiph. part. sing. masc. [with gutt. for מֵרֵעַ § 18. rem. 10] . . . . . . רעע
מֵרֵעַ וּ' pref. מֵ for ·מִ) (noun masc. s.; וּ bef. lab. רעע
מֵרָעָב[l] pref. id.) (noun masc. sing. dec. 4 a . . רעב
מֵרָעֵב[m] ‏וּ pref. id.) (adj. masc. sing.; וּ bef. lab. . רעב
מֵרָעָה pref. id.) (adj. or subst. fem. sing. dec. 10 [for רָעָה] from רַע masc. . . . רעע
מֵרֵעֶהָ[n] pref. id.) (noun masc. sing., suff. 3 pers. sing. fem. from רֵעַ (§ 36. rem. 4) . רעה
מֵרֵעֵה[o] / מֵרֵעָה וּ' } noun masc. sing., constr. and abs., dec. 9 a; וּ bef. lab. . . . . } רעה
מֵרֹעָה pref. מֵ for ·מִ) (Kal part. act. sing. m. d. 9 a רעה
מֵרֵעֵהוּ pref. id.) (noun masc. sing., suff. 3 pers. sing. masc. from רֵעַ (§ 36. rem. 4) . רעה
מֵרֵעֵהוּ[p] noun m. s., suff. 3 p. s. m. fr. [מֵרֵעַ] d. 1 b רעה
מֵרֵעֵהוּ[q] noun masc. sing., suff. 3 pers. sing. masc. from מֵרֵעָה dec. 9 a . . . . רעה
מֵרְעוֹת[r] pref. מֵ for ·מִ) (Kal inf. constr. . . רעה
מַרְעִיד[s] Hiph. part. sing. masc. . . . . רעד
מַרְעִידִים[t] id. pl., abs. st. . . . . . . רעד
מֵרְעֵיכֶם[u] noun masc. pl., suff. 2 pers. pl. masc. from מֵרֵעָה dec. 9 a . . . . . רעה

[a] 2 Sa. 6. 13, etc. [b] Eze. 39. 18. [c] Am. 5. 22. [d] Is. 1. 11. [e] Ex. 17. 7.
[f] 1 Sa. 2. 10. [g] Eze. 47. 19. [h] 2 Sa. 22. 48. [i] Da. 7. 4. [k] De. 31. 27.
[l] Da. 5. 19. [m] Ex. 15. 23. [n] Ps. 3. 4. [o] Is. 10. 15. [p] La. 3. 42.
[q] Ezr. 3. 13. [r] Ge. 42. 35. [s] De. 32. 24. [t] I Ki. 13. 21. [u] De. 28. 56.
[x] Le. 26. 36. [y] Na. 3. 2. [z] Ca. 3. 10. [a] Ex. 15. 4. [b] 2 Ch. 35. 7.
[c] Ps. 31. 21. [d] Ps. 35. 20. [e] Pr. 8. 2; 9. 3, 14. [f] Is. 33. 3. [g] Da. 8. 13.
[h] Is. 9. 16. [i] Job 28. 28. [k] Pr. 17. 4. [l] Eze. 12. 16. [m] Job 22. 7.
[n] Je. 3. 20. [o] Is. 32. 14. [p] Ge. 26. 26; 2 Sa. 3. 8; Pr. 19. 7. [pp] Job 14. 9.
[q] Job 39. 8. [r] Eze. 34. 10. [s] Da. 10. 11. [t] Ezr. 10. 9. [u] Eze. 34. 18.

מְרֵעִים[a] noun masc. pl. of [מֵרֵעַ] dec. 1b . . רעה

מְרֵעִים Hiph. part. pl. m. [for מְרִעִים] fr. מֵרַע (q. v.) רעע

מַרְעִישׁ Hiph. part. sing. masc. . . . . רעשׁ

מַרְעִיתוֹ noun f. s., suff. 3 p. s. m. fr. [מַרְעִית] d. 1b רעה

מַרְעִיתִי id., suff. 1 pers. sing. . . . רעה

מַרְעִיתֶךָ id., suff. 2 pers. sing. masc. [for מַרְעִיתְךָ] . רעה

מַרְעִיתָם id., suff. 3 pers. pl. masc. . . . רעה

מַרְעֲלָה וּ pr. name of a place; וּ bef. lab. . . רעל

מֵרַעְמְסֵס pref. מֵ for מִ·) pr. n. of a place, see רַעְמְסֵס

מְרָעֵעַ[b] Chald. Pael part. sing. m. (§ 49. Nos. 3 & 4) רעע

מֵרַעַשׁ[c] pref. מֵ for מִ·) noun masc. sing. . . רעשׁ

מֵרָעַת pref. id.) noun fem. sing., constr. of רָעָה dec. 10 [for רַעָה] from רַע masc. . . רעע

מֵרָעָתוֹ pref. id.) id., suff. 3 pers. sing. masc. . . רעע

מֵרָעָתָם[d] pref. id.) id., suff. 3 pers. pl. masc. . . רעע

מַרְפֵּא וּ noun masc. sing.; וּ bef. lab. . . רפא

מְרַפֵּא[e] Piel part. sing. m. [for מְרַפֶּה § 24. r. 19c] רפה

מַרְפֵּה[f] noun masc. sing. for מַרְפֵּא (§ 23. rem. 10) רפא

מֵרְפִידִים / מֵרְפִדִם } pref. מֵ for מִ·) pr. name of a place . רפד

מֵרִפְיוֹן[g] pref. id.) noun masc. sing. . . . רפה

מְרַפִּים[h] Piel part. masc. pl. [of מְרַפֶּה] dec. 9a . רפה

מִרְפַּשׂ[i] וּ noun masc. sing., constr. of [מִרְפָּשׂ] dec. 2b; וּ bef. lab. . . . . רפשׂ

מָרַץ Kal not used; Arab. *to be diseased, weak,* in body or mind. Niph. *to be weak,* ironically, Job 6. 25; part. *diseased, pernicious, foul,* Mi. 2. 10; 1 Ki. 2. 8. Hiph. *to make weak, foolish,* Job 16. 3.—Note. Kimchi, on the contrary, ascribes to this verb the signification of *being strong, forcible, vehement,* which Gesenius supports by making it cogn. with פָּרַץ q. v. comp. also Eng. vers.

מְרַצְּחִים[k] Piel part. masc. pl. of מְרַצֵּחַ' dec. 7b . רצח

מַרְצֶפֶת[l] noun fem. sing. . . . . . רצף

[מָרַק] *to make clean, bright by rubbing, to polish, furbish.* Pu. *to be cleansed,* Le. 6. 21.

מָרָק masc. dec. 4a, *broth.*

מְרוּקִים m. pl. (of מָרוּק) *purification,* Est. 2. 12.

תַּמְרוּק masc. dec. 1b, *purification,* Est. 2. 12. Meton. *precious ointments, perfumes,* Est. 2. 3, 9.

תַּמְרִיק masc. *cleansing, remedy,* Pr. 20. 30 Kh., תַּמְרוּק K.

מֹרַק[m] וּ Pual part. sing. masc.; וּ for וְ, conv. . מרק

מְרַקֵּד[n] Piel part. sing. masc. . . . . רקד

מְרַקֵּדָה[o] id. part. sing. fem. . . . . רקד

מִרְקוּ[p] Kal imp. pl. masc. . . . . . מרק

מֶרְקָחִים[q] noun masc. pl. [of מֶרְקָח] . . . רקח

מְרֻקָּחִים[r] Pual part. masc. pl. [of מְרֻקָּח] . . רקח

מִרְקַחַת[s] noun fem. sing. . . . . . רקח

מְרֻקָּע[t] Pual part. sing. masc. . . . . רקע

מָרַר fut. יֵמַר (§ 18. rem. 6).—I. *to be bitter;* impers. מַר לִי *it is bitter to me, it grieves me.*—II. *to be embittered, exasperated,* 1 Sa. 30. 6.—III. Arab. *to flow, drop,* whence derivv. מַר, מֹר q. v. Pi. I. *to make bitter, to embitter;* מָרֵר בַּבְּכִי *to weep bitterly.*—II. *to irritate, provoke,* Ge. 49. 23. Hiph. הֵמַר (§ 18. rem. 10).—I. *to embitter,* with נֶפֶשׁ Job 27. 2; ellipt. הֵ' לִי *has embittered me,* sc. life, Ruth 1. 20.—II. *to weep bitterly,* Zec. 12. 10.

מַר masc.—I. *a drop,* Is. 40. 15.—II. adj. (pl. מָרִים, c. מָרֵי § 37. rem. 7) fem. מָרָה dec. 10; *bitter;* neut. as subst. *bitterness.* Metaph. for (*a*) *sad, sorrowful;* subst. *sadness, grief;* (*b*) *bitter, lamentable,* of a cry, grief; (*c*) *violent, cruel;* (*d*) *deadly, pernicious;* (*e*) adv. *bitterly,* of lamentation.

מוֹר, מֹר masc. (with suff. מוֹרִי) *myrrh.*

מָרָא (*bitter, sad*) pr. name fem. Ruth 1. 20.

מָרָה (*bitterness*) pr. name of a fountain in the desert of Sinai.

מֹרָה fem. dec. 10, *bitterness,* Pr. 14. 10.

מֹרָה fem. dec. 10, *bitterness, grief.* Ge. 26. 35.

מָרוֹת (prob. *bitter fountains*) pr. name of a place in the tribe of Judah, Mi. 1. 12.

מְרֵרָה fem. dec. 10, *gall,* Job 16. 13.

מְרֹרָה fem. dec. 10.—I. *bitterness,* De. 32. 32; metaph. pl. *bitter, severe things,* Job 13. 26.—II. *gall,* Job 20. 25.—III. *poison,* Job 20. 14.

מְרֹרִים masc. pl. (of מָרוֹר dec. 3a) *bitter herbs.*

מְרָרִי (*bitter, sad*) pr. name of a son of Levi; also patronym. Nu. 26. 57.

מְרִירִי adj. masc. *bitter, poisonous,* De. 32. 24.

מְרִירוּת f. *bitterness, sorrow, trouble,* Eze. 21. 11.

מֶמֶר masc. *grief, sorrow,* Pr. 17. 25.

מַמְרֹרִים m. pl. (of מַמְרֹר *bitter things,* Job 9. 18.

תַּמְרוּרִים masc. pl. (of תַּמְרוּר) *bitterness;* adv. *bitterly,* Ho. 12. 15.

מְרֹרוֹת[u] noun fem. pl. of [מְרוֹרָה] dec. 10 . . מרר

מְרָרִי וּ' pr. name masc.; וּ bef. lab. . . מרר

מְרֹרִים[x] [y]וּ' noun masc. pl. of [מָרוֹר] dec. 3a; וּ id. מרר

מְרֹרֹת[z] defect. for מְרוֹרוֹת (q. v.) . . . מרר

מְרֵרָתִי[a] noun fem. s., suff. 1 pers. s. fr. [מְרֵרָה] d. 10. מרר

מָרֵשָׁה pr. name of a place, see מָרֵאשָׁה . . ראשׁ

[a] Ju. 14. 11. [b] Da. 2. 40. [c] Je. 47. 3. [d] Je. 44. 5. [e] Je. 38. 4. [f] Je. 8. 15. [g] Je. 47. 3. [h] Ezr. 4. 4. [i] Eze. 34. 19. [k] Is. 1. 21. [l] 2 Ki. 16. 17. [m] Le. 6. 21. [n] 1 Ch. 15. 29. [o] Na. 3. 2. [p] Je. 46. 4. [q] Ca. 5. 13. [r] 2 Ch. 16. 14. [s] Ex. 30. 25. [t] Je. 10. 9. [u] Job 13. 26. [x] Ex. 12. 8. [y] Nu. 9. 11. [z] De. 32. 32. [a] Job 16. 13.

מַרְשִׁיעַ[a] וּ Hiph. part. sing. masc. dec. 1b; וּ bef. lab. . רשע
מַרְשִׁיעֵי[b] וּ id. pl., constr. st.; וּ id. . . . רשע
מַרְשִׁית[c] defect. for מַרְאשִׁית (q. v.) . . . . ראש
מֵרָשָׁע[d] pref. מֵ for ·מִ) adj. masc. sing. dec. 4a . רשע
מֵרֶשַׁע[e] pref. id.) noun masc. sing. d. 6a (§ 35. r. 5) רשע
מֵרִשְׁעוֹ pref. id.) id. with suff. 3 pers. sing. masc. רשע
מֵרְשָׁעִים pref. id.) adj. masc. pl. of רָשָׁע dec. 4a רשע
מֵרִשְׁעָתוֹ pref. id.) noun fem. sing., suff. 3 pers. sing. masc. from רִשְׁעָה (no pl.) . . . רשע
מֵרֶשֶׁת pref. id.) noun fem. s. (suff. רִשְׁתִּי) d. 13b ירש
מָרַת[f] adj. fem. sing., constr. of מָרָה dec. 10 [for מָרָּה] from מַר masc. . . . מרר
מֹרַת[g] noun fem. sing. constr. [of מֹרָּה fr. מֹר m.] מרר
מֹרַת[h] noun fem. sing. constr. [of מֹרָה fr. מֹר m.] מרר
מָרָתָה pr. name of a place (מָרָה) with loc. ה מרר
מָרָתָה[i] } Kal pret. 3 pers. sing. fem. (§ 8. rem. 7) מרה
מָרָתָה[k] }
מָרָתַיִם[l] noun fem. du. from [מָרָה] dec. 11a . מרה
מֵרִתְמָה pref. מֵ for ·מִ) pr. name of a place . רתם
מָשׁ[m] וּ Kal pret. 3 pers. sing. m.; וּ for וְ, conv. מוש
מַשׁ וְ pr. name of a son of Aram, Ge. 10. 23.
מַשָּׂא ״וּ noun m. s. d. 1b, also pr. name; וּ bef. lab. נשא
מַשָּׁא[o] ״וּ noun masc. sing.; וּ id. . . . נשא
[מֵשָׁא] pr. name, *Mesha*, one of the boundaries of the district inhabited by the descendants of Joktan, Ge. 10. 30.
מַשָּׁא[p] וּ noun masc. sing.; וּ bef. lab. . . נשא
מַשְׁאַבִּים[q] noun masc. pl. of [מַשְׁאָב] dec. 8a . שאב
מַשָּׂאָה[r] noun fem. sing. . . . . . נשא
מְשׁוֹאָה[s] וּ defect. for מְשׁוֹאָה (q. v.); וּ bef. lab. . שוא
מַשָּׂאוֹ[t] noun masc. sing., suff. 3 pers. sing. masc. from מַשָּׂא dec. 1b . . . נשא
מִשָּׁאוּל pref. ·מִ) pr. name masc. . . . שאל
מִשְּׁאוֹל pref. id.) noun com. sing. dec. 1a . שאל
מַשָּׂאוֹת[u] noun fem. pl. abs. from מַשָּׂאָה dec. 11a . נשא
מַשְּׂאוֹת noun fem. pl. of מַשְׂאֵת (q. v.) . . נשא
מַשְׂאוֹתֵיכֶם[v] id. with suff. 2 pers. pl. masc. . . נשא
מִשְּׁאֵיהֶם[w] pref. ·מִ) noun masc. pl., suff. 3 pers. pl. masc. from [שׁוֹא] dec. 1a . . . שוא
מַשַּׂאֲכֶם[x] וּ noun masc. sing., suff. 2 pers. pl. masc. from מַשָּׂא dec. 1b (§ 21. rem. 1); וּ bef. lab. . נשא
מִישָׁאֵל ״וּ pr. name masc.; וּ id. . . . . שאל
מִשְׁאֲלוֹת[a] noun fem. pl. constr. from [מִשְׁאָלָה] d. 11a שאל
מִשְׁאֲלֹתֶיךָ[b] id. with suff. 2 pers. sing. masc. . . שאל
מַשָּׂאָם[c] noun m. s., suff. 3 pers. pl. m. fr. מַשָּׂא d. 1b נשא
מִשְּׁאָר[d] pref. ·מִ) noun masc. sing. dec. 1a . שאר

מִשְׁאַרְתֵּךְ[e] וּ noun fem. sing., suff. 2 pers. sing. masc. from [מִשְׁאֶרֶת] dec. 13a; וּ bef. lab. . שאר
מִשְׁאֲרֹתָם[f] id. pl. with suff. 3 pers. pl. masc. . שאר
מַשְׂאַת[g] [for מַשְׂאַת] n. m. s. constr. of [מַשָּׂאָה] d. 11a נשא
מַשְׂאַת[h] ״וּ [for מַשְׂאַת] noun fem. constr. as if from מַשָּׂאָה, see מַשְׂאֵת; וּ bef. lab. . . נשא
מַשְׂאֵת ״וּ n. f. s. [for מַשְׂאֶת § 39. No. 4. r. 2]; וּ id. נשא
מִשְּׁאַת[k] וּ pref. ·מִ) n. f. s., constr. of שׁוֹאָה d. 10; וּ id. שוא
מִשְּׂאֵתוֹ[l] ״וּ pref. id.) noun fem. sing., suff. 3 pers. sing. m. from שְׂאֵת (§ 39. No. 4. r. 2); וּ id. נשא
מִשָּׁב וּ pref. id.) Kal part. sing. masc. dec. 1a (§ 30. No. 3); וּ id. . . . שוב
מִשְּׁבָא pref. id.) pr. name of a region . שבא
מְשֻׁבָה noun fem. sing. [for מְשׁוּבָה] dec. 10 . שוב
מְשֻׁבוֹתֵיהֶם[m] id. pl., suff. 3 pers. pl. masc. . שוב
מְשֻׁבוֹתַיִךְ[n] וּ id. pl., suff. 2 pers. sing. masc.; וּ bef. lab. שוב
מִשְׁבוֹתָם[p] וּ defect. for מוֹשְׁבוֹתָם q. v.; וּ id. . ישב
מְשַׁבֵּחַ[q] וּ Ch. Pael part. sing. m. (§ 49. No. 4); וּ id. שבח
מִשֵּׁבֶט[r] pref. ·מִ) Seg. n. as if for שֵׁבֶט=שֵׁבֶט see שֵׁבֶט שבט
מִשִּׁבְטֵי pref. id.) n. com. pl. constr. fr. שֵׁבֶט d. 6b שבט
מִשֶּׁבִי pref. id.) noun masc. sing. d. 6i (§ 35. r. 14) שבה
מַשְׁבִּיחַ[s] Hiph. part. sing. masc. . . . שבח
מַשְׂבִּיעַ[t] וּ Hiph. part. sing. masc.; וּ bef. lab. . שבע
מַשְׁבִּעֵךְ Hiph. part. sing. masc., suff. 2 pers. sing. masc. [for מַשְׁבִּיעֲךָ, from מַשְׁבִּיעַ] dec. 1b
מַשְׁבִּיר[u] Hiph. part. sing. masc. . . . . שבר
מַשְׁבִּית Hiph. part. sing. masc. . . . . שבת
מִשִּׁבֹּלֶת[x] pref. ·מִ) noun fem. sing., pl. שִׁבֳּלִים d. 13c שבל
מִשִּׁבְעָה pref. id.) num. card. m., constr. שִׁבְעַת fr. שֶׁבַע f. שבע
מִשְּׁבֻעָהּ[y] pref. id.) noun masc. sing., suff. 3 pers. s. f. שבע
מִשְּׁבֻעָתִי[z] pref. id.) n. f. s., suff. 1 p. s. fr. שְׁבוּעָה d. 10 שבע
מִשְּׁבֻעָתֵךְ[a] pref. id.) id., suff. 2 pers. sing. fem. . שבע
מִשְׁבְּצוֹת[b] noun fem. pl. of [מִשְׁבֶּצֶת] dec. 13 . שבץ
מְשֻׁבָּצִים[c] Pual part. masc. pl. [of מְשֻׁבָּץ] . . שבץ
מִשְׁבְּצֹת defect. for מִשְׁבְּצוֹת (q. v.) . . שבץ
מַשְׁבֵּר noun masc. sing., constr. מִשְׁבַּר (§ 36. r. 1) שבר
מְשַׁבֵּר[d] וּ Piel part. sing. masc.; וּ bef. lab. . שבר
מִשֶּׁבֶר[e] וּ pref. ·מִ) n. m. s. (suff. שִׁבְרוֹ) d. 6a; וּ id. שבר
מִשְׁבְּרֵי noun masc. pl. constr. from [מִשְׁבָּר] dec. 2b שבר
מִשִּׁבְרִי[f] pref. ·מִ) n. m. s., suff. 1 p. s. fr. [שֶׁבֶר] d. 6b שבר
מִשְׁבָּרֶיךָ noun m. pl., suff. 2 p. s. m. fr. [מִשְׁבָּר] d. 2b שבר
מִשְּׁבָרִים[g] pref. ·מִ) noun masc. pl. of שֶׁבֶר dec. 6b שבר
מִשַּׁבָּת[h] pref. id.) n. com. s. (suff. שַׁבַּתּוֹ, pl. שַׁבָּתוֹת) שבת
מִשֶּׁבֶת pref. id.) Kal inf. constr. (suff. שִׁבְתִּי) d. 13a ישב
מִשְׁבַּתֶּהָ[i] [for ־תֶיהָ § 4. rem. 1] noun masc. pl., suff. 3 pers. sing. fem. from [מִשְׁבָּת] dec. 8a שבת

[a] Pr. 17. 15. [b] Da. 11. 32. [c] De. 11. 12. [d] Ps. 17. 13. [e] Job 34. 10. [f] 1 Sa. 1. 10. [g] Pr. 14. 10. [h] Ge. 26. 35. [i] Je. 4. 17. [k] Ho. 14. 1. [l] Je. 50. 21. [m] Zec. 14. 4. [n] Je. 23. 36. [o] Ne. 5. 7, 10; 32. [p] 2 Ch. 19. 7. [q] Ju. 5. 11. [r] Is. 30. 27. [s] Job 30. 3. [t] Nu. 4. 19, 49. [u] Pr. 22. 26. [x] Eze. 20. 40. [y] Ps. 35. 17. [z] De. 1. 12. [a] Ps. 37. 4. [b] Ps. 20. 6. [c] Nu. 4. 27, 31, 32. [d] Le. 25. 49. [e] De. 28. 5, 17. [f] Ex. 12. 34. [g] De. 24. 10. [h] Am. 5. 11. [i] Je. 40. 5. [k] Pr. 3. 25. [l] Ps. 62. 5. [m] Job 31. 23. [n] Je. 5. 6. [o] Je. 2. 19. [p] 1 Ch. 7. 28. [q] Da. 2. 23; 4. 34. [r] Jos. 4. 2, 4. [s] Ps. 65. 8. [t] Ps. 145. 16. [u] Pr. 11. 26. [x] Is. 27. 12. [y] Ru. 2. 18. [z] Ge. 24. 8. [a] Jos. 2. 17, 20. [b] Ex. 28. 11. [c] Ex. 28. 20. [d] 1 Ki. 19. 11. [e] Is. 65. 14. [f] Ps. 119. 116. [g] Job 41. 17. [h] Is. 58. 13. [i] La. 1. 7.

וּמִשַּׁבְּתוֹתַי [a] וּ pref. ·מִ)(noun com. pl., suff. 1 pers. sing. from שַׁבָּת, comp. מִשְׁבָּת; וּ bef. lab. . . . שבת
מִשְׁבְּתֵיכֶם defect. for מוֹשְׁבוֹתֵיכֶם (q. v.) . . . ישב
מִשְׂגָּב noun masc. sing. dec. 8a . . . שגב
מִשְׂגַּב [b] id., constr. st. . . . . . שגב
מִשְׂגַּבּוֹ [c] id., suff. 3 pers. sing. masc. . . . שגב
מִשְׂגַּבִּי id., suff. 1 pers. sing. . . . . שגב
מַשְׁגֶּה [d] 'וּ Hiph. part. sing. masc.; וּ bef. lab. . . שגה
מִשְׁגֶּה [e] noun masc. sing. . . . . . שגה
מַשְׁגִּיא [f] Hiph. part. sing. masc. . . . . שגה
מַשְׁגִּיחַ [g] Hiph. part. sing. masc. . . . . שגח
מְשֻׁגָּע Pual part. sing. masc. dec. 2b . . . שגע
מְשֻׁגָּעִים [h] id. pl., abs. st. . . . . . שגע
מַשֶּׂגֶת [i] Hiph. part. sing. f. [of מַשִּׂיג § 39. No. 4 d] נשג
מִשֹּׁד [k] pref. ·מִ)(noun masc. sing. . . . . שדה
מִשֹּׁד pref. id.)(noun masc. sing. . . . . שדד
מְשַׁדֶּד־ [l] Piel part. s. m. [for מְשַׁדֵּד comp. § 10. r. 4] שדד
מִשְּׂדֵה [m] 'וּ n. m. s., constr. of שָׂדֶה d. 9b; וּ bef. lab. שדה
וּמִשְּׂדוֹת [n] וּ pref. id.)(id. with pl. fem. term., constr. of שָׂדוֹת; וּ id. . . . . . . שדה
מִשַּׁדַּי pref. ·מִ)(name of God, *the Almighty*, שַׁד with the pl. term. ־ַי . . . . . שדד
מִשְּׂדֵי pref. id.)(noun masc. pl. constr. fr. שָׂדֶה d. 9b שדה
מִשָּׁדָיִם [o] pref. id.)(for שָׁדַיִם, noun masc. du., constr. שְׁדֵי from שַׁד (§ 31. rem. 5) . . . שדה
וּמִשַּׁדְמֹת [p] וּ pref. id.)(noun fem. pl. constr. from שְׁדֵמָה dec. 11c (§ 42. rem. 4); וּ bef. lab. . . שדם

[מָשָׁה] *to draw out*, Ex. 2. 10. Hiph. id. 2 Sa. 22. 17; Ps. 18. 17.

מֹשֶׁה (*drawing out, deliverer*; or, in a passive sense, *drawn out*) pr. name, *Moses*, the great leader, lawgiver and prophet of the Israelites, the son of Amram, of the tribe of Levi.

מֶשִׁי masc. *silk*, Eze. 16. 10, 13.

נִמְשִׁי (*drawn out*) pr. name masc. 1 Ki. 19. 16; 2 Ki. 9. 2.

מַשֵּׁה [q] noun masc. sing., constr. of [מַשֶּׁה] dec. 9a נשה
מִשֶּׂה [r] pref. ·מִ)(noun masc. sing. irr. (§ 45) . שיה
מֹשֶׁה 'וּ pr. name masc.; וּ bef. lab. . . . משה
מָשׁוּ [s] Kal pret. 3 pers. pl. . . . . . מוש
מְשׁוֹאָה וּ noun fem. sing; וּ bef. lab. . . . שוא
מִשּׁוּב [t] pref. ·מִ)(Kal inf. constr. dec. 1a . . שוב
מְשׁוֹבָב וּ pr. name masc.; וּ bef. (:) . . . שוב
מְשׁוֹבֵב [u] Pilel part. sing. masc. . . . . שוב
מְשׁוֹבֶבֶת [w] Pulal part. sing. fem. [of מְשׁוֹבָב § 39. No. 4] שוב
מְשׁוּבַת [y] noun fem. sing. constr. of [מְשׁוּבָה] dec. 10 שוב
מְשׁוּבֹתֵיכֶם [z] id. pl., suff. 2 pers. pl. masc. . . שוב

מְשׁוּבֹתֵינוּ [a] id. pl., suff. 1 pers. pl. . . . שוב
מְשׁוּבָתָם [b] id. sing., suff. 3 pers. pl. masc. . . שוב
מְשׁוּגָתִי [c] noun fem. s., suff. 1 pers. s. fr. [מְשׁוּגָה] d. 10 שוג
מִשּׁוֹד [d] in full for מִשֹּׁד (q. v.) . . . . שדד
מַשְׁוֶה Hiph. part. sing. masc. . . . . . שוה
מָשׁוֹחַ [e] וּ Kal inf. abs.; וּ bef. lab. . . . משח
מָשׁוּחַ [f] וּ id. part. pass. sing. masc.; וּ id. . . משח
מָשׁוֹט [g] noun masc. sing. . . . . . שוט
מִשּׁוּט [qq] pref. ·מִ)(Kal inf. constr. . . . . שוט
מְשׁוֹטְטִים [h] Pilel part. masc. pl. [of מְשׁוֹטֵט] dec. 7b . שוט
מְשׁוֹטַיִךְ [i] noun masc. pl., suff. 2 pers. sing. fem. from [מָשׁוֹט] dec. 1b . . . . . שוט
מְשׂוּכָּתוֹ [k] noun fem. sing., suff. 3 pers. sing. masc. [from מְשׂוּכָה for מְשֻׂכָּה] . . . . שכך
מָשׁוֹל [l] Kal inf. abs. . . . . . . משל
מִשּׁוּמִי [m] pref. ·מִ)(Kal inf., suff. 1 pers. s. d. 1a שום
מְשׁוֹמֵם Poel part. sing. masc. . . . . . שמם
מְשַׁוֵּעַ Piel part. sing. masc. [for מְשַׁוֵּעַ § 15. rem. 1] שוע
מִשּׁוּר pref. ·מִ)(noun masc. sing. . . . . שור
מְשׂוּרָה [n] noun fem. sing. . . . . . משר
מְשׁוֹרֵר [o] Pilel part. sing. masc. dec. 7b . . . שיר
מָשׂוֹשׂ noun masc. sing. dec. 3a . . . . שוש
מְשׂוֹשׂ 'וּ id., constr. st.; וּ bef. lab. . . . שוש
מְשׂוֹשָׂהּ [p] id., suff. 3 pers. sing. fem. . . . שוש
מְשׂוֹשִׂי [q] id., suff. 1 pers. sing. . . . . שוש
מָשְׁזָר Hoph. part. sing. masc. . . . . . שזר

מָשַׁח [r] 'וּ fut. יִמְשַׁח, inf. מְשֹׁחַ, מָשְׁחָה, prop. as in Arab. *to draw the hand over* anything; hence Syr. *to measure*.—I. *to smear* or *rub over*; with oil, *to anoint*; with paint, *to paint*, Je. 22. 14.—II. *to anoint, to consecrate by unction*.—III. *to consecrate, appoint, constitute*.—IV. *to anoint oneself*, with בְּ Am. 6. 6. Niph. *to be anointed*.

מְשַׁח Chald. masc. *oil*, Ezr. 6. 9; 7. 22.

מָשִׁיחַ masc. dec. 3a.—I. adj. *anointed*.—II. subst. *the anointed*, applied to priests, kings; hence the *Messiah, Christ*.

מִשְׁחָה fem. constr. מִשְׁחַת (no vowel change). —I. *an anointing, unction*.—II. *portion*, Le. 7. 35.

מָשְׁחָה fem. *part, portion*, Nu. 18. 8, and perh. so in Ex. 40. 15.

מִמְשַׁח masc. *extension, spreading out*, Eze. 28. 14.

מְשַׁח [s] 'וּ Chald. noun masc. sing.; וּ id. . . משח
מְשָׁחֵהוּ [t] Kal imp. masc. sing. [מְשַׁח], suff. 3 pers. sing. masc. (§ 16. rem. 11) . . . משח
מָשְׁחוֹ [u] id. inf., suff. 3 pers. sing. masc. . . משח

[a] Eze. 22. 26. [b] Is. 25. 12. [c] Is. 33. 16. [d] Job 12. 16. [e] Ge. 43. 12. [f] Job 12. 23. [g] Ca. 2. 9. [h] 1 Sa. 21. 16. [i] Le. 14. 21. [k] Job 24. 9; Is. 66. 11. [l] Pr. 19. 26. [m] Le. 27. 28. [n] Ne. 12. 29. [o] Is. 28. 9. [p] De. 32. 32. [q] De. 15. 2. [r] Ex. 12. 4. [s] Nu. 14. 44. [t] 2 Ch. 36. 13. [u] Is. 58. 12. [w] Eze. 38. 8. [y] Pr. 1. 32. [z] Je. 3. 22. [a] Je. 14. 7. [b] Ho. 14. 5. [c] Job 19. 4. [d] Job 5. 21. [e] Je. 22. 14. [f] 2 Sa. 3. 39. [g] Eze. 27. 29. [h] Zec. 4. 10. [i] Eze. 27. 6. [k] Is. 5. 5. [l] Ge. 37. 8. [m] Is. 44. 7. [n] 1 Ch. 23. 29. [o] 2 Ch. 29. 28. [p] Ho. 2. 13. [q] Je. 49. 25. [qq] Job 1. 7. [r] 1 Ki. 1. 34. [s] Ezr. 6. 9; 7. 22. [t] 1 Sa. 16. 12. [u] Le. 7. 36.

מְשָׁחוּ id. pret. 3 pers. pl. . . . . . משח

מְשָׁחוֹ[a] id. pret. 3 pers. sing. m., suff. 3 pers. sing. m. משח

מִשְׁחוּ[b] id. imp. pl. masc. . . . . . משח

מִשְּׂחוֹק[c] pref. ·מִ) noun masc. sing. . . . שחק

מִשְּׁחוֹר[d] pref. id.) noun masc. sing. . . . שחר

מְשֻׁחִים Kal part. pass. masc. pl. of מָשׁוּחַ dec. 3 a . משח

מֹשְׁחִים[e] id. part. act. masc. pl. [of מֹשֵׁחַ] dec. 7 b משח

מַשְׂחִיקִים[f] Hiph. part. masc. pl. [of מַשְׂחִיק] dec. 1 b שחק

מַשְׁחִית[g] ו׳ Hiph. part. or subst. m. d. 1 b; וּ bef. lab. שחת

מִשְּׁחִיתוֹתָם[h] pref. ·מִ) noun fem. pl., suff. 3 pers. pl. masc. from [שְׁחִית] dec. 1 a . . שחה

מַשְׁחִיתִים Hiph. part. masc. pl. of מַשְׁחִית dec. 1 b שחת

מַשְׁחִיתָם[i] id. sing., suff. 3 pers. pl. masc. . . שחת

מַשְׁחִיתִם defect. for מַשְׁחִיתִים (q. v.) . . שחת

מְשָׁחֲךָ Kal pret. 3 pers. sing. m., suff. 2 pers. sing. m. משח

מָשַׁחְנוּ[k] id. pret. 1 pers. pl. . . . . משח

מְשַׂחֵק[l] ו׳[m] Piel (§ 14. r. 1) part. s. m. d. 7 b; וּ bef. lab. שחק

מִשְׂחָק[n] noun masc. sing. . . . . . שחק

מְשַׂחֲקִים Piel (§ 14. r. 1) part. masc. pl. of מְשַׂחֵק d. 7 b שחק

מְשַׂחֶקֶת id. part. sing. fem. dec. 13 . . . שחק

מִשְׁחָר[o] noun masc. sing. . . . . . שחר

מְשַׁחֲרִי[p] וּ the foll. with suff. 1 pers. sing.; וּ bef. lab. שחר

מְשַׁחֲרֵי[q] Piel part. pl. constr. [fr. מְשַׁחֵר § 14. r. 1] d. 7 b שחר

מָשַׁחְתָּ } Kal pret. 2 pers. sing. masc.; acc. shifted by conv. וּ, bef. lab. for וְ (§ 8. r. 7) } משח

וּמָשַׁחְתָּ }

מִשַּׁחַת pref. ·מִ) noun fem. sing. dec. 13 a . . שחת

מִשְׁחַת ו׳[r] noun fem. sing., constr. of מִשְׁחָה (no pl.); וּ bef. lab. . . . . . משח

מִשְׁחַת[s] noun masc. sing., constr. of [מִשְׁחָת] dec. 2 b שחת

מָשְׁחָת[t] Hoph. part. sing. masc. dec. 2 b . . שחת

מָשְׁחַת[u] id., constr. st. . . . . . שחת

מַשְׁחֵתוֹ[x] noun masc. sing., suff. 3 pers. sing. masc. [from מַשְׁחֵת] . . . . . שחת

מְשַׁחְתּוֹ[y] וּ Kal pret. 2 pers. sing. masc., suff. 3 pers. sing. masc.; וּ for וְ, conv. . . . משח

מְשַׁחְתִּיו[z] id. pret. 1 pers. sing., suff. 3 pers. sing. masc. משח

מְשַׁחְתִּיךָ id. id., suff. 2 pers. sing. masc. . . משח

מַשְׁחִתִים defect. for מַשְׁחִיתִים (q. v.) . . שחת

מָשְׁחָתָם[a] noun m. sing., suff. 3 pers. pl. m. [fr. מָשְׁחָת] שחת

מָשְׁחָתָם[b] Kal inf. [מָשְׁחָה § 8. r. 10], suff. 3 p. pl. m. משח

מִשַּׁחֲתָם[c] pref. ·מִ) Piel inf. (שַׁחֵת § 14. rem. 1), suff. 3 pers. pl. masc. dec. 7 b . . שחת

מִשּׁוּט[ee] pref. id.) Kal inf. constr. defect. for שׁוּט שוט

מִשְׁטוֹחַ[d] noun masc. sing. . . . . . שטח

מִשְׁטַח[e] noun masc. sing., constr. of [מִשְׁטָח] d. 2 b שטח

מְשֹׁטְטוֹת[f] Pilel part. fem. pl. [of מְשׁוֹטֶטֶת dec. 13, from מְשׁוֹטֵט masc.] . . . שוט

מַשְׂטֵמָה[g] noun fem. sing. . . . . שטם

מִשְׁטָרוֹ[h] noun m. s., suff. 3 pers. s. m. [fr. מִשְׁטָר] שטר

מֶשִׁי[i] וָ׳ n. m. s. [for מְשִׁי § 35. r. 14]; for וָ see lett. ו משה

מֻשִׁי וּ pr. name masc., see מוּשִׁי; וּ bef. lab. מוש

מֵשִׁיב Hiph. part. sing. masc. dec. 3 b . . שוב

מִשֵּׁיבוֹ[k] pref. ·מִ) noun masc. sing., suff. 3 pers. sing. masc. [fr. שֵׂיב or שַׂיִב] . . שיב

מְשִׁיבֵי constr. of the foll. . . . . שוב

מְשִׁיבִים[l] Hiph. part. masc. pl. of מֵשִׁיב dec. 3 b . שוב

מְשִׁיבַת[m] id. part. sing. fem. constr. [of מְשִׁיבָה] dec. 10 שוב

מַשִּׂיג[n] Hiph. part. sing. masc. dec. 1 b . נשג

מַשִּׂיגֵהוּ[o] id. with suff. 3 pers. sing. masc. . . נשג

מְשֵׁיזַב[p] Ch. Peil part. sing. masc. (§ 48) . שזב

מְשֵׁיזַבְאֵל pr. name masc. . . . . . שזב

מָשִׁיחַ noun masc. sing. dec. 3 a . . . משח

מְשִׁיחַ id., constr. st. . . . . . משח

מְשִׁיחוֹ id., suff. 3 pers. sing. masc. . . משח

מְשִׁיחִי[q] id., suff. 1 pers. sing. . . . . משח

מְשִׁיחֶךָ id., suff. 2 pers. sing. masc. [for מְשִׁיחֲךָ] משח

מֵשִׂים[r] Hiph. part. sing. masc. . . . שום

מַשִּׁיקוֹת[s] Hiph. part. fem. pl. [of מַשִּׁיקָה dec. 10, from מַשִּׁיק masc.] . . . . נשק

מִשִּׁיר[t] pref. ·מִ) noun masc. sing. dec. 1 a . שיר

.מִשִּׁירִי[u] וּ pref. ·מִ) id., suff. 1 pers. sing.; וּ bef. lab. שיר

מְשִׁיתִהוּ[x] Kal pret. 1 p. s. [מָשִׁיתִי] with suff. 3 p. s. m. משה

מָשַׁךְ ו׳[y] fut. יִמְשֹׁךְ.—I. *to draw; to draw* any one to a place, with אֶל, בְּ of the place; with מִן *to draw out;* espec. מָ׳ הַקֶּשֶׁת *to draw the bow;* מָ׳ הַיּוֹבֵל *to draw,* i. e. *to sound the trumpet,* perh. in *protracted* sounds.—II. *to draw out, stretch, hold out* the hand, in token of fellowship, Ho. 7. 5.—III. *to draw out, prolong, continue* a kindness to any one.—IV. *to make durable, strengthen,* Ec. 2. 3.—V. *to scatter,* as seed, Am. 9. 13; intrans. *to spread out.*—VI. *to seize, take,* Ex. 12. 21; *to hold,* with בְּ Ju. 5. 14.—VII. *to draw, take away, remove.* Niph. *to be protracted, delayed.* Pu. I. *protracted, deferred,* Pr. 13. 12.—II. Is. 18. 2, 7, Eng. vers. "*scattered;*" Lee, *spoiled;* Gesenius (who refers this prophecy to the Ethiopians) *stout, strong.*

מֶשֶׁךְ masc.—I. *acquisition,* Job 28. 18.—II. *a scattering,* Ps. 126. 6.—III. pr. name of a son of Japhet, and a people descended from him.

מֹשְׁכוֹת fem. pl. (of מוֹשְׁכָה or מוֹשֶׁכֶת) *cords, bands,* Job 38. 31, Lee, *attractions, influences.*

מֶשֶׁךְ וָ׳ pr. name of a people; for וָ see lett. ו . משך

[a] 2 Ch. 22. 7. [b] Is. 21. 5. [c] Ec. 7. 3. [d] La. 4. 8. [e] Ju. 9. 15. [ee] Job 2. 2. [f] 2 Ch. 30. 10. [g] Je. 4. 7. [h] Ps. 107. 20. [i] Ge. 6. 13. [k] 2 Sa. 19. 11. [l] Pr. 26. 19. [m] 1 Ch. 15. 29. [n] Hab. 1. 10. [o] Ps. 110. 3. [p] Pr. 8. 17. [q] Job 24. 5. [r] Le. 7. 35. [s] Is. 52. 14. [t] Pr. 25. 26. [u] Mal. 1. 14 [x] Eze. 9. 1. [y] 1 Sa. 9. 16. [z] Ps. 89. 21. [a] Le. 22. 25. [b] Ex. 40. 15. [c] Eze. 20. 17. [d] Eze. 47. 10. [e] Eze. 26. 5, 14. [f] 2 Ch. 16. 9. [g] Ho. 9. 7, 8. [h] Job 38. 33. [i] Eze. 16. 10, 13. [k] 1 Ki. 14. 4. [l] Ju. 11. 9. [m] Ps. 19. 8. [n] 1 Sa. 14. 26. [o] Job 41. 18. [p] Da. 6. 28. [q] 1 Sa. 2. 35. [r] Job 4. 20. [s] Eze. 3. 13. [t] Ps. 137. 3. [u] Ps. 28. 7. [x] Ex. 2. 10. [y] Job 24. 22.

מֶשֶׁךְ[a] — [b]וְ noun masc. sing.; וּ bef. lab. — משך
מְשֹׁךְ[c] — Kal imp. sing. masc. — משך
מֹשֵׁךְ[d] — id. part. sing. masc. dec. 7 b — משך
מִשְׁכָּב — noun masc. sing. dec. 2 b — שכב
מִשְׁכַּב — id., constr. st. — שכב
מֻשְׁכָּב[e] — Hoph. part. sing. masc. (§ 11. rem. 10) — שכב
מִשְׁכְּבֵהּ[f] — Chald. noun masc. sing., suff. 3 pers. sing. masc. from [מִשְׁכַּב] dec. 2 a — שכב
מִשְׁכָּבוֹ — noun m. s., suff. 3 p. s. m. fr. מִשְׁכָּב d. 2 b — שכב
מִשְׁכְּבוֹתָם — id. pl. fem., suff. 3 pers. pl. masc. — שכב
מִשְׁכָּבִי — id. sing., suff. 1 pers. sing. — שכב
מִשְׁכְּבֵי — id. pl., constr. st. — שכב
מִשְׁכְּבִי[g] — Ch. noun m. s., suff. 1 p. s. fr. [מִשְׁכַּב] d. 2 a — שכב
מִשְׁכָּבֵךְ[h] — noun m. s., suff. 2 pers. s. f. fr. מִשְׁכָּב d. 2 b — שכב
מִשְׁכָּבֶךָ[i], מִשְׁכָּבְךָ — } id., suff. 2 pers. sing. masc. — שכב
מִשְׁכְּבָךְ[k] — Chald. noun masc. sing., suff. 2 pers. sing. masc. from [מִשְׁכַּב] dec. 2 a — שכב
מִשְׁכַּבְכֶם[l] — noun m. s., suff. 2 p. pl. m. fr. מִשְׁכָּב d. 2 b — שכב
מִשְׁכָּבָם[m] — id. with suff. 3 pers. pl. masc. — שכב
מִשֹּׁכֶבֶת[n] — pref. ·מִ)(Kal part. act. fem. from שֹׁכֵב masc. — שכב
מָשְׁכָה[o] — Kal pret. 3 pers. sing. fem. — משך
מִשְׁכוּ[p], מְשֹׁכוּ[q] — } id. imp. pl. masc. (§ 8. rem. 12) — משך
מֹשְׁכֵי[r] — id. part. act. pl. constr. masc. fr. מֹשֵׁךְ d. 7 b — משך
מַשְׂכִּיּוֹת[s] — noun fem. pl. of מַשְׂכִּית (q. v.) — שכה
מַשְׂכִּיל — Hiph. part. sing. masc. — שכל
מַשְׂכִּיל — Hiph. part. sing. masc. dec. 1 b — שׂכל
מַשְׂכִּלֵי[t] — וּ id. pl. constr.; וּ bef. lab. — שׂכל
מַשְׁכִּים — Hiph. part. sing. masc. dec. 1 b — שכם
מַשְׁכֵּים[u] — id. id. *adverbially*; or perhaps Hiph. part. pl. [of מַשְׁכֶּה] dec. 9 a — שכה
מֹשְׁכִים[x] — Kal part. act. masc. pl. of מֹשֵׁךְ dec. 7 b — משך
מַשְׁכִּימֵי — Hiph. part. pl. constr. masc. fr. מַשְׁכִּים d. 1 b — שכם
מַשְׂכִּית[y] — n. f. s., pl. מַשְׂכִּיּוֹת (§ 39. No. 4. r. 1 note) — שכה
מַשְׂכִּיתוֹ[z] — id., suff. 3 pers. sing. masc. — שכה
מַשְׂכִּיֹּתָם[a] — id. pl., suff. 3 pers. pl. masc. — שכה
מִשֶּׂכֶל[b] — pref. ·מִ)(for שֶׂכֶל, noun m. s. see under שֵׂכֶל — שכל
מְשַׁכֵּלָה[c] — Piel part. sing. f. [of מְשַׁכֵּל] comp. מְשַׁכֶּלֶת — שכל
מַשְׂכִּלִים[d] — וּ Hiph. part. masc. pl. of מַשְׂכִּיל dec. 1 b; וּ bef. lab. — שכל
מַשְׂכָּלֶת[e] — [for כֶּלֶת'] Hiph. part. sing. fem. of מַשְׂכִּיל (§ 39. No. 4 d) — שכל
מְשַׁכָּלֶת[f] וּ, מְשַׁכֶּלֶת[g] וּ — } Piel part. sing. fem. [of מְשַׁכֵּל] comp. מְשַׁכֵּלָה; וּ bef. lab. — שכל
מִשְּׁכֶם — pref. ·מִ)(pr. name of a place — שכם

מִשִּׁכְמָהּ[h] — pref. ·מִ)(noun masc. sing., suff. 3 pers. sing. fem. (§ 3. r. 3) fr. שְׁכֶם (§ 35. r. 10) — שכם
מִשִּׁכְמוֹ — pref. id.)(id. with suff. 3 pers. sing. masc. — שכם
מִשְׁכָּן[i] — noun masc. sing. dec. 2 b — שכן
מִשְׁכַּן — [k]וּ id., constr. st.; וּ bef. lab. — שכן
מִשְׁכְּנֵהּ[l] — Chald. noun masc. sing., suff. 3 pers. sing. masc. from [מִשְׁכַּן] dec. 2 a — שכן
מִשְׁכָּנוֹ[m] — noun m. s., suff. 3 p. s. m. from מִשְׁכָּן d. 2 b — שכן
מִשְׁכָּנוֹת — id. pl. abs. fem. comp. מִשְׁכְּנֵי — שכן
מִשְׁכְּנוֹת — id. pl. constr. fem. — שכן
מִשְׁכְּנוֹתָיו — וּ id. pl., suff. 3 pers. sing. masc.; וּ bef. lab. — שכן
מִשְׁכְּנוֹתַיִךְ[n] — id. pl., suff. 2 pers. sing. fem. — שכן
מִשְׁכְּנוֹתֶיךָ — id. pl., suff. 2 pers. sing. masc. — שכן
מִשְׁכְּנוֹתֵינוּ[o] — id. pl., suff. 1 pers. pl. — שכן
מָשְׁכֵנִי[p] — Kal imp. sing. masc., suff. 1 pers. sing. — משך
מִשְׁכָּנִי — noun masc. sing., suff. 1 p. s. fr. מִשְׁכָּן d. 2 b — שכן
מִשְׁכְּנֵי[q] — id. pl. constr. [of מִשְׁכָּנִים] comp. מִשְׁכָּנוֹת — שכן
מִשְׁכְּנֵיהֶם[r] — id. pl., suff. 3 pers. pl. masc. — שכן
מִשְּׁכֶנְתָּהּ[s] — pref. ·מִ)((prop. adj.) subst. fem. sing., suff. 3 pers. s. f. [fr. שְׁכֶנֶת d. 13 b] fr. שָׁכֵן m. — שכן
מִשְׁכְּנֹתֶיהָ[t] — noun masc. with pl. fem. term. and suff. 3 pers. sing. fem. from מִשְׁכָּן dec. 2 b — שכן
מִשְׁכְּנֹתֶיךָ[u] — id., suff. 2 pers. sing. masc. see מִשְׁכְּנוֹתֶיךָ — שכן
מִשְׁכְּנֹתָם[x] — id., suff. 3 pers. pl. masc. (§ 4. rem. 2) — שכן
מְשַׁכֶּרֶת[y] — Piel part. sing. fem. [of מְשַׁכֵּר] — שכר
מַשְׂכֻּרְתִּי[z] — noun f. s., suff. 1 pers. s. fr. [מַשְׂכֹּרֶת] d. 13 c (comp. § 35. rem. 8) — שכר
מַשְׂכֻּרְתֶּךָ[a] — id., suff. 2 pers. sing. masc. (for תְּךָ') — שכר
מַשְׂכֻּרְתֵּךְ[b] — id., suff. 2 pers. sing. fem. — שכר
מָשַׁכְתָּ[c] — וּ Kal pret. 2 pers. sing. masc.; acc. shifted bef. וּ, for וְ, conv. (§ 8. rem. 7) — משך
מָשַׁכְתִּי[d] — וּ id. pret. 1 pers. sing.; acc. id. — משך
מְשַׁכְתִּיךְ[e] — id. id. with suff. 1 pers. sing. — משך

מָשַׁל וּ fut. יִמְשֹׁל.—I. *to rule, have dominion*; with בְּ, עַל of that *over* which one rules.—II. *to have power* to do anything, Ex. 21. 8. Part. מֹשֵׁל *ruler, prince*. Hiph. *to cause to rule, give dominion to, appoint ruler*. Inf. הַמְשֵׁל *dominion*, Job 25. 2.

מֹשֶׁל masc. dec. 7 c, *dominion*, Zec. 9. 10.

מִמְשָׁל masc. (no vowel change) *dominion*, Da. 11. 3, 5; pl. concr. *rulers*, 1 Ch. 26. 6.

מֶמְשָׁלָה fem. constr. מֶמְשֶׁלֶת, with suff. מֶמְשַׁלְתּוֹ (§ 42. rem. 5).—I. *dominion, rule*.—II. *dominion, kingdom*, 2 Ki. 20. 13.—III. meton. *rulers, lords*, 2 Ch. 32. 9.

---

[a] Ps. 126. 6. [b] Job 28. 18. [c] Ps. 36. 11. [d] Ps. 109. 12. [e] 2 Ki. 4. 32. [f] Da. 7. 1. [g] Da. 4. 2, 7, 10. [h] Is. 57. 7, 8. [i] 2 Ki. 6. 12. [k] Da. 2. 28, 29. [l] Ps. 4. 5. [m] Is. 57. 8. [n] Mi. 7. 5. [o] De. 21. 3. [p] Ex. 12. 21. [q] Eze. 32. 20. [r] Is. 5. 18; 66. 19. [s] Ps. 73. 7. [t] Da. 11. 33. [u] Je. 5. 8. [x] Ju. 5. 14. [y] Le. 26. 1. [z] Eze. 8. 12. [a] Nu. 33. 52. [b] Job 17. 4. [c] Ex. 23. 26. [d] Da. 1. 4. [e] Pr. 19. 14. [f] 2 Ki. 2. 19, 21. [g] Eze. 36. 13. [h] Job 31. 22. [i] Is. 22. 16. [k] 1 Ch. 21. 29. [l] Ezr. 7. 15. [m] Jos. 22. 29. [n] Is. 54. 2. [o] Je. 9. 18. [p] Ca. 1. 4. [q] Ps. 46. 5. [r] Eze. 25. 4. [s] Ex. 3. 22. [t] Je. 51. 30. [u] Nu. 24. 5. [x] Ps. 49. 12. [y] Je. 51. 7. [z] Ge. 31. 7, 41. [a] Ge. 29. 15. [b] Ru. 2. 12. [c] Ju. 4. 6. [d] Ju. 4. 7. [e] Je. 31. 3.

מָשָׁל[a] וּ׳ masc. dec. 4a.—I. *similitude, parable.*—II. *sentiment, sententious saying, maxim.*—III. *proverb.*—IV. *by-word; subject of a taunting proverb.*

מָשַׁל.—I. *to utter a comparison* or *similitude*, with עַל ,אֶל ,בְּ *concerning* any one in derision, Joel 2. 17.—II. *to use a proverb.* Part. מֹשְׁלִים *using similitudes, poets*, Nu. 21. 27. Niph. *to be* or *become like, similar*, with אֶל ,עִם ,כְּ. Pi. *to use a parable*, Eze. 21. 5. Hiph. *to compare*, Is. 46. 5. Hithp. *to become like, similar*, Job 30. 19.

מֹשֶׁל masc. *something like, similar*, Job 41. 25.

מְשֹׁל masc. *taunt, by-word*, Job 17. 6.

מָשָׁל[b] וּ׳ Kal pret. 3 pers. sing. masc. for מָשַׁל (§ 8. rem. 7); וּ bef. lab. — משל

מְשַׁל[c] noun masc. sing., constr. of מָשָׁל dec. 4a — משל

מְשֹׁל / מְשָׁל־[d] וּ׳ } Kal inf. constr. or imp. sing. masc. (§ 8. rem. 18); וּ bef. lab. — משל

מֹשֵׁל וּ׳ id. part. act. sing. masc. dec. 7b; וּ id. — משל

מְשֻׁלָּבֹת Pual part. fem. pl. [of מְשֻׁלֶּבֶת fr. מְשֻׁלָּב m.] — שלב

מִשָּׁלֶג[e] / מִשֶּׁלֶג[f] וּ׳[g] } pref. מִ) noun masc. sing. (§ 35. rem. 2); וּ bef. lab. — שלג

מָשְׁלָה[h] Kal pret. 3 pers. s. f. [for מָשְׁלָה § 8. r. 7] — משל

מִשִּׁלֹה pref. מִ) pr. name of a place, see שִׁילֹה — שלה

מֹשְׁלָה[i] Kal part. sing., fem. of מוֹשֵׁל — משל

מָשְׁלוּ id. pret. 3 pers. pl. — משל

מֹשְׁלוֹ[k] וּ id. part. act. sing. masc., suff. 3 pers. sing. masc. from מוֹשֵׁל dec. 7b; וּ bef. lab. — משל

מֶשְׁלוֹ[l] [m] וּ׳ n.m.s., suff. 3 p.s.m. fr. [מֶשֶׁל] d. 6c; וּ id. — משל

מֹשְׁלָיו[n] Kal part. pl., suff. 3 p.s.m. (§ 4. r. 1) fr. מוֹשֵׁל d. 7b — משל

מְשָׁלוֹ noun m. s., suff. 3 pers. s. m. fr. מָשָׁל d. 4a — משל

מִשִּׁלוֹ pref. מִ) pr. name of a place, see שִׁילֹה — שלה

מִשְׁלוֹחַ[o] וּ׳[p] noun masc. sing.; וּ bef. lab. — שלח

מִשָּׁלוֹם[q] pref. מִ) noun masc. sing. dec. 3a — שלם

מְשַׁלֵּחַ[r] וּ׳ Piel part. sing. masc. dec. 7b; וּ bef. lab. — שלח

מְשֻׁלָּח Pual part. sing. masc. — שלח

מִשְׁלַח noun masc. sing., constr. of [מִשְׁלָח] dec. 2b — שלח

מִשְּׁלֹחַ[s] pref. מִ) Kal inf. constr. — שלח

מִשְׁלַח[t] וּ defect. for מִשְׁלוֹחַ (q. v.) — שלח

מְשַׁלְּחֵי[u] / מְשַׁלְּחִים } Piel part. pl. masc. constr. and abs. from מְשַׁלֵּחַ dec. 7b — שלח

מְשַׁלֵּחֲךָ[y] id. sing., suff. 2 pers. sing. masc. (§ 16. r. 15) — שלח

מִשְׁלַחַת noun fem. sing. — שלח

מִשְׁלֵי noun masc. pl. constr. from מָשָׁל dec. 4a — משל

מֹשְׁלֵי[x] Kal part. pl. constr. masc. from מוֹשֵׁל d. 7b — משל

מַשְׁלִיחַ[a] Hiph. part. sing. masc. — שלח

מַשְׁלִיךְ Hiph. part. sing. masc. dec. 1b — שלך

מַשְׁלִיכֵי[b] id. pl., constr. st. — שלך

מְשָׁלִים noun masc. pl. of מָשָׁל dec. 4a — משל

מֹשְׁלִים Kal part. act. masc. pl. of מוֹשֵׁל dec. 7b — משל

מֻשְׁלָךְ[c] Hoph. part. sing. masc. (§ 11. rem. 10) — שלך

מֻשְׁלָכִים[d] id. pl., abs. st. — שלך

מֻשְׁלֶכֶת id. part. sing. fem. — שלך

מִשָּׁלָל[e] וּ pref. מִ) noun masc. s. d. 4a; וּ bef. lab. — שלל

מִשְּׁלַל[f] וּ׳ pref. id.) id., constr. st.; וּ id. — שלל

מְשַׁלֵּם וּ׳ Piel part. sing. masc. dec. 7b; וּ id. — שלם

מְשֻׁלָּם וּ׳ pr. name masc.; וּ id. — שלם

מִשְּׁלֹמֹה pref. מִ) pr. name masc. — שלם

מְשִׁלֵּמוֹת pr. name masc. — שלם

מְשַׁלְּמֵי[g] וּ Piel part. pl., constr. masc. from מְשַׁלֵּם dec. 7b; וּ bef. lab. — שלם

מְשֶׁלֶמְיָה / מְשֶׁלֶמְיָהוּ } pr. name masc. — שלם

מְשַׁלְּמִים[h] Piel part. masc., pl. of מְשַׁלֵּם dec. 7b — שלם

מְשִׁלֵּמִית pr. name masc. — שלם

מְשֻׁלֶּמֶת pr. name fem. — שלם

מִשֶּׁלָּנוּ[i] preff. שֶׁ & מִ (for מִן אֲשֶׁר)) pref. prep. לְ with suff. 1 pers. pl. (§ 5) — ל

מְשֻׁלָּשׁ[k] Pual part. sing. masc. — שלש

מְשֻׁלָּשׁוֹת[l] id. part. pl. fem. [prop. from מְשֻׁלָּשָׁה see מְשֻׁלֶּשֶׁת (§ 44. rem. 5) — שלש

מִשִּׁלְשֹׁם[m] pref. מִ) adv. — שלש

מְשֻׁלֶּשֶׁת[n] Pual part. s., fem. of מְשֻׁלָּשׁ, comp. מְשֻׁלָּשׁוֹת — שלש

מָשַׁלְתָּ[o] / מָשַׁלְתָּ[p] וּ } Kal pret. 2 pers. sing. masc.; acc. shifted by וּ, for וְ conv. (§ 8. rem. 7) — משל

מִשָּׁם וּ׳ pref. מִ) adv.; וּ bef. lab. — שם

מִשְּׂמֹאול[q] / מִשְּׂמֹאל } pref. id.) noun masc. sing. dec. 1a — שמאל

מִשְּׂמֹאלוֹ[r] וּ׳ pref. id.) id., suff. 3 p. s. m.; וּ bef. lab. — שמאל

מַשְׂמְאִלִים[s] וּ Hiph. part. pl. m. [for מַשְׂמְאִילִים]; וּ id. — שמאל

מִשְּׂמֹאלָם[t] וּ pref. מִ) noun masc. sing., suff. 3 pers. pl. masc. from שְׂמֹאל dec. 1a; וּ id. — שמאל

מְשַׁמָּה וּ noun fem. sing. dec. 10; וּ id. — שמם

מִשֻּׂמוֹ[u] pref. מִ) Kal inf. constr. (שׂוּם), suff. 3 pers. sing. masc. dec. 1a — שום

מִשְׁמוֹעַ in full for מִשְׁמַע (q. v.) — שמע

מִשְּׁמוּעָה[x] pref. מִ) noun fem. sing. dec. 10 — שמע

[a] Pr. 26. 7, 9. [b] Da. 11. 4, 5. [c] 1 Sa. 24. 14. [d] Ju. 8. 22. [e] Pr. 31. 21. [f] La. 4. 7. [g] Ps. 51. 9. [h] Ps. 103. 19. [i] Is. 40. 10. [k] Je. 30. 21. [l] Job 41. 25. [m] Zec. 9. 10. [n] Is. 52. 5. [o] Is. 11. 14. [p] Est. 9. 22. [q] La. 3. 17. [r] Pr. 6. 19. [s] 1 Sa. 26. 11. [t] Est. 9. 19. [u] Is. 32. 20. [x] 1 Sa. 6. 3. [y] Je. 28. 16. [z] Is. 28. 14. [a] Ex. 8. 17. [b] Is. 19. 8. [c] 2 Sa. 20. 21. [d] Je. 14. 16. [e] 1 Sa. 30. 19. [f] 2 Sa. 8. 12. [g] Ps. 38. 21. [h] Joel 4. 4. [i] 2 Ki. 6. 11. [k] Ge. 15. 9. [l] Eze. 42. 6. [m] Ex. 4. 10. [n] Ge. 15. 9. [o] Is. 63. 19. [p] De. 15. 6. [q] 2 Ch. 4. 6, 7, 8. [r] 1 Ki. 7. 39. [s] 1 Ch. 12. 2. [t] Ex. 14. 22, 29. [u] Nu. 24. 23. [x] Ps. 112. 7.

מְשַׁמּוֹת[a]	noun fem. pl. of מְשַׁמָּה dec. 10	שמם
מְשַׂמְּחֵי[b]	Piel part. pl. constr. masc. from מְשַׂמֵּחַ d. 7b	שמח
מִשְּׁמֵי[c]	pref. ·מִ)(noun masc. pl., constr. of שָׁמַיִם [from שָׁמַי § 38. rem. 2]	שמה
מַשְׁמִים[d]	Hiph. part. sing. masc.	שמם
מִשָּׁמַיִם / מִשָּׁמָיִם	pref. ·מִ)(noun masc. pl. [of שָׁמַי § 38. rem. 2]	שמה
מַשְׁמִיעַ[e]	ו׳ Hiph. part. sing. masc. dec. 1b; וּ bef. lab.	שמע
מַשְׁמִיעִים[f]	id. pl., abs. st.	שמע
מִשִּׁמְךָ[g] / מִשִּׁמְךְ[h]	pref. ·מִ)(noun masc. sing., suff. 2 pers. sing. masc. from שֵׁם dec. 7a	שם
מְשֹׁמֵם	defect. for מְשׁוֹמֵם (q. v.)	שמם
מִשֶּׁמֶן / ו׳ מִשָּׁמֶן[i]	pref. ·מִ)(noun masc. sing. dec. 6a (§ 35. rem. 2); וּ bef. lab.	שמן
מִשְׁמַן[k]	וּ noun masc. sing., constr. of [מִשְׁמָן] dec. 8a (pl. c. מִשְׁמַנֵּי); וּ id.	שמן
מִשַּׁמְנָהּ	וּ pref. ·מִ)(noun masc. sing., suff. 3 pers. sing. fem. from שֶׁמֶן dec. 6a; וּ id.	שמן
מִשְׁמַנָּה	pr. name masc.	שמן
מִשְּׁמַנֵּי[l]	ו׳ pref. מִ [for מִמִּשְׁמַנֵּי])(noun m. pl. constr. fr. [מִשְׁמָן] dec. 8a (§ 37. No. 3 c); וּ bef. lab.	שמן
מַשְׁמַנִּים[m]	noun masc. pl. of [מִשְׁמָן] dec. 8a	שמן
מִשְׁמָע	ו׳ pr. name masc.; וּ bef. lab.	שמע
מִשְּׁמֹעַ	pref. ·מִ)(Kal inf. constr.	שמע
מִשִּׁמְעוֹן	וּ pref. id.)(pr. name of a tribe; וּ bef. lab.	שמע
מַשְׁמִעִים[n]	defect. for מַשְׁמִיעִים (q. v.)	שמע
מִשְׁמַעְתּוֹ	noun f. s., suff. 3 p. s. m. fr. [מִשְׁמַעַת] d. 13a	שמע
מִשְׁמַעְתֶּךָ[o]	id., suff. 2 pers. sing. masc. [for ־תְּךָ]	שמע
מִשְׁמַעְתָּם[p]	id., suff. 3 pers. pl. masc.	שמע
מִשְׁמָר	noun masc. sing. dec. 2b	שמר
מִשָּׁמְרוֹ[q]	וּ pref. ·מִ)(Kal inf., suff. 3 p. s. m.; וּ bef. lab.	שמר
מִשֹּׁמְרוֹן	ו׳ pref. id.)(pr. name of a country; וּ id.	שמר
מִשְׁמָרוֹת	noun fem., pl. abs. from מִשְׁמֶרֶת (§ 44. r. 5)	שמר
מִשְׁמְרוֹת[r]	id. pl., constr. st.	שמר
מִשְׁמְרוֹתָם	id. pl., suff. 3 pers. pl. masc. (§ 4. rem. 2)	שמר
מִשֹּׁמְרֵי	pref. ·מִ)(Kal part. act. pl. constr. masc. from שֹׁמֵר dec. 7b	שמר
מְשַׁמְּרִים[s]	Piel part. masc. pl. of [מְשַׁמֵּר] dec. 7b	שמר
מִשֹּׁמְרִים[t]	pref. ·מִ)(noun masc. pl. of שֹׁמֵר dec. 7b	שמר
מִשְׁמַרְכֶם[u]	noun masc. sing., suff. 2 pers. pl. masc.	שמר
מִשְׁמֶרֶת	ו׳ noun f. s. d. 13a, comp. מִשְׁמָרוֹת; וּ bef. lab.	שמר
מִשְׁמַרְתּוֹ	id., suff. 3 pers. sing. masc.	שמר
מִשְׁמַרְתִּי	id., suff. 1 pers. sing.	שמר
מִשְׁמַרְתֶּךָ[v]	id., suff. 2 pers. sing. masc.	שמר
מִשְׁמַרְתָּם	וּ id., suff. 3 pers. pl. masc.; וּ bef. lab.	שמר
מִשְּׁמֹתָם[w]	pref. ·מִ)(noun masc. with pl. fem. term. and suff. 3 pers. pl. m. (§ 4. r. 2) from שֵׁם d. 7a	שם

מְשַׂנְאַי[z]	ו׳ Piel part. pl. masc., suff. 1 pers. sing. [fr. מְשַׂנֵּא § 10. rem. 7] dec. 7b; וּ bef. lab.	שנא
מְשַׂנְאֵי[a]	id. pl., constr. st.	שנא
מְשַׂנְאִי	id. sing. with suff. 1 pers. sing.	שנא
מִשֹּׂנְאַי[b] / ו׳ מִשֹּׂנְאַי[c]	pref. ·מִ)(Kal part. act. pl., suff. 1 pers. sing. from שֹׂנֵא dec. 7b; וּ bef. lab.	שנא
מְשַׂנְאָיו[d]	ו׳ Piel part. pl. masc., suff. 3 pers. sing. masc. [from מְשַׂנֵּא § 10. rem. 7] dec. 7b; וּ id.	שנא
מְשַׂנְאֶיךָ[e]	ו׳ id. pl., suff. 2 pers. pl. masc.; וּ id.	שנא
מְשַׂנְאֵינוּ[f]	וּ id. pl., suff. 1 pers. pl.; וּ id.	שנא
מִשִּׂנְאָתוֹ[g]	וּ pref. ·מִ)(noun fem. sing., suff. 3 pers. sing. masc. from שִׂנְאָה (no pl.); וּ id.	שנא
מִשִּׂנְאָתְךָ[h]	id. sing. (§ 4. r. 3), suff. 2 pers. sing. masc.	שנא
מְשַׁנֶּה[i]	Piel part. sing. masc.	שנה
מִשְׁנֶה	ו׳ noun masc. sing. dec. 9a; וּ bef. lab.	שנה
מִשְׁנֵה	id., constr. st.	שנה
מִשְׁנֵהוּ[k]	ו׳ id. with suff. 3 pers. sing. masc.; וּ bef. lab.	שנה
מִשְּׁנֵי	pref. ·מִ)(num. card. masc., constr. of שְׁנַיִם	שנה
מְשַׁנְּיָה[l]	Chald. Pael part. sing. fem. [of מְשַׁנֵּא]	שנה
מִשְּׁנֵיהֶם	pref. ·מִ)(num. card. masc. (שְׁנַיִם) with suff. 3 pers. pl. masc.	שנה
מִשִּׁנָּיו[m]	וּ pref. id.)(noun com. du., suff. 3 pers. sing. masc. from שֵׁן dec. 2b; וּ bef. lab.	שנן
מִשְׁנִים[n]	noun masc., pl. of מִשְׁנֶה dec. 9a	שנה
מִשְּׂנִיר	pref. ·מִ)(pr. name of a mount, see שְׂנִיר	
מִשִּׁנְעָר	וּ pref. id.)(pr. name of a country, see שִׁנְעָר; וּ bef. lab.	
מִשְּׁנַת	pref. ·מִ)(noun fem. sing., constr. of שָׁנָה d. 11a	שנה
מִשְּׁנָתוֹ	pref. id.)(noun fem. s., constr. of שֵׁנָה d. 11b	ישן
מִשְּׁנָתֶךָ[o]	pref. id.)(id., suff. 2 pers. sing. m. [for שְׁנָתְךָ]	ישן
מִשְּׁנָתָם[p]	pref. id.)(id., suff. 3 pers. pl. masc.	ישן
מְשִׁסָּה[q]	noun fem. sing. dec. 10	שסס

מָשַׁע Root not used; Arab. *to cleanse*.

מֶשִׁי masc. *a cleansing*, with pref. לְ adv. *clean*, Eze. 16. 4.

מִשְׁעָם (*cleansing*) pr. name masc. 1 Ch. 8. 12.

מֹשִׁעִי[r]	Hiph. part. sing. masc., suff. 1 pers. sing. [for מוֹשִׁיעִי] from מוֹשִׁיעַ dec. 1b	ישע
מִשְּׂעִיר	pref. ·מִ)(pr. name of a country	שער
מִשְׁעָם	וּ pr. name masc.; וּ bef. lab.	משע
מִשְׁעָן[s]	noun masc. sing.	שען
מַשְׁעֵן[t]	noun masc. sing. dec. 2a	שען
מִשְׁעַן[u]	id., constr. st.	שען
מַשְׁעֵנָה[v]	וּ noun fem. sing.; וּ bef. lab.	שען
מִשְׁעֶנֶת	noun fem. sing. dec. 13a	שען
מִשְׁעַנְתּוֹ	id., suff. 3 pers. sing. masc.	שען

a Is. 15. 6. b Ps. 19. 9. c Ps. 20. 7. d Eze. 3. 15. e Je. 4. 15. f 1 Ch. 15. 16. g 1 Ki. 1. 47. h Na. 1. 14. i Ex. 29. 21. k Is. 17. 4. l Ge. 27. 28, 39. m Ne. 8. 10. n 1 Ch. 15. 28. o 1 Sa. 22. 14. p Is. 11. 14. q De. 7. 8. r Ne. 7. 3. s Jon. 2. 9. t Ps. 130. 6. u Ge. 42. 19. v Nu. 18. 3. w Ex. 28. 10. z Ps. 18. 41. a Ps. 81. 16. b Ps. 9. 14. c Ps. 18. 18. d Ps. 68. 2. e Ps. 83. 3. f Ps. 44. 8, 11. g De. 9. 28. h Eze. 35. 11. i Job 14. 20. k 1 Sa. 8. 2. l Da. 7. 7. m Job 29. 17. n Ezr. 1. 10. o Pr. 6. 9. p Job 14. 12. q Is. 42. 22. r 2 Sa. 22. 3. s Is. 3. 1. t 2 Sa. 22. 19. u Is. 3. 1. v Is. 3. 1.

מִשְׁעַנְתִּי[a] id., suff. 1 pers. sing. . . . . שׁען

מִשְׁעַנְתֶּךָ[b] וּ id., suff. 2 pers. sing. m. [for ־תֵּךְ]; וּ bef. lab. . שׁען

מִשַּׁעַר [c] 'וּ pref. ·מִ)(noun fem. sing. dec. 6d; וּ id. שׁער

מִשְּׂעַר[d] pref. id.)(noun m. sing. constr. of שֵׂעָר d. 4d שׂער

מִשַּׂעֲרוֹת pref. id.)(noun fem. pl. constr. from שַׂעֲרָה (no pl. abs.) . . . . . שׂער

מִשַּׁעֲרֵי[e] pref. id.)(noun fem. pl. constr. of שַׁעַר d. 6d שׁער

מִשַּׂעֲרַת pref. id.)(n. f. s., constr. of שַׂעֲרָה (no pl. abs.) שׂער

מִשַּׂעֲרָתוֹ[f] pref. id.)(id., suff. 3 pers. sing. masc. . שׂער

מִשְׂפָּח[g] noun masc. sing. . . . . . שׂפח

מִשְׁפָּחָה [h] 'וּ noun fem. sing., constr. מִשְׁפַּחַת dec. 11 & 13 (§ 42. rem. 5); וּ bef. lab. . שׁפח

מִשְׁפָּחוֹת [i] 'וּ id. pl., abs. st.; וּ id. . . . שׁפח

מִשְׁפְּחוֹת [k] 'וּ id. pl., constr. st.; וּ id. . . . שׁפח

מִשְׁפְּחוֹתֶיהָ[l] id. pl., suff. 3 pers. sing. fem. . . שׁפח

מִשְׁפָּחֹת[m] id. pl., abs. st. . . . . . שׁפח

מִשְׁפַּחַת [n] 'וּ id. sing., constr. st.; וּ bef. lab. . שׁפח

מִשְׁפְּחֹת [o] 'וּ id. pl., constr. st.; וּ id. . . . שׁפח

מִשְׁפַּחְתּוֹ id. sing., suff. 3 pers. sing. masc. . שׁפח

מִשְׁפַּחְתִּי[p] [q] 'וּ id. sing., suff. 1 pers. sing.; וּ bef. lab. שׁפח

מִשְׁפַּחְתָּם[r] id. sing., suff. 3 pers. pl. masc. . . שׁפח

מִשְׁפְּחֹתָם[s] id. pl., suff. 3 pers. pl. masc. (§ 4. rem. 2) שׁפח

מִשְׁפָּט 'וּ noun masc. sing. dec. 2b; וּ bef. lab. . שׁפט

מִשְׁפַּט 'וּ id., constr. st.; וּ id. . . . . שׁפט

מִשְׁפָּטָהּ[t] id., suff. 3 pers. sing. fem. . . . שׁפט

מִשְׁפָּטָו id. pl., suff. 3 pers. sing. masc. (§ 4. rem. 1) שׁפט

מִשְׁפָּטוֹ id. sing., suff. 3 pers. sing. masc. . . שׁפט

מִשְׁפָּטַי 'וּ id. pl., suff. 1 pers. sing.; וּ bef. lab. . שׁפט

מִשְׁפָּטִי [u] 'וּ id. sing., suff. 1 pers. sing.; וּ id. . שׁפט

מִשֹּׁפְטִי[x] pref. ·מִ)(Kal part. act. sing. masc. (שׁוֹפֵט), suff. 1 pers. sing. dec. 7b . . . שׁפט

מִשְׁפְּטֵי 'וּ n. m. pl. constr. fr. מִשְׁפָּט d. 2b; וּ bef. lab. שׁפט

מִשֹּׁפְטֵי[y] pref. ·מִ)(Kal part. act. pl. constr. masc. from שׁוֹפֵט dec. 7b . . . . שׁפט

מִשְׁפְּטֵיהֶם[z] noun masc. pl., suff. 3 pers. pl. masc. from מִשְׁפָּט dec. 2b . . . . . שׁפט

מִשְׁפָּטָיו 'וּ id. pl., suff. 3 pers. sing. masc.; וּ bef. lab. שׁפט

מִשְׁפָּטֶיךָ [a] 'וּ id. pl., suff. 2 pers. sing. masc.; וּ id. . שׁפט

מִשְׁפָּטַיִךְ[b] id. pl., suff. 2 pers. sing. fem. . . שׁפט

מִשְׁפָּטִים 'וּ id. pl., abs. st.; וּ bef. lab. . . שׁפט

מִשְׁפָּטֶךָ[c] 'וּ id. s., suff. 2 p. s. mas. [for מִשְׁפָּטְךָ]; וּ id. שׁפט

מִשְׁפָּטָם id. sing., suff. 3 pers. pl. masc. . . שׁפט

מִשְׁפָּטָן[d] id. sing., suff. 3 pers. pl. fem. . . שׁפט

מַשְׁפִּיל Heb. & Chald. def. Da. 5. 19. Hiph. part. s. m. שׁפל

מִשְׁפָם pref. ·מִ)(pr. name of a place . . שׁפה

מִשִּׁפְעַת[e] pref. id.)(n. f. s. constr. [of שִׁפְעָה, no pl.] שׁפע

מִשְּׂפַת[f] pref. ·מִ)(noun f. s., constr. of שָׂפָה d. 11a שׂפה

מִשְּׂפָתוֹ pref. id.)(id., suff. 3 pers. sing. masc. . שׂפה

מֶשֶׁק

masc. i. q. מֶשֶׁךְ *possession*, Ge. 15. 2, בֶּן־מֶ׳ *son possession, possessor*. R. מָשַׁק i. q. מָשַׁךְ.

מִמְשָׁק masc. dec. 2 b, *possession*, Zep. 2. 9. Le *overspreading*.

מְשֻׁקָּדִים Pual part. masc. pl. [of מְשֻׁקָּד] . . שׁקד

מַשְׁקֶה [g] 'וּ Hiph. part. or subst. m. d. 9 a; וּ bef. lab. שׁקה

מַשְׁקֵה id., constr. st. . . . . . שׁקה

מַשְׁקֵהוּ[h] id., suff. 3 pers. sing. masc. . . . שׁקה

מַשְׁקָיו וּ id. (subst.) pl., suff. 3 p. s. m.; וּ bef. lab. שׁקה

מִשְׁקָל [i] 'וּ noun masc. sing. dec. 2 b; וּ id. . שׁקל

מִשְׁקַל 'וּ id., constr. st.; וּ id. . . . . שׁקל

מִשְׁקָלָהּ [k] 'וּ id., suff. 3 pers. sing. masc.; וּ id. . שׁקל

מִשְׁקָלוֹ id., suff. 3 pers. sing. masc. . . . שׁקל

מִשְׁקָלָם[l] id., suff. 3 pers. pl. masc. . . . שׁקל

מִשְׁקֹלֶת[m] noun fem. sing. . . . . . . שׁקל

מִשְׁקַע[n] וּ noun masc. sing., constr. of [מִשְׁקָע] dec. 2 b; וּ bef. lab. . . . . . שׁקע

מְשַׂקְּרוֹת[o] וּ Piel part. fem. pl. [of מְשַׂקֶּרֶת dec. 13, from מְשַׂקֵּר masc.]; וּ id. . . . שׂקר

מֶשֶׁר

Root not used, Arab. *to divide*.

מְשׂוּרָה fem. *measure* for liquids. Others, deriv it from שׂוּר *to divide, saw*.

מִשָּׂר[p] pref. ·מִ)(noun masc. sing. d. 8 (§ 37. r. 7) שׂרר

מְשָׁרֵא[q] וּ Ch. Pa. part. sing. masc.; וּ bef. lab. . שׁרא

מַשְׁרוֹקִיתָא[r] Ch. noun f. s., emph. of [מַשְׁרוֹקִי] d. 8 b שׁרק

מִשָּׂרֵי pref. ·מִ)(noun masc. pl. constr. [for שָׂרֵי] from שַׂר dec. 8 e (§ 37. rem. 7) . שׂרר

מִשָּׂרִיד pref. id.)(pr. name of a place . . שׂרד

מְשָׁרִים[s] וּ defect. for מֵישָׁרִים (q. v.) . . . ישׁר

מַשְׁרִישׁ[t] Hiph. part. sing. masc. . . . . שׁרשׁ

מְשָׂרֶכֶת[u] Piel part. sing. [from מְשָׂרֵךְ masc.] . שׂרך

[מִשְׁרָעִי] gent. noun from an unknown town מִשְׁרָע 1 Ch. 2. 53.

מִשְּׂרֵפָה[x] pref. ·מִ)(noun fem. sing. dec. 10 . שׂרף

מִשְׂרְפוֹת noun fem. pl. constr. fr. [מִשְׂרָפָה] dec. 11a, also pr. name in compos. מִ׳ מַיִם . שׂרף

מְשֹׁרְרוֹת וּ Pilel part. fem. pl. [of מְשׁוֹרֶרֶת] dec. 10, fr. מְשׁוֹרֵר masc.; וּ bef. lab. . . שׁיר

מְשֹׁרְרִים id. part. masc. pl. of מְשׁוֹרֵר dec. 7 b שׁיר

מִשֹּׁרֶשׁ pref. ·מִ)(noun masc. sing. dec. 6 c . שׁרשׁ

מִשָּׁרָשֶׁיהָ[y] pref. id.)(id. pl., suff. 3 pers. s. f. (§ 35. r. 9) שׁרשׁ

מִשָּׁרָשָׁיו[z] pref. id.)(id. pl., suff. 3 pers. sing. masc. שׁרשׁ

[a] 2 Ki. 4. 29. [b] Ps. 23. 4. [c] Ru. 4. 10. [d] Ezr. 9. 3. [e] Ps. 9. 14. [f] 1 Ki. 1. 52. [g] Is. 5. 7. [h] Est. 9. 28. [i] Na. 3. 4. [k] 1 Ch. 2. 53, 55. [l] Jos. 6. 23. [m] Zec. 12. 12, 14. [n] Nu. 3. 21, 27, 33. [o] 1 Ch. 4. 8, 21. [p] Ge. 24. 38, 41. [q] 1 Sa. 9. 21. [r] 1 Ch. 4. 27. [s] Nu. 1. 18. [t] Je. 51. 9. [u] Is. 51. 4. [x] Job 23. 7. [y] Ps. 109. 31. [z] Eze. 20. 18. [a] Ps. 119. 108, etc. [b] Zep. 3. 15. [c] 1 Ki. 20. 40. [d] Nu. 27. 5. [e] Eze. 26. 10. [f] Ps. 120. 2. [g] Is. 32. 6. [h] Ge. 40. 13, 21. [i] Nu. 7. 13, 19, &c. [k] 2 Sa. 12. 30. [l] Ge. 24. 22. [m] 2 Ki. 21. 13. [n] Eze. 34. 18. [o] Is. 3. 16. [p] Da. 1. 8. [q] Da. 5. 12. [r] Da. 3. 5, 7, 10, 15. [s] Pr. 1. 3. [t] Job 5. 3. [u] Je. 2. 23. [x] Am. 4. 11. [y] Eze. 17. 9. [z] Is. 11. 1.

[מַשְׂרֵת] m. *frying-pan*, 2 Sa. 13. 3. Etymology doubtful.

מְשָׁרֵת Piel part. sing. masc. dec. 7 b . . . שרת

מְשָׁרַ֫תְ [a] id. fem. [for מְשָׁרֶ֫תֶת] . . . שרת

מִשְׁרַת [b] noun fem. sing., constr. of [מִשְׁרָה] dec. 10 שרה

מְשָׁרְתוֹ [c] וּ Piel part. sing. masc. (מְשָׁרֵת), suff. 3 pers. sing. masc. dec. 7 b; וּ bef. lab. . שרת

מְשָׁרְתַי [d] id. pl., suff. 1 pers. sing. for תַי' . . שרת

מְשָׁרְתֵי id. pl., abs. st. . . . . . שרת

מְשָׁרְתָיו id. pl., suff. 3 pers. sing. masc. . . שרת

מְשָׁרְתִים [e] וּ id. pl., abs. st.; וּ bef. lab. . . שרת

[מָשַׁשׁ] *to touch, feel*, Ge. 27. 12, 22. Pi. I. *to feel, examine by feeling*.—II. *to feel one's way, grope*. Hiph. *to grope*, with acc. Ex. 10. 21.

מִשַּׁשְׁתָּ [f] Piel pret. 2 pers. sing. masc. . . . משש

מִשְׁתָּאֵה [g] Hithpa. part. s. m. [for מִתְשָׁאֵה § 12. r. 3] שאה

מִשְׁתַּבְּשִׁין [h] Chald. Ithpa. part. masc. pl. [of מִשְׁתַּבַּשׁ for מִתְשַׁבַּשׁ § 12. rem. 3] dec. 2 b . שבש

מִשְׁתַּגֵּעַ [i] Hithpa. part. sing. masc. [for מִתְשַׁגֵּעַ v. id.] שגע

מִשֶּׁתִּדּוֹר [k] preff. מִ· & שֶׁ·) Kal fut. 2 pers. sing. masc. נדר

מִשְׁתַּדַּר [l] Ch. Ithpa. part. s. m. [for מִתְשַׁדַּר § 12. r. 3] שדר

מִשְׁתֶּה וּ noun masc. sing. dec. 9 a; וּ bef. lab. . שתה

מִשְׁתֵּה id., constr. st. . . . . . . שתה

מִשְּׁתוֹ [m] pref. מִ·) for שְׂאֵתוֹ, noun fem. sing., suff. 3 pers. sing. m. fr. שְׂאֵת (§ 39. No. 4. r. 2) נשא

מִשְׁתּוֹלֵל [n] Hithpoel part. s. m. [for מִתְשׁוֹלֵל § 12. r. 3] שלל

מִשְׁתַּחֲוֶה [o] וּ [for מִתְשׁ' § 12. r. 3] Hithpal. (3rd rad. ה doubled, for חֲוֶהֶ) part. s. m. d. 9 a; וּ bef. lab. שחה

מִשְׁתַּחֲוִים וּ id. pl., abs. st.; וּ id. . . . שחה

מִשְׁתַּחֲוִיתֶם [p] prob. an error for מִשְׁתַּחֲוִים, as some MSS. read . . . . שחה

מַ֫שְׁתִּי [q] וּ Kal pret. 1 pers. sing.; acc. shifted by וּ, for וְ, conv. (comp. § 8. rem. 7) מוש

מִשְּׁתֵּי [r] pref. מִ·) num. card. fem., constr. of שְׁתַּיִם, from שְׁנַיִם masc. . . . . . שנה

מִשְׁתְּיָא [s] Chald. noun masc. s., emph. of [מִשְׁתֵּי] d. 6 b שתה

מִשְׁתֵּיהֶם pref. מִ·) noun masc. pl. or sing. (§ 38. rem. 1), suff. 3 pers. s. m. fr. מִשְׁתֶּה d. 9 a שתה

מִשְׁתָּיו [t] pref. id.) id., suff. 3 pers. sing. masc. . שתה

מִשְׁתֵּיכֶם [u] pref. id.) id., suff. 2 pers. pl. masc. . שתה

מִשְּׁתַּיִם [x] pref. id.) num. card. fem., constr. of שְׁתַּיִם שנה

מַשְׁתִּין Hiph. part. sing. masc. . . . . . שתן

מִשְׁתַּכַּל [y] Ch. Ithpa. part. s. m. [for מִתְשַׂכַּל § 12. r. 3] שכל

מִשְׁתַּכֵּר [z] Hithpa. part. sing. masc. [for מִתְשַׁכֵּר v. id.] שכר

מִשְׁתָּרַיִן [a] Chald. Ithpa. part. masc. pl. [of מִשְׁתָּרֵא for מִתְשָׁרֵא § 12. rem. 3] dec. 6 a . שרא

מֵת וְ', וּ' Kal pret. 3 pers. sing. masc.; or part. (§ 21. rem. 2); וּ bef. lab., for וְ see lett. ו מות

מֻת [b] וּ, [c] וְ' id. imp. s. m. (§ 21. r. 5); preff. id. מות

מְתָאֵב [d] Piel part. sing. masc. . . . . תאב

מִתְאַבֵּל Hithpa. part. sing. masc. dec. 7 b . . אבל

מִתְאַבְּלִים [e] id. pl., abs. st. . . . . . אבל

מִתְאַבֶּלֶת [f] id. part. sing. fem. . . . . אבל

מִתְאַוָּה [g] Hithpa. part. sing. fem. [of מִתְאַוֶּה] . אוה

מִתַּאֲוָתָם [h] pref. מִ·) noun fem. sing., suff. 3 pers. pl. masc. from תַּאֲוָה dec. 10 . . . אוה

מַתְאִימוֹת Hiph. part. f. pl. [of מַתְאִימָה, fr. מַתְאִים m.] תאם

מִתְאַמֶּצֶת Hithpa. part. sing. fem. [of מִתְאַמֵּץ] . אמץ

מִתְאַנֶּה [k] Hithpa. part. sing. masc. . . . אנה

מִתַּאֲנָה [l] pref. מִ·) noun fem. sing. dec. 10 . . תאן

מִתְבָּהַל [m] Ithpa. part. sing. masc. (§ 49. rem. 3) . בהל

מִתְּבוּאַת [n] pref. מִ·) noun f. s., constr. of תְּבוּאָה d. 10 בוא

מִתְּבוּאֹתֵיכֶם [o] pref. id.) id. pl., suff. 2 pers. pl. masc. בוא

מִתְבּוֹסֶסֶת [p] Hithpal. part. sing. masc. . . . בוס

מִתֵּבֵל [q] וּ pref. מִ·) noun fem. sing.; וּ bef. lab. . יבל

מַתְבֵּן [r] noun masc. sing. . . . . . . תבן

מִתְבְּנֵא [s] Chald. Ithpe. part. sing. masc. R. בְּנָא see בנה

מֶתֶג masc. dec. 6 a (with suff. מִתְגִּי) *a bridle*.

מִתְגֹּדְדִים [t] וּ Hithpoel part. masc. pl. [of מִתְגֹּדֵד] dec. 7 b; וּ bef. lab. . . . . . נדד

מִתְגּוֹרֵר [u] Hithpalel part. sing. masc. . . . גור

מִתְגּוֹרֵר [x] Hithpoel part. sing. masc. . . . גרר

מִתְגִּי וּ noun masc. sing., suff. 1 pers. sing. from מֶתֶג dec. 6 a; וּ bef. lab. . . . מתג

מִתְגֹּלֵל [y] Hithpoel part. sing. masc. . . . גלל

מִתִּגְרַת [z] pref. מִ·) noun f. s., constr. of [תִּגְרָה] d. 10 גרה

מִתְדַּפְּקִים [a] Hithpa. part. masc. pl. [of מִתְדַּפֵּק] dec. 7 b דפק

מָתָה Root not used; Arab. מתי, מתא, *to extend*; cogn. מָתַח.

מַת masc. *man* (prop. *adult*); only pl. מְתִים, constr. מְתֵי (§ 36. rem. 5) *men*; מְתֵי מִסְפָּר *men of number*, i. e. that can be numbered, *a few*; מְ' אֹהֶל *men of tent*, i. e. *domestics*; others, *tent-companions*.

מְתוּשָׁאֵל (*man of God*; מְתוּ-שַׁ-אֵל) pr. name of one of the descendants of Cain.

מְתוּשֶׁלַח (*man of dart*) pr. name of the son of Enoch.

מָתַי adv. *when?* Also without interrog. Pr. 23.

---

a 1 Ki. 1. 15. b Nu. 6. 3. c Ex. 33. 11. d Je. 33. 21. e Eze. 44. 11. f Ge. 31. 37. g Ge. 24. 21. h Da. 5. 9. i 1 Sa. 21. 15. k Ec. 5. 4. l Da. 6. 15. m Job 41. 17. n Is. 59. 15. o Est. 3. 5. p Eze. 8. 16. q Zec. 3. 9. r Ju. 16. 28. s Da. 5. 10. t Da. 1. 5, 8. u Da. 1. 10. x Jon. 4. 11. y Da. 7. 8. z Hag. 1. 6. a Da. 5. 6. b De. 32. 50. c Job 2. 9. d Am. 6. 8. e 2 Ch. 35. 24. f 2 Sa. 14. 2. g Pr. 13. 4. h Ps. 78. 30. i Ru. 1. 18. k 2 Ki. 5. 7. l Is. 34. 4. m Da. 5. 9. n Jos. 5. 12. o Je. 12. 13. p Eze. 16. 6, 22. q Job 18. 18. r Is. 25. 10. s Ezr. 5. 8, 16. t Je. 41. 5. u 1 Ki. 17. 20. x Je. 30. 23. y 2 Sa. 20. 12. z Ps. 39. 11. a Ju. 19. 22.

35; עַד מָתַי, לְמָתַי *how long?* אַחֲרֵי־מָתַי *after how long?*

מְתֹם perh. adv. *all, every one*, Ju. 20. 48; comp. the forms שִׁלְשֹׁם, פִּתְאֹם.

וְ מַתָּה[a] Kal pret. 2 pers. sing. masc. [for מַתְּתָּה, מַתְתָּ § 25. r.]; וָ bef. dist. acc. for וְ conv. — מות

מֵתָה[b] וָ, וָ׳[c] Kal pret. 3 pers. s. f. (§ 21. r. 2); וָ id. — מות

מֵתָה[d] id. part. sing. fem. of מֵת masc. — מות

מִתְּהוֹם[e] וּ pref. מִ) noun com. sing. d. 1a; וּ bef. lab. — הום

מִתְּהוֹמוֹת[f] וּ pref. id.) id. pl. fem.; וּ id. — הום

מִתְהַלֵּךְ Hithpa. part. sing. masc. dec. 7b — הלך

מִתְהַלֶּכֶת[g] id. part. sing. fem. — הלך

מִתְהַלֵּל[h] Hithpa. part. sing. masc. dec. 7b — הלל

מִתְהַפֵּךְ Hithpa. part. sing. masc. — הפך

מֵתוֹ[i] Kal part. sing. masc. (מֵת § 21. rem. 2), suff. 3 pers. sing. masc. dec. 1a (§ 30. No. 3) — מות

מֵתוּ וּ׳, וָ׳, וְ id. pret. 3 pers. pl.; וּ bef. lab., & וָ bef. pause & dist. acc., for וְ, conv. — מות

מֹתוֹ[k] defect. for מוֹתוֹ (q. v.) — מות

מִתּוּגָה[l] pref. מִ) noun fem. sing. dec. 10 — יגה

מִתְוַדֶּה וּ Hithpa. (§ 20. No. 1) part. sing. masc. dec. 9a; וּ bef. lab. — ידה

מִתְוַדִּים[m] וּ׳[n] id. pl., abs. st.; וּ id. — ידה

מִתֹּךְ[o] pref. מִ) noun masc. sing. for תֹּךְ — תכך

מִתּוֹךְ pref. id.) noun masc. sing., constr. of תָּוֶךְ dec. 6g (as a *prep.*) — תוך

מִתּוֹכָהּ וּ׳[p] pref. id.) id., suff. 3 p. s. f.; וּ bef. lab. — תוך

מִתּוֹכֵךְ pref. id.) id., suff. 2 pers. sing. masc. — תוך

מִתּוֹכְכֶם[q] pref. id.) id., suff. 2 pers. pl. masc. — תוך

מִתּוֹכָם pref. id.) id., suff. 3 pers. pl. masc. — תוך

מָתוֹק וּ׳ adj. masc. sing.; וּ bef. lab. — מתק

מְתוּקָה[r] id. fem. (§ 39. No. 3. rem. 1) — מתק

מְתוּקִים[s] וּ id. pl. masc. (§ 32. rem. 5); וּ bef. lab. — מתק

מִתּוּר[t] pref. מִ) Kal inf. constr. — תור

מִתּוֹרָתֶךָ[u], מִתּוֹרָתְךָ[x] וּ׳[w] } pref. id.) noun fem. sing., suff. 2 pers. sing. m. fr. תּוֹרָה d. 10; וּ bef. lab. — ורה

מְתוּשָׁאֵל וּ׳, מְתוּשֶׁלַח & מְתוּשָׁאֵל pr. names masc. — מתה

מִתַּזְנוּתַיִךְ[y] pref. מִ) Kh. תֵּךְ׳, K. תַיִךְ׳, noun fem. sing. or pl., suff. 2 pers. sing. f. fr. תַּזְנוּת d. 1b. — זנה

[מָתַח] *to stretch out*, Is. 40. 22.

אַמְתַּחַת fem., with suff. אַמְתַּחְתִּי׳ (dec. 13a) *a sack* or *bag*.

מִתְחַבֵּא Hithpa. part. sing. masc. dec. 7b — חבא

מִתְחַבְּאִים[a] id. pl., abs. st. — חבא

מִתְחוֹלֵל Hithpal. part. sing. masc. — חול

מִתְחַזֵּק Hithpa. part. sing. masc. dec. 7b — חזק

מִתְּחִלַּת[b] pref. מִ) noun f. sing., constr. of תְּחִלָּה d. 10 — חלל

מִתְחַנַּן[c] וּ Ch. Ithpa. part. s. m.; וּ bef. lab. — חנן

מִתְּחִנָּתִי[d] pref. מִ) noun f. sing., constr. of תְּחִנָּה d. 10 — חנן

מִתְחָרֶה[e] Tiphal part. sing. masc. (§ 6. No. 5) — חרה

מִתַּחַת[f], מִתַּחַת וּ׳ } pref. id.) adv. (see the foll.), also pr. name; וּ bef. lab. — תחת

מִתַּחְתֶּהָ[g] וּ pref. id.) id. with suff. 3 pers. sing. fem. Kh. מִתַּחְתָּהּ וּ; id. — תחת

מִתַּחְתָּיו[h] וּ׳ pref. id.) id. pl. with suff. 3 p. s. m.; וּ id. — תחת

מִתַּחְתִּיּוֹת[i] pref. id.) adj. fem. pl. of תַּחְתִּית [from תַּחְתִּי § 39. No. 4. rem. 1 note] masc. — תחת

מִתַּחְתֶּיךָ[k] pref. id.) adv. (תַּחַת) with pl. suff. 2 p. s. m. — תחת

מָתַי, מָתָי וּ׳[m] } adv. interr.; וּ bef. lab. — מתה

וְ מַתִּי[n] Kal pret. 1 pers. sing. [for מַתְתִּי § 25. rem.]; וָ bef. pause for וְ, conv. — מות

מֵתֵי[o] id. part. pl. constr. masc. from מֵת (§ 21. rem. 2, & § 30. No. 3) dec. 1a — מות

מֵתִי[p] id. sing. with suff. 1 pers. sing. — מות

מְתֵי n. m. pl., constr. of מְתִים [fr. מַת § 36. r. 5] — מתה

מִתְיְהֵב Chald. Ithpe. part. sing. masc. dec. 2b — יהב

מִתְיַהֲבָא[q] Chald. id. part. sing. fem. — יהב

מִתְיַהֲבִין[r] Chald. id. part. pl. masc. dec. 2b — יהב

מִתְיַהֲדִים[s] Hithpa. (§ 14. rem. 1) part. masc. pl. [of מִתְיַהֵד] dec. 7b — ידה

מְתָיו[t] noun masc. pl. (מְתִים), suff. 3 pers. sing. masc. [from מַת § 36. rem. 5] — מתה

מְתַיִךְ[u] id. pl. with suff. 2 pers. sing. fem. — מתה

מֵתֶיךָ[w] the foll. with suff. 2 pers. sing. masc. — מות

מֵתִים Kal part. masc. pl. of מֵת (§ 21. rem. 2, & § 30. No. 3) dec. 1a — מות

מְתִים noun masc. pl. [of מַת § 36. rem. 5] — מתה

מִתֵּימָן וּ׳[y] noun masc. s., also pr. name; וּ bef. lab. — ימן

מַתִּיר[z] Hiph. part. sing. masc. — נתר

מֵתְךָ[a], מֵתֶךָ[b] } Kal part. sing. masc., suff. 2 pers. s. m. from מֵת (§ 21. r. 2, & § 30. No. 3) d. 1a — מות

מִתְכַּנְּשִׁין[c] וּ׳ Chald. Ithpa. part. m. pl. [of מִתְכַּנֵּשׁ] d. 2b — כנש

מַתְכֹּנֶת[d] noun fem. sing. dec. 13c — תכן

מַתְכֻּנְתּוֹ id., suff. 3 pers. sing. masc. (§ 44. rem. 4) — תכן

מִתְכַּסֶּה[e] Hithpa. part. sing. masc. dec. 9a — כסה

מִתְכַּסִּים id. pl., abs. st. — כסה

מִתֵּל pref. מִ) pr. name in compos. תֵּל מֶלַח — תלל

מַתְּלָאָה[aa] for מַה־תְּלָאָה (comp. מַזֶּה), see מָה; תְּלָאָה noun fem. sing. — לאה

[a] Eze. 28. 8. [b] Ge. 35. 18; 48. 7; Ex. 7. 21; [c] De. 22. 21. [d] Ge. 30. 1. [e] De. 33. 13. [f] Ps. 71. 20. [g] Eze. 1. 13. [h] Pr. 25. 14. [i] Ge. 23. 3. [k] 2 Ki. 15. 5. [l] Ps. 119. 28. [m] Ne. 9. 3. [n] 2 Ch. 30. 22. [o] Ps. 72. 14. [p] Eze. 1. 4, 5. [q] 1 Sa. 7. 3. [r] Ec. 5. 11. [s] Ps. 19. 11. [t] Nu. 13. 25. [u] Ps. 119. 18. [x] Ps. 119. 51, 150. [y] Ps. 94. 12. [z] Eze. 16. 20. [a] 1 Ch. 21. 20. [b] 2 Sa. 21. 10. [c] Da. 6. 12. [d] Ps. 55. 2. [e] Je. 22. 15. [f] Ex. 20. 4, etc. [g] Eze. 42. 9. [h] Ex. 10. 23. [i] Zec. 6. 12. [k] Ne. 4. 7. [l] Pr. 22. 27. [m] Ne. 2. 6. [n] Ge. 19. 19. [o] Is. 22. 2. [p] Ge. 23. 4, 8, 13. [q] Ezr. 6. 8. [r] Ezr. 7. 19. [s] Est. 8. 17. [t] De. 33. 6. [u] Is. 3. 25. [w] Is. 26. 19. [y] Jos. 12. 3. [z] Ps. 146. 7. [aa] Mal. 1. 13. [a] Ge. 23. 6, 11. [b] Ge. 23. 15. [c] Da. 3. 3, 27. [d] Ex. 5. 8. [e] 1 Ki. 11. 29.

מְתַלְחֲשִׁים[a] Hithpa. part. pl. masc. [from מִתְלַחֵשׁ § 14. rem. 1] dec. 7b . . . . לחשׁ

מְתַלְּעוֹת[b] [c] וּ n. f. pl. constr., by transp. for מַלְתְּעוֹת (q.v.) לתע

מְתֻלָּעִים[d] Pual part. masc. pl. [of מְתֻלָּע] . תלע

מְתַלְּעֹתָיו[e] noun fem. pl., suff. 3 pers. s. m., see מְתַלְּעוֹת לתע

מִתְלַקַּחַת Hithpa. part. sing. fem. [of מִתְלַקֵּחַ masc.] לקח

מְתִם defect. for מְתִים (q. v.) . . . מתה

מְתֹם noun masc. sing. . . . . תמם

מִתְמַהְמֵהַּ[f] Hithpalp. part. sing. masc. (§ 6. rem. 4) . מהה

מִתְּמוֹל pref. מִ)(adv. . . . . מול

מִתְּמֹךְ[g] pref. id.)(Kal inf. constr. . . . תמך

מִתְּמֹל defect. for מִתְּמוֹל (q. v.) . . . מול

מִתָּמָר pref. מִ)(pr. name of a place . . תמר

מָתַן Root not used; Arab. *to be firm*.

מֹתֶן only du. מָתְנַיִם (dec. 6c) *loins*.

מִתְנִי gent. noun elsewhere unknown, 1 Ch. 11. 43.

אֵמְתָּנִי Chald. fem. *strong*, Da. 7. 7.

מַתָּן[h] [i] וּ' noun m. s. d. 2b, also pr. n.; וּ bef. lab. נתן

מֻתָן[j] [for מוּתָן] Kal inf. constr. (מוּת), suff. 3 pers. pl. fem. dec. 1a . . . . מות

מִתְנַבֵּא[k] [l] וּ' Hithpa. part. sing. m. d. 7b; וּ bef. lab. נבא

מִתְנַבְּאִים id. pl., abs. st. . . . . נבא

מִתְנַדַּב[l] Chald. Ithpa. part. sing. masc. dec. 2a . נדב

מִתְנַדֵּב Hithpa. part. sing. masc. dec. 7b . נדב

מִתְנַדְּבִין[m] Chald. Ithpa. part. masc., pl. of מִתְנַדַּב d. 2a נדב

מַתָּנָה noun fem. sing. dec. 11a; also pr. name נתן

מַתְנוּ[n] וָ' / מָתְנוּ[o] וָ" } Kal pret. 1 pers. pl.; וָ conv. see lett. ו מות

מִתְּנוּבוֹת[p] pref. מִ)(noun fem. pl. of תְּנוּבָה dec. 10 נוב

מִתְנוֹדֵד[q] Hithpal. part. sing. masc. . . נוד

מִתְנוֹסְסוֹת[r] Hithpoel part. fem. pl. [from מִתְנוֹסֶסֶת, from מִתְנוֹסֵס masc.] . . . . נסס

מַתָּנוֹת[s] וּ' noun fem. pl. abs. from מַתָּנָה dec. 11a נתן

מַתְּנוֹתֵיכֶם[t] id. pl. with suff. 2 pers. pl. masc. . נתן

מִתְנַחֵם[u] Hithpa. part. sing. masc. (§ 14. rem. 1) . נחם

מָתְנַי[x] / מָתְנָי[y] } noun masc. du. (מָתְנַיִם), suff. 1 pers. sing. from [מֹתֶן] dec. 6c . . . . מתן

מָתְנֵי[z] [a] וּ' id. du., constr. st.; וּ bef. lab. . מתן

מַתְּנַי, מַתַּנְיָה וּ' pr. names masc.; וּ id. . . נתן

מָתְנֶיהָ[b] noun m. du., suff. 3 p. s. f. fr. [מֹתֶן] d. 6c מתן

מַתַּנְיָהוּ pr. name masc., see מַתַּנְיָה . . נתן

מָתְנֵיהֶם[c] [d] וּ' noun masc. du., suff. 3 pers. pl. masc. from [מֹתֶן] dec. 6c; וּ bef. lab. . מתן

מָתְנָיו[e] וּ' id. du., suff. 3 pers. sing. masc.; וּ id. מתן

מָתְנֶיךָ id. du., suff. 2 pers. sing. masc. . . מתן

מָתְנֵיכֶם[f] id. du., suff. 2 pers. pl. masc. . . מתן

מָתְנַיִם / מָתְנָיִם } id. du., abs. st. . . . . מתן

מִתְנַכְּרָה[g] Hithpa. part. s. f. [of מִתְנַכֵּר § 39. No. 3. r. 4.] נכר

מַתְּנָם[h] noun masc. sing., suff. 3 pers. pl. masc. fr. מַתָּן נתן

מַתְּנָן[i] [j] וּ' Chald. noun fem. pl. of [מַתְּנָא] dec. 8a; וּ bef. lab. . . . . . . נתן

מִתְנַפֵּל[k] וּ Hithpa. part. sing. masc.; וּ id. . נפל

מִתְנַצַּח[l] Chald. Ithpa. part. sing. masc. . . נצח

מִתְנַקֵּם וּ Hithpa. part. sing. masc.; וּ bef. lab. . נקם

מִתְנַקֵּשׁ[m] Hithpa. part. sing. masc. . . . נקשׁ

מִתְנַשֵּׂא[ss] Hithpa. part. sing. masc. . . . נשׂא

מִתְנַשְּׂאָה[n] Chald. Ithpa. part. sing. fem. of מִתְנַשֵּׂא נשׂא

מַתָּנֹת noun fem. pl. of מַתָּנָה dec. 11a נתן

מַתְּנֹת[o] id. pl., constr. st. . . . . נתן

מַתְּנֹתֵיכֶם id. pl., suff. 2 pers. pl. masc. . . נתן

מַתְּנָתָךְ[p] Chald. noun fem. pl., suff. 2 pers. sing. masc. from [מַתְּנָא] dec. 8a . . . נתן

מִתְעֲבֵד[q] / מִתְעֲבֶד־[r] } Chald. Ithpe. part. sing. masc. . עבד

מִתְעַבְדָא[s] Chald. id. part. sing. fem. . . . עבד

מִתְעַבֵּר Hithpa. part. sing. masc. . . . עבר

מִתְעַבְּרוֹ[t] id. with suff. 3 pers. sing. masc. . עבר

מַתְעֶה Hiph. part. sing. masc. dec. 9a . . תעה

מִתְעוֹרֵר[u] Hithpal. part. sing. masc. . . עור

מַתְעִים Hiph. part. masc. pl. of מַתְעֶה dec. 9a . תעה

מִתַּעֲנִיתִי[x] pref. מִ)(noun fem. sing., suff. 1 pers. sing. from [תַּעֲנִית] dec. 1b . . . ענה

מִתְעָרַב[y] Chald. Ithpa. part. sing. masc. dec. 2a . ערב

מִתְעָרְבִין[z] Chald. id. pl., abs. st. . . . ערב

מִתַּעְרָהּ pref. מִ)(noun masc. sing., suff. 3 pers. sing. fem. from תַּעַר [for תַּעְרָה] . . . ערה

מִתְעָרֶה[a] וּ Hithpa. part. sing. masc.; וּ bef. lab. ערה

מִתְעַשֵּׁר[b] Hithpa. part. sing. masc. . . . עשׁר

מְתַעְתְּעִים[c] וּ Hithpal. part. pl. masc. [from מְתַעְתֵּעַ for מִתְתַּעְתֵּעַ] dec. 7b; וּ bef. lab. . . תעע

מִתַּפּוּחַ pref. מִ)(pr. name of a place . . נפח

מִתְפַּלֵּל וּ' Hithpa. part. sing. masc. dec. 7b; וּ bef. lab. פלל

מִתְפַּלְלִים[d] וּ id. pl., abs. st.; וּ id. . . . פלל

מִתִּפְסַח pref. מִ)(pr. name of a place . . פסח

מְתֹפְפוֹת[e] Hithpoel part. pl. fem. [from מְתֹפֶפֶת d. 13, from מְתֹפֵף masc.] . . . תפף

[מָתַק] fut. יִמְתַּק.—I. *to be* or *become sweet*.—II. i. q. Syr. *to suck, to feed upon with relish*, Job 24. 20.

---

[a] 2 Sa. 12. 19. [b] Job 29. 17. [c] Joel 1. 6. [d] Na. 2. 4. [e] Pr. 30. 14. [f] 2 Sa. 15. 28. [g] Is. 33. 15. [h] Ge. 34. 12. [i] 2 Sa. 20. 3. [k] Je. 29. 26. [l] Ezr. 7. 13. [m] Ezr. 7. 16. [n] Nu. 14. 2. [o] 2 Ki. 7. 4. [p] La. 4. 9. [q] Je. 31. 18. [r] Zec. 9. 16. [s] Est. 9. 22. [t] Le. 23. 38. [u] Ge. 27. 42. [x] Je. 13. 2. [y] Is. 21. 3. [z] Je. 13. 11. [a] Is. 45. 1. [b] Pr. 31. 17. [c] Eze. 44. 18. [d] Ps. 69. 24. [e] Da. 10. 5. [f] Ex. 12. 11. [g] 1 Ki. 14. 5, 6. [h] Nu. 18. 11. [i] Da. 2. 6, 48. [k] Ezr. 10. 1. [l] Da. 6. 4. [m] 1 Sa. 28. 9. [n] Ezr. 4. 19. [o] Ex. 28. 38. [p] Da. 5. 17. [q] Ezr. 7. 26. [r] Ezr. 4. 19. [s] Ezr. 5. 8. [ss] 1 Ki. 1. 5. [t] Pr. 20. 2. [u] Is. 64. 6. [x] Ezr. 9. 5. [y] Da. 2. 43. [z] Da. 2. 43. [a] Ps. 37. 35. [b] Pr. 13. 7. [c] 2 Ch. 36. 16. [d] Is. 45. 20. [e] Na. 2. 8.

Hiph. I. *to make sweet*, Ps. 55. 15. הַמְתִּיק סוֹד *to take sweet counsel.*—II. *to be sweet*, Job 20. 12.

מָתוֹק, masc. pl. מְתוּקִים, fem. מְתוּקָה (§ 32. r.5) adj. *sweet*; neut. *sweet, sweetness; pleasantness.*

מֶתֶק masc. *sweetness*, Pr. 16. 21; 27. 9.

מֹתֶק masc. dec. 6e, id. Ju. 9. 11.

מִתְקָה (*sweetness*) pr. name of a station of the Israelites in the desert, Nu. 33. 28.

מַמְתַּקִּים masc. pl. (of מַמְתָּק dec. 8a) *sweet things.*

וּמֶתֶק noun masc. sing.; וּ bef. lab. . . מתק

מִתְקַדֶּשֶׁת[a] Hithpa. part. sing. fem. [of מִתְקַדֵּשׁ m.] קדשׁ

מָתְקוּ[b] Kal pret. 3 pers. pl. . . . . מתק

מְתָקוֹ[c] id. pret. 3 pers. sing. m., suff. 3 pers. sing. m. מתק

מִתְקוֹמְמָה[d] Hithpal. part. sing. fem. [of מִתְקוֹמֵם comp. § 12. rem. 1] . . . . . קום

וּמִתְקוֹמְמַי[e] id. masc. with suff. 1 pers. sing. [from מִתְקוֹמֵם dec. 7b; וּ bef. lab. . . . קום

מִתְּקוֹעַ pref. מִ)(pr. name of a place . תקע

מִתְקַטְּלִין[f] Chald. Ithpa. part. pass. masc. pl. [of מִתְקַטֵּל] dec. 2a . . . . קטל

מָתְקִי[g] noun m. sing., suff. 1 pers. s. fr. [מֹתֶק] d. 6c מתק

וּמְתֻרְגָּם[h] Pual part. sing. masc. (§ 7); וּ bef. lab. תרגם

מִתְרְדָת (Mithra-dat (-datus), *given* or *dedicated to Mithra*, the genius of the sun) pr. name—I. of a treasurer of Cyrus, Ezr. 1. 8.—II. of an officer of Artaxerxes, Ezr. 4. 7.

מִתְּרוּמַת[i] pref. מִ)(noun fem. s., constr. of תְּרוּמָה d. 10 רום

מִתְרוֹנֵן[k] Hithpal. part. sing. masc. . . . . דון

מִתְרוֹשֵׁשׁ[l] Hithpal. part. sing. masc. . . . רושׁ

מִתֶּרַח pref. מִ)(pr. name masc. for תֶּרַח (§ 35. r. 2) תרח

מִתְרַפֶּה[m] Hithpa. part. sing. masc. dec. 9a . . רפה

מִתְרַפִּים[n] id. pl., constr. st. . . . . . רפה

מִתְרַפֵּס[o] Hithpa. part. sing. masc. . . . רפס

מִתְרַפֶּקֶת[p] Hithpa. part. sing. fem. [of מִתְרַפֵּק masc.] רפק

מִתִּרְצָה pref. מִ)(pr. name of a place . . רצה

מִתַּרְשִׁישׁ pref. id.)(pr. name of a place, see תַּרְשִׁישׁ.

מִתֹּשָׁבֵי[q] pref. id.)(noun masc. pl. constr. from תּוֹשָׁב dec. 1b (§ 31. rem. 1) . . . ישׁב

מִתְּשָׂם[r] Chald. Ithpe. part. sing. masc. . . שׂום

מַתַּת[s], מַתַּת } noun fem. sing. [contr. for מַתֶּנֶת] . נתן

מִתֵּת pref. מִ)(Kal inf. constr. [for תֶּנֶת § 17. r. 9] נתן

מַתַּתָּה pr. name masc. . . . . . . נתן

מִתִּתִּי pref. id.)(Kal inf. (תֵּת for תֶּנֶת), suff. 1 pers. sing. (§ 17. rem. 9) . . . . . נתן

מֹתָתִי[t] Pilel [מוֹתֵת] pret. 1 p. s. [for מוֹתַתְתִּי § 25. r.] מות

וּמַתִּתְיָה, וּמַתִּתְיָהוּ } pr. name masc.; וּ bef. lab. . . נתן

וּמֹתְתֵנִי[u] Pilel imp. s. m., suff. 1 pers. sing.; וּ id. מות

נ

נָא interj. noting respectful entreaty or exhortation, *I pray!* used—I. with the imp. optat. and fut. with and without negation, as אִמְרִי נָא *say, I pray thee!* יֻקַּח נָא *let there be taken, I pray thee!* אֵלְכָה־נָּא *let me go, I pray thee!* אַל־נָא תַעֲבֹר *pass not away, I pray thee!*—II. with conj. and interj. אַל־נָא *nay*, or *not so, I pray thee!* הִנֵּה־נָא *behold, I pray thee!* In many instances the word *now* may be substituted, as אִם־נָא *if now*, or *if indeed;* אוֹי־נָא *woe now! alas!* comp. also Ex. 3. 3. אָסוּרָה־נָּא *let me go now*, comp. No. I.

נָא[x] adj. masc. sing. . . . . . . ניא

נֹא ׳ו fully נֹא אָמוֹן pr. name of an Egyptian city, supposed to be *Thebes*.

נֹאבֵד Kal fut. 1 pers. pl. . . . . . אבד

נֹאבְדָה[y] id. with parag. ה (§ 8. rem. 13) . . אבד

נֹאד[z] ׳ו masc. dec. 1a (pl. נֹאדוֹת), *bottle, skin-bottle.* Arab. נאד *to yield water.*

נֹאדוֹת[a] ׳ו id. pl. with fem. term. . . . . נאד

נֶאְדָּר[b] Niph. part. sing. masc. (§ 13. rem. 7) . אדר

נֶאְדָּרִי[c] id. with parag. י (comp. § 8. rem. 19) . אדר

נָאָה Kal not used; i. q. נָוָה *to sit, dwell*, comp. deriv. נָאָה. Pil. נַאֲוָה (§ 24. rem. 25).—I. *to be suitable, becoming*, with לְ Ps. 93. 5; prop. *to sit well* (Gesenius).—II. *to be comely, beautiful*, cogn. יָאָה.

נָאָה fem. dec. 11a, only pl. c.—I. *seats, dwellings, habitations.*—II. flocks and herds, *pastures;* נְאוֹת דֶּשֶׁא *green pastures.*

נָאוֶה (for נַאֲוָה) adj. fem. נָאוָה.—I. *suitable, becoming.*—II. *comely, beautiful.*

נְאוֹד[d] with ו *in otio* for נאד (q. v.) . . . נאד

---

[a] 2 Sa. 11. 4. [b] Job 21. 33. [c] Job 24. 20. [d] Job 20. 27. [e] Job 27. 7. [f] Da. 2. 13. [g] Ju. 9. 11. [h] Ezr. 4. 7. [i] Eze. 48. 12. [k] Ps. 78. 65. [l] Pr. 13. 7. [m] Pr. 18. 9. [n] Jos. 18. 3. [o] Ps. 68. 31. [p] Ca. 8. 5. [q] 1 Ki. 17. 1. [r] Ezr. 5. 8. [s] 1 Ki. 13. 7. [t] 2 Sa. 1. 16. [u] 1 Sa. 1. 9. [x] Ex. 12. 9. [y] Jon. 1. 14. [z] 1 Sa. 16. 20. [a] Jos. 9. 4, 13. [b] Ex. 15. 11. [c] Ex. 15. 6. [d] Ju. 4. 19.

נָאוָה[a] וְ' fem. of the foll. . . . . . נאה
נָאוֶה adj. masc. sing. [for נָאֲוֶה], comp. the foll. נאה
נַאֲוָה[b] Pilel pret. 3 p. s. m. (§ 6. No. 2, & § 24. r. 22) נאה
נָאווּ id. pret. 3 pers. pl. [for נָאֲווּ] . . נאה
נָאוֹף[c] Kal inf. abs. . . . . . . נאף
נָאוֹר[d] Niph part. sing. masc. . . . . אור
נֵאוֹת[e] Niph [for נֵאוֹת], or Kal (comp. יֵבוֹשׁ from בּוֹשׁ) fut. 1 pers. pl. . . . . אות
נְאוֹת noun fem. pl. constr. from [נָאָה] dec. 11 a נאה
נֵאוֹתָה[f] Niph. or Kal fut. 1 pers. pl. with parag. ה comp. נֵאוֹת . . . . . יאת
נֶאֱזָר[g] Niph. part. sing. masc. (§ 13. rem. 7) . אזר
נֶאֱחָז[h] Niph. part. sing. masc. . . . . אחז
נֵאחֲזוּ[i] [k]וְ' id. pret. 3 pers. pl. (§ 19. rem. 7) . אחז
נֶאֱכַל[l] וְ Niph. pret. 3 pers. sing. masc. . . אכל
נֹאכַל
נֹאכֵל } Kal fut. 1 pers. pl. (§ 19. rem. 1) . אכל
נֹאכְלָה[m] וְ
נֹאכֵלָה וְ } id. with parag. (ה § 8. rem. 13) . אכל
נֹאכְלֵהוּ[n] וַ
נֹאכְלֶנּוּ[o] וְ } id. with suff. 3 pers. sing. masc.; וַ com. אכל
נֹאלוּ[p] וְ in pause and defect. for נוֹאֲלוּ (q. v.) . יאל
נֶאֱלָח[q] וְ Niph. part. sing. masc. . . . . אלח
נֶאֱלָחוּ id. pret. 3 pers. pl. [for נֶאֶלְחוּ comp. § 8. r. 7] אלח
נֶאֱלָמָה[r] Niph. pret. 3 pers. sing. fem. [for נֶאֶלְמָה § 13. rem. 7, comp. § 8. rem. 7] . אלם
נֶאֱלַמְתָּ[s] וְ id. pret. 2 pers. sing. masc. . . . אלם
נֶאֱלַמְתִּי[t] וְ' id. pret. 1 p. s. [for נֶאֱלַמְתִּי comp. § 8. r. 7] אלם

[נָאַם]

to utter, speak, declare, Je. 23. 31; elsewhere in the part. pass. constr. נְאֻם prop. *declared of, by*, as a subst. *declaration, dictum of*; נְאֻם יְהוָה *a declaration of the Lord*, Eng. vers. *saith the Lord*.

נְאֻם וּ' Kal part. pass. sing. masc. constr. [of נָאוּם] dec. 3 a; וּ bef. (:) . . . נאם
נֶאֱמָן[u] וְ' Niph. part. sing. masc. dec. 2 b . . אמן
נֶאֱמַן[x] וְ' id. id., constr. st. or pret. 3 pers. sing. m. אמן
נֶאֱמָנָה id. part. sing. fem. . . . . אמן
נֶאֶמְנָה[y] id. pret. 3 pers. sing. fem. . . . אמן
נֶאֶמְנוּ[z]
נֶאֱמָנוּ } id. pret. 3 pers. pl. (comp. § 8. rem. 7) אמן
נֶאֱמָנוֹת[a] וְ id. part. fem. pl. of נֶאֱמָנָה . . . אמן
נֶאֱמָנִים[b] וְ' id. part. masc. pl. of נֶאֱמָן dec. 2 b . אמן
נֶאֱמֶנֶת[c] id. part. sing. fem., comp. נֶאֱמָנָה . . אמן
נֶאֱמַר[d] Niph. pret. 3 pers. sing. masc. . . . אמר

נֵאמַר[e] Chald. Peal fut. 1 pers. pl. (§ 53) . . אמר
נֹאמַר[f] וְ' Kal fut. 1 pers. pl. (§ 19. rem. 1) . אמר
נֹּאמֶר וַ id.; acc. drawn back by conv. וַ . אמר
נֶאֱנָח[g] Niph. part. sing. masc. (§ 13. rem. 7) . אנח
נֶאֱנָחָה[h] id. part. sing. fem. . . . . אנח
נֶאֶנְחָה id. pret. 3 pers. sing. fem. . . . אנח
נֶאֱנָחוּ[i] id. pret. 3 pers. pl. . . . . אנח
נֶאֱנָחִים[k] id. part. masc., pl. of נֶאֱנָח . . . אנח
נֶאֱסָף[l] Niph. part. sing. masc. . . . . אסף
נֶאֱסַף[m] וְ' id. pret. 3 pers. sing. masc. . . . אסף
נֶאֱסֹף[n] Kal fut. 1 pers. pl. . . . . אסף
נֶאֶסְפָה[o] וְ Niph. pret. 3 pers. sing. fem. . . אסף
נֶאֶסְפוּ[p] וְ'[q]
נֶאֱסָפוּ וְ' } id. pret. 3 pers. pl. . . . אסף
נֶאֱסָפִים id. part. masc. pl. of נֶאֱסָף . . . אסף
נֶאֱסַפְתָּ וְ id. pret. 2 pers. sing. masc., acc. shifted by conv. וְ (§ 8. rem. 7) . . . אסף
נֶאֱסַפְתֶּם[r] וְ id. pret. 2 pers. pl. masc. . . . אסף
נֶאֱסָרְךָ[s] Kal fut. 1 pers. pl., suff. 2 pers. sing. masc. אסר

[נָאַף]

fut. יִנְאַף *to commit adultery*; const. with an acc. נֹאֵף אִשָּׁה *he that committeth adultery with a woman*, Pr. 6. 32. Trop. applied to apostacy from the true God to idolatry. Pi. נִאֵף (§ 14. r. 1) idem.

נִאֻף m. d. 1 b, *adultery*, Je. 13. 27; Eze. 23. 43.

נַאֲפוּף masc. dec. 1 b, id. Ho. 2. 4.

נָאוֹף[t] וְ Kal inf. abs. . . . . . נאף
נֹאֵף id. part. act. sing. masc. . . . . נאף
נִאֲפָה[u] Piel pret. 3 pers. sing. fem. (§ 14. rem. 1) נאף
נִאֵפוּ[x] id. pret. 3 pers. pl. [for נִאֲפוּ comp. § 8. r. 7] נאף
נַאֲפוּפֶיהָ[y] וְ n. m. pl., suff. 3 p. s. f. fr. [נַאֲפוּף] d. 1 b נאף
נֹאֲפוֹת Kal part. act. fem., pl. of נֹאֶפֶת' dec. 13 נאף
נִאֻפַיִךְ[z] the foll. with suff. 2 pers. sing. fem. . נאף
נִאֻפִים[a] noun masc. pl. [of נִאוּף, נִאֻף] . . נאף

נָאַץ[b]

fut. יִנְאַץ *to deride, despise, contemn, reject.* Pi. נִאֵץ (§ 14. rem. 1).—I. *to despise, contemn.*—II. *to give occasion for blasphemy*, 2 Sa. 12. 14. Hiph. intrans. *to be despised*, Ec. 12. 5. Hithpo. *to be despised, contemned*, Is. 52. 5.

נְאָצָה fem. *reproach, insult.*

נֶאָצָה fem. id. pl. נֶאָצוֹת Ne. 9. 18, 26. נֶאָצוֹתֶיךָ Eze. 35. 12.

נִאֵץ[c] Piel (§ 14. rem. 1) pret. 3 pers. sing. masc.; or, 2 Sa. 12. 14, inf. (§ 10. rem. 2) נאץ
נְאָצָה וּ noun fem. sing.; וּ bef. (:) . . נאץ

[a] Ca. 1. 5. [b] Ps. 93. 5. [c] Je. 23. 14. [d] Ps. 76. 5. [e] Ge. 34. 15. [f] Ge. 34. 23. [g] Ps. 65. 7. [h] Ge. 22. 13. [i] Jos. 22. 9. [k] Nu. 32. 30. [l] Ex. 22. 5. [m] Nu. 11. 18. [n] 2 Ki. 6. 29. [o] 2 Ki. 6. 28, 29. [p] Je. 50. 36. [q] Job 15. 16. [r] Is. 53. 7. [s] Eze. 3. 26. [t] Da. 10. 15. [u] Je. 42. 5. [x] 2 Sa. 7. 16; Pr. 11. 13. [y] Ps. 78. 8. [z] Je. 15. 18.

[a] De. 28. 59. [b] De 28. 59. [c] Ps. 89. 29. [d] Da. 8. 26. [e] Da. 2. 36. [f] Is. 41. 26. [g] Eze. 21. 12. [h] La. 1. 21. [i] Is. 24. 7. [k] La. 1. 4, 11. [l] Ge. 49. 29. [m] Is. 16. 10. [n] Le. 25. 20 [o] Je. 48. 33. [p] Ps. 47. 10. [q] Ps. 35. 15. [r] Le. 26. 25. [s] Ju. 15. 13. [t] Je. 7. 9; Ho. 4. 2. [u] Je. 3. 8. [x] Eze. 23. 37. [y] Ho. 2. 4. [z] Je. 13. 27. [a] Eze. 23. 43. [b] Pr. 5. 12. [c] Ps. 10. 3, 13.

נָאֲצוּ[a] / נָאֲצוּ[b] } Kal pret. 3 pers. pl. (§ 8. rem. 7) . נאץ

נִאֲצוּ / נִאֲצוּ[c] } Piel pret. 3 pers. pl. (§ 14. rem. 1) . נאץ

נִאֲצוּנִי[d] וְ id. with suff. 1 pers. sing. . . . נאץ

נֶאָצוֹת[e] noun f. pl. of [נֶאָצָה] d. 10 (§ 42. No. 3 note) נאץ

נָאֲצוֹתֶיךָ[f] id. with suff. 2 pers. sing. masc. (vowel under נ lengthened instead of (ִ) and dag. forte impl. in א) . . . . נאץ

נֶאֱצַל[g] Niph. pret. 3 pers. sing. masc. . . אצל

נִאַצְתָּ[h] Piel (§ 14. rem. 1) pret. 2 pers. sing. masc. נאץ

נָאַק וְ fut. יִנְאַק, *to groan, lament.*

נְאָקָה fem. dec. 11 c (constr. נַאֲקַת § 42. r. 1) *a groaning, lamentation.*

נַאֲקוֹת[k] n. f. pl. constr. fr. [נְאָקָה] d. 11 c (§ 42. r. 1) נאק

נַאֲקַת[l] id. sing., constr. st. . . . . נאק

נַאֲקָתָם[m] id. sing., suff. 3 pers. pl. masc. . . נאק

נֵאֵר[n] Pi. (§ 14. rem. 1) *to abhor, reject.*

נָאֳרְבָה[o] Kal fut. 1 p. pl. [נָאֱרֹב] with opt. ה (§ 8. r. 13) ארב

נֵאָרִים[p] Niph. part. m. pl. [of נֵאָר, for נָאָר § 18. r. 14] ארר

נֵאַרְתָּה[q] Piel pret. 2 pers. sing. masc. (comp. § 8. r. 5) נאר

נֶאְשְׁאַר[r] וְ anom. form prob. made up from two readings, נִשְׁאָר Niph. part. & אֶשְׁאַר Kal fut. שאר

נֶאְשָׁם[s] Kal fut. 1 pers. pl. [for נֶאְשַׁם § 13. rem. 5] אשם

נֶאְשָׁמוּ[t] Niph. pret. 3 pers. pl. [for נֶאֶשְׁמוּ § 13. rem. 7, comp. § 8. rem. 7] . . אשם

נֹב pr. name of a place . . . . . נבה

נָבָא. Niph. נִבָּא *to announce, to prophesy,* i. e. to foretell future events, and also generally to teach the Divine will; const. with אֶל, עַל, לְ *concerning* whom, with בְּ in whose name one prophesies. Hithp. idem.

נְבָא Chald. Ithpa. id. Ezr. 5. 1.

נָבִיא masc. dec. 3a, *prophet,* one inspired and commissioned of God to instruct the people and foretell future events; בְּנֵי הַנְּבִיאִים *the sons of the prophets,* i. e. the disciples of the prophets.

נְבִיא Chald. masc. idem. See § 68.

נְבִיאָה fem.—I. *prophetess.*—II. *a prophet's wife,* Is. 8. 3.

נְבוּאָה fem. dec. 10.—I. *prophecy, prediction.*—II. *prophetical book,* 2 Ch. 9. 29.

נְבוּאָה Chald. fem. id. Ezr. 6. 14.

נְבוֹ (for נְבוֹא) pr. name of an idol worshipped by the Chaldeans, supposed to have been *Mercury,* as the *interpreter* of the gods, Is. 46. 1, see also נְבוֹ under נָבָה. Hence also the following compounds with נְבוֹ as נְבוּכַדְנֶאצַּר, נְבוּזַרְאֲדָן, נְבוּשַׁזְבָּן which see in their order.

נָבוֹא וַנָּ׳ Kal fut. 1 pers. pl. (§ 25. No. 2 f); ־ַ conv. בוא

נִבָּא Niph. pret. 3 pers. sing. masc.; or part. . נבא

נָבוֹאָה[u] וְ Kal fut. 1 p. pl. with parag. ה (§ 25. No. 2 f) בוא

נִבְּאוּ[x] / נִבְּאוּ[y] וְ׳[z] } id. pret. 3 pers. pl. . . . נבא

נִבְּאֵי[ii] constr. of נִבְּאִים (q. v.) . . . נבא

נְבִאִים defect. for נְבִיאִים (q. v.) . . . נבא

נִבְּאִים Niph. part. masc. pl. [of נִבָּא § 23. rem. 9] comp. הַנִּבְּאִים . . . . . נבא

נִבְאַשׁ[a] Niph. pret. 3 pers. sing. masc. . . באש

נִבְאֲשׁוּ[b] id. pret. 3 pers. pl. . . . . באש

נִבְאַשְׁתָּ[c] id. pret. 2 pers. sing. masc. . . באש

נִבֵּאתָ / נִבֵּאתָ[d] וְ } Niph. pret. 2 pers. sing. masc.; acc. shifted by conv. וְ (comp. § 8. r. 7) } נבא

נִבֵּאתִי וְ id. pret. 1 pers. sing. . . . . נבא

נָבַב *to bore through, to make hollow;* only part. נָבוּב *hollow;* Metaph. *empty, stupid, foolish,* Job 11. 12.

נְבַגֵּד[e] Kal fut. 1 pers. pl. . . . . בגד

נִבְדְּלוּ[f] Niph. pret. 3 pers. pl. . . . . בדל

נָבָה Root not used; i. q. Arab. נבא *to be high.*

נְבוֹ (*height*) pr. name—I. of a mountain and a city in the land of Moab.—II. of a town in the tribe of Judah.

נֹב (for נֹבֶה *height*) pr. name of a city of the Levites near Jerusalem; with ה parag. נֹבֶה.

נְבָיוֹת (*heights*) pr. name of a people descended from Ishmael.

נֹבֶה pr. name (נֹב) with ה parag. . . . נבה

נִבְהָל Niph. part. sing. masc. . . . . בהל

נִבְהַל[g] id. pret. 3 pers. sing. masc. . . . בהל

נִבְהָלָה[h] id. part. sing. fem. of נִבְהָל . . . בהל

נִבְהֲלָה[i] id. pret. 3 pers. sing. fem. . . . בהל

נִבְהֲלוּ[nn] וְ׳[k] / נִבְהָלוּ וְ׳[l] } Niph. pret. 3 pers. pl. (comp. § 8. rem. 7) . . . . } בהל

נִבְהָלְנוּ[m] id. pret. 1 pers. pl. [for נִבְהַלְנוּ v. id.] . בהל

נִבְהַלְתִּי[n] / נִבְהַלְתִּי[o] וְ } id. pret. 1 pers. sing. (v. id.) . בהל

[a] Ps. 107. 11. [b] Pr. 1. 30. [c] Is. 5. 24. [d] De. 31. 20. [e] Ne. 9. 18, 26. [f] Eze. 35. 12. [g] Eze. 42. 6. [h] 2 Sa. 12. 14. [i] Eze. 30. 24. [ii] Je. 23. 26, 32. [k] Eze. 30. 24. [l] Ex. 6. 5. [m] Ex. 2. 24. [n] La. 2. 7. [nn] Jer. 51. 32. [o] Pr. 1. 11. [p] Mal. 3. 9. [q] Ps. 89. 40. [r] Eze. 9. 8. [s] Je. 50. 7. [t] Joel 1. 18. [u] 2 Ki. 7. 9. [x] Je. 23. 21. [y] Je. 37. 19, etc. [z] Joel 3. 1. [a] 1 Sa. 13. 4. [b] 2 Sa. 10. 6. [c] 2 Sa. 16. 21. [d] Eze. 4. 7. [e] Mal. 2. 10. [f] Ps. 30. 8; Pr. 28. 22. [g] 1 Sa. 28. 21. [h] Zep. 1. 18. [i] Ps. 6. 4. [k] Is. 13. 8. [l] Eze. 26. 18. [m] Ps. 90. 7. [n] Job 21. 6. [o] Is. 21. 3.

נְבוֹ pr. name of an idol . . . . . נבא

נְבוֹ וּ׳ pr. name of a place; וּ bef. (:) . . . נבה

נְבוֹ pr. name, see סַמְגַּר נְבוֹ.

נָבוֹא[a] וָ׳, וַנָּ׳ Kal fut. 1 p. pl. (§ 25. No. 2f); ·ַו conv. בוא

נָבוֹאָה[b] וְ׳[c] id. with parag. ה (§ 8. rem. 13) . . בוא

נְבוּאַת[d] noun fem. sing., constr. of נְבוּאָה dec. 10 נבא

נָבוּב Kal part. p. s. m. (or Niph. part. of בוב) d. 3a נבב

נְבוּב id., constr. st. . . . . נבב

נְבוּזַרְאֲדָן (*of Nebo prince and lord*; compnd. of נְבוֹ q. v. Root נבא, זַר i. q. שַׂר, & אֲדָן i. q. אָדוֹן) pr. name of one of Nebuchadnezzar's generals.

נְבוּכַדְנֶאצַּר וּ׳, נְבוּכַדְנֶצּוֹר, נְבוּכַדְנֶצַּר וּ׳, נְבוּכַדְרֶאצּוֹר, נְבוּכַדְרֶאצַּר } pr. name, *Nebuchadnezzar*, king of Babylon. It is variously interpreted. According to Gesenius: *of Nebo the god, prince*, i. e. *prince of the god Nebo*, comp. the preced.; *chodna* or *chodan* is in the Pers. god; *Zar*, prince. Or נְבוּךְ אֶדֶר אֲצַר *Nebo, god of splendour*.

נָבוֹכָה[e] Niph. pret. 3 pers. sing. fem. . . . בוך

נָבוֹן וְ׳ Niph. part. sing. masc. dec. 3a . . . בין

נְבוֹן וּ id., constr. st.; וּ bef. (:) . . . . בין

נְבוֹנִים id. pl., abs. st. . . . . . . בין

נָבוּס[f] Kal fut. 1 pers. pl. . . . . . בוס

נְבוּשַׁזְבָּן וּ (*adorer of Mercury*; Gesenius. Comp. נְבוֹ R. נָבָא) pr. name of a prince of Assyria, Je. 39. 13.

נָבוֹת pr. name of a man . . . . . נוב

נְבִזְבָּה וּ Chald. fem. *gift*, Da. 2. 6; pl. נְבִזְבְּיָן (from נְבִזְבִּיָה dec. 9b), Da. 5. 17. This word is supposed to be of Pers. origin.

נְבִזְבְּיָתָךְ[g] וּ Chald. noun fem. pl., suff. 2 pers. sing. masc., see the preced.; וּ bef. (:)

נָבֹזָּה[h] וְ Kal fut. 1 pers. plur. com. [נָבֹז] with parag. ה (§ 8. rem. 13) . . . . בזז

נִבְזֶה[i] וְ׳ Niph. part. sing. masc. dec. 9a . . בזה

נָבֹזּוּ[k] וְ Niph. pret. 3 pers. pl. . . . . בזז

נִבְזִים[l] Niph. part. masc. pl. of נִבְזֶה dec. 9a . בזה

[נָבַח] *to bark*, Is. 56. 10. Hence

נֹבַח וְ׳ (*a barking*) pr. name—I. of a man, Nu. 32. 42.—II. of a city, Ju. 8. 11 . נבח

נִבְחַז pr. name of an idol of the Avites, 2 Ki. 17. 31.

נִבְחָר Niph. part. sing. masc. . . . . . בחר

נִבְחַר[m] וְ id. pret. 3 pers. sing. masc. . . . בחר

נִבְחֲרָה[n] Kal fut. 1 pers. plur. [נִבְחַר] with parag. ה (§ 8. rem. 13) . . . . בחר

נָבַט וְ. Pi. only Is. 5. 30, and Hiph. הִבִּיט.—I. *to look*, abs.—II. *to behold, look at* or *towards*, with אֶל, לְ, עַל of the place.—III. with בְּ, *to look upon with pleasure*, Ps. 92. 12.—IV. *to regard, have respect to*, with acc., לְ, אֶל.—V. *to look towards with expectation*, with אֶל.

נְבָט (*aspect*) pr. name of the father of Jeroboam.

מַבָּט masc. dec. 1b (with suff. also מֶבָּטָה), *expectation, hope*, Zec. 9. 5; meton. *object of expectation*.

נְבָט pr. name masc. . . . . . . נבט

נָבִיא[o] וְ׳ Hiph. fut. 1 pers. pl. . . . . בוא

נָבִיא וְ׳ noun masc. sing. dec. 3a . . . . נבא

נְבִיאָה Chald. noun m. s. emph. [of נְבִיא irr. § 68] נבא

נְבִיאָה[p] noun fem. sing. from נָבִיא masc. . . נבא

נְבִיאָו[q] Kh. נְבִיאוֹ for נְבִיאָיו q. v.; K. נְבִיאַי (q. v.) נבא

נְבִיאַי וּ׳ noun m. pl. constr. fr. נָבִיא d. 3a; וּ bef. (:) נבא

נְבִיאַיָּא[r], נְבִיאַיָּה[s] } Chald. noun masc. pl. emph. [from נְבִיא irr. § 68] . . . . נבא

נְבִיאֶיהָ וּ׳ noun masc. pl., suff. 3 pers. sing. fem. from נָבִיא dec. 3a; וּ bef. (:) . . . נבא

נְבִיאֵיהֶם וּ id. pl., suff. 3 pers. pl. masc.; וּ id. . נבא

נְבִיאָיו id. pl., suff. 3 pers. sing. masc. . . . נבא

נְבִיאַיִךְ[t] id. pl., suff. 2 pers. sing. fem. . . . נבא

נְבִיאֶיךָ id. pl., suff. 2 pers. sing. masc. . . . נבא

נְבִיאֵיכֶם id. pl., suff. 2 pers. pl. masc. . . . נבא

נְבִיאִים id. pl., abs. st. . . . . . . נבא

נְבִיאֶךָ[u] id. sing., suff. 2 pers. sing. masc. (for נְבִיאֲךָ) נבא

נְבִיאֲכֶם[x] id. sing., suff. 2 pers. pl. masc. . . נבא

נְבִיאֵם[y] וְ׳ Hiph. fut. 1 pers. plur. (נָבִיא), suff. 3 pers. pl. masc.; וְ for וַ, conv. . . . בוא

נְבָיוֹת, נְבָית } pr. name of a man and a people . נבה

נִבֵּיתָ[z] Niph. pret. 2 p. s. m. for נִבֵּאתָ (§ 23. r. 11) נבא

נָבַךְ Root not used; prob. i. q. Chald. נְבַג *to spring, gush forth*.

נֵבֶךְ m. d. 6b, *fountain*, Job 38. 16, so the Sept.

נְבֻכַדְנֶאצַּר, נְבֻכַד־נֶאצַּר, נְבֻכַדְנֶצַּר } pr. name masc. defect., see נְבוּכַד׳

נָבֹכוּ[a] Niph. pret. 3 pers. pl. . . . . בוך

נִבְכֵי[b] noun masc. pl. constr. of [נֵבֶךְ] dec. 6b . נבך

נְבֻכִים[c] Niph. part. masc. pl. [of נָבוֹךְ § 32. rem. 5] בוך

[a] 1 Sa. 10. 14. [b] Ps. 132. 7. [c] Je. 4. 5. [d] 2 Ch. 9. 29. [e] Est. 3. 15. [f] Ps. 44. 6. [g] Da. 5. 17. [h] 1 Sa. 14. 36. [i] Ps. 119. 141. [k] Am. 3. 11. [l] Mal. 2. 9. [m] Je. 8. 3. [n] Job 34. 4. [o] Ps. 90. 12. [p] Ju 4. 4. [q] 2 Ki. 17. 13. [r] Ezr. 5. 1. [s] Ezr. 5. 2. [t] La. 2. 14. [u] Ex. 7. 1. [x] Nu. 12. 6. [y] 2 Ch. 2. 15. [z] Je. 26. 9. [a] Joel 1. 18. [b] Job 38. 16. [c] Ex. 14. 3.

נָבֵל fut. יִבֹּל.—I. *to wither, fade, fall off,* of leaves and flowers.—II. trop. *to wear, waste, fall away.*—III. *to be weak, to act foolishly,* Pr. 30. 32. Hiph. *to wither, fade,* Is. 64. 5. Pi. נִבֵּל, *to lightly esteem, despise, contemn.*

נָבָל, fem. נְבָלָה (Job 2. 10) adj.—I. *foolish.*—II. *wicked, impious, ungodly.*

נֶבֶל, נֵבֶל masc. dec. 6b or a.—I. *bottle, skin-bottle,* as being shrivelled, flaccid.—II. any kind of *vessel* or *jar,* made of earthenware.—III. *a musical instrument,* perhaps so called from its shape; generally considered to have been a kind of *lute.*

נְבָלָה fem.—I. *folly.*—II. *impiety, wickedness.*—III. *disgraceful action, crime.*—V. meton. *punishment,* for such an action, Job 42. 8.

נְבֵלָה fem. dec. 11c (with suff. נִבְלָתוֹ, once נְבֵלָתִי § 42. rem. 4), *corpse, carcase,* of men and animals; trop. of idols, Je. 16. 18.

נַבְלוּת fem. dec. 1b, *shame, nakedness,* Ho. 2. 12.

נָבָל [a] ׳וְ adj. masc. sing. dec. 4a; also pr. name . נבל

נָבֶל Seg. noun in pause for נֶבֶל (§ 35. rem. 2) נבל

נַּבֶל[b] וַ [for נַבֵּל] Hiph. fut. 1 p. pl. ap. [fr. נַבִּיל], acc. drawn back by conv. וַ [for וַנַבֵּל] נבל

נָבוֹל[c] Kal inf. abs. . . . . . . נבל

נֵבֶל ׳וְ / נֶבֶל[d] [e]׳וֶ } noun masc. sing. dec. 6b or a; for וְ see lett. ו . . . . } נבל

נֹבֵל[f] Kal part. sing. masc. . . . נבל

נָבְלָה[xx] id. pret. 3 pers. sing. fem. . . . . נבל

נָבְלָה[g] וְ Kal fut. 1 pers. pl. with parag. ה [for נָבֹלָּה § 18. rem. 15, & § 8. rem. 13] . בלל

נְבָלָה ׳וּ n. f. s. (no pl. or sing. constr.); וּ bef. (:) נבל

נְבֵלָה [h]׳וּ noun fem. s. d. 11c (§ 42. rem. 4); וּ id. נבל

נְבַלָּט pr. name of a town in the tribe of Benjamin, Ne. 11. 34.

נִבְלֵי[i] [k]׳וְ noun masc. pl. constr. from נֵבֶל dec. 6b נבל

נִבְלֵיהֶם[l] וְ id. pl., suff. 3 pers. pl. masc. . . . נבל

נְבָלֶיךָ id. pl., suff. 2 pers. sing. masc. . . . נבל

נְבָלִים ׳וּ id. pl., abs. st.; וּ bef. (:) . . . נבל

נִבְלַע[m] Niph. pret. 3 pers. sing. masc. . . בלע

נִבְלְעוּ[n] id. pret. 3 pers. pl. . . . . בלע

נְבַלְּעֵם[o] Kal fut. 1 pers. pl. [נְבַלַּע], suff. 3 pers. pl. masc. (§ 16. rem. 12) . . . בלע

נֹבֶלֶת[p] Kal part. act. sing. fem. of נֹבֵל . נבל

נָבַלְתָּ[q] id. pret. 2 pers. sing. masc. . . . נבל

נִבְלַת noun f. s. constr. of נְבֵלָה d. 11c (§ 42. r. 4) נבל

נַבְלֻתָהּ[r] noun f. s., suff. 3 pers. s. f. fr. [נַבְלוּת] d. 1b נבל

נִבְלָתָהּ[s] noun fem. sing., suff. 3 pers. sing. fem. from נְבֵלָה dec. 11c (§ 42. rem. 4) . . נבל

נִבְלָתוֹ [t]׳וְ id., suff. 3 pers. sing. masc. . . . נבל

נְבֵלָתִי[u] id., suff. 1 pers. sing. (..) immut. § 42. r. 4) נבל

נִבַּלְתִּיךְ[x] וְ Piel pret. 1 pers. sing., suff. 2 pers. sing. f. נבל

נִבְלָתְךָ noun fem. sing., suff. 2 pers. sing. masc. from נְבֵלָה dec. 11c (§ 42. rem. 4) . . נבל

נִבְלָתָם id., suff. 3 pers. pl. masc. . . . . נבל

נִבְנָה Niph. pret. 3 pers. sing. masc. . . . בנה

נִבְנֶה [y]וַנִּ ,׳וְ Kal fut. 1 pers. pl.; ־וַ conv. . בנה

נִבְנוּ[z] ׳וְ Niph. pret. 3 pers. pl. . . . בנה

נְבֻנוֹתִי[a] Niph. pret. 1 pers. sing. . . . . בין

נְבֹנָיו[b] id. part. pl., suff. 3 pers. s. m. fr. נָבוֹן d. 3a בין

נְבֹנִים[c] וּ id. id., abs. st.; וּ bef. (:) . . . בין

נִבְנֵית[d] וְ Niph. pret. 2 pers. sing. fem. . . בנה

נִבְנְתָה ׳וְ id. pret. 3 pers. sing. fem. . . . בנה

[נָבַע] *to gush out, bubble out* or *up,* Pr. 18. 4. Hiph. הִבִּיעַ.—I. *to pour forth, to utter, declare.*—II. *to cause to bubble up,* as fermenting matter, *to render putrid,* Ec. 10. 1.

מַבּוּעַ masc. dec. 1b, *spring* or *fountain.*

נֹבֵעַ[e] Kal part. sing. masc. . . . . נבע

נִבְעֶה[f] Niph. part. sing. masc. . . . . בעה

נִבְעוּ[g] id. pret. 3 pers. pl. . . . . בעה

נִבְעַר[h] Niph. pret. 3 pers. sing. masc. . . . בער

נִבְעָרָה[i] id. part. sing. fem. . . . . בער

נְבַעֲרָה[k] וּ Piel (§ 14. rem. 1) fut. 1 pers. pl. with parag. ה; וּ bef. (:) . . . . בער

נִבְעָרוּ[l] Niph. pret. 3 pers. pl. . . . . בער

נִבְעַת Niph. pret. 3 pers. sing. masc. . . . בעת

נִבְעָתִּי[m] id. pret. 1 pers. s. [for נִבְעַתְּתִּי § 25. rem.] בעת

נִבְקָה[n] וְ Niph. pret. 3 p. s. f. [for נִבְקְקָה § 18. r. 15] בקק

נְבַקִיעֶנָּה[o] וְ Hiph. fut. 1 pers. pl., suff. 3 pers. sing. f. בקע

נִבְקַע[p] [q]׳וְ Niph. pret. 3 pers. sing. masc. . בקע

נִבְקְעוּ / נִבְקָעוּ } id. pret. 3 pers. pl. (comp. § 8. rem. 7) בקע

נְבַקֵּשׁ[r] Piel fut. 1 pers. pl. . . . . בקש

נְבַקְשָׁה[s] וַ id. with parag. ה (§ 8. rem. 13); ־וַ conv. בקש

נְבַקְשֶׁנּוּ[t] וּ id. with suff. 3 pers. sing. masc.; וּ bef. (:) בקש

נָבָר Niph. part. sing. masc. . . . . ברר

נִבְרָא[u] Niph. part. sing. masc. . . . . ברא

נִבְרָאוּ[v] / נִבְרָאוּ וְ } id. pret. 3 pers. pl. (comp. § 8. rem. 7) ברא

[a] Pr. 30. 22. [b] Is. 64. 5. [c] Ex. 18. 18. [d] Ps. 71. 22. [e] Is. 5. 12.
[f] Is. 28. 1. 4. [g] Ge. 11. 7. [h] Eze. 4. 14. [i] 1 Sa. 15. 18. [k] Job 38. 37.
[l] Je. 48. 12. [m] Ho. 8. 8. [n] Is. 28. 7. [o] Pr. 1. 12. [p] Is. 1. 30.
[q] Pr. 30. 32. [r] Ho. 2. 12. [s] Le. 11. 40. [t] Je. 36. 30. [u] Is. 26. 19.
[x] Na. 3. 6. [y] Ne. 3. 38. [z] Mal. 3. 15. [a] Is. 10. 13. [b] Is. 29. 14.
[c] De. 1. 13. [d] Je. 31. 4. [e] Pr. 18. 4. [f] Is. 30. 13. [g] Ob. 1, 6.
[h] Je. 10. 14. [i] Is. 19. 11. [k] Ju. 20. 13. [l] Je. 10. 21. [m] Da. 8. 17.
[n] Is. 19. 3. [o] Is. 7. 6. [p] Job 26. 8. [q] Zec. 14. 4. [r] Ne. 5. 12.
[s] Ezr. 8. 23. [t] Ca. 6. 1. [u] Ps. 102. 19. [v] Ps. 148. 5. [xx] Is. 24. 4.

נִבְרֵאת[a] id. pret. 2 pers. sing. fem. . . . ברא

נִבְרְחָה[b] וְ Kal fut. 1 pers. pl. with parag. ה (§ 8. r. 13) ברח

נְבָרֵךְ[c] Piel fut. 1 pers. pl. . . . . ברך

נִבְרְכָה[d] Kal fut. 1 pers. pl. with parag. ה (§ 8. r. 13) ברך

נִבְרְכוּ וְ Niph. pret. 3 pers. pl. . . . ברך

נֶבְרַשְׁתָּא Ch. f., emph. [of נֶבְרַשָׁא d. 9a] *lamp*, Da. 5. 5.

נְבַשֵּׁל[e] וַ Piel fut. 1 pers. pl.; ·וַ conv. . . בשל

נִגְאַל[f] וְ Niph. pret. 3 pers. sing. masc. [for נִגְאַל] גאל

נִגְאָלָה[g] וְ id. part. sing. fem. . . . . גאל

נְגֹאַלוּ pret. 1 pers. sing. (§ 6. No. 10 note) . גאל

נָגַב Root not used; Syr. & Chald. *to be dry*. Hence

נֶגֶב masc.—I. *the desert* tract of land to the *south* of Judea.—II. *the south*; with ה parag. נֶגְבָּה (§ 35. rem. 3) *towards the south, southward*; לְנֶגְבָּה, בְּנֶגְבָּה in the region lying *towards the south*; מִנֶּגֶב *from the south*; simply נֶגֶב *south, on the south*, comp. Zec. 14. 10 . . . . . נגב

נֶגְבָּה[h] ,וְ ,וָ ,ו׳ id. with loc. ה; for וָ see lett. ו נגב

נַגְבִּיר[i] Hiph. fut. 1 pers. pl. . . . . גבר

נָגַד Kal not used; Arab. *to be clear and manifest*. Hiph. הִגִּיד.—I. *to declare, show, tell, announce*, with לְ of the pers. to whom.—II. *to publish, proclaim with commendation, to praise*.—III. *to betray*, Job 17. 5. Hoph. הֻגַּד *to be shown, told*.

נְגַד Chald. *to flow*, Da. 7. 10.

נֶגֶד with suff. נֶגְדִּי (§ 35. rem. 3) prep.—I. *before, in the presence* or *sight of*.—II. *over against, in front of, opposite to*.—III. *in comparison with*, Is. 40. 17.—IV. *straight, forwards*, comp. Jos. 6. 5, 20. —V. with prepositions. כְּנֶגֶד Ge. 2. 18, 20. כְּנֶגְדּוֹ *as over against him*, i. e. *corresponding to him*, his counterpart; or, *one like him* (Lee);—לְנֶגֶד *before, in the presence of; over against; against, in opposition to; for, appointed to; before*, proceeding on a journey;—מִנֶּגֶד *from before, away from, aloof from; before, in the presence of, over against, opposite*, const. with לְ; *against, in opposition to*, with לְ.

נֶגֶד Chald. prep. *towards*, Da. 6. 11.

נָגִיד masc. dec. 3a. — I. *leader, chief, prefect, overseer*.—II. *prince*.—III. pl. *nobles*; neut. *noble, excellent thing*, Pr. 8. 6.

נָגֵד[k] Chald. Peal part. sing. masc. . . . נגד

נַגֵּד[l] וְ Hiph. fut. 1 pers. pl., ap. & conv. from נַגִּיד . . . . . נגד

נֶגֶד[m] ,וְ ו׳ (prop. subst. m. d. 6) as a *prep.* (§ 35. r. 3) נגד

נְגִד defect. for נָגִיד (q. v.) . . . . נגד

נֶגְדָּהּ[l] prep. (נֶגֶד) with suff. 3 p. s. f. (§ 35. r. 3) נגד

נֶגְדָּה־[m] id. with loc. ה . . . . . נגד

נֶגְדּוֹ id., suff. 3 pers. sing. masc. . . . נגד

נֶגְדִּי id., suff. 1 pers. sing. . . . . נגד

נֶגְדְּךָ, נֶגְדֶּךָ } id., suff. 2 pers. sing. masc. . . . נגד

נֶגְדָּם[n] וְ ו׳ id., suff. 3 pers. pl. masc. . . . נגד

נִגְדַּע[o], נִגְדָּע[p] } Niph. pret. 3 p. s. m. (the reading נִגְדַּע in Je. 50. 23 is only confined to *some* copies) } גדע

נִגְדְּעָה[q] וְ ו׳ id. pret. 3 pers. sing. fem. . . . גדע

נִגְדָּעוּ וְ id. pret. 3 pers. pl. . . . . גדע

נִגְדַּעְתָּ[s] id. pret. 2 pers. sing. masc. . . . . גדע

נָגַהּ fut. יִגַּהּ *to shine, give light*. Hiph. הִגִּיהַּ.—I. *to cause to shine*, Is. 13. 10.—II. *to make light, enlighten*.

נֹגַהּ masc. dec. 6c (§ 35. rem. 5).—I. *shining, brightness, splendour*.—II. pr. name of a son of David.

נֹגַהּ Chald. masc. dec. 3e, *light*, Da. 6. 20.

נְגֹהָה fem. dec. 10, *shining brightness*, Is. 59. 9.

נֹגַהּ ו׳ noun m. s. d. 6c (§ 35. r. 5), also pr. name נגה

נָגְהָם id., suff. 3 pers. pl. masc. . . . . נגה

נְגוֹ, נְגוֹא } pr. name in compos. עֲבֵד נְגוֹ see. . . עבד

נָגֹזּוּ[t] Niph. pret. 3 pers. pl. [for נָגֹזּוּ comp. § 18. r. 2] גזז

נָגוּעַ Kal part. pass. sing. masc. . . . . נגע

נִגּוֹף[u] Niph. inf. abs. (§ 9. rem. 2, & § 17. rem. 4) נגף

נִגְזְלָה[w] וְ Niph. pret. 3 pers. sing. fem. . . . גזל

נִגְזַר Niph. pret. 3 pers. sing. masc. . . . גזר

נִגְזָרוּ[y] id. pret. 3 pers. pl. [for נִגְזְרוּ comp. § 8. r. 7] גזר

נִגְזָרְנוּ[z] id. pret. 1 pers. pl. . . . . גזר

נִגְזָרְתִּי[a] id. pret. 1 pers. s. [for נִגְזַרְתִּי comp. § 8. r. 7] גזר

[נָגַח] fut. יִגַּח *to push, butt* with the horns, Ex. 21. 28, 31, 32. Pi. id. trop. of a conqueror prostrating nations. Hithp. with עִם *to engage in conflict with* any one, Da. 11. 40.

נַגָּח masc. *addicted to push* or *butt* with the horns, Ex. 21. 29. 36.

נַגָּח[b] noun masc. sing. . . . . . נגח

נָגִיד[c] ו׳ noun masc. sing. dec. 3a . . . נגד

נַגִּיד[d] Hiph. fut. 1 pers. pl. . . . . נגד

[a] Eze. 21. 35. [b] 2 Sa. 15. 14. [c] Ps. 115. 18. [d] Ps. 95. 6. [e] 2 Ki. 6. 29. [f] Le. 25. 49. [g] Zep. 3. 1. [h] Eze. 48. 10, 17. [i] Ps. 12. 5. [k] Da. 7. 10. [l] Am. 4. 3. [m] Ps. 116. 14, 18. [n] Ne. 12. 37. [o] Je. 50. 23. [p] Ju. 21. 6. [q] Je. 48. 25. [r] Is. 22. 25. [s] Is. 14. 12. [t] Na. 1. 12. [u] Ju. 20. 39. [w] Pr. 4. 16. [y] Ps. 88. 6. [z] Eze. 37. 11. [a] La. 3. 54. [b] Ex. 21. 29, 36. [c] 2 Ch. 32. 21. [d] Je. 36. 16.

נְגִיד noun masc. sing., constr. of נָגִיד dec. 3a . . . נגד
נַגִּידָה[a] וְ Hiph. fut. 1 p. pl. with parag. ה (comp. § 8. r. 13) נגד
נְגִידֵי[b] / נְגִידִים } noun masc. pl. constr. & abs. from נָגִיד dec. 3a . . . . . } נגד
נַגִּידֶנּוּ[c] וְ Hiph. fut. 1 pers. pl., suff. 3 pers. sing. m. נגד
נָגִילָה Kal fut. 1 p. pl. with parag. ה (comp. § 8. r. 13) גול
נְגִינוֹת[d] וּ noun fem. pl. of [נְגִינָה] dec. 10; וּ bef. (:) נגן
נְגִינוֹתַי[e] וּ id. pl., suff. 1 pers. sing.; וּ id. . . נגן
נְגִינַת[f] id. sing., constr. st. . . . . נגן
נְגִינָתִי[g] id. sing., suff. 1 pers. sing. . . . נגן
נְגִינָתָם id. sing., suff. 3 pers. pl. . . . נגן

נָגַל Root not used; Arab. *to cut, wound.*
מַגָּל masc. *sickle*, Je. 50. 16; Joel 4. 13.

נִגְלָה וְ' Niph. pret. 3 pers. sing. masc., or part. fem. dec. 10 [from נִגְלֶה masc.] . . . גלה
נָגֹלּוּ[h] וְ Niph. pret. 3 pers. pl. . . . . גלל
נִגְלוּ Niph. pret. 3 pers. pl. . . . . גלה
נִגְלוֹת[i] id. inf. constr. . . . . . גלה
נִגְלִינוּ[k] וְ id. pret. 1 pers. pl. (§ 24. rem. 8) . . גלה
נִגְלֵיתִי[l] id. pret. 1 pers. sing. . . . . גלה
נִגְלָתָה[m] id. pret. 3 p. s. fem. [for נִגְלְתָה comp. § 8. r. 7] גלה

[נָגַן] Ps. 68. 26, and Pi. נִגֵּן *to play on a stringed instrument.*

נְגִינָה fem. dec. 10.—I. *music.*—II. *a song;* meton. *subject of a song.*

מַנְגִּינָה fem. d. 10, *song of derision, satire,* La. 3. 62.

נַגֵּן Piel inf. constr. . . . . . נגן
נִגֵּן[n] וְ id. pret. 3 pers. sing. masc. . . . נגן
נִגְנֹב[o] Kal fut. 1 pers. pl. . . . . . גנב
נֹגְנִים[p] Kal part. act. masc. pl. [of נֹגֵן] dec. 7b . נגן

נָגַע[q] וְ' fut. יִגַּע, inf. c. נְגֹעַ, גַּעַת.—I. *to touch, meddle with;* const. with בְּ, אֶל, עַל; metaph. *to touch, affect* the heart.—II. *to touch, to reach, come to, arrive at,* with בְּ, עַד, אֶל, עַל; abs. of time, *to arrive.*—III. *to touch with force and violence, to strike, smite.* Niph. *to be smitten, beaten* in battle, Jos. 8. 15. Pi. *to smite,* as God does, with disease and calamities. Pu. pass. Ps. 73. 5. Hiph. הִגִּיעַ.—I. *to cause to touch;* הִ' בַּיִת בְּבַיִת *to cause house to touch house,* i. e. to join house to house; הִ' לָאָרֶץ *to cause to touch* (i. e. cast down to) *the ground.*—II. *to touch,* with עַל, אֶל, לְ.—III. *to reach to,* with עַד, לְ.—IV. *to come to,* with אֶל, עַד, לְ; hence, *to come upon, happen to;* with לְ *to attain to,* Est. 4. 14; abs. *to come, arrive.*

נֶגַע masc. dec. 6a (§ 35. rem. 5; with suff. נִגְעִי).—I. *stroke, blow,* comp. De. 17. 8.—II. *infliction of evil, calamity, plague,* espec. as a divine judgment.—III. *spot, mark,* as of leprosy.

גַּעְתָּם (for נֶגַע תַּם *calamity is ended*) pr. name masc. Ge. 36. 11, 16.

נֶגַע / נָגַע[r] וְ' } noun masc. sing. (suff. נִגְעִי) dec. 6a (§ 35. rem. 2 & 5) . . } נגע
נֹגֵעַ[s] וְ' Kal part. act. sing. masc. dec. 7b . נגע
נְגֹעַ[t] וּ id. inf. constr.; וּ bef. (:) . . . נגע
נָגְעָה[u] וְ' id. pret. 3 pers. sing. fem. . . . נגע
נָגְעוּ id. pret. 3 pers. pl. [for נָגְעוּ § 8. rem. 7] נגע
נִגְּעוֹ[x] Piel pret. 3 pers. s. m. [נִגַּע], suff. 3 pers. s. m. נגע
נִגְעוֹ noun masc. sing., suff. 3 pers. sing. masc. from נֶגַע dec. 6a (§ 35. rem. 5) . . נגע
נִגְעִי[y] id. with suff. 1 pers. sing. . . . . נגע
נְגָעִים[z] id. pl., abs. st. . . . . . נגע
נָגְעֵךְ[a] Kal inf., suff. 2 pers sing. fem. . . . נגע
נִגְעֵךְ[b] noun masc. sing., suff. 2 pers. sing. masc. [for נִגְעֲךָ] from נֶגַע dec. 6a (§ 35. rem. 5) נגע
נִגְעַל[c] Niph. pret. 3 pers. sing. masc. . . . געל
נְגַעֲנוּךָ[d] Kal pret. 1 pers. pl., suff. 2 pers. sing. masc. נגע
נֹגַעַת / נֹגְעֹת[e] } id. part. sing. and pl. fem. dec. 13 from נֹגֵעַ masc. (§ 39. No. 4b) . . } נגע

נָגַף[g] וְ' fut. יִגֹּף.—I. *to strike, smite,* with the hand, a sword, &c.—II. *to smite,* as God does, with disease and calamities, *to plague.*—III. *to thrust, push.*—IV. *to strike, stumble against.* Niph. *to be smitten, defeated.* Hithp. *to strike oneself, stumble against,* Je. 13. 16.

נֶגֶף masc.—I. *infliction of disease, plague,* as a divine judgment.—II. *a stumbling,* Is. 8. 14.

מַגֵּפָה fem. dec. 10.—I. *a plague* or *pestilence.*—II. *a beating,* defeat in battle.

נָגֹף[h] Kal inf. abs. . . . . . נגף
נֶגֶף noun masc. sing. . . . . . נגף
נִגָּף Niph. part. sing. masc. . . . . נגף
נִגַּף[i] id. pret. 3 pers. sing. masc. . . . נגף
נֹגֵף id. part. act. sing. masc. . . . . נגף
נִגְּפוּ[k] וְ id. pret. 3 pers. pl. . . . . נגף
נְגָפוֹ[l] id. pret. 3 pers. sing. m., suff. 3 pers. sing. m. נגף
נִגְּפוּ[m] / נִגְּפוּ } Niph. pret. 3 pers. pl. (comp. § 8. rem. 7) נגף
נִגָּפִים id. part., pl. of נִגָּף . . . . נגף

[a] 2 Ki. 7. 9. [b] 2 Ch. 35. 8. [c] Je. 20. 10. [d] Ps. 69. 13. [e] Is. 38. 20. [f] Ps. 61. 1. [g] Ps. 77. 7. [h] Is. 34. 4. [i] 2 Sa. 6. 20. [k] 1 Sa. 14. 8. [l] 1 Sa. 2. 27. [m] Is. 53. 1. [n] 1 Sa. 16. 16, 23. [o] Ge. 44. 8. [p] Ps. 68. 26. [q] Hag. 2. 12. [r] Ps. 91. 10. [s] Le. 11. 36. [t] Ex. 19. 12. [u] Je. 4. 10. [x] 2 Ch. 26. 20. [y] Ps. 38. 12. [z] Ge. 12. 17. [a] Ru. 2. 9. [b] Ps. 39. 11. [c] 2 Sa. 1. 21. [d] Ge. 26. 29. [e] 1 Ki. 6. 27. [f] 2 Ch. 13. 15. [g] Is. 19. 22. [h] Is. 19. 22. [i] 2 Sa. 10. 15. [k] Ex. 21. 22. [l] 2 Ch. 21. 18. [m] Ju. 20. 36.

[a]נְגָפָנוּ Kal pret. 3 pers. sing. masc., suff. 1 pers. pl. נגף

[b]נִגַּפְתֶּם וְ Niph. pret. 2 pers. pl. masc. . . . נגף

נָגַר. Niph. נִגַּר.—I. *to be poured out, to flow out.*—II. *to flow, run,* as a wound, Ps. 77. 3. יָדִי נִגְּרָה *my hand* (i. e. *the hand upon me*), *my wound runs*; others, *my hand is put forth, stretched out.* Hiph. הִגִּיר.—I. *to pour out,* Ps. 75. 9.—II. *to pour, thrust down,* Mi. 1. 6.—III. trop. *to deliver up, give over.* Hoph. *to be poured down,* Mi. 1. 4.

נִגָּרָה Niph. pret. 3 pers. sing. fem. . . . נגר

[c]נִגָּרוֹת Niph. part. fem. pl. [of נִגָּרָה from נִגָּר masc. § 18. rem, 14] . . . . . גרר

[d]נִגְרַזְתִּי Niph. pret. 1 pers. sing. . . . גרז

[e]נִגָּרַע Niph. fut. 1 pers. pl. . . . גרע

[f]נִגְרָע id. part. sing. masc. . . . . גרע

[g]וְ נִגְרַע id. pret. 3 pers. sing. masc. . . . גרע

[h]וְ נִגְרְעָה id. pret. 3 pers. sing. fem. . . . גרע

[i]נִגְרָשׁ Niph. part. sing. masc. . . . גרש

[k]וְ נִגְרְשָׁה id. pret. 3 pers. sing. fem. . . . גרש

[l]נִגְרַשְׁתִּי id. pret. 1 pers. sing. . . . גרש

נָגַשׂ[m] fut. יִגֹּשׂ.—I. *to impel, drive,* Job 39. 7.—II. *to urge* any one, *to exact,* a task, debt or tax from him; part. נֹגֵשׂ *an exactor, task-master.*—III. *to oppress;* part. נֹגֵשׂ *oppressor.* Niph. I. *to be oppressed.*—II. *to be wearied, distressed,* 1 Sa. 14. 24.

[נָגַשׁ] fut. יִגַּשׁ, imp. גַּשׁ, גֶּשׁ, inf. c. גֶּשֶׁת; and Niph. נִגַּשׁ *to draw* or *come near, to approach,* constr. with עַל, עַד, לְ, בְּ, אֶל *to* any person or thing. Hiph. הִגִּישׁ.—I. *to bring near.*—II. *to offer, present,* espec. a sacrifice.—III. *to approach,* Am. 9. 10. Hoph. הֻגַּשׁ.—I. *to be brought, placed, put,* 2 Sa. 3. 34. —II. *to be offered,* Mal. 1. 11. Hithp. *to approach,* Is. 45. 20.

[n]נִגַּשׂ וְ״ Niph. pret. 3 pers. sing. masc. . . . נגשׂ

נִגַּשׁ וְ׳ Niph. pret. 3 pers. sing. masc. . . . נגשׁ

נֹגֵשׂ Kal part. act. masc. dec. 7b . . . נגשׂ

[o]וְ נִגְּשָׁה Niph. pret. 3 pers. sing. fem. . . . נגשׁ

וְ׳ נִגְּשׁוּ id. pret. 3 pers. pl. . . . נגשׁ

[p]נֹגְשֵׂי Kal part. pl. constr. masc. from נֹגֵשׂ dec. 7b נגשׂ

נֹגְשָׂיו id. pl., suff. 3 pers. sing. masc. . . . נגשׂ

[q]וְ נֹגְשַׂיִךְ id. pl., suff. 2 pers. sing. fem. . . . נגשׂ

[r]נְגַשְׁשָׁה
[s]נְגַשְׁשָׁה
} Piel fut. 1 pers. pl. with parag. ה (comp. § 8. rem. 13 & 15) . . . } גשש

[t]נִגַּשְׁתֶּם Niph. pret. 2 pers. pl. masc. . . . נגשׁ

[u]וָ נָד Kal part. act. sing. masc.; for וָ comp. lett. ו נוד

נֵד noun masc. sing.; or (Is. 17. 11) Kal pret. 3 pers. sing. masc. (§ 21. rem. 2) . נדד

[נָדָא] i.q. נָדָה Hiph. *to remove, separate,* 2 Ki. 17. 21. Kh.

נָדַב[x] *to impel, make willing.* Hithp. I. *to show oneself willing, to act voluntarily.*—II. *to give, offer willingly.*

נְדַב Chald. Ithpa. i. q. Heb. Hithp. inf. הִתְנַדָּבוּת as subst. *free-will offering,* Ezr. 7. 16.

נָדָב (*liberal*) pr. name masc. of several persons, espec. (*a*) son of Jeroboam; (*b*) son of Aaron.

נְדָבָה fem. dec. 11c.—I. *willingness, free will;* Ps. 110. 3, עַמְּךָ נְדָבוֹת *thy people will be willingness,* i. e. *willing.*—II. *voluntary offering.*—III. *liberality, abundance,* Ps. 68. 10.

נָדִיב masc. dec. 3a, fem. נְדִיבָה adj.—I. *willing, ready.*—II. *liberal.*—III. *noble, noble-minded.*—IV. *noble,* as a subst. *a noble, a prince.*—V. prob. *libertine,* Job 21. 8 (Lee).

נְדִיבָה fem. d. 10, *nobility, excellency,* Job 30. 15.

נוֹדָב (*noble*) pr. name masc. 1 Ch. 5. 19.

נְדַבְיָה (*noble of the Lord*) pr. name masc. 1 Ch. 3. 18.

נָדָב וְ׳ pr. name masc. . . . . . נדב

[y]נָדְבָה Kal pret. 3 pers. sing. fem. . . . נדב

נְדָבָה noun fem. sing. dec. 11a . . . . נדב

נְדָבוֹת id. pl., abs. st. . . . . . נדב

נִדְבוֹת id. pl., constr. st. . . . . . נדב

[z]נִדְבוֹתָם id. pl., suff. 3 pers. pl. masc. . . . נדב

נְדַבְיָה וּ pr. name masc.; וּ bef. (:) . . . נדב

[a]וְ נִדְבָּךְ Chald. noun masc. sing. dec. 1a . . דבך

[b]נִדְבָּכִין Chald. id. pl., abs. st. . . . . דבך

נְדַבֵּר Piel fut. 1 pers. pl. . . . . . דבר

[c]נִדְבְּרוּ
[d]נִדְבָּרוּ
} Niph. pret. 3 pers. pl. (comp. § 8. rem. 7) דבר

[e]נִדְבַּרְנוּ id. pret. 1 pers. pl. . . . . דבר

[f]נִדְבַת noun fem. pl. abs. from נְדָבָה d. 11c, see נְדָבוֹת נדב

[g]נִדְבַת id. sing., constr. st. . . . . נדב

[dd]נְדִבָתִי adj. fem. sing., suff. 1 pers. sing. from נְדִיבָה dec. 10, from נָדִיב masc. . . . נדב

[h]וְ נִדְבֹתֶיךָ noun fem. pl., suff. 2 p. s. m. fr. נְדָבָה d. 11c נדב

[i]וְ׳ נִדְבֹתֵיכֶם id. pl., suff. 2 pers. pl. masc. . . . נדב

[k]נִדְגֹּל Kal fut. 1 pers. pl. . . . . דגל

[נָדַד] fem. נָדְדָה, fut. יִדֹּד, יִדַּד.—I. *to move,* as the wing, Is. 10. 14.—II. *to move, wander about.*—III.

[a] 1 Sa. 4. 3. [b] Le. 26. 17. [c] Job 20. 28. [d] Ps. 31. 23. [e] Nu. 9. 7. [f] Ex. 5. 11. [g] Le. 27. 18. [h] Nu. 36. 3. [i] Is. 57. 20. [k] Am. 8. 8. [l] Jon. 2. 5. [m] 2 Ki. 23. 35. [n] Is. 3. 5. [o] De. 25. 9. [p] Ex. 5. 10, 14. [q] Is. 60. 17. [r] Is. 59. 10. [s] Is. 59. 10. [t] 2 Sa. 11. 20, 21. [u] Ge. 4. 12, 14. [x] Ex. 35. 29. [y] Ex. 35. 29. [z] Le. 22. 18. [a] Ezr. 6. 4. [b] Ezr. 6. 4. [c] Ps. 119. 23. [d] Mal. 3. 16. [dd] Job 30. 15. [e] Mal. 3. 13. [f] Ps. 110. 3. [g] De. 16. 10. [h] De. 12. 17. [i] Le. 23. 38. [k] Ps. 20. 6.

to flee; of a bird, to fly away. Po. to flee away, Na. 3. 17. Hiph. הֵנֵד to chase away, Job 18. 18. Hoph. הֻנַּד (§ 18. rem. 14) fut. יֻנַּד to be made to wander, be driven to and fro. Hithpo. to flee, or be agitated, Ps. 64. 9.

נְדַד Chald. to flee, Da. 6. 19.

נְדֻדִים masc. pl. agitation, restlessness, Job 7. 4.

נֵד masc. heap, mound; Is. 17. 11 נֵד קָצִיר the heap of the harvest; but see R. נוד.

נִדָּה fem. dec. 10.—I. uncleanness, impurity, of the female menses.—II. unclean, filthy thing, of idols, of incest.

נִידָה fem. (for נִדָּה dag. forte resolved in Yod) uncleanness, La. 1. 8; but comp. R. נוד.

נְדֹד[a] Kal inf. constr. . . . . . נדד

נֹדֵד id. part. sing. masc. dec. 7b . . . נדד

נָדְדָה id. pret. 3 pers. sing. fem. . . . . נדד

נָדְדוּ / נָדָדוּ } Kal pret. 3 pers. pl. (§ 8. rem. 7) . נדד

נְדֻדִים[b] noun masc. pl. abs. . . . . . נדד

נֹדְדִים[u] Kal part. act. masc. pl. of נוֹדֵד dec. 7b נדד

I. נָדָה. Pi. נִדָּה to remove, put away or thrust out.

II. נָדָה Root not used; to give.

נֵדֶה masc. gift, Eze. 16. 33.

נָדָן masc. dec. 4a, id. Eze. 16. 33.

נֵדֶה[c] noun masc. sing. . . . . . נדה

נִדָּה noun fem. sing. dec. 10 . . . . נדד

נִדְהָם[d] Niph. part. sing. masc. . . . . . דהם

נָדוּ[e] Kal pret. 3 pers. pl. . . . . . נוד

נֻדוּ id. imp. pl. masc. . . . . . . נוד

נָדוֹן[f] Niph. part. sing. masc. . . . . . דון

נָדוֹשׁ[g] וְ Niph. pret. 3 pers. sing. masc. . . דוש

[נָדַח] fut. יַדַּח.—I. to impel, force, thrust, De. 20. 19.—II. to expel, thrust out, 2 Sa. 14. 14. Niph. נִדַּח.—I. to be impelled, as the hand in striking with an axe, De. 19. 5.—II. to be expelled, driven or cast out.—III. to be impelled, incited, induced to an action. Pu. to be thrust, driven forth, Is. 8. 22. Hiph. הִדִּיחַ.—I. to thrust, cast down, with מִן Ps. 62. 5.—II. to draw or bring down, with עַל 2 Sa. 15. 14.—III. to thrust, drive out, expel.—IV. to urge, seduce, with מִן away from. Hoph. to be driven, chased, Is. 13. 14.

מַדּוּחַ masc. dec. 1b, seduction, La. 2. 14.

נִדָּח[h] Niph. part. sing. masc. dec. 2b . . . נדח

נִדָּחָה[i] id. part. sing. fem. . . . . . נדח

נִדְּחָה[k] וְ׳ id. pret. 3 pers. sing. fem. . . . נדח

נִדָּחוֹ[m] id. part. sing. masc., suff. 3 pers. sing. masc. [as if from נִדֶּה dec. 7b, § 15. rem. 2] נדח

נִדְּחוּ id. pret. 3 pers. pl. . . . . . נדח

נִדָּחַי[n] id. part. pl., suff. 1 pers. sing. fr. נִדָּח d. 2b נדח

נִדְּחֵי[o] / נִדְחֵי } id. id. pl., constr. st. . . . . נדח

נִדָּחִים id. id. pl., abs. st. . . . . . נדח

נִדָּחֲךָ[p] id. id. sing., suff. 2 pers. sing. masc. [as if from נִדֶּה dec. 7b, § 15. rem. 2] . נדח

נִדַּחֲכֶם[q] id. id. sing., suff. 2 pers. pl. masc. (v. id.) נדח

נִדְחָף Niph. pret. 3 pers. sing. masc. . . . דחף

נִדַּחְתָּ וְ Niph. pret. 2 pers. sing. masc.; acc. shifted by conv. וְ (comp. § 8. rem. 7) . נדח

נִדַּחְתֶּם[r] וְ id. pret. 2 pers. pl. masc. . . . נדח

נִדִי[s] noun masc. sing., suff. 1 pers. sing. from [נוֹד] dec. 1a . . . . . . נוד

נָדִיב[t] וְ׳ adj. or subst. masc. sing. dec. 3a . נדב

נְדִיב id. constr. st. . . . . . . נדב

נְדִיבָה[u] id. sing. fem. dec. 10 . . . . נדב

נְדִיבוֹת[x] id. pl. fem. . . . . . . נדב

נְדִיבֵי id. pl. constr. masc. dec. 3a . . . נדב

נְדִיבִים[y] וּ׳ id. pl. abs. masc.; וּ bef. (:) . . . נדב

נְדִיבֵמוֹ[z] id. pl. masc. with suff. 3 pers. pl. masc. . נדב

נִדְכָּאִים[a] Niph. part. masc. pl. [of נִדְכָּא] . . דכא

נִדְכֶּה[b] וְ Niph. part. sing. masc. . . . . דכה

נִדְכֵּיתִי[c] וְ id. pret. 1 pers. sing. . . . . דכה

נִדְמָה Niph. pret. 3 pers. sing. masc. . . . דמה

נִדְּמָה[d] וְ Kal fut. 1 pers. pl. with opt. ה [for נָדֹמָּה § 18. rem. 14 & 15, comp. § 8. rem. 13] דמם

נִדְמֶה[e] וְ׳ Kal fut. 1 pers. pl. or Niph. part. sing. m. דמה

נִדְמֹה[f] Niph. inf. abs. . . . . . . דמה

נָדַמּוּ[g] וְ Niph. pret. 3 pers. pl. . . . . דמם

נִדְמוּ Niph. pret. 3 pers. pl. . . . . . דמה

נִדְמֵיתָ[h] / נִדְמִיתָה[i] } id. pret. 2 pers. sing. masc. (comp. § 8. rem. 5) . . . . } דמה

נִדְמֵיתִי[k] id. pret. 1 pers. sing. . . . . . דמה

נִדְמְתָה[l] id. pret. 3 pers. sing. fem. . . . . דמה

[נָדָן] masc. dec. 4a, sheath of a sword, 1 Ch. 21. 27.

נִדְנֶה Ch. masc. sheath, trop. of the body, Da. 7. 15.

נְדָנָהּ[m] noun masc. sing., suff. 3 pers. sing. fem. from [נָדָן] dec. 4a . . . . . נדן

נִדְנֶה[n] Ch. noun masc. sing. . . . . . נדן

[a] Ps. 55. 8. [b] Job 7. 4. [c] Eze. 16. 33. [d] Je. 14. 9. [e] Je. 50. 3. [f] 2 Sa. 19. 10. [g] Is. 25. 10. [h] 2 Sa. 14. 14. [i] Je. 30. 17. [u] Hos. 9. 17. [k] Job 6. 13. [l] De. 19. 5. [m] 2 Sa. 14. 13. [n] Is. 16. 4. [o] Je. 49. 36. [p] De. 30. 4. [q] Ne. 1. 9. [r] Je. 49. 5. [s] Ps. 56. 9. [t] Is. 32. 8. [u] Ps. 51. 14. [x] Is. 32. 8. [y] Pr. 8. 16. [z] Ps. 83. 12. [a] Is. 57. 15. [b] Ps. 51. 19. [c] Ps. 38. 9. [d] Je. 8. 14. [e] Ho. 10. 15; Is. 46. 5. [f] Ho. 10. 15. [g] Je. 25. 37. [h] Eze. 32. 2. [i] Ob. 5. [k] Is. 6. 5. [l] Je. 47. 5. [m] 1 Ch. 21. 27. [n] Da. 7. 15.

נְדָנַיִךְ[a] noun masc. pl., suff. 2 pers. sing. fem. fr. [נָדָן] dec. 4 a . . . . . . נדה

נֵדַע, נֵדָע } Kal fut. 1 pers. pl. (§ 20. rem. 1) . ידע

נֵדְעָה וְ, נֵדְעָה[b] וְ' } id. with opt. ה (§ 8. rem. 13) . ידע

נִדְעָכוּ[c] Niph. pret. 3 pers. pl. . . . . . דעך

נֵדָעֵם[d] וְ Kal fut. 1 pers. sing. (נֵדַע), with suff. 3 pers. pl. masc. (§ 16. rem. 12) . ידע

נֵדָעֶנּוּ[e] וְ id. with suff. 3 pers. sing. masc. . . ידע

נָדַף fut. יִדֹּף, יִנְדֹּף (§ 17. rem. 3).—I. *to drive about, scatter*.—II. *to put to flight, to rout*, an enemy, Job 32. 13. Niph. נִדַּף, inf. c. הִנָּדֵף *to be driven about, away*.

נִדָּף Niph. part. sing. masc. . . . . נדף

נִדַּף[f] id. pret. 3 pers. sing. masc. . . . . נדף

I. נָדַר fut. יִדֹּר, יִדַּר (§ 17. rem. 3) *to vow*; נָדַר נֶדֶר *to make a vow*.

נֶדֶר, נֵדֶר masc. dec. 6 b.—I. *a vow*.—II. *thing vowed*.

II. נָדַר Root not used; Arab. *to cut off*.

אִדַּר Ch. masc. dec. 2 b, *threshing-floor*, Da. 2. 35. But this word is more likely to be derived from אָדַר (q. v.) from the *large* space the threshing-floor occupies.

נָדְרָה[g] Kal pret. 3 pers. sing. m. for נָדַר (§ 8. r. 7) נדר

נֶדֶר, נֵדֶר[h] וְ' } noun masc. sing. dec. 6 b or a . נדר

נֹדֵר[i] וְ Kal part. act. sing. masc. . . . נדר

נָדְרָה[k] id. pret. 3 pers. sing. f. [for נָֽדְרָה § 8. r. 7] נדר

נִדְרָהּ[l] noun masc. sing., suff. 3 pers. sing. fem. from נֶדֶר dec. 6 b . . . . . נדר

נָדְרוּ[m] וְ Kal pret. 3 pers. pl. . . . . נדר

נִדְרוֹ noun masc. sing., suff. 3 pers. sing. masc. from נֶדֶר dec. 6 b . . . . . נדר

נִדְרוּ[n] Kal imp. pl. masc. . . . . . נדר

נִדְרוֹשׁ[o] Kal fut. 1 pers. pl. (§ 8. rem. 18) . . דרש

נִדְרִי, נְדָרַי } noun masc. pl., suff. 1 pers. sing. from נֶדֶר dec. 6 b . . . . } נדר

נִדְרִי[p] id. sing., suff. 1 pers. sing. . . . נדר

נְדָרֶיהָ[q] וּ' id. pl., suff. 3 pers. sing. fem.; וּ bef. (:) נדר

נִדְרֵיהֶם[r] id. pl., suff. 3 pers. pl. masc. . . נדר

נְדָרָיִךְ[s] id. pl., suff. 2 pers. sing. fem. [for ־רַיִךְ] נדר

נְדָרֶיךָ וּ' id. pl., suff. 2 pers. sing. masc.; וּ bef. (:) נדר

נִדְרֵיכֶם[t] וְ' id. pl., suff. 2 pers. pl. masc. . . נדר

נְדָרִים id. pl., abs. st. . . . . . נדר

נְדָרֵינוּ[u] id. pl., suff. 1 pers. pl. . . . . נדר

נָדַרְנוּ[x] Kal pret. 1 pers. pl. . . . . נדר

נִדְרָשׁ[ss] Niph. pret. 3 pers. sing. masc. [for נִדְרַשׁ comp. § 8. rem. 7] . . . . דרש

נִדְרְשָׁה וְ Kal fut. 1 pers. pl. with parag. ה (§ 8. r. 13) דרש

נִדְרָשׁוּ[y] Niph. pret. 3 p. pl. [for נִדְרְשׁוּ comp. § 8. r. 7] דרש

נִדְרַשְׁתִּי[z] id. pret. 1 pers. sing. . . . . דרש

נָדַרְתָּ Kal pret. 2 pers. sing. masc. . . . נדר

נָדַרְתִּי id. pret. 1 pers. sing. . . . . נדר

נַדַּת[a] Chald. Pael pret. 3 pers. sing. fem. . . נדד

נִדַּת[b] noun fem. sing., constr. of נִדָּה dec. 10 . נדד

נִדָּתָהּ[c] id., suff. 3 pers. sing. fem. . . . נדד

נֹהַּ masc. Eze. 7. 11, according to some, *lamentation*, from נָהָה; others (with the Sept.) *ornament, beauty*, from נוּהַּ, i. q. נָאָה, Arab. *to be high, magnificent*.

I. נָהַג[d] fut. יִנְהַג.—I. *to drive*, as beasts, a vehicle.—II. *to lead, conduct*.—III. *to lead, carry away*, as a spoil.—IV. with בְּ *to guide into, accustom to*, Ec. 2. 3. Pi. נִהַג (§ 14. rem. 1).—I. *to cause to drive*, Ex. 14. 25.—II. *to lead, bring*.—III. *to take away*, Ge. 31. 26.

מִנְהָג masc. dec. 2 b, *a driving of a chariot*, 2 Ki. 9. 20.

II. נָהַג. Pi. *to sigh*, Na. 2. 8.

נְהַג[e] Kal imp. sing. masc. . . . . נהג

נִהַג[f] Piel pret. 3 pers. sing. masc. (§ 14. rem. 1) נהג

נֹהֵג Kal part. sing. masc. dec. 7 b . . . נהג

נֶהְגֶּה[g] Kal fut. 1 pers. pl. (§ 13. rem. 5) . הגה

נָהֲגוּ[h] Kal pret. 3 pers. pl. . . . . נהג

נֹהֲגִים id. part. act. masc. pl. of נֹהֵג dec. 7 b . נהג

נִהַגְתָּ[i] Piel 2 pers. sing. masc. (§ 14. rem. 1) נהג

נֶהְדָּרוּ[k] Niph. pret. 3 pers. pl. [for נֶהֶדְּרוּ § 13. rem. 7] הדר

נָהָה[l] וְ *to wail, lament*. Niph. *to lament*, 1 Sa. 7. 2.

נְהִי masc. *lamentation*.

נִהְיָה fem. id. Mi. 2. 4.

נִי masc. (for נְהִי) id. Eze. 27. 32

הִי masc. (for נְהִי) id. Eze. 2. 10.

נְהֵה[m] Kal imp. sing. masc. . . . . נהה

נְהוּגִים[n] Kal part. pass. masc. pl. of [נָהוּג] dec. 3 a נהג

נְהוֹרָא[o] וּ Ch. n. m. s., emph. of [נְהוֹר] d. 1 a; וּ bef. (:) נהר

נְהַחֲוֵה[p] Chald. Pael fut. 1 pers. pl. . . . חוה

---

[a] Eze. 16. 33. [b] Job 34. 4. [c] Job 6. 17. [d] Ps. 78. 3. [e] Ju. 19. 22.
[f] Is. 19. 7. [g] Ju. 11. 39. [h] Nu. 30. 10. [i] Mal. 1. 14. [k] Nu. 30. 11.
[l] Nu. 30. 5, 9. [m] Is. 19. 21. [n] Ps. 76. 12. [o] Ezr. 4. 2. [p] 2 Sa. 15. 7.
[q] Nu. 30. 5, 6, 7, 8, 12, 15. [r] Le. 22. 18. [s] Na. 2. 1. [ss] Gen. 42. 22.
[t] De. 12. 6. [u] Je. 44. 25. [x] Je. 44. 25. [y] 1 Ch. 26. 31.
[z] Is. 65. 1. [a] Da. 6. 19. [b] Le. 12. 2. [c] Le. 15. 24, 25, 26.
[d] La. 3. 2. [e] 2 Ki. 4. 24. [f] Ex. 10. 13. [g] Is. 59. 11.
[h] 1 Sa. 30. 20. [i] Is. 63. 14. [k] La. 5. 12. [l] Mi. 2. 4.
[m] Eze. 32. 18. [n] Is. 60. 11. [o] Da. 2. 22. [p] Da. 2. 7.

נָהִי [a] וְ' / נְהִי — noun masc. sing. (§ 35. rem. 14); for וְ see lett. ו — נהה

נְהִי — וַ Kal fut. 1 pers. pl., ap. for נִהְיֶה (§ 24. rem. 3c); ·וַ conv. — היה

נִהְיָה — Niph. pret. 3 pers. sing. masc., or (Pr. 13. 19) part. fem. [of נִהְיֶה] — היה

נִהְיָה [b] — noun fem. sing. — נהה

נִהְיֶה [c] — וְ', וַנְּ' Kal fut. 1 pers. pl.; ·וַ conv. — היה

נִהְיֵיתָ [d] — Niph. pret. 2 pers. sing. masc. — היה

נִהְיֵיתִי — id. pret. 1 pers. sing. — היה

נְהִירָא [hh] — ו Ch., נְהִירָא Cheth., n. m. s. emph. [of נְהִיר], K. נְהוֹרָא (q.v.) — נהר

נַהִירוּ [f] — וְ Chald. noun fem. sing. — נהר

נִהְיְתָה / נִהְיָתָה — וְ' Niph. pret. 3 pers. sing. fem. (comp. § 8. rem. 7) — היה

נָהַל. Pi. נִהַל, נֵהֵל (§ 14. rem. 1).—I. *to lead, conduct.*—II. *to sustain, provide.* Hithp. *to proceed,* Ge. 33. 14.

נַהֲלֹל m. d. 1b.—I. *pasture,* Is. 7. 19.—II. pr.n. of a city in Zebulun, Ju. 1. 30, called נַהֲלָל in Jos. 19. 15.

נְהַלֵּךְ [g] — Piel fut. 1 pers. pl. — הלך

נֶהֱלַכְתִּי [h] — Niph. pret. 1 pers. sing. [for נֶהֱלַכְתִּי § 13. r. 7] — הלך

נַהֲלָל — וְ' pr. name of a place — נהל

נַהֲלֹל — pr. name of a place — נהל

נֵהַלְתָּ [i] — Piel pret. 2 pers. sing. masc. — נהל

[נָהַם] fut. יִנְהֹם.—I. *to grumble* or *growl,* as a lion.—II. *to murmur,* as the sea, Is. 5. 30.—III. *to groan, moan,* as one in distress.

נַהַם m. *a growling,* as of a lion, Pr. 19. 12; 20. 2.

נְהָמָה fem. dec. 11c (constr. נַהֲמַת § 42. r. 1).—I. *a murmuring, roaring* of the sea, Is. 5. 30.—II. *groaning, moaning* of one in affliction, Ps. 38. 9.

נַהַם — noun masc. sing. — נהם

נֹהֵם [k] — Kal part. act. sing. masc. — נהם

נֶהֱמֶה [l] — Kal fut. 1 pers. pl. — המה

נָהַמְתָּ [m] — וְ Kal pret. 2 pers. sing. masc.; acc. shifted by conv. וְ (§ 8. rem. 7) — נהם

נְהַמְתֶּם [n] — ו id. pret. 2 pers. pl. masc.; ו for וְ, conv. — נהם

נַהֲפוֹךְ [o] — וְ Niph. inf. abs. (§ 9. rem. 1) — הפך

נֶהְפַּךְ [p] / נֶהְפָּךְ — וְ' Niph. pret. 3 pers. sing. masc. (§ 13. r. 7) — הפך

נֶהְפְּכָה [q] — id. pret. 3 pers. sing. fem. — הפך

נֶהְפְּכוּ / נֶהְפָּכוּ — וְ' id. pret. 3 pers. pl. (§ 13. rem. 7, comp. rem. 4, 5, 6) — הפך

נֶהְפֶּכֶת [r] — id. part. fem. sing. [for פֶּכֶת' from נֶהְפָּךְ m.] — הפך

נֶהְפַּכְתָּ [s] — וְ id. pret. 2 pers. sing. masc.; acc. shifted by conv. וְ (comp. id. & § 8. rem. 7) — הפך

נֶהְפַּכְתְּ [t] — id. pret. 2 pers. sing. fem. — הפך

[נָהַק] fut. יִנְהַק *to bray,* as the ass, Job 6. 5; 30. 7.

[נָהַר] I. *to flow, run.*—II. *to shine, be bright.*

נָהָר masc. dec. 4a (pl. נְהָרִים, נְהָרוֹת, constr. נַהֲרֵי, נַהֲרוֹת).—I. *current, stream.*—II. *stream, river.* Du. נַהֲרַיִם (from a sing. נַהַר) *the two rivers,* i. e. Tigris and Euphrates, whence אֲרַם נַ' *Mesopotamia.*

נְהַר Ch. m. emph. נַהֲרָא, נַהֲרָה (d. 3a) *a river.*

נְהוֹר Chald. masc. dec. 1a, *light,* Da. 2. 22, Keri; נְהִיר Kh.

נַהִירוּ or נַהִירוּ Ch. fem. *light, wisdom,* Da. 5. 11, 14.

נְהָרָה fem. *light, daylight,* Job 3. 4.

מִנְהָרָה fem. only pl. מִנְהָרוֹת Ju. 6. 2, *clefts* in the mountains, serving as canals to the mountain torrents (Lee).

נָהָר — וְ' noun masc. sing. dec. 4a — נהר

נְהַר [u] — ו' id. constr. st.; & (Da. 7. 10) Chald. noun masc. dec. 3a — נהר

נַהֲרָא [x] — Chald. id. emph. st., see the preced. — נהר

נַהֲרֹג [y] — Kal fut. 1 pers. pl. — הרג

נַהַרְגֵהוּ [z] — וְ id., suff. 3 pers. sing. masc. — הרג

נַהֲרָה — Chald. for נַהֲרָא (q. v.) — נהר

נְהָרָה [a] — noun fem. sing. — נהר

נָהֲרוּ [b] / נָהָרוּ — וְ Kal pret. 3 pers. pl. (§ 8. rem. 7) — נהר

נְהָרוֹת / נַהֲרוֹת [c] — ו' n. m. with pl. f. term. constr. & abs. st. fr. נָהָר d. 4a (comp. § 42. r. 1); ו bef. (:) — נהר

נַהֲרוֹתֶיהָ [d] — id. pl. fem., suff. 3 p. s. fem. (comp. § 42. r. 1) — נהר

נַהֲרוֹתָם [e] — וְ id. pl. fem., suff. 3 pers. pl. masc. (§ 4. r. 2) — נהר

נַהֲרֵי [f] — id. pl. masc., constr. of נְהָרִים. — נהר

נַהֲרַיִם / נַהֲרָיִם — id. du., pr. name in compos. אֲרַם נַ' — ארם

נְהָרִים — id. pl., abs. st. — נהר

נֶהֶרְסָה [g] — Niph. pret. 3 pers. sing. fem. [for נֶהֶרְסָה comp. § 8. rem. 7] — הרס

נֶהֶרְסוּ — וְ' id. pret. 3 pers. pl. — הרס

נָהַרְתְּ [h] — וְ Kal pret. 2 pers. sing. fem. — נהר

נַהֲרֹתֶיהָ — noun m., pl. f. term., suff. 3 pers. sing. fem. from נָהָר dec. 4a (comp. § 42. rem. 1) — נהר

נַהֲרֹתַיִךְ [k] — וְ id., suff. 2 pers. sing. fem. — נהר

נַהֲרֹתָם — id., suff. 3 pers. pl. masc. (§ 4. rem. 2) — נהר

נְהַשְׁכַּח [l] — Chald. Aph. fut. 1 pers. pl. (§ 47. rem. 4) — שכח

[a] Je. 9. 9. [b] Mi. 2. 4. [c] Ge. 47. 19. [d] De. 27. 9. [e] Da. 8. 27. [f] Da. 5. 11, 14. [g] Is. 59. 9; Ps. 55. 15. [h] Ps. 109. 23. [i] Ex. 15. 13. [k] Pr. 28. 15. [l] Is. 59. 11. [m] Pr. 5. 11. [n] Eze. 24. 23. [o] Est. 9. 1. [p] Job 20. 14. [q] La. 5. 2. [r] Jon. 3. 4. [s] 1 Sa. 10. 6. [t] Je. 2. 21. [u] 1 Ch. 5. 26. [x] Ezr. 4. 16. [y] Ge. 37. 26. [z] Ge. 37. 20. [a] Job 3. 4. [b] Ps. 34. 6. [c] Ca. 8. 7. [d] Eze. 31. 15. [e] Eze. 32. 14. [f] Job 20. 17. [g] Pr. 24. 31. [h] Is. 60. 5. [hh] Da. 2. 22. [i] Eze. 31. 4. [k] Is. 44. 27. Da. 6. 6.

נוּא Kal not used (except Nu. 32. 7, Kh.) Hiph. הֵנִיא.—I. *to refuse, decline*, Ps. 141. 5.—II. *to hinder, restrain, prohibit*, Nu. 30. 6, 9, 12.—III. *to dissuade, discourage*, with מִן Nu. 32. 7, 9.—IV. *to frustrate*, Ps. 33. 10.

תְּנוּאָה fem. dec. 10, *hinderance, opposition, hostility*, Nu. 14. 34; Job 33. 10.

נוֹאֲלוּ Niph. pret. 3 pers. pl. . . . . יאל

נוֹאַלְנוּ[a] id. pret. 1 pers. pl. . . . . יאל

נוֹאָשׁ Niph. part. sing. masc. (adverbially) . יאש

נוֹאָשׁ[b] וְ id. pret. 3 pers. sing. masc. . . יאש

[נוּב] fut. יָנוּב.—I. *to put forth shoots*, Ps. 92. 15.—II. *to increase*, Ps. 62. 11.—III. *to produce, utter*, Pr. 10. 31.

נוֹב masc. Is. 57. 19. Kh. and

נִיב m. d. 1 a, *produce, fruit*, Is. 57. 19; Mal. 1. 12.

נֵיבַי (*prosperous*) pr. name masc. Ne. 10. 20.

נָבוֹת (*produce, fruit*) pr. name m. 1 Ki. 21. 1, sq.

תְּנוּבָה fem. dec. 10, *produce, increase, fruit*.

נוֹב[c] Kh. נוֹב, K. נִיב noun masc. sing. dec. 1 a . נוב

נוֹבַי Kh. נוֹבַי, K. נֵיבַי pr. name masc. . נוב

נוּגוֹת[d] Niph. part. fem. pl. [of נוּגָה from נוּגֶה masc. § 20. rem. 5] . . . . יגה

נוּגַי[e] id. part. pl. constr. masc. [from נוּגֶה] d. 9 a יגה

נוֹגֵעַ[f] Kal part. act. sing. masc. dec. 7 b . נגע

נוֹגֵשׂ Kal part. act. sing. masc. dec. 7 b . . נגש

[נוּד] fut. יָנוּד, ap. תָּנֹד.—I. *to move, be agitated, shaken*.—II. *to be driven about, to wander as a fugitive*; part. נָד *a fugitive*.—III. *to remove, depart, flee*; Is. 17. 11 נֵד קָצִיר *the harvest fleeth*, according to some; but see נֵד.—IV. *to shake* the head, as an expression of pity, *to console, comfort*, with לְ of the person; hence—V. *to deplore, bemoan*, Je. 22. 10. Hiph. הֵנִיד.—I. *to move, shake* the head, with בְּ, Je. 18. 16.—II. *to cause to move, wander*, 2 Ki. 21. 8.—III. *to move, disturb*, Ps. 36. 12. Hithpal.—I. *to shake oneself*, i. e. shake one's head in derision, Je. 48. 27.—II. *to be shaken to and fro, to reel*, Is. 24. 20.—III. *to bemoan oneself*, Je. 31. 18.

נוּד Chald. *to depart, flee*, Da. 4. 11.

נוֹד masc. dec. 1 a.—I. *wandering*, Ps. 56. 9.—II. pr. name of the region whither Cain fled, Ge. 4. 16.

נִיד masc. *a moving* of the lips, Job 16. 5.

נִידָה fem. *a wandering*, La. 1. 8; but see R. נָדַד.

מָנוֹד masc. dec. 3 a, *a shaking* of the head, i. e. the object of it, Ps. 44. 15.

נוֹד pr. name of a region . . . . נוד

נוֹדָב וְ pr. name masc. . . . . נדב

נוֹדַד[g] וְ Poal pret. 3 pers. sing. masc. . . נדד

נוֹדֵד Kal part. act. sing. masc. dec. 7 b . . נדד

נוֹדֶדֶת[h] id. part. sing. fem. . . . . נדד

נוֹדֶה Hiph. fut. 1 pers. pl. (§ 25. No. 2e) . ידה

נוּדוּ[i] Kh. נוּדוּ Kal imp. pl. masc., K. נוּדִי sing. fem. נוד

נוֹדִיעָה[k] וְ Hiph. fut. 1 pers. pl. with parag. ה (comp. § 8. rem. 13) . . . . ידע

נוֹדָע וְ'' Niph. part. sing. masc. . . . ידע

נוֹדַע וְ' id. pret. 3 pers. sing. masc. . . ידע

נוֹדְעָה וְ id. pret. 3 pers. sing. fem. . . . ידע

נוֹדָעוּ[m] id. pret. 3 pers. pl. [for נוֹדְעוּ comp. § 8. r. 7] ידע

נוֹדַעְתִּי
וְנוֹדַעְתִּי[n] id. pret. 1 pers. sing.; acc. shifted by conv. וְ (comp. § 8. r. 7) . . ידע

נוֹדַעְתִּי[o] וְ id. id.; with conv. וְ, acc. retained bef. monos. (בָּם), comp. the preced. . . ידע

[נָוָה] *to sit, dwell quietly*, Hab. 2. 5. Hiph. *to prepare a dwelling*, Ex. 15. 2. Others, *to adorn*, נָוָה i. q. נָאָה q. v.

נָוֶה masc. dec. 9 b, fem. נָוָה dec. 11 a—I. adj. (*a*) *inhabiting*, Ps. 68. 13; (*b*) *comely*, Je. 6. 2; comp. נָאָה.—II. subst. (*a*) *dwelling, habitation*; (*b*) *fold* for cattle; others, *pasture*.

נָוָה fem. dec. 11 a, i. q. נָוֶה No. II. Job 8. 6; Zep. 2. 6.

נָוְיֹת (*habitations*) pr. name of a dwelling-place of the prophets near Ramah, 1 Sa. 19. 18, 19, 22, 23; 20. 1, Kh., in Keri נָיוֹת.

נָוֶה noun masc. sing. dec. 9 a . . . נוה

נְוֵה וּ'[p] id., constr. st.; וּ bef. (:) . . . נוה

נָוֵהוּ id., suff. 3 pers. sing. masc. . . נוה

נְוֵהֶם id., suff. 3 pers. pl. masc. . . . נוח

נוֹזְלֵיהֶם[q] וְ the foll. with suff. 3 pers. pl. masc. . נזל

נוֹזְלִים וְ' Kal part. act. masc. pl. [of נוֹזֵל] dec. 7 b נזל

[נוּחַ, נוֹחַ] fut. יָנוּחַ, ap. וַיָּנַח (§ 21. rem. 9).—I. *to rest, settle down, alight*, with בְּ, עַל.—II. *to rest, be at rest, have repose*. Hence—III. *to abide, continue*.—IV. *to rest, to cease, leave off* speaking, 1 Sa. 25. 9. Hiph. 1. הֵנִיחַ, fut. יָנִיחַ, ap. יָנַח (§ 21. rem. 19).—I. *to set, put, lay* or *let down*; *to let fall*.—II. *to cause to rest*; *to give rest, repose*. 2. הִנִּיחַ, fut. יַנִּיחַ, ap. יַנַּח (§ 21. rem. 24).—I. *to set, put* or *lay down, to place, deposit*.—II. *to let rest, remain*.—III. *to permit, suffer, let alone*.—IV. *to leave behind*. Hoph. I. הוּנַח *rest*

[a] Nu. 12. 11. [b] 1 Sa. 27. 1. [c] Is. 57. 19. [d] La. 1. 4. [e] Zep. 3. 18. [f] Da. 8. 5. [g] Na. 3. 17. [h] Pr. 27. 8. [i] Ps. 11. 1. [k] 1 Sa. 14. 12. [l] Ec. 6. 10. [m] Ps. 77. 20. [n] Eze. 38. 23. [o] Eze. 35. 11. [p] Pr. 3. 33. [q] Ps. 78. 44.

is given, La. 5. 5.—II. הֻנַּח to be set, placed; part. מֻנָּח something left, Eze. 41. 9, 11.

נוֹחַ masc.—I. rest, quiet, Est. 9. 16, 17, 18; with suff. נוֹחֶךָ (§ 30. rem. 4), 2 Ch. 6. 41.—II. נֹחַ pr. name, Noah.

נוֹחָה (rest) pr. name masc. 1 Ch. 8. 2.

נַחַת fem.—I. a setting, letting down, Job 36. 16; Is. 30. 30, which may consistently be derived from נָחַת.—II. rest, quiet.—III. pr. name m. 1 Ch. 6. 11, called תּוֹחַ in ver. 19.

נִיחוֹחַ masc. dec. 1b (prop. acquiescence) satisfaction, delight; רֵיחַ נִ׳ savour of delight, i. e. pleasant, sweet savour.

נִיחוֹחַ Chald. masc. dec. 1a, sweet odour, incense.

הֲנָחָה fem. rest, release, Est. 2. 18.

יָנוֹחַ (rest) pr. name of a town on the confines of Ephraim and Manasseh.

מָנוֹחַ masc. dec. 3a (with suff. מְנוּחֵךְ § 30. r. 4). —I. rest, quiet.—II. resting-place.—III. pr. name of the father of Samson.

מְנוּחָה f. d. 10.—I. rest, quiet.—II. resting-place.

מָנַחַת (rest) pr. name—I. of a man, Ge. 36. 23. —II. of a place, 1 Ch. 8. 6.

נֹחַ[a] וְ noun masc. sing., suff. נוֹחֶךָ (§ 30. rem. 4) נוח

נֹחָה pr. name masc. . . . . . נוח

נוֹחֲלָה[b] Niph. pret. 3 pers. sing. fem. . . יחל

[נוּט] to move, be shaken, Ps. 99. 1.

נוֹטֶה Kal part. sing. masc. dec. 9 . . . נטה

נוֹטֵיהֶם[c] וְ id. sing., suff. 3 pers. pl. masc. from נוֹטֶה dec. 9a (§ 38. r. 1, comp. also § 24. r. 21b) נטה

נוֹטֵל[d] Kal part. act. sing. masc. . . . . נטל

נְוִיהֶן[e] noun masc. pl. (but comp. נוֹטֵיהֶם), suff. 3 pers. pl. fem. from נָוֶה dec. 9b . נוה

נָוֹית Kh. נְוָית, K. נָיוֹת pr. name of a place נוה

נָוֶךָ[f] noun masc. sing., suff. 2 p. s. m. fr. נָוֶה d. 9b נוה

נוֹטֵר[g] וְ Kal part. act. sing. masc. dec. 7b . נטר

נוֹכָח[h] Niph. part. sing. masc. . . . . יכח

נִוָּכְחָה[i] וְ id. fut. 1 pers. pl. [נִוָּכַח] with parag. ה (comp. § 8. rem. 13) . . . יכח

נוֹכֵל[k] Kal part. act. sing. masc. . . . נכל

נוּכַל Hoph. fut. 1 pers. pl. . . . . יכל

נוּכְלָה[l] וְ id. with parag. ה (comp. § 8. rem. 13) יכל

נָוֶל Root not used; Chald. Pa. to dirty, soil.

נְוָלִי, נְוָלוּ Chald. fem. dunghill, Da. 2. 5; 3. 29; Ezr. 6. 11.

נוֹלָד Niph. part. sing. masc. dec. 2b . . ילד

נוֹלַד id. pret. 3 pers. sing. masc. . . . ילד

נוּלְּדוּ[m] id. pret. 3 pers. pl. with euph. dag. [for נוֹלְדוּ § 20. rem. 5] . . . . ילד

נְוָלוּ[n] Chald. noun fem. sing. . . . . נול

נְוָלִי[o] Chald. noun fem. sing. . . . נול

[נוּם] fut. יָנוּם, to slumber.

נוּמָה fem. slumber, Pr. 23. 21.

יָנוּם (slumber) pr. name of a place in the tribe of Judah, Jos. 15. 53, Kh., יָנוּם Keri.

תְּנוּמָה fem. dec. 10, slumber.

נוּמָה[p] noun fem. sing. . . . . . . נום

נוּן Niph. in Keri, or Hiph. in Kheth. Ps. 72. 17, to sprout, flourish; others, to propagate. Comp. derivv. Lee, drawn out, perpetuated. The versions seem to have read here יִכּוֹן.

נוּן (fish; so Syr. and Chald.) pr. name of the father of Joshua; once נוֹן 1 Ch. 7. 27.

נִין masc. dec. 1a, offspring, posterity.

מָנוֹן masc. Pr. 29. 21, child, son, comp. Eng. vers. Yarchi, young master or lord. Others, from מָנַן, ingratitude; Lee, despiser.

נוּן pr. name masc. . . . . . נון

נוֹן pr. name masc. . . . . . . נון

[נוּס] fut. יָנוּס.—I. to flee, flee away, escape from a person, place or thing, with לִפְנֵי, מִפְּנֵי, מִן.—II. to proceed, ride swiftly, Is. 30. 16. Pil. נוֹסֵס to impel, drive, Is. 59. 19. Hiph. הֵנִיס.—I. to cause to flee for refuge or shelter.—II. to put to flight, De. 32. 30.

נִיס masc. fleeing, Je. 48. 44, Kh.; Keri נָס part.

מָנוֹס masc. (with suff. מְנוּסִי § 30. rem. 4).— I. flight, Je. 46. 5.—II. place of flight, refuge.

מְנוּסָה fem. d. 10, flight, Le. 26. 36; Is. 52. 12.

נוֹס[q] Kal inf. abs. . . . . . . נוס

נוֹסְדוּ[r] Niph. pret. 3 pers. pl. . . . . יסד

נוֹסָף[s] וְ Niph. part. sing. masc. . . . יסף

נוֹסַף[t] וְ׳ id. pret. 3 pers. sing. masc. . . יסף

נוֹסְפָה[u] וְ id. pret. 3 pers. sing. fem. . . . יסף

נוֹסָפוֹת[x] id. part. fem. pl. [of נוֹסָפָה] as a subst. . יסף

נִוַּסְּרוּ[y] וְ [for נִתְיַסְּרוּ] Nithpa. pret. 3 pers. pl. (§ 20. No. 1, & § 7. No. 10) . . . יסר

[נוּעַ, נוֹעַ Is. 7. 2.] fut. יָנוּעַ, ap. יָנַע (§ 21. rem. 9).— I. to move to and fro, be agitated, shaken.—II. to

[a] Est. 9. 16, 17, 18. [b] Eze. 19. 5. [c] Is. 42. 5. [d] 2 Sa. 24. 12. [e] Je. 23. 3. [f] Job 5. 24. [g] Na. 1. 2. [h] Job 23. 7. [i] Is. 1. 18. [k] Mal. 1. 14. [l] Je. 20. 10. [m] 1 Ch. 3. 5; 20. 8. [n] Ezr. 6. 11. [o] Da. 2. 5; 3. 29. [p] Pr. 23. 21. [q] 2 Sa. 18. 3. [r] Ps. 2. 2. [s] Pr. 11. 24. [t] Je. 36. 32. [u] Nu. 36. 4. [x] Is. 15. 9. [y] Eze. 23. 48.

stagger, as a drunken man.—III. *to move, be moved*, of the lips.—IV. *to be changeable, variable*, Pr. 5. 6.—V. *to wander, wander about*. Niph. *to be shaken*. Hiph. הֵנִיעַ.—I. *to shake*, as the head or hand.—II. *to agitate, shake, disturb*.—III. *to cause to reel, tremble*, Da. 10. 10.—IV. *to cause to wander about*.

נֵעָה (*a shaking*) pr. name of a place in Zebulun, Jos. 19. 13.

נֹעָה (*moving, motion*) pr. name fem. Nu. 26. 33.

מְנַעַנְעִים masc. pl. (of מְנַעֲנַע, נִעַ׳ § 36. rem. 5) 2 Sa. 6. 5, the name of a musical instrument. Vulg. sistra, *sistrums*, a kind of *timbrel*, played upon by *shaking* it in cadence.

נוֹעַ[a] ו׳[b] Kal inf. abs. . . . . . . נוע

נִוָּעֵד[c] Niph. fut. 1 pers. pl. . . . . . יעד

נִוָּעֲדָה[d] וְ id. id. with parag. ה (comp. § 8. rem. 13) יעד

נוֹעֲדוּ[e], נֽוֹעֲדוּ[f] ו׳[g] } Niph. pret. 3 pers. pl. (comp. § 8. rem. 7) . . . . . יעד

נוֹעַדְיָה וְ pr. name masc. . . . . . . יעד

נוֹעַדְתִּי[h] וְ id. pret. 1 pers. s.; acc. shifted by conv. וְ יעד

נוֹעָז[i] Niph. pret. 3 pers. sing. masc. . . . יעז

נוֹעִיל[k] Hiph. fut. 1 pers. pl. . . . . . יעל

נוֹעַץ[l] Niph. pret. 3 pers. sing. masc. . . . יעץ

נִוָּעֲצָה[m] וְ id. fut. 1 pers. pl. with parag. ה (comp. § 8. rem. 13) . . . . . . יעץ

נוֹעֲצוּ id. pret. 3 pers. pl. . . . . . יעץ

נוֹעָצִים id. part. masc., pl. of נוֹעָץ . . . . יעץ

[נוּף] *to sprinkle*, which is done by *waving, shaking* the hand, Pr. 7. 17, comp. Hiph. הֵנִיף.—I. *to lift up*, as the hand an instrument, with אֶל, עַל *against, over*.—II. *to move to and fro, to wave, shake*, as the hand a sieve; espec. with reference to the priests' *waving* in the presentation of offerings.—III. *to sprinkle, scatter*, Ps. 68. 10. Hoph. *to be waved*, Ex. 29. 27. Pil. נוֹפֵף *to wave, shake* the hand, Is. 10. 32.

נוֹף masc. *elevation*, Ps. 48. 3.

נָפָה fem. dec. 10.—I. *a height*; only in the pr. name נְפוֹת דּוֹר, נָפַת דּוֹר *heights of Dor*, a place near Mount Carmel.—II. *sieve, fan*, Is. 30. 28.

נֶפֶת fem. *high place, height*, Jos. 17. 11.

נֹפֶת fem. *a dropping, distilling*; נֹפֶת צוּפִים *honey as dropped from the honeycomb*.

תְּנוּפָה fem. dec. 10.—I. *a lifting, waving* or *shaking* of the hand.—II. *a waving* of the priest in the presentation of offerings; meton. *wave-offering*.—III. *agitation, tumult*, Is. 30. 32.

נוֹף[n] noun masc. sing. . . . . . נוף

נוֹפֵל[o] Kal part. act. sing. masc. dec. 7b . . נפל

נוּץ. Hiph. הֵנֵץ (comp. § 21. rem. 14) *to flourish, blossom*, Ca. 6. 11; 7. 13.

נוֹצָה[p] noun fem. sing. . . . . . נצה

נוֹצִיא[q] Hiph. fut. 1 pers. pl. . . . . . יצא

נוֹצַר[r] Niph. pret. 3 pers. sing. masc. . . . יצר

נוֹצְרֵי[s] Kal part. sing. masc. dec. 7b . . . נצר

נֹצְרִים id. pl., abs. st. . . . . . נצר

נוּק i. q. יָנַק, only Hiph. *to give suck, to suckle*, Ex. 2. 9.

נוֹקֵשׁ[t] Kal part. sing. masc. . . . . . נקשׁ

נוֹקְשׁוּ וְ Niph. pret. 3 pers. pl. . . . . יקשׁ

נוֹקַשְׁתָּ[u] id. pret. 2 pers. sing. masc. . . . יקשׁ

נוּר Root not used; i. q. נָהַר, Arab. נאר *to shine*.

נוּר Chald. masc. dec. 1a, *fire*.

נִיר, נֵר (once) masc. dec. 1a.—I. *light, lamp*; trop. *prosperity, happiness*.—II. pr. name of the grandfather of Saul.

נִיר, נֵר masc. *light, lamp*, only metaph.

נֵרִיָּה (*light of the Lord*) pr. name—I. of the father of Baruch, companion of Jeremiah.—II. Je. 51. 59.

מְנוֹרָה fem. dec. 10, *candlestick* or *chandelier*.

נוּר Chald. noun masc. sing. dec. 1a . . . נור

נוֹרָא ו׳ Niph. part. sing. masc. (§ 25. No. 2d) . ירא

נוּרָא Chald. noun masc. sing., emph. of נוּר dec. 1a נור

נוֹרָאָה[x] Niph. part. sing. fem. dec. 11a, fr. נוֹרָא m. ירא

נוֹרָאוֹת ו׳[y] id. pl., abs. st. . . . . . ירא

נוֹרְאוֹתֶיךָ[z] id. pl. with suff. 2 pers. sing. masc. . . ירא

[נוּשׁ] i. q. אָנַשׁ *to be sick*, Ps. 69. 21.

נוֹשְׂאֵי Kal part. act. pl. constr. masc. from נֹשֵׂא (q. v.) dec. 7b . . . . . נשׂא

נוֹשָׁבָה[a] Niph. pret. 3 pers. sing. fem. [for נוֹשְׁבָה comp. § 8. rem. 7] . . . . ישׁב

נוֹשָׁבָה[b] Kh. נוֹשָׁבָה q. v., K. נוֹשָׁבוּ (q. v.) . ישׁב

נוֹשָׁבוּ[c], וְ נוֹשָׁבוּ[d] } Niph. pret. 3 pers. pl. (comp. § 8. rem. 7) . . . . ישׁב

נוֹשָׁבוֹת[e] Niph. part. fem. pl. of the foll. . . ישׁב

נוֹשָׁבֶת[f], נוֹשֶׁבֶת[g] } id. part. sing. fem., pl. נוֹשָׁבוֹת (§ 44. rem. 5) . . . . ישׁב

נוֹשֶׁה[h] Kal part. act. sing. masc. dec. 9a . . נשׁה

---

[a] Is. 24. 20. [b] Ps. 109. 10. [c] Ne. 6. 10. [d] Ne. 6. 2. [e] Am. 3. 3. [f] Ps. 48. 5. [g] Nu. 10. 4. [h] Ex. 25. 22. [i] Is. 33. 19. [k] Job 21. 15. [l] Is. 40. 14. [m] Ne. 6. 7. [n] Ps. 48. 3. [o] Job 14. 18. [p] Eze. 17. 7. [q] Nu. 20. 10. [r] Is. 43. 10. [s] Pr. 28. 7. [t] Ps. 9. 17. [u] Pr. 6. 2. [x] Is. 21. 1. [y] 1 Ch. 17. 21. [z] Ps. 145. 6. [a] Je. 6. 8. [b] Je. 22. 6. [c] Eze. 26. 19. [d] Eze. 36. 10. [e] Eze. 38. 12. [f] Ex. 16. 35. [g] Eze. 26. 17. [h] Ps. 109. 11.

[a]נוֹשָׁן Niph. part. sing. masc. . . . . . . ישן
[b]נוֹשֶׁנֶת id. part. sing. fem. . . . . . ישן
[c]נוֹשַׁנְתֶּם ְ id. pret. 2 pers. pl. masc. . . . . ישן
[d]נוֹשָׁע ו׳ְ Niph. part. sing. masc. . . . . . ישע
נוֹשַׁע id. pret. 3 pers. sing. masc. . . . . . ישע
[f]נִוָּשֵׁעַ ְ id. fut. 1 pers. pl. [for נִוָּשֵׁעַ § 15. rem. 1] ישע
[g]נִוָּשֵׁעָה ְ id. id. with opt. ה [for נִוָּשְׁעָה v. i. and § 8. rem. 13] . . . . . ישע
[h]נוֹשָׁעְנוּ id. pret. 1 pers. pl. . . . . . ישע
[i]נוֹשַׁעְתֶּם ְ id. pret. 2 pers. pl. masc. . . . . ישע
[ii]נוֹשְׁקֵי Kal part. act. pl. constr. m. [fr. נוֹשֵׁק d. 7b] נשק
[k]נְוַת ו׳י adj. or subst. fem., constr. of נָוָה׳ dec. 11a, from נָוֶה masc.; ו bef. (:) . . . נוה
[m]נְוֹת noun fem. pl. constr. of נָוָה, see the preced. נוה
נוֹתֵן ו׳״ Kal part. act. sing. masc. dec. 7b . . נתן
[o]נוֹתַר, נוֹתָר } Niph. pret. 3 pers. sing. masc. (comp. § 8. rem. 7) . . . . . יתר
נוֹתְרָה ו׳[p] id. pret. 3 pers. sing. fem. . . . . יתר
נוֹתְרוּ id. pret. 3 pers. pl. . . . . . יתר
נוֹתַרְתִּי id. pret. 1 pers. sing. . . . . . יתר
[q]נוֹתַרְתֶּם id. pret. 2 pers. pl. masc. . . . . יתר
[r]נִזְבַּח Kal fut. 1 pers. pl. . . . . . זבח
[s]נִזְבְּחָה ו׳ id. with parag. ה (§ 8. rem. 13) . . . זבח

נָזָה only fut. יִזֶּה, ap. יִז וַיִּז (§ 25. No. 2e) *to spatter, be sprinkled*, with אֶל, עַל upon anything. Hiph. הִזָּה, fut. יַזֶּה, ap. וַיַּז.—I. *to sprinkle*, with acc. of the liquid or מִן some of it, and עַל upon whom. —II. *to sprinkle, besprinkle, expiate*, with acc. of the person, Is. 52. 15. But this passage seems rather to indicate the Messiah's exaltation in judgment (comp. Ps. 2), and this word may be rendered, *to scatter*; comp. נוּף Kal and Hiph. According to Schultens, *to cause to leap* or *exult*, coll. with the Arab.

יִזִּיָּה (*exults in the Lord*; comp. Hiph.) pr. name masc. Ezr. 10. 25.

נִזְהָר Niph. part. sing. masc. . . . . . זהר
נָזִיד noun masc. sing. dec. 3a . . . . . זוד
[t]נְזִיד ו id., constr. st.; ו bef. (:) . . . זוד
[nn]נָזִיר noun masc. sing. dec. 3a . . . . נזר
נְזִיר id., constr. st. . . . . . נזר
[u]נְזִירֶיהָ id. pl., suff. 3 pers. sing. fem. . . . נזר
[w]נְזִירֶךָ id. pl., suff. 3 pers. s. m. [for ־ירֶיךָ § 4. r. 1] נזר
נַזְכִּיר, [y]נַזְכִּירָה } Hiph. fut. 1 pers. pl. (§ 8. rem. 13) . זכר
[z]נִזְכָּרִים Niph. part. masc. pl. [of נִזְכָּר] . . . זכר

[a]נִזְכַּרְתֶּם ְ id. pret. 2 pers. pl. masc. . . . זכר

[נָזַל] fut. יִזַּל.—I. *to sink down*, Ju. 5. 5.—II. *to drop down, distil, flow*. Hiph. הִזִּיל *to cause to flow*, Is. 48. 21.

מַזָּל masc. *wandering star, planet*; like Gr. πλανήτης from πλανάω; only pl. מַזָּלוֹת 2 Ki. 23. 5.

[b]נָזְלוּ Kal pret. 3 pers. pl. R. נזל; or Niph. for נָזֹלּוּ (§ 18. rem. 15) R. . . . . . זלל
נָזֹלּוּ Niph. pret. 3 pers. pl. . . . . . זלל
[c]נֹזְלִים ו׳[d] defect. for נוֹזְלִים (q. v.) . . . . נזל

נֶזֶם ו׳[e] masc. dec. 6a (with suff. נִזְמָהּ).—I. *nosering*. —II. *earring*.

[f]נִזְמָהּ id. with suff. 3 pers. sing. fem. . . . נזם
נִזְמֵי ו׳[g] id. pl., constr. st. . . . . . נזם
[h]נְזַמְּרָה ו Piel fut. 1 pers. pl. with parag. ה (comp. § 8. rem. 13) . . . . . זמר
[i]נִזְעָכוּ Niph. pret. 3 p. pl. [for נִזְעֲכוּ comp. § 8. r. 7] זעך
[k]נִזְעָמִים Niph. part. masc. pl. [of נִזְעָם] . . . זעם
[l]נִזְעַק ְ Kal fut. 1 pers. pl. . . . . . זעק
[m]נִזְעֲקוּ Niph. pret. 3 pers. pl. . . . . . זעק
[n]נִזְעַקְתָּ id. pret. 2 p. s. m. [for נִזְעַקְתָּ comp. § 8. r. 7] זעק

[נְזַק] Chald. *to suffer loss, injury*, Da. 6. 3. Aph. *to cause loss, endamage*, Ezr. 4. 13, 15, 22.

נֵזֶק masc. *injury, damage*, Est. 7. 4.

[o]נָזִק Chald. Peal part. act. sing. m. (§ 47. r. 1a) נזק

נָזַר. Niph. I. *to separate, withdraw oneself*, with מֵאַחֲרֵי, Eze. 14. 7.—II. *to restrict oneself*, Zec. 7. 3.—III. *to abstain from*, with מִן, Le. 22. 2.—IV. *to devote, consecrate oneself*, with לְ to anything, Ho. 9. 10. Hiph. הִזִּיר.—I. *to set apart*, with לְ Nu. 6. 12.—II. *to cause to avoid, restrict from*, with מִן.—III. intrans. *to abstain from*, with מִן Nu. 6. 3.—IV. *to devote, consecrate oneself*, with לְ, Nu. 6. 2, 5, 6.

נָזִיר masc. dec. 3a.—I. *a Nazarite*, one *separated* and *consecrated* to God, comp. Nu. 6.—II. *the unpruned vine*, by application from the *unshorn* head of the Nazarite, Le. 25. 5, 11.—III. *prince*, comp. נֵזֶר.

נֵזֶר masc. dec. 6b.—I. *separation, consecration*. —II. sign or mark of separation, consecration or distinction; (*a*) *the long hair* of the Nazarite; (*b*) *crown, diadem*, whether priestly or regal.

מִנְּזָרִים masc. pl. (of מִנְּזָר) *princes*, Na. 3. 17.

[a] Le. 26. 10. [b] Le. 13. 11. [c] De. 4. 25. [d] Ps. 33. 16. [e] Zec. 9. 9. [f] Is. 64. 4. [g] Ps. 80. 4, 8, 20. [h] Je. 8. 20. [i] Nu. 10. 9. [ii] Ps. 78. 9. [k] Job 8. 6. [l] Ps. 68. 13. [m] Zep. 2. 6. [n] Ps. 37. 21. [nn] Nu. 6. 2. [o] Ps. 106. 11. [p] Is. 1. 8. [q] Is. 30. 17. [r] Ex. 8. 22. [s] Ex. 5. 8, 17. [t] Ge. 25. 34. [u] La. 4. 7. [w] Le. 25. 5. [y] Ca. 1. 4. [z] Est. 9. 28. [a] Nu. 10. 9. [b] Ju. 5. 5. [c] Ex. 15. 8. [d] Ca. 4. 15. [e] Ex. 35. 22. [f] Ho. 2. 15. [g] Is. 3. 21. [h] Ps. 21. 14. [i] Job 17. 1. [k] Pr. 25. 23. [l] 2 Ch. 20. 9. [m] Ju. 18. 22. [n] Ju. 18. 23. [o] Da. 6. 3.

נֵזֶר / [a] נֵזֶר } noun masc. sing. dec. 6b & a . . נזר

[b] נָזֹרוּ Niph. pret. 3 pers. pl. . . . זור

נִזְרוֹ noun masc. sing., suff. 3 pers. sing. masc. from נֵזֶר dec. 6b . . . . נזר

[c] נְזִרָה defect. for נְזִירָה (q. v.) . . . נזר

[d] נִזְרֵךְ noun masc. sing., suff. 2 p. s. f. fr. נֵזֶר d. 6b נזר

[e] נִזְרָע Kal fut. 1 pers. pl. [for נִזְרַע comp. § 8. r. 15] זרע

[f] נִזְרְעָה וְ Niph. pret. 3 pers. sing. fem. . . . זרע

[g] נִזְרַעְתֶּם וְ id. pret. 2 pers. pl. masc. . . . זרע

נֹחַ וְ' pr. name masc. . . . . נוח

נֶחְבָּא Niph. pret. 3 p. s.; or part. m. (§ 13. r. 7) חבא

[h] נֶחְבָּאוּ / [i] נֶחְבָּאוּ } וְ' id. pret. 3 pers. pl. (v. i. & § 8. rem. 7) חבא

[k] נֶחְבָּאִים id. part. masc. pl. [of נֶחְבָּא or בָא' § 23. rem. 6 & 9] . . . חבא

[l] נַחְבֵּאתָ [m] וְ' id. pret. 2 pers. sing. m. (§ 13. r. 7, note) חבא

[n] נֵחָבֵה וְ Niph. inf. (v. i. & § 24. rem. 9) . . חבה

[o] נַחְבֵּתֶם וְ id. pret. 2 pers. pl. masc. [for נֶחְבֵּאתֶם § 23. rem. 5, & § 13. rem. 7] . חבא

נַחְבִּי pr. name masc. . . . . חבה

[p] נֶחְדָּל Kal fut. 1 pers. pl. (§ 13. rem. 7) . חדל

[q] נְחַדֵּשׁ וּ Piel fut. 1 pers. pl.; וּ bef. (:) . חדש

[נָחָה] *to lead, conduct.* Hiph. I. *to lead, conduct, guide.*—II. *to lead back,* Job 12. 23.

נָחָה / [r] נָחָה וְ } Kal pret. 3 pers. sing. fem.; acc. shifted by conv. וְ (comp. § 8. rem. 7) נוח

[s] נְחֵה Kal imp. sing. masc. . . . נחה

[t] נָחוּ / [u] נָחוּ וְ } Kal pret. 3 pers. pl.; acc. shifted by conv. וְ (comp. § 8. rem. 7) נוח

[x] נְחַוֵּא Chald. Pael fut. 1 pers. pl. . חוה

נַחוּם, נְחוּם pr. names masc. . . . נחם

[y] נִחוּמָי noun masc. pl., suff. 1 p. s. fr. [נִחוּם] d. 1b נחם

[z] נָחוּץ Kal part. pass. sing. masc. . . נחץ

נָחוֹר וְ' pr. name masc. . . . נחר

[a] נָחוּשׁ adj. masc. sing. . . . נחש

נְחוּשָׁה id. sing. fem. . . . נחש

[b] נֶחֱזֶה וְ Kal fut. 1 pers. pl. . . . חזה

[c] נֶחֱזַק Kal fut. 1 pers. pl. . . . חזק

[d] נֶחֱטָא וַ Kal fut. 1 pers. pl.; וַ conv. . חטא

נִחְיֶה וְ' Kal fut. 1 pers. pl. . . . חיה

נְחַיֶּה וּ Piel fut. 1 pers. pl.; וּ bef. (:) . חיה

נָחִיתָ Kal pret. 2 pers. sing. masc. . . נחה

[e] נָחֲךָ וְ id. pret. 3 pers. sing. masc. [נָחָה], suff. 2 pers. sing. masc. (§ 24. rem. 21) . נחה

נָחַל [f] וְ fut. יִנְחַל.—I. *to obtain, acquire a possession, to possess.*—II. *to obtain by inheritance, to inherit.*—III. *to divide for a possession, to apportion,* with acc. and also לְ of the thing, acc. of the person. Pi. נִחַל (§ 14. rem. 1) *to give, distribute for a possession,* with double acc., also לְ of the person. Hiph. הִנְחִיל.—I. *to cause to possess, give as a possession,* with double acc.—II. *to cause to inherit, give* or *leave as an inheritance,* with double acc., also לְ of the person. Hoph. *to be made to possess,* Job 7. 3. Hithp. I. *to receive as one's own possession, to possess for oneself,* with acc.—II. *to leave as an inheritance,* with acc. of the thing, and לְ of the person.

נַחֲלָה fem. dec. 12 d.—I. *the act of taking possession,* perh. so Is. 17. 11.—II. *possession, property, estate.*—III. *inheritance.*—IV. *portion, lot,* Job 20. 29; 27. 13; 31. 2.

נַחֲלָת fem. *portion, lot,* Ps. 16. 6.

נַחַל [g] וְ' masc. dec. 6 d (with ה parag. נַחְלָה).—I. *stream, river* or *brook.*—II. *torrent.*—III. *valley* through which streams run.—IV. *shaft* of a mine, so, according to some, in Job 28. 4.

נַחֲלִיאֵל (*valley of God*) pr. name of a station of the Israelites in the desert, Nu. 21. 19.

נַחַל [h] וְ' / נָחַל [i] וְ' } noun masc. sing. dec. 6 d (§ 35. rem. 2) . . . נחל

[k] נִחַל Niph. pret. 3 p. s. m. [for נִחַל, נֵחַל § 18. r. 14] חלל

[l] נִחַל Piel pret. 3 pers. sing. masc. (§ 14. rem. 1) נחל

נַחֲלָה וְ' noun fem. sing. dec. 12 d . . . נחל

נַחְלָה noun masc. sing. (נַחַל) with parag. ה . נחל

נַחֲלָה Niph. part. sing. fem. [from נֶחֱלָה § 13. rem. 7, & § 24. rem. 18] . . . חלה

נָחֲלוּ [m] וְ' Kal pret. 3 pers. pl. . . . נחל

נֶחֱלוּ Niph. pret. 3 pers. pl. (§ 13. rem. 7) . חלה

נִחֲלוּ Piel pret. 3 pers. pl. (§ 14. rem. 1) . נחל

[n] נִחֲלוּ וְ Niph. pret. 3 pers. pl. (§ 18. rem. 8 & 14) חלל

[o] נְחָלוֹת noun fem. pl. abs. fr. נַחֲלָה dec. 12 d . נחל

נַחֲלֵי [p] וְ' noun masc. pl. constr. from נַחַל dec. 6 d נחל

נַחֲלִיאֵל pr. name masc. . . . . נחל

[q] נְחָלֶיהָ noun m. pl., suff. 3 pers. s. m. fr. נַחַל d. 6 d נחל

[r] נַחֲלַיִם id. du., abs. st. . . . נחל

נְחָלִים וּ' id. pl., abs. st.; וּ bef. (:) נחל

[a] Ex. 39. 30. [b] Is. 1. 4; Eze. 14. 5. [c] Le. 25. 11. [d] Je. 7. 29. [e] Le. 25. 20. [f] Nu. 5. 28. [g] Eze. 36. 9. [h] Job 29. 8, 10. [i] Jos. 10. 27. [k] Jos. 10. 17. [l] Ge. 31. 27. [m] 1 Sa. 19. 2. [n] Je. 49. 10. [o] Jos. 2. 16. [p] 1 Ki. 22. 15. [q] 1 Sa. 11. 14. [r] Is. 11. 2. [s] Ex. 32. 34. [t] Est. 9. 22. [u] Is. 7. 19. [x] Da. 2. 4. [y] Ho. 11. 8. [z] 1 Sa. 21. 9. [a] Job 6. 12. [b] Ca. 7. 1. [c] 1 Ki. 20. 23. [d] Is. 64. 4. [e] Is. 58. 11. [f] Zec. 2. 16. [g] Ps. 36. 9. [h] Ps. 74. 15. [i] Ps. 36. 9. [k] Eze. 25. 3. [l] Jos. 13. 32. [m] Ex. 32. 13. [n] Eze. 7. 24. [o] Is. 49. 8. [p] Ps. 18. 5. [q] Is. 34. 9. [r] Eze. 47. 9.

נַחֲלִיף[a] Hiph. fut. 1 pers. pl. . . . . . חלף

נַחֲלֵיתִי[b] וְ Niph. pret. 1 pers. sing. . . . חלה

נַּחְלְמָה[c] וַ Kal fut. 1 pers. pl. [נַחֲלֹם] with parag. ה (§ 8. rem. 13); וַ conv. . . . חלם

נֵחָלֵץ[d] Niph. fut. 1 pers. pl. . . . . חלץ

נֶחֱלָץ[e] id. part. sing. masc. . . . . חלץ

נָחַלְתָּ[f] וְ Kal pret. 2 pers. sing. masc.; acc. shifted by conv. וְ (§ 8. rem. 7) . . נחל

נַחֲלָת[g] noun fem. sing. . . . . . נחל

נַחֲלַת וְ' noun fem. sing., constr. of נַחֲלָה d. 12 d נחל

נִחַלְתְּ[h] וְ Niph. pret. 2 pers. sing. fem. [dag. forte impl. for נִחַלּוֹת, נִחַלְתְּ § 18. rem. 14] חלל

נַחֲלָתוֹ וְ' noun fem. sing., suff. 3 pers. sing. masc. from נַחֲלָה dec. 12 d . . . נחל

נָחַלְתִּי[i] Kal pret. 1 pers. sing. . . . נחל

נַחֲלָתִי וְ' noun f. s., suff. 1 pers. s. fr. נַחֲלָה d. 12d נחל

נַחֲלָתֶךָ, נַחֲלָתְךָ [k]וְ', וְ' } id., suff. 2 pers. sing. masc. . . נחל

נַחֲלַתְכֶם id., suff. 2 pers. pl. masc. . . . נחל

נַחֲלָתָם [l]וְ' id., suff. 3 pers. pl. masc. . . נחל

נְחַלְתֶּם[m] וּ Kal pret. 2 pers. pl. masc.; וּ for וְ conv. נחל

נְחַלְתָּנוּ[n] וּ id. pret. 2 pers. s. m., suff. 1 pers. pl.; וּ id. נחל

נַחֲלָתָן[o] noun masc. sing., suff. 3 pers. pl. fem. fr. נַחֲלָה dec. 12 d . . . . נחל

נַחֲלָתֵנוּ id., suff. 1 pers. pl. . . . . נחל

נָחַם Kal not used; as in the Arab. *to sigh*, cogn. נָהַם; hence Niph. נִחַם (comp. § 14. rem. 1).—I. *to mourn, grieve over*, with עַל, לְ, אֶל, Ju. 21. 6, 15; Eze. 32. 31.—II. *to grieve, feel compassion for, pity*, with עַל, אֶל, לְ, מִן.—II. *to feel regret, to repent* (with עַל, אֶל) so as to produce either a change of *conduct* or of *purpose*, which latter case is inapplicable to God, comp. 1 Sa. 15. 29; Ps. 110. 4.—III. *to ease, free oneself* of any displeasing object, with מִן.—IV. *to be comforted, to console oneself*, with עַל, אַחֲרֵי. Pi. נִחַם (§ 14. rem. 1) *to sympathize with, to console, comfort*, with acc. of the pers., with עַל, מִן concerning which. Pu. נֻחַם *to be consoled, comforted*. Hithp. הִתְנַחֵם, הִנֶּחָם (contr.) i. q. Niph. Nos. II, III, IV, const. with עַל, לְ.

נַחַם (*consolation*) pr. name masc. 1 Ch. 4. 19.

נֹחַם masc. *repentance*, Ho. 13. 14.

נֶחָמָה fem. dec. 10, *consolation*, Job 6. 10; Ps. 119. 50.

נַחוּם (*compassionate*) pr. name, *Nahum*, the prophet, Na. 1. 1.

נִחוּם masc. dec. 1b, only pl.—I. *compassion*, Ho. 11. 8.—II. *consolations*.

נְחֶמְיָה (*consolation of the Lord*) pr. name of a governor of Judea under Artaxerxes, and other persons.

נַחֲמָנִי (*compassionate*) pr. name masc. Ne. 7. 7.

מְנַחֵם (*consoler*) pr. name of a king of Israel, *Menahem*.

תַּנְחוּם m. d. 1b, only pl. *consolations, comforts*.

תַּנְחוּמָה fem. dec. 10, only pl. id. Job 21. 2.

תַּנְחֻמֶת (*consolation*) pr. name of a man.

נָחָם[p] Kal pret. 3 pers. sing. masc. [נָחָה], suff. 3 pers. pl. masc. (§ 24. rem. 21) . נחה

נַחַם pr. name masc. . . . . . נחם

נִחָם וְ' Niph. part. masc.; or נִחַם pret., in pause for the foll. . . . . . נחם

נִחַם וְ' id.; or Piel pret. 3 p. s. m. (dag. f. impl. in ח) נחם

נֹחַם[q] noun masc. sing. . . . . . נחם

נֶחְמָד [r]וְ' Niph. part. sing. masc. (§ 13. rem. 7) חמד

נַחְמְדֵהוּ[s] וְ Kal fut. 1 p. pl., suff. 3 p. s. m. (§ 13. r. 5) חמד

נֻחָמָה[t] Pual pret. 3 pers. sing. fem. (§ 14. rem. 1) נחם

נַחֲמוּ[u] Piel imp. pl. masc. (§ 14. rem. 1) . נחם

נִחֲמוּ[x] וְ id. pret. 3 pers. pl. . . . . נחם

נְחֶמְיָה pr. name masc. . . . . . נחם

נִחֻמִים noun masc. pl. [of נִחוּם] dec. 1b . . נחם

נַחֲמָנִי pr. name masc. . . . . . נחם

נֶחְמְסוּ[y] Niph. pret. 3 pers. pl. (§ 13. rem. 7) . חמס

נֶחָמָתִי noun fem. sing., suff. 1 p. s. fr. [נֶחָמָה] d. 10 נחם

נִחַמְתִּי[z], נִחָמְתִּי } Niph. pret. 1 pers. sing. (§ 14. rem. 1, comp. § 8. rem. 7) . . . } נחם

נִחַמְתִּי וְ id. id.; acc. shifted by conv. וְ (comp. § 8. r. 7) נחם

נִחַמְתִּים[a] וְ Piel (§ 14. r. 1) pret. 1 p. s., suff. 3 p. pl. m. נחם

נִחַמְתֶּם[b] וְ Niph. (comp. § 14. r. 1) pret. 2 p. pl. m. נחם

נִחַמְתָּנִי[zz] [cc]וְ' Piel (§ 14. r. 1) pret. 2 p. s. m., suff. 1 p. s. נחם

נַּחֲנֶה[c] וַ Kal fut. 1 pers. pl.; וַ conv. . . . חנה

נַחְנוּ[d], נָחְנוּ } pers. pron. 1 pers. pl., by aphaer. for אֲנַחְנוּ q. v.

נָחָנִי Kal pret. 3 pers. sing. masc. [נָחָה], suff. 1 pers. sing. (§ 24. rem. 21) . . נחה

נְחֵנִי[e] וּ' id. imp. s. m. (נְחֵה), suff. 1 p. s.; וּ bef. (:) נחה

נֶחֱנַנְתְּ[f] Kh. נֶחֱנַנְתִּי, K. נֶחֱנַנְתְּ Niph. pret. 2 pers. sing. fem. [for נֶחֱנוֹת, נֶחֱנַנְתְּ § 18. rem. 14] חנן

נֶחְפָּה[g] Niph. part. sing. fem. [of נֶחְפֶּה § 13. r. 7] חפה

נֶחְפָּז[h] Niph. part. sing. masc. (§ 13. rem. 7) . חפז

נֶחְפָּזוּ[i] id. pret. 3 pers. pl. [for נֶחְפְּזוּ v. i. & § 8. r. 7] חפז

---

[a] Is. 9. 9. [b] Da. 8. 27. [c] Ge. 41. 11. [d] Nu. 32. 17. [e] Pr. 11. 8. [f] Ex. 23. 30. [g] Ps. 16. 6. [h] Eze. 22. 16. [i] Ps. 119. 111. [k] De. 9. 29. [l] Ps. 37. 18. [m] Eze. 47. 14. [n] Ex. 34. 9. [o] Nu. 36. 3, 4, 12. [p] Ex. 13. 17. [q] Ho. 13. 14. [r] Ge. 3. 6. [s] Is. 53. 2. [t] Is. 54. 11. [u] Is. 40. 1. [x] Eze. 14. 23. [y] Je. 13. 22. [z] Zec. 8. 14. [zz] Ru. 2. 13. [a] Je. 31. 13. [b] Eze. 14. 22. [c] Ezr. 8. 15. [cc] Ps. 86. 17. [d] Ge. 42. 11. [e] Ps. 5. 9. [f] Je. 22. 23. [g] Ps. 68. 14. [h] 1 Sa. 23. 26. [i] Ps. 48. 6.

[a] נַחְפְּשָׂה Kal fut. 1 pers. pl. [נַחְפֹּשׂ] with parag. ה (§ 13. rem. 5, & § 8. rem. 13) . חפשׂ

[b] נֶחְפְּשׂוּ Niph. pret. 3 pers. pl. (§ 13. rem. 7) . חפשׂ

נָחַץ only part. pass. *urgent*, 1 Sa. 21. 9.

נֶחְקַר Niph. pret. 3 pers. sing. masc. (§ 13. rem. 7) חקר

[c] נַחְקְרָה וְ Kal fut. 1 pers. pl. [נַחְקֹר] parag. ה (§ 13. rem. 5, & § 8. rem. 13) . . חקר

נָחַר Root not used; Arab. *to snort*.

נַחַר masc. dec. 6 d, *a snorting*, Job 39. 20.

נַחֲרָה fem. id. only נַחֲרַת Je. 8. 16.

נַחְרַי, נַחֲרַי (*snorer*) pr. name masc. 2 Sa. 23. 37; 1 Ch. 11. 39.

נָחוֹר (*snoring*) pr. name masc.—I. Ge. 11. 22.—II. of a brother of Abraham, Ge. 11. 26, 27, &c.

נְחִירַיִם masc. du. *nostrils*, Job 41. 12.

חַרְנֶפֶר (*snorer*, for נָחַר, & נפר Syr. *to breathe hard*) pr. name masc. 1 Ch. 7. 36.

[d] נִחַר, [e] נִחָר } Niph. pret. 3 pers. sing. masc. (comp. § 8. rem. 7) . . . . } חרר

[f] נִחַרָ id., dag. forte impl. [for נִחַּר § 18. rem. 14] חרר

[g] נֶחֶרְבוּ Niph. pret. 3 pers. pl. . . . . חרב

[h] נֶחֱרָבוֹת, [i] נֶחֱרֶבֶת } id. part. pl. & sing. [from נֶחֱרָב masc. § 44. rem. 5, & § 13. rem. 7] . } חרב

[k] נַחְרוֹ noun fem. sing., suff. 3 pers. sing. masc. from נַחַר dec. 6 d [for נַחֲרוֹ § 35. rem. 5] . נחר

[l] נִחָרוּ, [m] נִחֲרוּ } Niph. pret. 3 pers. pl. [dag. f. impl. for נִחַּרוּ § 18. rem. 14, comp. § 8. rem. 7] } חרר

נַחְרַי pr. name masc. . . . . . נחר

וַנַּחֲרִם Hiph. fut. 1 pers. pl. ap. [fr. נַחֲרִים]; וַ conv. חרם

[n] נֶחֱרֶפֶת Niph. part. sing. fem. [of נֶחֱרָף] . . חרף

[o] נֶחֱרָצָה וְ', [p] נֶחֱרָצֶת } Niph. part. sing. fem. [of נֶחֱרָץ] . חרץ

[q] נַחֲרַת noun fem. sing. constr. [of נַחֲרָה, no pl.] נחר

נָחָשׁ [r] וְ' masc. dec. 4 a.—I. *serpent*.—II. pr. name; (*a*) of a place, 1 Ch. 4. 12; (*b*) of a king of the Ammonites; (*c*) 2 Sa. 17. 27; (*d*) 2 Sa. 17. 25.

נִחֵשׁ Pi. (§ 14. rem. 1) denom. of נָחָשׁ ὀφιομαντεία divination by serpents.—I. *to use enchantment, divination*.—II. *to perceive, observe*.

נַחַשׁ masc. d. 6 d, *enchantment*, Nu. 23. 23; 24. 1.

נַחְשׁוֹן (*enchanter*) pr. name of a man.

נְחָשׁ [s] וּ' Chald. masc. dec. 1 a, *copper, brass*.

נְחֹשֶׁת fem. dec. 13 c (with suff. נְחֻשְׁתָּה, נְחָשְׁתִּי).—I. *brass*.—II. *fetter, chain*, La. 3. 7; du. נְחֻשְׁתַּיִם *fetters*.—III. *money*, Eze. 16. 36.

נְחֻשְׁתָּא (*brass*) pr. name fem. 2 Ki. 24. 8.

נְחֻשְׁתָּן masc. adj. *brazen* serpent, 2 Ki. 18. 4.

נָחוּשׁ masc. adj. *brazen*, Job 6. 12.

נְחוּשָׁה fem. *brass*.

[t] נַחַשׁ noun masc. sing. dec. 6 d . . . נחשׁ

[u] נַחֵשׁ Piel inf. constr. for abs. (§ 14. rem. 1) . נחשׁ

נִחֵשׁ וְ id. pret. 3 pers. sing. masc. . . . נחשׁ

נְחַשׁ noun masc. sing., constr. of נָחָשׁ dec. 4 a . נחשׁ

נְחָשָׁא Chald. noun masc. sing., emph. of נְחָשׁ d. 1 a נחשׁ

[x] נֶחְשָׁב Niph. part. sing. masc. (§ 13. rem. 7) . חשׁב

[y] נֶחְשָׁב, [z] וְ נֶחְשַׁב } id. pret. 3 pers. sing. masc. (comp. § 8. r. 7) חשׁב

[a] וְ נַחְשְׁבָה Kal fut. 1 pers. pl. with parag. ה (§ 13. rem. 5, comp. § 8. rem. 13) . . חשׁב

נֶחְשְׁבוּ, נֶחְשָׁבוּ } Niph. pret. 3 pers. pl. (§ 13. rem. 7, comp. § 8. rem. 7) . . . } חשׁב

נֶחְשַׁבְנוּ id. pret. 1 pers. pl. . . . . חשׁב

[b] נֶחְשַׁבְתִּי id. pret. 1 pers. sing. . . . חשׁב

נַחְשׁוֹן וְ' pr. name masc. . . . . נחשׁ

[c] נְחָשִׁים noun masc. pl. of נָחָשׁ dec. 4, or נַחַשׁ dec. 6 a נחשׁ

נְחֹשֶׁת וּ' noun fem. sing. dec. 13 c; וּ bef. (:) . נחשׁ

נְחֻשְׁתָּא pr. name fem. . . . . . נחשׁ

[d] נְחֻשְׁתָּהּ noun fem. sing., suff. 3 pers. sing. fem. from נְחֹשֶׁת dec. 13 c (§ 44. rem. 4) . נחשׁ

[e] נְחֻשְׁתִּי id. with suff. 1 pers. sing. (v. id.) . נחשׁ

[f] נִחַשְׁתִּי Piel pret. 1 pers. sing. (§ 14. rem. 1) . נחשׁ

[g] נְחֻשְׁתֵּךְ noun fem. sing., suff. 2 pers. sing. fem. from נְחֹשֶׁת dec. 13 a (§ 44. rem. 4) . נחשׁ

נְחֻשְׁתָּם id. with suff. 3 pers. pl. masc. . . נחשׁ

[h] נְחֻשְׁתָּן noun masc. sing. from נְחֹשֶׁת with the term. ־ָן . . . . . נחשׁ

נָחַת only fut. יֵחַת, יִנְחַת, *to come down, descend*, with עַל *upon* any one; with בְּ *into* any, *to penetrate* him. Niph. נִחַת (comp. § 14. rem. 1) id. with בְּ *to penetrate*, Ps. 38. 3. Pi. נִחַת (§ 14. rem. 1).—I. *to press, bend down*, as a bow.—II. *to level*, as furrows, Ps. 65. 11. Hiph. *to cause to come down, to prostrate*, Joel 4. 11.

נְחַת Chald. *to come down, descend*, Da. 4. 10, 20. Aph. (§ 51. rem. 1).—I. *to bring* or *carry down*, Ezr. 5. 15.—II. *to lay down, deposit, place*, Ezr. 6. 1, 5. Hoph. הָנְחַת *to be deposed*, Da. 5. 20.

נָחֵת adj. *coming down*, only pl. נְחִתִּים (with dag. euph. for נְחֵתִים) 2 Ki. 6. 9.

La. 3. 40. · Ob. 6. · La. 3. 40. · Eze. 15. 4. · [e] Je. 6. 29. · [f] Ps. 69. 4. · [g] 2 Ki. 3. 23. · [h] Eze. 30. 7. · [i] Eze. 26. 19. · [k] Job 39. 20. · [l] Ps. 102. 4. · [m] Ca. 1. 6. · [n] Le. 19. 20. · [o] Da. 11. 36. · [p] Da. 9. 26. · [q] Je. 8. 16. · [r] Is. 65. 25. · [s] Da. 4. 12, 20. · [t] Nu. 23. 23. · [u] Ge. 44. 5, 15. · [x] 2 Ch. 9. 20; Is. 2. 22. · [y] 1 Ki. 10. 21. · [z] Nu. 18. 27, 30. · [a] Je. 18. 18. · [b] Ps. 88. 5. · [c] Nu. 24. 1; Je. 8. 17. · [d] Eze. 24. 11. · [e] La. 3. 7. · [f] Ge. 30. 27. · [g] Eze. 16. 36. · [h] 2 Ki. 18. 4.

נָחַת / וְ' נַ֫חַת } pr. name masc. . . . . . נוח

נַחַת / [a]נַ֫חַת ,וְ' ,וָ'[b] } noun fem. sing.; for וָ see lett. ו נוח

[c]נָחֵת Chald. Peal part. act. sing. masc. (§ 47. r. 1a) נחת

[d]נַחֵת Piel imp. sing. masc. (§ 14. rem. 1) . נחת

[e]נִחַת Niph. pret. 3 pers. sing. masc. [dag. forte impl. for נִחַת ,נִחַּת § 18. rem. 14] . חתת

[f]נִחַת וְ Piel pret. 3 pers. sing. masc. (§ 14. rem. 1) נחת

[g]נִחֲתָה וְ id. pret. 3 pers. sing. fem. . . . נחת

[h]נִחֲתוּ Niph. pret. 3 pers. pl. for [נִנְחֲתוּ ,נִחַתּוּ dag. forte impl.] . . . . . . נחת

[i]נַחְתּוֹם וְ Niph. inf. abs. (§ 9. rem. 1) . . חתם

[k]נְחָתִּי for נַחְתִּי (as some read) Niph. pret. 1 pers. s. נוח

[l]נְחִתִּים adj. masc. pl. [for נְחֵתִים from נָחֵת] . נחת

[m]נֶחְתַּךְ Niph. pret. 3 pers. sing. masc. (§ 13. rem. 7) חתך

[n]נֶחְתָּם וְ Niph. part. sing. masc. (§ 13. rem. 7) חתם

[o]נִטְבְּלוּ Niph. pret. 3 pers. pl. . . . טבל

נָטָה וְ' fut. יִטֶּה, ap. יֵט (§ 25. No. 2b).—I. *to stretch out, extend*, as the hand, a measure, &c.—II. *to stretch, spread out, expand*, as a tent.—III. *to incline, bow*.—IV. *to turn, lead to*; and intrans. *to turn away, decline*; with אֶל ,אַחֲרֵי *to, after*, מִן ,מֵעִם *from* any one.—V. *to go away, depart*, 1 Sa. 14. 7. Niph. נִטָּה *to be stretched out, extended*. Hiph. הִטָּה, fut. יַטֶּה, ap. יַט.—I. *to stretch out, extend*.—II. *to spread out, expand*.—III. *to decline, bow down, lower*, with לְ to any one.—IV. *to turn, lead away*; and intrans. *to decline, depart*; with אֶל ,לְ ,אַחֲרֵי.—V. *to wrest, pervert*.

יֻטָּה ,יוּטָּה (*spread out*) pr. name of a city in the tribe of Judah, Jos. 15. 55; 21. 16.

מַטֶּה masc. dec. 9a (pl. מַטּוֹת, once מַטִּים Hab. 3. 14).—I. *branch, bough*, Eze. 19. 11, sq.—II. *rod, staff*; מַ' לֶחֶם *staff of bread*, i. e. bread which supports and strengthens.—III. *sceptre*.—IV. *tribe*.

מַט only with ה loc. מַטָּה adv. *downwards*, De. 28. 43; (*a*) *beneath*, Pr. 15. 24; לְמַטָּה *downwards*; (*b*) *below, beneath*; (*c*) *below, under*, e. g. twenty years וּלְמַטָּה *and under*; מִלְמַטָּה *from below, underneath*.

מִטָּה fem. dec. 10.—I. *couch, bed*.—II. *a bier*, for dead bodies, 2 Sa. 3. 31.

מֻטֶּה masc. *a wresting* of right and judgment, Eze. 9. 9.

מֻטָּה fem. d. 10, *a spreading out, expansion*, Is. 8. 8.

וּנְטֵה Kal imp. s. masc.; וּ bef. (:) . . . טה

נִטֶּה id. fut. 1 pers. pl. (§ 25. No. 2b) . טה

נֹטֶה id. part. act. sing. masc. dec. 9a . טה

נָטוּ id. pret. 3 pers. pl. . . . . טה

[p]נְטוּוֹת Kh. Niph. part. fem. pl. [of נְטוּוָה from נָטוּ § 24. rem. 4] K. נְטוּיוֹת pl. of נְטוּיָה (q. v.) טה

[q]נָטְוּי Kh. נְטוּי, constr. of נָטוּי q. v.; K. נָטָיוּ Kal pret. 3 pers. pl. (§ 24. rem. 5) . . טה

נָטוּי Kal part. pass. sing. masc. dec. 3a . טה

נְטוּיָה id. part. sing. fem. dec. 10 . . . טה

[r]נָטוּעַ Kal part. pass. sing. masc. dec. 3a . טע

[s]נְטוּעִים id. pl., abs. st. . . . . . טע

נְטוֹפָתִי וּ' gent. noun from נְטֹפָה (q v.); וּ bef. (:) טף

[t]נְטוֹשׁ Kal imp. sing. masc. . . . . טש

[u]נְטוּשָׁה id. part. pass. sing. fem. [of נָטוּשׁ] . טש

[x]נְטוֹת id. inf. constr. . . . . . טה

[y]נִטָּיוּ Niph. pret. 3 pers. pl. (§ 24. r. 8, & § 25. No. 2) טה

[uu]נְטִילֵי noun masc. pl. constr. [from נָטִיל or נְטִיל] טל

[z]נְטִילַת וּ Peal part. pass. 3 pers. sing. fem. (§ 47. rem. 11); וּ bef. (:) . . . . טל

[a]נְטִישׁוֹתֶיהָ noun fem. pl., suff. 3 pers. sing. fem. from [נְטִישָׁה] dec. 10 . . . . טש

[b]נְטִישׁוֹתַיִךְ id., suff. 2 pers. sing. fem. . . . טש

[c]נָטִיתָ Kal pret. 2 pers. sing. masc. . . . טה

נָטִיתִי וְ' id. pret. 1 pers. sing. . . . . טה

נָטַל[d] fut. יִטּוֹל.—I. *to lift, take up*, Is. 40. 15.—II. *to lay, impose upon*, with עַל. Pi. *to take up*, Is. 63.

נְטַל Chald. *to lift up*, Da. 4. 31; pret. pas Da. 7. 4.

נֵטֶל masc. *burden*, Pr. 27. 3.

נָטִיל adj. masc. dec. 3a, *laden*, Zep. 1. 11.

[e]נֵטֶל וְ noun masc. sing. . . . . . טל

[f]נִטְלֵת Chald. Peal pret. 1 pers. sing. . . טל

נִטְמָא Niph. pret. 3 pers. sing. masc. . . מא

[g]וְ' נִטְמְאָה / [aa]נִטְמָאָה } id. pret. 3 pers. sing. fem. (comp. § 8. r. 7) מא

[h]נִטְמְאוּ id. pret. 3 pers. pl. . . . . מא

[i]נִטְמְאִים id. part. m., pl. of [נִטְמָא or נִטְמֶא § 23. r. 6 & 9] מא

נִטְמֵאת id. pret. 3 pers. sing. fem. . . . מא

[k]נִטְמֵאתִי id. pret. 1 pers. sing. . . . . מא

[l]נִטְמֵאתֶם id. pret. 2 pers. pl. masc. . . . מא

[m]נִטְמֵינוּ Niph. pret. 1 pers. pl. (§ 23. rem. 11) מא

[n]נִטְמֵתֶם וְ defect. for נִטְמֵאתֶם q. v. (§ 23. rem. 5) מא

נָטַע fut. יִטַּע, inf. נְטוֹעַ ,טַעַת.—I. *to plant*, as tre gardens, &c.—II. trop. *to plant* or *settle* a peo

---

[a] Ec. 6. 5. [b] Is. 30. 15. [c] Da. 4. 10, 20. [d] Ps. 65. 11. [e] Mal. 2. 5. [f] 2 Sa. 22. 35. [g] Ps. 18. 35. [h] Ps. 38. 3. [i] Est. 8. 8. [k] Job 3. 26. [l] 2 Ki. 6. 9. [m] Da. 9. 24. [n] Est. 3. 12. [o] Jos. 3. 15. [p] Is. 3. 16. [q] Ps. 73. 2. [r] Ec. 3. 2. [s] Ec. 12. 11. [t] Pr. 17. 14. [u] Is. 21. 15. [uu] Zep. 1. 11. [x] Ju. 19. 8. [y] Nu. 24. 6. [z] Da. 7. 4. [a] Je. 5. 10. [aa] Nu. 5. 27, 28. [b] Je. 48. 32. [c] Ex. 15. 12. [d] La. 3. 28. [e] Pr. 27. 3. [f] Da. 4. 31. [g] Nu. 5. 29. [h] Le. 18. 24. [i] Eze. 20. 30, 31. [k] Je. 2. 23. [l] Eze. 20. 43 [m] Job 18. 3. [n] Le. 11. 43.

in a particular country.—III. *to plant, pitch a tent,* Da. 11. 45.—IV. *to fix, fasten* a nail, Ec. 12. 11.—V. *to fix, set up* an image, De. 16. 21. Niph. *to be planted, established,* Is. 40. 24.

נֶטַע masc. dec. 6 (constr. נְטַע, with suff. נִטְעֵךְ § 35. rem. 5 & 7).—I. *a planting,* Is. 17. 11.—II. *a plant,* Job 14. 9.—III. *place planted, plantation.*

נָטִיעַ m. *something planted, a plant,* Ps. 144. 12.

מַטָּע masc. dec. 2b (pl. c. מַטָּעֵי § 31. rem. 1) *a planting, plantation.*

נָטָ֫עַ[a] Kal pret. 3 pers. sing. masc. for נָטַע (§ 8. r. 7) נטע
נָטַע[b] Seg. noun as if for נַטְע=נֶטַע but pl. c. נִטְעֵי (§ 35. rem. 2) . . . . נטע
נְטָעָ֑[c] Kh. נָטַע q. v.; K. נְטָעָה (q. v.) . . נטע
נְטַע[d] noun masc. sing., constr. [of נֶטַע comp. נֶטַע § 35. rem. 6] . . . נטע
נָטְעָה[e] Kal pret. 3 pers. sing. fem. . . . נטע
נָטְעוּ[f] 'וְ id. pret. 3 pers. pl. . . . נטע
נִטָּעוּ[g] Niph. pret. 3 pers. pl. [for נִטְּעוּ comp. § 8. r. 7] נטע
נִטְעוּ וְ Kal imp. pl. masc. . . . . . נטע
נִטְעֵי[h] }
נְטָעִים[i] } noun masc. pl. constr. & abs. from [נֶטַע] dec. 6a (§ 35. rem. 5) . . נטע
נֹטְעִים[k] Kal part. masc. pl. of 'נוֹטֵעַ dec. 7b . . נטע
נִטְעֵךְ[l] noun masc. sing., suff. 2 pers. sing. fem. from [נֶטַע] dec. 6a (§ 35. rem. 5) . נטע
נָטָעְתָּ[dd] Kal pret. 2 pers. s. m. [for נָטַעְתָּ § 8. r. 7] נטע
נָטַעְתִּי }
נְטַעְתִּי וְ } id. pret. 1 pers. sing.; acc. shifted by conv. וְ (§ 8. rem. 7) . . נטע
נְטַעְתִּיהוּ[m] וּ }
נְטַעְתִּיו[n] וּ } id. id., suff. 3 pers. sing. masc.; וּ for וְ, conv. . . . . . נטע
נְטַעְתִּיךְ[o] id. id., suff. 2 pers. sing. fem. . . . נטע
נְטַעְתִּים וּ id. id., suff. 3 pers. pl. masc.; וּ for וְ, conv. נטע
נְטַעְתָּם[p] id. pret. 2 pers. sing. masc., suff. 3 p. pl. m. נטע
נְטַעְתֶּם 'וּ[q] id. pret. 2 pers. pl. masc.; וּ for וְ, conv. נטע

[נָטַף] fut. יִטֹּף.—I. *to drop, distil;* metaph. of discourse.—II. *to drop with, let fall in drops.* Hiph. הִטִּיף *to let drop, distil,* Am. 9. 13; elsewhere metaph. of *dropping* sentiments, prophetic declarations, for *to prophesy.*

נָטָף masc. dec. 4a.—I. *a drop,* Job 36. 27.—II. Sept. στακτή, *myrrh,* Ex. 30. 34.

נְטֹפָה (*a dropping, distilling*) pr. name of a town near Bethlehem in Judea. Gent. n. נְטוֹפָתִי

נְטִיפָה fem. dec. 10, only pl. *drops, pendants* or *earrings.*

טָפַת (*drop;* for נְטָפַת) pr. name of a daughter of Solomon, 1 Ki. 4. 11.

נָטָף[r] noun masc. sing. dec. 4a . . . נטף
נְטֹפָה 'וּ pr. name of a place; וּ bef. (:) . . נטף
נָטָפוּ }
נָטְפוּ } Kal pret. 3 pers. pl. (§ 8. rem. 7) . נטף
נֹטְפוֹת[s] id. part. act. fem. pl. [נֹטֶפֶת from נוֹטֵף m.] נטף
נִטְפֵי[t] noun masc. pl., constr. of נָטָף dec. 4a . נטף
נְטֹפָתִי gent. noun, from נְטֹפָה . . . נטף

[נָטַר] fut. יִנְטוֹר, יִטֹּר.—I. *to watch, guard.*—II. *to keep, retain,* sc. anger, אַף being implied, with לְ, אֵת of the person.

נְטַר Chald. *to keep, preserve,* Da. 7. 28.

מַטָּרָא, מַטָּרָה fem.—I. *place of custody, a prison.*—II. *mark* or *butt,* aimed and shot at.

נֹטֵרָה[u] Kal part. act. s., f. of נוֹטֵר (§ 39. No. 3. r. 4) נטר
נִטְרֵת[x] Chald. Peal pret. 1 pers. sing. . . נטר
נָטָרְתִּי[y] Kal pret. 1 pers. sing. [for נָטַרְתִּי § 8. r. 7] נטר

נָטַשׁ[z] fut. יִטּוֹשׁ, יִטֹּשׁ.—I. *to leave, forsake, abandon.*—II. *to leave* in charge of any one, with עַל.—III. *to let alone without using,* as a field.—IV. *to let be, to remit* a debt, Ne. 10. 32.—V. *to let be, to allow, permit,* Ge. 31. 28.—VI. *to let out, draw out* a sword, Is. 21. 15.—VII. *to spread, scatter* intrans. *to spread itself,* 1 Sa. 4. 2. Niph. I. *to be left, forsaken,* Am. 5. 2.—II. *to be loosened,* Is. 33. 23.—III. *to spread itself.* Pu. *to be forsaken,* Is. 32. 14.

נְטִישׁוֹת fem. pl. (of נְטִישָׁה dec. 10).—I. *shoots* of a vine.—II. Je. 5. 10, perhaps, *bulwarks;* Prof. Lee, "*smaller towns,* considered as shoots of the capital."

נֻטָּשׁ[a] Pual pret. 3 pers. sing. masc. [for נֻטַּשׁ comp. § 8. rem. 7] . . . . . נטשׁ
נִטֹּשׁ[b] וְ Kal fut. 1 pers. pl. . . . נטשׁ
נִטְּשָׁה[c] Niph. pret. 3 pers. sing. masc. . . נטשׁ
נִטְּשׁוּ id. pret. 3 pers. pl. . . . . נטשׁ
נְטֻשִׁים[d] Kal part. pass. masc., pl. of נָטוּשׁ dec. 3a . נטשׁ
נְטָשָׁנוּ[e] id. pret. 3 pers. sing. masc., suff. 1 pers. pl. נטשׁ
נָטַשְׁתָּ[f] id. pret. 2 pers. sing. masc. . . נטשׁ
נָטַשְׁתְּ[g] id. pret. 2 pers. sing. fem. . . . נטשׁ
נָטַשְׁתָּה[h] id. pret. 2 pers. sing. masc. (§ 8. rem. 5) נטשׁ
נְטַשְׁתָּהּ[i] וּ id. id., suff. 3 pers. sing. fem.; וּ for וְ conv. נטשׁ
נָטַשְׁתִּי[k] }
נְטַשְׁתִּי וְ } id. pret. 1 pers. sing.; acc. shifted by conv. וְ (§ 8. rem. 7) . . נטשׁ

[a] Ps. 104. 16. [b] Job 14. 9. [c] Pr. 31. 16. [d] Is. 5. 7. [e] Ps. 80. 16. [f] Je. 31. 5. [g] Is. 40. 24. [h] Is. 17. 10. [i] 1 Ch. 4. 23. [k] Je. 31. 5. [l] Is. 17. 11. [m] 1 Ch. 17. 9. [n] 2 Sa. 7. 10. [o] Je. 2. 21. [p] Je. 12. 2. [q] Le. 19. 23. [r] Ex. 30. 34. [s] Ca. 5. 13. [t] Job 36. 27. [u] Ca. 1. 6. [x] Da. 7. 28. [y] Ca. 1. 6. [z] 1 Sa. 10. 2. [a] Is. 32. 14. [b] Ne. 10. 32. [c] Am. 5. 2. [d] 1 Sa. 30. 16. [dd] De. 6. 11. [e] Ju. 6. 13. [f] 1 Sa. 17. 28. [g] Je. 15. 6. [h] Is. 2. 6. [i] Ex. 23. 11. [k] Je. 12. 7.

נְטַשְׁתִּיךָ וֹ id. id., suff. 2 pers. sing. masc.; וֹ for וְ conv. נטש
[a]נְטַשְׁתַּנִי id. pret. 2 pers. sing. masc., suff. 1 pers. sing. נטש
[b]נָטְתָה Kal pret. 3 pers. sing. fem. . . . נטה

נָיא Root not used; Arab. *to be raw.*

נָא adj. masc. *raw, half-boiled,* Ex. 12. 9.

[c]נִיבוֹ וְ noun m. s., suff. 1 pers. s. fr. [נִיב] d. 1 a נוב
[d]נִיד וְ noun masc. sing. . . . . נוד
נִיָה וַ see וַנִיָה under lett. ו.
נִיחוֹחַ noun masc. sing. dec. 1 b . . . נוח
[e]נִיחוֹחֵיהֶם id. pl., suff. 3 pers. pl. masc. . . נוח
[f]נִיחוֹחִין [g]וְ' Chald. id. pl., abs. st. dec. 1 a . נוח
נִיחֹחַ noun masc. sing. dec. 1 b for נִיחוֹחַ . נוח
[h]נִיחֹחִי id., suff. 1 pers. sing. . . . . נוח
[i]נִיחֹחֲכֶם id., suff. 2 pers. pl. masc. . . . נוח
[k]נִין [l]וְ' noun masc. sing. dec. 1 a . . . נון
נִינְוֵה וְ' pr. name, *Nineveh,* the ancient capital of Assyria.
[m]נִינֵם Kal fut. 1 pers. pl. [נִינֶה], suff. 3 pers. pl. masc. (§ 25. No. 2 e) . . . . ינה
נִיסָן m. *Nisan,* the first month of the Hebrew year, called also אָבִיב. Etymology not defined.

[נוּר, נִיר] I. *to break up the ground, to till,* Je. 4. 3. —II. *to cultivate,* Ho. 10. 12.

נִיר masc. *fallow-ground, land first broken up.*

מָנוֹר masc. dec. 3, *beam* (prop. *yoke*; comp. Lat. jugum, a yoke, a beam) only in the phrase מְנוֹר אֹרְגִים *a weaver's beam.*

נִיר noun masc. sing. R. ניר or . . . נור
נִירָא [n]וַנִּ' Kal fut. 1 pers. pl.; וַ· conv. . . ירא
נִירוּ Kal imp. pl. masc. . . . . . ניר
[o]נֵירִי noun masc. s., suff. 3 p. s. m. fr. [נֵיר] d. 1 a נור
[p]נִּירָם וַ Kal fut. 1 pers. pl. [נִירֶה], suff. 3 pers. pl. masc. (§ 25. No. 2 e); וַ· conv. . ירה
[q]נִירָשׁ Kal fut. 1 pers. pl. [for נִירַשׁ § 8. rem. 15] ירש
[r]נִירָשָׁה id. with parag. ה (§ 8. rem. 13) . . ירש
[s]נַךְ וַ Hiph. fut. 1 pers. pl., ap. from נַכֶּה (§ 25. No. 2 a); וַ· conv. . . . . נכה

נָכָא Kal not used; i. q. נָכָה *to smite.* Niph. *to be beaten,* Job 30. 8 נִכְּאוּ, which some render, *they were frightened,* supposing it to stand for נִכְאוּ from כָּאָה.

נָכָא adj. masc. dec. 4 a, *smitten, afflicted,* Is. 16. 7.

נָכֵא adj. masc. dec. 5 a, id. רוּחַ נְכֵאָה *an afflicted mind, broken spirit.*

נְכֹאת fem. with suff. נְכֹאתֹה (prop. *something crushed, bruised*) *spicery, spices;* בֵּית נְכֹתֹה *house of his spices, his perfume house.*

נְכֵאָה adj. fem. sing. [for נָכֵא masc.] . . נכא
[t]נִכְאָה וְ Niph. pret. 3 pers. sing. masc. . . כאה
[u]נִכְאֵה וְ id. part. sing. m. constr. [of נִכְאֶה] d. 9 a כאה
[v]נִכְּאוּ Niph. pret. 3 pers. pl. . . . . נכא
[y]נְכָאִים adj. masc. pl. of [נָכָא] dec. 4 a . . נכא
נְכֹאת noun fem. sing. (with suff. נְכֹתֹה) . נכא
נִכְבָּד [z]וְ' Niph. part. sing. masc. (§ 37. rem. 5) . כבד
[a]נִכְבַּד id. pret. 3 p. s. m., or (2 Sa. 13. 25) Kal fut. 1 p. pl. כבד
[b]נִכְבָּדוֹת id. part. fem. pl. [of נִכְבָּדָה fr. נִכְבָּד masc.] כבד
נִכְבַּדֵּי id. part. pl. constr. masc. from נִכְבָּד dec. 8 a (§ 37. rem. 5) . . . . כבד
[c]נִכְבַּדֶּיהָ id. id., suff. 3 pers. sing. fem. . . כבד
[d]נִכְבַּדֵּיהֶם וְ id. id., suff. 3 pers. pl. masc. dec. 2 b . כבד
[e]נִכְבָּדִים וְ id. id. pl. abs. dec. 2 b . . . כבד
[f]נִכְבַּדְתְּ, [g]נִכְבַּדְתָּ id. pret. 2 pers. sing. masc. (comp. § 8. rem. 7) . . . . כבד
[h]נִכְבַּדְתִּי וְ id. pret. 1 pers. sing.; acc. shifted by conv. וְ (§ 8. rem. 7) . . . כבד
נִכְבְּשָׁה [i]וְ' Niph. pret. 3 pers. sing. fem. . . כבש
[k]נִכְבָּשׁוֹת id. part. fem. pl. [of נִכְבָּשָׁה fr. נִכְבָּשׁ masc.] כבש

נֶכֶד [m]וְ' masc. with suff. נֶכְדִּי (§ 35. rem. 3) *progeny;* always with נִין.

נָכָה Niph. נִכָּה (§ 25. No. 2 b) *to be smitten,* 2 Sa. 11. 15. Pu. נֻכָּה *to be beaten down,* Ex. 9. 31, 32. Hiph. הִכָּה; imp. הַכֵּה, הַךְ; fut. יַכֶּה, ap. וַיַּךְ.—I. *to smite, strike,* e. g. with the fist, a stick, sling, arrow, &c.; also with the horn, *to push;* moreover of the rays of the sun, of the cold. Espec. (*a*) הִכָּה כַף *to clap the hands,* in derision, but also in exultation; (*b*) trop. of the heart, i. e. the conscience reproving one; (*c*) with the tongue, *to taunt;* (*d*) frequently of God's judgments, as disease, pestilence; (*e*) of enemies, *to vanquish.* —II. *to strike, smite down, beat in pieces,* as hail; *to kill, slay;* הִ' נֶפֶשׁ *to strike* (as to) *life, to kill;* הִ' לְפִי חֶרֶב *to smite with the edge of the sword.*—III. *to strike* root, Ho. 14. 6. Hoph. הוּכָּה, הֻכָּה *to be smitten,* &c. pass. of Hiph.

נָכֶה adj. masc. dec. 9 b, *smitten.*—I. נְכֵה רַגְלַיִם *injured as to the feet,* i. e. *lame.*—II. נְכֵה רוּחַ *afflicted, contrite in spirit.*

נֵכִים masc. pl. (of נֵכֶה) *smiters,* sc. with t[...]

[a] Ge. 31. 28. [b] Nu. 22. 33. [c] Mal. 1. 12. [d] Job 16. 5. [e] Eze. 20. 28. [f] Ezr. 6. 10. [g] Da. 2. 46. [h] Nu. 28. 2. [i] Le. 26. 31. [k] Job 18. 19. [l] Is. 14. 22. [m] Ps. 74. 8. [n] Jos. 9. 24. [o] 2 Sa. 22. 29. [p] Nu. 21. 30. [q] Ju. 11. 24. [r] Ps. 83. 13. [s] De. 2. 33. [t] Da. 11. 30. [u] Ps. 109. 16. [x] Job 30. 8. [y] Is. 16. 7. [z] 1 Sa. 22. 14. [a] 2 Sa. 6. 20. [b] Ps. 87. 3. [c] Na. 3. 10. [d] Ps. 149. 8. [e] Nu. 22. 15. [f] Is. 26. 15. [g] Is. 43. 4. [h] Eze. 28. 22. [i] Jos. 18. 1. [k] Ne. 5. 5. [l] Job 18. 19. [m] Is. 14. 22.

tongue, *slanderers*, Ps. 35. 15. Others take it as the pl. of נָךְ *a jester*, from נוּךְ i. q. Arab. נאך *to jest*.

מַכָּה fem. dec. 10 (pl. מַכִּים, מַכּוֹת).—I. *a smiting, beating*.—II. *stroke, blow, wound*.—III. *slaughter*.—IV. *calamity* from God.

נַכֶּה[a] [b]וְ'ו Hiph. fut. 1 pers. pl. (§ 25. No. 2 b) נכה

נִכָּה[c] וְ Niph. pret. 3 pers. sing. masc. . . נכה

נְכוֹ, נְכֹה *Pharaoh Necho*, pr. name of a king of Egypt.

נְכֵה [d]וּ'ו adj. masc. sing., constr. of [נָכֶה] dec. 9 b; וּ bef. (:) . . . . נכה

נַכֵּהוּ[e] וַ, [f]וַנַּ'ו Hiph. fut. 1 pers. pl. (נָכָה), suff. 3 pers. sing. masc. (§ 25. No. 2 b); וַ conv. נכה

נְכוֹ pr. name masc. see נְכֹה.

נֻכּוּ[g] Hoph. pret. 3 pers. pl. (§ 25. No. 2 b) . נכה

נָכוֹן Niph. part. s. m. d. 3 a (also pr. name m.) כון

נְכוֹן[h] id., constr. st. . . . . . כון

נָכוֹנָה[i] id. pret. 3 pers. sing. fem. . . . כון

נְכוֹנָה id. part. fem of נָכוֹן . . . . כון

נָכוֹנוּ[k] id. pret. 3 pers. pl. . . . . . כון

נִכְזָבָה[l] Niph. pret. 3 pers. sing. fem. [for נִכְזְבָה comp. § 8. rem. 7] . . . . כזב

נִכְזָבְתָּ[m] וְ id. pret. 2 p. s. m. [for נִכְזַבְתָּ comp. § 8. r. 7] כזב

נֹכַח prep.—I. *opposite, over against*.—II. *before, in sight of*.—III. with other prep. אֶל נֹכַח *towards*, Nu. 19. 4. לְנֹכַח (*a*) adv. *straight forward*, Pr. 4. 25; (*b*) *before*, Ge. 30. 38; (*c*) *in behalf of*, Ge. 25. 21, עַד נֹכַח *as far as, in front of*.

נָכֹחַ masc. dec. 3 a.—I. adj. *straight, right, upright*, Pr. 8. 9; Is. 57. 2, הֹלֵךְ נְכֹחוֹ *he that walketh in what is right with him*, sc. God.—II. fem. נְכֹחָה *right, righteousness*.

נֵכַח i. q. נֹכַח, with suff. נִכְחוֹ (dec. 6 b) *over against*.

נְכַחֵד Piel fut. 1 pers. pl. (§ 14. rem. 1) . כחד

נִכְחַד Niph. pret. 3 pers. sing. masc. . . כחד

נִכְחֲדוּ id. pret. 3 p. pl. [for נִכְחֲדוּ comp. § 8. r. 7] כחד

נִכְחָדוֹת[n] id. part. fem. pl., sing. נִכְחֶדֶת (§ 44. r. 5) כחד

נְכֹחָה[o] [p]וּ'ו adj. fem. s. d. 10 [fr. נָכֹחַ m.]; וּ bef. (:) נכח

נְכֹחוֹ[q] id. masc., suff. 3 pers. s. m. fr. [נָכֹחַ] d. 3 a נכח

נִכְחוֹ prep. [נֵכַח] with suff. 3 pers. sing. m. d. 6 e נכח

נְכֹחוֹת adj. fem., pl. of נְכֹחָה d. 10 [fr. נָכֹחַ masc.] נכח

נַכְחִידֵם[r] וְ Hiph. fut. 1 pers. pl., suff. 3 pers. pl. m. כחד

נְכֹחִים [s]וּ'ו adj. masc. pl. of [נָכֹחַ] d. 3 a; וּ bef. (:) נכח

נֹכַחַת[t] וְ Niph. part. sing. fem. [of נוֹכַח] . יכח

נֵכִים[u] adj. masc. pl. of [נָכֶה] dec. 9 . . נכה

[נָכַל] *fraudulently to withhold*, Mal. 1. 14. Pi. *to act deceitfully*, Nu. 25. 18. Hithp. *to plot together against*, with בְּ, אֶת.

נֵכֶל masc. dec. 6 b, *craft, deceit*, Nu. 25. 18.

כֵּלַי, כִּילַי m. *churl, miser, niggard*, Is. 32. 5, 7.

נִכְּלוּ[x] Piel pret. 3 pers. pl. . . . . נכל

נִכְלָם[y] Niph. part. sing. masc. . . . . כלם

נִכְלָמוּ id. pret. 3 pers. pl. . . . . . כלם

נִכְלָמִים id. part. masc. pl. of נִכְלָם . . . כלם

נִכְלַמְתְּ וְ id. pret. 2 pers. sing. fem. . . . כלם

נִכְלָמְתִּי[z], נִכְלַמְתִּי[a] [b]וְ'ו } id. pret. 1 pers. sing. (comp. § 8. r. 7) כלם

נַכֵּם[c] וְ Hiph. fut. 1 pers. pl. (נָכָה), suff. 3 pers. pl. masc. (§ 25. No. 2 b); וַ conv. . נכה

נִכְמָרוּ[d], נִכְמְרוּ } Niph. pret. 3 pers. pl. (comp. § 8. rem. 7) . . . . } כמר

נְכֹנוּ[e] defect. for נְכוֹנוּ (q. v.) . . . . כון

נַכֶּנּוּ[f] Hiph. fut. 1 pers. pl. (נָכָה), suff. 3 pers. sing. masc. (§ 25. No. 2 b) . . נכה

נְכֹנִים Niph. part. masc., pl. of נָכוֹן dec. 3 a . כון

נִכְנַע Niph. pret. 3 pers. sing. masc. . . . כנע

נִכְנָעוּ[g], נִכְנְעוּ } id. pret. 3 pers. pl. (comp. § 8. rem. 7) . . . } כנע

[נֶכֶס] masc. dec. 6 a, only pl. *riches, treasures*.

נְכַס Chald. masc. dec. 3 b, pl. id.

נְכָסִים[h] וּ'ו noun masc. pl. of [נֶכֶס] dec. 6; וּ bef. (:) נכס

נִכְסִין[i] Chald. noun masc. pl. of [נְכַס] dec. 3 b נכס

נִכְסָף[k] Niph. part. sing. masc. . . . . כסף

נִכְסֹף[l] id. inf. abs. . . . . . . כסף

נִכְסְפָה[m] id. pret. 3 pers. sing. fem. . . . כסף

נִכְסַפְתָּה[n] id. pret. 2 pers. sing. masc. (§ 8. rem. 5) כסף

נִכְסָתָה[o] Niph. pret. 3 p. s. f. [for סְתָה' comp. § 8. r. 7] כסה

נִכַּפֵּר[p] וְ Nithpa. pret. 3 pers. sing. masc. [for נִתְכַּפֵּר § 7. No. 10] . . . כפר

נָכַר Pi. נִכֵּר.—I. *to estrange, alienate*, Je. 9. 4.—II. *to seem strange*, hence (*a*) *to gaze at, admire*, Job 34. 19; (*b*) *to mistake*, De. 32. 27; Job 21. 29; (*c*) *to reject*, 1 Sa. 23. 7. Hiph. הִכִּיר.—I. *to gaze at, regard, have respect to*, with פָּנִים.—II. *to be concerned, care for* any one.—III. *to recognise; to acknowledge; to know, be acquainted*

[a] Nu. 22. 6. [b] Jos. 10. 4. [c] 2 Sa. 11. 15. [d] Is. 66. 2. [e] Je. 18. 18. [f] De. 3. 3. [g] Ex. 9. 32. [h] Pr. 4. 18. [i] 1 Ki. 2. 46. [k] Pr. 19. 29. [l] Job 41. 1. [m] Pr. 30. 6. [n] Job 15. 28. [o] Am. 3. 10. [p] Is. 59. 14. [q] Is. 57. 2. [r] Ps. 83. 5. [s] 2 Sa. 15. 8. [t] Ge. 20. 16. [u] Ps. 35. 15. [x] Nu. 25. 18. [y] Ps. 74. 21. [z] Is. 50. 7. [a] Je. 31. 19. [b] Ezr. 9. 6. [c] De. 29. 6. [d] La. 5. 10. [e] Eze. 16. 7. [f] Ge. 37. 21. [g] 2 Ch. 12. 7. [h] 2 Ch. 1. 11. [i] Ezr. 7. 26. [k] Zep. 2. 1. [l] Ge. 31. 30. [m] Ps. 84. 3. [n] Ge. 31. 30. [o] Je. 51. 42. [p] De. 21. 8.

with. — IV. *to know, discriminate,* Ezr. 3. 13. Niph. נִכַּר.—I. *to feign oneself a stranger,* Pr. 26. 24.—II. *to be recognised, known,* La. 4. 8. Hithp. I. *to feign, dissemble.*—II. *to be recognised, known,* Pr. **20.** 11.

נֵכָר masc. constr. נֵכַר (§ 33. rem. 3) *what is strange, foreign,* comp. Ne. 13. 30; *strange, foreign part* (comp. Germ. die Fremde). בֶּן־נֵכָר *son of a foreign land, a stranger, foreigner.*

נֵכֶר masc. *alienation,* Job 31. 3.

נֹכֶר masc. dec. 6c, id. Ob. 12.

נָכְרִי masc. pl. נָכְרִים; fem. נָכְרִיָּה, pl. נָכְרִיּוֹת. —I. adj. *strange, foreign.*—II. *strange, new, singular,* Is. 28. 21.—III. *stranger, foreigner.*

הַכָּרָה fem. (verbal of Hiph.) *respect, regard,* Is. 3. 9, הַכָּרַת פְּנֵיהֶם *the respect of persons,* sc. in judgment. Others, *acknowledgment of their face,* i. e. the indication in their looks.

מַכָּר masc. dec. 1b, *acquaintance, friend,* 2 Ki. **12.** 6, 8.

נֵכָר noun masc. sing. dec. 2b . . . . נכר

נֵכַר[a] id., constr. st. (§ 33. rem. 3) . . . נכר

נִכַּר[b] Piel pret. 3 pers. sing. masc. (§ 10. rem. 1) נכר

נֵכֶר[c] וְ noun masc. sing. . . . . . נכר

נָכְרוֹ[d] noun m. s., suff. 3 p. s. m. fr. [נֹכֶר] d. 6c נכר

נִכְּרוּ[e] Niph. pret. 3 pers. pl. . . . . . נכר

נָכְרִי[ee] וְ' adj. masc. sing., pl. נָכְרִים . . . נכר

נָכְרִיָּה id. fem. sing. dec. 10 . . . . נכר

נָכְרִיּוֹת id. fem. pl. . . . . . . נכר

נָכְרִים[f] וְ[g] id. masc. pl. of נָכְרִי . . . נכר

נָכְרִיִּם[h] Kh. נָכְרִים q. v.; K. נָכְרִיָּה (q. v.) . נכר

נַכְרִית[i] Hiph. fut. 1 pers. pl. . . . . כרת

נַכְרִיתֶנָּה[k] וְ id., suff. 3 pers. sing. fem. . . . כרת

נִכְרְעָה[l] וְ Kal fut. 1 pers. pl. with opt. ה [for נִכְרְעָה § 8. rem. 13 & 15] . . . . כרע

נִכְרַתָּ[kk] וְ Niph. pret. 2 pers. sing. masc. [for נִכְרַתְתָּ § 25. rem.] . . . . . כרת

נִכְרַת, נִכְרָת } וְ' Niph. pret. 3 pers. sing. masc. (comp. § 8. rem. 7) . . . . כרת

נִכְרַת[m], נִכְרָת־[n] } Kal fut. 1 pers. pl. (§ 8. rem. 18) . כרת

נִכְרָתָה[o] Niph. pret. 3 p. s. f. [for נִכְרְתָה comp. § 8. r. 7] כרת

נִכְרְתָה[pp] וְ' Kal fut. 1 pers. pl. ה parag. (§ 8. rem. 13), or Niph. pret. 3 pers. sing. fem. . . כרת

נִכְרָתוּ[p], נִכְרְתוּ } וְ' Niph. pret. 3 pers. pl. (comp. § 8. rem. 7) כרת

נִכְרְתֶנּוּ[q] וְ Kal fut. 1 pers. pl. (נִכְרֹת), suff. 3 p. s. m. כרת

נִכְשַׁל[r] וְ Niph. pret. 3 pers. sing. masc. . . כשל

נִכְשָׁלוּ[s], נִכְשְׁלוּ[t] } וְ Niph. pret. 3 pers. pl. (comp. § 8. rem. 7) כשל

נִכְשָׁלִים[u] וְ id. part. masc. pl. [of נִכְשָׁל] . . . כשל

נִכְתָּב וְ'[x] Niph. part. sing. masc. . . . . כתב

נִכְתֻּב[y] Ch. Peal fut. 1 pers. pl. . . . . כתב

נְכֹאתֹה[z], נְכֹתֹה[a] } noun fem. sing., suff. 3 pers. sing. masc. from נְכֹאת . . . . } נכא

נֻכְּתָה[b] Pual pret. 3 p. s. f. [for נֻכְּתָה comp. § 8. r. 7] נכה

נִכְתָּם[c] Niph. part. sing. masc. . . . . כתם

נִלְאָה וְ[d] Niph. pret. 3 pers. sing. fem. . . . לאה

נִלְאוּ[e] וְ[f] id. pret. 3 pers. pl. . . . . . לאה

נִלְאֵית[g] id. pret. 2 pers. sing. fem. . . . . לאה

נִלְאֵיתִי וְ[h] id. pret. 1 pers. sing. . . . . . לאה

נִלְבְּנָה[i] Kal fut. 1 pers. pl. with parag. ה (§ 8. r. 13) לבן

נִלְבַּשׁ[k] Kal fut. 1 pers. pl. [for נִלְבַּשׁ § 8. rem. 15] לבש

נָלָה Kal not used; prob. i. q. Arab. נאל *to complete* hence Hiph. *to complete, accomplish,* Is. 33. 1.

מִנְלָה masc. dec. 9a, *possession, wealth,* Job 15. 29

נִלְוָה[l] וְ[m] Niph. pret. 3 pers. sing. masc. . . . לוה

נִלְווּ וְ id. pret. 3 pers. pl. . . . . . לוה

נָלוֹז[n] וְ[o] Niph. part. sing. masc. dec. 3a . . לוז

נְלוֹז[p] וּ id., constr. st.; וּ bef. (:) . . . לוז

נְלוֹזִים[q] וּ id. pl., abs. st. . . . . . לוז

נִלָּחֵם[r] Niph. fut. 1 pers. pl. . . . . . לחם

נִלְחָם id. part. sing. masc., or in pause for the foll. לחם

נִלְחַם וְ' id. pret. 3 pers. sing. masc. . . . . לחם

נִלְחֹם[s] id. inf. abs. . . . . לחם

נִלָּחֲמָה וְ id. fut. 1 pers. pl. (נִלָּחֵם) with parag. ה (comp. § 8. rem. 13) . . . . לחם

נִלְחֲמוּ[t], נִלְחָמוּ וְ' } id. pret. 3 pers. pl. (comp. § 8. rem. 7) לחם

נִלְחָמִים id. part. masc., pl. of נִלְחָם . . . לחם

נִלְחַמְנוּ[u] וְ id. pret. 1 pers. pl. . . . . . לחם

נִלְחַמְתָּ וְ id. pret. 2 pers. sing. masc.; acc. shifted by conv. וְ (§ 8. rem. 7) . . . . לחם

נִלְחַמְתִּי[x], נִלְחַמְתִּי וְ } id. pret. 1 pers. sing.; acc. shifted by conv. וְ (§ 8. rem. 7) . . . } לחם

נִלְחַמְתֶּם[y] וְ id. pret. 2 pers. pl. masc. . . . לחם

נָלִין[z], נָלִינָה[b] } וְ'[a] Kal fut. 1 pers. pl. (comp. § 8. rem. 13) R. לין see . . . . } לין

[a] De. 31. 16. [b] 1 Sa. 23. 7; Job 34. 19. [c] Job 31. 3. [d] Ob. 12. [e] La. 4. 8. [f] Is. 2. 6. [g] Ob. 11. [h] Pr. 20. 16. [i] 1 Ki. 18. 5. [k] Je. 48. 2. [l] Ps. 95. 6. [m] 2 Ch. 2. 15. [n] Ezr. 10. 3. [o] Ps. 37. 38. [p] Jos. 3. 16. [q] Je. 11. 19. [r] Da. 11. 19. [s] Da. 11. 14. [t] Da. 11. 33. [u] 1 Sa. 2. 4. [x] Est. 9. 32. [y] Ezr. 5. 10. [z] 2 Ki. 20. 13. [a] Is. 39. 2. [b] Ex. 9. 31. [c] Je. 2. 22. [d] Ps. 68. 10. [e] Je. 9. 4. [ee] Ps. 69. 9. [f] Ex. 7. 18. [g] Is. 47. 13. [h] Je. 20. 9. [i] Ge. 11. 3. [k] Is. 4. 1. [kk] Ob. 1. 10. [l] Ps. 83. 9. [m] Is. 14. 1. [n] Pr. 3. 32. [o] Is. 30. 12. [p] Pr. 14. 2. [pp] Ge. 31. 44. [q] Pr. 2. 15. [r] 1 Ki. 20. 23. [s] Ju. 11. 25. [t] Ju. 5. 19, 20. [u] De. 1. 41. [x] 2 Sa. 12. 27. [y] 1 Sa. 4. 9. [z] Ge. 19. 2. [a] Ju. 19. 11. [b] Ca. 7. 12.

Form	Analysis	Root
[a] וַנֵּ׳, [b] וְ׳ נֵלֵךְ / נֵלֶךְ־[u]	Kal fut. 1 pers. pl. (§ 20. rem. 4); וְ conv.	ילך
נִלְכַּד[c]	Niph. pret. 3 pers. sing. masc.	לכד
וְ נִלְכֹּד	Kal fut. 1 pers. pl.; וְ conv.	לכד
[d] וְ נִלְכְּדָה	Niph. pret. 3 pers. sing. fem.	לכד
וְ נִלְכָּדוּ / וְ נִלְכְּדוּ[e]	id. pret. 3 pers. pl. (comp. § 8. rem. 7)	לכד
נִלְכַּדְתָּ[f]	id. pret. 2 pers. sing. masc.	לכד
נִלְכַּדְתְּ[g]	id. pret. 2 pers. sing. fem.	לכד
וְ׳ נֵלְכָה[h] / וְ׳ נֵלֵכָה	Kal fut. 1 pers. pl. (נֵלֵךְ) with parag. ה (comp. § 8. rem. 13 & 15)	ילך
נִלְעַג[i]	Niph. part. sing. m. constr. [of נִלְעָג] d. 2b	לעג
נִלְקַח / נִלְקָח[k]	Niph. pret. 3 pers. sing. masc. (comp. § 8. rem. 7)	לקח
נִלְקָחָה[l]	id. pret. 3 pers. sing. fem. [for נִלְקְחָה v. id.]	לקח
נִמְאָס	Niph. part. sing. masc.	מאס
נִמְבְזָה[m]	Niph. part. formed from the subst. מִבְזָה	בזה
נָמֹגוּ	Niph. pret. 3 pers. pl.	מוג
נְמֹגִים[n]	id. part. masc. pl. [of נָמוֹג] dec. 3a	מוג
נִמְהָרָה[o]	Niph. pret. sing. [for נִמְהֲרָה comp. § 8. r. 7]	מהר
נִמְהָרִים[p]	id. part. pl. masc. from נִמְהָר dec. 2b	מהר
נָמוּ[q]	Kal pret. 3 pers. pl.	נום
נְמוּאֵל	pr. name masc. Nu. 26. 9; see also יְמוּאֵל. Patronym. נְמוּאֵלִי ver. 12.	
נָמוֹג	Niph. pret. 3 pers. sing. masc.	מוג
נָמוֹטּוּ[r]	Niph. pret. 3 pers. pl.	מוט
נְמוֹלִי[s]	Niph. pret. 3 pers. sing. masc., Chald. form for נָמוֹל (§ 21. rem. 24)	מול
נָמוּת	Kal fut. 1 pers. pl.	מות
וְ נִמְחוּ[t]	Niph. pret. 3 pers. pl.	מחה
נְמִיתֶךָ	Hiph. fut. 1 pers. pl. [נָמִית], suff. 2 pers. s. m.	מות
וּ נְמִיתֵם	id., suff. 3 pers. pl. masc.; וּ for וְ conv.	מות
וְ׳ נִמְכַּר	Niph. pret. 3 pers. sing. masc.	מכר
וְ נִמְכְּרוּ[u]	id. pret. 3 pers. pl.	מכר
נִמְכַּרְנוּ[x]	id. pret. 1 pers. pl.	מכר
וְ נִמְכְּרֶנּוּ[y]	Kal. fut. 1 pers. pl. [נִמְכֹּר], suff. 3 p. s. m.	מכר
נִמְכַּרְתֶּם	Niph. pret. 2 pers. pl. masc.	מכר

[נָמַל] *to circumcise*, Ge. 17. 11; so according to some, but see מָלַל.

נְמָלָה fem. *the ant*, Pr. 6. 6; from the idea of *cutting, consuming*. Pl. נְמָלִים Pr. 30. 25.

Form	Analysis	Root
נְמַלֵּא[z]	Piel fut. 1 pers. pl.	מלא
נִמְלָא[a]	Niph. part. sing. masc.	מלא
נְמָלָה[b]	noun fem. sing. (pl. נְמָלִים)	נמל
נָמֹלוּ[c]	Niph. pret. 3 p. pl. Ch. form [for נָמוֹלוּ § 21. r. 24]	מול
נִמְלָחוּ[d]	Niph. pret. 3 p. pl. [for נִמְלְחוּ comp. § 8. r. 7]	מלח
נִמָּלֵט[e]	Niph. fut. 1 pers. pl.	מלט
[g] וְ׳ נִמְלַט[f] / [h] וְ׳ נִמְלָט	Niph. pret. 3 pers. sing. masc. (§ 8. rem. 15)	מלט
וְ נִמְלָטָה[i]	id. part. sing. masc. with parag. ה	מלט
נִמְלְטָה[k]	id. pret. 3 pers. sing. fem.	מלט
[m] וְ׳ נִמְלָטוּ[l] / נִמְלְטוּ	id. pret. 3 pers. pl. (comp. § 8. rem. 7)	מלט
נִמְלָטְנוּ[n]	id. pret. 1 pers. pl. [for נִמְלַטְנוּ v. id.]	מלט
וְ נִמְלַטְתִּי[o] / וְ נִמְלַטְתִּי[p]	id. pret. 1 pers. sing.; acc. shifted by וְ conv. (comp. § 8. rem. 7)	מלט
וְ נַמְלִיךְ[q]	Hiph. fut. 1 pers. pl.	מלך
נְמֹלִים[r]	Niph. part. pl. m., from נָמוֹל (§ 21. rem. 24)	מול
נַמְלִךְ[s]	defect. for נַמְלִיךְ (q. v.)	מלך
נִמְלְצוּ[t]	Niph. pret. 3 pers. pl.	מלץ
וּ נְמַלֹּתֶם[u]	Niph. pret. 2 pers. pl. masc. for נְמַלְתֶּם (§ 18 rem. 15); וּ for וְ conv.	מלל
נִמְנָה[x]	Niph. pret. 3 pers. sing. masc.	מנה
נִמְנַע[y]	Niph. pret. 3 pers. sing. masc.	מנע
וְ נָמֵס	Niph. pret. 3 pers. sing. masc. [for נָמַס]	מסס
וְ׳ נָמֵס	id. id. (§ 18. rem. 7) and in pause נָמָס	מסס
וְ׳ נָמַסּוּ[z]	id. pret. 3 pers. pl.	מסס
וְ׳ נִמְצָא[rr]	Niph. pret. 3 pers. s. m.; or Kal fut. 1 pers. pl.	מצא
נִמְצָאָה[a]	Kh. נִמְצָאָה Niph. pret. 3 pers. sing. fem.; K. נִמְצָא (q. v.)	מצא
[b] וְ׳ נִמְצְאוּ / נִמְצָאוּ	Niph pret. 3 pers. pl. (comp. § 8. rem. 7)	מצא
נִמְצָאַיִךְ[c]	id. part. pl. masc., suff. 2 pers. s. f. fr. נִמְצָא	מצא
נִמְצֵאת[d]	id. pret. 2 pers. sing. fem.	מצא
[f] וְ׳ נִמְצֵאתִי[e]	id. pret. 1 pers. sing.	מצא
וְ נִמְצָה[g]	Niph. pret. 3 pers. sing. masc.	מצה
וְ׳ נָמַקּוּ[h]	Niph. pret. 3 pers. pl.	מקק
נְמַקִּים[i]	id. part. pl. masc. [fr. נָמַק d. 8. § 37. No. 2]	מקק
וּ נְמַקֹּתֶם[k]	id. pret. 2 pers. pl. masc.; וּ for וְ, conv.	מקק
וְ׳ נָמֵר[l]	masc. dec. 5a, *panther, leopard*. In the Arab. *to be spotted*; also *to be limpid*, comp. בֵּית נִמְרָה. נְמַר Chald. masc. id. Da. 7. 6.	נמר
נָמַר[m]	Niph. pret. 3 pers. sing. masc. [for נָמַר]	מור
נִמְרֹד	pr. name. masc.	מרד
וְ׳ נִמְרָה	pr. name in compos. בֵּית נִמְרָה see.	בית
נִמְרוֹד	pr. name masc., see נִמְרֹד	מרד

[a] Je. 51. 9. [b] De. 1. 19. [c] La. 4. 20. [d] Zec. 14. 2. [e] Je. 51. 56. [f] Pr. 6. 2. [g] Je. 50. 24.
[h] 1 Sa. 9. 10. [i] Is. 33. 19. [k] 1 Sa. 4. 22. [l] 1 Sa. 4. 17. [m] 1 Sa. 15. 9. [n] Ps. 75. 4. [o] Job 5. 13.
[p] Is. 32. 4. [q] Ps. 76. 6. [r] Ps. 17. 5. [s] Ge. 17. 26. [t] Eze. 6. 6. [u] Ne. 5. 8. [x] Est. 7. 4, 4.
[y] Ge. 37. 27. [z] Pr. 1. 13. [a] Ca. 5. 2. [b] Pr. 6. 6. [c] Ge. 17. 27. [d] Is. 51. 6. [e] Is. 20. 6.
[f] Pr. 11. 21. [g] Eze. 17. 15 [h] Job 22. 30. [i] Je. 48. 19. [k] Ps. 124. 7. [l] 2 Sa. 4. 6. [u] Je. 42. 3.
[m] Ps. 22. 6. [n] Ps. 124. 7. [o] 2 Sa. 1. 3. [p] 1 Sa. 27. 1. [q] Is. 7. 6. [r] Ge. 34. 22. [rr] 1 Sa. 15. 9.
[s] 2 Ki. 10. 5. [t] Ps. 119. 103. [u] Ge. 17. 11. [x] Is. 53. 12. [y] Joel 1. 13. [z] Ps. 97. 5.
[a] Je. 48. 27. [b] De. 22. 28. [c] Is. 22. 3. [d] Je. 50. 24. [e] Is. 65. 1. [f] Je. 29. 14.
[g] Le. 1. 15. [h] Ps. 38. 6. [i] Eze. 33. 10. [k] Eze. 24. 23. [l] Je. 5. 6. [m] Je. 48. 11.

נְמֵרִים[a] noun masc. pl. of נָמֵר dec. 5 a . . . נמר
נִמְרִים pr. name of a place, see בֵּית נִמְרָה . בית
נִמְרָץ[b] Niph. part. sing. masc. . . . . . מרץ
נִמְרְצוּ[c] id. pret. 3 pers. pl. . . . . . מרץ
נִמְרֶצֶת[d] id. part. sing. fem. . . . . . מרץ
נִמְשַׁח[e] Niph. pret. 3 pers. sing. masc. . . משח
נִמְשִׁי pr. name masc. . . . . . . משה
נִמְשַׁל[f] Niph. pret. 3 pers. sing. masc. . . . משל
נִמְשַׁלְתָּ[g] id. pret. 2 pers. sing. masc. [for נִמְשַׁלְתָּ comp. § 8. rem. 7] . . . משל
נִמְשַׁלְתִּי וְ id. pret. 1 pers. sing. . . . משל
נְמִתֵהוּ[h] וּ Hiph. fut. 1 pers. pl. [נָמִית], suff. 3 pers. sing. masc.; וּ for וְ conv. . . . מות
נַמְתִּיק[i] Hiph. fut. 1 pers. pl. . . . . . מתק
נְנַגֵּחַ[k] Piel fut. 1 pers. pl. (§ 15. rem. 1) . . נגח
נְנַגֵּן[l] Piel fut. 1 pers. pl. . . . . . נגן
נָנוּס Kal fut. 1 pers. pl. . . . . . נוס
נָנוּסָה[m] id. with parag. ה (comp. § 8. rem. 13) . נוס
נִנְחָל[n] Kal fut. 1 pers. pl. . . . . . נחל
נִנְעַרְתִּי[o] Niph. pret. 1 pers. sing. . . . . נער
נְנַתְּקָה[p] Piel fut. 1 pers. pl. with parag. ה (comp. § 8. r. 13) . . . . . . נתק
נָס וְ' Kal pret 3 p. s. m.; or part. masc. d. 1 a נוס
נַס[q] Piel imp. sing. masc. ap. [fr. נַסֵּה § 24. r. 11] נסה
נֵס noun masc. sing. dec. 8 b . . . . נסס
נָסַב וְ Niph. pret. 3 pers. sing. masc. . . סבב
נָסֵב[r] וְ Hiph. fut. 1 pers. pl. . . . . סבב
נָסֹב[s] }
וַנִּסֹּב[s] } Kal fut. 1 pers. pl. (§ 18. rem. 5) . סבב
נְסֻבְּאָה[u] וְ Kal fut. 1 p. pl. with parag. ה (§ 8. r. 13) סבא
נָסַבָּה[x] Niph. pret. 3 pers. sing. fem. (§ 18. rem. 7) סבב
נְסֻבָּה[y] וְ Hiph. fut. 1 pers. pl. (נָסֵב) with parag. ה סבב
נָסַבָּה[z] וְ Niph. pret. 3 p. s. f. [for נָסַבָּה § 18. r. 15] סבב
נְסִבָּה* noun fem. sing. *2 Ch. 10. 15 . . סבב
נָסַבּוּ וְ' Niph. pret. 3 pers. pl. . . . . סבב

[נָסַג] fut. יִסַּג to recede, depart, Is. 59. 13; Mi. 2. 6. Hiph. הִסִּיג.—I. to remove a boundary.—II. to take away, Mi. 6. 14. Hoph. הֻסַּג, to be turned back, be perverted, Is. 59. 14.

נִסְגֻּד[a] Chald. Peal fut. 1 pers. pl. . . . סגד
נָסֹגוּ Niph. pret. 3 pers. pl. . . . . סוג
נִסְגַּר[b] Niph. pret. 3 pers. sing. masc. . . . סגר
נִסְגְּרָה[c] וְ Kal fut. 1 pers. pl. with parag. ה (§ 8. r. 13) סגר

נָסָה. Pi. נִסָּה.—I. *to try, prove, tempt.*—II. *to try, attempt, essay.*

מַסָּה fem. d. 10.—I. *trial, temptation.*—II. *trial, calamity*, Job 9. 23.

נָסָה[d] Kal pret. 3 pers. sing. fem. . . . נוס
נְסָה[e] Kal imp. s. m., for נְשָׂא, or better *inf.* (c. מְרָדָה) נשא
נִסָּה Piel pret. 3 pers. sing. masc. . . . נסה
נִסָּהוּ[f] id., suff. 3 pers. sing. masc. . . . נסה
נָסוּ }
וְנָסוּ } Kal pret. 3 pers. pl.; acc. shifted by conv. וְ (comp. § 8. rem. 7) . . . נוס
נֻסוּ[g] וְ' id. imp. pl. masc. . . . . . נוס
נָסוֹג Niph. pret. 3 pers. sing. masc.; or (Ps. 80. 19) Kal fut. 1 pers. pl. . . . . . סוג
נָסוֹג[h] וְ Kal inf. abs. . . . . . . נסג
נְסוֹגִים[i] Niph. part. pl. masc. [from נָסוֹג] dec. 3 a סוג
נְסוּגֹתִי[k] id. pret. 1 pers. sing. . . . . סוג
נִסּוּנִי[l] Piel pret. 3 pers. pl., suff. 1 pers. sing. . נסה
נָסוֹעַ[m] וְ Kal inf. abs. . . . . . . נסע
נָסוּר Kal fut. 1 pers. pl. . . . . . סור
נָסוּרָה[n] וְ id. with parag. ה (comp. § 8. rem. 13) . סור
נַסּוֹת Piel inf. constr. dec. 1 b . . . . נסה

נָסַח only fut. יִסַּח, *to pluck, tear away*, spoken of a house, Pr. 15. 25, of a person, Ps. 52. 7; Pr. 2. 22. Niph. *to be plucked up*, De. 28. 63.

נְסַח Chald. Ithpe. id. pass. Ezr. 6. 11.

מַסָּח masc. *removing*, i. e. *a changing* or *relieving* of guards, adverbially 2 Ki. 11. 6. Others, *a keeping off.*

נִסְחַף[o] Niph. pret. 3 pers. sing. masc. . . סחף
נִסַּחְתֶּם[p] וְ Niph. pret. 2 pers. pl. masc. . . נסח
נִסִּי noun masc. sing., suff. 1 pers. s. fr. נֵס d. 8 b נסס
נְסִיכֵי noun masc. pl. constr. from [נָסִיךְ] dec. 3 a נסך
נְסִיכָם[q] id. sing., suff. 3 pers. pl. masc. . . נסך
נְסִיכֵמוֹ[r] id. pl., suff. 3 pers. pl. masc. [for נְסִיכֵימוֹ] נסך
נָסִים Kal part. act. masc., pl. of נָס dec. 1 a . נוס
נִסִּיתוֹ[s] Piel pret. 2 p. s. m. [נִסִּיתָ], suff. 3 p. s. m. נסה
נִסִּיתִי id. pret. 1 pers. sing. . . . . נסה
נִסִּיתֶם[t] id. pret. 2 pers. pl. masc. . . . נסה

I. נָסַךְ I. *to pour, pour out*, Is. 29. 10.—II. *to pour out, make a libation.*—III. *to melt, cast, found.*—IV. *to anoint* a king, Ps. 2. 6. Niph. *to be appointed*, Pr. 8. 23. Pi. 1 Ch. 11. 18, and Hiph. הִסִּיךְ *to pour out a libation.* Hoph. pass. Ex. 25. 29; 37. 16; these passages, however, may fairly be referred to סָכַךְ *to cover.*

נְסַךְ Ch. Pa. *to pour out, make a libation*, Da. 2. 46.

[a] Ca. 4. 8. [b] Mi. 2. 10. [c] Job 6. 25. [d] 1 Ki. 2. 8. [e] 1 Ch. 14. 8. [f] Ps. 49. 13, 21. [g] Is. 14. 10. [h] 2 Sa. 14. 7. [i] Ps. 55. 15. [k] Ps. 44. 6. [l] Is. 38. 20. [m] Ju. 20. 32. [n] Nu. 32. 19. [o] Ps. 109. 23. [p] Ps. 2. 3. [q] Da. 1. 12. [r] 2 Ch. 14. 6. [s] 1 Sa. 16. 11. [t] De. 2. 1. [u] Is. 56. 12. [x] Eze. 26. 2. [y] 1 Ch. 13. 3. [z] Eze. 41. 7. [a] Da. 3. 18. [b] 1 Sa. 23. 7. [c] Ne. 6. 10. [d] Is. 10. 29. [e] Ps. 4. 7. [f] Ex. 15. 25. [g] Zec. 2. 10. [h] Is. 59. 13. [i] Je. 46. 5. [k] Is. 50. 5. [l] Ps. 95. 9. [m] Ge. 12. 9. [n] Ju. 19. 11. [o] Je. 46. 15. [p] De. 28. 63. [q] De. 32. 38. [r] Ps. 83. 12. [s] De. 33. 8. [t] De. 6. 16.

נֶסֶךְ, נֵסֶךְ masc. dec. 6b.—I. *libation, drink-offering.*—II. *molten image.*

נְסַךְ Chald. masc. dec. 3b, *libation, drink-offering*, Ezr. 7. 17.

נָסִיךְ m. d. 3a.—I. *drink-offering*, De. 32. 38.—II. *molten image*, Da. 11. 8.—III. *one appointed, a prince.*

מַסֵּכָה fem. dec. 10.—I. *a fusing*; אֱלֹהֵי מַ׳ *molten gods, images.*—II. *libation*, meton. for *truce, league*, Is. 30. 1.

II. נָסַךְ *to cover*, only part. pass. Is. 25. 7. Arab. *to weave.*

מַסֵּכָה fem. *a covering*, Is. 25. 7; 28. 20.

מַסֶּכֶת fem. *a web*, Ju. 16. 13, 14.

נָסַךְ[a] Kal pret. 3 pers. sing. masc. for נָסַךְ (§ 8. r. 7) . נסך

נֶסֶךְ[b] וְ / נֵסֶךְ וְ׳ noun masc. sing. (suff. נִסְכּוֹ) dec. 6a (comp. § 35. rem. 2); for וְ see lett. ו . נסך

נֶסֶךְ וְ noun masc. sing. dec. 6b . . . נסך

נֻסְךָ[c] Kal inf. (נוּס), suff. 2 pers. sing. masc. d. 1a . נוס

נִסְכָּהּ וְ noun masc. s., suff. 3 p. s. f. fr. נֶסֶךְ d. 6b . נסך

נִסְכֹּה[d] וְ id., suff. 3 pers. sing. masc., Keri נִסְכּוֹ . נסך

נִסְכֵּהֶם[e] וְ id. pl., suff. 3 pers. pl. masc. for נִסְכֵּיהֶם . נסך

נִסְכּוֹ וְ׳ id. sing., suff. 3 pers. sing. masc. . . נסך

נִסְכִּי[f] וְ id. sing., suff. 1 pers. sing. . . . נסך

נִסְכֶּיהָ[g] וּ id. pl., suff. 3 pers. sing. fem.; וּ bef. (:) . נסך

נִסְכֵּיהוֹן[h] וְ Ch. id. pl., suff. 3 p. pl. m. fr. [נְסַךְ] d. 3b . נסך

נְסִיכֵיהֶם[i] noun m. pl., suff. 3 p. pl. m. fr. [נָסִיךְ] d. 3a . נסך

נִסְכֵּיהֶם וְ׳ the foll. with suff. 3 pers. pl. masc. . נסך

נְסָכִים[k] וּ׳ noun masc., pl. of נֶסֶךְ dec. 6b; וּ bef. (:) . נסך

נִסְכַּלְתָּ[l] / נִסְכַּלְתָּ[m] Niph. pret. 2 pers. sing. masc. (comp. § 8. rem. 7) . . . סכל

נִסְכַּלְתִּי id. pret. 1 pers. sing. . . . סכל

נָסַכְתִּי[n] Kal pret. 1 pers. sing. . . . . נסך

נִסַּכְתִּי[o] Piel pret. 1 pers. sing. . . . . נסך

נִסְלַח וְ Niph. pret. 3 pers. sing. masc. . . סלח

נִסְמְכוּ[p] Niph. pret. 3 p. pl. [for נִסְמְכוּ comp. § 8. r. 7] סמך

נִסְמַכְתִּי[q] id. pret. 1 pers. sing. . . . סמך

נִסְמָן[r] Niph. part. sing. masc. . . . . סמן

נַסְנוּ[s] וְ׳[t] Kal pret. 1 pers. pl. . . . . נוס

נַסֵּנִי[u] וְ Piel imp. sing. masc. [נַסֵּה], suff. 1 pers. sing. (§ 24. rem. 21, & § 25) . . נסה

I. נָסַס *to pine, waste away*, only part. נֹסֵס Is. 10. 18; cogn. נָסַס.

II. נָסַס. Hithpo. I. *to lift, raise oneself up*, Zec. 9. 16. Others, *to glitter, shine*, i. q. נָצַץ q. v. where the two ideas seem to be combined.—II. denom. of נֵס, *to rally round a standard*, Ps. 60. 6.

נֵס masc. dec. 8b.—I. *a standard, banner.*—II. *sail*, Is. 33. 23; Eze. 27. 7; others, *flag* of a ship.—III. *pole*, Nu. 21. 8, 9.—IV. *sign, token*, Nu. 26. 10.

נֹסֵס[x] Kal part. act. sing. masc. . . . נסס

נֹסְסָה[y] Pilel pret. 3 pers. sing. fem. . . . נוס

נָסַע וְ׳ fut. יִסַּע, imp. סְעוּ, inf. נְסֹעַ.—I. *to pull, pluck up* or *out*, as tent pins, &c.—II. *to break up* a camp, castra movere.—III. generally, *to remove, depart.*—IV. *to travel, journey.* Niph. *to be torn away.* Hiph. הִסִּיעַ.—I. *to tear up*; also *to quarry stones.*—II. *to cause to depart*, Ex. 15. 22.—III. *to lead, guide.*—IV. *to put away, remove*, 2 Ki. 4. 4.

מַסָּע, מַסַּע masc. dec. 2b (§ 31. rem. 5).—I. *a removing*, 1 Ki. 6. 7, אֶבֶן מַסָּע *stone* (ready) *for removing*; Gesenius, *stone of the quarry.*—II. *journey, march.*

מַסָּע masc. *missile, weapon*, Job 41. 18.

נִסַּע Piel pret. 3 pers. sing. masc. . . . נסע

נִסַּע וְ Kal fut. 1 pers. pl.; וַ conv. . . . נסע

נֹסֵעַ id. part. act. sing. masc. dec. 7b . . נסע

נִסְעָה[z] וַנִּ׳[a] id. fut. 1 pers. pl. with parag. ה; וַ conv. נסע

נָסְעוּ[b] / נָסָעוּ וְ׳ id. pret. 3 pers. pl. (§ 8. rem. 7) . נסע

נֹסְעִים[c] id. part. act. masc., pl. of נֹסֵעַ dec. 7b . נסע

נִסְפֶּה[d] וְ Niph. pret. 3 pers. sing. masc. . . ספה

נִסְפֶּה id. part. sing. masc. . . . . ספה

נִסְפְּחוּ[e] וְ Niph. pret. 3 pers. pl. . . . ספח

נְסַפֵּר[f] וַנְּ׳[g] Piel fut. 1 pers. pl.; וַ conv. . . ספר

נְסַפְּרָה[h] וּ id. with parag. ה; וּ bef. (:) . . ספר

נָסַק only fut. יִסַּק, *to go up, ascend*, Ps. 139. 8.

נְסַק Chald. Aph. *to cause to ascend, to take* or *bring up.* Hoph. pass. Da. 6. 24.

נִסְרְחָה[i] Niph. pret. 3 pers. sing. fem. . . . סרח

נִסְרֹךְ pr. name, *Nisroch*, an idol of the Ninevites.

נַסְתָּה[k] וְ Kal pret. 2 pers. sing. masc. (§ 8. rem. 5) נוס

נִסְּתָה[l] Piel pret. 3 pers. sing. fem. . . . נסה

נַסְתִּי[m] Kal pret. 1 pers. sing. . . . . נוס

נַסֹּתְךָ[n] Piel inf. (נַסּוֹת), suff. 2 pers. sing. m. d. 1b נסה

נַסֹּתָם[o] id., suff. 3 pers. pl. masc. . . . נסה

נַסְתֶּם[p] וְ׳ Kal pret. 2 pers. pl. masc. . . . נוס

נִסָּתֵר[q] Niph. fut. 1 pers. pl. . . . . סתר

נִסְתָּר id. part. sing. masc. . . . . סתר

---

[a] Is. 44. 10. [b] Joel 1. 13. [c] 2 Sa. 24. 13. [d] Le. 23. 13. [e] Nu. 29. 33. [f] Is. 48. 5. [g] Nu. 29. 31. [h] Ezr. 7. 17. [i] Da. 11. 8. [k] Le. 23. 37. [l] 1 Sa. 13. 13. [m] 2 Ch. 16. 9. [n] Ps. 2. 6. [o] Pr. 8. 23. [p] Is. 48. 2. [q] Ps. 71. 6. [r] Is. 28. 25. [s] Is. 20. 6. [t] Jos. 8. 5, 6. [u] Ps. 26. 2. [x] Is. 10. 18. [y] Is. 59. 19. [z] Ge. 33. 12.

[a] Ezr. 8. 31. [b] Nu. 9. 21. [c] Nu. 10. 29. [d] 1 Sa. 26. 10. [e] Is. 14. 1. [f] Ps. 79. 13. [g] Ge. 41. 12. [h] Je. 51. 10. [i] Je. 49. 7. [k] 2 Ki. 9. 3. [l] De. 28. 56. [m] 1 Sa. 4. 16. [n] De. 8. 16. [o] Ex. 17. 7. [p] Zec. 14. 5. [q] Ge. 31. 49.

נִסְתָּרָה } Niph. pret. 3 pers. sing. fem. (comp. } סתר
נִסְתָּרָה[a] וְ׳[b] } § 8. rem. 7) . . . }

נִסְתְּרוּ id. pret. 3 pers. pl. . . . . סתר

נִסְתָּרְנוּ[c] id. pret. 1 p. pl. [for נִסְתַּרְנוּ comp. § 8. r. 7] סתר

נִסְתַּרְתָּ[d] } id. pret. 2 pers. sing. masc.; acc. shifted } סתר
נִסְתַּרְתָּ[e] וְ } by conv. וְ (comp. § 8. rem. 7) . }

נִסְתַּרְתִּי[f] וְ id. pret. 1 pers. sing.; acc. id. . . סתר

נָע Kal part. act. sing. masc. . . . נוע

נַעֲבֹד וַנַּ׳ Kal fut. 1 pers. pl.; ·נַ conv. . . . עבד

נֶעֱבָד[g] Niph. pret. 3 p. s. m. [for נֶעֱבַד § 13. r. 7] עבד

נַעַבְדָה וְ Kal fut. 1 pers. pl. (נַעֲבֹד) with parag. ה
(comp. § 8. rem. 13) . . . עבד

נַעַבְדֶךָּ וְ id., suff. 2 pers. sing. masc. . . . עבד

נָעָבְדֵם[h] וְ Hoph. fut. 1 pers. pl., suff. 3 pers. pl. masc. עבד

נַעַבְדֶנּוּ Kal fut. 1 pers. pl. [נַעֲבֹד], suff. 3 pers. s. m. עבד

נֶעֱבַדְתֶּם[i] וְ Niph. pret. 2 pers. pl. masc. . . עבד

נַעֲבֹר וַנַּ׳ Kal fut. 1 pers. pl.; ·נַ conv. . . . עבר

נַעַבְרָה[k] וְ } id. with parag. ה (§ 8. rem. 13, & § 13. } עבר
נַעְבְּרָה וְ׳ } rem. 7) . . . }

נֶעְדָּר } Niph. pret. 3 pers. sing. masc. (comp. } עדר
נֶעְדָּר[l] } § 8. rem. 7, & § 13. rem. 7) }

נֶעְדָּרָה[m] id. pret. 3 pers. sing. fem. [for נֶעֶדְרָה comp.
§ 8. rem. 7] . . . . עדר

נֶעְדֶּרֶת[n] id. part. sing. fem. [from נֶעְדָּר masc.] . עדר

נֹעַדְתִּי[o] וְ defect. for נוֹעַדְתִּי (q. v.) . . יעד

נֹעָה וְ׳ pr. name fem. . . . . . נוע

נָעוּ } Kal pret. 3 pers. pl.; acc. shifted by } נוע
נָעוּ וְ } conv. וְ (comp. § 8. rem. 7) . . }

נַעֲוֵה[p] וְ Niph. part. sing. m., constr. [of נַעֲוֶה] d. 9a עוה

נַעֲוֵיתִי id. pret. 1 pers. sing. (§ 13. rem. 7, note) . עוה

נָעוּל[q] Kal part. pass. sing. masc. . . . . נעל

נָעוּר[r] Kal part. pass. sing. masc. . . . . נער

נֵעוֹר[s] Niph. pret. 3 pers. sing. masc. (§ 21. rem. 11) עור

נְעוּרַי } noun masc. pl., suff. 1 pers. sing. from } נער
נְעוּרַי[t] } [נְעוּר] dec. 1a . . . . }

נְעוּרֶיהָ id., suff. 3 pers. sing. fem. . . . . נער

נְעוּרַיִךְ } id. with suff. 2 pers. sing. fem. . . . נער
נְעוּרָיִךְ }

נְעוּרֶיךָ id., suff. 2 pers. sing. masc. . . . נער

נְעוּרֵיכִי[u] id., suff. 2 pers. sing. fem. (§ 4. rem. 4) נער

נְעוּרִים[x] id. pl., abs. st. . . . . . נער

נָעוֹת[y] Kal part. act. fem. pl. [of נָעָה dec. 10]
from נָע masc. . . . . נוע

נַעֲוַת[z] Niph. part. sing. fem. constr. [of נַעֲוָה dec. 10,
from נַעֲוֶה masc.] . . . . עוה

נַעֲזֹב[a] Kal fut. 1 pers. pl. . . . . עזב

נֶעֱזָב[b] וְ׳[c] Niph. part. sing. masc. . . . עזב

נֶעֱזַב[d] id. pret. 3 pers. sing. masc. . . . עזב

נַעַזְבָה[e] Kal fut. 1 pers. pl. (נַעֲזֹב) with parag. ה
(comp. § 8. rem. 13) . . . עזב

נֶעֱזָבָה[f] Niph. pret. 3 pers. sing. fem. [for נֶעֶזְבָה
comp. § 8. rem. 7] . . . . עזב

נֶעֱזַרְתִּי[g] וְ Niph. pret. 1 pers. sing. . . . עזר

נְעִיאֵל וּ pr. name of a place in the tribe of Asher,
Jos. 19. 27.

נָעִים וְ׳[h] adj. masc. sing. dec. 3a . . . נעם

נְעִים[i] וּ id., constr. st.; וּ bef. (:) . . . נעם

נֶעְכָּר[k] Niph. part. sing. masc. (§ 13. rem. 7) . עכר

נֶעְכָּרֶת[l] id. part. sing. fem. [for נֶעְכֶּרֶת comp. § 35. r. 2] עכר

נָעַל[m] וְ fut. יִנְעַל.—I. *to fasten with a bolt* or *bar, to bolt.*
—II. *to tie* or *latch the sandals* for any one, with
acc. of the person, Eze. 16. 10.

נַעַל fem. dec. 6d (pl. נְעָלוֹת, נְעָלִים) *sandal,
shoe;* שְׂרוֹךְ נַ׳ *shoe-latchet;* du. נַעֲלַיִם *a pair
of shoes.*

מַנְעוּל masc. dec. 1b, *bolt, bar.*

מִנְעָל masc. dec. 2b, id. De. 33. 25.

נָעַל[n] וְ Kal pret. 3 pers. sing. masc. for נָעַל (§ 8. r. 7) נעל

נָעַל[o] noun fem. sing. dec. 6d . . . . נעל

נַעַל[p] וַ Kal fut. 1 pers. pl., ap. from נַעֲלֶה ; ·נַ conv. עלה

נְעָל[q] וּ Kal imp. sing. masc.; וּ bef. (:) . . נעל

נַעֲלָה[r] וְ׳ Niph. pret. 3 pers. sing. m. (§ 13. r. 7, note) עלה

נַעֲלֶה וְ׳ Kal fut. 1 pers. pl. (v. id.) . . . עלה

נַעֲלוֹ noun fem. sing., suff. 3 pers. sing. masc. from
נַעַל dec. 6d . . . . . נעל

נְעֻלוֹת[s] Kal part. fem. pl. [of נְעוּלָה d. 10] fr. נָעוּל m. נעל

נְעָלוֹת[t] וּ noun fem. pl. abs. from נַעַל d. 6d; וּ bef. (:) נעל

נַעֲלִי id. sing., suff. 1 pers. sing. . . . נעל

נְעָלָיו[u] id. pl. (נְעָלִים׳), suff. 3 pers. sing. masc. נעל

נְעָלֶיךָ[x] וּ׳[y] id. pl., suff. 2 pers. sing. masc.; וּ bef. (:) נעל

נַעֲלֵיכֶם[z] וְ׳[a] id. pl., suff. 2 pers. pl. masc. . . נעל

נַעֲלַיִם id. du., abs. st. [for נַעֲלַיִם] . . . נעל

נְעָלֵינוּ[b] וּ id. pl. (נְעָלִים׳), suff. 1 pers. pl.; וּ bef. (:) נעל

נַעֲלֵיתָ[c] Niph. pret. 2 pers. sing. masc. (§ 13. r. 7 note) עלה

נַעֲלֵךְ[d] וְ׳ noun fem. sing., suff. 2 pers. sing. masc.
from נַעַל dec. 6d . . . . נעל

נֶעְלָם Niph. part. sing. masc., pl. נֶעֱלָמִים (§ 13. r. 7) עלם

נֶעְלַם[e] וְ׳ id. pret. 3 pers. sing. masc. . . . עלם

נַעֲלָמָה[f] id. part. sing. fem. . . . . עלם

---

[a] Is. 40. 27. [b] Nu. 5. 13. [c] Is. 28. 15. [d] 1 Sa. 20. 19. [e] 1 Ki. 17. 3. [f] 1 Sa. 20. 5.
[g] Ec. 5. 8. [h] De. 13. 3. [i] Eze. 36. 9. [k] Is. 51. 23. [l] 1 Sa. 30. 19. [m] Is. 34. 16.
[n] Is. 59. 15. [o] Ex. 29. 43. [p] Pr. 12. 8. [q] Ca. 4. 12. [r] Ne. 5. 13. [s] Zec. 2. 17.
[t] Ps. 25. 7. [u] Ps. 103. 5. [x] Is. 54. 6. [y] 1 Sa. 1. 13. [z] 1 Sa. 20. 30. [a] Ne. 10. 40.
[b] Ps. 37. 25. [c] Is. 27. 10. [d] Ne. 13. 11. [e] Ne. 5. 10. [f] Is. 62. 12. [g] Ps. 28. 7.
[h] Pr. 24. 4. [i] 2 Sa. 23. 1. [k] Ps. 39. 3. [l] Pr. 15. 6. [m] 2 Sa. 13. 18. [n] Ju. 3. 23.
[o] Ge. 14. 23. [p] De. 3. 1. [q] 2 Sa. 13. 17. [r] Nu. 9. 21. [s] Ju. 3. 24. [t] Jos. 9. 5.
[u] Is. 5. 27. [x] Ex. 3. 5. [y] Eze. 24. 17. [z] Ex. 12. 11. [a] Eze. 24. 23.
[b] Jos. 9. 13. [c] Ps. 97. 9. [d] Jos. 5. 15. [e] 2 Ch. 9. 2. [f] Na. 3. 11.

[a] נֶעְלְמָה ְ Niph. pret. 3 pers. sing. masc. . . עלם
[b] נֶעֱלָמִים id. part. masc., pl. of נֶעְלָם (q. v.) . עלם
[c] נֶעֶלְסָה Niph. pret. 3 pers. sing. fem. [for נֶעֶלְסָה comp. § 8. rem. 7] . . . . עלם

[נָעֵם] fut. יִנְעַם *to be pleasant, agreeable, lovely.*

נָעִים masc. dec. 3a, adj.—I. *pleasant, agreeable, sweet.*—II. *lovely, amiable.* Pl. נְעִימִים *pleasant places,* Ps. 16. 6; נְעִימוֹת, נְעִימִים *delights, pleasures.*

נַעַם (*pleasantness*) pr. name masc. 1 Ch. 4. 15.

נֹעַם masc.—I. *pleasantness.*—II. *beauty, glory,* Ps. 27. 4.—III. *kindness, grace,* Ps. 90. 17.

נַעֲמָה (*pleasant*) pr. name—I. of a daughter of Lamech, Ge. 4. 22.—II. of the mother of Rehoboam.—III. of a place in the tribe of Judah, Jos. 15. 41.—IV. of another unknown place, whence the gent. n. נַעֲמָתִי, comp. Job 2. 11.

נַעֲמִי patronym. of pr. name נַעֲמָן (q.v.) Nu. 26. 40.

נָעֳמִי (*my pleasantness;* or perh. for נָעֳמִיָּה (*pleasantness of the Lord;* or for נָעֳמִית *pleasant*) pr. name of the mother-in-law of Ruth.

נַעֲמָן masc.—I. pl. נַעֲמָנִים *pleasantness,* Is. 17. 10. —II. pr. name masc. of several persons.

מַנְעַמִּים masc. pl. of (מַנְעָם dec. 8a) *delicacies,* Ps. 141. 4.

נָעַם ְ pr. name masc. [for נַעַם § 35. rem. 2]; ְ see lett. ו . . . . . נעם
נֹעַם noun masc. sing. . . . . . נעם
[d] נַעֲמֹד Kal fut. 1 pers. pl. . . . . . עמד
נַעַמְדָה id. with parag. ה (§ 8. rem. 13) . . עמד
נַעֲמָה ו' pr. name of a woman and a place . נעם
[e] נָעֲמָה Kal pret. 3 pers. s. fem. [for נָעֲמָה § 8. r. 1a] נעם
[f] נָעֵמוּ id. pret. 3 pers. pl. [for נָעֲמוּ v. i.] . . נעם
[g] נְעִמוֹת adj. fem. pl. [of נְעִימָה dec. 10] from נָעִים m. נעם
נָעֳמִי pr. name fem. . . . . . נעם
[h] נַּעֲמִיד ַ Hiph. fut. 1 pers. pl.; ַ conv. . . עמד
נַעֲמָן ו' pr. name masc. . . . . . נעם
[i] נַעֲמָנִים noun masc., pl. of [נַעֲמָן] dec. 2b . . נעם
[k] נָעַמְתָּ, [l] נָעַמְתָּ } Kal pret. 2 pers. sing. masc. (§ 8. rem. 7) נעם
[m] נָעַמְתְּ id. pret. 2 pers. sing. fem. . . . . נעם
[n] נַעֲנָה, נַעֲנֶה } Niph. part. sing. fem. & masc. . . ענה
נַעֲנֵיתִי id. pret. 1 pers. sing. (§ 13. rem. 7, note) ענה
[o] נֶעֶנְשׁוּ ו' Niph. pret. 3 pers. pl. [for נֶעֶנְשׁוּ comp. § 8. rem. 7] . . . . . ענש

[p] נָעֻפָה ַ Kal fut. 1 pers. pl. with parag. ה (comp. § 8. rem. 13); ַ conv. . . . . עוף

נָעַץ Root not used; Chald. *to prick.*

נַעֲצוּץ masc. d. 1b, *thorn-bush,* Is. 7. 19; 55. 13.

נֶעֱצַב Niph. pret. 3 pers. sing. masc. . . עצב
[q] נַעְצֹר Kal fut. 1 pers. pl. (§ 13. rem. 5) . עצר
[r] נֶעְצָר Niph. part. sing. masc. (§ 13. rem. 7) . עצר
[s] נַעְצְרָה Kal fut. 1 pers. pl. with parag. ה (§ 8. rem. 13, & § 13. rem. 5) . . . עצר
[t] נֶעֶצְרָה Niph. pret. 3 pers. sing. fem. [for נֶעֶצְרָה] עצר
[u] נֶעְקַשׁ ְ Niph. part. sing. masc., constr. of [נֶעְקָשׁ § 13. rem. 7] dec. 2b . . . . עקש

I. [נָעַר] *to roar,* as a young lion, Je. 51. 38.

II. [נָעַר] cogn. עוּר, עָרָה.—I. *to shake, shake out.*—II. *to shake off,* i. e. cast off foliage, Is. 33. 9. Niph. I. *to be shaken, cast out.*—II. *to shake* or *rouse oneself,* Ju. 16. 20. Pi. נִעֵר (§ 14. rem. 1) *to shake, throw out.* Hithp. *to shake oneself,* Is. 52. 2.

נַעַר m. *that which is cast* or *driven out,* Zec. 11. 16.

נְעֹרֶת fem. *tow,* Ju. 16. 9; Is. 1. 31.

נַעַר ו' masc. dec. 6d.—I. *a male infant,* comp. Ex. 2. 6. —II. *boy, lad.*—III. *a youth.*—IV. *servant.*

נֹעַר masc. *childhood, youth.*

נַעֲרָה fem. dec. 12a.—I. *a girl, maiden.*—II. *a young woman.*—III. *handmaid.*—IV. pr. name of a woman, 1 Ch. 4. 5.—V. pr. name of a town on the borders of Ephraim, Jos. 16. 7, called נַעֲרָן in 1 Ch. 7. 28.

נְעוּרִים masc. pl. (of נְעוּר dec. 1a).—I. *childhood,* Ge. 46. 34.—II. *youth, early life.*

נְעוּרוֹת fem. pl. (of נְעוּרָה dec. 10) id. Je. 32. 30.

נַעַרְיָה (*servant of the Lord*) pr. name masc.— I. 1 Ch. 3. 22.—II. 1 Ch. 4. 42.

[a] נַעַר Kh. נַעַר (q. v.) com. gen.; K. נַעֲרָה (q. v.) נער
[y] נָעַר ו' in pause for נַעַר (§ 35. r. 2); for ְ see lett. ו נער
[z] נִעֵר ְ Piel pret. 3 pers. sing. masc. (§ 14. rem. 1) נער
[a] נֹעֵר ו' Kal part. sing. masc. . . . . נער
[b] נַעֲרָה ְ noun fem. sing. d. 12d (also pr. name fem.) נער
[c] נַעֲרָהּ noun masc. sing., suff. 3 pers. sing. fem. from נַעַר dec. 6d . . . . . נער
[d] נָעֲרוּ ו' Kal pret. 3 pers. pl. . . . . נער
נַעֲרוֹ ו' n. m. s., suff. 3 pers. sing. masc. fr. נַעַר d. 6d נער
[e] נַעֲרוֹת constr. of the foll. . . . . . נער

[a] Job 28. 21. [b] Ps. 26. 4. [c] Job 39. 13. [d] 2 Ki. 10. 4. [e] Ge. 49. 15. [f] Ps. 141. 6. [g] Ps. 16. 11. [h] Ne. 4. 3. [i] Is. 17. 10. [k] Ex. 32. 19. [l] 2 Sa. 1. 26. [m] Ca. 7. 7. [n] Is. 58. 10. [o] Pr. 22. 3; 27. 12. [p] Ps. 90. 10. [q] 1 Ch. 29. 14. [r] 1 Sa. 21. 8. [s] Ju. 13. 15. [t] Nu. 17. 15. [u] Pr. 28. 18. [x] De. 22. 23, 28. [y] Je. 51. 22. [z] Ps. 136. 15. [a] Is. 33. 9, 15. [b] Est. 2. 12. [c] 2 Ki. 4. 24. [d] Je. 51. 38. [e] Est. 4. 4.

נְעָרוֹת noun fem. pl. abs. from נַעֲרָה dec. 12d . . נער
נַעֲרֹתֶיהָ id. pl., suff. 3 pers. sing. fem. . . נער
נַעֲרוֹתָיו id. pl., suff. 3 pers. sing. masc. . . נער
נַעֲרַי pr. name masc. . . . נער
נַעֲרֵי noun masc. pl. constr. from נַעַר dec. 6d נער
נְעָרַי[a] / נְעָרָי } id. pl., suff. 1 pers. sing.; ו' bef. (:) . נער
נְעֻרַי[b] defect. for נְעוּרַי (q. v.) . . נער
נְעַרְיָה ו' pr. name masc.; ו bef. (:) . . נער
נַעֲרֵיהֶם[c] noun masc. pl., suff. 3 p. pl. m. fr. נַעַר d. 6d נער
נְעָרָיו id. pl., suff. 3 pers. sing. masc. . . נער
נְעָרֶיךָ[d] id. pl., suff. 2 pers. sing. masc. . . נער
נְעָרִים ו' id. pl., abs. st.; ו bef. (:) . . נער
נַעֲרֹךְ[e] Kal fut. 1 pers. pl. . . . ערך
נַעַרְךָ[f] noun masc. s., suff. 2 pers. s. m. fr. נַעַר d. 6g נער
נֶעֶרְמוּ[g] Niph. pret. 3 pers. pl. . . ערם
נַעֲרָן pr. name of a place, see נַעֲרָה . . נער
נַעֲרָץ[h] Niph. part. sing. masc. . . . ערץ
נַעֲרָתָה וְ pr. name of a place נַעֲרָה with parag. ה . נער
נִעַרְתִּי[i] Kal pret. 1 pers. sing. . . נער
נַעֲרֹתַי[k] / נַעֲרֹתַי[l] } noun fem. pl., suff. 1 pers. sing. from וְ נַעֲרָה dec. 12d } נער
נַעֲרֹתֶיהָ[m] וְ' id., suff. 3 pers. sing. fem. . . נער
נַעַשׂ[n] וַ Kal fut. 1 pers. pl., ap. fr. נַעֲשֶׂה; וַ conv. עשה
נַעֲשָׂה וְ'[o] Niph. pret. 3 pers. sing. m. (§ 13. r. 7, note) עשה
נַעֲשֶׂה וְ', נַעַ'[p] Kal fut. 1 pers. pl.; or (Ne. 5. 18) Niph. part. dec. 9a . . . עשה
נַעֲשׂוּ Niph. pret. 3 pers. pl. (§ 13. rem. 7, note) עשה
נַעֲשִׂים[uu] וְ'[aa] id. part. masc., pl. of נַעֲשָׂה dec. 9a . עשה
נַעֲשֶׂנָּה[q] וְ Kal fut. 1 pers. pl. (נַעֲשֶׂה), suff. 3 p. s. f. עשה
נַעַשְׂתָה[r] / נַעַשְׂתָה } Niph. pret. 3 pers. sing. fem. (comp. § 8. rem. 7) } עשה
נֵעָתוֹר[s] וְ Niph. inf. abs. (§ 9. rem. 1, & § 13. rem. 7) עתר
נֶעְתַּם[t] Niph. pret. 3 pers. sing. masc. (§ 13. rem. 7) עתם
נֶעְתַּר[u] וְ Niph. pret. 3 pers. sing. masc. (§ 13. r. 7) עתר
נַעְתָּרוֹת[x] וְ id. part. pl. fem. (§ 13. rem. 7) עתר
נֹף pr. name, *Memphis*, see נֹף.
נֶפֶג וְ', וָ' (*sprout*) pr. name masc. of two different persons.
נִפְגַּע[y] Kal fut. 1 pers. pl. . . . פגע
נִפְגְּשׁוּ Niph. pret. 3 p. pl. [for נִפְגְּשׁוּ comp. § 8. r. 7] פגש
נִפְדָּתָה[z] Niph. pret. 3 pers. sing. fem. [for נִפְדְּתָה comp. § 8. rem. 7] . . . פדה
נְפוּגֹתִי[a] Niph. pret. 1 pers. sing. . . . פוג
נָפוּחַ Kal part. pass. sing. masc. . . . נפח
נָפוֹל[b] Kal inf. abs. . . . . נפל
נָפוֹץ[c] וְ Kal inf. abs. . . . . נפץ

נָפוּץ[d] id. part. pass. sing. masc. . . . נפץ
נָפוּץ[e] Kal fut. 1 pers. pl. . . . . פוץ
נָפוֹצָה[f] Niph. pret. 3 pers. sing. fem. . . פוץ
נְפוֹצוֹתֶם[g] id. pret. 2 pers. pl. masc. (§ 21. rem. 12) פוץ
נְפוֹצִים[h] id. part. masc. pl. [of נָפוֹץ] dec. 3a . פוץ
נְפוּשְׁסִים Kh. נְפוּשְׁסִים, K. נְפִישְׁסִים see נְפִיסִים.
נִפְזְרוּ[i] Niph. pret. 3 pers. pl. . . . פזר

[נָפַח] fut. יִפַּח.—I. *to blow, breathe* a breath, or abs. *to blow*; with בְּ *into* or *upon*.—II. *to blow* a fire, with acc., בְּ; and עַל upon a thing or person; דּוּד נָפוּחַ *a seething pot*.—III. with נֶפֶשׁ *to expire*, Je. 15. 9. Pu. *to be blown*, of a fire, Job 20. 26. Hiph. I. *to cause to breathe out, cause to pant*, Job 31. 39.—II. *to puff at, despise*, Mal. 1. 13.

נֹפַח (*a blowing*) pr. name of a town in Moab, Nu. 21. 30.

מַפָּח masc. dec. 2b, *an expiring*, with נֶפֶשׁ, Job 11. 20.

מַפֻּחַ masc. *bellows*, Je. 6. 29.

תַּפּוּחַ masc.—I. *apple*.—II. *apple-tree*.—III. pr. name (*a*) of a town in Judah; (*b*) of another between Ephraim and Manasseh, Jos. 16. 8; (*c*) of a man, 1 Ch. 2. 43.

נֹפַח pr. name of a place . . . . נפח
נֹפֵחַ[k] Kal part. act. sing. masc. . . . נפח
נֻפַּח[l] Pual pret. 3 p. s. m. [for נֻפַּח comp. § 8. r. 7] נפח
נָפְחָה[m] Kal pret. 3 pers. sing. fem. . . נפח
נָפַחְתִּי וְ id. pret. 1 pers. sing.; acc. shifted by conv. וְ (§ 8. rem. 7) . . . נפח
נַפִּילָה[n] וְ Hiph. fut. 1 p. pl. with parag. ה (comp. § 8. r. 13) נפל
נְפִיסִים Kh. נְפִיסִים, K. נְפוּסִים pr. name masc. Ezr. 2. 50, for which in Ne. 7. 52 נְפוּשְׁסִים Kh. נְפִישְׁסִים K.
נָפִישׁ וְ' pr. name masc. . . . . נפש

נֹפֶךְ masc. name of a precious stone; kind uncertain. LXX. ἄνθρακα, *carbuncle*; Eng. vers. *emerald*; marg. *chrysoprase*, Eze. 28. 13.

נָפַל וְ' fut. יִפֹּל, inf. נְפֹל.—I. *to fall*, of persons and things.—II. *to fall* in battle, by the sword, *to be killed*.—III. *to fall down, to alight, dismount*.—IV. *to be fallen, to lie*, 1 Sa. 19. 24; and so frequently in the part. נֹפֵל *fallen, lying*.—V. *to fall, hang down*, as the arms from weakness; as the countenance in sorrow or anger.—VI. trop. *to fall* to

[a] Job 29. 5. [b] Je. 3. 4. [c] Ne. 5. 15. [d] 1 Sa. 25. 8. [e] Job 37. 19. [f] Ju. 7. 10. [g] Ex. 15. 8. [h] Ps. 89. 8. [i] Ne. 5. 13. [k] Ru. 2. 8. [l] Est. 4. 16. [m] Pr. 9. 3. [n] Je. 35. 10. [o] Eze. 15. 5. [p] Jos. 9. 24. [q] De. 30. 12, 13. [r] Da. 11. 36. [s] 1 Ch. 5. 20. [t] Is. 9. 18. [u] Is. 19. 22. [uu] Ec. 4. 1. [x] Pr. 27. 6. [y] Job 21. 15. [z] Le. 19. 20. [a] Ps. 38. 9. [aa] Es. 9. 28. [b] Est. 6. 13. [c] Ju. 7. 19. [d] Je. 22. 28. [e] Ge. 11. 4. [f] Je. 10. 21. [g] Eze. 20. 34. [h] 2 Ch. 18. 16. [i] Ps. 141. 7. [k] Is. 54. 16. [l] Job 20. 26. [m] Je. 15. 9. [n] Jon. 1. 7.

the ground, come to nothing, comp. 2 Ki. 10. 10. —VII. *to fall out, terminate*, Ru. 3. 18.—VIII. with עַל (*a*) *to fall upon*, as sleep, terror, divine revelation; (*b*) upon the sword; (*c*) upon the neck of any one, to embrace him; (*d*) upon the face, *to prostrate oneself* before any one; (*e*) upon any one, *to attack* him; (*f*) נָ׳ גּוֹרָל עַל *the lot fell upon*.—IX. with מִן *to fall away from* one party to another, with אֶל, עַל.—X. with לְ (*a*) *to fall to*, of an inheritance; (*b*) נָ׳ לְמִשְׁכָּב *to fall upon a sick-bed, to fall sick*.—XI. with מִן *to fall, sink down*; trop. from counsels, Ps. 5. 11. Hiph. הִפִּיל.—I. *to cause, make to fall*; hence, *to cast, throw down*; הִ׳ גּוֹרָל *to cast lots*; with לְ *to assign to* any one.—II. הִ׳ פְּנֵי פ׳ *to cause* the countenance of any one *to fall*, i. e. to make sad; הִ׳ פָּנָיו בְּ *to drop* one's countenance at any one, to be angry with him; הִ׳ תְּחִנָּה לִפְנֵי *to lay down* one's prayer, petition before any one; הִ׳ עַיִן *to knock out* an eye.—III. הִפִּיל מִן *to desist from*; הִ׳ אַרְצָה *to let fall* to the ground, not to fulfil.—IV. *to cast, bear, bring forth*. Hithp. I. *to prostrate oneself*.—II. with עַל, *to throw oneself upon, to attack*, Ge. 43. 18. Pil. נִפֵּל i. q. Kal, Eze. 28. 23.

נְפַל Ch. fut. יִפֵּל.—I. *to fall*.—II. *to fall down, prostrate oneself*.—III. *to be cast down*, Da. 3. 23. —IV. *to fall out, happen*, Ezr. 7. 20.

נֵפֶל masc. *an untimely birth*.

נְפִיל masc. only pl. נְפִילִים *giants*.

מַפָּל masc. dec. 2 b.—I. *refuse* of corn, Am. 8. 6. —II. *pendulous, flaccid parts* of the flesh, Job 41. 15.

מַפֵּלָה, מַפָּלָה fem. *ruins*.

מַפֶּלֶת fem. dec. 13 a (with suff. מַפַּלְתּוֹ).—I. *fall, ruin*, spoken of a man, a kingdom, a fallen trunk.—II. *a carcase*, Ju. 14. 8.

נָפָל Kal pret. 3 pers. sing. m. for נָפַל (§ 8. r. 7) — נפל

נְפַל Chald. Peal pret. 3 pers. sing. masc. . . — נפל

[a] נֵפֶל noun masc. sing. . . . . . — נפל

[b] וְ׳ נֹפֵל Kal part. sing. masc. . . . . — נפל

[c] נִפְלְאוּ Niph. pret. 3 pers. pl. . . . . — פלא

[d] וְ׳ נִפְלָאוֹת id. part. pl. abs. fem. [from נִפְלָאָה dec. 11 a, in use נִפְלֵאת q. v. . . . — פלא

[dd] נִפְלְאוֹת id. pl., constr. st. . . . . . — פלא

[e] וְ׳ נִפְלְאוֹתָיו id. pl., suff. 3 pers. sing. masc. . . — פלא

נִפְלְאוֹתֶיךָ id. pl., suff. 2 pers. sing. masc. . . — פלא

[f] נִפְלָאִים id. part. pl. masc. [from נִפְלָא . . — פלא

[g] נִפְלָאת id. pret. 3 pers. sing. fem. (§ 23. rem. 5) — פלא

[h] נִפְלָאֹת id. part. pl. abs. fem. see נִפְלָאוֹת . . — פלא

[i] נִפְלֵאת id. part. sing. fem. [for נִפְלֵאָת § 23. rem. 5] — פלא

[k] נִפְלְאַתָה id. pret. 3 pers. sing. fem. with parag. ה — פלא

[l] נִפְלְאֹתַי id. part. pl. fem., suff. 1 pers. sing. [from נִפְלָאָה dec. 11 b] . . . . — פלא

וְ׳ נִפְלְאֹתָיו id. pl., suff. 3 pers. sing. masc. . . — פלא

נִפְלְאֹתֶיךָ id. pl., suff. 2 pers. sing. masc. . . — פלא

נִפְלְגָה Niph. pret. 3 pers. sing. fem. . . . — פלג

[m] נָפְלָה, וְ׳ נָפְלָה } Kal pret. 3 pers. sing. fem. (§ 8. rem. 7) — נפל

[n] וְ׳[o] נִפְּלָה id. fut. 1 p. pl. with parag. ה (comp. § 8. r. 13) — נפל

וְ׳ נָפְלוּ, וְ׳ נָפְלוּ } id. pret. 3 pers. pl. (§ 8. rem. 7) — נפל

[p] נְפַלוּ Chald. Peal pret. 3 pers. pl. masc. . . — נפל

[q] נָפְלוֹ Kal inf. [נְפֹל], suff. 3 p. s. m. (§ 16. r. 10) — נפל

[r] נָפְלוֹ id. inf. (נְפֹל), suff. 3 pers. s. m. (§ 16. r. 7) — נפל

[s][t] וְ׳ נִפְלוּ id. imp. pl. masc. . . . . — נפל

[u] נְפַלוּ ו Ch. Peal pret. 3 p. pl., Kh. נְפַלוּ m., K. נְפַלָה f. — נפל

נֹפְלִים Kal part. act. masc. pl. of נֹפֵל dec. 7 b . — נפל

[x] נָפְלִין Ch. Peal part. act. masc. pl. [of נָפֵל] d. 2 b — נפל

[y] וְ נִפְלִינוּ Niph. pret. 1 pers. pl. (§ 24. rem. 8) — פלה

[z] נִפְלֵיתִי id. pret. 1 pers. sing. . . . . — פלה

[a] וְ נִפְלַל Pilel pret. 3 pers. sing. masc. (§ 6. No. 2) — נפל

[b] נָפְלָם Kal inf. [נְפֹל], suff. 3 p. pl. m. (§ 16. r. 10) — נפל

[c] נָפַלְתָּ, [d] נָפַלְתָּ, [e] וְ נָפַלְתָּ } id. pret. 2 pers. sing. masc. (§ 8. r. 7) — נפל

נֹפֶלֶת id. part. sing., fem. of נֹפֵל . . . — נפל

[f] וְ נָפַלְתָּה id. pret. 2 pers. sing. masc. (§ 8. rem. 5) — נפל

[g] נָפַלְתִּי, [h] וְ נָפַלְתִּי } id. pret. 1 pers. sing.; acc. shifted by conv. וְ (§ 8. rem. 7) . . — נפל

ו נְפַלְתֶּם id. pret. 2 pers. pl. masc.; ו for וְ, conv. — נפל

וְ נֵפֶן Kal fut. 1 pers. pl., ap. [fr. נִפְנֶה] (§ 24. rem. 3); וַ conv. . . . . — פנה

[i] נִפְעַמְתִּי Niph. pret. 1 pers. sing. . . . — פעם

[k] נָפַץ I. *to break, dash in pieces*.—II. *to disperse, scatter*, Is. 11. 12.—III. of a people, *to disperse themselves, be scattered abroad*. Pi. i. q. Kal No. I & II. Pu. *to be dashed* or *broken down*, Is. 27. 9.

נֶפֶץ masc. *a violent shower, flood*, Is. 30. 30.

[a] Ps. 58. 9. [b] 2 Sa. 3. 29. [c] Pr. 30. 18. [d] Da. 8. 24, etc. [e] Ps. 96. 3. [f] Ps. 139. 14. [g] Ps. 118. 23. [h] Ex. 34. 10. [i] De. 30. 11. [k] 2 Sa. 1. 26. [l] Ex. 3. 20. [m] Je. 51. 44. [n] 2 Sa. 24. 14. [o] 2 Ki. 7. 4. [p] Da. 3. 23. [q] 2 Sa. 1. 10. [r] 1 Sa. 29. 3. [s] Ho. 10. 8. [t] Je. 25. 27. [u] Da. 7. 20. [x] Da. 3. 7. [y] Ex. 33. 16. [z] Ps. 139. 14. [a] Eze. 28. 23. [b] Je. 49. 21. [c] 2 Sa. 3. 34. [d] Is. 14. 12. [dd] Job. 37. 14. [e] 2 Ch. 25. 19. [f] 2 Ki. 14. 10. [g] Mi. 7. 8. [h] Ju. 15. 18. [i] Ps. 77. 5. [k] 1 Sa. 13. 11.

מַפָּץ masc. *a bruising*, only מַפָּצוֹ Eze. 9. 2.

מַפֵּץ m. *hammer*, Je. 51. 20. Eng. vers. "battleaxe."

נַפֵּץ[a] Piel inf. constr. . . . . . נפץ

נֶפֶץ[b] noun masc. sing. . . . . . . נפץ

נִפֵּץ[c] וְ' Piel pret. 3 pers. sing. masc. . . . נפץ

נָפְצָה[d] Kal pret. 3 pers. sing. fem. . . . . נפץ

נָפְצוּ[e] id. pret. 3 pers. pl. . . . . . נפץ

נָפֹצוּ[f] וְ' Niph. pret. 3 pers. pl. . . . . פוץ

נְפֻצוֹת[g] Kh. נְפֻצוֹת q. v.; K. נְפוֹצֶת Niph. part. fem. פוץ

נְפֻצוֹת[h] וּ Kal part. pass. fem. pl. [of נְפוּצָה] from נָפוּץ; וּ bef. (:) . . . . . . נפץ

נְפֹצוֹתֵם[i] defect. for נְפוֹצוֹתֵם (q. v.) . . . . פוץ

נְפֹצִים[k] defect. for נְפוֹצִים (q. v.) . . . . פוץ

נִפַּצְתִּי[l] וְ Piel pret. 1 pers. sing.; acc. shifted by conv. וְ (comp. § 8. rem. 7) . . . . נפץ

נִפַּצְתִּים וּ id., suff. 3 pers. pl. masc.; וּ for וְ, conv. נפץ

נְפֹצֹתֶם[m] defect. for נְפוֹצוֹתֶם (q. v.) . . . . פוץ

נְפַק[n] Chald. *to go forth.* Aph. *to bring forth* or *out.*

נִפְקָא Chald. fem. dec. 8 a, *expense*, Ezr. 6. 4, 8.

נָפֵק[o] וְ Ch. Peal part. act. sing. masc. dec. 2 b נפק

נִפְקַד Niph. pret. 3 pers. sing. masc. . . . פקד

נִפְקַדְתָּ[p] וְ id. pret. 2 pers. sing. masc.; acc. shifted by conv. וְ (comp. § 8. rem. 7) . . פקד

נְפַקוּ[q] Ch. Peal pret. 3 p. pl., Kh. נְפַקוּ m., K. נְפַקָה f. נפק

נִפְקְחוּ[r] וְ Niph. pret. 3 pers. pl. . . . . . פקח

נָפְקִין[s] Ch. Peal part. act. masc., pl. of נָפֵק dec. 2 b נפק

נֶפְקַת[t] Ch. id. pret. 3 pers. sing. fem. [for נִפְקַת] נפק

נִפְקְתָא[u] וְ' Ch. noun fem. s., emph. of [נִפְקָא] d. 8 a נפק

נִפְרָד Niph. part. sing. masc. dec. 2 b . . . פרד

נִפְרְדוּ[x] נִפְרָדוּ[y] } id. pret. 3 pers. pl. (comp. § 8. rem. 7) פרד

נִפְרָדִים[z] id. part. masc., pl. of נִפְרָד . . . . פרד

נִפְרָץ[a] Niph. part. sing. masc. . . . . . פרץ

נִפְרְצָה[b] Kal fut. 1 pers. pl. with parag. ה (§ 8. r. 13) פרץ

נִפְרֹשׂ[c] וַ Kal fut. 1 pers. pl.; וַ conv. . . . פרשׂ

נִפְרָשׁוֹת[d] Niph. part. f. pl. [of נִפְרָשָׁה, fr. נִפְרָשׁ m.] פרשׁ

נָפַשׁ *to respire, take breath, refresh oneself.*

נֶפֶשׁ com. dec. 6 a (with suff. נַפְשִׁי, pl. נְפָשׁוֹת once נְפָשִׁים).—I. *breath;* also *odour, perfume*, Is. 3. 20, בָּתֵּי נֶפֶשׁ *perfume boxes;* and so perhaps in Pr. 27. 9, see עֵצָה R. עָצָה.—II. meton. any thing that breathes, *an animal.*—III. *person;* שִׁבְעִים נֶ' *seventy persons;* נֶ' מֵת *one dead, a dead body;* טָמֵא לָנֶפֶשׁ *polluted by a dead body.*—IV. *soul*, as the principle of life.—V. *life.*—VI. *self*, as נַפְשִׁי *myself*, נַפְשְׁךָ *thyself.*—VI. *feelings, spirit*, e. g. Ex. 23. 9, נֶפֶשׁ הַגֵּר *the feelings of a stranger*, also used for the *feelings* of an animal, Pr. 12. 10 —VII. *desire, inclination.*

נָפִישׁ (*refreshed, recreated*) pr. name of a man.

נֶפֶשׁ וְ' נָפֶשׁ } noun com. sing. dec. 6 a (§ 35. rem. 2) נפשׁ

נַפְשָׁהּ id., suff. 3 pers. sing. fem. . . . נפשׁ

נָפֹשׁוּ[e] Niph. pret. 3 pers. pl. . . . . פושׁ

נַפְשׁוֹ[f] Kh. נַפְשׁוֹ q. v.; K. נַפְשִׁי (q. v.) . נפשׁ

נַפְשׁוֹ וְ' noun com. s., suff. 3 pers. s. m. fr. נֶפֶשׁ d. 6 a נפשׁ

נַפְשׁוֹת[g] וְ' id. pl. constr. fem. . . . . נפשׁ

נְפָשׁוֹת[h] וּ' id. pl. abs. fem.; וּ bef. (:) . . . נפשׁ

נַפְשׁוֹתֵינוּ[i] id. pl. fem., suff. 1 pers. pl. . . . נפשׁ

נַפְשִׁי וְ' id. sing., suff. 1 pers. sing. . . . נפשׁ

נְפָשִׁים[k] id. pl. abs. masc. . . . . . נפשׁ

נַפְשְׁךָ נַפְשֶׁךָ } id. sing., suff. 2 pers. sing. masc. . נפשׁ

נַפְשֵׁךְ id. sing., suff. 2 pers. sing. fem. . . נפשׁ

נַפְשְׁכֶם[l] וְ' id. sing., suff. 2 pers. pl. masc. . . נפשׁ

נַפְשָׁם[m] וְ' id. sing., suff. 3 pers. pl. masc. . . נפשׁ

נַפְשֵׁנוּ[n] וְ' id. sing., suff. 1 pers. pl. . . . נפשׁ

נִפְשָׁע[o] Niph. part. sing. masc. . . . . פשׁע

נַפְשֹׁת[p] noun com. pl. constr. fr. נֶפֶשׁ dec. 6 a . נפשׁ

נְפָשֹׁת id. pl., abs. st. . . . . . . נפשׁ

נַפְשֹׁתֵיכֶם id. pl., suff. 2 pers. pl. masc, def. Je. 44. 7. נפשׁ

נַפְשֹׁתֵינוּ id. pl., suff. 1 pers. pl. . . . . נפשׁ

נָפַת[q] noun fem. sing., constr. of [נָפָה] dec. 10 נוף

נֹפֶת וְ' noun fem. sing. . . . . . . נוף

נִפְתָּה[r] Niph. pret. 3 pers. sing. masc. . . . פתה

נֶפְתּוֹחַ pr. name of a place. . . . . . פתח

נַפְתּוּלֵי[s] noun masc. pl. constr. of [נַפְתּוּל] dec. 1 b. פתל

נִפְתָּח[t] Niph. part. sing. masc. . . . . . פתח

נִפְתַּח[u] id. pret. 3 pers. sing. masc. . . . . פתח

נִפְתְּחָה וַנִּ'[x] ,וְ'[y] Kal fut. 1 pers. pl. with parag. ה (comp. § 8. rem. 13); וַ conv. . . . פתח

נִפְתְּחוּ נִפְתָּחוּ } Niph. pret. 3 pers. pl. (comp. § 8. rem. 7) . . . . . . } פתח

נַפְתֻּחִים pr. name of an Egyptian people.

נַפְתִּי[z] Kal pret. 1 pers. sing. . . . . . נוף

נִפְתָּל[a] Niph. part. sing. masc. . . . . . פתל

נַפְתָּלִי וְ' pr. name of a man and a tribe . . פתל

נִפְתָּלִים[b] Niph. part. masc., pl. of נִפְתָּל . . פתל

נִפְתַּלְתִּי[c] id. pret. 1 pers. sing . . . . . פתל

נֵץ[d] noun masc. sing. dec. 8 b . . . . נצץ

[a] Da. 12. 7. [b] Is. 30. 30. [c] Ps. 137. 9. [d] Ge. 9. 19. [e] Is. 33. 3. [f] Je. 40. 15. [g] 2 Sa. 18. 8. [h] Is. 11. 12. [i] Eze. 11. 17. [k] 1 Ki. 22. 17. [l] Je. 51. 20, 21, 22, 23. [m] Eze. 20. 41. [n] Da. 2. 14. [o] Da. 7. 10. [p] 1 Sa. 20. 18. [q] Da. 5. 5. [r] Ge. 3. 5. [s] Da. 3. 26. [t] Da. 2. 13. [u] Ezr. 6. 4, 8. [x] 2 Sa. 1. 23. [y] Ge. 10. 5, 32. [z] Ne. 4. 13. [a] 1 Sa. 3. 1. [b] 1 Ch. 13. 2. [c] Ps. 44. 21. [d] Eze. 34. 12. [e] Na. 3. 18. [f] Ps. 24. 4. [g] Ps. 72. 13. [h] Eze. 13. 18. [i] Je. 26. 19. [k] Eze. 13. 20. [l] 1 Ch. 22. 19. [m] Is. 46. 2. [n] Nu. 21. 5. [o] Pr. 18. 19. [p] Le. 21. 11. [q] 1 Ki. 4. 11. [r] Job 31. 9. [s] Ge. 30. 8. [t] Zec. 13. 1. [u] Is. 5. 27. [x] Am. 8. 5. [y] Ge. 43. 21. [z] Pr. 7. 17. [a] Pr. 8. 8. [b] Job 5. 13. [c] Ge. 30. 8. [d] Job 39. 26.

נָצָה.—I. *to contend with one another, to quarrel.*—II. *to be desolated.*

נָצָה, נוֹצָה fem. *feather, pinion.*

מַצָּה fem. *contention, quarrel.*

מַצּוּת fem. dec. 1 b, id. Is. 41. 12.

נִצָּה[h] noun fem. sing. dec. 10 . . . נצץ

נִצָּהּ[i] noun masc. sing., suff. 3 pers. sing. fem. fr. נֵץ dec. 8 b . . . . . נצץ

נֹצָה[k] וְ defect. for נוֹצָה (q. v.) . . . נצה

נָצוּ[l] Kal pret. 3 pers. pl. R. נצה or . . נוץ

נָצוּמָה[m] וַ Kal fut. 1 pers. pl. with parag. ה (comp. § 8 rem. 13); וַ· conv. . . . . צום

נָצוֹר[n] Kal inf. abs. . . . . . . נצר

נָצוּר[o] Kal fut. 1 pers. sing. . . . . צור

נְצוּרָה[p] Kal part. pass. sing. fem. dec. 10, fr. נָצוּר' m. נצר

נָצַח Kal not used; Arab. *to be pure, innocent, faithful;* Syr. *to conquer;* hence Pi. I. *to excel;* especially *to be* or *preside over, to superintend;* part. מְנַצֵּחַ *overseer.*—II. *to lead in music,* 1 Ch. 15. 21; part. מְנַצֵּחַ *leader of music, precentor, chorister.* Niph. *to be entire, perfect, complete,* Je. 8. 5.

נְצַח Chald. Ithpa. *to conquer, surpass,* Da. 6. 4.

נֵצַח, נֶצַח masc. dec. 6 e.—I. *truth, uprightness, faithfulness;* 1 Sa. 15. 29, for concr. *the truthful, faithful,* sc. God. — II. *permanency, perpetuity, eternity;* לָנֶצַח, עַד נֶצַח, and נֶצַח adv. *for ever;* לָנֶצַח נְצָחִים *for ever and ever.*—III. *confidence, trust.*—IV. *excellency, glory,* 1 Ch. 29. 11.—V. *completeness, entireness,* לָנֶצַח, and נֶצַח adv. *wholly, entirely.*—VI. *juice,* Is. 63. 3, 6; Arab. נצח *to spatter.*

נְצִיחַ (*excellent;* Syr. נציחא) pr. name of a man.

נֵצַח / נֶצַח } noun masc. sing. dec. 6 e (§ 35. rem. 5) נצח

נִצְחִי[q] id. with suff. 1 pers. sing. . . . נצח

נְצָחִים[r] id. pl., abs. st. . . . . . נצח

נִצְחָם[s] id. sing., suff. 3 pers. pl. masc. . . נצח

נִצַּחַת[t] Niph. part. sing. fem. [of נִצָּח] . . נצח

נִצְטַדָּק[u] Hithpa. fut. 1 pers. pl. [for נִתְצַדֵּק § 12. r. 3] צדק

נְצִיב וּ' noun m. sing. d. 1 a, also pr. n.; וּ bef. (:) נצב

נְצִיבִים id. pl., abs. st. . . . . . נצב

נְצִיחַ pr. name masc. . . . . . נצח

נִצִּים Niph part. masc. pl. [of נִצָּה] dec. 9 a . נצה

נְצִירֵי[x] וּ Kh. נְצִירֵי adj. pl. constr. masc. [fr. נָצִיר]; K. נְצוּרֵי Kal part. pass. pl. constr. masc., from נָצוּר' dec. 3 a; וּ bef. (:) . . נצר

נָצָא inf. abs. Je. 48. 9, *to fly away.*

נֵצֵא וְ' Kal fut. 1 pers. pl. . . . . יצא

נָצַב Kal not used; i. q. יָצַב q. v. Niph. נִצַּב.—I. *to be set, placed* or *appointed,* with עַל *over* any one; part. נִצָּב *one set over, an officer.*—II. *to place, station oneself; to stand.* Hiph. הִצִּיב.—I. *to set, place.*—II. *to set up, erect.*—III. *to fix, appoint.* Hoph. הֻצַּב.—I. *to be set, placed, fixed.*—II. *to be set, planted,* Ju. 9. 6.

נִצָּב masc. *handle, haft,* Ju. 3. 22.

נִצְבָּא Ch. f. d. 8 a, *firmness, strength,* Da. 2. 41.

נְצִיב masc. dec. 1 a.—I. *a statue, pillar,* Ge. 19. 26. —II. *garrison.*—III. *officer, overseer,* 1 Ki. 4. 7, 19. —IV. pr. name of a place in the tribe of Judah, Jos. 15. 45.

צוֹבָה, צֹבָה, צֹבָא (for נְצוֹבָה *station*) pr. name of a region in Syria, whence the two cities אֲרַם צוֹבָה & חֲמַת צוֹבָה.

צִיבָא (for נְצִיבָא *statue*) pr. name of a servant of Saul.

מַצָּב masc. d. 2 b.—I. *standing-place,* Jos. 4. 3, 9. —II. *station, office,* Is. 22. 19.—III. *military station, garrison.*

מֻצָּב masc. *station, garrison,* Is. 29. 3.

מַצָּבָה, מִצָּבָה fem. id. 1 Sa. 14. 12; Zec. 9. 8.

מַצֵּבָה fem. dec. 11 b (but pl. with suff. invariably retaining *Tseri,* comp. § 42. rem. 4).—I. *pillar, monument.*—II. *statue, image of an idol.*

מַצֶּבֶת fem. dec. 13 a.—I. *pillar, monument.*—II. *stem, root,* Is. 22. 19.

נִצָּב Niph. part. sing. masc. . . . נצב

נִצָּבָה / נִצָּבָה[a] } id. pret. 3 pers. sing. fem. (comp. § 8. rem. 7) . . . . } נצב

נִצָּבוּ[b] וְ'[c] id. pret. 3 pers. pl. . . . . נצב

נְצִבֵי[d] noun masc. pl., constr. of נְצִיב dec. 1 a . נצב

נְצִבִים id. pl. abs. (comp. נְצִיבִים) . . . נצב

נִצָּבִים Niph. part. masc. pl. of נִצָּב . . . נצב

נִצַּבְתָּ וְ id. pret. 2 pers. sing. masc.; acc. shifted by conv. וְ (comp. § 8. rem. 7) . . נצב

נִצְבְּתָא[e] Ch. noun fem. sing., constr. of [נִצְבָּא] d. 8 a נצב

נִצְדּוּ[f] Niph. pret. 3 pers. pl. . . . . צדה

נִצְדַּק[g] וְ' Niph. pret. 3 pers. sing. masc. . צדק

[נָצָה] I. *to fly,* La. 4. 15.—II. *to be desolate, laid waste,* Je. 4. 7. Hiph. הִצָּה *to strive, contend.* Niph.

[a] Ps. 45. 10. [b] Ex. 15. 8. [c] Ex. 33. 8. [d] 1 Sa. 10. 5. [e] Da. 2. 41. [f] Zep. 3. 6. [g] Da. 8. 14. [h] Is. 18. 5. [i] Ge. 40. 10. [k] Job 39. 13. [l] La. 4. 15. [m] Ezr. 8. 23. [n] Na. 2. 2. [o] Ca. 8. 9. [p] Is. 1. 8. [q] La. 3. 18. [r] Is. 34. 10. [s] Is. 63. 3, 6. [t] Je. 8. 5. [u] Ge. 44. 16. [x] Is. 49. 6.

נָצַל. Pi. נִצֵּל.—I. *to strip off, take away*, 2 Ch. 20. 25. —II. *to snatch away, deliver*, Eze. 14. 14.—III. *to spoil, plunder* any one. Hiph. הִצִּיל.—I. *to take away*; with בֵּין *to part, separate*, 2 Sa. 14. 6.— II. *to deliver, rescue*, with מִכַּף, מִיַּד, מִן. Hoph. הֻצַּל *to be delivered, rescued*. Niph. נִצַּל.—I. *to be delivered, rescued*.—II. *to deliver oneself, to escape*. Hithp. *to strip oneself of* any thing, with acc. Ex. 33. 6.

נְצַל Ch. Aph. *to deliver, rescue*.

הַצָּלָה fem. *deliverance*, Est. 4. 14.

נִצַּלְנוּ[a] Niph. pret. 1 pers. pl. . . . . נצל
נִצַּלְתֶּם[b] וְ Pi. pret. 2 pers. pl. masc. . . . נצל
נִצְמְתוּ[c] Niph. pret. 3 p. pl. [for נִצַּמְּתוּ comp. § 8. r. 7] צמת
נִצְמַתִּי[ss] id. pret. 1 pers. sing. [for נִצְמַתְּתִּי § 25. r.] צמת
נִצְעַק וְ Kal fut. 1 pers. pl.; וַ· conv. . . . צעק
נִצְפַּן[d] Niph. pret. 3 pers. sing. masc. . . . צפן
נִצְפְּנָה[e] Kal fut. 1 pers. pl. [נִצְפֹּן] with parag. ה (§ 8. rem. 13) . . . צפן
נִצְפְּנוּ Niph. pret. 3 pers. pl. . . . . צפן

[נָצַץ] *to glitter, shine*, Eze. 1. 7. In the derivv. also *to flourish, to fly*.

נֵץ masc. dec. 8b.—I. *flower, blossom*, Ge. 40. 10. —II. *a hawk*.

נִצָּה fem. dec. 10, *flower, blossom*.

נִצָּן masc. id. Ca. 2. 12.

נִיצוֹץ masc. *a spark*, Is. 1. 31.

נֹצְצִים[f] וְ Kal part. act. masc. pl. [of נוֹצֵץ] dec. 7b נצץ

[נָצַר] fut. יִנְצֹר, יִצֹּר.—I. *to watch, guard, keep, preserve*, Is. 49. 6, נְצוּרֵי יִשְׂרָאֵל *the preserved of Israel*, Kh.; K. נְצִירֵי from a pass. form נָצִיר *preserved*.—II. *to keep, observe*, as a law; *to observe* mercy, truth; *to observe, scrutinize*, Job 7. 20.—III. *to shut up, conceal, hide*.—IV. *to besiege*.

נֵצֶר[g] וְ[h] masc. *shoot, branch*; Arab. نضر *to shine*; *to be green*.

נְצֹר Kal imp. sing. masc. . . . . נצר
נֹצֵר וְ[i] id. part. act. sing. masc. dec. 7b . נצר
נִצְרְבוּ[k] וְ Niph. pret. 3 pers. pl. . . . צרב
נִצְּרָה[l] Kal imp. sing. masc. with parag. ה (§ 8. r. 13) נצר
נִצְּרֶהָ[m] id. id. with suff. 3 pers. sing. fem. . . נצר
נֹצְרָהּ[n] id. part. act. sing. masc., suff. 3 pers. sing. fem. from נֹצֵר dec. 7b . . . . נצר

נָצְרוּ[o] id. pret. 3 pers. pl. . . . . . נצר
נְצֻרוֹת[p] וּ id. part. pass. fem. pl. of נְצוּרָה dec. 10, from נָצוּר masc.; וּ bef. (:) . . . נצר
נֹצְרֵי[q] id. part. act. pl. constr. masc. fr. נֹצֵר dec. 7b נצר
נֹצְרִים id. id. pl., abs. st. . . . . . נצר
נְצֻרַת[r] וּ id. part. pass. sing. fem., constr. of נְצוּרָה dec. 10, from נָצוּר masc.; וּ bef. (:) . נצר
נָצַרְתִּי[s] id. pret. 1 pers. sing. [for נָצַרְתִּי § 8. r. 7] נצר
נְצָרָתַם[t] id. pret. 3 pers. sing. fem., suff. 3 pers. pl. m. נצר
נִצְּתָה וְ[u] Niph. pret. 3 pers. sing. fem. (§ 20. rem. 16) יצת
נִצְּתָה[u] Kh. נִצְּתָה q. v.; K. נִצְּתוּ q. v. . . יצת
נִצָּתוֹ[w] noun fem. sing., suff. 3 pers. sing. masc. fr. נִצָּה dec. 10 . . . . . נצץ
נִצְּתוּ Niph. pret. 3 pers. pl. (§ 20. rem. 16) יצת
נְקֵא[y] Ch. Peal part. pass. sing. masc. R. נקא see נקה

[נָקַב] fut. יִקֹּב, יִנְקֹב.—I. *to bore, bore through, pierce*. —II. *to mark out, to determine, specify, name*.— III. i. q. קָבַב *to execrate, curse, blaspheme*. Niph. *to be specified*, by name.

נֶקֶב masc. dec. 6a.—I. *a bezel*, the cavity in which a gem is set, Eze. 28. 13, Eng. vers. *pipes*. —II. pr. name of a place in the tribe of Naphtali, Jos. 19. 33.

נְקֵבָה fem. *female*, both of man and beast.

קֵבָה fem. (for נְקֵבָה) *the stomach* or *maw* of a beast, De. 18. 3.

קֹבָה fem. (for נְקֹבָה) *the womb*, Nu. 25. 8. Others make it, i. q. קֻבָּה *a tent*.

מַקָּבָה fem. *hammer*, only in the pl. מַקָּבוֹת.

מַקֶּבֶת fem.—I. *hammer*, Ju. 4. 21.—II. *hollow* or *shaft* of a rock, Is. 51. 1.

נֹקֵב[z] וְ Kal part. act. sing. masc. . . . . נקב
נְקָבָהּ וּ id. pret. 3 pers. sing. masc., suff. 3 pers. sing. fem.; וּ for וְ, conv. . . . . נקב
נְקֵבָה וּ' noun fem. sing.; וּ bef. (:) . . . נקב
נָקְבָה[a] Kal imp. sing. masc. with parag. ה (§ 8 r. 11) נקב
נִקְּבוּ Niph. pret. 3 pers. pl. . . . . נקב
נְקֻבֵי[b] Kal part. pass. pl. constr. masc. from נָקוּב dec. 3a . . . . . . נקב
נְקָבֶיךָ[c] וּ noun masc. pl., suff. 2 pers. sing. masc. fr. נֶקֶב dec. 6; וּ bef. (:) . . . . נקב
נְקַבֵּל[d] Piel fut. 1 pers. pl. . . . . קבל
נִקְבָּצוּ[e] וְ Niph. pret. 3 pers. pl. (comp. § 8. rem. 7) . . . . קבץ
נִקְבְּצוּ וְ'[f]
נָקַבְתָּ[g] Kal pret. 2 pers. sing. masc. . . . נקב

[a] Je. 7. 10. [b] Ex. 3. 22. [c] Job 6. 17. [d] Je. 16. 17. [e] Pr. 1. 11. [f] Eze. 1. 7. [g] Is. 60. 21. [h] Is. 11. 1. [i] Pr. 24. 12. [k] Eze. 21. 3. [l] Ps. 141. 3. [m] Pr. 4. 13. [n] Is. 27. 3. [o] Pr. 22. 12. [p] Is. 48. 6. [q] Ps. 119. 2. [r] Pr. 7. 10. [s] Ps. 119. 22, 56, 100. [ss] Job. 23. 17. [t] Ps. 119. 129. [u] Je. 2. 15. [w] Job 15. 33. [y] Da. 7. 9. [z] Le. 24. 16. [a] Ge. 30. 28. [b] Am. 6. 1. [c] Eze. 28. 13. [d] Job 2. 10. [e] Joel 4. 11. [f] Ho. 2. 2. [g] Hab. 3. 14.

נָקֹד [a] וְ׳ pl. נְקֻדִּים (§ 37. No. 3) fem. נְקֻדּוֹת adj. *spotted, speckled*, spoken of sheep and goats.

נְקוֹדָא (*marked*) pr. name of a man.

נֹקֵד m. d. 7 b, *shepherd, herdsman* (Arab. נקאד).

נְקֻדָּה fem. dec. 10, *point, stud*, Ca. 1. 11.

נִקֻּדִים masc. pl. (of נִקּוּד).—I. *spots, specks* of mould, Jos. 9. 5, 12. Others, *crumbs*.—II. a kind of *cake*, 1 Ki. 14. 3.

מַקֵּדָה (*place of herdsmen?*) pr. name of a town in the tribe of Judah.

נֹקֵד [b] noun masc. sing. dec. 7 b . . . נקד
נְקֻדּוֹת [c] noun fem. pl. of [נְקֻדָּה] dec. 10 . . נקד
נְקֻדִּים adj. masc. pl. of נָקֹד dec. 8 c (§ 37. No. 3) נקד
נִקֻּדִים [d] [e] וְ׳ noun masc. pl. of [נִקּוּד] dec. 1 b . נקד
נְקַדְּמָה [f] Kal fut. 1 pers. pl. with parag. ה (comp. § 8. rem. 13) . . . . קדם
נִקְדַּשׁ [g] [h] וְ׳ Niph. pret. 3 pers. sing. masc. . . קדשׁ
נִקְדַּשְׁתִּי וְ id. pret. 1 pers. sing.; acc. shifted by conv. וְ (except bef. monos. comp. § 8. rem. 7) קדשׁ

[נָקָה] *to be pure, innocent*, Je. 49. 12. Niph. נִקָּה.—I. *to be pure, innocent, blameless*, with מִן from a crime, or regarding a person.—II. *to be clear, free* from punishment, an obligation.—III. *to be cleared, empty, desolate*, of a city, Is. 3. 26; of persons, *to be destroyed*, Zec. 5. 3. Pi. I. *to cleanse*, Joel 4. 21.—II. *to pronounce innocent, to acquit*.—III. *to let go unpunished, to pardon*.

נְקָא Ch. *to be pure, white*, Da. 7. 9.

נָקִי, constr. נְקִי, pl. נְקִיִּם (§ 37. No. 4) adj.—I. *pure, innocent, free from guilt*.—II. *clear, free* from an obligation.

נָקִיא id. Joel 4. 19; Jon. 1. 14. Kh.

נִקָּיוֹן masc. dec. 3 c.—I. *cleanness*, Am. 4. 6.—II. *innocency*.

מְנַקִּית fem. only pl. מְנַקִּיּוֹת (§ 39. No. 4. rem. 1) *bowls* used in making libations. (Syr. מניקיתא id.)

נַקֹּה [i] Kal inf. abs. . . . . . . נקה
נַקֵּה וְ Piel inf. abs. . . . . . . נקה
נִקָּה [k] וְ׳ Niph. pret. 3 pers. sing. masc. . . נקה
נִקְהֲלוּ Niph. pret. 3 pers. pl. . . . . קהל
נָקוּב [l] Kal part. pass. sing. masc. dec. 3 a . נקב
נְקוֹדָא pr. name masc. . . . . . נקד
נְקַוֶּה [m] וּ׳ Piel fut. 1 pers. pl.; וּ bef. (:) . קוה
נִקְווּ [n] וְ Niph. pret. 3 pers. pl. . . . . קוה
נָקוּם [o] Kal fut. 1 pers. pl. . . . . קום
נָקוּמָה וְ id. with parag. ה (comp. § 8. rem. 13) . קום

נִקַּח וַנִּ׳ Kal fut. 1 pers. pl. (§ 17. rem. 8); ־ַ conv. לקח
נִקְחָה [p] וְ׳ id. with parag. ה (comp. § 8. rem. 13) לקח

נָקַט *to be weary of, to loathe*, only in the following form.
נָקְטָה [q] Kal pret. 3 pers. sing. fem. . . . נקט
נָקֹטּוּ [r] וְ Niph. pret. 3 pers. pl. . . . קטט
נְקֹטֹתֶם [s] וּ Niph. pret. 2 pers. pl. masc. (§ 21. rem. 12); וּ for וְ conv. . . . . . קוט
נָקִי וְ׳ adj. masc. sing. d. 8 (pl. נְקִיִּם § 37. rem. 4) נקה
נְקִי [t] id., constr. st. . . . . . . נקה
נָקִיא adj. masc. sing., א added to נָקִי . . נקה
נִקְיוֹן [u] noun masc. sing., constr. of נִקָּיוֹן dec. 3 c נקה
נְקִיִּם [x] נְקִיִם } adj. masc. pl. of נָקִי dec. 8 (§ 37 rem. 4) . . . . . } נקה
נִקָּיֹן [y] noun masc. sing. dec. 3 c . . . נקה
נְקִיצֶנָּה [z] וּ Hiph. fut. 1 pers. pl. [נָקִיץ], suff. 3 pers. sing. fem.; וּ bef. (:) . . . . קוץ
נִקֵּיתָ [a] וְ Niph. pret. 2 pers. sing. masc. (§ 24. r. 8) נקה
נִקֵּיתִי וְ׳ id. pret., or Piel pret. 1 pers. s. (§ 24. r. 11) נקה
נָקַל [b] נָקֵל [c] נָקֵל } וְ Niph. pret. 3 pers. sing. m. (§ 18. r. 7) קלל
נְקַלָּה id. pret. 3 pers. sing. fem. . . . קלל
נִקְלָה וְ Niph. pret. 3 pers. sing. masc. . . קלה
נִקְלֶה [d] וְ׳ id. part. sing. masc. . . . . קלה
נְקַלֹּתִי [e] וּ Niph. pret. 1 pers. sing.; וּ bef. (:) . קלל

[נָקַם] fut. יִקֹּם, inf. נְקוֹם.—I. *to avenge, take vengeance for*, with acc.—II. *to take revenge on*, with acc., also לְ.—III. *to revenge* a person, with the acc.; with מִיַּד, מֵאֵת, מִן, עַל on whom. Niph. *to be avenged, to avenge oneself*, with בְּ, מִן on whom. Pi. i. q. Kal No. 1. Hoph. *to be avenged*. Hithp. *to avenge oneself*; part. מִתְנַקֵּם *avenger*.

נָקָם masc. dec. 4 a, and נְקָמָה fem. dec. 11 c.—I. *vengeance*; הֵשִׁיב נָקָם לְ *to render vengeance to*, i. e. to repay an injury; לָקַח, עָשָׂה נָ׳ *to take vengeance*; נָתַן נְקָמוֹת לְ *to avenge* any one, *to give* him *satisfaction*.—II. *desire of revenge, vindictiveness*.

נָקָם [f] וְ׳ noun masc. sing. dec. 4 a . . . נקם
נָקֹם [g] Kal inf. abs. . . . . . נקם
נְקַם noun masc., constr. of נָקָם dec. 4 a . . נקם
נְקֹם [h] Kal imp. sing. masc. . . . . נקם
נִקָּם [i] וְ׳ id. part. sing. masc. . . . . נקם
נְקָמָה noun fem. sing. dec. 11 c . . . נקם
נִקְמוּ [k] וְ Niph. pret. 3 pers. pl. . . . נקם

[a] Ge. 30. 32, 33. [b] 2 Ki. 3. 4. [c] Ca. 1. 11. [d] Jos. 9. 5, 12. [e] 1 Ki. 14. 3. [f] Ps. 95. 2. [g] Is. 5. 16. [h] Ex. 29. 43. [i] Je. 49. 12. [k] Zec. 5. 3. [l] Hag. 1. 6. [m] Je. 14. 22. [n] Je. 3. 17. [o] Ne. 2. 18, 20. [p] 1 Sa. 4. 3. [q] Job 10. 1. [r] Eze. 6. 9. [s] Eze. 20. 43; 36. 31. [t] Ps. 24. 4. [u] Am. 4. 6. [x] Je. 2. 34. [y] Ho. 8. 5. [z] Is. 7. 6.

[a] Ge. 24. 8. [b] Pr. 14. 6. [c] 2 Ki. 3. 18. [d] 1 Sa. 18. 23. [e] 2 Sa. 6. 22. [f] De. 32. 43. [g] Ex. 21. 20. [h] Nu. 31. 2. [i] Na. 1. 2. [k] Eze. 25. 12.

נְקָמוֹת noun fem. pl., abs. from נְקָמָה dec. 11c נקם

נְקָמַנִי[a] וּ Kal pret. 3 p. s. m., suff. 1 p. s.; וּ bef. (:) נקם

נְקָמֹת[b] noun fem. pl. abs., from נְקָמָה dec. 11c נקם

נִקְמַת id. sing., constr. st. . . . . נקם

נֹקֶמֶת[c] Kal part. sing. fem. from נֹקֵם masc. . . נקם

נִקַּמְתִּי[d] Niph. pret. 1 pers. sing. . . . . נקם

נִקַּמְתִּי[e] וְ Piel, or (1 Sa. 14. 24) Niph. pret. 1 pers. sing.; acc. shifted by conv. וְ (comp. § 8. r. 7) נקם

נִקְמָתִי noun fem. s., suff. 1 pers. s. fr. נְקָמָה d. 11c נקם

נִקְמָתֵךְ[f] id., suff. 2 pers. sing. fem. . . . . נקם

נִקְמָתְךָ id., suff. 2 pers. sing. masc. . . . נקם

נִקְמָתָם[g] id., suff. 3 pers. pl. masc. . . . נקם

נִקְמָתֵנוּ[h] id., suff. 1 pers. pl. . . . . . נקם

נִקְנָה[i] וְ Niph. pret. 3 pers. sing. masc. . . . קנה

נַקֵּנִי[k] Piel imp. s. m. (נַקֵּה), suff. 1 p. s. (§ 24. r. 21) נקה

נָקַע *to be removed, alienated* (comp. יָקַע), only in the following form.

נָקְעָה[l] Kal pret. 3 pers. sing. fem. . . . נקע

נָקַף Kal, only Is. 29. 1, חַגִּים יִנְקֹפוּ let the feasts *go* or *come round*; so Vulg. solennitates evolutæ sunt, *the solemn feasts are rolled by*, comp. Hiph.; others, "*let them kill* the sacrifices;" as in the Chald. and Arab. *to smite, hew*. Pi. I. *to cut down*, Is. 10. 34.—II. *to destroy*, Job 19. 26. Hiph. הִקִּיף.—I. *to surround, compass*, with acc., עַל.—II. *to go* or *come round*, of time.

נֹקֶף masc. *a beating* or *shaking* of an olive-tree.

נִקְפָּה fem. Is. 3. 24, Eng. vers. "rent." Others, after the Sept. and Vulg. *a rope, cord*. According to the Rabbis, *a bruising, wounding*.

נִקַּף[m] וְ Piel pret. 3 pers. sing. masc. . . . נקף

נִקְפָּה[n] noun sing. fem. . . . . . . נקף

נִקְּפוּ[o] Piel pret. 3 pers. pl. . . . . . נקף

נָקַק Root not used; whence

נָקִיק or נְקִיק masc. *cleft* of a rock.

[נָקַר] I. *to bore, dig* or *put out* an eye, 1 Sa. 11. 2.—II. *to pick out*, as a bird, Pr. 30. 17. Pi. I. *to pierce*, Job 30. 17.—II. *to put out* an eye. Pu. *to be dug out*, Is. 51. 1.

נְקָרָה fem. dec. 11c, *cleft* of a rock.

נִקַּר[p] Piel pret. 3 pers. sing. masc. . . . נקר

נִקְרָא וְ' Kal fut. 1 pers. pl.; or Niph. 3 pers. s. m. קרא

נִקְרֹא[q] Niph. inf. abs. . . . . . . קרא

נִקְרְאָה[r] וְ id. pret. 3 pers. sing. fem. . . . קרא

נִקְרָאוּ[s] id. pret. 3 p. pl. [for נִקְרְאוּ comp. § 8. r. 7] קרא

נִקְרָאִים[yy] id. part. masc. pl. of נִקְרָא . . . קרא

נִקְרֵאתִי[t] id. pret. 1 pers. sing. . . . . קרא

נַקְרִב[u] וְ Hiph. fut. 1 p. pl. ap. [fr. קָרִיב]; וְ conv. קרב

נִקְרַב[x] וְ' Kal fut. 1 p. pl.; or Niph. pret. 3 p. s. m. קרב

נִקְרְבָה[y] } id. fut. 1 pers. pl. (נִקְרַב) with parag. ה (§ 8. rem. 13 & 15) . קרב

נִקְרָבָה[z] וְ' }

נִקְרַבְתֶּם[b] וְ' Niph. pret. 2 pers. pl. masc. . . . קרב

נִקְרָה[c] Niph. pret. 3 pers. sing. masc. . . . קרה

נִקְרֵיתִי[d] id. pret. 1 pers. sing. . . . . . קרה

נִקְרָע[e] Niph. part. sing. masc. . . . . קרע

נֻקַּרְתֶּם[f] Pual pret. 2 pers. pl. masc. . . . קר

[נָקַשׁ] *to lay snares, to ensnare*, Ps. 9. 17. Niph. *to be ensnared, enticed*, De. 12. 30. Pi. *to lay snares* with לְ for any one. Hithp. id. with בְּ 1 Sa. 28. 9

נְקַשׁ Chald. *to smite, strike*, Da. 5. 6.

נִקְשֶׁה[g] Niph. part. sing. masc. . . . . קשה

נַקְשִׁיב[h] Hiph. fut. 1 pers. sing. . . . . קשב

נַקְשִׁיבָה[i] id. with parag. ה (§ 8. rem. 13) . . קשב

נָקְשָׁן[k] Chald. Peal part. act. fem. pl. [of נָקְשָׁא dec. 8a, נָקֵשׁ masc.] . . . . . נקש

נִקְשְׁרָה[l] Niph. pret. 3 pers. sing. fem. . . . קשר

נִקָּתָה[m] וְ } Niph. pret. 3 pers. sing. fem. (comp. § 8. rem. 7) נקה

נִקָּתָה[n] וְ }

נֵר וְ' noun masc. sing. dec. 1a, also pr. name . נור

נִר[o] defect. for נִיר (q. v.) . . . . . ניר

נֵרָא[p] וְ Kh. נֵרָא, ap. form from K. נִרְאֶה (q. v.) ראה

נִרְאָה וְ' Niph. pret. 3 pers. sing. masc. . . . ראה

נִרְאֶה וְ', וַנִּ'[q] Kal fut. 1 pers. pl.; וַ conv. . . ראה

נִרְאֵהוּ[r] וְ id. with suff. 3 pers. sing. masc. . . ראה

נִרְאוּ Niph. pret. 3 pers. pl. . . . . ראה

נֹרָאוֹת[s] וְ defect. for נוֹרָאוֹת (q. v.) . . . ירא

נִרְאֲתָה[t] וְ'[u] Niph. pret. 3 pers. sing. fem. . . ראה

נֵרְגַל וְ' pr. name of an idol, 2 Ki. 17. 30.

נֵרְגַל שַׁרְאֶצֶר pr. name masc. Je. 39. 3, 13.

נָרַג Root not used; Arab. נירג *calumniator, whisperer* hence

נִרְגָּן[x] וְ' masc. *whisperer, slanderer, talebearer* . רגן

נֵרְדְּ[y] masc. dec. 6b (§ 35. rem. 6) *spikenard*.

נֵרֵד[z] } Kal fut. 1 pers. pl. (§ 20. rem. 4) . ירד

נֵרֲדָה[a] וְ' }

a 1 Sa. 24. 13. b 2 Sa. 22. 48. c Le. 26. 25. d Ju. 15. 7. e 2 Ki. 9. 7; Je. 51. 36. f Je. 51. 36. g La. 3. 60. h Je. 20. 10. i Je. 32. 43. k Ps. 19. 13. l Eze. 23. 18, 22, 28. m Is. 10. 34. n Is. 3. 24. o Job 19. 26. p Job 30. 17. q 2 Sa. 1. 6. r Is. 48. 2. s Est. 4. 11. t Nu. 31. 50. u Jos. 8. 5. x Ex. 22. 7. y Is. 41. 1. yy Est. 6. 1. z 1 Sa. 14. 36. a Ju. 19. 13. b Jos. 7. 14. c Ex. 3. 18. d 2 Sa. 1. 6. e 1 Ki. 13. 3, 5. f Is. 51. 1. g Is. 8. 21. h Je. 6. 17. i Je. 18. 18. k Da. 5. 6. l 1 Sa. 18. 1. m Is. 3. 26. n Nu. 5. 28. o Pr. 21. 4. p Is. 41. 23. q 1 Sa. 10. 14. r Is. 53. 2. s 2 Sa. 7. 23. t Ju. 19. 30. u Ge. 9. 14. x Pr. 16. 28. y Ca. 4. 14. z Ge. 43. 5. a 2 Ki. 10. 13.

נֵרֵדָה	id. with parag. ה (comp. § 8. rem. 13) .	ירד
נִרְדִּי	n. m. s., suff. 1 p. s. from נֵרְדְּ d. 6 (§ 35. r. 6)	נרד
[b] נְרָדִים	id. pl. abs. state . .	נרד
נִרְדָּם	Niph. part. sing. masc.	רדם
[cc] נִרְדַּם	id. pret. 3 pers. sing. masc. . . .	רדם
[c] נִרְדַּמְתִּי	id. pret. 1 pers. sing.	רדם
[d] נִרְדָּף	Niph. part. sing. masc.	רדף
[ff] נִרְדְּף־	Kal fut. 1 pers. pl. [for נִרְדֹּף § 8. rem. 18]	רדף
[e] נִרְדְּפָה	id. with parag. ה (§ 8. rem. 13) .	רדף
[f] נִרְדָּפְנוּ	Niph. pret. 1 pers. pl. [for נִרְדַּפְנוּ § 8. r. 7]	רדף
[g] נֵרָהּ	noun masc. sing., suff. 3 p. s. f. fr. נֵר d. 1a	נור
נֵרוֹ	[h] וְ׳ id., suff. 3 pers. sing. masc. . .	נור
נִרְוֶה	Kal fut. 1 pers. pl.	רוה
[k] נְרוֹמְמָה	וּ Pil. fut. 1 pers. pl. [נְרוֹמֵם] with parag. ה (comp. § 8. rem. 13); וּ bef. (:) .	רום
נָרוּצָה	Kal fut. 1 pers. pl. [נָרוּץ] with parag. ה (comp. § 8. rem. 13) . . .	רוץ
[l] נִרְחָב	Niph. part. sing. masc.	רחב
[m] נֵרִי	noun masc. sing., suff. 1 pers. s. fr. נֵר d. 1a	נור
נֵרִיָּה / נֵרִיָּהוּ	} pr. name masc.	נור
[n] נָרִיעַ	Hiph. fut. 1 pers. pl.	רוע
[o] נָרִיעָה	id. with parag. ה (comp. § 8. rem 13) .	רוע
נִרְכַּב	Kal fut. 1 pers. pl. [for נִרְכַּב § 8. rem. 15]	רכב
נְרַנְּנָה	[p] וּ׳ Piel fut. 1 pers. pl. [נְרַנֵּן] with parag. ה (comp. § 8. rem. 13); וּ bef. (:) .	רנן
[q] נָרַע	Hiph. fut. 1 pers. pl., with gutt. [for נָרֵעַ]	רעע
[r] נִרְעָב	Kal fut. 1 pers. s. [for נִרְעַב § 8. rem. 15]	רעב
[s] נִרְעֲשָׁה	Niph. pret. 3 pers. sing. fem. . . .	רעש
נִרְפָּא	[t] וְ׳ Niph. pret. 3 pers. sing. masc. . .	רפא
[u] נִרְפָּאוּ	וְ id. pret. 3 pers. pl. (§ 23. rem. 3) .	רפא
[x] נִרְפִּים	Niph. part. masc. pl. [of נִרְפֶּה] dec. 9a .	רפה
[y] נִרְפָּשׂ	Niph. part. sing. masc. R. רפשׂ see .	רפס
[z] נִרְפְּתָה	Niph. pret. 3 pers. sing. fem. [for נִרְפְּאָה § 23. rem. 11] as if from R. רפה .	רפא
[a] נָרֹץ	וְ Niph. pret. 3 pers. sing. masc. (§ 18. r. 7)	רצץ
[b] נִרְצָה	[c] וְ׳ Niph. pret. 3 pers. sing. m. . .	רצה
[d] נֵרֹת	noun masc. with pl. fem. term. from נֵר d. 1a	נור
נֵרֹתֶיהָ	וְ׳ id., suff. 3 pers. sing. fem. . .	נור
נֵרֹתֵיהֶם	וְ id., suff. 3 pers. pl. masc. . . .	נור

נָשָׂא וְ׳ (§ 25. No. 2a) fut. יִשָּׂא, inf. c. שְׂאֵת, שׂוֹא, נְשֹׂא, שְׂאֵת.—I. *to lift* or *raise up*; נָ׳ יָד *to lift up the hand,* as in a solemn promise or prayer, with לְ *for* any one; with בְּ *against* any one, to do him violence; נָ׳ רֹאשׁוֹ *to lift up one's head,* to become cheerful, happy, &c.; *to lift up the head* of another, to give him his liberty; with מֵעַל, to behead him; נָ׳ פָּנָיו *to lift up one's countenance,* of one conscious of innocence; נָ׳ עֵינָיו לְ, אֶל־ *to lift up, cast one's eyes upon,* espec. with longing desire; נָ׳ נֶפֶשׁ אֶל־ *to set one's affection upon* any thing; נָ׳ לִבּוֹ *to be willing;* נָ׳ רַגְלָיו *to lift up one's feet,* i. e. to set out upon a journey; נָ׳ קוֹל *to lift up the voice,* of weeping, rejoicing, calling aloud; hence *to utter,* as a parable, prayer.—II. *to bear, carry,* as an infant in the arms, garments *to wear,* a tree its fruit; also *to bear, take away;* hence *to bear, endure, suffer;* נָ׳ עֲוֹן פ׳ *to bear the guilt of* any one; but also *to forgive, pardon sin;* נְשׂוּא עָוֹן *whose sins are forgiven.*—III. *to lead, bring.*—IV. *to take up, to take;* נָ׳ אִשָּׁה *to take a wife;* נָ׳ פָּנִים *to take, accept the person* of any one, i. e. to act with partiality; נָ׳ רֹאשׁ *to take the sum* of anything. Niph. I. *to be lifted up, raised;* part. נִשָּׂא *lifted up, lofty.*—II. *to raise oneself.*—III. *to be borne, carried, carried away.* Pi. נִשֵּׂא, נִשָּׂא.—I. *to lift up, exalt;* נִ׳ נֶפֶשׁ לְ *to set* one's *heart upon.*—II. *to aid, assist.*—III. *to present a gift,* with לְ 2 Sa. 19. 43.—IV. *to carry away,* Am. 4. 2. Hiph. הִשִּׂיא.—I. *to cause to bear* sin, Le. 22. 16.—II. *to bring,* 2 Sa. 17. 13. Hithp. I. *to be elevated, exalted,* with עַל above any thing.—II. *to lift up, exalt oneself* in strength or pride, *to rise.*

נְשָׂא Chald.—I. *to bear* or *carry away,* Da. 2. 35.—II. *to take,* Ezr. 5. 15. Ithpa. *to rise up,* with עַל against, Ezr. 4. 19.

נְשֵׂאת fem. *a gift,* 2 Sa. 19. 43.

נְשׂוּאָה fem. dec. 10, *burden,* Is. 46. 1.

נָשִׂיא masc. dec. 3a.—I. *chief.*—II. *prince.*—III. pl. *vapours;* hence *clouds.*

שִׂיא masc. dec. 1a (for נְשִׂיא) *elevation, dignity,* Job 20. 6.

שִׂיאֹן (*elevated*) pr. name of one of the peaks of Hermon, De. 4. 48

שְׂאֵת fem. dec. 1a.—I. *a lifting up* of the countenance, Ge. 4. 7; according to the Eng. vers. *acceptance.*—II. *a swelling* in the skin.—III. *exaltation, dignity.*—IV. *judgment, sentence,* Hab. 1. 7.

שֵׂת fem. dec. 1a (for שְׂאֵת) *a lifting up, rising,* Job 41. 17.

מַשָּׂא masc. dec. 1b.—I. *a lifting up, carrying,* Eze. 24. 25, מַ׳ נֶפֶשׁ *that on which the heart is set.*

[a] Ca. 1. 12. [b] Ca. 4. 13. [c] Da. 8. 18. [cc] Ju. 4. 21. [d] Ec. 3. 15. [e] Ho. 6. 3. [f] La. 5. 5. [ff] Job 19. 28. [g] Pr. 31. 18. [h] Job 18. 6. [i] Pr. 7. 18. [k] Ps. 34. 4. [l] Is. 30. 23. [m] Ps. 18. 29. [n] Ps. 95. 2. [o] Ps. 95. 1. [p] Ps. 90. 14. [q] Ge. 19. 9. [r] Je. 42. 14. [s] Je. 50. 46. [t] Le. 13. 18. [u] Eze. 47. 8. [x] Ex. 5. 8, 17. [y] Pr. 25. 26. [z] Je. 51. 9. [a] Ec. 12. 6. [b] Is. 40. 2. [c] Le. 1. 4. [d] Ex. 39. 37.

—II. *burden, load; anything burdensome.*—III. *a lifting up of the voice in singing, a singing,* 1 Ch. 15. 27; שַׂר הַמַּשָּׂא *master of song*; but according to Hengstenberg (Christ. vol. ii. p. 78) master *of burden.*—IV. something uttered, *a saying; a solemn declaration; a prophecy;* but according to Hengstenberg (in l. c.) *burden, burdensome prophecy,* in general, and also *a weighty, important sentence.*—V. *tribute,* 2 Ch. 17. 11.—VI. pr. name of a son of Ishmael.

מַשֹּׂא masc. 2 Ch. 19. 7 מַ׳ פָּנִים *preference, respect of persons.*

מַשָּׂאָה fem. *a rising of a flame, a burning, conflagration,* Is. 30. 27. Others, *burden.*

מַשְׂאֵת (for מַשָּׂאַת) fem. constr. מַשְׂאַת (as if from מַשָּׂאָה), pl. מַשְׂאוֹת.—I. *a lifting up,* Ps. 141. 2; *a rising, ascending* of smoke, Ju. 20. 38, 40.—II. *signal,* Je. 6. 1.—III. *burden,* Zep. 3. 18.—IV. *a prophecy,* La. 2. 14; but comp. מַשָּׂא Nos. II & III.—V. *gift, present.*—VI. *tribute,* 2 Ch. 24. 6, 9.

I. [נָשָׁא] *to err, go astray,* Je. 23. 39. Hiph. הִשִּׁיא.—I. *to lead astray, deceive,* const. with acc., לְ.—II. *to come suddenly upon,* with עַל Ps. 55. 16.—III. *to seduce, corrupt.* Niph. *to be deceived,* Is. 19. 13.

מַשָּׁאוֹן masc. *deceit,* Pr. 26. 26.

II. [נָשָׁא] *to lend* on usury, with בְּ, Ne. 5. 9; part. נשֶׁא (§ 23. rem. 9) *a creditor.* Hiph. *to exact,* with בְּ, Ps. 89. 23.

מַשָּׁא masc.—I. *usury,* Ne. 5. 7, 10.—II. *debt,* Ne. 10. 32.

מַשָּׁאָה fem. constr. מַשַּׁאת (for מַשְׁאַת, pl. מַשָּׁאוֹת, *debt.*

נָשֹׂא Kal inf. abs. . . . . נשא
נָשֹׂא[a] Kal inf. abs. [for נָשֹׂה § 24. rem. 18] . נשה
נְשָׂא[b] וּ׳[c] id. imp. s. m.; or Ch. Peal pret. 3 p. s. m. נשא
נְשֹׂא[d] id. inf. constr. . . . . נשא
נְשֹׂא[e] וּ׳[f] defect. for נְשׂוֹא (q. v.) . . . נשא
נִשָּׂא וְ׳ Kal fut. 1 pers. pl. (La. 3. 41); Niph. pret. 3 pers. sing. or part. masc.; Piel pret. 3 pers. sing. masc. (1 Ki. 9. 11; Am. 4. 2) נשא
נִשֵּׂא[g] Piel pret. 3 pers. sing. masc. . . נשא
נֹשֵׂא וְ׳ Kal part. sing. masc. dec. 7b . . נשא
נֹשֶׁא Kal part. sing. masc. (§ 23. rem. 9) . נשא
נָשְׂאָה[h] Kal pret. 3 pers. sing. fem. . . . נשא
נִשָּׂאָה[i] Niph. part. sing. fem. . . . נשא

נָשָׂאוּ וְ׳[k] } Kal pret. 3 pers. pl. (§ 8. rem. 7) . נשא
נָשְׂאוּ וְ׳ }
נְשָׂאוֹ וּ׳ id. pret. 3 pers. s. m., suff. 3 p. s. m.; וּ bef. (:) נשא
נִשְּׂאוֹ[l] Piel pret. 3 pers. s. m. (נִשֵּׂא), suff. 3 pers. s. m. נשא
נִשְּׂאוּ[m] Niph. pret. 3 pers. pl. . . . נשא
נִשְּׂאוּ[n] וְ Niph. pret. 3 pers. sing. masc. . . נשא
נִשָּׂאוּם[o] וּ Kal fut. 1 pers. pl., suff. 3 p. pl. m; וּ bef. (:) נשא
נֹשְׂאוֹת[p] id. part. act. f., pl. of נֹשֵׂאת [for נֹשֶׂאֶת § 23. r. 4] נשא
נְשָׂאֵי[q] Kh. נֹשְׂאֵי q. v.; K. נָשְׂאוּ (q. v.) . . נשא
נֹשְׂאֵי Kal part. act. pl. constr. masc. fr. נוֹשֵׂא d. 7b נשא
נֹשְׂאֵי[r] Kh. נְשִׂאֵי q. v.; K. נֹשֵׂא (q. v.) . . נשא
נְשִׂאִים defect. for נְשִׂיאִים (q. v.) . . . נשא
נֹשְׂאִים וְ׳[s] Kal part. act. masc. pl. of נוֹשֵׂא dec. 7b נשא
נְשָׂאִים[t] Kh. נְשָׂאִים, pl. of נְשָׂא q. v.; K. נָשִׁים (q. v.) נשה
נְשָׂאֲךָ[u] וּ׳ Kal pret. 3 p. s. m., suff. 2 p. s. m.; וּ bef. (:) נשא
נִשְׁאַל[x] Niph. pret. 3 pers. sing. masc. . . שאל
נִשְׁאֹל[y] id. inf. abs. . . . . . שאל
נִשְׁאֲלָה[z] וְ Kal fut. 1 pers. pl., with parag. ה (§ 8. r. 7) שאל
נִשְׁאַלְתִּי[a] Niph. pret. 1 pers. sing. . . . שאל
נַשְּׂאֵם[b] וְ Piel imp. sing. m. [נַשֵּׂא], suff. 3 pers. pl. m. נשא
נַשְׁאֵר[c] Hiph. fut. 1 pers. pl. ap. [from נַשְׁאִיר] . שאר
נִשְׁאָר[d] } Niph. pret. 3 pers. sing. masc. (comp. } שאר
נִשְׁאַר וְ׳ } § 8. rem. 7) . . . . }
נִשְׁאֲרָה[e] } id. pret. 3 pers. sing. fem. (v. id.) . שאר
נִשְׁאֲרָה }
נִשְׁאָרוּ } id. pret. 3 pers. pl. (v. id.) . . שאר
נִשְׁאֲרוּ וְ׳[f] }
נִשְׁאַרְנוּ id. pret. 1 pers. pl. . . . . שאר
נִשְׁאַרְתִּי id. pret. 1 pers. sing. . . . שאר
נִשְׁאַרְתֶּם וְ id. pret. 2 pers. pl. masc. . . . שאר
נָשָׂאתָ וְ׳ Kal pret. 3 pers. sing. masc. . . נשא
נֹשֵׂאת[g] id. part. act. s. f. [for נֹשֶׂאֶת § 23. r. 4] fr. נוֹשֵׂא m. נשא
נְשֹׂאת[h] id. pl., comp. dec. 13 . . . . נשא
נֹשֵׂאת[i] id. sing. [for נֹשֶׂאֶת] . . . . נשא
נִשֵּׂאת[k] Niph. part. sing. fem. [for נִשֶּׂאֶת comp. § 23. rem. 4]; subst. 2 Sa. 19. 43 . . נשא
נָשָׂאתָה[l] Kal pret. 2 pers. sing. masc. (§ 8. rem. 5) נשא
נָשָׂאתִי וְ׳[m] id. pret. 1 pers. sing. . . . נשא
נְשׂאֹתֵיכֶם[n] noun f. pl., suff. 2 p. pl. m. [fr. נְשׂוּאָה] d. 10 נשא
נְשָׂאתִים[o] Kal pret. 2 pers. sing. fem., suff. 3 pers. pl. m. נשא
נְשָׂאתֶם וּ׳[p] id. pret. 2 pers. pl. masc.; וּ for וְ, conv. נשא
נְשָׂאַתְנִי id. pret. 3 pers. sing. fem., suff. 1 pers. sing. נשא
נְשָׂאתַנִי[q] וּ׳[r] id. pret. 2 p. s. m., suff. 1 p. s.; וּ for וְ, conv. נשא

[נָשַׁב] *to blow,* with בְּ, Is. 40. 7. Hiph. I. *to cause to blow,* Ps. 147. 18.—II. Ge. 15. 11, *to drive away*

[a] Je. 23. 39. [b] Ps. 10. 12. [c] Da. 2. 35. [d] Is. 1. 14. [e] Is. 33. 24. [f] 2 Ki. 5. 1. [g] 2 Sa. 5. 12. [h] Est. 5. 2. [i] Is. 30. 25. [k] Mi. 2. 2. [l] Est. 5. 11. [m] Is. 19. 13. [n] Ezr. 8. 36. [o] 2 Ch. 12. 11. [p] 2 Ch. 9. 21. [q] Ezr. 10. 44. [r] 2 Sa. 23. 37. [s] Mal. 2. 9. [t] Ne. 5. 7. [u] De. 1. 31. [x] 1 Sa. 20. 6, 28. [y] 1 Sa. 20. 6, 28. [z] Ge. 24. 57. [a] Ne. 13. 6. [b] Ps. 28. 9. [c] 1 Sa. 14. 36. [d] Ge. 42. 38. [e] 2 Sa. 14. 7. [f] Je. 37. 10. [g] 1 Ki. 10. 22. [h] Ge. 45. 23. [i] Est. 2. 15. [k] Zec. 5. 7; 1 Ch. 14. 2. [l] Nu. 14. 19. [m] Ge. 18. 26. [n] Is. 46. 1. [o] Eze. 16. 58. [p] Eze. 36. 6. [q] Ps. 102. 11. [r] Ge. 47. 30.

or *frighten away*, as birds, with a kind of *puffing* noise.

נָּשֶׁב[a] וַ Hiph. fut. 1 p. pl., ap. & conv. (§ 21. r. 18) שוב

נֵשֵׁב[b] / וַנֵּשֶׁב } Kal fut. 1 pers. pl. (§ 20. rem. 4); ·וַ conv. ישב

נָּשֶׁב[c] וַ Hiph. fut. 1 pers. pl. ap. & conv. [from נוֹשִׁיב § 20. rem. 9] . . . . ישב

נָשְׁבָה[d] Kal pret. 3 pers. sing. fem. . . . . נשב

נָשֻׁבָה[e] וְ defect. for נָשׁוּבָה (q. v.) . . . . שוב

נִשְׁבָּה Niph. pret. 3 pers. sing. masc. . . . שבה

נִשְׁבּוּ id. pret. 3 pers. pl. . . . . . שבה

נַשְׁבִּיר[f] Hiph. fut. 1 pers. pl. . . . . . שבר

נַשְׁבִּירָה[g] וְ id. with parag. ה (§ 8. rem. 13) . שבר

נִשָּׁבַע[h] / וַנִּשָּׁבַע[i] } Kal fut. 1 pers. pl. (§ 8. rem. 15); ·וַ conv. שבע

נִשְׁבַּע וְ׳[k] Niph. pret. 3 pers. sing. masc. . . שבע

נִשָּׁבְעָה[l] Kal fut. 1 pers. pl. with parag. ה (§ 8. rem. 13) שבע

נִשְׁבְּעוּ / נִשְׁבָּעוּ } Niph. pret. 3 pers. pl. (comp. § 8. rem. 7) שבע

נִשְׁבָּעוֹת[m] וְ id. part. fem. pl. [of נִשְׁבָּעָה] fr. נִשְׁבָּע m.׳ שבע

נִשְׁבַּעְנוּ id. pret. 1 pers. pl. . . . . שבע

נִשְׁבַּעְתָּ וְ׳[n] id. pret. 2 pers. sing. masc. . . . שבע

נִשְׁבַּעְתִּי id. pret. 1 pers. sing. . . . . שבע

נִשְׁבַּעְתֶּם[o] id. pret. 2 pers. pl. masc. . . . שבע

נִשְׁבָּר[p] Niph. part. sing. m. d. 2b; or in pause for foll. שבר

נִשְׁבַּר וְ׳[q] id. pret. 3 pers. sing. masc. . . . שבר

נִשְׁבָּרָה[r] id. part. sing. fem. of נִשְׁבָּר . . . שבר

נִשְׁבְּרָה / נִשְׁבָּרָה וְ׳ { id. pret. 3 pers. sing. fem.; or (Ge. 43. 4) Kal fut. 1 pers. pl. (§ 8. rem. 7 & 15) } שבר

נִשְׁבְּרָהּ[s] Kh. נִשְׁבְּרָה q. v.; K. נִשְׁבְּרוּ (q. v.) . שבר

נִשְׁבְּרוּ וְ / נִשְׁבָּרוּ וְ׳ } Niph. pret. 3 pers. pl. (comp. § 8. rem. 7) שבר

נִשְׁבָּרִים[t] id. part. masc. pl. of נִשְׁבָּר dec. 2b . . שבר

נִשְׁבֶּרֶת[u] id. part. sing. fem. . . . . . שבר

נִשְׁבַּרְתִּי[x] id. pret. 1 pers. sing. . . . . שבר

נִשְׁבַּת וְ Niph. pret. 3 pers. sing. masc. . . . שבת

נִשְׁבְּתוּ[y] וְ id. pret. 3 pers. pl. . . . . שבת

נָשַׂג Kal not used; cogn. נָסַג, סוּג. Hiph. הִשִּׂיג.—I. *to reach*, as the hand to the mouth, 1 Sa. 14. 26.—II. *to reach, attain to, overtake.*—III. *to come upon, befall.*—IV. *to acquire, obtain.*—V. *to overpass, go beyond*, Job 24. 2. Others, *to remove*, i. q. סוּג.

נִשְׂגָּב וְ׳ Niph. part. sing. masc., or (Pr. 18. 10) pret. 3 pers. masc. sing. in pause . . שגב

נִשְׂגַּב[z] וְ id. pret. 3 person. sing. masc. . . . שגב

נִשְׂגָּבָה id. part. sing. fem. of נִשְׂגָּב . . . שגב

נִשְׂגְּבָה[a] id. pret. 3 pers. sing. fem. . . . שגב

נְשַׁדֵּנוּ[b] Niph. pret. 1 pers. pl. [for נְשַׁדַּדְנוּ § 18. r. 16] שדד

I. **[נָשָׁה]** I. *to forget*, La. 3. 17.—II. *to neglect*, Je. 23. 39. Niph. id. Is. 44. 21. Pi. *to cause to forget*, Ge. 41. 51. Hiph. הִשָּׁה id. Job 11. 6; 39. 17.

נְשִׁיָּה fem. *forgetfulness*, Ps. 88. 13.

מְנַשֶּׁה (*causing to forget*) pr. name, Manasseh.—I. a son of Joseph.—II. a king of Judah.—III. Ju. 18. 30. Kh.—IV. Ezr. 10. 30.—V. Ezr. 10. 33.

II. **[נָשָׁה]** I. *to lend* on usury, with בְּ of *the person*; נֹשֶׁה *a lender, creditor.*—II. *to borrow* on usury, const. abs. Je. 15. 10; Is. 24. 2; נֹשֶׁה *a usurer.*—III. *to take as usury*, Ne. 5. 11. Hiph. *to lend* on usury, with בְּ of the person.

נְשִׁי masc. dec. 6i, *debt*, 2 Ki. 4. 7.

יִשִּׁיָּה (whom *the Lord lendeth*) pr. name masc. of several individuals.

יִשִּׁיָּהוּ (id.) pr. name masc. 1 Ch. 12. 6.

מַשֶּׁה masc. dec. 9a, *debt*, De. 15. 2.

נָשֶׁה masc. *the ischiatic nerve*, extending through the thigh and leg to the ankles, Ge. 32. 33. Etymology not known.

נֹשֶׁה[c] Kal part. act. sing. masc. dec. 9a . נשה

נָשׁוּ[d] id. pret. 3 p. pl.; acc. drawn back bef. monos. נשה

נָשׁוּ[e] וְ Kal pret. 3 pers. pl. for נָשְׂאוּ (§ 23. r. 11) נשא

נָשׂוֹא[f] Kal inf. abs. . . . . . נשא

נָשׂוּא[g] id. pret. 3 pers. pl. (§ 23. r. 11, & § 8. r. 4) נשא

נְשׂוּא וּ id. part. pass. sing. masc. constr. [of נָשׂוּא] dec. 3a; וּ bef. (:) . . . . נשא

נָשׁוּב[h] וַ Kh. וְנָשׁוּב; K. וַנָּשָׁב ap. from נָשׁוּב (q. v.) שוב

נָשׁוּבָ[i] וְ Kh. נָשׁוּב q. v.; K. נָשׁוּבָה (q. v.) שוב

נָשׁוּב וְ׳ Kal fut. 1 pers. pl. . . . שוב

נָשׁוּבָה וְ Kal fut. 1 pers. pl. (נָשׁוּב) with parag. ה (comp. § 8. rem. 13) . . . . שוב

נָשׁוֹג[k] Niph. pret. 3 pers. sing. masc. . . שוג

נְשׂוּי[l] Kal part. pass. sing. masc., constr. of נָשׂוּי (§ 23. rem. 11) see . . . . נשא

נַשְׁחִיתָה[m] וְ׳[n] Hiph. fut. 1 pers. pl. with parag. ה (comp. § 8. rem. 13) . . . . שחת

נִשְׁחַת[o] וְ׳[p] Niph. pret. 3 pers. sing. masc. . . שחת

נִשְׁחָתָה[zz] id. pret. 3 pers. sing. fem. [for נִשְׁחֲתָה comp. § 8. rem. 7] . . . שחת

נָשַׁי[q] the foll. with suff. 1 pers. sing. . אנש

---

[a] Ge. 43. 21. [b] Je. 42. 13, 14. [c] Ezr. 10. 2. [d] Is. 40. 7. Je. 46. 16. [f] Am. 8. 6. [g] Am. 8. 5. [h] Job 31. 31. [i] Je. 44. 17. [k] Le. 5. 22. [l] Ps. 65. 5. [m] Is. 19. 18. [n] Je. 4. 2. [o] Jos. 6. 22. [p] Ps. 51. 19; 124. 7. [q] Ex. 22. 13. [r] Ps. 51. 19. [s] 1 Ki. 22. 49. [t] Je. 2. 13. [tt] Mal. 1. 4. [u] Eze. 27. 34. [x] Eze. 6. 9. [y] Eze. 6. 6. [z] Is. 2. 11, 17. [zz] Ge. 6. 12.

[a] Ps. 139. 6. [b] Mi. 2. 4. [c] De. 24. 11. [d] Je. 15. 10. [e] Eze. 39. 26. [f] Je. 10. 5. [g] Ps. 139. 20. [h] Ne. 4. 9. [i] La. 5. 21. [k] 2 Sa. 1. 22. [l] Ps. 32. 1. [m] Je. 11. 19. [n] Je. 6. 5. [o] Je. 13. 7. [p] Je. 18. 4. [q] Ge. 30. 26.

נָשֵׁי ו׳ n. fem. with pl. masc. term., constr. of נָשִׁים, irr. of אִשָּׁה (§ 45); וּ bef. (:) . אנש

נָשִׂיא וְ noun masc. sing. dec. 3 a . . . . נשא

נְשִׂיא ו׳ id., constr. st.; וּ bef. (:) . . . נשא

נְשִׂיאֵהֶם[a] id. pl., suff. 3 pers. pl. masc. . . . נשא

נְשִׂיאַי[xx] id. pl., suff. 1 pers. sing. . . . נשא

נְשִׂיאֵי ו׳ id. pl., constr. st.; וּ bef. (:) . . . נשא

נְשִׂיאֶיהָ[b] id. pl., suff. 3 pers. sing. fem. . . . נשא

נְשִׂיאֵיהֶם id. pl., suff. 3 pers. pl. masc. . . . נשא

נְשִׂיאִם / נְשִׂאִם[c] } id. pl., abs. st. . . . . . נשא

נָשִׁיב וְ׳ Hiph. fut. 1 pers. pl. . . . . שוב

נְשִׁיָּה* noun fem. sing.*Ps. 88. 13. . . . . נשה

נְשֵׁיהוֹן[e] וּ Chald. noun fem. with pl. m. term. [נְשִׁין], suff. 3 pers. pl. masc., see the foll. . אנש

נְשֵׁיהֶם ו׳ noun f. with pl. m. term. (נָשִׁים), suff. 3 pers. pl. m., irr. of אִשָּׁה (§ 45); וּ bef. (:) אנש

נָשָׁיו[f] וְ׳ id. pl., suff. 3 pers. sing. masc. . . אנש

נָשֶׁיךָ[g] וְ id. pl., suff. 2 pers. sing. masc. . . אנש

נְשִׁיֵכִי[h] noun masc. sing., suff. 2 pers. sing. fem., Kh. נְשִׁיֵכִי, K. נִשְׁיֵךְ [fr. נְשִׁי] dec. 6 i נשה

נְשֵׁיכֶם[i] ו׳ the foll. with suff. 2 p. pl. m.; וּ bef. (:) אנש

נָשִׁים וְ׳ noun fem. with pl. masc. term. irr. of אִשָּׁה (§ 45) . . . . . אנש

נָשִׂים[k] וְ Kal fut. 1 pers. pl. R. שִׂים, see . . שום

נַשִּׁים[l] וַ Hiph. fut. 1 pers. pl., for נַשֵּׁם (§ 18. rem. 12, & § 21. rem. 24); ־ַ conv. . שמם

נֹשִׁים[m] Kal part. masc. pl. of נוֹשֶׁה dec. 9 a . נשה

נָשִׂימָה[n] ו׳[o] Kal fut. 1 pers. pl. with parag. ה (comp. § 8. rem. 13) R. שִׂים, see . . . שום

נָשֵׁינוּ[p] וְ׳ noun fem. with pl. masc. term. (נָשִׁים), suff. 1 pers. pl., irr. of אִשָּׁה (§ 45) . אנש

נְשִׁיקוֹת[q] noun fem. pl. of [נְשִׁיקָה] dec. 10 . נשק

נָשִׁיר[r] Kal fut. 1 pers. pl. . . . . שיר

נָשִׁירָה[s] id. with parag. ה (comp. § 8. rem. 13) שיר

נָשִׂישׂ[t] Kal fut. 1 pers. pl. R. שִׂישׂ, see . . שוש

נָשִׁיתִי[u] וְ׳ Kal pret. 1 pers. sing. . . . . נשה

נָשַׁךְ[x] fut. יִשֹּׁךְ, יִשַּׁךְ.—I. *to bite.*—II. *to vex, oppress,* Hab. 2. 7.—III. *to lend on usury,* De. 23. 20. Pu. *to bite.* Hiph. *to take usury, exact interest,* De. 23. 20, 21. Hence

נֶשֶׁךְ masc. *usury, interest* . . . נשך

נִשְׁכְּבָה[y] וְ׳[z] Kal fut. 1 pers. pl. with parag. ה (§ 8. rem. 13) . . . . . שכב

נִשְׁכָּה[a] fem. dec. 12 d, for לִשְׁכָּה *a chamber* (q. v.) לשך

נִשְּׁכוּ[b] וְ Piel pret. 3 pers. pl. . . . . נשך

נְשָׁכוֹ[c] וּ Kal pret. 3 pers. sing. masc., suff. 3 pers. sing. masc.; וּ bef. (:) . . . נשך

נִשְׁכָּח[d] / נִשְׁכַּח[e] } וְ׳[f] Niph. pret. 3 pers. s. m. (comp. § 8. r. 7) שכח

נִשְׁכָּחָה[g] id. part. sing. fem. . . . . שכח

נִשְׁכָּחוּ[h] id. pret. 3 pers. pl. . . . . שכח

נִשְׁכַּחַת[i] וְ id. part. sing. fem. . . . . שכח

נִשְׁכַּחְתִּי[k] id. pret. 1 pers. sing. . . . . שכח

נֹשְׁכֶיךָ[l] Kal part. act. pl. masc., suff. 2 pers. sing. masc. from נֹשֵׁךְ dec. 7 b . . . נשך

נַשְׁכִּימָה[m] Hiph. fut. 1 p. pl. with parag. ה (§ 8. r. 13) שכם

נְשָׁכָם[n] וּ Kal pret. 3 pers. sing. masc., suff. 3 pers. pl. masc.; וּ for וְ conv. . . . נשך

נִשְׂכָּרוּ[o] Niph. pret. 3 pers. pl. [for נִשְׂכְּרוּ comp. § 8. rem. 7] . . . . . שכר

נִשְׁכָּתוֹ[p] noun fem. sing., suff. 3 pers. sing. masc. fr. נִשְׁכָּה dec. 12 d, for לִשְׁכָּה q. v. . לשך

נָשַׁל וְ fut. יִשַּׁל.—I. *to fall* or *drop off,* De. 28. 40.—II. trans. *to draw* or *put off,* as a shoe.—III. *to cast* or *drive out* a nation, De. 7. 1, 22. Pi. *to cast, drive out,* 2 Ki. 16. 6.

נִשְׁלוֹחַ[q] וְ Niph. inf. abs. . . . . . שלח

נִשְׁלָחָה[r] וְ׳ Kal fut. 1 p. pl. with parag. ה (§ 8. r. 13) שלח

נְשַׁלְּחֶךָ[s] וַ Piel fut. 1 pers. pl., 2 pers. sing. masc. (§ 16. rem. 15); ־ַ conv. . . . שלח

נְשַׁלְּחֶנּוּ id. with suff. 3 pers. sing. masc. . . שלח

נַשְׁלִיכָה[t] וְ Hiph. fut. 1 p. pl. with parag. ה (§ 8. r. 13) שלך

נַשְׁלִכֵהוּ[u] וְ id. with suff. 3 pers. sing. masc. . . שלך

נְשַׁלְּמָה[x] וּ Piel fut. 1 pers. pl. with parag. ה (§ 8. rem. 13); וּ bef. (:) for : . . . שלם

[נָשַׁם] *to breathe, pant,* perhaps so אֶשֹּׁם Is. 42. 14; but which may be from שָׁמֵם.

נְשָׁמָה fem. d. 11 c.—I. *breath.*—II. *life;* meton *a living thing.*—III. *mind, spirit.*—IV. *anger.*

נִשְׁמָא Ch. fem. dec. 8 a, *breath, life,* Da. 5. 23

תִּנְשֶׁמֶת f. a species of *animal,* enumerated among the *lizards,* Le. 11. 30, according to Bochart, the *chameleon.* In Le. 11. 18; De. 14. 16, it occurs among the *waterfowls,* according to some, the *swan;* others, *seagull;* Sept. πορφυρίον, the creste purple *heron.*

נִשְׁמַד וְ Niph. pret. 3 pers. sing. masc. . . שמד

---

a Nu. 17. 17. b Eze. 32. 29. c Nu. 17. 21. d Ge. 25. 16. e Da. 6. 25.
f 2 Ch. 21. 17. g 1 Ki. 20. 3, 5. h 2 Ki. 4. 7. i Je. 44. 25. k 2 Ki. 4. 10.
l Nu. 21. 30. m Ne. 5. 10, 11. n 1 Ki. 20. 31. o Is. 41. 22. p 2 Ch. 29. 9.
q Pr. 27. 6. r Ps. 137. 4. s Ps. 21. 14. t Eze. 21. 15. u Je. 23. 39.
x Nu. 21. 9. y Je. 3. 25. z Ge. 19. 32. a Ne. 13. 7. b Je. 8. 17.
c Am. 5. 19. d Ec. 2. 16. e Ec. 9. 5. f Ge. 41. 30. g Is. 23. 16.
h Is. 65. 16. i Is. 23. 15. k Ps. 31. 13. l Hab. 2. 7. m Ca. 7. 13.
n Am. 9. 3. o 1 Sa. 2. 5. p Ne. 3. 30. q Est. 3. 13. r Ge. 26. 29.
s 1 Sa. 6. 2. t Ps. 2. 3. u Ge. 37. 20. x Ho. 14. 3. xx Eze. 45. 8.

[a] נִשְׁמְדָה id. pret. 3 pers. sing. fem. . . שמד

[b] נִשְׁמְדוּ וְ' id. pret. 3 pers. pl. . . . שמד

[c] נִשְׁמַדְנוּ id. pret. 1 pers. pl. . . . שמד

[d] נִשְׁמַדְתִּי וְ id. pret. 1 pers. sing.; acc. shifted by conv. וְ (comp. § 8. rem. 7) . . . שמד

נָשַׁמָּה Niph. pret. 3 pers. sing. fem. . . שמם

[e] נְשָׁמָה וּ' noun fem. sing. dec. 11 c; וּ bef. (:) . נשם

[f] נְשַׁמָּה [g] וּ' Niph. part. sing. fem. [fr. נָשַׁם m.]; וּ id. שמם

נָשַׁמּוּ וְ' id. pret. 3 pers. pl. . . . שמם

[h] נְשָׁמוֹת וּ noun f. pl. abs. fr. נְשָׁמָה d. 11 c; וּ bef. (:) נשם

נְשַׁמּוֹת Niph. part. fem. pl. of נְשַׁמָּה (q. v.) . שמם

[i] נִשְׂמְחָה וְ' Kal fut. 1 pers. pl. with parag. ה (§ 8. r. 13) שמח

[k] נִשְׁמְטוּ Niph. pret. 3 pers. pl. . . . שמט

[l] נַשְׁמִידָה וְ Hiph. fut. 1 p. pl. with parag. ה (§ 8. r. 13) שמד

נִשְׁמָע [m] וְ' / נִשְׁמַע וַנִּ', וְ' } Kal fut. 1 pers. pl.; ־ַנִּ conv.; or Niph. pret. 3 pers. s. m. (§ 8. r. 7 & 15) } שמע

[n] נִשְׁמְעָה וְ / [o] נִשְׁמָעָה וְ } id. fut. 1 pers. pl. with parag. ה (§ 8. rem. 13 & 15) . . . } שמע

[p] נִשְׁמְעוּ Niph. pret. 3 pers. pl. . . . שמע

[q] נִשְׁמָעִים id. part. masc. pl. [of נִשְׁמָע] . . שמע

[r] נִשְׁמָעֶנָּה וְ Kal fut. 1 pers. pl., suff. 3 pers. sing. fem. שמע

[s] נִשְׁמָר / [t] נִשְׁמַר [u] וְ' } Niph. pret. 3 pers. sing. masc. (comp. § 8. rem. 7) . . . } שמר

[x] נִשְׁמֹר Kal fut. 1 pers. pl. . . . . שמר

[y] נִשְׁמָרוּ / [z] נִשְׁמְרוּ } Niph. pret. 3 pers. pl. (comp. § 8. rem. 7) . . . . } שמר

[a] נִשְׁמַרְתָּ וְ id. pret. 2 pers. sing. masc.; acc. shifted by conv. וְ (comp. § 8. rem. 7) . . שמר

נִשְׁמַרְתֶּם וְ id. pret. 2 pers. pl. masc. . . שמר

נִשְׁמַת וְ' noun fem. sing., constr. of נְשָׁמָה d. 11 c נשם

[b] נִשְׁמָתוֹ וְ id., suff. 3 pers. sing. masc. . . נשם

[c] נִשְׁמָתִי id., suff. 1 pers. sing. . . . נשם

[d] נִשְׁמָתָךְ Ch. n. f. s., suff. 2 pers. s. f., fr. [נִשְׁמָא] d. 8 a נשם

[e] נַשַּׁנִי Piel pret. 3 p. s. m., suff. 1 p. s. [for נִשַּׁנִי § 10. r. 1] נשה

[f] נָשַׁמּוּ וְ Niph. pret. 3 pers. pl. . . . שסס

נִשְׁעָן Niph. part. sing. masc. . . . שען

נִשְׁעַן [g] וְ id. pret. 3 pers. sing. masc. . . שען

[h] נִשְׁעַנּוּ id. pret. 1 pers. pl. [for נִשְׁעַנְנוּ § 25. rem.] שען

[i] נִשְׁעֲנוּ id pret. 3 pers. pl. . . . . שען

[k] נִשְׁעַנְתָּ id. pret. 2 pers. sing. masc. . . שען

[l] נִשְׂעֲרָה Niph. pret. 3 pers. sing. fem. . . שער

[m] נָשַׁף *to breathe, blow.*

נֶשֶׁף masc. dec. 6 a (with suff. נִשְׁפּוֹ) *twilight,* supposed to be so called from the refreshing breezes of that time.—I. *dawn, morning twilight.*—II. *dusk, evening twilight.*—III. *darkness, night.*

יַנְשׁוֹף, יַנְשׁוּף masc. the name of an unclean bird, Sept. & Vulg. *ibis,* the Egyptian *heron.* Ch. & Syr. *the owl.*

נָשֶׁף / נֶשֶׁף } in pause, as if for נַשְׁף = נֶשֶׁף (comp. § 35. r. 2) noun masc. sing. (suff. נִשְׁפּוֹ) dec. 6 a } נשף

[n] נִשְׁפֶּה Niph. part. sing. masc. . . . שפה

[o] נִשְׁפּוֹ noun m. s., suff. 3 pers. s. m. fr. נֶשֶׁף d. 6 a נשף

נִשְׁפָּט Niph. part. sing. masc. . . . שפט

[p] נִשָּׁפְטָה id. fut. 1 pers. pl. [נִשָּׁפֵט] with parag. ה (comp. § 8. rem. 15) . . . שפט

[q] נִשְׁפַּטְתִּי / נִשְׁפַּטְתִּי וְ } id. pret. 1 pers. sing.; acc. shifted by conv. וְ (§ 8. rem. 7) . . } שפט

[r] נִשְׁפַּךְ [s] וְ' Niph. pret. 3 pers. sing. masc. . . שפך

[t] נִשְׁפַּכְתִּי id. pret. 1 pers. sing. . . . שפך

[u] נָשַׁפְתָּ Kal pret. 2 pers. sing. masc. . . . נשף

נָשַׂק. Hiph. *to kindle, set on fire.* Niph. pass. Ps. 78. 21.

[x] נָשַׁק fut. יִשַּׁק, יִשַּׁק, in the Arab. *to join, to arrange;* hence Heb.—I. intrans. *to be arranged, to regulate oneself,* Ge. 41. 40.—II. *to arm oneself.*—III. *to kiss* (i. e. join mouth to mouth), const. with לְ of the person. Pi. *to kiss.* Hiph. *to join, touch,* with אֶל, Eze. 3. 13.

נֵשֶׁק, נֶשֶׁק, masc.—I. *battle array,* Job 39. 21.—II. *battle,* Ps. 140. 8.—III. *arms, armour.*—IV. *armoury, arsenal.*

נְשִׁיקָה fem. dec. 10, *a kiss.*

[y] נָשַׁק וְ Kal pret. 3 p. s. m. before monos. for נָשַׁק נשק

נֵשֶׁק / [z] נֶשֶׁק } noun masc. sing. (§ 35. rem. 2) . נשק

[a] נֶשֶׁק [b] וְ noun masc. sing. . . . . נשק

[c] נִשְׁקַד Niph. pret. 3 pers. sing. masc. . . שקד

[d] נָשְׁקָה וְ Kal pret. 3 pers. sing. fem. . . . נשק

[e] נַשְׁקֶה Hiph. fut. 1 pers. pl. . . . שקה

[f] נִשְּׂקָה Niph. pret. 3 pers. sing. fem. . . . נשק

[g] נִשְׁקְעָה וְ Kh. נִשְׁקָה, K. נִשְׁקְעָה Niph. pret. 3 pers. sing. fem. R. שקה or . . . שקע

[kk] נָשָׁקוּ Kal pret. 3 pers. pl. [for נָשְׁקוּ § 8. rem. 7] נשק

[h] נַשְּׁקוּ Piel imp. pl. masc. . . . . נשק

נֹשְׁקֵי Kal part. act. pl. constr. m. [fr. נֹשֵׁק] d. 7 b נשק

[i] נִשְׁקָל Niph. pret. 3 pers. sing. masc. . . שקל

[k] נַשְׁקֶנּוּ Hiph. fut. 1 pers. pl. (נַשְׁקֶה), suff. 3 pers. sing. masc. (§ 24. rem. 21) . . . שקה

[l] נִשְׁקָף Niph. pret. 3 p. s. m. [for נִשְׁקַף comp. § 8. r. 7] שקף

---

[a] Ju. 21. 16. [b] Ho. 10. 8. [c] 2 Sa. 21. 5. [d] Ge. 34. 30. [e] Da. 10. 17. [f] Ps. 69. 26. [g] Eze. 32. 15.
[h] Is. 57. 16. [i] Ps. 66. 6. [k] Ps. 141. 6. [l] 2 Sa. 14. 7. [m] Ex. 24. 7. [n] Ex. 20. 19. [o] 2 Sa. 17. 5.
[p] Da. 10. 12. [q] Ec. 9. 16, 17. [r] Ju. 14. 13. [s] Ho. 12. 14. [t] 2 Sa. 20. 10. [u] 2 Ki. 6. 10. [x] De. 6. 25.
[y] Ps. 37. 28. [z] 1 Sa. 21. 5. [a] De. 23. 10. [b] Job 34. 14. [c] Job 27. 3. [d] Da. 5. 23. [e] Ge. 41. 51.
[f] Zec. 14. 2. [g] Nu. 21. 15; Is. 10. 20. [h] 2 Ch. 14. 10. [i] 2 Ch. 13. 18. [k] 2 Ch. 16. 7. [kk] Ps. 85. 11.
[l] Ps. 50. 3. [m] Is. 40. 24. [n] Is. 13. 2. [o] Job 3. 9. [p] Is. 43. 26. [q] Eze. 20. 36.
[r] La. 2. 11. [s] 1 Ki. 13. 3. [t] Ps. 22. 15. [u] Ex. 15. 10. [x] 1 Ki. 19. 18. [y] 2 Sa. 15, 5.
[z] 2 Ch. 9. 24. [a] Is. 22. 8. [b] 1 Ki. 10. 25. [c] La. 1. 14. [d] Pr. 7. 13. [e] Ge. 19. 32.
[f] Ps. 78. 21. [g] Am. 8. 8. [h] Ps. 2. 12. [i] Ezr. 8. 33. [k] Ge. 19. 34. [l] Ps. 85. 12.

נִשְׁקְפָה[a] } וְ id. pret. 3 pers. sing. fem. (v. id.) . שקף
נִשְׁקָפָה }

נִשְׁקַפְתִּי[b] id. pret. 1 pers. sing. [for נִשְׁקַפְתִּי v. id.] שקף

נָשַׁר Root not used; i. q. Chald. נְסַר *to saw*.

מַשּׂוֹר masc. *a saw*, Is. 10. 15.

נֶשֶׁר masc. dec. 6a (pl. c. נִשְׁרֵי) *an eagle*.

נְשַׁר[c] Chald. masc. dec. 3b, id.

נָשֶׁר noun masc. s., in pause for נֶשֶׁר (§ 35. r. 2) נשר

נְשָׁרִים[d] id. pl., abs. st. . . . . . נשר

נִשְׂרֹף Kal fut. 1 pers. pl. . . . . . שרף

נִשְׂרְפָה[e] וְ id. with parag. ה (§ 8. rem. 13) . שרף

[נָשַׁת] I. *to dry up*, of the tongue from thirst, *to be parched*, Is. 41. 17.—II. *to fail, waste away*, of strength, Je. 51. 30. Niph. *to dry up*, Is. 19. 5.

נָשַׁתָּה[f] } Kal pret. 3 pers. sing. fem. (§ 8. rem. 3) נשת
נָשְׁתָה[g] }

נִשְׁתֶּה וְ' Kal fut. 1 pers. pl. . . . . שתה

נִשְּׁתוּ[h] וְ Niph. pret. 3 pers. pl. . . . . נשת

נִשְׁתָּוָה[i] Nithpa. pret. 3 pers. sing. masc. [for נִתְשַׁוָּה § 7. No. 10, & § 12. rem. 3] . . שוה

[נִשְׁתְּוָן] masc. *epistle, letter*. Chald. id.

נִשְׁתְּוָנָא Chald. id. emph. state.

נִשְׁתַּחֲוֶה וְ'[k] [for נִתְשַׁ § 12. rem. 3] Hithpalel (3rd rad. doubled for תַּחֲוֶה') fut. 1 pers. pl. (§ 24. rem. 22, & § 6. rem. No. 2) . שחה

נִשְׁתָּעָה[l] וְ [for נִתְשַׁ § 12. rem. 3] Hithpa. fut. 1 pers. pl. [נִשְׁתָּעָה] with parag. ה [for נִשְׁתַּעְהָה] שעה

נָתַב Root not used; Arab. *to be high, raised*; meaning uncertain as regards its connection with the derivatives. Gesenius and Fürst ascribe to it the signification of *treading*.

נָתִיב masc. dec. 3a, fem. נְתִיבָה dec. 10.—I. adj. *trodden*, Pr. 12. 28, דֶּרֶךְ נְתִיבָה *a trodden way, beaten path* (Gesenius), comp. the Root.—II. *path, by-way*; metaph. *course of life*.

נָתוֹן וְ' Kal inf. abs. . . . . . . נתן

נָתוּן id. part. pass. sing. masc. dec. 3a . . נתן

נְתוּנִים[m] } id. pl. abs. st. . . . . . נתן
נְתוּנִם[n] }

נְתוֹץ[o] Kal imp. sing. masc. . . . . נתץ

נָתוּק[p] וְ Kal part. pass. sing. masc. . . . נתק

נָתוֹשׁ[q] Kal inf. abs. . . . . . . נתש

נָתַח. Pi. נִתַּח, *to divide, cut in pieces*. Hence

נֵתַח[r] masc. dec. 6e, *a piece* . . . . נתח

נִתַּח[s] וְ' Piel pret. 3 pers. sing. masc. . . נתח

נִתְחַזֵּק[t] וְ Hithpa. fut. 1 pers. pl. (§ 12. rem. 1) . חזק

נִתְחַזְּקָה[u] וְ id. with parag. ה (comp. § 8. rem. 13) חזק

נְתָחֶיהָ[x] noun masc. pl., suff. 3 pers. sing. fem. from נֵתַח dec. 6e . . . . . נתח

נְתָחָיו[y] id. pl., suff. 3 pers. sing. masc. . . נתח

נְתָחִים[z] id. pl., abs. st. . . . . . נתח

נִתְחַכְּמָה[a] Hithpa. fut. 1 pers. pl. [נִתְחַכֵּם] with parag. ה (comp. § 8. rem. 13) . . . חכם

נָתִיב noun masc. sing. dec. 3a . . . נתב

נְתִיבָה[b] noun fem. sing. dec. 10; or (Pr. 12. 28) adj., fem. of נָתִיב . . . . . נתב

נְתִיבוֹת id., pl. of the preced. . . . נתב

נְתִיבוֹתַי id. pl., suff. 1 pers. sing. . . . נתב

וּנְתִיבוֹתֶיהָ[c] id. pl. with suff. 3 pers. sing. fem.; וּ bef. (:) נתב

נְתִיבוֹתֵיהֶם[d] id. pl., suff. 3 pers. pl. masc. . . נתב

נְתִיבָתִי id. sing., suff. 1 pers. sing. . . . נתב

נְתִיבֹתֶיהָ[e] id. pl., suff. 3 pers. sing. fem. . . נתב

נְתִינַיָּא[f] Chald. noun masc. pl. emph. fr. [נְתִין] d. 1a נתן

נְתִינִים[g] noun masc. pl. of [נָתִין] dec. 3a . . נתן

[נָתַךְ] fut. יִתַּךְ *to be poured out, to flow*, as water, Job 3. 24; elsewhere metaph. of anger, curses. Niph. I. i. q. Kal No. 1.—II. *to flow down, be melted*. Hiph. I. *to pour out*.—II. *to melt*, Eze. 22. 20. Hoph. *to be melted*, Eze. 22. 22.

הִתּוּךְ masc. *a melting*, Ezr. 22. 22.

נִתַּךְ Niph. pret. 3 pers. sing. masc. . . . נתך

נִתְּכָה וְ'[h] id. pret. 3 pers. sing. fem. . . . נתך

נִתְכְּנוּ[i] Niph. pret. 3 pers. pl. . . . . תכן

נִתֶּכֶת[k] Niph. part. sing. fem. [of נִתָּךְ] . . נתך

נִתַּכְתֶּם[l] וְ id. pret. 2 pers. pl. masc. . . . נתך

נִתְלוּ[m] Niph. pret. 3 pers. pl. . . . . תלה

נָתַן וְ' fut. יִתֵּן, imp. תֵּן, inf. נְתוֹן more frequently תֵּת (§ 17. rem. 9).—I. *to give*, with the acc. of the thing and לְ of the person; מִי יִתֵּן *who will give?* a formula of wishing, for *O that!*—II. *to grant, permit, suffer*.—III. *to give forth*, an odour, *to emit*; fruit, *to yield, bear*; the voice, *to speak aloud*; the hand, *to put forth*, Ps. 81. 3, נָ' תֹּף *to strike the timbrel*.—IV. *to render, ascribe*.—V. *to place, set, lay, put*, with עַל, לְ, בְּ, אֶל; hence *to impose* any thing *upon*; נָ' פָּנָיו בְּ *to set his face against* any one; נָ' לִבּוֹ לְ *to apply his heart, mind,*

[a] Nu. 21. 20. [b] Pr. 7. 6. [c] Da. 7. 4. [d] Ex. 19. 4. [e] Ge. 11. 3. [f] Is. 41. 17. [g] Je. 51. 30. [h] Is. 19. 5. [i] Pr. 27. 15. [k] Ge. 22. 5. [l] Is. 41. 23. [m] 1 Ch. 6. 33. [n] Nu. 3. 9. [o] Ps. 58. 7. [p] Le. 22. 24. [q] Je. 12. 17. [r] Eze. 24. 4. [s] Le. 1. 6, 12; 8, 20. [t] 2 Sa. 10. 12. [u] 1 Ch. 19. 13. [x] Eze. 24. 4. [y] Ex. 29. 17. [z] Ju. 19. 29. [a] Ex. 1. 10. [b] Is. 43. 16. [c] Ho. 2. 8. [d] Is. 59. 8. [e] Pr. 3. 17. [f] Ezr. 7. 24. [g] Ezr. 8. 20. [h] Eze. 24. 11 [i] 1 Sa. 2. 3. [k] Je. 7. 20. [l] Eze. 22. 21. [m] La. 5. 12.

to any thing.—VI. *to appoint*, with עַל over any one.—VII. *to make, to do; to make, constitute*; with כְּ *to make like* something else; also *to hold, regard* or *treat* as such. Niph. I. *to be given, delivered*.—II. *to be made*. Hoph. *to be given*.

נְתַן Chald. fut. יִנְתֵּן, יִנְתֵּן *to give*.

נָתָן (*giver*) pr. name masc. of several persons, espec.—I. of a prophet in the time of David.—II. of a son of David, 2 Sa. 5. 14.

נְתַן־מֶלֶךְ (*king's gift*) pr. name m. 2 Ki. 23. 11.

נְתִינִים masc. pl. (of נָתִין dec. 3a) *Nethinim*, servants *devoted* to the service of the temple in waiting upon the Levites; once נְתוּנִים Kh. Ezr. 8. 17.

נְתִינִין Chald. id. Ezr. 7. 24.

נְתַנְאֵל (*gift of God*) pr. name masc. of several persons.

נְתַנְיָה, נְתַנְיָהוּ (*gift of the Lord*) pr. name masc. of several persons.

מַתָּן masc. dec. 1b.—I. *gift*; אִישׁ מַתָּן *liberal man*.—II. pr. name masc. (*a*) of a priest of Baal; (*b*) Je. 38. 1.

מַתָּנָה fem. dec. 11a.—I. *gift, present*.—II. pr. name of a place on the borders of Moab.

מַתְּנָא Chald. fem. dec. 8a, *gift, present*.

מַתַּנְיָה, מַתַּנְיָהוּ (*gift of the Lord*) pr. name masc. of several persons.

מַתְּנַי (id.) pr. name of several men.

מַתָּת fem. (contr. from מַתֶּנֶת) *gift, present*.

מַתַּתָּה (contr. fr. מַתִּתְיָה) pr. n. m. Ezr. 10. 33.

מַתִּתְיָה, מַתִּתְיָהוּ (*gift of the Lord*) pr. name masc. of several persons.

נָתָן וְ׳ pr. name masc. . . . . נתן

נָתָן Kal pret. 3 pers. sing. m. for נָתַן (§ 8. r. 7) נתן

נָתוֹן וְ׳ id. inf. abs., comp. נָתוֹן . . . נתן

נָתָן pr. name in compos. נְתַן מֶלֶךְ . . נתן

נָתוֹן[a] / נְתָן־[b] } Kal inf. constr. (§ 8. rem. 18) . . נתן

נִתָּן Niph. part. sing. masc. . . . נתן

נִתַּן וְ׳ id. pret. 3 pers. sing. masc.; or (Ju. 16. 5) with Mak. for the foll. . . . נתן

נִתֵּן Kal fut. 1 pers. pl. . . . . נתן

נֹתֵן[c] וְ׳ id. part. act. sing. masc. dec. 7b . נתן

נְתַנְאֵל וּ׳ pr. name masc.; וּ bef. (:) . . נתן

נָתְנָה[d] / וְ׳ נָתְנָה } Kal pret. 3 pers. sing. fem. (§ 8. rem. 7) נתן

נְתָנָהּ וּ׳ id. pret. 3 pers. sing. masc., suff. 3 pers. sing. fem.; וּ bef. (:) . . . נתן

נִתְּנָה / וְ׳ נִתְּנָה } Niph. pret. 3 p.s.fem., or Kal fut. 1 p.pl., ה parag. (comp. § 8. rem. 7, 13 & 15) } נתן

נִתְּנֶהָ[e] וַ Kal fut. 1 pers. pl., suff. 3 p. s. f.; וַ conv. נתן

נָתַנּוּ* / וְ׳ נָתַנּוּ[f] } id. pret. 1 pers. pl. [for נָתַנְנוּ § 17. rem. 9] *Eze. 27. 19 . . } נתן

נָתְנוּ וְ׳ id. pret. 3 pers. pl. . . . . . נתן

נְתָנוֹ[g] וּ׳ id. pret. 3 p. s. m., suff. 3 p. s. m.; וּ bef. (:) נתן

נִתְּנוּ[h] Niph. pret. 3 pers. pl. for נִתְּנוּ (comp. § 8. r. 7) נתן

נִתַּנּוּ[i] id. pret. 1 pers. pl. [for נִתַּנְנוּ § 17. rem. 9] נתן

נִתְּנוּ id. pret. 3 pers. pl. . . . . . נתן

נֹתְנוֹ[k] Kal part. act. sing. masc. (נֹתֵן), suff. 3 pers. sing. masc. dec. 7b . . . . . נתן

נְתַנּוּךָ[l] וּ׳[m] id. pret. 1 pers. pl. (נָתַנּוּ q. v.), suff. 2 pers. sing. masc.; וּ bef. (:) . . . נתן

נְתֻנוֹת[n] id. part. pass. fem. pl. [of נְתוּנָה] fr. נָתוּן m. נתן

נֹתְנֵי[o] id. part. act. pl. constr. masc., from נוֹתֵן d. 7b נתן

נְתַנְיָה וּ׳ / נְתַנְיָהוּ וּ׳ } pr. name masc. . . . . נתן

נְתִנִים defect. for נְתוּנִים (q. v.) . . . נתן

נֹתְנִים Kal part. act. masc. pl. of נוֹתֵן dec. 7b . נתן

נְתָנְךָ וּ׳ id. pret. 3 pers. sing. masc., suff. 2 pers. sing. masc.; וּ bef. (:) . . . . נתן

נֹתְנֵךְ id. part. act. sing. masc. (נֹתֵן), suff. 2 pers. sing. fem. (for ךְ— § 3. rem. 2) dec. 7b נתן

נֹתֶנְךָ[p] id. id., suff. 2 pers. sing. masc. . . נתן

נְתָנָם וּ׳ id. pret. 3 pers. sing. masc., suff. 3 pers. pl. masc.; וּ bef. (:) . . . . נתן

נְתָנָנוּ[q] id. id., suff. 1 pers. pl. . . . נתן

נְתָנַנִי[r] / נְתָנַנִי } id. id., suff. 1 pers. sing. (§ 2. rem. 1) נתן

[נָתַס] *to tear up, destroy*, only in the foll. form.

נָתְסוּ[s] Kal pret. 3 pers. pl. . . . . נתס

נָתַע. Niph. *to be broken out*, Job 4. 10, cogn. נָתַץ.

נִתְעָב Niph. part. sing. masc. . . . . . תעב

נִתְעָב[t] id. pret. 3 pers. sing. masc. . . . תעב

נִתְעָה[u] Niph. pret. 3 pers. sing. masc. . . תעה

נִתָּעוּ[cc] Niph. pret. 3 p. pl. [for נִתְּעוּ comp. § 8. r. 7] נתע

נִתְעוֹדָד[x] וַ Hithpal. fut. 1 p. pl. (comp. § 12. r. 1); וַ conv. עוד

נִתְעַלְּסָה[y] Hithpa. fut. 1 pers. pl. with parag. ה (comp. § 8. rem. 13) . . . . עלס

נִתְפַּלֵּל[z] וַ Hithpa. fut. 1 pers. pl.; וַ conv. . . פלל

נִתְפָּשׂ[a] / וְ׳ נִתְפָּשׂ[b] } Niph. pret. 3 pers. sing. masc. (comp. § 8. rem. 7) . . } תפש

נִתְפָּשָׂה / נִתְפָּשָׂה[c] } id. pret. 3 pers. sing. fem. (v. id.) . תפש

[a] Nu. 20. 21. [b] Ge. 38. 9. [c] Da. 1. 16. [cc] Job 4. 10. [d] Ju. 5. 25. [e] De. 29. 7. [f] Ge. 34. 16. [g] De. 21. 10. [h] Ge. 9. 2; Eze. 47. 11. [i] Ezr. 9. 7. [k] 1 Ki. 20. 13. [l] 2 Ch. 25. 16. [m] Ju. 15. 13. [n] De. 28. 31. [o] Ho. 2. 7. [p] Je. 20. 4. [q] Ps. 124. 6. [r] Ps. 118. 18. [s] Job 30. 13. [t] 1 Ch. 21. 6. [u] Job 15. 31. [x] Ps. 20. 9. [y] Pr. 7. 18. [z] Ne. 4. 3. [a] Eze. 19. 8. [b] Eze. 19. 4. [c] Je. 50. 46.

נִתְפָּשׂוּ[a] id. pret. 3 pers. pl. [for נִתְפְּשׂוּ v. id.] . תפשׂ

נִתְפְּשֵׂם[b] וְ Kal fut. 1 pers. pl. [נִתְפֹּשׂ], suff. 3 pers. pl. masc. . . . . . . תפשׂ

נִתְפַּשְׂתְּ[c] Niph. pret. 2 pers. sing. fem. . . . תפשׂ

נָתַץ וְ' fut. יִתֹּץ, inf. נְתֹץ.—I. *to tear* or *break down, destroy*, as houses, &c.; trop. of persons.—II. *to break out* the teeth, Ps. 58. 7. Pi. *to break down, destroy*. Niph. Pu. and Hoph. *to be broken, thrown down*.

נָתָץ Kal pret. 3 pers. sing. masc. for נָתַץ (§ 8. r. 7) נתץ

נִתַּץ[d] Piel pret. 3 pers. sing. masc. (§ 10. rem. 1) נתץ

נֻתַּץ[e] Pual pret. 3 pers. sing. masc. . . . נתץ

נָתָצוּ[f] / נָתְצוּ } Kal pret. 3 pers. pl. (§ 8. rem. 7) . נתץ

נִתְּצוּ וְ'[g] Niph. pret. 3 pers. pl. . . . נתץ

נִתַּצְתֶּם[h] וְ Piel pret. 2 pers. pl. masc. . . . נתץ

נָתַק I. *to pluck, draw off* or *away*.—II. part. נָתוּק *castrated*, Le. 22. 24. Niph. נִתַּק.—I. *to be torn, broken*, as a string; metaph. Job 17. 11.—II. *to be plucked* or *drawn away, withdrawn*. Pi. נִתֵּק.—I. *to pull up, uproot*, Eze. 17. 9.—II. *to tear* or *break*, as cords, the breasts, a yoke. Hiph. *to draw away* or *out*. Hoph. pass. Ju. 20. 31. Hence

נֶתֶק[i] masc. *a kind of leprosy, a scall* (prop. *a plucking off of hair*) . . . . . נתק

נִתַּק[k] Niph. pret. 3 pers. sing. masc. . . . נתק

נִתָּקוּ / נִתְּקוּ } id. pret. or (Je. 5. 5) Piel 3 pers. pl. (comp. § 8. rem. 7) . . } נתק

נְתַקְּנוּהוּ[l] וּ Kal pret. 1 pers. pl., with dag. euph. & suff. 3 pers. sing. masc.; וּ for וְ, conv. . נתק

נִתַּקְתִּי[m] Piel pret. 1 pers. sing. . . . . נתק

נָתַר in Kal only fut. יִתַּר *to tremble*, of the heart, *to palpitate*, Job 37. 1.—Pi. *to spring, leap*, of the locust, Le. 11. 21. Hiph. הִתִּיר.—I. *to cause to tremble*.—II. *to let loose, loosen*.

נְתַר Chald. Aph. *to shake off*, Da. 4. 11.

[נֶתֶר] masc.—I. *nitre*, Pr. 25. 20.—II. *soap* made of *nitre* and oil, Je. 2. 22.

נָתֶר[n] noun masc. sing. for נֶתֶר׳ (§ 35. rem. 2) נתר

נִתְרָאֶה Hithpa. fut. 1 pers. pl. . . . ראה

נָתַשׁ[o] וְ fut. יִתּשׁ, inf. נְתוֹשׁ.—I. *to tear, pluck up*, only metaph. of a people *to be expelled* from a land, comp. Je. 24. 6.—II. *to tear down, destroy*. Niph. I. i. q. Kal No. 1.—II. *to fail*, spoken of water, Je. 18. 14. Hoph. *to be torn, plucked up*, Eze. 19. 12.

נֹתֵשׁ[p] Kal part. act. sing. masc. dec. 7 b . . נתשׁ

נָתְשִׁי[q] id. inf. with suff. 1 pers. sing. . . נתשׁ

נֹתְשָׁם[r] id. part. act. sing. masc. (נֹתֵשׁ), suff. 3 pers. pl. masc. dec. 7 b . . . . נתשׁ

נָתַשְׁתָּ[s] id. pret. 2 pers. sing. masc. . . נתשׁ

נָתַשְׁתִּי וְ id. pret. 1 pers. sing.; acc. shifted by conv. וְ (§ 8. rem. 7) . . . נתשׁ

נְתַשְׁתִּים[t] וּ id. id., suff. 3 pers. pl. masc.; וּ for וְ, conv. נתשׁ

נָתַתָּ וְ' Kal pret. 2 pers. s. m. [for נָתַנְתָּ § 17. r. 9] נתן

נָתַתְּ[u] id. pret. 2 pers. sing. fem. . . . נתן

נָתַתָּה וְ' id. pret. 2 pers. sing. masc. (§ 8. rem. 5) נתן

נָתָתִּי[x] וְ' / נָתַתִּי / נָתַתִּי וְ } id. pret. 1 pers. sing. (§ 17. rem. 9, & § 8. rem. 7) . . } נתן

נָתַתְּי[y] id. pret. 2 pers. sing. fem., Kh. נָתַתִּי, K. נָתַתְּ (§ 8. rem. 5) . . . נתן

נְתַתִּיהָ וּ' id. pret. 1 pers. sing., suff. 3 pers. sing. fem.; וּ for וְ, conv. . . . . נתן

נְתַתִּיהוּ[zz] וּ / נְתַתִּיו וּ' } id. id., or (Eze. 16. 19) pret. 2 pers. fem. sing. suff. 3 pers. sing. masc.; וּ id. } נתן

נְתַתִּיךָ וּ' id. id., suff. 2 pers. sing. masc.; וּ id. נתן

נְתַתִּיךְ וּ' id. id., suff. 2 pers. sing. fem.; וּ id. . נתן

נְתַתִּים וּ' id. id., suff. 3 pers. pl. masc.; וּ id. . נתן

נִתַּתֶּם[z] וְ Niph. pret. 2 p. pl. m. [for נִתַּנְתֶּם § 17. r. 9] נתן

נְתַתָּם וּ Kal pret. 2 pers. sing. masc., suff. 3 pers. pl. m. [for נְתַנְתָּם § 17. r. 9]; וּ for וְ, conv. נתן

נְתַתֶּם וּ' id. pret. 2 pers. pl. masc.; וּ id. . נתן

נְתַתָּנִי id. pret. 2 pers. sing. masc., suff. 1 pers. sing. [for ־תַנִי׳ § 2. rem. 1] . . נתן

ס

סְאָה[a] וּ' fem. pl. סְאִים, du. סָאתַיִם (for סְאָתַיִם) *a seah*, a measure of capacity for dry things, containing the third part of an ephah. Arab. סאא *to extend, expand*.

סַאסְּאָה fem. contr. from סְאָה סְאָה *measure* (and) *measure*, Is. 27. 8.

סְאוֹן[bb] noun masc. sing. . . . . סאן

סְאִים noun fem. with pl. masc. term. fr. סְאָה (q. v.) סאה

---

[a] Je. 51. 32. [b] 2 Ki. 7. 12. [c] Je. 50. 24. [d] 2 Ch. 33. 3. [e] Ju. 6. 28. [f] Je. 39. 8. [g] Eze. 16. 39. [h] De. 12. 3. [i] Le. 13. 30. [k] Is. 5. 27. [l] Ju. 20. 32. [m] Je. 2. 20. [n] Pr. 25. 20. [o] 1 Ki. 14. 15. [p] Je. 45. 4. [q] Je. 12. 15. [r] Je. 12. 14. [s] Ps. 9. 7. [t] 2 Ch. 7. 20. [u] Eze. 16. 33. [x] Eze. 17. 22. [y] Eze. 16. 18, 36. [z] Le. 26. 25. [zz] Ju. 4. 7. [a] 2 Ki. 7. 1, 16. [b] 2 Ki. 7. 18. [bb] Is. 9. 4.

סָאֹן part. only Is. 9. 4, *one shod with a warrior's shoe* or *greaves*, i. e. a warrior, soldier. Syr. סאן *to shoe.*

סְאוֹן masc. *a warrior's shoe* or *greaves*, an armour for the legs, ibid.

סָאתַיִם [a] וְ׳ noun fem. du. by Syriasm [for סְאָתַיִם] from סְאָה (q. v.) . . . . סאה

סֹב Kal imp. sing. m.; or (De. 2. 3) inf. constr. סבב

[סָבָא] *to drink to excess,* Is. 56. 13; part. סֹבֵא *a drunkard;* pass. סָבוּא *drunken,* Na. 1. 10, *for as thorns folden together* וּכְסָבְאָם סְבוּאִים, *the drunken, like their wine, shall be consumed.*

סָבָא masc. *drunkard,* Eze. 23. 42 Keri.

סֹבֶא masc. dec. 6c.—I. *wine,* or perhaps any other *strong, inebriating drink.*—II. *carouse, drinking bout,* Ho. 4. 18.

סְבָא וּ׳ pr. name—I. of a son of Cush, Ge. 10. 7. —II. of a people descended from him; pl. סְבָאִים *Sabeans.*

סֹבֵא[b] [c]וְ׳ Kal part. act. sing. masc. dec. 7b . סבא

סְבָאִים וּ gent. noun pl. from סְבָא q. v. . . סבא

סָבְאֵךְ[d] noun m. s., suff. 2 pers. s. f. fr. [סֹבֶא] d. 6c סבא

סָבְאָם[e] id., suff. 3 pers. pl. masc. . . . סבא

סָבַב[f] וְ׳ pl. סַבּוֹתֶם, סַבּוּ, סָבְבוּ ; inf. סֹב, סְבֹב (§ 18. r. 13); imp. סֹב (§ 18. r. 3); fut. יָסֹב, יָסֹב (r. 14).—I. *to turn oneself, to turn,* with אֶל, לְ, עַל *to* any one, and מִן, מִפְּנֵי, מֵעַל *from* any one; with אֶל־אַחֲרֵי *after* any one, to follow him; absol. *to return;* also absol. *to turn to, set about* doing any thing, as 1 Sa. 22. 17, 18; of things, *to be turned, brought to, conferred upon.* —II. *to turn, go about* in a place, *to go over, go round* a place, with אֶת, בְּ.—III. *to surround, encompass,* with acc., also אֶל, עַל; absol. *to surround, sit round* a table, 1 Sa. 16. 11.—IV. *to be turned, changed,* with כְּ Zec. 14. 10.—V. *to be the cause* or *occasion* of anything, with בְּ 1 Sa. 22. 22. Niph. נָסַב, נָסֵב (§ 18. r. 7), fut. יִסַּב.—I. *to turn oneself, to turn;* hence *to be turned, transferred,* with לְ Je. 6. 12.—II. *to surround,* with עַל. Pi. סִבֵּב *to change,* 2 Sa. 14. 20. Po. סוֹבֵב.—I. *to go about,* with בְּ *in* a place, with acc. *over* a place, with עַל *to go round* a place.—II. *to surround, encompass.* Hiph. הֵסֵב, fut. יָסֵב, יַסֵּב (§ 18. r. 3).—I. *to cause to turn;* trans. *to turn;* hence *to transfer.*—II. *to cause to go about, to lead about, around;* hence, *to carry round* a wall, 2 Ch. 14. 6.—III. *to surround, encompass.*—IV. *to change, alter.*—V. intrans. 2 Sa. 5. 23. Hoph. הוּסַב, fut. יוּסַב (§ 18. r. 3).—I. *to turn,* intrans.; also *to roll.*—II. *to be surrounded.* —III. *to be changed,* Nu. 32. 38.

סִבָּה fem. *a turn of events, a change,* 1 Ki. 12. 15.

סָבִיב masc. dec. 3a.—I. *a circuit;* מִסָּבִיב, *from around, around, round about;* סָבִיב סָבִיב, סָבִיב, סָבִיב לְ adv. and prep. *round about, around.*—II. pl. סְבִיבִים *round about,* of persons, *neighbours;* of place, *places round about* or *circumjacent, environs.* With suff. as a prep. סְבִיבָיו, סְבִיבֶיךָ *round about thee, him,* Je. 46. 14; Ps. 50. 3.—III. pl. סְבִיבוֹת (*a*) *circuits, orbits,* Ec. 1. 6; (*b*) i. q. סְבִיבִים *places round about, environs;* prep. *round about, around.*

מֵסַב masc. with suff. מְסִבּוֹ dec. 8d.—I. *couches ranged round* for reclining on, Ca. 1. 12.—II. *environs,* 2 Ki. 23. 5.—III. adv. *round about,* 1 Ki. 6. 29.

מְסִבָּה fem. dec. 10, *revolution,* Job 37. 12.

מוּסַב masc. *circuit* of a house, Eze. 41. 7.

נְסִבָּה f. *a turn of events, a change,* 2 Ch. 10. 15.

סַבֵּב[g] Piel inf. constr. . . . . סבב

סֹבֵב[h] Kal part. act. sing. masc. dec. 7b . סבב

סְבָבֻהוּ[i] id. pret. 3 pers. pl., suff. 3 pers. sing. masc. סבב

סָבְבוּ[k] וְ׳ id. pret. 3 pers. pl. . . . סבב

סְבָבוּם[l] id. id., suff. 3 pers. pl. masc. . . סבב

סְבָבוּנִי[m] id. id., suff., Kh. נִי׳ 1 pers. s., K. נוּ׳ 1 p. pl. סבב

סְבָבוּנִי id. id., suff. 1 pers. sing. . . . סבב

סֹבְבִים[o] id. part. act. masc., pl. of סֹבֵב dec. 7b . סבב

סְבָבֻנִי[p] id. pret. 3 pers. pl., suff. 1 pers. sing. . סבב

סִבָּה[q] noun fem. sing. . . . . . סבב

סֹבּוּ [r]וְ׳ Kal imp. pl. masc. . . . . סבב

סְבוּאִים[s] Kal part. pass. masc. pl. [of סָבוּא] dec. 3a סבא

סַבּוּנִי Kal pret. 3 pers. pl., suff. 1 pers. sing. . סבב

סַבּוֹתִי[t] וְ׳ id. pret. 1 pers. sing. . . . . סבב

סֹבִּי[u] id. imp. sing. fem. . . . . . סבב

סָבִיב וְ׳ (prop., noun m. s. d. 3a) as an *adv.* & *prep.* סבב

סְבִיב[x] וּ id. constr. st. (subst.); וּ bef. (:) . . סבב

סְבִיבוֹת וּ׳ id. pl. fem. as a *prep.*; וּ id. . . סבב

סְבִיבוֹתָי id. pl. fem., suff. 1 pers. sing., *prep.* . . סבב

סְבִיבוֹתֶיהָ[y] וּ׳ id. pl. f., suff. 3 p. s. f., *prep.*; וּ bef. (:) סבב

סְבִיבוֹתֵיהֶם id. pl. fem., suff. 3 pers. pl. masc., *subst.* (Ezr. 1. 6) and *prep.* . . . . . סבב

סְבִיבוֹתָיו id. pl. fem., suff. 3 pers. sing. masc., *subst.* (Je. 50. 32) and *prep.* . . . . . סבב

[a] 2 Ki. 7. 1, 16. [b] Pr. 23. 21. [c] De. 21. 20. [d] Is. 1. 22. [e] Ho. 4. 18. [f] Eze. 42. 19. [g] 2 Sa. 14. 20. [h] Ec. 1. 6. [i] 1 Ki. 5. 17. [k] Jos. 6. 15. [l] Ec. 12. 5. [m] Ho. 7. 2. [n] Ps. 17. 11. [o] 1 Ki. 7. 24. [p] Ho. 12. 1. [q] 1 Ki. 12. 15. [r] Jos. 6. 7. [s] Na. 1. 10. [t] Ec. 2. 20; 7. 25. [u] Is. 23. 16. [x] Am. 3. 11. [y] Eze. 5. 5.

סְבִיבוֹתַיִךְ[a] id. pl. fem., suff. 3 pers. sing. fem., *prep.* סבב
סְבִיבוֹתֶיךָ id. pl. fem., suff. 2 pers. sing. masc., *prep.* סבב
סְבִיבוֹתֵיכֶם id. pl. fem., suff. 2 pers. pl. masc., *prep.* סבב
סְבִיבֶיהָ[b] id. pl. masc., suff. 3 pers. sing. fem., *subst.* סבב
סְבִיבָיו[ff] c ו׳ id. pl. masc., suff. 3 pers. sing. masc., *subst.* and *prep.*; וּ bef. (:) . . . . סבב
סְבִיבַיִךְ[d] id. pl. masc., suff. 2 pers. sing. fem., *subst.* סבב
סְבִיבֶיךָ id. pl. masc., suff. 2 pers. sing. masc., *subst.* סבב
סְבִיבֹת id. pl. fem., *prep.* . . . . סבב
סְבִיבֹתָו[e] id. pl. f., suff. 3 pers. s. m. (§ 4. r. 1), *prep.* סבב
סְבִיבֹתַי[f] id. pl. fem., suff. 1 pers. sing. for ־ֹתַי, *prep.* סבב
סְבִיבֹתֶיהָ id. pl. fem., suff. 3 pers. sing. fem., *prep.* . סבב
סְבִיבֹתֵיהֶם id. pl. fem., suff. 3 pers. pl. masc., *prep.* סבב
סְבִיבֹתָיו id. pl. fem., suff. 3 pers. sing. masc., *subst.* (Ecc. 1. 6) and *prep.* . . . . סבב
סְבִיבֹתֵיכֶם id. pl. fem., suff. 2 pers. pl. masc., *prep.* . סבב
סְבִיבֹתֵינוּ id. pl. fem., suff. 1 pers. pl., *subst.* (Nu. 22. 4; Da. 9. 16) and *prep.* . . . סבב
סְבִיבֹתָם[g] id. pl. f., suff. 3 p. pl. (§ 4. r. 2) *subst.* and *prep.* סבב

סָבַךְ *to interweave, entwine, fold together,* Na. 1. 10. Pu. pass. Job 8. 17.
סְבַךְ masc. *thicket*, Ge. 22. 13.
סְבֹךְ masc. id. Ps. 74. 5.
סְבָךְ or סֹבֶךְ masc. dec. 6b (§ 35. rem. 10, but comp. rem. 9, note) id. Is. 9. 17; 10. 34.
סֻבְּךְ masc. dec. 6c, id. Je. 4. 7.
סִבְּכַי (for סְבַךְ יָהּ *perplexity, confusion from the Lord*) pr. name of one of David's chiefs, for which מְבֻנַּי 2 Sa. 23. 27, comp. 2 Sa. 21. 18.

סַבְּכָא Chald. fem. the name of a certain *stringed instrument*, Da. 3. 5, elsewhere שַׂבְּכָא.
סִבְּכַי pr. name masc. . . . . סבב
סִבְכֵי[h] noun m. pl. constr. [for סִבְּכֵי without Meth. from סְבָךְ dec. 6b, or סְבֹךְ § 35. rem. 10] סבך
סְבֻכִים[i] Kal part. pass. masc. pl. [of סָבוּךְ] dec. 3a סבך

[סָבַל] fut. יִסְבֹּל *to bear, carry,* as a heavy load; metaph. of sin. Pu. part. *laden,* i. e. *big with young,* Ps. 144. 14. Hithp. הִסְתַּבֵּל *to become a burden,* Ecc. 12. 5.
סְבַל Chald. in the Targums, *to lift up, erect*; in the Bible only Poal part. *erected, built,* Ezr. 6. 3; Prof. Lee, *brought*.
סֵבֶל masc. *a burden*.
סֹבֶל masc. with suff. סֻבֳּלוֹ (with dag. forte euphonic) *burden,* Is. 9. 3; 10. 27; 14. 25.

סַבָּל masc. dec. 1b, *porter*.
סִבְלוֹת fem. pl. c. (from סְבָלָה or סִבְלָה) *burdens, labours, tasks*.

סַבָּל noun masc. sing. (pl. סַבָּלִים) dec. 1b . סבל
סֵבֶל[k] noun masc. sing. . . . . סבל
סֻבֳּלוֹ[l] ו׳ noun masc. sing., suff. 3 pers. sing. masc., dag. euph. [from סֹבֶל § 35. rem. 17] סבל
סִבְלוֹת[m] noun fem. pl. constr. [from סִבְלָה or סְבָלָה] סבל
סְבָלָם[n] Kal pret. 3 pers. sing. m., suff. 3 pers. pl. m. סבל
סְבָלְנוּ[o] id. pret. 1 pers. pl. [for סְבַלְנוּ § 8. rem. 7] סבל
סִבְלֹת[p] defect. for סִבְלוֹת (q. v.) . סבל
סִבֹּלֶת[q] in the dialect of the Ephraimites for שִׁבֹּלֶת (q.v.) שבל
סַבֻּנִי[r] defect. for סַבּוּנִי (q. v.) . . סבב

[סְבַר] Chald. *to hope, purpose,* Da. 7. 25. Hence
סִבְרַיִם pr. name of a city in Syria, Eze. 47. 16 . סבר
סַבְתָּא ו׳ / סַבְתָּה ו׳ } pr. name of a son of Cush and the people descended from him.
סַבֹּתִי[s] Kal pret. 1 pers. sing. . . . סבב
סַבְתְּכָא ו׳ pr. name of a son of Cush, Ge. 10. 7.
סַבֹּתֶם[t] ו׳ Kal pret. 2 pers. pl. masc. . סבב
סָג[u] Kal pret. 3 pers. sing. masc. . . סוג

[סָגַד] fut. יִסְגֹּד *to fall down, to worship,* with לְ, used in reference to idols only. Hence
סְגִד[x] Chald. Peal pret. 3 pers. sing. masc. (§ 47. rem. 6) fut. יִסְגֻּד, id. . . סגד
סָגְדִין[y] Chald. id. part. act. masc. pl. of [סָגֵד] d. 2b סגד
סָגוּר Kal part. pass. sing. masc. . . סגר
סְגוֹר noun masc. sing., comp. סְגֹר . . סגר
סִגַּיִךְ[z] [for סִגַיִךְ] the foll. with suff. 2 pers. sing. fem. סוג
סִגִים[a] noun masc. pl. [as if fr. סֵג R. סגג], see סִיג סוג

סָגַל Root not used; Chald. סְגַל *to gain, acquire.* Hence
סְגֻלָּה fem. dec. 10, *peculiar property* or *treasure* . סגל
סְגֻלַּת[b] ו׳ id., constr. st.; וּ bef. (:) . . סגל

[סָגָן] or [סֶגֶן] masc. dec. 6 (§ 35. rem. 10) only pl. סְגָנִים *chiefs* or *prefects* among the Babylonians and Persians, and among the Jews after the return from Babylon.
סְגַן Chald. masc. dec. 3b, idem.

סִגְנַיָּא Chald. noun masc. pl. emph. from [סְגַן] d. 3b סגן
סְגָנֶיהָ[c] ו׳ the foll. with suff. 3 pers. sing. f.; וּ bef. (:) סגן

a Eze. 5. 12, 14, 15. b Je. 21. 14. c Ps. 50. 3. d Je. 49. 5. e 1 Sa. 26. 5, 7. f De. 17. 14. ff Je. 46. 14. g 2 Ki. 17. 15; Eze. 28. 24. h Is. 10. 34. i Na. 1. 10. k 1 Ki. 11. 28. l Is. 14. 25. m Ex. 6. 7. n Is. 53. 4. o La. 5. 7. p Ex. 6. 6. q Ju. 12. 6. r 2 Sa. 22. 6. s 1 Sa. 22. 22. t Jos. 6. 3. u Ps. 53. 4. x Da. 2. 46. y Da. 3. 7, 12, 14. z Is. 1. 25. a Eze. 22. 18. b Ec. 2. 8. c Je. 51. 28, 57.

[a]סְגָנִים ו׳ noun masc. pl. [of סְגַן or סֶגֶן § 35. r. 10] סגן

[b]סִגְנִין Chald. noun masc. pl. of [סְגַן] dec. 3 b . סגן

סָגַר ו׳ fut. יִסְגֹּר.—I. *to shut* a door.—II. *to shut up*, const. with בְּעַד, עַל; Ps. 35. 3, וּסְגֹר לִקְרַאת רֹדְפָי *and shut up* (the way) *against my persecutors*. III.—*to close* a breach, 1 Ki. 11. 27. Part. pass. סָגוּר *shut up*; hence *precious*, זָהָב סָגוּר *precious gold*, i. e. pure, unadulterated. Niph. pass. of Kal Nos. I & II; also *to shut up oneself*. Pi. סִגֵּר *to deliver up*, with בְּיַד. Pu. to be *shut up*. Hiph. I. *to shut up*.—II. *to deliver up*, with בְּיַד, לְ, אֶל.

סְגַר Chald. *to shut, close*, Da. 6. 23.

סְגוֹר masc.—I. *enclosure*, Ho. 13. 8.—II. *precious, fine gold*, Job 28. 15, comp. the verb.

סוּגַר masc. *close confinement*; perhaps *a cage*, only Eze. 19. 9.

מַסְגֵּר masc. prop. part. Hiph. I. *a locksmith*; Prof. Lee, *joiner*.—II. that which shuts up, *a prison*.

מִסְגֶּרֶת fem. dec. 13 a (with suff. ׳גַּרְתּוֹ).—I. *close, confined place*.—II. *border, ridge*, as an enclosure.

סַגְרִיר masc. *rain*, Pr. 27. 15. Syr. סגרא id. Arab. שׂגר to fill with water.

[c]סְגַר ו׳ Ch. Peal pret. 3 pers. sing. masc.; ו׳ bef. (־) סגר

סִגֵּר Piel pret. 3 pers. sing. masc. (§ 10. rem. 1) סגר

[d]סֹגֵר Kal part. act. sing. masc. . . . סגר

סְגֹר ו׳ id. imp. sing. masc. (Is. 26. 20); Ps. 35. 3, perh. subst., defect. for סְגוֹר (q. v.); ו׳ bef. (:) סגר

[e]סֻגַּר Pual pret. 3 pers. sing. masc. . . סגר

סָגְרוּ / סָגָרוּ } Kal pret. 3 pers. pl. (§ 8. rem. 7) סגר

[f]סִגְרוּ id. imp. pl. masc. . . . . סגר

[g]סֻגְּרוּ ו׳ Pual pret. 3 pers. pl. . . . סגר

[h]סַגְרִיר noun masc. sing. . . . . סגר

סִגְּרַנִי Piel pret. 3 pers. sing. masc., suff. 1 pers. sing. סגר

[k]סָגַרְתְּ ו׳ Kal pret. 2 pers. sing. fem. . . . סגר

[kk]סֹגֶרֶת id. part. act. sing. fem. of סֹגֵר masc. . סגר

סָדַד Root not used; Arab. *to shut, stop up*.

סַד masc. *stocks*, a wooden frame or block in which the feet of prisoners were *inserted*, Job 13. 27; 33. 11. Prof. Lee, *fetters*.

[l]סָדִין noun masc. sing. dec. 3 a . . . סדן

[m]סְדִינִים id. pl., abs. st. . . . . . סדן

סְדֹם pr. name, *Sodom*, one of the four cities in the vale of Siddim, which were destroyed for their wickedness in the time of Abraham and Lot. Signification uncertain. Simonis, *dew*, or *plentiful waters*. Arab. סדא *rore aspersa fuit, maduit terra*. Gesenius, *conflagration*.

סְדֹמָה id. with parag. ה.

סָדַן Root not used; Arab. *to loosen, to let a garment hang loose*.

סָדִין masc. dec. 3 a, *a wide linen under-garment*, worn next to the body.

סָדַר, שָׂדַר Root not used; i. q. Syr. & Chald. סדר *to set in order*.

סֵדֶר masc. dec. 6 b, *order, orderly arrangement*, Job 10. 22.

שְׂדֵרָה fem. dec. 10, *order, row* of soldiers, *suite* of chambers.

מִסְדְּרוֹן masc. *porch, portico*, Ju. 3. 23.

[mm]סְדָרִים noun masc. pl. of [סֵדֶר] dec. 6 b . סדר

סָהַר, שָׂהַר Root not used; i. q. Samar. סחר *to surround, to be round*.

סַהַר masc. *roundness*, Ca. 7. 2.

סֹהַר masc. only בֵּית הַסֹּהַר *a prison*, from the *round* form of the building, q. d. *a round-house*; Gesenius, *house of the round-tower*.

שַׂהֲרֹנִים masc. pl. (of שַׂהֲרוֹן) *little moons*, as an ornament.

סוֹא pr. name of an Egyptian king, 2 Ki. 17. 4.

[n]סֻוֹבָאִים Kh. סוֹבְאִים, pl. of סֹבֵא q. v.; K. סְבָאִים noun masc. pl. [of סָבָא] . . סבא

[o]סוֹבֵב ו׳ Kal part. act. sing. masc. dec. 7 b . סבב

[p]סוֹבְבִים id. pl., abs. st. . . . . . סבב

I. **[סוּג]** *to slide back, depart*, espec. from God; part. pass. Pr. 14. 14. סוּג לֵב *backslider in heart*. Niph. נָסוֹג, נָשׂוֹג.—I. *to be turned, driven back*.—II. *to decline, fall away*, espec. from God.

סוּג masc. *dross*, Eze. 22. 18. Kheth.

סִיג masc. pl. סִיגִים, סִגִים, that which goes off from metal, *dross*.

שִׂיג masc. *retirement*, 1 Ki. 18. 27.

II. **[סוּג]** *to fence, hedge about*, Ca. 7. 3.

[q]סוּגָה Kal part. pass. sing. masc. . . . סוג

[r]סוּגָה id. part. pass. sing. fem. . . . סוג

[s]סוֹד ו׳ noun masc. sing. dec. 1 a [for יְסוֹד] . יסד

---

[a] Is. 41. 25. [b] Da. 2. 48. [c] Da. 6. 23. [d] Is. 22. 22. [e] Is. 24. 10. [f] 2 Ki. 6. 32. [g] Je. 13. 19. [h] Pr. 27. 15. [i] 1 Sa. 24. 19. [k] 2 Ki. 4. 4. [kk] Jos. 6. 1. [l] Pr. 31. 24. [m] Ju. 14. 12, 13. [mm] Job 10. 22. [n] Eze. 23. 42. [o] Ec. 1. 6. [p] 2 Ch. 4. 3. [q] Pr. 14. 14. [r] Ca. 7. 3. [s] Pr. 25. 9.

סוֹדוֹ id., suff. 3 pers. sing. masc. . . . . יסד

סוֹדִי pr. name masc. . . . . . יסד

[a]סוֹדִי noun masc. sing., suff. 1 pers. sing. from סוֹד dec. 1a [for יְסוֹד] . . . יסד

סָוָה Root not used; prob. *to cover*, cogn. צָפָה, זָוָה.
מַסְוֶה masc. *covering, veil*, Ex. 34. 33, 34, 35.
סוּת fem. *a garment*, Ge. 49. 11; but see כְּסוּת Root כָּסָה.

סוּחַ Root not used; i. q. סָחָה *to sweep away*.
סוּחָה fem. *sweepings, filth*, Is. 5. 25.
סִיחוֹן (*sweeping away*) pr. name of a king of the Amorites.

סוּחַ pr. name masc. 1 Ch. 7. 36.

[b]סוֹחֵר Kal part. act. sing. masc. dec. 7b . . סחר

סוֹטַי (*departing* סוּט i. q. שׂוּט) pr. name of a man, Ezr. 2. 55; Ne. 7. 57.

[סוּךְ] I. *to anoint*.—II. *to anoint oneself*. Hiph. *to anoint oneself*, 2 Sa. 12. 20.
אָסוּךְ masc. *oil-flask*, 2 Ki. 4. 2.

[c]סוֹךְ ֽ Kal inf. abs. . . . . . סוך

[d]סוֹלֲלָה noun fem. sing. dec. 10 . . סלל

[e]סוֹמֵךְ ֽ' Kal part. act. sing. dec. 7b . . סמך

[f]סוּמְפֹּנְיָה, סוּמְפּוֹנְיָה Chald. fem. Da. 3. 5, 15; but in ver. 10 סִיפֹּנְיָה συμφωνία, a musical instrument, supposed to be *a bagpipe*.

סְוֵנֵה pr. name of a city in Egypt, Eze. 29. 10; 30. 6.

סוּס ֽ', ֽ masc. dec. 1a.—I. *a horse*.—II. *a swallow*, Is. 38. 14, & Je. 8. 7, where the Khethib has סִיס.
סוּסָה fem. dec. 10, *a mare*, Ca. 1. 9. Others, after the Sept. & Vulg. in a collective sense, *horses*.
סוּסִי (*horseman*) pr. name masc. Nu. 13. 11.

[g]סוּס ֽ Kh. סוּס q. v.; K. סִיס noun masc. sing. סוס

סוּסָה pr. name in compos. חֲצַר סוּסָה see חצר חצר

סוּסִי pr. name masc. . . . . סוס

[h]סוּסֵי ֽ noun masc. pl. constr. from סוּס dec. 1a סוס

[i]סוּסֵיהֶם ֽ' id. pl., suff. 3 pers. pl. masc. . . סוס

סוּסָיו id. pl., suff. 3 pers. sing. masc. . . סוס

סוּסֶיךָ id. pl., suff. 2 pers. sing. masc. . . סוס

[k]סוּסֵיכֶם id. pl., suff. 2 pers. pl. masc. . . סוס

סוּסִים id. pl., abs. st. . . . סוס

[סוּף] *to come to an end, to cease, perish*. Hiph. *to make an end of, destroy*.
סוּף Chald. id. of prophecy, *to be accomplished, fulfilled*, Da. 4. 30. Aph. *to make an end of, destroy*, Da. 2. 44.
סוֹף masc. d. 1a.—I. *end, extremity*, 2 Ch. 20. 16.—II. *the rear* of an army.—III. *end, termination*.—IV. *end, completion*, Ec. 3. 11.
סוֹף Chald. m. d. 1a, i. q. Heb. Nos. I, III & IV.
סוּפָה fem. dec. 10, *whirlwind, hurricane*.

סוּף ֽ' masc.—I. *sea-weed, sedge*, Jon. 2. 6; יַם־סוּף *the sea of weed, Red Sea*.—II. *reed, rush, bulrush*.—III. pr. name of a place, De. 1. 1.

סוֹף noun masc. sing. dec. 1a . . . סוף

סוֹפָא Chald. noun masc. sing., emph. of סוֹף dec. 1a סוף

סוּפָה noun fem. sing. dec. 10 . . . סוף

[m]סוֹפֵר ֽ' Kal part. act. sing. masc. dec. 7b . ספר

[n]סוֹפְרִים id. pl, abs. st. . . . . ספר

[o]סוּפָתָה ֽ noun fem. sing. (סוּפָה q. v.) with parag. ה סוף

סוּר fut. יָסוּר, ap. וַיָּסַר (§ 21. rem. 9).—I. *to turn aside* or *away, to depart*, e. g. from a way; const. with מִן, מֵעַל, מֵאַחֲרֵי, בְּ; espec. *to turn away* from God and His laws, *to apostatize, degenerate*. Part. Pr. 11. 22, סָרַת טָעַם *deviating as to* (i. e. *lacking*) *understanding*.—II. *to be removed*; also *to pass away*.—III. *to turn aside* to any person or thing, *to approach, draw near*, with עַל; with אֶל *to turn in* to any one, to lodge with him. Hiph. הֵסִיר; fut. יָסִיר ap. וַיָּסַר (§ 21. rem. 19).—I. *to remove. put away*.—II. *to take off*, e. g. a ring from the finger, the head from any one.—III. *to lay, set, put aside*; hence, *to omit, neglect*.—IV. *to turn, lead away* any one, with מֵאַחֲרֵי De. 7. 4.—V. *to let* any thing *be brought*, with אֵלָיו *to oneself*, 2 Sa. 6. 10. Hoph. *to be removed*. Pil. *to turn aside, cause to deflect*, spoken of a way, La. 3. 11.
סוּר masc. dec. 1a, properly part. pass.—I. adj. *removed, driven out*.—II. Je. 2. 21, סוּרֵי הַגֶּפֶן *degenerate* (shoots) *of the vine*.—III. pr. name of one of the gates of the temple, 2 Ki. 11. 6; called יְסוֹד in 2 Ch. 23. 5.
סָרָה fem.—I. *a turning, departing* from God; *apostasy*.—II. *falsehood*, De. 19. 16.
סִרָה (*recession*) pr. name of a cistern, 2 Sa. 3. 26.
יָסוּר masc. *one departing*, Je. 17. 13. Kheth.

סוּר pr. name of a gate . . . . סור

[p]סוּר ֽ Kal inf. constr. . . . . סור

סוּר ֽ' id. inf. constr., or imp. sing. masc. . סור

[nn]סוּרָה, [oo]סוּרָה id. imp. with parag. ה (§ 8. rem. 11) סור

[a] Job 19. 19. [b] Pr. 31. 14. [c] Da. 10. 3. [d] Da. 11. 15. [e] Ps. 37. 17. [f] Da. 3. 5, 15. [g] Je. 8. 7. [h] 2 Ki. 2. 11. [i] Is. 31. 3. [k] Am. 4. 10. [l] Is. 19. 6. [m] 1 Ch. 27. 32. [n] 2 Ch. 34. 13. [nn] Ru. 4. 1. [o] Ho. 8. 7. [oo] Ju. 4. 18. [p] Da. 9. 5, 11.

סֹרָה[a] וְ Kal part. pass. or adj. fem. from סוּר masc. . סור
סֹרוּ id. imp. pl. masc. . . . . . סור
סוּרֵי[b] adj. pl. masc. from [סוּר] dec. 1 a . . סור
סוֹרֵר[c] Pilel pret. 3 pers. sing. masc. . . סור
סוֹרֵר Kal part. act. sing. masc. dec. 7 b . . סרר
סוֹרְרִים id. pl., abs. st. . . . . . סרר
סוֹרֶרֶת[d] id. part. sing. fem. . . . . סרר

סוּת. Hiph. הֵסִית, הִסִּית ; fut. יָסִית, יַסִּית (§ 21. r. 24) *to urge, excite, induce, persuade.*

סוּתֹה[e] noun fem. sing., suff. 3 pers. sing. masc. [from סוּת] R. סָוָה, or by aphaeresis for כְּסוּת R. כסה

[סָחַב] *to draw* or *drag along the ground.*
סְחָבָה fem. only pl. בְּלוֹיֵ הַסְּחָבוֹת *old torn clothes, rags.*

סְחַבְנוּ[f] וְ Kal pret. 1 pers. sing. . . . סחב

סָחָה. Pi. *to sweep away,* Eze. 26. 4.
סְחִי masc. *sweepings, offscouring,* La. 3. 45.
סָחוֹב[g] Kal inf. abs. . . . . . סחב
סְחִי[h] noun masc. sing. . . . . סחה
סָחִישׁ[i] 2 Ki. 19. 29, & שָׁחִיס Is. 37. 30, *that which grows of itself the third year after sowing.* Etymology uncertain . . . . סחש
סְחַבְנוּ[k] וְ Kal pret. 1 pers. pl. . . . סחב
סְחֵיתִי[l] וְ Piel pret. 1 pers. sing. (§ 14. rem. 1) ; acc. shifted by conv. וְ (comp. § 8. rem. 7) . סחה

סֹחֵף[m] Kal part. *sweeping, driving,* as a violent shower of rain, Pr. 28. 3. Niph. נִסְחַף *to be swept away, destroyed,* Je. 46. 15.

[סָחַר] I. *to go, travel about,* Je. 14. 18.—II. with אֶת *to go round* or *over, traverse* a country for the sake of *traffic,* Ge. 34. 21 ; 42. 34 ; סֹחֵר *a travelling merchant* or *trader.* Pilp. (§ 6. No. 3) *to go about in quick motion,* of the heart, *to palpitate,* Ps. 38. 11.
סַחַר masc. dec. 4 a.—I. *seat of commerce, mart,* Is. 23. 3.—II. *wealth, profit* acquired by commerce.
סַחַר masc. (with suff. סַחְרָהּ § 35. rem. 5) *profit, gain,* either as acquired by trading, or in general.
סְחֹרָה fem. dec. 10, *traffic, trade.*
סֹחֵרָה fem. *shield,* Ps. 91. 4. Others, *a tower* ; Syr. סחרתא id.
סֹחֶרֶת fem. Est. 1. 6, a kind of valuable stone. According to some, *black marble* ; according to others, *tortoise-shell.*
מִסְחָר masc. dec. 2 a, *traffic, trade,* 1 Ki. 10. 15.

סְחַר[n] וּ׳ noun masc. sing., constr. of [סַחַר] dec. 4 a סחר
סֹחֵר[o] Kal part. act. sing. masc. dec. 7 b . . סחר
סַחְרָהּ noun masc. sing., suff. 3 pers. sing. fem. [for סַחְרָהּ § 35. rem. 5] from סַחַר dec. 6 d סחר
וְסֹחֵרָה[p] וְ noun fem. sing. . . . . סחר
סְחָרוּ[q] Kal pret. 3 pers. pl. . . . . סחר
סְחָרוּהָ[r] וּ id. with suff. 3 pers. sing. fem. ; וּ for וְ, conv. סחר
סְחַרְחַר[s] Pilp. pret. 3 pers. sing. masc. (§ 6. No. 3) סחר
סֹחֲרֵי[t] וְ׳ Kal part. act. pl. constr. m. from סוֹחֵר d. 7 b סחר
סֹחֲרֶיהָ[u] id. pl., suff. 3 pers. sing. fem. . . סחר
סֹחֲרַיִךְ[x] / סֹחֲרָיִךְ[y] } id. pl., suff. 2 pers. sing. fem. . . סחר
סֹחֲרִים id. pl., abs. st. . . . . . סחר
סֹחֶרֶת[z] וְ noun fem. sing. [for סֹחֶרֶת comp. § 35. r. 2] סחר
סְחֹרַת[a] noun fem. sing., constr. of [סְחֹרָה] dec. 10 סחר
סֹחַרְתֵּךְ[b] Kal part. act. sing. fem. [סֹחֶרֶת], suff. 2 pers. sing. fem. dec. 13 a, from סֹחֵר masc. סחר
סֹטַי pr. name masc. for סוֹטַי q. v.
סֵטִים[c] noun masc. pl. for שֵׂטִים (q. v.) . . שוט
סִיגִים noun masc. pl. of סִיג׳ dec. 1 a . . סיג
סִיוָן (prob. *bright, splendid* סִיו i. q. זִיו) name of the third month of the Jewish year, Est. 8. 9.
סִיחוֹן / סִיחֹן } pr. name masc. . . . . סוח
סִין (*mire,* סִין Chald., סינא Syr. id.) pr. name *Sin.* —I. a city in the north-eastern extremity of Egypt, according to Jerome, *Pelusium.* Eze. 30. 15, 16.—II. a desert westward of Mount Sinai.
סִינַי / סִינָי { (*miry* ; others, *thorn-bush,* i. q. סְנֶה) pr. name, *Sinai,* a mountain in Arabia Deserta, where the Mosaic law was given.
[סִינִי׳] pr. name, *Sinite,* a people of Canaan, Ge. 10. 17 ; 1 Ch. 1. 15.
סִינִים pr. name of a people, Is. 49. 12. According to some, the inhabitants of *Pelusium,* see סִין ; according to Gesenius, the *Chinese.*
סִיסְרָא וְ׳ (*battle-array* ; Syr. סיסרתא id.) pr. name, *Sisera.*—I. a general under Jabin, king of the Canaanites, comp. Ju. 4. 2.—II. of a Jew, Ezr. 25. 53 ; Ne. 7. 55.
סִיעָא, סִיעֲהָא pr. name masc. Ne. 7. 47 ; Ezr. 2. 44.
סִיפְּנְיָא[d] וְ Kh. for סוּמְפֹּנְיָא q. v.

---

[a] Is. 49. 21. [b] Je. 2. 21. [c] La. 3. 11. [d] Ne. 9. 29. [e] Ge. 49. 11. [f] 2 Sa. 17. 13. [g] Je. 22. 19. [h] La. 3. 45. [i] 2 Ki. 19. 29. [k] 2 Sa. 17. 13. [l] Eze. 26. 4. [m] Pr. 28. 3. [n] Is. 23. 3 ; 45. 14. [o] Is. 23. 2. [p] Ps. 91. 4. [q] Je. 14. 18. [r] Ge. 34. 10. [s] Ps. 38. 11. [t] Eze. 38. 13. [u] Is. 23. 8. [x] Eze. 27. 21. [y] Is. 47. 15. [z] Est. 1. 6. [a] Eze. 27. 15. [b] Eze. 27. 12, 16, 18. [c] Ps. 101. 3. [d] Da. 3. 10.

סִיר com. dec. 1a (pl. ־ִים, ־וֹת).—I. *a pot, vessel.*—II. *thorn.*—III. *hook, fishhook.* Gesenius compares the Root סִיר with the Arab. שׂאר *to spring up, boil up; to rage* as a fever.

סִירִים id. pl. masc., abs. st. . . . סיר

סִירֹתָיו[a] id. pl. fem., suff. 3 pers. sing. masc. . סיר

סִירֹתֵיכֶם[b] id. pl. fem., suff. 2 pers. pl. masc. . סיר

סֻכָּה[c] וְ[d] noun fem. sing. dec. 10 . . . סכך

סֻכּוֹ noun m. s., suff. 3 pers. s. m. fr. [סֹךְ] d. 8c סכך

סִכּוּת[e] noun fem. sing. . . . . סכך

סֻכּוֹת וְ noun fem., pl. of סֻכָּה dec. 10, also pr. name, and in compos. סֻכּוֹת בְּנוֹת . סכך

סֻכּוֹתָה full form for סֻכֹּתָה (q. v.) . . . סכך

סֻכִּיִּים pr. name of a people . . . . סכך

[סָכַךְ, שָׂכַךְ] I. *to cover,* with acc., עַל of the object covered; intrans. *to cover, conceal oneself,* La. 3. 43, 44.—II. *to protect,* with לְ; part. סוֹכֵךְ *that which protects, defends, a defence.*—III. *to place as a covering,* with עַל Ex. 33. 22; 40. 3.—IV. Ps. 139. 13, *to interweave, weave.* Prof. Lee, *to compact, put together.* Hiph. הֵסַךְ.—I. *to cover, protect,* with עַל.—II. *to hedge in* (comp. Kal No. IV), or *to shut in, confine,* with בְּעַד, Job 3. 23; 38. 8. Hoph. pass. see נָסַךְ. Pilp. סִכְסֵךְ (§ 6. No. 3) *to cover with arms,* Is. 9. 10; 19. 2. Others, *to mingle together,* comp. Kal No. IV.

סְכָכָה (*enclosure*) pr. name of a town in Judah, Jos. 15. 61.

סָךְ masc. *crowd, multitude,* Ps. 42. 5.

סֹךְ, שֹׂךְ masc. dec. 8c.—I. *booth, hut.*—II. *thicket,* as the *covert* of wild beasts.

סֻכָּה fem. dec. 10.—I. *booth, tent, tabernacle,* made of boughs and branches.—II. *thicket,* Job 38. 40.—III. *a dwelling.*

סֻכּוֹת (*booths*) pr. name—I. of a station of the Israelites in the desert.—II. of a town in the tribe of Gad.—III. סֻכּוֹת בְּנוֹת 2 Ki. 17. 30, *booths of the daughters,* supposed to be *booths* made by the Babylonian colonists for the idolatrous worship of their *daughters.*

סִכּוּת fem. *shrine,* Am. 5. 26.

סֻכִּיִּים (*tent-dwellers*) pr. name of a people, 2 Ch. 12. 3.

מָסָךְ masc. constr. מְסַךְ, *a covering;* used espec. of the *curtain* in the tabernacle.

מְסֻכָּה fem. dec. 10, *a covering,* Eze. 28. 13.

מוּסָךְ masc. *a covering, porch,* 2 Ki. 16. 18, Kh. מֵיסַךְ.

סְכָכָה ‏· pr. name of a place; ‏· bef. (:) . סכך

סֹכְכִים וְ, סֹכְכִים[f] וְ[g, h] } Kal part. act. masc., pl. of סֹכֵךְ dec. 7b . . . . } סכך

סָכַל Kal not used; Syr. *to be foolish.* Niph. *to act foolishly, wickedly.* Pi. *to render foolish, to frustrate.* Hiph. *to act foolishly.*

סָכָל masc. dec. 4a, *fool, foolish.*

סֶכֶל masc. *folly,* Ecc. 10. 6.

סִכְלוּת, שִׂכְלוּת fem. *folly.*

סָכָל noun masc. sing. dec. 4a . . . סכל

סַכֶּל־[i] Piel imp. sing. masc. [for סַכֵּל § 10. rem. 4] סכל

סִכְלוּת[k] וְ noun fem. sing. . . . סכל

סְכָלִים[l] noun masc. pl. of סָכָל dec. 4a . . סכל

[סָכַן] fut. יִסְכֹּן. Arab. שׁכן *to sit still; to dwell* with any one. Hence in the Heb.—I. Job 34. 9, *to be prosperous* (Lee); but see No. III.—II. part. סֹכֵן *associate, companion,* e. g. of a king, Is. 22. 15; fem. סֹכֶנֶת *a female companion, attendant,* 1 Ki. 1. 2, 4. Others, *steward,* fem. *nurse,* from the following signification.—III. *to be beneficial, profitable* to any one, with לְ, עַל, Job 22. 2; 35. 3; abs. Job 15. 3. Perh. intrans. *to profit,* Job 34. 9; but comp. No. I. Niph. Ecc. 10. 9, *to be endangered;* so in the Chald. Pu. part. מְסֻכָּן, Is. 40. 20, *brought down, reduced, poor,* from the primary idea of *sitting;* or perh. as *being benefitted by receiving the bounty of* others. Hiph. I. *to become familiar, acquainted with,* const. with עִם, Job 22. 21; with acc. *to know,* Ps. 139. 3.—II. *to be accustomed, be wont,* Nu. 22. 30.

מִסְכֵּן masc. *poor.*

מִסְכֵּנֻת fem. *poverty,* De. 8. 9.

מִסְכְּנוֹת fem. pl. (of מִסְכֶּנֶת) *stores, treasuries,* transp. for מִכְנְסוֹת from כָּנַס q. v.

סֹכֶנֶת[m] Kal part. act. sing. fem. of סֹכֵן . . סכן

וְסִכְסַכְתִּי[n] Pilp. pret. 1 pers. sing. (§ 6. rem. 4); acc. shifted by conv. וְ (comp. § 8. rem. 7) . סכך

סָכַר. Niph. *to be shut, stopped.* Pi. *to deliver up,* Is. 19. 4, comp. סָגַר.

סֹכְרִים[o] וְ Kal part. act. pl. masc. for שֹׂכְרִים (q. v.) שׂכר

וְסִכַּרְתִּי[p] Piel pret. 1 pers. sing.; acc. shifted by conv. וְ (comp. § 8. rem. 7) . . סכר

[a] Ex. 27. 3. [b] Ps. 58. 10. [c] Jon. 4. 5. [d] Is. 4. 6. [e] Am. 5. 26. [f] Ex. 37. 9. [g] Ex. 25. 20. [h] 1 Ch. 28. 18. [i] 2 Sa. 15. 31. [k] Ec. 2. 12; 10. 1, 13. [l] Je. 4. 22. [m] 1 Ki. 1. 2, 4. [n] Is. 19. 2. [o] Ezr. 4. 5. [p] Is. 19. 4.

סָכַת. Hiph. *to be silent*, De. 27. 9.

[a]סַכְתְּ וְ Kal pret. 2 pers. sing. fem.; for וְ see lett. ו . סוך

[b]סַכֹּתָ וְ Kal pret. 2 pers. sing. masc.; acc. shifted by conv. וְ (comp. § 8. rem. 7) . . סכך

[c]סֻכַּת noun fem. sing., constr. of סֻכָּה dec. 10 . סכך

סֻכֹּת id. pl. defect. for סֻכּוֹת . . . . סכך

[d]סַכֹּתָה Kal pret. 2 pers. sing. masc. (§ 8. rem. 5) סכך

סֻכֹּתָה pr. name of a place (סֻכּוֹת) with parag. ה סכך

סֻכָּתוֹ noun fem. s., suff. 3 pers. s. m. fr. סֻכָּה d. 10 סכך

[e]סַכְתִּי Kal pret. 1 p. s. [for סַכְתִּי comp. § 8. r. 15] סוך

[f]סַל וְ noun masc. sing. dec. 8d . . סלל

סָלָא. Pu. *to be weighed*, La. 4. 2. Cogn. סָלָה, סָלַל *to lift up*.

סָלוּא (*weighed*) pr. name masc. Nu. 25. 14.

סַלּוּא, סַלָּא (id.) pr. name masc. 1 Ch. 9. 7; Ne. 11. 7.

סַלּוּ (id.) pr. name masc. Ne. 12. 7, for which סַלַּי ver. 20.

סִלָּא, סִלָּא pr. names of a man and a place . סלל

סָלַד Kal not used; Arab. *to leap* (whence prob. Rabbin. *to praise*); also *to be hard*; Chald. סְלַד *to burn*. Hence Pi. only Job 6. 10, וַאֲסַלְּדָה בְחִילָה לֹא יַחְמוֹל כִּי וגו׳ is variously rendered: (*a*) *and I will exult even under pain* which *does not spare, that,* &c. (*b*) *and I will praise under pain* Him who *spares not*, &c. (*c*) *and I will harden myself in pain*, &c. (*d*) *though I burn* or *be consumed with pain*, &c. Hence

סֶלֶד pr. name of a place

[סָלָה] prop. *to lift up, raise*; hence—I. *to bear, carry away*, Ps. 119. 118. Others, as in the Syr. and Chald. *to reject, despise*. Pi. id. La. 1. 15.—II. Pu. *to be weighed*, Job 28. 16, 19. Hence

סֶלָה a musical note or term in the Psalms and Hab. and everywhere in pause for סֶלָה (comp. § 35. rem. 14) imp. with ה parag. from סָלָה *raise!* sc. the voice in response to the instrument; or, according to others who take שָׁלָה=סָלָה, *to rest*: hence, *rest! pause!*

[g]סִלָּה Piel pret. 3 pers. sing. masc. . . . סלה

סַלּוּ pr. name masc. . . . . . סלא

סֹלּוּ Kal imp. pl. masc. . . . . סלל

סַלּוּא pr. name masc. . . . . . סלא

סָלוּא pr. name masc. . . . . . סלא

[h]סֹלּוּהָ Kal imp. pl. masc. (סֹלּוּ), suff. 3 pers. sing. masc. (§ 18. rem. 4) . . . סלל

[i]סְלוּלָה id. part. pass. sing. fem. [from סָלוּל] masc. סלל

[k]סִלּוֹן noun masc. sing. . . . . . סלל

[l]סַלּוֹנִים וְ noun masc. pl. of [סַלּוֹן] dec. 1b . סלל

[סָלַח] fut. יִסְלַח (once אֶסְלוֹחַ Je. 5. 7, Kh.) *to forgive, pardon*, with לְ of the person. Niph. *to be forgiven*.

סַלָּח masc. *forgiving, placable*, Ps. 86. 5.

סְלִיחָה fem. dec. 10, *forgiveness*.

[m]סַלָּח וְ noun masc. sing. . . . . סלח

סְלַח Kal imp. sing. masc. . . . . סלח

[n]סְלֹחַ id. inf. constr. . . . . . סלח

[o]סְלָחָה id. imp. sing. masc. ((סְלַח)) with parag. ה (§ 8. rem. 11 & 12) . . . סלח

[p]סָלַחְתָּ, וְסָלַחְתָּ } Kal pret. 2 pers. sing. masc.; acc. shifted by conv. וְ (§ 8. rem. 7) . } סלח

[q]סָלַחְתִּי, וְסָלַחְתִּי } id. pret. 1 pers. sing. (v. id.) . . סלח

סַלַּי pr. name masc. for סַלַּי . . . סלל

[r]סַלֵּי noun masc. pl. constr. from סַל dec. 8d . סלל

[s]סְלִיחוֹת noun fem. pl. of סְלִיחָה dec. 10 . . סלח

[t]סְלִיקוּ accord. to some copies, סְלִקוּ (q. v.) . סלק

[u]סָלִיתָ Kal pret. 2 pers. sing. masc. . . . סלה

סַלְכָה pr. name of a city in the kingdom of Bashan.

[סָלַל] fut. יָסֹל.—I. *to raise, cast up* into a heap or mound, Je. 50. 26; specially *to cast up, prepare, make* a way.—II. in the Arab. *to connect, knit, link together*, comp. derivv. סַל, סַלְסִלּוֹת. Pilp. (§ 6. No. 3) *to raise, exalt*, Pr. 4. 8. Hithpo. הִסְתּוֹלֵל *to oppose oneself, to resist*, with בְּ Ex. 9. 17.

סֹלְלָה fem. dec. 10, *a mound, rampart*.

סַל masc. dec. 8d, *basket*.

סִלָּא (*elevation* or *way*) pr. name of a town near Jerusalem, 2 Ki. 12. 21.

סִלּוֹן, סַלּוֹן masc. dec. 1b, *thorn*, Eze. 28. 24; metaph. *a wicked man*, Eze. 2. 6.

סַלַּי (*elevated, exalted*) pr. name masc. Ne. 11. 8; see also R. סָלָה סַלּוּ.

סֻלָּם masc. *a ladder*, Ge. 28. 12.

סַלְסִלּוֹת fem. pl. *baskets*, Je. 6. 9.

מְסִלָּה fem. dec. 10.—I. *a raised way, highway*;

Ru. 3. 3. Ex. 40. 3. Am. 9. 11. [d] La. 3. 44. [e] Da. 10. 3. [f] Nu. 6. 15. [g] La. 1. 15. [h] Je. 50. 26. [i] Je. 18. 15. [k] Eze. 28. 24. [l] Eze. 2. 6. [m] Ps. 86. 5. [n] De. 29. 19. [o] Da. 9. 19. [p] La. 3. 42. [q] Nu. 14. 20. [r] Ge. 40. 16. [s] Ne. 9. 17. [t] Ezr. 4. 12. [u] Ps. 119. 118.

trop. *manner of life.*—II. *steps, stairs,* 2 Ch. 9. 11. Prof. Lee, *terraces.*

מַסְלוּל masc. *highway,* Is. 35. 8.

סְלָלָה[a] defect. for סְלוּלָה (q. v.) . . . . סלל

סֹלְלָה noun sing. fem. dec. 10 . . . . סלל

סֻלָּם[b] noun masc. sing. [סֹל] with the term. ־ָם. סלל

סַלְסְלֶהָ[c] Pilp. imp. sing. masc. (§ 6. No. 4) . סלל

סַלְסִלּוֹת[d] noun fem. pl. of סַלְסִלָּה . . . . סלל

סֶלַע masc. dec. 6 (with suff. סַלְעִי § 35. rem. 5).—I. *a rock.*—II. pr. name, *Sela,* i. e. Petra, in Edom.

סָלַע id. in pause (§ 35. rem. 2) . . . סלע

סַלְעוֹ[e] וְ id. with suff. 3 pers. sing. masc. . . סלע

סַלְעִי id., suff. 1 pers. sing. . . . . סלע

סְלָעִים id. pl., abs. st. . . . . . סלע

[סָלְעָם] masc. a species of *locust,* Le. 11. 22.

סָלַף. Pi.—I. *to subvert, overthrow.*—II. *to pervert.* Hence

סֶלֶף וְ masc. *perverseness,* Pr. 11. 3; 15. 4 . סלף

[סְלִק] Chald. *to go* or *come up.*

סְלִקוּ[f] Chald. Peal pret. 3 pers. pl. masc. (§ 47. r. 6) סלק

סָלְקָן[g] Chald. id. part. act. fem. pl. [of סָלְקָה] d. 8a סלק

סִלְקַת[h]
סִלְקָת[i] } Chald. Peal pret. 3 pers. sing. fem. . סלק

סֹלֶת [k]וְ' com. *fine meal, flour.*

סַמְגַּר נְבוֹ pr. name of a Babylonian general, Je. 39. 3.

סְמָדַר[l] masc. *a vine blossom.*

סָמוּךְ Kal part. pass. sing. masc. dec. 3a . . סמך

סְמוּכִים[m] id. pl., abs. st. . . . . . סמך

סַמִּים noun masc. pl. of [סַם] dec. 8d . . סמם

סָמַךְ וְ' fut. יִסְמֹךְ.—I. *to lean* or *lay, to impose,* as the hand, with עַל *upon* any thing.—II. intrans. *to lean, rest heavily upon,* with עַל Ps. 88. 8.—III. *to uphold, support.*—IV. *to advance, draw near,* with אֶל Eze. 24. 2. Niph.—I. *to lean upon.*—II. metaph. *to trust in.* Pi. *to stay, refresh,* Ca. 2. 5.

סְמַכְיָהוּ (whom *the Lord upholds*) pr. name masc. 1 Ch. 26. 7.

יִסְמַכְיָהוּ (*the Lord uphold* him) pr. name masc. 2 Ch. 31. 13.

שְׂמִיכָה fem. *mattress, covering,* Ju. 4. 18 (some MSS. read סְמִיכָה).

סָמְכָה[n] Kal pret. 3 pers. sing. fem. . . סמך

סָמְכוּ וְ id. pret. 3 pers. pl. . . . . סמך

סַמְּכוּנִי[o] Piel pl. with suff. 1 pers. sing. . . סמך

סֹמְכֵי[p] Kal part. act. pl. constr. m. from סוֹמֵךְ d. 7b סמך

סְמַכְיָהוּ וּ pr. name masc.; וּ bef. (:) . . . סמך

סָמְכֵנִי[q] id. inf., suff. 1 pers. sing. . . . סמך

סָמַכְתָּ[r] וְ id. pret. 2 pers. sing. masc.; acc. shifted by conv. וְ (§ 8. rem. 7) . . . . סמך

סְמָכַתְהוּ[s] id. pret. 3 pers. sing. fem., suff. 3 pers. sing. masc. [for כַתְהוּ'] . . . . סמך

סְמַכְתִּיו[t] id. pret. 1 pers. sing., suff. 3 pers. sing. masc. סמך

סְמָכָתְנִי[u] id. pret. 3 pers. sing. fem., suff. 1 pers. sing. סמך

סֶמֶל[x] masc. *a figure, image,* with the art. הַסֶּמֶל.

סָמֶל[y] in pause for סֶמֶל' (§ 35. rem. 2) . . סמל

סמם Root not used; Arab. *to smell.*

סַמִּים masc. pl. (of סַם) *sweet spices, aromatics*

סָמַן. Niph. *to be marked off, appointed,* Is. 28. 25.

סָמַר *to shudder,* Ps. 119. 120. Pi. *to bristle up, stand on end,* of the hair, Job 4. 15.

סָמָר masc. *bristly, having bristly hairs,* Je. 51. 27.

מַסְמֵר, מַשְׂמֵר, מִסְמֵר masc. only pl. מְרִים' מְרוֹת' *nails.*

סָמָר[z] noun masc. sing. . . . . . מר

סנא Root not used; prob. i. q. סָנָה (whence סְנֶה) *to be thorny, prickly,* cogn. Syr. סְנָא, Heb. שָׂנֵא *to hate.*

סְנָאָה (*thorny*) pr. name of a town in Judah.

סְנוּאָה (*hated*) pr. name probably of a woman, Ne. 11. 9.

סְנָאָה pr. name of a place . . . . נא

סַנְבַלַּט וְ' (*hatred in secret*; comp. סְנָא) pr. name, *Sanballat,* a Persian governor in Samaria.

סְנֶה[a] masc. *a bush, thorn-bush.* For the Root see סנא.

סֶנֶּה (for סְנֶה § 35. rem. 14) pr. name of a rock, 1 Sa. 14. 4.

סַנָּה pr. name, see קִרְיַת סַנָּה . . . . דה

סנור Root not used; Chald. *to blind, dazzle.*

סַנְוֵרִים m. pl. *blindness,* Ge. 19. 11; 2 Ki. 6. 18

---

[a] Pr. 15. 19. [b] Ge. 28. 12. [c] Pr. 4. 8. [d] Je. 6. 9. [e] Is. 31. 9. [f] Da. 2. 29; Ezr. 4. 12. [g] Da. 7. 3. [h] Da. 7. 8. [i] Da. 7. 20. [k] Le. 7. 12. [l] Ca. 2. 13, 15. [m] Ps. 111. 8. [n] Ps. 88. 8. [o] Ca. 2. 5. [p] Eze. 30. 6. [q] Ps. 119. 116. [r] Nu. 27. 18. [s] Is. 59. 16. [t] Ge. 27. 37. [u] Is. 63. 5. [x] Eze. 8. 3, 5. [y] De. 4. 16. [z] Je. 51. 27. [a] De. 33. 16.

סַנְחֵרָב
סַנְחֵרִיב } pr. name, *Sennacherib*, king of Assyria.

סנן Root not used; signification uncertain.

סַנְסַנָּה (*palm-branch;* others, *full of thorns,* comp. סְנֶה) pr. name of a town in the tribe of Judah, Jos. 15. 31.

סַנְסִנִּים masc. pl. (of סַנְסַן) *palm-branches,* Ca. 7. 8, according to the Sept. *tops.*

סַנְסַנָּה וְ pr. name of a place . . . . סנן

סְנַפִּיר masc. *fin* of a fish, Le. 11. 9, 10; De. 14. 9, 10.

סָס masc. *a moth,* an insect that eats cloth, Is. 51. 8.

סֻסִים[a] וְ defect. for סוּסִים q. v. . . . . סוס

סִסְמַי וְ' pr. name masc. 1 Ch. 2. 40.

סָעַד[b] וְ fut. יִסְעַד.—I. *to support, uphold.*—II. *to stay, aid.*—III. *to stay, refresh,* the heart.

סְעַד Ch. Pa. *to assist, aid,* with לְ, Ezr. 5. 2.

מִסְעָד masc. *prop, support,* 1 Ki. 10. 12.

סְעָד[c] Kal imp. sing. masc. . . . . סעד

סְעָד־[rr] id. id. bef. Mak. [for סְעֹד § 8. rem. 18] . סעד

סַעֲדָה[d] וּ id. id. with parag. ה [for סְעָדָה, for סְעֹדָה, fr. סְעַד comp. § 8. r. 11]; the (ֲ) under ס seems to result from the influence of the following guttural, and the preceding *u* sound, comp. לְקָחָה, וּצְעָקִי . . . סעד

סַעֲדוּ[e] וְ id. imp. pl. masc. . . . . . סעד

סְעָדֵנִי[f] id. imp. s. m. (סְעָד), suff. 1 p. s. (§ 16. r. 11) סעד

[סָעָה] *to run, rush,* Ps. 55. 9.

סֹעָה[g] Kal part. act. sing. fem. [of סֹעֶה] . סעה

סְעוּ[h] וּ' Kal imp. pl. masc.; וּ bef. (:) . נסע

סְעִיף[i] noun masc. sing. dec. 1 a . . . סעף

סָעַף, שָׂעַף Kal not used; prob. i. q. Arab. שאב *to divide.* Pi. (denom. fr. סָעִיף) *to cut off branches,* Is. 10. 33.

סֵעֵף adj. masc. dec. 7 b, *divided,* i. e. as to mind, *doubting,* only Ps. 119. 113.

סְעַפָּה fem. dec. 10, *branch,* Eze. 31. 6, 8.

סַרְעַפָּה fem. id. (with ר inserted) Eze. 31. 5.

סְעִפָּה fem. *division, party,* 1 Ki. 18. 21, *how long will ye halt* עַל־שְׁתֵּי הַסְּעִפִּים *between two parties;* others, *upon two boughs,* like a bird *hopping* backwards and forwards.

סָעִיף masc. dec. 1 a.—I. *cleft, fissure.*—II. *branch, bough.*

שְׂעִפִּים masc. pl. (of שָׂעִף) *thoughts,* prob. *distracting thoughts,* Job 4. 13; 20. 2.

שַׂרְעַפִּים m. pl. (of שַׂרְעַף) id. Ps. 94. 19; 139. 23.

סְעִפֵּי[k] n. m. pl. constr. [for סְעִיפֵי] from סָעִיף dec. 1 a סעף

סְעִפֶּיהָ[l] id. pl., suff. 3 pers. sing. fem. [for סְעִיפֶיהָ] סעף

סֵעֲפִים[m] noun masc. pl. of [סֵעֵף] dec. 7 b . סעף

סַעֲפֹּתָיו[n] noun fem. pl., suff. 3 pers. sing. masc. from [סְעַפָּה] dec. 10 . . . . סעף

[סָעַר] I. *to be tempestuous, tossed* by a tempest, as the sea, Jon. 1. 11, 13; metaph. *to be agitated* by adversity, Is. 54. 11.—II. *to rage,* as a foe, Hab. 3. 14. Niph. *to be agitated, disquieted,* 2 Ki. 6. 11. Pi. *to scatter,* Zec. 7. 14. Po. *to be scattered,* Hos. 13. 3.

סַעַר masc. dec. 6 d, *storm, tempest.*

סְעָרָה f. d. 11 c (constr. סַעֲרַת § 42. r. 1) id.

סַעַר וְ' noun masc. sing. dec. 6 d . . . סער

סֹעֵר[o] וְ Kal part. act. sing. masc. . . . סער

סְעָרָה וּ' noun f. s. d. 11 c (constr. סַעֲרַת § 42. r. 1) סער

סֹעֲרָה[p] Kal part. act. sing. fem. of סֹעֵר . סער

סְעָרוֹת[q] noun fem. pl. abs. from סְעָרָה dec. 11 c . סער

סַעֲרַת id. sing., constr. st. (§ 42. rem. 1) . סער

סַף[r] וְ' n. m. s. (suff. סִפִּי) d. 8 e, also pr. name ספף

ספא Root not used; Arab. *to satiate;* Chald. *to feed.*

מִסְפּוֹא masc. *provender, fodder.*

[סָפַד] fut. יִסְפֹּד *to mourn, lament, bewail,* const. with לְ, עַל, לִפְנֵי. Niph. *to be lamented.*

מִסְפֵּד m. d. 7 c (comp. § 36. r. 1) *lamentation.*

סָפְדָה[s] וְ Kal pret. 3 pers. sing. fem. . . ספד

סָפְדוּ וְ id. pret. 3 pers. pl. . . . ספד

סִפְדוּ[t] וְ' id. imp. pl. masc. . . . ספד

סֹפְדִים[u] id. part. masc. pl. [of סֹפֵד] dec. 7 b . ספד

סְפֹדְנָה[x] id. imp. pl. fem. . . . . ספד

[סָפָה] I. *to take off,* as the beard; *to take away,* as life; hence, *to destroy.*—II. intrans. *to be taken away, to perish.*—III. i. q. יָסַף *to add; to increase.* Niph. I. *to betake, withdraw oneself,* Is. 13. 15.—II. *to be taken away, destroyed, to perish.* Hiph. *to heap up, accumulate,* De. 32. 23.

סָפוּ[y]
וְסָפוּ[z] } Kal pret. 3 pers. pl.; acc. shifted by conv. וְ (comp. § 8. rem. 7) . . } סוף

---

a 2 Sa. 15. 1. b Pr. 20. 28. c Ju. 19. 5. d 1 Ki. 13. 7. e Ge. 18. 5. f Ps. 119. 117. g Ps. 55. 9. h De. 2. 24. i Ju. 15. 11. k Is. 57. 5. l Is. 27. 10. m Ps. 119. 113. n Eze. 31. 8. o Jon. 1. 11, 13. p Is. 54. 11. q Eze. 13. 11, 13. r Eze. 40. 7. rr Ju. 19. 8. s Zec. 12. 12. t Je. 4. 8. u Is. 32. 12. x Je. 49. 3. y Ps. 73. 19. z Am. 3. 15.

[a]סֻפוֹ ְ noun m. s., suff. 3 pers. s. m. fr. סוּף d. 1 a סוף
סְפוּ Kal imp. pl. masc. . . . . . ספה
[b]סָפוֹד ְ Kal inf. abs. . . . . . ספד
[c]סְפוֹד id. inf. constr. (§ 8. rem. 18) . . . ספד
[d]סָפוּן [e]ְ'' Kal part. pass. sing. masc. dec. 3 a . ספן
[f]סְפוּנִים id. pl., abs. st. . . . . . ספן
סְפוֹת Kal inf. constr. . . . . . ספה
[g]סִפּוֹת, [h]סַפּוֹת ְ n. m. with pl. f. term. fr. סַף d. 8 e ספף

[סָפַח] *to join*, or *admit*, 1 Sa. 2. 36. Niph. *to be joined*, Is. 14. 1. Pi. *to pour out*, Hab. 2. 15. Pu. *to be scattered*, Job 30. 7; others, *to be joined, gathered together*. Hithpa. *to join oneself*, with בְּ 1 Sa. 26. 19.

סָפִיחַ masc. dec. 3 a.—I. *an overflowing*, Job 14. 19.—II. produce of grain accidentally *spilt*, instead of being sown, *self-sown grain* (Prof. Lee).

סַפַּחַת fem. *scurf, scab*, Le. 13. 2; 14. 56.

מִסְפַּחַת fem. id. Le. 13. 6, 7, 8.

מִסְפָּחָה fem. dec. 11 a, *cushion, quilt, coverlet*, from the idea of *spreading*, Eze. 13. 18, 21.

[i]סְפָחֵנִי Kal imp. s. m. [סְפַח], suff. 1 p. s. (§ 16. r. 11) ספח
[k]סַפַּחַת noun fem. sing. . . . . . ספח
סַפַּי pr. name masc., see סַף . . . . ספף
[l]סִפִּי noun masc. sing., suff. 1 pers. s. fr. סַף d. 8 e ספף
סָפִיחַ noun masc. sing. dec. 3 a . . . ספח
[m]סְפִיחַ id., constr. st. . . . . . ספח
סְפִיחֶיהָ id. pl., suff. 3 pers. sing. fem. . . . ספח
סַפִּיר [n]ְ'' noun masc. sing. dec. 1 b . . . ספר
[o]סַפִּירִים id. pl., abs. st. . . . . . ספר

[סֵפֶל] masc. *dish, bowl*, Ju. 5. 25; 6. 38.

[p]סִפָּם noun masc. sing., suff. 3 pers. pl. masc. from סַף dec. 8 e . . . . . ספף

[סָפַן] fut. יִסְפֹּן.—I. *to cover*, spec. with *boards* or *planks*.—II. *to hide, preserve*, De. 33. 21.

סִפּוּן masc. *ceiling*, 1 Ki. 6. 15.

סְפִינָה fem. *ship*, Jon. 1. 5.

[q]סָפֻן ְ defect. for סָפוּן (q. v.) . . . . ספן

סָפַף Kal not used; Ethiop. *to extend, expand*. Hithpo. הִסְתּוֹפֵף (denom. from סַף q. v.) *to stand at the threshold*, as a door-keeper, Ps. 84. 11.

סַף masc. dec. 8 e (pl. סִפִּים, סִפּוֹת).—I. *dish, basin*.—II. *threshold*.—III. pr. name masc. 2 Sa. 21. 18, for which סִפַּי in 1 Ch. 20. 4.

[r]**סָפַק** ְ fut. יִסְפֹּק.—I. *to strike, smite* or *clap*, as the hands together, whether in anger, exultation, insolence or derision; אֶל יָרֵךְ or עַל ס' *to smite oneself on the thigh*, sc. in indignation or mourning.—II. *to smite, chastise*, Job 34. 26.—III. Je. 48. 26 *to throw oneself about*, as a drunken man (Eng vers. *wallow*). So Kimchi. Rabbin. סָפַק in Pu and Ithp. *to waver, doubt*.

סֶפֶק masc. dec. 6 b, *abundance, sufficiency*, Job 20. 22. Syr. ספק *to suffice*.

[s]סְפֹק Kal imp. sing. masc. . . . . . ספק
[t]סָפְקוּ id. pret. 3 pers. pl. . . . . . ספק
[u]סִפְקוֹ noun m. s., suff. 3 p. s. m. fr. [סֶפֶק] d. 6 b ספק
[v]סְפָקָם Kal pret. 3 pers. sing. m., suff. 3 pers. pl. m. ספק
[y]סָפַקְתִּי id. pret. 1 pers. sing. . . . . ספק

[z]**סָפַר** [a]ְ'' fut. יִסְפֹּר.—I. *to write*, only in part. סֹפֵר *writer, scribe*.—II. *to number, count*. Niph. *to be numbered*. Pi.—I. *to number, count*.—II. *to recount, relate, tell*.—III. *to speak, talk*. Pu. *to be related, told*.

סָפַר Chald. masc. dec. 2 a (prop. part. act.) *scribe*.

סֵפֶר masc. dec. 6 b.—I. *writing*, art of writing comp. Is. 29. 11.—II. *a writing, something written letter, epistle*.—III. *a book*.—IV. *enumeration*, Ge 5. 1 (Lee).

סְפַר Chald. masc. dec. 3 b, *a book*.

סְפָר masc.—I. *a numbering*, 2 Ch. 2. 16.—II. pr name of a city, Ge. 10. 30.

סִפְרָה fem. *a book*, Ps. 56. 9.

סְפֹרָה fem. dec. 10, *number*, Ps. 71. 15.

סֹפֶרֶת (*scribe*) pr. name masc. Ezr. 2. 55; Ne 7. 57.

מִסְפָּר masc. dec. 2 b.—I. *number*; אֵין מ' *without number, innumerable*; אַנְשֵׁי מ' or מְתֵי *men of number*, i. e. who can be numbered, *a few*.—II *relation, narration*, Ju. 7. 15.—III. pr. name masc Ezr. 2. 2, for which מִסְפֶּרֶת in Ne. 7. 7.

סַפִּיר masc. dec. 1 b, *a sapphire*. Etymology uncertain.

[b]סָפַר Chald. noun masc. sing. dec. 2 a . . ספר
סַפֵּר Piel imp. sing. m. (Is. 43. 26), inf. Ex. 9. 16 ספר
[c]סְפַר Ch. noun masc. sing. dec. 3 b . . ספר
[d]סְפֹר ְ Kal imp. sing. masc.; ְ bef. (:) . . ספר
[e]סֵפֶר ְ'' noun masc. sing. dec. 6 b . . . ספר
סֹפֵר Kal part. act. sing. masc. dec. 7 b . . ספר

[a] Joel 2. 20. [b] Zec. 7. 5. [c] Ec. 3. 4. [d] De. 33. 21. [e] Je. 22. 14. [f] Hag. 1. 4. [g] 2 Ki. 12. 14. [h] 2 Sa. 17. 28. [i] 1 Sa. 2. 36. [k] Le. 13. 2. [l] Eze. 43. 8. [m] Le. 25. 5. [n] Job 28. 16. [o] Ca. 5. 14. [p] Eze. 43. 8. [q] 1 Ki. 7. 3, 7. [r] Je. 48. 26. [s] Eze. 21. 17. [t] La. 2. 15. [u] Job 20. 22. [v] Job 34. 26. [y] Je. 31. 19. [z] 2 Sa. 24. 10. [a] Le. 15. 13. [b] Ezr. 7. 12, 21. [c] Ezr. 6. 18. [d] Ge. 15. 5. [e] Job 31. 35.

סִפַּר[a] Pual pret. 3 pers. sing. masc. . . ספר

סִפְרָא Ch. noun masc. sing., emph. of [סְפַר] d. 2 a ספר

סְפָרַד pr. name of a region, Ob. 20.

סָפְרָה[b] וְ Kal pret. 3 pers. sing. fem. . . . ספר

סַפְּרָה[c] Piel imp. sing. masc. (סַפֵּר) with parag. ה (comp. § 8. rem. 11) . . . ספר

סְפָרָה pr. name of a place (סְפָר) with parag. ה . ספר

סַפְּרוּ[d] / סַפְּרוּ } Piel imp. pl. masc. (comp. § 8. rem. 7, 12, 15) . . . } ספר

סִפְרוּ Kal imp. pl. masc. . . . . ספר

סִפְּרוּ Piel pret. 3 pers. pl. . . . . ספר

סְפַרְוַיִם וּ׳ pr. name of a city in Assyria. Gent. n. סְפַרְוִים 2 Ki. 17. 31; וּ bef. (:)

סְפֹרוֹת[e] noun fem. pl. of [סְפֹרָה] dec. 10 . ספר

סֹפְרֵי Kal part. act. pl. constr. masc. fr. סוֹפֵר d. 7b ספר

סִפְרַיָּא[f] Ch. noun masc. pl. emph. from סְפַר dec. 3b ספר

סְפָרִים[g] וּ׳ noun masc., pl. of סֵפֶר d. 6b; וּ bef. (:) ספר

סְפַרְוָיִם Kh. סְפָרִים, K. סְפַרְוַיִם q. v.

סֹפְרִים Kal part. act. masc. pl. of סוֹפֵר dec. 7b ספר

סִפְרִין[h] וְ Chald. noun masc., pl. of סְפַר dec. 3b ספר

סִפְרְךָ[i] noun m. s., suff. 2 pers. s. m. fr. סֵפֶר d. 6b ספר

סְפָרָם[k] Kal pret. 3 pers. sing. m., suff. 3 pers. pl. m. ספר

סָפַרְתָּ[l] וְ id. pret. 2 pers. sing. masc.; acc. shifted by conv. וְ (§ 8. rem. 7) . . . ספר

סֹפֶרֶת pr. name masc. . . . . ספר

סָפַרְתָּה[m] Kal pret. 2 pers. sing. masc. (§ 8. rem. 5) ספר

סִפַּרְתִּי[n] Piel pret. 1 pers. sing. . . . ספר

סְפַרְתֶּם[o] וּ׳[p] Kal pret. 2 pers. pl. masc.; וּ for וְ conv. ספר

סָפַת[q] Chald. Peal pret. 3 pers. sing. fem. . . סוף

סָפְתָה[r] Kal pret. 3 pers. sing. fem. . . . ספה

סָקוֹל Kal inf. abs. . . . . . . סקל

[סָקַל] *to stone.* Niph. *to be stoned.* Pi. I. *to stone,* 2 Sa. 16. 6, 13.—II. *to clear of stones.* Pu. *to be stoned,* 1 Ki. 21. 14, 15.

סֻקַּל[s] Pual pret. 3 pers. sing. masc. . . . סקל

סְקָלֻהוּ[t] וְ Kal imp. pl. masc., suff. 3 pers. sing. masc. סקל

סַקְּלוּ[u] Piel imp. pl. masc. . . . . סקל

סְקָלוּהָ[x] וּ Kal pret. 3 p. pl. m., suff. 3 p. s. f.; וּ bef. (:) סקל

סְקָלֻנִי[y] וּ id. id., suff. 1 pers. sing.; וּ id. . . סקל

סְקַלְתּוֹ[z] וּ id. pret. 2 pers. s. m., suff. 3 p. s. m.; וּ id. סקל

סְקָלְתָם[a] וּ id. id., suff. 3 pers. pl. masc.; וּ id. . סקל

סְקַלְתֶּם[b] וּ id. pret. 2 pers. pl. masc.; וּ id. . . סקל

סָר וְ׳ Kal pret. 3 p. s., or part. act. s. m. d. 1a סור

סַר adj. masc. sing. fem. סָרָה . . . סרר

סָרַב Root not used; Chald. *to be refractory.* Hence

סָרָבִים m. pl. [of סָרָב for סָרָב] *rebellious,* Eze. 2. 6

סַרְבֵּל Root not used; Chald. *to cover, clothe.* סַרְבָּלִין masc. pl. *trowsers,* Da. 3. 21, 27.

סַרְבָּלֵיהוֹן[c] וְ Ch. noun m. pl. [סַרְבָּלִין], suff. 3 p. pl. m. סרבל

סַרְגוֹן pr. name of a king of Assyria, Is. 20. 1.

סֶרֶד (*fear*) pr. name masc. Ge. 46. 14. Patronym. סַרְדִּי Nu. 26. 26.

סָרָה[d] וְ׳ Kal pret. 3 pers. sing. fem. . . . סור

סָרָה[e] adj. fem. [for סָרָה from סַר masc. . סרר

סָרָה[f] וְ׳ noun fem. sing. . . . . סור

סָרוּ[g] וְ׳ Kal pret. 3 pers. pl. . . . . סור

סֻרוּ[h] defect. for סוּרוּ (q. v.) . . . . סור

סָרוּחַ[i] Kal part. pass. sing. masc. dec. 3a . . סרח

סְרוּחֵי[k] / סְרוּחִים[l] } id. pl., constr. and abs. . . . . סרח

[סָרַח] I. *to be stretched out,* Am. 6. 4, 7.—II. *to spread forth,* of a *luxuriant* vine, Eze. 17. 6.—III. *to be redundant, to hang over* or *loose,* Ex. 26. 12, 13; Eze. 23. 15: סְרוּחֵי טְבוּלִים *redundant as to turbans,* i. e. wearing turbans long and hanging down. Niph. *to be poured out, spilt,* trop. of wisdom, Je. 49. 7; or, as in the Syr. and Chald. *to have an ill savour.* Hence

סֶרַח וְ m. *superfluous part, remainder,* Ex. 26. 12

סֶרַח pr. name, see תִּמְנַת ס׳.

סְרֻחִים[m] וּ defect. for סְרוּחִים (q. v.); וּ bef. (:) . סרח

סֹרַחַת[n] Kal part. act. sing. fem. [of סוֹרֵחַ] . סרח

סָרֵי[o] Kal part. act. pl. constr. masc. from סָר dec. 1a (§ 30. No. 3) . . . סור

סָרִיס noun masc. s. d. 1b, or 3a (comp. the foll.) סרס

סְרִיס id., constr. st. . . . . . סרס

סָרִיסֵי[p] / סְרִיסֵי[q] וְ׳ } id. pl., constr. st. . . . סרס

סָרִיסֶיהָ[r] וְ id. pl., suff. 3 pers. sing. fem. . סרס

סָרִיסָיו[s] וְ׳ id. pl., suff. 3 pers. sing. masc. . סרס

סָרִיסִים id. pl., abs. st. . . . . . סרס

[סָרַךְ] Chald. masc. dec. 2b, only in the pl., *superintendents,* Da. 6. 3—8.

סָרְכֵי[t] Chald. noun masc. pl. constr. fr. [סָרַךְ] d. 2b סרך

סָרְכַיָּא[u] Chald. id. pl., emph. st. . . . סרך

סָרְכִין[x] Chald. id. pl., abs. st. . . . . סרך

---

a Is. 52. 15. b Le. 15. 28. c 2 Ki. 8. 4. d Joel 1. 3. e Ps. 71. 15. f Ezr. 6. 1. g 2 Ch. 32. 17. h Da. 7. 10. i Ps. 139. 16. k 2 Ch. 2. 16. l Le. 25. 8. m Ps. 56. 9. n Ps. 119. 13, 26. o Is. 22. 10. p Le. 23. 15. q Da. 4. 30. r Je. 12. 4. s 1 Ki. 21. 14, 15. t 1 Ki. 21. 10. u Is. 62. 10. x De. 22. 21. y Ex. 17. 4. z De. 13. 11. a De. 17. 5. b De. 22. 24. c Da. 3. 27. d 1 Sa. 16. 14. e 1 Ki. 21. 5. f Is. 59. 13. g Ex. 8. 7. h 1 Sa. 15. 6. i Ex. 26. 13. k Eze. 23. 15. l Am. 6. 7. m Am. 6. 4. n Eze. 17. 6. o Je. 6. 28. p Est. 6. 14. q Ge. 40. 7. r Est. 4. 4. s 2 Ki. 24. 12. t Da. 6. 8. u Da. 6. 4, 5, 7. x Da. 6. 3.

[סֶרֶן] masc. dec. 6a (pl. c. סַרְנֵי) only in the pl.—I. *axles*, 1 Ki. 7. 30.—II. *princes, lords.*

סַרְנֵי ו׳ id. pl., constr. st. . . . . . סרן

סָרַס Root not used; Syr. and Chald. *to castrate.*

סָרִיס masc. constr. סְרִיס, pl. סָרִיסִים, constr. סְרִיסֵי, סָרִיסֵי (§ 32. rem. 2).—I. *an eunuch*, one castrated.—II. *courtier, chamberlain*, or *any chief officer*, as *eunuchs* were commonly entrusted with the most important offices at court; hence the Syriac everywhere renders this word by מְהֵימְנָא *faithful.*

סָרִסִים[a] וְ defect. for סָרִיסִים (q. v.) . . . סרס

סַרְעַפֹּתָיו[b] n. f. pl., suff. 3 p. s. m. fr. [סַרְעַפָּה] d. 10 סעף

סָרַף Kal not used; i. q. שָׂרַף *to burn.* Pi. id. Am. 6. 10.

[סִרְפָּד] masc. Is. 55. 13, the name of a plant; species uncertain; Eng. vers. *brier*; most of the old versions, *nettle.*

סָרַר[c] *to be refractory, rebellious, perverse.* Arab. *bad, evil.*

סַר masc. סָרָה fem. (§ 37. rem. 7) adj. *sad, sullen, angry.*

סֹרֵרָה[d] } וְ׳ Kal part. act. sing. fem. of סוֹרֵר . סרר
סֹרֶרֶת[e] }

סָרַת[g] וְ Kal part. f. constr. [of סָרָה d. 10] fr. סָר m. סור

סַרְתִּי[h] Kal pret. 1 pers. s. [for סַרְתִּי comp. § 8. r. 7] סור

סַרְתֶּם ו׳ id. pret. 2 pers. pl. masc. . . . סור

סָתָה *Root not used*; Arab. שתא *to winter.*

סְתָו masc. *winter*, Ca. 2. 11, Kh., סְתָיו Keri.

סָתוּם[i] Kal part. pass. sing. masc. . . . סתם

סְתוּר pr. name masc. . . . . . סתר

סָתַם[k] I. *to stop up, obstruct.*—II. *to shut up, conceal.* Niph. *to close, repair* a breach, Ne. 4. 1. Pi. *to stop up*, Ge. 26. 15, 18.

סְתֹם Kal imp. sing. masc. . . . . . סתם

סִתְּמוּם[l] Piel pret. 3 pers. pl., suff. 3 pers. pl. masc. (for ן fem. § 2. rem. 5) . . . סתם

סְתֻמִים[m] Kal part. pass. pl. masc. from סָתוּם dec. 3a סתם

[סָתַר] *to hide, conceal oneself*, Pr. 22. 3. Niph. I. *to be hid, to lie hidden* or *concealed, secreted*; hence *to be unknown*; part. נִסְתָּרוֹת *hidden, secret things*.—II. *to hide oneself.* Pi. *to hide, conceal*, Is. 16. 3. Pu. *to be hid, secret*, Pr. 27. 5. Hiph. הִסְתִּיר.—I. *to hide, cover*, as the face; hence, *to hide one's face*, i. e. to disregard.—II. *to hide, conceal*, with מִפְּנֵי, מִן from any one.—III. *to protect, defend.* Hithp. הִסְתַּתֵּר (for הִתְסַתֵּר) *to hide oneself.*

סְתַר Chald. Pa. id.—I. part. pass. pl. *hidden secret things*, Da. 2. 22.—II. *to destroy*, prop. *to put out of sight*, Ezr. 5. 12.

סֵתֶר masc. dec. 6b.—I. prop. *a hiding*, hence *secrecy*; בַּסֵּתֶר *secretly.*—II. *a covering, hiding place, secret place.*—III. *shelter, protection.*

סִתְרָה fem. *shelter, protection*, De. 32. 38.

סִתְרִי (for סִתְרִיָּה *protection of the Lord*) pr. name masc. Ex. 6. 22.

סְתוּר (*hidden, protected*) pr. name m. Nu. 13. 13.

מִסְתּוֹר masc. *hiding place*, Is. 4. 6.

מִסְתָּר m. dec. 2b.—I. *secret place.*—II. *lurking place, an ambush.*

סָתֶר[n] in pause [for סֵתֶר § 35. rem. 2] Seg. noun masc. see סֵתֶר . . . . . סתר

סֵתֶר וְ׳ noun masc. sing. dec. 6b . . . סתר

סַתְרֵהּ[o] Chald. Peal pret. 3 p. s. m., suff. 3 p. s. m. סתר

סִתְרָה[p] noun fem. sing. . . . . . סתר

סִתְרוֹ[q] noun m. s., suff. 3 pers. s. m. fr. סֵתֶר d. 6b סתר

סַתְּרִי[r] Piel imp. sing. fem. . . . . סתר

סִתְרִי וְ pr. name masc. . . . . . סתר

סִתְרִי[s] noun masc. s., suff. 1 pers. s. fr. סֵתֶר d. 6b סתר

סְתָרִים[t] id. pl. abs. st. . . . . . . סתר

ע

עָב ו׳ n. m. s. d. 1 (§30. No.3, yet once עַב constr.) עוב

עָב[u] וְ noun masc. sing. comp. עֻבִּים . . עבב

עָבַב Root not used; Chald. *to cover, hide.*

עָב masc. a term in architecture, *a covering* of planks. Vulg. *epistylium*, a roof supported on columns so as to form a portico. Gesenius, *thresholds, steps.* 1 Ki. 7. 6; Eze. 41. 25; pl. עֻבִּים (from עֹב) ver. 26.

עָבַד[x] וְ׳ fut. יַעֲבֹד.—I. *to work, labour*, variously; when spoken of the ground, *to till, cultivate*; of a vine

---

[a] Je. 41. 16. [b] Eze. 31. 5. [c] Ho. 4. 16. [d] Ho. 4. 16. [e] Zec. 7. 11. [f] Pr. 7. 11. [g] Pr. 11. 22. [h] Ps. 119. 102. [i] Eze. 28. 3. [k] 2 Ch. 32. 30. [l] Ge. 26. 15. [m] Da. 12. 9. [n] Pr. 25. 23. [o] Ezr. 5. 12. [p] De. 32. 38. [q] Ps. 18. 12. [r] Is. 16. 3. [s] Ps. 119. 114. [t] Pr. 9. 17. [u] 1 Ki. 7. 6; Eze. 41. 25. [x] Nu. 18. 23.

yard, *to dress it*, De. 28. 39.—II. *to serve, work for* another, const. with acc., לְ, עִם of the person served; *to serve* God, or idols, i. e. *to worship* them.—III. with בְּ *to impose servitude upon, make to serve.* Niph. I. *to be cultivated, tilled.*—II. *to be served*, Ec. 5. 8. Pu. with בְּ *labour to be imposed upon.* Hiph. I. *to cause* or *compel to work* or *labour.*—II. *to cause to serve*; also, *to reduce to servitude.*—III. *to weary*, Is. 43. 23, 24. Hoph. הָעֳבַד *to be made to serve.*

עֲבַד Chald. *to make* or *do.* Ithpe. pass.

עֶבֶד masc. dec. 6 a (with suff. עַבְדִּי).—I. *a servant, slave*; also applied to *a vassal*, and any one employed in the service of a king; frequently used as a submissive epithet in addressing a superior; עֶבֶד יְהוָֹה *servant of the Lord*, one *doing* the will of God, as a true worshipper; or one *executing* the purpose of God, as a mere instrument, comp. Je. 25. 9.—II. pr. name masc. of two different persons.

עֶבֶד־מֶלֶךְ (*servant of the king*) pr. name of an Ethiopian in the service of Zedekiah. Je. 38. 7; 39. 16.

עֲבֵד נְגוֹ, עֲבֵד נְגוֹא (*servant of Nego*, i. e. *of expedition*; Simonis, coll. Arab.) pr. name given in Babylon to Azariah one of Daniel's companions.

עֲבַד Chald. masc. dec. 3 a, i. q. עֶבֶד, *servant.*

עֲבָד masc. dec. 1 a, *work, deed*, Ec. 9. 1.

עוֹבֵד (*serving*) pr. name masc. of several persons.

עֹבֵד אֱדֹם (*serving Edom*) pr. name of a Levite.

עַבְדָּא (*servant*) pr. name masc.—I. 1 Ki. 4. 6. —II. Ne. 11. 17, for which עֹבַדְיָה in 1 Ch. 9. 16.

עַבְדְּאֵל (*servant of God*) pr. name masc. Je. 36. 26.

עֲבֹדָה, עֲבוֹדָה fem. dec. 10.—I. *work, labour.* —II. *tillage, agriculture.*—III. *work, employment, business.*—IV. *service*; also *religious service.*—V. *service, use, benefit.*

עֲבֻדָּה fem. coll. *body of servants, domestics.*

עַבְדּוֹן (*servile*) pr. name of a city of the Levites in the tribe of Asher.

עַבְדוּת fem. dec. 10, *servitude, bondage.*

עַבְדִּי (for עַבְדִּיָּה *servant of the Lord*) pr. name masc. of three different persons.

עַבְדִּיאֵל (*servant of God*) pr. name m. 1 Ch. 5. 15.

עֹבַדְיָה, עֹבַדְיָהוּ (*servant of the Lord*) pr. name masc. of several persons, especially of a prophet at the time of Jeremiah.

עֲבִידָא Chald. fem. dec. 8 a.—I. *work, labour.*—II. *business, public business.*—III. *service, worship*, Ezr. 6. 18.

מַעְבָּד masc. dec. 1 b (Heb. & Chald.) *work, doing*, Job 34. 25; Da. 4. 34.

עָבֶד in pause for עֶבֶד (q. v. and § 35. rem. 2) עבד

עָבֵד[a] וְ׳ Chald. Peal part. act. sing. masc. . עבד

עֲבַד Chald. Peal pret. 3 pers. sing. masc.; or (Da. 6. 21) noun masc. dec. 3 a . . . עבד

עֲבֵד וְ׳ pr. name in compos. עֲבֵד נְגוֹ; וַ bef. (-:) עבד

עֲבֹד Kal imp. s. m. (1 Sa. 26. 19); or inf. constr. עבד

עֲבָד־[b] id. inf. with Mak. (§ 8. rem. 18) . . עבד

עֶבֶד וְ׳ noun masc. sing. (suff. עַבְדִּי) dec. 6 a, also pr. name, and in compos. עֶבֶד מֶלֶךְ . עבד

עֹבֵד וְ׳ Kal part. act. sing. masc.; also pr. name in compos. עֹבֵד אֱדֹם . . . עבד

עֻבַּד Pual pret. 3 pers. sing. masc. . . . עבד

עָבְדָא[c] Chald. Peal part. act. sing. fem. of עָבֵד עבד

עַבְדָּא וְ׳, עַבְדְּאֵל pr. names masc. . . . עבד

עֲבָדָהּ[d] וַ Kal pret. 3 pers. sing. masc., suff. 3 pers. sing. fem.; וַ bef. (-:) . . . עבד

עֲבֹדָה[e] וַ׳ noun fem. sing. dec. 10; וַ id. . עבד

עֲבֻדָּה וַ noun fem. sing.; וַ id. . . . עבד

עֲבָדָהוּ[f] וַ defect. for עֲבָדוּהוּ (q. v.) . . עבד

עָבְדֵהוּ[g] וְ Kal imp. sing. masc., suff. 3 pers. sing. m. עבד

עִבְדֻהוּ[h] וְ id. imp. pl. m. (עִבְדוּ), suff. 3 pers. s. m. עבד

עֲבָדָו[i] וַ׳[k] Kh. for עֲבָדָיו (q. v.) . . . עבד

עָבְדוּ[l] וְ / עָבְדוּ וְ׳ Kal pret. 3 pers. pl. (§ 8. rem. 7) . עבד

עֲבָדוֹ וַ׳ id. pret. 3 p. s. m., suff. 3 p. s. m.; וַ bef. (-:) עבד

עֲבַדוּ[m] וַ׳ Chald. Peal pret. 3 pers. pl. masc.; וַ id. עבד

עַבְדּוֹ וְ׳ noun m. s., suff. 3 p. s. m. fr. עֶבֶד d. 6 a עבד

עַבְדָּו[n] Kh. עַבְדּוֹ q. v., K. עַבְדֶּךָ (q. v.) . עבד

עֲבֹדוּ[o] / עִבְדוּ וְ׳ Kal imp. pl. masc. (§ 8. rem. 12) . עבד

עֲבָדוּהוּ[p] id. pret. 3 pers. pl., suff. 3 pers. sing. masc. עבד

עַבְדוֹהִי Chald. noun masc. pl., suff. 3 pers. sing. masc. from עֲבַד dec. 3 a . . . . עבד

עֲבָדוּךָ[q] וַ׳[r] Kal pret. 3 p. pl., suff. 2 p. s. m.; וַ bef. (-:) עבד

עֲבָדוּם[s] וַ׳ id., suff. 3 pers. pl. masc.; וַ id. עבד

עַבְדּוֹן pr. name of a man or place . . עבד

עֲבָדַי וַ׳ the foll. with suff. 1 pers. sing.; וַ bef. (-:) עבד

עַבְדֵי וְ׳ noun masc. pl. constr. from עֶבֶד dec. 6 a עבד

עַבְדִּי וְ׳ pr. name masc. . . . עבד

עַבְדִּי וְ׳ noun m. s., suff. 1 pers. s. fr. עֶבֶד d. 6 a עבד

עֹבְדֵי Kal part. act. pl. constr. masc. fr. עֹבֵד d. 7 b עבד

עַבְדִּיאֵל, עֹבַדְיָה וְ׳, עֹבַדְיָהוּ וְ׳ pr. names masc. . עבד

עֲבָדֶיהָ וַ noun masc. pl., suff. 3 pers. sing. fem. from עֶבֶד dec. 6 a; וַ bef. (-:) . . עבד

---

[a] Da. 6. 28. [b] Je. 34. 9, 10. [c] Da. 7. 21. [d] Je. 27. 11. [e] Nu. 8. 26. [f] Je. 28. 14. [g] 1 Ch. 28. 9. [h] 1 Sa. 7. 3. [i] 1 Sa. 18. 22. [k] Je. 22. 4. [l] Nu. 4. 26. [m] Ezr. 6. 16. [n] 2 Sa. 14. 22. [o] Eze. 20. 39. [p] Ju. 10. 6. [q] Ne. 9. 35. [r] De. 20. 11. [s] Je. 8. 2.

עַבְדֵיהֶם id. pl., suff. 3 pers. pl. masc. . . עבד

עֲבָדֵיהֶם[i] וַ noun masc. pl. with suff. 3 pers. sing. m. fr. [עֲבָד] d. 1 a (§ 30. No. 3); וַ bef. (-:) עבד

עֲבָדָיו וַ' noun masc. pl., suff. 3 pers. sing. masc. from עֶבֶד dec. 6 a; וַ id. . . . עבד

עֹבְדָיו[k] Kal part. act. pl. masc., suff. 3 pers. sing. masc. from עֹבֵד dec. 7 b . . . עבד

עֲבָדֶיךָ וַ' noun masc. pl., suff. 2 pers. sing. masc. from עֶבֶד dec. 6 a; וַ bef. (-:) . . עבד

עַבְדָיךְ[e] Chald. noun masc. pl., suff. 2 pers. sing. masc. from עֲבַד dec. 3 a . . . עבד

עַבְדֵיכֶם וְ'[d] noun masc. pl., suff. 2 pers. pl. masc. from עֶבֶד dec. 6 a . . . . עבד

עֲבָדִים וַ' id. pl., abs. st.; וַ bef. (-:) . . עבד

עֹבְדִים וְ'[e] Kal part. act. masc., pl. of עֹבֵד dec. 7 b עבד

עָבְדִין[f] Chald. Peal part. act. m., pl. of עָבֵד d. 2 b עבד

עֲבָדְךָ[g] וַ' Kal pret. 3 pers. sing. masc., suff. 2 pers. sing. masc.; וַ bef. (-:) . . . עבד

עַבְדְּךָ / עַבְדֶּךָ וְ' } noun masc. sing., suff. 2 pers. sing. masc. from עֶבֶד dec. 6 a . } עבד

עָבְדֶךָ[h] Kal inf. [for עָבְדְךָ], suff. 2 pers. sing. masc. עבד

עַבְדְּכֶם noun m. s., suff. 2 pers. pl. m. fr. עֶבֶד d. 6 a עבד

עֲבָדִם[i] וַ defect. for עֲבָדִים (q. v.) . . . עבד

עָבַדְתָּ[k] וְ / עָבַדְתָּ[l] / עָבַדְתָּ וְ } Kal pret. 2 pers. sing. masc. (§ 8. r. 7) עבד

עֲבַדְתְּ[m] Chald. Peal pret. 2 pers. sing. masc. . עבד

עַבְדֵת Chald. id. pret. 1 pers. sing. . . עבד

עֲבֹדַת וַ'[n] noun f. s., constr. of עֲבוֹדָה d. 10; וַ bef. (-.) עבד

עֲבֹדָתוֹ id., suff. 3 pers. sing. masc. . . עבד

עָבַדְתִּי / עָבַדְתִּי[o] וְ } Kal pret. 1 pers. sing.; acc. shifted by conv. וְ (§ 8. rem. 7) . . } עבד

עֲבֹדָתִי[p] noun f. sing., suff. 1 pers. s. fr. עֲבוֹדָה d. 10 עבד

עֲבַדְתִּיךָ Kal pret. 1 pers. sing., suff. 2 pers. sing. m. עבד

עֲבֹדַתְכֶם noun f. s., suff. 2 pers. pl. fr. עֲבוֹדָה d. 10 עבד

עֲבַדְתָּם וַ Kal pret. 2 pers. sing. masc., suff. 3 pers. pl. masc.; וַ for וְ, conv. . . עבד

עֲבַדְתֶּם וַ id. pret. 2 pers. pl. masc.; וַ id. . . עבד

עֲבֹדָתָם noun masc. sing., suff. 3 pers. pl. masc. from עֲבוֹדָה dec. 10 . . . . עבד

עֲבֹדָתֵנוּ[r] id., suff. 1 pers. pl. . . . עבד

עֲבַדְתַּנִי[s] וַ Kal pret. 2 pers. sing. masc., suff. 1 pers. sing.; וַ for וְ, conv. . . . עבד

עָבָה *to be thick, gross.*

עֳבִי masc. *density, compactness.*

עֳבִי masc. dec. 6 k, *thickness.*

מַעֲבֶה masc. dec. 9 a, *density, compactness,* 1 Ki. 7. 46.

עֲבוֹדָה[t] וַ' noun fem. sing. dec. 10; וַ bef. (-:) . עבד

עֲבוֹדַת וַ'[pp] id., constr. st.; וַ id. . . . עבד

עֲבוֹדָתִי[u] id., suff. 1 pers. sing. . . . עבד

עֲבוֹדָתָם[x] id., suff. 3 pers. pl. masc. . . . עבד

עָבוֹר[y] Kal inf. abs. . . . . . עבר

עֲבוֹר id. inf. constr. (§ 8. rem. 18) . . עבר

עָבוֹת noun com., pl. of עָב dec. 1 (§ 30. No. 3, yet once, constr. עָב) . . . עבה

עָבֹת[z] adj. masc. sing. comp. עָבֹת . . עבת

עֲבוֹת[a] noun com. sing. dec. 1 a . . . עבת

עֲבוֹתִים id. pl., abs. st. . . . . עבת

[עָבַט] fut. יַעֲבֹט *to give a pledge,* De. 24. 10; hence, *to borrow* upon a pledge, De. 15. 6. Pi. *to change, alter,* a course, Joel 2. 7. Prof. Lee, *to break the ranks.* Hiph. *to lend* upon a pledge, De. 15. 6, 8.

עֲבוֹט masc. dec. 1 a, *a pledge,* De. 24. 10, 11, 12.

עַבְטִיט masc. *an accumulation of debts,* Hab. 2. 6. Eng. vers. "thick clay."

עֲבֹטוֹ[b] noun m. s., suff. 3 pers. s. m. fr. עֲבוֹט d. 1 a עבט

עַבְטִיט[c] noun masc. sing. . . . עבט

עָבֵי noun masc. pl. constr. fr. עָב d. 1 a (§ 30. No. 3) עוב

עֲבִידַת Ch. noun fem. sing., constr. of [עֲבִידָא] d. 8 a עבד

עֲבִידְתָּא[d] וַ'[e] Chald. id., emph. st.; וַ bef. (-:) . עבד

עָבָיו[f] noun masc. pl., suff. 3 pers. sing. masc. from עָב dec. 1 a (§ 30. No. 3) . . עוב

עָבְיוֹ וְ noun masc. sing., suff. 3 pers. sing. masc. [from עֳבִי] dec. 6 k . . . עבה

עָבִים noun masc. pl. of עָב dec. 1 a (§ 30. No. 3) עוב

עָבִיתָ[g] Kal pret. 2 pers. sing. masc. . . עבה

עָבַל Root not used; Arab. (conj. IV) *to be leafless, stripped of leaves.*

עוֹבָל (*stripped of foliage*) pr. name of a region, and a people descended from Joktan.

עֵיבָל (id.) pr. name of a rock in the northern part of mount Ephraim.

עָבַר וְ' fut. יַעֲבֹר.—I. *to pass over,* as a river, a sea, const. with acc., or בְּ; and with אֶל of the place to which; *to pass over* any thing, and hence *to transgress;* spoken of water, *to overflow;* of an army, *to overwhelm; to pass over* to the side or cause of any one, with עַל, Is. 45. 14.—II. *to pass through* a place, country, &c. with acc., בְּ,

---

[a] Ec. 9. 1. [b] 2 Ki. 10. 19. [c] Ezr. 4. 11. [d] De. 12. 12. [e] 1 Ki. 5. 1. [f] Ezr. 4. 15. [g] De. 15. 18. [h] Job 39. 9. [i] Ge. 24. 35. [k] De. 28. 39. [l] De. 28. 47. [m] Da. 4. 32. [n] Nu. 4. 47; Is. 32. 17. [o] 2 Sa. 15. 8. [p] Ge. 30. 26. [pp] 2 Ch. 31. 21. [q] Nu. 18. 31. [r] Ne. 10. 38. [s] Ge. 29. 15. [t] 1 Ch. 28. 14, 21. [u] 2 Ch. 12. 8. [x] 1 Ch. 6. 17. [y] 2 Sa. 17. 16. [z] Eze. 20. 28. [a] Ps. 129. 4. [b] De. 24. 10. [c] Hab. 2. 6. [d] Da. 2. 49. [e] Ezr. 5. 8. [f] Ps. 18. 13. [g] De. 32. 15.

בֵּין, בְּתוֹךְ, also absolutely; Ge. 23. 16, כֶּסֶף עֹבֵר *money passing, current.*—III. *to pass by, along* a place or person, with לִפְנֵי, עַל פְּנֵי, מֵעַל, עַל; metaph. *to pass by,* i. e. *forgive* transgression.—IV. *to pass away,* of time; *to pass away, vanish; to pass away, perish.*—V. *to pass, pass on, move on, go further,* with אַחֲרֵי, לִפְנֵי, מִן from, before, after any one; עָבַר וְשָׁב *to pass on and return;* עָבַר בִּבְרִית *to enter into a covenant.*—VI. const. with עַל (rarely acc.) *to pass, go* or *come upon* any one, *to overwhelm, overcome, assail.*—VII. *to drop* as a liquid, Ca. 5. 5, 13. Niph. *to be passed,* Eze. 47. 5. Pi. I. *to cause to pass,* as a bar, bolt; hence *to bar, bolt,* 1 Ki. 6. 21.—II. *to conceive, become pregnant,* Job 21. 10. Hiph. הֶעֱבִיר.—I. *to cause to pass over, send* or *conduct over,* e. g. a river; *to transfer* from place to place; *to cause to transgress* a law, 1 Sa. 2. 24; ה׳ תַּעַר עַל *to cause a razor to pass upon, to shave,* Nu. 8. 7.—II. *to cause to pass through;* ה׳ קוֹל בְּ *to cause to proclaim throughout.*—III. *to cause to pass by;* trop. of sin, *to remit, forgive.*—IV. *to cause to pass, go* or *come, to bring, offer.*—V. *to lead, take* or *put away, to remove;* hence *to avert* evil, reproach. Hithpa. *to be angry,* prop. *to allow oneself to go beyond proper limits,* to give way to one's feelings; with acc., בְּ, עִם, עַל; also *to be proud,* Pr. 14. 16.

עֵבֶר masc. dec. 6b (with suff. עֶבְרוֹ § 35. rem. 6).—I. *passage* of a river, *a ford.*—II. *a mountain pass,* 1 Sa. 26. 13.—III. *a region* or *country near* a river or sea on either *side.*—IV. *a side;* אֶל־עֵבֶר *beyond, over,* De. 30. 13; *over against,* Jos. 22. 11; *towards,* Ex. 28. 26; אֶל־עֵבֶר פְּנֵי *in front of,* Ex. 25. 37; אֶל־עֵבֶר פָּנָיו *forwards, straight forwards;* לְעֶבְרוֹ *straight forwards;* מֵעֵבֶר *from the other side; on the other side; beyond.*—V. pr. name, *Eber;* (*a*) the grandson of Shem, and progenitor of Abraham; (*b*) Ne. 12. 20; (*c*) 1 Ch. 8. 12; (*d*) 1 Ch. 8. 22; (*e*) 1 Ch. 5. 13.

עֲבַר Chald. i. q. עֵבֶר No. III.

עֲבָרָה fem. dec. 11c (§ 42. rem. 1).—I. *a ferry-boat,* 2 Sa. 19. 19.—II. עֲבָרוֹת 2 Sa. 15. 28, Kh. for עַרְבוֹת Keri q. v.

עֶבְרָה fem. dec. 12b (pl. c. עֶבְרוֹת, עַבְרוֹת).—I. *anger,* comp. Hithpa.—II. *pride, haughtiness.*

עִבְרִי noun gent. masc. *a Hebrew,* pl. עִבְרִים, עִבְרִיִּים; fem. עִבְרִיָּה, pl. עִבְרִיּוֹת.

עֲבָרִים (*regions beyond*) pr. name, *Abarim,* Je. 22. 20; fully הַר־הָעֲבָרִים or הָרֵי הָעֲ׳ a range of hills beyond Jordan over against Jericho.

עַבְרֹנָה (*passage*) pr. name of a station of the Israelites, Nu. 33. 34.

עָבוּר masc. only constr. עֲבוּר *produce* of the ground, Jos. 5. 11, 12.

עָבוּר prop. subs. *transition;* always with בְּ pref. בַּעֲבוּר.—I. prep. *because of; for, in return for.*—II. conj. *because; that, for the purpose that; while,* 2 Sa. 12. 21; לְבַעֲבוּר, בַּ׳ אֲשֶׁר *for the purpose that.*

מַעֲבָר masc. dec. 2b.—I. *place of passing,* Is. 30. 32.—II. *ford,* Ge. 32. 23.—III. *mountain pass,* 1 Sa. 13. 23.

מַעְבָּרָה fem. dec. 11a.—I. *ford.*—II. *mountain pass.* Pl. abs. מַעְבָּרוֹת prop. from מַעְבֶּרֶת.

עָבַר ו׳ Kal pret. 3 p. s. m. for עָבַר (comp. § 8. r. 7) עבר
עֲבַר Chald. noun masc. sing. . . . עבר
עֲבֹר ו׳ Kal inf., or imp. sing. masc. . . עבר
יַעֲבֹר[a] Kh. עָבַר q. v., K. יַעֲבֹר (q. v.) . עבר
עֵבֶר ו׳ noun masc. sing. dec. 6 (§ 35. rem. 6), also pr. name . . . . עבר
עִבַּר[b] Piel pret. 3 pers. sing. masc. (§ 10. rem. 1) עבר
עֹבֵר ו׳[c] Kal part. sing. masc. dec. 7 b . . עבר
עָבְרָה ו׳[d] id. pret. 3 pers. sing. fem. . . עבר
עֶבְרָה ו׳[e] noun fem. sing. dec. 12 b . . . עבר
עָבְרוּ / עָבְרוּ ו׳ } Kal pret. 3 pers. pl. (§ 8. rem. 7) . עבר
עָבְרוֹ id. inf., suff. 3 pers. sing. masc. . . עבר
עֲבָרוֹ ו׳[f] id. pret. 3 pers. sing. m., suff. 3 pers. s. m. עבר
עִבְרוּ ו׳ id. imp. pl. masc. . . . . עבר
עֲבָרוֹת[g] noun fem. pl. abs. from עֲבָרָה dec. 12 b (comp. § 35. rem. 6) . . . עבר
עֶבְרוֹת[h] id. pl., constr. st. . . . . עבר
עָבְרִי Kal inf., suff. 1 pers. sing. . . . עבר
עִבְרִי[i] / עִבְרִי } id. imp. sing. fem. (§ 8. rem. 12) . עבר
עִבְרִי ו׳ gent. noun from עֵבֶר (q. v.) . . עבר
עֹבְרֵי Kal part. act. pl. constr. masc. fr. עוֹבֵר d. 7b עבר
עֶבְרֵיהֶם[k] noun masc. pl., suff. 3 pers. pl. masc. from עֵבֶר dec. 6d (§ 35. rem. 6) . . עבר
עֲבָרָיו id. pl. with suff. 3 pers. sing. masc. . עבר
עִבְרִים ו׳ gent. noun, pl. of עִבְרִי from עֵבֶר . עבר
עֹבְרִים Kal part. act. masc., pl. of עוֹבֵר dec. 7b . עבר
עָבְרְכֶם[l] id. inf., suff. 2 pers. pl. masc. . . עבר
עֶבְרֹן ו pr. name of a place, see עַבְדּוֹן. R. . עבר
עָבַרְנוּ ו׳[m] Kal pret. 1 pers. pl. . . . עבר
עָבְרֵנוּ[n] id. inf., with suff. 3 pers. pl. masc. . עבר

[a] Is. 28. 15. [b] Job 21. 10. [c] Mi. 7. 18. [d] 2 Sa. 19. 19. [e] Is. 13. 9. [f] Je. 23. 9. [g] Job 21. 30. [h] Job 40. 11. [i] Is. 23. 12. [k] Ex. 32. 15. [l] Jos. 4. 23. [m] Ju. 19. 12. [n] Jos. 4. 23.

[a] עֲבָרְנוּ id. with suff. 1 pers. pl., Kh. עֲבָרֵנוּ, or suff. 3 pers. pl. masc., K. עֲבָרָם . . . עבר

עֲבַרְתָּ / [b] וְעָבַרְתָּ } id. pret. 2 pers. sing. masc.; acc. shifted by conv. וְ (§ 8. rem. 7) . . עבר

עֶבְרַת noun fem. sing., constr. of עֶבְרָה dec. 12 b (comp. § 35. rem. 6) . . עבר

עֶבְרָתוֹ וְ׳ id., suff. 3 pers. sing. masc. . . עבר

עָבַרְתִּי / [c] וְעָבַרְתִּי } Kal pret. 1 pers. sing.; acc. shifted by conv. וְ (§ 8. rem. 7) . . עבר

עֶבְרָתִי noun fem. sing., suff. 1 pers. sing. from עֶבְרָה dec. 12 b (comp. § 35. rem. 6) . . עבר

עֶבְרָתֶךָ id., suff. 2 pers. sing. masc. [for עֶבְרָתְךָ] . עבר

עֲבַרְתֶּם [d] וַ׳ Kal pret. 2 pers. pl. masc.; וַ for וְ, conv. עבר

[e] עֶבְרָתָם וְ noun fem. sing., suff. 3 pers. pl. masc. from עֶבְרָה dec. 12 b (comp. § 35. rem. 6) . עבר

[עָבַשׁ] *to dry up*, Joel 1. 17; others, *to rot*.

[f] עָבְשׁוּ Kal pret. 3 pers. pl. . . . . . עבש

עָבַת Kal not used; prob. *to be twisted* or *interwoven*, cogn. עָבַט, עָוַת. Pi. *to perplex, complicate*, sc. oppression, Mi. 7. 3; others, *to pervert*, sc. the cause in judgment. Hence the two following.

עָבֹת adj., f. עֲבֻתָּה *interwoven, thick, bushy*, of trees.

עֲבֹת com. dec. 1 a (pl. ־ִים, ־וֹת).—I. *wreathen work*, Ex. 28. 14, 24.—II. *a cord, line*, Ju. 15. 13, 14; hence pl. *bands*.—III. *branches with thick, entangled foliage*.

[g] עֲבֻתָּה adj. fem. sing. from עָבֹת masc. . . . עבת

[h] עֲבֹתוֹ noun com. sing., suff. 3 p. s. m. fr. עֲבֹת d. 1 a עבת

עֲבֹתִים id. pl., abs. st. . . . . . . עבת

[i] עֲבֹתֵימוֹ id. pl., suff. 3 pers. pl. masc. . . . עבת

[k] עֲבֹתֹת id. with pl. fem. term. . . . . עבת

עָג וְ pr. name masc., see עוֹג . . . עוג

[עָגַב] fut. יַעְגַּב (§ 13. rem. 5) *to love*, espec. in a bad sense, const. with acc., עַל.

עֲגָבִים masc. pl. (of עֶגֶב) *love*, Eze. 33. 31, 32.

עֲגָבָה fem. dec. 11 c (§ 42. rem. 1) *inordinate love*, Eze. 23. 11.

עוּגָב, עֻגָב, עֻגָּב masc. (once with suff. עֻגָּבִי) a kind of musical instrument supposed to be *a flute* or *organ*.

[l] עֻגָּב· וְ or accord. to some עֻגָב see עוּגָב . . עגב

[m] עָגְבָה / [n] עָגְבָה } Kal pret. 3 pers. sing. fem. (§ 8. rem. 7) עגב

[o] עֲגָבִים noun masc. pl. [of עֶגֶב] dec. 6 a . . עגב

[oo] עֻגָבִי וְ noun masc. s., suff. 1 pers. s. fr. עוּגָב d. 2 b עגב

[p] עֹגְבִים Kal part. act. masc. pl. [of עֹגֵב] dec. 7 b . עגב

[q] עַגְבָתָהּ noun fem. sing., suff. 3 pers. sing. fem. from [עֲגָבָה] dec. 11 c (§ 42. rem. 1) . עגב

עֻגָה noun fem. sing. dec. 10 [for עֻגָה, עוּגָה] . עוג

עָגוֹל in full for עָגֹל (q. v.) . . . עגל

[r] עָגוּר וְ׳ noun masc. sing. . . . . עגר

עֻגוֹת noun fem., pl. of עֻגָה (q. v.) . . עוג

[s] עֲגִיל noun masc. sing. dec. 3 a . . . עגל

[t] עֲגִילִים וַ id. pl. abs.; וַ bef. (־ֲ) . . . עגל

עָגַל Root not used; Syr. *to roll, revolve*.

עָגֹל masc. עֲגֻלָּה fem. *round, circular*.

עָגִיל masc. dec. 3 a, *earring*.

עֵגֶל masc. dec. 6 b (with suff. עֶגְלִי § 35. rem. 6).—I. *a calf, young bullock*; עֵ׳ מַסֵּכָה *a molten calf*.—II. metaph. *prince, leader*, Ps. 68. 31.

עֶגְלָה fem. dec. 12 b.—I. *cow-calf, heifer*; more fully עֶגְלַת בָּקָר prop. *a calf of the beeves*, in contradistinction to neat cattle; עֶגְלַת שְׁלִשִׁיָּה *a heifer three years old*.—II. pr. name of a wife of David.

עֲגָלָה fem. dec. 11 c (with suff. עֶגְלָתוֹ § 42. rem. 1).—I. *cart* or *waggon*.—II. *threshing-dray*, Is. 28. 27, 28.—III. *war-chariot*, Ps. 46. 10.

עֶגְלוֹן (*vitulinus*) pr. name—I. of a king of Moab, Ju. 3. 12.—II. of a city in the tribe of Judah.

מַעְגָּל masc. dec. 2 b.—I. *a track*, in which wheels roll.—II. *way, path*; hence, *way, manner of life*.—III. *a barricade of waggons*, 1 Sa. 26. 5, 7.

מַעְגָּלָה fem. dec. 11 a, i. q. מַעְגָּל Nos. II & III.

עָגֹל adj. masc. sing., pl. fem. עֲגֻלּוֹת . . עגל

עֵגֶל וְ׳ noun masc. sing. dec. 6 (§ 35. rem. 6) . עגל

עֲגָלָה noun fem. sing. dec. 11 c (§ 42. rem. 1) . עגל

עֶגְלָה noun fem. sing. (no pl. abs.) . . . עגל

עֶגְלוֹן וְ׳ pr. name of a man and a place . . עגל

עֲגָלוֹת noun fem. pl. abs. from עֲגָלָה dec. 11 c עגל

[u] עֲגֻלֹּת adj. fem. pl. [of עֲגֻלָּה] from עָגֹל masc. . עגל

עֶגְלֵי constr. of the foll. . . . . עגל

[x] עֲגָלִים וַ׳ noun masc., pl. of עֵגֶל dec. 6 (§ 35. rem. 6); וַ bef. (־ֲ) . . . . עגל

עֶגְלַיִם id. du., pr. name in compos. עֵין עֶ׳ . עין

[y] עֶגְלֵךְ id. sing. with suff. 2 pers. sing. fem. . עגל

עֶגְלָתָה pr. name of a place (עֶגְלוֹן) with parag. ה עגל

עֶגְלַת noun fem. sing., constr. of עֶגְלָה (no pl. abs.) עגל

[a] Jos. 5. 1. [b] 1 Ki. 2. 37. [c] Ex. 12. 12. [d] De. 12. 10. [e] Ge. 49. 7. [f] Joel 1. 17. [g] Eze. 6. 13. [h] Job 39. 10. [i] Ps. 2. 3. [k] Ex. 28. 24. [l] Ps. 150. 4. [m] Eze. 23. 12. [n] Eze. 23. 7, 9. [o] Eze. 33. 31, 32. [oo] Job 30. 31. [p] Je. 4. 30. [q] Eze. 23. 11. [r] Je. 8. 7; Is. 38. 14. [s] Nu. 31. 50. [t] Eze. 16. 12. [u] 1 Ki. 7. 31. [x] Am. 6. 4. [y] Ho. 8. 5.

[a]עֶגְלֹת noun fem. pl. constr. from עֶגְלָה dec. 11c (§ 42. rem. 1) . . . . . עגל

[b]עֶגְלָתוֹ id. sing. with suff. 3 pers. sing. masc. . עגל

[עָגַם] *to be sad, to grieve for* any one, with לְ only in the following form.

[c]עָגְמָה Kal pret. 3 pers. sing. fem. . . . עגם

עָגַן. Niph. *to be shut up, prevented* from marrying, Ru. 1. 13.

עָגַר Root not used; perh. i. q. נָעַר, as in the Ethiop., *to cry out;* Arab. *flexit, inflexit.*

עָגוּר masc. *the crane,* Is. 38. 14; Je. 8. 7. Gesenius takes it as an epithet of the swallow, signifying *turning round, flying in a circle.*

[d]עֻגַת [e]וְ noun fem. sing., constr. of עֻגָּה (q. v.) עוג

[f]עֻגֹת pl. of the preced. . . . . עוג

עַד וְ / עַד וָ noun m. s.; also a *prep.*, pl. c. עֲדֵי, suff. עָדֶיךָ (§ 31. rem. 5); for וָ see lett. ו — עדה

עֵד וְ, [g]וָ noun masc. sing. dec. 1a (§ 30. No. 3); וָ id. . . . . . עוד

עֹד defect. for עוֹד (q. v.) . . . . עוד

עִדֹּא pr. name masc., see עִדּוֹ . . . עדד

עָדַד Root not used; Arab. *to number, compute,* espec. time.

עֵד masc. dec. 8b, only pl. עִדִּים Is. 64. 5, *stated times,* of the *monthly courses* of women, Arab. עִדָּה.

עִדּוֹא, עִדּוֹ (*timely*) pr. name masc.—I. of a prophet, 2 Ch. 12. 15; 13. 22.—II. of the grandfather of the prophet Zechariah.

עִדָּן Chald. masc. dec. 1a, *time;* used also of *a prophetic period.*

עַדְעָדָה (*festival;* Syr. id.) pr. name of a town in the tribe of Judah, Jos. 15. 22.

עֹדֵד pr. name masc. . . . . . עוד

[h]עָדָה I. *to go* or *pass by,* with עַל, Job 28. 8.—II. *to put on,* sc. an ornament; also *to deck, adorn oneself.* Hiph. I. *to remove, put away,* a garment, Pr. 25. 20.

עֲדָה, עֲדָא Chald.—I. *to pass upon* any one, with בְּ, Da. 3. 27.—II. *to pass away, depart,* with מִ, Da. 4. 28; hence, *to be abolished.* Aph. *to take away, remove.*

עָדָה (*ornament*) pr. name—I. of a wife of Lamech.—II. of a wife of Esau, Ge. 36. 4, 12.

עַד masc.—I. *prey, spoil,* from the idea of *rushing upon,* Ge. 49. 27; Is. 33. 23; Zep. 3. 8.—II. *perpetuity, eternity;* לְעוֹלָם וָעֶד, לָעַד (for לְעֹ' וָלָעַד), עֲדֵי עַד *for ever, for ever and ever.*—III. (pl. עֲדֵי, with suff. עָדֶיךָ, § 31. rem. 5) prep. (*a*) *while, as long as;* (*b*) *to, unto, as far as;* (*c*) *until;* עַד הֵנָּה, עַד כֹּה, עַד עַתָּה *hitherto;* עַד־אָנָה, עַד־מָה, עַד־מָתַי *until when? how long?*—IV. conj. (*a*) *while, during,* with the pret. and participle; עַד־אֲשֶׁר, עַד שֶׁ *while;* עַד לֹא, עַד אֲשֶׁר לֹא *while not, while as yet not, before;* (*b*) *until;* עַד אֲשֶׁר, עַד כִּי, עַד אִם, עַד אֲשֶׁר אִם *until that;* (*c*) *so that, even so that.*

עַד Chald.—I. prep. (*a*) *during, within,* Da. 6. 8, 13; (*b*) *until;* עַד כְּעַן *until now;* (*c*) *to, for,* of purpose; עַד דִּבְרַת דִּי *to the intent that,* Da. 4. 14.—II. conj. עַד דִּי; (*a*) *while, when, meantime,* Da. 6. 25; (*b*) *until.*

עֲדֶן, עֲדֶנָּה contr. from עַד־הֵנָּה *hitherto, as yet.*

עֲדִי masc. dec. 6i (with suff. עֶדְיִי § 35. rem. 14).—I. *age,* Ps. 103, 5.—II. *ornaments.*—III. *trappings* of a horse, Ps. 32. 9.

עֲדִיאֵל (*ornament of God*) pr. name masc. of three different persons.

עֲדָיָה, עֲדָיָהוּ (whom *the Lord adorns*) pr. name masc. of several persons.

עֲדִיתַיִם (*double ornament*) pr. name of a town in the tribe of Judah, Jos. 15. 36.

עֵת com. dec. 8b (contr. from עֶדֶת) *time, season;* adv. *a long time;* כָּעֵת *at this time, now;* כָּעֵת מָחָר *about this time to-morrow;* pl. עִתִּים, עִתּוֹת *times, vicissitudes;* עִתִּים רַבּוֹת *many times, repeatedly,* Ne. 9. 28.

עֵת קָצִין (*time of the prince*) pr. name of a town in Zebulon, with ה local עִתָּה קָצִין, Jos. 19. 13.

עַתָּה adv.—I. *at this time, now;* עַד־עַתָּה *until now;* מֵעַתָּה *from this time.*—II. *soon, shortly, presently.*

עַתַּי (*opportune*) pr. name masc. of three different persons.

עִתִּי masc. adj. *fit, opportune,* Le. 16. 21.

יֶעְדּוֹ pr. name masc. 2 Ch. 9. 26, Keri.

מַעַדְיָה (*ornament of the Lord*) pr. name masc. Ne. 12. 5, for which מוֹעַדְיָה ver. 17.

מַעֲדַי (for מַעֲדְיָה) pr. name masc. Ezr. 10. 34.

עָדָה pr. name fem. . . . . . עדה

עֵדָה וְ noun fem. sing. dec. 11b . . יעד

[i]עֵדָה וְ noun fem. sing. dec. 10 (comp. § 30. No. 3) עוד

[k]עֲדֵה Kal imp. sing. masc. . . . . עדה

[a] Nu. 7. 3. [b] Is. 28. 28. [c] Job 30. 25. [d] 1 Ki. 19. 6. [e] Eze. 4. 12. [f] Ex. 12. 39. [g] Je. 29. 23. [h] Job 28. 8. [i] Ge. 31. 52. [k] Job 40. 10.

עִדּוֹ ,עִדּוֹא 'וְ } pr. name masc. . . . . . עדד

עֵדוּת n. f. s. [pl. עֵדְוֹת comp. Ch. d. 8], see the foll. עוד

עֵדְוֹתָיו 'וְ id. pl., suff. 3 pers. sing. masc. . . . עוד

עֵדוֹתָיו[a] וְ noun fem. pl., suff. 3 p. s. m. fr. עֵדָה d. 10 עוד

עֵדְוֹתֶיךָ noun f. s., suff. 2 pers. s. m. fr. עֵדוּת (q. v.) עוד

עָדַי prep. (עַד) pl. with suff. 1 p. s. (§ 31. r. 5) עדה

עֲדֵי id. pl., constr. st. . . . . . . עדה

עֲדִי noun masc. s. (suff. עֶדְיוֹ) d. 6i (§ 35. r. 14) עדה

עֵדַי[b], עֵדָי[c] } the foll. with suff. 1 pers. sing. . . . עוד

עֵדֵי noun m. pl. constr. fr. עֵד d. 1a (§ 30. No. 3) עוד

עֵדִי[d] id. sing., suff. 1 pers. sing. . . . . עוד

עֶדִי in pause for עֲדִי q. v. (§ 35. rem. 14) . עדה

עֲדִיאֵל 'וְ, עֲדָיָה 'וְ, וַ pr. names masc.; וַ bef. (-:) . עדה

עָדֶיהָ[e] prep. (עַד) pl. with suff. 3 p. s. f. (§ 31. r. 5) עדה

עֶדְיָהּ[f] n. m. s., suff. 3 p. s. f. fr. עֲדִי d. 6i (§ 35. r. 14) עדה

עֲדָיָהוּ pr. name masc., see עֲדָיָה . . . . עדה

עֵדֵיהֶם[g] 'וְ noun masc. pl., suff. 3 pers. pl. masc. from עֵד dec. 1a (§ 30. No. 3) . . . . עוד

עָדָיו[h] prep. (עַד) pl. with suff. 3 p. s. m. (§ 31. r. 5) עדה

עֶדְיוֹ n. m. s., suff. 3 p. s. m. fr. עֲדִי d. 6i (§ 35. r. 14) עדה

עֲדָיִים[i] id. pl., abs. st. . . . . . . עדה

עָדֶיךָ [k]'וְ prep. (עַד) pl. with suff. 2 p. s. m. (§ 31. r. 5) עדה

עֵדֶיךָ[l] n. m. pl., suff. 2 p. s. m. fr. עֵד d. 1a (§ 30. No. 3) עוד

עֶדְיֵךְ[m] n. m. s., suff. 2 p. s. f. fr. עֲדִי d. 6i (§ 35. r. 14) עדה

עֶדְיֵךְ[n] id. with suff. 2 pers. sing. masc. . . . עדה

עֲדֵיכֶם[o] וְ prep. (עַד) with suff. 2 pers. pl. masc. retaining (-:) against anal. (§ 31. rem. 5) עדה

עֶדְיָם[p] n. m. s., suff. 3 p. pl. m. fr. עֲדִי d. 6i (§ 35. r. 14) עדה

עֵדִים noun masc., pl. of עֵד dec. 1a (§ 30. rem. 3) עוד

עִדִּים[q] noun masc., pl. of [עִד] dec. 8b . . עדד

עָדִין pr. name masc. . . . . . . עדן

עֲדִינָא pr. name masc. . . . . . . עדן

עֲדִינָה[r] adj. fem. sing. [from עָדִין masc.] . . עדן

עֲדִינוֹ pr. name masc.; see this form under the R. עדן

עָדִית[s] וְ Kal pret. 2 pers. sing. fem. . . . עדה

עֲדִיתַיִם וַ pr. name of a place; וַ bef. (-:) . . עדה

עֵדְךָ[t] defect. for עוֹדְךָ (q. v.) . . . . עוד

עָדַל Root not used; Arab. *to be just*. Hence

עַדְלַי (for עֲדַלְיָה=עַדְלַי *justice of God*) pr. name masc. 1 Ch. 27. 29 . . . . עדל

עֲדֻלָּם וַ (*justice of the people*) pr. name of a city in Judah, in the vicinity of which was the *cave of Adullam*. Hence the foll. . עדל

עֲדֻלָּמִי gent. noun from the preced.

עָדַן Kal not used; Arab. *to be soft, lax, pliant*. Hithp. *to live luxuriously*, Ne. 9. 25.

עָדִין masc.—I. adj. *luxurious, delicate*, fem. עֲדִינָה Is. 47. 8.—II. pr. name masc. Ezr. 2. 15; Ne. 7. 20.

עֲדִינָא (*pliability*, or *voluptuousness*) pr. name masc. 1 Ch. 11. 42.

עֲדִינוֹ (for עֲדִינוֹן *pliant*, or *voluptuous*) pr. name masc. 2 Sa. 23. 8. According to Gesenius, as an appellative, *his vibration*, i. e. *brandishing* of the spear, comp. the Root. Simonis, *his smiting*, from עדן Arab. *to smite with a pointed weapon*.

עֵדֶן masc. dec. 6b.—I. *delight, pleasure*.—II. pr. name, *Eden*, the pleasant region in which the garden, גַּן עֵדֶן, the abode of our first parents, was placed.

עֶדֶן (*pleasantness*) pr. name of a region in Mesopotamia.

עַדְנָא (*pleasure*) pr. name masc. Ezr. 10. 30.

עַדְנָה (id.) pr. name masc.—I. 1 Ch. 12. 20.—II. 2 Ch. 17. 14.

עֶדְנָה fem. *pleasure*, Ge. 18. 12.

מַעֲדָן masc. only pl. מַעֲדַנִּים, מַעֲדַנּוֹת.—I. *delights, pleasure*, Pr. 29. 17; adv. *cheerfully, willingly*, 1 Sa. 15. 32.—II. *delicacies, dainties*.

עֲדֶן[u] contr. from עַד־הֵנָּה . . . . . עדה

עֵדֶן 'וְ pr. name masc. (and in compos. see בֵּית) עדן

עֶדֶן 'וְ pr. name masc.; for וָ see lett. ו . . עדן

עִדָּן[x] 'וְ Chald. noun masc. sing. dec. 1a . . עדד

עַדְנָא pr. name masc. . . . . . . עדן

עִדָּנָא[y] Chald. noun masc. sing., emph. of עִדָּן d. 1a עדד

עַדְנָה pr. name masc. . . . . . . עדן

עֲדֶנָּה[z] contr. from עַד־הֵנָּה . . . . עדה

עֶדְנָה[a] noun fem. sing. . . . . . עדן

עֹדֶנּוּ[b] 'וְ defect. for עוֹדֶנּוּ (q. v.) . . . עוד

עִדָּנַיָּא[c] Chald. noun masc. pl. emph. from עִדָּן d. 1a עדד

עֲדָנֶיךָ[d] the foll. with suff. 2 pers. sing. masc. . עדן

עֲדָנִים[e] noun masc., pl. of עֵדֶן dec. 6b . . עדן

עִדָּנִין [f]'וְ Chald. noun masc. pl. of עִדָּן dec. 1a עדד

עַדְעָדָה וְ pr. name of a place . . . . עדד

[עָדַף] I. *to be over, superabundant*, or *superfluous*.—II. *to exceed*, Nu. 3. 46, 48, 49. Hiph. *to cause to superabound, to have over*, Ex. 16. 18.

[עָדַר] *to set in order, arrange, array*. Niph. I. *to be cleansed* or *cleared*, as a vineyard, by hoeing or

[a] Ps. 78. 56. [b] Is. 44. 8. [c] Is. 43. 10, 12. [d] Job 16. 19. [e] Job 6. 20. [f] Je. 2. 32. [g] Is. 43. 9; 44. 9. [h] Is. 45. 24. [i] Eze. 16. 7. [k] Mi. 7. 12. [l] Job 10. 17. [m] Ps. 103. 5. [n] Ex. 33. 5. [o] Job 32. 12. [p] Ex. 33. 6. [q] Is. 64. 5. [r] Is. 47. 8. [s] Eze. 23. 40. [t] Job 2. 9. [u] Ec. 4. 3. [x] Da. 7. 12, 25. [y] Da. 2. 8, 9. [z] Ec. 4. 2. [a] Ge. 18. 12. [b] Job 2. 3; 8. 12. [c] Da. 2. 21. [d] Ps. 36. 9. [e] 2 Sa. 1. 24. [f] Da. 7. 25.

raking, Is. 5. 6; 7. 25.—II. *to be missing* in a mustering, comp. פָּקַד.—III. *to be left behind.* Pi. *to omit, neglect,* 1 Ki. 5. 7.

עֵדֶר masc. dec. 6b (with suff. עֶדְרוֹ § 35. rem. 6).—I. *flock, herd.*—II. pr. name of a town in the tribe of Judah, Jos. 15. 21.—III. pr. name of a man.

עֵדֶר (*flock*) pr. name masc. 1 Ch. 8. 15.

עַדְרִיאֵל (*flock of God*) pr. name of a son-in-law of king Saul.

מַעְדֵּר masc. *a rake,* Is. 7. 25.

עֵדֶר וְ pr. name m. for עֵדֶר (§ 35. r. 2); for וְ see ו — עדר
עֵדֶר וְ', וְ noun m. s. d. 6 (§ 35. r. 6), also pr. n. — עדר
עֶדְרוֹ [a] וְ' id. with suff. 3 pers. sing. masc. — עדר
עֹדְרֵי [b] Kal part. act. pl. constr. masc. [fr. עֹדֵר] d. 7b — עדר
עֶדְרֵי noun m. pl. constr. fr. עֵדֶר d. 6 (§ 35. r. 6) — עדר
עֶדְרֵיהֶם [c] וְ id. with suff. 3 p. pl. m. — עדר
עֲדָרִים [d] וַ' id. pl., abs. st.; וַ bef. (-:) — עדר
עֲדָשִׁים וַ' pl. m. *lentils.* In the Talm. the sing. is עֲדָשָׁה.
עֲדַת Chald. Peal pret. 3 pers. sing. fem. — עדה
עֲדַת וַ' noun f. s., constr. of עֵדָה d. 11b; וַ bef. (-:) — יעד
עֲדָתוֹ [e] [f] וַ' id., suff. 3 pers. sing. masc.; וַ id. — יעד
עֲדָתִי [g] id., suff. 1 pers. sing. — יעד
עֵדֹתַי [h] וְ noun fem. pl., suff. 1 pers. sing. [for עֵדְוֹתַי] (§ 4. r. 2) fr. עֵדָה d. 10 (comp. § 30. No. 3) — עוד
עֵדֹתָיו וְ' id. pl., suff. 3 pers. sing. masc. — עוד
עֵדֹתֶיךָ [i] וְ' id. pl., suff. 2 pers. sing. masc. — עוד
עֲדָתְךָ noun fem. sing., suff. 2 pers. sing. masc. from עֵדָה dec. 11b — יעד

עוּב. Hiph. *to cover with darkness, darken* (Syr. Aph. *to obscure*), La. 2. 1.

עָב masc. dec. 1a (pl. עָבִים, עָבוֹת).—I. *darkness,* chiefly of clouds.—II. *thick cloud.*—III. *a thicket,* Je. 4. 29.

עוֹבֵד וְ', עֹבַדְיָהוּ pr. names masc. — עבד
עוֹבָל pr. name masc. — עבל
עוֹבֵר Kal part. act. sing. masc. dec. 7b — עבר
עוֹבְרֵי [k] id. pl., constr. st. — עבר

עוּג *to bake cakes,* Eze. 4. 12.

עֻגָה, עֻגָּה fem. *cake, bread-cake.*

מָעוֹג masc. id. 1 Ki. 17. 12; Ps. 35. 16.

עוֹג וְ' pr. name of a king of Bashan, famous for his gigantic stature. עוֹג supposed to stand for עֲנַג, עֲנָק *long-necked, gigantic.*

עוּגָב [l] [m] וְ' noun masc. sing. dec. 2b — עגב

עוּד in Kal only, La. 2. 13 Kethib, *to say again and again, to testify.* Pi. *to surround,* Ps. 119. 61. Hiph. הֵעִיד.—I. *to call* or *take as a witness,* with בְּ *against* any one.—II. *to testify, bear witness,* with acc. *against* or *for* any one.—III. *to protest, affirm solemnly,* with בְּ of the person.—IV. *to exhort, admonish,* with בְּ, עַל.—V. *to enjoin, command.* Hoph. הוּעַד *to be testified, warning be given to,* with בְּ, Ex. 21. 29. Pil. *to set up, confirm.* Hithpal. *to keep oneself erect, upright,* Ps. 20. 9.

עוֹד, עֹד adv.—I. *again.*—II. *again and again, repeatedly.*—III. *further, besides.*—IV. *yet, as yet, still;* עוֹדֶנָּה, עוֹדֶנּוּ, עוֹדְךָ, עוֹדֶנִּי *I am, thou art, he, she is as yet* or *still.*—V. with prefixes; (*a*) בְּעוֹד, בְּעֹד *while, while yet;* בְּעֹדִי *while yet I am, while I yet have being; within yet;* (*b*) מֵעוֹד *since;* מֵעוֹדִי *since, ever since, I am.*

עוֹד Chald. *while,* Da. 4. 23.

עֹדֵד (*setting up;* for מְעוֹדֵד) pr. name masc. —I. 2 Ch. 15. 1, 8.—II. 2 Ch. 28. 9.

עֵד masc. dec. 1a (comp. § 30. rem. 3).—I. *a witness.*—II. *testimony.*—III. *proof.*

עֵדָה fem. dec. 10 (comp. עֵד).—I. *a witness* (fem.) Ge. 31. 52.—II. *testimony;* frequently of *the precepts* of God.

עֵדוּת fem. dec. 1b, pl. עֵדְוֹת (comp. Chald. d. 8, מַלְכוּ, pl. מַלְכְוָן).—I. *testimony* or *witness,* i. e. that which *testifies* or *witnesses* to the will and requirements of God; it is applied to the law, the decalogue, and the sacred rites; אֲרוֹן הָעֵדוּת *the ark of testimony,* as containing the tables of stone on which the decalogue was written; אֹהֶל הָעֵדוּת *the tabernacle of testimony,* where the sacred rites were performed.—II. the titles of Psalms 60 and 80.

תְּעוּדָה fem. *testimony* (comp. עֵדוּת No. 1) applied to the law or precepts of God, Is. 8. 16, 20; and *to custom,* Ru. 4. 7.

עוֹד וְ' (prop., inf. abs.) only as an *adv.* — עוד
עוֹדֵד pr. name masc. — עוד
עוֹדִי וְ adv. (עוֹד) with suff. 1 pers. sing. — עוד
עוֹדֵינָה [n] id. pl., suff., Kh. נָה' 3 p. pl. f., K. נוּ' 1 p. pl. — עוד
עוֹדֵךְ [o] id. sing., suff. 2 pers. sing. fem. — עוד
עוֹדְךָ [p] וְ' id. sing., suff. 2 pers. sing. masc. — עוד
עוֹדָם [q] id. sing., suff. 3 pers. pl. masc. — עוד
עוֹדֶנָּה [r] id. sing., suff. 3 pers. sing. fem. — עוד
עוֹדֶנּוּ [s] וְ' id. sing., suff. 3 pers. sing. masc. — עוד

[a] Je. 51. 23. [b] 1 Ch. 12. 38. [c] Je. 6. 3. [d] 2 Ch. 32. 28. [e] Nu. 16. 5, 6. [f] Je. 30. 20. [g] Job 16. 7. [h] Ps. 132. 12. [i] Ps. 119. 168. [k] Job 21. 29. [l] Job 21. 12. [m] Ge. 4. 21. [n] La. 4. 17. [o] 1 Ki. 1. 14. [p] Ex. 9. 2. [q] Est. 6. 14. [r] 1 Ki. 1. 22. [s] Je. 40. 5.

עִוְּדֻנִי[a] Piel pret. 3 pers. pl., suff. 1 pers. sing. . עוד

עוֹדֶנִּי adv. (עוֹד) with suff. 1 pers. sing. . עוד

[עָוָה] *to deal perversely, to sin.* Niph. I. *to be bent* with pain, Is. 21. 3.—II. *to be bowed down* with sorrow, Ps. 38. 7.—III. *to be perverse.* Pi. עִוָּה. —I. *to make crooked,* La. 3. 9.—II. *to overturn, turn upside down,* Is. 24. 1. Hiph. הֶעֱוָה.—I. *to make crooked, pervert* one's way.—II. *to act perversely.*

עַוָּא, עִוָּה (*overturning, ruin*) pr. name, *Ivvah* or *Avvah*, an Assyrian city.

עַוָּה fem. *overturning, overthrow,* Eze. 21. 32.

עַוִּי, pl. עַוִּים.—I. gent. noun, *Avites* the earliest inhabitants of Philistia.—II. the inhabitants of the city עַוָּא or עִוָּה q. v. 2 Ki. 17. 31.—III. הָעַוִּים a city in the tribe of Benjamin, Jos. 18. 23.

עָוֹן, עָווֹן masc. dec. 3 a (pl. עֲוֹנִים, עֲוֹנוֹת).—I. *iniquity, sin.*—II. *guilt.*—III. *punishment for sin.*

עֲוָיָא Chald. fem. dec. 8 a, *iniquity, sin,* Da. 4. 24.

עֲוִית (*ruins*) pr. name of a town in Edom, Ge. 36. 35.

עִוְעֶה masc. dec. 9 a, *perversity,* Is. 19. 14.

עִי masc. (for עֲוִי; pl. עִיִּים § 37. No. 4).—I. *ruin, heap of ruins.*—II. עִיִּים pr. name of a part of mount Abarim.—III. עִיִּים pr. name of a city in Judah, Jos. 15. 29.

עַי (for עֲוִי *heap of ruins*) pr. name of a Canaanitish city in the northern part of the tribe of Benjamin; called also עַיָּא, עַיָּה, עַיַּת.

עִיּוֹן (*a ruin*) pr. name of a city in the tribe of Naphtali.

מְעִי (for מְעֲוִי) masc. *a heap of ruins,* Is. 17. 1.

עַוָּה[b] noun fem. sing. . . . . . עוה

עִוָּה ןְ pr. name of a place . . . . עוה

עִוָּה[c] וְ[d] Piel pret. 3 pers. sing. masc. . . עוה

עָוֹן[e] noun masc. sing. dec. 3 a, comp. עָוֹן . עוה

עֲוֹן[f] id., constr. st. . . . . . עוה

עֲוֹנוֹתָיו[g] id. pl. fem., suff. 3 pers. sing. masc. . עוה

[עוּז] or [עָוֹז] *to flee for refuge,* with בְּ to any one, Is. 30. 2. Arab. עאז id. Hiph. *to cause to flee for refuge, safety,* with acc. Ex. 9. 19; acc. implied, *to save by flight,* sc. one's effects.

עוֹז noun masc. sing. for עֹז, (suff. עֻזִּי & עָזִּי) d. 8 c עזז

עוּזָּה[h] Kal imp. sing. masc. [עֹז] with parag. ה, [§ 18. rem. 2 & 4, for עֻזָּה] . . עזז

עוּזֵּנוּ[i] n. m. s. with suff. 1 pers. pl. fr. עֹז d. 8 c [for עֻזֵּנוּ] עזז

עוֹזֵר Kal part. act. sing. masc. dec. 7 b . עזר

עוּט Root not used; Arab. *to impress, dig in.*

עֵט masc.—I. *style, graver.*—II. *pen.*

עֲוִיל[k] noun masc. sing. . . . . . עול

עֲוִילֵיהֶם[l] noun m. pl., suff. 3 p. pl. m. fr. [עֲוִיל] d. 3 a עול

עֲוִילִים[m] id. pl., abs. st. . . . . . עול

עֲוִינוּ[n] וְ Kal pret. 1 pers. pl. . . . . עוה

עַוִּית pr. name of a place . . . . . עוה

עֲוָיָתָךְ[o] וְ Ch. noun fem. pl., suff. 2 pers. sing. masc. from [עֲוָיָא] dec. 8 a; וְ bef. (-:) . . עוה

עוֹכֵר[p] Kal part. act. sing. masc. dec. 7 b . עכר

עָוַל Kal not used; Arab. *to decline, turn aside.* Pi. *to deal unrighteously, unjustly.*

עַוָּל masc. *unjust, wicked.*

עָוֶל masc. (constr. עֲוֶל, with suff. עַוְלוֹ § 35. rem. 11) *iniquity, injustice.*

עַוְלָה fem. (with ה parag. עַוְלָתָה, contr. עֹלָתָה, pl. עֹלוֹת) *iniquity, wickedness.*

עַלְוָה fem. id. Ho. 10. 9, transp. for עַוְלָה.

עַלְוָן (*unjust*) pr. name masc. Ge. 36. 23, for which עַלְיָן 1 Ch. 1. 40.

עֲוִיל m. *wicked,* Job 16. 11; another under עול.

עוּל only in part. pl. fem. עָלוֹת.—I. *being with young.* —II. *milk-giving, milch.*

עוּל masc. (prop., part. pass. *suckled*) *suckling, child,* Is. 49. 15; 65. 20.

עֲוִיל masc. dec. 3 a (pass. § 26. No. 5; and comp. עוּל subst.) id. Job 21. 11; 19. 18.

עָוֶל noun masc. sing. with suff. עַוְלוֹ (§ 35. r. 11) עול

עַוָּל noun masc. sing. . . . . . עול

עוֹל noun masc. sing., for עֹל dec. 8 c . עלל

עוּל[q] noun masc. sing. dec. 1 a . . . עול

עַוְלָה[r] וְ noun fem. sing. (§ 43. rem.) . . עול

עוֹלָה noun fem. sing. dec. 10 . . . עלה

עוֹלֶה Kal part. act. sing. masc. dec. 9 a . עלה

עוּלָהּ[r] noun m. s., suff. 3 pers. s. f. fr. עוּל d 1 a עול

עוֹלוֹת[s] noun fem. pl. of עוֹלָה dec. 10 . . עלה

עוֹלֹתֵיכֶם[hh] id. with suff. 2 pers. pl. masc. . . עלה

עוֹלָל noun masc. sing. dec. 2 b . . . עלל

עוֹלַל[t] Poal (pass.) pret. 3 pers. sing. masc. . עלל

עוֹלֵל[u] וְ Poel inf. (Je. 6. 9; La. 1. 22); or n. m. s. d. 7 b עלל

[a] Ps. 119. 61. [b] Eze. 21. 32. [c] La. 3. 9. [d] Is. 24. 1. [e] 2 Ki. 7. 9. [f] 1 Ch. 21. 8. [g] Pr. 5. 22. [h] Ps. 68. 29. [hh] Eze. 43. 27. [i] Ps. 81. 2. [k] Job 16. 11. [l] Job 21. 11. [m] Job 19. 18. [n] Da. 9. 5. [o] Da. 4. 24. [p] 1 Ch. 2. 7. [q] Is. 65. 20. [r] Is. 49. 15. [s] Am. 5. 22. [t] La. 1. 12. [u] La. 1. 22.

עוֹלְלָה[a] id. pret. 3 pers. sing. masc. . . . . עלל

עוֹלָלוֹת[b] noun fem. pl., comp. עֹלֵלוֹת . . עלל

עוֹלְלֵי[c] noun masc. pl. constr. fr. עוֹלָל dec. 7 b . עלל

עוֹלָלֶיהָ[d] noun masc. pl., suff. 3 pers. sing. fem. from עוֹלָל dec. 2 b . . . . עלל

עוֹלָלַיִךְ id. pl., suff. 2 pers. sing. fem. . . . עלל

עוֹלָלִים id. pl., abs. st. . . . . עלל

עֹלְלִים[e] noun masc. pl. of עוֹלֵל dec. 7 b . . עלל

עוֹלַלְתָּ Poel pret. 3 pers. sing. masc. . . . עלל

עוֹלָם Kh. עוֹלָם, K. עֵילָם, pr. name of a man and a province . . . . . . עלם

עוֹלָם noun masc. sing. dec. 2 b . . . עלם

עוֹלָמֵי[f] id. pl., constr. st. . . . . עלם

עוֹלָמִים id. pl., abs. st. . . . . עלם

עוֹלַת[g] noun fem. sing., constr. of עוֹלָה dec. 10 עלה

עוֹלֹת[h] id. pl. comp. עוֹלוֹת & עֹלֹת . . . עלה

עוֹלֹת noun fem., pl. of עַוְלָה (§ 43. rem.) . עול

עַוְלָתָה id. sing. with parag. ה . . . עול

עוֹלָתוֹ[i] noun fem. sing., suff. 3 pers. sing. masc. from עוֹלָה dec. 10 . . . . עלה

עוֹלֹתֵיהֶם[k] id. pl., suff. 3 pers. pl. masc. . . עלה

עוֹלֹתֶיךָ[l] וְ id. pl., suff. 2 pers. sing. masc. . . עלה

עוֹלֹתֵיכֶם id. pl., suff. 2 pers. pl. masc. . . עלה

עוֹלָתְךָ[m] וְ id. sing., suff. 2 pers. sing. masc. . . עלה

עוֹמֵד Kal part. act. sing. masc. dec. 7 b . . עמד

עוֹמֶדֶת[n] id. part. sing. fem. dec. 13 . . . עמד

עָוַן Root not used; *to dwell.* Arab. عني *to stay;* also *to take a wife;* עאן *to be married.*

עֹנָה fem. dec. 10, *cohabitation, conjugal rights,* Ex. 21. 10.

מָעוֹן masc. dec. 3 a (pl. מְעוֹנִים § 32. rem. 5). —I. *habitation, dwelling.*—II. *refuge,* Ps. 71. 3; 90. 1; 91. 9.—III. pr. name (*a*) of a town in the tribe of Judah; (*b*) of a people, Ju. 10. 12; pl. מְעוּנִים, 2 Ch. 26. 7; (*c*) of a man, 1 Ch. 2. 45.

מְעֹנָה, מְעוֹנָה fem. d. 10.—I. *habitation, dwelling.* —II. *den* of wild beasts.—III. *refuge,* De. 33. 27.

מְעוּנִים pr. name—I. see מָעוֹן No. III (*b*).—II. of a man, Ezr. 2. 50; Ne. 7. 52.

מְעוֹנֹתַי (*my habitations*) pr. name m. 1 Ch. 4. 14.

מְעִינִים pr. name, 1 Ch. 4. 41, Kheth. i. q. מְעוּנִים No. I.

עָוֹן noun masc. sing. dec. 3 a . . . עוה

עֲוֹן id., constr. st. . . . . . עוה

עוֹיֵן[o] K. עֹיֵן, Kal part. act. sing. masc. . . עין

עֲוֹנָהּ / עֲוֹנָה[p] noun masc. sing., suff. 3 pers. sing. fem. (§ 3. rem. 3) from עָוֹן dec. 3 a . . עוה

עוֹנֶה[q] Kal part. act. sing. masc. dec. 9 a . . ענה

עֲוֹנוֹ noun masc. sing., suff. 3 pers. sing. masc. from עָוֹן dec. 3 a . . . . עוה

עֲוֹנוֹת[r] וַ֫ id. pl. fem.; וַ bef. (-:) . . . עוה

עֲוֹנוֹתֵיהֶם[s] id. pl. fem., suff. 3 pers. pl. masc. . עוה

עֲוֹנֹתָיו[t] id. pl. fem., suff. 3 pers. sing. masc. . עוה

עֲוֹנוֹתֵיכֶם id. pl. fem., suff. 2 pers. pl. masc. . עוה

עֲוֹנֹתָם[u] id. pl. fem., suff. 3 pers. pl. masc. (§ 4. r. 2) עוה

עֲוֹנִי[x] וַ id. sing., suff. 1 pers. sing.; וַ bef. (-:) . עוה

עֲוֹנֶיךָ[y] id. pl. masc., suff. 2 pers. sing. masc. . עוה

עֲוֹנֵינוּ id. pl. masc., suff. 1 pers. pl. . . עוה

עֲוֹנֶךָ / עֲוֹנְךָ id. sing., suff. 2 pers. sing. masc. . עוה

עֲוֹנֵךְ id. sing., suff. 2 pers. sing. fem. . . עוה

עֹנֶךָ[z] Kal part. act. sing. masc., suff. 2 pers. sing. masc. from עוֹנֶה dec. 9 a . . ענה

עֲוֹנֵכִי[a] noun masc. sing., suff. 2 pers. sing. fem. (§ 4. rem. 2) from עָוֹן dec. 3 a . . עוה

עֲוֹנְכֶם[b] id., suff. 2 pers. pl. masc. . . . עוה

עֲוֹנָם id., suff. 3 pers. pl. masc. . . . עוה

עוֹנֵן וְ Kal part. act. sing. masc. dec. 7 b . . ענן

עֲוֹנֵנוּ[c] [d]וַ noun masc. sing., or pl. (for עֲוֹנֵינוּ), suff. 1 pers. pl. from עָוֹן dec. 3 a; וַ bef. (-:) . עוה

עֲוֹנֹת [e]וַ id. pl. fem.; וַ id. . . . עוה

עֲוֹנֹתַי id. pl. fem., suff. 1 pers. sing. . . עוה

עֲוֹנֹתֵיהֶם[f] id. pl. fem., suff. 3 pers. pl. masc. . עוה

עֲוֹנֹתֵיכֶם id. pl. fem., suff. 2 pers. pl. masc. . עוה

עֲוֹנֹתֵינוּ [g]וַ id. pl. fem., suff. 1 pers. pl.; וַ bef. (-:) עוה

עֲוֹנֹתָם[h] [i]וַ id. pl. fem., suff. 3 pers. pl. m. (§ 4. r. 2) עוה

עִוְעִים[k] noun masc. pl. of [עִוְעֶה] dec. 9 a . עוה

עוּף[l] cogn. עוב q. v. fut. יָעוּף, ap. וַיָּעַף.—I. *to cover with the wings,* as a bird its young, Is. 31. 5; *to cover with darkness* (Syr. id.), but only intrans. and trop. of calamity, Job 11. 17.—II. *to fly, fly away,* of birds; trop. of ships, of an army; with בְּ perh. *to fly upon, attack,* Is. 11. 14 (Prof. Lee).— III. *to fly away, vanish,* of a dream, of human life.— IV. fut. ap. וַיָּעַף (§ 21. rem. 9) *to be faint, weary,* cogn. יָעַף, עָיֵף, comp. עָטַף. Pil. עוֹפֵף.—I. *to fly.*—II. *to cause to fly, brandish,* a sword, Eze. 32. 10. Hiph. *to make fly, turn quickly* the eyes, Pr. 23. 5. Hithpal. *to fly away, vanish,* Ho. 9. 11.

---

[a] La. 3. 51. [b] Je. 49. 9. [c] La. 2. 20. [d] La. 1. 5. [e] Ps. 8. 3. [f] Is. 45. 17. [g] Nu. 28. 24. [h] De. 27. 6. [i] Eze. 46. 2. [k] Is. 56. 7. [l] Ps. 50. 8. [m] Ps. 20. 4. [n] Ps. 19. 10. [o] 1 Sa. 18. 9. [p] Nu. 15. 31. [q] Is. 66. 4. [r] Ne. 9. 2. [s] Je. 33. 8. [t] Ps. 130. 8. [u] Eze. 32. 27. [x] Ps. 32. 5. [y] Eze. 28. 18. [z] Job 5. 1. [a] Ps. 103. 3. [b] Eze. 21. 29. [c] Je. 16. 10. [d] Is. 64. 5. [e] Is. 65. 7. [f] La. 5. 7. [g] Is. 59. 12. [h] Le. 16. 22. [i] Is. 53. 11. [k] Is. 19. 14. [l] Job 5. 7.

עוֹף masc. collect. *birds, fowls.*

עוֹף Chald. masc. id. Da. 2. 38; 7. 6.

עֵיפָה fem.—I. *darkness.*—II. pr. name (*a*) of a son of Midian and the tribe descended from him; (*b*) of a man, 1 Ch. 2.47; (*c*) of a woman, 1 Ch. 2.46.

עַפְעַפַּיִם masc. du. (of עַפְעַף dec. 8d) *eyelids;* poet. for *the eyes.*

מָעוּף masc. dec. 3a, *darkness*, Is. 8. 22.

מוּעָף masc. id. Is. 8. 23.

עוֹף ,וְ[a]'וְ noun masc. sing.; וְ see lett. ו . עוף

עֵוֹפַי Kh. עוֹפַי, K. עֵיפַי pr. name masc. . עוף

עוֹפֶרֶת וְ noun fem. sing., comp. עֹפֶרֶת . . עפר

[עוּץ] *to consult, take counsel*, Ju. 19. 30; Is. 8. 10.

יְעוּץ (*counsellor*) pr. name masc. 1 Ch. 8. 10.

עוּץ וְ' pr. name—I. of a son of Aram, Ge. 10. 23. —II. of a son of Nahor, Ge. 22. 21, from whom the land of *Uz* is supposed to derive its name, viz. *Ausitis*, a district of Arabia. —III. masc. Ge. 36. 28.

עוּק. Hiph. *to press, press down.*

עָקָה fem. dec. 10, *oppression*, Ps. 55. 4.

מוּעָקָה fem. *oppressive burden, affliction* or *pain*, Ps. 66. 11.

עָוַר Kal not used; *to dig, dig out*, i. q. חוּר. Pi. עִוֵּר *to blind, make blind.*

עִוֵּר adj. masc. d. 7b, *blind;* also, *mentally blind.*

עִוָּרוֹן masc. *blindness*, De. 28. 28; Zec. 12. 4.

עַוֶּרֶת fem. idem, Le. 22. 22.

מְעָרָה fem. dec. 10, *cave, cavern.*

I. עוּר (inf. does not occur) *to awake, rouse oneself, rise;* part. עָר (§ 21. rem. 2) *waking, watching.* Niph. נֵעוֹר (§ 21. rem. 11).—I. *to be awakened, roused.* —II. *to be stirred* or *raised up, to arise.* Pil. עוֹרֵר.—I. *to awaken, rouse.*—II. *to stir up, excite.* —III. *to raise, lift up* a sword, a scourge. Pilp. (§ 6. No. 4) *to excite* a cry, Is. 15. 5. Hiph. הֵעִיר. —I. *to awaken, rouse.*—II. *to stir up, excite.*—III. intrans. *to awake, bestir oneself*, with עַל *for* any one. Hithpal. I. *to raise* or *rouse oneself.*—II. perh. *to be elated*, Job 31. 29.

עָר masc. (*city;* whence properly pl. עָרִים, see עִיר) pr. name of the metropolis of Moab, עָר־מוֹאָב *Ar of Moab*, otherwise called רַבָּה.

עֵר (*waking, watchful*) pr. name—I. of a son of Judah.—II. 1 Ch. 4. 21.

עֵרִי (for עֵרִיָּה *watching*, i. e. serving *the Lord*) pr. name of a son of Gad, Ge. 46. 16. Patronym. עֵרִי (for עֵרִיִּי) Nu. 26. 16.

עֵרָן (*watchful*) pr. name masc. Nu. 26. 36. Patronym. עֵרָנִי ibid.

עִיר fem. irr. (§ 45).—I. *a city, town*, prop. *a watching*, a place fortified and watched.—II. in composition with pr. names: עִיר הַמֶּלַח (*city of salt*) in the desert of Judah, near the Salt Sea, Jos. 15. 62;—עִיר נָחָשׁ (*city of serpents*) 1 Ch. 4. 12; —עִיר שֶׁמֶשׁ (*city of the sun*) in the tribe of Dan, Jos. 19. 41;—עִיר הַתְּמָרִים (*city of palm-trees*) for Jericho, abounding with palm-trees.—III. pr. name of a man, 1 Ch. 7. 12, for which עִירִי ver. 7.

עִיר Ch. m. d. 1a, *a watcher*, Da. 4. 10, 14, 20.

עִירָא (*watch*) pr. name masc.—I. 2 Sa. 20. 26. —II. 2 Sa. 23. 26.—III. 2 Sa. 23. 28.

עִירוּ (*a watching*) pr. name masc. 1 Ch. 4. 15.

עִירָם (*citizen* or *watchman*) pr. n. m. Ge. 36. 43.

יָעִיר (whom *He stirs up*) pr. name masc. 1 Ch. 20. 5, Keri; Kh. יָעוּר.

II. עוּר Kal not used; i. q. עָרָה ,עָרַר. Niph. *to be made bare*, Hab. 3. 9.

עוֹר masc. dec. 1a (pl. עוֹרוֹת), *skin* of man or of animals, prob. so called from the idea of *nakedness;* Job 19. 20, עוֹר שִׁנָּיִם *skin of the teeth*, i. e. *the gums.*

מְעוֹרִים m. pl. (of מָעוֹר) *nakedness*, Hab. 2. 15.

עוּר Chald. masc. *chaff*, only כְּעוּר, Da. 2. 35.

עִוֵּר [b]'וְ Piel pret. 3 pers. sing. m.; or adj. m. d. 7b עור

עוֹר noun masc. sing. dec. 1a . . . עור

עוֹרֵב pr. name of a man and a rock . . ערב

עוּרָה [c]'וְ Kal imp. sing. masc. with parag. ה (§ 21. rem. 5, comp. § 8. rem. 11) . . עור

עוֹרוֹ noun masc. sing., suff. 3 p. s. m. fr. עוֹר d. 1a עור

עִוְרוֹת[d] adj. fem. pl. [of עַוֶּרֶת dec. 13], fr. עִוֵּר masc. עור

עוֹרִי [e]'וְ noun masc. sing., suff. 1 pers. sing. from עוֹר dec. 1a . . . . . . עור

עוּרִי Kal imp. sing. fem. . . . . . עור

עֲיָרִים[f] Kh. for עֲיָרִים K. (q. v.) . . . עיר

עִוְרִים adj. masc. pl. of עִוֵּר dec. 7b . . עור

עוֹרָם [g]'וְ noun masc. sing., suff. 3 pers. pl. masc. from עוֹר dec. 1a . . . . . עור

עוֹרֵנוּ[h] id. sing., suff. 1 pers. pl. . . . עור

עוֹרֵר [i]'וְ Pilel pret. 3 pers. sing. masc. . . עור

[a] Je. 12. 4. [b] Is. 42. 19. [c] Ps. 7. 7. [d] Is. 42. 7. [e] La. 3. 4. [f] Is. 30. 6. [g] Mi. 3. 3. [h] La. 5. 10. [i] Is. 10. 26.

עֽוּרָה id. imp. sing. masc. with parag. ה (comp. § 21. rem. 5, & § 8. rem. 11) . . עור
עֽוֹרְרוּ[a] Poel pret. 3 pers. pl. . . . . ערר
עֽוֹרַרְתִּי[c] וְ Pilel pret. 1 pers. sing.; acc. shifted by conv. וְ (comp. § 8. rem. 7) . . עור
עֽוֹרַרְתִּיךָ[d] id. with suff. 2 pers. sing. masc. . . עור
עֽוֶרֶת[e] noun fem. sing. . . . . עור
עוֹרֹת[f] noun masc. with pl. fem. term. fr. עוֹר d. 1a עור

[עוּשׁ] i. q. חוּשׁ *to hasten, make haste,* Joel 4. 11.
יְעוּשׁ (*hastener*) pr. name m. of several persons.

עוֹשֶׂה Kal part. act. sing. masc. dec. 9a . . עשה
עוֹשֵׂה וְ id., constr. st. . . . . . עשה
עוּשׁוּ[g] Kal imp. pl. masc. . . . . עוש
עוֹשֵׂי Kal part. act. pl. c. from עוֹשֶׂה dec. 9a. . עשה
עוֹשֵׁק Kal part. act. sing. masc. dec. 7b . עשק

עָוַת. Pi. עִוֵּת.—I. *to make crooked,* Ec. 7. 13.—II. *to pervert, subvert*; of judgment, *to wrest.* Pu. part. *crooked,* Ec. 1. 15. Hithpa. *to bend oneself, bow down,* Ec. 12. 3.
עַוָּתָה fem. dec. 10, *oppression,* La. 3. 59.

עוּת *to aid, help,* with acc. of the pers. and thing, only לָעוּת Is. 50. 4.
עוּתַי (for עוּתְיָה *succoured of the Lord*) pr. name masc. of two persons, 1 Ch. 9. 4; Ezr. 8. 14.

עָוְתָה[h] Kal pret. 3 pers. sing. fem. . . . עוה
עִוְּתוֹ[i] Piel pret. 3 p. s. m. [עִוֵּת], suff. 3 p. s. m. עות
עִוְּתוּנִי[k] id. pret. 3 pers. pl., suff. 1 pers. sing. עות
עוּתַי pr. name masc. . . . . . עות
עִוְּתָנִי[l] Piel pret. 3 pers. sing. m. [עִוֵּת], suff. 1 p. s. עות
עַוָּתָתִי[m] noun fem. sing., suff. 1 pers. sing. [fr. עַוָּתָה] עות
עַז, עָז } adj. masc. sing. dec. 8a; subst. Ge. 49. 3 עזז
עֵז [n]וְ, [o]וְ noun f. sing. d. 8b; for וָ see lett. ו עזז
עֹז, עָז־[p] וְ, וְ } noun masc. sing. dec. 8c (§ 37. rem. 2); וָ id. . . . עזז
עֻזָּא וְ pr. name masc. . . . . עזז
[עֲזָאזֵל] masc. *the scape-goat,* Le. 16. 8, 10, 26, lit. *goat of departure,* comp. of עֵז & אָזַל q. v. Hengstenberg, who with some of the Jews, takes this word to signify *a demon* or *devil,* supposes the act of sending the goat to have been a symbol by which the kingdom of darkness and its prince were renounced, and the sins sent back to him by which he had sought to enslave the people.

עָזַב [q]וְ fut. יַעֲזֹב.—I. *to leave, forsake, desert.*—II. *to leave, leave behind.*—III. *to leave, commit* to any one, with לְ, אֶל, עַל; intrans. Ps. 10. 14.—IV. *to leave off, cease from, give up.*—V. *to set free* or *loose,* Ex. 23. 5; part. עָזוּב *set free.* Niph. *to be left, forsaken, deserted;* with לְ *to be left, given over to,* Is. 18. 6. Pu. id. Is. 32. 14.
עֲזוּבָה fem. dec. 10.—I. *a forsaking,* Is. 6. 12.—II. *ruins.*—III. pr. name (*a*) of the mother of Jehoshaphat, 1 Ki. 22. 42; (*b*) of the wife of Caleb, 1 Ch. 2. 18, 19.
עִזָּבוֹן masc. dec. 3c.—I. *a market, market-place,* Eze. 27. 12, 14, 16, 19, 22.—II. *merchandise,* Eze. 27. 27, 33.

עָזָב[r] Kal pret. 3 pers. s. m. for עָזַב (comp. § 8. r. 7) עזב
עָזֹב[s] id. inf. abs. (§ 8, rem. 8) . . . עזב
עֲזֹב[t] וַ id. imp. sing. masc.; וַ bef. (-:) . . עזב
עֹזֵב וְ id. part. act. sing. masc. dec. 7b . . עזב
עֻזָּב[u] Pual pret. 3 p. s. m. [for עֻזַּב comp. § 8. r. 7] עזב
עָזָבָה[x] Kal pret. 3 pers. sing. f. [for עָזְבָה § 8. r. 7] עזב
עָזְבָה[y] id. imp. sing. masc. with parag. ה (§ 8. r. 11) עזב
עָזְבָהּ[z] id. inf. with suff. 3 pers. sing. fem. . . עזב
עֻזָּבָה[a] Pual pret. 3 pers. sing. fem. . . עזב
עָזָבוּ, עָזְבוּ [b]וְ } Kal pret. 3 pers. pl. (§ 8. rem. 7) . עזב
עֲזָבוֹ id. pret. 3 pers. sing. masc., suff. 3 pers. s. m. עזב
עִזְבוּ id. imp. pl. masc. . . . . עזב
עֲזָבוּהָ[c] id. id., suff. 3 pers. sing. fem. . . עזב
עֲזָבוּךְ[d] וַ id. pret. 3 p. pl., suff. 2 p. s. f.; וַ bef. (-:) עזב
עֲזָבוּנִי id. id., suff. 1 pers. sing. . . עזב
עִזְבוֹנַיִךְ[e], עִזְבוֹנַיִךְ[f] וְ } noun masc. pl., suff. 2 pers. sing. fem. from [עִזָּבוֹן] dec. 3c . . . } עזב
עַזְבּוּק pr. name masc. . . . . . עזז
עֲזֻבוֹת Kal part. pass. fem. pl. of עֲזוּבָה dec. 10, from עָזוּב masc. . . . . . עזב
עֹזְבֵי [g]וְ id. part. act. pl. constr. m. fr. עֹזֵב d. 7b עזב
עֹזְבִי[h] id. sing., suff. 1 pers. sing. . . . עזב
עֹזְבָיו[i] id. pl., suff. 3 pers. sing. masc. . . עזב
עֹזְבֶיךָ[k] id. pl., suff. 2 pers. sing. masc. . . עזב
עָזְבֵךְ[l] id. inf., suff. 2 pers. sing. fem. . . עזב
עָזְבָם[m] id. id., suff. 3 pers. pl. masc. . . עזב
עֲזַבְנֻהוּ[n] id. pret. 1 pers. pl. (עָזַבְנוּ), suff. 3 p. s. m. עזב
עֲזָבָנוּ[o] id. pret. 3 pers. sing. masc., suff. 1 pers. pl. עזב
עָזַבְנוּ id. pret. 1 pers. pl. . . . . עזב

[a] Ps. 80. 3. [b] Is. 23. 13. [c] Zec. 9. 13. [d] Ca. 8. 5. [e] Le. 22. 22. [f] Ex. 39. 34. [g] Joel 4. 11. [h] Est. 1 16. [i] Ec. 7. 13. [k] Ps. 119. 78. [l] Job 19. 6. [m] La. 3. 59. [n] Ge. 15. 9. [o] Le. 7. 23. [p] Is. 26. 1. [q] Ge. 44. 22. [r] Is. 58. 2. [s] Ex. 23. 5. [t] Ps. 37. 8. [u] Is. 32. 14. [x] Eze. 23. 8. [y] Je. 49. 11. [z] 2 Ki. 8. 6. [a] Je. 49. 25. [b] Ps. 49. 11. [c] Je. 51. 9. [d] Eze. 23. 29. [e] Eze. 27. 12, 14, 22. [f] Eze. 27. 27, 33. [g] Is. 1. 28. [h] Zec. 11. 17. [i] Ezr. 8. 22. [k] Je. 17. 13. [l] Je. 2. 17, 19. [m] Je. 9. 12. [n] 2 Ch. 13. 10. [o] Ezr. 9. 9.

עֲזָבַנִי[a] } id. pret. 3 pers. sing. masc., suff. 1 pers. sing.; ךָ bef. (-:) } עזב
עֲזָבָנִי[b] ךָ'

עֲזָבֽוּנִי[c] id. pret. 3 pers. pl. (עָזְבוּ), suff. 1 pers. sing. עזב

עָזַבְתָּ[d] id. pret. 2 pers. sing. masc. . . . עזב

עָזַבְתִּי id. pret. 1 pers. sing. . . . . עזב

עֲזַבְתִּיךְ[e] id. id., suff. 2 pers. sing. fem. . . . עזב

וַעֲזַבְתִּים[f] [g]וְ' id. id., suff. 3 pers. pl. m.; וַ for וְ, conv. עזב

עֲזַבְתֶּם[h] id. pret. 2 pers. sing. m., suff. 3 pers. pl. m. עזב

וַעֲזַבְתֶּם וְ' id. pret. 2 pers. pl. masc.; וַ for וְ, conv. עזב

עֲזַבְתֶּן[i] id. pret. 2 pers. pl. fem. . . . עזב

עֲזַבְתָּנִי id. pret. 2 pers. sing. masc., suff. 1 pers. sing. (for תַּנִי' § 2. rem. 1) . . . עזב

עַזְגָּד pr. name masc. . . . . . עזז

עָזָה Root not used; Arab. عزي to console.

יַעֲזִיאֵל (whom *God consoles*) pr. name masc. 1 Ch. 15. 18; for which עֲזִיאֵל ver. 20.

יַעֲזִיָּהוּ (whom *the Lord consoles*) pr. name masc. 1 Ch. 24. 26, 27.

מַעַזְיָה ,מַעַזְיָהוּ (*consolation of the Lord*) pr. name masc. 1 Ch. 24. 18; Ne. 10. 9.

עַזָּה וְ' adj. fem. s. d. 10, fr. עַז m.; also pr. name עזז

עֻזָּה pr. name masc. . . . . . עזז

עֻזָּהּ noun masc. sing., suff. 3 pers. sing. fem. from עֹז dec. 8 c . . . . . עזז

עֻזֹּה[k] } id., suff. 3 pers. sing. masc. . . עזז
עֻזּוֹ וְ'

עָזוֹב[l] וְ Kal inf. abs. . . . . עזב

עָזוּב[m] וְ' id. part. pass. sing. masc. . . עזב

עֲזוּבָה id. id. fem.; also pr. name . . עזב

עִזּוּז[n] [o]וְ' adj. masc. sing. . . . . עזז

עֱזוּז וֶ noun masc. sing. dec. 1 a; וֶ bef. (-:) . עזז

עֱזוּזוֹ[p] וֶ id. with suff. 3 pers. sing. masc.; וֶ id. עזז

עַזּוּר pr. name masc. . . . . . עזר

עַזּוֹת[q] adj. fem., pl. of עַזָּה from עַז masc. . עזז

[עָזַז] fut. יָעֹז, inf. עֻזּוֹ.—I. *to make strong, to strengthen*, const. with לְ Ec. 7. 19.—II. *to be* or *wax strong*; hence, *to prevail*.—III. *to be*, or *show oneself strong, powerful, mighty*. Hiph. הֵעֵז *to make bold*, with בְּפָנִים ,פָּנִים Pr. 7. 13; 21. 29.

עָזָז (*strong*) pr. name masc. 1 Ch. 5. 8.

עִזּוּז masc. *strong, mighty*, Ps. 24. 8; collect. *strong men*, Is. 43. 7.

עֱזוּז masc. dec. 1 a, *strength, might*.

עֲזִיזָא (*strength*) pr. name masc., Ezr. 10. 27.

עַז masc. dec. 8 d, עַזָּה fem. dec. 10, adj.—I. *strong, vehement, fierce*.—II. *strong, fortified*, Nu. 21. 24.—III. *harsh, cruel, hardened*, Is. 19. 4; עַז־פָּנִים *bold, impudent*.

עֵז fem. dec. 8 b.—I. *goat*; גְּדִי עִזִּים *a kid of the goats*; שֵׂה עִזִּים *an animal* of the goat kind.—II. pl. *goat's-hair*.

עֵז Chald. id., Ezr. 6. 17.

עֹז, עוֹז masc. dec. 8 c (§ 37. rem. 2).—I. *strength, might, power*; concr. *strong ones*, Ju. 5. 21.—II *refuge, defence*.—III. *ascription of power, praise*.

עֻזָּא ,עֻזָּה (*strength*) pr. name m. of several men.

עַזָּה (*strong, fortified*) pr. name, *Gaza*, a city of the Philistines. Gent. noun עַזָּתִי.

מָעוֹז ,מָעֹז masc. dec. 8 c (with suff. מָעֻזִּי ,מָעֻוזִּי § 37. rem. 2 & 4).—I. *place of strength, stronghold, fortress*.—II. *refuge, asylum*.

עֲזַזְיָהוּ (whom *the Lord strengthens*) pr. name masc. of several persons.

עֻזִּי (for עֻזִּיָּה q. v.) pr. name masc. of several persons.

עֻזִּיאֵל (*strength of God*) pr. name masc. of several persons. Patronym.—

עָזִּיאֵלִי Nu. 3. 27.

עֻזִּיָּה ,עֻזִּיָּהוּ pr. name, *Uzziah*, king of Judah, called also עֲזַרְיָה ,עֲזַרְיָהוּ; also the name of several other persons.

עַזְבּוּק (*strength exhausted*) pr. name masc., Ne. 3. 16

עַזְגָּד (*strength of fortune*) pr. name masc.

עַזְמָוֶת (*strength of death*) pr. name masc.—I. 2 Sa. 23. 31.—II. 1 Ch. 27. 25; see also בַּיִת.

עֲזַזְיָהוּ ,עָזָז וַ' וְ pr. names masc.; וַ bef. (-:) . . עזז

עֻזִּי noun masc. sing., suff. 1 pers. sing. from עֹז dec. 8 c (§ 37. rem. 2) . . . עזז

עַזֵּי adj. pl. constr. masc. from עַז dec. 8 d . עזז

עֻזִּי noun masc. sing., suff. 1 pers. sing. fr. עֹז d. 8 c עזז

עֻזִּי עֻזִּיָּא ,וְ' (for עֻזִּיָּה) pr. names masc. . עזז

עֲזִיאֵל וַ pr. name masc.; וַ bef. (-:) . . . עזה

עֻזִּיאֵל עֻזִּיָּה ,וְ' עֻזִּיָּהוּ ,וְ' עֲזִיזָא ,וַעֲזִיזָא pr. names masc. עזז

עִזַּיִךְ[r] וְ noun fem. pl., suff. 2 pers. s. m. fr. עֵז dec. 8 b עזז

עַזִּים adj. pl. abs. masc. from עַז dec. 8 d . עזז

עִזִּים וְ' noun fem., pl. of עֵז dec. 8 b . . עזז

עִזִּין[s] Chald. id. pl. abs. dec. 5 b . . . עזז

עֻזְּךָ noun masc. s., suff. 2 pers. s. m. fr. עֹז d. 8 c עזז

עֻזֶּךָ } id., suff. 2 pers. sing. masc. . . . עזז
עֻזְּךָ

[a] Ps. 40. 13. [b] De. 31. 16. [c] Je. 19. 4. [d] Ps. 9. 11. [e] Is. 54. 7. [f] Is. 42. 16. [g] De. 31. 17. [h] Ne. 9. 17, 19, 31. [i] Ex. 2. 20. [k] Hab. 3. 4. [l] Je. 14. 5. [m] 2 Ki. 14. 26. [n] Ps. 24. 8. [o] Is. 43. 17. [p] Ps. 78. 4. [q] Pr. 18. 23. [r] Is. 56. 11. [s] Ge. 31. 38. [t] Ezr. 6. 17.

עֻזְּכֶם id., suff. 2 pers. pl. masc. . . . . עזז

עֻזָּמוֹ[a] id., suff. 3 pers. pl. masc. . . . עזז

עַזְמָוֶת וְ' pr. name masc. (in compos. see בֵּית) עזז

עַזָּן pr. name masc. Nu. 34. 26.

[עָזְנִיָּה] fem. a species of *eagle*, according to the Sept. and Jerome, *the ospray*, or *the sea-eagle*, Le. 11. 13; De. 14. 12.

עָזַק. Pi. עִזֵּק *to dig*, Is. 5. 2.

עִזְקָא Chald. fem. dec. 8 a, *engraved ring, seal*, Da. 6. 18.

עֲזֵקָה (*dug up* or *over*) pr. name of a city in the plain of Judah.

עֲזֵקָה וְ' pr. name of a place; וַ bef. (-:) . . עזק

[עָזַר] fut. יַעֲזֹר pl. יַעְזְרוּ (§ 13. rem. 5) *to help, assist, aid*, const. with acc., לְ, עִם, אַחֲרֵי; part. עֹזֵר *helper*; in war, *an ally*. Niph. *to be helped, to obtain help*. Hiph. i. q. Kal.

עֵזֶר masc. dec. 6 b (with suff. עֶזְרִי § 35. rem. 6). —I. *help*; also as a concr. *helper*.—II. pr. name m.—(*a*) 1 Ch. 4. 4, for which עֶזְרָה ver. 17; (*b*) 1 Ch. 12. 9; (*c*) Ne. 3. 19.

עֵזֶר (*help*) pr. name masc.—I. Ne. 12. 42.—II. 1 Ch. 7. 21.

עַזּוּר, עַזֻּר (*helper*) pr. name masc.—I. Je. 28. 1. —II. Eze. 11. 1.—III. Ne. 10. 18.

עֶזְרָא (*help*) pr. name, *Ezra*.—I. a priest and scribe, who led up a colony of Jews from Babylon to Jerusalem.—II. Ne. 12. 1, 13.

עֶזְרָה fem. (with suff. עֶזְרָתִי; no pl.).—I. *help*. —II. pr. name masc.; see עֵזֶר.

עֲזָרָה fem.—I. *a court* of the temple.—II. *a settle* or *inbenching* in the altar of *burnt-offerings*, Eze. 43. 14, 17, 20; עָזַר i. q. חָצַר *to enclose*.

עֶזְרַת fem. with ה parag. עֶזְרָתָה, *help*.

עֲזַרְאֵל (*whom God helps*) pr. name masc. of several persons.

עֶזְרִי (for עֲזַרְיָה *help of the Lord*) pr. name masc., 1 Ch. 27. 26.

עַזְרִיאֵל (*help of God*) pr. name masc.—I. 1 Ch. 5. 24.—II. 1 Ch. 27. 19.—III. Je. 36. 26.

עֲזַרְיָה, עֲזַרְיָהוּ (whom *the Lord helps*) pr. name masc. of several persons; it stands also for עֻזִּיָּה king of Judah, q. v.

עַזְרִיקָם (*help against the enemy*) pr. name masc. —I. 1 Ch. 3. 23.—II. 1 Ch. 8. 38; 9. 44.—III. 1 Ch. 9. 14.—IV. 2 Ch. 28. 7.

יַעְזֵר, יַעְזֵיר (*He will help*) pr. name of a city in the tribe of Gad.

עֵזֶר וְ' for עֵזֶר (§ 35. rem. 2) pr. name masc. (see also רֹמַמְתִּי־עֶזֶר. R. רום) . . עזר

עָזֻר[b] Kal part. pass. sing. masc. [for עָזוּר] . עזר

עֶזֶר pr. name masc. . . . . עזר

עֵזֶר וְ' pr. name m. (see also רֹמַמְתִּי־עֶזֶר. R. רום) עזר

עֵזֶר[c] וְ'' noun m. s. d. 6 (§ 35. r. 6), also pr. name עזר

עֹזֵר Kal part. act. sing. masc. dec. 7 b . . עזר

עֶזְרָא וְ' עֲזַרְאֵל, וְ' עֶזְרָה (see עֵזֶר) pr. names masc. עזר

עֶזְרָה[d] noun fem. sing. (no pl.) . . . עזר

עֶזְרֹה[e] noun masc. sing., suff. 3 pers. sing. masc. (K. וֹ for ־ו) from עֵזֶר dec. 6 (§ 35. rem. 6) . עזר

עֲזָרוֹ[f] Kal pret. 3 pers. sing. m., suff. 3 pers. sing. m. עזר

עָזְרוּ id. pret. 3 pers. pl. . . . . עזר

עֶזְרִי pr. name masc. . . . . עזר

עֶזְרִי noun masc. sing., suff. 1 pers. sing. from עֵזֶר dec. 6 (§ 35. rem. 6) . . . עזר

עֹזְרֵי Kal part. act. pl. constr. masc. fr. עֹזֵר d. 7 b עזר

עַזְרִיאֵל וְ' עֲזַרְיָה, וְ' pr. names masc.; וַ bef. (-:) . עזר

עֹזְרֶיהָ[g] Kal part. act. pl., suff. 3 pers. sing. fem. from עֹזֵר dec. 7 b . . . עזר

עֲזַרְיָהוּ וְ' pr. name masc., see עֲזַרְיָה . . עזר

עֹזְרָיו[h] Kal part. act. pl., suff. 3 pers. sing. masc. from עֹזֵר dec. 7 b . . . עזר

עַזְרִיקָם וְ' pr. name masc. . . . . עזר

עֲזָרְךָ[i] Kal pret. 3 pers. sing. m., suff. 2 pers. sing. m. עזר

עֶזְרֶךָ[k] / עֶזְרְךָ[l] } noun masc. sing., suff. 2 pers. sing. masc. from עֵזֶר dec. 6 (§ 35. rem. 6) } עזר

עֲזָרֻם Kal pret. 3 pers. pl. (עָזְרוּ), suff. 3 pers. pl. m. עזר

עֶזְרָם noun masc. sing., suff. 3 pers. pl. masc. from עֵזֶר dec. 6 (§ 35. rem. 6) . . . עזר

עֲזָרָנוּ[m] Kal pret. 3 pers. sing. masc., suff. 1 pers. pl. עזר

עֶזְרֵנוּ noun masc. sing., suff. 1 pers. pl. fr. עֵזֶר dec. 6 (§ 35. rem. 6) . . . . עזר

עָזְרֵנוּ וְ''[n] Kal imp. sing. masc. with suff. 1 pers. pl. עזר

עִזְרוּנִי[o] וְ' id. imp. pl. masc. [עִזְרוּ], suff. 1 pers. sing. עזר

עָזְרֵנִי id. imp. sing. masc., suff. 1 pers. sing. . עזר

עֲזָרָנִי[p] id. pret. 3 pers. sing. masc., suff. 1 pers. sing. (§ 2. rem. 1) . . . . עזר

עֶזְרַת noun fem. sing. . . . עזר

עֶזְרַת[q] noun fem. sing., constr. of עֶזְרָה (no pl.) עזר

עָזַרְתָּ[r] Kal pret. 2 pers. sing. masc. . . עזר

עֶזְרָתָה noun fem. sing. (עֶזְרַת) with parag. ה עזר

עֶזְרָתִי noun fem. s., suff. 1 pers. s. fr. עֶזְרָה (no pl.) עזר

עֲזַרְתִּיךָ Kal pret. 1 pers. sing., suff. 2 pers. sing. masc. עזר

[a] Ps. 89. 18. [b] Is. 31. 3. [c] De. 33. 7. [d] Ps. 46. 2. [e] Eze. 12. 14. [f] 2 Ch. 18. 31. [g] Eze. 30. 8. [h] Eze. 32. 21. [i] 1 Ch. 12. 18. [k] De. 33. 29. [l] Ps. 20. 3. [m] 1 Sa. 7. 12. [n] Jos. 10. 6. [o] Jos. 10. 4. [p] Ps. 118. 13. [q] Is. 31. 2. [r] Job 26. 2.

עֲזַרְתִּיךְ[a] id. id., suff. 2 pers. sing. fem. . . עזר
עֲזַרְתֶּם[b] וְ id. pret. 2 pers. pl. masc.; וַ for וְ, conv. עזר
עֶזְרָתֵנוּ[c] noun fem. s., suff. 1 pers. pl. fr. עֶזְרָה (no pl.) עזר
עֲזַרְתַּנִי[d] Kal pret. 2 pers. sing. masc., suff. 1 pers. s. עזר
עַזָּתָה pr. name of a place (עַזָּה) with parag. ה . עזז
עֵט noun masc. sing. . . . . עוט
עֵטָא[e] Chald. noun fem. sing. . . . יעט

עָטָה[f] וְ fut. יַעְטֶה, ap. יַעַט (§ 24. rem. 3).—I. *to cover*, with עַל, *to cover over*.—II. *to cover oneself, put on*.—III. *to wrap* or *roll up*, Is. 22. 17; intrans. *to wrap oneself up in* any thing, Je. 43. 12.—IV. *to become languid, to faint* (comp. עָטַף) Ca. 1. 7. Hiph. הֶעֱטָה *to cover*, with acc., עַל.

מַעֲטֶה masc. dec. 9a, *covering, garment*, Is. 61. 3.

עָטֹה[g] Kal inf. abs. . . . . . עטה
עֹטֶה id. part. act. sing. masc. dec. 9a . . עטה
עָטוּ[h] וְ id. pret. 3 pers. pl. . . . . עטה
עֲטִינָיו[i] noun masc. pl., suff. 3 p. s. m. fr. [עָטִין] d. 3a עטן
עֲטִישֹׁתָיו[pp] noun f. pl., suff. 3 p. s. m. fr. [עֲטִישָׁה] d. 10 עטש
עֹטְךָ[qq] וְ Kal part. act. sing., suff. 2 pers. sing. masc. from עֹטֶה dec. 9a . . . . . עטה

[עֲטַלֵּף] masc. dec. 1b, *bat*.

עָטַן Root not used; Arab. *to dress skins*.

עָטִין masc. dec. 3a, *skin-bottle* for holding milk or water, Job 21. 24.

[עָטַף] fut. יַעֲטֹף, יַעֲטֹף (§ 13. rem. 5).—I. *to cover, to clothe*.—II. *to cover oneself, to be covered*.—III. *to languish, faint*, comp. עָטָה; part. עָטוּף *languid, faint; weak, feeble*. Niph. *to languish, faint*, La. 2. 11. Hiph. *to be weak, feeble*, Ge. 30. 42. Hithpa. *to faint*, of the mind.

מַעֲטָפָה fem. *mantle*, Is. 3. 22.

[עָטַר] *to surround, encompass*, with acc., לְ. Pi. עִטֵּר *to crown*, with acc., לְ. Hiph. *to crown, distribute crowns*, Is. 23. 8.

עֲטָרָה fem. constr. עֲטֶרֶת pl. עֲטָרוֹת (§ 42. r. 5).—I. *crown, diadem*.—II. pr. name fem. 1 Ch. 2. 26.

עֲטָרוֹת (*crowns*) pr. name—I. of a city in the tribe of Gad, Nu. 32. 3, 34.—II. of a city in Ephraim, Jos. 16. 7, called also עַטְרוֹת אַדָּר (*crowns of Addar*).—III. עַ׳ בֵּית יוֹאָב (*crowns of the house of Joab*) a city in the tribe of Judah, 1 Ch. 2. 54.—IV. עַ׳ שׁוֹפָן a city in Gad, Nu. 32. 35.

עֲטָרָה pr. name fem. . . . . עטר
עֲטָרוֹת noun fem. pl. abs., from עֲטָרָה constr. עֲטֶרֶת (§ 42. rem. 5); also pr. name . עטר
עַטְרוֹת pr. name in compos. as עַטְ׳ אַדָּר &c. . עטר
עֹטְרִים[k] Kal part. act. masc., pl. of עֹטֵר dec. 7b . עטר
עֲטֶרֶת וַ׳ noun fem. sing., used as the constr. of עֲטָרָה (§ 42. rem. 5); וַ bef. (ֲ) . . עטר
עַטְרֹת pr. name in compos. עַטְרֹת שׁוֹפָן . עטר
עִטַּרְתָּ[l] Piel pret. 2 pers. sing. masc. . . עטר

עָטַשׁ Root not used; Arab. *to sneeze*.

עֲטִישָׁה fem. dec. 10, *a sneezing*, Job 41. 10.

עַי, עַיָּא, וְעַיָּא (see עַי) pr. name of place . . עוה
עֵיבָל וְ׳ pr. name of a man and a mount . עבל
עִידִי[m] in some copies for עֲדִי (q. v.) . . עוד
עִיּוֹן pr. name of a place . . . . . עוה
עַיּוֹת Kh. עיות, K. עֲוִית pr. name of a place . עוה

עִיט or עוּט only fut. ap. וַיַּעַט, also וַתַּעַט (§ 22. rem. 3, & § 21. rem. 8).—I. *to be angry with*, with בְּ 1 Sa. 25. 14.—II. *to rush, fall upon with fury*. Hence

עַיִט[n] / עָיִט[o] } masc. dec. 6h, *rapacious bird* or *beast*. Coll. *birds of prey* . . . } עיט
עֵיטָם (*place of rapacious beasts*) pr. name of a town and hill in the tribe of Judah . . עיט
עִיִּים[p] / עִיִּין[q] } וְ׳ noun masc. pl. of עִי׳ dec. 8 (§ 8. No. 4), also pr. name . . . } עוה
עִילַי pr. name masc. . . . . . עלה
עֵילָם וְ׳ pr. name—I. of a son of Shem, Ge. 10. 22, and a Persian province called after him *Elam*, i. e. *Elymaïs*. Gent. noun Chald. עֵלְמָיֵא *Elamites*.—II. Ezr. 2. 7; 8. 7; 10. 2. —III. Ezr. 2. 31.

[עַיָּם] m. *ardour, violence*, Is. 11. 15. Prof. Lee, *drought*.

עַיִן וְ׳ com. dec. 6h (du. עֵינַיִם).—I. *eye*; לְעֵינֵי פ׳ *before the eyes of* any one, in his presence; בְּעֵינֵי פ׳ *in the eyes of* any one, in his opinion, judgment; hence, טוֹב בְּעֵינַי *it seemeth good to me*, i. e. it pleases me; חָכָם בְּעֵינָיו *wise in his own estimation, conceited*; מֵעֵינֵי פ׳ *away from the eyes of* any one, i. e. behind his back; בֵּין עֵינַיִם *between the eyes*, i. e. on the forehead; הָיָה לְעֵינַיִם לְ *to be for eyes to* any one, i. e. to lead him the right way; עַיִן בְּעַיִן *eye with eye*, with both eyes, plainly; עֵינַיִם רָמוֹת *lofty eyes*, i. e. pride.—

[a] Is. 41. 14. [b] Jos. 1. 14. [c] La. 4. 17. [d] Ps. 86. 17. [e] Da. 2. 14. [f] Je. 43. 12. [g] Is. 22. 17. [h] Mi. 3. 7. [i] Job 21. 24. [k] 1 Sa. 23. 26. [l] Ps. 65. 12. [m] Ps. 27. 12. [n] Job 28. 7. [o] Is. 46. 11. [p] Je. 26. 18. [pp] Job 41. 10. [q] Mi. 3. 12. [qq] Is. 22. 17.

II. *face, surface.*—III. *face, appearance.*—IV. *fountain*; pl. עֲיָנוֹת, constr. עֵינוֹת (§ 35. rem. 12).—V. pr. name of a city of the Levites in the tribe of Simeon.—VI. pr. name of a place in the north of Palestine, Nu. 34. 11.—VII. עֵין גֶּדִי (*fountain of the kid*) a city in the desert of Judah.—עֵין גַּנִּים (*fountain of gardens*) a city of Judah, Jos. 15. 34; also a city of the Levites in Issachar.—עֵין דּאר, עֵין דּוֹר (*fountain of the dwelling*) a city in the tribe of Manasseh.—עֵין חַדָּה (*sharp* or *swift fountain*) a city of Issachar, Jos. 19. 21.—עֵין חָצוֹר (*fountain of the court* or *village*) a city in Naphtali, Jos. 19. 37.—עֵין מִשְׁפָּט (*fountain of judgment*) i. q. קָדֵשׁ Ge. 14. 7; comp. Nu. 20. 13.—עֵין עֶגְלַיִם (*fountain of the two calves*) a city in Moab, Eze. 47. 10.—עֵין רֹגֵל (*fountain of the fuller*) a fountain in the confines of Judah and Benjamin.—עֵין רִמּוֹן (*fountain of pomegranates*) a city of Judah, Ne. 11. 28.—עֵין שֶׁמֶשׁ (*fountain of the sun*) a city on the confines of Judah and Benjamin, Jos. 15. 7.—עֵין תַּנִּים (*fountain of dragons*) a fountain near Jerusalem, Ne. 2. 13.—עֵין תַּפּוּחַ (*fountain of the city* תַּפּוּחַ) in the tribe of Manasseh, Jos. 17. 7.

עֵין Chald. dec. 3 d, id.

עֹיֵן part. (denom. of עַיִן) *to eye, view with envy*, 1 Sa. 18. 9, Kh. עָוֹן.

עֵינַיִם (*two fountains*) pr. name of a town in the tribe of Judah, Ge. 38. 21; contr. עֵינָם Jos. 15. 34.

עֵינָן (*having eyes*) pr. name of a man.

עָנִים (contr. from עֵינַיִם *fountains*) pr. name of a town in Judah, Jos. 15. 50.

עָנֵם (contr. for עֵינַיִם *two fountains*) pr. name of a city in Issachar, 1 Ch. 6. 58, elsewhere called עֵין גַּנִּים.

מַעְיָן masc. dec. 2b (with ו parag. מַעְיְנוֹ; pl. מַעְיָנוֹת, מַעְיָנִים) *fountain, well of water.*

עַיִן וְ noun fem. sing. dec. 6h, for עַיִן (§ 35. rem. 2); also pr. name; for וָ see lett. ו . . . עין

עֵין וְ id., constr. st., also in compos. with pr. name, as עֵין גֶּדִי &c. . . . . עין

עֵינָהּ[a] id., suff. 3 pers. sing. fem. . . . . עין

עֵינָו וְ id. du., suff. 3 pers. sing. masc. (§ 4. r. 1) . עין

עֵינוֹ[b] וְ id. sing., suff. 3 pers. sing. masc. . . עין

עֵינוֹן pr. name, see חֲצַר עֵינוֹן under . . חצר

עֵינוֹת[c] noun fem. pl., constr. of עֲיָנֹת, from עַיִן dec. 6 h (§ 35. rem. 12) . . עין

עַיְנַי[d] Chald. id. pl. (עַיְנִין), suff. 1 pers. sing. d. 3 d . עין

עֵינַי, עֵינָי וְ } id. du., suff. 1 pers. sing. . . . עין

עֵינֵי וְ id. du., constr. st. . . . . עין

עֵינִי[e] וְ id. sing., suff. 1 pers. sing. . . . עין

עֵינֶיהָ id. du., suff. 3 pers. sing. fem. . . . עין

עֵינֵיהוּ[f] וְ id. du., suff. 3 pers. sing. masc. (§ 4. r. 5) . עין

עֵינֵיהֶם id. du., suff. 3 pers. pl. masc. . . . עין

עֵינָיו וְ id. du., suff. 3 pers. sing. masc. . . עין

עֵינָוֹ[g] id. du. (Kh. עֵינָיו q. v.), or sing. (K. עֵינוֹ), suff. 3 pers. sing. masc. . . . עין

עֵינַיִךְ[h] וְ id. du., suff. 2 pers. sing. fem. . . עין

עֵינֶיךָ וְ id. du., suff. 2 pers. sing. masc. . . עין

עֵינֵיכֶם[i] id. du. (Kh. עֵינֵיכֶם), or sing. (K. עֵינְכֶם), suff. 2 pers. pl. masc. . . . עין

עֵינֵיכֶם וְ id. du., suff. 2 pers. pl. masc. . . עין

עֵינַיִם, עֵינָיִם וְ } id. du., abs. st.; also pr. name . . עין

עַיְנִין[k] וְ Chald. id. pl., abs. st. dec. 3 d . . עין

עֵינֵינוּ[l] וְ id. du., suff. 1 pers. pl. . . . עין

עֵינְךָ, עֵינֶךָ } id. sing., suff. 2 pers. sing. masc.; the first form also def. for עֵינֶיךָ . } עין

עֵינֵךְ[m] id. sing., suff. 2 pers. sing. fem. . . . עין

עֵינְכֶם[n] וְ id. sing., suff. 2 pers. pl. masc. . . עין

עֵינָם, עֵינֵמוֹ[o] } id. sing., suff. 3 pers. pl. masc. . . עין

עֵינָן pr. name masc. (see also חֲצַר עֵ׳. R. חצר) . עין

עֵינֵנוּ noun fem. sing., suff. 1 pers. pl. fr. עַיִן d. 6h . עין

עֲיָנֹת[p] id. pl. abs. fem. (§ 35. rem. 12) . . עין

עֵינֹת id. pl. constr. fem. . . . . עין

עֵינֹתָם[q] Kh. עֵינֹתָם noun fem. pl. with suff. from עַיִן q. v.; K. עוֹנֹתָם [from עוֹנָה] see . עון

[עָיֵף] *to be weary*, Je. 4. 31.

עָיֵף masc. dec. 5 c, עֲיֵפָה fem. adj. *weary, exhausted*, of fatigue, hunger, thirst; trop. of a land.

עֵיפַי (*weary*) pr. name m. Je. 40. 8; Kh. עוֹפַי.

עָיֵף וְ adj. masc. sing. dec. 5 c . . . עיף

עָיְפָה[rr] Kal pret. 3 pers. sing. fem. . . . עיף

עֲיֵפָה adj. fem. sing. from עָיֵף masc. . . עיף

עֵיפָה[r] וְ noun fem. sing., also pr. name masc. . עוף

עֲיֵפִים adj. masc., pl. of עָיֵף dec. 5 c . . עיף

[עִיר] *to heat* an oven, Ho. 7. 4. Arab. עאר *to be hot, ardent.*

עִיר masc.—I. *heat, anger*, Ho. 11. 9, perh. also Ps. 73. 20.—II. *fear, terror*, Je. 15. 8; perh. also, with the Syr., Job 24. 12, מֵעִיר מְתִים

[a] De. 28. 56. [b] Nu. 11. 7. [c] Pr. 8. 28. [d] Da. 4. 31. [e] Je. 8. 23. [f] Job 24. 23. [g] Ec. 4. 8. [h] Je. 31. 16. [i] Eze. 9. 5. [k] Da. 7. 8, 20. [l] De. 21. 7. [m] La. 2. 18. [n] Ge. 45. 20. [o] Ps. 73. 7. [p] De. 8. 7. [q] Ho. 10. 10. [r] Am. 4. 13. [rr] Je. 4. 31.

יִנְאָקוּ׃ *from terror* (agony of death) *the dying groan*, reading מֵתִים for מְתִים.

עָר masc. dec. 1 a, *an enemy*, 1 Sa. 28. 16; Is. 14. 21; Ps. 139. 20.

עָר Chald. masc. id. Da. 4. 16.

[ff]עַיִר ו״ן masc. dec. 6 h (pl. עֲיָרִים § 35. rem. 12) *a young ass, an ass colt*; also *a full grown ass*.

[a]עִיר noun masc. sing. . . . . . עיר

[b]עִיר Chald. noun masc. sing. dec. 1 a . עור

עִיר ן, ו׳ noun fem. sing. irr., pl. עָרִים, once עֲיָרִים (§ 45); also pr. name . . עור

עִירָא pr. name masc. . . . . . עור

עִירָד ו׳ pr. name masc. . . . . . ערד

[c]עִירָהּ noun masc. sing., suff. 3 pers. sing. fem. from עִיר irr. (§ 45) . . . עור

[d]עִירֹה noun masc. sing., suff. 3 p. s. m. fr. עַיִר d. 6 h עיר

עִירוֹ noun fem. sing., suff. 3 pers. sing. masc. from עִיר irr. (§ 45) . . . . עור

עִירוּ pr. name masc. . . . . . עור

עִירִי ו pr. name masc., see עִיר . . . . עור

עִירִי noun m. s., suff. 1 pers. s. fr. עִיר irr. (§ 45) עור

[e]עֲיָרִים id. pl., abs. st. . . . . . עור

עֲיָרִים noun masc. pl. of עַיִר dec. 6 h (§ 35. r. 12) עיר

[f]עִירִין Chald. noun masc. pl. of עִיר dec. 1 a . עור

[g]עִירְךָ noun f. s., suff. 2 p. s. m. fr. עִיר irr. (§ 45) עור

[h]עֲיָרִם ן defect. for עֲיָרִים; ן bef. (-:) . . . עיר

[i]עֵירֹם ו׳ adj. masc. sing., pl. עֵירֻמִּם, dec. 8 c . ערם

עִירָם pr. name masc. . . . . . עור

עִירָם noun f. s., suff. 3 p. pl. m. fr. עִיר irr. (§ 45) עור

[k]עֵירֻמִּם adj. masc. pl. of עֵירֹם dec. 8 c . . ערם

[l]עַיִשׁ ן the name of a constellation, Job 38. 32, supposed to be *the Great Bear, Arcturus*, בָּנֶיהָ (her sons) being the three stars in its tail. It is also called עָשׁ q. v.

עַיָּת pr. name of a place, see עַי . . . עוה

עַכְבּוֹר ו׳ pr. name masc. . . . . עכבר.

עַכָּבִישׁ masc. *a spider*, Job 8. 14; Is. 59. 5.

[עַכְבָּר] masc. dec. 2 b, *mouse*; Prof. Lee, *jerboa*.

עַכְבּוֹר (*mouse*) pr. name masc. of two different persons.

[m]עַכְבְּרֵי ו׳ noun masc. pl. constr. from עַכְבָּר' dec. 2 b עכבר

[n]עַכְבְּרֵיכֶם id. pl., suff. 2 pers. pl. masc. . . עכבר

עַכּוֹ pr. n. of a city in the tribe of Asher, Ju. 1. 31.

עָכוֹר pr. name of a valley . . . . עכר

עָכָן (*troubler*, i. q. עָכָר, comp. 1 Ch. 2. 7) pr. name masc. comp. Jos. 7. 1.

יַעְכָּן (id.) pr. name masc. 1 Ch. 5. 13.

עכס Kal not used; Arab. *to bind*. Pi. (denom. of עֶכֶס q. v.) *to wear anklets*, or *to make a tinkling* with them.

עֶכֶס masc. dec. 6 a.—I. *fetter*, Pr. 7. 22.—II. pl. *anklets, ornamental foot-rings* or *chains*, Is. 3. 18. Hence

עַכְסָה (*anklet*) pr. name of the daughter of Caleb, Jos. 15. 16; Ju. 1. 12; 1 Ch. 2. 49.

[o]עָכַר *to trouble, cause sorrow*. Niph. *to be irritated, excited*, Ps. 39. 3; part. fem. *confusion*, Pr. 15. 6.

עָכוֹר (*causing sorrow*) pr. name of a valley near Jericho.

עָכָר (*troubler*) pr. name m., elsewhere עָכָן q. v.

עָכְרָן (*troubled*) pr. name m. Nu. 1. 13; 2. 27.

עָכָר pr. name masc. . . . . . עכר

[p]עֹכֵר ו׳ן Kal part. act. sing. masc. dec. 7 b . עכר

עָכְרָן pr. name masc. . . . . . עכר

[q]עֲכַרְתִּי Kal pret. 1 pers. sing. . . . . עכר

[r]עֲכַרְתֶּם ו׳ id. pret. 2 pers. pl. masc.; וַ for וְ, conv. עכר

[s]עֲכַרְתָּנוּ id. pret. 2 pers. sing. masc., suff. 1 pers. pl. עכר

עַכְשׁוּב masc. *an asp*, Ps. 140. 4.

[t]עָל noun m. s. (Ho. 7. 16); or *adv.* (2 Sa. 23. 1) עלה

[u]עָל־ noun masc. sing. . . . . . עלה

עַל ו׳ prep., pl. c. עֲלֵי, with suff. עָלַי (§ 31. r. 5) עלה

[v]עַל Chald. Peal pret. 3 pers. sing. masc. . עלל

[w]עֲלֵ־ Kh. עַל prep. q. v., K. עֲלֵי (q. v.) . . עלה

[x]עֲלֵ־ Kh. עַל prep. R. עלה, K. אֶל (q. v.) R. . אלה

עֹל noun masc. sing. dec. 8 c . . . עלל

עֻלָּא pr. name masc. . . . . . עלל

[y]עֵלָּא ן Ch. עַל with parag. א, comp. [מַעְלָה] *adv.* עלה

עַלְבוֹן pr. name, see אֲבִי עַל . . . . . אב

עלג Root not used; i. q. לָעַג q. v. Hence

[c]עִלְּגִים masc. pl. [of עִלֵּג d. 7 b] *stammerers*, Is. 32. 4 עלג

עָלָה ו׳ן fut. יַעֲלֶה, ap. יַעַל (§ 24. rem. 3).—I. *to go* or *come up, to ascend, mount up*, with עַל, אֶל, לְ, בְּ also acc. of the place.—II. *to arise*, of the dawn. —III. *to spring* or *grow up*; Ge. 40. 10, עָלְתָה נִצָּהּ *it* (the vine) *sprang up into its blossom*, i. e. put

[a] Je. 15. 8. [b] Da. 4. 10, 20. [c] De. 22. 21. [d] Ge. 49. 11. [e] Ju. 10. 4. [f] Da. 4. 14. [ff] Ze. 9. 9. [g] Da. 9. 19. [h] Ge. 32. 16. [i] Eze. 18. 7, 16. [k] Job 11. 12. [l] Ge. 3. 7. [l] Job 38. 32. [m] 1 Sa. 6. 4, 11, 18. [n] 1 Sa. 6. 5. [o] 1 Sa. 14. 29. [p] Pr. 11. 17. [q] 1 Ki. 18. 18. [r] Ge. 34. 30. [s] Jos. 6. 18. [t] Jos. 7. 25. [u] 2 Sa. 23. 1; Ho. 7. 16. [w] Ho. 11. 7. [y] Da. 2. 16, 24. [x] Job 7. 1. [a] 1 Ki. 1. 33. [b] Da. 6. 3. [c] Is. 32. 4.

forth blossoms, comp. Pr. 24. 31; hence part. עֹלֶה, Job 36. 33, *the rising*, sc. plant.—IV. *to rise, increase*. Niph. נַעֲלָה (§ 13. rem. 7, note).—I. *to be brought up*, Ezr. 1. 11.—II. *to be led* or *driven away*.—III. *to be exalted*. Hiph. הֶעֱלָה; fut. יַעֲלֶה, ap. יַעַל (§ 24. rem. 16).—I. *to cause to go up, to lead, bring* or *carry up*.—II. *to put* or *set up*.—III. *to bring, offer*, or *present* an offering upon the altar.—IV. *to bring* into an account, *to enrol*, 1 Ki. 9. 21. Hoph. pass. of Hiph. Nos. I, III & IV. Hithp. *to exalt oneself*, Je. 51. 3.

עָלֶה masc. dec. 9 b, *a leaf*; collect. *foliage*.

עַל, עָל masc.—I. *high, the Most High*, Ho. 7. 16; 11. 7.—II. adv. *on high*, 2 Sa. 23. 1; מֵעָל *from above*, Ge. 27. 39; 49. 25; *above*, Ps. 50. 4.

עַל (prop. constr. of עָל dec. 2 a) pl. c. עֲלֵי, with suff. עָלַי, עָלֶיךָ, עָלָיו, &c. prep.—I. noting a state of rest, of one thing *upon, on, over, above* another, to the question *where?* as he sits עַל הַמִּטָּה *upon the bed*; espec. (*a*) with words which imply clothing, covering, protecting; and intellectually, trusting, sparing, pitying, pleasing; (*b*) with the idea of burden, trouble, and hence, duty or obligation; הָיוּ עָלַי לָטֹרַח *they are a burden upon me*; עָלַי לָתֵת *it lay on me to give*; then of hostility, as חָרָה עַל, קָצַף עַל *to be wrath against*; קוּם עַל *to rise against*; moreover with verbs of commissioning, ruling, commanding, as פָּקַד עַל, מָלַךְ עַל; (*c*) of the objects, means, instruments by which any thing is effected; as, to live עַל הַחֶרֶב *by the sword*; עַל הַלֶּחֶם *by bread*; frequently in the titles of the Psalms, e. g. עַל הַגִּתִּית *upon Gittith*; (*d*) of norm, rule, standard and cause, עַל דִּבְרָתִי מַ׳ *after* the manner of Melchizedek; עַל־כָּכָה *in this manner*; עַל־דְּבַר *because of, on account of*; עַל־מָה *wherefore?* with inf. *because that*.—II. noting contiguity, (*a*) *at, by, near*; (*b*) *with*; e. g. flesh עַל־הַדָּם *with the blood*; (*c*) as a periphrase for adverbs, עַל יֶתֶר *with abundance, abundantly*; עַל נְקַלָּה *lightly*.—III. with idea of motion, to the question *whither? upon, down upon, to, towards*, after verbs of laying, casting, raining; hence—IV. frequently i. q. אֶל, לְ marking the dative, *to, for*.—V. conj. (*a*) *though, although*, i. q עַל אֲשֶׁר; (*b*) *because that, because*; more fully עַל אֲשֶׁר, עַל כִּי.—VI. with other particles. כְּעַל *according to*; as a conj. *accordingly*, Is. 59. 18. מֵעַל *from upon, from above*; also *from* (being) *near, at*, hence simply *away from, from*, after verbs of passing, moving, turning. מֵעַל לְ *above, over*; also, *at, by, near, by the side of*.

עַל Chald. with suff. עֲלוֹהִי, עֲלַיְנָא, עֲלֵיהוֹן.—I. *upon, above, over*; עַל דְּנָה *therefore*.—II. i. q. אֶל *to*; and for לְ marking the dative.

עֹלָה, עוֹלָה fem. dec. 10.—I. *a step*, Eze. 40. 26. —II. *a burnt-offering*, a sacrifice which is wholly consumed.

עֵלָּא Chald. with מִן *above*, Da. 6. 3.

עֲלָוָה Chald. fem. *burnt-offering*, only pl. עֲלָוָן (comp. dec. 8 c) Ezr. 6. 9.

עֱלִי masc. *pestle*, Pr. 27. 22.

עֵלִי (*exalted*) pr. name, *Eli*, the high-priest.

עִלַּי Chald. masc. *the Supreme, Most High*, only emph. st. עִלָּיָא Kh. עִלָּאָה K.

עִלִּי adj. only fem. עִלִּית *upper*, Ju. 1. 15; pl. עִלִּיּוֹת Jos. 15. 19.

עִלִּי Chald. fem. dec. 8 c, *upper chamber*, Da. 6. 11.

עִילַי (*supreme*, i. q. Chald. עִלַּי) pr. name masc. 1 Ch. 11. 29, called צַלְמוֹן in 2 Sa. 23. 28.

עֲלִיָּה fem. dec. 10.—I. *upper room, chamber*.—II. *ascent, staircase*, 2 Ch. 9. 4.

עֶלְיוֹן masc. עֶלְיוֹנָה fem. adj.—I. *very high, lofty*, 1 Ki. 9. 8; 2 Ch. 7. 21.—II. *higher, upper*.—III. *high, exalted*.—IV. *the Supreme, Most High*.

עֶלְיוֹן Chald. masc. only pl. עֶלְיוֹנִין prob. *high places*, comp. מְרוֹמִים; others, *the Most High*, Da. 7. 18, 22, 25, 27.

מַעֲלֶה masc. dec. 9 a.—I. *ascent, place of ascent*. —II. *stage, platform*, Ne. 9. 4.—III. *ascent, acclivity, hill*; מַעֲלֵה אֲדֻמִּים *hill of the red ones*, on the confines of Judah and Benjamin; מַ׳ עַקְרַבִּים *hill of scorpions*, in the south of Palestine.

מַעַל, adv. *above*; but only in composition.—I. מִמַּעַל *from above*, Is. 45. 8; also simply *above*; מִמַּעַל לְ *above, upon*.—II. מַעְלָה (with parag. ה) *upwards*; מַעְלָה מַעְלָה *higher and higher*; also *upward, above*, mostly of time; also *forward, onward*, 1 Sa. 16. 13.—III. לְמַעְלָה *upwards*; also *upward, above*; עַד לְמַעְלָה *to a high degree, exceedingly*.—IV. מִלְמַעְלָה *from above*.

מֹעַל *a lifting up, elevating*, Ne. 8. 6.

מַעֲלָה fem. dec. 10.—I. *ascent, going up*, Ezr. 7. 9; metaph. *suggestion*, Eze. 11. 5.—II. *step* of a stair.—III. *degree* of a sundial.—IV. שִׁיר הַמַּעֲלוֹת *song of degrees* in the title of fifteen psalms, prob. so called from having been sung upon the *steps* of the temple.

תְּעָלָה fem. dec. 10.—I. *channel* for water, *a*

conduit.—II. *plaster, bandage*, something *placed upon* a wound, Je. 30. 13; 46. 11. Others, *a recovery, a getting up* from illness.

עָלֶה noun masc. sing. dec. 9b . . . עלה

עֲלֵה[a] וַ' id. constr. st.; or Kal imp. s. m.; וַ bef. (-:) עלה

עָלֶהָ[b] id. with suff. 3 pers. sing. fem. . . עלה

עָלֹה Kal inf. abs. . . . . . עלה

עָלֶה[c] Kh. עָלָה q. v.; K. עָלוּ (q. v.) . . עלה

עִלָּה Chald. noun fem. sing. . . . . עלל

עֹלָה וְ' noun fem. sing.; or fem. of the foll. עלה

עֹלֶה Kal part. act. sing. masc. dec. 9a . עלה

עָלֵהוּ וְ' noun masc. sing., suff. 3 pers. sing. masc. from עָלֶה dec. 9b . . . עלה

עֲלֹהִי[d] Chald. prep. (עַל) with suff. 3 pers. sing. m. עלה

עֲלֵהֶם defect. for עֲלֵיהֶם (q. v.) . . . עלה

עֲלֵהֶן defect. for עֲלֵיהֶן (q. v.) . . . עלה

עָלוֹ[e] [f]וְ' Kh. for עָלָיו K. (q. v.) . . עלה

עָלוּ וְ' Kal pret. 3 pers. pl. . . . עלה

עֲלוּ וַ' id. imp. pl. masc.; וַ bef. (-:) . . עלה

עֻלּוֹ [g]וְ' noun masc. sing., suff. 3 pers. sing. masc. from עֹל dec. 8e . . . . עלל

עַלְוָה[h] noun f. s. by transp. for עַוְלָה; also pr. n. m. עול

עֲלוֹהִי Chald. prep. (עַל) with suff. 3 pers. sing. masc. עלה

עֲלוּמָיו[i] / עֲלוּמָיו } noun masc. pl. [עֲלוּמִים], suff. 3 pers. sing. masc. (§ 4. rem. 1) . . עלם

עֲלוּמַיִךְ[k] id. with suff. 2 pers. sing. fem. . . עלם

עַלְוָן pr. name masc. [for עַלְיָן] . . . עול

עָלוֹת Kal part. act. fem. pl. [of עָלָה fr. עָל masc.] עול

עֲלוֹת Kal inf. constr. . . . . עלה

עֹלוֹת[pp] id. part. act. f., pl. of עֹלָה d. 10, fr. עֹלֶה m. עלה

עֹלוֹת וְ' noun fem. pl. of עֹלָה dec. 10 . . עלה

עֲלוֹתָהּ[l] Kal inf. (עֲלוֹת), suff. 3 pers. sing. fem. dec. 1 a עלה

עֹלֹתָיו[m] noun fem. pl., suff. 3 pers. sing. masc. from עֹלָה dec. 10 . . . עלה

עֹלוֹתֵיכֶם id. with suff. 2 pers. pl. masc. . . עלה

[עָלַז] fut. יַעֲלֹז *to exult, rejoice*, with בְּ of the object of joy.

עָלֵז masc. dec. 1 b, *one rejoicing, expressing joy.*

And the following.

עָלֵז[n] וְ adj. masc. *one exulting, rejoicing* . עלז

עִלְזוּ[o] וְ Kal imp. pl. masc. . . . . עלז

עִלְזִי[p] וְ id. imp. sing. fem. (§ 8. rem. 12) . עלז

עָלַט Root not used; Arab. *to be dense*, and transp. עטל *to be dark.* Hence

עֲלָטָה[q] וַ fem. *thick darkness*; וַ bef. (-:) . . עלט

עָלַי / וְ' עָלַי } prep. (עַל) pl. with suff. 1 pers. sing. (§ 31. rem. 5) . . . עלה

עֲלַי Ch. id. with suff. 1 pers. sing. . . עלה

עֲלֵי וַ' id. pl. constr.; or noun masc. pl. c. fr. עָלֶה dec. 9 b; וַ bef. (-:) . . עלה

עֲלִי Kal imp. sing. fem. . . . עלה

עֵלִי וְ' pr. name masc. . . . . עלה

עִלָּאָה Chald. Kh. עִלָּיָא by Syriasm, K. עִלָּאָה adj. masc. sing. emph. [of עִלַּי comp. § 63] . עלה

עָלֶיהָ וְ' prep. (עַל) pl. with suff. 3 pers. sing. fem. (§ 31. rem. 5) . . . עלה

עַלְיָה Kh., עַלְוָה K. pr. name masc. . עלה

עֲלַיהּ Ch. prep. (עַל) pl. with suff. 3 pers. sing. fem. עלה

עֲלֵיהוֹן[r] Ch. id. with suff. 3 pers. pl. masc. . עלה

עֲלֵיהֶם וַ' id. with suff. 3 pers. pl. masc.; וַ bef. (-:) עלה

עֲלֵיהֹם[s] Ch. id. with suff. 3 pers. pl. masc. . עלה

עֲלֵיהֶן id. with suff. 3 pers. pl. fem. . . עלה

עָלָיו וְ' id. with suff. 3 pers. sing. masc. (§ 31. r. 5) עלה

עֶלְיוֹן וְ' adj. masc. sing. . . . עלה

עֶלְיוֹנִין[t] Ch. id. pl. abs. dec. 1 a . . . עלה

עֶלְיוֹת[u] adj. fem., pl. of עִלִּית [from עִלִּי masc.] . עלה

עֲלִיּוֹת[x] וַ noun fem., pl. of עֲלִיָּה dec. 10; וַ bef. (-:) עלה

עֲלִיּוֹתָיו[y] [z]וַ' id., suff. 3 pers. sing. masc.; וַ id. . עלה

עַלִּיזָה adj. fem. sing. [from עַלִּיז masc.] . עלז

עַלִּיזֵי / עַלִּיזִים[a] } id. pl., constr. and abs. masc. . . עלז

עֲלָיִךְ Ch. prep. (עַל) pl. with suff. 2 pers. sing. masc. עלה

עָלַיִךְ / [b]וְ' עָלַיִךְ } id. with suff. 2 pers. sing. f. (§ 31. r. 5) עלה

עָלֶיךָ id. with suff. 2 pers. sing. masc. . . עלה

עָלָיְכִי[c] id. with suff. 2 pers. sing. f. [עָלַיִךְ § 4. r. 4] עלה

עֲלֵיכֶם id. with suff. 2 pers. pl. masc. . . עלה

עֲלִילָה noun fem. sing. dec. 10 . . . עלל

עֲלִילוֹתָיו id. pl., suff. 3 pers. sing. masc. . . עלל

עֲלִילוֹתַיִךְ[d] id. pl., suff. 2 pers. sing. fem. . . עלל

עֲלִילוֹתֵיכֶם id. pl., suff. 2 pers. pl. masc. . . עלל

עֲלִילוֹתָם id. pl., suff. 3 pers. pl. (§ 4. rem. 2) . עלל

עֲלִילֹת[e] id. pl., comp. עֲלִלוֹת . . . עלל

עֲלִילֹתָיו[f] id. pl., suff. 3 pers. sing. masc. . . עלל

---

a De. 10. 1. b Is. 1. 30. c 2 Ki. 24. 10. d Ezr. 6. 11. e 1 Sa. 2. 10. f 2 Sa. 20. 8. g Is. 10. 27. h Ho. 10. 9. i Job 20. 11. k Is. 54. 4. l Ho. 2. 17. m Eze. 40. 26. n Is. 5. 14. o Ps. 68. 5. p Zep. 3. 14. pp Ge. 41. 3, 5. q Ge. 15. 17. r Ezr. 5. 1, 3. s Ezr. 7. 24. t Da. 7. 18, 22, 25, 27. u Jos. 15. 19. x Je. 22. 14. y Ps. 104. 3. z Je. 22. 13. a Is. 24. 8. b Is. 60. 2. c Ps. 116. 7. d Zep. 3. 11. e De. 22. 14, 17. f 1 Ch. 16. 8; Is. 12. 4.

עֹלִים Kal part. act. masc., pl. of עֹלֶה dec. 9a — עלה

עֲלֵימוֹ [a]וְ' prep. (עַל) pl. with suff. 3 p. pl. m. (§31. r. 5) — עלה

עַלְיָן pr. name masc., see עַלְוָן . . . — עול

עֲלַיְנָא[b] / עֲלֶינָא } Chald. prep. (עַל) pl. with suff. 1 pers. pl. — עלה

עָלֵינוּ Heb. id. with suff. 1 pers. pl. (§ 31. rem. 5) — עלה

עָלִינוּ וְ' Kal pret. 1 pers. pl. . . . . — עלה

עֲלִיצֻתָם[c] noun f. s., suff. 3 p. pl. m. fr. [עֲלִיצוּת] d. 10 — עלץ

עָלִיתָ וְ' Kal pret. 2 pers. sing. masc. . . — עלה

עָלִית id. pret. 2 pers. sing. fem. . . . — עלה

עֲלִיַּת noun fem. sing., constr. of עֲלִיָּה dec. 10 — עלה

[d]עִלִּית adj. fem. sing. [from עִלִּי masc.] . . — עלה

[e]עֲלִיָּתוֹ וַ noun fem. sing., suff. 3 pers. sing. masc. from עֲלִיָּה dec. 10; וַ bef. (-:) . . — עלה

[f]וְ' עָלִיתִי Kal pret. 1 pers. sing. . . . — עלה

[g]עֲלִיֹּתָיו וַ id. pl. with suff. 3 pers. sing. m.; וַ bef. (-:) — עלה

עֲלִיתֶם וַ' Kal pret. 2 pers. pl. masc.; וַ for וְ conv. — עלה

עֻלֵּךְ noun masc. s., suff. 2 pers. s. f. fr. עֹל d. 8c — עלל

עֻלְּכֶם id. with suff. 2 pers. pl. masc. . . — עלל

עָלַל Kal not used; i. q. גָּלַל *to roll* (comp. Fürst in concord.), hence *to repeat an action, to do habitually* or *effectually* (comp. Prof. Lee s. v.). Po. עוֹלֵל.—I. *to roll* any thing in the dust, Job 16. 15.—II. *to glean*, prop. to repeat an action, to go over again.—III. with לְ, *to treat, to act towards*, espec. *to maltreat; hence to affect painfully*, La. 3. 51.—IV. *to act as a child*, only part. מְעוֹלֵל *a child*, Is. 3. 12. Hithpa. with בְּ.—I. *to exert oneself against* any one.—II. *to abuse, insult*. Hithpo. *to practise*, Ps. 141. 4.

עֲלַל Chald. *to go in, to enter*. Aph. הַנְעֵל (§ 47. rem. 4, comp. § 52. rem. 2) *to bring in*. Hoph. *to be brought in*, Da. 5. 13, 15.

עוֹלֵל, עוֹלָל masc. dec. 7b & 2b, *a child, boy*, comp. Poel No. IV.

עֹלֵלוֹת, עוֹלֵלוֹת fem. pl. dec. 11b, *gleanings*.

עֹל masc. dec. 8c, *a yoke*; trop. *servitude*.

עֻלָּא (*yoke*) pr. name masc. 1 Ch. 7. 39.

עִלָּה Chald. fem. *pretext, pretence*, Da. 6. 5, 6.

עֲלִיל masc. *crucible*, Ps. 12. 7.

עֲלִילָה fem. *work, deed, action*.

עֲלִילִיָּה fem. id. Je. 32. 19.

מֶעָל Ch. pl. מֶעָלִין *a setting* of the sun, Da. 6. 15.

מַעֲלָל masc. dec. 2b, only pl. *works, deeds*.

מְעֻלָּל masc. id. Zec. 1. 4, Kh.

תַּעֲלוּל masc. dec. 1b, only pl.—I. *children, boys*, Is. 3. 4, comp. Poel No. IV, and עוֹלֵל.—II. *vexations, adversities*, Is. 66. 4.

עֲלָלוֹת defect. for עֲלִילֹת (q. v.) . . . — עלל

עֹלֵלוֹת noun fem. pl. abs. dec. 11b . . . — עלל

[h]עֹלְלוֹת id. pl., constr. state . . . . — עלל

[gg]עֹלֲלֵי noun masc. pl. constr. from עוֹלָל dec. 7b — עלל

עוֹלָלֶיהָ noun masc. pl., suff. 3 p. s. f. fr. עוֹלָל d. 2b — עלל

[i]עֹלְלֵיהֶם וְ' id. pl., suff. 3 pers. pl. masc. . . — עלל

[k]עָלְלִין Chald., Kh. עָלְלִין Peal part. act. masc. pl. [of עָלֵל] dec. 2b; K. עָלִּין contr. . . — עלל

[l]עַלְּלַת Ch., Kh. עַלְלַת id. pret. 3 p. s. f.; K. עַלַּת contr. — עלל

[m]עֹלַלְתִּי וְ Poel pret. 1 pers. sing. . . . — עלל

[עָלַם] I. *to hide, conceal*, only part. pass. עֲלֻמִים *hidden, secret*, sc. sins.—II. Arab. *to grow ripe of age and desirous of marriage*; hence derivv. עַלְמָה, עֶלֶם, עֲלוּמִים. Niph. נֶעְלָם *to be hidden*; part. נַעֲלָמִים *hidden*, i. e. *crafty dissemblers*, Ps. 26. 4. Hiph. הֶעְלִים *to hide, conceal*, with מִן (once בְּ) *from* any one; with עֵינַיִם, אֹזֶן *to turn* one's eyes or ears from any one, so as not to see or hear. Hithp. *to hide oneself, to be hidden*.

עוֹלָם, עֹלָם masc. dec. 2b, *a time hidden, indefinite* or *unlimited*.—I. of the past; (*a*) *antiquity, ancient times*; מֵעוֹלָם *of old, from ancient times*; (*b*) *time everlasting, without beginning*; מֵעוֹלָם *from everlasting*, comp. Ps. 90. 2; 93. 2; Pr. 8. 23.—II. of the future; (*a*) *very long, indefinite duration to come*; לְעוֹלָם *for ever*, not endless, comp. Ex. 21. 6; 1 Ki. 1. 31; (*b*) *eternity, everlasting duration*; לְעוֹלָם *for ever*; עַד עוֹלָם id. comp. Ps. 90. 2; 103. 17; Ps. 10. 16, מֶלֶךְ עוֹלָם וָעֶד *king of eternity and perpetuity*, i. e. *king for ever and ever*.—III. pl. עוֹלָמִים i. q. sing. Nos. I & II, comp. Ps. 77. 6; 145. 13; Is. 26. 4;—adv. *for ever*.

עֵילוֹם masc. i. q. עוֹלָם 2 Ch. 33. 7.

עָלַם Chald. masc. dec. 2a, id.

עֶלֶם m. *a youth, young man*, 1 Sa. 17. 56; 20. 22.

עַלְמָה fem. dec. 12a.—I. *a maiden, virgin, marriageable* but *not married* (comp. the Root No. II), so in the seven passages of its occurrence, viz. Ge. 24. 43; Ex. 2. 8; Is. 7. 14; Ps. 68. 26; Pr. 30. 19; Ca. 1. 3; 6. 8.—II. pl. עַל עֲלָמוֹת in the title of

[a] Job 29. 22. [b] Ezr. 4. 12. [c] Hab. 3. 14. [d] Ju. 1. 15. [e] 2 Ch. 9. 4. [f] 2 Ki. 20. 8. [g] 1 Ch. 28. 11. [gg] La. 2. 20. [h] Ju. 8. 2. [i] Ho. 14. 1. [k] Da. 4. 4; 5. 8. [l] Da. 5. 10. [m] Job 16. 15.

Ps. 46, upon *Alamoth*, prob. the name of a musical instrument; others, with *female voices*.

עֲלוּמִים masc. pl. (of עֲלוּם dec. 1 a) *youth, youthful age*; trop. for *vigour*, Job 20. 11.

עַלְמוֹן (*concealment*) pr. name—I. of a town in the tribe of Benjamin, Jos. 21. 18; for which עָלֶמֶת in 1 Ch. 6. 45.—II. עַ׳ דִּבְלָתַיְמָה a station of the Israelites in the desert, Nu. 33. 46.

עָלֶמֶת (*covering*) pr. name masc. of two different persons.

יַעְלָם (whom *He hides, protects*) pr. name masc. Ge. 36. 5, 14.

תַּעֲלֻמָה fem. dec. 10, *hidden thing, secret*.

עָלַם Chald. noun masc. sing. dec. 2 a . . . עלם

עֻלָּם[a] noun masc. s., suff. 3 p. pl. m. fr. עֹל d. 8 c עלל

עָלְמָא Chald. noun masc. sing., emph. of עָלַם d. 2 a עלם

עֹלָמוֹ[b] noun masc. s., suff. 3 p. s. m. fr. עוֹלָם d. 2 b עלם

עַלְמוֹן pr. name of a place . . . . עלם

עֲלָמוֹת [c] וְ noun f. pl. abs. fr. עַלְמָה d. 12 a; וַ bef. (-:) עלם

עָלְמַיָּא[d] Chald. noun masc. pl. emph. from עָלַם d. 2 a עלם

עֵלְמָיֵא Chald. gent. noun masc. pl. from עֵילָם q. v.

עֹלָמִים defect. for עוֹלָמִים (q. v.) . . . עלם

עֲלֻמֵנוּ[e] Kal part. pass. pl. masc., suff. 1 pers. pl. [from עָלוּם] dec. 3 a . . . עלם

עָלֶמֶת וְ׳ }
עַלֶּמֶת וְ׳ } pr. name masc. (comp. § 35. r. 2) . עלם

עַלֶּמֶת pr. name of a place, see עַלְמוֹן . . עלם

עֻלֵּנוּ noun masc. sing., suff. 1 pers. pl. fr. עֹל d. 8 c עלל

[עָלַס] *to exult, rejoice*, Job 20. 18. Niph. id. Job 39. 13. Hithp. *to delight oneself*, Pr. 7. 18.

עָלַע. Pi. *to sip, suck up*, Job 39. 30.

עֲלַע Chald. masc. *a rib*, only in the following form.

עִלְעִין[f] Chald. noun masc. pl. of [עֲלַע] dec. 3 b . עלע

עָלַף. Pu. I. *to be covered over*, Ca. 5. 14.—II. *to be languid, faint*, Is. 51. 20. Hithp. I. *to veil oneself*, Ge. 38. 14.—II. *to become languid, faint*. Hence

עֻלְפֶּה masc. *languor, fainting*, Eze. 31. 15 . עלף

עֻלְּפוּ[g] Pual pret. 3 pers. pl. . . . . עלף

עָלַץ׳ fut. יַעֲלֹץ *to exult, rejoice*, with בְּ in one, with לְ over one, *to triumph* over him.

עֲלִיצוּת fem. *exultation, rejoicing*, Hab. 3. 14.

עָלַק Root not used; Arab. *to adhere*.

עֲלוּקָה fem. *leech*, Pr. 30. 15.

עֲלֹתִי defect. for עֲלוֹת (q. v.) . . . עלה

עֹלַת וְ׳ noun fem. sing., constr. of עֹלָה dec. 10 עלה

עֹלֹת [h] וְ׳ id. pl.; or (Ge. 41. 2, 22) part. comp. עֹלוֹת עלה

עָלְתָה }
עָלָתָה וְ׳ } Kal pret. 3 pers. sing. fem. (comp. § 8. rem. 7) . . . . עלה

עַוְלָתָה[i] וְ noun fem. sing. (עַוְלָה) with parag. ה (§. 43. rem.) . . . . . עול

עֹלָתָה[m] defect. for עוֹלָתָה (q. v.) . . עלה

עַ׳לָתָה[n] Kh. עֹלָתָה q. v.; K. עַוְלָתָה (q. v.) . עול

עֲלֹתוֹ[o] Kal inf. (עֲלוֹת), suff. 3 pers. sing. masc. dec. 1 a . . . . עלה

עֹלָתוֹ [p] וְ׳ noun fem. sing., suff. 3 pers. sing. masc. from עֹלָה dec. 10 . . . עלה

עֹלֹתֶיךָ id. pl., suff. 2 pers. sing. masc. . . עלה

עֹלֹתֵיכֶם id. pl., suff. 2 pers. pl. masc. . . עלה

עֹלָתֶךָ id. sing., suff. 2 pers. sing. masc. . עלה

עֹלָתָם[q] id. sing., suff. 3 pers. pl. masc. . . עלה

עַם וְ׳ עָם וְ׳ וְ׳ עָם, (with distinct. acc.) noun com. sing., pl. עַמִּים dec. 8 d, also pl. עֲמָמִים (§ 45) . . . . . . עמם

עִם וְ׳ prep. with suff. עִמִּי ,עִמְּךָ (§ 5) . עמם

עַמָּא[r] Chald. noun com. sing., emph. of עַם dec. 5 a, but pl. עַמְמַיָּא (§ 68) . . . עמם

I. עָמַד וְ׳ fut. יַעֲמֹד—I. *to stand*, spoken of animate and inanimate things; with לִפְנֵי *to stand before* any one, *to serve, minister to him*; with עַל *to stand, be set over; to stand upon, confide in*, Eze. 33. 26; *to stand by* or *for*, i. e. *to defend*.—II. *to stand, stand firm, endure*; with לִפְנֵי ,בִּפְנֵי ,נֶגֶד ,בְּ before or against any one.—III. *to stay, remain*; hence, *to remain alive*, Ex. 21. 21.—IV. *to stand still, stop*; hence, *to desist, leave off*; with מִן from any thing. —V. *to stand up, arise*; with עַל *against* any one. Hiph. הֶעֱמִיד—I. *to cause to stand*.—II. *to set up, erect*.—III. *to set, place*.—IV. *to set, establish, appoint*, e. g. an ordinance, with לְ ,עַל for any one; also *to appoint, constitute* to an office.—V. *to confirm, accomplish*.—VI. intrans. *to stand still*, 2 Ch. 18. 34. Hoph. הָעֳמַד—I. *to be set, placed*, Le. 16. 10.—II. *to remain*, 1 Ki. 22. 35.

II. עָמַד once by transp. for מָעַד in Hiph. Eze. 29. 7, *to make to tremble*.

[a] Eze. 34. 27. [b] Ec. 12. 5. [c] Ca. 6. 8. [d] Da. 7. 18. [e] Ps. 90. 8. [f] Da. 7. 5. [g] Is. 51. 20. [h] 1 Sa. 2. 1. [i] Ne. 3. 19. [k] Ex. 10. 25. [l] Job 5. 16. [m] 1 Sa. 1. 7. [n] Ps. 92. 16. [o] Is. 11. 16. [p] 1 Ki. 10. 5. [q] Le. 10. 19. [r] Ezr. 7. 13, 16, 25.

עֹמֶד prop. *standing, being*; hence, with the suff. of 1 pers. (only) עִמָּדִי *with me*.

עֹמֶד masc. dec. 6 c, *a standing place, station*.

עֶמְדָּה fem. *a place for stopping*, only sing. Mi. 1. 11.

עַמּוּד masc. dec. 1 b.—I. *column, pillar*.—II. *stage, scaffold*.

מַעֲמָד masc. dec. 2 b.—I. *standing, order*, 1 Ki. 10. 5.—II. *station, place of standing*.

מָעֳמָד masc. *place for standing, bottom*, Ps. 69. 3.

עָמַד [a] וְ' Kal pret. 3 pers. s. masc. for עָמַד (§ 8. r. 7) עמד
עָמֹד [b] וְ id. inf. abs. . . . . . עמד
עֲמֹד [c] וְ' id. imp. s. masc.; or inf. constr.; וְ bef. (-:) . עמד
עֲמָד־ [d] id. imp. (§ 8. rem. 18) . . . עמד
עֹמֵד וְ' id. part. act. sing. masc. dec. 7 b . עמד
עָמְדָה [e] וְ' id. pret. 3 pers. sing. fem. . . עמד
עַמֻּדָו [f] וְ defect. for עַמּוּדָיו (q. v.) . . . עמד
עָמְדוּ / וְ' עָמָדוּ } Kal pret. 3 pers. pl. (§ 8. rem. 7) . עמד
עָמְדוֹ id. inf. or, 2 Ch. 34. 31, subst. [עֹמֶד dec. 6c], suff. 3 pers. sing. masc. . . . עמד
עִמְדוּ [g] / וְ' [h] עִמְדוּ } id. imp. pl. masc. (§ 8. rem. 12) . עמד
עֹמְדוֹת [i] id. part. act. fem., pl. of עֹמֶדֶת dec. 13, from עֹמֵד masc. . . . עמד
עָמְדִי noun m. s., suff. 1 pers. sing. fr. [עֹמֶד] d. 6c עמד
עַמֻּדֵי [k] [l] וְ' defect. for עַמּוּדֵי (q. v.) . . . עמד
עִמָּדִי [m] וְ' prep. [עֹמֶד] with suff. 1 pers. sing. עמד
עִמְדִי Kal imp. sing. fem. . . . . עמד
עַמֻּדֶיהָ [n] noun masc. pl., suff. 3 pers. sing. masc. from עַמּוּד dec. 1b . . . . עמד
עַמֻּדֵיהֶם [o] וְ' id. pl., suff. 3 pers. pl. masc.; id. . עמד
עַמֻּדָיו וְ' id. pl., suff. 3 pers. sing. masc.; id. . עמד
עַמֻּדִים [p] וְ' id. pl., abs. st. . . . . עמד
עֹמְדִים Kal part. act. masc., pl. of עֹמֵד dec. 7b . עמד
עָמְדְךָ [q] id. inf., suff. 2 pers. sing. masc. . . עמד
עָמְדֶךָ [r] noun masc. sing., suff. 2 pers. sing. masc. from [עֹמֶד] dec. 6c . . . . עמד
עָמְדָם id. id., suff. 3 pers. pl. masc. . . . עמד
עָמַדְנוּ [ii] וְ id. pret. 1 pers. pl. . . . עמד
עָמַדְתָּ [s] / וְ עָמַדְתָּ } id. pret. 2 pers. sing. masc.; acc. shifted by conv. וְ . . } עמד
עֹמֶדֶת [t] / עֹמֶדֶת } id. part. act. sing. fem. dec. 13, from עֹמֵד masc. (§ 8. rem. 19) . } עמד
עֶמְדָּתוֹ [u] noun fem. s., suff. 3 pers. s. m. [from עֶמְדָּה] עמד
עָמַדְתִּי / וְ עָמַדְתִּי [x] } Kal pret. 1 pers. sing.; acc. shifted by conv. וְ . . . . } עמד

עֲמַדְתֶּם [y] [z] וְ' id. pret. 2 pers. pl. masc.; וְ for וְ, conv. עמד

עמה Root not used; cogn. עָמַם q. v.

עָמִית fem. dec. 3 a, *society, fellowship*, Zec. 13. 7; then for the concr. *fellow-man, neighbour*.

עַמָּה [a] וְ Chald. emph. of עַם irr. (§ 68) . . עמם
עַמָּהּ [b] וְ' noun com. sing., suff. 3 pers. sing. fem. from עַם dec. 8 d (exc. pl. עֲמָמִים § 45) עמם
עִמָּהּ prep. (עִם) with suff. 3 pers. sing. fem. (§ 5) עמם
עִמֵּהּ [c] Chald. id. with suff. 3 pers. sing. masc. . עמם
עֻמָּה וְ pr. name of a place . . . עמם
עִמְּהוֹן [d] וְ Ch. prep. (עִם) with suff. 3 pers. pl. masc. עמם
עִמָּהֶם וְ' Heb. id. with suff. 3 pers. pl. masc. . עמם
עַמּוֹ וְ' noun com. sing., suff. 3 pers. sing. masc. from עַם dec. 8 d (exc. עֲמָמִים § 45) . עמם
עִמּוֹ וְ' prep. (עִם) with suff. 3 pers. sing. m. (§ 5) עמם
עַמּוּד [e] וְ' noun masc. sing. dec. 1 b . . . עמד
עַמּוּדוֹ [f] id., suff. 3 pers. sing. masc. . . עמד
עַמּוּדֵי וְ' id. pl., constr. st. . . . . עמד
עַמּוּדֶיהָ [g] וְ' id. pl., suff. 3 pers. sing. fem. . . עמד
עַמּוּדֵיהֶם [h] id. pl., suff. 3 pers. pl. masc. . . עמד
עַמּוּדָיו וְ' id. pl., with suff. 3 pers. sing. masc. . עמד
עַמּוּדִים id. pl., abs. st. . . . . . עמד
עַמּוֹן וְ' pr. name of a people . . . עמם
עַמּוֹנִי gent. noun from עַמּוֹן . . . . עמם
עַמּוֹנִיּוֹת / עַמֳּנִיּוֹת } id. fem., pl. of עַמּוֹנִית (§ 39, 4, rem. 1, note), K. עַמֳּנִיּוֹת . . . } עמם
עָמוֹס pr. name masc. . . . . . עמס
עֲמוּסוֹת [i] Kal part. pass. f. pl. [of עֲמוּסָה fr. עָמוּס m.] עמס
עָמוֹק pr. name masc. . . . . . עמק
עֲמֻקָּה [k] adj. fem. sing. fr. עָמֹק masc. (§ 39, 3. r. 1) עמק
עַמֵּי [l] וְ' noun com. pl. constr. from עַם dec. 8 d (exc. עֲמָמִים § 45) . . . עמם
עַמִּי וְ' id. sing. with suff. 1 pers. sing. . . עמם
עִמִּי prep. (עִם) with suff. 1 pers. sing. . . עמם
עַמִּיאֵל pr. name masc. . . . . . עמם
עַמֶּיהָ [m] noun com. pl., suff. 3 pers. sing. fem. fr. עַם dec. 8 d (exc. עֲמָמִים § 45) . . עמם
עַמִּיהוּד pr. name masc. . . . . . עמם
עַמָּיו noun com. pl., suff. 3 pers. sing. masc. fr. עַם dec. 8 d (exc. עֲמָמִים § 45) . עמם
עַמִּיזָבָד pr. name masc. . . . . . עמם
עַמִּיחוּר Kh., עַמִּיהוּד K. q. v. . . . עמם
עַמֶּיךָ noun com. pl., suff. 2 pers. s. m. fr. עַם d. 8 d עמם
עַמִּים וְ' id. pl., abs. st., comp. עֲמָמִים (§ 45) . עמם
עַמִּינָדָב וְ' pr. name masc. . . . . עמם
עֲמִיקְתָא [n] Ch. adj. f. s. emph. [of עֲמִיקָא, fr. עֲמִיק m.] עמק

a 2 Sa. 20. 12. b Est. 9. 16. c Da. 10. 11. d 2 Sa. 1. 9. e 1 Ki. 1. 2. f Ex. 27. 11. g Na. 2. 9. h 2 Ch. 35. 5. i Ps. 122. 2. ii Sa. 14. 9. k Ex. 38. 17. l Nu. 3. 37. m Ru. 1. 8. n Ex. 39. 40. o Ex. 38. 19. p 1 Ki. 7. 41. q Ob. 11. r Da. 10. 11. s De. 4. 10. t Ec. 1. 4. u Mi. 1. 11. x 1 Sa. 19. 3. y Eze. 33. 26. z Je. 7. 10. a Ezr. 5. 12. b Is. 65. 18. c Da. 2. 22. d Ezr. 5. 2. e Ex. 13. 22. f 2 Ch. 23. 13. g Job 9. 6. h Ex. 38. 10, 11, 12, 14. i Is. 46. 1. k Pr. 23. 27. l Ne. 10. 32. m Ex. 31. 14. n Da. 2. 22.

עָמִיר[a] noun masc. sing. . . . . . עמר

עַמִּישַׁדָּי pr. name masc. . . . . . עמם

עֲמִיתוֹ noun fem. sing., suff. 3 pers. sing. masc. from [עָמִית] dec. 3 a . . . עמה

עֲמִיתִי[b] id., suff. 1 pers. sing. . . . . עמה

עֲמִיתֶךָ, עֲמִיתְךָ[c] } id., suff. 2 pers. sing. masc. . . עמה

עַמֶּךָ וְ׳, עַמְּךָ וְ׳ } noun com. sing., suff. 2 pers. sing. m. from עַם dec. 8 a (exc. עֲמָמִים § 45) } עמם

עַמֵּךְ[d] וְ׳ id. with suff. 2 pers. sing. fem. . עמם

עִמָּךְ prep. (עִם) with suff. 2 pers. sing. fem. (Chald. masc.), or in pause for the foll. עמם

עִמְּךָ וְ׳, עִמְּכָה[e] } id. with suff. 2 pers. sing. masc. (§ 3. rem. 2) . . . } עמם

עִמָּכֶם וְ׳ id. with suff. 2 pers. pl. masc. (§ 5) . עמם

עָמַל[f] fut. יַעֲמֹל *to toil, labour, travail.* Hence the two following.

עָמָל וְ׳ masc. dec. 4c.—I. *labour, toil.*—II. *travail, vexation, sorrow.*—III. *fruit of labour.*—IV. *mischief, iniquity, sin,* Nu. 23. 1, perh. also Is. 10. 1.—V. pr. name m. 1 Ch. 7. 35 עמל

עָמֵל adj. masc. dec. 5c.—I. *labouring, toiling*; pl. *labourers, workmen,* Ju. 5. 26.—II. *weary, wretched* . . עמל

עֲמַל[g] בַּ׳, וַ׳ n. m. s., constr. of עָמָל d. 4c; וַ bef. (ֲ) עמל

עָמְלָה[h] Kal pret. 3 pers. sing. fem. . . עמל

עֲמָלוֹ[i] וַ׳ n. m.s., suff. 3 p. s. m. fr. עָמָל d. 4c; וַ bef. (ֲ) עמל

עָמְלוּ[k] Kal pret. 3 pers. pl. . . . . עמל

עֲמָלִי[n] וַ׳ n. m. s., suff. 1 p. s. fr. עָמָל d. 4c; וַ bef. (ֲ) עמל

עֲמֵלִים[l] adj. masc., pl. of עָמֵל dec. 5c . . עמל

עֲמָלֵנוּ[m] noun masc. s., suff. 1 pers. pl. fr. עָמָל d. 4c עמל

עֲמָלֵק וַ׳ pr. name—I. of a grandson of Esau, Ge. 36. 12, 16.—II. of a people who inhabited the south of Palestine, and the borders of the desert of Sinai. Hence

עֲמָלֵקִי וַ׳ gent. noun from the preceding, *Amalekite.*

עָמַלְתָּ[n] Kal pret. 2 pers. sing. masc. . . . עמל

עָמַם I. *to hide, conceal,* Eze. 31. 8; intrans. *to be hidden,* Eze. 28. 3.—II. as in the Arab. *to be common, in common,* whence derivv. עַם, עִם, עֻמָּה. Hoph. הוּעַם *to become obscured, dim,* La. 4. 1.

עַם, עָם com. dec. 8a or d (pl. עַמִּים, עֲמָמִים § 45).—I. *people, nation*; most frequently of Israel opposed to גּוֹיִם *gentiles*; pl. עַמִּים is also used for other nations; בְּנֵי עַמִּי *the children of my people,* i. e. my countrymen; בַּת עַמִּי *the daughter of my people,* i. e. my people or country; it is applied to a *tribe,* comp. Ju. 5. 18; also to *family, kindred, relatives,* comp. Le. 21. 1, 4; 19. 16.—II. of animals, *a swarm* or *flock.*

עַם Chald. id. pl. עַמְמִין (§ 68).

עִם prep. (with suff. עִמִּי, עִמְּךָ, &c. § 5).—I. *with, along with*; Ne. 5. 18, עִם־זֶה *with this, notwithstanding*; Ps. 72. 5, עִם־שֶׁמֶשׁ *with the sun,* i. e. *as long as the sun endures*; עָשָׂה חֶסֶד עִם *to do kindness with* any one, i. e. to show him kindness.—II. *at, by, near.*—III. *like as,* comp. Ec. 2. 16; Ps. 73. 5.—IV. *with, amid.*—V. מֵעִם prop. *from* (being) *with, at, by*; hence (*a*) simply *from*; Job 34. 33 מֵעִמְּךָ *from with thee,* i. e. according as it proceeds from thy mind or judgment; (*b*) *from among,* Ru. 4. 10.

עִם Chald. i. q. Heb. *with, along with*; עִם־לֵילְיָא *in the night*; עִם־דָּר וְדָר *during* generation and generation, as long as the generations of men endure.

עֻמָּה fem. dec. 10.—I. prop. *union, connexion*; as a prep. לְעֻמּוֹת, לְעֻמַּת, עֻמַּת, (*a*) *by, at, near*; (*b*) *against,* Eze. 3. 8; (*c*) *opposite to,* 1 Ch. 26.16; *like, even as*; כָּל־עֻמַּת *wholly as,* Ec. 5. 15; מִלְּעֻמַּת *near by.*—II. pr. name of a town in the tribe of Asher, Jos. 19. 30.

עַמּוֹן (*of* or *from the people* or *kindred,* i. q. בֶּן־עַמּוֹן Ge. 19. 38) pr. name of the son of Lot's daughter and his descendants. Gent. noun עַמּוֹנִי, fem. עַמּוֹנִית *Ammonite,* pl. fem. עַמּוֹנִיּוֹת.

עַמְעָד (*people of duration*) pr. name of a town of Asher, Jos. 19. 26.

עַמְרָם (*the people is exalted*) pr. name—I. of the father of Moses. Patronym. עַמְרָמִי.—II. Ezr. 10. 34.

עַמִּיאֵל (*kindred of God*) pr. name masc. of several persons.

עַמִּיהוּד (*kindred of Judah,* for עַמִּי יְהוּד) pr. name masc. of several persons.

עַמִּיזָבָד (*kindred of the Giver*) pr. name masc. 1 Ch. 27. 6.

עַמִּיחוּר (*kindred of nobility*) pr. name masc. 2 Sa. 13. 37, Kh.

עַמִּינָדָב (*kindred of the prince*) pr. name masc. of several persons.

עַמִּישַׁדָּי (*kindred of the Almighty*) pr. name masc. Nu. 1. 12; 2. 25.

---

[a] Am. 2. 13. [b] Zec. 13. 7. [c] Le. 18. 20. [d] Is. 60. 21. [e] 1 Sa. 1. 26. [f] Ec. 2. 21. [g] Ps. 105. 44. [h] Pr. 16. 26. [i] Pr. 31. 7. [n] Ps. 25. 18. [k] Ps. 127. 1. [l] Ju. 5. 26. [m] De. 26. 7. [n] Jon. 4. 10.

עִמָּנוּאֵל (*God with us*) a prophetic title of the Messiah, Is. 7. 14; 8. 8.

עַמָּם noun com. sing. with suff. 3 pers. pl. masc. from עַם dec. 8d (exc. עֲמָמִים § 45) . עמם

עִמָּם prep. (עִם) with suff. 3 pers. pl. masc. (§ 5) עמם

עֲמָמֻהוּ[a] Kal pret. 3 pers. pl. [עָמְמוּ], suff. 3 p. s. m. עמם

עֲמָמוּךָ[b] id., suff. 2 pers. sing. masc. . . עמם

עַמְמֵי[c] constr. of עֲמָמִים (q. v.) . . . עמם

עַמְמַיָּא Ch. noun com. pl. emph., irr. of עַם (§ 68) עמם

עֲמָמִים[d] וְ‚ noun com. pl., irr. of עַם (§ 45); וְ bef. (-:) עמם

עַמֵּנוּ id. sing. with suff. 1 pers. pl. dec. 8d . עמם

עִמָּנוּ וְ‚ prep. (עִם) with suff. 1 pers. pl. (§ 5) . עמם

עִמָּנוּאֵל prophetic name . . . . עמם

עַמֹּנִים gent. noun, pl. of עַמּוֹנִי from עַמּוֹן . . עמם

[עָמַס, עָמַשׂ] fut. יַעֲמֹס.—I. *to take* or *lift up*, Zec. 12. 3.—II. *to bear, carry*, Is. 46. 3.—III. *to load, lay a burden upon*, with עַל, לְ. Hiph. *to load, burden*, with עַל.

עָמוֹס (*bearer* of burden) pr. name, *Amos*, the prophet.

עֲמָשָׂא (*burden*) pr. name masc. of two different persons.

עֲמָשַׂי (*burdensome*) pr. name of three different persons.

עֲמַסְיָה (*the Lord bears* him *up*) pr. name masc. 2 Ch. 17. 16.

מַעֲמָסָה fem. *burden*, Zec. 12. 3.

עֲמַסְיָה pr. name masc. . . . . . עמם

עֹמְסֶיהָ[e] the foll. with suff. 3 pers. sing. fem. . עמם

עֹמְסִים[f] וְ Kal part. act. masc. pl. [of עוֹמֵס] dec. 7b עמם

עַמְעָד וְ pr. name masc. . . . . . עמם

[עָמַק] *to be deep, unsearchable*, Ps. 92. 6. Hiph. *to make deep*; Je. 49. 8, 30 הֶעְמִיקוּ לָשֶׁבֶת *make deep to dwell*, i. e. make your dwellings deep in the earth; metaph. *to act deeply, lay deep designs*.

עָמֵק adj. masc. dec. 5, *deep, profound*, only pl. c. עִמְקֵי שָׂפָה *of unintelligible speech*.

עָמֹק masc. pl. עֲמֻקִּים, fem. עֲמֻקָּה.—I. *deep*.—II. metaph. *unsearchable*.

עָמוֹק (*deep*) pr. name masc. Ne. 12. 7, 20.

עֲמִיק Chald. only fem. עֲמִיקָא (dec. 8a) adj. *deep, profound, unsearchable*, Da. 2. 22.

עֵמֶק masc. dec. 6b.—I. *deep place*, Pr. 9. 18.—II. *valley* or *vale*.—III. עֵ׳ הָאֵלָה *valley of terebinths*, near Bethlehem; עֵ׳ בְּרָכָה *valley of blessing*, 2 Ch. 20. 26; עֵ׳ הַמֶּלֶךְ *the king's valley*, not far from the Dead Sea; עֵ׳ רְפָאִים *valley of the Rephaim*, south-west of Jerusalem.—IV. עֵ׳ קְצִיץ (*valley of cutting*) pr. name of a town in Benjamin, Jos. 18. 21.

עֹמֶק fem. *depth*, Pr. 25. 3.

מַעֲמָק masc. dec. 8a, only pl., *depths*.

עָמֹק וְ׳ adj. m. s., pl. עֲמֻקִּים d. 8c (§ 37. No. 3c) עמק

עֵמֶק וְ׳ noun masc. sing. dec. 6b . . . עמק

עֲמֻקָּה adj. fem. sing. dec. 10, from עָמֹק masc. (q. v.) עמק

עָמְקוּ[g] Kal pret. 3 pers. pl. . . . . עמק

עֲמֻקּוֹת[h] adj. fem., pl. of עֲמֻקָּה fr. עָמֹק masc. (q. v.) עמק

עִמְקֵי adj. pl. constr. masc. from [עָמֵק] dec. 5 . עמק

עֲמָקַיִךְ[i] the foll. with suff. 2 pers. sing. fem. . עמק

עֲמָקִים[k] וְ׳ noun masc., pl. of עֵמֶק dec. 6b; וַ bef. (-:) עמק

עֲמֻקִּים adj. masc., pl. of עָמֹק dec. 6c (§ 37. No. 3c) עמק

עִמְקֵךְ[l] noun masc. sing., suff. 2 pers. s. f. עֵמֶק d. 6b עמק

עִמְקָם[m] id., suff. 3 pers. pl. masc. . . . עמק

עָמַר. Pi. *to bind* sheaves, Ps. 129. 7. Hithp. with בְּ *to serve oneself with* any one, *treat* him *as a slave*.

עֲמַר Chald. *wool*, i. q. Heb. צֶמֶר Da. 7. 9.

עָמִיר masc. *a sheaf*. See also the three following.

עֹמֶר masc. dec. 6c.—I. *sheaf*.—II. *Omer*, a measure of things dry, tenth part of an ephah . עמר

עֲמֹרָה וְ׳ pr. name, *Gomorrah*, one of the four cities of the valley of Siddim, destroyed in the time of Lot and Abraham . עמר

עָמְרִי וְ׳ (for עָמְרִיָּה *servant of the Lord*) pr. name —I. *Omri*, king of Israel.—II. of three other men . . . . . . עמר

עַמְרָם pr. name masc. . . . . . עמם

עֲמָשָׂא pr. name masc. . . . . . עמם

עֲמָשַׂי, עֲמָשָׂי וְ׳ } pr. name masc.; וַ bef. (-:) . . עמם

עֹמְשִׂים[n] Kal part. act. pl. masc. for עֹמְסִים . עמם

עֲמַשְׁסַי וְ pr. name masc. Ne. 11. 13.

עֻמַּת[o] (prop. noun fem. sing., constr. of עֻמָּה) *adv*. עמם

ענב Root not used; Chald. *to bind together*.

עָנוּב (*bound together*) pr. name masc. 1 Ch. 4. 8. Also the two following.

עֲנָב וְ׳ (i. q. עֵנָב *cluster*) pr. name of a town in Judah, Jos. 11. 21; 15. 50 . . ענב

עֵנָב[p] masc. dec. 4b, *clusters of grapes* . ענב

עִנְּבֵי id. pl. constr. with dag. euph. (§ 33. rem. 1) ענב

עֲנָבִים[q] וְ׳ id. pl. abs.; וַ bef. (-:) . . . ענב

עִנְּבֵמוֹ[r] id. pl., suff. 3 pers. pl. masc. . . ענב

---

[a] Eze. 31. 8. [b] Eze. 28. 3. [c] Ne. 9. 24. [d] Ne. 9. 22. [e] Zec. 12. 3. [f] Ne. 13. 15. [g] Ps. 92. 6. [h] Job 12. 22. [i] Is. 22. 7. [k] Ps. 65. 14. [l] Je. 49. 4. [m] Je. 47. 5. [n] Ne. 4. 11. [o] Ec. 5. 15. [p] De. 32. 14. [q] Nu. 6. 3. [r] De. 32. 32.

עָנַג Pu. part. *delicately brought up*, Je. 6. 2. Hithp. I. *to be delicate*, De. 28. 56.—II. *to delight oneself, to rejoice in* any thing, with עַל, also מִן.—III. *to sport oneself* against any, with עַל Is. 57. 4.

עָנֹג masc. עֲנֻגָּה fem. adj. *delicate, tender.*

עֹנֶג masc. *delight, pleasure*, Is. 13. 22; 58. 13.

תַּעֲנוּג masc. dec. 1 b (pl. ־ִים, ־וֹת) *delight, pleasure, enjoyment, luxury.*

עֹנֶג noun masc. sing. . . . . . ענג

וַעֲנֻגָּה[a] adj. fem. sing. from עָנֹג masc. (§ 37. No. 3 c); וַ bef. (־ֲ) . . . ענג

[עָנַד] *to bind on.*

מַעֲדַנּוֹת (for מַעֲנַדּוֹת) fem. pl. *bands*, Job 38. 31.

עָנְדֵם[b] Kal imp. sing. masc., suff. 3 pers. pl. masc. (ם for ן fem. § 2. rem. 5) . . . ענד

***I.* עָנָה** וֹ fut. יַעֲנֶה, ap. וַיַּעַן (§ 24. rem. 3).—I. *to answer*, const. with acc. of the thing answered, also with acc. of the person; *to answer* God, is to dispute with him; it is spec. spoken (*a*) of judges, Ex. 23. 2; (*b*) of those who *answer* to inquiries of the judge, *to give testimony, to testify*, with בְּ *for*, but more frequently *against* any one; (*c*) frequently of God, *to answer* prayer; hence *to impart* or *grant* any thing; Ec. 10. 19, הַכֶּסֶף יַעֲנֶה אֶת־הַכֹּל *money answers (serves) all* sc. purposes.—II. *to answer in singing, sing alternately, in response*; hence *to sing to* any one, with לְ *to celebrate* him; also *to cry, call, shout*, as soldiers in battle, or the jackals in the desert, Is. 13. 22.—III. *to speak, begin to speak*; of God, *to announce, declare* an oracle. Niph. I. *to be answered.*—II. *to be induced to answer*, Eze. 14. 4, 7. Pi. *to sing.* Hiph. *to answer favourably, grant, impart.*

עֲנָה, עֲנָא Chald. *to answer, speak, begin to speak.*

***II.* [עָנָה]** I. *to bestow labour upon, to exercise oneself*, with בְּ, Ec. 1. 13; 3. 10.—II. *to be afflicted, depressed, humbled.* Niph. *to be afflicted, humbled*; with מִפְּנֵי *to humble oneself before* any one, Ex. 10. 3. Pi. *to oppress, subdue, afflict, humble*; with אִשָּׁה *to ravish a woman*; with נֶפֶשׁ *to fast.* Pu. *to be afflicted, humbled.* Hiph. *to oppress, afflict.* Hithp. I. *to humble, submit oneself.*—II. *to be afflicted*, 1 Ki. 2. 26.

עֲנָה Chald. *to be afflicted.*

עֲנָה (*answer* sc. to prayer) pr. name—I. of a son of Seir, and his descendants.—II. of a son of Zibeon, grandson of Seir.

עָנָו masc. dec. 4 c, *humble, meek, poor, afflicted.*

עֲנָוָה fem. dec. 11 c (§ 42. r. 1) *humility, meekness.*

עַנְוָה fem. id. Ps. 45. 5.

עֱנוּת fem. *affliction*, Ps. 22. 25; others, *cry.*

עָנִי masc. dec. 8 f. עֲנִיָּה fem. adj. *afflicted, distressed, poor, needy.*

עֳנִי masc. dec. 6 k, *affliction, misery.*

עֻנִּי (*depressed*) pr. name of a man.

עֲנָיָה (whom *the Lord answers*) pr. name masc. Ne. 8. 4; 10. 23.

עָנָיו masc. frequently in Keri for עֲנָו in Khethib.

עִנְיָן masc. dec. 2 b, *business, affair, matter, thing.*

עֲנָת (*answer*) pr. name masc. Ju. 3. 31; 5. 6.

עֲנָתוֹת (*answers*) pr. name—I. of a city of the Levites in the tribe of Benjamin. Gent. noun עַנְּתֹתִי.—II. of two men, 1 Ch. 7. 8; Ne. 10. 20.

עַנְתֹתִיָּה (*answer from the Lord*) pr. name masc. 1 Ch. 8. 23.

יַעַן I. prep. *on account of, because of.*—II. conj. *because that, because*; יַעַן אֲשֶׁר (*a*) *because that*; (*b*) *to the intent that*, Eze. 12. 12; יַעַן כִּי *because that*; יַעַן בְּיַעַן, יַעַן וּבְיַעַן *because, even because.*

יַעְנַי (for יַעֲנְיָה *the Lord answers*) pr. name masc. 1 Ch. 5. 12.

מַעֲנֶה masc. dec. 9 a.—I. *answer.*—II. *intent, end, purpose*, Pr. 16. 4.

מַעַן prop. for מַעֲנֶה *intent, purpose*, only in the combination לְמַעַן, with suff. לְמַעֲנִי, לְמַעַנְךָ, &c. (comp. dec. 6 d).—I. prep. *on account of, because of, for the sake of.*—II. conj. *in order that, so that*; לְמַעַן אֲשֶׁר *to the end that, in order that*; also *because that.*

מַעֲנָה fem. *furrow*, 1 Sa. 14. 14.

מַעֲנִית fem. dec. 1 b, id. Ps. 129. 3. Keri.

תַּעֲנִית f. d. 1 b, *self-humiliation, fasting*, Ezr. 9. 5.

וַעֲנָה וֹ pr. name masc.; וַ bef. (־ֲ) . . . . ענה

עָנֵה Chald. Peal part. act. s. m. d. 6 a (§ 55, note) ענה

עַנֵּה[c] Piel inf. abs. . . . . . ענה

עֲנֵה Kal imp. sing. masc. . . . . . ענה

עִנָּה Piel pret. 3 pers. sing. masc. . . . ענה

עֹנֶה וֹ"ד[d] Kal part. act. sing. masc. dec. 9 a . ענה

עָנָהוּ id. pret. 3 p. s. m., suff. 3 p. s. m. (§ 24. r. 21) ענה

עֹנֵהוּ[e] id. part. act. s. m., suff. 3 p. s. m. fr. עֹנֶה d. 9 a ענה

עָנָו[f] adj. masc. sing. dec. 4 c; Cheth. עָנָיו . ענה

עֲנוֹ Chald. Peal pret. 3 pers. pl. masc. . ענה

עָנוּ וֹ Kal pret. 3 pers. pl. . . . . ענה

עֲנוּ[gg] id. imp. pl. masc. . . . . . ענה

[a] Is. 47. 1. [b] Pr. 6. 21. [c] Ex. 22. 22. [d] Mal. 2. 12. [e] 1 Sa. 14. 39. [f] Nu. 12. 3. [gg] 1 Sa. 12. 3.

עַנּוּ [a] [b] ו׳ Piel imp. pl. masc. . . . ענה
עֲנוּ Kal imp. pl. masc. . . . ענה
עִנּוּ ו׳ Piel pret. 3 pers. pl. . . . ענה
עֲנוֹ וּ Kh. עָנוֹ, K. עָנִו pr. name masc. . . ענה
עָנוּב pr. name masc. . . . ענב
עֲנָוָה noun fem. sing. dec. 11c (§ 42. rem. 1) ענה
עַנְוָה [c] וּ noun fem. sing. . . . ענה
עַנְוֵי noun masc. pl. constr. from עָנָו dec. 4c . ענה
עֲנָוֵי Kh. עֲנָוֵי q. v., K. עֲנִיֵּי (q. v.) . . ענה
עֲנָוִים [d] ו׳ adj. masc., pl. of עָנָו dec. 4c; וַ bef. (-:) ענה
עֲנָוִים Kh. עֲנָוִים q. v., K. עֲנִיִּים (q. v.) . ענה
עָנוֹשׁ [e] Kal inf. abs. . . . ענש
עֲנוֹשׁ [f] id. inf. constr. . . . ענש
עֲנוּשִׁים [g] id. part. pass. masc. pl. [of עָנוּשׁ] dec. 3a . ענש
עֲנוֹת [h] Kal inf. constr. (and pr. name in compos. see בֵּית) . . ענה
עַנּוֹת Piel inf. constr. . . . ענה
עֱנוּת [i] noun fem. sing. . . . ענה
עֻנּוֹתוֹ [k] Pual inf. (עֻנּוֹת), suff. 3 pers. sing. m. d. 1b ענה
עַנְוַתְךָ [l] וּ noun fem. sing. with suff. 2 pers. sing. masc. from עֲנָוָה dec. 11c (§ 42. rem. 1) . ענה
עָנִי ו׳ adj. masc. sing., pl. עֲנִיִּים d. 8 (§ 37. No. 4) ענה
עָנִי [m] Kh.; עֵינֵי K. (q. v.) . . . עין
עֳנִי / עֳנִי } noun masc. sing. dec. 6k (§ 35. rem. 14) ענה
עֻנִּי וּ pr. name masc. . . . ענה
עֲנָיָה ו׳ pr. name masc.; וַ bef. (-:) . . ענה
עָנְיָהּ [n] noun masc. sing., suff. 3 pers. sing. fem. from עֳנִי dec. 6k . . . ענה
עֲנִיָּה adj. fem. sing. from עָנִי masc. . . ענה
עֲנִיָּיו [o] וַ adj. pl. masc., suff. 3 pers. sing. masc. from עָנִי dec. 8 (§ 37. No. 4); וַ bef. (-:) . ענה
עָנְיִי noun masc. s., suff. 1 pers. sing. fr. עֳנִי d. 6k ענה
עֲנִיֵּי adj. pl. constr. masc. fr. עָנִי d. 8 (§ 37. No. 4) ענה
עֲנִיֶּיךָ [p] ו׳ וַ id. pl. with suff. 2 pers. sing. m.; וַ bef. (-:) ענה
עֲנִיִּים id. pl., abs. st. Kh. עֲנִיִּים, but עֲנָוִים K. (q. v.) ענה
עֲנִיִּים [q] ו׳ id. pl., abs. st.; וַ bef. (-:) . ענה
עָנְיֵךְ [r] noun masc. sing., suff. 2 pers. s. m. fr. עֳנִי d. 6k ענה
עָנְיָם [s] id. with suff. 3 pers. pl. masc. . . ענה
עֲנִים וּ pr. name of a place . . . עין
עֲנַיִן [t] Chald. Peal part. act. masc., pl. of עָנֵה [for עָנֵא] dec. 6a . . . . ענה
עֲנַיִן [u] Ch. id. part. pass. m. pl. [of עֲנֵה for עֲנֵא] d. 6a ענה
עִנְיָן noun masc. sing. dec. 2b . . . ענה
עִנְיַן [x] ו׳ id., constr. st. . . . ענה
עָנְיֵנוּ noun masc. sing., suff. 1 pers. pl. fr. עֳנִי d. 6k ענה

עִנְיָנוֹ [y] noun masc. s., suff. 3 pers. sing. m. fr. עִנְיָן d. 2b ענה
עִנִּינוּ [z] Piel pret. 1 pers. pl. . . . ענה
עָנִיתָ [a] וּ Kal pret. 2 pers. sing. masc. . . ענה
עִנִּיתָ [b] Piel pret. 2 pers. sing. masc. . . ענה
עִנִּיתָהּ [c] id. with suff. 3 pers. sing. fem. . . ענה
עָנִיתִי Kal pret. 1 pers. sing. . . . ענה
עִנֵּיתִי [d] Piel pret. 1 pers. sing. (§ 24. rem. 11) . ענה
עֻנֵּיתִי [e] Pual pret. 1 pers. sing. . . . ענה
עֲנִיתִיךָ [f] Kal pret. 1 pers. sing. (עָנִיתִי), suff. 2 pers. s. m. ענה
עֲנִיתָם [g] [h] ו׳ id. pret. 2 pers. sing. masc. (עָנִיתָ), suff. 3 pers. pl. masc.; וַ for וְ, conv. . ענה
עֲנִיתֶם id. pret. 2 pers. pl. masc. . . ענה
עִנִּיתֶם וּ Piel pret. 2 pers. pl. masc. . . ענה
עִנִּיתָנוּ id. pret. 2 pers. sing. masc., suff. 1 pers. pl. ענה
עֲנִיתָנִי Kal pret. 2 pers. s. m. (עָנִיתָ), suff. 1 pers. s. ענה
עִנִּיתָנִי [k] Piel pret. 2 pers. sing. masc., suff. 1 pers. sing. ענה
עֲנָךְ Kal pret. 2 pers. sing. masc. (עָנָה), suff. 2 p. s. m. (§ 2 rem. 2 and 24. rem. 21). ענה
עָנָם id., suff. 3 pers. pl. masc. . . . ענה
עָנֵם pr. name of a place . . . עין
עֲנָמִים pr. name of a people, not definitely known, Ge. 10. 13.
עֲנַמֶּלֶךְ וּ pr. name of an idol of the Sepharvites, 2 Ki. 17. 31.

עָנָן ו׳ masc. dec. 4c.—I. *a cloud.*—II. pr. name masc. Ne. 10. 27.

עִנֵּן Pi. *to cloud, bring a cloud,* Ge. 9. 14. Poel. עוֹנֵן *to divine,* by the *clouds* or perh. the sky generally; part. מְעוֹנֵן, *a diviner, meteorologist;* fem. עֹנְנָה for מְעוֹנְנָה.

עֲנַן Chald. masc. dec. 1a, *cloud,* Da. 7. 13.

עֲנָנָה fem. id. Job 3. 5.

עֲנָנִי (for עֲנַנְיָה, q. v.) pr. name masc. 1 Ch. 3. 24.

עֲנַנְיָה (whom *the Lord covers, protects*) pr. name —I. of a man, Ne. 3. 23.—II. of a town in the tribe of Benjamin, Ne. 11. 32.

עֲנַן [l] ו׳ וַ id., constr. st.; וַ bef. (-:) . . ענן
עֲנָנָה [m] noun fem. sing. . . . ענן
עֹנְנָה [n] Kal part. act. fem. from עוֹנֵן masc. . ענן
עֲנָנוֹ noun masc. sing., suff. 3 pers. sing. masc. from עָנָן dec. 4c . . . ענן
עֲנָנוֹ וַ Kh. עֲנָנוֹ q. v., K. עֲנָנִי (q. v.) . ענה
עֲנֵנוּ [o] Kal imp. sing. masc. (עֲנֵה), suff. 1 pers. pl. (§ 24. rem. 21) . . ענה
עֲנָנִי [p] ו׳ id. pret. 3 p. s. m. (עָנָה), suff. 1 p. s. (§ 24. r. 2) ענה

[a] Is. 27. 2. [b] Ju. 19. 24. [c] Ps. 45. 5. [d] Ps. 37. 11. [e] Ex. 21. 22. [f] Pr. 17. 26. [g] Am. 2. 8. [h] Ex. 32. 18. [i] Ps. 22. 25. [k] Ps. 132. 1. [l] Ps. 18. 36. [m] Is. 3. 8. [n] La. 1. 7. [o] Is. 49. 13. [p] Ps. 72. 2; 74. 19. [q] Is. 58. 7. [r] Ge. 16. 11. [s] Ex. 4. 31. [t] Da. 3. 24. [u] Da. 4. 24. [x] Ec. 1. 13; 4. 8. [y] Ec. 2. 23. [z] Is. 58. 3. [a] De. 26. 5. [b] Ps. 88. 8. [c] De. 21. 14. [d] Ps. 35. 13. [e] Ps. 119. 71. [f] Is. 49. 8. [g] Ps. 99. 8. [h] 1 Ki. 12. 7. [i] Ps. 90. 15. [k] Ps. 119. 75. [l] Nu. 10. 34. [m] Job 3. 5. [n] Is. 57. 3. [o] 1 Ki. 18. 26. [p] Ps. 34. 5.

עֲנָנִי וְ' pr. name masc.; וּ bef. (-:) . . . ענן

עֲנָנֵי[a] Chald. noun masc. pl. constr. fr. [עֲנָן] dec. 1 a ענה

עֲנֵנִי וַ' Kal imp. sing. masc. (עֲנֵה), suff. 1 pers. sing. (§ 24. rem. 21); וּ bef. (-:) . . . ענה

עֲנָנְיָה pr. name of a man and a place . . . ענן

עֹנְנֵיכֶם[b] the foll. with suff. 2 pers. pl. masc. . . ענן

עֹנְנִים[c] וְ Kal part. act. masc. pl. of עוֹנֵן dec. 7 b ענן

עֲנָנְךָ[d] וַ noun masc. sing., suff. 2 pers. sing. masc. from עָנָן q. v.; וּ bef. (-:) . . . ענן

עָנָף וְ'[e] masc. dec. 4 a, *branch, bough.*

עָנֵף fem., עֲנֵפָה adj., *full of branches,* Eze. 19. 10.

עֲנַף Chald. masc. dec. 3 a, *branch, bough,* Da. 4. 9, 11, 18.

עֲנַף[f] וַ id., constr. st.; וּ bef. (-:) . . . ענף

עֲנֵפָה[g] וַ adj. fem. sing. [from עָנֵף masc.]; וּ id. ענף

עַנְפּוֹהִי[h] Chald. noun masc. pl., suff. 3 pers. sing. masc. from [עֲנַף] dec. 3 a . . . ענף

עֲנָפֶיהָ[i] וַ noun masc. pl., suff. 3 pers. sing. fem. from עָנָף dec. 4 c; וּ bef. (-:) . . . ענף

עַנְפְּכֶם[k] id. sing., suff. 2 pers. pl. masc. . . ענף

עֲנָק masc. dec. 1 a (pl. ־ִים, ־וֹת).—I. *a necklace, neck-chain* or *collar.*—II. (*long-necked*; Arab. id.) pr. name, *Anak,* the father of the *Anakim* (בְּנֵי עֲנָק, בְּנֵי עֲנָקִים, or עֲנָקִים, יְלִידֵי הָעֲ', בְּנֵי הָעֲנָק), a Canaanitish people, who were giants.

עָנַק (denom. of עֲנָק) *to adorn with a necklace,* Ps. 73. 6, *pride surrounds them, like a necklace.* Hiph. הֶעֱנִיק *to lay upon the neck of* any one, *to lade him liberally,* De. 15. 14.

עֲנוֹק i. q. עֲנָק No. II, Jos. 21. 11.

עֲנָקִים וְ'[l] id. pl., also pr. name; וּ bef. (-:)

עֲנָקַתְמוֹ[m] Kal pret. 3 pers. s. fem. with suff. 3 pers. pl. m. ענק

עָנֵר pr. name—I. of a Canaanite, Ge. 14. 13, 24. —II. of a city, 1 Ch. 6. 55; elsewhere תַּעְנָךְ q. v.

[עָנַשׁ] fut. יַעֲנֹשׁ.—I. *to tax.*—II. *to fine in money,* with לְ. Niph. *to be fined, mulcted.*

עֲנָשׁ Chald. masc. *fine, mulct,* Ezr. 7. 26. Also the following.

עֹנֶשׁ masc. *fine, mulct,* 2 Ki. 23. 33; Pr. 19. 19 ענש

עָנְשׁוּ[n] וְ Kal pret. 3 pers. pl. . . . ענש

עֲנָת pr. name masc. (and in compos. see בַּיִת) ענה

עֲנָת[o] Chald. Peal pret. 3 pers. sing. fem. . ענה

עָנְתָה וְ' Kal pret. 3 pers. sing. fem. . . . ענה

עֹנָתָהּ[p] וְ noun fem. sing., suff. 3 pers. sing. fem. from [עוֹנָה] dec. 10 . . . עון

עַנּוֹתוֹ Piel inf. (עַנּוֹת), suff. 3 pers. s. masc. dec. 1 b ענה

עֲנָתוֹת וְ' pr. name of a man and a place; וּ bef. (-:) ענה

עַנֹּתְךָ[q] Piel inf. (עַנּוֹת), suff. 2 pers. s. masc. dec. 1 b ענה

עֲנֹתְךָ[r] וַ contr. from עֲנָוֹתְךָ (q. v.) . . . ענה

עִנִּתִךְ[s] וְ Piel pret. 1 pers. s. (עִנִּיתִי), suff. 2 pers. s. f. ענה

עֲנָתֹת pr. name of a place . . . ענה

עַנְתֹתִיָּה וְ pr. name masc. . . . ענה

עַסּוֹתֶם[t] וְ Kal pret. 2 pers. pl. masc. . . עסס

עָסִיס noun masc. sing. dec. 3 a . . . עסס

[עָסַס] *to tread down,* Mal. 3. 21.

עָסִיס masc. dec. 3 a, *must, new wine.*

עֳפָאיִם[u] noun masc. pl. of [עֳפִי] dec. 6 k . . עפה

עָפָה Root not used; Syr. *to flourish.*

עֳפִי masc. only pl. עֳפָאיִם (§ 35. rem. 15) *branches, boughs.*

עֳפִי Chald. *branch, bough,* with suff. עָפְיֵהּ (comp. dec. 6 k) Da. 4. 9, 11, 18.

עָפָה[x] Kal part. act. fem. [of עָף masc.] . . עוף

עָפוּ[y] וְ id. pret. 3 pers. pl.; acc. shifted by conv. וְ (comp. § 8. rem. 7) . . . עוף

עָפוֹת[z] id. part. act. fem., pl. of עָפָה [fr. עָף masc.] עוף

עָפְיֵהּ[a] וְ' Chald. noun masc. sing., suff. 3 pers. sing. masc. [from עֳפִי comp. Heb. dec. 6 k] עפה

עָפַל Pu. *to be swollen,* metaph. *elated, proud,* Hab. 2. 4. Hiph. *to act arrogantly, presumptuously,* Nu. 14. 44. Hence

עֹפֶל masc. dec. 6 c.—I. *swelling, tumour.*—II. *mount, hill* . . . . עפל

עֻפְּלָה[b] Pual pret. 3 pers. sing. fem. . . עפל

עֳפָלִים[c] Kh. עֳפָלֵי n. m. pl. c. fr. עֹפֶל d. 6 c (K. טְחֹרֵי q. v.) עפל

עֳפְלֵיכֶם[d] Kh. עֳפָלֵיכֶם id. pl. with suff. 2 pers. pl. masc. (K. טְחֹרֵיכֶם) . . . עפל

עֳפָלִים[e] Kh. עֳפָלִים id. pl., abs. st. (K. טְחֹרִים) . עפל

[עָפְנִי] only in the form הָעָפְנִי (כְּפַר) *village of the Ophnite,* pr. name of a town in Benjamin, Jos. 18. 24.

עַפְעַפָּי[f] noun du. [עַפְעַפַּיִם], suff. 1 pers. sing. [from עַפְעַף dec. 8 d] . . . עוף

עַפְעַפָּיו[g] וְ'[h] id. du., suff. 3 pers. sing. masc. . עוף

עַפְעַפֶּיךָ[i] וְ id. du., suff. 2 pers. sing. masc. . עוף

עַפְעַפֵּינוּ[k] וְ id. du., suff. 1 pers. pl. . . . עוף

[a] Da. 7. 13. [b] Je. 27. 9. [c] Is. 2. 6. [d] Nu. 14. 14. [e] Mal. 3. 19. [f] Le. 23. 40. [g] Eze. 19. 10. [h] Da. 4. 11. [i] Ps. 80. 11. [k] Eze. 36. 8. [l] Pr. 1. 9. [m] Ps. 73. 6. [n] De. 22. 19. [o] Da. 5. 10. [p] Ex. 21. 10. [q] De. 8. 2, 16. [r] 2 Sa. 22. 36. [s] Na. 1. 12. [t] Mal. 3. 21. [u] Ps. 104. 12. [x] Zec. 5. 1, 2. [y] Is. 11. 14. [z] Is. 31. 5. [a] Da. 4. 9, 11, 18. [b] Hab. 2. 4. [c] 1 Sa. 6. 4. [d] 1 Sa. 6. 5. [e] 1 Sa. 5. 9. [f] Job 16. 16. [g] Ps. 11. 4. [h] Pr. 30. 13. [i] Pr. 4. 25. [k] Je. 9. 17.

עָפָר וְ' masc. dec. 4c (pl. c. עַפְרוֹת).—I. *dust, dry earth.* —II. *earth, mould, clay.*—III. *the earth.*—IV. pl. *clods, lumps.*

עִפֵּר Pi. (denom. of עָפָר) *to dust, throw dust at* any one, 2 Sa. 16. 13.

עֵפֶר (i. q. עֹפֶר) pr. name masc.—I. Ge. 25. 4.—II. 1 Ch. 4. 17.—III. 1 Ch. 5. 24.

עֹפֶר masc. dec. 6c, *fawn,* i. e. young deer, roe, gazelle.

עָפְרָה (*female fawn*) pr. name—I. of a city in the tribe of Benjamin, called also בֵּית לְעַפְרָה (*house of the fawn*) Mi. 1. 10.—II. of another in Manasseh.—III. of a man, 1 Ch. 4. 14.

עֶפְרוֹן (*vitulinus*) pr. name—I. of a city on the borders of Ephraim, 2 Ch. 13. 19, in Keri עֶפְרַיִן.—II. of a mountain on the confines of Judah and Benjamin, Jos. 15. 9.—III. of a Hittite, comp. Ge. 23. 8.

עוֹפֶרֶת, עֹפֶרֶת fem. *lead;* אֶבֶן הָעֹ' *a stone,* i. e. weight, *of lead.*

עֲפַר[a] וְ' noun m. s., constr. of עָפָר d. 4c; וַ bef. (-:) . . . עפר
עִפַּר[b] וְ Piel pret. 3 pers. sing. masc. . . . עפר
עֵפֶר וְ', וָ pr. name masc.; for וָ see letter ו . . . עפר
עָפְרָה וְ' pr. name of a man and a place . . . עפר
עֲפָרָהּ[c] וַ' n. m. s., suff. 3 p. s. f. fr. עָפָר d. 4c; וַ bef. (-:) . . . עפר
עֶפְרוֹ[d] id. with suff. 3 pers. sing. masc. . . . עפר
עֶפְרוֹן וְ' pr. name of a man and a place . . . עפר
עֶפְרוֹן Kh. עֶפְרוֹן, K. עֶפְרַיִן pr. name of a place . . . עפר
עַפְרוֹת[e] [f]וְ' noun m. with pl. constr. fem. fr. עָפָר d. 4c . . . עפר
עֳפָרִים noun masc. pl. of עֹפֶר dec. 6c . . . עפר
עֲפָרְךָ[g] וַ n. m. s., suff. 2 p. s. m. fr. עָפָר d. 4c; וַ bef. (-:) . . . עפר
עֲפָרָם[h] וַ' id., suff. 3 pers. pl. masc. . . . עפר
עֶפְרֹן pr. name masc. . . . עפר
עֹפֶרֶת[i] [k]וְ' / עֹפֶרֶת[l] } noun fem. sing. (comp. § 35. rem. 2) . . . עפר
עָפְרָתָה pr. name (עָפְרָה) with parag. ה . . . עפר
עֵפָתָה[m] noun fem. sing. (עֵיפָה) with parag. ה . . . עוף
עֵץ וְ', [n]וְ' noun masc. sing. d. 7a (§ 36. r. 2 & 4) . . . עצה

[עָצַב] I. *to travail, suffer pain.*—II. *to pain, grieve.* Niph. *to be pained, grieved,* with בְּ, אֶל, עַל with any thing. Pi. I. *to form, fashion,* Job 10. 8.—II. *to pain, grieve.* Hiph. I. *to serve, worship,* Je. 44. 19.—II. *to grieve, provoke,* Ps. 78. 40. Hithp. *to grieve oneself, be grieved.*

עֲצִיב Chald. part. pass. *grieved, afflicted,* Da. 6. 21.

עָצָב masc. dec. 8a (pl. עֲצַבִּים) *images, idols.*

עֶצֶב, עֶצֶב masc. dec. 6b.—I. *earthen vessel,* Je. 22. 28; Prof. Lee, *tendon, sinew;* Eng. vers. "idol." —II. *labour, travail.*—III. *pain;* also *grief.*

עֹצֶב masc. dec. 6c.—I. *image, idol.*—II. *pain, grief.*

עִצָּבוֹן masc. dec. 3c.—I. *labour, toil, travail.*—II. *pain, sorrow,* Ge. 3. 16.

עַצֶּבֶת fem. dec. 13a (constr. עַצְּבַת prop. from עַצָּבָה or עַצֶּבָה) *pain, grief, sorrow.*

מַעֲצֵבָה fem. *labour, affliction,* Is. 50. 11.

עֶצֶב noun masc. sing. dec. 6a . . . עצב
עֹצֶב[o] noun masc. sing. dec. 6c . . . עצב
עֲצָבוֹ[p] Kal pret. 3 pers. sing. m., suff. 3 pers. s. m. . . . עצב
עִצְּבוּ[q] וְ Piel pret. 3 pers. pl. . . . עצב
עִצְּבוּנִי[r] id., suff. 1 pers. sing. . . . עצב
עִצְּבוֹנֵךְ[s] noun masc. s., suff. 2 p. s. f. fr. עִצָּבוֹן d. 3c . . . עצב
עַצְּבוֹתָם[t] noun f. pl., suff. 3 p. pl. m. fr. עַצֶּבֶת (q. v.) . . . עצב
עֲצַבֵּי[u] n. m. pl. constr. fr. [עָצָב] d. 8a (§ 37. No. 3c) . . . עצב
עָצְבִּי[x] Kal inf., or noun masc. sing., suff. 1 pers. sing. from עֹצֶב dec. 6c . . . עצב
עֲצַבֶּיהָ[y] noun masc. pl., suff. 3 pers. sing. fem. from [עָצָב] dec. 8a (§ 37. No. 3c) . . . עצב
עֲצַבֵּיהֶם id., suff. 3 pers. pl. masc. . . . עצב
עֲצָבֶיךָ[z] וַ noun masc. pl., suff. 2 pers. sing. masc. from עֶצֶב dec. 6a; וַ bef. (-:) . . . עצב
עַצְּבֵיכֶם[a] id., suff. 2 pers. pl. masc. and dag. euph. . . . עצב
עֲצַבִּים noun m. pl. [of עָצָב] d. 8a (§ 37. No. 3c) . . . עצב
עַצֶּבֶת[b] [for עַצֶּבֶת] noun fem. sing., constr. עַצְּבַת', pl. עַצְּבוֹת . . . עצב
עַצְּבֹתָי[c] id. pl., suff. 1 pers. sing. [for עַצְּבֹתַי] . . . עצב

עָצַד Root not used; Arab. *to cut with an axe.*

מַעֲצָד masc. *an axe,* Is. 44. 12; Je. 10. 3.

עָצָה *to close* the eyes, Pr. 16. 30. Arab. also *to be hard, firm,* hence עֵץ, עָצֶה.

עָצֶה masc. *back-bone, spine.*

עֵץ masc. dec. 7a (with suff. עֵצִי, pl. עֵצִים, c. עֲצֵי § 26. rem. 2 & 4).—I. *tree;* עֵץ פְּרִי *fruit trees.*—II. *wood;* pl. עֵצִים *wood,* i. e. sticks for fuel, or *timber* for building.—III. *stake, gibbet, gallows.*

עֵצָה fem. *wood, timber,* Je. 6. 6; according to Gesenius also Pr. 27. 9, עֲצַת נֶפֶשׁ *fragrant wood*(?).

עֶצְיוֹן גֶּבֶר (*back-bone of a man*) pr. name of a seaport in the Red Sea.

עֵצָה[d] noun fem. sing. (comp. מַעֲצַת) . . . עצה

[a] Is. 49. 23. [b] 2 Sa. 16. 13. [c] Is. 34. 9. [d] De. 9. 21. [e] Pr. 8. 26. [f] Job 28. 6. [g] Eze. 26. 12. [h] Is. 34. 7. [i] Je. 6. 29. [k] Job 19. 24. [l] Zec. 5. 7. [m] Job 10. 22. [n] 1 Ch. 22. 15. [o] Ps. 139. 24. [p] 1 Ki. 1. 6. [q] Is. 63. 10. [r] Job 10. 8. [s] Ge. 3. 16. [t] Ps. 16. 4. [u] Ps. 135. 15. [x] 1 Ch. 4. 10; Is. 48. 5. [y] Je. 50. 2; Mi. 1. 7. [z] Pr. 5. 10. [a] Is. 58. 3. [b] Pr. 10. 10. [c] Job 9. 28. [d] Je. 6. 6.

עֵצָה וְ' noun fem. sing. dec. 11 b . . . יעץ

[a]עֵצָהּ noun masc. sing., suff. 3 pers. sing. fem. from עֵץ (§ 36. rem. 2) . . . . עצה

[b]עֹצֶה Kal part. act. sing. masc. . . . . עצה

עֻצוּ Kal imp. pl. masc. . . . . . עוץ

[c]עֲצוּבַת וַ Kal part. pass. sing. masc. constr. [of עֲצוּבָה from עָצוּב masc.]; וַ bef. (-:) . עצב

עָצוּם וְ' adj. masc. sing. dec. 3 a . . . עצם

עֲצוּמִים וַ id. pl. abs.; וַ bef. (-:) . . . עצם

עָצוּר וְ' Kal part. pass. sing. masc. . . . עצר

עֵצוֹת noun fem. pl. abs. from עֵצָה dec. 11 b . יעץ

עֲצֵי וַ' noun m. pl. constr. fr. עֵץ d. 7 a; וַ bef. (-:) עצה

[d]עֲצִיב Chald. Peal part. pass. sing. masc. . עצב

עֵצֶיהָ noun masc. pl., suff. 3 pers. sing. fem. from עֵץ (§ 36. rem. 2 & 4) . . . עצה

עֵצָיו id. pl., suff. 3 pers. sing. masc. . . . עצה

[e]עֵצַיִךְ וַ id. pl., suff. 2 pers. sing. fem. . . עצה

[f]עֵצֶיךָ id. pl., suff. 2 pers. sing. masc. . . עצה

עֵצִים וְ' id. pl., abs. st. . . . . עצה

[g]עֵצֵינוּ id. pl., suff. 1 pers. pl. . . . עצה

[h]עֵצְךָ id. sing., suff. 2 pers. sing. masc. . . עצה

עָצַל. Niph. *to be sluggish, slothful*, Ju. 18. 9. Hence

[i]עָצֵל וְ' adj. masc. *sluggard, slothful man* . עצל

[k]עַצְלָה fem. *sloth, indolence*; du. עֲצַלְתַּיִם [fr. עֲצֶלֶת] *great slothfulness* . . . . עצל

עַצְלוּת idem, Pr. 31. 27 . . . . . עצל

[l]עָצַם וְ I. *to close* the eyes (prop., as in the Arab., *to tie* or *bind up*), Is. 33. 15.—II. intrans. [עָצֵם] *to be* or *become strong, mighty, powerful, great.*—III. *to be strong in number, be numerous, many.* Pi. I. *to close* or *bind up* the eyes, Is. 29. 10.—II. (denom. of עֶצֶם) *to break the bones*, Je. 50. 17; others, *to gnaw the bones.* Hiph. *to make strong*, Ps. 105. 24.

עָצוּם adj. masc. dec. 3 a.—I. *strong, mighty, great.*—II. *strong, numerous.*

עֲצוּמִים masc. pl. (of עָצוּם) *strength, power*, Ps. 10. 10.

עֲצֻמוֹת fem. pl. *strong defence*, trop. of arguments, Is. 41. 21.

עֶצֶם fem. dec. 6 a (pl. עֲצָמִים, עַצְמֵי, also עֲצָמוֹת).—I. *bone.*—II. *body*, La. 4. 7.—III. *self, self-same.*—IV. pr. name of a city in the tribe of Simeon.

עֹצֶם masc. dec. 6 c.—I. *strength.*—II. *body, substance*, Ps. 139. 15.

עָצְמָה fem. (constr. עָצְמַת).—I. *strength.*—II. *number, multitude*, Na. 3. 9.

עַצְמוֹן (*strong*) pr. name of a town in the south of Canaan.

תַּעֲצֻמוֹת f. pl. (of תַּעֲצוּמָה) *strength*, Ps. 68. 36

[m]עֶצֶם וְ' noun fem. sing. dec. 6 a (§ 35. rem. 2), עֶצֶם וְ' also pr. name . . . עצם

[n]עֹצֵם וְ Kal part. act. sing. masc. . . . עצם

[o]עֹצֶם וְ noun masc. sing. dec. 6 c . . . עצם

עָצְמָה noun fem. sing. (no pl.) . . . עצם

[p]עָצְמוּ, עָצְמוּ Kal pret. 3 pers. pl. (§ 8. rem. 1 a) . עצם

עַצְמוֹ noun fem. sing., suff. 3 pers. sing. masc. from עֶצֶם dec. 6 a . . . . עצם

[q]עִצְּמוֹ Piel pret. 3 pers. sing. masc. [עִצֵּם], suff. 3 pers. sing. masc. . . . עצם

עַצְמוֹנָה pr. name of a place (עַצְמוֹן), with parag. ה עצם

עֲצָמוֹת noun fem. pl. abs. from עֶצֶם dec. 6 a . עצם

עַצְמוֹת וְ' id. pl., constr. st. . . . . עצם

עַצְמוֹתַי, [r]עַצְמוֹתָי וְ id. pl. with suff. 1 pers. sing. . . עצם

[s]עַצְמוֹתֵיהֶם id. pl., suff. 3 pers. pl. masc. . . עצם

עַצְמוֹתָיו id. pl., suff. 3 pers. sing. masc. . . עצם

[t]עַצְמוֹתֵיכֶם [u]וְ' id. pl., suff. 2 pers. pl. masc. . . עצם

[x]עֲצֻמוֹתֵיכֶם noun fem. pl. [עֲצֻמוֹת], suff. 2 pers. pl. m. עצם

[y]עַצְמוֹתֵינוּ noun fem. pl., suff. 1 pers. pl. from עֶצֶם d. 6a עצם

[z]עַצְמוֹתָם id. pl., suff. 3 pers. pl. masc. (§ 4. rem. 2) עצם

עֲצָמַי, [a]עֲצָמָי [b]וַ' id. pl. m., suff. 1 pers. sing.; וַ bef. (-:) עצם

[c]עָצְמִי noun masc. sing., suff. 1 pers. s. fr. עֹצֶם d. 6c עצם

עַצְמִי [d]וְ' noun fem. sing., suff. 1 pers. s. fr. עֶצֶם d. 6a עצם

[e]עֲצָמֶיהָ id. pl., suff. 3 pers. sing. fem. . . עצם

עֲצָמָיו id. pl., suff. 3 pers. sing. masc. . . עצם

עֲצָמִים id. pl., abs. st. . . . . עצם

[f]עֲצֻמִים וַ' defect. for עֲצוּמִים (q. v.) . . עצם

[g]עֲצָמֵינוּ noun fem. pl., suff. 1 pers. pl. from עֶצֶם d. 6a עצם

עָצְמְךָ id. sing., suff. 2 pers. sing. masc. . . עצם

[h]עַצְמְכֶם id. sing., suff. 2 pers. pl. masc. . . עצם

[i]עַצְמָם id. sing., suff. 3 pers. pl. masc. . . עצם

עַצְמֹנָה pr. name of a place (עַצְמוֹן) with local ה עצם

[k]עָצַמְתָּ Kal pret. 2 pers. sing. masc. . . עצם

[l]עַצְמֹתַי, עַצְמֹתָי noun fem. pl., suff. 1 pers. sing. from עֶצֶם dec. 6 . . . . עצם

[m]וְ' עַצְמֹתֵיהֶם id. pl., suff. 3 pers. sing. masc. . עצם

עַצְמֹתָיו id. pl., suff. 3 pers. sing. masc. . . עצם

[n]עַצְמֹתֶיךָ וְ id. pl., suff. 2 pers. sing. masc. . . עצם

[o]עַצְמֹתָם id. pl., suff. 3 pers. pl. masc. (§ 4. rem. 2) עצם

[a] De. 20. 19. [b] Pr. 16. 30. [c] Is. 54. 6. [d] Da. 6. 21. [e] Eze. 26. 12. [f] De. 29. 10. [g] La. 5. 4. [h] De. 28. 42. [i] Pr. 26. 14. [k] Pr. 19. 15. [l] Da. 8. 24; 11. 23. [m] Pr. 15. 30. [n] Is. 33. 15. [o] De. 8. 17. [p] Ps. 38. 20. [q] Je. 50. 17. [r] Ps. 102. 4. [s] 1 Ch. 10. 12. [t] Eze. 6. 5. [u] Is. 66. 14. [x] Is. 41. 21. [y] Eze. 37. 11. [z] Mi. 3. 2. [a] Job 30. 17. [b] Ps. 31. 11. [c] Ps. 139. 15. [d] Job 30. 30. [e] Eze. 24. 5. [f] Mi. 4. 3. [g] Ps. 141. 7. [h] Ju. 9. 2. [i] La. 4. 8. [k] Ge. 26. 16. [l] 1 Ki. 13. 31. [m] Nu. 24. 8. [n] Is. 58. 11. [o] Eze. 32. 27.

עָצַן Root not used; whence

עֲצְנוֹ 2 Sa. 23. 8 (Keri עֶצְנִי), *Eznite*, one of David's heroes. According to Simonis and Gesenius, an appellative, *spear* (Arab. עצן *branch*), hence *his spear*, according to Khethib. Comp. עֲדִן.

עָצַר [a]וְ״ fut. יַעְצֹר, יַעֲצֹר (§ 13. rem. 5).—I. *to shut, close up.*—II. *to hold back, restrain, detain.*—III. *to retain* strength.—IV. *to rule, reign,* with בְּ 1 Sa. 9. 17. Niph. I. *to be shut up.*—II. *to be restrained, detained, stayed.*—III. *to be assembled,* 1 Sa. 21. 8.

עֶצֶר masc. *rule, dominion,* Ju. 18. 7.

עֹצֶר masc.—I. *a shutting up, restraining* the womb from childbearing, Pr. 30. 16.—II. *oppression, vexation,* Ps. 107. 39; perh. *prison,* Is. 53. 8.

עֲצָרָה fem. dec. 11 c (§ 42. rem. 1) and עֲצֶרֶת, *assembly;* frequently of the *solemn assemblies* when the people came together for the celebrating of festivals.

מַעְצוֹר masc. *restraint, hinderance,* 1 Sa. 14. 6.

מַעְצָר m. *restraint, power of restraint,* Pr. 25. 28.

עָצֹר[b] Kal inf. abs. . . . . . עצר
עָצֻר[c] defect. for עָצוּר (q. v.) . . . עצר
עֶצֶר[d] noun masc. sing. . . . . . עצר
עֹצֶר[e] וְ noun masc. sing. . . . . עצר
עְצֹר[f] וַ Kal inf. constr. [for וַעְצֹר comp. § 13. r. 1 & 2] עצר
עֲצָרָה[g] וְ״ noun fem. s. d. 11 c (§ 24. r. 1); וַ bef. (-:) עצר
עֲצֻרָה[h] Kal part. pass. sing., fem. of עָצוּר . עצר
עָצְרוּ id. pret. 3 pers. pl. . . . . עצר
עֲצָרַנִי[i] id. pret. 3 pers. sing. masc., suff. 1 pers. sing. עצר
עֲצֶרֶת[k] / עֲצֶרֶת } noun fem. sing., see under עֲצָרָה . עצר
עָצַרְתִּי[l] [m]וְ״ Kal pret. 1 pers. sing. . . . עצר
עֲצַת וְ״ noun fem. s. constr. of עֵצָה d. 11 b; וַ bef. (-:) יעץ
עֲצָתוֹ [n]וְ״ id., suff. 3 pers. sing. masc.; וַ id. . יעץ
עֲצָתוֹ[o] id., suff., Kh. תוֹ׳ 3 pers. sing. masc., K. תִי׳ 1 pers. sing. . . . . . יעץ
עֲצָתִי id., suff. 1 pers. sing. . . . . יעץ
עֲצָתַיִךְ[p] id. pl., suff. 2 pers. sing. fem. . . . יעץ
עֲצָתְךָ[q] id. sing., suff. 2 pers. sing. masc. . . יעץ
עֲצָתָם id. sing., suff. 3 pers. pl. masc. . . יעץ

עָקֵב[r] fut. יַעְקֹב.—I. *to take by the heel,* Ho. 12. 4.—II. *to supplant, circumvent, defraud.* Pi. *to hold back, retard,* Job 37. 4; Prof. Lee, *to trace,* comp. עָקֵב.

עָקֵב masc. dec. 5 c (pl. עֲקֵבִים, constr. עִקְבֵי, עִקְּבוֹת, עִקְּבֵי, § 34. rem. 4, comp. § 33. rem. 1).—I. *heel.*—II. *hoof* of a horse.—III. *rear* of an army.—IV. *impression of the heel, trace, track, footstep.*—V. *a supplanter, insidiator,* Ps. 49. 6.

עָקֹב masc.—I. *crooked place,* Is. 40. 4; Gesenius, *steep place.*—II. adj. *fraudulent, deceitful,* Je. 17. 9.—III. fem. עֲקֻבָּה (denom. of עָקֵב) *traced, marked,* Ho. 6. 8.

עַקּוּב (*insidious*) pr. name masc. of three different persons.

עֵקֶב masc.—I. *end,* only as an adv. *to the end,* Ps. 119. 33, 112.—II. *recompense, reward.*—III. עֵקֶב, עַל עֵקֶב (*a*) adv. *on account of, because;* (*b*) conj. *because;* עֵ׳ כִּי, עֵ׳ אֲשֶׁר idem.

יַעֲקֹב (*taking by the heel, supplanter*) pr. name, *Jacob,* son of Isaac, called also *Israel;* hence the Israelites, his descendants, are called בֵּית יַעֲקֹב; it is likewise simply applied to them and their land.

יַעֲקֹבָה (id.) pr. name masc. 1 Ch. 4. 36.

עָקֵב noun masc. sing. dec. 5 (§ 34. rem. 4) . עקב
עָקֹב[s] adj. masc. sing., comp. עֲקֻבָּה . . . עקב
עֵקֶב noun masc. sing., also as an *adv.* . . עקב
עֲקֻבָּה[t] adj. fem. s. fr. עָקֹב m. (comp. § 37. No. 3) עקב
עֲקֵבוֹ[u] noun masc. sing., suff. 3 pers. sing. masc. from עָקֵב dec. 5 . . . . . עקב
עִקְּבוֹת[x] id. pl. constr. fem., dag. euph. (§ 34. rem 4) עקב
עִקְּבוֹתֶיךָ[y] וְ id. pl. fem., suff. 2 pers. s. masc., dag. euph. עקב
עֲקֵבָי id. pl. masc., suff. 1 pers. sing. . . עקב
עִקְּבֵי id. pl., constr. masc., dag. euph. (§ 34. rem. 4) עקב
עֲקֵבַיִךְ[z] id. pl. masc., suff. 2 pers. sing. fem. . עקב

[עָקַד] *to bind,* Ge. 22. 9. Hence

עָקֹד[a] adj. m. *striped, ring-streaked;* pl. עֲקֻדִּים (q. v.) עקד
עֵקֶד pr. name, see בֵּית עֵקֶד הָרֹעִים under . בית
עֲקֻדִּים adj. masc., pl. of עָקֹד (§ 37. No. 3 c) . עקד

עָקָה Root not used; Arab. *to retain, detain.*

מַעֲקֶה masc. *parapet, battlement,* De. 22. 8.

עָקוֹב[b] Kal inf. abs. . . . . . עקב
עַקּוּב וְ׳ pr. name masc. . . . . עקב

עָקַל only Pu. part. *perverted,* Hab. 1. 4.

עֲקַלְקַל adj. only pl. f. עֲקַלְקַלּוֹת *crooked, perverted.*

עֲקַלָּתוֹן masc. *crooked,* Is. 27. 1.

עֲקַלְקַלּוֹת[c] adj. pl. fem. [from עֲקַלְקַל dec. 8] . עקל
עֲקַלְקַלּוֹתָם[d] id. pl., suff. 3 pers. pl. masc. . עקל

---

a De. 11. 17. b Ge. 20. 18. c Je. 20. 9. d Ju. 18. 7. e Pr. 30. 16. f Job 4. 2. g Is. 1. 13. h 1 Sa. 21. 6. i Ge. 16. 2. k 2 Ch. 7. 9. l Da. 10. 8, 16. m Is. 66. 9. n Is. 19. 3. o Is. 46. 11. p Is. 47. 13. q Ps. 20. 5. r Ho. 12. 5. s Je. 17. 9. t Ho. 6. 8. u Jos. 8. 13. x Ps. 89. 52. y Ps. 77. 20. z Je. 13. 22. a Ge. 30. 40. b Je. 9. 3. c Ju. 5. 6. d Ps. 125. 5.

[a]עֲקַלָּתוֹן noun masc. sing. . . . . עקל

עֲקָן ןָ pr. name m. Ge. 36. 27, elsewhere called יַעֲקָן.

[עָקַר] *to root out, pluck up*, Ec. 3. 2. Niph. *to be rooted up, destroyed*, Zep. 2. 4. Pi. *to hough* or *hamstring* horse.

עֲקַר Chald. Ithpe. *to be rooted out*, Da. 7. 8.

עָקָר masc. עֲקָרָה, עֲקֶרֶת fem. *barren, sterile.*

עֵקֶר masc.—I. *root*, only trop. for *stock, family*, Le. 25. 47.—II. pr. name masc. 1 Ch. 2. 27.

עִקַּר Chald. masc. dec. 1 b, *stump, trunk*, Da. 4. 12, 20.

עֶקְרוֹן (*eradication*) pr. name of one of the principal cities of the Philistines. Gent. noun עֶקְרֹנִי.

[b]עָקָר adj. masc. sing., fem. עֲקָרָה, עֲקֶרֶת . . עקר

[c]עִקַּר Chald. noun masc. sing. constr. [of עִקָּר] עקר

[d]עִקֵּר Piel pret. 3 pers. sing. masc. . . עקר

עֵקֶר ןְ pr. name masc.; for ןְ see lett. ו . . עקר

עַקְרָב ןְ masc. dec. 8a.—I. *scorpion.*—II. a kind of *scourge*, armed with knots and thorns.

עַקְרַבִּים id. pl., abs. st., (Eze. 2. 7.); also pr. name עקרב

עֲקָרָה ןְ adj. fem. sing. from עָקָר masc. . . עקר

[f]עִקְּרוּ Piel pret. 3 pers. pl. . . . עקר

עֶקְרוֹן ןְ pr. name of a place . . . עקר

[g]עֲקֶרֶת adj. fem. sing. from עָקָר masc. . . עקר

עָקַשׁ *to convict of perverseness*, Job 9. 20. Niph. *to be perverse*, Pr. 28. 18. Pi. *to pervert.*

עִקֵּשׁ adj. masc. dec. 7 b.—I. *perverse, false, deceitful.*—II. pr. name masc. 2 Sa. 23. 26.

עִקְּשׁוּת fem. *perverseness*, Pr. 4. 24; 6. 12.

מַעֲקַשִּׁים masc. pl. (of מַעֲקָשׁ), *crooked ways*, Is. 42. 16.

עִקֵּשׁ pr. name masc. . . . . . עקשׁ

עִקֵּשׁ[h] } adj. masc. sing. dec. 7 b (§ 36. rem. 3) עקשׁ
עִקֶּשׁ־[i]

[k]עִקְּשׁוּ Piel pret. 3 pers. pl. . . . . עקשׁ

עִקְּשׁוּת noun fem. sing. . . . . . עקשׁ

[l]עִקְּשֵׁי } adj. masc. pl. constr. and abs. from עִקֵּשׁ dec. 7 b } עקשׁ
[m]עִקְּשִׁים

[n]עָקַת noun fem. sing., constr. of [עָקָה] dec. 10 (comp. § 30. No. 3) . . . . עוק

עָר pr. name of a place . . . . עור

[o]עֵר Kal part. act. s. m. (§ 21. r. 2); also pr. name עור

I. עָרַב inf. עֲרֹב.—I. *to exchange, barter*, Eze. 27. 9, 27. —II. *to become surety, to pledge oneself for* another, const. with acc. of pers.—III. *to pledge, give as pledge.*—IV. [עָרֵב] intrans. fut. יֶעֱרַב *to be agree able, pleasant, sweet*, with לְ, עַל of pers. Hithp I. *to intermix, intermeddle, interfere*, Pr. 14. 10.— II. *to have intercourse, be familiar with* any one with בְּ, לְ, עִם.—III. *to enter into a negociation* with אֶת.

עֲרַב Chald. Pa. *to mix*, only part. pass. Da. 2. 43 Ithpa. *to be mixed*, ibid.

עָרֵב adj. masc. *agreeable, sweet.*

עָרֹב masc. *gadfly.* Sept. κυνόμυια.

עֵרֶב masc.—I. *woof*, Le. 13. 48—59.—II. collect *foreigners, strangers* (Arab. ערב *to travel in foreig lands*), Ex. 12. 38; Ne. 13. 3; with the art. הָעֶרֶב 1 Ki. 10. 15; Je. 25. 20, 24; 50. 37; Eze. 30. 5

עֲרֻבָּה fem. dec. 10.—I. *surety, security*, Pr. 17. 18 —II. *pledge*, 1 Sa. 17. 18.

עֵרָבוֹן masc. *pledge*, Ge. 38. 17, 18, 20.

מַעֲרָב masc. dec. 2 b, *wares, merchandise*, Eze 27, 19, &c. Another under No. *II.*

תַּעֲרֻבָה fem. dec. 10, *suretyship*; בְּנֵי תַ׳ *hostages*

II. עָרַב (Arab. *to be black*) *to become dark, drawing toward evening*, inf. Ju. 19. 9, and 3 pers. fem. metaph Is. 24. 11. Hiph. inf. הַעֲרֵב adv. *at evening* 1 Sa. 17. 16, comp. Hiph. of שָׁכַם.

עֹרֵב masc. dec. 7 b.—I. *a raven.*—II. pr. nam (*a*) of a prince of Midian; (*b*) of a rock beyon Jordan.

עֶרֶב com. d. 6 a.—I. *evening*; לָעֶרֶב, בָּעֶרֶב, als עֶרֶב *in the evening, at evening*; du. בֵּין הָעַרְבַּיִם *between the two evenings*, the time between th declining and the setting of the sun.—II. pl. עֲרָבִים c. עַרְבֵי, *oziers, willows*; נַחַל הָעֲ׳ *brook of willow* —III. see עֲרָב under R. No. *I.*

מַעֲרָב masc. *the west.* Another under No. *I.*

מַעֲרָבָה fem. id. Is. 45. 6.

III. עָרַב Root not used; i. q. חָרֵב *arid, sterile.*

עֲרָב, עֲרַב pr name, *Arabia.* Gent. noun עַרְבִי עַרְבִי *Arab, Arabian*; pl. עֲרָבִים, עַרְבִיאִים *Arab Arabians.*

עֲרָבָה fem. dec. 11 c (§ 42. rem. 1).—I. *ar tract, desert.*—II. *plain, open country*; in Ps. 68. perh. metaph. for *the heavens*, see Buxtorf on th word.—III. הָעֲרָבָה the country between the Dea Sea and the Elantic Gulf; יָם הָעֲ׳ *the sea of t desert* or *plain*, the Dead Sea; נַחַל הָעֲ׳ *the bro*

---

[a] Is. 27. 1. [b] De. 7. 14. [c] Da. 4. 12, 20, 23. [d] Jos. 11. 9. [e] De. 8. 15. [f] Ge. 49. 6. [g] Ps. 113. 9. [h] Pr. 8. 8. [i] Pr. 17. 20. [k] Is. 59. 8. [l] Pr. 11. 20. [m] Pr. 2. 15. [n] Ps. 55. 4. [o] Ca. 5. 2; Mal. 2. 12.

of Kedron; עֲ׳ מוֹאָב, עַרְבוֹת יְרֵחוֹ *the plains of Jericho, Moab*.—IV. pr. name of a town in Benjamin; gent. noun עַרְבָתִי, see under בַּיִת.

עֲרָב / עֲרָב } pr. name of a country . . . ערב
עָרֵב adj. masc. sing. . . . . . ערב
עָרֵב in pause for עָרֵב (q. v. & § 35. rem. 2) . ערב
עָרֹב noun masc. sing. . . . . . ערב
עֲרֹב[a] Kal imp. sing. masc. . . . . . ערב
עֶרֶב noun masc. sing. . . . . . ערב
עֶרֶב ו׳[b] וָ noun masc. sing. (pl. c. עַרְבֵי) dec. 6a; for וָ see lett. ו . . . . . ערב
עֹרֵב pr. name masc. . . . . . ערב
עֹרֵב ו׳ noun masc.; or (Pr. 17. 18) Kal part. act. sing. masc. dec. 7b . . . . . ערב
עֲרָבָה וַ׳ noun fem. s. d. 11c (§ 42. r. 1); וַ bef. (-:) ערב
עָרְבָה וְ׳ Kal pret. 3 pers. sing. fem. . . . ערב
עֲרֵבָה[c] noun fem. sing. dec. 10 . . . . . ערב
עָרְבוּ[d] Kal pret. 3 pers. sing. . . . . ערב
עֵרָבוֹן[e] noun masc. sing. . . . . . . ערב
עֲרָבוֹת[f] noun m. with pl. f. term., abs. fr. עֶרֶב d. 6a ערב
עַרְבוֹת[g] noun f. pl. constr. fr. עֲרָבָה d. 11c (§ 42. r. 1) ערב
עֲרָבִי gent. noun from עֲרָב . . . ערב
עַרְבֵי[h] וְ׳[i] noun masc. pl. constr. from עֶרֶב dec. 6a ערב
עֹרְבֵי[k] וְ׳[l] Kal part. act., or noun masc. pl. c. from עֹרֵב dec. 7b . . . . . ערב
עֲרָבִים[m] noun masc., pl. of עֶרֶב dec. 6a . . . ערב
עֹרְבִים[n] Kal part. act. masc., pl. of עֹרֵב dec. 7b . ערב
עָרְבֵנִי id. imp. sing. masc., suff. 1 pers. sing. . ערב
עָרַבְתָּ[o] id. pret. 2 pers. sing. masc. . . . ערב
עָרַבְתְּ[p] id. pret. 2 pers. sing. fem. . . . . ערב
עַרְבֹת[q] defect. for עַרְבוֹת (q. v.) . . . ערב
עַרְבָתָהּ[r] וְ noun fem. sing., suff. 3 pers. sing. fem. from עֲרָבָה dec. 11c (§ 42. rem. 1) . ערב
עֲרֻבָּתָם[s] noun fem. sing., suff. 3 pers. pl. masc. from עֲרֻבָּה dec. 10 . . . . . ערב

[עָרַג] fut. תַּעֲרֹג.—I. *to low, bleat*, as an animal *from desire, longing*, Joel 1. 20.—II. *to desire, to long for*, with אֶל, עַל Ps. 42. 2.

עֲרוּגָה fem. dec. 10, *a raised bed* in a garden. Arab. ערג *to rise, ascend*.

עֲרֻגֹת[t] noun fem. pl. of [עֲרוּגָה] dec. 10 . . ערג

עָרַד Root not used; Arab. *to flee*; Syr. *to be wild*.

עָרוֹד masc. *wild ass*, Job 39. 5.

עִירָד (*wild ass*) pr. name masc. Ge. 4. 18.

עֲרָד masc. dec. 1a, *wild ass*, Da. 5. 21. Also the following.

עֲרָד וְ׳ (*wild ass*) pr. name—I. of a man, 1 Ch. 8. 15.—II. of a town in the southern part of Palestine . . . . . ערד

עֲרָדַיָּא[u] Chald. noun masc. pl. emph. of [עֲרָד] d. 1a ערד

עָרָה Pi. עֵרָה, inf. עָרוֹת, fut. ap. וַתְּעַר.—I. *to make naked* or *bare, to uncover*.—II. *to empty, pour out*. Hiph. הֶעֱרָה.—I. *to make bare, to expose, uncover*, Le. 20. 18, 19.—II. *to pour out*, Is. 53. 12. Niph. *to be poured*, Is. 32. 15. Hithp. I. *to make oneself naked*, La. 4. 21.—II. *to spread oneself abroad*, Ps. 37. 35.

עָרָה fem. only pl. עָרוֹת, *bare places, pastures*, Is. 19. 7.

עֶרְוָה fem. dec. 10.—I. *nakedness*, Hos. 2. 11; metaph. of *an unfortified part of a country*, Ge. 42. 9, 12.—II. *nudity* of a person, male or female.—III. *offensiveness, shamefulness; disgrace*.

עַרְוָא Chald. fem. dec. 8a, *damage, detriment*, Ezr. 4. 14.

עֶרְיָה fem. *nakedness, need, destitution*.

מַעֲרֶה masc. dec. 9a, *a bare place, a plain* or *moor*, Ju. 20. 33.

מַעַר masc.—I. *nudity*, Na. 3. 5.—II. *naked, empty space*, 1 Ki. 7. 36.

מַעֲרָת (*naked, bare place*) pr. name of a town in the tribe of Judah, Jos. 15. 59.

תַּעַר masc. (with suff. תַּעְרָהּ).—I. *razor*.—II. *penknife*, Je. 36. 23.—III. *scabbard, sheath of a sword*.

עֵרָה Piel pret. 3 pers. sing. masc. . . . ערה
עֹרָהּ[x] noun masc. s., suff. 3 pers. s. fem. fr. עוֹר d. 1a עור
עֹרָה[y] וְ Kal imp. sing. masc. with parag. ה (comp. § 8. rem. 11, & § 18. rem. 4) . . ערר
עָרוּ[z] Piel imp. pl. masc. . . . . ערה
עֹרוֹ noun masc. s., suff. 3 pers. s. m. fr. עוֹר d. 1a עור
עָרוֹד[a] noun masc. sing. . . . . ערד
עֶרְוָה noun fem. sing. (no pl.) . . . ערה
עָרוּךְ Kal part. pass. sing. masc. dec. 3a . ערך
עֲרוּךְ[b] id., constr. st. . . . . . ערך
עֲרוּכָה[c] id. part. sing. fem. dec. 10 . . . ערך
עָרוֹם וְ׳[d] adj. m. sing., pl. עֲרוּמִּים (§ 37. rem. 2) ערם
עָרוּם וְ׳[e] adj. masc. sing. dec. 3a . . . ערם
עֲרוּמִּים adj. masc. pl. of עָרוֹם (§ 37. rem. 2) . ערם
עֲרוּמִים וַ׳[f] adj. masc. pl. of עָרוּם dec. 3a; וַ bef. (-:) ערם

[a] Ps. 119. 122. [b] Ps. 65. 9. [c] Pr. 17. 18. [d] Je. 6. 20. [e] Ge. 38. 17. [f] Je. 5. 6. [g] Jos. 4. 13. [h] Job 40. 22. [i] Le. 23. 40. [k] Pr. 30. 17. [l] Eze. 27. 27. [m] Ps. 137. 2. [n] Ne. 5. 3. [o] Pr. 6. 1. [p] Eze. 16. 37. [q] Nu. 31. 12. [r] Is. 51. 3. [s] 1 Sa. 17. 18. [t] Eze. 17. 10. [u] Da. 5. 21. [x] Nu. 19. 5. [y] Is. 32. 11. [z] Ps. 137. 7. [a] Job 39. 5. [b] Joel 2. 5. [c] 2 Sa. 23. 5. [d] Mi. 1. 8. [e] Pr. 14. 15. [f] Pr. 14. 18.

עֲרוֹעֵר pr. name of a place . . . . ערר
עָרוֹת[a] noun fem. pl. abs. [from עָרָה] . . . ערה
עָרוֹת[b] Piel inf. constr. . . . . ערה
עֶרְוַת[c] וְ Chald. noun fem. sing. constr. of [עַרְוָא] d. 8a ערה
עֶרְוַת וְ' noun fem. sing. constr. of עֶרְוָה (no pl.) ערה
עֶרְוָתָהּ id., suff. 3 pers. sing. fem. . . . ערה
עֶרְוָתוֹ[d] id., suff. 3 pers. sing. masc. . . . ערה
עֶרְוָתְךָ id., suff. 2 pers. sing. masc. . . . ערה
עֶרְוָתֵךְ id., suff. 2 pers. sing. fem. . . . ערה
עֶרְוָתָן[e] id., suff. 3 pers. pl. fem. . . . ערה
עָרַי[f] n. f., pl. (עָרִים), suff. 1 p. s., irr. of עִיר (§ 45) עור
עָרֵי וְ' id. pl., constr. st. . . . . עור
עֵרִי pr. name masc. . . . . . עור
עָרֶיהָ וְ' noun fem. pl., (עָרִים), suff. 3 pers. sing. fem., irr. of עִיר (§ 45) . . . עור
עֲרִיָּה וְ' noun fem. sing. . . . . ערה
עָרֵיהֶם וְ' noun fem. pl., (עָרִים), suff. 3 pers. pl. masc., irr. of עִיר (§ 45) . . . . עור
עָרָיו וְ' id. pl., suff. 3 pers. sing. masc. . . עור
עָרַיִךְ id. pl., suff. 2 pers. sing. fem. . . . עור
עָרֶיךָ[g] וְ' id. pl., suff. 2 pers. sing. masc. . . עור
עָרֶיךָ[h] noun masc. pl., suff. 2 pers. s. m. fr. [עָר] d. 1a עיר
עָרֵיכֶם וְ' the foll. with suff. 2 pers. pl. masc. . עור
עָרִים וְ' noun fem. pl. properly of עָר see עִיר (§ 45) עור
עָרִים[k] noun masc. pl. of [עָר] dec. 1a . . . עיר
עֲרִסֹתֵיכֶם[l] noun f. pl., suff. 2 p. pl. m. fr. עֲרִיסָה d. 10 ערס
עֲרִיסֹתֵינוּ[m] id. pl., suff. 1 pers. pl. . . . ערס
עָרִיץ noun masc. sing. [for עַרְיָץ] dec. 1b . ערץ
עָרִיצֵי id. pl., constr. st. . . . . ערץ
עָרִיצִים וְ' id. pl., abs. st. . . . . ערץ
עֲרִירִי adj. masc. sing. dec. 1b . . . ערר
עֲרִירִים[n] id. pl., abs. st. . . . . ערר

עָרַךְ[o] וְ' fut. יַעֲרֹךְ.—I. *to set in order, to arrange, dispose*; hence, *to prepare* a table; *to array* a battle, with אֵת, לִקְרַאת *against* any one; part. עֹרְכֵי מִלְחָמָה, עֲרוּךְ מ׳, or simply עָרוּךְ *arrayed for battle*; עָרַךְ מִלִּין, and simply עָרַךְ *to set in order, prepare* or *utter a speech*, with לְ *to*, with אֶל *against* any one; עָ׳ מִשְׁפָּט *to prepare a cause* for judgment.—II. *to place together, to compare*, with לְ, אֶל.—III. *to estimate, value*, Job 36. 19. Hiph. *to estimate, value.*

עֵרֶךְ masc. dec. 6 (with suff. עֶרְכִּי § 35. rem. 6).—I. *row, pile*, of the shew-bread, Ex. 40. 23.—II. *a preparation*, i. e. *suit* of clothes.—III. *valuation, estimation.*

מַעֲרָךְ masc. dec. 2 b, *arrangement, disposing*, only pl. c. מַעַרְכֵי Pr. 16. 1.

מַעֲרָכָה, מַעֲרֶכֶת fem. (pl. מַעֲרָכוֹת, constr. מַעַרְכוֹת).—I. *arrangement, disposition, order*.—II. *row, pile, heap*.—III. *array* of battle.

עֶרְךָ[p] noun masc. sing., suff. 2 pers. sing. masc. from [עָר] dec. 1a (§ 30. No. 3) . . עיר
עָרֹךְ[q] Kal inf. abs. . . . . . ערך
עֲרֹךְ[r] id. inf. constr. . . . . . ערך
עֵרֶךְ[s] / וְ עֶרֶךְ[t] } noun masc. sing. dec. 6 (§ 35. rem. 6) ערך
עָרְכָה[u] Kal pret. 3 pers. sing. fem. . . . ערך
עֶרְכָּהּ[v] n. m. s., suff. 3 p. s. f. fr. עֵרֶךְ d. 6 (§ 35. r. 6) ערך
עָרְכָה[w] Kal imp. sing. m. with parag. ה (§ 8. r. 11) ערך
עָרְכוּ[x] וְ' id. pret. 3 pers. pl. . . . . ערך
עֶרְכּוֹ noun masc. sing., suff. 3 pers. sing. masc. from עֵרֶךְ dec. 6 (§ 35. rem. 6) . ערך
עִרְכוּ Kal imp. pl. masc. . . . . ערך
עֹרְכֵי id. part. act. pl. constr. m. [fr. עֹרֵךְ] d. 7b ערך
עֶרְכְּךָ[a] / עֶרְכְּךָ[b] } noun masc. sing., suff. 2 pers. sing. masc. from עֵרֶךְ dec. 6 (§ 35. rem. 6) . } ערך
עָרַכְתָּ[c] וְ Kal pret. 2 pers. sing. masc.; acc. shifted by conv. וְ (§ 8. rem. 7) . . ערך
עָרַכְתִּי id. pret. 1 pers. sing. . . . . ערך

ערל עָרֵל[d] וְ' adj. masc. dec. 5c (constr. עֲרַל, עָרֵל § 34. No. 2) *uncircumcised*; עֲרַל שְׂפָתַיִם *uncircumcised*, i. e. *dull of speech*, hesitating or stammering; used also of the ear, the heart.

עָרֵל (denom.) *to regard as uncircumcised, profane*, Le. 19. 23. Niph. *to show oneself uncircumcised*, Hab. 2. 16.

עָרְלָה fem. dec. 12c.—I. *foreskin*; עָרְלַת לֵב *uncircumcision of the heart*.—II. applied to the fruit of the three first years, Le. 19. 23.—III. pl. עֲרָלוֹת pr. name of a place near Gilgal, Jos. 5. 3.

עֲרַל[e] / וְ' עֲרַל[f] } adj. masc. sing., constr. of עָרֵל dec. 5c (§ 34. No. 2) . . . } ערל
עָרְלָה[g] noun fem. sing., pl. abs. עֲרָלוֹת dec. 12c . ערל
עֲרֵלָה[h] adj. fem. sing. from עָרֵל masc. . . ערל
עָרְלוֹת noun fem. pl. constr. from עָרְלָה dec. 12c ערל
עַרְלֵי[i] / עֲרֵלִים } adj. masc. pl. constr. & abs. from עָרֵל dec. 5c . . . } ערל
עָרְלַת noun fem. sing. constr. of עָרְלָה dec. 12c . ערל
עָרְלָתוֹ id., suff. 3 pers. sing. masc. . . . ערל
עָרְלֹתֵיהֶם[k] id. pl., suff. 3 pers. pl. masc. . . ערל

[a] Is. 19. 7. [b] Hab. 3. 13. [c] Ezr. 4. 14. [d] Le. 20. 17. [e] Le. 18. 9, 10. [f] Zec. 1. 17. [g] Eze. 35. 9. [h] Ps. 139. 20. [i] Le. 26. 33. [k] Is. 14. 21. [l] Eze. 44. 30. [m] Ne. 10. 38. [n] Le. 20. 20, 21. [o] Job 32. 14. [p] 1 Sa. 28. 16. [q] Is. 21. 5. [r] Ps. 40. 6. [s] Ex. 40. 23. [t] Ju. 17. 10. [u] Pr. 9. 2. [v] Job 28. 13. [w] Job 33. 5. [x] Ju. 20. 22. [y] Le. 27. 13. [a] Le. 27. 3, 7, 15, 16, 19, 25. [b] Ex. 40. 4. [c] Ge. 17. 14. [d] Ex. 6. 12, 30. [e] Eze. 44. 9, 9. [f] Ge. 34. 14. [g] Je. 6. 10. [h] Eze. 44. 7. [i] 1 Sa. 18. 27.

[a] עָרְלַתְכֶם id. sing., suff. 2 pers. pl. masc. . . . ערל

[b] עָרְלָתָם id. pl., suff. 3 pers. pl. masc. . . . ערל

[c] וַעֲרַלְתֶּם וְ Kal pret. 2 pers. pl. masc.; וַ for וְ conv. ערל

I. עָרַם I. *to be cunning, subtle,* only inf. עָרֹם 1 Sa. 23. 22. —II. Arab. *to make bare,* see derivv. Hiph. I. *to make crafty,* with סוֹד *to devise crafty counsel,* Ps. 83. 4.—II. *to act cunningly, craftily,* 1 Sa. 23. 22. —III. *to act prudently, wisely.*

עָרוֹם, עָרֹם masc. pl. עֲרוּמִּים, fem. עֲרֻמָּה (§ 37. No. 3c) adj. *naked, stripped.*

עָרוּם adj. masc. dec. 3 a.—I. *crafty, cunning, subtle.*—II. *prudent, cautious.*

עֵירֹם, עֵרֹם masc. pl. עֵירֻמִּים (§ 37. No. 3c).— I. adj. *naked,* Ge. 3. 7, 10, 11.—II. subst. *nakedness.*

עָרְם masc. dec. 6c, *craftiness, cunning,* Job 5. 13.

עָרְמָה f.—I. *craftiness, cunning.*—II. *prudence.*

עַרְמוֹן masc. dec. 1b, *plane tree.*

מַעֲרֻמִּים masc. pl. (of מַעֲרֹם § 37. No. 3c) *nakedness,* 2 Ch. 28. 15.

II. עָרַם *to become heaped up,* Ex. 15. 8.

עֲרֵמָה fem. dec. 10 (pl. ־ִים, ־וֹת), *a heap,* e. g. of rubbish, of grain.

[d] עָרֹם וְ Kal inf. abs. (1 Sa. 23. 22); or defect. for עָרוֹם (q. v.) . . . . ערם

[e] עֵרֹם וְ defect. for עֵירֹם (q. v.) . . . . ערם

עָרְמָה noun fem. sing. . . . . . . ערם

[f] עֲרֻמָּה adj. fem. sing. from עָרֹם masc. (§ 37. No. 3c) ערם

[g] עַרְמוֹן וְ noun masc. sing. dec. 1b . . . . ערם

[h] עֲרֵמוֹת, [i] עֲרֵמִים } noun fem., pl. of עֲרֵמָה dec. 10 . . . ערם

[k] עַרְמֹנִים וְ noun masc., pl. of עַרְמוֹן dec. 1b . . ערם

עֲרֵמַת noun fem. sing., constr. of עֲרֵמָה dec. 10 . ערם

עָרַס Root not used; prob. *to break, pound,* comp. גָּרַס.

עֲרִיסָה fem. dec. 10, only pl. *groats, grits.* Others, *dough,* coll. with Chald. עֲרַס *to mix.*

[bb] עֲרִסֹתֵיכֶם, [dd] עֲרִסֹתֵכֶם } noun fem. pl. with suff. 2 pers. pl. masc. [from עֲרִיסָה] dec. 10 . . } ערס

עַרְעֵר Pilp. (§ 6. No. 4) inf. abs. (Je. 51. 58) . ערר

עֲרֹעֵר pr. n. of a place (Is. 17. 2), defect. for עֲרוֹעֵר ערר

עָרַף only fut. יַעֲרֹף *to drop, distil,* De. 32. 2; 33. 28.

עֲרִיפִים m. pl. (of עָרִיף) *clouds, for the skies,* Is. 5. 30.

עֲרָפֶל masc. *thick clouds, darkness, gloom.*

עֹרֶף masc. d. 6c, *neck*; נָתַן ע׳, פָּנָה ע׳ *to turn the back,* with אֶל to any, i. e. to turn away from him; פָּנָה ע׳, הָפַךְ ע׳ *to turn the back,* i. e. flee.

עָרַף (denom.) *to break the neck* of an animal; metaph. *to throw down, destroy* an altar, Ho. 10. 2.

[l] עֹרֵף Kal part. act. sing. masc. . . . . ערף

עָרְפָּה (for עָפְרָה *fawn*) pr. name fem. Ru. 1. 4, 14.

[m] עָרְפוּ וְ Kal pret. 3 pers. pl. . . . . ערף

עָרְפּוֹ noun m. s., suff. 3 pers. s. m. fr. עֹרֶף d. 6c ערף

[n] עָרְפְּךָ, [o] עָרְפְּךָ } id., suff. 2 pers. sing. masc. . . ערף

[p] עָרְפְּכֶם [q] וְ id., suff. 2 pers. pl. masc. . . . ערף

[r] עֲרָפֶל וְ noun masc. sing.; וֲ bef. (־ֲ) . . ערף

עָרְפָּם וְ[s] noun masc. sing., suff. 3 pers. pl. masc. from עֹרֶף dec. 6c . . . . ערף

וַעֲרַפְתּוֹ וַ Kal pret. 2 pers. sing. masc., suff. 3 pers. sing. masc.; וַ for וְ, conv. . . ערף

[עָרַץ] fut. יַעֲרֹץ.—I. *to terrify, make afraid.*—II. intrans. *to tremble, fear, be afraid,* with מִפְּנֵי before or of any one. Niph. part. נַעֲרָץ *terrible.* Hiph. I. *to make afraid,* Is. 8. 13.—II. *to fear,* with acc.

עֲרוּץ masc. *horror,* Job 30. 6.

עָרִיץ masc. dec. 1b.—I. *strong, mighty.*—II. *violent, fierce, a tyrant.*

מַעֲרָצָה fem. *terror,* Is. 10. 33.

[עָרַק] I. *to flee,* Job 30. 3.—II. (as in Syr.) *to gnaw,* Job 30. 7, part. עֹרְקַי *my gnawers,* i. e. my gnawing pains; others, *my nerves.*

עַרְקִי gent. noun, *an Arkite,* an inhabitant of the city *Arca* or *Arce,* in Syria, Ge. 10. 17.

[עָרַר] *to be naked,* Is. 32. 11. Po. עוֹרֵר *to make naked, bare,* of a foundation, *to demolish,* Is. 23. 13. Pilp. עַרְעֵר and Hithpalp. הִתְעַרְעֵר (§ 6. No. 4) *to be laid bare, exposed, demolished.*

עֲרִירִי adj. masc. dec. 1b, *solitary, forsaken,* hence *childless.*

עַרְעָר adj. *naked, destitute, poor.*

עֲרוֹעֵר, עֲרֹעֵר masc.—I. *naked, bare,* prob. of a leafless tree, Je. 48. 6. Gesenius, *needy, outcast.* Eng. vers. "heath."—II. pr. name, *Aroer,* a city on the banks of Arnon, called also עֲרֹעוֹר, comp. Jos. 12. 2 with Ju. 11. 26.—III. pr. name, *Aroer,* a city near Rabbath-Ammon, on the brook of Jabbok. —IV. pr. name, *Aroer,* a city in the tribe of Judah, 1 Sa. 30. 28. Gent. noun עֲרֹעֵרִי, 1 Ch. 11. 44.

[a] Ge. 17. 11. [b] Ge. 17. 23. [bb] Nu. 15. 21. [c] Le. 19. 23. [d] Job 1. 21. [dd] Nu. 15. 20. [e] Eze. 18. 7, 16. [f] Ho. 2. 5. [g] Ge. 30. 37. [h] 2 Ch. 31. 6. [i] Je. 50. 26. [k] Eze. 31. 8. [l] Is. 66. 3. [m] De. 21. 4. [n] Is. 48. 4. [o] De. 31. 27. [p] 2 Ch. 30. 8. [q] De. 10. 16. [r] Job 22. 13. [s] Ne. 9. 29.

[a]עֲרָקַי וְ Kal part. act. pl., suff. 1 pers. sing. [from עֹרֵק] dec. 7b . . . . ערק

[b]עֹרֵר Pilel inf. constr. . . . . . עור

עֶרֶשׂ fem. dec. 6a (pl. עֲרָשׂוֹת) *couch, bed.*

[c]עָרֶשׂ id. in pause (§ 35. rem. 2) . . . ערשׂ

[d]עַרְשׂוֹ id. with suff. 3 pers. sing. masc. . . ערשׂ

עַרְשִׂי id., suff. 1 pers. sing. . . . ערשׂ

[e]עַרְשֵׂנוּ id., suff. 1 pers. pl. . . . . ערשׂ

[f]עַרְשׂוֹתָם id. pl. fem., suff. 3 pers. pl. masc. (§ 4. r. 2) ערשׂ

עֹרֹת וְ' noun masc. with pl. f. term. fr. עוֹר d. 1a עור

[g]עֹרֹתָם id. with suff. 3 pers. pl. masc. (§ 4. rem. 2) עור

עָשׁ the name of a constellation, Job 9. 9, supposed to be the *Great Bear, Arcturus,* called also עַיִשׁ (q. v.)

עָשׁ noun masc. sing. . . . . . . עשש

עֵשֶׂב וְ' masc. dec. 6 (suff. עֶשְׂבָּם § 35. rem. 6; pl. c. עִשְׂבוֹת) *green herb;* collect. *herbs, vegetables.*

עֲשַׂב Chald. dec. 3b, idem. Da. 4. 12, 21, 22, 29, 30; 5, 21.

[h]עִשְׂבָּא וְ' Chald. noun m. s., emph. of עֲשַׂב d. 3b עשב

[i]עִשְּׂבוֹת noun fem. pl. constr. dag. euph. from עֵשֶׂב dec. 6 (§ 35. rem. 17) . . . עשב

[k]עֶשְׂבָּם id. sing., suff. 3 pers. pl. masc. (§ 35. rem. 6) עשב

עָשָׂה וְ' fut. יַעֲשֶׂה, ap. יַעַשׂ (§ 24. rem. 3).—I. *to work, labour,* with בְּ.—II. *to make, fabricate,* with acc.; *into* anything, with לְ & acc.; *to make* a thing into something, with double acc.; spoken of God, *to create:* hence part. עֹשֶׂה *maker, creator,* עֹשַׂי, עֹשֵׂהוּ *my, his maker, creator.*—III. *to produce, yield,* as fruit, flour, milk.—IV. *to make, get, acquire;* עָ' חַיִל, עָ' שֵׁם *to get riches, a name.*—V. *to make ready, prepare, dress,* as a meal, feast, the beard, a sacrifice.—VI. *execute, accomplish, perform,* a command, order; עָ' שַׁבָּת, עָ' פֶּסַח *to keep* or *celebrate the Sabbath, Passover,* with לְ to the Lord.—VII. *to make, do, act,* with בְּ, לְ, also acc.; עָ' רָעָה, עָ' חֶסֶד with לְ, עִם, אֶת *to show kindness* or *unkindness to* any one; עָ' מִלְחָמָה *to make war.* Niph. נַעֲשָׂה *to be made, be done.* Pi. *to press, squeeze,* Eze. 23. 3, 8. Pu. *to be made, created,* Ps. 139. 15.

עֲשָׂהאֵל (whom *God made, constituted*) pr. name masc. of three different persons.

עֲשִׂיאֵל (*made, constituted of God*) pr. name masc. 1 Ch. 4. 35.

עֲשָׂיָה (whom *God made, constituted*) pr. name masc. of several persons.

יַעֲשַׂי (for יַעֲשָׂיָה *may the Lord constitute* him) pr. name masc. Ezr. 10. 37 Kheth.

יַעֲשִׂיאֵל (*may God constitute* him) pr. name masc. 1 Ch. 11. 47.

מַעֲשֶׂה masc. dec. 9a.—I. *work* of an artificer.—II. *labour, business, occupation.*—III. *deed, act.*—IV. *work,* the fruit of one's labour, *goods, property;* also *fruits, produce.*

מַעֲשַׂי (for מַעֲשֵׂיָה) pr. name masc. 1 Ch. 9. 12.

מַעֲשֵׂיָה, מַעֲשֵׂיָהוּ (*work of the Lord*) pr. name of several men.

עֲשָׂה וְ' pr. name in compos. עֲשָׂהאֵל see עֲשָׂה אֵל עשה

עָשֹׂה וְ' id. inf. abs. . . . . . עשה

עֲשׂה id. inf. constr. . . . . . עשה

עֲשֵׂה וְ' id. imp. sing. masc.; וַ bef. (-:) . . עשה

עֹשָׂה id. part. act. fem. from עֹשֶׂה masc. . . עשה

עֹשֶׂיהָ [m]וְ' id. part. act. masc. (עֹשֶׂה), suff. 3 pers. sing. fem. dec. 9a . . . . . עשה

עֹשֵׂה [n]וְ' id. id., constr. st. . . . . עשה

עֹשֶׂה וְ' id. id., abs. st. . . . . . עשה

עֲשָׂהאֵל וַ' pr. name masc.; וַ bef. (-:) . . . עשה

עָשָׂהוּ [o]וְ' Kal pret. 3 pers. sing. m., suff. 3 pers. s. m. עשה

[p]עֲשׂהוּ id. inf. constr. (עֲשׂה), suff. 3 pers. sing. masc. (§ 24. rem. 2) . . . . . . עשה

עֹשֵׂהוּ id. part. act. sing. masc. (עֹשֶׂה), suff. 3 pers. sing. masc. dec. 9a . . . . . עשה

עֵשָׂו וְ' (*hairy;* coll. Arab.) pr. name, *Esau,* the son of Isaac; בֵּית עֵשָׂו, בְּנֵי עֵשָׂו, and simply עֵשָׂו *the Esauites,* i. e. the Edomites, הַר עֵשָׂו *mountain of Esau* or *Edom.*

עָשׂוֹ Kal inf. abs. (§ 24. rem. 2) . . . עשה

עָשׂוּ וְ' id. pret. 3 pers. pl. . . . . עשה

[q]עָשׂוּ Kh. עָשׂוּ q. v., K. עָשׂוּי (q. v.) . . עשה

[r]עֲשׂוֹ Kal inf. constr. (§ 24. rem. 2) . . . עשה

עֲשׂוּ וַ' id. imp. pl. masc.; וַ bef. (-:) . . . עשה

[s]עֲשׂוּ וַ Kh. וַעֲשׂוּ q. v.; K. יַעֲשׂוּ Kal fut. 3 p. pl. m. עשה

[t]עִשּׂוּ Piel pret. 3 pers. pl. . . . . עשה

[u]עָשׂוּהוּ Kal pret. 3 pers. pl., suff. 3 pers. sing. masc. עשה

[x]עֲשׂוּוֹת id. part. pass. pl. fem. from עָשׂוּ masc. (§ 24. rem. 4); K. עֲשׂוּיוֹת from עָשׂוּי . עשה

עָשׂוּי [y]וְ' id. id. masc. dec. 3a . . . עשה

[z]עֲשׂוּיָה [a]וַ' id. id. fem. dec. 10; וַ bef. (-:) . . עשה

עֲשׂוּיִם id. id. pl. masc. from עָשׂוּי dec. 3a . עשה

[b]עָשׂוּנִי id. pret. 3 pers. pl., suff. 1 pers. sing. . עשה

[c]עָשׁוֹק noun masc. sing. . . . . עשק

עָשׁוּק Kal part. pass. sing. masc. dec. 3a . עשק

---

[a] Job 30. 17. [b] Job 3. 8. [c] Am. 3. 12. [d] De. 3. 11. [e] Ca. 1. 16. [f] Am. 6. 4. [g] Le. 16. 27. [h] Da. 4. 22, 30. [i] Pr. 27. 25. [k] Is. 42. 15. [l] Je. 33. 2. [m] Is. 45. 18. [n] Is. 64. 4. [o] Le. 16. 9. [p] Ex. 18. 18. [q] Is. 16. 3. [r] Ge. 31. 28. [s] Eze. 46. 15. [t] Eze. 23. 3, 8. [u] Ec. 2. 12. [x] 1 Sa. 25. 18. [y] Eze. 41. 18. [z] Eze. 21. 20. [a] Eze. 41. 25. [b] Ps. 119. 73. [c] Je. 22. 3.

עֲשׁוּקִים[a] [b]וַ׳ id. pl. (Je. 50. 33; Ps. 103. 6); or noun m. pl. עשק

עָשׁוֹר noun masc. sing. . . . עשר

עָשׁוֹת[rr] adj. masc. sing. . . . עשת

עַשְׁוָת וְ pr. name masc. 1 Ch. 7. 33.

עֲשׂוֹת Kal inf. constr. . . . . . עשה

עֹשׂוֹת[c] וְ id. part. act. fem., pl. of עֹשָׂה d. 10, fr. עֹשֶׂה m. עשה

עֲשׂוֹתָהּ[d] id. inf. (עֲשׂוֹת), suff. 3 pers. sing. fem. dec. 1 a עשה

עֲשׂוֹתְכֶם[e] id. id., suff. 2 pers. pl. masc. . . . עשה

עֲשִׂי וַ׳ id. imp. sing. fem.; וַ bef. (-:) עשה

עֹשָׂי[f] id. part. act. pl. masc., suff. 1 pers. sing. from עֹשֶׂה dec. 9 a . . . עשה

עֹשֵׂי וְ׳ id. id., constr. st. . . . . עשה

עֲשִׂיאֵל, וַ׳ עֲשָׂהאֵל pr. names masc.; וַ bef. (-:) . עשה

עֹשֶׂיהָ[g] Kal part. act. pl., suff. 3 p. s. fem. fr. עֹשֶׂה d. 9 a עשה

עֹשֵׂיהֶם id. pl., suff. 3 pers. pl. masc. . . . עשה

עֹשַׂיִךְ[h] id. pl., suff. 2 pers. sing. fem. . . . עשה

עֹשִׂים [i]וְ׳ id. pl., abs. st. . . . . עשה

עָשִׂינוּ וְ׳ id. pret. 3 pers. pl. . . . . עשה

עָשִׁיר [k]וְ׳ noun masc. sing. dec. 3 a . . . עשר

עֲשִׁירֵי[l] id. pl., constr. st. . . . . עשר

עֲשִׂירִי adj. ord. masc. from עֶשֶׂר . . . עשר

עֲשִׁירֶיהָ[m] noun masc. pl., suff. 3 pers. sing. fem. from עָשִׁיר dec. 3 a . . . . . עשר

עֲשִׂירִיָּה[n] adj. ord. fem. from עֲשִׂירִי masc. . . עשר

עֲשִׁירִים[o] וַ noun masc., pl. of עָשִׁיר dec. 3 a; וַ bef. (-:) עשר

עֲשִׂירִית[p], עֲשִׂרִת — וַ, [q]וַ׳ — adj. ord. fem., from עֲשִׂירִי masc.; וַ id. עשר

עָשִׂיתָ וְ׳ Kal pret. 2 pers. sing. masc. . . . עשה

עָשִׂיתִ°[r] וְ Kh. עָשִׂית q. v., K. עָשִׂיתִי (q. v.) . . עשה

עָשִׂית Kal pret. 2 pers. sing. fem. . . . עשה

עֲשִׂית[s] Chald. Peal pret. 3 pers. sing. masc. (§ 47. r. 6) עשת

עָשִׂיתָה Kal pret. 2 pers. sing. masc. (§ 8. rem. 5) עשה

עֲשִׂיתָהּ[t] id. id., suff. 3 pers. sing. fem. . . . עשה

עָשִׂיתִי וְ׳ id. pret. 1 pers. sing. . . . עשה

עָשִׂיתִי°[u] Kh. עָשִׂיתִי, K. עָשִׂית Kal pret. 2 pers. sing. fem. (comp. § 8. rem. 5) . . עשה

עָשִׂיתָי°[x] Kh. עָשִׂיתִי q. v., K. עָשִׂיתָ (q. v.) . . עשה

עֻשֵּׂיתִי[y] Pual part. 1 pers. sing. . . . עשה

עֲשִׂיתִיהוּ[z] וַ Kal pret. 1 pers. sing., suff. 3 pers. sing. masc.; וַ for וְ, conv. . . . עשה

עֲשִׂיתִיו [a]וַ׳ id. id., suff. 3 pers. sing. masc.; וַ id. עשה

עֲשִׂיתָם[b] [c]וַ׳ id. pret. 2 p. s. m., suff. 2 pers. pl. m.; וַ id. עשה

עֲשִׂיתֶם וַ׳ id. pret. 2 pers. pl. masc.; וַ id. . עשה

עֲשִׂיתִם [d]וַ׳ id. pret. 1 pers. sing., suff. 3 pers. pl.; וַ id. עשה

עֲשִׂיתֶן id. pret. 2 pers. pl. fem. . . . עשה

עֲשִׂיתַנִי[e] id. pret. 2 pers. s. m., suff. 1 pers. s. (§ 2. r. 1) עשה

עֲשִׂיתִנִי[f] id. pret. 1 pers. sing., suff. 1 pers. sing. . עשה

עָשְׂךָ[g] id. pret. 3 pers. sing. masc. (עָשָׂה), suff. 2 pers. sing. masc. (§ 24. rem. 21) עשה

עֹשֶׂךָ id. part. act. sing. masc., suff. 2 pers. sing. masc. from עֹשֶׂה dec. 9 a . . עשה

עָשָׂם[h] id. pret. 3 pers. sing. masc. (עָשָׂה), suff. 3 pers. pl. masc. (§ 24. rem. 21) . . עשה

עָשֵׁן[i] fut. יֶעְשַׁן (§ 13. rem. 5) *to smoke.* Hence the two foll.

עָשָׁן [k]וְ׳ masc. dec. 4 c (constr. עֲשַׁן, עָשָׁן, § 33. r. 3), *a smoke*; metaph. of *anger*, of a *cloud* עשן

עָשֵׁן[l] adj. masc. dec. 5 c, *smoking* . . עשן

עֲשַׁן noun masc. sing. constr. of עָשָׁן dec. 4 c . עשן

עֲשָׁנָהּ[m] id. with suff. 3 pers. sing. fem. . . עשן

עֲשָׁנוֹ[n] id. with suff. 3 pers. sing. masc. . . עשן

עָשָׂנוּ[o] Kal pret. 3 pers. sing. masc. (עָשָׂה), suff. 1 pers. pl. (§ 24. rem. 21) . . עשה

עֹשֵׂנוּ[p] id. part. act. s. m., suff. 1 p. pl. fr. עֹשֶׂה d. 9 a עשה

עָשָׂנִי[q] id. pret. 3 p. s. m. (עָשָׂה), suff. 1 p. s. (§ 24. r. 21) עשה

עֹשֵׂנִי id. part. act. sing. masc., suff. 1 pers. sing. (§ 2. rem. 7) from עֹשֶׂה dec. 9 a . . עשה

עָשַׁנְתָּ[r] Kal pret. 2 pers. sing. masc. . . . עשן

עָשַׂק Hithp. *to strive, contend,* Ge. 26. 20. Hence

עֵשֶׂק (*strife*) pr. name of a well near Gerar, Ge. 26. 20 עשק

עָשַׁק fut. יַעֲשֹׁק.—I. *to oppress, treat with violence and injustice.*—II. *to defraud, extort by fraud.*—III. *to press upon.*

עָשׁוֹק masc. *oppressor,* Je. 22. 3.

עֲשׁוּקִים masc. pl. *oppressions, acts of violence,* Job 35. 9; Am. 3. 9.

עֵשֶׁק (*oppression*) pr. name masc. 1 Ch. 8. 39.

עֹשֶׁק masc.—I. *violence, oppression, injury.*—II. *something extorted by fraud and violence, unjust gain.*

עָשְׁקָה fem. *pressure, distress, anguish,* Is. 38. 14.

מַעֲשַׁקּוֹת fem. pl. *oppressions, exactions,* Pr. 28. 16.

עָשָׁק[xx] Kal pret. 3 pers. sing. masc. for עָשַׁק (§ 8. r. 7) עשק

עָשֻׁק[s] defect. for עָשׁוּק (q. v.) . . . עשק

עֵשֶׁק pr. name masc. . . . . עשק

עֹשֵׁק [t]וְ׳ Kal part. sing. masc. dec. 7 b . . עשק

עֹשֶׁק noun masc. sing. . . . . עשק

עָשְׁקָה[u] noun fem. sing. . . . . עשק

עֲשָׁקוֹ[x] Kal pret. 3 pers. sing. m., suff. 3 pers. sing. m. עשק

עָשְׁקוּ[y] [z]וְ׳ id. pret. 3 pers. pl. . . . עשק

[a] Job 35. 9. [b] Am. 3. 9. [c] Eze. 13. 18. [d] Je. 11. 15. [e] Je. 7. 13. [f] Job 35. 10. [g] Is. 22. 11. [h] Is. 54. 5. [i] Eze. 33. 32. [k] Pr. 18. 23. [l] Ps. 45. 13. [m] Mi. 6. 12. [n] Is. 6. 13. [o] Ec. 10. 6. [p] Nu. 28. 5. [q] Eze. 45. 11. [r] Eze. 16. 59. [rr] Eze. 27. 19. [s] Da. 6. 4. [t] Ps. 109. 27. [u] Eze. 16. 31, 43, 47, 51. [x] 2 Sa. 14. 21. [xx] Le. 5. 23. [y] Ps. 139. 15. [z] 1 Ki. 17. 12. [a] Eze. 12. 25. [b] Ne. 9. 31. [c] Ex. 4. 21. [d] Eze. 37. 19. [e] Job 10. 9. [f] Eze. 29. 3. [g] De. 32. 6. [h] Is. 48. 5. [i] Ex. 19. 18. [k] Is. 4. 5. [l] Ex. 20. 18. [m] Is. 34. 10. [n] Ex. 19. 18. [o] Ps. 100. 3. [p] Ps. 95. 6. [q] Is. 29. 16. [r] Ps. 80. 5. [s] Pr. 28. 17. [t] Pr. 28. 3. [u] Is. 38. 14. [x] Is. 52. 4. [y] Eze. 22. 29. [z] Mi. 2. 2.

עֲשֻׁקֵיהֶם[a] id. part. pl., suff. 3 pers. pl. masc. fr. עָשֻׁק d. 7 b — עשק
עֲשַׁקְתִּי[b] id. pret. 1 pers. sing. — עשק
עֲשַׁקְתָּנוּ[c] id. pret. 2 pers. sing. masc., suff. 1 pers. pl. — עשק

עֶשֶׂר ,'וְ ,'נ fem. עֲשָׂרָה ,עֲשֶׂרֶת masc. *ten;* pl. עֲשָׂרוֹת *tens, decades.*

עָשָׂר masc. עֶשְׂרֵה fem. *ten,* used only in composition with other numbers, as אַחַד־עָשָׂר *eleven,* אַרְבָּעָה עָשָׂר *fourteen,* שִׁשָּׁה עָשָׂר *sixteen;* also as ordinals, *eleventh, fourteenth, sixteenth;* fem. אַחַת עֶשְׂרֵה, אַרְבַּע עֶשְׂרֵה, &c. Pl. עֶשְׂרִים (of עֶשֶׂר § 35. rem. 16) com. *twenty;* also *twentieth.*

עֲשַׂר Ch. fem. עַשְׂרָה m. *ten.* Pl. עֶשְׂרִין *twenty.*

עָשַׂר fut. יַעְשֹׂר (§ 13. rem. 5) *to tithe, take the tenth part,* 1 Sa. 8. 15, 17. Pi. *to give the tenth part, pay tithe.* Hiph. id.

עָשׂוֹר masc. *ten,* בֶּעָשׂוֹר לַחֹדֶשׁ *in the tenth* [day] *of the month;* נֵבֶל עָ׳, and simply עָשׂוֹר *a lyre of ten strings.*

עֲשִׂירִי adj. ordinal, *tenth;* fem. עֲשִׂירִיָּה, עֲשִׂירִית *the tenth,* sc. part.

עִשָּׂרוֹן masc. dec. 3 c (pl. עֶשְׂרֹנִים) a measure of things dry, *the tenth part* of an ephah.

מַעֲשֵׂר masc. dec. 7 c (constr. מַעְשַׂר, מַעֲשַׂר; pl. מַעְשְׂרוֹת) *tithe.*

עָשָׂר num. card. masc. — עשר
עֲשַׂר Chald. num. card. masc. — עשר
עָשָׂר in pause for עֶשֶׂר (q. v. § 35. rem. 2) — עשר
עַשֵּׂר Piel inf. constr. used as an abs. — עשר

[עָשַׁר] fut. יַעְשִׁר (§ 13. rem. 5) *to be rich.* Pi. I. *to make rich, to enrich.*—II. *to be* or *become rich.* Hithp. *to feign oneself rich,* Pr. 13. 7.

עָשִׁיר masc. d. 3 a.—I. *rich.*—II. *proud, arrogant.* Also

עֹשֶׁר ,וְ' ,וָ'[d] masc. dec. 6 c, *riches;* for וָ see lett. ו — עשר
עֲשָׂרָה 'וַ num. card. masc. from עֶשֶׂר fem.; וַ bef. (-:) — עשר
עַשְׂרָה[e] Chald. num. card. masc. from עֲשַׂר fem. — עשר
עֶשְׂרֵה num. card., fem. of עָשָׂר masc. — עשר
עָשְׁרוֹ noun masc. sing., suff. 3 pers. sing. masc. from עֹשֶׁר dec. 6 c — עשר
עִשָּׂרוֹן 'וְ noun m. sing., pl. עֶשְׂרֹנִים d. 3 c (§ 32. r. 3) — עשר
עֶשְׂרִים 'וְ num. card. com. gend., pl. of עֶשֶׂר (§ 35. r. 16) — עשר
עֶשְׂרִין[f] וְ Chald. num. card. com. pl. — עשר
עֲשִׂרִית[g] defect. for עֲשִׂירִית (q. v.) — עשר
עָשְׁרָם noun masc. sing. with suff. 3 pers. pl. masc. from עֹשֶׁר dec. 6 c — עשר
עִשָּׂרֹן[h] וְ defect. for עִשָּׂרוֹן noun masc. sing. dec. 3 c — עשר

עֶשְׂרֹנִים id. pl. abs. st. — עשר
עֲשָׂרֹת num. card. masc. pl. of עֲשָׂרָה — עשר
עֲשֶׂרֶת 'וַ id. constr. (§ 42. rem. 5); וַ bef. (-:) — עשר
עִשַּׂרְתִּי[i] Kal pret. 1 pers. sing. — עשר

[עָשֵׁשׁ] *to waste away, become old.*

עָשׁ masc. *moth.*

עָשְׁשָׁה Kal pret. 3 pers. sing. fem. — עשש
עָשְׁשׁוּ[k] id. pret. 3 pers. pl. [for עָשְׁשׁוּ § 8. rem. 1] — עשש

[עָשַׁת] *to be made smooth, bright, polished,* hence, metaph. of the skin, *to shine,* Je. 5. 28. Hithp. *to think of, remember,* Jon. 1. 6, see Chald. עֲשִׁת.

עֲשִׁת, עֲשִׁית Chald. (§ 47. rem. 6) *to think, intend, purpose,* Da. 6. 4.

עָשׁוֹת adj. m. *shining, bright,* of iron, Eze. 27. 19; others, *forged, wrought.*

עֶשֶׁת fem. dec. 6 a.—I. *something wrought, artificial work.*—II. *thought, opinion,* only pl. עַשְׁתּוֹת Job 12. 5, where many MSS. read עֶשְׁתּוֹת.—III. pl. c. עַשְׁתֵּי only in combination with the number *ten,* as עַשְׁתֵּי עָשָׂר, עַשְׁתֵּי עֶשְׂרֵה to express the number *eleven,* also *eleventh.* Etymology uncertain.

עֶשְׁתֹּנוֹת fem. pl. *thoughts, devices,* Ps. 146. 4.

עֶשֶׁת[l] noun fem. sing. [for עֶשֶׁתֶת] — עשת
עָשְׂתָה[m] וְ Kal pret. 3 pers. sing. fem. (§ 24. rem. 1) — עשה
עֲשׂתָה, 'וַ עֲשׂתָה id. pret. 3 pers. sing. fem. (comp. § 8. rem. 7) — עשה
עֲשֹׂתָהּ[n] id. inf. (עֲשׂוֹת), suff. 3 pers. sing. fem. dec. 1 a — עשה
עָשְׁתוּ[o] Kal pret. 3 pers. pl. — עשת
עֲשֹׂתוֹ Kal inf. (עֲשׂוֹת), suff. 3 pers. sing. m. d. 1 a — עשה
עַשְׁתֵּי noun masc. pl. constr. from עֶשֶׁת dec. 6 a — עשת
עָשָׂתְנִי[pp] Kal pret. 3 pers. sing. fem. (עָשְׂתָה), suff. 1 pers. sing. — עשה
עֶשְׁתֹּנֹתָיו[qq] noun f. pl., suff. 3 pers. s. m. [fr. עֶשְׁתֹּנֶת] — עשת
עַשְׁתָּרוֹת 'וְ, עַשְׁתָּרוֹת וְ noun fem. pl. abs. & constr. from עַשְׁתֹּרֶת q. v. (§ 44. rem. 5).

עַשְׁתֹּרֶת fem.—I. Gr. Ἀστάρτη, *Astarte,* perhaps the deified planet Venus, worshipped by the Phœnicians and Philistines.—II. pl. עַשְׁתָּרוֹת (§ 44. rem. 5) *images* or *statues of Astarte.*—III. עַשְׁתְּרוֹת צֹאן (amours) *offspring* or *increase of the flock.*—IV. *Ashtaroth,* pr. name of a city of Bashan, De. 1. 4; Jos. 13. 12; called עַשְׁתְּרוֹת קַרְנַיִם (*Astarte with horns*) Ge. 14. 5, and בְּעֶשְׁתְּרָה q. v. Gent. noun עַשְׁתְּרָתִי 1 Ch. 11. 44.

עֵת[p] 'וְ[q] Kh., עַתָּה K., *adv.* — עדה

[a] Ec. 4. 1. [b] 1 Sa. 12. 3. [c] 1 Sa. 12. 4. [d] 2 Ch. 1. 12. [e] Da. 7. 24. [f] Da. 6. 2. [g] Ex. 16. 36. [h] Ex. 29. 40. [i] Ho. 12. 9. [k] Ps. 31. 11. [l] Ca. 5. 14. [m] Le. 25. 21. [n] Je. 3. 7. [o] Je. 5. 28. [p] Eze. 23. 43. [pp] Job 33. 4. [q] Ps. 74. 6. [qq] Ps. 146. 4.

עֵת / עֶת־ } ו׳ noun com. sing. dec. 8b . . עדה

עָתַד. Pi. *to make ready, prepare*, Pr. 24. 27. Hithp. *to be ready, destined*, Job 15. 28.
עָתוּד i. q. עָתִיד Is. 10. 13; Est. 8. 13 Kheth.
עָתִיד m. d. 3a, adj. *ready, prepared*. Pl. עֲתִידוֹת.—I. *things ready, destined to take place*, De. 32. 35.—II. *things prepared, acquired*, i.e. *riches*, Is. 10. 13.
עֲתִיד Chald. dec. 1a, *ready*, Da. 3. 15.
עַתּוּד masc. dec. 1b.—I. *he-goat*.—II. metaph. *leader, prince*.

עַתְּדֶהָ[a] ו׳ Piel imp. sing. m. [עַתֵּד], suff. 3 pers. s. f. עתד
עַתֻּדִים defect. for עַתּוּדִים (q. v.) . . . עתד
עֲתִדֹת[b] adj. fem. pl. [of עֲתִידָה] from עָתִיד masc. עתד
עַתָּה / עַתָּה ו׳ } adv. . . . . . עדה
עִתָּהּ noun com. s., suff. 3 pers. s. f. fr. עֵת d. 8b עדה
עִתּוֹ[c] noun com. s., suff. 3 pers. s. m. fr. עֵת d. 8b עדה
עַתּוּדֵי[d] noun masc. pl. constr. from [עַתּוּד] dec. 1b עתד
עֲתוּדִים[e] Kh. עֲתוּדִים adj. masc., pl. of [עָתוּד] dec. 3a; K. עֲתִידִים (q. v.) . . . . עתד
עַתּוּדִים ו׳ noun masc. pl. [of עַתּוּד] dec. 1b . עתד
עַתַּי / עַתָּי ו׳ } pr. name masc. . . . . . עדה
עִתִּי[f] adj. masc. sing. . . . . . עדה
עָתִיד[g] adj. masc. sing. dec. 3a . . . . עתד
עֲתִידִים[h] id. pl., abs. st. . . . . . עתד
עֲתִידִין[i] Chald., adj. masc., pl. of [עֲתִיד] dec. 1a . עתד
עֲתִידוֹתֵיהֶם[k] וְ Kh. עֲתִי׳, K. עֲתוּ׳ adj. pl. fem., suff. 3 pers. pl. masc. fr. עָתִיד [or עָתוּד] d. 3a עתד
עֲתָיָה pr. name masc. Ne. 11. 4.
עִתֶּיךָ[l] n. com. pl. with suff. 2 p. s. m. fr. עֵת d. 8b עדה
עִתִּים id. pl., abs. st. . . . . . עדה
עָתִיק[m] adj. masc. sing. . . . . . עתק
עַתִּיק[n] ו׳ Chald., adj. masc. sing. . . . עתק
עַתִּיקֵי[o] / עַתִּיקִים[p] } adj. masc. pl. abs. & constr. from עַתִּיק dec. 1b . . . . } עתק
[עֲתָךְ] pr. name of a town in the tribe of Judah, 1 Sa. 30. 30.
עִתֵּךְ[q] noun com. s., suff. 2 pers. s. f. fr. עֵת d. 8b עדה
עִתְּךָ[r] id., suff. 2 pers. sing. masc. . . . עדה
עַתְלַי [for עֲתַלְיָה, ap. fr. [עֲתַלְיָה] pr. n. m. Ezr. 10. 28.
עֲתַלְיָה / עֲתַלְיָהוּ וְ׳ } (whom *the Lord has afflicted*; coll. Arab.) pr. name—I. of a man, 1 Ch. 8. 26.—II. of a man, Ezr. 8. 7.—III. of a queen of Judah.

עָתַם. Niph. *to be burned, consumed*, Is. 9. 18. Others, *to be darkened*.
עִתָּם[s] noun com. sing., 3 pers. pl. masc. fr. עֵת d. 8b עדה
עָתְנִי (for עָתְנִיָה *lion of the Lord*; Arab. עתון *lion*) pr. name masc. 1 Ch. 26. 7.
עָתְנִיאֵל (*lion of God*) pr. name of a judge of Israel.

[עָתַק] fut. יֶעְתַּק (§ 13. rem. 3).—I. *to be removed, transferred* from place to place.—II. *to advance in age, grow old*. Hiph. הֶעְתִּיק (§ 13. rem. 9).—I. *to remove, take away*.—II. *to remove, break up* a camp.—III. *to transfer, transcribe*, Pr. 25. 1.
עָתָק adj. masc. *bold, insolent, wicked*.
עָתֵק adj. m. *beautiful, shining*, Pr. 8. 18. Vulg. *opes superbæ*. Prof. Lee, subst. *freedom, liberty*.
עָתִיק adj. masc. *neat, elegant, splendid*, Is. 23. 18.
עַתִּיק adj. masc. dec. 1 b.—I. *removed, taken away*, sc. from the mother's breast, *weaned*, Is. 28. 9.—II. *ancient*, 1 Ch. 4. 22.
עַתִּיק Ch. *ancient*, Da. 7. 9, 13, 22.

עָתָק noun masc. sing. . . . . . עתק
עָתֵק[t] adj. masc. sing. . . . . . עתק
עָתְקָה[u] Kal pret. 3 pers. sing. fem. . . . עתק
עָתְקוּ[x] id. pret. 3 pers. pl. . . . . עתק

I. **עָתַר** only fut. יֶעְתַּר *to entreat, supplicate*, with אֶל, לְ. Niph. *to be prevailed upon by entreaty, to become propitious*; part. pl. fem. נַעְתָּרוֹת *seemingly propitious, false*, Pr. 27. 6 (Prof. Lee), see No. *II*. Hiph. *to entreat, supplicate*, with לְ, בְּעַד for any one.

II. **עָתַר**. Niph. *to be rich, abundant*, only part., Pr. 27. 6, comp. Niph. of No. *I*. Hiph. *to make abundant, to multiply*, Eze. 35. 13.
עָתָר masc. dec. 4 c.—I. *suppliant*, Zep. 3. 10.—II. *abundance*, Eze. 8. 11. Gesenius, *incense, perfumed smoke, fragrant vapour*.
עֶתֶר (*abundance*) pr. name of a town in the tribe of Simeon.
עֲתֶרֶת fem. *abundance, riches*, Je. 33. 6.

עֲתַר[y] ו noun m. s. constr. [of עָתָר] d. 4c; ו bef. (-:) עתר
עֶתֶר ו pr. name of a place . . . עתר
עֲתָרַי[z] noun masc. pl. with suff. 1 pers. sing. from [עָתָר] dec. 4c . . . . עתר
עֲתֶרֶת[a] noun fem. sing. . . . . עתר
עִתֹּתַי[b] noun com. pl. with suff. 1 pers. sing. from עֵת dec. 8 b . . . . . עדה

---

[a] Pr. 24. 27. [b] De. 32. 35. [c] Ec. 9. 12. [d] Is. 14. 9. [e] Est. 8. 13. [f] Le. 16. 21. [g] Job 15. 24. [h] Est. 3. 14. [i] Da. 3. 15. [k] Is. 10. 13. [l] Is. 33. 6. [m] Is. 23. 18. [n] Da. 7. 9, 13, 22. [o] Is. 28. 9. [p] 1 Ch. 4. 22. [q] Eze. 16. 8. [r] Ec. 7. 17. [s] Ps. 81. 16. [t] Pr. 8. 18. [u] Ps. 6. 8. [x] Job 21. 7. [y] Eze. 8. 11. [z] Zep. 3. 10. [a] Je. 33. 6. [b] Ps. 31. 16.

פ

פָּא ־ adv. i. q. פֹּה *here*, Job 38. 11; ־ bef. lab.

פָּאָה Kal not used; "to which I do not hesitate to assign the signification of *breathing*, *blowing*, like the cogn. פָּעָה (פָּהָה), also פּוּחַ, פּוּהַ, פּוּא" (Gesenius). Hiph. *to blow away*, i. e. scatter like the wind, De. 32. 26.

פֵּאָה fem. dec. 11 b.—I. *side, quarter* of the heavens (prop. wind, comp. רוּחַ).—II. *side, district, region*.—III. *corner*, e. g. of a field; פְּאַת הַזָּקָן *corner* or *extremity of the beard*, i. e. *whiskers*; קְצוּצֵי פֵאָה *men having their whiskers clipped*.

פֶּה masc. (for פֵּאָה, § 45).—I. *mouth*; פֶּה אֶל־פֶּה *mouth to mouth*, i. e. without the intervention of any one; פֶּה אֶחָד *with one mouth*, i. e. *unanimously*.—II. *mouth, aperture, entrance*.—III. *edge* of a sword.—IV. *edge, border, side*; פֶּה לָפֶה *from one side* or *end to the other*.—V. *part, portion*; פִּי שְׁנַיִם *portion of two*, i. e. *two parts*.—VI. *word, command*; *expression, tenor*; כְּפִי *according to the word* or *command of*, also, *in proportion, according to*; Job 33. 6 כְּפִיךָ *as thou art*; כְּפִי אֲשֶׁר *according as, even as* (and אֲשֶׁר omitted), *so as, so that*; לְפִי *in proportion, according to*; עַל פִּי *according to the word* or *command*; also *according to*.

פִּיָּה fem. (for פֵּאָה) *edge* of a sword, only pl. פֵּיוֹת Ju. 3. 16.

פִּיפִיּוֹת fem. pl. *edges, two edges*; בַּעַל פ׳ *having many edges*.

פִּי־בֶסֶת pr. name of a city in Egypt, Eze. 30. 17.

פִּי־הַחִירֹת (*mouth of the caverns*) pr. name of a place on the Red Sea.

פִּיכֹל (*all-commanding*) pr. name of the chief of Abimelech's troops.

פִּינְחָס (*mouth of brass*) pr. name, *Phinehas*.—I. a son of Eleazar, son of Aaron.—II. son of the high priest, Eli.—III. Ezr. 8. 33.

פֵּאָה noun fem. sing. dec. 11 b . . . פאה

I. פָּאַר Pi. פֵּאֵר.—I. *to adorn, beautify, honour*.—II. *to glean*, comp. פֹּארָה, De. 24. 20. Hithp. I. *to be adorned, honoured, glorified*, with בְּ in any one.—II. *to vaunt, boast oneself*, with עַל *against* any one.

פְּאֵר masc. dec. 1 a (but pl. c. פַּאֲרֵי, § 35. rem. 10), *ornamental headdress, turban*.

פֹּארָה fem. dec. 10, *a green bough*; *branch*.

פֻּארָה fem. idem, Is. 10. 33.

פֻּרָה (for פֻּארָה *bough*) pr. name masc. Ju. 7. 10, 11.

פָּארוּר masc. *beauty, brightness*; קִבֵּץ פ׳ *to gather in*, i. e. lose one's *brightness*, to grow pale.

פָּרוּר masc. (פָּארוּר, פָּרוּר) *pot for boiling*; Arab. פאר *to be hot, to boil*.

תִּפְאָרָה, תִּפְאֶרֶת fem. dec. 13 a (with suff. תִּפְאַרְתִּי).—I. *ornament, beauty, splendour*.—II. *glory, honour*.—III. *glorying, boasting*; also *the object of glorying*.

II. פָּאַר Kal not used; Arab. *to dig down*, cogn. בָּאַר. Hithp. *to explain, declare oneself*, Ex. 8. 5.

פֵּרוֹת (for פְּאֵרוֹת) *holes*, see under R. חָפַר.

פָּארָן (*abounding in caverns*) pr. name of a desert and somewhat mountainous tract between Egypt and Palestine.

פְּאֵר[a] noun masc. sing. . . . . . פאר

פֻּארָה[b] noun fem. sing. . . . . . פאר

פָּארוּר noun masc. sing. . . . . . פאר

פַּאֲרֵי noun masc. pl. constr. from פְּאֵר (§ 35. r. 10) פאר

פֵּאֲרָךְ[c] Piel pret. 3 pers. sing. masc. [פֵּאֵר], suff. 2 pers. sing. fem. . . . . . פאר

פְּאֵרְךָ[d] noun masc. sing., suff. 2 pers. sing. masc. from פְּאֵר (§ 35. rem. 10) . . . פאר

פְּאֵרֵכֶם[e] ־ id. pl., suff. 2 pers. pl. masc. [for פַּאֲרֵיכֶם]; ־ bef. lab. . . . . . פאר

פָּארָן pr. name of a region . . . . פאר

פֹּארֹת[f] noun fem. pl. of [פֹּארָה] dec. 10 . . פאר

פֹּארֹתָיו[g] id. pl., suff. 3 pers. sing. masc. . . פאר

פְּאַת ־[i] noun fem. sing., constr. of פֵּאָה dec. 11 b; ־ bef. lab. . . . . . פאה

פַּאֲתֵי[h] id. du. constr. [of פֵּאָתַיִם] . . . פאה

פָּגַג Root not used; Arab. *to be unripe*.

פַּג masc. dec. 8 d, *unripe fig*, Ca. 2. 13.

פִּגּוּל noun masc. sing. dec. 1 b . . . פגל

פָּגוֹשׁ[i] Kal inf. abs. . . . . . . פגש

פַּגֶּיהָ[k] noun masc. pl., suff. 3 pers. sing. fem. from [פַּג] dec. 8 d . . . . . . פגג

[a] Is. 61. 3, 10. [b] Is. 10. 33. [c] Is. 55. 5; 60. 9. [d] Eze. 24. 17. [e] Eze. 24. 23. [f] Eze. 17. 6. [g] Eze. 31. 5, 6. [h] Nu. 24. 17. [i] Pr. 17. 12. [k] Ca. 2. 13.

פָּגַל Root not used; Eth. *to be impure.*

פִּגּוּל masc. dec. 1 b, *something impure, abominable.*

פִּגֻּלִים[a] noun masc., pl. of פִּגּוּל dec. 2 b . . . פגל

פָּגַע fut. יִ׳ I. *to meet, meet with, light upon,* with acc., בְּ.—II. *to fall upon* any one, in a hostile sense.—III. *to reach unto, border upon,* with אֶל, בְּ.—IV. *to assail* with petitions, *to urge, entreat, supplicate,* with בְּ, לְ.—V. *to meet, regard with favour,* Is. 47. 3; 64. 4. Hiph. I. *to cause to fall upon, to lay upon,* Is. 53. 6.—II. *to cause to entreat, supplicate,* Je. 15. 11.—III. intrans. *to fall upon,* only Job 36. 32 מַפְגִּיעַ *assailant, enemy.*—IV. *to entreat, supplicate,* with בְּ, לְ.

פֶּגַע masc. *occurrence, incident, event.*

פַּגְעִיאֵל (*event of God*) pr. n. of a prince of Asher.

מִפְגָּע masc. *attack, object of attack,* Job 7. 20.

פֶּגַע[b] וָ[c] noun masc. sing.; for וָ see lett. ו . . פגע

פְּגַע וּ Kal imp. sing. masc.; וּ bef. lab. . . . פגע

פְּגָעוֹ[d] וּ id. pret. 3 pers. sing. masc., suff. 3 pers. sing. masc.; וּ id. . . . . . פגע

פִּגְעוּ[e] וּ id. imp. pl. masc.; וּ id. . . . . פגע

פַּגְעִיאֵל pr. name masc. . . . . . . פגע

פָּגַעְתָּ[f] } Kal pret. 2 pers. sing. masc.; acc. shifted
פָּגַעְתָּ[g] וּ } by conv. וּ bef. lab. (§ 8. rem. 7) } פגע

פָּגַר Pi. *to become weary, exhausted,* 1 Sa. 30. 10, 21. Hence

פֶּגֶר[h] } masc. dec. 6 a (pl. com. פְּגָרִי), *corpse,*
פָּגֶר[i] } *carcase,* of man or beast . . } פגר

פִּגְּרוּ[k] Piel pret. 3 pers. pl. . . . . . פגר

פִּגְרֵי וּפ׳ n. m. pl. constr. fr. פֶּגֶר d. 6 a; וּ bef. lab. פגר

פִּגְרֵיהֶם[m] וּ id. pl., suff. 3 pers. pl.; וּ id. . . . פגר

פִּגְרֵיכֶם וּפ׳[n] id. pl., suff. 2 pers. pl. masc.; וּ id. . פגר

פְּגָרִים וּפ׳[o] id. pl., abs. st.; וּ id. . . . . פגר

[פָּגַשׁ] fut. יִפְגֹּשׁ.—I. *to meet, fall in with,* with acc., בְּ.—II. *to fall upon,* in a hostile sense. Niph. *to meet each other.* Pi. *to light upon, meet with,* Job 5. 14.

פָּגְשׁוּ[p] וּ Kal pret. 3 pers. pl.; וּ bef. lab. . . פגשׁ

פָּגַשְׁתִּי[q] id. pret. 1 pers. sing. [for פָּגַשְׁתִּי] . . פגשׁ

פָּדָה fut. יִ׳ I. *to redeem, ransom.*—II. *to set free, let go.*—III. *to deliver, preserve.* Niph. *to be redeemed.* Hiph. *to cause to be redeemed,* Ex. 21. 8. Hoph. *to be redeemed,* Le. 19. 20.

פְּדוּיִ masc. only pl. פְּדוּיִם *price of redemption, ransom,* Nu. 3. 46, 48, 49, 51; 18. 16.

פָּדוֹן (*deliverance*) pr. name masc. Ezr. 2. 44; Ne. 7. 47.

פְּדוּת fem.—I. *deliverance.*—II. *distinction,* Ex. 8. 19, Sept. διαστολή.

פִּדְיוֹן, פִּדְיוֹם masc. *price of redemption, ransom.*

פְּדַהְאֵל (whom *God has delivered*) pr. name masc. Nu. 34. 28.

פְּדָהצוּר (whom *the Rock has delivered*) pr. name masc. Nu. 1. 10; 2. 20.

פְּדָיָה, פְּדָיָהוּ (whom *the Lord has delivered*) pr. name masc. of several persons.

יִפְדְיָה (whom *the Lord delivers*) pr. name masc. 1 Ch. 8. 25.

פָּדֹה Kal inf. abs. . . . . פדה

פְּדֵה[r] id. imp. sing. masc. . . . . . פדה

פְּדַהְאֵל, פְּדָהצוּר pr. names masc. . . . . פדה

פְּדוּיָו[s] וּ noun masc. pl., suff. 3 pers. sing. masc. from [פְּדוּי] dec. 1 a; וּ bef. lab. . . . פדה

פְּדוּיֵי[t] id. pl., constr. st. . . . . . . פדה

פְּדוּיֵי וּ Kal part. pass. pl. constr. [from פָּדוּי] dec. 3 a; וּ bef. lab. . . . . . פדה

פָּדוֹן pr. name masc. . . . . פדה

פְּדוּת noun fem. sing. . . . . פדה

פְּדָיָה, פְּדָיָהוּ pr. names masc. . . . . . פדה

פִּדְיוֹן[x] }
פִּדְיֹן[y] } noun masc. sing. . . . . . . פדה

פָּדִיתָ }
פָּדִיתָה[z] } Kal pret. 2 pers. sing. masc. (§ 8. r. 5) פדה

פְּדִיתִיךָ[a] id. pret. 1 pers. sing., suff. 2 pers. sing. masc. פדה

פְּדִיתִים[b] id., suff. 3 pers. pl. masc. . . . . פדה

פָּדְךָ[c] id. pret. 3 pers. sing. masc. (פָּדָה), suff. 2 pers. sing. masc. (§ 24. rem. 21) . . . פדה

פָּדָם[d] id. id., suff. 3 pers. pl. masc. . . . . פדה

[פַּדָּן] masc. *field, plain;* פַּדַּן־אֲרָם *Padan-aram,* the plain of Syria, i. e. Mesopotamia.

אַפֶּדֶן masc. dec. 6 a, *palace,* Da. 11. 45.

פַּדֶּנָה pr. name [פַּדָּן] with parag. ה . . . פדן

פְּדֵנוּ[e] וּ Kal imp. sing. masc. (פְּדֵה), suff. 1 pers. pl. (§ 24. rem. 21); וּ bef. lab. . . . פדה

פְּדֵנִי id. id., suff. 1 pers. sing. . . . . . פדה

[פָּדַע] *to redeem, deliver,* Job 33. 24.

פְּדָעֵהוּ[f] Kal imp. sing. masc. [פְּדַע], suff. 3 pers. sing. masc. (§ 16. rem. 12) . . . פדע

---

[a] Is. 65. 4. [b] 1 Ki. 5. 18. [c] Ec. 9. 11. [d] Am. 5. 19. [e] Ge. 23. 8. [f] Is. 64. 4. [g] 1 Sa. 10. 5. [h] Na. 3. 3. [i] 1 Sa. 17. 46. [k] 1 Sa. 30. 10, 21. [l] Eze. 43. 9. [m] Is. 34. 3. [n] Nu. 14. 32. [o] 2 Ch. 20. 25. [p] Is. 34. 14. [q] Ge. 33. 8. [r] Le. 27. 27. [s] Ps. 25. 22. [t] Nu. 18. 16. [u] Nu. 3. 46, 48, 49. [x] Ps. 49. 9. [y] Ex. 21. 30. [z] Ps. 31. 6. [a] Mi. 6. 4. [b] Zec. 10. 8. [c] Job 5. 20. [d] Ps. 78. 42. [e] Ps. 44. 27. [f] Job 33. 24.

[פֶּדֶר] masc. dec. 6 a (with suff. פִּדְרוֹ), *fat, grease.*

פִּדְרוֹ[a] id. with suff. 3 pers. sing. masc. . . פדר

פְּדֻת[b] defect. for פְּדוּת (q. v.) . . . פדה

פְּדִתֶיךָ[c] וּ defect. for פְּדִיתֶיךָ q. v.; וּ bef. lab. . פדה

פֹּה[d] וֹ adv.—I. *here, in this place.*—II. *hither;* מִפֹּה, מִפּוֹ *from here, hence.*

פֶּה[e] וּ noun masc. sing. irr. (§ 45); וּ bef. lab. פאה

פּוּאָה וּ pr. name masc.—I. 1 Ch. 7. 1, elsewhere פֻּוָּה.—II. Ju. 10. 1.

[פּוּג] *to become chilled, languid; to cease to act.* Niph. *to be languid,* Ps. 38. 9.

פּוּגָה fem. dec. 10, *intermission, rest,* La. 2. 18.

הֲפוּגָה fem. dec. 10, idem, La. 3. 49.

פוּגַת[f] noun fem. sing. constr. [of פּוּגָה] dec. 10 פוג

פּוֹדֶה[g] Kal part. act. sing. masc. dec. 9a . . פדה

[פּוּחַ] *to blow, breathe,* Ca. 2. 17; 4. 6, *the day blows,* i. e. grows cool by the evening *breeze.* Hiph. I. *to blow upon,* with acc. Ca. 4. 16.—II. *to blow, kindle* a fire, with בְּ, Eze. 21. 36; metaph. *to inflame, excite,* Pr. 29. 8.—III. *to puff at, rail at,* with בְּ, לְ.—IV. *to breathe out, utter, speak.*

פִּיחַ masc. *dust, ashes,* Ex. 9. 8, 10.

פּוֹחֲזִים[h] Kal part. act. masc. pl. [of פּוֹחֵז] dec. 7b . פחז

פֻּוָּה וּ pr. name masc. Ge. 46. 13; Nu. 26. 23, see פּוּאָה.

פּוּט וּ (*afflicted*) pr. name of one of the sons of Ham and his descendants, according to the Sept. & Vulg. *the Libyans.*

פּוֹטִי פֶרַע pr. n., *Potipherah,* the father-in-law of Joseph.

פּוּטִיאֵל (*afflicted of God*) pr. name masc. Ex. 6. 25.

פּוֹטִיפַר pr. name, *Potiphar,* a chief of Pharaoh's guard, Ge. 39. 1.

פּוֹטֵר[i] Kal part. act. sing. masc. . . . פטר

פּוּךְ[k] masc.—I. *eye-paint, stibium,* prepared from antimony; see also קֶרֶן־.—II. אַבְנֵי פוּךְ a kind of costly stone or species of marble, 1 Ch. 29. 2.

פּוֹל וּ masc. *beans,* 2 Sa. 17. 28; Eze. 4. 9.

פּוּל pr. name—I. of a people and region in Africa, Is. 66. 19.—II. of a king of Assyria, 2 Ki. 15. 19; 1 Ch. 5. 26.

פּוּם only defect. פֻּם Chald. dec. 1 a.—I. *mouth.*—II. *aperture,* Da. 6. 18.

[פּוּן] *to be perplexed, distracted,* Ps. 88. 16.

פּוּנִי patronym. from an unknown person (*distracted*) Nu. 26. 23. פון

פּוּנֹן (*perplexed;* Gesenius, *darkness*) pr. name of a city of Idumea, Nu. 33. 42.

פִּינֹן (id.) pr. n. of an Idumean prince, Ge. 36. 41.

פּוּעָה pr. name of a woman . . . יפע

[פּוּץ] I. *to disperse themselves, be scattered;* part. pass. פּוּץ *dispersed,* Zep. 3. 10.—II. *to overflow,* Pr. 5. 16; metaph. Zec. 1. 17. Niph. *to be scattered.* Pil. פּוֹצֵץ *to break, shatter in pieces,* Je. 23. 29. Pilp. פִּצְפֵּץ (§ 6. No. 4) id. Job 16. 12. Hiph. I. *to disperse, scatter, confuse.*—II. *to pour abroad,* Job 40. 11.—III. intrans. *to spread abroad, be scattered.* Hithpal. (§ 6. No. 4) *to be scattered,* Hab. 3. 6.

מֵפִיץ masc. *battle-hammer, maul,* Pr. 25. 18.

פּוּצַי[l] Kal part. pass. pl., suff. 1 p. s. fr. [פּוּץ] d. 1 a פוץ

[פּוּק] I. *to move to and fro, to waver, be unsteady,* Is. 28. 7.—II. i. q. Chald. נְפַק *to go out,* see Hiph. Hiph. I. *to move, be moved,* Je. 10. 4.—II. causat. (comp. Kal No. II.) (*a*) *to give out, furnish, supply;* (*b*) *to get, obtain* from any one; (*c*) *to further, let succeed,* Ps. 140. 9.

פּוּקָה fem. *stumblingblock,* 1 Sa. 25. 31.

פִּיק masc. tottering, Na. 2. 11.

פּוֹקֵד Kal part. act. sing. masc. . . . פקד

פּוּקוּ[m] Chald. Peal imp. pl. masc. . . . נפק

פּוּר *to break in pieces,* Is. 24. 19. Hiph. הֵפִיר.—I. *to break, violate,* Eze. 17. 19.—II. *to frustrate,* 2 Sa. 15. 34; Ps. 33. 10.

פּוּרָה fem. *wine-press,* Is. 63. 3; Hag. 2. 16.

פּוּר[n] masc. dec. 1 a, *lot;* pl. פּוּרִים (*a*) *lots;* (*b*) *the feast of Purim.*

פּוֹר[o] Kal inf. abs. R. פּוּר, or [for פֹּר] R. . פרר

פּוּרָה noun fem. sing. . . . . פור

פּוּרִים[p] noun masc., pl. of פּוּר dec. 1 a . . פור

פּוֹרֵעַ Kal part. act. sing. masc. . . . פרע

פּוֹרַרְתָּ[q] Poel pret. 2 pers. sing. masc. . . . פרר

פֹּרֵשׂ[r] Kal part. act. sing. masc. dec. 7 b . פרשׂ

פּוֹרָתָא pr. name of one of the sons of Haman, Est. 9. 8.

[פּוּשׁ] I. *to spread, thrive, grow fat.*—II. *to spread themselves,* Hab. 1. 8. Niph. *to be scattered,* Na. 3. 18.

[a] Le. 1. 12. [b] Ex. 8. 19. [c] Je. 15. 21. [d] Jos. 18. 8. [e] Pr. 26. 28. [f] La. 2. 18. [g] Ps. 34. 23. [h] Zep. 3. 4. [i] Pr. 17. 14. [k] 1 Ch. 29. 2. [l] Zep. 3. 10. [m] Da. 3. 26. [n] Est. 3. 7. [o] Is. 24. 19. [p] Est. 9. 26. [q] Ps. 74. 13. [r] Pr. 29. 5.

פַּשׁ masc. Job 35. 15, perh. *excess*; others, *multitude*; Gesenius, *arrogance, wickedness*, or, as apoc. from פֶּשַׁע, פֶּשַׁע *transgression*.

פִּישׁוֹן (*spreading, overflowing*) pr. name, *Pishon*, one of the rivers issuing from the garden of Eden, Ge. 2. 11.

פּוֹשְׁעִים[a] Kal part. act. masc., pl. of פֹּשֵׁעַ dec. 7b . פשע

פּוּת Root not used; prob. *to be spread open*, cogn. פָּתַח, פָּתָה, פּוּשׁ.

פֹּת masc.—I. *nakedness, pudendum muliebre*, with suff. פָּתְהֵן, Is. 3. 17.—II. pl. פֹּתוֹת *hinges*, 1 Ki. 7. 50.

פּוּתִי patronym. 1 Ch. 2. 53.

פִּיתוֹן pr. name masc. 1 Ch. 8. 35; 9. 41.

פּוֹתָה[b] Kal part. act. sing., fem. of פֹּתֶה masc. . פתה

פּוֹתֵחַ[c] Kal part. act. sing. masc. dec. 7b . . פתח

פּוֹתֵר[d] Kal part. act. sing. masc. . . . פתר

פָּז noun masc. sing. . . . . . . פזז

[פָּזַז] I. *to be light, active, agile*, Ge. 49. 24. Pi. *to leap*, 2 Sa. 6. 16.—II. i. q. Arab. פצץ *to purify* metals, Heb. only Hoph. part. זָהָב מוּפָז *purified, pure gold*, 1 Ki. 10. 18, for which 2 Ch. 9. 17, זָהָב טָהוֹר.

פָּז adj. masc. *purified, pure*, an epithet of gold, Ca. 5. 11; then for *refined, pure gold*.

פְּזוּרָה[e] Kal part. pass. sing. fem. [of פָּזוּר masc.] פזר

[פָּזַר] *to disperse, scatter*, Je. 50. 17. Pi. I. *to disperse, scatter*.—II. *to distribute liberally*. Niph. & Pu. *to be scattered*.

פִּזַּר Piel pret. 3 pers. sing. masc. (§ 10. rem. 1) פזר

פִּזְּרוּ[f] id. pret. 3 pers. pl. . . . . פזר

פִּזַּרְתָּ[g] id. pret. 2 pers. sing. masc. . . . פזר

פַּח, פָּח ,וָ׳} noun masc. sing., pl. פַּחִים (§ 37. rem. 7); for וָ see lett. ו . . } פחח

פָּחַד[h] ,וּ׳ fut. יִפְחַד.—I. *to tremble, fear, be afraid*, with מִפְּנֵי *before* any one.—II. *to be agitated* with wonder and joy, Is. 60. 5; Je. 33. 9.—III. *to hasten, make haste*, Ho. 3. 5. Pi. *to fear greatly, continually*, Is. 51. 13; hence, *to be very careful, solicitous*, Pr. 28. 14. Hiph. *to cause to tremble, to terrify*, Job 4. 14.

פַּחַד masc. dec. 6d (with suff. פַּחְדּוֹ § 35. r. 5).—I. *fear, dread*.—II. *fear, reverence*, Ps. 36. 2.—III. *object of fear* or *reverence*.—IV. *thigh*, Job 40. 17, so Schultens and Prof. Lee, coll. with the Arab. פַּחְדָּה f. *fear, terror*, only פַּחְדָּתִי Je. 2. 19.

פָּחָד Kal pret. 3 pers. sing. m. for פָּחַד (§ 8. r. 7) פחד

פַּחַד ,וּ׳ ,וָ׳ n. m. s. d. 6d; וּ bef. lab., for וָ see lett. ו פחד

פָּחֲדוּ[i], וּפָחֲדוּ ,וּ׳} Kal pret. 3 pers. pl. (§ 8. rem. 7); וּ bef. lab. . . . } פחד

פְּחָדָיו[k] noun masc. pl., suff. 3 pers. sing. masc. from פַּחַד dec. 6d . . . פחד

פַּחְדּוֹ[l] ,וּ׳[m] id. sing., suff. 3 pers. sing. masc. (§ 35. rem. 5); וּ bef. lab. . . . . פחד

פְּחָדִים[n] id. pl., abs. st. . . . . . פחד

פַּחְדְּךָ[o] id. sing., suff. 2 pers. sing. masc. (§ 35. r. 5) פחד

פַּחְדְּכֶם id. sing., suff. 2 pers. pl. masc. . . פחד

פַּחְדָּם id. sing., suff. 3 pers. pl. masc. . . פחד

וּפָחַדְתָּ[p] Kal pret. 2 pers. sing. masc.; acc. shifted by וּ, for וָ, conv. (§ 8. rem. 7) . . פחד

פָּחַדְתִּי[q] id. pret. 1 pers. sing. . . . . פחד

פַּחְדָּתִי[r] noun fem. sing., suff. [from פַּחְדָּה no pl.] פחד

פֶּחָה[s] Heb. & Chald. masc. irr. (§ 45) *governor, deputy* of a province.

פַּחַת masc. idem, Ne. 5. 14, see § 45.

פַּחַת־מוֹאָב (*governor of Moab*) pr. name of a man.

פַּחוֹת[t], פַּחֲווֹת ,וּ׳[u]} noun masc. with pl. fem. term. from פֶּחָה irr. (§ 45); וּ bef. lab. . } פחה

פַּחֲוָתָא ,וּ Ch. id. pl., emph. st.; וּ id. . . . פחה

פַּחוֹתֶיהָ[v] id. pl., suff. 3 pers. sing. fem. . . פחה

[פָּחַז] in the Chald. *to boil up* or *over*, hence—I. *to be wanton, rash*, Ju. 9. 4.—II. *to be proud, vainglorious*, Zep. 3. 4.

פַּחַז masc. *wantonness, arrogance*, Ge. 49. 4.

פַּחֲזוּת f. d. 10, *boasting, vain-glory*, Je. 23. 32.

פַּחַז[y] noun masc. sing. . . . . . פחז

וּפֹחֲזִים[z] Kal part. act. m. pl. [of פֹּחֵז] d. 7b; וּ bef. lab. פחז

פָּחַח. Hiph. הָפֵחַ (denom. from פַּח) *to spread a net, ensnare*, Is. 42. 22.

פַּח masc. pl. פַּחִים (dag. forte impl. § 37. r. 7).—I. *snare, gin*; metaph. *cause of ruin, destruction*; hence, *ruin, destruction*.—II. pl. פַּחִים *plates of metal*.—III. Ps. 11. 6, פַּחִים *snares*, for *crooked lightnings*; others take it as a sing. i. q. פֶּחָם *coal, coals*.

פַּחֵי[a] noun masc. pl. constr. from פַּח (§ 37. r. 7) פחח

[a] Is. 46. 8. [b] Ho. 7. 11. [c] Ps. 145. 16. [d] Ge. 41. 8. [e] Je. 50. 17. [f] Joel 4. 2. [g] Ps. 89. 11. [h] Ps. 119. 161. [i] Ps. 78. 53. [k] Job 40. 17. [l] 1 Ch. 14. 17. [m] Job 13. 11. [n] Job 15. 21. [o] De. 2. 25. [p] De. 28. 66. [q] Job 3. 25. [r] Je. 2. 19. [s] Ezr. 5. 14. [t] Ne. 2. 7, 9. [u] Ezr. 8. 36. [v] Je. 51. 28, 57. [y] Ge. 49. 4. [z] Ju. 9. 4. [a] Ex. 39. 3.

פְּחִי[a] וּ Kal imp. sing. fem.; וּ bef. lab. . . . נפח

פְּחִים[b] וּ׳ noun masc. pl. of פַּח (§ 37. r. 7); וּ id. פחח

פֶּחָם masc. *coal, charcoal,* Pr. 26. 21; also *burning coal,* Is. 44. 12; 54. 16.

פַּחִים masc. id. so according to some in Ps. 11. 6, see פַּח.

פֶּחָם[c] noun masc. sing., suff. 3 pers. pl. masc. [as if from פַּח], see פֶּחָה irr. (§ 45) . פחה

פֶּחָר Ch. masc. *potter,* Da. 2. 41. Syr. פחרא id.

פָּחַת Root not used; Syr. *to dig, excavate.*

פַּחַת m. d. 6 d, *pit; metaph. ruin destruction.*

פְּחֶתֶת fem. *corrosion, inward fretting* of the leprosy in a garment, Le. 13. 55.

פַּחַת[d] / וְ פַחַת } noun masc. sing. dec. 6 d; for וְ see lett. ו . . . . } פחת

פַּחַת noun masc. with fem. term., constr. of פֶּחָה irr. (§ 45), and pr. n. in compos. פ׳ מוֹאָב פחה

פְּחֶתֶת[e] noun fem. sing., from פַּחַת masc. . פחת

פִּטְדָה fem. a precious stone, according to most of the ancient versions the *topaz.*

פִּטְדַת[f] id., constr. st. . . . . . פטדה

פְּטוּרֵי[g] וּ Kal part. pass. pl. constr. [from פָּטוּר] dec. 3 a; וּ bef. lab. . . . . פטר

פְּטֻרִים[h] Kh. פְּטִירִים adj. masc. pl. of [פָּטִיר]; K. פְּטוּ׳ part. pass. pl. masc., dec. 3 a . פטר

פַּטִּישׁ noun masc. sing. . . . . פטשׁ

פַּטִּישֵׁיהוֹן[i] Ch. noun masc. pl., suff. 3 pers. pl. masc. Keth. פַּטִּישֵׁיהוֹן [from פַּטִּישׁ dec. 1]; K. פַּטְשֵׁיהוֹן [from פְּטַשׁ dec. 3 a] . פטשׁ

פָּטַר[k] fut. יִפְטַר.—I. *to burst open,* only part. pass. פְּטוּרֵי צִצִּים *bursted ones of the flowers,* i. e. *open flowers.*—II. *to let out* water, Pr. 17. 14.—III. *to let go, dismiss, exempt from duty.*—IV. *to slip away,* 1 Sa. 19. 10.

פָּטִיר masc. *free, exempt from duty,* 1 Ch. 9. 33, Keth.

פֶּטֶר masc. *a breaking forth, opening,* פֶּטֶר רֶחֶם *firstborn,* so also without רֶחֶם.

פִּטְרָה fem. dec. 10, idem, Nu. 8. 16.

פֶּטֶר[l] וּ׳ noun masc. sing.; וּ bef. lab. . . פטר

פְּטֻרֵי[m] וּ defect. for פְּטוּרֵי (q. v.) . . . פטר

פִּטְרַת[n] noun fem. sing. constr. [of פִּטְרָה no pl.] פטר

פָּטַשׁ Root not used; Arab. *to hammer,* also *to spread out.*

פַּטִּישׁ masc. *a hammer.*

פַּטִּישׁ Chald. masc. dec. 1 a, *a tunic,* Da. 3. 21.

פִּי וּ׳ noun masc. sing. constr. st. or with suff. 1 pers. sing. from פֶּה irr. (§ 45); also pr. name in compos., as פִּי־בֶסֶת, &c.; וּ bef. lab. פאה

פִּיד Root not used; Arab. *to disappear, die.* Hence

פִּיד[o] וּ masc. sing. dec. 1 a, *calamity;* וּ bef. lab. . פיד

פִּיהָ[p] וּ׳ noun masc. sing., suff. 3 pers. sing. fem. from פֶּה irr. (§ 45); וּ id. . . פאה

פִּיהוּ וּ׳ id., suff. 3 pers. sing. masc.; וּ id. . פאה

פִּיהֶם[q] וּ id., suff. 3 pers. pl. masc.; וּ id. . פאה

פִּיו[r] וּ׳ id., suff. 3 pers. sing. masc.; וּ id. . פאה

פֵּיוֹת[s] noun fem. pl. of [פֵּיָה] dec. 10 . . פאה

פִּיוֹת[t] noun m. with pl. f. term. fr. פֶּה irr. (§ 45) פאה

פִּיחַ[u] noun masc. sing. . . . . . פוח

פִּיךָ noun masc. s., suff. 2 p. s. m. fr. פֶּה (§ 45) פאה

פִּיכֹל וּ pr. name masc.; וּ bef. lab. . . פאה

פִּילֶגֶשׁ (for פִּלֶּגֶשׁ dag. forte resolved in י) noun fem. sing. dec. 6a (§ 35. rem. 16) . פלגשׁ

פִּילַגְשֵׁהוּ[x] וּ id., suff. 3 pers. sing. masc.; וּ bef. lab. פלגשׁ

פִּילַגְשׁוֹ וּ׳ id., suff. 3 pers. sing. masc.; וּ id. . פלגשׁ

פִּילַגְשִׁי[y] וּ׳ id., suff. 1 pers. sing.; וּ id. . . פלגשׁ

פִּילַגְשָׁיו[z] וּ id. pl., suff. 3 pers. sing. masc.; וּ id. . פלגשׁ

פִּילַגְשִׁים וּ׳ id. pl., abs. st.; וּ id. . . פלגשׁ

פִּים Root not used; Arab. *to be fat.*

פִּימָה fem. *fat, fatness,* Job 15. 27.

פִּים[a] noun masc. pl. of פֶּה irr. (§ 45) . . פאה

פִּימָה[b] noun fem. sing. . . . . פים

פִּימוֹ noun masc. sing., suff. 3 pers. sing. masc. from פֶּה irr. (§ 45) . . . . פאה

פִּינוּ[c] id. with suff. 1 pers. pl. . . . פאה

פִּינְחָס וּ׳ pr. name masc.; וּ bef. lab. . . . פאה

פִּינֹן pr. name of a place, see פּוּנֹן . . פון

פִּיפִיּוֹת noun masc. with pl. fem. term. [from פִּיפֶה] comp. פִּיּוֹת . . . . . פאה

פִּיק[d] וּ noun masc. sing.; וּ bef. lab. . . פוק

פִּישׁוֹן pr. name of a river . . . . פושׁ

פִּיתוֹן / פִּיתֹן } pr. name of a place . . . פות

פַּךְ noun masc. sing. . . . . . פכה

פָּכָה. Pi. *to flow out,* Eze. 47. 2.

פַּךְ masc. *flask, cruse.*

---

[a] Eze. 37. 9. [b] Je. 18. 22. [c] Ne. 5. 14. [d] Je. 48. 28. [e] Le. 13. 55. [f] Job 28. 19. [g] 1 Ki. 6. 18, 29, 32. [h] 1 Ch. 9. 33. [i] Da. 3. 21. [k] 2 Ch. 23. 8. [l] Ex. 34. 20. [m] 1 Ki. 6. 35. [n] Nu. 8. 16. [o] Pr. 24. 22. [p] 1 Ki. 7. 31. [q] Job 29. 23. [r] Pr. 18. 6. [s] Ju. 3. 16. [t] Pr. 5. 4. [u] Ex. 9. 8, 10. [x] Ju. 19. 24. [y] Ju. 20. 4, 5. [z] 2 Ch. 11. 21. [a] 1 Sa. 13. 21. [b] Job 15. 27. [c] Ps. 126. 2. [d] Na. 2. 11.

פֹּכֶרֶת הַצְּבָיִים (*snaring the gazelles*) pr. name m. Ezr. 2. 57; Ne. 7. 59.

פָּלָא Kal not used; i. q. פָּלָה *to separate, distinguish.* Niph. I. *to be extraordinary, great,* 2 Sa. 1. 26; part. נִפְלָאוֹת *great things,* Da. 11. 36.—II. *to be or appear hard, difficult,* with בְּעֵינֵי in the eyes of any one.—III. *to be wonderful, marvellous;* part. נִפְלָאוֹת *wonderful, marvellous things* or *deeds,* also adv. *wonderfully, marvellously.* Pi. *to set apart, dedicate,* with נֶדֶר a thing vowed. Hiph. I. i. q. Pi.—II. *to make extraordinary, great,* e. g. kindness, to show great kindness; inf. הַפְלֵא adv. *exceedingly, very.*—III. *to make wonderful, admirable;* with אֶת *to act wonderfully;* inf. לְהַפְלִיא adv. *wonderfully.* Hithp. *to show oneself wonderful,* Job 10. 16.

פַּלּוּא (*distinguished*) pr. name of a son of Reuben. Patronym. פַּלֻּאִי, Nu. 26. 5.

פֶּלִיא, fem. פְּלִיאָה adj. *wonderful,* only Ps. 139. 6, Keri.

פֶּלֶא masc. dec. 6a (with suff. פִּלְאֲךָ).—I. *something wonderful, a miracle;* pl. פְּלָאִים adv. *wonderfully;* פְּלָאוֹת *wonderful things.*—II. *the wonderful,* Is. 9. 5.

פִּלְאִי, fem. פִּלְאִיָּה adj. *wonderful,* only in Kheth. Ju. 13. 18; Ps. 139. 6.

פְּלָאיָה (whom *the Lord separated*) pr. name of a man.

פְּלָיָה (id.) pr. name masc. 1 Ch. 3. 24.

מִפְלָאָה fem. dec. 11a, *miracle,* Job 37. 16.

[a] וָ׳פֶּלֶא noun masc. sing. (suff. פִּלְאֲךָ) dec. 6a; for וָ see lett. ו . . . . . פלא

[b] פְּלָאוֹת id. with pl. fem. term., abs. st. . . פלא

[c] פִּלְאִי Kh. פִּלְאִי adj. from פֶּלֶא with the adj. term. ◌ִי, K. פֶּלִי by contraction . . . פלא

פְּלָאיָה pr. name masc. . . . . פלא

[d] פְּלִאיָה Kh. פִּלְאִיָּה adj., fem. of פִּלְאִי; K. פְּלִיאָה fem. of an obsol. פֶּלִיא . . פלא

[e] פְּלָאִים noun masc., pl. of פֶּלֶא dec. 6a . . פלא

[f] פִּלְאֲךָ, פִּלְאֲךָ } id. sing., suff. 2 pers. sing. masc. . . פלא

פִּלְאֶסֶר see תִּגְלַת פִּלְ׳.

פָּלַג. Niph. *to be divided.* Pi. I. *to cut out, form,* Job 38. 25.—II. *to divide,* Ps. 55. 10.

פְּלַג Chald. *to divide,* Da. 2. 41.

פְּלַג Chald. masc. *half,* Da. 7. 25.

פֶּלֶג masc. dec. 6a (pl. c. פַּלְגֵי).—I. *brook, stream.*—II. pr. name of a son of Eber.

פְּלַגָּה fem. dec. 10, *brook.*

פְּלֻגָּה fem. dec. 10, *division,* 2 Ch. 35. 5.

פְּלֻגָּא Chald. fem. dec. 8a, idem, Ezr. 6. 18.

מִפְלַגָּה fem. dec. 10, idem, 2 Ch. 35. 12.

[g] פַּלַּג Piel imp. sing. masc. (§ 10. rem. 3) . פלג

פֶּלֶג, פָּלֶג } pr. name masc. (§ 35. rem. 2) . פלג

[h] פֶּלֶג noun masc. sing. (pl. c. פַּלְגֵי) dec. 6a . פלג

[i] פִּלַּג Piel pret. 3 pers. sing. masc. (§ 10. rem. 1) פלג

[k] וּפְלַג Chald. noun masc. sing.; וּ bef. lab. . פלג

פַּלְגֵי noun masc. pl. constr. from פֶּלֶג dec. 6a פלג

[l] פְּלָגָיו id. pl., suff. 3 pers. sing. masc. . . פלג

[m] פְּלָגִים id. pl., abs. st. . . . . . פלג

פִּילֶגֶשׁ, פִּלֶגֶשׁ fem. d. 6a (with suff. ׳לַגְשׁוֹ § 35. r. 16), *concubine.*

[n] פִּלַגְשֵׁי id. pl., constr. st. . . . . פלגש

[o] פִּלַגְשֵׁיהֶם id. pl., suff. 3 pers. pl. masc. . . פלגש

[p] פִּלַגְשֶׁיךָ id. pl., suff. 2 pers. sing. masc. . . פלגש

פִּלַגְשִׁים id. pl., abs. st. . . . . פלגש

פָּלַד Root not used; Arab. *to cut up.*

פְּלָדָה fem. dec. 12a, *iron, steel,* Na. 2. 4.

פִּלְדָּשׁ pr. name masc. Ge. 22. 22.

[q] פְּלָדֹת noun fem. pl. abs. from [פְּלָדָה] dec. 12a פלד

פָּלָה. Niph. I. *to be separated, distinguished,* Ex. 33. 16.—II. *to be made wonderful,* i. e. *wonderfully made,* Ps. 139. 14. Hiph. I. *to set apart.*—II. *to separate, distinguish.*

פְּלֹנִי masc.—I. *a certain one,* always followed by אַלְמֹנִי, *such an one, such and such* place.—II. gent. noun, *Pelonite,* 1 Ch. 11. 27, 36.

פַּלְמֹנִי masc. id. by contr. for פְּלֹנִי אַלְמֹנִי.

וּ׳ פַּלּוּא pr. name masc.; וּ bef. lab. . . פלא

[פָּלַח] *to cut, cleave,* Ps. 141. 7. Pi. I. *to cut in pieces,* 2 Ki. 4. 39.—II. *to cleave.*—III. *to let break forth, to bring forth,* Job 39. 3.

פְּלַח Chald. *to serve, worship.*

פֶּלַח masc.—I. *slice, piece.*—II. *millstone;* פֶּ׳ רֶכֶב *upper millstone;* פֶּ׳ תַּחְתִּית *nether millstone.*

פִּלְחָא (*slice*) pr. name masc. Ne. 10. 25.

פָּלְחָן Chald. m. d. 1b, *service, worship,* Ezr. 7. 19.

---

[a] Is. 29. 14. [b] Ps. 119. 129. [c] Ju. 13. 18. [d] Ps. 139. 6. [e] La. 1. 9. [f] Ps. 89. 6. [g] Ps. 55. 10. [h] Ps. 65. 10. [i] Job 38. 25. [k] Da. 7. 25. [l] Ps. 46. 5. [m] Is. 30. 25. [n] 2 Sa. 16. 21, 22. [o] Eze. 23. 20. [p] 2 Sa. 19. 6. [q] Na. 2. 4.

פָּלַח[a] Ch. Peal part. act. s. m. (§ 49. rem. 4) d. 2a פלח

פִּלְחָה noun fem. sing. . . . . . . פלח

פֹּלֵחַ[b] Kal part. act. sing. masc. . . . . פלח

פִּלְחָא pr. name masc. . . . . . . פלח

פָּלְחֵי[c] וְ | פָּלְחִין } Chald. Peal part. act. masc. pl. constr. & abs. from פְּלַח (§ 49. rem. 4) dec. 2a } פלח

[פָּלַט] *to slip away, escape*, Eze. 7. 16. Pi. I. *to escape, be delivered*, Job 23. 7.—II. *to let escape, deliver*; hence—III. *to bring forth*, Job 21. 10. Hiph. I. *to deliver*, Mi. 6. 14.—II. *to carry away safely*, Is. 5. 29.

פָּלֵט adj. masc. dec. 5, *escaped by flight.*

פָּלִיט adj. masc. dec. 3a, idem.

פְּלֵטָה, פְּלֵיטָה fem. dec. 10.—I. *escape, deliverance.*—II. *that which escapes*; collect. *those escaped, remnant.*

פָּלִיט adj. masc. dec. 3a, *one escaped by flight.*

פַּלֵּט masc. *deliverance*, Ps. 32. 7.

פֶּלֶט (*deliverance*) pr. name masc.—I. 1 Ch. 2. 47. —II. 1 Ch. 12. 3.

פַּלְטִי (for פְּלַטְיָה *deliverance of the Lord*) pr. name masc.—I. Nu. 13. 9.—II. 1 Sa. 25. 44, called פַּלְטִיאֵל 2 Sa. 3. 15.

פִּלְטַי (for פְּלַטְיָה) pr. name masc. Ne. 12. 17.

פְּלַטְיָהוּ, פְּלַטְיָה (whom *the Lord delivers*) pr. name masc. of several persons.

מִפְלָט masc. *escape, safety*, Ps. 55. 9.

פֶּלֶט pr. name, see בֵּית פֶּלֶט . . . . בית

פַּלֵּט[d] (prop. Piel inf.) as a subst. . . . פלט

פַּלֶּט־[e] Piel imp. sing. masc. [for פַּלֵּט § 10. rem. 4] פלט

פֶּלֶט וָ pr. name masc.; for וָ see lett. ו . . פלט

פַּלְּטָה[f] Piel imp. s. m. with parag. ה (comp. § 8. r. 11) פלט

פְּלֵטָה[g] noun fem. sing. dec. 10 . . . . פלט

פָּלְטוּ[h] וּ Kal pret. 3 pers. pl.; וּ, for וְ, conv. . פלט

פַּלְּטוּ[i] Piel imp. pl. masc. . . . . . פלט

פַּלְטִי, פִּלְטַי (for פְּלַטְיָהוּ, וּ׳ פְּלַטְיָה, פַּלְטִיאֵל ,(מַי) pr. names masc.; וּ bef. lab. . . . פלט

פְּלֵטִים[k] וּ׳ adj. masc. pl. of פָּלֵט dec. 5a; וּ bef. lab. פלט

פַּלְּטֵנִי[l] Piel imp. sing. masc., suff. 1 pers. sing. . פלט

פְּלִיגָה[m] Chald. Peal part. pass. sing. fem. [of פְּלִיג] פלג

פְּלָיָה וּ pr. name masc.; וּ bef. lab. . . . פלא

פָּלִיט וּ׳ adj. masc. sing. dec. 3a; וּ id. . . פלט

פְּלֵיטָה וּ׳ noun fem. sing. dec. 10; וּ id. . . פלט

פְּלִיטֵי[n] וּ׳ adj. pl. constr. masc. from פָּלִיט dec. 3a פלט

פְּלִיטֵיהֶם[o] id. pl., suff. 3 pers. pl. masc. . . . פלט

פְּלִיטָיו[p] id. pl., suff. 3 pers. sing. masc. . . . פלט

פְּלִיטֵיכֶם[q] id. pl., suff. 2 pers. pl. masc. . . . פלט

פְּלֵיטִים[r] | פְּלֵיטִם[s] } adj. masc., pl. of [פָּלִיט] dec. 3a . פלט

פְּלֵיטַת[t] וּ׳ n. f. s., constr. of פְּלֵיטָה d. 10; וּ bef. lab. פלט

פְּלִילָה[u] noun fem. sing. . . . . . . פלל

פְּלִילִי[x] | פְּלִילִיָּה[y] } adj. masc. and fem. sing. . . . פלל

פְּלִלִים noun masc., pl. of [פָּלִיל] dec. 3a . . פלל

פָּלַךְ Root not used; Arab. *to be round.* Hence

פֶּלֶךְ[z] | פֶּלֶךְ { masc. d. 6a (but with suff. פִּלְכּוֹ § 35. r. 2 & 3).—I. *circuit, district.*—II. *distaff*, Pr. 31. 19.—III. *staff*, 2 Sa. 3. 29; according to others, *distaff* } פלך

פָּלַל. Pi. פִּלֵּל—I. *to judge*, 1 Sa. 2. 25.—II. *to adjudge*, with לְ, Eze. 16. 52.—III. *to execute judgment, inflict judicial punishment*, Ps. 106. 30.—IV. *to judge, suppose*, Ge. 48. 11. Hithp. I. *to intercede, supplicate, pray for* any one, with בְּעַד ,עַל ,לְ *for* whom, with אֶל *with* whom one intercedes.—II. generally *to supplicate, pray*, with לִפְנֵי ,לְ ,אֶל *to whom*, with אֶל *for* which one prays.

פָּלָל (*judge*) pr. name masc. Ne. 3. 25.

פָּלִיל masc. dec. 3a, *a judge.*

פְּלִילָה fem. *justice*, Is. 16. 3.

פְּלִילִי masc. adj. *judicial*, Job 31. 28; fem. פְּלִילִיָּה *what is judicial, for judgment*, Is. 28. 7 (Gesenius, *judgment-seat, tribunal*).

פְּלַלְיָה (whom *the Lord judges*) pr. n. m. Ne. 11. 12.

אֶפְלָל (*judgment*) pr. name masc. 1 Ch. 2. 37.

תְּפִלָּה fem. dec. 10.—I. *intercession.*—II. *supplication, prayer.*

פָּלָל pr. name masc. . . . . . . פלל

פִּלְלוֹ[a] וּ Piel pret. 3 pers. s. m. [פִּלֵּל], suff. 3 pers. sing. m. (comp. § 10. r. 7); וּ, for וְ, conv. פלל

פְּלַלְיָה pr. name masc. . . . . . פלל

פִּלַּלְתְּ[b] id. pret. 2 pers. sing. fem. . . . פלל

פִּלָּלְתִּי[c] id. pret. 1 pers. sing. [for פִּלַּלְתִּי] . פלל

פַּלְנִי adj. masc. sing. . . . . . פלה

פִּלְנְאֶסֶר | פִּלְנֶסֶר } pr. name, see תִּגְלַת פִּל׳.

[a] Da. 6. 17, 21. [b] Ps. 141. 7. [c] Ezr. 7. 24. [d] Ps. 32. 7. [e] Ps. 56. 8. [f] Ps. 17. 13. [g] Eze. 14. 22. [h] Eze. 7. 16. [i] Ps. 82. 4. [k] Je. 50. 28. [l] Ps. 31. 2; 71. 4. [m] Da. 2. 41. [n] Je. 44. 28. [o] Eze. 7. 16. [p] Ob. 14. [q] Eze. 6. 9. [r] Is. 66. 19. [s] Nu. 21. 29. [t] Is. 10. 20. [u] Is. 16. 3. [x] Job 31. 28. [y] Is. 28. 7. [z] Pr. 31. 19. [a] 1 Sa. 2. 25. [b] Eze. 16. 52. [c] Ge. 48. 11.

פָּלַס. Pi. I. *to make level, plain,* a way.—II. *to weigh,* trop. Ps 58. 3; hence *to ponder, consider,* Pr. 5. 21.

פֶּלֶס m. *balance, steelyard,* Pr. 16. 11; Is. 40. 12.

מִפְלָשׂ m. d. 2 b, *a poising, balancing,* Job 37. 16.

[a] פַּלֵּס Piel imp. sing. masc. . . . . פלס

[b] פֶּלֶס noun masc. sing. . . . . . פלס

פִּלְאֶסֶר pr. name, see תִּגְלַת פִּלְ׳.

פָּלַץ. Hithp. *to shake, tremble,* Job 9. 6.

פַּלָּצוּת fem. *trembling, fear.*

מִפְלֶצֶת fem. dec. 13a (with suff. מִפְלַצְתָּהּ), *fear, object of fear,* used of *images, idols.*

תִּפְלֶצֶת fem. dec. 13a, *fear, terror,* Je. 49. 16.

פַּלָּצוּת noun fem. sing. . . . . פלץ

פָּלַשׁ. Hithp. *to roll oneself, to wallow* sc. in the dust.

פְּלֶשֶׁת / פְּלָשֶׁת { pr. name, *Philistia,* a country west and south-west of Palestine. Gent. n. פְּלִשְׁתִּי *Philistine* . . } פלש

פְּלִשְׁתִּיִּים וְ / פְּלִשְׁתִּים וְ { *Philistines,* pl. of פְּלִשְׁתִּי see the preceding . . . . . } פלש

פָּלַת Root not used; Arab. *to escape, flee,* comp. פָּלַט.

פְּלֵתִי masc. collect. *public runners, couriers.* According to others, one of the tribes of the Philistines, *Pelethites,* employed as mercenary soldiers, which is very improbable. Hence also

פֶּלֶת (*swiftness*) pr. name masc.—I. Nu. 16. 1.—II. 1 Ch. 2. 33 . . . . . פלת

[d] פֻּם [e] וְ Chald. noun masc. sing. d. 1 a; וּ bef. lab. פום

פֶּן־ וְ only with Mak.; conj.; וּ id. . . פנה

פַּנַּג וְ masc. Eze. 27. 17, prob. *some delicate spice* or *gum;* Chald. פְּנַק *to be delicate.* Sept. *μύρων,* or *κασίας.* Vulg. *balsamum.* Gesenius, *pastry* or *sweet cake.*

פָּנָה וְ fut. יִפְנֶה.—I. *to turn, turn oneself,* in order to go or look away; with בְּ, לְ, אֶל *to turn to* or *towards;* with אַחֲרֵי *to follow* any one; with מֵעִם *to turn away from* any one.—II. of time, *to turn, decline;* לִפְנוֹת בֹּקֶר *at the turning,* i. e. *approach* of the morning; לִפְנוֹת עֶרֶב *at the approach of evening.*—III. trans. *to turn,* only in the phrase פָּנָה עֹרֶף *to turn the neck.* Pi. I. *to remove.*—II. *to clear,* a house or a road, i. e. to prepare it. Hiph. I. *to turn.*—II. intrans. *to turn oneself.* Hoph. *to be turned, to turn oneself.*

פָּנֶה masc. dec. 9 b, only pl. פָּנִים.—I. *face, countenance;* also pl. *faces;* פָּ׳ בְּפָנִים, פָּנִים אֶל־פָּנִים *face to face;* עַל־פְּנֵי פְ׳ or אֶל *to the face of* any one, i. e. freely, frankly, or insolently, so also בְּפָנָיו; שׂוּם פָּנִים with אֶל, עַל, לְ *to set one's face towards* any quarter, or, followed by an inf., *to intend* to do any thing; id. with בְּ *to set one's face in anger against* any one, and so נָתַן פָּנִים בְּ.—II. *person, presence;* פָּנַי *my person, myself.*—III. *face, surface,* hence *appearance.*—IV. *fore part, front;* of a sword, *the edge,* Ec. 10. 10; Eze. 21. 21. Adv. פָּנִים *in front;* לְפָנִים (*a*) *forwards;* (*b*) *before, of old;* מִלְּפָנִים *from of old, from ancient times;* מִפָּנִים *in front, before.*—V. with prepositions: אֶל־פְּנֵי (*a*) *in presence of, before,* implying either motion or rest; (*b*) *upon the surface of;* אֶת־פְּנֵי *before;* מֵאֵת פְּנֵי *from before;* בִּפְנֵי *in front of, before;* לִפְנֵי with suff. לְפָנַי, לְפָנֶיךָ, &c. (*a*) *in the presence of;* (*b*) *in the presence, as long as endures,* Ps. 72. 5, 17; (*c*) *in front of, before;* (*d*) *before, preceding,* of time; מִלִּפְנֵי (*a*) *from before, from the presence of;* (*b*) *because of,* 1 Ch. 16. 33; מִפְּנֵי (*a*) *from the face, presence, front of,* hence *from, away from;* (*b*) *before;* (*c*) *because of, on account of,* and with אֲשֶׁר *because that;* (*d*) *towards,* Je. 1. 13; עַל פְּנֵי (*a*) *upon* or *above, the surface,* implying either motion or rest; hence *along, towards, against,* but also *at, before;* (*b*) *above, besides,* Ex. 20. 3.

פְּנִיאֵל, פְּנוּאֵל (*face of God*) pr. name—I. of a place beyond Jordan.—II. of two men.

פֵּן prop. *a turning to, regarding, considering,* hence פֶּן־ as a conj. *lest, lest perhaps, for fear that, beware, lest.*

יְפֻנֶּה (*turned, removed*) pr. name—I. of the father of Caleb.—II. 1 Ch. 7. 38.

לִפְנַי adj. *anterior, front, in front,* 1 Ki. 6. 17.

[f] פָּנֹה Kal inf. abs. . . . . . פנה

[g] פִּנָּה [bb] וְ Piel pret. 3 p. s. m. R. פנה; also subs. f. R. פנן

[h] פִּנָּהּ noun m. s., suff. 3 pers. s. fem. fr. [פֵּן] d. 8 b פנן

פְּנֵה Kal imp. sing. masc. . . . . פנה

פֹּנֶה id. part. sing. masc. dec. 9 a . . . פנה

פָּנוּ id. pret. 3 pers. pl. . . . . פנה

פַּנּוּ Piel imp. pl. masc. . . . . פנה

פִּנּוּ וּ id. pret. 3 pers. pl.; וּ, for וְ, conv. . פנה

פְּנוּ וְ Kal imp. pl. masc.; וּ bef. lab. . . פנה

פְּנוּאֵל וְ pr. name masc.; וּ id. . . . פנה

פְּנוֹת Kal inf. constr. . . . . פנה

---

[a] Pr. 4. 26. [b] Pr. 16. 11. [bb] Mal. 3. 1. [c] Am. 9. 7. [d] Da. 6. 18, 23. [e] Da. 7. 8, 20. [f] Hag. 1. 9. [g] Zep. 3. 15. [h] Pr. 7. 8. [i] Le. 14. 36.

פִּנּוֹת noun fem. pl. of פִּנָּה dec. 10 . . פנן

פִּנּוֹתָם[a] id. pl., suff. 3 pers. pl. masc. (§ 4. rem. 2) פנן

פִּנְחָס 'ו pr. name masc., see פִּינְחָס ;ו bef. lab. פאה

פָּנָי / פָּנַי 'ו } the foll. with suff. 1 pers. sing; ו id. פנה

פְּנֵי 'ו noun masc. pl., constr. of פָּנִים [fr. [פָּנֶה dec. 9 b ; ו id. . . . . . פנה

פִּנּוֹ[b] ו Kh. פְּנֵי q. v., K. פִּי noun masc. sing. constr. of פֶּה irr. (§ 45) . . . . פאה

פְּנִיאֵל pr. name masc., see פְּנוּאֵל . . . פנה

פָּנֶיהָ 'ו[c] noun masc. pl., (פָּנִים), suff. 3 pers. sing. fem. [from [פָּנֶה dec. 9 b ; ו bef. lab. . פנה

פְּנֵיהֶם 'ו id. pl., suff. 3 pers. pl. masc.; ו id. פנה

פָּנָיו 'ו id. pl., suff. 3 pers. sing. masc.; ו id. פנה

פָּנָיִךְ / פָּנַיִךְ } id. pl., suff. 3 pers. sing. fem. . פנה

פָּנֶיךָ 'ו[d] id. pl., suff. 2 pers. sing. masc.; ו bef. lab. פנה

פְּנֵיכֶם id. pl., suff. 2 pers. pl. masc. . . . פנה

פָּנִים 'ו[e] id. pl., abs. st.; ו bef. lab. . . . פנה

פֹּנִים Kal part act. masc., pl. of פֹּנֶה dec. 9 a . פנה

פְּנִימָה noun masc. sing. [פְּנִים] with loc. ה . פנם

פְּנֵימוֹ[f] noun masc. pl., (פָּנִים), suff. 3 pers. pl. masc. from [פָּנֶה] dec. 9 b . . . . פנה

פָּנֵינוּ[g] id. pl. with suff. 1 pers. pl. . . . פנה

פָּנִינוּ[h] Kal pret. 1 pers. pl. . . . . . פנה

פְּנִינִים[cc] noun masc. pl. [from [פְּנִין . . . פנן

פָּנִיתָ 'ו[i] Kal pret. 2 pers. sing. masc.; ו, for וְ, conv. פנה

פִּנִּיתָ[k] Piel pret. 2 pers. sing. masc. . . . פנה

פָּנִיתִי ו Kal pret. 1 pers. sing.; ו bef. lab. . פנה

פִּנִּיתִי[l] Piel pret. 1 pers. sing. . . . . פנה

פָּנַם doubtful Root; according to Fürst (in concord.), *to hide, conceal.*

פְּנִים masc. prop. *interior, inner part,* only as an adv. מִלִּפְנִים *within,* 1 Ki. 6. 29; with ה parag. פְּנִימָה; (*a*) *to the inside, inward;* (*b*) *within, inside* a house or palace; (*c*) *within, on the inside.* לִפְנִימָה *to the inside, inward,* Eze. 41. 3; also *within, on the inside;* מִפְּנִימָה *on the inside, within.*

פְּנִימִי fem. פְּנִימִית (pl. פְּנִימִיּוֹת) adj. *inner.*

פָּנַן Root not used; Arab. *to divide.*

פֵּן masc. dec. 8 b, *corner,* Pr. 7. 8; Zec. 14. 10.

פִּנָּה f. d. 10.—I. *corner;* אֶבֶן פִּ׳, רֹאשׁ פִּ׳ *corner-stone.*—II. *battlement, parapet.*—III. *chief, prince.*

פְּנִינִים m. pl. *pearls;* others, *red corals.* Hence also

פְּנִנָּה (*pearl*) pr. name fem. 1 Sa. 1. 2, 4 . פנן

פִּנֵּק Pi. *to bring up, train delicately,* Pr. 29. 21.

פִּנַּת noun fem. sing., constr. of פִּנָּה dec. 10 . פנן

פִּנָּתָהּ[m] id., suff. 3 pers. sing. fem. . . . פנן

פִּנֹּתָיו[n] id. pl., suff. 3 pers. sing. masc. . . פנן

פַּס[o] Chald. noun masc. sing. dec. 5 a . . . פסס

פַּסָּא[p] Chald. id., emph. st. . . . . פסס

פִּסֵּג Pi. prop. *to divide,* hence *to distinguish, view* or *consider,* Ps. 48. 14.

פִּסְגָּה (*part, piece*) pr. name of a mountain ridge in the territory of Moab.

פַּסְּגוּ[q] Piel imp. pl. masc. . . . . פסג

פַּסּוּ[r] Piel pret. 3 pers. pl. . . . . פסס

פָּסוֹחַ[s] Kal inf. abs. . . . . . פסח

פָּסַח 'ו I. *to leap* or *pass over* or *by, to spare,* with עַל.—II. *to halt, limp,* 1 Ki. 18. 21. Niph. *to become lame,* 2 Sa. 4. 4. Pi. *to leap about,* 1 Ki. 18. 26.

פָּסֵחַ (*lame*) pr. name masc. of three different persons.

פֶּסַח masc. dec. 6 (§ 35. rem. 5) *the passover;* (*a*) *the paschal lamb;* (*b*) *the festival of the passover.*

פִּסֵּחַ masc. dec. 7 b, adj. *lame.*

תִּפְסַח (*passage*) pr. name of a city on the Euphrates, *Thapsacus.*

פָּסֵחַ pr. name masc. . . . . . פסח

פֶּסַח noun masc. sing. dec. 6 a . . . פסח

פִּסֵּחַ 'ו adj. masc. sing. dec. 7 b ; ו bef. lab. . פסח

פִּסְחִים[u] id. pl., abs. st. . . . . . פסח

פֹּסְחִים[w] Kal part. act. masc. pl. [of [פּוֹסֵחַ dec. 7 b פסח

פָּסַחְתִּי[y] ו id. pret. 1 pers. sing.; acc. shifted by ו, for וְ, conv. (§ 8. rem. 7) . . . . פסח

פִּסִּי וְ pr. name, see וָפְסִי under lett. ו.

פְּסִילֵי 'ו[z] n. m. pl. constr. fr. [פָּסִיל] d. 3 a; ו bef. lab. פסל

פְּסִילֶיהָ id. pl., suff. 3 pers. sing. fem. . . פסל

פְּסִילֵיהֶם 'ו[a] id. pl., suff. 3 pers. pl. masc.; ו bef. lab. פסל

פְּסִילֶיךָ[b] id. pl., suff. 2 pers. sing. masc. . . פסל

פְּסִילִים[c] id. pl., abs. st. . . . . . פסל

פַּסִּים noun masc. pl. of פַּס dec. 8 d . . פסס

פִּסְפָּה pr. name masc. 1 Ch. 7. 33.

[פָּסַל] fut. יִפְסֹל *to cut* or *hew,* espec. stones; *to carve* wood.

פָּסִיל masc. dec. 3 a.—I. *a carved image.*—II. *quarry,* Ju. 3. 19, 26, and the following.

[a] Zep. 3. 6. [b] Pr. 15. 14. [c] 1 Sa. 1. 18. [d] 2 Sa. 17. 11. [e] Pr. 25. 23. [f] Ps. 11. 7. [g] Je. 51. 51. [h] Is. 53. 6. [i] 2 Sa. 9. 8 [k] Ps. 80. 10. [l] Ge. 24. 31. [m] Job 38. 6. [n] Ex. 27. 2; 38. 2. [o] Da. 5. 5. [p] Da. 5. 24. [q] Ps. 48. 14. [r] Ps. 12. 2. [s] Is. 31. 5. [t] Ex. 12. 23, 27. [u] Is. 33. 23. [w] 1 Ki. 18. 21. [y] Ex. 12. 13. [x] De. 12. 3. [z] 2 Ki. 17. 41. [b] Mi. 5. 12. [c] Je. 50. 38. [cc] Pr. 20. 15.

פֶּסֶל ו׳ masc. dec. 6a (suff. פִּסְלִי), *carved image or idol; also for a molten image*; ו bef. lab. פסל

פְּסָל־ Kal imp. sing. masc. [for פְּסֹל § 8. rem. 18] פסל

פְּסָלוֹ[a] id. pret. 3 pers. sing. m., suff. 3 pers. s. m. פסל

פִּסְלִי[b] ו n. m. s., suff. 1 p. s. fr. פֶּסֶל d. 6a; ו bef. lab. פסל

פִּסְלָם[c] id. with suff. 3 pers. pl. masc. . פסל

פְּסַנְטֵרִין, פְּסַנְתֵּרִין, פְּסַנְתְּרִין } Chald. a musical instrument, *ψαλτήριον, psaltery*, Da. 3. 5, 7, 10, 15.

[פָּסַס] *to cease, fail, have an end*, Ps. 12. 2.

פַּס masc. *extremity*; only in the phrase כְּתֹנֶת פַּסִּים a long dress with sleeves covering the hands.

פַּס Chald. dec. 5a, *extremity* of the hand, Da. 5. 5, 24.

פִּסָּה fem. dec. 10, *abundance*, Ps. 72. 16.

פִּסְפָּה ו pr. name masc. 1 Ch. 7. 38.

פִּסַּת[d] noun fem. sing., constr. of [פִּסָּה] dec. 10 פסס

[פָּעָה] *to cry out*, only Is. 42. 14. Syr. *to bleat, low*; Arab. *to hiss*, of a serpent (Gesenius). Hence

פָּעוּ (*a bleating*) pr. name of a place in Edom, Ge. 36. 39, called פָּעִי 1 Ch. 1. 50.

אֶפְעֶה com. *adder, viper*.

אֶפַע masc. id. Is. 41. 24, מֵאָפַע (worse) *than vipers*. Others regard it as a corrupt reading for מֵאֶפֶס *than nothing*.

פְּעוֹר pr. name (see בֵּית & בַּעַל פְּעוֹר) . . פער

פָּעִי pr. name of a place, see פָּעוּ . . פעה

פָּעַל[e] ו׳ fut. יִפְעַל, יִפְעָל (Job 35. 6).—I. *to work*.—II. *to make, form*.—III. *to do, perform*.—IV. *to practise*.

פֹּעַל masc. dec. 6f.—I. *work, a thing made*.—II. *deed, action*.—III. *acquisition*, Pr. 21. 6.—IV. *wages*.

פְּעֻלָּה fem. dec. 10.—I. *work, employment, business*.—II. *reward, wages*.

פְּעֻלְּתַי (for פְּעֻלְּתְיָה *reward of the Lord*) pr. name masc. 1 Ch. 26. 5.

מִפְעָל masc. dec. 2b, & מִפְעָלָה fem. dec. 11a, *work, doing* of God.

פָּעָל[f] Kal pret. 3 pers. sing. masc. for פָּעַל (§ 8. rem. 7) . . . . פעל

פֹּעַל ו׳ noun masc. s. d. 6f (§ 35. r. 8); ו bef. lab. פעל

פֹּעֵל[g] ו׳ Kal part. act. sing. masc. dec. 7b; ו id. פעל

פָּעָלוּ[h], פָּעֲלוּ } id. pret. 3 pers. pl. (§ 8. rem. 7) . פעל

פָּעֳלוֹ, פָּעֳלוֹ } ו noun masc. sing., suff. 3 pers. sing. masc. fr. פֹּעַל d. 6f (§ 35. rem. 8); ו bef. lab. פעל

פֹּעֲלֵי[i] ו׳ Kal part. act. pl. constr. masc. from פֹּעֵל dec. 7b; ו id. . . . . פעל

פָּעֳלִי[k] noun masc. sing., suff. 1 pers. s. fr. פֹּעַל d. 6f פעל

פְּעָלִים id. pl., abs. st. . . . . . פעל

פָּעָלְךָ[l], פָּעֳלֶךָ[m] } ו׳ id. sing., suff. 2 pers. sing. masc.; ו bef. lab. . . . . פעל

פָּעֳלֵךְ[n] id. sing., suff. 2 pers. sing. fem. . . פעל

פָּעָלְכֶם[o] ו id. sing., suff. 2 pers. pl. masc.; ו bef. lab. פעל

פָּעֳלָם[p] id. sing., suff. 3 pers. pl. masc. . . פעל

פָּעַלְתָּ Kal pret. 2 pers. sing. masc. . . פעל

פְּעֻלַּת noun fem. sing., constr. of [פְּעֻלָּה] dec. 10 פעל

פְּעֻלֹּת[q] id. pl. . . . . . . פעל

פְּעֻלָּתוֹ[r] ו׳ id. sing., suff. 3 pers. sing. masc.; ו bef. lab. פעל

פָּעַלְתִּי Kal pret. 1 pers. sing. . . . פעל

פְּעֻלָּתִי[s] ו noun fem. sing., suff. 1 pers. sing. from [פְּעֻלָּה] dec. 10; ו bef. lab. . . . פעל

פְּעֻלְּתַי pr. name masc. . . . . . פעל

פְּעֻלָּתָם noun fem. sing., suff. 3 pers. pl. masc. from פְּעֻלָּה dec. 10 . . . . . פעל

[פָּעַם] *to impel, urge, move*, Ju. 13. 25. Niph. *to be moved, disturbed*. Hithp. id. Da. 2. 1.

פַּעַם fem. (masc. Ju. 16. 28) dec. 6d, prop. *a striking* or *stamping*, hence—I. *an anvil*, Is. 41. 7; others, *hammer*.—II. *step, footstep*; metaph. of the *progress* of a chariot, Ju. 5. 28; hence *foot, pedestal*, Ex. 25. 12.—III. פַּעַם, פ׳ אַחַת *once*, פַּעֲמַיִם *twice*, שָׁלֹשׁ פְּעָמִים *three times*; הַפַּעַם *this time, now*; כְּפַעַם בְּפַעַם *as at other times*; פַּעַם—פַּעַם *at one time—at another*, Pr. 7. 12.

פַּעֲמוֹן masc. dec. 1b, *a bell*.

פָּעַם[t], פָּעַם } noun fem. sing. dec. 6d (§ 35. rem. 2) פעם

פַּעֲמֵי id. pl., constr. st. . . . . . פעם

פְּעָמַי, פְּעָמַי } id. pl., suff. 1 pers. sing. . . . פעם

פְּעָמָיו id. pl., suff. 3 pers. sing. masc. . . פעם

פְּעָמַיִךְ[u] id. pl., suff. 2 pers. sing. fem. . . פעם

פְּעָמֶיךָ[v] id. pl., suff. 2 pers. sing. fem. . . . פעם

פַּעֲמַיִם, פַּעֲמָיִם } id. du., abs. st. . . . . . פעם

פְּעָמִים id. pl., abs. st. . . . . . פעם

פַּעֲמֹן noun masc. sing. dec. 1b . . . . פעם

---

[a] Hab. 2. 18. [b] Is. 48. 5. [c] Is. 45. 20. [d] Ps. 72. 16. [e] Is. 44. 12. [f] Ps. 11. 3. [g] Ps. 15. 2. [h] Zep. 2. 3. [i] Mi. 2. 1. [k] Ps. 95. 9. [l] Hab. 3. 2. [m] Is. 45. 9. [n] Ru. 2. 12. [o] Is. 41. 24. [p] Job 36. 9. [q] Ps. 28. 5. [r] Eze. 29. 20. [s] Is. 49. 4. [t] Is. 41. 7. [u] Ca. 7. 2. [v] Ps. 74. 3.

פַּעֲמֹנֵי[a] וּ id. pl., constr. st.; וּ bef. lab. . . פעם

פַּעֲמֹתָיו noun fem. pl., suff. 3 pers. sing. masc. from פַּעַם dec. 6 d . . . . . פעם

פַּעְנֵחַ pr. name, see צָפְנַת פַּעְנֵחַ.

[פָּעַר] *to open wide* the mouth, *to gape.*

פְּעוֹר (*a gap*) pr. name of a mountain in Moab. בַּעַל פְּעוֹר, also simply פְּעוֹר, an idol of the Moabites.

פַּעֲרַי pr. name masc. 2 Sa. 23. 35, for which נַעֲרַי 1 Ch. 11. 37.

פָּעֲרָה[b] וּ Kal pret. 3 pers. sing. fem.; וּ, for וְ, conv. פער

פָּעֲרוּ id. pret. 3 pers. pl. . . . . . פער

פַּעֲרַי pr. name masc. . . . . . פער

פָּעַרְתִּי[c] id. pret. 1 pers. pl. . . . . . פער

[פָּצָה] I. *to open* the mouth; with עַל *to gape upon.*—II. *to tear away, save, deliver.*

פְּצֵה[d] Kal imp. sing. masc. . . . . . פצה

פֹּצֶה[e] וּ id. part. act. sing. masc.; וּ bef. lab. . פצה

פָּצוּ id. pret. 3 pers. pl. . . . . . פצה

פֻּצוּ[f] Kal imp. pl. masc. [for פּוּצוּ] . . . פוץ

פְּצוּעַ[g] Kal part. pass. s. m. constr. [of פָּצוּעַ] dec. 3 a פצע

[פָּצַח] *to break forth* into singing, rejoicing. Pi. *to break in pieces,* Mi. 3. 3.

פִּצְחוּ[h] Kal pret. 3 pers. pl. . . . . פצח

פִּצֵּחוּ[ll] Piel pret. 3 p. pl. [for פִּצְּחוּ, comp. § 8. r. 7] פצח

פִּצְחוּ Kal imp. pl. masc. . . . . . פצח

פִּצְחִי[i] id. imp. sing. fem. . . . . . פצח

פָּצִיתָה[k] Kal pret. 2 pers. sing. masc. (comp. § 8. r. 5) פצה

פָּצִיתִי[l] id. pret. 1 pers. sing. . . . . פצה

פִּצֵּל[m] Pi. *to peel,* Ge. 30. 37, 38. פָּצַל i. q. בָּצַל. Hence

פְּצָלוֹת fem. pl. *parts peeled* or *stripped of the bark,* Ge. 30. 37 . . . . . פצל

פָּצַם *to break, rend,* only in the foll. form.

פְּצַמְתָּהּ[n] Kal pret. 3 pers. s. masc., suff. 3 pers. s. fem. פצם

פְּצֵנִי[o] Kal imp. sing. masc., (פְּצֵה), suff. 1 pers. sing. (§ 24. rem. 21) . . . . . פצה

[פָּצַע] *to wound;* פְּצוּעַ דַּכָּה *eunuch,* see דָּכָה. Hence

פֶּצַע[p], פָּצַע } masc. dec. 6 a (with suff. פִּצְעִי, § 35. r. 5), *a wound* . . . . } פצע

פָּצוֹעַ[q] וּ Kal inf. abs.; וּ bef. lab. . . . פצע

פְּצָעוּנִי[r] id. pret. 3 pers. pl., suff. 1 pers. sing. . פצע

פְּצָעַי[s] noun masc. pl., suff. 1 pers. sing. from פֶּצַע dec. 6 a (§ 35. rem. 5) . . . פצע

פִּצְעֵי[t] id. pl., constr. st. . . . . פצע

פְּצָעִים[u] id. pl., abs. st. . . . . . פצע

פָּצַץ Root not used; i. q. פּוּץ *to disperse.*

פִּצֵּץ (*dispersion*) pr. name masc. 1 Ch. 24. 15.

פִּצֵּץ pr. name, see בֵּית פ׳ . . . . בית

[פָּצַר] fut. יִפְצַר.—I. *to press upon,* with בְּ Ge. 19. 3.—II. *to press, urge.* Hiph. *to be stubborn, wilful,* 1 Sa. 15. 23.

פְּצִירָה fem. *pressed,* 1 Sa. 13. 21, פְּצִירָה פִּים *pressed* or *rubbed* (upon) *edges,* i. e. *a file* for sharpening or setting edges

פָּצְתָה[x] וּ׳ Kal pret. 3 pers. sing. fem.; וּ, for וְ, conv. פצה

פָּקַד fut. יִפְקֹד.—I. *to visit, go* or *come to see.*—II. *to examine, prove.*—III. *to visit, punish,* with עַל, also אֶל, בְּ, acc. of the person.—IV. *to review, muster, number.*—V. *to miss,* sc. in reviewing.—VI. *to look after, to take care of.*—VII. *to set over, appoint,* with אֶת, עַל part. pass. פְּקוּדִים *officers.*—VIII. *to charge with, enjoin upon* the care of any one, with עַל.—IX. *to deposit, lay up,* 2 Ki. 5. 24. Niph. I. *to be missed.*—II. *to be visited, punished.*—III. *to be set over, appointed.* Pi. *to muster,* Is. 13. 4. Pu. I. *to be mustered, numbered,* Ex. 38. 21.—II. *to be missed,* Is. 38. 10; Eng. vers. "deprived." Hiph. I. *to set over, appoint,* with בְּ, לְ, עַל.—II. *to charge with, to commit* to the care of any one, with בְּיַד, עַל יְדֵי.—III. *to deposit, lay.* Hoph. I. *to be set over, have the oversight of.*—II. *to be visited, punished,* Je. 6. 6.—III. *to be deposited,* Le. 5. 23. Hothpa. (§ 6. No. 10, note) *to be mustered, numbered.*

פְּקוֹד masc.—I. *visitation, punishment,* allegorically for Babylon, Je. 50. 21.—II. *dominion,* Eze. 23. 23.

פְּקֻדָּה fem. dec. 10.—I. *care, providence.*—II. *visitation, punishment.*—III. *oversight, office, charge.*—IV. *custody;* בֵּית הַפְּקֻדּוֹת *prison.*—V. *store, treasure,* Is. 15. 7.

פָּקִיד masc. dec. 3 a, *overseer, chief officer.*

פִּקְדוֹת fem. *oversight, office,* Je. 37. 13.

פִּקּוּדִים masc. pl. (of פִּקּוּד dec. 1 b) *commands, precepts.*

[a] Ex. 28. 33; 39. 25. [b] Is. 5. 14. [c] Ps. 119. 131. [d] Eze. 2. 8. [e] Is. 10. 14. [f] 1 Sa. 14. 34. [g] De. 23. 2. [h] Is. 14. 7. [i] Is. 54. 1. [k] Ju. 11. 36. [l] Ju. 11. 35. [ll] Mi. 3. 3. [m] Ge. 30. 38. [n] Ps. 60. 4. [o] Ps. 144. 7, 11. [p] Ex. 21. 25. [q] 1 Ki. 20. 37. [r] Ca. 5. 7. [s] Job 9. 17. [t] Pr. 27. 6. [u] Pr. 23. 29. [x] Nu. 16. 30.

פִּקָּדוֹן masc. *what is laid up, a deposit.*

מִפְקָד masc. dec. 2 b.—I. *a numbering, census,* 2 Sa. 24. 9.—II. *appointment, arrangement,* 2 Ch. 31. 13.—III. *appointed place,* Eze. 43. 21.—IV. שַׁעַר הַמִּפְקָד name of a gate in Jerusalem, Ne. 3. 31.

פָּקֹד Kal inf. abs. . . . . . פקד
[a] פְּקֹד [b] וּ id. imp. sing. masc.; וּ bef. lab. . . פקד
פֹּקֵד id. part. act. sing. masc. dec. 7 b . . . פקד
[c] פֻּקַּד Pual pret. 3 pers. sing. masc. . . . פקד
[d] פְּקֻדָּה noun fem. sing. dec. 10 . . . . פקד
[e] פָּקְדוּ } Kal pret. 3 pers. pl. (§ 8. rem. 7); } פקד
[f] פָּקְדוּ [g] וּ } וּ bef. lab. . . . }
פִּקְדוּ [h] וּ id. imp. pl. masc.; וּ id. . . . פקד
[i] פְּקָדוּךָ id. pret. 3 pers. pl., suff. 2 pers. sing. masc. פקד
פְּקֻדּוֹת noun fem., pl. of פְּקֻדָּה dec. 10 . . פקד
פָּקְדִי Kal inf., suff. 1 pers. sing. . . . . פקד
[k] פְּקֻדֵי id. part. pass. pl. constr. m. [fr. פָּקוּד] dec. 3 a פקד
פְּקֻדֵיהֶם וּ id. pl., suff. 3 pers. pl. masc.; וּ bef. lab. . פקד
פְּקֻדָיו וּ id. pl., suff. 3 pers. sing. masc.; וּ id. . פקד
[l] פִּקֻּדָיו noun masc. pl., suff. 3 pers. sing. masc. from [פִּקּוּד] dec. 1 b . . . . . פקד
[m] פִּקֻּדֶיךָ id. pl., suff. 2 pers. sing. masc. . . . פקד
[n] פְּקֻדֵיכֶם Kal part. pass. pl. masc., suff. 2 pers. pl. masc. [from פָּקוּד] dec. 3 a . . . פקד
פְּקִדִים noun masc., pl. of פָּקִיד dec. 3 a . . פקד
[o] פָּקַדְנוּ Kal pret. 1 pers. pl. . . . . . פקד
[p] פָּקְדֵנִי [q] וּ id. imp. s. m., suff. 1 pers. s.; וּ bef. lab. פקד
פָּקַדְתָּ } id. pret. 2 pers. sing. masc.; acc. shifted } פקד
[r] פָּקַדְתָּ וּ } by וּ, for וְ, conv. (§ 8. rem. 7) . }
פְּקֻדַּת וּ noun fem. sing., constr. of פְּקֻדָּה dec. 10; וּ bef. lab. . . . . פקד
[s] פְּקִדֻת noun fem. sing. [defect. for פְּקִידוּת] . . פקד
[t] פְּקֻדֹּת noun fem., pl. of פְּקֻדָּה dec. 10 . . . פקד
[u] פְּקֻדָּתוֹ id. sing., suff. 3 pers. sing. masc. . . . פקד
פָּקַדְתִּי } Kal pret. 1 pers. sing.; acc. shifted by וּ, } פקד
פָּקַדְתִּי וּ } for וְ, conv. (§ 8. rem. 7) . . }
[x] פֻּקַּדְתִּי Pual pret. 1 pers. sing. . . . . . פקד
[y] פְּקַדְתִּיו Kal pret. 1 pers. sing., suff. 3 pers. sing. m. פקד
[z] פְּקַדְתִּיךָ id. id., suff. 2 pers. sing. masc. . . . פקד
[a] פְּקַדְתִּים id. id., suff. 3 pers. pl. masc. . . . פקד
[b] פְּקֻדָּתֵךְ noun fem. s., suff. 2 p. s. f. fr. פְּקֻדָּה d. 10 פקד
[c] פְּקֻדָּתְךָ [d] וּ id., suff. 2 pers. sing. masc.; וּ bef. lab. . פקד
פְּקֻדָּתָם [e] וּ id., suff. 3 pers. pl. masc.; וּ id. . . פקד
[f] פְּקַדְתֶּם [g] וּ Kal pret. 2 pers. pl. masc.; וּ id. . . פקד
[h] פָּקוּ Kal pret. 3 pers. pl. . . . . . . פוק
פָּקוֹד noun masc. sing. . . . . פקד

פְּקוּדֵי noun masc. pl. constr. from [פָּקוּד] dec. 1 b פקד
פְּקוּדֵי וּ Kal part. pass. pl. constr. masc. [from פָּקוּד] dec. 3 a; וּ bef. lab. . . . פקד
[i] פִּקּוּדָיו noun masc. pl., suff. 3 pers. sing. masc. from [פִּקּוּד] dec. 1 b . . . . . פקד
[k] פִּקּוּדֶיךָ id., suff. 2 pers. sing. masc. . . . פקד

פָּקַח[l] fut. יִפְקַח *to open,* espec. the eyes, also the ears. Niph. *to be opened.*

פֶּקַח (*opening,* sc. of the eyes) pr. name of a king of Israel.

פִּקֵּחַ masc. dec. 7 b, *seeing, having the eyes open.*

פְּקַחְיָה (*the Lord has opened,* sc. his eyes) pr. name of a king of Israel.

פְּקַח־קוֹחַ masc. *opening,* sc. of the prison, *deliverance,* Is. 61. 1.

[m] פָּקוֹחַ Kal inf. abs. . . . . פקח
פְּקַח id. imp. sing. masc. (see also פְּקַח־קוֹחַ) . פקח
פֶּקַח וּ pr. name masc.; וּ bef. lab. . . . . פקח
[n] פִּקֵּחַ adj. masc. sing. dec. 7 b . . . . פקח
[o] פֹּקֵחַ Kal part. act. sing. masc. . . . . פקח
[p] פְּקָחָה Kh. פְּקָחָה, K. פְּקַח, Kal imp. sing. masc. (§ 8. rem. 11) . . . . . . פקח
[q] פְּקֻחוֹת Kal part. pass. fem. pl. [of פְּקוּחָה for פָּקוּחַ] פקח
פְּקַחְיָה pr. name masc. . . . . . . פקח
[r] פִּקְחִים adj. masc., pl. of פִּקֵּחַ dec. 7 b . . . פקח
[s] פָּקַחְתָּ Kal pret. 2 pers. sing. masc. . . . פקח
פָּקִיד [t] וּ noun masc. sing. dec. 3 a; וּ bef. lab. . פקד
פְּקִיד וּ id., constr. st.; וּ id. . . . . . פקד
[u] פְּקִידוֹ id., suff. 3 pers. sing. masc. . . . . פקד
פְּקִידִים id. pl., abs. st. . . . . פקד

פָּקַע Root not used; Syr. *to split,* i. q. בָּקַע. Hence

פְּקָעִים וּ masc. pl. [of פֶּקַע § 35. r. 5] *wild cucumbers;* others, *mushrooms,* as an architectural ornament, 1 Ki. 6. 18; 7. 24 . . פקע
פַּקֻּעֹת fem. pl. id. 2 Ki. 4. 39 . . . . פקע
פַּר } noun masc. sing., pl. פָּרִים, dec. 8 (§ 37. } פרר
פַּר וּ } rem. 7); וּ bef. lab. . . . }

פָּרָא. Hiph. *to be fruitful,* Ho. 13. 15.

פֶּרֶא, פֶּרֶה masc. dec. 6 a, *wild ass.*

פִּרְאָם (*like a wild ass*) pr. name of a king of Canaan, Jos. 10. 3.

פְּרָאִים [x] וּ id. pl., abs. st.; וּ bef. lab. . . פרא

---

[a] Nu. 3. 15, 40. [b] Ps. 80. 15. [c] Ex. 38. 21. [d] Is. 10. 3. [e] Is. 34. 16. [f] Nu. 26. 63, 64. [g] De. 20. 9. [h] 2 Sa. 24. 2. [i] Is. 26. 16. [k] 2 Ki. 11. 15. [l] Ps. 103. 18. [m] Ps. 119. 4, 45, 56, 87, 93, 100, 141. [n] Nu. 14. 29. [o] 1 Sa. 25. 15. [p] Ps. 106. 4. [q] Je. 15. 15. [r] Job 5. 24. [s] Je. 37. 13. [t] 2 Ki. 11. 18, etc. [u] Ps. 109. 8. [x] Is. 38. 10. [y] Je. 49. 8. [z] Je. 50. 31. [a] Je. 6. 15. [b] Is. 60. 17. [c] Mi. 7. 4. [d] Job 10. 12. [e] Is. 15. 7. [f] Je. 23. 2. [g] Nu. 4. 27. [h] Is. 28. 7. [i] Ps. 111. 7. [k] Ps. 119. 27, 63, 69, 94, 134, 159, 168, 173. [l] Job 27. 19. [m] Is. 42. 20. [n] Ex. 4. 11. [o] Ps. 146. 8. [p] Da. 9. 18. [q] Je. 32. 19. [r] Ex. 23. 8. [s] Job 14. 3. [t] Ne. 11. 14. [u] Ju. 9. 28. [x] Je. 14. 6.

פְּרָאם pr. name masc. . . . . . פרא

פְּרֹאתָיו[a] transp. for פֹּארֹתָיו (q. v.) . . פאר

[פַּרְוָר, פַּרְבָּר] masc. *suburb*, 2 Ki. 23. 11; 1 Ch. 26. 18.

[פָּרַד] *to separate, spread* the wing, Eze. 1. 11. Niph. *to be separated, divided; also to separate oneself*, with מִן, מֵעַל *from* any one. Pi. *to go aside*, Ho. 4. 14. Pu. part. *separated, singular*, Est. 3. 8; others, *dispersed*. Hiph. I. *to separate*.—II. *to scatter, disperse*, De. 32. 8; others, *to separate, divide*. Hithp. I. *to separate oneself, to be sundered*.—II. *to be dispersed, scattered*, Job 4. 11.

פֶּרֶד masc. dec. 6 a (with suff. פִּרְדּוֹ), *a mule*.

פִּרְדָּה fem. *she-mule*, 1 Ki. 1. 33, 38, 44.

פְּרוּדָא (*seed*) pr. name masc. Ezr. 2. 55, for which פְּרִידָא Ne. 7. 57.

פְּרֻדוֹת f. pl. *seeds scattered, corn sown*, Joel 1. 17.

פָּרֶד[b] ן noun masc. sing. dec. 6 a; for ן see lett. ו פרד

פִּרְדּוֹ[c] id. with suff. 3 pers. sing. masc. . . פרד

פְּרֻדוֹת[d] Kal part. pass. or (Joel 1. 17) subst. fem. pl. [of פְּרוּדָה from פָּרוּד masc.] . פרד

פִּרְדֵיהֶם the foll. with suff. 3 pers. pl. masc. . פרד

פְּרָדִים[e] ו׳ noun masc., pl. of פֶּרֶד dec. 6 a; ו bef. lab. פרד

פַּרְדֵּס[f] masc. dec. 1 b, *garden, park*.

פַּרְדֵּסִים[g] ו id. pl. abs.; ו bef. lab. . . . פרדס

פִּרְדַּת[h] noun fem. sing., constr. of פִּרְדָּה׳ (no pl.) פרד

[פָּרָה] fut. יִפְרֶה *to be fruitful, to bear fruit*; part. fem. פֹּרָת, פֹּרִיָּה *fruit-bearing*, fruitful, sc. tree. Hiph. *to make fruitful*.

פְּרִי masc. d. 6 i (with suff. 3 pers. pl. פִּרְיָם). —I. *fruit, produce*; עֵץ פְּרִי *fruit-tree*.—II. *fruit of the body, offspring*.—III. metaph. *result, consequence, reward*.

אַפִּרְיוֹן masc. *sedan, litter*, Ca. 3. 9.

פָּרָה[i] ו׳ noun fem. sing. dec. 10 [for פַּרָּה comp. § 37. rem. 7] from פַּר masc.; ו bef. lab. פרר

פֶּרֶה[k] for פֶּרֶא (q. v.) . . . . . . פרא

פְּרֵה[l] Kal imp. sing. masc. . . . . . פרה

פֹּרֶה[m] id. part. sing. masc. . . . . . פרה

פָּרָה ו pr. name masc., see פֹּארָה; ו bef. lab. פאר

פָּרוּ[n] ו׳ id. pret. 3 pers. pl.; ו, for ן, conv. . פרה

פְּרוּ id. imp. pl. masc. . . . . . . פרה

פְּרוּדָא pr. name masc. . . . . . . פרד

פָּרוֹחַ[o] Kal inf. abs. . . . . . . פרח

פָּרוּחַ pr. name masc. . . . . . . פרח

פַּרְוָיִם pr. name of a country, 2 Ch. 3. 6.

פָּרוּעַ[p] Kal part. pass. sing. masc. . . . פרע

פְּרוּצָה[q] Kal part. pass. sing. fem. [of פָּרוּץ] . פרץ

פְּרוּצִים[r] id. part. pass. masc. pl. [of פָּרוּץ] dec. 3 a פרץ

פְּרוּשָׂה[s] Kal part. pass. sing. fem. from פָּרוּשׂ masc. פרשׂ

פָּרוֹת noun fem., pl. of פָּרָה d. 10, from פַּר masc. פרר

פֵּרוֹת[t] see חֲפַר־פֵּרוֹת . . . . . חפר

פָּרַז Root not used; Arab. *to separate*, i. q. פָּרַד, פָּרַשׂ; hence perh. *to scatter*, see פְּרָזָה.

פָּרָז masc. dec. 4 a, *ruler, leader*, Hab. 3. 14.

פִּרְזוֹן masc. d. 3 c (§ 32. r. 2) id., Ju. 5. 7, 11.

פְּרָזָה f. *a scattered place, unwalled town, village*.

פְּרָזִי masc. *one living in an unwalled town or village*.

פְּרוֹזִי masc. id. Est. 9. 19, Kheth.

פְּרִזִּי pr. name collect. *Perizzites*, a people of Canaan.

פְּרָזָיו[u] noun m. pl., suff. 3 p. s. m. fr. [פָּרָז] d. 4 a פרז

פִּרְזוֹן[x] noun masc. sing., comp. dec. 3 c . . פרז

פִּרְזוֹנוֹ[y] id. with suff. 3 pers. sing. masc. . . פרז

פְּרָזוֹת noun fem. pl. abs. [from פְּרָזָה] . . פרז

פַּרְזֶל Chald. masc. i. q. Heb. בַּרְזֶל *iron*.

פַּרְזְלָא Chald. id., emph. st. . . . . . פרזל

פָּרַח ו׳ fut. יִפְרַח.—I. *to sprout, flourish, blossom*.—II. *to break out*, as ulcers, leprosy.—III. *to fly*, only part. Eze. 13. 20 לְפֹרְחוֹת *that they fly away* (for לִהְיוֹת פֹּרְחוֹת lit. *that they become flying ones*); Gesenius, *as flying ones*, i. e. *birds*. Hiph. I. *to cause to flourish*.—II. intrans. *to flourish, blossom*.

פֶּרַח masc. dec. 6 a (with suff. פִּרְחוֹ § 35. r. 5). —I. *young shoot*, Na. 1. 4.—II. *flower, blossom*.—III. as an artificial ornament, Ex. 25. 33.

פִּרְחַח fem. *brood*, Job 30. 12; comp. אֶפְרוֹחַ.

פָּרוּחַ (*flourishing*) pr. name masc. 1 Ki. 4. 17.

אֶפְרוֹחַ masc. dec. 1 b, *the young* of birds, *a brood*.

פָּרַח ן in pause for פֶּרַח (q. v.) . . . פרח

פָּרֹחַ[z] Kal inf. abs. . . . . . . פרח

פֶּרַח[a] ו׳, ן noun masc. sing. (suff. פִּרְחָהּ) dec. 6 a (§ 35. rem. 5); ו bef. lab., for ן see lett. ו פרח

פֹּרֵחַ[b] Kal part. act. sing. masc. . . . . פרח

פָּרְחָה[c]
פָּרָחָה[d] } id. pret. 3 pers. sing. fem. (§ 8. rem. 7) פרח

---

[a] Eze. 31. 12, 13. [b] 1 Ki. 18. 5. [c] 2 Sa. 13. 29. [d] Eze. 1. 11. [e] 2 Ki. 5. 17. [f] Ca. 4. 13. [g] Ec. 2. 5. [h] 1 Ki. 1. 38, 44. [i] Nu. 19. 2; Is. 11. 7. [k] Je. 2. 24. [l] Ge. 35. 11. [m] De. 29. 17. [n] Ex. 1. 7. [o] Le. 13. 12. [p] Le. 13. 45. [q] Pr. 25. 28. [r] Ne. 2. 13. [s] Ho. 5. 1. [t] Is. 2. 20. [u] Hab. 3. 14. [x] Ju. 5. 7. [y] Ju. 5. 11. [z] Is. 35. 2. [a] Na. 1. 4. [b] Ex. 9. 9, 10. [c] Le. 13. 20, 25. [d] Ca. 7. 13.

פִּרְחָהּ[a] noun masc. sing., suff. 3 pers. sing. fem. from פֶּרַח dec. 6a (§ 35. rem. 5) . פרח

פִּרְחָה[b] noun fem. sing. . . . . . פרח

פְּרָחֶיהָ ‏ו noun masc. pl., suff. 3 pers. sing. fem. from פֶּרַח dec. 6a (§ 35. rem. 5) ; ‏וּ bef. lab. פרח

פִּרְחָם[c] ‏ו id. sing., suff. 3 pers. pl. masc. ; ‏וּ id. . פרח

פֹּרַחַת[d] Kal part. act. sing. fem. from פֹּרֵחַ masc. . פרח

[פָּרַט] prob. *to cut, divide,* cogn. פָּרַד ; hence *to sing* (comp. Pi. of זָמַר) Am. 6. 5. Hence

פֶּרֶט[e] ‏ו grapes fallen off of themselves and lying about *scattered* or *strewed,* Le. 19. 10 . פרט

פְּרִי } noun masc. sing. dec. 6 i (§ 35. rem. 14); } פרה
פֶּרִי ‏ו'} ‏וּ bef. lab. . . . . }

פְּרִידָא pr. name masc. . . . . פרד

פְּרִיהָ[f] n. m. pl., suff. 3 p. s. f. fr. פַּר d. 8 (§ 37. r. 7) פרר

פִּרְיָהּ noun masc. sing., suff. 3 p. s. f. fr. פְּרִי d. 6 o פרה

פֹּרִיָּה Kal part. act. s. f. [as if fr. פּוֹרִי § 24. r. 4] פרה

פִּרְיָהֶם[g] noun masc. s., suff. 3 p. pl. m. fr. פְּרִי d. 6i פרה

פִּרְיָהֶן[h] id., suff. 3 pers. pl. fem. . . . פרה

פִּרְיוֹ ‏ו' id., suff. 3 pers. sing. fem. ; ‏וּ bef. lab. פרה

פִּרְיִי[i] id., suff. 1 pers. sing. . . . . פרה

פִּרְיְךָ[k] id., suff. 2 pers. sing. masc. . . . פרה

פִּרְיֵךְ[l] id., suff. 2 pers. sing. fem. . . . פרה

פֶּרְיְכֶם[m] ‏ו id., suff. 2 pers. pl. masc. ; ‏וּ bef. lab. . פרה

פָּרִים ‏ו' noun masc. pl. of פַּר d. 8 (§ 37. r. 7); ‏וּ id. פרר

פִּרְיָם noun masc. s., suff. 3 p. pl. m. fr. פְּרִי d. 6i פרה

פִּרְיָמוֹ[n] id., suff. 3 pers. pl. masc. . . . פרה

פִּרְיָן[o] id., suff. 3 pers. pl. fem. . . . . פרה

פָּרִינוּ[p] ‏ו Kal pret. 1 pers. pl. ; ‏וְ, for ‏וָ, conv. . פרה

פְּרִיסַת[q] Ch. Peal part. pass. 3 pers. s. f. (§ 47. r. 11) פרס

פָּרִיץ noun masc. sing. [for פַּרְיִץ] dec. 1b . פרץ

פְּרִיץ[r] ‏ו id. constr. st. (accord. to dec. 3a, § 32. rem. 2) ; ‏וּ bef. lab. . . . . . פרץ

פָּרִיצֵי[s] id. pl., constr. st. . . . . . פרץ

פָּרִיצִים[t] id. pl., abs. st. . . . . . פרץ

פְּרִיתֶם[u] ‏ו Kal pret. 2 pers. pl. masc. ; ‏וְ, for ‏וָ, conv. פרה

פָּרַךְ Root not used ; i. q. פָּרַק *to break.*
פֶּרֶךְ m. *oppression, rigour.* Also the following.

פָּרֹכֶת fem. *the vail* or *curtain* which *separated* the holy place from the holy of holies . . פרך

פָּרַם fut. יִפְרֹם *to rend, tear,* as a garment.

פְּרֻמִים[v] Kal part. pass. masc. pl. [of פָּרוּם] dec. 3a פרם

פַּרְמַשְׁתָּא pr. name of a son of Haman, Est. 9. 9.

פַּרְנָךְ pr. name masc. Nu. 34. 25.

[פָּרַס] *to break* bread, to any one, *to give* or *distribute to.* Hiph. *to cleave, divide* the hoof.
פְּרַס Chald. *to divide,* Da. 5. 25, 28.
פֶּרֶס masc. a species of eagle, the *osprey.*
פַּרְסָה fem. dec. 12a (pl. ‏ִ־ים, ‏וֹת), *hoof.*

פָּרַס ‏ו'} Heb. & Chald. pr. name, *Persia, Persians.*
פָּרָס ‏ו'} Gent. noun פַּרְסִי *Persian.*

אֲפָרְסָיֵא pr. name of an unknown tribe, Ezr. 4. 9.

אֲפַרְסַתְכָיֵא, אֲפַרְסְכָיֵא pr. name of two Syrian tribes, Ezr. 4. 9 ; 5. 6.

פָּרֹס[w] Kal inf. abs. . . . . . פרס

פְּרִיס[x] Peal part. pass. sing. masc. (§ 47. rem. 1) פרס

פַּרְסָה ‏ו' noun fem. sing. dec. 12a ; ‏וּ bef. lab. . פרס

פַּרְסוֹת[a] ‏ו' id. pl., constr. st. ; ‏וּ id. . . . פרס

פְּרָסוֹת[b] id. pl., abs. st. . . . . . פרס

פַּרְסָיָא Ch., K. פַּרְסָאָה gent. n., emph. of פַּרְסִי d. 7, fr. פָּרַס.

פַּרְסֵיהֶן[c] ‏ו noun f. with pl. m. term. [פְּרָסִים], and suff. 3 p. pl. fem. from פַּרְסָה d. 12a; ‏וּ bef. lab. פרס

פַּרְסִין[aa] ‏ו Ch. Peal part. act. m. pl. [for פָּרְסִין § 58. r. 1]; ‏וּ id. פרס

פְּרָסֹת[d] noun fem., pl. of פַּרְסָה dec. 12a . . פרס

פַּרְסֹתֶיהָ[e] ‏ו id. pl. fem., suff. 2 pers. s. fem.; ‏וּ bef. lab. פרס

פָּרַע[f] ‏ו fut. יִפְרַע.—I. *to free, exempt* from punishment, Eze. 24. 14.—II. *to free, deliver,* Ju. 5. 2, בִּפְרֹעַ פְּרָעוֹת *for working deliverance* ; Gesenius, *in leading on the leaders,* and so the LXX. Eng. Vers. "for avenging," from the Chald. פְּרַע *to retribute.*—III. *to let go loose, in a state of disorder,* Ex. 32. 25. —IV. *to neglect, reject,* e. g. counsel.—V. *to make bare* the head, espec. by cutting off the hair. Niph. *to become lawless,* Pr. 29. 18. Hiph. I. *to set loose, disengage,* Ex. 5. 4.—II. *to cause disorder, lawlessness,* 2 Ch. 28. 19.
פֶּרַע masc. dec. 6 (§ 35. rem. 5).—I. *the hair* or *locks* as growing *loose and free.*—II. pl. fem. פְּרָעוֹת Ju. 5. 2, *deliverance* ; others, *leaders, princes* ; or *revenges,* see the Root No. II ; constr. פַּרְעוֹת De. 32. 42.
פִּרְעָתוֹן (perh. *principal,* or *free-town*) pr. name of a city of Ephraim, Ju. 12. 13. Gent. noun פִּרְעָתֹנִי.

פָּרֻעַ[g] defect. for פָּרוּעַ (q. v.) . . . . פרע

פֶּרַע[h] ‏ו' noun masc. sing. ; ‏וּ bef. lab. . . פרע

פַּרְעֹה ‏ו' (*king*) the title of all monarchs of Egypt down to the time of the Persian invasion.

פְּרָעֹה[k] Kal pret. 3 pers. sing. m., suff. 3 pers. sing. m. פרע

פְּרָעֵהוּ[l] id. imp. s. m. [פְּרַע], suff. 3 p. s. m. (§ 16. r. 12) פרע

[a] Nu. 8. 4. [b] Job 30. 12. [c] Is. 5. 24. [d] Le. 13. 42, 57. [e] Le. 19. 10. [f] Je. 50. 27. [g] Am. 9. 14. [h] Je. 29. 28. [i] Pr. 8. 19. [k] Ho. 14. 9. [l] Eze. 25. 4. [m] Eze. 36. 8. [n] Ps. 21. 11. [o] Je. 29. 5. [p] Ge. 26. 22. [q] Da. 5. 28. [r] Is. 35. 9. [s] Da. 11. 14. [t] Eze. 7. 22. [u] Je. 3. 16. [v] Le. 13. 45. [w] Is. 58. 7. [x] Da. 5. 28. [a] Eze. 32. 13. [b] De. 14. 6. [c] Zec. 11. 16. [d] Le. 11. 3. [e] Mi. 4. 13. [f] Nu. 5. 18. [g] Ex. 32. 25. [h] Nu. 6. 5. [aa] Da. 5. 25. [i] Eze. 44. 20. [k] Ex. 32. 25. [l] Pr. 4. 15.

פְּרָעוֹת[a] פְּרָעוֹת[b] } noun masc. with pl. fem. term., constr. and abs., from פֶּרַע d. 6 (§ 35. rem. 5) } פרע

פַּרְעֹשׁ masc.—I. *a flea*, 1 Sa. 24. 15; 26. 20.—II. pr. name of a man.

פִּרְעָתֹנִי gent. noun from פִּרְעָתוֹן . . . פרע

פַּרְפַּר וּ pr. name of a river; וּ bef. lab. . . פרר

פָּרַץ fut. יִפְרֹץ[c] וּ.—I. *to break* or *tear down, demolish*, e. g. a wall.—II. *to break asunder*, i. e. *to disperse, scatter*.—III. *to break, afflict*, Job 16. 14.—IV. *to break forth*, as a child from the womb, Ge. 38. 29; of water, *to burst forth*, Job 28. 4, פָּ׳ נַחַל *a torrent bursts forth* (but according to Gesenius, *he breaks a mine through, sinks a shaft*); also *to break out, act with violence*, Ho. 4. 2; with בְּ *to break forth upon, break in upon, cause an overthrow among*; hence *to press upon, urge*.—V. *to spread abroad, to increase*; also *to overflow, abound with*, Pr. 3. 10. Niph. part. *spread abroad, common*, 1 Sa. 3. 1. Pu. *to be broken down*, Ne. 1. 3. Hithp. *to break away, loose*, 1 Sa. 25. 10.

פָּרִיץ masc. constr. פְּרִיץ, pl. פָּרִיצִים, constr. פָּרִיצֵי.—I. *violent, rapacious*.—II. *ravenous, wild, wild beast*, Is. 35. 9.

פֶּרֶץ masc. dec. 6a (pl. with suff. פִּרְצֵיהֶן).—I. *a breaking forth*, Ge. 38. 29; of water, *a bursting forth*, 2 Sa. 5. 20.—III. *a breach* of a wall.—IV. *overthrow, calamity, affliction*.—V. pr. name masc. Patronym. פַּרְצִי.—VI. פֶּרֶץ עֻזָּא pr. name of a place, 2 Sa. 6. 8; 1 Ch. 13. 11.

מִפְרָץ masc. dec. 2b, *creek* or *haven*, Ju. 5. 17.

פָּרוֹץ[d] Kal inf. abs. . . . . . פרץ

פֶּרֶץ, פָּרֶץ וָ׳ } noun masc. sing. (pl. & suff. פִּרְצֵיהֶם) d. 6a; also pr. name; for וָ see lett. ו } פרץ

פֹּרֵץ[e] וּ Kal part. act. sing. masc.; וּ bef. lab. . פרץ

פָּרְצוּ, פָּרָצוּ[f] } Kal pret. 3 pers. pl. (§ 8. rem. 7) . פרץ

פִּרְצֵיהֶן[g] noun m. pl., suff. 3 pers. s. fem. fr. פֶּרֶץ d. 6a פרץ

פָּרִצִים[h] defect. for פָּרִיצִים (q. v.) . . . פרץ

פְּרָצִים[i] וּ noun masc., pl. of פֶּרֶץ dec. 6a; also pr. name; וּ bef. lab. . . . . . פרץ

פָּרַצְתָּ, פָּרַצְתָּ[k] וּ } Kal pret. 3 pers. sing. masc.; acc. shifted by וּ, for וְ, conv. (§ 8. rem. 7) . } פרץ

פְּרַצְתָּנוּ[l] id. id. with suff. 1 pers. pl. . . . פרץ

[פָּרַק] I. *to break off*, Ge. 27. 40.—II. *to break, crush*, as a wild beast the limbs, Ps. 7. 3.—III. *to tear away, rescue, deliver*. Pi. I. *to break* or *tear off*.—II. *to break* or *rend in pieces*, 1 Ki. 19. 11. Hithp. I. *to break* or *tear off from oneself*, Ex. 32. 3, 24.—II. *to be broken in pieces*, Eze. 19. 12.

פְּרַק Chald. *to break off, expiate*, Da. 4. 24.

פָּרָק masc. dec. 4a, *broth*, from the *fragments* it contains, Is. 65. 4, Kh.

פֶּרֶק masc.—I. *violence, rapine*, Na. 3. 1.—II. *cross-way*, Ob. 14.

מַפְרֶקֶת fem. dec. 13a, *the vertebra of the neck*, 1 Sa. 4. 18.

פֶּרֶק[m] noun masc. sing. . . . . פרק

פְּרַק[n] וּ noun masc. sing., constr. of [פָּרָק] dec. 4a; וּ bef. lab. . . . . . פרק

פְּרֻק[o] Chald. Peal imp. sing. masc. . . . פרק

פֹּרֵק Kal part. act. sing. masc. . . . . פרק

פָּרְקוּ[p] Piel imp. pl. masc. . . . . פרק

פָּרַקְתָּ[q] וּ id. pret. 2 pers. sing. masc.; acc. shifted by וּ, for וְ, conv. (§ 8. rem. 7) . . פרק

[פָּרַר] I. *to break in pieces*, Is. 24. 19; but see פּוּר.—II. Arab. *to be borne swiftly, to run*, see derivv. Hiph. הֵפַר, הֵפֵר (§ 18. r. 10).—I. *to break, violate*.—II. *to frustrate* a counsel; *to declare void* a vow, Nu. 30. 9, 13.—III. *to annul, abolish*.—IV. intrans. *to fail*, Ec. 12. 5. Hoph. *to come to nought, be frustrated*. Po. פּוֹרֵר *to cleave, rend*, Ps. 74. 13. Hithpo. *to be broken, rent*, Is. 24. 19. Pilp. (§ 6. No. 4) *to shake, agitate violently*.

פַּר masc. with the art. הַפָּר (pl. פָּרִים § 37. rem. 7) *a young bull, bullock*.

פָּרָה fem. (for פַּרָּה § 37. rem. 7) dec. 10.—I. *young cow, heifer*.—II. הַפָּרָה pr. name of a town in the tribe of Benjamin, Jos. 18. 23.

פַּרְפַּר (*swift*) pr. name of a small stream which flows into the Amana near Damascus, 2 Ki. 5. 12.

פָּרַשׂ fut. יִפְרֹשׂ וּ׳.—I. i. q. פָּרַס *to break* bread, with לְ *to give* or *distribute* (it) *to*.—II. *to spread*, e. g. a garment; metaph. Pr. 13. 16.—III. *to stretch out* the hands. Niph. *to be scattered*, Eze. 17. 21. Pi. I. *to spread out* the hands.—II. *to disperse, scatter*.

מִפְרָשׂ masc. dec. 2b.—I. *a spreading out, expansion*, Job 36. 29.—II. *sail* of a ship, Eze. 27. 7.

[פָּרַשׁ] prop. *to divide*; hence, *to decide, determine, declare*, Le. 24. 12. Niph. *to be dispersed, scattered*, Eze.

[a] De. 32. 42. [b] Ju. 5. 2. [c] Ne. 3. 35. [d] Is. 5. 5. [e] Ec. 10. 8. [f] Ho. 4. 2. [g] Am. 9. 11. [h] Je. 7. 11. [i] Am. 4. 3. [k] Ge. 28. 14. [l] Ps. 60. 3. [m] Na. 3. 1. [n] Is. 65. 4. [o] Da. 4. 24. [p] Ex. 32. 2. [q] Ge. 27. 40.

34. 12. Pu. *to be made clear, declared,* Nu. 15. 24; part. מְפֹרָשׁ *distinctly,* Ne. 8. 8. Hiph. *to sting, wound,* Pr. 23. 32.

פְּרַשׁ Chald. Pa. part. pass. מְפָרַשׁ *distinctly, accurately,* Ezr. 4. 18.

פֶּרֶשׁ masc. dec. 6a (with suff. פִּרְשׁוֹ).—I. *dung.* —II. pr. name masc. 1 Ch. 7. 16.

פָּרָשָׁה fem. (for פְּרָשָׁה) dec. 10, *distinct declaration, specification,* Est. 4. 7; 10. 2.

פָּרָשׁ masc. (for פָּרָּשׁ) dec. 1b (but constr. פָּרַשׁ § 30. rem. 1).—I. *horseman, rider.*—II. *horse for riding.*

[a] פָּרַשׁ id., constr. st. . . . . . . פרש

[b] פָּרֻשׁ Kal part. pass. sing. masc. [for פָּרוּשׁ] . פרש

[c] פֵּרַשׂ וּ Piel pret. 3 pers. sing. masc. (comp. § 10. rem. 1); וּ, for וְ, conv. . . . . פרש

[d] פֶּרֶשׁ noun m. s. (suff. פִּרְשׁוֹ) d. 6a, also pr. name פרש

[e] פֹּרַשׁ Pual pret. 3 pers. sing. masc. . . . פרש

[f] פֹּרֵשׂ Kal part. act. sing. masc. dec. 7b . . פרש

פַּרְשֶׁגֶן, פַּתְשֶׁגֶן masc. Heb. & Chald. *transcript, copy of a writing.*

פרשד Root not used; Arab. *to separate* or *spread out the feet.*

פַּרְשְׁדֹן masc. *the interstice of the legs,* Ju. 3. 22.

[g] פָּרְשָׂה Kal pret. 3 pers. sing. fem. . . . פרש

[h] פֵּרְשָׂה Piel pret. 3 pers. sing. fem. . . . פרש

[i] פִּרְשָׁהּ noun masc. s., suff. 3 p. s. f. fr. פֶּרֶשׁ d. 6a פרש

פָּרְשׂוּ וּ' Kal pret. 3 pers. pl.; וּ bef. lab. . . פרש

[k] פִּרְשׁוֹ וּ' noun masc. sing., suff. 3 pers. sing. masc. from פֶּרֶשׁ dec. 6a; וּ id. . . . . פרש

[l] פְּרֻשׂוֹת Kal part. pass. fem., pl. of פְּרוּשָׂה [from פָּרוּשׂ masc.] . . . . . . פרש

פרשז *to spread out, expand,* Job 26. 9.

[m] פֹּרְשֵׂי וּ' Kal part. act. pl. constr. masc. from פֹּרֵשׂ dec. 7b; וּ bef. lab. . . . . פרש

פֹּרְשָׂיו וּ' the foll. with suff. 3 pers. sing. m.; וּ id. פרש

פָּרָשִׁים וּ' noun masc., pl. of פָּרָשׁ dec. 1b . . פרש

פֹּרְשִׂים Kal part. act. pl. masc. from פֹּרֵשׂ dec. 7b פרש

[n] פִּרְשָׁם noun masc. s., suff. 3 p. pl. m. fr. פֶּרֶשׁ d. 6a פרש

פַּרְשַׁנְדָּתָא pr. name of one of Haman's sons, Est. 9. 7.

[o] פָּרָשַׁת וּ' noun fem. sing., constr. of [פָּרָשָׁה] dec. 10 פרש

פָּרַשְׂתָּ וּ } Kal pret. 1 & 2 pers. sing. masc.; acc. shifted by וּ, for וְ, conv. (§ 8. rem. 7) } פרש

פָּרַשְׂתִּי וּ

פֵּרַשְׂתִּי Piel pret. 1 pers. sing. . . . . . פרש

[p] פְּרָת defect. for פָּרוֹת (q. v.) . . . . פרר

פְּרָת (*sweet water*) pr. name, the river *Euphrates.*

[q] פֹּרָת Kal part. act. sing. fem. [for פֹּרָה comp. § 24. rem. 1] from פֹּרֶה masc. . . . פרה

פְּרָתָה pr. name of a river (פְּרָת) with parag. ה פרת

[r] פָּרָתוֹ noun fem. sing., suff. 3 pers. sing. masc. from פָּרָה dec. 10, from פַּר masc. . . . פרר

פַּרְתְּם masc. only pl. פַּרְתְּמִים' *nobles, princes,* Est. 1. 3; 6. 9; Da. 1. 3.

פָּשָׂה fut. יִפְשֶׂה *to spread,* as the leprosy.

[s] פָּשֹׂה Kal inf. abs. . . . . . . פשה

[t] פָּשׁוּ וּ Kal pret. 3 pers. pl.; וּ, for וְ, conv. . פוש

פִּשַּׁח Pi. *to tear in pieces,* La. 3. 11.

פַּשְׁחוּר וּ' pr. name masc. of several persons, espec. a priest contemporary with Jeremiah, Je. 20. 3; 38. 1.

פָּשַׁט וּ' fut. יִפְשֹׁט.—I. *to strip* or *put off* a garment.—II. *to spread oneself out,* of a hostile troop, with בְּ, אֶל, עַל *to invade.* Pi. *to strip, pillage, plunder.* Hiph. I. *to strip* a person.—II. *to strip off* a garment.—III. *to flay, skin.* Hithp. *to strip oneself,* 1 Sa. 18. 4.

[u] פְּשֹׁטָה Kal imp. s. m. [פְּשֹׁט] with parag. ה (§ 8. r. 12) פשט

פָּשְׁטוּ id. pret. 3 pers. pl. . . . . . פשט

[x] פֹּשְׁטִים id. part. act. masc. pl. [of פּוֹשֵׁט] dec. 7b פשט

[y] פָּשַׁטְנוּ id. pret. 1 pers. pl. . . . . . פשט

[z] פָּשַׁטְתָּ וּ id. pret. 2 pers. sing. masc., acc. shifted by וּ, for וְ, conv. (§ 8. rem. 7) . . פשט

[a] פָּשַׁטְתִּי id. pret. 1 pers. sing. . . . . פשט

[b] פְּשַׁטְתֶּם id. pret. 2 pers. pl. masc. . . . פשט

פָּשַׂע only fut. יִפְשַׂע, *to step, pass through,* with בְּ, Is. 27. 4.

פֶּשַׂע masc. *step, stride,* 1 Sa. 20. 3.

מִפְשָׂעָה fem. *the buttocks,* 1 Ch. 19. 4.

פָּשַׁע fut. יִפְשַׁע.—I. *to revolt, rebel,* with בְּ, מִתַּחַת.— II. *to transgress, sin,* with עַל *against* any one. Niph. part. *transgressed against, offended,* Pr. 18. 19.

פֶּשַׁע masc. dec. 6 (with suff. פִּשְׁעִי § 35. rem. 5). —I. *rebellion, defection.*—II. *trespass, fault.*—III. *transgression, sin.*—IV. perh. *offering for sin,* Mi. 6. 7

[c] פֶּשַׁע וָ' for פֶּשַׁע (q. v. § 35. rem. 2) . . פשע

[d] פָּשֹׁעַ Kal inf. abs. . . . . . . פשע

פֶּשַׁע וָ' noun masc. sing. (suff. פִּשְׁעִי) dec. 6a (§ 35. rem. 5); for וָ see lett. ו . . . פשע

[a] Eze. 26. 10. [b] Joel 2. 2. [c] Is. 25. 11. [d] Mal. 2. 3, 3. [e] Nu. 15. 34. [f] La. 4. 4. [g] Pr. 31. 20. [h] La. 1. 17. [i] Nu. 19. 5. [k] Le. 4. 11. [l] 1 Ki. 8. 54. [m] Is. 19. 8. [n] Le. 16. 27. [o] Est. 4. 7; 10. 2. [p] Ge. 41. 26. [q] Ge. 49. 22. [r] Job 21. 10. [s] Le. 13. 7, 22, 27, 35. [t] Hab. 1. 8. [u] Is. 32. 11. [x] Ne. 4. 17. [y] 1 Sa. 30. 14. [z] Ju. 9. 33. [a] Ca. 5. 3. [b] 1 Sa. 27. 10. [c] Nu. 14. 18. [d] Is. 59. 13.

פֹּשֵׁעַ[a] וּ Kal part. act. sing. masc. d. 7b; וּ bef. lab. פשע

פִּשְׁעָהּ[b] noun masc. sing., suff. 3 pers. sing. fem. from פֶּשַׁע dec. 6a (§ 35. rem. 5) . . פשע

פָּשְׁעוּ[c] / פָּשָׁעוּ } Kal pret. 3 pers. pl. (§ 8. rem. 7) . . פשע

פִּשְׁעוֹ noun masc. sing., suff. 3 pers. sing. masc. from פֶּשַׁע dec. 6a (§ 35. rem. 5) . פשע

פִּשְׁעוּ[d] וּ Kal imp. pl. masc.; וּ bef. lab. . . פשע

פִּשְׁעִי / פְּשָׁעַי } [e] וּ the foll. with suff. 1 pers. sing.; וּ id. פשע

פִּשְׁעֵי noun m. pl. constr. from פֶּשַׁע d. 6a (§ 35. r. 5) פשע

פִּשְׁעִי id. sing., suff. 1 pers. sing. . . . פשע

פְּשָׁעֶיהָ[f] id. pl., suff. 3 pers. sing. fem. . . פשע

פִּשְׁעֵיהֶם[g] וּ id. pl., suff. 3 pers. pl. masc.; וּ bef. lab. פשע

פְּשָׁעָיו id. pl., suff. 3 pers. sing. masc. . . פשע

פְּשָׁעֶיךָ id. pl., suff. 2 pers. sing. masc. . . פשע

פִּשְׁעֵיכֶם id. pl., suff. 2 pers. pl. masc. . . . פשע

פְּשָׁעִים[h] id. pl., abs. st. . . . . פשע

פֹּשְׁעִים וּ Kal part. act. m. pl. of פֹּשֵׁעַ d. 7b; וּ bef. lab. פשע

פְּשָׁעֵינוּ n. m. pl., suff. 1 p. pl. fr. פֶּשַׁע d. 6a (§ 35. r. 5) פשע

פִּשְׁעָם id. sing., suff. 3 pers. pl. masc. . . פשע

פָּשַׁעְנוּ[i] Kal pret. 1 pers. pl. . . . . פשע

פָּשַׁעַתְּ[k] / פָּשַׁעַתְּ[l] } id. pret. 2 pers. sing. fem. (§ 8. rem. 7) פשע

פְּשַׁעְתֶּם id. pret. 2 pers. pl. masc. . . . פשע

[פָּשַׂק] *to distend, open wide* the lips, Pr. 13. 3. Pi. id. of the feet, Eze. 16. 25.

פֹּשֵׂק[m] Kal part. act. sing. masc. . . . פשק

[פְּשַׁר] Chald. i. q. Heb. פָּתַר *to interpret, explain*, Da. 5. 16. Hence the two foll.

פְּשַׁר[n] וּ Chald. m. d. 3b, *interpretation, explanation* פשר

פֵּשֶׁר masc. id. Ec. 8. 1 . . . . פשר

פִּשְׁרָא וּ Ch. n. m. s., emph. of פְּשַׁר d. 3b; וּ bef. lab. פשר

פִּשְׁרֵא[o] וּ Chald. id. with suff. 3 pers. sing. masc. for פִּשְׁרֵהּ; וּ id. . . . . פשר

פִּשְׁרָה וּ Chald. id. emph. st. for פִּשְׁרָא; וּ id. . פשר

פִּשְׁרֵהּ[p] וּ id. with suff. 3 pers. sing. masc.; וּ id. פשר

פִּשְׁרִין[q] id. pl., abs. st. . . . . פשר

פשת obsolete and doubtful Root, whence

פִּשְׁתָּה fem. with suff. פִּשְׁתִּי, pl. פִּשְׁתִּים, constr. פִּשְׁתֵּי.—I. *flax*; Jos. 2. 6 פִּשְׁתֵּי הָעֵץ *flax of the tree*, i. e. *cotton*.—II. *linen*.—III. *wick* of a lamp, Is. 42. 3; 43. 17.

פָּשְׂתָה[r] / פָּשָׂתָה[s] } Kal pret. 3 pers. sing. fem. (comp. § 8. rem. 7) . . } פשה

פִּשְׁתָּה[t] וּ noun fem. sing.; וּ bef. lab. . . פשת

פִּשְׁתִּי[u] וּ id. with suff. 1 pers. sing.; וּ id. . פשת

פִּשְׁתִּים וּ id. pl., abs. st.; וּ id. . . . פשת

פַּשְׁתֶּם[x] וּ Kal pret. 2 pers. pl. masc. [for פַּשְׁתֶּם § 21. rem. 2]; וּ, for וְ, conv. . . פוש

פַּת noun fem. sing. (suff. פִּתִּי) dec. 8e . פתת

פִּתְאוֹם adv. [for פִּתְעֹם] see . . . פתע

פְּתָאִים noun masc., pl. of [פֶּתִי] d. 6i (§ 35. r. 15) פתה

פִּתְאֹם[y] וּ adv. [for פִּתְעֹם]; וּ bef. lab. . פתע

פַּתְבַּג[z] masc. [constr. of פַּתְבָּג dec. 2b] *delicate food, dainties*; prob. compounded of פַּת (R. פָּתַת) & בַּג (q. v.); but modern interpreters assign to it a Persian origin.

פַּתְבָּגוֹ[a] id. with suff. 3 pers. sing. masc.

פַּתְבָּגָם[b] id. with suff. 3 pers. pl. masc.

פִּתְגָּם masc.—I. Chald. & Heb. *word, sentence, decree*.—II. Chald. *epistle, letter*, Ezr. 5. 7.—III. Chald. *thing, matter*, Ezr. 6. 11.

פִּתְגָּמָא Chald. id. emph. st. . . . פתגם

[פָּתָה] fut. יִפְתֶּה.—I. *to open wide*, Pr. 20. 19 פֹּתֶה שְׂפָתָיו *babbler*.—II. prop. to be open, ingenuous; hence *to be* (easily) *persuaded, enticed*, De. 11. 16; part. act. *simple, silly*. Pi. I. *to persuade, entice*.—II. *to deceive, seduce*. Pu. pass. of Piel. Hiph. *to make wide, to enlarge*, with לְ, Ge. 9. 27.

פְּתָי Chald. masc. dec. 1a, *breadth*.

פֶּתִי masc. dec. 6i (pl. פְּתָאִים, פְּתָיִם § 35. rem. 15).—I. *simplicity, folly*, Pr. 1. 22.—II. *simple, inexperienced, ignorant*.

פְּתַיּוּת fem. *folly*, for concr. *foolish*, Pr. 9. 13.

פְּתוּאֵל (*enlarged of God*) pr. name m. Joel 1. 11.

יֶפֶת (*enlargement*) pr. n. *Japheth*, son of Noah.

פֹּתֶה[c] וּ Kal part. act. sing. masc.; וּ bef. lab. . פתה

פְּתֹתֶהָ[d] noun m. s., suff. 3 pers. s. f. [§ 3. r. 5; fr. פַּת, like בָּשְׁתִּי fr. בֹּשֶׁת, comp. § 39. No. 4d] פות

פְּתוּאֵל pr. name masc. . . . . . פתה

פָּתוֹחַ[e] Kal inf. abs. . . . . . פתח

פָּתוּחַ id. part. pass. sing. masc. . . . פתח

פִּתּוּחַ[f] noun masc. sing. dec. 1b . . . פתח

פְּתוּחָה Kal part. pass. sing. fem. from פָּתוּחַ masc. פתח

פְּתוּחוֹת id. pl., comp. פְּתֻחוֹת & פְּתֻחֹת . . פתח

פִּתּוּחֵי noun masc. pl. constr. from פִּתּוּחַ dec. 1b פתח

פִּתּוּחֶיהָ[g] id. pl., suff. 3 pers. sing. fem. . . פתח

---

[a] Is. 48. 8. [b] Is. 24. 20. [c] Ho. 8. 1. [d] Am. 4. 4. [e] Ps. 25. 7. [f] La. 1. 5. [g] Job 36. 9. [h] Pr. 10. 12. [i] La. 3. 42. [k] Je. 3. 13. [l] Zep. 3. 11. [m] Pr. 13. 3. [n] Da. 7. 16. [o] Da. 4. 15. [p] Da. 2. 9, 45. [q] Da. 5. 16. [r] Le. 13. 23. [s] Le. 13. 8, 28. [t] Is. 42. 3. [u] Ho. 2. 7, 11. [x] Mal. 3. 20. [y] Mal. 3. 1. [z] Da. 1. 13, 15. [a] Da. 11. 26. [b] Da. 1. 16. [c] Job 5. 2. [d] Is. 3. 17. [e] Na. 3. 13. [f] 2 Ch. 2. 13. [g] Ps. 74. 6.

[a]פְּתוּחִים id. pl., abs. st. . . . . פתח

פְּתוֹרָה pr. name of a place (פְּתוֹר) with parag. ה פתר

[b]פָּתוֹת Kal inf. abs. . . . . פתת

פָּתַח ו׳ fut. יִפְתַּח.—I. *to open*, as a door, window, the womb, sack, roll, &c.; פ׳ יָד *to open the hand*, with לְ, to act liberally to any one; פ׳ אָזְנֵי פ׳ *to open the ears* of any one, i. e. to reveal anything to him.—II. *to cleave* a rock, Ps. 105. 41.—III. *to loosen, untie*.—IV. *to draw, unsheath* a sword.—V. *to open, begin*, Ps. 49. 5. Niph. pass. of Kal Nos. I & II. Pi. I. *to open*; intrans. *to open itself, to be open*.—II. *to loosen, untie*.—III. *to plough*, Is. 28. 24.—IV. *to engrave, carve, sculpture*. Pu. *to be engraved*, Ex. 39. 6. Hithp. *to loose oneself*, Is. 52. 2.

פְּתַח Chald. *to open*, Da. 6. 11; 7. 10.

פֶּתַח masc. dec. 6 (with suff. פִּתְחִי § 35. rem. 5). —I. *opening, entrance*.—II. *door, gate*.

פֵּתַח masc. *opening, laying open*, Ps. 119. 130.

פִּתְחוֹן masc. dec. 3c, *an opening* of the mouth, Eze. 16. 63; 29. 21.

פִּתּוּחַ masc. dec. 1b, *engraving, carving*.

פְּתִיחָה f. d. 10, only pl. *drawn swords*, Ps. 55. 22.

פְּתַחְיָה (whom *the Lord liberates*) pr. name masc. of several persons.

יִפְתָּח (*opening*) pr. name—I. of a place in the tribe of Judah, Jos. 15. 43.—II. of a judge in Israel, *Jephtha*.

מַפְתֵּחַ masc. *key*.

מִפְתָּח masc. dec. 2b, *an opening*, Pr. 8. 6.

[c]פָּתַח in pause for פֶּתַח (q. v. § 8. rem. 7) . פתח

[d]פָּתָח Kal pret. 3 pers. sing. masc. for פָּתַח (§ 8. rem. 7) . . . . פתח

[e]פָּתֹחַ id. inf. abs. . . . . פתח

[f]פַּתֵּחַ Piel inf. constr. . . . . פתח

[g]פֶּתַח noun masc. sing. . . . . פתח

פֶּתַח ו׳ noun masc. s. (suff. פִּתְחִי) d. 6a (§ 35. r. 5) פתח

פְּתַח Kal imp. sing. masc. . . . . פתח

פִּתַּח / פִּתֵּחַ ו׳[h] } Piel pret. 3 pers. sing. masc. (§ 15. rem. 1); ו bef. lab. } פתח

פֹּתֵחַ Kal part. act. sing. masc. dec. 7b . . פתח

[k]פָּתְחָה ו׳ id. pret. 3 pers. sing. fem.; וְ, for וָ, conv. פתח

[l]פִּתְּחָה Piel pret. 3 pers. sing. fem. . . פתח

[m]פִּתְחָהּ ו noun masc. sing., suff. 3 pers. sing. fem. from פֶּתַח (§ 35. rem. 5) d. 6a; ו bef. lab. פתח

[n]פִּתֻּחָהּ noun masc. s., suff. 3 p. s. f. fr. פִּתּוּחַ d. 1b פתח

[o]פָּתְחוּ / [p]פִּתְּחוּ } Kal pret. 3 pers. pl. (§ 8. rem. 7) . פתח

[q]פִּתְחוֹ n. m. s., suff. 3 p. s. m. fr. פֶּתַח (§ 35. r. 5) d. 6a פתח

פִּתְחוּ Kal imp. pl. masc. . . . פתח

[r]פַּתְּחוּ ו Piel imp. pl. masc.; ו bef. lab. . פתח

פִּתְחוֹן noun masc. sing., constr. of [פִּתָּחוֹן] dec. 3c פתח

[s]פְּתָחוֹת noun fem., pl. of [פְּתִיחָה] dec. 10 . פתח

[t]פִּתֻּחוֹת defect. of פִּתּוּחוֹת (q. v.) . . פתח

[u]פְּתָחַי the foll. with suff. 1 pers. sing. . . פתח

פִּתְחֵי noun m. pl. constr. fr. פֶּתַח d. 6a (§ 35. r. 5) פתח

[x]פִּתְחִי Kal imp. sing. fem. . . . פתח

[y]פְּתָחֶיהָ noun masc. pl., suff. 3 pers. sing. fem. from פֶּתַח dec. 6a (§ 35. rem. 5) . . פתח

פְּתַחְיָה ו׳ pr. name masc.; ו bef. lab. . . פתח

[z]פִּתְחֵיהֶם ו noun masc. pl., suff. 3 pers. pl. masc. from פֶּתַח dec. 6a (§ 35. rem. 5); ו id. . פתח

[a]פְּתָחִים id. pl., abs. st. . . . . פתח

[b]פְּתָחֵינוּ id. pl., suff. 1 pers. sing. . . . פתח

[c]פְּתָחֹת defect. for פְּתוּחוֹת (q. v.) . . . פתח

[d]פָּתַחְתָּ ו Kal pret. 2 p. s. m.; וְ, for וָ, conv. (§ 8. r. 7) פתח

פִּתַּחְתָּ ו׳ Piel pret. 2 pers. sing. masc.; ו id. . פתח

פָּתַחְתִּי Kal pret. 1 pers. sing. . . . פתח

[e]פִּתַּחְתִּיךָ Piel pret. 1 pers. sing., suff. 2 pers. sing. m. פתח

פַּתְּחִי Piel imp. sing. fem. . . . . פתח

פֶּתִי ו׳[f] n. m. s. [for פֶּתִי § 35. r. 14] d. 6i; ו bef. lab. פתה

[g]פִּתִּי noun fem. sing., suff. 1 pers. s. fr. פַּת d. 8e פתת

[h]פְּתִיגִיל masc. Is. 3. 24, Eng. vers. "stomacher;" according to others, *a wide mantle*. Etymology obscure.

פְּתָיֵהּ Ch. noun m. s., suff. 3 p. s. m. fr. [פְּתָי] d. 1a פתה

[i]פְּתִיחוּ Ch. Peal part. pass. 3 p. pl. m. (§ 47. r. 11) פתח

[k]פְּתַיּוּת noun fem. sing. . . . . פתה

[l]פְּתִיחָן Ch. Peal part. pass. fem. pl. [of פְּתִיחָא from פְּתִיחַ masc.] . . . . פתח

[m]פְּתָיִים ו׳[n] noun masc., pl. of [פֶּתִי] d. 6i; ו bef. lab. פתה

[o]פָּתִיל noun masc. sing. dec. 3a . . . פתל

פְּתִיל ו׳[p] id., constr. st.; ו bef. lab. . . פתל

[q]פְּתִילְךָ ו id., suff. 2 pers. s. m. [for פְּתִילְךָ]; ו id. פתל

[r]פְּתִילִם id. pl., abs. st. . . . . פתל

[s]פְּתָיִם defect. for פְּתָיִים (q. v.) . . . פתה

פִּתִּים noun fem., pl. of פַּת dec. 8e . . פתת

[t]פִּתֵּיתִי Piel pret. 1 pers. sing. (§ 24. rem. 11) . פתה

[u]פִּתִּיתַנִי id. pret. 2 pers. sing. masc., suff. 1 pers. s. פתה

[x]פִּתְּךָ noun fem. sing., suff. 2 pers. sing. masc. from פַּת dec. 8e . . . . פתת

[y]פִּתֵּךְ id. with suff. 2 pers. sing. fem. . . פתת

---

a 2 Ch. 2. 6. b Le. 2. 6. c Job 31. 34, etc. d Ps. 78. 23. e De. 15. 8, 11. f Is. 58. 6. g Ps. 119. 130. h 2 Ch. 3. 7. i Pr. 31. 26. k De. 20. 11. l Is. 48. 8. m Ez. 40. 38. n Zec. 3. 9. o Ps. 109. 2. p Ps. 37. 14. q Pr. 17. 19. r Is. 60. 11. s Ps. 55. 22. t 2 Ch. 6. 40; 7. 15. u Pr. 8. 34. x Ca. 5. 2. y Is. 3. 26. z Eze. 42. 4. a Pr. 8. 3. b Ca. 7. 14. c 1 Ki. 8. 29, 52. d 2 Ki. 9. 3. e Je. 40. 4. f Pr. 19. 25. g Job 31. 17. h Is. 3. 24. i Da. 7. 10. k Pr. 9. 13. l Da. 6. 11. m Ps. 119. 130. n Pr. 22. 3. o Nu. 19. 15. p Eze. 40. 3. q Ge. 38. 18. r Ex. 39. 3. s Pr. 1. 22, 32. t Eze. 14. 9. u Je. 20. 7. x Pr. 23. 8. y Ru. 2. 14.

פָּתַל. Niph. I. prop. *to be twisted*, only metaph. *to be perverse, false, deceitful.*—II. *to wrestle, struggle*, Ge. 30. 8. Hithp. *to show oneself false*, Ps. 18. 27; 2 Sa. 22. 27; Prof. Lee, *to struggle.*

פָּתִיל masc. dec. 3a, *thread, string, cord*; also *a string for a signet-ring*, Ge. 38. 18, 25.

פְּתַלְתֹּל masc. *crooked, perverse*, De. 32. 5.

נַפְתּוּל masc. dec. 1b, only pl. *wrestlings, struggles*, De. 32. 5.

נַפְתָּלִי (*my wrestling*, Ge. 30. 8) pr. name, *Naphtali*, son of Jacob by Bilhah.

פְּתַלְתֹּל[a] וּ adj. masc. sing.; וּ bef. lab. . . . פתל

פִּתֹם pr. name, *Pithom*, a city in Egypt, on the eastern bank of the Nile, Ex. 1. 11.

פֶּתֶן[b] ן״ו masc. dec. 6a, *asp.* פֶּתֶן prob. i. q. פָּתַל *to twist.*

מִפְתָּן masc. dec. 2b, *threshold.* Arab. פתן *to be strong, firm* (Gesenius).

פָּתֶן[d] noun masc. sing. dec. 6, for פֶּתֶן (§ 35. rem. 2); for ךָ see lett. ו . . . . . פתן

פְּתָנִים id. pl., abs. st. . . . . . פתן

פֶּתַע masc. *suddenness*, hence—I. פֶּתַע, בְּפֶתַע adv. *suddenly.*—II. בְּפֶתַע, *accidentally, undesignedly*, Nu. 35. 22.

פִּתְאֹם (for פִּתְעֹם) adv. *suddenly*; בְּפִתְאֹם id. פֶּתַע פִּ׳, בְּפֶתַע פִּ׳, לְפֶתַע פִּ׳, לְפֶתַע פִּ׳ *very suddenly.*

פָּתַר fut. יִפְתֹּר *to interpret, explain.*

פְּתוֹר (*interpretation*) pr. name of the residence of Balaam.

פִּתְרוֹן masc. dec. 1b, *interpretation.*

פָּתַר Kal pret. 3 pers. sing. m. for פָּתַר (§ 8. r. 7) פתר

פֹּתֵר וּ id. part. act. sing. masc.; וּ bef. lab. . פתר

פַּתְרוֹס pr. name of a country in Egypt; according to some, *Upper Egypt.* Gent. n. פַּתְרֻסִים.

פִּתְרֹנוֹ[e] noun m. s., suff. 3 p. s. m. fr. פִּתְרוֹן d. 1b פתר

פִּתְרֹנִים[f] id. pl., abs. st. . . . . . פתר

פַּתְרֹס pr. name of a region, see פַּתְרוֹס.

פַּתְרֻסִים gent. noun, pl. from the preced.

פַּתְשֶׁגֶן noun masc. i. q. פַּרְשֶׁגֶן (q. v.).

[פָּתַת] *to break*, Le. 2. 6.

פַּת fem. d. 8e, *piece, crumb, morsel*, sc. of bread.

פְּתוֹת masc. dec. 1a, id. Eze. 13. 19.

צ

צֵא ן׳ Kal imp. sing. masc. . . . . . יצא

צְאָה[g] ן id. with parag. ה [for צְאָה]; for ן see let. ו יצא

צֹאָה[h] noun fem. sing. dec. 10 . . . . יצא

צְאוּ / צְאוּ ו׳ } Kal imp. pl. masc.; וּ bef. (:) . . יצא

צאוננו[i] Kh. צְאוֹנֵנוּ noun com. sing., suff. 1 pers. pl. [from צְאוֹן]; K. צֹאנֵנוּ (q. v.) . . . צאן

צְאִי[k] Kal imp. sing. fem. . . . . . יצא

צְאֶינָה[l] id. imp. pl. fem. (§ 23. rem. 3) . . יצא

צֶאֱלִים m. pl. Job 40. 21, 22, *lotus bushes*, coll. with the Arab. צאל, so Schultens; others, *shades*, i. e. *shady trees* [for צְלָלִים].

צֹאן ן׳, ו׳ (for צְאֹן) com. dec. 1a, collect.—I. *small cattle, sheep and goats.*—II. *flock, flocks of sheep and goats*; metaph. of a people.

צְאוֹן idem, Ps. 144. 13, Khethib.

צַאֲנָן (*place of flocks*; others, *fertile*) pr. name of a place in the tribe of Judah, Mi. 1. 11.

צֹאנוֹ id. with suff. 3 pers. sing. masc. . . צאן

צֹאנִי[m] ן״ו id., suff. 1 pers. sing. . . . צאן

צֹאנֵנוּ[n] ן id. pl. or sing. (for צֹאנֵנוּ), suff. 1 pers. pl. צאן

צֹאנְךָ ן׳ / צֹאנֶךָ ן׳ } id., suff. 2 pers. sing. masc. . צאן

צֹאנְכֶם[oo] ן׳ id., suff. 2 pers. pl. masc. . . . צאן

צֹאנָם ן׳ id., suff. 3 pers. pl. masc. . . . צאן

צַאֲנָן pr. name of a place . . . . . צאן

צֶאֱצָאַי[o] ן the foll. with suff. 1 pers. sing. . . יצא

צֶאֱצָאֵי[p] ן noun masc. pl. constr. fr. [צֶאֱצָא] dec. 1b יצא

צֶאֱצָאֶיהָ[q] ן׳ id. pl., suff. 3 pers. sing. fem. . . יצא

צֶאֱצָאֵיהֶם ן id. pl., suff. 3 pers. pl. masc. . . יצא

צֶאֱצָאָיו[r] ן id. pl., suff. 3 pers. sing. masc. . . יצא

צֶאֱצָאֶיךָ[s] ן״ו[t] id. pl., suff. 2 pers. sing. masc. . . יצא

צֹאַת[u] noun fem. sing., constr. of [צֹאָה] dec. 10 יצא

צֵאת Kal inf. constr. [for צֶאֱת § 25. No. 2 d] יצא

צֹאַת[x] noun fem. sing., constr. of צֹאָה dec. 10 יצא

צֵאתוֹ Kal inf. [צֵאת for צֶאֱת § 25. No. 2d], suff. 3 pers. sing. masc. . . . . . יצא

צֵאָתְךָ[y] noun fem sing., suff. 2 pers. sing. masc. [for צֹאָתְךָ] from צֹאָה dec. 10 . . יצא

[a] De. 32. 5. [b] Ps. 58. 5. [c] Ps. 91. 13. [d] Is. 11. 8. [e] Ge. 40. 12, 18. [f] Ge. 40. 8. [g] Ju. 9. 29. [h] Is. 28. 8. [i] Ps. 144. 13. [k] Ca. 1. 8. [l] Ca. 3. 11. [m] Eze. 34. 19. [n] Ne. 10. 37. [o] Job 31. 8. [oo] De. 12. 6. [p] Is. 48. 19. [q] Is. 34. 1; 42. 5. [r] Job 27. 14. [s] Is. 44. 3. [t] Job 5. 25. [u] Eze. 4. 12. [x] Is. 4. 4. [y] De. 23. 14.

צֵאתְךָ 'וְ Kal inf. (צֵאת for צְאֵת § 25. No. 2 d), suff. 2 pers. sing. masc. . . . . יצא

צֵאתָם[a] id., suff. 3 pers. pl. masc. . . . . יצא

צֵאתֵנוּ[b] id., suff. 1 pers. pl. . . . . . יצא

צָב[c] noun masc. sing. dec. 8 a . . . צבב

[צָבָא] I. *to go forth to war, to carry on war,* with עַל against any one.—II. *to go forth to service, to serve in the temple.* Hence

צָבָא 'וְ masc. (fem. Is. 40. 2; Da. 8. 12) dec. 4 a, constr. צְבָא (§ 33. rem. 2), pl. צְבָאִים, צְבָאוֹת (Ps. 103. 21; 148. 2).—I. *army, host;* אַנְשֵׁי צָ׳ *warriors, soldiers;* שַׂר הַצָּ׳ *captain of the host, commander in chief;* צְבָא הַשָּׁמַיִם *host of heaven,* i. e. *the angels,* sometimes also *the sun, moon and stars;* hence the epithet יְהוָֹה צְבָאוֹת, אֱלֹהֵי צְ׳.—II. *warfare, military service;* trop. *struggle, trial, affliction.*

[צְבָא] Chald. *to will, please, choose.*

צְבוּ Chald. fem. *determination, resolution, purpose,* Da. 6. 18.

צָבֵא[d] Chald. Peal part. act. sing. masc. . . . צבא

צְבָא [e]'וּ noun masc. sing., constr. of צָבָא dec. 4 a (§ 33. rem. 2); וּ bef. (:) . . . צבא

צְבָאָהּ id. with suff. 3 pers. sing. fem. . . . צבא

צָבְאוּ Kal pret. 3 pers. pl. . . . . צבא

צְבָאָיו[f] n. m. pl. with suff. 3 p. s. m. from צָבָא dec. 4 a צבא

צְבָאוֹ '׳וּ id. sing., suff. 3 pers. sing. masc.; וּ bef. (:) צבא

צְבָאוֹת id. pl. abs. fem. . . . . . צבא

צִבְאוֹת id. pl. constr. fem. . . . . צבא

צִבְאוֹתֵיכֶם[g] id. pl. fem., suff. 2 pers. pl. masc. . צבא

צְבָאִי[h] id. sing., suff. 1 pers. sing. . . . צבא

צְבָאָיו[i] id. pl. masc., suff. 3 pers. sing. masc. . צבא

צְבָאֲךָ[k] id. sing., suff. 2 pers. sing. masc. . . צבא

צְבָאָם id. sing., suff. 3 pers. pl. masc. . . . צבא

צִבְאֹתַי[l] id. pl. fem., suff. 1 pers. sing. . . . צבא

צִבְאֹתָם id. pl. fem., suff. 3 pers. pl. masc. (§ 4. rem. 1) צבא

צָבַב Root not used; Arab. *to cover.*

צָב masc. dec. 8 a.—I. *covering,* עֶגְלֹת צָב *covered waggon,* Nu. 7. 3, and (without עֲגָלָה) Is. 66. 20, id.—II. a species of *lizard,* Le. 11. 29.

צֹבֵבָה (*stout, fat,* Simonis) pr. name f. 1 Ch. 4. 8.

[צָבָה] *to swell,* Nu. 5. 27. Arab. *to shine,* comp. צְבִי, perh. prim. *to be prominent.*

צָבֶה, fem. צָבָה adj. *swelling,* Nu. 5. 21.

צְבִי masc. dec. 6 i.—I. *splendour, beauty, glory.*—II. *gazelle;* pl. צְבָאוֹת, צְבָאִים, צְבָיִים (§ 35. r. 15).

צִבְיָא (*gazelle*) pr. name masc. 1 Ch. 8. 9.

צִבְיָה (id.) pr. name of the mother of king Josiah.

צְבִיָּה fem. *female gazelle,* Ca. 4. 5; 7. 4.

צְבֹאִים, צְבֹיִם, צְבִיִּם, צְבֹיִים (*gazelles*) pr. name of one of the cities destroyed with Sodom.

צָבָה[m] adj. fem. sing. [from צָבֶה masc.] . . צבה

צְבוּ[n] Ch. noun fem. sing. . . . . צבה

צָבוּעַ[rr] noun masc. sing. . . . . צבע

[צָבַט] *to reach* or *hold out,* Ru. 2. 14.

צְבִי 'וּ noun masc. sing. dec. 6 i; וּ bef. (:) . צבה

צִבְיָא pr. name masc. . . . . . צבה

צְבִיָּה noun fem. sing. from צְבִי masc. . . צבה

צִבְיָה pr. name fem. . . . . . צבה

צֹבֶיהָ[o] Kal part. act. pl. masc., suff. 3 pers. sing fem. [for צֹבְאֶיהָ from צָבָא] . . . צבא

צְבֹיִים 'וּ} צְבֹיִם 'וּ} pr. name of a place; וּ bef. (:) . צבה

צְבִית[p] Chald. Peal pret. 1 pers. sing. . . . צבא

צָבַע Root not used; Arab. *to dip in, to tinge, dye.*

צְבַע Chald. Aph. *to wet, moisten,* Da. 4. 22. Ithp. אִצְטַבַּע pass.

צֶבַע masc. *dyed garments,* Ju. 5. 30; pl. צְבָעִים.

צָבוּעַ masc. *hyena,* Je. 12. 9. Arab. ضَبُعٌ id.

צְבֹעִים (*hyenas*) pr. name, *Zeboim,* a valley and town in the tribe of Benjamin.

צִבְעוֹן (*coloured*) pr. name of a son of Seir.

אֶצְבַּע fem. dec. 2 b (pl. אֶצְבָּעוֹת § 31. rem. 5).—I. *finger,* espec. *forefinger;* pl. *fingers,* poet. for *hand,* Ps. 8. 4; 144. 1.—II. *a digit,* a measure, Je. 52. 21.—III. with רַגְלַיִם, *a toe.*

אֶצְבַּע Chald. dec. 2 a, only אֶצְבְּעָן *fingers,* Da. 5. 5; *toes,* Da. 2. 41, 42.

צֶבַע[q] noun masc. sing. dec. 6 (§ 35. rem. 5) . צבע

צִבְעוֹן 'וְ pr. name masc. . . . . צבע

צְבָעִים[r] noun masc., pl. of צֶבַע dec. 6 (§ 35. rem. 5) צבע

צְבֹעִים pr. name of a valley . . . . צבע

צָבַר only fut. יִצְבֹּר.—I. *to heap up.*—II. *to lay, treasure up.* Hence

צִבֻּרִים noun masc. pl. [of צִבּוּר] *heaps,* 2 Ki. 10. 8 צבר

צָבַת Root not used; Arab. *to bind,* also *to take in the hand.*

צֶבֶת m. *bundle, sheaf,* Ru. 2. 16; others, *handful.*

---

[a] 1 Sa. 18. 30. [b] Jos. 9. 12. [c] Nu. 7. 3. [d] Da. 5. 19. [e] Ne. 9. 6. [f] Ps. 148. 2. [g] Ex. 12. 17. [h] Job 14. 14. [i] Ps. 103. 21. [k] Ju. 9. 29. [l] Ex. 7. 4. [m] Nu. 5. 21. [n] Da. 6. 18. [o] Is. 29. 7. [p] Da. 7. 19. [q] Ju. 5. 30. [r] Ju. 5. 30. [rr] Je. 12. 9.

צָבְתָה[a] וְ Kal pret. 3 pers. sing. fem. . . . צבה

צָד noun masc. sing. (suff. צִדּוֹ) dec. 8e . צדד

צָדַד Root not used; Arab. *to turn away;* Talm. צַדֵּד *to turn one's side* to any one.

צַד masc. dec. 8e.—I. *side;* with ה parag. צִדָּה *to* or *at the side,* 1 Sa. 20. 20; מִצַּד *at the side of;* עַל צַד *on the side,* i. e. where a child is carried upon the arm, comp. Is. 60. 4.—II. *adversary,* Ju. 2. 3.

צַד Chald. *side;* מִצַּד *on the side of, in reference to,* Da. 6. 5; לְצַד *against,* Da. 7. 25.

צִדִּים (*sides*) pr. name of a town in Naphtali, Jos. 19. 35. Also

צְדָדָה pr. name [צְדָד] with local ה, a place in the north of Palestine, Nu. 34. 8; Eze. 47. 15 צדד

צָדָה[b] *to lie in wait for.* Niph. *to be destroyed, desolated,* Zep. 3. 6.

צְדָא Chald. *purpose, intention,* Da. 3. 14, הַצְדָא *was it on purpose?* According to Fürst, *it is derision, mockery,* for אַצְדָּא (§ 47. rem. 4) Targ. אַצְדִּי Aph. *to deride,* R. צְדָא.

צְדִיָּה fem. *purpose, design,* Nu. 35. 20, 22.

צֵדָה defect. for צֵידָה (q. v.) . . . צוד

צִדָּה[c] noun masc. sing. (צַד) with parag. ה dec. 8e צדד

צֹדֶה[d] Kal part. act. sing. masc. . . . צדה

צָדוּ[e] Kal pret. 3 pers. pl. . . . . . צוד

צָדוּם[f] וְ id., suff. 3 pers. pl. masc. . . . צוד

צָדוּנִי[g] id., suff. 1 pers. sing. . . . . צוד

צָדוֹק וְ pr. name masc. . . . . . צדק

צִדֵּי[h] noun masc. pl. constr. from צַד dec. 8e . צדד

צְדִיָּה[i] noun fem. sing. . . . . . צדה

צִדָּיו noun m. pl., suff. 3 pers. s. m. fr. צַד d. 8e צדד

צַדִּיק וְ adj. masc. sing. dec. 1b . . . צדק

צַדִּיקִים / צַדִּקִם } וְ' id. pl., abs. st. . . . . צדק

צִדְּךָ[k] / צִדֶּךָ[l] } noun masc. sing., suff. 2 pers. sing. masc. from צַד dec. 8e . . . } צדד

צִדֹנִי gent. noun from צִידוֹן . . . . צוד

צִדֹנִים / צִדֹנִין } id. pl. masc. . . . . . צוד

צִדֹנִית id. pl. fem. . . . . . צוד

[צָדַק] fut. יִצְדַּק.—I. *to be just, righteous, equitable.*—II. *to be in the right, to have a just cause.*—III. *to be right, correct,* Job 33. 12.—IV. *to be declared righteous, be justified.* Niph. Da. 8. 14, *to be purified,* so the Sept. and Vulg. Others, *to be justified, vindicated,* sc. from injury. Pi. *to justify.* Hiph. I. *to make righteous, lead to righteousness* or *justification,* Da. 12. 3.—II. *to do justice to,* 2 Sa. 15. 4. —III. *to pronounce just, righteous, to justify,* with acc. לְ. Hithp. *to justify oneself,* Ge. 44. 16.

צָדוֹק (*just*) pr. name of the father-in-law of king Josiah and several other men.

צַדִּיק adj. masc. dec. 1b.—I. *just, equitable* in the administration of justice.—II. *just, righteous* in character and general conduct.—III. *having a just cause.*—IV. *blameless, innocent.*—V. *true,* Is. 41. 26.

צֶדֶק masc. dec. 6a (with suff. צִדְקִי), & צְדָקָה dec. 11c.—I. *justice, equity* in the administration of justice.—II. *righteousness, justice* of character and conduct.—III. *right, what is right, fair.*—IV. *truth,* comp. Ps. 52. 5.—V. *justification, acquittal,* Job 6. 29; Da. 9. 24.—VI. pl. צְדָקוֹת *righteous acts, righteousness.*

צִדְקָה Chald. fem. *equity, righteousness,* Da. 4. 24.

צִדְקִיָּהוּ (*justice of the Lord*) pr. name—I. of a king of Judah.—II. of a false prophet under Ahab, called also צִדְקִיָּה, 1 Ki. 22. 11.—III. of three other men.

צֶדֶק וְ, וְ'[m] noun masc. sing. (suff. צִדְקִי) dec. 6a; for וָ see lett. ו . . . . צדק

צָדְקָה[n] Kal pret. 3 pers. sing. fem. . . . צדק

צְדָקָה וְ' noun fem. sing. dec. 11c; וּ bef. (:) . צדק

צִדְּקָה[o] Piel pret. 3 pers. sing. fem. . . . צדק

צִדְקָהּ[p] noun masc. sing., suff. 3 pers. sing. fem. from צֶדֶק dec. 6a . . . . צדק

צָדְקוּ[q] Kal pret. 3 pers. pl. . . . . צדק

צַדְּקוֹ[r] Piel inf. (צַדֵּק), suff. 3 pers. sing. m. d. 7b צדק

צִדְקוֹ noun m. s., suff. 3 pers. s. m. fr. צֶדֶק d. 6a צדק

צְדָקוֹת noun fem. pl. abs. from צְדָקָה dec. 11c צדק

צִדְקוֹת id. pl., constr. st. . . . . צדק

צִדְקִי noun m. sing., suff. 1 pers. sing. fr. צֶדֶק d. 6a צדק

צִדְקִיָּה / צִדְקִיָּהוּ } וְ' pr. name masc. . . . . צדק

צַדִּקִים וְ'[s] defect. for צַדִּיקִים (q. v.) . . . צדק

צַדְּקֶךָ[t] Piel inf. (צַדֵּק), suff. 2 pers. sing. masc. [for צַדֶּקְךָ dec. 7b. § 16. rem. 15] . . צדק

צִדְקֵךְ[n] noun m. s., suff. 2 pers. s. fem. fr. צֶדֶק d. 6a צדק

צִדְקְךָ id., suff. 2 pers. sing. masc. for צִדְקֶךָ' . צדק

צִדְקֵנוּ id., suff. 1 pers. pl. . . . . צדק

צָדַקְתָּ Kal pret. 1 pers. sing. . . . צדק

צִדְקַת וְ'[u] noun fem. sing., constr. of צְדָקָה dec. 11c צדק

[a] Nu. 5. 27. [b] Ex. 21. 13. [c] 1 Sa. 20. 20. [d] 1 Sa. 24. 12. [e] La. 4. 18. [f] Je. 16. 16. [g] La. 3. 52. [h] Ex. 26. 13. [i] Nu. 35. 22. [k] Eze. 4. 8. [l] Eze. 4. 4, 6, 9. [m] Ps. 85. 12. [n] Ge. 38. 26. [o] Je. 3. 11. [p] Is. 62. 1. [q] Ps. 19. 10. [r] Job 32. 2. [s] Ho. 14. 10. Job 33. 32. [t] Is. 62. 2. [u] Is. 5. 23.

צִדְקָתוֹ וְ' id., suff. 3 pers. sing. masc. . . . צדק
צִדְקֹתָו id. pl., suff. 3 pers. sing. masc. . . צדק
צָדַקְתִּי [a]וְ' Kal pret. 1 pers. sing. . . צדק
צִדְקָתִי וְ' noun fem. s., suff. 1 pers. s. fr. צְדָקָה d. 11 c צדק
צִדְקֹתֶיךָ[b] id. pl., suff. 2 pers. sing. masc. . . צדק
צִדְקֹתֵינוּ id. pl., suff. 1 pers. pl. . . . צדק
צִדְקָתֵךְ[c] id. sing., suff. 2 pers. sing. fem. . . צדק
צִדְקָתְךָ / צִדְקָתֶךָ וְ' } id. sing., suff. 2 pers. sing. masc. . צדק
צִדְקָתָם[d] וְ id. sing., suff. 3 pers. pl. masc. . . צדק

צָהַב, only Hoph. part. *shining like gold*, or perh. *gold-coloured*, Ezr. 8. 27. Hence

צָהֹב adj. *gold-coloured, yellow*, Le. 13. 30, 32 . צהב

[צָהַל] I. *to neigh*, of a horse, Je. 5. 8; of persons, *to shout for joy;* also *for fear*, Is. 10. 30.—II. i. q. זָהַר *to shine*, only Hiph. *to cause to shine*, Ps. 104. 15.

מִצְהָלָה fem. d. 11 a, *a neighing*, Je. 8. 16; 13. 27.

צָהֲלָה[e] Kal pret. 3 pers. sing. fem. . . . צהל
צָהֲלוּ[f] id. pret. 3 pers. pl. . . . . צהל
צַהֲלוּ[g] וְ id. imp. pl. masc. . . . . צהל
צַהֲלִי[h] וְ' id. imp. sing. fem. . . . . צהל

צָהַר Kal not used; i. q. זָהַר *to shine*. Hiph. (denom. from יִצְהָר) *to make* or *press out oil*, Job 24. 11.

צֹהַר masc. dec. 6 f.—I. *a light, window*, Ge. 6. 16. —II. du. צָהֳרַיִם (§ 35. rem. 9 & 16) *noon;* metaph. of great prosperity.

יִצְהָר masc. dec. 2 b.—I. *oil*, espec. *new oil*.—II. pr. name of a son of Kohath. Patronym. יִצְהָרִי.

צַר masc. (for צֹהַר, צָהַר splendour) *the moon*, so according to some, in Is. 5. 30.

צֶרֶת (for צֶהֶרֶת *splendour*) pr. name—I. of a man, 1 Ch. 4. 7.—II. צֶרֶת הַשַּׁחַר (*splendour of the dawn*) of a city in Reuben, Jos. 13. 19.

צֹהַר[i] noun fem. sing. dec. 6 f . . . צהר
צָהֳרַיִם / צָהֳרָיִם[k] וְ } id. du., abs. st. . . . . צהר
צָו[l] noun masc. sing. for צַו . . . צוה
צַו [m]וְ' ap. for צַוֵּה q. v.; or (Is. 28. 10, 13) n. m. צוה
צוֹאִים[n] adj. masc., pl. of [צוֹא] dec. 1 a . . יצא
צַוָּאר noun masc. sing. dec. 2 b . . . צור
צַוַּאר id., constr. st. . . . . . צור
צַוָּארָהּ[o] id., suff. 3 pers. sing. fem. . . . צור
צַוְּארֵהּ[p] Ch. id., suff. 3 pers. sing. masc. . . צור
צַוָּארָו[q] id. pl., suff. 3 p. s. m. for צַוָּארָיו (§ 4. rem. 1) צור

צַוָּארוֹ id. sing., suff. 3 pers. sing. masc. . . . צור
צַוָּארִי[r] id. sing., suff. 1 pers. sing. . . . צור
צַוְּארֵי id. pl., constr. st. . . . . . צור
צַוְּארֵיהֶם[s] id. pl., suff. 3 pers. pl. masc. . . . צור
צַוָּארָיו id. pl., suff. 3 pers. sing. masc. . . . צור
צַוְּארֵיכֶם[t] id. pl., suff. 2 pers. pl. masc. . . . צור
צַוָּארֵךְ id. sing., suff. 2 pers. sing. fem. . . . צור
צַוְּארָךְ[u] Ch. id. sing., suff. 2 pers. sing. masc. . צור
צַוָּארֶךָ id. sing., suff. 2 pers. sing. m. [for צַוָּארְךָ] צור
צַוָּארֵנוּ[x] id. sing., suff. 1 pers. pl. . . . . צור
צַוְּארֹתֵיכֶם[y] id. pl. fem., suff. 2 pers. pl. masc. . . צור
צוֹבָא / צוֹבָה } pr. name of a place . . . . . נצב

[צוּד] *to hunt* wild beasts; *to lay snares* for birds; metaph. *to hunt, pursue* men. Pil. *to ensnare, beguile*, Eze. 13. 18, 20. Hithp. הִצְטַיֵּד (denom. from צַיִד) *to furnish oneself with provision*, Jos. 9. 12.

צַיִד masc. dec. 6 h.—I. *a hunting*, Ge. 10. 9.—II. *game, venison*, Ge. 25. 28.—III. *provision, food.*

צֵדָה, צֵידָה fem. *provision, food.*

צַיָּד masc. dec. 1 b, *hunter*, Je. 16. 16.

צִידוֹן, צִידֹן (*fishery*) pr. name, *Zidon*, an ancient city of Phœnicia.—Gent. noun צִידֹנִי, pl. f. צִדְנִית.

מְצָד masc. dec. 1 a (pl. מְצָדוֹת abs. & constr.) *strong place, citadel, fortress.*

מָצוֹד masc. dec. 3 a (with suff. מְצוּדוֹ § 32. rem. 5).—I. *capture, prey*, Pr. 12. 12.—II. *net* of hunters.—III. *fortress*, Ec. 9. 14.

מְצוֹדָה fem. d. 10.—I. *net*, Ec. 9. 12.—II. *citadel, fortress.*

מְצוּדָה f. d. 10.—I. *capture, prey*, Eze. 13. 21.—II. *net* of a hunter, Eze. 12. 13.—III. *citadel, fortress.*

צוֹד[z] Kal inf. abs. . . . . . . צוד
צוּדָה[a] וְ id. imp. sing. masc. with parag. ה . צוד

צָוָה Kal not used; Syr. *to set up, erect*. Pi. צִוָּה.—I. *to set over, appoint, constitute*, with acc. of the person and עַל of the thing.—II. *to appoint, determine, decree.*—III. *to charge, command*, with acc., also עַל, אֶל, לְ.—IV. *to send with orders, to commission*, with לְ, אֶל, עַל *to* or *concerning* whom; צִוָּה לְבֵיתוֹ *to give one's last orders to his family.* Pu. *to be commanded, charged.*

צַו, צָו masc. *command, precept.*

צִיּוּן masc. dec. 1 b.—I. *pillar, monument.*—II. *way-mark*, Je. 31. 21.

מִצְוָה fem. dec. 10, *commandment, precept.*

[a] Job 10. 15. [b] Da. 9. 16. [c] Is. 57. 12. [d] Is. 54. 17. [e] Est. 8. 15. [f] Is. 24. 14. [g] Je. 31. 7. [h] Is. 54. 1. [i] Ge. 6. 16. [k] Ps. 55. 18. [l] Ho. 5. 11. [m] De. 8. 28. [n] Zec. 3. 3. [o] Ho. 10. 11. [p] Da. 5. 7, 29. [q] Ge. 33. 4. [r] La. 1. 14. [s] Jos. 10. 24. [t] Je. 27. 12. [u] Da. 5. 16. [x] La. 5. 5. [y] Mi. 2. 8. [z] La. 3. 52. [a] Ge. 27. 3.

צַוֵּה Piel imp. sing. masc. . . . צוה

צִוָּה 'וְ id. pret. 3 pers. sing. masc. . . . צוה

צֻוָּה Pual pret. 3 pers. sing. masc. . . . צוה

צִוָּהוּ Piel pret. 3 pers. sing. m., suff. 3 pers. s. m. צוה

צַוּוּ וְ id. imp. pl. masc. . . . . צוה

[צָוַח] *to cry, shout for joy,* Is. 42. 11. Hence

צְוָחָה fem. dec. 11 c, *a cry* for joy or sorrow . צוח

צִוְחַת[a] וְ id., constr. st. . . . . . צוח

צִוְחָתֵךְ[b] וְ id., suff. 2 pers. sing. fem. . . . צוח

צִוִּיתָ, צִוִּיתָ[c] וְ, צִוִּיתָה, צִוִּיתָה[d] וְ } Piel pret. 2 pers. sing. masc. (comp. § 8. rem. 5 & 7) . . . } צוה

צֻוֵּיתָה[e] Pual pret. 2 pers. sing. masc. (comp. § 8. r. 5) צוה

צִוֵּיתִי, צִוִּיתִי 'וְ[f] } Piel pret. 1 pers. sing. (§ 24. rem. 11) צוה

צֻוֵּיתִי Pual pret. 1 pers. sing. . . . . צוה

צִוִּיתִיהָ[g] Piel pret. 1 pers. sing., suff. 3 pers. sing. fem. צוה

צִוִּיתִיו[h] id. id., suff. 3 pers. sing. masc. . . . צוה

צִוִּיתִיךָ id. id., suff. 2 pers. sing. masc. . . . צוה

צִוִּיתִים id. id., suff. 3 pers. pl. masc. . . . צוה

צִוִּיתִךָ defect. for צִוִּיתִיךָ (q. v.) . . . צוה

צִוִּתִם defect. for צִוִּיתִים (q. v.) . . . צוה

צִוִּיתָנוּ[i] Piel pret. 2 pers. sing. masc., suff. 1 pers. pl. צוה

צִוִּיתָנִי id. id., suff. 1 pers. sing. [for תָּנִי' § 2. r. 1] צוה

צִוְּךָ, צִוְּךָ 'וְ } id. pret. 3 pers. sing. masc. (צִוָּה), suff. 2 pers. sing. masc. (§ 24. rem. 21) } צוה

צוּל Root not used; prob. i. q. צָלַל *to sink.*

צוּלָה fem. *the deep,* Is. 44. 27.

מְצוֹלָה, מְצוּלָה fem. dec. 10, *depth, deep place.*

[צוּם] *to fast.* Hence

צוֹם 'וְ masc. dec. 1 a (pl. צוֹמוֹת), *a fast, fasting* צום

צִוָּם Piel pret. 3 pers. sing. masc. (צִוָּה), suff. 3 pers. pl. masc. (§ 24. rem. 21) . צוה

צוּמוּ[k] וְ Kal imp. pl. masc. . . . . צום

צוֹמֵחַ[l] Kal part. act. sing. masc. . . . צמח

צִוָּנוּ Piel pret. 3 pers. sing. masc., (צִוָּה), suff. 1 pers. pl. (§ 24. rem. 21) . . . צוה

צִוַּנִי, צִוָּנִי } id. id. with suff. 1 pers. sing. . . צוה

צוּעַ Root not used; *to form, design.*

צַעֲצֻעִים masc. pl. *carved work,* 2 Ch. 3. 10.

צוֹעַר pr. name of a place . . . . צער

צוּעָר pr. name masc. . . . . צער

[צוּף] *to overflow, overwhelm,* La. 3. 54. Hiph. I. *to cause to overflow,* De. 11. 4.—II. *to cause to swim,* 2 Ki. 6. 6.

צוּף masc. dec. 1 a.—I. *honeycomb.*—II. pr. name masc. 1 Sa. 1. 1; also 1 Ch. 6. 20, Kh. for which צוֹפַי, 1 Ch. 6. 11.

צָפָה fem. dec. 10, *an overflowing,* Eze. 32. 6

צַפְצָפָה fem. *a willow,* Eze. 17. 5.

צוּף[m] noun masc. sing. dec. 1 a, also pr. name . צוף

צוֹפֶה Kal part. act. sing. masc. dec. 9 a, comp. צָפָה צפה

צוֹפוֹת[n] id. pl. fem. [from צוֹפָה] dec. 10 . . צפה

צוֹפַח, צוֹפָח } pr. name masc. . . . . צפח

צוֹפַי pr. name masc., see צוּף . . . צוף

צוֹפִיָּה[o] Kal part. act. sing. fem. [as if from a masc. צוֹפִי § 24. rem. 4] . . . . צפה

צוֹפִים pr. name in compos., רָמָתַיִם צוֹפִים, see under רום

צוּפִים[p] noun masc., pl. of צוּף dec. 1 a . . צוף

צוֹפַר 'וְ pr. name masc. . . . . צפר

[צוּץ] *to flower, flourish,* Eze. 7. 10. Hiph. I. *to glitter shine.*—II. *to flower, blossom.*

צִיץ masc.—I. *a shining plate* of gold on the forehead of the high priest.—II. *flower;* pl. צִצִּים —III. *plumage, wing,* Je. 48. 9.—IV. pr. name of a place, 2 Ch. 20. 16.

צִיצָה fem. dec. 10, *a flower,* Is. 28. 4.

צִיצִת fem.—I. *a lock* of hair, Eze. 8. 3.—II. *fringe,* Nu. 15. 38, 39.

I. צוּק Hiph. הֵצִיק.—I. *to straiten, distress;* part. *oppressor* Is. 51. 13.—II. *to press, urge,* with acc. לְ.

צוֹק masc. *distress, oppression, trouble,* Da. 9. 25

צוּקָה fem. id. Pr. 1. 27; 30. 6.

מָצוֹק masc. and מְצוּקָה fem. dec. 10, idem.

מוּצָק masc.—I. something *narrow, scanty,* Job 36. 16; 37. 10.—II. *straitness, distress,* Is. 8. 23

II. צוּק *to pour out,* only צָקוּן (for צָקוּ) Is. 26. 16; fut. צוק Job 28. 2; 29. 6.

מָצוּק masc. dec. 3 a.—I. *pillar, column,* 1 Sa. 2. 8 (צוּק i. q. הֵצִיק *to set up,* R. יָצַק).—II. metaph. *a precipitous rock,* 1 Sa. 14. 5.

צוּקָה[q] 'וְ noun fem. sing. . . . . צוק

[צוּר] fut. יָצוּר, ap. וַיָּצַר (see analyt. order).—I. *to bind up.*—II. *to press, besiege,* with acc. אֶל, עַל.—III. *to press upon, beset, assail.*—IV. with acc. and לְ *to press* or *thrust forward, to cause to advance,*

[a] Je. 14. 2. [b] Je. 46. 12. [c] Je. 27. 4. [d] Nu. 27. 19. [e] Ge. 45. 19. [f] Le. 25. 21. [g] Ju. 13. 14. [h] De. 18. 20. [i] Jos. 1. 16. [k] Est. 4. 16. [l] Ec. 2. 6. [m] Pr. 16. 24. [n] Pr. 15. 3. [o] Pr. 31. 27. [p] Ps. 19. 11. [q] Is. 8. 22.

troops against a city, Is. 29. 3; or, *to stir* a city, i. e. *to urge* it to sedition, Ju. 9. 31.—V. *to form, fashion.*

צַוָּר, צַוָּאר (Ne. 3. 5) masc. dec. 2 b (constr. צַוַּאר; pl. צַוָּארִים, constr. צַוְּארֵי, צַוְּארוֹת), *the neck*; sometimes also for the *back*; pl. *necks*, but more frequently in the sense of the singular, *neck.* Chald. id.

צַוְּרֹן masc. dec. 3 c, only pl. Ca. 4. 9, *the neck.*

צוּר masc. dec. 1 a (pl. ־ִים, ־וֹת).—I. *a rock*; metaph. of God, *strength* or *refuge.*—II. *a stone.* —III. *sharp stone* used as a knife, Jos. 5. 2, 3; hence, *an edge* of a sword, Ps. 89. 44.—IV. *form, shape*, Ps. 49. 15.—V. pr. name m. of two persons.

צֹר, צוֹר masc.—I. *a rock*, Eze. 3. 9.—II. *a sharp stone*, Ex. 4. 25.—III. pr. name, *Tyre*, the capital of Phœnicia. Gent. noun, צֹרִי *a Tyrian.*

צוּרָה fem. dec. 10, *form*, Eze. 43. 11.

צוּרִיאֵל (*my rock is God*) pr. name masc. Nu. 3. 35.

צוּרִישַׁדָּי (*my rock is the Almighty*) pr. name of a man, comp. Nu. 1. 6; 2. 12.

צִיר masc. dec. 1 a.—I. *figure, image*, Is. 45. 16. —II. *form, shape*, Ps. 49. 15.

מָצוֹר masc. dec. 3 a (with suff. מְצוֹרֵךְ § 32. rem. 5).—I. *straitness, distress.*—II. *siege.*—III. *mound, bulwark.*—IV. *fortification, fortress.*

מְצוּרָה fem. dec. 10.—I. *mound, entrenchment*, Is. 29. 3.—II. *fortress, fortified city.*

צוּר וְ׳ noun masc. sing. dec. 1 a, also pr. name in compos. (see בַּיִת) . . . צור

צוֹר וְ׳ pr. name of a place . . . . צור

צוֹר[a] [for צֹר] Kal imp. sing. masc. . . צרר

צוּרֵי[b] noun masc. pl. constr. from צוּר dec. 1 a צור

צוּרִי id. sing. with suff. 1 pers. sing. . . צור

צוּרִי[c] Kal imp. sing. masc. . . . צור

צוּרִיאֵל, צוּרִישַׁדָּי pr. names masc. . . . צור

צַוָּרָם[d] defect. for צַוָּארָם (q. v.) . . . צור

צוּרָם noun masc. sing., suff. 3 pers. pl. masc. from צוּר dec. 1 a . . . . . צור

צוֹרֵף Kal part. act. sing. masc. dec. 7 b . צרף

צוֹרְפִים[e] id. pl., abs. st. . . . . . צרף

צוֹרְפָם[f] id. sing., suff. 3 pers. pl. masc. . . צרף

צוֹרְרַי, צוֹרְרַי[g] Kal part. act. pl. masc., suff. 1 pers. sing. from צֹרֵר dec. 7 b . . . צרר

צוֹרְרִי[h] id. sing., suff. 1 pers. sing. . . . צרר

צוֹרְרָיו[i] id. pl., suff. 3 pers. sing. masc. . . צרר

צוֹרְרֶיךָ id. pl., suff. 2 pers. sing. masc. . . צרר

צוּרַת[k] noun fem. sing., constr. of [צוּרָה] dec. 10 צור

צוּרָתוֹ[l] id., suff. 3 pers. sing. masc. . . . צור

צוּרֹתָו[m] id. pl., suff. 3 pers. sing. masc., K. ־ָיו׳ . צור

צוּת. Hiph. הֵצִית *to set on fire, kindle*, Is. 27. 4.

צִוְּתָה[n] the foll. with suff. 3 pers. sing. f. (§ 24. r. 21) צוה

צִוְּתָה[o] Piel pret. 3 pers. sing. fem. . . . צוה

צַוֹּתוֹ[p] id. inf. (צַוֹּת), suff. 3 pers. sing. masc. d. 1 b צוה

צַח adj. masc. sing. . . . . צחח

צִחָא pr. name masc. . . . . . צחה

צָחָה Root not used; Chald. *to thirst, be dry.*

צִחָא (*dryness*) pr. name of a man. Also

צִחֵה adj. masc. [constr. of צָחֶה dec. 9 a] *dry*, sc. from thirst, Is. 5. 13 . . . צחה

צַחוּ[q] Kal pret. 3 pers. pl. (dag. forte impl. in ח) צחח

צַחוֹת[r] adj. pl. fem. from צַח masc. (§ 37. rem. 7) צחח

[צָחַח] *to be bright, white*, La. 4. 7.

צַח masc. adj.—I. *bright, white*, Ca. 5. 10.—II. *bright, serene*; metaph. *clear, plain*, Is. 32. 4.

צְחִיחַ masc. *dry, parched.*

צְחִיחָה fem. *dry, parched land*, Ps. 68. 7.

צְחִיחִי masc. pl. צְחִיחִיִּים *dry places*, Ne. 4. 7.

צַחְצָחוֹת fem. pl. id. Is. 58. 11.

צְחִיחַ[s] noun masc. sing. . . . . צחח

צְחִיחָה[t] noun fem. sing. . . . . . צחח

צָחַן Root not used; prob. *to be foul, stinking* (cogn. זָנַח). Syr. *to be filthy.*

צַחֲנָה fem. dec. 10, *stench*, Joel 2. 20.

צַחֲנָתוֹ[u] noun fem. s., suff. 3 pers. s. m. [fr. צַחֲנָה] צחן

[צָחַק] fut. יִצְחַק *to laugh*, with לְ at any one. Pi. I. *to play, sport, jest.*—II. *to laugh, mock at, insult*, with בְּ Ge. 39. 14, 17.

צְחֹק m. *laughter, ridicule*, Ge. 21. 6; Eze. 23. 32.

יִצְחָק (*laughter*, or *he laughs*) pr. name, *Isaac*, the patriarch, son of Abraham and Sarah; sometimes written יִשְׂחָק.

צְחֹק[x] noun masc. sing. . . . . . צחק

צָחֲקָה[y] Kal pret. 3 pers. sing. fem. . . . צחק

צָחָקְתְּ[z] id. pret. 2 pers. sing. f. [for צָחַקְתְּ § 8. r. 7] צחק

צָחָקְתִּי[a] id. pret. 1 pers. sing. . . . צחק

צַחַר [for צֹחַר] masc. *whiteness*, Eze. 27. 18. Hence the two following.

[a] Is. 8. 16. [b] 1 Sa. 24. 3. [c] Is. 21. 2. [d] Ne. 3. 5. [e] Ne. 3. 8. [f] Je. 9. 6. [g] Ps. 31. 12. [h] Ps. 7. 5. [i] Ps. 10. 5. [k] Eze. 43. 11. [l] Eze. 43. 11. [m] Eze. 43. 11. [n] Ru. 3. 6. [o] Est. 4. 17. [p] Le. 7. 38. [q] La. 4. 7. [r] Is. 32. 4. [s] Eze. 24. 7, 8. [t] Ps. 68. 7. [u] Joel 2. 20. [x] Ge. 21. 6. [y] Ge. 18. 13. [z] Ge. 18. 15. [a] Ge. 18. 15.

צֹחַר ו' (*whiteness*) pr. name masc. of several persons, espec. of a son of Simeon, called also זֶרַח comp. Nu. 26. 13, with Ge. 46. 12 . צחר

צְחֹרוֹת adj. fem. pl. [of צְחֹרָה from צָחֹר masc.] *white*, Ju. 5. 10 . . . . צחר

צִי[a] ו noun masc. sing., pl. צִים & צִיִּים . ציה

צִיבָא ו' pr. name masc. . . . . נצב

צַיִד / צֵיד } noun masc. sing. dec. 6h (comp. § 35. rem. 2) . . } צוד

צֵיד[b] id., constr. st. . צוד

צֵידָה[c] Kh. צֵידָה q. v., K. צַיִד (q. v.) . . צוד

צֵידָה ו'[d] noun fem. sing. . . . צוד

צֵידָהּ[e] noun masc. s., suff. 3 pers. s. f. fr. צַיִד d. 6h צוד

צֵידוֹ id. with suff. 3 pers. sing. masc. . . צוד

צִידוֹן ו' pr. name of a place . . . צוד

צִידוֹנִים ו gent. noun pl. from the preced. . . צוד

צַיָּדִים[f] noun masc., pl. of [צַיָּד] dec. 1b . . צוד

צֵידָם[g] noun masc. s., suff. 3 p. pl. m. fr. צַיִד d. 6h צוד

צִידֹן pr. name of a man and a place . . צוד

צִידֹנִים gent. noun pl. from the preced. . . צוד

צִיָּה Root not used; i. q. Arab. צוה Chald. & Syr. צוא *to dry up*.

צִי masc. (for צִיִּי) pl. צִים & צִיִּים, *a ship*.

צִיָּה fem. dec. 10, *drought*; אֶרֶץ צִיָּה *land of drought*, i. e. *dry land, a desert*.

צָיוֹן masc. *dry, parched land*, Is. 25. 5; 32. 2.

צִיּוֹן (*parched place*; others *citadel*) pr. name, *Zion*, the most southern and highest of the hills on which Jerusalem was built, often put for Jerusalem itself.

צִיִּי masc. (denom. from צִי, צִיָּה *desert*) only pl. צִיִּים *inhabitants of the desert*, men or beasts.

צִיָּה ו'[h] noun fem. sing. dec. 10 . . ציה

צִיּוֹן pr. name of a place . . . ציה

צִיּוּן[i] noun masc. sing. dec. 1b . . . צוה

צִיּוֹנָה pr. name of a place (צִיּוֹן) with parag. ה ציה

צִיחָא ו' pr. name masc., see צְחָא . . צחח

צִיִּים noun masc., pl. of צִיִּי, or (Da. 11. 30) of צִי ציה

צִיִּים[k] ו noun masc., pl. of צִי . . . ציה

צִיֻּנִים[l] noun masc., pl. of צִיּוּן dec. 1b . . צוה

צִיעֹר ו pr. name of a place . . . צער

צִיף Kh. צִיף, K. צוּף, pr. name masc. . צוף

צִיץ ו'[m] noun masc. sing. dec. 1a . . צוץ

צִיצַת[n] noun fem. sing., constr. of [צִיצָה] dec. 10 צוץ

צִיצִת[o] noun fem. sing. . . . . צוץ

צִיקְלַג pr. name of a place, see צִקְלַג.

צִיר Kal not used;—I. Arab. *to go*. Hithp. הִצְטַיֵּר *t*
prepare for a journey, Jos. 9. 4.—II. *to go roun*
revolve; Arab. צאר *to writhe with pain* (Gesenius)
only in the following deriv.

צִיר[p] ו' masc. dec. 1 a.—I. *hinge* of a door, Pr. 26. 14.—II. pl. *writhings, pains, pangs*.—III. *messenger* . . . . יר

צִירָהּ[q] id., suff. 3 pers. sing. fem. . . יר

צִירַי[r] id. pl., suff. 1 pers. sing. . . . יר

צִירַיִךְ[s] id. pl., suff. 2 pers. sing. fem. . . יר

צִירִים id. pl., abs. st. . . . . יר

צִירִים[t] noun masc., pl. of [צִיר] dec. 1 a . ור

צִירָם[u] ו id. sing., suff. 3 pers. pl. masc. (Kh. צִירָם; K. צוּרָם (q. v.) . . . . ור

צֵל noun masc. sing. dec. 8 b . . . לל

צְלָא Ch. only Pa. *to pray*, Da. 6. 11; Ezr. 6. 10.

[צָלָה] *to roast*.

צָלִי masc. dec. 3 a, *roasted, a roast*.

צִלָּה ו' pr. name fem. . . . . לל

צִלָּהּ noun masc. sing., suff. 3 pers. sing. fem. from צֵל dec. 8 b . . . . לל

צְלוֹל[v] Kh. צְלוּל, K. צְלִיל noun masc. sing. . לל

[צָלַח] fut. יִצְלַח.—I. *to pass over* or *cross* a river, 2 S
19. 18.—II. *to come, fall* or *descend upon*, wi
עַל, אֶל.—III. *to advance, flourish, prosper*.—I
to be fit for any thing, with לְ. Hiph. I. *to cau*
or *make to prosper*.—II. *to accomplish prosperous*
successfully.—III. *to have success, be prosperous*.

צְלַח Ch. Aph. I. *to prosper, promote*, Da. 3. 3
to accomplish prosperously, Ezr. 6. 14.—II. *to pro*
per, be promoted, Da. 6. 29; *to be prosperous, su*
cessful, Ezr. 5. 8.

צַלַּחַת, צְלֹחִית, צְלֹחָה fem. *dish, bowl*.

צְלַח[y] Kal imp. sing. masc. . . . לח

צָלְחָה[z] / צָלֵחָה[a] ו } Kal pret. 3 pers. sing. fem. (§ 8. rem. 1 & 7) . . . } לח

צָלְחוּ[b] ו id. pret. 3 pers. pl. . . . לח

צְלֹחִית[c] noun fem. sing. . . . . לח

צָלִי[d] adj. masc. sing. (comp. § 37. No. 4) dec. 3a לה

צְלִי[e] id., constr. st. . . . . לה

צִלֵּךְ[f] noun masc. sing., suff. 2 pers. sing. fem. from צֵל dec. 8 b . . . לל

צִלְּךָ[g] id. with suff. 2 pers. sing. masc. . . לל

---

[a] Is. 33. 21. [b] Le. 17. 13. [c] Ge. 27. 3. [d] 1 Sa. 22. 10.
[e] Ps. 132. 15. [f] Je. 16. 16. [g] Jos. 9. 5. [h] Is. 35. 1.
[i] Eze. 39. 15. [k] Nu. 24. 24. [l] Je. 31. 21. [m] Is. 28. 1.
[n] Is. 28. 4. [o] Nu. 15. 38. [p] Pr. 25. 13.
[q] Pr. 26. 14. [r] Da. 10. 16. [s] Is. 57. 9.
[t] Is. 45. 16. [u] Ps. 49. 15. [v] Ju. 7. 13.
[y] Ps. 45. 5. [z] Je. 12. 1. [a] 1 Sa. 10. 6.
[b] 2 Sa. 19. 18. [c] 2 Ki. 2. 20. [d] Is. 44. 16.
[e] Ex. 12. 8, 9 [f] Is. 16. 3. [g] Ps. 121. 5.

[צָלַל] I. *to tingle*, of the ears; trop. of the lips, *to quiver*, Hab. 3. 16. Hiph. *to tingle*, 1 Sa. 3. 11.—II. Kal *to roll* or *tumble down*, i. e. *sink*, Ex. 15. 10. —III. Kal *to be shaded, dark*, Ne. 13. 19. Hiph. *to shadow*, Eze. 31. 3.

צְלוּל masc. *a cake*, Ju. 7. 13 (Keri צְלִיל) from its *roundness*, comp. R. No. II.

צֶלֶל masc. dec. 6 b, *shade, shadow*.

צֵל m. d. 8 b, *shade, shadow*; metaph. *covering, shelter*; hence *protection, defence*.

צִלָּה (*shade*) pr. name of a wife of Lamech, Ge. 4. 19, 22, 23.

צִלְּתַי (for צִלַּת יָהּ *shadow of the Lord*) pr. name of two men, 1 Ch. 8. 20; 12. 20.

צְלָצַל m. (constr. צִלְצַל).—I. *rattling, rustling*, Is. 18. 1.—II. *fishing instrument, harpoon*, Job 40. 31. —III. pl. צֶלְצְלִים, constr. צִלְצְלֵי (comp. dec. 8, § 36. rem. 5, & dec. 4) *cymbals*.—IV. a species of *locust*, De. 28. 42; others, *crickets*.

מְצִלָּה fem. only pl. מְצִלּוֹת *bells*, Zec. 14. 20.

מְצֻלָּה fem. *a shady place*, Zec. 1. 8.

מְצֵלֶת fem. (§ 39. No. 4. rem. 1) dual מְצִלְתַּיִם dec. 13 b, *cymbals*.

צַלְמָוֶת masc. *shadow of death*, poet. for *thick darkness*.

צַלְמֻנָּע (*shade withheld* from him) pr. name of a prince of Midian.

צֶלְצַח (*shade from the sun*) pr. name of a place in Benjamin, 1 Sa. 10. 2.

צְלֶלְפּוֹנִי (*shade turned towards me*) pr. name masc. 1 Ch. 4. 3.

בְּצַלְאֵל (*in the shadow of God*) pr. name masc. *Bezaleel*.—I. a famous artificer appointed by God to the work of the tabernacle.—II. Ezr. 10. 30.

צָלֲלוּ[a] צָלְלוּ } Kal pret. 3 pers. pl. . . . . צלל

צִלְלוֹ[b] noun masc. sing., suff. 3 pers. sing. masc. from [צֶלֶל] dec. 6 b . . . . צלל

צִלְלֵי[c] id. pl., constr. st. . . . . . צלל

צלם Root not used; Arab. *to be obscure, dark*; Syr. *to figure, delineate*.

צֶלֶם masc. dec. 6 a (with suff. צַלְמִי).—I. *shade, shadow*, Ps. 39. 7; metaph. *shadow, illusion*, Ps. 73. 20.—II. *image, likeness*.

צְלֵם, צְלֶם Ch. masc. dec. 3 a, *image, idol*.

צַלְמוֹן (*shady*) pr. name, *Salmon*—I. of a mountain of Ephraim near Shechem.—II. of a man, 2 Sa. 23. 28.—III. *shade, gloom, darkness*, so, according to Kimchi, in Ps. 68. 15, *it shone like snow in darkness*, comp. שָׁלַג.

צַלְמֹנָה (*shady*) pr. name of a station of the Israelites in the desert, Nu. 33. 41.

צְלֵם[d] ו׳ Ch. noun masc. sing. dec. 3 a; וּ bef. (:) צלם

צִלָּם[e] noun masc. sing., suff. 3 pers. pl. masc. from צֵל dec. 8 b . . . . . צלל

צַלְמָא Ch. noun masc. sing., emph. of צְלֵם dec. 3 a צלם

צַלְמוֹן pr. name of a man and a place . . צלם

צַלְמָוֶת ו׳ noun m. s., compnd. of צל & מָוֶת, see under צלל

צַלְמֵי ו׳ noun masc. pl. constr. from צֶלֶם dec. 6 a צלם

צְלָמָיו id. pl., suff. 3 pers. sing. masc. . . צלם

צַלְמֵיכֶם[f] id. pl., suff. 2 pers. pl. masc. . . צלם

צַלְמָם[g] id. sing., suff. 3 pers. pl. masc. . . צלם

צַלְמֻנָּע ו׳ pr. name of a man . . . צלל

צֶלַע[h] ו׳[i] fem. constr. צֵלַע, צֶלַע with suff. צַלְעִי (§ 33. rem. 3).—I. *rib*; pl. צְלָעוֹת *ribs* of a building, *planks for wainscotting*, 1 Ki. 6. 15; 7. 3.—II. *side* of a man, also of inanimate things; pl. צְלָעוֹת, constr. צַלְעוֹת *sides*; pl. צְלָעִים *sides* or *leaves* of a double door.—III. *a side-chamber*; also *a series of side-chambers*.—IV. pr. name of a city in Benjamin where Saul was buried.

צָלַע (denom. from צֶלַע) *to lean on one side*, q. d. *to halt, limp*.

צֶלַע masc. dec. 6 (with suff. צַלְעִי § 35. rem. 5), *a halting, falling*, Ps. 35. 15; 38. 18, and perh. Je. 20. 10.

צֵלַע noun fem., constr. of צֶלַע (q. v.) . . צלע

צֹלֵעַ[k] Kal part. act. sing. masc. . . . צלע

צַלְעוֹ noun fem. sing., suff. 3 pers. sing. masc. from צֶלַע dec. 4 (§ 33. rem. 2) . . צלע

צְלָעוֹת id. pl. fem., abs. st. . . . . צלע

צַלְעוֹת[l] וְ id. pl. fem., constr. st. . . . צלע

צַלְעִי[m] id. sing. with suff. 1 pers. sing. . . צלע

צְלָעִים[n] id. (masc. gen.) with pl. masc. term. . צלע

צַלְעֹת id. pl. fem., constr. st., comp. צַלְעוֹת . צלע

צַלְעֹתָיו id. pl. fem., suff. 3 pers. sing. masc. . צלע

צָלָף (*fracture, wound*) pr. name of a man, Ne. 3. 30.

צְלָפְחָד ו׳ (*first rupture*) pr. name of a man; וּ bef. (:)

צִלְצַל[o] noun m. s., constr. of צְלָצַל (comp. d. 4 & 11 c) צלל

צֶלֶק (*fissure*) pr. n. of one of David's military chiefs.

[a] Ex. 15. 10. [b] Job 40. 22. [c] Je. 6. 4. [d] Da. 3. 19. [e] Nu. 14. 9. [f] Am. 5. 26. [g] Ps. 73. 20. [h] Eze. 41. 6. [i] Jos. 18. 27. [k] Ge. 32. 32. [l] Eze. 41. 26. [m] Je. 20. 10. [n] 1 Ki. 6. 34. [o] Is. 18. 1.

צִלְּתַי ׳ pr. name masc. for צִלְּתַי . . . צלל

צָם Kal part. act. sing. masc. . . . צום

[צָמֵא] fut. יִצְמָא *to thirst*; metaph. *to desire earnestly*.

צָמָא masc. dec. 4 a (§ 33. rem. 2), *thirst*.

צָמֵא masc. dec. 5 a, fem. צְמֵאָה adj. *thirsty*.

צִמְאָה fem. *thirst*, Je. 2. 25.

צִמָּאוֹן masc. *thirsty land*.

צָמָא[a] [b]׳ ׳ noun masc. sing. dec. 4 a (§ 33. rem. 2) צמא

צָמֵא [c]׳ ׳ adj. masc. sing. dec. 5 a . . . צמא

צָמְאָה Kal pret. 3 pers. sing. fem. . . . צמא

[d]צָמְאוּ ׳ id. pret. 3 pers. pl. . . . . . צמא

צִמָּאוֹן ׳ noun masc. sing. . . . . . צמא

צְמֵאִים[e] adj. masc., pl. of צָמֵא dec. 5 a . . . צמא

צְמָאָם[f] noun masc. sing., suff. 3 pers. pl. masc. from צָמָא dec. 4 a . . . . . . צמא

צָמַד. Niph. *to be bound to, joined to*, with לְ. Pu. *to be bound, fastened*, 2 Sa. 20. 8. Hiph. *to contrive, frame*, Ps. 50. 19.

צָמִיד masc. dec. 3 a.—I. *band, bracelet*.—II. *lid* or *cover* of a vessel, Nu. 19. 15. Also the one following.

צֶמֶד ׳ masc. sing. dec. 6 a.—I. *pair, couple, yoke* of oxen, mules, horsemen.—II. a quantity of land ploughed in a day by a pair of oxen, *an acre* . . . . . צמד

[g]צִמְדּוֹ ׳ id., suff. 3 pers. sing. masc. . . . צמד

[h]צִמְדֵּי id. pl., constr. st. . . . . . צמד

צְמָדִים id. pl., abst. st. . . . . . . צמד

צִמּוּקִים[i] noun masc., pl. of [צִמּוּק] dec. 1 b . . צמק

צָמַח[k] fut. יִצְמַח *to shoot, spring, grow up*; metaph. *to spring up, arise, begin*, of events. Pi. *to grow*, of hair. Hiph. *to cause to spring up, make to grow*. Hence

צֶמַח [l]׳ ׳ noun masc. sing. (suff. צִמְחָהּ) dec. 6 a, *a shooting, springing up*.—I. *shoot*.—II. *plant*.—III. *branch* . . . . . צמח

צִמֵּחַ[m] Piel pret. 3 pers. sing. [for צִמַּח § 15. rem. 1] צמח

צִמְחָהּ noun masc. sing., suff. 3 pers. sing. fem. from צֶמַח dec. 6 a (§ 35. rem. 5) . . . צמח

[n]צָמְחוּ ׳ Kal pret. 3 pers. pl. . . . . צמח

צֹמְחוֹת[o] id. part. act. fem. pl. [of צֹמַחַת dec. 13] from צוֹמֵחַ masc. . . . . . צמח

[p]צָמִיד ׳ ׳ noun masc. sing. dec. 3 a . . . צמד

צְמִידִים id. pl., abst. st. . . . . . . צמד

צַמִּים[q] noun masc. sing. . . . . . צמם

צֹמְכֶם[r] noun m. s., suff. 2 pers. pl. m. fr. צוֹם d. 1 a צום

צָמַם Root not used; Arab. صمّ, ضمّ *to braid, plait, bind*.

צַמָּה fem. dec. 10, *a veil*.

צַמִּים masc. *a noose, snare*, Job 18. 9; metaph. *destruction*, Job 5. 5.

צַמְנוּ[s] Kal pret. 1 pers. pl. . . . . . צום

[צָמַק] *to be dried up*, Ho. 9. 14.

צִמּוּק masc. dec. 1 b, *dried grapes* or *raisins*.

צִמֻּקִים [t]׳ ׳ defect. for צִמּוּקִים (q. v.) . . . צמק

צֹמְקִים[u] Kal part. act. masc. pl. [of צָמַק] dec. 7 b . צמק

צֶמֶר [x]׳ ׳ masc. dec. 6 a (with suff. צַמְרִי), *wool*; also *woollen garments*, Eze. 34. 3; 44. 17. R. צָמַר perh. i. q. סָמַר *to stand out, bristle up*.

צַמֶּרֶת fem. dec. 13 a (with suff. צַמַּרְתּוֹ), *foliage*.

צְמָרִי pr. name of a Canaanitish tribe, Ge. 10. 18.

צְמָרַיִם (*two hills?*) pr. name of a city in the tribe of Benjamin, Jos. 18. 22; hence הַר צ׳ in the mountains of Ephraim, 2 Ch. 13. 4.

צֶמֶר[y] noun masc. sing. dec. 6 a (for צֶמֶר § 35. r. 2) צמר

צַמְרִי[z] id. with suff. 1 pers. sing. . . . צמר

צְמָרַיִם ׳ו pr. name of a place; ו bef. (:) . . צמר

צַמֶּרֶת[a] noun fem. sing. dec. 13 a . . . צמר

צַמַּרְתּוֹ[b] id., suff. 3 pers. sing. masc. . . . צמר

צַמַּרְתָּם[c] id., suff. 3 pers. pl. masc. . . . צמר

[צָמַת] *to cut off, destroy*, La. 3. 53. Niph. *to be cut off to perish*. Pi. Ps. 119. 139. Hiph., & Pilp. Ps. 88. 17 *to cut off, destroy*.

צְמִיתֻת fem. *cutting off, extinction*, hence לִצְמִיתֻת *until extinction*, i. e. so long as the thing lasts, i. e. *for ever*, Le. 25. 23, 30 (Gesenius). Others, *absolutely, entirely*.

[d]צָמִת ׳ Kal pret. 2 pers. sing. fem. (§ 23. rem. 11) צמא

צַמְתֶּ[e] Kal pret. 2 pers. sing. masc. . . . צום

צָמְתוּ[f] Kal pret. 3 pers. pl. . . . . צמת

צָמִתִי[g] Kal pret. 1 pers. sing. (§ 23. rem. 10) צמא

צַמְתִּי[h] Kal pret. 1 pers. sing. . . . . צום

צַמָּתֵךְ[i] noun fem. s., suff. 2 p. s. fem. fr. [צַמָּה] d. 10 צמם

צַמְתֶּם[k] Kal pret. 2 pers. pl. masc. . . . צום

צַמְתֻּנִי[l] id. id. with suff. 1 pers. sing. . . . צום

צִמְּתֻתוּנִי[m] [reduplicated for צִמְּתוּנִי] Piel pret. 3 pers. pl., suff. 1 pers. sing. . . . . צמת

צִמְּתָתְנִי[n] Piel pret. 3 pers. s. fem. [צִמְּתָה], suff. 1 p. s. צמת

---

[a] Am. 8. 11. [b] Eze. 19. 13. [c] 2 Sa. 17. 29. [d] Is. 48. 21. [e] Ps. 107. 5. [f] Ps. 104. 11. [g] Je. 51. 23. [h] Is. 5. 10. [i] 2 Sa. 16. 1. [k] Le. 13. 37. [l] Ge. 19. 25. [m] Eze. 16. 7. [n] Is. 44. 4. [o] Ge. 41. 6, 23. [p] Nu. 19. 15; 31, 50. [q] Job 5. 5; 18. 9. [r] Is. 58. 3. [s] Is. 58. 3. [t] 1 Ch. 12. 40. [u] Ho. 9. 14. [x] Eze. 27. 18. [y] 2 Ki. 3. 4. [z] Ho. 2. 7, 11. [a] Eze. 17. 3. [b] Eze. 31. 3, 10. [c] Eze. 31. 14. [d] Ru. 2. 9. [e] 2 Sa. 12. 21. [f] La. 3. 53. [g] Ju. 4. 19. [h] 2 Sa. 12. 22. [i] Is. 47. 2. [k] Zec. 7. 5. [l] Zec. 7. 5. [m] Ps. 88. 17. [n] Ps. 119. 139.

צִן pr. name of the desert between Palestine and Idumea, with ה parag. צִנָה.

[צֹנֶא] com. d. 7 b, & צֹנֶה i. q. צֹאן *flocks*, Nu. 32. 24; Ps. 8. 8.

צִנָה pr. name (צִן q. v.) with parag. ה.

צִנָּה וְ' noun fem. sing. dec. 10 . . . צנן

צֹנֶה[a] noun com. sing., see . . . . צנא

צְנוּעִים[b] Kal part. pass. masc. pl. [of צָנוּעַ] dec. 3 a צנע

צָנוֹף[c] Kal inf. abs. . . . . . צנף

צָנוֹף[d] וְ Kh. צָנוּף, K. צָנִיף, noun masc. sing. constr. [of צָנוּף or צָנִיף dec. 3 a] . . . צנף

צִנּוֹרֶיךָ[e] noun m. pl., suff. 2 pers. s. m. fr. צִנּוֹר d. 1 b צנר

צִנּוֹת[f] noun fem., pl. of צִנָּה dec. 10 . . צנן

[צָנַח] I. *to alight*, Jos. 15. 18; Ju. 1. 14.—II. *to go down*, i. e. penetrate, Ju. 4. 21.

צִנִּים[g] noun masc., pl. of [צֵן] dec. 8 b . . צנן

צָנִיף[h] וְ'[i] noun masc. sing. dec. 3 a . . צנף

צָנַם prob. *to be hard*, *dry*, only in the foll. form.

צְנֻמוֹת[k] Kal part. pass. fem. pl. [of צְנוּמָה fr. צָנוּם m.] צנם

צָנַן Root not used; prob.—I. i. q. שָׁנַן *to be sharp*; Chald. צְנַן *to be cold*.—II. i. q. Arab. צאן *to keep*, also *to lay up*, Heb. גָּנַן *to protect*.

צָנִין masc. only pl. צְנִינִים *thorns*.

צֵן masc. only pl. צִנִּים id. Pr. 22. 5; Job 5. 5.

צִנָּה fem. dec. 10.—I. *thorn*; trop. צִנּוֹת *hooks*, *fish-hooks*.—II. *a cooling*, *refreshing*, Pr. 25. 13; Prof. Lee, *a vessel* for containing snow, comp. צִנְצֶנֶת.—III. *a shield*.

צִנְצֶנֶת fem. *urn*, *vase*, Ex. 16. 33; others, *basket*.

צְנָן pr. name of a place, see צַאֲנָן . . . צאן

[צָנַע] i. q. כָּנַע *to be bowed down*, *humble*, *lowly*, cogn. צָנַח, Pr. 11. 2. Hiph. *to act humbly*, Mi. 6. 8.

[צָנַף] *to wind* or *wrap round*.

צְנֵפָה fem. *a winding* or *wrapping round*, Is. 22. 18; Gesenius, *a ball*.

צָנִיף masc. dec. 3 a (pl. צְנִיפוֹת), *turban*.

צָנוּף masc. id. Is. 62. 3, Kh.

מִצְנֶפֶת fem. *turban*, espec. of the high priest.

צְנֵפָה[l] noun fem. sing. . . . . . צנף

צִנְצֶנֶת[m] noun fem. sing. . . . . . צנן

צָנַק Root not used; Samar. *to shut up*.

צִינֹק masc. *fetters*, Arab. זנאק *compedes*, Je. 29. 26 (Prof. Lee); others, *a prison*.

צָנַר Root not used; meaning uncertain.

צִנּוֹר masc. dec. 1 b, *waterfall*, *cataract*.

צַנְתְּרוֹת pl. fem. [constr. of צַנְתָּרוֹת] *pipes*, *tubes*, Zec. 4. 12. Etymology uncertain.

[צָעַד] fut. יִצְעַד.—I. *to step*, *walk*, *advance*; poet. for *to shoot*, Ge. 49. 22.—II. *to pass through*, with acc. Hab. 3. 12. Hiph. *to cause to march*, *to chase*, Job 18. 14.

צַעַד masc. d. 6 d.—I. *a stepping*, *going*, Pr. 30. 29.—II. *step*, *pace*; metaph. *conduct*.

צְעָדָה fem.—I. *a going*, *marching*.—II. pl. צְעָדוֹת *ornamental chains worn at the ankles*, *ankle chains*, Is. 3. 20.

אֶצְעָדָה fem. *bracelet*; pl. אֶצְעָדוֹת.

מִצְעָד masc. dec. 2 b, *step*, *walk*.

צָעַד[n] noun masc. sing. dec. 6 d [for צַעַד § 35. r. 2] צעד

צָעֲדָה[o] Kal pret. 3 pers. sing. fem. . . . צעד

צְעָדָה[p] noun fem. sing. . . . . . צעד

צָעֲדוּ[q] Kal pret. 3 pers. pl. . . . . צעד

צַעֲדוֹ noun m. sing., suff. 3 pers. s. m. fr. צַעַד d. 6 d צעד

צַעֲדֵי[r] id. pl., constr. st. . . . . צעד

צַעֲדִי id. sing., suff. 1 pers. sing. . . . צעד

צְעָדַי id. pl., suff. 1 pers. sing. . . . צעד

צְעָדֶיהָ[s] id. pl., suff. 3 pers. sing. fem. . . צעד

צְעָדָיו[t] id. pl., suff. 3 pers. sing. masc. . . צעד

צְעָדִים[u] id. pl., abs. st. . . . . . צעד

צְעָדֵינוּ[x] id. pl., suff. 1 pers. pl. . . . . צעד

צַעֲדֶךָ[y] id. sing., suff. 2 pers. sing. masc. [for צַעַדְךָ] צעד

[צָעָה] cogn. טָעָה, צָעַן, צָעַד.—I. *to step*, *stride*, Is. 63. 1.—II. *to wander*, *to emigrate*; part. צֹעֶה (*a*) *an exile*; (*b*) *wanderer*, *stranger*, Je. 2. 20; 48. 12. Pi. *to make* or *induce to wander*, *emigrate*, Je. 48. 12.

צֹעָה[z] / צֹעֶה } Kal part. act. sing. fem. and masc. . צעה

צֵעֲהוּ[a] וְ Piel pret. 3 pers. pl. [צֵעוּ], suff. 3 pers. s. m. צעה

צְעוֹרֶיהָ[b] Kh. צְעוֹ', K. צְעִי' adj. pl. masc., suff. 3 pers. sing. fem. from צָעוּר or צָעִיר dec. 3 a . צער

צְעוֹרֵיהֶם[c] Kh. צְעוֹ', K. צְעִי', id. pl., with suff. 3 p. pl. m. צער

צֹעִים[d] Kal part. act. masc., pl. of צֹעֶה dec. 9 a . צעה

צְעִיפָהּ[e] noun m. s., suff. 3 pers. s. fem. fr. צָעִיף d. 3 a צעף

צָעִיר adj. masc. sing. dec. 3 a . . . צער

צָעִירָה pr. name of a place (צָעִיר) with parag. ה צער

צְעִירוֹ[f] adj. m. s., suff. 3 pers. sing. m. fr. צָעִיר d. 3 a צער

---

a Ps. 8. 8. b Pr. 11. 2. c Is. 22. 18. d Is. 62. 3. e Ps. 42. 8. f 2 Ch. 11. 12. g Pr. 22. 5. h Zec. 3. 5. i Job 29. 14. k Ge. 41. 23. l Is. 22. 18. m Ex. 16. 33. n Pr. 30. 29. o Ge. 49. 22. p 2 Sa. 5. 24. q 2 Sa. 6. 13. r Job 18. 7. s Pr. 5. 5. t Job 34. 21. u 2 Sa. 6. 13. x La. 4. 18. y Pr. 4. 12. z Je. 2. 20. a Je. 48. 12. b Je. 48. 4. c Je. 14. 3. d Je. 48. 12. e Ge. 38. 19. f 1 Ki. 16. 34.

צְעִירֵי id. pl., constr. st. . . . . . צער

צְעִירִים[a] id. pl., abs. st. . . . . . צער

[צָעַן] *to wander, remove*, Is. 33. 20.

צַעֲנַנִּים (*wanderings*) pr. name of a city of the Kenites, in the tribe of Naphtali.

צֹעַן pr. name, *Zoan*, an ancient city in Lower Egypt.

צָעַף Root not used; Arab. *to double*.

צָעִיף masc. dec. 3 a, *a veil*.

צֶאֱצָאִים[b] noun masc. pl. [of צֶעֱצַע] dec. 1 b . . צוע

צָעַק fut. יִצְעַק *to cry out*, espec. for help. Pi. *to cry out, exclaim*, 2 Ki. 2. 12. Hiph. *to call together, convoke*. Niph. *to be called*, or *to come, together*.

צְעָקָה fem. dec. 11 c (constr. צַעֲקַת § 42. rem. 1), *a cry* for help.

צָעֹק[c] Kal inf. abs. . . . . . . צעק

צָעֲקָה id. pret. 3 pers. sing. fem. . . . . צעק

צְעָקָה noun fem. sing. dec. 11 c (§ 42. rem. 1) צעק

צָעֲקוּ[d] / צָעֲקוּ } Kal pret. 3 pers. pl. (§ 8. rem. 7) . צעק

צַעֲקִי[e] וְ / צַעֲקִי[f] וּ } id. imp. fem. sing. for the latter form comp. וְצַעֲרָה . . . } צעק

צֹעֲקִים id. part. act. masc. pl. [of צֹעֵק] dec. 7 b צעק

צְעַקְנָה[g] id. imp. pl. fem. . . . . . צעק

צַעֲקַת[h] ו' n. fem. s., constr. of צְעָקָה d. 11 a (§ 42. r. 1) צעק

צֹעֶקֶת[i] Kal part. act. sing. fem. [of צֹעֵק] . . צעק

צַעֲקָתוֹ noun fem. sing., suff. 3 pers. sing. masc. from צְעָקָה dec. 11 c (§ 42. rem. 1) . צעק

צָעַקְתִּי[k] Kal pret. 1 pers. sing. . . . . צעק

צַעֲקָתָם noun fem. sing., suff. 3 pers. pl. masc. from צְעָקָה dec. 11 c (§ 42. rem. 1) . צעק

[צָעַר] *to be small*; metaph. *to be brought low*.

צָעִיר masc. dec. 3 a, fem. צְעִירָה.—I. *small*.—II. *young*.—III. pr. name of a place, 2 Ki. 8. 21.

צְעִירָה fem. dec. 10, *smallness*, sc. in age, *youth*.

צָעוֹר i. q. צָעִיר Je. 14. 3; 48. 4, Kh.

צֹעַר (*smallness*) pr. name, *Zoar*, a town near the Dead Sea.

צוּעָר (*reduced*) pr. name of a man.

צִיעֹר (*smallness*) pr. name of a place of Judah, Jos. 15. 54.

מִצְעָר masc. dec. 2 b, *smallness*, hence—I. *small, little*.—II. *few*, 2 Ch. 24. 24.—III. *short time*, Is. 63. 18.

מִצְעִירָה fem. *very small*, Da. 8. 9.

צֹעַר pr. name of a place . . . . צער

צֹעֲרָה id. with parag. ה . . . . צער

צָפַד *to adhere, cleave*, La. 4. 8.

I. [צָפָה] I. *to look about, keep watch*; part. צוֹפֶה *a watchman*.—II. *to look out for, await*; hence with לְ *to lie in wait for*, Ps. 37. 32.—III. *to watch, observe closely*, with acc., בֵּין, בְּ.—IV. *to look out, select*, Job 15. 22. Pi. I. i. q. Kal No. I.—II. *to look out for, expect* help, with אֶל, בְּ, and abs. Ps. 5. 4.

צְפוֹ (*watch-tower*) pr. name m. Ge. 36. 11, 15, called צְפִי 1 Ch. 1. 36.

צְפִיָּה fem. dec. 10, *watch-tower*, La. 4. 17.

צִפְיוֹן (*expectation*) pr. name m. Ge. 46. 16, for which צְפוֹן Nu. 26. 15, and patronym. צְפוֹנִי ibid.

צָפִית fem. *a watching, watch*, Is. 21. 5.

צְפַת (*watch-tower*) pr. name of a city of Canaan, Ju. 1. 17.

צְפָתָה (id.) pr. name of a valley near Maresha in Judah, 2 Ch. 14. 9.

מִצְפֶּה masc. dec. 9 a.—I. *watch-tower*, Is. 21. 8; 2 Ch. 20. 24.—II. pr. name (*a*) of a town in Judah, Jos. 15. 38; (*b*) in Moab; (*c*) in Gad, Ju. 11. 29; (*d*) in Benjamin, Jos. 18. 26; (*e*) a valley in the region of Lebanon, Jos. 11. 8.

מִצְפָּה (*watch-tower*) pr. name—I. of a town in Gilead, the same as מִצְפֵּה־גִלְעָד.—II. of a town in Benjamin, called מִצְפֶּה Jos. 18. 26.

II. [צָפָה] Pi. צִפָּה *to cover, overlay*, as with wood, metal. Pu. pass.

צִפּוּי masc. *a covering* or *overlaying* of metal.

צֶפֶת fem. *a chapiter, capital* of a column, 2 Ch. 3. 15.

צָפֹה[l] Kal inf. abs. . . . . . . צפה

צַפֵּה[m] Piel imp. sing. masc. . . . . . צפה

צִפָּה ו' id. pret. 3 pers. sing. masc. . . . צפה

צֹפֶה Kal part. act. sing. masc. dec. 9 a . . צפה

צָפוּ[n] Kal pret. 3 pers. pl. . . . . צוף

צָפוּי[o] וְ Kal part. pass. sing. masc. (§ 24. rem. 4) צפה

צְפוֹ pr. name masc. . . . . . . צפה

צֹפָיו[p] Kal part. act. pl. masc., suff. 3 pers. sing. masc. from צֹפֶה dec. 10 . . צפה

צִפּוּי[q] ו' noun masc. sing. . . . . . צפה

צָפוֹן ו' noun masc. sing. dec. 3 a, also pr. name צפן

צְפוֹן pr. name, see צִפְיוֹן R. צפה, & בַּעַל צְפוֹן R. בעל.

[a] Job 30. 1. [b] 2 Ch. 3. 10. [c] Ex. 22. 22. [d] 2 Ki. 4. 40. [e] Je. 22. 20. [f] Je. 22. 20. [g] Je. 49. 3. [h] Job 34. 28. [i] 2 Ki. 8. 5. [k] Ps. 88. 2. [l] Is. 21. 5. [m] Na. 2. 2. [n] La. 3. 54. [o] Job 15. 22. [p] Is. 56. 10. [q] Ex. 38. 17, 19.

[a] צָפוּן וְ Kal part. pass. sing. masc. dec. 3 a . . צפן
צָפ֫וֹנָה וְ׳ noun masc. sing. (צָפוֹן) with parag. ה — צפן
[b] צְפוּנָה Kal part. pass. sing., fem. of צָפוּן . . צפן
[c] צְפוּנַי id. m. with suff. 1 pers. sing. fr. צָפוּן d. 3 a — צפן
[d] צְפוּנֶיךָ id. pl. masc. with suff. 2 pers. sing. masc. — צפן
[e] צְפוּעֵי Kh. צְפוּ׳, K. צְפִי׳, noun masc. pl. constr. [fr. צָפוּעַ or צָפִיעַ] dec. 3 a . . צפע
[f] צִפּוֹר וְ׳ noun com. sing., pl. צִפֳּרִים (§ 30. rem. 1); also pr. name . . . . צפר

צָפַח Root not used; Arab. *to be spread out.*

צוֹפַח (*cruse*) pr. name masc. 1 Ch. 7. 35, 36.

צַפִּיחִת fem. *a flat cake*, Ex. 16. 31. Also

צַפַּחַת וְ׳ noun fem. *a cruse* or *flask* . . צפח
[g] צַפִּי וְ Piel imp. sing. fem. . . . . צפה
צְפִי, צִפְיוֹן } pr. names masc. . . . . צפה
[h] צֹפַיִךְ the foll. with suff. 2 pers. sing. masc. . צפה
[i] צֹפִים Kal part. act. masc., pl. of צֹפֶה dec. 9 a . צפה
[k] צִפִּינוּ Piel pret. 1 pers. pl. . . . . צפה
[l] צְפִינְךָ וּ Kh. צְפִי׳, K. צְפוּ׳ adj. or Kal part. p. m., with suff. 2 pers. s. m. [fr. צָפִין] or צָפוּן d. 3 a — צפן
[m] צְפִיר וּ׳ noun m. s., constr. of צָפִיר d. 3 a; וּ bef. (:) — צפר
[n] צְפִירֵי [o] וּ׳ id. pl., constr. st.; once Chald. Ezr. 6. 17, [from צְפִיר]; וּ id. . . . צפר
צָפִיתָ וְ Kal pret. 2 pers. sing. masc.; acc. shifted by conv. וְ (comp. § 8. rem. 7) . . צפה

צָפַן[p] fut. יִצְפֹּן.—I. *to hide, conceal.*—II. *to lay, treasure up*; part. pass. *a treasure.*—III. *to keep back, restrain.*—IV. *to lie hid, lurk* in ambush, with לְ. Niph. I. *to be hidden*, with מִן.—II. *to be laid up, destined*, with לְ, Job 15. 20. Hiph. *to hide.*

צָפוֹן com. dec. 3a.—I. *the north*, prop. *hidden, dark quarter*; מִצָּפוֹן לְ, צָפוֹן לְ *on the north of*; צָפוֹנָה, לַצָּפוֹנָה *northward, towards the north*; מִצָּפוֹנָה *on the north side*; מִצָּפוֹנָה לְ *on the north side of* any place.—II. pr. name of a town in Gad, Jos. 13. 27.

צְפוֹנִי adj. masc. *northern*, Joel 2. 20.

צָפִין masc. dec. 3a, *a treasure*, Ps. 17. 14, Kh.

צְפַנְיָה (whom *the Lord has hidden*) pr. name masc.—I. the prophet *Zephaniah.*—II. a priest in the time of Jeremiah, called also צְפַנְיָהוּ.—III. Zec. 6. 10, 14.—IV. 1 Ch. 6. 21, called also אוּרִיאֵל comp. ver. 9.

מַצְפּוּן masc. d. 1 b, only pl. *hidden places*, Ob. 6.

צְפֹן pr. name in compos. בַּעַל צְפוֹן see under — בעל
[q] צְפֹּן וְ Kheth. וְצָפַן q. v., K. יִצְפֹּן Kal fut. 3 p. s. m. — צפן
צְפֹנָה וְ׳[r] defect. for צָפוֹנָה (q. v.) . . צפן
צְפַנְיָה pr. name masc. . . . . . צפן
צֹפְנֶיהָ[s] Kal part. act. pl. masc., suff. 3 pers. sing. [from צֹפֵן] dec. 7 b . . . צפן
צְפַנְיָהוּ pr. name masc., see צְפַנְיָה . . . צפן
צָפַנְתָּ Kal pret. 2 pers. sing. masc. . . . צפן
צָפְנַת פַּעְנֵחַ an Egyptian title given to Joseph, Ge. 41. 45, according to Jablonsky and others, *Saviour of the age.*
צָפַנְתִּי Kal pret. 1 pers. sing. . . . . צפן

צָפַע Root not used; Arab. דפע *to emit, thrust out.*

צָפוּעַ or צָפִיעַ m. d. 3 a, *excrement, dung*, Eze. 4. 15.

צְפִיעָה fem. dec. 10, pl. *shoots*, trop. for *lower offspring*, Is. 22. 24.

צֶפַע masc. *basilisk*, Is. 14. 29. Also

צִפְעֹנִי masc. i. q. צֶפַע *a basilisk* . . . צפע
[t] צִפְעֹנִים id. pl., abs. st. . . . . . צפע

צִפְצֵף only Pilp. (§ 6. rem. 4).—I. *to pip, chirp.*—II. *to speak in a low, whispering voice.*

[u] צַפְצָפָה noun fem. sing. . . . . . צוף

צָפַר only fut. יִצְפֹּר *to turn, return*, Ju. 7. 3. For the derivv. comp. the Arab. I. *to dance, leap, spring.*—II. *to chirp.*—III. i. q. טפר *to scratch* (Gesenius).

צָפִיר masc. dec. 3 a, *goat, he-goat.*

צְפִיר Chald. masc. dec. 1 a, idem. Ezr. 6. 17.

צְפִירָה fem. dec. 10.—I. *crown*, Is. 28. 5.—II. *circle, turn*, Eze. 7. 7, 10; Eng. vers. "morning."

צִפּוֹר com. (pl. צִפֳּרִים § 30. rem. 2).—I. *bird*; espec. *a sparrow.*—II. pr. name of the father of Balak, king of Moab.

צִפַּר Chald. com. dec. 2 a, *bird*; pl. צִפְּרִין, c. צִפְּרֵי, Da. 4. 9, 11, 18, 30.

צִפֹּרָה (*bird*) pr. name of the wife of Moses.

צוֹפַר pr. name of one of Job's friends.

צִפֹּרֶן masc. dec. 6 c.—I. *nail* of the finger, De. 21. 12.—II. *point* of a graver, Je. 17. 1.

צִפֹּר pr. name masc., see צִפּוֹר . . . . צפר
צֹפַר pr. name masc., see צוֹפַר . . . . צפר

[v] צְפַרְדֵּעַ וּ masc. dec. 7 b, *frog*; collect. *frogs.*

צְפַרְדְּעִים id. pl., abs. st. . . . . צפרדע

---

[a] Pr. 13. 22. [b] Ho. 13. 12. [c] Eze. 7. 22. [d] Ps. 83. 4. [e] Eze. 4. 15. [f] Ps. 148. 10. [g] Je. 48. 19. [h] Is. 52. 8. [i] Je. 6. 17. [k] La. 4. 17. [l] Ps. 17. 14. [m] Da. 8. 5, 8. [n] Ezr. 8. 35. [o] 2 Ch. 29. 21. [p] Pr. 27. 16. [q] Pr. 2. 7. [r] Ge. 28. 14. [s] Pr. 27. 16. [t] Je. 8. 17. [u] Eze. 17. 5. [v] Ps. 78. 45.

צִפֹּרָה pr. name fem. . . . . . צפר
צִפְּרֵי[a] Chald. noun com. pl. constr. fr. [צִפַּר] d. 1 b צפר
צִפְּרַיָּא[b] וְ Chald. id., pl. emph. st. . . . צפר
צִפֳּרִים[c] וְ׳ noun com., pl. of צִפּוֹר (§ 30. rem. 1) . צפר
צִפָּרְנֶיהָ[d] noun masc. pl., suff. 3 pers. sing. fem. from
צִפֹּרֶן dec. 6c (§ 35. rem. 16) . . צפר

צָפַת Root not used; Syr. צַפְתָּא *ornament.*
צֶפֶת masc. *chapiter, capital* of a column, 2 Ch. 3. 15.

צְפַת pr. name of a place . . . . צפה
צְפָתָה pr. name of a valley . . . . צפה
צְפָתְךָ[e] noun fem. sing., suff. 2 pers. sing. masc. [from
צָפָה dec. 10, comp. § 30. No. 3] . . צוף
צָץ[f] Kal pret. 3 pers. sing. masc. . . ציץ
צִצִּים [for צִיצִים] noun masc., pl. of צִיץ dec. 1a ציץ
צַק[g] Kal imp. sing. masc. . . . . יצק
צָקוּן[h] Kal pret. 3 p. pl. [צָקוּ] with parag. ן (§ 8. r. 4) יצק

צָקַל Root not used; meaning uncertain.
צִקְלוֹן masc. dec. 1 b, *bag, scrip,* 2 Ki. 4. 42; others, *husk.*

צִקְלַג } pr. name of a city of the Philistines in the
צִקְלָג וְ׳ } territory of Simeon; written also צִיקְלַג.
צַר } adj. or subst. masc. sing. dec. 8. § 37. r. 7 } צרר
צָר } (for this form in Is. 5. 30, see R. צָהַר) }
צֵר pr. name of a place . . . . צרר
צֹר noun masc. sing. (Ex. 4. 25); also pr. name צור

צָרַב Niph. *to be scorched,* Eze. 21. 3. Hence the two following.
צָרֶבֶת [for צָרֶבֶת from צָרֵב masc.] adj. *scorching, burning,* Pr. 16. 27 . . . צרב
צָרֶבֶת fem. *inflammation,* Le. 13. 23, 28 . . צרב

צָרַד Root not used; Arab. *to cool.*
צְרֵדָה (*cooling*) pr. name of a town in the tribe of Manasseh, prob. the same with צְרֵרָה, צָרְתָן.
צְרֵדָתָה id. with parag. ה . . . . צרד

צָרָה Root not used; Arab. צרי *to flow.*
צְרִי, צֳרִי masc.—I. *balsam,* distilling from a tree or shrub growing in Gilead.—II. pr. name, 1 Ch. 25. 3, for יִצְרִי, see יָצַר.
צְרוּיָה, צְרֻיָה (*fragrant*) pr. name of the mother of Joab.

צָרָה[i] Kal pret. 3 pers. sing. fem. [for צָרָה] . צרר
צָרָה וְ׳[k] adj. or subst. fem. sing. dec. 10 [for צָרָּה]
from צַר masc. . . . . . צרר
צְרוּיָה pr. name fem. . . . . . צרה
צָרוּעַ Kal part. pass. sing. masc. . . . צרע
צְרוּעָה pr. name fem. . . . . . צרע
צָרוֹף[l] Kal inf. abs. . . . . . צרף
צָרוּף[m] id. part. sing. masc. . . . . צרף
צָרְופָה[n] id. imp. sing. masc. with parag. ה, צָרְופָה,
K. צָרְפָה (§ 8. rem. 11) . . . צרף
צְרוּפָה id. part. pass. sing. fem. from צָרוּף masc. צרף
צָרוֹר[o] Kal inf. abs. . . . . . צרר
צָרוּר[p] id. part. pass. sing. masc. . . . צרר
צְרוֹר noun masc. sing. dec. 1 a; also pr. name צרר
צְרוּרָה[q] Kal part. pass. sing. fem. from צָרוּר masc. צרר
צָרוֹת וְ׳[pp] noun fem., pl. of צָרָה dec. 10, from צַר
masc. (comp. § 30. No. 3) . . צרר
צָרוֹתָיו id. pl., suff. 3 pers. sing. masc. . . צרר
צָרוֹתָם[r] id. pl., suff. 3 pers. pl. masc. (§ 4. rem. 2) צרר

[צָרַח] *to cry aloud,* Zep. 1. 14. Hiph. *to shout,* Is. 42. 13.
צְרִיחַ masc. dec. 1 a, *tower, watch-tower.*

צֹרֵחַ[s] Kal part. act. sing. masc. . . . צרח
צָרַי וְ׳[t] } the foll. with suff. 1 pers. sing. . . צרר
צָרָי }
צָרֵי noun m. pl. constr. from צַר d. 8 (§ 37. r. 7) צרר
צָרִי[u] id. sing. with suff. 1 pers. sing. . . צרר
צֹרִי gent. noun from צוֹר . . . . צור
צֹרִי[x] וָ } noun masc. sing. (§ 35. rem. 14); for וָ } צרה
צְרִי } see lett. ו . . . . }
צְרִי[y] וּ noun m. s., or pr. name (1 Ch. 25. 3); וּ bef. (:) צרה
צָרֶיהָ[z] noun masc. pl., suff. 3 pers. sing. fem. from
צַר dec. 8 (§ 37. rem. 7) . . . צרר
צִירֶיהָ[a] noun masc. pl., suff. 3 pers. sing. masc. from
צִיר dec. 1 a . . . . ציר
צָרֵיהֶם וְ׳[b] noun masc. pl., suff. 3 pers. pl. masc.
from צַר dec. 8 (§ 37. rem. 7) . . צרר
צָרָיו id. pl. with suff. 3 pers. sing. masc. . צרר
צְרִיחַ[c] noun masc. sing. dec. 1 a . . . צרר
צָרַיִךְ[d] } noun masc. pl., suff. 2 pers. sing. fem. } צרר
צָרָיִךְ[e] } from צַר dec. 8 (§ 37. rem. 7) . }
צָרֶיךָ id. pl. with suff. 2 pers. sing. masc. . צרר
צָרִים[f] id. pl., abs. st. . . . . צרר
צֻרִים noun masc. pl., of צוּר dec. 1 a . צור
צָרֵימוֹ[g] noun masc. pl., suff. 3 pers. pl. masc. from
צַר dec. 8 (§ 37. rem. 7) . . . צרר
צָרֵינוּ id. pl. with suff. 1 pers. pl. . . . צרר

---

a Da. 4. 9, 18. b Da. 4. 11. c Ne. 5. 18. d De. 21. 12. e Eze. 32. 6. f Eze. 7. 10. g 2 Ki. 4. 41. h Is. 26. 16. i Is. 28. 20. k Ps. 78. 49. l Je. 6. 29. m Ps. 12. 7. n Ps. 26. 2. o Nu. 25. 17. p Ho. 13. 12. pp De. 30. 17, 21. q 1 Sa. 25. 29. r Ps. 34. 18. s Zep. 1. 14. t Ps. 119. 157. u Job 16. 9. x Eze. 27. 17. y Ge. 37. 25. z La. 1. 5. a 1 Sa. 4. 19. b Je. 50. 7. c Ju. 9. 46. d La. 2. 17. e Je. 30. 16. f La. 1. 7. g De. 32. 27.

צֹרֶךְ masc. *need, necessity*, only in the following form.

[a] צָרְכֶּךָ noun masc. sing., suff. 2 pers. sing. masc. from [צֹרֶךְ] dec. 6 c . . . צרך

צָרַע only part. pass. צָרוּעַ, and Pu. part. מְצֹרָע *struck with leprosy, leprous*.

צְרוּעָה (*leprous*) pr. name of the mother of Jeroboam, 1 Ki. 11. 26.

צִרְעָה fem. collect. *wasps* or *hornets*. Also the two following.

צָרְעָה 'ו (*smiting, defeat*; Gesenius, *place of hornets*) pr. name of a town of the Danites in Judah. Gent. noun צָרְעָתִי ,צָרְעִי . צרע

צָרַעַת / [b] צָרָעַת 'ו — fem. dec. 13 a [for צָרַעַת, hence with suff. צָרַעְתּוֹ] *leprosy*, of men, houses, garments . . . צרע

[c] **צָרַף** fut. יִצְרֹף.—I. *to refine* metals; part. צֹרֵף *refiner*; also *goldsmith, silversmith*.—II. metaph. *to purify*, Da. 11. 35; part. pass. צָרוּף *purified, pure*.—III. metaph. *to try, prove*.

צֹרְפִי (*goldsmith*) pr. name masc. Ne. 3. 31.

צָרְפַת (*fusion*) pr. name of a town between Tyre and Zidon.

[zz] צֹרֵף 'ו Kal part. act. sing. masc. dec. 7 b . צרף

צָרְפַת pr. name of a place . . . . . צרף

צָרְפָתָה id. with parag. ה . . . . . צרף

[d] צְרָפָתְהוּ Kal pret. 3 pers. sing. fem., suff. 3 pers. s. m. צרף

[e] צְרַפְתִּיךָ id. pret. 1 pers. sing., suff. 2 pers. sing. masc. צרף

[f] צְרַפְתִּים ו id. id., suff. 3 pers. pl. masc.; וּ, for וְ, conv. צרף

[g] צְרַפְתָּנוּ id. pret. 2 pers. sing. masc., suff. 1 pers. pl. צרף

[h] צְרַפְתַּנִי id. id., suff. 1 pers. sing. . . . צרף

צָרַר I. *to tie* or *bind up*; metaph. of the wind, Ho. 4. 19.—II. *to shut up*, 2 Sa. 20. 3.—III. *to be hostile to*; part. צֹרֵר *adversary*.—IV. intrans. *to be straitened, distressed*, only impers. צַר לִי *I am distressed, in a strait; I grieve*; fut. וַיֵּצֶר לִי (§ 18. rem. 6) id. Pu. part. *bound up*. Hiph. הֵצַר, inf. הָצֵר.—I. *to straiten, distress, vex*.—II. *to be distressed, in pains, pangs*, Je. 48. 41; 49. 22.

צַר masc. dec. 8 (§ 37. rem. 7).—I. adj. *strait, narrow*; fem. צָרָה Pr. 23. 27.—II. subst. *adversary, enemy*.—III. subst. *distress, adversity*.—IV. *stone, flint*, Is. 5. 28.

צֵר (*flint*) pr. name of a place in Naphtali, Jos. 19. 35.

צָרָה fem. dec. 10 (for צָרָה, comp. צַר).—I. *female adversary, a rival*, 1 Sa. 1. 6.—II. *distress, adversity*; with ה parag. צָרָתָה.—III. *anguish*.

צְרוֹר masc. (pl. צְרֹרוֹת).—I. *bundle*.—II. *bag, purse*.—III. *a small stone, a grain, kernel*, 2 Sa. 17. 13; Am. 9. 9.—IV. pr. name masc. 1 Sa. 9. 1.

מֵצַר masc. dec. 8 (§ 37. rem. 7; pl. מְצָרִים), *straitness, distress*.

צֹרֵר Kal part. act. sing. masc. dec. 7 b . . צרר

[i] צָרֲרוּ ןְ id. pret. 3 pers. pl. . . . . צרר

[k] צְרָרוּנִי id. id., suff. 1 pers. sing. . . . צרר

[l] צְרֹרוֹת noun m. with pl. fem. term. fr. צְרוֹר dec. 1 a צרר

[m] צֹרְרָי the foll. with suff. 1 pers. sing. . . צרר

[n] צֹרְרֵי 'ו Kal part. act. pl. constr. masc. from צוֹרֵר dec. 7 b . . . . . צרר

צֹרְרֶיךָ id. pl., suff. 2 pers. sing. masc. . . צרר

[o] צֹרְרִים id. pl., abs. st. . . . . . צרר

צְרֻרֹת id. part. pass. fem. pl. of צְרוּרָה fr. צָרוּר masc. צרר

צַרְתָּ ןְ Kal pret. 2 pers. sing. masc.; acc. shifted by conv. ןְ (comp. § 8. rem. 7) . צור

[p] צָרַת noun fem. sing., constr. of צָרָה dec. 10, from צַר masc. . . . . צרר

צֶרֶת 'ו pr. name [for צֹהֶרֶת] . . . צהר

[q] צָרָתָהּ adj. fem. sing., suff. 3 pers. sing. fem. from צָרָה dec. 10, from צַר masc. (§ 30. No. 3) צרר

צָרָתִי noun fem. sing., suff. 1 pers. s. fr. צָרָה d. 10 צרר

צַרְתִּי ןְ Kal pret. 1 pers. sing.; acc. shifted by conv. ןְ (comp. § 8. rem. 7) . . צור

[r] צָרוֹתֵיכֶם ןְ noun fem. pl., suff. 2 pers. pl. masc. from צָרָה dec. 10, from צַר masc. (§ 30. No. 3) צרר

[s] צָרַתְכֶם id. sing., suff. 2 pers. pl. masc. . . צרר

צָרָתָם id. sing., suff. 3 pers. pl. masc. . . צרר

צָרְתָן pr. name of a place, see צְרֵדָה under . צרד

צָרְתָנָה id. with parag. ה.

[t] צַרְתָּנִי Kal pret. 2 pers. sing. masc., suff. 1 pers. sing. צור

ק

[u] קָאָה Kal pret. 3 pers. sing. fem. . . . קוא

[x] קֵאוֹ noun masc. s., suff. 3 p. s. m. fr. [קֵא] d. 1 a קוא

[y] קָאֵם Chald. Peal part. act. sing. masc. dec. 2 b קום

[z] קָאם ןְ Kal pret. 3 pers. s. m. for קָם (§ 21. r. 1) קום

[a] קָאֲמַיָּא Ch. Peal part. act. pl. emph. m. fr. קָאֵם d. 2 b קום

[b] קָאֲמִין ןְ Chald. id. pl. abs.; K. קָיְמִין from קָיֵם . קום

[a] 2 Ch. 2. 15. [b] 2 Ki. 5. 27. [c] Jc. 6. 29. [d] Ps. 105. 19. [e] Is. 48. 10. [f] Zec. 13. 9. [g] Ps. 66. 10. [h] Ps. 17. 3. [i] Nu. 33. 55. [k] Ps. 129. 1, 2. [l] Ge. 42. 35. [m] Ps. 23. 5. [n] Is. 11. 13. [o] Nu. 25. 18. [p] Ge. 42. 21. [q] 1 Sa. 1. 6. [r] 1 Sa. 10. 19. [s] Ju. 10. 14. [t] Ps. 139. 5. [u] Le. 18. 28. [x] Pr. 26. 11. [y] Da. 2. 31. [z] Ho. 10. 14. [zz] Is. 40. 19. [a] Da. 7. 16. [b] Da. 3. 3.

קָאַת noun fem. sing. (constr. קְאַת) . . . קוא

קֹב[a] Kal inf. abs. . . . . . . קבב

[קָבַב] *to curse.* According to the derivv. *to hollow out; to arch, vault,* Arab. id.

קַב masc. *a cab,* a measure containing the sixth part of a סְאָה, 2 Ki. 6. 25.

קֻבָּה fem. dec. 10, *alcove, tent,* Nu. 25. 8.

קָבָה־[b] id. imp. sing. masc. [קֹב] with parag. ה . קבב

קַבֹּה[c] id. pret. 3 pers. s. m. [קַב], suff. 3 p. s. m. קבב

קִבּוּצַיִךְ[d] noun m. pl., suff. 2 pers. s. f. fr. [קִבּוּץ] d. 1 b קבץ

קְבוּצִים[e] Kal part. pass. masc. pl. [of קָבוּץ] dec. 3 a . קבץ

קָבוֹר[f] id. inf. abs. . . . . . . קבר

קָבוּר[g] id. part. pass. sing. masc. dec. 3 a . . קבר

קְבוּרָה[h] noun fem. sing. dec. 10 . . . קבר

קְבוּרַת id., constr. st. . . . . . קבר

קָבַל Kal not used; prob. *to be before, in front;* Arab. *to meet.* Pi. קִבֵּל.—I. *to receive,* sc. a person who comes to meet one, 1 Ch. 12. 18; hence *to receive, accept* instruction, Pr. 19. 20.—II. *to take.*—III. *to undertake,* Est. 9. 23; with עַל *to take upon* oneself, ver. 27. Hiph. *to stand over against each other.*

קַבֵּל Chald. Pa. *to receive.*

קֹבֶל masc. (prop. *something opposed*) poet. for *battering-ram,* Eze. 26. 9. And the foll.

קָבָל Heb. (only 2 Ki. 15. 10) קֳבֵל ,קֳבָל Chald. —I. prep. לָקֳבֵל ,לְקֳבָל (*a*) *over against,* Da. 5. 5; (*b*) *before,* with suff. לָקֳבְלָךְ; and without ל 2 Ki. 15. 10, *in the presence of;* (*c*) *on account, because of,* Da. 5. 1; Ezr. 4. 16; (*d*) with דִּי, conj. *because that,* Ezr. 6. 13.—II. כָּל־קֳבֵל־דְּנָה conj. lit. *wholly on account of this,* i. e. *for this cause;* כָּל־קֳבֵל דִּי, *because that, since.*

קַבֵּל[i] [k] וְ' Chald. Peal 3 p. s. m.; Heb. Piel imp. s. m. קבל

קַבֶּל־[l] Piel imp. sing. masc. for קַבֵּל (§ 10. rem. 4) קבל

קִבֵּל[m] וְ' id. pret. 3 pers. sing. masc. . . קבל

קִבְּלוּ[n] וְ'} id. pret. 3 pers. pl. . . . קבל
קִבְּלוּ[o] וְ'}

קָבְלוֹ[p] noun masc. sing., suff. 3 pers. s. m. [fr. קֹבֶל].

A composite sheva to be followed by dag. forte, as is the case in this word and in קָטֳנִּי, is contrary to the principles of Heb. syllabication; and since the copies vary in both these instances, the forms קָבְלוֹ, קָבֳלוֹ ,קָטְנִי or קָטֳנִי are to be preferred, comp. § 35. rem. 8, & § 37. No. 3 . קבל

קָבְנוֹ[q] וְ Kal imp. sing. masc. [קֹב] with epenth. נ and suff. 3 pers. sing. masc. (§ 16. r. 13) קבב

קָבַע[r] וְ fut. יִקְבַּע. (Arab. *to cover, hide;* hence) *to defraud, rob.*

קוֹבַע m. (constr. קוֹבַע, comp. § 31. r. 5) *helmet.*

קֻבַּעַת fem. *cup, goblet,* Is. 51. 17, 22.

קֹבְעֵיהֶם[s] the foll. with suff. 3 pers. pl. masc. . קבע

קֹבְעִים[t] Kal part. act. masc. pl. [of קֹבֵעַ] dec. 7 b . קבע

קְבַעֲנוּךָ[u] id. pret. 1 pers. pl., with suff. 1 pers. pl. קבע

קֻבַּעַת[w] noun fem. sing. . . . . קבע

קָבַץ[y] fut. יִקְבֹּץ.—I. *to collect, gather.*—II. *to gather together, assemble.* Niph. pass. Pi. I. *to take into* one's arms, Is. 40. 11.—II. *to collect, gather.*—III. *to gather together, assemble.*—IV. *to gather to oneself, draw in,* Joel 2. 6; Na. 2. 11. Pu. pass. Hithp. reflex.

קִבּוּץ masc. dec. 1 b, *company, troop,* Is. 57. 13.

קְבֻצָה fem. dec. 10, *collection, heap,* Eze. 22. 20.

קִבְצַיִם (*two heaps*) pr. n. of a town in Ephraim, Jos. 21. 22.

קַבְצְאֵל ,יְקַבְצְאֵל (which *God shall gather*) pr. name of a town in Judea.

קַבֵּץ[z] Piel inf. constr. for abs. . . . קבץ

קְבֹץ[a] Kal imp. sing. masc. . . . . קבץ

קֹבֵץ[b] [c] וְ' id. part. act. sing. masc. . . . קבץ

קַבְצְאֵל pr. name masc., see יְקַבְצְאֵל (q. v.) . קבץ

קִבְּצָה[d] Piel pret. 3 pers. s. f. [for קִבְּצָה as if fr. a s. קָבֵץ comp. § 10. r. 1, & § 8. r. 1 & 7] קבץ

קִבְּצוּ id. pret. 3 pers. pl. . . . . קבץ

קִבְצוּ[e] וְ' Kal imp. pl. masc. . . . . קבץ

קַבְּצִי[f] Piel inf. (קַבֵּץ), suff. 1 pers. sing. dec. 7 b קבץ

קִבְצַיִם pr. name of a place . . . . קבץ

קִבֶּצְךָ[g] וְ Piel pret. 3 p. s. m. [קִבֵּץ], suff. 2 p. s. m. קבץ

קִבְּצָם} id. id., suff. 3 pers. pl. masc. & fem. . קבץ
קִבְּצָן[h]}

קַבְּצֵנוּ וְ id. imp. sing. masc. [קַבֵּץ], suff. 1 pers. pl. קבץ

קְבֻצַת[i] noun fem. sing., constr. of [קְבוּצָה] dec. 10 קבץ

קִבַּצְתִּי וְ Piel pret. 1 p. s.; acc. shifted by conv. וְ (§ 8. r. 7) קבץ

קִבַּצְתִּים וְ id. id., suff. 3 pers. pl. masc. . . קבץ

קָבַר[k] fut. יִקְבֹּר *to bury.* Niph. pass. Pi. *to bury.* Pu. pass. Ge. 25. 10.

קְבוּרָה f. d. 10.—I. *burial.*—II. *burial-place.* Also

[a] Nu. 23. 25. [b] Nu. 22. 11, 17. [c] Nu. 23. 8. [d] Is. 57. 13. [e] Ne. 5. 16. [f] De. 21. 23. [g] 1 Ki. 13. 31. [h] Ec. 6. 3. [i] Da. 6. 1. [k] Pr. 19. 20. [l] 1 Ch. 21. 11. [m] Est. 4. 4; 9. 23. [n] Est. 9. 27. [o] Ezr. 8. 30. [p] Eze. 26. 9. [q] Nu. 23. 13. [r] Pr. 22. 23. [s] Pr. 22. 23. [t] Mal. 3. 8, 9. [u] Mal. 3. 8. [w] Is. 51. 17, 22. [y] 1 Ki. 20. 1. [z] Mi. 2. 12. [a] 1 Ki. 18. 19. [b] Eze. 22. 19. [c] Pr. 13. 11. [d] Mi. 1. 7. [e] 2 Ch. 24. 5. [f] Zep. 3. 20. [g] De. 30. 3. [h] Is. 34. 16. [i] Eze. 22. 20. [k] Ge. 23. 19.

קֶבֶר / קֶ֫בֶר — m. d. 6a (with suff. קִבְרִי, though in pause קָבֶר § 35. rem. 2, & pl. קְבָרִים, ־וֹת).—I. *sepulchre*.—II. קִבְרוֹת הַתַּאֲוָה (*sepulchres of lust*) pr. name of a place in the desert of Sinai . — קבר

קְבֹר[a] וְ Kal imp. sing. masc.; וּ bef. (:) . . — קבר
קֹבֵר[b] id. part. act. sing. masc. dec. 7b . . — קבר
קֻבַּר[c] Pual pret. 3 pers. sing. masc. . . — קבר
קְבָרֻהוּ[d] Kal pret. 3 pers. pl. (קָבְרוּ), suff. 3 pers. s. m. — קבר
קָבְרוֹ id. inf., suff. 3 pers. sing. masc. . . — קבר
קָבְרוּ וְ id. pret. 3 pers. pl. . . . — קבר
קִבְרוֹ noun m. s., suff. 3 pers. sing. m. fr. קֶבֶר d. 6a — קבר
קִבְרוּ[e] Kal imp. pl. masc. . . . — קבר
קְבָרוּהָ[f] וְ id. id., suff. 3 pers. sing. fem. . . — קבר
קְבָרוּם[g] וּ id. pret. 3 p. pl., suff. 3 p. pl. m.; וּ bef. (:) — קבר
קִבְרוֹת noun masc. with pl. fem. term., constr. st. fr. קֶבֶר d. 6a, & pr. name in compos. ק׳ הַתַּאֲוָה — קבר
קִבְרוֹתֶיהָ[i] id. pl., suff. 3 pers. sing. fem. — קבר
קִבְרוֹתֶיךָ[k] id. pl., suff. 2 pers. sing. masc. . . — קבר
קִבְרוֹתֵיכֶם[l] id. pl., suff. 2 pers. pl. masc. . . — קבר
קִבְרֵי id. pl., constr. masc. . . . — קבר
קִבְרִי[m] id. sing., suff. 1 pers. sing. . . . — קבר
קְבָרִים id. pl., abs. masc. . . . — קבר
קְבֻרִים[n] Kal part. pass. masc., pl. of קָבוּר dec. 3a — קבר
קֹבְרִים[o] id. part. act. masc., pl. of קֹבֵר dec. 7b . — קבר
קְבָרֵינוּ[p] noun masc. pl., suff. 1 pers. pl. from קֶבֶר d. 6a — קבר
קִבְרֶךָ[q] id. sing., suff. 2 pers. sing. masc. . — קבר
קְבֻרַת[r] n. f. s., constr. of קְבוּרָה d. 10, comp. קְבוּרַת — קבר
קְבֻרָתָהּ id. with suff. 3 pers. sing. fem. . . — קבר
קִבְרֹתֶיהָ[s] defect. for קִבְרוֹתֶיהָ (q. v.) . . — קבר
קְבֻרָתוֹ[t] noun fem. s., suff. 3 pers. s. m. fr. קְבוּרָה d. 10 — קבר
קְבַרְתּוֹ[u] וְ Kal pret. 2 pers. sing. masc., suff. 3 pers. sing. masc.; וְ, for וְ, conv. . . — קבר
קָבַרְתִּי[w] id. pret. 1 pers. sing. . . . — קבר
קִבְרֹתֶיהָ[y] noun masc., with pl. fem. term. & suff. 3 pers. sing. fem. from קֶבֶר dec. 6a . . — קבר
קִבְרֹתָיו[z] id. pl. with suff. 3 pers. sing. masc. . — קבר
קִבְרֹתֶיךָ[a] id. pl. with suff. 2 pers. sing. masc. . — קבר
קְבַרְתֶּם[b] וּ Kal pret. 2 pers. pl. masc.; וּ, for וְ, conv. — קבר
קְבַרְתַּנִי[c] וּ id. pret. 2 pers. s. m. with suff. 1 p. s.; וּ id. — קבר
קֳבָתָהּ[d] noun fem. s., suff. 3 p. s. f. [fr. קֹבָה for נִקְבָה] — נקב
קַבֹּתוֹ[e] וְ Kal pret. 2 p. s. m. [קַבּוֹתָ], suff. 3 pers. s. m. — קבב

קָדַד only fut. יִקֹּד (§ 18. rem. 14) *to bow the head*, demon. of

קָדְקֹד masc. (with suff. קָדְקֳדוֹ § 36. rem. 6) *crown of the head.*

קִדָּה וְ fem. *cassia*, Ex. 30. 24; Eze. 27. 19.

קְדוּמִים[f] noun masc. pl. . . . . . — קדם
קָדוֹשׁ וְ adj. masc. sing. dec. 3a . . . — קדש
קְדוֹשׁ וּ id., constr. st.; וּ bef. (:) . . — קדש
קְדוֹשׁוֹ[g] וּ id., suff. 3 pers. sing. masc.; וּ id. . — קדש
קְדוֹשִׁים id. pl., abs. st. . . . . — קדש
קְדוֹשְׁכֶם[h] id. sing., suff. 2 pers. pl. masc. . . — קדש

[קָדַח] I. *to kindle*.—II. *to be kindled, to burn.*

קַדַּחַת fem. *burning fever.*

אֶקְדָּח masc. prob. *the carbuncle*, Is. 54. 12.

קָדְחָה Kal pret. 3 pers. sing. fem. . . . — קדח
קֹדְחֵי[i] id. part. act. pl. c. masc. [from קֹדֵחַ] dec. 7b — קדח
קְדַחְתֶּם[k] id. pret. 2 pers. pl. masc. . . — קדח
קָדִים noun masc. sing. . . . . — קדם
קָדִימָה וְ id. with loc. ה . . . . — קדם
קַדִּישׁ[l] וְ Chald. adj. masc. sing. dec. 1a . — קדש
קַדִּישֵׁי[m] Chald. id. pl., constr. st. . . . — קדש
קַדִּישִׁין Chald. id. pl., abs. st. . . . — קדש

קָדַם. Pi. קִדֵּם.—I. *to go before, precede*.—II. *to be beforehand, prevent, anticipate*; hence *to be early*, Ps. 119. 147.—III. *to meet* any one with an offering, for succour, also in a hostile manner. Hiph. I. *to come before, anticipate*, Job 41. 3.—II. *to come upon*, as calamity, Am. 9. 10.

קֶדֶם masc. dec. 6a, strictly *what is before, in front*.—I. adv. *before*, Ps. 139. 5.—II. *the east*; מִקֶּדֶם *on the east*; מִקֶּדֶם לְ *on the east of*.—III. *olden time*; מִקֶּדֶם *of old*; adv. *formerly*.—IV. *beginning*, Pr. 8. 23.

קֵדֶם masc. only with ה loc. קֵדְמָה *eastward.*

קָדִים masc.—I. *the front*, only קָדִימָה *forwards*, Hab. 1. 9.—II. *the east*.—III. *east wind.*

קְדוּמִים masc. pl. *ancients*, Ju. 5. 21.

קֳדָם, קֳדָם Chald. *before*; מִן־קֳדָם *from before, from the presence of, by order of*; with suff. קֳדָמַיִךְ, קֳדָמוֹהִי, קֳדָמֵיהוֹן.

קַדְמָה fem. (constr. קַדְמַת, pl. קַדְמוֹת, no pl. abs.)—I. *beginning, origin*.—II. *former state.*

קַדְמָה Chald. *former time*; מִן־קַדְמַת דְּנָה *aforetime, formerly.*

קֵדְמָה (*eastward*) pr. name masc. Ge. 25. 15.

קִדְמָה fem. only constr. קִדְמַת *eastward of.*

קַדְמוֹן adj. masc. *eastern*, Eze. 47. 8.

קְדֵמוֹת (*origin*) pr. name of a city of Reuben and an adjacent desert.

[a] Ge. 23. 11, 15; 50. 6. [b] 2 Ki. 9. 10. [c] Ge. 25. 10. [d] 2 Ch. 24. 25. [e] Ge. 49. 29. [f] 2 Ki. 9. 34. [g] Eze. 39. 12. [i] Eze. 32. 26. [k] 2 Ch. 34. 28. [l] Eze. 37. 12, 13. [m] Je. 20. 17. [n] Ec. 8. 10. [o] 2 Ki. 13. 21. [p] Ge. 23. 6. [q] Na. 1. 14. [r] Ge. 35. 20. [s] Eze. 32. 25. [t] De. 34. 6. [u] 1 Ki. 2. 31. [w] Ge. 49. 31. [y] Eze. 32. 23. [z] Eze. 32. 22. [a] 2 Ki. 22. 20. [b] 1 Ki. 13. 31. [c] Ge. 47. 30. [d] Nu. 25. 8. [e] Nu. 23. 27. [f] Ju. 5. 21. [g] Is. 10. 17; 49. 7. [h] Is. 43. 15. [i] Is. 50. 11. [k] Je. 17. 4. [l] Da. 4. 10, 20. [m] Da. 7. 18, 27.

קַדְמֹנִי masc. adj.—I. *front, anterior*, Eze. 10. 19; 11. 1. — II. *eastern*. — III. *former, ancient*; pl. קַדְמֹנִים *ancients*; fem. קַדְמֹנִיּוֹת *former things*.—IV. pr. name of a Canaanitish tribe, Ge. 15. 19.

קַדְמַי Chald. masc. dec. 7, *first, former*.

קַדְמִיאֵל (*one in the presence of God*) pr. name of a man.

קֳדָם Chald. (prop. subs. masc.) as a *prep*. dec. 1a קדם

קֶדֶם [cc] וְ׳ noun masc. & *prep*. d. 6a; for וְ see lett. ו קדם

קֵדְמָה [a] defect. for קָדִימָה (q. v.) . . . . קדם

קַדְּמָה [b] Piel imp. sing. masc. [קַדֵּם] with parag. ה קדם

קֵדְמָה וְ׳ noun masc. sing. [קֶדֶם] with loc. ה, also pr. name; for וְ see lett. ו . . . . קדם

קִדְּמוּ Piel pret. 3 pers. pl. . . . . . קדם

קֳדָמוֹהִי, קֳדָמוֹהִי [c] וּ Chald. prep. (קֳדָם, קֳדָם) pl. with suff. 3 pers. sing. masc. dec. 1a; וּ bef. (:) קדם

קִדְּמוּנִי Piel pret. 3 pers. pl., suff. 1 pers. sing. . קדם

קַדְמוֹנִים [d] adj. masc. pl. [of קַדְמוֹנִי] . . . . קדם

קְדֵמוֹת. וּ׳ pr. name of a place; וּ bef. (:) . . . קדם

קָדָמַי, קֳדָמַי Chald. prep. (קֳדָם) pl. with suff. 1 pers. sing. dec. 1 . . . . . קדם

קַדְמָיָא [e] Chald. adj. pl. emph. masc. [fr. קַדְמַי comp. dec. 7 & § 63] . . . . . . קדם

קַדְמִיאֵל pr. name masc. . . . . . קדם

קָדָמַיהּ [f], קֳדָמוֹהּ [g] Chald. prep. (קֳדָם) pl. with suff. 3 pers. sing. fem. dec. 1a . . . . קדם

קֳדָמֵיהוֹן [h] Chald. id. pl., suff. 3 pers. pl. masc. . קדם

קֳדָמָיךְ [i] Chald. id. pl., suff. 2 pers. sing. masc. . קדם

קַדְמָיָתָא [k] Chald. adj. pl. fem. emph. [of קַדְמָאָה dec. 11, from קַדְמַי masc.] . . . . קדם

קַדְמָיְתָא [l] Chald. id. sing., emph. st. . . . . קדם

קֳדָמָךְ [m] Chald. prep. (קֳדָם) pl. with suff. 2 p. s. m. קדם

קַדְמֹנִי defect. for קַדְמוֹנִי (q. v.) . . . . קדם

קַדְמֹנִיּוֹת [n] [o] וְ׳ adj. fem. pl. [of ־נִיָּה, from קַדְמוֹנִי masc.] קדם

קַדְמֹנִים [p] וְ defect. for קַדְמוֹנִים (q. v.) . . . קדם

קַדְמַת [q] Chald. noun f. s. constr. [of קַדְמָה, no pl.] קדם

קִדְמַת noun fem. sing. constr. [of קִדְמָה] as a *prep*. קדם

קַדְמָתָהּ [r] noun fem. sing., suff. 3 pers. sing. fem. [from קַדְמָה, no pl.] . . . . . קדם

קִדַּמְתִּי Piel pret. 1 pers. sing. . . . . קדם

קָדְקֹד [s] וְ׳ noun masc. sing. (§ 36. r. 6, & § 30. r. 2) קדד

קָדְקֳדוֹ, קָדְקֳדוֹ id., suff. 3 pers. sing. masc. . . . קדד

קָדְקֳדֶךָ [u] id., suff. 2 pers. sing. masc. . . . קדד

קָדַר [v] וְ I. *to be turbid*, Job 6. 16.—II. *to be black, dark*. — III. part. act. *mourning*. Hiph. I. *to darken, obscure*, Eze. 32. 7, 8.—II. *to cause to mourn*, Eze. 31. 15. Hithp. *to become darkened*, 1 Ki. 18. 45.

קֵדָר (*dark-skinned*) pr. name of a son of Ishmael; also a tribe descended from him, more fully בְּנֵי קֵדָר.

קִדְרוֹן (*turbid*) pr. name, *Kedron*, a brook between Jerusalem and the mount of Olives.

קַדְרוּת fem. *darkness*, Is. 50. 3.

קְדֹרַנִּית adv. *mournfully*, Mal. 3. 14.

קֵדָר וְ׳ pr. name of a tribe . . . . . קדר

קֹדֵר Kal part. act. sing. masc. dec. 7b . . קדר

קָדְרוּ, קָדָרוּ [y] וְ׳ [x] Kal pret. 3 pers. pl. (§ 8. rem. 7) . קדר

קִדְרוֹן pr. name of a brook . . . . . קדר

קַדְרוּת [a] noun fem. sing. . . . . . קדר

קֹדְרִים [b] וְ Kal part. act. masc., pl. of קֹדֵר dec. 7b קדר

קְדֹרַנִּית [f] adv. after the form אֲחֹרַנִּית . . . קדר

קָדַרְתִּי [c] Kal pret. 1 pers. sing. . . . . קדר

קָדַשׁ [d] וְ, also קָדֵשׁ (Nu. 17. 2) fut. יִקְדַּשׁ.—I. *to be holy*, spoken of a man who devotes himself to God, and thus *separates* himself from the rest of the people, comp. Is. 65. 5; Syr. ܩܕܫ *to separate, devote, consecrate*.—II. *to be sacred*, of things *set apart* for God; also *to be consecrated, rendered sacred*, either by touching sacred things, or by being destined for the sacred worship. Niph. I. *to be rendered holy, consecrated*, Ex. 29. 43.—II. *to be regarded as holy, to be sanctified, reverenced*. Pi. I. *to set apart for sacred use, to consecrate, hallow, sanctify*. —II. *to regard as sacred, to keep holy*.—III. *to hallow, sanctify, reverence*, sc. God.—IV. *to render sacred*, by contact.—V. *to appoint* a fast or religious festival.—VI. *to prepare* by sacred rites; hence, *to purify*. Pu. pass. of Pi. No. I, also II, Is. 13. 3. Hiph. i. q. Pi. Nos. I, II & III. Hithp. I. *to consecrate oneself*; espec. *to prepare oneself before approaching something sacred*; hence, *to purify oneself*.—II. *to sanctify oneself, cause to be reverenced*, Eze. 38. 23. — III. *to be celebrated, kept holy*, Is. 30. 29.

קָדֵשׁ masc.—I. *a male prostitute, sodomite*; fem. קְדֵשָׁה *prostitute, harlot*; prop. one *devoted* to prostitution in honour of idols.—II. קָדֵשׁ, קָ׳ בַּרְנֵעַ pr. name of a city in the desert, south of Palestine, between Idumea and Egypt.

קָדוֹשׁ adj. masc. dec. 3a.—I. *holy*, of God.—II.

[a] Ez. 48. 4, 5, 23. [b] Ps. 17. 13. [c] Da. 7. 13. [cc] Ps. 139. 5. [d] Eze. 38. 17. [e] Da. 7. 24. [f] Da. 7. 7, 8. [ff] Mal. 3. 14. [g] Da. 7. 20. [h] Da. 4. 4. [i] Da. 6. 23. [k] Da. 7. 8. [l] Da. 7. 4. [m] Da. 5. 23. [n] Mal. 3. 4. [o] Is. 43. 18. [p] Job 18. 20. [q] Da. 6. 11. [r] Is. 23. 7. [s] Je. 48. 45. [t] Job 2. 7. [u] De. 28. 35. [x] Mi. 3. 6. [y] Je. 14. 2. [z] Je. 4. 28. [a] Is. 50. 3. [b] Job 5. 11. [c] Je. 8. 21. [d] Ex. 29. 21.

set apart, sacred, holy to God; pl. קְדֹשִׁים (*a*) of God; (*b*) of angels; (*c*) of men, *saints.*

קַדִּישׁ Chald. masc. dec. 1a, *holy,* of God; of angels; of men, *saints.*

קֶדֶשׁ (*sanctuary*) pr. name—I. of a town in Judah, Jos. 15. 23.—II. of another in Naphtali.—III. of a third in Issachar, 1 Ch. 6. 57, called also קִשְׁיוֹן Jos. 19. 20; 21. 28.

קֹדֶשׁ (once קוֹדֶשׁ) masc. dec. 6c (comp. § 35. rem. 8).—I. *holiness.*—II. *that which is holy, sacred, consecrated* to God.—III. *holy place;* קֹדֶשׁ קֳדָשִׁים (*a*) *something most holy;* (*b*) *Holy of Holies,* the place within the vail of the tabernacle.

מִקְדָּשׁ masc. dec. 2b.—I. *any thing sacred,* Nu. 18. 29.—II. *holy place, sanctuary.*—III. *asylum, place of refuge.*

קָדֵשׁ noun masc. sing. dec. 4a . . . קדשׁ
קָדֵשׁ pr. name of a place, and in compos. קָ׳ בַּרְנֵעַ קדשׁ
קָדוֹשׁ adj. masc. sing. dec. 3a . . . . קדשׁ
קַדֵּשׁ[a] / קַדֶּשׁ־[b] } Piel imp. sing. masc. (§ 10. rem. 4) . קדשׁ
קֶדֶשׁ וְ׳ pr. name of a place . . . קדשׁ
קְדוֹשׁ adj. masc. sing., constr. of קָדוֹשׁ dec. 3a . קדשׁ
קִדֵּשׁ[c] וְ׳[d] Piel pret. 3 pers. sing. masc. (§ 10. r. 1) קדשׁ
קֹדֶשׁ וְ׳[e] noun masc. sing. dec. 6c . . . קדשׁ
קֶדְשָׁה pr. name of a place (קֶדֶשׁ) with loc. ה . קדשׁ
קֵדְשָׁה / קֶדְשָׁה } pr. name of a place (קֶדֶשׁ) with loc. ה . קדשׁ
קְדֵשָׁה noun fem. sing., pl. קְדֵשׁוֹת, from קָדֵשׁ masc. קדשׁ
קָדְשׁוּ[f] Kal pret. 3 pers. pl. [for קָדְשׁוּ § 8. r. 1 & 7] קָדֵשׁ
קַדְּשׁוּ[g] / קַדֵּשׁוּ וְ׳[h] } Piel imp. pl. masc. (v. id.) . קדשׁ
קִדְּשׁוֹ[i] וְ id. pret. 3 pers. sing. masc., suff. 3 p. s. m. קדשׁ
קִדְּשׁוּ[k] וְ׳[l] id. pret. 3 pers. pl. . . . קדשׁ
קָדְשׁוֹ noun m. s., suff. 3 pers. s. m. fr. קֹדֶשׁ d. 6c קדשׁ
קָדְשׁוֹ[m] וְ Kh. קָדְשׁוֹ q. v., K. קָדְשֵׁי (q. v.) קדשׁ
קִדְּשׁוּהוּ[n] Piel pret. 3 pers. pl., suff. 3 pers. sing. masc. קדשׁ
קָדָשַׁי[o] / קָדָשַׁי } noun masc. pl., suff. 1 pers. sing. from קֹדֶשׁ dec. 6c . . . . קדשׁ
קָדְשֵׁי[p] וְ׳ id. pl., constr. st. . . . . קדשׁ
קָדְשִׁי id. sing., suff. 1 pers. sing. . . . קדשׁ
קְדֹשִׁי[q] adj. masc. s., suff. 1 pers. s. fr. קָדוֹשׁ d. 3a קדשׁ
קָדְשֵׁיהֶם noun m. pl., suff. 3 p. pl. m. fr. קֹדֶשׁ d. 6c קדשׁ
קֳדָשָׁיו / קֳדָשָׁיו[r] וְ } id. pl. suff. 3 pers. sing. masc. (§ 35. rem. 8) . . . . קדשׁ
קְדֹשָׁיו adj. pl. masc., suff. 3 pers. sing. masc. from קָדוֹשׁ dec. 3a . . . . קדשׁ

קֳדָשֶׁיךָ[s] noun masc. pl., suff. 2 pers. sing. masc. from קֹדֶשׁ dec. 6c (§ 35. rem. 8) . . קדשׁ
קָדְשֵׁיכֶם[t] id. pl., suff. 2 pers. pl. masc. . . קדשׁ
קֳדָשִׁים id. pl., abs. st. (§ 35. rem. 8) . . . קדשׁ
קְדֹשִׁים adj. masc., pl. of קָדוֹשׁ dec. 3a . . קדשׁ
קָדְשְׁךָ / קָדְשֶׁךָ } noun masc. sing., suff. 2 pers. sing. masc. from קֹדֶשׁ dec. 6c . . . קדשׁ
קָדְשֵׁנוּ[u] id. with suff. 1 pers. pl. . . . קדשׁ
קִדַּשְׁתָּ וְ Piel pret. 2 pers. sing. masc.; acc. shifted by conv. וְ (comp. § 8. rem. 7) . . קדשׁ
קִדַּשְׁתּוֹ וְ id. id., suff. 3 pers. sing. masc. . . קדשׁ
קִדַּשְׁתִּי וְ id. pret. 1 pers. sing.; acc. shifted by conv. וְ (comp. § 8. rem. 7) . . קדשׁ
קְדַשְׁתִּיךָ[x] Kal pret. 1 pers. sing., suff. 2 pers. sing. m. קדשׁ
קִדַּשְׁתָּם[y] וְ Piel pret. 2 pers. s. m., suff. 3 pers. pl. m. קדשׁ
קִדַּשְׁתֶּם[z] וְ׳ id. pret. 2 pers. pl. masc. . . קדשׁ

[קָהָה] *to be blunt,* of the teeth, *to be set on edge.* Pi. *to be blunt,* only in the foll. form.

קֵהָה[a] Piel pret. 3 pers. sing. masc. . . . קהה

קָהַל. Hiph. הִקְהִיל *to call together, assemble.* Niph. *to assemble, come together.*

קָהָל masc. dec. 4a.—I. *a meeting.*—II. *congregation, assemblage of persons.*—III. *multitude.*

קְהֵלָתָה (*convocation*) pr. name of a station of the Israelites in the wilderness, Nu. 33. 22.

קְהִלָּה fem. dec. 10, *assembly, congregation.*

קֹהֶלֶת masc. (fem. Ec. 7. 27) *preacher,* properly *convoker;* pr. name applied to Solomon in the book of Ecclesiastes.

מַקְהֵלִים pl. masc. *congregations,* Ps. 26. 12.

מַקְהֵלוֹת pl. fem.—I. *congregations,* Ps. 68. 27.—II. pr. name of a station of the Israelites in the desert, Nu. 33. 25.

קָהָל וְ׳[b] noun masc. sing. dec. 4a . . . קהל
קְהַל וּ׳[c] id., constr. st.; וּ bef. (:) . . . קהל
קְהָלָהּ[d] id. with suff. 3 pers. sing. fem. . . קהל
קְהִלָּה[e] noun fem. sing. dec. 10 . . . קהל
קְהָלַיִךְ[f] noun masc. pl., suff. 2 p. s. m. fr. קָהָל d. 4a קהל
קְהָלֵךְ[g] id. sing., suff. 2 pers. sing. masc. [for קְהָלְךָ] קהל
קְהָלֵךְ[h] id. sing., suff. 2 pers. sing. fem. . . קהל
קְהַלְכֶם[i] id. sing., suff. 2 pers. pl. masc. . . קהל
קְהִלַּת[k] noun fem. sing., constr. of קְהִלָּה dec. 10 קהל
קֹהֶלֶת noun fem. sing. . . . . קהל

[a] Jos. 7. 13. [b] Ex. 13. 2. [c] 1 Ki. 8. 64. [d] Nu. 6. 11. [e] Da. 8. 13. [f] Nu. 17. 2. [g] Eze. 20. 20. [h] 2 Ch. 29. 5. [i] Le. 16. 19. [k] 1 Sa. 7. 1. [l] Mi. 3. 5. [m] 1 Ki. 15. 15. [n] Ne. 3. 1. [o] Eze. 44. 8. [p] 2 Ch. 31. 14. [q] Hab. 1. 12. [r] 2 Ch. 15. 18. [s] De. 12. 26. [t] Eze. 20. 40. [u] Is. 64. 10. [x] Is. 65. 5. [y] Ex. 19. 10. [z] De. 32. 51. [a] Ec. 10. 10. [b] Eze. 26. 7. [c] Ge. 35. 11. [d] Eze. 32. 22, 23. [e] Ne. 5. 7. [f] Eze. 38. 7. [g] Eze. 38. 13. [h] Eze. 27. 27, 34. [i] De. 5. 19. [k] De. 33. 4.

קְהָת, קְהָת ו׳ { (*assembly*; קְהַת i. q. Chald. קְהָא *to assemble*, to which Root יִקְּהַת Ge. 49. 10, has been referred by some) pr. name of a son of Levi. Patronym. קְהָתִי . . . } קהת

תָּקְהַת (*assembly*) pr. n. m. 2 Ch. 34. 22, Keri.

קָו ו׳, קַו } noun masc. sing. dec. 8 (§ 37. No. 4) . קוה

[קוֹא] *to spew out, vomit*, only metaph. for, *to reject*, Le. 18. 28. Hiph. id.

קֵא masc. dec. 1 a, *vomit*, Pr. 26. 11.

קִיא masc. dec. 1 a, idem.

קָיָה (secondary Root) *to vomit*, only Je. 25. 27.

קָאַת fem. with the art. הַקָּאַת, constr. קְאַת (contrary to the analogy of derivv. from ע״ו § 30. No. 2) *the pelican*, so called from its *vomiting* the things which it has too voraciously swallowed (Gesenius).

קוֹבַע[a], קוֹבַע[b] ו׳ } noun masc. sing. (comp. § 31. rem. 5) קבע

קוֹבֵר[c] Kal part. act. sing. masc. dec. 7 b . . קבר

קוֹדֶשׁ[d] fully for קֹדֶשׁ (q. v.) . . . . קדש

[קָוָה] I. *to wait for, hope in*.—II. Arab. *to twist, wind, bind*; hence, *to be strong*, comp. derivv. תִּקְוָה, קַו. Pi. I. *to wait for, confide in*, with אֶל, לְ.—II. *to wait, lie in wait for*, with לְ, acc. Niph. *to gather themselves together*.

קָוֶה or קָוָה masc. *a cord*, only in Kheth. 1 Ki. 7. 23; Je. 31. 39; Zec. 1. 16.

קָו, קַו masc. with suff. קַוָּם (dec. 8).—I. *cord, line*, 1 Ki. 7. 23.—II. *measuring line*.—III. *cord, string*, Ps. 19. 5.—IV. *rule, direction*, Is. 28. 10. —V. *strength, might*, Is. 18. 2, 7, גּוֹי קַו־קָו, *a nation most mighty*, so, those who refer this prophecy to Egypt; others, *a land of rule upon rule*, meaning Judah; Eng. vers. "meted out," comp. No. II.

מִקְוֶה masc. dec. 9 a.—I. *expectation, hope, confidence*.—II. *collection* of waters, of men, or animals, *company, band*, 1 Ki. 10. 28.

מִקְוָה fem. *place of collecting, reservoir*, Is. 22. 11.

תִּקְוָה fem. dec. 10.—I. *cord, line*, Jos. 2. 18, 21. —II. *expectation, hope*.—III. pr. name masc. 2 Ki. 22. 14, for which תָּקְהַת in 2 Ch. 34. 22.

קַוֵּה ו׳ Piel inf. constr. or imp. sing. masc. . קוה

קַוֹּה[e] id. inf. abs. . . . . . קוה

קוּהּ[f] ו׳ Kh. קָוֶה noun masc. sing., K. קָו (q. v.) קוה

קִוּוּ Piel pret. 3 pers. pl. . . . . . קוה

קוֹחַ[g] see פְּקַח־קוֹחַ . . . . . פקח

[קוּט] *to loath, abhor, be grieved with*, with בְּ. Niph. and Hithpal. id.

קְוֵי[h] [for קֹוֵי] the foll. with suff. 1 pers. sing. קוה

קֹוֵי ו Kal part. act. pl. c. masc. [fr. קֹוֶה] d. 9 a קוה

קֹוֶיךָ id. pl., suff. 2 pers. sing. masc. . . קוה

קִוִּינוּ Piel pret. 1 pers. pl. . . . . קוה

קִוִּינוּךָ[i] id. id., suff. 2 pers. sing. masc. . קוה

קִוִּיתִי[k] ו׳, קִוִּיתִי } id. pret. 1 pers. sing. (§ 24. rem. 11) קוה

קִוִּיתִיךָ[l] id. id., suff. 2 pers. sing. masc. . . קוה

קִוִּיתֶם[m] ו id. pret. 2 pers. pl. masc. . . . קוה

קוֹל ו׳, ו״, ו masc. dec. 1 a (pl. וֹת).—I. *voice*.—II. *cry* of animals.—III. *sound, noise*.—IV. *thunder*.—V. *rumour, report*.

קָל Ch. masc. *a voice*.

קוֹלָיָה (*voice of the Lord*) pr. name masc.—I. Je. 29. 21.—II. Ne. 11. 7.

קוֹלָהּ[o] ו׳ id., suff. 3 pers. sing. fem. . . קול

קוֹלוֹ[p] ו׳ id., suff. 3 pers. sing. masc. . . קול

קוֹלוֹת id. pl. fem. . . . . . . קול

קוֹלִי[q] ו׳ id. sing., suff. 1 pers. sing.; or (Ps. 116. 1) with י parag. . . . . . קול

קוֹלָיָה pr. name masc. . . . . . קול

קוֹלֵךְ noun masc. sing., suff. 2 p. s. f. fr. קוֹל d. 1 a קול

קוֹלְךָ, קוֹלֶךָ[r] } id. sing., suff. 2 pers. sing. masc. . . קול

קוֹלְכֶם id. sing., suff. 2 pers. pl. masc. . . קול

קוֹלָם id. sing., suff. 3 pers. pl. masc. . . קול

קוֹלָן id. sing., suff. 3 pers. pl. fem. . . קול

קוֹלֵעַ[s] Kal part. act. sing. masc. . . . קלע

קוּם ו׳ (inf. & imp.) fut. יָקוּם, יָקֻם, ap. וַיָּקָם, יָקֹם; once pret. קָאם.—I. *to rise, arise*, e. g. from bed, a seat; frequently pleonastically וַיָּקָם וַיֵּלֶךְ *and he arose and went*.—II. with עַל, אֶל, בְּ *to rise up against* any one; part. קָמַי, קָמָיו *those that rise up against me, him*.—III. *to rise, appear*, e. g. light. —IV. *to rise, flourish, prosper*, Pr. 28. 12.—V. *to stand, stand firm*; also, *to be fixed*, of the eyes.—VI. *to remain, endure, be established*; hence *to stand good, be valid*. Pi. קִיֵּם.—I. *to strengthen*,

a 1 Sa. 17. 38. b Eze. 23. 24. c Ps. 79. 3. d Da 11. 30. e Ps. 40. 2. f Je. 31. 39. g Is. 61. 1. h Is. 49. 23. i Is. 26. 8. k Is. 5. 4; 8. 17. l Ps. 25. 21. m Je. 13. 16. n Job 4. 16. o 1 Sa. 1. 13. p Eze. 43. 2. q Pr. 8. 4. r Ju. 18. 25. s Je. 10. 18.

Ps. 119. 28; hence *to confirm.*—II. *to enjoin,* with עַל a thing upon any one; קִיֵּם עָלָיו *to take upon oneself.*—III. *to keep, fulfil, perform,* Ps. 119. 106. Pil. קוֹמֵם.—I. *to raise up, restore.*—II. *to rise up,* Mi. 2. 8. Hiph. הֵקִים.—I. *to cause to rise up.*—II. *to raise, lift up.*—III. *to raise, set* or *rear up.*—IV. *to raise up, constitute, appoint.*—V. *to raise up, bring into existence.*—VI. *to cause* or *make to stand.*—VII. *to make to stand still,* Ps. 107. 29.—VIII. *to confirm, establish.*—IX. *to fulfil, perform.* Hoph. pass. of Hiph. Nos. III, IV & VIII. Hithpal. הִתְקוֹמֵם with לְ *to rise up against*; part. *adversary.*

קוּם Chald.—I. *to arise.*—II. *to stand up.*—III. *to stand*; hence *to remain, endure.* Pa. קַיֵּם *to confirm, establish,* Da. 6. 8. Aph. הֲקִים, אֲקִים; fut. יְהָקִים, יְקִים.—I. *to set up, erect.*—II. *to constitute, appoint.* Hoph. *to be made to stand,* Da. 7. 4.

קָמָה fem. dec. 10, *standing corn.*

קָמוֹן (*standing firm*) pr. name of a town in Gilead, Ju. 10. 5.

קוֹמָה fem. dec. 10, *stature, height.*

קוֹמְמִיּוּת adv. *upright, erect,* Le. 26. 13.

קִים masc. dec. 1a, *adversary,* Job 22. 20.

קִימָה fem. dec. 10, *a rising up,* La. 3. 62.

קְיָם Chald. masc. *statute, edict,* Da. 6. 8, 16.

קַיָּם Chald. masc. adj. *enduring, sure.*

יָקִים (*He will establish* him) pr. name masc. of two persons, 1 Ch. 8. 19; 24. 12.

יְקוּם masc. *whatever exists, lives; a being.*

מָקוֹם com. dec. 3a (pl. מְקוֹמוֹת).—I. *place, room, space.*—II. *habitation, abode, home.*—III. *place, town.*

תְּקוּמָה f. *power of standing, resisting,* Le. 26. 37.

תְּקוֹמֵם masc. dec. 7b, *adversary,* Ps. 139. 21.

קָוָם[a] noun masc. sing., suff. 3 pers. pl. masc. from קַו dec. 8 (§ 37. No. 4) . . . . קוה

קוֹם[b] Kal inf. abs. . . . . . . קום

קוֹמָה וְ' noun fem. sing. dec. 10 . . . . קום

קוֹמָה[c] Kh. קוֹמָה q. v., K. קוֹמַת (q. v.) . . . קום

קוֹמָה, קוּמָה[d] וְ' Kal imp. s. m. (קוּם) with parag. ה . קום

קוּמוּ וְ' id. imp. pl. masc. . . . . . . קום

קוּמִי id. imp. sing. fem. & Chald. Da. 7. 5 . . קום

קוּמִי[f] וְ' id. inf. constr., suff. 1 p. s. fr. קוּם d. 1a . קום

קוֹמְמִיּוּת[g] (prop. noun fem. sing.) *adv.* . . . קום

קוֹמַת וְ' noun fem. sing., constr. of קוֹמָה dec. 10 . קום

קוֹמָתָהּ id., suff. 3 pers. sing. fem. . . . . קום

קוֹמָתוֹ id., suff. 3 pers. sing. masc. . . . . קום

קוֹמָתֵךְ[h] id., suff. 2 pers. sing. fem. . . . . קום

I. קוּן. Pil. קוֹנֵן *to utter a lamentation, to lament,* with עַל, אֶל *over* a person or thing.

קִינָה fem. dec. 10 (pl. ־ִים, ־וֹת).—I. *lamentation.*—II. pr. name of a town in Judah, Jos. 15. 22.

II. קוּן Root not used; Arab. קאן *to form, forge*; Heb. also i. q. קָנָה, whence pr. n. קַיִן (*acquisition*) Ge. 4. 1.

קַיִן masc. dec. 6h.—I. *lance, spear,* 2 Sa. 21. 16.—II. pr. name, *Cain,* the son of Adam.—III. pr. name of the tribe of the Kenites.—IV. הַקַּיִן pr. name of a town in Judah, Jos. 15. 57.

קֵינִי, קֵנִי, קִינִי gent. noun, *Kenite, Kenites,* one of the tribes of Canaan.

קֵינָן (*smith*) pr. name masc. Ge. 5. 9; 1 Ch. 1. 2.

קוֹנֶה[i] Kal part. act. sing. masc. dec. 9a . . קנה

קוֹנְנוּ[k] וְ Pilel pret. 3 pers. pl. . . . . קון

קוֹנְנוּהָ[l] וְ id., with suff. 3 pers. sing. fem. . . קון

קוּעַ Root not used; prob. i. q. קוּר *to dig,* cogn. Arab. וקע *to wound, mark, brand*; Talm. קַעְקַע *to cauterize.*

קַעֲקַע masc. *a mark cut into the skin,* Le. 19. 28.

קוֹעַ וְ masc. *prince*; Eze. 23. 23; so Vulg. and others; others again take it as a pr. name.

קוּף Root not used; i. q. נָקַף *to go round.*

קוֹף dec. 1a, *an ape.*

תְּקוּפָה fem. dec. 10.—I. *circuit, orbit* of the sun, Ps. 19. 7.—II. *revolution* of time.

קוֹפִים[m] וְ noun masc., pl. of קוֹף dec. 1a . . קוף

I. קוּץ (inf. does not occur).—I. *to loathe, abhor,* with בְּ.—II. *to fear,* with מִפְּנֵי. Hiph. הֵקִיץ *to put in fear,* i. e. *besiege,* Is. 7. 6.

II. קוּץ i. q. יָקַץ only Hiph. הֵקִיץ.—I. *to awake* from sleep, death.—II. *to awake, arise.*

III. קוּץ Root not used; perh. i. q. קָצַץ *to cut, cut off.*

קוֹץ masc. dec. 1a.—I. *thorn, thorn-bush.*—II. pr. name masc. of several persons.

קְוֻצּוֹת fem. pl. *locks* of hair, so called from being *cut* (Gesenius).

קַיִץ masc. dec. 6h.—I. *fruit-harvest,* q. d. the time for cutting and gathering the fruits, Is. 16. 9; 28. 4.—II. *summer-fruit.*—III. *summer.*

קוּץ (denom. fr. קַיִץ) *to pass the summer,* Is. 18. 6.

קוֹץ[n] וְ' noun masc. sing. dec. 1a, also pr. name . קוֹץ

[a] Ps. 19. 5. [b] Je. 44. 29. [c] Je. 52. 21. [d] Ps. 35. 2. [e] Zep. 3. 8. [f] Ps. 139. 2. [g] Le. 26. 13. [h] Ca. 7. 8. [i] Pr. 15. 32. [k] Eze. 27. 32. [l] Eze. 32. 16. [m] 2 Ch. 9. 21. [n] Is. 32. 13, etc.

קְוֻצּוֹתַי[a] noun fem. pl., suff. 1 pers. s. fr. [קְוֻצָּה] d. 10 קוץ
קְוֻצּוֹתָיו[b] id. pl., suff. 3 pers. sing. masc. . . קוץ
קוֹצֵי[c] } constr. of the foll. . . . } קוץ
קוֹצִים[d] } noun masc. pl. constr.&abs. fr. קוֹץ dec. 1 a }
קוֹצֵר[e] Kal part. act. sing. masc. dec. 7 b . . קצר

[קוּר] *to dig a well*, 2 Ki. 19. 24; Is. 37. 25; Hiph. *to let spring up* water, Je. 6. 7. Pilp. קַרְקַר (§ 6. No. 4).—I. *to dig under* a wall, Is. 22. 5.—II. *to destroy*, Nu. 24. 17.

מָקוֹר masc. dec. 3 a, *spring, fountain.*

קַרְקֹר (*foundation*) pr. name of a place beyond Jordan, Ju. 8. 10.

[קוּר] m. dec. 1 a, *thin thread* of a spider's web, Is. 59. 5, 6.
קוֹרָא[dd] Pual pret. 3 pers. masc. sing. for קֹרָא . קרא
קוֹרֵא וְ' Kal part. act. sing. m. d. 7 b, also pr. name קרא
קוֹרָה[f] noun fem. sing. dec. 10 . . . קרה
קוּרֵי[g] וְ' noun masc. pl. constr. from [קוּר] dec. 1 a קור
קוּרֵיהֶם[h] id. pl., suff. 3 pers. pl. masc. . . קור
קוֹרֵץ[i] Kal part. act. sing. masc. . . קרץ

[קוֹשׁ] *to lay snares*, Is. 29. 21. Arab. *to be curved, bent.*

קוּשָׁיָהוּ (*bow of the Lord*) pr. name masc. 1 Ch. 15. 17; called קִישִׁי in 1 Ch. 6. 29.

קִישׁ (*bow*) pr. name of the father of Saul, and of several other men.

קִישׁוֹן (*winding*) pr. name of a stream near mount Tabor.

קֶשֶׁת com. (with suff. קַשְׁתִּי dec. 13 a; but pl. קְשָׁתוֹת. c. קַשְׁתוֹת, ת treated as if radical).—I. *a bow* for shooting arrows; meton. for *archer.*—II. *rainbow.*

קַשָּׁת masc. *archer*, Ge. 21. 20.

קוֹשׁוּ[k] וְ Kal imp. pl. masc.; for וְ see lett. ו . קשש
קוּשָׁיָהוּ pr. name masc. . . . . קוש
קִוְּתָה[l] Piel pret. 3 pers. sing. fem. . . . קוה
קָח[m] Kal pret. 3 p. s. m. for לָקַח (comp. § 17. r. 8) לקח
קַח[n] } id. imp. sing. masc. . . . . לקח
וְ' קַח }
קְחָה[o] id. id. with parag. ה . . . . לקח
קָחֻהוּ[p] id. imp. pl. masc. (קְחוּ), suff. 3 pers. sing. masc. (§ 16. rem. 11) . . . לקח
קְחוּ[q] } id. imp. pl. masc.; וּ bef. (:) . לקח
וּ' קְחוּ }
קְחִי[r] וּ' id. imp. sing. fem.; וּ id. . . לקח
קַחְתָּם[s] id. inf., or perh. pret. 3 pers. sing. masc. (comp. קָח), suff. 3 pers. pl. masc. . לקח

קָחֶם־[t] id. imp. sing. masc. (קַח), suff. 3 pers. pl. masc. [for קָחֵם; § 16. rem. 11] . לקח
קָחֶנָּה[u] id. id., suff. 3 pers. sing. fem. . . לקח
קָחֶנּוּ[x] וְ' id. id., suff. 3 pers. sing. masc. . לקח
קַחַת } id. inf. constr. . . . . לקח
קַחַת־[y] }
קַחְתִּי[z] id. id. with suff. 1 pers. sing. dec. 13 a . לקח
קַחְתֵּךְ[a] id. id. with suff. 2 pers. sing. fem. . לקח
קָט[b] Kal pret. 3 pers. sing. masc. . . . קוט

קָטַב Root not used; Arab. & Chald. *to cut*, hence, to cut off.

קֹטֶב masc. dec. 6 c, *destruction*, Ho. 13. 14. Also

קֶטֶב[c] } (§ 35. rem. 2) masc.—I. *destruction*, Is. 28. 2.—II. *contagion, pestilence* } קטב
וְ' קֶטֶב[d] }
קָטָבְךָ[e] noun masc. sing. with suff. 2 pers. sing. masc. from [קֹטֶב] dec. 6 c (§ 35. rem. 8) קטב
קְטוֹרָה[f] noun fem. sing. . . . . קטר
קְטוּרָה pr. name fem. . . . . . קטר

[קָטַט] *to be cut off*, Job 8. 14. Arab. trans.
קְטִיל[g] Chald. Peal part. pass. sing. masc. . קטל
קְטִילַת[h] Chald. id. id. with afformative 2 pers. sing. fem. (§ 47. rem. 11) . קטל

[קָטַל] fut. יִקְטֹל *to kill, slay.*

קְטַל Chald. id. Pa. id. intens. *to slay many.* Ithpe. & Ithpa. *to be slain.*

קֶטֶל masc. *slaughter*, Ob. 9.

קָטֵל[i] Chald. Peal part. act. sing. masc. . קטל
קַטֵּל[k] Chald. Pael pret. 3 pers. s. masc. (§ 47. r. 1) קטל

[קָטֹן] (§ 8. rem. 1) fut. יִקְטַן.—I. *to be little, small.*—II trop. *to be of no account, unworthy.*

קָטֹן masc. dec. 8 a (with suff. קְטַנִּי), קְטַנָּה fem. dec. 10, adj.—I. *little, small.*—II. *young, younger.*—III. trop. *small, least, unimportant.*—IV. הַקָּטָן pr. name masc. Ezr. 8. 12.

קָטָן masc. dec. 3 a, idem.

קֹטֶן masc. *the little finger*, 1 Ki. 12 10; 2 Ch. 10. 10.

קַטָּת (for קְטַנַּת *small*) pr. name of a town in Zebulon, Jos. 19. 15.

יָקְטָן (*diminished*) pr. name of a son of Eber, progenitor of several Arabian tribes.

קָטֹן adj. m. s. with suff. קְטַנָּם d. 8 a (§ 37. No. 2) קטן
קָטֹן adj. masc. sing. dec. 3 a . . . קטן

[a] Ca. 5. 2. [b] Ca. 5. 11. [c] Ju. 8. 7, 16. [d] Ps. 18. 12; Is. 33. 12. [e] Ps. 129. 7. [f] 2 Ki. 6. 2. [g] Is. 59. 5. [h] Is. 59. 6. [i] Pr. 6. 13. [k] Zep. 2. 1. [l] Ps. 130. 5. [m] Eze. 17. 5. [n] 1 Sa. 21. 10. [o] Ge. 15. 9. [p] 1 Ki. 20. 33. [q] Ge. 43. 13. [r] Je. 46. 11. [s] Ho. 11. 3. [t] Ge. 48. 9. [u] Je. 36. 14. [x] 1 Sa. 16. 11. [y] 2 Ki. 12. 9. [z] Eze. 24. 25. [a] Ge. 30. 15. [b] Eze. 16. 47. [c] Is. 28. 2. [d] De. 32. 24. [dd] Eze. 10. 13. [e] Ho. 13. 14. [f] De. 33. 10. [g] Da. 5. 30. [h] Da. 7. 11. [i] Da. 5. 19. [k] Da. 3. 22.

קָטֹן[a] id.; constr. st. . . . . קטן

קְטַנָּה ו׳ / קְטַנּוֹת } adj. fem. sing. & pl. dec. 10, from קָטָן masc.; וּ bef. (:) . . . קטן

קָטְנִי noun m. s., suff. 1 p. s. [fr. קֹטֶן comp. קָבְלוֹ] קטן

קְטַנֵּי[b] / קְטַנִּים[c] ו׳ } adj. masc. pl. constr. & abs. from קָטָן dec. 8a (§ 37. No. 2); וּ bef. (:) קטן

קְטַנָּם[d] id. sing., suff. 3 pers. pl. masc. . . קטן

קָטֹנְתִּי[e] Kal pret. 1 pers. sing. (§ 8. rem. 1) . . קטן

[קָטַף] fut. יִקְטֹף *to pluck off*. Niph. pass. Job 8. 12.

קָטַף[f] Kal pret. 3 pers. sing. m. [for קָטַף § 8. r. 7] קטף

קָטַפְתָּ[g] וְ id. pret. 2 pers. sing. masc.; acc. shifted by conv. וְ (§ 8. rem. 7) . . . קטף

I. קָטַר. Pi. קִטֵּר *to raise an odour by burning, to burn incense*, also *fat*; part. מְקַטְּרוֹת *altars of incense*. Pu. *to be perfumed*, Ca. 3. 6. Hiph. *to burn incense*, also *sacrifices*. Hoph. pass. Le. 6. 15; *part.* מֻקְטָר *incense*, Mal. 1. 11.

קְטוֹרָה fem. *incense*, De. 33. 10.

קְטֹרֶת fem. dec. 13c, *incense; also the fat* of a victim burned as incense, Ps. 66. 15.

קְטוּרָה (*incense*) pr. name of a wife of Abraham.

קִטֵּר masc. *a burning of incense*, Je. 44. 21.

קִיטוֹר masc.—I. *smoke*.—II. *vapour*, Ps. 148. 8.

מִקְטָר masc. dec. 2b, *incense*, Ex. 30. 1.

מִקְטֶרֶת fem. dec. 13 (with suff. ־טַרְתִּי), *a censer*.

II. קָטַר *to bind*, only part. קְטֻרוֹת *bound, joined*, Eze. 46. 22.

קְטַר Chald. masc. dec. 3b, only pl.—I. *joints, ligatures*, Da. 5. 6.—II. *knots, difficult questions*, Da. 5. 12, 16.

קַטְּרוֹן (*knotty*) pr. name of a town in Zebulun, Ju. 1. 30.

קַטֵּר וְ Piel inf. abs., used also as an abs. . קטר

קִטְּרוּ id. pret. 3 pers. pl. . . . . קטר

קִטְרוֹן pr. name of a place . . . . קטר

קְטֻרוֹת[h] Kal part. pass. pl. fem. [from קָטוּר masc.] קטר

קִטְרֵי[i] וְ / קִטְרִין[k] וְ׳ } Chald. noun masc. pl. constr. & abs. from [קְטַר] dec. 3b . . . קטר

קְטֹרֶת ו׳ noun fem. sing. dec. 13d; וּ bef. (:) . קטר

קְטָרְתִּי וּ id. with suff. 1 pers. sing.; וּ id. . קטר

קִטַּרְתֶּם Piel pret. 2 pers. pl. masc. . . . קטר

קַטָּת וְ pr. name of a place . . . קטן

קִיא[l] noun masc. sing. dec. 1a . . . קוא

קִיוּ[m] וּ Kal imp. pl. masc.; וּ bef. (:) comp. R. קיא

קִיט[n] Chald. noun masc. sing. . . . קוט

קִיטוֹר[o] וְ / קִיטֹר[p] } noun masc. sing. . . . . קטר

קְיָם[q] ו׳ Chald. noun masc. sing.; וּ bef. (:) . קום

קַיָּם[r] וְ Chald. adj. masc. sing. . . . קום

קִיֵּם[s] Piel pret. 3 pers. sing. masc. (§ 10. rem. 1) קום

קַיָּמָא[t] Chald. adj. fem. sing., from קַיָּם masc. . קום

קִיְּמוּ[u] Piel pret. 3 pers. pl. . . . . קום

קִימוֹשׁ[x] noun masc. sing., for קִמּוֹשׁ (q. v.) . קמש

קִימָנוּ[y] n.m.s., suff. 1 p. pl. [for קִימֵנוּ, fr. קִים, § 3. r. 4] קום

קַיְּמֵנִי[z] Piel imp. sing. masc. [קַיֵּם], suff. 1 pers. s. קום

קִימָתָם[a] וְ noun f. s., suff. 3 p. pl. m. fr. [קִימָה] d. 10 קום

קַיִן / קָיִן וְ׳ } pr. name of a man and a people . קון

קִינָה וְ׳ noun fem. sing. dec. 10, also pr. name וְ . קון

קֵינוֹ[b] noun m. s., suff. 3 pers. s. m. fr. [קַיִן] d. 6h קון

קֵינִי pr. name of a people . . . . קון

קִינִים[c] noun fem. with pl. masc. term. fr. קִינָה d. 10 קון

קֵינָן pr. name masc. . . . . . קון

קַיִץ / קָיִץ וָ׳, וְ׳[d] } noun masc. sing. dec. 6h; for וָ see lett. ו . . . קוץ

קִיצֵךְ id. with suff. 2 pers. sing. fem. . . קוץ

קִיקָיוֹן[e] masc. Jon. 4. 6, 7, 9, 10, the name of a plant, according to the Syr. and Jerome, the *palma Christi, ricinus communis*, called in Egypt **KIKI**; Sept. κολόκυνθα *gourd*.

קִיקָלוֹן[f] וְ noun masc. sing. . . . . קלל

קִיר[g] וְ׳ masc. dec. 1a (pl. קִירוֹת).—I. *a wall*, of a city, of a house.—II. *side* of an altar; applied to the *sides* of the heart, Je. 4. 19.—III. pr. name קִיר חֲרֶשֶׂת, קִיר חֶרֶשׂ, קִיר מוֹאָב a city in the territory of Moab.—IV. pr. name of a people and region of Assyria.

קִירָה pr. name of a place (קִיר) with loc. ה . קיר

קִירוֹת noun masc. with pl. fem. term. from קִיר d. 1a קיר

קִירוֹתֶיהָ[h] וְ id. pl., suff. 3 pers. sing. fem. . . קיר

קִירוֹתָיו[i] וְ id. pl., suff. 3 pers. sing. masc. . . קיר

קֵירֹס pr. name masc. see קֵרֹס . . . קרס

קִירֹתָיו[k] וְ׳ defect. for קִירוֹתָיו (q. v.) . . קיר

קִישׁ וְ׳ pr. name masc. . . . . קוש

קִישׁוֹן pr. name of a stream . . . קוש

קִישִׁי pr. name masc., see קוּשָׁיָהוּ . . . קוש

קִיתְרֹס[l] Chald. masc. Kheth. קִיתָרֹס, Keri קַתְרֹס, *harp, lyre*, Gr. Κίθαρις *cithara*. Da. 3. 5, 7, 10, 15.

קָל Chald. noun masc. sing. . . . . קול

קַל[m] וְ׳ adj. masc. sing. dec. 8d . . . קלל

קֹל[n] וְ defect. for קוֹל (q. v.) . . . קול

[a] 2 Ch. 21. 17. [b] Pr. 30. 24. [c] Je. 16. 6. [d] Jon. 3. 5. [e] Ge. 32. 11. [f] Eze. 17. 4. [g] De. 23. 26. [h] Eze. 46. 22. [i] Da. 5. 6. [k] Da. 5. 12, 16. [l] Is. 28. 8. [m] Je. 25. 27. [n] Da. 2. 35. [o] Ps. 148. 8. [p] Ge. 19. 28. [q] Da. 6. 8, 16. [r] Da. 6. 27. [s] Est. 9. 31, 32. [t] Da. 4. 23. [u] Est. 9. 27, 31. [x] Ho. 9. 6. [y] Job 22. 20. [z] Ps. 119. 28. [a] La. 3. 63. [b] 2 Sa. 21. 16. [c] Eze. 2. 10. [d] Je. 40. 12. [e] Jon. 4. 6. [f] Hab. 2. 16. [g] Eze. 41. 12, 20. [h] Eze. 41. 13. [i] 2 Ch. 3. 7. [k] Eze. 41. 22. [l] Da. 3. 5, 7, 10, 15. [m] Am. 2. 15. [n] Ex. 19. 16.

קָהָה perh. i. q. קָהַל, only Niph. *to be assembled,* 2 Sa. 20. 14, Kheth.

I. **[קָלָה]** I. *to roast, parch,* e. g. corn.—II. *to burn,* Je. 29. 22. Niph. part. *burning disease,* Ps. 38. 8.

קָלִיא, קָלִי m. *corn roasted* or *parched in the ear.*

II. **[קָלָה]** Kal not used; i. q. קָלַל. Niph. *to be made light of, to be despised;* part. *despised, mean.* Hiph. *to make light of, to despise,* De. 27. 16.

קָלוֹן masc. dec. 3 a.—I. *shame, contempt.*—II. *shameful deed.*—III. *shame, pudenda.*

[a]קַלָּה adj. fem. sing. from קַל masc. . . . קלל

[b]קֹלָה defect. for קוֹלָה (q. v.) . . . קול

[c]קַלּוּ וְ Kal pret. 3 pers. pl. . . . קלל

קֹלוֹ noun masc. sing., suff. 3 pers. sing. masc. from קוֹל dec. 1 a . . . . קול

[d]קָלוּט וְ Kal part. pass. sing. masc. . . . קלט

[e]קָלוּי [f]וְ Kal part. pass. sing. . . . קלה

קָלוֹן וְ noun masc. sing. dec. 3 a . . . קלה

[g]קְלוֹן id., constr. st. . . . . קלה

קְלוֹנֵךְ id., suff. 2 pers. sing. fem. . . . קלה

[h]קַלּוֹתָ Kal pret. 2 pers. sing. masc. . . . קלל

קֹלוֹת noun masc. with pl. fem. term. from קוֹל d. 1 a קול

קָלַח Root not used; Talm. *to flow.*

קַלַּחַת [for קְלַחַת] fem. *pot, kettle* . . . קלח

קָלַט (Arab. קלץ *to contract*) only part.; קָלוּט *contracted, dwarfish,* Le. 22. 23.

קְלִיטָא (*dwarfish*) pr. name masc., called also קְלָיָה, comp. Ezr. 10. 23.

מִקְלָט masc. dec. 2 b, *refuge, asylum.* Chald. קְלַט *to receive to oneself.*

קָלִי וְ noun masc. sing. . . . . קלה

קַלַּי pr. name masc. . . . . קלל

קְלָיָה וְ pr. name masc., see קְלִיטָא . . . קלט

קְלִיטָא pr. name masc. . . . . קלט

קַלִּים adj. masc. pl. of קַל dec. 8 d . . . קלל

[k]קֹלִךְ noun m. sing., suff. 1 pers. sing. m. fr. קוֹל d. 1 a קול

[קָלַל] fut. יֵקַל (§ 18. rem. 6) *to be light,* i. e. not heavy, hence—I. *to be swift.*—II. *to be lessened, diminished, abated,* Ge. 8. 8, 11.—III. *to be lightly esteemed, be despised, mean.* Niph. נָקַל, נָקֵל (§ 18. rem. 7).—I. *to be light, slight;* עַל נְקַלָּה *slightly;* hence, *to be easy.*—II. *to be swift,* Is. 30. 16.—III. *to be small, unimportant.*—IV. *to be despised,* 2 Sa. 6. 22. Pi. קִלֵּל *to revile, curse,* with בְּ, with לְ *to bring a curse upon oneself,* 1 Sa. 3. 13. Pu. *to be cursed, accursed.* Hiph. הֵקַל.—I. *to lighten, remove,* a burden מֵעַל, מִן from any one.—II. *to make light of, to despise; to bring into contempt,* Is. 8. 23. Pilp. (§ 6. No. 4).—I. *to shake together,* sc. arrows in divination, Eze. 21. 26.—II. *to polish, sharpen,* Ec. 10. 10. Hithpalp. *to be shaken,* Je. 4. 24.

קָלָל adj. masc. *polished, shining.*

קְלָלָה fem. dec. 11 c.—I. *a reviling, cursing.*—II. *curse, imprecation;* an object *of curse.*

קַל masc. dec. 8 d, קַלָּה fem. adj.—I. *light, swift.*—II. adv. *swiftly.*

קַלָּי (*swift*) pr. name masc. Ne. 12. 20.

קְלֹקֵל masc. *light, mean, vile,* Nu. 21. 5.

קִיקָלוֹן (for קְלַקְלוֹן) masc. *ignominy, shame,* Hab. 2. 16. Eng. vers. after the Vulg. "shameful spewing," as compnd. of קִי & קָלוֹן.

קָלָל adj. sing. masc. . . . . קלל

קַלֵּל Piel imp. sing. masc. . . . קלל

[l]קִלֵּל [m]וְ id. pret. 3 pers. sing. masc. . . . קלל

[n]קְלָלָה וּ noun fem. sing. dec. 11 c; וּ bef. (:) . קלל

[o]קִלְלַנִי Piel pret. 3 p. s. m. (קִלֵּל), suff. 1 p. s. (§ 10. r. 7) קלל

[p]קִלַּלְתָּ id. pret. 2 pers. sing. masc. . . . קלל

קִלְלַת noun fem. sing., constr. of קְלָלָה dec. 11 c קלל

[q]קִלְלָתוֹ id., suff. 3 pers. sing. masc. . . . קלל

[r]קִלְלָתְךָ id., suff. 2 pers. sing. masc. . . . קלל

[s]קָלָם Kal pret. 3 pers. sing. masc. [קָלָה], suff. 3 pers. pl. masc. (§ 24. rem. 21) . . קלה

קֹלֵנוּ noun masc. s., suff. 1 pers. pl. fr. קוֹל dec. 1 a קול

קָלַס. Pi. *to mock, scorn,* Eze. 16. 31. Hithp. id. with בְּ. Hence

[t]קֶלֶס וְ masc. *scorn, derision.*

[u]קַלָּסָה fem. id.

קָלַע [v]וְ I. *to sling, throw with a sling;* trop. *to cast out, reject,* Je. 10. 18.—II. *to cut out, carve.* Pi. i. q. Kal No. I.

קֶלַע masc. dec. 6 a (with suff. קַלְעִי § 35. rem. 5).—I. *a sling.*—II. *curtain, hanging.*

קַלָּע masc. dec. 1 b, *slinger,* 2 Ki. 3. 25.

מִקְלַעַת fem. dec. 13 a, *carving, sculpture.*

קַלְעוֹ noun masc. sing., suff. קַלְעוֹ dec. 6 a (§ 35. r. 5) קלע

---

[a] Je. 2. 23. [b] Ge. 21. 16. Hab. 1. 8. [d] Le. 22. 23. [e] Le. 2. 14. [f] Jos. 5. 11. [g] Is. 22. 18. [h] Na. 1. 14. [i] Mi. 3. 3. [k] Ge. 3. 10. [l] 2 Sa. 16. 10. [m] Is. 8. 21. [n] De. 11. 26. [o] 1 Ki. 2. 8. [p] Ec. 7. 22. [q] 2 Sa. 16. 12. [r] Ge. 27. 13. [s] Je. 29. 22. [t] Ps. 44. 14. [u] Eze. 22. 4. [v] 1 Ki. 6. 29, 32, 35.

קְלַע[a] Kal part. act. sing. masc. . . . קלע
וְ קַלְעוֹ[b] noun masc. sing., suff. 3 pers. sing. masc. from קֶלַע dec. 6 a (§ 35. rem. 5) קלע
קְלָעֵי[c] וְ׳ id. pl., constr. st. . . . קלע
קְלָעִים id. pl., abs. st. . . . . קלע
קִלְקַל Pilp. pret. 3 pers. sing. masc. (§ 6. rem. 4) קלל

קָלַשׁ Root not used; meaning uncertain. Hence
קִלְשׁוֹן[d] masc. שְׁלֹשׁ קְ׳ a three-pronged pitchfork.
קָלֹת noun masc. with pl. fem. term. fr. קוֹל dec. 1 a קול
קַלֹּתִי[e] Kal pret. 1 pers. sing. . . . קלל
קָם וְ׳, וְ׳[f] Kal pret. 3 pers. sing. masc., Chald. Da. 3. 24; for וְ see lett. ו . . קום
קֻם[g] id. imp. s. masc. for קוּם (but comp. § 21. r. 5) קום

קָמָה Root not used; Arab. קמא *to heap together, to collect.*
קְמוּאֵל (*assembly of God*) pr. name masc.—I. Ge. 22. 21.—II. Nu. 34. 24.—III. 1 Ch. 27. 17.
יְקַמְיָה (*the Lord shall gather together*) pr. name masc.—I. 1 Ch. 2. 41.—II. 1 Ch. 3. 18.
יְקַמְעָם (*he shall gather the people*) pr. name masc. 1 Ch. 23. 19; 24. 23.
יָקְמְעָם (*the people shall be gathered*) pr. name of a city in Ephraim.

קָמָה[h] וְ׳ Kal pret. 3 pers. sing. fem. . . . קום
קָמָה[i] id. part. sing. fem. . . . . קום
קָמָה noun fem. s. dec. 10 (constr. קָמַת § 30. No. 3) קום
קֻמָה[k] וְ defect. for קוּמָה (q. v.) . . . קום
קָמוּ וְ׳, וְ׳[l] Kal pret. 3 pers. pl., Chald. Ezr. 5. 2; וְ bef. pause . . . . . קום
קֻמוּ[m] id. imp. pl. masc. (for קוּמוּ) . . . קום
קְמוּאֵל pr. name masc. . . . . . קמה
קִמּוֹשׂ[n] noun masc. sing., comp. קִימוֹשׂ . . . קמש

קֶמַח וְ׳[o] masc. *flour*. Talm. קמח *to grind*.
קָמַח id. in pause (§ 35. rem. 2) . . . קמח

[קָמַט] *to bind*, Job 16. 8; so according to the Arab.; others, *to seize firmly*, cogn. קָפַץ, קָבַץ, קָמַץ. Pu. *to be taken away*, Job 22. 16.
קֻמְּטוּ[p] Pual pret. 3 pers. pl. . . . . קמט
קָמַי[q], קָמַי } Kal part. act. pl. masc., suff. 1 pers. sing. [from קָם] dec. 1 a (§ 30. No. 3) . } קום
קָמָיו[r] id. pl., suff. 3 pers. sing. masc. . . . קום
קָמֶיךָ id. pl., suff. 2 pers. sing. masc. . . . קום

קָמִים[s] id. pl., abs. st. . . . . . קום
קָמֵינוּ[dd] id. pl., suff. 1 pers. pl. . . . . קום

קָמַל *to wither*, Is. 33. 9, and the foll. form.
קָמְלוּ[t] Kal pret. 3 pers. pl. for [קָמְלוּ § 8. r. 1 & 7] קמל
קָמְנָה[u] Kal pret. 3 pers. pl. fem. . . . . קום
קַמְנוּ[v] id. pret. 1 pers. pl. . . . . . קום

קָמַץ וְ *to grasp, take a grasp.*
קֹמֶץ masc. dec. 6 c, *a handful*; לִקְמָצִים *by handfuls*, i. e. abundance.
קֻמְצוֹ noun masc. sing., suff. 3 pers. sing. masc. from [קֹמֶץ] dec. 6 c (§ 35. rem. 8) . קמץ

קָמַשׁ Root not used; Arab. *to heap together.*
קִמּוֹשׁ, קִימוֹשׁ m. *nettles*, Is. 34. 13; Ho. 9. 6.
קִמְּשׁוֹן masc. dec. 3 c, idem, Pr. 24. 31.
קִמְּשׂנִים[y] noun masc. pl. of [קִמְּשׁוֹן] dec. 3 c . קמש
קָמַת[z] noun fem. sing., constr. of קָמָה dec. 10 (comp. § 30. No. 3) . . . קום
קַמְתָּ[a], וְקַמְתָּ } Kal pret. 2 pers. sing. masc.; acc. shifted by conv. וְ (comp. § 8. rem. 7) . } קום
קֹמָתוֹ noun fem. s., suff. 3 pers. s. m. fr. קוֹמָה d. 10 קום
קַמְתִּי[b], קַמְתִּי, וְקַמְתִּי } Kal pret. 1 pers. sing.; acc. shifted by conv. וְ (comp. § 8. rem. 7) . } קום
קַמְתֶּם id. pret. 2 pers. pl. masc. . . . קום
קַן[c], קֵן } noun masc. sing., constr. & abs. dec. 8 b (§ 37. rem. 1) . . . } קנן

קָנָא[d] וְ׳[e] Pi. I. *to be jealous*, with acc., בְּ, of a wife, rival.—II. *to provoke to jealousy, anger*, with בְּ *by* or *with*.—III. *to envy*, with בְּ, acc., לְ of the person.—IV. *to be jealous* or *zealous for*, with לְ. —V. *to emulate*, with בְּ Pr. 3. 31. Hiph. *to provoke to jealousy*.
קַנָּא adj. masc. *jealous*, of God.
קַנּוֹא id. Jos. 24. 19; Na. 1. 2.
קִנְאָה fem. dec. 12 b.—I. *jealousy*.—II. *envy*; also *object of envy*, Ec. 4. 4.—III. *zeal, ardour*.—IV. *ardour, anger*.

קַנָּא noun masc. sing. . . . . . קנא
קַנֹּא[f] Piel inf. abs. . . . . . קנא
קִנֵּא[g] וְ׳ id. pret. 3 pers. sing. masc. . . . קנא
קִנְאָה[h] וְ׳ noun fem. sing. dec. 12 b . . . קנא
קִנְאוּנִי[i] Piel pret. 3 pers. pl., suff. 1 pers. s. (§ 10. r. 7) קנא
קְנָאֹת[k] noun fem. pl. abs. from קִנְאָה dec. 12 b . קנא

[a] Ju. 20. 16. [b] 1 Sa. 17. 40. [c] Nu. 3. 26. [d] 1 Sa. 13. 21. [e] Job 40. 4. [f] Pr. 24. 16. [g] Jos. 7. 10, 13. [h] 1 Sa. 24. 21. [i] Mi. 7. 6. [k] Ex. 27. 18. [l] Is. 49. 7. [m] De. 2. 13. [n] Is. 34. 13. [o] 2 Sa. 17. 28. [p] Job 22. 16. [q] Je. 51. 1. [r] De. 33. 11. [s] Ps. 3. 2. [t] Is. 19. 6. [u] Is. 32. 9. [x] Ps. 20. 9. [y] Pr. 24. 31. [z] De. 23. 26. [a] 2 Sa. 12. 21. [dd] Ps. 44. 6. [b] Mi. 7. 8. [c] De. 22. 6. [d] Nu. 25. 13. [e] Nu. 5. 14. [f] 1 Ki. 19. 10, 14. [g] Nu. 5. 14; 25. 13. [h] Eze. 16. 38. [i] De. 32. 21. [k] Nu. 5. 15, 18.

קִנְאַת id. sing., constr. st. . . . . . קנא

קִנְאָתוֹ[a] וְ[b] id. sing., suff. 3 pers. sing. masc. . קנא

קִנְאָתִי id. sing., suff. 1 pers. sing. . . . קנא

קִנֵּאתִי, וְקִנֵּאתִי[c] } Piel pret. 1 pers. sing.; acc. shifted by conv. וְ (comp. § 8. rem. 7) . . } קנא

קִנְאָתְךָ[d], קִנְאָתְךָ[e] } noun fem. sing., suff. 2 pers. sing. masc. from קִנְאָה dec. 12 b . . . . } קנא

קִנְאָתָם[f] id., suff. 3 pers. pl. masc. . . . קנא

קָנָה fut. יִקְנֶה.—I. *to form, create.*—II. *to get, acquire;* also *to obtain,* Ge. 4. 1.—III. *to buy, purchase;* hence *to redeem.*—IV. *to possess.* Niph. *to be acquired, purchased.* Hiph. *to buy,* Zec. 13. 5.

קְנָא Ch. *to buy,* Ezr. 7. 17.

קִנְיָן masc. dec. 2 b.—I. *creature,* Ps. 104. 24.—II. *acquisition, purchase.*—III. *possession, wealth.*

קְנָת (*possession*) pr. name of a city in the country of Gilead.

יָקְנְעָם (*gotten by the people*) pr. name of a town in the tribe of Zebulun.

מִקְנֶה masc. dec. 9 a (comp. § 38. rem. 1).—I. *purchase,* Ge. 49. 32.—II. *possession, riches, wealth,* but chiefly consisting in *cattle;* אַנְשֵׁי מ׳ *men of* (i. e. possessing) *cattle;* אֶרֶץ מ׳ *a place for cattle,* adapted for pasturage.

מִקְנָה fem. dec. 10.—I. *purchase.*—II. *thing purchased,* Ge. 17. 12, 13, 23.—III. *price of purchase.*—IV. *possession,* Ge. 23. 18.

מִקְנֵיָהוּ (*possession of the Lord*) pr. name masc. 1 Ch. 15. 18, 21.

קָנֶה וְ masc. dec. 9 b (pl. קָנִים, קָנוֹת).—I. *reed, cane.*—II. *sweet cane.*—III. *stalk* of wheat, Ge. 41. 5, 22.—IV. *a measuring reed.*—V. *beam of a balance,* Is. 46. 6.—VI. *branch* of a candlestick.—VII. *arm-bone* above the elbow, Job 31. 22. Hence

קָנָה וְ (*place of reeds*) pr. name—I. of a stream on the borders of Ephraim and Manasseh.—II. of a town in Asher, Jos. 19. 28.

קָנָהּ וְ noun masc. sing. with suff. 3 pers. sing. fem. from קָנֶה dec. 9 b . . . . קנה

קָנֹה Kal inf. abs. . . . . . . קנה

קְנֵה id. imp. sing. masc. . . . . . קנה

קְנֵה[uu] וּ noun masc. sing., constr. of קָנֶה d. 9 b; וּ bef. (:) . . . . קנה

קְנֹה[g] Kal inf. constr. (§ 24. rem. 2) . . קנה

קִנָּהּ[h] noun masc. s., suff. 3 pers. s. fem. fr. קֵן d. 8 b קנן

קֹנֵה[i], קֹנֶה } Kal part. act. sing. masc. constr. & abs. dec. 9 a . . . . . } קנה

קָנָהוּ[k] id. pret. 3 pers. sing. m., suff. 3 pers. sing. m. קנה

קֹנֵהוּ id. part. sing. masc., suff. 3 pers. sing. masc. from קֹנֶה dec. 9 a . . . . קנה

קָנֹה[l] id. inf. abs. (§ 24. rem. 2) . . . קנה

קִנּוֹ noun m. sing., suff. 3 pers. sing. m. fr. קֵן d. 8 b קנן

קַנּוֹא noun masc. sing. . . . . . קנא

קְנוֹת[m] לִ Kal inf. constr. dec. 1; לִ bef. (:) . . קנה

קְנוֹתְךָ[n] id., suff. 2 pers. sing. masc. . . קנה

קְנַז וּ pr. name—I. of a descendant of Esau, from whom an Arabian country derived its name, Ge. 36. 11, 15.—II. the father of Othniel the judge. Patronym. קְנִזִּי.—III. of a grandson of Caleb, 1 Ch. 4. 15.

קְנִזִּי pr. name, *Kenizzite,* a people of Canaan. For another, see קְנַז.

קְנֵי noun masc. pl. constr. from קָנֶה dec. 9 b . קנה

קִנִּי[o] noun m. sing., suff. 1 pers. sing. fr. קֵן d. 8 b קנן

קֹנֵיהֶן[p] Kal part. act. pl. masc., suff. 3 pers. pl. fem. from קֹנֶה dec. 9 a . . . . קנה

קָנִים noun masc. pl. of קָנֶה dec. 9 b . . קנה

קִנִּים[q] noun masc., pl. of קֵן dec. 8 b . . קנן

קִנְיָן[r] וְ noun masc. sing. dec. 2 b . . . קנה

קִנְיַן[s] id., constr. st. . . . . . קנה

קָנִינוּ[t] Kal pret. 1 pers. pl. . . . . קנה

קִנְיָנוֹ noun m. sing., suff. 3 pers. s. m. fr. קִנְיָן d. 2 b קנה

קִנְיָנֶיךָ[u], קִנְיָנֶךָ[x] } id., pl. and sing. suff. 2 pers. sing. masc. קנה

קִנְיָנָם[y] וְ id., suff. 3 pers. pl. masc. . . . קנה

קָנִיתָ, וְקָנִיתָ } Kal pret. 2 pers. sing. masc.; acc. shifted by conv. וְ (comp. § 8. rem. 7) . } קנה

קָנִיתִי[z] Kh. קָנִיתִי q. v. K. קָנִיתָ (q. v.) . . קנה

קָנִיתִי Kal pret. 1 pers. sing. . . . . קנה

קָנֶךָ[z] id. pret. 3 pers. sing. masc. (קָנָה), suff. 2 pers. sing. masc. (§ 24. rem. 21) . . . קנה

קִנֶּךָ noun m. sing., suff. 2 pers. sing. m. fr. קֵן d. 8 b קנן

קִנָּמוֹן[yy] וְ m. d. 3 c, *cinnamon,* only Ca. 4. 14, and the foll.

קִנְּמָן[a] וְ id. constr. st. with mak. [for קִנָּמוֹן § 32. r. 7].

קָנַן Pi. קִנֵּן *to nest, build a nest.* Pu. *to have one's nest built,* Je. 22. 23.

קֵן masc. dec. 8 b (constr. קַן § 37. rem. 1).—I. *a nest;* meton. *young birds of a nest,* Is. 16. 2; metaph. (*a*) *a dwelling;* (*b*) meton. *family,* Job 29. 18.—II. pl. קִנִּים *cells, chambers,* Ge. 6. 14.

---

[a] Zep. 1. 18. [b] De. 29. 19. [c] Eze. 39. 25. [d] Ps. 79. 5. [e] Is. 63. 15. [f] Ec. 9. 6. [g] Pr. 16. 16. [h] Pr. 27. 8. [i] Ge. 14. 19, 22. [k] Le. 27. 24. [l] 2 Sa. 24. 24. [m] Pr. 16. 16. [n] Ru. 4. 5. [o] Job 29. 18. [p] Zec. 11. 5. [q] Ge. 6. 14. [r] Eze. 38. 12, 13. [s] Le. 22. 11. [t] Ne. 5. 8, 16. [u] Ps. 104. 24. [uu] Eze. 40. 3, 5. [x] Pr. 4. 7. [y] Ge. 34. 23. [yy] Pr. 7. 17. [z] De. 32. 6. [a] Ex. 30. 23.

קִנְּנָה[a] Piel pret. 3 pers. sing. fem. . . קנן

קִנְּנוּ[b] id. pret. 3 pers. pl. (§ 10. rem. 7) . . קנן

קָנָנִי[c] Kal pret. 3 pers. sing. masc. (קָנָה), suff. 1 pers. sing. (§ 24. rem. 21) . . קנה

קִנְצֵי[d] noun masc. pl. c. [for קִצֵּי dag. forte resolved in נ] from קֵץ dec. 8b . . . קצץ

קָנָת / קְנָת } pr. name of a place . . . קנה

קָנְתָה[e] Kal pret. 3 pers. sing. fem. . . . קנה

קְנוֹתָם ו noun masc. with pl. fem. term. and suff. 3 pers. pl. masc. from קָנֶה d. 9b; ו bef. (:) קנה

קָסֳמִי[f] Kh. קְסוּמִי, K. קָסֳמִי Kal imp. sing. fem. (§ 8. rem. 12 & 14) . . . קסם

[קָסַם] fut. יִקְסֹם to divine, spoken espec. of false prophets.
קֶסֶם masc. dec. 6a.—I. *divination*; trop. *decision, certainty*, Pr. 16. 10.—II. meton. *reward of divination*, Nu. 22. 7.
מִקְסָם masc. d. 2b, *divination*, Eze. 12. 24; 13. 7.

קֶסֶם[g] / וְ קֶסֶם } noun masc. sing. dec. 6a (§ 35. rem. 2) קסם

קֹסֵם[h] ו'[i] Kal part. act. sing. masc. dec. 7b . קסם

קֹסְמֵיכֶם[k] וְ' id. pl., suff. 2 pers. pl. masc. . . קסם

קְסָמִים ו'[l] noun masc., pl. of קֶסֶם dec. 6a; ו bef. (:) קסם

קֹסְמִים[m] וְ' Kal part. act. masc., pl. of קֹסֵם dec. 7b . קסם

קָסַס only Po. קוֹסֵס *to cut off*, comp. קָצַץ, Eze. 17. 9.

קֶסֶת[n] וְ' noun masc. sing. . . . . קשה

קְעִילָה ו' / קְעִלָה } pr. name of a city in the tribe of Judah.

קַעֲקַע[o] noun masc. sing. . . . . קוע

קָעַר Root not used; Arab. *to be deep*; cogn. קוּר.
קְעָרָה fem. (§ 42. rem. 1 & 3) *a dish, charger*.

קַעֲרַת[p] noun f. s., constr. of קְעָרָה d. 11c (§ 42. r. 1) קער

קַעֲרֹת[q] id. pl., constr. st. . . . . קער

קַעֲרֹתָיו id. pl., suff. 3 pers. sing. masc. (§ 42. rem. 3) קער

[קָפָא] *to congeal, become condensed*, Ex. 15. 8; perh. also Zec. 14. 6, Kheth. יְקָרוֹת יִקְפָּאוּן *the splendid ones*, i. e. stars, *shall become condensed*, shall contract their light. Metaph. Zep. 1. 12, *to be congealed upon the lees*, i. e. to sit quiet, indifferent. Hiph. *to make to curdle*, Job 10. 10.
קִפָּאוֹן masc. *a congealing, denseness*, Zec. 14. 6, Keri, see the verb.

קָפְאוּ[r] Kal pret. 3 pers. pl. . . . . קפא

קָפַד Kal not used; Ch. קְפַד *to cut off*. Pi. id. Is. 38. 12.
קְפָדָה masc. *destruction*, Eze. 7. 25.
קִפֹּד, קִפּוֹד masc. *hedgehog*. (Arab. קנפד id.)

קִפֹּד noun masc. sing. . . . . קפד

קְפָדָה[s] noun masc. sing. [קְפָד or קִפֹּד] with parag. ה קפד

קִפַּדְתִּי[t] Piel pret. 1 pers. sing. . . . קפד

קִפּוֹד[u] וְ noun masc. sing. . . . . קפד

קִפּוֹז[v] noun masc. sing. . . . . קפז

קָפַז Root not used; Arab. *to leap, spring*, comp. Pi. of קָפַץ.
קִפּוֹז masc. *the arrow-snake*, Is. 34. 15.

קֹפִים[w] וְ noun masc., pl. of קוֹף dec. 1a . . קוף

קָפַץ[x] fut. יִקְפֹּץ *to contract, close, shut*, as the mouth, hand. Niph. *to be shut up*, sc. in the grave, Job 24. 24. Others, *to be contracted, to die*. Pi. *to leap, spring*, Ca. 2. 8.

קָפְצָה Kal pret. 3 pers. sing. fem. . . . קפץ

קָץ[y] וְ Kal pret. 3 p. s. m. (see קוּץ), or part. m. קוץ

קֵץ noun masc. sing. dec. 8b . . . קצץ

[קָצַב] fut. יִקְצֹב.—I. *to cut off* or *down*, e. g. wood or a tree, 2 Ki. 6. 6.—II. *to shear sheep*, Ca. 4. 2. Hence

קֶצֶב[z] וְ masc. dec. 6a (pl. c. קִצְבֵי).—I. *form, shape*.—II. *end, extremity*, Jon. 2. 7; Prof. Lee, *cleft* . . . . . קצב

[קָצָה] *to cut off, destroy*, Hab. 2. 10. Pi. *to cut off*. Hiph. *to scrape off*, Le. 14. 41, 43.
קָצֶה masc. dec. 9b.—I. *end, limit*, of space or time; Ge. 19. 4, מִקָּצֶה *from every end*, i. e. from all parts, מִקְצֵה שְׁלֹשֶׁת יָמִים *at the end of three days*.—II. *the whole, the sum*.
קָצָה fem. dec. 11a.—I. *end, extremity* of space; מִקְצָה *at the extreme part*.—II. *the whole, the sum, mass*, e. g. of people.
קָצֵה masc. *end, limit*.
קָצוּ masc. dec. 6a, קַצְוֵי אֶרֶץ *ends of the earth*.
קָצָת fem. i. q. קָצָה, קָצֶה; pl. קְצָווֹת with suff. קְצוֹתָיו (comp. כְּנָת § 45).
קְצָת Chald. fem. constr. קְצָת, idem.
קָצִין masc. dec. 3a.—I. *a judge*.—II. *leader, chief*.—III. *prince*.

קָצָה[c] Kal pret. 3 pers. sing. fem. . . . קוץ

קָצֶה noun masc. sing. . . . . קצה

קְצֵה noun masc. sing., constr. of קָצֶה dec. 9b . קצה

---

[a] Is. 34. 15. [b] Eze. 31. 6. [c] Pr. 8 22. [d] Job 18. 2. [e] Ps. 78. 54. [f] 1 Sa. 28. 8. [g] Eze. 21. 26. [h] De. 18. 10. [i] Is. 3. 2. [k] Je. 29. 8, 9. [l] Nu. 22. 7. [m] De. 18. 14. [n] Eze. 9. 2, 3. [o] Le. 19. 28. [p] Nu. 7. 13, 19, &c. [q] Nu. 7. 84. [r] Ex. 15. 8. [s] Eze. 7. 25. [t] Is. 38. 12. [u] Is. 34. 11. [v] Is. 34. 15. [w] 1 Ki. 10. 22. [x] Ps. 77. 10. [y] Is. 18. 6; 7. 16. [z] 1 Ki. 6. 25; 7. 37. [c] Nu. 21. 5.

קְצָהּ[zz] Kh. for קִצּוֹ (q. v.) . . . . קצץ
קָצֵהוּ noun masc. sing., suff. 3 pers. sing. masc. from קָצֶה dec. 9b . . . קצה
קִצּוֹ [a] וְ' noun masc. sing., suff. 3 pers. sing. masc. from קֵץ dec. 8b . . . קצץ
קְצוֹוֹתָיו[b] Kh. קְצוֹוֹתָיו noun fem. pl. with suff., see קָצוֹת ; K. קְצוֹתָיו (q. v.) . . קצה
קְצְוֵי noun masc. pl. constr. from [קָצוֹ] dec. 6a קצה
קְצוּצֵי Kal part. pass. pl. c. masc. [fr. קָצוּץ] d. 3a קצץ
קְצוֹת[c] noun fem. pl. abs., fr. קָצָת' (comp. מְנָת § 45) קצה
קְצוֹת noun fem. pl. constr. from קָצָה' dec. 11a; or (Hab. 2. 10) inf. constr. . . . קצה
קְצוֹתָיו id. pl., suff. 3 pers. sing. masc. . . . קצה
קְצוֹתָם[d] id. pl., suff. 3 pers. pl. masc. (§ 4. rem. 2) קצה

קֶצַח masc. *black cummin*, Is. 28. 25, 27.

קִצִּי noun masc. sing., suff. 1 pers. s. fr. קֵץ d. 8b קצץ
קֵצִים [e] וְ' noun masc., pl. of קוֹץ dec. 1a . . קוץ
קָצִין noun masc. sing. dec. 3a . . . . קצה
קְצִין' id., constr. st. . . . . . קצה
קְצִינֵי [g] וּ' id. pl., constr. st.; וּ bef. (:) . . קצה
קְצִינַיִךְ[h] id. pl., suff. 2 pers. sing. fem. . . . קצה
קְצִיעָה pr. name masc. . . . . . קצע
קְצִיעוֹת[i] noun fem., pl. of קְצִיעָה dec. 10 . . קצע
קְצִיץ pr. name in compos. עֵמֶק קְ' . . . עמק
קָצִיר וְ' noun masc. sing. dec. 3a . . . קצר
קְצִיר [k] וּ' id., constr. st.; וּ bef. (:) . . . קצר
קְצִירָהּ id., suff. 3 pers. sing. fem. . . . קצר
קְצִירוֹ id., suff. 3 pers. sing. masc. . . . קצר
קְצִירֶיהָ[l] id. pl., suff. 3 pers. sing. fem. . . קצר
קְצִירְךָ id. sing., suff. 2 pers. sing. masc. . . . קצר
קְצִירֵךְ[m] id. sing., suff. 2 pers. sing. fem. . . קצר
קְצִירְכֶם[n] id. sing., suff. 2 pers. pl. masc. . . . קצר
קִצֵּךְ[o] noun masc. s., suff. 2 pers. s. f. fr. קֵץ d. 8b קצץ
קִצֵּנוּ[p] id. with suff. 1 pers. pl. . . . . קצץ

קָצַע Kal not used; i. q. קָצָה, קָצַץ *to cut*; also *to break*, comp. derivv. Hiph. *to scrape off*. Pu. and Hoph. part. מְהֻקְצָעוֹת, מְקֻצָעוֹת *angles, corners*.

קְצִיעָה fem. dec. 10.—I. *cassia*, Ps. 45. 9.—II. pr. name of one of Job's daughters, Job 42. 14.

מִקְצוֹעַ masc. dec. 1b (pl. וֹת—, ים—) *angle, corner*.

מַקְצוּעָה fem. dec. 10, *a plane*, Is. 44. 13.

קָצַף fut. יִקְצֹף *to be angry, wroth*, with אֶל, עַל of the person. Hiph. *to provoke to anger*. Hithp. *to become angry*.

קְצַף Chald. *to be angry*, Da. 2. 12.

קֶצֶף masc. dec. 6a (with קִצְפִּי, קֶצֶפְךָ).—I. *chip, splinter*, Hos. 10. 7.—II. *anger, wrath*.—III. *strife*, Est. 1. 18.

קְצַף Chald. masc. *anger*, Ezr. 7. 23.

קְצָפָה f. *a breaking*, Joel 1. 7. Sept. συγκλασμός, *splinter*; comp. κλασμός, *fragment*.

קֶצֶף וְ' } noun masc. sing. (suff. קִצְפִּי) dec. 6a
קָצֶף וּ'[q] } (§ 35. rem. 2) . . . . קצף
קְצַף[s] וּ' Ch. Peal pret. 3 p. s. m. or n. m.; וּ bef. (:) קצף
קֹצֵף[t] Kal part. act. sing. masc. . . . קצף
קִצְפְּךָ[u] וְ noun m. s., suff. 2 pers. s. m. fr. קֶצֶף d. 6a קצף
קָצַפְתָּ Kal pret. 2 pers. sing. masc. . . . קצף
קָצַפְתִּי id. pret. 1 pers. sing. . . . קצף

[קָצַץ] *to cut off*. Pi. קִצֵּץ, קִצֵּץ (§ 10. rem. 1).—I. *to cut off*; also *to cut asunder* or *in pieces*.—II. *to cut up*, as plates *into* wires, Ex. 39. 3. Pu. pass. Ju. 1. 7.

קַצֵּץ Chald. Pa. *to cut off*, Da. 4. 11.

קֵץ masc. dec. 8b.—I. *end, limit*, of space, time, condition, or circumstances; מִקֵּץ, לְקֵץ *at the end of, after*.—II. *end, termination, destruction*.

קִיצוֹן (for קִצּוֹן) only fem. קִיצוֹנָה *the last, extreme*.

מָקַץ (*end*) pr. name of a place, 1 Ki. 4. 9.

קִצֵּץ[v] }
קִצֵּץ[y] וְ' } Piel pret. 3 pers. sing. masc. (§ 10. r. 1) קצץ
קַצִּצוּ[z] וְ Ch. Pael pret. 3 pers. pl. masc. (§ 47. r. 1c) קצץ

קָצַר[a] I. fut. יִקְצֹר, *to cut down, reap*; part. קוֹצֵר *reaper*.—II. fut. יִקְצַר (once יִקְצֹר Pr. 10. 27) *to be shortened, short*; trop. of one's hand, *to be shortened*, i. e. *to be deficient, unable*; and so of one's spirit, soul, *to be impatient, grieved, vexed*. Pi. *to shorten*, Ps. 102. 24. Hiph. I. *to reap*, Job 24. 6, Kh.—II. *to shorten*, Ps. 89. 46.

קָצֵר adj. m. dec. 5a, *short*, Eze. 42. 5; קְצַר יָד *short of hand*, i. e. *weak, feeble*, Is. 37. 27; קְ' רוּחַ *impatient, passionate*; קְ' אַפַּיִם Pr. 14. 17, 29; קְ' יָמִים *short-lived*, Job 14. 1.

קֹצֶר masc. *shortness* of spirit, i. e. *impatience*, Ex. 6. 9.

קָצִיר masc. dec. 3a.—I. *fruits cut down, harvest*; hence *time of harvest*; meton. for *harvest-men*, Is. 17. 5.—II. *branch, bough*.

קְצַר [b] וּ' adj. m. s., constr. of [קָצֵר] d. 5a; וּ bef. (:) קצר

[a] Da. 9. 26. [b] Ex. 37. 8; 39. 4. [c] Ps. 65. 9. [d] Ps. 19. 7. [e] Je. 12. 13. [f] Is. 3. 7. [g] Mi. 3. 1, 9. [h] Is. 22. 3. [i] Ps. 45. 9. [k] Ru. 2. 23. [l] Ps. 80. 12. [m] Is. 16. 9. [n] Le. 23. 10. [o] Je. 51. 13. [p] La. 4. 18. [q] Zec. 1. 15. [r] Ezr. 7. 23. [s] Da. 2. 12. [t] Zec. 1. 15. [u] Ps. 102. 11. [v] 2 Ki. 18. 16. [y] Ps. 129. 4. [z] Da. 4. 11. [aa] 2 Ki. 19. 23. [a] Is. 28. 20. [b] Pr. 14. 29.

קִצֵּר[a] Piel pret. 3 pers. sing. masc. (§ 10. rem. 1) קצר

קָצְרָה Kal pret. 3 pers. sing. fem. . . קצר

קָצָרוּ[zz] id. pret. 3 pers. pl. [for קָצְרוּ § 8. rem. 7] קצר

קִצְרוּ[b] וְ׳ id. imp. pl. masc. . . . . קצר

קְצֻרוֹת[c] id. part. pass. f. pl. [of קְצוּרָה fr. קָצוּר m.] קצר

קִצְרֵי adj. pl. constr. masc. from [קָצֵר] dec. 5a קצר

קֹצְרִים[d] Kal part. act. masc., pl. of קוֹצֵר dec. 7b קצר

קְצַרְתֶּם[e] וּ׳[f] id. pret. 2 pers. pl. masc.; וּ, for וְ, conv. קצר

קְצָת[g] Chald. noun fem. sing. (constr. קְצַת) . קצה

קַצֹּתָה[h] וְ Kal pret. 2 pers. sing. masc. (§ 8. rem. 5); acc. shifted by conv. וְ (§ 8. rem. 7) . קצץ

קַצְתִּי[i] Kal pret. 1 pers. sing. . . . . קוץ

קַר־[k] וְ Kh. adj. masc., pl. קָרִים, q. v.; K. יְקַר, constr. of יָקָר (q. v.) . . . יקר

קָרִי[l] defect. for קִיר (q. v.) . . . . קיר

קֹר[m] וְ noun masc. sing. . . . . קרר

I. קָרָא וְ׳ fut. יִקְרָא.—I. *to cry, call out, shout*, with אֶל, אַחֲרֵי, עַל *to, after* any one.—II. *to cry* for help, *to call upon, invoke*, with אֶל, בְּשֵׁם.—III. *to cry, proclaim, publish*; Ex. 33. 19, קָ׳ בְּשֵׁם *to proclaim the name of*; hence *to praise, celebrate*.—IV. *to call, call for*, either *summon* or *invite*; hence *to call together, convoke*; also *to call* to an office, with acc. קָ׳ בְּשֵׁם פְּ׳ *to call one by his name*, i. e. *to nominate, constitute him*, Is. 43. 1; 45. 3, 4.—V. *to call, to name*, with acc. of the name, and לְ of the person or thing named, also both in the acc.—VI. *to read aloud, recite*. Niph. I. *to be called for, summoned; to be called together, convoked*.—II. *to be called, named*, const. i. q. Kal No. V.—III. *to be read aloud*. Pu. I. *to be called, chosen*, Is. 48. 12.—II. *to be called, named*.

קְרָא Chald.—I. *to call out, proclaim*.—II. *to read aloud*. Ithpe. *to be called*, Da. 5. 12.

קֹרֵא masc.—I. *partridge*.—II. pr. name of a man.

קָרִיא masc. dec. 3a, *called, selected*.

קְרִיאָה fem. *proclamation*, Jon. 3. 2

מִקְרָא masc. d. 1b.—I. *a calling together, convocation*.—II. *convocation, assembly*.—III. *a reading, reciting*, Ne. 8. 8.

II. קָרָא *to meet, befall, happen*. Niph. I. *to meet, happen to meet*, with לִפְנֵי, עַל.—II. *to happen*. Hiph. *to cause to happen* or *befall*, Je. 32. 23.

קְרָאָה fem. *a meeting*, everywhere with לְ pref. לִקְרַאת (constr. st. for לִקְרְאַת § 23. rem. 2, comp. מְלֶאכֶת for מַלְאֲכַת, מְלָאכָה for מְלָאכָה) *for meeting, to meet* (with suff. לִקְרָאתִי, לִקְרַאתְכֶם), as a prep.—I. *towards*; in a hostile sense *against*.—II. *over against*.

קָרֵא Chald. Peal part. act. sing. masc. . . קרא

קְרָא וּ׳ Kal imp. sing. masc.; וּ bef. (:) . קרא

קְרֹא id. inf. constr. . . . . . קרא

קֹרָא וְ׳ Pual pret. 3 pers. sing. masc. . . קרא

קֹרֵא Kal part. act., or (Je. 17. 11) subst. masc. dec. 7b; also pr. name . . . קרא

קָרְאָה id. pret. 3 pers. sing. fem. . . . קרא

קְרָאָהוּ[n] וּ id. pret. 3 pers. sing. masc., suff. 3 pers. sing. masc.; וּ, for וְ, conv. . . קרא

קְרָאֻהוּ[o] id. imp. pl. masc., suff. 3 pers. sing. masc. (§ 16. rem. 11) . . . . קרא

קָרָאוּ, וְ׳ קָרְאוּ } id. pret. 3 pers. pl. . . . . קרא

קִרְאוּ[p] וּ, וְ׳ קִרְאוּ } id. imp. pl. masc. (§ 8. rem. 12); וּ bef. (:) . . . . } קרא

קְרֹאות[q] id. inf. constr. (§ 23. rem. 2, comp. rem. 9) קרא

קְרִאֵי[r] adj. pl. constr. masc. [from קָרִיא] dec. 3a קרא

קְרֻאֶיהָ[s] Kal part. pass. pl., suff. 3 pers. sing. fem. from קָרוּא dec. 3a . . . קרא

קְרֻאָיו[t] id. id. pl., suff. 3 pers. sing. masc. . . קרא

קֹרְאָיו[u] id. part. act. pl. masc., suff. 3 pers. sing. masc. from קֹרֵא dec. 7b . . . קרא

קֹרְאֶיךָ[x] id. id., suff. 2 pers. sing. masc. . . קרא

קְרֻאִים[y] id. part. pass. masc., pl. of קָרוּא dec. 3a קרא

קֹרְאִים[z] id. part. act. pl. masc. from קֹרֵא dec. 7b קרא

קְרָאָךְ[a] id. pret. 3 pers. sing. m., suff. 2 pers. sing. fem. קרא

קָרְאָם id. inf., suff. 3 pers. pl. masc. . . קרא

קְרֶאןָ[b], קְרֶאןָ[c] } id. imp. pl. fem. (comp. § 8. rem. 16) . קרא

קְרָאֶנָּה[d] וּ id. imp. sing. masc. (קְרָא), suff. 3 pers. sing. fem. (§ 16. rem. 11); וּ bef. (:) . . קרא

קְרָאֵנִי[e] וּ id. id., suff. 1 pers. sing.; וּ id. . . קרא

קָרְאֵנוּ id. inf., suff. 1 pers. pl. . . . קרא

קְרָאַנִי[f], קְרָאַנִי[g] } id. pret. 3 pers. sing. masc., suff. 1 pers. sing. (§ 2. rem. 1) . . } קרא

קְרָאֻנִי[h] id. pret. 3 pers. pl. (קָרְאוּ), suff. 1 pers. sing. קרא

קָרָאתָ וְ׳ id. pret. 2 pers. sing. masc. . . קרא

קָרָאת וְ׳ id. pret. 2 pers. sing. fem., or 3 pers. sing. fem. [for קָרְאַת § 23. rem. 1] . . קרא

קָרָאתִי[i] Kh. קָרָאתִי q. v., K. קָרָאת (q. v.) . קרא

קָרָאתִי וְ׳ Kal pret. 1 pers. sing. . . . קרא

קְרָאתִיו id. id., suff. 3 pers. sing. masc. . . קרא

קְרָאתִיךָ id. id., suff. 2 pers. sing. masc. . . קרא

---

[a] Ps. 102. 24. [b] Ho. 10. 12. [c] Eze. 42. 5. [d] 1 Sa. 6. 13. [e] Ho. 10. 13. [f] Le. 23. 10. [g] Da. 2. 42. [h] De. 25. 12. [i] Ge. 27. 46. [k] Pr. 17. 27. [l] Is. 22. 5. [m] Ge. 8. 22. [n] Ge. 42. 38. [o] Is. 55. 6. [p] Is. 34. 16. [q] Ju. 8. 1. [r] Nu. 16. 2. [s] Pr. 9. 18. [t] Zep. 1. 7. [u] Ps. 145. 18. [x] Ps. 86. 5. [y] 2 Sa. 15. 11. [z] Ps. 99. 6. [zz] Je. 12. 13. [a] Is. 54. 6. [b] Ru. 1. 20. [c] Ex. 2. 20. [d] Je. 36. 15. [e] Ps. 50. 15. [f] Is. 49. 1. [g] Job 4. 14. [h] Je. 13. 22. [i] Je. 3. 4.

קְרֹאתַיִךְ[a] id. part. act. pl. fem., suff. 2 pers. sing. fem. [fr. קֹרְאָה or קֹרֵאת sing. § 8. rem. 19] קרה

קְרָאתֶם[b] וּ׳ id. pret. 2 pers. pl. masc.; וּ, for וְ, conv. קרא

קָרַב [also קָרֵב according to Zep. 3. 2] fut. יִקְרַב; inf. קְרֹב, imp. קְרַב.—I. *to draw* or *come near, approach,* with בְּ, לְ, אֶל.—II. *to advance* in order to attack, with אֶל, עַל.—III. *to keep by oneself,* with אֶל, Is. 65. 5, comp. נִגְּשָׁה־הָלְאָה. Niph. *to draw near, approach.* Pi. קֵרַב.—I. *to bring near, cause to approach* or *advance.*—II. intrans. *to be near,* Eze. 36. 8. Hiph. I. *to cause to come near, to allow* or *let approach.*—II. *to bring* or *join together,* Is. 5. 8.—III. *to bring, offer* or *present* a gift, offering.—IV. *to remove,* with מִן, 2 Ki. 16. 14. —V. intrans. *to draw near, approach.*

קְרֵב Chald. *to come near.* Pa. *to bring, offer,* Ezr. 7. 17. Aph. I. *to bring near,* Da. 7. 17.—II. *to bring, offer,* Ezr. 6. 10, 17.

קָרֵב masc. dec. 5 a, *drawing near, approaching.*

קָרוֹב masc. dec. 3 a, קְרוֹבָה fem. dec. 10, adj.—I. *near,* of place or time; De. 32. 17, מִקָּרוֹב *from near, from the vicinity.*—II. *kindred.*—III. *short, of short continuance,* Job 17. 12; מִקָּרוֹב adv. (*a*) *for a short time,* Job 20. 5; (*b*) *shortly, soon,* Eze. 7. 8.

קְרָב masc. (pl. קְרָבוֹת) *encounter, battle, war.*

קְרָב Chald. id. Da. 7. 21.

קִרְבָה fem. dec. 11 c, *approach, access.*

קָרְבָּן masc. dec. 2 b, and קֻרְבָּן (Eze. 40. 43), *an offering, oblation, sacrifice.*

קֻרְבָּן masc. dec. 2 b, id. Ne. 10. 35; 13. 31.

קֶרֶב[c] וְ masc. dec. 6 a (with suff. קִרְבִּי).—I. *inward part, inwards, bowels;* hence *the heart.*—II. *the inner part, middle, midst;* בְּקֶרֶב *in the midst, middle, among;* and of time, *within,* Hab. 3. 2.

קָרֵב[d] וְ Piel imp. sing. masc. (§ 10. rem. 1) קרב

קָרֵב וְ adj. masc. sing. dec. 5 a . . . קרב

קְרָב[e] וּ׳ noun masc. s. d. 1 a (§ 30. No. 3); וּ bef. (:) קרב

קְרַב Kal imp. sing. masc. . . . . קרב

קְרֵב[f] Chald. Peal pret. 3 pers. sing. m. (§ 47. r. 6) קרב

קָרְבָה[g], וְ׳ קָרֵבָה[h] } Kal pret. 3 pers. sing. fem. (§ 8. rem. 1 & 7) . . . . } קרב

קָרְבָה[i] id. imp. 2 pers. s. m. parag. ה (§ 8. rem. 11) קרב

קְרֹבָה adj. fem. sing. dec. 10, from קָרוֹב masc. . קרב

קָרְבוּ[k] וְ׳ Kal pret. 3 pers. pl. קרב

קָרְבוּ וְ Piel imp. pl. masc. . . . קרב

קָרְבוּ id. pret. 3 pers. pl. . . . . קרב

קְרִבוּ Chald. Peal pret. 3 pers. pl. masc. (§ 47. r. 6) קרב

קְרֹבוֹ adj. masc. sing., suff. 3 pers. sing. masc. from קָרוֹב dec. 3 a . . קרב

קִרְבּוֹ וְ noun masc. sing., suff. 3 pers. sing. masc from קֶרֶב dec. 6 a . . . קרב

קִרְבוּ Kal imp. pl. masc. . . . . קרב

קְרָבוֹת[m] noun masc. with pl. fem. term. from קְרָב dec. 1 a (§ 30. No. 3) . . . קרב

קִרְבִּי[n] וְ noun masc. sing., suff. 1 pers. sing. from קֶרֶב dec. 6 a . . . . . קרב

קְרָבַי[o] id. pl. with suff. 1 pers. sing. . . קרב

קְרֵבִים[p] adj. masc., pl. of קָרֵב dec. 5 a . . קרב

קְרֹבִים adj. masc., pl. of קָרוֹב dec. 3 a . . קרב

קִרְבָּם noun masc. sing., suff. 3 pers. pl. masc. from קֶרֶב dec. 6 a . . . . קרב

קָרְבָּן noun masc. sing. dec. 2 b (but comp. § 30. r. 3) קרב

קָרְבַּן id., constr. st. . . . . קרב

קֻרְבָּן[q] Chald. noun masc. sing. . . . קרב

קָרְבָּנָהּ[r] noun masc. sing., suff. 3 pers. sing. fem. from קָרְבָּן dec. 2 b . . . . קרב

קִרְבָּנָה[s] noun masc. sing., suff. 3 pers. sing. fem. (§ 3. rem. 5) from קֶרֶב dec. 6 a . . קרב

קָרְבָּנוֹ וְ׳ noun masc. sing., suff. 3 pers. sing. masc. from קָרְבָּן dec. 2 b . . . . קרב

קָרְבָּנִי[u] id., suff. 1 pers. sing. . . . קרב

קָרְבָּנֵיהֶם[v] id. pl., suff. 3 pers. pl. masc. (others read קָרְבְּנֵיהֶם) . . . . . קרב

קָרְבָּנְךָ[w], קָרְבָּנֶךָ[x] } id. sing., suff. 2 pers. sing. masc. . קרב

קָרְבַּנְכֶם[a] id. sing., suff. 2 pers. pl. masc. . . קרב

קָרְבָּנָם id. sing., suff. 3 pers. pl. masc. . . קרב

קָרַבְתָּ[b], קָרַבְתָּ[c], וְקָרַבְתָּ[d] } Kal pret. 2 pers. sing. masc.; acc. shifted by conv. וְ (§ 8. rem. 7) . } קרב

קִרְבַת noun fem. sing., constr. of [קִרְבָה] dec. 11 c קרב

קִרְבֵת[e] Chald. Peal pret. 1 pers. sing. . . קרב

וְקָרַבְתִּי[f] וְ Kal pret. 1 pers. sing.; acc. shifted by conv. וְ (§ 8. rem. 7) . . . . קרב

קֵרַבְתִּי[g] Piel pret. 1 pers. sing. . . . . קרב

[קַרְדֹּם] masc. dec. 8 c (pl. קַרְדֻּמּוֹת, ־דֻּמִּים), *an axe.*

קַרְדֻּמּוֹ[h] id. with suff. 3 pers. sing. masc.

קַרְדֻּמּוֹת[i] id. with pl. fem. term.

[קָרָה] fut. יִקְרֶה.—I. *to meet, to go* or *come to meet.*— II. *to befall, happen* to any one, with acc., לְ, of

---

[a] Is. 51. 19. [b] Ju. 14. 15. [c] Ps. 64. 7. [d] Eze. 37. 17. [e] Ps. 55. 22. [f] Da. 3. 26. [g] Zep. 3. 2. [h] De. 15. 9; 25. 11. [i] Ps. 69. 19. [k] Eze. 42. 14. [l] Is. 41. 21. [m] Ps. 68. 31. [n] Is. 16. 11. [o] Ps. 103. 1. [p] De. 20. 3. [q] Ne. 10. 35. [r] Nu. 5. 15. [s] Ge. 41. 21. [t] Nu. 7. 13. [u] Nu. 28. 2. [w] Le. 7. 38. [x] Le. 2. 5, 7. [z] Le. 2. 13. [a] Le. 1. 2. [b] De. 2. 37. [c] La. 3. 57. [d] De. 2. 19. [e] Da. 7. 16. [f] Mal. 3. 5. [g] Is. 46. 13. [h] 1 Sa. 13. 20. [i] Ps. 74. 5.

the person. Niph. I. *to meet, fall in with*, with אֶל, עַל.—II. *to happen, chance*, 2 Sa. 1. 6. Pi. קֵרָה *to join* or *lay beams* or *rafter*; hence *to frame, build*, Ps. 104. 3. Hiph. I. *to cause to meet, to let occur.*—II. *to make suitable, convenient*, Nu. 35. 11.

קָרֶה masc. dec. 9b, *accident*, De. 23. 11.

קוֹרָה fem. dec. 10.—I. *a beam.*—II. *a roof*, Ge. 19. 8.

קְרִי masc. only in pause קֶרִי (§ 35. rem. 14), *contrariness, opposition*; with הָלַךְ *to walk contrary, in opposition.*

קִרְיָה fem. (no pl.)—I. *city, town.*—II. combined in pr. names of cities or towns. קִרְיַת אַרְבַּע (*city of Arba*) the ancient Hebron in Judah, comp. Ge. 23. 2.—קִ׳ בַּעַל (*city of Baal*) i. q. קִ׳ יְעָרִים.—קִ׳ חֻצוֹת (*city of streets*) in Moab, Nu. 22. 39.—קִ׳ יְעָרִים, קִ׳ עָרִים (*city of forests*) in the confines of Judah and Benjamin.—קִ׳ סַנָּה (*city of palms*) & קִ׳ סֵפֶר (*city of the book*) in Judah, also called דְּבִיר.—קִרְיָתַיִם (*double-city*) one in the tribe of Reuben; and another in Naphtali, 1 Ch. 6. 61, also called קַרְתָּן.

קִרְיָה, קִרְיָא Chald. fem. dec. 8 a, idem, Ezr. 4. 10, 12, 13, 15.

קְרִיּוֹת (*cities*) pr. name—I. of a city in Judah, Jos. 15. 25.—II. of another in Moab.

קֶרֶת fem. poet. i. q. קִרְיָה *a city.*

קַרְתָּה (*city*) pr. name of a town in Zebulun, Jos. 21. 34.

קַרְתָּן pr. name of a town, Jos. 21. 32, the same as קִרְיָתַיִם see קִרְיָה.

מִקְרֶה masc. dec. 9a.—I. *chance, accident.*—II. *event, result.*

מְקָרֶה masc. *building, edifice*, Ec. 10. 18.

קָרָה noun fem. sing. dec. 10 [for קָרָה fr. קַר m.] . קרר

קָרֵהוּ[a] וְ׳ Kal pret. 3 pers. sing. masc. [קָרָה], suff. 3 pers. sing. masc. (§ 24. rem. 21) . קרה

קָרוּא[b] Kal part. pass. sing. masc. dec. 3a . . קרא

קְרוּאֵי Kh. קְרוּאֵי constr. of the foll.; K. קְרִיאֵי adj. pl. constr. masc. [from קָרִיא] dec. 3a . קרא

וּקְרוּאִים[c] Kal part. pass. pl. m. fr. קָרוּא d. 3a; וּ bef. (:) קרא

קָרוֹב וְ׳ adj. masc. sing. dec. 3a . . . קרב

קְרוֹב[d] Kal inf. constr. . . . . . קרב

קְרוֹבָה adj. fem. sing. dec. 10, from קָרוֹב masc. קרב

קְרוֹבַי[e], וּקְרוֹבַי[f] } id. pl. masc., suff. 1 pers. pl.; וּ bef. (:) קרב

קְרוֹבִים id. pl. masc., abs. st. . . . . קרב

קְרוּהוּ[g] Piel pret. 3 pers. pl., suff. 3 pers. sing. masc. קרה

קָרוּעַ[h] Kal part. pass. sing. masc. dec. 3a . . קרע

קְרוּעֵי id. pl., constr. st. . . . . . קרע

קֹרוֹת[i] noun fem., pl. of קוֹרָה dec. 10 . . קרה

[קָרַח] *to make* (smooth) *bald.* Niph. *to be made bald*, Je. 16. 6. Hiph. i. q. Kal, Eze. 27. 31. Hoph. pass. Eze. 29. 18. Hence the following.

קֶרַח, וְקֶרַח[k] } masc. (§ 35. rem. 2).—I. *ice.*—II. *cold.*—III. *crystal*, Eze. 1. 22 . . } קרח

קָרֵחַ (*bald-head*) pr. name m. 2 Ki. 25. 23; Je. 40. 8 קרח

קֵרֵחַ masc. [for קֵרֵחַ § 26. No. 9] one *bald* on the crown of the head . . . . קרח

קֹרַח וְ׳ masc. dec. 6c (§ 35. rem. 5).—I. *ice*, Ps. 147. 17.—II. pr. name, *Korah*, a son of Esau, Ge. 36. 5, 14.—III. a son of Eliphaz, and a tribe descended from him.—IV. a Levite who conspired against Moses. Patronym. קָרְחִי . . . . . קרח

קָרְחָא[l], קָרְחָה { fem. dec. 10, & קָרַחַת dec. 13a (with suff. קָרַחְתּוֹ).—I. *baldness, bald part* on the crown or front part of the head.—II. trop. *bareness, threadbare spot*, only Le. 13. 55 } קרח

קָרְחוֹ[m] noun m. s., suff. 3 p. s. m. fr. [קֹרַח] d. 6c קרח

קָרְחִי[n] Kal imp. sing. fem. (§ 8. rem. 12) . קרח

קָרְחָתֵךְ[o] noun fem. sing., suff. 2 pers. sing. fem. from קָרְחָה (no pl.) . . . . . קרח

קֶרִי[p] noun masc. sing. [for קְרִי § 35. rem. 14] קרה

קְרֵי[q] Chald. Peal part. pass. sing. masc. (§ 35. r. 4) קרא

קִרְיָא[r] Chald. noun fem. sing. dec. 8a . . קרה

קְרִיאֵי[s] Kh. קְרִיאֵי adj. pl. constr. masc. [from קָרִיא dec. 3a, K. קְרוּאֵי (q. v.) . . . קרא

קִרְיָה noun fem. sing. (no pl.) . . . קרה

קְרִיּוֹת וּ׳ pr. name of a place; וּ bef. (:) . . קרה

קָרִים adj. masc. pl., of קַר dec. 8 (§ 37. rem. 7) קרר

קִרְיַת וְ׳ noun fem. s., constr. of קִרְיָה (no pl.); also pr. name, and in compos. as קִ׳ אַרְבַּע &c. קרה

קִרְיְתָא[t] וְ׳ Chald. noun fem. s., emph. of קִרְיָא d. 8a קרה

קִרְיָתַיִם, קִרְיָתָיִם וְ׳ } pr. name of a place, see קִרְיָה . . קרה

קִרְיַת יְעָרִים וְ׳ id. with parag. ה, K. תִימָה׳ . . קרה

קָרְךָ[u] Kal pret. 3 pers. sing. masc. (קָרָה), suff. 2 pers. sing. masc. (§ 24. rem. 21) . קרה

[קָרַם] *to cover*, with עַל, Eze. 37. 6; intrans. ver. 8.

וְקָרַמְתִּי[x] Kal pret. 1 pers. sing.; acc. shifted by conv. וְ (§ 8. rem. 7) . . . . קרם

---

[a] Ge. 44. 29. [b] Est. 5. 12. [c] Eze. 23. 23. [d] Ps. 32. 9. [e] Job 19. 14. [f] Ps. 38. 12. [g] Ne. 3. 3, 6. [h] 2 Sa. 15. 32. [i] Ca. 1. 17. [k] Ge. 31. 40. [l] Eze. 27. 31. [m] Ps. 147. 17. [n] Mi. 1. 16. [o] Mi. 1. 16. [p] Le. 26. 21, 23, 28. [q] Ezr. 4. 18, 23. [r] Ezr. 4. 15. [s] Nu. 1. 16. [t] Ezr. 4. 12, 13, 15, 16, 19, 21. [u] De. 25. 18. [x] Eze. 37. 6.

קֶרֶן ו׳ fem. dec. 6a (du. קַרְנַיִם, קַרְנָיִם; pl. קְרָנוֹת, c. קַרְנוֹת).—I. *horn* of an animal.—II. *horn*, as a vessel for oil.—III. *horn, wind instrument*, Jos. 6. 5.—IV. *horn*, as a symbol of *strength, power* in men or state; הֵרִים קֶרֶן *to lift up, exalt the horn*, i. e. to strengthen.—V. *peak, summit of a mountain*, Is. 5. 1.—VI. pl. *horns* or the projecting points on the four corners of an altar.—VII. du. *beams, rays* of light, Hab. 3. 4.—VIII. קֶרֶן הַפּוּךְ (*paint-horn*), pr. name fem. Job 42. 14.

קֶרֶן Chald. d. 3a (du. קַרְנַיִן § 59), idem. Hence

קָרַן *to emit rays, to shine*, Ex. 34. 29, 30, 35.
Hiph. *to have horns*, Ps. 69. 32.

קָרֶן	in pause for קֶרֶן (§ 35. rem. 2) . .	קרן
קַרְנָא[a] ו׳	Ch. noun f. s., emph. of קֶרֶן dec. 3a (§ 59)	קרן
קַרְנוֹ	Heb. id., suff. 3 pers. sing. masc. dec. 6a	קרן
קַרְנוֹת	id. pl., constr. st.	קרן
קְרָנוֹת[b]	id. pl. fem., abs. st.	קרן
קַרְנוֹתָיו[c]	id. pl. fem., suff. 3 pers. sing. masc. .	קרן
קַרְנֵי[d] ו׳	id. du., constr. of קַרְנַיִם . . .	קרן
קַרְנִי	id. sing., suff. 1 pers. sing. . .	קרן
קַרְנַיָּא[e] ו׳	Ch. id. du., emph. of קַרְנַיִן . .	קרן
קַרְנָיו[f]	Heb. id. du., suff. 3 pers. sing. masc. .	קרן
קַרְנָיו[g]	id. du. (קַרְנַיִם q. v.), suff. 3 pers. sing. masc.	קרן
קַרְנַיִם[h] / קַרְנָיִם[i]	id. du., abs. st.	קרן
קְרָנַיִם[k]	id. du. [for קַרְנַיִם as if from קָרָן]	קרן
קַרְנַיִן[l] ו	Chald. id. du., abs. st. . . .	קרן
קַרְנְךָ[m]	Heb. id. sing., suff. 2 pers. sing. masc. .	קרן
קַרְנֵךְ[n]	id. sing., suff. 2 pers. sing. fem. . .	קרן
קַרְנְכֶם[o]	id. sing., suff. 2 pers. pl. masc. . .	קרן
קַרְנֵנוּ[p]	id. sing., suff. 1 pers. pl. . . .	קרן
קַרְנֹת	id. pl. fem., constr. st. . . .	קרן
קַרְנֹתָיו	id. pl. fem., suff. 3 pers. sing. masc. . .	קרן

[קָרַס] *to bend, stoop*.

קֶרֶס masc. dec. 6a (pl. c. קַרְסֵי), *hook, tache*.

קֵרֹס, קֵירֹס (*weaver's comb*; from the Chald.) pr. name masc. Ezr. 2. 44; Ne. 7. 47.

קַרְסֹל masc. du. קַרְסֻלַּיִם *ankles*, 2 Sa. 22. 37; Ps. 18. 37.

קֵרֹס	pr. name masc.	קרס
קֹרֵס[q]	Kal part. act. sing. masc. . . .	קרס
קָרְסוּ[r]	id. pret. 3 pers. pl.	קרס
קַרְסֵי	noun masc. pl., constr. from [קֶרֶס] dec. 6a .	קרס
קְרָסָיו	id. pl., suff. 3 pers. sing. masc. . .	קרס
קַרְסֻלָּי	noun du., suff. 1 pers. sing. fr. [קַרְסֹל] dec. 8c	קרס

קָרַע ו׳ I. *to tear, rend*.—II. *to tear off* or *away*.—III *to cut in pieces*, Je. 36. 23.—IV. *to cut out*. Niph. *to be rent, torn*.

קֶרַע masc. only pl. קְרָעִים *rendings, rags*.

קָרֹעַ[s]	Kal inf. abs.	קרע
קֹרֵעַ	id. part. act. sing. masc. . . .	קרע
קָרְעָה[t]	id. pret. 3 pers. sing. fem. [for קָרְעָה § 8. r. 7]	קרע
קָרְעוּ	id. pret. 3 pers. pl.	קרע
קִרְעוּ[u] ו׳	id. imp. pl. masc.	קרע
קִרְעִי[w] ו׳	defect. for קִרְעוּ (q. v.) . . .	קרע
קְרָעִים[a] ו׳	noun masc., pl. of [קֶרַע] dec. 6 (§ 35. rem. 5); ו bef. (:) . . .	קרע
קְרֻעִים	Kal part. pass. pl. masc. from קָרוּעַ dec. 3a	קרע
קָרַעְתָּ	id. pret. 2 pers. sing. masc. . .	קרע
קָרַעְתִּי[b] / וְקָרַעְתִּי[c]	id. pret. 1 pers. sing.; acc. shifted by conv. ו (§ 8. rem. 7) . .	קרע

[קָרַץ] *to close, press together*, as the lips or eyes, denoting fraud, cunning, &c. (Prof. Lee). Others, *to cut, bite* the lips; this is however unsuitable of the eyes. Pu. *to be cut out*, Job 33. 6.

קְרַץ Chald. masc. dec. 3a, *a piece*; only in the phrase אֲכַל קַרְצֵי דִּי *to eat the pieces of* any one, q. d. *to eat him up in piece-meal*, metaph. for *to slander*. The figure is taken from various dogs devouring a corpse; comp. the English *backbite*. Also

קֶרֶץ[d]	masc. *destruction*, Je. 46. 20 . . .	קרץ
קֹרֵץ	Kal part. act. sing. masc. . . .	קרץ
קַרְצוֹהִי[e]	Chald. noun masc. pl., suff. 3 pers. sing. masc. from [קְרַץ] dec. 3a .	קרץ
קַרְצֵיהוֹן[f]	Chald. id. pl., suff. 3 pers. pl. masc. .	קרץ
קֹרַצְתִּי[g]	Pual pret. 1 pers. sing. . . .	קרץ

קַרְקַע[h] masc.—I. *floor, bottom*.—II. *bottom* of the sea, Am. 9. 3.—III. pr. n. of a town in Judah, Jos. 15. 3.

וְקַרְקַר[i]	Piel inf. abs. (§ 6. No. 4) . .	קור

קָרַר Root not used; Syr. *to be cold*; Arab. *to be cool, quiet*.

קַר masc. (pl. קָרִים § 37. rem. 7) adj.—I. *cold, cool*.—II. *cool, quiet*, Pr. 17. 27.

קֹר masc. *cold*, Ge. 8. 22.

קָרָה fem. dec. 10, idem.

מְקֵרָה fem. *a cooling, refreshing*, Ju. 3. 20, 24.

---

[a] Da. 7. 20, 21. [b] Zec. 2. 1. [c] Eze. 43. 20. [d] De. 33. 17. [e] Da. 7. 8, 20, 24. [f] De. 33. 17. [g] Da. 8. 7. [h] Am. 6. 13. [i] Hab. 3. 4. [k] Da. 8. 3. [l] Da. 7. 7. [m] 1 Sa. 16. 1. [n] Mi. 4. 13. [o] Ps. 75. 6. [p] Ps. 89. 18. [q] Is. 46. 1. [r] Is. 46. 2. [s] 1 Ki. 11. 11. [t] 2 Sa. 13. 19. [u] 2 Sa. 3. 31. [w] Joel 2. 13. [y] 2 Sa. 13. 31. [z] Je. 41. 5.

[a] Pr. 23. 21. [b] Ezr. 9. 3. [c] Eze. 13. 20, 21. [d] Je. 46. 20. [e] Da. 6. 25. [f] Da. 3. 8. [g] Job 33. 6. [h] 1 Ki. 6. 15, 30. [i] Nu. 24. 17.

קֶרֶשׁ Root not used; Arab. *to cut.* Hence

קֶרֶשׁ[a] קָרֶשׁ } masc. dec. 6a (with suff. קַרְשֵׁךְ).—I. *board, plank.*—II. *bench* of a ship.

קַרְשֵׁי id. pl., constr. st. . . . . . קרש

קְרָשָׁיו id. pl., suff. 3 pers. sing. masc. . . . קרש

קְרָשִׁים id. pl., abs. st. . . . . . קרש

קַרְשֵׁךְ[b] id. sing., suff. 2 pers. sing. fem. . . . קרש

קֶרֶת noun fem. sing. [for קָרֶת comp. § 35. r. 2] קרה

קַרְתָּה pr. name of a place . . . . . קרה

קָרָתוֹ[c] noun fem. sing., suff. 3 pers. sing. masc. from קָרָה [for קִרָּה] dec. 10 . . . קרר

קַרְתִּי Kal pret. 1 pers. sing. . . . . . קור

קוֹרָתִי[d] noun fem. sing., suff. 1 pers. s. fr. קוֹרָה d. 10 קרה

קַרְתָּן pr. name of a place . . . . . קרה

קַשׁ[e] קָשׁ } noun masc. sing. . . . . קשש

קָשָׁא Root not used; prob. i. q. קָשָׁה *to be hard.*

קִשֻּׁא masc. d. 1a, *cucumber* or *melon,* Nu. 11. 5.

מִקְשָׁה fem. (for מִקְשָׁאָה) *field* or *garden of cucumbers,* Is. 1. 8.

[קָשַׁב] fut. יִקְשַׁב *to attend, listen,* Is. 32. 3. Hiph. *to attend to, hearken,* with בְּ, עַל, אֶל, לְ.

קַשָּׁב fem. קַשֶּׁבֶת adj. *attentive,* Ne. 1. 6, 11.

קַשֻּׁב adj. id. Ps. 130. 2. Also

קֶשֶׁב[f] קָשֶׁב } masc. (§ 35. rem. 2) *attention* . . . קשב

קַשֻּׁבוֹת adj. pl. fem. [from קַשָּׁב masc.] . . . קשב

קַשֶּׁבֶת[g] adj. fem. sing. from קַשָּׁב masc. (§ 39. No. 4) קשב

[קָשָׂה] fem. dec. 11a, *dish, bowl.*

קְשָׂוָה fem. dec. 12a, id.

קֶסֶת fem. *a vessel for ink, inkhorn,* Eze. 9. 2, 3, 11.

קַשְׂקֶשֶׂת fem. (pl. קַשְׂקְשׂוֹת, קַשְׂקַשִּׂים § 39. No. 4. rem. 1).—I. *scales* of a fish.—II. *scale armour,* 1 Sa. 17. 5.

[קָשָׁה] I. *to be hard, harsh, severe.*—II. *to be hard, difficult.* Niph. part. נִקְשָׁה *subject to hardships,* Is. 8. 21. Pi. *to labour hard, have hard labour,* of a parturient woman, Ge. 35. 16. Hiph. הִקְשָׁה.—I. *to harden* sc. the neck, the heart, make stubborn, obdurate. —II. *to make hard, grievous,* a yoke.—III. *to make hard, difficult.*—IV. i. q. Pi. Ge. 35. 17.

קָשֶׁה masc. dec. 9b, קָשָׁה fem. dec. 11a; adj.— I. *hard, firm, unyielding;* with לֵב, עֹרֶף *stiff-necked, hard-hearted, stubborn, obstinate;* with פָּנִים *impudent.*—II. *hard, vehement, strong.*—III. *hard, severe, grievous.*—IV. *hard, difficult,* Ex. 18. 26.— V. *heavy, depressed,* 1 Sa. 1. 15.

קְשִׁי masc. *stubbornness,* De. 9. 27.

קִשְׁיוֹן (*hardness*) pr. name of a place in Issachar, Jos. 19. 20; 21. 28; called also קֶדֶשׁ, 1 Ch. 6. 57.

מִקְשֶׁה masc. *a wreathing, plaiting* of the hair, Is. 3. 24 (Prof. Lee), comp. the following.

מִקְשָׁה fem. *turned work, opus turnatum.* Arab. קשא *to take off the bark,* espec. by *turning* (Gesenius); *opere tornatili elaboravit* (Prof. Lee).

קָשָׁה[h] וְ fem. of the foll., dec. 10 . . . קשה

קָשֶׁה adj. masc. sing. dec. 9b . . . . קשה

קְשֵׁה id., constr. st. . . . . . קשה

קְשׁוֹט[i] Chald. noun masc. sing. . . . . קשט

קְשׁוּרָה Kal part. pass. sing. fem. [of קָשׁוּר masc.] קשר

קָשׁוֹת[k] adj. fem. pl. abs. of קָשָׁה d. 11a, fr. קָשֶׁה m. קשה

קְשׂוֹת[l] noun fem. pl. constr. from [קָשָׂה] dec. 11a קשה

קְשׂוֹתָיו[m] וּ id., suff. 3 pers. sing. masc.; וּ bef. (:) קשה

קָשַׁח. Hiph. I. *to harden, make obdurate* the heart, Is. 63. 17.—II. *to treat harshly,* Job 39. 16.

קָשַׂט Root not used; Arab. *to divide,* whence, keston, *pair of scales.*

קְשִׂיטָה fem. *something weighed,* a certain coin or weight of this name.

קָשַׁט Root not used; Arab. *to divide out equally; to be equal, right.* Hence

קֹשְׁט קֹשֶׁט } masc. *truth,* Ps. 60. 6; Pr. 22. 21 . קשט

קְשֹׁט[n] Chald. m. id. Da. 2. 47, and קְשׁוֹט Da. 4. 34 קשט

קְשֵׁי[o] וְ adj. pl. constr. masc. from קָשֶׁה dec. 9b קשה

קְשִׁי[p] noun masc. sing. . . . . . קשה

קִשְׁיוֹן וְ pr. name of a place . . . . קשה

קְשִׂיטָה noun fem. sing. . . . . . קשט

קָשִׁים[q] adj. masc., pl. of קָשֶׁה dec. 9b . . קשה

קַשְׂקַשִּׂים[r] noun fem. with pl. masc. term. from the foll. קשה

קַשְׂקֶשֶׂת וְ noun fem. sing. (§ 39. No. 4. rem. 1) קשה

קָשַׁר fut. יִקְשֹׁר.—I. *to bind, tie.*—II. *to conspire against,* with עַל.—III. part. pass. קָשׁוּר *bound, firm, strong,* Ge. 30. 42. Niph. I. *to be bound,* metaph. 1 Sa. 18. 1. —II. *to be joined, closed,* Ne. 3. 38. Pi. *to bind,* Job 38. 31; *to bind on* oneself, Is. 49. 18. Pu. part. *strong,* Ge. 30. 41. Hithp. i. q. Kal No. II.

קֶשֶׁר masc. dec. 6a (with suff. קִשְׁרוֹ), *conspiracy.*

קִשֻּׁר masc. dec. 1b, *band, girdle.*

[a] Ex. 26. 18, 20. [b] Eze. 27. 6. [c] Ps. 147. 17. [d] Ge. 19. 8. [e] Joel 2. 5. [f] Is. 21. 7. [g] Ne. 1. 6, 11. [h] Ju. 4. 24. [i] Da. 4. 34. [k] Ge. 42. 7, 30. [l] Nu. 4. 7. [m] Ex. 25. 29. [n] Da. 2. 47. [o] Eze. 2. 4; 3. 7. [p] De. 9. 27. [q] 2 Sa. 3. 39. [r] 1 Sa. 17. 5.

קָשָׁר Kal pret. 3 pers. sing. masc. for קָשַׁר (§ 8. r. 7) קשר

קֶשֶׁר, קָשֶׁר, קָשֶׁר } noun masc. sing. dec. 6a (§ 35. rem. 2), yet see the foll. . . . } קשר

קִשְׁרוֹ וְ id. with suff. 3 pers. sing. masc. . . קשר

קְשָׁרֶיהָ[a] noun masc. pl., suff. 3 pers. sing. fem. from [קֶשֶׁר] dec. 1b . . . קשר

קָשְׁרֵם Kal imp. sing. masc., suff. 3 pers. pl. masc. (ם for ן fem. in Pr. 6. 21; 7. 3, § 2. rem. 5) קשר

קָשַׁרְתִּי[b] id. pret. 1 pers. sing. . . . . קשר

קְשַׁרְתָּם[c] וּ id. pret. 2 pers. sing. masc., suff. 3 pers. pl. masc.; וּ, for וְ, conv. . . קשר

קְשַׁרְתֶּם[d] וּ,[e] id. pret. 2 pers. pl. masc.; וּ id. . . קשר

[קָשַׁשׁ] *to collect, assemble together*, Zep. 2. 1. Po. *to collect, gather*, as stubble, wood. Hithpo. *to assemble themselves*, Zep. 2. 1.

קַשׁ masc.—I. *stubble*.—II. *chaff*.

קֹשְׁשׁוּ[f] וְ Poel pret. 3 pers. pl. . . . . קשש

קָשֶׁת in pause for קֶשֶׁת (q. v. comp. § 35. rem. 2) קוש

קַשָּׁת[g] noun fem. sing. . . . . קוש

קְשַׁת[h] adj. fem. s., constr. of קָשָׁה d. 11a, fr. קָשֶׁה m. קשה

קֶשֶׁת וְ[i] noun com. sing., suff. קַשְׁתִּי, pl. קְשָׁתוֹת, c. קַשְׁתוֹת, ת treated as if radical, comp. d. 6a קוש

קָשְׁתָה[k], קָשָׁתָה[l] } Kal pret. 3 pers. sing. fem. (comp. § 8. rem. 7) . . . } קשה

קַשְׁתּוֹ noun com. s., suff. 3 pers. s. m. fr. קֶשֶׁת (q.v.) קוש

קְשָׁתוֹת וּ id. pl., abs. st.; וּ bef. (:) . . קוש

קַשְּׁתוֹתָם[m] וְ[n] id. pl., suff. 3 pers. sing. masc. . קוש

קַשְׁתִּי[o] וְ[p] id. sing., suff. 1 pers. sing. . . קוש

קַשְׁתֶּךָ[q], קַשְׁתְּךָ[s] } וְ[r] id. sing., suff. 2 pers. sing. masc. . קוש

קַשְׁתָּם id. sing., suff. 3 pers. pl. masc. . . קוש

קַשְּׁתֹתֵיהֶם[t] וְ id. pl., suff. 3 pers. pl. masc. . . קוש

קַשְּׁתֹתָיו[u] id. pl., suff. 3 pers. sing. masc. . . קוש

ר

רָאָה וְ fut. יִרְאֶה, ap. יֵרֶא, וַיַּרְא, וַתֵּרֶא (§ 24. rem. 3). —I. *to see*, generally, const. with acc., once לְ (Ps. 64. 6); espec. *to see* the sun, *to live*, Ec. 7. 11; and simply, *to see, exist, live*, Ge. 16. 13; *to see* a vision, hence part. רֹאֶה *a seer, prophet*.—II. *to see, look at, view, regard, observe*; hence *to see* either *with delight*, to rejoice in, or *with grief*, usually with בְּ; also *to care for*.—III. *to visit*.—IV. *to look out, provide, choose*, with לְ for oneself.—V. *to have in view*, Ge. 20. 10.—VI. *to perceive, experience*; hence *to perceive, understand*.—VII. *to discern, discriminate*. Niph. נִרְאָה.—I. *to be seen*. —II. *to appear*, with אֶל, לְ, אֶת־פְּנֵי.—III. *to be provided*, Ge. 22. 14. Pu. *to be seen*, Job 33. 21. Hiph. הִרְאָה, הֶרְאָה, fut. יַרְאֶה, ap. וַיַּרְא (§ 11. rem. 1; § 24. rem. 16).—I. *to cause to see, to show*.—II. *to cause to see* or *experience*, with בְּ. Hoph. I. *to be shown*.—II. *to be shown, be made to see*. Hithp. *to look at each other*.

רָאֶה adj. masc. dec. 9b, *seeing*, Job 10. 15.

רָאָה fem. the name of an unclean bird, De. 14. 13, for which in the parallel passage, Le. 11. 14, it is דָּאָה *a kite*.

רֹאֶה masc. dec. 9.—I. part. act. *seer, prophet*.—II. *vision*, Is. 28. 7, comp. חֹזֶה.

רְאוּת fem. *a seeing, viewing*, Ec. 5. 10, Keri.

רְאִי masc. *mirror*, Job 37. 18.

רֳאִי masc. (in pause רֹאִי, § 35. rem. 14).—I. *vision, revelation*, Ge. 16. 13.—II. *sight, view*.—III. *spectacle, gazing-stock*, Ne. 3. 6.

רְאִית fem. *a seeing*, Ec. 5. 10, Kheth.

רֵו Chald. masc. dec. 1a (for רְאֵו), *aspect, appearance*, Da. 2. 31; 3. 25.

רְאוּבֵן (*behold a son!*) pr. name, *Reuben*, the eldest son of Jacob, and head of the tribe which was named from him. Patronym. רְאוּבֵנִי.

רְאָיָה (*the Lord looks upon* him) pr. name masc. of three different men, for which also הָרֹאֶה, comp. 1 Ch. 4. 2, with 1 Ch. 2. 52.

יִרְאִיָּה (*the Lord shall look upon* him) pr. name masc. Je. 37. 13, 14.

מַרְאֶה masc. dec. 9a.—I. *a seeing, looking*.—II. *sight, vision*.—III. *appearance, form*.

מַרְאָה fem. dec. 10.—I. *vision*.—II. *mirror*, Ex. 38. 8.

רָאָהּ[x] Kal pret. 3 pers. sing. masc., suff. 3 pers. sing. fem. (§ 24. rem. 21). . . ראה

רָאֹה וְ[y] id. inf. abs. . . . . ראה

רְאֵה וּ id. imp. sing. masc.; וּ bef. (:) . . ראה

רְאֵה[z] וּ adj. m. s., constr. of [רָאֶה] dec. 9b; וּ id. ראה

---

[a] Je. 2. 32. [b] 2 Ki. 10. 9. [c] De. 6. 8. [d] 1 Sa. 22. 8, 13. [e] De. 11. 18. [f] Ex. 5. 7. [g] Ge. 21. 20. [h] 1 Sa. 1. 15. [i] Ho. 2. 20. [k] Ge. 49. 7. [l] 1 Sa. 5. 7. [m] Je. 51. 56. [n] Ps. 37. 15. [o] Ge. 9. 13. [p] Job 29. 20. [q] Hab. 3. 9. [r] Ge. 27. 3. [s] Eze. 39. 3. [t] Ne. 4. 7. [u] Is. 5. 28. [x] Job 28. 27. [y] Ec. 9. 11. [z] Job 10. 15.

[a]רְאֹה Kal inf. constr. ראה
[b]רֹאָה id. part. act. sing. fem. dec. 10, fr. רֹאֶה masc. ראה
[c]רֹאֵה } id. part. act. sing. masc. constr. & abs. } ראה
רֹאֶה [d]וְ' } dec. 9 a }
רָאָהוּ וְ' id. pret. 3 pers. sing. masc., suff. 3 pers. sing. masc. (§ 24. rem. 21) ראה
רָאוֹ id. inf. abs. for רָאֹה (§ 24. rem. 2) ראה
רָאוּ וְ' id. pret. 3 pers. pl. ראה
רְאוּ וּ' id. imp. pl. masc.; וּ bef. (:) ראה
[e]רֹאוּ Pual pret. 3 pers. pl. (note א with dag.) ראה
רְאוּבֵן וּ' pr. name of a man and a tribe; וּ bef. (:) ראה
רָאוּהָ Kal pret. 3 pers. pl., suff. 3 pers. sing. fem. ראה
רָאוּךָ id. id., suff. 2 pers. sing. masc. ראה
רְאוּמָה pr. name fem. ראם
רָאוּנִי[f] Kal pret. 3 pers. pl., suff. 1 pers. sing. ראה
רְאוֹת id. inf. constr. ראה
רֹאוֹת id. part. act. fem. pl. of רֹאָה d. 10, fr. רֹאֶה m. ראה
[g]רְאוֹתִי id. inf. (רְאוֹת), suff. 1 pers. sing. dec. 1 a ראה
רְאִי וּ' id. imp. sing. fem.; וּ bef. (:) ראה
רֹאַי id. part. act. pl. masc., suff. 1 pers. sing. from רֹאֶה dec. 9 a ראה
[h]רֹאֵי id. id. pl., constr. st. ראה
רֳאִי } noun masc. sing. (§ 35. rem. 14) ראה
רְאִי }
רְאָיָה וּ' pr. name masc.; וּ bef. (:) ראה
[k]רֹאֶיהָ Kal part. act. pl. masc., suff. 3 pers. sing. fem. from רֹאֶה dec. 9 a ראה
[l]רֹאֵיהֶם id. pl., suff. 3 pers. pl. masc. ראה
[m]רֹאָיו id. pl., suff. 3 pers. sing. masc. ראה
[n]רֹאַיִךְ id. pl., suff. 2 pers. sing. fem. ראה
רֹאֶיךָ id. pl., suff. 2 pers. sing. masc. ראה
רֹאִים id. pl., abs. st. ראה
[o]רְאֶינָה וּ id. imp. pl. fem. (§ 23. rem. 3); וּ bef. (:) ראה
רָאִינוּ id. pret. 1 pers. pl. ראה
[p]רִאישֹׁנָה Kh. רִאישֹׁנָה adj. fem.; K. רִאשֹׁנָה (q. v.) ראש
רָאִיתָ וְ' Kal pret. 2 pers. sing. masc. ראה
[q]רָאִית id. pret. 2 pers. sing. fem. ראה
[r]רָאִית Kh. רָאִיתָ q. v., K. רָאוֹת Kal inf. abs. (§ 24. rem. 2) ראה
[s]רְאִית Kh. רְאִית, K. רְאוּת noun fem. sing. ראה
רָאִיתָה וְ' Kal pret. 3 pers. sing. masc. (§ 8. rem. 5) ראה
רָאִיתִי וְ' id. pret. 1 pers. sing. ראה
[u]רְאִיתִיהָ וּ id. id., suff. 3 pers. sing. f.; וּ, for וְ, conv. ראה
רְאִיתִיו [x]וּ' id. id., suff. 3 pers. sing. masc.; וּ bef. (:) ראה
[y]רְאִיתִיךָ id. id., suff. 2 pers. sing. masc. ראה
רְאִיתֶם וּ' id. pret. 2 pers. pl. masc.; וּ, for וְ, conv. ראה
[z]רְאִיתֶן וּ id. pret. 2 pers. pl. fem.; וּ id. ראה

[a]רְאִיתָנִי וּ id. pret. 2 pers. sing. masc., suff. 1 pers. sing.; וּ, for וְ, conv. ראה
[b]רָאֲךָ וְ id. pret. 3 pers. sing. masc. (רָאָה), suff. 2 pers. sing. masc. (§ 24. rem. 21) ראה

[רָאַם] *to be high*, Zec. 14. 10.

רֵים ,רְאֵים ,רְאֵם masc. dec. 1 a, according to Bochart, *oryx*. A. Schultens, *buffalo* (and so Gesenius and Prof. Lee). Sept. *μονόκερως*, *unicorn*.

רָאמוֹת fem. pl.—I. *high, sublime things*, Pr. 24. 7.—II. *precious things*.—III. pr. name (*a*) of a town in Gilead, the same as רָמוֹת, רָמַת מִצְפֶּה; (*b*) of another in Issachar, 1 Ch. 6. 58.

רָאמַת נֶגֶב (*height of the south*) pr. name of a town in Simeon, Jos. 20. 8, for which רָמוֹת נֶגֶב 1 Sa. 30. 27.

רְאוּמָה (*high*) pr. name fem. Ge. 22. 24.

רָאָם Kal pret. 3 pers. sing. masc. (רָאָה), suff. 3 pers. pl. masc. (§ 24. rem. 21) ראה
רְאֵם noun masc. sing., pl. רְאֵמִים ראם
[c]וְרָאֲמָה Kal pret. 3 pers. sing. fem. ראם
רָאמוֹת [d]וְ' noun f. pl. of [רָאמָה] d. 10; also pr. name ראם
רְאֵמִים noun masc. pl. of רְאֵם ראם
רָאמֹת pr. name of a place, see רָאמוֹת ראם
[e]רֹאֵנוּ Kal part. act. sing. masc., suff. 1 pers. pl. from רֹאֶה dec. 9 a ראה
רֹאֵנִי[f] id. with suff. 1 pers. sing. (§ 2. rem. 1 & 7) ראה

ראשׁ רֹאשׁ וְ' m. irr. (§ 45).—I. *head* of men and animals.—II. *head, chief, leader*; ר' אָבוֹת, ר' בֵּית אָבוֹת *chief of a family*; כֹּהֵן הָרֹאשׁ *chief priest, high priest*.—III. *chief city, metropolis*.—IV. *chief, top, summit*, of a mountain, column.—V. *first, chief, principal* of anything; ר' פִּנָּה *head-stone of the corner*; ר' שִׂמְחָה *chief, highest joy*; רָאשֵׁי בְשָׂמִים *most precious spices*.—I. *head, first, foremost, beginning*; Ge. 2. 10, רָאשִׁים *beginnings of streams*; ר' דֶּרֶךְ *beginning of the ways, cross-ways*; of time, ר' חֳדָשִׁים *first of the months*; מֵרֹאשׁ *from the beginning*.—VI. *whole number, capital, amount, sum*, נָשָׂא ר' *to take the sum*, to number.—VII. *body, band, company*.—VIII. *a poisonous plant*; according to some, *hemlock*; others, *colocynth*. Gesenius, *the poppy*, whence מֵי ר' *opium*; and then for poison in general.

רֵאשׁ Chald. masc. dec. 1 a (pl. once רָאשִׁין § 68).—I. *head*.—II. *sum, amount*, Da. 7. 1.

a Ge. 48. 11. b Pr. 20. 12. c Ps. 64. 9. d Ec. 11. 4. e Job 33. 21. f Job 29. 8. g Ge. 46. 30. h Est. 1. 14. i Ge. 16. 13. k Est. 2. 15. l Is. 61. 9. ll La. 3. 19. m Job 20. 7. n Na. 3. 7. o Ca. 3. 11. p Jos. 21. 10. q 1 Sa. 28. 13. r Is. 42. 20. s Ec. 5. 10. t Nu. 27. 13. u Ge. 9. 16. x Da. 8. 7. y Job 8. 18. z Ex. 1. 16. a 1 Ch. 17. 17. b Ex. 4. 14. c Zec. 14. 10. d Eze. 27. 16. e Is. 29. 15. f Is. 47. 10.

רְאִשָׁה f. d. 10 (for רְאִישָׁה), *beginning*, Eze. 36. 11.

רֹאשָׁה fem. הָאֶבֶן הָרֹאשָׁה *the head-stone*, Zec. 4. 7.

רִאשׁוֹן (for רְאִישׁוֹן), רִישׁוֹן masc. d. 1 b, רִאשֹׁנָה fem. dec. 10.—I. adj. *first*, in time, order or dignity; pl. רִאשֹׁנִים *ancestors*; הָרִאשֹׁנוֹת *the former things*. —II. רִאשֹׁנָה adv. *first, foremost*; of time, *at first, before*; בָּרִאשֹׁנָה *first*, in order and time; *aforetime, formerly*; לָרִאשֹׁנָה *at the first*.

רִאשֹׁנִי fem. ־ִית *first*, Je. 25. 1.

רֵאשִׁית, רֵשִׁית fem. dec. 1 b.—I. *a beginning; former time, former state*.—II. *the first* of its kind, in respect to time, rank and worth, hence *firstling*.

רַאֲשֹׁות fem. pl., only constr. רַאֲשֹׁתֵי (with double plural, comp. § 37. rem. 5, & § 4. rem. 2) *the part about the head*, 1 Sa. 26. 12.

מָרֵאשָׁה, מָרֵשָׁה (*what is at the head*) pr. name —I. of a city in the plains of Judah.—II. of a man, 1 Ch. 2. 42.

מְרַאֲשֹׁות fem. pl. *place of* or *about the head*, hence מְרַאֲשֹׁתָיו *at his head*.

מְרַאֲשֹׁות fem. pl. (dec. 11 a) idem, Je. 13. 18.

רֹאשׁ וְ׳ pr. name of a northern nation, supposed to be the *Russians*, Eze. 38. 2, 3; 39. 1.

רָאשׁ Kal part. act. sing. masc. dec. 1 a (§ 21. r. 1) רוש

רָאשֵׁ[a] Kh. ראש q. v. K. רָאשֵׁי (q. v.) . . ראש

רֵאשׁ[b] Chald. noun masc. sing. irr. (§ 68) . ראש

רֵאשׁ[c] noun masc. sing. dec. 1 (for רֵישׁ) . . רוש

רֵאשָׁה[d] Ch. noun masc. sing. emph. of רֵאשׁ irr. (§ 68) ראש

רֵאשֵׁהּ Chald. id., suff. 3 pers. sing. masc. . ראש

רֹאשָׁהּ noun masc. sing., suff. 3 pers. sing. fem. from ראש irr. (§ 45) . . . . ראש

רֵאשְׁהוֹן[e] Chald. noun masc. sing., suff. 3 pers. pl. masc. from רֵאשׁ irr. (§ 68) . . ראש

רֹאשׁוֹ וְ׳ noun masc. sing., suff. 3 pers. sing. masc. from ראש irr. (§ 45) . . . ראש

רִאשׁוֹן adj. masc. sing. dec. 1 a . . . ראש

רִאשׁוֹנָה id. fem. as an *adv*. . . . . ראש

רָאשֵׁי וְ׳ noun masc. pl. constr. fr. ראש irr. (§ 45) ראש

רֵאשִׁי Ch. noun m. s., suff. 1 p. s. fr. רֵאשׁ irr. (§ 68) ראש

רֹאשִׁי noun m. s., suff. 1 p. s. fr. ראש irr. (§ 45) ראש

רָאשֶׁיהָ[f] id. pl., suff. 3 pers. sing. fem. . . ראש

רָאשֵׁיהֶם id. pl., suff. 3 pers. pl. masc. . . ראש

רָאשֵׁיהֶן[g] id. pl., suff. 3 pers. pl. fem. . . ראש

רָאשָׁיו[h] id. pl., suff. 3 pers. sing. masc. . . ראש

רָאשֵׁיכֶם id. pl., suff. 2 pers. plur. masc. . . ראש

רָאשִׁים id. pl., abs. st. . . . . . ראש

רָאשִׁים[i] Kal part. act. m. pl. of רָאשׁ d. 1 a (§ 21. r. 1) רוש

רֵאשִׁין[k] Ch. noun masc. pl. of רֵאשׁ irr. (§ 68) . ראש

רֵאשִׁית וְ׳ noun fem. sing. dec. 1 a . . . ראש

רֵאשִׁיתְךָ[l] id., suff. 2 pers. sing. masc. . . ראש

רֵאשִׁיתָם[m] id., suff. 3 pers. pl. masc. . . ראש

רֵאשָׁךְ[n] Ch. n. m. s., suff. 2 p. s. m. fr. רֵאשׁ irr. (§ 68) ראש

רֵאשֶׁךָ[o] noun masc. s., suff. 2 p. s. m. fr. רָאשׁ d. 1 a רוש

רֹאשְׁךָ / רֹאשֶׁךָ } noun masc. sing., suff. 2 pers. sing. masc. from ראש irr. (§ 45) . . ראש

רֹאשֵׁךְ id., suff. 2 pers. sing. fem. . . . ראש

רָאשְׁכֶם[u] id., suff. 2 pers. pl. masc. . . . ראש

רֹאשָׁם וְ׳[p] id., suff. 3 pers. pl. masc. . . . ראש

רֹאשָׁן[q] id., suff. 3 pers. pl. fem. . . . ראש

רִאשֹׁנָה adj. fem., as an *adv*. from רִאשׁוֹן m. . ראש

רֹאשֵׁנוּ[r] noun m. s., suff. 1 p. pl. fr. ראש irr. (§ 45) ראש

רִאשֹׁנוֹת וְ׳[s] / רִאשֹׁנִים } adj. pl. fem. & masc. from רִאשׁוֹן . ראש

רָאֲתָה[t] / רָאֲתָה וְ׳[w] } Kal pret. 3 pers. sing. fem. (comp. § 8. rem. 7) . . . ראה

רָאָתָה[x] defect. for רָאֲתָה (q. v.) . . . ראה

רָאָתְךָ[y] Kal pret. 3 p. s. f., suff. 2 p. s. m. (§ 24. r. 21) ראה

רְאֹתְךָ[z] id. inf. (רְאוֹת), suff. 2 pers. sing. masc. d. 1 a ראה

רָב וְ׳[a] Kal pret. 3 pers. sing. masc., or part. act. masc.; for וְ see lett. ו . . . ריב

רַב[b] Kal pret. 3 pers. sing. masc. [for רָבַב] רבב

רַב וְ׳ / רָב וְ׳, [c] } adj. & subst. (also *adv.*) masc. sing. d. 8 d (Ch. d. 5); for וְ see lett. ו רבב

רִב[d] וְ׳[e] defect. for רִיב (q. v.) . . . ריב

רַב[f] וְ K. יָרֵב q. v. R. רבה; Kh. וְרֹב (q. v.) . רבב

רֹב וְ׳ / רֹב־ וְ׳ } noun masc. sing. dec. 8 c (§ 37. rem. 2) רבב

רַבָּא Ch. adj. & subst. masc. s. emph. of רַב d. 5 a רבב

רִבֹּאוֹת[g] / רִבֹּאוֹת[h] } noun fem. pl. of רִבּוֹא see רִבּוֹ . רבב

I. [רָבַב] *to be* or *become many, numerous*. Pu. (denom. from רְבָבָה) *to increase to myriads*, Ps. 144. 13.

רַב masc. dec. 8 d, רַבָּה fem. dec. 10, adj.—I. *much, many, numerous*; adv. *much, abundantly, enough*.—II. *great, vast*.—III. *mighty, powerful*.—IV. *elder*, Ge. 25. 23; *aged*, Job 32. 9.—V. *chief, captain, leader*; hence, *a master*, one skilled in any art, Pr. 26. 10.—VI. neut. & subst. *greatness*, Ps. 145. 7; Is. 63. 7.

רַב Chald. masc. dec. 5 a, רַבָּא fem. dec. 8 a (only Da. 4. 27), adj.—I. *great, large*.—II. subst. *chief head, prince*.

---

[a] Ne. 12. 46. [b] Da. 7. 1. [c] Pr. 30. 8. [d] Da. 2. 38. [e] Da. 3. 27. [f] Mi. 3. 11. [g] Eze. 23. 42. [h] Is. 15. 2. [i] Pr. 13. 23. [k] Da. 7. 6. [l] Job 8. 7. [m] Nu. 18. 12. [n] Da. 2. 28. [o] Pr. 6. 11. [p] Eze. 44. 20. [q] La. 2. 10. [r] La. 5. 16. [s] Is. 43. 9. [t] Is. 64. 3. [u] Le. 19. 27. [w] 2 Ki. 11. 1. [x] Ps. 10. 14. [y] Job 42. 5. [z] Ex. 10. 28. [a] Is. 19. 20. [b] Ps. 18. 15. [c] De. 2. 10, 21. [d] Ex. 23. 2. [e] Job 29. 16. [f] 2 Ch. 24. 27. [g] Da. 11. 12. [h] Ezr. 2. 69.

רֹב masc. dec. 8c (also רוֹב).—I. *multitude, abundance*.—II. *greatness*.

רַבָּה (*metropolis*) pr. name—I. of the capital of the Ammonites, fully רַבַּת בְּנֵי עַמּוֹן.—II. of a city in Judah, Jos. 15. 60.

רְבָבָה fem. dec. 11c, *myriad, ten thousand*; pl. רְבָבוֹת *myriads*.

רִבְּבָא Chald. fem. dec. 8a, id. Da. 7. 10, Keri.

רִבּוֹא, רִבּוֹ fem. id. du. רִבּוֹתַיִם *two myriads*; pl. רִבּוֹת, רִבֹּאוֹת, רִבְּאוֹת *myriads*.

רִבּוֹ Chald. fem. id. pl. רִבְּוָן (dec. 8c) Da. 7. 10, Khethib.

רַבִּית (*multitude*) pr. name of a city in Issachar, Jos. 19. 20.

רְבִיבִים masc. pl. *showers of rain*.

רַבְרַב Chald. masc. dec. 2b, רַבְרְבָא fem. dec. 8a, adj. *great*, Da. 2. 48; 3. 33; 7. 3, 7, 11, 17; pl. fem. רַבְרְבָן *great* (boasting) *things*, Da. 7. 8, 20.

רַבְרְבָן Chald. masc. dec. 1a, *great, noble, prince*.

רַבְשָׁקֵה (*chief cup-bearer*) pr. name of a military chief of the Assyrians.

יָרָבְעָם (whose *people is numerous*, for יָרֹב עָם) pr. name, *Jarobeam*, commonly, *Jeroboam*, two kings of Israel, one, the son of Nebat, the other, the son of Joash.

מֵרַב (*increase*) pr. name of a daughter of Saul.

II. [רָבַב] *to shoot arrows*, Ge. 49. 23; Ps. 18. 15; unless the latter passage be rendered וּבְרָקִים רָב *and lightnings in abundance*, see רַב No. I, R. *I*.

רַב masc. dec. 8d, *arrow*, Job 16. 13.

רְבָבָה[a] וּ' noun fem. sing. dec. 11c; וּ bef. (:) . רבב
רְבָבוֹת[b] id. pl., abs. st. . . . . רבב
רִבְבוֹת[c] / רִבְבוֹת[d] } id. pl., constr. st. . . . . רבב
רְבִבִים[e] defect. for רְבִיבִים (q. v.) . . . רבב

[רָבַד] *to spread, strew, make up* a bed, Pr. 7. 16. Arab. *to bind*.

רָבִיד masc. dec. 3a, *collar, neck-chain*.

מַרְבַדִּים masc. pl. (of מַרְבָד) *coverlets*, Pr. 7. 16; 31. 22.

רְבִד[f] [for רְבִיד] noun m. s., constr. of רָבִיד d. 3a רבד
רָבַדְתִּי[g] Kal pret. 1 pers. sing. . . . . רבד

[רָבָה] fut. יִרְבֶּה, ap. יִרֶב, יֶרֶב (§ 24. rem. 3).—I. *to be* or *become many, numerous, to multiply*.—II. *to be* or *become great*, or *greater*; hence *to grow up*; also *to be mighty, powerful*. Pi. רִבָּה.—I. *to make much, to increase, multiply*.—II. *to let grow up, bring up*. Hiph. הִרְבָּה; fut. יַרְבֶּה, ap. יֶרֶב; inf. abs. הַרְבֵּה, הַרְבָּה, constr. הַרְבּוֹת.—I. *to make* or *do much, to increase*; הִרְבָּה לַעֲשׂוֹת *to increase doing*, i. e. *to do much*; הִ' לְהָבִיא *to bring much*; inf. הַרְבֵּה, rarely הַרְבּוֹת adv. *much*; לְהַרְבֵּה *plentifully*.—II. *to increase, multiply*.—III. *to have much* or *many*.—IV. *to give much*, Ex. 30. 15.—V. *to make great, enlarge*.

רְבָה Ch. *to become great, to grow*, Da. 4. 8, 19. Pa. *to make great, exalt*, Da. 2. 48.

רְבוּ Chald. fem. dec. 9b, *greatness*.

אַרְבֶּה masc. a species of *locust*.

מַרְבֶּה masc. dec. 9a, *increase, abundance*.

מִרְבָּה fem. *largeness, amplitude*, Eze. 23. 32.

מַרְבִּית fem. dec. 1b.—I. *multitude*, 2 Ch. 30. 18.—II. *greatness*, 2 Ch. 9. 6.—III. *the greater part*, 1 Ch. 12. 29.—IV. *increase, offspring*, 1 Sa. 2. 33.—V. *increase, interest, usury*, Le. 25. 37.

תַּרְבּוּת fem. *progeny*, Nu. 32. 14.

תַּרְבִּית fem. *interest, usury*.

רַבָּה[h] Kal pret. 3 pers. sing. fem. [for רָבְבָה] . רבב
רַבָּה וְ' adj. fem. s. d. 10, fr. רַב m. (also pr. name) רבב
רַבֵּה[i] Piel inf. abs. [for רַבֵּה] . . . רבה
רְבָה[k] Chald. Peal pret. 3 pers. sing. masc. . רבה
רְבֵה[l] וּ Kal imp. sing. masc.; וּ bef. (:) . . רבה
רֹבֶה[m] id. part. act. sing. masc. . . . רבה
רָבוּ Kal pret. 3 pers. pl. . . . . ריב
רָבוּ וְ' Kal pret. 3 pers. pl. . . . רבה
רַבּוּ / וְ' רָבּוּ } Kal pret. 3 pers. pl. . רבב
רִבּוֹ[ll] וְ' noun fem. sing. dec. 1b (Chald. dec. 8c) רבב
רַבּוּ[n] וָ Kal pret. 3 pers. pl.; for וָ see lett. ו . רבב
רִבּוֹ[o] Kh. רִבּוֹ q. v., K. רֻבֵּי n. m. pl. c. fr. רֹב d. 8c רבב
רְבוּ וּ Kal imp. pl. masc.; וּ bef. (:) . . רבה
רְבוּ[p] וּ Chald. noun fem. sing. dec. 8c; וּ id. . רבה
רִבּוֹא noun fem. sing. dec. 1b . . רבב
רִבְּוָן[q] Ch. Kh., pl. of רִבּוֹ; K. רִבְבָן, pl. of רְבָבָה רבב
רָבוּעַ Kal part. pass. sing. masc. dec. 3a . רבע
רַבּוֹת[nn] וְ'' adj. fem. pl. of רַבָּה dec. 10, fr. רַב masc. רבב
רְבוֹת[r] Kal inf. constr. . . . . רבה
רִבּוֹת[s] noun fem. pl. of רִבּוֹ dec. 1b . . רבב
רִבוֹת[t] וְ noun masc. with pl. f. term. fr. רִיב dec. 1a ריב
רְבוּתָא[pp] וּ' Ch. noun f. s., emph. of רְבוּ d. 8c; וּ bef. (:) רבה
רְבוּתָךְ[u] וּ Chald. noun fem. sing., suff. 2 pers. sing. masc. from רְבוּ dec. 9b; וּ id. . רבה
רַבֵּי[x] וְ' noun masc. pl. constr. from רַב dec. 8d רבב

[a] Ps. 91. 7. [b] 1 Sa. 18. 8. [c] Nu. 10. 36. [d] De. 33. 17. [e] Je. 3. 3. [f] Ge. 41. 42. [g] Pr. 7. 16. [h] Ge. 18. 20. [i] Ju. 9. 29. [k] Da. 4. 8, 17, 30. [l] Ge. 35. 11. [ll] Da. 7. 10. [m] Ge. 21. 20. [n] Ge. 49. 23. [nn] Da. 11. 41. [o] Ho. 8. 12. [p] Da. 4. 33. [pp] Da. 5. 19. [q] Da. 7. 10. [r] Ex. 11. 9. [s] Ne. 7. 71. [t] Job 13. 6. [u] Da. 4. 19. [x] Je. 39. 13; 41. 1.

רִבִּי[a] Chald. Pael pret. 3 pers. sing. masc. . רבה
רְבִיבִים[b] noun masc. pl. abs. . . . . . רבב
רָבִיד[c] וְ noun masc. sing. dec. 3 a . . . רבד
רִבָּיו[d] noun masc. pl., suff. 3 pers. sing. masc. from רַב dec. 8 d . . . . . רבב
רַבִּים וְ' adj. & subst. masc. pl. of רַב dec. 8 d . רבב
רְבִיעִי adj. ord. masc. from אַרְבַּע . . . רבע
רְבִיעָאָה[e] Chald. Kh. רְבִיעָיָא, K. רְבִיעָאָה adj. ord. sing. masc., emph. [of רְבִיעַי dec. 7. § 63] רבע
רְבִיעָאָה[f] Chald. Kh. רְבִיעָיָא, K. רְבִיעָאָה id. fem. abs. dec. 11 [from רְבִיעַי masc.] . רבע
רְבִיעִים[g] adj. ord. masc., pl. of רְבִיעִי . רבע
רְבִיעִית[h] וְ' id. sing. fem. from רְבִיעִי masc.; וּ bef. (:) רבע
רְבִיעָיְתָא[i] Chald. adj. ord. sing. fem., emph. of רְבִיעָאָה dec. 11 [from רְבִיעַי masc.] . רבע
רְבִיעִת[k] וּ defect. for רְבִיעִית (q. v.) . רבע
רְבִית[l] Chald. Kh. רְבַיְתָ, K. contr. רְבַת Peal pret. 2 pers. sing. masc. . . . . רבה
רָבִיתָ[m] וְ Kal pret. 2 pers. sing. masc. . . רבה
רִבִּיתָ[n] Piel pret. 2 pers. sing. masc. . . רבה
רִבִּיתִי[o] וְ id. pret. 1 pers. sing. . . . רבה
רִבִּיתֶם[p] וּ id. pret. 2 pers. pl. masc.; וּ, for וְ, conv. רבה

רָבַךְ Kal not used; Arab. *to mix*. Hoph. part. מֻרְבֶּכֶת *mixed, saturated*.

רָבַל Root not used. Arab. *to be much, fertile, abundant*.
רִבְלָה (*fertility*) pr. name of a city on the northern borders of Palestine.

רִבְלָתָה id. with parag. ה.

I. **[רָבַע]** *to lie with*, carnally. Hiph. *to copulate*, Le. 19. 19.
רֶבַע masc. *a lying down*, only רִבְעִי, Ps. 139. 3.

II. **[רָבַע]** Kal only in part. pass. רָבוּעַ (denom. from אַרְבַּע *four*) *four-sided, four-square*. Pu. part. מְרֻבָּע idem.
אַרְבַּע fem. אַרְבָּעָה, constr. אַרְבַּעַת masc.—I. num. card. *four*; rarely for the ordinal, *fourth*; with suff. אַרְבַּעְתָּם *they four*; du. אַרְבַּעְתַּיִם *four-fold*; pl. אַרְבָּעִים com. *forty*.—II. *Arba*, pr. name of a giant.
אַרְבַּע Chald. fem. אַרְבְּעָה masc. *four*.
רֶבַע masc. dec. 6 a (pl. with suff. רִבְעֵיהֶן § 35. rem. 5).—I. *a fourth part*.—II. *a side*, i. e. one side of four.—III. pr. name of a king of the Midianites.
רֹבַע masc. *the fourth part*.
רִבֵּעַ masc. only pl. רִבֵּעִים *posterity in the fourth generation*.
רְבִיעִי masc. רְבִיעִית fem. adj. ordinal, *fourth* בְּנֵי רְבִיעִים *children of the fourth generation*; fem. רְבִיעִית *the fourth part*.
רְבִיעַי Chald. id., רְבִיעָיָא Kh., רְבִיעָאָה K. emph. or fem. abs., רְבִיעָיְתָא pl. fem. emph.

רֶבַע noun masc. sing. (suff. רִבְעִי) dec. 6 a (§ 35. rem. 5); also pr. name . . . בע
רֹבַע[q] וְ' noun masc. sing. . . . . בע
רֹבְעָה[r] Kal part. act. sing. fem., of רֹבֵעַ masc. בע
רִבְעִי[s] וְ noun masc. sing., suff. 1 pers. sing. from רֶבַע dec. 6 a (§ 35. rem. 5) . . בע
רִבְעֶיהָ[t] id. pl., suff. 3 pers. sing. fem. . . בע
רִבְעֵיהֶם[u] id. pl., suff. 3 pers. pl. masc. . . בע
רִבְעֵיהֶן[v] id. pl., suff. 3 pers. pl. fem. . . בע
רְבָעָיו[w] id. pl., suff. 3 pers. sing. masc. . . בע
רְבִעִים[x] defect. for רְבִיעִים (q. v.) . . בע
רְבֻעִים[y] Kal part. pass. masc., pl. of רָבוּעַ dec. 3 a בע
רִבֵּעִים noun masc., pl. of [רִבֵּעַ] dec. 1 b . בע
רְבִעִית[z] defect. of רְבִיעִית (q. v.) . . . בע

רָבַץ[d] fut. יִרְבַּץ *to lie down* for repose, spoken of quadrupeds; metaph. of men, waters, a curse. Hiph. I. *to cause to lie down*.—II. *to set*, of precious stones, Is. 54. 11.
רֵבֶץ masc. dec. 6 b.—I. *place of lying down* for animals.—II. *resting place* for man, Pr. 24. 15.
מַרְבֵּץ masc. *a place for lying down, couching place*, Zep. 2. 15; constr. מִרְבַּץ (§ 36. rem. 1) Eze. 25. 5.

רֹבֵץ Kal part. act. sing. masc. dec. 7 b . . בץ
רָבְצָה[e] } id. pret. 3 pers. sing. fem. (§ 8. rem. 7) בץ
רָבָצָה[f] וְ }
רִבְצָהּ[g] noun masc. sing., suff. 3 pers. sing. fem. from רֵבֶץ' dec. 6 b . . . בץ
רָבְצוּ וְ Kal pret. 3 pers. pl. . . . . בץ
רִבְצוֹ[h] noun masc. sing., suff. 3 p. s. m. fr. רֵבֶץ' d. 6 b בץ
רֹבְצִים[i] Kal part. act. masc., pl. of רֹבֵץ dec. 7 b בץ
רִבְצָם[k] noun masc. sing., suff. 3 p. pl. m. fr. רֵבֶץ d. 6 b בץ
רֹבֶצֶת Kal part. act. s., fem. of רֹבֵץ m. (§ 8. r. 19) בץ
רָבַצְתָּ[l] וְ id. pret. 2 pers. sing. masc., acc. shifted by conv. וְ (§ 8. rem. 7) . . . בץ

רָבַק Root not used; Arab. *to tie, fasten*, espec. an animal.
רִבְקָה (*binding*, i. e. *engaging, captivating*) pr. name, *Rebecca*, the wife of Isaac.

[a] Da. 2. 48. [b] Je. 14. 22. [c] Eze. 16. 11. [d] Job 16. 13. [e] Da. 3. 25. [f] Da. 2. 40; 7. 7, 23. [g] 2 Ki. 15. 12. [h] Ne. 9. 3. [i] Da. 7. 19, 23. [k] Nu. 28. 14. [l] Da. 4. 19. [m] De. 30. 16. [n] Ps. 44. 13. [o] La. 2. 22. [p] De. 8. 1. [q] Nu. 23. 10. [r] 2 Ki. 6. 25. [s] Eze. 41. 21. [t] Ps. 139. 3. [u] Eze. 43. 17. [v] Eze. 1. 8; 10. 11. [w] Eze. 1. 17. [x] Eze. 43. 16. [y] 2 Ki. 10. 30. [z] 1 Ki. 7. 5. [c] 1 Ki. 6. 33. [d] Ge. 49. 9. [e] Eze. 19. 2. [f] De. 29. 19. [g] Is. 35. 7. [h] Pr. 24. 15. [i] Ge. 29. 2. [k] Je. 50. 6. [l] Job 11. 19.

מַרְבֵּק masc. *a stall*, in which cattle are *tied* for fattening; עֵגֶל מַ׳ *a calf of the stall*, i. e. a fatted calf.

רִבְקָה ׳ן pr. name fem. . . . . . רבק
רַבְרְבִין[a] Chald. adj. masc. pl. [of רַבְרַב] dec. 2 a . רבב
רַבְרְבָן Chald. id. fem. pl. [of רַבְרְבָא] dec. 9 a . רבב
רַבְרְבָנוֹהִי[b] ׳ן Chald. noun masc. pl., suff. 3 pers. sing. masc. from [רַבְרְבָן] dec. 1.a . . רבב
רַבְרְבָנַי[c] ן Chald. id. pl., suff. 1 pers. sing. . . רבב
רַבְרְבָנָיךְ[d] ן Chald. id. pl., suff. 2 pers. s. masc., Keri ־נָךְ רבב
רַבְרְבָתָא[e] Chald. adj. pl. emph. fem. [from רַבְרְבָא dec. 9a, from רַבְרַב masc.] . . . רבב
רִבְשָׁקֵה pr. name masc. . . . . . רבב
רַבְתָּ[f] Kal pret. 2 pers. sing. masc. . . . רוב
רַבַּת pr. name, constr. of רַבָּה . . . . רבב
רַבַּת[g] ׳ן adj. (also as an *adv.*) fem. sing., constr. of רַבָּה dec. 10, from רַב masc. . . רבב
רְבָת[h] Chald. Peal pret. 3 pers. sing. fem. . רבה
רַבְּתָא[i] Ch. adj. f. s. emph. [of רַבָּא d. 8a] fr. רַב m. רבב
רַבָּתָה pr. name of a place (רַבָּה) with parag. ה . רבב
רָבְתָה[k] Kal pret. 3 pers. sing. fem. . . . רבה
רִבְּתָה[l] Piel pret. 3 pers. sing. fem. . . . רבה
רַבָּתִי[m] adj. רַבָּה (q. v.) with parag. י . . . רבב
רִבֹּתַיִם[n] noun fem. du. of רִבּוֹ dec. 1 b . . רבב

רָגַב Root not used; cogn. רָגַם *to heap together* stones, lumps, clods, &c.

רֶגֶב masc. dec. 6 b, *a clod of earth*.

אַרְגֹּב (*heap of stones*) pr. name—I. of a region beyond Jordan subject to Og, king of Bashan.—II. of a man, 2 Ki. 15. 25.

רִגְבֵי[o] constr. of the foll. . . . . . רגב
רְגָבִים[p] וּ noun masc. pl. of [רֶגֶב] dec. 6 b; וּ bef. (:) רגב
רָגוֹם[q] Kal inf. abs. . . . . . . רגם

רָגַז ן fut. יִרְגַּז.—I. *to shake, tremble.*—II. *to be moved, agitated*, with anger, grief. Hiph. I. *to make tremble, shake.*—II. *to move, disquiet*, with acc. לְ.—III. *to agitate, excite to anger*, Job 12. 6. Hithp. *to rage, rave against*, with אֶל.

רְגַז Chald. Aph. *to excite to anger*, Ezr. 5. 12.

רְגַז Chald. masc. *anger*, Da. 3. 13.

רַגָּז masc. *trembling*, De. 28. 65.

רֹגֶז masc. dec. 6 c.—I. *disquiet, perturbation, trouble.*—II. *a raging*, of thunder, of a horse.—III. *anger, fury*, Hab. 3. 2.

רָגְזָה fem. *trembling, perturbation*, Eze. 12. 18.

אַרְגָּז masc. *box, chest, coffer*, hanging from the side of a cart or waggon, 1 Sa. 6. 8, 11, 15.

רַגָּז[r] noun masc. sing. . . . . . רגז
רֹגֶז[s] ׳ן noun masc. sing. dec. 6 c . . . רגז
רָגְזָה[t] Kal pret. 3 pers. sing. fem. . . . רגז
רְגָזָה[u] id. imp. s. m. [רְגַז] with parag. ה (§ 8. r. 12) רגז
רָגְזוּ ן id. pret. 3 pers. pl. . . . . רגז
רִגְזוּ[x] id. imp. pl. masc. . . . . . רגז

רֶגֶל ׳ן fem. dec. 6 a (with suff. רַגְלִי).—I. *foot*, of man or beast; בְּרֶגֶל *on foot*; לְרַגְלֵי פ׳, בְּרַגְלֵי פ׳ *at the foot* or *in the track of any*, i. e. behind or after him; הִשְׁקָה בָרֶגֶל *to water* (sc. land) *with the foot*, by means of a machine trodden with the feet, De. 11. 10; מֵימֵי רַגְלַיִם *water of the feet*, urine. —II. *step, pace*, Ge. 33. 14; לְרַגְלִי Ge. 30. 30, *at my proceeding, as I proceeded*, sc. in the service; pl. רְגָלִים (*steps*) *times*, comp. פַּעַם.

רְגַל Chald. fem. dec. 3 a, *foot*. Also

רָגַל (denom. fr. רֶגֶל) *to go about slandering, backbiting*, Ps. 15. 3. Pi. I. i. q. Kal, with בְּ, 2 Sa. 19. 28.—II. *to explore, spy out*; part. מְרַגֵּל *a spy*. Tiph. (§ 6. No. 5) *to teach to walk, to lead by the hand* (a child), Ho. 11. 3.

רֹגֵל (*fuller*) pr. name—I. see under עַיִן.—II.

רֹגְלִים (*fullers' place*) a town in Gilead.

רַגְלִי masc. (pl. רַגְלִים) *footman, foot soldier.*

מַרְגְּלוֹת fem. pl. (of מַרְגֶּלֶת) *what is at the feet of any one*; adv. *at the feet*, Ru. 3. 8.

רָגֶל noun fem. sing. dec. 6 a, for רֶגֶל (§ 35. r. 2) רגל
רֹגֵל pr. name, see עֵין רֹגֵל under . . . עין
רַגְלָהּ noun fem. sing., suff. 3 pers. s. f. fr. רֶגֶל d. 6 a רגל
רַגְלָו[y] id. du., suff. 3 pers. s. m.; K. ־לָיו . . רגל
רַגְלוֹ id. sing., suff. 3 pers. sing. masc. . . רגל
רַגְּלוּ[z] ן Piel imp. pl. masc. . . . . רגל
רַגְלוֹהִי[a] Chald. noun fem. du., suff. 3 pers. sing. masc. from [רְגַל] dec. 3 a . . . רגל
רַגְלַי / רַגְלָי[b] ׳ן noun fem. du., suff. 1 pers. sing. from רֶגֶל dec. 6 a . . . רגל
רַגְלֵי ׳ן id. du., constr. st. . . . . רגל
רַגְלִי id. s., suff. 1 p. s.; or noun m. (pl. רַגְלִים) רגל
רַגְלַיָּא[c] Chald. noun fem. du. emph. from רְגַל d. 3 a רגל
רַגְלֶיהָ noun fem. du. (רַגְלַיִם), suff. 3 pers. sing. fem. from רֶגֶל dec. 6 a . . . רגל
רַגְלֵיהֶם ׳ן id. du., suff. 3 pers. pl. masc. . . רגל
רַגְלָיו ׳ן id. du., suff. 3 pers. sing. masc. . . רגל

---

[a] Da. 3. 33. [b] Da. 5. 2, 3, 9, 10; 6. 18. [c] Da. 4. 33. [d] Da. 5. 23. [e] Da. 7. 11, 17. [f] La. 3. 58. [g] 1 Sa. 2. 5. [h] Da. 4. 19. [i] Da. 4. 27. [k] 1 Sa. 14. 30. [l] Eze. 19. 2. [m] La. 1. 1. [n] Ps. 68. 18. [o] Job 21. 33. [p] Job 38. 38. [q] Le. 24. 16. [r] Pr. 29. 9. [s] De. 28. 65. [t] Job 39. 24. [u] Is. 32. 11. [x] Ps. 4. 5. [y] 1 Ki. 5. 17. [z] Jos. 7. 2. [a] Da. 2. 33, 34. [b] Ps. 22. 17. [c] Da. 2. 41, 42.

רַגְלָיו[a] id. du., suff. 3 p.s.m. (read לָיו׳) K. רַגְלַי (q.v.) רגל

רַגְלָיו[b] id. du., suff. 3 pers. sing. masc. (Kh. לָיו׳ but K. רַגְלוֹ q. v.) . . . . רגל

רַגְלַיִךְ id. du., suff. 2 pers. sing. fem. . . רגל

רַגְלֶיךָ ו׳[c] id. du., suff. 2 pers. sing. masc. . . רגל

רַגְלֶיךָ[d] id. du., suff. 2 pers. sing. masc. (Kh. לֶיךָ׳ but K. רַגְלְךָ q. v.) . . . . רגל

רַגְלֵיכֶם id. du., suff. 2 pers. pl. masc. . . . רגל

רַגְלַיִם, וְ׳[e] רַגְלָיִם } id. du., abs. st. . . . . רגל

רַגְלִים[f] noun masc., pl. of רַגְלִי . . . . רגל

רְגָלִים noun fem., pl. of רֶגֶל dec. 6a . . . רגל

רַגְלַיִן[g] Chald. noun fem., du. of רְגַל dec. 3a . רגל

רַגְלֵינוּ noun fem. du. (רַגְלַיִם), suff. 1 p. pl. fr. רֶגֶל d. 6a רגל

רַגְלְךָ, וְ׳ רַגְלֶךָ } id. sing., suff. 2 pers. sing. masc. . רגל

רַגְלֵךְ[h] id. sing., suff. 2 pers. sing. fem. . . . רגל

רַגְלְכֶם id. sing., suff. 2 pers. pl. masc. . . . רגל

רַגְלָם id. sing., suff. 3 pers. pl. masc. . . . רגל

רַגְלֵנוּ[i] id. sing., suff. 1 pers. pl. . . . . רגל

[רָגַם] *to stone to death*, const. with עַל, בְּ.

רִגְמָה fem. *crowd, throng, band*, Ps. 68. 28.

מַרְגֵּמָה fem. *heap of stones*, Pr. 26. 8.

רֶגֶם (*friend*; Arab. id.) pr. name m. 1 Ch. 2. 47.

רֶגֶם מֶלֶךְ (*friend of the king*) pr. name masc. Zec. 7. 2 . . . . . רגם

רָגוֹם[k] Kal inf. abs. . . . . . . רגם

וְרָגְמֻהוּ[l] וּ id. pret. 3 pers. pl. [רָגְמוּ], suff. 3 pers. sing. masc.; וּ, for וְ, conv. . . . רגם

רָגְמוּ וְ id. pret. 3 pers. pl. . . . . רגם

רִגְמָתָם[m] noun fem. s., suff. 3 p. pl. m. [fr. רִגְמָה no pl.] רגם

[רָגַן] *to murmur, rebel*, Is. 29. 24. Niph. id. De. 1. 27; Ps. 106. 25.

רָגַע cogn. רָגַז, רָגַשׁ, רָעַשׁ, רָעַע.—I. *to be in a commotion, make a noise*, spoken of the sea, Job 26. 12; Is. 51. 15; Je. 31. 35.—II. *to tremble*, or perh. *shrink* (Ethiop. *to contract, curdle*), Job 7. 5.

רֶגַע masc. dec. 6a (§ 35. rem. 5), *a moment* (prop. *a twinkling*, sc. *of the eye*, comp. *moment* for *movement*; רֶגַע, כְּרֶגַע, בְּרֶגַע *in a moment, suddenly*; לִרְגָעִים *every moment, repeatedly*; also *suddenly*, Eze. 26. 16.

רָגַע Kal not used; *to rest, be quiet*, comp. adj. רָגֵעַ. Niph. id. Je. 47. 6. Hiph. I. *to cause to rest, giv[e]* or *restore rest, quiet*; Je. 49. 19, אַרְגִּיעָה אֲרִיצֶנּוּ *[I] will restore rest, I will cause him to run*; whic[h] Gesenius renders, *I will wink*, &c.—II. intrans. *t[o] have rest, dwell quietly*, De. 28. 65; Is. 34. 14.

רָגֵעַ adj. masc. dec. 5a, *still, quiet*, Ps. 35. 20

מַרְגּוֹעַ masc. *a rest*, Je. 6. 16.

מַרְגֵּעָה fem. id. Is. 28. 12.

רֶגַע, וְ׳[n] רָגַע } noun masc. sing. dec. 6 (§ 35. rem. 5) [ר]גע

רֹגַע Kal part. act. sing. (§ 36. rem. 1) . [ר]גע

רִגְעֵי[o] adj. pl. constr. masc. [from רָגֵעַ] dec. 5a . [ר]גע

[רָגַשׁ] *to rage, make a noise, tumult*, Ps. 2. 1.

רְגַשׁ Ch. *to run together in a tumult*, Da. 6. 7, 12, 16

רֶגֶשׁ masc. *a bustling crowd, multitude*, Ps. 55. 15

רִגְשָׁה fem. id. only constr. רִגְשַׁת Ps. 64. 3.

רָגְשׁוּ[p] Kal pret. 3 pers. pl. . . . . [ר]גש

רָד[q] Kal pret. 3 pers. sing. masc. . . . [ר]וד

רַד[r] Kal pret. 3 pers. sing. masc. by aphaer. for יָרַד [י]רד

רֵד וְ׳[s] id. imp. sing. masc.; for וְ see lett. ו [י]רד

[רָדַד] (prop. *to spread out*) *to prostrate, subdue*, Ps. 144. 2 Is. 45. 1. Hiph. *to overlay with metal*, 1 Ki. 6. 32

רְדִיד masc. dec. 3a, *a wide mantle*.

רַדַּי (*subduing*) pr. name masc. 1 Ch. 2. 14.

רָדָה fut. יִרְדֶּה, ap. וַיֵּרְדְּ (§ 24. rem. 3).—I. *to tread* winepress, Joel 4. 13; with בְּ *upon* any one Ps. 49. 15; with acc. Is. 14. 6; perh. also *to trea[d]*, *walk*, Je. 5. 31, *and the priests* יִרְדּוּ עַל־יְדֵיהֶם *wal[k] at their side*, i. e. assist them; this is usuall[y] referred either to No. II or III.—II. *to subdue rule over*; poet. of a spreading fire, La. 1. 13.— III. *to take*, Ju. 14. 9; others, *to break*. Pi. *t[o] tread under foot, break*, or *subdue*, only fut. ap יְרַד Ju. 5. 13, 13; according to others imp. o[f] יָרַד. Hiph. *to cause to rule*, Is. 41. 2.

רְדָה[t], רֵדָה } Kal imp. sing. masc. (רֵד) with parag. ה (§ 20. rem. 3) . . . . [י]רד

רְדֵה[u] id. imp. sing. masc. . . . . [ר]דה

רֹדֶה id. part. act. sing. masc. dec. 9a . . [ר]דה

רָדוּ וְ id. pret. 3 pers. pl. . . . . [ר]דה

רְדוּ וּ׳[w] Kal imp. pl. masc.; וּ bef. (:) . . . [י]רד

רְדוּ וּ׳[x] Kal imp. pl. masc.; וּ id. . . . [ר]דה

רָדְפִי[b] Kal inf., suff. 1 pers. sing. Kh. רְדוֹפִי, K. רָדְפִי (§ 8. rem. 12) acc. retracted bef. monos. [ר]דף

[a] 2 Sa. 22. 34. [b] Ps. 105. 18. [c] 2 Sa. 3. 34. [d] Ec. 4. 17. [e] Job 29. 15. [f] Je. 12. 5. [g] Da. 7. 4. [h] Je. 2. 25. [i] Ps. 66. 9. [k] Nu. 15. 35. [l] De. 21. 21. [m] Ps. 68. 28. [n] Je. 18. 9. [o] Ps. 35. 20. [p] Ps. 2. 1. [q] Ho. 12. 1. [r] Ju. 19. 11. [s] 1 Ki. 18. 44. [t] Ju. 14. 9. [u] 2 Ki. 1. 9, 11. [w] Ps. 110. 2. [y] Am. 6. 2. [x] Joel 4. 13. [a] Ge. 1. 28. [b] Ps. 38. 21.

רְדוֹת[a] Kal inf. constr. . . . . . . רדה
רַדַּי pr. name masc. . . . . . רדד
רְדִי Kal imp. sing. fem. . . . . . ירד
רְדִידִי[b] noun m. s., suff. 1 pers. s. fr. [רָדִיד] d. 3 a רדד
רְדִיתֶם[c] Kal pret. 2 pers. pl. masc. . . . רדה

רָדַם. Niph. נִרְדַּם.—I. *to lie in a deep sleep.*—II. *to sink down stupified* or *senseless.*

תַּרְדֵּמָה fem. dec. 10.—I. *deep sleep.*—II. *sluggishness, inactivity.*

רֹדֵם[d] Kal part. act. sing. masc., suff. 3 pers. pl. masc. from רֹדֶה dec. 9 a . . . רדה
רַדְנוּ[e] Kal pret. 1 pers. pl. . . . . רוד

רָדַף fut. יִרְדֹּף.—I. *to follow after.*—II. *to pursue, persecute,* with acc., לְ, אֶל, אַחֲרֵי.—III. *to put to flight, to chase,* Le. 26. 36. Niph. *to be pursued;* part. נִרְדָּף *that which is past,* Ec. 3. 15. Pi. i. q. Kal Nos. I & II. Pu. *to be chased, driven away,* Is. 17. 13. Hiph. *to persecute,* Ju. 20. 43. Hoph. part. מֻרְדָּף *persecuted,* Is. 14. 6, according to Gesenius, as a subst. *persecution.*

רְדֹף [f] וּ Kal imp. sing. masc.; וּ bef. (:) . . רדף
רֹדֵף וְ id. part. act. sing. masc. dec. 7 b . רדף
רֻדַּף[g] וְ Pual pret. 3 pers. sing. masc. . . . רדף
רִדְּפָה[h] וְ Piel pret. 3 pers. sing. fem. . . . רדף
רָדְפֵהוּ[i] וְ Kal imp. sing. masc., suff. 3 pers. sing. m. רדף
רָדְפוּ[k] / רָדָפוּ וְ[l] } id. pret. 3 pers. pl. (§ 8. rem. 7) רדף
רִדְפוּ id. imp. pl. masc. . . . . רדף
רָדְפוֹ[m] id. inf. with suff. 3 pers. sing. masc. . רדף
רְדָפוּךָ[n] וּ id. pret. 3 pers. pl., suff. 2 pers. sing. masc.; וּ, for וְ, conv. . . . . רדף
רְדָפוּם[o] id. id., suff. 3 pers. pl. masc. . . . רדף
רְדָפוּנִי[p] id. id., suff. 1 pers. sing. . . . רדף
רֹדְפַי[q] / רֹדְפַי } id. part. act. pl. masc., suff. 1 pers. sing. from רֹדֵף dec. 7 b . . } רדף
רֹדְפֵי id. pl., constr. st. . . . . רדף
רֹדְפֶיהָ[r] id. id. with suff. 3 pers. sing. fem. . . רדף
רֹדְפֵיהֶם[s] id. id., suff. 3 pers. pl. masc. . . רדף
רֹדְפֵיכֶם[t] id. id., suff. 2 pers. pl. masc. . . . רדף
רֹדְפִים[u] וְ id. id., abs. st. . . . . רדף
רֹדְפֵינוּ[x] id. id. with suff. 1 pers. pl. . . . רדף
רֹדְפֶךָ[y] id. id. sing. with suff. 2 pers. sing. masc. רדף
רֹדְפָם[z] id. id. sing., suff. 3 pers. pl. masc. . רדף
רָדַפְתִּי[a] וְ id. pret. 1 pers. sing.; acc. shifted by conv. וְ (§ 8. rem. 7) . . . . . רדף
רְדַפְתֶּם[b] וּ id. pret. 2 pers. pl. masc.; וּ, for וְ, conv. רדף
רֶדֶת[c] Kal inf. constr. dec. 13 (§ 44. rem. 1) . ירד
רִדְתָּהּ[d] id., suff. 3 pers. sing. fem. . . . ירד
רִדְתּוֹ[e] id., suff. 3 pers. sing. masc. . . ירד

[רָהַב] I. *to act insolently* (Syr. *to make a noise*), with בְּ, *against,* Is. 3. 5.—II. *to urge, press upon,* Pr. 6. 3. Hiph. I. *to embolden,* Ps. 138. 3.—II. *to overcome,* trop. Ca. 6. 5.

רָהָב masc. dec. 4 a, *insolent, proud,* Ps. 40. 5.

רַהַב masc.—I. *insolence, pride.*—II. *Rahab,* a poetic name for Egypt.

רֹהַב masc. dec. 6 f, *pride,* Ps. 90. 10.

רָהַב / רַהַב } noun masc. sing. . . . . רהב
רְהַב[f] וּ Kal imp. sing. masc.; וּ bef. (:) . רהב
רְהָבִים[g] adj. masc. pl. of [רָהָב] dec. 4 a . . רהב
רָהְבָּם[h] וְ noun masc. sing., suff. 3 pers. pl. masc. from רֹהַב dec. 6 (§ 35. rem. 5) . רהב

רָהָה a spurious Root, to which is ascribed the signification of *to fear,* on account of תִּרְהוּ Is. 44. 8; but see יָרָה.

רָהַט Root not used; Syr. *to run, flow.*

רַהַט masc. d. 6 d, only pl.—I. *watering-troughs.*—II. *locks, curls,* so called from their *flowing* down the neck, Ca. 7. 6.

רָהִיט masc. dec. 1 b, *a ceiling done with fretwork,* resembling little channels or troughs, Ca. 1. 17. Vulg. laquearia. Sept. φατνώματα. The Khethib has רָחִיטִים; but a Root רָחַט is not extant.

רוֹנְנִים[i] וְ Kal part. act. masc. pl. [of רֹנֵן dec. 7 b] רגן

[רוּד] I. *to wander, rove,* Je. 2. 31; Arab. ראד *to run about.*—II. in a good sense, *to walk,* sc. עִם־אֵל with God, Ho. 12. 1. Hiph. *to wander,* as nomades, Ge. 27. 40; *to wander, go about,* of one in affliction, Ps. 55. 3.

אַרְוָד (*a wandering*) pr. name of a Phœnician city, Eze. 27. 8, 11. Gent. noun אַרְוָדִי.

מָרוּד masc. dec. 3 a, *a wandering, erring about;* pl. מְרוּדִים Is. 58. 7, for concr. *wanderers.*

רוֹדָנִים וְ pr. name of a people, 1 Ch. 1. 7, supposed to be the *Rhodians;* elsewhere it is דֹּדָנִים.

רוֹדֵף[k] Kal part. act. sing. masc. dec. 7 b . רדף

---

[a] Eze. 29. 15. [b] Ca. 5. 7. [c] Eze. 34. 4. [d] Ps. 68. 28. [e] Je. 2. 31. [f] 2 Sa. 20. 6. [g] Is. 17. 13. [h] Ho. 2. 9. [i] Ps. 34. 15. [k] Ps. 69. 27. [l] Le. 26. 8. [m] Am. 1. 11. [n] De. 28. 22, 45; 30. 7. [o] Jos. 8. 24. [p] Ps. 119. 86, 161. [q] Ps. 35. 3. [r] La. 1. 3. [s] Ne. 9. 11. [t] Is. 30. 16. [u] Ju. 8. 4. [x] La. 4. 19. [y] 2 Sa. 24. 13. [z] Ps. 35. 6.

[a] Je. 29. 18. [b] Le. 26. 7. [c] De. 28. 52. [d] De. 20. 20. [e] Eze. 31. 15. [f] Pr. 6. 3. [g] Ps. 40. 5. [h] Ps. 90. 10. [i] Is. 29. 24. [k] La. 1. 6.

[רָוָה] to be or become satiated with drink (Syr. to be drunken), also with fat; metaph. with unlawful love; const. with acc., מִן. Pi. I. to be satiated, filled, soaked.—II. to cause to drink in, i. e. to water.—III. to satiate, with fatness; metaph. to satisfy, delight, Pr. 5. 19. Hiph. I. to give to drink, to water.—II. to satiate, with fatness, Is. 43. 24.

רָוֶה masc. רָוָה fem. adj. satiated with drink, De. 29. 18; also soaked, well watered, of gardens.

רְוָיָה fem. abundance, plenty of drink.

רִי m. (for רְוִי) a watering, irrigation, Job 37. 11.

רָוֶה adj. masc. sing. . . . . . רוה

רַוֵּה[a] Piel imp. sing. masc. . . . . רוה

רֵוֵהּ ן Ch. n. m. sing., suff. 3 pers. sing. masc. [from רֵו for רְאוּ] . . . . ראה

רֻוֹהֲגָה ן Kh. רוֹהֲגָה, K. רָהֲגָּה pr. n. m. 1 Ch. 7. 34.

רוז Root not used; Syr. רוז, רזז to hide, keep secret.

רָז Chald. masc. dec. 1 a, a secret.

רוֹזְנִים[b] ו׳ Kal part. act. masc. pl. [of רוֹזֵן] dec. 7 b רזן

רָוַח[c] ן cogn. רוּחַ (prop. to be airy, spacious, wide); only impers. יְרוַּח לִי I am relieved. Pu. part. spacious, wide, Je. 22. 14.

רֶוַח masc.—I. relief, enlargement, Est. 4. 14.—II. space, distance, Ge. 32. 17.

רְוָחָה fem. dec. 11 c, relief, enlargement.

רוּחַ Kal not used. Hiph. הֵרִיחַ.—I. to smell; metaph. to smell, touch fire, Ju. 16. 9; also to scent, perceive, as a horse the battle, Job 39. 25.—II. const. with בְּ to smell with pleasure; hence generally, to enjoy, delight in.

רוּחַ com. dec. 1 a (pl. רוּחוֹת, רֻחוֹת).—I. air, breeze; רוּחַ הַיּוֹם cool air of the day, i. e. evening. —II. breath; metaph. vanity, folly.—III. spirit, soul.—IV. mind, spirit, disposition; אֶרֶךְ רוּחַ patience; קְצַר רוּחַ impatience; גְּבַהּ רוּחַ proud of spirit; קְשֵׁה רוּחַ sorrowful of spirit.—V. the spirit of God.—VI. wind; also tempest, hurricane.—VII. wind, side, quarter of the heavens.—VIII. anger, wrath, from the idea of breathing, snuffing.

רוּחַ Chald. com. dec. 1 a.—I. wind.—II. spirit, mind.—III. spirit of God.

רֵיחַ masc. dec. 1 a, odour, scent, smell.

רֵיחַ Chald. masc. id. Da. 3. 27.

רַחַת fem. winnowing fan, Is. 30. 24.

יְרִיחוֹ, יְרֵחוֹ, יְרִיחֹה (place of fragrance) pr. name, Jericho, a city in Palestine, in the territory of Benjamin.

רֶוַח[d] ו׳[e] noun masc. sing. . . . . רוח

רוּחַ ו׳ noun com. sing. dec. 1 a . . . . רוח

רוּחָא[f] Ch. id., emph. st. . . . . . רוח

רוּחָה[g] Heb. id. with parag. ה . . . . . רוח

רוּחֵהּ[h] ן Ch. id. with suff. 3 pers. sing. masc. . . רוח

רוּחוֹ ו׳ id. with suff. 3 pers. sing. masc. . . . רוח

רוּחוֹת id. pl. with fem. term. . . . . . רוח

רוּחֵי[i] Ch. id. pl. constr. masc. . . . . . רוח

רוּחִי ו׳[k] id. sing. with suff. 1 pers. sing. . . רוח

רוּחֲךָ, **רוּחֶךָ**[m] ו׳[l] } id. sing. with suff. 2 pers. sing. masc. רוח

רוּחֲכֶם id. sing. with suff. 2 pers. pl. masc. . . . רוח

רוּחָם id. sing. with suff. 3 pers. pl. masc. . . . רוח

רְוָיָה[n] noun fem. sing. . . . . . . רוה

רִוֵּיתִי[o] ן Piel pret. 1 pers. sing.; acc. shifted by conv. ן (comp. § 8. rem. 7) . . . רוה

רוֹכֵל[p] Kal part. act. sing. masc. dec. 7 b . . רכל

רוּם[q] fut. יָרוּם, ap. יָרֹם, וַיָּרָם.—I. to be high, lofty.—II. to raise oneself, to rise, be lifted up, Job 22. 12; hence to rise, grow, of worms, Ex. 16. 20.—III. to be raised, made high, Is. 49. 11.—IV. metaph. to be high, exalted, in power or rank; to be lifted up, elated with pride. Part. רָם, fem. רָמָה (a) high, lofty, tall; (b) lifted up; of the voice, loud; (c) metaph. high, powerful, mighty; elated with pride, haughty; high, difficult, Pr. 24. 7; pl. רָמִים heights of heaven, Ps. 78. 69. Pil. רוֹמֵם.—I. to raise a building, Ezr. 9. 9; a plant, to make to grow, Eze. 31. 4; children, to bring up.—II. to lift up, set on a high place.—III. metaph. to exalt; with praises to extol. Pul. רוֹמַם pass. Hiph. הֵרִים.—I. to lift up, raise. —II. to set up, erect.—III. to take away.—IV. to take up for an offering, to offer. Hoph. הוּרַם pass. of Hiph. Nos. III & IV. Hithpal. to exalt oneself.

רוּם Chald. to be lifted up, Da. 5. 20. Pal. to exalt, extol, Da. 4. 34. Aph. to exalt in dignity, Da. 5. 19. Ithpal. to lift up oneself, rise up against, with עַל, Da. 5. 23.

רוּם masc.—I. height, elevation, Pr. 25. 3.—II. a lifting up of the eyes, the heart, i. e. haughtiness, pride.

רוּם Chald. masc. dec. 1 a, height.

רוֹם masc. height, Hab. 3. 10; which others take as an adv. on high.

רוֹמָה f. haughtiness, as an adv. haughtily, Mi. 2. 3.

---

[a] Ps 65. 11. [b] Is. 40. 23. [c] 1 Sa. 16. 23. [d] Est. 4. 14. [e] Ge. 32. 17. [f] Da. 2. 35. [g] Je. 52. 23. [h] Da. 5. 20. [i] Da. 7. 2. [k] Hag. 2. 5. [l] Ne. 9. 20. [m] Job 15. 13. [n] Ps. 23. 5. [o] Je. 31. 14. [p] Ca. 3. 6. [q] De. 17. 20.

רוֹמָה (*lofty*) pr. name of a place, 2 Ki. 23. 36.

רוֹמָם masc. *exaltation, praise*, Ps. 66. 17; pl. constr. רוֹמְמוֹת Ps. 149. 6.

רוֹמֵמוּת fem. dec. 3 b, *a lifting up*, Is. 33. 3.

רָם I. part. *high*, see the verb.—II. pr. name masc. of several persons.

רָמָה fem. dec. 10.—I. *high place*, 1 Sa. 22. 6; espec. for the worship of idols, Eze. 16. 24, 25, 39. —II. pr. name, *Ramah*, (*a*) a city in Benjamin; (*b*) a city in the mountains of Ephraim, called also רָמָתַיִם צוֹפִים; (*c*) a city in the tribe of Naphtali, Jos. 19. 36; (*d*) a city in Gilead, 2 Ki. 8. 29, called also רָמַת הַמִּצְפֶּה Jos. 13. 26, and רָאמוֹת, רָמוֹת; (*e*) רָמַת לְחִי i. q. לְחִי q. v. Gent. n. רָמָתִי 1 Ch. 27. 27.

רָמוֹת (*heights*) pr. name—I. of a city in Gilead, called also רָאמוֹת.—II. רָמוֹת נֶגֶב i. q. רָאמוֹת נֶגֶב (q. v.) 1 Sa. 30. 27.

רָמוּת fem. dec. 1 b, *heap, pile*, Eze. 32. 5.

רֶמֶת (*height*) pr. name of a city in Issachar, Jos. 19. 21.

רֹמַמְתִּי עֶזֶר (*I have raised help*) pr. name masc. 1 Ch. 25. 4, 31.

מָרוֹם masc. dec. 3 a.—I. *height, altitude*; בַּמָּרוֹם, מָרוֹם *on high*; concr. *the Most High*, Ps. 92. 9; also collect. *high ones, princes*, Is. 24. 4.—II. *height, high place*.—III. *haughtiness*, only as an adv. *haughtily*, Ps. 56. 3.

מֵרוֹם (*height*) pr. name מֵי מֵרוֹם *the waters of Merom*, a lake at the foot of Mount Lebanon. Gr. Σαμοχονίτις.

מְרֵמוֹת (*elevations*) pr. name m. of two persons.

תְּרוּמָה fem. dec. 10.—I. *an offering, present, gift*; espec. an *oblation* to the temple and the priests; 2 Sa. 1. 21 שְׂדֵי תְרוּמוֹת *a field of oblation*, i. e. fertile and producing fruits fit for oblations.—II. *heave-offering*, a sacrifice consecrated by *elevating* it; שׁוֹק הַתְּרוּמָה *heave-shoulder*.

תְּרוּמִיָּה fem. *an offering*, Eze. 48. 12.

רוֹם[a] (prop. subst.) as an *adv*. . . . רום

רוּם Kal inf. constr. (De. 17. 20) or subst. רום

רוֹמָה[b] (prop. subst.) as an *adv*. . . . רום

רוּמָה pr. name of a place . . . . רום

רוּמָה Kal imp. sing. masc. with parag. ה . רום

רוּמֵהּ[c] וְ' Chald. noun masc. sing., suff. 3 pers. sing. masc. from רוּם dec. 1 a . . . רום

רוֹמֵי[d] Kal part. act. pl. constr. m. [fr. רֹמֶה] d. 9 a רמה

רוֹמָם[e] וְ noun masc. sing. dec. 2 b . . . רום

רוֹמֵמָה[f] Kal part. act. sing. fem. . . . . רמם

רוֹמְמוּ[g] Pilel imp. pl. masc. . . . . רום

רוֹמְמוֹת[h] noun pl. constr. fem. from רוֹמָם dec. 2 b רום

רוֹמַמְתִּי[i] וְ' Pilel pret. 1 pers. sing. . . . רום

רוֹמֵשׂ Kal part. act. sing. masc. . . . רמשׂ

רוּן Kal not used; Arab. *to conquer*. Hithp. *to be overcome* of wine, Ps. 78. 65.

רוּעַ Kal not used; (cogn. Arab. רעא) *to make a loud noise*. Niph. fut. יֵרוֹעַ.—I. *to become evil, be made worse*, Pr. 13. 20.—II. *to suffer evil, injury*, Pr. 11. 15. Hiph. הֵרִיעַ.—I. *to cry aloud*, Job 30. 5.—II. *to shout*, in joy, alarm, or war.—III. *to sound* a trumpet, with בְּ; espec. *to sound an alarm*. Pul. fut. יְרֹעַע *there shall be shouting*, for joy, Is. 16. 10. Hithpal. הִתְרוֹעַע *to shout* for joy.

רֵעַ masc. dec. 1 a, *noise, outcry*; perh. of *the noise of thunder*, Job 36. 33.

תְּרוּעָה fem. dec. 10.—I. *a shout*, of joy, or of battle.—II. *a sound* of a trumpet.

רוֹעֶה[k] וְ Kal part. act. sing. masc. d. 10, comp. רֹעֶה רעה

רוֹעֵי[l] id. pl., constr. st. comp. רֹעֵי . . רעה

I. רוּף Pul. *to be agitated, shaken*, Job 26. 11

II. רוּף Root not used; cogn. Arab. רפת *to bruise, pound*, Eng. *rub*; perh. also i. q. רָפָא *to heal*.

רִיפוֹת pl. fem. *bruised corn, grits*.

תְּרוּפָה fem. *medicine*, or *healing, cure*, Eze. 47. 12.

[רוּץ] *to run*; with בְּ *into*, for refuge; with אֶל, עַל *to run, rush upon, assail*. Part. pl. *runners, couriers*. Pil. רוֹצֵץ *to run swiftly*, Na. 2. 5. Hiph. I. *to cause to run*.—II. *to bring quickly*.—III. *to let make haste*, sc. the hands in work, service, Ps. 68. 32.

מֵרוֹץ masc. *a running, race*, Ec. 9. 11.

מְרוּצָה fem. d. 10, idem. Another under רָצַץ.

רוּץ Kal imp. sing. masc. . . . . רוץ

רוֹצֶה Kal part. act. sing. masc. dec. 9 a . רצה

רוֹצֵחַ Kal part. act. sing. masc., comp. רֹצֵחַ . רצח

רוּק Hiph. I. *to empty*, e. g. a vessel, sack.—II. *to pour out*.—III. *to draw out*, a sword, spear.—IV. *to draw, lead out*, sc. troops, Ge. 14. 14. Hoph. *to be poured out*, Ca. 1. 3.

רֵיק masc.—I. adj. *empty*, Je. 51. 34: hence *vain*,

[a] Hab. 3. 10. [b] Mi. 2. 3. [c] Da. 4. 17. [d] Ps. 78. 9. [e] Ps. 66. 17. [f] Ps. 118. 16. [g] Ps. 99. 5, 9. [h] Ps. 149. 6. [i] Is. 1. 2; 23. 4. [k] Eze. 37. 24. [l] Eze. 34. 2.

רְזַיָּא[i] } Chald. noun masc. pl., emph. & abs., } רוז
רָזִין[k] } from רָז dec. 1 a . . .

[רָזַם] *to wink* with the eyes; Job 15. 12 (i. q. Aram. רְמַז); Prof. Lee, *to be fixed, fastened.*

רָזַן (Arab. *to be weighty*) only part. רוֹזֵן *chief, prince.*

רָזוֹן masc. *prince,* Pr. 14. 28.

רְזוֹן (*prince*) pr. name masc. 1 Ki. 11. 23.

רוֹזְנִים[l] ו׳[m] Kal part. act. pl. masc. [from רוֹזֵן] dec. 7 b רזן

רֵחַ or רֵחֶה masc. only du. רֵחַיִם (*a pair of millstones*) *a hand-mill.* R. uncertain.

רָחַב[n] ו׳[o] *to be* or *become wide, large, spacious.* Niph. part. *large, extended,* Is. 30. 23. Hiph. הִרְחִיב.—I. *to make wide, broad, enlarge,* with נֶפֶשׁ *to enlarge oneself.*—II. with לְ *to make room for.*—III. *to open wide,* as the mouth; trop. the heart, for instruction.—IV. intrans. *to be enlarged, great,* Ps. 25. 17; except we render הִרְחִיבוּ *they enlarged,* sc. the ensnaring enemies.

רָחָב masc. dec. 4 a, רְחָבָה fem. dec. 11 c.—I. adj. *wide, broad, large, spacious;* רְחַב יָדַיִם, רַחֲבַת יָדַיִם *large on both sides, very large;* רְחַב לֵב, ר׳ נֶפֶשׁ *puffed up, proud, arrogant;* also as a subst. *arrogance,* Pr. 21. 4.—II. רָחָב pr name, *Rahab,* a harlot of Jericho.

רַחַב masc. dec. 6 d, *wide place,* Job 36. 16; 38. 18.

רֹחַב masc. dec. 6 c (§ 35. rem. 5).—I. *width, breadth.*—II. *largeness,* with לֵב *largeness of understanding, comprehensive understanding,* 1 Ki. 5. 9.

רְחֹב, רְחוֹב fem. dec. 1 a (pl. רְחֹבוֹת).—I. *a wide open place, a street, square, market-place.*—II. pr. name, see בַּיִת.

רְחֹבוֹת (*wide, open places*) pr. name—I. of a well, Ge. 26. 22.—II. ר׳ עִיר, a city in Assyria, Ge. 10. 11.—III. ר׳ הַנָּהָר, a city on the Euphrates, Ge. 36. 37.

רְחַבְיָה, רְחַבְיָהוּ (*enlargement of* [from] *the Lord*) pr. name of a man.

רְחַבְעָם (*enlargement of the people*) pr. name, *Rehoboam,* son and successor of king Solomon.

מֶרְחָב masc. dec. 2 b, *wide place;* metaph. of freedom, deliverance.

רָחָב[p] adj. masc. sing. dec. 4 c; also pr. name רחב
רַחַב[q] noun masc. sing. dec. 6 g . . . רחב
רְחַב[r] ו׳ adj. m. sing., constr. of רָחָב d. 4 c; וּ bef. (: רחב

vain thing.—II. adv. *in vain;* more fully לָרִיק, בְּדֵי רִיק, לְרִיק.

רֵיק masc. dec. 1 a, רֵיקָה fem. dec. 10, adj.—I. *empty;* hence *vain,* De. 32. 47.—II. *emptied, impoverished, poor,* Ne. 5. 13.—III. *worthless, wicked.*

רֵיקָם adv.—I. *emptily,* Je. 14. 3.—II. *empty handed.*—III. *without effect, in vain.*—IV. *without a cause.*

רוֹקֵחַ Kal part. act. sing. masc. dec. 7 b, comp. רֹקֵחַ רקח

[רוּר] *to flow,* with an acc. *to emit,* Le. 15. 3.

רִיר masc. dec. 1 a, *saliva, spittle,* 1 Sa. 21. 14; poet. *slaver* or *slime* of a yolk, i. e. the white of an egg, Job 6. 6. Prof. Lee, *whey,* comp. חַלָּמוּת.

[רוּשׁ] *to be poor, in want;* part. רָשׁ, רָאשׁ *poor, needy.* Hithpal. *to feign oneself poor,* Pr. 13. 7.

רִישׁ, רֵישׁ, רֵאשׁ masc. dec. 1 a, *poverty.*

רוּשׁ[a] noun masc. sing. for רֵאשׁ . . . ראש

רוּת ו׳ (contr. for רְעוּת *friend,* R. רָעָה; or for רְאוּת *appearance,* R. רָאָה) pr. name *Ruth,* the wife of Chilion, afterwards of Boaz, whose history is contained in the book of *Ruth.*

רָוְתָה[b] וְ Kal pret. 3 pers. sing. fem. . . . רוה
רִוְּתָה[c] ו׳ Piel pret. 3 pers. sing. fem. . . . רוה
רָז[d] Chald. noun masc. sing. dec. 1 a . . רוז
רָזָא[e] Chald. id., emph. st. . . . רוז

רָזָה *to attenuate, cause to waste away,* Zep. 2. 11. Niph. *to become lean, to waste away.*

רָזֶה, fem. רָזָה.—I. *lean,* Eze. 34. 20.—II. *barren* of land, Nu. 13. 20.

רָזוֹן masc.—I. *a wasting, consumption.*—II. *diminution, scantiness,* Mi. 6. 10.

רָזִי masc. *destruction, woe,* only Is. 24. 16, רָזִי לִי *woe unto me!*

רָזָה adj. fem. sing. [from רָזֶה masc.] . . רזה
רָזוֹן noun masc. sing. . . . . רזה
רְזוֹן[g] noun masc. sing. . . . . רזן
רְזוֹן pr. name masc. . . . . רזן

רָזַח Root not used; Arab. *to raise the voice.*

מַרְזֵחַ masc. *outcry,* either for joy or sorrow, Je. 16. 5; constr. מִרְזַח (§ 36. rem. 1), Am. 6. 7.

רָזִי[h] noun masc. sing. . . . . רזה

[a] De. 32. 32. [b] Je. 46. 10. [c] Is. 34. 5, 7. [d] Da. 4. 6. [e] Da. 2. 18, 19, 27, 30, 47. [g] Pr. 14. 28. [h] Is. 24. 16. [i] Da. 2. 29. [k] Da. 2. 47. [l] Ju. 5. 3. [m] Pr. 8. 15. [n] 1 Sa. 2. 1. [o] Is. 60. 5. [p] Job 30. 14. [q] Job 36. 16. [r] Pr. 28. 25.

רְחֹב וּ pr. name of a man and a place (see also בֵּית ; וּ bef. (:) . . . רחב

רְחַב וְ noun m. s. with suff. רָחְבּוֹ d. 6 (§ 35. r. 5) רחב

רָחֲבָה[a] וְ Kal pret. 3 pers. sing. masc. . . רחב

רְחָבָה[b] וּ adj. fem. sing. (constr. רַחֲבַת) dec. 11 c, from רָחָב masc.; וּ bef. (:) . . . רחב

רְחֹבָהּ[c] noun fem. sing. with suff. 3 pers. sing. fem. from רְחוֹב dec. 1 a . . . רחב

רָחְבָּהּ[d] וְ noun masc. sing. with suff. 3 pers. sing. fem. from רֹחַב dec. 6 (§ 35. rem. 5) רחב

רָחְבּוֹ וְ id. with suff. 3 pers. sing. masc. . . רחב

רְחֹבוֹת[e] וּ noun fem., pl. of רְחוֹב dec. 1 a; וּ bef. (:) רחב

רַחֲבֵי adj. (Is. 33. 21), or subst. (Job 38. 18) pl. c. fr. רָחָב or רַחַב (q. v.) . . . רחב

רְחַבְיָה / רְחַבְיָהוּ } pr. name masc. . . . . רחב

רָחְבָּן[f] noun masc. sing. with suff. 3 pers. pl. fem. from רֹחַב dec. 6 (§ 35. rem. 5) . רחב

רְחַבְעָם וּ pr. name masc.; וּ bef. (:) . . . רחב

רַחֲבַת adj. fem. sing., constr. of רְחָבָה, dec. 11 c (§ 42. rem. 1), from רָחָב masc. . . רחב

רְחֹבֹת pr. name of a place . . . . רחב

רְחוֹב וּ noun fem. sing., pl. רְחֹבוֹת dec. 1 a, also pr. name; וּ bef. (:) . . . . רחב

רַחוּם וְ adj. masc. sing. . . . . רחם

רְחוּם pr. name masc. . . . . . רחם

רָחוֹק[g] וְ adj. or subst. (Jos. 3. 4) masc. dec. 3 a רחק

רְחוֹקָה / רְחוֹקוֹת[h] } adj. fem. sing. & pl. dec. 10, from רָחוֹק masc. . . . . רחק

רְחוֹקִים וּ adj. masc. pl. of רָחוֹק dec. 3 a; וּ bef. (:) רחק

רְהִיטֵנוּ[i] K. רָהִיטֵנוּ noun masc. sing., suff. 1 pers. pl. [from רָהִיט or רַהִיט] see . . . רהט

רֵחַיִם noun masc. du. of [רֵחֶה] dec. 9 a . . רח

רַחִיקִין[k] Chald. adj. masc. pl. of [רַחִיק] dec. 1 a . רחק

[רָחֵל] fem. dec. 5 a, *a ewe*; then *a sheep* generally.

רָחֵל וְ (*ewe*) pr. name, *Rachel*, wife of Jacob.

רְחֵלֶיךָ[l] the foll. with suff. 2 pers. sing. masc. . רחל

רְחֵלִים[m] noun fem. pl. of רָחֵל dec. 5 a . . רחל

[רָחַם] *to love*, Ps. 18. 2. Pi. רִחַם (§ 14. rem. 1) *to love tenderly, to pity, to have compassion* or *mercy upon* any one, with acc., עַל of pers. Pu. רֻחַם *to obtain mercy*.

רָחָם, רָחָמָה masc. a small species of vulture, *the aquiline vulture*, Le. 11. 18; De. 14. 17.

רֶחֶם com. dec. 6 a (with suff. רַחְמִי), *the womb*.

רַחַם fem. dec. 6 d.—I. *the womb*.—II. *a maiden*, Ju. 5. 30.—III. pr. name masc. 1 Ch. 2. 44.—IV. pl. רַחֲמִים (§ 35. rem. 16); (*a*) *the intestines*, Pr. 12. 10; (*b*) *tender affection, love*; (*c*) *compassion, pity, mercy*.

רַחֲמִין Ch. masc. pl. *compassion, mercy*, Da. 2. 18.

רַחֲמָה fem. *a maiden*, only du. רַחֲמָתַיִם Ju. 5. 30.

רַחֲמָנִי adj. masc. *merciful, compassionate*, La. 4. 10.

רַחוּם adj. id. used only of God.

רְחוּם (*merciful*) pr. name of a Persian governor in Samaria, Ezr. 4. 8; also of several other persons.

יְרֹחָם (*he shall obtain mercy*) pr. name masc. of several persons.

יְרַחְמְאֵל (whom *the Lord will pity*) pr. name masc. of several persons. Patronym. יְרַחְמְאֵלִי.

רֶחֶם[n] וְ / רָחֶם[o] } noun masc. sing., pl. רַחֲמִים [for רְחָמִים § 35. r. 16]; for וָ see lett. ו } רחם

רַחַם pr. name masc. . . . . . רחם

רַחֵם Piel inf. constr. (§ 14. rem. 1) . . . רחם

רֶחֶם noun masc. sing. (suff. רַחְמָהּ) dec. 6 a . רחם

רֶחֶם pr. name masc., see רְחוּם . . . רחם

רִחַם[p] וְ Piel pret. 3 pers. sing. (§ 14. rem. 1) . רחם

רַחְמָהּ[q] וְ noun masc. (fem. Je. 20. 17), suff. 3 pers. sing. fem. from רֶחֶם dec. 6 a . . . רחם

רֻחָמָה Pual (§ 14. r. 1) pret. 3 pers. f. s. [for רֻחֲמָה] רחם

רַחֲמָו Kh., רַחֲמָיו K. (q. v.) . . . . רחם

רִחֲמוּם[r] וְ Piel (§ 14. r. 1) pret. 3 p. pl., suff. 3 p. pl. m. רחם

רַחֲמֵי[s] וְ noun m. pl., constr. of רַחֲמִים [for רְחָמִים § 36. rem. 16] from רֶחֶם . . . רחם

רַחֲמֶיהָ[t] id. pl., suff. 3 pers. sing. fem. . . רחם

רַחֲמָיו[u] וְ id. pl., 3 pers. sing. masc. . . רחם

רַחֲמֶיךָ[w] וְ id. pl., 2 pers. sing. masc. . . רחם

רַחֲמִים וְ id. pl. abs. [for רְחָמִים § 36. rem. 16] . רחם

רַחֲמִין[y] וְ Chald. id. pl. abs. . . . . רחם

רַחֲמָנִיּוֹת[z] adj. pl. fem. [from רַחֲמָנִי masc.] . רחם

רִחַמְךָ[a] וְ / רִחַמְתִּךְ[b] וְ } Piel (§ 14. rem. 1) pret. 3 pers. sing. masc., suff. 2 pers. sing. masc. . } רחם

רִחַמְתִּי וְ id. pret. 1 pers. sing.; acc. shifted by conv. וְ (comp. § 8. rem. 7) . . . . רחם

רִחַמְתִּיךְ id. id., with suff. 2 pers. sing. fem. . רחם

רַחֲמָתַיִם[c] noun fem. dual of [רַחֲמָה] dec. 10 . רחם

רִחַמְתִּים[d] וְ Piel (§ 14. r. 1) pret. 1 p. s. with suff. 3 p. pl. m. רחם

[רָחַף] *to shake, tremble*, Je. 23. 9. Pi. רִחֵף (§ 14. rem. 1) *to flutter, hover, brood*.

רָחֲפוּ[e] Kal pret. 3 pers. pl. . . . . רחף

[a] Eze. 41. 7. [b] Ps. 119. 96. [c] De. 13. 17. [d] Zec. 5. 2. [e] Zec. 8. 5. [f] Eze. 42. 11. [g] Je. 12. 2. [h] Eze. 12. 27. [i] Ca. 1. 17. [k] Ezr. 6. 6. [l] Ge. 31. 38. [m] Ge. 32. 15. [n] Ge. 49. 25. [o] Ju. 5. 30. [p] Ps. 103. 13. [q] Je. 20. 17. [r] 1 Ki. 8. 50. [s] Pr. 12. 10. [t] 1 Ki. 3. 26. [u] Ps. 145. 9. [w] Is. 63. 15. [y] Da. 2. 18. [z] La. 4. 10. [a] De. 30. 3. [b] De. 13. 18. [c] Ju. 5. 30. [d] Zec. 10. 6. [e] Je. 23. 9.

רָחַץ וְ fut. יִרְחַץ, inf. רְחֹץ.—I. *to wash*, in reference to the body or other flesh.—II. *to wash away*, Is. 4. 4.—III. *to wash oneself*, *to bathe*. Pu. רֻחַץ (§ 14. rem. 1) *to be washed*, Pr. 30. 12. Hithp. *to wash oneself*, *to bathe*, Job 9. 30.

רַחַץ masc. dec. 6d, *a washing*.

רַחְצָה f. *a washing-place* for sheep, Ca. 4. 2; 6. 6.

רְחַץ Chald. only Ithpa. *to trust on* or *in* any one, with עַל Da. 3. 28.

רְחַץ[a] ו' [b] Kal imp. sing. masc.; וּ bef. (:) . . . רחץ

רֻחָץ[c] Pual pret. 3 p. s. m. in pause (§ 14. rem. 1) רחץ

רָחֲצוּ[d] }

וְרָחֲצוּ } Kal pret. 3 pers. pl. (§ 8. rem. 7) . רחץ

רַחֲצוּ[e] וְ id. imp. pl. masc. . . . . רחץ

רֹחֲצוֹת[f] id. part. act. f., pl. of רֹחֶצֶת d. 13 [fr. רֹחֵץ m.] רחץ

רַחְצִי noun masc. sing., suff. 1 pers. sing. from [רַחַץ] dec. 6d (§ 35. rem. 5) . . רחץ

רָחַצְתָּ וְ Kal pret. 2 pers. sing. masc.; acc. shifted by conv. וְ (§ 8. rem. 7) . . . רחץ

רָחַצְתְּ[g] [h] וְ' id. pret. 2 pers. sing. fem. . . . רחץ

רֹחֶצֶת[i] id. part. sing. fem. dec. 13 . . . רחץ

רֻחַצְתְּ[k] Pual pret. 2 pers. sing. fem. (§ 14. rem. 1) רחץ

רָחַצְתִּי[l] Kal pret. 1 pers. sing. . . . . רחץ

רָחַק fut. יִרְחַק.—I. *to go far away*, *to recede*, with מִן.—II. *to be far off*, *distant*, *remote*, with מֵעַל, מִן. Niph. *to be removed*, Ec. 12. 6, Kheth. Pi. רִחַק (§ 14. rem. 4) *to put far away*, *to remove*. Hiph. I. *to put far away*, *to remove*; הִרְחִיק לָלֶכֶת *to go far away*, Ex. 8. 24; inf. הַרְחֵק adv. *afar off*, Ge. 21. 16.—II. *to go far away*.

רָחֵק adj. masc. dec. 5a, *going far away*, *departing*, Ps. 73. 27.

רָחוֹק masc. dec. 3a, רְחוֹקָה fem. dec. 10.—I. *far off*, *remote*, *distant*, of space and time; neut. *remoteness*, *distance*, Jos. 3. 4; בְּרָחוֹק *at a distance*; מֵרָחוֹק *from a distance*, *from afar*; also *afar off*, and of time, *long ago*; עַד מֵרָחוֹק *far off*; לְמֵרָחוֹק *from afar*, and of time *long ago*.—II. *far above*, sc. in value, Pr. 31. 10.

רַחִיק Chald. masc. dec. 1a, *distant*, Ezr. 6. 6.

מֶרְחָק masc. pl. מֶרְחַקִּים, מֶרְ', *distance*, *distant part*; מִמֶּרְחָק *from afar*, also Is. 17. 13, *while yet far off*; אֶרֶץ מֶרְחָק *a distant land*; pl. מֶרְחַקִּים, אֶרֶץ מֶרְ', מֶרְחַקֵּי אֶרֶץ *distant lands*.

רָחֹק[m] וְ defect. for רָחוֹק (q. v.) . . . רחק

רִחַק[n] וְ' Piel pret. 3 pers. sing. masc. (§ 14. r. 1) רחק

רָחֲקָה Kal pret. 3 pers. sing. fem. . . רחק

רְחֹקָה defect. for רְחוֹקָה (q. v.) . . . רחק

רָחֲקוּ[o] }

וְרָחֲקוּ[p] } Kal pret. 3 pers. pl. (§ 8. rem. 7) . רחק

רַחֲקוּ[q] id. imp. pl. masc. . . . . רחק

רַחֲקִי[r] id. imp. sing. fem. . . . . רחק

רְחֵקֶיךָ[s] adj. pl. masc., suff. 2 pers. sing. masc. from [רָחֵק] dec. 5a . . . . . רחק

רְחֹקִים defect. for רְחוֹקִים (q. v.) . . . רחק

רִחַקְתָּ[t] Piel pret. 2 pers. sing. masc. (§ 14. rem. 1) רחק

רָחַשׁ *to boil up*, *throw up* as a fountain, metaph. Ps. 45. 2.

מַרְחֶשֶׁת fem. *pot*, *kettle* for boiling, Le. 2. 7; 7. 9.

[רָטַב] *to be wet*, Job 24. 8. Hence

רָטֹב adj. masc. *moist*, *fresh*, Job 8. 16 . . רטב

רָטָה perh. i. q. Arab. רטא *to throw*, hence יִרְטֵנִי Job 16. 11, *they give me over*; but see יָרַט.

רֶטֶט וְ masc. *trembling*, *fear*, Je. 49. 24. Syr. & Chald. רְטַט *to tremble*, *be terrified*.

רֻטֲפַשׁ *to grow moist*, *fresh*, *to revive*, Job 33. 25.

רָטַשׁ Pi. I. *to dash in pieces* against a rock.—II. *to strike to the ground* with arrows, Is. 13. 18. Pu. pass. of Piel, No. I.

רֻטָּשָׁה[u] Pual pret. 3 pers. sing. fem. [for רֻטְּשָׁה, comp. § 8. rem. 7] . . . רטש

רִיב[x] [also רוּב, comp. ירוב, Pr. 3. 30, Kh. and pr. names יְרֻבַּעַל, [יְרֻבֶּשֶׁת] pret. רָב, רַבְתָּ, רִיבוֹתָ; inf. abs. רֹב, constr. and imp. רִיב; fut. יָרִיב, ap. יָרֵב (§ 22. rem. 1, sq.).—I. *to contend*, *strive*, *quarrel*, with עִם, אֶת, אֶל, בְּ, rarely acc. *with whom*, with לְ, עַל *for what* one contends.—II. *to plead* or *defend a cause*, with acc. of the person whose cause is sustained, also acc. of the cause; part. רָב *defender*, Is. 19. 20.—III. *to decide a cause favourably*. Hiph. part. מֵרִיב *contending*, hence *adversary*.

רִיב masc. dec. 1a (pl. ־ִים, ־וֹת).—I. *contention*, *strife*, *quarrel*; אִישׁ רִיב *an adversary*.—II. *controversy*, *suit*, *cause*; אִישׁ רִיב *one who has a cause*.

רִיבַי (perh. for יְרִיבַי q. v.) pr. name of a man.

---

[a] 2 Ki. 5. 13. [b] 2 Sa. 11. 8. [c] Pr. 30. 12. [d] 1 Ki. 22. 38. [e] Is. 1. 16. [f] Ca. 5. 12. [g] Eze. 23. 40. [h] Ru. 3. 3. [i] 2 Sa. 11. 2. [k] Eze. 16. 4. [l] Ca. 5. 3. [m] Pr. 31. 10. [n] Is. 6. 12; 26. 15. [o] Ps. 119. 150. [p] Is. 49. 19. [q] Eze. 11. 15. [r] Is. 54. 14. [s] Ps. 73. 27. [t] Is. 26. 15. [u] Ho. 10. 14. [x] Je. 50. 34.

יָרִיב masc. dec. 3a.—I. *adversary.*—II. pr. name masc. Ezr. 8. 16; see also יָכִין. R. כּוּן.

יְרִיבַי (for יְרִיבְיָה whom *the Lord defends*) pr. name masc. 1 Ch. 11. 46.

יְרֻבַּעַל (for יָרֹב בַּעַל *let Baal contend*) a surname of Gideon, the judge of Israel, comp. Ju. 6. 32. Called also

יְרֻבֶּשֶׁת (*let the idol contend*) in 2 Sa. 11. 21; comp. the preced.

יָרָבְעָם (who *contends with the people*) pr. name of two kings of the ten tribes, Jeroboam, son of Nebat, and Jeroboam, son of Joash.

מְרִיבָה fem. dec. 10.—I. *contention, strife.*—II. pr. name, *Meribah*, a fountain in the desert of Sin. —III. מֵי מְרִיבָה (*waters of strife*) pr. name of a fountain at Kadesh in the desert of Zin; fully מֵי מְרִיבוֹת קָדֵשׁ, Eze. 47. 19.

רִיב וְ' Kal imp.; or subst. masc. sing. dec. 1a . ריב
רִיבָה [a] וְ' id. imp. sing. masc. with parag. ה . ריב
רִיבוּ id. imp. pl. masc. . . . . ריב
רִיבוֹתָ [b] id. pret. 3 pers. sing. masc. . . ריב
רִיבַי pr. name masc. . . . . . ריב
רִיבֵי [c] noun masc. pl. constr. from רִיב dec. 1a . ריב
רִיבִי id. sing., suff. 1 pers. sing. . . . ריב
רִיבֶךָ, רִיבְךָ [d] id. sing., suff. 2 pers. sing. masc. . ריב
רִיבֵךְ [e] id. sing., suff. 2 pers. sing. fem. . . ריב
רִיבְכֶם [f] וְ' [g] id. sing., suff. 2 pers. pl. masc. . ריב
רִיבָם id. sing., suff. 3 pers. pl. masc. . . ריב
רִיבֹת [h] id. with pl. fem. term. . . . ריב
רֵיחַ וְ' noun masc. sing. dec. 1a . . . רוח
רֵיחוֹ וְ' [k] id., suff. 3 pers. sing. masc. . . רוח
רֵיחֵנוּ [i] id., suff. 1 pers. pl. . . . . רוח
רֵים noun masc. sing. dec. 1a, for רְאֵם . ראם
רֵיעֲכֶם [m] [for רֵעֲכֶם] noun masc. sing., suff. 2 pers. pl. masc. from רֵעַ dec. 1a . רעה
רִיפַת וְ pr. name of a son of Gomer, and of a people descended from him, Ge. 10. 3.
רִיק [n] וְ' noun masc. sing., used also as an *adv.*; for וְ see lett. ו . . . . רוק
רֵיקָה [o] וְ adj. fem. sing. dec. 10, from רֵיק masc. . רוק
רֵיקִים id. pl. masc. from רֵיק dec. 1a . . ריק
רֵיקָם [p] וְ' *adv.* from רֵיק with the term. ־ָם . ריק
רִירוֹ [q] noun masc. s., suff. 3 p. s. m. fr. רִיר d. 1a רור
רֵישׁ [r] noun masc. sing. dec. 1a . . . רושׁ
רִישׁ [s] noun masc. sing. dec. 1a . . . רושׁ
רִישׁוֹ [t] id. with suff. 3 pers. sing. masc. . . רושׁ

רִישׁוֹן [u] adj. masc. sing. [for רִאשׁוֹן] . . ראשׁ
רֵישְׁךָ [x] noun m. s., suff. 2 pers. s. m. fr. רֵישׁ d. 1a רושׁ
רֵישָׁם [y] id., suff. 3 pers. pl. masc. . . . רושׁ
רַךְ וְ, רָךְ וְ' Kal pret. 3 p.s.m. 2 Ki. 22. 19; 2 Ch. 34. 27, or adj. masc. s. dec. 8d; for וְ see lett. ו רכך

רָכַב [z] fut. יִרְכַּב, inf. רְכֹב *to ride* either on the back of an animal or in a chariot, const. with בְּ, עַל, also acc.; part. רֹכֵב *a rider, horseman*; metaph. of God *riding*, being borne upon the clouds, &c. Hiph. I. *to cause* or *make to ride* upon an animal, also *to carry* in a chariot.—II. *to place, put,* or *lay upon*, 2 Ki. 13. 16.—III. *to cause to be ridden*, Ho. 10. 10.

רֶכֶב masc. dec. 6a (with suff. רִכְבִּי).—I. *a rider*, perh. so 2 Ki. 7. 14; collect. *riders, cavalry*, Is. 21. 7.—II. *chariot*, collect. *chariots.*—III. also *chariot horses*, 2 Sa. 8. 4.—IV. *the upper millstone*, lit. *the rider*.

רַכָּב masc. dec. 1b.—I. *a horseman*, 2 Ki. 9. 17. —II. *charioteer*.

רֵכָב (*rider*) pr. name—I. of the father of Jonadab, the progenitor of a wandering tribe called after him רֵכָבִים *Rechabites*, comp. Je. 35. 24, seq. —II. of two other men, 2 Sa. 4. 2; Ne. 3. 14.

רִכְבָּה fem. *a riding*, Eze. 27. 20.

רְכוּב masc. dec. 1a, *vehicle, chariot*, Ps. 104. 3.

מֶרְכָּב masc. dec. 2b.—I. *a chariot.*—II. *the seat of a chariot*.

מֶרְכָּבָה fem. constr. מִרְכֶּבֶת, with suff. מֶרְכַּבְתּוֹ (§ 42. rem. 5) pl. abs. מַרְכָּבוֹת, constr. מַרְכְּבוֹת, *a chariot*.

רכב Root not used; prob. i. q. בָּרַךְ *to bend* (comp. Fürst. in concord.)

אַרְכֻּבָה Chald. fem. dec. 8a, *a knee*, Da. 5. 6. Targ. רְכוּב id.

רַכָּב [a] noun masc. sing. dec. 1b (§ 37. No. 3) . רכב
רֶכֶב וְ', רָכֶב וְ', וְ' noun masc. sing. dec. 6a (§ 35. r. 2, but with suff. רִכְבּוֹ); for וְ see lett. ו רכב
רֵכָב וְ' pr. name masc. . . . . . רכב
רְכַב [b] Kal imp. sing. masc. . . . . רכב
רֹכֵב וְ' id. part. act. sing. masc. dec. 7b . . רכב
רִכְבָּהּ [c] noun masc. sing., suff. 3 p. s. f. fr. רֶכֶב d. 6a רכב
רָכְבוּ [d] Kal pret. 3 pers. pl. . . . . רכב
רִכְבּוֹ noun masc. sing., suff. 3 pers. sing. masc. from רֶכֶב dec. 6a . . . . . רכב

[a] Ps. 43. 1. [b] Job 33. 13. [c] La. 3. 58. [d] Pr. 25. 9. [e] Je. 51. 36. [f] Is. 41. 21. [g] De. 1. 12. [h] De. 17. 8. [i] Ca. 1. 12. [k] Je. 48. 11. [l] Ex. 5. 21. [m] Job 6. 27. [n] Is. 30. 7. [o] Is. 29. 8. [p] Ru. 1. 21. [q] 1 Sa. 21. 14. [r] Pr. 13. 18. [s] Pr. 28. 19. [t] Pr. 31. 7. [u] Job 8. 8. [x] Pr. 24. 34. [y] Pr. 10. 15. [z] Est. 6. 8. [a] 2 Ki. 9. 17. [b] Ps. 45. 5. [c] Na. 2. 14. [d] 1 Sa. 30. 17.

רֹכְבוֹ[a] וְ Kal part. act. sing. masc., suff. 3 pers. sing. masc. from רֹכֵב dec. 7b . . רכב

רִכְבִּי[b] noun masc. sing., suff. 1 pers. sing. from רֶכֶב dec. 6a . . . . רכב

רֹכְבֵי Kal part. act. pl. constr. masc. fr. רֹכֵב d. 7b רכב

רֹכְבֶיהָ[c] וְ id. pl., suff. 3 pers. sing. fem. . . רכב

רֹכְבֵיהֶם[d] וְ id. pl., suff. 3 pers. pl. masc. . . רכב

רֹכְבִים id. pl., abs. st. . . . . . רכב

רָכַבְתָּ[e] id. pret. 2 pers. sing. masc. . . . רכב

רֹכֶבֶת[f] id. part. act., fem. of רֹכֵב (§ 8. rem. 19) רכב

רַכָּה adj. fem. sing. from רַךְ masc. . . רכך

רֵכָה pr. name masc. 1 Ch. 4. 12.

רַכּוּ[g] Kal pret. 3 pers. pl. . . . . . רכך

רְכוּבוֹ[h] noun masc. sing., suff. 3 pers. sing. masc. from רְכוּב dec. 1a . . . . רכב

רְכוּשׁ וּ׳ noun masc. sing. dec. 1a; וּ bef. (:) . רכש

רְכוּשׁוֹ id., suff. 3 pers. sing. masc. . . . רכש

רְכוּשְׁךָ[i] id., suff. 2 pers. sing. masc. [for רְכוּשְׁךָ] רכש

רְכוּשָׁם id., suff. 3 pers. pl. masc. . . . רכש

רְכוּשֵׁנוּ[k] id., suff. 1 pers. pl. . . . . . רכש

רַכּוֹת adj. fem., pl. of רַכָּה dec. 10, from רַךְ masc. רכך

רָכִיל noun masc. sing. . . . . . רכל

רַכִּים[l] adj. pl. masc. from רַךְ dec. 8d . . . רכך

[רָכַךְ] fut. יֵרַךְ (§ 18. rem. 6).—I. *to be tender*, of the heart, *contrite*, 2 Ki. 22. 19; hence, *to be timid, faint*.—II. *to be soft*, of words, Ps. 55. 22. Pu. *to be softened*, Is. 1. 6. Hiph. *to make timid*, the heart, Job 23. 16.

רַךְ masc. dec. 8d, רַכָּה fem. dec. 10.—I. *tender, young*.—II. *tender, delicate, effeminate*.—III. *soft, gentle*, of words.—IV. *tender, weak, sore*, of the eyes.—V. *faint, timid*, of the heart.

רֹךְ masc. *delicateness, effeminacy*, De. 28. 56.

מֹרֶךְ m. *softness, timidity, cowardice*, Le. 26. 36.

רֻכְּכָה[m] Pual pret. 3 pers. sing. fem. . . . רכך

[רָכַל] *to go about*, particularly as a trader for traffic, hence (and only) part. רֹכֵל, fem. רֹכֶלֶת *trader, merchant*.

רָכָל (*traffic*) pr. name of a town in Judah, 1 Sa. 30. 29.

רְכֻלָּה fem. dec. 10, *trade, traffic*.

רָכִיל masc. *talebearing, slandering*; אַנְשֵׁי רָ׳ *talebearers, slanderers*; הָלַךְ רָ׳ *to go about talebearing*.

מַרְכֹּלֶת fem. dec. 13c, *market, mart*, Eze. 27. 24.

רֹכְלֵי[n] Kal part. act. pl. constr. masc. from רֹכֵל d. 7b רכל

רֹכְלַיִךְ[o] } id. pl., suff. 2 pers. sing. fem. . . . רכל
רֹכְלַיִךְ

רֹכְלִים[p] id. pl., abs. st. . . . . . . רכל

רֹכֶלֶת[q] id. sing. fem. (§ 8. rem. 19) dec. 13a . רכל

רְכֻלָּתֵךְ[r] noun fem. s., suff. 2 pers. s. fem. [רְכֻלָּה] d. 10 רכל

רְכֻלָּתְךָ[s] id. with suff. 2 pers. sing. masc. . . רכל

רֹכַלְתֵּךְ[t] Kal part. act. sing. fem., suff. 2 pers. sing. fem. from רֹכֶלֶת (q. v.) . . . רכל

[רָכַס] *to bind on* or *to* any thing.

רֶכֶס masc. only pl. רְכָסִים *difficult, rugged places*, Is. 40. 4.

רֹכֶס masc. dec. 6c, *conspiracy, plot*, Ps. 31. 21.

רָכַשׁ *to get, gain, acquire*.

רְכֻשׁ, רְכוּשׁ m. d. 1a, *substance, property, wealth*.

[רֶכֶשׁ] masc. a species of *swift horse*. Syr. רכשא *a horse*, espec. *a stallion*.

רָכַשׁ[u] } Kal pret. 3 pers. sing. masc. (§ 8. rem. 7) רכש
רָכָשׁ

רְכֻשׁ[x] defect. for רְכוּשׁ (q. v.) . . . . רכש

רָכְשׁוּ[y] } Kal pret. 3 pers. pl. (§ 8. rem. 7) . רכש
רָכָשׁוּ[z]

רְכֻשׁוֹ[a] וּ׳ defect. for רְכוּשׁוֹ (q. v.) . . . רכש

רָם וְ׳ pr. name masc. . . . . . רום

רָם וָ׳, וְ׳ Kal pret. 3 pers. sing. masc.; or part. dec. 1a (§ 30. No. 3); for וָ see lett. ו . רום

רָם[b] Chald. part. Peil pret. 3 pers. s. m. (§ 54. r. 6) רום

רָם[c] וְ defect. for רוּם subst. (q. v.) . . . רום

רָמָה[d] I. *to cast, throw*.—II. *to shoot* with a bow. Pi. רִמָּה *to deceive* (prop. *to make fall*).

רְמָה, רְמָא Chald.—I. *to cast, throw*.—II. *to set, place*, Da. 7. 9.—III. *to impose* tribute, Ezr. 7. 24. Ithpe. *to be cast, thrown*, Da. 3. 6, 15.

רַמְיָה (whom *the Lord has set, appointed*) pr. name masc. Ezr. 10. 25.

רְמִיָּה fem.—I. *slackness, remissness* (prop. *a letting fall* of the hands); adv. *remissly*, Je. 48. 10. —II. *deceit*.

יִרְמְיָה, יִרְמְיָהוּ (whom *the Lord sets, appoints*) pr. name, *Jeremiah*.—I. the prophet, son of Hilkiah a priest.—II. pr. name of several other men.

מִרְמָה fem. dec. 10.—I. *deceit, fraud*; אִישׁ מִ׳ *fraudulent man*; אַבְנֵי מִ׳ *false weights*; meton. *goods obtained by fraud*.—II. pr. name m. 1 Ch. 8. 10.

---

[a] Ge. 49. 17. [b] 2 Ki. 19. 23; Is. 37. 24. [c] Hag. 2. 22. [d] Hag. 2. 22. [e] Nu. 22. 30. [f] 1 Sa. 25. 20. [g] Ps. 55. 22. [h] Ps. 104. 3. [i] 2 Ch. 21. 14. [k] Ezr. 8. 21. [l] Ge. 33. 13. [m] Is. 1. 6. [n] Eze. 27. 22, 23. [o] Eze. 27. 13, 17, 22. [p] Eze. 17. 4. [q] Eze. 27. 3. [r] Eze. 26. 12. [s] Eze. 28. 16, 18. [t] Eze. 27. 20, 23. [u] Ge. 31. 18. [x] Ge. 14. 11. [y] Ge. 12. 5. [z] Ge. 46. 6. [a] Ge. 14. 16. [b] Da. 5. 20. [c] Je. 48. 29. [d] Ex. 15. 1, 21.

תַּרְמָה fem. *deceit, craft*, Ju. 9. 31.
תַּרְמוּת fem. Je. 14. 14 Kh., and
תַּרְמִית fem. dec. 1 b, *deceit, craft*.

רָמָה Kal pret. 3 pers. sing. fem. . . . רום
רָמָה id. part. s. fem. or subst. f., d. 10; also pr. name רום
[a]רָמָה Kal pret. 3 pers. sing. masc. . . . רמה
רִמָּה ו' noun fem. sing. . . . . רמם
[b]רִמָּה Piel pret. 3 pers. sing. masc. . . . רמה
[c]רֹמֵה וְ Kal part. act. sing. masc., constr. of רֹמֶה d. 9 a רמה
רָמוּ Kal pret. 3 pers. pl., and in pause רָמוּ . רום
[d]רְמוֹ ו' Peal pret. 3 pers. pl. masc.; וּ bef. (:) רמה
[e]רֹמּוּ Kal pret. 3 pers. pl. . . . רמם
רִמּוֹן ו' noun masc. sing. dec. 1 b; also pr. name רמם
רִמּוֹנוֹ pr. name of a place, see רִמּוֹן . רמם
[f]רִמּוֹנֵי noun masc. pl. constr. from רִמּוֹן dec. 2 b רמם
[g]רִמּוּנִי Piel pret. 3 pers. pl. with suff. 1 pers. sing. רמה
רִמֹּנִים[h] ו' noun masc., pl. of רִמּוֹן dec. 1 b רמם
רָמוֹת Kal part. act. fem., pl. of רָמָה, dec. 10, from רָם masc. (§ 30. No. 3) . . רום
רָמוּתֶךָ noun fem. sing., suff. 2 pers. sing. masc. from [רָמוּת, comp. § 30. No. 3] dec. 1 b רום

רֹמַח ו' masc. dec. 6 c (§ 35. rem. 5), *lance, spear*.
[k]רָמְחֵיהֶם id. pl. with suff. 3 pers. pl. masc. . רמח
רְמָחִים וּ id. pl., abs. st. (§ 35. rem. 9); וּ bef. (:) רמח
רָמֵי וְ Kal part. act. pl. c. masc. from רָם dec. 1 a (§ 30. No. 3) . . . רום
רְמְיָה pr. name masc. . . . . רמה
רְמִיָּה ו' noun fem. sing; וּ bef. (:) . . . רמה
[n]רְמִיו ו' Chald. Peal pret. 3 pers. pl. masc. (§ 55. rem. 1); וּ id. . . . . רמה
רָמִים Kal part. act. m., pl. of רָם d. 1 a (§ 30. No. 3) רום
[o]רֵמִים for רְאֵמִים noun masc., pl. of רְאֵם dec. 1 a ראם
[p]רְמֵינָא Chald. Peal pret. 1 pers. pl. . . . רמה
[q]רִמִּיתֶם Piel pret. 2 pers. pl. masc. . . . רמה
רִמִּיתָנִי id. pret. 2 pers. sing. masc., suff. 1 pers. sing. רמה
רִמִּיתִנִי[r] id. pret. 2 pers. sing. fem., suff. 1 pers. sing. רמה

[רַמָּךְ] fem. dec. 1 b, *a mare*, Est. 8. 10.
רְמַלְיָהוּ (whom *the Lord has adorned*, coll. with the Arab.) pr. name of the father of Pekah, king of Israel.

[רָמַם] I. i. q. רום *to be high, lofty*.—II. Arab. *to rot*, hence deriv. רִמָּה. Niph. *to lift oneself up, to rise up*.
רִמָּה fem. *worm*, collect. *worms*.
רִמּוֹן masc. dec. 1 b.—I. *pomegranate*; also as an artificial ornament.—II. *pomegranate tree*.—III. pr. name (*a*) of a city in the tribe of Simeon; (*b*) of another in the tribe of Zebulun, Jos. 19. 13; called רִמּוֹנוֹ 1 Ch. 6. 62; (*c*) of a rock near Gibeah; (*d*) of a Syrian idol, 2 Ki. 5. 18; (*e*) of a man, 2 Sa. 4. 2; (*f*) רִמֹּן פֶּרֶץ of a station of the Israelites in the desert, Nu. 33. 19.

[zz]רֹמְמַתְהוּ Pilel pret. 3 pers. sing. fem. [רוֹמְמָה] with suff. 3 pers. sing. masc. . . . רום
רִמֹּן ו' noun masc. sing., also pr. name; see רִמּוֹן רמם
רִמָּנִי Piel pret. 3 pers. sing. masc. (רִמָּה), suff. 1 pers. sing. (§ 24. rem. 21) . . רמה
[u]רִמֹּנֵי noun masc. pl. constr. masc. fr. רִמּוֹן dec. 1 b רמם
[x]רִמֹּנִי id. sing., suff. 1 pers. sing. . . . רמם
[y]רִמֹּנִים וְ[z] id. pl., abs. st. . . . . רמם

[a]רָמַס וְ fut. יִרְמֹס.—I. *to tread* with the feet, e. g. as the potter the clay, with acc. בְּ.—II. with עַל *to tread upon, walk over* any thing, Ps. 91. 13.—III. *to tread down, trample under foot*; part. רֹמֵס *a treader down, oppressor*, Is. 16. 4. Niph. *to be trodden down*, Is. 28. 3.
מִרְמָס masc. dec. 2 b, *a treading down, something trodden under foot*.
[b]רְמֹס Kal inf. constr. . . . . רמס
[c]רֹמֵס id. part. act. sing. masc. . . . . רמס
[d]רִמְסִי וְ id. imp. sing. fem. . . . . רמס

[רָמַשׂ] fut. יִרְמֹשׂ.—I. *to creep*, of reptiles.—II. *to move*, of any living creature; Ge. 9. 2, אֲשֶׁר תִּרְמֹשׂ הָאֲדָמָה *with which the earth moves*, for, *which moves upon the earth*. Hence
רֶמֶשׂ [e]ו', [f]וְ' masc.—I. *reptile*, collect. *reptiles*.—II. *that which moves* (on the earth), *any land animal*, in opposition to *fowls*; once of *water animals*, Ps. 104. 25 . . רמשׂ
רֹמֵשׂ Kal part. act. sing. masc. . . . רמשׂ
רָמַת pr. name in compos. as רָ' לְחִי &c. . רום
רָמַת, וְרָמֶת pr. names of places . . . רום
[g]רָמֹתַיִךְ noun fem. pl., suff. 2 pers. sing. fem. from רָמָה dec. 10 (comp. § 30. No. 3) . רום
[h]רָמָתֵךְ ו' id. sing., suff. 2 pers. sing. fem. . . רום

[רָנָה] *to rattle*, Job 39. 23.
רִנָּה ו' noun fem. sing. dec. 10, also pr. name רנן
רָנּוּ Kal imp. pl. masc. (§ 18. rem. 14) רנן

[a] Ex. 15. 1. 21. [b] Pr. 26. 19. [c] Je. 4. 29. [d] Da. 6. 17, 25. [e] Job 24. 24. [f] Ex. 39. 24. [g] La. 1. 19. [h] Je. 52. 22. [i] Eze. 32. 5. [k] Ne. 4. 7. [l] Is. 10. 33. [m] Pr. 12. 24. [n] Da. 3. 21; 7. 9. [o] Ps. 22. 22. [p] Da. 3. 24. [q] Jos. 9. 22. [r] 1 Sa. 19. 17. [s] Ex. 39. 26. [t] 2 Sa. 19. 27. [u] Ex. 28. 33. [x] Ca. 8. 2. [y] 1 Ki. 7. 42. [z] 2 Ki. 25. 17. [zz] Eze. 31. 4. [a] Mi. 5. 7. [b] Is. 1. 12. [c] Is. 16. 4. [d] Na. 3. 14. [e] Ho. 2. 20. [f] Ge. 1. 24. [g] Eze. 16. 39. [h] Eze. 16. 25, 31.

רָנִּי Kal imp. sing. fem. (§ 18. rem. 4); רנן
[a] וְ׳ רָנִּי for וְ see lett. ו . . .

[b] רָנֵּי noun masc. pl. constr. from [רֹן] dec. 8 c (comp. § 37. rem. 2) . . . . . רנן

[רָנַן] fut. יָרֹן, also יָרוּן (§ 18. rem. 12).—I. *to shout for joy*, and hence frequently *to sing*.—II. *to call out* in invitation, Pr. 1. 20; 8. 3.—III. *to cry out* for help, La. 2. 19; Gesenius, *to wail*. Piel רִנֵּן.—I. *to shout, sing, rejoice*, with בְּ, עַל *over*.—II. *to sing, celebrate, praise*, with acc. לְ, אֶל of the person or thing. Hiph. I. *to cause to sing or rejoice*.—II. *to shout for joy*.

רְנָנָה fem. dec. 11 c.—I. *singing, rejoicing*.—II. pl. רְנָנִים *ostriches*, Job 39. 13.

רֹן masc. dec. 8 c, *a shouting, rejoicing*, Ps. 32. 7.

רִנָּה fem. dec. 10.—I. *shouting, singing, rejoicing*.—II. *outcry, cry for help*.—III. pr. name masc. 1 Ch. 4. 20.

אַרְנוֹן (*rushing, roaring*) pr. name, *Arnon*, a torrent flowing from the eastward into the Dead Sea.

[c] רַנֵּן [d] וְ׳ Piel inf. constr. . . . . . רנן
[e] רְנָנָה noun fem. sing. dec. 11 c . . . . רנן
רַנְּנוּ וְ׳ Piel imp. pl. masc. . . . . . רנן
[f] רִנְּנוּ וְ id. pret. 3 pers. pl. . . . . . רנן
[g] רְנָנוֹת, [h] רְנָנִים noun fem. pl. abs. from רְנָנָה dec. 11 a רנן
[i] רִנְנַת id. sing., constr. st. . . . . . רנן
רִנָּתִי noun fem. sing., suff. 1 pers. s. fr. רִנָּה d. 10 רנן
רִנָּתָם id., suff. 3 pers. pl. masc. . . . . רנן
[k] רְסִיסֵי, [l] רְסִיסִים noun masc. pl. constr. & abs. [from רָסִים or רְסִים] . . . . . רסס

רָסַן Root not used; Arab. رسن *to bind*. Hence

[m] רֶסֶן, [n] וְ׳ masc. dec. 6 a.—I. *bridle, halter*.—II. *the inner part of the mouth, the jaws*, Job 41. 5, בְּכֶפֶל רִסְנוֹ *into the jaws*, the double row of the teeth of the crocodile (Gesenius, and so most of the modern interpreters).

[ll] רִסְנוֹ id. with suff. 3 pers. sing. masc. . . . רסן

[רָסַס] I. *to moisten, sprinkle*, Eze. 46. 14.—II. in the deriv. i. q. רָצַץ *to break in pieces*.

רְסִיסִים masc. pl. (of רָסִים or רְסִים).—I. *dew-drops*, Ca. 5. 2.—II. *fractures*, Am. 6. 11.

רִסָּה (*fracture, ruins*) pr. name of a station of the Israelites in the desert, Nu. 33. 21, 22.

רָע וְ׳, רַע וְ׳ Kal pret. 3 pers. s. m.; & adj. or subst. m. d. 8 (§ 37. r. 7); for וְ see lett. ו רעע
רֵעַ [n] וְ׳, [o] וְ׳ noun masc. s. d. 1 a (§ 36. r. 2); וְ id. רעה
[p] רֵעַ noun masc. sing. dec. 1 a (§ 30. No. 3) . רוע
רֹעַ noun masc. sing. . . . . . רעע

[רָעֵב] I. *to be hungry*.—II. *to suffer from famine, to famish*.—III. with לְ *to hunger after*, Je. 42. 14. Hiph. *to cause to hunger*.

רָעָב masc. dec. 4 a.—I. *hunger*.—II. *famine*.

רָעֵב masc. dec. 5 a, רְעֵבָה fem. adj.—I. *hungry*.—II. *famishing*, Job 18. 12.

רְעָבוֹן masc. dec. 3 c (§ 32. No. 3), *famine*.

רָעָב וְ׳ noun masc. sing. dec. 4 a . . . רעב
רָעֵב וְ׳ adj. masc. sing. dec. 5 a . . . . רעב
רְעֵבָה fem. of the preced. . . . . . רעב
[q] רָעֵבוּ וְ Kal pret. 3 pers. pl. [for רָעֲבוּ § 8. rem. 1] רעב
[r] רַעֲבוֹן, [s] רְעָבוֹן noun masc. sing., constr. & abs. dec. 3 c (§ 32. No. 2) . . . . רעב
רְעֵבִים וּ׳ adj. masc. pl. of רָעֵב dec. 5 a; וּ bef. (:) רעב

[רָעַד] *to tremble, quake*, Ps. 104. 32. Hiph. *to tremble, shake*. Hence

[t] רַעַד, [u] וְ רָעַד masc. *a trembling, awe*; for וְ see lett. ו.
רְעָדָה [v] וּ׳ fem. *a trembling, awe*; וּ bef. (:).

רָעָה וְ fut. יִרְעֶה, ap. יֵרַע (§ 24. rem. 3).—I. *to feed, pasture* a flock, with acc., בְּ; part. רֹעֶה *a shepherd, herdsman*, fem. רֹעָה *shepherdess*.—II. trop. *to lead, rule, govern*; also *to feed, nourish*.—III. intrans. *to feed, pasture, graze*, as does a flock.—IV. *to feed down, consume, devastate*.—V. *to feed upon*, i. e. *to delight, take pleasure in*.—VI. *to associate with*. Pi. רֵעָה *to treat as a friend, make a companion of*, Ju. 14. 20. Hithp. *to make friendship, hold intercourse with*, Pr. 22. 24.

רֵעֶה masc. dec. 9 a (Tseri unchangeable), *acquaintance, companion, friend*.

רֵעַ masc. dec. 1 a (for רֵעֶה).—I. *acquaintance, companion, friend*.—II. *one beloved, lover*.—III. *neighbour, fellow*; אִישׁ אֶל־רֵעֵהוּ *one to another*; used also of inanimate things.—IV. *thought, will*, Ps. 139. 2, 17; Chald. רְעָה *to will*, Syr. ܪܥܐ *to think*.

רֵעָה fem. dec. 10, *a female companion*.

רְעוּ (*friendship, friend*) pr. name masc. Ge. 11. 18.

---

[a] Is. 12. 6; La. 2. 19. [b] Ps. 32. 7. [c] Ps. 132. 16. [d] Is. 35. 2. [e] Job 3. 7. [f] Je. 31. 12; 51. 48. [g] Ps. 63. 6. [h] Job 39. 13. [i] Job 20. 5. [k] Ca. 5. 2. [l] Am. 6. 11. [ll] Job 41. 5. [m] Ps. 32. 9. [n] Job 30. 29. [o] Ps. 88. 19. [p] Mi. 4. 9. [q] Ps. 34. 11. [r] Ge. 42. 19, 33. [s] Ps. 37. 19. [t] Ex. 15. 15. [u] Ps. 55. 6. [v] Job 4. 14.

רְעוּאֵל (*friend of God*) pr. name—I. of a son of Esau, Ge. 36. 4, 10.—II. of the father of Jethro.—III. 1 Ch. 9. 8.—IV. Nu. 2. 14, elsewhere דְּעוּאֵל comp. Nu. 1. 14.

רְעוּת fem. dec. 1 a.—I. prop. *friendship*, used for *female friend* or *companion*, אִשָּׁה—רְעוּתָהּ *one another*.—II. רְעוּת רוּחַ *a feeding upon the wind*; others, *desire after the wind*, i. e. something vain, comp. רֵעַ No. IV.

רְעוּת Chald. fem. (prop. constr. of רְעוּ dec. 8 c) *will, wish*, Ezr. 5. 17; 7. 18, comp. רֵעַ No. IV.

רְעִי masc. *pasture*, 1 Ki. 5. 3.

רֵעִי (*social*) pr. name masc. 1 Ki. 1. 8.

רֹעִי masc.—I. adj. (denom. of רֹעֶה) *of a shepherd, pastoral*, Is. 38. 12.—II. subst. *shepherd*, Zec. 11. 17.

רַעְיוֹן m. *desire, pursuit, striving*, comp. רֵעַ No. IV.

רַעְיוֹן Chald. masc. dec. 1 a, *thought*.

מִרְעֶה masc. dec. 9 a, *pasture* for cattle.

מַרְעִית fem. dec. 1 b.—I. *a pasturing, feeding*.—II. *flock*, Je. 10. 21.

מֵרֵעַ masc. dec. 1 b (Tseri unchangeable), *companion, friend*.

רָעָה וְ' Kal pret. 3 pers. sing. fem.; adj. or subst. fem. dec. 10 [for רַעָה], from רַע masc. — רעע

רָעָה[a] Kh. רָעָה q. v., K. רַע (q. v.) — רעע

רִעָה[b] Piel pret. 3 pers. sing. masc. — רעה

רֵעָה[c] וְ Kh. רֵעָה q. v., K. רֵעַ (q. v.) — רעה

רֵעֵה[d], רֵעֶה } noun masc. sing. constr. & abs. dec. 9 a — רעה

רְעֵה[e] וּ' Kal imp. sing. masc.; וּ bef. (:) — רעה

רֹעָה[f] id. part. sing. fem. dec. 10, from רֹעֶה masc. — רעה

רָעָה[g] n. f. s., & רֹעָה (Is. 24. 19) Kal inf. with parag. ה — רעע

רֹעֵה, וְ' רֹעֶה } Kal part. sing. masc. constr. & abs. d. 9 a — רעה

רֵעֵהוּ[h] וְ' noun masc. sing., or (Job 42. 10) pl., for רֵעֵיהוּ, suff. 3 p. s. m. fr. רֵעַ d. 1 a (§ 36. r. 2) — רעה

רָעוּ וְ' Kal pret. 3 pers. pl. — רעה

רָעוּ[i] וְ Kal pret. 3 pers. pl., for רַעוּ=רָעוּ acc. shifted by conv. וְ (comp. § 8. rem. 7) — רעע

רֵעוֹ[k] וְ noun masc. sing., suff. 3 pers. sing. masc. from רֵעַ dec. 1 (§ 36. rem. 2) — רעה

רֵעוֹ[l] noun masc. sing. with suff. 3 pers. sing. masc. from רֵעַ dec. 1 a (§ 30. No. 3) — רוע

רְעוּ pr. name masc. — רעה

רְעוּ[m] Kal imp. pl. masc. — רעה

רֹעוּ[n] Kal imp. pl. masc. — רעע

רְעוּאֵל pr. name masc. — רעה

רָעוּם[o] וְ Kal pret. 3 pers. pl., suff. 3 pers. pl. masc. — רעה

רָעוֹת וְ' adj. or subst. fem., pl. of רָעָה dec. 10 [for רַעָה], from רַע masc. — רעע

רֹעוֹת[p] Kal part act. fem. pl. of רֹעָה d. 10, fr. רֹעֶה m. — רעה

רְעוּת וּ noun fem. sing. dec. 1 a; וּ bef. (:) — רעה

רְעוּתָהּ id., suff. 3 pers. sing. fem. — רעה

רְעוֹתֶיהָ[q] וְ'[r] noun fem. pl., suff. 3 pers. sing. fem. from [רֵעָה] dec. 10 (comp. § 36. rem. 2) — רעה

רָעוֹתֵיכֶם noun fem. pl., suff. 2 pers. pl. masc. from רָעָה dec. 10 [for רַעָה], from רַע masc. — רעע

רָעֵי[s] adj. pl. constr. masc. fr. רַע d. 8 e (§ 37. r. 7) — רעע

רְעִי[t] וְ', רֵעִי[u] וְ } the foll. with suff. 1 pers. sing. — רעה

רֵעֵי[x] noun m. pl. constr. fr. רֵעַ d. 1 a (§ 36. r. 2) — רעה

רֵעִי וְ' id. sing. with suff. 1 pers. s.; also pr. name — רעה

רְעִי[y] וּ'[z] Kal imp. sing. fem., or subst.; וּ bef. (:) — רעה

רֹעִי the foll. with suff. 1 pers. sing. — רעה

רֹעֵי Kal part. act. pl. constr. masc. fr. רֹעֶה d. 9 a — רעה

רֹעִי id. sing., suff. 1 pers. sing.; or רֹעִי adj. (Is. 38. 12) and subst. (Zec. 11. 17) — רעה

רֵעֶיהָ[a] noun masc. pl., suff. 3 pers. sing. fem. from רֵעַ dec. 1 a (§ 36. rem. 2) — רעה

רֵעֵיהֶם id. pl., suff. 3 pers. pl. masc. — רעה

רֹעֵיהֶם[b] וְ'[c] Kal part. act. pl. masc., suff. 3 pers. pl. masc. from רֹעֶה dec. 9 a — רעה

רֵעָיו[d] noun masc. pl., suff. 3 pers. sing. masc. from רֵעַ dec. 1 a (§ 36. rem. 2) — רעה

רַעְיוֹן[e] וְ' noun masc. sing. dec. 1 a — רעה

רַעְיוֹנַי[f] Chald. id. pl., suff. 1 pers. sing. — רעה

רַעְיוֹנֵי[g] וְ Chald. id. pl., constr. st. — רעה

רַעְיוֹנָךְ[h] Chald. id. pl., suff. 2 pers. sing. masc. — רעה

רֵעַיִךְ[i] noun masc. pl., suff. 2 pers. sing. fem. from רֵעַ dec. 1 a (§ 36. rem. 2) — רעה

רֵעֶיךָ וְ'[k] id. pl., suff. 2 pers. sing. masc.; Pr. 6. 3, sing. with suff. from רֵעָה (§ 38. rem. 1) — רעה

רֹעַיִךְ[l] Kal part. act. pl. masc., suff. 2 pers. sing. fem. from רֹעֶה dec. 9 a — רעה

רֹעֶיךָ id. pl. with suff. 2 pers. sing. masc. — רעה

רָעִים וְ' adj. or subst. (Ps. 78. 49) masc., pl. of רַע dec. 8 (§ 37. rem. 7) — רעע

רֵעִים noun masc., pl. of רֵעַ dec. 1 a (§ 36. rem. 2) — רעה

רֹעִים וְ'[m] Kal part. act. masc., pl. of רֹעֶה dec. 9 a — רעה

רַעְיֹנֹהִי וְ Chald. noun masc. pl., suff. 3 pers. sing. masc. from רַעְיוֹן dec. 1 a — רעה

רַעְיָתִי noun fem. sing., suff. 1 pers. sing. from [רַעְיָה] dec. 10 — רעה

---

[a] Mi. 3. 2. [b] Ju. 14. 20. [c] Pr. 27. 10. [d] 2 Sa. 16. 16. [e] Ps. 37. 3. [f] Ge. 29. 9. [g] Pr. 25. 19. [h] 1 Ki. 16. 11. [i] Je. 11. 16. [k] Je. 6. 21. [l] Job 36. 33. [m] Ge. 29. 7. [n] Is. 8. 9. [o] Je. 23. 4. [p] Job 1. 14. [q] Ps. 45. 15. [r] Ju. 11. 38. [s] Eze. 7. 24. [t] Ps. 122. 8. [u] Ps. 38. 12. [x] Job 2. 11. [y] 1 Ki. 5. 3. [z] Ca. 1. 8. [a] La. 1. 2. [b] Je. 50. 6. [c] Zec. 11. 5. [d] Job 32. 3. [e] Ec. 1. 17; 4. 16. [f] Da. 7. 28. [g] Da. 2. 30. [h] Da. 2. 29; 5. 10. [i] Eze. 22. 12. [k] Zec. 3. 8. [l] Je. 22. 22. [m] Is. 13. 20.

וְ רַעֲנַן Ch. m. id. metaph. *flourishing, prosperous*, Da. 4. 1.

רַעֲנָנָה [for רַעֲנְנָה] Pilel (§ 6. No. 2) pret. 3 pers. sing. fem., or fem. of the preced. . רען

רַעֲנַנִּים[h] וְ adj. masc. pl., of רַעֲנָן dec. 8a . . רען

[רָעַע] fut. יָרֹעַ.—I. *to break, break in pieces.*—II. i. q. רוּעַ *to make a loud noise*, Is. 8. 9; where Gesenius prefers to render רֹעוּ עַמִּים וָחֹתּוּ *be evil, O ye people, ye shall be broken.*—III. fut. יֵרַע (§ 18. rem. 6) intrans. (*a*) *to be evil*; with לוֹ, לִי *it is evil, it goes ill with me*, him; (*b*) וַיֵּרַע בְּעֵינַי *and it was evil in my eyes*, it displeased me; (*c*) *to be hurtful*, 2 Sa. 20. 6; of the eyes, *to be envious, malignant*; of the countenance, the heart, *to be sad, sorrowful.* Hiph. הֵרַע, הֵרֵעַ *to make evil*, Mi. 3. 4; *to do evil*; הֵ׳ לַעֲשׂוֹת *to act wickedly*; const. with בְּ, עִם, עַל, לְ *to do evil to any one*; part. מֵרַע *an evil-doer.* Hithpo. הִתְרוֹעַע.—I. *to be broken in pieces*, Is. 24. 19.—II. *to be destroyed, to perish*, Pr. 18. 24.

רְעַע Chald. *to break in pieces*, Da. 2. 40.

רַע masc. (pl. רָעִים § 37. rem. 7).—I. adj. (רָעָה fem. dec. 10) *evil, bad, worthless.*—II. *evil, wicked.*—III. *noxious, hurtful*; רַע עַיִן *of an evil eye*, i. e. envious, malignant.—IV. *ill-favoured*, with מַרְאֶה Ge. 41. 3.—V. *ill, calamitous.*—VI. *sad, sorrowful.*—VII. subst. (*a*) *evil, wickedness*; (*b*) *evil, harm, injury, calamity.*

רֹעַ masc. rarely רוֹעַ masc.—I. *badness, bad quality.*—II. *wickedness.*—III. *sadness* of heart, countenance.

[רָעַף] fut. יִרְעַף *to drop, distil.* Hiph. *to let drop*, Is. 45. 8.

[רָעַץ] *to break, crush*, Ex. 15. 6; metaph. *to oppress*, Ju. 10. 8.

[רָעַשׁ] *to be moved, to shake, tremble.* Niph. *to quake*, of the earth, Je. 50. 46. Hiph. I. *to move, shake.*—II. *to cause to tremble, to terrify*, Eze. 31. 16.—III. *to cause to leap*, Job 39. 20. Hence

רַעַשׁ וְ׳׳ masc.—I. *a shaking.*—II. *earthquake.*—III. *a tumult.*—IV. *a rattling, rushing* רעשׁ

רָעֲשָׁה[i] / רָעֲשָׁה } Kal pret. 3 pers. sing. fem. (§ 8. rem. 7) רעשׁ

רָעֲשׁוּ[k] וְ׳ id. pret. 3 pers. pl. . . . רעשׁ

רֹעֲשִׁים[l] id. part. act. masc. pl. [of רֹעֵשׁ] dec. 7b . רעשׁ

רֵעוּתָי[a] וְ Kh. וְרֵעוּתִי, K. וְרֵעוֹתָי noun fem. pl. with suff. 1 pers. sing. from רְעוּת or רֵעָה . רעה

רְעִיתִים[b] וְ Kal pret. 1 pers. sing., suff. 3 pers. pl. masc.; וּ, for וְ, conv. . . . רעה

רֵעֲךָ / רֵעֶךָ } noun masc. sing., suff. 2 pers. sing. masc. from רֵעַ dec. 1a (§ 36. rem. 2) . } רעה

רָעַל. Hoph. *to be shaken, to tremble*, Na. 2. 4.

רַעַל masc. dec. 6d.—I. *a reeling*, from intoxication, Zec. 12. 2.—II. pl. רְעָלוֹת *veils*, prob. from their tremulous motion, Is. 3. 19.

רְעֵלָיָה (*terror of the Lord*) pr. name masc. Ezr. 2. 2, for which רַעַמְיָה Ne. 7. 7.

מַרְעֲלָה (*a trembling, quaking*) pr. name of a place in the tribe of Zebulun, Jos. 19. 11.

תַּרְעֵלָה fem. *a reeling, staggering*, from intoxication.

רַעַל[c] noun masc. sing. . . . . . רעל

רְעֵלָיָה pr. name masc. . . . . . רעל

[רָעַם] fut. יִרְעַם.—I. *to rage, roar*, of the sea.—II. *to tremble, quake*, Eze. 27. 35. Hiph. I. *to thunder, cause thunder.*—II. *to irritate, vex*, 1 Sa. 1. 6.

רַעַם masc. dec. 6d.—I. *tumult, rage*, Job 39. 25.—II. *thunder.*

רַעְמָה fem.—I. *a trembling, shivering*, poet. for the mane of a horse, Job 39. 19.—II. pr. name of a son of Cush, Ge. 10. 7, for which also רַעְמָא 1 Ch. 1. 9, and a city so called after him, Eze. 27. 22.

רַעַם[d] וְ noun m. s. dec. 6d, pause רָעַם, Ps. 81. 8. רעם

רְעֵם[e] וּ Kal imp. sing. masc. (רְעֵה), suff. 3 pers. pl. masc. (§ 24. rem. 21); וּ bef. (:) . רעה

רַעְמָא וְ׳ / רַעְמָה[f] וְ׳ } noun fem. sing., also pr. name . רעם

רָעֲמוּ[g] Kal pret. 3 pers. pl. . . . . . רעם

רַעַמְיָה pr. name masc., see רְעֵלָיָה under . . רעל

רַעַמְךָ noun m. s., suff. 2 pers. s. m. fr. רַעַם d. 6d רעם

רַעְמְסֵס / רַעַמְסֵס } (*son of the sun*) pr. name of a city and country in Lower Egypt, or Goshen.

רָעַן. Pil. רַעֲנַן (§ 6. No. 2) *to be green, covered with leaves*, Job 15. 32; Ca. 1. 16, in both of which passages, however, it may be taken as an adjective. Hence

רַעֲנָן masc. pl. רַעֲנַנִּים adj.—I. *green, flourishing*, of trees; metaph. of prosperity.—II. *fresh*, spoken of oil, Ps. 92. 11.

[a] Ju. 11. 37. [b] Eze. 34. 13. [c] Zec. 12. 2. [d] Job 26. 14; 39. 25. [e] Ps. 28. 9. [f] Job 39. 19. [g] Eze. 27. 35. [h] Ps. 92. 15. [i] Je. 10. 22. [k] Ps. 68. 9. [l] Je. 4. 24.

רָעַת [a] וְ noun fem. sing., constr. of רָעָה dec. 10 [for רַעַת], from רַע masc. . . . רעע
רָעֹת [b] id. pl. constr. . . . . רעע
רָעָתָהּ [c] id. sing., suff. 3 pers. sing. fem. . רעע
רָעָתוֹ [d] וְ id. sing., suff. 3 pers. sing. masc. . רעע
רָעָתִי id. sing., suff. 1 pers. sing. . . רעע
רָעֹתֵיכֶם [e] id. pl., suff. 2 pers. pl. masc. . . רעע
רָעָתְךָ / רָעָתֶךָ } id. sing., suff. 2 pers. sing. masc. . רעע
רָעָתֵךְ id. sing., suff. 2 pers. sing. fem. . . רעע
רָעָתֵכִי [f] id. sing., suff. 2 pers. sing. fem. (§ 3. rem. 2) רעע
רָעַתְכֶם id. sing., suff. 2 pers. pl. masc. . . רעע
רָעָתָם id. sing., suff. 3 pers. pl. masc. . . רעע

רָפָא [g] וְ (Milêl bef. monos.)—I. *to heal, cure*; part. רֹפֵא *a physician.*—II. metaph. (*a*) *to restore* to prosperity; (*b*) *to restore* in a spiritual sense, from a state of habitual neglect of God's commandments, for, *to pardon, forgive*; (*c*) for, *to restore, to comfort, console*, Job 13. 4. Niph. I. *to be repaired*, Je. 19. 11.—II. *to be healed, cured*; of waters, *to be made wholesome*; metaph. *to be restored* to prosperity, Is. 53. 5. Pi. I. *to repair*, 1 Ki. 18. 30.—II. *to heal, cure*; of waters, *to render wholesome*, 2 Ki. 2. 21; metaph. *to comfort, console*, Je. 8. 11.—III. *to cause to be healed*, Ex. 21. 19. Hithp. *to get oneself cured*, 2 Ki. 8. 29.

רָפָא masc.—I. only in the pl. רְפָאִים *the quiet*, comp. the verb No. II. (*c*); or רָפָה=רָפָא, *the languid, feeble*, poet. for *the dead, the departed.*—II. pr. name, *Rapha*, (*a*) the progenitor of the tribe Rephaim, comp. 1 Ch. 20. 4, also רָפָה; (*b*) two other persons, 1 Ch. 4. 12; 8. 2.

רְפָאִי, only pl. רְפָאִים pr. name of a people beyond Jordan, celebrated for their gigantic stature, the descendants of רָפָא, רָפָה.

רָפוּא (*healed*) pr. name masc. Nu. 13. 9.

רְפָאָה fem. only pl. רְפֻאוֹת *medicines*.

רִפְאוּת fem. *healing, health*, Pr. 3. 8.

רְפָאֵל (whom *God healed*) pr. name m. 1 Ch. 26. 7.

רְפָיָה (*whom the Lord healed*) pr. name masc. of several persons.

יִרְפְּאֵל (which *God heals*) pr. name of a place in Benjamin, Jos. 18. 27.

מַרְפֵּא, מַרְפֵּה masc.—I. *healing, cure.*—II. *remedy*, means of cure, Je. 33. 6.—III. trop. *refreshment, recreation*; also *relief* from calamity.—IV. *calmness, tranquillity* (comp. verb No. II. (*c*)), Pr. 14. 30; 15. 4; Ec. 10. 4.

רָפָא וְ pr. name masc. . . . רפא
רְפָא [h] Kal imp. sing. masc. . . . רפא
רַפֹּא [i] וְ Piel inf. abs. . . . רפא
רֹפֵא Kal part. act. sing. masc. dec. 7b . רפא
רְפָאָה [k] id. imp. s. m., with parag. ה (§ 8. rem. 12) רפא
רְפֻאוֹת noun fem., pl. of [רְפָאָה] dec. 10 . רפא
רִפְאוּת [l] noun fem. sing. . . . רפא
רֹפְאֵי [m] Kal part. act. pl. constr. masc. from רֹפֵא d. 7b רפא
רְפָאִים noun masc. pl., also pr. name . רפא
רֹפְאֶךָ [n] Kal part. act. sing. masc., suff. 2 pers. sing. [for רֹפַאֲךָ] from רֹפֵא dec. 7b . . רפא
רְפָאֵל וּ pr. name masc.; וּ bef. (:) . רפא
רְפָאָם [o] וּ Kal pret. 3 pers. sing. masc., suff. 3 pers. pl. masc.; וּ, for וְ, conv. . . רפא
רִפִּאנוּ [p] Piel pret. 1 pers. pl. (§ 23. rem. 9) רפא
רְפָאֵנִי Kal imp. sing. masc., suff. 1 pers. sing. . רפא
רִפֵּאתִי [q] Piel pret. 1 pers. sing. (§ 23. rem. 9) רפא
רְפָאתִיו [r] וּ Kal pret. 1 pers. sing., suff. 3 pers. sing. masc.; וּ, for וְ, conv. . . . רפא
רְפָאתִים / וּרְפָאתִים [s] } id., suff. 3 pers. pl. masc.; וּ id. . רפא
רִפֵּאתֶם [t] Piel pret. 2 pers. pl. masc. . . רפא

[רָפַד] *to strew, spread*, Job 41. 22. Pi. I. *to spread a bed*, Job 17. 13.—II. *to stay, refresh*, Ca. 2. 5.

רְפִידָה fem. dec. 10, *support*, prob. *the sides and back* of a portable couch, Ca. 3. 10.

רְפִידִים (*couches*) pr. name of a station of the Israelites in the desert.

אַרְפָּד (*support*) pr. name of a city of Syria.

רַפְּדוּנִי [u] Piel imp. pl. masc., suff. 1 pers. sing. . רפד
רִפַּדְתִּי [x] id. pret. 1 pers. sing. . . . . רפד

רָפָה [y] fut. יִרְפֶּה, ap. יִרֶף.—I. *to hang down* the hands, *to become relaxed, feeble.*—II. *to decline*, of the day, Ju. 19. 9.—III. *to sink down*, of straw in the fire, Is. 5. 24.—IV. *to relax, abate, to desist* from a person or thing, with מִן. Niph. *to be remiss, idle, lazy*, Ex. 5. 8, 17. Pi. I. *to let down* the wings, Eze. 1. 24, 25.—II. *to relax, loosen*, Job 12. 21.—III. *to relax, weaken.* Hiph. הִרְפָּה.—I. *to slacken* the hand, *to desist* from smiting, 2 Sa. 24. 16; with מִן *from* any one, i. e. *to desert* him, Jos. 10. 6.—II. (without יָד) *to let alone, cease from*, with מִן.—III. *to leave off, cease.*—IV. *to*

a Zec. 7. 10. b Je. 44. 9. c Je. 6. 7. d Je. 48. 16. e Je. 44. 9. f Je. 11. 15. g Is. 6. 10. h Nu. 12. 13. i Ex. 21. 19. k Ps. 41. 5. l Pr. 3. 8. m Job 13. 4. n Ex. 15. 26. o Is. 19. 22. p Je. 51. 9. q 2 Ki. 2. 21. r Is. 57. 19. s Je. 33. 6 t Eze. 34. 4. u Ca. 2. 5. x Job 17. 13. y Ju. 19. 9.

give up, forsake.—V. *to let go, dismiss.* Hithp. *to relax oneself, be slothful.*

רָפָה pr. name—I. of a giant, whose descendants are called יְלִידֵי הָרָפָה; also רְפָאִים, see רְפָאִי.—II. 1 Ch. 8. 37, for which רָפָיָה 1 Ch. 9. 43.

רָפֶה masc. dec. 9 b, pl. fem. רָפוֹת, adj. *relaxed, weak, feeble.*

רִפְיוֹן masc. *weakness,* Je. 47. 3.

רָפָה pr. name masc. . . . . . רפה

רְפָה[a] Kal imp. sing. masc. for רְפָא (§ 23. rem. 10) רפא

רְפֵה[b] ו adj. masc. sing., constr. of רָפֶה dec. 9 b; ו bef. (:) . . . . . . רפה

רִפָּה[c] Piel pret. 3 pers. sing. masc. . . . רפה

רָפוּ[d] וְ Kal pret. 3 pers. pl. . . . . רפה

רָפוּא pr. name masc. . . . . . רפא

רָפוֹא[e] וְ Kal inf. abs. . . . . . רפא

רָפוֹת adj. fem. pl. [of רָפָה] from רָפֶה masc. רפה

רֶפַח וְ (*riches*) pr. name masc. 1 Ch. 7. 25.

רְפִידָתוֹ[f] noun fem. s., suff. 3 p. s. from [רְפִידָה] d. 10 רפד

רְפָיָה וּ pr. name masc.; וּ bef. (:) . . . רפא

[רָפַשׂ, רָפַס] *to tread, trample upon,* espec. of water, troubled, made turbid, Eze. 34. 18; 32. 2. Niph. part. נִרְפָּשׂ *troubled, made turbid by trampling,* Pr. 25, 26. Hithpa. הִתְרַפֵּס *to humble, submit oneself.*

רְפַס Chald. *to trample down, stamp upon,* Da. 7. 7.

מִרְפָּשׂ masc. dec. 2 b, *water made turbid by trampling,* Eze. 34. 19.

רַפְסֹדוֹת fem. pl. *floats, rafts,* 2 Ch. 2. 15. Etymology uncertain.

רָפְסָה[g] Chald. Peal part. sing. fem. [of רָפֵס masc.] רפס

רָפַק Hithp. *to support oneself, to lean,* Ca. 8. 5.

רֶפֶשׁ masc. *mud, mire,* Is. 57. 20.

[רֶפֶת] masc. dec. 6 a, *a stall* for cattle, Hab. 3. 17.

רָפְתָה Kal pret. 3 pers. sing. fem. . . . רפה

רָץ Kal pret. 3 pers. sing. masc.; or part. act. dec. 1 a (§ 30. No. 3) . . . רוץ

רֻץ id. imp. sing. masc. (§ 21. rem. 5) . . רוץ

[רָצָא] i. q. רוּץ *to run,* Eze. 1. 14.

רָצָאתִי[h] וְ Kal pret. 1 pers. s. [for רָצִיתִי § 24. r. 19] רצה

רָצַד Kal not used; Arab. *to observe, watch narrowly.* Pi. id. Ps. 68. 17. Others, after the Targ. (טְפַז), i. q. רָקַד *to leap, spring.*

רָצָה fut. יִרְצֶה.—I. *to delight, take pleasure in, to be well pleased with,* const. with בְּ, acc.—II. *to accept kindly* or *graciously;* part. pass. רָצוּי *accepted, acceptable.*—III. *to associate, be in friendship with,* const. with עִם.—IV. *to be pleased* to do any thing, followed by an inf.—V. *to satisfy, discharge, make compensation for.* Niph. I. *to be graciously received.*—II. *to be paid off, compensation made for,* Is. 40. 2. Pi. *to satisfy, conciliate,* Job 20. 10. Hiph. *to satisfy, make compensation for,* Le. 26. 34. Hithp. *to make oneself acceptable, pleasing,* 1 Sa. 29. 4.

רָצוֹן masc. dec. 3 a.—I. *delight, satisfaction, acceptance;* לְרָצוֹן, עַל־רָצוֹן *acceptable, well pleasing.*—II. *object of delight, acceptance.*—III. *will, pleasure;* hence *wantonness,* Ge. 49. 6.—IV. *good-will, favour, grace;* meton. *favours, benefits.*

רִצְיָא (*delight*) pr. name masc. 1 Ch. 7. 39.

רְצִין (*accepted, beloved;* or i. q. רָזוֹן *prince,* Arab *stable, firm*) pr. name—I. of a king of Damascus.—II. Ezr. 2. 48; Ne. 7. 50.

תִּרְצָה (*delight*) pr. name—I. of a royal city in the kingdom of Israel.—II. of a daughter of Zelophehad.

רְצֵה Kal imp. sing. masc. . . . . רצה

רָצוּ[i] id. pret. 3 pers. pl. . . . . רצה

רָצוּ[k] / וְרָצוּ[l] } Kal pret. 3 pers. pl.; acc. shifted by conv. וְ (comp. § 8. rem. 7) . . רוץ

רָצוֹא[m] Kal inf. abs. . . . . . רצא

רָצוּי[n] וְ Kal part. pass. sing. masc. dec. 3 a . רצה

רְצוּי[o] id., constr. st. . . . . . רצה

רָצוֹן noun masc. sing. dec. 3 a . . . רצה

רְצוֹן[p] וּ id., constr. st.; וּ bef. (:) . . . רצה

רְצוֹנוֹ וּ id., suff. 3 pers. sing. masc.; וּ id. . רצה

רְצוֹנֶךָ[q] / רְצוֹנְךָ[r] } id., suff. 2 pers. sing. masc. . . רצה

רְצוֹנָם[s] id., suff. 3 pers. pl. masc. . . . רצה

רָצוּף[t] Kal part. pass. sing. masc. . . . רצף

רָצוּץ[u] וְ Kal part. pass. sing. masc. dec. 3 a . רצץ

רְצוּץ[y] id. id., constr. st. . . . . רצץ

רְצוּצִים[z] id. id. pl., abs. st. . . . . רצץ

רַצּוֹתִי[a] id. pret. 1 pers. sing. . . . . רצץ

רַצּוֹתָנוּ[zz] id. pret. 2 pers. sing. masc., suff. 1 pers. pl. רצץ

רָצַח[b] וְ *to kill, slay;* רָ׳ נֶפֶשׁ *to smite dead;* part. רֹצֵחַ *manslayer, homicide.* Niph. pass. Ju. 20. 4. Pi. I. *to dash in pieces.*—II. *to murder, be a murderer.*

רֶצַח masc.—I. *a crushing,* Ps. 42. 11.—II. *a killing, slaughter,* Eze. 21. 27.

[a] Ps. 60. 4. [b] 2 Sa. 17. 2. [c] Job 12. 21. [d] Je. 6. 24. [e] Is. 19. 22. [f] Ca. 3. 10. [g] Da. 7. 7, 19. [h] Eze. 43. 27. [i] Ps. 102. 15. [k] Je. 23. 21. [l] 1 Sa. 8. 11. [m] Eze. 1. 14. [n] Est. 10. 3. [o] De. 33. 24. [p] De. 33. 16. [q] Ps. 143. 10. [r] Ps. 40. 9. [s] 2 Ch. 15. 15. [t] Ca. 3. 10. [u] Is. 42. 3. [x] De. 28. 33. [y] Ho. 5. 11. [z] Is. 58. 6. [zz] 1 Sa. 12. 4. [a] 1 Sa. 12. 3. [b] Nu. 35. 27.

רָצֹחַ [b]ו' Kal inf. abs. . . . . . רצח
רֹצֵחַ id. part. act. sing. masc. . . . רצח
רְצָחוֹ[c] וּ id. pret. 3 pers. sing. masc., suff. 3 pers. sing. masc.; וּ bef. (:) . . . רצח
רִצְיָא ו pr. name masc. . . . . רצה
רָצִים Kal part. act. masc. pl. of רָץ d. 1 a (§ 30. No. 3) רוץ
רְצִין pr. name masc. . . . . . רצה
רָצִיתָ[d] Kal pret. 2 pers. sing. masc. . . . רצה
רְצִיתָם[e] [f]ו' וּ id. id., suff. 3 pers. pl. m.; וּ, for וְ, conv. רצה
רָצָם id. pret. 3 pers. sing. masc. (רָצָה), suff. 3 pers. pl. masc. (§ 24. rem. 21) . . רצה
רֹצָם[g] id. part. act. sing. masc., suff. 3 p. pl. m. from רוֹצֶה dec. 9 a . . . רצה

רָצַע ו to pierce, bore through, Ex. 21. 6.

מַרְצֵעַ masc. an awl.

[רָצַף] *to range stones artificially*, e. g. in a pavement or inlaid work, *to checker*; only part. pass. *checkered, tesselated*, Ca. 3. 10 (Gesenius). Some regard רָצַף=צָרַף *to burn*.

רֶצֶף masc. dec. 6 a.—I. *hot stone*, 1 Ki. 19. 6; others, *coals*.—II. pr. name of a city subject to the Assyrians, Is. 37. 12.

רִצְפָּה fem.—I. *hot stone* or *coal*, Is. 6. 6.—II. *tesselated pavement*.—III. pr. name of a woman.

מַרְצֶפֶת fem. *pavement*, 2 Ki. 16. 17.

רֶצֶף ו pr. name of a place . . . רצף
רִצְפָּה[h] ו' noun fem. sing. (no pl.); also pr. name רצף
רְצָפִים[i] noun masc. pl. of [רֶצֶף] dec. 6 a . . רצף
רִצְפַּת[k] noun fem. sing., constr. of רִצְפָּה (no pl.) רצף

[רָצַץ] fut. יָרוּץ (§ 18. rem. 12).—I. *to break, bruise, crush*.—II. trop. *to treat with violence, to oppress*.—III. intrans. *to be broken*, Ec. 12. 6. Niph. נָרוֹץ *to be broken, bruised*. Pi. רִצַּץ intens. of Kal Nos. I & II. Po. רוֹצֵץ *to oppress*, Ju. 10. 8. Hiph. *to break in pieces*, Ju. 9. 53. Hithpo. *to struggle together*, Ge. 25. 22.

רַץ masc. dec. 8 d, *a fragment, piece*, Ps. 68. 31.

מְרוּצָה fem. (for מְרֻצָּה) *oppression*, Je. 22. 17.

רִצַּץ Piel pret. 3 pers. sing. masc. (§ 10. rem. 1) רצץ
רִצַּצְתָּ[m] id. pret. 2 pers. sing. masc. . . . רצץ
רָצְתָה Kal pret. 3 pers. sing. fem. . . . רצה
רַצְתָּה[n] id. pret. 2 pers. sing. masc. (comp. § 8. r. 5) רוץ
רַצְתִּי[o] id. pret. 1 pers. sing. . . . . רוץ

רַק ו' *adv.* . . . . רקק
רַק [gg]ו' adj. masc. sing. dec. 1 a; for ו see lett. ו רוק
רֹק[p] [q]ו' noun masc. sing. dec. 8 c; ו id. . . רקק

[רָקַב] fut. יִרְקַב *to rot, decay*. Hence

רָקָב[r] masc. dec. 4 a, and רִקָּבוֹן (Job 41. 19) *decay, rottenness* . . . . . . רקב
רְקַב[s] וּ id., constr. st.; וּ bef. (:) . . . רקב
רִקָּבוֹן[t] noun masc. sing. . . . . . רקב

[רָקַד] *to leap, skip, dance*. Pi. id.; also trop. of the *jolting* of a chariot. Hiph. *to cause to leap*, Ps. 29. 6.

רָקְדוּ[u] Kal pret. 3 pers. pl. . . . . רקד
רַקָּה[x] adj. fem. sing. dec. 10, from רַק masc. . רוק
רְקוֹד[y] Kal inf. constr. . . . . . רקד
רַקּוֹת[z] ו adj. fem. pl. of רַקָּה from רַק masc. . רקק

[רָקַח] *to compound* or *prepare* ointment, Ex. 30. 33; part. רֹקֵחַ *perfumer* or *apothecary*. Pu. pass. 2 Ch. 16. 14. Hiph. *to spice, season*, Eze. 24. 10.

רֶקַח masc. *a spicing*, Ca. 8. 2.

רֹקַח masc. *ointment, perfume*, Ex. 30. 25.

רַקָּח masc. dec. 1 b, *perfumer* or *apothecary*. Fem. רַקָּחָה, 1 Sa. 8. 13.

רִקּוּחַ masc. dec. 1 b, *ointment, perfume*, Is. 57. 9.

מֶרְקָח masc. only pl. מֶרְקָחִים *aromatic herbs*, Ca. 5. 13.

מֶרְקָחָה fem.—I. *ointment*, Eze. 24. 10.—II. *pot of ointment*, Job 41. 23.

מִרְקַחַת fem.—I. *preparation of ointments*.—II. *ointment*, 1 Ch. 9. 30.

רֶקַח[kk] noun masc. sing. . . . . . רקח
רֹקֵחַ Kal part. act. sing. masc. dec. 7 b . . רקח
רֹקְחֵי[a] id. pl., constr. st. . . . . . רקח
רִקֻּחַיִךְ[b] noun masc. pl., suff. 2 pers. sing. fem. from [רִקֻּחַ] dec. 1 b . . . . . רקח
רֻקִּי[c] noun masc. s., suff. 1 pers. s. fr. רֹק d. 8 c רקק
רֵקִים adj. masc., pl. of רֵק dec. 1 a . . . רוק
רָקִיעַ noun masc. sing. dec. 3 a . . . רקע
רְקִיעַ[d] id., constr. st. . . . . . רקע
רָקִיק ו noun masc. sing. dec. 3 a . . . רקק
רְקִיק[e] וּ id., constr. st.; וּ bef. (:) . . . רקק
רְקִיקֵי וּ id. pl., constr. st.; וּ id. . . . רקק

[רָקַם] *to embroider*, or *to weave with threads of different colours*, only part. רֹקֵם *an embroiderer*, or *a weaver*

---

[a] Je. 7. 9. [b] Ho. 4. 2. [c] De. 22. 26. [d] Ps. 85. 2. [e] Ps. 44. 4. [f] 2 Ch. 10. 7. [g] Je. 14. 12. [gg] Ne. 5. 13. [h] Eze. 40. 17. [i] 1 Ki. 19. 6. [k] Est. 1. 6. [kk] Ex. 30. 25, 35. [l] Job 20. 19. [m] Ps. 74. 14. [n] Je. 12. 5. [o] 2 Ki. 5. 20. [p] Job 30. 10. [q] Is. 50. 6. [r] Hab. 3. 16. [s] Pr. 14. 30. [t] Job 41. 19. [u] Ps. 114. 4. [x] Eze. 24. 11. [y] Ec. 3. 4. [z] Ge. 41. 19. [a] 1 Ch. 9. 30. [b] Is. 57. 9. [c] Job 7. 19. [d] Ge. 1. 20. [e] Nu. 6. 19.

in colours. Pu. *to be curiously wrought* or *woven*, metaph. Ps. 139. 15.

רֶקֶם (*variegated*) pr. name—I. of a city in Benjamin, Jos. 18. 27.—II. of a king of the Midianites.—III. of two men, 1 Ch. 2. 43; 7. 16.

רִקְמָה fem. d. 12 b.—I. *a variegation* or *variety of colour.*—II. *variegated work*, or *embroidery*; du. רִקְמָתַיִם prob. *stuff worked on both sides*, Ju. 5. 30.

רָקֶם וְ׳} pr. name of a man and a place; for וְ} see lett. ו . . . . . רקם
רֶקֶם וְ׳}
רֹקֵם וְ׳ Kal part. act. sing. masc. . . . רקם
רִקְמָה וְ׳ noun fem. sing. dec. 12 b . . . רקם
רֻקַּמְתִּי[a] Pual pret. 1 pers. sing. . . . רקם
רִקְמָתַיִם[b] noun fem., du. of רִקְמָה dec. 12 b . . רקם
רִקְמָתֵךְ[c] id. sing., suff. 2 pers. sing. fem. . . רקם
רִקְמָתָם[d] id. sing., suff. 3 pers. pl. masc. . . רקם

[רָקַע] I. *to stamp* with the feet.—II. *to stamp, tread down*, 2 Sa. 22. 43.—III. *to stretch, spread out, expand.* Pi. I. *to beat into thin plates.*—II. *to cover* with metallic plates, Is. 40. 19. Pu. part. *beaten* or *spread* into plates, Je. 10. 9. Hiph. *to stretch out, expand*, Job 37. 18.

רָקִיעַ m. d. 3 a, *the expanse.* Vulg. *firmamentum.*

רִקֻּעִים m. pl. (of רִקֻּעַ) *plates of metal*, Nu. 17. 3.

יָרְקְעָם (for יָרְקַע עָם *the people is spread abroad*) pr. name of a town in Judea, 1 Ch. 2. 44.

רֹקַע Kal part. act. sing. masc. (§ 36. rem. 1) רקע
רְקַע׳ וּ id. imp. sing. masc.; וּ bef. (:) . . רקע
רִקֻּעֵי[e] noun masc. pl. constr. from [רִקֻּעַ] dec. 1 b רקע
רִקְעֲךָ[g] וְ Kal inf. [רְקַע], suff. 2 pers. s. m. (§ 16. r. 10) רקע

***I.* רָקַק** Root not used; Arab. *to be thin.*

רַק masc.—I. adj. *thin, lean*, Ge. 41. 19, 20, 27.—II. adv. (*a*) *only, alone*; (*b*) *surely, certainly*; (*c*) *save, except.*

רַקָּה fem. dec. 10.—I. *the temple* of the head.—II. poet. for *the cheek*, Ca. 4. 3; 6. 7.

רַקַּת (*thinness*; Chald. רַקְּתָא *shore*) pr. name of a city in the tribe of Naphtali, Jos. 19. 35.

רַקּוֹן (id.) pr. name of a city in Dan, Jos. 19. 46.

רָקִיק masc. dec. 3 a, *a thin cake.*

***II.* רָקַק** i. q. יָרַק *to spit*, only fut. יָרֹק Le. 15. 8.

רֹק masc. dec. 8 c, *spittle.*

רַקַּת pr. name of a place . . . . רקק

רַקָּתוֹ[h] noun f. s., suff. 3 pers. s. m. fr. [רַקָּה] d. 10 רקק
רַקָּתֵךְ id., suff. 2 pers. sing. fem. . . . רקק
רָר[i] Kal pret. 3 pers. sing. masc. . . . רור
רָשׁ וְ׳, וָ׳[k] Kal part. act. sing. masc. dec. 1 a (§ 30. rem. 3); for וָ see lett. ו . . . רוש
רָשׁ[l] f. רְשִׁי} Kal imp. sing. masc. (§ 20. rem. 2) ירש
רֵשׁ}

רָשָׁה Root not used; Chald. רְשָׁא *to be able, have permission.*

רִשְׁיוֹן masc. *grant, permission*, Ezr. 3. 7.

רָשׁוּ[m] Kal pret. 3 pers. pl. . . . רוש
רְשׁוּ וּ Kal imp. pl. masc.; וּ bef. (:) . . ירש
רְשִׁים Ch. Peal part. pass. sing. masc. . . רשם

[רְשַׁם] *to write down, record*, Da. 10. 21. Hence

רְשַׁם[n] Ch. fut. יִרְשֻׁם idem.
רְשַׁמְתָּ[o] Ch. Peal pret. 2 pers. sing. masc. . . רשם

[רָשַׁע] fut. יִרְשַׁע.—I. *to be wicked, to act wickedly, unjustly, impiously.*—II. *to be guilty, have an unjust cause*, Job 9. 29; 10. 7, 15. Hiph. הִרְשִׁיעַ.—I. *to declare guilty, to condemn.*—II. *to cause mischief, disquiet* (Syr. רתע *to be restless, to disturb*), 1 Sa. 14. 47.—III. *to be wicked, act wickedly.*

רָשָׁע masc. d. 4 a, רְשָׁעָה fem. adj.—I. *wicked, ungodly, impious.*—II. *having an unjust cause.*—III. *guilty, punishable.*

רֶשַׁע masc. dec. 6 a (with suff. רִשְׁעוֹ § 35. r. 5).—I. *wickedness, ungodliness.*—II. *injustice*, מֹאזְנֵי רֶ׳ *unjust*, i. e. *false balances.*—III. perh. pl. רְשָׁעִים *wicked deeds*, Job 34. 26.

רִשְׁעָה fem. (constr. רִשְׁעַת, no pl.).—I. *wickedness, ungodliness.*—II. *guilt, fault*, De. 25. 2.

מִרְשַׁעַת fem. *wickedness*, for concr. *wicked person*, 2 Ch. 24. 7.

רָשָׁע וְ׳ adj. masc. sing. dec. 4 a . . . רשע
רֶשַׁע noun masc. sing. (suff. רִשְׁעוֹ) d. 6 (§ 35. r. 5) רשע
רִשְׁעָה וְ׳[p] noun fem. sing. (no pl.) . . . רשע
רִשְׁעוֹ[q] noun masc. sing., suff. 3 pers. sing. masc. from רֶשַׁע dec. 6 (§ 35. rem. 5) . . רשע
רִשְׁעֵי constr. of the foll. . . . . רשע
רְשָׁעִים וּ׳ adj. masc., pl. of רָשָׁע dec. 4 a; or perh. (Job 34. 26) pl. of רֶשַׁע q. v.; וּ bef. (:) רשע
רִשְׁעֶךָ[r] noun masc. sing., suff. 2 pers. sing. masc. from רֶשַׁע dec. 6 (§ 35. rem. 5) . . . רשע
רָשָׁעְנוּ וְ׳[s] Kal pret. 1 pers. pl. [for רָשַׁעְנוּ] . . רשע

[a] Ps. 139. 15. [b] Ju. 5. 30. [c] Eze. 16. 18. [d] Eze. 26. 16. [e] Eze. 6. 11. [f] Nu. 17. 3. [g] Eze. 25. 6. [h] Ju. 5. 26. [i] Le. 15. 3. [k] Pr. 13. 8. [l] De. 2. 24, 31. [m] Ps. 34. 11. [n] Da. 6. 10. [o] Da. 6. 13, 14. [p] Pr. 13. 6. [q] De. 9. 27. [r] Job 35. 8. [s] 2 Ch. 6. 37.

רְשָׁעֵנוּ[a] noun masc. sing., suff. 1 pers. sing. from
 רֶשַׁע dec. 6 (§ 35. rem. 5) . . . רשע

רִשְׁעַת ן noun fem. sing., constr. of רִשְׁעָה (no pl.) רשע

רִשְׁעָתוֹ[b] id. with suff. 3 pers. sing. masc. . . רשע

רָשַׁעְתִּי Kal pret. 1 pers. sing. . . . רשע

רִשְׁעָתַיִם } pr. name masc., see כּוּשַׁן ר׳.
רִשְׁעָתַיִם

רֶשֶׁף ן׳ masc. dec. 6a (pl. c. רִשְׁפֵּי).—I. *a flame*, Ca. 8. 6; others, *burning coal*.—II. *lightning*, Ps. 78. 48; metaph. Ps. 76. 4 רִשְׁפֵי קָשֶׁת *lightnings of the bow*, for *arrows*; Job 5. 7 בְּנֵי רֶ׳ *sons of lightning*, i. e. *arrows*, or (according to Gesenius) birds of prey which fly swift as the lightning; others, *sons of the flame*, i. e. *sparks*.—III. *burning disease*.—IV. pr. name masc. 1 Ch. 7. 25.

רִשְׁפֵּי noun masc. pl., constr. st. . . . רשף

רְשָׁפֶיהָ[c] id. pl., suff. 3 pers. sing. fem. . . רשף

רָשַׁשׁ Kal not used; cogn. רָצַץ. Po. *to break in pieces, to destroy*, Je. 5. 17. Pu. pass. Mal. 1. 4.
 תַּרְשִׁישׁ.—I. pr. name, *Tarshish*, supposed to be a city and kingdom in Spain; אֳנִיּוֹת תַּ׳ *Tarshish ships*, prop. ships employed by the Tyrians in voyages to and from Tarshish; but also generally for all large merchant ships bound on long voyages, though to other countries.—II. a precious stone brought from Tarshish, according to some the *chrysolite*, others *amber*.—III. pr. name of a Persian king, Est. 1. 14, and another person, 1 Ch. 7. 10.

רֻשַּׁשְׁנוּ[d] Pual pret. 1 pers. pl. . . . רשש

שׁ

שֶׁ less frequently שַׁ· (before gutturals dag. forte is omitted, once שָׁ) and rarely שְׁ, a pref. i. q. אֲשֶׁר fr. which it is abbreviated, אֲ being dropped by aphaeresis and ר assimilated to the next letter.—I. a relative pronoun (*a*) *who, which, what*; (*b*) as a mere sign of relation, as שֶׁ—שָׁם *whither*, comp. Ec. 1. 7; (*c*) followed by לְ, שֶׁל equivalent to the genitive, Ca. 1. 6; 3. 7.—II. as a relative conj. (*a*) *that*; עַד שֶׁ· *till that*; כִּמְעַט שֶׁ· *scarcely that*; (*b*) *so that*, Ec. 3. 14; (*c*) *because that, for*; שַׁלָּמָה *for why?*—III. with prefixes, בְּשֶׁ· *because that*; כְּשֶׁ· *as*, also *as, when*.

רֶשֶׁת[e] ן׳ noun fem. sing. dec. 13 (§ 44. rem. 1 & 2) ירש

רִשְׁתּוֹ[f] ן id., suff. 3 pers. sing. masc. . . ירש

רִשְׁתִּי id., suff. 1 pers. sing. . . . ירש

רִשְׁתָּם id., suff. 3 pers. pl. masc. . . . ירש

רָתַח. Pi. *to make boil*, Eze. 24. 5. Pu. *to boil*, metaph. for *to be agitated*, Job 30. 27. Hiph. i. q. Pi. Job 41. 23.
 רֶתַח masc. d. 6 (§ 35. r. 5), *a boiling*, Eze. 24. 5.

רַתַּח[g] Piel imp. sing. masc. . . . רתח

רֻתְּחוּ[h] Pual pret. 3 pers. pl. . . . רתח

רְתָחֶיהָ[i] noun masc. pl., suff. 3 pers. sing. fem. from
 [רֶתַח § 35. rem. 5] dec. 6 . . רתח

[רָתַם] *to bind, yoke*, or *harness*, Mi. 1. 13.
 רֹתֶם masc. (pl. רְתָמִים) *the broom*, Spanish *retama*. Jerome *the juniper*.
 רִתְמָה (*broom*) pr. name of a station of the Israelites in the desert, Nu. 33. 18, 19.

רְתֹם[k] Kal imp. sing. masc. . . . רתם

רֹתֶם[l] noun masc. sing. dec. 6c . . . רתם

רְתָמִים id. pl., abs. st. (§ 35. rem. 9) . . רתם

רָתַק. Niph. *to be bound*, Ec. 12. 6, Keri. Pu. id. Na. 3. 10.
 רַתּוֹק masc. *a chain*, Eze. 7. 23.
 רַתּוּקָה fem. id. 1 Ki. 6. 21, K., in Kh. רַתִּיקָה.
 רְתֻקוֹת fem. pl. *chains*, Is. 40. 19.

רֻתְּקוּ[m] Pual pret. 3 pers. pl. . . . רתק

רְתֻקוֹת[n] וּ noun fem. pl. of [רְתֻקָה] dec. 10; וּ bef. (:) רתק

רְתֵת masc. i. q. רֶטֶט *trembling, terror*, Ho. 13. 1.

שׁ

שֶׁל, a particle made up of שֶׁ· q. v. & לְ, occurs only with prefix.—I. בְּשֶׁל *on account of, because*; בְּשֶׁלְּמִי *on whose account*; בְּשֶׁלִּי *on my account*.—II. בְּשֶׁל אֲשֶׁר *in whatsoever*, or *how much soever*, Ec. 8. 17.

שָׂא ן׳ Kal imp. sing. masc. . . . נשא

שְׂא[o] Chald. Peal imp. sing. masc. . . נשא

[שָׁאַב] fut. יִשְׁאַב *to draw* water.
 מַשְׁאָב masc. only pl. מַשְׁאַבִּים *watering-troughs*, or *watering places*, Ju. 5. 11.

שֹׁאֵב[p] Kal part. act. sing. masc. dec. 7b . . שאב

[a] Je. 14. 20. [b] De. 25. 2. [c] Ca. 8. 6. [d] Mal. 1. 4. [e] Ho. 5. 1. [f] Ps. 35. 8. [g] Eze. 24. 5. [h] Job 30. 27. [i] Eze. 24. 5. [l] 1 Ki. 19. 4,5. [k] Mi. 1. 13. [m] Na. 3. 10. [n] Is. 40. 19. [o] Ezr. 5. 15. [p] De. 29. 10.

שַׁאֲבִי[a] id. imp. sing. fem. . . . . . שאב

שֹׁאֲבֵי[b] וְ id. part. act. pl. constr. masc. fr. שֹׁאֵב d. 7 b שאב

שְׁאַבְתֶּם[c] וּ id. pret. 2 pers. pl. masc.; וּ, for וְ, conv. שאב

שָׁאַג[d] (§ 8. rem. 2) fut. יִשְׁאַג.—I. *to roar*, as a lion, thunder, &c.—II. *to groan*, Ps. 38. 9.

שְׁאָגָה fem. dec. 11 c (§ 42. rem. 1).—I. *a roaring*, of a lion, Is. 5. 29.—II. *a groaning, groan.*

שָׁאֹג[e] Kal inf. abs. . . . . . . שאג

שָׁאַג[f] וְ Kh. יִשְׁאַג, Kal fut., K. וְשָׁאַג pret. 3 p. s. m. שאג

שֹׁאֵג[g] וְ'[h] Kal part. act. sing. masc. dec. 7 b . שאג

שַׁאֲגָה[i] noun fem. sing. dec. 11 c (§ 42. rem. 1) . שאג

שָׁאֲגוּ[k] Kal pret. 3 pers. pl. . . . . . שאג

שֹׁאֲגִים id. part. act. masc. pl. of שֹׁאֵג dec. 7 b . שאג

שַׁאֲגַת noun fem. sing., constr. of שְׁאָגָה dec. 11 c (§ 42. rem. 1) . . . . . שאג

שַׁאֲגָתוֹ[l] id. with suff. 3 pers. sing. masc. . . שאג

שָׁאַגְתִּי[m] Kal pret. 1 pers. sing. . . . . שאג

שַׁאֲגָתִי[n] noun fem. sing., suff. 1 pers. sing. from שְׁאָגָה dec. 11 c (§ 42. rem. 1) . . שאג

שַׁאֲגֹתָי[o] id. pl., suff. 1 pers. sing. . . . . שאג

[שָׁאָה] *to be desolate* (prob. *to fall with a crash*), Is. 6. 11. Niph. I. *to make a noise, rushing*, Is. 17. 12, 13; Prof. Lee, *to be dashed together*.—II. *to be laid waste*, Is. 6. 11. Hiph. *to lay waste*. Hithp. הִשְׁתָּאָה *to be confused, astonished*, Ge. 24. 21; others, *to gaze at*; Sept. καταμανθάνω, Vulg. *contemplor*, as synonymous with הִשְׁתָּעָה R. שָׁעָה.

שַׁאֲוָה fem. *tempest*, Pr. 1. 27, Kh.

שָׁאוֹן masc. dec. 3 a.—I. *a noise, tumult, bustle, shouting*, Je. 48. 45; בְּנֵי שָׁ' *tumultuous warriors*.—II. *destruction*, Ps. 40. 3.

שְׁאִיָּה fem. *a crash* or *destruction*, Is. 24. 12.

שֵׁאת fem. *desolation*, La. 3. 47.

שֵׁת fem. (for שֵׁאת) *noise, tumult*, Nu. 24. 17; according to others, a pr. name.

שֹׁאָה defect. for שׁוֹאָה (q. v.) . . . . שוא

שֶׁאָהֲבָה pref. שֶׁ (q. v.))(Kal pret. 3 pers. sing. fem. אהב

שָׂאֵהוּ Kal imp. sing. masc. (שָׂא), suff. 3 pers. sing. masc. (§ 25. No. 2 a) . . . . נשא

שָׁאוּ[p] Kal pret. 3 pers. pl. . . . . . שאה

שְׂאוּ וּ' Kal imp. pl. masc.; וּ bef. (:) . . . נשא

שָׁאוֹל[q] וְ Kal inf. abs. . . . . . שאל

שָׁאוּל וְ' id. part. pass. sing. masc.; also pr. name שאל

שְׁאוֹל noun masc. sing. dec. 1 a . . . . שאל

שְׁאוֹלָה[r] id. with parag. ה . . . . . שאל

שָׁאוֹן noun masc. sing. dec. 3 a . . . . שאה

שְׁאוֹן[s] וּ' id. constr. st.; וּ bef. (:) . . . . שאה

שְׁאוֹנָהּ[t] וּ id., suff. 3 pers. sing. fem.; וּ id. . שאה

שְׂאוּנִי Kal imp. pl. masc. (שְׂאוּ), suff. 1 pers. sing. (comp. § 16. rem. 11) . . . . נשא

שָׁאַט Root not used; prob. i. q. שׁוּט *to contemn, despise*.

שְׁאָט masc. *contempt* (for another); with suff. see the following.

שָׁאטְךָ[u] noun masc. sing., suff. 2 pers. sing. masc. [for שְׁאָטְךָ] from שְׁאָט' . . . . שאט

שְׂאִי וּ' Kal imp. sing. fem.; וּ bef. (:) . . . נשא

שְׁאִיָּה[x] וּ noun fem. sing.; וּ id. . . . . שאה

שֶׁאֵין[y] pref. שֶׁ (q. v.))(*adv.*, constr. of אַיִן dec. 6 h אין

שָׁאַל וְ' [also שָׁאֵל, comp. Ge. 32. 18; 1 Sa. 12. 13] fut. יִשְׁאַל.—I. *to ask, inquire of, interrogate*, with לְ, עַל *concerning* any one, with בְּ *to inquire of, consult*, e. g. God; שָׁ' לְרֵעֵהוּ לְשָׁלוֹם *to ask after the welfare of any one, to salute him*.—II. *to ask, demand, require*, with מִן, מֵאֵת *of* any one.—III. *to request, petition*, with מִן, מֵאֵת, מֵעִם; abs. *to beg*, Pr. 20. 4.—IV. *to ask as a loan, to borrow*; with לְ *to lend*, 1 Sa. 2. 20. Niph. *to ask for oneself, to ask leave*. Pi. שִׁאֵל (§ 14. rem. 1).—I. *to beg*, Ps. 109. 10.—II. *to ask, inquire*, 2 Sa. 20. 18. Hiph. *to lend*.

שְׁאֵל Chald.—I. *to ask, interrogate*, with לְ, acc. of pers. Ezr. 5. 9, 10.—II. *to ask, demand*.

שְׁאָל (*petition*) pr. name masc. Ezr. 10. 29.

שֵׁלָה, שְׁאֵלָה fem. (§ 42. rem. 4).—I. *request, petition*.—II. *thing lent, a loan*, 1 Sa. 2. 20.

שְׁאֵלָא Chald. fem. dec. 8 a, *subject of inquiry, matter, affair*, Da. 4. 14.

שְׁאֹל, שְׁאוֹל masc.—I. *grave*; hence—II. *the abode of the departed souls*; Sept. mostly ᾍδης, *Hades*. It is so called either from its devouring and ever craving character, Pr. 15. 11, or the Root שָׁאַל may be in signification i. q. שָׁעַל *to be hollow*.

שָׁאוּל (*asked for* or *lent*) pr. name, *Saul*.—I. the first king of the Israelites, from the tribe of Benjamin.—II. a king of Edom, Ge. 36. 37.—III. Ge. 46. 10, patronym. שָׁאוּלִי Nu. 26. 13.—IV. 1 Ch. 6. 9.

שַׁלְתִּיאֵל, שְׁאַלְתִּיאֵל (*I have asked him of God*) pr. name of a man.

אֶשְׁתָּאוֹל (*petition*) pr. name of a city in Dan. Gent. noun אֶשְׁתָּאֻלִי.

[a] Na. 3. 14. [b] Jos. 9. 21, 23, 27. [c] Is. 12. 3. [d] Am. 3. 8. [e] Je. 25. 30. [f] Is. 5. 29. [g] Ju. 14. 5. [h] Ps. 22. 14. [i] Is. 5. 29. [k] Ps. 74. 4. [l] Eze. 19. 7. [m] Ps. 38. 9. [n] Ps. 22. 2. [o] Job 3. 24. [p] Is. 6. 11. [q] 1 Sa. 22. 13. [r] Ge. 42. 38. [s] Is. 17. 12. [t] Is. 5. 14. [u] Eze. 25. 6. [x] Is. 24. 12. [y] Ps. 146. 3.

מִשְׁאָל (*petition*) pr. name of a city in the tribe of Asher.

מִשְׁאָלָה fem. dec. 12 a, *petition, request*, Ps. 20. 6; 37. 4.

שָׁאַל Kal pret. 3 pers. s. m. for שָׁאֵל (§ 8. rem. 7) אשל
שְׁאֵל[a] Chald. Peal part. act. sing. masc. . . שאל
שְׁאָל וּ pr. name masc.; וּ bef. (:) . . . שאל
שְׁאַל Kal imp. sing. masc. . . . . . שאל
שְׁאֵל[b] Chald. Peal pret. 3 pers. sing. masc. . . שאל
שֶׁאֵל[c] pref. שֶׁ (q. v.)) (noun masc. sing. dec. 1 a (§ 30. No. 3) . . . אול
שְׁאֹל defect. for שְׁאוֹל (q. v.) . . . . שאל
שֹׁאֵל[d] וְ׳ Kal part. act. sing. masc. dec. 7 b . . שאל
שָׁאֲלָה / וְשָׁאֲלָה[e] } id. pret. 3 pers sing. fem. (§ 8. rem. 7) שאל
שְׁאָלָה[f] id. imp. sing. masc. (שְׁאַל) with parag. ה (§ 8. rem. 12) . . . . שאל
שְׁאֵלָה noun fem. sing. dec. 10 & 11 c (§ 42. rem. 4) שאל
שְׁאֹלָה defect. for שְׁאוֹלָה (q. v.) . . . שאל
שָׁאֲלוּ / שָׁאֲלוּ[g] וְ׳ } Kal pret. 3 pers. pl. (§ 8. rem. 7) . שאל
שַׁאֲלוּ[h] וְ׳ id. imp. pl. masc. . . . . . שאל
וְשִׁאֲלוּ[i] Piel pret. 3 pers. pl. [for שִׁאֲלוּ § 14. rem. 1, comp. § 8. rem. 7] . . . . שאל
שְׁאֵלוּנוּ[k] Kal pret. 3 pers. pl., suff. 1 pers. pl. (§ 16. r. 1) שָׁאַל
שְׁאֵלוּנִי[l] id. id. with suff. 1 pers. sing. . . . שָׁאַל
שַׁאֲלִי[m] וְ׳ id. imp. sing. fem. . . . . . שאל
שְׁאֵלְךָ[n] וּ id. pret. 3 pers. sing. m. [שָׁאֵל], suff. 2 pers. sing. masc. (§ 16. rem. 1); וּ bef. (:) שאל
שְׁאֵלֵךְ[o] וּ id. id., suff. 2 pers. sing. fem.; וּ id. . שאל
שְׁאֵלְנָא[p] Chald. Peal pret. 1 pers. pl. . . . שאל
שָׁאַלְתָּ / שָׁאַלְתָּ } Kal pret. 2 pers. sing. masc. (§ 8. rem. 7) שאל
וְשָׁאַלְתָּ[q] / וְשָׁאַלְתָּ[r] } id. id.; acc. shifted by conv. וְ, retained bef. monos. (§ 8. rem. 7) . . } שאל
שָׁאַלְתְּ[s] id. pret. 2 pers. sing. fem. . . . שאל
שֹׁאֶלֶת[t] id. part. act. sing., fem. of שֹׁאֵל (§ 8. rem. 19) שאל
שְׁאֶלְתָּא[u] Chald. noun fem. sing., emph. of [שְׁאֵלָא] d. 8 a שאל
שָׁאַלְתִּי Kal pret. 1 pers. sing. . . . . שאל
שְׁאֵלָתִי / שֶׁאֱלָתִי[x] } noun fem. sing., suff. 1 pers. sing. from שְׁאֵלָה (§ 42. rem. 4) . . } שאל
שְׁאַלְתִּיאֵל pr. name masc. . . . . . שאל
שְׁאִלְתִּיהוּ[y] Kal pret. 1 pers. s., suff. 3 p. s. m. (§ 8. r. 1 b) שאל
שְׁאִלְתִּיו[z] id. id., suff. 3 pers. sing. masc. . . שאל

שְׁאֵלָתֵךְ noun fem. s., suff. 2 p. s. fem. fr. שְׁאֵלָה d. 10 שאל
שֶׁאֱלָתְכֶם[a] id. with suff. 3 pers. pl. dec. 11 c (§ 42. r. 4) שאל
שְׁאֶלְתֶּם[b] וְ׳ Kal pret. 2 pers. pl. masc. (§ 8. rem. 1 b); וּ, for וְ, conv. . . . . . . שאל

שָׁאַן Kal not used; i. q. שָׁעַן *to lean, rest*. Pil. שַׁאֲנַן (§ 6. No. 2), *to be quiet, live quietly*.

בֵּית שְׁאָן (*quiet*) pr. name, see בֵּית שְׁ.

שׁוּנִי (for שְׁאוּנִי *quiet*) pr. name masc. Ge. 46. 16; also patronym. (for שׁוּנִיִּי) Nu. 26. 15.

שׁוּנֵם (perh. *two resting places*, comp. עָנֵם for עֵינַיִם Gesen.) pr. name of a city in the tribe of Issachar. Gent. noun fem. שׁוּנַמִּית.

שַׁאֲנָן masc. שַׁאֲנַנָּה fem. adj.—I. *quiet, living in quiet, peace.*—II. *at ease, careless, proud.*—III. subst. *wantonness, pride*.

שַׁלְאֲנָן (with ל inserted) *at ease*, Job 21. 23.

שְׁאָן pr. name, see בֵּית שְׁאָן . . . . בית
שֶׁאֲנִי[c] pref. שֶׁ (q. v.)) (pron. pers. com. sing. . אני
שֶׁאֲנִיחֶנּוּ[d] pref. id.) (Hiph. fut. 1 pers. sing. [אַנִיחַ § 21. rem. 24], suff. 3 pers. sing. masc. נוח
שַׁאֲנָן adj. masc. sing. (pl. שַׁאֲנַנִּים׳) dec. 8 a . שאן
שַׁאֲנַן[e] וְ׳ Pilel pret. 3 pers. sing. masc. (§ 6. No. 2) שאן
שַׁאֲנַנּוּ[f] id. pret. 3 pers. pl. [for שַׁאֲנְנוּ comp. § 8. r. 7] שאן
שַׁאֲנַנּוֹת adj. pl. fem. from שַׁאֲנָן masc. . . שאן
שַׁאֲנַנְךָ וְ id. masc. sing., suff. 2 pers. sing. masc. [for נַנְךָ׳] from שַׁאֲנָן dec. 8 a . . . שאן
שֹׁאסַיִךְ[g] Kal part. act. pl. masc., suff. 2 pers. sing. fem. [by Syr. for שֹׁסַיִךְ § 18. rem. 17] . ששס

שָׁאַף[h] וְ *to draw in*, sc. the air, wind, cogn. שָׁאַב; hence —I. abs. *to pant, gasp*, Ps. 119. 131; of one in anger, *to breathe hard, puff*, Is. 42. 14; hence *to hasten*, Ec. 1. 5.—II. *to breathe in, snap, snuff up*, the air, wind, with acc.; trop. *to pant for, desire eagerly*; once with עַל Am. 2. 7; metaph. of savage enemies, *to swallow up, destroy*.

שָׁאֹף[i] וְ Kal inf. abs. . . . . . . שאף
שָׁאֲפָה[k] id. pret. 3 pers. sing. fem. . . . . שאף
שָׁאֲפוּ id. pret. 3 pers. pl. . . . . . שאף
שֹׁאֲפִי[l] id. part. act. s. m., suff. 1 p. s. fr. שׁוֹאֵף d. 7 b שאף
שְׁאָפַנִי[m] id. pret. 3 pers. sing. masc., suff. 1 pers. sing. שאף

שָׁאַר, שְׁאַר Roots not used; Arab. שׁאר, תאר *to be hot, to boil up* (Gesenius).

שְׂאֹר masc. *leaven*.

מִשְׁאֶרֶת fem. dec. 13 a, *a kneading-trough*.

---

a Da. 2. 11, 27. b Da. 2. 10. c Ps. 146. 5. d De. 18. 11. e Ex. 3. 22. f Is. 7. 11. g 1 Sa. 10. 4. h Je. 6. 16. i Ps. 109. 10. k Ps. 137. 3. l Is. 45. 11. m 1 Ki. 2. 22. n Ge. 32. 18. o Ju. 4. 20. p Ezr. 5. 9, 10. q De. 13. 15. r 1 Ki. 3. 11. s 1 Sa. 1. 17. t 1 Ki. 2. 20, 22. u Da. 4. 14. x Job 6. 8. y Ju. 13. 6. z 1 Sa. 1. 20. a Ps. 106. 15. b 1 Sa. 25. 5. c Ca. 1. 6; Ec. 2. 18. d Ec. 2. 18. e Je. 48. 11. f Job 3. 18. g Je. 30. 16. h Job 5. 5. i Eze. 36. 3. k Je. 2. 24. l Ps. 57. 4. m Ps. 56. 2.

שָׁאַר[a] to remain, 1 Sa. 16. 11. Niph. I. to remain, be left over.—II. to remain, be left behind. Hiph. I. to let remain, to leave.—II. to leave behind, Joel 2. 14. —III. to have left, to retain.

שְׁאָר masc. remainder, remnant.

שְׁאָר Chald. masc. dec. 1 b, idem.

שְׁאָר יָשׁוּב (a remnant shall return) pr. name of a son of Isaiah, Is. 7. 3.

שְׁאֵרִית, contr. שֵׁרִית fem. dec. 1 b, remainder, remnant.

שְׁאֵר masc. dec. 1 a.—I. flesh.—II. blood-relation, kindred. —III. food, aliment, Ex. 21. 10; Prof. Lee, a right arising from marriage.

שַׁאֲרָה fem. blood-relationship, concr. near relative, Le. 18. 17.

שֶׁאֱרָה (id.) pr. name fem. 1 Ch. 7. 24.

שְׁאָר 'ו n. m. s., constr. שְׁאָר Ezr. 7. 20.; ו bef. (:) . . . שאר

שְׁאָר noun masc. sing. . . . . . שאר

שְׁאָר יָשׁוּב ו pr. name masc.; ו bef. (:) . . . שאר

שְׁאָרָא[b] ו Ch. noun m. sing., emph. of שְׁאָר d. 1 b; ו id. שאר

שַׁאֲרָה[c] noun fem. sing. . . . . . שאר

שְׁאֵרָהּ[d] noun m. s., suff. 3 pers. s. fem. fr. שְׁאֵר d. 1 a שאר

שֶׁאֱרָה pr. name fem. . . . . . שאר

שְׁאֵרוֹ noun m. sing., suff. 3 pers. s. m. fr. שְׁאֵר d. 1 a שאר

שְׁאֵרִי[e] ו/f id., suff. 1 pers. sing.; ו bef. (:) . . שאר

שְׁאֵרִית 'ו noun fem. sing. dec. 1 b; ו id. . . שאר

שְׁאֵרִיתוֹ[g] ו id., suff. 3 pers. sing. masc; ו id. . . שאר

שְׁאֵרִיתֵךְ[h] 'ו ו id., suff. 2 pers. sing. fem.; ו id. . . שאר

שְׁאֵרִיתָם[k] ו id., suff. 3 pers. pl. masc.; ו id. . . שאר

שְׁאֵרֶךָ[l] ו noun masc. sing., suff. 2 pers. sing. masc. from שְׁאֵר dec 1; ו id. . . . שאר

שְׁאֵרָם[m] ו id., suff. 3 pers. pl. masc.; ו id. . . שאר

שְׂאֵת Kal inf. constr., or subst. fem. dec. 1 [for שְׂאֵת § 25, No. 2 a] . . . . . נשא

שָׁאַתָּה[n] pref. שֶׁ (q. v.)) (pron. pers. masc. sing. . אנת

שְׂאֵתוֹ[o] 'ו Kal inf. (De. 14. 24), or subst. fem., suff. 3 pers. sing. masc. fr. שְׂאֵת (q. v.); ו bef. (:) נשא

שְׂאֵתִי id. inf. with suff. 1 pers. sing. . . . נשא

שָׁב[p] Kal part. sing. masc. . . . . . שיב

שָׁב 'וְ Kal pret. 3 pers. sing. masc. . . . שוב

שָׁב[q] 'וְ id. part. act. sing. masc. dec. 1 a (§ 30. No. 3); for וְ see lett. ו . . . . שוב

שֵׁב 'וְ, שֶׁב־[r] 'וְ } Kal imp. sing. masc. . . . . ישב

שֻׁבִי[s] defect. for שׁוּבִי (q. v.) . . . . שוב

שֻׁב Kal imp. sing. masc. (§ 21. rem. 5) . . שוב

שְׁבָא pr. name—I. of a son of Raamah, grandson of Cush, comp. Ge. 10. 7.—II. of a son of Joktan, Ge. 10. 28.—III. of a grandson of Abraham by Keturah.—IV. of a people and a country in Arabia Felix.

שֶׁבָּאוּ[t] pref. שֶׁ) (Kal pret. 3 pers. sing. masc. . . בוא

שְׁבָאֵל ו pr. name masc., see שְׁבוּאֵל . . . שבה

שְׁבָבִים[u] noun masc. pl. . . . . . שבב

שָׁבַב Root not used.—I. Arab. to kindle.—II. Chald. שְׁבַב, to break.

שָׁבִיב masc. dec. 3 a, a flame, Job 18. 5.

שְׁבִיב Chald. masc. 1 a, idem, Da. 3. 22; 7. 9.

שְׁבָבִים masc. pl. fragments, Ho. 8. 6.

שֹׁבַבְתִּי[x] וְ Pilel pret. 1 pers. sing.; acc. shifted by conv. וְ (§ 8. rem. 7) . . . . שוב

שֹׁבַבְתִּיךָ[y] וְ id. id., suff. 2 pers. sing. masc. . . שוב

שָׁבָה[z] fut. apoc. יִשְׁבְּ (§ 24. rem. 3), to take prisoner, to carry away captive, to carry off; part. pass. שְׁבוּיִם, שְׁבוּיוֹת captives. Niph. pass.

שְׁבוּאֵל (captive of God) pr. name masc. of two persons, also written שׁוּבָאֵל.

שְׁבוּת fem. dec. 1 a.—I. captivity; meton. captives.—II. trop. a state of great affliction and misery, Job 42. 10.

שְׁבִי masc. dec. 6 i (§ 35. rem. 14).—I. captivity; meton. captives.—II. a captive, Ex. 12. 29; fem. שְׁבִיָּה, Is. 52. 2.

שֹׁבִי (one who takes captive) pr. name of a man.

שֹׁבִי (id.) pr. name of a man, 2 Sa. 17. 27.

שִׁבְיָה fem. captivity; meton. captives.

שְׁבִית fem. dec. 1 a, captivity.

תִּשְׁבִּי gentile noun of the prophet Elijah, Tishbite, from a city of Naphtali, called תִּשְׁבֶּה or תִּשְׁבָּה (captivity).

שָׁבָה[a] Kal part. act. sing., fem. of שָׁב . . . שוב

שָׁבָה, וְשָׁבָה } id. pret. 3 pers. sing. fem.; acc. shifted by conv. וְ . . . . . } שוב

שְׁבָה Kal imp. sing. masc. (שֵׁב) with parag. ה (§ 20. rem. 3) . . . . . . ישב

שָׁבָה[b] 'וְ[c] defect. for שׁוּבָה (q. v.) . . . שוב

שְׁבֵה[d] וְ Kal imp. sing. m.; (comp. the form וְזֵהַב) שבה

שְׁבוֹ masc. an agate; Sept. ἀχάτης, Ex. 28. 19; 39. 12.

שָׁבוּ[e] 'וְ, 'וְ Kal pret. 3 pers. pl.; for וְ see lett. ו שוב

שָׁבוּ Kal pret. 3 pers. pl. . . . . . שבה

---

[a] 1 Sa. 16. 7. [b] Da. 7. 7, 19. [c] Le. 18. 17. [d] Ex. 21. 10. [e] Ps. 73. 26. [f] Je. 51. 35. [g] Is. 44. 17. [h] Eze. 5. 10. [i] Is. 14. 30. [k] Je. 15. 9. [l] Pr. 5. 11. [m] Mi. 3. 2. [n] Ju. 6. 17. [o] Hab. 1. 7. [p] Job 15. 10. [q] Je. 30. 18. [r] Ge. 35. 1. [s] Jos. 2. 16. [t] Ec. 5. 15; 11. 8. [u] Ho. 8. 6. [x] Je. 50. 19. [y] Eze. 39. 2. [z] Je. 41. 14. [a] Est. 2. 14. [b] 2 Sa. 15. 27. [c] Je. 40. 5. [d] Ju. 5. 12. [e] Zec. 10. 9.

שְׁבוּ[a] וְ' / שְׁבוּ וּ } Kal imp. pl. masc.; וּ bef. (:) . . . ישב

שָׁבוּ defect. for שׁוּבוּ (q. v.) . . . . שוב

שְׁבוּאֵל pr. name masc. . . . . . שבה

שְׁבוּלֵי[b] Kh. שְׁבוּלֵי, K. שִׁבְּלֵי, noun masc. pl. constr. [from שְׁבוּל or שְׁבִיל] . . . שבל

שָׁבוּם וְ Kal pret. 3 pers. pl., suff. 3 pers. pl. masc. שבה

שָׁבוֹעַ וְ Kal inf. abs. . . . . . שבע

שָׁבוּעַ[c] noun masc. sing., constr. שְׁבֻעַ pl. שָׁבֻעִים, dec. 3a & 1b (§ 32. rem. 1) . . . . שבע

שְׁבוּעָה noun fem. sing. dec. 10 . . . שבע

שְׁבוּעַת[d] id., constr. st. . . . . . שבע

שְׁבוּעָתוֹ וּ id., suff. 3 pers. sing. masc.; וּ bef. (:) שבע

שֹׁבוּר[e] Kal part. act. sing. masc. . . . שבר

שְׁבוֹר[f] id. inf. constr. . . . . . שבר

שְׁבוּת[g] Kh. שְׁבוּת; K. שְׁבִית noun fem. sing. d. 1 a שבה

שְׁבוּת[h] Kal inf. constr. . . . . . שבה

שְׁבוּת noun fem. sing. dec. 1 a . . . שבה

שְׁבוּתְהֶן[i] id., suff. 3 pers. pl. fem. (Kh. שְׁבוּתְהֶן), K. שְׁבִיתְהֶן from שְׁבִית . . . שבה

שְׁבוּתֵיכֶם id. pl., suff. 2 pers. pl. masc. . . . שבה

שְׁבוּתֵךְ[l] id. sing., suff. 2 pers. sing. masc. . . שבה

שְׁבוּתָם[m] / שְׁבוּתָם } id. sing., suff. 3 pers. pl. masc., K. שְׁבִיתָם from שְׁבִית } שבה

שְׁבוּתֵנוּ[n] id. sing., suff. 1 pers. pl. (Kh. שְׁבוּתֵנוּ), K. שְׁבִיתֵנוּ from שְׁבִית . . . שבה

שָׁבַח Pi. שִׁבַּח.—I. *to soothe, calm, quiet,* Ps. 89. 10; Pr. 29. 11.—II. *to praise, laud.*—III. *to pronounce happy,* Ec. 4. 2. Hiph. *to still, calm,* Ps. 65. 8. Hithp. *to praise oneself, to boast of,* with בְּ.

שְׁבַח Ch. Pa. *to praise, laud.*

יִשְׁבָּח (*soothing*) pr. name masc. 1 Ch. 4. 17.

שַׁבֵּחַ[o] וְ Piel part. sing. masc. [for מְשַׁבֵּחַ comp. § 10. rem. 6] . . . . . שבח

שַׁבַּחוּ[p] וְ Ch. Pael pret. 3 pers. pl. masc. . . שבח

שַׁבְּחוּהוּ[q] Piel imp. pl. masc., suff. 3 pers. sing. masc. שבח

שַׁבְּחִי[r] id. imp. sing. fem. . . . . שבח

שַׁבַּחְתָּ[s] Ch. Pael pret. 2 pers. sing. masc. . . שבח

שַׁבְּחֵת[t] Ch. id. pret. 1 pers. sing. . . . שבח

שִׁבַּחְתִּי[u] וְ Piel pret. 1 pers. sing. . . . שבח

שֵׁבֶט וְ' m. dec. 6 b (in pause שָׁבֶט, from שַׁבְטְ=שֵׁבֶט § 35. rem. 2).—I. *staff.*—II. *rod,* for punishment; also as *a measure,* and meton. *a portion measured off.*—III. *a sceptre,* of a leader, chief, king.—IV. *a tribe.*—V. *a spear, lance,* 2 Sa. 18. 14.

שְׁבַט Ch. 3 b, *tribe.*

שַׁרְבִיט masc. i. q. שֵׁבֶט (with ר inserted) *a sceptre.*

שְׁבָט the eleventh month of the Hebrew year, corresponding to February and March, Zec. 1. 7.

שָׁבֶט [for שֵׁבֶט § 35. r. 2] Seg. noun, see שֵׁבֶט שבט

שִׁבְטוֹ noun masc. sing., suff. 3 pers. sing. masc. from שֵׁבֶט dec. 6 b . . . . שבט

שִׁבְטֵי[x] וְ' id. pl., constr. st. [Chald. Ezr. 6. 17] שבט

שְׁבָטֶיהָ[y] id. pl., suff. 3 pers. sing. fem. . . שבט

שְׁבָטֶיךָ id. pl., suff. 2 pers. sing. masc. . . שבט

שִׁבְטֵיכֶם id. pl., suff. 2 pers. pl. masc. . . שבט

שְׁבָטִים id. pl., abs. st. . . . . . שבט

שִׁבְטְךָ[z] id. sing., suff. 2 pers. sing. masc. . . שבט

שָׁבֵי[a] וְ' Ch. Peal part. act. pl. c. from שָׁב dec. 1 a (comp. § 30. No. 3) . . . . שיב

שְׁבִי[b] וּ' Kal imp. sing. fem.; וּ bef. (:) . . ישב

שְׁבִי / שֶׁבִי } noun masc. sing. dec. 6 i (§ 35. rem. 14) שבה

שֹׁבִי pr. name masc. for שְׁבִי . . . . שבה

שֹׁבַי וְ pr. name masc. . . . . . שבה

שׁבִי[c] defect. for שׁוּבִי (q. v.) . . . שוב

שׁבִי[d] וְ for Keri שְׁבוּ (q. v.) . . . שוב

שְׁבִיב[e] noun masc. sing., constr. of [שָׁבִיב] dec. 3 a שבב

שְׁבִיבָא[f] Ch. noun masc. sing., emph. of [שְׁבִיב] d. 1 a שבב

שְׁבִיבִין[g] Ch. id. pl., abs. st. . . . . שבב

שָׁבֶיהָ[h] וְ Kal part. act. pl. masc., suff. 3 pers. sing. fem. from שָׁב dec. 1 a (§ 30. No. 3) שוב

שִׁבְיָה[i] noun fem. sing. . . . . . שבה

שִׁבְיָה[k] וְ' noun fem. sing. . . . . . שבה

שִׁבְיָהּ[l] noun masc. sing., suff. 3 pers. sing. fem. from שְׁבִי dec. 6 i . . . . שבה

שֹׁבֵיהֶם Kal part. act. pl. masc., suff. 3 pers. pl. masc. from שֹׁבֶה dec. 9 a . . שבה

שִׁבְיוֹ[m] noun m. s., suff. 3 pers. s. m. fr. שְׁבִי d. 6 i שבה

שִׁבְיֵךְ[n] id. with suff. 2 pers. sing. masc. . . שבה

שִׁבְיְכֶם[cc] וּ id., suff. 2 p. pl. m. (§ 35. r. 14); וּ bef. (:) שבה

שְׁבִילֶיךָ[o] וּ Kh. ־לֶיךָ, K. ־לְךָ noun masc. pl. or sing., suff. 2 pers. sing. m. fr. [שְׁבִיל] d. 1 a; וּ id. שבל

שָׁבִים Kal part. act. m., pl. of שָׁב d. 1 a (§ 30. No. 3) שוב

שִׁבְיָם noun m. s., suff. 3 pers. pl. m. fr. שְׁבִי d. 6 i שבה

שֹׁבִים[p] Kal part. act. masc. pl. [of שֹׁבֶה] dec. 9 a . שבה

שָׁבִיתָ[q] וְ' id. pret. 2 pers. sing. masc. . . שבה

שְׁבִית[r] וּ' n. f. s. d. 1 a; Kh. שְׁבִית, K. שְׁבוּת; וּ bef. (:) שבה

---

[a] Je. 13. 18; 29. 5, 28.
[b] Je. 18. 15.
[c] Da. 9. 27.
[d] Ec. 8. 2.
[e] Le. 22. 22.
[f] Je. 28. 12.
[g] Ps. 85. 2.
[h] Ob. 11.
[i] Eze. 16. 53.
[k] Zep. 3. 20.
[l] De. 30. 3.
[m] Zep. 2. 7.
[n] Ps. 126. 4.
[o] Ec. 4. 2.
[p] Da. 5. 4.
[q] Ps. 117. 1.
[r] Ps. 147. 12.
[s] Da. 5. 23.
[t] Da. 4. 31.
[u] Ec. 8. 15.
[x] Eze. 37. 19.
[y] Is. 19. 13.
[z] Ps. 23. 4.
[a] Ezr. 6. 14.
[b] Is. 47. 1.
[c] Je. 31. 21.
[d] Job 6. 29.
[e] Job 18. 5.
[cc] Nu. 31. 19.
[f] Da. 3. 22.
[g] Da. 7. 9.
[h] Is. 1. 27.
[i] Is. 52. 2.
[k] De. 32. 42.
[l] De. 21. 13.
[m] De. 21. 10.
[n] Ju. 5. 12.
[o] Ps. 77. 20.
[p] Is. 14. 2.
[q] De. 21. 10.
[r] Eze. 16. 53.

שְׁבִיתֵךְ[a] id. pl., suff. 2 pers. sing. fem. . . . שבה
שְׁבִיתֵךְ[b] id. sing., suff. 2 p. s. f. Kh. שְׁבוּתֵךְ, K. שְׁבִיתֵךְ שבה
שְׁבִיתְכֶם[c] id. sing., suff. 2 p. pl. m., Kh. שְׁבִי', K. שְׁבוּ' שבה
שְׁבִיתֶם[d] Kal pret. 2 pers. pl. masc. . . . שבה

שָׂבַךְ Root not used; i. q. סָבַךְ *to interweave.*

שְׂבָךְ masc. only pl. שְׂבָכִים *ornaments of net-work,* 1 Ki. 7. 17.

שְׂבָכָה fem.—I. *a net,* Job 18. 8.—II. *network,* ornamenting the capitals of pillars.—III. *lattice* of a window, 2 Ki. 1. 2.

שׂוֹבֶךְ masc. *thick branches, thicket,* 2 Sa. 18. 9.

שַׂבְּכָא[ii] Chald. noun fem. sing. see סַבְּכָא.
שְׂבָכָה ו' noun fem. sing., pl. שְׂבָכוֹת; ו bef. (:) . שבך
שְׂבָכִים[e] noun masc., pl. of [שְׂבָךְ] d. 6 (§ 35. r. 10) שבך
שֶׁבַּכְּרָמִים[f] preff. שֶׁ, & בַּ for בְּהַ) n. m. pl. of כֶּרֶם d. 6 a כרם

שָׁבַל Root not used; according to Gesenius, coll. with the Arab., (*a*) *to go;* (*b*) *to rise, grow;* (*c*) *to flow copiously.*

שׁוֹבֶל masc. *a train* of a robe, Is. 47. 2, Eng. vers. "*locks*" of hair, both from the idea of *flowing.*

שַׁבְּלוּל masc. *a snail,* so called from the slimy trail it leaves as it goes along, Ps. 58. 9.

שִׁבֹּלֶת fem. (pl. שִׁבֳּלִים § 44. No. 2; constr. שִׁבֲּלֵי Zec. 4. 12, where most codices read שִׁבֳּלֵי, from a form שִׁבֶּלֶת).—I. *an ear of corn.*—II. *a branch,* Zec. 4. 12.—III. *stream, flood.*

שׁוֹבָל (*shoot*) pr. name m. of two different persons.

שְׁבוּל Kh., שְׁבִיל K. masc. dec. 1 a, *way, path.*

שֻׁבֶל[g] noun masc. sing. . . . . שבל
שַׁבְּלוּל[h] noun masc. sing. . . . . שבל
שִׁבֲּלֵי[i] or שִׁבֳּלֵי noun fem. pl. constr. see שִׁבֹּלֶת under the R. . . . . שבל
שִׁבֳּלִים noun fem., pl. of the foll. . . . שבל
שִׁבֹּלֶת ו'[k] noun fem. sing. dec. 13 c (§ 44. No. 2) שבל
שָׁבָם[l] ו Kal pret. 3 pers. sing. masc. (שָׁבָה), suff. 3 pers. pl. masc. (§ 24. rem. 21) . . שבה

שְׂבָם ו' } pr. name of a city in the tribe of Reuben;
שִׂבְמָה ו' } ו bef. (:).

שָׁבַן Root not used; Arab. *to be tender, delicate.*

שֶׁבְנָה, שֶׁבְנָא (*tenderness, tender*) pr. name of a scribe or secretary of king Hezekiah.

שְׁבַנְיָה (*tender one of the Lord*) pr. name masc. of several persons; the one of Ne. 10. 5; 12. 14, is written שְׁכַנְיָה in Ne. 12. 3.

שֶׁבֶּן[m] pref. שֶׁ) noun m. s., constr. of בֵּן irr. (§ 45) בנה
שֶׁבְנָא ו' } pr. name masc. . . . . בן
שֶׁבְנָה ו' }
שְׁבֹנָה[n] Kal imp. pl. fem. . . . . שוב
שַׁבְנוּ id. pret. 1 pers. pl. . . . . שוב
שְׁבַנְיָה ו } pr. name masc.; ו bef. (:) . . בן
שְׁבַנְיָהוּ }

שָׁבַס Root not used; perh. i. q. שָׁבַץ *to mingle, interweave.*

שְׁבִיסִים masc. pl. (of שָׁבִים) *cap of network, cauls,* Is. 3. 18; others (i. q. Arab. שבישא), *little suns,* as an ornament, comp. שַׂהֲרֹנִים.

שָׂבַע ו [also שָׂבֵעַ, comp. Is. 9. 19; De. 14. 29; 26. 12] fut. יִשְׂבַּע *to be* or *become satiated, satisfied, filled,* espec. with food, less frequently with drink; with acc., בְּ, מִן of the thing *with* which; metaph. *to be satisfied* with any thing, *to have enough.* Pi. *to satisfy, satiate.* Hiph. *to satisfy, satiate,* with acc., בְּ, מִן of the thing, acc., לְ of the person, metaph. Ps. 91. 16.

שָׂבָע masc. *abundance, plenty.*

שָׂבֵעַ masc. d. 5 a, *satiated, satisfied, full;* metaph. *enough, abounding, rich.*

שֹׂבַע masc. dec. 6 c (§ 35. rem. 5), *satiety, fulness, abundance;* לָשֹׂבַע *to the full.*

שָׂבְעָה, שִׂבְעָה fem. (no pl.) idem.

שֶׁבַע ו', ו' (constr. שְׁבַע § 35. rem. 7) fem. שִׁבְעָה masc. (constr. שִׁבְעַת).—I. num. card. *seven;* שֶׁבַע שָׁנִים *seven years,* and with the constr. שִׁבְעַת יָמִים *seven days;* less frequently preceded by the noun, as אֵילִים שִׁבְעָה *seven rams;* also as an ordinal when preceded by a noun in the construct state, as שְׁנַת שֶׁבַע *seventh year;* שִׁבְעָה שִׁבְעָה *by sevens;* שְׁבַע עֶשְׂרֵה fem. & שִׁבְעָה עָשָׂר masc. *seventeen.*—II. (שֶׁבַע) adv. *seven times,* Ps. 119. 164; Pr. 24. 16. Du. שִׁבְעָתַיִם *sevenfold.* Pl. שִׁבְעִים (§ 35. rem. 16) *seventy.* For another שֶׁבַע (& שִׁבְעָה) see below.

שִׁבְעָה Chald. masc. *seven.*

שִׁבְעָנָה masc. *seven,* Job 42. 13.

שָׁבוּעַ masc. (constr. שְׁבוּעַ, pl. c. שְׁבֻעוֹת, du. שְׁבֻעַיִם d. 3 a; but also pl. (abs.) שָׁבֻעוֹת, שָׁבֻעִים with suff. שָׁבֻעֹתֵיכֶם § 32. rem. 1).—I. *a week,* seven days; חַג שָׁבֻעוֹת *the feast of weeks, pentecost.*—II. *a week of years,* comp. Da. 9. 24, seq.

[a] Eze. 16. 53. [b] La. 2. 14. [c] Je. 29. 14. [d] 2 Ch. 28. 11. [e] 1 Ki. 7. 17. [f] 1 Ch. 27. 27. [g] Is. 47. 2. [h] Ps. 58. 9. [i] Zec. 4. 12. [ii] Da. 3. 7, 10, 15. [k] Ps. 69. 3. [l] Je. 43. 12. [m] Jon. 4. 10. [n] Ru. 1. 8, 11, 12.

שְׁבִיעִי masc. **שְׁבִיעִית** fem. adj. ordin. from שֶׁבַע, *seventh*.

שָׁבַע *to swear* (since oaths were usually confirmed by seven victims), Eze. 21. 28. Niph. נִשְׁבַּע *to swear*, with בְּ *by*, לְ *to*, any thing or any one; with acc. *to promise with an oath*, comp. Ge. 50. 24. Hiph. I. *to cause to swear*.—II. *to adjure charge solemnly*.

שֶׁבַע (*oath*) pr. name—I. of two men, 2 Sa. 20. 1; 1 Ch. 5. 13.—II. of a town in the tribe of Simeon, Jos. 19. 2.—III. see under בְּאֵר.—IV. **שִׁבְעָה** Ge. 26. 33, i. q. בְּאֵר שֶׁבַע.

שְׁבֻעָה, שְׁבוּעָה fem. dec. 10.—I. *an oath*.—II. *oath of imprecation, curse*.

אֱשְׁבֵּעַ (*adjuration*) pr. name masc. 1 Ch. 4. 21.

שֶׁבַע noun masc. sing. . . . . שבע
שֶׁבַע for שֶׁבַע (§ 35. r. 2) pr. n. in compos. בְּאֵר שֶׁבַע באר
שָׂבֵעַ וְ adj. masc. sing. dec. 5 a . . . . שבע
שְׁבַע[a] וּ, שֶׁבַע וּ' { num. card., constr. of שֶׁבַע (§ 35. rem. 7); וּ bef. (:), for the form וְשֶׁבַע comp. וְשָׂדֶה, וְזָהָב } שבע
שְׂבַע[ll] וּ'‎ Kal imp. or adj. m. s., con. of שָׂבֵעַ d. 5 a; וּ id. שבע
שְׁבֻעַ[b] noun masc. sing., constr. of שָׁבוּעַ dec. 3 a שבע
שֹׂבַע[c] noun masc. sing. dec. 6 c (§ 35. rem. 5) . שבע
שָׂבְעָה[d] וְ' Kal pret. 3 pers. sing. fem. . . . שבע
שָׂבְעָה[e] noun fem. sing. (no pl.) . . . שבע
שְׂבֵעָה[f] adj. fem. sing., from שָׂבֵעַ masc. . שבע
שְׁבֻעָה[g] defect. for שְׁבוּעָה (q. v.) . . . שבע
שִׁבְעָה וְ' num. card. masc., from שֶׁבַע fem. . שבע
שָׂבְעוּ[h] וְ', שָׂבֵעוּ[i] } Kal pret. 3 pers. pl. (§ 8. rem. 7) . שָׂבַע
שָׁבֻעוֹת[k] noun masc. pl. abs. from שָׁבוּעַ (§ 32. rem. 1) שבע
שְׁבֻעוֹת id. constr. st. (Eze. 45. 21); or pl. of שְׁבוּעָה שבע
שְׁבֻעֵי[l] Kal part. pass. pl. constr. masc. [from שָׁבוּעַ] dec. 3 a . . . . . שבע
שָׁבֻעִים[m] וְ' noun masc., pl. of שָׁבוּעַ (§ 32. rem. 1) שבע
שְׂבֵעִים[n] adj. masc., pl. of שָׂבֵעַ dec. 5 a . . שבע
שְׁבֻעַיִם[o] noun masc., du. of שָׁבוּעַ dec. 3 a . שבע
שִׁבְעִים וְ' num. card. com., pl. of שֶׁבַע fem. . שבע
שָׂבְעֲךָ[p] noun masc. sing., suff. 2 pers. sing. masc. from שֹׂבַע dec. 6 c (§ 35. rem. 5) . . . שבע
שִׁבְעָנָה[q] num. i. q. שִׁבְעָה . . . . . . שבע
שָׂבָעְנוּ[r] Kal pret. 1 pers. pl. . . . . . שבע
שַׂבְּעֵנוּ[s] Piel imp. sing. masc. [שַׂבַּע], suff. 1 pers. pl. שבע
שָׂבַעְתָּ וְ', שָׂבָעְתָּ[t] } Kal pret. 2 pers. sing. masc. (§ 8. rem. 7) . . . . . } שבע
שָׂבַעַתְּ[u] id. pret. 2 pers. sing. fem. . . . שבע

שְׁבֻעֹת[oo] defect. for שְׁבוּעוֹת (q. v.) . . . שבע
שְׁבֻעַת[x] וּ' defect. for שְׁבוּעַת (q. v.) . . שבע
שְׁבֻעֹת[y] pl. c. of שָׁבוּעַ, see שְׁבֻעוֹת . . . שבע
שִׁבְעַת וְ' num. card. masc., constr. of שִׁבְעָה from שֶׁבַע fem. . . . . . . שבע
שִׁבְעַת[z] noun fem. sing., constr. of שִׁבְעָה . . שבע
שָׂבַעְתִּי[a] וְ'[b] Kal pret. 1 pers. sing. . . . . שבע
שִׁבְעָתַיִם[c] Kh. שִׁבְעָתַיִם q. v.; K. שָׁבְעָתָם, num. [prop. fr. שִׁבְעַת i. q. שִׁבְעָה] with suff. 3 pers. pl. m. שבע
שִׁבְעָתַיִם, שִׁבְעָתָיִם } du. of שִׁבְעָה num. . . . . שבע
שָׂבְעָתֵךְ[d] noun fem. s., suff. 2 p. s. fem. fr. שָׂבְעָה (no pl.) שבע
שְׂבַעְתֶּם וּ Kal pret. 2 pers. pl. masc.; וּ, for וְ, conv. שבע

שָׁבַץ Root not used; Syr. *to mingle, interweave*; Arab. (conj. V) *to be interwoven, intricate* (Gesenius, Winer, and others), only Pi. *to work* or *weave in checker-work*, Ex. 28. 39; Eng. vers. "embroider." Pu. *to be set, enchased*, of precious stones, Ex. 28. 20.

שָׁבָץ masc. *perplexity, terror*, 2 Sa. 1. 9; others, *giddiness*; according to the Rabbins, *the cramp*.

מִשְׁבֶּצֶת fem. only pl. מִשְׁבְּצוֹת.—I. *textures, cloth interwoven* or *embroidered* with gold threads, Ps. 45. 14.—II. *settings* or *bezels* for precious stones.

תַּשְׁבֵּץ masc. *checker-work* or *embroidery*, Ex. 28. 4.

שִׁבַּצְתָּ[e] וְ Piel pret. 2 pers. sing. masc. . . שבץ

[שְׁבַק] *to leave*. Ithpe. *to be left*, Da. 2. 44.

שׁוֹבֵק (*forsaking*) pr. name masc. Ne. 10. 21.

יִשְׁבָּק (id.) pr. name of a son of Abraham by Keturah.

שְׁבֻקוּ[f] Chald. Peal imp. pl. masc. . . . שבק

[שָׂבַר] *to view, examine*, with בְּ, Ne. 2. 13, 15. Pi. *to look, wait for, hope*, with אֶל, לְ.

שֵׂבֶר masc. dec. 6 b, *hope*, Ps. 119. 116; 146. 5.

שָׁבַר fut. יִשְׁבֹּר.—I. *to break, break in pieces*; metaph. *to break, quench* the thirst, Ps. 104. 11; *to break, afflict* the heart.—II. *to tear*, as a wild beast.—III. *to break down, destroy*.—IV. *to define, assign*, with עַל *to* or *for*, Job 38. 10.—V. (denom. from שֶׁבֶר q. v.) *to buy* or *sell corn*. Niph. pass. of Kal, Nos. I, II & III. Pi. שִׁבֵּר, שַׁבֵּר (§ 10. rem. 1) *to break, shiver in pieces*. Hiph. I. *to cause to break through*, of the fœtus, Is. 66. 9.—II. *to sell corn*. Hoph. *to be broken, afflicted, distressed*, Je. 8. 21.

---

[a] 1 Ki. 14. 21. [b] Ge. 29. 27, 28. [c] Ps. 16. 11. [d] Jer. 46. 10. [e] Is. 56. 11. [f] Pr. 27. 7. [g] Nu. 30. 3. [h] Is. 9. 19. [i] Ho. 13. 6. [k] De. 16. 9, 10. [l] Eze. 21. 28. [ll] Pr. 20. 13. [m] Da. 9. 25. [n] 1 Sa. 2. 5. [o] Le. 12. 5. [oo] Ex. 34. 22. [p] De. 23. 25. [q] Job 42. 13. [r] Ps. 123. 3. [s] Ps. 90. 14. [t] Hab. 2. 16. [u] Eze. 16. 28, 29. [x] Zec. 8. 17. [y] Je. 5. 24. [z] Eze. 16. 49. [a] Is. 1. 11. [b] Job 7. 4. [c] 2 Sa. 21. 9. [d] Eze. 16. 28. [e] Ex. 28. 39. [f] Da. 4. 12, 20.

שֶׁבֶר masc. dec. 6 b (in pause שָׁבֶר, from שֶׁבֶר = שֶׁבֶר § 35. rem. 2).—I. *a breaking, breach, fracture;* metaph. *sorrow, vexation, calamity.*—II. (prop. *definition,* comp. Kal. No. IV) *solution, interpretation,* Ju. 7. 15.—III. *destruction, ruin.*—IV. *terror,* Job 41. 17.

שֶׁבֶר masc. dec. 6 a (with suff. שִׁבְרוֹ), *grain, corn.* Etym. uncertain.

שִׁבָּרוֹן masc. dec. 3 c.—I. *breaking, pain,* Eze. 21. 11.—II. *destruction, ruin,* Je. 17. 18.

מַשְׁבֵּר masc. *matrix;* constr. מִשְׁבַּר (§ 36. r. 1).

מִשְׁבָּר masc. dec. 2 b, *waves, breakers.*

שָׁבָר[a] Kal pret. 3 pers. s. masc. for שָׁבַר (§ 8. r. 7) שבר

שָׁבֶר[b] for שֶׁבֶר (q. v.) Seg. noun masc., see שֶׁבֶר under the R. . . . . . שבר

שַׁבֵּר[c] וְ Piel inf. constr. . . . . . שבר

שֶׁבֶר[d] noun masc. sing. dec. 6 b . . . שבר

שֶׁבֶר וְ, וְ/ noun masc. sing. (suff. שִׁבְרִי) d. 6 a; also pr. name; for וְ see lett. ו . . שבר

שְׁבֹר[e] Kal imp. sing. masc. . . . . שבר

שִׁבַּר / שִׁבֵּר[f] וְ/ } Piel pret. 3 pers. sing. masc. (§ 15. rem. 1) . . . . . } שבר

שֹׁבֵר Kal part. act. sing. masc. dec. 7 b . . שבר

שֹׁבֵר Kal part. act. sing. masc. . . . שבר

שָׁבְרָה[g] id. pret. 3 pers. sing. fem. . . . שבר

שְׁבָרָהּ[h] וּ id. pret. 3 pers. sing. masc., suff. 3 pers. sing. fem.; וּ, for וְ, conv. . . . שבר

שִׁבְרָהּ[i] noun masc. sing., suff. 3 pers. sing. fem. from שֶׁבֶר dec. 6 b . . . . שבר

שָׁבְרוּ[k] Kal pret. 3 pers. pl. . . . . שבר

שִׁבְרוֹ noun masc. sing., suff. 3 pers. sing. masc. from שֶׁבֶר or שֵׁבֶר dec. 6 b . . . שבר

שִׁבְרוֹ[l] noun masc. sing., suff. 3 pers. sing. masc. from [שֵׁבֶר] dec. 6 b . . . . שבר

שִׁבְּרוּ[m] / שִׁבְּרוּ } Piel pret. 3 pers. pl. (comp. § 8. rem. 7) שבר

שִׁבְּרוּ[n] Piel pret. 3 pers. pl. . . . . שבר

שִׁבְרוּ[o] וְ/ Kal imp. pl. masc. . . . . שבר

שִׁבָּרוֹן[p] noun masc. sing. dec. 3 c . . . שבר

שִׁבְרִי[q] noun masc. sing., suff. 1 pers. sing. from שֶׁבֶר dec. 6 b . . . . . שבר

שְׁבָרֶיהָ[r] id. pl., suff. 3 pers. sing. fem. . . . שבר

שֹׁבְרִים[s] Kal part. act. masc., pl. of שֹׁבֵר dec. 7 b שבר

שְׁבָרֵךְ[t] id. pret. 3 pers. s. masc., suff. 2 pers. s. fem. שבר

שִׁבְרֵךְ noun masc. sing., suff. 2 pers. sing. fem. from שֶׁבֶר dec. 6 b . . . . שבר

שִׁבְרְךָ[u] id., suff. 2 pers. sing. masc. . . . שבר

שִׁבְרָם[x] noun masc. s., suff. 3 pers. pl. m. fr. שֶׁבֶר d. 6 a שבר

שְׁבָרֵם[y] Kal imp. sing. masc., suff. 3 pers. pl. masc. שבר

שָׁבַרְתָּ[z] / שָׁבַרְתָּ[a] וְ } id. pret. 3 pers. s. m., acc. shifted by conv. וְ (§ 8. rem. 7) . . } שבר

שִׁבַּרְתָּ Piel pret. 2 pers. sing. masc. . . . שבר

שָׁבַרְתִּי[b] / שָׁבַרְתִּי / וְ שָׁבַרְתִּי } Kal pret. 1 pers. sing., acc. shifted by conv. וְ (§ 8. rem. 7) . . } שבר

שִׁבַּרְתִּי[c] Piel pret. 1 pers. sing. . . . שבר

שִׁבַּרְתֶּם[d] וְ Piel pret. 2 pers. pl. masc. . . . שבר

שָׁבַשׁ. Chald. Ithpa. *to be perplexed,* Da. 5. 9.

שֶׁבְּשִׁפְלֵנוּ[e] preff. בְּ & שֶׁ) (noun masc. sing., suff. 1 pers. pl. from שֵׁפֶל dec. 6 b . . . שפל

שָׁבַת fut. יִשְׁבֹּת, יִשְׁבַּת.—I. *to rest* from labour, with מִן; of land, *to lie uncultivated.*—II. *to cease, desist,* with מִן & inf., from doing any thing.—III. *to cease, be interrupted,* Ne. 6. 3.—IV. *to cease to be, have an end.*—V. with שַׁבָּת *to keep the sabbath,* Le. 23. 32. Niph. *to cease, have an end.* Hiph. I. *to make* or *let rest* from labour; of work, *to intermit.*—II. *to restrain, still,* Ps. 8. 3.—III. *to cause to cease* from doing any thing, with מִן, לְבִלְתִּי & inf.—IV. *to make to cease, to interrupt, put an end to.*—V. *to put away, remove.*

שֶׁבֶת masc. dec. 6 a (with suff. שִׁבְתּוֹ).—I. *a ceasing, cessation.*—II. *interruption, loss of time,* Ex. 21. 19.

שַׁבָּת com. (constr. שַׁבַּת, with suff. שַׁבַּתּוֹ; pl. שַׁבָּתוֹת, constr. שַׁבְּתוֹת) *day of rest, sabbath;* שַׁבַּת שָׁנִים *a sabbath of years,* every seventh year.

שַׁבָּתוֹן masc. id.; שַׁבַּת שַׁבָּתוֹן *a great sabbath.*

שַׁבְּתַי (*sabbath-born*) pr. name of a man.

מִשְׁבָּת m. pl. מִשְׁבַּתֶּיהָ *destruction, ruin,* La. 1. 7.

שָׁבַת[f] וְ Kal pret. 3 pers. sing. fem. for שָׁבָה, (comp. § 8. rem. 3 & § 24. rem. 1) שוב

שָׁבֶת[g] for שֶׁבֶת Seg. n. [as if from שֶׁבֶת § 35. rem. 2 & 3, but see under the R.] . שבת

שַׁבָּת וְ/ noun com. sing. (see the inflexion of this word in its place under the R.) . שבת

שַׁבַּת id., constr. st. . . . . . שבת

שַׁבְתָּ[h] / וְ שַׁבְתָּ } Kal pret. 2 pers. sing. masc.; acc. shifted by conv. וְ (comp. § 8. rem. 7) } שוב

שֶׁבֶת Kal inf. constr. (suff. שִׁבְתִּי § 35. rem. 3) d. 13 ישב

שֶׁבֶת[i] noun masc. sing. (suff. שִׁבְתּוֹ) dec. 6 a שבת

---

a Ps. 105. 16. b Pr. 17. 19. c Ex. 23. 24. d Am. 6. 6. e Ps. 10. 15. f Ex. 9. 25. g Ps. 69. 21. h Is. 30. 14. i Is. 30. 13. k Je. 5. 5. l Ps. 146. 5. m 2 Ch. 28. 17. n Est. 9. 1. o Ge. 42. 2. p Je. 17. 18. q Je. 10. 19. r Ps. 60. 4. s Ge. 47. 14. t Eze. 27. 26. u Eze. 32. 9. x Ge. 42. 26. y Je. 17. 18. z Je. 28. 13. a Je. 19. 10. b Eze. 30. 21. c Ps. 119. 166. d De. 12. 3. e Ps. 136. 23. f Eze. 46. 17. g Is. 30. 7. h Ps. 85. 2. i Pr. 20. 3.

שַׁבְּתָה[a] / שָׁבְתָה[b] } וְ Kal pret. 3 pers. sing. fem. (§ 8. rem. 7) שבת
שַׁבַּתָּהּ[c] וְ noun com. sing., suff. 3 pers. sing. fem. from שַׁבָּת (q. v.) . . . . שבת
שִׁבְתָּהּ[d] Kal inf. (שֶׁבֶת), suff. 3 pers. sing. fem. dec. 13 (§ 35. rem. 3) . . . . ישב
שָׁבְתוּ[e] Kal pret. 3 pers. pl. [for שָׁבְתוּ § 8. rem. 7] שבת
שִׁבְתּוֹ[f] וְ noun masc. sing., suff. 3 pers. sing. masc. from שֶׁבֶת dec. 6a . . . . שבת
שִׁבְתּוֹ Kal inf. (שֶׁבֶת), suff. 3 pers. sing. masc. dec. 13 (§ 35. rem. 3) . . . . ישב
שַׁבָּתוֹן noun masc. sing. . . . . . . שבת
שַׁבָּתוֹת[g] noun com. pl. abs. from שַׁבָּת (q. v.) . שבת
שַׁבְּתוֹתַי id. pl., suff. 1 pers. sing. . . . . שבת
שַׁבְּתוֹתֶיהָ[h] id. pl., suff. 3 pers. sing. fem. . . שבת
שַׁבְּתַי וְ pr. name masc. . . . . . שבת
שַׁבְתִּי / שַׁבְתִּי } Kal pret. 1 pers. sing.; acc. shifted by conv. וְ (§ 8. rem. 7) . . . שוב
שַׁבְתִּי[i] וְ for יָשַׁבְתִּי Kal pret. 1 pers. sing. (comp. רֵד for יְרַד) . . . . . . ישב
שַׁבְתִּי[k] וָ Kal pret. 1 pers. sing.; for וָ see lett. ו שיב
שִׁבְתִּי Kal inf. (שֶׁבֶת), suff. 1 p. s. d. 13 (§ 35. r. 3) ישב
שִׁבְתְּךָ / שִׁבְתֵּךְ } וְ id. with suff. 2 pers. sing. masc. . ישב
שַׁבַּתְּכֶם[l] noun com. sing., suff. 2 pers. pl. masc. from שַׁבָּת (q. v.) . . . . . . שבת
שַׁבְתֶּם וְ Kal pret. 2 pers. pl. masc. . . . שוב
שִׁבְתָּם Kal inf. (שֶׁבֶת), suff. 3 pers. pl. masc. dec. 13 (§ 35. rem. 3) . . . . ישב
שַׁבְּתֹת n. com. pl., constr. of שַׁבָּתוֹת, fr. שַׁבָּת (q. v.) שבת
שַׁבְּתֹתַי id. pl., suff. 1 pers. sing. . . . שבת
שַׁבְּתֹתֶיהָ id. pl., suff. 3 pers. sing. fem. . . שבת

[שָׂגָא] Kal not used; i. q. שָׂגָה *to be* or *become great*. Hiph. I. *to make great*, with לְ, Job 12. 23.—II. *to magnify, laud*, Job 36. 24.
שְׂגָא Chald. *to become great, to increase*.
שַׂגִּיא masc. *great*.
שַׂגִּיא Chald. masc., שַׂגִּיאָה fem. dec. 8a, adj.—I. *great*.—II. *much, many*.—III. adv. *greatly*.

שָׁגָא Root not used; i. q. שָׁגָה *to err*.
שְׁגִיאָה fem. dec. 10, *error, sin through ignorance*, Ps. 19. 13. Also
שָׁגֵא (*erring*) pr. name masc. 1 Ch. 11. 34.

[שָׂגַב] I. *to be lifted, raised up*, Job 5. 11.—II. *to be high, inaccessible*, De. 2. 36. Niph. I. *to be high*, Pr. 18. 11.—II. *to be exalted*.—III. *to be high, secure, safe*, Pr. 18. 10.—IV. *to be high, difficult to comprehend*, Ps. 139. 6. Pi. I. *to raise, set in security*.—II. *to make powerful, to strengthen*, Is. 9. 10. Pu. pass. of Pi. No. I, Pr. 29. 25. Hiph. *to be exalted*, Job 36. 22.
שְׂגוּב (*elevated*) pr. name masc.—I. 1 Ch. 2. 21, 22.—II. 1 Ki. 16. 34, K., שְׂגִיב Kh.
מִשְׂגָּב masc. dec. 8a.—I. *hill, rock, strong place*.—II. *refuge*.—III. pr. name of a town in Moab, Je. 48. 1.
שָׂגְבָה[m] Kal pret. 3 pers. sing. fem. . . . שגב
שָׂגְבוּ[n] id. pret. 3 pers. pl. . . . . . שגב

שָׁגַג[o] (§ 8. rem. 7) *to err, commit an error*; inf. שַׁג, Ge. 6. 3.
שְׁגָגָה fem. d. 11c, *error, sin through ignorance*.
שֹׁגֵג Kal part. act. sing. masc. . . . שגג
שְׁגָגָה noun fem. sing. dec. 11c . . . שגג
שִׁגְגָתוֹ[p] id., suff. 3 pers. sing. masc. . . שגג
שִׁגְגָתָם[q] id., suff. 3 pers. pl. masc. . . . שגג

[שָׂגָה] *to become great*. Hiph. *to increase*, Ps. 73. 12.

[שָׁגָה] I. *to wander, go astray*.—II. *to err, sin through ignorance*. Hiph. I. *to cause to go astray*.—II. *to let err*, Ps. 119. 10.
שִׁגָּיוֹן masc. dec. 3c, *a psalm*, perh. composed on an occasion of *wandering and persecution*, or apostacy from God, Ps. 7. 1; Hab. 3. 1.
מִשְׁגֶּה masc. *error, mistake*, Ge. 43. 12.
שֹׁגֶה Kal part. act. sing. masc. dec. 9a . שגה
שָׁגוּ[r] Kal pret. 3 pers. pl. . . . . שגה
שְׂגוּב וּ pr. name masc.; וּ bef. (:) . . שגב

שָׁגַח. Hiph. *to look*.
שַׂגִּיא Heb. & Chald. adj. masc. sing. . . שגא
שְׁגִיאוֹת[s] noun fem., pl. of [שְׁגִיאָה] dec. 10 . שגא
שַׂגִּיאָן Ch. adj. f. pl. [of שַׂגִּיאָה or שַׂגִּיאָא fr. שַׂגִּיא m.] שגא
שִׁגָּיוֹן[t] noun masc. sing. dec. 3c . . . שגה
שִׁגְיֹנוֹת[u] pl. of the preced. . . . . שגה
שָׁגִיתִי Kal pret. 1 pers. sing. . . . . שגה

[שָׁגַל] *to lie with a woman*. Niph. & Pu. pass. Hence
שֵׁגַל[x] Heb. & Chald. fem. *a queen* . . שגל
שֶׁגָּלְשׁוּ pref. שֶׁ) Kal pret. 3 pers. pl. . . גלש
שֻׁגַּלְתְּ[y] Pual pret. 2 pers. sing. fem. (K. שֻׁכַּבְתְּ) שגל

[a] 2 Ch. 36. 21. [b] Le. 25. 2. [c] Ho. 2. 13. [d] Ru. 2. 7. [e] La. 5. 14. [f] Ex. 21. 19. [g] Le. 23. 15. [h] 2 Ch. 36. 21. [i] Ps. 23. 6. [k] 1 Sa. 12. 2. [l] Le. 23. 32. [m] De. 2. 36. [n] Job 5. 11. [o] Le. 5. 18. [p] Le. 5. 18. [q] Nu. 15. 25. [r] Is. 28. 7. [s] Ps. 19. 13. [t] Ps. 7. 1. [u] Hab. 3. 1. [x] Ps. 45. 10. [y] Je. 3. 2.

שֵׁגְלָתֵהּ[a] Ch. noun fem. pl., suff. 3 pers. sing. m. fr. שֵׁגַל שגל

שֵׁגְלָתָךְ[b] Ch. id. pl., suff. 2 pers. sing. fem. . שגל

שֶׁגַּם[c] pref. ·שֶׁ)(conj. . . . . . . גמם

שֶׁגָּמַלְתְּ[d] pref. id.)(Kal pret. 2 pers. sing. fem. . גמל

שָׁגַע. Pu. part. מְשֻׁגָּע *maddened, mad;* also applied contemptuously to prophets. Hithp. *to act, behave like a madman,* 1 Sa. 21. 15, 16.

שִׁגָּעוֹן masc. *madness; impetuosity,* 2 Ki. 9. 20.

שֶׁגֶר, שְׁגַר[e] (constr. § 35. rem. 7) masc. *the young, offspring.* Chald. שְׁגַר *to cast forth, eject.*

שַׁד[f] noun m. s., du. שָׁדַיִם, c. שְׁדֵי d. 2 (§ 31. r. 5) שדה

שֹׁד ו׳, וְ׳ noun masc. sing.; for וְ see lett. ו שדד

שֹׁד[g] וְ noun masc. sing. (i. q. שַׁד) . . . שדה

שָׁדַד Kal not used; coll. with the Arab. *to be straight, even.* Pi. *to harrow.*

שִׂדִּים (*plains*) pr. name, עֵמֶק הַשִּׂדִּים, the plain of the cities, Sodom and Gomorrah.

[שָׁדַד] pl. שָׁדְּדוּ ,שַׁדּוּ, fut. with suff. יְשָׁדֵּם ,יְשָׁדְּדֵם (§ 18. rem. 13 & 15).—I. *to treat with violence, to oppress.* —II. *to attack, invade.*—III. *to plunder;* part. שֹׁדֵד *a plunderer.*—IV. *to lay waste, destroy,* e. g. a land; part. pass. שָׁדוּד *destroyed, dead,* of a person, Ju. 5. 27. Niph. *to be laid waste.* Pi. *to spoil, waste, ruin.* Pu. pass. Po. i. q. Pi. Ho. 10. 2. Hoph. *to be spoiled, laid waste.*

שֹׁד ,שׁוֹד masc.—I. *violence, oppression.*—II. *wealth obtained by violence, extortion,* Am. 3. 10.— III. *devastation, ruin, destruction.*

שִׁדָּה fem. dec. 10, prop. *mistress, lady,* hence, *a wife,* Ec. 2. 8 (Arab. שידה *mistress*); others *female cupbearers* (comp. Chald. שְׁדָא *to pour out*). Eng. vers. *"musical instruments"* (Arab. שדא, שדו *to sing*).

שַׁדַּי masc. pl. *The Almighty; Omnipotent* (Arab. שדיד *strong, vehement*).

אַשְׁדּוֹד (*strong-hold*) pr. name, *Ashdod,* one of the principal cities of the Philistines. Gent. n. אַשְׁדּוֹדִי *Ashdodite,* fem. ־ִית *women of Ashdod;* the latter also as an adv., *in the language of Ashdod,* Ne. 13. 23.

שֹׁדֵד Kal part. act. sing. masc. dec. 7b . . שדד

שֻׁדַּד[h], שֻׁדַּד } Pual pret. 3 pers. sing. masc. . . שדד

שָׁדְדָה[i], שֻׁדְּדָה[k], שֻׁדָּדָה } id. pret. 3 pers. sing. fem. (§ 10. rem. 5, comp. § 8. rem. 7) . . . . } שדד

שָׁדְדוּ[l] וְ Kal pret. 3 pers. pl. . . . . שדד

שָׁדְדוּ[m] וְ id. imp. pl. masc. [for שֹׁדּוּ § 18. rem. 13] שדד

שֻׁדְּדוּ[n], שֻׁדָּדוּ[o] } Pual pret. 3 pers. pl. (comp. § 8. rem. 7) שדד

שֹׁדְדֵי[p], שֹׁדְדִים } Kal part. act. pl. masc., constr. and abs. from שֹׁדֵד dec. 7b . . . . } שדד

שֻׁדַּדְנוּ Pual pret. 1 pers. pl. [for שֻׁדַּדְנוּ] . . שדד

שָׂדֶה וְ׳ masc. dec. 9b (pl. שָׂדוֹת, constr. שְׂדֵי, שְׂדוֹת). —I. *plain, level tract of country;* שְׂדֵה אֲרָם *the plain of Syria,* i. e. Mesopotamia.—II. *field, piece of cultivated ground.*—III. collect. *the fields, the country.*—IV. *country, territory.*

שָׂדַי masc. poet. for שָׂדֶה *plain, field.*

שָׁדָה Root not used; Arab. שדא *to moisten, irrigate;* Chald. *to cast, shoot, pour out.*

שַׁד masc. (du. שָׁדַיִם, constr. שְׁדֵי § 35. rem. 1), *the breast, teat,* spoken of men and animals.

שֹׁד masc. idem. Job 24. 9; Is. 60. 16.

שְׁדֵיאוּר (*shedding* or *darting light*) pr. name masc. Nu. 1. 5; 2. 10.

שָׂדָהּ[q] id. with suff. 3 pers. sing. fem. . . שדה

שְׂדֵה[r], שְׂדֵה } id. constr. st. (for the first form comp. (וּשְׂבַע, וְזָהָב . . . } שדה

שִׁדָּה[s] noun fem. sing. dec. 10 . . . שדד

שָׂדֵהוּ noun m. s., suff. 3 pers. sing. m. fr. שָׂדֶה d. 9b שדה

שָׁדוֹד[t] Kal inf. constr. . . . . . שדד

שָׁדוּד id. part. pass. sing. masc. . . . שדד

שַׁדּוּנִי[u] id. pret. 3 pers. pl., suff. 1 pers. sing. . שדד

שְׁדוּפֹת[w] וּ Kal part. pass. pl. fem. [from שָׁדוּף masc.] שדף

שָׂדוֹת וְ׳[y] noun masc. with pl. fem. term., abs. st., from שָׂדֶה dec. 9b . . . . שדה

שִׁדּוֹת[z] וְ noun fem., pl. of שִׁדָּה dec. 10 . . שדד

שְׂדוֹתֵיהֶם[a] noun masc. with pl. fem. term. and suff. 3 pers. pl. masc. from שָׂדֶה dec. 9b . שדה

שְׂדוֹתֵיכֶם[b] id. pl. fem., suff. 2 pers. pl. masc. . שדה

שָׂדַי, שָׂדָי } noun masc. sing., poet. for שָׂדֶה . שדה

שָׁדַי[c] וְ׳ n. m. pl., suff. 1 p. s. fr. שַׁד d. 2 (§ 31. r. 5) שדה

שַׁדַּי וְ׳ noun masc. [שַׁד] with the pl. term. ־ַי שדד

שָׂדִי[d] noun masc. s., suff. 1 pers. s. fr. שָׂדֶה d. 9b שדה

שְׂדֵי[e] וּ׳ id. pl. constr. [of שָׂדִים] comp. שָׂדוֹת שדה

שְׁדֵי n. m. du., constr. of שָׁדַיִם, fr. שַׁד d. 2 (§ 31. r. 5) שדה

---

[a] Da. 5. 2, 3.
[b] Da. 5. 23.
[c] Ec. 1. 17; 2. 15; 8. 14.
[d] Ps. 137. 8.
[e] Ex. 13. 12.
[f] La. 4. 3.
[g] Is. 60. 16.
[h] Je. 10. 20.
[i] Na. 3. 7.
[k] Je. 48. 1.
[l] Eze. 32. 12.
[m] Je. 49. 28.
[n] Zec. 11. 2.
[o] Je. 4. 20.
[p] Ob. 5.
[q] 2 Ki. 8. 3, 5.
Le. 25. 34.
[s] Ec. 2. 8.
[t] Mi. 2. 4.
[u] Ps. 17. 9.
[w] Ge. 41. 6.
[y] Je. 32. 15.
[z] Ec. 2. 8.
[a] Je. 8. 10.
[b] 1 Sa. 8. 14.
[c] Ca. 1. 13; 8. 10.
[d] Je. 32. 7, 8.
[e] 2 Sa. 1. 21.

שְׁדֵיאוּר pr. name masc. . . . . . שדה

[a]שָׁדֶיהָ n. m. du., suff. 3 p. s. f. fr. שַׁד d. 2 (§ 31. r. 5) שדה

[b]שְׁדֵיהֶן id. du., suff. 3 pers. pl. fem. . . . שדה

שָׁדַיִךְ וְ' id. du., suff. 2 pers. sing. fem. . . . שדה

[c]שָׂדֶיךָ noun m. pl., suff. 2 p. s. m. fr. שָׂדֶה d. 9b שדה

[d]שָׁדַיִם, שָׁדָיִם וְ' } noun masc., du. of שַׁד dec. 2 (§ 31. rem. 5) . . . . } שדה

[e]שַׁדִּין pref. ·שַׁ) Kh. דִּין q. v.; K. דּוּן n. m. s., see דון

[f]שָׂדֵינוּ noun masc. pl., suff. 1 pers. pl. fr. שָׂדֶה d. 9b שדה

[g]שָׂדְךָ, שָׂדֶךָ } id. sing., suff. 2 pers. sing. masc. . . שדה

שָׁדַם Root not used; signification uncertain. Hence

שְׁדֵמָה fem. dec. 11c (§ 42. rem. 4).—I. *blasted corn*, i. q. שְׁדֵפָה Is. 37. 27.—II. pl. שְׁדֵמוֹת *fields; espec. corn fields*; also *vineyards*, De. 32. 32.

[h]שָׁדֵּם וְ Kh. וְשָׁדֵּם Kal pret. 3 pers. sing. masc. [שַׁד] with suff.; K. יְשָׁדֵּם fut. 3 pers. sing. masc. [יָשֹׁד], suff. 3 pers. pl. masc. (§ 18. r. 5) שדד

[i]שְׁדֵמָה וּ noun fem. sing. dec. 11c (§ 42. rem. 4); וּ bef. (:) . . . . . . שדם

[k]שַׁדְמוֹת id. pl., constr. st. . . . . . שדם

[l]שְׁדֵמוֹת וּ id. pl., abs. st.; וּ bef. (:) . . . שדם

[שָׁדַף] *to blight*, as the east wind corn, Ge. 41. 6, 23, 27. Hence the two following.

שְׁדֵפָה וּ fem. *blight* in corn, 2 Ki. 19. 26; וּ bef. (:) שדף

שִׁדָּפוֹן masc. the same . . . . . שדף

[m]שְׁדֻפוֹת Kal part. pass. pl. fem. [from שָׁדוּף masc.] שדף

שְׁדַר Chald. Ithpa. *to exert oneself*, Da. 6. 15.

אֶשְׁתַּדּוּר Chald. masc. *rebellion*, Ezr. 4. 15, 19.

שַׁדְרַךְ Chald. pr. name, *Shadrach*, given to Hananiah, one of Daniel's companions at the court of Babylon.

[n]שְׂדֵרֹת וּ noun f. pl. abs. [fr. שְׂדֵרָה]; וּ bef. (:) see סדר

[o]שַׂרְתָּ וְ Kal pret. 2 pers. sing. masc.; acc. shifted by conv. וְ (§ 8. rem. 7) . . . . שיר

[p]שְׂדֹתֶיהָ וּ noun masc. with pl. fem. term. & suff. 3 pers. sing. fem. from שָׂדֶה dec. 9; וּ bef. (:) שדה

[q]שְׂדֹתֵיהֶם id. pl., suff. 3 pers. pl. masc. . . . שדה

[r]שְׂדֹתֵינוּ וּ' id. pl., suff. 1 pers. pl.; וּ bef. (:) . . שדה

[s]שֵׂה וְ', שֶׂה וְ', וָ' } noun masc. s. constr. & abs. (§ 45); for וָ see lett. ו } שיה

[t]שֶׁהֲבֵאתִיו K., שֶׁהֲבִיאֹתִיו Kh. } pref. שֶׁ) Hiph. pret. 1 pers. sing., suff. 3 p. s. m. (§ 21. r. 13 & 14) } בוא

שָׂהֵד Root not used; Syr. & Chald. סְהֵד *to testify, bear witness*.

שָׂהֵד masc. dec. 5a, *a witness*.

שָׂהֲדוּ fem. (a Chald. & Syr. word, dec. 9b) *testimony*, Ge. 31. 47.

[שָׁהָה] prob. i. q. Arab. שהא *to forget, neglect*, De. 32. 18, but comp. שָׁיָה.

[u]שָׂהֲדוּתָא noun f. s. emph. [of שָׂהֲדוּ] comp. Ch. d. 9b שהד

[x]שָׂהֲדַי וְ better שָׂהֲדִי n. m. s., suff. 1 p. s. [fr. שָׂהֵד] שהד

[y]שֶׁהוּא pref. שֶׁ) pron. pers. 3 pers. sing. masc. . הוא

שֶׁהָיָה pref. id.) Kal pret. 3 pers. sing. masc. . היה

[z]שֶׁהָיוּ pref. id.) id. pret. 3 pers. pl. . . היה

[a]שֶׁהַיָּמִים preff. שֶׁ & ·הַ) noun m. pl., irr. of יוֹם (§ 45) יום

[b]שֶׁהִכָּה pref. שֶׁ) Hiph. pret. 3 pers. sing. masc. נכה

שֹׁהַם [c]וְ' masc.—I. *the onyx*, or *sardonyx*.—II. pr. name masc. 1 Ch. 24. 27.

[d]שֶׁהֵם, [e]שֶׁהֵם, [f]שֶׁהֵם־ } pref. שֶׁ or שֶׁ) pron. pers. masc. pl. הם

[g]שֶׁהַמֶּלֶךְ preff. שֶׁ & ·הַ) noun masc. sing. dec. 6a מלך

[h]שֶׁהַנְּחָלִים preff. id.) noun masc., pl. of נַחַל dec. 6d נחל

[i]שֶׁהַתַּקִּיף preff. id. (Kh. שֶׁהַ')) adj. masc. sing. . תקף

שׁוֹא Root not used; i. q. שָׁאָה, *to make a noise, crashing*; Arab. שׁא *to be evil*, comp. רָעַע, רוּעַ.

שׁוֹא masc. dec. 1a, *destruction*, Ps. 35. 17; Prof. Lee, *mischievous design*, or *raging*.

שׁוֹאָה fem. dec. 10.—I. *storm, tempest*.—II. *destruction, ruin*.—III. *ruins, desolate places*.

שָׁוְא masc.—I. *evil, iniquity, wickedness*.—II. *evil, calamity, destruction*.—III. *worthlessness, vanity*; לַשָּׁוְא *in vain*.—IV. *falsehood, lie*; שֵׁמַע שָׁוְא *false report*; לְשָׁוְא *in vain*.

שְׁוָא (*vanity*) pr. name masc.—I. 1 Ch. 2. 49.—II. 2 Sa. 20. 25, see שְׁוָיָה.

שַׁו masc. i. q. שָׁוְא, Job 15. 31, Keth.

שִׁיאֹן (*desolation, ruins*) pr. name of a city in Issachar, Jos. 19. 19.

מְשׁוֹאָה fem. *desolation*, Zep. 1. 15; also *desolate places, ruins*.

מַשּׁוּאוֹת fem. pl. *desolations*, Ps. 73. 18; 74. 3.

תְּשֻׁאָה fem. *noise, tumult, clamour*.

שָׁוְא וְ' noun masc. sing. . . . . שוא

שְׁוָא pr. name masc. . . . . . שוא

[a] Ho. 2. 4. [b] Eze. 23. 3. [c] 1 Ki. 2. 26. [d] Joel 2. 16. [e] Job 19. 29. [f] Mi. 2. 4. [g] Le. 25. 3. [h] Pr. 11. 3. [i] Is. 37. 27. [k] Is. 16. 8. [l] Hab. 3. 17. [m] Ge. 41. 23, 27. [n] 1 Ki. 6. 9. [o] De. 27. 2, 4. [p] Ne. 11. 30. [q] Ne. 5. 11. [r] Ne. 5. 3, 4, 5. [s] De. 14. 4. [t] Ca. 3. 4. [u] Ge. 31. 47. [x] Job 16. 19. [y] Ec. 2. 22. [z] Ec. 2. 7. [a] Ec. 7. 10. [b] Ps. 135. 8, 10. [c] Ex. 28. 20. [d] Ca. 6. 5. [e] La. 4. 9. [f] Ec. 3. 18. [g] Ca. 1. 12. [h] Ec. 1. 7. [i] Ec. 6. 10.

מְשׁוּבָה fem. dec. 10, *a returning, defection, apostacy*; as a concr. *rebellious, apostate*, Je. 3. 6, 8, 11, 12.
תְּשׁוּבָה fem. d. 10.—I. *a return*.—II. *an answer*.

שׁוּב	[d] וְ׳, וָ Kal inf. abs.; for וָ see lett. ו	שוב
שׁוֹב[e]	Kal inf. abs. for יָשׁוֹב	ישב
שׁוּב	[f] וְ׳, וָ Kal imp. s. m.; or inf. d. 1 a; for וָ see lett. ו	שוב
שׁוּבָאֵל	pr. name masc., see שְׁבוּאֵל	שבה
שׁוֹבָב[g]	וְ adj. masc. sing. dec. 2 b, also pr. name	שוב
שׁוֹבְבָה[h]	Pilel pret. 3 pers. sing. fem.	שוב
שׁוֹבָבִים[i]	adj. masc., pl. of שׁוֹבָב dec. 2 b	שוב
שׁוֹבְבִים[k]	K. שׁוֹבְבוּם Pil. pret. 3 pers. pl., suff. 3 pers. pl. masc., Kh. שׁוֹבְבִים (q. v.)	שוב
שׁוֹבַבְתִּיךָ[l]	וְ id. pret. 1 pers. s. with suff. 2 pers. s. m.	שוב
שׁוֹבְבָתֶךְ[m]	id. pret. 3 pers. sing. fem. (שׁוֹבְבָה), suff 2 pers. sing. fem. (§ 16. rem. 2)	שוב
שׁוּבָה	Kal imp. sing. masc. (שׁוּב) with parag. ה	שוב
שׁוּבוֹ	id. inf. (שׁוּב), suff. 3 pers. sing. masc. d. 1 a	שוב
שׁוּבוּ	[n] וְ, וָ id. imp. pl. masc.; for וָ see lett. ו	שוב
שׁוּבֵי[o]	id. part. pass. pl. constr. m. [fr. שׁוּב] d. 1 a	שוב
שׁוּבִי	id. imp. sing. fem.	שוב
שׁוּבִי	id. inf. (שׁוּב), suff. 1 pers. sing. dec. 1 a	שוב
שׁוֹבֵיהֶם	Kal part. act. pl. m., suff. 3 p. pl. m. fr. שֹׁבֶה d. 9 a	שבה
שׁוֹבֵינוּ[p]	id. pl. with suff. 1 pers. pl.	שבה
שׁוֹבַךְ / שׁוֹבַךְ	וְ} pr. name masc., see שׁוֹפַךְ under	שפך
שׁוֹבֶךְ[q]	noun masc. sing.	שבך
שׁוּבְךָ[r] / שׁוּבְךָ[s]	Kal inf. (שׁוּב), suff. 2 pers. sing. masc. dec. 1 a	שוב
שׁוֹבָל	וְ׳ pr. name masc.	שבל
שׁוֹבָל	pr. name masc.	שבל
שׁוּבֵנוּ[t]	Kal imp. sing. masc., suff. 1 pers. pl.	שוב
שׁוֹבֵק	pr. name masc.	שבק

שׁוּג Kal not used; i. q. סוּג *to hedge about*. Pilp. שִׂגְשֵׂג (§ 6. No. 4) *to hedge about*, Is. 17. 11; others *to cause to grow*, from שָׂנָא, שָׂנָה = שָׂנַג.

שׁוּג Root not used; i. q. שָׁגָה, שָׁגַג.
מְשׁוּגָה fem. dec. 10, *error*, Job 19. 4.

שׁוֹגִים[u]	Kal part. act. masc., pl. of שֹׁגֶה dec. 9 a	שגה

[שׁוּד] i. q. שָׁדַד *to lay waste*, Ps. 91. 6.
שֵׁד masc. dec. 1 a, *demon*. Syr. שארא id.

שׁוֹדֵד	Kal part. act. sing. masc. dec. 7 b	שדד

שָׁוָה[v] (Milêl bef. monos.)—I. *to be equal* in value, with בְּ.—II. *to countervail, be sufficient* for a damage, sc.

שׁוֹאָה	noun fem. sing. dec. 10	שוא
שׁוֹאֵג[a]	Kal part. act. sing. masc. dec. 7 b	שאג
שׁוֹאֵל[b]	Kal part. act. sing. masc. dec. 7 b	שאל
שׁוֹאֵף[c]	Kal part. act. sing. masc. dec. 7 b	שאף

שׁוּב fut. יָשׁוּב, יָשֹׁב, וַיָּשָׁב, ap. יָשֹׁב.—I. *to turn, turn back, return*, const. with מִן *from*, מֵאַחֲרֵי *from following*, אֶל *to*, any one; with לְ, ה (local) *to* a place. Trop. *to return*, to God, with עַד, אֶל, לְ, בְּ, and without addition, *to be converted*.—II. *to return, go back, be restored*, as a field to the former possessor; a thing to its former state.—III. *to turn away, cease, desist*, with מֵעַל, מֵאַחֲרֵי from any one.—IV. *to return to the doing of* any thing, joined with another verb, e. g. אָשׁוּבָה אֶרְעֶה *I will feed again*, Ge. 30. 31; comp. 2 Ki. 1. 11; Job 7. 7.—V. *to lead* or *bring back*. Pil. שׁוֹבֵב.—I. *to cause to return, bring back*, Je. 50. 19; trop. *to convert*, Is. 49. 5.—II. *to restore, renew*; with נֶפֶשׁ *to refresh*, Ps. 23. 3.—III. *to turn, take away*, Mi. 2. 4; trop. Is. 47. 10. Pul. part. *brought back*, Eze. 38. 8. Hiph. הֵשִׁיב.—I. *to cause to return, to bring* or *lead back*; hence *to drive back, repulse*; הֵ׳ חֵמָה *to turn away, avert anger*, also *to withdraw, appease anger*; הֵ׳ יָד *to withdraw the hand*; הֵ׳ פְּנֵי פ׳ *to turn away the face* of any one, to repulse him, deny his request; הֵ׳ נֶפֶשׁ *to restore life*, to revive, refresh; הֵ׳ רוּחַ *to draw breath*.—II. *to return, give back, restore*; hence *to requite*; הֵ׳ דָּבָר *to return word, to answer*, and so with מִלִּין, אֲמָרִים, and simply הֵשִׁיב *to answer*.—III. *to recall, revoke* a declaration.—IV. *to bring, pay* tribute, offering.—V. *to turn, direct, apply*; with הֵ׳ יָדוֹ עַל or אֶל־לֵב *to lay to heart, to consider*; עַל *to turn one's hand against* any one; with מֵעַל, מִן *to turn away from*. Hoph. הוּשַׁב *to be brought, led, given back*.

שׁוּבָה fem. *returning*, sc. to God, Is. 30. 15.
שִׁיבָה fem. dec. 10, *a return*, concr. *those that return*, Ps. 126. 1.
שׁוֹבָב masc.—I. adj. *turning away, rebellious*.—II. pr. name (*a*) of a son of David; (*b*) 1 Ch. 2. 18.
שׁוֹבֵב, f. שׁוֹבֵבָה adj. *rebellious*, Je. 31. 22; 49. 4.
יָשׁוּב (*turning himself*) pr. name masc.—I. Nu. 26. 24; patronym. יָשֻׁבִי.—II. Ezr. 10. 29.
יָשָׁבְעָם (*the people shall return*) pr. name of a man.
מְשׁוֹבָב (*restored*) pr. name masc. 1 Ch. 4. 34.

[a] Eze. 22. 25. [b] Mi. 7. 3. [c] Ec. 1. 5. [d] Je. 3. 1. [e] Je. 42. 10. [f] Pr. 3. 28. [g] Is. 57. 17. [h] Je. 8. 5. [i] Je. 3. 14, 22. [k] Je. 50. 6. [l] Eze. 38. 4. [m] Is. 47. 10. [n] Ex. 32. 27. [o] Mi. 2. 8. [p] Ps. 137. 3. [q] 2 Sa. 18. 9. [r] Ju. 6. 18. [s] Ge. 3. 19. [t] Ps. 85. 5. [u] Ps. 119. 118. [v] Job 33. 27.

to make it good, Est. 7. 4; hence, *to be sufficient, enough,* Est. 5. 13; impers. שָׁוֶה לִי *it satisfied me,* Job 33. 27; which latter Prof. Lee regards as a subst. *equity.*—III. *to be fitting, proper,* with לְ, Est. 3. 8.—IV. *to be like, to resemble,* with לְ. Pi. שִׁוָּה.—I. *to make level, even,* Is. 28. 25.—II. *to make similar, like,* Ps. 18. 34; 131. 2; also *to make oneself like,* Is. 38. 13, unless שִׁוִּיתִי, in this passage, stands for שִׁוַּעְתִּי (Prof. Lee).—III. *to put, set, place,* with עַל *to bestow upon.*—IV. *to put forth, yield,* fruit, Ho. 10. 1.—V. see Nithpa. Hiph. *to liken, compare,* La. 2. 13. Nithpa. נִשְׁתָּוָה (§ 6. No. 10) *to be compared, considered like,* Pr. 27. 15; others, *to be feared,* as the Ithp. signifies in the Chald.; and hence render the Pi. Job 30. 22, Kheth. *to terrify.*

שַׁוִּי or שַׁוִּא Ch. Pa. *to set, place,* with עִם *to place with, make equal with,* Da. 5. 21. Ithpa. *to be made into,* Da. 3. 29.

שָׁוֵה (*plain*) pr. name—I. of a valley north of Jerusalem.—II. שָׁוֵה קִרְיָתַיִם a plain near Kiriathaim in the tribe of Reuben, Ge. 14. 5.

יִשְׁוָה (*likeness, similarity*) pr. name m. Ge. 46. 17.

יִשְׁוִי (*like, similar*) pr. name masc.—I. Ge. 46. 17. —II. 1 Sa. 14. 49.

שָׁוֵה pr. name of a valley . . . . שוה

[a] שִׁוָּה Piel pret. 3 pers. sing. masc. . . . שוה

שֹׁוֶה Kal part. act. sing. masc. . . . שוה

[שׂוּחַ] *to meditate,* i. q. שִׂיחַ, Ge. 24. 63; others, *to walk,* or *to converse.*

[שׁוּחַ] I. *to sink down,* Pr. 2. 18.—II. *to be bowed down, depressed.*

שׁוּחַ (*pit*) pr. name of a son of Abraham by Keturah, Ge. 25. 2; 1 Ch. 1. 32. Patronym. שׁוּחִי, comp. Job 2. 11; 8. 1, &c.

שׁוּחָה fem.—I. *a pit.*—II. pr. name masc. 1 Ch. 4. 11, for which חוּשָׁה ver. 4.

שׁוּחָם (*pit-digger;* Simonis, *haste,* for חוּשָׁם) pr. name masc. Nu. 26. 24, called חֻשִׁים Ge. 46. 23.

שִׁיחָה fem. dec. 10, *a pit.*

שַׁחַת fem. (once with suff. שַׁחְתָּם).—I. *pit;* also a *pitfall,* metaph. for plot, treachery, destruction.—II. *dungeon,* Is. 51. 14.—III. *grave, sepulchre.* See also שָׁחַת.

יְשׁוֹחָיָה (whom *the Lord bows down*) pr. name masc. 1 Ch. 4. 36.

שׁוּחַ ן' pr. name masc. . . . . . שוח

[b] שׁוּחָה ו' noun fem. sing., also pr. name . . שוח

[c] שׁוֹחֵט Kh. שׁוֹחֵט q. v., K. שָׁחוּט (q. v.) . . שחט

שֹׁחֵט Kal part. act. sing. masc. dec. 7 b . . שחט

[שׂוּט] *to go* or *turn aside,* Ps. 40. 5.

שֵׂט, סֵט masc. dec. 1 a, *one who turns aside,* Ho. 5. 2; Ps. 101. 3.

I. [שׁוּט] I. *to row* (prop. *to lash* the water with oars, Arab. שׁאט *to whip*) only part. *rower,* Eze. 27. 8, 26. —II. *to go, run to and fro.* Pil. שׁוֹטֵט i. q. Kal No. II; metaph. *to run through* or *over* a book, i. e. to examine it thoroughly, Da. 12. 4; so most of the moderns, but not necessarily so. Hithpal. i. q. Pil. Je. 49. 3.

II. [שׁוּט] i. q. שָׁאַט *to contemn, despise,* Eze. 16. 57; 28. 24, 26.

שׁוֹט masc. d. 1 a, *a whip, scourge;* trop. *scourge, calamity.*

שַׁיִט masc.—I. *scourge,* Is. 28. 15, Kheth.—II. *oar, oars,* Is. 33. 21.

שֹׁטֵט masc. *scourge,* Jos. 23. 13.

מָשׁוֹט masc. *an oar,* Eze. 27. 29.

מִשּׁוֹט masc. dec. 1 b, id. Eze. 27. 6.

שׁוֹט noun masc. sing. dec. 1 a . . . . שוט

[d] שׁוּט Kal imp. sing. masc. . . . . שוט

[e] שׁוֹטְטוּ Pilel imp. pl. masc. . . . שוט

[f] שׁוֹטְנַי Kal part. act. pl. m., suff. 1 p. s. fr. שֹׂטֵן d. 7 b שטן

שׁוֹטֵף Kal part. act. sing. masc. dec. 7 b . שטף

[g] שַׁוִּי Ch. Pael pret. 3 pers. sing. masc. . שוה

שִׁוִּיתִי Piel pret. 1 pers. sing. . . . . שוה

[סוּךְ, שׂוּךְ] *to hedge in, to fence* (prop. with a thorn-hedge), Job 1. 10; Ho. 2. 8. Pil. id. Job 10. 11; others, *to twist, weave,* comp. Ps. 139. 13.

שׂוֹךְ m. d. 1 a, *a bough,* Ju. 9. 49. (Syr. & Ch. id.)

שׂוֹכָה fem. dec. 10, id. Ju. 9. 48.

שׂוֹכֹה, שׂוֹכוֹ (*hedge, fence*) pr. name of a town in Judah.

שׂוּכָתִי gent. noun, *Suchathite,* of an unknown place שׂוֹכָה, 1 Ch. 2. 55.

מְסוּכָה, מְשׂוּכָה fem. d. 10, *hedge, thorn-hedge.*

[h] שֹׁכֵב Kal part. act. sing. masc. dec. 7 b . שכב

שׂוֹכֹה ן' / שׂוֹכוֹ } pr. name of a place . . . שוך

[i] שׂוֹכֹה noun m. sing., suff. 3 pers. s. m. fr. [שׂוֹךְ] d. 1 a שוך

[a] Is. 28. 25. [b] Je. 2. 6. [c] Je. 9. 7. [d] 2 Sa. 24. 2. [e] Je. 5. 1. [f] Ps. 109. 29. [g] Da. 5, 21. [h] Eze. 4. 9. [i] Ju. 9. 49.

שׂוֹכַת[a] noun fem. sing., constr. of [שׂוֹכָה] dec. 10 . . . שׂוך

שׂוֹכָתִים gent. noun pl. [from שׂוֹכָה] . . . שׂוך

שׁוֹל masc. dec. 1 a, only found in the pl.—I. *train* of a robe.—II. *hem* of a garment, Ex. 28. 33, 34.

שׁוֹלֵחַ[b] Kal part. act. sing. masc. dec. 7 b . . . שׁלח

שׁוּלֵי noun masc. pl. constr. from [שׁוּל] dec. 1 a . . . שׁול

שׁוּלָיו[c] [d]וְ׳ id. pl., suff. 3 pers. sing. masc. . . . שׁול

שׁוּלַיִךְ id. pl., suff. 2 pers. sing. fem. . . . שׁול

שׁוֹלָל[e] adj. masc. sing. . . . . . שׁלל

שׂוּם[f], שִׂים[g] fut. יָשׂוּם (only Ex. 4. 11), יָשִׂים, ap. יָשֵׂם, וַיָּשֶׂם; inf. abs. שׂוֹם; imp. שִׂים.—I. *to put, set, place*, of persons and things made to *stand* erect; hence—II. *to set* a plant.—III. with בָּנִים *to set children*, sc. into the world, i. e. *to beget* them, Ezr. 10. 44.—IV. *to set in array* an army.—V. *to set, constitute, appoint*, with acc., לְ; with עַל *to set over*.—VI. *to set up*, e. g. a pillar; hence, *to found, establish*; with שְׁמוֹ, of God, *to establish* his name, the true worship; and, *to set, fix* a law, a place.—VII. *to put, set, lay*, of inanimate things; e. g. שׂוּם יָד עַל פֶּה *to lay* the hand upon the mouth; שׂ׳ אֵשׁ *to set* or *lay* a fire; with שֵׁם לְ *to set a name*, i. e. give a name to any one; trop. שׂ׳ בְּאָזְנֵי פ׳ *to put into the ear*, i.e. to recite to or tell any one; שׂ׳ עַל לֵב, or בְּלֵב, אֶל לֵב *to lay to heart*, also *to purpose*; שׂ׳ לֵב לְ *to set the heart upon, to attend, consider*; with פָּנִים, עַיִן *to set* or *direct* the face, eye, with עַל, לְ, בְּ.—VIII. *to lay up, preserve*, Job 36. 13.—IX. with עַל *to lay* or *put on* a garment.—X. *to put, lay, impose upon*; hence *to impute*, e. g. guilt; const. with עַל, לְ, בְּ.—XI. *to set* in a position or state, hence *to make*, espec. into any thing; rarely *to do, perform*, as שׂ׳ אֹתוֹת *to perform miracles*.—XII. with לְ *to render, give, bestow*; with רַחֲמִים *to show mercy*. Hiph. *to mark, attend, notice* (לֵב implied), Job 34. 23; Eze. 21. 21. Hoph. *to be set*, Ge. 24. 33.

שׂוּם Ch. *to put, set, place*; hence the phrases שׂ׳ שֵׁם *to name*; שׂ׳ בָּל לְ *to set the heart upon, to purpose*, comp. Heb. No. VII; שׂ׳ טְעֵם *to put forth, give out a decree*; שׂ׳ טְעֵם עַל *to regard*, Da. 3. 12. Ithpe. I. *to be put, placed*, Ezr. 5. 8; of a decree, *to be put forth* or *given*, Ezr. 4. 21.—II. *to be made*, Da. 2. 5.

יְשִׂימִאֵל (*whom God constitutes*) pr. name masc. 1 Ch. 4. 36.

תְּשׂוּמֶת fem. with יָד *a deposit*, Le. 5. 21.

[שׁוּם] masc. *garlic*, Nu. 11. 5.

שֻׁמָתִי patronym. *Shumathite*, 1 Ch. 2. 53, from an unknown שׁוּמָה (*garlic*).

שׂוּם[h] Kh. שׂוּם, K. שִׂים (q. v.) . . . . שׂום

שׂוֹם וְ׳[i] Kal inf. abs., or (Ne. 8. 8) constr. . . שׂום

שׂוּם[k] id. inf. constr. . . . . . שׂום

שֹׁמֵם Kal part. act. sing. m., pl. שֹׁמֲמִים (q. v.) שׁמם

שֹׁמֵמָה id. fem. dec. 11 b . . . . . שׁמם

שֹׁמְמִים[l], שֹׁמֲמִין[m] } id. masc., pl. of שֹׁמֵם comp. dec. 7 a . שׁמם

שׁוֹמֵעַ[n] Kh. שֹׁמֵעַ [rr]Kal part. masc. s. K. שָׁמוּעַ (q.v.) שׁמע

שׁוֹמֵר Kal part. act. sing. m. d. 7 b, also pr. name שׁמר

שׁוּן Root not used; Syr. תון *mingere*.

שַׁיִן masc. dec. 6 h, only pl. *urine*, 2 Ki. 18. 27; Is. 36. 12, Kheth.

שׂוֹנֵא וְ׳ Kal part. act. sing. masc. dec. 7 b . שׂנא

שׁוֹנֶה[o] Kal part. act. sing. masc. dec. 9 a . שׁנה

שׁוּנִי pr. name masc. [for שְׁאוּנִי] . . . שׁאן

שׁוֹנִים Kal part. act. masc., pl. of שׁוֹנֶה dec. 9 a שׁנה

שׁוּנֵם וְ׳ pr. name of a place [for שְׁאוּנֵם] . שׁאן

שׁוֹסֵינוּ[p] Kal part. act. pl. masc., suff. 1 pers. pl. [from שֹׁסֶה] dec. 9 a . . . שׁסה

שָׁוַע only Pi. שִׁוַּע *to cry for help*.

שֶׁוַע masc. dec. 6 a (§ 35. rem. 5), *a cry for help*, Ps. 5. 3.

שׁוֹעַ masc. id. Is. 22. 5.

שׁוּעַ masc. id. Job 30. 24.

שַׁוְעָה fem. (constr. שַׁוְעַת; no pl.) id.

שׁוּעַ Root not used; i. q. יָשַׁע q. v.

שׁוֹעַ masc.—I. *rich, opulent*.—II. *liberal, noble* Is. 32. 5.

שׁוּעַ m. d. 1 a.—I. *riches, wealth*, Job 36. 19.—II. pr. name masc. 1 Ch. 7. 32.

שׁוּעָא (*riches*) pr. name masc. 1 Ch. 7. 32.

תְּשׁוּעָה fem. dec. 10, *salvation, deliverance*.

שׁוֹעַ וְ׳ noun masc. sing. . . . . שׁוע

שׁוּעַ[q] noun masc. sing. dec. 1 a, also pr. name . שׁוע

שׁוּעָא pr. name masc. . . . . . שׁוע

שַׁוְעִי[r] noun masc. sing., suff. 1 pers. sing. [from שֶׁוַע § 35. rem. 5] dec. 6 a . . . שׁוע

[a] Ju. 9. 48. [b] Eze. 2. 3, 4. [c] Ex. 28. 33. [d] Is. 6. 1. [e] Job 12. 17, 19. [f] Hag. 2. 15. [g] Job 20. 4. [h] 2 Sa. 14. 7. [i] Ne. 8. 8. [k] Hag. 2. 15. [l] La. 1. 16. [m] La. 1. 4. [n] Je. 17. 23. [o] Pr. 26. 11. [p] Is. 17. 14. [q] Job 30. 24. [r] Ps. 5. 3. [rr] Je. 50. 10.

[a] שׁוּעֲךָ noun masc. sing., suff. 2 pers. sing. masc. from שׁוּעַ dec. 1a . . . . שוע
[b] שׁוּעָל וְ' noun m. s. (no vowel change); also pr. name שעל
שׁוּעָלִים id. pl., abs. st. . . . . שעל
[c] שֹׁעֲרִים וְ' noun masc., pl. of שַׁעַר dec. 7b . שער
שַׁוְעַת noun fem. sing. constr. [of שַׁוְעָה, no pl.] שוע
[d] שַׁוְעָתִי וְ' id. with suff. 1 pers. sing. . . שוע
שִׁוַּעְתִּי Piel pret. 1 pers. sing. . . . . שוע
שַׁוְעָתָם noun masc. sing., suff. 3 pers. pl. masc. [from שַׁוְעָה, no pl.] . . . שוע

שׁוּף I. *to bruise, wound,* Ge. 3. 15; Job 9. 17.—II. *to cover with darkness* (comp. נֶשֶׁף), Ps. 139. 11.

שֹׁפֵט Kal part. act. sing. masc. dec. 7b . . שפט
שׁוֹפָךְ וְ' pr. name masc. . . . . . שפך
[e] שֹׁפֵךְ Kal part. act. sing. masc. dec. 7b . . שפך
שׁוֹפָן pr. name, see עַטְרֹת שׁוֹ'.
שׁוֹפָר noun masc. sing. dec. 2b . . . . שפר
[f] שׁוֹפַר id., constr. st. . . . . . שפר
[g] שׁוֹפָרוֹת id. pl., abs. st. . . . . . שפר
[h] שׁוֹפְרוֹת id. pl., constr. st. . . . . . שפר
[i] שׁוֹפְרֹתֵיהֶם id. pl., suff. 3 pers. pl. masc. . . שפר

שׁוּק Kal not used; cogn. שָׁקַק *to run;* hence *to run after, to desire.* Hiph. *to run over, to overflow,* Joel 2.24; 4.13. Pil. שׁוֹקֵק *to cause to overflow,* Ps. 65.10.
שׁוֹק com. dec. 1a, *a leg* of a man or animal.
שׁוּק masc. (pl. שְׁוָקִים § 35. rem. 13) *a street.*
שָׁק Chald. masc. dec. 1a, *leg.*
תְּשׁוּקָה fem. dec. 10, *desire, longing.*

שׁוֹק noun fem. sing. dec. 1a . . . . שוק
[k] שׁוֹקָיו id. pl., suff. 3 pers. sing. masc. . . שוק
[l] שׁוֹקֵק Kal part. act. sing. masc. . . . . שקק
[m] שׁוֹקֵקָה id. part. act. sing. fem. (§ 39. No. 3. rem. 4) שקק

[שׂוּר] fut. וַיָּשַׂר (§ 21. rem. 9). I. i. q. שָׂרַר, שָׂרָה, (1) *to contend, strive,* Ho. 12. 5; (2) *to be prince, to have dominion,* Ju. 9. 22. Hiph. *to appoint princes,* Ho. 8. 4. II. *to saw,* 1 Ch. 20. 3. III. i. q. סוּר *to go away, depart.*

I. [שׁוּר] I. *to see, view, behold.*—II. *to watch for.*
שׁוּר m. d. 1a, *a lyer-in-wait, enemy,* Ps. 92. 12.

II. [שׁוּר] *to go, travel,* espec. for traffic, Is. 57. 9; part. fem. שָׁרָה *a travelling company, caravan,* Eze. 27. 25.
תְּשׁוּרָה fem. *gift, present,* 1 Sa. 9. 7.

III. שׁוּר masc. dec. 1a (pl. שׁוּרוֹת).—I. *wall* (perh. from שׁוּר, No. II, *to go round,* comp. תּוּר).—II. pr. name of a place in the desert between Egypt and Palestine; מִדְבַּר שׁוּר the desert extending from the borders of Palestine to Shur.
שׁוּר Chald. m. d. 1a, *a wall,* Ezr. 4. 12, 13, 16.
שֹׁרָה fem. dec. 10, id. Je. 5. 10.

שׁוֹר וְ',וְ״ masc. dec. 1a (pl. שְׁוָרִים § 35. rem. 13). —I. *an ox.*—II. *herd of oxen.*

שׁוּר noun masc. sing. dec. 1b, also pr. name שור
[o] שׁוּר וְ Kal imp. sing. masc. . . . . שור
[p] שׁוּרָה noun fem. sing. . . . . . שור
שׁוּרָה pr. name of a place (שׁוּר) with parag. ה שור
[q] שׁוֹרוֹ וְ' noun masc. sing., suff. 3 pers. sing. masc. from שׁוֹר (q. v.) . . . . שור
[r] שׁוּרַיְּ וְ Kh. for שׁוּרַיָּא K. (q. v.) . . . שור
[s] שׁוּרַיָּא וְ, [t] שׁוּרַיָּה וְ } Chald. noun masc. pl. emph. from שׁוּר dec. 1 . . . . } שור
[u] שְׁוָרִים noun masc., pl. of שׁוֹר (q. v.) . . שור
[zz] שׁוֹרְךָ, [x] שׁוֹרֶךָ וְ״ } id. sing., suff. 2 pers. sing. masc. . שור
[y] שׁוֹרֵק noun masc. sing.; also pr. name . . שרק
[z] שׁוֹרְרַי, [a] שׁוֹרְרָי } Kal part. act. pl. masc., suff. 1 pers. sing. from שֹׁרֵר dec. 7b . . } שור
[b] שׁוּרֹתָם noun masc. with pl. fem. term. & suff. 3 pers. pl. masc. from שׁוּר dec. 1a . . שור

[שׂוּשׂ, שִׂישׂ] fut. יָשִׂישׂ (only Is. 35. 1) יְשֻׂשׂוּם; inf. abs. שׂוֹשׂ; imp. שִׂישׂ *to exult, be glad, rejoice,* with עַל, בְּ.
שָׂשׂוֹן masc. dec. 3a (§ 32. rem. 5), *joy, gladness.*
מָשׂוֹשׂ m. d. 3a, *joy, rejoicing;* also, *object of joy.*

שׁוּשׁ Root not used; prob. *to be white.*
שַׁיִשׁ masc. *white marble,* 1 Ch. 29. 2.
שֵׁשׁ masc.—I. *white marble.*—II. *fine linen, byssus.*
שֵׁשַׁי (*white*) pr. name of an Anakite, comp. Nu. 13. 22.
שָׁשַׁי (id.) pr. name masc. Ezr. 10. 40.
שֵׁשָׁן (id., or i. q. שׁוּשַׁן) pr. name masc. 1 Ch. 2. 31, 34, 35.
שׁוּשַׁן masc.—I. *a lily, artificial lily,* 1 Ki. 7. 19. —II. שׁוּשַׁן עֵדוּת prob. the name of a musical instrument, resembling a lily, Ps. 60. 1.—III. pr. name, *Susa,* the capital of Persia.
שׁוֹשָׁן masc.—I. *a lily.*—II. *an artificial lily,*

[a] Job 36. 19. [b] Ne. 3. 35. [c] 2 Ch. 34. 13 [d] Ps. 40. 2. [e] Job 12. 21. [f] Le. 25. 9. [g] Ju. 7. 16. [h] Jos. 6.4,6,8,13. [i] Ju. 7. 8. [k] Ca. 5. 15. [l] Pr. 28. 15. [m] Is. 29. 8. [n] Ju. 6. 4. [o] Job 35. 5. [p] Is. 28. 25. [q] Ex. 20. 17. [r] Ezr. 4. 12. [s] Ezr. 4. 13. [t] Ezr. 4. 16. [u] Ho. 12. 12. [x] De. 5. 14. [y] Je. 2. 21. [z] Ps. 5. 9. [zz] De. 15. 19. [a] Ps. 56. 3. [b] Job 24. 11

1 Ki. 7. 22, 26.—III. pl. שׁוֹשַׁנִּים the name of a musical instrument, Ps. 45. 1; 69. 1; 80. 1, comp. שׁוּשַׁן.

שׁוֹשַׁנָּה fem. dec. 10, *a lily*.

שׁוּשַׁנְכָיֵא Chald. gent. noun pl. *inhabitants of Susa*, Ezr. 4. 9.

שׁוֹשׁ[a] Kal inf. abs. . . . . . שוש

שַׁוְשָׁא ן pr. name masc., see שְׂרָיָה under . שרה

שׁוֹשָׁן[b] noun masc. sing., pl. שׁוֹשַׁנִּים dec. 8a . שוש

שׁוּשַׁן / שׁוּשָׁן } pr. name of a place . . . שוש

שׁוּשַׁן noun masc. sing. . . . . . שוש

שׁוֹשַׁנָּה[c] noun fem. sing. dec. 10 . . . שוש

שׁוֹשַׁנִּים noun masc., pl. of שׁוֹשָׁן dec. 8a . . שוש

שׁוּשַׁנְכָיֵא Chald. gent. noun pl. from שׁוּשַׁן (q. v.) שוש

שׁוֹשַׁנַּת[d] noun fem. sing., constr. of שׁוֹשַׁנָּה dec. 10 שוש

שׁוֹשֵׁק Kh. שׁוֹשֵׁק, K. שִׁישַׁק q. v.

שׁוֹשֵׂתִי[e] Poel (§ 6. No. 1) pret. 1 p. s. [for שׁוֹסַתִּי] שסה

שׁוֹתֵי[f] / שׁוֹתִים[g] } Kal part. act. masc., pl. constr. & abs. from שֹׁתֶה dec. 9a . . . . } שתה

שׁוּתֶלַח / שׁוּתֶלַח } pr. name — I. Nu. 26. 35. Patronym. שֻׁתַלְחִי ibid.—II. 1 Ch. 7. 20, 21.

שֵׁזַב Chald. only Peil שֵׁיזִיב; fut. יְשֵׁיזִב; inf. שֵׁיזָבוּת (§ 68 d) *to deliver, rescue*.

מְשֵׁיזַבְאֵל (whom *God delivers*) pr. name masc. Ne. 3. 4; 10. 22; 11. 24.

שֵׁיזִיב[h] ן Ch. Peil pret. 3 pers. sing. masc. (§ 48) . שזב

[שָׁזַף] *to see, look upon, behold*; metaph. of the sun, Ca. 1. 6, which some render *the sun has scorched me*; regarding שָׁזַף i. q. שְׁדַף Chald. *to scorch, burn*; and thence derive the signification of *looking, casting a glance*.

שְׁזָפַתְנִי Kal pret. 3 pers. fem. with suff. 3 pers. s. m. שזף

שָׁזַר Kal not used; Arab. *to twist*; hence Hoph. part. שֵׁשׁ מָשְׁזָר *twined linen*.

שַׁח[i] ן Kal pret. 3 p. s. m.; or (Job 22. 29) adj. m. שחח

שֶׁחֻבְּרָה[k] pref. שֶׁ) (Pual pret. 3 pers. sing. fem. . חבר

[שָׁחַד] *to give presents, to bribe*. Hence

שֹׁחַד ן masc.—I. *gift, present*.—II. *a bribe*.—III. *bribery*, Job 15. 34 . . . . שחד

שִׁחֲדוּ[l] Kal imp. pl. masc. [for שִׁחֲדוּ or שְׁחַדוּ] שחד

[שָׂחָה] *to swim*, Is. 25. 11. Hiph. *to make to swim, overflow*, Ps. 6. 7.

שָׂחוּ fem. *a swimming*, Ezr. 47. 5.

[שָׁחָה] *to bow, stoop down*, Is. 51. 23. Hiph. הִשְׁחָה *to bow down, depress*, Pr. 12. 25. Hithpal. הִשְׁתַּחֲוָה (§ 6. No. 2, & § 24. rem. 25).—I. *to bow down, prostrate oneself*, with לְ, לִפְנֵי *before* any one, once עַל Le. 26. 1.—II. *to worship*.

שְׁחוּת fem. dec. 1a, *a pit*, Pr. 28. 10.

שְׁחִית fem. dec. 1a (pl. שְׁחִיתוֹת), id.

שָׁחָה Kal pret. 3 pers. sing. fem. . . שוח

שָׂחוּ[m] noun fem. sing. (after the form אָחוּ) . שחה

שָׁחוּ Kal pret. 3 pers. pl. [for שַׁחּוּ dag. f. impl.] שחח

שֵׂחוֹ[n] noun m. s., suff. 3 pers. s. m. fr. [שֵׂחַ] d. 1a שיח

שְׁחוֹחַ[o] Kal inf. constr., others, subst. masc. שחח

שָׁחוּט[p] Kal part. pass. sing. masc. . . שחט

שֶׁחוֹלַת[q] pref. שֶׁ) (Kal part. act. sing. fem., constr. of חֹלָה dec. 10, from חֹלֶה masc. . . חלה

שְׂחוֹק noun masc. sing. . . . . שחק

שִׁחוֹר pr. name of a river . . . . שחר

שְׁחוֹרָה[r] adj. fem. sing. dec. 10, from שָׁחֹר masc. . שחר

שַׁחוֹתִי Kal pret. 1 pers. sing. (dag. forte impl. in ח) שחח

[שָׁחַח] pl. שַׁחוּ, שָׁחֲחוּ (§ 18. rem. 13).—I. *to bow, stoop down*.—II. *to be bowed down, brought low, be depressed*.—III. *to humble oneself, to submit*. Niph. *to be bowed down, brought low, be depressed*. Hiph. הֵשַׁח *to bring low, cast down*. Hithpo. הִשְׁתּוֹחֵחַ *to be brought low, be cast down*, of the soul.

שַׁח adj. masc. *cast down*, with עֵינַיִם *cast down as to the eyes*, i. e. *with cast down eyes*, Job 22. 29.

שְׁחוֹחַ masc. *a bowing down, submission*, Is. 60. 14; others regard it as an inf. and render it: they shall come *to submit themselves*.

שָׁחֲחוּ[s] Kal pret. 3 pers. pl. (also שַׁחוּ § 18. rem. 13) שחח

[שָׂחַט] *to squeeze, press out*, Ge. 40. 11.

שָׁחַט ן fut. יִשְׁחַט.—I. *to slaughter, kill* animals.—II. *to kill, slay* persons.—III. part. זָהָב שָׁחוּט *alloyed* gold (Arab. שחט to dilute wine). Niph. *to be slaughtered*.

שְׁחִיטָה fem. dec. 10, *a slaughtering* of victims, 2 Ch. 30. 17.

שָׁחֹט[t] ן Kal inf. abs. . . . . שחט

שַׁחֲטָה[u] ן id. inf. constr. (§ 8. rem. 10) . . שחט

---

[a] Is. 61. 10. [b] 1 Ki. 7. 22, 26. [c] 2 Ch. 4. 5. [d] Ca. 2. 1. [e] Is. 10. 13. [f] Ps. 69. 13. [g] 1 Ch. 12. 39. [h] Da. 3. 28; 6. 28. [i] Is. 2. 11, 17. [k] Ps. 122. 3. [l] Job 6. 22. [m] Eze. 47. 5. [n] Am. 4. 13. [o] Is. 60. 14. [p] 2 Ch. 9. 15, 16. [q] Ca. 5. 8. [r] Ca. 1. 5. [s] Job 9. 13. [t] Is. 22. 13. [u] Ho. 5. 2.

שָׁחֲטוּ[a] ‏וְ[b]׳ id. pret. 3 pers. pl. . . . שחט
שַׁחֲטוּ ‏וְ id. imp. pl. masc. . . . . שחט
שְׁחָטוֹ[c] ‏וּ id. pret. 3 pers. sing. masc., suff. 3 pers. sing. masc.; ‏וּ, for ‏וְ, conv. . . שחט
שֹׁחֲטֵי[d] id. part. act. pl. c. masc. from שֹׁחֵט dec. 7b שחט
שָׁחַטְתָּ[e] ‏וְ id. pret. 2 pers. sing. masc.; acc. shifted by conv. ‏וְ (§ 8. rem. 7) . . . שחט
שְׁחַטְתֶּם[f] ‏וּ id. pret. 2 pers. pl. masc.; ‏וּ, for ‏וְ, conv. שחט
שְׁחִי[g] Kal imp. sing. fem. . . . . שחה
שִׂחִי[h] defect. for שִׂיחִי (q. v.) . . . . שיח
שְׁחִיטַת[i] noun fem. sing., constr. of [שְׁחִיטָה] dec. 10 שחט
שְׁחִין noun masc. sing. . . . . שחן
שָׁחִים[k] noun masc. sing. see סָחִישׁ.
שְׁחִיף[l] noun masc. sing. constr. [from שָׁחִיף or שְׁחִיף] שחף
שְׁחִיתָה ‏וּ Ch. Peal part. pass. s. f. [of שְׁחִית]; ‏וּ bef. (:) שחת
שֶׁחָכַמְתִּי[m] ‏וְ pref. שֶׁ) (Kal pret. 1 pers. sing. . . חכם

שַׁחַל, שָׁחַל (§ 35. rem. 2) masc. *lion.*

שְׁחֵלֶת ‏וּ fem. *onyx, an odoriferous shell,* Ex. 30. 34. Arab. שחל *to peel, shell.*

שָׁחַן Root not used; Arab. *to be hot, inflamed.*

שְׁחִין masc. *boil, sore, ulcer.*

שָׁחַף Root not used; Arab. *to be thin.*

שָׁחִיף or שְׁחִיף masc. *thin board,* Eze. 41. 16.

שַׁחַף masc. *the seagull,* Le. 11. 16; De. 14. 15.

שַׁחֶפֶת fem. *consumption,* Le. 26. 16; De. 28. 22.

שָׁחַץ Root not used; Arab. *to lift up oneself.*

שַׁחַץ masc. *elation, pride,* hence בְּנֵי שׁ׳ *sons of pride,* for the larger and stronger kind of wild beasts, Job 28. 8; 41. 26.

שַׁחֲצִים (*heights*) pr. name of a place in Issachar, Jos. 19. 22.

שָׁחַץ noun masc. sing. [for שַׁחַץ § 35. rem. 2] שחץ
שַׁחֲצוֹמָה ‏וְ Kh. שַׁחֲצוֹמָה, K. שַׁחֲצִימָה pr. name שַׁחֲצוֹם or שַׁחֲצִים with parag. ה . . . שחץ

שָׂחַק" ‏וְ I. *to laugh,* abs.—II. with אֶל *to smile upon, approve,* Job 29. 24.—III. with לְ, עַל *to laugh at, deride, scorn.*—IV. *to make sport,* Ju. 16. 27. Pi. שִׂחֵק (§ 14. rem. 1).—I. *to rejoice,* Je. 15. 17; Pr. 8. 30, 31.—II. *to sport, play.*—III. *to make sport;* hence *to skirmish,* 2 Sa. 2. 14.—IV. *to play* on a musical instrument. Hiph. *to laugh at, to scorn* with עַל 2 Ch. 30. 10.

שְׂחֹק, שְׂחוֹק masc.—I. *laughter.*—II. *object of laughter, scorn.*—III. *jest, sport,* Pr. 10. 23.

יִשְׂחָק put poetically for יִצְחָק *Isaac,* q. v.

מִשְׂחָק m. *object of laughter, derision,* Hab. 1. 10.

[שָׁחַק] I. *to bruise, pound, reduce to dust.*—II. *to wear away,* Job 14. 19.

שַׁחַק masc. dec. 6d.—I. *dust,* Is. 40. 15.—II. *cloud;* pl. שְׁחָקִים *clouds.*—III. *the sky.*

שְׂחֹק noun masc. sing., comp. שְׂחוֹק . . שחק
שָׂחֲקוּ Kal pret. 3 pers. pl. . . . . שחק
שָׁחֲקוּ[o] Kal pret. 3 pers. pl. . . . . שחק
שְׁחָקִים ‏וּ׳ noun masc., pl. of שַׁחַק׳ dec. 6d; ‏וּ bef. (:) שחק
שָׁחַקְתָּ[p] ‏וְ Kal pret. 2 pers. sing. masc.; acc. shifted by conv. ‏וְ (§ 8. rem. 7) . . שחק
שִׂחַקְתִּי[q] ‏וְ Piel (§ 14. rem. 1) pret. 1 pers. sing.; acc. shifted by conv. ‏וְ (comp. § 8. rem. 7) . שחק

שָׁחַר I. *to be black,* Job 30. 30.—II. (denom. from שַׁחַר q. v.) prop. *to do early,* comp. הִשְׁכִּים, hence *to seek early, diligently,* Pr. 11. 27. Pi. שִׁחֵר (§ 14. rem. 1) *to seek early,* also *diligently,* const. with acc., לְ, אֶל with inf.

שָׁחֹר masc. d. 3a, שְׁחֹרָה fem. d. 10, adj. *black.*

שְׁחוֹר masc. *blackness,* La. 4. 8.

שַׁחַר masc. dec. 6d (with suff. שַׁחְרָהּ § 35. r. 5).—I. *the dusk* of the morning; hence *dawn, morning;* בֶּן־שַׁחַר *son of the dawn,* i. e. *the Morning Star, Lucifer.*—II. adv. *at dawn, early.*—III. *rise, origin,* Is. 47. 11.—IV. perh. *dawn* for *light,* and metaph. for *sense, reason,* Is. 8. 20, which passage may be rendered: *by the law and the testimony* (I declare) *that they shall say* (comp. אִם) *such a thing as this* (see the preeding ver. 19) *in which there is no light.*

שַׁחֲרוּת fem. *dawn of life,* i. e. *youth,* Ec. 11. 10.

שְׁחַרְחֹר, only fem. שְׁחַרְחֹרֶת adj. *blackish, swarthy* (§ 26. Nos. 21, 22, 23), Ca. 1. 6.

שְׁחַרְיָה (*whom the Lord seeks*) pr. name masc. 1 Ch. 8. 26.

שַׁחֲרַיִם (*two dawns, twilights*) pr. name masc. 1 Ch. 8. 8.

שִׁחֹר, שִׁחוֹר, שִׁיחוֹר (*black, turbid*) pr. name—I. the Hebrew appellation for the *Nile.*—II. שִׁיחוֹר לִבְנָת a small river in the tribe of Asher, Jos. 19. 26.

אַשְׁחוּר (*blackness*) pr. name m. 1 Ch. 2. 24; 4. 5.

מִשְׁחָר masc. *the dawn, morning,* Ps. 110. 3.

---

[a] 2 Ki. 25. 7. [b] Ex. 12. 6. [c] Le. 3. 2. [d] Is. 57. 5. [e] Ex. 29. 11, 16, 20. [f] 1 Sa. 14. 34. [g] Is. 51. 23. [h] Job 23. 2. [i] 2 Ch. 30. 17. [k] Is. 37. 30. [l] Eze. 41. 16. [m] Ec. 2. 19. [n] Pr. 29. 9. [o] Job 14. 19. [p] Ex. 30. 36. [q] 2 Sa. 6. 21.

שְׁחַר / שַׁחַר } noun masc. sing. dec. 6d (§ 35. rem. 2) שחר

[a]שָׁחֹר adj. masc. sing. dec. 3a . . . שחר

שִׁחוֹר pr. name of a river . . . . שחר

[b]שֹׁחֵר Kal part. act. sing. masc. . . . . שחר

[c]שַׁחְרָהּ noun masc. sing., suff. 3 pers. sing. fem. from שַׁחַר dec. 6d [for שַׁחֲרָהּ § 35. rem. 5] שחר

[d]שִׁחֲרוֹ Piel (§ 14. rem. 1) pret. 3 pers. sing. masc. [שִׁחֵר], suff. 3 pers. sing. masc. . שחר

[e]שִׁחֲרוּ וְ id. pret. 3 pers. pl. . . . . . שחר

[f]שְׁחֹרוֹת adj. fem., pl. of שְׁחוֹרָה d. 10, from שָׁחֹר masc. שחר

[g]שְׁחַרְחֹרֶת adj. fem. sing. from שְׁחַרְחֹר masc. שחר

שְׁחַרְיָה, וּ שְׁחַרַיִם וְ pr. names masc.; וּ bef. (:) . שחר

[h]שְׁחֹרִים adj. masc., pl. of שָׁחֹר dec. 3a . . שחר

[i]שִׁחַרְתַּנִי וְ Piel pret. 2 pers. s. m., suff. 1 p. s. (§ 14. r. 1) שחר

שָׁחַת . Niph. I. *to be marred* or *spoiled by rotting*, Je. 13. 7. —II. *to be corrupted*, morally, Ge. 6. 11, 12.—III. *to be laid waste*, Ex. 8. 20. Pi. שִׁחֵת (§ 14. rem. 1). —I. *to destroy, ruin*, e. g. land, persons; metaph. of compassion, Am. 1. 11, of wisdom, Eze. 28. 17, of a covenant, prob. *to corrupt, pervert*, Mal. 2. 8.—II. *to act corruptly, wickedly*. Hiph. I. i. q. Pi. No. I.—II. *to corrupt, pervert*, as one's way, actions. Hoph. *to be corrupted, spoiled*.

שְׁחַת Chald. part. pass. fem. שְׁחִיתָה *corrupt*, of words, Da. 2. 9; neut. *corrupt deed, crime*, Da. 6. 5.

שַׁחַת masc. *corruption, putridity*, Job 17. 14; Ps. 16. 10.

מַשְׁחִית masc. dec. 1b.—I. *destruction, ruin*.—II. *snare, trap*, Je. 5. 26.

מַשְׁחֵת masc. dec. 1b, *destruction*, Eze. 9. 1.

מָשְׁחַת m. d. 2b, *corruption, defilement*, Le. 22. 25.

[k]שָׁחַת noun masc. sing. [for שַׁחַת § 35. rem. 2] . שחת

שַׁחַת / שָׁחַת } noun fem. sing. dec. 13a (comp. § 35. r. 2) שוח

[l]שַׁחֵת Piel inf. constr. (§ 14. rem. 1) . . שחת

[m]שִׁחַתָּ וְ id. pret. 2 pers. sing. m. [for שִׁחַתְתָּ § 25. r.] שחת

שִׁחֵת וְ id. pret. 3 pers. sing. masc. . . שחת

[n]שַׁחֲתָהּ id. inf. (שַׁחֵת), suff. 3 pers. sing. fem. dec. 7b שחת

[o]שִׁחֲתָהּ וְ id. pret. 3 pers. sing. masc. (שִׁחֵת), suff. 3 pers. sing. fem. . . . . . . שחת

[p]שַׁחֲתוּ וְ id. imp. pl. masc. [for שַׁחֲתוּ comp. § 8. r. 7] שחת

שִׁחֲתוּ / שִׁחֵתוּ [q] וְ } id. pret. 3 pers. pl. (comp. id.) . שחת

[r]שִׁחֶתְךָ id. pret. 3 pers. sing. masc. (שִׁחֵת § 14. r. 1), suff. 2 pers. sing. masc. (§ 16. r. 15) שחת

[s]שִׁחַתֶּם וְ id. pret. 2 p. pl. m. [for שִׁחַתְתֶּם § 25. r.] שחת

[שָׂטָה] fut. יִשְׂטֶה, ap. יֵשְׂטְ (§ 24. rem. 3), *to turn aside, go astray*.

שִׁטָּה[u] fem.—I. *acacia*, Is. 41. 19; pl. שִׁטִּים *acacia wood*. —II. שִׁטִּים pr. name of a valley in Moab on the borders of Palestine.

[x]שְׂטֵה Kal imp. sing. masc. . . . . . שטה

[y]שָׁטוּ Kal pret. 3 pers. pl. . . . . שוט

[z]שֶׁטּוֹב pref. ·שֶׁ) (adj. masc. sing. dec. 1a . . טוב

[a]שָׁטוֹחַ Kal inf. abs. . . . . . שטח

[שָׁטַח] I. *to spread abroad, expand, enlarge*.—II. *to strew, scatter*.

מִשְׁטָח m. d. 2b, *a place for spreading*, Eze. 26. 5, 14.

מִשְׁטוֹחַ masc. id. Eze. 47. 10.

[b]שֹׁטֵחַ Kal part. act. sing. masc. . . . שטח

[c]שְׁטָחוּם וּ id. pret. 3 pers. pl. masc., suff. 3 pers. pl. masc.; וּ, for וְ, conv. . . . שטח

[d]שִׁטַּחְתִּי Piel pret. 1 pers. sing. . . . . שטח

[e]שָׁטֵי וְ Kal part. act. pl. constr. masc. [from שָׁט dec. 1a, § 30. No. 3] . . . . שוט

[f]שָׁטִים Kal part. act. pl. m. [fr. שָׁט d. 1a, § 30. No. 3] שוט

[g]שֵׂטִים noun masc. pl. [of שֵׂט] . . שוט

שִׁטִּים noun fem., pl. of שִׁטָּה dec. 10 . . שטה

[h]שָׂטִית Kal pret. 2 pers. sing. fem. . . . שטה

[שָׂטַם] fut. יִשְׂטֹם *to hate, persecute*; others, coll. with the Syr., *to lay snares for*.

מַשְׂטֵמָה fem. *hatred, persecution*, Ho. 9. 7, 8; others, *snares, destruction*.

[שָׂטַן] *to be hostile, to oppose*; part. שֹׂטֵן *adversary*. Hence the two following.

שָׂטָן [i] וְ masc.—I. *adversary, opponent*.—II. הַשָּׂטָן *the adversary, the devil, Satan* . שטן

שִׂטְנָה fem.—I. *accusation*, Ezr. 4. 6.—II. pr. name of a well, Ge. 26. 21 . . . שטן

[k]שִׂטְנִי the foll. with suff. 1 pers. sing. . . שטן

[l]שֹׂטְנֵי Kal part. act. pl. constr. m. [fr. שֹׂטֵן] d. 7b שטן

שָׁטַף [m] וְ I. *to wash away*, Eze. 16. 9.—II. *to wash, rinse, cleanse by washing*, Le. 15. 11; 1 Ki. 22. 38. —III. *to overflow, inundate, overwhelm*; hence metaph. *to sweep away as with a flood*. Niph.

[a] Le. 13. 31, 37. [b] Pr. 11. 27. [c] Is. 47. 11. [d] Pr. 13. 24. [e] Ps. 78. 34. [f] Ca. 5. 11. [g] Ca. 1. 6. [h] Zec. 6. 2. [i] Job 7. 21. [k] Ps. 16. 10. [l] Ge. 13. 10. [m] Pr. 23. 8 [n] Eze. 22. 30. [o] Ex. 21. 26. [p] Je. 5. 10. [q] Eze. 26. 4. [r] Ho. 13. 9. [s] Mal. 2. 8. [t] Nu. 32. 15. [u] Is. 41. 19. [x] Pr. 4. 15. [y] Nu. 11. 8. [z] Ec. 2. 26. [a] Nu. 11. 32. [b] Job 12. 23. [c] Je. 8. 2. [d] Ps. 88. 10. [e] Ps. 40. 5. [f] Eze. 27. 8. [g] Ho. 5. 2. [h] Nu. 5. 19, 20. [i] Ps. 109. 6. [k] Ps. 109. 20. [l] Ps. 71. 13. [m] Da. 11. 10, 40.

pass. of Kal Nos. II & III. Pu. *to be washed, rinsed*, Le. 6. 21. Hence

שֶׁטֶף[a] ,ְ שֶׁטֶף masc.—I. *an overflowing* of water, metaph. of an effusion of anger, of the devastation of an army:—II. *flood, inundation.*

שֹׁטֵף Kal part. act. sing. masc. dec. 7 b . . שטף

שֻׁטַּף[b] ְ Pual pret. 3 pers. sing. masc. . . שטף

שְׁטָפוּנוּ[c] Kal pret. 3 pers. pl. with suff. 1 pers. pl. שטף

שֹׁטְפִים[d] id. part. act. masc., pl. of שֹׁטֵף dec. 7 b . שטף

שְׁטָפָתְנִי[e] id. pret. 3 pers. sing. fem., suff. 1 pers. sing. שטף

[שָׁטַר] Arab. (שׂטר) *to write*; whence part. שֹׁטֵר *officer, overseer* or *magistrate*.

שְׂטַר Ch. m. *a side*, Da. 7. 5. Targ. סְטַר id.

שִׁטְרַי (*writer*) pr. name m. 1 Ch. 27. 29, Kh.

מִשְׁטָר masc. dec. 2 a, *dominion*, Job 38. 33.

שֹׁטֵר[f] Kal part. act. sing. masc. dec. 7 b . שטר

שִׁטְרַי pr. name masc. . . . . . שטר

שֹׁטְרֵי Kal part. act. pl. c. masc. from שֹׁטֵר d. 7 b שטר

שֹׁטְרֵיהֶם[g] ְ id. pl., suff. 3 pers. pl. masc. . . שטר

שֹׁטְרָיו[h] 'ְ id. pl., suff. 3 pers. sing. masc. . . שטר

שֹׁטְרֵיכֶם ְ id. pl., suff. 2 pers. pl. masc. . . שטר

שֹׁטְרִים ְ id. pl., abs. st. . . . . שטר

שַׁי / שַׁי } masc. *present, gift*. Etym. uncertain.

שְׁיָא ׳ pr. name, see שְׁוָיָה, under . . שרה

שִׂיאוֹ[k] noun masc. sing., suff. 3 pers. sing. masc. [from שִׂיא for נְשִׂיא] . . . . נשא

שִׁיאוֹן ְ pr. name of a place . . . . שוא

שֶׁיֹּאחֵז[l] pref. ·שֶׁ) Kal fut. 3 pers. sing. masc. . אחז

שֶׁיֹּאכַל[m] pref. id.) Kal fut. 3 pers. sing. masc. . אכל

שֶׁיֹּאמַר[n] pref. id.) Kal fut. 3 pers. sing. masc. . אמר

שֶׁיֹּאמְרוּ[o] pref. id.) id. fut. 3 pers. pl. masc. . אמר

שִׂיאֹן pr. name of a mountain . . . נשא

[שִׂיב] *to be grey-headed*, 1 Sa. 12. 2; part. שָׂב *grey-headed, old man.*

שִׂיב Chald. id. only in the participle, Ezr. 5. 5, 8, 9; 6. 7, 14.

שֵׂיב masc. dec. 1 a, *grey hairs, old age*, 1 Ki. 14. 4. Also

שֵׂיבָה[p] 'ו fem. dec. 10, *grey hair* . . . שיב

שֶׁיָּבוֹא[q] pref. ·שֶׁ) Kal fut. 3 pers. sing. masc. . בוא

שֵׂיבַת[r] noun fem. sing., constr. of שֵׂיבָה dec. 10 . שיב

שִׁיבַת[s] noun fem. sing., constr. of [שִׁיבָה] dec. 10 שוב

שֵׂיבָתוֹ[t] noun fem. sing., suff. 3 pers. sing. masc. from שֵׂיבָה dec. 10 . . . שיב

שֵׂיבָתִי id., suff. 1 pers. sing. . . . . שיב

שֵׂיבָתֵךְ[u] id., suff. 2 pers. sing. fem. . . . שיב

שִׂיג[x] noun masc. sing., see . . . . סוג

שִׂיד[y] masc. *lime, plaster.*

שִׂיד *to cover with lime, to plaster*, De. 27. 2, 4.

שֶׁיְּדֻבַּר[z] pref. ·שֶׁ) Pual fut. 3 pers. sing. masc. . דבר

[שָׁיָה] (cogn. שָׁהָה, Arab. שׂהא) *to forget, neglect*, De. 32. 18, but comp. שָׁהָה.

[שֶׂיֶה] De. 22. 1; 1 Sa. 14. 34, elsewhere by contr. שֶׂה com., constr. שֵׂה (comp. § 45) *one of the flock, a sheep* or *goat.*

שֵׂיֵהוּ[a] id. with suff. 3 pers. sing. masc. . . שיה

שֶׁיְהֹוָה[b] pref. שֶׁ) the most sacred name of God, יהוה with the vowels of אֲדֹנָי . הוה

שֶׁיִּהְיֶה[c] pref. ·שֶׁ) Kal fut. 3 pers. sing. masc. . היה

שֶׁיִּהְיוּ[d] pref. id.) id. fut. 3 pers. pl. masc. . היה

שֵׂיוֹ[e] noun masc. sing., suff. 3 pers. sing. masc. from שֶׂה irr. (§ 45) . . . שיה

שִׁיזָא pr. name of a man, 1 Ch. 11. 42.

שֶׁיָּזֻעוּ[f] pref. ·שֶׁ) Kal fut. 3 pers. pl. masc. . זוע

[שִׂיחַ] I. *to speak*, const. with לְ, acc. (Pr. 6. 22) *with,* with בְּ *of* any one.—II. *to complain, lament.*—III. *to meditate,* with בְּ. Pil. שׂוֹחֵחַ.—I. *to tell, declare,* Is. 53. 8.—II. *to meditate,* Ps. 143. 5.

שִׂיחַ masc. dec. 1 a.—I. *speech, discourse,* 2 Ki. 9. 11.—II. *complaint.*—III. *meditation* or *talk,* 1 Ki. 18. 27.

שֵׂחַ masc. dec. 1 a, *thought, purpose,* Am. 4. 13.

שִׂיחָה fem. dec. 10, *meditation,* espec. *pious meditation.*

שִׂיחַ masc. dec. 1 a, *plant, shrub, bush.*

שִׂיחַ[g] Kal imp. sing. masc. . . . . שיח

שִׁיחָה[h] / שִׁיחָה[i] } noun fem. sing. dec. 10 (K. שׁוּחָה) . שוח

שִׂיחָה noun fem. sing. dec. 10 . . . שיח

שִׂיחוֹ noun masc. sing., suff. 3 pers. sing. masc from שִׂיחַ dec. 1 a . . . שיח

שִׂיחוּ Kal imp. pl. masc. . . . . שיח

שִׁיחוֹר pr. name of a river . . . שחר

שִׁיחוֹת[k] noun fem., pl. of שִׁיחָה dec. 10 . שוח

שִׂיחִי noun masc. sing., suff. 1 pers. sing. from שִׂיחַ dec. 1 a . . . . שיח

[a] Pr. 27. 4. [b] Le. 6. 21. [c] Ps. 124. 4. [d] Is. 28. 2. [e] Ps. 69. 3. [f] Pr. 6. 7. [g] 1 Ch. 27. 1. [h] Ex. 5. 6. [i] Ps. 68. 30. [k] Job 20. 6. [l] Ps. 137. 9. [m] Ec. 2. 24; 3. 13. [n] Ec. 1. 10. [o] La. 2. 15. [p] Ps. 71. 18. [q] Ec. 2. 12. [r] Ge. 44. 31. [s] Ps. 126. 1. [t] 1 Ki. 2. 6, 9. [u] Ru. 4. 15. [x] 1 Ki. 18. 27. [y] Is. 33. 12. [z] Ca. 8. 8. [a] 1 Sa. 14. 34. [b] Ps. 144. 15. [c] Ec. 1. 9; 10. 14, etc. [d] Ec. 1. 11. [e] De. 22. 1. [f] Ec. 12. 3. [g] Job 12. 8. [h] Je. 18. 22. [i] Ps. 57. 7. [k] Ps. 119. 85.

שִׂיחִים[a] id. pl., abs. st. . . . . . שיח

שֶׁיְּחָנֵּנוּ[b] pref. ·שֶׁ)(Kal fut. 3 pers. sing. masc. (יָחֹן), suff. 1 pers. pl. (§ 18. rem. 5) . . חנן

שִׂיחָתִי[c] noun fem. s., suff. 1 pers. s. fr. שִׂיחָה dec. 10 שיח

שַׁיִט[d] noun masc. sing. . . . . שוט

שַׁיִט[e] Kh. שַׁיִט q. v., K. שׁוֹט (q. v.) . . שוט

שֶׁיִּירָאוּ[f] pref. ·שֶׁ)(Kal fut. 3 pers. pl. masc. . ירא

שִׁילֹה[g] noun masc. sing. (or it is to be read (שֶׁלּוֹ=שֶׁלֹּה), see R. . . . . שלה

שֶׁיֹּלֵךְ[h] pref. ·שֶׁ)(Hiph. fut. 3 pers. sing. masc., ap. & defect. for יוֹלִיךְ . . . . ילך

שֵׁילָל[i] Kh. שֵׁילָל, Keri שׁוֹלָל adj. masc. sing. . שלל

שִׂים וְ׳ Kal inf. c. (Job 20. 4), or imp. sing. masc. R. שִׂים, see . . . שום

שִׂים Chald. Peal part. pass. sing. masc. R. שִׂים (§ 54. rem. 6), see . . . . שום

שִׂימָה Kal imp. sing. masc. (שִׂים) with parag. ה, see שום

שִׂימֶהָ[k] id. id. with suff. 3 pers. sing. fem. . . שום

שׂוּמָה[l] id. part. pass. sing. fem., Kh. שִׂימָה from שִׂים, K. שׂוּמָה from שׂוּם . . . שום

שִׂימוּ וְ׳ id. imp. pl. masc.; Chald. Ezr. 4. 21 . שום

שִׁימוֹן pr. name masc. . . . . . ישם

שִׂימֵנִי[m] Kal imp. sing. masc. (שִׂים), suff. 1 p. s., see שום

שֶׁיָּמֻתוּ[n] pref. ·שֶׁ)(Kal fut. 3 pers. pl. masc. מות

שֵׁינֵיהֶם Kh. שֵׁינֵיהֶם n. m. pl. with suff. from an obsol. שַׁיִן (K. מֵימֵי רַגְלֵיהֶם) 2 Ki. 18. 27; Is. 36. 12. שון

שֶׁיַּעֲמֹל pref. ·שֶׁ)(Kal fut. 3 pers. sing. masc. . עמל

שֶׁיֵּעָשֶׂה[o] pref. id.)(Niph. fut. 3 pers. sing. masc. עשה

שֶׁיָּפוּחַ pref. id.)(Kal fut. 3 pers. sing. masc. פוח

שֶׁיִּפּוֹל[p], שֶׁיִּפֹּל[q] } pref. id.)(Kal fut. 3 pers. sing. masc. נפל

שֶׁיֹּצָא[r] pref. id.)(Kal part. act. sing. fem. [for יֹצְאָה] contr. for יֹצֵאָה (comp. § 23. rem. 11) יצא

שֵׁיצִיא[s] וְ Chald. Shaph. pret. 3 pers. sing. masc. (§ 48) יצא

[שׁוּר, שִׁיר] fut. יָשִׁיר, ap. וַיָּשַׁר (§ 22. rem. 3) once יָשֹׁר Job 33. 27 (?), *to sing*, with לְ *to* or *concerning*, with בְּ *of* any one; part. שָׁר, pl. שָׁרִים, fem. שָׁרוֹת *singers*. Pil. שׁוֹרֵר *to sing*; part. מְשֹׁרֵר *a singer*. Hoph. הוּשַׁר *to be sung*, Is. 26. 1.

שִׁיר masc. dec. 1a.—I. *a singing, song*; כְּלֵי שִׁיר *musical instruments*.—II. *sacred song, hymn*.

שִׁירָה fem. dec. 10, *a song*.

שִׁיר וְ׳ (Ne. 12. 46) noun masc. sing. dec. 1a . שיר

שֶׁיֹּרֵד[t] pref. ·שֶׁ)(Kal part. act. sing. masc. dec. 7b ירד

שִׁירֹה[u], שִׁירוֹ[x] } noun masc. sing., suff. 3 pers. sing. masc. from שִׁיר dec. 1a . . } שיר

שִׁירוּ Kal imp. pl. masc. . . . . . שיר

שִׁירוֹת[y] noun fem., pl. of שִׁירָה dec. 10 . שיר

שִׁירַיִךְ[z] noun masc. pl., suff. 2 pers. sing. fem. from שִׁיר dec. 1a . . . . . שיר

שִׁירֵיכֶם[a] id. pl., suff. 2 pers. pl. masc. . . שיר

שִׁירַת[b] noun fem. sing., constr. of שִׁירָה dec. 10 שיר

שַׁיִשׁ[c] noun masc. sing. . . . . שוש

שֶׁיֵּשׁ[d] pref. ·שֶׁ)(adv. . . . . . ישה

שִׁישָׁא pr. name, see שְׂרָיָה, under . . שרה

שִׂישׂוּ Kal imp. pl. masc., R. שִׂישׂ, see . . שוש

שִׂישִׂי[e] id. imp. sing. fem., R. שִׂישׂ, see . . שוש

שֶׁיְּשַׁלֶּם־[f] pref. ·שֶׁ)(Piel fut. 3 pers. sing. masc. for יְשַׁלֵּם (§ 10. rem. 4) . . . . שלם

שִׁישַׁק, שִׁישָׁק } pr. name of a king of Egypt, contemporary with Jeroboam.

שִׁית [also שׁוּת, Is. 22. 7] fut. יָשִׁית, ap. וַיָּשֶׁת, יָשֶׁת. —I. *to put, set, place*, of persons or things made to stand or regarded as erect.—II. *to set in array*, מַחֲנֶה implied; i. e. *to set oneself in array*.—III. *to constitute, appoint*, with acc., לְ; with עַל *to set over*.—IV. *to set* a limit, a term; ellipt. & impers. Job 38. 11.—V. *to put, set, lay*; שׁ׳ יָד עַל *to lay the hand upon* any, in protection; שׁ׳ יָד עִם *to join hands*.—VI. *to set, direct, turn*; שׁ׳ פָּנִים אֶל *to set* or *turn the face towards*, Nu. 24. 1; שׁ׳ עֵינַיִם *to set* or *turn the eyes*, i. e. to intend doing any thing, Ps. 17. 11; שׁ׳ לֵב *to lay to heart, to regard*.—VII. *to put* or *lay on* an ornament, Ex. 33. 4.—VIII. perh. *to cast, throw*, Job 22. 24; others, *to lay up*.—IX. to set in a position or state, hence *to make*, with לְ *into*, with כְּ *as* any thing; rarely *to do, perform*.—X. *to render, give*. Hoph. הוּשַׁת, with עַל *to be laid, imposed upon*, Ex. 21. 30.

שִׁית masc. *attire, dress*, Pr. 7. 10; Ps. 73. 6.

שָׁת masc. dec. 1a (pl. שָׁתוֹת), *foundation*; others, *pillars*.

שֵׁת masc. dec. 7a (pl שְׁתוֹת).—I. *buttock*.—II. (*gift*, or *compensation*, Ge. 4. 25) pr. name of the third son of Adam.

שַׁיִת[g] וְ׳ in pause שָׁיִת masc. (with suff. שִׁיתוֹ) *thorn*, collect. *thorns*, everywhere coupled with שָׁמִיר. Etym. doubtful.

שָׁיִת וְ noun masc. sing. dec. 6h; for וְ see lett. ו שית

שִׁית[h] וְ׳ Kal inf. (Job 22. 24), or imp. sing. masc. (Pr. 27. 23), or subst. m., Ps. 73. 6; Pr. 7. 10. שית

a Job 30. 7. b Ps. 123. 2. c Ps. 119. 97. d Is. 33. 21. e Is. 28. 15. f Ec. 3. 14. g Ge. 49. 10. h Ec. 5. 14. i Mi. 1. 8. k De. 31. 19. l 2 Sa. 13. 32. m Ca. 8. 6. n Ec. 9. 5. o Ec. 1. 9. p Ec. 11. 3. q Ec. 4. 10. r Ec. 10. 5. s Ezr. 6. 15. t Ps. 133. 2, 3. u Ps. 42. 9. x 1 Ki. 5. 12. y Am. 8. 3. z Eze. 26. 13. a Am. 8. 10. b Is. 5. 1. c 1 Ch. 29. 2. d Ec. 2. 13. e La. 4. 21. f Ps. 137. 8. g Is. 27. 4. h Job 22. 24.

שִׁיתָה id. imp. sing. masc. (שִׁית) with parag ה . שית

[a] שִׁיתוֹ noun masc. sing., suff. 3 pers. sing. masc. from שַׁיִת dec 6h . . . . . שית

[b] שִׁיתוּ Kal imp. pl. masc. . . . . . . שית

[c] שִׁיתִי id. imp. sing. fem. . . . . . . שית

[d] שִׁיתֵמוֹ id. imp. sing. masc. (שִׁית), suff. 3 pers. pl. m. שית

[e] שָׁךְ Kal part. act. sing. masc. . . . . שוך

שָׁכַב fut. יִשְׁכַּב .—I. *to lie down*; espec. *to lie down to sleep* or *to rest oneself*.—II. *to lie, keep one's bed.*—III. *to lie*, of one slain; שָׁ׳ עִם אֲבֹתָיו *to lie* or *sleep with his fathers*, i. e. *to die*.—IV. *to lie with* carnally, with אֶת, עִם. Niph. *to be lain with, ravished*, Is. 13. 16; Zec. 14. 2. Pu. id. Je. 3. 2. Hiph. הִשְׁכִּיב .—I. *to cause to lie, to lay down.*—II. *to stop*, Job 38. 37; others, *to pour out* (Arab. שכב id.). Hoph. *to be laid, to lie.*

שְׁכָבָה fem. dec. 11c.—I. *the act of lying with.*—II. *a layer* of dew.

שְׁכֹבֶת fem. dec. 13c, *the act of lying with.*

מִשְׁכָּב masc. dec. 2b (pl. ־ִים, ־וֹת).—I. *a lying down.*—II. *a lying with.*—III. *couch, bed*, 2 Sa. 17. 28.—IV. *a bier.*

מִשְׁכַּב Chald. masc. dec. 2a, *couch, bed.*

[f] שָׁכָב Kal pret. 3 pers. sing. m. for שָׁכַב (§ 8. r. 7) שכב

[g] שָׁכֹב id. inf. abs. . . . . . . שכב

שְׁכַב / שְׁכָב } id. inf. constr.; or imp. sing. masc. . שכב

שֹׁכֵב id. part. act. sing. masc. dec. 7b . . שכב

[h] שָׁכְבָה id. pret. 3 pers. sing. fem. . . . . שכב

[i] שִׁכְבָה id. imp. s. m. (שְׁכַב) with parag. ה (§ 8. r. 11) שכב

שָׁכְבוּ id. pret. 3 pers. pl. . . . . שכב

שִׁכְבִי id. imp. sing. fem. . . . . . שכב

[k] שֹׁכְבֵי id. part. act. pl. constr. masc. from שֹׁכֵב d. 7b שכב

שֹׁכְבִים id. pl., abs. st. . . . . . שכב

שֶׁכְּבָר pref. שֶׁ) (adv. . . . . . כבר

[l] שָׁכַבְתָּ / [m] שָׁכַבְתָּ } Kal pret. 2 pers. sing. masc.; acc. shifted by conv. וְ (§ 8. rem. 7) . . } שכב

שִׁכְבַת noun fem. sing., constr. of [שְׁכָבָה] dec. 11c שכב

[n] שֹׁכֶבֶת Kal part. act. sing., fem. of שֹׁכֵב . . שכב

שְׁכָבְתּוֹ noun fem. s., suff. 3 p. s. m. fr. [שְׁכֹבֶת] d. 13c שכב

[o] שָׁכַבְתְּי Kal pret. 2 pers. sing. fem. (§ 8. r. 5) Kh. ־תִּי ,וְ שכב

שָׁכַבְתִּי / [p] וְשָׁכַבְתִּי } id. pret. 1 pers. sing.; acc. shifted by conv. וְ (§ 8. rem. 7) . . } שכב

[q] שְׁכָבְתְּךָ noun fem. s., suff. 2 pers. sing. masc. from [שְׁכֹבֶת] dec. 13c . . . . . שכב

[r] שְׁכַבְתֶּם Kal pret. 2 pers. pl. masc.; וּ, for וְ, conv. שכב

שָׂכָה Root not used; סְכָא Syr. *to look for*; Chald. *to view, regard.*

שֵׂכוּ (*watch-tower*; Chald. סְכוּת id.) pr. name of a place near Ramah, 1 Sa. 19. 22.

שֶׂכְוִי masc. *intelligence*, only meton. the seat of it, *the heart, mind*; Targ. לִבָּא, Job 38. 36; some Jewish commentators regard it as an epithet for the *cock*.

שְׂכִיָּה fem. dec. 10, *a sight*, an object gazed upon, Is. 2. 16.

מַשְׂכִּית fem. (מַשְׂכִּיּוֹת).—I. *image, figure.*—II. *imagination, idea, thought.*

שָׁכָה Kal not used; perh. i. q. שָׁגָה (Ethiop. שכי) *to wander, rove.* Hiph. *to wander about lasciviously*, Je. 5. 8.

שָׁכְיָה (*wandering*) pr. name masc. 1 Ch. 8. 10.

שֹׂכֹה pr. name of a place, see שׂוֹכֹה . . שוך

שֻׂכּוֹ noun masc. sing., suff. 3 pers. sing. masc. from [שֹׂךְ] dec. 8c, see סֹךְ . . . סכך

שָׁכוּל adj. masc. sing. . . . . . שכל

שְׁכוֹל noun masc. sing. . . . . . שכל

[s] שְׁכוּלָה Kal part. pass. sing. fem. [of שָׁכוּל masc.] שכל

[u] שָׂכוּר Kal part. pass. sing. masc. . . . שכר

שִׁכּוֹר adj. masc. sing. dec. 1b . . . . שכר

[x] שִׁכּוֹרֵי id. pl., constr. st. . . . . שכר

[y] שִׁכּוֹרִים id. pl., abs. st. . . . . שכר

שָׁכַח fut. [also שָׁכֵחַ, comp. Pr. 2. 17; Is. 49. 14] fut. יִשְׁכַּח .—I. *to forget.*—II. *to leave from forgetfulness*, De. 24. 19.—III. *to forget, disregard, neglect.* Niph. I. *to be forgotten.*—II. *to be forgotten, neglected*, Job 28. 4. Pi. & Hiph. causative. Hithp. הִשְׁתַּכַּח *to be forgotten*, Ec. 8. 10.

שָׁכֵחַ masc. dec. 5a (but pl. c. שִׁכְחֵי § 34. rem. 2), *forgetting, neglecting.*

שְׁכַח Chald. Ithpe. הִשְׁתְּכַח (§ 47. rem. 4) *to be found.* Aph. הַשְׁכַּח (§ 47. rem. 4).—I. *to find.*—II. *to get, obtain*, Ezr. 7. 16.

[a] שָׁכֹחַ Kal inf. abs. . . . . . . שכח

[b] שִׁכַּח Piel pret. 3 pers. sing. masc. . . . שכח

[c] שָׁכְחָה / [d] שָׁכֵחָה } Kal pret. 3 pers. sing. fem. (§ 8. rem. 1 & 7) שכח

שָׁכְחוּ id. pret. 3 pers. pl. . . . . . שכח

[cc] שְׁכֵחוּךְ id. id., suff. 2 pers. sing. fem. (§ 16. rem. 1) שָׁכַח

שְׁכֵחוּנִי id. id., suff. 1 pers. sing. . . . שָׁכַח

---

[a] Is. 10. 17. [b] Ps. 48. 14. [c] Is. 16. 3. [cc] Je. 30. 14. [d] Ps. 83. 12, 14. [e] Ho. 2. 8. [f] Ju. 5. 27. [g] Le. 15. 24. [h] 1 Ki. 1. 2; 3, 19. [i] Ge. 39. 7, 12. [k] Ps. 88. 6. [l] Ec. 4. 2. [m] Is. 14. 8. [n] Ru. 3. 8. [o] Ru. 3. 4. [p] Ge. 47. 30. [q] Le. 18. 20, 23. [r] Le. 26. 6. [s] La. 2. 6. [t] Is. 49. 21. [u] Ne. 6. 13. [x] Is. 28. 3. [y] Joel 1. 5. [z] Ge. 27. 45. [a] De. 8. 19. [b] La. 2. 6. [c] Pr. 2. 17. [d] Ho. 2. 15.

[a]שְׁכְחֵי adj. pl. constr. masc. [from שָׁכֵחַ] dec. 5a . שכח

[b]שִׁכְחִי וְ Kal imp. sing. fem. . . . שכח

שֹׁכְחֵי id. part. act. pl. constr. masc. [fr. שֹׁכֵחַ] d. 7b שכח

[c]שְׁכַחְנוּ id. pret. 1 pers. pl. . . . . שכח

[d]שְׁכַחֲנוּךָ id. id., suff. 2 pers. sing. masc. . . שכח

[e]שְׁכֵחָנִי id. pret. 3 pers. sing. masc. [שָׁכַח], suff. 1 pers. sing. (§ 16. rem. 1) . שכח

[f]שְׁכֵחֻנִי id. pret. 3 pers. pl., suff. 1 pers. sing. (v. id.) שכח

שָׁכַחַתְּ id. pret. 2 pers. sing. fem. . . . שכח

שָׁכַחְתָּ וְ id. pret. 2 pers. sing. masc.; acc. shifted by conv. וְ (§ 8. rem. 7) . . . שכח

שָׁכַחְתִּי, [g]שָׁכַחְתִּי } id. pret. 1 pers. sing. (§ 8. rem. 7) . שכח

[h]שְׁכַחְתָּנִי id. pret. 2 pers. sing. masc., suff. 1 pers. sing. שכח

שָׁכְיָה pr. name masc. . . . . . שכה

[i]שְׂכִיּוֹת noun fem., pl. of [שְׂכִיָּה] dec. 10 . שכה

שַׂכִּין masc. *a knife*, Pr. 23. 2; Chald. סַכִּין. Etym. doubtful, comp. however שָׂכַךְ.

שָׂכִיר וְ' noun masc. sing. dec. 3a . . . שכר

[שָׂכַךְ] *to cover*, Ex. 33. 22. In the derivv. i. q. שׂוּךְ *to weave, to hedge*; but perh. also *to cut* (comp. Lat. *secare*), whence שַׂכִּין, and then *to be sharp, pointed.*

שֵׂךְ masc. dec. 8b, *thorn*, Nu. 33. 55.

שֹׂךְ masc. dec. 8c, *hedge, fence*, La. 2. 6.

שֻׂכָּה fem. dec. 10, *a spear*, Job 40. 31.

מְשׂוּכָה fem. dec. 10, *hedge, fence*, Is. 5. 5.

[שָׁכַךְ] I. *to bow, stoop down*, Je. 5. 26.—II. *to lower itself, abate*. Hiph. *to cause to abate, to quiet, still*, Nu. 17. 20.

שֵׁשַׁךְ *Sheshach*, a name for Babylon, Je. 25. 26; 51. 41. According to C. B. Michaelis for שְׁכַשְׁךְ (comp. בָּבֶל, שָׁשַׁק) χαλκόπυλος *having brazen gates*, from שך Arab. to overlay a gate with iron or brass; according to Hengstenberg, *a sinking down*, with reference to its future destiny.

[k]שָׁכָכָה Kal pret. 3 pers. sing. fem. [for שָׁכְכָה § 8. r. 7] שכך

שֶׁכָּכָה pref. שֶׁ)(adv. see כָּכָה.

שָׂכַל *to act wisely, prudently*, 1 Sa. 18. 30. Pi. *to act wisely, wittingly*, Ge. 48. 14. Hiph. I. *to look at*, Ge. 3. 6.—II. *to consider, attend to*, with בְּ, אֶל, עַל (Da. 9. 13).—III. *to be* or *become intelligent, wise*, or *prudent*; also *to act wisely, prudently*; part. מַשְׂכִּיל *wise, prudent, godly, pious*; as a title of several Psalms (besides Ps. 47. 8) prob. *a devout poem*, which others render *a didatic poem* (comp. No. V), not alike suitable to all those Psalms; inf. הַשְׂכִּיל, הַשְׂכֵּל as a subst. *intelligence, wisdom, prudence.*—IV. *to prosper, have success.*—V. *to make wise, teach, instruct.*—VI. *to cause to prosper*, 1 Ki. 2. 3.

שְׂכַל Chald. Ithpa. אִשְׂתַּכַּל *to consider*, Da. 7. 8.

שֶׂכֶל masc. & שֵׂכֶל (in pause שָׂכֶל § 35. rem. 2). —I. *regard, estimation*, Pr. 3. 4.—II. *intelligence, understanding.*—III. *signification*, Ne. 8. 8.—IV. *craft, cunning*, Da. 8. 25.

שׇׂכְלְתָנוּ Chald. fem. *intelligence, understanding*, Da. 5. 11, 12, 14.

[שָׁכֹל § 8. rem. 1] fut. יִשְׁכַּל *to lose children, to become childless*; part. pass. שְׁכוּלָה *childless*, Is. 49. 21. Pi. שִׁכֵּל.—I. *to make childless, to bereave.*—II. *to cause abortion*, 2 Ki. 2. 19.—III. *to produce an abortion, to miscarry*; part. מְשַׁכֶּלֶת as a subst. *abortion*, 2 Ki. 2. 21.—IV. metaph. of a vine, *to be unfruitful*. Hiph. i. q. Pi. Nos. I & III, Je. 50. 9; Ho. 9. 14.

שְׁכוֹל masc.—I. *loss of children, bereavement.*—II. *destitution*, Ps. 35. 12.

שַׁכּוּל adj. masc.—I. *bereaved* of children; *deprived* of the young.—II. *without young*, Ca. 4. 2; 6. 6.

שִׁכֻּלִים m. pl. *bereavement, childless state*, Is. 49. 20.

אֶשְׁכֹּל masc. (pl. אַשְׁכְּלוֹת, אֶשְׁכֹּלוֹת § 36. rem. 6, & § 44. rem. 5).—I. *a cluster, bunch of grapes* or *flowers* (Ca. 1. 14; 7. 8). Arab. שכל *to bind.*—II. pr. name of a valley in the south of Palestine. —III. pr. name masc. Ge. 14. 13, 24.

שֶׂכֶל, שֵׂכֶל [l]וְ' } noun masc. sing. dec. 6b & a . . שכל

[m]שִׁכֵּל Piel pret. 3 pers. sing. masc. . . שכל

שַׁכֻּלָה וְ adj. fem. sing. dec. 10, from שַׁכּוּל masc. שכל

שִׁכְּלָה [n]וְ' Piel pret. 3 pers. sing. fem. . . שכל

[o]שִׁכֵּלוּ id. pret. 3 pers. pl. [for שִׁכְּלוּ comp. § 8. r. 7] שכל

שִׂכְלוֹ noun m. sing., suff. 3 pers. s. m. fr. שֶׂכֶל d. 6b שכל

[p]שַׁכֻּלוֹת adj. fem., pl. of שַׁכֻּלָה d. 10, from שַׁכּוּל masc. שכל

[q]שִׂכְלוּת וְ noun fem. sing., see . . . סכל

[r]שִׁכֻּלַיִךְ noun m. pl. [שִׁכֻּלִים], suff. 2 pers. sing. fem. שכל

[s]שִׁכְּלֻךְ וְ Piel pret. 3 pers. pl., suff. 2 pers. sing. fem. שכל

[t]שַׁכְלְלֵהּ וְ Chald. Shaph. pret. 3 pers. sing. masc., suff. 3 pers. sing. masc. (§ 48) . . . כלל

[u]שַׁכְלִלוּ וְ Chald. id. pret. 3 pers. pl. masc. . כלל

[x]שִׁכְּלָתָּה וְ Piel pret. 3 pers. s. fem., suff. 3 pers. s. fem. שכל

---

a Ps. 9. 18. b Ps. 45. 11. c Ps. 44. 21. d Ps. 44. 18. e Is. 49. 14. f Je. 18. 15. g Ps. 102. 5. h Ps. 42. 10. i Is. 2. 16. k Est. 7. 10. l Pr. 3. 4. m Ge. 48. 14. n Le. 26. 22. o Ge. 31. 38. p Je. 18. 21. q Ec. 1. 17. r Is. 49. 20. s Eze. 5. 17. t Ezr. 5. 11. u Ezr. 6. 14. x Eze. 14. 15.

[a]שֶׁכֻּלָּם pref. שֶׁ· (שֶׁ) noun masc. sing., suff. 3 pers. pl. masc. from כֹּל dec. 8c . . . כלל

[b]שָׁכָלְתִּי Kal pret. 1 pers. sing. for שָׁכַלְתִּי R. . שכל

[c]שָׁכֹלְתִּי id. pret. 1 pers. sing. (§ 8. rem. 1) R. . שכל

[d]שִׁכַּלְתִּי Piel pret. 1 pers. sing. . . . שכל

[e]שִׁכַּלְתִּים ·ְ id. id., suff. 3 pers. pl. masc. . . שכל

[f]שִׁכַּלְתֶּם id. pret. 2 pers. pl. masc. . . שכל

[g]שָׁכְלְתָנוּ ·ְ Chald. noun fem. sing. . . . שכל

שָׁכַם. Hiph. הִשְׁכִּים.—I. *to rise early* in the morning, with or without בַּבֹּקֶר.—II. *to get early to* a place, with לְ, comp. Ge. 19. 27, or perh. וַיֵּלֶךְ is to be implied.—III. inf. הַשְׁכֵּם adv. *in the morning*, 1 Sa. 17. 16; hence, *early, without delay*; part. מַשְׁכִּים *early*, Ho. 6. 4.

שְׁכֶם ·ו masc. dec. 6b (§ 35. rem. 10).—I. *shoulder, shoulders*.—II. *part, portion*, Ge. 48. 22.—III. pr. name, *Shechem*, a city in the mountains of Ephraim, pertaining to the Levites; with ה parag. שְׁכֶ֫מָה.—IV. pr. name of a Canaanite, comp. Ge. 33. 19.

שֶׁכֶם (*portion*) pr. name masc.—I. Nu. 26. 31; Jos. 17. 2, where his brother's name is said to be חֵלֶק; patronym. שִׁכְמִי, Nu. 26. 31.—II. 1 Ch. 7. 19.

שִׁכְמָה fem. *shoulder*, Job 31. 22.

[h]שְׁכֶם ,וָ· ,וְ· / שֶׁכֶם ·ו } noun masc. sing., suff. שִׁכְמִי dec. 6 (§ 35. rem. 10), also pr. name } שכם

שְׁכֶ֫מָה / שְׁכֶמָה } id. (pr. name) with parag. ה . . שכם

שִׁכְמָהּ id., suff. 3 pers. sing. fem. . . שכם

שִׁכְמוֹ id., suff. 3 pers. sing. masc. . . שכם

[i]שִׁכְמִי id., suff. 1 pers. sing. . . . שכם

[k]שִׁכְמֶךָ id., suff. 2 pers. sing. masc. . . שכם

[l]שִׁכְמָם id., suff. 3 pers. pl. masc. . . . שכם

שָׁכֵן, שָׁכַן ·וְ fut. יִשְׁכֹּן.—I. *to lie down, to rest*.—II. *to rest, abide, continue*.—III. *to dwell*; part. שָׁכוּן *settled, dwelling*.—IV. *to inhabit*. Pi. שִׁכֵּן.—I. *to cause to dwell*.—II. *to place, fix*. Hiph. i. q. Pi.

שְׁכַן Chald. id. Da. 4. 18. Pa. *to cause to dwell*, Ezr. 6. 12.

שָׁכֵן masc. dec. 5a, fem. שְׁכֶנֶת (§ 44. rem. 3), pl. שְׁכֵנוֹת.—I. *inhabitant*.—II. *neighbour*.

שֶׁכֶן masc. dec. 6a, *a dwelling*, De. 12. 5.

שְׁכַנְיָה (*dweller with the Lord*) pr. name masc. of several persons.

שְׁכַנְיָהוּ (id.) pr. name masc. 2 Ch. 31. 15.

מִשְׁכָּן masc. dec. 2b (pl. ־ִים, ־וֹת).—I. *habitation, dwelling*; also habitation of God, *the temple*.—II. *tent*, Ca. 1. 8.—III. *the sacred tabernacle* of the Israelites.—IV. *lair of beasts*, Job 39. 6.

מִשְׁכַּן Chald. masc. dec. 2a, *habitation*, Ezr. 7. 15.

שָׁכֵן adj. masc. sing. dec. 5a . . . . שכן

[m]שַׁכִּן Chald. Pael pret. 3 pers. sing. masc. (§ 47. r. 1) שכן

[n]שְׁכַן adj. masc., constr. of שָׁכֵן dec. 5a . שכן

[o]שְׁכָן / [q]שְׁכָן־ [p]·ו } Kal imp. sing. masc. (§ 8. rem. 18); ·ו bef. (:) . . . } שכן

[r]שִׁכֵּן Piel pret. 3 pers. sing. masc. . . שכן

שֹׁכֵן Kal part. act. sing. masc. dec. 7b . שכן

שָׁכְנָה id. pret. 3 pers. sing. fem. . . . שכן

[s]שָׁכְנוּ ·וְ id. pret. 3 pers. pl. . . . שכן

[t]שִׁכְנוּ ·ְ id. imp. pl. masc. . . . שכן

[u]שְׁכֵנוֹ ·ו adj. masc. sing., suff. 3 pers. sing. masc. from שָׁכֵן dec. 5a; ·ו bef. (:) . . שכן

[x]שְׁכֵנַי id. pl. with suff. 1 pers. sing. . . שכן

[y]שֹׁכְנֵי ·וְ Kal part. act. pl. c. masc. from שֹׁכֵן dec. 7b שכן

שֹׁכְנִי id. sing., with parag. ·י (§ 8. rem. 19) . שכן

[z]שְׁכֵנֶיהָ ·ו adj. pl. masc., suff. 3 pers. sing. fem. from שָׁכֵן dec. 5a; ·ו bef. (:) . . . שכן

שְׁכַנְיָה / שְׁכַנְיָהוּ ·ו } pr. name masc.; ·ו id. . . . שכן

[a]שֹׁכְנֵיהֶם ·ְ Kal part. act. pl., suff. 3 pers. pl. masc. from שֹׁכֵן dec. 7b . . . . שכן

[b]שְׁכֵנָיו [c]·ו adj. pl. m., suff. 3 pers. s. m. fr. שָׁכֵן d. 5a שכן

[d]שְׁכֵנַיִךְ id. pl., suff. 2 pers. sing. fem. . . שכן

[e]שְׁכֵנַיִכִי id. pl., suff. 2 p. s. f., Kh. ־ַיִכִי, K. ־ַיִךְ (§ 4. r. 4) שכן

[f]שָׁכַנְתָּ Kal pret. 2 pers. sing. masc. . . . שכן

[g]שָׁכַנְתְּ ·ְ id. pret 2 pers. sing. fem. . . . שכן

שָׁכַנְתִּי / שָׁכַנְתִּי ·ְ } id. pret. 1 pers. sing.; acc. shifted by conv. ·ְ (§ 8. rem. 7) . . } שכן

[h]שִׁכַּנְתִּי ·וְ Piel pret. 1 pers. sing. . . . שכן

[i]שֹׁכַנְתִּי Kh. שֹׁכַנְתִּי, K. שֹׁכַנְתְּ Kal part. act. sing. fem. (§ 39. No. 4. rem. 3, also § 8. rem. 5) שכן

שָׂכַר fut. יִשְׂכֹּר.—I. *to hire*.—II. *to bribe*. Niph. *to hire out oneself*, 1 Sa. 2. 5. Hithp. הִשְׂתַּכֵּר id. Hag. 1. 6.

שָׂכָר masc. dec. 4a.—I. *hire, wages, reward*.—II. pr. name of two men, 1 Ch. 11. 35 (for which שָׁרָר 2 Sa. 23. 33), & 26. 4.

שֶׂכֶר masc. *hire, wages*.

שָׂכִיר masc. dec. 3a, *hired labourer, hireling*.

שְׂכִירָה fem. *a hiring*, Is. 7. 20.

יִשָּׂשכָר (Kh. יִשָּׂשְׂכָר for יִשָּׂא שָׂכָר *he brings*

a Ca. 4. 2; 6. 6. b Ge. 43. 14. c Ge. 43. 14. d Je. 15. 7. e Ho. 9. 12. f Ge. 42. 36. g Da. 5. 11, 12. 14. h Ps. 21. 13. i Job 31. 36. k Is. 10. 27. l Ex. 12. 34. m Ezr. 6. 12. n Ho. 10. 5. o Ge. 26. 2. p Ps. 37. 27. q Ps. 37. 3. r Ps. 78. 60. s Ps. 68. 7. t Je. 48. 28. u Ex. 12. 4. x Je. 12. 14. y Is. 18. 3. z Je. 49. 18; 50. 40. a Job 26. 5. b De. 1. 7. c Je. 49. 10. d Eze. 16. 26. e 2 Ki. 4. 3. f Ps. 74. 2. g Mi. 4. 10. h Je. 7. 7, 12. i Je. 51. 13.

reward; invariably in Keri יִשָּׂכָר *gotten by hire*, comp. Ge. 30. 16) pr. name of the fifth son of Jacob and the tribe descended from him.

מַשְׂכֹּרֶת fem. dec. 13 c, *wages*.

[שָׁכַר] fut. יִשְׁכַּר.—I. *to drink to the full, drink to hilarity*. —II. *to be intoxicated*; metaph. *to be giddy*. Pi. & Hiph. *to make drunken*. Hithp. *to act like one drunken*, 1 Sa. 1. 14.

שֵׁכָר masc. *strong, intoxicating drink*.

שִׁכּוֹר, שִׁכֹּר masc. dec. 1 b, *drunken, intoxicated*; fem. שִׁכֹּרָה 1 Sa. 1. 13.

שִׁכָּרוֹן masc. *drunkenness*, Eze. 23. 33; 39. 19.

שִׁכְּרוֹן (*drunkenness*) pr. name of a place in Judah, Jos. 15. 11.

אֶשְׁכָּר masc. *gift, present*. Arab. شكر *to give a reward, a present*.

שָׂכָר [a] וְ noun masc. sing. dec. 4 a; also pr. name . שכר
שַׂכֵּר [b] Piel inf. constr. . . . . . שכר
שָׂכֹר [c] Kal inf. abs. . . . . . שכר
שֵׂכָר וְ noun masc. sing. . . . . . שכר
שְׂכַר וּ noun m. s., constr. of שָׂכָר d. 4 a; וּ bef. (:) שכר
שֵׁכָר noun masc. sing. . . . . . שכר
שֹׁכֵר [d] וְ Kal part. act. sing. masc. dec. 7 b . שכר
שִׁכֹּר [e] defect. for שִׁכּוֹר (q. v.) . . . שכר
שְׂכָרָהּ [f] noun masc. sing., suff. 3 pers. sing. fem. from שָׂכָר dec. 4 a . . . . שכר
שָׁכְרוּ [g] Kal pret. 3 pers. pl. . . . . שכר
שְׂכָרוֹ [h] id. pret. 3 pers. s. masc., suff. 3 pers. s. masc. שכר
שְׂכָרוֹ noun masc. sing., suff. 3 pers. sing. masc. from שָׂכָר dec. 4 a . . . . שכר
שִׁכְרוּ וְ Kal imp. pl. masc. . . . . שכר
שִׁכָּרוֹן [i] noun masc. sing. . . . . . שכר
שִׁכְּרוֹנָה pr. name of a place [שִׁכְּרוֹן] with parag. ה שכר
שְׂכָרִי noun masc. s., suff. 1 pers. s. fr. שָׂכָר dec. 4 a שכר
שִׁכֹּרֵי [k] defect. for שִׁכּוֹרֵי (q. v.) . . . שכר
שְׂכִירֶיהָ [l] noun m. pl., suff. 3 pers. s. fem. fr. שָׂכִיר d. 3 a שכר
שֹׂכְרִים [m] Kal part. act. masc., pl. of שֹׂכֵר dec. 7 b . שכר
שְׂכָרֵךְ [n] noun masc. sing., suff. 2 pers. sing. fem. from שָׂכָר dec. 4 a . . . . שכר
שְׂכָרְךָ [o], שְׂכָרֶךָ } id., suff. 2 pers. sing. masc. . . שכר
שְׁכֻרַת [p] וּ Kal part. pass. constr. [of שְׁכוּרָה from שָׁכוּר masc.]; וּ bef. (:) . . . . שכר
שְׂכַרְתִּיךָ [q] id. pret. 1 pers. sing., suff. 2 pers. sing. masc. שכר
שַׂכֹּתָ [r] Kal pret. 2 pers. sing. masc. . . שוך
שַׂכֹּתִי [s] וְ Kal pret. 1 pers. sing.; acc. shifted by conv. וְ (comp. § 8. rem. 7) . . . סכך

שַׁל Kal imp. sing. masc. . . . . נשל
שֹׁל [t] Kal inf. abs. . . . . . שלל
שֶׁלֹּא pref. שֶׁ) adv. . . . . . לא
שַׁלְאֲנָן [u] adj. masc. sing., שַׁאֲנָן with ל inserted . שאן

[שָׁלַב] Kal not used; Chald. שַׁלֵּב Pa. *to join together*. Pu. part. מְשֻׁלָּבוֹת *joined together*, Ex. 26. 17; 36. 22.

שְׁלַבִּים masc. pl. *joinings, edges, borders*, 1 Ki. 7. 28, 29.

שֶׁלֶג, שָׁלַג (§ 35. r. 2) masc. *snow*. הִשְׁלִיג Hiph. *to be white as snow*, of the bones of the slain, only Ps. 68. 16; or perh. causative like הִמְטִיר, *to cause to snow* (תַּשְׁלֵג 2 pers.), in allusion to some destructive snowfall; see also צַלְמוֹן.

[שָׁלָה, שָׁלֵו] pret. 1 pers. שָׁלַוְתִּי, 3 pers. pl. שָׁלוּ; ap. יֵשֶׁל. —I. *to be quiet, at ease, to enjoy prosperity*.—II. *to make prosperous*, Job 27. 8; others, *to draw out*, i. q. שָׁלַל, נָשַׁל; or the form יֵשֶׁל l. c. is supposed to stand for יִשְׁאַל *he shall require*. Niph. *to become negligent*, 2 Ch. 29. 11; others, *to go astray, err*, i. q. Chald. שְׁלָה. Hiph. 2 Ki. 4. 28, *to deceive*, either from the idea of *quieting, flattering*, by promise of happiness, or *leading astray*, comp. Niph.

שְׁלָה Chald. *to be at ease*, Da. 4. 1.

שַׁל masc. *fault, error*, 2 Sa. 6. 7, comp. Niph.

שָׁלֵו, שָׁלֵיו, שְׁלֵיו (pl. c. שַׁלְוֵי dec. 5, comp. § 33, rem. 1), fem. שְׁלֵוָה.—I. adj. *at ease, prosperous*. —II. *careless, unmindful* of God, Eze. 23. 42.—III. subst. *quiet, prosperity*, Job 20. 20.

שֶׁלֶו masc. dec. 6 a (with suff. שַׁלְוִי), *quiet, prosperity*, Ps. 30. 7.

שָׁלוּ Chald. fem. *failure, negligence*, or *error, fault* (comp. Niph.), Da. 6. 5; Ezr. 4. 22; 6. 9; & Da. 3. 29, where Khethib has שָׁלָה.

שַׁלְוָה fem. (constr. שַׁלְוַת; no pl. abs.).—I. *quiet, prosperity*.—II. *carelessness, negligence* of God, Pr. 1. 32.

שְׁלֵוָא Chald. fem. d. 8 a, *quiet, prosperity*, Da. 4. 24.

שְׁלִי masc. *quiet, stillness*, 2 Sa. 3. 27.

שִׁלְיָה fem. *the after-birth*.

שִׁילֹה I. *Shiloh*, Ge. 49. 10, *pacificator*, or *bringer of peace*, i. e. the Messiah; but the ancient versions have evidently read here שֶׁלֹּה (שֶׁלּוֹ) *whose it is*; שֶׁ, i. q. אֲשֶׁר, & לֹה, לוֹ *to him*, comp. Eze. 21. 32. —II. שִׁלֹה, שִׁלוֹ, שִׁילֹה, שִׁילוֹ pr. name of a city

[a] Eze. 29. 18. [b] Hab. 2. 15. [c] Ge. 30. 16. [d] Pr. 26. 10. [e] 1 Sa. 25. 36. [f] Jon. 1. 3. [g] Is. 29. 9. [h] Ne. 6. 12. [i] Je. 13. 13; Eze. 23. 33. [k] Is. 28. 1. [l] Je. 46. 21. [m] 2 Ch. 24. 12. [n] Ex. 2. 9. [o] Ge. 31. 8, 8. [p] Is. 51. 21. [q] Ge. 30. 16. [r] Job 1. 10. [s] Ex. 33. 22. [t] Ru. 2. 16. [u] Job 21. 23.

in the tribe of Ephraim, north of Bethel, where the tabernacle remained for a long time. Gent. noun שִׁלֹנִי *Shilonite.*

שְׁלָה[a] Chald. Kh. שְׁלָה, K. שָׁלוּ, noun fem. sing. . שלה

שֵׁלָה וְ׳ pr. name masc. (for שְׁאֵלָה) . . שאל

שְׁלֵה[b] Chald. Peal part. pass. sing. masc. (§ 55, note) שלה

שִׁלֹה pr. name, see תַּאֲנַת שׁ׳.

שַׁלְהֶבֶת[c] / שַׁלְהֶבֶת[d] } noun fem. sing. . . . . . להב

שְׂלָו[e] masc. (pl. שַׂלְוִים § 35. rem. 10) *quails.* In the sing. the Keri has everywhere שְׂלָיו.

שָׁלֵו adj. m. sing., pl. c. שַׁלְוֵי d.5 (comp. § 35. r. 1) שלה

שָׁלוּ Kal pret. 3 pers. pl., or Chald. noun fem. sing. שלה

שִׁלוֹ pr. name of a place, see שִׁילֹה . . שלה

שַׁלְוָה[f] וְ׳[g] noun fem. sing. (no pl.) . . . שלה

שְׁלֵוָה וּ adj. fem. sing. from שָׁלֵו masc.; וּ bef. (:) שלה

שָׁלוֹחַ וְ׳ Kal inf. abs. . . . . . שלח

שָׁלוּחַ id. part. pass. sing. masc. . . . שלח

שְׁלוּחָה id. part. pass. sing. fem. . . . שלח

שְׁלוּחֶיהָ[h] the foll. with suff. 3 pers. sing. fem. . שלח

שִׁלּוּחִים[i] noun masc., pl. of [שִׁלּוּחַ] dec. 1b . שלח

שַׁלְוֵי[k] וְ adj. pl. constr. masc. see שָׁלֵו dec. 5 (comp. § 33. rem. 1) . . . . . שלה

שַׂלְוִים[l] noun masc., pl. of שְׂלָו dec. 6 (§ 35. rem. 16, comp. rem. 10) . . . . שלו

שָׁלוֹם וְ׳ adj. or subst. masc. dec. 3a . . שלם

שַׁלּוּם וְ׳ pr. name masc. . . . . . שלם

שְׁלוֹם noun masc. sing., constr. of שָׁלוֹם dec. 3a שלם

שְׁלוֹמִי id. with suff. 1 pers. sing. . . . שלם

שְׁלוֹמִים[m] adj. masc., pl. of שָׁלוֹם dec. 3a . . שלם

שִׁלּוּמִים[n] noun masc., pl. of שִׁלּוּם dec. 1b . שלם

שְׁלוֹמִית pr. name masc. . . . . . שלם

שְׁלוֹמֶךָ[o] noun masc. sing., suff. 2 pers. sing. masc. from שָׁלוֹם dec. 3a . . . . שלם

שְׁלוֹמֵנוּ[p] id. with suff. 1 pers. pl. . . . שלם

שַׁלּוּן pr. name masc. . . . . . שלל

שְׁלוּפָה Kal part. pass. sing. fem. [of שָׁלוּף] . שלף

שָׁלוֹשׁ וְ׳ num. card. fem. sing. . . . שלש

שְׁלוֹשׁ[q] id. constr. st. . . . . . שלש

שְׁלוֹשָׁה וּ׳ (2 Ch. 4. 4.) id. masc.; וּ bef. (:) שלש

שְׁלוֹשִׁים[r] id. com. gen. pl. . . . . שלש

שַׁלְוַת וְ noun fem. sing., constr. of שַׁלְוָה (no pl.) שלה

שָׁלוֹתָ[s] Kal pret. 2 pers. sing. masc. . . שלל

שָׁלַוְתִּי[t] Kal pret. 1 pers. sing. R. שלו see . . שלה

שָׁלַח וְ׳ fut. יִשְׁלַח; inf. c. שְׁלֹחַ, שְׁלֹחַ.—I. *to send* a person or thing, with אֶל, עַל of the person *to* whom; with לְ and inf. *to send* to do any thing; with בְּיַד *by* whom; שְׁלַח לְךָ *send for thyself,* Nu. 13. 2.—II. *to send word, a message, a charge.* —III. *to send, commission,* comp. 2 Sa. 11. 22.— IV. *to send away,* i. e. *to let loose, let go,* Ps. 50. 19; שָׁלַח יָד מִן *to let go the hand from* any thing, i. e. to withdraw it, 1 Ki. 13. 4; Ca. 5. 4.—V. *to put forth, stretch out, extend;* שׁ׳ יָד בְּ *to lay hand on* a person or thing, i. e. *to injure,* or *on* a thing, *to take it unjustly,* and is const. also with אֶל, עַל; part. שָׁלוּחַ *stretched out, slim, slender,* Ge. 49. 21. Niph. *to be sent,* Est. 3. 13. Pi. שִׁלַּח.—I. *to send,* with עַל *to* whom; espec. in reference to calamities which God sends, with עַל, אֶל, בְּ *on* whom.—II. *to send away, let go, dismiss;* e. g. one on his way, *to accompany him;* a husband his wife, *to divorce.*—III. *to let loose, set free, set at liberty;* שׁ׳ מְדוֹן *to let loose, occasion strife.*—IV. *to give up, deliver up,* with בְּ, בְּיַד, Job 8. 4; Ps. 81. 13.—V. *to let down* by a cord, Je. 38. 6, 11; *to let hang down* the hair, Eze. 44. 20.—VI. *to cast, throw, shoot;* also *to cast down, cast off, cast forth.*—VII. שׁ׳ בָּאֵשׁ *to set on fire.*—VIII. *to put forth, stretch out, extend,* espec. the hand. Pu. I. *to be sent.*—II. *to be sent away, let go, dismissed;* of a woman, *to be divorced;* hence *to be left, forsaken.*—III. *to be cast out, driven out.* Hiph. *to send,* e. g. plagues, &c. with בְּ *on* any one.

שְׁלַח Chald. fut. יִשְׁלַח.—I. *to send.*—II. *to put forth* the hand.

שֶׁלַח masc. dec. 6 (with suff. שִׁלְחוֹ, but in pause שָׁלַח § 35. rem. 2 & 5).—I. a *missile, weapon,* as a *dart, javelin, spear.*—II. *shoot, sprout.*—III. pr. name masc. Ge. 10. 24; 11. 12.—IV. pr. name of a pool near mount Zion, called also שִׁלֹחַ Ne. 3. 15.

שִׁלֹחַ (*a sending forth,* sc. of water) pr. name, *Siloah,* a spring and conduit on the south-west of Jerusalem.

שִׁלּוּחִים masc. pl. (of שִׁלּוּחַ dec. 1b) prop. *a sending away.*—I. *divorce,* Ex. 18. 2; *bill of divorce,* Mi. 1. 14.—II. *presents, dowry.*

שְׁלֻחוֹת f. pl. (of שְׁלוּחָה dec. 10) *shoots,* Is. 16. 8.

שִׁלְחִי (*armed,* comp. שֶׁלַח) pr. name of a man.

[a] Da. 3. 29. [b] Da. 4. 1. [c] Job 15. 30. [d] Ca. 8. 6; Eze. 21. 3. [e] Ps. 105. 40. [f] Ps. 122. 7. [g] Pr. 17. 1. [h] Ex. 18. 2. [i] Mi. 1. 14. [k] Ps. 73. 12. [l] Nu. 11. 31. [m] Je. 13. 19. [n] Is. 34. 8. [o] Is. 48. 18. [p] Is. 53. 5. [q] Eze. 40. 11. [r] Est. 4. 11; 2 Ch. 16. 12. [s] Hab. 2. 8. [t] Job 3. 26.

שִׁלְחִים (*armed men*) pr. name of a city in the tribe of Judah, Jos. 15. 32.

שֻׁלְחָן masc. dec. 2b (pl. שֻׁלְחָנוֹת), *a table*; שֻׁלְחָן הַפָּנִים, *to spread, prepare a table*; עָרַךְ שׁ׳ שׁ׳ הַמַּעֲרֶכֶת *table of shewbread.*

מִשְׁלָח masc. dec. 2b.—I. *a sending forth* of cattle for grazing, Is. 7. 25.—II. *a putting forth* of the hand, i.e. *that to which the hand is put, business.*

מִשְׁלוֹחַ masc. *a sending*, Est. 9. 19, 22; with יָד *that on which the hand is laid, prey, booty.*

מִשְׁלַחַת fem.—I. *a sending*, Ps. 78. 49.—II. *a dismission, discharge*, Ec. 8. 8.

שֶׁלַח pr. name masc. for שֶׁלַח (§ 35. rem. 2) . שלח

[a]שָׁלֹחַ וְ׳ Kal inf. abs. . . . . . שלח

שַׁלַּח וְ׳ Piel inf. constr. or imp. sing. masc. . שלח

שַׁלֵּחַ id. inf. abs. . . . . . שלח

[b]שֶׁלַח וְ׳ noun masc. sing. (suff. שִׁלְחוֹ) dec. 6 (§ 35. rem. 5), also pr. name . . . . שלח

שְׁלַח וּ׳ Kal imp. s. m. or (Is. 58. 9) inf.; וּ bef. (:) שלח

שְׁלַח Chald. Peal pret. 3 pers. sing. masc. . שלח

שְׁלֹחַ Kal inf. constr. . . . . שלח

שִׁלַּח וְ׳ Piel pret. 3 pers. sing. masc. . . שלח

[c]שֹׁלֵחַ וְ׳ Kal part. act. sing. masc. dec. 7b . שלח

[d]שֻׁלַּח / שֻׁלָּח } Pual pret. 3 pers. sing. masc. . . שלח

[e]שָׁלְחָה וְ׳ Kal pret. 3 pers. sing. fem. . . שלח

[f]שַׁלְּחָהּ Piel inf. (שַׁלַּח), suff. 3 pers. sing. fem. d. 7b שלח

[g]שְׁלֻחָה defect. for שְׁלוּחָה (q. v.) . . . שלח

שִׁלְחָה Kal imp. s. m. (שְׁלַח) with parag. ה (§ 8. r. 11) שלח

שִׁלְּחָה Piel pret. 3 pers. sing. fem. for which שִׁלְּחָה Eze. 17. 7; 34. 4 (§ 10. rem. 7) . שלח

[h]שִׁלְּחָהּ וְ׳ id. pret. 3 p. s. m. (שִׁלַּח), suff. 3 p. s. f. שלח

[i]שֻׁלְּחָה Pual pret. 3 pers. sing. fem. . . שלח

[k]שִׁלְּחֻהוּ Piel pret. 3 pers. pl. (שִׁלְּחוּ), suff. 3 p. s. m. שלח

שָׁלְחוּ וְ׳ Kal pret. 3 pers. pl. . . . . שלח

[l]שַׁלְּחוּ Piel imp. pl. masc. . . . . שלח

שְׁלָחוֹ Kal pret. 3 pers. sing. m., suff. 3 pers. s. m. שלח

[m]שָׁלֵחוּ in pause for שָׁלְחוּ (§ 8. rem. 12) . . שלח

שְׁלַחוּ Chald. Peal pret. 3 pers. pl. masc. . . שלח

שָׁלֵחוּ in pause for שָׁלְחוּ (§ 8. rem. 12) . שלח

שִׁלְחוֹ n. m. s., suff. 3 p. s. m. fr. שֶׁלַח d. 6 (§ 35. r. 5) שלח

[n]שִׁלְּחוֹ וְ׳ Piel pret. 3 p. s. m. (שִׁלַּח), suff. 3 p. s. m. שלח

[o]שִׁלְחוּ וְ׳ Kal imp. pl. masc. . . . . שלח

[p]שִׁלְּחוּ, שִׁלְּחוּ Piel pret. 3 pers. pl. (§ 10. rem. 7) שלח

[q]שֻׁלְּחוּ Pual pret. 3 pers. pl. . . . . שלח

[r]שִׁלְּחוּךָ Piel pret. 3 pers. pl., suff. 2 pers. sing. masc. שלח

שַׁלְּחוּנִי id. imp. pl. masc., suff. 1 pers. sing. . שלח

שִׁלְחִי pr. name masc. . . . . שלח

שֹׁלְחִי Kal part. act. s. m., suff. 1 p. s. fr. שֹׁלֵחַ d. 7b שלח

שְׁלָחַיִךְ n. m. pl., suff. 2 p. s. f. fr. שֶׁלַח d. 6 (§ 35. r. 5) שלח

[u]שְׁלֻחִים defect. for שְׁלוּחִים (q. v.) . . . שלח

שִׁלְחִים וְ pr. name of a place . . . שלח

שֹׁלְחִים Kal part. act. masc., pl. of שֹׁלֵחַ dec. 7b שלח

[x]שָׁלְחֲךָ id. inf., suff. 2 pers. sing. masc. . . שלח

שְׁלָחֲךָ id. pret. 3 pers. sing. m., suff. 2 pers. s. m. שלח

[y]שְׁלָחֵךְ id. id., suff. 2 pers. sing. fem. . . שלח

[z]שִׁלַּחֲךָ Piel pret. 3 pers. sing. m., suff. 2 pers. s. m. שלח

[a]שֹׁלֵחֲךָ Kal part. act. sing. masc., suff. 2 pers. sing. masc. from שֹׁלֵחַ dec. 7b (§ 36. rem. 3) שלח

שַׁלְּחָם Piel inf. (שַׁלַּח), suff. 3 pers. pl. masc. d. 7b שלח

[b]שְׁלָחָם Kal pret. 3 pers. sing. m., suff. 3 pers. pl. m. שלח

[c]שִׁלְּחָם Piel pret. 3 p. pl. m. (שִׁלַּח), suff. 3 p. pl. m. שלח

שֻׁלְחָן וְ׳ noun masc. sing. dec. 2b . . שלח

שֻׁלְחַן id., constr. st. . . . . . שלח

[d]שְׁלַחְנָא Chald. Peal pret. 1 pers. pl. . . שלח

[e]שֻׁלְחָנָהּ noun m. s., suff. 3 pers. s. f. fr. שֻׁלְחָן d. 2b שלח

[f]שָׁלַחְנוּ Kal pret. 1 pers. pl. [for שָׁלַחְנוּ] . שלח

[g]שְׁלָחָנוּ id. pret. 3 pers. sing. masc., suff. 1 pers. pl. שלח

[h]שִׁלַּחְנוּ Piel pret. 1 pers. pl. . . . . שלח

שֻׁלְחָנוֹ noun m. s., suff. 3 pers. s. m. fr. שֻׁלְחָן d. 2b שלח

שֻׁלְחָנוֹת id. with pl. fem. term., abs. st. . . שלח

שַׁלְּחֵנִי Piel imp. sing. masc. (שַׁלַּח), suff. 1 pers. s. שלח

[i]שַׁלְּחֻנִי defect. for שַׁלְּחוּנִי (q. v.) . . שלח

שְׁלָחַנִי / שְׁלָחַנִי } Kal pret. 3 pers. sing. masc. with suff. 1 pers. sing. . . . . } שלח

[k]שַׁלְּחֵנִי id. imp. sing. masc. (שַׁלַּח), suff. 1 pers. s. שלח

שֻׁלְחָנִי noun m. s., suff. 1 pers. s. fr. שֻׁלְחָן d. 2b שלח

שֻׁלְחָנְךָ / [l]שֻׁלְחָנֶךָ } id. with suff. 2 pers. sing. masc. . שלח

[m]שֻׁלְחָנָם id. with suff. 3 pers. pl. masc. . . שלח

[n]שָׁלַחְתָּ / שָׁלַחְתָּ } Kal pret. 2 pers. sing. masc. (§ 8. rem. 7) . . . . } שלח

שִׁלַּחְתָּ Piel pret. 2 pers. sing. masc. . . שלח

[o]שִׁלַּחְתָּהּ וְ id. id., suff. 3 pers. sing. fem. . שלח

[p]שִׁלַּחְתּוֹ [q]וְ׳ id. id., suff. 3 pers. sing. masc. . שלח

[a] Nu. 22. 37. [b] 2 Ch. 32. 5. [c] Job 5. 10. [d] Ob. 1. [e] De. 25. 11. [f] De. 22. 29. [g] Ge. 49. 21. [h] De. 24. 1, 3, 4. [i] Is. 50. 1. [k] 1 Ch. 12. 19. [l] 1 Sa. 5. 11. [m] 2 Ki. 2. 17. [n] 1 Sa. 24. 20. [o] Ne. 8. 10. [p] Ps. 74. 7. [q] Ge. 44. 3. [r] Ob. 7. [s] Ge. 24. 56. [t] Ca. 4. 13. [u] 1 Ki. 9. 16. [x] Ge. 38. 17. [y] 1 Sa. 25. 32. [z] 1 Sa. 20. 22. [a] 1 Sa. 21. 3. [b] Eze. 13. 6. [c] Jos. 22. 7. [d] Ezr. 4. 14. [e] Pr. 9. 2. [f] Jos. 6. 17. [g] 1 Sa. 25. 40. [h] Ex. 14. 5. [i] Ge. 24. 54. [k] Is. 6. 8. [l] Job 36. 16. [m] Ps. 69. 23. [n] 1 Sa. 25. 25. [o] De. 21. 14. [p] 2 Sa. 3. 24. [q] Je. 34. 14.

שְׁלַחְתּוּן[a] Ch. Peal pret. 2 pers. pl. masc. . שלח

שְׁלַחְתִּי, וְשָׁלַחְתִּי } Kal pret. 1 pers. sing.; acc. shifted by conv. וְ (§ 8. rem. 7) . . שלח

שִׁלַּחְתִּי, וְשִׁלַּחְתִּי } Piel pret. 1 pers. sing.; acc. shifted (v. i.) . . . . שלח

שֻׁלַּחְתִּי[b] Pual pret. 1 pers. sing. . . . שלח

שְׁלֻחוֹתֶיהָ[c] noun f. pl., suff. 3 pers. s. f. fr. [שְׁלֻחָה] d. 10 שלח

שִׁלַּחְתִּיהָ Piel pret. 1 pers. sing., suff. 3 pers. sing. fem. שלח

שְׁלַחְתִּיו Kal pret. 1 pers. sing., suff. 3 pers. sing. m. שלח

שְׁלַחְתִּיךָ id. id., suff. 2 pers. sing. masc. . שלח

שִׁלַּחְתִּיךָ וְ Piel pret. 1 pers. sing., suff. 2 pers. sing. m. שלח

שְׁלַחְתִּים Kal pret. 1 pers. sing., suff. 3 pers. pl. masc. שלח

שִׁלַּחְתָּם[d] וְ Piel pret. 2 pers. s. m., suff. 3 pers. pl. m. שלח

שְׁלַחְתֶּם[e] וְ Kal pret. 2 pers. pl. masc.; וּ, for וְ, conv. שלח

שִׁלַּחְתֶּם[f] וְ[g] Piel pret. 2 pers. pl. masc. . . שלח

שְׁלַחְתָּנוּ[h] Kal pret. 2 pers. sing. masc., suff. 1 pers. pl. שלח

שְׁלַחְתַּנִי[i] id. id., suff. 1 pers. sing. [for תָּנִי] . שלח

שִׁלַּחְתָּנִי[k], וְשִׁלַּחְתָּנִי[l] } Piel pret. 2 pers. sing. masc., suff. 1 pers. sing. . . . שלח

שָׁלַט[m] fut. יִשְׁלַט *to rule, have dominion* or *power over*, with בְּ, עַל. Hiph. I. *to let rule, let have dominion*, Ps. 119. 133.—II. *to give permission, to permit*, Ec. 5. 18; 6. 2.

שְׁלֵט Ch.—I. *to rule, have dominion* or *power over*, with בְּ.—II. *to get the mastery of, to seize*, Da. 6. 25. Aph. *to cause to rule, appoint ruler*, with בְּ, Da. 2. 38, 48.

שֶׁלֶט masc. dec. 6 a (pl. c. שִׁלְטֵי), *a shield*.

שַׁלִּיט masc. dec. 1 b, שַׁלֶּטֶת fem. adj.—I. *imperious, impudent*, Eze. 16. 30.—II. *having power, bearing rule*, Ec. 8. 8.—III. subst. *ruler, magistrate*.

שַׁלִּיט Ch. masc. dec. 1 a.—I. *powerful, mighty, having power*.—II. *being permitted, lawful*, לָא שַׁ׳ *it is not lawful*, Ec. 7. 24.—III. *ruler, prince*.

שִׁלְטוֹן m. *power, authority*, Ec. 8. 4, 8; others, adj. *powerful, potent*.

שִׁלְטוֹן Ch. m. d. 1 a, *ruler, magistrate*, Da. 3. 2, 3.

שָׁלְטָן Ch. masc. d. 1 b, *dominion, power, empire*.

שְׁלֵט[n] Ch. Peal pret. 3 pers. sing. masc. . שלט

שָׁלְטוּ[o] Kal pret. 3 pers. pl. . . . . שלט

שְׁלִטוּ[p] Ch. Peal pret. 3 pers. pl. masc. . . שלט

שִׁלְטוֹן noun masc. sing. . . . . שלט

שִׁלְטוֹנֵי[q] Ch. id. pl., constr. st. dec. 1 a . . שלט

שִׁלְטֵי noun masc. pl. constr. fr. [שֶׁלֶט] dec. 6 a שלט

שִׁלְטֵיהֶם[r] id. pl., suff. 3 pers. pl. masc. . . שלט

שָׁלְטָן וְ[s] Chald. noun masc. sing. dec. 1 b . שלט

שָׁלְטָן[t] Chald. id., constr. st. . . . שלט

שָׁלְטָנָא[u] וְ Chald. id., emph. st. . . . שלט

שָׁלְטָנֵהּ[x] וְ Chald. id., suff. 3 pers. sing. masc. . שלט

שָׁלְטָנְהוֹן[y] Chald. id., suff. 3 pers. pl. masc. . שלט

שִׁלְטֹנֵי[z] defect. for שִׁלְטוֹנֵי (q. v.) . . שלט

שָׁלְטָנַיָּא[a] Chald. noun masc. pl., emph. st. fr. שָׁלְטָן d. 1 b שלט

שָׁלְטָנָךְ[b] וְ Chald. id. sing., suff. 2 pers. sing. masc. . שלט

שַׁלֶּטֶת[c] adj. fem. sing. [for שַׁלֶּטֶת] from שַׁלִּיט masc. (§ 39. No. 4 d) . . . . שלט

שֶׁלִּי[d] pref. ·שֶׁ & pref. prep. לְ with suff. 1 pers. sing. לי

שְׁלֵיו[e] וְ in full for שָׁלֵו (q. v.) . . . שלה

שְׁלֵיו[f] adj. masc. sing., see שָׁלֵו under . שלה

שְׁלִיחַ Chald. Peal part. pass. sing. masc. . שלח

שַׁלִּיט וְ[g] adj. or subst. masc. dec. 1 b . . שלט

שַׁלִּיטָא[h] Chald. id., emph. st. . . . שלט

שַׁלִּיטִים[i] id. pl., abs. st. . . . . שלט

שַׁלִּיטִין[k] וְ[l] Ch. id. pl., abs. st. . . . שלט

שְׁלִים[m] Chald. Peal part. pass. sing. masc. . שלם

שָׁלִישׁ[n] noun masc. sing. (§ 32. rem. 1) . שלש

שָׁלִישׁוֹ[o] id. with suff. 3 pers. sing. masc. . . שלש

שְׁלִישִׁי, שְׁלִישִׁיָּה } adj. ord. masc. & fem. sing. from שָׁלֹשׁ שלש

שָׁלִישָׁיו[p] the foll. with suff. 3 pers. sing. masc. . שלש

שָׁלִישִׁים[q] noun masc. pl. of שָׁלִישׁ dec. 1 b (§ 32. r. 1) שלש

שְׁלִישִׁית, שְׁלִשִׁת[r] } adj. ord. fem. from שְׁלִישִׁי masc.; וּ bef. (:) . . . . שלש

שְׁלִשְׁתָּה[s] id. with parag. ה, *adv.* . . . שלש

שָׁלַךְ Hiph. הִשְׁלִיךְ.—I. *to throw, cast*, with אֶל *into*, עַל, בְּ *upon*, מִן *from*; הִ׳ אַחֲרָיו *to cast behind him*, i. e. *to despise*.—II. *to cast off*, as a *plant* its flowers, Job 15. 33.—III. *to cast out, expel, banish*.—IV. *to cast down, overthrow, destroy*. Hoph. הָשְׁלַךְ, הֻשְׁלַךְ (§ 11. rem. 10).—I. *to be thrown, cast*.—II. *to cast forth*.—III. *to be cast down, overthrown*, Da. 8. 11.

שָׁלָךְ masc. *the gannet*, a sea-fowl, Le. 11. 17; De. 14. 17. Also

שַׁלֶּכֶת fem.—I. *a felling* of a tree, Is. 6. 13.—II. pr. name of a gate of the temple, 1 Ch. 26. 16 שלך

---

[a] Ezr. 4. 18. [b] Da. 10. 11. [c] Is. 16. 8. [d] Je. 27. 3. [e] 2 Sa. 15. 36. [f] Je. 34. 16. [g] 1 Sa. 6. 8. [h] Nu. 13. 27. [i] Ex. 5. 22. [k] Ge. 31. 42. [l] 1 Sa. 20. 5. [m] Ec. 8. 9. [n] Da. 3. 27. [o] Ne. 5. 15. [p] Da. 6. 25. [q] Da. 3. 3. [r] Eze. 27. 11. [s] Da. 7. 6. [t] Da. 4. 31; 7. 14. [u] Da. 7. 27. [x] Da. 4. 31; 7. 14. [y] Da. 7. 12. [z] Da. 3. 2. [a] Da. 7. 27. [b] Da. 4. 19. [c] Eze. 16. 30. [d] Ca. 1. 6; 8. 12. [e] Job 21. 23. [f] Je. 49. 31. [g] Da. 2. 10. [h] Da. 2. 15. [i] Ec. 7. 19. [k] Da. 4. 23. [l] Ezr. 4. 20. [m] Ezr. 5. 16. [n] Ps. 80. 6. [o] 2 Ki. 15. 25. [p] 2 Ch. 8. 9. [q] Eze. 23. 15, 23. [r] Nu. 28. 14. [s] Eze. 21. 19.

שָׁלַל[a] pret. שָׁלוּתִי, שָׁלְלוּ; inf. שֹׁל, שָׁלֹל (§ 18. rem. 13). —I. *to draw out*, Ru. 2. 16; Arab. id.—II. *to plunder, spoil.*—III. *to carry off* spoil, Is. 10. 6; Eze. 29. 19. Hithpo. אֶשְׁתּוֹלַל (Chald. form for הִשְׁתּוֹלֵל) *to be spoiled, become a prey*, Ps. 76. 6; Is. 59. 15.

שָׁלָל masc. dec. 4 a.—I. *spoil, plunder, booty.*—II. *gain, profit*, Pr. 31. 11.

שׁוֹלָל m.—I. *stripped, naked*, Mi. 1. 8; Sept. & Syr. *barefoot.*—II. *captive, prisoner*, Job 12. 17, 19.

שָׁלוּן (*spoil*) pr. name masc. Ne. 3. 15.

שָׁלָל	noun masc. sing. dec. 4 a . . .	שלל
שְׁלַל	id., constr. st.; ו bef. (:) . . .	שלל
שְׁלָלָהּ	id. with suff. 3 pers. sing. fem. . .	שלל
שָׁלְלוּ	Kal pret. 3 pers. pl.	שלל
שְׁלָלוֹ[b]	noun m. s., suff. 3 pers. s. m. fr. שָׁלָל dec. 4 a	שלל
שֹׁלְלֶיהָ[c]	Kal part. act. pl. masc., suff. 3 pers. sing. fem. from שֹׁלֵל dec. 7 b	שלל
שֹׁלְלֵיהֶם[d]	id. pl., suff. 3 pers. pl. masc. . . .	שלל
שְׁלָלֵךְ[e]	noun masc. s., suff. 2 pers. s. fem. fr. שָׁלָל d. 4 a	שלל
שְׁלַלְכֶם[f]	id., suff. 2 pers. pl. masc.; ו bef. (:) .	שלל
שְׁלָלָם	id., suff. 3 pers. pl. masc.; ו id. . .	שלל

שׁלם a Root which does not exist, the following being a mere transposition of letters.

שַׂלְמָה fem. dec. 12 a (transp. for שִׂמְלָה, see שׂמל).—I. *a garment.*—II. pr. name of the father of Boaz, called also שַׂלְמוֹן, comp. Ru. 4. 20, 21, & שַׂלְמָא 1 Ch. 2. 11.

שַׂלְמָא (*garment*) pr. name of a son of Caleb, 1 Ch. 2. 51, 54, see also the preced.

[שָׁלֵם] fut. יִשְׁלַם.—I. *to be entire*, i. e. *sound, safe*, Job 9. 4; 22. 21.—II. *to be completed, finished.*—III. *to be at peace*, only part. Ps. 7. 5, שׁוֹלְמִי *one at peace with me, my friend*; pass. שְׁלוּם *peaceable*, 2 Sa. 20. 19. Pi. שִׁלֵּם, שִׁלַּם (§ 10. rem. 1).—I. *to preserve, keep uninjured*, Job 8. 6.—II. *to complete, finish*, 1 Ki. 9. 25.—III. *to restore, make good.*—IV. *to repay, pay* a debt.—V. *to pay, perform*, as a vow.—VI. *to requite, recompense*, with acc. of the thing, and with לְ, also acc. of person. Pu. I. *to be perfected*, only part. *perfect*, Is. 42. 19, of the servant of God, comp. ver. 1.—II. *to be paid, performed*, as a vow, Ps. 65. 2.—III. *to be requited, recompensed.* Hiph. I. *to complete, execute, perform.*—II. *to make peace with* any one, with עִם, אֶת; with אֶל *to submit oneself in peace to* any one, Jos. 11. 19.—III. *to cause to be at peace with*, with עִם, Pr. 16. 7. Hoph. *to be at peace with*, with לְ, Job 5. 23.

שְׁלֵם Ch. *to complete, finish*, Ezr. 5. 16. Aph. I. *to make an end of*, Da. 5. 26.—II. *to restore*, Ezr. 7. 19.

שָׁלֵם masc. dec. 5 a, fem. שְׁלֵמָה adj.—I. *whole*, אֲבָנִים שְׁלֵמוֹת; *whole, unhewn stones.*—II. *perfect, complete, full*, e. g. אֶבֶן שְׁלֵמָה *full weight*; גָּלוּת שְׁלֵמָה *captives in full number*, Am. 1. 6, 9.—III. *complete, finished*, 2 Ch. 8. 16.—IV. *safe, uninjured*, Ge. 33. 18.—V. *peaceable, at peace with*, with אֵת, Ge. 34. 21, לֵב שָׁלֵם עִם יְהוָֹה *a heart at peace with God*; better with others, *whole, perfect, sincere* with God.—VI. pr. name, *Salem*, i. q. Jerusalem.

שָׁלוֹם masc. dec. 3 a.—I. adj. *sound, well* in health.—II. *the whole*, only pl. adverbially, *wholly*, Je. 13. 19.—III. *safe, secure, enjoying peace.*—IV. *peaceably, friendlily disposed*, Ps. 55. 21.—V. subst. *health, welfare, prosperity, peace*; הֲשָׁלוֹם לוֹ *is it well with him?* שָׁאַל לוֹ לְשָׁלוֹם *to inquire after the welfare* of any one; שָׁלוֹם לְךָ *peace be to thee*; or affirmatively, *it is well with thee*; לֵךְ לְשָׁלוֹם *go in peace.*—VI. *peace*, as opposed to war; קָרָא לְשָׁלוֹם לְ *to offer peace*, or *make peaceable proposals*; עָנָה שָׁלוֹם אֵת *to give a peaceable answer*, i. e. to accept peace offered; עָשָׂה שָׁלוֹם לְ *to make peace* with any one.—VII. *friendship*; אִישׁ שְׁלֹמִי *my friend.*

שְׁלָם Chald. masc. dec. 1 a, *peace, prosperity.*

שֶׁלֶם masc. dec. 6 a (pl. with suff. שַׁלְמֵיכֶם), *peace-offering*; perh. also *thank-offering.*

שִׁלֵּם masc.—I. *retribution*, De. 32. 35.—II. pr. name masc. Ge. 46. 24, for which שַׁלּוּם 1 Ch. 7. 13. Patronym. שִׁלֵּמִי Nu. 26. 49.

שִׁלֻּם, שִׁלּוּם masc. dec. 1 b, *retribution.*

שַׁלֻּם, שַׁלּוּם (*retribution*) pr. name—I. of a king of Israel.—II. of a king of Judah, son of Josiah, Je. 22. 11.—III. of several other men.

שִׁלֻּמָה fem. d. 10, *retribution, punishment*, Ps. 91. 8.

שְׁלֹמֹה (*peaceable*) pr. name, *Solomon*, son of David and king of Israel.

שְׁלֹמִי (*peaceable*) pr. name masc. Nu. 34. 27.

שַׁלְמַי (for שֶׁלֶמְיָה q. v.) pr. name masc. Ne. 7. 48; Ezr. 2. 46, where Khethib has שַׁמְלַי.

שְׁלֻמִיאֵל (*at peace with God*, or *friend of God*) pr. name masc. Nu. 1. 6; 2. 12.

[a] Eze. 29. 19. [b] Ju. 8. 24, 25. [c] Je. 50. 10. [d] Eze. 39. 10. [e] Zec. 14. 1. [f] Is. 38. 4.

שֶׁלֶמְיָהוּ, שֶׁלֶמְיָה (*retribution of the Lord*) pr. name masc. of several men.

שְׁלֹמִית (*peaceable*) pr. name—I. of two women, Le. 24. 11 & 1 Ch. 3. 19.—II. of several men, called also שְׁלֹמוֹת 1 Ch. 24. 22, and so in Khethib, 1 Ch 23. 9; 26. 25.

שׁוּלַמִּית (*peaceable*) pr. name of a maiden celebrated in the book of Canticles.

שַׁלְמֹן masc. dec. 1 b, *reward, gift,* Is. 1. 23.

מְשֻׁלָּם (*rewarded,* i. e. *given as a reward*) pr. name masc. of several persons.

מְשִׁלֵּמוֹת (*retributions*) pr. name masc.—I. 2 Ch. 28. 12.—II. Ne. 11. 13, for which מְשִׁלֵּמִית 1 Ch. 9. 12.

מְשֶׁלֶמְיָהוּ, מְשֶׁלֶמְיָה (for מְשֻׁלֶּמְיָה whom *the Lord repays,* or *gives as a reward*) pr. name masc. 1 Ch. 9. 21; 26. 1, 9, called שֶׁלֶמְיָהוּ 1 Ch. 26. 14.

מְשֻׁלֶּמֶת (fem. of מְשֻׁלָּם q. v.) pr. name of the wife of king Manasseh, 2 Ki. 21. 19.

שָׁלֵם adj. masc. sing. dec. 5 a, also pr. name . שלם
שָׁלֵם defect. for שָׁלוֹם (q. v.) . . . שלם
שַׁלֵּם[a] ו׳ Piel imp. s. masc.; or inf. constr. as an abs. שלם
שֶׁלֶם[b] וְ noun masc. sing. (pl. c. שַׁלְמֵי) dec. 6 a שלם
שֶׁלֶם pr. name masc. . . . שלם
שִׁלֵּם[c] וְ׳ Piel pret. 3 pers. sing. masc. (§ 10 r. 1) שלם
שִׁלֵּם[d] וְ noun masc. sing., also pr. name : שלם
שְׁלָם[e] Chald. noun masc. sing. dec. 1 a . . שלם
שְׁלַם[f] וּ [for שְׁלַם] Kal imp. sing. masc.; וּ bef. (:) שלם
שַׁלְמָא ו׳ pr. name masc. . . . שלם
שְׁלָמָא[g] Chald. noun masc. sing., emph. of שְׁלָם d. 1 a שלם
שַׁלָּמָה[h] pref. שֶׁ)(adv. . . . מה
שַׂלְמָה noun fem. sing. dec. 12 a, also pr. name שלם
שְׁלֵמָה adj. fem. sing. from שָׁלֵם masc. . . שלם
שְׁלֹמֹה וּ׳ pr. name masc.; וּ bef. (:) . שלם
שָׁלְמוּ[i] וְ Kal pret. 3 pers. pl. . . . שלם
שַׁלְּמוּ[k] [l]ו׳ Piel imp. pl. masc. . . . שלם
שִׁלְּמוּ[m] וְ id. pret. 3 pers. pl. [for שִׁלְּמוּ comp. § 8. r. 7] שלם
שַׁלְמוֹן וְ pr. name masc. . . . שלם
שְׂלָמוֹת וּ noun f. pl. abs. fr. שַׂלְמָה d. 12 a; וּ bef. (:) שלם
שְׁלֵמוֹת adj. fem., pl. of שְׁלֵמָה, from שָׁלֵם masc. שלם
שְׁלֹמוֹת pr. name masc. . . . שלם
שְׁלֹמוֹת ו׳ Kh. שְׁלֹמוֹת q. v., K. שְׁלֹמִית (q. v.) שלם
שַׂלְמוֹתַי[n] noun fem. pl., suff. 1 pers. s. fr. שַׂלְמָה d. 12 a שלם
שַׂלְמוֹתֵינוּ[o] id. with suff. 1 pers. pl. . . שלם

שַׁלְמַי pr. name masc. . . . . שלם
שַׁלְמֵי[p] noun masc. pl. constr. from שֶׁלֶם dec. 6 a שלם
שַׁלְּמִי[q] [r]ו׳ Piel imp. sing. fem. . . . שלם
שְׁלֹמִי pr. name masc. . . . . שלם
שְׁלֹמִי[s] defect. for שְׁלוֹמִי (q. v.) . . . שלם
שְׁלֻמֵי[t] Kal part. p. pl. constr. m. [fr. שָׁלוּם] d. 3 a שלם
שֹׁלְמִי[u] id. part. act. s. m., suff. 1 p. s. [fr. שֹׁלֵם] d. 7 b שלם
שֶׁלֶמְיָהוּ וְ׳, שֶׁלֶמְיָה וְ׳, שְׁלֻמִיאֵל, pr. names masc. . שלם
שַׁלְמֵיהֶם noun m. pl., suff. 3 p. pl. m. fr. שֶׁלֶם d. 6 a שלם
שְׁלָמָיו id. pl., suff. 3 pers. sing. masc. . . שלם
שְׁלָמֶיךָ[v] id. pl., suff. 2 pers. sing. masc. . . שלם
שַׁלְמֵיכֶם id. pl., suff. 2 pers. pl. masc. . . שלם
שְׁלָמִים וּ׳ id. pl., abs. st.; וּ bef. (:) . שלם
שְׁלֵמִים adj. masc. pl. of שָׁלֵם dec. 5 a . . שלם
שְׁלֹמִית וּ׳ pr. name masc. & fem.; וּ bef. (:) . שלם
שְׁלֹמֶךָ[y] defect. for שְׁלוֹמֶךָ (q. v.) . . . שלם
שְׁלָמְכוֹן Ch. n. m. s., suff. 2 p. pl. m. fr. שְׁלָם d. 1 a שלם
שְׁלֹמָם noun m. s., suff. 3 p. pl. m. fr. שָׁלוֹם d. 3 a שלם
שַׁלְמַן Ho. 10. 14, elsewhere שַׁלְמַנְאֶסֶר pr. name of a king of Assyria, who carried away the ten tribes into captivity.
שַׁלְמֹנִים[z] noun masc., pl. of [שַׁלְמֹן] dec. 1 b . שלם
שַׂלְמַת[a] noun fem. sing., constr. of שַׂלְמָה dec. 12 a שלם
שִׁלֻּמַת[b] וְ noun fem. sing., constr. of [שִׁלֻּמָה] dec. 10 שלם
שַׂלְמֹתַי[c] noun fem. pl., suff. 1 pers. s. fr. שַׂלְמָה d. 12 a שלם
שִׁלַּמְתִּי / וְשִׁלַּמְתִּי } Piel pret. 1 pers. sing.; acc. shifted by conv. וְ (comp. § 8. rem. 7) . } שלם
שַׂלְמֹתֵיהֶם[d] noun fem. pl., suff. 3 pers. pl. masc. from שַׂלְמָה dec. 12 a . . . שלם
שַׂלְמֹתַיִךְ[e] id. pl., suff. 2 pers. sing. fem. . . שלם
שַׂלְמֹתֵיכֶם[f] id. pl., suff. 2 pers. pl. masc. . . שלם
שִׁלַּמְתֶּם[g] Piel pret. 2 pers. pl. masc. . . שלם

שָׁלַף fut. יִשְׁלֹף.—I. *to draw* a sword; שֹׁלֵף חֶרֶב *one drawing the sword,* i. e. armed man.—II. *to pull off* a shoe, Ru. 4. 7, 8.—III. *to pluck up* grass, Ps. 129. 6.

שֶׁלֶף [for שָׁלֶף] pr. name of an Arabian tribe, Ge. 10. 26; 1 Ch. 1. 20 . . . שלף
שְׁלֹף Kal imp. sing. masc. . . . שלף
שֹׁלֵף id. part. act. sing. masc. dec. 7 b . . שלף
שְׁלֻפָה[h] defect. for שְׁלוּפָה (q. v.) . . . שלף
שֹׁלְפֵי[i] Kal part. act. pl. c. masc. from שֹׁלֵף dec. 7 b שלף

[a] Ps. 50. 14. [b] Am. 5. 22. [c] Ju. 1. 7. [d] De. 32. 35. [e] Ezr. 4. 17. [f] Job 22. 21. [g] Ezr. 5. 7. [h] Ca. 1. 7. [i] Is. 60. 20. [k] Je. 50. 29. [l] Ps. 76. 12. [m] Is. 19. 21. [n] Job 9. 31. [o] Jos. 9. 13. [p] Le. 10. 14. [q] Na. 2. 1. [r] 2 Ki. 4. 7. [s] Je. 20. 10. [t] 2 Sa. 20. 19. [u] Ps. 7. 5. [v] Ex. 20. 24. [y] Je. 38. 22; Ob. 7. [z] Is. 1. 23. [a] Ex. 22. 25. [b] Ps. 91. 8. [c] Job 9. 31. [d] Ne. 9. 21. [e] Ca. 4. 11. [f] De. 29. 4. [g] Ge. 44. 4. [h] Nu. 22. 31. [i] Ju. 20. 25.

שָׁלֹשׁ, שָׁלוֹשׁ ו׳ (constr. שְׁלֹשׁ, שְׁלשׁ) fem.; שְׁלֹשָׁה (constr. שְׁלֹשֶׁת § 42. rem. 5) masc.—I. num. card. *three*; שָׁלֹשׁ שָׁנִים *three years*; rarely preceded by the noun, עָרִים שָׁלֹשׁ *three cities*; as an ordinal when preceded by a noun in the constr. st. בִּשְׁנַת שָׁלֹשׁ *in the third year*, prop. *in the year three*; שְׁלֹשׁ עֶשְׂרֵה fem., שְׁלֹשָׁה עָשָׂר masc. *thirteen*; שְׁלָשְׁתְּכֶם *ye three*; שְׁלָשְׁתָּם *they three*.—II. *thrice*, Job 33. 29. Pl. שְׁלֹשִׁים *seventy*.

שִׁלֵּשׁ Pi. I. *to divide into three parts*, De. 19. 3. —II. *to do a third time*, 1 Ki. 18. 34.—III. *to do on the third day*, 1 Sa. 20. 19. Pu. part. מְשֻׁלָּשׁ. —I. *threefold*.—II. *three years old*, Ge. 15. 9.

שִׁלֵּשׁ (*triad*) pr. name masc. 1 Ch. 7. 35.

שְׁלִישִׁי masc., שְׁלִישִׁיָּה, שְׁלִישִׁית fem., pl. שְׁלִישִׁים. —I. adj. ord. *third*.—II. pl. *chambers of the third story*, Ge. 6. 16.—III. fem. (*a*) *third, third part*; (*b*) adv. *third time*, Eze. 21. 19; (*c*) *third year*, Is. 15. 5; 48. 34, see עֶגְלָה.

שָׁלִשׁ, שָׁלִישׁ masc. (§ 32. rem. 1).—I. *a measure*, prob. *the third part* of an Ephah.—II. a musical instrument, either *a triangle*, or *a harp with three strings*, pl. 1 Sa. 18. 6.—III. *an officer of high* (prob. *the third*) *rank*.—IV. *a peculiar class of soldiers*, supposed to have been *chariot-warriors*, three of whom were contained in one chariot.

שִׁלֵּשִׁים masc. pl. *descendants of the third generation, great-grandchildren*; בְּנֵי שׁ׳ *children of great-grandchildren*.

שָׁלִשָׁה (*in a triangle*) pr. name of a district in Palestine, 1 Sa. 9. 4.

שִׁלְשָׁה (*triad*) pr. name masc. 1 Ch. 7. 37.

שִׁלְשֹׁם, שִׁלְשׁוֹם adv. *three days ago, the day before yesterday*; תְּמוֹל שׁ׳ *yesterday and the day before*; כִּתְמוֹל שׁ׳ גַּם אֶתְמוֹל גַּם שׁ׳ *heretofore, formerly*; *as before*; מִתְּמוֹל שׁ׳ *before, in time past*.

מְשֻׁלָּשׁ masc. *a triad*, כְּמִשְׁלֹשׁ חֳדָשִׁים *about three months after*, Ge. 38. 24.

שְׁלשׁ ו׳ } id., constr. st. (§ 32. rem. 7); ו bef. (:) שלש
שְׁלָשׁ־[a] ו׳ }
שָׁלִשָׁה pr. name of a region . . . . שלש
שְׁלִשָׁהּ[b] Kh., but K. שְׁלִישׁוֹ (q. v.) . . . שלש
שִׁלְשָׁה ן pr. name masc. . . . . שלש
שְׁלֹשָׁה ו׳ num. card. masc., constr. שֶׁת׳ from שָׁלוֹשׁ masc.; ו bef. (:) . . . . . שלש
שַׁלְּשׁוּ[c] Piel imp. pl. masc. [for שַׁלְּשׁוּ comp. § 8. r. 7] שלש

שָׁלִשׁוֹם[d] Kh. שָׁלִשׁוֹם q. v., K. שָׁלִישִׁים (q. v.) . שלש
שִׁלְשׁוֹם adv. [from שָׁלֹשׁ] with term. ־וֹם . . שלש
שְׁלִשִׁיָּה[e] defect. for שְׁלִישִׁיָּה (q. v.) . . . שלש
שָׁלִשָׁיו[f] ן׳[g] defect. for שָׁלִישָׁיו (q. v.) . . . שלש
שָׁלִשִׁים[h] defect. for שָׁלִישִׁים (q. v.) . . . שלש
שְׁלֹשִׁים[i] Kh. שְׁלֹשִׁים q. v., K. שְׁלֹשָׁה (q. v.) . שלש
שְׁלִשִׁים ו׳ adj. ord. masc., pl. of שְׁלִישִׁי; ו bef. (:) שלש
שְׁלֹשִׁים ו׳ num. card. com., pl. of שָׁלוֹשׁ; ו id. . שלש
שִׁלֵּשִׁים noun masc., pl. of [שִׁלֵּשׁ] dec. 1 b . . שלש
שְׁלִשִׁית defect. for שְׁלִישִׁית (q. v.) . . . שלש
שֶׁלִּשְׁלֹמֹה preff. ·שׁ, שֶׁ, & לִ bef. (:) (pr. name masc. שלם
שָׁלִשֵׁם[k] ן defect. for שָׁלִישִׁים (q. v.) . . . שלש
שִׁלְשֹׁם adv., defect. for שִׁלְשׁוֹם (q. v.) . . . שלש
שִׁלַּשְׁתָּ ן Piel pret. 2 pers. sing. masc.; acc. shifted by conv. ן (comp. § 8. rem. 7) . . שלש
שְׁלֹשֶׁת ו׳ num. card. masc., constr. of שְׁלֹשָׁה (§ 42 rem. 5) from שָׁלֹשׁ masc.; ו bef. (:) . שלש
שְׁלִשִׁתֵיךְ[l] adj. ord. fem. sing., suff. 2 pers. sing. fem. (§ 3. rem. 2) from שְׁלִישִׁית (q. v.) . . שלש
שְׁלָשְׁתְּכֶם[m] num. card. (שְׁלֹשֶׁת q. v.), suff. 2 pers. pl., comp. dec. 13 c . . . . . . שלש
שְׁלָשְׁתָּם[n] id. with suff. 3 pers. pl. masc. . . . שלש
שַׁלְתִּיאֵל pr. name, see שְׁאַלְתִּיאֵל . . . . שאל
שֵׁלָתֵךְ[o] contr. for שְׁאֵלָתֵךְ (q. v.) . . . . שאל

שָׁם ן׳ adv.—I. *there, in that place*; אֲשֶׁר שָׁם, אֲשֶׁר—שָׁם *where*; שָׁם—שָׁם *here—there*; מִשָּׁם *thence*; אֲשֶׁר—מִשָּׁם *whence*.—II. *thither*, after verbs of motion; אֲשֶׁר—שָׁם *whither*.—III. *then, at that time*.—IV. with ה parag. שָׁמָּה *thither*; rarely i. q. שָׁם *there*; שָׁמָּה *whither*,—rarely *where*.

שֵׁם ו׳, ן׳, ן׳[p] masc. dec. 7 a (pl. שֵׁמוֹת).—I. *a name*.—II. *fame, renown, reputation*; אַנְשֵׁי שֵׁם *men of renown*; שֵׁם רַע *ill report*.—III. *a name after death, memory*.—IV. perh. *a monument*, 2 Sa. 8. 13; Is. 55. 13.—V. שֵׁם יְהוָֹה, and by way of eminence הַשֵּׁם, שֵׁם *the name of the Lord*.—VI. pr. name, *Shem*, the eldest son of Noah.

שֻׁם Chald. masc. irr. (§ 68) *a name*.

שְׁמִידָע (*fame of knowledge*) pr. name masc. Patronym. שְׁמִידָעִי, Nu. 26. 32.

שְׁמִירָמוֹת (*name of exaltation*; others, *a watching of the heights*, for שְׁמִירָמוֹת) pr. name of two Levites.

[a] Ex. 21. 11. [b] 2 Ki. 9. 25. [c] 1 Ki. 18. 34. [d] Pr. 22. 20. [e] Is. 15. 5. [f] Ex. 15. 4. [g] 1 Ki. 9. 22. [h] Eze. 23. 23. [i] 2 Sa. 23. 13. [k] Ex. 14. 7. [l] Eze. 5. 12. [m] Nu. 12. 4. [n] Nu. 12. 4. [o] 1 Sa. 1. 17. [p] Is. 56. 5.

שָׂם וְ' Kal (Chald. Peal) pret. 3 pers. sing. masc.; or part. act. dec. 1a (§ 30. No. 3) . שום

שָׁם֯[a] Kh. שָׁם q. v., K. שַׁמָּה (q. v.) . . שם

שֶׁם־ with Makkeph for שֵׁם q. v. (§ 36. rem. 3) שם

שֻׁם[yy] Chald. noun masc. sing. irr. (§ 68) . שם

שַׁמָּא וְ pr. name masc. . . . . שמם

שֶׁמְאֵבֶר וְ pr name masc. . . . שמה

שִׁמְאָה (perh. for שִׁמְעָא *fame*) pr. name m. 1 Ch. 8. 32, called שִׁמְאָם 1 Ch. 9. 38.

שְׂמֹאול וּ' noun masc. sing. dec. 1a; וּ bef. (:) . שמאל

שְׂמֹאולָהּ[b] id., suff. 3 pers. sing. fem. . . שמאל

שְׂמֹאולֵךְ[c] id., suff. 2 pers. sing. fem. . . שמאל

שְׂמֹאולָם[d] id., suff. 3 pers. pl. masc. . . שמאל

שְׂמֹאל, שְׂמֹאול וּ' masc. dec. 1a.—I. *the left, left side*; עַל שְׂ׳, שְׂמֹאל *to the left*; מִשְּׂמֹאל *on the left*; יַד שְׂ׳ *the left hand*.—II. (without יָד) *the left hand*.—III. *the north*, Job 23. 9; Ge. 14. 15.

הִשְׂמִיל, הִשְׂמְאִיל, הַשְׂמְאִיל Hiph. I. *to turn or go to the left*.—II. *to use the left hand*, 1 Ch. 12. 2.

שְׂמָאלִי, שְׂמָלִי masc., שְׂמָאלִית fem. adj. *left, on the left*.

שְׂמֹאלָהּ[e] id. with suff. 3 pers. sing. fem. . שמאל

שְׂמֹאלוֹ וּ' id., suff. 3 pers. sing. masc.; וּ bef. (:) שמאל

שְׂמֹאלֶךָ id., suff. 2 pers. sing. masc. . . שמאל

שִׁמְאָם pr. name masc., see שִׁמְאָה.

שֶׁמַּגִּיעַ[f] pref. שֶׁ׳) Hiph. part. sing. masc. dec. 1b . נגע

שַׁמְגַּר pr. name of a judge of Israel, Ju. 3. 31; 5. 6.

שָׁמַד. Hiph. I. *to destroy, lay waste*.—II. *to destroy, cut off* persons, nations. Inf. הַשְׁמֵד *destruction*. Niph. pass. of Hiph.

שְׁמַד Chald. Aph. *to destroy*, Da. 7. 26.

שָׁמָה Root not used; Arab. שמא *to be high*.

שָׁמַי masc. only pl. שָׁמַיִם (constr. שְׁמֵי, with suff. שָׁמֶיךָ § 38. rem. 2) *heaven, the heavens*; הַשָּׁמַיְמָה, שָׁמַיִם, הַשָּׁמַיִם *towards heaven, heavenward*.

שְׁמַי Chald. masc. only pl. emph. שְׁמַיָּא *heaven*.

שֶׁמְאֵבֶר (*soaring on high*, for שַׁמְאֵבֶר from שָׁמֶה=שָׁם *height*, and אֵבֶר) pr. name of a king of Zeboim, Ge. 14. 2.

שָׂמָה[g] Kal pret. 3 pers. sing. fem. . . שום

שָׂמָהּ וְ'[h] id. pret. 3 pers. s. m. (שָׂם), suff. 3 p. s. fem. שום

שָׁמָּה וְ' adv. (שָׁם) with parag. ה . . . שם

שַׁמָּה noun fem. sing. dec. 10, also pr. name . שמם

שָׂמֵהּ[i] Ch. Peal pret. 3 pers. s. m. (שָׂם), suff. 3 p.s.m. שום

שְׁמָהּ וּ' noun masc. sing., suff. 3 pers. sing. fem. from שֵׁם dec. 7; וּ bef. (:) . . שם

שְׁמֵהּ[k] Chald. noun masc. sing., suff. 3 pers. sing. masc. (prop. from שְׁם, see שֻׁם § 68) . שם

שָׂמְהוּ וְ'[l] Kal pret. 3 pers. sing. m. (שָׂם), suff. 3 pers. s. m. שום

שַׁמְהוּת pr. name masc., see שַׁמָּה . . . שמם

שְׁמָהָת[m] Chald. noun masc. pl. constr., irr. of שֻׁם (§ 68) שם

שְׁמָהָתְהֹם[n] Chald. id. pl., suff. 3 pers. pl. masc. . שם

שָׂמוֹ וְ'[o] Kal pret. 3 pers. sing. m., suff. 3 pers. s. m. שום

שָׂמוּ, וְשָׂמוּ } id. pret. 3 pers. pl.; acc. shifted by conv. וְ (comp. § 8. rem. 7) . } שום

שָׂמוּ[p] וְ defect. for שִׂימוּ (q. v.) . . . שום

שְׁמוֹ וּ' noun masc. sing., suff. 3 pers. sing. masc. from שֵׁם dec. 7a; וּ bef. (:) . . שם

שֹׁמּוּ[q] Kal imp. pl. masc. . . . . שמם

שְׁמוּאֵל וּ' pr. name masc.; וּ bef. (:) . . שמע

שָׁמוֹט[r] Kal inf. abs. . . . . שמט

שָׂמוּךָ[s] Kal pret. 3 pers. pl., suff. 2 pers. sing. masc. שום

שְׁמוֹנָה וּ', שְׁמֹנָה וּ' } num. card. fem. & masc.; וּ bef. (:) שמן

שְׁמוֹנִים וּ' id. com. gen. pl.; וּ id. שמן

שְׁמוֹנַת[t] וּ id. fem. sing., constr. of שְׁמוֹנָה; וּ id. . שמן

שָׁמוֹעַ Kal inf. abs. . . . . שמע

שַׁמּוּעַ pr. name masc. see שִׁמְעָא . . . שמע

שְׁמוֹעַ Kal inf. constr. . . . . שמע

שְׁמוּעָה וּ'[u] noun fem. sing. dec. 10; וּ bef. (:) . שמע

שָׁמוֹר Kal inf. abs. . . . . שמר

שָׁמוּר id. part. pass. sing. masc. . . . שמר

שָׁמְוֹר pr. name masc. Kh. שָׁמוּר, K. שָׁמִיר (q. v.) שמר

שְׁמוֹר[x] Kal imp. sing. masc. . . . . שמר

שַׁמּוֹת[y] Kal inf. (§ 18. rem. 3), or noun fem. pl. of שַׁמָּה dec. 10; also pr. name (see שַׁמָּה) שמם

שֵׁמוֹת noun m. with pl. fem. term., abs. st. fr. שֵׁם d. 7a שם

שְׁמוֹת id. pl., constr. st. . . . שם

שְׁמוֹתָם id. pl., suff. 3 pers. pl. masc. (§ 4. rem. 2) שם

שְׁמוֹתָן[z] וּ id. pl., suff. 3 pers. pl. fem.; וּ bef. (:) שם

שָׂמַח וְ' [also שָׂמֵחַ comp. Ne. 12. 43] fut. יִשְׂמַח.—I. *to shine cheerfully*, of a candle, Pr. 13. 9.—II. *to be joyful, glad*.—III. *to express joy*, const. with בְּ, עַל, לְ. Pi. שִׂמַּח *to cheer, gladden, cause to rejoice*, with עַל, לְ, מִן. Hiph. id. Pr. 89. 43.

שָׂמֵחַ masc. dec. 5a, שְׂמֵחָה fem. adj. *joyful, glad, rejoicing*.

שִׂמְחָה fem. dec. 12b.—I. *joy, rejoicing*.—II. *loud expressions of joy, festivity, mirth*.

שָׂמֵחַ וְ'[a] adj. masc. sing. dec. 5a (§ 34. rem. 2) שמח

שַׂמַּח וְ Piel imp. sing. masc. . . . שמח

[a] 2 Sa. 21. 12. [b] Zec. 4. 11. [c] Eze. 16. 46. [d] Ju. 7. 20. [e] Zec. 4. 3. [f] Ec. 8. 14. [g] 1 Sa. 19. 13. [h] Je. 13. 16. [i] Ezr. 5. 14. [k] Da. 2. 20, etc. [l] Eze. 7. 20. [m] Ezr. 5. 4. [n] Ezr. 5. 10. [o] Le. 6. 3. [p] Je. 40. 10. [q] Je. 2. 12. [r] De. 15. 2. [s] Ps. 88. 14. [t] 1 Ch. 29. 7. [u] Pr. 25. 25. [x] Ec. 12. 13. [y] Ps. 46. 9; Eze. 36. 3. [yy] Ezr. 5. 10. [z] Eze. 23. 4. [a] Pr. 29. 6.

שְׂמַח id. id. (Ps. 86. 4); or inf. abs. (Je. 20. 15) שמח

שָׂמֵחַ[a] וְ id. pret. 3 pers. sing. masc. . . שמח

שְׂמַח[b] וּ׳ Kal imp. sing. masc.; וּ bef. (:) . שמח

שָׂמֵחָה[c] וְ id. pret. 3 p. s. fem. [for שָׂמְחָה § 8. r. 1 & 7] שמח

שְׂמֵחָה[d] adj. fem. sing. from שָׂמֵחַ masc. . . שמח

שִׂמְחָה וְ׳ noun fem. sing. dec. 12b . . שמח

שִׂמְּחָהוּ[e] Piel pret. 3 pers. s. m. (שִׂמַּח), suff. 3 pers. s. m. שמח

שָׂמְחוּ[f] וְ׳ / שָׂמֵחוּ[g] וְ׳ } Kal pret. 3 pers. pl. (§ 8. rem. 1 & 7) שמח

שִׂמְחוּ[h] וְ׳ id. imp. pl. masc. . . . . שמח

שִׂמְּחוּךָ[i] Piel pret. 3 pers. pl., suff. 2 pers. sing. masc. שמח

שְׂמָחוֹת[k] noun fem. pl. abs. for שִׂמְחָה dec. 12b . שמח

שְׂמֵחָי[l] וּ in pause for שְׂמֵחִי (§ 8. rem. 12); וּ bef. (:) שמח

שְׂמֵחֵי[m] / שְׂמֵחֵי[n] } adj. pl. constr. masc. from שָׂמֵחַ (§ 34. r. 2) שמח

שִׂמְחִי[o] וְ׳ Kal imp. sing. fem. . . . שמח

שְׂמֵחִים וּ׳ adj. masc., pl. of שָׂמֵחַ dec. 5a; וּ bef. (:) שמח

שִׂמְּחָם Piel pret. 3 pers. s. m. (שִׂמַּח), suff. 3 p. pl. m. שמח

שַׂמְּחֵנוּ[p] id. imp. sing. masc. (שַׂמַּח), suff. 1 pers. pl. שמח

שָׂמַחְתָּ וְ Kal pret. 2 pers. sing. masc.; acc. shifted by conv. וְ (§ 8, rem. 7) . . . . שמח

שִׂמַּחְתָּ[q] Piel pret. 2 pers. sing. masc. . . . שמח

שִׂמְחַת וְ׳ noun fem. sing., constr. of שִׂמְחָה d. 12 b שמח

שָׂמַחְתִּי Kal pret. 1 pers. sing. . . . . שמח

שִׂמְחָתִי[r] noun f. s., suff. 1 pers. s. fr. שִׂמְחָה d. 12 b שמח

שִׂמַּחְתִּים וְ Piel pret. 1 pers. sing., suff. 3 pers. pl. m. שמח

שִׂמְחַתְכֶם[s] noun f. s., suff. 2 pers. pl. m. fr. שִׂמְחָה d. 12b שמח

שְׂמַחְתֶּם וּ Kal pret. 2 pers. pl. masc.; וּ, for וְ, conv. שמח

שִׂמַּחְתַּנִי[t] Piel pret. 2 pers. sing. masc., suff. 1 pers. s. שמח

[שָׁמַט] I. *to let go, release, remit*, a debt, De. 15. 2.—II. *to let lie uncultivated*, Ex. 23. 11.—III. *to cease from*, with מִן Je. 17. 4.—IV. *to throw down*, 2 Ki. 9. 33.—V. intrans. *to set oneself free, to break loose*, 2 Sa. 6. 6; others, *to kick* (Arab. שמץ *to strike, smite*); or, *to stick fast*; others again, *to drop, slip, stumble*. Niph. *to be thrown down*, Ps. 141. 6. Hiph. *to release, remit*, De. 15. 3. Hence

שְׁמִטָּה fem. *a remission, release*, De. 15. 1, 2; שְׁנַת הַשְּׁמִטָּה *the year of release*, De. 15. 9; 31. 10 . . . . . שמט

שָׁמְטוּ Kal pret. 3 pers. pl. . . . . שמט

שִׁמְטוּהוּ[u] id. imp. pl. m., suff. הוּ or הָ 3 pers. s. m. or f. שמט

שָׁמַטְתָּה[v] וְ Kal pret. 2 pers. sing. masc.; acc. shifted by conv. וְ (§ 8. rem. 7) . . . . שמט

שַׁמַּי / שַׁמַּי } pr. name masc. . . . . שמם

שְׁמֵי וּ׳ noun masc. pl., constr. of שָׁמַיִם [fr. שְׁמַי § 38. rem. 2]; וּ bef. (:) . . . שמה

שְׁמִי וּ׳ noun masc. sing. with suff. 1 pers. sing. from שֵׁם dec. 7 a; וּ id. . . . שם

שִׂימִי[y] Kal imp. sing. fem. R. שׂים see שום

שְׁמַיָּא Ch. noun masc. pl. emph. [of שְׁמַיִן fr. שְׁמַי sing. comp. § 38. rem. 2] . . . שמה

שְׁמִידָע וּ׳ pr. name masc.; וּ bef. (:) . . . שם

שָׁמָיו[z] noun masc. pl. (שָׁמַיִם) with suff. 3 pers. sing. masc. [from שְׁמַי § 38. rem. 2] שמה

שָׁמֶיךָ id. pl., suff. 2 pers. sing. masc. . . שמה

שְׁמֵיכֶם[a] id. pl., suff. 2 pers. pl. masc. . . שמה

שָׁמַיִם וְ׳ / שָׁמָיִם וְ׳ } id. pl., abs. st. . . . . שמה

שָׂמִים Kal part. act. m., pl. of שָׂם d. 1 a (§ 30. No. 3) שום

שָׁמִיר noun masc. sing. dec. 3 a, also pr. name שמר

שְׁמִירוֹ[dd] וּ id., suff. 3 pers. sing. masc.; וּ bef. (:) שמר

שְׁמִירָמוֹת וּ pr. name masc.; וּ id. . . . שם

שָׂמְךָ Kal pret. 3 pers. sing. m., suff. 2 pers. s. m. שום

שְׁמֵךְ noun m. s., suff. 2 pers. s. f. fr. שֵׁם d. 7 a שם

שִׁמְךָ / שְׁמֶךָ וְ׳ } id., suff. 2 pers. sing. masc. . . שם

שִׁמְכֶם[b] וְ׳ id., suff. 2 pers. pl. masc. . . . שם

שָׂמַל Root not used; Arab. *to cover with a garment* conj. IV *to wrap oneself in a garment* (Gesenius) Hence the two following.

שִׂמְלָה וְ fem. dec. 12 b, *a garment*; espec. a wide outer garment or mantle; frequently by transposition שַׂלְמָה q. v.

שַׂמְלָה (*garment*) pr. name of a king of Edom, Ge. 36. 36; 1 Ch. 1. 47; see a similar form under שָׁלַם.

שַׂמְלַי Kh. for שַׁלְמַי (q. v.) . . . . שלם

שֶׁמַּלְכֵּךְ[c] pref. שֶׁ) noun masc. sing., suff. 2 pers. sing. masc. from מֶלֶךְ dec. 6 a . . מלך

שִׂמְלַת noun fem. sing., constr. of שִׂמְלָה dec. 12 b שמל

שְׂמָלוֹת[d] וּ id. pl., abs. st.; וּ bef. (:) . . . שמל

שִׂמְלָתוֹ[e] id. sing., suff. 3 pers. sing. masc. . . שמל

שִׂמְלֹתָו[f] / שִׂמְלֹתָיו } id. pl., suff. 3 pers. sing. masc. (§ 4. r. 1) שמל

שִׂמְלֹתַיִךְ[g] id. pl., suff. 2 pers. sing. fem. . . . שמל

שִׂמְלֹתֵיכֶם[h] id. pl., suff. 2 pers. pl. masc. . . . שמל

שִׂמְלָתְךָ[i] id. sing., suff. 2 pers. sing. masc. . . שמל

שִׂמְלֹתָם id. pl., suff. 3 pers. pl. masc. (§ 4. rem. 2) . שמל

שִׂמְלָתֵנוּ[k] וְ id. sing., suff. 1 pers. pl. . . . שמל

---

[a] De. 24. 5. [b] Pr. 5. 18. [c] Est. 8. 15. [d] Ps. 113. 9. [e] Je. 20. 15. [f] Zec. 4. 10. [g] Zec. 10. 7; Ne. 12. 43. [h] Joel 2. 23. [i] Ps. 45. 9. [k] Ps. 16. 11. [l] Joel 2. 21. [m] Ps. 35. 26. [n] Is. 24. 7. [o] Zep. 3. 14. [p] Ps. 90. 15. [q] Ps. 30. 2. [r] Ps. 137. 6. [s] Nu. 10. 10. [t] Ps. 92. 5. [u] 2 Ki. 9. 33. [x] Je. 17. 4. [y] Je. 31. 21. [z] De. 33. 28. [a] Le. 26. 19. [b] Is. 65. 15; 66. 22. [c] Ec. 10. 16, 17. [d] Ge. 45. 22. [dd] Is. 10. 17. [e] Ex. 22. 26. [f] 2 Sa. 12. 20. [g] Ru. 3. 3. [h] Ge. 35. 2. [i] De. 8. 4. [k] Is. 4. 1.

שָׁמַם Root not used; Arab. *to poison.*
שְׂמָמִית fem. a species of *poisonous lizard,* Pr. 30. 28 (Bochart).

[שָׁמֵם] fut. יֵשֹׁם, pl. יָשֹׁמּוּ (perh. also תֵּשַׁם q. v.).—I. *to be desolate, laid waste;* part. שׁוֹמֵם *desolate,* and of persons, (*a*) *wasted, perishing,* La. 1. 13, 16; (*b*) *solitary.*—II. less frequently trans. *to lay waste, make desolate;* part. שׁוֹמֵם *desolator.*—III. *to be astonished, amazed,* with עַל, לְ. Niph. נָשַׁם, i. q. Kal Nos. I & III. Po. I. part. מְשׁוֹמֵם *desolator.* —II. *to be astonished,* Ezr. 9. 3. Hiph. הֵשֵׁם (fut. יַשִּׁים; inf. הַשֵׁמֵּם § 18. rem. 13 & 14).—I. *to make desolate, to lay waste.*—II. *to astonish,* Eze. 32. 10; also intrans. *to be astonished.* Hoph. הָשַּׁם (for הֻשַּׁם, הָשַׁם § 8. rem. 13).—I. *to be laid waste.*—II. *to be astonished,* Job 21. 5. Hithpo. הִשְׁתּוֹמֵם.—I. *to destroy oneself,* Ec. 7. 16.—II. *to be astonished, amazed, confounded.*
שְׁמַם Chald. Ithpo. *to be astonished,* Da. 4. 16.
שָׁמֵם masc., שְׁמֵמָה fem. adj. *laid waste, desolate.*
שְׁמָמָה fem. dec. 11 c.—I. *desolation, waste, desert.* —II. *astonishment,* Eze. 7. 27.
שִׁמְמָה fem. *desolation,* Eze. 35. 7, 9.
שִׁמָּמוֹן masc. *astonishment, amazement,* Eze. 4. 16; 12. 19.
שַׁמָּה fem. dec. 10.—I. *desolation.*—II. *astonishment,* Je. 8. 21; meton. *object of astonishment.*— III. pr. name masc. (*a*) Ge. 36. 13, 17; (*b*) of a brother of David, 1 Sa. 16. 9; 17. 13, called also שִׁמְעָה 2 Sa. 13. 3, & שִׁמְעָא 1 Ch. 2. 13; (*c*) 2 Sa. 23. 25, for which שַׁמּוֹת 1 Ch. 11. 27, & שַׁמְהוּת 1 Ch. 27. 8; (*d*) of two other persons, 2 Sa. 23. 11, 33.
שַׁמָּא (*desert*) pr. name masc. 1 Ch. 7. 37.
שַׁמַּי (*desolated*) pr. name of three men, 1 Ch. 2. 28, 44; 4. 17.
מְשַׁמָּה fem. dec. 10.—I. *desolation.*—II. *astonishment, amazement.*

שְׁמָם noun m. s., suff. 3 pers. pl. m. fr. שֵׁם d. 7 a שם
שֹׁמֵם Kal part. act. sing. masc. dec. 7 b . שמם
שָׁמֵמָה[a] id. pret. 3 p. s. f. [for שָׁמְמָה § 8. r. 1 & 7] שמם
שָׁמֵמָּה[b] Kh. שְׁמֵמָה q. v., K. שָׁמֵמוּ for שָׁמְמוּ (q. v.) שמם
שֹׁמֵמָה[c] וְ Kal part. act. s. f. fr. שׁוֹמֵם m. (§ 39. No. 3. r. 4) שמם
שְׁמָמָה וּ noun fem. sing. dec. 11 c; וּ bef. (:) שמם
שְׁמֵמָה[d] adj. fem. sing. from שָׁמֵם masc. . . שמם
שָׁמֵמוּ וְ Kal pret. 3 pers. pl. . . . . שמם
שִׁמְמוֹת[e], שִׁמְמוֹת } noun fem. pl. constr. from שְׁמָמָה dec. 11 c שמם

שֹׁמְמוֹת[f] constr. of the foll. . . . . . שמם
שֹׁמֵמוֹת Kal part. act. fem., pl. of שֹׁמֵמָה fr. שׁוֹמֵם m. שמם
שְׂמָמִית[g] noun fem. sing. . . . . . שמם
שֹׁמְמֹתַיִךְ[h] וְ Kal part. act. pl. fem., suff. 2 pers. sing. fem. from שֹׁמֵמָה (q. v.) . . . . שמם
שֹׁמְמֹתֵינוּ[i] id. pl. with suff. 1 pers. pl. שמם

[שָׁמַן] or [שָׁמֵן] fut. יִשְׁמַן, *to be* or *become fat.* Hiph. I. *to make fat,* metaph. Is. 6. 10.—II. *to become fat,* Ne. 9. 25.
שָׁמֵן masc. שְׁמֵנָה fem. *fat;* spoken of persons, *stout, robust;* of land, *fertile;* of food, *nourishing.*
שֶׁמֶן masc. dec. 6 a (with suff. שַׁמְנִי).—I. *fatness; spoken of food, richness, delicacy;* of land, *fertility;* metaph. *prosperity,* Is. 10. 27.—II. *oil;* עֵץ שֶׁמֶן *wild olive tree.*—III. *ointment.*
שְׁמַנִּים masc. pl. *fatness, rich production* of the earth, Ge. 27. 28.
אַשְׁמַנִּים masc. pl. *fatness, fertile fields,* Is. 59. 10; others, *darkness* (Syr. אותמניא id.). Eng. vers. "*desolate places*" (Syr. אשימון *desert,* Heb. יְשִׁימוֹן).
מִשְׁמָן masc. dec. 8 a.—I. *fatness,* Is. 17. 4.— II. pl. מִשְׁמַנִּים *fat, fertile places,* Da. 11. 24.— III. pl. concr. *fat, stout,* of warriors.
מַשְׁמַנָּה (*fatness*) pr. name masc. 1 Ch. 12. 10.
מַשְׁמַנִּים masc. pl. *rich, delicate food,* Ne. 8. 10.

שְׁמֹנֶה fem. שְׁמֹנָה masc. constr. שְׁמֹנַת, *eight.* Pl. שְׁמֹנִים *eighty.*
שְׁמִינִי masc. שְׁמִינִית fem. adj. ord. *eighth.* Fem. שְׁמִינִית prob. a musical instrument with *eight strings;* others, *the octave* in music.

שָׁמֵן וְ adj. masc. sing. from שְׁמֵנָה . . שמן
שֶׁמֶן, שָׁמֶן } noun masc. sing. dec. 6 a (§ 35. r. 2); for וָ, וְ see lett. ו . . . שמן
שַׁמְנָהּ[k] id. with suff. 3 pers. sing. fem. . . שמן
שְׁמֵנָה adj. fem. sing. from שָׁמֵן masc. . . שמן
שְׁמֹנָה, שְׁמֹנֶה } וּ num. card. masc. & fem.; וּ bef. (:) . שמן
שַׂמְנוּ[pp] Kal pret. 1 pers. pl. [for שַׂמְנוּ] . . שום
שָׁמְנוּ[l] Kal pret. 3 pers. pl. . . . . שמן
שְׁמֵנוּ[m] noun masc. s., suff. 1 pers. pl. fr. שֵׁם d. 7 a שם
שָׂמַנִי Kal pret. 3 pers. s. m. (שָׂם), suff. 1 pers. s. שום
שָׂמֻנִי[n] id. pret. 3 pers. pl. (שָׂמוּ), suff. 1 pers. sing. שום
שַׁמְנִי[o] וְ noun masc. s., suff. 1 pers. s. fr. שֶׁמֶן d. 6 a שמן
שְׁמָנַיִךְ[p] id. pl., suff. 2 pers. sing. fem. . . שמן
שְׁמָנֶיךָ[q] id. pl., suff. 2 pers. sing. masc. . . שמן
שְׁמָנִים id. pl., abs. st. . . . . . שמן

[a] Eze. 35. 15. [b] Eze. 35. 12. [c] 2 Sa. 13. 20. [d] Je. 12. 11. [e] Eze. 35. 9. [f] Is. 61. 4. [g] Pr. 30. 28. [h] Is. 49. 19. [i] Da. 9. 18. [k] Nu. 4. 9. [l] Je. 5. 28. [m] Jos. 7. 9. [n] Ca. 1. 6. [o] Ho. 2. 7. [p] Ca. 4. 10. [pp] Is. 28. 15. [q] Ca. 1. 3.

שְׁמֹנִים ו׳ num. card. com., pl. of שְׁמֹנֶה ; וּ bef. (:) שמן
שָׁמַנְתָּ[a] Kal pret. 2 pers. sing. masc. . . . שמן
שְׁמֹנַת[b] ו׳ ,ל׳ num. card. m., constr. of שְׁמֹנָה fr. שְׁמֹנֶה f. שמן

שָׁמַע ו׳ in pause שָׁמֵעַ Ps. 22. 25 (comp. also Ju. 2. 17; Je. 13. 11, &c.) fut. יִשְׁמַע.—I. *to hear.*—II. *to listen, give attention,* with acc. אֶל, לְ, בְּ *to* any one.—III. *to hear, accept prayer,* of God.—IV. *to hearken, obey.*—V. *to understand*; לֵב שֹׁמֵעַ an understanding heart. Niph. I. *to be heard.*—II. *to show oneself obedient* or *submissive,* Ps. 18. 45.—III. *to be understood,* Ps. 19. 4. Pi. *to cause to hear, to summon.* Hiph. I. *to cause to hear* or *be heard.*—II. *to proclaim.*—III. *to call, summon.*—IV. *to sing* or *play aloud.*

שְׁמַע Chald. *to hear,* Da. 5. 14, 16. Ithpe. *to show oneself obedient, to obey,* Da. 7. 27.

שָׁמָא (*hearing*) pr. name masc. 1 Ch. 11. 44.

שֵׁמַע masc. dec. 6e.—I. *the act of hearing.*—II. *report, rumour.*—III. *sound, music,* Ps. 150. 5.

שֶׁמַע (*report*) pr. name masc.—I. 1 Ch. 2. 43, 44. —II. 1 Ch. 5. 8.—III. Ne. 8. 4.—IV. 1 Ch. 8. 13.

שְׁמַע (*fame*) pr. name of a city in the tribe of Judah, Jos. 15. 26.

שֹׁמַע masc. dec. 6c (§ 35. rem. 5), *fame.*

שִׁמְעָא (*report*) pr. name—I. of a son of David, 1 Ch. 3. 5, elsewhere called שַׁמּוּעַ.—II. 1 Ch. 6. 15. —III. 1 Ch. 6. 24.—IV. of a son of Jesse, 1 Ch. 2. 13, elsewhere שַׁמָּה (q. v.) & שִׁמְעָה 2 Sa. 13. 3, 32; patronym. שִׁמְעָתִי 1 Ch. 2. 55.

שְׁמָעָה (*obedience*) pr. name masc. 1 Ch. 12. 3.

שִׁמְעוֹן (*a hearing, accepting*) pr. name, *Simeon.* —I. a son of Jacob by Leah's handmaid, and of the tribe descended from him. Patronym. שִׁמְעֹנִי.—II. Ezr. 10. 31.

שִׁמְעִי (*renowned*) pr. name masc. of several persons. Patronym. שִׁמְעִי for שִׁמְעִיִי.

שְׁמַעְיָה ,שְׁמַעְיָהוּ (*the Lord has heard,* i. e. answered prayer) pr. name, *Shemaiah.*—I. a prophet, 1 Ki. 12. 22.—II. another, Je. 29. 31.—III. of several other men.

שִׁמְעָת (*report*) pr. n. f. 2 Ki. 12. 22; 2 Ch. 24. 26.

שְׁמוּעָה ,שְׁמֻעָה fem. dec. 10.—I. *news, tidings.* —II. *information, report,* 2 Ch. 9. 6.—III. *information, teaching, doctrine,* Is. 28. 9.

שְׁמוּאֵל (for שְׁמוּעַ אֵל *heard of God,* comp. 1 Sa. 1. 20) pr. name, *Samuel.*—I. the judge and prophet of the Israelites.—II. three other persons; (*a*) 1 Ch. 6. 13, 18; (*b*) Nu. 34. 20; (*c*) 1 Ch. 7. 2.

אֶשְׁתְּמוֹעַ (*obedience*) pr. name of a city of the Levites in the tribe of Judah; once written אֶשְׁתְּמֹה Jos. 15. 50.

הַשְׁמָעוּת fem. *a causing to hear, information,* Eze. 24. 26.

יִשְׁמָעֵאל (*God hears*) pr. name, *Ishmael.*—I. son of Abraham by Hagar, the progenitor of several Arabian tribes. Patronym. יִשְׁמְעֵאלִי *Ishmaelite.*—II. the murderer of Gedaliah, comp. Je. 40. 8, and several other persons.

יִשְׁמַעְיָה (*the Lord hears*) pr. name m. 1 Ch. 12. 4.

יִשְׁמַעְיָהוּ (id.) pr. name masc. 1 Ch. 27. 19.

מִשְׁמָע masc. dec. 2b.—I. *a hearing,* Is. 11. 3.—II. pr. name of two men, Ge. 25. 14; 1 Ch. 4. 25.

מִשְׁמַעַת fem. dec. 13a (with suff. מִשְׁמַעְתּוֹ, comp. § 35. rem. 5).—I. *a hearing, audience.*—II. *obedience,* as a concr. & collect. *subjects,* Is. 11. 14.

שָׁמָע pr. name masc. . . . . שמע
שָׁמָע[c] ו׳ in pause for שֵׁמַע (§ 35. r. 2 & 5) see שֵׁמַע שמע
שָׁמוֹעַ Kal inf. abs. . . . . שמע
שֵׁמָע ,וּ / שְׁמָע ,וּ } in pause for שֶׁמַע q. v. (comp. וְזָהָב, וּשְׁבַע ,וּשְׂדֵה); וּ bef. (:) . . } שמע
שְׁמָע ,וּ pr. name of a place; וּ id. . . . שמע
שְׁמַע[d] Chald. Peal pret. 3 pers. sing. masc. . . שמע
שְׁמַע ,וּ Kal imp. sing. masc.; וּ bef. (:) . . שמע
שֵׁמַע noun masc. sing. dec. 6e . . . שמע
שֶׁמַע ו׳ pr. name masc. . . . . שמע
שְׁמֹעַ Kal inf. constr. . . . . שמע
שֹׁמֵעַ ו׳ id. part. act. sing. masc. dec. 7b . . שמע
שִׁמְעָא ו׳ pr. name masc. . . . . שמע
שָׁמְעָה ו׳[e] Kal pret. 3 pers. sing. fem. . . . שמע
שְׁמָעָה[f] in pause for שְׁמַעָה q. v. (§ 8. rem. 12) . שמע
שְׁמֻעָה[g] ו׳ ,וּ[h] defect. for שְׁמוּעָה (q. v.) . . שמע
שִׁמְעָה pr. name masc. . . . . שמע
שִׁמְעָה Kal imp. s. m. (שְׁמַע) with parag. ה (§ 8. r. 11) שמע
שִׁמְעָהּ[i] noun masc. sing., suff. 3 pers. s. f. שֵׁמַע d. 6e שמע
שֹׁמְעָהּ[k] Kal part. act. sing. masc., suff. 3 pers. sing. fem. from שֹׁמֵעַ dec. 7b . . שמע
שָׁמְעוֹ ו׳ id. inf. (Nu. 30. 6, 8, 13, 15), or subst. masc. [שֹׁמַע], with suff. 3 pers. sing. masc. שמע
שָׁמֵעוּ / שָׁמְעוּ ו׳ } id. pret. 3 pers. pl. (§ 8. rem. 1 & 7) . שמע
שְׁמָעוּ[l] וּ / שִׁמְעוּ ו׳ } id. imp. pl. masc. (§ 8. r. 12); וּ bef. (:) שמע
שֹׁמְעוֹ[m] id. part. a. s. m., suff. 3 p. s. m. fr. שֹׁמֵעַ d. 7b שמע
שִׁמְעוֹן ו׳ pr. name of a man and a tribe . . שמע
שְׁמָעוּנִי Kal imp. pl. m. (שִׁמְעוּ), suff. 1 p. s. (§ 16. r. 11) שמע

[a] De. 32. 15. [b] Nu. 2. 24. [c] Ps. 150. 5. [d] Da 6. 15. [e] Le. 5. 1. [f] Da. 9. 19. [g] Je. 49. 23. [h] Eze. 7. 26. [i] Job 28. 22. [k] Je. 19. 3. [l] Is. 42. 18. [m] 1 Sa. 3. 11.

שְׁמֻעוֹת[a] וּ noun fem., pl. of שְׁמוּעָה dec. 10; וּ bef. (:) שמע

שִׁמְעָי° Kh. שִׁמְעִי, K. שִׁמְעָה pr. name masc. . שמע

שִׁמְעִי וְ׳ pr. name masc. . . . . שמע

שִׁמְעִי Kal imp. fem. sing.; or (Is. 66. 19) noun masc. with suff. from שֵׁמַע dec. 6e . שמע

שֹׁמְעֵי id. part. act. pl. c. masc. from שֹׁמֵעַ dec. 7b שמע

שְׁמַעְיָה וּ׳ / שְׁמַעְיָהוּ וּ׳ } pr. name masc.; וּ bef. (:) . . שמע

שִׁמְעָיו[b] the foll. with suff. 3 p. s. m. K. שִׁמְעָה (q. v.) שמע

שֹׁמְעִים וְ׳[c] Kal part. act. masc., pl. of שֹׁמֵעַ dec. 7b שמע

שָׁמְעִין Chald. Peal part. act. pl. m. [fr. שָׁמַע] d. 2b שמע

שִׁמְעֲךָ noun masc. sing. with suff. 2 pers. sing. masc. from שֵׁמַע dec. 6e . . . . שמע

שִׁמְעָם id. with suff. 3 pers. pl. masc. . . . שמע

שְׁמַעַן[d] Kal imp. pl. fem. for שְׁמַעְנָה (comp. § 8. r.16) שמע

שְׁמָעֶנָּה[e] id. imp. sing. masc. (שְׁמַע), suff. 3 pers. sing. fem. (§ 16. rem. 11) . . שמע

שְׁמַעְנָה id. imp. pl. fem. . . . . . שמע

שָׁמַעְנוּ / שָׁמָעְנוּ וְ׳[f] } id. pret. 1 pers. pl. (§ 8. rem. 7) . שמע

שְׁמָעֵנוּ[g] id. imp. s. m. (שְׁמַע), suff. 1 p. pl. (§ 16. r. 11) שמע

שְׁמַעֲנוּהָ[h] id. pret. 1 pers. pl. (שָׁמַעְנוּ), suff. 3 pers. s. fem. שמע

שְׁמָעֵנִי[i] id. imp. s. m. (שְׁמַע), suff. 1 p. s. (§ 16. r. 11) שמע

שָׁמַעְתָּ וְ׳[k] / שָׁמָעְתָּ / שָׁמַעְתָּ וְ } id. pret. 2 pers. sing. masc.; acc. shifted by conv. וְ (§ 8. rem. 7) . } שמע

שָׁמַעַתְּ id. pret. 2 pers. sing. fem. . . . שמע

שִׁמְעַת[l] noun fem. sing., constr. of שְׁמוּעָה dec. 10 שמע

שִׁמְעָת pr. name masc. . . . . . שמע

שִׁמְעֵת וְ׳[m] Chald. Peal pret. 1 pers. sing. . . שמע

שֹׁמַעַת[n] / שֹׁמַעַת } Kal part. act. sing., fem. of שֹׁמֵעַ (§ 8. r. 19) שמע

שָׁמַעַתִּי°[o] id. pret. 2 p. s. f., Kh. תִּי׳, K. שָׁמַעַתְּ (§ 8. r. 5) שמע

שָׁמַעְתִּי / שָׁמָעְתִּי / שָׁמַעְתִּי וְ } id. pret. 1 pers. sing.; acc. shifted by conv. וְ (§ 8. rem. 7) . . } שמע

שְׁמַעְתִּיו[p] וּ id. id., suff. 3 pers. sing. masc.; וּ, for וְ, conv. שמע

שְׁמַעְתִּיךָ id. id., suff. 2 pers. sing. masc. . . שמע

שִׁמְעָתִים patronym. pl. from שִׁמְעָה . . . שמע

שְׁמַעְתָּם[q] Kal pret. 2 pers. sing. masc., suff. 3 pers. pl. m. שמע

שְׁמַעְתֶּם וּ׳ id. pret. 2 pers. pl. masc.; וּ, for וְ, conv. שמע

שָׁמַץ Root not used; Arab. *to impel, drive, thrust;* also *to speak rapidly.* Hence the two foll.

שֶׁמֶץ masc. *a short, gentle sound, a whispering,* Job 4. 12; 26. 14; Prof. Lee, *a hint;* others regard it i. q. שֵׁמַע *report.* And

שִׁמְצָה fem. Ex. 32. 25, *a whispering, muttering;* others, *rout, overthrow;* or *ill fame, reproach,* i. q. שִׁמְעָה.

שֶׁמְּצָאתִי[r] pref. ·שֶׁ) Kal pret. 1 pers. sing. . . מצא

שֶׁמִּקְרֶה[s] pref. id.) noun masc. sing. dec. 9a . קרה

שָׁמַר וְ׳ fut. יִשְׁמֹר.—I. *to keep, watch, guard;* part שֹׁמֵר *a watchman.*—II. *to keep safe, preserve, protect,* with acc., בְּ, אֶל, עַל of the object, with מִן *from* or *against* anything.—III. *to keep, retain, reserve.*—IV. *to keep, observe, mark,* with acc., אֶל, עַל.—V. *to keep, observe,* as the commandments of God.—VI. *to take heed,* with לְ and inf. to do anything.—VII. *to regard, reverence.*—VIII. *to keep oneself from,* with מִן, Jos. 6. 18. Niph. I. *to be kept, preserved,* Ps. 37. 28.—II. *to keep oneself from,* with מִן.—III. *to take heed, beware,* with לְ, בְּ, מִן. Pi. *to regard,* Jon. 2. 9. Hithpa. הִשְׁתַּמֵּר.—I. *to be kept, observed,* Mi. 6. 16.—II. *to take heed to oneself, to beware,* Ps. 18. 24.

שָׁמִיר masc. dec. 3a.—I. *thorn;* collect. *thorns.*—II. *diamond.*—III. pr. name (*a*) of a city in Judah, Jos. 15. 48; (*b*) of a city in Ephraim, Ju. 10. 1, 2; (*c*) of a man, 1 Ch. 24. 24 Keri, שָׁמוּר Kh.

שֶׁמֶר masc. dec. 6a (pl. with suff. שִׁמְרֵיהֶם).—I. pl. *sediment, lees* of wine.—II. pr. name of several men.

שֹׁמֵר (*keeper*) pr. name.—I. masc. 1 Ch. 7. 32, for which שֶׁמֶר ver. 34.—II. fem. 2 Ki. 12. 22, for which שִׁמְרִית 2 Ch. 24. 26.

שְׁמֻרָה fem. *a watching,* poet. for *eyelid,* Ps. 77. 5.

שָׁמְרָה fem. *watch, guard,* Ps. 141. 3.

שִׁמֻּרִים masc. pl. *observance, keeping of a festival,* Ex. 12. 42.

שִׁמְרוֹן (*watch, guard*) pr. name—I. of a son of Issachar, Ge. 46. 13. Patronym. שִׁמְרֹנִי Nu. 26. 24.—II. pr. name of a town of Zebulun, Jos. 11. 1; 19. 15, called שִׁ מְרֹאוֹן Jos. 12. 20.

שֹׁמְרוֹן (*watch-hill* or *height*) pr. name, *Samaria.*—I. the capital of the kingdom of Israel.—II. the kingdom of Israel or the ten tribes. Gent. n. שֹׁמְרֹנִי 2 Ki. 17. 29.

שִׁמְרִי (*watchful*) pr. name masc. of several men.

שְׁמַרְיָה (whom *the Lord keeps*) pr. name—I. of a son of Rehoboam, 2 Ch. 11. 19.—II. of two other men, Ezr. 10. 32, 41.

שְׁמַרְיָהוּ (id.) pr. name masc. 1 Ch. 12. 5.

שָׁמְרַיִן Ch. i. q. Heb. שֹׁמְרוֹן, Ezr. 4. 10, 17.

[a] Da. 11. 44. [b] 2 Ki. 21. 12. [c] 2 Ch. 9. 7. [d] Ge. 4. 23. [e] Job 5. 27. [f] De. 5. 24. [g] Ge. 23. 6. [h] Ps. 132. 6. [i] Ge. 23. 11, 13, 15. [k] De. 17. 4. [l] 2 Sa. 4. 4. [m] Da. 5. 14, 16. [n] Pr. 25. 12. [o] Je. 4. 19. [p] De. 1. 17. [q] Is. 48. 7. [r] Ca. 3. 4. [s] Ec. 2. 14.

שִׁמְרָת (*watch, guard*) pr. name m. 1 Ch. 8. 21.

אַשְׁמֹרֶת, אַשְׁמוּרָה fem. (§ 39. No. 4 d), pl. אַשְׁמֻרוֹת *night-watch.*

יִשְׁמְרַי (for יִשְׁמְרְיָה whom *the Lord keeps*) pr. name masc. 1 Ch. 8. 18.

מִשְׁמָר masc. dec. 2 b.—I. *a watching, guarding,* Pr. 4. 23.—II. *a watch,* i. e. *place of watching;* also *a watch, persons watching, guards.*—III. *custody, prison.*—IV. *observance, rite,* Ne. 13. 14.

מִשְׁמֶרֶת fem. dec. 13 a (with 'מַרְתִּי; pl. מִשְׁמָרוֹת § 44. r. 5).—I. *a watching, guarding,* 2 Ki. 11. 5, 6, meton. *an object guarded,* 1 Sa. 22. 23.—II. *place of watching, post, station;* also *a watch, persons keeping watch.*—III. *a keeping, preservation.*—IV. *observance* or *performance.*—V. *what is to be observed, a charge, law, usage, rite.*—VI. *adherence to* any one, 1 Ch. 12. 29.

שָׁמָר Kal pret. 3 pers. sing. m. for שָׁמַר (§ 8. r. 7) שמר

שָׁמֶר 'ן pr. n. m. for שֶׁמֶר (§ 35. r. 2); for ן see lett. ו שמר

שָׁמוֹר Kal inf. abs. . . . . . שמר

שֶׁמֶר pr. name masc. . . . . שמר

שְׁמֹר 'וּ } Kal imp. sing. masc., or (De. 8. 11)
שְׁמָר־ } inf. constr. (§ 8. r. 18); וּ bef. (:) } שמר

שֹׁמֵר 'ן id. part. act. sing. m. d. 7 b, also pr. name שמר

שָׁמְרָה id. pret. 3 pers. sing. fem. . . . שמר

שָׁמְרָה id. imp. (§ 8. rem. 11), or (Ps. 141. 3) n. f. s. שמר

שְׁמָרָהּ[a] id. pret. 3 pers. sing. masc. (שָׁמַר), suff. 3 pers. sing. fem., acc. drawn back before penacute (נֶצַח) for שְׁמָרָהּ (§ 2. rem. 3) שמר

שְׁמֻרָה[b] וּ id. part pass., fem. of שָׁמוּר; וּ bef. (:) שמר

שָׁמָרוּ[c] 'ן }
שָׁמְרוּ 'ן } id. pret. 3 pers. pl. (§ 8. rem. 7) . שמר

שִׁמְרוּ 'ן id. imp. pl. masc. . . . . שמר

שְׁמָרוֹ[d] וּ id. pret. 3 p. s. m., suff. 3 p. s. m.; וּ bef. (:) שמר

שֹׁמְרוֹן 'ן pr. name of a place, also in compos. שִׁ' מְראוֹן שמר

שֹׁמְרוֹן 'ן pr. name of a place . . . שמר

שֹׁמְרוֹנָה id. with parag. ה . . . . שמר

שְׁמֻרוֹת[e] noun fem., pl. of [שְׁמֻרָה] dec. 10 . שמר

שִׁמְרִי pr. name masc. . . . . . שמר

שֹׁמְרֵי 'ן Kal part. act. pl. c. masc. fr. שֹׁמֵר d. 7 b שמר

שְׁמַרְיָה pr. name masc. . . . . שמר

שְׁמָרֶיהָ[f] noun m. pl., suff. 3 pers. s. f. fr. [שֶׁמֶר] d. 6 a שמר

שְׁמַרְיָהוּ וּ pr. name masc. see שְׁמַרְיָה; וּ bef. (:) . שמר

שִׁמְרֵיהֶם[g] noun m. pl., suff. 3 pers. pl. m. fr. [שֶׁמֶר] d. 6 a שמר

שְׁמָרָיו[h] id. pl., suff. 3 pers. sing. masc. . . שמר

שְׁמָרִים[i] id. pl., abs. st. . . . . . שמר

שִׁמֻּרִים[k] noun masc. pl. . . . . שמר

שֹׁמְרִים Kal part. act. masc., pl. of שֹׁמֵר dec. 7 b . שמר

שְׁמָרִימוֹת וּ Kh. for שְׁמִירָמוֹת (q. v.) . . שם

שָׁמְרָיִן Ch. pr. name of a place . . . שמר

שִׁמְרִית pr. name masc. see שֹׁמֵר . . . שמר

שֹׁמְרֶךָ[l] Kal part. act. sing. masc., suff. 2 pers. sing. masc. from שֹׁמֵר dec. 7 b . . . שמר

שָׁמְרֵם[m] id. imp. sing. masc., suff. 3 pers. pl. masc. שמר

שִׁמְרֹן ן pr. name masc. . . . . שמר

שֹׁמְרֹנָה pr. name of a place (שֹׁמְרוֹן) with parag. ה שמר

שָׁמַרְנוּ Kal pret. 1 pers. pl. . . . . שמר

שְׁמָרַנִי[n] וּ id. pret. 3 pers. sing. masc., suff. 1 pers. sing.; וּ, for ן, conv. . . . . שמר

שָׁמְרֵנִי id. imp. sing. masc., suff. 1 pers. sing. . שמר

שָׁמַרְתָּ } id. pret. 2 pers. sing. masc.; acc. shifted
שָׁמַרְתָּ ן } by conv. ן (§ 8. rem. 7) . . } שמר

שִׁמְרַת ן pr. name masc. . . . . שמר

שָׁמָרְתִּי[o] }
שָׁמַרְתִּי } Kal pret. 1 pers. sing. (§ 8. rem. 7) . שמר

שְׁמַרְתִּיךָ[p] וּ id. id., suff. 2 pers. sing. masc.; וּ, for ן, conv. שמר

שְׁמַרְתֶּם 'וּ id. pret. 2 pers. pl. masc.; וּ id. . . שמר

שְׁמַרְתָּנִי[q] וּ id. pret. 2 pers. sing. masc., suff. 1 pers. sing. for 'תַּנִי; וּ id. . . . שמר

[שְׁמַשׁ] Ch. *to attend, serve,* Da. 7. 10.

שֶׁמֶשׁ com. dec. 6 a (with suff. שִׁמְשֵׁךְ).—I. *the sun.*—II. pl. שְׁמָשׁוֹת *windows,* Is. 54. 12; others, *notched battlements.*

שִׁמְשׁוֹן (*sun-like*) pr. name, *Samson,* a judge of Israel, celebrated for his strength.

שִׁמְשַׁי (id.) pr. name masc. Ezr. 6. 8, 17.

שָׁמֶשׁ 'ן id. in pause (§ 35. rem. 2); for ן see lett. ו שמש

שִׁמְשָׁא[r] Ch. id. emph. st. dec. 3 b . . . שמש

שִׁמְשָׁהּ[s] id., suff. 3 pers. sing. fem. . . . שמש

שִׁמְשׁוֹן pr. name masc. . . . . . שמש

שִׁמְשַׁי ן pr. name masc. . . . . שמש

שִׁמְשֵׁךְ[t] noun com. sing., suff. 2 pers. sing. fem. from שֶׁמֶשׁ dec. 6 a . . . . . שמש

שַׁמְשְׁרַי ן pr. name masc. 1 Ch. 8. 26.

שִׁמְשֹׁתַיִךְ[u] id. noun c. with pl. fem. & suff. 2 pers. s. fem. שמש

שָׂמְתָּ[w] Ch. Peal pret. 2 pers. sing. masc. . . שום

שָׂמֶת[y] Ch. id. pret. 1 pers. sing. . . . שום

שַׂמְתָּ } Kal pret. 2 pers. sing. masc.; acc.
שַׂמְתָּ ן } shifted by conv. ן (comp. § 8. rem. 7) } שום

שַׂמְתְּ id. pret. 2 pers. sing. fem. . . . שום

שָׂמַת[z] ן Ch. part. pass. with afform. 3 pers. sing. fem. (§ 54. rem. 2) . . . . שום

---

[a] Am. 1. 11. [b] 2 Sa. 23. 5. [c] Ge. 41. 35. [d] Je. 31. 10. [e] Ps. 77. 5. [f] Ps. 75. 9. [g] Zep. 1. 12. [h] Je. 48. 11. [i] Is. 25. 6. [k] Ex. 12. 42. [l] Ps. 121. 3, 5. [m] Pr. 4. 21. [n] Ge. 28. 20. [o] Ps. 119. 67. [p] Ge. 28. 15. [q] Job 10. 14. [r] Da. 6. 15. [s] Je. 15. 9. [t] Is. 60. 20. [u] Is. 54. 12. [w] Da. 3. 10. [y] Ezr. 6. 12. [z] Da. 6. 18.

שֵׁמֹת noun masc. with pl. fem. term. abs. fr. שֵׁם d. 7 a . שם
שְׁמֹת id., constr. st. comp. שְׁמוֹת ,שֵׁמוֹת . שם
שָׂמַתְהוּ Kal pret. 3 pers. s. f. (שָׂמָה), suff. 3 pers. s. m. שום
שַׂמְתּוֹ[a] וְ[b]׳ id. pret. 2 pers. s. masc., suff. 3 pers. s. m. שום
שַׂמְתִּי[c], שַׂמְתִּי וְ׳, שַׂמְתִּי וְ } id. pret. 1 pers. sing.; acc. shifted by conv. וְ (comp. § 8. rem. 7) . } שום
שַׂמְתִּי[d] וְ id. pret. 2 pers. sing. fem., Kh. שַׂמְתִּי, K. שַׂמְתְּ (§ 8. rem. 5) . . . שום
שַׂמְתִּיהָ[e] וְ׳ id. pret. 1 pers. sing., suff. 3 pers. sing. masc. שום
שַׂמְתִּיו[f] id. id., suff. 3 pers. sing. masc. . . שום
שַׂמְתִּיךָ וְ id. id., suff. 2 pers. sing. m. . . שום
שַׂמְתִּיךְ[g] וְ׳ id. id., suff. 2 pers. sing. fem. . . שום
שַׂמְתִּים וְ id. id., suff. 3 pers. pl. masc. (ם for ן fem. in Ho. 2. 14, § 2. rem. 5) . . שום
שְׁמֹתָם defect. for שְׁמוֹתָם (q. v.) . . . שם
שַׂמְתָּם וְ Kal pret. 2 pers. s. masc., suff. 3 pers. pl. m. שום
שַׂמְתֶּם וְ׳ id. pret. 2 pers. pl. masc. . . שום
שָׂמַתְנִי[h] id. pret. 3 pers. s. fem. (שָׂמָה), suff. 1 pers. s. שום
שַׂמְתַּנִי[i] id. pret. 2 pers. sing. masc., suff. 1 pers. sing. שום
שָׁן pr. name, see בֵּית שְׁאָן.
שֵׁן וְ[k]׳, שֶׁן־[l] וְ[m]׳ } noun com. sing. dec. 8 b (§ 36. rem. 3) שנן

שָׂנֵא fut. יִשְׂנָא *to hate*; part. שֹׂנֵא, *hater, enemy*. Niph. *to be hated*, Pr. 14. 17, 20. Pi. part. מְשַׂנֵּא *hater, enemy*.

שְׂנֵא Chald. only part. *hater*, Da. 4. 16.

שִׂנְאָה fem. (constr. שִׂנְאַת; no pl.) *hatred*.

שָׂנִיא only fem. שְׂנִיאָה adj. *hated*, De. 21. 15.

שָׂנֹא[n] Kal inf. abs. . . . . . שנא
שֵׁנָא[o] noun fem. sing. for שֵׁנָה (q. v.) . . ישן
שִׁנָּא[p] וְ Piel pret. 3 pers. s. masc. for שִׁנָּה (§ 24. r. 19) שנה
שְׂנֹא[q] Kal inf. constr. . . . . . שנא
שֹׂנֵא id. part. act. sing. masc. dec. 7 b . . שנא
שִׁנְאָב pr. name masc. . . . . . שנן
שָׂנְאָה Kal pret. 3 pers. sing. fem. . . שנא
שְׂנֵאָהּ[r] וּ׳ id. pret. 3 pers. sing. masc. (שָׂנֵא), suff. 3 pers. s. fem. (§ 16. r. 1); וּ, for וְ, conv. שנא
שִׂנְאָה וְ׳ noun fem. sing. (no pl. abs.) . . שנא
שְׂנֵאָהוּ[s] the foll. with suff. 3 pers. s. masc. (§ 16. r. 1) שנא
שָׂנְאוּ Kal pret. 3 pers. pl. . . . שנא
שְׂנֻאָי[t] Kh. שְׂנֻאוּ q. v.; K. שְׂנוּאֵי; Kal part. pass. pl. c. from שָׂנוּא dec. 3 a . . . שנא
שִׂנְאוּ Kal imp. pl. masc. . . . . . שנא
שְׂנֵאוּנִי[u] id. pret. 3 p. pl. (שָׂנְאוּ), suff. 1 p. s. (§ 16. r. 1) שנא

שֶׁנֶּאֱחָזִים[x] pref. ·שֶׁ)(Niph. part. pl. m. [fr. נֶאֱחָז § 13. r. 7] אחז
שֹׂנְאַי[y], שֹׂנְאַי } the foll. with suff. 1 pers. sing. . שנא
שֹׂנְאֵי וְ[z]׳ Kal part. act. pl. c. masc. from שֹׂנֵא d. 7 b שנא
שֹׂנְאִי[a] id. sing., with parag. י (Kh. שֹׂנְאֵי (§ 8. r. 19); K. שֹׂנֵא (q. v.) . . . . שנא
שֹׂנְאֵיהֶם[b] id. pl., suff. 3 pers. pl. masc. . . שנא
שֹׂנְאָיו[c] id. pl., suff. 3 pers. sing. masc. . . שנא
שֹׂנְאֶיךָ id. pl., suff. 2 pers. sing. masc. . . שנא
שֹׂנְאֵיכֶם id. pl., suff. 2 pers. pl. masc. . . . שנא
שֹׂנְאֵינוּ[d] id. pl., suff. 1 pers. pl. . . . שנא
שֹׂנַאֲךָ id. sing., suff. 2 pers. sing. masc. . . שנא
שְׂנֵאֶךָ[e] וּ id. pret. 3 pers. sing. masc. (שָׂנֵא), suff. 2 pers. sing. masc. (§ 16. rem. 1); וּ bef. (:) שנא
שַׁאֲנָן[f] noun masc. sing. . . . . . שנה
שֶׁנְאַצַּר וְ pr. name masc. 1 Ch. 3. 18.
שָׂנֵאתָ Kal pret. 2 pers. sing. masc. (§ 23. rem. 1) שנא
שָׂנֵאת id. pret. 2 pers. sing. fem. . . . שנא
שְׂנֹאת[g] id. inf. constr. (§ 23. rem. 2) . . שנא
שִׂנְאַת[h] וְ noun fem. sing., constr. of שִׂנְאָה (no pl. abs.) שנא
שְׂנֵאתָהּ[i] Kal pret. 2 pers. sing. masc., suff. 3 pers. sing. fem. (§ 23. rem. 1) . . . שנא
שָׂנֵאתִי, שָׂנֵאתִי[k] וְ } id. pret. 1 pers. sing.; acc. shifted by conv. וְ (§ 8. rem. 7) . . } שנא
שְׂנֵאתִיהָ[l] id. id., suff. 3 pers. sing. fem. . . שנא
שְׂנֵאתִיהוּ[m] id. id., suff. 3 pers. sing. masc. . . שנא
שְׂנֵאתִיו[n] id. id., suff. 3 pers. sing. masc. . . שנא
שֹׂנְאֹתַיִךְ[o] id. part. act. fem. pl., suff. 2 pers. sing. fem. [from שֹׂנְאָה or שֹׂנֵאת] . . . שנא
שְׂנֵאתִים id. pret. 1 pers. s., suff. 3 pers. pl. m. (§ 23. r. 1) שנא
שִׂנְאָתָם[p] noun fem. sing., suff. 3 pers. pl. masc. from שִׂנְאָה (no pl. abs.) . . . . שנא
שְׂנֵאתֶם Kal pret. 2 pers. pl. masc. (§ 23. rem. 1) שנא
שְׂנֵאתַנִי[q] id. pret. 2 pers. sing. masc., suff. 1 pers. sing. שנא

שָׂנַב Root not used; Arab. *to be cool*.

אֶשְׁנָב masc. dec. 8 a, *a latticed window*.

שָׁנָה[r] (Milêl bef. monos.) fut. יִשְׁנֶה.—I. *to repeat, to do the second time* or *again*.—II. *to be different from*, with מִן, Est. 1. 7; 3. 8.—III. *to alter, change, be changed*; part. שֹׁנִים *changeable, given to change, unsteady*, Pr. 24. 21. Niph. *to be repeated*, Ge. 41. 32. Pi. שִׁנָּה.—I. *to change*, e. g. a garment.—II. *to change, alter* a promise, one's way.—III. *to change, disfigure* the countenance, Job 14. 20; with טַעְמוֹ *one's* (own) *understanding*, i. e. *to feign oneself mad*.

[a] Hab. 1. 12. [b] Je. 13. 1. [c] Je. 33. 25. [d] Ru. 3. 3. [e] Eze. 5. 5.
[f] Ge. 27. 37. [g] Is. 41. 15. [h] Ca. 6. 12. [i] Job 7. 20. [k] 1 Sa. 14. 4.
[l] Job 39. 28. [m] De. 32. 24. [n] Ju. 15. 2. [o] Ps. 127. 2. [p] 2 Ki. 25. 29.
[q] Ge. 37. 5, 8. [r] 2 Sa. 13. 15. [s] Pr. 19. 7. [t] 2 Sa. 5. 8. [u] Ps. 25. 19.
[x] Ec. 9. 12. [y] Ps. 41. 8. [z] Ps. 34. 22. [a] Pr. 28. 16.
[b] Ps. 106. 41. [c] Ge. 24. 60. [d] Ex. 1. 10. [e] Pr. 25. 17.
[f] Ps. 68. 18. [g] Pr. 8. 13. [h] Ps. 25. 19. [i] Ju. 15. 2.
[k] Ec. 2. 17, 18. [l] Je. 12. 8. [m] 2 Ch. 18. 7. [n] 1 Ki. 22. 8.
[o] Eze. 16. 27. [p] Ec. 9. 6. [q] Ju. 14. 16. [r] 2 Sa. 20. 10.

IV. *to transfer* or *remove* to another place, Est. 2. 9. Pu. *to be changed, altered,* Ec. 8. 1. Hithpa. *to change, disguise oneself,* 1 Ki. 14. 2.

שְׁנָא Chald.—I. *to be changed, altered.*—II. *to be different from,* with מִן. Pa. I. *to change, make different to,* with מִן, Da. 4. 13; part. passive, *different,* Da. 7. 7.—II. *to change, violate,* Da. 3. 28. Ithpa. *to be changed, altered.* Aph. I. *to change, alter.*—II. *to transgress,* Ezr. 6. 11, 12.

שָׁנָה fem. dec. 11 a (pl. שָׁנוֹת, שָׁנִים).—I. *a year;* מִדֵּי שָׁ׳ בְּשָׁנָה, שָׁ׳ בְּשָׁנָה, שָׁנָה שָׁנָה *every year, from year to year;* pl. שָׁנִים *years,* also indef. *some years;* dual שְׁנָתַיִם *two years.*—II. trop. *the produce of a year,* Joel 2. 25.

שְׁנָה or שְׁנָא Chald. fem. (constr. שְׁנַת; pl. שְׁנִין) *year.*

שָׁנִי masc. (constr. שְׁנִי, pl. שָׁנִים) *bright, scarlet colour* (Arab. שנא *to shine, be bright*) obtained from the *coccus* תּוֹלַעַת; pl. *scarlet clothes,* or *garments.*

שְׁנַיִם masc. du. constr. שְׁנֵי; fem. שְׁתַּיִם (prob. for שְׁנָתַיִם, to distinguish it from the du. of שָׁנָה *a year*), constr. שְׁתֵּי.—I. num. card. *two;* שְׁנַיִם שְׁנַיִם *two and two, by pairs;* שְׁתֵּיהֶם, שְׁנֵיהֶם *they two, both of them.*—II. fem. *a second time,. again,* Ne. 13. 20; בִּשְׁתַּיִם id. Job 33. 14.—III. שְׁנֵים עָשָׂר masc. שְׁתֵּים עֶשְׂרֵה fem. *twelve;* also *twelfth.*

שֵׁנִי masc. שֵׁנִית fem.—I. adj. ord. *second.*—II. pl. שְׁנִיִּים *chambers of the second story,* Ge. 6. 16; but in Nu. 2. 16, *the second.*—III. fem. also as an adv. *the second time, again.*

שִׁנְאָן m. Ps. 68. 18, Eng. vers. *"angels;"* perh. *changed, glorified ones;* others, אַלְפֵי שִׁ׳ *thousand of repetition,* i. e. *thousands upon thousands.*

מִשְׁנֶה masc. dec. 9 a.—I. *second rank,* in order or dignity; כֹּהֵן הַמִּשְׁנֶה *the priest next* to the high priest.—II. *second in rank,* in succession, dignity or quality, *second, next, the next;* אֲחֵיהֶם הַמִּשְׁנִים *their younger brethren,* 1 Ch. 15. 18; מִשְׁנֵה הַמֶּלֶךְ *the one next to the king;* 1 Ch. 15. 18 *silver cups of* (מִשְׁנִים) *second quality,* 1 Sa. 15. 9.—III. *a doubling, double.*—IV. *a duplicate, copy.*—V. *a division of* Jerusalem, so called 2 Ki. 22. 14; 2 Ch. 34. 22; Zep. 1. 10.

שָׁנָה וְ׳ noun fem. sing. dec. 11 a . . . שנה
שָׁנָה[a] Kh. שָׁנָה subst. q. v., K. שָׁנִים (q. v.) . שנה
שֵׁנָה noun fem. sing. dec. 11 b [for יְשֵׁנָה] . ישן
שִׁנָּה[b] וְ Piel pret. 3 pers. sing. masc. . . שנה
שֹׁנֶה[c] וְ Kal part. act. sing. masc. dec. 9 a . שנה

שֶׁנְהַבִּים noun masc. pl. . . . . . שנן
שְׁנוֹ[d] Ch. Peal pret. 3 pers. pl. masc. . . שנה
שְׁנוּ[e] Kal imp. pl. masc. . . . שנה
שִׁנּוֹ[f] noun com. sing., suff. 3 pers. s. m. fr. שֵׁן d. 8 b שנן
שְׂנוּאָה[g] ו׳ Kal part. pass. fem. sing. [from שָׂנוּא m.] שנא
שְׁנוֹהִי[h] Ch. Peal pret. 3 pers. pl. m., suff. 3 pers. s. m. שנה
שָׁנוּן[i] Kal part. pass. sing. masc. dec. 3 a . שנן
שְׁנוּנִים id. pl., abs. st. . . . . . שנן
שֵׁנוֹת noun fem. pl. abs. from שֵׁנָה dec. 11 b . ישן
שְׁנוֹת ו׳ noun f. pl., constr. of שָׁנוֹת fr. שָׁנָה d. 11 a שנה
שֹׁנוֹת[k] Kal part. act. pl. fem. [fr. שֹׁנָה] fr. שֹׁנֶה m. שנה
שִׁנּוֹתִי[l] Kal pret. 1 pers. sing. . . . שנן
שְׁנוֹתָי[m] / שְׁנוֹתַי[n] ו׳ [o] { noun fem. pl., suff. 1 pers. sing. from שָׁנָה dec. 11 a; ו bef. (:) . } שנה
שְׁנוֹתָיו[p] id. pl., suff. 3 pers. sing. masc. . שנה
שְׁנוֹתָיִךְ[q] id. pl., suff. 2 pers. sing. fem. [for ־תַיִךְ] שנה
שְׁנוֹתֶיךָ[r] ו׳ id. pl., suff. 2 pers. sing. masc.; ו bef. (:) שנה
שְׁנוֹתֵינוּ[s] id. pl., suff. 1 pers. pl. . . . שנה
שְׁנוֹתָם[t] ו id. pl., suff. 3 p. pl. m. (§ 4. r. 2); ו bef. (:) שנה
שָׁנִי noun masc. sing., constr. שְׁנִי, pl. שָׁנִים . שנה
שְׁנֵי ו׳ noun f. with pl. m. term., constr. of שָׁנִים, fr. שָׁנָה d. 11 a; or constr. of שְׁנַיִם (q. v.) שנה
שֵׁנִי adj. ord. m. s. (pl. שֵׁנִים d. 8 f) fr. שְׁנַיִם card. שנה
שְׁנִי[u] ו׳ noun masc., constr. of שָׁנִי; ו bef. (:) . שנה
שְׁנִי see וּשְׁנִי under lett. ו.
שִׁנַּי [for שִׁנַּיִ] the foll. with suff. 1 pers. sing. . שנן
שִׁנֵּי וְ׳ noun com. du., constr. of שִׁנַּיִם fr. שֵׁן d. 8 b שנן
שָׁנְיָה[x] Ch. Peal part. act. f. [fr. שְׁנֵא m.] R. שנא under שנה
שִׁנַּיהּ[y] Ch. noun com. du. (שִׁנַּיִן), suff. 3 pers. sing. fem. from שֵׁן dec. 5 b . . . שנן
שְׁנֵיהֶם ו׳ num. card. masc. (שְׁנַיִם) with suff. 3 pers. pl. masc.; ו bef. (:) . . . שנה
שְׁנֵיהֶם[z] ו noun fem. pl. (שָׁנִים) with suff. 3 pers. pl. masc. from שָׁנָה dec. 11 a; ו id. שנה
שִׁנֵּיהֶם noun com. pl., suff. 3 pers. pl. m. fr. שֵׁן d. 8 b שנן
שָׁנָיו noun f. pl. (שָׁנִים), suff. 3 p. s. m. fr. שָׁנָה d. 11 a שנה
שַׁנִּיו[a] Ch. Pael pret. 3 pers. pl. masc. . שנה
שִׁנָּיו noun com. pl., suff. 3 pers. s. m. fr. שֵׁן d. 8 b שנן
שִׁנַּיִךְ id. pl., suff. 2 pers. sing. fem. . . שנן
שְׁנֵיכֶם[b] num. card. m. (שְׁנַיִם) with suff. 2 pers. pl. m. שנה
שָׁנִים[c] noun masc., pl. of שָׁנִי (q. v.) . . . שנה
שָׁנִים וְ׳ noun f. with pl. m. term. fr. שָׁנָה d. 11 a שנה
שְׁנָיִם ו׳ / שְׁנַיִם ו׳ { num. card. masc. du., constr. שְׁנֵי & שְׁנֵים, fem. שְׁתַּיִם; ו bef. (:) . } שנה
שִׁנַּיִם noun com., dual of שֵׁן dec. 8 b . . שנן
שְׁנֵים ו׳ card. num. masc., constr. of שְׁנַיִם (q. v.) שנה
שֵׁנִים[d] ו׳ [e] adj. ord. masc., pl. of שֵׁנִי dec. 8 f; ו bef. (:) שנה

[a] 2 Ki. 8. 17. [b] Je. 52. 33. [c] Pr. 17. 9. [d] Da. 3 27. [e] 1 Ki. 18. 34. [f] Ex. 21. 27. [g] Is. 60. 15. [h] Da. 5. 6. [i] Pr. 25. 18. [k] Est. 3. 8. [l] De. 32. 41. [m] Is. 38. 10. [n] Is. 38. 15. [o] Ps. 31. 11. [p] Ps. 61. 7. [q] Eze. 22. 4. [r] Ps. 102. 28. [s] Ps. 90. 10. [t] Ps. 78. 33. [u] Le. 14. 6, 51. [x] Da. 7. 19. [y] Da. 7. 5, 19. [z] Job 36. 11. [a] Da. 3. 28. [b] Ge. 27. 45. [c] Pr. 31. 21. [d] Ge. 6. 16. [e] Nu. 2. 16.

שְׁנֵּימוֹ noun com. dual, suff. 3 pers. pl. m. fr. שֵׁן d. 8 b — שנן
שָׁנַיִן[a] Ch. Peal part. act. pl. m. [fr. שְׁנָא] d. 6 a — שנה
שָׁנְיָן[b] Ch. id. part. a. f., pl. of שָׁנְיָה [for שָׁנְיָא] d. 10 — שנה
שִׁנַּיִן[c] ן׃ Ch. noun com., dual of שֵׁן dec. 5 b . — שנן
שְׁנִין Ch. noun f. with pl. m. term. fr. [שְׁנָה] d. 9 a — שנה
שָׁנֵינוּ[d] noun f. pl. (שָׁנִים), suff. 1 p. pl. fr. שָׁנָה d. 11 a — שנה
שְׁנֵינוּ num. card. m. du. (שְׁנַיִם) with suff. 1 pers. pl. — שנה
שְׂנִיר ו׳ pr. name of mount Hermon among the Amorites.
שֵׁנִית adj. ord., fem. of שֵׁנִי, as an *adv.* . . — שנה
שָׁנִיתִי[e] Kal pret. 1 pers. sing. . . . — שנה

[שָׁנַן] I. *to sharpen,* e. g. a sword; part. שָׁנוּן *sharp.*—II. metaph. *to sharpen* the tongue, to utter sharp and insulting words. Pi. *to inculcate, teach diligently,* De. 6. 7. Hithpo. הִשְׁתּוֹנֵן *to be pricked, pierced* with pain, Ps. 73. 21.

שֵׁן com. dec. 8 b.—I. *a tooth.*—II. *ivory.*—III. *tooth* or *prong* of a fork, 1 Sa. 2. 13.—IV. *a sharp cliff.*—V. pr. name of a place, 1 Sa. 7. 12.

שִׁנְאָב (*father's tooth*) pr. name of a Canaanitish king, Ge. 14. 2.

שֶׁנְהַבִּים masc. pl. *ivory,* 1 Ki. 10. 22; 2 Ch. 9. 21. הַבִּים is supposed to be a contraction for הָאֶבִּים *the elephants.* Sansc. *ibha,* id.

שְׁנִינָה fem. *sharp* or *pointed saying, a taunt.*

שָׁנְנוּ Kal pret. 3 pers. pl. . . . . — שנן
שִׁנַּנְתָּם[f] ן׃ Piel pret. 2 pers. s. masc., suff. 3 pers. pl. m. — שנן

שִׁנֵּס Pi. *to gird up* the loins, 1 Ki. 18. 46.

שִׁנְעָר pr. name, *Shinar,* the country round Babylon.
שֶׁנַּעֲשָׂה[g] pref. ·שֶׁ (Niph. pret. 3 pers. sing. masc. — עשה
שֶׁנַּעֲשׂוּ[h] pref. id. (id. pret. 3 pers. pl. . . — עשה
שְׁנָת noun fem. sing. Ps. 132. 4. . . — ישן
שְׁנַת noun fem. sing., constr. of שֵׁנָה dec. 11 b — ישן
שְׁנַת ו׳ noun f. s., constr. of שָׁנָה d. 11 a; ו׳ bef. (:) — שנה
שְׁנָתָהּ id. with suff. 3 pers. sing. fem. . . — שנה
שִׁנְתֵּהּ[k] ן׃ Ch. noun fem. sing., suff. 3 pers. sing. masc. from [שְׁנָא] dec. 9 a . . . — ישן
שְׁנָתוֹ noun fem. sing., suff. 3 pers. sing. masc. from שָׁנָה dec. 11 a . . . — שנה
שְׁנָתוֹ ו׳ noun fem. sing., suff. 3 pers. sing. masc. from שֵׁנָה dec. 11 b; ו׳ bef. (ּ) . — ישן
שְׁנָתִי[m] ו׳ id., suff. 1 pers. sing.; ו׳ id. . — ישן
שְׁנָתַיִם / שְׁנָתָיִם } noun fem., du. of שָׁנָה dec. 11 a . — שנה
שְׁנֹתֶךָ[o] ו׳ id. pl., suff. 2 p. s. m. שְׁנוֹתֶיךָ; ו׳ bef. (:) — שנה

שְׁנָתְךָ[p] noun fem. s., suff. 2 pers. s. m. fr. שֵׁנָה d. 11 b — ישן
שְׁנָתָם id., suff. 3 pers. pl. masc. . . . — ישן
שֶׁנָּתַן[q] pref. ·שֶׁ (Kal pret. 3 pers. sing. masc. . — נתן

[שָׁסָה] *to plunder, spoil;* part. שֹׁסִים *spoilers.* Po. שׁוֹשָׂה (for שׁוֹסָה) id. Is. 10. 13.

שַׁסּוּהוּ[r] Kal pret. 3 pers. pl. [שַׁסּוּ], suff. 3 pers. s. m. — שסס
שֹׁסֵהוּ[s] Kal part. act. sing. masc., suff. 3 pers. sing. masc. [from שֹׁסֶה] dec. 9 a . . — שסה
שָׁסוּ[t] id. pret. 3 pers. pl. . . . . — שסה
שְׁסוּיִ[u] ן׃ id. part. pass. sing. masc. . . — שסה
שֹׁסֵי[v] id. part. act. pl. constr. masc. fr. שֹׁסֶה dec. 9 a — שסה
שֹׁסֵיהֶם[y] id. id. pl., suff. 3 pers. pl. masc. . — שסה
שֹׁסִים id. id. pl., abs. st. . . . . — שסה

[שָׁסַס] fut. יָשֹׁס *to plunder, spoil.* Niph. נָשַׁס *to be plundered, spoiled.*

מְשִׁסָּה fem. dec. 10, *prey, booty.*

[שָׁסַע] *to cleave, divide;* שֹׁסַע שֶׁסַע פַּרְסָה *cleaving the cleft of the hoof,* i. e. *having a divided hoof.* Pi. I. *to cleave,* Le. 1. 17.—II. *to rend, tear asunder,* Ju. 14. 6.—III. *to chide, rebuke,* 1 Sa. 24. 8; others, *to keep off, withhold, stay.* Hence

שֶׁסַע[z] ן׳ masc. *cleft, division* in a hoof . — שסע
שִׁסַּע[a] ן׃ Piel pret. 3 pers. sing. masc. . — שסע
שֹׁסַעַת[b] / שֹׁסַעַת[c] } Kal part. act. sing. masc. & fem. (§ 36. rem. 1) . . — שסע

שִׁסֵּף Pi. *to cut* or *hew in pieces,* 1 Sa. 15. 33.

שֶׁעָבַרְתִּי[d] pref. שֶׁ (Kal pret. 1 pers. sing. . — עבר

שָׁעָה I. *to look at, regard with attention,* with בְּ, Ex. 5. 9; Ps. 119. 117.—II. *to look at with favour, regard graciously,* with אֶל.—III. *to look out* or *about* for help, 2 Sa. 22. 42; and perh. also Is. 32. 3 (to which is assigned the sense of שָׁעַע; Syr. שׁעא *to be blinded*), with עַל ,אֶל *to look to* any one, expecting help.—IV. *to look away from, allow respite to,* with מֵעַל ,מִן. Hiph. *to look away from,* with מִן, Ps. 39. 14. Hithpa. הִשְׁתָּעָה.—I. *to look about with alarm,* Is. 41. 10.—II. *to be dismayed,* Is. 41. 23; others, *to look at* or *face one another.*

שָׁעָה or שְׁעָא Chald. (only emph. שַׁעֲתָא ,שַׁעְתָּא) *a moment of time;* whence in the Targums and elsewhere, *an hour.*

[a] Da. 5. 9. [b] Da. 7. 3. [c] Da. 7. 7. [d] Ps. 90. 9. [e] Mal. 3. 6. [f] De. 6. 7. [g] Ec. 1. 9; 2. 17. [h] Ec. 1. 14. [i] Is. 63. 4. [k] Da. 6. 19. [l] Da. 2. 1. [m] Ge. 31. 40. [n] Je. 31. 26. [o] Pr. 5. 9. [p] Pr. 3. 24. [q] Ezr. 8. 20. [r] Ps. 89. 42. [s] 1 Sa. 14. 48. [t] Ps. 44. 11. [u] Is. 42. 22. [x] Je. 50. 11. [y] Ju. 2. 16. [a] Le. 11. 26. [a] Le. 1. 17. [b] Le. 11. 7. [c] Le. 11. 26. [d] Ca. 3. 4. [e] Ge. 4. 5.

שְׁעֵה[a] Kal imp. sing. masc. . . . . . שעה
שָׁעוּ[b] id. pret. 3 pers. pl. . . . . . שעה
שְׁעוּ[c] id. imp. pl. masc. . . . . . שעה
שְׁעוּ[d] וְ Kal imp. pl. masc.; for וְ see lett. ו . . שעע
שְׂעֹרָה[rr] noun fem. sing. dec. 10 . . . . שער
שְׂעֹרִים ו' (2 Ch. 27. 5) id. pl., abs. st.; ו bef. (:) שער

שָׁעַט Root not used; Arab. תעט *to stamp, pound in pieces.*

שְׁעָטָה fem. dec. 11 c (§ 42. rem. 1), *a stamping* of the horse hoofs, Je. 47. 3.

שַׁעַטְנֵז *a cloth made of different threads,* Le. 19. 19; De. 22. 11, in which latter passage the word is explained by a mixture *of wool and flax together.* According to Bochart it is compounded of שַׁעַט i. q. Arab. שׁאט *to mix,* and the Chald. נוז *to twist threads together.* Others compare it with the Egyptian שָׁנְטְנָז a kind of linen.

שֶׁעִטְּרָה[e] pref. שֶׁ) Piel pret. 3 pers. sing. fem. . עטר
שַׁעֲטַת[f] noun fem. sing., constr. of [שְׁעָטָה] dec. 11 c שעט
שָׂעִיר[g] וְ noun masc. sing. dec. 3 a . . . שער
שְׂעִיר ו' id., constr. st.; ו bef. (:) . . . שער
שֵׂעִיר וְ' pr. name of a man and a country . שער
שֵׂעִירָה id. with parag. ה . . . . שער
שְׂעִירֵי[h] [i]ו' noun masc. pl. constr. fr. שָׂעִיר dec. 3 a שער
שְׂעִירִים[k] ו id. pl., abs. st.; ו bef. (:) . . שער
שְׂעִירַת noun fem. sing., constr. of [שְׂעִירָה] dec. 10 שער

שָׁעַל Root not used; to which the idea of *hollowness* is ascribed, as it appears from some of the derivatives.

שֹׁעַל m. d. 6 f, *the hollow hand, palm,* Is. 40. 12.

שַׁעַל masc. dec. 6 d, *a handful.*

שַׁעֲלִים (*foxes;* שַׁעַל i. q. שׁוּעָל) pr. name of a district, 1 Sa. 9. 4.

שׁוּעָל masc. (pl. שׁוּעָלִים).—I. *a fox.*—II. pr. name, (1) of a man, 1 Ch. 7. 36; (2) of a district in Benjamin, 1 Sa. 13. 17.

שַׁעַלַבִּין, שַׁעַלְבִים (*foxes;* Arab. תעלב *fox*) pr. name of a city in the tribe of Dan. Gent. noun שַׁעַלְבֹנִי.

מִשְׁעוֹל m. *a narrow path, a hollow way,* Nu. 22. 24.

שֶׁעָלַי pref. שֶׁ) prep., with suff. עָלַי (§ 31. rem. 5) עלה
שַׁעֲלַבִּים וְ pr. name of a place . . . שעל
שֶׁעָלוּ pref. id.) Kal pret. 3 pers. pl. . . עלה
שַׁעֲלִים pr. name of a district . . . שעל
שְׁעָלִים defect. for שׁוּעָלִים (q. v.) . . . שעל
שֶׁעֹמְדִים[m] pref. שֶׁ) Kal part. act., pl. of עֹמֵד dec. 7 b עמד

שֶׁעִמָּהֶם[n] pref. id.) prep. (עִם) with suff. 3 pers. pl. masc. (§ 5) . . . . עמם
שֶׁעֲמָלוֹ[o] pref. id.) noun masc. sing., suff. 3 pers. sing. masc. from עָמָל dec. 4 c . . . עמל
שֶׁעָמַלְתִּי[p] pref. id.) Kal pret. 1 pers. sing. . . . עמל

שָׁעַן. Niph. נִשְׁעַן.—I. *to lean, rest upon,* with עַל.—II. metaph. *to rely upon, to trust in,* with בְּ, אֶל, עַל.—III. *to touch, border upon, be adjacent to,* with לְ, עַל.—IV. *to recline,* abs. Ge. 18. 4.

אֶשְׁעָן (*support*) pr. name of a city in the tribe of Judah, Jos. 15. 52.

מִשְׁעָן masc. dec. 2 b, *a stay, support.*

מַשְׁעֵן masc., מַשְׁעֵנָה fem. id. Is. 3. 1.

מִשְׁעֶנֶת fem. dec. 13 a (with suff. 'עַנְתּוֹ), *a staff.*

[שָׁעַע] *to be overspread, to be closed* (Syr. & Chald. שְׁעַע, שׁוּעַ trans. *to spread over;* also, *to stroke, caress, flatter*); of the eyes, *to be blinded,* Is. 29. 9. Hiph. *to cover, blind* the eyes, Is. 6. 10. Pilp. שִׁעֲשַׁע (§ 6. No. 4).—I. *to delight, rejoice,* Ps. 94. 19.—II. *to delight oneself, be delighted.* Pulp. שֳׁעֳשַׁע *to be fondled, caressed,* Is. 66. 12. Hithpalp. הִשְׁתַּעֲשַׁע *to delight oneself,* with בְּ in any one, Ps. 119. 16, 47; abs. i. q. *to indulge oneself,* Is. 29. 9; others, *to be dazzled* or *blinded.*

שַׁעֲשֻׁעִים masc. pl. (of שַׁעֲשׁוּעַ dec. 1 b) *delight, pleasure.*

שָׁעַף וְ } pr. name masc. of two persons, 1 Ch.
שַׁעַף } 2. 47, 49; for וְ see lett. ו.
שְׂעִפַּי[q] noun masc. pl., suff. 1 pers. sing. from [שָׂעִף] dec. 8 b (§ 37. No. 2), see . . . סעף

[שָׂעַר] I. *to shudder.*—II. *to fear, reverence,* De. 32. 17.—III. *to sweep, tear away with a tempest,* Ps. 58. 10. Niph. impers. *it is tempestuous,* Ps. 50. 3. Pi. *to sweep away with a tempest,* Job 27. 21. Hithpa. *to rage against,* or *rush upon like a tempest,* with עַל, Da. 11. 40.

שַׂעַר masc.—I. *a storm, tempest,* Is. 28. 2.—II. *a shuddering, horror.* See also under the foll. R.

שְׂעָרָה fem. id. Job 9. 17; Na. 1. 3.

שְׂעִירִים masc. pl. *showers,* De. 32. 2.

שֵׂעָר [r]וְ' masc. dec. 4 b, *a hair;* collect. *hair.*

שַׂעַר masc. dec. 6 d, *the hair,* Ca. 4. 1; 6. 5; Is. 7. 20. For another, see above.

שְׂעַר Chald. id. Da. 3. 27; 7. 9.

[a] Job 14. 6. [b] Is. 31. 1. [c] Is. 22. 4. [d] Is. 29. 9. [e] Ca. 3. 11. [f] Je. 47. 3. [g] Is. 34. 14. [h] Le. 16. 5; 2 Ch. 29. 23. [i] Nu. 7. 87. [k] Is. 13. 21. [l] Ju. 7. 12; 8. 26. [m] Ps. 135. 2. [n] 1 Ch. 5. 20. [o] Ec. 2. 21. [p] Ec. 2. 11, 19, 20. [q] Job 20. 2. [r] Le. 13. 3, 31, 37. [rr] Joel. 1. 11.

שַׂעֲרָה fem. dec. 12 d, *a hair*; collect. *the hair.*

שְׂעוֹרָה, שְׂעֹרָה fem. *barley*, the plant as it grows; pl. שְׂעֹרִים *barley*, of the grain.

שְׂעֹרִים (*barley*) pr. name masc. 1 Ch. 24. 8.

שָׂעִיר masc. dec. 3 a.—I. adj. *hairy*, Ge. 27. 11, fem. שְׂעִרָה ver. 23.—II. *he-goat*; שְׂעִיר עִזִּים *a buck of the goats*.—III. pl. *demons*, prob. worshipped under the figure of *goats*, Le. 17. 7; 2 Ch. 11. 15.

שֵׂעִיר (*hairy*) pr. name, *Seir*.—I. a chief of the Horites, comp. Ge. 36. 20, 30.—II. a mountainous country east and south of the Dead Sea, inhabited first by the Horites, and afterwards by the posterity of Esau, comp. De. 2. 12.—III. a mountain in Judah, Jos. 15. 10.

שְׂעִירָה fem. dec. 10.—I. *she-goat*.—II. pr. name of a place in Ephraim, Ju. 3. 26.

I. שָׁעַר *to estimate the value*, abs. Pr. 23. 7; prob. from the primary signification *to cleave, divide* (whence *to decide, determine*, &c.), Arab. תער intrans. *to be cleft*; Chald. תַּרְעָא by transp. *an aperture*, and then *a gate*.

שַׁעַר com. dec. 6 d.—I. *gate* of a camp, a palace, a temple, but espec. of a city; meton. for the *city* itself, comp. De. 12. 17; 17. 2.—II. *gate*, as the place for administering justice, and for any public business; meton. for *the people assembled at the gate*, Ru. 3. 11.—III. *a measure*, Ge. 26. 12.

שַׁעֲרַיִם (*two gates*) pr. name of a city in the tribe of Judah.

שׁוֹעֵר masc. dec. 7 b, *gate-keeper, porter*.

שְׁעַרְיָה (*whom the Lord values*) pr. name masc. 1 Ch. 8. 38; 9. 44.

II. שָׁעַר Root not used; prob. i. q. שָׂעַר *to shudder*.

שֹׁעָר adj. *horrid, bad*, of figs, Je. 29. 17; Prof. Lee, *blighted figs* (Arab. שער *to infect with a contagion*).

שַׁעֲרוּר, fem. שַׁעֲרוּרָה adj. *horrible*, Je. 5. 30; 23. 14.

שַׁעֲרוּרִי, fem. ־רִיָּה, ־רִית adj. Ho. 6. 10; neut. *a horrible thing*, Je. 18. 13.

[a]שָׁעַר	in pause for שַׁעַר (q. v. & § 35. rem. 2)	שער
שַׁעַר ,ו׳ / שַׁעַר ,ו׳	noun fem. sing. dec. 6 d (§ 35. rem. 2)	שער
[b]שַׂעַר ,ו׳	noun masc. sing. dec. 6 d	שער
[c]שָׂעִר	adj. masc. sing., defect. for שָׂעִיר	שער
שֵׂעָר ,ו׳	noun masc. sing. dec. 4 d	שער
שְׂעַר ,ו׳	id., constr. st.; or Chald. noun masc. dec. 3 a; ו bef. (:)	שער
שֹׁעָר	noun masc. sing. dec. 7 b	שער
[d]שַׁעְרָה	noun fem. s. (שַׁעַר) with loc. ה [for שַׁעֲרָה]	שער
[e]שַׂעְרֵהּ	Ch. n. m. s., suff. 3 p. s. m. from שְׂעַר dec. 3 a	שער
[f]שְׂעָרָהּ ,ו׳ / [g]שְׂעָרָהּ ,ו	noun masc. sing., suff. 3 pers. sing. fem. from שֵׂעָר dec. 3 d (§ 3. r. 3); ו bef. (:)	שער
[h]שְׂעֹרָה ,ו׳	noun fem. sing., pl. שְׂעֹרִים; ו id.	שער
[i]שָׂעֲרוּ	Kal pret. 3 pers. pl.	שער
[k]שַׂעֲרוּ ,וְ	id. imp. pl. masc.	שער
[l]שְׁעָרוֹ	Kh. for שְׁעָרָיו K. (q. v.)	שער
[m]שְׂעָרוֹ	noun masc. sing., suff. 3 pers. sing. masc. from שֵׂעָר dec. 4 d	שער
[n]שְׂעָרוּם	Kal pret. 3 pers. pl. with suff. 3 pers. pl. masc.	שער
[o]שַׁעֲרוּרָה ,וְ׳	adj. fem. sing. [from שַׁעֲרוּר masc.]	שער
שַׁעֲרֵי ,וְ׳	noun fem. pl., constr. from שַׁעַר dec. 6 d	שער
שְׁעָרֶיהָ ,ו׳	id. pl., suff. 3 pers. sing. fem.; ו bef. (:)	שער
שְׁעַרְיָה ,ו	pr. name masc.; ו id.	שער
שַׁעֲרֵיהֶם	noun fem. pl., suff. 3 pers. pl. masc. from שַׁעַר dec. 6 d	שער
שְׁעָרָיו	id. pl., suff. 3 pers. sing. masc.	שער
[p]שְׁעָרַיִךְ ,וּ / [q]שְׁעָרַיִךְ ,וּ׳	id. pl., suff. 2 pers. sing. fem.; ו bef. (:)	שער
שְׁעָרֶיךָ	id. pl., suff. 2 pers. sing. masc.	שער
שַׁעֲרַיִם ,וְ׳	id. du. as a pr. name	שער
שְׁעָרִים ,ו׳	id. pl., abs. st.; ו bef. (:)	שער
שְׂעֹרִים ,ו׳	noun fem. with pl. m. term. from שְׂעֹרָה d. 10	שער
[r]שֹׁעֲרִים	noun masc., pl. of שֹׁעֵר dec. 7 b	שער
[s]שַׁעֲרִירִיָּה	Kh. שַׁעֲרִירִיָּה, K. שַׁעֲרוּרִיָּה, adj. fem. from שַׁעֲרוּרִי or שַׁעֲרִרִי	שער
[t]שְׂעָרֵךְ / [u]שְׂעָרֵךְ	noun masc. sing., suff. 2 pers. sing. fem. from שֵׂעָר dec. 6 d (§ 35. rem. 5)	שער
[x]שְׂעָרֵךְ	ו noun masc. sing., suff. 2 pers. sing. fem. from שְׂעַר dec. 3 d; ו bef. (:)	שער
[y]שַׁעֲרֻרִת	adj. fem. sing. [from שַׁעֲרוּרִי masc.]	שער
[z]שַׂעֲרַת	noun fem. sing., constr. of שַׂעֲרָה (no pl. abs.)	שער
[a]שְׂעִירֹת	adj. fem., pl. of שְׂעִירָה, from שָׂעִיר masc.	שער
שַׁעַשְׁגַז	pr. name of a Persian eunuch, Est. 2. 14.	
[b]שֶׁעָשׂוּ	pref. שֶׁ)(Kal pret. 3 pers. pl.	עשה
[c]שִׁעֲשַׁע ,וְ	Pilp. pret. 3 pers. sing. masc. (§ 6. No. 4)	שעע
[d]שַׁעֲשֻׁעָיו	the foll. with suff. 3 pers. sing. masc.	שעע
שַׁעֲשֻׁעִים	noun masc., pl. of [שַׁעֲשׁוּעַ] dec. 1 b	שעע
שַׁעֲשֻׁעָי / [f]שַׁעֲשֻׁעָי ,ו׳	id. pl. with suff. 1 pers. sing.	שעע
[g]שִׁעֲשָׁעְתִּי	Pilp. pret. 1 pers. sing.	שעע
שַׁעְתָּא / [h]שַׁעְתָּא	Chald. noun fem., emph. of שָׁעָה	שעה

[a] Job 18. 20. [b] Is. 7. 20. [c] Ge. 27. 11. [d] Is. 28. 6. [e] Da. 4. 30. [f] Le. 13. 4. [g] Le. 13. 20. [h] Job 31. 40. [i] Eze. 27. 35. [k] Je. 2. 12. [l] Ob. 11. [m] Le. 14. 8, 9. [n] De. 32. 17. [o] Je. 5. 30; 23. 14. [p] Ps. 147. 13. [q] Is. 60. 11. [r] 1 Ch. 23. 5. [s] Ho. 6. 10. [t] Ca. 6. 5. [u] Ca. 4. 1. [x] Eze. 16. 7. [y] Je. 18. 13. [z] Job 4. 15. [a] Ge. 27. 23. [b] Ec. 2. 11. [c] Is. 11. 8. [d] Is. 5. 7. [e] Ps. 119. 24. [f] Pr. 8. 31. [g] Ps. 119. 70. [h] Da. 3. 6.

שָׂפָה [a] ו׳ fem. dec. 11a (du. שְׂפָתַיִם, pl. c. שִׂפְתוֹת).—I. *lip;* אִישׁ שְׂפָתַיִם *a loquacious man;* דְּבַר שׂ׳ *talk of the lips,* i. e. vain words, idle talk.—II. *speech, words.*—III. *language, dialect;* עִמְקֵי שָׂפָה *men of unintelligible language, barbarians.*—IV. *brim* of a vessel.—V. *shore* of the sea; *bank* of a river.—VI. *edge, edging, border.*—VII. *border, boundary,* Ju. 7. 22.

שָׂפָם masc. dec. 4a, *the lower part of the face, the chin, the beard;* עָשָׂה שְׂפָמוֹ *to trim one's beard.*

שָׁפָה Kal not used; Arab. שפא *to appear, become visible.* Niph. part. *conspicuous, lofty,* Is. 13. 2. Pu. *to become prominent, to stand out,* of the bones, Job 33. 21.

שָׁפָה or שְׁפָה fem. dec. 11, *cheese,* 2 Sa. 17. 29 (Syr. שפא to cleanse from the dregs).

שְׁפוֹ (*eminent, excellent*) pr. name masc. Ge. 36. 23, for which שְׁפִי 1 Ch. 1. 40.

שְׁפִי masc. dec. 6i.—I. *eminence, elevated place.*—II. pr. name, see שְׁפוֹ.

שָׁפָם (*eminent, excellent*) pr. name m. 1 Ch. 5. 12.

שְׁפָם (*elevated place*) pr. name of a town in Judah, Nu. 34. 10, 11; called שִׁפְמוֹת 1 Sa. 30. 28. Gent. n. שִׁפְמִי 1 Ch. 27. 27.

יִשְׁפָּה (*eminent*) pr. name masc. 1 Ch. 8. 16.

יִשְׁפָּן (prob. id.) pr. name masc. 1 Ch. 8. 22.

שְׁפוֹ	pr. name masc.	שפה
שָׁפוֹט [b]	Kal inf. abs.	שפט
שְׁפוֹט [c] / שְׁפוֹטִים [d] ו	noun masc. sing., & pl. abs. (§ 30. rem. 4); ו bef. (:)	שפט
שְׁפֹךְ [e]	Kal imp. sing. masc.	שפך
שְׁפוּכָה [f]	id. part. pass., fem. of שָׁפוּךְ	שפך
שְׁפוּפָן	ו pr. name masc.; ו bef. (:)	שפף
שְׁפוֹת [g]	ו noun f. pl. constr. [fr. שָׁפָה or שְׁפָה]; ו id.	שפה

שָׂפַח. Kal not used; *to pour out,* comp. סָפַח. Pi. *to make to fall off,* sc. the hair by disease, scab, &c. hence, *to make bald,* Is. 3. 17.

מִשְׂפָּח masc. *a shedding of blood,* Arab. שפח *to shed blood,* Is. 5. 7; Prof. Lee, *violence,* Arab. שפע *to strike,* and then *to propel, drive away.* It may be worth inquiry, whether *confusion,* so closely allied to the signification of *pouring* (comp. נָסַךְ I & II), may not be intended in this passage?

שָׁפַח Root not used; perh. to join, associate, cogn. סָפַח (comp. Fürst in conc.)

שִׁפְחָה fem. dec. 12b, *female servant, handmaid;* Lat. *famula,* "as if, one of the family." (Gesen.)

מִשְׁפָּחָה fem. (constr. מִשְׁפַּחַת, with suff. ׳פַּחְתִּי pl. ׳פָּחוֹת § 42. rem. 5).—I. *family, household* comp. Ex. 12. 21.—II. *family, clan,* comp. Jos. 7. 14 —III. *tribe,* comp. Ju. 18. 2; also for a whole *nation* —IV. *race, kind,* of animals.

שִׂפַּח [h]	ו Piel pret. 3 pers. sing. masc.	שפח
שִׁפְחָה	ו׳ noun fem. sing. dec. 12b	שפח
שְׁפָחוֹת	ו id. pl., abs. st.; ו bef. (:)	שפח
שִׁפְחוֹתֵיכֶם [i]	id. pl., suff. 2 pers. pl. masc.	שפח
שְׁפָחֹת	ו id. pl., abs. st.; ו bef. (:)	שפח
שִׁפְחַת	id. sing., constr. st.	שפח
שִׁפְחָתָהּ	id. sing., suff. 3 pers. sing. fem.	שפח
שִׁפְחָתוֹ	id. sing., suff. 3 pers. sing. masc.	שפח
שִׁפְחָתִי	id. sing., suff. 1 pers. sing.	שפח
שִׁפְחֹתָיו [k]	id. pl., suff. 3 pers. sing. masc.	שפח
שִׁפְחָתְךָ / שִׁפְחָתֶךָ	id. sing., suff. 2 pers. sing. masc.	שפח
שִׁפְחָתֵךְ [l]	id. sing., suff. 2 pers. sing. fem.	שפח
שִׁפְחֹתֶךָ [m]	id. pl., suff. 2 pers. sing. masc. (§ 4. rem. 2)	שפח

שָׁפַט ו׳ fut. יִשְׁפֹּט.—I. *to judge, administer justice;* with בֵּין—לְ, בֵּין—וּבֵין *to decide between;* part. שׁוֹפֵט *a judge.*—II. *to judge, do justice to, to defend* or *vindicate the cause of* any one.—III. *to condemn, punish.*—IV. *to rule;* שֹׁפֵט *a judge, ruler.* Niph. נִשְׁפַּט.—I. *to be judged.*—II. *to litigate, contend before a judge,* with אֵת, עִם, לְ, of the person *with* whom, with acc., עַל of the thing *about* which. Po. part. *a judge,* Job 9. 15.

שְׁפַט Chald. part. שָׁפֵט *a judge,* Ezr. 7. 25.

שָׁפָט (*judge*) pr. name masc. of several persons

שֶׁפֶט masc. dec. 6a, only pl. שְׁפָטִים *judgments, punishments.*

שְׁפוֹט masc. *judgment, punishment,* 2 Ch. 20. 9; pl. שְׁפוּטִים (§ 30. rem. 4) Eze. 23. 10.

שִׁפְטָן (*judicial*) pr. name masc. Nu. 34. 24.

שְׁפַטְיָה (whom *the Lord judges, defends*) pr. name —I. of a son of David, 2 Sa. 3. 4.—II. of several other men.

שְׁפַטְיָהוּ (id.) pr. name—I. of a son of Jehoshaphat, 2 Ch. 21. 2.—II. of two other men, 1 Ch. 12. 5; 27. 16.

מִשְׁפָּט masc. dec. 2b.—I. *judgment, the act of judging.*—II. *judgment, sentence, decision.*—III. *punishment.*—IV. *place of judgment, court of justice.* —V. *cause, suit;* בַּעַל מִ׳ *opponent, adversary;* דִּבֶּר מִשְׁפָּטִים אֵת *to litigate, contend with* any one, also (comp. No. II.) *to pronounce severe judg-*

[a] Ge. 11. 6. [b] Ge. 19. 9. [c] 2 Ch. 20. 9. [d] Eze. 23. 10. [e] Ju. 6. 20. [f] Eze. 20. 33, 34. [g] 2 Sa. 17. 29. [h] Is. 3. 17. [i] 1 Sa. 8. 16. [k] Ge. 32. 23. [l] Ge. 16. 6. [m] Ru. 2. 13.

ments upon any one.—VI. *justice, equity, right.*—VII. *right, privilege.*—VIII. *law, institution.*—IX. *custom, usage.*—X. *mode, manner.*

שָׁפָט וְ pr. name masc. . . . . שפט

שָׁפַט[a] Kal pret. 3 pers. sing. masc. (§ 8. rem. 2) שפט

שְׁפֹט[b] id. inf. constr. . . . . . שפט

שְׁפָט־[c] id. imp. sing. masc. (for שְׁפֹט § 8. rem. 18) שפט

שֹׁפֵט[d] וְ id. part. act. sing. masc. dec. 7b . שפט

שָׁפְטָה id. imp. s. m. [שְׁפֹט] with parag. ה (§ 8. r. 11) שפט

שֹׁפְטָה[e] id. part. act. sing., fem. of שֹׁפֵט (§ 8. rem. 19) שפט

שְׁפָטֻהוּ[f] וְ id. pret. (Kh. וּשְׁפָטֻהוּ), or fut. (K. וְיִשְׁפְּטֻהוּ), 3 pers. pl. masc, suff. 3 pers. sing. masc. . שפט

שָׁפְטוּ[g], שָׁפָטוּ[h] וְ } id. pret. 3 pers. pl. (§ 8. rem. 7) . שפט

שְׁפָטוֹ[i] id. pret. 3 pers. sing. m., suff. 3 pers. sing. m. שפט

שִׁפְטוּ[k], שִׁפְטוּ } id. pret. 3 pers. pl. (§ 8. rem. 12) . שפט

שְׁפָטוּךְ[l] וּ id. pret. 3 p. pl., suff. 2 p.s.f.; וּ, for וְ, conv. שפט

שְׁפָטוּם[m] וּ id. id., suff. 3 pers. pl. masc.; וּ id. שפט

שְׁפָטוּנוּ[n] id. id., suff. 1 pers. pl. . . . שפט

שְׁפָטַי[o] noun m. pl., suff. 1 pers. s. from [שֶׁפֶט] d. 6a שפט

שֹׁפְטֵי Kal part. act. pl. c. masc. from שֹׁפֵט dec. 7b שפט

שְׁפַטְיָה pr. name masc. . . . . . שפט

שֹׁפְטֶיהָ[p] וְ Kal part. act. pl., suff. 3 pers. sing. fem. from שֹׁפֵט dec. 7b . . . . שפט

שְׁפַטְיָהוּ pr. name masc. . . . . . שפט

שֹׁפְטֵיהֶם Kal part. act. pl., suff. 3 p. pl. m. fr. שֹׁפֵט d. 7b שפט

שֹׁפְטָיו[q] וְ id. pl., suff. 3 pers. sing. masc. . . שפט

שֹׁפְטַיִךְ[r] id. pl., suff. 2 pers. sing. fem. . . שפט

שֹׁפְטֶיךָ וְ id. pl., suff. 2 pers. sing. masc. . . שפט

שֹׁפְטֵיכֶם[s] id. pl., suff. 2 pers. pl. masc. . . שפט

שְׁפָטִים noun masc., pl. of [שֶׁפֶט] dec. 6a . . שפט

שֹׁפְטִים וְ Kal part. act. masc., pl. of שֹׁפֵט dec. 7b שפט

שָׁפְטִין[t] Ch. Peal part. act. pl. masc. [from שָׁפֵט] d. 2b שפט

שֹׁפְטֵינוּ[u] Kal part. act. pl. m., suff. 1 p. pl. fr. שֹׁפֵט d. 7b שפט

שְׁפָטְךָ[x] id. pret. 3 pers. sing. m., suff. 2 pers. sing. m. שפט

שִׁפְטָן pr. name masc. . . . . . שפט

שְׁפָטָנוּ[y] וּ Kal pret. 3 pers. sing. masc., suff. 1 pers. pl.; וּ, for וְ, conv. . . . . שפט

שֹׁפְטֵנוּ[z] id. part. act. s. m., suff. 1 p. pl. fr. שֹׁפֵט d. 7b שפט

שָׁפְטֵנִי id. imp. sing. masc., suff. 1 pers. sing. . שפט

שָׁפַטְתָּ וְ id. pret. 2 pers. sing. masc.; acc. shifted by conv. וְ (§ 8. rem. 7) . . . . שפט

שָׁפַטְתִּי וְ id. pret. 1 pers. sing.; acc. id. . . שפט

שְׁפַטְתִּיךְ וּ id. id., suff. 2 pers. sing. fem.; וּ, for וְ, conv. שפט

שְׁפַטְתִּים[a] id. id., suff. 3 pers. pl. masc. . . שפט

שְׁפַטְתֶּם[b] וּ id. pret. 2 pers. pl. masc.; וּ, for וְ, conv. שפט

שְׁפִי[c], שֶׁפִי } noun masc. sing., pl. שְׁפָיִים dec. 6i (§ 35. rem. 14), also pr. name . . } שפה

שֻׁפּוּ[d] וְ Kh. שְׁפִי q. v.; K. שֻׁפּוּ Pual pret. 3 pers. pl. שפה

שְׁפָיִים, שְׁפָיִם } noun masc., pl. of שְׁפִי dec. 6i . . שפה

שְׁפִיפֹן noun masc. sing. . . . . . שפף

שָׁפִיר pr. name of a place . . . . שפר

שַׁפִּיר[e] Ch. adj. masc. sing. l suff. 3 pers. sing. m.' שפר

שָׁפַךְ וְ fut. יִשְׁפֹּךְ.—I. *to pour out;* metaph. *to pour out* one's prayer, soul, heart, before the Lord; also *to pour out* one's anger upon any one; moreover, God is said *to pour out, bestow in profusion,* the Spirit.—II. *to shed* blood.—III. *to throw up* a mound, Eze. 26. 8. Niph. I. *to be poured out, shed;* metaph. of a person in extreme weakness, Ps. 22. 15.—II. *to be profusely expended,* of money, Eze. 16. 36. Pu. I. *to be shed.*—II. of steps, *to slip,* Ps. 73. 2. Hithpa. הִשְׁתַּפֵּךְ *to be poured out,* La. 4. 1; metaph. of the soul, life.

שֶׁפֶךְ masc. *place of pouring out,* Le. 4. 12.

שָׁפְכָה fem. *membrum virile,* De. 23. 2.

שׁוֹפָךְ (*effusion, increase*) pr. name masc. 1 Ch. 19. 16, 18, for which שׁוֹבָךְ 2 Sa. 10. 16, 18 (Arab. שבך *to pour out*).

שָׁפָךְ Kal pret. 3 pers. sing. m. for שָׁפַךְ (§ 8. r. 7) שפך

שֶׁפֶךְ[f] noun masc. sing. . . . . . שפך

שֹׁפֵךְ Kal part. act. sing. masc. dec. 7b . . שפך

שְׁפֹךְ id. imp. sing. masc. . . . . שפך

שְׁפָךְ־ id. id. (Ps. 69. 25), or inf. constr. . שפך

שֻׁפַּךְ[g] [h] וְ Pual pret. 3 pers. sing. masc. . . שפך

שָׁפְכָה[i] noun fem. sing. . . . . . שפך

שָׁפְכָה[k] Kh. שָׁפְכָה, K. שָׁפְכוּ, Kal pret. 3 pers. sing. fem., or 3 pers. pl. . . . . שפך

שֻׁפְּכָה[l] Kh. שֻׁפְּכָה, K. שֻׁפְּכוּ, Pual pret. 3 pers. sing. fem., or 3 pers. pl. . . . שפך

שָׁפְכוּ[m] וְ Kal pret. 3 pers. pl. . . . שפך

שִׁפְכוּ[n] [o] וְ id. imp. pl. masc. . . . . שפך

שֹׁפְכוֹ[p] id. part. act. sing. masc., suff. 3 pers. sing. masc. from שֹׁפֵךְ dec. 7b . . . שפך

שֹׁפְכוֹת id. part. act. s. f. fr. שֹׁפֶכֶת (§ 8. r. 19) d. 13a שפך

שִׁפְכִי[q] id. imp. sing. masc. . . . . שפך

שָׁפַכְתָּ[r], שָׁפַכְתְּ[s], וְשָׁפַכְתָּ } id. pret. 2 pers. sing. masc.; acc. shifted by conv. וְ (§ 8. rem. 7) } שפך

a 1 Sa. 7. 17.
b Ru. 1. 1.
c Pr. 31. 9.
d Ex. 2. 14.
e Ju. 4. 4.
f Eze. 44. 24.
g Je. 5. 28.
h 2 Ki. 23. 22.
i 2 Sa. 18. 19.
k Zec. 7. 9.
l Eze. 23. 24; 24. 14.
m De. 25. 1.
n Da 9. 12.
o Eze. 14. 21.
p Ezr. 10. 14.
q Jos. 8. 33.
r Is. 1. 26.
s De. 1. 16.
t Ezr. 7. 25.
u Da. 9. 12.
x 2 Sa. 18. 31.
y 1 Sa. 8. 20.
z Is. 33. 22.
a Eze. 36. 19.
b De. 1. 16.
c Nu. 23. 3.
d Job 33. 21.
e Da. 4. 9, 18.
f Le. 4. 12.
g Nu. 35. 33.
h Zep. 1. 17.
i De. 23. 2.
k De. 21. 7.
l Ps. 73. 2.
m Le. 14. 41.
n Ps. 62. 9.
o Je. 6. 6.
p Nu. 35. 33.
q La. 2. 19.
r 1 Ch. 28. 3.
s 1 Ch. 22. 8.

שָׁפַכְתְּ id. pret. 2 pers. sing. fem. . . . שפך

[a] שֹׁפֶכֶת id. part. act. sing. fem. (§ 8. r. 19) fr. שֹׁפֵךְ m. שפך

[b] שֹׁפְכוֹת וְ id. id. pl. dec. 13a . . . שפך

שְׁפָכַתְהוּ [c] id. pret. 3 pers. sing. fem., suff. 3 pers. sing. m. שפך

שָׁפַכְתִּי, וְשָׁפַכְתִּי } id. pret. 1 pers. sing.; acc. shifted by conv. וְ (§ 8. rem. 7) . . . } שפך

[d] שָׁפֵל וְ׳ fut. יִשְׁפַּל.—I. *to be made low, to be lowered.*—II. *to be depressed,* of the voice, Ec. 12. 4.—III. *to be humbled;* inf. שְׁפַל רוּחַ *to be humble* in spirit, Pr. 16. 19. Hiph. I. *to bring low, throw down.*—II. *to humble.*—III. intrans. *to humble oneself,* Job 22. 29; Is. 57. 9 (trans. according to Prof. Lee, rendering the latter passage, *to send down*); with other verbs adverbially, Je. 13. 18; הַשְׁפִּילוּ שֵׁבוּ *sit down low,* Ps. 113. 6.

שְׁפַל Chald. Aph. *to bring down, to humble.*

שָׁפָל m. d. 4a, שְׁפָלָה fem. d. 11c, adj.—I. *low.*—II. *low, mean, contemptible.*—III. *humble, lowly.*

שְׁפַל Chald. *low, humble,* Da. 4. 14.

שֵׁפֶל masc. d. 6b, *lowness, low place* or *condition.*

שִׁפְלָה fem. id. Is. 32. 19.

שְׁפֵלָה f. d. 10, *low country;* הַשְּׁפֵלָה *the low country* or *plain* along the Mediterranean from Joppa to Gaza.

שִׁפְלוּת fem. *lowness* of the hands, *remissness, idleness,* Ec. 10. 18.

שָׁפָל [e] וְ׳ adj. masc. sing. dec. 4a . . . שפל

שְׁפַל [f] וְ׳ adj. masc. sing., constr. of שָׁפָל dec. 4a (perh. inf. Pr. 16. 19); וּ bef. (:) . . . שפל

[g] שְׁפַל וּ Chald. adj. sing. masc.; וּ id. . . . שפל

שְׁפָלָה [h] וְ׳ adj. sing. fem. d. 11c, from שָׁפָל m.; וּ id. שפל

שְׁפָלִים [i] וְ׳ id. masc., pl. of שָׁפָל dec. 4a; וּ id. . . שפל

[k] שָׁפַלְתְּ וְ Kal pret. 2 pers. sing. fem. . . . שפל

[l] שִׁפְלַת adj. fem. s., constr. of שְׁפָלָה d. 11c, fr. שָׁפָל m. שפל

[m] שְׁפֵלָתָהּ וּ noun fem. sing., suff. 3 pers. sing. masc. from שְׁפֵלָה dec. 10; וּ bef. (:) . . . שפל

שָׂפָם noun masc. sing. dec. 4a . . . . שפה

שָׁפָם וְ pr. name masc. . . . . שפה

שֻׁפָּם וְ pr. name masc., for שְׁפִים . . . שפף

שִׁפְמָה pr. name (שָׁפָם) with parag. ה . . . שפה

[n] שְׂפָמוֹ noun m. sing., suff. 3 pers. s. m. fr. שָׂפָם d. 4a שפה

[שָׂפַן] *to cover, hide,* De. 33. 19.

שָׁפָן וְ׳ masc. dec. 8a.—I. *the jerboa;* Sept. χοιρογρύλλιος; Rabbins, *the coney.*—II. pr. name of the scribe or secretary of king Josiah; also of another man.

[o] שְׂפֻנֵי וּ Kal part. p. pl. c. m. [fr. שָׂפוּן] d. 3a; וּ bef. (:) שפן

[p] שְׁפַנִּים noun masc., pl. of שָׁפָן dec. 8a (§ 37. No. 2) שפן

שֶׁפַע masc. *an overflowing, abundance,* De. 33. 19.

שִׁפְעָה fem. (only constr. שִׁפְעַת).—I. *overflowing, abundance* of water.—II. *multitude* of camels. Also (*abundant*) pr. name masc. 1 Ch. 4. 37 . שפע

שִׁפְעִי

שִׁפְעַת וְ׳ noun fem. sing. constr. [of שִׁפְעָה no pl.] שפע

שפף Root not used; Syr. *to creep.*

שְׁפִיפֹן masc. a species of *serpent,* Ge. 49. 17 (Arab. سَفَّ *a speckled serpent*).

שְׁפוּפָם (perh. *serpent*) pr. name masc. Nu. 26. 39. Patronym. שׁוּפָמִי ibid.

שְׁפוּפָן (id.) pr. name masc. 1 Ch. 8. 5.

שֻׁפִּים (*serpents*) pr. name of two men, 1 Ch. 7. 12. 15, & 26. 16.

[שָׂפַק] I. *to smite, clap the hands,* Job 27. 23.—II. *to suffice,* 1 Ki. 20. 10, comp. סָפַק. Hiph. *to strike,* or *make a league with,* with בְּ Is. 2. 6; better perh. *to applaud,* or *to abound with.*

שֶׂפֶק masc. *a smiting, chastisement,* Job 36. 18; Prof. Lee, *contempt.*

[שָׁפַר] prop. *to be bright,* see Pi.; hence, *to be pleasant, acceptable to,* with עַל Ps. 16. 6. Pi. *to make bright, beautiful,* Job 26. 13; but the word שִׁפְרָה is best taken as a subst., *brightness, beauty.*

שְׁפַר Chald. (*to be fair*) *to please, be acceptable to,* with קֳדָם, עַל.

שֶׁפֶר masc.—I. *beauty, pleasantness,* Ge. 49. 21.—II. pr. name of a mountain in the Arabian desert, Nu. 33. 23, 24.

שִׁפְרָה fem.—I. *brightness, beauty,* see Pi.—II. pr. name fem. Ex. 1. 15.

שׁוֹפָר m. d. 2b (pl. שׁוֹפָרוֹת), *trumpet, curved horn.*

שָׁפִיר (*fair*) pr. name of a place, Mi. 1. 11.

שַׁפִּיר Ch. masc. *beautiful, pleasing,* Da. 4. 9, 18.

שַׁפְרוּר or שַׁפְרִיר masc. *royal canopy,* Je. 43. 10.

שְׁפַרְפָּר Chald. masc. d. 2a, *the dawn,* Da. 6. 20.

אֶשְׁפָּר masc. *a measure;* etym. uncertain.

[q] שָׁפֶר noun m. s. [for שֶׁפֶר § 35. r. 2], also pr. name שפר

שְׁפַר Chald. Peal pret. 3 pers. sing. masc. . שפר

שֹׁפָר defect. for שׁוֹפָר (q. v.) . . . שפר

[r] שָׁפְרָה Kal pret. 3 pers. sing. fem. . . . שפר

שִׁפְרָה pr. name fem. . . . . . שפר

[s] שִׁפְרָה subst. f. or Piel pret. 3 p. s. f. [for שִׁפְּרָה § 10. r. 7] שפר

[a] Eze. 22. 3. [b] Eze. 16. 38. [c] Eze. 24. 7. [d] Is. 2. 11, 12, 17. [e] Ps. 138. 6. [f] Pr. 16. 19. [g] Da. 4. 14. [h] Le. 13. 21, 26. [i] Mal. 2. 9. [k] Is. 29. 4. [l] Eze. 17. 6. [m] Jos. 11. 16. [n] 2 Sa. 19. 25. [o] De. 33. 19. [p] Pr. 30. 26. [q] Ge. 49. 21. [r] Ps. 16. 6. [s] Job 26. 13.

שִׁפְרוּרוֹ[a] Kh. שִׁפְרוּרוֹ, K. שַׁפְרִירוֹ noun masc. with suff. [from שִׁפְרוּר or שַׁפְרִיר] . . שׁפר

[שָׁפַת] fut. יִשְׁפֹּת.—I. *to set, put, place*.—II. *to give*, Is. 26. 12.

שְׁפַתַּיִם masc. du. *stalls, folds* for cattle, Ps. 68. 14; Eze. 40, 43; others, *pots, cooking vessels*.

מִשְׁפְּתַיִם masc. du. *folds, enclosures for cattle*, Ge. 49. 14; Ju. 5. 16.

שְׂפַת noun fem. sing., constr. of שָׂפָה dec. 11 a . שׂפה

שְׁפֹת Kal imp. sing. masc. . . . . שׁפת

שְׂפָתָהּ[b] noun fem. sing., suff. 3 pers. sing. fem. from שָׂפָה dec. 11 a . . . שׂפה

שְׂפָתוֹ ו׳ id., suff. 3 pers. sing. masc.; וּ bef. (:) . שׂפה

שִׂפְתוֹת[c] וְ id. pl. constr. [of שְׂפָתוֹת] . . שׂפה

שִׂפְתוֹתָיו[d] id. pl., suff. 3 pers. sing. masc. . . שׂפה

שִׂפְתוֹתַיִךְ[e] id. pl., suff. 2 pers. sing. fem. . . שׂפה

שִׂפְתוֹתֵיכֶם[f] id. pl., suff. 2 pers. pl. masc. . . שׂפה

שְׂפָתִי } id. du. (שְׂפָתַיִם), suff. 1 pers. sing. . שׂפה
שְׂפָתָי

שִׂפְתֵי וְ׳ id. du., constr. st. . . . . שׂפה

שְׂפָתֶיהָ id. du., suff. 3 pers. sing. fem. . . שׂפה

שִׂפְתֵיהֶם[a] id. du., suff. 3 pers. pl. masc. . . שׂפה

שְׂפָתָיו [g]ו׳ id. du., suff. 3 pers. sing. masc.; וּ bef. (:) שׂפה

שְׂפָתָיו[h] id. id. Kh. שְׂפָתָיו, K. שְׂפָתוֹ (q. v.) . שׂפה

שְׂפָתֶיךָ ו׳ id. du., suff. 2 pers. sing. masc.; וּ bef. (:) שׂפה

שְׂפָתַיִם } id. du., abs. st. . . . . שׂפה
שְׂפָתָיִם

שְׁפַתַּיִם[i] noun m., du. of [שֶׁפֶת § 37. Nos. 2 & 3) d. 8 שׁפת

שְׂפָתֵימוֹ noun fem. du. (שְׂפָתַיִם), suff. 3 pers. pl. masc. from שָׂפָה dec. 11 a . . שׂפה

שְׂפָתֵינוּ id. du., suff. 1 pers. pl. . . . שׂפה

שְׂפָתָם[k] id. sing., suff. 3 pers. pl. masc. . . שׂפה

[שֶׁצֶף] masc. i. q. שֶׁטֶף *an overflowing*, Is. 45. 8.

שַׂק } noun masc. sing. dec. 8 d . . שׂקק
וְ׳ שָׂק

שָׂקַד. Niph. *to be bound, fastened*, La. 1. 14.

שָׁקַד[l] fut. יִשְׁקֹד.—I. *to wake, be sleepless*.—II. *to watch*, with עַל *over* any thing, or *for* any thing, *to lie in wait for*, Je. 5. 6.

שָׁקֵד[m] masc. dec. 5 a.—I. *almond tree*, Je. 1. 11, 12. —II. *almond*. Pu. part. מְשֻׁקָּדִים *formed like almonds*, Ex. 25. 33, 34 . . שׁקד

שֹׁקֵד Kal part. act. sing. masc. dec. 7 b . . שׁקד

שִׁקְדוּ[n] id. imp. pl. masc. . . . . . שׁקד

שֹׁקְדֵי[o] id. part. act. pl. c. masc. from שֹׁקֵד dec. 7 b שׁקד

שְׁקֵדִים[p] [q]ו׳ noun masc., pl. of שָׁקֵד dec. 5 a; וּ bef. (:) שׁקד

שֶׁקַּדְמַת[r] pref. שֶׁ)(noun f. s. constr. [of קַדְמָה, no pl.] קדם

שָׁקַדְתִּי Kal pret. 1 pers. sing. . . . . שׁקד

שָׁקָה. Hiph. הִשְׁקָה.—I. *to give to drink, to let drink*, with double acc. of pers. and thing; with מִן ,בְּ *out of* anything; מַשְׁקֶה *cupbearer, butler*.—II. *to water* cattle.—III. *to water, irrigate* the ground. Niph. *to be overflown*, Am. 8. 8, Kh. Pu. *to be moistened, refreshed*, Job 21. 24.

שֹׁקֶת f. *drinking-trough*, Ge. 24. 20; pl. שִׁקֲתוֹת (as if from שֶׁקֶת § 35. rem. 9, note) Ge. 30. 38.

שִׁקּוּי masc. dec. 1 b.—I. *drink*, Ho. 2. 7.—II. *moistening, refreshment*, Pr. 3. 8.

שִׁקֻּוִים masc. pl. (of שִׁקּוּ) *drink*, Ps. 102. 10.

מַשְׁקֶה masc. d. 9 a.—I. *drink*.—II. *a well-watered country*.

שָׁקָה[s] וְ Kal imp. sing. masc. with parag. ה, comp. וְשָׁבְעָה ,וְשִׁבְעָה ,וְזָהָב ; וּ bef. (:) . נשק

שַׂקּוֹ noun m. s., suff. 3 pers. s. m. fr. שַׂק d. 8 d שׂקק

שָׁקוֹהִי[t] Ch. n. m. pl., suff. 3 p. s. m. fr. [שָׁק] d. 1 a שׁוק

שִׁקּוּי[u] וְ noun masc. sing. dec. 1 b . . . שׁקה

שִׁקּוּיָי[x] וְ noun masc. pl., suff. 1 pers. sing. [fr. שִׁקּוּ] שׁקה

שִׁקּוּיָי[y] וְ noun m. pl., suff. 1 pers. s. fr. שִׁקּוּי d. 1 b שׁקה

שֶׁקִּוִּינֻהוּ[z] pref. שֶׁ)(Piel pret. 1 p. pl. with suff. 3 p. s. m. קוה

שָׁקוֹל[a] Kal inf. abs. . . . . . . שׁקל

שִׁקּוּץ[b] noun masc. sing. dec. 1 b . . . שׁקץ

שִׁקּוּצֵי[c] id. pl., constr. st. . . . . . שׁקץ

שִׁקּוּצֶיהָ[d] id. pl., suff. 3 pers. sing. fem. . . שׁקץ

שִׁקּוּצֵיהֶם id. pl., suff. 3 pers. pl. masc. . . שׁקץ

שִׁקּוּצַיִךְ[e] } id. pl., suff. 2 pers. sing. fem. . . שׁקץ
שִׁקּוּצַיִךְ[f]

שִׁקּוּצֶיךָ[g] id. pl., suff. 2 pers. sing. masc. . . שׁקץ

שִׁקּוּצִים id. pl., abs. st. . . . . . שׁקץ

שָׁקַט וְ fut. יִשְׁקֹט.—I. *to rest, be quiet, undisturbed*.—II. *to rest, be free from*, with מִן.—III. *to be inactive*. —IV. *to be silent*, Ps. 76. 9. Hiph. I. *to give rest*. —II. *to quiet, still*, Pr. 15. 18.—III. *to keep quiet, be quiet*; inf. הַשְׁקֵט *rest, quiet*. Hence.

שֶׁקֶט[h] וְ masc. *rest, quiet*, 1 Ch. 22. 9. . שׁקט

שֹׁקֵט[i] [k]וְ׳ Kal part. act. sing. masc. dec. 7 b . שׁקט

---

[a] Je. 43. 10. [b] Eze. 43. 13. [c] Ec. 10. 12. [d] Ca. 5. 13. [e] Ca. 4. 3, 11. [f] Is. 59. 3. [g] Pr. 18. 7. [h] Pr. 16. 27. [i] Ps. 68. 14. [k] Ge. 11. 7. [l] Ps. 127. 1. [m] Je. 1. 11. [n] Ezr. 8. 29. [o] Is. 29. 20. [p] Nu. 17. 23. [q] Ge. 43. 11. [r] Ps. 129. 6. [s] Ge. 27. 26. [t] Da. 2. 33. [u] Pr. 3. 8. [x] Ps. 102. 10. [y] Ho. 2. 7. [z] La. 2. 16. [a] Job 6. 2. [b] Da. 12. 11. [c] Eze. 20. 7, 8. [d] Eze. 11. 18. [dd] Pr. 24. 2. [e] Je. 13. 27. [f] Eze. 5. 11. [g] Je. 4. 1. [h] 1 Ch. 22. 9. [i] Ju. 18. 7, 27. [k] Je. 48. 11.

שָׁקְטָה[a] שָׁקָטָה } וְ id. pret. 3 pers. sing. fem. (§ 8. rem. 7) שקט

שֹׁקֶטֶת[b] שֹׁקָטֶת[c] } וְ id. part. act. sing., fem. of שֹׁקֵט (§ 8. r. 19) שקט

שָׁקַטְתִּי[d] שָׁקַטְתִּי[e] } id. pret. 1 pers. sing.; acc. shifted by conv. וְ . . . . } שקט

שַׂקִּי[f] noun masc. sing., suff. 1 pers. s. fr. שַׂק d. 8 d שקק

שַׂקֵּיהֶם[g] id. pl., suff. 3 pers. pl. masc. . . שקק

שַׂקִּים id. pl., abs. st. . . . . . שקק

שֹׁקַיִם[h] noun fem., du. of שׁוֹק dec. 1 a . . שוק

שָׁקַל fut. יִשְׁקֹל.—I. *to weigh.*—II. *to weigh out, to pay,* with לְ, עַל *to* any one.—III. trop. *to examine, try,* Job 6. 2; 31. 6. Niph. pass. of Kal Nos. II & III.

שֶׁקֶל masc. dec. 6 a (pl. c. שִׁקְלֵי), *a shekel,* a standard weight for weighing gold or silver. Two kinds of shekels are distinguished in Ex. 30. 13, & 2 Sa. 14. 26.

אַשְׁקְלוֹן (*migration,* Syr. שְׁקַל *to migrate,* Simonis) pr. name, *Askelon,* a city of the Philistines. Gent. noun אַשְׁקְלוֹנִי Jos. 13. 3.

מִשְׁקָל masc. dec. 2 b.—I. *the act of weighing.*—II. *weight.*

מִשְׁקוֹל masc. *weight,* Eze. 4. 10.

מִשְׁקֹלֶת, מִשְׁקֶלֶת *plummet*; Sept. *στάθμιον, balance.* Is. 28. 17; 2 Ki. 21. 13.

שֶׁקֶל שָׁקֶל } noun masc. sing. (pl. c. שִׁקְלֵי § 35. rem. 2) dec. 6 a . . . . } שקל

שֹׁקֵל Kal part. act. sing. masc. . . . שקל

שִׁקְלֵי שְׁקָלִים } noun masc. pl. constr. & abs. from שֶׁקֶל dec. 6 a . . . . } שקל

שִׁקְמָה f. only in the pl. שִׁקְמוֹת, שִׁקְמִים *sycamore trees.*

שִׁקְמוֹתָם[k] וְ noun f. pl., suff. 3 p. pl. m. fr. [שִׁקְמָה] d. 10 שקם

שִׁקְמִים id. with pl. masc. term. abs. st. . . שקם

שַׁקַּמְתִּי[l] pref. ·שַׁ)(Kal pret. 1 pers. sing. . . קום

[שָׁקַע] I. *to sink in water,* Je. 51. 64.—II. *to be overflown,* Am. 9. 5.—III. *to subside, abate,* of fire, Nu. 11. 2. Niph. *to be submerged, overflown,* Am. 8. 8, K. Hiph. I. *to cause to sink, depress,* Job 40. 25.—II. *to cause to subside,* Eze. 32. 14.

מִשְׁקָע masc. dec. 2 b, *a pool, pond,* Eze. 34. 18.

שָׁקְעָה[m] וְ Kal pret. 3 pers. sing. fem. . . . שקע

שְׁקַעֲרוּרֹת fem. pl. *hollow places* in a wall, Le. 14. 37, compounded of שָׁקַע & קָעַר q. v.

שָׁקַף Kal not used; Arab. שקף *to cover* (Gr. *σκεπάω*), also *to be long and bending from length* (Gesen.). Niph. (prop. *to bend forward in order to see*).—I. *to look out, abroad,* e. g. through *a window,* with בְּעַד.—II. of a mountain, *to overhang, to look towards,* with עַל פְּנֵי.—III. metaph. *to impend, threaten,* Je. 6. 1. Hiph. id. *to look,* La. 3. 50; with בְּעַד *through,* אֶל, עַל *towards,* מִן *from.*

שֶׁקֶף masc. *covering, coping,* 1 Ki. 7. 5.

שְׁקֻפִים m. pl. *coped, having copings,* 1 Ki. 7. 4; 6. 4.

מַשְׁקוֹף masc. *lintel,* the timber over the door-posts, Ex. 12. 7, 22, 23.

שָׁקֶף[ee] noun masc. sing. [for שֶׁקֶף § 35. rem. 2] שקף

שְׁקֻפִים[n] ו׳ noun masc., pl. of [שָׁקוּף] d. 3 a; ו bef. (:) שקף

שָׁקַץ Pi. I. *to contaminate, pollute.*—II. *to loathe, abominate, abhor.*

שֶׁקֶץ masc. *abominable thing.*

שִׁקּוּץ m. dec. 1 b, *abomination, abominable thing.*

שַׁקֵּץ[o] Piel inf. constr. as an *abs.* . . . שקץ

שֶׁקֶץ וְ׳ (Le. 11. 11.) noun masc. sing. . . שקץ

שִׁקַּץ[p] Piel pret. 3 pers. sing. masc. (§ 10. rem. 1) שקץ

שִׁקֻּץ noun masc. sing. dec. 1 b, comp. שִׁקּוּץ . שקץ

שִׁקֻּצָיו[q] וְ id. pl., suff. 3 pers. sing. masc. . . שקץ

שִׁקֻּצִים[r] id. pl., abs. st. . . . . שקץ

שָׁקַק Root not used; prob. i. q. זָקַק q. v. Gr. *σακκίζω,* Lat. *saccavit,* i. e. *to strain* (Gese.). Ethiop. סַקְסַק *lattice* (Fürst in conc.).

שַׂק m. d. 8 d.—I. *sackcloth.*—II. *a sack* for grain.

[שָׁקַק] fut. יָשֹׁק.—I. *to run to and fro.*—II. *to be eager, greedy.* Hithpalp. הִשְׁתַּקְשֵׁק (§ 6. No. 4) *to run to and fro,* Na. 2. 5.

שָׁשַׁק (*for* שַׁקְשַׁק *eagerness,* comp. בָּבֶל, שֵׁשַׁךְ) pr. name masc. 1 Ch. 8. 14, 25.

מַשָּׁק masc. d. 2 b; *a running to and fro,* Is. 33. 4.

שֹׁקֵק[s] Kal part. act. sing. masc. . . . שקק

שֹׁקֵקָה[t] id. fem. comp. שׁוֹקֵקָה . . . שוק

שָׁקַר Kal not used; Chald. סְקַר *to look*; also, *to stain, paint.* Pi. *to wink* with the eyes, or, *to paint* the eyes, Is. 3. 16.

שָׁקַר (only fut. יִשְׁקֹר) *to act falsely towards,* with לְ Ge. 21. 23. Pi. I. *to lie, speak falsehood,* 1 Sa. 15. 29.—II. with בְּ *to deceive.*—III. with בְּ *to act falsely to, to violate* a covenant. Hence

[a] Ps. 76. 9. [b] Zec. 1. 11. [c] 1 Ch. 4. 40. [d] Job 3. 26. [e] Eze. 16. 42. [ee] 1 Ki. 7. 5. [f] Ps. 30. 12. [g] Ge. 42. 35. [h] Pr. 26. 7. [i] 1 Ch. 21. 25. [k] Ps. 78. 47. [l] Ju. 5. 7. [m] Am. 9. 5. [n] 1 Ki. 6. 4; 7. 4. [o] De. 7. 26. [p] Ps. 22. 25. [q] Zec. 9. 7. [r] Na. 3. 6. [s] Is. 33. 4. [t] Ps. 107. 9.

שֶׁקֶר, שָׁקֶר [a] וְ masc. dec. 6 a (§ 35. rem. 2; but pl. with suff. שִׁקְרֵיהֶם).—I. *lie, falsehood*; אִישׁ שֶׁקֶר *a liar*; עֵד שֶׁ׳ *a false witness*; בַּשֶּׁקֶר, לַשֶּׁקֶר *falsely*. —II. *deceitful, vain thing*; לַשֶּׁקֶר, & שֶׁקֶר adv. *in vain*.

שְׁקָרִים id. pl., abs. st. . . . . . . שקר

שִׁקַּרְנוּ [b] Piel pret. 1 pers. pl. . . . . שקר

שָׁר [c] וְ [d] Kal pret. 3 pers. sing. masc., or part. act. dec. 1 a . . . . שיר

שַׂר, שָׂר [e] וְ [f] noun masc. sing., pl. שָׂרִים dec. 8 (§ 37. rem. 7) . . . . שרר

שְׁרָא [g] Ch. Peal pret. 3 pers. sing. masc. (§ 47. r. 6) שרה

שַׁרְאֶצֶר וְ pr. name—I. of a son of Sennacherib.—II. Zec. 7. 2.

שֶׁרֹאשִׁי [h] pref. שֶׁ) noun masc. sing. ראשׁ irr. (§ 45) ראשׁ

שָׁרָב masc.—I. *heat* of the sun, or *drought*, Is. 49. 10. Syr. & Chald. שְׁרַב *to be hot, dry*.—II. *the mirage*, a phenomenon frequent in Arabia and Egypt, when the desert presents the appearance of a sea or a lake (Arab. שׂראב), Is. 35. 7.

שֵׁרֵבְיָה (*heat of the Lord*) pr. name of a man.

שַׁרְבִט [i] defect. for שַׁרְבִיט (q. v.) . . . . שבט

שֵׁרֵבְיָה וְ pr. name masc. . . . . . שרב

שַׁרְבִיט noun masc. sing. . . . . . שבט

שָׂרַג. Pu. *to be interwoven*, Job 40. 17. Hithpa. הִשְׂתָּרֵג id. La. 1. 14.

שְׂרוּג (*branch*, i. q. שָׂרִיג) pr. name m. Ge. 11. 20.

שָׂרִיג masc. dec. 1 b, only pl. *branches* of a vine.

[שָׂרַד] *to flee, escape*, Jos. 10. 20.

שָׂרִיד masc. dec. 3 a.—I. *one left, escaped*.—II. *remnant*.

שְׂרָד [k] masc. prob. *colour*; בִּגְדֵי שְׂ׳ *coloured garments*. Samar. שרדה *varie picta, et colorata vestis* (Prof. Lee). Sept. στολαί λειτουργικαί, *ministering apparel*, i. q. שָׁרֵת.

שֶׂרֶד masc. *red chalk* or *ochre*, Is. 44. 33; Gesenius (Coll. Arab.), *style, graver*.

שָׂרְדוּ [l] Kal pret. 3 pers. pl. . . . . . שרד

שָׂרָה *to contend, wrestle*, with עִם, אֶת, Ge. 32. 29; Ho. 12. 4. Others, *to be a prince with, to prevail*; but against the context, on account of וַתּוּכָל in Gen. l. c.

שׂוֹרָה fem. *row*, adverbially *in a row*, Is. 28. 25. (Arab. id.)

שָׂרַי (*contentious?*) pr. name, *Sarai*, the wife of Abraham, afterwards called שָׂרָה q. v. R. שָׂרַר.

שְׂרָיָהוּ, שְׂרָיָה pr. name, *Seraiah*.—I. of the scribe or secretary of David, 2 Sa. 8. 17; for which שְׁוָא (Kh. שְׁיָא) 2 Sa. 20. 25, שַׁוְשָׁא 1 Ch. 18. 16, שִׁישָׁא 1 Ki. 4. 3. Simonis compares, for these three variations, the Arab. שׂוי and the Syr. שׁוּשׁ *to dwell*, and assigns to them the signification of *habitation*; for שְׂרָיָה he reads with the Syr. שְׁרָיָה *habitation of God*, comp. R. שָׁרָה.—II. of the father of Ezra, Ezr. 7. 1.—III. of several other men.

יִשְׂרָאֵל (*wrestler with God*; others, *prince with God*) pr. name, *Israel*, the new name given to Jacob, Ge. 32. 29, afterwards employed as the name of his descendants, and after the division of the kingdom under Rehoboam, to *the kingdom of the ten tribes* in opposition to that of Judah.

מִשְׂרָה fem. *government*, Is. 9. 5, 6.

שָׁרָה. Pi. שֵׁרָה *to loose, set free*, Je. 15. 11.

שְׁרָא, שְׁרָא Ch.—I. *to loose, untie, solve*.—II. *to lodge, dwell* (comp. Gr. καταλύω, *to unloose*, whence κατάλυμα, *a lodging*), Da. 2. 22. Pa. I. *to solve*, Da. 5. 12.—II. *to begin*, Ezr. 5. 2. Ithpa. אִשְׁתְּרָא *to be loosened*, Da. 5. 6.

שֵׁרוּת fem. dec. 1 b, *beginning*, Je. 15. 11, Kh.

שָׁרוּחֶן (for שְׁרוּת חֵן *pleasant lodging*) pr. name of a town in Simeon, Jos. 19. 6.

שָׁרַי (*beginning*) pr. name masc. Ezr. 10. 40.

שִׁרְיָה fem. *coat of mail*, Job 41. 18 (Arab. שׁרי *to glitter*).

שִׁרְיוֹן m., also סִרְיֹן Je. 46. 4, d. 1 b.—I. *coat of mail*, see שִׁרְיָה.—II. pr. name, *Sirion*, the name of mount Hermon among the Sidonians, De. 3. 9.

שִׁרְיָן masc. i. q. שִׁרְיוֹן No. I.

מִשְׁרָה fem. dec. 10, *solution, maceration*, Nu. 6. 3, מִשְׁרַת עֲנָבִים *maceration of grapes*, a drink prepared from macerated grapes.

שָׂרָה וְ pr. name fem. . . . . . שרר

שְׂרוּג pr. name masc. . . . . . שרג

שָׁרוּחֶן וְ pr. name of a place . . . . שרה

שָׂרוֹט [m] Kal inf. abs. . . . . . שרט

שְׂרוֹךְ noun masc. sing. . . . . . שרך

שָׁרוֹן pr. name of a region . . . . ישר

שָׂרוּעַ Kal part. pass. sing. masc. . . . שרע

[a] Mi. 2. 11. [b] Ps. 44. 18. [c] Ps. 7. 1. [d] Pr. 25. 20. [e] Ho. 3. 4. [f] 2 Ch. 32. 21. [g] Da. 2. 22. [h] Ca. 5. 2. [i] Est. 8. 4. [k] Ex. 39. 1. [l] Jos. 10. 20. [m] Zec. 12. 3.

שָׂרוֹף[a] Kal inf. abs. . . . . . שׂרף

שְׂרוּפָה[b] id. part. pass. sing. fem. from שָׂרוּף masc. שׂרף

שְׂרוּפוֹת[c] id. id. pl. dec. 10 . . . . שׂרף

שְׂרוּקֶּיהָ[d] noun masc. pl. [שְׂרוּקִּים], suff. 3 pers. s. f. שׂרק

שְׂרֻקֹּת[e] Kh. שְׂרוּקֹּת noun fem. pl. [of שְׂרוּקָּה], K. שְׂרֵקוֹת (q. v.) . . . . שׂרק

שָׂרוֹת ְ Kal part. act. f. pl. [of שָׂרָה], fr. שָׂר m. שׂיר

שָׂרוֹת noun f. pl. of [שָׂרָה] d. 10 [for שַׂרָּה], fr. שַׂר m. שׂרר

שָׂרוֹתֶיהָ[f] id. pl., suff. 3 pers. sing. fem. . . שׂרר

שָׂרוֹתֵיהֶם[n] ְ id. pl., suff. 3 pers. pl. masc. . . שׂרר

שָׂרוֹתַיִךְ[g] Kal part. fem. pl., suff. 2 pers. sing. fem. [fr. שָׂרָה d. 10, fr. שָׂר masc. § 30. No. 3] שׂיר

שֵׂרוֹתְךָ[h] Kh. שֵׂרוּתְךָ noun fem. sing. with suff. [fr. שֵׂרוּת]; K. שֵׂרִיתְךָ Piel pret. 1 pers. sing., suff. 2 pers. sing. masc. . . . שׂאר

שָׂרַח, שָׂרַח ְ } (*abundance*, comp. סֶרַח) pr. name masc. Ge. 46. 17; 1 Ch. 7. 30.

[שָׂרַט] *to cut*, *make incisions* in the body. Niph. *to tear* or *hurt oneself* by lifting, Zec. 12. 3. Hence

שֶׂרֶט[i] ְ masc. שָׂרֶטֶת fem. *an incision* in the body.

שָׂרָטֶת[k] noun fem. sing. [for שָׂרֶטֶת] . . שׂרט

שָׂרָי pr. name masc. for שָׂרַי . . . שׂרה

שָׂרָי, שָׂרַי ְ' } pr. name fem. . . . . שׂרה

שָׂרַי[l] ְ'[m] the foll. with suff. 1 pers. sing. . . שׂרר

שָׂרֵי ְ' noun m. pl. constr. fr. שַׂר m. d. 8 (§ 37. r. 7) שׂרר

שָׂרִיגֶיהָ[n] the foll. with suff. 3 pers. sing. fem. . שׂרג

שָׂרִיגִם[o] noun masc., pl. of [שָׂרִיג] dec. 1 b . . שׂרג

שָׂרִיד ְ' noun masc. sing. dec. 3 a, also pr. name שׂרד

שְׂרִידֵי[p] id. pl., constr. st. . . . . שׂרד

שְׂרִידָיו id. pl., suff. 3 pers. sing. masc. . . שׂרד

שָׂרֶיהָ ְ'[q] noun masc., pl., suff. 3 pers. sing. fem. from שַׂר dec. 8 (§ 37. rem. 7) . שׂרר

שְׂרָיָה, שְׂרָיָהוּ ו' } pr. name masc.; ו bef. (:) . . שׂרה

שִׂרְיָה[r] ְ noun fem. sing. . . . . שׂרה

שָׂרֵיהֶם ְ'[s] noun masc. pl., suff. 3 pers. pl. masc. from שַׂר dec. 8 (§ 37. rem. 7) . . שׂרר

שָׂרָיו ְ' id. pl., suff. 3 pers. sing. masc. . שׂרר

שָׂרִיו[t] ְ Chald. Pael pret. 3 pers. pl. m. (§ 49. No. 3) שׂרא

שִׂרְיוֹן[u] ְ' noun masc. sing. dec. 1 b . . . שׂרה

שָׂרַיִךְ[x] ְ'[y] noun masc. pl., suff. 2 pers. sing. fem. from שַׂר dec. 8 (§ 37. rem. 7) . . שׂרר

שָׂרֶיךָ[z] noun masc. pl., suff. 2 pers. sing. masc. from שִׁיר dec. 1 a . . . . . שׂיר

שָׂרֵיכֶם[a] ְ the foll. with suff. 2 pers. pl. masc. . שׂרר

שָׂרִים ְ' noun masc., pl. of שַׂר dec. 8 (§ 37. rem. 7) שׂרר

שָׂרִים ְ[b] Kal part. act. masc., pl. of שָׂר dec. 1 a שׂיר

שְׂרַיִן[c] Chald. Peal part. pass. pl. m. [fr. שְׂרֵא] d. 6 a שׂרה

שִׂרְיֹן ְ' pr. name of a mount . . . שׂרה

שָׂרֵינוּ ְ[d] noun masc. pl., suff. 1 pers. pl. from שַׂר dec. 8 (§ 37. rem. 7) . . . שׂור

שִׂרְיֹנוֹת[e] ְ noun m. with pl. fem. term. fr. שִׂרְיוֹן d. 1 b שׂרה

שְׂרִיקוֹת[f] adj. fem. pl. [of שְׂרִיקָה from שָׂרִיק masc.] שׂרק

שָׂרִיתָ[g] Kal pret. 2 pers. sing. masc. . . . שׂרה

שֵׂרִית[h] noun fem. sing., contr. for שְׁאֵרִית . שׂאר

שָׂרַךְ. Pi. part. מְשָׂרֶכֶת *twisting*, *winding* her course, Je. 2. 23, cog. שָׂרַג.

שְׂרוֹךְ masc. *a shoe-latchet*.

שָׂרֵךְ[i] noun masc. sing., suff. 2 pers. sing. masc. from [שֹׂר] dec. 8 c (§ 37. rem. 7) . שׂרר

שַׂרְכֶם[k] noun masc. sing., suff. 2 pers. pl. masc. from שַׂר dec. 8 (§ 37. rem. 7) . . שׂרר

שַׂרְסְכִים pr. name of a chief of the eunuchs, in the army of Nebuchadnezzar, Je. 39. 3.

שָׂרַע only part. שָׂרוּעַ *stretched out*, *prolonged*, i. e. *having any member too long*, *unnaturally grown out*, Le. 21. 18; 22. 23. Hithpa. הִשְׂתָּרֵעַ *to stretch oneself out*, Is. 28. 20.

שַׂרְעַפַּי[l], שַׂרְעַפַּי[m] } noun masc. pl., suff. 1 pers. sing. from [שַׂרְעָף] dec. 8 d, see . . } סעף

שָׂרַף ְ' I. *to burn*, *consume*.—II. *to burn* lamps or torches for the dead, a rite still existing among the Jews, with לְ, 2 Ch. 16. 14; Je. 34. 5.—III. *to burn* or *bake* bricks, Ge. 11. 3. Niph. *to be burned*. Pi. id. Le. 10. 16.

שָׂרָף masc. dec. 4 a.—I. a species of *venomous serpent*.—II. pl. שְׂרָפִים *seraphim*, an order of angelic beings attending upon the divine majesty, represented in the vision, Is. 6. 2, 6, as having six wings.—III. pr. name masc. 1 Ch. 4. 22.

שְׂרֵפָה fem. dec. 10.—I. *a burning*, *conflagration*.—II. *a funeral-burning*, *a burning* for the dead, comp. שָׂרַף, No. II.

מִשְׂרָפָה fem. dec. 11 a.—I. *a burning* of lime, Is. 33. 12; *a funeral-burning*, Je. 34. 5.—II. מִשְׂרְפוֹת מַיִם (*flowings of water*; Chald. שְׂרַף Ithpe. *to drop*), pr. name of a town near Sidon.

[a] 2 Sa. 23. 7. [b] 1 Sa. 30. 3. [c] Ne. 3. 34. [d] Is. 16. 8. [e] Je. 18. 16. [f] Ju. 5. 29. [g] Eze. 27. 25. [h] Je. 15. 11. [i] Le. 19. 28. [k] Le. 21. 5. [l] Is. 10. 8. [m] Ju. 5. 15. [n] Joel 1. 7. [o] Ge. 40. 10. [p] Je. 31. 2. [q] La. 2, 2, 9. [r] Job 41. 18. [s] Je. 17. 25. [t] Ezr. 5. 2. [u] 1 Sa. 17. 5, 38. [x] Is. 1. 23. [y] Ec. 10. 16, 17. [z] Am. 5. 23. [a] Je. 44. 21. [b] Ps. 87. 7. [c] Da. 3. 25. [d] Je. 44. 17. [e] 2 Ch. 26. 14. [f] Is. 19. 9. [g] Ge. 32. 29. [h] 1 Ch. 12. 38. [i] Eze. 16. 4. [k] Da. 10. 21. [l] Ps. 139. 23. [m] Ps. 94. 19. [mm] Is. 49. 23.

שְׂרָף[a] ו׳ noun masc. sing. dec. 4 a . . . שרף

שְׂרֹף[b] Kal inf. constr. . . . . שרף

שֹׂרַף[c] Pual pret. 3 pers. sing. masc. [for שֹׂרַף] שרף

שְׂרָפָהּ וּ Kal pret. 3 pers. sing. masc., suff. 3 pers. sing. fem.; וּ, for וְ, conv. . . . שרף

שְׂרָפֻהָ וּ id. pret. 3 pers. pl. (שָׂרְפוּ), suff. 3 pers. sing. fem.; וּ id. . . . שרף

שְׂרֵפָה noun fem. sing. (constr. שְׂרֵפַת) dec. 10 . שרף

שְׂרֵפָה[d] defect. for שְׂרוּפָה (q. v.) . . . שרף

שָׂרְפוֹ[e] Kal inf., suff. 3 pers. sing. masc. . . שרף

שָׂרְפוּ וְ׳ id. pret. 3 pers. pl. . . . . שרף

שְׂרָפוֹ[f] וּ id. pret. 3 pers. sing. masc., suff. 3 pers. sing. masc.; וּ, for וְ, conv. . . . שרף

שְׂרָפוּהָ וּ id. pret. 3 pers. pl., suff. 3 pers. sing. fem.; וּ id. . . . . שרף

שְׂרֻפוֹת[g] defect. for שְׂרוּפוֹת (q. v.) . . . שרף

שְׂרָפִים[h] noun masc. pl. of שָׂרָף dec. 4 a . . שרף

שֹׂרְפִים[i] Kal part. act. masc. pl. of שׂוֹרֵף dec. 7 b . שרף

שְׂרָפָם[k] ו׳[l] id. pret. 3 pers. sing. masc., suff. 3 pers. pl. masc.; וּ, for וְ, conv. . . . שרף

שָׂרַפְנוּ[m] id. pret. 1 pers. pl. . . . . שרף

שָׂרַפְתָּ[n] } id. pret. 2 pers. sing. masc.; acc. shifted } שרף
שָׂרַפְתָּ וְ } by conv. וְ . . . . }

שְׂרֵפַת[ll] noun fem. sing., constr. of שְׂרֵפָה dec. 10 . שרף

שָׂרַפְתִּי[o] Kal pret. 1 pers. sing. . . . שרף

שְׂרָפָתַם[p] id. pret. 3 pers. sing. fem., suff. 3 pers. pl. m. שרף

שָׁרַץ[q] ו׳ ר׳ I. *to creep*, of reptiles and smaller aquatic animals.—II. *to abound, swarm with.*—III. *to produce abundantly, to multiply.* Hence

שֶׁרֶץ masc. collect.—I. *reptiles, creeping things.*—II. *the smaller aquatic animals*, Ge. 1. 20; Le. 11. 10 . . . . . . שרץ

שָׁרְצוּ[r] וְ Kal pret. 3 pers. pl. . . . . שרץ

שִׁרְצוּ[t] id. imp. pl. masc. . . . . שרץ

שָׂרַק Root not used; i. q. שָׂרַג, שָׂרַךְ *to interweave*; Syr. סְרַק *to comb* flax, prop. *to disentangle*.

שֹׂרֵק masc. שֹׂרֵקָה fem.—I. *a vine* of a choice quality.—II. pr. name, *Sorek*, a valley between Askelon and Gaza, Ju. 16. 4.

שְׂרוּקִים m. pl. *shoots, tendrils* of a vine, Is. 16. 8.

שָׂרִיק, fem. שְׂרִיקָה adj. *combed*, Is. 19. 9.

מַשְׂרֵקָה (*vineyard*) pr. name of a place in Edom, Ge. 36. 36; 1 Ch. 1. 47.

שָׂרֹק adj. *bay*, of horses, only pl. שְׂרֻקִּים, Zec. 1. 8.

שָׁרַק[u] וְ fut. יִשְׁרֹק.—I. *to hiss, to lure by hissing or whistling*, with לְ.—II. *to hiss at* in contempt, with עַל.

שְׁרֵקָה fem. *a hissing, derision; object of contempt.*

שְׁרִיקָה fem. dec. 10.—I. *a hissing, derision*, Je. 18. 16.—II. *whistling, piping*, Ju. 5. 16.

מַשְׁרוֹקִי Chald. masc. dec. 8 b, *pipe, flute*, Da. 3. 5, 7, 10, 15.

שָׁרַק[x] וְ Kal pret. 3 pers. sing. m. for שָׁרַק (§ 8. r. 7) שרק

שֹׂרֵק[y] noun masc. sing. . . . . . שרק

שְׁרֵקָה[z] וּ noun fem. sing.; וּ bef. (:) . . . שרק

שָׁרְקוּ Kal pret. 3 pers. pl. . . . . שרק

שְׁרִקוֹת[a] noun fem., pl. of [שְׁרִיקָה] dec. 10 . שרק

שְׂרֻקִּים[b] adj. masc. pl. [of שָׂרֹק dec. 8 c, § 37. No. 3 c] שרק

[שָׂרַר] *to have dominion, to rule, be a prince.* Hithpa. הִשְׂתָּרֵר *to make oneself a ruler, prince*, Nu. 16. 13.

שַׂר masc. dec. 8 (pl. שָׂרִים § 37. rem. 7).—I. *commander, chief.*—II. *noble, prince.*

שָׂרָה fem. dec. 10 (for שָׂרָּה).—I. *princess, noble lady.*—II. pr. name, *Sarah*, the wife of Abraham, see שָׂרַי R. שרה.

שָׁרַר only part. שֹׁרֵר *adversary, enemy.* Syr. *to be firm.* Pa. *to make firm.* Gesenius supposes the primary meaning to be, *to twist, press together*, comp. צָרַר, hence *to oppress.* Here may suitably be referred Job 33. 27, יָשֹׁר עַל־אֲנָשִׁים *if he acts as an enemy* or *oppressor towards men.*

שָׁרָר (*firm*) pr. name masc. 2 Sa. 23. 33, for which שָׂכָר 1 Ch. 11. 35.

שֹׁרֶר masc. d. 6 c, *navel* (prop. *navel-cord*, Gesen.), Ca. 7. 3.

שֹׁר masc. dec. 8 c (with suff. שָׁרֵּךְ).—I. *sinew, muscle*, collect. Pr. 3. 8.—II. *navel*, Eze. 16. 4.

שָׁרִיר masc. dec. 3 a, *firm part*, Job 40. 16.

שְׁרִירוּת fem. *firmness*, everywhere with לֵב *stubbornness, obstinacy* of heart.

שֵׁרָה fem. dec. 10 (for שְׁרָרָה), *a chain*, Is. 3. 19.

שַׁרְשְׁרָה fem. dec. 10, id., and by contraction שַׁרְשָׁה Ex. 28. 22.

שָׁרָר pr. name masc. . . . . . שרר

שֹׂרֵר[c] Kal part. act. sing. masc. . . . . שרר

שֹׁרְרוּ[d] Pilel pret. 3 pers. pl. . . . . שיר

שְׁרִרוּת noun fem. sing. . . . . . שרר

שֹׁרְרָי[e] defect. for שׁוֹרְרַי (q. v.) . . . שרר

שָׁרְרֵךְ[f] noun m. s., suff. 2 pers. s. f. fr. [שֹׁרֶר] d. 6 c שרר

[a] Is. 30. 6. [b] Je. 36. 25, 27. [c] Le. 10. 16. [d] Ps. 80. 17. [e] Am. 2. 1. [f] Eze. 43. 21. [g] Is. 1. 7. [h] Is. 6. 2. [i] 2 Ki. 17. 31. [k] Jos. 11. 13. [l] Je. 43. 12. [ll] Nu. 19. 6, 17. [m] 1 Sa. 30. 14. [n] Je. 36. 29. [o] Is. 44. 19. [p] Is. 47. 14. [q] Ps. 105. 30. [r] Ex. 7. 28. [s] Ge. 1. 21; 8. 17. [t] Ge. 9. 7. [u] Is. 5. 26. [x] 1 Ki. 9. 8. [y] Is. 5. 2. [z] Je. 51. 37. [a] Ju. 5. 16. [b] Zec. 1. 8. [c] Est. 1. 22. [d] Job 36. 24. [e] Ps. 27. 11. [f] Ca. 7. 3.

שֹׁ֫רֶשׁ וְ masc. dec. 6c (pl. שָׁרָשִׁים § 35. rem. 9).—I. *root*.—II. *what springs up from the root, shoot, sprout*, Is. 53. 2; 11. 10.—III. *foot* of a mountain, Job 28. 9.—IV. *the bottom* of the sea, Job 36. 30. —V. *the sole* of the foot, Job 13. 27.—VI. *origin, source, cause*.

שֹׁרֶשׁ Chald. masc. dec. 3e, *root*, Da. 4. 12, 20, 23. Hence the three foll.

שֶׁ֫רֶשׁ [for שֹׁרֶשׁ *root*] pr. name masc. 1 Ch. 7. 16.

שָׁרַשׁ Po. *to take root*, Is. 40. 24. Poal id. Je. 12. 2. Pi. שֵׁרֵשׁ *to root out, extirpate*. Pu. שֹׁרַשׁ pass. Job 31. 8. Hiph. הִשְׁרִישׁ *to strike, take root*.

שְׁרֹשׁוּ or שְׁרֹשִׁי Ch. fem. *a rooting out*, Ezr. 7. 26.

שָׁרְשׁוֹ noun m. s., suff. 3 pers. s. m. from שֹׁרֶשׁ d. 6c . שרש
שֹׁרָ֫שׁוּ[a] Poal (pass.) pret. 3 p. pl. [for שֹׁרְשׁוּ, s. שֹׁרַשׁ] . שרש
שָׁרְשׁוֹהִי[b] Ch. noun masc. pl., suff. 3 pers. sing. masc. from שֹׁרֶשׁ (§ 59b) . שרש
שָׁרְשֵׁי[c] וְ' noun masc. pl. constr. from שֹׁרֶשׁ dec. 6c . שרש
שָׁרְשִׁי[d] id. sing., suff. 1 pers. sing. . שרש
שָׁרָשֶׁיהָ id. pl., suff. 3 pers. sing. fem. (§ 35. rem. 9) . שרש
שָׁרָשָׁיו וְ' id. pl., suff. 3 pers. sing. masc. . שרש
שָׁרְשֵׁךְ[e] id. sing., suff. 2 pers. sing. fem. . שרש
שֵׁרַשְׁךָ[f] וְ Piel pret. 3 p. s. m. [שֵׁרֵשׁ], suff. 2 p. s. m. . שרש
שָׁרְשָׁם noun masc. sing., suff. 3 pers. pl. masc. from שֹׁרֶשׁ dec. 6c . שרש
שַׁרְשְׁרוֹת, שַׁרְשְׁרֹת[g] וְ' } noun fem., pl. of [שַׁרְשְׁרָה] dec. 10 . שרר
שַׁרְשֹׁת[h] noun fem. pl. [of שַׁרְשָׁה for שַׁרְשְׁרָה] . שרר

שָׁרַת a doubtful Root; whence appears to be derived מַשְׂרֵת masc. *a frying-pan*, 2 Sa. 13. 9; Chald. מַסְרֵיתָא, מַסְרֵת id.

שָׁרַת Pi. שֵׁרֵת.—I. *to wait upon, to serve, minister*, with אֵת, לְ.—II. *to minister, perform the service of the sanctuary*.—III. *to worship*, Eze. 20. 32. Part. מְשָׁרֵת *minister, attendant*. Hence

שָׁרֵת[i] masc. *service, ministry* . שרת
שֵׁרֵת וְ Piel pret. 3 pers. sing. masc. . שרת
שֵׁרְתוּ[k] וְ id. pret. 3 pers. pl. . שרת
שָׂרָתִי[l] noun fem. sing. [שָׂרָה] with parag. י . שרר

שֵׁשׁ וְ, וְ' fem. שִׁשָּׁה masc. (constr. שֵׁשֶׁת § 39. No. 4, rem. 1) *six*. Pl. שִׁשִּׁים *sixty*.

שִׁשָּׁה Pi. *to give the sixth part*, Eze. 45. 13.

שִׁשִּׁי masc. שִׁשִּׁית adj. ord. *sixth*; fem. *sixth part*.

שָׂשׂ[m] וְ' Kal pret. 3 pers. sing. masc. or part. . שוש
שֵׁשׁ וְ', וְ[n] noun masc. sing. . שוש
שֶׁשׁ־[o] with Mak. for שֵׁשׁ (§ 36. rem. 3) . שוש

שָׁשָׁא Pi. *to lead*, only in the following form.

שִׁשֵּׁאתִיךָ[p] וְ Piel pret. 1 pers. sing., suff. 2 pers. sing. m. ששא
שֵׁשְׁבַּצַּר pr. name masc. Ezr. 1. 8; 5. 14.
שִׁשָּׁה וְ' num. card. m., constr. שֵׁשֶׁת from שֵׁשׁ fem. שש
שָׂשׂוּ[q] Kal pret. 3 pers. pl. . שוש
שָׂשׂוֹן[r] וְ' noun masc. sing. dec. 3a (§ 32. rem. 6) שוש
שְׂשׂוֹן id. constr. st. . שוש
שֶׁשְּׁזָפַתְנִי[s] pref. שֶׁ) Kal pret. 3 p. s. f. [שָׁזְפָה], suff. 1 p. s. שזף
שָׁשַׁי, שֵׁשַׁי pr. names masc. . שוש
שֵׁשִׁי[t] Kh. שֵׁשִׁי for שֵׁשׁ subst. . שוש
שִׁשִּׁי[u] adj. ord. masc. sing., fem. שִׁשִּׁית, from שֵׁשׁ שש
שִׁשִּׁים וְ' num. card. com. gen., pl. of שֵׁשׁ . שש
שִׁשִּׁית adj. ord. fem. sing. from שִׁשִּׁי masc. . שש
שִׁשִּׁיתֶם[v] וְ Piel pret. 2 pers. pl. masc. [from שִׁשָּׁה] R. שש
שֵׁשַׁךְ a name of Babylon . שכך
שֶׁשָּׁם[y] pref. שֶׁ) adv. . שם
שֶׁשָּׁמֵם[x] pref. id.) Kal pret. 3 pers. sing. masc. . שמם
שָׂשֹׂן[a] וְ defect. for שָׂשׂוֹן q. v. . שוש
שֵׁשָׁן pr. name masc. . שוש
שֹׁשַׁנִּים[b] defect. for שׁוֹשַׁנִּים (q. v.) . שוש
שָׁשָׁק, שָׁשַׁק } pr. name masc. . שקק

[שָׁשֵׁר] masc. *red colour, red ochre*, Je. 22. 14; Eze. 23. 14.

שֵׁשֶׁת וְ' num. card. masc., constr. of שִׁשָּׁה (§ 39. No. 4, rem. 1) from שֵׁשׁ fem. . שש
שַׂשְׂתִּי[c], וְשַׂשְׂתִּי } Kal pret. 1 pers. sing.; acc. shifted by conv. וְ (comp. § 8. rem. 7) . } שוש

שֵׁת, שֵׁת Chald. i. q. Heb. שֵׁשׁ *six*, Da. 3. 1; Ezr. 6. 15. Pl. שִׁתִּין *sixty*.

שָׁת Kal pret. 3 pers. sing. masc. . שית
שַׁתָּ[d] id. pret. 2 pers. sing. masc. [for שַׁתָּה § 25. r.] שית
שֵׁת[e] noun fem. sing. contr. for שְׂאֵת . שאה
שֵׁת[f] noun masc. sing., pl. with suff. שְׁתוֹתֵיהֶם; also pr. name . שית
שֹׁת[g] Kal inf. abs. (§ 22. rem. 2) . שית

שָׁתָה וְ' fut. יִשְׁתֶּה, ap. יֵשְׁתְּ (§ 24. rem. 3).—I. *to drink*, with acc. of the drink, with בְּ, מִן of the vessel; metaph. Job 15. 16.—II. *to banquet*, Est. 7. 1. Niph. *to be drunk*, Le. 11. 34.

שְׁתָה, שְׁתָא Chald. *to drink*, Da. 5. 1—4, 23.

[a] Je. 12. 2. [b] Da. 4. 12, 20, 23. [c] Job 13. 27; 36. 30. [d] Job 29. 19. [e] Is. 14. 30. [f] Ps. 52. 7. [g] 2 Ch. 3. 5. [h] Ex. 28. 22. [i] 2 Ch. 24. 14. [k] Nu. 3. 6. [l] La. 1. 1. [m] Is. 66. 14. [n] Est. 1. 6. [o] Pr. 6. 16. [p] Eze. 39. 2. [q] La. 1. 21. [r] Est. 8. 17. [s] Ca. 1. 6. [t] Eze. 16. 13. [u] Ge. 30. 19. [v] Eze. 45. 13. [y] Ps. 122. 4. [x] La. 5. 18. [a] Est. 8. 16. [b] Ps. 45. 1. [c] Ps. 119. 14. [d] Ps. 90. 8. [e] Nu. 24. 17. [f] Is. 20. 4. [g] Is. 22. 7.

שְׁתִי masc.—I. *a drinking*, Ec. 10. 17.—II. *the warp* of a web, Le. 13. 48, 49, sq.; שתי Arab. *to fix the warp to the loom*; Syr. *to weave*.

שְׁתִיָּה fem. *a drinking*, Est. 1. 8.

מִשְׁתֶּה masc. dec. 9 a.—I. *a drinking*.—II. *drink*.—III. *banquet, feast*.

מִשְׁתֵּי Chald. masc. dec. 6 b, id. Da. 5. 10.

שָׁתָה Kal pret. 3 pers. sing. fem. . . . . שית

[a] שָׁתֵה Chald. Peal part. act. sing. masc. d. 6a (§ 62) שתה

[b] שַׁתָּה Kal pret. 2 pers. s. m. [for שַׁתְּתָּה § 25. rem.] שית

[c] שַׁתָּהּ וְ id. pret. 1 pers. sing., suff. 3 pers. sing. fem. [for שַׁתִּתִּיהָ] . . . . שית

שָׁתֹה Kal inf. abs. . . . . . שתה

שְׁתֵה וּ id. imp. sing. masc.; וּ bef. (:) . . שתה

[d] שֹׁתָה id. part. act. sing., fem. of שֹׁתֶה . . שתה

שֹׁתֶה id. part. act. sing. masc. dec. 9 a . שתה

שָׁתוֹ וְ id. inf. abs. for שָׁתֹה (§ 24. rem. 2) שתה

שָׁתוּ וְ id. pret. 3 pers. pl. . . . . שתה

שָׁתוּ Kal pret. 3 pers. pl. . . . . שית

שָׁתּוּ Kal pret. 3 pers. pl. . . . . שתת

[e] שְׁתוֹ Kal inf. constr., comp. שָׁתוֹ (§ 24. rem. 2) שתה

שְׁתוּ וּ id. imp. pl. masc.; וּ bef. (:) . . שתה

שָׁתוּל Kal part. pass. sing. masc. dec. 3 a שתל

שְׁתוּלָה id. part. pass. sing. fem. . . . שתל

[f] שְׁתוּלִים id. part. pass. masc., pl. of שָׁתוּל dec. 3 a שתל

[g] שָׁתוֹת וְ Kal inf. abs. (§ 24. rem. 2) . . שתה

[qq] שְׁתוֹת id. inf. constr. dec. 1 a . . . שתה

[h] שְׁתוֹתוֹ id. id., suff. 3 pers. sing. masc. . . שתה

[i] שְׁתוֹתֵיהֶם noun pl. fem., suff. 3 pers. pl. masc. from שֵׁת שית

שֶׁתֶּחְפָּץ pref. שֶׁ) Kal fut. 3 pers. s. fem. [for תֶּחְפַּץ] חפץ

[k] שַׁתִּי [l] וְ Kal pret. 1 pers. s. [for שַׁתְּתִּי § 25. rem.] שית

שַׁתִּי וַ pr. name, see וַשְׁתִּי under lett. ו.

שְׁתֵּי וּ num. card. f., constr. of שְׁתַּיִם q.v.; וּ bef. (:) שנה

[m] שִׁתִי Kal inf. (שִׁית), suff. 1 pers. s., or imp. s. fem. שית

שֹׁתֵי Kal part. act. pl. c. masc. from שֹׁתֶה dec. 9 a שתה

שְׁתֵּיהֶם num. card. fem. (שְׁתַּיִם q. v.), suff. 3 pers. pl. masc. from שְׁנַיִם masc. . . שנה

[n] שְׁתֵּיהֶן id. id., suff. 3 pers. pl. fem. . . . שנה

שֹׁתִים וְ Kal part. act. masc., pl. of שֹׁתֶה dec. 9 a שתה

[o] שְׁתַּיִם וּ / שְׁתַּיִם וּ } num. card. du. [for שְׁנְתַּיִם], fem. of שְׁנַיִם; וּ bef. (:) . . . } שנה

שְׁתֵּים וּ id., constr. st., followed by עָשָׂר, otherwise שְׁתֵּי; וּ id. . . . . שנה

[p] שָׁתַיִן Ch. Peal part. act. m., pl. of שָׁתֵה d. 6a (§ 62) שתה

שִׁתִּין Chald. num. card. com. gen., pl. of שֵׁת . שת

[q] שָׁתִינוּ Kal pret. 1 pers. pl. . . . . שתה

[r] שָׁתִית וְ id. pret. 2 pers. sing. fem. . . שתה

שָׁתִיתִי וְ id. pret. 1 pers. sing. . . . . שתה

שְׁתִיתֶם וּ id. pret. 2 pers. pl. masc.; וּ bef. (:) . שתה

[שָׁתַל] fut. יִשְׁתֹּל *to plant*.

שָׁתִיל masc. dec. 3 a, *shoot, branch*, Ps. 128. 3.

[s] שְׁתַלְתִּי וְ Kal pret. 1 pers. sing. . . . שתל

שָׁתַם (comp. § 8. rem. 7) *to stop, shut out*, La. 3. 8.

שָׁתַם *to open*, only part. שְׁתֻם הָעָיִן *having his eyes opened*, Nu. 24. 3, 15; Chald. *to bore through*.

[t] שָׁתָם Kal pret. 3 pers. s. m. (שָׁת), suff. 3 pers. pl. m. שית

[u] שְׁתֻם Kal part. pass. sing. masc. constr. [fr. שָׁתוּם] dec. 3 a . . . . שתם

שָׁתַן Hiph. *to make water*, only part. מַשְׁתִּין *mingens* against the wall, i. e. a male child; according to others, a dog.

[x] שַׁתַּנִי Kal pret. 2 pers. s. m. (שַׁתָּ q. v.), suff. 1 p. s. שית

[שָׁתַק] fut. יִשְׁתֹּק *to be still, to rest, to abate*, of waves, of strife.

שָׁתַר Niph. *to break forth*, 1 Sa. 5. 9. Arab. שתר *to split, burst* (Gesen.).

שֵׁתָר (*star*) pr. name of a Persian prince, Est. 1. 14.

שְׁתַר בּוֹזְנַי וּ (*shining star*) pr. name of a Persian governor, Ezr. 5. 3; 6. 6.

[שָׁתַת] i. q. שִׁית *to set, place, put*.

[y] שָׁתֹתֶיהָ noun pl. fem., suff. 3 pers. sing. fem. from [שֵׁת] dec. 1 a (§ 30. No. 3) . שית

ת

תָּא noun masc. sing. dec. 1a . . . . תוה

I. [תָּאַב] i. q. אָוָה *to desire, long for*, with לְ Ps. 119. 40, 174.

תַּאֲבָה fem. *desire*, Ps. 119. 20.

II. [תָּאַב] i. q. תָּעַב only Pi. part. מְתָאֵב *abhorring*, Am. 6. 8.

תְּאַבֵּד וְ Piel fut. 2 pers. sing. masc., or (2 Ki. 11. 1) 3 pers. sing. fem.; וַ conv. . אבד

---

[a] Da. 5. 1. [b] Ps. 8. 7. [c] Ho. 2. 5. [d] Job 6. 4. [e] Pr. 31. 4. [f] Ps. 92. 14. [g] Is. 22. 13. [h] 1 Ki. 13. 23. [i] 2 Sa. 10. 4. [k] Ps. 73. 28. Je. 31. 21. [l] Ex. 23. 31. [m] Ex. 10. 1; [n] 1 Sa. 25. 43. [o] Ne. 13. 20. [p] Da. 5. 23. [q] La. 5. 4. [qq] Je. 35. 8, 14. [r] Is. 51. 17. [s] Eze. 17. 22. [t] Ge. 30. 40. [u] Nu. 24. 3, 15. [x] Ps. 88. 7, 9. [y] Is. 19. 10.

תֹּאבַד, תֹּאבֵד } Kal fut. 3 pers. sing. fem. (§ 19. rem. 1) אבד
תְּאַבְּדוּ[a] Piel fut. 2 p. pl. m. [for תְּאַבְּדוּ comp. § 8. r. 15] אבד
תֹּאבֵדוּ[b], וְתֹאבְדוּ[c] } Kal fut. 2 pers. pl. masc. (§ 8. rem. 15) אבד
תְּאַבְּדוּן[d] Piel fut. 2 pers. pl. masc. with parag. ן . אבד
תֹּאבֵדוּן Kal fut. 2 pers. pl. masc. with parag. ן [for תֹּאבְדוּן comp. § 8. rem. 7] . . אבד
תְּאַבְּדֵם[e] Piel fut. 3 pers. sing. fem., suff. 3 pers. pl. m. אבד
תֹּאבַדְנָה[f] וַ Kal fut. 3 pers. pl. fem.; וַ conv. . . אבד
תֹּאבֶה Kal fut. 2 pers. sing. masc., or (Ge. 24. 5, 8) 3 pers. sing. fem. . . . . אבה
תֹּאבוּ id. fut. 2 pers. pl. masc. (§ 25. No. 2c) . אבה
תֶּאֱבַל[g], תֶּאֱבָל } Kal fut. 3 pers. sing. fem. (§ 8. rem. 15) אבל
תָּאַבְתִּי[h] Kal pret. 1 pers. sing. . . . תאב
תֶּאֱגֹר[i] Kal fut. 2 pers. sing. masc. (§ 13. rem. 4) אגר

תָּאָה Pi. *to mark out*, Nu. 34. 7, 8.

תְּאוֹ, תּוֹא masc. a species of *gazelle*, De. 14. 5; Is. 51. 20 (Arab. תְּאִי *to outrun*); Vulg. *oryx*.

תֶּאֱהַב[k], תֶּאֱהָב[l] } Kal fut. 2 pers. sing. masc. (§ 8. rem. 15, & § 13. rem. 5) . . . אהב
תֶּאֱהַב[m] וַ id. fut. 3 pers. sing. fem.; וַ conv. . אהב
תֶּאֱהָבוּ[n] id. fut. 2 pers. pl. masc. [for תֶּאֱהְבוּ § 8. r. 15] אהב
תְּאֵהֲבוּ[o] id. id., Aram. form [for תֶּאֱהְבוּ] . . אהב
תֶּאֱהָבוּן[p] id. id. with parag. ן (§ 8. rem. 17) . אהב
תָּאָו[q] וְ' noun m. pl., suff. 3 pers. s. m. fr. תָּא d. 1a תוה
תְּאוֹ[r] וּ noun masc. sing.; וּ bef. (:) . . תאה
תַּאֲוָה noun fem. sing. dec. 10 . . . אוה
תְּאַוֶּה Piel fut. 3 pers. sing. fem. . . . אוה
תְּאוֹמֵי[s], תְּאוֹמִים[t] } noun masc. pl. constr. & abs. from [תְּאוֹם] dec. 3a . . תאם
תַּאֲוַת[u] וְ' noun fem. sing., constr. of תַּאֲוָה dec. 10 אוה
תַּאֲוָתִי[x] id., suff. 1 pers. sing. . . . אוה
תַּאֲוָתָם[y] וְ id., suff. 3 pers. pl. masc. . . אוה
תֶּאְזוֹר[z] Kal fut. 2 pers. sing. masc. (§ 13. rem. 4) אזר
תְּאַזְּרֵנִי וַ Piel fut. 2 pers. s. m., suff. 1 pers. s.; וַ conv. אזר
תֶּאֱחֹז[a] Kal fut. 2 pers. sing. masc. (§ 13. rem. 4) אחז
תֹּאחֵז[b] וְ, תֹּאחַז[c] וַ } id. fut. 3 pers. s. fem. (§ 19. r. 4); וַ conv. אחז
תֹּאחֲזֵנִי[d] וְ id. id. with suff. 1 pers. sing. . . אחז
תְּאַחֵר, תְּאַחַר } Piel fut. 2 pers. sing. masc., or (Is. 46. 13) 3 pers. sing. fem. (§ 14. rem. 1) . אחר
תְּאַחֲרוּ[e] id. fut. 2 pers. pl. masc. . . . אחר

תֹּאמַר[f] Kal fut. 3 pers. sing. fem. (§ 13. rem. 5) אמר
תְּאֵי[g] וְ noun masc. pl. constr. from תָּא dec. 1a תוה
תָּאִיצוּ[h] Hiph. fut. 2 pers. pl. masc. . . . אוץ
תָּאִיר[i] Hiph. fut. 2 pers. sing. m., or 3 pers. sing. fem. אור
תָּאִירוּ[k] id. fut. 2 pers. pl. masc. . . . אור
תַּאֲכִל[l] Hiph. fut. 2 pers. sing. masc. ap. [from תַּאֲכִיל] אכל
תֵּאָכֵל Niph. fut. 3 pers. sing. fem. . . אכל
תֹּאכַל, תֹּאכֵל } וַ, וְ, Kal fut. 2 pers. sing. masc., or 3 pers. sing. fem. (§ 10. rem. 1); וַ conv. אכל
תֵּאכֻל[m] וְ Chald. Peal fut. 3 pers. sing. fem. . . אכל
תְּאַכְּלֵהוּ[n] Piel fut. 3 pers. sing. fem. with suff. 3 pers. sing. masc. [for תְּאַכְּלֵהוּ § 10. rem. 7] אכל
תֹּאכְלֻהוּ[o] Kal fut. 2 pers. pl. masc., suff. 3 pers. sing. m. אכל
תְּאֻכְּלוּ[p] Pual fut. 2 pers. pl. masc. . . אכל
תֹּאכֵלוּ, תֹּאכְלוּ } Kal fut. 2 pers. pl. masc. (§ 19. rem. 1) אכל
תֹּאכְלוּם[q] id. id., suff. 3 pers. pl. masc. . . . אכל
תֹּאכְלוּן[r] id. id. with parag. ן . . . . אכל
תֹּאכְלִי id. fut. 2 pers. sing. fem. . . . אכל
תֹּאכְלֵךְ[s] id. fut. 3 pers. sing. fem., suff. 2 pers. sing. fem. אכל
תֹּאכַלְכֶם[t] id. id., suff. 2 pers. pl. masc. . . . אכל
תֹּאכְלֵם[u] וַתּ'[x], וְ' id. id., suff. 3 pers. pl. masc.; וַ conv. אכל
תֵּאָכַלְנָה[y] Niph. fut. 3 pers. pl. fem. . . . אכל
תֹּאכַלְנָה[z] וַ' Kal fut. 3 pers. pl. fem.; וַ conv. . אכל
תֹּאכְלֶנָּה id. fut. 2 pers. sing. m., suff. 3 pers. sing. fem. אכל
תֹּאכְלֶנּוּ[a] id. id., suff. 3 pers. sing. masc. . . אכל
תֹּאכְלֵנוּ[b] id. fut. 3 pers. sing. fem., suff. 1 pers. pl. . אכל
תֹּאכְלֶנּוּ id. fut. 2 p. s. m., or 3 p. s. f., suff. 3 p. s. m. אכל
תֵּאָלֵם[c] Niph. fut. 2 pers. sing. masc. . . אלם
תֵּאָלַמְנָה[d] id. fut. 3 pers. pl. fem. . . . . אלם
תֶּאֱלַף[e] Kal fut. 2 pers. sing. masc. (§ 13. rem. 5) אלף
תְּאַלְצֵהוּ[f] וַ Piel fut. 3 pers. sing. fem. [תְּאַלֵּץ], suff. 3 pers. sing. masc. (§ 10. rem. 7); וַ conv. אלץ
תַּאֲלָתְךָ[g] noun f. s., suff. 2 p. s. m. fr. [תַּאֲלָה] d. 10 אלה

תָּאַם *to be double*, only part. תֹּאֲמִים *doubled, coupled*. Hiph. *to bear twins*.

תְּאֹם masc. dec. 6f, *twin*, Ca. 7. 4.

תְּאוֹם masc. dec. 3a, id., pl. תְּאוֹמִים, תֹּמִים.

תָּאֳמֵי[h] noun masc. pl. constr. from [תְּאֹם] dec. 6f תאם
תַּאֲמִין[i] Hiph. fut. 2 pers. sing. masc. . . אמן
תַּאֲמִינוּ[k] וְ' id. fut. 2 pers. pl. masc. . . . אמן
תַּאֲמִינוּ[l] Hiph. fut. 2 pers. pl. masc. [for תֵּימִינוּ] ימן

[a] Nu. 33. 52. [b] Est. 4. 14. [c] Ps. 2. 12. [d] De. 12. 2. [e] Pr. 1. 32. [f] 1 Sa. 9. 3. [g] Job 14. 22. [h] Ps. 119. 40, 174. [i] De. 28. 39. [k] 2 Ch. 19. 2. [l] Pr. 20. 13. [m] 1 Sa. 18. 20. [n] Zec. 8. 17. [o] Pr. 1. 22. [p] Ps. 4. 3. [q] Eze. 40. 21, 29, 33, 36. [r] De. 14. 5. [s] Ca. 4. 5. [t] Ge. 38. 27. [u] Pr. 10. 24. [x] Ps. 38. 10. [y] Ps. 78. 29. [z] Je. 1. 17. [a] Ec. 7. 18. [b] De. 32. 41. [c] Ru. 3. 15. [d] Ps. 139. 10. [e] Ge. 24. 56. [f] Ps. 69. 16. [g] Eze. 40. 10. [h] Is. 22. 4. [i] Ps. 18. 29; Ec. 8. 1. [k] Mal. 1. 10. [l] Eze. 3. 3. [m] Da. 7. 23. [n] Job 20. 26. [o] Le. 7. 24. [p] Is. 1. 20. [q] Le. 11. 42. [r] Nu. 11. 19. [s] Na. 3. 15. [t] Is. 33. 11. [u] Ps. 21. 10. [x] Job 1. 16. [y] Je. 24. 2. [z] Ge. 41. 4, 20. [a] Eze. 4. 9, 10. [b] De. 5. 25. [c] Eze. 24. 27. [d] Ps. 31. 19. [e] Pr. 22. 25. [f] Ju. 16. 16. [g] La. 3. 65. [h] Ca. 7. 4. [i] De. 28. 66. [k] Is. 43. 10. [l] Is. 30. 21.

תְּאֻמִם[a] defect. for תּוֹאֲמִים (q. v.) . . . . תאם

תָּאֲמֵן[b] / תַּאֲמֵן[c] Hiph. fut. 2 pers. sing. masc., ap. from תַּאֲמִין . . . . אמן

תֵּאָמַנָּה[d] Niph. fut. 3 pers. pl. fem. [for תֵּאָמַנָּה, תֵּאָמַנְנָה § 9. rem. 4, comp. § 25. rem.] . אמן

תַּאֲמִינוּ[e] וְ׳[f] id. fut. 2 pers. pl. masc. . . . אמן

תְּאַמֵּץ וַ׳[g] Piel fut. 2 pers. sing. masc., or (Pr. 31. 17) 3 pers. fem. sing.; וַ conv. . . . . אמץ

תְּאַמְּצֶנּוּ[h] id. fut. 3 pers. sing. fem., suff. 3 pers. s. m. אמץ

תֹּאמַר / תֹּאמֵר Kal fut. 2 pers. sing. masc., or 3 pers. sing. fem. (§ 19. rem. 1) . . . אמר

וַתֹּאמַר / וַתֹּאמֶר id. id. with conv. וַ (§ 19. rem. 2) . אמר

תֹּאמְרוּ[k] / וַ׳ תֹּאמְרוּ id. fut. 2 pers. pl. masc.; וַ conv. . אמר

תֵּאמְרוּן[l] Chald. Peal fut. 2 pers. pl. masc. (§ 53) אמר

תֹּאמְרוּן Kal fut. 2 pers. pl. masc. with parag. ן . אמר

תֹּאמְרִי וַ׳ id. fut. 2 pers. sing. fem.; וַ conv. . אמר

תֹּאמְרֻן[m] id. fut. 2 pers. pl. masc. for תֹּאמְרוּן . אמר

תֹּאמַרְןָ וַ / תֹּאמַרְנָה וַ׳ id. fut. 3 pers. pl. fem. (§ 8. rem. 16); וַ conv. . . . אמר

תְּאֵנָה ו׳ f. (pl. תְּאֵנִים) *fig tree*; also *fig*. R. doubtful.

תְּאֻנֶּה[n] Pual fut. 3 pers. sing. fem. . . . אנה

תַּאֲנָה[o] noun fem. sing. . . . . אנה

תֵּאָנַח[p] Niph. fut. 2 pers. sing. masc. . . אנח

תַּאֲנִיָּה noun fem. sing. . . . . . אנה

תְּאֵנֵיכֶם[q] וּ the foll. with suff. 2 pers. pl. m.; וּ bef. (:) תאן

תְּאֵנִים ו׳[r] noun fem. with pl. masc. term. from תְּאֵנָה dec. 10; וּ id. . . . . תאן

תְּאֹנִים[s] noun masc. pl. . . . . און

תֶּאֱנַף Kal fut. 2 pers. sing. masc. . . . אנף

תַּאֲנַת pr. name in compos. תַּאֲנַת שִׁלֹה . אנה

תַּאֲנָתָהּ[t] noun f. s., suff. 3 pers. s. f. fr. [תַּאֲנָה] d. 10 אנה

תְּאֵנָתָהּ[u] וּ noun fem. sing., suff. 3 pers. sing. fem. from תְּאֵנָה dec. 10; וּ bef. (:) . . תאן

תְּאֵנָתוֹ id., suff. 3 pers. sing. masc. . . . תאן

תְּאֵנָתִי[x] וּ id., suff. 1 pers. sing.; וּ bef. (:) . תאן

תְּאֵנָתְךָ[y] וּ id., suff. 2 pers. sing. masc.; וּ id. . תאן

תְּאֵנָתָם[z] וּ id., suff. 3 pers. pl. masc.; וּ id. . תאן

תֵּאָסֵף[a] Niph. fut. 3 pers. sing. fem. . . . אסף

תֶּאֱסֹף Kal fut. 2 p. s. m., or 3 p. s. f. (§ 13. r. 4.) אסף

תַּאַסְפוּן[b] Hiph. fut. 2 p. pl. m. [for תּוֹסִיפוּן]; ן parag. יסף

תַּאַסְפִי[c] Kal fut. 2 pers. sing. fem. (§ 13. rem. 6) אסף

תֵּאָסֵר[d] Niph. fut. 2 pers. sing. masc. . . אסר

תַּאַסְרֵהוּ[e] וַ Kal fut. 3 pers. sing. fem. [תֶּאֱסֹר], suff. 3 pers. sing. masc. (§ 13. rem. 6); וַ conv. אסר

תֵּאָפֶה Niph. fut. 3 pers. sing. fem. . . . אפה

תֹּאפוּ[f] Kal fut. 2 pers. pl. masc. (§ 25. No. 2c) . אפה

תֵּאָפֶינָה[g] Niph. fut. 3 pers. pl. fem. . . . אפה

תָּאַר[h] וַ *to be drawn, marked out.* Pi. *to mark out, delineate*, Is. 44. 13. Pu. part. מְתֹאָר *marked off*, Jos. 19. 13 render, *which is marked off* (i. e. pertains) *to Neah*; others take it as a proper name. Hence

תֹּאַר masc. d. 6f (§ 35. r. 8).—I. *form, personal appearance*.—II. *handsome form, beauty*.

תָּאֹר Kal fut. 2 pers. sing. masc. . . . ארר

תֶּאֱרֹב[i] Kal fut. 2 p. s. m. or (Pr. 7. 12; 23. 28) 3 p. s. f. ארב

תַּאַרְגִי[k] Kal fut. 2 pers. sing. fem. (§ 13. rem. 6) ארג

תָּאֳרוֹ[l] / וְ תָּאֳרוֹ[m] noun masc. sing., suff. 3 pers. sing. masc. from תֹּאַר dec. 6 (§ 35. rem. 8) תאר

תַּאֲרִיךְ[n] Hiph. fut. 2 pers. sing. masc. . . ארך

תַּאֲרִיכוּ id. fut. 2 pers. pl. masc. . . . ארך

תַּאֲרִיכֻן id. id. with parag. ן . . . ארך

תֶּאֱרַכְנָה[o] וַ Kal fut. 3 pers. pl. f. (§ 13. r. 4); וַ conv. ארך

תָּאֳרָם[p] noun masc. sing., suff. 3 pers. pl. masc. from תֹּאַר dec. 6f . . . . תאר

תַּאְרֵעַ וְ pr. name masc. 1 Ch. 8. 35, called תַּחְרֵעַ in 1 Ch. 9. 41.

תְּאָרֵשׂ[q] Piel fut. 2 pers. sing. masc. . . ארש

תְּאַשּׁוּר וּ noun masc. sing.; וּ bef. (:) . . אשר

תֶּאְשַׁם[r] Kal fut. 3 pers. sing. fem. (§ 13. rem. 5) אשם

תֶּאְשָׁמוּ id. fut. 2 pers. pl. masc. [for תֶּאְשְׁמוּ v. id. & § 8. rem. 15] . . . . אשם

תְּאַשֵּׁר[s] Piel fut. 2 pers. sing. masc. . . אשר

תְּאַשְּׁרֵנִי[t] וַ id. fut. 3 pers. sing. fem., suff. 1 pers. sing.; וַ conv. . . . . . אשר

תֶּאֱתֶה[u] Kal fut. 3 pers. sing. fem. [for תֶּאֱתֶה § 13. rem. 4, § 19. rem. 3, & § 25. No. 2c] אתה

תָּבֵא וַ Hiph. fut. 3 p. s. f., ap. fr. תָּבִיא; וַ conv. בוא

תָּבֹא וַתָּ׳, וְ׳[x] id. fut. 2 pers. sing. masc., or 3 pers. sing. fem. (§ 25. No. 2b); וַ id. . בוא

תֹּבֵא[y] Kal fut. 2 pers. sing. masc. Chaldaism for תֹּבֶה (§ 24. r. 19), for תֹּאבֶה (§ 19. r. 5) אבה

תְּבִאֵהוּ[z] וַ׳ Hiph. fut. 2 pers. s. m. (Je. 13. 1), or 3 pers. sing. fem. (תָּבִיא), suff. 3 p. s. m.; וַ conv. בוא

תָּבֹאוּ וַ׳ Kal fut. 2 pers. pl. masc.; וַ id. . בוא

תָּבֹאִי[a] וַ id. fut. 2 pers. sing. fem.; וַ id. . בוא

תָּבֹאינָה[b] / תְּבֹאֶינָה[c] id. fut. 3 pers. pl. fem., Kh. תָּבֹאנָה (§ 21. rem. 10, & § 25. No. 2f) . בוא

תְּבִאֵמוֹ[d] Hiph. fut. 2 p. s. m. (תָּבִיא), suff. 3 p. pl. m. בוא

---

a Ex. 26. 24. b Je. 12. 6. c Pr. 26. 25. d Is. 60. 4. e Is. 7. 9. f 2 Ch. 20. 20. g Pr. 31. 17. h Ps. 89. 22. i 1 Ki. 5. 20; Pr. 1. 21. k Je. 23. 38. l Je. 10. 11. m Je. 21. 3. n Ps. 91. 10. o Ju. 14. 4. p Eze. 21. 11. q Am. 4. 9. r Ne. 13. 15. s Eze. 24. 12. t Je. 2. 24. u Ho. 2. 14. x Joel 1. 7. y Je. 5. 17. z Ps. 105. 33. a Nu. 12. 14. b Ex. 5. 7. c Jos. 2. 18. d Ju. 16. 6, 10, 13. e Ju. 16. 8, 12. f Ex. 16. 23. g Le. 23. 17. h Jos. 15. 9, 11; 18. 14, 17. i Pr. 24. 15. k Ju. 16. 13. l 1 Sa. 28. 14. m Is. 52. 14. n De. 4. 40. o Eze. 31. 5. p La. 4. 8. q De. 28. 30. r Ho. 14. 1. s Pr. 4. 14. t Job 29. 11. u Mi. 4. 8. x Is. 47. 11. y Pr. 1. 10. z Je. 13. 1. a Ex. 16. 7. b 1 Sa. 10. 7. c Ps. 45. 16. d Ex. 15. 17.

תָּבֹאןָ[a] / תָּבֹאנָה, וַתָּ', וְ'[b] } Kal fut. 3 pers. pl. fem. (§ 21. rem. 10, & § 25. No. 2f); ·וַ conv. בוא

תְּבֹאֶנּוּ[c] id. fut. 3 pers. s. m. (תָּבוֹא), suff. 3 p. s. m. בוא

תְּבִאֵנִי וַ Hiph. fut. 3 pers. sing. fem. (תָּבִיא), suff. 1 pers. sing.; ·וַ conv. . . . בוא

תִּבְאַשׁ[d] וַ'[e] Kal fut. 3 pers. sing. fem.; ·וַ id. . באשׁ

תָּבֹאתִי[f] וַ Kal fut. 2 pers. sing. fem., Kh. תָּבֹאתִי, K. תָּבֹאת for תָּבֹאִי, an anom. form, perhaps a fut. with both the preformative and afformative of the fem., comp. pret. בָּאת; for תִי comp. § 8. rem. 5 . . בוא

תִּבְגְּדוּ[g] Kal fut. 2 pers. pl. m. [for תִּבְגְּדוּ § 8. r. 15] בגד

תִּבְגּוֹד[h] id. fut. 2 pers. sing. masc. (§ 8. rem. 18) בגד

תַּבְדִּיל[i] Hiph. fut. 2 pers. sing. masc. . . בדל

[תֵּבָה] fem. dec. 10, strictly *a chest, box*; it is used for—I. *the ark* of Noah, built in the form of a chest.—II. *the ark* in which Moses was exposed, Ex. 2. 5.

תְּבַהֵל Piel fut. 2 pers. sing. masc. (§ 14. rem. 1) . בהל

תִּבָּהֵל[k] וַ'[l] Niph. fut. 2 pers. sing. masc.; ·וַ conv. בהל

תְּבַהֲלֵם[m] Piel fut. 2 pers. sing. masc. (תְּבַהֵל § 14. rem. 1), suff. 3 pers. pl. masc. . . בהל

תִּבָּהַלְנָה[n] Niph. fut. 3 pers. pl. fem. . . בהל

תָּבוֹא וַ' / תָּבוֹאָה[o] וַ } Kal fut. 2 pers. sing. masc., or 3 pers. sing. fem. (§ 8. rem. 13); ·וַ conv. בוא

תְּבוּאָה noun fem. sing. dec. 10 . . . בוא

תְּבוֹאֵהוּ[p] וַ' Kal fut. 3 pers. sing. fem. (תָּבוֹא), suff. 3 pers. sing. masc.; ·וַ conv. . . בוא

תְּבוּאוֹת noun fem., pl. of תְּבוּאָה dec. 10 . בוא

תָּבוֹאִי Kal fut. 2 pers. sing. fem. (§ 25. No. 2f) בוא

תָּבוֹאינָה[q] וַ / תְּבוֹאֶינָה[r] וּ } id. fut. 3 pers. pl. fem., K. תָּבוֹאנָה (§ 21. rem. 10); ·וַ conv., וּ bef. (:) בוא

תְּבוֹאֶךָּ[s] id. fut. 3 pers. s. f. (תָּבוֹא), suff. 2 p. s. m. בוא

תָּבוֹאנָה[t] וְ'[u] id. fut. 3 pers. pl. fem. (§ 21. rem. 10) בוא

תְּבוֹאֶנּוּ id. fut. 3 p. s. f. (תָּבוֹא), suff. 3 pers. s. m. בוא

תְּבוֹאֵנִי[x] id. id. with suff. 1 pers. sing. . . בוא

תְּבוּאַת וּ'[y] noun f. s., constr. of תְּבוּאָה d. 10; וּ bef. (:) בוא

תְּבוּאֹת id. pl., comp. תְּבוּאוֹת . . . בוא

תָּבוֹאתָה[z] Kal fut. 3 pers. sing. fem. for תָּבוֹא, an anom. form with the parag. syllable תָה, perh. intended for an afform. of the fem., comp. תְּבוֹאָתֶךָ & תָּבֹאתִי . . . בוא

תְּבוּאָתָהּ וּ'[a] n.f.s., suff. 3 p.s.f. fr. תְּבוּאָה d. 10; וּ bef. (:) בוא

תְּבוּאָתֹה id., suff. 3 pers. sing. masc., K. 'אָתוֹ . בוא

תְּבוּאָתוֹ[b] id., suff. 3 pers. sing. masc. . . בוא

תְּבוּאָתִי[c] וּ[d] id., suff. 1 pers. sing.; וּ bef. (:) בוא

תְּבוֹאָתֶךָ[e] made up from the form תָּבוֹאתָה (q. v.) & suff. 2 pers. sing. masc. . . . בוא

תְּבוּאָתֶךָ[f] / תְּבוּאָתְךָ } noun fem. sing., suff. 2 pers. sing. masc. from תְּבוּאָה dec. 10 . . בוא

תְּבוּאָתֵנוּ[g] id., suff. 1 pers. pl. . . . בוא

תָּבוּז[h] Kal fut. 2 pers. sing. masc. . . בוז

תִּבּוֹז Niph. fut. 3 pers. sing. fem. (§ 18. rem. 7) בזז

תְּבוּנָה וּ' noun fem. sing. dec. 10; וּ bef. (:) בין

תְּבוּנוֹת[i] id., pl. of the preced. . . בין

תְּבוּנוֹתֵיכֶם[k] id. pl., suff. 2 pers. pl. masc. . בין

תָּבוּס[l] Kal fut. 3 pers. sing. fem. . . בוס

תְּבוּסַת[m] noun fem. sing., constr. of תְּבוּסָה dec. 10 בוס

תִּבּוֹק[n] Niph. fut. 3 pers. sing. fem. (§ 18. rem. 7) בקק

תָּבוֹר pr. name of a place . . . תבר

תֵּבוֹשׁ[o] Kal fut. 3 pers. sing. fem. (§ 21. rem. 6) בושׁ

תֵּבוֹשִׁי id. fut. 2 pers. sing. fem. . . בושׁ

תָּבֹז[p] Kal fut. 2 pers. sing. masc. . . בזז

תִּבֶז וַ Kal fut. 3 pers. s. fem., ap. fr. תִּבְזֶה; ·וַ conv. בזה

תָּבֹז[q] וַ Kal fut. 3 pers. sing. fem. (§ 21. rem. 7) בזז

תִּבְזֶה Kal fut. 2 pers. sing. masc. . . בזה

תָּבֹזּוּ[r] Kal fut. 2 pers. pl. masc. . . בזז

תִּבְחַן Kal fut. 3 pers. s. fem. [for תִּבְחַן § 8. r. 15] בחן

תִּבָּחֵנוּ[s] Niph. fut. 2 p. pl. m. [for תִּבָּחֲנוּ comp. § 8. r. 15] בחן

תִּבְחָנֶנּוּ[t] Kal fut. 2 pers. sing. masc. (תִּבְחַן), suff. 3 pers. sing. masc. (§ 16. rem. 12) בחן

תִּבְחַר וַתִּ'[u], וְ'[v] Kal fut. 2 pers. sing. masc., or (Job 7. 15) 3 pers. sing. fem.; ·וַ conv. בחר

תַּבֵּט[y] וַ' Hiph. fut. 2 pers. sing. masc., or 3 pers. sing. fem., ap. from תַּבִּיט; ·וַ id. . נבט

תִּבְטַח וַ Kal fut. 2 pers. sing. masc.; ·וַ id. בטח

תִּבְטְחוּ / תִּבְטְחוּ[z] וְ' } id. fut. 2 pers. pl. masc. (§ 8. rem. 15); ·וַ id. . בטח

תִּבְטְחִי וַ id. fut. 2 pers. sing. fem.; ·וַ id. . בטח

תָּבִיא Hiph. fut. 2 pers. sing. masc., or 3 pers. s. fem. בוא

תְּבִיאֵהוּ[a] וַ id. fut. 3 pers. sing. fem., suff. 3 pers. sing. masc.; ·וַ conv. . . . בוא

תָּבִיאוּ id. fut. 2 pers. pl. masc. . . בוא

תְּבִיאֶינָה[b] id. fut. 3 pers. pl. fem. . . בוא

תְּבִיאֵם[c] וַ id. fut. 2 pers. sing. masc., suff. 3 pers. pl. masc.; ·וַ conv. . . . בוא

תְּבִיאֶנָּה[d] id. id., suff. 3 pers. sing. fem. . בוא

תְּבִיאֶנּוּ[e] id. id., suff. 3 pers. sing. masc. . בוא

תְּבִיאֵנִי[f] id. id., suff. 1 pers. sing. . . בוא

תַּבִּיט Hiph. fut. 2 pers. sing. masc. . נבט

תָּבִין Kal fut. 2 pers. sing. masc. . . בין

תָּבִינוּ וְ[g] id. fut. 2 pers. pl. masc. . . בין

---

[a] Ge. 30. 38. [b] Is. 47. 9. [c] Job 20. 22. [d] Is. 50. 2. [e] Ex. 8. 10. [f] 1 Sa. 25. 34. [g] Mal. 2. 16. [h] Is. 48. 8. [i] De. 19. 27. [k] Ec. 8. 3. [l] Job 4. 5. [m] Ps. 83. 16. [n] Eze. 7. 27. [o] Is. 5. 19. [p] Ps. 35. 8; 109. 17. [q] Est. 4. 4. [r] Je. 9. 16. [s] Eze. 32. 11. [t] 2 Ch. 9. 21. [u] Je. 9. 16. [x] Ps. 36. 12. [y] De. 22. 9. [z] De. 33. 16. [a] Ne. 9. 37. [b] Le. 19. 25. [c] Job 31. 12. [d] Pr. 8. 19. [e] Job 22. 21. [f] Pr. 3. 9. [g] Le. 25. 20. [h] Pr. 23. 22. [i] Is. 24. 3. [k] Job 32. 11. [l] Pr. 27. 7. [m] 2 Ch. 22. 7. [n] Is. 24. 3. [o] Je. 51. 47. [p] De. 20. 14. [q] Pr. 30. 17. [r] Jos. 8. 2. [s] Ge. 42. 15. [t] Job 7. 18. [u] Job 15. 5. [v] Job 7. 15. [y] 1 Sa. 16. 7 [z] Is. 30. 12. [a] Ju. 19. 3. [b] Le. 7. 30. [c] Ne. 9. 23. [d] Le. 6. 14. [e] De. 33. 7. [f] 1 Sa. 20. 8. [g] Is. 43. 10.

[a]תְּבִינֵם Hiph. fut. 3 pers. s. fem., suff. 3 pers. pl. masc. . בין

[b]תְּבִירָה Ch. Peal part. pass. sing. fem. [of תְּבִיר masc.] תבר

[c]תֵּבֹשׁוּ Hiph. fut. 2 pers. pl. masc. . . . בושׁ

[d]תְּבִישֵׁנִי id. fut. 2 pers. sing. masc., suff. 1 pers. sing. בושׁ

תֵּבְךְּ וַ ap. from the foll. (§ 24. rem. 3) . . בכה

תִּבְכֶּה ו' Kal fut. 2 pers. sing. masc., or 3 pers. sing. fem.; ·וַ conv. . . . . . בכה

תִּבְכּוּ ו' id. fut. 2 pers. pl. masc.; ·וַ id. . . בכה

[e]תִּבְכִּי id. fut. 2 pers. sing. fem. . . . . בכה

[f]תִּבְכֶּינָה / [h]תִּבְכֶּנָה [g]ו'} id. fut. 3 pers. pl. fem.; ·וַ conv. . . בכה

תֵּבֵל ו' noun fem. sing. . . . . . יבל

תֶּבֶל noun masc. sing. . . . . . בלל

[i]תִּבֹּל Kal fut. 2 pers. sing. masc. (§ 17. rem. 3) נבל

תֻּבַל ו' pr. name of a people, see תּוּבַל . . יבל

[k]תִּבְלֶה Kal fut. 3 pers. sing. fem. . . . בלה

[l]תַּבְלִיתָם noun fem. sing., suff. 3 pers. pl. masc. from [תַּבְלִית] dec. 1 b . . . . בלה

[m]תַּבְלֻל noun masc. sing. . . . . . בלל

[n]תְּבַלַּע Piel fut. 2 pers. sing. masc. . . . בלע

תִּבְלַע וַ Kal fut. 3 pers. sing. fem.; ·וַ conv. . . בלע

[o]תִּבְלָעֵם וַ id., suff. 3 pers. pl. masc. (§ 16. r. 12); ·וַ id. בלע

[p]תִּבְלָעֵמוֹ id., suff. 3 pers. pl. masc. . . . בלע

[q]תִּבְלַעְןָ וַ / [r]תִּבְלַעְנָה וַ } Kal fut. 3 pers. pl. fem. (§ 8. rem. 16); ·וַ conv. . . . } בלע

[s]תְּבַלְּעֶנּוּ Piel fut. 3 pers. sing. fem., suff. 3 pers. sing. m. בלע

[t]תִּבְלָעֵנוּ Kal fut. 3 pers. sing. fem. (תִּבְלַע), suff. 1 pers. pl. (§ 16. rem. 12) . . . בלע

[u]תִּבְלָעֵנִי id. with suff. 1 pers. sing. . . . בלע

[x]תְּבַלְּעֵנִי וַ Piel fut. 2 pers. s. m., suff. 1 pers. s.; ·וַ conv. בלע

תֶּבֶן [y]ו'' masc. *straw.*

מַתְבֵּן masc. *straw, heap of straw*, Is. 25. 10.

[z]תָּבֶן וַ Kal fut. 3 pers. sing. fem. ap. and conv. from תָּבִין . . . . . . בין

תִּבֶן וַ Kal fut. 3 pers. s. fem., ap. fr. תִּבְנֶה; ·וַ conv. בנה

תִּבָּנֶה Niph. fut. 2 pers. sing. masc. (Job 22. 23), or 3 pers. sing. fem. . . . . בנה

תִּבְנֶה Kal fut. 2 pers. sing. masc. . . . בנה

תִּבְנוּ id. fut. 2 pers. pl. masc. . . . . בנה

תִּבְנִי pr. name masc. . . . . . בנה

[a]תִּבְנִי וַ Kal fut. 2 pers. sing. fem.; ·וַ conv. . . בנה

תִּבָּנֶינָה Niph. fut. 3 pers. pl. fem. . . . בנה

תַּבְנִית [b]ו'' noun fem. sing. dec. 10 . . . . בנה

[c]תַּבְנִיתוֹ id., suff. 3 pers. sing. masc. . . . בנה

[d]תִּבְעֶה Kal fut. 3 pers. sing. fem. . . . בעה

[e]תִּבְעֲטוּ Kal fut. 2 pers. pl. masc. . . . בעט

[f]תִּבְעָיוּן Kal fut. 2 pers. pl. m. with parag. ן (§ 24. r. 5) בעה

[g]תַּבְעִיר Hiph. fut. 2 pers. sing. masc. . . . בער

תִּבָּעֵל Niph. fut. 3 pers. sing. fem. . . . בעל

[h]תַּבַּעְנָה Hiph. fut. 3 pers. pl. fem. . . . נבע

[i]תְּבַעֵר Piel fut. 2 pers. sing. masc. (§ 14. rem. 1) בער

תִּבְעַר ו' Kal fut. 3 pers. sing. fem.; ·וַ conv. . בער

תַּבְעֵרָה pr. name of a place . . . . בער

[k]תְּבַעֲרוּ Piel fut. 2 pers. pl. masc. (§ 14. rem. 1) בער

[l]תְּבַעֵת Piel fut. 3 pers. sing. fem. (§ 14. rem. 1) בעת

[m]תְּבַעֲתֶךָּ id., suff. 2 pers. sing. masc. [for 'עִתְךָ § 2. r. 3] בעת

[n]תְּבַעֲתַנִּי id. fut. 2 pers. sing. masc. (Job 7. 14), or 3 pers. sing. fem., suff. 1 pers. sing. . בעת

תֵּבֵץ pr. name of a place near Shechem, Ju. 9. 50; 2 Sa. 11. 21.

[o]תְּבַצְּעִי וַ Piel fut. 2 pers. sing. fem.; ·וַ conv. . בצע

[p]תִּבְצַעְנָה id. fut. 3 pers. pl. fem. . . . בצע

[q]תְּבַצֵּר Piel fut. 2 pers. sing. masc. . . . בצר

תִּבְצֹר Kal fut. 2 pers. sing. masc. . . . בצר

[r]תִּבְצְרוּ id. fut. 2 pers. pl. masc. . . . בצר

[s]תְּבַקַּע / [t]תְּבַקֵּעַ } Piel fut. 2 pers. sing. masc., or 3 pers. sing. fem. (§ 15. rem. 1) . } בקע

[u]תִּבָּקַע ו' Niph. fut. 3 pers. sing. fem.; ·וַ conv. . בקע

[x]תְּבַקְּעֵם Piel fut. 3 pers. sing. fem., suff. 3 pers. pl. masc. . . . . . . בקע

[y]תְּבַקַּעְנָה וַ id. fut. 3 pers. pl. fem.; ·וַ conv. . בקע

תְּבַקֵּשׁ Piel fut. 2 pers. sing. masc. . . . בקשׁ

[z]תְּבַקֶּשׁ־ id., id., or (Pr. 18. 15) fut. 3 p. s. f. (§ 10. r. 4) בקשׁ

תְּבַקְשׁוּ id. fut. 2 pers. pl. masc. (§ 10. rem. 7) . בקשׁ

[a]תְּבַקְשׁוּן id. id. with parag. ן [for תְּבַקְּשׁוּן § 10. r. 4] בקשׁ

[b]תְּבַקְשִׁי id. fut. 2 pers. sing. fem. (§ 10. rem. 7) בקשׁ

[c]תְּבֻקְשִׁי ו' Pual fut. 2 pers. sing. fem. (§ 10. rem. 7); ו bef. (:), comp. וּשְׁבַע . . . . בקשׁ

תְּבַקְשֵׁם Piel fut. 2 pers. sing. masc. (תְּבַקֵּשׁ), suff. 3 pers. pl. masc. (§ 10. rem. 7) . בקשׁ

תְּבַקְשֶׁנָּה id. id., suff. 3 pers. sing. fem. . . בקשׁ

[d]תְּבַקְשֶׁנּוּ id. id., suff. 3 pers. sing. masc. . . בקשׁ

תְּבַר Ch. i. q. Heb. שְׁבַר *to break*, only part. pass. תְּבִיר *fragile, brittle*, Da. 2. 42.

תָּבוֹר (*quarry*; or i. q. טַבּוּר *height*) pr. name, *Tabor*.—I. a mountain in Galilee, on the confines of Zebulun and Naphtali.—II. a grove of oaks, in Benjamin, 1 Sa. 10. 3.—III. a city of the Levites, in Benjamin, 1 Ch. 6. 62.

---

[a] Job 32. 8. [b] Da. 2. 42. [c] Ps. 14. 6. [d] Ps. 119. 31, 116. [e] 1 Sa. 1. 8. [f] Ps. 78. 64. [g] Ru. 1. 9, 14. [h] Job 27. 15. [i] Ex. 18. 18. [k] Is. 51. 6. [l] Is. 10. 25. [m] Le. 21. 20. [n] 2 Sa. 20. 19. [o] De. 11. 6. [p] Ex. 15. 12. [q] Ge. 41. 24. [r] Ge. 41. 7. [s] Ec. 10. 12. [t] Nu. 16. 34. [u] Ps. 69. 16. [x] Job 10. 8. [y] Ex. 5. 18. [z] Job 13. 1. [a] Eze. 16. 24. [b] 1 Ch. 28. 12. [c] 2 Ki. 16. 10. [d] Is. 64. 1. [e] 1 Sa. 2. 29. [f] Is. 21. 12. [g] Eze. 5. 2. [h] Ps. 119. 171. [i] De. 21. 9. [k] Ex. 35. 3. [l] Job 13. 11. [m] Job 33. 7. [n] Job 9. 34; 13. 21. [o] Eze. 22. 12. [p] Zec. 4. 9. [q] Je. 51. 53. [r] Le. 25. 11. [s] Hab. 3. 9. [t] 2 Ki. 8. 12; Eze. 13. 11. [u] Is. 59. 5. [x] Ho. 13. 8. [y] 2 Ki. 2. 24. [z] Je. 45. 5. [a] 2 Ki. 6. 19. [b] Na. 3. 11. [c] Eze. 26. 21. [d] Ge. 43. 9.

תָּבֹר pr. name, כִּסְלוֹת תָּ׳ under . . . כסל

תִּבְרַח[a] וַ Kal fut. 3 pers. sing. fem.; וַ conv. . ברח

תְּבָרֵךְ Piel fut. 2 pers. sing. masc. . ברך

תְּבֹרַךְ / תְּבֹרַךְ[b] } Pual fut. 3 pers. sing. fem. . ברך

תְּבָרְכוּ[c] Piel fut. 2 pers. pl. masc. . . ברך

תְּבָרֶכְךָ[d] id. fut. 3 pers. sing. fem., suff. 2 pers. s. m. ברך

תְּבָרְכֶנּוּ[e] id. id., suff. 3 pers. sing. masc. . ברך

תְּבָרְכֶנּוּ[f] id. id., suff. 3 pers. sing. masc. . ברך

תְּבָרְכֵנִי[g] id. id., suff. 1 pers. sing. . . ברך

תְּבָרְכֵנִי[h] id. fut. 2 pers. sing. masc., suff. 1 pers. sing. ברך

תַּבְרֵנִי[i] וַ Hiph. fut. 3 pers. sing. fem. [תַּבְרֶה], suff. 1 pers. sing. (§ 24. rem. 21) . ברה

תֵּבֹשׁוּ Kal fut. 2 pers. pl. masc. (§ 21. rem. 6) . בוש

תֵּבֹשִׁי id. fut. 2 pers. sing. fem. . . בוש

תְּבַשֵּׁל[k] וַ׳ Piel fut. 2 pers. sing. masc., or (2 Sa. 13. 8) 3 pers. sing. fem. . . . בשל

תְּבֻשַּׁל[l] Pual fut. 3 pers. sing. fem. . . בשל

תְּבַשְּׁלוּ[m] Piel fut. 2 pers. pl. masc. . . בשל

תְּבַשֵּׂר Piel fut. 2 pers. sing. masc. . . בשר

תְּבַשְּׂרוּ[n] id. fut. 2 pers. pl. masc. . . בשר

תֵּבַת noun fem. sing., constr. of תֵּבָה dec. 10 תבה

תִּגְאַל[o] Kal fut. 2 pers. sing. masc. . . גאל

תִּגָּאֵלוּ[p] Niph. fut. 2 pers. pl. masc. [for תִּגָּאֲלוּ comp. § 8. rem. 15] . . . . גאל

תִּגְבַּהּ[q] וַ Kal fut. 3 pers. sing. fem.; וַ conv. . גבה

תִּגְבְּהוּ[u] id. fut. 2 pers. pl. m. [for תִּגְבְּהוּ § 8. r. 15] גבה

תִּגְבְּהֶינָה[r] וַ id. fut. 3 pers. pl. f. (§ 8. r. 16); וַ conv. גבה

תַּגְבִּיהַּ Hiph. fut. 2 pers. sing. masc. . . גבה

תִּגְבַּל[s] Kal fut. 3 pers. s. f. [for תִּגְבֹּל § 8. r. 18] גבל

וַתַּגֵּד / וַתַּגֶּד־ } Hiph. fut. 3 pers. sing. fem. ap. from תַּגִּיד (§ 11. rem. 4); וַ conv. . נגד

תַּגְדִּילוּ[t] וַ׳[u] Hiph. fut. 2 pers. pl. masc.; וַ id. . גדל

תַּגְדֵּל־ וַ׳[v] id. fut. 2 pers. s. m. ap. [fr. תַּגְדִּיל]; וַ id. גדל

תִּגְדַּל וַ׳[y] Kal fut. 3 pers. sing. fem.; וַ id. . גדל

תִּגְדְּלִי[z] וַ id. fut. 2 pers. sing. fem.; וַ id. . גדל

תְּגַדְּלֶנּוּ[a] Piel fut. 2 pers. sing. m., suff. 3 pers. s. m. גדל

תְּגַדֵּעוּן Piel fut. 2 pers. pl. masc. with parag. ן [for תְּגַדְּעוּ § 10. rem. 4] . . . גדע

תִּגְדְּרוּ[b] וַ Kal fut. 2 pers. pl. masc.; וַ conv. . גדר

תִּגּוֹף Kal fut. 2 pers. sing. masc. (§ 17. rem. 3) . נגף

תָּגוּר[c] Kal fut. 2 pers. sing. masc. . . גור

תָּגוּרוּ[d] id. fut. 2 pers. pl. masc. . . . גור

תָּגוּרִי[e] id. fut. 2 pers. sing. fem. . . . גור

תָּגֹז[f] Kal fut. 2 pers. sing. masc. . . . גזז

תִּגְזֹל / תִּגְזָל־[g] } Kal fut. 2 pers. sing. masc. (§ 8. rem. 18) גזל

תִּגְזַר[h] וְ Kal fut. 2 pers. sing. masc. . . גזר

תָּגַח[i] וַ Kal fut. 2 p. s. m., ap. & conv. (§ 22. r. 3) גיח

תַּגִּיד / וְתַגִּיד[k] } Hiph. fut. 2 p. s. m., or (Est. 2. 10) 3 p. sing. f.; second form *plene* for תַּגֵּד ap. נגד

תַּגִּידוּ id. fut. 2 pers. pl. masc. . . . נגד

תַּגִּידִי[l] id. fut. 2 pers. sing. fem. . . . נגד

תָּגִיל[m] Kal fut. 2 pers. sing. masc., or 3 pers. s. f. גיל

תַּגִּיעַ[n] Hiph. fut. 3 pers. sing. fem. . . נגע

תַּגִּישׁ[o] Hiph. fut. 3 pers. sing. fem. . . נגש

תַּגִּישׁוּ[p] / וְ׳[r] תַּגִּשׁוּן[q] } id. fut. 2 pers. pl. masc. . . . נגש

תָּגֵל וְ׳ Hiph. fut. 3 pers. sing. fem., ap. fr. תָּגִיל גיל

תְּגַל[s] / וְ תְּגַל } Piel fut. 2 pers. sing. masc., or 3 pers. sing. fem. ap. from תְּגַלֶּה . גלה

תִּגָּל[t] Niph. fut. 3 pers. sing. fem., ap. from תִּגָּלֶה גלה

תְּגַלֶּה[u] / תְּגַלֶּה } Piel fut. 2 pers. sing. masc. (comp. § 24. rem. 20) . . . גלה

תִּגָּלֶה וְ׳[x] Niph. fut. 3 pers. sing fem; וְ conv. . גלה

תְּגַלַּח[y] וַ Piel fut. 3 pers. sing. fem.; וַ id. . גלח

תְּגַלִּי[z] Piel fut. 2 pers. sing. fem. . . גלה

תָּגֵלְנָה וַ׳[a] Kal fut. 3 pers. pl. fem.; וַ conv. . גיל

תִּגְלַת פִּלְאֶסֶר / תִּגְלַת פִּלֶסֶר } also written תִּ׳ פִּלְנְאֶסֶר and פִּלְנֶסֶר pr. n. *Tiglath-pileser*, a king of Assyria.

תַּגְמוּלוֹהִי[b] noun m. pl., suff. 3 p. s. m. (§ 4. r. 5), fr. תַּגְמוּל גמל

תִּגְמֹל[c] וַ׳[d] Kal fut. 2 p. s. m., or 3 p. s. f.; וַ conv. גמל

תִּגְמְלֵהוּ[e] וַ id. fut. 3 pers. s. f., suff. 3 p. s. m.; וַ id. גמל

תִּגְמְלוּ[f] id. fut. 2 pers. pl. masc. . . . גמל

תִּגְנֹב וַ׳[g] Kal fut. 2 pers. sing. masc.; וַ conv. גנב

תִּגְנֹב וַ id. fut. 3 pers. sing. fem.; וַ id. . גנב

תִּגְנֹבוּ[h] id. fut. 2 pers. pl. m. [for תִּגְנְבוּ § 8. r. 15] גנב

תַּגַּע[aa] וַ Hiph. fut. 3 p. s. f., ap. fr. תַּגִּיעַ; וַ conv. נגע

תִּגָּע[i] / וַ׳ תִּגַּע } Kal fut. 3 pers. sing. fem. (§ 8. rem. 15); וַ conv. . . . . . נגע

תִּגָּעוּ / תִּגְּעוּ } id. fut. 2 pers. pl. masc. . . . נגע

תִּגְעַל[k] Kal fut. 3 pers. sing. fem. . . . געל

תִּגְעֲרוּ[l] Kal fut. 2 pers. pl. masc. . . . גער

תִּגְעַשׁ[m] וַ Kal fut. 3 pers. sing. fem.; וַ conv. . געש

תִּתְגָּעַשׁ[n] וַ Kh. תִּגְעַשׁ q. v., K. וַיִּתְגָּעַשׁ Hithp. fut. 3 pers. sing. masc.; וַ conv. . . געש

תָּגָר[o] וַ Kal fut. 3 pers. sing. f., ap. & conv. fr. תָּגוּר גור

תַּגֵּר[p] וַ Hiph. fut. 2 pers. sing. masc. ap. [from תַּגִּיר]; וַ conv. נגר

---

[a] Ge. 16. 6. [h] 1 Ch. 4. 10. [p] Is. 52. 3. [y] Ge. 19. 19. [f] De. 15. 19. [m] Is. 41. 16; Ps. 35. 9. [s] Pr. 25. 9. [b] Ps. 116. 12. [i] Le. 12. 4.
[b] Ju. 5. 24. [i] 2 Sa. 13. 5. [q] Eze. 19. 11. [z] Eze. 16. 7. [g] Pr. 22. 22. [t] Is. 47. 3. [c] Ps. 142. 8. [k] Le. 26. 11, 15.
[c] Nu. 6. 23. [k] 2 Sa. 13. 8. [r] Eze. 16. 50. [a] Job 7. 17. [h] Job 22. 28. [n] Le. 5. 7. [u] Le. 18. 7, 8, 11, 15. [d] Ho. 1. 8. [l] Ru. 2. 16.
[d] Ge. 27. 4, 25. [l] Le. 6. 21. [s] Zec. 9. 2. [b] Eze. 13. 5. [i] Eze. 32. 2. [o] Am. 9. 10. [x] Eze. 16. 36. [e] 1 Ki. 11. 20. [m] Ps. 18. 8.
[e] Nu. 23. 25. [m] Ex. 16. 23. [t] Job 19. 5. [c] De. 18. 22. [k] Ex. 19. 3. [p] Mal. 1. 8. [y] Ju. 16. 19. [f] De. 32. 6. [n] 2 Sa. 22. 8.
[f] 2 Ki. 4. 29. [n] 2 Sa. 1. 20. [u] Eze. 35. 13. [d] De. 1. 17. [l] Jos. 2. 20. [q] Mal. 1. 8. [z] Is. 16. 3. [g] Ge. 31. 26, 27. [o] 2 Ki. 8. 2.
[g] Ge. 27. 19, 31. [o] Ru. 4. 4. [v] Ob. 12. [e] 2 Ki. 8. 1. [u] Je. 13. 15. [r] Am. 6. 3. [a] Ps. 97. 8. [aa] Ex. 4. 25. [h] Le. 19. 11. [p] Eze. 35. 5.

וְ תְּגַרְמָה Ge. 10. 3; elsewhere תּוֹגַרְמָה pr. name of a son of Gomer, Ge. 10. 3; 1 Ch. 1. 6, and his descendants inhabiting a region north of Palestine, Eze. 38. 6; 27. 14.

תְּגָרְמִי[b] Piel fut. 2 p. s. f. [for תְּגָרְמִי comp. § 8. r. 15] גרם
תִּגְרַע[c] וְ'י Kal fut. 2 pers. sing. masc. . . . גרע
תִּגְרְעוּ id. fut. 2 pers. pl. masc. . . . . גרע
תְּגָרֵשׁ[d] / וַתְּגָרֵשׁ[e] } Piel fut. 2 pers. sing. masc.; וַ conv. (§ 10. rem. 4) . . . } גרש
תְּגָרְשׁוּן[f] id. fut. 2 pers. pl. masc. with parag. ן . גרש
וַ תְּגָרְשׁוּנִי[g] id. id., suff. 1 pers. sing.; וַ conv. . גרש
וַ תַּגֵּשׁ Hiph. fut. 3 pers. s. f., ap. fr. תַּגִּישׁ; וַ id. נגש
תִּגַּשׁ[h] וְ'י Kal fut. 2 pers. s. m., or 3 p. s. f.; וַ id. נגש
תִּגַּשׁ[k] Kal fut. 2 pers. sing. masc. (§ 17. rem. 3) . נגש
תִּגְּשׁוּ[l] / תִּגָּשׁוּ[m] } Kal fut. 2 pers. pl. masc. (§ 8. rem. 15) נגש
וַ תִּגַּשְׁןָ[n] id. fut. 3 pers. pl. fem. (§ 8. r. 16); וַ conv. נגש
תִּדְבַּק[o] Kal fut. 2 pers. sing. masc., or 3 pers. sing. f. דבק
וַ'וְ תִּדְבַּק id. fut. 3 pers. sing. fem.; וַ conv. . דבק
תִּדְבְּקוּ[p] id. fut. 2 pers. pl. masc. [for תִּדְבְּקוּ § 8. r. 15] דבק
תִּדְבְּקוּן[q] id. id. with parag. ן [for תִּדְבָּקוּן § 8. r. 17] דבק
תִּדְבָּקִין[r] id. fut. 2 p. s. f. with parag. ן [for תִּדְבְּקִין] דבק
תִּדְבָּקֵנִי[s] id. fut. 3 p. s. f. (תִּדְבַּק), suff. 1 p. s. (§ 16. r. 12) דבק
וַ'וְ תְּדַבֵּר[t] Piel fut. 3 pers. sing. fem.; וַ conv. דבר
וַתְּ'וּ תְּדַבֵּר id. fut. 2 p. s. m.; וּ bef. (:); וַ id. דבר
תְּדַבֶּר־[u] וּ'וְ[x] id. fut. 3 pers. s. f. for תְּדַבֵּר (§ 10. r. 4); וַ id. דבר
תְּדַבְּרוּ id. fut. 2 pers. pl. masc. . . . דבר
תְּדַבֵּרוּן[y] / תְּדַבְּרוּן[z] } id. id., ן parag. (§ 10. rem. 4) . . דבר
תְּדַבֵּרִי id. fut. 2 p. s. f. [for תְּדַבְּרִי comp. § 8. r. 15] דבר
וַ'וְ תְּדַבֵּרְנָה id. fut. 2 p. pl. f. (Je. 44. 25), or 3 p. pl. f.; וַ conv. דבר
וַ תִּדֹּד[a] Kal fut. 3 pers. sing. fem.; וַ id. נדד
תִּדְהָר noun masc. sing. . . . . דהר
תָּדוּץ[b] Kal fut. 3 pers. sing. fem. . . . דוץ
תְּדוּר[c] Chald. Peal fut. 3 pers. sing. fem. . . דור
תָּדוּשׁ Kal fut. 2 pers. sing. masc. . . . דוש
תְּדוּשֶׁהָ[d] id. fut. 3 pers. sing. fem., suff. 3 pers. s. f. דוש
וּ תְּדוּשִׁנַּהּ[e] Ch. Peal fut. 3 p. s. f., suff. 3 p. s. f.; וּ bef. (:) דוש
וַ תַּדִּחוּם[f] Hiph. fut. 2 p. pl. m., suff. 3 p. pl. m.; וַ conv. נדח
תַּדִּיחֶנּוּ[pp] id. fut. 3 pers. sing. f. with suff. 3 pers. s. m. נדח
תָּדִין[g] Kal fut. 2 pers. sing. masc. R. דִּין see . דון
תְּדִינֵנִי[h] id. with suff. 1 pers. sing. R. דִּין see . דון
תְּדַכֵּא[i] Piel fut. 2 pers. sing. masc. . . . דכא
תְּדַכְּאוּ[k] id. fut. 2 pers. pl. masc. . . . דכא
וּ תְּדַכְּאוּנַנִי[l] id. id., suff. 1 pers. sing.; וּ bef. (:) דכא
וַ תִּדְלַח[m] Kal fut. 2 pers. sing. masc.; וַ conv. דלח

תִּדְלָחֵם[n] id. fut. 3 p. s. f., suff. 3 p. pl. m. (§ 16. r. 12) דלח
וַ תִּדְלֶנָה[o] Kal fut. 3 pers. pl. f. (§ 24. r. 7); וַ conv. דלה
תִּדֹּם[p] Kal fut. 3 pers. s. fem. [for תִּדֹּם § 18. r. 14] דמם
תִּדְמֶה[q] Kal fut. 3 pers. sing. fem. . . . דמה
תִּדַּמּוּ[r] Niph. fut. 2 pers. pl. masc. . . . דמם
תְּדַמִּי[s] Piel fut. 2 pers. sing. fem. . . . דמה
תִּדֹּמִּי[t] Niph. fut. 2 pers. sing. fem. (§ 18. rem. 7) דמם
תְּדַמְּיוּן[u] Piel fut. 2 pers. pl. masc., ן parag. (§ 24. r. 13) דמה
תְּדַמְּיוּנִי id. with suff. 1 pers. sing. . . דמה
תִּדְמֶינָה[x] Kal fut. 3 pers. pl. fem. . . . דמה
תִּדְמַע[y] Kal fut. 3 pers. sing. fem. . . . . דמע
תַּדְמֹר (*city of palm trees*) pr. name, *Tadmor*, a city in the Syrian desert between Damascus and the Euphrates, founded by Solomon, 2 Ch. 8. 4; Gr. *Palmyra*. The same is called תָּמֹר (*palm*) in 1 Ki. 9. 18, Khethib.
תֵּדַע וְ'י[z] / וְ'י תֵּדַע } Kal fut. 2 pers. sing. masc. (§ 20. rem. 1); וַ conv. . . } ידע
וַ תֵּדָעֵהוּ[a] id. id., suff. 3 pers. s. m. (§ 16. r. 12); וַ id. ידע
תֵּדָעוּ[b] / תֵּדְעוּ } id. fut. 2 pers. pl. masc. (§ 8. rem. 15) ידע
תֵּדָעוּהָ[c] id. id., suff. 3 pers. sing. fem. (§ 16. rem. 12) ידע
תֵּדְעוּן id. id. with parag. ן . . . . ידע
תֵּדְעִי[d] / תֵּדְעִי } id. fut. 2 pers. sing. fem. (§ 8. rem. 15) ידע
תֵּדְעִין[e] id. with parag. ן . . . . . ידע
וְ תִּדְעָל (*fear; from* דעל Samar. & Syr. *to fear*) pr. name masc. Ge. 14. 1.
תִּדְּפֶנּוּ[f] Kal fut. 3 pers. s. fem. [תִּדֹּף], suff. 3 p. s. m. נדף
וְ תָּדֹק[g] Kal fut. 2 pers. sing. masc. . . דקק
תַּדִּק[h] Ch. Aph. fut. 3 pers. sing. fem. . . דקק
וְ תַּדְקִנַּהּ[i] id., suff. 3 pers. sing. fem. . . דקק
תִּדֹּר וְ'י[k] Kal fut. 2 p. s. m., or 3 p. s. f. (§ 17. r. 3); וַ conv. נדר
תִּדְּרוּ[l] id. fut. 2 p. pl. m. [for תִּדְּרוּ, comp. § 10. r. 1] נדר
תִּדְרוֹשׁ[m] Kal fut. 2 pers. sing. masc. . . . דרש
תִּדְרֹךְ Kal fut. 2 pers. sing. masc., or 3 pers. s. fem. דרך
תִּדְרְכוּ[n] id. fut. 2 pers. pl. masc. . . . דרך
תִּדְרְכִי[o] id. fut. 2 pers. sing. fem. . . . דרך
תִּדְרֹשׁ Kal fut. 2 pers. sing. masc. . . . דרש
תִּדְרְשֻׁהוּ[p] id. fut. 2 pers. pl. masc., suff. 3 pers. s. masc. דרש
תִּדְרְשׁוּ id. fut. 2 pers. pl. masc. . . . דרש
תִּדְרְשֶׁנּוּ id. fut. 2 pers. s. masc., suff. 3 pers. s. masc. דרש
תִּדְרְשֻׁנִי[q] id. fut. 2 pers. pl. m. (תִּדְרְשׁוּ), suff. 1 pers. s. דרש
תַּדְשֵׁא[r] Hiph. fut. 3 pers. sing. fem., ap. [fr. תַּדְשִׁיא דשא
תְּדַשֶּׁן־[s] Piel fut. 3 pers. s. fem. [for תְּדַשֵּׁן § 10. r. 4] דשן
תְּדֻשָּׁן Pual fut. 3 pers. s. f. [for תְּדֻשַּׁן comp. § 8. r. 15] דשן

---

[b] Eze. 23. 34. [c] Job 15. 4, 8. [d] Ps. 80. 9. [e] Jos. 24. 12. [f] Mi. 2. 9. [g] Ju. 11. 7. [h] Is. 65. 5. [i] Ge. 33. 7.
[k] De. 15. 3. [l] Eze. 9. 6. [m] Ex. 19. 15. [n] Ge. 33. 6. [o] De. 10. 20; Eze 29. 4. [p] Jos. 23. 8. [pp] Pr. 7. 21.
[q] De. 13. 5. [r] Ru. 2. 8, 21. [s] Ge. 19. 19. [t] Ps. 37. 30. [u] 2 Sa. 14. 12. [x] 1 Sa. 25. 24. [y] Ps. 58. 2.
[z] Ge. 32. 20. [a] Ge. 31. 40. [b] Job 41. 14. [c] Da. 4. 18. [d] Job 39. 15. [e] Da. 7. 23. [f] Je. 23. 2.
[g] Zec. 3. 7. [h] Ps. 54. 3. [i] Pr. 22. 22. [k] Is. 3. 15. [l] Job 19. 2. [m] Eze. 32. 2. [n] Eze. 32. 13.
[o] Ex. 2. 16. [p] La. 2. 18. [q] La. 3. 49. [r] Je. 51. 6. [s] Est. 4. 13. [t] Je. 48. 2. [u] Is. 40. 18.
[x] Je. 14. 17. [y] Je. 13. 17. [z] Ps. 139. 1. [a] Ps. 144. 3. [b] Is. 6. 9. [c] Is. 43. 19. [d] Is. 47. 11.
[e] Ru. 3. 18. [f] Ps. 1. 4. [g] Is. 41. 15. [h] Da. 2. 40, 44. [i] Da. 7. 23. [k] 1 Sa. 1. 11. [l] De. 12. 11.
[m] Job 10. 6. [n] De. 11. 25. [o] Ju. 5. 21. [p] 2 Ch. 15. 2. [q] Je. 29. 13. [r] Ge. 1. 11. [s] Pr. 15. 30.

תְּהַבְּלוּ Kal fut. 2 pers. pl. masc. [for תֶּהְבְּלוּ § 8. rem. 15, & § 13. rem. 5 & 6] . הבל

תֶּהְגֶּה Kal fut. 3 pers. sing. fem. (§ 13. rem. 5) הגה

תֶּהְגּוּ[a] id. fut. 2 pers. pl. masc. . הגה

תֶּהְדְּפוּ[b] Kal fut. 2 pers. pl. masc. [for תֶּהֶדְפוּ § 8. rem. 15, & § 13. rem. 5] . הדף

תֶּהְדַּר Kal fut. 2 pers. sing. masc. (§ 13. rem. 5) הדר

תָּהָה Root not used; Chald. תְּהָא *to be waste, desolate,* whence תְּהָא, תְּהֵי, *waste, desert,* Arab. tahiy-you, *empty, chaos.* Hence

תֹּהוּ[c] וְ׳ masc. (Seg. n. for תֹּהֶו).—I. *desolation.*—II. *a desert.*—III. *emptiness,* Ge. 1. 2.—IV. *vanity, a vain, worthless thing.*—V. לְתֹהוּ, תֹּהוּ adv. *in vain.*

תֶּהֱוֵא Chald. Peal fut. 3 pers. sing. fem. . . הוה

תְּהוֹבֵד[d] Chald. Aph. fut. 2 pers. sing. masc. (§ 52. r. 2) אבד

תְּהוֹדְעוּן[e] Chald. Aph. fut. 2 pers. pl. masc. (§ 47. r. 4) ידע

תְּהוֹדְעוּנַּנִי[f] / תְּהוֹדְעֻנַּנִי[g] } Chald. id. with suff. 1 pers. sing. . ידע

תֶּהֱוֵה Chald. Peal fut. 3 pers. sing. masc. for תֶּהֱוֵא הוה

תְּהוֹם noun com. sing. dec. 1 a . . הום

תְּהוֹמוֹת id. with pl. fem. term. . . . תהם

תְּהוֹתְתוּ[h] Pilel fut. 2 pers. pl. masc. . . הות

תְּהַחֲוֹן[i] Chald. Pael (dag. forte impl.) fut. 2 pers. pl. m. חוה

תְּהַחֲוֻנַּנִי[k] Chald. id. with suff. 1 pers. sing. חוה

תְּהִי[l] וַ / וַתְּ׳, וּ׳ תְּהִי } Kal fut. 2 p. m. or, 3 p. s. f. ap. fr. תִּהְיֶה (§ 24. r. 3 e); וַ׳ conv., וּ bef. (:) היה

תִּהְיֶה־[m] / תִּהְיֶה } id. fut. 2 pers. sing. masc., or 3 pers. sing. fem. (§ 14. rem. 13, & § 24. rem. 20) היה

תִּהְיוּ[n] וְ׳ / תִּהְיוּן[o] } id. fut. 2 pers. pl. masc.; וַ׳ conv. . היה

תִּהְיִי[p] וַ׳[q] id. fut. 2 pers. sing. fem.; וַ׳ id. היה

תִּהְיֶין וַ׳ / תִּהְיֶינָה וַ׳ } id. fut. 3 pers. pl. fem. (comp. § 8. rem. 16); וַ׳ id. . היה

תְּהִימֶנָּה[r] Hiph. fut. 3 pers. pl. fem. (§ 21. rem. 13) הום

תִּהְיֶנָה וַ, וַתְּ׳[s] defect. for תִּהְיֶינָה (q. v.) . היה

תָּהִינוּ[t] וַ Hiph. fut. 2 pers. pl. masc.; וַ׳ conv. הון

תַּהְכְּרוּ[u] Kal or Hiph. fut. 2 pers. pl. masc. [for תַּהַכִּירוּ § 11. rem. 7] . . הכר

תָּהֵל[x] Hiph. fut. 3 pers. sing. fem. bef. monos. [for תָּהֵל § 18. rem. 11] . הלל

תְּהִלָּה[y] noun fem. sing. . . הלל

תְּהִלָּה וּ׳ noun fem. sing. dec. 10; וּ bef. (:) הלל

תְּהַלְלוּ[z] Kal fut. 2 pers. pl. masc. . הלל

תְּהִלּוֹת[a] וּ׳ noun fem., pl. of תְּהִלָּה dec. 10; וּ bef. (:) הלל

תְּהַלֵּךְ[b] וַ׳[c] Kal fut. 3 pers. sing. masc. for תֵּהָלֵךְ (§ 13. rem. 12); וַ׳ conv. . הלך

תַּהֲלֻכוֹת[d] וְ noun fem., pl. of [תַּהֲלוּכָה] dec. 10 . הלך

תְּהַלֵּל[e] Piel fut. 3 pers. sing. fem. . הלל

תְּהַלְלֶךָּ[f] וּ id., suff. 2 pers. sing. masc. for תְּהַלֶּלְךָ (§ 10. rem. 7, & § 2. rem. 2); וּ, for וְ, conv. הלל

תְּהִלַּת noun fem. sing., constr. of תְּהִלָּה dec. 10 הלל

תְּהִלֹּת id. pl., comp. תְּהִלּוֹת הלל

תְּהִלָּתוֹ וּ׳ id. sing., suff. 3 pers. sing. masc.; וּ bef. (:) הלל

תְּהִלָּתִי וּ׳ id. sing., suff. 1 pers. sing.; וּ id. הלל

[g] תְּהִלֹּתֶיךָ id. pl., suff. 2 pers. sing. masc., but see § 4. r. 4 הלל

תְּהִלָּתֶךָ / תְּהִלָּתֶךָ[h] } id. sing., suff. 2 pers. sing. masc. . הלל

תָּהֹם וַ Kal fut. 3 pers. sing. fem. [for תָּהֹם; § 18. rem. 7]; וַ׳ conv. . המם

תְּהֹמוֹת noun com., pl. of תְּהוֹם dec. 10 תהם

תֶּהֱמִי וְ׳[i] Kal fut. 2 pers. sing. fem.; וְ׳ conv. המה

תְּהֻמֵּם[k] וּ Kal fut. 2 pers. sing. masc. [תָּהֹם], suff. 3 pers. pl. masc. (§ 18. rem. 5); וּ bef. (:) המם

תְּהֹמֹת וּ׳[l] defect. comp. תְּהֹמֹת, תְּהוֹמוֹת תהם

תְּהַנְזִק[m] Ch. Pael fut. 2 pers. sing. m. (§ 47. r. 1 & 4) נזק

תַּהֲפֹךְ[n] וַ Kal fut. 3 pers. sing. fem.; וַ׳ conv. הפך

תֵּהָפֵךְ Niph. fut. 2 pers. sing. masc. הפך

תַּהְפֻּכוֹת / תַּהְפֻּכֹת[o] } noun fem., pl. of [תַּהְפּוּכָה] dec. 10 הפך

תַּהַר וַ Kal fut. 3 pers. sing. fem. ap. [for תַּהֲרֶה § 24. rem. 3]; וַ׳ conv. . הרה

תַּהֲרֹג Kal fut. 2 pers. sing. masc. הרג

תַּהַרְגֵהוּ[p] id. fut. 3 pers. sing. fem., suff. 3 pers. sing. m. הרג

תַּהַרְגוּ[q] וְ׳ / תַּהַרְגוּ[r] } id. fut. 2 pers. pl. masc. (§ 8. rem. 15) וַ׳ conv. הרג

תַּהַרְגֵם[s] id. fut. 2 pers. sing. masc., or (Pr. 1. 32) 3 pers. sing. fem., suff. 3 pers. pl. masc. הרג

תֵּהָרַגְנָה[t] Niph. fut. 3 pers. pl. fem. (§ 9. rem. 4) הרג

תַּהַרְגֵנוּ[u] Kal fut. 2 pers. s. m. (תַּהֲרֹג), suff. 3 pers. s. m. הרג

תַּהֲרוּ[x] Kal fut. 2 pers. pl. masc. הרה

תַּהֲרֶין[y] וַ id. fut. 3 p. pl. fem. (comp. § 8. r. 16); וַ׳ conv. הרה

תַּהֲרֹס[z] Kal fut. 2 pers. sing. masc. הרס

תֵּהָרֵס[a] Niph. fut. 3 pers. sing. fem. הרס

תְּהָרְסֵם[b] Piel fut. 2 pers. s. m. [תְּהָרֵס], suff. 3 p. pl. m. הרס

תֶּהֶרְסֶנּוּ[c] Kal fut. 3 pers. sing. fem. (תַּהֲרֹס), suff. 3 pers. sing. masc. (contrary to § 13. rem. 6) . הרס

תְּהַשְׁכַּח[d] וּ׳ Chald. Aph. fut. 2 pers. sing. masc. (§ 47. rem. 4); וּ bef. (:) שכח

---

[a] Is. 16. 7. [b] Eze. 34. 21. [c] Is. 40. 17; 41. 29. [d] Da. 2. 24. [e] Ezr. 7. 25. [f] Da. 2. 5. [g] Da. 2. 9. [h] Ps. 62. 4. [i] Da. 2. 6. [k] Da. 2. 9. [l] La. 3. 37. [m] Je. 17. 17. [n] Am. 4. 11. [o] Ex. 22. 30. [p] Ho. 3. 3. [q] Eze. 16. 8. [r] Mi. 2. 12. [s] 1 Ch. 7. 15. [t] De. 1. 41. [u] Job 19. 3. [x] Job 41. 10. [y] Job 4. 18. [z] Ps. 75. 5. [a] Is. 60. 6. [b] Ps. 73. 9. [c] Ex. 9. 23. [d] Ne. 12. 31. [e] Ps. 150. 6. [f] Ps. 119. 175. [g] Ps. 9. 15. [h] De. 10. 21. [i] Ps. 42. 6. [k] Ps. 144. 6. [l] De. 8. 7. [m] Ezr. 4. 13. [n] 2 Ch. 9. 12. [o] De. 32. 20. [p] Job 20. 16. [q] Eze. 9. 6. [r] Le. 20. 15. [s] Ps. 59. 12. [t] Eze. 26. 6. [u] De. 13. 10. [x] Is. 33. 11. [y] Ge. 19. 36. [z] Ex. 15. 7. [a] Pr. 11. 11. [b] Ex. 23. 24. [c] Pr. 14. 1. [d] Ezr. 4. 15; 7. 16.

תְּהָתֵלּוּ[a] Piel fut. 2 pers. pl. masc. R. התל see . תלל
תָּו[pp] noun masc. sing. [for תָּוֶה] . . תוה
תְּוֹאֲמִם[b] Kal part. act. masc. pl. [of תֹּוֹאֵם] dec. 7b תאם

תּוּב Chald. only fut. יְתוּב, i. q. Heb. שׁוּב *to return*, Da. 4. 31, 33. Aph. הֲתִיב (§ 47. rem. 4) *to return, give* or *send back*; הֲתִיב פִּתְגָּם *to return an answer, to answer*.

תּוּבַל ו׳ pr. name masc., and in compos. תּוּ׳ קַיִן יבל
תּוּבַל[c] Hoph. fut. 3 pers. sing. fem. . . . יבל
תּוּבְלוּן[d] id. fut. 2 pers. pl. masc., ן parag. [for תּוּבְלוּ § 8. rem. 17] . . . יבל
תּוּבַלְנָה[e] id. fut. 3 pers. pl. fem. . . . . יבל
תּוּגָה[f] noun fem. sing. dec. 10 . . . יגה
תְּוֹגְיוּן[g] Kal fut. 2 pers. pl. masc., ן parag. (§ 24. r. 5) יגה
תּוֹגַרְמָה ו׳ pr. name, see תֹּגַרְמָה.
תּוּגַת[h] noun fem. sing., constr. of תּוּגָה dec. 10 . יגה
תּוֹדָה ו׳ noun fem. sing. dec. 10 . . . ידה
תּוֹדוֹת[i] ו׳[k] id. pl., comp. תּוֹדֹת . . . . ידה
תּוֹדִיעֵנִי Hiph. fut. 2 pers. sing. masc. . . ידע
תּוֹדִיעֵנִי id. with suff. 1 pers. sing. . . . ידע
תּוֹדֶךָּ Hiph. fut. 3 pers. sing. fem. [תּוֹדֶה], suff. 2 pers. sing. masc. (§ 24. rem. 20) . ידה
תִּוָּדֵעַ[m] Niph. fut. 3 pers. s. f. [for תִּוָּדַע § 15. r. 1] ידע
תִּוָּדְעִי[n] id. fut. 2 pers. sing. fem. . . . ידע
תּוֹדַת[o] noun fem. sing., constr. of תּוֹדָה dec. 10 ידה
תּוֹדֹת[p] id. pl. comp. תּוֹדוֹת . . . . ידה

תְּוַהּ Ch. *to be astonished, amazed*, Da. 3. 24.

I. **תָּוָה** Pi. תִּוָּה *to make marks, to scribble*, 1 Sa. 21. 14, cog. תָּאָה, תָּאַר. Hiph. I. *to mark, set a mark upon*, with עַל Eze. 9. 4.—II. *to limit*, Ps. 78. 41, comp. תָּאַר; others, *to grieve* (Syr. *to repent, be grieved*).

תָּו masc.—I. *a mark, sign*, Eze. 9. 4.—II. *signature, subscription*, Job 31. 35, תָּוִי *my subscription*, q. d. affixed to my pleadings. Others take תָּוִי as a contraction תַּאֲוִי *my desire*, R. אָוָה.

II. **תָּוָה** Root not used; i. q. Arab. توى *to abide, dwell*.

תָּא masc. dec. 1a (for תָּוָא ,תָּוֶה), pl. ים—, ות—, *a chamber*, Ch. תָּוָא.

תּוֹחַ Root not used; Arab. تاح *to descend, sink down*.

תּוֹחַ (*lowness, low*) pr. name masc. 1 Ch. 6. 19, for which נַחַת ver. 11, & תֹּחוּ 1 Sa. 1. 1.

תַּחַת fem. (with suff. chiefly attached to the plural, תַּחְתֵּינוּ, תַּחְתֶּיהָ, תַּחְתָּיו, תַּחְתֶּיךָ, תַּחְתַּי, with the singular only, תַּחְתִּי, תַּחְתָּם, תַּחְתֵּיהֶם (תַּחְתֶּנָּה prop. *what is below, underneath*, hence *a place*.—I. adv. *below, beneath*.—II. prep. *under*.—III. *in place of, instead of*.—IV. *in return for*.—V. *on account of*.—VI. תַּחַת אֲשֶׁר (a) *instead that*; (b) *because that, because*.—VII. with prefixes, (a) מִתַּחַת *from under, from beneath*; also simply, *under*; (b) מִתַּחַת לְ *below, under* anything; (c) לְמִתַּחַת לְ *under*, after a verb of motion, 1 Ki. 7. 32; (d) אֶל־תַּחַת *under* of the place *whither*; also of the place *where*, 1 Sa. 21. 4.—VIII. (*place, station*) pr. name (a) of a station of the Israelites in the desert, Nu. 33. 26; (b) of two men, 1 Ch. 6. 9, 22; 7. 20.

תְּחֹת Da. 4. 11, elsewhere תְּחוֹת Ch. prep. *under*.

תַּחְתִּי masc. תַּחְתִּיָּה, תַּחְתִּית fem. adj. *lower, lowest*; pl. תַּחְתִּיִּים, תַּחְתִּיּוֹת *lowest parts* or *places*.

תַּחְתּוֹן masc. תַּחְתּוֹנָה fem. adj. *lower, lowest*.

תּוֹחַ pr. name masc. . . . . . תוח
תּוֹחֶל[q] Hiph. fut. 2 pers. sing. masc. ap. [fr. תּוֹחִיל] יחל
תּוֹחֶלֶת ו׳[r] noun fem. sing. dec. 13a . . . יחל
תּוֹחַלְתּוֹ[s] id., suff. 3 pers. sing. masc. . . . יחל
תּוֹחַלְתִּי[t] ו׳[u] id., suff. 1 pers. sing. . . . יחל
תָּוִי[w] noun masc. sing., suff. 1 pers. sing. from תָּו [for תָּוֶה] . . . . . תוה

תָּוֶךְ׳ (in this form only with pref.) masc. dec. 6g, *the middle, midst*; בְּתוֹךְ (a) *in the midst of*; (b) *in, within*; (c) *among*; מִתּוֹךְ *from the midst of*, also simply *out of, from*; אֶל־תּוֹךְ *into the midst of*.

תִּיכוֹן masc. תִּיכוֹנָה fem. adj. *middle*.

תּוֹךְ ו׳[y] noun masc. sing., constr. of תָּוֶךְ׳ dec. 6g תוך
תּוֹכוֹ ו׳[z] id., suff. 3 pers. sing. masc. . . . תוך
תּוֹכַח[a] Hiph. fut. 2 pers. sing. masc., ap. fr. תּוֹכִיחַ יכח
תּוֹכֵחָה[b] ו׳ noun fem. sing. dec. 10 (§ 39. No. 3. r. 4) יכח
תּוֹכָחוֹת noun fem. pl. abs., from תּוֹכַחַת (§ 44. r. 5) יכח
תּוֹכֵחוֹת[c] noun f., pl. of תּוֹכֵחָה d. 10 (§ 39. No. 3. r. 4) יכח
תּוֹכְחוֹת[d] noun fem. pl., constr. of תּוֹכָחוֹת (q. v.) יכח
תּוֹכִחֵךְ[e] Hiph. fut. 3 pers. sing. fem. (תּוֹכִיחַ for תּוֹכַחְנָה), suff. 2 pers. sing. fem. . יכח
תּוֹכַחַת ו׳ noun fem. sing. dec. 13a, but pl. תּוֹכָחוֹת (§ 44. rem. 5) . . . יכח
תּוֹכַחְתִּי ו׳ id. with suff. 1 pers. sing. . . . יכח
תּוֹכִיחַ[f] Hiph. fut. 2 pers. sing. masc. . . . יכח
תּוֹכִיחוּ[g] ן id. fut. 2 pers. pl. masc. . . . יכח

[a] Job 13. 9. [b] Ex. 36. 29. [c] Ps. 45. 15. [d] Is. 55. 12. [e] Ps. 45. 16. [f] Pr. 14. 13. [g] Job 19. 2. [h] Pr. 10. 1. [i] Ps. 56. 13. [k] 2 Ch. 29. 31. [l] Hab. 3. 2. [m] Pr. 14. 33. [n] Ru. 3. 3. [o] Le. 7. 13, 15. [p] Ne. 12. 31. [pp] Eze. 9. 4. [q] 1 Sa. 10. 8. [r] Pr. 11. 7. [s] Job 41. 1. [t] Ps. 39. 8. [u] La. 3. 18. [w] Job 31. 35. [y] Jos. 12. 2. [z] Eze. 15. 4. [a] Pr. 9. 8. [b] Ho. 5. 9. [c] Ps. 149. 7. [d] Pr. 6. 23. [e] Je. 2. 19. [f] Le. 19. 17. [g] Job 19. 5.

Word	Analysis	Root
תְּוֹכִיחֵנִי	id. fut. 2 pers. s. m. (תּוֹכִיחַ), suff. 1 pers. s.	יכח
תֻּוּכִּיִּים[a]	וְ noun masc. pl. see	תכי
תּוֹכְךָ[b]	noun masc. sing., suff. 2 pers. sing. masc. from תָּוֶךְ' dec. 6g . . .	תוך
תּוֹכָל[c]	Kh. תּוּכַל Hoph., K. תְּכוּל Peal, fut. 2 pers. sing. masc. (§ 52. rem. 2) . . .	יכל
תּוּכָל תּוּכַל	וַ' Hoph. fut. 2 pers. sing. masc., or 3 pers. sing. fem.; ·וַ conv. . .	יכל
תּוּכְלוּ	id. fut. 2 pers. pl. masc.	יכל
תּוּכְלִי[d]	id. fut. 2 pers. sing. fem.	יכל
תּוֹכָם[e]	noun masc. sing., suff. 3 pers. pl. masc. from תָּוֶךְ dec. 6g	תוך
תִּוָּלֵד	Niph. fut. 2 pers. sing. masc. . .	ילד
תּוֹלְדוֹת תּוֹלְדֹת	noun fem. pl. constr. [from תּוֹלָדָה or תּוֹלֶדֶת . . .	ילד
תּוֹלְדֹתָם	id. pl., suff. 3 pers. pl. masc. . .	ילד
תּוֹלִיד	Hiph. fut. 2 pers. sing. masc. . . .	ילד
תּוֹלוֹן	וְ Kh. תּוּלוֹן, K. תִּילוֹן pr. name masc. 1 Ch. 4. 20.	
תּוֹלָלֵינוּ[f]	וְ noun masc. pl. suff. 1 pers. pl. [fr. תּוֹלָל]	ילל
תּוֹלָע	pr. name masc.	תלע
תּוֹלָע[g]	noun masc. sing. (pl. תּוֹלָעִים) . . .	תלע
תּוֹלֵעָה	noun fem. sing.	תלע
תּוֹלָעִים[h]	noun masc., pl. of תּוֹלָע . . .	תלע
תּוֹלַעַת[i] תּוֹלַעַת	וְ' noun fem. sing. dec. 13 a . .	תלע
תּוֹלַעְתָּם[k]	id., suff. 3 pers. pl. masc. (§ 35. rem. 5) .	תלע
תּוֹמִיךְ[l]	Kal part. act. sing. masc. for תּוֹמֵךְ (§ 8. r. 19)	תמך
תּוֹמֵךְ[m]	וְ Kal part. act. sing. masc. dec. 7b .	תמך
תּוֹמִם[n]	by contr. for תְּאוֹמִים (q. v.) . . .	תאם
תֵּוֹמָן	Kh. תּוּמָן, K. תֵּימָן pr. name masc. .	ימן
תּוּמַת[o]	וַ' Hoph. fut. 3 pers. sing. fem.; ·וַ conv. .	מות
תּוֹנֶה[p]	Hiph. fut. 2 pers. sing. masc. (§ 25. No. 2 e)	ינה
תּוֹנוּ	id. fut. 2 pers. pl. masc. . . .	ינה
תּוֹנֶנּוּ[q]	id. fut. 2 pers. sing. masc. (תּוֹנֶה), suff. 3 pers. sing. masc. (§ 24. rem. 21) .	ינה
תִּוָּסֵד[r]	Niph. fut. 2 pers. sing. masc. . .	יסד
תּוֹסִיף	Hiph. fut. 2 pers. sing. masc., or 3 pers. s. fem.	יסף
תּוֹסִיפוּ[s]	id. fut. 2 pers. pl. masc.	יסף
תּוֹסִיפִי	id. fut. 2 pers. sing. fem.	יסף
תּוֹסַף[t] תּוֹסֶף[u]	id. fut. 2 pers. sing. masc., ap. from תּוֹסִיף (comp. § 19. rem. 2) .	יסף
תּוֹסֶף	וַ id. fut. 3 pers. sing. fem. ap.; ·וַ conv.	יסף
תּוֹסְףְ[x]	id. fut. 2 pers. sing. masc. ap. (§ 20. rem. 9)	יסף
תּוֹסִף	id. fut. 2 pers. sing. masc., or 3 pers. sing. fem., defect. for תּוֹסִיף . . .	יסף
תּוֹסִפִי[y]	defect. for תּוֹסִיפִי (q. v.) . . .	יסף
תִּוָּסְרוּ[z]	Niph. fut. 2 pers. pl. masc. . .	יסר
תּוֹעֵבָה	וְ'[a] noun fem. sing. dec. 11 b . . .	תעב
תּוֹעֲבוֹת	id. pl., constr. st.	תעב
תּוֹעֵבוֹת	id. pl., abs. st.	תעב
תּוֹעֲבוֹתֶיהָ	id. pl., suff. 3 pers. sing. fem. . . .	תעב
תּוֹעֲבוֹתֵיהֶם[b]	וְ id. pl., suff. 3 pers. pl. masc. . .	תעב
תּוֹעֲבוֹתֵיהֶן[c]	id. pl., suff. 3 pers. pl. fem. . .	תעב
תּוֹעֲבוֹתָיו[d]	וְ id. pl., suff. 3 pers. sing. masc. . .	תעב
תּוֹעֲבוֹתַיִךְ[e] תּוֹעֲבוֹתַיִךְ[f]	וְ' id. pl., suff. 2 pers. sing. fem. .	תעב
תּוֹעֲבוֹתָם[g]	וְ' id. pl., suff. 3 pers. pl. masc. (§ 4. rem. 2)	תעב
תּוֹעֲבַת	וְ' id. sing., constr. st.	תעב
תּוֹעֲבֹתֶיהָ[h]	id. pl., suff. 3 pers. sing. fem. . .	תעב
תּוֹעֲבֹתֵיהֶם[i]	id. pl., suff. 3 pers. pl. masc. . .	תעב
תּוֹעֲבֹתַיִךְ תּוֹעֲבֹתַיִךְ[k]	וְ' id. pl., suff. 2 pers. sing. fem. .	תעב
תּוֹעֲבֹתֵיכֶם	id. pl., suff. 2 pers. pl. masc. . .	תעב
תּוֹעֲבֹתָם	id. pl., suff. 3 pers. pl. masc. (§ 4. rem. 2)	תעב
תּוֹעָה	noun fem. sing.	תעה
תּוֹעֶה[l]	Kal part. act. sing. masc. dec. 9a . .	תעה
תּוֹעָפוֹת[m]	noun fem. pl. abs. from [תּוֹעָפָה] dec. 11a	יעף
תּוֹעֲפוֹת[n]	וְ id. pl., constr. st.	יעף

תֹּוף Root not used; Arab. *to spit out with contempt.* תֹּפֶת f.—I. *a spitting*, Job 17. 6, תּ' לְפָנִים אֶהְיֶה *I am become a spitting in the face,* i. e. as one before whose face men spit.—II. pr. name of a place in the valley of the sons of Hinnom, near Jerusalem, noted for the abominations committed there in the service of Moloch; with ה parag. תָּפְתֶּה Is. 30. 33 (§ 39. No. 4d).

Word	Analysis	Root
תּוֹפַע[o]	Hiph. fut. 3 pers. sing. fem. ap. [fr. תּוֹפִיעַ]	יפע
תֹּופְפוֹת[p]	Kal part. act. f. pl. [of תּוֹפֵפָה fr. תּוֹפֵף m.]	תפף
תּוֹצֵא[q]	וַ' Hiph. fut. 3 pers. sing. fem., ap. fr. תּוֹצִיא	יצא
תּוֹצָאוֹת[r]	noun fem. pl. abs. from תּוֹצָאָה dec. 11a .	יצא
תּוֹצְאוֹת	id. pl., constr. st.	יצא
תּוֹצְאוֹתָיו[s]	id. pl., suff. 3 pers. sing. masc. (read. 'תָיו), K. תּוֹצְאוֹת (q. v.)	יצא
תּוֹצְאוֹתָם[t]	id. pl., suff. 3 pers. pl. masc. (§ 4. rem. 2)	יצא
תּוֹצְאֹת	id. pl., constr. st.	יצא
תּוֹצְאֹתָיו	id. pl., suff. 3 pers. sing. masc. . .	יצא
תּוֹצִיא	Hiph. fut. 2 pers. sing. masc., or 3 pers. s. f.	יצא
תּוֹצִיאוּ	id. fut. 2 pers. pl. masc. . . .	יצא

[a] 2 Ch. 9. 21. [b] Eze. 28. 16. [c] Da. 5. 16. [d] Is. 47. 11, 12. [e] Ne. 4. 5. [f] Ps. 137. 3. [g] La. 4. 5. [h] Ex. 16. 20. [i] Nu. 19. 6. [k] Is. 66. 24. [l] Ps. 16. 5. [m] Am. 1. 5, 8. [n] Ge. 25. 24. [o] 2 Ki. 11. 15, 16. [p] Ex. 22. 20. [q] De. 23. 17. [r] Is. 44. 28. [s] Is. 1. 5, 13. [t] Job 40. 32. [u] De. 3. 26. [x] Pr. 30. 6. [y] Zep. 3. 11. [z] Le. 26. 23. [a] Mal. 2. 11. [b] Eze. 12. 16. [c] Eze. 23. 36. [d] 2 Ch. 36. 8. [e] Eze. 7. 8. [f] Eze. 7. 4; 16. 36, 51, 58. [g] Eze. 7. 20; 44. 13. [h] Eze. 11. 18. [i] Eze. 6. 9. [k] Eze. 7. 9; 16. 22, 51. [l] Pr. 21. 16. [m] Job 22. 25. [n] Ps. 95. 4. [o] Job 3. 4. [p] Ps. 68. 26. [q] Ge. 1. 24. [r] Ps. 68. 21. [s] Jos. 18. 19. [t] 1 Ch. 5. 16.

תְּוֹצִיאֵנוּ[a] וַ id. fut. 2 pers. s. m., suff. 1 p. pl.; ·וַ conv. יצא
תּוֹצִיאֵנִי[b] id. id., suff. 1 pers. sing. . . . יצא
תּוּקַד / תּוּקָד } Hoph. fut. 3 pers. sing. fem. (comp. § 8. rem. 15) . . . . } יקד
תָּקְהַת Kh. תּוֹקַהַת, K. תָּקְהַת pr. name masc. . קהת
תּוֹקֵעַ[c] וְ Kal part. act. sing. masc. dec. 7 b . תקע
תּוֹקְעִים[d] id. pl., abs. st. . . . . . תקע
תִּוָּקֵשׁ[e] Niph. fut. 2 pers. sing. masc. . . יקשׁ

[תּוּר] *to go round*, or *about*, cogn. דּוּר, hence—I. *to go* or *travel about*, as a merchant, 1 Ki. 10. 15.—II. *to go about as a spy, to spy out*.—III. *to search out, explore, investigate*.—IV. *to think of, to purpose*, Ec. 2. 3.—V. *to go astray*, metaph. Nu. 15. 39. Hiph. I. *to send spies, to spy out*, Ju. 1. 23.—II. *to lead* or *direct aright*, Pr. 12. 26; 2 Sa. 22. 33.

תּוֹר masc. dec. 1 a.—I. *turn, order*, Est. 2. 12, 15.—II. *row* or *string* of beads, Ca. 1. 10, 11.

יְתוּר masc. (after the form יְקוּם) *a searching out*, meton. *that which is sought, found* by search, Job 39. 8; others, *abundance*, from יָתַר.

תּוֹר[f] וְ masc. dec. 1 a, *a turtle-dove*.

תּוֹר Chald. masc. only pl. תּוֹרִין *oxen*, i. q. Heb. שׁוֹר.

תִּוָּרֵא[g] Niph. fut. 2 pers. sing. masc. . . ירא
תּוֹרֵד[h] Hiph. fut. 2 pers. sing. masc. ap. [fr. תּוֹרִיד] ירד
תּוֹרֶד[ee] וַ id. fut. 3 pers. sing. fem., ap. & conv. ירד
תּוּרַד[i] Hoph. fut. 2 pers. sing. masc. . . ירד
תּוֹרִדֵם[k] [l]וַ' Hiph. fut. 2 p. s. m., or 3 p. s. f., suff. 3 p. pl. m. ירד
תּוֹרָה וְ' noun fem. sing. dec. 10 . . . ירה
תּוֹרוֹת[m] וְ id. pl., comp. תּוֹרֹת . . . ירה
תּוֹרֵי[n] noun masc. pl. constr. from תּוֹר dec. 1 a . תור
תּוֹרִין Chald. noun masc., pl. of [תּוֹר] dec. 1 a תור
תּוֹרִישׁ[o] Hiph. fut. 2 pers. sing. masc. . . ירשׁ
תּוֹרִישׁוּ[p] id. fut. 2 pers. pl. masc. . . . ירשׁ
תּוֹרִישֵׁמוֹ id. fut. 3 pers. sing. fem., suff. 3 pers. pl. m. ירשׁ
תּוֹרִישֵׁנִי וְ id. fut. 2 pers. sing. masc., suff. 1 pers. s. ירשׁ
תּוֹרֶךָ[s] noun m. s., suff. 2 pers. s. m. fr. תּוֹר d. 1 a תור
תּוֹרְךָ[t] וְ Hiph. fut. 3 pers. sing. fem. [תּוֹרֶה], suff. 2 pers. sing. masc. (§ 25. No. 2 e) . ירה
תּוֹרֵם id. fut. 2 pers. sing. masc., suff. 3 p. pl. m. ירה
תּוּרַק[u] Hoph. fut. 3 pers. sing. fem. . . . רוק
תִּוָּרֵשׁ Niph. fut. 2 pers. sing. masc. . . ירשׁ
תּוֹרַת וְ' noun fem. sing., constr. of תּוֹרָה dec. 10 . ירה
תּוֹרֹת[x] id. pl., comp. תּוֹרוֹת . . . . ירה

תּוֹרֹתָו id. pl., suff. 3 pers. sing. masc. . . ירה
תּוֹרָתִי וְ' id. sing., suff. 1 pers. sing. . . ירה
תּוֹרֹתָי / תּוֹרֹתַי[y] וְ } id. pl., suff. 1 pers. sing. . . . ירה
תּוֹרֹתָיו[z] [a]וְ' id. pl., suff. 3 pers. sing. masc. . ירה
תּוֹרָתֶךָ / תּוֹרָתְךָ וְ' } id. sing., suff. 2 pers. sing. masc. . ירה
תּוֹשָׁב וְ' noun masc. sing. dec. 2 b . . ישׁב
תּוֹשַׁב[b] id., constr. st. . . . . . ישׁב
תּוֹשֶׁב[c] וַ Hiph. fut. 2 pers. sing. masc., ap. & conv. [from תּוֹשִׁיב] . . . . ישׁב
תּוּשַׁב[d] Hoph. fut. 3 pers. sing. fem. [for תּוּשַׁב] . ישׁב
תּוֹשָׁבִים וְ noun masc., pl. of תּוֹשָׁב, q. v. . . ישׁב
תּוּשַּׁד[e] Hoph. fut. 2 pers. sing. masc. . . שׁדד
תּוֹשִׁיבֵנִי[f] Hiph. fut. 2 pers. sing. masc., suff. 1 pers. sing. ישׁב
תּוּשִׁיָּה וְ' noun fem. sing. . . . . ישׁה
תּוֹשִׁיעַ [g]וְ' Hiph. fut. 2 pers. sing. masc., or (Job 40. 14) 3 pers. sing. fem. . . . ישׁע
תּוֹשִׁיעוּן[h] id. fut. 2 pers. pl. masc. with parag. ן . ישׁע
תּוֹשִׁיעֵנוּ[i] id. fut. 2 pers. sing. masc., suff. 1 pers. pl. ישׁע
תּוֹשִׁיעֵנִי[k] וְ' id. fut. 3 pers. sing. fem., suff. 1 pers. sing. ישׁע
תִּוָּשַׁע Niph. fut. 3 pers. sing. fem. . . . ישׁע
תּוֹשַׁע וַ Hiph. fut. 3 pers. sing. fem., ap. from תּוֹשִׁיעַ ישׁע
תִּוָּשֵׁעוּן[l] Niph. fut. 2 pers. pl. masc., ן parag. [for תִּוָּשְׁעוּן, comp. § 10. rem. 4] . . ישׁע
תִּוָּשֵׁעִי[m] id. fut. 2 pers. s. f. [for תִּוָּשְׁעִי, comp. § 8. r. 7] ישׁע
תּוֹתָח[kk] noun masc. sing. . . . . יתח
תּוֹתִירוּ Hiph. fut. 2 pers. pl. masc. . . יתר
תּוֹתַר[n] Hiph. fut. 2 pers. sing. masc. ap. [for תּוֹתֶר comp. § 19. rem. 2, from תּוֹתִיר] . . יתר
תִּזְבַּח Kal fut. 2 pers. sing. masc. . . זבח
תִּזְבָּחֵהוּ[o] וַ id. fut. 3 pers. sing. fem., suff. 3 pers. sing. masc. (§ 16. rem. 12); ·וַ conv. . . זבח
תִּזְבָּחֻהוּ[p] id. fut. 2 pers. pl. masc., suff. 3 pers. s. masc. זבח
תִּזְבָּחוּ / תִּזְבְּחוּ } id. fut. 2 pers. pl. masc. (§ 8. rem. 15) זבח
תִּזְבָּחִים[q] וַ id. fut. 2 pers. sing. fem. [תִּזְבְּחִי], suff. 3 pers. pl. masc. (§ 16. rem. 12); ·וַ conv. זבח
תִּזְבָּחֶנּוּ[r] id. fut. 2 pers. s. masc., suff. 3 pers. s. masc. זבח
תָּזִדוּ[s] וַ Hiph. fut. 2 pers. pl. masc.; ·וַ conv. . זוד
תָּזוּב[t] Kal fut. 3 pers. sing. fem. . . . זוב
תְּזוּרֶהָ[u] Kal fut. 3 pers. s. fem. [תָּזוּר], suff. 3 p. s. fem. זור
תִּזְכֶּה[x] Kal fut. 2 pers. sing. masc. . . זכה
תִּזְכּוֹר Kal fut. 2 pers. sing. masc. (§ 8. rem. 18) . זכר
תַּזְכִּירוּ Hiph. fut. 2 pers. pl. masc. . . זכר
תִּזָּכֵר[y] Niph. fut. 3 pers. sing. fem. (denom. of זָכָר) זכר

---

[a] Ps. 66. 12. [b] Ps. 31. 5. [c] 2 Ch. 23. 13. [d] Pr. 11. 15. [e] De. 7. 25. [ee] Ge. 24. 46. [f] Le. 12. 6. [g] Ps. 130. 4. [h] 1 Ki. 2. 6. [i] Is. 14. 15. [k] Ps. 55. 24. [kk] Job 41. 21. [l] Jos. 2. 15. [m] Ne. 9. 13. [n] Ca. 1. 11. [o] Jos. 17. 18. [p] Nu. 33. 55. [q] Ex. 15. 9. [r] Job 13. 26. [s] Ps. 74. 19. [t] Ps. 45. 5. [u] Ca. 1. 3. [x] Is. 24. 5. [y] Eze. 44. 24. [z] Ex. 18. 16. [a] Ps. 105. 45. [b] Le. 22. 10. [c] 2 Ki. 17. 26. [d] Is. 44. 26. [e] Is. 33. 1. [f] Ps. 4. 9. [g] 2 Ch. 20. 9. [h] Ju. 6. 31. [i] Jos. 22. 22. [k] Ps. 44. 7; 138. 7. [l] Is. 30. 15. [m] Je. 4. 14. [n] Ge. 49. 4. [o] 1 Sa. 28. 24. [p] Le. 19. 5. [q] Eze. 16. 20. [r] De. 15. 21. [s] De. 1. 43. [t] Le. 15. 25. [u] Job 39. 15. [x] Ps. 51. 6. [y] Ex. 34. 19.

Word	Analysis	Root
תִּזָּכֵר[a]	id. fut. 3 pers. sing. fem. . . .	זכר
תִּזְכֹּר / תִּזְכָּר־[b]	id. fut. 2 pers. sing. masc. (§ 8. rem. 18)	זכר
תִּזְכְּרוּ	id. fut. 2 pers. pl. masc. . . .	זכר
תִּזָּכְרִי	Niph. fut. 2 p. s. f. [for תִּזָּכֵרִי comp. § 8. r. 15]	זכר
תִּזְכְּרִי	Kal fut. 2 pers. sing. fem. . . .	זכר
תִּזָּכַרְןָ / תִּזָּכַרְנָה	Niph. fut. 3 pers. pl. fem. (comp. § 8. rem. 16, & § 9. rem. 4) . .	זכר
תִּזְכְּרֶנּוּ[c]	Kal fut. 2 pers. sing. masc., suff. 3 pers. s. m.	זכר
תִזְכְּרֵנִי[d]	וְ id. with suff. 1 pers. sing. . . .	זכר
תִּזַּל[e]	Kal fut. 3 pers. sing. fem. . . .	נזל
תֵּזְלִי[f]	Kal fut. 2 pers. s. f. [for תֵּאזְלִי § 19. r. 3]	אזל
תִּזְמֹר[g]	Kal fut. 2 pers. sing. masc. . . .	זמר
תִּזֶן	וַ Kal fut. 3 pers. sing. fem., ap. from תִּזְנֶה	זנה
תַּזְנֶה[h]	וַ Hiph. fut. 3 pers. sing. fem.; וַ conv. .	זנה
תִּזְנֶה	ו׳ Kal fut. 3 pers. sing. fem.; וַ id. .	זנה
תַּזְנוּתֶיהָ	noun fem. pl., suff. 3 p. s. f. fr. [תַּזְנוּת] d. 1b	זנה
תַזְנוּתַיִךְ[i] / תַּזְנוּתַיִךְ[k]	ו׳ id. pl., suff. 2 pers. sing. fem. . .	זנה
תַּזְנוּתָךְ[l]	id. sing., suff. 2 pers. sing. fem. (read תַּזְנוּתֵךְ; K. תַּזְנוּתַיִךְ (q. v.) . . .	זנה
תַּזְנוּתֵךְ[m]	id. sing., suff. 2 pers. sing. fem. . .	זנה
תַּזְנוּתָם[n]	id. sing., suff. 3 pers. pl. masc. (§ 4. rem. 2)	זנה
תִּזְנַח	[o] ו׳ Kal fut. 2 pers. sing. masc.; וַ conv.	זנח
תִּזְנִי[p]	[q] ו׳ Kal fut. 2 pers. sing. fem.; or (Je. 3. 6) 3 pers. s. f. for תִּזְנֶה (§ 24. rem. 18); וּ id.	זנה
תִּזְנִים[r]	וַ id. fut. 2 pers. s. f., suff. 3 p. pl. m.; וַ id.	זנה
תִּזְנֶינָה[s]	ו׳ id. fut. 3 pers. pl. fem.; וַ id. .	זנה
תַזְנֻתַיִךְ[t]	וְ defect. for תַּזְנוּתַיִךְ (q. v.) . .	זנה
תַּזְנֻתֵךְ[u]	defect. for תַּזְנוּתֵךְ (q. v.) . .	זנה
תִּזְעַק / תִּזְעָק	ו׳ Kal fut. 3 p. sing. fem., or (Je. 30. 15) 2 pers. sing. masc. (§ 8. r. 15); וַ conv.	זעק
תִּזְרֶה[y]	Kal fut. 2 pers. sing. masc. . . .	זרה
תִּזְרַח[z]	Kal fut. 3 pers. sing. fem. . . .	זרח
תַּזְרִיעַ[a]	Hiph. fut. 3 pers. sing. fem. . .	זרע
תִּזְרֵם	Kal fut. 2 pers. sing. masc. (תִּזְרֶה), suff. 3 pers. pl. masc. (§ 24. rem. 21)	זרה
תְּזַרֵנִי[b]	וַ Piel fut. 2 pers. sing. masc., suff. 1 pers. sing. for תְּאַזְּרֵנִי (§ 19. rem. 10); וַ conv.	אזר
תִּזָּרֵעַ[c]	Niph. fut. 3 pers. sing. fem. . . .	זרע
תִּזְרַע / תִּזְרָע	Kal fut. 2 pers. sing. masc. (§ 8. rem. 15)	זרע
תִּזְרָעוּ / תִּזְרְעוּ[d]	id. fut. 2 pers. pl. masc. . .	זרע
תִּזְרָעֶנּוּ[e]	id. fut. 3 p. s. f., suff. 3 p. s. m. (§ 16. r. 12)	זרע
תִּזְרֹק	Kal fut. 2 pers. sing. masc. . . .	רק
תַּחְבִּא[f]	וַ Hiph. fut. 3 pers. sing. fem.; וַ conv. .	בא
תֵּחָבֵא[g]	Niph. fut. 2 pers. sing. masc. . . .	בא
תַּחְבֹּט[h]	ו׳ Kal fut. 2 pers. sing. masc., or 3 pers. sing. fem. (§ 13. rem. 5); וַ conv. . .	בט
תַּחְבֹּל[k] / תַּחֲבֹל	Kal fut. 2 pers. sing. masc. (§ 13. rem. 5)	בל
תְּחַבֵּל[l]	Piel fut. 3 pers. sing. fem. . . .	בל
תַּחְבֻּלוֹת	noun fem., pl. of [תַּחְבּוּלָה] dec. 10	בל
תְּחַבֵּק[m]	וּ Piel fut. 2 pers. sing. masc.; וּ bef. (:)	בק
תְּחַבְּקֶנָּה[n]	id. id., suff. 3 pers. sing. fem. . .	בק
תְּחַבְּקֵנִי	id. fut. 3 pers. sing. fem., suff. 1 pers. sing.	בק
תַּחֲבֹשׁ[o]	וַ Kal fut. 3 pers. sing. fem.; וַ conv. .	בש
תָּחֹג	Kal fut. 2 pers. sing. masc. . . .	גג
תְּחָגֵּהוּ[p]	the foll. with suff. 3 pers. sing. masc.	גג
תָּחֹגּוּ[q]	Kal fut. 2 pers. pl. masc. (§ 18. rem. 5)	גג
תַּחְגֹּר[r]	Kal fut. 2 pers. sing. masc. (§ 13. rem. 5)	גר
תַּחְגְּרוּ[s]	וַ id. fut. 2 pers. pl. masc. (§ 13. r. 6); וַ conv.	גר
תַּחְגֹּרְנָה[t]	id. fut. 3 pers. pl. fem. . . .	גר
תֶּחַד[u]	Kal fut. 2 pers. sing. masc., or 3 pers. s. fem.	חד
תְּחַדֵּהוּ[x]	Piel fut. 2 pers. sing. masc., suff. 3 pers. s. m.	דה
תֶּחְדַּל[y] / תֶּחְדָּל	[a] ו׳ id. fut. 2 pers. sing. masc., or 3 pers. s. f. (§ 8. r. 15, & § 13. r. 5); וַ conv.	דל
תְּחַדֵּשׁ[b]	[c] וּ Piel fut. 2 pers. sing. masc.; וּ bef. (:)	דש
תָּחוּ	pr. name masc., see תּוֹחַ . . .	וח
תְּחוֹלֵל[d]	[e] [f] וַתְּ׳, וּ׳ Pilel fut. 2 pers. sing. masc., or 3 pers. sing. fem.; וּ bef. (:); וַ conv.	ול
תְּחוֹלֶלְכֶם[g]	id. fut. 3 pers. s. fem. with suff. 2 pers. pl. m.	ול
תָּחוֹס / תָּחוֹס[h]	Kal fut. 3 pers. sing. fem. (§ 21. rem. 3 & 7) . . .	וס
תְּחוֹת	Chald. prep., with suff. תְּחֹתוֹהִי .	חת
תַּחַז[i]	וַ Kal fut. 3 p. s. f. for תֹּאחַז (§ 19. r. 5); וַ conv.	חז
תֶּחֱז[k]	וְ Kal fut. 3 p. s. f., ap. for the foll. (§ 24. r. 3)	זה
תֶּחֱזֶה[l]	id. fut. 2 pers. sing. masc. . .	זה
תֶּחֱזוּ	id. fut. 2 pers. pl. masc. . . .	זה
תֶּחֱזֶינָה	id. fut. 3 pers. pl. fem. . . .	זה
תַּחֲזֵק[m] / תַּחֲזֶק־[n]	וַ Hiph. fut. 3 pers. sing. fem. ap. [for תַּחֲזִיק § 11. rem. 7]; וַ conv.	זק
תְּחַזֵּק[o]	Piel fut. 2 pers. sing. masc. . .	זק
תֶּחֱזַק	[p] ו׳ Kal fut. 3 pers. sing. fem.; וַ conv.	זק
תֶּחֶזְקוּ	id. fut. 2 pers. pl. masc. . .	זק
תֶּחֱזַקְנָה	id. fut. 3 pers. pl. fem. . . .	זק
תַּחֲטָא	וַ defect. for תַּחֲטִיא q. v.; וַ conv. .	טא
תֶּחֱטָא	Kal fut. 3 pers. sing. fem. . . .	טא
תֶּחֱטָא[q]	ו׳ id. fut. 2 pers. sing. masc.; וַ conv. .	טא

[a] Eze. 25. 10. [b] Ps. 79. 8. [c] Ps. 8. 5. [d] Job 14. 13. [e] De. 32. 2. [f] Je. 2. 36. [g] Le. 25. 3, 4. [h] 2 Ch. 21. 13.
[i] Eze. 23. 29, 35. [k] Eze. 16. 15. [l] Eze. 16. 25. [m] Eze. 16. 29. [n] Eze. 23. 8. [o] La. 3. 17. [p] Ho. 3. 3.
[q] Eze. 16. 15, 16, 17, 26, 28. [r] Eze. 16. 28. [s] Ho. 4. 13, 14. [t] Eze. 23. 3. [u] Eze. 16. 22. [x] Eze. 16. 26. [y] Eze. 5. 2.
[z] Ps. 104. 22. [a] Le. 12. 2. [b] 2 Sa. 22. 40. [c] De. 29. 22. [d] Je. 4. 3. [e] Is. 17. 10. [f] 2 Ki. 6. 29. [g] Job 5. 21.
[h] De. 24. 20. [i] Ru. 2. 17. [k] De. 24. 17. [l] Mi. 2. 10. [m] Pr. 5. 20. [n] Pr. 4. 8. [o] 2 Ki. 4. 24.
[p] Ex. 12. 14. [q] Le. 23. 39, 41. [r] Ps. 76. 11. [s] De. 1. 41. [t] Ps. 65. 13. [u] Ge. 49. 6; Is. 14. 20.
[x] Ps. 21. 7. [y] Job 14. 7. [z] De. 23. 23. [a] Ru. 1. 18. [b] Job 10. 17. [c] Ps. 104. 30. [d] Pr. 25. 23.
[e] Job 35. 14. [f] Ps. 90. 2. [g] Is. 51. 2. [h] Is. 13. 18. [i] 2 Sa. 20. 9. [k] Mi. 4. 11. [l] Ex. 18. 21.
[m] 2 Ki. 4. 27. [n] 2 Ki. 4. 8. [o] Job 4. 3. [p] Ex. 12. 33. [q] 1 Sa. 19. 5; Job 5. 24. [r] Eze. 28. 16.

תֶּחֶטְאוּ / תֶּחֶטְאוּ } id. fut. 2 pers. pl. masc. (§ 8. rem. 15) חטא

תְּחַטְּאֵנִי[a] Piel fut. 2 pers. sing. masc., suff. 1 pers. sing. חטא

תַּחֲטִיא[b] Hiph. fut. 2 pers. sing. masc. . חטא

תְּחִי ,וַתְּ'[c]וּ' Kal fut. 3 pers. sing. fem., ap. for תִּחְיֶה (§ 24. rem. 3 e) ; וּ bef. (:) ; ·וַ conv. חיה

תְּחַיֶּה Piel fut. 2 pers. sing. masc., or (Ec. 7. 12) 3 pers. sing. fem. . . . . חיה

תִּחְיֶה Kal fut. 2 pers. sing. masc., or (Jos. 6. 17) 3 pers. sing. fem. (§ 13. rem. 13) . חיה

תִּחְיוּ id. fut. 2 pers. pl. masc. . . . . חיה

תְּחַיּוּן[d] Piel fut. 2 pers. pl. masc. with parag. ן . חיה

תִּחְיוּן Kal fut. 2 p. pl. m. with parag. ן (§ 13. r. 13) חיה

תִּחְיִי[e] id. fut. 2 pers. sing. fem. . . . חיה

תְּחַיֶּיןָ[f] וַ Piel fut. 2 pers. pl. fem., or 3 pers. pl. fem. (§ 8. rem. 16) ; ·וַ conv. . . חיה

תְּחַיֶּינָה[g] id. fut. 2 pers. pl. fem. . . . חיה

תִּחְיֶינָה[h] Kal fut. 3 pers. pl. fem. (§ 13. rem. 13) . חיה

תְּחַיֵּנוּ Piel fut. 2 pers. sing. masc., suff. 1 pers. pl. חיה

תְּחַיֵּנוּ[i] id. with suff. (Kh. 'נוּ 1 p. pl. (K. 'נִי 1 p. s. חיה

תָּחִיל [k]'וְ Hiph. fut. 3 pers. sing. fem. . . חול

תָּחִיל[l] Kh. תָּחִיל, K. תָּחוּל Hiph. or Kal fut. 3 p. s. f. חול

תָּחִילוּ[m] Hiph. fut. 2 pers. pl. masc. . . . חול

תְּחִילִין[n] id. fut. 2 pers. s. f. with parag. ן (§ 8. r. 17) חול

תְּחַיֵּנִי Piel fut. 2 pers. s. m., or (Job 33. 4) 3 pers. s. f. (תְּחַיֶּה) with suff. 1 p. s. (§ 24. r. 21) חיה

תְּחַכֶּה[o] Piel fut. 2 pers. sing. masc. . . חכה

תֶּחְכַּם[p] Kal fut. 2 pers. sing. masc. (§ 13. rem. 5) חכם

תַּחְכְּמֹנִי pr. name masc. . . . . . חכם

תְּחַכְּמֵנִי[q] Piel fut. 2 pers. s. m. [תְּחַכֵּם], suff. 1 pers. s. חכם

תָּחֵל[r] Hiph. fut. 2 pers. sing. masc. . . . חלל

תָּחֶל[s] וַ Hiph. fut. 3 pers. s. f., ap. fr. תָּחִיל ; ·וַ conv. חול

תָּחֶל וַ Hiph. fut. 3 pers. sing. fem., acc. drawn back by conv. ·וַ for תָּחֵל . . . חלל

תָּחֶל[t] וַ Kal fut. 3 pers. s. f. ap. [fr. תָּחוּל] ; ·וַ conv. חול

תֵּחֵל[u] Niph. fut. 3 pers. s. f. [for תֵּחַל § 18. r. 7] חלל

תַּחֲלֻאֶיהָ[x] the foll. with suff. 3 pers. sing. fem. חלא

תַּחֲלֻאִים[y] noun masc., pl. of [תַּחֲלוּא] dec. 1 b . חלא

תְּחַלּוּ[z] Kal fut. 2 pers. pl. masc. . . . . חלל

תַּחֲלוּאֵי[a] noun masc. pl. constr. from [תַּחֲלוּא] d. 1 b חלא

תַּחֲלוּאָיְכִי[b] id. pl., suff. 2 pers. sing. fem. (§ 4. rem. 4) חלא

תַּחֲלִימֵנִי[c] וְ Hiph. fut. 2 pers. sing. m., suff. 1 pers. s. חלם

תְּחִלֶּינָה[d] וַ Hiph. fut. 3 pers. pl. fem. ; ·וַ conv. חלל

תַּחֲלִיף[e] Hiph. fut. 3 pers. sing. fem. . . חלף

תַּחֲלִיפֵם[f] id. fut. 2 pers. sing. masc., suff. 3 pers. pl. m. חלף

תְּחַלֵּל Piel fut. 2 pers. sing. masc. . . חלל

תְּחַלְּלֶהָ[g] וַ id. id., suff. 3 pers. s. f. (§ 10. r. 7) ; ·וַ conv. חלל

תְּחַלֶּלְנָה[h] וַ id. fut. 2 pers. pl. fem. ; ·וַ id. . חלל

תְּחַלְּלוּ 'וַ id. fut. 2 pers. pl. masc. ; ·וַ id. . חלל

תְּחַלְּלֶנּוּ[k] id. fut. 2 pers. sing. masc., suff. 3 pers. s. m. חלל

תַּחֲלֵף[l] וַ Hiph. fut. 2 pers. sing. masc. ap. [from תַּחֲלִיף] ; ·וַ conv. . . . חלף

תַּחֲלְפֵהוּ[m] Kal fut. 3 pers. sing. fem. [תַּחֲלֹף], suff. 3 pers. sing. masc. (§ 13. rem. 5) . חלף

תַּחֲלֹץ[n] Kal fut. 2 pers. sing. masc. . . . חלץ

תֵּחָלְצוּ[o] Niph. fut. 2 pers. pl. masc. . . . חלץ

תֵּחָלֵק[p] Niph. fut. 3 pers. sing. fem. . . . חלק

תְּחַלֵּק[q] Piel fut. 2 pers. sing. masc. . . . חלק

תְּחֻלָּק[r] Pual fut. 3 pers. sing. fem. . . . חלק

תַּחְלְקוּ[s] Kal fut. 2 pers. pl. masc. (§ 13. rem. 5 & 6) חלק

תַּחְלְקֵם[t] וַ id. fut. 2 p. s. m., suff. 3 p. pl. m. ; ·וַ conv. חלק

תְּחִלַּת noun fem. sing., constr. of תְּחִלָּה dec. 10 חלל

תֵּחַם[u] Kal fut. 3 pers. sing. fem. (§ 18. rem. 6) חמם

תַּחְמֹד Kal fut. 2 pers. sing. masc. (§ 13. rem. 5) חמד

תַּחְמֹל[x] 'וַ Kal fut. 2 pers. sing. masc., or (Ex. 2. 6) 3 pers. sing. fem. (§ 13. rem. 5) ; ·וַ conv. חמל

תַּחְמְלוּ / תַּחְמֹלוּ[y] } id. fut. 2 pers. pl. masc. (§ 8. rem. 15) . חמל

תְּחַמֵּם[z] Piel fut. 3 pers. sing. fem. . . . חמם

תַּחְמְסוּ Kal fut. 2 pers. pl. m. [for תַּחְמְסוּ § 8. rem. 15, & § 13. rem. 5] . . חמס

תַּחְמְרָה[a] וַ Kal fut. 3 pers. sing. fem. with parag. ה (§ 8. rem. 13, & § 13. rem. 5) ; ·וַ conv. חמר

תָּחֹן[b] Kal fut. 2 pers. sing. masc. . . . חנן

תַּחֲנֶה[c] Kal fut. 3 pers. sing. fem. . . . חנה

תְּחִנָּה noun fem. sing. dec. 10, pr. name . חנן

תַּחֲנוּ[d] Kal fut. 2 pers. pl. masc. . . . חנה

תַּחֲנוּנוֹתָי[nn] noun masc. with pl. fem. term. & suff. 1 pers. sing. from [תַּחֲנוּן] dec. 1 b . חנן

תַּחֲנוּנָי / תַּחֲנוּנַי } id. pl. masc. with suff. 1 pers. sing. חנן

תַּחֲנוּנֵי id. pl. masc., constr. st. . . . חנן

תַּחֲנוּנָיו[e] id. pl. masc. with suff. 3 pers. sing. masc. . חנן

תַּחֲנוּנֶיךָ[f] id. pl. masc. with suff. 2 pers. sing. masc. חנן

תַּחֲנוּנִים 'וְ id. pl. masc., abs. st. . . חנן

תַּחֲנוּנֵינוּ[g] id. pl. masc. with suff. 1 pers. pl. . חנן

תַּחֲנִיפוּ[h] Hiph. fut. 2 pers. pl. masc. . . . חנף

תַּחֲנִיפִי[i] וַ id. fut. 2 pers. sing. fem. ; ·וַ conv. חנף

[a] Ps. 51. 9. [b] De. 24. 4. [c] Ge. 45. 27. [d] Ex. 1. 22. [e] 2 Ki. 4. 7. [f] Ex. 1. 17, 18. [g] Eze. 13. 18. [h] Eze. 13. 19. [i] Ps. 71. 20. [k] Zec. 9. 5. [l] Eze. 30. 16. [m] Je. 5. 22. [n] Is. 45. 10. [nn] Ps. 86. 6. [o] 2 Ki. 9. 3. [p] Pr. 19. 20. [q] Ps. 119. 98. [r] De. 16. 9. [s] Ps. 97. 4. [t] Je. 51. 29. [u] Le. 21. 9. [x] De. 29. 21. [y] Je. 16. 4. [z] Eze. 9. 6. [a] Je. 14. 18. [b] Ps. 103. 3. [c] Is. 38. 16. [d] Ge. 41. 54. [e] Job 29. 20. [f] Ps. 102. 27. [g] Ex. 20. 25. [h] Eze. 13. 19. [i] Je. 34. 16. [k] De. 28. 30. [l] Ge. 31. 41. [m] Job 20. 24. [n] Is. 20. 2. [o] Nu. 32. 20. [p] Nu. 26. 53, 56. [q] Ps. 68. 13. [r] Am. 7. 17. [s] 2 Sa. 19. 30. [t] Ne. 9. 22. [u] Eze. 24. 11. [x] Ex. 2. 6. [y] Eze. 9. 5. [z] Job 39. 14. [a] Ex. 2. 3. [b] Ps. 59. 6. [c] Ps. 27. 3. [d] Ex. 14. 2. [e] Da. 9. 17. [f] Da. 9. 23. [g] Da. 9. 18. [h] Nu. 35. 33. [i] Je. 3. 2.

תְּחָנֵּם[a] Kal fut. 2 pers. sing. masc. (תָּחֹן), suff. 3 pers. pl. masc. (§ 18. rem. 5) . . . חנן

תֶּחֱנַף[b], וַ' תֶּחֱנַף[c] } Kal fut. 3 pers. sing. fem. (§ 8. rem. 15); וַ· conv. . . . } חנף

תְּחִנַּת noun fem. sing., constr. of תְּחִנָּה dec. 10 . חנן

תְּחִנָּתוֹ id. with suff. 3 pers. sing. masc. . . חנן

תַּחֲנֹתַי[d] noun fem. pl., suff. 1 pers. sing. [fr. תַּחֲנָה; for תַּחֲנֹתַי § 4. rem. 2] . . . חנה

תְּחִנָּתִי noun fem. sing., suff. 1 p. s. fr. תְּחִנָּה d. 10 חנן

תְּחִנֹּתֵיהֶם[e] id. pl., suff. 3 pers. pl. masc. . . חנן

תְּחִנָּתְךָ[f] id. sing., suff. 2 pers. sing. masc. . . חנן

תְּחִנַּתְכֶם[g] id. sing., suff. 2 pers. pl. masc. . . חנן

תְּחִנָּתָם id. sing., suff. 3 pers. pl. masc. . . חנן

תְּחִנָּתֵנוּ[h] id. sing., suff. 1 pers. pl. . . . חנן

תָּחֹס[i], וַ תָּחָס } Kal fut. 3 pers. s. f., ap. & conv. fr. תָּחוּס the acc. drawn back by conv. וַ . } חוס

תֶּחְסֶה[k] Kal fut. 2 pers. sing. masc. (§ 13. rem. 5) חסה

תַּחְסֹם[l] Kal fut. 2 pers. sing. masc. (§ 13. rem. 5) חסס

תֶּחְסַר, תֶּחְסָר } Kal fut. 3 pers. sing. fem. (§ 8. rem. 5), 1 Ki. 17. 14; Pr. 13. 25; or 2 p. m. De. 8. 9 } חסר

וַ תְּחַסְּרֵהוּ[m] Piel fut. 2 pers. sing. masc. [תְּחַסֵּר], suff. 3 pers. sing. masc.; וַ· conv. . . חסר

תַּחְפְּזוּ[n] Kal fut. 2 pers. pl. masc. (§ 13. rem. 5 & 6) חפז

תַּחְפִּירִי[o] Kal fut. 2 pers. sing. fem. (§ 13. rem. 5) חפר

תַּחְפַּנְחֵס, תַּחְפַּנְחֵס, תַּחְפְּנֵס pr. name of a city in Egypt, *Daphne*, near Pelusium.

תַּחְפְּנֵיס pr. name of an Egyptian queen, 1 Ki. 11. 19, 20.

תַּחְפֹּץ Kal fut. 2 pers. sing. masc. (§ 13. rem. 5) חפץ

וְ תַּחְפְּרוּ[p] Kal fut. 2 pers. pl. masc. (§ 13. rem. 5 & 6) חפר

תַּחְפְּשֶׂנָּה[q] Kal fut. 2 pers. sing. fem., suff. 3 pers. sing. fem. (§ 13. rem. 5) . . . חפש

וְ תֵּחָץ[r] Niph. fut. 3 pers. sing. fem., ap. [fr. תֵּחָצֶה] חצה

תַּחְצֹב[s] Kal fut. 2 pers. sing. masc. (§ 13. rem. 5) חצב

תַּחְקְרוּן[t] Kal fut. 2 pers. pl. masc., ן parag. (§ 13. rem. 5 & 6, & § 8. rem. 17) . . חקר

תַּחְרָא noun masc. sing. . . . . חרה

תֶּחֱרַב[u], תֶּחֱרַב[x] } Kal fut. 3 pers. sing. fem. (§ 8. rem. 15) חרב

תֶּחֱרַבְנָה id. fut. 3 pers. pl. fem. . . . חרב

תַּחֲרִים[y] Hiph. fut. 2 pers. sing. masc. . . חרם

תַּחֲרִימוּ id. fut. 2 pers. pl. masc. . . . חרם

תַּחֲרִימֵם[z] id. fut. 2 pers. s. masc., suff. 3 pers. pl. masc. חרם

תַּחֲרִישׁ[a] Hiph. fut. 2 pers. sing. masc. . . חרש

תַּחֲרִישׁוּן[b] id. fut. 2 pers. pl. masc. with parag. ן . חרש

תַּחֲרִישִׁי[c] id. fut. 2 pers. sing. fem. . . . חרש

וְ תַּחְרֵעַ pr. name masc., see תַּאְרֵעַ.

תֶּחֱרַף[d] Kal fut. 3 pers. sing. fem. [for תֶּחֱרַף § 8. r. 15] חרף

תֶּחֱרַץ[e] Kal fut. 2 pers. s. masc. [for תֶּחֱרַץ § 8. r. 15] חרץ

תַּחֲרֵשׁ[f] Hiph. fut. 2 pers. sing. masc. ap. [fr. תַּחֲרִישׁ] חרש

תַּחֲרֹשׁ Kal fut. 2 pers. sing. masc. . . . חרש

תֵּחָרֵשׁ Niph. fut. 3 pers. sing. fem. . . . חרש

תֶּחֱרשׁ, תֶּחֱרָשׁ } Kal fut. 2 pers. sing. masc. (§ [illegible]. rem. 15) חרש

תַּחֲרִשׁוּן[g] defect. for תַּחֲרִישׁוּן (q. v.) . . . חרש

תֶּחֱרַשְׁנָה[h] Kal fut. 3 pers. pl. fem. . . . חרש

תַּחַשׁ, תָּחַשׁ[i] masc. dec. 6 d.—I. *badger*; עוֹר תַּחַשׁ עוֹרוֹת תְּחָשִׁים *badgers' skins.*—II. pr. name masc Ge. 22. 24.

וַ תָּחַשׁ[k] Kal fut. 3 pers. sing. fem., dag. forte impl. [for תָּחֻשׁ § 21. rem. 24] . . . חוש

תֵּחָשֵׁב, וַ'[m] תֵּחָשֶׁב[l] } Niph. fut. 3 pers. sing. fem. (§ 9. rem. 3) חשב

תַּחְשֹׁב[n] Kal fut. 3 pers. sing. fem. (§ 13. rem. 5 & 6) חשב

תַּחְשְׁבוּ, תַּחְשֹׁבוּ[o] } id. fut. 2 pers. pl. masc. (v. i. & § 8. rem. 15) . . . . } חשב

וַ תְּחַשְּׁבֵהוּ[p] Piel fut. 2 p. s. m., suff. 3 p. s. m.; וַ· conv. חשב

תַּחְשְׁבוּן[q] id. fut. 2 p. pl. m. with parag. ן (§ 10. r. 4) חשב

וְ תַּחְשְׁבֵנִי[r] Kal fut. 2 pers. sing. masc., suff. 1 pers. sing. (§ 13. rem. 5 & 6); וַ· conv. . חשב

תַּחְשְׁבֻנִי[s] id. fut. 2 pers. pl. masc., suff. 1 pers. sing. חשב

תֶּחֱשֶׁה Kal fut. 2 pers. sing. masc. . . חשה

תַּחְשׂוֹךְ[t] Kal fut. 2 pers. s. masc. (§ 8. r. 18, & § 13. r. 5) חשך

תְּחָשִׁים noun masc., pl. of תַּחַשׁ dec. 6 d . . תחש

תַּחְשֹׂךְ[u] Kal fut. 2 pers. sing. masc. (§ 13. rem. 5) חשך

תֶּחְשַׁךְ[x] וַ'[y] Kal fut. 3 pers. sing. f. (§ 13. r. 5); וַ· conv. חשך

תַּחְשְׂכִי[z] Kal fut. 2 p. s. f. (§ 8. r. 15, comp. § 13. r. 6) חשך

תֶּחְשַׁכְנָה[a] Kal fut. 3 pers. sing. fem. (§ 13. rem. 5) חשך

תַּחַת[b], וְ' תַּחַת } adv. & prep., also pr. name . . וח

וְ תַּחֵת[c] Chald. Aph. fut. 2 pers. s. m. (§ 51. r. 1) חת

תֵּחַת, תֵּחַת } Kal fut. 2 pers. sing. masc., or (Is. 51. 6) 3 pers. sing. fem. (§ 18. rem. 6) } תת

תֵּחַת[d] Kal fut. 3 pers. sing. fem. (for תִּנְחַת) . חת

תַּחְתָּו Kh. for תַּחְתָּיו Keri (q. v.) . . וח

תֵּחַתּוּ, תֵּחַתּוּ } Kal fut. 2 pers. pl. masc. (§ 18. rem. 6) . תת

תַּחְתּוֹהִי[e] Ch. prep. (תַּחַת) pl. with suff. 3 pers. s. m. וח

תְּחֹתוֹהִי[f] Ch. prep. (תְּחוֹת) pl. with suff. 3 pers. s. m. וח

תַּחְתּוֹן[g] adj. masc. sing. . . . . וח

תַּחְתַּי, וְ תַּחְתַּי[h] } adv. or prep. (תַּחַת) pl. with suff. 1 pers. sing. . . . . . } וח

---

[a] De. 7. 2. [b] Mi. 4. 11. [c] Je. 3. 1. [d] 2 Ki. 6. 8. [e] 2 Ch. 6. 39. [f] 1 Ki. 9. 3.
[g] Je. 42. 9. [h] Je. 42. 2. [i] Ge. 45. 20. [k] Ps. 91. 4. [l] De. 25. 4. [m] Ps. 8. 6.
[n] De. 20. 3. [o] Is. 54. 4. [p] Is. 1. 29. [q] Pr. 2. 4. [r] Da. 11. 4. [s] De. 8. 9.
[t] Job 32. 11. [u] Is. 34. 10. [x] Je. 26. 9. [y] De. 7. 2. [z] De. 20. 17. [a] Hab. 1. 13.
[b] Job 13. 5. [c] Est. 4. 14. [d] Is. 18. 6. [e] 2 Sa. 5. 24. [f] 1 Sa. 7. 8. [g] Ex. 14. 14.
[h] Mi. 7. 16. [i] Nu. 4. 6, 14. [k] Job 31. 5. [l] Pr. 27. 14. [m] Ps. 106. 31. [n] Ps. 52. 4.
[o] Job 6. 26. [p] Ps. 144. 3. [q] Na. 1. 9. [r] Job 13. 24. [s] Job 19. 15. [t] Pr. 24. 11.
[u] Is. 58. 1. [x] Ec. 12. 2. [y] Ex. 10. 15. [z] Is. 54. 2. [a] Ps. 69. 24. [b] Ge. 49. 25; De. 33. 13.
[c] Ezr. 6. 5. [d] Pr. 17. 10. [e] Da. 4. 11. [f] Da. 4. 9, 18. [g] Jos. 18. 13. [h] Hab. 3. 16, et

תַּחְתֶּיהָ[a] וְ' id. with suff. 3 pers. sing. fem. . . תוח
תַּחְתִּיָּה[b] adj. fem. sing. [from תַּחְתִּי masc.] . . תוח
תַּחְתֵּיהֶם prep. (תַּחַת) pl. with suff. 3 pers. pl. masc. תוח
תַּחְתֵּיהֶן id. with suff. 3 pers. pl. fem. . . תוח
תַּחְתָּיו id. (adv. & prep.), suff. 3 pers. sing. masc. תוח
תַּחְתִּיּוֹת adj. fem., pl. of תַּחְתִּיָּה [from תַּחְתִּי masc.] תוח
תַּחְתֶּיךָ prep. (תַּחַת) pl. with suff. 2 pers. sing. m. תוח
תַּחְתֵּיכֶם id. with suff. 2 pers. pl. masc. . . תוח
תַּחְתִּים חָדְשִׁי pr. name of an unknown region, mentioned only in 2 Sa. 24. 6.
תַּחְתִּיִּם[d] adj. masc. pl. [of תַּחְתִּי] dec. 8f . . תוח
תַּחְתֵּינוּ[e] adv. (תַּחַת), pl. with suff. 1 pers. pl. . תוח
תַּחְתִּית adj. fem. sing. [from תַּחְתִּי masc.] . . תוח
תַּחְתָּם adv. or prep. (תַּחַת) with suff. 3 pers. pl. m. תוח
תַּחְתֹּם[f] וַ Kal fut. 3 pers. s. fem. (§ 13. r. 5); וַ· conv. חתם
תַּחְתֶּנָּה[g] (prep. תַּחַת) with suff. 3 pers. sing. fem. תוח
תַּחְתָּנִי id. with suff. 1 pers. sing. . . . תוח
תַּט Hiph. fut. 2 pers. sing. masc., ap. from תַּטֶּה (§ 25. No. 2b) . . . . נטה
תֵּט וְ' Kal fut. 2 pers. sing. masc., or 3 pers. sing. fem., ap. from תִּטֶּה (§ 25. No. 2b); וַ· conv נטה
תִּטְבְּלֵנִי[h] Kal fut. 2 pers. sing. m. (תִּטְבֹּל), suff. 1 pers. s. טבל
תִּטְבַּע[i] וַ Kal fut. 3 pers. sing. fem.; וַ· conv. . טבע
תַּטֶּה Hiph. fut. 2 pers. sing. masc. (§ 25. No. 2b) נטה
תִּטֶּה[k] Kal fut. 3 pers. sing. fem. (§ 25. No. 2b) נטה
תַּטֵּהוּ[l] וַ Hiph. fut. 3 pers. sing. fem., suff. 3 pers. sing. masc. (§ 24. r. 21, & § 25. No. 2b); וַ· conv. נטה
תִּטְהָר[m] Kal fut. 3 pers. sing. m. [for תִּטְהַר § 8. r. 15] טהר
תִּטְהָרוּ[n] id. fut. 2 pers. pl. masc. [for תִּטְהֲרוּ] . טהר
תִּטְהֲרִי id. fut. 2 pers. sing. fem. . . . טהר
תְּטַהֲרֵם[o] וַ Piel (§ 14. rem. 1) fut. 3 pers. sing. fem., suff. 3 pers. pl. masc.; וַ· conv. . טהר
תִּטְחַן[p] Kal fut. 3 pers. sing. fem. . . . טחן
תִּטְחָנוּ[q] id. fut. 2 pers. pl. masc. [for תִּטְחֲנוּ § 8. r. 15] טחן
תֵּטִיב[r] Hiph. fut. 2 pers. s. m. (better תֵּיטִיב q.v.) יטב
תַּטִּיף[s] Hiph. fut. 2 pers. sing. masc. . . . נטף
תַּטִּיפוּ[t] id. fut. 2 pers. sing. masc. . . . נטף
תַּטְלֵל[u] Chald. Aph. fut. 3 pers. sing. fem. . . טלל
תְּטַמֵּא Piel fut. 2 pers. sing. masc. . . . טמא
תִּטְמָא וַ' Kal fut. 3 pers. sing. fem.; וַ· conv. . טמא
תְּטַמְּאוּ[x] וַ'[y] Piel fut. 2 pers. pl. masc.; וַ· id. . טמא
תִּטַּמָּאוּ / תִּטַּמְּאוּ } Hithpa. fut. 2 pers. pl. m. [for תִּתְטַמְּאוּ § 12. rem. 2, comp. § 8. rem. 15] } טמא
תִּטְמְנֵם[z] וַ Kal fut. 3 pers. sing. fem. [תִּטְמֹן], suff. 3 pers. pl. masc.; וַ· conv. . . . טמן
תִּטַּע Kal fut. 2 pers. sing. masc. . . . נטע

תִּטָּעֶהָ[a] וַ the foll. with suff. 3 pers. sing. fem. (§ 16. rem. 12); וַ· conv. . . . . נטע
תִּטָּעוּ[b] id. fut. 2 pers. pl. masc. [for תִּטְּעוּ § 8. r. 15] נטע
תִּטְּעִי id. fut. 2 pers. sing. fem. . . . נטע
תִּטָּעֵם[c] וַ id. fut. 2 pers. sing. masc., suff. 3 pers. pl. masc. (§ 16. rem. 12); וַ· conv. . . נטע
תִּטָּעֵמוֹ[d] וַ id. id., suff. 3 pers. pl. masc. . . נטע
תִּטֹּף[e] Kal fut. 3 pers. sing. fem. . . . נטף
תִּטְפֹּל[f] וַ Kal fut. 2 pers. sing. masc.; וַ· conv. . טפל
תִּטֹּפְנָה Kal fut. 3 pers. pl. fem. . . . נטף
תִּטֹּר[g] Kal fut. 2 pers. sing. masc. (§ 17. rem. 3) נטר
תִּטֹּשׁ וַ'[h] Kal fut. 2 pers. sing. masc., or (1 Sa. 4. 2) 3 pers. sing. fem.; וַ· conv. . . . נטש
תִּטְּשֵׁנִי[i] id. fut. 2 pers. sing. masc., suff. 1 pers. sing. נטש
תְּיַבֵּב[k] וַ Piel fut. 3 pers. sing. fem.; וַ· conv. . יבב
תְּיַבֵּשׁ[l] / תְּיַבֶּשׁ־[m] } Piel fut. 3 pers. sing. fem. (§ 10. rem. 4) יבש
תִּיבָשׁ / תִּיבַשׁ וַ'[n] } Kal fut. 3 pers. sing. fem. (§ 8. rem. 16); וַ· conv. . . . . } יבש
תְּיַגֵּעַ[o] Piel fut. 2 pers. sing. masc. . . . יגע
תִּיגַע[p] Kal fut. 2 pers. sing. masc. . . . יגע
תְּיַגְּעֵנוּ[q] Piel fut. 3 pers. s. fem. (תְּיַגַּע), suff. 3 p. s. m. יגע
תִּיז. Hiph. *to cut off*, Is. 18. 5.
תִּיטַב[r] וַתִּ', וְ' Kal fut. 3 pers. sing. fem.; וַ· conv. יטב
תֵּיטֶב[s] וַ Hiph. fut. 3 pers. sing. fem., ap. and conv. from תֵּיטִיב . . . . . יטב
תֵּיטְבִי[t] id. fut. 2 pers. sing. masc. . . . יטב
תֵּיטִיב[u] id. fut. 2 p. s. m., or 3 p. s. f. (see also תֵּטִיב) יטב
תֵּיטִיבוּ id. fut. 2 pers. pl. masc. . . . יטב
תְּיֵלִילוּ[x] Hiph. fut. 2 p. pl. m. [for תְּהֵילִילוּ § 20. r. 15] ילל
תֵּימָא וְ' pr. name of a son of Ishmael, Ge. 25. 15, and of his posterity called *Tema* after him.
תֵּימָן noun masc. sing., also pr. name . . ימן
תֵּימָנָה וְ'[y] id. with loc. ה . . . . ימן
תֵּימָנִי patronym., see תֵּימָן . . . . ימן
תֵּינִק[z] וְ Hiph. fut. 3 pers. sing. fem. . . . ינק
תֵּינֶק[a] וַ id. ap. and conv. . . . . ינק
תִּינְקוּ[b] Kal fut. 2 pers. pl. masc. . . . ינק
תִּינְקִי[c] id. fut. 2 pers. sing. fem. [for תִּינָקִי § 8. r. 15] ינק
תְּיַסְּרֵךְ[d] Piel fut. 3 pers. sing. fem. [תְּיַסֵּר], suff. 2 pers. sing. fem. . . . . יסר
תְּיַסְּרֶנּוּ[e] id. fut. 2 pers. sing. m., suff. 3 pers. sing. m. יסר
תְּיַסְּרֵנִי id. id., suff. 1 pers. sing. . . . יסר
תֵּיעָשֶׂה[f] Niph. fut. 3 pers. s. fem. (for תֵּעָשֶׂה § 13. r. 8) עשה
תִּיפִי[g] וַ Kal fut. 2 p. s. fem. (§ 25. No. 2e); וַ· conv. יפה

[a] Job 28. 5. [b] Ps. 86. 13. [c] Je. 28. 13. [d] Ge. 6. 16. [e] 1 Sa. 14. 9; Ps. 47. 4. [f] 1 Ki. 21. 8. [g] Ge. 2. 21. [h] Job 9. 31. [i] 1 Sa. 17. 49. [k] Job 31. 7. [l] 2 Sa. 21. 10. [m] Le. 15. 28. [n] Le. 16. 30. [o] Job 37. 21. [p] Job 31. 10. [q] Is. 3. 15. [r] Ge. 4. 7. [s] Am. 7. 16. [t] Mi. 2. 6. [u] Da. 4. 9. [x] Le. 11. 44. [y] Je. 2. 7. [z] Jos. 2. 6. [a] Ps. 80. 9. [b] Je. 35. 7. [c] Ps. 44. 3. [d] Ex. 15. 17. [e] Job 29. 22. [f] Job 14. 17. [g] Le. 19. 18. [h] 1 Sa. 4. 2. [i] Ps. 27. 9. [k] Ju. 5. 28. [l] Job 15. 30. [m] Pr. 17. 22. [n] 1 Ki. 13. 4. [o] Jos. 7. 8. [p] Pr. 23. 4. [q] Ec. 10. 15. [r] Est. 2. 4, 9; Ps. 69. 32. [s] 2 Ki. 9. 30. [t] Je. 2. 33. [u] Ps. 49. 19; Pr. 15. 2. [x] Is. 65. 14. [y] De. 3. 27. [z] Ex. 2. 7. [a] 1 Sa. 1. 23. [b] Is. 66. 11. [c] Is. 60. 16. [d] Je. 2. 19. [e] Ps. 94. 12. [f] Ex. 25. 31. [g] Eze. 16. 13.

[תִּיצִי] gent. noun 1 Ch. 11. 45, from a place תִּיץ otherwise unknown.

תִּיקַד[a] וַ Kal fut. 3 pers. sing. fem.; ·וַ conv. . — יקד

תִּיקַר Kal fut. 3 pers. sing. fem. . . . — יקר

תִּירָא[b] וְ׳ Kal fut. 2 pers. sing. masc., or (Zec. 9. 5) 3 pers. sing. fem. . . . — ירא

תִּירְאוּ[c] וְ׳, תִּירָאוּ[d] וַ׳ } Kal fut. 2 pers. pl. masc. (§ 8. rem. 15); ·וַ conv. . . . — ירא

תִּירָאוּם[e] id. id., with suff. 3 p. pl. m. (comp. § 16. r. 12) — ירא

תִּירָאוּן id. id. with parag. ן . . . — ירא

תִּירְאִי, תִּירָאִי וַ } id. fut. 2 pers. sing. fem.; ·וַ conv. . — ירא

תִּירָאֻם[f] defect. for תִּירָאוּם (q. v.) . . — ירא

תִּירֶאןָ[g] וַ Kal fut. 3 pers. pl. fem. (§ 8. r. 16); ·וַ conv. — ירא

תִּירוֹשׁ וְ׳ noun masc. sing. dec. 1b . . — ירש

תִּירוֹשִׁי[h] וְ׳[i] id., suff. 1 pers. sing. . . — ירש

תִּירוֹשֵׁךְ[k] id., suff. 2 pers. sing. fem. . . — ירש

תִּירוֹשָׁם[l] וְ id., suff. 3 pers. pl. masc. . — ירש

תִּירְיָא pr. name masc. . . . . — ירא

תִּירָס וְ pr. name of a son of Japhet, Ge. 10. 2; 1 Ch. 1. 5.

תִּירַשׁ[m] Kal fut. 2 pers. sing. masc. (§ 8. rem. 15) — ירש

תִּירַשׁ[n] id. fut. 3 pers. sing. fem. . . . — ירש

תִּירֹשׁ[o] וְ׳[p] defect. for תִּירוֹשׁ (q. v.) . . — ירש

תִּירָשׁוּ[q], תִּירְשׁוּ וַ׳[r] } Kal fut. 2 pers. pl. masc. (§ 8. rem. 15); ·וַ conv. . . . . — ירש

תִּירָשׁוּן[s] id. id. with parag. ן [for תִּירְשׁוּן § 8. rem. 17] — ירש

תִּירֹשֵׁךְ וְ׳ noun masc. sing., suff. 2 pers. sing. fem. from תִּירוֹשׁ dec. 1b . . — ירש

תִּירָשֶׁנּוּ[t] Kal fut. 2 pers. sing. masc. (תִּירַשׁ), suff. 3 pers. sing. masc. (§ 16. rem. 12) . — ירש

תַּיִשׁ[u] [for תַּיִשׁ] masc., pl. תְּיָשִׁים (§ 35. rem. 12) *a he-goat* or *ram*.

תֵּישַׁבְנָה[x] Kh. תֵּישַׁבְנָה, K. תָּשֹׁבְנָה Kal fut. 3 pers. pl. fem. R. ישב or . . . . — שוב

תְּיָשִׁים וּ noun masc., pl. of תַּיִשׁ dec. 6h; וּ bef. (:) — תיש

תִּישַׁמְנָה[y] Kal fut. 3 pers. pl. fem. [for תִּישָׁמְנָה] — ישם

תִּישָׁן[z] Kal fut. 2 pers. sing. masc. . . . — ישן

תְּיַשְּׁנֵהוּ[a] וַ Piel fut. 3 pers. sing. fem. [תְּיַשֵּׁן], suff. 3 pers. sing. masc.; ·וַ conv. . . — ישן

תְּיַשֵּׁר[b] Piel fut. 2 pers. sing. masc. . . . — ישר

תִּישַׁר[c] וַ Kal fut. 3 pers. sing. fem.; ·וַ conv. . — ישר

תַּךְ[d] וַ Hiph. fut. 3 pers. sing. fem., ap. from תַּכֶּה (§ 25. No. 2b); ·וּ id. . . . — נכה

תֹּךְ[e] וָ׳ noun masc. sing.; for וָ see lett. ו . — תכך

תְּכָאֲבוּ[f] Hiph. fut. 2 pers. pl. masc. . . — כאב

תְּכַבֵּד[g] וַ Piel fut. 2 pers. sing. masc.; ·וַ conv. . — כבד

תִּכְבַּד וַ׳ Kal fut. 3 pers. sing. fem.; ·וַ id. . — כבד

תְּכַבְּדוּ[h] Piel fut. 2 pers. pl. masc. . . — כבד

תִּכְבְּדִי[i] וַ Kal fut. 2 pers. sing. fem.; ·וַ conv. . — כבד

תְּכַבְּדֶךָּ[k] id. fut. 3 pers. sing. fem., suff. 2 pers. s. m. — כבד

תְּכַבְּדֵנִי[l] וּ׳[m] id. fut. 2 pers. sing. masc., or (Is. 43. 20) 3 pers. s. f., suff. 1 pers. s.; וּ, for וְ, conv. — כבד

תְּכַבֶּה[n] Piel fut. 2 pers. sing. masc. . . — כבה

תִּכְבֶּה Kal fut. 2 pers. sing. masc. . . . — כבה

תְּכַבֵּס Piel fut. 2 pers. sing. masc. . . — כבס

תְּכַבְּסִי[o] id. fut. 2 pers. sing. fem. . . . — כבס

תְּכַבְּסֵנִי[p] id. fut. 2 pers. sing. masc., suff. 1 pers. sing. — כבס

תִּכְבְּשׁוּ[q] וַ Kal fut. 2 pers. pl. masc.; ·וַ conv. . — כבש

תָּכָה Kal not used; Arab. תכא *to lean upon.* Pu. *to be laid down*, De. 33. 3.

תַּכֶּה Piel fut. 2 pers. sing. masc. (§ 25. No. 2b) — נכה

תֵּכַהּ[r] וַ ap. & conv. from the foll. (§ 24. rem. 3) . — כהה

תִּכְהֶה[s] Kal fut. 3 pers. sing. fem. . . . — כהה

תִּכְהֶין[t] וַ id. fut. 3 pers. pl. fem. (§ 8. r. 16); ·וַ conv. — כהה

תֻּכּוּ[u] Pual pret. 3 pers. pl. . . . — תכה

תֻּכּוּ[x] Hoph. fut. 2 pers. pl. masc. (§ 25. No. 2b) — נכה

תִּכָּוֶה[y] Niph. fut. 2 pers. sing. masc. . . — כוה

תִּכָּוֶינָה[z] id. fut. 3 pers. pl. fem. . . . . — כוה

תִּכּוֹן וַ׳ Niph. fut. 2 pers. sing. masc. (1 Sa. 20. 31), or 3 pers. sing. fem.; ·וַ conv. . . — כון

תְּכוֹנֵן[a] וּ׳, וַתְּ׳[b] Pilel fut. 2 p. s. m.; וּ for וְ; ·וַ id. — כון

תִּכּוֹנֵן[c] וְ Hithpal fut. 3 pers. sing. fem. [for תִּתְכּוֹנֵן § 12. rem. 3] . . . . — כון

תְּכוֹנְנִי[d] id. fut. 2 pers. s. f. [for תְּכוֹנְנִי § 21. r. 21] — כון

תְּכוּנָתוֹ[e] noun fem. sing., suff. 3 pers. sing. masc. from [תְּכוּנָה] dec. 10 . . — כון

תְּכֻנָתוֹ[f] וּ noun fem. sing., suff. 3 pers. sing. masc. from תְּכוּנָה׳ dec. 10; וּ bef. (:) . — תכן

תְּכַזֵּב[g] Piel fut. 2 pers. sing. masc. . . — כזב

תְּכַזְּבִי[h] id. fut. 2 p. s. f. [for תְּכַזְּבִי comp. § 8. r. 15] — כזב

תְּכַחֵד Piel (§ 14. rem. 1) fut. 2 pers. sing. masc. . — כחד

תִּכָּחֵד[i] וַ׳[k] Niph. fut. 2 pers. sing. masc., or (Zec. 11. 9) 3 pers. sing. fem.; ·וַ conv. . — כחד

תְּכַחֲדוּ[l] Piel (§ 14. rem. 1) fut. 2 pers. pl. masc. [for תְּכַחְדוּ comp. § 8. rem. 15] . — כחד

תְּכַחֲדִי[m] id. fut. 2 pers. sing. fem. . . . — כחד

תְּכַחֵשׁ[n] וַ Piel fut. 3 pers. s. f. (§ 14. r. 1); ·וַ conv. — כחש

תְּכַחֲשׁוּ[o] id. fut. 2 pers. pl. masc. . . . — כחש

---

[a] De. 32. 22. [b] Zec. 9. 5. [c] Job 6. 21. [d] Je. 51. 46. [e] De. 3. 22. [f] Nu. 14. 9. [g] Ex. 1. 17.
[h] Ju. 9. 13. [i] Ho. 2. 11. [k] Is. 62. 8. [l] Ps. 4. 8. [m] Ju. 11. 24. [n] Pr. 30. 23. [o] Je. 31. 12.
[p] Ge. 27. 28, 37. [q] Eze. 33. 25, 26. [r] Jos. 24. 8. [s] De. 5. 33. [t] Ju. 11. 23. [u] Pr. 30. 31. [x] Eze. 35. 9.
[y] Eze. 6. 6. [z] Ps. 44. 24. [a] Ju. 16. 19. [b] Pr. 11. 5. [c] Ju. 14. 7. [d] Jon. 4. 7, 8. [e] Ps. 10. 7; 55. 12.
[f] 2 Ki. 3. 19. [g] 1 Sa. 2. 29. [h] 1 Sa. 6. 6. [i] Eze. 27. 25. [k] Pr. 4. 8. [l] Is. 43. 20. [m] Ps. 50. 15.
[n] 2 Sa. 21. 17. [o] Je. 2. 22. [p] Ps. 51. 9. [q] Je. 34. 16. [r] Job 17. 7. [s] Zec. 11. 17. [t] Ge. 27. 1.
[u] De. 33. 3. [x] Is. 1. 5. [y] Is. 43. 2. [z] Pr. 6. 28. [a] Ps. 7. 10; 21. 13. [b] 2 Sa. 7. 24.
[c] Nu. 21. 27. [d] Is. 54. 14. [e] Job 23. 3. [f] Eze. 43. 11. [g] 2 Ki. 4. 16. [h] Is. 57. 11.
[i] Zec. 11. 9. [k] Ex. 9. 15. [l] Je. 50. 2. [m] 2 Sa. 14. 18. [n] Ge. 18. 15. [o] Le. 19. 11.

תְּכַחֲשׁוּן[a] id. id. with parag. ן (§ 10. rem. 4) . . כחש

תֻּכִּי masc. only pl. תֻּכִּיִּים, תּוּכִּיִּים, *peacocks*, 1 Ki. 10. 22; 2 Ch. 9. 21.

תָּכִין Hiph. fut. 2 pers. sing. masc., or 3 pers. s. f. כון

תְּכִינֶהָ[b] id. fut. 2 pers. sing. masc., suff. 3 pers. s. f. כון

תַּכִּיר[c] Hiph. fut. 2 pers. sing. masc. . . . נכר

תַּכִּירוּ[d] id. fut. 2 pers. pl. masc. . . . . נכר

תָּכַךְ Root not used; Arab. *to cut, cut off*; Ch. תּוּךְ *to injure*.

תּוֹךְ, תֹּךְ masc. *violence, oppression*. Also,

תְּכָכִים masc. pl. *oppressions, injuries*, Pr. 29. 13.

תָּכַל Root not used; prob. *to peel, shell*, comp. שְׁחֵלֶת.

תְּכֵלֶת fem. a colour obtained from a mussel (helix janthina) *cerulean purple*, and hence any material dyed of this colour.

תְּכַל[f] וַתְּ׳, וּ Piel fut. 2 pers. sing. masc., or 3 pers. sing. fem., ap. from תְּכַלֶּה; וּ, for וַ ·וְ conv. . . . . . כלה

תֵּכֶל[g] וַ Kal fut. 3 pers. sing. fem., ap. fr. תִּכְלֶה (§ 24. rem. 3); וַ· id. . . . . כלה

תִּכְלָא[h] Kal fut. 2 pers. sing. masc. . . . כלא

תִּכְלָאִי[i] id. fut. 2 pers. s. f. [for תִּכְלְאִי § 8. r. 15] כלא

תְּכַלֶּה Piel fut. 2 pers. sing. masc. . . . כלה

תִּכְלֶה[k] Kal fut. 3 pers. sing. fem. (§ 24. r. 19); or (Ps. 119. 96) noun fem. sing. . . . כלה

תַּכְלִימוּהָ[l] Hiph. fut. 2 pers. pl. masc., suff. 3 pers. s. f. כלם

תַּכְלִימוּנִי[m] id. id., suff. 1 pers. sing. . . . כלם

תַּכְלִימֵנוּ[n] וַ id. fut. 2 p. s. m., suff. 1 pers. pl.; וַ· conv. כלם

תִּכְלֶינָה וַ׳[o] Kal fut. 3 pers. pl. fem.; וַ· id. . . כלה

תִּכְלִית noun fem. sing. . . . . . כלה

תִּכָּלֵם[p] Niph. fut. 3 pers. sing. fem. . . . כלם

תִּכָּלְמוּ[q] id. fut. 2 pers. pl. masc. . . . . כלם

תִּכָּלְמִי[r] id. fut. 2 pers. sing. fem. . . . . כלם

תְּכַלֶּנָּה[s] Piel fut. 2 pers. sing. masc. (תְּכַלֶּה), suff. 3 pers. sing. fem. (§ 24. rem. 21) . . כלה

תִּכְלֶנָה[t] defect. for תִּכְלֶינָה (q. v.) . . . . כלה

תְּכֵלֶת וּ׳ noun fem. sing.; וּ bef. (:) . . . תכל

[תָּכַן] *to weigh*, metaph. *to ponder, examine, try*. Niph. I. *to be weighed, examined*, 1 Sa. 2. 3.—II. *to be equal, fair, just*. Pi. תִּכֵּן.—I. *to weigh*, Job 28. 25. —II. *to measure*, Is. 40. 12.—III. *to fix*, Ps. 75. 4. —IV. *to direct*, Is. 40. 13. Pu. *to weigh out* money, 2 Ki. 12. 12.

תֹּכֶן masc.—I. *a fixed quantity*, Ex. 5. 18.—II. *measure*, Eze. 45. 11.—III. pr. name of a place, in the tribe of Simeon, 1 Ch. 4. 32.

תְּכוּנָה fem. dec. 10.—I. *arrangement, structure*, Eze. 43. 11.—II. *proportion, measure*, Na. 2. 10; others, *costly furniture*.

תָּכְנִית fem.—I. *arrangement, structure*, Eze. 43. 10.—II. *perfect form, perfection of beauty*, Eze. 28. 12.

מַתְכֹּנֶת fem. dec. 13 c, *measure, proportion*.

תָּכֵן[u] Hiph. fut. 2 pers. sing. m., defect. for תָּכִין כון

תִּכֵּן Piel pret. 3 pers. sing. masc. . . . . תכן

תִּכֹּן וַ Niph. fut. 3 pers. sing. fem., defect. for תִּכּוֹן; וַ· conv. . . . . . כון

תֹּכֵן[w] וְ׳ Kal part. act. sing. masc. . . . . תכן

תֹּכֶן[y] וְ׳[z] noun masc. sing., also pr. name . . תכן

תַּכֶּנּוּ[a] Hiph. fut. 2 pers. sing. masc. (תַּכֶּה), suff. 3 pers. sing. masc. (§ 25. No. 2 b) . . נכה

תַּכְנִיעַ[b] Hiph. fut. 2 pers. sing. masc. . . . . כנע

תָּכְנִית noun fem. sing. . . . . . . תכן

תַּכְנַע[c] וַ ap. & conv. from תַּכְנִיעַ q. v. . . . כנע

תִּכָּנַע וַ Niph. fut. 2 pers. sing. masc., or (Ju. 3. 30) 3 pers. sing. fem.; וַ· conv. . . . כנע

תִּכַּנְתִּי[d] Piel pret. 1 pers. sing. . . . . . תכן

תְּכַס[e] וַ׳ ap. from the foll.; וַ· conv. . . . כסה

תְּכַסֶּה Piel fut. 2 pers. sing. masc., or 3 pers. sing. f. כסה

תְּכַסֶּהָ[f] וּ id. fut. 3 p. s. f., suff. 3 p. s. f.; וּ bef. (:) כסה

תִּכַּסֶּה[g] Hithpa. fut. 3 p. s. f. [for תִּתְכַּסֶּה § 12. r. 3] כסה

תְּכַסֵּהוּ[h] וַ Piel fut. 3 p. s. f., suff. 3 p. s. m.; וַ· conv. כסה

תָּכֹסּוּ[i] Kal fut. 2 pers. pl. masc. . . . . כסס

תְּכַסִּי[k] Piel fut. 2 pers. sing. fem. . . . . כסה

תְּכַסִּים[l] וַ id. id., suff. 3 pers. pl. masc.; וַ· conv. . כסה

תְּכַסֵּךְ / תְּכַסֵּךְ[m] } id. fut. 3 pers. sing. fem. (תְּכַסֶּה) with suff. 2 pers. sing. masc. . . } כסה

תְּכַסֵּךְ[n] id. id., suff. 2 pers. sing. fem. . . . כסה

תְּכַסֵּנוּ[o] וּ id. id., suff. 1 pers. pl.; וּ bef. (:) . כסה

תְּכַסֵּנִי[p] וַ id. id., suff. 1 pers. sing.; וַ· conv. . כסה

תִּכְסֹף[q] Kal fut. 2 pers. sing. masc. . . . . כסף

תַּכְעִיסוּ[r] Hiph. fut. 2 pers. pl. masc. . . . כעס

תַּכְעִסֶנָּה[s] id. fut. 3 pers. s. f. [תַּכְעִיס], suff. 3 p. s. fem. כעס

תִּכָּפֵל[t] וְ Niph. fut. 3 pers. sing. fem. . . . כפל

תְּכַפֵּר Piel fut. 2 pers. sing. masc. . . . . כפר

תְּכֻפַּר[u] Pual fut. 3 pers. sing. fem. [for תְּכֻפַּר] . כפר

---

[a] Jos. 24. 27. [b] Ps. 65. 10. [c] De. 16. 19. [d] De. 1. 17. [f] Nu. 17. 25.
[g] Ex. 39. 32. [h] Ps. 40. 12. [i] Is. 43. 6. [k] 1 Ki. 17. 14. [l] Ru. 2. 15.
[m] Job 19. 3. [n] Ps. 44. 10. [o] Ge. 41. 53. [p] Nu. 12. 14. [q] Is. 45. 17.
[r] Is. 54. 4. [s] Ge. 6. 16. [t] Job 17. 5. [u] Ps. 89. 3. [w] Pr. 24. 12.
[y] Eze. 45. 11. [z] Ex. 5. 18. [a] Pr. 23. 13, 14. [b] Is. 25. 5. [c] Ne. 9. 24.
[d] Ps. 75. 4. [e] Ne. 3. 37. [f] Mi. 7. 10. [g] Pr. 26. 26. [h] Ju. 4. 18. 19.
[i] Ex. 12. 4. [k] Job 16. 18. [l] Eze. 16. 18. [m] Ob. 10.
[n] Is. 60. 6. [o] Je. 3. 25. [p] Ps. 55. 6. [q] Job 14. 15.
[r] Je. 25. 6. [s] 1 Sa. 1. 7. [t] Eze. 21. 19. [u] Is. 6. 7.

תְּכַפְּרֵם[a] Piel fut. 2 pers. s. m. (תְּכַפֵּר), suff. 3 p. pl. m. — כפר

תִּכְרוּ[b] וְ[c] Kal fut. 2 pers. pl. masc. . . . — כרה

תַּכְרִיךְ[d] וְ noun masc. sing. . . . . . — כרך

תַּכְרִיעַ Hiph. fut. 2 pers. sing. masc. . . . — כרע

תַּכְרִית Hiph. fut. 2 pers. sing. masc. . . . — כרת

תַּכְרִיתוּ[e] id. fut. 2 pers. pl. masc. . . . . — כרת

תַּכְרִיתֵךְ[f] id. fut. 3 pers. sing. fem., suff. 2 pers. s. fem. — כרת

תִּכְרַע[g] וְ[h] Kal fut. 3 pers. sing. fem.; וַ conv. — כרע

תִּכְרְעוּ[i] id. fut. 2 pers. pl. masc. [for תִּכְרְעוּ § 8. r. 15] — כרע

תִּכְרַעְנָה[k] id. fut. 3 pers. pl. fem. . . . . — כרע

תִּכָּרֵת Niph. fut. 3 pers. sing. fem. . . . . — כרת

תִּכְרֹת וְ[l] Kal fut. 2 pers. sing. masc., or (Ex. 4. 25) 3 pers. sing. fem.; וַ conv. . — כרת

תִּכְרָת־[m] וְ id. fut. 2 pers. sing. masc. with Mak. (§ 8. rem. 18); וַ id. . . . — כרת

תִּכְרְתוּ[n] וְ[o] id. fut. 2 pers. pl. masc.; וַ id. . . — כרת

תִּכְרֹתוּן[p] id. id., ן parag. [for תִּכְרְתוּן § 8. rem. 17] — כרת

תִּכָּשֵׁל[q] Niph. fut. 2 pers. sing. masc. . . . — כשל

תַּכְשִׁלִי[r] Hiph. fut. 2 pers. sing. fem. . . . — כשל

תְּכַשְּׁלִי[s] Piel fut. 2 pers. s. f., R. כשל, K. תְּשַׁכְּלִי R. — שכל

תִּכָּתֵב[t] Niph. fut. 3 pers. sing. fem., bef. a monos. [for תִּכָּתֵב § 9. rem. 3] . . . — כתב

תִּכְתֹּב וְ[u] Kal fut. 2 pers. sing. masc., or 3 pers. sing. fem.; וַ conv. . . . — כתב

תִּכְתְּבוּ[x] id. fut. 2 pers. pl. masc. . . . . — כתב

תִּכְתּוֹשׁ[y] Kal fut. 2 pers. sing. masc. (§ 8. rem. 18) — כתש

תֵּל noun masc. sing. dec. 8 b, and pr. name in compos. as תֵּל אָבִיב, &c. . . . — תלל

תָּלָא only part. תְּלוּאִים.—I. *suspended, placed in suspense* or *uncertainty*, De. 28. 66.—II. *hanging after*, i. e. *bent upon, addicted to*, with לְ, Ho. 11. 7.

תֵּלֶא[y] וְ ap. fr. תִּלְאֶה q. v. (§ 24. rem. 3); וַ conv. — לאה

תְּלָאָה[z] וּ noun fem. sing.; וּ bef. (:) . . . — לאה

תִּלְאֶה[a] Kal fut. 2 pers. sing. masc. . . . . — לאה

תַּלְאוּ[b] Hiph. fut. 2 pers. pl. masc. . . . — לאה

תַּלְאֻבֹת[c] noun fem., pl. of [תַּלְאוּבָה] dec. 10 . — לאב

תְּלֻאִים[d] defect. for תְּלוּאִים (q. v.) . . . — תלא

[תְּלַאשָּׂר, תְּלַשָּׂר] pr. name of a region in Syria or Mesopotamia, 2 Ki. 19. 12; Is. 37. 12.

תְּלַבֵּב[e] וּ, וַתְּ Piel fut. 3 pers. s. fem.; וּ, for וְ; וַ conv. — לבב

תַּלְבִּישׁ[f] Hiph. fut. 3 pers. sing. fem. . . . — לבש

תַּלְבִּישֵׁנִי[g] id. fut. 2 pers. sing. masc., suff. 1 pers. sing. — לבש

תַּלְבֵּשׁ[h] וְ ap. from תַּלְבִּישׁ q. v.; וַ conv. . — לבש

תִּלְבַּשׁ[i], תִּלְבָּשׁ[k] וְ Kal (Ch. Da. 5. 16) fut. 2 p. s. m., or 3 pers. s. fem. (§ 8. r. 15); וַ conv. — לבש

תִּלְבְּשׁוּ[l] id. fut. 2 pers. pl. m. [for תִּלְבְּשׁוּ § 8. r. 15] — לבש

תִּלְבְּשִׁי[m], תִּלְבָּשִׁי[n] id. fut. 2 pers. sing. fem. . . . — לבש

תִּלְבַּשְׁנָה[o] id. fut. 3 pers. pl. fem. . . . — לבש

תִּלְבֹּשֶׁת[p] noun fem. sing. . . . . . — לבש

[תְּלַג] Chald. i. q. Heb. שֶׁלֶג *snow*.

תְּלַגַּת pr. name in compos. see תִּגְלַת.

תֵּלֶד, תֵּלֵד וְ[q], וַ Kal fut. 3 pers. sing. fem. (§ 20. rem. 4); וַ conv. . . — ילד

תֵּלְדוּ[r] id. fut. 2 pers. pl. masc. . . . — ילד

תֹּלְדוֹת defect. for תּוֹלְדוֹת (q. v.) . . . — ילד

תֵּלְדִי[s] Kal fut. 2 pers. sing. fem. . . . — ילד

תֵּלַדְןָ[t] וַ, תֵּלַדְנָה וַתֵּ[z], וְ[u] Kal fut. 3 pers. pl. fem. (§ 8. rem. 16); וַ conv. . — ילד

תֹּלְדֹת[v] defect. for תּוֹלְדוֹת (q. v.) . . . — ילד

תָּלָה וְ[z] I. *to hang, suspend*.—II. *to hang, execute*. Niph. pass. La. 5. 12. Pi. *to hang, suspend*, Eze. 27. 10, 11.

תְּלִי masc. dec. 6 i, *a quiver*, as being suspended, Ge. 27. 3.

יִתְלָה (*hanging, lofty*) pr. name of a place in the tribe of Dan, Jos. 19. 42.

תַּלְפִּיּוֹת fem. pl. *armoury, a place where weapons were hung up*, from תֵּל, & פִּיּוֹת *edges*, sc. of swords, Ca. 4. 4; others, *deadly things*, i. e. *weapons* (Arab. תלף *to perish*; conj. IV. *to destroy*).

תֵּלַהּ[a] וַ Kal fut. 3 pers. sing. fem., ap. [fr. תִּלְהֶה § 24. rem. 3]; וַ conv. . . . — להה

תִּלָּהּ[b] noun masc. s., suff. 3 pers. s. f. fr. תֵּל d. 8 b — תלל

תֹּלֶה[c] Kal part. act. s. m., bef. penacute [for תֹּלֶה] — תלה

תְּלֻהוּ[d] id. imp. pl. masc., suff. 3 pers. sing. masc. — תלה

תְּלַהֵט וַתְּ[e], וּ[f] Piel fut. 3 pers. sing. fem. (§ 14. rem. 1); וּ bef. (:) for וְ, וַ conv. . — להט

תְּלַהֲטֵהוּ[g] וַ id. with suff. 3 pers. sing. masc.; וַ id. — להט

תָּלוּ וְ[h] Kal pret. 3 pers. pl. . . . . — תלה

תִּלּוּ[h] Piel fut. 3 pers. pl. . . . . — תלה

תְּלוּאִים[i] Kal part. pass. masc. pl. [of תָּלוּא] dec. 3 a — תלא

תַּלְוֶה[k] Hiph. fut. 2 pers. sing. masc. . . — לוה

---

a Ps. 65. 4. b De. 2. 6. c Job 6. 27. d Est. 8. 15. e Nu. 4. 18. f Na. 3. 15. g Is. 45. 23. h 1 Sa. 4. 19. i Is. 65. 12. k Job 39. 3. l Ex. 4. 25. m Is. 57. 8. n Ju. 2. 2. o Je. 34. 15. p Ex. 34. 13. q Pr. 4. 12. r Eze. 36. 15. s Eze. 36. 14. t Ps. 102. 19. u Jos. 18. 6. x Pr. 27. 22. y Job 4. 5. z La. 3. 5. a Job 4. 2. b Is. 7. 13. c Ho. 13. 5. d De. 28. 66. e 2 Sa. 13. 6, 8. f Pr. 23. 21. g Job 10. 11. h Ge. 27. 15. i Job 40. 10. k De. 22. 11. l Eze. 34. 3. m Is. 49. 18. n Je. 4. 30. o 2 Sa. 13. 18. p Is. 59. 17. q Ge. 30. 3. r Is. 33. 11. s Ge. 3. 16. t Ge. 30. 39. u Je. 29. 6. x Eze. 23. 4. y Ge. 25. 12. z Ge. 40. 19. a Ge. 47. 13. b Je. 30. 18. c Job 26. 7. d Est. 7. 9. e Ps. 97. 3. f De. 32. 22. g Is. 42. 25. h Eze. 27. 10, 11. i Ho. 11. 7. k Ex. 22. 24.

תַּלְוֶה[a] Kal fut. 2 pers. sing. masc. . . . . . לוה

תָּלוּי Kal part. pass. sing. masc. dec. 3a . . תלה

תְּלוּיִם[b] id. pl., abs. st. . . . . תלה

וְ תָלוּל[c] Kal part. pass. sing. masc. . . . תלל

תְּלָוָם[d] Kh. תְּלוּם Kal pret. 3 pers. pl., suff. 3 pers. pl. masc., R. תלה, K. תְּלָאוּם, R. . תלא

תַּלְוֶנּוּ[e] Hiph. fut. 2 pers. sing. masc. (תַּלְוֶה), suff. 3 pers. sing. masc. (§ 24. rem. 21) . לוה

תַּלּוֹנוּ Kh. תַּלּוֹנוּ Niph., K. תַּלִּינוּ Hiph. fut. 2 pers. pl. masc. (§ 21. rem. 24) . . . לון

תְּלוּנֹּת[f] noun fem., pl. of [תְּלוּנָּה] dec. 10 לון

תְּלוּנֹּתָם[g] id., suff. 3 pers. pl. masc. (§ 4. rem. 2) . לון

וַ תָּלוֹשׁ[h] Kh. תָּלְוֹשׁ Kal fut. 3 pers. sing. fem. K. תָּלֹשׁ ap. (§ 21. rem. 7); וַ conv. . לוש

וְ תֶּלַח (*breach*) pr. name masc. 1 Ch. 7. 25.

תִּלָּחֵם[i] Niph. fut. 3 pers. sing. fem. . . . לחם

תִּלְחַם[k] Kal fut. 2 pers. sing. masc. . . . לחם

תִּלָּחֲמוּ Niph. fut. 2 pers. pl. masc. . . . לחם

תִּלָּחֲמוּן[l] id. with parag. ן . . . . . לחם

וַ תִּלָּחֵץ[m] Niph. fut. 3 pers. sing. fem.; וַ conv. . לחץ

תִּלְחַץ[n] / וַ תִּלְחַץ[o] } Kal fut. 2 pers. sing. masc., or 3 pers. sing. fem. (§ 8. rem. 15); וַ id. . } לחץ

תִּלְחָצֶנּוּ[p] id. fut. 2 p. s. m., suff. 3 p. s. m. (§ 16. r. 12) לחץ

תֶּלְיְךָ[q] noun m. s., suff. 2 pers. s. m. fr. [תְּלִי] d. 6i תלה

תָּלִין Kal fut. 3 pers. sing. fem., R. לין see . לון

תָּלִינוּ id. fut. 2 pers. pl. masc. . . . . לון

תָּלִינוּ[r] Kal pret. 1 pers. pl. . . . . . תלה

תָּלִינִי[s] Kal fut. 2 pers. sing. fem., R. לין see . לון

וְ תָּלִיתָ[t] Kal pret. 2 pers. sing. masc. . . . תלה

תְּלִיתָאָה[u] Ch. adj. ord. fem. [of תְּלִיתַי masc. comp. d. 7] תלת

תֵּלֵךְ / וַ תֵּלֶךְ[mm] } Kal fut. 2 pers. sing. masc., or 3 pers. sing. fem. (§ 20. rem. 4); וַ conv. } ילך

תִּלָּכֵד[x] וַ[y] Niph. fut. 3 pers. sing. fem.; וַ id. . לכד

תִּלְכְּדוֹ[z] Kal fut. 3 pers. s. f. [תִּלְכֹּד], suff. 3 p. s. m. לכד

תִּלָּכֵדִי[a] Niph. fut. 2 pers. sing. fem. [for תִּלָּכְדִי comp. § 8. rem. 15] . . . לכד

תֵּלְכוּ / וַ תֵּלְכוּ } Kal fut. 2 pers. pl. masc. (comp. id.); וַ conv. . . . . } ילך

תֵּלֵכוּן / תֵּלֵכוּן[b] } id. id. with parag. ן (comp. § 8. rem. 17) ילך

תֵּלְכִי[c] Kh. תֵּלְכִי q. v., K. תֵּלְכוּ (q. v.) . . ילך

תֵּלְכִי / וַ תֵּלְכִי[d] } Kal fut. 2 pers. sing. fem. (comp. § 8. rem. 15); וַ conv. . . } ילך

וְ תֵּלַכְנָה id. fut. 2 pers. pl. fem. (Ru. 1. 11), or 3 pers. pl. fem.; וַ conv. . . . ילך

[תָּלַל] I. *to raise* or *heap up*, as a mound, only part. pass. *raised, lofty*, Eze. 17. 22.—II. in the derivv. *to vibrate, wave*, Arab. id., cogn. תָּלָה, סָלָה, סָלַל. Hiph. הֵתֵל (inf. הָתֵל; fut. יְהַתֵּל, יְהָתֵלּוּ, q. v.) —I. *to mock, deride*, 1 Ki. 18. 27, comp. זָלַל.—II. *to deceive, delude*, with בְּ. Hoph. הוּתַל *to be deceived*, Is. 44. 20.

תֵּל masc. dec. 8b.—I. *heap* of ruins.—II. *hill, mound*, Jos. 11. 13.—III. pr. name תֵּל אָבִיב (*hill of corn-ears*) a city in Mesopotamia, Eze. 3. 15.—תֵּל חַרְשָׁא (*hill of the forest*) a city in Babylonia.—תֵּל מֶלַח (*hill of salt*) another city in Babylonia.

תַּלְתַּלִּים masc. pl. *waving palm-branches*, comp. זַלְזַלִּים, Ca. 5. 11. Sept. ἐλάται. Vulg. *elatæ palmarum* (*the clusters* or *strings of embryo fruits* after they have burst the sheaths of the female *palm-tree*, and which then *hang down* and resemble locks of flowing hair).

הֲתֻלִּים masc. pl. *mockings*, poet. for *mockers*, Job 17. 2.

מַהֲתַלּוֹת fem. pl. *delusions*, Is. 30. 10.

תָּלַם Root not used; Arab. *to break, break open.*

תֶּלֶם masc. dec. 6a (pl. c. תַּלְמֵי), *a furrow.*

תַּלְמַי (*full of furrows?*) pr. name—I. of a king of Geshur, father-in-law of David, 2 Sa. 3. 3; 13. 37.—II. of an Anakite, comp. Nu. 13. 22.

תִּלָּם[e] noun m. s., suff. 3 pers. pl. m. fr. תֵּל d. 8b תלל

תִּלְמַד Kal fut. 2 pers. sing. masc. . . . למד

תִּלְמְדוּ[f] id. fut. 2 pers. pl. m. [for תִּלְמְדוּ § 8. r. 15] למד

תְּלַמְּדֵם[g] Piel fut. 2 pers. s. m. [תְּלַמֵּד], suff. 3 p. pl. m. למד

תְּלַמְּדֶנּוּ[h] id., suff. 3 pers. sing. masc. . . למד

תְּלַמְּדֵנִי id., suff. 1 pers. sing. . . . . למד

תַּלְמַי / וְ תַּלְמַי } pr. name masc. . . . . . תלם

תַּלְמֵי noun masc. pl. constr. from תֶּלֶם dec. 6a . תלם

תַּלְמִיד[i] noun masc. sing. . . . . . למד

תְּלָמֶיהָ noun m. pl., suff. 3 pers. s. f. fr. תֶּלֶם d. 6a תלם

תָּלַן[k] / תָּלֶן[l] } Kal fut. 3 pers. sing. fem., or 2 pers. sing. fem., ap. fr. תָּלִין (§ 22. r. 3) R. לין see } לון

תְּלֻנּוֹת noun fem., pl. of [תְּלֻנָּה] dec. 10 . . לון

תְּלֻנֹּתֵיכֶם[m] id. pl., suff. 2 pers. pl. masc. . . . לון

[a] De. 28. 12. [b] Jos. 10. 26. [c] Eze. 17. 22. [d] 2 Sa. 21. 12. [e] De. 28. 44. [f] Ex. 16. 12. [g] Nu. 17. 25. [h] 2 Sa. 13. 8. [i] Zec. 14. 14. [k] Pr. 23. 6. [l] 1 Ki. 12. 24. [m] Nu. 22. 25. [n] Ex. 23. 9. [o] Nu. 22. 25. [p] Ex. 22. 20. [q] Ge. 27. 3. [r] Ps. 137. 2. [s] Ru. 1. 16. [t] De. 21. 22. [u] Da. 2. 39. [x] Je. 50. 9. [y] 1 Sa. 10. 21. [z] Ps. 35. 8. [a] Je. 48. 7. [b] De. 6. 14. [c] Je. 6. 25. [d] Ru. 2. 11. [e] Jos. 11. 13. [f] Je. 10. 2. [g] De. 5. 28. [h] Ps. 94. 12. [i] 1 Ch. 25. 8. [k] Ju. 19. 20; Job 17. 2. [l] 2 Sa. 17. 16. [m] Ex. 16. 7, 8, 9. [mm] Je. 48. 2.

תֻּלָּע Pu. part. *clothed in scarlet*, denom. of תּוֹלָע q. v. Na. 2. 4.

תּוֹלָע masc. (pl. תּוֹלָעִים).—I. *a worm*.—II. espec. *the worm used in dying scarlet, the coccus*; hence *scarlet colour*, also *scarlet cloths* or *garments*.—III. pr. name (*a*) of a son of Issachar; Patronym. תּוֹלָעִי; (*b*) of a judge in Israel, Ju. 10. 1.

תּוֹלֵעָה fem. *a worm*, Job 25. 6; Is. 14. 11.

תּוֹלַעַת fem. dec. 13a (with תּוֹלַעְתָּם) i. q. תּוֹלָע q. v. & שָׁנִי.

תִּלְעַג [a] וַ' Kal fut. 2 p. s. m., or (Pr. 30. 17) 3 p. s. f. — לעג

תַּלְעִיג [b] Hiph. fut. 2 pers. sing. masc. . . . — לעג

תֹּלַעַת [c] וְ defect. for תּוֹלַעַת (q. v.) . . . — תלע

תִּלָּקַח [d] וַ Niph. fut. 3 pers. sing. fem.; וַ conv. . — לקח

תְּלַקֵּט [e] וַ' Piel fut. 2 pers. s. m., or 3 pers. s. fem.; וַ id. — לקט

תִּלְקְטֵהוּ Kal fut. 3 pers. pl. masc., suff. 3 pers. s. masc. — לקט

תְּלֻקְּטוּ [f] Pual fut. 2 pers. pl. masc. . . . . — לקט

תָּלֹשׁ [g] וַ Kal fut. 3 p. s. fem. [for תָּלוּשׁ], ap. & conv. — לוש

תַּלְשֵׁן [h] Hiph. fut. 2 pers. sing. masc. ap. [fr. תַּלְשִׁין] — לשן

תְּלָת וּ' Ch. fem. תְּלָתָא, תְּלָתָה masc. i. q. Heb. שָׁלֹשׁ *three*; pl. תְּלָתִין *thirty*.

תְּלָת Ch. adj. masc. dec. 3 a, ord. *third in rank*, Da. 5. 16, 29.

תַּלְתִּי Ch. *third*, Da. 5. 7.

תְּלִיתָי Ch. masc. dec. 7, *third*, Da. 2. 39.

תַּלְתָּא [k] וּ' Ch. adj. ord. emph. masc. [from תְּלָת], comp. dec. 3 a . . . . . — תלת

תְּלָתָאי [l] / **תְּלָתָה** [ff] וּ' Ch. num. card. masc. from תְּלָת fem.; וּ bef. (:) . . . . — תלת

תְּלָתְהוֹן [m] Ch. id. fem. (תְּלָת) with suff. 3 pers. pl. masc. — תלת

תַּלְתִּי [n] וְ Ch. adj. ord. masc. . . . . — תלת

תְּלָתִין [o] Ch. num. card. com. gen., pl. of תְּלָת fem. — תלת

תַּלְתַּלִּים [p] noun masc., pl. of [תַּלְתַּל] dec. 8 a . . — תלל

תַּם Ch. i. q. Heb. שָׁם *there*, only with ה parag. תַּמָּה

תָּם adj. masc. sing. . . . . . — תמם

תַּם [q] וְ' Kal pret. 3 pers. sing. masc. . . — תמם

תֹּם [r] וְ' / **תָּם־** [s] Kal inf., or subst. masc. dec. 8 c — תמם

תֵּמָא pr. name, see תֵּימָא.

תְּמָאֵן [t] וַ Piel fut. 2 p. s. m. or 3 pers. s. fem.; וַ conv. — מאן

תְּמָאֲנוּ [u] / **תְּמָאֵנוּ** [v] וַ id. fut. 2 pers. pl. masc. (comp. § 8. rem. 15); וַ id. . . . — מאן

תִּמָּאֵס [y] Niph. fut. 3 pers. sing. fem. . . — מאס

תִּמְאָס [z] וַ' / **תִּמְאַס** [*] Kal fut. 2 pers. sing. masc. (§ 8. rem. 15); וַ conv. . . — מאס

תִּמְאָסוּ [a] id. fut. 2 pers. pl. masc. [for תִּמְאֲסוּ] . — מאס

תְּמֹגְגֵנִי [b] וּ Pilel fut. 2 pers. sing. masc., suff. 1 pers. sing.; וּ bef. (:) . . . . — מוג

תְּמַגְּנֶךָּ [c] Piel fut. 3 pers. s. fem. [תְּמַגֵּן], suff. 2 pers. s. masc. [for תְּמַגֶּנְךָ § 2. r. 2, & § 16. r. 15] — מגן

תָּמֹדּוּ [d] Kal fut. 2 pers. pl. masc. . . — מדד

[תְּמַהּ] I. *to wonder, be astonished, be amazed*.—II. *to look with astonishment* or *surprise*. Hithp. הִתַּמָּה (for הִתְתַּמָּה), i. q. Kal No. I, Hab. 1. 5.

תְּמַהּ Ch. masc. dec. 3 b, *wonder, miracle*.

תִּמָּהוֹן masc. dec. 3 c, *astonishment, consternation*.

תַּמָּה Ch. adv. [תַּם] with loc. ה . . — תם

תָּמְהוּ [e] Kal pret. 3 pers. pl. [for תָּמֲהוּ § 8. rem. 7] — תמה

תְּמָהוּ [g] וּ' [h] id. imp. pl. masc. [for תְּמַהוּ, from sing. תְּמַהּ § 8. rem. 11]; וּ bef. (:) . . — תמה

תִּמְהוֹהִי [i] וְ Ch. noun masc. pl., suff. 3 pers. sing. masc. from [תְּמַהּ] dec. 3 b . . . — תמה

תִּמְהַיָּא [k] וְ Ch. id. pl., emph. st. . . . — תמה

תִּמְהִין [l] וְ Ch. id. pl., abs. st. . . . — תמה

תְּמַהֵר [m] וַ' Piel fut. 3 pers. s. fem. (§ 14. r. 1); וַ conv. — מהר

תְּמַהֲרוּ [n] id. fut. 2 pers. pl. masc. . . . — מהר

תְּמַהֵרְנָה [o] וּ id. fut. 3 pers. pl. fem.; וּ bef. (:) . — מהר

תַּמּוּ [p] / **תַּמּוּ** [q] וְ' Kal pret. 3 pers. pl. . . — תמם

תֻּמּוֹ Kal inf., or subst. masc., suff. 3 pers. sing. masc. from תֹּם dec. 8 c. . . . — תמם

תָּמוֹג [r] וַ / **תָּמוּג** [s] Kal fut. 3 pers. sing. fem.; וַ conv. (§ 21. rem. 7) . . — מוג

תְּמוֹגְגֶנָּה [t] Pilel fut. 2 pers. sing. masc. [תְּמוֹגֵג], suff. 3 pers. sing. fem. (§ 2. rem. 2) . — מוג

תְּמוּגֵנוּ [u] וַ Kal fut. 2 pers. sing. masc. (תָּמוּג), suff. 1 pers. pl.; וַ conv. . . . — מוג

תָּמוֹד [x] Kal fut. 2 pers. s. masc. [for תָּמֹד § 18. r. 2] — מדד

[תַּמּוּז] pr. name, *Tammuz*, an Assyrian idol, Eze. 8. 14.

תָּמוּט Kal fut. 3 pers. sing. fem. . . . — מוט

תִּמּוֹט Niph. fut. 3 pers. sing. fem. . . . — מוט

תְּמוּטֶינָה [y] Kal fut. 3 pers. pl. fem. . . . — מוט

תְּמוֹל adv. . . . . . . — מול

תְּמוּנָה [z] וּ' noun fem. sing. dec. 10; וּ bef. (:) — מון

תְּמוּנַת [a] id., constr. st. . . . . — מון

תְּמוּנָתֶךָ [b] id., suff. 2 pers. sing. masc. [for תְּמוּנָתְךָ] — מון

תְּמוּרָתָהּ [c] וּ noun fem. sing., suff. 3 pers. sing. fem. from תְּמוּרָה dec. 10; וּ bef. (:) — מור

[a] Job 11. 3. [b] Job 21. 3. [c] Ex. 26. 1. [d] Est. 2. 8, 16. [e] Ex. 16. 26. [f] Is. 27. 12. [g] 1 Sa. 28. 24. [h] Pr. 30. 10. [i] Da. 7. 5, 8, 20. [k] Da. 5. 16, 29. [l] Ezr. 6. 4. [m] Da. 3. 23. [n] Da. 5. 7. [o] Da. 6. 8, 13. [p] Ca. 5. 11. [q] Le. 26. 20. [r] Job 4. 6. [s] Pr. 13. 6. [t] Ex. 4. 23; Est. 1. 12. [u] Is. 1. 20. [v] Pr. 1. 24. [y] Is. 54. 6. [z] Ps. 89. 39. [*] Job 10. 3. [a] Le. 26. 15. [b] Job 30. 22. [c] Pr. 4. 9. [d] Eze. 47. 18. [e] Ps. 48. 6. [ff] Da. 7. 24. [g] Hab. 1. 5. [h] Is. 29. 9. [i] Da. 3. 33. [k] Da. 3. 32. [l] Da. 6. 28. [m] Is. 32. 4. [n] 2 Ch. 24. 5. [o] Je. 9. 17. [p] 2 Ki. 7. 13. [q] Je. 44. 12, 27. [r] Am. 9. 5. [s] Ps. 46. 7. [t] Ps. 65. 11. [u] Is. 64. 6. [x] Eze. 45. 3. [y] Is. 54. 10. [z] De. 4. 12. [a] De. 4. 16, 23, 25. [b] Ps. 17. 15. [c] Job 28. 17.

תְּמֽוּרָתוֹ[a]	וּ' id., suff. 3 pers. sing. masc.; וּ bef. (:)	מור
תָּמוּשׁ[b]	Kal fut. 3 pers. sing. fem. . . .	מושׁ
תָּמוּת	Kal fut. 2 pers. sing. masc., or 3 pers. sing. fem.	מות
תְּמוּתָה	noun fem. sing.	מות
תָּמוּתוּ	Kal fut. 2 pers. pl. masc. . . .	מות
תְּמוּתוּן[kk]	id. id. with parag. ן	מות
תָּמוּתִי[c]	id. fut. 2 pers. sing. fem. . . .	מות
תְּמוּתֶנָה[cc]	id. fut. 3 pers. pl. fem., defect. for 'תֶינָה	מות
תְּמוֹתֵת[d]	Pilel fut. 3 pers. sing. fem. . .	מות
תֶּמַח	[for תֶּמַח] pr. name m. Ezr. 2. 53; Ne. 7. 55.	
תֶּמַח[e]	Hiph. fut. 2 p. s. m., ap. [fr. תַּמְחֶה § 24. r. 16]	מחה
תִּמָּח[f]	ap. from the foll.	מחה
תִּמָּחֶה	Niph. fut. 3 pers. sing. fem. . .	מחה
תִּמְחֶה[g]	Kal fut. 2 pers. sing. masc. . . .	מחה
תֶּמְחִי[h]	Hiph. fut. 2 pers. sing. masc. (§ 24. r. 18)	מחה
תִּמְחַץ[i]	Kal fut. 2 pers. sing. masc. . .	מחץ
תַּמְטִיר[k]	Hiph. fut. 2 pers. sing. m. . . .	מטר
תִּמָּטֵר[l]	Niph. fut. 3 pers. sing. fem. . .	מטר
תֻּמִּי[m]	Kal inf. (תֹּם), suff. 1 pers. sing. dec. 8c .	תמם
תָּמִיד	וְ' noun masc. sing., also as an *adv.* .	תמד
תֻּמֶּיךָ[n]	noun m. pl., suff. 2 pers. sing. m. fr. תֹּם d. 8c	תמם
תָּמִים	adj. masc. sing. dec. 3a . . .	תמם
תַּמִּים[ee]	adj. pl. [for תְּאֹמִים] *joined, coupled,* comp.	תאם
תֻּמִּים[o]	וְ noun masc., pl. of תֹּם dec. 8c . .	תמם
תְּמִים	adj. masc. sing., constr. of תָּמִים dec. 3a	תמם
תְּמִימָה	id. fem. sing. dec. 10 . . .	תמם
תְּמִימֵי	id. masc., pl. constr. from תָּמִים dec. 3a .	תמם
תְּמִימִים / תְּמִימִם	וּ' } id. masc. pl. abs.; וּ bef. (:) . .	תמם
תְּמִימֹת[p]	id. fem., pl. of תְּמִימָה dec. 10 . .	תמם
תָּמִישׁ[q]	Kh. תָּמִישׁ Hiph., K. תָּמוּשׁ Kal, fut. 3 p. s. fem.	מושׁ
תָּמִישׁוּ[r]	Hiph. fut. 2 pers. pl. masc. . .	מושׁ
תָּמִית[s]	Hiph. fut. 2 pers. sing. m., or 3 pers. sing. fem.	מות
תְּמִיתֻהוּ[t]	id. fut. 2 pers. pl. masc., suff. 3 pers. sing. m.	מות
תְּמִיתוּהָ[u]	id. id., suff. 3 pers. sing. fem. . .	מות
תְּמִיתֶנּוּ[x]	id. fut. 3 pers. sing. fem., suff. 3 pers. sing. m.	מות
תְּמִיתֵנִי[y]	id. fut. 2 pers. sing. masc., suff. 1 pers. sing.	מות

[תָּמַךְ] fut. יִתְמֹךְ.—I. *to take hold of,* with acc., בְּ.—II. *to obtain, acquire.*—III. *to hold fast,* with acc.; metaph. *to retain,* Pr. 4. 4.—IV. *to hold up, support,* with בְּ.—V. recipr. *to hold together, follow each other,* Job 36. 17. Niph. *to be holden,* Pr. 5. 22.

תָּמוֹךְ[z]	Kal inf. abs.	תמך
תָּמְכָה[a]	id. pret. 3 pers. sing. fem. . . .	תמך
תָּמְכוּ	id. pret. 3 pers. pl.	תמך
תֹּמְכֶיהָ[rr]	וְ id. part. act. pl. masc., suff. 3 pers. sing. fem. from תֹּמֵךְ dec. 7b . . .	תמך
תִּמָּכֵר[b]	Niph. fut. 3 pers. sing. fem. . .	מכר
תִּמְכֹּר	וַ'[c] Kal fut. 2 p. s. m., or (Pr. 31. 24) 3 p. s. fem.	מכר
תִּמְכְּרוּ	id. fut. 2 pers. pl. masc. . . .	מכר
תִּמְכְּרֶנָּה[d]	id. fut. 2 pers. sing. m., suff. 3 pers. sing. fem.	מכר
תָּמַכְתָּ[e]	Kal pret. 2 pers. sing. masc. . .	תמך
תְּמַכְתִּיךָ[f]	id. pret. 1 pers. sing., suff. 2 pers. sing. masc.	תמך
תְּמַלֵּא	וַ' Piel fut. 2 pers. s. m., or 3 p. s. fem.; ·וַ conv.	מלא
תִּמָּלֵא	וַ' Niph. fut. 3 pers. sing. fem.; ·וַ id.	מלא
תִּמָּלְאִי[g] / וַ תִּמָּלְאִי[h]	} Niph. fut. 2 pers. sing. fem. (comp. § 8. rem. 15); ·וַ id. . . .	מלא
תִּמְלָאֵמוֹ[i]	Kal fut. 3 pers. sing. fem., suff. 3 pers. pl. m.	מלא
תְּמַלֶּאנָה[k]	וַ'[l] Piel fut. 3 pers. pl. fem.; ·וַ conv. .	מלא
תִּמְלוֹךְ[m]	Kal fut. 2 pers. sing. masc. (§ 8. rem. 18)	מלך
תִּמְלָח[n]	Kal fut. 2 pers. sing. m. [for תִּמְלַח § 8. r. 15]	מלח
תִּמָּלֵט	Niph. fut. 2 p. s. m., or (Je. 48. 8) 3 p. s. fem.	מלט
תְּמַלֵּט[o]	וַ Piel fut. 3 pers. sing. fem.; ·וַ conv. .	מלט
תַּמְלִיכוּ[p]	וַ Hiph. fut. 2 pers. pl. masc.; ·וַ id. .	מלך
תִּמְלֹךְ[q]	Kal fut. 2 pers. sing. masc., or 3 pers. sing. fem.	מלך
תְּמַלֶּל־[r]	Piel fut. 2 pers. sing. m. [for תְּמַלֵּל § 10. r. 4]	מלל

[תָּמַם] fut. יִתֹּם, יִתּוֹם, pl. יִתַּמּוּ.—I. *to be completed, ended;* also trans. *to complete, finish,* Ps. 64. 7; with לְ and inf. *to cease* doing.—II. *to be complete, whole,* in number.—III. *to be perfect, upright,* (*integer*), Ps. 19. 14.—IV. *to cease, be ended, come to an end.*—V. *to be consumed, exhausted, spent;* עַד תֻּמָּם *until they were consumed, destroyed.* Niph. (fut. pl. יִתַּמּוּ).—I. *to be ended, come to an end,* Ps. 102. 28.—II. *to be consumed.* Hiph. הֵתֵם (fut. יַתֵּם § 18. rem. 14).—I. *to complete, make ready,* Eze. 24. 10.—II. *to complete, make perfect, upright,* Job 23. 3.—III. *to complete, execute, finish,* 2 Sa. 20. 18.—IV. *to finish, cease,* Is. 33. 1; causat. *to cause to cease, to remove,* with מִן, Eze. 22. 15.—V. *to take the sum, count,* 2 Ki. 22. 4; others, *pay out,* i. q. שִׁלֵּם.—VI. intrans. *to be consumed,* Da. 8. 23; or perh. *be made* or *declared perfect* (?). Hithp. הִתַּמָּם (for הִתְתַּמֵּם) *to show oneself perfect, upright,* Ps. 18. 26.

תָּמִים masc. dec. 3a, תְּמִימָה fem. dec. 10, adj.—I. *complete, perfect.*—II. *whole, entire.*—III. *sound, without blemish, defect.*—IV. *perfect, upright, sincere,* (*integer*).—V. subst. *integrity.*

---

[a] Le. 27. 10, 33. [b] Is. 22. 25. [c] Ru. 1. 17. [d] Ps. 34. 22. [e] Ne. 13. 14. [cc] Ex. 26. 24; 36. 29. [f] Ps. 109. 14. [g] De. 25. 19. [h] Je. 18. 23. [i] Ps. 68. 24. [k] Am. 4. 7. [l] Am. 4. 7. [m] Je. 27. 8. [n] De. 33. 8. [o] Ne. 7. 65. [p] Le. 23. 15. [q] Pr. 17. 13. [r] Mi. 2. 3. [s] Ge. 42. 37; Job 5. 2. [t] 1 Ki. 3. 26, 27. [u] 2 Ch. 23. 14. [x] Pr. 21. 25. [y] 1 Sa. 30. 15; Je. 38. 15. [z] Ps. 17. 5. [a] Ps. 63. 9. [b] Le. 25. 23. [c] Pr. 31. 24. [d] De. 21. 14. [e] Ps. 41. 13. [f] Is. 41. 10. [g] Eze. 23. 33. [h] Eze. 27. 25. [i] Ex. 15. 9. [k] Job 39. 2. [kk] Ps. 82. 7. [l] Ex. 2. 16. [m] 1 Sa. 24. 21. [n] Le. 2. 13. [o] Is. 34. 15. [oo] Eze. 13. 19. [p] Ju. 9. 16, 18. [q] Ge. 37. 8; 1 Sa. 23. 17; Est. 2. 4. [r] Job 8. 2. [rr] Pr. 3. 18.

תָּם masc. תַּמָּה fem. dec. 10, adj.—I. *whole, perfect, sincere, honest.*—II. subst. *integrity*, Ps. 37. 37.

תֹּם, תּוֹם masc. dec. 8c.—I. *completeness, fulness* in number, Is. 47. 9.—II. *welfare, prosperity.*—III. *integrity, uprightness, sincerity.*—IV. pl. תֻּמִּים *truth.*

תֻּמָּה fem. dec. 10, *integrity, sincerity, innocence.*

מְתֹם masc. *soundness*, Ps. 38. 4, 8; Is. 1. 6.

תֻּמָּם Kal inf. (תֹּם), suff. 3 pers. pl. masc. dec. 8c תמם
תֵּמָן[a] defect. for תֵּימָן (q. v.) . . . ימן
תִּמְנָה pr. name of a place . . . . מנה
תִּמְנֶה[nn] Kal fut. 2 pers. sing. masc. . . מנה
תַּמְנוּ, תַּמְנוּ } Kal pret. 1 pers. pl. [for תַּמּוֹנוּ § 18. r. 16] תמם
תִּמָּנַע[b] Niph. fut. 2 pers. sing. masc. . . . מנע
תִּמְנָע ן' pr. name masc. and fem. . . מנע
תִּמְנַע Kal fut. 2 pers. sing. masc. . . . מנע
תִּמְנַת pr. name in compos. תִּ' סֶרַח . . מנה
תְּמֻנַת[c] וּ noun f. s., constr. of תְּמוּנָה d. 10; וּ bef. (:) מון
תִּמְנָתָה ן' pr. name (תִּמְנָה) with parag. ה . . מנה
תֶּמֶס[d] noun masc. sing. . . . . מסס
תֶּמֶס[e] וַ Hiph. fut. 2 p. s. m. ap. [fr. תַּמְסֶה]; וַ· conv. מסה
תִּמְעַד[f] Kal fut. 3 pers. sing. fem. . . . מעד
תִּמְעֲטוּ[g] Kal fut. 2 p. pl. m. [for תִּמְעֲטוּ § 8. r. 15] מעט
תַּמְעִטֵנִי[h] the foll. with suff. 1 pers. sing. . . מעט
תַּמְעִיט Hiph. fut. 2 pers. sing. masc. . . . מעט
תַּמְעִיטוּ[i] id. fut. 2 pers. pl. masc. . . . מעט
תַּמְעִיטִי[k] id. fut. 2 pers. sing. fem. . . . מעט
תִּמְעֹל[l] וַ'[m] Kal fut. 3 pers. sing. fem.; וַ· conv. מעל
תִּמְעֲלוּ[n] id. fut. 2 pers. pl. m. [for תִּמְעֲלוּ § 8. r. 15] מעל
תִּמָּצֵא וַ'[o] Niph. fut. 3 pers. sing. fem.; וַ· conv. מצא
תִּמְצָא וַ'[p] Kal fut. 2 pers. sing. masc., or 3 pers. sing. masc.; וַ· id. . . . מצא
תִּמְצָאֻהוּ[q] id. fut. 2 p. pl. m., suff. 3 p. s. m. (§ 16. r. 12) מצא
תִּמְצָאוּ[r], תִּמְצְאוּ } id. fut. 2 pers. pl. masc. (§ 8. rem. 15) מצא
תִּמְצְאוּן[s] id. with parag. ן (§ 8. rem. 17) . . מצא
תִּמָּצְאִי[t] Niph. fut. 2 pers. sing. fem. . . . מצא
תִּמָּצֶאינָה[u] id. fut. 3 pers. pl. fem. (comp. § 23. rem. 3) מצא
תִּמְצָאֵךְ[x] Kal fut. 3 pers. sing. fem., suff. 2 pers. sing. masc. (§ 16. rem. 12) . . . מצא
תִּמְצָאֵם[y] id. fut. 2 pers. sing. m., suff. 3 pers. pl. m. מצא
תִּמְצֶאןָ[z] id. fut. 3 pers. pl. fem. (§ 8. rem. 16) . מצא
תִּמְצָאֶנּוּ[a] id. fut. 2 p. s. m., suff. 3 p. s. m. (§ 16. r. 12) מצא
תָּמֹצּוּ[b] Kal fut. 2 pers. pl. masc. . . . מצץ
תִּמַּק[c] Niph. fut. 3 pers. sing. fem. . . מקק
תִּמַּקְנָה[d] id. fut. 3 pers. pl. fem. (§ 18. rem. 16) . מקק

תָּמָר[e] ן' m. d. 4a.—I. *palm-tree.*—II. pr. name of a town in the south of Palestine.—III. pr. name of another town, 1 Ki. 9. 18, i. q. תַּדְמֹר q. v.—IV. pr. name fem. (*a*) of a daughter-in-law of Judah; (*b*) of a daughter of David, 2 Sa. 13. 1; (*c*) of a daughter of Absalom, 2 Sa. 14. 27.

תֹּמֶר masc. *palm-tree*, Ju. 4. 5; Je. 10. 5.

תִּמֹּרָה fem. dec. 10 (pl. תִּמֹּרִים, תִּמֹּרוֹת) *artificial palm-trees.*

תִּימָרָה fem. dec. 11a, *pillar* of smoke.

תַּמְרוּר masc. dec. 1b, *column, pillar*, Je. 31. 21.

תַּ ְמֹר Kh. תָּמָר, see תַּדְמֹר.
תָּמֵר[f] Hiph. fut. 2 p. s. m. [for תָּמֵר § 18. r. 14] מרר
תֶּמֶר[g] וַ Hiph. fut. 3 p. s. f., ap. [for תַּמְרֶה]; וַ· conv. מרה
תֹּמֶר[h] noun masc. sing. . . . . תמר
תִּמְרֹדוּ, תִּמְרְדוּ[i] } Kal fut. 2 pers. pl. masc. (§ 8. rem. 15) מרד
תִּמֹּרָה[k] וְ noun fem. sing. dec. 10 . . . תמר
תַּמְרוּ[l] וַ' Hiph. fut. 2 pers. pl. masc.; וַ· conv. מרה
תִּמֹּרָו[m] וְ n. f. with pl. m. term., suff. 3 p. s. m. fr. תִּמֹּרָה d. 10 (others read תִּמֹּרָו, as if from תִּימֹרָה תמר
תֹּמְרוּ[n] Kal fut. 2 pers. pl. m. for תֹּאמְרוּ (§ 19. r. 5) אמר
תַּמְרוּקֶיהָ[o] n. m. pl., suff. 3 p. pl. f. fr. [תַּמְרוּק] d. 1b מרק
תַּמְרוּרִים noun masc., pl. of [תַּמְרוּר] dec. 1b . מרר
תַּמְרוּרִים[p] noun masc., pl. of [תַּמְרוּר] dec. 1b . תמר
תִּמְרוֹת[u] וְ noun fem. pl. constr. of [תִּימָרָה] dec. 12a תמר
תִּמֹּרוֹת[q] וְ noun fem., pl. of תִּמֹּרָה dec. 10 . תמר
תַּמְרִיא[r] Hiph. fut. 3 pers. sing. fem. . . מרא
תְּמָרִים noun masc., pl. of תָּמָר dec. 4a . . תמר
תִּמֹּרִים ן' noun fem. with pl. m. term. fr. תִּמֹּרָה d. 10 תמר
תַּמְרִ֫יק[s] Kh. תַּמְרִיק, K. תַּמְרוּק noun masc. sing. d. 1b מרק
תַּמְרֻקֵיהֶן[t] noun m. pl., suff. 3 p. pl. f. fr. [תַּמְרוּק] d. 1b מרק
תִּמֹּרֹת וְ noun fem., pl. of תִּמֹּרָה dec. 10 . . תמר
תָּמִישׁ[u] Kal fut. 2 pers. sing. masc. (§ 21. rem. 7) מוש
תִּמְשׁוֹל[x] Kal fut. 3 pers. sing. fem. (§ 8. rem. 18) משל
תִּמְשָׁח[y], תִּמְשַׁח } Kal fut. 2 pers. sing. masc. (§ 8. rem. 15) משח
תַּמְשִׁילֵהוּ[z] Hiph. fut. 2 pers. sing. m., suff. 3 pers. s. m. משל
תִּמָּשֵׁךְ[a] Niph. fut. 3 pers. sing. fem. . . . משך
תִּמְשֹׁךְ וַ'[b] Kal fut. 2 pers. sing. masc.; וַ· conv. . משך
תִּמְשְׁכֵנִי[c] id. fut. 2 pers. sing. masc., suff. 1 pers. sing. משך
תִּמְשֹׁל[d], תִּמְשָׁל־[e] } Kal fut. 2 pers. sing. masc. (§ 8. rem. 18) משל
תַּמְשִׁלֻנִי[f] וְ Hiph. fut. 2 p. pl. m. [תַּמְשִׁילוּ], suff. 1 p. s. משל
תָּמֹת וַתָּ'[h], וְ'[g]; תָּמֹת וַ } Kal fut. 3 pers. sing. fem., ap. & conv. fr. תָּמוּת (§ 21. r. 7 & 8) מות
תֻּמַּת[i] noun fem. sing., constr. of [תֻּמָּה] dec. 10 . תמם

[a] Job 9. 9. [b] Nu. 22. 16. [c] Nu. 12. 8. [d] Ps. 58. 9. [e] Ps. 39. 12. [f] Ps. 37. 31. [g] Je. 29. 6.
[h] Je. 10. 24. [i] Nu. 35. 8. [k] 2 Ki. 4. 3. [l] Le. 5. 15. [m] Nu. 5. 27. [n] Ne. 1. 8. [nn] 1 Ki. 20. 25.
[o] 1 Sa. 13. 22. [p] Is. 10. 14. [q] Ex. 16. 25. [r] Ex. 5. 11. [s] 1 Sa. 9. 13. [t] Eze. 26. 21. [tt] Joel 3. 3.
[u] Je. 50. 20. [x] 1 Sa. 23. 17. [y] Is. 41. 12. [z] De. 31. 21. [a] Ec. 11. 1. [b] Is. 66. 11.
[c] Zec. 14. 12. [d] Zec. 14. 12. [e] Joel 1. 12. [f] Ex. 23. 21. [g] Eze. 5. 6. [h] Ju. 4. 5.
[i] Jos. 22. 18. [k] Eze. 41. 18. [l] 1 Sa. 12. 14. [m] Eze. 40. 22. [n] 2 Sa. 19. 14. [o] Est. 2. 9.
[p] Je. 31. 21. [q] 1 Ki. 6. 35. [r] Job 39. 18. [s] Pr. 20. 30. [t] Est. 2. 3. [u] Ju. 6. 18.
[x] Pr. 12. 24. [y] Ex. 30. 30. [z] Ps. 8. 7. [a] Eze. 12. 25, 28. [b] Ne. 9. 30. [c] Ps. 28. 3.
[d] Ge. 37. 8. [e] Ge. 4. 7. [f] Is. 46. 5. [g] Is. 50. 2. [h] Ju. 20. 5. [i] Pr. 11. 8.

תְּמֻתוּ defect. for תְּמוּתוּ (q. v.) . . . מות

תְּמֻתוּן defect. for תְּמוּתוּן (q. v.) . . . מות

תַּמָּתִי adj. fem. sing., suff. 1 pers. sing. [from תַּמָּה dec. 10] from תָּם masc. . . תמם

תֻּמָּתִי noun fem. sing., suff. 1 pers. s. fr. [תֻּמָּה] d. 10 תמם

תַּמְתִּיק[a] Hiph. fut. 3 pers. sing. fem. . . . מתק

תְּמִתֵנוּ[b] Hiph. fut. 2 pers. s. m. (תָּמִית), suff. 1 p. pl. מות

תֵּן, וְ' תֶּן־ } Kal imp. sing. masc. (§ 17. rem. 2) . . נתן

תְּנָא Ch. Root not used; i. q. Heb. שְׁנָה *to repeat.*
 תִּנְיָן Ch. *second,* Da. 7. 5.
 תִּנְיָנוּת Ch. *a second time,* Da. 2. 7.

תִּנְאַף, וַ תִּנְאַף[c] } Kal fut. 2 pers. sing. masc., or 3 pers. sing. fem.; וַ· conv. . . נאף

תְּנָאַפְנָה[d] Piel fut. 3 pers. pl. fem. . . . נאף

תִּנְאָץ[e] Kal fut. 2 pers. sing. masc. . . . נאץ

תִּנָּבֵא Niph. fut. 2 pers. sing. masc. . . . נבא

תִּנָּבְאוּ[f] id. fut. 2 pers. pl. masc. . . . נבא

תְּנַבֵּל[g] Piel fut. 2 pers. sing. masc. . . . נבל

תְּנַגֵּחַ Piel fut. 2 pers. sing. masc. . . . נגח

תְּנַגְּחוּ[h] id. fut. 2 pers. pl. masc. . . . נגח

תִּנָּגְפוּ Niph. fut. 2 pers. pl. masc. . . . נגף

תִּנְגֹּשׂוּ[i] Kal fut. 2 pers. pl. m. [for תִּנְגְּשׂוּ § 8. r. 15] נגש

תָּנֹד[k] Kal fut. 2 pers. sing. masc., ap. from תָּנוּד נוד

תְּנֻד[l] Ch. Peal fut. 3 pers. sing. fem. . . . נוד

תָּנֻדוּ[m] Kal fut. 2 pers. pl. masc. [for תָּנוּדוּ] . נוד

תַּנְדֵנִי[n] Hiph. fut. 2 pers. s. m. [תָּנִיד], suff. 1 p. s. נוד

תִּנְדַּע[o], תִּנְדַּע[p] וְ'[q] } Ch. Peal fut. 2 pers. sing. m., dag. forte resolved in נ [for תִּדַּע § 52. r. 2] ידע

תִּנְדֹּף[r] Kal fut. 2 pers. sing. masc. . . . נדף

[תָּנָה] *to give presents, distribute gifts* in order *to hire* any one, Ho. 8. 10. Pi. *to praise, celebrate,* with acc., לְ. Hiph. *to hire,* Ho. 8. 9.
 אֶתְנָה fem. *gift, wages* of prostitution, Ho. 2. 14.
 אֶתְנִי (*giving, munificent*) pr. name m. 1 Ch. 6. 26.
 אֶתְנַן masc. dec. 8 a.—I. *gift, wages* of prostitution.—II. pr. name masc. 1 Ch. 4. 7.
 יַתְנִיאֵל (whom *God bestows,* i. e. given of God) pr. name masc. 1 Ch. 26. 2.
 יִתְנָן (*gift*) pr. name of a city in Judah, Jos. 15. 23.

תְּנָה Kal imp. s. m. (תֵּן), with parag. ה (§ 17. r. 2) נתן

תְּנַהֵג[s] וַ Piel fut. 2 pers. s. m. (§ 14. r. 1); וַ· conv. נהג

תְּנֵהוּ[t] וּ'[u] Kal imp. sing. masc. (תֵּן), suff. 3 pers. sing. masc.; וּ bef. (:) . . . נתן

תְּנַהֲלֵנִי[x] וּ Piel (§ 14. rem. 1) fut. 2 pers. sing. masc., suff. 1 pers. sing.; וּ bef. (:) . . נהל

תְּנוּ וּ' Kal imp. pl. masc.; וּ id. . . . נתן

תְּנוֹאוּן[y] Kh. תְּנוּאוּן Kal, K. תְּנִיאוּן Hiph. fut. 2 pers. pl. masc.; ן parag. . . . נוא

תְּנוּאוֹת[z] noun fem., pl. of [תְּנוּאָה] dec. 10 . נוא

תְּנוּאָתִי[a] id. sing., suff. 1 pers. sing. . . . נוא

תְּנוּבָה[b] noun masc. sing. dec. 10 . . . נוב

תְּנוּבַת[c] וּ id., constr. st.; וּ bef. (:) . . נוב

תְּנוּבֹת[d] id. pl. . . . . . נוב

תְּנוּבָתִי[e] id. sing., suff. 1 pers. sing. . . . נוב

תָּנוּד[f] Kal fut. 2 pers. sing. masc. . . . נוד

תָּנוּחַ[g] וְ' Kal fut. 2 p. s. m. (Da. 12. 13), or 3 p. s. f. נוח

תָּנוּט[h] Kal fut. 2 pers. sing. fem. . . . נוט

תְּנוּךְ noun masc. sing. . . . . תנך

תְּנוּמָה[i] וּ'[k] noun fem. sing. dec. 10; וּ bef. (:) . נום

תְּנוּמוֹת[l] id. pl. . . . . . נום

תָּנוּם Kal fut. 2 pers. sing. masc. . . . נום

תְּנוּסוּ[m], תְּנוּסוּן[n] } id. fut. 2 pers. pl. masc.; ן parag. נוס

תָּנוּעַ[o] Kal fut. 3 pers. sing. fem. . . . נוע

תְּנוּפָה noun fem. sing. dec. 10 . . . נוף

תְּנוּפַת id., constr. st. . . . . נוף

תְּנוּפֹת[p] id. pl. . . . . . נוף

תַּנּוּר[q] וְ' noun masc. sing. dec. 1 b . . תנר

תָּנַח וַ Kal fut. 3 pers. sing. fem., ap. and conv. from תָּנוּחַ (§ 21. rem. 9); וַ· conv. . נוח

תַּנַּח[r] וַ' Hiph. fut. 2 p. s. m., or (Ge. 39. 16) 3 p. s. f., ap. & conv. [fr. תָּנִיחַ=תַּנִּיחַ § 21. r. 24] נוח

תַּנְחֶה[s] Hiph. fut. 3 pers. sing. fem. . . . נחה

תַּנְחוּמוֹת[t] noun pl. fem. from [תַּנְחוּם] dec. 1 a נחם

תַּנְחוּמֶיךָ[u] id. pl. masc., suff. 2 pers. sing. masc. נחם

תַּנְחוּמִים[x] id. id., abs. st. . . . . נחם

תַּנְחוּמֹתֵיכֶם[y] id. pl. fem., suff. 2 pers. pl. masc. נחם

תַּנְחִיל[z] Hiph. fut. 2 pers. sing. masc. . . . נחל

תַּנְחִילֶנָּה[a] id., suff. 3 pers. sing. fem. . . . נחל

תִּנְחַל[b], תִּנְחָל } Kal fut. 2 pers. sing. masc. (§ 8. r. 15) נחל

תַּנְחֵם Hiph. fut. 2 pers. sing. masc., or (Pr. 11. 3) 3 pers. sing. fem. [תַּנְחֶה], suff. 3 pers. pl. masc. (§ 24. rem. 21) . . נחה

תְּנֻחָמוּ[c] Pual (§ 14. rem. 1) fut. 2 pers. pl. masc. [for תְּנֻחֲמוּ comp. § 8. rem. 15] . . נחם

תְּנַחֲמוּנִי[d] Piel (§ 14. rem. 1) fut. 2 pers. pl. masc., suff. 1 pers. sing. . . . נחם

תַּנְחֻמֶיהָ[e] noun m. pl., suff. 3 p. s. f. fr. [תַּנְחוּם] d. 1 b נחם

---

a Job 20. 12. b Je. 41. 8. c Je. 3. 9. d Ho. 4. 13, 14. e Je. 14. 21. f Am. 2. 12.
g Je. 14. 21. h Eze. 34. 21. i Is. 58. 3. k Je. 16. 5. l Da. 4. 11. m Je. 22. 10.
n Ps. 36. 12. o Da. 2. 30. p Da. 4. 22, 23, 29. q Ezr. 4. 15. r Ps. 68. 3. s Ge. 31. 26.
t 1 Ch. 21. 22. u Ne. 1. 11. x Ps. 31. 4. y Nu. 32. 7. z Job 33. 10. a Nu. 14. 34.
b Is. 27. 6. c Eze. 36. 30. d De. 32. 13. e Ju. 9. 11. f Je. 4. 1. g Da. 12. 13.
h Ps. 99. 1. i Ps. 132. 4. k Pr. 6. 4. l Pr. 6. 10; 24. 33. m Is. 10. 3. n Is. 30. 16.
o Is. 24. 20. p Nu. 18. 11. q Is. 31. 9. r Ge. 39. 16. s Pr. 6. 22.
t Job 15. 11. u Ps. 94. 19. x Je. 16. 7. y Job 21. 1. z Jos. 1. 6.
a De. 31. 7. b Nu. 18. 20. c Is. 66. 13. d Job 21. 34. e Is. 66. 11.

תְּנַחֲמֵנוּ[a] Piel fut. 3 pers. sing. masc. [תְּנַחֵם § 14. rem. 1], suff. 3 pers. sing. masc. . . נחם

תְּנַחֲמֵנִי[b] וּ/ id. fut. 2 pers. sing. masc., or (Job 7. 13) 3 pers. sing. f., suff. 1 pers. s.; וּ bef. (:) נחם

תַּנְחֻמֶת pr. name masc. . . . . . נחם

תַּנְחֵנוּ[c] Hiph. fut. 2 pers. sing. masc. [תַּנִּיחַ § 21. rem. 24], suff. 1 pers. pl. . . . נוח

תַּנְחֵנִי Hiph. fut. 2 pers. sing. masc., or (Ps. 139. 10) 3 pers. sing. fem. [תַּנְחֶה], suff. 1 pers. sing. (§ 24. rem. 21) . . נחה

תְּנַחֲשׁוּ[d] Piel fut. 2 pers. pl. masc. (§ 14. rem. 1) . נחש

תִּנְחַת[e] וַ Kal fut. 3 pers. sing. fem.; וַ conv. . נחת

תְּנִי[f] / תְּנִי } Kal imp. sing. fem. (comp. § 8. rem. 12) נתן

תְּנִיחֶנּוּ[g] Hiph. fut. 3 pers. sing. fem. [תָּנִיחַ], suff. 3 pers. sing. masc. . . . . . נוח

תַּנִּיחֵנִי[h] id. fut. 2 pers. sing. masc. [תַּנִּיחַ § 21. rem. 24], suff. 1 pers. sing. . . ינח

תַּנִּים[i] noun m. s. for תַּנִּין by interch. of the liquids תנן

תַּנִּים וְ[k] noun masc., pl. of [תַּן] dec. 8 d . . תנן

תַּנִּין[l] id. pl. with Chald. term. . . . . תנן

תַּנִּין וְ[m] noun masc. sing., pl. תַּנִּינִים dec. 1 b . תנן

תִּנְיָנָה[n] Ch. adj. ord. fem. sing. [from תִּנְיָן masc.] תנא

תִּנְיָנוּת[o] Ch. noun fem. sing. . . . . . תנא

תַּנִּינִים / תַּנִּינִם[p] } noun masc., pl. of תַּנִּין dec. 1 b . תנן

תְּנִיעֵנִי[q] וַ Hiph. fut. 3 pers. sing. fem. (תָּנִיעַ), suff. 1 pers. sing.; וַ conv. . . . . נוע

תָּנִיף Hiph. fut. 2 pers. sing. masc. . . . נוף

תְּנִיקֵהוּ[r] וַ Hiph. fut. 3 pers. sing. fem. [תָּנִיק], suff. 3 pers. sing. masc.; וַ conv. . . . נוק

תָּנַךְ Root not used; Syr. Ethpe. *to come to an end.*
תְּנוּךְ masc. *extremity, tip* of the ear.

תְּנַכְּרוּ[s] Piel fut. 2 p. pl. m. [for תְּנַכְּרוּ comp. § 8. r. 15] נכר

תְּנֵם[t] וּ Kal imp. sing. masc. (תֵּן), suff. 3 pers. pl. masc.; וּ bef. (:) . . . . נתן

תָּנַן Root not used; to which is ascribed the sense of *stretching out, extending.*

תַּן or תָּן masc. only pl. תַּנִּים, תַּנִּין *huge serpents*; others, *jackals.*

תַּנִּים masc. for תַּנִּין *a great serpent, sea monster*, Eze. 29. 3.

תַּנָּה fem. dec. 10, *serpent*, Mal. 1. 3; others, *dwelling, habitation.* (Arab. תנא *to abide, dwell.*)

תַּנִּין masc. (pl. תַּנִּינִים).—I. *serpent.*—II. *a large fish, sea monster.*—III. *crocodile.*

אַתּוּן Ch. masc. dec. 1 a, *furnace*, for אַתְנוּן, Ch. תְּנַן *to smoke.* According to some also תַּנּוּר q. v. R. תָּנַר.

תְּנֶנָּה[u] Kal imp. s. masc. with suff. 3 pers. sing. fem. נתן

תָּנֹס[x] וַ Kal fut. 3 pers. sing. fem., ap. & conv. [from תָּנוּס § 21. rem. 7 & 8] . נוס

תְּנֻסוּ[y] id. fut. 2 pers. pl. masc. defect. for תָּנוּסוּ . נוס

תְּנַסּוּ[z] / תְּנַסּוּן[a] } Piel fut. 2 pers. pl. masc., ן parag. . נסה

תְּנַפְּצֵם[b] Piel fut. 2 pers. sing. masc. [תְּנַפֵּץ], suff. 3 pers. pl. masc. . . . . נפץ

תִּנָּצֵל[c] וְ/ Niph. fut. 2 pers. sing. fem., or (Ge. 32. 31) 3 pers. sing. fem.; וַ conv. . נצל

תִּנָּצְלִי[d] id. fut. 2 pers. s. f. [for תִּנָּצֵלִי comp. § 8. r. 15] נצל

תִּנְצְרֶכָּה[e] Kal fut. 3 pers. sing. fem. [תִּנְצֹר], suff. 2 pers. sing. masc. [for תִּנְצָרְךָ § 2. r. 2] נצר

תִּנְצְרֵנִי[f] id. fut. 2 pers. sing. masc., suff. 1 pers. sing. נצר

תִּנָּקֶה Niph. fut. 2 pers. sing. masc. . . נקה

תְּנַקֵּהוּ[g] Piel fut. 2 pers. s. masc., suff. 3 pers. s. masc. נקה

תִּנָּקוּ[ll] Niph. fut. 2 pers. pl. masc. . . נקה

תְּנַקֵּנִי Piel fut. 2 pers. sing. masc. [תְּנַקֶּה], suff. 1 pers. sing. (§ 24. rem. 21) . נקה

תְּנַקֵּר[h] Piel fut. 2 pers. sing. masc. . . נקר

תִּנָּקֵשׁ[i] Niph. fut. 2 pers. sing. masc. . . נקש

תָּנַר Root not used; whence apparently

תַּנּוּר masc. dec. 1 b, *oven, furnace.* Some derive it from נוּר *to shine*, Chald. subst. *fire*; others regard it as a compounded word from תַּן, Chald. תְּנַן *to smoke*, & נוּר; comp. אַתּוּן, R. תָּנַן.

תִּנַּשֵּׂא[k] וְ Hithpa. fut. 3 pers. sing. fem. [for תִּתְנַשֵּׂא § 12. rem. 3] . . . . . נשא

תִּנָּשְׂאוּ[l] Niph. fut. 2 pers. pl. masc. [for תִּנָּשְׂאוּ, comp. § 8. rem. 15] . . . נשא

תִּנָּשֶׂאנָה[m] id. fut. 3 pers. pl. fem. . . . . נשא

תִּנָּשֵׁנִי[n] Niph. fut. 2 pers. sing. masc. [תִּנָּשֶׁה], suff. 1 pers. sing. (§ 24. rem. 21) . נשה

תְּנַתֵּחַ[o] Piel fut. 2 pers. s. masc. [for תְּנַתַּח § 15. r. 1] נתח

תִּנָּתֵן[p] וְ, [q] וַתִּ Niph. fut. 2 pers. sing. masc., or 3 pers. sing. fem.; וַ conv. . . נתן

תִּנָּתֶן[r] וְ id. fut. 3 pers. s. fem. (bef. monos. § 9. r. 3) נתן

תִּנְתֵּן[s] Chald. Peal fut. 2 pers. sing. masc. . נתן

תְּנַתְּקוּ[t] Piel fut. 2 pers. pl. masc. [for תְּנַתְּקוּ, comp. § 8. rem. 15] . . . . נתק

---

a Is. 66. 13. b Is. 12. 1. c Je. 14. 9. d Le. 19. 26. e Ps. 38. 3.
f Is. 43. 6. g Is. 63. 14. h Ps. 119. 121. i Eze. 29. 3. k Is. 13. 22.
l La. 4. 3. m Ps. 91. 13. n Da. 7. 5. o Da. 2. 7. p De. 32. 33.
q Da. 10. 10. r Ex. 2. 9. s Job 21. 29. t Ne. 3. 36. u 1 Sa. 21. 10.
x 2 Sa. 4. 4. y Is. 30. 17. z De. 6. 16. a Ex. 17. 2. b Ps. 2. 9.
c Ge. 32. 31. d Mi. 4. 10. e Pr. 2. 11. f Ps. 140. 2, 5. g 1 Ki. 2. 9.
h Nu. 16. 14. i De. 12. 30. k Nu. 24. 7. l Is. 66. 12. ll Je. 25. 29.
m Is. 49. 22. n Is. 44. 21. o Ex. 29. 17. p Da. 11. 6.
q Est. 9. 14. r Est. 7. 2, 3. s Ezr. 7. 20. t Eze. 23. 34.

תְּנַתְּקִי[a] id. fut. 2 pers. s. f. [for תְּנַתְּקִי comp. § 8. r. 15] נתק
תִּנָּתֵשׁ[b] Niph fut. 3 pers. sing. fem. נתשׁ
תָּסֹב וְ'[c], וַתִּ'[d] Kal fut. 2 pers. sing. masc., or 3 pers. sing. fem. [for תָּסֹב § 18. rem. 14]; וַ· conv. סבב
תָּסֹבּוּ[e] id. fut. 2 pers. pl. masc. סבב
תְּסֻבֶּינָה[f] id. fut. 3 pers. pl. fem. סבב
תַּסֵּג וְ'[g] ap. from תַּסִּיג (q. v.) נסג
תִּסְגְּדוּן[h] וְ' Chald. Peal fut. 2 pers. pl. masc. סגד
תַּסְגִּיר[i] / תַּסְגֵּר[k] } Hiph. fut. 2 pers. sing. masc. סגר
תִּסָּגֵר[l] וַ' Niph. fut. 3 pers. sing. fem.; וַ· conv. סגר
תִּסְגֹּר[m] וַ Kal fut. 3 pers. sing. fem.; וַ· id. סגר
תַּסְגִּרֵנִי[n] Hiph. fut. 2 pers. s. m. (תַּסְגִּיר), suff. 1 pers. s. סגר
תִּסּוֹב Kal fut. 3 pers. sing. fem., comp. תִּסֹּב סבב
תְּסוֹבֵב[o] Pilel fut. 3 pers. sing. fem. סבב
תְּסוֹבְבֶךָּ[p] id. id., suff. 2 pers. sing. masc. [for תְּסוֹבֶבְךָ § 2. rem. 2, comp. § 16. rem. 15] סבב
תְּסוֹבְבֵנִי[q] id. fut. 2 pers. sing. with suff. 1 pers. sing. סבב
תָּסוּךְ Kal fut. 2 pers. sing. masc. סוך
תָּסוּכִי[r] id. fut. 2 pers. sing. fem. סוך
תָּסוּר Kal fut. 2 pers. sing. masc., or 3 pers. s. fem. סור
תָּסוּרוּ id. fut. 2 pers. pl. masc. סור
תִּסְחָרוּ[s] Kal fut. 2 pers. pl. m. [for תִּסְחֲרוּ § 8. rem. 15] סחר
תַּסִּיג[t] Hiph. fut. 2 pers. sing. masc. נסג
תַּסִּיעַ[u] Hiph. fut. 2 pers. sing. masc. נסע
תַּסִּיעִי[x] id. fut. 2 pers. sing. fem. נסע
תֹּסִיף Hiph. fut. 2 pers. sing. masc. defect. for תּוֹסִיף יסף
תָּסִיר Hiph. fut. 2 pers. sing. masc. סור
תְּסִיתֵהוּ וַ Hiph. fut. 3 pers. sing. fem. [תָּסִית], suff. 3 pers. sing. masc.; וַ· conv. סות
תְּסִיתֵנִי[y] וַ id. fut. 2 pers. s. masc., suff. 1 pers. s.; וַ· id. סות
תָּסֵךְ[z] וְ Hiph. fut. 2 pers. sing. masc. סכך
תִּסְּכוּ[a] Kal fut. 2 pers. pl. masc. נסך
תְּסֻכֵּנִי[b] Kal fut. 2 pers. sing. masc. [תָּסֹךְ], suff. 1 pers. sing. (§ 18. rem. 5) סכך
תְּסֻלֶּה[c] Pual fut. 3 pers. sing. fem. סלה
תְּסַלֵּף Piel fut. 3 pers. sing. fem. סלף
תִּסְמְכֵנִי[d] Kal fut. 2 pers. sing. masc., or 3 pers. sing. fem., suff. 1 pers. sing. סמך
תְּסַמֵּר[e] Piel fut. 3 pers. sing. fem. סמר
תִּסְעָדֵנִי[f] Kal fut. 3 pers. sing. fem. [תִּסְעַד], suff. 1 pers. sing. (§ 16. rem. 12) סעד
תִּסְעוּ[g] Kal fut. 2 p. pl. m. [for תִּסְּעוּ, comp. § 10. r. 7] נסע
תָּסֵף[h] וְ Chald. Aph. fut. 3 pers. sing. fem. סוף
תֹּסֵף[i] Kal fut. 2 pers. s. m. [for תֶּאֱסֹף § 19. r. 4 & 5] אסף

תֹּסֵף[k] / תֹּסֶף וַ' } Hiph. fut. 2 pers. sing. masc., or 2 pers. sing. fem., ap. conv. & defect. for תּוֹסִיף } יסף
תֹּסֵף[l] id. fut. 3 pers. sing. fem. defect. for תּוֹסִיף יסף
תִּסְפֹּד[m] וַ'[n] Kal fut. 2 pers. s. m., or 3 p. s. f.; וַ· conv. ספד
תִּסְפְּדוּ[o] id. fut. 2 pers. pl. masc. ספד
תִּסָּפֶה[p] Niph. fut. 2 pers. sing. masc. ספה
תִּסְפֶּה[q] Kal fut. 2 pers. s. m., or (Is. 7. 20) 3 p. s. fem. ספה
תִּסָּפוּ Niph. fut. 2 pers. pl. masc. ספה
תֹּסִפוּ / תֹּסִפוּן } Hiph. fut. 2 pers. pl. masc. defect. for תּוֹסִיפוּ; ן parag. } יסף
תִּסְפּוֹר[r] Kal fut. 2 pers. sing. masc. (§ 8. r. 18) ספר
תְּסַפֵּר[s] Piel fut. 2 pers. sing. masc. ספר
תְּסַפֶּר־[t] וַ id. fut. 3 pers. s. fem. (§ 10. r. 4); וַ· conv. ספר
תִּסְפֹּר[u] / תִּסְפָּר־[x] } Kal fut. 2 pers. sing. masc. (§ 8. rem. 18) ספר
תְּסַפְּרוּ[y] Piel fut. 2 pers. pl. masc. ספר
תִּסְפְּרוּ[z] Kal fut. 2 pers. pl. masc. ספר
תָּסַר[a] וַ Hiph. fut. 3 pers. sing. fem., ap. & conv. [from תָּסִיר § 21. rem. 9] סור
תָּסֵר[b] וְ id. fut. 3 pers. sing. fem. ap. [from תָּסִיר] סור
תָּסֻרוּ[c] defect. for תָּסוּרוּ (q. v.) סור
תִּסְרַח[d] Kal fut. 2 pers. sing. masc. סרח
תַּסְתִּיר Hiph. fut. 2 pers. sing. masc. סתר
תַּסְתִּירֵהוּ[e] וַ id. fut. 3 pers. s. fem., suff. 3 p. s. m.; וַ· conv. סתר
תַּסְתִּירֵם[f] id. fut. 2 pers. s. masc., suff. 3 pers. pl. masc. סתר
תַּסְתִּירֵנִי id. id. with suff. 1 pers. sing. סתר
תִּסְתְּמוּ[g] Kal fut. 2 pers. pl. m. [for תִּסְתְּמוּ § 8. r. 15] סתם
תַּסְתֵּר Hiph. fut. 2 pers. sing. masc., ap. from תַּסְתִּיר סתר
תִּסָּתֵר[h] Niph. fut. 2 pers. sing. masc. סתר
תִּסָּתְרוּ[i] id. fut. 2 pers. pl. masc. סתר
תִּסְתַּתָּר[k] Hithpa. fut. 3 p. s. f. [for תִּתְסַתַּר § 12. r. 1 & 3] סתר

תָּעַב. Pi. תִּעֵב (§ 14. rem. 1).—I. *to abhor.*—II. *to render abominable, cause to be abhorred,* Eze. 16. 25.—III. *to excite abhorrence, be an object of abhorrence,* Is. 49. 7. Hiph. *to make abominable, to act abominably.* Niph. *to be abhorred, detested.*

תּוֹעֵבָה fem. dec. 11 b.—I. *abomination, abominable thing, object of abomination.*—II. *abominable act* or *practice.*

תַּעֵב[l] וְ Piel inf. abs. (§ 14. rem. 1) תעב
תַּעֲבֹד Kal fut. 2 pers. sing. masc. עבד
תֵּעָבֵד[m] Niph. fut. 3 pers. sing. fem. עבד
תַּעַבְדוּ / תַּעֲבֹדוּ וַ' } Kal fut. 2 pers. pl. masc. (§ 8. rem. 15); וַ· conv. } עבד

[a] Eze 23. 34. [b] Da. 11. 4. [c] Ps. 71. 21. [d] 1 Ki. 2. 15. [e] Jos. 6. 4. [f] Ge. 37. 7. [g] Mi. 6. 14. [h] Da. 3. 5, 15. [i] De. 23. 16. [k] Ob. 14. [l] Nu. 12. 14, 15. [m] 2 Ki. 4. 5, 21. [n] 1 Sa. 30. 15. [o] Je. 31. 22. [p] Ps. 7. 8. [q] Ps. 32. 7. [r] 2 Sa. 14. 2. [s] Ge. 42. 34. [t] De. 19. 14. [u] Ps. 80. 9. [x] 2 Ki. 4. 4. [y] Job 2. 3. [z] Ps. 5. 12. [a] Ex. 30. 9. [b] Ps. 139. 13. [c] Job 28. 16, 19. [d] Ps. 51. 14. [e] Job 4. 15. [f] Ps. 18. 36. [g] Jos. 3. 3. [h] Da. 2. 44. [i] Ps. 104. 29. [k] Ge. 4. 12; De. 13. 1. [l] Ex. 11. 6. [m] Eze. 24. 16. [n] 2 Sa. 11. 26. [o] Eze. 24. 23. [p] Ge. 19. 15, 17. [q] Ge. 18. 23, 24. [r] Job 14. 16. [s] Ex. 10. 2. [t] 2 Ki. 8. 6. [u] Job 39. 2. [x] De. 16. 9. [y] Ps. 48. 14. [z] Le. 23. 16. [a] Ge. 38. 14, 19. [b] Ho. 2. 4. [c] De. 5. 29. [d] Ex. 26. 12. [e] 2 Ch. 22. 11. [f] Ps. 31. 21. [g] 2 Ki. 3. 19. [h] Ps. 89. 47. [i] Zep. 2. 3. [k] Is. 29. 14. [l] De. 7. 26. [m] Eze. 36. 34.

תַּעַבְדוּם id. id., suff. 3 pers. pl. masc. . . עבד
תַּעַבְדוּן[a] } id. id. with parag. ן (§ 4. rem. 17); Chald. Ezr. 6. 8; 7. 18 . . . עבד
תַּעַבְדוּן[b]
תָּעָבְדֵם Hoph. fut. 2 pers. sing. m., suff. 3 pers. pl. m. עבד
תִּעֲבוּנִי [c]וְ׳ Piel (§ 14. r. 1) pret. 3 pers. pl., suff. 1 p. s. תעב
תַּעֲבוֹר[d] Kal fut. 2 pers. sing. masc. (§ 8. rem. 18) עבר
תַּעֲבוּרִי[e] id. fut. 2 pers. sing. fem. (§ 8. rem. 14) . עבר
תִּעֲבוֹת[f] defect. for תּוֹעֲבוֹת (q. v.) . . . תעב
תַּעֲבֹט[g] Kal fut. 2 pers. sing. masc. . . . עבט
תַּעֲבִיטֶנּוּ[h] Hiph. fut. 2 pers. sing. m., suff. 3 pers. sing. m. עבט
תַּעֲבִיר[i] וְ Hiph. fut. 2 pers. sing. masc. . . עבר
תַּעֲבִירוּ id. fut. 2 pers. pl. masc. . . . עבר
תַּעֲבֹר וַ׳ } Kal fut. 2 pers. sing. masc., or 3 pers. sing. fem. (§ 8. rem. 18); ·וַ conv. עבר
תַּעֲבָר־
תַּעַבְרוּ } id. fut. 2 pers. pl. masc. (§ 8. rem. 15); ·וַ id. . . . עבר
תַּעַבְרוּ [k]וַ׳
תַּעֲבֹרְנָה id. fut. 3 pers. pl. fem. . . . עבר
תַּעֲבִרֵנוּ[l] Hiph. fut. 2 pers. s. m. [תַּעֲבִיר], suff. 1 pers. pl. עבר
תַּעְגְּבָה[m] וַ Kh. תַּעְגַּב q. v., K. תַּעְגְּבָה (q. v.) . ענב
תַּעְגַּב[n] וַ Kal fut. 3 pers. s. fem. (§ 13. r. 5); ·וַ conv. ענב
תַּעְגְּבָה[o] וַ id. fut. 3 pers. sing. fem. with parag. ה (§ 8. rem. 13); ·וַ id. . . . ענב
תֵּעָגֵנָה[p] Niph. fut. 3 pers. pl. fem. (§ 8. rem. 13, note) ענן
תְּעֻגֶנָּה[q] Kal fut. 2 p. s. m., suff. 3 p. s. f., denom. fr. עֻגָּה עוג
תָּעַד[zz] וַ Hiph. fut. 2 pers. sing. masc. ap. & conv. for תָּעִיד (§ 21. rem. 9) . . . עוד
תַּעַד[r] וַ Kal fut. 3 pers. sing. fem. ap. from תַּעְדֶּה (§ 24. rem. 3); ·וַ conv. . . עדה
תֶּעְדֵּא[s] Chald. Peal fut. 3 pers. sing. fem. (§ 49. r. 2) עדה
תַּעְדֶּה[t] Kal fut. 3 pers. sing. fem. (§ 13. rem. 5) עדה
תַּעְדִּי [u]וַ׳ id. fut. 2 pers. sing. fem.; ·וַ conv. . עדה

תָּעָה[x] fut. יִתְעֶה, ap. יֵתַע (§ 24. rem. 3).—I. *to wander, go astray.*—II. *to stagger* through drunkenness, Is. 28. 7.—III. trop. *to stray, err,* with מֵעַל away from, מֵאַחֲרֵי from following.—IV. perh. *to perish,* Pr. 14. 22, comp. אָבַד. Niph. I. *to stagger,* Is. 19. 14.—II. *to be led astray, to be deceived,* Job 15. 31. Hiph. הִתְעָה.—I. *to cause to wander,* or *go astray.*—II. *to lead astray, to seduce.*—III. *to commit error, to err.*

תּוֹעָה fem.—I. *error,* or *apostacy,* Is. 32. 6.—II. *hurt, injury,* Ne. 4. 2.

תֹּעוּ (*error*) pr. name of a king of Hamath, 1 Ch. 18. 9, 10; called תֹּעִי 2 Sa. 8. 9, 10.

תֹּעֶה Kal part. act. sing. masc. dec. 9a . תעה
תָּעוּ id. pret. 3 pers. pl. . . . . תעה
תֹּעוּ pr. name masc. . . . . תעה
תְּעוּדָה[y] noun fem. sing. . . . . . עוד
תְּעוֹלֵל Poel fut. 2 pers. sing. masc. . . עלל
תְּעוֹנֵנוּ[z] Poel fut. 2 pers. pl. masc. [for תְּעוֹנְנוּ comp. § 8. rem. 15] . . . . . ענן
תָּעוּף[a] Kal fut. 3 pers. sing. fem. . . . עוף
תְּעוּפֶינָה[ee] id. fut. 3 pers. pl. fem. . . . עוף
תֵּעוֹר[b] Niph. fut. 3 pers. sing. fem. . . עור
תְּעוֹרְרוּ Pilel fut. 2 pers. pl. masc. . . . עור
תָּעֹז } Kal fut. 2 pers. sing. fem. (§ 18. rem. 5); ·וַ conv. . . . עזז
תָּעָז וַ
תַּעֲזֹב [c]וְ׳ Kal fut. 2 pers. sing. masc., or (Job 39. 14) 3 pers. sing. fem. . . . . עזב
תֵּעָזֵב[d] } Niph. fut. 3 pers. sing. fem. (§ 9. rem. 4) עזב
תֵּעָזֵב
תַּעַזְבֶהָ[e] Kal fut. 2 pers. s. m. (תַּעֲזֹב), suff. 3 p. s. fem. עזב
תַּעַזְבֻהוּ[f] id. fut. 2 pers. pl. masc., suff. 3 pers. sing. m. עזב
תַּעַזְבוּ } id. fut. 2 pers. pl. masc. (§ 8. rem. 15) עזב
תַּעֲזֹבוּ[g]
תַּעַזְבִי[h] וַ id. fut. 2 pers. sing. fem.; ·וַ conv. . עזב
תַּעַזְבֵם[i] וַ id. fut. 2 pers. sing. masc. (תַּעֲזֹב), suff. 3 pers. pl. masc.; ·וַ id. . . . עזב
תַּעַזְבֵנוּ[k] id. id., suff. 1 pers. pl. . . . עזב
תַּעַזְבֶנּוּ id. id., suff. 3 pers. sing. masc. . . עזב
תַּעַזְבֵנִי id. id., suff. 1 pers. sing. . . . עזב
תַּעַט[l] וַ Hiph. fut. 3 p. s. f. ap. & conv. (§ 21. r. 24) עיט
תַּעֲטֶה[m] Kal fut. 2 pers. sing. masc. . . . עטה
תַּעְטוּ[n] id. fut. 2 pers. pl. masc. (§ 13. rem. 5 & 6) עטה
תְּעַטְּרֵהוּ[o] Piel fut. 3 p. s. fem. [תְּעַטֵּר], suff. 3 p. s. m. עטר
תַּעְטְרֶנּוּ[p] Kal fut. 2 pers. sing. masc. [תַּעֲטֹר], suff. 3 pers. sing. masc. [for תַּעַטְרֶנּוּ § 13. rem. 5] . עטר
תֹּעֵי Kal part. act. pl. constr. masc. from תֹּעֶה d. 9a תעה
תֹּעִי [for תֹּעְי] pr. name masc., see תֹּעוּ . תעה
תָּעִיד[q] Hiph. fut. 2 pers. sing. masc. . . עוד
תְּעִידֵנִי[r] וַ id. fut. 3 pers. s. fem., suff. 1 p. s.; ·וַ conv. עוד
תָּעִינוּ[s] Kal fut. 1 pers. pl. . . . . תעה
תָּעִיק[t] Hiph. fut. 3 pers. sing. fem. . . . עוק
תָּעִירוּ Hiph. fut. 2 pers. pl. masc. . . . עור
תָּעִיתִי[u] Kal pret. 1 pers. sing. . . . . תעה
תְּעַכַּסְנָה[x] Piel fut. 3 pers. pl. f. [for תְּעַכֵּסְנָה § 10. r. 4] עכס
תַּעַל[y] וַ } Kal fut. 3 pers. sing. fem., ap. from תַּעֲלֶה (§ 24. r. 3 & 16); ·וַ conv. עלה
תַּעַל[z] וַתַּ׳, וְ׳
תַּעַל[a] וַ Hiph. fut. 2 pers. sing. masc., or 3 pers. sing. fem., ap. from תַּעֲלֶה (§ 24. r. 3 & 16); ·וַ id. עלה
תַּעֲלֶה וַ׳ Kal fut. 2 pers. sing. masc., or 3 pers. sing. fem.; or Hiph. fut. 2 pers. sing. m.; ·וַ id. עלה

[a] Ex. 3. 12. [b] Jos. 24. 15. [c] Job 9. 31. [d] 2 Sa. 17. 16. [e] Ru. 2. 8. [f] 2 Ch. 36. 14.
[g] De. 15. 6. [h] De. 15. 8. [i] Job 7. 21. [k] Jos. 24. 11. [l] Nu. 32. 5. [m] Eze. 23. 16.
[n] Eze. 23. 5. [o] Eze. 23. 20. [p] Ru. 1. 13. [q] Eze. 4. 12. [r] Ho. 2. 15. [s] Da. 6. 9, 13.
[t] Is. 61. 10. [u] Eze. 16. 13. [x] Is. 21. 4. [y] Is. 8. 16. [z] Le. 19. 26. [zz] Ne. 9. 29, 30.
[a] De. 4. 17. [b] Hab. 3. 9. [c] Job 39. 11. [d] Job 18. 4. [e] Pr. 4. 6. [ee] Is. 60. 8.
[f] 2 Ch. 15. 2. [g] Pr. 4. 2. [h] Ru. 2. 11. [i] Ne. 9. 28. [k] La. 5. 20.
[l] 1 Sa. 15. 19. [m] Eze. 24. 17. [n] Eze. 24. 22. [o] Ps. 8. 6. [p] Ps. 5. 13.
[q] 1 Sa. 8. 9. [r] Job 29. 11. [s] Is. 53. 6. [t] Am. 2. 13. [u] Ps. 119. 110, 176.
[x] Is. 3. 16. [y] Ge. 24. 16. [z] Joel 2. 20. [a] Eze. 19. 3; Jon. 2. 7.

תְּעָלָה	noun fem. sing., constr. תְּעָלַת, dec. 10 .	עלה
תַּעֲלֵהוּ[a]	וַ Hiph. fut. 3 pers. sing. fem., suff. 3 pers. sing. masc.; ·וַ conv. . .	עלה
תַּעֲלוּ[b]	וְ׳ Kal or Hiph. fut. 2 pers. pl. masc.; ·וְ id.	עלה
תֵּעָלוּ[c]	וְ Niph. fut. 2 pers. pl. masc.; ·וְ id. .	עלה
תַּעֲלוּלִים[d]	וְ noun masc., pl. of [תַּעֲלוּל] dec. 1 b .	עלל
תַּעַלְזִי[e]	Kal fut. 2 pers. sing. fem. for תַּעֲלְזִי (§ 8. r. 15)	עלז
תַּעַלְזוּ[f]	id. id. (Kh. תַּעֲלְזִי; K. תַּעַלְזוּ fut. 2 pers. pl. m.	עלז
תַּעֲלֹזְנָה[g]	וְ׳[h] id. fut. 3 pers. sing. fem. . .	עלז
תַּעֲלִי[i]	וַ Kal fut. 2 pers. sing. fem.; ·וַ conv. .	עלה
תַּעֲלִים[k]	Hiph. fut. 2 pers. sing. masc. (§ 13. rem. 5)	עלם
תַּעֲלֶינָה[l]	וַ׳[m] Kal fut. 3 pers. pl. fem.; ·וַ conv. .	עלה
תַּעְלֵם[n]	ap. from תַּעֲלִים q. v. (§ 13. rem. 5) .	עלם
תַּעֲלֻמָה[o] וְ, תַּעֲלֻמוֹת	noun fem. sing. and pl. dec. 10 .	עלם
תַּעֲלֶנָּה[p]	Hiph. fut. 2 pers. sing. masc. (תַּעֲלֶה) with suff. 3 pers. sing. fem. (§ 24. rem. 21)	עלה
תַּעֲלֵנוּ[q]	id. with suff., Kh. נוּ׳ 1 pers. pl., K. נִי׳ 1 pers. s.	עלה
תַּעֲלֵנוּ[r]	id., suff. 1 pers. pl.	עלה
תַּעֲלֵנִי[s]	id., suff. 1 pers. sing. . . .	עלה
תַּעֲלֹץ[t]	Kal fut. 3 pers. sing. fem. . . .	עלץ
תְּעָלַת[u]	noun fem. sing., constr. of תְּעָלָה dec. 10	עלה
תְּעָלֹתֶיהָ[v]	id. pl., suff. 3 pers. sing. fem. . .	עלה
תַּעֲמֹד	וַתַּ׳, וְ׳[y] Kal fut. 2 pers. sing. masc., or 3 pers. sing. fem.; ·וַ conv. . . .	עמד
תַּעַמְדוּ	id. fut. 2 pers. pl. masc. [for תַּעַמְדוּ § 8. r. 15]	עמד
תַּעַמְדוּן[z]	וַ id. id. with parag. ן; ·וַ conv. . .	עמד
תַּעֲמֹדְנָה	וַ id. fut. 3 pers. pl. fem.; ·וַ id. . .	עמד
תַּעֲמִדֵנִי	וַ Hiph. fut. 3 pers. sing. fem. [תַּעֲמִיד], suff. 1 pers. sing.; ·וַ id. . . .	עמד
תַּעֲמוֹד[a]	וַ Kal fut. 3 pers. sing. fem. (§ 8. r. 18); ·וַ id.	עמד
תַּעַן	וַ׳ ap. from תַּעֲנֶה q. v.; ·וַ id. . .	ענה
תַּעֲנֻגוֹת[b]	וְ noun fem. pl. [of תַּעֲנֻגָה] . .	ענג
תַּעֲנֻגֶיהָ[c]	noun m. pl., suff. 3 pers. s. f. fr. תַּעֲנוּג d. 1 b	ענג
תַּעֲנֶה	Kal fut. 2 pers. s. m., or (Ho. 2. 24) 3 p. s. f.	ענה
תְּעַנֶּהָ[d]	וַ Piel fut. 3 pers. s. f., suff. 3 p. s. f.; ·וַ conv.	ענה
תֵּעָנֶה	id. fut. 2 pers. sing. masc. . . .	ענה
תְּעֻנֶּה[e]	Pual fut. 3 pers. sing. fem. . . .	ענה
תַּעֲנֵהוּ	the foll. with suff. 3 pers. sing. masc. .	ענה
תַּעֲנוּ[f]	וַ Kal fut. 2 pers. pl. masc.; ·וַ conv. .	ענה
תְּעַנּוּ[g]	Piel fut. 2 pers. pl. masc. . . .	ענה
תַּעֲנוּג[h]	noun masc. sing. dec. 1 b . . .	ענג
תַּעֲנוּגַיִךְ[i]	id. pl., suff. 2 pers. sing. fem. . .	ענג
תְּעַנּוּן[k]	Piel fut. 2 pers. pl. masc. with parag. ן .	ענה
תַּעֲנֶינָה	וַ Kal fut. 3 pers. pl. fem.; ·וַ conv. .	ענה
תַּעֲנִיק[l]	Hiph. fut. 2 pers. sing. masc. . .	ענק
תַּעְנָךְ, תַּעֲנָךְ	pr. name of a city of the Manassites in the territory of Issachar.	
תְּעַנֵּךְ[m]	Kal fut. 3 pers. sing. fem. (תַּעֲנֶה), suff. 2 pers. sing. masc. (§ 24. rem. 21) .	ענה
תַּעֲנֵם	id. fut. 2 pers. sing. masc., suff. 3 pers. pl. m.	ענה
תַּעֲנֶנָּה[n]	id. fut. 3 pers. pl. fem. (§ 24. rem. 6) .	ענה
תַּעֲנֵנוּ[o]	id. fut. 2 pers. sing. masc., suff. 1 pers. pl.	ענה
תַּעֲנֶנּוּ[p]	id. id., suff. 3 pers. sing. masc. .	ענה
תְּעַנֵּנוּ[q]	וּ Piel fut. 2 pers. sing. masc. (תְּעַנֶּה), suff. 1 pers. pl. (§ 24. rem. 21); וּ bef. (:)	ענה
תַּעֲנֵנִי	וַ׳ Kal fut. 2 pers. sing. masc. (תַּעֲנֶה), suff. 1 pers. sing. (§ 24. rem. 21); ·וַ conv.	ענה
תְּעַנֵּנִי[r]	Piel fut. 2 pers. sing. masc. (תְּעַנֶּה), suff. 1 pers. sing. (§ 24. rem. 21) .	ענה

תָּעַע. Pil. תִּעְתַּע (§ 6. rem. 4) *to mock, scoff*, Ge. 27. 12. Hithpal הִתַּעְתֵּעַ (for הִתְתַּעְתֵּעַ) *to mock, scoff at,* with בְּ 2 Ch. 36. 16.

תַּעְתֻּעִים masc. pl. *mockeries, delusions,* Je. 10. 15; 51. 18.

תָּעֻפָה[s]	Kal fut. 2 pers. sing. masc. [תָּעוּף] with parag. ה (comp. § 8. rem. 13) .	עוף
תֵּעָצְבוּ[t], תֵּעָצְבוּ[u]	Niph. fut. 2 pers. pl. masc. (comp. § 8. rem. 15)	עצב
תֵּעָצֵלוּ[v]	Niph. fut. 2 pers. pl. masc. . . .	עצל
תַּעֲצֻמוֹת[y]	וְ noun fem. pl. [of תַּעֲצֻמָה] . .	עצם
תַּעְצֹר[z]	Kal fut. 3 pers. sing. fem. (§ 13. rem. 5)	עצר
תַּעְצָר[a]	id. fut. 2 pers. s. m. (§ 8. r. 18, & § 13. r. 5)	עצר
תֵּעָצַר	וַתֵּ׳, וְ Niph. fut. 3 p. s. f. (§ 9. r. 4); ·וַ conv.	עצר
תַּעְצְרֵנִי[b]	Kal fut. 2 pers. s. m., suff. 1 p. s. (§ 13. r. 5)	עצר
תֵּעָקֵר[c]	Niph. fut. 3 pers. sing. fem. . .	עקר
תְּעַקֵּר[d]	Piel fut. 2 pers. sing. masc. . .	עקר
תַּעַר	noun masc. sing. [for תַּעְרָה] . .	ערה
תְּעַר[e]	וַ׳[f] Piel fut. 2 pers. sing. masc., or 3 pers. sing. fem. ap. [from תְּעָרֶה]; ·וַ conv.	ערה
תֶּעֱרַב[g]	Kal fut. 3 pers. sing. fem. . . .	ערב
תַּעֲרֹג[h]	Kal fut. 3 pers. sing. fem. . . .	ערג
תַּעְרָהּ[i]	noun masc. sing., suff. 3 pers. sing. fem. from תַּעַר [for תַּעְרָה comp. § 35 r. 5] .	ערה
תַּעֲרוֹג[k]	Kal fut. 3 pers. sing. fem. (§ 8. rem. 18)	ערג
תַּעֲרוֹץ[l]	Kal fut. 2 pers. sing. masc. (§ 8. rem. 18)	ערץ
תַּעֲרוּצִי[m]	id. fut. 2 pers. s. f. [for תַּעַרְצִי § 8. r. 18]	ערץ

[a] 1 Sa. 1. 24. [b] De. 1. 43. [c] Eze. 36. 3. [d] Is. 3. 4. [e] Je. 11. 15. [f] Je. 50. 11. [g] 2 Sa. 1. 20. [h] Pr. 23. 16. [i] Is. 57. 8. [k] Ps. 10. 1. [l] Is. 65. 17. [m] Da. 8. 8. [n] La. 3. 56. [o] Job 28. 11. [p] Ju. 13. 16. [q] Ps. 71. 20. [r] Ex. 33. 15. [s] Ps. 102. 25. [t] Pr. 11. 10. [u] Is. 7. 3. [v] Eze. 31. 4. [y] Da. 12. 13. [z] De. 4. 11. [a] Ru. 2. 7. [b] Ec. 2. 8. [c] Mi. 2. 9. [d] Ge. 16. 6. [e] Le. 23. 29. [f] De. 1. 14, 41. [g] Le. 16. 29. [h] Pr. 19. 10. [i] Mi. 1. 16. [k] Ex. 22. 21. [l] De. 15. 14. [m] De. 20. 11. [n] Ju. 5. 29. [o] Ps. 65. 6. [p] 2 Ki. 4. 29. [q] Is. 64. 11. [r] 2 Sa. 13. 12. [s] Job 11. 17. [t] Ne. 8. 10, 11. [u] Ge. 45. 5. [v] Ju. 18. 9. [y] Ps. 68. 36. [z] Da. 11. 6. [a] 2 Ki. 4. 24. [b] Ju. 13. 16. [c] Zep. 2. 4. [d] Jos. 11. 6. [e] Ps. 141. 8. [f] Ge. 24. 20. [g] Pr. 13. 19. [h] Ps. 42. 2. [i] Eze. 21. 35. [k] Joel 1. 20. [l] Job 13. 25. [m] Is. 47. 12.

תַּעֲרִיצוּ[a] Hiph. fut. 2 pers. pl. masc. . . . ערץ
תַּעֲרֵךְ[b] noun masc. sing., suff. 2 pers. sing. masc. from תַּעַר [for תַּעַרְךָ comp. § 35 r. 5] . ערה
תַּעֲרֹךְ[c] [d]וַ׳ Kal fut. 2 pers. sing. masc., or 3 pers. sing. fem.; ·וַ conv. . . . ערך
תַּעַרְכוּ[e] id. fut. 2 pers. pl. masc. . . . ערך
תַּעֲרֹץ Kal fut. 2 pers. sing. masc. . . ערץ
תַּעַרְצוּ
תַּעַרְצוּן[f] } id. fut. 2 pers. pl. masc., ן parag. . ערץ
תְּעֹרֵר[g] Pilel fut. 3 pers. sing. fem. . . עור
תְּעֹרְרוּ[h] id. fut. 2 pers. pl. masc. . . . עור
תַּעַשׂ וַ׳ ap. from תַּעֲשֶׂה (q. v.) . . . עשׂה
תַּעַשׂ[i] Kh. תַּעַשׂ q. v., K. תַּעֲשֶׂה (q. v.) . . עשׂה
תֵּעָשׂ וְ ap. from תֵּעָשֶׂה (q. v.) . . . עשׂה
תַּעֲשֶׂהָ[k] Kal fut. 2 pers. sing. masc. (תַּעֲשֶׂה), suff. 3 pers. sing. fem. (§ 24. rem. 21) . עשׂה
תַּעֲשֶׂה id. fut. 2 pers. sing. masc. (§ 24. rem. 20) עשׂה
תַּעֲשֶׂה וַ׳ id. fut. 2 pers. s. m., or 3 p. s. f.; ·וַ conv. עשׂה
תֵּעָשֶׂה Niph. fut. 3 pers. sing. fem. . . עשׂה
תַּעֲשׂוּ
תַּעֲשׂוּן } וַ׳ Kal fut. 2 pers. pl. masc., ן parag.; ·וַ conv. עשׂה
תַּעֲשִׂי
תַּעֲשִׂין[l] } וַ׳ id. fut. 2 pers. sing. fem., ן parag.; ·וַ id. עשׂה
תַּעֲשֶׂינָה [m]וַ׳ id. fut. 2 p. (Je. 44. 25) or 3 p. pl. f.; ·וַ id. עשׂה
תֵּעָשֶׂינָה Niph. fut. 3 pers. pl. fem. . . . עשׂה
תַּעֲשִׁיר[n] Hiph. fut. 3 pers. sing. fem. . . עשׁר
תַּעֲשֶׂנָה[o] defect. for תַּעֲשֶׂינָה (q. v.) . . . עשׂה
תַּעֲשֶׂנּוּ[p] Kal fut. 2 pers. sing. masc. (תַּעֲשֶׂה), suff. 3 pers. sing. masc. (§ 24. rem. 21) . עשׂה
תַּעֲשֹׁק Kal fut. 2 pers. sing. masc. . . . עשׁק
תַּעֲשֹׁקוּ id. fut. 2 pers. pl. m. [for תַּעַשְׁקוּ § 8. r. 15] עשׁק
תְּעַשֵּׂר[q] Piel fut. 2 pers. sing. masc. . . עשׂר
תַּעְשְׁרֶנָּה[r] [for תַּעֲשִׁירֶנָּה] Hiph. fut. 2 pers. sing. masc. [תַּעְשֵׁר], suff. 3 pers. sing. f. (§ 16. r. 16) עשׁר
תַּעְתִּירִי[s] Hiph. fut. 2 pers. sing. masc. (§ 13. rem. 9) עתר
תַּעְתֻּעִים noun masc. pl. [of תַּעְתֻּעַ] . . . תעע
תֹּף [t]וְ׳ noun masc. sing. dec. 8 c . . . תפף
תְּפָאֵר[u] Piel fut. 2 pers. sing. masc. . . . פאר
תִּפְאָרָה noun fem. sing. (§ 42. rem. 5) . . . פאר
תִּפְאֶרֶת
תִּפְאֶרֶת } וְ׳ id., constr. st. . . . . פאר
תִּפְאַרְתּוֹ וְ׳ id., suff. 3 pers. sing. masc. . . . פאר
תִּפְאַרְתִּי id., suff. 1 pers. sing. . . . . פאר
תִּפְאַרְתֶּךָ
תִּפְאַרְתְּךָ[y] } [x]וְ׳ id., suff. 2 pers. sing. masc. . . פאר
תִּפְאַרְתֵּךְ id., suff. 2 pers. sing. fem. . . . פאר

תִּפְאַרְתְּכֶם[z] id., suff. 2 pers. pl. masc. . . . פאר
תִּפְאַרְתָּם id., suff. 3 pers. pl. masc. . . . פאר
תִּפְאַרְתֵּנוּ[a] וְ id., suff. 1 pers. pl. . . . פאר
תִּפְגַּע Kal fut. 2 pers. sing. masc. . . . פגע
תִּפְגְּעוּן[b] id. fut. 2 pers. pl. masc. with parag. ן . פגע
תִּפְגְּעִי[c] id. fut. 2 pers. sing. fem. . . . פגע
תִּפְגֹּשׁ[d] וַ Kal fut. 3 pers. sing. fem.; ·וַ conv. . פגשׁ
תִּפָּדֶה[e] Niph. fut. 3 pers. sing. fem. . . . פדה
תִּפְדֶּה Kal fut. 2 pers. sing. masc. . . . פדה
תֹּפֵהוּ[f] וַ Kal fut. 3 pers. sing. fem., suff. 3 pers. sing. masc. [for תֹּאפֵהוּ § 19. rem. 5]; ·וַ conv. אפה
תִּפְדּוּנִי[g] Kal fut. 2 pers. pl. masc., suff. 1 pers. sing. פדה
תָּפוּג Kal fut. 3 pers. sing. fem. . . . פוג
תַּפּוּחַ[h] וְ׳ noun masc. sing., also pr. name (& in compos. see בַּיִת) . . . . נפח
תַּפּוּחֵי[i] id. pl., constr. st. . . . . נפח
תִּפּוֹל Kal fut. 2 pers. s. m., or 3 p. s. fem. (§ 17. r. 3) נפל
תְּפוֹצוֹתֵיכֶם[k] וּ noun fem. pl., suff. 2 pers. pl. masc. [from תְּפוֹצָה]; וּ bef. (:) . . פוץ
תְּפוּצֶיןָ[l] וּ
תְּפוּצֶינָה[m] וַ
תְּפוּצֶנָה[n] } Kal fut. 3 pers. pl. fem. (comp. § 8. rem. 16, & § 24. rem. 6); וּ, for וְ; ·וַ conv. . . . . . פוץ
תָּפוּשׂ[o] Kal part. pass. sing. masc. . . תפשׂ
תָּפוּשׁ[p] Kh. תָּפוּשִׁי, K. תָּפוּשׁוּ, Kal fut. 2 pers. sing. fem., or 2 pers. pl. masc. . . . פושׁ
תְּפַזְּרִי[q] וַ Piel fut. 2 pers. sing. fem.; ·וַ conv. . פזר
תַּפֻּחַ וְ pr. name masc., see תַּפּוּחַ . . . נפח
תְּפַחֵד[r] וַ Piel fut. 2 pers. s. masc. (§ 14. r. 1); ·וַ conv. פחד
תִּפְחָד Kal fut. 2 pers. s. masc. [for תִּפְחַד § 8. r. 15] פחד
תִּפְחֲדוּ[s] id. fut. 2 pers. pl. masc. . . . פחד
תֻּפַּיִךְ[t] noun m. pl., suff. 2 pers. s. fem. fr. תֹּף dec. 4 c תפף
תֻּפֶּיךָ[u] id. pl., suff. 2 pers. sing. masc. . . תפף
תַּפִּיל Hiph. fut. 2 p. s. m., or (Pr. 19. 15) 3 p. s. fem. נפל
תַּפִּילוּ id. fut. 2 pers. pl. masc. . . . נפל
תֻּפִּים[x] noun masc., pl. of תֹּף dec. 8 c . . תפף
תֻּפִינֵי[y] noun masc. pl. constr. [from תֻּפִין] . . אפה
תָּפִיץ[z] Hiph. fut. 3 pers. sing. fem. . . . פוץ
תְּפִיצֵם[a] וּ id. fut. 2 pers. s. m., suff. 3 p. pl. m.; וּ bef. (:) פוץ

תָּפֵל [b]וְ׳ masc.—I. *any thing unseasoned, unsavoury,* Job 6. 6.—II. metaph. *insipid, foolish,* La. 2. 14.—III. *lime, mortar.*

תֹּפֶל (*lime*) pr. name of a place in the desert of Sinai, De. 1. 1.

תִּפְלָה fem. *insipidity, folly, impiety.*

---

[a] Is. 8. 12. [b] Je. 47. 6. [c] Ps. 23. 5. [d] 1 Sa. 17. 21. [e] Is. 40. 18. [f] De. 1. 29. [g] Pr. 10. 12. [h] Ca. 8. 4. [i] Je. 40. 16. [k] Ge. 6. 16. [l] Ru. 3. 4. [m] Eze. 16. 50. [n] Pr. 10. 4, 22. [o] Job 5. 12. [p] Ex. 28. 15. [q] De. 14. 22. [r] Ps. 65. 10. [s] Job 22. 27. [t] 1 Sa. 10. 5. [u] De. 24. 20. [x] Is. 63. 15. [y] Ju. 4. 9. [z] Je. 13. 18. [a] Is. 64. 10. [b] Ju. 15. 12. [c] Ru. 1. 16. [d] 1 Sa. 25. 20. [e] Is. 1. 27. [f] 1 Sa. 28. 24. [g] Job 6. 23. [h] Joel 1. 12. [i] Pr. 25. 11. [k] Je. 25. 34. [l] Zec. 13. 7. [m] Eze. 34. 5. [n] Zec. 1. 17. [o] Hab. 2. 19. [p] Je. 50. 11. [q] Je. 3. 13. [r] Is. 51. 13. [s] Is. 44. 8. [t] Je. 31. 4. [u] Eze. 28. 13. [x] Is. 24. 8. [y] Le. 6. 14. [z] Is. 41. 16. [a] Ps. 144. 6. [b] La. 2. 14.

תַּפֵּל[b] [c]וְ׳ Hiph. fut. 2 pers. sing. masc., or 3 pers. sing. fem., ap. from תַּפִּיל; ·וַ conv. — נפל

תִּפֹּל וַתִּ׳, [zz]וְ׳ Kal fut. 2 pers. sing. masc. (Je. 39. 18), or 3 pers. s. f. (§ 17. r. 3); ·וַ id. — נפל

תִּפָּל־ id. fut. 3 p. s. fem. with Mak. (comp. § 8. r. 18) — נפל

תֹּפֶל pr. name of a place — תפל

תְּפִלָּה וּ׳ noun fem. sing. dec. 10; וּ bef. (:) — פלל

תִּפְלָה noun fem. sing. — תפל

תִּפְּלוּ[d] defect. for תַּפִּילוּ (q. v.) — נפל

תִּפְּלוּ Kal fut. 2 pers. pl. masc. [for תִּפְּלוּ § 8. r. 15] — נפל

תִּפְּלוּן[e] Chald. Peal fut. 2 pers. pl. masc. — נפל

תְּפִלּוֹת[f] noun fem., pl. of תְּפִלָּה dec. 10 — פלל

תְּפַלַּחְנָה[g] Piel fut. 3 pers. pl. fem. — פלח

תְּפַלֵּט[h] Piel fut. 2 pers. sing. masc., or 3 pers. s. fem. — פלט

תְּפַלְּטֵמוֹ[i] וַ id. fut. 2 pers. s. m., suff. 3 p. pl. m.; ·וַ conv. — פלט

תְּפַלְּטֵנִי [k]וּ׳, [l]וַתְּ׳ id. id., suff. 1 pers. s.; וּ for וְ, ·וַ id. — פלט

תַּפְלִיט[m] Hiph. fut. 2 pers. sing. masc. — פלט

תִּפֹּלְנָה Kal fut. 3 pers. pl. fem. — נפל

תְּפַלֵּס Piel fut. 2 pers. sing. masc. — פלס

תְּפַלֵּסוּן[n] id. fut. 2 pers. pl. masc., ן parag. [for תְּפַלְּסוּן § 8. rem. 17] — פלס

תִּפְלַצְתְּךָ[o] noun fem. sing., suff. 2 pers. sing. masc. from [תִּפְלֶצֶת] dec. 13 a — פלץ

תְּפִלַּת וּ׳ noun fem. s., constr. of תְּפִלָּה d. 10; וּ bef. (:) — פלל

תְּפִלָּתוֹ[p] וּ׳ id., suff. 3 pers. sing. masc.; וּ id. — פלל

תְּפִלָּתִי וּ׳ id., suff. 1 pers. sing.; וּ id. — פלל

תְּפִלָּתְךָ, תְּפִלָּתֶךָ[q] } id., suff. 2 pers. sing. masc. — פלל

תְּפִלָּתָם id., suff. 3 pers. pl. masc. — פלל

תֵּפֶן וַ ap. from the foll. (§ 24. rem. 3); ·וַ conv. — פנה

תִּפְנֶה Kal fut. 2 pers. s. m., or (Le. 20. 6) 3 p. s. fem. — פנה

תִּפְנוּ[r] id. fut. 2 pers. pl. masc. — פנה

תִּפְסַח pr. name of a place — פסח

תֹּפַע[s] וַ Hiph. fut. 3 p. s. fem., ap. & conv. [fr. תּוֹפִיעַ] — יפע

תִּפְעָל[t] Kal fut. 2 pers. s. masc. [for תִּפְעַל § 8. r. 15] — פעל

תִּפְעָל־[u] id. with Mak. [for תִּפְעַל § 8. rem. 18] — פעל

תִּפְעָלוּן[x] id. fut. 2 pers. pl. masc., ן parag. [for תִּפְעֲלוּן § 8. rem. 17] — פעל

תִּפָּעֶם וַ Niph. fut. 3 pers. sing. fem.; (§ 9. rem. 3) ·וַ conv. — פעם

[תָּפַף] *to beat* the tabret, Ps. 68. 26. Pu. *to smite upon* the breast, with עַל, Na. 2. 8.

תֹּף masc. dec. 8 c, *drum, tabret.*

תָּפֵק[y] [z]וְ׳ Hiph. fut. 2 pers. s. masc. ap. [fr. תָּפִיק] — פוק

תִּפָּקֵד[a] Niph. fut. 2 pers. sing. masc., or 3 pers. s. fem. — פקד

תִּפְקֹד [b]וְ׳ Kal fut. 2 pers. sing. masc.; ·וַ conv. — פקד

תִּפְקְדוּ id. fut. 2 pers. pl. masc. — פקד

תִּפְקְדִי[c] וַ id. fut. 2 pers. sing. fem.; ·וַ conv. — פקד

תִּפְקְדֵם id. fut. 2 pers. sing. m., suff. 3 pers. pl. m. — פקד

תִּפְקְדֶנּוּ[d] [e]וַ׳ id. id., suff. 3 pers. sing. masc.; ·וַ conv. — פקד

תִּפָּקַחְנָה[f] [g]וַ׳ Niph. fut. 3 pers. pl. fem.; ·וַ id. — פקח

[תָּפַר] *to sew, join together.* Pi. id. Eze. 13. 18.

תָּפֵר [h]וְ׳ Hiph. fut. 2 pers. sing. masc., or (Ec. 12. 5) 3 pers. sing. fem. — פרר

תֻּפַר וְ, תֻּפַר[k] [l]וְ׳ } Hoph. fut. 3 pers. sing. fem. [defect. for תּוּפַר]; ·וַ conv. — פרר

תִּפְרֶה[m] Kal fut. 2 pers. sing. masc. — פרה

תָּפֵרוּ[n] Hiph. fut. 2 p. pl. masc. — פרר

תִּפְרַח[o], תִּפְרַח [p]וְ׳ } Kal fut. 3 pers. sing. fem. (§ 8. rem. 15) — פרח

תִּפְרַחְנָה[q] id. fut. 3 pers. pl. fem. — פרח

תַּפְרִיחִי[r] Hiph. fut. 2 pers. sing. fem. — פרח

תַּפְרִיעוּ[s] Hiph. fut. 2 pers. pl. masc. — פרע

תִּפְרְמוּ[t] Kal fut. 2 pers. s. m. [for תִּפְרְמוּ § 8. r. 15] — פרם

תִּפְרָעוּ[u], תִּפְרָעוּ[x] וַ } Kal fut. 2 pers. pl. masc. (§ 8. rem. 15); ·וַ conv. — פרע

תִּפְרֹץ[y] וַ Kal fut. 3 pers. sing. fem. [for תִּפְרֹץ § 8. rem. 18]; ·וַ id. — פרץ

תִּפְרְצִי[z] id. fut. 2 pers. s. f. [for תִּפְרְצִי § 8. rem. 15] — פרץ

תְּפָרֵשׂ[a] Piel fut. 3 pers. sing. fem. — פרש

תִּפְרֹשׂ[b] וַ Kal fut. 3 pers. sing. fem.; ·וַ conv. — פרש

תָּפַרְתִּי[c] Kal pret. 1 pers. sing. — תפר

תָּפַשׂ [d]וְ׳ fut. יִתְפֹּשׂ.—I. *to lay hold of, to seize,* with acc., בְּ.—II. *to take, capture.*—III. *to handle,* e. g. a bow, harp, &c.; metaph. *to handle, administer* the law, Je. 2. 8; of the name of God, *to use irreverently,* Pr. 30. 9.—IV. part. pass. *held, set* in gold, Hab. 2. 19. Niph. *to be taken, caught, captured.* Pi. *to take hold,* Pr. 30. 28.

תָּפוֹשׂ[e] Kal inf. abs. — תפש

תְּפֹשׂ[f] id. inf. constr. — תפש

תֹּפֵשׂ[g] וְ׳ id. part. act. sing. masc. dec. 7 b — תפש

תְּפָשָׂהּ[h] וּ id. pret. 3 pers. sing. masc., suff. 3 pers. sing. fem.; וּ, for וְ, conv. — תפש

תִּפְשֶׂה[i] Kal fut. 3 pers. sing. fem. — פשה

תְּפָשָׂהוּ[k] defect. for תְּפָשׂוּהוּ (q. v.) — תפש

תָּפְשׂוּ[l] [m]וְ׳ Kal pret. 3 pers. pl. — תפש

---

[b] Est. 6. 10. [c] Da. 8. 10. [d] Eze. 47. 22. [e] Da. 3. 5, 15. [f] Ps. 72. 20. [g] Job 39. 3. [h] Mi. 6. 14; Job 21. 10. [i] Ps. 22. 5. [k] Ps. 71. 2. [l] 2 Sa. 22. 44. [m] Mi. 6. 14. [n] Ps. 58. 3. [o] Je. 49. 16. [p] Pr. 28. 9. [q] 1 Ki. 9. 3. [r] Le. 19. 4, 31. [s] Job 10. 22. [t] Job 11. 8. [u] Job 35. 6. [x] Ps. 58. 3. [y] Ps. 140. 9. [z] Is. 58. 10. [a] Is. 29. 6; Eze. 38. 8. [b] 2 Sa. 3. 8. [c] Eze. 23. 21. [d] Ps. 8. 5. [e] Job 7. 18. [f] Is. 35. 5. [g] Ge. 3. 7. [h] Ec. 12. 5. [i] Is. 8. 10. [k] Je. 33. 21. [l] Zec. 11. 11. [m] Ex. 23. 30. [n] Je. 33. 20. [o] Hab. 3. 17. [p] Is. 35. 1. [q] Is. 66. 14. [r] Is. 17. 11. [s] Ex. 5. 4. [t] Le. 10. 6. [u] Le. 10. 6; Pr. 8. 33. [x] Pr. 1. 25. [y] Ps. 106. 29. [z] Is. 54. 3. [zz] Is. 47. 11. [a] Je. 4. 31. [b] 2 Sa. 17. 19. [c] Job 16. 15. [d] 2 Ki. 14. 7. [e] Je. 34. 3. [f] Eze. 14. 5. [g] Ge. 4. 21. [h] De. 22. 28. [i] Le. 13. 7, 22, 27. [k] 1 Ki. 13. 4. [l] Jos. 8. 23. [m] De. 21. 19.

Word	Analysis	Root
תָּצוּד[f]	Kal fut. 3 pers. sing. fem.	צוד
תְּצוֹדֵדְנָה[g]	Pilel fut. 2 pers. pl. fem. . . .	צוד
תְּצוּדֵנִי[h]	Kal fut. 2 pers. s. m. [תָּצוּד], suff. 1 pers. s.	צוד
תְּצַוֶּה	Piel fut. 2 pers. sing. masc. . . .	צוה
תְּצַוֵּהוּ[i]	וַ id. fut. 3 pers. sing. fem. with suff. 3 pers. sing. masc.; וַ conv.	צוה
תְּצַוֵּם[k]	id. fut. 2 pers. pl. masc., suff. 3 pers. pl. masc. (§ 24. rem. 21)	צוה
תָּצוּמוּ[l]	Kal fut. 2 pers. pl. masc.	צום
תְּצַוֶּנּוּ[m]	Piel fut. 2 pers. sing. masc. (תְּצַוֶּה), suff. 3 pers. sing. masc. (§ 24. rem. 21)	צוה
תְּצַוֻּנִי[n]	id. fut. 2 pers. pl. m. [תְּצַוּוּ], suff. 1 pers. s.	צוה
תָּצוּר[o]	Kal fut. 2 pers. sing. masc. . . .	צור
תִּצְחַק[p]	וַ Kal fut. 3 pers. sing. fem.; וַ conv. .	צחק
תַּצִּיבֵנִי[q]	וַ Hiph. fut. 2 p. s. m., suff. 1 p. s.; וַ id.	נצב
תַּצִּיג[r]	Hiph. fut. 2 pers. sing. masc. (§ 20. r. 16)	יצג
תַּצִּיל	Hiph. fut. 2 pers. sing. masc., or 3 pers. s. f.	נצל
תַּצִּילֵם[s]	וְ, וַ id. id., suff. 3 pers. pl. masc. . .	נצל
תַּצִּילֶנּוּ[u]	id. fut. 2 pers. sing. masc., suff. 3 pers. s. m.	נצל
תַּצִּילֵנִי	id. id., suff. 1 pers. sing. . . .	נצל
תִּצֶּינָה[x]	Kal fut. 3 pers. pl. fem. (§ 25. No. 2 b)	נצה
תַּצִּיתוּ[bb]	Hiph. fut. 2 pers. pl. masc. (§ 20. rem. 16)	יצת
תַּצֵּל[y]	Hiph. fut. 2 pers. sing. masc., ap. from תַּצִּיל	נצל
תִּצְלַח / וַתִּצְלַח	Kal fut. 3 pers. sing. fem. (§ 8. rem. 15); וַ conv.	צלח
תִּצְלְחִי[z]	וַ id. fut. 3 pers. sing. fem.; וַ id.	צלח
תַּצְלִיחַ[a]	Hiph. fut. 2 pers. sing. masc.	צלח
תַּצְלִיחוּ	id. fut. 2 pers. pl. masc. .	צלח
תַּצְלִיחִי[b]	id. fut. 2 pers. sing. fem. .	צלח
תְּצִלֶּינָה[c]	Hiph. fut. 3 pers. pl. fem. .	צלל
תִּצַּלְנָה	Kal fut. 3 pers. pl. fem. (§ 18. rem. 16)	צלל
תִּצְמְאוּ[d]	Kal fut. 2 pers. pl. m. [for תִּצְמְאוּ § 8. r. 15]	צמא
תַּצְמִחַ[e]	defect. for תַּצְמִיחַ (q. v.)	צמח
תִּצְמַח	Kal fut. 3 pers. s. fem. [for תִּצְמַח § 8. r. 15]	צמח
תִּצְמַחְנָה[f]	id. fut. 3 pers. pl. fem.	צמח
תַּצְמִיד[g]	Hiph. fut. 3 pers. sing. fem.	צמד
תַּצְמִיחַ	Hiph. fut. 3 pers. sing. fem. . .	צמח
תַּצְמִית[h]	Hiph. fut. 2 pers. sing. masc. . .	צמת
תִּצְנַח	וַ Kal fut. 3 pers. sing. fem.; וַ conv. .	צנח
תִּצְעַד[i]	Kal fut. 3 pers. sing. fem. . .	צעד
תַּצְעִידֵהוּ[k]	וַ Hiph. fut. 3 pers. s. f. with suff. 3 p s m.	צעד
תִּצְעַק[l]	Kal fut. 2 pers. sing. masc. . .	צעק
תִּצְעֲקוּ[m]	וְ, וַ[n] id. fut. 2 pers. pl. masc.; וַ conv. .	צעק
תְּצַפֶּה[o]	Piel fut. 2 pers. sing. masc.	צפה

Word	Analysis	Root
תִּפְשׂוּ[a]	id. imp. pl. masc.	תפש
תְּפָשׂוּהוּ[b]	וְ id. id., suff. 3 pers. sing. masc. . . .	תפש
תְּפָשׂוּם	id. id., suff. 3 pers. pl. masc. . . .	תפש
תַּפְשִׁטוּן[c]	Hiph. fut. 2 pers. pl. masc. with parag. ן	פשט
תֹּפְשֵׂי	וְ[d] Kal part. act. pl. constr. m. fr. תֹּפֵשׂ d. 7 b	תפש
תֹּפְשִׂי[e]	id. sing. with parag. י (§ 8. rem. 19) .	תפש
תַּפְשִׁיט[f]	Hiph. fut. 2 pers. sing. masc. . . .	פשט
תִּפְשַׁע	Kal fut. 3 pers. sing. fem. . . .	פשע
תְּפַשְּׂקִי[g]	וַ Piel fut. 2 pers. sing. fem.; וַ conv. .	פשק
תָּפַשְׂתִּי[h]	וְ Kal pret. 1 pers. sing.	תפש
תְּפַשְׂתֶּם[i]	id. pret. 2 pers. pl. masc. . . .	תפש
תֹּפֶת[k]	וְ noun fem. sing.	תוף
תָּפְתֶּה[l]	noun masc. sing.	תוף
תְּפַתֶּה	Piel fut. 2 pers. sing. masc. . . .	פתה
תְּפַתַּח[m] / תְּפַתֵּחַ[n]	Piel fut. 2 pers. sing. masc. (§ 15. rem. 1)	פתח
תִּפָּתַח[o]	Niph. fut. 3 pers. sing. fem. . . .	פתח
תִּפְתַּח[p] / וַתִּפְתַּח	Kal fut. 2 pers. sing. masc., or 3 pers. sing. fem. (§ 8. rem. 15); וַ conv.	פתח
תִּפָּתַחְנָה[q]	Niph. fut. 3 pers. pl. fem. (§ 10. rem. 4)	פתח
תִּפְתָּיֵא[r]	Chald. masc. pl. emph. [of תִּפְתָּי § 63] *lawyers* or *judges*, Da. 3. 2, 3. Etymology doubtful.	
תֵּצֵא	וַתֵּ, וְ Kal fut. 2 pers. sing. masc., or 3 pers. sing. fem.; וַ conv.	יצא
תֹּצֵא[s]	וַ Hiph. fut. 2 pers. sing. masc., ap. & defect. for תּוֹצִיא; וַ id.	יצא
תֵּצְאוּ / תֵּצֵאוּ	Kal fut. 2 pers. pl. masc. (comp. § 8. rem. 15)	יצא
תֹּצְאוֹת	defect. for תּוֹצָאוֹת (q. v.)	יצא
תֵּצְאִי[u]	Kh. תֵּצְאִי q. v., K. תֵּצְאוּ (q. v.)	יצא
תֵּצְאִי	Kal fut. 2 pers. sing. fem. . . .	יצא
תֵּצֶאןָ[x]	וַ id. fut. 3 pers. pl. fem.; וַ conv.	יצא
תֵּצֶאנָה[y]	וְ id. fut. 2 pers. pl. fem. (Am. 4. 3), or 3 pers. pl. fem. (§ 25. No. 2 d); וַ id. .	יצא
תֹּצְאֹתָו[z] / תֹּצְאֹתָיו	noun fem. pl., suff. 3 pers. sing. masc. (§ 3. rem. 1) from תּוֹצָאָה dec. 11 a	יצא
תִּצְבָּר־[a]	וַ Kal fut. 3 pers. sing. fem. [for תִּצְבֹּר § 8. rem. 18]; וַ conv.	צבר
תִּצְדָּק / תִּצְדַּק[b]	Kal fut. 2 pers. sing. masc. (§ 8. r. 15)	צדק
תְּצַדְּקִי[c]	וַ Piel fut. 2 pers. sing. fem.; וַ conv. .	צדק
תִּצְדַּקְנָה[d]	Kal fut. 3 pers. pl. fem.	צדק
תִּצְהֲלִי[e]	וַ Kh. תִּצְהֲלִי Kal fut. 2 pers. sing. fem., K. תִּצְהֲלוּ 2 pers. pl. masc.; וַ conv. .	צהל

[a] 1 Ki. 18. 40. [b] Ps. 71. 11. [c] Mi. 2. 8. [d] Je. 2. 8. [e] Je. 49. 16. [f] Job 22. 6. [g] Eze. 16. 25. [h] Pr. 30. 9. [i] Je. 40. 10. [k] Job 17. 6. [l] Is. 30. 33. [m] Job 38. 31. [n] Ex. 28. 11. [o] Je. 1. 14. [p] Ps. 51. 17. [q] Is. 35. 5. [r] Da. 3. 2, 3. [s] Ju. 9. 20. [t] Je. 32. 21. [u] Je. 6. 25. [x] Ex. 15. 20. [y] Am. 4. 3. [z] Jos. 16. 3. [a] Zec. 9. 3. [b] Ps. 51. 6. [c] Eze. 16. 51. [d] Eze. 16. 52. [e] Je. 50. 11. [f] Pr. 6. 26. [g] Eze. 13. 18. [h] Job 10. 16. [i] Est. 4. 5, 10. [k] De. 32. 46. [l] Is. 58. 4. [m] Jos. 1. 18. [n] Is. 45. 11. [o] De. 20. 19. [p] Ge. 18. 12. [q] Ps. 41. 13. [r] Ju. 7. 5. [s] Pr. 11. 6. [t] Ne. 9. 28. [u] Eze. 33. 12. [x] Je. 4. 7. [y] Ps. 119. 43. [z] Eze. 16. 13. [a] De. 28. 29. [b] Je. 2. 37. [bb] Jos. 8. 8. [c] 1 Sa. 3. 11. [d] Is. 65. 13. [e] De. 29. 22. [f] Is. 42. 9. [g] Ps. 50. 19. [h] Ps. 143. 12. [i] Hab. 3. 12. [k] Job 18. 14. [l] Ex. 14. 15. [m] Is. 65. 14. [n] Ju. 10. 12. [o] Ex. 26. 29.

תִּצְפֶּינָה[a] Kal fut. 3 pers. pl. fem. . . . צפה
תִּצְפֹּן Kal fut. 2 pers. sing. masc. . . צפן
תִּצְפְּנֵהוּ[b] וַ id. fut. 3 pers. sing. fem., suff. 3 pers. sing. masc.; וַ· conv. . . . צפן
תְּצַפֶּנּוּ[c] Piel fut. 2 pers. sing. masc. (תְּצַפֶּה), suff. 3 pers. sing. masc. (§ 24. rem. 21) . צפה
תִּצְפְּנוֹ[d] וַ Kal fut. 3 p. s. fem., suff. 3 p. s. m.; וַ· conv. צפן
תִּצְפְּנֵם[e] id. fut. 3 pers. sing. fem., suff. 3 pers. pl. m. צפן
תַּצְפִּנֵנִי[f] Hiph. fut. 2 pers. s. m. [תַּצְפִּין], suff. 1 p. s. צפן
תְּצַפְצֵף[g] Pilp. fut. 3 pers. sing. fem. (§ 6. No. 4) . צפף
תִּצֹּק[h] וַ Kal fut. 3 p. s. fem. (§ 20. r. 16); וַ· conv. יצק
תָּצַר[i] Kal fut. 2 pers. sing. masc. ap. (§ 21. rem. 9) צור
תִּצֶר וַ Kal fut. 3 pers. sing. fem.; וַ· conv. . יצר
תִּצֹּר Kal fut. 2 p. s. m., or (Pr. 13. 6) 3 p. s. fem. נצר
תִּצְּרִי[k] Kal fut. 2 pers. sing. fem. . . . יצר
תְּצֻרֵם[l] Kal fut. 2 pers. sing. masc. (תָּצוּר) with suff. 3 pers. pl. masc. . . . . צור
תִּצְּרֶךָּ[m] וְ Kal fut. 3 pers. sing. fem. (תִּצֹּר), suff. 2 pers. sing. masc. [for תִּצָּרְךָ § 2. rem. 2] . נצר
תִּצְּרֶנּוּ[n] id. fut. 2 pers. sing. masc., suff. 3 pers. sing. m. נצר
תִּצְּרֵנִי[o] id. id., suff. 1 pers. sing. . . . נצר
תִּצַּת[p] וַ Kal fut. 3 pers. s. fem. (§ 20. r. 16); וַ· conv. יצת
תִּצַּתְנָה[q] id. fut. 3 pers. pl. fem. . . . יצת
תָּקֵא[r] וַ defect. for תָּקִיא q. v.; וַ· conv. . קוא
תִּקֹּב[dd] Kal fut. 2 pers. sing. masc. . . . נקב
תְּקַבְּלוּן[s] Chald. Pael fut. 2 pers. pl. masc. . קבל
תִּקָּבֶנּוּ[t] Kal fut. 2 pers. sing. masc. (תִּקֹּב), suff. 3 pers. sing. masc. (§ 8. rem. 14) . . . נקב
תִּקָּבֵץ[u] Niph. fut. 2 pers. sing. masc. . . קבץ
תִּקְבֹּץ[x] Kal fut. 2 pers. sing. masc. . . . קבץ
תִּקְבְּצוּ[y] Kal fut. 2 pers. pl. masc. . . . קבץ
תְּקַבְּצוּ[z] וַ Piel fut. 2 pers. pl. masc.; וַ· conv. . קבץ
תְּקַבְּצֵם[a] id. fut. 3 pers. s. f. [תְּקַבֵּץ], suff. 3 pers. pl. m. קבץ
תִּקָּבֵר וַ' Niph. fut. 2 p. s. m., or 3 pers. s. f.; וַ· conv. קבר
תִּקְבְּרוּ[b] וַ Kal fut. 2 pers. pl. masc.; וַ· id. . קבר
תְּקַבְּרֵם[c] Piel fut. 3 pers. s. f. [תְּקַבֵּר], suff. 3 pers. pl. m. קבר
תִּקְבְּרֶנּוּ[d] Kal fut. 2 pers. sing. masc. [תִּקְבֹּר], suff. 3 pers. sing. masc. . . . . קבר
תִּקְבְּרֵנִי id. with suff. 1 pers. sing. . . . קבר
תִּקֹּד[kk] וַ Kal fut. 3 pers. sing. fem.; וַ· conv. . קדד
תַּקְדִּים[e] וַ Hiph. fut. 3 pers. sing. fem.; וַ· id. . קדם
תַּקְדִּישׁ[f] Hiph. fut. 2 pers. sing. masc. . . . קדש
תַּקְדִּישׁוּ[g] id. fut. 2 pers. pl. masc. . . . קדש
תְּקַדְּמֶךָּ[h] Piel fut. 3 pers. s. f. [תְּקַדֵּם], suff. 2 pers. s. m. [fr. תְּקַדֶּמְךָ § 2. r. 2, & § 16. r. 15] קדם
תְּקַדְּמֶנּוּ[i] id. fut. 2 pers. sing. masc., suff. 3 pers. s. m. קדם

תִּקְדַּשׁ[k] Kal fut. 3 pers. sing. fem. . . . קדש
תִּקְהֶינָה Kal fut. 3 pers. pl. fem. . . . קהה
תִּקָּהֵל וַ Niph. fut. 3 pers. sing. fem.; וַ· conv. . קהל
תִּקְוָה וְ'[l] noun fem. sing. dec. 10, pr. name קוה
תָּקוּם Kal fut. 2 pers. sing. masc., or 3 pers. s. f. קום
תְּקוּם[m] Chald. Peal fut. 3 pers. sing. fem. . קום
תְּקוּמָה[n] noun fem. sing. . . . . . קום
תָּקוּמוּ[o] Kal fut. 2 pers. pl. masc. . . . קום
תְּקוֹמֵם[p] Pilel fut. 2 pers. sing. masc. . . . קום
תְּקוֹנֵנָּה Pilel fut. 3 pers. pl. fem. (§ 18. r. 15, note) קון
תָּקוֹעַ[q] וְ Kal inf. abs. . . . . תקע
תְּקוֹעַ pr. name of a place . . . . תקע
תְּקוֹעָה id. with parag. ה . . . . תקע
תְּקוּפַת[r] noun fem. sing., constr. of [תְּקוּפָה] dec. 10 קוף
תְּקוּפָתוֹ[s] וּ id., suff. 3 pers. sing. masc.; וּ bef. (:) . קוף
תִּקְוַת וְ' noun fem. sing., constr. of תִּקְוָה dec. 10 קוה
תִּקְוָתָהּ[t] id., suff. 3 pers. sing. fem. . . . קוה
תִּקְוָתִי וְ' id., suff. 1 pers. sing. . . . קוה
תִּקְוָתְךָ[u] וְ' id., suff. 2 pers. sing. masc. . . קוה
תִּקְוָתָם[x] וְ id., suff. 3 pers. pl. masc. . . . קוה
תִּקְוָתֵנוּ[y] id., suff. 1 pers. pl. . . . . קוה
תִּקָּח } Kal fut. 2 pers. s. m., or 3 pers.
תִּקַּח וְ'[z], וַתִּ' } s. f. (§ 17. rem. 8); וַ· conv. } לקח
תֻּקַּח[a] וַ Hoph. fut. 3 pers. s. f. (§ 17. r. 8); וַ· id. לקח
תִּקָּחֵהוּ וַ Kal fut. 3 pers. sing. fem. (תִּקַּח), suff. 3 pers. sing. masc. (§ 16. r. 12, & § 17. r. 8); וַ· id. לקח
תִּקָּחֶהָ[qq] וַ id., suff. 3 pers. sing. fem.; וַ· id. . . לקח
תִּקָּחוּ } id. fut. 2 pers. pl. masc. (§ 8. rem. 15,
תִּקְחוּ } comp. § 10. rem. 7) . . . } לקח
תִּקְחִי[b] וַ' id. fut. 2 p. s. m. (comp. § 10. r. 7); וַ· conv. לקח
תִּקָּחֵךְ[c] id. fut. 3 pers. sing. fem., suff. 2 pers. sing. masc. (§ 16. rem. 12) . . . לקח
תִּקָּחֵם[d] וַ'[e] id. id., suff. 3 pers. pl. masc.; וַ· conv. לקח
תִּקָּחֶנָּה[f] id. fut. 2 pers. sing. masc., suff. 3 pers. s. f. לקח
תִּקָּחֶנּוּ id. id., suff. 3 pers. sing. masc. . . לקח
תִּקָּחֵנִי וַ'[g] id. fut. 2 pers. sing. masc., or (Eze. 3. 14) 3 pers. sing. fem.; וַ· conv. . . . לקח
תַּקְטִיר Hiph. fut. 2 p. s. m. (Nu. 18. 17) or 3 p. f. s.[yy] קטר
תַּקְטִירוּ id. fut. 2 pers. pl. masc. . . . קטר
תִּקְטֹל[h] Kal fut. 2 pers. sing. masc. . . קטל
תִּקְטַן וַ Kal fut. 3 pers. sing. fem.; וַ· conv. . קטן
תָּקְטָרִ[i] Hoph. fut. 3 pers. sing. fem. [for תָּקְטַר comp. § 8. rem. 15] . . . קטר
תָּקִיא Hiph. fut. 3 pers. sing. fem. . . . קוא
תְּקִיאֶנָּה[k] id. fut. 2 pers. sing. masc., suff. 3 pers. s. f. קוא
תְּקִילְתָּא[l] Chald. Peil pass. 2 pers. s. m. (§ 47. r. 11) תקל

[a] Ps. 66. 7. [b] Ex. 2. 2. [c] Ex. 25. 11. [d] Jos. 2. 4. [e] Ps. 31. 21. [f] Job 14. 13. [g] Is. 29. 4.
[h] 2 Sa. 13. 9. [i] De. 2. 9. [k] Is. 49. 19. [l] De. 2. 19. [m] Pr. 4. 6. [n] Ps. 12. 8. [o] Ps. 32. 7.
[p] Is. 9. 17. [q] Je. 49. 2. [r] Le. 18. 25. [s] Da. 2. 6. [t] Nu. 23. 25. [u] Eze. 29. 5. [x] De. 13. 17.
[y] Ne. 4. 14. [z] Is. 22. 9. [a] Ho. 9. 6. [b] 2 Sa. 2. 5. [c] Ho. 9. 6. [d] De. 21. 23. [dd] Job 40. 26.
[e] Am. 9. 10. [f] De. 15. 19. [g] Is. 8. 13. [h] Ps. 88. 14. [i] Ps. 21. 4. [k] De. 22. 9. [kk] 1 Ki. 1. 16, 31.
[l] Je. 29. 11. [m] Da. 2. 39, 44. [n] Le. 26. 37. [o] Je. 25. 27. [p] Is. 58. 12. [q] Jos. 6. 13. [qq] Ex. 2. 5.
[r] Ex. 34. 22. [s] Ps. 19. 7. [t] Eze. 19. 5. [u] Job 4. 6. [x] Job 11. 20. [y] Eze. 37. 11. [yy] Ho. 2. 15.
[z] Je. 9. 19. [a] Ge. 12. 15. [b] Zep. 3. 7. [c] Pr. 6. 25. [d] Am. 9. 2. [e] Job 1. 15.
[f] Eze. 5. 1. [g] Eze. 3. 14. [h] Ps. 139. 19. [i] Le. 6. 15. [k] Pr. 23. 8. [l] Da. 5. 27.

תָּקִים Hiph. fut. 2 pers. sing. masc. . . . קום
תְּקִים[a] Chald. Aph. fut. 2 pers. sing. masc. . קום
תָּקִימוּ Hiph. fut. 2 pers. pl. masc. . . . . קום
תְּקִימֶנָה[b] id. fut. 2 pers. pl. fem. (for תָּקֵמְנָה) . קום
תַּקִּיפָא[c] / תַּקִּיפָה[d] ו׳ } Chald. adj. fem. sing. from תַּקִּיף masc. תקף
תַּקִּיפִין[e] Chald. id. masc., pl. of תַּקִּיף dec. 1a . תקף

[תְּקַל] Chald. *to weigh*, Da. 5. 25, 27. Peil pret. *to be weighed*, Da. 5. 27.

תֵּקַל[f] וַ Kal fut. 3 pers. s. f. (§ 18. r. 6); וַ· conv. קלל
תְּקֵל[g] Ch. Peal part. pass. s. m. [for תְּקִיל § 47. r. 1] תקל
תְּקַלֵּל Piel fut. 2 pers. sing. masc. . . . קלל
תְּקֻלַּל[h] Pual fut. 3 pers. sing. fem. . . . . קלל
תָּקֶם[gg] וַ Hiph. fut. 2 p. s. m. ap. & conv. from תָּקִים קום
תָּקָם וַ Kal fut. 3 pers. s. f. ap. & conv. from תָּקוּם קום
תִּקֹּם[i] Kal fut. 2 pers. sing. masc. . . . נקם
תָּקֻמוּ[k] defect. for תָּקוּמוּ (q. v.) . . . קום
תִּקְמְטֵנִי[l] וַ Kal fut. 2 pers. s. m., suff. 1 p. s.; וַ· conv. קמט

[תָּקַן] *to be arranged, straight*, Ec. 1. 15. Pi. I. *to make straight*, Ec. 7. 13.—II. *to set in order, compose*, Ec. 12. 9.

תְּקַן Chald. Hoph. *to be established*, Da. 4. 33.

תִּקֵּן[m] Piel pret. 3 pers. sing. masc. . . . תקן
תְּקַנֵּא[n] וַ ו׳ Piel fut. 2 pers. sing. masc., or (Ge. 30. 1) 3 pers. sing. fem.; וַ· conv. . . . . קנא
תִּקְנֵא[o] Chald. Peal fut. 2 pers. sing. m. R. קנא see קנה
תִּקְנֶה Kal fut. 2 pers. sing. masc. . . . קנה
תִּקְנוּ[p] id. fut. 2 pers. pl. masc. . . . קנה
תְּקַנֵּן[q] Piel fut. 3 pers. sing. fem. . . . קנן
תִּקְסַמְנָה[r] Kal fut. 2 pers. pl. fem. . . . . קסם

תָּקַע ו׳[s] I. *to smite, clap* the hands, as a sign of joy.—II. *to strike hands*, as a sign of surety.—III. *to strike, drive, fix in*, as a nail.—IV. *to fasten with nails*.—V. *to pitch* a tent.—VI. *to thrust in*, e. g. a spear.—VII. *to cast, throw in*, Ex. 10. 19.—VIII. with שׁוֹפָר, בַּשּׁוֹפָר *to strike* for *to blow the trumpet*; with תְּרוּעָה *to sound an alarm*. Niph. I. *to strike hands, become surety*, with לְיַד of the person with whom, Job 17. 3.—II. with שׁוֹפָר *to be blown*.

תָּקוֹעַ masc. *a blast with the trumpet*, Eze. 7. 14.

תְּקוֹעַ pr. name of a city in the tribe of Judah. Gent. noun תְּקוֹעִי, fem. תְּקֹעִית.

תֵּקַע masc. *blast* of the trumpet, Ps. 150. 3.

תֵּקַע[t] וַ ו׳ Kal fut. 3 pers. sing. fem.; וַ· conv. . יקע
תֹּקֵעַ[u] וְ ו׳[x] defect. for תּוֹקֵעַ (q. v.) . . . תקע
תָּקְעוּ וְ ו׳ Kal pret. 3 pers. pl. . . . תקע
תִּקְעוּ וְ ו׳[y] id. imp. pl. masc. . . . . תקע
תֹּקְעוּ[z] id. pret. 3 pers. pl. (Kh. תָּקְעוּ); K. תֹּקְעֵי part. act. pl. constr. m. from תּוֹקֵעַ dec. 7b תקע
תִּתְקַע[a] id. fut. 2 pers. sing. masc. . . . תקע
תָּקַעְתִּי[b] וְ id. fut. 1 pers. sing.; acc. shifted by conv. וְ (§ 8. rem. 7) . . . תקע
תְּקַעְתִּיו[c] וּ id. id., suff. 3 pers. sing. m.; וּ, for וְ, conv. תקע
תְּקַעְתֶּם וּ id. fut. 2 pers. pl. masc.; וּ id. . . תקע

[תָּקַף] *to overpower, prevail over, oppress*.

תְּקֵף Chald.—I. *to be* or *become great, strong, powerful*.—II. *to become firm, obstinate*, Da. 5. 20. Pa. *to make strong*, Da. 6. 8.

תֹּקֶף masc. dec. 6 c, *might, power, authority*.

תְּקֹף Chald. m. (emph. תָּקְפָּא) id. Da. 2. 37; 4. 27.

תַּקִּיף adj. masc. *strong, mighty*, Ec. 6. 10.

תַּקִּיף Chald. masc. dec. 1 a, adj.—I. *strong, hard*, Da. 2. 40, 42.—II. *mighty, powerful*, Da. 3. 33.

תֹּקֶף[d] noun masc. sing. dec. 6 c . . . תקף
תְּקֵף[e] וּ Chald. Peal pret. 3 pers. sing. masc. (§ 47. rem. 6); וּ bef. (:) . . . תקף
תָּקְפָּא[f] וְ Chald. noun masc. s., emph. of תְּקֹף (§ 59) תקף
תָּקְפּוֹ[g] noun masc. s., suff. 3 pers. s. m. fr. תֹּקֶף dec. 6c תקף
תַּקִּפוּ[h] Hiph. fut. 2 pers. pl. masc. . . . נקף
תַּקְפִּיאֵנִי[i] Hiph. fut. 2 pers. sing. masc., suff. 1 pers. s. קפא
תִּקְפֹּץ[k] Kal fut. 2 pers. sing. masc. . . . קפץ
תְּקִפַת[l] Ch. Peal pret. 3 pers. sing. fem. . . . תקף
תְּקִפְתְּ[m] וּ Ch. id. pret. 2 pers. sing. masc.; וּ bef. (:) תקף
תָּקֹץ[kk] Kal fut. 2 pers. sing. masc. ap. [from תָּקוּץ] קוץ
תִּקְצוֹר Kal fut. 2 pers. sing. masc. (§ 8. rem. 18) קצר
תִּקְצֹף Kal fut. 2 pers. sing. masc. . . . קצף
תִּקְצַר[n] / תִּקְצַר[o] ו׳ } Kal fut. 3 pers. sing. masc. (§ 8. rem. 15); וַ· conv. . . . } קצר
תִּקְצֹר[p] id. fut. 2 pers. sing. m. . . . קצר
תִּקְצְרוּ[q] id. fut. 2 pers. pl. masc. . . . קצר
תִּקְצֹרְנָה[r] id. fut. 3 pers. pl. fem. . . . קצר
תַּקְרֵא[s] וַ Hiph. fut. 2 pers. sing. masc. ap. [from תַּקְרִיא]; וַ· conv. . . . . קרא
תִּקְרָא וַ ו׳ Kal fut. 2 pers. sing. masc., or 3 pers. sing. fem.; וַ· id. . . . . . קרא
תִּקְרְאוּ id. fut. 2 pers. pl. masc. . . . קרא
תִּקָּרֵאוּ[oo] Niph. fut. 2 pers. pl. masc. [for תִּקָּרְאוּ, comp. § 8. rem. 15] . . . קרא

[a] Da. 6. 9. [b] Je. 44. 25. [c] Da. 2. 42; 7. 7. [d] Da. 2. 40. [e] Da. 3. 33, etc.
[f] Ge. 16. 4. [g] Da. 5. 25, 27. [h] Job 24. 18. [i] Le. 19. 18. [k] Jos. 8. 7.
[l] Job 16. 8. [m] Ec. 12. 9. [n] Ge. 30. 1. [o] Ezr. 7. 17. [p] Le. 25. 44, 45.
[q] Je. 48. 28. [r] Eze. 13. 23. [s] Eze. 33. 3. [t] Je. 6. 8. [u] Pr. 17. 18.
[x] 2 Ki. 11. 14. [y] Je. 4. 5. (Kh.) [z] Jos. 6. 9. [a] Pr. 6. 1. [b] Ju. 7. 18.
[c] Is. 22. 23. [d] Est. 9. 29. [e] Da. 4. 8, 17. [f] Da. 2. 37. [gg] Ne. 9. 8.
[g] Est. 10. 2. [h] Le. 19. 27. [i] Job 10. 10. [k] De. 15. 7. [kk] Pr. 3. 11.
[l] Da. 5. 20. [m] Da. 4. 19. [n] Nu. 11. 23. [o] Job 21. 4. [oo] Is. 61. 6.
[p] De. 24. 19. [q] Le. 25. 11. [r] Pr. 10. 27. [s] Je. 32. 23.

תִּקְרְאִי Kal fut. 2 pers. sing. fem. . . . קרא
תִּקְרָאֻם[a] id. fut. 2 pers. sing. masc., suff. 3 pers. pl. masc. (comp. § 16. rem. 12) . . קרא
תִּקְרֶאןָ[b] וַ id. fut. 3 p. pl. fem. (comp. § 8. r. 16); ·וַ conv. קרא
תִּקְרֶאנָה וַ׳ id. fut. 2 or 3 pers. pl. fem. (for Ex. 1. 10, see § 2. rem. 4); ·וַ id. . . . קרא
תַּקְרֵב[c] Hiph. fut. 2 pers. s. masc., defect. for תַּקְרִיב קרב
תִּקְרַב[d] / תִּקְרָב וַתִּ׳, וְ׳[e] } Kal fut. 2 pers. s. masc., or 3 pers. sing. fem. (§ 8. r. 15); ·וַ conv. } קרב
תְּקָרֵב[f] וּ Piel (Chald. Pael.) fut. 2 pers. s. m.; וּ bef. (:) קרב
תִּקְרְבוּ[g] וַ Kal fut. 2 pers. pl. masc.; ·וַ conv. . קרב
תַּקְרִבוּן[h] Hiph. fut. 2 pers. pl. masc. (תַּקְרִיב), ן parag. (comp. § 8. rem. 17) . . . קרב
תִּקְרְבוּן וַ Kal fut. 2 pers. pl. masc., ן parag. (§ 8. rem. 17); ·וַ conv. . . . . קרב
תִּקְרַבְנָה וַ id. fut. 3 pers. pl. fem.; ·וַ id. . . קרב
תַּקְרִיב Hiph. fut. 2 pers. sing. masc., or 3 pers. s. fem. קרב
תַּקְרִיבוּ id. fut. 2 pers. pl. masc. . . . קרב
תַּקְרִיבִי[i] וַ id. fut. 2 pers. sing. fem.; ·וַ conv. . קרב
תִּקְרֶינָה[k] Kal fut. 3 pers. pl. fem. . . . קרה
תִּקְרַע וַ Kal fut. 2 pers. s. m., or 3 p. s. fem.; ·וַ conv. קרע
תִּקְרְעִי[l] id. fut. 2 pers. sing. fem. . . . קרע
תְּקַשׁ[m] וַ Piel fut. 3 p. s. fem. ap. [fr. תְּקַשֶּׁה]; ·וַ conv. קשה
תִּקְשַׁבְנָה[n] Kal fut. 3 pers. pl. fem. . . . קשב
תַּקְשׁוּ Hiph. fut. 2 pers. pl. masc. . . קשה
תַּקְשִׁיב[o] Hiph. fut. 3 pers. sing. fem. . . . קשב
תַּקְשִׁיחַ[p] Hiph. fut. 2 pers. sing. masc. . . קשח
תִּקָּשֵׁר[q] וַ Niph. fut. 3 pers. sing. fem.; ·וַ conv. . קשר
תִּקְשֹׁר[r] וַ׳ Kal fut. 2 pers. sing. masc. (Je. 51. 63), or 3 pers. sing. fem.; ·וַ id. . . קשר
תִּקְשְׁרִי[s] id. fut. 2 pers. sing. fem. . . . קשר
תְּקַשְּׁרִים[t] וּ Piel fut. 2 p. s. f., suff. 3 p. pl. m.; וּ bef. (:) קשר
תִּקְשְׁרֶנּוּ[u] וְ Kal fut. 2 p. s. m. (תִּקְשֹׁר), suff. 3 p. s. m. קשר
תֹּר וְ׳[x] defect. for תּוֹר (q. v.) . . . תור
תֵּרֶא וַתֵּ׳, וְ׳[y] ap. fr. תִּרְאֶה q. v. (§ 24. r. 3); ·וַ conv. ראה
תֵּרָאֶה וְ׳[z] Niph. fut. 3 pers. sing. fem. . . ראה
תֵּרֶאהָ[a] וַ Kh. תִּרְאֶה q. v. K. תֵּרֶא (q. v.) . ראה
תִּרְאֶה[b] Kal fut. 2 pers. sing. masc. (§ 24. rem. 20) ראה
תִּרְאֶה id. fut. 2 pers. sing. masc., or 3 pers. sing. f. ראה
תִּרְאֵהוּ[c] וַ id. fut. 3 pers. sing. fem., suff. 3 pers. sing. masc. (§ 24. rem. 21); ·וַ conv. . . ראה
תִּרְאוּ וַ׳ id. fut. 2 pers. pl. masc.; ·וַ id. . ראה
תִּרְאִי[d] Kal fut. 2 p. s. m. for תִּירְאִי R. ירא, or for תִּרְאִי R. ראה
תִּרְאִי[e] id. fut. 2 pers. sing. fem. . . . ראה
תִּרְאֶינָה וַ׳ id. fut. 3 pers. pl. fem.; ·וַ conv. . ראה
תַּרְאֲלָה וְ pr. name of a town in Benjamin, Jos. 18. 27.

תְּרָאֶנָה[f] וַ Kal fut. 3 pers. pl. f. (Kh. תִּרְאֶנָה R. ראה), K. תָּאֹרְנָה Root . . . . אור
תִּרְאֶנּוּ[g] Kal fut. 2 pers. sing. masc. (תִּרְאֶה), suff. 3 pers. sing. masc. (§ 24. rem. 21) . . ראה
תַּרְאֵנִי[h] Hiph. fut. 2 pers. sing. masc. [תַּרְאֶה], suff. 1 pers. sing. (§ 24. rem. 21) . . ראה
תִּרְאַנִי[i] וַ Kal fut. 3 pers. sing. fem. (תִּרְאֶה), suff. 1 pers. sing. (§ 24. rem. 21); ·וַ conv. ראה
תִּרְאֵנִי[k] id. fut. 2 pers. s. m., or 3 pers. s. f., suff. 1 p. s. ראה
תִּרְאֻנִי[m] id. fut. 2 pers. pl. m. (תִּרְאוּ), suff. 1 pers. s. ראה
תֵּרֶב וַ Kal fut. 3 pers. sing. fem., ap. fr. תִּרְבֶּה (§ 24. rem. 3); ·ו conv. . . . . רבה
תֶּרֶב[n] וְ׳[o] Hiph. fut. 2 pers. sing. m., ap. fr. תַּרְבֶּה רבה
תַּרְבֶּה וַ׳[p] id. fut. 2 pers. sing. masc., or (Eze. 23. 19) 3 pers. sing. fem.; ·וַ conv. . . רבה
תִּרְבֶּה[q] וְ׳[r] Kal fut. 3 pers. sing. fem. . . רבה
תַּרְבּוּ Hiph. fut. 2 pers. pl. masc. . . . רבה
תִּרְבּוּ[s] Kal fut. 2 pers. pl. masc. . . . רבה
תִּרְבּוּן[t] id. with parag. ן (comp. § 8. rem. 17) רבה
תַּרְבּוּת[u] noun fem. sing. . . . . . רבה
תַּרְבִּי[x] וַתַּ׳, וְ Hiph. fut. 2 pers. sing. fem.; ·וַ conv. רבה
תִּרְבִּי[y] וַ Kal fut. 2 pers. sing. fem.; ·וַ id. . רבה
תִּרְבֶּינָה[z] וַ id. fut. 3 pers. pl. fem.; ·וַ id. . . רבה
תַּרְבִּיעַ[a] Hiph. fut. 2 pers. sing. masc. . . רבע
תַּרְבִּיץ[b] Hiph. fut. 2 pers. sing. masc. . . . רבץ
תַּרְבִּית וְ noun fem. sing. . . . . רבה
תַּרְבֵּנִי Hiph. fut. 3 p. s. f. (תַּרְבֶּה), suff. 1 p. s. (§ 24. r. 21) רבה
תִּרְבַּץ[pp] וַ Kal fut. 3 pers. sing. fem. . . . רבץ
תִּרְבַּצְנָה[c] id. fut. 3 pers. pl. fem. . . . רבץ
תִּרְגַּז[d] וַ׳ Kal fut. 3 pers. sing. fem.; ·וַ conv. . רגז
תִּרְגְּזוּ[e] id. fut. 2 pers. pl. masc. . . . רגז
תִּרְגְּזִי[f] וַ id. fut. 2 pers. sing. fem.; ·וַ conv. . רגז
תִּרְגַּזְנָה[g] id. fut. 2 pers. pl. fem. . . . רגז
תַּרְגִּיעַ[h] Hiph. fut. 2 pers. sing. masc. . . . רגע
תִּרְגַּלְתִּי[i] Tiph. pret. 1 pers. sing. (§ 6. No. 5) . רגל

תַּרְגֵּם Chald. *to interpret, translate,* only part. pass. מְתֻרְגָּם Ezr. 4. 7.

תֵּרָנְנוּ[k] וַ Niph. fut. 2 pers. pl. masc.; ·וַ conv. . רנן
תֵּרֵדִי[l] וְ׳[m] / תֵּרֵד וְ׳[n] } Kal fut. 2 pers. sing. masc., or 3 pers. sing. fem. (§ 20. rem. 2) . . } ירד
תֵּרֶד[o] וַ׳ id. fut. 3 pers. sing. fem. bef. monos. or conv. ·וַ (§ 20. rem. 4) . . . ירד
תֹּרֶד וַ Hiph. fut. 3 pers. sing. fem., ap. & defect. for תּוֹרֶד; ·וַ conv. . . . ירד
תִּרְדֶּה[p] Kal fut. 2 pers. sing. masc. . . . רדה

[a] Je. 36. 6. [b] Nu. 25. 2. [c] Le. 2. 4. [d] Le. 18. 14. [e] Is. 5. 19. [f] Ps. 65. 5; Ezr. 7. 17. [g] Eze. 37. 7. [h] De. 1. 17. [i] Eze. 22. 4. [k] Is. 41. 22. [l] Je. 4. 30. [m] Ge. 35. 16. [n] Is. 32. 3. [o] Ps. 10. 17. [p] Is. 63. 17. [q] Ne. 3. 38. [r] Je. 51. 63. [s] Jos. 2. 18. [t] Is. 49. 18. [u] Job. 40. 29. [x] Ge. 15. 9. [y] Mi. 7. 10. [z] Ge. 1. 9. [a] Je. 3. 7. [b] Da. 1. 13. [c] Ex. 2. 6. [d] Is. 60. 5. [e] Zep. 3. 15 [f] 1 Sa. 14. 27. [g] Nu. 23. 13. [h] Hab. 1. 3. [i] Nu. 22. 33. [k] Je. 12. 3; Job 10. 18. [m] Ca. 1. 6. [n] Ps. 71. 21. [o] Job 10. 17. [p] Eze. 23. 19. [q] De. 7. 22. [r] Da. 12. 4. [s] Je. 3. 16. [t] De. 6. 3. [u] Nu. 32. 14. [x] Je. 2. 22. [y] Eze. 16. 7. [z] Eze. 31. 5. [a] Le. 19. 19. [b] Ca. 1. 7. [c] Eze. 34. 14. [d] Am. 8. 8. [e] Ge. 45. 24. [f] Eze. 16. 43. [g] Is. 32. 10. [h] De. 28. 65. [i] Ho. 11. 3. [k] De. 1. 27. [l] La. 3. 48. [m] Je. 13. 17. [n] Ps. 144. 5. [o] 2 Ki. 1. 10, 12. [p] Le. 25. 43, 46. [pp] Nu. 22. 27.

תַּרְדֵּמָה	[a] וְ' noun fem. sing. dec. 10	רדם
תַּרְדֵּמַת[b]	id., constr. st.	רדם
תֵּרַדְנָה	[c] וְ' Kal fut. 3 pers. pl. fem. (§ 2. r. 4, note)	ירד
תְּרַדֵּף[d]	Piel fut. 3 pers. sing. fem.	רדף
תִּרְדֹּף	Kal fut. 2 p. s. m., or (Job 30. 15) 3 p. s. f.	רדף
תִּרְדְּפֵם[e]	id. fut. 2 pers. sing. m., suff. 3 pers. pl. m.	רדף
תִּרְדְּפֵנוּ[f]	וַ id. id., suff. 1 pers. pl.; ·ַ conv.	רדף
תִּרְדְּפֻנִי[g]	id. fut. 2 pers. pl. m. [תִּרְדְּפוּ], suff. 1 pers. s.	רדף
תַּרְהִבֻנִי[h]	Hiph. fut. 2 pers. s. m. [תַּרְהִיב], suff. 1 p. s.	רהב
תִּרְהָיוּ[i]	Kal fut. 2 pers. pl. masc. R. רהה, or תִּרְהוּ, for תִּירְאוּ. R.	ירא
תִּרְהָקָה	pr. name of a king of Egypt and Ethiopia, 2 Ki. 19. 9; Is. 37. 9.	
תָּרוּ[k]	Kal pret. 3 pers. pl.	תור
תָּרוֹב[l]	Kal fut. 2 pers. sing. masc., Kh. תָּרוּב, R. רוב, K. תָּרִיב. R. ריב see both under	ריב
תָּרוּם	Kal fut. 3 pers. sing. fem.	רום
תְּרוּמָה / תְּרוּמוֹת	ו'[m] noun fem. sing. and pl. dec. 10; ו bef. (:)	רום
תְּרוּמִיָּה[n]	noun fem. sing.	רום
תְּרוֹמֵם	[o] וְ' Pilel fut. 2 pers. sing. masc. (Job 17. 4), or 3 pers. sing. fem.; ·ְ conv.	רום
תְּרוֹמְמֶךָּ[p]	ו id. fut. 3 pers. sing. fem., suff. 2 pers. sing. masc. [for תְּרוֹמֶמְךָ § 2. rem. 2]; ו bef. (:)	רום
תְּרוֹמַמְנָה[q]	Pilal (pass.) fut. 3 pers. pl. fem.	רום
תְּרוֹמְמֵנִי	Pilel fut. 2 pers. sing. masc., suff. 1 pers. s.	רום
תְּרוּמַת	ו' noun f. s., constr. of תְּרוּמָה d. 10; ו bef. (:)	רום
תְּרוּמֹת[r]	id. pl.	רום
תְּרוּמָתִי[s]	id. sing., suff. 1 pers. sing.	רום
תְּרוּמֹתַי[t]	id. pl., suff. 1 pers. sing.	רום
תְּרוּמֹתֵיכֶם	id. pl., suff. 2 pers. pl. masc.	רום
תְּרוּמֹתֵינוּ[u]	ו id. pl., suff. 1 pers. pl.; ו bef. (:)	רום
תְּרוּמַתְכֶם[v]	id. sing., suff. 2 pers. pl. masc.	רום
תְּרוּמָתָם[w]	id. sing., suff. 3 pers. pl. masc. (§ 4. rem. 2)	רום
תְּרוּעָה	ו' noun fem. sing. dec. 10; ו bef. (:)	רוע
תְּרוּעַת	[y] ו' id., constr. st.; ו id.	רוע
תָּרוּץ[a]	Kal fut. 2 pers. sing. masc.	רוץ
תֵּרוֹץ[b]	Niph. fut. 2 pers. sing. masc. (§ 18. r. 7)	רצץ
תִּרְזָה	fem. a species of *hard tree*; Vulg. *ilex*, Is. 44. 14.	
תֶּרַח / תָּרַח	pr. name—I. of a station of the Israelites in the desert, Nu. 33. 27.—II. of the father of Abraham.	
תַּרְחִיב	Hiph. fut. 2 pers. sing. masc.	רחב
תַּרְחִיבוּ[c]	id. fut. 2 pers. pl. masc.	רחב
תַּרְחִיק[d]	Hiph. fut. 2 pers. sing. masc.	רחק
תַּרְחִיקוּ	id. fut. 2 pers. pl. masc.	רחק
תְּרַחֵם	Piel fut. 2 pers. sing. masc. (§ 14. rem. 1)	רחם
תִּרְחֲנָה	pr. name masc. 1 Ch. 2. 48.	
תִּרְחַק / תִּרְחָק	[e] וַ' Kal fut. 2 pers. sing. masc., or 3 pers. sing. fem. (§ 8. rem. 15); ·ַ conv.	רחק
תְּרַטֵּשׁ[f]	Piel fut. 2 pers. sing. masc.	רטש
תְּרַטַּשְׁנָה[g]	id. fut. 3 pers. pl. fem. (§ 10. rem. 4)	רטש
תְּרֵי	Chald. num. card. masc., constr. of תְּרֵין q. v.	
תְּרִיבֵהוּ[h]	Kal fut. 2 pers. s. m. (תָּרִיב), suff. 3 pers. s. m.	ריב
תָּרִיבוּ[i]	id. fut. 2 pers. pl. masc.	ריב
תְּרִיבוּן	id. id. with parag. ן (comp. § 8. rem. 17)	ריב
תְּרִיבֶנָּה[k]	id. fut. 2 pers. sing. m., suff. 3 pers. sing. fem.	ריב
תְּרִיבֵנִי[l]	id. id., suff. 1 pers. sing.	ריב
תָּרִיד[m]	Hiph. fut. 2 pers. sing. masc.	רוד
תָּרִים[n]	Kh. תָּרִים Hiph. fut. 2 pers. sing. masc., K. תָּרוּם Kal fut. 3 pers. sing. fem.	רום
תָּרִים	noun masc., pl. of תּוֹר dec. 1 a	תור
תָּרִימוּ	Hiph. fut. 2 pers. pl. masc.	רום
תְּרֵין	Chald. only constr. תְּרֵי masc. and תַּרְתֵּין fem. *two*.	
תָּרִיעוּ	Hiph. fut. 2 pers. pl. masc.	רוע
תָּרִיעִי[o]	id. fut. 2 pers. sing. fem.	רוע
תָּרִיץ[p]	Hiph. fut. 3 pers. sing. fem.	רוץ
תֹּרֶךָּ[q]	וְ defect. and with epenth. נ for תּוֹרְךָ q. v. (§ 2. rem. 2)	ירה
תִּרְכַּב[r]	וַ'[s] Kal fut. 2 pers. s.m., or 3 p. s.fem.; ·ַ conv.	רכב
תִּרְכַּבְנָה[t]	וַ id. fut. 3 pers. pl. fem.; ·ַ id.	רכב
תַּרְכִּבֵנִי[u]	Hiph. fut. 2 pers. sing. masc., suff. 1 pers. sing.	רכב
תָּרֶם[w]	וַ Hiph. fut. 3 pers. s. fem., ap. & conv. fr. תָּרִים	רום
תָּרֹם[y] / תָּרָם[z]	וַ Kal fut. 3 pers. sing. fem., ap. & conv. from תָּרוּם	רום
תַּרְמוּת[a]	וְ noun fem. sing., Kh. תַּרְמוּת, K. תַּרְמִית q.v.	רמה
תַּרְמִית[b]	noun fem. sing. dec. 1 b	רמה
תַּרְמִיתָם[c]	id., suff. 3 pers. pl. masc.	רמה
תִּרְמֹס[d]	וַ' Kal fut. 2 pers. sing. masc. (Ps. 91. 13), or 3 pers. sing. fem.; ·ַ conv.	רמס
תִּרְמְסוּ[e]	id. fut. 2 pers. pl. masc.	רמס
תִּרְמְסֵם[f]	וַ id. fut. 3 p. s. fem., suff. 3 p. pl. m.; ·ַ conv.	רמס
תֵּרָמַסְנָה[g]	Niph. fut. 3 p. pl. f. (§ 2. r. 4, note, & § 10. r. 4)	רמס
תִּרְמְסֶנָּה[h]	Kal fut. 3 p. s. fem. [תִּרְמֹס], suff. 3 p. s. fem.	רמס
תִּרְמֹשׂ	Kal fut. 3 pers. sing. fem.	רמש
תַּרְמִת[i]	defect. for תַּרְמִית (q. v.)	רמה
תְּרֻמַת[k]	ו defect. for תְּרוּמַת (q. v.); ו bef. (:)	רום
תָּרֹן[l]	וַ' Kal fut. 3 pers. sing. fem.	רנן

a Ge. 15. 12. b 1 Sa. 26. 12. c Je. 9. 17. d Pr. 13. 21. e Ps. 83. 16. f La. 3. 43. g Job 19. 22.
h Ps. 138. 3. i Is. 44. 8. k Nu. 13. 32. l Pr. 3. 30. m Ex. 29. 28. n Eze. 48. 12. o Ps. 107. 25.
p Pr. 4. 8. q Ps. 75. 11. r Nu. 18. 19. s Ex. 25. 2. t Nu. 18. 8. u Ne. 10. 38. w Nu. 18. 27.
y Ex. 29. 2. z Nu. 23. 21. a Pr. 4. 12. b Eze. 29. 7. c Is. 57. 4. d Job 22. 23.
e Ps. 109. 17. f 2 Ki. 8. 12. g Is. 13. 18. h De. 33. 8. i Je. 2. 29. k Is. 27. 8.
l Job 10. 2. m Ge. 27. 40. n Ps. 89. 18. o Mi. 4. 9. p Ps. 68. 32. q Job 12. 7, 8.
r Hab. 3. 8. s 1 Sa. 25. 42. t Ge. 24. 61. u Job 30. 22. w Ps. 92. 11. y Mi. 5. 8.
z Ge. 7. 17. a Je. 14. 14. b Zep. 3. 13. c Ps. 119. 118. d Ps. 91. 13. e Eze. 34. 18.
f Da. 8. 10. g Is. 28. 3. h Is. 26. 6. i Je. 23. 26. k De. 12. 11. l Is. 35. 6.

תֹּרֶן[a] masc. dec. 6c.—I. *mast*.—II. *banner*, Is. 30. 17.

תָּרֹנָּה Kal fut. 3 pers. pl. fem. with parag. ה (comp. § 8. rem. 13) . . . . רנן

תִּרְנֶה[b] Kal fut. 3 pers. sing. fem. . . . . רנה

תַּרְנִין[c] Hiph. fut. 2 pers. sing. masc. . . . . רנן

תָּרְנָם[d] noun m. sing., suff. 3 pers. pl. m. fr. תֹּרֶן d. 6c תרן

תְּרַנֵּן[e] Piel fut. 3 pers. sing. fem. . . . . רנן

תְּרַנֵּנָּה[f] id. fut. 3 pers. pl. fem. [for תְּרַנֵּנְנָה § 18. rem. 15, note] . . . . רנן

[תְּרַע] Chald. masc.—I. *a door*, Da. 3. 26.—II. *gate* of the king, for royal palace, Da. 2. 49.

תָּרָע Ch. m. d. 1 a, *doorkeeper*, *porter*, Ezr. 7. 24.

תִּרְעָתִי gent. noun, 1 Ch. 2. 55, from a place תִּרְעָה (*gate*) otherwise unknown.

תָּרַע[g], וַתָּרַע[h] } Hiph. fut. 2 pers. sing. masc. ap. & conv. (§ 18. rem. 11) . . . . } רעע

תֵּרֹעַ[i] Kal fut. 3 pers. sing. fem. (§ 18. rem. 6) רעע

וְתֵרֹעַ[k] Chald. Peal fut. 3 pers. sing. fem. . . רעע

תִּרְעָב[l], וַתִּרְעַב[m] } Kal fut. 3 pers. sing. fem. (§ 8. rem. 15); וַ conv. . . . . } רעב

תִּרְעָבוּ[n] id. fut. 2 pers. pl. masc. [for תִּרְעֲבוּ v. id.] רעב

וַתִּרְעַד[o] Kal fut. 3 pers. sing. fem. [for תִּרְעַד § 8. rem. 15]; וַ conv. . . . . רעד

תִּרְעֶה Kal fut. 2 pers. s. m., or (Je. 22. 22) 3 p. s. fem. רעה

תָּרֹעוּ[p] וְ' Hiph. fut. 2 pers. pl. masc. . . . רעע

תִּרְעוּ[q] Kal fut. 2 pers. pl. masc. . . . . רעה

תַּרְעַיָּא[r] noun masc. pl. emph. from [תְּרַע] dec. 1 תרע

תִּרְעֶינָה[s] וְ' Kal fut. 3 pers. pl. fem.; וַ conv. . רעה

תַּרְעֵלָה[t] noun fem. sing. . . . . . רעל

תַּרְעֵם[u] Hiph. fut. 2 pers. sing. masc. ap. [fr. תַּרְעִים] רעם

תְּרֹעֵם[x] Kal fut. 2 pers. s. m. [תָּרֹעַ], suff. 3 pers. pl. m. רעע

תִּרְעַץ[y] Kal fut. 3 pers. sing. fem. . . . . רעץ

תִּרְעַשׁ[z] וַתִּ', וְ'[a] Kal fut. 3 pers. sing. fem.; וַ conv. רעשׁ

תִּרְעַשְׁנָה[b] id. fut. 3 pers. pl. fem. . . . . רעשׁ

תִּרְעָתִים gent. noun pl. from תִּרְעָה . . . . תרע

תֶּרֶף Hiph. fut. 2 pers. sing. masc. ap. [fr. תַּרְפֶּה] רפה

תֵּרָפֵא[c] Niph. fut. 2 pers. sing. masc. . . . רפא

תֵּרָפְאוּ[d] id. fut. 2 pers. pl. masc. . . . . רפא

וַתִּרְפָּאֵנִי[e] Kal fut. 2 pers. sing. masc., suff. 1 pers. sing. (comp. § 16. rem. 12); וַ conv. רפא

תְּרָפִים ו masc. pl. *Teraphim*, a kind of penates or household gods.

תְּרַפֶּינָה[f] Piel fut. 3 pers. pl. fem. . . . . רפה

תִּרְפֶּינָה Kal fut. 3 pers. pl. fem. . . . . רפה

תִּרְפֶּינָה[g] Kal fut. 3 pers. pl. fem. (§ 23. rem. 11) . רפא

תַּרְפֵּנִי[h] Hiph. fut. 2 pers. sing. masc. [תַּרְפֶּה], suff. 1 pers. sing. (§ 24. rem. 21) . . רפה

וַתִּרְפֹּשׂ[i] Kal fut. 2 pers. sing. masc.; וַ conv. see רפס

תִּרְפְּשׂוּן[k] id. fut. 2 pers. pl. masc., ן parag. [for תִּרְפְּשׂוּן § 8. rem. 17] . . . . . רפס

וַתָּרֶץ[l] Hiph. fut. 3 p. s. fem. (§ 18. r. 12); וַ conv. רצץ

וַתָּרָץ Kal fut. 3 pers. s. fem. ap. & conv. fr. תָּרוּץ רוץ

וְתָרֹץ[m] Kal fut. 3 pers. sing. fem. (§ 18. rem. 12) רצץ

תֶּרֶץ[n] וַתֶּ', וְ'[o] ap. from תִּרְצֶה q. v.; וַ conv. . רצה

תְּרַצְּדוּן[p] Piel fut. 2 pers. pl. masc. with parag. ן . רצד

תִּרְצָה pr. name fem., also of a place . . . רצה

תִּרְצֶה Kal fut. 2 pers. s. m., or (Le. 26. 34) 3 p. s. fem. רצה

תִּרְצָח[q], תִּרְצָח } Kal fut. 2 pers. sing. masc. (§ 8. rem. 15) רצח

תְּרַצְּחוּ[r] Piel fut. 2 pers. pl. masc. [for תְּרַצְּחוּ § 10. r. 7] רצח

תִּרְצֶנָה[s] Kal fut. 3 pers. pl. fem., Kh. תִּרְצֶנָה (§ 24. rem. 7) R. רצה, K. תִּצֹּרְנָה R. . . נצר

וַתִּרְצֵנִי[t] Kal fut. 2 pers. sing. masc. (תִּרְצֶה), suff. 1 pers. sing. (§ 24. rem. 21); וַ conv. רצה

תִּרְצָתָה pr. name (תִּרְצָה) with parag. ה . . רצה

תִּרְקְדוּ[u] Kal fut. 2 pers. pl. masc. . . . . רקד

תַּרְקִיעַ[x] Hiph. fut. 2 pers. sing. masc. . . . רקע

תֶּרֶשׁ וָ pr. name of a eunuch at the court of Ahasuerus, Est. 2. 21; 6. 2.

תַּרְשִׁיעַ[y] Hiph. fut. 2 pers. sing. masc. . . . רשׁע

תַּרְשִׁיעִי[z] id. fut. 2 pers. sing. fem. . . . . רשׁע

תַּרְשִׁיעֵנִי id. fut. 2 pers. sing. masc., suff. 1 pers. sing. רשׁע

תַּרְשִׁישׁ וְ' pr. name of a place . . . . רשׁשׁ

תַּרְשִׁישׁ noun masc. sing. . . . . . רשׁשׁ

תַּרְשִׁישָׁה וְ' pr. name (תַּרְשִׁישׁ) with parag. ה . רשׁשׁ

תִּרְשֻׁם[a] וְ Ch. Peal fut. 2 pers. sing. masc. . . רשׁם

תִּרְשַׁע[b] Kal fut. 2 pers. sing. masc. . . . רשׁע

תַּרְתִּי Kal pret. 1 pers. sing. . . . . . תור

תַּרְתֵּין[c] וְ'[d] Ch. num. card. fem., from תְּרֵין masc. q. v.

תַּרְתֶּם[e] Kal pret. 2 pers. pl. masc. . . . . תור

תַּרְתָּן pr. name of an Assyrian general.

תַּרְתָּק pr. name of an idol of the Arvadites, 2 Ki. 17. 31.

תִּשָּׂא וַתִּ', וְ'[f] Kal fut. 2 pers. sing. masc., or 3 pers. sing. fem.; וַ conv. . . . נשׂא

וַתִּשְׁאַב[g], וַתִּשְׁאַב[h] } Kal fut. 3 pers. sing. fem. (§ 8. rem. 15); וַ conv. . . } שׁאב

תִּשָּׁאֶה[i] Niph. fut. 3 pers. sing. fem. . . . שׁאה

וַתִּשָּׂאֵהוּ[k] Kal fut. 3 pers. sing. fem., suff. 3 pers. sing. masc. (§ 16. rem. 12); וַ conv. נשׂא

תַּשִּׂאוּ[l] Hiph. fut. 2 pers. pl. masc. . . . נשׂא

[a] Eze. 27. 5. [b] Job 39. 23. [c] Ps. 65. 9. [d] Is. 33. 23. [e] Ps. 51. 16. [f] Ps. 71. 23. [g] Ps. 44. 3. [h] 1 Ki. 14. 9. [i] De. 28. 54, 56. [k] Da. 2. 40. [l] Pr. 19. 15. [m] Ge. 41. 55. [n] Is. 65. 13. [o] Ps. 104. 32. [p] Is. 41. 23. [q] Eze. 34. 3, 18. [r] Ezr. 7. 24. [s] Ge. 41. 2, 18. [t] Ps. 60. 5. [u] Job 40. 9. [x] Ps. 2. 9. [y] Ex. 15. 6. [z] Je. 10. 10. [a] Is. 13. 13. [b] Eze. 26. 10. [c] Je. 51. 8. [d] 1 Sa. 6. 3. [e] Ps. 30. 8.

[f] Eze. 1. 24, 25. [g] Job 5. 18. [h] Job 7. 19. [i] Eze. 32. 2. [k] Eze. 34. 18. [l] Ju. 9. 53. [m] Ec. 12. 6. [n] Le. 26. 43. [o] Ps. 50. 18. [p] Ps. 68. 17. [q] Ex. 20. 13; De. 5. 17. [r] Ps. 62. 4. [s] Pr. 23. 26. [t] Ge. 33. 10. [u] Ps. 114. 6. [x] Job 37. 18. [y] Job 34. 17. [z] Is. 54. 17. [a] Da. 6. 9. [b] Ec. 7. 17. [c] Ezr. 4. 24. [d] Da. 6. 1. [e] Nu. 14. 34. [f] Job 22. 26. [g] Ge. 24. 45. [h] Ge. 24. 20. [i] Is. 6. 11. [k] 2 Sa. 4. 4. [l] Je. 37. 9.

תִּשָּׂאוּ[a] / תִּשְׂאוּ } Kal fut. 2 pers. pl. masc. (§ 8. rem. 15, comp. § 10. rem. 7) . . . } נשא

תִּשָּׂאוּן[b] id. with parag. ן [for תִּשְׂאוּן § 8. rem. 17] נשא

תְּשֻׁאוֹת noun fem., pl. of [תְּשׁוּאָה] dec. 10 . שוא

תִּשְׂאִי Kal fut. 2 pers. sing. fem. . . . נשא

תִּשֶּׂאינָה[c] id. fut. 2 pers. pl. fem. (§ 23. rem. 3) . נשא

תַּשְׁאִיר[d] Hiph. fut. 3 pers. sing. fem. . . . שאר

תִּשְׁאַל וַ׳[e] Kal fut. 2 pers. sing. masc.; וַ· conv. שאל

תִּשְׁאָלְךָ[f] Kal fut. 3 pers. sing. fem. (תִּשְׁאַל), suff. 2 pers. sing. masc. (§ 16. rem. 12) . שאל

תִּשְׁאָלֵנִי[g] id. fut. 2 pers. sing. masc., suff. 1 pers. sing. שאל

תִּשָּׂאֵם Kal fut. 3 pers. sing. fem., suff. 3 pers. pl. masc. (comp. § 16. rem. 12) . נשא

תִּשֶּׂאנָה[h] וַ id. fut. 3 pers. pl. fem.; וַ· conv. נשא

תִּשָּׂאֵנִי[i] וַ׳ id. fut. 2 pers. sing. masc. (Job 30. 22), or 3 pers. sing. fem., suff. 1 pers. sing. (comp. § 16. rem. 12); וַ· id. . נשא

תִּשְׁאַף[k] Kal fut. 2 pers. sing. masc. . . שאף

תִּשָּׁאֵר[l] וַ׳[m] Niph. fut. 3 pers. sing. fem.; וַ· conv. שאר

תִּשָּׁאַרְנָה[n] id. fut. 3 pers. pl. fem. . . . שאר

תָּשֵׁב / תָּשֶׁב[o] } Hiph. fut. 2 pers. sing. masc., ap. fr. תָּשִׁיב (§ 21. rem. 18) } שוב

תָּשֹׁב[p] וְ / תָּשָׁב[q] וַ׳ } Kal fut. 2 pers. sing. masc., or 3 pers. sing. fem., ap. & conv. from תָּשׁוּב } שוב

תֵּשֵׁב / תֵּשֶׁב וַ } Kal fut. 2 pers. sing. masc., or 3 pers. sing. fem.; וַ· conv. . } ישב

תָּשֻׁבוּ[r] וְ defect. for תָּשִׁיבוּ q. v.; וְ· id. . . שוב

תָּשֻׁבוּ וַ׳ defect. for תָּשׁוּבוּ q. v.; וַ· id. . . שוב

תֵּשְׁבוּ[s] / תֵּשֵׁבוּ וַ׳ } Kal fut. 2 pers. pl. masc. (comp. § 8. rem. 15); וַ· id. . . . } ישב

תְּשֻׁבוּן[t] defect. for תְּשׁוּבוּן (q. v.) . . . שוב

תְּשַׁבְּחֵם[u] Piel fut. 2 pers. s. m. [תְּשַׁבַּח], suff. 3 p. pl. m. שבח

תָּשִׁבִי[x] Hiph. fut. 2 pers. sing. fem. . . שוב

תֵּשְׁבִי[y] / תֵּשֵׁבִי[z] } Kal fut. 2 pers. sing. fem. (comp. § 8. rem. 15) . . . . } ישב

תְּשׁוּבֶינָה[a] Kal fut. 3 pers. pl. fem. . . . שוב

תַּשְׂבִּיעַ[b] Hiph. fut. 2 pers. sing. masc. . . שבע

תַּשְׂבִּיעוּ[c] Hiph. fut. 2 pers. pl. masc. . . שבע

תַּשְׁבִּית[d] Hiph. fut. 2 pers. sing. masc. . . שבת

תַּשְׁבִּיתוּ[e] id. fut. 2 pers. pl. masc. . . . שבת

תִּשְׁבֵּךְ[f] Kal fut. 3 pers. sing. fem. [תִּשְׁבֶּה], suff. 2 pers. sing. masc. (§ 24. rem. 21) . שבה

תְּשֻׁבֶן[g] Kal fut. 3 pers. pl. fem. (§ 21. rem. 10) שוב

תְּשִׁיבֶנָה[h] Hiph. fut. 3 pers. pl. fem. . . . שוב

תָּשֹׁבְנָה[i] וַ Kal fut. 3 pers. pl. fem. (§ 21. r. 10); וַ· conv. שוב

תְּשַׁבְנִי[k] defect. for תְּשִׁיבֵנִי (q. v.) . . שוב

תִּשָּׁבַע / תִּשָּׁבֵעַ } Niph. fut. 2 pers. sing. masc., or 3 pers. sing. fem. (§ 15. rem. 1) . . } שבע

תִּשְׂבָּע / תִּשְׂבַּע וַ׳[m] } Kal fut. 2 pers. sing. masc., or 3 pers. sing. fem. (§ 8. rem. 15); וַ· conv. } שבע

תִּשָּׁבְעוּ Niph. fut. 2 pers. pl. masc. . . שבע

תִּשְׂבָּעוּ / תִּשְׂבְּעוּ[n] } Kal fut. 2 pers. pl. masc. (§ 8. rem. 15) שבע

תִּשְׂבַּעְנָה id. fut. 3 pers. pl. fem. . . . שבע

תִּשְׂבָּעֶנּוּ[o] id. fut. 2 pers. s. m., suff. 3 p. s. m. (§ 16. r. 12) שבע

תַּשְׁבֵּץ[p] noun masc. sing. . . . . שבץ

תְּשַׁבֵּר Piel fut. 2 pers. sing. masc. שבר

תִּשָּׁבֵר[q] Niph. fut. 2 pers. sing. masc. (§ 10. rem. 4) שבר

תִּשָּׁבֵר וַ׳ id. fut. 2 pers. sing. masc. (Eze. 29. 7), or 3 pers. sing. fem.; וַ· conv. . שבר

תִּשָּׁבֶר[r] וְ id. fut. 3 pers. s. fem. bef. monos. (§ 9. r. 3) שבר

תִּשְׁבַּר[s] Kal fut. 3 pers. s. fem. [for תִּשְׁבֹּר § 8. r. 18] שבר

תְּשַׁבֵּרוּ[t] Piel fut. 2 pers. pl. masc. [for תְּשַׁבְּרוּ, comp. § 8. r. 15] . . . שבר

תִּשְׁבֹּרוּ[u] / תִּשְׁבְּרוּ } Kal fut. 2 pers. pl. masc. (§ 8. rem. 15) שבר

תְּשַׁבֵּרוּן[v] Piel fut. 2 pers. pl. masc., ן parag. [for תְּשַׁבְּרוּן § 10. rem. 4] . . . שבר

תְּשַׁבֵּרְנָה[y] Piel fut. 2 pers. pl. fem. . . שבר

תִּשָּׁבַרְנָה וַ׳[z] Niph. fut. 3 pers. pl. fem.; וַ· conv. שבר

תַּשְׁבִּרֵנִי[a] Hiph. fut. 2 pers. sing. masc., suff. 1 pers. s. שבר

תְּשֻׁבֹת[b] noun fem., pl. of [תְּשׁוּבָה] dec. 10 . שוב

תִּשְׁבֹּת Kal fut. 3 pers. sing. fem. (§ 8. rem. 13) . שבת

תִּשְׁבַּת id. fut. 2 pers. sing. masc., or (Le. 26. 35) 3 pers. sing. fem. (§ 8. rem. 13) . שבת

תִּשְׁבְּתוּ[c] id. fut. 2 pers. pl. masc. . . שבת

תְּשֻׁבָתוֹ[d] וּ noun fem. sing., suff. 3 pers. sing. masc. from [תְּשׁוּבָה] dec. 10; וּ bef. (:) . שוב

תְּשַׂגְּבֵנִי Piel fut. 2 pers. sing. masc., or 3 pers. sing. fem. [תְּשַׂגֵּב], suff. 1 pers. sing. (§ 10. r. 7) שגב

תִּשְׁגֶּה[e] Kal fut. 2 pers. sing. masc. . . . שגה

תִּשְׁגּוּ[f] id. fut. 2 pers. pl. masc. . . . שגה

תַּשְׂגִּיא[g] Hiph. fut. 2 pers. sing. masc. . . שגא

תִּשָּׁגַלְנָה Niph. fut. 3 pers. pl. fem. (K. תִּשָּׁכַבְנָה q. v.) שגל

תַּשְׁגֵּנִי[h] Hiph. fut. 2 pers. sing. masc. [תַּשְׁגֶּה], suff. 1 pers. sing. (§ 24. rem. 21) . . שגה

תְּשַׁגְשֵׁגִי[i] Pilpel fut. 2 pers. sing. fem. (§ 6. No. 4) . שוג

תְּשַׁדֵּד[k] Piel fut. 2 pers. sing. masc. . . שדד

תַּשֶּׁה[l] Hiph. fut. 2 pers. sing. masc. . . נשה

תָּשׁוּב Kal fut. 2 pers. sing. masc., or 3 pers. sing. f. שוב

תְּשׁוֹבֵב[m] Pilel fut. 2 pers. sing. masc. . . שוב

תָּשׁוּבוּ Kal fut. 2 pers. pl. masc. . . . שוב

[a] Mi. 6. 16. [b] Job 13. 8, 10. [c] Eze. 23. 49. [d] Am. 5. 3. [e] 2 Ch. 1. 11. [f] De. 14. 26. [g] 1 Sa. 28. 16. [h] Ru. 1. 9. [i] Job 30. 22. [k] Job 36. 20. [l] Ex. 10. 26. [m] Ru. 1. 3, 5. [n] Ex. 8. 5, 7. [o] 1 Ki. 2. 20. [p] 1 Ki. 13. 6; Job 10. 16. [q] 1 Ki. 17. 21. [r] Je. 34. 16. [s] Ge. 34. 10. [t] 1 Ki. 9. 6. [u] Ps. 89. 10. [x] 1 Ki. 2. 16. [y] Eze. 26. 20. [z] Ho. 3. 3. [a] Eze. 16. 55. [b] Is. 58. 10. [c] Jos. 23. 7. [d] Le. 2. 13. [e] Ex. 12. 15. [f] Nu. 24. 22. [g] Eze. 16. 55. [h] Job 20. 10. [i] 1 Sa. 7. 14. [k] Je. 37. 20. [l] Mi. 6. 14. [m] Ru. 2. 14. [n] Ex. 16. 12. [o] Pr. 25. 16. [p] Ex. 28. 4. [q] Eze. 32. 28. [r] Ec. 12. 6. [s] Pr. 25. 15. [t] De. 7. 5. [u] Le. 11. 33. [x] Ex. 34. 13. [y] Ru. 1. 13. [z] Eze. 31. 12. [a] De. 2. 28. [b] Job 34. 36. [c] Le. 23. 32. [d] 1 Sa. 7. 17. [e] Pr. 5. 19, 20. [f] Nu. 15. 22. [g] Job 36. 24. [h] Ps. 119. 10. [i] Is. 17. 11. [k] Pr. 24. 15. [l] De. 24. 10. [m] Ps. 60. 3.

תְּשׁוּבוּ[a] Kh. תְּשׁוּבוּ q. v. K. תָּשׁוּבִי Kal fut. 2 p. s. f. שׁוב
תְּשׁוּבוּן[b] תְּשׁוּבֻן[c] } Kal fut. 2 pers. pl. masc. with parag. ן (comp. § 8. rem. 17) . . . שׁוב
תְּשׁוּבַת[d] noun fem. sing., constr. of [תְּשׁוּבָה] dec. 10 שׁוב
תְּשׁוּבֹתֵיכֶם[e] וּ id. pl., suff. 2 pers. pl. masc.; וּ bef. (:) שׁוב
תְּשַׁוֶּה[f] Piel fut. 2 pers. sing. masc. . . . שׁוה
תְּשֻׁוָּה[g] Kh. תְּשֻׁוָּה q. v., K. תְּשִׁיָּה for תּוּשִׁיָּה (q. v.) ישׁה
תִּשְׁוֶה[h] Kal fut. 2 pers. sing. masc. . . . שׁוה
תַּשְׁווּ[i] וְ Hiph. fut. 2 pers. pl. masc. . . . שׁוה
תִּשּׁוֹמֵם[k] Hithpoel fut. 2 p. s. m. [for תִּתְשׁוֹמֵם § 12. r. 3] שׁמם
תְּשַׁוַּע[l] תְּשַׁוַּע[m] } Piel fut. 2 pers. sing. masc., or 3 pers. sing. fem. (§ 15. rem. 1) . . שׁוע
תְּשׁוּעָה וּ'[n] noun fem. sing. dec. 10; וּ bef. (:) שׁוע
תְּשׁוּעַת וּ'[n] id. constr. st.; וּ id. . . . שׁוע
תְּשׁוּעָתִי וּ'[o] id., suff. 1 pers. sing.; וּ id. . . שׁוע
תְּשׁוּעָתֶךָ תְּשׁוּעָתְךָ[p] } id. with suff. 2 pers. sing. masc.; וּ' וּ id. . . . . שׁוע
תְּשׁוּפֶנּוּ[q] Kal fut. 2 p. s. m. [תְּשׁוּף], suff. 3 p. s. m. שׁוף
תְּשׁוּקָתוֹ noun f. s., suff. 3 p. s. m. fr. [תְּשׁוּקָה] d. 10 שׁוק
תְּשׁוּקָתֵךְ[r] id., suff. 2 pers. sing. fem. . . . שׁוק
תְּשׁוּרָה[s] וּ noun fem. sing.; וּ bef. (:) . . שׁור
תָּשׁוּרִי[t] Kal fut. 2 pers. sing. fem. . . . שׁור
תְּשׁוּרֶנּוּ[u] id. fut. 2 p. s. m., or 3 p. s. f., suff. 3 p. s. m. שׁור
תְּשׁוּרֵנִי id. fut. 2 pers. sing. masc., or 3 pers. sing. fem., suff. 1 pers. sing. . . . שׁור
תִּשַּׁח[x] Niph. fut. 3 pers. sing. fem. . . . שׁחח
תִּשְׁחָדִי[y] וַ Kal fut. 2 pers. s. f. (§ 8. r. 14); וַ conv. שׁחד
תִּשָּׁחֵט[z] Niph. fut. 3 pers. sing. fem. . . . שׁחט
תִּשְׁחַט[a] Kal fut. 2 pers. sing. masc. . . . שׁחט
תִּשְׁחֲטוּ[b] id. fut. 2 pers. pl. masc. . . . שׁחט
תִּשְׁחֲטִי[c] וַ id. fut. 2 pers. sing. fem.; וַ conv. . שׁחט
תַּשְׁחִית Hiph. fut. 2 pers. sing. masc. . . . שׁחת
תַּשְׁחִיתֵהוּ id., suff. 3 pers. sing. masc. . . . שׁחת
תַּשְׁחִיתֵם[d] וַ id., suff. 3 pers. pl. masc.; וַ conv. . שׁחת
תִּשְׂחַק[e] Kal fut. 2 pers. sing. masc. (§ 8. rem. 15) שׂחק
תִּשְׂחָק וַ'[f] id. fut. 2 pers. sing. masc. (Ps. 59. 9), or 3 pers. sing. fem.; וַ conv. . . שׂחק
תְּשַׁחֵר[g] Piel fut. 2 pers. sing. masc. (§ 14. rem. 1) שׁחר
תַּשְׁחֵת וַ'[h] Hiph. fut. 2 pers. sing. masc., or (Eze. 23. 11) 3 pers. sing. fem.; וַ conv. . שׁחת
תִּשָּׁחֵת[i] וַ'[k] Niph. fut. 3 pers. sing. fem.; וַ id. . שׁחת
תַּשְׁחִתוּן Hiph. fut. 2 pers. pl. masc. [תַּשְׁחִיתוּ], ן parag. (comp. § 8. rem. 17) . . שׁחת
תַּשְׁחִתִי[l] וַ id. fut. 2 pers. sing. fem.; וַ conv. . שׁחת
תִּשְׂטֶה[m] Kal fut. 3 pers. sing. fem. . . . שׂטה
תִּשְׁטְפֵנִי[n] וַ Kal fut. 3 pers. sing. fem.; וַ conv. . שׁטח

תִּשְׂטְמֵנִי[o] Kal fut. 2 pers. s. m. [תִּשְׂטֹם], suff. 1 pers. s. שׂטם
תִּשְׁטֹף[p] Kal fut. 2 pers. sing. masc. . . . שׁטף
תִּשְׁטְפֵנִי[q] id. fut. 3 pers. sing. fem., suff. 1 pers. sing. שׁטף
תֶּשִׁי[r] Kal fut. 2 pers. sing. masc. ap. for תֶּשְׁי R. שָׁיָה (§ 24. r. 3 e, comp. § 35. r. 14), or תֶּשִׁי may be contracted fr. תִּשְׁהִי, תֶּשְׁהִי (after the analogy of זוֹ for זְהִיַן, נִי for נְהִי) R. שׁהה
תָּשִׁיב Hiph. fut. 2 p. s. m., or (Ju. 5. 29) 3 p. s. f. שׁוב
תֹּשִׁיבוּ[s] וַ Hiph. fut. 2 pers. pl. masc.; וַ conv. . ישׁב
תָּשִׁיבוּ Hiph. fut. 2 p. pl. masc. . . . שׁוב
תְּשִׁיבֵם[t] id. fut. 2 pers. sing. masc., suff. 3 pers. pl. m. שׁוב
תְּשִׁיבֶנּוּ id. id., suff. 3 pers. sing. masc. . . שׁוב
תְּשִׁיבֵנוּ[u] id. id., suff. 1 pers. pl. . . . שׁוב
תְּשִׁיבֵנִי id. id., suff. 1 pers. sing. . . . שׁוב
תַּשִּׂיג Hiph. fut. 2 p. s. m. (1 Sa. 30. 8), or 3 p. s. fem. נשׂג
תַּשִּׂיגֵהוּ[x] id. fut. 3 pers. sing. fem., suff. 3 pers. sing. m. נשׂג
תַּשִּׂיגוּם[y] id. fut. 2 pers. pl. masc., suff. 3 pers. pl. masc. נשׂג
תַּשִּׂיגֵם[z] id. fut. 3 pers. sing. fem., suff. 3 pers. pl. m. נשׂג
תַּשִּׂיגֵנוּ[a] id. id., suff. 1 pers. pl. . . . נשׂג
תָּשִׂיחַ[b] וְ Kh. תָּשִׂיחַ, K. תָּשׁוּחַ Hiph. or Kal fut. 3 p. s. f. שׁוח
תְּשִׂיחֶךָ[c] Kal fut. 3 pers. s. fem. [תָּשִׂיחַ], suff. 2 p. s. m. שׂיח
תַּשִּׁיךְ[d] Hiph. fut. 2 pers. sing. masc. . . . נשׁך
תָּשִׂים Kal fut. 2 pers. sing. masc. R. שִׂים see . שׂום
תָּשִׂימוּ id. fut. 2 pers. pl. masc. . . . שׂום
תְּשִׂימוּן וַ'[e] id. id. with parag. ן . . . שׂום
תָּשִׂימִי[f] וַ id. fut. 2 pers. sing. fem.; וַ conv. שׂום
תְּשִׂימֵנוּ id. fut. 2 pers. sing. masc., suff. 1 pers. pl. שׂום
תְּשִׂימֵנִי id. id., suff. 1 pers. sing. . . . שׂום
תְּשִׂימֻנִי[g] id. fut. 2 pers. pl. masc., suff. 1 pers. sing. שׂום
תָּשִׂישׂ[h] Kal fut. 3 pers. sing. fem., R. שִׂישׂ, see שׂושׂ
תָּשִׁית Kal fut. 2 pers. sing. masc. . . . שׁית
תְּשִׁיתֵהוּ[i] id. id., suff. 3 pers. sing. masc. . . שׁית
תָּשִׁיתוּ[k] id. fut. 2 pers. pl. masc. . . . שׁית
תָּשִׁיתִי[l] id. fut. 2 pers. sing. fem. . . . שׁית
תְּשִׁיתֵמוֹ id. fut. 2 pers. s. masc., suff. 3 pers. pl. masc. שׁית
תִּשְׁכַּב וַ'[m] תִּשְׁכַּב וַתִּ', וַ'[n] } Kal fut. 2 pers. s. masc., or 3 pers. sing. fem. (§ 8. r. 15); וַ conv. שׁכב
תַּשְׁכִּבֵהוּ[o] וַ defect. for תַּשְׁכִּיבֵהוּ q. v. . . שׁכב
תִּשְׁכָּבוּן[p] תִּשְׁכְּבוּן[q] } Kal fut. 2 pers. pl. masc., ן parag. (§ 8. rem. 17) . . . שׁכב
תִּשְׁכַּבְנָה Keri, Niph. fut. 3 pers. pl. fem. (§ 10. r. 4) שׁכב
תִּשְׁכּוֹן id. fut. 2 pers. s. m. (Is. 13. 20), or 3 p. s. fem. שׁכן
תִּשָּׁכַח[r] תִּשָּׁכַח } Niph. fut. 3 pers. sing. fem. (§ 15. rem. 1) . . . שׁכח
תִּשְׁכַּח תִּשְׁכַּח וַ' } Kal fut. 2 pers. sing. masc., or 3 pers. sing. fem. (§ 8. rem. 15); וַ conv. שׁכח

[a] Je. 3. 19. [b] 2 Ch. 7. 19. [c] Nu. 32. 15. [d] 1 Ch. 20. 1. [e] Job 21. 34. [f] Ps. 21. 6. [g] Job 30. 22.
[h] Pr. 26. 4. [i] Is. 46. 5. [k] Ec. 7. 16. [l] Is. 58. 9. [m] Job 24. 12. [n] Ps. 37. 39. [o] Is. 46. 13.
[p] Ps. 40. 11; 119. 41. [q] Ge. 3. 15. [r] Ge. 3. 16. [s] 1 Sa. 9. 7. [t] Ca. 4. 8. [u] Job 29. 9; 35. 14. [x] Is. 29. 4.
[y] Eze. 16. 33. [z] Le. 6. 18. [a] Ex. 34. 25. [b] Le. 22. 28. [c] Eze. 16. 21. [d] Ps. 78. 45. [e] Job 5. 22.
[f] Pr. 31. 25. [g] Job 8. 5. [h] Eze. 23. 11. [i] Ex. 8. 20. [k] Ge. 6. 11. [l] Eze. 16. 47. [m] Nu. 5. 12, 29.
[n] 2 Sa. 17. 19. [o] Job 30. 21. [p] Job 14. 19. [q] Ps. 69. 16. [r] De. 32. 18. [s] Ezr. 10. 10. [t] De. 22. 1.
[u] Ps. 44. 11. [x] Job 27. 20. [y] Jos. 2. 5. [z] Ho. 10. 9. [a] Is. 59. 9. [b] La. 3. 20. [c] Pr. 6. 22.
[d] De. 23. 20, 21. [e] Eze. 44. 8. [f] Is. 51. 23. [g] Is. 3. 7. [h] Ps. 35. 9. [i] Ps. 21. 7. [k] Ps. 62. 11.
[l] 2 Sa. 13. 20. [m] Ru. 3. 7. [n] Eze. 32. 28. [o] 2 Ki. 4. 21. [p] Is. 50. 11. [q] Ps. 68. 14. [r] De. 31. 21.

תִּשְׁכְּחוּ[a], תִּשְׁכָּחוּ[b] } id. fut. 2 pers. pl. masc. . . . שכח

תִּשְׁכְּחִי[c], תִּשְׁכָּחִי[d] } id. fut. 2 pers. sing. fem. . . . שכח

תִּשְׁכַּחְנָה[e] id. fut. 3 pers. pl. fem. . . . שכח

תִּשְׁכָּחֵנוּ[f] id. fut. 2 pers. s. m., suff. 1 p. pl. (§ 16. r. 12) שכח

תִּשְׁכָּחֵנִי[g] id. id. with suff. 1 pers. sing. . . . שכח

תַּשְׁכִּיבֵהוּ[h] וַ Hiph. fut. 3 pers. sing. fem., suff. 3 pers. sing. masc.; וַ· conv. . . . שכב

תַּשְׂכִּיל Hiph. fut. 2 pers. sing. masc. . . . שכל

תַּשְׂכִּילוּ id. fut. 2 pers. pl. masc. . . . שכל

תַּשְׁכִּים[i] Hiph. fut. 2 pers. sing. masc. . . . שכם

תְּשֹׂכְכֵנִי[k] Pilel fut. 2 pers. sing. masc., suff. 1 pers. sing. שוך

תַּשְׂכֵּל[l] וַ ap. from תַּשְׂכִּיל (q. v.) . . . שכל

תְּשַׁכֵּל ־תְּשַׁכֶּל (De. 32. 25) Piel fut. 3 p. s. f. . שכל

תִּשְׁכַּל[m] Kal fut. 3 pers. sing. fem. . . . שכל

תַּשְׁכֵּן[n] Hiph. fut. 2 pers. sing. masc. ap. [fr. תַּשְׁכִּין] שכן

תִּשְׁכֹּן, תִּשְׁכָּן־[o] } Kal fut. 3 pers. sing. fem. (§ 8. rem. 18) שכן

תִּשְׁכֹּנָּה[p] id. fut. 3 pers. pl. fem. [for תִּשְׁכֹּנְנָה comp. § 18. rem. 15, note] . . . שכן

תִּשְׁכְּרִי Kal fut. 2 pers. sing. fem. . . . שכר

תַּשְׁלֵג[q] Hiph. fut. 2 pers. sing. masc. ap. [fr. תַּשְׁלִיג] שלג

תַּשְׁלֶה[r] Hiph. fut. 2 pers. sing. masc. . . . שלה

תָּשֹׁלּוּ[s] Kal fut. 2 pers. pl. masc. . . . שלל

תִּשָּׁלוּ[t] Niph. fut. 2 pers. pl. masc. . . . שלה

תְּשַׁלַּח Piel fut. 2 pers. sing. masc. . . . שלח

תִּשְׁלַח[u] [x] וַ' id. fut. 3 pers. sing. fem.; וַ· conv. . שלח

תִּשְׁלָח[y] Kal fut. 2 pers. sing. masc. (§ 8. rem. 15) שלח

תִּשְׁלַח וַ' id. id., or fut. 3 p. s. fem.; וַ· conv. . שלח

תְּשַׁלְּחֵהוּ[z] וַ Piel fut. 2 pers. sing. masc. (תְּשַׁלַּח), suff. 3 pers. sing. masc. (§ 10. rem. 7); וַ· id. שלח

תְּשַׁלְּחוּ[a], תְּשַׁלֵּחוּ } id. fut. 2 pers. pl. masc. (comp. § 8. r. 15) שלח

תִּשְׁלְחוּ, תִּשְׁלָחוּ } Kal fut. 2 pers. pl. masc. (§ 8. rem. 15) . שלח

תְּשַׁלְּחוּם[b] Piel fut. 2 pers. pl. m., suff. 3 pers. pl. m. שלח

תְּשַׁלְּחוּנִי[c] וַ id. id., suff. 1 pers. sing.; וַ· conv. שלח

תְּשַׁלְּחִי וַ id. fut. 2 pers. sing. fem.; וַ· id. . שלח

תְּשַׁלְּחֵם[d] וַ id. fut. 2 pers. sing. masc., or 3 pers. sing. fem., suff. 3 pers. pl. masc.; וַ· id. . שלח

תִּשְׁלָחֵם Kal fut. 2 pers. sing. masc. (תִּשְׁלַח), suff. 3 pers. pl. masc. (§ 16. rem. 12) . שלח

תְּשַׁלַּחְנָה[e] Piel fut. 3 pers. pl. fem. . . . שלח

תִּשְׁלַחְנָה Kal fut. 3 or 2 pers. pl. fem. (§ 2. r. 4, note) שלח

תְּשַׁלְּחֶנּוּ[f] Piel fut. 2 p. s. m. (תְּשַׁלַּח), suff. 3 p. s. m. שלח

תִּשְׁלָחֵנוּ[g] Kal fut. 2 pers. sing. masc. (תִּשְׁלַח), suff. 1 pers. pl. (§ 16. rem. 12) . . שלח

תְּשַׁלְּחֵנִי[h] Piel fut. 2 pers. s. m. (תְּשַׁלַּח), suff. 1 p. s. שלח

תִּשְׁלָחֵנִי[i] Kal fut. 2 pers. sing. masc. (תִּשְׁלַח), suff. 1 pers. sing. (§ 16. rem. 12) . שלח

תַּשְׁלֵט־[k] Hiph. fut. 2 p. s. m. ap. [for תַּשְׁלִט § 11. r. 7] שלט

תִּשְׁלַט[l], תִּשְׁלָט[m] } Chald. Peal fut. 2 pers. sing. masc., or 3 pers. sing. fem. (§ 8. rem. 15) } שלט

תַּשְׁלִיךְ[n] וְ Hiph. fut. 2 pers. sing. masc. . שלך

תַּשְׁלִיכֵהוּ[o] וְ id. fut. 3 pers. sing. f., suff. 3 pers. s. m. שלך

תַּשְׁלִיכֻהוּ[p] id. fut. 2 pers. pl. masc., suff. 3 pers. s. m. שלך

תַּשְׁלִיכִי[q] וַ id. fut. 2 pers. sing. fem.; וַ· conv. . שלך

תַּשְׁלִיכֵנִי וַ' id. fut. 3 pers. sing. f., suff. 1 pers. s.; וַ· id. שלך

תַּשְׁלִים[r] Hiph. fut. 3 pers. sing. fem. . . שלם

תַּשְׁלִימֵנִי[s] id. fut. 2 pers. sing. masc., suff. 1 pers. sing. שלם

תַּשְׁלֵךְ[t] וַתַּ', וְ Hiph. fut. 2 pers. sing. masc. (Ps. 50.17), or 3 p. s. f., ap. fr. תַּשְׁלִיךְ; וַ· conv. שלך

תַּשְׁלִכוּן[u] Hiph. fut. 2 pers. pl. masc. with parag. ן (comp. § 8. rem. 17) . . שלך

תֻּשְׁלְכִי[x] וַ Hoph. fut. 2 p. s. f. (§ 11. r. 10); וַ· conv. שלך

תְּשַׁלֵּם Piel fut. 2 pers. sing. masc. . . שלם

תִּשְׁלַם וַ Kal fut. 3 pers. sing. fem.; וַ· conv. . שלם

תָּשֵׂם[y] וְ Kal fut. 2 p. s. m. ap. fr. תָּשִׂים R. שים see שום

תָּשֶׂם[z] וַ' id. fut. 2 pers. sing. masc. (1 Sa. 9. 20), or 3 pers. sing. fem.; וַ· conv. . שום

תֵּשָׁם[a], תֵּשַׁם[b] וַ' } Kal fut. 3 pers. sing. fem. R. שמם (§ 18. rem. 6) or . . } ישם

תַּשְׂמְאִילוּ[c] Hiph. fut. 2 pers. pl. masc. . . שמאל

תִּשָּׁמֵדוּן[d] Niphal fut. 2 p. pl. masc. parag. ן [for תִּשָּׁמְדוּן comp. § 8. rem. 17] . שמד

תְּשִׂמוּן[e] defect. for תְּשִׂימוּן (q. v.) . . שום

תִּשְׁמוֹר[f] וְ Kal fut. 2 pers. sing. masc. (§ 8. rem. 18) שמר

תִּשְׁמוּרֵם[g] id. fut. 3 p. s. f., suff. 3 p. pl. m. (§ 8. r. 14) שמר

תִּשְׂמַח[h], תִּשְׂמָח וַ' } Kal fut. 2 pers. sing. masc., or 3 pers. sing. fem. (§ 8. rem. 15); וַ· conv. } שמח

תִּשְׂמְחִי id. fut. 2 pers. sing. fem. . . שמח

תִּשְׂמְחִי[k] id. fut., Kh. 'מְחִי 2 pers. sing. fem., K. 'מְחוּ 2 pers. pl. masc. . . . שמח

תִּשְׂמַחְנָה[l] id. fut. 3 pers. pl. fem. . . שמח

תַּשְׁמֵט[m] Hiph. fut. 2 pers. sing. m. ap. [fr. תַּשְׁמִיט] שמט

תִּשְׁמְטֶנָּה[n] Kal fut. 2 p. s. m. [תִּשְׁמֹט], suff. 3 p. s. f. שמט

a 2 Ki. 17. 38. b De. 4. 23. c Is. 54. 4. d Ps. 103. 2. e Is. 49. 15. f La. 5. 20. g Ps. 13. 2.
h 1 Ki. 3. 20. i Ju. 9. 33. k Job 10. 11. l Da. 9. 25. m 1 Sa. 15. 33. n Job 11. 14. o Job 3. 5.
p Eze. 17. 23. q Ps. 68. 15. r 2 Ki. 4. 28. s Ru. 2. 16. t 2 Ch. 29. 11. u Ps. 80. 12. x Eze. 17. 6.
y Ex. 4. 13. z Job 14. 20. a Nu. 5. 3. b Nu. 5. 3. c Ge. 26. 27. d Jos. 2. 21; Ps. 44. 3.
e Job 39. 3. f De. 15. 12, 13. g Jos. 1. 16. h 1 Ki. 11. 22. i Ne. 2. 5. k Ps. 119. 133. l Da. 5. 16.
m Da. 2. 39. n Mi. 7. 19. o Job 18. 7. p Ex. 1. 22. q Eze. 23. 35. r De. 20. 12. s Is. 38. 12, 13.
t Da. 8. 12. u Ex. 22. 30. x Eze. 16. 5. y Job 13. 27. z 1 Sa. 9. 20. a Ge. 47. 19.
b Eze. 12. 19; 19. 7. c Is. 30. 21. d De. 4. 26. e Je. 42. 15. f Job 13. 27. g Pr. 14. 3.
h Pr. 24. 17. i 1 Sa. 19. 5. k Je. 50. 11. l 2 Sa. 1. 20. m De. 15. 3. n Ex. 23. 11.

תַּשְׁמִיד[a] Hiph. fut. 2 pers. sing. masc. . . . שמד

תַּשְׁמִידוּ id. fut. 2 pers. pl. masc. . . . שמד

תַּשְׁמִידֵם[b] וַתַּ׳[c], וְ id. fut. 2 pers. sing. masc., suff. 3 pers. pl. masc.; ־וַ conv. . . . שמד

תַּשְׁמִיעוּ[d] Hiph. fut. 2 pers. pl. masc. . . . שמע

תַּשְׁמִיעֵנִי[e] id. fut. 2 pers. sing. masc., suff. 1 pers. sing. שמע

תְּשִׂמֵם[f] וְ Kal fut. 3 pers. sing. fem. (תָּשִׂים), suff. 3 pers. pl. masc. R. שִׂים see . . שום

תַּשְׁמַע[g] Hiph. fut. 2 pers. sing. m. ap. [from תַּשְׁמִיעַ] שמע

תִּשָּׁמַע[h] וַ׳[i] Niph. fut. 3 pers. sing. fem.; ־וַ conv. שמע

תִּשְׁמַע, תִּשְׁמָע וַתִּ׳, וְ Kal fut. 2 pers. sing. masc., or 3 pers. s. f. (§ 8. r. 15); ־וַ id. שמע

תִּשְׁמְעוּ, תִּשְׁמָעוּ וַ׳[k] Kal fut. 2 pers. pl. masc.; ־וַ id. שמע

תִּשְׁמָעוּהָ[l] id., suff. 3 pers. sing. fem. (§ 16. rem. 12) שמע

תִּשְׁמְעוּן, תִּשְׁמָעוּן id. fut. 2 pers. pl. masc., ן parag. (§ 8. rem. 17) . . . שמע

תִּשְׁמְעוּן[m] Peal fut. 2 pers. pl. masc. . . . שמע

תִּשְׁמַעְנָה וְ[n] Kal fut. 3 pers. pl. fem. . . . שמע

תִּשָּׁמֵר[o] Niph. fut. 3 pers. sing. fem. . . . שמר

תִּשְׁמֹר, תִּשְׁמָר־[p] וְ, וַ׳[q] id. fut. 2 pers. sing. masc., or 3 pers. sing. fem. (§ 8. r. 18); ־וַ conv. שמר

תִּשָּׁמְרוּ[r] Niph. fut. 2 pers. pl. masc. [for תִּשָּׁמְרוּ comp. § 8. rem. 15] . . . שמר

תִּשְׁמְרוּ, תִּשְׁמָרוּ וַ׳ Kal fut. 2 pers. pl. masc. (§ 8. r. 15); ־וַ conv. . . . שמר

תִּשְׁמְרוּן id. id. with parag. ן (§ 8. rem. 17) . . שמר

תִּשְׁמְרֶךָּ[s] וְ id. fut. 3 pers. sing. fem. (תִּשְׁמֹר), suff. 2 pers. sing. masc. [for תִּשְׁמָרְךָ] . . שמר

תִּשְׁמְרֵם id. fut. 2 pers. sing. masc., suff. 3 pers. pl. m. שמר

תִּשְׁמְרֵנִי[u] id. id., suff. 1 pers. sing. . . . שמר

תִּשְׂנָא[x] וַ׳[y] Kal fut. 2 pers. sing. masc.; ־וַ conv. שנא

תִּשְׁנֵא Ch. Peal fut. 3 pers. sing. fem. . . . שנה

תִּשְׁנוּ[z] Kal fut. 2 pers. pl. masc. . . . שנה

תִּשֶּׂנָה וַתִּ׳[b], וְ[a] Kal fut. 3 pers. pl. fem. for תִּשֶּׂאנָה (§ 23. rem. 10); ־וַ conv. . . נשא

תֵּשַׁע וְ, וָ constr. תְּשַׁע (§ 35. rem. 7) fem., תִּשְׁעָה, constr. תִּשְׁעַת m. *nine;* also *ninth,* בְּתִשְׁעָה לַחֹדֶשׁ *on the ninth* day *of the month.* Pl. תִּשְׁעִים com. *ninety.*

תְּשִׁיעִי masc. תְּשִׁיעִית fem. *ninth.*

תְּשַׁע וְ[c] id. constr. st. (§ 35. rem. 7); וּ bef. (:) תשע

תִּשְׁעָה וְ[d] id. masc., abs. . . . . תשע

תִּשְׁעֶה[e] Kal fut. 2 pers. sing. masc. . . . שעה

תִּשְׁעִים וְ num. card. com. gen., pl. of תֵּשַׁע (§ 35. r. 16) תשע

תִּשְׁעֶינָה[f] Kal fut. 3 pers. pl. fem. . . . שעה

תִּשָּׁעֵן[g] Niph. fut. 2 pers. sing. masc. . . . שען

תִּשָּׁעֲנוּ[h] וְ id. fut. 2 pers. pl. masc.; ־וַ conv. . שען

תּוֹשִׁיעֵנִי[i] Hiph. fut. 2 pers. s. m. (תּוֹשִׁיעַ), suff. 1 pers. s. ישע

תִּשְׁתַּעַשְׁעוּ[k] Pulpal (§ 6. No. 4) fut. 2 pers. pl. masc. [for תְּשֻׁעַשְׁעוּ from שִׁעֲשַׁע] . . שעע

תִּשְׁפּוֹט[l], תִּשְׁפֹּט, תִּשְׁפָּט־[m] Kal fut. 2 pers. sing. masc. (§ 8. r. 18) שפט

תִּשְׁפְּטוּ id. fut. 2 pers. pl. masc. . . . שפט

תַּשְׁפִּיל Hiph. fut. 2 pers. sing. masc. . . . שפל

תַּשְׁפִּילִי[n] וְ id. fut. 2 pers. sing. fem.; ־וַ conv. שפל

תַּשְׁפִּילֶנּוּ[o] id. fut. 3 pers. sing. fem., suff. 3 pers. s. m. שפל

תִּשְׁפֹּךְ[p] Kal fut. 2 pers. sing. masc. . . . שפך

תִּשְׁפְּכוּ[q], תִּשְׁפָּכוּ id. fut. 2 pers. pl. masc. (§ 8. rem. 15) שפך

תִּשְׁפְּכִי[r] וְ id. fut. 2 pers. sing. masc.; ־וַ conv. . שפך

תִּשְׁפְּכֶנּוּ id. fut. 2 pers. sing. masc., suff. 3 pers. s. m. שפך

תִּשְׁפַּל[s] Kal fut. 3 pers. sing. fem. . . . שפל

תִּשְׁפַּלְנָה[t] id. fut. 3 pers. pl. fem. . . . שפל

תִּשְׁפֹּת[u] Kal fut. 2 pers. sing. masc. . . . שפת

תִּשְׁפְּתֵנִי[x] id. with suff. 1 pers. sing. . . . שפת

תַּשְׁקְ[y] וְ Hiph. fut. 3 pers. sing. f. ap. [from תַּשְׁקֶה § 24. rem. 16]; ־וַ conv. . . . שקה

תִּשַּׁק וְ Kal fut. 3 pers. sing. fem.; ־וַ id. . נשק

תַּשְׁקֶה[z] Hiph. fut. 2 pers. sing. masc. . . . שקה

תַּשְׁקֵהוּ וְ id. fut. 3 p. s. fem., suff. 3 p. s. m.; ־וַ conv. שקה

תַּשְׁקוּ[a] וְ id. fut. 2 pers. pl. masc.; ־וַ id. . שקה

תִּשְׁקוֹל[b] Kal fut. 2 pers. sing. masc. (§ 8. rem. 18) שקל

תִּשְׁקֹט[c] וַ׳ Kal fut. 2 pers. sing. masc. (Ps. 83. 2), or 3 pers. sing. fem.; ־וַ conv. . . . שקט

תִּשְׁקְטִי[d] id. fut. 2 pers. sing. f. [for תִּשְׁקֹטִי § 8. r. 15] שקט

תַּשְׁקֶין[e] וְ Hiph. fut. 3 pers. pl. fem. (comp. § 8. rem. 16); ־וַ conv. . . . . שקה

תַּשְׁקִיעַ[f] Hiph. fut. 2 pers. sing. masc. . . . שקע

תִּשְׁקְלוּ Kal fut. 2 pers. pl. masc. . . . שקל

תַּשְׁקֵם[g] Hiph. fut. 2 pers. sing. masc. (תַּשְׁקֶה), suff. 3 pers. pl. masc. (§ 24. rem. 21) . שקה

תַּשְׁקֵמוֹ[h] וְ id., suff. 3 pers. plur. masc.; ־וַ conv. . שקה

תִּשְׁקַע וַ׳[k] Kal fut. 3 pers. sing. fem.; ־וַ id. . שקע

תַּשְׁקֵף[l] וְ Hiph. fut. 3 p. s. f. ap. [fr. תַּשְׁקִיף]; ־וַ id. שקף

תְּשַׁקְּצוּ[m], תְּשַׁקֵּצוּ Piel fut. 2 pers. pl. masc. (comp. § 8. r. 15) שקץ

תְּשַׁקְּצֶנּוּ[n] id. fut. 2 pers. sing. masc., suff. 3 pers. s. m. שקץ

תְּשֹׁקְקֶהָ[o] וְ Pilel fut. 2 pers. sing. masc. [תְּשֹׁקֵק], suff. 3 pers. sing. fem.; ־וַ conv. . . שוק

[a] 1 Sa. 24. 22. [b] La. 3. 66. [c] Is. 26. 14. [d] Jos. 6. 10. [e] Ps. 51. 10. [f] Ge. 31. 34. [g] Ju. 18. 25. [h] Je. 18. 22. [i] Ne. 12. 43. [k] Jos. 22. 2. [l] Je. 13. 17. [m] Da. 3. 5, 15. [n] Mi. 6. 1. [o] Ju. 13. 13. [p] Ps. 130. 3. [q] 1 Ki. 3. 6. [r] Ex. 23. 13. [s] Je. 35. 18. [t] Pr. 4. 6. [u] 2 Sa. 22. 44. [x] Le. 19. 17. [y] Ps. 45. 8. [z] Ne. 13. 21. [a] Je. 9. 17. [b] Ru. 1. 14; Ze. 5. 9. [c] Ge. 5. 8, 11, 14, 20, 27. [d] Ezr. 2. 42. [e] Job 7. 19. [f] Is. 32. 3. [g] Pr. 3. 5. [h] Is. 30. 12. [i] 2 Sa. 22. 3. [k] Is. 66. 12. [l] 2 Ch. 1. 11. [m] 2 Ch. 20. 12. [n] Is. 57. 9. [o] Pr. 29. 23. [p] Ex. 29. 12. [q] Eze. 33. 25. [r] Eze. 16. 15. [s] Is. 32. 19. [t] Is. 5. 15. [u] Is. 26. 12. [x] Ps. 22. 16. [y] Ge. 21. 19. [z] Job 22. 7. [a] Am. 2. 12. [b] 1 Ki. 20. 39. [c] Ps. 83. 2. [d] Je. 47. 6, 7. [e] Ge. 19. 33, 35. [f] Job 40. 25. [g] Ps. 36. 9. [h] Ps. 80. 6. [i] Je. 51. 64. [k] Nu. 11. 2. [l] 2 Ki. 9. 30. [m] Le. 11. 11. [n] De. 7. 26. [o] Ps. 65. 10.

תִּשְׁקֹר[a] Kal fut. 2 pers. sing. masc. . . שקר

תְּשַׁקְּרוּ[b] Piel fut. 2 pers. pl. masc. . . . שקר

תָּשַׁר[c] וַ Kal fut. 3 pers. s. f. ap. & conv. (§ 22. r. 3) שיר

תְּשֻׁרִי[d] וַ defect. for תְּשׁוּרִי (q. v.) . . . שור

תִּשָּׂרֵף[e] וְ' Niph. fut. 3 pers. sing. fem. . . שרף

תִּשְׂרֹף Kal fut. 2 pers. sing. masc. . . . שרף

תִּשְׂרְפוּ id. fut. 2 pers. pl. m. [for תִּשְׂרְפוּ § 8. r. 15] שרף

תִּשְׂרְפוּן id. id. with parag. ן (§ 8. rem. 17) . . שרף

תִּשָּׂרַפְנָה[f] Niph. fut. 3 pers. pl. fem. . . . שרף

תִּשְׂרְפֶנּוּ[g] Kal fut. 2 p. s. m. (תִּשְׂרֹף), suff. 3 p. s. m. שרף

תַּשְׁרֵשׁ[h] וַ Hiph. fut. 3 p. s. f. ap. [fr. תַּשְׁרִישׁ]; וַ conv. שרש

תְּשָׁרֵשׁ[i] Piel fut. 3 pers. sing. fem. . . . שרש

תְּשָׁרְתֵהוּ[k] וַ Piel fut. 3 pers. sing. fem. [תְּשָׁרֵת], suff. 3 pers. sing. masc.; וַ conv. . . שרת

תָּשֶׁת[l] / תָּשֶׁת וְ' / וַ' } Kal fut. 2 pers. sing. masc. ap. & conv. for תָּשִׁית . . . } שית

תֵּשְׁתְּ וַ' Kal fut. 2 pers. s. m., or (Nu. 20. 11) 3 pers. sing. fem. ap. fr. תִּשְׁתֶּה (§ 24. r. 3); וַ conv. שתה

תִּשְׁתְּבֵק[m] Ithpe. fut. 3 pers. sing. fem. Chald. [for תִּתְשְׁבֵק comp. § 12. rem. 3] . שבק

תִּשְׁתֶּה Kal fut. 2 pers. sing. masc. . . שתה

תְּשִׁתֵהוּ[n] וַ Kal fut. 3 person. sing. fem. [תָּשִׁית], suff. 3 pers. sing. masc.; וַ conv. . שית

תִּשְׁתּוּ Kal fut. 2 pers. pl. masc. . . . שתה

תִּשְׁתּוֹחֲחִ[o] Hithpo. fut. 3 pers. sing. fem. [for תִּתְשׁוֹחֵחַ comp. § 12. rem. 3] . . שחח

תִּשְׁתּוֹחֲחִי id. fut. 2 pers. sing. fem. . . . שחח

תִּשְׁתַּחוּ[p] וַ / תִּשְׁתַּחוּ וַ } 3 pers. sing. fem. ap. from the foll. . שחה

תִּשְׁתַּחֲוֶה [transp. for תִּתְשַׁ' § 12. rem. 3] Hithpalel fut. 2 pers. sing. masc., 3d rad. ה doubled [for תִּשְׁתַּחְוֶה § 6. No. 2, & § 24. rem. 22] שחה

תִּשְׁתַּחֲווּ id. fut. 2 pers. pl. masc. . . . שחה

תִּשְׁתַּחֲוֶיןָ וַ id. fut. 3 p. pl. f. (comp. § 8. r. 16); וַ conv. שחה

תִּשְׁתִּי Kal fut. 2 pers. sing. fem. . . . שתה

תִּשְׁתֶּינָה[q] id. fut. 3 pers. pl. fem. . . . שתה

תִּשְׁתַּכָּרִין[r] Hithpa. fut. 2 pers. sing. fem., ן parag. [for תִּתְשַׁכְּרִין § 12. rem. 3, & § 8. rem. 17] . שכר

תִּשְׁתָּע[s] [for תִּתְשָׁע § 12. rem. 3] Hithpa. fut. 2 pers. sing. masc. ap. [from תִּשְׁתָּעֶה § 24. r. 12] שעה

תִּשְׁתַּפֵּךְ[t] Hithpa. fut. 3 p. s. f. [for תִּתְשַׁפֵּךְ § 12. r. 3] שפך

תִּשְׁתַּפֵּכְנָה[u] id. fut. 3 pers. pl. masc. . . . שפך

תִּשְׂתָּרֵר[x] Hithpa. fut. 2 p. s. m. [for תִּתְשָׂרֵר § 12. r. 3] שרר

תֵּת Kal inf. constr. (suff. תִּתִּי) dec. 13 [for תֵּנֶת=תְּנֶת § 17. rem. 9, & § 44. rem. 1] . נתן

תִּתְאַבְּלוּ[y] Hithpa. fut. 2 pers. pl. masc. . . אבל

תְּתָאוּ[z] Piel fut. 2 pers. pl. masc. . . . תאה

תִּתְאָו ap. from the foll. (§ 24. rem. 12) אוה

תִּתְאַוֶּה[a] Hithpa. fut. 2 pers. sing. masc. . . אוה

תִּתְאַפַּק[b] Hithpa. fut. 2 pers. sing. masc. (§ 12. rem. 1) אפק

תִּתְבּוֹנֵן[c] וַ Hithpal. fut. 2 pers. sing. masc. (§ 12. rem. 4); וַ conv. . . . בין

תִּתְבּוֹנְנוּ id. fut. 2 pers. pl. masc. . . . בין

תִּתְבַּלַּע[d] Hithpa. fut. 3 pers. sing. fem. . . בלע

תִּתְבְּנֵא[e] Chald. Ithpe. fut. 3 pers. sing. fem. . בנה

תִּתְבֹּנָנוּ[f] defect. & in pause for תִּתְבּוֹנְנוּ (q. v.) בין

תִּתְבָּרָר[g] / תִּתְבָּרַר[h] } Hithpa. fut. 2 pers. sing. masc. (§ 18. rem. 18) . . . . } ברר

תִּתְגֹּדְדוּ[i] Hithpo. fut. 2 pers. pl. masc. . . גדד

תִּתְגֹּדְדִי[k] / תִּתְגוֹדָדִי[l] } id. fut. 2 pers. sing. fem. (comp. § 21. r. 20) גדד

תִּתְגָּר[rr] ap. from the foll. (§ 24. rem. 12) . גרה

תִּתְגָּרֶה Hithpa. fut. 2 pers. sing. masc. . גרה

תִּתְגָּרוּ[m] id. fut. 2 pers. pl. masc. . . . גרה

תָּתָּה[n] Kal pret. 2 pers. sing. masc. for נָתַתָּה (comp. רֵד for יְרַד) see § 17 r. 9. . . נתן

תִּתְהַדַּר[yy] Hithpa. fut. 2 pers. sing. masc. . הדר

תִּתְהַלַּכְנָה[o] וַ Hithpa. fut. 3 pers. pl. fem.; וַ conv. הלך

תִּתְהַלָּל[p] / תִּתְהַלֵּל } Hithpa. fut. 2 pers. sing. masc., or (Ps. 34. 3) 3 pers. sing. fem. (§ 12. rem. 1) } הלל

תִּתְהַלְלִי[q] id. fut. 2 pers. sing. fem. . . . הלל

תִּתְהַפֵּךְ[r] Hithpa. fut. 3 pers. sing. fem. . . הפך

תִּתּוֹ Kal inf. (תֵּת § 17. rem. 9), suff. 3 pers. sing. masc. dec. 13 (§ 44. rem. 1) . . נתן

תְּתוּרוּ[s] Kal fut. 2 pers. pl. masc. . . . תור

תִּתְחַבַּל Chald. Ithpa. fut. 3 pers. sing. fem. חבל

תִּתְחַדֵּשׁ[t] Hithpa. fut. 3 pers. sing. fem. . . חדש

תִּתְחַטָּאוּ[u] / תִּתְחַטְּאוּ[x] } Hithpa. fut. 2 pers. pl. masc. (comp. § 8. rem. 15) . . . } חטא

תִּתְחַכַּם[y] Hithpa. fut. 2 pers. sing. masc. (§ 12. rem. 1) חכם

תִּתְחַלְחַל[z] וַ Hithpalp. fut. 3 pers. sing. fem.; וַ conv. חול

תִּתְחַמָּקִין[a] Hithpa. fut. 2 pers. sing. fem., ן parag. [for תִּתְחַמְּקִין § 8. rem. 17] . . . חמק

תִּתְחַנָּן[b] Hithpa. fut. 2 pers. sing. masc. (§ 12. rem. 1) חנן

תִּתְחַנֶּן[c] וַ id. fut. 3 pers. s. fem. (§ 12. r. 4); וַ conv. חנן

תִּתְחַסָּד Hithpa. fut. 2 pers. sing. masc. (§ 12. rem. 1) חסד

תִּתְחַקֶּה[d] Hithpa. fut. 2 pers. sing. masc. . . חקה

תִּתְחַר Hithpa. fut. 2 pers. sing. masc. ap. [from תִּתְחָרֶה § 24. rem. 12] . . . חרה

---

a Ge. 21. 23. b Le. 19. 11. c Ju. 5. 1. d Is. 57. 9. e Ge. 38. 24. f Pr. 6. 27. g Le. 13. 55, 57. h Ps. 80. 10. i Job 31. 12. k 1 Ki. 1. 4. l Nu. 12. 11. m Da. 2. 44. n Ru. 4. 16. o Ps. 42. 7. p 2 Sa. 14. 4. q Eze. 34. 19. r 1 Sa. 1. 14. s Is. 41. 10. t Job 30. 16. u La. 4. 1. x Nu. 16. 13. y Ne. 8. 9. z Nu. 34. 7, 8. a De. 5. 21.

b Is. 64. 11. c Job 30. 20. d Ps. 107. 27. e Ezr. 4. 13, 21. f Is. 43. 18. g 2 Sa. 22. 27. h Ps. 18. 27. i De. 14. 1. k Mi. 4. 14. l Je. 47. 5. m De. 2. 5. n 2 Sa. 22. 41. o Zec. 6. 7. p Is. 41. 16; Pr. 31. 30. q Je. 49. 4. r Job 38. 14. rr De. 2. 9, 19. s Nu. 15. 39. t Ps. 103. 5. u Nu. 31. 20. x Nu. 31. 19. y Ec. 7. 16. yy Pr. 25. 6. z Est. 4. 4. a Je. 31. 22. b Job 8. 5. c Est. 8. 3. d Job 13. 27.

תִּתְחָרֶה[a] Tiphal fut. 2 pers. sing. masc. (§ 6. No. 5) חרה

תִּתְחַתֵּן Hithpa. fut. 2 pers. sing. masc. . חתן

תִּתִּי Kal inf. (תֵּת § 17. rem. 9), suff. 1 pers. sing. dec. 13 (§ 44. rem. 1) . . נתן

תִּתְיְהֵב[b] Chald. Ithpe. fut. 3 pers. sing. fem. . יהב

תַּתִּיכֵנִי[c] Hiph. fut. 2 pers. sing. masc., suff. 1 pers. sing. נתך

תִּתְיַמָּרוּ[d] Hithpa. fut. 2 p. pl. m. [for תִּתְיַמְּרוּ § 12. r. 1] ימר

תִּתְיַפֵּחַ[e] Hithpa. fut. 3 p. s. fem. [for תִּתְיַפַּח § 15. r. 1] יפח

תִּתְיַפִּי[f] Hithpa. fut. 2 pers. sing. fem. . . יפה

תִּתְיַצֵּב[g] Hithpa. fut. 2 pers. sing. masc. . . יצב

תִּתַּךְ וַ' Kal fut. 3 pers. sing. fem.; וַ conv. . נתך

תִּתְּךָ[h] Kal inf. (תֵּת § 17. rem. 9), suff. 2 pers. sing. masc. dec. 13 (§ 44. rem. 1) . . נתן

תֻּתְּכוּ[i] Hoph. fut. 2 pers. pl. masc. . . נתך

תִּתְכָּס[k] וַ Hithpa. fut. 3 pers. sing. fem. ap. [from תִּתְכַּסֶּה § 24. rem. 12]; וַ conv. כסה

תִּתְלוֹצָצוּ[l] Hithpal. fut. 2 pers. pl. masc. [for תִּתְלוֹצְצוּ § 21. rem. 20] . . . לוץ

תַּתֵּם[m] Hiph. fut. 2 pers. s. m. [for תָּתֵם § 18. r. 14] תמם

תִּתָּם[n] Kal inf. (תֵּת § 17. rem. 9), suff. 3 pers. pl. masc. dec. 13 (§ 44. rem. 1) . . נתן

תִּתֹּם וַ' / תִּתֹּם[o] Kal fut. 3 pers. sing. fem. [for תִּתֹּם § 18. rem. 14]; וַ conv. . . תמם

תִּתְמַהּ[p] Kal fut. 2 pers. sing. masc. . . . תמה

תִּתְמוֹגָג[q] Hithpal. fut. 3 pers. sing. fem. (§ 21. rem. 20) מוג

תִּתְמוֹגַגְנָה[r] id. fut. 3 pers. pl. fem. . . . . מוג

תִּתְמֹךְ[s] Kal fut. 3 pers. sing. fem. . . . תמך

תִּתַּמָּם Hithpa. fut. 2 p. s. m. [for תִּתְתַּמָּם § 12. r. 1] תמם

תִּתֵּן[t] Kh. תִּתֵּן for תִּנְתֵּן, inf. of a reduplicated form, K. תֵּן Kal inf. . . . . נתן

תִּתֵּן וַ' / תִּתֶּן־ וַ' Kal fut. 3 pers. sing. masc., or 3 pers. sing. fem.; וַ conv. . . נתן

תִּתְּנֶהָ[u] וַ id. fut. 2 p. s. m., suff. 3 pers. s. fem.; וַ id. נתן

תִּתְּנֵהוּ[x] וַ'[y] id. fut. 2 pers. sing. masc., or 3 pers. sing. fem., suff. 3 pers. sing. masc.; וַ id. . נתן

תִּתְּנֻהוּ[z] id. fut. 2 pers. pl. masc., suff. 3 pers. sing. m. נתן

תִּתְּנוֹ[a] id. fut. 2 pers. sing. m., suff. 3 pers. sing. m. נתן

תִּתְּנוּ / תִּתֵּנוּ id. fut. 2 pers. pl. masc. (comp. § 8. r. 15) נתן

תִּתְנוֹדֵד[b] Hithpal. fut. 2 pers. sing. masc. (§ 21. rem. 20) נוד

תִּתְּנוּם[c] Kal fut. 2 pers. pl. masc., suff. 3 pers. pl. m. נתן

תִּתְנַחֲלוּ[d] / תִּתְנַחֲלוּ Hithpa. fut. 2 pers. pl. masc. (§ 14. rem. 1, & § 12. rem. 1) נחל

תַּתְּנַי pr. name of a Persian noble, Ezr. 5. 3; 6. 6.

תִּתְּנִי Kal fut. 2 pers. sing. fem. . . . נתן

תִּתְּנֵים[e] וַ id. id., suff. 3 pers. pl. masc.; וַ conv. נתן

תִּתְּנֵם[f] וַ id. fut. 2 pers. sing. masc. (תִּתֵּן), suff. 3 pers. pl. masc.; וַ id. . . . נתן

תִּתְּנֶנָּה[g] id. id., suff. 3 pers. sing. fem. . נתן

תִּתְּנֵנוּ[h] id. id., suff. 1 pers. pl. . . . . נתן

תִּתְּנֶנּוּ[i] id. id., suff. 3 pers. sing. masc. . . נתן

תִּתְּנֵנִי[k] id. id., suff. 1 pers. sing. . . . נתן

תִּתְנַקֵּם Hithpa. fut. 3 pers. sing. fem. . . נקם

תִּתְנַשֵּׂא[l] Hithpa. fut. 2 pers. sing. masc. . . נשא

תִּתְנַשְּׂאוּ[m] id. fut. 2 pers. pl. masc. . . . נשא

תֵּתַע[n] וַ'[o] Kal fut. 2 pers. sing. masc., or 3 pers. sing. fem. ap. [fr. תִּתְעֶה § 24. rem. 3]; וַ conv. תעה

תְּתַעֵב[p] Piel fut. 2 pers. sing. masc., or 3 pers. sing. fem. (§ 14. rem. 1) . . . תעב

תִּתְעַבְדוּן[r] Chald. Ithpa. fut. 2 pers. pl. masc. . עבד

תְּתַעֲבִי[s] וַ Piel fut. 2 pers. s. fem. (§ 14. r. 1); וַ conv. תעב

תְּתַעֲבֶנּוּ[t] id. fut. 2 pers. sing. m., suff. 3 pers. sing. m. תעב

תִּתְעַטֵּף[u] / וַתִּ', וַ תִּתְעַטֵּף[x] Hithpa. fut. 3 pers. sing. fem. (§ 12. rem. 1); וַ conv. . עטף

תִּתְעַלָּם[y] / תִּתְעַלָּם[z] Hithpa. fut. 2 pers. sing. masc. (§ 12. r. 1) עלם

תִּתְעַלָּף[a] וַ Hithpa. fut. 3 pers. s. f. (§ 12. r. 1); וַ conv. עלף

תִּתְעַלַּפְנָה[b] id. fut. 3 pers. pl. fem. . . . עלף

תְּתָעֵם[c] Hiph. fut. 3 pers. sing. fem. [תַּתְעֶה], suff. 3 pers. pl. masc. (§ 24. rem. 21) . תעה

תִּתְעַמָּר[d] Hithpa. fut. 2 pers. sing. masc. . . עמר

תִּתְעַנַּג[e] / וְ' תִּתְעַנָּג[f] id. fut. 2 pers. sing. masc., or 3 pers. sing. fem. (§ 12. rem. 1) . . ענג

תִּתְעַנְּגוּ[g] id. fut. 2 pers. pl. masc. [for תִּתְעַנְּגוּ] . ענג

תַּתְעֵנוּ[h] Hiph. fut. 2 pers. sing. masc. [תַּתְעֶה], suff. 1 pers. pl. (§ 24. rem. 21) . . תעה

תִּתְעָרָב Hithpa. fut. 2 pers. sing. masc. (§ 12. r. 1) ערב

תִּתְעָרִי[i] וְ Hithpa. fut. 2 pers. sing. fem. . . ערה

תִּתְעַרְעָר[k] Hithpalp. fut. 3 pers. sing. fem. (§ 6. No. 4) ערר

תִּתַּפָּל[l] by contr. and transp. for תִּתְפַּתָּל Hithpa. fut. 2 pers. sing. masc. (§ 18. rem. 18) פתל

תִּתְפַּלָּא[m] Hithpa. fut. 2 pers. sing. masc. . . פלא

תִּתְפַּלֵּל וַ' Hithpa. fut. 2 pers. sing. masc., or 3 pers. sing. fem.; וַ conv. . . . . פלל

תִּתְפָּעֶם[n] וַ Hithpa. fut. 3 pers. sing. fem. (§ 12. rem. 4); וַ id. . . . . . פעם

תִּתָּפֵשׂ וַ'[o] Niph. fut. 2 pers. sing. masc., or (Je. 51. 41) 3 pers. sing. fem.; וַ id. . . תפש

תְּתַפֵּשׂ[p] Piel fut. 3 pers. sing. fem. . . תפש

---

[a] Je. 12. 5. [b] Ezr. 6. 4. [c] Job 10. 10. [d] Is. 61. 6. [e] Je. 4. 31. [f] Je. 4. 30. [g] 2 Sa. 18. 13.
[h] Eze. 28. 6. [i] Eze. 22. 22. [k] Ge. 24. 65. [l] Is. 28. 22. [m] Job 22. 3. [n] 2 Ch. 25. 20. [o] Eze. 24. 11.
[p] Ec. 5. 7. [q] Ps. 107. 26. [r] Am. 9. 13. [s] Pr. 11. 16. [t] 1 Ki. 17. 14. [u] 2 Ch. 20. 7. [x] Ps. 41. 3.
[y] Ju. 17. 4. [z] 2 Ki. 12. 8. [a] Ex. 22. 29. [b] Je. 48. 27. [c] Jos. 10. 19. [d] Nu. 33. 54. [e] Eze. 16. 21.
[f] Ne. 9. 24, 27, 30. [g] De. 14. 21. [h] Ps. 44. 12. [i] Ps. 74. 14. [k] Ps. 27. 12. [l] Eze. 29. 15. [m] Nu. 16. 3.
[n] Pr. 7. 25. [o] Ge. 21. 14. [p] De. 23. 8; Ps. 107. 18. [r] Da. 2. 5. [s] Eze. 16. 25. [t] De. 7. 26.
[u] Ps. 107. 5. [x] Ps. 77. 4; 143. 4. [y] Is. 58. 7. [z] Ps. 55. 2. [a] Ge. 38. 14. [b] Am. 8. 13. [c] Pr. 12. 26.
[d] De. 21. 14. [e] Job 22. 26. [f] Is. 55. 2; 58. 14. [g] Is. 57. 4. [h] Is. 63. 17. [i] La. 4. 21.
[k] Je. 51. 58. [l] 2 Sa. 22. 27. [m] Job 10. 16. [n] Da. 2. 1. [o] Je. 51. 41. [p] Pr. 30. 28.

[a]תִּתְפְּשֵׂהוּ וַ Kal fut. 3 p. s. f., suff. 3 p. s. m.; וַ· conv. תפשׂ

[b]תִּתָּפֵשׂוּ Niph. fut. 2 pers. pl. masc. [for תִּתָּפְשׂוּ, comp. § 8. rem. 15] . . . . תפשׂ

[c]תִּתְפַּתָּל Hithp. fut. 2 pers. sing. masc. (§ 12. rem. 1) פתל

[d]תֵּתַצַּב וַ Hithpa. fut. 3 pers. sing. fem. (for תִּתְיַצֵּב § 20. rem. 13 and § 12 r. 1); וַ· conv. יצב

[e]תִּתֹּצוּ } Kal fut. 2 pers. pl. masc. (§ 8. r. 15);
[f]וַתִּתְּצוּ } וַ· id. . . . . } נתץ

תִּתֹּצוּן id. with parag. ן [for תִּתְּצוּן § 8. rem. 17] נתץ

תִּתְקַע וַ Kal fut. 3 pers. sing. fem.; וַ· conv. . תקע

[g]תִּתְקְעוּ id. fut. 2 pers. pl. masc. . . . תקע

תִּתְקְפֵהוּ Kal fut. 2 p. s. m., or 3 p. s. f., suff. 3 p. s. m. תקף

[h]תֹּתַר וַ Hiph. fut. 3 pers. sing. fem. ap. & conv. [for וַתּוֹתֶר § 20. r. 9, comp. § 9. r. 3 & 4] יתר

[i]תִּתְרָאוּ Hithpa. fut. 2 p. pl. m. [for תִּתְרְאוּ § 8. r. 15] ראה

[k]תִּתְרְמוֹן Ch. Ithpe. fut. 2 pers. pl. masc. R. רְמָא, see רמה

[l]תִּתְרַע Hithpa. fut. 2 pers. sing. m. ap. [fr. תִּתְרָעֶה] רעה

[m]תֻּתַּשׁ וַ Hoph. fut. 3 pers. sing. fem.; וַ· conv. נתשׁ

[a] Ge. 39. 12. [b] Eze. 21. 29. [c] Ps. 18. 27. [d] Ex. 2. 4. [e] De. 7. 5. [f] Is. 22. 10. [g] Nu. 10. 7. [h] Ru. 2. 14. [i] Ge. 42. 1. [k] Da. 3. 15. [l] Pr. 22. 24. [m] Eze. 19. 12.